WORLD RADIO TV HANDBOOK

WRTH

THE DIRECTORY OF GLOBAL BROADCASTING

2016

REFERENCE AND INFORMATION
DAW | £35.00
18.2.2016.

WORLD RADIO TV HANDBOOK
WRTH
THE DIRECTORY OF GLOBAL BROADCASTING

70TH ANNIVERSARY EDITION

VOLUME 70 – 2016

Publisher
Nicholas Hardyman

International Editor
Sean Gilbert

'A' Schedule & Web Updates Editor
Mauno Ritola

Television Editor
Bernd Trutenau

Technical Editor
John Nelson

Contributing Editors
George Jacobs
Bengt Ericson
Dave Kenny
Mauno Ritola
Bernd Trutenau
Torgeir Woxen

Cover Design
Richard Boxall Design Associates

WRTH Publications Limited
PO Box 290
Oxford OX2 7FT
United Kingdom
Tel: +44 (0) 1865 339355
Fax: +44 (0) 1865 339301
Email: wrth@wrth.com
Web: www.wrth.com
ISBN 978-0-9555481-8-5

Printed and bound in the UK by CPI William Clowes, Beccles NR34 7TL

WORLD RADIO TV HANDBOOK

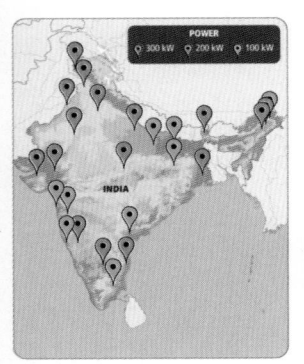
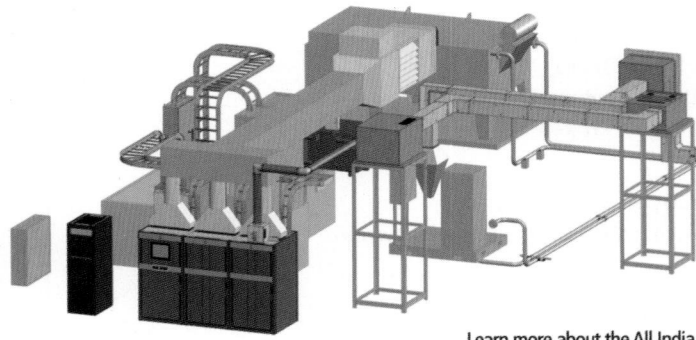

CONTENTS

Section Contents

Features & Reviews

National Radio

International Radio

Frequency Lists

National Television

Reference

Editorial

NEW WAVES

We are very pleased to welcome you to the 70th edition of *WRTH,* which has now been published for longer than any other comparable directory. We are sure that the founder of *WRTH*, Mr O. Lund Johanssen, would be delighted to know that the book he created is still providing accurate broadcasting information to professionals and enthusiasts alike seventy years after the first publication of *World Radio Handbook*.

We are proud to provide the most comprehensive and up-to-date information on global broadcasting available anywhere in the world. This book is of course the result of the hard work and dedication of our team of editors and contributors without whom the compilation and correction of all the data would not be possible. In this anniversary year we would particularly like to thank them, our readers and our advertisers for their loyalty to this unique publication.

There have been no new desktop receivers of note this year but a glimpse into a possible direction for the future of this market is provided by the AOR AR-DV1. This very interesting unit combines for the first time conventional manual control and much of the functionality of an SDR over the HF portion of its very wide coverage. There have however been some intriguing small portables. We particularly enjoyed testing the very capable new Satellit 'Grundig edition' from Etón – which offers a capable DAB+ implementation for the very first time in a small receiver – and the CC Skywave from C. Crane. It would have been gratifying this year finally to see a capable production-ready DRM receiver but we were again disappointed. The AV DVR 1401 DRM from Avion Electronics, which we hoped to see in 2014, was scheduled for release in October 2015 but was still not available as we went to press.

We are sad to report the imminent closure of the Danish Short Wave Club International. Under the expert guidance of Anker Petersen the DSWCI has for many years been providing an excellent forum for many DXers, and invaluable information on domestic SW broadcasting.

AM BROADCASTING

Sadly but perhaps inevitably there has been a further reduction in shortwave broadcasting over the past year. There has also been a marked decrease in transmissions on MW and LW and the consequent dismantling of AM transmitter stations. In acknowledgement of these changes, Dave Porter looks back on 95 years of MW and LW transmissions by the BBC, and Thomas Witherspoon laments the decline in SW. But the outlook is not as gloomy as it may at first appear. As state broadcasters leave the AM airwaves, many private and commercial stations are use-

ing the vacated frequencies to provide interesting and innovative programming. In addition to this, as many enthusiasts have pointed out to us, DXing and listening have become more exciting as it has become possible to hear smaller or more distant stations that were previously swamped by the transmissions of the larger broadcasters.

WRTH FREQUENCY BARGRAPH

The bargraph frequency CDs we produced this year were as popular as ever, and we will be producing them for the B15 and A16 seasons. The download facility once again proved to be extremely popular. The CDs and the downloads will again only be available from our website.

WEBSITE UPDATES

We will as usual be uploading free pdf updates to our website. Updates to the B15 season will be available in February 2016. The full schedules for the A16 season will be posted in May 2016 with an update in July 2016. We will also continue to provide updates to the National Radio section on the *WRTHmonitor* page on our website.

PRIZE DRAW RESULTS

These winners were again drawn by members of the British DX Club. We have decided that we will no longer print the Questionnaire in the book. It will instead be available for downloading from our website and can then be emailed to us.

RESULTS OF THE
WRTH 2015 PRIZE DRAW

First prize: Tecsun PL-600

FIRST PRIZE
A. Dean, UK

RUNNERS-UP PRIZES (copies of WRTH 2016)
R. Burket, USA
J. Galante, USA
M. Gerbault, France
M. Halford, UK
N. Salis, Switzerland

I hope you will enjoy reading and using this new edition of *WRTH*

Nicholas Hardyman
Publisher

WRTH Contributors 2016

The *WRTH* contributors come from all walks of life; yet share a common fascination with all aspects of global broadcasting. Each year we profile one of the people whose dedicated enthusiasm makes possible the enormous task of updating *WRTH* each year. This year it is the turn of Dave Kenny to give us an insight into what makes a *WRTH* contributor.

Dave Kenny at his receiving station

My interest in radio started as a schoolboy in the late 1960s, I was fascinated by all things electrical and especially the glow of the dial on my grandparent's valve radio. It was around 1970 that I acquired my first radio, it too was an old bakelite set make by Ekco, which I bought from a local junk shop with my pocket money. As well as the standard medium and long wave bands, it had a short-wave band covering 16 to 49 metres. Scanning the SW band I was intrigued to hear all sorts of exotic-sounding stations and interval signals, which I gradually managed to identify. So began a lifetime interest in short wave radio. At school in 1972 I started circulating a typewritten sheet listing stations I had heard on SW, and then in 1974, with a couple of school friends who were equally fascinated by radio, we set up the Twickenham DX Club. Membership grew rapidly and spread worldwide so in 1979 it was renamed the British DX Club (BDXC-UK), the club celebrated its 40th anniversary in 2014. For many years the club has published a guide to Radio Stations in the UK every two years or so, which I have compiled and continue to do so. In more recent years I have taken on the editing the UK and Ireland sections in the *WRTH* as well as several of the international schedules.

After a series of domestic valve sets my first communications receiver was an RCA AR88D which despite being almost an antique by the 70s, worked very well and lead to my discovering the tropical bands and even more exotic stations. Nowadays I use an AOR AR7030+, supplemented by some listening online. I have not yet got an SDR receiver as I generally prefer to listen in real-time.

I was very fortunate in that my interest in radio lead to a career at the BBC Monitoring Service, initially as a World Schedules Monitor - literally tuning the bands to build up schedules of stations that were being monitored at that time, and arranging the signal feeds to the various language monitors. This was during the cold war when the bands were full of competing signals from east and west, accompanied by much jamming. Later I spent several years on the editorial side at BBC Monitoring as a chief sub editor, working mostly on World Broadcasting Information (later World Media), which may be familiar to some readers as it was available on subscription, along with the schedules. After a career spanning almost 25 years I took early retirement from the BBC in 2003, but have continued with my work for BDXC and the *WRTH*.

I bought my first *WRTH* in 1972 and have every issue since then, along with several earlier editions, which between them make up an invaluable resource chronicling the history of national and international broadcasting. I used *WRTH* professionally for many years at BBC Monitoring and I still find the book to be an invaluable reference guide. It comes in particularly useful to me while listening away from home or when travelling abroad. Since the early '90s I have been going on regular DXpditions to the far north of Scotland where reception conditions are so much better than here in the south of England and there is more room to put up long 500m "Beverage" aerials. But I am lucky to still have fairly good reception conditions at home, despite living in a built-up area: I have a variety of aerials to chose from including a 25m long wire, a Wellbrook ALA 1530 loop and a mini Beverage which despite being on the ground and much shorter than a typical Beverage, works surprisingly well on medium wave. Selecting different aerials can sometimes help to minimise local electrical interference.

Despite all the closures of SW and MW stations in recent years I still get immense pleasure from the hobby. Although sadly it is inevitable that more SW and MW stations will close over the coming years, on the positive side there have been a number of new private SW broadcasters opening up from countries such as Australia, Germany, Finland, Sweden, USA, and elsewhere. There has also been a move to SDR receivers and many online receivers have become available, which can be a great help to anyone with difficult local reception. So while things will evolve I am hopeful that there will continue to be plenty to listen to on the bands.

Dave Kenny
WRTH Contributing Editor for UK, Ireland and Gibraltar, and International Radio

A large project such as WRTH could not be produced without the help of many people from all over the world. The following organisations and publications give invaluable help:

Asian Broadcasting Institute, BC-DX Top News, British DX Club, DX-Listening Digest, Electronic DX Press, Grupo Radioescucha Argentino, National Radio Club Inc (USA listings), Radio Heritage Foundation, International Radio Club of America

our Country Contributors provide us with updated entries for the countries for which they are responsible:

Herman Boel, Luís Carvalho, Swopan Chakroborty, Svetomir Cuckovic, Alan Davies, Alok Dasgupta, Bengt Ericson, David Foster, Stig Hartvig Nielsen, István Hegedüs, Karel Honzík, Jose Jacob, Richard Jary, Dave Kenny, Tetsuya Kondo, Vashek Korinek, Kai Ludwig, Dario Monferini, Andy Reid, David Ricquish, Mauno Ritola, Roberto Scaglione, Bernd Trutenau, Max van Arnhem, Thierry Vignaud, Tore B Vik, Torgeir Woxen

they and we are greatly aided by our other major contributors:

Pedro Arrunátegui, Ian Baxter, Carlos Benoit, Erich Bergmann, Dino Bloise, Héctor García Bojorge, Jordi Brunet, Mustafa Cancurt, Alfredo Cañote, Julio Pineda Cordón, Marcelo Cornachioni, Fredrik Dourén, Samir Elahcene, Santiago San Gil, Dan Goldfarb, Victor Goonetilleke, Noel Green, Chris Greenway, Rudolf Walter Grimm, Alokesh Gupta, Tom Hägg, Wolf Harranth, Glenn Hauser, Aslam Javaid, Hans Johnson, Dave Kernick, Henrik Klemetz, Anatoly Klepov, Andrej Kuznecov, Miller Liu, William López, James MacDonell, Alexander Mak, Humberto Molina, Adán Mur, Michael Nevradakis, Horacio Nigro, Samuel Ouma, Anker Petersen, Mieczyslaw Pietruski, Arnulf Piontek, Rimantas Pleikys, Patrick Robic, Rafael Rodríguez, Daniel Rosenzweig, Ibrahim Rustamov, Victor Rutkovsky, David Sharp, Zhang ShiFeng, David Stanley, Luis Toranzo, Tarek Zeidan

We thank them, and also all our readers who have written or emailed us with useful ideas and information. Please keep sending your thoughts and updates to:

wrth@wrth.com

or write to:
WRTH Publications Limited, PO Box 290, Oxford OX2 7FT, UK

WRTH Receiver Reviews 2016

For this 70th edition we invited Thomas Witherspoon to join John Nelson, as a guest reviewer

John Nelson (GW4FRX) is an author, editor and consultant specialising in audio, radio and communications technology. After graduation John worked for the BBC and the Radio Society of Great Britain before forming his own company and has written, edited and contributed to a wide variety of publications. He is the managing director of Crew Green Consulting Ltd (www.crew-green.com), which carries out electronic and communications systems design and assessment for an international client base.

Thomas Witherspoon (K4SWL) is the owner of *The SWLing Post*, curator of the Shortwave Radio Audio Archive and founder/director of the charity Ears To Our World.

C. Crane CC Skywave

US$90   £65   €85

While electronics manufacturer and retailer C. Crane offers a number of AM/FM radios, among them some of the best portable MW receivers currently on the market, they've traditionally only had two models of shortwave radio, namely the CCRadio-SW, and the CCRadio-SWP. Late last year, however, C. Crane announced a new portable receiver: the CC Skywave

FIRST IMPRESSIONS

The compact form factor of the Skywave is very similar to C.Crane's CCRadio-SWP pocket radio. The Skywave's backlit LCD display is small, but readily viewable from several angles. All of the buttons on the front of the Skywave have a tactile response, which is again similar to the CCRadio-SWP. The buttons require slightly more pressure to activate than Tecsun and Degen models, but I find this preferable, especially for a travel radio as it makes it much less likely that the radio will turn on accidentally during transit.

Once the radio is on, the main displays shows

either the time or frequency. While the Skywave defaults to a time display, I found that the lock button toggles the display between time and frequency for ten seconds. You can also change the default display mode to either time or frequency

The Skywave's memory allocation is very straightforward. Simply tune to the desired station, then press and hold a number button for two seconds to save the frequency. Press a button quickly to recall. The memory holds the bandwidth, stereo or mono (if FM), and any voice or music audio filters that you utilized!

The Skywave has five bandwidth selections on shortwave, mediumwave, and air bands: 6, 4, 3, 2, and 1 kHz. By pressing the bandwidth button, you can cycle through these from widest to narrowest. The bandwidth defaults to 3kHz, but the default can be changed by holding down the bandwidth button for five seconds (this has to be performed with the radio powered off).

To enter a frequency in AM/FM/SW, you simply press the FREQ button and then key in the frequency. To scan through the band, press and hold one of the up/down arrow buttons. The Skywave's scan function is one of the fastest I have ever seen in a portable.

On the topic of scanning, and since this is a travel radio, I would have liked C.Crane to include an ETM function like that found in the Tecsun PL-310ET and PL-380. It's quite a handy function for auto-populating temporary memories from a simple band scan. I assume this is not an option on the DSP chip powering the Skywave.

It's a easy process to change the tuning speed – and frequency step-spacing on the tuning knob (which has an option of 5 or 1kHz steps) – just by pressing the knob itself. I much prefer this to using a front-panel tuning step button because it's so simple to operate in low-light settings.

PERFORMANCE

As mentioned earlier, C.Crane radios tend to lead the pack in terms of mediumwave performance and the CC Skywave is no exception to this rule. I've spent a great deal of time listening to the Skywave on the this band and I can recommend the CC Skywave to both the casual MW listener and the MW DXer with confidence. It has above-average sensitivity and selectivity on the band and it's *automatic gain control* (AGC) handles nighttime choppy propagation conditions better than some of my other ultralight DSP portables.

While I'm not a dedicated FM DXer, I can confirm that the CC Skywave receives my "benchmark" FM stations with ease. Sensitivity also seems to be on par with my other DSP based portables – it's excellent in this respect.

Of course, being a shortwave enthusiast, I've spent the bulk of my listening time on the shortwave bands. The CC Skywave has excellent sensitivity and selectivity for a radio of its size and price. When I compared the Skywave with my trusty Tecsun PL-310ET – also a strong performer among the ultra-portables – they performed equally well in almost every situation, which means they are both very good indeed.

Several readers on the *SWLing Post* have in the past noted significant receiver overloading and imaging when in the presence of strong local broadcasters. Fortunately the C. Crane company has announced that units produced after October 1, 2015 have been updated and are no longer prone to this overloading

NOAA WEATHER RADIO

Those of us living or traveling in North America will appreciate the Skywave's built-in NOAA weather radio functionality. Indeed, not only does the Skywave have NOAA weather radio, but it also has SAME weather alerts. What's so great about that? Imagine that you're travelling to a rural area and weather is looking ominous; in this case, you can simply set the Skywave to the strongest NOAA channel and activate the weather alert (choose options for 4, 8, or 16 hours). If severe weather is reported for your geographic area, the Skywave will alert you. I'm very pleased with the NOAA weather radio reception as well as the the Skywave receives NOAA stations even better than one of my dedicated weather radios.

AIR BAND

C.Crane included the Air band for travelers, as a means to listen to air traffic control while in an airport or awaiting a flight's arrival. I have several portables with the AIR band, but most lack an autoscan ability (Grundig G3, G6), and performance on these tends to be mediocre at best. While the Skywave's AIR reception can't compare with a dedicated triple-conversion scanner, it is quite good. Since I like listening to aviation traffic, I've used it to hear local air traffic control on several trips. What really separates the Skywave from my other shortwave portable with the AIR band is that it also features an adjustable squelch mode which is a very nice feature.

ACCESSORIES

Unlike Tecsun portables which typically ship with batteries, an external antenna wire, chargers, travel cases, and the like, the CC Skywave comes with very few included accessories—just a carry case, an owner's manual, and earphones.

CONCLUSION

C. Crane has few shortwave radios in their product line, and all perform rather well for their price point; I know, as I have owned all of them and even purchased them as gifts in the past. I was concerned, in early 2014, when I noted the similarity between the CC Skywave and the poorly-reviewed Digitech AR1733, sold in Australia and New Zealand by Jaycar.

Fortunately, it's clear that C. Crane noticed the shortcomings of the AR1733 and has modified the Skywave's design and firmware accordingly, which may account for the delayed roll-out of the receiver. The Skywave's ACG circuit has obviously been tweaked to cope with mediumwave and shortwave listening, since a poor ACG circuit is one of the shortcomings of the AR1733.

All in all, the CC Skywave is a excellent little radio. Indeed, in terms of the ultra-compact portable market on which I have done several comparative tests, I think it's one of the best performers I've seen in the past few years.

In conclusion, the CC Skywave has now replaced the Tecsun PL-310ET and PL-380 as my one-bag travel companion, for both domestic and international journeys. The CC Skywave is also especially well-suited for the "go" bags and "bug-out" bags used in evacuations and other emergencies. Indeed, with AM/FM/SW/AIR plus functional NOAA radio, this little radio packs a lot; it's a veritable "Swiss Army Knife" of a radio. and will certainly get packed in my bag.   **TW**

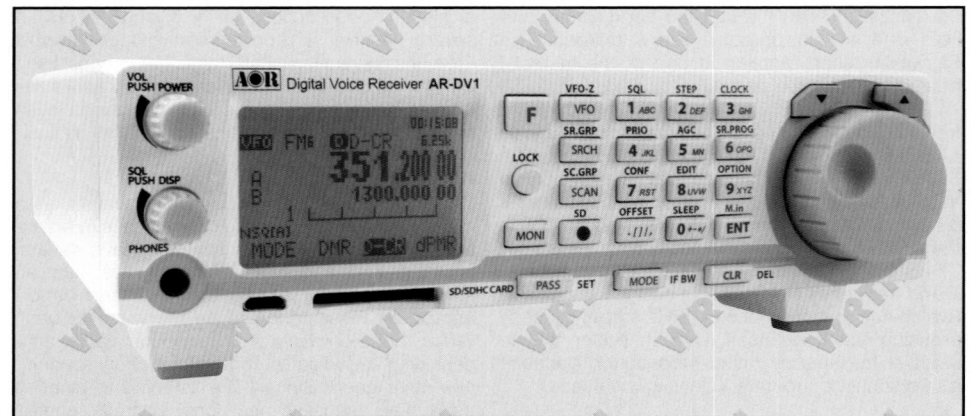

AOR AR-DV1

US$1220   £1200   €1550

OVERVIEW

The Japanese company AOR – the letters standing for "Authority on Radio" and apparently derived from the amateur callsign of the founder, JA1AOR – is well known for innovative radio communications equipment for the professional and consumer market. The AR-DV1 is its newest receiver and although not at first glance aimed principally at the market represented by *WRTH* readers, it offers a fascinating insight into the possibilities of combining an SDR with a conventional front-panel interface and adding a great deal of leading-edge digital decoding technology.

FEATURES

In a sense the AR-DV1 is two receivers in one. Covering 100kHz to 1.3GHz, it is a direct-conversion design from its low-frequency limit to 18MHz. Between 18 and 180MHz it is a conventional up-converting double-conversion superheterodyne with intermediate frequencies of 393 and 31MHz. From 180MHz to 1.3GHz the first IF becomes an up-converted 1705MHz with the second and third IFs as before. We would imagine that some form of SAW filter is used in the 1705MHz IF sub-system. The specification states that the IF bandwidths are 200 and 500Hz and 1.8, 2.6, 3.8, 5.5, 6, 8, 15, 30, 100 and 200kHz and these appear to be digitally implemented although no information is given in the manual. The available analogue receive modes are FM, AM, synchronous AM, USB, LSB and CW but in addition the AR-DV1 can cater for a wide variety of commercial digital modes. Some of these are used by radio amateurs and others are in wide use by private mobile radio systems of various types. From the point of view of broadcast reception it is a little unfortunate that modes such as DRM and some flavour of DAB are not available.

However, it would presumably not be difficult for the manufacturer to add them in future via a firmware update if it so chose. There are no less than four distinct squelch modes based on noise and level together with an auto notch facility, three selectable AGC speeds, three separate 'VFOs' and an effective noise-reduction mode available in AM only.

Physically the AR-DV1 measures 180 x 50 x 220mm and weighs about 1.5kg, from which it may be inferred that it is a very substantially made (and beautifully finished) package. The front panel is remarkably small and densely packed and the entire receiver is raised to a convenient height above whatever surface it is mounted on by two tilt-out feet. The left-hand side of the front panel is taken up with a small orange-backlit display with volume and squelch controls adjacent. A 4 x 4 matrix keypad is to the right of the display with most numeric keys having second functions. They keys themselves have short travel and quite high breakout force with rather too much lost motion for their size. Consequently they feel slightly "rattly" in use. A 'VFO' knob with up/down keys is at the right of the panel. In contrast with the keypad buttons, the breakout force here is very low and there is some lost motion around the detents. One of our few consistent criticisms of AOR receivers over the years is that their ergonomics are not particularly well thought out and implemented; accepting that modern receivers are complex and contain a good deal of functionality, many of them could easily be made more pleasant to use. Learning one's way around the AR-DV1 is likely to be rather a protracted exercise, not helped by the relatively low display contrast and somewhat idiosyncratic interface.

Beneath the display is a Micro-B USB socket and a slot for an SD card. The latter can be used for both voice recording and back-up memory management. The receiver has a comprehensive configuration and option menu for various user-selectable parameters and these can also be backed up on the card. As would be expected, the AR-DV-1's memory functions are very comprehensive. In effect there are 2,000 memories organised as 40 banks of 50 channels. Each memory location is capable of holding frequency, mode, tuning step and a text comment of up to 12 characters. The contents are held in an EEPROM so that no backup battery is required for memory retention and can also be stored on the SD card if required. The principal use of the USB socket is to form an interface to a PC and the manual gives a clear and comprehensive guide to how this function can be used. Unfortunately the review sample of the AR-DV1 receiver – which was kindly loaned to us by Messrs Waters & Stanton – was only available for a relatively short period and we did not have time to test this aspect of the unit's capabilites in any depth.

On the rear drop is a BNC antenna connector and a standard 12V DC power socket. The specification states that the receiver can run off any DC voltage between 10.8 and 16 and draws 750mA. The supplied PSU runs quite warm, as indeed does the receiver as a whole. Auxiliary and extension-speaker sockets are available on the rear. Given the receiver's wide coverage it would have been useful and convenient to have separate antenna input sockets available for different portions of the frequency range.

PERFORMANCE

We took the view that *WRTH* readers would be chiefly interested in the AR-DV-1's potential as an MF and HF broadcast receiver with a look at its FM capabilities in passing. We mostly used a Wellbrook *Imperium* loop antenna together with assorted dipoles and random wires and a TH7DXX seven-element tri-band Yagi, the latter being used to generate some very strong signals from local amateurs. We used a Racal RA3791 and a WinRadio 'Excalibur Pro' for comparative evaluation. In general terms the AR-DV1 exhibited good sensitivity in the MF and HF bands. The specification states that from 530kHz to 18MHz the figure is 0.71μV for 12dB SINAD but no bandwidth is given. Our measurements suggested that this figure was a little pessimistic and the true figure was about 0.5 μV for 12dB SINAD at 17.9MHz in a 2.6kHz bandwidth in USB mode and was essentially independent of frequency elsewhere in the specified range. In the narrower CW bandwidths the MDS was found to be about -122dBm which more or less equates to the measured figure above. As such, the AR-DV1 could be said to be about 8dB worse than either the Racal or the WinRadio receivers but the actual sensitivity will be more than enough for real-world MF and HF reception. Above 18MHz, incidental-

ly, the sensitivity improved by about 4dB overall. Below 18MHz the strong-signal performance of the AR-DV1 approximated to that of a good portable receiver. It was happy enough with reasonably small antennas and input levels below about -14dBm but very strong signals in the MF and HF region (and in particular the 7MHz band at night when fed from a half-wave dipole) caused noticeable front-end distress and on occasions actual blocking. The switchable AGC worked fairly well although in the slow position there was a degree of audible 'pumping' on strong SSB and CW signals and none of the settings was quite ideal for utility SSB speech transmissions. Our guess is that the AR-DV1 would greatly benefit from the addition of an external preselector if it is fed from large antennas or used in a hostile RF environment. On balance it seemed to be happiest with the Wellbrook loop. Sensitivity in the 88-108MHz FM broadcast region was adequate for good reception with the supplied telescopic antenna and the IF filtering was very effective. Many FM receivers at the elevated test location suffer from adjacent-channel interference and noise caused by sub-par IF filter passband and stopband shapes but the AR-DV1 is certainly not one of them. Tests on non-broadcast frequencies suggested that this excellent performance is maintained elsewhere, for which air-band and utility UHF listeners in particular will be grateful.

CONCLUSION

Summing up the AR-DV1 is rather difficult. Clearly the AM broadcast listener is not the primary user at which the receiver is aimed. But for those wanting wide coverage of the RF spectrum together with the ability to decode various amateur and commercial digital modes, the AOR product might be an attractive choice. The inclusion of DAB and other digital broadcast modes in future models would be very useful. The wider significance of receivers of this general type is that they represent the convergence of SDR technology and the conventional dial-and-keypad interface and there is little doubt that this is how receiver technology of the future will develop. **JN**

Rating table for AOR AR-DV1

Constructional quality	★★★★
Sensitivity	★★★★
Dynamic range	★★★★
RF intermodulation	★★★
Versatility	★★★★
VFM	★★★★

Overall rating ★★★★

Key:
★ = Poor   ★★ = Fair   ★★★ = Average
★★★★ = Good   ★★★★★ = Excellent
VFM = Value for money

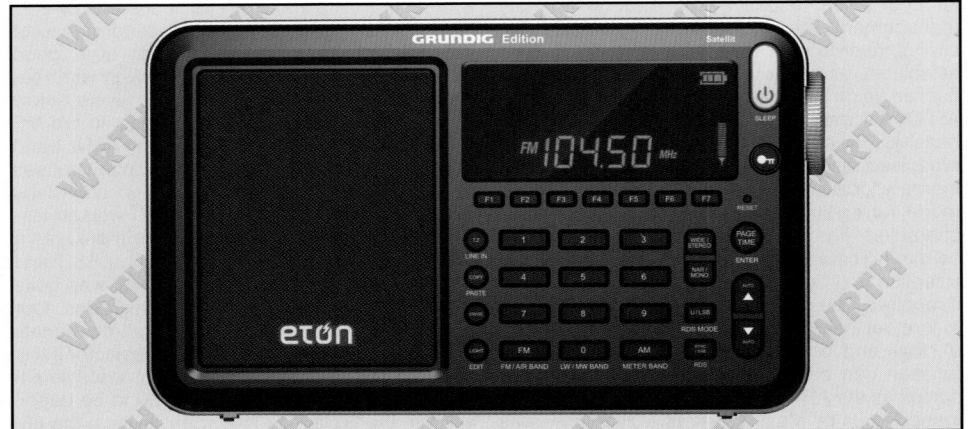

Etón Satellit Grundig Edition

US$200 £125 €165

Etón and Lextronix are familiar names to radio enthusiasts in various parts of the world. The holding company owns the Grundig brand name in the USA and the new Etón 'Satellit' portable receiver is also referred to as the 'Grundig Edition', presumably in homage to the much-loved Satellit family of high-grade portable radios produced by Grundig for many years.

OVERVIEW

Unlike Grundig Satellit receivers of yore the modern-day Satellit is a small portable in the mould of the popular Tecsun 660 and 880 but offering some rather unusual functionality. In particular it incorporates DAB+ which as far as we are aware is currently unique amongst portables. It also provides coverage of the 117-137MHz VHF aeronautical band although rather unfortunately in 25kHz steps instead of the 8.33kHz steps in which much of the band is nowadays channelized. The squelch is selectable in three discrete levels and can also be disabled. Standard FM broadcast reception is augmented by optional mono/stereo switching and partial RDS and the lower limit of the FM broadcast coverage can be set to 64, 76, 87 or 87.5MHz.

The AM band offers continuous coverage of 150kHz-30MHz in switchable 9 or 10kHz steps and short-wave broadcast bands can be directly selected. There are five separate AM bandwidth settings (2, 2.5, 3, 4 and 6kHz) and the shape of the passbands suggest that these are implemented via digital filters. Interestingly the quality of FM reception suggests that the intermediate-frequency filtering in this mode is also carried out in the digital domain and the resulting reception quality is noticeably better than is usually the case with low-cost portable receivers. A very useful SSB mode with selectable 10Hz tuning steps is available, as is fine tuning and optional synchronous detection on AM.

FEATURES

The Satellit measures 175 x 115 x 32mm and weighs just under 1kg with four AA cells (not supplied) installed. Our unit came with an American-style mains PSU which the manual implies can be used to charge nickel-metal hydride cells but the write-up suggests this requires the charge time to be set manually on the basis of the cell capacity. This is at best misleading and at worst could cause damage. We strongly recommend that NiMH cells are only ever recharged by a properly designed unit incorporating delta-V control of the charge rate. The orange-hued display at upper right is clear and legible and has three switchable levels of backlighting. Two thoughtful mechanical design details in the Satellit are the fold-out stand on the rear and the "double-jointed" telescopic antenna allowing the latter to be mounted vertically when the former is in use. The keys all have quite high breakout force, short travel and nicely weighted tactile feedback, making them feel pleasant and positive in operation. There are comprehensive clock and alarm facilities together with selectable time zones. One minor 'glitch' is that selecting automatic RDS-derived clock updating always resulted in the hour being reset either to zero or some arbitrary number and subsequent manual adjustment of the displayed time was required.

The Satellit offers a total of 700 memories configured as 100 pages each with seven presets. Each page can be copied and pasted and labelled with up to eight alphanumeric symbols; the procedure is somewhat cumbersome but no more so than in some scanning receivers of yore. Other useful features include local/DX switching, an 3.5mm auxiliary antenna input (which for some reason does not work on AM but does when individual SW bands are selected) and a line-level output socket.

PERFORMANCE

We tested the Satellit in conjunction with a Wellbrook *Imperium* loop and a variety of wire dipoles as well as its integral antennas. First impressions were of very good sensitivity and selectivity performance on the AM bands with pleasant audio and no obviously audible digital artefacts. In the higher HF bands the Satellit's telescopic antenna did it no favours, with the unit performing very much better on a 30ft random wire. In its SSB mode the Satellit proved to work very well, both on amateur and commercial SSB transmissions and when using the mode for ECSS reception. The AGC was not quite slow enough for good results on fading signals and a switchable AGC time-constant would have been a boon under some conditions but nevertheless the results were very creditable for a low-cost portable receiver. Much time was spent exploring the Satellit's capabilities on weak AM broadcast signals using SSB and the synchronous detector and the overall performance was judged to be very good although the audio quality with synchronous detection was noticeably degraded with audible distortion on strong signals. One oddity is that antennas with coaxial feed where the outer is grounded do not work well with the Satellit. Pushing the connecting plug all the way home results in a chronic loss of signal and there is evidently something unusual or non-standard about the design of the input circuitry.

On the brighter side, the performance on FM was very good throughout. Sensitivity was well up to that of other high-grade portables, selectivity was excellent and the audio quality was very good. On stereo headphones the audio sounded a trifle 'toppy' but there was no distortion. Multipath was very well handled. The RDS information was limited to PS name and programme type and no programme text or data was seen. This may reflect the fact that the Satellit's main market is expected to be the USA where the RBDS specification is slightly different from the original EBU RDS standard. The 'icing on the cake' would have been for the Satellit to make use of RDS EON information but very few portables have this capability.

Perhaps the Satellit's most intriguing feature is its implementation of DAB+. We should say straight away that the supplied manual was for the US version of the unit and did not mention DAB+ at all, so we may not have examined all the functionality available. The Satellit appeared to scan the available multiplexes correctly and after a short pause presented us with the stations it had found. Pressing the up/down button gave good-quality reception of each station in sequence and all the stations known to be in the two multiplexes available at the test location were audible. What we were not then able to do was to store and recall any of them in a preset; it seemed that if we wished to listen to DAB stations it was necessary to re-scan the multiplexes each time and step through the results sequentially until we reached the desired station. Curiously, however, the DAB stations in the multiplexes were clearly retained somewhere in switch-off. On switching on and selecting DAB it was possible to step through the stations in the multiplex until the required one was reached. This is perfectly acceptable if perhaps a little unusual, and in the absence of the correct manual it is quite possible that we have overlooked something. Incidentally the manual is not at all well written and some of the receiver's ancillary functionality (e.g. alarm setting, timezone selection and son on) appears not to operate in the manner described. Consequently there is rather a steep learning curve involved in getting to grips with the Satellit although this is not – alas – untypical of small portables and indeed contemporary consumer electronics in general. The once-honourable profession of technical author appears to have become a casualty of corporate cost-cutting, to the detriment of the user.

CONCLUSION

We liked the Etón Satellit very much. It offers a good deal of functionality and generally convincing performance in a small portable package. The inclusion of DAB+ makes it particularly attractive and high-quality FM reception is an added bonus. In general terms the AM performance is good with the digital IF filters and selectable bandwidths being particularly well implemented. The audio is above-average for a small portable and notably unfatiguing to listen to for extended periods. Some aspects of its ergonomics are a little unintuitive and the manual could be considerably improved but overall the Satellit is an excellent receiver which deserves to be very popular. **JN**

Rating table for Etón Satellit Grundig

Constructional quality	★★★★
Sensitivity	★★★★
Dynamic range	★★★★
RF intermodulation	★★★
Audio quality	★★★★
Versatility	★★★★
VFM	★★★★

Overall rating ★★★★

Key:
★ = Poor   ★★ = Fair   ★★★ = Average
★★★★ = Good   ★★★★★ = Excellent
VFM = Value for money

Tecsun PL-680

US$135 £90 €120

Tecsun is currently one of the most dynamic shortwave radio companies on the market and now produce some amazing portable receivers, some of which are considered to be among the best performers in their price class. I was interested to take a look at the PL-680.

FIRST IMPRESSIONS

Cosmetically, the Tecsun PL-680 looks like the PL-600, with PL-660 features and layout. Indeed, the buttons, switches and dials are identically positioned to those of the PL-660 and the new receiver appears to have no added features. The similarity is so striking, in fact, that I believe the PL-680 is the first radio I've ever turned on for the first time only to find that I immediately knew every single function.

So, what performance differences does the PL-680 have over the PL-660?

PERFORMANCE

In all of my comparisons, the PL-680 came out ahead of the venerable PL-660 in two respects: it features not only marginally better sensitivity, but also more stable AGC. While the PL-660 is a brilliant receiver, its soft muting and a sometimes overactive AGC equates to more listening fatigue – especially with weak-signal DXing.

While testing the PL-680 on the air, I haven't noticed any soft muting; the audio has been smooth and the AGC copes with fading much better than the PL-660. No doubt, these two improvements alone make the PL-680 a worthy portable for shortwave radio listening.

There is a downside to the improved sensitivity, however: the PL-680 has a slightly higher noise floor than the PL-660 which is most noticeable during weak-signal listening.

The PL-680 also has a better synchronous detector than the PL-660 and most other portables in its price class. I've always considered the PL-660 to have a strong sync lock, but after many comparative tests, and during periods of deep fading (QSB), the PL-680's lock was definitely of a much higher standard.

I've spent time listening to both radios in SSB mode and comparing the models. To my ear, both are very close in SSB performance, but again the PL-680 does have a slight edge on the PL-660 in terms of sensitivity and AGC performance. SSB audio fidelity is very similar in both radios.

In terms of FM reception, the PL-680 is a very capable performer and is sensitive enough to receive every one of my benchmark local and regional FM stations.

For mediumwave performance, however, the PL-680 is not as good as the PL-660. Although it is more sensitive on shortwave, it simply lacks that sensitivity on the mediumwave bands. While the PL-680 does a marginally better job than the PL-660 of handling the choppy conditions of nighttime MW DX, the PL-660 still pulled voices and music out of the static and made them noticeably more intelligible.

SUMMARY

If you're a shortwave radio listener, you'll be pleased with the Tecsun PL-680. In all of my comparison tests between the two, the PL-680 tended to edge out the PL-660 performance-wise. But if you are a mediumwave DXer, you might prefer to skip over the PL-680, although a casual listener will probably be pleased with it.

All in all, I like the Tecsun PL-680 and I see myself using it more than the PL-660 when I'm on the move. If you are primarily a shortwave radio listener, then the PL-680 may well be worth the upgrade. It is certainly good value. **TW**

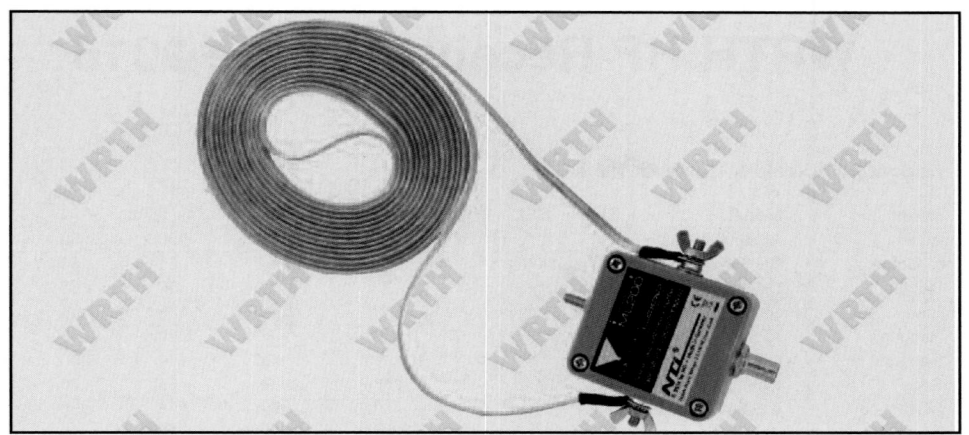

Nti ML200 Megaloop
US$350   £220   €370

The active loop antenna combines some form of radially disposed element with an electronic package consisting of a wideband amplifier and an impedance transformer to match the connecting cable (almost always 50ohm coaxial) over the frequency range of interest. Many loops consist of aluminium-tubing elements of a fixed diameter but it is perfectly feasible to form it from flexible wire or cable. As might be expected, the low-frequency performance of the antenna is a function of the size of the loop.

The new Nti ML200 'Megaloop' make this very simple. The kit consists of a small plastic antenna amplifier and matching box with a BNC connector for the output and two nutted studs for connection of the wire element, for which there are two options. One is a 5m loop made from Litz wire and intended for internal installation. The other uses a substantial PVC-coated stainless-steel element available in both 5m and 10m lengths for external use. We tried the 10m version of the latter arranged as a delta loop using a tree and the top of a mast as anchor points. The upper portion of the result was about 10m above ground.

The quality of the associated amplifier is crucial to the overall performance of a wideband loop antenna. The ML200's amplifier gain can be reduced by 9dB by an internal switch to cater for the 10m loop. Its frequency range to the -3dB points is 9kHz-170MHz in low-gain mode with a reduced upper limit of 110MHz in high gain. This is combined with a claimed IPI_3 of +40dBm and an IPI_2 of +85dBm, both with 200kHz spacing at 7MHz, and our testing gave us no grounds to doubt these excellent figures.

The ML200 invites comparison with one or two of the Wellbrook loop family and we trialled it against both an *Imperium* and an ALA1530S. We used a WinRadio Excalibur Pro as the test receiver since its S-meter calibration is known to be highly accurate and its ability to behave as a spectrum analyser gave some illuminating insights. The essence of the results could be summed up in a few sentences. The ML200 is better than the Wellbrook loops at very low frequencies insofar as it delivers between 10 and 16dB more to the receiver for similar noise levels. In the long-wave broadcast band the advantage again lies with the ML200 by perhaps 6-10dB. These results are entirely in line with expectation in view of the larger size (and hence larger aperture) of the ML200. In the MF region the performance of both antennas at our test location was generally very similar. Interestingly, however, above about 2MHz the Wellbrook loops proved to be slightly better – not because they produced stronger signals but because the signal/noise ratio was higher. Some considerable time was spent adjusting the orientation and location of the Wellbrook loops to ensure that this was not a function of the antennas' comparative positions. The conclusion after a good deal of testing was that the ML200 was consistently about 3dB worse than either Wellbrook loop in the shortwave region. However, we would not advance that figure with any certainty.

What we can reliably say is that the ML200 is a very good antenna indeed for general listening. If VLF and LF reception is one of your primary interests, a large-aperture loop such as the ML200 will deliver excellent results. Elsewhere in the AM broadcast spectrum it will also work extremely well. Both the antenna proper and the amplifier box are very well made and our only caveat is that we wish the manual gave advice on long-term weatherproofing of the connections. But overall the ML200 is an excellent antenna which should find a wide market.   **JN**

WRTH HF Receiver Guide 2016

Budget, Hand-held & Travel Portables

Maker	Model	Size	SEL	DR	OV	US$	£	€
AOR	AR8200D	H	***	***	***	750	450	580
C. Crane	CC Skywave	S	****	****	****	90	65	85
Degen	DE-1103	S	***	***	**	90	50	65
Eton	Satellit Grundig	S	****	****	****	200	125	165
Sangean	ATS-404	S	***	***	***	80	60	75
Sangean	ATS-909X	S	****	****	****	220	170	200
Sony	ICF-SW11	S	***	***	***	90	55	70
Sony	ICF-SW7600GR	S	****	****	****	118	115	150
Tecsun	PL-380	S	****	****	*****	40	40	50
Tecsun	PL-600	S	****	***	****	60	65	80
Tecsun	PL-660	S	***	****	****	118	108	140
Tecsun	PL-680	S	***	***	***	135	90	120

SDRs, Serious Shortwave & Semi-pro Receivers

Maker	Model	Size	SEL	DR	OV	US$	£	€
Afedri	SDR-Net	C	***	***	***	259	160	185
Alinco	DX-R8E	M	****	****	****	520	550	640
AOR	AR5001D	M	*****	****	****	4290	2990	3900
AOR	AR6000	L	****	*****	****	6500	5000	6500
AOR	AR8600	L	**	***	***	960	590	770
AOR	AR-DV1	M	****	****	****	1120	1200	1550
Apach Labs	ANAN-10	M	*****	****	****	1680	1395	1810
Bonito	1102S Radiojet	C	****	****	****	650	430	560
CommRadio	CR-1A	M	*****	****	*****	600	530	670
Cross Country	SDR-4+	C	****	****	****	295	180	220
Elad	FDM77	C	****	****	****	670	410	640
Etón	Satellit 750	L	***	***	***	300	260	320
FlexRadio	FLEX-1500	C	****	****	***	700	600	550
FunCube Dongle	Pro+	C	****	***	****	270	160	200
Icom	IC-718	L	***	****	****	665	590	770
Icom	IC-7600	L	*****	****	****	3400	2950	3800
Icom	IC-R9500	L	*****	*****	*****	13300	10700	13910
Microtelecom	Perseus	C	*****	*****	*****	1000	600	800
Palstar	R30	M	*****	*****	****	860	730	950
Reuter Elektronik	RDR54C	M	*****	*****	*****	4600	2730	3550
RFSpace	SDR-IQ	C	****	****	****	500	490	570
SDRplay	SDRplay	C	****	***	****	300	175	220
Ten-Tec	RX340	L	*****	*****	*****	4450	4000	5200
WinRadio	G31 Excalibur	C	*****	****	*****	950	585	710
WinRadio	G33 Excalibur Pro	C	*****	*****	*****	1650	1600	1900
WinRadio	G35 Excalibur Ultra	C	*****	*****	*****	5000	3800	4200
WinRadio	G313i	C	*****	****	*****	1200	1110	1440
WinRadio	G313e	C	*****	*****	*****	1200	1110	1440
WinRadio	G305e	C	****	****	****	750	700	910

KEY: SEL = Selectivity, DR = Dynamic Range, OV = Overall Value. C = SDR, H = Hand-held, L = Large, table top use, M = Medium, suitcase size, S = Small, easily portable.　　* = Avoid　** = Poor　*** = Fair　**** = Very Good　***** = Outstanding.
NOTE: Prices vary due to exchange rate fluctuations. Some models may be unavailable in certain markets.

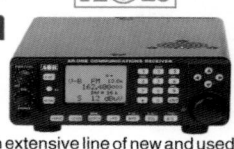

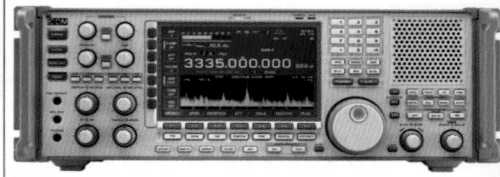

70TH
ANNIVERSARY
EDITION

A Brief History of
World Radio TV Handbook

Lund Johanssen to inform him. Lund Johanssen replied that he was planning to publish a whole book of information, and offered Frost the chance to help. Jens Frost readily agreed and initially worked for a few hours a day in the early morning before starting his job on the newspaper.

When the *World-Radio Handbook for Listeners* was published, its success was immediate. The first edition was intended only for readers in Denmark, but once its existence became known outside Denmark, there was a steady demand for it, and Lund Johanssen's company, World Publications, found itself dealing

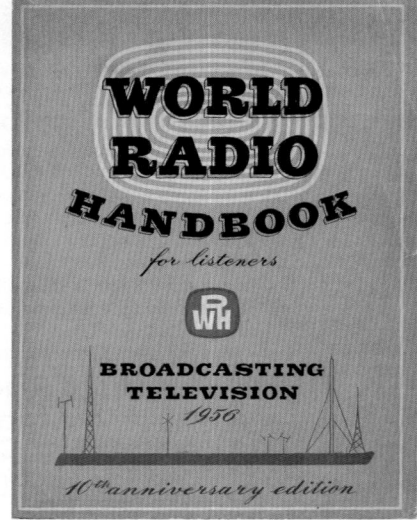

World Radio TV Handbook began as a result of the Nazi occupation of Denmark in World War II. Listening to foreign radio stations was forbidden, but many Danes tuned into the BBC and other broadcasters to find out what was really happening in the world. These broadcasts from overseas continued after the war ended, and so did the interest in shortwave listening. As a result, Mr 0. Lund Johanssen, who had published some early schedule guides before the war and provided information during it, started a newspaper column listing the schedules of the various stations.

A young journalist on a provincial newspaper, Jens Frost, noticed some errors in the listings based on his own observations, and wrote to Mr

1960s and early 1970s there was a *Summer Supplement*, a reduced version of *WRTH* that listed the summer schedules of the international broadcasters, and other revised data since that years' *WRTH* was published. Unfortunately this did not sell well, and had to be discontinued. The idea was later revived with a simple typed newsletter called *Downlink*, which continued until the end of the 1980s. Several editions of a book of articles called *How To Listen to the World* were also produced, but sales did nor justify a continuation of this title, and the articles were later absorbed into *WRTH*.

During the 1970s *WRTH* continued to increase in size as many new radio and TV stations came on air, or were reported to *WRTH* for the first time by a growing number of contributors. Eventually Jens Frost, who had worked alone

with orders from many other countries. As more television stations began to broadcast, TV listings were added to the *World Radio Handbook* and its title was changed to *World Radio TV Handbook*; soon to be known to everyone as 'WRTH'.

When Lund Johanssen retired in 1964, Jens Frost became Editor of the book, and an American involved in the TV business bought *WRTH* and attempted to increase sales in the TV industry. When this idea failed, he in turn looked for a new buyer, and *WRTH* was bought by the Billboard Corporation, who published the music industry reference *Billboard* magazine.

WRTH was not the only title produced in the Danish editorial office. For several years in the

since 1964, decided he needed some help. Andy Sennitt, who had been working at BBC Monitoring, was appointed as Assistant Editor in 1978. At the same time Jens Frost persuaded Larry Magne to write a regular article in *WRTH* reviewing and testing the latest shortwave receivers. This was a valuable addition to *WRTH*, and after Larry Magne left to work on his own publication, the equipment reviews were continued by Jonathan Marks. They are now produced by the Technical Editor of *WRTH*, John Nelson.

When Jens Frost retired, Andy Sennitt was appointed Editor and moved *WRTH* to the offices of a magazine owned by Billboard in The Netherlands. There he appointed Bart Kuperus as Assistant and later Managing Editor. Bart Kuperus's interest in TV and satellite broadcasting led him to write and produce the *WRTH Satellite Broadcasting Guide*. He also developed, together with Andy Sennitt, *The Travelers Guide*

to *World Radio,* showing SW broadcasts in major cities, and the *WRTH Equipment Buyers Guide.*

In 1994 Billboard, which had published *WRTH* for almost 30 years, became part of the VNU media group. VNU continued to publish *WRTH* until 1998 when Andy Sennitt and Bart Kuperus left the company. A new company in England, WRTH Publications, took over production of *WRTH* and appointed David Bobbett as Editor. Sean Gilbert joined him as Assistant Editor and, when David Bobbett left the company in 2002, Sean Gilbert was promoted to the new post of International Editor. *WRTH* is now run by Nicholas Hardyman as Publisher and National

Editor. In 2002 the latest in the long list of volumes of summer updates was produced in the form of *The Shortwave Guide* which showed the 'A' season schedules as colour bar graphs. Unfortunately sales did not grow and publication ceased after only one further volume. However, the bargraph was revived in 2011 in the form of the *WRTH Bargraph Frequency Guide,* available as a download or on CD for both the 'A' and 'B' seasons. Details of the 'A' season schedules and updated broadcaster information are also published as free pdf downloads on the website.

The *WRTH* editorial team has always been surprisingly small for such a detailed and authoritative reference book, but there is a good reason for this. *WRTH* relies on the hard work and good

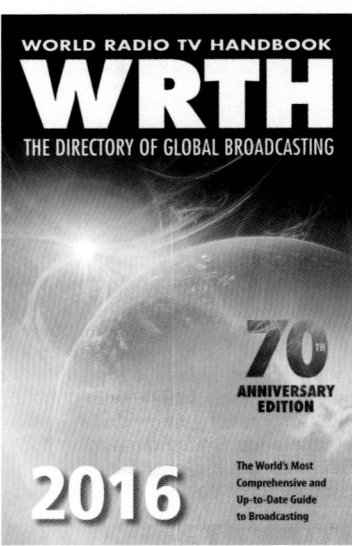

will of a large team of contributors throughout the world. Most of these dedicated enthusiasts work for no reward other than serving the radio community through their contributions. They are assisted in turn by information from many other industry specialists, enthusiasts and listeners.

These contributors are extremely loyal, and some have contributed to *WRTH* for over 60 years. The editorial team is further strengthened by Contributing Editors Mauno Ritola, Bernd Trutenau and Dave Kenny.

The editorial team at *WRTH* believes that the book only exists to serve its readers, and continually reviews the content and format to make it as accurate and easy to use as possible.

There have been a lot of changes over the past 70 years, and *WRTH* has had to change with them. But it has continued, and that continuity is a tribute to all the people, readers, contributors and editors, who have been involved with this extraordinary book.

Authority On Radio Communications

AR-DV1

SDR Digital Voice Receiver

The first software defined receiver of its kind to receive and decode virtually ALL popular digital modes.

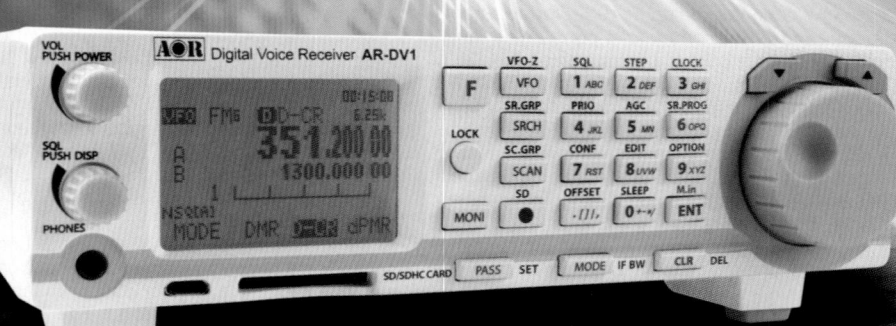

MOTOTRBO™ DMR™ dPMR™ APCO P25
NXDN™ Icom D-Star™ Digital CR
Yaesu Kenwood® Alinco EJ-47U

UK MW & LW Broadcasting: the first 95 years

Former BBC Senior Transmitter Engineer **Dave Porter,** *G4OYX, outlines the history and current use of MW & LW broadcasting in the UK*

Lisnagarvey in 1949 showing the impressive Blaw-Knox mast (Picture courtesy of Norman Marsden, G4BQN)

Experimental sound broadcasting was begun in the British Isles by the Marconi Company and other large electrical engineering manufacturers as far back as 1919. The British Broadcasting Company came into being in 1922, formed from Marconi and other commercial companies, and took over three 1.5 kilowatt transmitters: 2LO in London, 5IT in Birmingham and 2ZY in Manchester. Regular daily broadcasting on MW started from these stations during November 1922. A period of expansion followed and by 1925 over 20 MW stations were in operation. These were all low-power local services; situated in large towns and cities.

In July 1924 the first LW transmitter, 5XX, opened at Chelmsford. It was transferred to Daventry a year later to carry a nascent national service. Coverage initially extended to 150 miles or so on crystal set receivers from this 25kW service, but 5XX later provided a national service – programmed from London and available to the majority of the population – which was the forerunner of the National Programme.

On 1 January 1927 the British Broadcasting Company was dissolved and the British Broadcasting Corporation was constituted under Royal Charter. It was decided to combine the local stations in each area into one regional station, with an underlying programme support from London. This was known as the Regional Scheme. The scheme was executed with low-power stations being replaced by new studio centres and high-power transmitters, initially serving five regions of the British Isles. In 1927 the prototype of these regional transmitters, Daventry 5GB with a 50kW MW transmitter, was established in the Midlands.

THE REGIONAL SCHEME

Brookmans Park, 25 miles north of London, opened in 1929 as the first true regional centre. Operating two 50kW MW services from the same site was uncharted territory. The Regional Service ran from the north side of the building, with the National Service from the south side, and there was no direct connection between the two as there were concerns about the possibilities of cross-modulation. In the event this was not a problem and a common earth system could be used at all future stations.

In 1931 the second regional centre was set up at Moorside Edge covering Manchester, Leeds and the industrial parts of Northern England. As at Brookmans Park, this new site generated its own 220 VDC electricity supply by diesel engines since at that time there was no public electricity supply to the site.

A service for Central Scotland was started in 1932 at Westerglen, near Falkirk, followed in 1933 by its twin at Washford in Somerset to cover the west of England, and also Wales by direct sea path. The last of the main five regional centres was inaugurated at Wychbold, near Droitwich, in 1934. The 5XX 200kHz Daventry service was transferred to a 150kW transmitter with 700-foot masts, and the 5GB 50kW MW service acquired a newly-developed directional antenna aimed at Birmingham.

Lisnagarvey, near Lisburn in Northern Ireland, followed in 1936 with a Marconi 100kW transmitter and a US-manufactured 'Blaw-Knox' mast radiator of two pyramids each 250 feet long joined at their bases. This site was the first to have mains electricity from the start, with diesel alternators as back-up.

Expansion continued with Burghead (100kW: 1936) on the Moray Firth, then Penmon (8kW: 1937) on Anglesey for North Wales. Later that year Stagshaw, near Newcastle-upon-Tyne, commenced with a 100kW STC transmitter. Redmoss (10kW: 1938) near Aberdeen was followed by Start Point (100kW: 1939) in Devon; Clevedon (20kW: 1939) near Bristol was the twelfth and final station.

THE SECOND WORLD WAR

The Scheme was now complete but regrettably did not last long as from 3 September 1939 the UK was at war with Nazi Germany and two national Home Service synchronised groups were set up on 767kHz (Northern transmitters) and 668kHz (Southern transmitters). Eight transmitters also used 877kHz for the Forces Programme. The groups were intended to prevent the enemy using solo stations for direction-finding. The BBC also used Redmoss, Clevedon and Penmon on 565kHz synchronised with the Radio Eireann service from Athlone for the same purpose. Sixty-one so-called 'H Group' sites were used for Civil Defence broadcasts, with transmitter powers from 50W to 1kW. All these were on 1474kHz. Longwave was not in use.

The BBC had until now used LW and MW only for domestic services and were against the idea of using them for external services. But with the Nazis utilising their LW 'Deutschlandsender' for propaganda purposes, permission was given for external broadcasting on LW and MW in addition to the SW Overseas Service.

In 1939 an STC 140kW unit destined for Lithuania was commandeered for Brookmans Park, with two Marconi 150kW units for Moorside Edge. Westerglen and Moorside Edge each benefitted from the installation of RCA-50E 50kW units via the US Lend-Lease programme.

The Overseas Service Extension programme was started pre-war and OSE6 at Droitwich started broadcasting in February 1940 from a new building with a paralled pair of Marconi 200kW transmitters on 1149kHz into a horizontally polarised antenna for maximum skywave during darkness. Start Point on 1050kHz was also used at 180kW during darkness for the European service, and after the Allied invasion of occupied Europe the antenna pattern was altered for maximum radiation into France.

The four English Electric diesel alternators at Droitwich in 1935 (Picture courtesy of John Phillips)

Three 50kW Marconi Doherty transmitters at Droitwich in 1978 for 693kHz (Picture courtesy of John Phillips)

Featuring heavily protected accommodation, OSE5 at Ottringham near Hull was on air by 1943 with four 200kW transmitters. Three were combined for 600kW on LW with one at 200kW on 977kHz. It was on a direct sea path to the Third Reich. The Political Warfare Executive also had the 600kW MW 'Aspidistra' station at Crowborough which was used by the BBC when it was not required for 'black' and 'grey' broadcasting.

POST WAR DEVELOPMENTS

Peace-time broadcasting restarted on 29 July 1945 with the continuation of the Home Service and the new Light Programme. By May 1946 the Third Programme had started from Droitwich with MW fill-in services from some of the wartime H Group sites. A 10kW service from Bartley near Southampton was added in 1946 to improve Home Service coverage. In 1948 new STC 100kW transmitters were installed at Washford and Westerglen. The Overseas Services continued from Ottringham and Crowborough.

Implementation of the Copenhagen Plan, a new wavelength plan for Europe, confirmed Daventry as the home of the Third Programme with a new 150kW transmitter. A 725-foot mast radiator at Dodford some 2.4 km away ensured both an anti-fading service and one not affected by the antennas and masts on the HF site. Despite the new plan there was serious competition for channels in Europe and interference was evident, so the decision was taken to build a VHF/FM transmission system at 88-108MHz. Wrotham in Kent was first on-air in May 1955 followed by many other FM transmitters to achieve national coverage within ten years. Each site radiated the Home, Light and Third Programmes at high quality and free of interference.

This development of FM could have spelled the end for MW and LW operations, but the Cold War, the transistor portable and offshore pirate

stations ensured otherwise. The Cold War meant that many of the unused H Group stations and some new sites were established with pairs of BBC-modified RCA ET-4336 250W transmitters as 'Deferred Facility' sites for Civil Defence use in case of a nuclear attack. The early transistors used in portable radios could not function at VHF so these receivers revolutionised listening at home and on the move, but only on LW and MW. The offshore pirate-radio stations of the mid-1960s were extremely popular and, following their closure by the UK government, the BBC was asked to launch a similar MW service. Called Radio 1, this station began in September 1967, broadcast by 17 transmitters on the former Light Programme MW channel, and proved as popular as its pirate predecessors.

Apart from the installation of some in-house units at Burghead, Droitwich, Lisnagarvey, Stagshaw and Start Point in the early 1970s, no more money was spent on AM sites until the Geneva Plan was implemented in 1978 when many 50kW and 10kW Doherty transmitters were commissioned country-wide. But for the BBC and independent local radio throughout the 1970s, MW services were considered paramount' preference being given on air to the MW outlet over the parallel VHF/FM one.

Since the transfer of BBC local and regional services to FM and DAB many of the former BBC regional stations, with their three high-powered MW transmitters, have been taken over by commercial services. Many countries in Europe have been closing their MW and LW services over the past decade, but in the UK only Orfordness has been closed. The BBC continues to use many sites for Radio 5, the Asian Network and local radio, and of course Droitwich on LW.

After 95 years it looks very likely that MW and LW services in the UK will be in fine shape to celebrate their 100th anniversary.

70 Years of Reception

To mark our sixtieth edition ten years ago we attempted an overview of receiver history and technology during the life of *WRTH*, i.e. from the 1940s to the present day. We looked in detail at particular receivers which seemed to us to represent important turning points in design or caught the spirit of their times. For our seventieth edition we have tried to bring the story up to date and to reflect the extraordinary scale and scope of technological change taking place over the period.

When *WRTH* was first published the *superheterodyne* technique was well established and the majority of new receivers coming on to the commercial and military markets made use of it. In the "superhet" a particular band of incoming radio transmissions is mixed with the output of a variable-frequency oscillator to produce a single frequency – the *intermediate frequency* or IF – which is amplified, filtered and detected. The result is a receiver which is much easier to use and with considerably better selectivity than earlier *tuned radio frequency* (TRF) units.

By the beginning of World War II there were three main types of receiver. Mass-produced products for domestic broadcast listening shared the market with rather more elaborate items intended mainly for short-wave broadcast and amateur reception. Notable examples of the latter were the National SW3 and the Eddystone 'AllWorld' series, both of which used pre-superhet TRF technology, and the superheterodyne Hammarlund HQ and Hallicrafters 'Sky' family. The marketing men of the day referred to them as "communications receivers" and the terminology was soon extended to the later professional and military models. There was also a smaller number of higher-performance receivers intended for military or professional purposes. Many of the latter, such as the National HRO (rumour has it that the letters stood for "Hell of a Rush Order") and early Hallicrafters were American.

The wartime period saw many advances in electronic technology, some of which were associated with the need to mass-produce rugged and reliable high-grade receivers in large quantities for military communications and surveillance purposes. Typical examples were the Marconi R1155 and CR100 from the UK and the AR88, BC312, BC342 and BC348 from the USA. Many later found their way on to the surplus market.

The invention of the point-contact transistor in 1947 marked a profoundly important new stage in electronic development. Initially these devices did not find their way into radio receivers and the better examples of the 1950s were still based on thermionic valves. Arguably the classic receivers

The 1940s – RCA AR88

The AR88 was introduced in 1941 as a potential replacement for the HRO in intercept applications. It was produced in very large quantities by RCA and several sub-contractors. The original version was the AR88D with the AR88LF following about a year later. The main differences between them are the intermediate frequencies (455 and 735kHz respectively) and coverage although for some reason they also have different audio output valves. Both weigh about 45kg.

The original specifications quoted a sensitivity of 5mV for a 20dB S/N ratio in CW mode and a well-cared-for example will probably display very good sensitivity and selectivity, at least on the lower bands. By Band 6 (22-32MHz in the D, 19-30.5MHz in the LF) the tuning rate is becoming a little fast for comfort and the sensitivity is deteriorating somewhat as the noise figure starts to increase. However, the very well-weighted tuning knob and a front-panel layout conducive to ease of use over long periods mean that the AR88 is still delightfully easy to operate and can produce very pleasant audio quality from AM broadcast stations. If you have the room to house it and the strength to lift it, an AR88 in good condition is a pleasure to own and use.

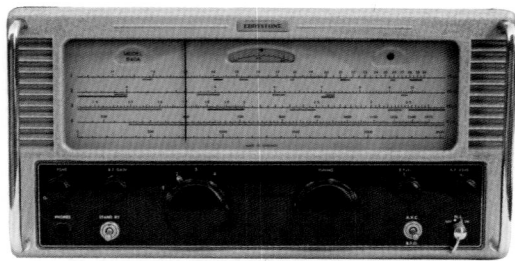

The 1950s – Eddystone 840A

The Eddystone 840A is a relatively simple receiver covering 480kHz-30MHz in four bands. It was introduced in 1954 as a development of the 740 and used a similar single-conversion architecture with a 1.6MHz intermediate frequency. It was marketed as a 'cabin receiver' and designed for both AC and DC mains supplies.

To modern eyes the most noticeable feature of the 840A is its extremely slow tuning. The dial pointer only moves about 5mm for each rotation of the tuning knob and it is a little unfortunate that the implied accuracy of the frequency readout is rather optimistic. However, the provision of

a logging scale at the top of the dial allows the user to return to a frequency quite easily.

Although by modern standards a little short of sensitivity, an 840A in good condition is a delight to use with its large and well-weighted tuning control placed adjacent to the equally large bandswitch knob. A little practice is needed to make CW and SSB reception possible, with careful use of the RF gain and BFO controls being required to obtain good-quality results. On SSB the receiver is not really stable enough and frequent adjustments are required. That said, the 840A was a classic and many remain in service.

of the period were the Collins 75-series marketed for the radio amateur and largely based on the professional 51-J and R390. These introduced for the first time the combination of a crystal-controlled first oscillator and variable first IF using permeability tuning. Amongst other advantages this allowed a similar degree of bandspreading on all bands irrespective of absolute frequency. In the 75A-3 Collins also introduced the *mechanical filter* offering important improvements in the shape of the IF filter passband.

Another line of development began in the 1950s and its consequences are very much with us today. One of the main problems of communications receivers is the achievement of *frequency stability*. In essence this is the property whereby a receiver can be tuned to a particular frequency and remain there without 'drifting' away from it. In the conventional superheterodyne this was a difficult issue requiring an alarming and expensive amount of mechanical precision. In fact at very high frequencies – an area of the RF spectrum which was becoming more interesting in the 1950s – the conventional superhet becomes unworkable. The advent of the crystal-controlled local oscillator and tunable first IF relieved the situation to some extent but it is difficult to maintain good performance over a very large tuning range. Generally speaking, a conventional tunable IF is restricted to a usable range of about 500kHz. This implies that coverage of the 3-30MHz HF spectrum would require 27 crystal oscillators and the concomitant switching, which is bordering on the impractical. Happily a brilliant insight by Dr Trevor Wadley during the wartime development of a

wavemeter led to the development of an exceedingly elegant system for drift cancellation. Known then as the *Wadley Loop* and a precursor of today's *phase-locked loop* or PLL, this made use of the harmonics of a 1MHz crystal oscillator together with a combination of mixers and bandpass filters. At the cost of some rather complex circuitry the result was that drift could be reduced to the negligible drift of a single crystal oscillator.

While Wadley's ideas were taking shape, a small British company called Racal (an acronym derived from the names of its founders, Raymond Brown and George Calder Cunningham) had expressed a wish to acquire manufacturing rights to the Collins 51-J in the UK. On this basis the company had been awarded a contract with the Royal Navy in 1953 for the supply of 200. Racal initially proposed to use a substantial portion of British components but Collins insisted that only American parts were to be used. The situation was only resolved after a visit by Collins to Racal's then-primitive manufacturing facility, after which they decided that Racal was not in any position to undertake manufacture of the 51-J and withdrew the rights. This left Racal still holding the contract with the Royal Navy and with no very obvious way of fulfilling it.

Nowadays a PLL and associated circuitry can be easily implemented in a single integrated circuit, but in the 1950s it was a formidably difficult undertaking to design and build a Wadley-loop receiver using valves. In a remarkable sequence of coincidences Racal's founders and Dr Wadley met, exchanged ideas and quickly decided that a receiver using the Wadley loop was feasible.

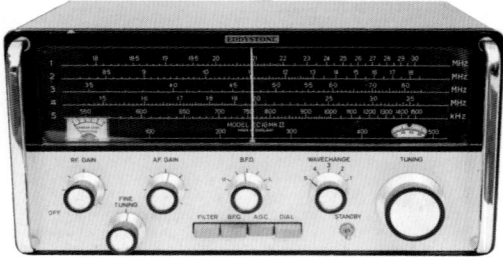

The 1960s – Eddystone EC-10

By modern standards a rather indifferent performer, the Eddystone EC10 is important because it was one of the first communications receivers to use semiconductors throughout. Introduced late in 1963 as a single-conversion design with a 465kHz intermediate frequency, the battery-powered EC10 covered 550kHz-30MHz in five ranges. Regrettably its germanium transistors had (and have) numerous drawbacks compared to modern silicon devices.

There were several variants of the EC10 offering options such as LF reception and the 'Mk II' version marketed in 1969 featured an additional fine-tuning control and an S-meter (rather grandly entitled a 'Carrier Level Meter' by the manufacturer). Even with these refinements a present-day user will find the EC10 decidedly short of sensitivity and probably also rather noisy. The lack of pre-selection and low IF give rise to noticeable image problems at the higher frequencies and Eddystone's claimed figure of 20dB at 20MHz rather glosses over the fact that on the highest band it is considerably worse! At the higher frequencies there is also a considerable shortage of dial bandspread.

Although not the most outstanding item ever manufactured by Eddystone, the EC10 is a good example of an early transistorized communications receiver. Some 17,000 examples were made until production ceased in 1977.

Racal assembled a prototype in record time and demonstrated it to the Royal Navy in May 1954. Notwithstanding its protracted and difficult birth, the resulting RA17 was the finest HF receiver of its era and its lineal descendants are still with us. Production began in 1955 and continued until 1967 with something in excess of 10,000 units being manufactured.

The Wadley-loop scheme and indeed phase-locked loop systems in general do not readily lend themselves to low-cost mass production using discrete components. In consequence receivers incorporating such architectures initially remained relatively uncommon outside professional and military environments. However, the invention of the integrated circuit in 1959 and the enormously rapid expansion of interest in digital techniques best suited to exploit the properties of ICs changed this situation remarkably quickly. By the early 1970s the essential portions of a PLL-based receiver were readily available as low-cost integrated circuits. At the same time as these were beginning to make their mark, another development of great importance to receiver technology took place. This was the realisation that a phase-locked loop could form the heart of what came to be known as a *synthesizer*. Reduced to its lowest terms, the essence of a PLL is the comparison between the phase of a signal from some form of reference and the signal from a *voltage-controlled oscillator* (VCO). The *phase comparator* generates a signal proportional to the phase difference and applies it to the VCO in such a way as to reduce it. So if the VCO frequency drifts, the phase comparator will drive it in the opposite direction so as to reduce the error. By this means the VCO output is phase-locked to the reference frequency. Since the latter can be derived from a high-stability source such as a quartz crystal, the result is a very stable free-running oscillator.

The key to the ability of a frequency synthesizer to generate multiple frequencies is a circuit element called a *divider* which is placed between the VCO output and the input of the phase comparator. Nowadays this usually takes the form of a digital counter known as a *programmable divider* which in a receiver is linked to the tuning control. With the addition of the divider the loop still functions as described above but the VCO will now be running at a frequency multiplied by the division ratio, which changes as the receiver is tuned. Described in this way the system sounds rather complicated and the mathematics of phase-locked loops and synthesizers are certainly rather daunting. However, they are easy to implement using modern integrated circuits and because the divider is 'digital' in nature it then becomes simple to integrate the synthesizer with other digital elements or a microprocessor.

One might think that the invention of the synthesizer and the consequent ability to generate accurate and exact frequencies was a matter of more interest to transmitter engineers than receiver designers. It is certainly the case that synthesizers were enthusiastically adopted by transmitter manufacturers as the solution to a good many problems. However, the potential of the synthesizer for forming a repeatable and almost drift-free receiver local oscillator was also immensely attractive. This was especially the case when it was realized by the receiver industry that synthesizers naturally operated in fixed step sizes. These could be made to correspond to the 'channels' in which radio broadcasts normally take place. Another advantage was the ease with which a little additional circuitry enables direct display of the tuned frequency. In consequence the vast majority of modern television and radio receivers use digitally controlled synthesizers as the tunable elements. Amongst other things this allows the required frequency to be directly selected by a tuning knob, keypad, PC interface or a remote data stream. It also allows for very easy implementation of a variety of scanning, search and memory functions. Here again, it would be rather difficult to implement a synthesizer and all its control and display circuitry in discrete components but it is almost trivially simple to do so with the aid of integrated circuits.

A curious consequence of these developments was that the overall quality of most receivers intended for the consumer market deteriorated in the 1970s and 1980s. The older generation of receivers required high standards of mechanical design in order to work at all well whereas synthesizer-based receivers are not reliant on mechanical ruggedness in the same way. For example, the Eddystone dial drive of

yore was a beautifully made item of solid precision equipment which was a joy to behold and no doubt horribly expensive to manufacture. A contemporary digital display provided much more information at a much lower price but by comparison was light and relatively fragile. Hence receivers of the period tended to be much more mechanically lightweight than their predecessors and had tuning mechanisms that could perhaps be best described as adequate. Equally, strong-signal handling had seldom been an issue with valve-based receivers whereas it became a very large issue with early transistorised units and an even larger one with many of their successors. Even professional receivers were not exempt. Although considerably smaller and lighter, Racal's successor to the RA17 family – the RA217 – displayed a considerable propensity to front-end overload which did not endear it to its users. It was not until the late 1970s that the limitations of discrete transistor circuitry began to be successfully addressed and some elaborate and costly techniques had to be introduced to address them. The excellent Racal RA1772 introduced in 1975 showed the way forward. It used a hard-driven quad-FET mixer and elaborate synthesiser circuitry to minimise reciprocal mixing problems and provide the highest possible dynamic range. It remains a classic which can still out-perform many modern receivers.

With the advent of the personal computer in the 1980s, interest began to be expressed in the possibilities of interfacing the PC with a receiver.

The 1970s – Barlow Wadley XCR-30

The Barlow Wadley XCR-30 was produced by the Barlows Manufacturing Company Ltd of New Germany, Natal between 1969 and 1981, with some 20,000 being made. At first glance the receiver looks like any other multi-band portable of its era. However, internally the unit uses the Wadley-loop principle to give a combination of frequency stability, accuracy and resettability which was unprecedented for its day. The XCR-30 tunes in 1MHz segments from 500kHz to 30MHz and caters for AM, SSB and CW.

Performance at the lower frequencies with the supplied telescopic whip antenna is not very

good but sensitivity and selectivity in the HF region are excellent and lack of drift is very noticeable compared with its contemporaries. Even SSB reception remains stable for quite long periods. The calibration is fairly accurate.

The XCR-30's internal architecture was revolutionary for its day and although resembling other receivers of its era in being prone to front-end overload, it can still turn in a very good performance in comparison with contemporary transportable receivers of the same size. Only the lack of a digital display and the slightly counter-intuitive tuning procedure hint at its age.

The 1980s – Kenwood R-1000

Introduced in 1980 as a consumer-grade receiver, the R-1000 embodies many of the modern techniques discussed in the main article. It covers 200kHz to 30MHz in thirty 1MHz bands, making use of a rotary 1MHz band-selector control similar to that in the XCR-30 but adding a digital readout of the frequency selected by the 'tuning' knob.

High sensitivity across its coverage quickly endeared the R-1000 to users, as did the remarkable lack of drift and the ease with which stations could be tuned. A striking feature of the R-1000 was the noise blanker which dealt effectively with repetitive short-pulse interference. More or less standard nowadays on reasonably high-grade receivers, the noise blanker was still something of a novelty in the early 1980s.

The R-1000 holds up well when compared with today's products and only a slight shortage of strong-signal performance and a rather indifferent signal/noise ratio betray its age. The latter is a consequence of the synthesizer being somewhat noisy by modern standards, the importance of low phase noise not having been fully appreciated. The lack of a notch filter and passband tuning is a little limiting but for its price the R-1000 represented very good value and it is still a useful receiver.

Amongst many other things this conferred almost unlimited memory space and hence the facility for labelling, logging and instant store and recall of essentially any amount of frequencies. It also allowed long-term logging of signal strength, a wide variety of scanning and searching modes and – in later iterations – real-time decoding of a wide variety of special modes such as RTTY, data, fax and the like. The Drake R8 and its successors were amongst the earliest receivers to embody the facility for remote software control via the industry-standard RS-232 interface although others soon followed. Today practically every amateur transceiver has comprehensive interface facilities, as do many semi-professional receivers.

With the falling cost of the microprocessor in the 1980s, it was logical for receiver manufacturers to take advantage of the extensive facilities which could be provided. Multiple VFOs, extensive memories, direct frequency entry via a keypad, assorted scan and search techniques and a variety of useful functionality became available.

The 1990s – Drake R8

The R8 was one of Drake's last products for the amateur and semi-professional market. It is a microprocessor-controlled, synthesized all-mode receiver designed with sensitivity and dynamic range very much in mind. The R8 covers 100kHz to 30MHz and provides AM, FM, USB, LSB, RTTY and CW reception. For AM reception there is a selectable synchronous detector. Other useful features included an RF preamplifier and attenuator, twin VFOs and 100 memories. Each of these stored a variety of information appropriate to the frequency, such as bandwidth, mode, AGC setting, notch filter state, and whether or not the synchronous detector was in or out of circuit.

The R8 is still a very good receiver and its combination of extensive functionality and fine performance remains attractive. Only a mild lack of mechanical ruggedness and rather indifferent ergonomics suggest that it was built down to a price rather than up to a specification. For some reason the R8 did not embody flywheel tuning and the knob feels a little spongy in consequence. Although the actual function is very smooth, rapid re-tuning is not a pleasurable experience. The R8 is perhaps at its best when connected to a PC, when some of its ergonomic shortcomings fade into the background and its excellent RF performance shines through.

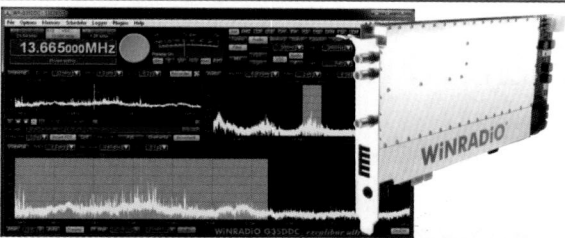

The modern age – WinRadio Excalibur Ultra

In the past ten years or so the software-defined receiver has advanced from being a laboratory curiosity to defining the current state of the art. Early SDRs could record and replay segments of the RF spectrum a few hundred kilohertz wide. Astonishingly the WinRadio Excalibur Ultra features a maximum selectable real-time recording and processing bandwidth of 32MHz. To put that into perspective, it amounts to the entire long-wave, MF and HF spectrum! As if that were not enough it can be configured as three separate receivers all capable of similar performance.

Physically the Excalibur Ultra is a nondescript internal PCIe card. Its useful frequency range is 3kHz-45MHz with a tuning resolution of 1Hz throughout. In the HF bands its MDS is between -127 and -131dBm in a 2.8kHz SSB bandwidth, entirely on a par with what would be expected with a very high-grade conventional professional receiver. The only drawback is that the computer used with the Excalibur Ultra SDR and its like can hardly have too much memory, hard-drive capacity or processor speed.

It is very difficult to imagine that in sheer performance terms a receiver of the calibre of the Excalibur Ultra will ever be supplanted.

For a time it seemed that 'bells and whistles' were more important than outright RF performance although some manufacturers remembered their priorities. By the late 1980s receivers such as the Kenwood R-5000 and Yaesu FRG-100 were offering very respectable performance and versatility for relatively low cost.

With the advent of the twenty-first century there has been a strong tendency for high-grade receivers to become almost fully digital in nature. In these units, what is usually referred to as *digital signal processing* or DSP takes over from some or almost all analogue functions. In principle this approach can confer many benefits. One is that the IF filters exist solely as software and it is consequently not difficult to arrange for as many as are required, with properties which can be easily defined and specified. By conventional standards the resulting shape factors of around 1·15 coupled with negligible passband ripple are astonishingly good, as is the phase linearity.

In the last few years DSP architectures have been augmented to produce the *software-defined receiver*. In the SDR the RF and mixer stages of a conventional superheterodyne give way to what is referred to as *direct down-conversion* (DDC). In effect the fixed IF generated by the RF and mixer stage is replaced by a technique in which the entire spectrum of interest is digitised as a whole. A SIGINT organisation with access to enough supercomputing power might well be able to process all the resulting signals simultaneously in real time. For the rest of us, a smaller portion is selected by a process known as *decimation* and down-converted for a PC to perform the filtering and demodulation functions using digital processing techniques implemented in software.

Given enough hard-drive capacity in the associated computer, large parts of the RF spectrum can be recorded en masse and subjected to off-line analysis as required. A high-performance modern SDR such as almost any of the WinRadio family represents the current apotheosis of the radio receiver designer's art.

Comparing an SDR such as the WinRadio Excalibur to a 1943-vintage AR88 is a fascinating exercise. In many ways the comparison shows how far we have come but it also reminds us of some eternal verities. Ergonomics still matters as much as outright capability. There have been several so-called 'professional' receivers that are not at all pleasant to operate for extended periods despite their excellent performance and many DSP receivers are needlessly difficult to use because of poor software design. Reliability and what might be called maintainability are both extremely important factors. Furthermore, it is very doubtful whether any contemporary receiver irrespective of its architecture will be either functional or repairable seventy years from now.

We naturally hope that *WRTH* will be extant in another seventy years and that 'broadcasting' will still exist in some form or other. But it requires more courage than we possess to attempt to predict the future of any product involving electronic technology. Both the nature of radio and broadcasting in general and social attitudes to them have changed enormously in the last seventy years and will undoubtedly continue to do so. What is very evident is that many radio receivers have already become classic artefacts which are a pleasure to own and operate, and it will be fascinating to see whether any of today's receivers become classics in the same way.

Radio in Timor-Leste

*WRTH contributor **David Foster** has been involved with Timor-Leste for many years and now raises funds for, and volunteers at, local community projects. Here he outlines the part radio played in the struggle for independence, and its continuing importance*

Looking down on Timor-Leste's capital city Dili

It took a failed rebellion in 1959 to kick start radio broadcasting in the neglected and almost forgotten colony of Portuguese Timor in South-East Asia. One of the ringleader's so-called crimes was to have listened to foreign broadcasts from Brazzaville, Moscow and Beijing. Belatedly realising that a radio vacuum existed in the territory, the Portuguese regime gave birth to Emissora de Radiodifusão de Timor in the capital city Dili.

Shortwave was the easiest way to cover the country and so a 1kW transmitter was established on 3268kHz. Reception of it overseas was always an achievement. In 1972 it was replaced by a 10kW unit on 3668kHz and by 1975 the station had added MW and FM transmitters on 1560kHz and 100MHz.

The Carnation Revolution in Portugal in 1974 led to the legalisation of political parties in Timor in the lead up to local elections planned for 1976. Parties were allowed airtime on the Dili station to announce their policies although they often descended into slanderous slanging matches.

Portuguese Timor's giant neighbour Indonesia did not stand idly by. In an effort to destabilise its small neighbour by claiming that most of the new parties were either communist, or fascist and neo-colonialist, the Indonesian secret service set up Operation Komodo. Masquerading as a trading company in Kupang in Indonesian West Timor, it commenced with the broadcast training of Timorese sympathetic to integration of Portuguese Timor into Indonesia.

Broadcasts got under way in January 1975 using a variety of station identifications which included Radio Ramelau (Timor's highest mountain), Radio Lorosae (Rising Sun, meaning East) and Radio Timor Liberdade. It was well heard on 3550kHz with a 10kW transmitter apparently borrowed from Radio Republik Indonesia Kupang which had previously utilised 3385 kHz. It was reported also to have used other frequencies and possibly to have attempted to jam the Dili station.

The psychological warfare propaganda must have worked its evil spell as discord was sown to the point that political party UDT staged a coup in Dili in August 1975, taking over the radio station from the Portuguese. The Fretilin party immediately staged a counter coup and soon seized control of the country but in the process the main transmitters were destroyed.

Fretilin had to resort to an ex-Portuguese Army low-power transmitter which was often barely audible even in nearby Darwin. Despite that, Radio Maubere (Radio of the Peasant-Folk), became Timor's tenuous link to the outside world.

East Timor, through the agency of Fretilin, unilaterally declared its independence on 28 November 1975. But celebrations were short-lived as Indonesia invaded nine days later, capturing Dili after a brief struggle.

The Indonesian propaganda station in Kupang on 3550kHz began to identify as Radio Dili and a puppet provisional government of East Timor was formed. It was the start of a very tough twenty-four years of resistance to occupation by the East Timorese people.

Radio Maubere was forced to head for the hills to become a clandestine operation. The 40 kilogram transmitter was either carried by Timor pony or a massive soldier who lugged it on his back through the rugged trails. When they reached a high enough point, they would transmit the latest developments then quickly flee before the Indonesian military could track them down. Frequency of choice was 3804kHz but other channels used were 5270 and 9965kHz. The broadcasts continued until the end of 1978 when the radio operators were eventually captured.

In the meantime the provisional government initiated its own shortwave activity on 3850kHz. When East Timor was integrated into Indonesia as its twenty-seventh province in July 1976, Radio Republik Indonesia took over the responsibility for broadcasting. The 3550kHz station straightaway began to identify as RRI Kupang, revealing the true nature of its whereabouts.

RRI Dili used various shortwave channels until 1995 including 2456kHz with 300 Watts, and

Mountain scenery with Timor ponies

3120 and 3305kHz each with 10kW. In the 1980s it even broadcast a 24-hour service. Medium wave was introduced in 1986 on 684kHz (variable) and FM was reported as arriving around 1990 on 88.2, 93.0 and 105.0MHz.

The only head of state to visit East Timor during the Indonesian occupation was Pope John Paul II in 1989. Perhaps not unconnected to that event, the Catholic Diocese of Dili was afterwards permitted to open Radio Timor Kmanek (Beautiful Timor) which broadcast on 1404kHz and 98.5MHz. In common with all other non-government stations in Indonesia at the time, the only news it could present was relayed from RRI.

Two other private stations in Dili received official sanction. One was Radio Suara Lorosae on 963kHz which formed a part of the Top FM network which was owned by the Armed Forces. The other was Radio Suara Beringin on 936kHz.

After staring defeat in the face for so many years, the East Timorese guerrilla resistance regrouped in 1997 to put Radio Falintil on the air. It broadcast on FM, powered by a car battery, from close by the village of Remexio near Dili.

Caving in to world opinion, the Indonesian government offered East Timor an independence referendum in 1999. In the three month lead-up, Radio UNAMET (United Nations Mission in East Timor) broadcast one-hour programmes over RRI Dili. In addition, student activists launched Radio Matebian Lian, meaning Radio Spirit Voice. After one or two nights in one place, they moved elsewhere, crisscrossing the mountainous terrain by foot. In August one of its journalists was shot dead by Indonesian police while covering the pro-independence campaign. Four days later the transmitter was destroyed in Maliana, and its official premises in Dili torched by Timorese militias.

Following the resounding vote in favour of independence, the Indonesian army and its militia supporters engaged in an orgy of destruction, with 80% of the country's infrastructure purposefully destroyed or damaged.

Staff at RRI Dili were evacuated to West Timor with any equipment they could carry before the studio buildings were gutted. An Australian-led international peace keeping force arrived shortly after, quelled the violence and paved the way for the United Nations to take charge.

Radio Timor Kmanek, which had amazingly escaped relatively unscathed, was first back on air. Radio UNAMET sprang back into action after the chaos, initially setting up studios in Darwin which then relayed programs via Radio Timor Kmanek. FM transmitters were then promptly put in place in Dili and Maliana and a 5kW unit commenced a 24-hour service on 684kHz. Radio Falintil returned triumphantly to Dili but was required to change its name to A Voz de Esperança, the Voice of Hope. Disturbingly, it was located in the Indonesia Special Services HQ, which had been used for interrogation and torture.

JOJO Radio, Dili

In quick succession UNAMET gave way to UNTAET (UN Transitional Administration in East Timor), and its broadcasting arm, Radio UNTAET, expanded the FM network so that after a year there were relays in all districts.

New found freedoms never before experienced allowed the development of community stations from the year 2000 onwards in Dili and all the regional centres. They were supported by a plethora of foreign government and non-government organisations. Starting from scratch was no easy task. Problems abounded, including lack of electricity and fuel for generators, limited training, equipment maintenance, volunteers leaving for paid employment, inability to obtain advertising revenue, loss of donors and uncertain media law. However, local communities were so keen to see them succeed that they resorted to ritual blessings so the stations could keep functioning. By and large they succeeded.

Student-focused Radio Rakambia in Dili was donated a handy mobile transmitter. It was used in 2000 to great effect at different points along the border to assure East Timorese taking refuge in West Timor that it was safe to return. Radio Comunidade Maliana's initial purpose was the same. A Dutch NGO had the idea of distributing wind-up radios in Viqueque but was told no stations were audible. Their answer was to build Radio Povo (Radio of the People).

In the meantime, foreign relays took to the airwaves. Australia's ABC-operated youth network JJJ plus the News and Parliamentary network were fired up quickly. The sessions of parliament were sufficiently unpopular with Australian peace keepers that it soon changed to relaying Radio Australia, and then ABC Perth. It also took a sprinkling of other station programmes such as Radio New Zealand, Radio Netherlands and even commercial 3AW from Melbourne. RDP Internacional from Portugal broadcast from Dili and Baucau, and RDP Antena 1 from Dili. A Voz de Esperança carried Voice of America programmes for a couple of hours a day. Finally, the BBC got into gear when Princess Anne opened its FM outlet in Dili in 2005.

On 20 May 2002 East Timor became the Democratic Republic of Timor-Leste. Since then the radio environment has continued to develop. Radio UNTAET has bequeathed all its facilities to Radio Timor-Leste. More community stations have taken off. A handful of quasi-commercial stations are trying their luck. Two universities have launched into the broadcasting field and a technical high school near Baucau broadcasts intermittent programmes.

Media organisations have branched out, not the least Radio STL, the radio arm of newspaper Suara Timor Lorosae, as well as Radio CRC from the Community Radio Centre, and Radio Liberdade, affiliated with the Timor-Leste Media Development Centre. Sixteen stations receive support from the Timor-Leste Community Radio Association. Apart from Radio Timor Kmanek, religious organisations are sending their messages through the Diocese of Baucau's Radio Fini Lorosae (Seed of the East), Christian Vision's Radio Voz in Dili and the Seventh Day Adventist Voice of Hope also in Dili.

In a significant development, the Fretilin party instituted a new version of Radio Maubere in 2011 with a nation-wide network to rival Radio Timor-Leste. It took over the political mantle from A Voz de Esperança which had been forced to close several years earlier after not being able to make ends meet.

Despite decades of occupation of one sort or another, along with war, destruction and poverty, independent Timor-Leste has defied expectations and is becoming a viable democratic community. As the key media in this developing new nation, radio has played a profoundly important role.

The Future of Shortwave

Shortwave enthusiast and advocate **Thomas Witherspoon** outlines the decline in international shortwave broadcasting, the loss that involves for both the developing and developed world, and the interest that can still be found by scanning the shortwave bands

I originally wrote this article for *The Spectrum Monitor* magazine and then published it on my blog, the *SWLing Post*. It has become one of my most popular (and controversial) articles: one which actually achieved traction among state and private broadcasters around the world. What follows is an updated version of that article.

DOES SHORTWAVE RADIO HAVE A FUTURE?
I'm frequently asked this question on my blog, and as I travel and speak about shortwave radio.

In my work, I continue to regard shortwave radio as a relevant and contemporary medium that conveys information to all parts of the globe, regardless of where one is born and, for the most part, regardless of one's income or status. I love the technology, the content, the variety, the affordability, the relevance, and (let's face it) the sheer magic of shortwave radio. I love that the medium can help people, teach people, move and inspire people, all around the world, everyday – even in the midst of famines, disasters, crises and wars.

One answer to the question is that the shortwaves will never disappear, even though international broadcasters may eventually fade into history. I often think of the shortwave spectrum as a global resource that will always be here, even if we humans are not. But on a brighter note, I expect the shortwave spectrum will be used for centuries to come, as we implement various technologies that make use of the medium in different ways. So, in the broadest sense, yes I do believe shortwave has a future.

But that's not really what most people are asking. They want to know if there is anything out there to listen to, and what if anything will continue to be out there.

Shortwave broadcasting is clearly on the decline. Just to be clear: when I refer to a shortwave broadcaster here, I mean large state-supported international broadcasters. There are also many private, non-profit, and clandestine broadcasters; these I will address separately.

If you're a dedicated shortwave radio listener, radio news in recent years has been enough to squelch anyone's optimism about the future of the hobby. The Voice of America, with very little warning, dropped many of their shortwave services in June 2014, and the Broadcasting Board of Governors' (BBG), according to their special committee report, regard shortwave radio as a 'legacy technology'. They cite plummeting listener numbers around the world, despite an acknowledgement that there are still communities throughout the world who rely on shortwave.

In 2014, after months of speculation, Voice of Russia suddenly dropped all of their shortwave radio services. VOR, and its predecessor, Radio Moscow, have long been dominant voices on the shortwaves. It was a shock when they fell silent.

Radio Australia has also been hit by budget cuts from their parent company, the Australian Broadcasting Corporation In January 2015 they announced the closure of the Brandon, Queensland transmission facility and, according to my contact at Radio Australia, also mothballed the newest Continental transmitters at the Shepparton site. RA consequently reduced their broadcast schedule for the B15 season.

Even the small non-profit clandestine station, Shortwave Radio Africa, sadly lost funding in August 2014, closing shop within the course of a few weeks. This was a particularly unfortunate event as this station provided an strong and necessary alternative voice to government propaganda.

Radio Exterior de España, a broadcaster I've listened to most of my life, announced their closure of shortwave services in October 2014. After a couple of months of silence, however, the Board of Directors of RTVE approved a proposal to re-open broadcasts on shortwave for a few hours a day. At the time of publication, REE is still on the air, albeit part-time.

Let's face it; shortwave radio broadcasting is on the decline. It simply is. There is no denying this unfortunate fact.

HITTING HOME
Clearly, there are not as many broadcasters on the air as there were in even the late 1990s, let alone as many as there were in the late 1970s and early 1980s, when as a child I began SWLing, and found the bands crowded with voices clamouring to be heard.

In the past five years I've had to say a painful goodbye to some of my favorite broadcasters: Radio Netherlands, Radio Canada International, and Radio Bulgaria; at the same time the BBC,

Deutsche Welle, Radio France International, and the VOA have all also substantially decreased broadcasting hours.

I find it sad to hear these stations fall silent, one by one. Perhaps because I'm something of an anachronism: a fellow who still uses short-wave radio as a means to understand the world, who still regards radio as a source of news that is ...well...from the source.

Perhaps this is why I feel so compelled to archive shortwave radio broadcasts on the Shortwave Radio Archive; why I especially want to hear the voice of each station preserved. I hope this archive will also serve as a reminder that wireless information has been crossing the planet for the better part of a century, even faster than the Internet can disseminate it now. Shortwave still has this power.

What about Private, independent broadcast-ers who often rely on revenue from content providers and advertising? While struggling in some respects in this economy, private broad-casters are still prominent on the shortwaves.

I asked Jeff White, president of the private shortwave broadcaster, WRMI, for his view on the current state of pri-vate broadcasting:

"There has been some decline in shortwave broadcasting among private broadcasters (primarily religious broadcasters). HCJB in Ecuador and FEBA in the Seychelles come to mind – Christian Vision in Chile. But most of the privately-owned broadcasters seem to be in a status quo situation – not any signifi-cant decline, and not any significant growth. Of course you also have to consider the gov-ernment broadcasters who have privatized their transmitter sites to separate companies, like Babcock, Media Broadcast, MGLOB in Madagascar, Sentech, TDF, etc. In that sense, there has been a great growth in private SW broadcasting, although Media Broadcast has closed a site or two and TDF closed their site in French Guiana (but they both are still very strong shortwave relay sites with lots of clients)."

A difficulty, inherent in private shortwave broadcasting is finding a way to fund it. Shortwave radio is difficult to monetize through promotional ads. After all, private stations typical-ly broadcast to a vast audience; it's hard to adver-tise a regional retailer or service when your foot-print covers up to a third of the entire planet. And shortwave listeners often have no means to pur-chase products. But conversely, the disadvantage is also an advantage: what media, apart from the Internet, is so widespread?

Private broadcasters get round this by broker-ing air-time to paying clients, many of whom have a religious affiliation, and by relaying language

services for government broadcasters who sim-ply purchase transmitter time. But there are oth-ers, such as WBCQ in Monticello, Maine. This station is all about free speech, and maintains its site on a shoestring budget. The number and vari-ety of shows they broadcast is nothing short of amazing. Looking at WRMI and WBCQ, it's clear that government broadcasters could learn from the example they set.

IS SHORTWAVE RELEVANT IN THE INTERNET AGE?

If you read the Shortwave Committee Report Fact Sheet the BBG published last year, you might be led to believe that shortwave should be replaced by more recent communications media. The BBG committee claims that listeners use mobile tech-nologies and computers to access broadcasters around the globe. There is some truth in this argument. If you surveyed people living in, for example, Seoul, Beijing, Bangkok and Singapore, you would likely find very few who still listen to shortwave radio. It's quite true that people gravi-tate towards the more accessible medium: in parts of the world where people live above the poverty line you will find the market flooded with smart-phones. In such cases, mobile Internet is of course financially and technologically accessible.

But although Internet penetration is increasing even in the developing world, there is inevitably a direct cor-relation between poverty and Internet usage. This is why my charity, Ears To Our World, distributes smartphones rather than radios.

Technological transitions can be difficult to implement even in the most developed countries, but imagine if you are in a developing country, liv-ing on less than one or two US dollars a day, in a village without mains power, and your news source on shortwave has been removed with only a few days notice. Your alternatives? To listen over the Internet (a service that requires a sub-scription you can ill afford), or pay-as-you-go access via an Internet café, a half-day's walk away? Suddenly, this "accessible technology" seems much less accessible.

It's easy to become complacent, and assume listeners have access to broadcasting content via the Internet, when you are a decision-maker liv-ing in a world where information is not only plen-tiful and ubiquitous, but even bombards us to the point that we simply tune it out.

There are also other advantages of shortwave radio over the Internet – especially in parts of the world where governments tightly control their country's media:

Shortwave radio cannot be easily monitored by governments. This is why shortwave radio remains a vital lifeline of information about the outside world. Censorship of shortwave radio is comparatively unsuccessful, while the Internet is often subject to total blocking.

Shortwave radio is the ultimate free speech medium, as it has no regard for national borders, nor for who is in power.

Shortwave radio is inexpensive to the listener, as radios are affordable and plentiful; no apps are required, and no subscription fees are needed.

Shortwave radio is fast. Information races over the shortwaves at the speed of light. No buffering is needed, and there is no speed difference between one area and another.

Shortwave radio works everywhere on the planet. You don't have to be within a local broadcast footprint or that of a satellite to receive broadcasts. Even in the most impoverished parts of the world you'll find shortwave radios and the batteries that run them.

Shortwave radio is a basic, simple technology, requiring little to no learning curve for use.

CAN WE STOP THE DECLINE SHORTWAVE RADIO BROADCASTING?

Large-scale, government-supported shortwave radio broadcasting has an inherent conundrum: those who fund the broadcasting do not directly benefit from it. Customers pay for private broadcaster airtime, but taxpayers pay for government broadcasting.

Without the catalyst and fuel of a World War or Cold War, government-supported international broadcasting becomes invisible to those who fund it. Politicians find it easy to cut, as few constituents understand the significance of broadcasting outside their own countries. And why should they? When one lives in a first-world country with an abundance of news sources, it's hard to relate to those who don't. Many people are not even aware that their country broadcasts to the world via shortwave radio, and that the world was listening to, even relying on, this service.

I'd like to think that if taxpayers knew about the real benefits of shortwave radio broadcasting to those in need, about the vital and even life-saving information broadcasters provide to vast reaches of the developing world, they would support it.

If you would like to advocate for the continuation of shortwave broadcasting, contact your local government representative and explain the benefits I've outlined. Use social media to spread the word. While I acknowledge that we may be fighting a losing battle, it's nonetheless worth making funders aware that first-world countries may one day regret the loss of this powerful form of outreach and diplomacy.

Even if broadcasts are terminated, broadcasters should not dismantle their transmission sites. Not only is the current service originating from these sites a more reliable form of emergency communications than the Internet should a

national disaster befall us, they also continue to provide a broad-spectrum mode of diplomacy, and some future communication mode may be developed to take advantage of the HF spectrum using these transmitter sites.

Let's assume for a moment that you're an international broadcaster who has decided to move your content to the Internet. You campaign for and attempt to promote this transition to your listeners, some of whom are living in impoverished areas and/or under repressive regimes (these frequently go hand-in-hand). Do you really think these people can: 1) Afford an Internet service and Internet capable device? 2) Surf anonymously with no chance of their government knowing about the content they research? 3) Ensure that their Internet sources aren't filtered by their government? 4) Feel confident that their Internet source won't be turned off at a moment's notice?

None of these points is a stretch. Many countries exercise control over the intereNet and turn it on or off at will. And it's worth making the point again that the disenfranchised, by and large, do not have free and open access to the Internet.

A (MODEST) POSITIVE SPIN ON THE DECLINE OF SHORTWAVE BROADCASTING

In this article I've focused on the negative implications of shortwave radio's decline, especially within the humanitarian context. The decline of shortwave radio is a fact I don't like to face, yet it's in front of me every day as a humanitarian and as a listener.

But somehow, I'm still an optimist. While others are loudly complaining there's nothing to listen to on the bands, I'll be quietly listening to those stations that they don't realize still exist.

While I penned the original version of this article, Radio Alcaravan was playing on my receiver, and as I wrote the update, Channel Africa kept me company in the background. It still amazes me that the relatively weak signal of Alcaravan punched through the ether during the night, filling my headphones with music. These signals, and others like them, play on in the pale glow of shortwave's "sundowning"; a decline mocked by the lively sound they transport on the airwaves.

LONG LIVE SHORTWAVE

If you feel so compelled, be an advocate for shortwave radio; it's something you can do for those who don't have a voice in this matter. Ask your local representative to maintain vital transmission sites and world broadcasts. Your voice can make a difference here – and across the planet, too.

And in the meanwhile, don't be discouraged by the doomsdayers. There's still much to be heard on the shortwaves right now ... simply by tuning in and listening.

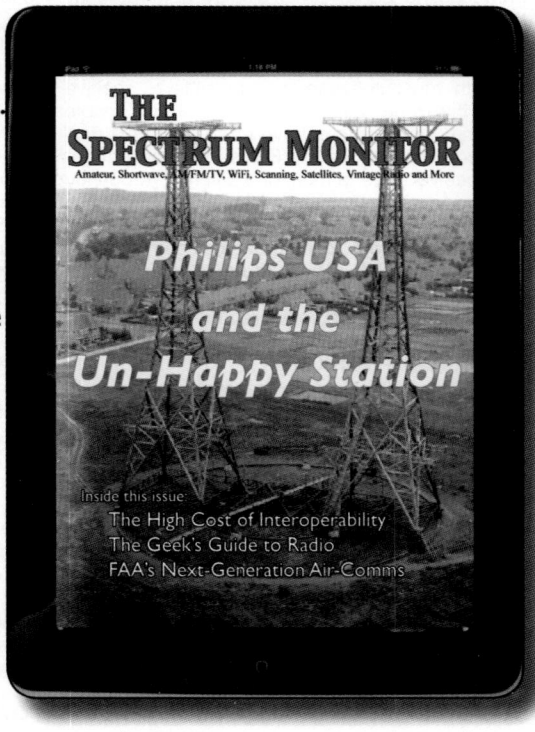

A Guide to SDRs

Everyone involved in DXing or hobby listening will have heard of and probably used an SDR. Here *WRTH* International Editor **Sean Gilbert** provides essential information on SDRs, including what they are and how they work.

INTRODUCTION

We have discussed *software-defined radio* (SDR) in previous editions of *WRTH*. In brief, an SDR is a radio in which most of the signal processing is carried out by software within a computer (be it a PC, tablet or smartphone) rather than by hardware within the radio itself. Whereas a conventional radio only presents one station at a time, an SDR provides a visual indication of every audible signal over a span of frequencies or even a whole broadcasting band. On a display generated by the software (sometimes referred to as an FFT or 'waterfall') it is possible to see every station, noise burst and fleeting signal over the entire span.

With most software it is feasible to receive more than one station at a time. SDR Console v2.3 can, for example, have up to six VFOs running concurrently. Each VFO is in effect a separate receiver, able to monitor a different frequency and mode within the currently selected frequency span of the SDR. The individual audio from each VFO can be sent to different devices such as soundcards which can route the audio into data decoding software. The only limiting factors are the capabilities of the software and the computer.

HOW AN SDR WORKS

An SDR uses the processing power of a computer to take over the majority of radio functions apart from signal acquisition. The signal is captured and processed in such a way that the software can demodulate the signal and present it in a usable manner. The signal flow from antenna to computer begins with the untuned, unfiltered wideband RF being fed from the antenna into the SDR. It then passes through various filtering and signal amplification stages which limit the frequency ranges to those required. Better-quality SDRs have a number of software-selected BPFs covering smaller sub-sets of frequencies. Each filter can be tailored to cover a specific narrow band rather than using a single filter to cover the entire range which would give lower performance.

The next stage in the signal path is a high-performance ADC which, in conjunction with a VFO or other form of oscillator such as a DCO, allows the selection of a single frequency within the span of the SDR. The ADC outputs a special type of wideband audio called 'baseband' which consists of two samples from the original signal. The 'in-phase' or 'I' channel is not phase-shifted relative to the original signal whereas the 'quadrature' phase or 'Q' channel is shifted by 90 degrees relative to the 'I' channel. Amongst other things this

shift is vital for the rejection of image signals.

The final stage is to transfer the I and Q channels into the computer where the associated monitor can display the signal. This connection is made via USB or Ethernet and also carries control information to and from the PC.

RECEIVING AND RECORDING SIGNALS

Modern low-end SDRs use ADCs with a resolution of 8 bits whereas the better-performing receivers use ADCs with 12 to 24 bits or more. ADC resolution dictates the overall dynamic range with more bits being preferable. Receivers using ADCs with more bits also have a lower noise floor, better image rejection and improved SNR. Recent SDR designs use specialist ADCs in the receiver hardware. In combination with high-quality DDSs these give more resistance to the effects of interference and noise and hence provide superior-quality signals.

'Sample rate' is a term commonly used when discussing SDR specifications and is the rate or speed at which the ADC is sampled. By undersampling or oversampling the signal it is possible to extend the tuning range of the receiver.

The total baseband audio bandwidth is governed by the sample rate and selected frequency span of the SDR. The more bandwidth covered, the larger the baseband audio file will be. For instance a 1MHz spectrum bandwidth recording would produce a file size in the order of 170GB or more over the course of a 24-hour recording period. Recording a 20MHz span for the same amount of time requires 3.4TB. The main reason for recording baseband audio is to capture a section of spectrum for later analysis. This is particularly useful if it is wished to record signals over night, either to fit in with other activities or to avoid interference from neighbouring devices which are likely to be dormant or switched off at night.

POWER SUPPLY

Some low-current SDRs are bus-powered, meaning that the USB connection supplies the necessary voltage and current to power the radio without the need for an external supply. An SDR with higher current drain will require an external power supply. If a bus-powered SDR is used with a tablet it would be worth investing in a powered USB hub. The reason is that the tablet battery may drain much faster than usual and also the tablet may not be able to supply enough current from its USB port to power the SDR. Some higher sample-rate SDRs such as the Airspy really need a USB3 connection from a powered hub to perform properly. A USB2 connection may work but it is unlikely that the full sample rate of the AirSpy could be used due to data-transfer limitations of the USB2 protocol.

RTL DONGLES

Some DXers are using adapted RTL dongles to achieve an output similar to that of an SDR. The RTL provides the flow of data from the receiver hardware to the host computer but all other functions – including baseband signal processing, gain control, AGC and demodulation – are catered for by the SDR control software. In order to persuade RTL devices to perform as wideband SDRs it is necessary to use specially engineered software drivers and DLLs. There is a great deal of information on the internet relating to the installation, set-up and use of these items. Some RTL-based SDRs shown in the table overleaf have the converter and dongle hardware built into a bespoke case. A degree of caution is needed, however, since many of the dongles sold on the internet contain non-compatible tuner ICs.

GLOSSARY OF TERMS

ADC: Analogue to digital converter: converts the analogue RF signal into a multi-bit digital audio stream for later processing.
Baseband: The wideband audio output from the ADC containing all the signal information for the entire block of captured spectrum.
BPF: Bandpass filter
DCO: Digitally controlled oscillator.
DDC: Digital down-conversion: a process which takes the high-speed output of the ADC and selects the frequency range of interest, then converts it down to baseband.
DDE: Dynamic Data Exchange: an inter-process communications protocol used by MS Windows.
DDS: Direct Digital Synthesizer; a proprietary form of digital signal synthesis.
DLL: Dynamic Link Library. A collection of coded instructions or data that can be accessed and used by several applications.
Dynamic Range: Loosely speaking the ratio of the weakest signal the receiver can detect to the strongest signal the receiver can handle, usually expressed in decibels. Good SDRs exhibit a dynamic range of over 100dB.
ENOB: Effective Number of Bits. This is a measure of the performance of an ADC compared to an 'ideal ADC' with the same resolution. .
FFT: Fast Fourier Transform: in this context related to the graphical 'waterfall' display common in SDR and audio processing software.
FPGA: Field Programmable Gate Array. A type of IC which can be configured after manufacture (i.e. "in the field")
I/Q signals: Two samples of the baseband audio shifted in phase by 90 degrees.
Image rejection: In general terms the ability of a receiver to reject unwanted copies of signals generated due to shortcomings in various circuit elements. I and Q channels can be used together to reject images.
Images or image signals: Duplicates of the original signal resulting from signal-mixing products within the ADC and elsewhere.
Panadaptor: A device plugged into the IF output of a conventional receiver to produce a visual display of a range or span of frequencies.
RTL dongle: Small low-cost USB device, usually the size of a flash drive, originally designed to receive off-air DTV and DAB signals. Certain chipsets have been found to make useful – if basic – SDRs.
Sampling rate: The speed at which the ADC is sampled. The higher the sample rate, the greater the amount of spectrum that can be displayed.
SNR: Signal to noise ratio. One factor in determining receiver performance.
Up-converter: In the context of an SDR, additional hardware allowing a receiver to cover frequencies it would otherwise not be able to tune. It operates by converting the incoming signal to a frequency within the receiver's coverage.
VFO: Variable frequency oscillator. Tunes the receiver by varying the local oscillator frequency.

SDR CONTROL SOFTWARE

There are various software controllers linked to specific receivers but the three most popular free SDR software programs are:

'SDR Console' by Simon Brown. This supports a large number of SDR types. It has a built-in decoder for several digital modes together with advanced satellite tracking and support for multiple memory channels. It supports external MIDI devices such as Hercules DJ controllers and the use of broadcast-schedule databases

'SDR Sharp (SDR#)' by Youssef Touil. This supports a number of different SDRs including the author's own AirSpy units. Several third-party plug-ins have been developed to enhance functionality including satellite trackers, digital audio processing and TV decoding.

'HDSDR'. Another popular SDR program supporting a large number of SDRs by the use of ExtIO DLLs. It has a DDE client for interfacing with other software. An advanced version of Winrad (I2PHD)

TYPES OF SDR AVAILABLE

Overleaf is a table of some popular SDRs in various price ranges. The list is not exhaustive and new receivers frequently appear. Equally SDR control software is under constant development and new and improved features are added over time to improve both performance and functionality. One of the delights of SDRs is that they are at the cutting edge of current radio technology and provide features and functionality that just a few years ago would have been impossible.

TABLE 1. Some of the more widely used SDRs

Maker	Model	Coverage	Bandwidth	Notes	Price
Afredi	SDR-Net	10kHz-36MHz	1.85MHz/230kHz [7]	12-bit ADC	$260
Airspy	Airspy	24-1750MHz	10MHz	12-bit ADC	£170
Alinco	DX-R8E	150kHz-35MHz	48kHz+ (PC audio b/w)	Conventional Rx with I/Q outputs	$500
AOR	AR2300	40kHz-3150MHz	15MHz	14-bit ADC	$3600
CommRadio	CR-1a	500kHz-512MHz [11]	200kHz	Conventional Rx with I/Q outputs	$600
Cross Country	SDR-4+	850kHz-70.5MHz	48/192kHz [8]	Internal soundcard-based	£180
CT1FFU	DX Patrol [3]	100kHz-2000MHz	2.4MHz	8-bit ADC	$105
Elad	FDM-S2	9kHz-174MHz [9]	6.1MHz	16-bit ADC	$499
Elad	FDM-S1	80kHz-30MHz	3MHz	Integral DRM decoder; no DRM software required.	$329
Enablia	TitanSDR	9kHz-32MHz	4 x wide, 8 x narrow	16-bit ADC	€1645
Enablia	TitanSDR Pro	0.009-40MHz	4 x wide, 40 x narrow	16-bit ADC	€2345
Expert Electronics	Colibri DDC	9kHz-55MHz	2 x 312kHz	14-bit ADC	€649
FiFi	SDR	200kHz-30MHz	192kHz	24-bit ADC + preselector	$169
FUNcube	Dongle Pro +	150kHz-2050MHz [4]	192kHz	16-bit ADC	£150
Hunter	SDR	1-30MHz [6]	48kHz+ (PC audio b/w)	PC soundcard-based	$130
Marty, KN0CK	Up-converting RTL	500kHz-54MHz	2.4MHz	LPF and preamp on R820T	$75
Microtelecom	Perseus	10kHz-40MHz	1.6MHz	14-bit ADC + 10 BPFs	$1100
NooElec	RTL R820T	24-1760MHz [1]	2.4MHz (stable)	8-bit ADC	£10
NooElec	RTL R820T2	24-1760MHz [1]	2.4MHz (stable)	Better RF performance	£18
RFSpace	Cloud-IQ	9kHz-56MHz	1.288MHz	12 ENOB ADC	$629
RFSpace	CloudSDR	9kHz-1200MHz	Up to 56MHz (10MHz remote, 8MHz @56MHz+)	12.55 ENOB ADC	$999
RFSpace	NetSDR	0.1kHz-32MHz	1.6MHz	16-bit ADC + 10 BPFs	$1450
RFSpace	SDR-IQ	0.1kHz-30MHz	192kHz	14-bit ADC	£450
Satrian	Andrus MK1.5	5kHz-30MHz [10]	400kHz	24-bit ADC	$480
SDRplay	SDRplay	100kHz-2000MHz	8MHz	12-bit ADC	£120
Soft66	LC4 [5]	500kHz-70MHz	48kHz+ (PC audio b/w)	PC soundcard-based	$98
Soft66	RTL2 [4]	0.1-30/50-1000MHz	2.4MHz	Preamp/gain control	$50
SRL	QS1R	10kHz-300MHz	4MHz	16-bit ADC	$900
USRP	B200	70MHz-6GHz	56MHz	12-bit ADC (USB3)	$675
USRP	B210	70MHz-6GHz	56MHz	2 Rx/Tx modules	$1100
WinRadio	G31 Excalibur	9kHz-50MHz	2MHz	16-bit ADC	£700
WinRadio	G33 Excalibur Pro	9kHz-50MHz	4MHz	16-bit ADC	£1600
WinRadio	G39 Excelsior	9kHz-3500MHz	2 x 4MHz + 16MHz span	16-bit ADC	$4700

Notes:
[1] Third-party up-converters can extend the tuning range to cover HF. Some have better filtering than others. Some R820Ts claim a coverage of 0.1-1750MHz without the need for an up-converter. These use the 'direct sampling' method, in which a direct feed is taken from the tuner IC without any filtering. Although these work, performance is poor compared with a standard R820T used with an up-converter. [2] Except for 260-410MHz. [3] R820T base with up-converter, filters and bespoke case. [4] Japanese-designed up-converting unit on R820T base and bespoke PCB with SMA sockets, inbuilt preamp and variable gain control. [5] Uses PC soundcard as ADC. Display bandwidth is restricted to the b/w of the soundcard (usually 48kHz, up to 192kHz for high-grade sound devices). [6] Comes in kit form with 6 switched BPFs. [7] Bandwidth 1.85MHz using Ethernet connection, or 230kHz using standard USB. [8] 48kHz bandwidth using built-in soundcard or 192kHz using an external higher-specification soundcard. [9] Covers 9kHz-52MHz (and 74-108 & 135-160MHz in undersampled mode). [10] Optional add-on daughterboard allows reception up to 2200MHz. [11] Actual coverage is 0.5-30MHz, 64-260MHz and 437-512MHz but the 50MHz band is not covered.

HF BROADCASTING RECEPTION CONDITIONS EXPECTED DURING 2016

*Likely listening conditions in the coming year by **Ulf-Peter Hoppe***

PASSED THE PEAK OF SOLAR CYCLE 24

The ongoing sunspot Cycle 24 had two peaks: the first was 66.9 in February 2012 and the second 75.4 in November 2013. Many cycles are double-peaked, but this is the first recorded instance of the second peak in sunspot numbers being larger than the first. Combined with little interference between stations, resulting from the reduced level of transmissions, we can expect to enjoy a generally good year of reception on the HF broadcasting bands.

The current sunspot cycle is the 24th observed since 1756, when telescopic observation of the sun began. Fig. 1, provided by NASA,

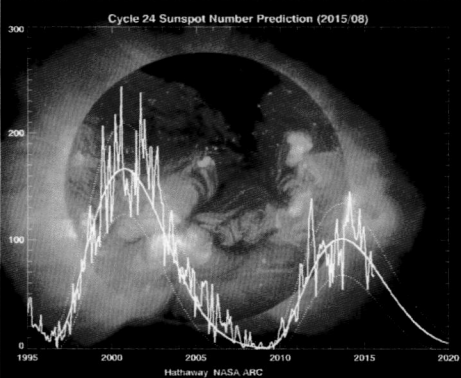

Fig. 1 Sunspot Cycles 23 and 24 (Hathaway/NASA/ARC)

charts the complete previous Cycle 23 and the progression of Cycle 24. NASA scientists estimate that the smoothed sunspot number will steadily decrease from about 44 in January to February 2016 to about 31 in November and over December. These numbers have been used for the prediction of the most suitable frequencies on the page facing this one.

Solar ultraviolet radiation creates the ionosphere, the ionized fraction of the earth's atmosphere. The F-region of the ionosphere starts about 150 km (93 miles) above the ground and constitutes the most important reflector for HF radio waves. The E-region at 100 to 120 km (62 to 74 miles) is weaker, but sometimes plays a role in HF radio communication.

The flux of ultraviolet light from the sun is greatest when the solar cycle is near its maximum, and decreases as the sunspot number decreases. The electron density in the ionosphere will decrease somewhat during the course of 2016. The best reception conditions in the

second half of 2016 may occur in the next lower band compared to the first half of the year, at least for some of the circuits.

Reception conditions in the HF bands will be similar to those in 2015. The ionospheric conditions at the reflection point halfway along the great circle from transmitter to receiver have the greatest influence on the best frequency to use, except for the rarer two-hop circuits and even rarer circuits taking the opposite direction, along the longest part of the great circle. When the reflection point is in daylight, the 17, 19, and 21 MHz bands often give the most stable reception conditions. When the reflection point is on the night side of the earth, the 11, 9, 7, 6, and 5 MHz bands give the best results.

The first *WRTH* appeared in 1947 near the maximum of solar cycle 18, six solar cycles ago. Since then, the largest maximum (since 1756!) occurred in Cycle 19 with a smoothed monthly sunspot number of 201.3. The last minimum in 2008 holds the record as the deepest and longest minimum known, 829 days without any sunspots being recorded at all.

Those six solar cycles varied in length between 9.7 years (Cycle 22) and 11.7 years (Cycles 20 and 23). Despite all the advances over the past 70 years in scientific knowledge and technological achievement, both the length of an ongoing solar cycle and its maximum value are still very difficult to predict.

Solar flares are an important phenomenon in solar activity, and they are related to sunspots. Depending on the direction of a solar flare, also known as a coronal mass ejection (CME), we can experience a subsequent polar cap absorption (PCA) event. Many CMEs miss the Earth, but if they don't, a PCA event may disrupt radio communication for many hours to several days. These events occur at any time during a solar cycle, but preferentially in the years following each maximum. For instance, the so-called superstorms in March 1989 and in October 2003 caused power failures and degradation of navigation networks for several hours to some days. Both of these events occurred on the decreasing flank of their sunspot number maximum.

Good listening on the HF broadcast bands in 2016!

ABOUT THE AUTHOR

Ulf-Peter Hoppe is an adjunct professor of physics at the Arctic University of Norway. He has used the WRTH since the late 1970s.

Most Suitable Frequencies 2016

Prepared by Prof. Dr. rer. nat. Ulf-Peter Hoppe, Chief Scientist
E-mail: ulf-peter.hoppe@tveco.net
Web: http://tinyurl.com/pg46arx

TRANSMITTING STATION LOCATION

LISTENER'S AREA	LOCAL TIME	APPROX. UTC TIME	JAN/FEB & NOV/DEC								MAR/APR & SEPT/OCT								MAY-AUGUST							
			EUR/NAF	N.AM(E)	N.AM(W)	C/S.AM	C/S.AF	ME/S.AS	E.AS	AUS/NZ	EUR/NAF	N.AM(E)	N.AM(W)	C/S.AM	C/S.AF	ME/S.AS	E.AS	AUS/NZ	EUR/NAF	N.AM(E)	N.AM(W)	C/S.AM	C/S.AF	ME/S.AS	E.AS	AUS/NZ
EUROPE AND NORTH AFRICA	00:00-04:00	23:00-03:00	7	7	11	11	7	7	9	15	7	9	11	11	9	9	11	15	9	9	15	11	7	11	13	13
	04:00-08:00	03:00-07:00	6	6	7	9	9	13	13	-	6	9	9	11	9	15	17	-	9	9	15	13	11	17	17	21
	08:00-12:00	07:00-11:00	13	9	9	11	17	17	17	25	15	9	-	13	17	21	17	25	11	11	15	13	15	21	17	25
	12:00-16:00	11:00-15:00	13	17	9	17	17	17	17	21	15	17	-	25	21	17	17	21	11	17	15	21	15	15	15	17
	16:00-20:00	15:00-19:00	7	15	9	21	13	13	13	11	11	21	11	21	15	9	13	13	15	17	15	21	15	13	11	11
	20:00-00:00	19:00-23:00	7	9	9	11	9	7	11	11	9	15	13	17	13	9	11	11	11	15	17	15	9	11	13	11
NORTH AMERICA (EAST)	22:00-02:00	03:00-07:00	6	6	6	9	9	-	-	-	7	6	9	9	11	-	-	-	9	7	11	9	9	-	15	17
	02:00-06:00	07:00-11:00	9	6	6	7	-	-	9	11	11	6	7	9	-	-	9	11	13	7	9	9	-	-	9	11
	06:00-10:00	11:00-15:00	13	11	6	17	21	15	9	9	17	11	7	15	21	17	13	13	17	17	11	15	21	17	15	15
	10:00-14:00	15:00-19:00	13	15	13	21	21	-	13	21	21	15	15	21	21	-	15	21	15	13	13	21	21	17	17	-
	14:00-18:00	19:00-23:00	9	13	17	17	17	11	9	15	11	11	17	17	17	13	13	-	-	17	17	17	17	15	17	-
	18:00-22:00	23:00-03:00	6	7	11	9	9	13	13	-	9	7	13	9	13	13	15	17	11	11	15	11	13	17	17	15
NORTH AMERICA (WEST)	00:00-04:00	08:00-12:00	9	7	6	7	-	11	9	9	9	7	6	9	-	11	9	11	11	7	7	9	-	-	11	11
	04:00-08:00	12:00-16:00	13	11	6	17	17	9	7	9	15	11	6	15	17	11	9	11	15	13	9	17	17	15	13	13
	08:00-12:00	16:00-20:00	13	15	11	25	21	11	11	15	15	15	15	25	21	13	13	15	17	17	11	21	17	17	15	-
	12:00-16:00	20:00-00:00	9	15	13	17	17	11	13	17	11	15	13	21	21	-	15	25	15	13	11	15	17	17	17	21
	16:00-20:00	00:00-04:00	9	7	9	9	11	13	15	-	6	9	11	11	13	17	17	21	11	11	11	13	13	17	17	21
	20:00-00:00	04:00-08:00	6	6	9	9	11	-	9	11	9	7	6	7	11	-	15	13	13	7	9	9	13	-	17	15
CENTRAL AND SOUTH AMERICA	00:00-04:00	04:00-08:00	9	7	9	9	11	-	15	15	9	9	11	11	11	-	17	21	11	9	9	9	-	17	13	-
	04:00-08:00	08:00-12:00	15	7	9	7	17	21	13	11	17	7	9	17	21	21	15	11	17	9	11	7	17	21	17	9
	08:00-12:00	12:00-16:00	25	17	-	17	25	21	-	-	25	17	-	21	25	25	-	-	21	15	15	17	21	25	21	-
	12:00-16:00	16:00-20:00	17	17	21	21	25	-	-	-	25	21	25	25	21	-	-	-	17	17	17	21	15	17	-	-
	16:00-20:00	20:00-00:00	11	13	25	17	11	11	-	21	11	15	21	11	13	13	15	21	11	15	17	11	11	15	17	17
	20:00-00:00	00:00-04:00	9	7	13	11	11	11	13	21	11	9	17	13	11	17	17	21	9	11	17	11	13	17	21	17
CENTRAL AND SOUTH AFRICA	00:00-04:00	22:00-02:00	11	13	15	13	9	9	13	9	11	17	17	13	9	9	17	11	9	15	15	9	7	9	15	7
	04:00-08:00	02:00-06:00	7	11	13	11	7	15	17	13	9	11	13	11	7	15	17	13	9	9	5	7	7	15	17	13
	08:00-12:00	06:00-10:00	17	-	-	15	15	21	21	21	21	-	-	15	17	25	25	21	21	13	-	-	17	25	25	21
	12:00-16:00	10:00-14:00	17	21	-	21	21	17	21	21	21	-	-	25	21	21	25	17	17	17	-	21	17	21	25	13
	16:00-20:00	14:00-18:00	17	21	9	21	15	11	11	11	17	25	11	21	17	13	15	9	17	21	15	21	13	11	13	7
	20:00-00:00	18:00-22:00	11	17	15	21	11	11	11	9	11	17	17	21	11	15	15	9	11	17	17	11	9	9	15	7
MIDDLE EAST AND SOUTH ASIA	00:00-04:00	21:00-01:00	7	11	11	13	9	9	7	-	7	13	13	17	11	9	9	13	9	15	15	13	9	9	13	9
	04:00-08:00	01:00-05:00	6	9	17	9	9	13	15	11	7	11	21	13	7	17	21	15	11	13	15	15	9	17	21	21
	08:00-12:00	05:00-09:00	17	-	-	17	21	21	25	-	17	-	17	-	21	25	25	-	15	-	17	-	17	21	21	-
	12:00-16:00	09:00-13:00	17	-	9	17	17	17	11	17	17	-	11	25	21	25	15	21	17	17	15	21	17	21	21	15
	16:00-20:00	13:00-17:00	11	15	9	25	15	11	7	13	13	17	9	25	17	13	11	17	15	21	13	21	17	15	15	13
	20:00-00:00	17:00-21:00	7	-	9	17	11	9	7	13	9	17	11	21	13	9	13	-	13	17	17	17	9	11	13	13
EAST ASIA AND FAR EAST	00:00-04:00	16:00-20:00	9	-	6	-	11	7	6	9	11	15	7	-	15	9	11	9	13	17	11	-	15	11	11	9
	04:00-08:00	20:00-00:00	9	15	11	11	9	6	6	15	9	17	15	11	13	7	9	15	13	15	17	15	15	11	11	13
	08:00-12:00	00:00-04:00	9	13	15	21	15	17	17	25	9	15	17	25	17	17	21	17	13	17	11	21	-	17	17	17
	12:00-16:00	04:00-08:00	15	9	7	15	15	21	15	21	17	11	11	17	21	17	21	21	17	15	13	17	25	17	13	17
	16:00-20:00	08:00-12:00	13	9	6	9	21	13	7	9	9	9	7	9	25	15	9	11	17	11	9	11	25	17	13	9
	20:00-00:00	12:00-16:00	9	11	7	-	11	7	6	9	13	11	7	-	17	9	11	11	15	15	9	17	21	15	13	9
AUSTRALIA AND NEW ZEALAND	00:00-04:00	14:00-18:00	13	17	-	13	13	9	6	-	17	17	-	13	9	9	6	-	13	-	11	-	11	11	9	6
	04:00-08:00	18:00-22:00	11	17	17	17	13	13	7	6	13	25	15	17	11	11	7	6	11	21	17	13	11	11	9	6
	08:00-12:00	22:00-02:00	-	21	25	21	17	15	21	6	-	25	25	21	15	17	21	6	15	21	21	21	17	-	7	7
	12:00-16:00	02:00-06:00	-	-	17	21	-	21	25	9	-	17	21	21	-	21	25	7	17	17	17	17	-	21	21	7
	16:00-20:00	06:00-10:00	25	11	9	13	21	17	17	9	25	13	11	15	21	21	21	9	21	11	11	9	17	17	15	7
	20:00-00:00	10:00-14:00	21	9	9	13	17	11	13	6	21	11	9	13	-	11	13	6	-	13	11	9	-	13	9	6

Band selections have been made according to predicted propagation conditions. Also check neighbouring bands of the most suitable bands shown here. A '-' means there is no reliable propagation in any frequency band.

How to use *WRTH*

ORGANISATION OF THE BOOK

The book consists of three main areas: **Features**, consisting of equipment reviews, broadcasting predictions and informative radio-related articles; **Directory**, which is further divided into *National Radio*, *International Radio* (including Clandestine and Other Target Broadcasts), *Frequency Lists* (which includes Mediumwave lists by region, Shortwave Stations of the World, International Broadcasts in selected languages and International DRM broadcasts), and *Terrestrial Television*; and finally **Reference** where a full country index, abbreviations used in WRTH and transmitter site location tables, as well as other useful information related to the world of radio broadcasting can be found.

Each section is identified by a unique 'side-bar', which can be found both on the main contents page and on each individual page throughout the book. Each section starts with an alphabetical country listing.

In the Directory, countries are listed alphabetically within each section so that they may be easily located by flicking forward to the relevant location. Alternatively, the index in the Reference section may be used to find the exact page number for a specific country of interest.

Under each country in the National Radio section, state broadcasters are listed first followed by major networks and then other stations. Armed forces stations and local relays of international stations are at the end of the entry. For all stations, mediumwave is listed first, followed by shortwave and finally FM. Many stations now only broadcast on FM. Details are given of digital radio multiplexes where appropriate.

OPERATING TECHNIQUES

When operating their receivers, the majority of listeners tend to operate in one of two main modes, switching between them as and when they deem appropriate. One method is to 'target' a given station or country by monitoring known frequencies and the other is simply to 'cruise' a specific band and identify each station as they occur (known as 'band scanning'). We have designed WRTH in such a way that either of these methods can be accommodated.

When operating in the targeting mode there are two ways to find a particular country. The first option is to go to the main contents page and use the section 'side-bars' to direct you to the right area of the book. Once there, you then only have to flick forward a few pages to locate the country of interest. Alternatively you can use the country index at the back of the book, which will tell you the

precise page number. As you develop a 'feel' for the book and get used to the alphabetical layout, you will probably find that the side-bar method is simpler and quicker than using the country index.

Should you prefer to use band-scanning, there are listings of both medium wave and international short-wave broadcasts available in the Frequency Listings. These can also be useful for casual listening, but in either case can help to identify a station by frequency – whereupon further details can be obtained using the country entry to identify alternative frequencies for the station of interest.

UTC

UTC (Coordinated Universal Time) is the current time standard used throughout the world by broadcasters and many other organisations. UTC replaced Greenwich Mean Time, GMT, as the world time standard some years ago. UTC, like its predecessor, is based on the Greenwich meridian at 0 degrees longitude (in London, England). To find out how many hours ahead or behind UTC your location is, refer to the World Time Table elsewhere in this section. If your location is ahead of UTC (indicated by a '+' sign in the table), you will need to add that number of hours to the time shown in the schedules. Likewise, if your location is behind UTC (indicated by '-'), you will need to subtract that many hours from the time shown in the schedules in order to find out at what time the broadcast can be heard at your location.

RECEPTION REPORTS

When requesting a verification of the reception report you sent (commonly referred to as a QSL-card), it is important that you include details of the programming heard (over a period of time, usually at least 15 minutes wherever possible); the date and time, in UTC (as explained above); how well you heard the broadcast and what receiver/antenna you were using. Where possible, try to use the language of the broadcast, rather than English, as there may be no English speakers available at the station. Be polite and do not demand a QSL card – stations on a tight budget may not have the resources to print QSL cards, but may send you promotional items and a verification letter instead.

It is courteous to enclose return postage when writing to small domestic broadcasters. This can be in the form of an International Reply Coupon (IRC) available from post offices. In all cases, when writing to radio stations you must write clearly. Remember, if the station cannot read your address, then you cannot expect to receive a reply!

Local Time, with respect to UTC

Population

Country

ANGOLA

Principal Language(s)

L.T: UTC +1h — **Pop:** 10 million — **Pr.L:** Portuguese + ethnic — **E.C:** 50Hz, 220V — **ITU:** AGL

Country Code

Electricity supply (Electric Current)

Address

RÁDIO NACIONAL DE ANGOLA (RNA)
✉ Rua Rainha Jinga, CP. 1329, Luanda ☎ +244 2 323172/321258
🖷 +244 2 324647/391234 **W:** www.rna.ao **E:** dgeral@rna.ao **L.P:** DG:
Filipe Diatezua. PD: Júlio Mendonça. TD: Cândido R. Pinto.

Telephone & Fax

Mediumwave Stations

MW:

Leading Personnel

SW Stations

Location	kHz	kW	Prgr.	H. of tr.
Mulenvos	1088	25	A	24h

Web & email

SW:

Frequency in kiloHertz

Location	kHz	kW	Prgr.	H. of tr.
Mulenvos	4950	25	A	24h
Mulenvos	7217v	15	N/A	24h

Hours of Transmission

FM Stations

FM (MHz): Luanda (4kW): 93.5 (A), 94.5 (5), 96.5MHz (FME), 99.9 (RL), 101.4MHz (N).

Power in kiloWatts

Announcement

Ann: "Rádio Nacional de Angola". **F.PI:** new 100kW tx on MW.

Programme decode

Prgrs: A=Canal A in Portuguese (general coverage): 24h. **N:** on the h. **N=Rádio N'Gola Yetu** (ethnic): 0000-2000. **N:** rel. Canal A. **FME=Rádio FM Estéreo** (music): 1000-2400. **RL=Rádio Luanda** (capital channel): 24h. **5=Rádio 5** (sports): 0500-2300.

Programme

Future Plans (F.PI)

NB: Not all entries are in the same format, example above is given for guidance and should cover most entries. If a country observes Daylight Savings Time/Summer Time, the effective dates are shown after the local time (**L.T**).

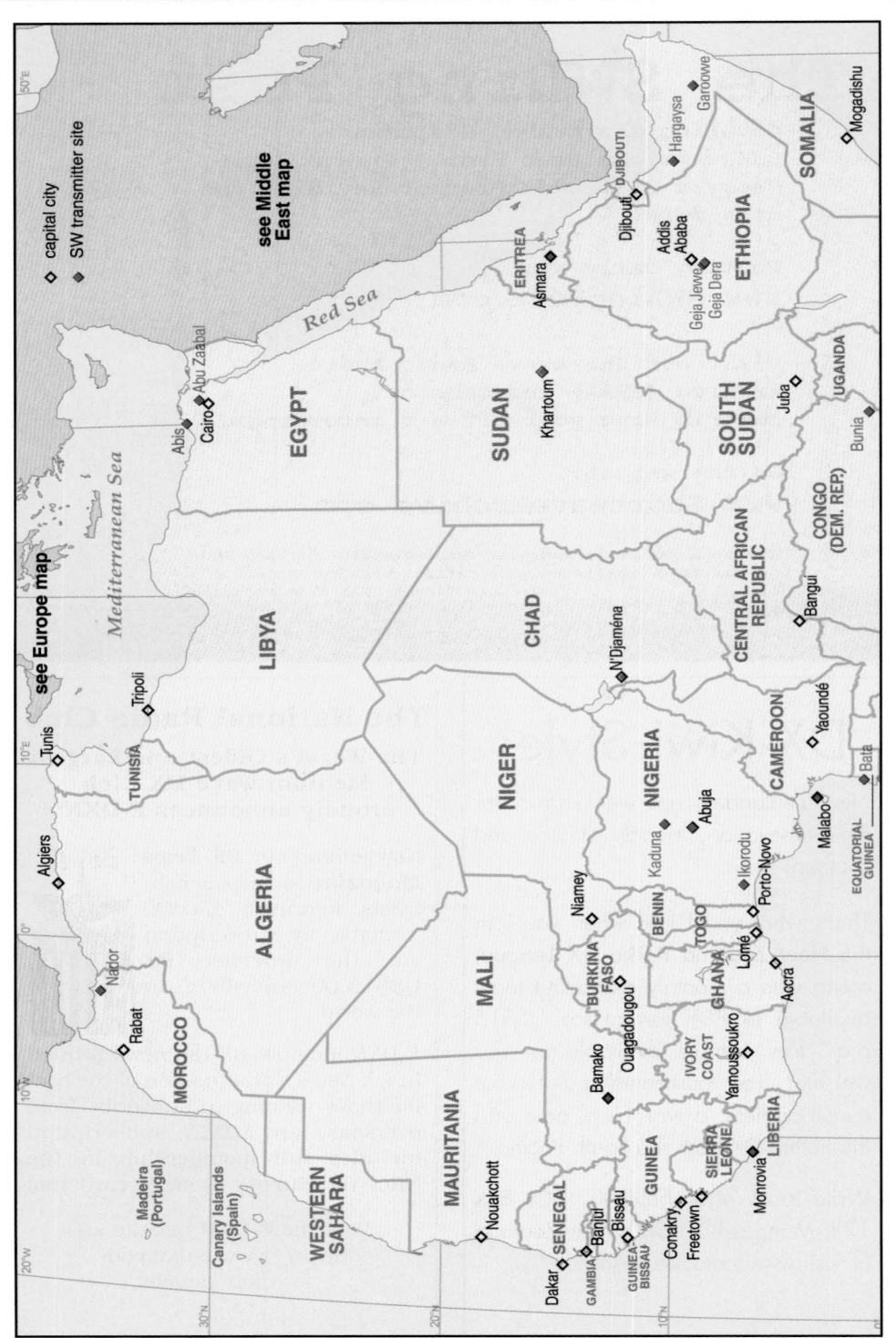

◇ capital city
◆ SW transmitter site

see Middle
East map

see Europe map

Red Sea

Mediterranean Sea

SOMALIA
Mogadishu
Garoowe
Hargaysa
DJIBOUTI
Djibouti
ETHIOPIA
Addis Ababa
Geja Jewe
Geja Dera
ERITREA
Asmara
Abu Zabal
Abis
Cairo
EGYPT
SUDAN
Khartoum
SOUTH SUDAN
Juba
UGANDA
CONGO (DEM. REP.)
Bunia
CENTRAL AFRICAN REPUBLIC
Bangui
LIBYA
Tripoli
TUNISIA
Tunis
Algiers
CHAD
N'Djaména
CAMEROON
Yaoundé
Bata
EQUATORIAL GUINEA
Malabo
NIGER
NIGERIA
Abuja
Kaduna
Ikorodu
Porto-Novo
BENIN
TOGO
Lomé
GHANA
Accra
ALGERIA
Niamey
BURKINA FASO
Ouagadougou
IVORY COAST
Yamoussoukro
Nador
Rabat
MOROCCO
MALI
Bamako
GUINEA
SIERRA LEONE
Freetown
LIBERIA
Monrovia
Conakry
MAURITANIA
Nouakchott
WESTERN SAHARA
SENEGAL
Dakar
Banjul
GAMBIA
GUINEA-BISSAU
Bissau
Madeira (Portugal)
Canary Islands (Spain)

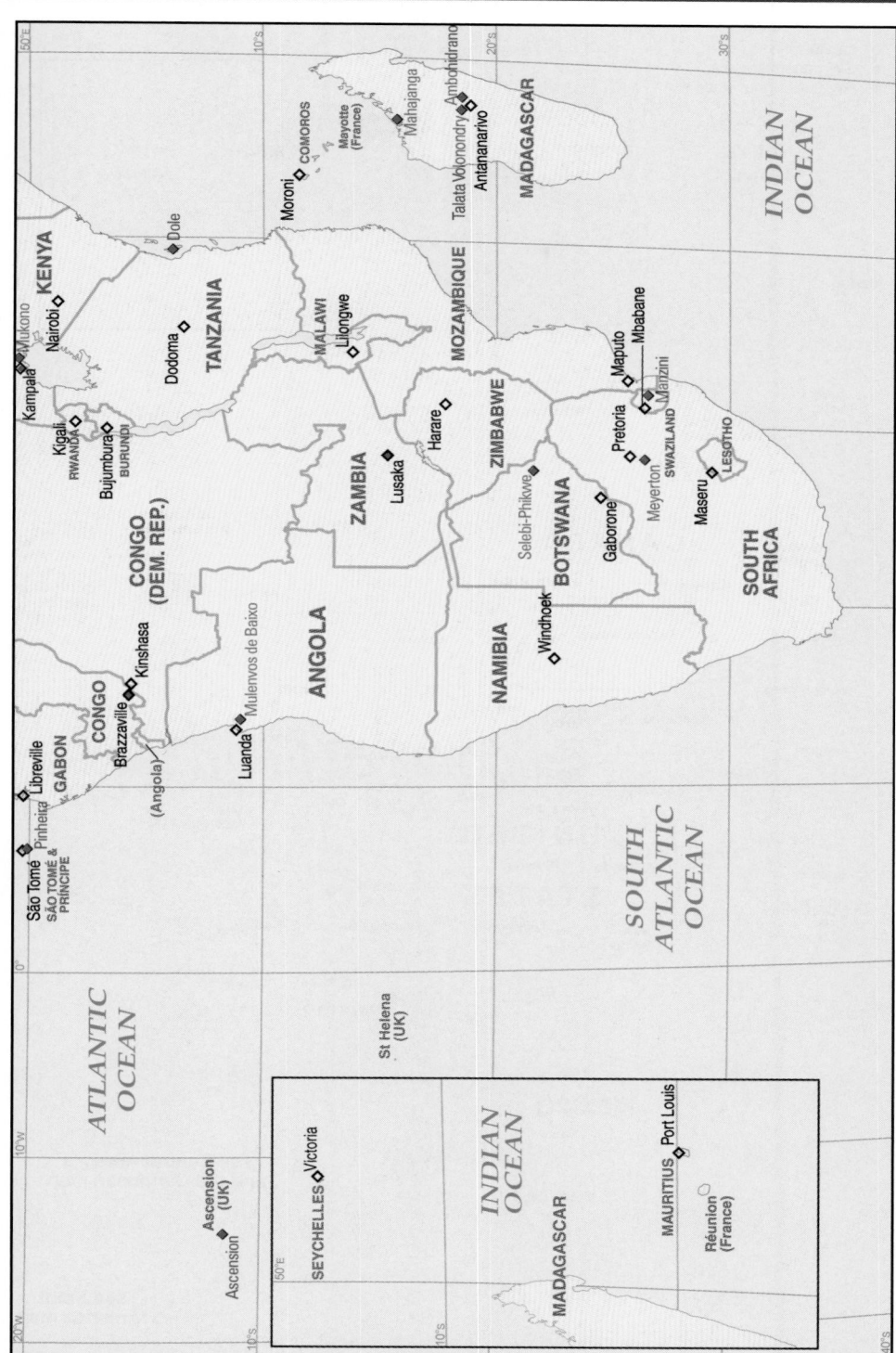

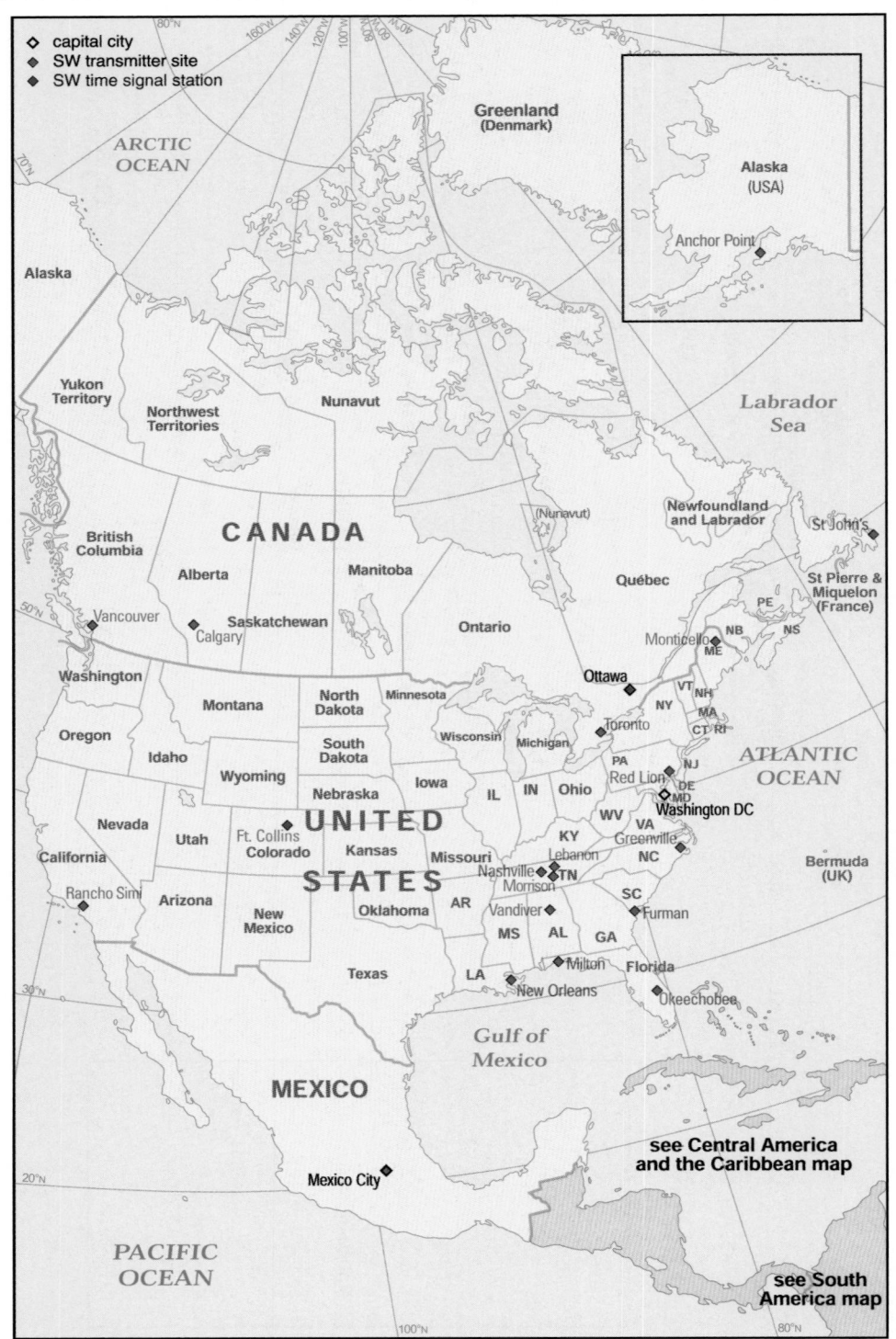

◇ capital city
◆ SW transmitter site
◆ SW time signal station

ARCTIC OCEAN

Greenland (Denmark)

Alaska (USA)

Anchor Point

Alaska

Yukon Territory

Northwest Territories

Nunavut

Labrador Sea

CANADA

British Columbia

Alberta

Manitoba

Québec

Newfoundland and Labrador

St John's

St Pierre & Miquelon (France)

Vancouver

Calgary

Saskatchewan

Ontario

PE

NB

NS

Monticello

ME

Ottawa

Washington

Montana

North Dakota

Minnesota

Wisconsin

Michigan

Toronto

VT

NY

NH

MA

CT RI

ATLANTIC OCEAN

Oregon

Idaho

Wyoming

South Dakota

Nebraska

Iowa

IL

IN

Ohio

PA

Red Lion

NJ

DE

MD

Washington DC

Nevada

Utah

Ft. Collins

Colorado

Kansas

Missouri

UNITED

WV

VA

KY

Greenville

NC

Bermuda (UK)

California

Rancho Simi

Arizona

New Mexico

STATES

Oklahoma

AR

Nashville

Morrison

Vandiver

Lebanon

TN

SC

Furman

MS

AL

GA

New Orleans

LA

Milton

Florida

Okeechobee

Texas

Gulf of Mexico

MEXICO

see Central America and the Caribbean map

Mexico City

PACIFIC OCEAN

see South America map

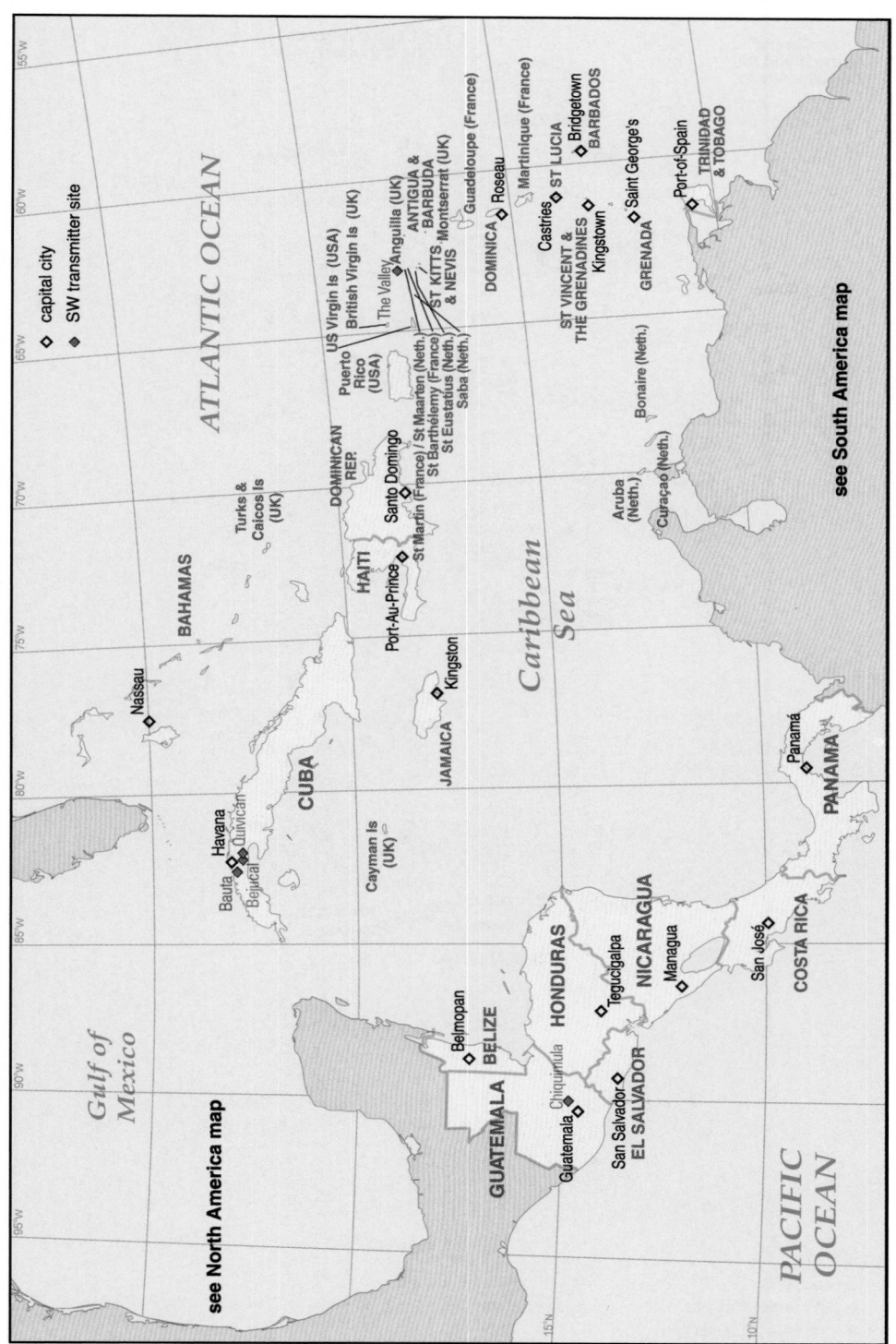

see Central America and the Caribbean map

see Central America and the Caribbean map

Caracas

VENEZUELA

Georgetown
Paramaribo

GUYANA

COLOMBIA

◇ Bogotá

SURINAME

French Guiana

NORTH ATLANTIC OCEAN

Puerto Lleras
San José del Guaviare

Boa Vista

Macapá

São Gabriel da Cachoeira

Bragança
Belém

Quito ◇

Tena
ECUADOR

Iquitos

Tefé

Manaus

Coari

Parintins

Santarém

Huancabamba

Saraguro

B R A Z I L

Chachapoyas

Cruzeiro do Sul

Araguaína

Chiclayo
Santiago de Chuco

Bolívar

PERU

Rio Branco

Porto Velho

Huaraz
Huanuco
Cerro de Pasco

Atalaya
Pichanaki

Xapuri

Junín

Quillabamba
Urubamba

Riberalta

Lima ◇

Cusco

Puerto Maldonado

Tarma
Huancavelica

Huanta
Sicuani

Tumupasa
Reyes

Santa Ana del Yacuma

Cuiabá

Trinidad

Brasília

BOLIVIA

S. Ignacio de Velasco

Arequipa

La Paz ◇

Goiânia

Cochabamba
Putre

Santa Cruz
Siglo Veinte

S. José de Chiquitos

Campo Grande

Belo Horizonte

Yura

Camargo

Ibitinga

Congonhas
São Gonçalo
Rio de Janeiro
Cachoeira Paulista

Uyuni

PARAGUAY

Araraquara

Asunción ◇

Londrina
Limeira

Aparecida

Foz de Iguaçu

São Paulo

Curitiba

SOUTH PACIFIC OCEAN

CHILE

Camboriú

Porto Alegre

Artigas

URUGUAY

Santiago ◇

General Pacheco

Castillos

Buenos Aires

Montevideo

ARGENTINA

Temuco

SOUTH ATLANTIC OCEAN

Falkland Is. (UK)

◇ capital city
◆ SW transmitter site
◆ SW time signal station

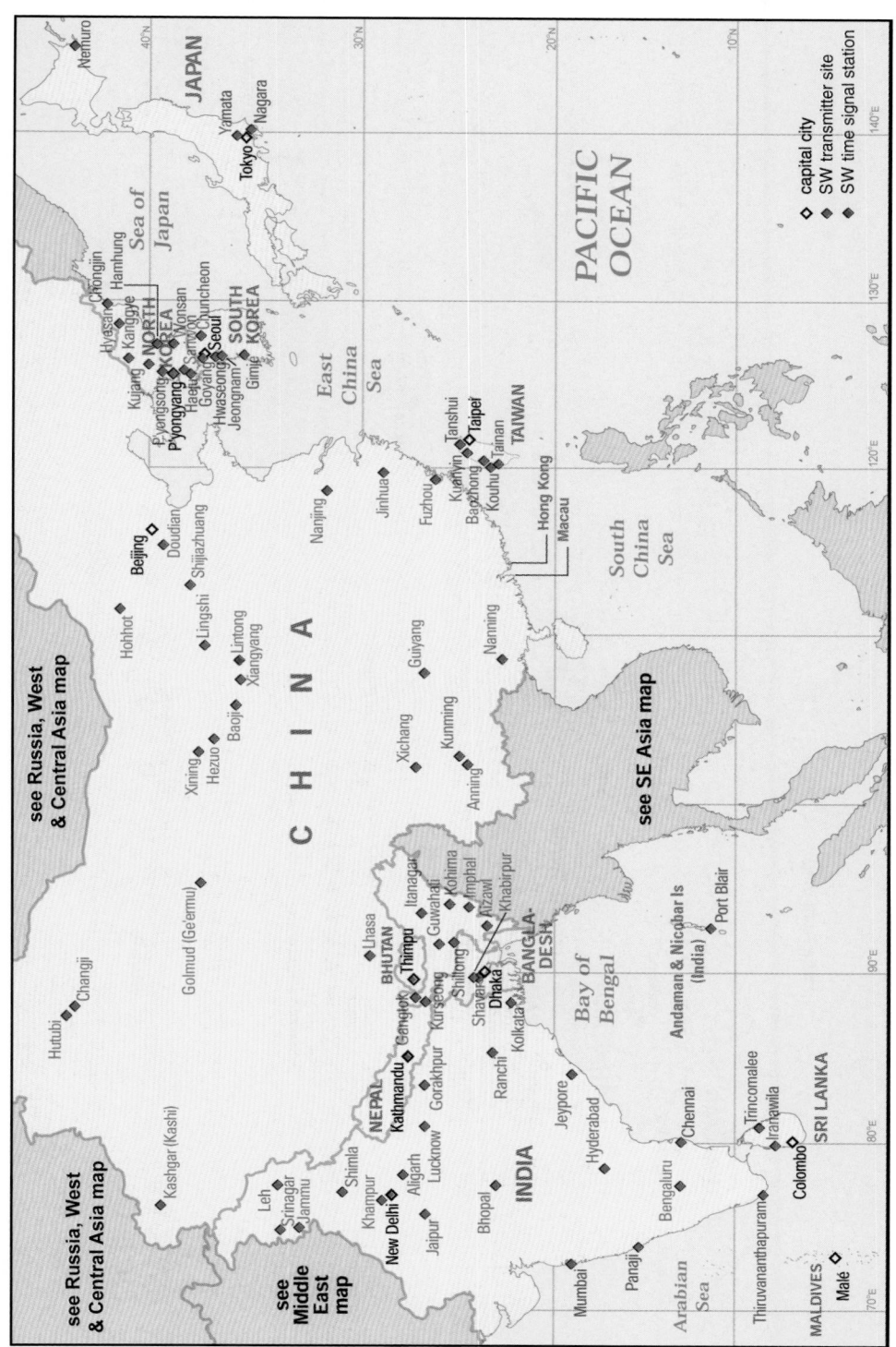

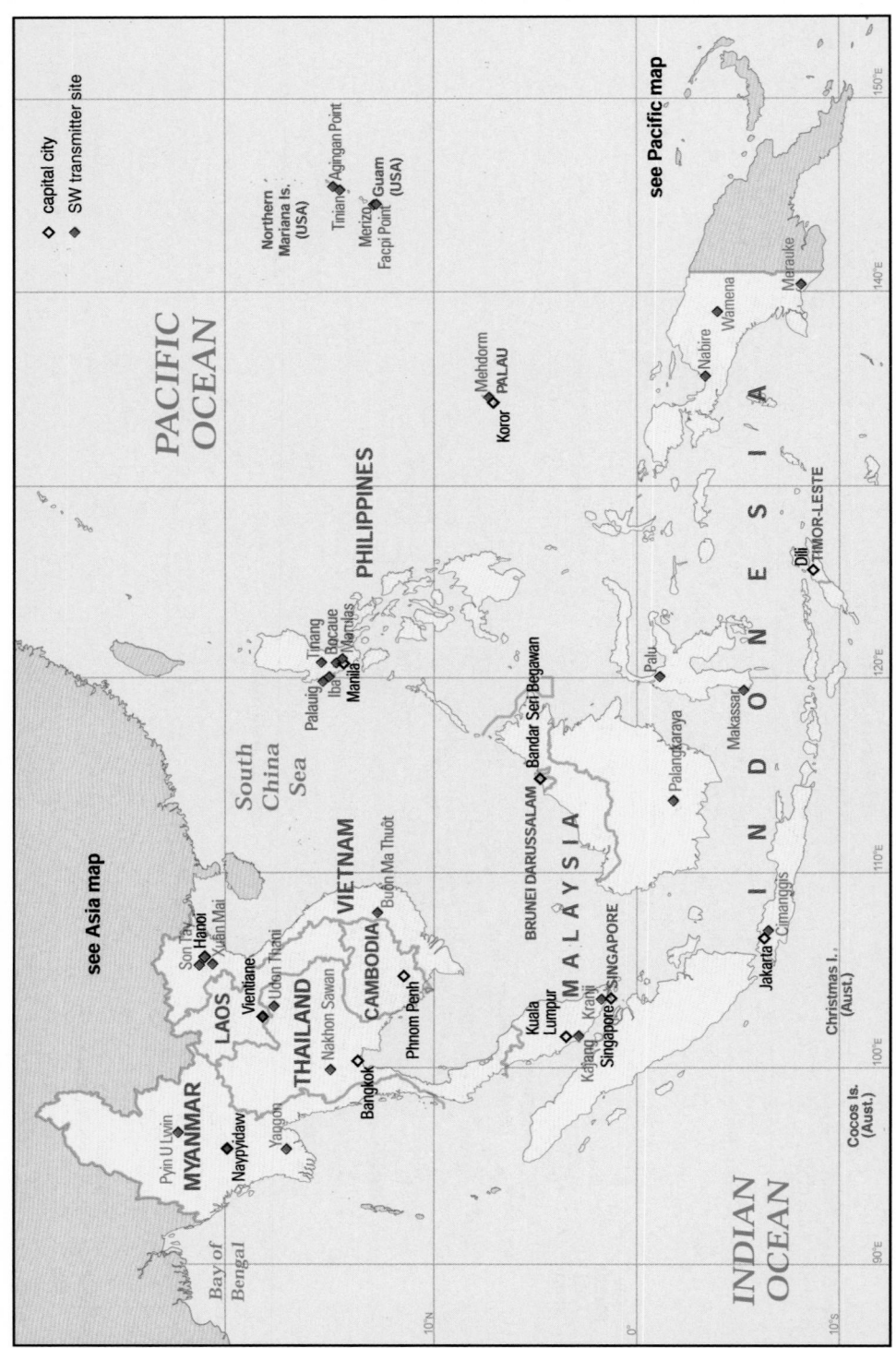

◇ capital city
◆ SW transmitter site

PACIFIC OCEAN

Northern Mariana Is. (USA)
Tinian Agingan Point
Merizo Guam (USA)
Facpi Point (USA)

Marauke

Warnena

Nabire

Mehdorm
Koror PALAU

PHILIPPINES

Tinang
Bocaue
Palauig Marulas
Iba Manila

Dili
TIMOR-LESTE

Palu

I N D O N E S I A

South China Sea

BRUNEI DARUSSALAM
Bandar Seri Begawan

Makassa

Palangkaraya

VIETNAM
Buôn Ma Thuột

see Asia map

Son Tay
Hanoi
Xuân Mai

LAOS
Vientiane
Ubon Thani

M A L A Y S I A

SINGAPORE

Jakarta
Cimanggis

CAMBODIA
Phnom Penh

THAILAND
Nakhon Sawan

Kuala Lumpur
Kranji
Kajang Singapore

Bangkok

Christmas I., (Aust.)

MYANMAR
Pyin U Lwin
Naypyidaw

Yangon

Cocos Is. (Aust.)

Bay of Bengal

INDIAN OCEAN

see Pacific map

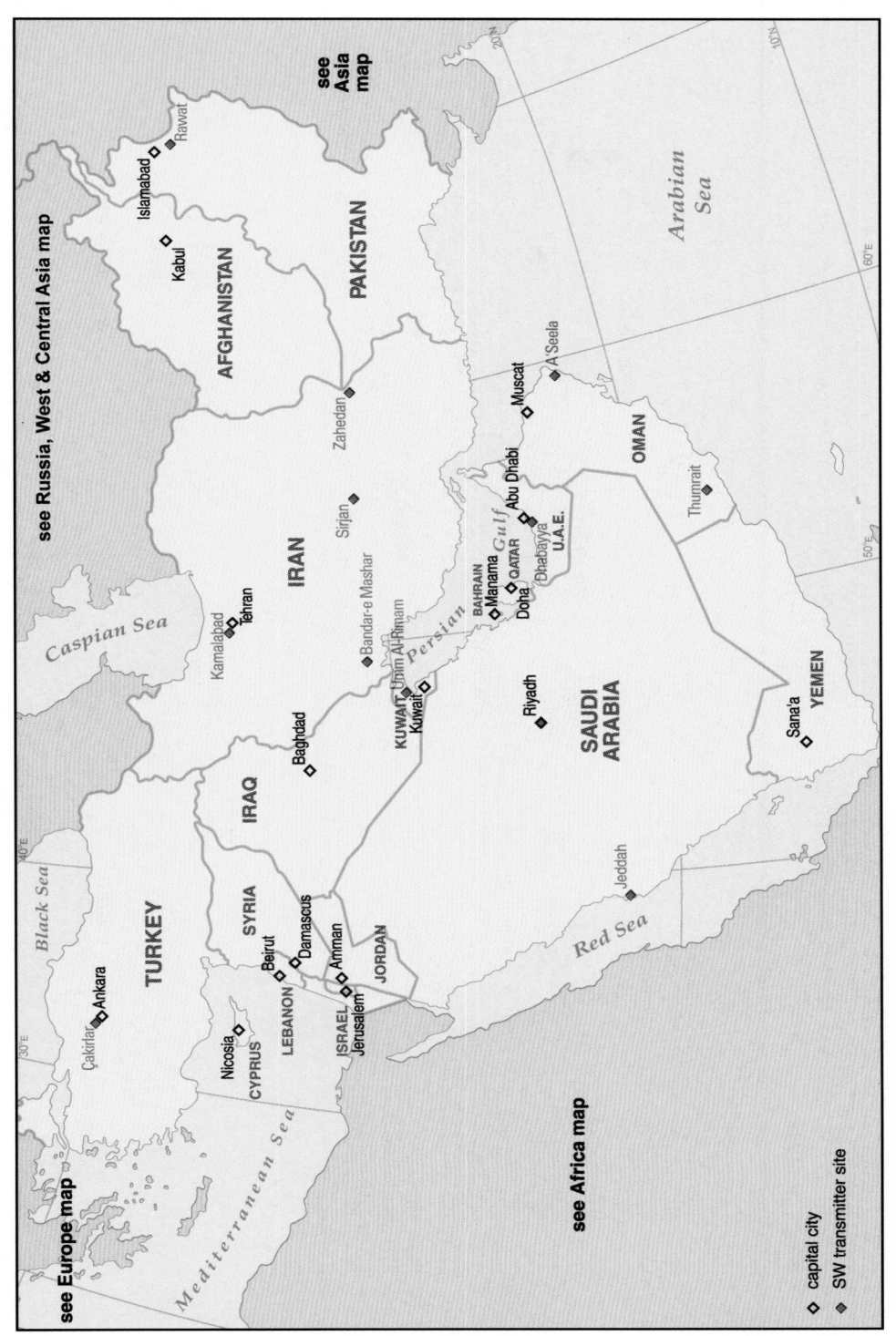

see Asia map

see Russia, West & Central Asia map

Rawat
Islamabad
Kabul
AFGHANISTAN
PAKISTAN

Zahedan

Arabian
Sea

Muscat
A'Seela
Abu Dhabi
OMAN
Thumrait

Sirjan
IRAN
Bandar-e Mashar
BAHRAIN
Manama
QATAR
Doha
Dhabayya
U.A.E.

Caspian Sea

Kamalabad
Tehran
Umm Al-Rimam
Kuwait
KUWAIT

Riyadh
SAUDI
ARABIA

YEMEN
Sana'a

Baghdad
IRAQ

Persian Gulf

Black Sea

TURKEY
Çakirlar Ankara

SYRIA
Damascus
Beirut
Amman
JORDAN

Nicosia
CYPRUS
LEBANON
ISRAEL
Jerusalem

Jeddah

Red Sea

Mediterranean Sea

see Europe map

see Africa map

◇ capital city
◆ SW transmitter site

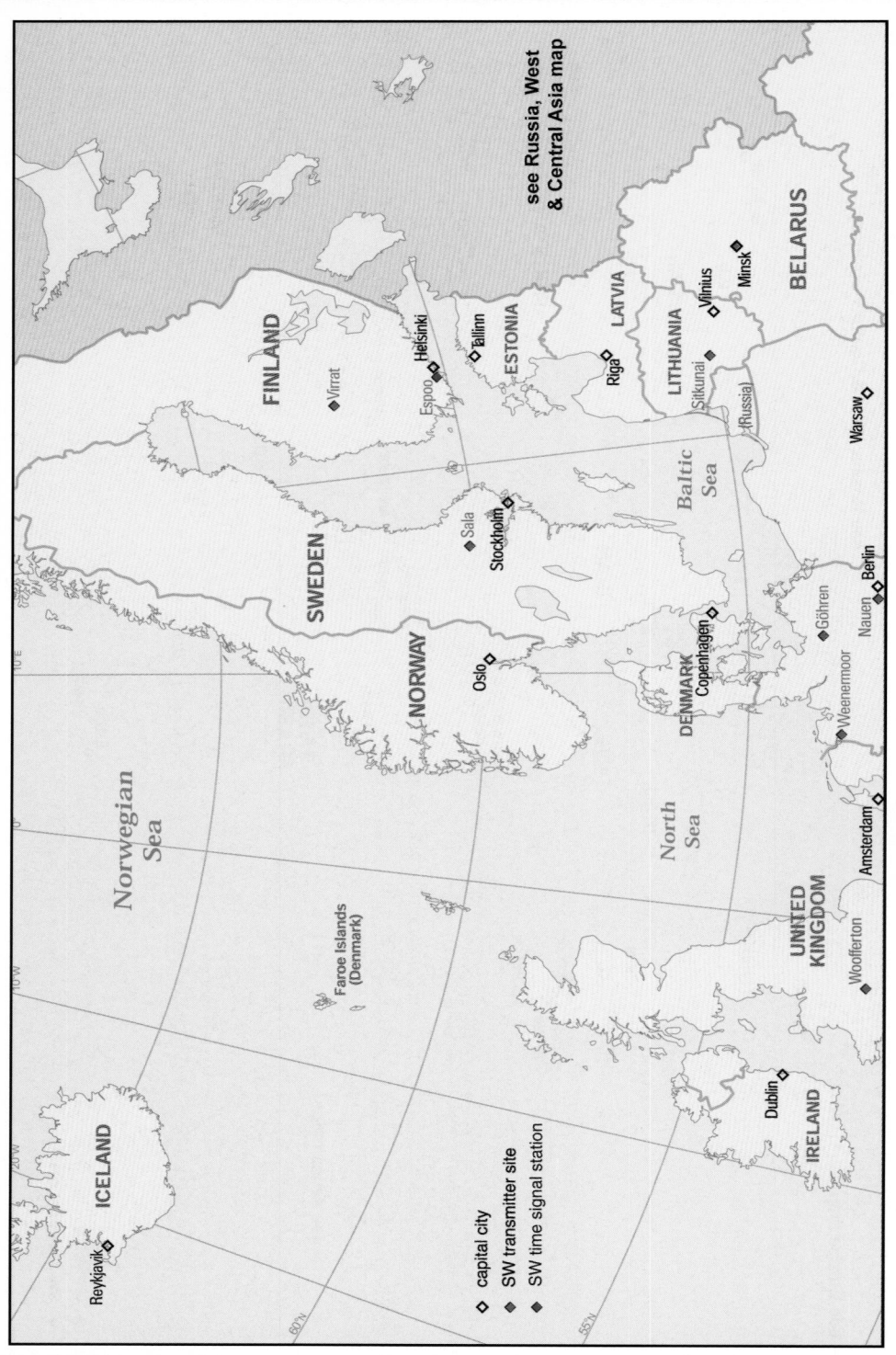

see Russia, West
& Central Asia map

BELARUS

Minsk ◆

Vilnius ◇

LITHUANIA

Šikūnai ◆

(Russia)

LATVIA

Riga ◇

Warsaw ◆

ESTONIA

Tallinn ◇

FINLAND

Virrat ◆

Helsinki ◇
Espoo ◆

SWEDEN

Sala ◆
Stockholm ◇

Baltic
Sea

Berlin ◇
Göhren ◆
Nauen ◆
Weenermoor ◆

NORWAY

Oslo ◇

DENMARK
Copenhagen ◇

North
Sea

Amsterdam ◇

Norwegian
Sea

Faroe Islands
(Denmark)

UNITED
KINGDOM

Woofferton ◆

ICELAND

Reykjavík ◇

Dublin ◇

IRELAND

◇ capital city
◆ SW transmitter site
◆ SW time signal station

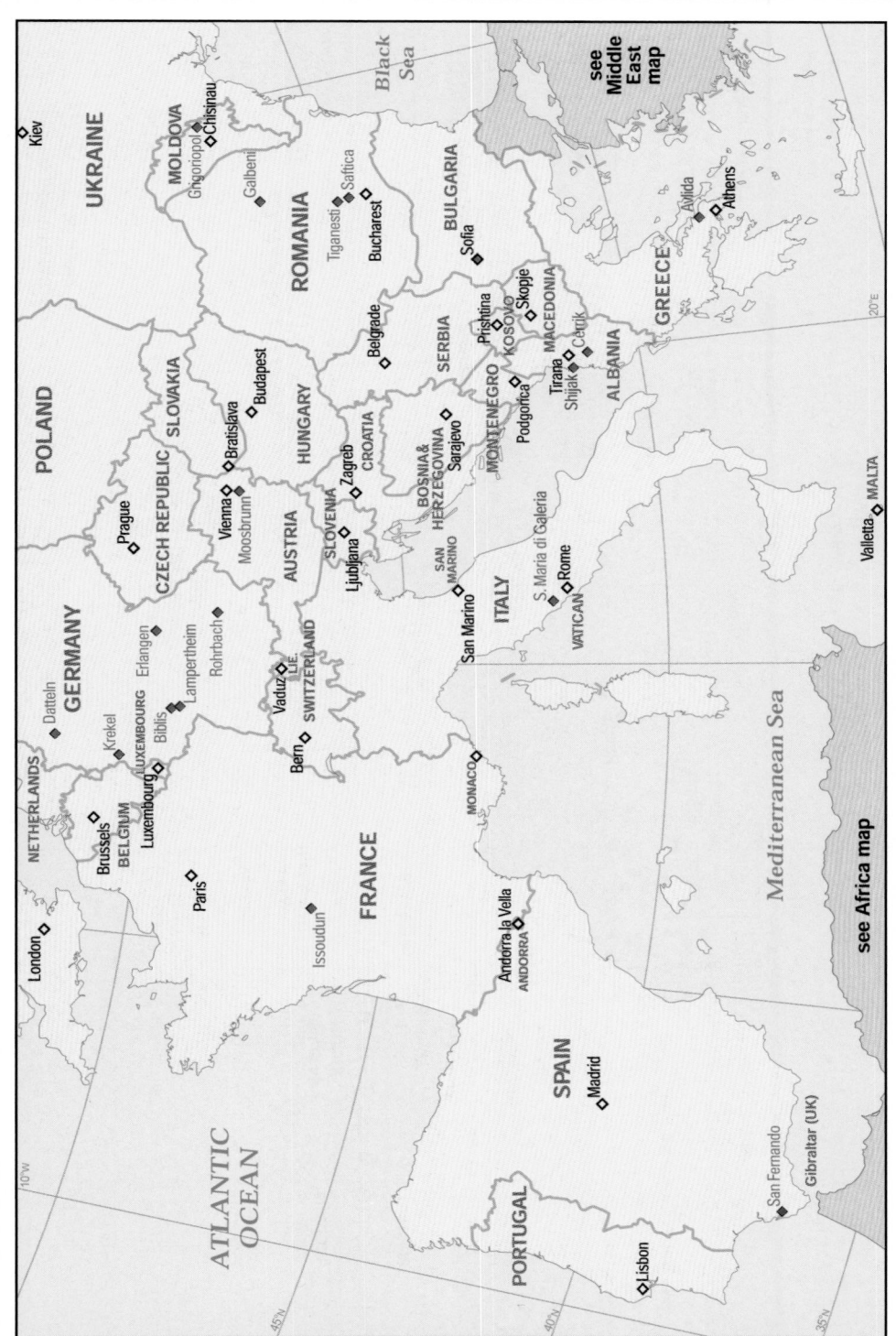

Black Sea

see Middle East map

Kiev

UKRAINE

MOLDOVA
Grigoriopol
Chisinau
Galbeni

ROMANIA
Tiganesti
Saftica
Bucharest

BULGARIA
Sofia

Avlida
Athens

GREECE

20°E

POLAND

SLOVAKIA
Budapest

HUNGARY

Bratislava

CZECH REPUBLIC
Prague

Vienna
Moosbrunn
AUSTRIA

SLOVENIA
Ljubljana

Zagreb

CROATIA

BOSNIA &
HERZEGOVINA
Sarajevo

Belgrade

SERBIA

Prishtina
KOSOVO
Skopje
MACEDONIA
Cerrik
Tirana
Shijak
Podgorica
MONTENEGRO
ALBANIA

GERMANY
Datteln
Krekel
LUXEMBOURG
Biblis
Lampertheim
Erlangen
Rohrbach

Vaduz
LIE.
SWITZERLAND
Bern

NETHERLANDS

Brussels
BELGIUM
Luxembourg

SAN
MARINO
San Marino

S. Maria di Galeria
Rome
VATICAN

ITALY

Valletta
MALTA

London

Paris

FRANCE

Issoudun

MONACO

Mediterranean Sea

see Africa map

ATLANTIC
OCEAN

Andorra la Vella
ANDORRA

SPAIN
Madrid

10°W

PORTUGAL

Lisbon

San Fernando

Gibraltar (UK)

45°N

40°N

35°N

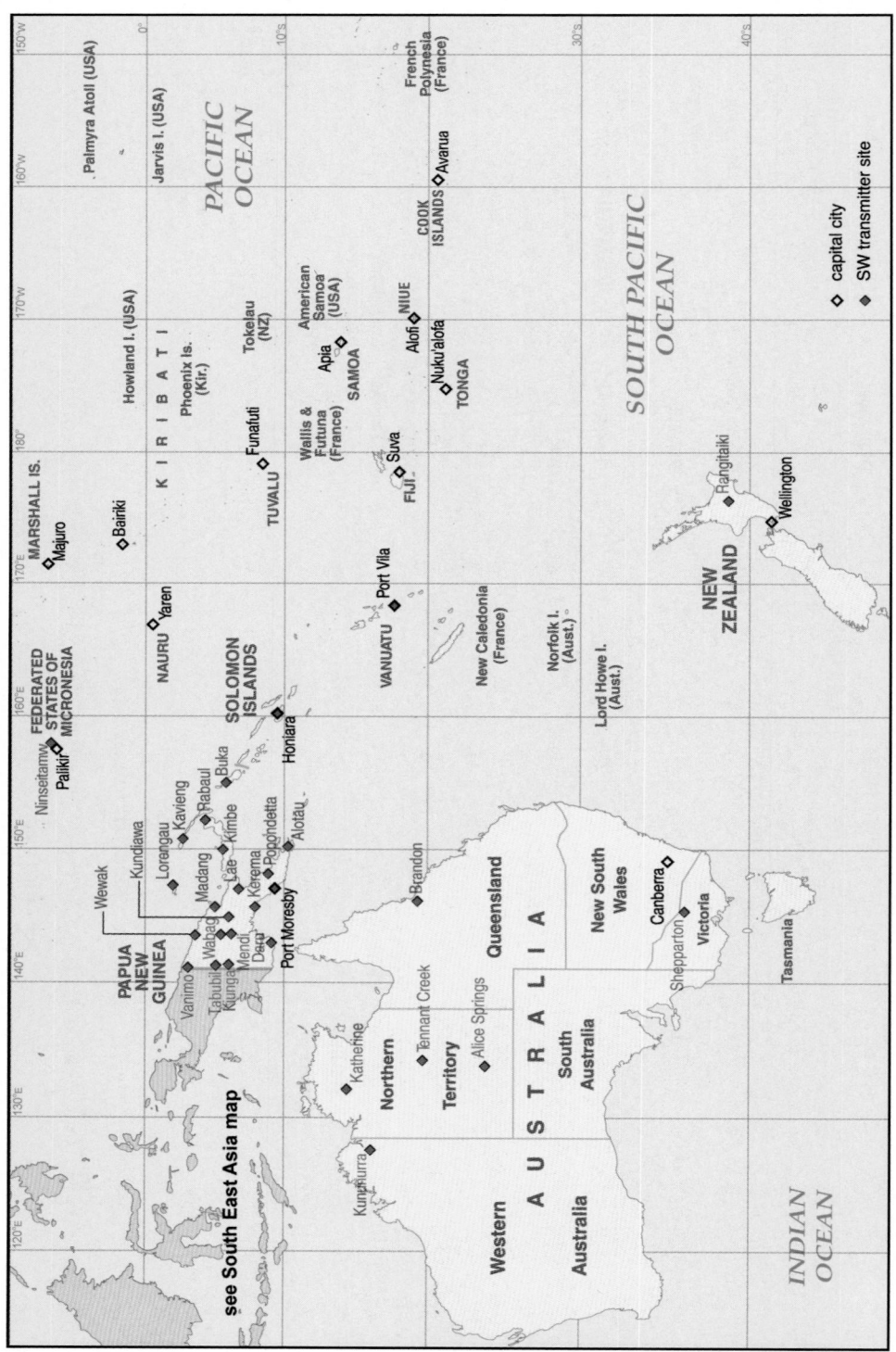

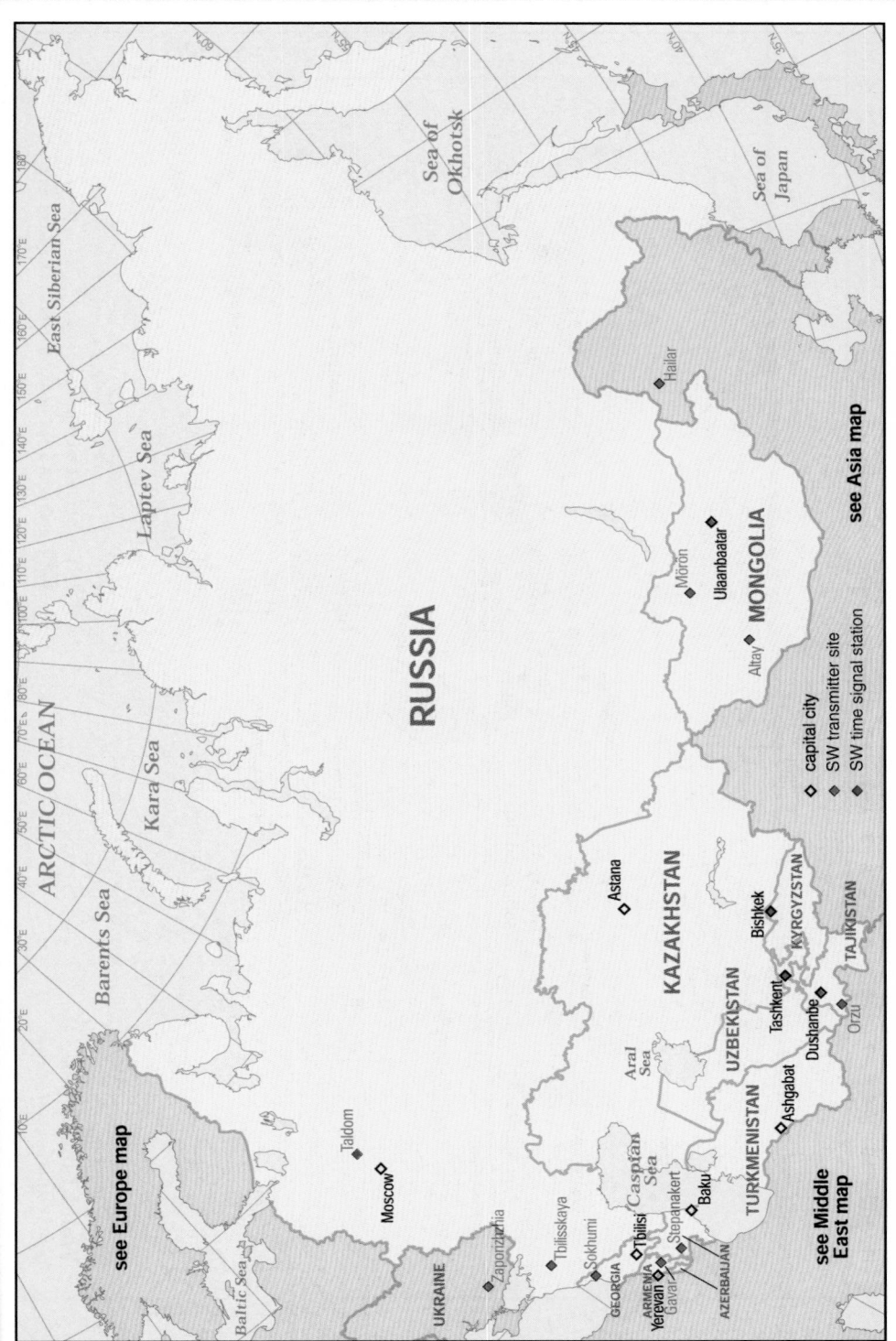

Sea of Okhotsk

Sea of Japan

East Siberian Sea

Laptev Sea

Kara Sea

Barents Sea

ARCTIC OCEAN

Baltic Sea

RUSSIA

Hailar

Mörön

Ulaanbaatar

MONGOLIA

Altay

see Asia map

◇ capital city
◆ SW transmitter site
◆ SW time signal station

Astana

KAZAKHSTAN

Bishkek

KYRGYZSTAN

Tashkent

Dushanbe

TAJIKISTAN

Orzu

UZBEKISTAN

Aral Sea

Ashgabat

TURKMENISTAN

Caspian Sea

Baku

AZERBAIJAN

Stepanakert

Sokhumi

Tbilisskaya

Tbilisi

GEORGIA

Gavar

Yerevan

ARMENIA

Taldom

Moscow

Zaporizhzhia

UKRAINE

see Europe map

see Middle East map

www.wrth.com

61

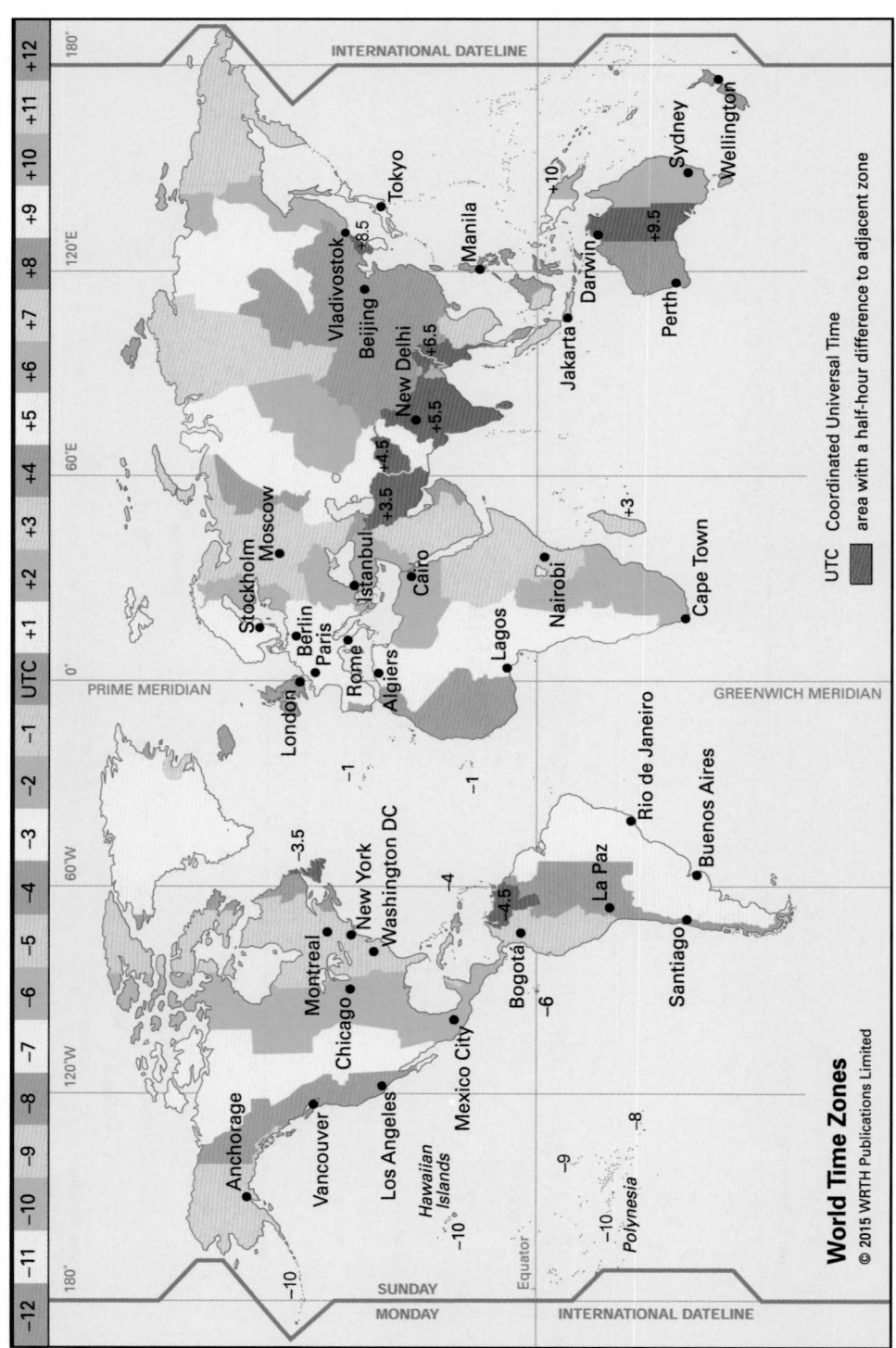

World Time Zones
© 2015 WRTH Publications Limited

UTC Coordinated Universal Time

area with a half-hour difference to adjacent zone

INTERNATIONAL DATELINE

PRIME MERIDIAN

GREENWICH MERIDIAN

INTERNATIONAL DATELINE

SUNDAY

MONDAY

Equator

-12 -11 -10 -9 -8 -7 -6 -5 -4 -3 -2 -1 UTC +1 +2 +3 +4 +5 +6 +7 +8 +9 +10 +11 +12

180° 120°W 60°W 0° 60°E 120°E 180°

Anchorage
Vancouver
Los Angeles
Hawaiian Islands
Mexico City
Chicago
Montreal
New York
Washington DC
Bogotá
La Paz
Santiago
Buenos Aires
Rio de Janeiro
Polynesia
London
Stockholm
Berlin
Paris
Rome
Algiers
Lagos
Nairobi
Cape Town
Moscow
Istanbul
Cairo
Vladivostok
Beijing
New Delhi
Tokyo
Manila
Jakarta
Darwin
Perth
Sydney
Wellington

-3.5
-4
-4.5
-6
-1
-1
-8
-9
-10
-10
+3
+3.5
+4.5
+5.5
+6.5
+8.5
+9.5
+10

WORLD TIME TABLE

Differences marked + or - show the number of hours ahead, or behind, UTC. Variations from Standard Time for part of the year (referred to as DST or Summer Time) are shown below; see the various country sections for the dates of operation. *) DST2016-2017 subject to confirmation
N=Normal (Standard) Time; **D**=Daylight Saving Time (DST) ¹) in parts of the territory ²) for other regions, see country section

Location	N	D
Afghanistan	+4½	+4½
Alaska	−9	−8
Aleutian Is	−10	−9
Albania	+1	+2
Algeria	+1	+1
American Samoa	−11	−11
Andorra	+1	+1
Angola	+1	+1
Anguilla	−4	−4
Antarctica		
(Argentine)	−3	−3
(Chilean)	−4	−4
(McMurdo)	+12	+13
Antigua	−4	−4
Argentina (B.Aires)²	−3	−3
Armenia	+4	+4
Aruba	−4	−4
Ascension I.	UTC	UTC
Australia		
We. Australia	+8	+8
No. Territory	+9½	+9½
So. Australia	+9½	+10½
Queensland	+10	+10
VIC, NSW, TAS	+10	+11
Austria	+1	+2
Azerbaijan (Baki)²	+4	+5
Azores	−1	UTC
Bahamas	−5	−4
Bahrain	+3	+3
Bangladesh	+6	+6
Barbados	−4	−4
Belarus	+3	+3
Belgium	+1	+2
Belize	−6	−6
Benin	+1	+1
Bermuda	−4	−3
Bhutan	+6	+6
Bolivia	−4	−4
Bonaire	−4	−4
Bosnia & Herzegovina	+1	+2
Botswana	+2	+2
Brazil (Brasília)²	−3	−2
British Ind. Oc. Terr.	+6	+6
British Virgin Is	−4	−4
Brunei	+8	+8
Bulgaria	+2	+3
Burkina Faso	UTC	UTC
Burundi	+2	+2
Cambodia	+7	+7
Cameroon	+1	+1
Canada		
NL (SE Labr. & Is)	−3½	−2½
NL¹, NB, NS, PE, QC¹	−4	−3
QC¹	−4	−4
NT¹, NU¹, ON¹, QC¹	−5	−4
NU¹	−5	−5
MB, NU¹, ON¹	−6	−5
SK¹	−6	−6
AB, BC¹, NT, NU¹, SK¹	−7	−6
BC¹	−7	−7
BC¹, YT	−8	−7
Canary Is	UTC	+1
Cape Verde	−1	−1
Cayman Is*	−5	−5
Ce. African Rep.	+1	+1
Chad	+1	+1
Chile	−4	−4
China (P.R.)	+8	+8
Christmas Is	+7	+7
Cocos (Keeling) Is	+6½	+6½
Colombia	−5	−5
Comoros	+3	+3
Congo (Kinshasa)²	+1	+1

Location	N	D
Congo (Rep.)	+1	+1
Cook Is	−10	−10
Costa Rica	−6	−6
Côte d'Ivoire	UTC	UTC
Croatia	+1	+2
Cuba	−5	−4
Curaçao	−4	−4
Cyprus	+2	+3
Akrotiri & Dhekelia	+2	+3
Czech Rep.	+1	+2
Denmark	+1	+2
Djibouti	+3	+3
Dominica	−4	−4
Dominican Rep.	−4	−4
Easter I.	−5	−5
Ecuador	−5	−5
Egypt*	+2	+3
El Salvador	−6	−6
Equatorial Guinea	+1	+1
Eritrea	+3	+3
Estonia	+2	+3
Ethiopia	+3	+3
Falkland Is*	−4	−3
Faroe Is	UTC	+1
Fiji	+12	+13
Finland	+2	+3
France	+1	+2
French Guiana	−3	−3
French Poly.(Tahiti)²	−10	−10
French So.& Ant. L.	+5	+5
Gabon	+1	+1
Galapagos Is	−6	−6
Gambia	UTC	UTC
Georgia (Tbilisi)²	+4	+4
Germany	+1	+2
Ghana	UTC	UTC
Gibraltar	+1	+2
Greece	+2	+3
Greenland (Nuuk)²	−3	−2
Grenada	−4	−4
Guadeloupe	−4	−4
Guam	+10	+10
Guatemala	−6	−6
Guinea	UTC	UTC
Guinea-Bissau	UTC	UTC
Guyana	−4	−4
Haiti	−5	−5
Hawaii	−10	−10
Honduras	−6	−6
Hong Kong	+8	+8
Hungary	+1	+2
Iceland	UTC	UTC
India	+5½	+5½
Indonesia (Jakarta)²	+7	+7
Iran	+3½	+4½
Iraq	+3	+3
Ireland	UTC	+1
Israel	+2	+3
West Bank & Gaza	+2	+3
Italy	+1	+2
Jamaica	−5	−5
Japan	+9	+9
Jordan	+2	+3
Kazakhstan (Astana)²	+6	+6
Kenya	+3	+3
Kiribati	+12	+12
Korea (North, DPR)	+8½	+8½
Korea (South, Rep.)	+9	+9
Kosovo	+1	+2
Kuwait	+3	+3
Kyrgyzstan	+6	+6
Laos	+7	+7
Latvia	+2	+3

Location	N	D
Lebanon	+2	+3
Lesotho	+2	+2
Liberia	UTC	UTC
Libya	+2	+2
Liechtenstein	+1	+2
Lithuania	+2	+3
Lord Howe I.	+10½	+11
Luxembourg	+1	+2
Macau	+8	+8
Macedonia	+1	+2
Madagascar	+3	+3
Madeira	UTC	+1
Malawi	+2	+2
Malaysia	+8	+8
Maldives	+5	+5
Mali	UTC	UTC
Malta	+1	+2
Marshall Is	+12	+12
Martinique	−4	−4
Mauritania	UTC	UTC
Mauritius	+4	+4
Mayotte	+3	+3
Mexico (Mexico City)²	−6	−5
Micronesia		
Chuuk, Yap	+10	+10
Kosrae, Pohnpei	+11	+11
Moldova	+2	+3
Monaco	+1	+2
Mongolia (U-baataar)²	+8	+8
Montenegro	+1	+2
Montserrat	−4	−4
Morocco	UTC	+1
Ceuta & Melilla	+1	+2
Mozambique	+2	+2
Myanmar	+6½	+6½
Namibia	+1	+2
Nauru	+12	+12
Nepal	+5¾	+5¾
Netherlands	+1	+2
New Caledonia	+11	+11
New Zealand	+12	+13
Nicaragua	−6	−6
Niger	+1	+1
Nigeria	+1	+1
Niue	−11	−11
Norfolk I.	+11	+11
No. Mariana Is	+10	+10
Norway	+1	+2
Oman	+4	+4
Pakistan	+5	+5
Palau	+9	+9
Panama	−5	−5
Papua New Guinea	+10	+10
Paraguay	−4	−3
Peru	−5	−5
Philippines	+8	+8
Pitcairn Is	−8	−8
Poland	+1	+2
Portugal	UTC	+1
Puerto Rico	−4	−4
Qatar	+3	+3
Réunion	+4	+4
Romania	+2	+3
Russia (Moscow)²	+3	+3
Rwanda	+2	+2
Saba	−4	−4
Samoa	+13	+14
San Marino	+1	+2
São Tomé & Prínc.	UTC	UTC
Saudi Arabia	+3	+3
Senegal	UTC	UTC
Serbia	+1	+2
Seychelles	+4	+4

Location	N	D
Sierra Leone	UTC	UTC
Singapore	+8	+8
Slovakia	+1	+2
Slovenia	+1	+2
Solomon Is	+11	+11
Somalia	+3	+3
South Africa	+2	+2
South Sudan	+3	+3
Spain	+1	+2
Sri Lanka	+5½	+5½
St. Barthélemy	−4	−4
St. Eustatius	−4	−4
St. Helena	UTC	UTC
St. Kitts & Nevis	−4	−4
St. Lucia	−4	−4
St. Martin	−4	−4
St. Pierre & Miq.	−3	−2
St. Vincent & Gren.	−4	−4
Sudan	+3	+3
Suriname	−3	−3
Swaziland	+2	+2
Sweden	+1	+2
Switzerland	+1	+2
Syria	+2	+3
Taiwan	+8	+8
Tajikistan	+5	+5
Tanzania	+3	+3
Thailand	+7	+7
Timor-Leste	+9	+9
Togo	UTC	UTC
Tokelau	+13	+13
Tonga	+13	+13
Trinidad	−4	−4
Tristan da Cunha	UTC	UTC
Tunisia	+1	+1
Turkey	+2	+3
Turkmenistan	+5	+5
Turks & Caicos Is	−5	−4
Tuvalu	+12	+12
Uganda	+3	+3
Ukraine (Kyiv)²	+2	+3
United Arab Em.	+4	+4
United Kingdom	UTC	+1
Uruguay*	−3	−2
USA		
Eastern Time (CT, DE, FL, GA, IN¹, KY, MA, MD, ME, MI, NC, NH, NJ, NY, OH, PA, RI, SC, VA, VT, WV)	−5	−4
Central Time (AL, AR, IA, IL, IN¹, KS, LA, MN, MO, MS, ND, NE, OK, SD, TN, TX, WI)	−6	−5
Mountain Timeª (N-E AZ, CO, ID, MT, NM, UT, WY)	−7	−6
ª) exc. most of AZ	−7	−7
Pacific Time (CA, NV, OR, WA)	−8	−7
Uzbekistan	+5	+5
Vanuatu	+11	+11
Vatican City State	+1	+2
Venezuela	−4½	−4½
Vietnam	+7	+7
Virgin Is	−4	−4
Wake I.	+12	+12
Wallis & Futuna	+12	+12
Yemen	+3	+3
Zambia	+2	+2
Zimbabwe	+2	+2

NATIONAL RADIO

Section Contents

Initial entries for each letter,
see Main Index for full details

Features & Reviews

National Radio

International Radio

Frequency Lists

National Television

Reference

AFGHANISTAN

LT: UTC +4½h — **Pop:** 33 million — **Pr.L:** Dari, Pashto, Turkmen, Uzbek — **E.C:** 50Hz, 220V — **ITU:** AFG

AFGHANISTAN TELECOM REGULATORY AUTHORITY (ARTA) ✉ Moh. Jan Khan Watt 10th floor MoCIT Building, Kabul ☎+93 20 2105361 **W:** atra.gov.af

RADIO TELEVISION AFGHANISTAN (RTA, Gov.)
✉ PO Box 544, Mohammad Akbar Khan Street 13, Kabul ☎+93 20 2102487 **W:** rta.org.af **E:** info@rta.org.af
LP: DG: Zarin Anzor. DG Radio: Abdul Ghaney Mudaqiq.
MW: Kabul (Pol-e-Charkhi) 1107kHz 400kW.
FM: Kabul 93.0 1kW, 105.2MHz 30W.
D.Prgr: 0100-1930. Main **N:** Pashto 1430, Dari 1530. **Ann:** "Radyo Afghanistan, Kabul". For Foreign Sce. see International Radio Section. Relayed also on 93.0MHz for Kabul.

PROVINCIAL STATIONS
R. Badakhshan, Faizabad: 584kHz‡ 5kW, 105.1MHz‡ 30W – **R. Badghis,** Qalay-e Naw: 1500kHz 6kW, 91.4MHz 250W. 0130-0330, 1330-1630, times vary – **R. Baghlan,** Pol-e-Khomri 103.0MHz, Baghlan: 106.6MHz 250W – **R. Balkh,** Mazar-e-Sharif: 1584kHz 10kW, 105.1MHz 0.1kW. In Dari/Pashto/Tajik/Uzbek: 0230-0430 (Fri 0430-0730), 1230-1530 – **R. Bamyan:** 96.0MHz 1kW – **R. Day Kundi:** Nili 1200kHz‡ 0.5kW, 103.2MHz 30W, Qalat 99.0MHz 0.5kW – **R. Farah,** Farah: 1044kHz‡ 7kW, 88.5MHz 1kW (F.P.I.). 0300-0430 – **R. Faryab,** Maimana: 594kHz 5kW, 104.3MHz 30W. 1230-1430 – **R. Ghazni** 1017kHz 10kW, 92.4MHz 30W. 0230-0330, 1130-1530 – **R. Ghor,** Chaghcharan: 1584kHz 0.5kW, 93.4MHz – **R. Helmand,** Lashkar Ga: 999kHz‡ 5kW, 96.1MHz 1kW. 0330-0730, 1130-1430 **W:** hrt.aft – **R. Herat** 1550kHz 0.1kW, 95.5MHz 250W. 0300-0500, 1130-1330 – **R. Jowzjan,** Sheberghan 106.6MHz 250W – **R. Kandahar:** 1305kHz 10kW, 90.6MHz 1kW. 0230-1430 **W:** kandahartv-gov.com – **R. Kapisa,** Mahmud-e-Raqi: 101.1MHz 600W – **R. Khost:** 91.2MHz 1kW – **R. Kunar,** Asadabad: 1575kHz 10kW, 100.5MHz 1kW.0330-0530, 0930-1500 – **R. Kunduz** 909kHz 10kW, 94.4MHz 250W – **R. Laghman,** Mehtarlam: 88.2MHz‡ 0.5kW – **R. Logar,** Pol-e-Alam: 92.7MHz – **R. Nangarhar,** Jalalabad: 1440kHz 10kW, 93.5MHz 250W. 0230-0730, 1030-1130 – **R. Nimroz,** Zaranj: 1584kHz 2kW, 90.0MHz 1kW. 0330-0530, 1230-1500 (Fri 1930) – **R. Nuristan,** Nuristan: 1500kHz 0.1kW, 88.5MHz 300W – **R. Paktia,** Gardez: 909kHz 50W, 104.2MHz 0.5kW – **R. Paktika,** Zareh Sharan: 93.2MHz – **R. Paktin Voice** (semi-gov), Shakin 1386kHz 5kW, 89.8MHz 150W. 0230-1730. **W:** paktinvoice. com – **R. Panjshir,** Bazarak: 88.0MHz 0.1kW – **R. Parwan,** Charikar: 88.9MHz – **R. Samangan,** Aybak: 1500kHz1 0.1kW, 90.4MHz‡ 150W – **R. Sar-e-Pol:** 89.9MHz – **R. Takhar,** Taloqan: 91.2MHz 30W – **R. Uruzgan,** Tarin Kowt: 93.0MHz 50W – **R. Wardak,** Meydan Shahr: 88.9MHz – **R. Zabul,** Qalat: 936kHz 10kW, 88.7MHz.
‡ = inactive

BBG–R. FREE AFGHANISTAN / R. MASHAAL / VOA ASHNA & DEEWA R. (US Gov.)
R. Free Afghanistan & VOA Ashna R:
MW: Kabul (Pol-e-Charkhi) 1296kHz 400kW 0030-1730. **FM:** Herat/ Jalalabad/Kabul/Kandahar/Mazar-e-Sharif 100.5MHz. 24h in Dari/ Pashto/English.
R. Mashal & VOA Deewa R: MW: Khost 621kHz 0100-1900. **FM:** Asadabad/Gardez/Khost 100.5MHz.
For SW broadcasts & more details see International R. section (USA).

Independent commercial stations:
Arman FM ✉ P.O. Box 1045, Central PO, Kabul **W:** arman.fm **E:** info@arman.fm **LP:** Dir: Saad Mohseni. **FM:** 98.1MHz in Kabul (2kW)/Ghazni/Herat/Jalalabad/Kandahar/Konduz/Lashkar Ga/ Mazar-e-Sharif – **Ariana R.** ✉ Darlaman St. (near Ministry of Trade), Kabul ☎+93 70 151515 **W:** arianatelevision.com **E:** marketing@arianatelevision.com **LP:** Dir: Ahmad Zubair. **FM:** Kabul 93.5MHz – **R. City** ✉ Karte 3, District 6, Street 3, House no. 96, Kabul ☎+93 0 2100995/77 7955955 **W:** citymedia.af **E:** info@citymedia.af **LP:** Saleem Totakhil, CEO. **FM:** Kabul/Mazar-i-Sharif: 95.5MHz 3.5/1kW – **R. Killid** ✉ The Killid Group, House no. 442, Street No. 6, Chardehi Watt, Near to Uzbekha Mosque, Karta-e-sea, Kabul 442 ☎+93 77 1088888 **W:** tkg. af **E:** info@killid.com **LP:** Dir: Najiba Ayubi. **FM:** Kabul 88.0MHz 4kW, Herat 88.0MHz 2kW, Khost 88.2MHz. **Kabul Rock R:** 108.0MHz – **R. Maiwand,** Kabul: 92.7MHz 1.5kW – **Nawa R. W:** sabacent.org **LP:** Dir: Mohammad Waqfi. **FM:** Kabul/Ghazni/Herat/Jalalabad/Kandahar/ Konduz/Mazar e-Sharif/Paktia: 103.1MHz.

Other stations (powers 50-500W if not stated otherwise, frqs in MHz):

Ayna R, Shahrak-e Shirpoor: 88.0 – **ERTV R,** (UNESCO), Kabul: 96.8 – **Gorbat FM,** Kabul: 91.8 – **Police FM,** Kabul: 96.5 **R. Abasin,** Jalalabad: 93.7 **W:** moi.gov.af/en/page/pfm – **R. Abasin,** Jalalabad: 93.7 – **R. Adib,** Shahr-e Jadid: 89.7 – **R. Aliksiz,** Kabul: 90.0 – **R. Amo,** Faizabad: 88.7 – **R. Amozgar,** Kabul: 101.3 – **R. Arghawan,** Ada-e Kabul: 90.1 – **R. Arkozia,** Charahi: 90.3 – **R. Armaghan,** Sheberghan: 89.9 – **R. Arya,** Kabul: 100.2 – **R. Arzu,** Mazar-e-Sharif: 91.8 – **R. Arzu ha FM,** Jada-e Sahat: 88.1 – **R. Aye Khanom,** Shahr-e Taliqan: 88.9 – **R. Azad Afgan,** Kandahar: 88.1 – **R. Azad Paktia Ghagh,** Gardez: 94.2 – **R. Armaghan,** Sheberghan: 89.9 – **R. Bakhtar,** Kabul: 99.2 – **R. Baran,** Herat: 98.4 1kW – **R. Biltoon,** Kabul: 104.9 – **R. Bustan,** Andkhoy: 87.7 – **R. Charchino,** Uruzgan prov: 88.1 – **R. Cheragh,** Kunduz: 87.4 – **R. Dahwat,** Kabul: 102.5 – **R. Daikundi,** Shahr-e Nili: 88.5 – **R. Darman,** Aqcha: 89.5 – **R. Dehkada,** Shahr-e Naw: 91.6 – **R. Dehrawod,** Uruzgan: 87.5 – **R. De Helo Karwan,** Khost: 90.6 – **R. Dunya-e-Naween,** Parwan: 87.9 – **R. Ejtima,** Logar: 88.5 – **R. Ertibat,** Malistan: 88.3 – **R. Faryad,** Herat: 87.8 – **R. Ghaznawiyan,** Ghazni: 89.3 – **R. Hamdard,** Ghazni prov: 94.9 – **R. Hamisha Bahar,** Nangarhar: 90.6 – **R. Hanzala,** Qalay-e Naw: 91.4 – **R. Humsada,** Takhar: 89.6 – **R. Istiqlal,** Baraki-Barak: 89.6 – **R. Jaghori,** Ghazni prov.: 90.9 – **R. Jaihoon,** Imam Shahib: 88.0 – **R. Javan,** Ghazni: 96.6 – **R. Jawanan,** Kabul: 97.5 – **R. Jurm,** Badakhshan prov: 98.0 – **R. Kaihan,** Tahmirat-e Spinzar: 88.4 – **R. Kalagush,** Nuristan prov: 90.0 – **R. Kawoon Voice,** Meterlam: 90.1 – **R. Khorasan,** Rokha: 89.3 – **R. Khushi,** Baghlan prov: 89.2 – **R. Kokcha,** Badakshan: 96.0 – **R. Meher,** Dasht-e Shor: 99.3 – **R. Milli e-Paygham,** Mohammad Agha: 94.5 – **R. Mirman,** Kandahar: 92.0 – **R. Mowj,** Kabul: 105.5 1kW – **R. Muram,** Nangarhar: 97.8 – **R. Muzdah,** Herat: 91.5MHz – **R. Nargis,** Jalalabad: 88.6 – **R. Nan:** Ghani Khel: 89.1 – **R. Naw-e-Bahar,** Balkh: 87.9 – **R. Nedaye Afghan,** Kabul: 99.6 – **R. Nedaye Solh,** Ghoreyan: 90.4 – **R. Nedaye Subh,** Ghoryan: 90.0 – **R. Nehad,** Mazar-e Sharif: 90.4MHz – **R. Nida,** Kabul: 97.2 – **R. Nin,** Khost: 89.1 – **R. Omid-e Jawan,** Ghazni: 96.9 – **R. Paiwastoon,** Terinkot: 89.9 – **R. Paktika Voice,** Zareh Sharan: 92.9 – **R. Payman,** Baghlan: 90.0 – **R. Pashtun Voice,** Shahr-e Sharan: 89.4 – **R. Payam,** Faizabad: 94.7 – **R. Qarabagh,** Kabul prov: 94.8 – **R. Qoyash,** Maimana: 89.0 – **R. Rabia-e Balkhi,** Mazar-e-Sharif: 89.7 – **R. Rah-e Farda,** Kabul: 92.0 – **R. Roshani,** Kunduz: 89.0 – **R. Rustam,** Aibak: 88.1 – **R. Sabawoon,** Lashkar Ga: 88.0 0.6kW – **R. Sadat,** Ghazni: 90.9 – **R. Safa,** Nangarhar prov: 89.7 – **R. Sahar,** Herat: 88.7 – **R. Samun,** Lashkar Ga: 88.6 – **R. Sana,** Pol-e Khumri: 87.8 – **R. Setara,** Kabul: 87.2 – **R. Setara-e Sahar,** Balkh: 91.3 – **R. Shahr,** Kabul: 95.5 – **R. Shahrwand,** Samangan prov: 87.8 – **R. Sharq,** Jalalabad: 91.3 – **R. Solh-e Paygham,** Khost: 88.8 – **R. Spin Ghar,** Ghani Khel: 89.4 – **R. Tahlim ul-Salaam,** Kandahar: 94.6 – **R. Takharistan,** Taloqan: 93.2 – **R. Tamana,** Faryab: 89.6 – **R. Tanin,** Shindan: 89.7 – **R. Tiraj Mir,** Pol-e Khumri: 89.4 – **R. Waranga,** Kandahar: 95.2 0.6kW – **R. Watan** Kabul: 100.8 – **R. Watandar:** Herat/Kabul 87.5 0.5/1kW – **R. VO Adalat,** Chagcharan: 90.3 – **R. VO Baharistan,** Baharak: 95.3 – **R. VO Haqiqat,** Aibaq: 90.0 – **R. VO Islam,** Kabul: 104.3 – **R. VO Jawan,** Herat University: 92.3 – **R. VO Kishm,** Badakhshan prov: 90.3 – **R. VO Najrab,** Kapisa prov: 96.0 – **R. VO Peace,** Naray: 94.0 – **R. VO Peace,** Jabul Saraj: 96.7 – **R. VO Wolas,** Khost: 96.4 – **R. Yawali Voice,** Sayedabad: 94.4 – **R. Zafar,** Paghman: 96.5 – **R. Zala Kunar,** Azadabad: 89.2 – **R. Zalah,** Kunduz prov.: 106.6 0.6kW – **R. Zhwandoon,** Kabul: 107.0 – **R. Zohra,** Kunduz: 89.8 – **R. Zrak,** Logar prov: 97.2 – **R. Zuhal,** Herat prov: 90.0 – **Rana FM,** Kandahar: 88.5. **W:** ranafm.org – **Salam Watandar,** Kabul: 98.9 1kW **W:** salamwatandar.com – **Saraish FM,** Sheberghan: 91.1 **W:** radiosaraish.webstarts.com – **Shamshod FM,** Ghanikhel: 101.1 – **Spogmai R,** Kabul: 102.2 – **University R.** (UNESCO), Kabul: 106.7 1.2kW, Herat 92.3 – **VO Afghan Women** (UNESCO), Kabul 96.3 10kW, Herat 88.7 – **Zala FM,** Naray: 89.2 60kW – **Zawon Voice R,** Khost: 99.7 – **Zenat R,** Pol-e Alam: 105.7.
NB: many stations are Internews affiliates and relay their news prgr: "Salam Watandar". **W:** internews.org

Relays of international stations:
BBC World Sce: in English/Pashto/Dari/Uzbek/Farsi: Kunar 87.5, Gardez 87.9, Konduz 88.1, Ghazni/Saloquan/Taloqan 88.3, Ghazni 88.3, Faizabad 88.4, Kabul/Bamian/Jalalabad/Pol-e-Khomri/Shebergan/ Zareh Sharan 89.0, Herat/Lashkar-Ga/Mazar-e-Sharif 89.2, Kandahar 90.0, Khost 90.1, Maimana 92.1, Jabal-os-Saraj 92.2, Kabul 101.6.
Deutsche Welle/Monte-Carlo Doualiya: Kabul: 90.5 1kW.
R. France Int: Kabul 89.5 0.2kW.
Many stns supporting the former Taliban gov. rep. to be in operation.

ALASKA (USA)

LT: UTC -9h (13 Mar-6 Nov -8h). Aleutian Is. UTC -10h (13 Mar-6 Nov -9h) — **Pop:** 735,000 — **Pr.L:** English — **E.C:** 60Hz, 120/240V — **ITU:** ALS

FEDERAL COMMUNICATIONS COMMISSION (FCC)
see USA for details

ALASKA BROADCASTERS ASSOCIATION
✉ 700 W 41st Ave, Anchorage AK 99503 ☎+1 907 258 2424 🖷+1 907 258 2414 **W:** alaskabroadcasters.org

MW	kHz	Call	kW	N	Location
2)	550	KTZN	3.1/5		Anchorage
3)	560	KVOK	1		Kodiak
4)	580	KRSA	5	d	Petersburg
5)	590	KHAR	5		Anchorage
6)	620	KGTL	5		Homer
7)	630	KJNO	5/1		Juneau
8)	630	KIAM	10/3.1		Nenana
9)	640	KYUK	10		Bethal
2)	650	KENI	50		Anchorage
11)	660	KFAR	10		Fairbanks
12)	670	KDLG	10		Dillingham
13)	680	KBRW	10		Barrow
14)	700	KBYR	10		Anchorage
15)	720	KOTZ	10		Kotzebue
5)	750	KFQD	50		Anchorage
17)	770	KCHU	9.7		Valdez
18)	780	KNOM	25/14		Nome
19)	790	KCAM	5		Glennallen
7)	800	KINY	10/7.6		Juneau
11)	820	KCBF	10		Fairbanks
22)	830	KSDP	1		Sand Point
24)	850	KICY	50	*	Nome
25)	870	KSKO	10		McGrath
26)	890	KBBI	10		Homer
27)	900	KZPA	5	r	Fort Yukon
28)	910	KIYU	5		Galena
29)	920	KSRM	5		Soldotna
30)	930	KTKN	5/1		Ketchikan
12)	930	KNSA	4.2	r	Unalakleet
32)	950	KSEW	1		Seward
33)	970	KFBX	10		Fairbanks
34)	1020	KVNT	10	d	Eagle River
34)	1080	KOAN	10		Anchorage
35)	1110	KAGV	10		Big Lake
29)	1140	KSLD	10		Soldotna
37)	1170	KJNP	50/21		North Pole
38)	1230	KIFW	1		Sitka
39)	1230	KVAK	1		Valdez
7)	1330	KXXJ	10/3		Juneau
41)	1430	KKNI	1		Wasilla
42)	1450	KLAM	0.25		Cordova

d=directional *=directional 0800-1200 (Summer -1h) r=relay

FM	Call	MHz	kW	Location	FM	Call	MHz	kW	Location
	KAKL	88.5	11	Anchorage		KYSC	96.9	5.8	Fairbanks
	KATB	89.3	4.9	Anchorage		KWLF	98.1	28	Fairbanks
	KNBA	90.3	100	Anchorage	33)	KAKQ-FM	101.1	50	Fairbanks
	KSKA	91.1	100	Anchorage	33)	KIAK-FM	102.5	100	Fairbanks
	KFAT	92.9	10	Anchorage	33)	KKED	104.7	50	Fairbanks
	KAFC	93.7	27	Anchorage		KEUL	88.9	1.4	Girdwood
	KEAG	97.3	55	Anchorage	19)	KCAM-FM	88.7	1.7	Glennallen
	KLEF	98.1	5	Anchorage	17)	KXGA	90.5	3.2	Glennallen
2)	KYMG	98.9	100	Anchorage		KHNS	102.3	3	Haines
2)	KBFX	100.5	25	Anchorage	6)	KWVV-FM	103.5	100	Homer
2)	KGOT	101.3	26	Anchorage		KBBO-FM	92.1	10	Houston
	KTMB	102.1	23	Anchorage	34)	KZND-FM	94.7	15	Houston
	KMXS	103.1	100	Anchorage		KXLW	96.3	10	Houston
5)	KBRJ	104.1	55	Anchorage		KAKI	88.1	1.7	Juneau
34)	KMVN	105.7	51	Anchorage		KLSF	89.7	1.7	Juneau
5)	KWHL	106.5	100	Anchorage		KXLL	100.7	6	Juneau
2)	KASH-FM	107.5	100	Anchorage		KRNN	102.7	6	Juneau
8)	KYKD	100.1	12	Bethel		KTOO	104.3	1.4	Juneau
	KJNR	91.9	3	Bethel	7)	KTKU	105.1	3.8	Juneau
	KCUK	88.1	6	Chevak		KSUP	106.3	10	Juneau
	K220CL	91.9	1	Chignik		KABN-FM	88.9	3.2	Kasilof
	KTDZ	103.9	28	College		KWJG	91.5	1	Kasilof
42)	KCDV	100.9	1.2	Cordova	29)	KFSE	106.9	8	Kasilof
	KRUP	99.1	6	Dillingham		KOGJ	88.1	1.1	Kenai
	KDJF	93.5	20.5	Ester		KDLL	91.9	4.9	Kenai
	KZVV	88.3	3.2	Fairbanks	29)	KWHQ-FM	100.1	25	Kenai
	KRFF	89.1	10	Fairbanks		KRBD	105.3	3.4	Ketchikan
	KUAC	89.9	38	Fairbanks		KRXX	101.1	3.1	Kodiak
	KSUA	91.5	3	Fairbanks		KYKA	104.9	19	Meadow Lk
	KQHE	92.7	1.2	Fairbanks		KAKN	100.9	3	Naknek
	KWDD	94.3	28	Fairbanks		KXBA	93.3	50	Nikiski
	KXLR	95.9	28	Fairbanks	18)	KNOM-FM	96.1	1	Nome

FM Call	MHz	kW	Location	FM Call	MHz	kW	Location
24) KICY-FM	100.3	1	Nome		KUHB-FM	91.9	15	St. Paul
37) KJNP-FM	100.3	25	North Pole		KKNI	105.3	7	Sterling
KFSK	100.9	2	Petersburg		KTNA	88.9	7.2	Talkeetna
KIBH-FM	91.7	1	Seward	39)	KVAK-FM	93.3	1.2	Valdez
KSBZ	103.1	3.1	Sitka		K220AD	91.9	1.1	Valdez
KCAW	104.7	3.6	Sitka		KMBQ-FM	99.7	51	Wasilla
29) KKIS-FM	96.5	10	Soldotna		KAYO	100.9	50	Wasilla
6) KPEN-FM	101.7	25	Soldotna		KSTK	101.7	3	Wrangell

NB: Txs 1kW and higher

Addresses:
2) 800 E Dimond Blvd, Ste. #3-370, Anchorage AK 99515-2058 – **3)** Box 708, Kodiak AK 99615-0708 – **4)** Box 650, Petersburg AK 99833-0650 – **5)** 301 Arctic Slope Ave #200, Anchorage AK 99518-3035 – **6)** Box 109, Homer AK 99603-0109 – **7)** 3161 Channel Dr #2, Juneau AK 99801-7815 – **8)** Box 474, Nenana AK 99760-0474 – **9)** Box 468, Bethel AK 99559-0468 – **11)** 819 1st Ave #A, Fairbanks AK 99701-4449 – **12)** Box 670, Dillingham AK 99576-0670 – **13)** Box 109, Barrow AK 99723-0109 – **14)** 833 Gambell St, Anchorage AK 99501-3756 – **15)** Box 78, Kotzebue AK 99752-0078 – **17)** Box 467, Valdez AK 99686-0467 – **18)** Box 988, Nome AK 99762-0988 – **19)** Box 249, Glennallen AK 99588-0249 – **22)** Box 328, Sand Point AK 99661 – **24)** Box 820, Nome AK 99762-0820. Russian 0800-1200 (Summer -1h) – **25)** Box 70, McGrath AK 99627-0070 – **26)** 3913 Kachemak Way, Homer AK 99603-7618 – **27)** Box 50, Fort Yukon AK 99740-0050 – **28)** Box 165, Galena AK 99741-0165 – **29)** 40960 Kalifornsky Beach Rd, Kenai AK 99611-6445 – **30)** 526 Stedman St, Ketchikan AK 99901-6629 – **32)** Box 2414, Seward AK 99664-2414 – **33)** 546 9th Ave, Fairbanks AK 99701-4902 – **34)** 4700 Business Park Blvd #E-44A, Anchorage AK 99503-7176 – **35)** 4723 King David St, Houston Park AK 99694 – **37)** Box 56359, North Pole AK 99705-1359 – **38)** 611 Lake St, Sitka AK 99835-7402 – **39)** Box 367, Valdez AK 99686-0367 – **41)** Box 4307, Soldotna AK 99669-4307 – **42)** Box 60, Cordova AK 99574-0060

EXTERNAL SERVICE: Radio Station KNLS
See International Broadcasting section

ALBANIA

L.T: UTC +1h (27 Mar-30 Oct +2h) — **Pop:** 3.6 million — **Pr.L:** Albanian — **E.C:** 50Hz, 220V — **ITU:** ALB

AUTORITETI I MEDIAVE AUDIOVIZIVE (AMA) (AUDIOVISUAL MEDIA AUTHORITY)
✉ Rruga "Abdi Toptani", Tirana. ☎+355 42 233599 🖷 +355 42 226288 **W:** ama.gov.al **E:** info@ama.gov.al **LP:** Chairman: Mesila Doda. Tech. Dir: Pirro Koci.

RADIOTELEVIZIONI SHQIPTAR (RTSH) ALBANIAN RADIO & TELEVISION (Pub.)
✉ Rruga Ismail Qemali 11, Tirana ☎ +355 4 2256059 🖷 +355 4 2227745 **W:** rtsh.al **E:** marketing@rtsh.al **LP:** DG: Petrit Beci. Tech. Dir: Mr. Ermir Agaci. Dir. Eng: Mr. Valmir Hajdari.

FM	MHz	kW	Ch	FM	MHz	kW	Ch
Llogora	88.3	1	1	Cervenake	99.1	1	1
Korce	89.5	1	2	Tirana(Dajt)	99.5	10	1
Tarabosh	91.0	1	1	Zvernec	99.8	3	1
Shkodra	92.0	2	R	Erseke	100.2	1	1
Mile	93.0	1	1	Kukesi	100.4	1	R
Ishem	95.4	1	1	Qafe Prush	100.7	1	1
Petresh	95.4	1	1	Homesh	102.2	1	1
Tirana(Dajt)	95.8	2	2	Gjirokastra	102.5	0.3	R
Mide	96.0	3	1	Sopot	107.0	1	1

+11 more txs under 1kW.
D.Prgr: 1st Ch.: 24h, **2nd Ch.:** 24h, **Regional Ch.:** 0600-2000.

EXTERNAL SERVICES: R. Tirana + TWR relays on MW 1395kHz (0900-1000,1925-2130), 1458kHz (1500-1700, 1930-2000 & 2115-2130) and SW: see International Broadcasting section.

Nationwide Private FM Stations:
+2 RADIO
✉ Rr. Aleksandër Moisiu Nr 76/1, ish kinostudjo Shqipëria e Re, Tirana ☎+355 4 2368490 **W:** plus2radio.com.al **E:** info@plus2radio.com.al **LP:** Mgr: Leonard Gremi.

FM	MHz	kW	FM	MHz	kW
Fushe Dajt	89.8	63	Zvernec	96.3	0.3
Cervenake	90.3	4	Gllave	97.6	3
Mide	94.3	6	Tirana/Dajt	101.6	89

TOP ALBANIA RADIO

Piramida QNK, Blvd. Dëshmorët e Kombit, Tirana. ☎+355 4 2247592 ▤ +355 4 2247493 **W**: topalbaniaradio.com **E**: contact@topalbaniaradio.com

FM	MHz	kW	FM	MHz	kW
Kerculle	93.0	1	Sarande	100.6	1
Shkoder	94.1	2	Mide	101.3	15
Korce	95.0	2	Elbasan	102.2	2
Gllave	96.0	1	Sopot	104.0	5
Dürres	99.0	1	Lezhe	104.3	1
Tirana/Dajt	100.0	15	Ardenice	104.5	2

Other Private FM Stations

FM Station	MHz	kW		FM Station	MHz	kW
1) R. Ngjallja	88.5	6	1)	R. Koha	98.1	2
1) R. New Planet	89.0	3	1)	R. Aldo 03	98.8	2
1) R. Kontakt	89.3	2	1)	R. Super Star	99.0	-
1) AMC Love R.	90.7	2	16)	R. Armonia	99.2	0.4
2) R. Alfa	90.9	1	10)	R. Saranda	100.0	0.5
3) R. Argjiropoli	91.0	1	1)	R. Club FM	100.4	13
1) R. Skorpion	91.4	0.3	11)	R. E Pare	100.4	0.1
4) R. +3	91.6	1	12)	R. Prespa	100.8	0.3
1) R. Italia	92.4	0.4	1)	R. Top Gold	100.8	56
5) R. 1	93.2	2	1)	R. Boom Boom	101.2	38
1) R. Nacional AH	93.4	1	1)	R. Alfa & Omega	102.6	6
6) R. Klea	93.9	1	14)	R. Val e Kalter	103.3	2
7) R. Alpo	94.1	0.1	2)	R. Club FM	104.3	1
1) R. Eurostar	94.5	2	1)	R. Rock	104.6	25
6) R. Fantasy	94.7	0.3	1)	R. Perla	105.0	1
8) R. Ruzvelt	94.8	0.1	1)	R. Ime	105.4	0.5
9) R. Emanuel	95.7	4	4)	R. Star	105.5	2
1) R. Oxygen	96.1	3	2)	R. Club Alsion	106.3	1
1) R. Real	96.4	2	15)	R. Perla	106.4	0.5
2) R. Eurostar	96.6	1	1)	R. NRG	106.6	2
1) R. Rash	97.0	3	1)	R. Stinet	106.9	1
1) R. Muzika Jone	97.3	2	9)	R. Magic Star	107.0	4
1) R. +7	97.7	6	4)	R. Fieri	107.4	2
9) R. ABC	98.0	2	1)	R. House of Arts	107.7	2

Locations: 1) Fushe Dajt, 2) Petresh, 3) Kerculle, 4) Fier, 5) Tirana, 6) Kavaje, 7) Kerculle, 8) Memaliaj, 9) Korce 10) Mile 11) Burrel, 12) Prespe, 13) Shkoder, 14) Zvernec, 15) Dürres, 16) Bularat.

Other FM stations

China R. Int.: Tirana 106.6MHz — **R. France International**: Fushe Dajt/Korca 102.0MHz 1kW, Shkodêr 103.5MHz 0.5kW — **VOA**: Tirana (Dajt) 107.4MHz 0.8kW — **BBC**: Tirana (Dajt) 103.9MHz 2.2kW

ALGERIA

L.T: UTC +1h — **Pop**: 35 million — **Pr.L**: Arabic, French, Tamazight — **E.C**: 50Hz, 230V — **ITU**: ALG

TÉLÉDIFFUSION D'ALGERIE (TDA)

Direction Générale, B.P. 50, Bouzaréah, Route de Baïnam, 16340 Algér ☎+213 21 901717 ▤ +213 21 902424 **W**: tda.dz **E**: contact@tda.dz **LP**: DG: Abdelmalek Houyou. Dir. Tech. Sces: Mohamed Hacine Ladj.

RADIO ALGÉRIENNE (RA, Pub.)

DCRR, 12 Rue Shakespeare, El Mouradia, Algér ☎+213 21 230805 ▤ +213 21 694620 **W**: radioalgerie.dz **E**: radionet@radioalgerie.dz **LP**: DG: Tewfik Khelladi.

	LW/MW	kHz	kW	Pr.	Hrs.
	Béchar	**153	2000	1	24h
	Ouargla	**198	2000	1	24h
	Tipaza	252	*1500	3	24h
	F'Kirina	531	600	J	24h
	Sidi Hamadouche	549	600	J	24h
20)	Touggourt	558	10	1/L	24h
4)	Béchar	576	*400	L	24h
30)	Tindouf	666	10	1/L	24h
	Aboudid (Ain el H.)	693	5	2	24h
1)	Reggane	693	10	1/L	24h
14)	Laghouat	702	25	3/L/Int	24h
12)	In Amenas	738	5	1/L	24h
12)	Djanet	783	5	1/L	24h
24)	El Oued	783	10	1/L	24h
	Béchar	837	5	3/Int	24h
10)	Ghardaïa	873	10	1/L	24h
	Ouled Fayet	**891	600	1	24h
	Tamanrasset	909	10	1	24h

	LW/MW	kHz	kW	Pr.	Hrs.
1)	Timimoun	927	10	1/L	24h
	Ouled Fayet	981	100	2	24h
20)	Hassi Messaoud	1026	10	1/L	24h
	Illizi	1071	5	1	24h
1)	Adrar	1089	10	1/L	24h
27)	In Salah	1161	5	1/L	24h
	Ouled Fayet	1422	50	C	24h

*) half-power 1900-0600.
**) irregular & running on low power.

FM (MHz)	1	2	3	I	J	kW(TRP)
Adrar			88.8			2
Aflou	90.7					10
Akfadou		91.8				10
Bains Romains			95.6			0.1
Bordj El Bahri	91.0		89.2	104.2		2
Chréa			88.4	101.5	94.7	2
Doukhane			91.0			2
Gara Djebilet	98.0					0.1
Kef El Akhal			87.6			10
Mahouna	97.6					2.5
M'cid	91.9					10
Mecheria	87.8					10
Meghriss	93.5					10
Nador		88.4	91.5			10
Puits des Zouaves					92.4	0.1
Tessala	102.7					2
Tiaret	89.4					2
Tizi Ouzou		88.0				0.1

Other Stations:

	FM Station, location	MHz	kW(TRP)	Ch.
14)	R. Laghouat, Aflou	87.6	10	3/L
5)	R. Chlef, Ain N'sour	87.7	10	1/L
28)	R. Tébessa, Doukhane	87.9	2	1/L
3)	R. Batna, Metlili	88.1	10	2/L
11)	R. El Tarf, Oum Ali	88.3	2.5	1/L
26)	R. Soummam, Akfadou	88.7	10	1/L
2)	R. Annaba, M'cid	88.8	10	1/L
4)	R. Béchar	89.3	5	1/L
39)	R. Tipaza	89.9		1/L
9)	R. Setif, Megriss	90.4	10	3/L
21)	R. Rélizane, Ain N'sour	90.8	10	1/L
18)	R. Naama, Mecheria	90.9	10	1/L
16)	R. Djelfa, Sbaa Mokrane	91.1	2	3/L
32)	R. Biskra, Metlili	91.2	10	1/L
7)	R. El Bahdja, Chréa	91.5	10	L
1)	R. Adrar	91.9	2	1/L
20)	R. Ouargla	92.1	3	1/L
29)	R. Tiaret	92.5	2	B/L
19)	R. Oran, Tessala	92.7	10	3/L
44)	R. Tizi Ouzou, Belloua	93.0	0.25	1/L
12)	R. Illizi	93.5	0.1	1/L
6)	R. Constantine, Kef El Akhal	93.9	10	1/L
7)	R. El Bahdja, Bordj el Bahri	94.2	2	L
32)	R. Tlemcen, Nador	94.7	10	1/L
23)	R. Skikda, Filfila	94.8	2.5	1/L
25)	R. Souk Ahras, M'cid	95.1	10	3/L
43)	R. Aïn Defla, Anneb	95.2	0.25	1/L
36)	R. Aïn Témouchent, Tessala	95.9	10	1/L
45)	R. Oum el Bouaghi, Chettaia	96.4	2.5	1/L
46)	R. Blida, Bordj el Bahri	97.5	2.5	1/L
47)	R. Guelma, Mahouna	97.6	2.5	1/L
10)	R. Ghardaïa, El Golea	98.0	2.5	1/L
14)	R. Laghouat, Hassi R'Mel	98.0	2.5	3/L
24)	R. El Oued, 3 locations	98.0		1/L
27)	R. Tamanrasset, 4 locations	98.0	1	3/L
30)	R. Tindouf	98.0	0.1	1/L
15)	R. Mascara, Chareb Rih	98.5	3	1/L
37)	R. Bordj Bou Arreridj, Tafartas	98.7	2.5	1/L
22)	R. Sidi Bel Abbés, Tessala	99.2	10	1/L
34)	R. Bouira, Dirah	99.8	2.5	1/L
8)	R. El Bayadh	100.1	0.1	1/L
40)	R. Médéa	100.7	0.1	1/L
41)	R. Saïda	101.3	0.1	1/L
42)	R. Boumerdes	102.6	0.1	1/L
38)	R. Mila, Kef Bouderga	102.7	2.5	1/L
13)	R. Jijel, Kern	103.0	2.5	1/L
33)	R. Tissemsilt	103.2	0.1	1/L
17)	R. Mostaganem	104.0	2.5	1/L
48)	R. M'Sila	104.5	1.5	1/L
35)	R. Khenchela, Chettaia	105.7	2.5	1/L

+25 more transmitters under 1kW.

D.Prgr: 1=Chaîne 1 in Arabic: 24h. **2=Chaîne 2** in Tamazight: 24h.
3=Chaîne 3 in French, 0500-0100. **Int=R. Algérie Internationale** in
Arabic, French, E. & Spanish: 0800-2300 and r. R. Quran 2300-0800. **C=**
consists of **R. Quran** 0100-1200, Chaîne 1 1200-1900, **R. Culture** in
Arabic: 1600-2200 Chaîne 3 2200-0100 on 1422kHz.
J: Jil FM: youth channel in Arabic, French & Tamazight: 24h.
L=Local stations: times of local prgrs vary by stn (may be
longer in summer than winter), but at least between 0800-1600.
Most local stns transmit Chaîne 1 at other times (Some stations
[693/927/1089/1161kHz] rep. also with R. Algérie Int, R. Quran and
Culture relay). Many local stns carry Arabic news from Chaîne 1 1100-
1200 and at other times.

Addresses and other information for local stations:
Audio feeds for local stations: **W:** radioalgerie.dz/player/fr
1) B.P. 309, Adrar – **2)** 7, Boulevard Radji Mokhtar, Quartier Annasr,
Annaba – **3)** B.P. 453, Batna **W:** radio-batna.dz – **4)** Cité Badr, B.P. 330,
Béchar **W:** radiobechar.com – **5)** Ain N'sour – **6)** B.P. 28B El Koudia,
Constantine **W:** radio-constantine.dz – **7) W:** facebook.com/pages/
Radio-El-Bahdja-FM/239397829331 – **8)** B.P. 195, El Bayadh – **9)** B.P.
54, Ain Tbinet, Sétif. **W:** radio-setif.com – **10)** B.P. 17, Ghardaïa – **11)**
El Tarf **W:** radio-eltarf.com – **12)** Route de l'aéroport, B.P. 230, Illizi
– **13)** B.P. 48, Jijel – **14)** B.P. 1410, Bd. de l'Indépendance Mamourah,
El Maqam, Laghouat **W:** radiolagh.voila.net – **15)** Place Mostfa
Ben Touhami, Mascara – **16)** Djelfa – **17)** Place El Matemar, B.P.
1014, Mostaganem 027000 **W:** radiomostaganem.net – **18)** Av. du 1
Novembre, BP 223, Naama **W:** radionaamafm.com – **19)** 4 place Aîssa
Messaoudi, Oran – **20)** Ruissat, B.P. 83, Ouargla – **21)** 15 Rue Ismail
Mustapha, Maison de Culture, Rélizane **W:** radiorelizane.net – **22)**
Ex Gare de l'État, Sidi Bel Abbés 022000 – **23)** Porte des Aurès, B.P.
55, Skikda **W:** facebook.com/pages/Radio-skikda/1625659967647250
– **24)** Cité Reml El Oued, B.P. 172, El Oued – **25)** Blvd. Messous Hamid,
Souk Ahras – **26)** Boulevard Youcef Bouchebah, Béjaia – **27)** B.P. 1080,
Tamanrasset – **28)** Unité de Tébéssa, Parc des Loisirs, Tébéssa – **29)**
Rue des Fréres Saim Tiaret, B.P. 671, Tiaret **W:** radiotiaret.dz – **30)** B.P.
213, Agence Enasr, Tindouf – **31)** B.P. 44K, Tlemcen – **32)** Av. Idriss
Mohamed, Biskra **W:** radiobiskra.com – **33)** Tissemsilt – **34)** Bouira
– **35)** Khenchela – **36)** Aïn Témouchent **W:** radioaintemouchent.com
– **37)** Bordj Bou Arreridj **W:** facebook.com/radio.bordj – **38)** Mila – **39)**
Tipaza – **40)** Médéa – **41)** Saïda **W:** saidafm.com – **42)** Boumerdes
– **43)** Aïn Defla – **44)** Tizi Ouzou – **45)** Boulevard Houari Boumédiène,
0400 Oum el Bouaghi **W:** facebook.com/radio – **46)** Blida – **47)**
Guelma **W:** facebook.com/radio.guelma.fm – **48)** M'Sila
Ann: Chaîne 1: "Al Kanet al Oula min Idha'at al-Djazairiyah.", 2:
"Radio Isnath", 3: "Algérie Chaîne trois", C: "Idha'atul-Thaqafiyah",
K:"Idha'atul-Koran al Karim". **IS:** Oriental Lute (Ud)

ANDORRA

L.T: UTC + 1h (27 Mar-30 Oct: + 2h) — **Pop:** 76.949 — **Pr.L:** Catalan,
French, Spanish — **E.C:** 50Hz, 230V — **ITU:** AND

ANDORRA TELECOM (Gov)
✉ Mn. Lluís Pujol 8-14, AD500 Santa Coloma (Admin.)
✉Av. Meritxell 112, AD500 Andorra la vella (Comm.)
☎+376 875000 ✆ +376 821414 **E:** comunicacio@andorratelecom.ad
W: andorratelecom.ad **L.P:** Admin Dir: Jordi Nadal Bentadé

RNA RÀDIO NACIONAL D'ANDORRA (Pub)
✉ RTVA Ràdio i Televisió d'Andorra S.A., Baixada del Molí 24, AD500
Andorra la Vella ☎+376 873777 ✆ +376 863242 **E:** web@rtva.ad **W:**
andorradifusio.ad **L.P:** DG: Xavier Mujal Closa

CADENA PIRENAICA DE RÀDIO I TELEVISIÓ (Comm.)
✉ Cadena Pirenaica de Ràdio i Televisió, SA, Av. Príncep Benlloch 24,
AD200 Encamp ☎+376 732000 ✆ +376 834831 - Av. Pau Claris 8,
ES-25700 Seu d'Urgell, Spain
E: info@cadenapirenaica.com **W:** cadenapirenaica.com

GRUP FLAIX ANDORRA (Comm.)
✉ Ràdio i Televisió de les Valls S.A., (GRUP FLAIX), Av. Meritxell 75,
3 - Edifici Quars, AD500 Andorra la Vella ☎+376 18020304 ✆ +376
862287 **W:** andorra1.fm **W:** flaixfmandorra.com

COPE- AD RÀDIO (Comm.)
✉ Avda Bonaventura Riberaygua, 39, 5 Pis, Edifici Alexandre, AD500
Andorra la Vella ☎+376 877477 **W:** diariandorra.ad **E:** laradio@
adradio.ad

SER PRINCIPAL D'ANDORRA (Comm.)
✉ C. Prat de la Creu, 32, AD500 Andorra la Vella ☎+376 808300
✆ +376 828301 **E:** informatiusserandorra@prisaradio.com
W: cadenaser.ad

FM	MHz	kW	Location	Station
2)	87.8	0.3	La Comella	R. María España
1)	88.1	0.3	Pic de Carroi	Cadena Dial
2)	89.0	0.3	Pic de Carroi	R7P - RAC1
2)	89.5	0.3	Pic de Carroi	Europa FM
2)	90.1	0.3	Valls Valira	R. Tele Taxi
7)	90.7	0.1	Pas de la Casa	Pyrénées FM
6)	91.4	0.1	Pic de Maià	RNA R. Nacional d'Andorra
1)	92.1	1	Pic de Carroi	Maxima FM
1)	92.6	1	Pic de Carroi	M80 R.
2)	93.3	0.3	Pic de Carroi	R. Valira - Onda Cero
10)	93.8	0.3	Pic de Carroi/ de Maià	Flaix FM Andorra
6)	94.2	1	Pic de Carroi/ de Maià	RNA R. Nacional d'Andorra
2)	94.6	0.3	Encamp	Pròxima FM
2)	95.0	0.3	Pic de Carroi	Gestiona R.
8)	95.6	0.1	Valls Valira	Catalunya Informació
10)	96.0	1	Pic de Carroi/ de Maià	Andorra 1 - R. Flaixbac
8)	96.5	0.1	Valls Valira	Catalunya Música
6)	97.0	1	Pic de Carroi/ de Maià	Andorra Música
3)	97.7	0.1	Sant Julià de Lòria	R. Festa Major
2)	98.1	0.1	Valls Valira	Gestiona R.
2)	98.5	0,1	La Comella	R. Valira - Onda Cero
2)	98.9	1	Pic de Carroi	Kiss FM
2)	100.2	0.1	Valls Valira	RAC 105
4)	100.6	0.3	Pic de Carroi	NRJ
9)	101.5	1	Pic de Carroi/de Maià	COPE - AD R.
4)	101.8	1	Pic de Carroi/de Maià	France Inter
2)	102.3	1	Pic de Carroi/ de Maià	R.SER Principat d'Andorra
4)	102.6	1	Pic de Carroi/ de Maià	France Musique
1)	103.3	1	Pic de Carroi/ de Maià	40 Principals Andorra
4)	104.1	1	Pic de Carroi/ de Maià	France Culture
8)	104.6	1	Pic de Carroi/ de Maià	Catalunya R.
4)	106.0	1.2	Pic de Carroi/ de Maià	RNE R. 4
4)	106.8	1.2	Pic de Carroi/ de Maià	RNE R. 1
5)	107.5	1.2	Valls Valira	R. Principat - R. Estel
4)	107.9	1.2	Pic de Carroi/ de Maià	RNE R. 3

Addresses & other information:
1) SER Principat d'Andorra ✉ C. Prat de la Creu, 32, AD500 Andorra la
Vella ☎+376 808300 ✆ +376 828301 **E:** informatiusserandorra@prisa-
radio.com **W:** cadenaser.ad – **2)** Cadena Pirenaica de Ràdio i Televisió,
SA, ✉ Av. Príncep Benlloch 24, AD200 Encamp ☎+376 732000 ✆
+376 834831 **E:** info@cadenapirenaica.com **W:** cadenapirenaica.com
– **3)** R. Festa Major, ✉ Plaça Major, 3, AD-600 Sant Julià de Lòria
☎+376 842601 (temporary station only last week of July) – **4)** Andorra
Telecom ✉ Mn. Lluís Pujol 8-14, AD500 Santa Coloma (Admin.)
☎+376 875000 ✆ +376 821414 **E:** comunicacio@andorratelecom.ad
W: andorratelecom.ad – **5)** R. Principat - R. Estel ✉ Pg del Parc 16-18,
ES-25700 La Seu d'Urgell, Spain. ☎+973 354400 **E:**radio@radioprin-
cipat.com – **6)** RTVA Ràdio i Televisió d'Andorra S.A., ✉ Baixada del
Molí 24, AD500 Andorra la Vella **W:** andorradifusio.ad – **7)** Pyrénées
FM ✉ Le barry d'en Fort 09110 Montaillou - 99 Route d'Espagne,
F-31100 Toulouse, France **W:** pyreneesfm.com – **8)** CCMA ✉ Av.
Diagonal 614-616, ES-08021 Barcelona, Spain ☎+34 933069200 **W:**
catradio.cat – **9)** COPE-AD Ràdio ✉ Avda Bonaventura Riberaygua,
39, 5 Pis, Edifici Alexandre, AD500 Andorra la Vella ☎+376 877477
W: diariandorra.ad **E:** laradio@adradio.ad – **10)** GRUP FLAIX ✉
Av. Meritxell 75, 3 - Edifici Quars, AD500 Andorra la Vella ☎+376
18020304 ✆ +376 862288 ✆ +376 862287 **E:** publicitat@andorra1.fm **W:**
andorra1.fm **W:** flaixfmandorra.com

ANGOLA

L.T: UTC +1h — **Pop:** 24 million — **Pr.L:** Portuguese + ethnic — **E.C:**
50Hz, 220V — **ITU:** AGL

MINISTÉRIO DA COMUNICAÇÃO SOCIAL (MCS)
✉ Av. Comandante Valódia 1°& 2° amdar , CP. 2608, Luanda ☎+244
22 2443495 ✆ +244 22 2392649 **W:** mcs.gov.ao **L.P:** Min: Carolina
Cerqueiro.

RÁDIO NACIONAL DE ANGOLA (RNA, Pub.)
✉ Av. Comandante Gika, CP. 1329, Luanda ☎+244 22 2323172
✆ +244 22 2324647 **W:** rna.ao **L.P:** CEO: Pedro Cabral. PD: Júlio
Mendonça. TD: Cândido R. Pinto.

MW	kHz	kW	Prgr.	H of tr
Mulenvos	945	25	N/E	24h
Mulenvos	1134	10	A	
SW	**kHz**	**kW**	**Prgr.**	**H of tr.**
Mulenvos	4950	25	A	24h

Ann: "Rádio Nacional de Angola".
Prgrs: A=Canal A in Portuguese (general coverage): 24h. **N:** on the h.

N=Rádio N'Gola Yetu (ethnic): 24h. **N**: rel. Canal A. **E=External service. RFM=Rádio FM Estéreo** (music): 1000-2400. **5=Rádio 5** (sports): 0500-2300. **P=Emissora Provincial:** 0400-2300, rel. A at night.

Provincial MW transmitters:

MW		kHz	kW	Pr	MW		kHz	kW	Pr
18)	Mbanza Congo	1152	10	P	13)	Saurimo	1386	10	P
7)	Huambo	1170	25	P	5)	Kuito	1404	10	P
14)	Malanje	1197	10	P	12)	Dundo	1440	10	P
8)	Lubango	1233	10	P	15)	Luena	1458	10	P
10)	N'dalatando	1260	10	P	9)	Menongue	1467	10	P
18)	Soyo	1290	5	P	11)	Sumbe	1485	10	P
17)	Uíge	1296	10	P	4)	Benguela	1503	10	P
16)	Namibe	1314	10	P	5)	Tenda	1530	10	P

N.B: Only R. Soyo 1290kHz reported active recently.

FM:

Prov.	Location	A	N	5	RFM	P	kW
1)	Luanda	93.5	101.4	94.5	96.5	99.9	4
1)	Viana	90.0	101.0	94.2		92.8/101.0	
2)	Caxito	91.5		88.2		87.9	4
3)	Lobito	93.5	104.9	101.0	98.5	89.1	1
3)	Benguela	91.5	90.4		92.3	92.9	2
3)	Bocoio	93.3				98.3	
3)	Ganda	90.0		93.1		95.1	
3)	Cubal	91.3		88.2		94.4	
3)	Canjala	100.0				98.0	
3)	Caimbambo	88.1				99.1	
3)	Balombo	95.3				93.1	
3)	Dombe Grande	88.5		98.0			
4)	Kuito	92.0	91.0	94.5		106.7	4
4)	Chinguar	101.8		88.9		98.5	
5)	Cabinda		98.8	95.0		88.2/91.3	4
5)	Malembo	97.7				90.8	
5)	Belize	102.5				100.0	
6)	Ondjiva	92.2	101.0	91.8		88.7	5
6)	Xangongo	98.9				94.7	
7)	Huambo	99.2	89.0	91.6		88.5/98.7	4
7)	Bailundo	95.9				99.2	
7)	Caála					94.8	
8)	Lubango	95.8	90.2	99.1	92.8	96.6	4
9)	Menongue	91.4	92.0	94.6	96.5	88.3	
9)	Kuito Kuanavale	91.1		88.0			
10)	N'dalatando	95.5	95.0	91.8		92.3/98.8	1
10)	Dondo	92.7				88.2	
10)	Golungo Alto	97.2		105.4			
10)	Camabatela	100.0		98.0			
11)	Sumbe	101.1	104.7	91.7		97.6	4
11)	Waco Cungo	100.7		97.2			
11)	Gabela	95.7				100.7	
11)	Porto Ambuim	90.0				93.3	
11)	Libolo	92.7		90.2			
11)	Kibala	94.7		91.7			
12)	Dundo	94.4		93.3		90.3/97.7	4
12)	Lucapa	88.7				91.7	
12)	Cafunfo	90.2		99.9			
13)	Saurimo	103.7	106.2	90.3		100.2	
14)	Malanje	92.0	93.7	90.9	94.8	100.7	4
15)	Luena	90.7	107.3	103.7		97.2	2
15)	Cazombo	87.9		90.3			
15)	Luau	90.2		93.3			
16)	Namibe	88.5	92.5	91.6	97.7	95.2	4
16)	Bibala	88.5		92.6			
16)	Camucuio	90.3		93.4			
16)	Tômbwa	87.7				95.9	
17)	Uíge	99.8	106.3	92.5		89.6/91.0	4
17)	Negage	94.4		88.0		103.0	
17)	Quitexi	99.3				92.4	
17)	Bungo					97.3	
18)	Mbanza Congo	101.9	97.1	92.7		95.1	2
18)	Soyo	103.7		88.7		92.3	

+50 more low power transmitters.

Provincial & local stations:
1) R. Luanda & R. Cacuaco 105.0MHz, R. Cazenga 102.1MHz – **2)** R. Bengo, Caxito – **3)** R. Benguela, R. Lobito. R. Ganda & R. Kubal are carried daytime on R. 5 fqs. – **4)** R. Bié, Kuito – **5)** R. Cabinda – **6)** R. Cunene, Ondjiva & R. Xangongo – **7)** R. Huambo & R. Caála – **8)** R. Huíla, Lubango – **9)** R. Cuando Cubango, Menongue – **10)** Cuanza Norte: R. N'dalatando & R. Dondo – **11)** Cuanza Sul: R. Sumbe – **12)** R. Lunda Norte, Lucapa – **13)** Lunda Sul: R. Saurimo – **14)** R. Malanje – **15)** R. Moxico, Luena – **16)** R. Namibe, R. Tombwa – **17)** R. Uíge, R. Negage, R. Quitexi, R. Bungo – **18)** R. Zaire, Mbanza Congo & R. Soyo.
Affiliated community stations on FM in Buco Zau, Camabatela,

Golungo Alto, Tombwa, Viana and Virei.

EXTERNAL SERVICE: Angolan National Radio
see International Radio section.

Other stations:
A Voz da Esperança, Luanda: 89.2MHz. **W:** insjcm-tokoistas.org
Luanda Antena Comercial, Luanda: 95.5MHz 5kW. **W:** lacluanda.com **E:** lac@lacluanda.com
Rádio Ecclesia (Rlg.), Rua Comandante Bula 118, São Paulo, CP. 3579, Luanda. **FM:** 97.5MHz 5kW. **W:** radioecclesia.org

ANGUILLA (UK)

LT: UTC -4h — **Pop:** 13,500 — **Pr.L:** English — **E.C:** 50Hz, 230V — **ITU:** AIA

RADIO ANGUILLA (Gov. Comm.)
✉ PO Box 60, The Valley ☎ +1 264 497 2218 🖷 +1 264 497 5432 **E:** radioaxa@anguillanet.com **W:** radioaxa.com
L.P: Dir.: Farrah Banks. PM: Keithstone Greaves. Eng.: Lester Richardson
FM: 95.5MHz, Crocus Hill.

THE CARIBBEAN BEACON (Rlg.)
✉ PO Box 690, The Valley ☎+1 264 497 4340 🖷 +1 264 497 4311
L.P: GM & CEN: Eddie Sutton
MW: 1610kHz 50kW
SW: 6090/11775kHz 100kW
FM: 100.1MHz 20kW
D.Prgr: 24h Owned by University Network

Private FM stations:
BLAZING FM, The Valley ☎ +1 264 462 9330 **W:** blazingfm.com **FM:** 93.3MHz — **KLASS FM**, Wilmot Estate Rock Farm, PO Box 339, AI-2640 The Valley ☎ +1 264 497 3791 **W:** klass929.com **FM:** 92.9MHz — **KOOL FM**, North Side, AI-2640 The Valley ☎ +1 264 497 0103 **W:** koolfm103.com **FM:** 103.3MHz. Format: Urban Caribbean – **NEW BEGINNING RADIO GRACE 99.3**, Shoal Bay, PO Box 1122, AI-2640 The Valley ☎+1 264 497 3629 **W:** nbr993.com **FM:** 99.3MHz. Format: Rlg – **RAINBOW FM**, The Quarter, PO Box 603, The Valley ☎ +1 264 498 9305. **FM:** 93.5MHz – **UP BEAT RADIO**, Cedar Av., Rey Hill, PO Box 5045, AI-2640 The Valley ☎ +1 264 498 3354 🖷 +1 264 497 5995 **W:** hbr1075.com **FM:** 97.7MHz – **VOICE OF CREATION RADIO**, Sachasses, The Valley ☎ +1 264 497 0106 **FM:** 106.7MHz **W:** creationradiofm.com Format: Gospel – **ZRON TRADEWINDS RADIO**, 398 East Dania Beach Blvd. Ste. 210, Dania Beach, FL 33004, USA. ☎ +1 305 459 1559 **W:** twrlive.net **FM:** 105.1MHz

ANTARCTICA

LT: Antártida Argentina: UTC -3h; Antártida Chilena: UTC -4h; Ross Dependency (NZL)/South Pole Station: UTC +12h (27 Sep 15-3 Apr 16, 25 Sep 16-2 Apr 17: +13h) — **Pop:** 4,120 (Su), 1,066 (Wi) — **ITU:** ATA

RADIO NACIONAL ARCANGEL SAN GABRIEL
✉ LRA36 Radio Nacional Arcangel San Gabriel, Base de Ejercito Esperanza, CP 9411-Antártida Argentina, Argentina. ☎+54 2974 44 5304, +54 810 222 0776 **E:** esperanzaantar@infovia.com.ar, lra36esperanza@yahoo.com.ar **L.P:** Dir: Guillermo Bolger, Op.: Pablo González
SW: see international section. **FM:** 97.6MHz 24h.

SOBERANIA FM, Villa Las Estrellas, Antarctica Chilena, Chile. **FM:** 90.5MHz 0.1kW.
ICE FM, McMurdo Station, Ross Dependency. **FM:** 104.5MHz 0.05kW. Rel AFRTS exc. some local prgrs
KOLD, South Pole Station, Ross Dependency. **FM:** 87.5MHz
88.7 FM, McMurdo Station, Ross Dependency. **FM:** 88.7MHz
SCOTT BASE R., Scott Base, Ross Dependency. **FM:** 97.0MHz
AMERICAN FORCES ANTARCTIC NETWORK, AFAN McMurdo, US Naval Support Force Antarctica, 651 Lyons Str, Port Hueneme, CA 93043-4345, USA. **FM:** 93.9MHz 0.03kW. **D.Prgr:** 24h.

ANTIGUA & BARBUDA

LT: UTC -4h — **Pop:** 86,500 — **Pr.L:** English — **E.C:** 60Hz, 110/220V — **ITU:** ATG

ANTIGUA & BARBUDA BROADCASTING SERVICE (Gov. Comm.)
✉ Cecil Charles Bldg, Cross Street, St. John's ☎ +1 268 462

2998 **W**: abstvradio.com **L.P**: SM: Dave Lester Payne. PM: Blondell Anthony. CEN: Denis Leandro
FM: 90.5/101.5MHz **D.Prgr**: **ABS Radio** 24h

CARIBBEAN RADIO LIGHTHOUSE (Rlg.)
✉ Jolly Hill, PO Box 1057, St.John's ☎ +1 268 462 1454 🖷 +1 268 462 7420/1452 **E**: info@radiolighthouse.org **W**: radiolighthouse.org **L.P**: SM: Jerry Baker. CE: Nathan Owens. Owned by Baptist International Missions Inc.
MW: 1160kHz 10kW **FM**: 92.3MHz 2kW **D.Prgr**: MW: 0925-0145. FM: 24h

GRENVILLE RADIO LTD. (Comm.)
✉ Bird Rd, PO Box 1100, St. John's ☎ +1 268 462 1116 🖷 +1 268 462 1101 **E**: mail@radiozdk.com **W**: radiozdk.com and sunfm1001.com
L.P: PD: Ivor Bird
FM: **Liberty Radio ZDK** 97.1MHz 1kW 24h – **Sun FM Power 100.1**: 100.1MHz 2.5kW 24h

OBSERVER MEDIA GROUP (Comm.)
✉ Ryans Place, High Street, PO Box 1318, St. John's ☎ +1 268 460 0911/481 9100 🖷 +1 268 725 9111 **W**: antiguaobserver.com
FM: **Observer Radio** 91.1MHz (News/talk) – **Hitz 91.9**: 91.9MHz

OTHER FM STATIONS:
ABUNDANT LIFE RADIO, Codrington Village, Barbuda ☎ +1 268 560 2676 🖷 +1 268 560 2676 **E**: info@abundantliferadioag.com **W**: abundantliferadioag.com **L.P**: MD: Clifton Francois. **FM**: Barbuda 103.1MHz 1kW, Antigua 103.9MHz 1kW. Format: Gospel – **BBC**, Caribbean Relay Co. Ltd., PO Box 1203, St. John's. ☎ +1 268 462 0994. **FM** 89.1MHz – **CATHOLIC RADIO,** Michaels Mount, PO Box 836, St. John's ☎ +1 268 562 6868 **E**: catholicradio@candw.ag **W**: s212802169.onlinehome.us **FM** 89.7MHz – **HEALTY CHOICE FM,** Ramco Bldg, Independence Ave, PO Box 1296, St. John's ☎ +1 268 462 2273 🖷 +1 268 462 2275 **W**: healtychoice.projectsdisplay.com **L.P**: CEO: Lester Storm. **FM** 94.9MHz – **NICE FM,** All Saints Rd, Clarkes Hill ☎ +1 268 462 4343 **W**: nicefmradio.com **FM** 104.3MHz – **RED HOT FLAMES RADIO.** Carlisle Estate ☎ +1 268 562 9805 🖷 +1 268 562 6693 **E**: redhotfm@hotmail.com **W**: redhotflames.com **FM** 98.5MHz – **ROGERS RADIO CARIBBEAN,** Rogers Media House, PO Box W1481, Scotts Hill, St. John's ☎ +1 268 736 2255 **W**: rogersradiocaribbean.com **L.P.** MD Julian Rogers, CCO Denise Francis. **FM** 94.1MHz. Format: News/talk/entertainment – **SECOND ADVENT RADIO,** America Rd, PO Box 109, St. John's ☎ +1 268 562 1015 **L.P.**: SM Necole Caleb. **W**: secondadventradio.org **FM** 101.5MHz. Format: Rlg. – **VARIETY RADIO,** Cooks Hill, Harbour View, St. John's ☎ +1 268 562 4835 **E**: varietyradio@hotmail.com **L.P**: SM: Kelvin Carter **FM** 102.3MHz 1kW – **VIBZ FM – FAMILY RADIO NETWORK,** Belmont School of Business, All Saints Rd, PO Box W1102, St. John's ☎ +1 268 560 7578/9 **W**: vibzfm.com **FM** 92.9MHz – **ZOOM RADIO,** Blackburn St. 5, Villa, St. John's ☎ +1 268 734 0485 **L.P.**: SM Andy Liburd. **W**: zoomradiofm.com **FM** 96.1MHz. Format: Classic soul and jazz.

ARGENTINA

L.T: UTC -3h; exc. SC: -4h — **Pop**: 42.7 million — **Pr.L**: Spanish — **E.C.**: 50Hz, 220V — **ITU**: ARG — **Int. dialling code**: +54

SECRETARIA DE COMUNICACIONES (SECOM)
✉ Tucúman 744, piso 4, (C1049AAP) Buenos Aires ☎11 4318 9400 **W**: secom.gov.ar **E**: usarios@secom.gov.ar
L.P: Lic. Arq.Carlos Lisandro Salas (Secretario de Comunicaciones)

COMISION NACIONAL DE COMUNICACIONES (C.N.C.)
✉ Perú 103, (C1067AAC) Buenos Aires ☎11 4347 9200 ✉ Perú 103, (C1067AAC) CA Buenos Aires **W**: cnc.gob.ar

AUTORIDAD FEDERAL DE SERVICIOS DE COMUNICACIÓN AUDIOVISUAL (AFSCA)
✉ Suipacha 765, 9° piso, (C1008AAO) Buenos Aires ☎11 4320 4900 **W**: afsca.gob.ar **E**: afsca@afsca.gov.ar. AFSCA controls certain technical aspects of broadcasting, and also controls the prgrs. trs over all kinds of broadcasting stns.

° = on-air stn name not confirmed, ‡ = inactive, ± = varying freq.

MW	Call	kHz	kW	Station, location and h of tr
CF34)		530	25/5	R. Madre, Buenos Aires: 24h
BA119)		540		R.Italia, Villa Martelli
SF01)	LRA14	540	25/1	R. Nal, Santa Fé
SA01)	LRA25	540	10	R. Nal,Tartagal: 0900-0300

MW	Call	kHz	kW	Station, location and h of tr
CB04)	LU17	540	10/5	R. Golfo Nuevo, Pto. Madryn: 24h
TF03)		‡540	25/5	Ushuaia (F.PI)
NE11)		550	5/0.5	AM 550 La Primera, Neuquen: 24h
CB01)	LRA9	560	25/1	R. Nal, Esquel: 24h
BA01)	LRA13	560	25/5	R. Nal., Bahia Blanca: 24h
ER01)	LT15	560	10/3	R. del Litoral, Concordia
SJ01)	LV1	560	25/5	R. Colón, San Juan: 24h
JU01)	LRA16	560	25/5	R. Nal., La Quiaca: 24h
CF30)		570	5	R. Argentina, Buenos Aires: 24h
CB02)	LU20	580	20	R. Chubut, Trelew: 24h
CO01)	LW1	580	25/5	R. Univ. Nal. de Córdoba, Córdoba
ME12)		580	3	R. Andina, San Rafael
CF01)	LS4	590	50	R. Continental, Buenos Aires: 24h
RN01)	LRA30	590	25/1	R. Nal., San Carlos de Bariloche: 24h
TU01)	LV12	590	4	R. Independencia, San Miguel de Tucumán: 24h
NE04)	LU5	600	25/1	R. Neuquén, Neuquén: 24h
SE03)	LRK201	610	1	R. Solidaridad, Añatuya
BA91)		610	5	R. General San Martin – "La Buena R. San Martin: 24h
ME07)	LV4	620	25/5	R. San Rafael, San Rafael: 1000-0400
SC01)	LRA18	620	25	R. Nal., Río Turbio: 24h
MS01)	LT17	620	25/5	R. Provincia de Misiones, Posadas: 24h
CH03)	LRA26	620	25	R. Nal,. Resistencia: 24h
CF02)	LS5	630	25/5	R. Rivadavia, Buenos Aires: 24h
JU03)	LW8	630	25/5	R. San Salvador de Jujuy: 0900-0500
CB05)	LU4	630	10/5	R. Patagonia Argentina, Comodoro Rivadavia: 24h
TF01)	LRA24	640	25/5	R. Nal., Río Grande: 24h
RN02)	LU18	640	10	R. El Valle, General Roca: 24h
SL01)	LV15	640	1	R. Villa Mercedes
CF38)		650	3	Belgrano AM 650, Buenos Aires: 24h
ER04)	LT41	660	1/0.5	R. LV del Sur Entrerriano, Gualeguaychú: 0830-0030 Sat: 0900-0000(Sun: -0400)
BA36)		660	1	Amplitud 660, Ciudad Evita
BA172)		670	4	R. Republica, Ciudad Evita
CB03)	LRA11	670	25/5	R. Nal., Comodoro Rivadavia: 24h
NE01)	LRA52	670	10	R. Nal., Chos Malal: 24h
MS02)	LT4	670	1	R. Dif. Misiones, Posadas: 0800-0200
BA02)	LRI209	670	25/5	R. Mar del Plata, Mar del Plata: 24h
BA68)		680	1	R. Popular, Claypole
BA173)		680	2	R. Magna, Villa Martelli
SF07)	LT3	680	5	R. Cerealista, Rosario: 24h
SC02)	LU12	680	25/5	R. Río Gallegos, Río Gallegos
ME01)	LV6	680	15	R. Nihuil, Mendoza: 24h
CF45)		690	2	R. AM 690 - K-24, Buenos Aires
SA02)	LRA4	690	25/5	R. Nal. Salta: 24h
RN03)	LU19	690	10/3	R. LV de Comahue, Cipolletti: 0900-0500
CO05)	LV3	700	25/5	Cadena 3 - R. Córdoba: 24h
NE02)	LRA17	710	25/1	R. Nal., Zapala: 0900-0300
MS03)	LRA19	710	25/1	R. Nal., Pto. Iguazú: 0900-0300
CF13)	LRL202	710	50	R. Diez, Buenos Aires: 24h
SC03)	LRA59	720	25/5	R. Nac., Gobernador Gregores: 1100-2300
ME02)	LV10	720	50/5	R. de Cuyo, Mendoza: 24h
LP01)	LRA3	730	20/5	R. Nal., Santa Rosa: 0900-0300
SC04)	LU23	730	25/5	R. Lago Argentino, El Calafate:1000-0300
CA01)	LRA27	730	25/5	R. Nal., Catamarca: 24h
CF27)		730		R. Concepto, Gregorio de Laferrere: 24h
CB07)	LRA55	740	1	R. Nal., Alto Río Senguer: 0900-0300
CF48)		740		R. Rebelde, Buenos Aires:1000-0200 (Sat: -0300) Sun: 1400-0100
SC05)	LRI200	740	10/1	R. Municipal: 24h
CH05)	LRH251	740	25/5	R. Provincia de Chaco, Resistencia
RN13)		740	10	AM 740 La Carretera, Allen
CF51)	LRL203	750	1/0.25	R. AM 7-50, Lomas de Zamora
CO02)	LRA7	750	100/10	R. Nal., Córdoba: 0900-0500
BA09)	LU6	760	25/5	Emisora Atlántica, Mar del Plata: 24h
CF21)		770	5/1	R. Cooperativa, Valentín Alsina: 24h
TF02)	LRA10	780	25/1	R. Nal., Ushuaia: 24h
CS01)	LRA12	780	25/5	R. Nal., Santo Tomé
ME03)	LV8	780	25/5	R. Libertador, Mendoza: 24h
CB06)	LRF210	780	10/5	R. Tres "Cadene Patagoni", Trelew: 24h
ME06)	LV19	790	10	R. Malargüe: 1100-0400
CF04)	LR6	790	25/5	R. Mitre "AM 80", Buenos Aires: 24h
JU02)	LRA22	790	25/5	R. Nal, San Salvador de Jujuy
RN04)	LU15	800	25/2	R. Viedma: 24h
ME04)	LV23	800	1/0.25	R. Rio Atuel, General Alvear:1000-0400
CH01)	LT43	800	5	R. Mocoví, Charata: 0900-0300
CF52)		810		R.Federal, CF Buenos Aires
CO16)		810	10/1	R. Mitre AM 810, Córdoba: 24h
FO01)	LRA8	820	25/5	R. Nal., Formosa: 0855-0400

MW Call	kHz	kW	Station, location and h of tr
BA04) LU24	820	5/1	R. Tres Arroyos : 0900-0400
BA33) LRI208	820	2/0.5	Estacion 820, Lomas de Zamora: 24h
CF24)	830	5	R. Del Pueblo, Villa Forito: 24h
SF02) LT8	830	10/5	R. Rosario "La Ocho", Rosario: 24h
ME08) LV18	830	25/5	R. Municipal, San Rafael: 1030-0230
SC06) LU14	830	25	R. Provincia de Santa Cruz,Río Gallegos: 0900-0500
CS05) LT21	840	1/0.5	R. Municipal, Alvear
CS02) LT12	840	10/5	R. General Madariaga, Paso de los Libres: 0900-0300
BA05) LU2	840	25/5	R. Bahía Blanca, Bahía Blanca: 24h
SA03) LV9	840	25/5	R. Salta AM 840, Salta: 1000-0500
CF18)	840	5	R. General Belgrano, Buenos Aires
BA182)	850	1	R. La Gauchita, Morón: 24h
BA139)	860	0.5	R. Digital, Lanus: 24h
SC07) LRA56	860	1	R. Nal., Perito Moreno: 0955-0300
CF05) LRA1	870	100	R. Nal., Buenos Aires: 24h
BA260)	880		R. Democracia, Longchamps
RN12)	‡880	1/0.25	R. Provincial de Sierra Colorada, Sierra Colorada (F.PI: move from 1580)
SC06) LU14	880	10	R. Provincia de Santa Cruz, Las Heras (//LU14 830): 1000-0300
BA183)	890	10	R.Libre, Villa Caraza: 1000-0400
LP02) LU33	890	25/1	Emisora Pampeana, Santa Rosa: 24h
SE01) LV11	890	25/5	Em. Santiago del Estero, Santiago del Estero: 24h
CS03) LT7	900	25/5	R. Provincia de Corrientes, Corrientes: 0900-0300
LP05)	900	1	R. Municipal, 25 de Mayo
SJ02) LRA23	910	50/5	R. Nal.,San Juan: 0855-0400
CF06) LR5	910	150	R. La Red, Ituzaingó: 24h
TU02) LV7	930	25/5	R. Tucumán, San Miguel de Tucumán: 24h
CO09) LV28	930	5/1	R. Villa María, Villa María: 24h
BA138)	930	5	R. Nativa, Ciudad Evita
BA56)	930	1.5	R. Excelsior, Monte Grande
SL03) LRJ241	940	20/5	R. Dimensión, San Luís: 0900-0400
ER07) LRH200	940	3/5	R. Chajarí, Chajarí: 24h
CF07) LR3	950	25/5	R. Belgrano, Buenos Aires: 24h
CH04) LT16	950	25/5	RSP - R. Sáenz Peña , Roque Saénz Peña: 0900-0300
ME05) LRA6	960	25/5	R. Nal., Mendoza: 24h
BA06) LU13	‡960	10/1	R. Necochea, Necochea: 0900-0400
CF35)	970	3	R. Génesis, Valentin Alsina
CO03) LV2	‡970	25/5	R. Cooperativa, Córdoba: 24h
CS07) LT25	970	1/0.25	R. Guaraní, Curuzú Cuatiá:0900-0300
NE12) LRA43	970	25	R. Nal., Neuquén (F.PI)
LP03) LU37	980	3/1	R. General Pico "Radio37": 0900-0300
ER06) LT39	980	5	R. Victoria, Victoria: 0900-0400
JU06)	980	5/1	San Salvador de Jujuy (F.PI.)
RN11) LRG387	980	1	R. Luján, Valcheta
SC08)	980	5	Rio Gallegos (F.PI.
CF12) LR4	990	25/5	R. Splendid AM 990, Villa Domínico: 24h
SJ03) LRJ201	990	1	R. Calingasta, Tamberías: 1000-0500
FO03) LRH203	990	25/5	AM 990, Formosa: 24h
BA120)	1000	1	R.Sintonia, José C.Paz: 24h
LR03)	1000	10/1	La Rioja (F.PI.)
RN05) LU16	1000	3	R. Río Negro, Villa Regina: 0900-0300
CS06) LT42	1000	5	R. Del Iberá, Mercedes: 0900-0400
CH09)	‡1000	5/1	Comodoro Rivadavia (FPI.)
CO04) LV16	1010	20/10	R. Rio Cuarto, Rio Cuarto: 0830-0500
SA05) LW2	1010	1/0.25	R. Emis. Tartagal: 1000-0300
CF15)	1010	4	R. Onda Latina, Buenos Aires: 24h
SJ07) LRJ214	1020	25/5	AM 1020, San Juan
SF03) LT10	1020	25/5	R. Univ. Nal. del Litoral, Santa Fé: 0800-0430
CH02) LRA58	1020	1	R. Nal., Río Mayo: 1100-2300
CF08) LS10	1030	25/5	R. del Plata, Buenos Aires: 24h
BA249)	1040		R. Revolution, Luján
CF50)	1050	1.3	R. General Güemes "La Radio Mundial", Villa Lynch
CO08) LV27	1050	10	R. San Francisco, San Francisco
BA186)	‡1060		R. Las Naciones, Monte Grande
CF09) LR1	1070	25/5	R. El Mundo, Buenos Aires: 24h
BA08) LU3	1080	25/5	Ondas del Sur, Bahía Blanca: 0900-0400
BA127)	1080		R. Claridad, Monte Grande: 24h
CO21)	‡1080	10/1	Paso de los Libres (FPI.)
SA06) LW4	1080	0.25	R. Orán/R.Maria: 24h
BA141)	1090		R. Décadas, José León Suárez
BA79)	1090	2	R. Popular, Valentín Alsina
SF17)	1090	1	Libertad AM 1100, Rosario: 24h
BA66)	1100	1	R. Estilo, Glew: 24h
CO17)	1100	10/0.5	R.Mitre, Corrientes
CF03) LS1	1110	25/5	R. de la Ciudad, Dique Luján: 24h:
BA184)	1120	1	R.Sudamericana, San Martin: 24h
BA198)	1120	1	Em. Santiago y Copla, Ciudad Evita: 24h
CF33)	1120	2	AM Tango "Nacional y Popular", Villa Dominico: 24h
SJ04) LV5	1120	25/5	R. Sarmiento, San Juan: 0900-0400
TU04) LRK204	1120	1	R. 21 (Cadena Eco), Yerba Buena: 24h
BA229)	1130	3	R. Show, Isidro Casanova
SE02) LRA21	1130	25/5	R. Nal., Santiago del Estero: 0900-0400
LP06) LRG203	1130	5/1	R. Capital "Antena 10", Santa Rosa
BA12) LU22	1140	10/1	R. Tandil, Tandil: 0830-0300
BA208)	1140	1	R. La Luna, El Palomar
RN06) LRA2	1140	25	R. Nal., Viedma: 0900-0400
SJ05) LRA51	1150	5	R. Nal., Jáchal: 1030-0300
SF04) LT9	1150	60	R. Brigadier López, Santa Fé: 24h
MS07) LRH202	1150	50	R. Tupá Mbaé, Posadas: 0900-0300
BA154)	1150	0.1	R. Sagrada Familia (R.Maria), Ciudad Madero
BA232)	1160		R. La Más Santiagueña, Gregorio de Laferrere: 0900-0300
RN07) LRA57	1160	5/1	R. Nal., El Bolsón: 0900-0300
MS04) LRH253	1160	5/10	R. Cataratas, Pto. Iguazú: 24h
BA10) LU32	1160	10/2.5	R. Coronel Olavarría, Olavarría: 0900-0300
BA185)	1160	1	R. Independencia, Remedios de Escalada
SA07)	‡1160	5/1	Salta. FPI
SL02) LRA29	1170	10	R. Nal., San Luis: 1000-0500
BA51)	1170	1	R. Luz del Mundo, Rafael Calzada
BA77)	1170	5	R. Mi País, Hurlingham: 24h
BA155) LRI230	1180		R. de la Sierra, Tandil
BA253)	1180	0.25	AM San Ponciano, Abasto
TU03) LRA15	1190	25	R. Nal., San Miguel de Tucumán: 24h
CF10) LR9	1190	25/5	R. América, Buenos Aires: 24h
BA250)	1200		La Radio del Chamamé, Morón
CB09) LRF203	1200	10/1	R. 3 "Cadena Patagonia": 24h
CS04) LT6	1200	1	R. Goya, Goya: 0900-0300
TF04)	‡1200	25/5	Rio Grande (F.PI)
BA29) LRI229	1210	1/0.5	R. Las Flores, Las Flores: 24h
BA54)	1210	5	R. La Luz "AM Doce Diez", Lomas de Mirador
BA200)	1210		R. Mailin, Gregorio de Laferrere
BA233)	1210		R. del Promesero, José C. Paz
BA83) LRI224	1220	10/5	R. Onda Marina, Mar del Plata (Cad. Eco)
CF16)	1220	5/1	Eco R. AM 1210, Buenos Aires: 24h
CH06)	1220	1	LRC Radio "La Radio de Chaco", Pres. Roque Sanez Peña
SF05) LT2	1230	25/5	R. Gen. San Martín "R.Dos", Rosario: 24h
JU05) LW5	1230	5/1	R. Libertador, General San Martin
BA89)	1230	1	R. Litoral, Ciudad Evita
CF44)	1230	1	R. Creativa, CA Buenos Aires: 24h
BA230) LRI218	1240	1	R. Universidad Nal. del Sur, Bahia Blanca
CF31)	1240	1	R. Cadena Uno, Paso del Rey: 24h
BA31)	1250	10	R. Estirpe Nacional., San Justo: 24h
CB10)	1250		Puerto Madryn
BA131)	1260	2	R. Amor, Villa Tesel: 24h
BA256)	1260		R. Sendero de Verdad, El Jagüel
CF36)	1260	9	R. Oliva "Unicon del Cielo", General Rodriguez
ER02) LT14	1260	10/5	R. General Urquiza, Paraná: 24h
NE10)	‡1260		R. y Television del Neuquén, Neuquén (F.PI)
FO02) LRA20	1270	25/5	R. Nal., Las Lomitas: 0900-0300
BA11) LS11	1270	100	R. Provincia de Buenos Aires, La Plata: 24h
BA15) LU11	1280	10/5	R. Trenque Lauquén, Tr. Lauquén: 0900-0300
CF17)	1280	6	R. Cadena Eco, CA Buenos Aires: 24h
BA244)	1280		AM 1280 El Sonido de la Gente, Gregorio de Laferrere
SF11) LRI371	1290	1/0.5	R. Amanecer, Reconquista: 0800-0400
BA72)	1290	1	R. Provinciana, San Miguel
BA53)	1290	1	R. Interactiva, Ciudad Madero
ME10) LRJ212	1290	5/1	R. Murialdo, Villa Nueva de Guaymallén: 24h
SF06) LRA5	1300	10/1	R. Nal., Rosario: 0853-0303
BA241)	1300		R. Juventud, Florencio Varela
BA63)	1300		Plus Radio, Lanús: 1100-0300
CF26)	1300	2	R. Identidad "La Salada", Buenos Aires: 24h
BA199)	1310	0.25	Gesell Radio, Villa Gesell
ER03) LRA42	1310	10	R. Nal., Gualeguaychú: 24h
NE06)	1310	0.5	R. Dr. Gregorio Alvarez (Cadena Eco) Piedra del Aguila: 24h
CF29)	1310	1	Rdif. Antártica Argentina, Buenos Aires: 24h
BA13) LU10	1320	10	R. Azul, Azul: 0900-0300
BA187)	1320	1	R. Máster, Luján
BA209)	1320		R.Area Uno, Caseros
ME09) LV24	1320	0.25	R. Andina, Tunuyán: 1000-0600
SF19)	1330	1/0.25	AM 1330, Rosario

MW	Call	kHz	kW	Station, location and h of tr
BA205)		1340	0.8	AM Renacer, Moreno
BA225)		1340		R.Tradicional Conurbano Norte, Florida (irr)
CS08)		‡1340	1/0.25	Goya (F.PI.)
ER13)		1340	1	R. Mediterránea, Rosario del Tala
CF11)	LS6	1340	10/5	R. Buenos Aires, Burzaco:24h
CH07)		‡1350	1/0.25	Juan José Castelli, Chaco (F.PI.)
CO13)	LRJ747	1350	5/1	R. Sucesos, Villa Carlos Paz
BA38)		1360	0.4	R. Nuestra Señora de Itatí - "R. Itati", Morón
ER15)		1360	1	AM 1360 R.Cooperativa Estirpe Entrerriana, Maria Grande: 0930-2300
RN08)	LRA54	1370	10	R. Nal., Ingeniero Jacobacci: 0900-0300
BA76)		1370	3	AM Trece-70, González Catan: 24h
BA226)		‡1370		Junin (F.PI.)
SF20)		1370	1/0.25	Aire de Santa FeRafaela
BA144)		1380	2	R. Buenas Nuevas, Merlo
BA179)		1380	0.5	R. AM Súper Sport, Temperley
BA189)		1380	0.5	R. Los Toldos, Los Toldos
BA190)	LRI231	1380	5/1	LV del Sudeste, Necochea
BA14)	LR11	1390	10	R. Univ. Nacional, La Plata: 24h
BA216)		1390		R. General Paz, José C. Paz
BA254)		1390		La Rocha Azul AM 1390, Libertad
BA255)		1400		AM 1400, Luján
NE07)	LRG202	1400	5/1	R. Cumbre, Neuquén: 24h
CF41)		1400		R. Punto, Buenos Aires
CH08)		1400	1/0.25	AM del NEA, Charata
SF23)		1400	0.25	Red 24, Rosario
BA42)		1410	5/1	R. Folclorismo, José Léon Suárez: 0900-0200
BA214)		1410	0.5	R. Fundacion, Rafael Calzada
BA218)		1410	1	R.Cope, Chivilcoy
ME14)		1410	1	R. Lider, Mendoza
SL04)		1410		R. María de La Paz, Villa Mercedes
BA108)		1420	1	R. Génesis 2000, General Conesa
CF28)	LRI220	1420	1/0.25	R. Dime, Villa Martelli
JU04)	LRK221	1420	1/0.25	R. Ciudad Perico, Perico: 1000-0400
BA16)	LT24	1430	1/0.25	SN24, San Nicolás
CO06)	LV26	1430	1/0.25	Cadena 26, Río Tercero: 24h
BA17)	LRI235	1430	0.25	R. Balcarce, Balcarce: 0900-0300
BA201)		1430	0.5	R. Shekinah, Merlo
BA212)		1430	1	R. Cunumi Guazú, Rafael Castillo: 24h
LP08)		1430	1	Red Pampeana, General Pico
BA146)		1440	0.25	R. Cristo Viene, Mar del Plata
BA257)		1440		R. FEDETUR Turismo, Mar de Ajó
NE03)	LRA53	1440	5	R. Nal., San Martín de los Andes: 0900-0500
BA18)	LU36	1440	1	R. Coronel Suárez, Coronel Suárez: 1000-0300
CO07)	LV20	1440	1/0.25	R. Laboulaye, Laboulaye
BA52)		1440	2	R. Impacto, Ciudad Madero: 24h
BA234)		‡1440	0.25	Villa Gesell (F.PI.)
SF12)	LRI221	1440	5/1	R. General Obligado, Reconquista: 0830-(SS 1000-)0300
BA235)		1450	5	R. Banderas, Moreno
CF37)	LRI213	1450	1.32	R. El Sol, Porción Quilmes
CS09)		‡1450	5/1	Corrientes (F.PI.)
SJ06)	LRI211	1450	1/0.25	R. Las 40, Villa Aberastain
SF08)	LT29	1460	1/0.25	R. Venado Tuerto, Venado Tuerto: 24h
BA19)	LU30	1460	0.25	R. Maipú (Cad. Eco), Maipú: 0900-0100 (Sat/Sun -2300)
BA20)	LU34	1460	0.1	R. Pigüé, Pigüé: 24h
BA41)		1460	1	R. Contacto, San Antonio de Padua: 1100-0300
BA191)		1460	1	R. Jerusalén, Monte Grande
BA21)	LT20	±1470	1/0.25	R. Junín, Junin
BA22)	LU26	1470	0.25	La Dorrego AM 1470, Coronel Dorrego: 24h (r. 1468)
BA174)		1470		R. Lider, Mariano Acosta
BA49)		1470	1	R. Mburucuya, José León Suarez
BA84)		1470	0.7	Cadena 1470, Remedios de Escalada: 1000-0200
ER05)	LT26	1470	1/0.25	R. Nuevo Mundo, Colón: 0900-0300
RN09)		‡1470	1	R. Municipal, Luis Beltrán: 1200-0100
SF09)	LT28	1470	1/0.25	R. Rafaela, Rafaela: 0900-0300
BA50)	LU27	1480	1	R. Centro, Dolores: 1100-0300
BA147)		1480	1	R. Sensaciones, Tapiales: 1000-0200
CO15)	LV22	1490	1/0.25	R. Huinca Renancó, Huinca Renancó:
BA67)		1490		AM Vida en el Espiritu, Mar del Plata(irr)
BA69)		1490	1.5	R. Gama, Lanús: 1000-0300
BA169)		1490		R. Dif, Emanuel, Partido de Ezieza
BA246)		1490		R. Ciudad de Caá Cati, José C. Paz
CO18)		1490		R. AM Vida, Córdoba
SJ08)		1490	1/0.25	R. Rivadavia (F.PI.)
BA07)	LRI214	‡1500	2	R. Bonaerense, Lavallol
BA23)	LT34	1500	0.25	R. Nuclear, Zárate
BA178)		1500	0.25	R. Olivera, General Rodriguez
BA236)		‡1500		Frecuencia On, La Reja
BA237)		1500		AM Entre Mares, San Clemente del Tuyú
BA239)		1500		R. 20 de Agosto, Longchamps
CO20)		1500		R.Vida, Río Cuarto
BA34)		1510		LV del Oeste,Libertad: 24h
BA220)		1510	1	R. RBN "Radio de las Buenas Nuevas", Lomas de Zamora
CF23)		1510	2	R. Nueva Bolivia, Ciudad Madero
BA74)		1510		R. Alabanza, Guernica
SF14)	LRI253	1510	1/0.25	R. Belgrano, Suardi: 0900-0400
ER08)	LT38	1520	0.25	R. Gualeguay, Gualeguay: 0900-0300
BA40)		1520	1	R. Metropolitana "R.Metro", Ciudadela
BA47)		1520	3	R. Cielo Nuevo, Isidro Casanova
BA92)		1520	5/1	R. Chascomús, Chascomús: 24h
BA145)		1520	2	R. Norteña, Los Polvorines: 0900-0100
BA148)		1520		Cadena D, Monte Chingolo
BA258)		1520	2	LV del Sur, Luis Guillón
BA192)		1530	1.5	R. Esencia "LV del Litoral", San Miguel Oeste
BA238)		1530	5	LV del Futuro, Merlo
CO12)	LRJ200	1530	1/0.25	R. Centro Morteros, Morteros: 0900-0300
BA25)	LT35	1540	0.25	R. Mon, Pergamino: 0900-0400
BA26)	LU28	1540	0.25	R. Tuyú:1000-0300
BA100)		1540	1	R. AM Líder, Benavidez
BA231)		1540		R. Zorobabel, Esteban Echeverría
CF43)		‡1540	1	R. Amanecer, Ciudad Evita
BA251)		1550		Estacion Quince Cincuenta, Villa Florito
SF10)	LT23	1550	5/0.25	R. Regional, San Jenaro Norte: 0900-0300
BA27)	LT32	1550	0.25	R. Chivilcoy, Chivilcoy: 1000-0400
ER09)	LT40	1550	1	R. LV de la Paz, La Paz: 0900-0100
BA175)		1550		R. Popular, José León Suárez
BA213)		1550		R. Esperanza, Gregorio de Laferrere
BA259)		1550		R. La Amistad, José C. Paz
ER10)	LT11	1560	2.5/1.5	R. Gral. Francisco Ramírez, Concepción del Uruguay (La R. Publica): 0900-0300
BA28)	LT33	‡1560	0.25	R. 9 de Julio, 9 de Julio: 0900-0300
BA44)		1560	1.5	R. Castañares, Ituzaingó
BA99)		1560		R. Restauración, Llavallol
BA194)		1560	0.5/0.25	AM 1560 "La R. de la Gente", Tandil
BA196)		1560	1	R. Antena, Lobos: 24h
ME13)		‡1560	1/0.25	Mendoza (F.PI.)
BA55)		1570	2.5	R. Melody, Remedios de Escalada: 1200-0300
BA71)		1570	1	R. AM Rocha, Tolosa: 24h
BA163)		1570		R. La Morena de Itati, Grand Bourg
SF22)		1570		R. Alegría Regional, Luis Palacio: 24h
ER11)	LT27	1580	1	R. LV del Montiel, Villaguay: 0900-0300
BA48)		1580	2	R. Tradición, San Martín
BA135)		1580	1	R. 26. de Julio, Longchamps: 0900-0100
BA176)	LT36	1580	0.25	R. Chacabuco, Chacabuco
BA247)		1580		R. Cóndor, Moreno
MS08)		1580	1	R. La Cueva, 25 de Mayo
RN12)		1580		R. Provincial de Sierra Colorada, Sierra Colorada (F.pl. move to 880)
BA223)		1590	1	R. Dolores, Dolores: 24h
BA240)		1590	1	R. Sin Fronteras, Merlo
CF49)		1590		R. Stentor, Buenos Aires
BA37)		1600	1	R. Armonia, Caseros: 24h
SF21)		1600	0.25	AM 1600 Del Centro, Montes de Oca: 24h
BA124)		1610	1	R. Guabiyú, Gregorio de Laferrere:24h
CO14)		1610	0.5	R. Comunitaria Regional, Laboulaye
SF18)		1610	0.2	R. Fósil, Rosario: irr active Sun to 2200
BA45)		1620	2	R. Vida, Monte Grande: 24h
BA180)		1620	10/1	AM 16-20 La Radio, Mar del Plata
BA224)		1620		R. Sentires,Merlo: 1100-0100
BA134)		1630	1	R. Restauración, Hurlingham
BA227)		‡1630	10	AM Diagonal, La Plata
ER12)		1630	1/0.25	R. America, San José: 24h
BA177)		1630	1	R. Hosanna Argentina, Isidro Casanova
BA181)	LRI227	1650	1/0.5	Antares AM 1650 "La R. de la Familia", Pilar (irr): 24h
BA195)		‡1650		R. Fenix. Temperley
BA245)		1650		R. El Mensajero, Rafael Castillo
BA156)		1660	1	R. Revivir, Gregorio de la Ferrere
ER14)		‡1660	5/0.25	Nogoyá (F.PI.)
CO19)		‡1660	1/0.25	Paso de los Libres (F.PI.)
BA167)		1670		R. Bethel, Banfield (r. v1672-1675)
BA242)		1670		R. Gratitud, Glew
BA261)		1680		R. Santa Fe, Canning
BA107)		1690	1	R. Cristo la Solución, San Justo: 24h
BA90)		1700		R. Imagen, Castelar: 0900-0100
CF47)		‡1700	5/1	R. Fantastico, Tigre
CF32)		‡1710	0.3	AM 1710/R.Urquiza, Buenos Aires

SW	Call	kHz	kW	Station, location and h of tr
CF05)	LRA31	6060	30	R. Nac., Buenos Aires: 2100-1500

ASOCIACION DE RADIODIFUSORAS PRIVADAS ARGENTINAS (ARPA)

✉ Tte. Gral. Juan D. Perón 1561, Piso 3, (C1037ACB) Buenos Aires ☎ 11 4371 5999 ▤ 11 4382 4483 **W:** arpa.org.ar **E:** arpaorg@arpa.org.ar **L.P:** Edmundo Omar RéboraARPA is an association of privately owned commercial stns.

ASOCIACION DE RADIODIFUSORES CATOLICOS ARGENTINOS (ARCA)

✉ Tucumán 1993, (C1050AAM) CA Buenos Aires ☎ 11 4375 0376 **W:** radiocatolicasarca.or.ar **E:** arcato@sminter.com.ar **L.P:** Presidente: Osvaldo Bufarini

Addresses and other information:
BA00) BUENOS AIRES (PROV.):
BA01) Moreno 30, 1° Piso, (B8000FWB) Bahía Blanca ☎ 291 453 2700 **W:** lra13.com.ar **E:** administracionlra13@radionacional.gov.ar – **FM:** 95.1 MHz – **BA02)** Hipólito Yrigoyen 2641, (B7600DPG) Mar del Plata ☎ 223 494 1039 ▤ 223 492 2020 **W:** lu9mardelplata.com.ar **E:** lu9-adm@lacapitalnet.com.ar - **FM:** 103.3MHz FM 103 Universo – **BA04)** Av. Belgrano 457, (B7500EBE) Tres Arroyos ☎ 2983 42 3504 ▤ 2983 42 7000 **W:** lu24.com.ar **E:** noticias@lu24.com.ar – **FM:** 95.3MHz FM Ilusiones – **BA05)** Rodriguez 55 (B8000HSA) Bahía Blanca ☎ 291 459 0002 ▤ 291 455 5556 **W:** lu2.com.ar **E:** radio@lu2.com.ar – **FM:** 94.7MHz FM Ciudad – **BA06)** Calle 64 N° 2946, Gran Galería Central, EP, (B7630CIR) Necochea ☎ 2262 42 0100 **W:** radionecochea.com.ar **E:** administracion@lu13radionecochea.com.ar – **FM:** 88.1MHz FM Oceánica – **BA07)** Doyhenard 316, (B1836EVH) Lavallol ☎ 11 4231 3225 **W:** am1500.com.ar **E:** radiobonarense@gmail.com – **BA08)** Av. Lamadrid 116, (B8000FKD) Bahía Blanca ☎ 291 452 0382 **W:** lu3ondas.com.ar **E:** radiolu3@yahoo.com.ar - **FM:** 94.3MHz FM Ondas – **BA09)** Córdoba 1865, (B7600DVM) Mar del Plata ☎ 223 491 7047 ▤ 223 491 2355 **W:** lu6.com.ar **E:** radioa@lu6.com.ar – **FM:** 93.3MHz FM – **BA10)** Alsina 3377, (B7400COW) Olavarría ☎ 2284 41 0911 **W:** lu32.com.ar **E:** administracion@lu32.com.ar – **FM:** 98.7MHz FM Cristal – **BA11)** Calle 53 N°. 810, (B1900BBQ) La Plata ☎ 221 424 9713 **W:** amprovincia.com.ar **E:** secretaria@amprovincia.com.ar – **FM:** 97.1MHz FM Provincia – **BA12)** Gral. Rodriguez 762, PA, (B7000AOP) Tandil ☎ 249 442 7493 **W:** lu22radiotandil.com.ar **E:** radiotandil@arnet.com.ar – **FM:** 97.1MHz Galática FM – **BA13)** Av. Bartolomé Mitre 819/21, (B7300IKQ) Azul ☎ 2281 42 4138 **E:** lu10radioazul@latinmail.com – **FM:** 89.5MHz FM Celestial – **BA14)** Plaza Rocha 133, 2°Piso, (B1900DVA) La Plata ☎ 221 422 0330 ▤ 221 422 4164 **W:** radiouniversidad.unlp.edu.ar/am-1390 **E:** administracion@radiouniversidad.unlp.edu.ar – **FM:** 107.5MHz – **BA15)** Av. Pedro García Salinas 1815, (B6400EIF) Trenque Lauquen ☎ 2392 42 5454 **W:** radiotrenquelauquen.com.ar **E:** radiolu11@speedy.com.ar – **FM:** 88.5MHz FM Proyección – **BA16)** Av. Moreno 124, (B2900GPO) San Nicolás ☎ 336 442 5222 ▤ 336 442 4479 **W:** sn24web.com.ar **E:** lt24@cablenet.com.ar – **FM:** 88.3MHz FM 88 – **BA17)** Av. San Martin 2700, (B7620) Balcarce ☎ 2266 43 0780 ▤ 2266 43 0779 **W:** //radiobalcarce.blogspot.com.ar **E:** radiobalcarce@telefax.com.ar – **FM:** 89.7MHz FM Balcarce – **BA18)** Garibaldi 71, (B7540DQA) Coronel Suárez ☎ 2926 43 2706 **W:** radiocoronelsuarez.com **E:** info@radiocoronelsuarez.com - **FM:** 100.5MHz "Frecuencia 36" – **BA19)** Lavalle Sud 312, (B7160BAH) Maipú ☎ 2268 42 1774 **W:** lu30radiomaipu.com.ar **E:** lu30rm@yahoo.com.ar – **FM:** 104.1 FM Cristal – **BA20)** Lavalle 210, (B8170CHF) Pigüé ☎ 2923 47 2205 **W:** radiopigue.com.ar **E:** radio-lu34@s8.coopenet.com.ar - **FM:** 96.3MHz FM Serrana – **BA21)** Hipólito Yrigoyen 86, (B6000DDB) Junín ☎ 236 444 3610 ▤ 236 444 3474 **W:** lt20radiojunin.com.ar **E:** gerente@lt20radiojunin.com.ar – **FM:** 89.1MHz Nova Retro – **BA22)** Uslenghi 592, 1° Piso, (B8150EGD) Coronel Dorrego ☎ 2921 45 3456 **W:** ladorrego.com.ar **E:** info@ladorrego.com.ar – **BA23)** Independencia 140, (B2800JIG) Zárate ☎ 3487 42 3116 ▤ 3487 43 9500 **W:** radionuclear.com.ar **E:** audioradionuclear@yahoo.com.ar – **FM:** 90.1MHz FM Top – **BA25)** Dr. Alem 340, (B2700LHH) Pergamino ☎ 2477 42 4022 **W:** lt35radiomon.com.ar **E:** lt35radiomon@speedy.com.ar - **FM:** 90.3MHz FM Mágica – **BA26)** Av. San Martín 366, (B7163EGQ) General Madariaga ☎ 2267 55 1540 **W:** radiotuyu.blogspot.com **E:** radiotuyu@telpin.com.ar – **FM:** 92.5MHz FMTuy – **BA27)** Av. Mitre 924. (B6620BMW) Chivilcoy ☎ 2346 43 0690 **E:** radiochivilcoy@speedy.com.ar – **FM:** 101.1MHz FM Sónica – **BA28)** Pte. Hipólito Yrigoyen 969, (B6500DJQ) 9 de Julio ☎ 2317 52 1333 **W:** cadenanueve.com **E:** lt33@cadenanueva.com - **FM:** 89.9MHz Maxima FM – **BA29)** Av. Avellaneda 793, (B7200AOH) Las Flores **W:** radiolasflores.com.ar **E:** am1210@s2coopnet.com.ar ☎ 2244 45 2320 - **FM:** 89.7MHz FM Condor – **BA31)** Juan Florio 3573, (B1754AJK) San Justo ☎ 11 4441 1400 **W:** estirpe1250.com.ar **E:** estirpe1250@yahoo.com.ar – **BA33)** Antonio Sáenz 572, 2° piso, (B1832HUL) Lomas de Zamora ☎ 11 4243 7891 ▤ 11 4292 5559 **W:** radioestacion820.com.webgte.alsolnet.com **E:** 820am@speedy.com.ar – **BA34)** Isla Soledad 2510, (B1716NXB) Libertad ☎ 220 497 4623 **W:** lavozdeloesteam1510.com.ar

E: oyentes@lavozdeloeste1510.com.ar – **BA36)** Dr. Ignacio Arieta 3950 (B1754AQT) San Justo ☎ 11 4651 0193 **W:** am660.com.ar– **BA37)** Wenceslao Paunero 2915, (B1678DSG) Caseros ☎ 11 4716 2279 **W:** am1600armonia.com.ar **E:** armoniaam1600@arnet.com.ar – **BA38)** San Luís 991, (B1708JUE) Morón ☎ 11 4627 7439 – **BA40)** Julio A. Roca 3414, (B1702BCL) Ciudadela ☎ 11 4488 3644. ▤ 11 4657 4098 **E:** amradiometro@gmail.com – **BA41)** Agustín Zárate 154, (B1718BPD) San Antonio de Padua ☎ 220 482 4526 **W:** amcontacto.blogspot.com.ar **E:** contacto1460@gmail.com – **BA42)** Lacroze 1871 –(Ex 7277)-, (B1655LVS) José León Suárez ☎ 11 4720 2688 **W:** radiofolclorisimo.com.ar **E:** folclorísimo@hotmail.com – **BA44)** 33 Orientales 1033, Villa Ariza, (B1714NOS) Ituzaingó ☎ 11 4623 7773 **W:** //radioam1560.blogspot.com.ar **E:** – **BA45)** Mariano Alegre 23, (B1842FSA) Monte Grande ☎ 11 4281 4094 – **BA47)** Juan Jofré 4243, (B1765MOY) Isidro Casanova ☎ 11 4694 8131 **W:** emisoracielonuevo.weebly.com **E:** radiocielonuevo@hotmail.com – **BA48)** Pueyrredón 3846, (B1650CVP) San Martín ☎ 11 4754 8784 **W:** amtradicion.com.ar **E:** amtradicion@gmail.com – **BA49)** Santa Cruz 1312, (B1655IHD) José León Suárez ☎ 11 4720 0059 **E:** radioam1470@gmail.com – **BA50)** Bartolomé Mitre 317, (B7100BNG) Dolores ☎ 2245 44 2175 **W:** radiocentrodolores.com.ar **E:** radiocentro97@gmail.com – **FM:** 97.1MHz R.Centro – **BA51)** Catamarca 2560, (B1847CXH) Rafael Calzada ☎ 11 4219 1150 **W:** //nuevaradio1170.es.tl **E:** radioluzdelmundo@hotmail.com – **BA52)** Juncal 12, 1° Piso, Of. "3", (B1770AOB) Tapiales ☎ 11 4442 6333 **W:** am-1440.com.ar **E:** impactoam@hotmail.com – **BA53)** Mariquita Sánches de Thompson 1850, (B1768BDP) Ciudad Madero ☎ 11 4622 1570 **W:** radiointeractiva.com.ar **E:** radiointeractiva1290@hotmail.com– **BA54)** Av.General Paz 13869, Villa Insuperable, (B1751BRG) Lomas del Mirador ☎ 11 4454 7799 **W:** Facebook **E:** amdocediez@gmail.com – **BA55)** Las Piedras 2447, (B1826DJO) Remedios de Escalada ☎ 11 4249 6047 **W:** radiomelody1570.com.ar **E:** melody1570@hotmail.es – **BA56)** Andrés Berasain 659, (B1842AMM) Monte Grande ☎ 11 4281 3740 **W:** amexcelsior.com.ar **E:** amexcelsior@gmail.com - **FM:** 91.7MHz FM Malvinas – **BA63)** Eva Perón 1169, (B1824IBI) Lanús ☎ 11 4247 3106 **W:** plusradioam1300.com **E:** plusradio1300@hotmail.com – **BA66)** Florencio Sánchez 119, Bo Los Alamos, (B1856FXE) Glew ☎ 11 4233 1323 **W:** am1100estilo.blogspot.com **E:** amestilo@hotmail.com – **BA67)** Gascón 6343, (B7604BGA) Mar del Plata ☎ 223 478 2947 **W:** radioamvida.com **E:** info@radioamvida.com – **BA68)** Potrerillos 1246, (B1849DVX) Claypole ☎ 11 4219 3850 **W:** am660popular.com.ar **E:** info@am660popular.com.ar – **FM:** 89.1MHz FM Popular – **BA69)** Choele Choel 1233, (B1822DPY) Valentín Alsina ☎ 11 4218 4860 **W:** radiogamaeninternet.com **E:** radiogama@hotmail.com – **BA71)** Calle 39 N° 256, 1° piso (B1902APL) La Plata ☎ 221 427 3360 **W:** radiorocha1570.tk **E:** rocha1570@yahoo.com.ar – **BA72)** Domingo F.Sarmiento 2220, (B1663GFX) San Miguel ☎ 11 4667 4460 **W:** radioprovinciana.com **E:** radioprovincianaam1290@hotmail.com – **BA74)** Santiago del Estero 73, (B1862SCA) Guernica ☎ 2224 47 6963 **W:** radioalabanzas.com.ar **E:** info@radioalabanzas.com.ar – **BA76)** Cristianía 3049 =3747=, (B1765HOG) Isidro Casanova ☎ 11 4694 5434 ▤ 11 4694 7222 **W:** la1370.com.ar **E:** am1370@yahoo.com.ar – **FM:** 92.1MHz R.Cosmos – **BA77)** Jauretche 1052, 1° Piso "B", (B1686FCD) Hurlingham ☎ 11 4662 5016 **W:** laradiodemipais.com.ar **E:** info@laradiodemipais.com.ar – **BA79)** Santander 892, 1° Piso, (C1424CSL) CA Buenos Aires ☎ 11 4296 1623 **W:**radio1090.com.ar **E:** mensajes@radio1090.com.ar – **BA83)** Llavalle 900. 9° Piso "B" (C1047AAR) Buenos Aires ☎ 11 4325 2020 **W:** ondamarinaam1220.com.ar **E:** radio@ondamarinaam1220.com.ar - **FM:** 89.1MHz – **BA84)** Carlos Gardel 599. (B1824NTK) Lanús ☎ 11 4225 7304 **W:** cadenaam1470.com **E:** info@cadenaam1470.com – **BA89)** Francisco Beazley 1209 (B1755CLY) Rafael Castillo ☎ 11 4697 7333 **W:** http://radiolitoral1230.blogspot.no/ **E:** litoral1230@gmail.com – **BA90)** Madrid 3987, Barrio San Juan, (B1712NMO) Castelar ☎ 11 4692 4412 **W:** facebook.com/amradio.imagen **E:** amradioimagen@hotmail.com – **BA91)** Av. General Paz 3755, (B1672AMA) Villa Lynch ☎ 11 4755 9061 **W:** radioam610.com.ar **E:** radioam610@gmail.com – **BA92)** Juarez 250, (B7130CWF) Chascomús ☎ 2241 42 5367 **E:** rch@radiochascomus.com.ar – **FM:** 90.9MHz – **BA99)** Av. Alte. Francisco Seguí 1059, (B1836BYK) Llavallol ☎ 11 4293 9904 **W:** restaurandote.com.ar **E:** restaurandote@hotmail.com – **BA100)** Pte Hipólito Yrigoyen 51, Oficina 303, (B1640HEA) Martinez ☎ 11 4793 7471 **W:** amlider.com.ar **E:** info@amlider.com.ar - **FM:** 99.3MHz – **BA107)** Av. Brig. Gral. Juan Manuel de Rosas 4357, (B1754FVB) San Justo ☎ 11 4484 4517 **W:** Facebook **E:** contacto@cristolasolucion.com– **FM:** 91.1MHz – **BA108)** Manuel Dorrego 292, (B7101) General Conesa ☎ 2245 49 2140 **W:** am1420.com.ar – **BA119)** Gral. Martín Miguel de Güemez 5025, (B1603CUE) Villa Martelli ☎ 11 4709 1172 **W:** amitalia.com.ar **E:** radioitalia.am@gmail.com – **BA120)** Domingo F.Sarmiento 4154, (B1665KON) José C.Paz ☎ 2320 42 3306 **W:** sintonia1000.com.ar **E:** sintonia1000@yahoo.com.ar – **BA124)** Soberanía Nacional 2945, (B1757KHY) Gregorio de Lafferrere ☎ 11 4457 3674 **W:** guabiyu1610.com.ar **E:** oyentes@guabiyu1600.com.ar –

BA127) Vicente López 235 2° Piso, (B1842AUE) Monte Grande ☎11 4284 3186 **W:** radioclaridad.com.ar **E:** radio@radioclaridad.com.ar – **BA131)** Cnl. Brandsen 1175, (B1646ABW) San Fernando ☎11 4746 6856 **W:** radiooasis92.com.ar **E:** angelbonarrico@yahoo.com.ar - **FM:** 92.5MHz FM Sencacion – **BA134)** Cuzco 2821, (B1681CGU) William C. Morris, Hurlingham ☎11 4662 6387 **W:** http://amrestauracion. blogspot.no/ **E:** restauracionam@hotmail.com – **BA135)** San Martin 513 (B1854FEM) Longchamps ☎11 4233 5560 **W:** radio26.com.ar **E:** radio26dejulio@gmail.com – **BA138)** Juan Florio 3573, (B1754AJK), San Justo ☎11 4484 0808 **W:**amnativa.com.ar – **BA139)** Fray Mamerto Esquiú 1161, (B1824BFQ) Lanús ☎11 4225 2256 **W:** digit-al860.blogspot.com **E:** digital860@hotmail.com – **BA141)** Jauretche 1052, 1° Piso "C", (B1686FCD) Hurlingham ☎11 4452 8688 **W:** deca-dasam1090.com.ar **E:** info@decadasam1090.com.ar – **BA144)** Santa Fe 2540, (B1722BGZ) Merlo ☎220 485 6696 **W:** buenasnuevasradio.com.ar **E:** radiobuenasnuevasam1380@yahoo.com.ar - **FM:** 92.5MHz – **BA145)** Ex. Combatientes de Malvinas 2053, (B1613ECO) Los Polvorines ☎2320 44 7711 **W:** radionorteña.com.ar **E:** radionortena@ hotmail.com **BA146)** Av Dr. Juan Héctor Jara 2075, (B7604EOE) Mar del Plata ☎223 506 3266 **W:** creedcristoviene.com - **FM:** 91.1MHz – **BA147)** Donovan 1433, (B1770AHK) Tapiales ☎11 4426 0185 **W:** am1480.com.ar **E:** sensacionesam@yahoo.com.ar – **BA148)** Victor Hugo 647, (B1825FBI) Monte Chingolo ☎11 4220 6822 **W:** cadenal. com **E:** director@cadenad.com – **BA154)** Salta 2641, (B1754IQS) San Justo ☎11 4441 8196 - **FM:** 104.5MHz FM Sintonia – **BA155)** Gral. Belgrano 531, (B7000GEK) Tandil ☎249 444 6383 **W:** am1180.com.ar **E:** am1180@speedy.com.ar - **FM:** 99.5MHz – **BA156)** Av Bdr. Juan Manuel de Rosas N° 10840, (B1757EPS) Gregorio de Laferrere ☎11 4640 1021 **W:** radiorevivir.net **E:** radiorevivir@gmail.com – **FM:** 89.7MHz – **BA163)** Juan F.Segui 895, (B1615MNA) Grand Bourg ☎23 2041 4426 – **BA167)** Benito Pérez Galdós 688, Villa Fiorito, (B1821EON) Banfield ☎11 4276 5194 – **BA169)** Yatay 628, (B1804CMH) Ezeiza ☎11 4232 7070 **W:** radiodifusoraemanuel.jimdo.com **E:** radiodifusor-aemanuel@hotmail.com – **BA172)** Juan Florio 3573, (B1754AJK) San Justo ☎11 4441 8200 **W:** radiorepublica.com.ar – **BA173)** Belgrano 4033, (B1650CCS) San Martin ☎11 4713 8808 **W:**am680.com.ar – **BA174)** Heredia 920, Augstín Ferrari, (B1724EOT) Mariano Acosta ☎220 498 1498 **W:** http://radioamlider.com **E:** laradiolider@hotmail. com – **BA175)** Av. Marquez 2468, (B1655MSS) José León Suárez ☎11 4729 1545 **W:** popular1550.com.ar **E:** radio1550popular@hotmail.com – **BA176)** Remedios de Escalada San Martin 76, (B6740ELB) Chacabuco ☎2352 42 6156 **W:**lt36radiochacabuco.com.ar **E:** radiochacabuco@ topmail.com.ar – **FM:** 91.7 MHz FM Universal – **BA177)** Zufriategui 871, (B1765CKQ) Isidro Casanova ☎11 4467 2468 **W:** hosanna.hol.es - **E:** hosannaam1640@hotmail.com – **BA178)** Pedro Laurenz 237, Las Malvinas (B1748), General Rodríguez ☎237 487 3200 **W:** http:// radioolivera.es.tl **E:** radioolivera@yahoo.com.ar – **BA179)** Bombero Ariño 1150, (B1834IAX) Temperley ☎11 5290 0075 **W:**lasupersport. com.ar **E:** lasuper@lasupersport.com.ar – **BA180)** Hipólito.Yrigoyen 2629, (B7600DPG) Mar del Plata ☎223 494 1428 **W:** 1620.com.ar **E:** am1620@yahoo.com.ar – **BA181)** Cjal. Manuel Martitegui 598, Fátima, (B1629JGL) Pilar ☎ 230 437 3150 **W:** am1650antares.com.ar **E:** info@1650antares.com.ar – **BA182)** Salta 138, 2° Piso "C", (B1708JOD) Morón ☎11 4489 2024 **W:** am850.com.ar **E:** lagauchita810@gmail. com – **BA183)** Av Cnl Ramón L. Falcón 6219 (C14085DRQ) CA Buenos Aires ☎11 4641 2821 **W:** am890.com.ar **E:** administracion@am890. com.ar – **BA184)** Santa Rosalía (Diagonal 78) 1465 (B1651CXE) San Andrés ☎11 4752 3245 **W:** sudamericana1120.com.ar **E:** info@suda-mericana1120.com.ar – **BA185)** Fray Mamerto Esquiú 2855, (B1826GBO) Remedios de Escalada ☎11 4225 3198 **W:** radioindependencia.com.ar **E:** radioindependencia@hotmail.com - **FM:** 99.3MHz R. G – **BA186)** Calle Angel Rotta 168, (B1842AED) Monte Grande ☎11 4296 0771 **W:** lasnaciones.org/radio – **BA187)** Las Heras 1478, (B6700AUO) Luján ☎2323 42 9595 **W:** masterradiolujan.com.ar **E:** master1310@ciudad. com.ar – **BA189)** Paso 1943, (B6015ASC) Los Toldos ☎2358 44 3954 **E:** radiolostoldos@hotmail.com – **BA190)** Avenida 59 N° 2465, PA, (B7630GYJ) Necochea ☎2262 52 0003 **W:** am1380.com.ar **E:** contac-to@am1380.com.ar – **FM:** 103.9MHz R.10 - Net – **BA191)** Florentino Ameginho 34, 1° Piso, Oficino 6, (B1842CAB) Monte Grande ☎11 4296 3890 **W:** jerusalenradio.com **E:** info@jerusalenradio.com.ar – **BA192)** Paula Albarracin 3957, Barrio Sarmiento (B1663CPE) San Miguel Oeste ☎2320 46 0649 **W:** amesencia.com.ar **E:** radioesencia@live.com.ar – **BA194)** Av. Aristóbulo del Valle 1202 (B7000HLN) Tandil ☎249 443 6006 **W:**lavozdetandil.com.ar **E:** lavozdetandil.com.ar – **BA195)** Coronel Suárez 554, (B1834GHL) Temperley ☎11 4244 1843 **W:** fenix1650.com.ar **E:** amradiofenix@hotmail.com – **BA196)** Aristóbulo del Valle 23, (B7240IXA) Lobos ☎2227 42 1211 **W:** amradioantena. com.ar **E:** info@amradioantena.com.ar – **BA198)** Luis Vernet 6654, (B1757MOB) Gregorio de Laferrere ☎11 4467 4224 **W:** la1120.com.ar – **BA199)** Av. Buenos Aires 735, Galeria Pinar, Local 11, (B7165JCH) Villa Gesell ☎2255 47 6749 **W:** am1310gesell.com.ar **E:**

am1310gesell@hotmail.com – **FM:** 89.9MHz – **BA200)** Fournier 4075, (B1757IDW) Gregorio de Laferrere ☎11 4457 7204 **W:** Facebook **E:** radiomailin@am1330radiomailin.com.ar – **BA201)** Burela 560, Bo Pompeya (B1722PHL) Merlo ☎220 489 8012 **W:** radioshekinah.es.tl **E:** am1430shekinah@hotmail.com – **BA205)** Dr. Eugenio Asconape 371, (B1744FIG) Moreno ☎237 460 0878 **W:** amrenacer.com.ar **E:** radiore-nacer1340@hotmail.com – **BA208)** Ramón L.Falcón 2193, (B1685BDY) El Palomar ☎11 4443 7424 **W:** radiolaluna.com.ar - **FM:** 90.5MHz – **BA209)** Dr.Rebizzo- (Calle 626) – N° 3917 (B1678BCC) Caseros ☎11 4578 5130 **W:** Facebook **E:** radioarea1@gmail.com – **BA212)** Marcelo T.de Alvear 650 (B1755JMN) Rafael Castillo ☎11 4697 4919 **W:** Facebook: Centro Los Cunumi Guasu **E:** cunumiguasu@hotmail.com – **BA213)** Mñor. López May 3372, (B1757DHJ) Gregorio de Laferre ☎11 4467 3600 **W:** radioesperanzaamyfm.com **E:** radioesperanza@gmail. com – **FM:** 88.3MHz – **BA214)** General Lavalle 2307, (B1847BQW) Rafael Calzada ☎11 4219 1903 **W:** radiofundacion.org.ar **E:** contacto@ radiofundacion.org.ar – **BA216)** Andrés Blanqui 4233, (B1666CZS) José C. Paz ☎2320 59 9321 **W:** radiogeneralpaz.com **E:** generalpazam1390@ hotmail.com – **BA218)** Av. Ceballos 241 (CB6620HQ) Chivilcoy ☎2346 42 4532 **W: E:** cope1410@gmail.com – **BA220)** Ejército de los Andes 5, Villa Florito, (B1821BWA) Banfield Oeste ☎11 4276 2423 **W:** rbn1510am.com.ar **E:** rbn_am1510@hotmail.com – **BA223)** Faustino Brughetti 1392, (B7100) Dolores ☎2245 44 3131 **W:** radiodolores.com. ar **E:** radiodolores@hotmail.com - **FM:** 94.9MHz – **BA224)** Mozart 1015, (B1721EUS) Parque San Martin, Merlo ☎220 470 4265 **W:** amsentires.com.ar **E:** sentires1620@hotmail.com – **BA225)** Av Maipú 18, L-28, (B1602AAN) Florida ☎11 4797 0687 **W:** amradiotradicional. jimdo.com **E:** amradiotradicional@yahoo.com.ar – **BA226)** Remedios de Escalada de San Martin 65, PB "1", (B6000CZA) Junin ☎236 444 4450 – **FM:** 96.5MHz – **BA227)** La Plata ☎221 410 4800 **W:** diago-nal1630.com.ar **E:** contacto@diagonal1630.com.ar – **BA229)** Lavalle 1625. P.B., Oficina 4 (C1048AAM) CA Buenos Aires ☎11 4371 2597 **W:** am1130.com.ar **E:** am1130radio@gmail.com – **BA230)** San Andrés 800, Barrio Altos de Palihue, (B8000FTN) Bahia Blanca ☎291 459 5190 **W:** radio.uns.edu.ar **E:** radio@.uns.edu.ar – **BA231)** Carmen de Areco 406 (B1841HHJ9 Monte Grande ☎11 4263 4108 – **BA232)** Hilario Ascasubi 4446 (B1757AZB) Gregorio de Laferrere ☎11 4457 1466 **W:** radioam1160.com.ar **E:** radiolas@live.com – **BA233)** Dr. Carlos Saavedra Lamas 3636, (B1666MDV) José C. Paz ☎2320 45 3200 **W:** laradiodelradiopromisero.blogspot.com.ar **E:** damianeliseoalvez@hot-mail.com – **FM:** 31.3MHz – **BA234)** Villa Gesell – **BA235)** Autopista Acceso Oeste –Colectora Lado Norte- N° 6589 (B1743NVD) Moreno ☎237 468 7766 **W:** ambanderas.com.ar – **BA236)** José Miró1453, (B1738BIC) La Reja ☎237 487 1145 - **FM:** 90.7 MHz – **BA237)** Calle 51 N° 559, (B7105BJK) San Clemente del Tuyú ☎2252 42 1228 **W:** http// amentremares.com.ar – **FM:** 101.7 MHz Cadena Virtual – **BA238)** Patricias Argentinas 456, (B1721BTD) Parque San Martin, Merlo ☎220 480 2134 **W:** am1530.com.ar **E:** infoam1530.com.ar – **BA239)** General San Martin 933, (B1854FFE) Longchamps ☎11 4233 7432 **E:** radio_ 20deagosto@hotmail.com – **BA240)** Av Hipólito Yrigoyen 1700, Depto. 1, (B1722JMP) Merlo ☎220 486 5767 **W:** radiosinfronterasam1590. blogspot.com.ar **E:** chamamesinfronteras@hotmail.com – **BA241)** Cjal. José Dans Rey –Calle 26- N° 742 (B1888ELF) Florencio Varela ☎11 4255 0739 **W:** siemprechamame.com.ar **E:** info@siemprechamame. com.ar - **FM:** 90.1MHz – **BA242)** Weiss de Rossi 3056, (B1856IBD) Glew ☎2224 43 6516 **W:** //radiogratitudunaradiocononda.webnode. es **E:** gratitudam1670@gmail.com – **BA244)** Soberania Nacional 2945, (B1757KHY) Gregorio de Laferrere ☎11 4457 3674 **W:** Facebook: El Sonido de la Gente – **BA245)** Cayetano Cazón 2338, (B1755HDH) Rafael Castillo ☎11 4698 3163 **W:** sendaantigua.com.ar **E:** radioel-mensajero@hotmail.com – **BA246)** Chaco 67 (B1620EOA) Maquinista Savio ☎348 448 3825 – **BA247)** Sófocles 4825, (B1743FFA) Moreno ☎237 468 7195 **W:** radiocondoram1580.com **E:** radiocondoram1580@ hotmail.com – **BA249)** Dr José Manuel Galvez 950, Bo Juan XXIII, (B6702COV) Luján ☎2323 15 642763 **W:** Facebook **E:** radiorevolu-tion1040@gmail.com – **BA250)** Salta 138, 2° piso "C", (B1708JOD) Morón ☎11 4628 3348 **W:** laradiodelchamame.com.ar – **BA251)** Oliden 2872, Villa Caraza, Lanus ☎11 4218 0549 **W:** am1550.com.ar **E:** estacion1550@gmail.com **BA253)** Call 515 s/n, e /Calles 203 y 204, (B1903) Abasto ☎221 491 6476 **W:** fmsanponciamo.com.ar **E:** fmsan-ponciamo@yahoo.com.ar – **FM:** 99.7MHz – **BA254)** Aconquija 1053 (B1716BNL) Libertad ☎220 494 2303 **W:** larocaazulradioam.com.ar **E:** dijitalradio@hotmail.com – **BA255)** 25 de Mayo 579, (B6700ALK) Luján ☎2323 44 2020 **E:** am1400lujan@yahoo.com.ar - **FM:** 91.9 MHz FM Fantástica – **BA256)** Isla Decepción 224, (B1805GAF) El Jagüel ☎11 4290 3299 **W:** amsenderodeverdad.com **E:** amsenderodeverdad.com – **BA257)** Azopardo 186, (B7109AHD) Mar de Ajó ☎257 60 4610 **W:** radio.fedetur.org,.ar **E:** secretaria@fedetur.com.ar **BA258)** Robertson 1249, 1° Piso, (B1838AIE) Luis Guillón radiometro1520.com.ar ☎11 4290 8007 **W:** lavozdelsur.com.ar **E:** amlavozdelsur@gmail.com – **BA259)** José C. Paz **W:** radioamistad.webnode.es **E:** radioamistad@hotmail.com –

BA260) Longchamps – **BA261)** Alvarez de Toledo 3150, (B1847GDR), Canning – **FM:** 95.3 MHz FM Alfa

CA00) CATAMARCA:
CA01) Chacabuco 762, (K4700BTP) S.F. del Valle de Catamarca ☎3833 42 4223 **W:** lra27.com.ar **W:** nacionalcatamarca.com.ar **E:** catamarca@radionacional.gov.ar - **FM:** 103.3MHz

CB00) CHUBÚT:
CB01) Av. Alvear 1180, (U9200AXY) Esquel ☎2945 45 1900 **W:** nacionalesquel.com.ar **E:** esquel@radionacional.gov.ar - **FM:** 88.7MHz – **CB02)** Av. Hipólito Yrigoyen 1735, (U9102BGM) Trelew ☎280 443 0580 ☐280 442 5457 **W:** radiochubut.com **E:** info@radiochubut.com - **FM:** 95.7MHz Galaxia – **CB03)** 25 de Mayo 453, (U9000CXC) Comodoro Rivadavia ☎297 447 2125 **W:** nacionalcomodoro.com.ar **E:** administracionlra11@radionacional.gov.ar - **FM:** 94.3MHz – **CB04)** Estivariz 226, (U9120KEF) Puerto Madryn ☎280 445 9200 **W:** lu17.com **E:** lu17@lu17.com - **FM:** 96.1MHz Paraiso FM – **CB05)** Av. Rivadavia 198, (U9000AKP) Comodoro Rivadavia ☎297 447 6561 **W:** lu4radio.com. ar **E:** direccion@lu4radio.com - **FM:** 101.7MHz FM Alfa – **CB06)** 25 de Mayo 740, (U9100BRP) Trelew ☎280 443 5221 **W:** radio3cadenapatagonia.com **E:** radiotres@speedy.com.ar – **CB07)** Av. Comandante Fontana y Dr. Mariano Moreno, (U9033) Alto Rio Senguer ☎2945 49 7050 **W:** nacionalriosenguer.com.ar **E:** direcciónlra55@radionacional. gov.ar - **FM:** 93.5MHz – **CB09)** Esquel **W:** radio3cadenapatagonia.com **E:** radiotres@speedy.com.ar – **CB10)** Puerto Madryn

CF00) CIUDAD AUTÓNOMA DE BUENOS AIRES (BUENOS AIRES):
CF01) Rivadavia 835, (C1002AAG) CA Buenos Aires ☎☐11 4338 4250 **W:** continental.com.ar **E:** info@continental.com.ar– **CF02)** Arenales 2467, (C1124AAM) CA Buenos Aires ☎11 5219 4744 ☐11 5219 4760 **W:** rivadavia.com.ar **E:** info@rivadavia.com.ar – **CF03)** Sarmiento 1551, 8° Piso, (C1042ABC) CA Buenos Aires ☎11 5371 4646 ☐11 5371 4613 **W:** buenosaires.gob.ar/radiociudad **E:** laoncediez@gmail.com – **CF04)** Gral. Mansilla 2668, 1° piso (C1425BPD) CA Buenos Aires ☎11 5777 1500 ☐11 5777 1504 **W:** radio-mitre.com.ar **E:** info@radiomitre.com.ar – **CF05)** Maipú 555, (C1006ACE) CA Buenos Aires ☎11 4327 3021. ☐11 4325 9433 **W:** radionacional.com.ar **E:** buenosaires@radionacional.gov. ar - **International Sce:** see International Broadcasting section – **CF06)** Fitz Roy 1460, (C1414CHT) CA Buenos Aires ☎11 4535 2011 **W:** lasenal. am **E:** info@radiolared.com.ar – **CF07)** Pedro Conde 935, (C1426AYS) CA Buenos Aires ☎11 4318 7888 **W:** am950belgrano.com **E:** info@am950belgrano.com – **CF08)** José Ignacio Gottiti 5963, (C1414BKK) CA Buenos Aires ☎11 4556 9200 ☐11 4556 9056 **W:** amdelplata. com **E:** gbray@amdelplata F.P.I.: 100 kW – **CF09)** Rivadavia 825, (C1002AAG) CA Buenos Aires ☎4121 8900 **W:** elmundo1070.com – **CF10)** José de Amenábar 23, (C1426AIA) CA Buenos Aires ☎11 4778 8500 **W:** 11090america.com **E:** contacto@amradioamerica.com – **CF11)** Av. Entre Ríos 1931, (C1133AAH) CA Buenos Aires ☎11 4307 2200 **W:** radiobuenosaires.com.ar **E:** am1350@radiobuenosaires.com. ar – **CF12)** Cap. Gral. Ramon Freire 932 (C1426AVT) CA Buenos Aires ☎11 4535 7625 **W:** splendid990.com **E:** info@splendid990.com.ar – **CF13)** Uriarte 1899, (C1414DAU) CA Buenos Aires ☎11 4535 2110 **W:** facebook.com/laradio/info **E:** comercial@radio10.com.ar – **CF15)** Sarmiento 1586, 6° Piso "E", 2° Cuerpo, (C1042ABD) CA Buenos Aires ☎11 4372 2841 **W:** am1010ondalatina.com.ar **E:** contactoam1010@yahoo.com.ar – **CF16)** Lavalle 900, 9° Piso B, (C1047AAR) CA Buenos Aires ☎11 4325 2020 **W:** ecomedios.com **E:** radio@cadenaeco. com.ar – **CF17)** Av.Rivadavia 10561, 3° Piso, (C1408AAF) CA Buenos Aires ☎11 5631 1000 **W:** cadenaradioeco.com.ar **E:** am1530@cadenaderadioeco.com.ar – **CF18)** Traful 3834, (C1437HML) CA Buenos Aires ☎11 4912 0497 **W:** am840generalbelgrano.com **E:** am840generalbelgrano@hotmail.com – **CF21)** Cerrito 242, PB "B", (C1010AAF) CA Buenos Aires ☎11 5275 0770 **W:** radiocooperativa. com.ar **E:** dirección@radiocooperativa.com.ar – **CF23)** Av. Larrazábal 4300, Casa 32, (C1439EDR) CA Buenos Aires ☎11 4638 7644 – **CF24)** Lavalle 1625, P.B., Oficina 4, (C1048AAMI) CA Buenos Aires ☎11 4371 2597 **W:** radiodelpueblo.com.ar **E:** gerencia@radiodelpueblo. com.ar – **CF26)** Bonpland 1114, (C1414CMJ) CA Buenos Aires ☎11 4856 8819 – **CF27)** Maipu 267 7° Piso, (C1084ABE) CA Buenos Aires ☎11 4136 1050 **W:** conceptoam.com.ar **E:** radio@conceptoam.com. ar – **CF28)** Humboldt 1477, (C1414CKT) CA Buenos Aires ☎11 4778 8200 **W:** la1420.com **E:** contacto@radiodime.com.ar – **CF29)** Santander 892, 1° Piso (C1424CSL) CA Buenos Aires ☎11 4926 0177 **W:** am1310.com.ar **E:** radioam1310@gmail.com – **CF30)** San Martin 569 2° Piso "7", (C1004AAK) CA Buenos Aires ☎11 4893 1701 **W:** am570radioargentina.com.ar **E:** am570radioargentina@hotmail. ar – **CF31)** Manzanares 4006, (C1430AEN) CA Buenos Aires ☎11 4541 0303 **W:** cadenauno.com.ar **E:** mensajes@cadenauno.com.ar – **CF32)** Av. Triunvirato 4671, (C1431FBJ) CA Buenos Aires ☎11 4521 3931 **W:** am1710.com **E:** mensajes@am1710.com.ar – **CF33)** Tacuari 1594, (C1139AAH) CA Buenos Aires ☎11 4307 1835 **W:** amtango. com.ar **E:** amtango@amtango.com.ar – **CF34)** Pte. Luis Sàenz Peña

210 (C1110AAF) CA Buenos Aires ☎11 4382 9327 **W:** madres.org **E:** radio@madres.org – **CF35)** Santander 892, 1° Piso (C1424CSL) CA Buenos Aires ☎11 4926 1622 **W:** radiogenesis970.com.ar **E:** mensajes@radiogenesis970.com.ar – **CF36)** Fonrouge 76, (C1408HFB) CA Buenos Aires ☎11 3979 5663 **W:** radiooliva.com **E:** radiooliva2006@hotmail.com – **CF37)** Alicia Moreau de Justo 2050, 1°P, Of. "132", (C1107AFP) CA Buenos Aires ☎11 4893 7555 **W:** radioelsol.com. ar **E:** trd@trdpublicidad.com.ar – **CF38)** San Martín 569, 2° Piso "6", (C1004AAK) CA Buenos Aires ☎11 4313 8575 **W:** belgrano650.com. ar **E:** info@belgrano650.com.ar – **CF41)** Tte. Gral. Juan Domingo Perón 1669, 4° Piso, Oficina 75 y 77 (C1037ACE) CA Buenos Aires ☎11 4372 2989 **W:** amradiopunto.com.ar **E:** contacto@amradiopunto.com. ar – **CF43)** Cnel. Martiniano Chilavert 5875, (C1439CLM) CA Buenos Aires ☎11 4605 4857 **W:** siembraelpan.com.ar/radio_amanecer.html **E:** radio_amanecer@hotmail.com – **CF44)** Av. Callao 449, 5° Piso "C", (C1022AAE) CA Buenos Aires ☎11 4372 5863 **W:** am1230creativa.wix. com **E:** am1230creativa@yahoo.com.ar – **CF45)** Ulrico Schmidt 6057, 4° Piso, (C1440CFS) CA Buenos Aires ☎11 4642 5533 **W:** am690k24. com.ar **E:** radioam690@yahoo.com.ar – **CF47)** Pje. Gibson 3999 (C1255AAA) CA Buenos Aires ☎11 4921 9999 **W:** radiofantastico.com. ar **E:** interior@radiofantastico.com.ar – **CF48)** Av.Pueyrrdeón 19, 2° Piso, (C1032ABA) CA Buenos Aires ☎11 4864 2230 **W:** radiorebelde. com.ar **E:** amrebelde@hotmail.com – **CF49)** Libertad 434, 1° Subsuelo, Of. 5, (C1012AAJ) CA Buenos Aires ☎11 4381 4305 **W:** am1590.com. ar – **CF50)** Santiago del Estero 79, Subsuelo, (C1427BDE) CA Buenos Aires ☎11 4381 1672 **W:** guemesam.com.ar **E:** guemes1050am@gmail.com – **CF51)** Venezuela 370, 2° piso, (C1095AAH) CA Buenos Aires ☎11 5354 6651 **W:** radioam750.com.ar **E:** web@radioam750. com.ar – **FM.** 89.1 R.Malena – **CF52)** Av Colonel Ramón L Falcón 6219 (C1408DRQ) CA Buenos Aires ☎11 4641 3920 **W:** 810am.com.ar **E** administracion@810am.com.ar

CH00) CHACO:
CH01) Av. General Güemes 1103, (H3730AML) Charata ☎3731 42 0150 ☐ 3731 42 0735 **W:** mocovi.com.ar **E:** am800@mocovi.com.ar - **FM:** 95.7MHz FM Lider – **CH02)** Acceso Ruta Nacional N° 40 s/n, Bo Gendarmería, (U9030) Río Mayo ☎2903 42 0099 **W.** Nacionalriomayo. com.ar **E:** direccionlra58@radionacional.gov.ar - **FM:** 88.1MHz – **CH03)** Av. Sarmiento 1201, (H3502COE) Resistencia ☎362 443 2920 – **W:** nacionalresistencia.com.ar **E:** resistencia@radionacional.com.ar Guaraní: Sat. 1800 - **FM:** 96.7MHz – **CH04)** Hermana Hortensia - Calle 19 - N° 151, (H3700ASC) Presidencia Roque Sáenz Peña ☎364 442 8047 **W:** radiorsp.comar **E:** lt16am950@yahoo.com.ar - **FM:** 93.3MHz FM Sentimientos – **CH05)** Casa de Las Culturas de Resistencia, Resistencia **W:** Facebook - **FM:** 101.5MHz FM Chaco – **CH06)** John F. Kennedy -Calle 9- 158, (H3700XXX) Presidencia Roque Sáenz Peña ☎364 442 7188 **W:** lrcradio.com.ar **E:** lrcradio@hotmail.com - **FM:** 107.9MHz – **CH07)** Juan José Castelli – **CH08)** Maipú 550 (H3730DPL) Charata ☎3731 42 0090 **W:** redtvsrl.com.ar **E:** administracion@iblast. com.ar – **CH09)** Comodoro Rivadavia

CO00) CORDOBA:
CO01) Fray Miguel de Mojica 1600, Bo Marquez de Sobremonte, (X5008CCN) Córdoba ☎351 410 5000 **W:** cba24n.com.ar **E:** am580@srt.com - **FM:** 102.3MHz Nuestra Radio – **CO02)** Santa Rosa 241, (X5000ESE) Córdoba ☎351 422 5664 ☐351 422 5665 **W:** nacionalcordoba.com.ar **E:** direccionlra7@radionacional.gov.ar - **FM:** 100.1 MHz – **CO03)** 27 de Abril 979, (X5000AES) Córdoba ☎351 526 5200 ☐351 526 5222 **W:** am970.com.ar **E:** info@am970.com.ar – **CO04)** Constitución 399, (X5800BBB) Río Cuarto ☎358 463 8255 **W:** lv16. com **E:** lv16@lv16.com - **FM:** 93.9, 106.9MHz – **CO05)** Alvear 139, (X5000ILC) Córdoba ☎351 526 0597 ☐351 526 0504 **W:** cadena3. com.ar **E:** info@cadena3.com.ar - **FM:** 92.3, 100.5, 106.9MHz – **CO06)** Libertad 455 2° Piso, (X5850KNI) Río Tercero ☎3571 42 1019 **W:** cadena26.com.ar **E:** cadena26comar@gmail.com - **FM:** 101.9 - 94.5MHz FM Libra – **CO07)** Tucumán 159, (X6120EOC) Laboulaye ☎3385 42 6259 ☐3385 42 5848 **W:** radiolv20.com **E:** info@radiolv20.com – **CO08)** Córdoba 51,"Edifico Reggio II", (X2400PQA) San Francisco ☎3564 42 2186 **W:** lavozdesanjusto.com.ar **E:** lavoz@lavozdesanjusto.com.ar - **FM:** 88.7MHz FM Galaxia – **CO09)** Santa Fe 1490, (X5900DTJ) Villa María ☎353 452 2699 **W:** radiovillamaria.com **E:** contame@radiovil-lamaria.com.ar - **FM:** 98.5MHz FM Record – **CO12)** Blvd. 25 de Mayo 133, PB, (X2421ABB) Morteros ☎☐3562 42 2148 **W:** radiomorteros. com **E:** info@diomorteros.com - **FM:** 90.3MHz FM Selección – **CO13)** Av. Concepción Arenal 1174, (X5004AAY) Córdoba ☎351 460 1010 **W:** radiosucesos.com **E:** audiencia@radiosucesos.com - **FM:** 104.7MHz – **CO14)** Pte.Gral. Julia A.Roca 36, (X6120CGB) Laboulaye ☎3385 42 5199 **W:** radio1610am.com.ar **E:** radio.luis@hotmail.com – **CO15)** Santa Fé 804, (X6270CWR) Huinca Renancó ☎2336 44 2007 **W:** lv22. com.ar **E:** lv22_1490@yahoo.com.ar – **CO16)** Av. Fernando Fader 3469, Bo Cerro de Las Rosas, (X5009ABB) Córdoba ☎351 526 1300 **W:** radio-mitre-cordoba.com.ar **E:** interstockbroker@gmail.com - **FM:** 97.9MHz – **CO17)** Pte. Hipólito Yrigoyen 1083, 1° Piso, (W3400ASU)

Corrientes ☎379 4340143 **W:** mitrecorrientes.com **E:** redaccion@mitrecorrientes.com – **FM:** 92.9MHz R.ciudad – **CO18)** Tolosa 2379, Bo Maipú, (X5014JSE) Córdoba ☎351 4117010 **W:** radioamvida.com.ar **E:** info@radioamvida.com.ar – **CO19)** Paso de los Libres – **CO20)** Florencio Sánches 450, (X5804HIH) Río Cuarto ☎358 4628179 **W:** misionvida.com.ar **E.** lausassa@gmail.com – **FM:** 89.3 MHz – **CO21)** Paso dos Libres

CS00) CORRIENTES:
CS01) Chacra 46, Km 3, La Tablada, (W3340) Santo Tomé ☎3756 42 0090 **W:** nacionalsantotome.com.ar **E:** santotome@radionacional. gov.ar - **FM:** 100.5MHz **CS02)** Juan Sitja Nin 941, (W3230GEQ) Paso de los Libres ☎3772 42 4332 **W:** radiolt12.com.ar **E:** contacto@radiolt12.com.ar - **FM:** 92.7MHz FM Confluencia – **CS03)** La Rioja 743, (W3400BZG) Corrientes ☎379 442 3560 **W:** radiolt7.com **E:** directorio@radiolt7.com – **FM:** 95.3MHz FM Capital – **CS04)** Mariano I. Loza 231, (W3450BXE) Goya ☎3777 42 2653 **W:** Facebook: LT6 Radio Goya **E:** lt6radiogoya@hotmail.com.ar - **FM:** 98.3MHz FM Esplendida – **CS05)** General Paz 903, (W3344AYQ) Alvear ☎3772 47 0699 **W:** lt21radiomunicipalalvear.blogspot.com.ar **E:** radiomunicipalvear@hotmail.com – **CS06)** Av. Atanaico Aguirre Km 2, (W3470EHA) Mercedes ☎3773 42 0087 **W:** radiodelibera.com.ar **E:** oyentes@lt42. net.ar - **FM:** 93.5MHz – **CS07)** San Martín 1380, (W3461AKA) Curuzú Cuatiá ☎3774 42 2634 **W:** lt25.com.ar **E:** info@lt25..com.ar - **FM:** FM Guarani 107.1MHz – **CS08)** Goya **CS09)** Corrientes

ER00) ENTRE RIOS:
ER01) San Martín 371, (E3202FUG) Concordia ☎345 421 5506 **W:** lt15concordia.com.ar **E:** lt15adm@arnet.com.ar - **FM:** 89.3MHz – **ER02)** Almeda de la Federacion 126, (E3100GNO) Paraná ☎343 423 0101 **W:** lt14.com.ar **E:** lt14web@gmail.com – **FM:** 93.1MHz Baxada del Paraná – **ER03)** Urquiza Oeste 4200, (E2820) Gualeguaychú ☎3446 42 6159 **W:** lra42.com.ar **E:** gualeguaychu@radionacional. gov.ar – **FM:** 98.7MHz – **ER04)** Carlos Pellegrini 106, (E2822EWD) Gualeguaychú ☎3446 43 7550 ≣3446 42 7088 **W:** radiolt41.com.ar **E:** info@radiolt41.com.ar – **FM:** 90.3 / 97.9MHz – **ER05)** Av. Pte. Juan D. Perón 117, (E3280CBS) Colón ☎3447 42 1067 **W:** nuevomundodigital. com.ar **E:** radionmundo@colonred.com.ar – **FM:** 93.7MHz FM Palmares – **ER06)** Blvd Eva Perón –Ex Sarmiento- 474, (E3153EZH) Victoria ☎3436 42 1285 **W:** lt39noticias.com.ar **E:** gerencia@lt39am980.com. ar - **FM:**90.3MHz FM Victoria – **ER07)** Pablo Stampa 2430, (E3228FDD) Chajarí ☎3456 42 0002 **W:** chajarialdia.com.ar **E:** info@multimedioschajari.com.ar – **FM** 107.7MHz – **ER08)** Chacabuco 38, 1° Piso, (E2840BFB) Gualeguay ☎3444 42 4915 **W:** radiogualeguay.com.ar **E:** info@radiogualeguay.com.ar – **FM:** 104.3MHz – **ER09)** Roque Sáenz Peña 1082, (E3190FZJ) La Paz ☎3437 42 1568 **W:** lt40.com.ar **E:** info@lt40.com.ar – **FM:** 91.3MHz FM La Paz – **ER10)** Onésimo Leguizamón 269, (E3260FQE) Concepción del Uruguay ☎3442 42 5661 **W:** lt11.com. ar **E:** direccion@eleteonce.com.ar – **FM:** 92.9MHz FM Arena – **ER11)** Av. Vélez Sársfield 1111, (E3240AUL) Villaguay ☎3455 42 1717 **W:** Facebook: R.LV del Montiel **E:** lt27villaguay@hotmail.com – **FM:** 88.7MHz – **ER12)** Chacabuco 1514, (E3283AWB) San José ☎3447 47 0998 **W:** 10tv.com.ar **E:** danycanal@hotmail.com - **FM:** 105.3 MHz R.Melody – **ER13)** Dr. Rozados 533, (E3174BEK) Rosario del Tala ☎344 542 3009 **W:** fmmediterranea.blogspot.no **E:** frecuenciamediterranea@gmail.com - **FM:** 102.5MHz – **ER14)** Nogoyá – **ER15)** Av.libertador Gral. San Martin 359, (E3133CXG) Maria Grande ☎343 494 0486 **W:** //am1360.com.ar **E:** comercialam1360@hotmail.com.ar

FO00) FORMOSA:
FO01) Junín 655, (P3600IDM) Formosa ☎3717 42 6197 **W:** nacionalformosa.com.art **E:** lra8@radionacional.gov.ar - **FM:** 94.1MHz – **FO02)** Ruta Nacional 81 y Ruta Provincial 32, (F3630) Las Lomitas ☎3715 43 2167 **W:** nacionallaslomitas.com.ar **E:** laslomitas@radionacional.gov. ar - **FM:** 93.5MHz – **FO03)** Av. 9 de Julio 165, (P3600BCB) Formosa ☎370 442 2590 **W:** am990formosa.com.ar **E:** info@am990formosa.com - **FM:** 98.9MHz FM Unica

JU00) JUJUY:
JU01) Av. España (Sur) 700, (Y4650ALN) La Quiaca ☎3885 42 2356 **E:** laquiaca@radionacional.gov.ar - **FM:** 92.5MHz – **JU02)** Rio Bermejo y Olavarria, (Y4600) San Salvador de Jujuy ☎388 422 2781 **E:** jujuy@radionacional.gov.ar - **FM:** 94.1MHz – **JU03)** Dr. Horacio Guzmán 496, (Y4600) San Salvador de Jujuy ☎388 423 0035 **W:** radiovisionjujuy. com.ar **E:** rvj@arnet.com.ar – **FM:** 97.7MHz FM Tropico – **JU04)** Av. Villafañe y Calilegua, (Y4608) Perico ☎388 491 1465 **W:** radiovisionjujuy.com.ar **E:** radiociudadperico@gmail.com – **JU05)** Jujuy 126, (Y4512DRJ) Libertador General San Martin ☎3886 42 6440 **W:** radiovisionjujuy.com.ar **E:** gerencia@grupovisionjujuy.com.ar - **FM:** 104.5MHz – **JU06)** San Salvador de Jujuy – **FM:** 92.1 MHz

LP00) LA PAMPA:
LP01) Rivadavia 202, 4° Piso, (L6300DWF) Santa Rosa ☎2954 42 2456 **W:** nacionalsantarosa.com.ar **E:** santarosa@radionacional.gov. ar - **FM:** 95.9MHz – **LP02)** Lisandro de la Torre 474, (L6300BQJ) Santa Rosa ☎2954 41 4015 **W:** lu33pampeana.com.ar **E:** publicidadlu33@

yahoo.com.ar - **FM:** 103.7MHz FM Power – **LP03)** Calle 40 No 1250, (L6360EVZ) General Pico ☎2302 43 0055 **W:** radiolu37.com.ar **E:** radiolu37@radiolu37.com.ar - **FM:** 88.9MHz Melodiás FM – **LP05)** General Pico 610, (L8201BIL) 25 de Mayo ☎299 494 8086 **W:** fmrio911. com.ar**E:** radiomuni@hotmail.com - **FM:** 91.1MHz FM Rio – **LP06)** Pasaje Rabinad 545, (L6304BJA) Santa Rosa ☎2954 42 7545 **W:** antena10.com.ar **E:** radioantena10@gmail.com – **FM:** 102.5MHz R.10 – **LP08)** Ca 105 Bis (Oeste) N° 546, (L6360FLL) General Pico ☎2302 43 2331 **W:** laredpampeana.com.ar **E:** contactto@laredpampeana.com. ar – **FM:** 95.7 MHz

LR00) LA RIOJA:
LR03) La Rioja

ME00) MENDOZA:
ME01) Manuel A.Sáez 2421, (M5539HSW) Las Heras ☎261 430 1600 **W:** radionihuil.com.ar **E:** radionihuil.com.ar – **FM:** 98.9MHz – **ME02)** Rioja 1093, (M5500ALU) Mendoza ☎261 521 5100 ≣261 521 5121 **W:** lvdiez.com.ar **E:** eleve10@infovia.com.ar or info@lvdiez.com. ar – **FM:** 100.9MHz Estacion del Sol – **ME03)** Rioja 1484, (M5500AMD) Mendoza ☎261 423 8872 **W:** nacionallibertado.com.ar **E:** contacto@radio-libertador.com.ar – **FM:** 92.7MHz – **ME04)** Bernado de Irigoyen 17, PA (M5620BDA) General Alvear ☎2625 42 6566 **E:** lv23@gmail. com – **FM:** 88.9MHz FM Paraiso – **ME05)** Emilio Civit 460, (M5502GVR) Mendoza ☎261 438 0596 **W:** radionacionalmendoza.blogspot.com.ar **E:** mendoza@radionacional.gov.ar - **FM:** 97.1MHz.ar – **ME06)** Esquivel Aldao 350, (M5613AEH) Malargüe ☎260 447 1160 ≣260 447 0658 **E:** nacionalmalargue.com.ar **E:** radiomalargue03@yahoo.com.ar - **FM:** 88.1MHz – **ME07)** Av. Hipólito Yrigoyen 223, (M5602HBC) San Rafael ☎260 443 0055 **W:** nacionalsanrafael.com.ar **E:** lv14@radiosanrafael.com.ar - **FM:** 97.3MHz – **ME08)** Comandante. Salas 150 1° Piso Of. 6, (M5600DJD) San Rafael ☎260 444 9276 **E:** lv18@sanrafael.gov.ar – **FM:** 98.7MHz – **ME09)** Av. Pellegrini 692, (M5560EMT) Tunuyán ☎2622 42 5588 **E:** lv24am1320@yahoo.com - **FM:** 104.5MHz – **ME10)** Av. Bandera de los Andes 4420, (M5521AXL) Villa Nueva de Guaymallén ☎261 421 3992 **W:** radiomurialdo.com.ar **E:** mensajes@radiomurialdo.com.ar – **FM:** 90.5MHz FM Familia. – **ME11)** Valle de Uspallata, Las Heras – **ME12)** Comandante Salas 200, (M5602AVD) San Rafael ☎260 442 4265 – **FM:** 104.5 FM Andina – **ME13)** Mendoza – **ME14)** General Gregorio Paz 25, 6° Piso (M5500GNA) Mendoza ☎261 637 2700 **W:** amlider. jimdo.com **E:** cumbre1410@gmail.com

MS00) MISIONES:
MS01) Cristóbal Colón 1452, (N3300LXF) Posadas ☎376 443 8727 **W:** lt17.com.ar **E:** info@radiolt17.com - **FM:** 107.3MHz FM Provincia – **MS02)** Félix de Azara 2440, (N3300LQZ) Posadas ☎376 443 0500 **W:** lt4digital.com.ar – **FM:** 104.5MHz – **MS03)** Av. Victoria Aguirre Sur 809, (N3370AYI) Puerto Iguazú ☎3757 420099 **W:** lra19.com.ar **E:** direccionlra19@radionacional.gov.ar- **FM:** 99.1MHz – **MS04)** Av. Las Calandrias y Las Golondrinas, Bo IPRODHA, (N3370) Puerto Iguazú ☎3757 42 0060 **W:** radiocataratas.com **E:** info@radiocataratas. com - **FM:** 94.7MHz – **MS07)** Domingo F.Sarmiento 1847, 7° Piso, (N3300HUM) Posadas ☎376 42 0203 ≣376 42 2758 **W:** radiotupambae.com.ar **E:** administracion@radiotupambae.com.ar – **FM:** 105.9MHz – **MS08)** Manantial (Ruta Provincial N° 8)s/n (N3363) 25 de Mayo ☎3755 49 3084 **E:** am_provincia@hotmail.com

NE00) NEUQUÉN:
NE01) Gral. Paz 536, (Q8353CGL) Chos Malal ☎2948 42 1198 **W:** nacionalchosmalal.com.ar **E:** chosmalal@radionacional.gov.ar - **FM:** 92.3MHz – **NE02)** Av. San Martín 324, (Q8340EYQ) Zapala ☎2942 42 2960 **W:** nacionalzapala.com.ar **E:** direccionlra17@radionacional. gov.ar - **FM:** 93.9MHz – **NE03)** Gral. Villegas 1375, (Q8370ELB) San Martín de los Andes ☎2972 42 7766 **E:** nacionalsmandes.com.ar **E:** lra53@smandes.com.ar - **FM:** 92.5MHz – **NE04)** Fotheringham 445, (Q8302HBI) Neuquén ☎299 449 0485 **W:** lu5am.com.ar **E:** info@lu5am.com.ar - **FM:** 88.7 MHz FM Ciudad – **NE06)** Las Rosas 81, Bo Jardín, (Q8315AYA) Piedra del Aguila ☎2942 49 3216 **W:** radiogregorioalvarez.net **E:** contactorga@gmail.com – **FM:** 99.5MHz – **NE07)** Pte. Bernardino Rivadavia 609, (Q8300HDM) Neuquén ☎299 443 0249 **W:** amcumbre.com **E:** info@cumbream.com.ar - **FM:** 89.9MHz FM Cumbre – **NE10)** Santa Cruz 679, (Q8300BNI) Neuquén ☎299 449 5109 ≣299 442 1568 **W:** rtnweb.gob.ar **E:** rtnweb@neuquen.gov.ar - **FM:** 104.9MHz – **NE11)** Montevideo 605 (Q8300LTM) Neuquen ☎299 443 4472 **W:** am550laprimera.com **E:** info@am550laprimera.com – **FM:** 90.7MHz – **NE12)** Maestro Thames Alderete 560, (Q8300HWL) Neuquén - **FM:** 103.3MHz

RN00) RIO NEGRO:
RN01) Av. 12 de Octubre 2421, (R8403AOH) San Carlos de Bariloche ☎294 4431856 **W:** nacionalbariloche.com.ar **E:** administracion-lra30@radionacional.gov.ar - **FM:** 93.5MHz – **RN02)** Tucumán 1074, (R8332HQV) General Roca ☎298 442 4715 **W:** radioelvalle.com **E:** buzon@radioelvalle.com - **FM:** 99.3MHz FM Color – **RN03)** Gral. Roca 365, 2° piso, (R8324BPG) Cipolletti ☎299 477 6333 ≣299 477 6800 **W:** lavozdelcomanhue.com.ar **E:** publicidadradiolu19@yahoo.com.

ar - **FM:** 102.9MHz FM Comanhue – **RN04)** Av. Alvaro Barros 1148, (R8500FFX) Viedma ☎2920 42 7700 **W:** lu15am.com **E:** radiolu15@ speedy.com - **Italian:** Sat 1500-1600. - **FM:** 94.3MHz FM Rio – **RN05)** Remedios de Escalada 52, (R8336FED) Villa Regina ☎298 446 1102 📠298 446 2620 **W:** lu16radiorn.com **E:** administracion@lu16radio. com.ar - **FM:** 92.7MHz FM Rio Negro – **RN06)** Gral. Manuel Belgrano 710, (R8500FAP) Viedma ☎2920 43 1697 **W:** nacionalviedma.com. ar **E:** viedma@radionacional.gov.ar - **FM:** 93.5MHz – **RN07)** Av. San Martín y Salta, (R8430) El Bolsón ☎2944 49 2350 **W:** nacionalbolson.com.ar **E:** elbolson@radionacional.gov.ar - **FM:** 92.3MHz – **RN08)** Martín Coronado y José Hernández, (R8418) Ingeniero Jacobacci ☎2940 43 2032 **W:** nacionaljacobacci.com.ar **E:** ingenierojacobacci@ radionacional.gov.ar - **FM:** 93.5MHz – **RN09)** Casa de Tucumán 481, (R8361BKO) Luis Beltrán ☎2946 41 3090 **W:** municipalam1470.com. ar **E:** contacto@lamunicipalam1470.com – **FM:** 96.5 MHz – **RN11)** Hipólito Yrigoyen y Remedios de Escalada, (R8536BBE) Valcheta ☎2934 49 3283 **E:** aznarezmarco@hotmail.com – **FM:** 105.3MHz FM Luján – **RN12)** Hipólito Yrigoyen 402, (R8534) Sierra Colorada ☎2940 49 5176 **W:** Facebook: R.Provincial **E:** am_provincia@hotmail.com – **RN13)** Ruta Nacional Nº 22, Km 1200 y Acceso Martin Fierr, (R8328) Allen ☎298 445 4000 **W:** radioam740.com.ar **E:** radioam740@ gmail.com

SA00) SALTA:
SA01) Ruta Nal. 34, Km. 1433, (A4560CJA) Tartagal ☎3875 421600 **W:** nacionaltartaggal.com.ar **E:** tartagal@radionacional.gov.ar - **FM:** 92.3MHz – **SA02)** Dr.Carlos Pellegrini 715, 1° piso, (A4402FYO) Salta ☎387 426 0243 📠387 426 0109 **W:** nacionalsalta.com.ar **E:** saltalra4@radionacional.gov.ar - **FM:** 102.7MHz – **SA03)** Av Ex Combatientes de Malvinas 3890, (A4412BYA) Salta ☎387 424 6234 📠378 431 1140 **W:** radiosalta.com **E:** contacto@radiosalta.com - **FM:** 96.9MHz FM Genesis –**SA05)** Gorriti 524, (A4560BRL) Tartagal ☎3873 42 4141 **E:** lw2@fullnet.com.ar - **FM:** 96.1 FM Tartagal – **SA06)** 9 de Julio 163, (A4530XBF) San Ramón de la Nueva Orán ☎3878 42 1026 **W:** radiomaria.org.ar **E:** oranradio@yahoo.com - **FM:** 90.9MHz FM Orán – **SA07)** Salta

SC00) SANTA CRUZ:
SC01) Comodoro Py 342, Casa 16, Dept. 1, Bo Las Lengas (Z9407BFH) Río Turbio ☎2902 421131 **W:** nacionalrioturbio.com.ar **E:** rioturbio@ radionacional.gov.ar - **FM:** 90.3MHz – **SC02)** Zapiola 25, (Z9400BCA) Río Gallegos ☎2966 42 0023 📠2966 42 2608 **W:** lu12.com.ar **E:** lu12_am680@speedy.com.ar - **FM:** 92.9MHz FM Laser – **SC03)** Av. San Martín 1114, (Z9311AVY) Gobernador Gregores ☎2962 49 1044 **W.** Nacionalgregores.com.ar **E:** direccionlra59@radionacional.gov.ar - **FM:** 99.9MHz – **SC04)** Hermanos Vidal 261, (Z9405) El Calafate **W:** nacionalcalafare.com.ar **E:** info@lu23.com.ar ☎2902 49 5580. - **FM:** 88.1MHz – Glaciar FM – **SC05)** Ramón Lista 36, (Z9050DLB) Puerto Deseado ☎297 487 1211 **E:** lri200@deseado.gov.ar – **SC06)** Av. Néstor Kirchner –Ex Roca- 823, 1°piso, (Z9400BAH) Río Gallegos **W:** santacruz.gov.ar/lu14 **E:** radiolu14@santacruz.gov.ar ☎2966 42 2315 📠2966 42 3510 - **FM:** 99.3MHz FM Provincia – **SC07)** Saavedra 1318, (Z9040BQN) Perito Moreno ☎2963 43 2233 **E:** administracionlra56@ radionacional.gov.ar - **FM:** 93.5MHz – **SC08)** Rio Gallegos

SE00) SANTIAGO DEL ESTERO:
SE01) 9 de Julio 390, (G4200DEH) Santiago del Estero ☎385 421 3230 **W:** radiolv11.com.ar **E:** lv11@radiolv11.com.ar - **FM:** 88.1, 89.5MHz FM Total – **SE02)** Urquiza 332, 1° Piso, (G4300DHH) Santiago del Estero ☎385 421 2565 **W:** nacionalsantiago.com.ar **E:** nacionalsantiago@hotmail.com- **FM:** 98.5MHz – **SE03)** Av. 25 de Mayo sur 69, (G3760AEA) Añatuya ☎3844 42 1661 **W:** radiosolidaridad.com.ar **E:** amsolidaridad@yahoo.com.ar

SF00) SANTA FE:
SF01) Juan de Gary 2960, (S3000CRL) Santa Fé ☎342 483 5327 **W:** nacionalsantafe.com.ar **E:** administracionlra14@radionacional.gov.ar - **FM:** 94.9MHz – **SF02)** Sarmiento 763, (S2000CMK) Rosario ☎341 422 9500 **W:** nacionalsanluis.com.ar **E:** info@lt8.com.ar - **FM:** 99.5MHz – **SF03)** 9 de Julio 3560, (S3002EXB) Santa Fé ☎342 452 0187 **W:** lt10digital.com.ar **E:** administracion@radiounl.com.ar - **FM:** 103.5MHz FM X – **SF04)** 4 de Enero 2153, (S3000FHY) Santa Fé ☎342 410 9999 **W:** lt9.com.ar **E:** info@lt9.com.ar - **FM:** 92.5MHz – **SF05)** Av. Pte. Juan Domingo Perón 8101, (S2010ACF) Rosario ☎341 457 5415 **W:** nacionaljachal.com.ar **E:** radio2@rosario3.com - **FM:** 97.9MHz – **SF06)** Córdoba 1331, 1° Piso, (S2000AWS) Rosario ☎341 440 2490 **W:** nacionalrosario.com.ar **E:** rosario@radionacional.gov.ar - **FM:** 104.5MHz – **SF07)** Balcarce 800, (S2000DNR) Rosario ☎341 528 2680 **W:** lt3.com.ar **E:** lt3@lt3.com.ar - **FM:** 102.7MHz – **SF08)** Av. Casey 642, (S2600FJN) Venado Tuerto ☎346 242 0777 **W:** radiovenadotuerto.com.ar **E:** lt29@radiovenadotuerto.com.ar - **FM:** 88.9MHz – **SF09)** Cornelia Saavedra 52, 1° piso, (S2300KJB) Rafaela ☎3492 42 0300 **W:** lt28rafaela.com **E:** hola@lt28rafaela.com - **FM:** 96.5MHz – **SF10)** Juan Chavarri 458, (S2147AUH) San Jenaro Norte ☎3401 49 3069 **W:** lt23.com.ar **E:** lt23@co19set.com.ar - **FM:** 92.1MHz FM Concierto

– **SF11)** Lucas Funes 1258, (S3560ETZ) Reconquista ☎3482 42 8945 **W:**radioamanecer.com.ar **E:** radioamanecer@radioamanecer.com.ar - **FM:** 92.7MHz FM Amanecer – **SF12)** Ludueña 661, (S3560EWM) Reconquista ☎3482 42 7830 **W:** am1440rqta.com.ar **E:** am1440rqta@ yahoo.com.ar - **FM:** 95.7MHz – **SF14)** Belgrano 470, (S2349AJJ) Suardi ☎3562 47 7612 **W:** radiobelgranosuardi.com.ar **E:** belgrano@suardi. com.ar - **FM:** 104.9MHz – **SF17)** San Luis 935, Oficina 7, (S2000BBK) Rosario ☎341 558 1090 **W:** amlibertad.com.ar **E:** am1100@argentina. com – **SF18)** José Grevasio Artigas 253, (S2013ALA) Rosario ☎ 341 455 4827 **W:** radiofosil.com.ar **E:** alfredo@iacom.com.ar – **SF19)** Av Carlos Pellegrini 168, (S2000BTO) Rosario ☎341 424 5259 **W:** am1330rosario.com.ar **E:** am1330rosario@gmail.com – **FM:** 105.9 MHz – **SF20)** 25 de Mayo 3255, (S3000FUI) Santa Fe ☎342 410 1370 **W:** airedesantafe.com.ar **E:** info@airedesantafe.com.ar - **FM:** 91.1MHz – **SF21)** Córdoba 662, 1° Piso, (S2521) Montes de Oca ☎3471 49 5143 **W:** amdelcentro.com.ar **E:** am1600@am1600.com.ar - **FM:** 102.7MHz FM La Red – **SF22)** Av.San Martín 710, (S3142XAC) Luis Palacios ☎3476 49 9249 **W:** radioalegria.supersitio.net **E:** radioalegriaregional@hotmail.com.ar - **FM:** 99.3MHz – **SF23)** Casilda 5670, (S2007CKN) Rosario ☎341 437 3431 **E:** amred24@hotmail.com - **FM:** 89.7 MHz Cadena Solidaria

SJ00) SAN JUAN:
SJ01) Mitre 50 Oeste, (J5402CXB) San Juan ☎264 427-6867 **W:** lv1radiocolon.com.ar **E:** colonsa@speedy.com.ar - **FM:** 105.7, 106.3MHz – **SJ02)** Av. Ignacio de la Roza 293 Este, 2° Piso, (J5402DBC) San Juan ☎264 421 4149 **W:** nacionalsanjuan.com.ar **E:** administracionlra23@ radionacional.gov.ar - **FM:** 101.9MHz – **SJ03)** General Soler s/n, (J5405AAA) Barreal ☎2648 44 1260 **E:** radiocalingasta@gmail.com - **FM:** FM Nuestra 103.5MHz – **SJ04)** Mendoza 452 Sur, (J5402GUJ) San Juan ☎264 420 4028 **W:** lv5sarmiento.com.ar **E:** contacto@lv5sarmiento.com.ar - **FM:** 102.3, 103.7, 104.3, 104.7MHz Sarmiento FM – **SJ05)** General Paz 631, (J5460BBM) San José de Jáchal ☎2647 42 0028. 📠2647 42 0561 **E:** jachal@radionacional.gov.ar - **FM:** 102.7MHz – **SJ06)** Mitre 11 este, (J5402CWA) San Juan ☎264 427 2740 **E:** amlas40@yahoo.com.ar - **FM:** 105.1 – **SJ07)** Santa Fe 668 oeste, (J5402ACN) San Juan ☎264 421 2443 **W:** am1020sj.com.ar **E:** info@ am1020sj.com.ar - **FM:** 96.3 – **SJ08)** Rivadavia

SL00) SAN LUIS:
SL01) Lavalle 291, PA, (D5732AEE) Villa Mercedes ☎📠2657 42 4400 **W:** radiolv15.com.ar **E:** lv15@speedy.com.ar - **FM:** 95.5MHz FM Unica – **SL02)** Av. Lafinur 488, (D5700DCR) San Luís ☎266 443 1318 **E:** administracionlra29@radionacional.gov.ar - **FM:** 96.7MHz – **SL03)** Belgrano 927, 1° piso, (D5700ISS) San Luís ☎266 442 7300 **W:** am940dimension.com.ar **E:** info@am940dimension.com.ar - **FM:** 94.7MHz – **SL04)** General Paz 1078, (D5732AGJ) Villa Mercedes ☎2657 43 7734 **W:** radiomariadelapaz.com.ar - **FM:** 105.3 MHz

TU00) TUCUMAN:
TU01) Lapride 530, (T4000IFL) San Miguel de Tucumán ☎381 484 5100 **W:** lv12.com.ar **E:** radiolv12@yahoo.com.ar - **FM:** 89.5MHz FM Independencia – **TU02)** Mendoza 273, (T4000DAE) San Miguel de Tucumán ☎381 497 5080 **W:** lv7.com.ar **E:** lv7@lv7.com.ar - **FM:** 102.7MHz – **TU03)** San Martín 251, 4° Piso, (T4000CVE) San Miguel de Tucumán ☎381 431 0131 **W:** nacionaltucuman.com.ar **E:** tucuman@ radionacional.gov.ar - **FM:** 98.7MHz – **TU04)** San Martín 610, Piso 6 "6", (T4000CVN) San Miguel de Tucumán ☎381 411 1247 **W:** radio-21tucuman.com.ar **E:** info@radio21tucuman.com.ar

TF00) TIERRA DEL FUEGO:
TF01) Leonardo Rosales 490, (V9420CMJ) Río Grande ☎2964 42 2176 **W:** nacionalriogrande.com.ar **W:** lra24.com.ar **E:** riogrande@radionacional.gov.ar - **FM:** 88.1MHz – **TF02)** Av. San Martín 331, (V9410BFD) Ushuaia ☎2901 42 1670 **W:** nacionalushuaia.com.ar **E:** lra10@radionacional.gov.ar **FM:** 92.1MHz – **TF03)** Ushuaia – **TF04)** Rio Grande

FM in Buenos Aires: CF16) 90.3 Eco Radio – **CF05)** 93.7 R.Pop Nac – 96.7 FM Clásica Nacional – 98.7 Folclórica FM – **CF22)** 89.1 – **CF28)** 89.9 FM La Isla – **CF16)** 90.3 Eco Radio, 91.1 R.Abierta, 92.1 Mambo, 92.3 La Radio – **CF03)** 92.7 La Ciudad – **CF37)** 93.1 R.Late 93.7, FM Federal – **CF04)** 94.3 Disney, 94.7 FM Palermo – **CF08)** 95.1 La Metro – **CF12)** 95.9 Rock & Pop, 96.3 R.Jai – **CF05)** 96.7 Clásica, 97.1 FM Europa, 97.3 Contacto FM, 97.9 R.Cultura – **CF13)** 98.3 Mega – **CF05)** 98.7 FM Folklorica, 99.1 Cadena 3 Argentina – **CF04)** 99.9 Cadena 100, 100.3 FM Cultural Musical – **CF07)** 100.7 Blue FM, 101.1 La Ciento Uno – **CF06)** 101.5 Pop Radio – **CF10)** 102.3 Aspen Classic – **CF02)** 103.1 R. Uno, 103.7 Amadadeus FM – **CF01)** 104.3 – **CF01)** 105.5 FM Hit – **CF11)** 106.3 R.Alfa, 106.7 X4, 107.3 Milenium, 107.9 Kabul Rock. In the city area there are over 150 unlicensed LP FM stns, about 900 in the rest of the country.

FM in Córdoba 88.1 FM Láser, 90.1FM Sur – **CO02)** 91.3 R.Nacional, 91.9 Hot FM – **CO05)** 92.3 R.Popular, 92.9 FM Logos, 93.7 R.Vital, 94.3 R.Universidad, 95.1 Radiocentro Bar, 96.1 FM Shopping Classics, 96.3 FM Norte, 96.5 R.Suquia, 96.9 CNI, 98.5 FM Latinoamericana, 99.1

FM Amistad, 99.3 FM Impacto – **CO03**) 99.7 Estacion Tierra – **CO05**) 100.5 FM Córdoba, 101.5 R.Maria – **CO01**) 102.3 Power 102, 102.7 FM Vision – **CO13**) 104.7, 105.5 FM Cielo, 107.5 Box Music Station, 107.9 FM Potencia

FM in Mar del Plata: 87.7 R.Urbana, 87.9 R. 87.9, 88.1 Graffiti FM, 88.3 LV del Puerto, 88.5 Onda Cero, 88.7 DeLaAzotea, 88.9 Mediterrano – **BA83**) 89.1 Red Impacto, 89.3 Láser, 89.7 d-Rock, 90.1 R. 90.1, 90.5 Kids, 90.7 Rural, 90.9 Concierto FM, 91.3 La Red, 91.7 K.L.A., 92.1 R. María, 92.3 Nova-92, 92.7 Líder – **BA09**) 93.3 Atlantica Latina, 93.7 Lisán, 94.1 R. 94-1 – **BA105**) 94.5 Latina, 94.9 Mega, 95.3 R. Uno, 95.9 Compacto, 96.5 Residencias, 96.9 Red 92, 97.1/ 97.5 R 97-1, 97.5 Popular, 97.6 R. 97.6, 97.7 Faro, 97.9 Estación 97, 98.1 R.Disney, 98.5 Brisas, 98.9 Rock'n Pop, 99.1 R. 99.1, 99.5 Más R., 99.9 Coast, 101.1 Cadena Musica, 100.3 Cadena Latina, 100.7 Del Sol, 101.1 Red Master, 101.5 Arena Sports, 101.7 La Ola, 101.9 Concierto, 102.1 Bristol, 102.1 R.10, 102.3 Municipal, 102.5 Nativa, 102.9 Ferimar, 102.9 Box, 102.9 La Nueva – **BA02**)103.3 Universo, 103.7 Premium, 103.9 Canaan, 104.1 FM 104-1, 104.5 Via, 104.7 Urbana, 104.9 LV Amiga, 104.9 Cosmos, 105.1 Señal, 105.5 Inolviable, 105.9 Coast-Melody, 106.3 Five, 106.5 Argentian, 106.7 Sur, 106.9 Veronica, 107.1 Cielo, 107.5 Radioactiva, 107.7 R.107.7, 107.9 Trinidad

FM in Rosario (Santa Fe): 89.5 R.Fisherton (CNN R.), 90.9 Uruguay – **SF05**) 92.3 FM Vida, 92.7 A-Z 927, 92.9 Radioactiva, 93.7 Cordial, 94.5 Latina, 95.5 Corazon, 96.6 Rio – **SF05**) 97.9 Vida, 98.5 Tango, 98.9 FM Si – **SF02**) 99.5 Estacion del Siglo, 100.5 Radiofónica, 100.9 Meridiano, 101.3 Hollywood – **SF02**) 102.3 FM No – **SF07**) 102.7 – **SF06**) 104.5 R.Nacional, 105.5 Tiempo Libre, 107.1 R.Universidad, 107.9 Cristal FM

FM in Santa Fe: 89.9 Federal, 90.7 Eclipse – **SF04**) 92.5 Láser, 93.1 Estacion Rock – **SF01**) 94.9 R.Nacional, 98.1 Santa Fe Capital, 101.7 Cielo, 104.3 Plenitud, 104.5 Sensación, 105.1 Hot 105, 105.5 News, 105.9 Ibiza FM – **SF03**) 107.3 FM X, 107.9 R.Antena (CNN R.)

ARMENIA

L.T: UTC +4h – **Pop:** 3.2 million – **Pr.L:** Armenian – **E.C:** 50Hz, 220V – **ITU:** ARM

NATIONAL COMMISSION ON TV AND RADIO (NCTR)
Isahakyan St. 28, 0009 Yerevan ☎ +374 10 528370 **E:** nctr@tvradio.am **W:** tvradio.am **L.P:** Chmn: Gagik Buniatyan
NB: NCTR is the licensing body for broadcasting.

HAYASTANI HANRAYIN RADIO (Public R. of Armenia)
A.Manoogian St. 5, 0025 Yerevan ☎ +374 10 551143 ≣ +374 10 554600 **E:** info@armradio.am **W:** armradio.am
L.P: Dir: Armen Amiryan

FM	1	2	kW	FM	1	2	kW
Jermuk	100.3	-	1	Vanadzor	103.7	-	1
Noyemberyan	101.7	-	5	Yerevan	107.6	103.8	1
Pushkin Pass	101.1	-	5	Zovashen	104.0	-	1

NB: Sites with only txs below 1kW not listed.
D.Prgr: Prgr 1 (Arajin tsragir) 24h. – **Prgr 2 (Im R.)** 24h.
International Service: see Int. Radio section.

OTHER STATIONS
FM	MHz	kW	Location	Station
4)	90.1	1	Yerevan	R. Shanson
5)	90.7	1	Yerevan	R. Jan
1A)	100.2	2	Dilijan	R. Hay
1A)	100.4	5	Armavir	R. Hay
8)	100.6	1	Yerevan	R. Aurora
11)	101.1	2	Amasia	R. Shirak
2)	101.9	2	Yerevan	R. Yerevan
9)	102.4	1	Yerevan	RFI Relay
3)	103.5	1	Yerevan	R. Ardzaganq
1A)	103.6	2	Noyemberyan	R. Hay
1A)	104.1	1	Yerevan	R. Hay
12)	104.1	1	Gyumri	R. Shant
2)	104.4	1	Charentsavan	R. Yerevan
2)	104.6	1	Vedi	R. Yerevan
7)	104.9	1	Yerevan	Russkoye R.
2)	105.4	5	Pushkin Pass	R. Yerevan
2)	105.2	1	Talin	R. Yerevan
1B)	105.5	1	Yerevan	FM 105.5
10)	106.0	1	Yerevan	City FM
2)	106.1	2	Noyemberyan	R. Yerevan
2)	106.8	1	Zovashen	R. Yerevan
6)	106.9	1	Yerevan	Lav R. 106.9
2)	107.2	1	Vanadzor	R. Yerevan

FM	MHz	kW	Location	Station
2)	107.3	1	Jermuk	R. Yerevan

NB: Txs below 1kW not listed.
Addresses & other information:
1A,B) Pavstos Buzandi St. 1/3, 0010 Yerevan info@hayfm.am – **2)** A.Manoogian St. 5, 0025 Yerevan **E:** aa@arradio.am – **3)** Armeniak Armenakyan St. 250, 0047 Yerevan **E:** ardzagank@ardzagank.com – **4)** A.Manoogian St. 5, 0025 Yerevan. R. Hay – **5)** Acharyan St. 42, 0040 Yerevan **E:** info@radiojan.am – **6)** Yeghvard Highway 1, 0054 Yerevan **E:** info@fm107.am – **7)** Khandjyan St. 13a, 0010 Yerevan **E:** radio_alfa@mail.ru – **8)** Nairi Zaryan St. 22, 0051 Yerevan **E:** radio-aurora@mail.ru – **9)** Ovsepyan St. 95, 0047 Yerevan. Rel. RFI (France) – **10)** Yerevan – **11)** 248 Abovyan St., Gyumri **E:** globus888@bk.ru – **12)** Gyumri.

Int. relays on MW: Gavar 864/1314/1350/1377kHz 1000kW, 1395kHz 500kW. See Int. Radio section

ARUBA (Netherlands)

L.T: UTC -4h – **Pop:** 101,480 – **Pr.L:** Dutch (official), Papiamentu, English, Spanish – **E.C:** 50+60Hz, 127/220V – **ITU:** ABW

DIRECTIE TELECOMMUNICATIE ZAKEN
Rumbastraat 19, Oranjestad ☎ +297-582-6069 ≣ +297-582-5307 **E:** dirtelza@setarnet.aw **W:** dtz.aw

FM	MHz	kW	Station, location
12)	88.1	1	Mega 88FM, Ponton
11)	88.9	0.1	Bo Guia, Jaburibari
3)	89.9	0.25	Canal 90FM, Ponton
14)	90.7	0.45	Caliente FM, Hooiberg
7)	91.5	0.125	Rumba 91.5 FM, Hooiberg
10)	92.3	0.1	Latina Tu FM, Hooiberg
1)	93.1	0.66	R. Victoria, Hooiberg (Rlg.)
12)	94.1	1	Hit 94 FM, Ponton
7)	95.1	0.325	Top 95 FM, Hooiberg
8)	96.5	0.2	Magic 96.5 FM, Hooiberg
6)	97.9	0.2	Easy FM ,Hooiberg
13)	98.9	0.75	Cool FM 98.9, Hooiberg
9)	99.9	0.5	R. Galactica 99.9 FM, Urataka
16)	100.9	0.85	Hits 100, Balashi
17)	101.7	0.7	Power 101.7 FM, Jaburibari
18)	104.3	0.6	Fresh FM
15)	105.3	0.5	Vision FM, Urataka
19)	106.7	0.6	I love Aruba FM, Oranjestad
2)	107.5	0.2	Blue FM 107.5

Addresses and other information
1) Washington 23 Noord, Oranjestad ☎ +297 587 3444 Mngr: Nico J. Arts. Rlg: 24h in English, Spanish, Papiamentu, Dutch, Creole, Tagalog and Cantonese **W:** srv931fm.org **E:** radiovictoria@setarnet.aw – **2)** Renaissance Market Place ☎ +297 588 2488 **W:** bluefm1075aruba. com **E:** info@bluefmaruba.com – **3)** Van Leeuwenhoekstraat 26, Oranjestad ☎+297 582 8952 ≣ +297 583 7340 Dir. Mrs Leoncita Arends Progranms; 24h in English, Papiamentu, Dutch and Spanish **W:** canal90fm.aw **E:** canal90fm@gmail.com –6) Sabana Basora 31-D, Oranjestad ☎+297 593 3637 ≣ +297 585 2639 GM: Wouter Gesterkamp 24h in English, Papiamentu, Spanish and Dutch **E:** easy-979fm@yahoo.com **W:** easyfm.aw – **7)** Santa Cruz 110, Oranjestad ☎+297 585 9500 ≣+297 585 0951 24h in Papiamentu on Top 95 FM and 24 h in Spanish on Rumba FM **W:** top95fm.aw **E:** solodipueblo@gmail.com Dir. Edmond Croes – **8)** Palm Beach 51 Lokaal 7-D ☎+297 586 5353 ≣ +297 586 5350 24h **E:** magicarubapromo@gmail.com **W:** magic96-5.com – **9)** Makapruimstraat 1-E, Oranjestad ☎+297 588 2534 ≣ +297 588 2536 Man. Dir: Richard A. Arends Stn Man.: Maikel Oduber 24h in Papiamentu, English and Dutch **W:** gfm999aruba.webs. com **E:** gfmgalactica@gmail.com – **10)** Tanki Leendert 8 ☎ +297 5942700 ≣ +297 583 3101 **E:** radio.latinaaruba@gmail.com – **11)** Tanki Flip 26B ☎+297 587 5000 ≣ +297 587 5889 **E:** radio.boguia@gmail.com – **12)** Caya Ernesto Petronia 68-A, Oranjestad. Mega 88 FM ☎ +297 582 6888 ≣ +297 582 0494 **W:** mega88fm.com **E:** mail@mega88fm.com **E:** hit94@hotmail.com 24h in Papiamentu, Spanish and English: Latin Caribbean R.; Hit 94 FM ☎ +297 582 0694 and +297 583 9494 ≣ +297 582 0494 **E:** hit94@gmail.com 24h in Papiamentu, Spanish and English. Dir: John A. Habibe – **13)** Caya G.F.(Betico) Croes 23 ☎ + 297 583 3111 ≣+ 297 583 3101 Dir. Alexander Ponson 24 prgr in Papiamentu, and English **W:** coolaruba.com **E:** info@coolaruba.com – **14)** Windstraat 29, Oranjestad ☎+ 297 582 2339 ≣+ 297 583 1515 **W:** calientefmaruba.com **E:** info@calientefmaruba.com – **15)** Cumana 20, Oranjestad ☎+ 297 583 5656 ≣+ 297 582 5477 Rlg prgr – **16)** Kolibristraat 2, Oranjestad, ☎+297 588 6100 **E:** contact@hits100.fm – **17)** Piedra Plat 44 C-D, Lok 12, Paradera, Oranjestad ☎+297 5851017

NATIONAL RADIO

E: info@powerfmaruba.com **W:**powerfmaruba.streamon.fm – **18)** Caya G.F. (Betico) Croes 19-23, Oranjestad ☎ +297 583 2220; Dir. Alexander Ponson 24 prgr in Dutch, **E:** info@fresharuba.com **W:** fresharuba.com – **19)** Pos Aboa 45, Oranjestad ☎ +297 5889096 **W:** Ilovearubafm.com **E:** info@ilovearubafm.com

ASCENSION ISLAND (UK)

L.T: UTC — **Pop:** 900 — **Pr.L:** English — **E.C:** 50Hz, 220V — **ITU:** ASC

VOLCANO RADIO (USAF)
✉ Ascension Radio Station, Ascension AAF, P.O. Box 4235, Patrick AFB, FL 32925-0235, USA.
FM: AFN, 98.7MHz 0.4kW 24h.
NB: MW service ZD8VR on 1602kHz currently inactive

BBC ATLANTIC RELAY STATION
✉ English Bay, Ascension Island, So. Atlantic.
Local Sce: FM: 93.2MHz 15W (24h relay of BBCWS in English plus occ. local prgrs). See International section for details of SW relays.

BRITISH FORCES BROADC. SCE: FM(MHz): Travellers Hill BFBS 1 100.9 BFBS 2 97.3, Green Mt BFBS 1 107.3 BFBS 2 105.3.

SAINT FM: Jamestown, 91.4 & 95.5MHz 25W

AUSTRALIA

L.T: See World Time Table. DST (where applicable): 4 Oct 15-3 Apr 16, 2 Oct 16-2 Apr 17 — **Pop:** 23 million — **Pr.L:** English — **E.C:** 50Hz, 230V — **ITU:** AUS

ABORIGINAL RESOURCE & DEVELOPMENT SERVICES
✉ Box 36921, Winnellie NT 0821 ☎+61 8 8984 4174 🖷 +61 8 8984 4192 **W:** ards.com.au **E:** info@ards.com.au
MW: 1530kHz Humpty Doo NT 2kW

AUSTRALIAN BROADCASTING CORP. (ABC)
HQ: Ultimo Centre, 700 Harris Str, Ultimo, NSW 2007; ✉ GPO Box 9994, Sydney NSW 2001) ☎+61 2 9333 1500 🖷 +61 2 9333 5305
MW: N = R. National, L = Local R, P = Parliamentary & News Netw. **Call letters:** 2 = NSW (exc. Canberra = A.C.T.), 3 = Victoria, 4 = Queensland, 5 = So. Australia, 6 = We. Australia, 7=Tasmania, 8=Northern Territory

MW	Call	kHz	kW	Netw	Location
46)	6DL	531	10	L	Dalwallinu
29)	4QL	540	10	L	Longreach
11)	2CR	549	50	L	Orange (Cumnock)
44)	6WA	558	50	L	Wagin
25)	4JK	567	10(d)	L	Julia Creek
47)	6MN	567	0.1	L	Newman
47)	6PN	567	0.1	L	Pannawonica
47)	6PU	567	0.1	L	Paraburdoo
47)	6TP	567	0.1	L	Tom Price
2)	2RN	576	50	N	Sydney
6)	6PB	585	10	P	Perth
7)	7RN	585	10	N	Hobart
42)	3WV	594	50	L	Horsham
2)	2RN	603	10(d)	N	Nowra
26)	4CH	603	10(d)	L	Charleville
47)	6PH	603	2	L	Port Hedland
4)	4QR	612	50	L	Brisbane
6)	6RN	612	10	N	Dalwallinu
3)	3RN	621	50	N	Melbourne
2)	2PB	630	10	P	Sydney
24)	4QN	630	50	L	Townsville (Brandon)
48)	6AL	630	5	L	Albany
7)	7RN	630	0.4	N	Queenstown
23)	4MS	639	1	L	Mossman
31)	5CK	639	10	L	Port Pirie (Crystal Brook)
8)	8RN	639	2	N	Katherine
14)	2NU	648	10	L	Tamworth (Manilla)
43)	6GF	648	2	L	Kalgoorlie
19)	2BY	657	10(d)	L	Byrock
8)	8RN	657	2	N	Darwin
1)	2CN	666	5	L	Canberra ACT
9)	2CO	675	10	L	Albury (Corowa)
45)	6BE	675	5	L	Broome
13)	2KP	684	10	L	Kempsey (Smithtown)
49)	6BS	684	5	L	Busselton
8)	8RN	684	1	N	Tennant Creek

MW	Call	kHz	kW	Netw	Location
34)	5SY	693	2(d)	L	Streaky Bay
2)	2BL	702	50	L	Sydney
47)	6KP	702	10	L	Karratha
26)	4QW	711	10(d)	L	Roma/St.George
16)	2ML	720	0.4	L	Murwillumbah
2)	2RN	720	0.05	N	Armidale
38)	3MT	720	2(d)	L	Omeo
23)	4AT	720	4	L	Atherton
6)	6WF	720	50	L	Perth
5)	5RN	729	50	N	Adelaide
16)	2NR	738	50	L	Grafton
49)	6MJ	738	5(d)	L	Manjimup
26)	4QS	747	10	L	Toowoomba (Dalby)
7)	7PB	747	3.5	P	Hobart
8)	8JB	747	0.2	L	Jabiru
13)	2TR	756	2(d)	L	Taree
3)	3RN	756	10(d)	N	Wangaratta
3)	3LO	774	50	L	Melbourne
20)	8AL	783	2	L	Alice Springs
4)	4RN	792	25	N	Brisbane
23)	4QY	801	2	L	Cairns
17)	2BA	810	10	L	Bega
6)	6RN	810	20	N	Perth
14)	2GL	819	10	L	Glen Innes
45)	6KW	819	5	L	Kununurra
38)	3GI	828	2(d)	L	Sale (Longford)
46)	6GN	828	10	L	Geraldton
21)	4RK	837	10	L	Rockhampton (Gracemore)
43)	6ED	837	1	L	Esperance
1)	2RN	846	10	N	Canberra
47)	6CA	846	2.5	L	Carnarvon
30)	4QB	855	10(d)	L	Pialba
30)	4QO	855	10	L	Eidsvold
45)	6DB	873	2	L	Derby
5)	5AN	891	50	L	Adelaide
4)	4PB	936	10	P	Brisbane
7)	7ZR	936	10(d)	L	Hobart
5)	5PB	972	2	P	Adelaide
3)	3RN	990	0.5	N	Albury-Wodonga
8)	8GO	990	0.5	L	Gove (Nhulunbuy)
10)	2NB	999	2(d)	L	Broken Hill
45)	6WH	1017	0.5	L	Wyndham
3)	3PB	1026	14.5	P	Melbourne
18)	2UH	1044	2(d)	L	Muswellbrook
23)	4WP	1044	0.5	L	Weipa
49)	6BR	1044	1	L	Bridgetown
23)	4TI	1062	2	L	Thursday Island
32)	5MV	1062	2	L	Renmark/Loxton
2)	2RN	1098	0.2	N	Goulburn
6)	6PB	1152	10(d)	P	Busselton
33)	5PA	1161	10(d)	L	Naracoorte
35)	7FG	1161	1(d)	L	Fingal
47)	6XM	1188	2	L	Exmouth
46)	6NM	1215	0.5	L	Northam
15)	2NC	1233	10	L	Newcastle
6)	6RN	1269	5	N	Busselton
6)	6RN	1296	10	N	Wagin
5)	5RN	1305	2	N	Renmark/Loxton
11)	2LG	1395	0.2	L	Lithgow
2)	2RN	1431	2	N	Wollongong
2)	2PB	1458	2	P	Newcastle
33)	5MG	1476	1(d)	L	Mt. Gambier
2)	2RN	1485	0.1	L	Wilcannia
24)	4HU	1485	0.05	L	Hughenden
34)	5LN	1485	0.2	L	Port Lincoln
2)	2RN	1512	10	N	Newcastle
21)	4QD	1548	50	L	Emerald
30)	4GM	1566	0.2	L	Gympie
10)	2WA	1584	0.1	L	Wilcannia
31)	5WM	1584	0.05	L	Woomera
7)	7SH	1584	0.1	L	St. Helens
17)	2CP	1602	0.05	L	Cooma
41)	3WL	1602	0.25	L	Warrnambool
31)	5LC	1602	0.2	L	Leigh Creek South

FM stations (txs of greater than 1kW)
Networks: N=Radio National, L=Local Radio, FM=Fine Music Network, JJJ=Triple J Network (alternative)

	FM Area	State	N	L	FM	JJJ
5)	Adelaide	SA			103.9	105.5
5)	Adel. Foothills	SA			97.5	95.9
39)	Alexandra	VIC	104.5	102.9		

FM	Area	State	N	L	FM	JJJ
14)	Armidale	NSW		101.9	103.5	101.1
3)	Bairnsdale	VIC	106.3			
36)	Ballarat	VIC		107.9	105.5	107.1
17)	Batemans Bay	NSW	105.1	103.5	101.9	
2)	Bega/Cooma	NSW	100.9		99.3	100.1
37)	Bendigo	VIC		91.1	92.7	90.3
4)	Blackwater	QLD	94.3			
17)	Bombala	NSW		94.1		
2)	Bourke	NSW	101.1			
4)	Brisbane	QLD			106.1	107.7
5)	Broken Hill	NSW	102.9		103.7	102.1
6)	Broome	WA	107.7			
6)	Bunbury	WA			93.3	94.1
35)	Burnie	TAS		102.5		
23)	Cairns	QLD	105.1	106.7	105.9	107.5
23)	Cairns North	QLD	93.9	95.5	94.7	97.1
1)	Canberra	ACT			102.3	101.5
6)	Cen.Agricult	WA			98.9	98.1
2)	Cen.Table'nds	NSW	104.3		102.7	101.9
11)	Cen. Western	NSW	107.9	107.1	105.5	102.3
4)	Darling Downs	QLD	105.7		107.3	104.1
8)	Darwin	NT		105.7	107.3	103.3
8)	Deniliquin	NSW	99.3			
35)	Devonport E	TAS		100.5		
19)	Dubbo City	NSW		95.9		
4)	Emerald	QLD	93.9		90.7	
6)	Esperance	WA	106.3		104.7	
6)	Geraldton	WA	99.7		94.9	98.9
2)	Glen Innes	NSW	105.1			
22)	Gold Coast	QLD	90.1	91.7	88.5	97.7
39)	Goulburn V.	VIC		97.7	96.1	94.5
13)	Grafton/Kemp.	NSW	99.5	92.3	97.9	91.5
30)	Gympie	QLD	96.9	95.3	93.7	
9)	Hay	NSW	88.9	88.1		
7)	Hobart	TAS			93.9	92.9
12)	Illawara	NSW		97.3	95.7	98.9
2)	Jerilderie	NSW	94.1			
6)	Kalgoorlie	WA	97.1		95.5	98.7
8)	Katherine	NT		106.1		
5)	Keith	SA	96.9			
35)	King Island	TAS		88.5		
38)	Latrobe Valley	VIC		100.7	101.5	96.7
35)	Lileah	TAS	89.7	91.3		
16)	Lismore	NSW	96.9	94.5	95.3	96.1
4)	Longreach	QLD	99.1			
28)	Mackay	QLD	102.7	101.1	97.9	99.5
13)	Manning River	NSW	97.1	95.5	98.7	96.3
35)	Maydena	TAS		89.7		
4)	Meandarra	QLD	104.3			
3)	Melbourne	VIC			105.9	107.5
40)	Mildura	VIC	105.9	104.3	102.7	101.1
23)	Mission Beach	QLD	90.9	89.3		
4)	Monto	QLD	101.9			
28)	Moranbah	QLD	106.5	104.9		
4)	Mossman	QLD	90.1			
25)	Mount Isa	QLD	107.3	106.5	101.7	104.1
5)	Mt Gambier	SA	103.3		104.1	102.5
39)	Murray Valley	VIC		102.1	103.7	105.3
9)	Murrumbidgee	NSW	98.9		100.5	97.3	96.5
18)	Muswellbrook	NSW		105.7		
27)	Nambour	QLD		90.3	88.7	89.5
6)	Narrogin	WA			92.5	
35)	NE Tas.	TAS	94.1	91.7	93.3	90.9
2)	Newcastle	NSW			106.1	102.1
3)	Nhill	VIC	95.7			
6)	Perth	WA			97.7	99.3
6)	Port Hedland	WA	95.7			
41)	Portland	VIC	98.5	96.9		
5)	Renmark	SA			105.1	101.9
5)	Rockhampton	QLD	103.1		106.3	104.7
6)	Roebourne	WA	107.5			
26)	Roma	QLD	103.7	105.7	97.7	
31)	Roxby Downs	SA	101.9	102.7	103.5	
6)	Salmon Gums	WA	100.7			
4)	S. Agricultural	WA	96.9		94.5	92.9
46)	South'n Cross	WA	107.9	106.3		
26)	South'n Downs	QLD	106.5	104.9	101.7	103.3
5)	Spencer Gulf N	SA	106.7		104.3	103.5
5)	Streaky Bay	SA	100.9			103.3
9)	SW Slopes	NSW	89.1	89.9	88.3	90.7
2)	Sydney	NSW			92.9	105.7
2)	Tamworth	NSW	93.9		103.1	94.7
4)	Townsville	QLD	104.7		101.5	105.5

FM	Area	State	N	L	FM	JJJ
5)	Tumby Bay	SA	101.9			
39)	Upper Murray	VIC		106.5	104.1	103.3
14)	Upper Namoi	NSW	100.7	99.1	96.7	99.9
3)	Warrnambool	VIC	101.7		92.1	89.7
42)	Western Vic.	VIC	92.5	94.1	93.3	94.9
30)	Wide Bay	QLD	100.9	100.1	98.5	99.3
4)	Winton	QLD	107.9			
5)	Wirrulla	SA	107.3			
5)	Wudinna	SA	107.7			105.3
6)	Wyndham	WA				98.9

Parliamentary News Network (MHz): 89.1 Emerald QLD (8d), 89.3 Horsham VIC (20), 89.5 Bendigo VIC (10), 89.7 Bega/Cooma NSW (112d), 90.5 Burnie TAS (1d), 90.7 Grafton/Kemspey NSW (20d), 90.9 Illawara NSW (150d), 91.3 Warrnambool VIC (3.2d), 91.5 SW Slopes/E Riverina NSW (80), 91.7 Tumby Bay SA (2), 91.7 Tamworth NSW (10), 91.7 Western Victoria (80d), 91.9 Central Tablelands NSW (5d), 92.1 Southern Agricultural WA (80), 92.5 NE Tasmania (192d), 93.5 Inverell NSW (10), 93.9 Renmark SA (150d), 94.3 Ballarat VIC (5d), 94.3 Townsville QLD (92d), 94.5 Gympie QLD (20d), 94.5 Nambour QLD (20d), 94.7 Manning River NSW (5), 94.9 Port Hedland WA (2), 95.1 Latrobe Valley VIC (200d), 95.7 Gold Coast (26d), 95.9 Murray Valley VIC (20), 96.3 Cairns North QLD (10d), 96.3 Warwick QLD (2), 96.3 Wagin WA (5), 96.7 Toowoomba QLD (2.5d), 97.7 Portland VIC (2.6d), 97.7 Wide Bay QLD (10d), 98.1 Murrumbidgee NSW (100), 98.5 Lismore NSW (100d), 99.7 Central Agricultural WA (80), 100.3 Mildura VIC (150d), 100.3 Kalgoorlie WA (6), 100.5 Batemans Bay NSW (40d), 100.9 Deniliquin NSW (2d), 100.9 Upper Murray VIC (2), 101.1 Cairns QLD (100), 101.3 Geraldton WA (10), 101.5 Upper Namoi NSW (20d), 102.1 Devonport East TAS (1.2), 102.5 Darwin (32d), 102.7 Armidale NSW (4), 102.7 Spencer Gulf North SA (70), 103.1 Esperance WA (5), 103.9 Canberra ACT (80), 104.1 Alice Springs NT (1), 104.3 Mackay QLD (100d), 104.5 Broken Hill NSW (4), 104.7 Colac VIC (10d), 104.9 Muswellbrook NSW (16), 104.9 Mount Isa QLD (10), 105.3 Katherine NT (1), 105.5 Rockhampton QLD (80), 105.7 Mt Gambier SA (240d), 106.3 Central West Slopes NSW (220d), 106.9 Broome WA (2), 107.7 Goulburn Valley VIC (5d), 107.9 Bairnsdale VIC (2d)

NB: Reports for R. National, Parliament, ABC-FM and Triple J should go to the capital city ABC office in that state (Addresses 1-8)

ABC local radio addresses:
1) ABC Canberra, GPO Box 9994, Canberra ACT 2601 – **2)** ABC Sydney, GPO Box 9994, Sydney NSW 2001 – **3)** ABC Melbourne, GPO Box 9994, Melbourne VIC 3001 – **4)** ABC Brisbane, GPO Box 9994, Brisbane QLD 4001 – **5)** ABC Adelaide, GPO Box 9994, Adelaide SA 5001 – **6)** ABC Perth, GPO Box 9994, Perth WA 6848 – **7)** ABC Hobart, GPO Box 9994, Hobart TAS 7001 – **8)** ABC Darwin, PO Box 9994, Darwin NT 0801 – **9)** ABC Riverina, 100 Fitzmaurice St, Wagga Wagga NSW 2650 – **10)** ABC Broken Hill, PO Box 315, Broken Hill NSW 2880 – **11)** ABC Central West, PO Box 8549, East Orange NSW 2800 – **12)** ABC Illawarra, PO Box 973, Wollongong NSW 2520 – **13)** ABC Mid North Coast, PO Box 42, Port Macquarie NSW 2444 – **14)** ABC New England / North West, PO Box 558, Tamworth NSW 2340 – **15)** ABC Newcastle, PO Box 2205, Dangar NSW 2309 – **16)** ABC North Coast, PO Box 908, Lismore NSW 2480 – **17)** ABC South East NSW, PO Box 336, Bega NSW 2550 – **18)** ABC Upper Hunter, PO Box 400, Muswellbrook NSW 2333 – **19)** ABC Western Plains, PO Box 985, Mudgee NSW 2830 – **20)** ABC Alice Springs, PO Box 1144, Alice Springs NT 0871 – **21)** ABC Capricornia, GPO Box 911, Rockhampton QLD 4700 - **22)** ABC Gold Coast, PO Box 217, Mermaid Beach QLD 4218 – **23)** ABC Far North, PO Box 932, Cairns QLD 4810 – **24)** ABC North Queensland, PO Box 694, Townsville QLD 4810 – **25)** ABC North West Queensland, 114 Camooweal St, Mount Isa QLD 4825 – **26)** ABC Southern Queensland, PO Box 358, Toowoomba QLD 4350 – **27)** ABC Sunshine Coast, PO Box 1212, Maroochydore QLD 4558 – **28)** ABC Tropical Queensland, PO Box 127, Mackay QLD 4740 – **29)** ABC Western Queensland, PO Box 318, Longreach QLD 4730 – **30)** ABC Wide Bay, PPO Box 1152, Bundaberg QLD 4670 – **31)** ABC North and West South Australia, PO Box 289, Port Pirie SA 5540 – **32)** ABC Riverland, PO Box 20, Renmark SA 5341 – **33)** ABC Southeast, PO Box 1448, Mount Gambier SA 5290 – **34)** ABC Eyre Peninsula, PO Box 679, Port Lincoln SA 5606 – **35)** ABC Northern Tasmania, PO Box 201, Launceston TAS 7250 – **36)** ABC Ballarat, PO Box 7, Ballarat VIC 3353 – **37)** ABC Central Victoria, PO Box 637, Bendigo VIC 3550 – **38)** ABC Gippsland, PO Box 330, Sale VIC 3850 – **39)** ABC Goulburn Murray, PO Box 1063, Wodonga VIC 3690 – **40)** ABC Mildura / Swan Hill, PO Box 10083, Mildura VIC 3502 – **41)** ABC South West Victoria, PO Box 310, Warrnambool VIC 3280 – **42)** ABC Western Victoria, PO Box 506, Horsham VIC 3402 – **43)** ABC Goldfields / Esperance, PO Box 125, Kalgoorlie WA 6430 – **44)** ABC Great Southern, 58 Tudhoe St, Wagin

WA 6315 – **45)** ABC Kimberley, PO Box 217, Broome WA 6725 – **46)** ABC Mid West & Wheatbelt, PO Box 211, Geraldton WA 6530 – **47)** ABC North West, PO Box 994, Karratha WA 6714 – **48)** ABC South Coast, 2 St Emilie Way, Albany WA 6330 – **49)** ABC South West, PO Box 242, Bunbury WA 6231

EXTERNAL SERVICE: Radio Australia
See International Broadcasting section

DAB: Now rolled out in capital cities: Channel 9A 202.928 MHz, 9B 204.64 MHz, 9C 206.352 MHz. All 50kW. Relays existing stns and some extra programming controlled by existing stns. All prgr also available at **W:** digitalradioplus.com.au. Sydney NSW, Melbourne VIC, Brisbane QLD all 9A, 9B and 9C. Adelaide SA and Perth WA 9B and 9C. Canberra ACT and Darwin NT trials on channel 10B 211.648 MHz.

NORTHERN TERRITORY SHORTWAVE SERVICE
Box 9994, Darwin, NT 0801
SW: VL8A Alice Springs: 4835kHz (24h) – **VL8T Tennant Creek:** 2325kHz (0830-2130), 4910kHz (2130-0830) – **VL8K Katherine:** 2485kHz (0830-2130), 5025kHz (2130-0830).

COMMUNITY SHORTWAVE:
OZY RADIO
E: 3210kHz@gmail.com
SW: Newcastle NSW 5055kHz 1kW (**F.PI**)

RADIO SYMBAN
887 New Canterbury Rd, Hurlstone Park, NSW 2193
SW: Leppington NSW 2368.5kHz 1kW **NB:** Temp. inactive

STATION X
E: admin@stationx.com.au
SW: 3210kHz & 5050kHz (**F.PI**)

COMMERCIAL RADIO AUSTRALIA
Abbreviations: The numeral preceding the call letters indicates the state: 2=New South Wales,. 3=Victoria, 4=Queensland, 5=South Australia, 6=Western Australia; 7=Tasmania, 8=Northern Territory. (t) is a designated translator station.
News: Additional newscasts are often carried during breakfast and drive times.

MW	Call	kHz	kW	Location
1)	2PM	531	5(d)	Kempsey
2)	3GG	531	5(d)	Warragul
3)	4KZ	531	5(d)	Innisfail
4)	7SD	540	5(d)	Scottsdale
5)	4AM	558	5(d)	Atherton
6)	4GY	558	5(d)	Gympie
7)	7BU	558	2	Burnie
8)	2BH	567	0.5	Broken Hill
164)	6EL	621	2	Bunbury
133)	2HC	639	5(d)	Coffs Harbour
33)	4CC(t)	666	2(d)	Biloela
103)	4LM	666	2	Mount Isa
160)	6LN	666	1	Carnarvon
105)	3AW	693	5(d)	Melbourne
9)	4KQ	693	10/5(d)	Brisbane
3)	4KZ(t)	693	0.5	Tully
103)	4LM(t)	693	0.5	Cloncurry
31)	6FMS	747	1	Exmouth
131)	6SE	747	5(d)	Esperance
166)	6TZ	756	2	Margaret River
10)	2EC	765	5(d)	Bega
73)	4GC(t)	765	0.5	Hughenden
134)	5CC	765	5(d)	Port Lincoln
88)	6SAT	765	0.1	Paraburdoo
88)	6SAT	765	0.1	Tom Price
147)	8HOT(t)	765	0.5	Katherine
13)	6VA	783	2	Albany
14)	5RM	801	2	Berri
73)	4GC	828	1	Charters Towers
16)	7XS	837	0.5	Queenstown
17)	4EL	846	5(d)	Cairns
18)	4GR	864	2	Toowoomba
19)	6AM	864	2	Northam
21)	2GB	873	5	Sydney
22)	3YB	882	2(d)	Warrnambool
24)	4BH	882	5(d)	Brisbane
23)	6PR	882	10	Perth
25)	2LM	900	5(d)	Lismore
107)	2LT	900	5(d)	Lithgow

MW	Call	kHz	kW	Location
58)	6BY	900	2	Bridgetown
27)	7AD	900	2	Devonport
28)	8HA	900	2	Alice Springs
29)	2XL	918	2	Cooma
153)	4VL	918	2/2.5	Charleville
164)	6NA	918	2	Narrogin
32)	3UZ	927	5	Melbourne
33)	4CC	927	5(d)	Gladstone
69)	4HI(t)	945	1(d)	Dysart
36)	2UE	954	5	Sydney
17)	4EL(t)	954	0.35	Gordonvale
38)	2RG	963	5(d)	Griffith
37)	4WK	963	5(d)	Warwick
93)	5SE	963	5(d)	Mt. Gambier
164)	6TZ	963	2	Bunbury
86)	2DU(t)	972	0.3	Cobar
39)	2MW	972	5(d)	Murwillumbah
112)	2NM	981	5(d)	Muswellbrook
41)	3HA	981	2	Hamilton
42)	6KG	981	2	Kalgoorlie
43)	4RO	990	5(d)	Rockhampton
45)	2ST	999	5(d)	Nowra
46)	4TAB	1008	10(d)	Brisbane
49)	2KY	1017	5	Sydney
139)	4AA	1026	5(d)	Mackay
52)	6NW	1026	2	Port Hedland
53)	5AU	1044	2	Port Pirie
54)	2CA	1053	5(d)	Canberra
55)	3EL	1071	5(d)	Maryborough
56)	4SB	1071	2	Kingaroy
151)	6WB	1071	2	Katanning
57)	2MO	1080	2	Gunnedah
167)	6IX	1080	2	Perth
59)	2EL	1089	5(d)	Orange
60)	3WM	1089	5(d)	Horsham
61)	4LG	1098	2	Longreach
62)	6MD	1098	2	Merredin
156)	3AK	1116	5(d)	Melbourne
65)	4BC	1116	6.3/17(d)	Brisbane
135)	6MM	1116	2	Mandurah
113)	5MU	1125	5(d)	Murray Bridge
66)	2AD	1134	2(d)	Armidale
67)	3CS	1134	5(d)	Colac
164)	6TZ(t)	1134	2	Collie
68)	2HD	1143	2	Newcastle
69)	4HI	1143	5(d)	Emerald
70)	2WG	1152	2	Wagga Wagga
30)	4FC	1161	2	Maryborough
72)	2CH	1170	5	Sydney
75)	2NZ	1188	2	Inverell
80)	2CC	1206	5/5(d)	Canberra
78)	2GF	1206	5(d)	Grafton
69)	4HI(t)	1215	0.25	Moranbah
82)	3GV	1242	5(d)	Sale
85)	4AK	1242	2	Toowoomba
84)	5AU	1242	2(d)	Port Augusta
86)	2DU	1251	2	Dubbo
32)	3SR	1260	2	Shepparton
88)	6KA	1260	1	Karratha
89)	2SM	1269	5	Sydney
90)	3EE	1278	5	Melbourne
91)	2TM	1287	2	Tamworth
32)	3BT	1314	5(d)	Ballarat
40)	5DN	1323	3.3/5	Adelaide
98)	3SH	1332	2	Swan Hill
99)	4BU	1332	5(d)	Bundaberg
102)	2LF	1350	5(d)	Young
37)	4WK(t)	1359	0.25	Toowoomba City
104)	2GN	1368	2	Goulburn
105)	3MP	1377	5(d)	Melbourne
106)	5AA	1395	5(d)	Adelaide
108)	2PK	1404	2	Parkes/Forbes
5)	4AM(t)	1422	1(d)	Port Douglas
111)	2MG	1449	5(d)	Mudgee
32)	3ML	1467	2	Mildura
115)	4ZR	1476	2	Roma
116)	2AY	1494	2	Albury
117)	2BS	1503	5(d)	Bathurst
142)	6BAY	1512	5	Morawa
119)	2QN	1521	2	Deniliquin
120)	2VM	1530	2	Moree
121)	2RE	1557	2	Taree
	3NE	1566	5(d)	Wangaratta
10)	2EC(t)	1584	0.2	Narooma
33)	4CC(t)	1584	0.5	Rockhampton

MW	Call	kHz	kW	Location		FM	Call	MHz	kW	Location
153)	4VL(t)	1584	0.2	Cunnamulla		93)	5SEF	96.1	20	Mount Gambier
FM stations (1kW and higher):						125)	6NOW	96.1	40(d)	Perth
FM	Call	MHz	kW	Location		29)	2XL(t)	96.3	2(d)	Jindabyne
117)	2BS(t)	88.1	2(d)	Burraga		8)	2HIL	96.5	4(d)	Broken Hill
3)	4KZ(t)	88.5	1(d)	Mission Beach		95)	2UUL	96.5	40(d)	Wollongong
165)	4RGC	88.5	1	Mossman		142)	6GGG	96.5	30(d)	Geraldton
170)	8SAT	88.7	1	Hawker SA		19)	6NAM	96.5	10	Northam
41)	3HFM	88.9	20(d)	Hamilton		170)	8SAT	96.5	4(d)	Pinnaroo (SA)
56)	4KRY	89.1	15	Kingaroy		40)	5ADD(t)	96.7	2(d)	Adelaide Foothills
117)	2BS(t)	89.3	1(d)	Blayney		161)	2SYD	96.9	150(d)	Sydney
63)	7LAA	89.3	5(d)	Launceston		118)	3SUN	96.9	100(d)	Shepparton
46)	4TAB	89.7	5(d)	Beaudesert		14)	5RIV	97.1	2.5(d)	Morgan
71)	5CCC	89.9	6(d)	Port Lincoln		159)	4BFM	97.3	12	Brisbane
48)	7EXX	90.1	5(d)	Launceston		135)	6CST	97.3	5(d)	Mandurah
69)	4HIT(t)	90.3	1	Blackwater		57)	2GGG	97.5	20(d)	Gunnedah
130)	5SSA (t)	90.3	2(d)	Adelaide Foothills		29)	2SKI	97.7	50(d)	Cooma
154)	4SEA	90.9	25(d)	Gold Coast		170)	8SAT	97.7	5(d)	Birchip VIC
170)	8SAT	90.9	4(d)	Maitland SA		170)	8SAT	97.7	3(d)	Coonalpyn SA
168)	4MCY	91.1	10(d)	Nambour		136)	3RMR	97.9	12(d)	Mildura
123)	2MAC	91.3	1	Campbelltown		5)	4AMM	97.9	5(d)	Atherton
120)	2NOW(t)	91.3	1	Lightning Ridge		42)	6KAR	97.9	6	Kalgoorlie
96)	4HIT	91.3	5	Moranbah		170)	8SAT	97.9	1.3(d)	Roxby Downs SA
148)	3PTV	91.5	56(d)	Melbourne		112)	2VLY	98.1	20(d)	Muswellbrook
29)	2SKI(t)	91.7	1	Bombala		123)	2WIN	98.1	40(d)	Wollongong
45)	2ST(t)	91.7	1(d)	St Georges Basin		142)	6BAY	98.1	30(d)	Geraldton
17)	4HOT(t)	91.7	1	Mossman		120)	2NOW	98.3	100(d)	Moree
52)	6HED	91.7	2	Port Hedland		11)	4TOO	98.3	2(d)	Bowen
55)	3BDG	91.9	120(d)	Bendigo		3)	4ZKZ	98.3	20(d)	Innisfail
18)	4RGD	91.9	2	Warwick		77)	5MMM(t)	98.3	2(d)	Adelaide Foothills
15)	4SEE	91.9	10(d)	Nambour		60)	3WWM(t)	98.5	1(d)	Ararat
169)	5ADL	91.9	20(d)	Adelaide		98)	3SHI(t)	98.7	1	Kerang
16)	7AUS	92.1	20(d)	Queenstown/Zeehan		158)	4RGM	98.7	100(d)	Mackay
29)	2XL(t)	92.5	1	Bombala		113)	5EZY	98.7	20(d)	Murray Bridge
96)	4CCA(t)	92.5	1	Mossman		170)	8SAT	98.9	10(d)	Minlaton SA
155)	4GLD	92.5	25(d)	Gold Coast		169)	5ADL(t)	99.1	2(d)	Adelaide Foothills
86)	2ZOO	92.7	10	Dubbo		117)	2BXS	99.3	10	Bathurst
15)	4SSS	92.7	10(d)	Nambour		170)	8SAT	99.3	4	Streaky Bay (SA)
29)	2SKI(t)	92.9	1	Thredbo		150)	4RBL	99.4	2(d)	Mt. Tamborine
91)	2TTT	92.9	20(d)	Tamworth		107)	2ICE	99.5	1(d)	Katoomba
120)	2VM(t)	92.9	1	Lightning Ridge		114)	3MDA	99.5	20(d)	Mildura
41)	3HA/t	92.9	1(d)	Portland		82)	3TFM	99.5	20(d)	Sale
44)	6PPM	92.9	40(d)	Perth		157)	4RGC	99.5	10(d)	Cairns
143)	2GEE	93.1	10	Mudgee		170)	8SAT	99.5	1(d)	Kapunda SA
70)	2WZD	93.1	80	Wagga Wagga		38)	2RGF	99.7	50	Griffith
154)	4RGB	93.1	3(d)	Bundaberg		113)	5EZY	99.7	1	Victor Harbour
14)	5RIV	93.1	10(d)	Renmark/Loxton		132)	6CAR	99.7	5	Carnarvon
163)	2DBO	93.5	10	Dubbo		154)	7RGS	99.7	5(d)	Scottsdale
1)	2PM(t)	93.5	3(d)	Port Macquarie		82)	3TFM(t)	99.9	5(d)	Bairnsdale
104)	2SNO	93.5	40	Goulburn		69)	4HI(t)	100.1	1(d)	Rolleston Mine
35)	3BBO	93.5	120(d)	Bendigo		147)	8HOT	100.1	16.6(d)	Darwin
43)	4ROK	93.5	1(d)	Gladstone		66)	2NEB	100.3	10	Armidale
41)	3HFM(t)	93.7	2	Portland		121)	2RE(t)	100.3	1.6	Forster
87)	3SUN(t)	93.7	1(d)	Alexandra/Eildon		172)	3MEL	100.3	56(d)	Melbourne
87)	3SUN(t)	93.7	1.2(d)	Mt. Buller		51)	4MKY	100.3	100(d)	Mackay
87)	3SUN(t)	93.7	1(d)	Yea		113)	5EZY(t)	100.3	1	Mount Barker
150)	4RBL	93.7	4	Tenterfield NSW		170)	8SAT	100.3	5(d)	Padthaway East (SA)
47)	6PER	93.7	40(d)	Perth		116)	2AAY(t)	100.5	1(d)	Falls Creek VIC
102)	2LFF	93.9	40	Young		88)	6BET	100.5	5	Bridgetown
101)	3BAY	93.9	55(d)	Geelong		164)	6NAN	100.5	5	Narrogin
99)	4RUM	93.9	3.2(d)	Bundaberg		150)	4BRZ	100.6	2(d)	Mt. Tamborine
83)	2BDR	94.1	1(d)	Falls Creek VIC		1)	2PQQ	100.7	20(d)	Port Macquarie
2)	3SEA(t)	94.3	7	Warragul		18)	4RGD	100.7	10(d)	Toowoomba
60)	3WWM(t)	94.5	2	Nhill/Lawloit		11)	4RGR	100.7	100(d)	Townsville
79)	6MIX	94.5	40(d)	Perth		25)	2ZZZ	100.7	32(d)	Lismore
29)	2SKI(t)	94.7	2	Jindabyne		144)	7TTT	100.9	36	Hobart
69)	4HIT	94.7	5	Emerald		107)	2LT/t	101.1	1(d)	Katoomba
45)	2WSK	94.9	50(d)	Nowra		50)	3TTT	101.1	56(d)	Melbourne
141)	4MIX	94.9	50(d)	Ipswich		140)	2CFM	101.3	16	Gosford
88)	6KAN	94.9	5	Katanning		60)	3WWM	101.3	20(d)	Horsham
75)	2GEM	95.1	10	Inverell		52)	6HED	101.3	2	Broome
43)	4RGK	95.1	1(d)	Gladstone		170)	8SAT	101.5	5(d)	Lake Cargellico NSW
115)	4ROM	95.1	1	Roma		43)	4RGK	101.5	10	Rockhampton
145)	2PTV	95.3	150(d)	Sydney		81)	2UUS	101.7	150(d)	Sydney
32)	3SRR	95.3	100(d)	Shepparton		33)	4CCC	101.7	2	Charleville
162)	3YFM	95.3	20(d)	Warrnambool		20)	7HHO	101.7	36	Hobart
13)	6AAY	95.3	50(d)	Albany		27)	7SEA(t)	101.7	20(d)	Burnie
170)	8SAT	95.3	2(d)	Karoonda SA		120)	2NOW(t)	101.9	1	Collarenebri
108)	2ROK	95.5	10	Parkes/Forbes		126)	3FOX	101.9	56(d)	Melbourne
101)	3CAT	95.5	55(d)	Geelong		149)	4CEE	101.9	10(d)	Maryborough
170)	8SAT	95.5	3(d)	Kingscote (SA)		139)	4MMK	101.9	100(d)	Mackay
151)	6BUN	95.7	40(d)	Bunbury		122)	3NNN	102.1	25(d)	Wangaratta
73)	4CHT	95.9	1.5	Charters Towers		1)	2ROX	102.3	20	Port Macquarie
12)	2ONE	96.1	5	Katoomba		94)	3RBA	102.3	20(d)	Ballarat
6)	4NNN	96.1	5(d)	Gympie		11)	4TOO	102.3	100(d)	Townsville
150)	4RBL	96.1	1	Weipa		40)	5ADD	102.3	20(d)	Adelaide

FM	Call	MHz	kW	Location
131)	6SEA	102.3	5	Esperance
10)	2EEE	102.5	5	Bega
119)	2MOR	102.5	50	Deniliquin
150)	4BRZ	102.5	4	Tenterfield NSW
150)	4BRZ	102.5	1	Childers
170)	8SAT	102.5	3	Bourke
96)	4CCA	102.7	10(d)	Cairns
75)	2GEM	102.9	2	Warialda
109)	2KKO	102.9	20(d)	Newcastle
45)	2ST	102.9	2	Bowral
76)	4HTB	102.9	25(d)	Gold Coast
52)	6NW	102.9	2	Broome
94)	3BBA	103.1	20(d)	Ballarat
34)	4RAM	103.1	100(d)	Townsville
120)	2VM(t)	103.5	1	Collarenebri
96)	4HOT	103.5	10(d)	Cairns
149)	4MBB	103.5	10(d)	Maryborough
78)	2GF(t)	103.9	5(d)	Maclean
128)	2DAY	104.1	150(d)	Sydney
39)	2MW(t)	104.1	1(d)	Gold Coast QLD
10)	2EEE	104.3	20(d)	Batemans Bay/Moruya
25)	2LM(t)	104.3	1(d)	Kyogle
74)	3KKZ	104.3	56(d)	Melbourne
171)	2GOS	104.5	16	Gosford
61)	4LRE	104.5	1(d)	Longreach
127)	4MMM	104.5	12	Brisbane
78)	2CLR	104.7	20(d)	Grafton
138)	2ROC	104.7	20	Canberra
77)	5MMM	104.7	20(d)	Adelaide
116)	2AAY	104.9	100(d)	Albury
129)	2MMM	104.9	150(d)	Sydney
150)	4RBL	104.9	3	Bourke NSW
146)	8MIX	104.9	16.6(d)	Darwin
120)	2NOW(t)	105.1	1	Walgett
59)	2OAG	105.1	5	Orange
1)	2ROX	105.1	10(d)	Kempsey
124)	3MMM	105.1	56(d)	Melbourne
62)	6MER	105.1	10	Merredin
139)	2NEW	105.3	20(d)	Newcastle
92)	4BBB	105.3	12	Brisbane
133)	2CSF	105.5	15	Coffs Harbour
10)	2EC(t)	105.5	1	Eden
120)	2VM(t)	105.5	1	Mungindi
83)	2BDR	105.7	100(d)	Albury
167)	6IX(t)	105.7	4(d)	Wanneroo
10)	2EC(t)	105.9	20(d)	Batemans Bay/Moruya
59)	2GZF	105.9	5	Orange
84)	5AUU	105.9	20	Spencer Gulf North
170)	8SAT	106.1	3	Ceduna/Smoky Bay (SA)
137)	1CBR	106.3	20	Canberra
133)	2CFS	106.3	15	Coffs Harbour
67)	3CCS	106.3	10(d)	Colac
11)	4RGT	106.3	100(d)	Townsville
64)	2WFM	106.5	150(d)	Sydney
88)	6RED	106.5	1	Karratha
1)	2PQQ	106.7	10(d)	Kempsey
45)	2ST(t)	106.7	1.6	Ulladulla
120)	2VM(t)	106.7	1	Walgett
150)	4RBL	106.7	1	Childers
100)	2XXX	106.9	20(d)	Newcastle
26)	4BNE	106.9	12	Brisbane
170)	8SAT	106.9	2	Minnipa SA
146)	8MIX	106.9	1	Katherine
120)	2NOW(t)	107.1	1	Mungindi
130)	5SSA	107.1	20(d)	Adelaide
121)	2MVB	107.3	10(d)	Taree
150)	4BRZ	107.3	1	Bourke (NSW)
152)	7XXX	107.3	36	Hobart
170)	8SAT	107.3	2(d)	Kingston SE (SA)
97)	2GGO	107.5	16	Gosford
98)	3SHI	107.7	10	Swan Hill
27)	7DDD	107.7	7(d)	Devonport
107)	2ICE	107.9	10(d)	Lithgow
34)	4RAM(t)	107.9	2(d)	Bowen
43)	4ROK	107.9	10	Rockhampton

Addresses and other information (ARN:Australian Radio Network)
NB: The term midnight-to-dawn refers to local time. Exact hrs vary from stn to stn

1) PO Box 1161, Port Macquarie NSW 2444 (DMG). Supplementary stn. on 102.3MHz and 105.1MHz – **2)** PO Box 253, Warragul Vic. 3820. (N-2) – **3)** PO Box 19, Innisfail, Qld. 4860 **E:** zedamfm@4kz.com.au (N-1: Translators: Tully 693kHz 0.5kW, Dunk Island 88.5MHz 0.5kW – **4)** PO Box 189, Scottsdale, TAS. 7254 (N-1).Part of TASmanian Broadcasting Network – **5)** PO Box 177, Mareeba, QLD 4880 (N-1) Translators: Port Douglas 1422kHz, Weipa 97.7MHz – **6)** PO Box 42, Gympie QLD 4370 (N-1) – **7)** PO Box 120, Burnie, TAS. 7320 (N-1) – **8)** 25 Garnet St, Broken Hill, NSW 2880 (N-3). Supplementary stn on 106.9MHz – **9)** PO Box 693, Newstead, QLD 4006 (N-1) – **10)** PO Box 471, Bega, NSW 2550. Translators: 1584=Narooma, 105.9MHz = Batemans Bay – **11)** PO Box 986, Townsville, QLD 4810 **E:** fourto@ultra.net.au **W:** ozemail.com.au/~asichter (N-1:) – **12)** PO Box 145, Penrith, NSW 2750 (N-1) – **13)** PO Box 293, Albany, WA 6330. (N-1) – **14)** PO Box 321, Berri SA 5343 **E:** fiverm@riverland.net. au **W:** riverland.net.au /~fiverm/ (N-1) – **15)** PO Box 828, Nambour, QLD 4560 (N-1) – **16)** PO Box 315, Queenstown, TAS 7467 (N-3). Translators at Strahan 105.1MHz 25w & Rosebery 107.1MHz 0.3kW – **17)** PO Box 6110, Cairns, QLD 4870. (N-1:Sky Radio) – **18)** PO Box 111, Toowoomba, QLD 4350 (N-1) – **19)** PO Box 256 Northam, WA 6401 – **20)** GPO Box 542F, Hobart, TAS 7001 (N-3) – **21)** GPO Box 4290, Sydney 2001 (N-3) – **22)** PO Box 485, Warrnambool, Vic. 3280 – **23)** GPO Box 6072, Perth, W.A. 6000 (N-1) – **24)** GPO Box 906, Brisbane, QLD 4001 (N-1) – **25)** PO Box 44, Lismore, NSW 2480. (N-1) – **26)** Locked Bag 1069, Fortitude Value BC, QLD 4006 – **27)** PO Box 635, Launceston TAS 7310 – **28)** PO Box 2106, Alice Springs 0871 (N-1).Translator at Yularaon 100.5MHz with 100w. Supplementary st. 8SUN on 96.9MHz with 300w at Alice Springs – **29)** PO Box 651, Cooma, NSW 2630 (N-1) Relays 2UE 9:00-10:00 and AUSTEREO 16:00-18:00. Translators: Thredbo 92.1MHz 1kW, Jindabyne 96.3MHz 2kW and Perisher 98.7MHz 1kW – **30)** 625 Wyndham St, Shepparton, VIC 3630 – **31)** PO Box 665, Carnarvon WA 6701 – **32)** 3UZ Pty Ltd, PO Box 927, Carlton, VIC 3053 (N-1). ID's as "Sport 927" – **33)** PO Box 420, Gladstone, QLD 4680. (N-1). Translator at Rockhampton on 1584 with 500w and at Biloela on 666kHz with 2.5 Kw – **34)** PO Box 986, Townsville, QLD 4810 (FM **E:** hotfm@ultra.net.au) (N-1). 4RR: Racing format, prgrs 8.00-24.00, also relays 4TAB 1008. 4RAM: Translator at Mt Stuart 107.9MHz 1kW, ID's as "103.1 Hot FM" – **35)** PO Box 108, Golden Square, Vic. 3555 (N-1) – **36)** PO Box 950, North Sydney, NSW 2059 (N-3) – **37)** PO Box 195, Warwick, QLD 4370 (N-1) Rel 2TM 1287 7:00pm to 6:00am. Translator: Toowoomba 1359kHz 0.3kW – **38)** PO Box 493, Griffith, NSW 2680 (N-10) – **39)** PO Box 97, Coolangatta, QLD 4225 (N-1). Ids as "Radio 97" – **40)** 201 Tynte St, Nth Adelaide SA 5006. **W:** 5dn.com.au (N-1) – **41)** PO Box 981, Hamilton, VIC 3300 (N-1) – **42)** PO Box 440, Kalgoorlie, WA 6430 (N-1) – **43)** PO Box 159, Rockhampton, QLD 4700 (N-1) – **44)** PO Box 157, Subiaco, WA 6008 (N-1) – **45)** PO Box 540, Nowra 2540 (N-1). Translators: Uladulla 106.7MHz. Supplementary stn on 94.9MHz. (N-1) – **46)** Radio 4TAB, PO Box 275, Albion, QLD 4010. Racing format – **47)** Level 1, 464 Hay St, Subiaco, WA 6008 – **48)** G.PO Box 572F, Hobart, TAS 7001 on 1008kHz & 1080kHz, 87.6MHz 1W narrowcast throughout Queenstown, Strahan, Zeehan, Roseberry, Tullah, Stanley& Smithton (N-1:Sky Radio). Racing format. Rel 2UE M-F – **49)** 79 Frenchs Forest Rd., Frenchs Forest NSW 2086 (N-3: Sky Sports) Provides relays to over 100 NSW stns carrying racing: – **50)** Private Bag 1011, Richmond Vic. 3121 (N-1) – **51)** PO Box 183, Mackay, QLD 4740 (N-1). Airlie Beach on 94.7MHz. Bowen on 107.9MHz – **52)** PO Box 2216, South Hedland, WA 6722 – **53)** PO Box 481, Pt. Pirie, SA 5540 (N-1) – **54)** PO Box 163, Canberra City, ACT 2601 **W:** 2ca.village.com.au (N-3) – **55)** PO Box 178, Bendigo VIC 3550 – **56)** PO Box 305, Kingaroy, QLD 4610 (N-1) ID's as "1071AM" and "Classic Gold" – **57)** PO Box 62, Gunnedah 2380 – **58)** 3 Gemmes Lane, Yornup WA 6256 – **59)** PO Box 88, Orange, NSW 2800. (N-1:Sky Radio) – **60)** PO Box 606, Horsham, VIC 3400. (N-1) – **61)** PO Box 20, Longreach, QLD 4730 – **62)** PO Box 264, Merredin, WA 6415. (N-1) – **63)** PO Box 835G, Launceston, TAS 7250 (N-1) – **64)** PO Box 1107, Neutral Bay NSW 2089 (N-1). ID's as "Mix 106.5 FM" – **65)** G.PO Box 95, Brisbane, QLD 4001 (N-1) – **66)** PO Box 270, Armidale, NSW 2350. **E:** 2AD@mpx.com.au (N-1 – **67)** PO Box 63, Colac, Vic. 3250 (N-1) – **68)** PO Box 19, Mayfield, NSW 2304 (N-3) – **69)** PO Box 267, Emerald, QLD 4720. (N-1). Translators: 945kHz 1kW, 1215kHz 0.1kW, 88.1MHz 30W, 92.5MHz 10W, 98.2MHz 0.1kW, 102.1MHz 0.25kW. Rel 4AM 558kHz, 4ZR 1476kHz, 4CC 927kHz – **70)** PO Box 480, Wagga Wagga, NSW 2650. (N-1). Translator at Tumut on 107.9MHz with 10w. Supplementary St. on 93.1MHz. Both stns – **71)** PO Box 143, Maryborough, QLD 4650. (N-1) – **72)** GPO Box 2516, Nth Sydney, NSW 2001 (N-1) – **73)** PO Box 381, Charters Towers, QLD 4820 Translator: Hughenden 765kHz 0.5kW – **74)** Private Bag 1043, Richmond Vic. 3121 ID's as "Gold FM" – **75)** PO Box 770, Inverell, NSW 2360. (N-3) – **76)** PO Box 10290, Southport BC, QLD 4215 – **77)** PO Box 1047, Unley, SA 5061 (N-1) Translator in Adelaide city on 98.3MHz 0.5kW – **78)** PO Box 276, Grafton, NSW 2460. (N-1) – **79)** PO Box 945, Subiaco, WA 6008 (N-1: BBC) – **80)** PO Box 1499, Canberra City, ACT 2601 (N-1) – **81)** PO Box 234, Seven Hills, NSW 2147 (N-1 – **82)** PO Box 160, Sale, Vic. 3850 (N-1) – **83)** 490 David Street, Albury NSW 2640 – **84)** PO Box 496, Port Augusta, SA 5700 (N-1) – **85)** PO Box 783, Toowoomba, QLD 4350 (N-1) – **86)** PO Box 1221, Dubbo, NSW 2830 **E:** 2du@lisp.com.au. (N-1) FM station "ZOO FM" Dubbo 92.7MHz, Cobar 103.7MHz – **88)** PO Box 153, Karratha, WA 6714. (N-1) – **89)** 8 Jones Bay Road, Pyrmont NSW 2009 **E:** contact@

kick-am.com.au. **W:** kick-am.com.au/ (N-1) ID's as "Kick AM" – **90)** GPO Box 369F, Melbourne 3001 **W:** 3aw.com.au/ – **91)** PO Box 497, Tamworth, NSW 2340 (N-1). Supplementary stn. on 92.9MHz – **92)** PO Box 105, Albion, QLD 4010 (N-1) ID's as "B105" – **93)** PO Box 500, Mt. Gambier, SA 5290 (N-1) – **94)** PO Box 360, Ballarat, VIC 3350. (N-1) – **95)** PO Box 1234, Wollongong, NSW 2500 **E:** mike@w151.aone.net.au (N-1) – **96)** 68 Abbott St Cairns QLD 4870 – **97)** PO Box 564, Gosford, NSW 2250 (N-1) – **98)** PO Box 504, Swan Hill, VIC 3585 (N-1) – **99)** PO Box 1059, Bundaberg, QLD 4670 (N-1) – **100)** PO Box 97, Charlestown, NSW 2290 (N-1) – **101)** PO Box 9550, Geelong, VIC 3220 **E:** krock@slanreach.au (N-1). ID's as "K-Rock" – **102)** PO Box 31, Young, NSW 2594 (N-1) – **103)** PO Box 780, Mount Isa, QLD 4825 (N-1). Relays to 4GC 828. Translator: Cloncurry 693kHz. Supplementary FM license at Mt. Isa. (N-1) – **04)** PO Box 115, Goulburn, NSW 2580 (N-1: Sky Radio) – **105)** PO Box 75, Frankston, Vic. 3199 **E:** magic@magic.com.au (N-1). 3EE ID's as "Magic" – **106)** GPO Box 5AA, Adelaide SA 5001 (N-1) – **107)** Mailbag 90, Lithgow, NSW 2790 **E:** 2lt@lisp.com.au. (N-1) (for QSL'ing purposes) c/o John Wright, 15 Olive Cres, Peakhurst NSW 2210 – **108)** PO Box 295, Parkes, NSW 2870. (N-1) – **109)** PO Box 606, Charlestown, NSW 2290. (N-1) – **111)** PO Box 17, Mudgee, NSW 2850 – **112)** PO Box 600, Muswellbrook, NSW 2333 (N-1) 2VLY 98.1 ID's as "Power FM" – **113)** PO Box 470, Murray Bridge, SA 5253 (N-1). Serves Murray Bridge, The Coorong and Meningie – **114)** PO Box 539, Mildura, VIC 3500 (N-1). 3MA 99.5 ID's as "Today's Music 99.5FM" – **115)** PO Box 22, Roma, QLD 4455. (N-1:Sky Radio) – **116)** PO Box 670, Albury, NSW 2640 **W:** albury.net.au/radio.albury.wodonga/2ay.html (N-1). Supplementary stn. on FM – **117)** PO Box 310, Bathurst, NSW 2795 **E:** stereo@2bs.ix.net.au or 2bs@csu.edu.au **W:** 2bs.ix.net.au (N-1) FM service on 99.3MHz – **118)** PO Box 195, Shepparton, Vic. 3630 – **119)** PO Box 312, Deniliquin, NSW 2710. (N-1) 2MOR 102.5 ID's as "Classic Rock 102.5" – **120)** PO Box 389, Moree, NSW 2400. (N-1). Supplementary license on 98.3MHz. Translator on 88.7MHz with 250w r. (N-1) – **121)** PO Box 275, Taree, NSW 2430 (N-1). Translator: Gloucester 100.1MHz and Forster on 100.3MHz – **122)** PO Box 449, Wangaratta, VIC 3677 (N-1). 3NE Translators: Mt. Hotham 89.3MHz 0.02kW, Mt. Buffalo 105.3MHz 0.2kW, Mt. Beauty 90.3MHz 10w. 3NNN ID's as "Edge FM" – **123)** Locked Bag 6198 Sth Coast Mail Centre NSW 2521 (N-1) ID's as "98FM" – **124)** GPO Box 105, Melbourne, VIC (N-1) – **125)** 111 Wellington Str, East Perth, WA 6004. (N-1) – **126)** PO Box 1019, St. Kilda, Vic. 3182 (N-1) – **127)** GPO Box 1041, Brisbane, QLD 4001. (N-1) – **128)** PO Box 920, Crows Nest, NSW 2065 **W:** 2dayfm.com.au (N-1) – **129)** GPO Box 442, Sydney, NSW 2001 (N-1). **W:** mrock.com.au – **130)** PO Box 1071, Unley, SA 5061.24h (N-1) Translator South Tce, Adelaide on 91.1MHz 1kW. ID's as "SAFM" – **131)** PO Box 527, Esperance, WA 6450. N-1. Rel. 6PPM-FM 1000-2200 – **132)** PO Box 665, Carnarvon, WA 6701. 2200-1500 (N-1). Translator: Exmouth – **133)** PO Box 1950, Coffs Harbour, NSW 2450 (N-1). Rp – **134)** PO Box 483, Port Lincoln, SA 5606. (N-1) – **135)** 141 Mandurah Tce, Mandurah, WA 6210 (N-1) – **136)** GPO Box 163, Canberra, ACT 2601. Belongs to 54). **F.PI:** translator for Tuggeranong area – **137)** PO Box 106, Dickson, ACT 2602. (N-1) ID's as "Mix 106.3" – **138)** GPO Box 163, Canberra, A.C.T. 2601 (N-1) – **139)** PO Box 185, Mackay QLD 4740 – **140)** PO Box 2101, Gosford, NSW 2250 (N-1) – **141)** PO Box 7, Ipswich, QLD 4305 (N-1) ID's as "Mix 106.9 QFM" – **142)** PO Box 128 Geraldton, WA 6530. 24h (N-1) – **143)** 15 Puttabucca Rd, Mudgee NSW 2850 – **144)** G.PO Box 1800, Hobart, TAS. 7001 (N-1) – **145)** Locked Bag 5000, Broadway NSW 2007 – **146)** GPO Box 2510, Darwin NT 0801 – **147)** 4 Peary St., Darwin, NT 0800 (N-1) Translators: Katherine 765kHz 0.5kW – **148)** 678 Victoria St, Richmond VIC 3121 – **149)** 403 The Esplanade, Torquay QLD 4655 – **150)** PO Box 332, Beaudesert QLD 4285 – **151)** PO Box 148, Bunbury WA 6231 – **152)** GPO Box 1345, Hobart TAS 7001 – **153)** PO Box 84, Charleville, QLD 4470 (N-1) ID's as "Outback Radio". Translator: Cunnamulla 1584kHz 0.2kW – **154)** PO Box 5910 Gold Coast Mail Centre Bundall QLD 4217 r. (N-1) – **155)** Private Bag 925 Gold Coast Mail Centre QLD 4215. (N-1) – **156)** Paul Taylor, 41 Allards Crt., Clifton Springs VIC 3222 – **157)** Sea FM, 320 Sheridan St Cairns QLD 4870 – **158)** Sea FM, Suncorp/Metway Building Suite 3, Level 3, 123 Victoria St Mackay QLD 4740 – **159)** 444 Logan Rd, Stones Corner QLD 4120 – **160)** PO Box 665 Carnarvon WA 6701 – **161)** 33 Saunders Road, Pyrmont NSW 2009 – **162)** Regional Communications Pty Ltd, PO Box 7515, St Kilda Road VIC 3004 – **163)** 47 Wingewarra St Dubbo NSW 2830 – **164)** DMG Regional Radio, Locked Bag 5000, Broadway NSW 2007 – **165)** 68 Abbott St, Cairns QLD 4870 – **166)** PO Box 112, Bunbury WA 6230 – **167)** PO Box 33, Tuart Hill WA 6060 **168)** cnr Plaza Pde & Carnaby St, Maroochydore QLD 4558 – **169)** Locked Bag 919, Adelaide SA 5001 – **170)** PO Box 579, Lilydale VIC 3140 – **171)** PO Box 3535, Erina NSW 2250, - **172)** Level 2, 678 Victoria Street, Richmond, Vic, 3121

COMMUNITY BROADCASTING ASSOCIATION OF AUSTRALIA

Suite One, Level Three, 44-54 Botany Rd. Alexandria, NSW 2015

☎ +61 (2) 9310 2999   +61 (2) 9319 4545

PRN: Public Radio Network, CBAA: Community Broadcasting Association of Australia. CBAA provides ComRadSat

PUBLIC BROADCASTING STATIONS

MW	Call	Location	kHz	kW
1)	2WEB	Bourke	585	10(d)
2)	6WR	Kununurra	693	5
3)	3CR	Melbourne	855	2(d)
4)	7RPH	Hobart	864	2
15)	6FX	Fitzroy Crossing	936	5
220)	6RPH	Perth	990	5
7)	1RPH	Canberra	1125	2(d)
9)	3RPH	Melbourne	1179	5
8)	4BI	Brisbane	1197	0.5/1
10)	5RPH	Adelaide	1197	2
11)	2RPH	Sydney	1224	5(d)
6)	4MW	Thursday Is.	1260	2
18)	4RPH	Brisbane	1296	5(d)
193)	3KND	Melbourne	1503	5(d)

FM	Call	MHz	kW	Location
151)	3MFM	88.1	2(d)	Leongatha
9)	3BPH	88.7	6.6	Bendigo
176)	3RUM	88.7	1	Walwa/Jingellic
13)	2RBR	88.9	1(d)	Coraki
14)	2YOU	88.9	1(d)	Tamworth
112)	7DBS	88.9	1(d)	Lileah
217)	4CCR	89.1	2(d)	Cairns
148)	5BBB	89.1	1	Barossa Valley
17)	4CRB	89.3	25(d)	Gold Coast
16)	4SDB	89.3	2	Warwick
149)	5EFM	89.3	1	Victor Harbour
150)	5GFM	89.3	10(d)	Arthurton
151)	3MFM	89.5	1(d)	Foster
218)	2HIM	89.7	1(d)	Tamworth
19)	2TEN	89.7	4	Tenterfield
147)	5TCB(t)	89.7	1.5	Naracoorte
158)	6TCR	89.7	2(d)	Wanneroo
152)	3TSC	89.9	56(d)	Melbourne
20)	4DDD	89.9	2	Dalby
153)	5GSFM	90.1	1	Victor Harbour
153)	3SYN	90.7	56(d)	Melbourne
21)	4CSB	90.7	5	Wondai
22)	5KIX	90.7	3(d)	Kangaroo Island
23)	1CMS	91.1	20	Canberra
24)	2CBD	91.1	5	Deepwater
1)	2WEB(t)	91.1	1(d)	Coonamble
25)	2MAX	91.3	10(d)	Narrabri
102)	4BRR	91.5	1	Gayndah
26)	4GCR	91.5	1	Gympie
27)	1WAY	91.9	20	Canberra
28)	4RGL	91.9	1	Gladstone
37)	2ARM	92.1	2	Armidale
30)	2MFM	92.1	6	Sydney
31)	6RTR	92.1	10(d)	Perth
33)	2MCE	92.3	1	Bathurst
34)	3ZZZ	92.3	56(d)	Melbourne
35)	1ART	92.7	20	Canberra
155)	5FBI	92.7	20(d)	Adelaide
36)	2NCR	92.9	6	Lismore
147)	5TCB	92.9	2	Kingston SE
38)	2BBB	93.3	3.2	Dorrigo
156)	2MNO	93.3	2	Monaro
157)	2SNR	93.3	2	Gosford
9)	3RPH	93.5	1	Warragul
39)	2BAR	93.7	1(d)	Bega
212)	2LND	93.7	50(d)	Sydney
40)	5DDD	93.7	6.3	Adelaide
226)	2CCM	94.1	2	Gosford
41)	2LIV	94.1	4(d)	Wollongong/Nowra
239)	4UMR	94.1	2	Cherbourg
43)	2DCB	94.3	10	Dubbo
213)	2FBI	94.5	150(d)	Sydney
9)	3RPH	94.5	5(d)	Warrnambool
44)	5CCR	94.5	1	Ceduna/Smoky Bay
45)	8KNB	94.5	15	Darwin
33)	2MCE	94.7	1(d)	Orange
228)	3PLS	94.7	56(d)	Geelong
47)	4BCR	94.7	3(d)	Bundaberg
194)	2GCB	94.9	2	Gosford
160)	2MIA	95.1	5	Griffith
229)	2TRR	95.3	2	Coolah
161)	6EBA	95.3	16(d)	Perth
12)	4BVR	95.9	1	Esk

FM	Call	MHz	kW	Location
229)	2TRR	96.1	1	Dunedoo
11)	7RPH	96.1	3.2	Devonport
32)	7THE	96.1	3(d)	Hobart
48)	2CCC	96.3	2	Gosford
49)	3GGR	96.3	56(d)	Geelong
240)	6PAC	96.3	6	Kalgoorlie
50)	2CHR	96.5	2(d)	Cessnock/Maitland
51)	3EON	96.5	1(d)	Bendigo (city)
52)	4FRB	96.5	12	Brisbane
46)	4RFM	96.9	5	Moranbah
219)	7MID	97.1	2	Oatlands
159)	2OLD	97.3	1	Lake Macquarie
54)	3HCR	97.3	1	Omeo
165)	7TAS	97.7	1	Tasman Peninsula
55)	8GGG	97.7	15	Darwin
56)	2LVR	97.9	4	Parkes/Forbes
57)	6DBY	97.9	2	Derby
58)	4EB	98.1	12	Brisbane
59)	1XXR	98.3	20	Canberra
60)	6MKA	98.3	1	Meekatharra
61)	2OOO	98.5	25(d)	Sydney
62)	3ONE	98.5	10(d)	Shepparton
167)	4YOU	98.5	1	Rockhampton
147)	5TCB	98.5	2	Padthaway
63)	6SON	98.5	16(d)	Perth
64)	2KRR	98.7	1	Kandos
65)	4CIM	98.7	10(d)	Cairns
66)	4AAA	98.9	12	Brisbane
29)	3SFM	99.1	1	Swan Hill
67)	3RPC	99.3	2(d)	Portland
168)	7EDG	99.3	1	Hobart South
68)	2RFM	99.7	10(d)	Newcastle
70)	3MCR	99.7	1	Mansfield
215)	4ACR	99.7	1	Woorabinda
169)	4RED	99.7	2(d)	Redcliffe
71)	6GME	99.7	2	Broome
170)	2BAY	99.9	3	Byron Bay
72)	2PMQ	99.9	3	Port Macquarie
73)	3BBB	99.9	3	Ballarat
74)	4TCB	99.9	20	Townsville
171)	5MBS	99.9	2.5	Adelaide Foothills
75)	2BCB	100.1	10	Bathurst
9)	3SPH	100.1	10(d)	Shepparton
172)	4RIM	100.1	1	Boonah
214)	5GTR	100.1	1	Mt. Gambier
5)	6NR	100.1	6.5(d)	Perth
76)	2TLC	100.3	1	Maclean
216)	2YAS	100.3	2	Yass
77)	4BAY	100.3	4(d)	Wynnum/Redlands
11)	2RPH	100.5	4	Newcastle
11)	2RPH	100.5	1(d)	Sydney Eastern Suburbs
1)	2WEB	100.7	1(d)	Nyngan
78)	3CH	100.7	1(d)	Kyneton
79)	4US	100.7	1	Rockhampton
211)	2PSR	100.9	1(d)	Port Stephens
80)	6CRA	100.9	10	Albany
166)	6NME	100.9	16(d)	Perth
81)	4CBL	101.1	4(d)	Logan
82)	3WPR	101.3	1	Wangaratta
85)	8KTR	101.3	1(d)	Katherine
83)	2GLA	101.5	10(d)	Forster
230)	3BBS	101.5	1	Bendigo
174)	4BSR	101.5	1	Beaudesert
84)	4OUR	101.5	3(d)	Caboolture
185)	5UV	101.5	20(d)	Adelaide
9)	2APH	101.7	2	Albury
231)	6SEN	101.7	8(d)	Perth
177)	2PAR	101.9	1	Ballina
86)	4ZZZ	102.1	12	Brisbane
87)	6WR	102.1	1	Wyndham
88)	2NIM	102.3	1	Nimbin
89)	2MBS	102.5	50(d)	Sydney
90)	3RRR	102.7	56(d)	Melbourne
178)	4DDB	102.7	4	Toowoomba
91)	2CVC	103.1	1	Grafton
92)	2WET	103.1	1	Kempsey
210)	3BBR	103.1	1	Warragul
93)	5EBI	103.1	20(d)	Adelaide
94)	2CBA	103.2	50(d)	Sydney
95)	2TLP	103.3	3(d)	Taree
97)	2CCB	103.5	5	Orange
98)	3MBR	103.5	4.8	Murrayville
99)	3MBS	103.5	56(d)	Melbourne
100)	2NUR	103.7	10(d)	Newcastle
53)	3WAY	103.7	5	Warrnambool
101)	4MBS	103.7	12	Brisbane
179)	7LTN	103.7	2(d)	Launceston
103)	2WAY	103.9	3	Port Macquarie
104)	3BGR	103.9	3	Ballarat
209)	3GCB	103.9	10(d)	Latrobe Valley
105)	4TTT	103.9	20	Townsville
106)	6ESP	103.9	5	Esperance
107)	2CHY	104.1	5	Coffs Harbour
69)	2UUU	104.5	2(d)	Nowra
147)	5TCB	104.5	1.6	Keith
180)	8KIN	104.5	1	Katherine
109)	2BOB	104.7	5	Taree
110)	3GCR	104.7	7.9(d)	Latrobe Valley
111)	3GRR	104.7	5(d)	Echuca
112)	7DBS	104.7	2	Devonport
181)	4SFM	104.9	3	Nambour
182)	5RCB	104.9	20	Mt. Gambier
113)	4WBR	105.1	10(d)	Maryborough
201)	5TRX	105.1	5	Port Pirie
114)	7WAY	105.3	3.2	Launceston
115)	4MET	105.7	10(d)	Gold Coast
24)	2CBD	105.9	3	Glen Innes
116)	2NVR	105.9	2(d)	Nambucca Heads
175)	4MUR	105.9	1	Mackay
147)	5TCB	106.1	1.6	Bordertown
112)	7DBS	106.1	10(d)	Wynyard
117)	2CUZ	106.5	10	Bourke
183)	4CLG	106.5	3	Nambour
96)	7HFC	106.5	36	Hobart
227)	3HOT	106.7	1	Mildura
118)	3PBS	106.7	56(d)	Melbourne
119)	2VOX	106.9	2(d)	Wollongong
120)	3UGE	106.9	1	Alexandra/Eildon
4)	7RPH	106.9	3.2	Launceston
121)	4KIG	107.1	16	Townsville
122)	2REM	107.3	2	Albury
123)	2SER	107.3	14	Sydney
124)	4CAB	107.3	10(d)	Gold Coast
125)	2EAR	107.5	1.6(d)	Moruya
173)	2OCB	107.5	5	Orange
9)	3MPH	107.5	1	Mildura
126)	4CRM	107.5	1	Mackay
176)	3RUM	107.7	1	Tumbarumba NSW
127)	2AIR	107.9	5	Coffs Harbour
128)	2COW	107.9	1	Casino
129)	5RAM	107.9	20(d)	Adelaide
130)	6CCR	107.9	1(d)	Fremantle

HIGH POWER OPEN NARROWCAST STATIONS

These stns are licenced for a specific market such as horseracing or for a certain local audience not catered for by commercial or other such radio stns. Official callsigns are not issued for these stns but may be used. **NB:** Many expanded band (1611-1701kHz) stations are licensed but may not be on air, confirming their status can be difficult. Additionally some stations in some centers may be off air for extended periods.

MW	Station	kHz	kW	Location
188)	R. Italiana 531	531	0.5	Adelaide SA
141)	Niche R. Network	657	2	Perth WA
141)	Niche R. Network	801	5(d)	Gosford NSW
189)	4AY	873	2	Innisfail QLD
138)	R. TAB	891	5(d)	Townsville QLD
146)	RSN	945	2	Bendigo VIC
241)	Sky Sports R.	1008	0.3	Canberra ACT
132)	TAB R. (WA)	1008	2	Geraldton WA
138)	R. TAB	1008	5(d)	Launceston TAS
164)	Vision Christian R.	1017	1	Bunbury WA
243)	R. Rhythm	1053	0.5	Brisbane QLD
138)	R. TAB	1080	5(d)	Hobart TAS
132)	TAB R. (WA)	1206	2	Perth WA
242)	KIX Country	1215	0.35	Bowral NSW
138)	R. TAB	1242	2	Darwin NT
241)	Sky Sports R.	1314	5(d)	Wollongong NSW
244)	Star AM	1323	0.4(d)	Canberra ACT
241)	Sky Sports R.	1341	5(d)	Newcastle NSW
192)	3CW 1341	1341	5(d)	Geelong VIC
146)	RSN	1359	0.2	Mildura VIC
132)	TAB R. (WA)	1404	4	Busselton WA
164)	Vision Christian R.	1413	0.5(d)	Shepparton VIC
195)	3XY R. Hellas	1422	5	Melbourne VIC

MW	Station	kHz	kW	Location
200)	R. Great Southern	1422	2	Wagin WA
164)	Vision Christian R.	1431	2	Kalgoorlie WA
132)	TAB R. (WA)	1449	2	Mandurah WA
141)	Niche R. Network	1539	1	Sydney NSW
138)	R. TAB	1539	5(d)	Adelaide SA
242)	KIX Country	1557	0.5(d)	Renmark/Loxton SA
141)	Niche R. Network	1575	5(d)	Wollongong NSW
241)	Sky Sports R.	1593	0.2	Murwillumbah NSW
141)	Niche R. Network	1593	5(d)	Melbourne VIC
164)	Vision Christian R.	1611	0.4	Grafton NSW
164)	Vision Christian R.	1611	0.4	Western Sydney NSW
164)	Vision Christian R.	1611	0.4	Tamworth NSW
199)	Old Gold 1611AM	1611	0.4	Mildura VIC
164)	Vision Christian R.	1611	0.4	Chiltern VIC
164)	Vision Christian R.	1611	0.4	Melbourne [Western] VIC
197)	KIK FM	1611	0.05	Croydon QLD
189)	4KZ	1611	0.4	Karumba QLD
245)	Hot Country	1611	0.4	Emerald QLD
245)	Hot Country	1611	0.4	Goondiwindi QLD
245)	Hot Country	1611	0.4	Roma QLD
245)	Hot Country	1611	0.4	St George QLD
164)	Vision Christian R.	1611	0.4	Adelaide SA
164)	Vision Christian R.	1611	0.4	Margaret River WA
200)	Easy Listening 1611	1611	0.4	Wagin WA
237)	Gold MX	1611	0.4	Albany WA
141)	Niche R. Netw.	1611	0.4	Esperance WA
141)	Niche R. Netw.	1611	0.4	Kalgoorlie WA
141)	Niche R. Netw.	1611	0.4	Devonport TAS (F.PI)
141)	Niche R. Netw.	1611	0.4	Hobart TAS
141)	Niche R. Netw.	1611	0.4	Launceston TAS (F.PI)
141)	Niche R. Netw.	1611	0.4	Darwin NT
190)	R. 2MORO	1620	0.4	Sydney NSW
192)	3CW 1620	1620	0.4	Melbourne VIC
141)	Niche R. Netw.	1620	0.4	Wangaratta VIC
141)	Niche R. Netw.	1620	0.4	Gladstone QLD (F.PI)
141)	Niche R. Netw.	1620	0.4	Gold Coast QLD
141)	Niche R. Netw.	1620	0.4	Sunshine Coast QLD
189)	4KZ	1620	0.4	Taylors Beach QLD
141)	Niche R. Netw.	1629	0.4	Canberra Nth ACT (F.PI)
203)	Unforgettable 1629	1629	0.1	Newcastle NSW
164)	Vision Christian R.	1629	0.4	Bathurst NSW
164)	Vision Christian R.	1629	0.4	Dubbo NSW
202)	ACR Huaxia	1629	0.4	Melbourne VIC
141)	Niche R. Netw.	1629	0.4	Shepparton VIC
245)	Hot Country	1629	0.4	Dalby QLD
246)	R. Italia Uno	1629	0.4	Adelaide SA
141)	Niche R. Netw.	1629	0.4	Mount Gambier SA
234)	3ABN	1629	0.4	Busselton WA
141)	Niche R. Netw.	1629	0.4	Albany WA
164)	Vision Christian R.	1638	0.4	Armidale NSW (F.PI)
187)	Niche R. Netw.	1638	0.4	Canberra ACT
222)	2ME	1638	0.4	Sydney NSW
222)	2ME	1638	0.4	Melbourne VIC
164)	Vision Christian R.	1647	0.4	Mackay QLD
205)	2MM	1656	0.4	Sydney NSW
223)	VAC Chinese R.	1656	0.4	Brisbane QLD
164)	Vision Christian R.	1656	0.4	Bundaberg QLD
204)	2MM	1656	0.4	Darwin NT
204)	2MM	1665	0.4	Sydney NSW
164)	Vision Christian R.	1665	0.4	East Melbourne VIC
225)	R. Haanji	1674	0.4	Melbourne VIC
164)	Vision Christian R.	1674	0.4	Brisbane QLD
207)	R. Club AM	1683	0.4	Sydney NSW
207)	R. Club AM	1683	0.4	Melbourne VIC
164)	Vision Christian R.	1692	0.06	Nanango QLD
198)	Station X	1692	0.1	Ashmore QLD
235)	Voice of Charity	1701	0.4	Sydney NSW
224)	Islamic Voice R.	1701	0.4	Somerton VIC
208)	R. Brisvaani	1701	0.1	Brisbane QLD

FM	MHz	kW	Location
189)	88.7	2(d)	Atherton QLD
132)	89.5	1.2	Esperance WA
141)	90.3	1	Griffith NSW
142)	90.5	1(d)	Barossa Valley SA
133)	90.5	1(d)	Tamworth NSW
232)	90.5	5(d)	Perth WA
134)	90.9	1	Mossman QLD
133)	90.9	1	Mudgee NSW
135)	91.5	1	Toowoomba QLD
154)	91.9	1(d)	Latrobe Valley VIC
136)	92.3	10(d)	Maryborough QLD
132)	92.5	2	Port Hedland WA
133)	92.7	1	Inverell NSW

FM	MHz	kW	Location
133)	92.7	3(d)	Port Macquarie NSW
164)	93.7	5	Albany WA
133)	94.3	1	Goulburn NSW
137)	94.9	4	Broken Hill NSW
133)	95.5	10(d)	Wagga Wagga NSW
138)	95.5	3(d)	Bundaberg QLD
138)	95.5	4.5(d)	Emerald QLD
139)	95.5	5(d)	Renmark/Loxton SA
133)	95.9	20(d)	Gunnedah NSW
138)	95.9	1	Alice Springs NT
133)	96.9	1(d)	Cooma NSW
164)	97.5	2(d)	Bairnsdale VIC
138)	97.5	1	Blackwater QLD
138)	97.7	1(d)	Burnie TAS
136)	98.1	1	Inglewood QLD
184)	98.7	1	Alice Springs NT
141)	99.1	2(d)	Atherton QLD
133)	99.9	10	Parkes/Forbes NSW
138)	99.9	1	Rockhampton QLD
133)	100.5	4	Broken Hill NSW
132)	100.5	1	Wyndham WA
133)	100.9	10	Bathurst NSW
142)	101.1	10(d)	Nowra NSW
138)	101.3	2	Devonport TAS
133)	101.5	1	Grafton NSW
133)	101.5	1	Kempsey NSW
132)	101.7	1	Karratha WA
164)	102.1	1	Hamilton VIC
133)	102.7	2(d)	Jindabyne NSW
164)	102.9	2	Horsham VIC
133)	103.3	1	Muswellbrook NSW
138)	103.5	100(d)	Mackay QLD
133)	103.7	1	Moree NSW
133)	103.7	2(d)	Nowra NSW
138)	103.7	1	Katherine NT
133)	104.3	10	Armidale NSW
138)	104.3	10(d)	Cairns QLD
164)	105.3	1	Portland NSW
144)	105.3	2(d)	Wollongong NSW
133)	105.7	5	Taree NSW
145)	106.1	1	Deniliquin NSW
133)	106.7	5	Orange NSW
146)	106.9	10	Swan Hill VIC
133)	107.1	1	Eden NSW
133)	107.5	3	Glen Innes NSW

NB: FM stns below 1kW are not mentioned. There have been allocations for a number of years for HF outlets but only one has ever made it to air.

Addresses and other information

1) Western Region Educational Broadc. Co. Ltd, PO Box 426, Bourke NSW 2840. Plus 5 FM translators. – **2)** Radio Station 6WR. PO Box 162 Kununurra WA 6743. (N-1:CBAA) Aboriginal prgrs from National Indigenous Radio Service – **3)** Community R. Federation Ltd, PO Box 277, Collingwood VIC 3066. Various foreign languages – **4)** Radio 7RPH Broadcasting Services for Handicapped Inc. 136 Davey St Hobart TAS. 7000. Information and reading service format. Relays BBCWS 11:00pm to 10:00am Mon-Sat, Sunday – **5)** Curtin Univ of Technology, GPO Box U1987, Perth WA 6001. Rel. CBAA Network at times and BBCWS overnight – **6)** PO Box 385, Thursday Island QLD 4875 – **7)** Print-Handicapped Radio of ACT Inc, Barton Highway, Gungahlin, ACT 2912 – relays BBCWS Mon-Fri 1:00pm to 6:00pm SA noon to Su 9:30am – **8)** Switch FM, PO Box 173, Fortitude Valley QLD, 4006 – **9)** Assoc. for the Blind, 454 Glenferrie Rd, Kooyong 3144. Relays BBCWS overnight – **10)** Radio 5RPH, 231 Morphett St. Adelaide SA 5000. Relays BBCWS overnight – **11)** R. for the Print-Handicapped (NSW) Co-op Ltd, 2/252 Illawarra Rd, Marrickville NSW 2204 – **12)** PO Box 148, Toogoolawah QLD 4313 – **13)** 50 Houghwood Rd, Bora Ridge NSW 2471 – **14)** PO Box 998, Tamworth NSW 2340 – **15)** PO Box 52, Fitzroy Crossing WA 6765 – **16)** Rainbow FM, PO Box 473, Warwick QLD 4370 – **17)** PO Box 86, Burleigh Heads QLD 4220 – **18)** Unit 3/17 Henry Street, Spring Hill QLD 4000 – **19)** PO Box 93, Tenterfield NSW 2372 – **20)** PO Box 483, Dalby QLD 4405 – **21)** Crow FM, PO Box 171, Emerald QLD 4606 – **22)** PO Box 90, Kingscote SA 5223 – **23)** PO Box 3882, Weston ACT 2611 (Ethnic) – **24)** Gough St, Deepwater NSW 2371 – **25)** PO Box 94, Narrabri NSW 2390 – **26)** The Positive Alternative, PO Box 774, Gympie QLD 4570 (Christian) – **27)** Canberra Christian Radio, PO Box 927, Fyshwick ACT 2609 (Christian) – **28)** 257 Goondoon St WArwick QLD 4680 (Christian) – **29)** PO Box 998, Swan Hill VIC 3585 – **30)** Muslim Community Radio, PO Box 969, Bankstown NSW 1885 (Ethnic) – **31)** Arts Radio, PO Box 949, Nedlands WA 6009 – **32)** GPO Box 1324, Hobart TAS 7001 – **33)** Charles Sturt University, Locked Bag 30, Bathurst NSW 2795 – **34)** PO Box 1106, Collingwood VIC 3066 (Ethnic) – **35)** Artsound, PO Box 87,

Curtin ACT 2605 – **36)** PO Box 5123, East Lismore NSW 2480 – **37)** PO Box 707, Armidale NSW 2350 – **38)** PO Box 304, Dorrigo NSW 2454 – **39)** Edge FM, PO Box 771, Bega NSW 2550 – **40)** 48 Nelson St, Stepney SA 5069 – **41)** Living Sound Broadcasters, PO Box 7, Coniston NSW 2500 (Christian) – **42)** Radio Hope Island, PO Box 16 Sanctuary Cove QLD 4212 – **43)** Radio Rhema, PO Box 1502, Dubbo NSW 2830 (Christian) – **44)** PO Box 271, Ceduna SA 5690 – **45)** Radio Larrakia, Shop 2, Alawa Shops, Alawa NT 0810 (Aboriginal) – **46)** PO Box 597, Moranbah QLD 4744 – **47)** PO Box 2678, Bundaberg QLD 4670 – **48)** PO Box 19, Gosford NSW 2250 – **49)** Rhema FM, PO Box 886, Belmont VIC 3216 (Christian) – **50)** PO Box 421, Cessnock NSW 2325 – **51)** Radio KLFM, PO Box 2997, Bendigo Delivery Centre VIC 3554 – **52)** Family Radio, PO Box 1700, Milton QLD 4064 – **53)** PO Box 752, Warrnambool VIC 3280 – **54)** PO Box 86, Omeo VIC 3898 – **55)** Darwin Christian Broadcasters, PO Box 43146, Casaurina NT 0810 (Christian) – **56)** Parkes Road, Forbes NSW 2871 – **57)** PO Box 655, Derby WA 6728 – **58)** 140 Main St, Kangaroo Point QLD 4169 – **59)** 2XX, GPO Box 812, Canberra ACT 2601 – **60)** PO Box 259, Meekatharra WA 6642 – **61)** Radio 2000, 2/25 Belmore Rd, Burwood NSW 2134 (Ethnic) – **62)** PO Box 6824, Shepparton VIC 3630 – **63)** Sonshine FM, PO Box 6340, Morley WA 6062 (Christian) – **64)** PO Box 99, Kandos NSW 2848 – **65)** PO Box 1856, Cairns QLD 4870 (Aboriginal) – **66)** Box 6229, Fairfield Gardens QLD 4103 (Aboriginal) – **67)** PO Box 450, Portland VIC 3305 – **68)** Rhema FM, PO Box 2000, Dangar NSW 2309 (Christian) – **69)** PO Box 884, Nowra NSW 2541 – **70)** PO Box 667, Mansfield VIC 3724 – **71)** PMB Turkey Creek, via Kununurra WA 6743 (Aboriginal) – **72)** Radio Rhema, PO Box 1537, Port Macquarie NSW 2444 (Christian) – **73)** Voice FM, PO Box 149, Ballarat VIC 3350 – **74)** Live FM, PO Box 332, Aitkenvale QLD 4814 (Christian) – **75)** Radio Rhema, PO Box 615, Bathurst NSW 2795 (Christian) – **76)** PO Box 601, Yamba NSW 2464 – **77)** PO Box 1003, Cleveland QLD 4163 – **78)** Central Highlands Broadc. Inc, PO Box 966, Woodend VIC 3442 – **79)** PO Box 663, Rockhampton QLD 4700 (Aboriginal) – **80)** 211-217 North Road, Albany WA 6330 – **81)** PO Box 2101, Logan City DC QLD 4114 – **82)** PO Box 605 Wangaratta VIC 3676 – **83)** PO Box 1015, Tuncurry NSW 2428 – **84)** PO Box 418, Caboolture QLD 4510 – **85)** PO Box 889, Katherine NT 0851 – **86)** PO Box 509, Fortitude Valley QLD 4006 – **87)** PO Box 815, Kununurra WA 6743 (Aboriginal) – **88)** PO Box 522, Nimbin NSW 2480 – **89)** 76 Chandos St, St Leonards NSW 2065 – **90)** PO Box 304, Fitzroy VIC 3065 – **91)** PO Box 115, Grafton NSW 2460 (Christian) – **92)** PO Box 200, West Kempsey NSW 2440 – **93)** 10 Byron Pl, Adelaide SA 5000 (Ethnic) – **94)** PO Box 54, Five Dock NSW 2046 – **95)** Ngarralinyi, The Listening Place, PO Box 657, Taree NSW 2430 (Aboriginal) – **96)** PO Box 1033, New Town TAS 7008 – **97)** Radio Rhema, PO Box 974, Orange NSW 2800 – **98)** PO Box 139, Murrayville NSW 3512 – **99)** 146 Cotham Road, Kew VIC 3101 – **100)** University Dr, Callaghan NSW 2308 – **101)** 384 Old Cleveland Rd, Coorparoo QLD 4151 – **102)** PO Box 915, Gayndah QLD 4625 – **103)** PO Box 603, Port Macquarie 2446 – **104)** Good News Radio, PO Box 312, Ballarat VIC 3350 – **105)** PO Box 1033, Townsville QLD 4810 – **106)** PO Box 2154, Esperance WA 6450 – **107)** PO Box J233, Coffs Harbour NSW 2450 – **108)** PO Box 40146, Casaurina NT 0810 – **109)** PO Box 400, Taree NSW 2430 – **110)** PO Box 579, Morwell VIC 3840 – **111)** 1/15 Matong Rd, Echuca VIC 3564 – **112)** PO Box 333, Wynyard TAS 7325 – **113)** Rhema FM, PO Box 384, Hervey Bay QLD 4655 (Christian) – **114)** 93 Reatta Rd, Trevallyn TAS 7250 (Christian) – **115)** Radio Metro, PO Box 6530, GCMC QLD 9726 – **116)** PO Box 69, Bowraville NSW 2449 – **117)** PO Box 363, Bourke NSW 2840 (Aboriginal) – **118)** PO Box 2917, Fitzroy VIC 3065 – **119)** PO Box 1663, Wollongong NSW 2500 – **120)** PO Box 270, Alexandra VIC 3714 – **121)** PO Box 5483, Townsville QLD 4810 (Aboriginal) – **122)** Garland Ave, North Albury NSW 2640 – **123)** PO Box 123, Broadway NSW 2007 – **124)** Life FM, PO Box 948, Southport QLD 4125 (Christian) – **125)** PO Box 86, Moruya NSW 2537 – **126)** PO Box 1075, Mackay QLD 4740 – **127)** PO Box 2028, Coffs Harbour NSW 2450 – **128)** PO Box 1149, Casino NSW 2470 – **129)** Radio Alta Mira, PO Box 1079, North Adelaide SA 5006 (Christian) – **130)** Unit 4, 153 Rockingham Rd, Hamilton Hill WA 6163 – **131)** KIK FM, PO Bpx 1434, Edge Hill QLD 4870 – **132)** TAB WA, 14 Hasler Rd, Osborne Park WA 6017 – **133)** 79 Frenchs Forest Rd, Frenchs Forest NSW 2086 – **134)** 90.9 FM, Mossman & Port Douglas PO Box 383, Whakatane NEW ZEALAND – **135)** PO Box 111, Toowoomba QLD 4350 – **136)** PO Box 1059, Bundaberg QLD 4670 – **137)** Cross FM, Broken Hill Church of Christ, 232 Lane St, Broken Hill NSW 2880 – **138)** Radio TAB, PO Box 275, Albion QLD 4010 – **139)** GPO Box 5AA, Adelaide SA 5001 – **140)** NT Racing Commission, PO Box 3170, Darwin NT 0800 – **141)** PO Box 159, Clifton Hill VIC 3068 – **142)** Ambersky, PO Box 540, Nowra NSW 2541 – **143)** PO Box 5109, GCMC, Bundall QLD 9726 – **144)** 63 Minimbah Rd, Northbridge NSW 2063 – **145)** Rich Rivers Radio, PO Box 312, Deniliquin NSW 2710 – **146)** PO Box 927, Carlton VIC 3053 – **147)** PO Box 526, Bordertown SA 5268 – **148)** PO Box 654, Tanunda SA 5352 – **149)** PO Box 591 Victor Harbour SA 5211 – **150)** PO Box 390, Kadina SA 5554 – **151)** PO Box 144,

Inverloch VIC 3996 – **151)** PO Box 899, Mont Albert VIC 3127 – **152)** PO Box 999, Victor Harbour SA 5211 – **153)** PO Box 12013, A'Beckett St, Melbourne VIC 3000 – **154)** PO Box 5910 Gold Coast Mail Centre Bundall QLD 4217 – **155)** Level 2, 230-232 Angas St, Adelaide SA 5000 – **156)** PO Box 28, Nimmitabel NSW 2631 – **157)** PO Box 2050, Gosford NSW 2250 – **158)** PO Box 281 Wanneroo WA 6946 – **159)** PO Box 205, Budgewoi NSW 2262 – **160)** PO Box 2122, Griffith NSW 2680 – **161)** PO Box 1005, Subiaco WA 6904 – **162)** c/- PO, Gordon St, Poatina TAS 7302 – **163)** PO Box 79, Earlwood NSW 2206 – **164)** Locked Bag 3, Springwood QLD 4127 – **165)** GPO Box 1345, Hobart TAS 7001 – **166)** PO Box 105, Bentley WA 6102 – **167)** PO Box 5035, North Rockhampton MC QLD 4701 – **168)** GPO Box 252-44, Hobart TAS 7001 – **169)** PO Box 139, Redcliffe QLD 4020 – **170)** PO Box 440, Byron Bay NSW 2481 – **171)** PO Box 7016, Hutt St, Adelaide SA 5000 – **172)** PO Box 243, Boonah QLD 4310 – **173)** PO Box 1031, Orange NSW 2800 – **174)** PO Box 235, Beaudesert QLD 4285 – **175)** PO Box 5337, Mackay MC QLD 4741 – **176)** 55 Main St Walwa VIC 3709 – **177)** PO Box 612, Ballina NSW 2478 – **178)** PO Box 400, Toowoomba QLD 4350 – **179)** 43 Tamar St, Launceston TAS 7250 – **180)** CAAMA, PO Box 2608, Alice Springs NT 0871 – **181)** 5 Desiree Cl, Buderim QLD 4556 – **182)** Radio Rhema, PO Box 1465, Mt. Gambier SA 5290 – **183)** Radio Rhema, PO Box 200, Woombye QLD 4559 – **184)** 17 North St, Frewville SA 5063 – **185)** 228-230 North Tce, Adelaide SA 5000 – **186)** 8/12 Mulloon St, Queanbeyan East NSW 2620 – **187)** c/- John Wright, 29 Milford Rd, Peakhurst NSW 2210 – **188)** GPO Box 1329, Adelaide SA 5001 (Italian) – **189)** PO Box 19, Innisfail QLD 4860 – **190)** 2MORO, Suite 1B, 9 Burwood Rd, Burwood NSW 2134 – **191)** GPO Box 572F, Hobart TAS 7001 – **192)** Suite 3, 15-29 Bank St, South Melbourne VIC 3205 – **193)** 48 Mary Street, Preston VIC 3072 – **194)** Radio Rhema, Suite 4, 162 The Entrance Road, Erina NSW 2250 – **195)** Level 2, 280 William St, Melbourne VIC 3000 – **196)** 5 Phoenix St, Castle Hill NSW 2154 – **197)** PO Box 177, Mareeba QLD 4880 – **198)** E: admin@stationx.com.au – **199)** PO Box 2181, Mildura VIC 3501 – **200)** PO Box 280, Wagin WA 6315 – **201)** Box 887, Port Pirie SA 5540 – **202)** Suite615, 343 Little Collins Street, Melbourne VIC 3000 – **203)** 70 Dawson St, Cooks Hill NSW 2300 – **204)** PO Box 163, Dulwich Hill NSW 2203 – **205)** 1 Woodley Close, Kariong NSW 2250 – **206)** Locked Bag 888, St. Peters NSW 2044 – **207)** 4/9 Mavis St, Revesby NSW 2212 – **208)** PO Box 1187, Oxley QLD 4075 – **209)** PO Box 124 Sale VIC 3853 – **210)** PO Box 995, Drouin VIC 3818 – **211)** PO Box 22 Salamander Bay NSW 2317 – **212)** PO Box 966, Strawberry Hills NSW 2012 – **213)** PO Box 1962, Strawberry Hills NSW 2012 – **214)** PO Box 2161, Mt Gambier SA 5290 – **215)** Rankin St, Woorabinda QLD 4702 – **216)** PO Box 51, Yass NSW 2582 – **217)** PO Box 891, Manunda QLD 4870 – **218)** PO Box 1527, Tamworth NSW –**219)** PO Box 21, Oatlands TAS 7120 – **220)** China Radio International, **E:**beyondbeijing@cri.com.cn – **221)** 12 Pickering Close Hoppers Crossing VIC 3029 – **222)** 5 Macquarie St, Parramatta NSW 2150 – **223)** Level 1, 25 Donkin St, West End QLD 4101 – **224)** PO Box 20, Campbellfield VIC 3061 – **225)** 1/203 William Street, St Albans VIC 3021 – **226)** PO Box 1042, Gosford NSW 2250 (country format) – **227)** PO Box 1067, Mildura VIC 3502 – **228)** 68-70 Little Ryrie Street, Geelong VIC 3220 – **229)** PO Box 1000, Dunedoo NSW 2844 – **230)** PO Box 1206, Bendigo Central VIC 3552 – **231)** PO Box 1388, Booragoon WA 6954 – **232)** 15 Peneral Way, Bulleen VIC 3105 – **233)** PO Box 1921, Southport BC QLD 4125 – **234)** PO Box 752, Morrisset NSW 2264 – **235)** 22 Frank St, Mt. Druitt NSW 2770 – **236)** 33-35 Saunders St, Pyrmont NSW 2009 – **237)** 36 Stead Road, Albany WA 6330 – **238)** 17D Chester St Oakleigh VIC 3166 – **239)** PO Box 403, Murgon QLD 4605 – **240)** PO Box 1049, Kalgoorlie WA 6433 – **241)** 79 Frenchs Forest Rd, Frenchs Forest NSW 2086 – **242)** PO Box 51, Yass NSW 2582 – **243) W:** http://radiorhythm.com.au ☎+61-7 3162 9282 – **244)** Nishi Building, Level 9, 2 Phillip Law Street, Acton ACT 2601 – **245)** PO Box 1172, Kingaroy QLD 4610 – **246)** 7/60 West Terrace, Adelaide SA 5000

SPECIAL BROADCASTING SERVICE (SBS)

✉ Locked Bag 028, Crows Nest, NSW 2065 ☎+61 (02) 9430 2828
🖶 +61 (02) 9430 3700

	MW	Call	kHz	kW	Service
1)	Wollongong	2EA	1035	2	National Prgr
1)	Sydney	2EA	1107	5	Sydney 1
2)	Melbourne	3EA	1224	5(d)	Melbourne 1
1)	Newcastle	2EA	1413	5(d)	National Prgr
1)	Canberra	1SBS	1440	2	National Prgr
1)	Shellharbour	2EA	1485	0.15	Sydney
	FM	**Call**	**MHz**	**kW**	**Service**
1)	Cairns	4SBS	90.5	1(d)	National Prgr
1)	Griffith	2SBS	92.7	1	National Prgr
2)	Melbourne	3SBS	93.1	100	Melbourne 2
1)	Brisbane	4SBS	93.3	96(d)	National Prgr
1)	Adel. Hills	5SBS	95.1	2(d)	National Prgr
2)	Ballarat	3SBS	95.9	1	National Prgr

FM	Call	MHz	kW	Service
1) Perth	6SBS	96.9	100	National Prgr
1) Sydney	2SBS	97.7	150(d)	Sydney 2
1) Lismore	2SBS	98.9	1	National Prgr
1) Wondai	4SBS	98.9	2	National Prgr
1) Renmark	5SBS	99.1	1	National Prgr
1) Darwin	8SBS	100.9	16.6(d)	National Prgr
1) Sapphire	4SBS	103.5	1	National Prgr
1) Canberra	2SBS	105.5	80	National Prgr
1) Hobart	7SBS	105.7	56	National Prgr
1) Adelaide	5SBS	106.3	32	National Prgr

Addresses and other information
1) Locked Bag 028, Crows Nest, NSW 2065
2) PO BOX 294, South Melbourne VIC 3205

AUSTRIA

L.T: UTC +1h (27 Mar-30 Oct: +2h) — **Pop:** 8.5 million — **Pr.L:** German — **E.C:** 50Hz, 230V — **ITU:** AUT

ORF - ÖSTERREICHISCHER RUNDFUNK
✉ ORF-Funkhaus, Argentinierstr. 30A, 1040 Wien ☎+43 1 50101 18699 🖷 +43 1 50101 82500 **W:** orf.at
L.P: DG: Dr. Alexander Wrabetz MD: Karl Amon Tech. Dir.: Michael Götzhaber

FM (MHz)	Ö-1	Ö-Reg	Ö-3	FM4	kW
Bad Gleichen		94.9a			6
Bludenz	87.6	96.0h	98.8		4
Bregenz	93.3	98.2h	89.6	102.1	50
Bruck/Mur	87.6	93.2f	98.7	102.1	20
Graz	91.2	95.4f	89.2	101.7	67
Innsbruck	92.5	96.4g	88.5	101.4	45
Klagenfurt	92.8	97.8b	90.4	102.9	100
Kufstein	97.5	95.4g	103.9	99.9	5
Lienz	89.3	93.8b	99.3	101.0	2.6
		95.9g			2.6
Linz	97.5	95.2d	88.0	104.0	100
		90.1c			10
Mattersburg	89.0	96.2a	100.9		0.6/3/0.6
Rechnitz	90.6	93.5a	87.9	97.4	6
		100.1f			3
Salzburg	90.9	94.8e	99.0	104.6	100
		101.2d			7
St. Pölten	97.0	91.5c	89.4	98.8	100
Schärding	92.5	99.5d	88.2		3/4/3
Schladming	94.3	96.3f	101.3	103.3	3
Semmering	90.3	95.8c	88.2	92.4	9
Spittal/Drau	91.6	100.4b	87.9	103.6	3
Weitra	92.7	95.7c	98.1	101.4	2
Wolfsberg	96.7	94.5b	99.5	102.3	1.5
Wien	92.0	89.9i	99.9	103.8	100
		97.9c			100
		94.7a			2.4

+ more than 500 low power txs
Österreich-1 (Ö1): 24h **N:** on the h
Österreich 2 (Ö2): Regional services
a) Burgenland – Buchgraben 51, 7001 Eisenstadt **W:** burgenland.orf.at b) Kärnten – Sponheimerstr. 13, 9010 Klagenfurt **W:** kaernten.orf.at c) Niederösterreich – Radioplatz 1, 3100 St. Pölten **W:** noe.orf.at d) Oberösterreich – Europaplatz 3, 4010 Linz **W:** ooe.orf.at e) Salzburg – Nonntaler-Haupstr. 49d, 5020 Salzburg **W:** salzburg.orf.at f) Steiermark – Marburgerstr. 20, 8042 Graz **W:** steiermark.orf.at g) Tirol – Rennweg 14, 6010 Innsbruck **W:** tirol.orf.at h) Vorarlberg – Höchsterstrasse 38, 6851 Dornbirn **W:** vorarlberg.orf.at i) Wien – Argentinierstr. 30a, 1040 Wien **W:** wien.orf.at
Österreich 3 (Ö3): 24h **N:** on the h
FM4: Prgrs in English (0000-1300), otherwise in German **W:** fm4.orf.at
Ann: "Österreich 1", "Ö2 (Wien, Niederösterreich, Tirol)", "Ö3"
IS: Österreich 1: composition by Werner Pirchner. Ö2: Composition by Bert Breit. Ö3: Electronic Music
F.PI: Permission to use the following freq for commercial radio (kHz): 585, 630, 774, 891, 963, 1026, 1125, 1143, 1314, 1458, 1485, 1548 & 1602

EXTERNAL SERVICES: Radio Ö1 International
see international radio section

PRIVATE STATIONS
KRONEHIT
Nationwide network with regional news windows
✉ Daumegasse 1, A-1100 Wien **W:** kronehit.at

FM	MHz	kW	FM	MHz	kW
Weitra	90.2	3	Schärding	104.9	8
Linz	92.6	14	St. Pölten	105.3	100
Semmering	102.9	8	Schladming	105.6	2
Bad Gleichenberg	103.2	1.5	Wien	105.8	100
Mattersburg	103.4	1	Innsbruck	106.5	32
Klagenfurt	103.7	2	Lienz	107.1	1
Rechnitz	104.1	6	Graz	107.5	1

+ 40 txs below 1kW

Other Private Stations by Area - FM (MHz):
BURGENLAND: Radio 88.6 Regional, 106.3 Mattersburg, 1kW; 105.5 Rechnitz, 1kW + 1rly

KÄRNTEN (Carinthia): Antenne Kärnten, 104.9 Klagenfurt, 100kW; 107.4 Spittal a.d.Drau, 3kW; 104.3 Wolfsberg, 2kW + 4rly – **Radio Dva (ORF)-Agora** (German/Slovenian progr), 105.5 Klagenfurt, 10kW; 106.8 Wolfsberg, 1kW + 7rly – **Welle 1 Kärnten,** 95.2 Klagenfurt, 2kW + 4rly – **Radio Maria,** 99.3 Spittal a.d. Drau, 0.2kW – **Lokalradio Spittal a.d.Drau,** 101.6 Spittal a.d.Drau, 1kW (F.PI.)

NIEDERÖSTERREICH (Lower Austria): Radio 88.6 Regional, 104.9 Weitra/Nebelstein, 3kW; 103.3 Melk, 3kW; 100.8 St. Pölten, 2kW; 106.7 Hornstein, 1kW – **Radio St. Pölten,** 94.4 St. Pölten, 0.2kW – **Radio Ypsilon Live,** 94.5 Hollabrunn, 0.1kW + 1rly – **Radio Maria,** 95.5 St. Pölten, 0.2kW; 104.7 Waidhofen a.d.Ybbs, 0.5kW; 93.4 Baden-Tattendorf, 0.4kW – **Radio Arabella NOE (Tulln),** 99.4 Tulln-Judenau, 0.3kW + 1rly – **Radio Arabella_NOE (Mostviertel),** 96.5 Ybbs a.d. Donau, 2kW + 2rly – **Radio Ö24,** 96.3 St.Pölten, 1kW

OBERÖSTERREICH (Upper Austria): Life Radio, 100.5 Linz, 100kW; 102.6 Schärding, 3kW; 102.2 Bad Ischl, 0.4kW + 7rly – **Welle 1 Linz,** 91.8 Linz, 0.3kW – **Welle 1 Steyr,** 102.6 Steyr, 1.4kW; 98.3 Wels, 0.1kW + 3 rly – **Radio Arabella Oö Live,** 96.7 Linz, 4kW – **Radio FRO,** 105.0 Linz, 0.3kW – **LoungeFM,** 102.0 Linz, 2.2kW; 95.8 Ried im Innkreis, 1kW (F.PI.); 95.8 Schärding, 1kW (F.PI.) + 2rly – **Freies Radio Salzkammergut,** 100.2 Bad Ischl, 1kW; 107.3 Gmunden, 0.1kW + 4rly – **FRF Freies Radio Freistadt** 107.1 Freistadt, 0.6kW + 1rly

SALZBURG: Antenne Salzburg, 101.8 Salzburg/Gaisberg, 10kW; 105.9 Zell am See, 1kW; 102.5 St. Michael i. Lungau, 0.5kW + 1rly – **Welle 1 Salzburg,** 106.2 Salzburg/Gaisberg, 2kW; 107.1 Zell am See, 0.3kW; 107.5 St. Johann Pongau, 0.2kW – **Radiofabrik LIVE Stream,** 107.5 Salzburg/Hochgitzen, 0.5kW – **Klassik Radio,** 102.5 Salzburg/Högl (D), 0.3kW – **Energy Salzburg,** 94.0 Salzburg/Gaisberg, 0.3kW – **LoungeFM,** 106.6 Salzburg/Hochgitzen, 0.5kW

STEIERMARK (Styria): Antenne Steiermark, 99.1 Graz/Schöckl, 80kW; 105.7 Bruck a.d. Mur, 20kW; 92.0 Schladming, 2kW – **Radio Grün-Weiss,** 106.3 Schladming 2kW, 106.6 Bruck a.d.Mur 1.2kW+3rly – **Radio West,** 107.3 Köflach, 0.1kW +1rly – **Radio Freequenns,** 100.8 Liezen/Salberg, 1kW – **Welle 1 Graz,** 104.6 Graz, 0.5kW – **LoungeFM Graz,** 89.6 Graz 1kW – **Lokalradio Schladming,** 88.5 Schladming, 3kW (F.PI.)

TIROL (Tyrol): Life Radio Tirol, 103.4 Inzing 8kW; 101.8 Innsbruck 1kW; 104.4 Lienz 1kW; 105.4 Haiming 1kW; 106.0 Landeck 1kW; 106.8 Kufstein 1kW + 8rly – **Antenne Tirol Livestream,** 100.8 Zirog (Italy) 1kW; 105.1 Innsbruck 0.2kW; 106.4 Lienz 0.5kW; 104.6 Jenbach 0.2kW; + 4rly – **Welle 1 Innsbruck,** 92.9 Innsbruck 0.3kW – **Welle 1 Oberland,** 103.9 Haiming (Telfs) 0.5kW; 104.3 Inzing 0.4kW; 107.1 Landeck 0.4kW + 5rly – **Welle 1 Ausserfern,** 104.0 Reutte 0.3kW + 2rly – **City-Radio U1 Tirol,** 97.0 Innsbruck 1kW; 89.2 Jenbach 0.4kW + 8rly – **City-Radio U1,** 101.6 Landeck 0.5kW; 104.8 Haiming 0.5kW – **FREIRAD - Freies Radio Innsbruck,** 105.9 Innsbruck 1kW – **Radio Osttirol,** 101.7 Matrei-Hopfgarten 1kW; 107.8 Lienz 0.4kW; + 6rly – **Energy Innsbruck,** 99.9 Innsbruck 0.3kW – **Klassik Radio,** 95.5 Innsbruck 0.3kW – **Radio Maria,** 91.1 Innsbruck 0.4kW; 107.9 Jenbach 0.2kW; 96.0 Mayrhofen 0.2kW – **LoungeFM,** 92.1 Innsbruck 0.4kW

VORARLBERG: Antenne Vorarlberg, 106.5 Bregenz/Pfänder, 5kW; 101.1 Bludenz, 1kW; 105.1 Feldkirch 0.2kW + 2rly – **Radio Proton,** 104.6 Bludenz 0.5kW; 95.9 Bregenz 0.3kW; 104.3 Feldkirch 1kW – **Lokalradio Bregenz,** 103.2 Bregenz/Pfänder, 1kW (F.PI.)

WIEN (Vienna): 88.6 Der Musiksender, 88.6 Wien/Kahlenberg, 10kW – **Radio Ö24,** 102.5 Wien/Kahlenberg, 10kW – **Radio Arabella Wien Live,** 92.9 Wien-Donauturm, 3kW – **Energy Wien,** 104.2 Wien/RiFu-Arsenal, 1kW – **Radio Klassik Stephansdom,** 107.3 Wien-Donauturm, 2kW – **Radio Orange 94.0,** 94.0 Wien/Donauturm, 1kW; **98.3 Superfly,** 98.3 Wien/Donauturm, 2kW

AZERBAIJAN

L.T: UTC +4h (27 Mar-30 Oct: +5h); Mountainous Karabagh (de facto): UTC +4h — **Pop:** 9.2 million — **Pr.L:** Azeri, Armenian — **E.C:** 50Hz, 220V — **ITU:** AZE

MILLI TELEVIZIYA VÄ RADIO SURASI (MTRS)
(National TV & Radio Council)
📧 Nizami küç. 145, AZ 1000 Baki ☎ +994 12 5983659 🖹 +994 12 4987668 **E:** office@ntrc.gov.az **W:** ntrc.gov.az
L.P: Chmn: Nusirävan Mähärrämov
NB: MTRS is the licensing body for broadcasting.

AZÄRBAYCAN TELEVIZIYA VÄ RADIO VERILISLÄRI
QSC (Azerbaijan TV and Radio Broadcasting CJSC) (Gov)
📧 Mehdi Hüseyn küç. 1, AZ 1011 Baki ☎ +994 12 4923807 🖹 +994 12 4972020 **E:** info@aztv.az **W:** aztv.az **L.P:** Chmn: Arif Alisanov

MW	kHz	kW	Prgr	MW	kHz	kW	Prgr
Gäncä	549	70	Resp.	Haciqabul (a)	1296	125	F
Haciqabul (a)	801	150	Resp.	Sixli	1476	1	Resp.
Baki	891	30	Resp.	(a) Pirsaat			

Resp.=Respublika F=International Service

FM (Resp.)	MHz	kW	FM (Resp.)	MHz	kW
Gülüstan	88.0	5	Danaçi	103.0	2
Astara	90.0	1	Ordubad*	103.0	1
Poylu	90.0	5	Säki	104.0	1
Daskäsän	101.5	2	Babäk*	104.5	1.5
Lerik	101.5	2	Särur*	105.0	1
Yergüc	101.5	2	Baki	105.0	5

NB: Txs below 1kW not listed.*) situated in the Naxçivan exclave
D.Prgr: Respublika Radiosu 24h.

ASAN RADIO (Gov)
📧 Akademik Häsän Äliyev küç. 36, AZ 1078 Baki ☎ +994 12 44474448 🖹 +994 12 5417663 **E:** info@asan.gov.az **W:** asan.gov.az
FM: Baki 100.0MHz (1kW) & nationwide network under construction.

ICTIMAI TELEVIZIYA VÄ RADIO YAYIMLARI SIRKÄTI
(Public TV and Radio Broadcasting Co.)
📧 Särifzadä küç. 241, AZ 1012 Baki ☎ +994 12 4313968 🖹 +994 12 4302958 **E:** info@itv.az **W:** itv.az **L.P:** DG: Cämil Quliyev

FM	MHz	kW	FM	MHz	kW
Daskäsän	88.3	1	Danaçi	100.6	1
Lerik	88.3	1	Gülüstan	102.5	5
Yergüc	88.3	1	Poylu	103.0	5
Baki	90.0	5	Babäk*	103.0	1
Säki	91.6	1			

NB: Txs below 1kW not listed.*) situated in the Naxçivan exclave
D.Prgr: Ictimai R. 24h.

OTHER STATIONS

FM	MHz	kW	Location	Station
1)	88.6	1	Danaçi	Bürc FM
7)	89.0	1	Gäncä	Xäzär FM
7)	89.0	1	Lerik	Xäzär FM
1)	91.0	1	Gülüstan	Bürc FM
3)	92.0	1	Lerik	R. ANS-ÇM
2)	100.0	1	Poylu	R. Antenn
2)	100.0	1	Lerik	R. Antenn
1)	100.7	1	Quba	Bürc FM
2)	101.0	1	Baki	R. Antenn
2)	101.2	1	Gülüstan	R. Antenn
3)	102.0	1	Baki	R. ANS-ÇM
3)	102.0	1	Säki	R. ANS-ÇM
1)	102.8	1	Lerik	Bürc FM
7)	103.0	2	Baki	Xäzär FM
10)	103.3	4	Baki	Araz FM
4)	104.0	2	Baki	R. Space
3)	104.5	1	Xizi	R. ANS-ÇM
6)	105.0	1	Gäncä	Lider Jazz FM
2)	105.3	2	Daskäsän	R. Antenn
8)	105.5	2.5	Baki	Media FM
5)	106.3	2	Baki	R. Azad Azärbaycan
6)	107.0	1	Baki	Lider Jazz FM
6)	107.0	1	Imisli	Lider Jazz FM
9)	107.7	1	Baki	Avto FM

NB: Txs below 1kW not listed.
Addresses & other information:
1) Atatürk pr. 28, AZ 1069 Baki – **2)** Azadliq pr. 189, AZ 1130 Baki **E:** info@antenn.az – **3)** Keçid 1128, 504-cü mähällä, AZ 1073 Baki **E:** info@ansradio.ws – **4)** C.Cabbarli küç. 33, AZ 1009 Baki **E:** radio@

spacetv.az – **5)** A.Abbaszadä küç. 8, AZ 1001 Baki **E:** info@atv.az – **6)** S. Mehdiyev küç. 83/23, AZ 1141 Baki **E:** radio@lidertv.com – **7)** Atatürk pr. 28, AZ 1069 Baki. **E:** info@xazar.tv – **8)** Teymur Äliyev küç. 25A, AZ 1130 Baki **E:** mediafm@mediafm.az – **9)** Närimanov Mämmäd Araz küç. 43, AZ 1106 Baki – **10)** Mätbuat pr. 23M, AZ 1100 Baki. **E:** info@arazfm.az. Incl. rel. R. Sputnik (Russia).

HD Radio Transmitter (Trial)
Tx Operator: Teleradio IB **M:** Ictimai R. **Tx:** Baki 105.0MHz (5kW). As analogue simulcast, the tx carries R. Respublika.

MOUNTAINOUS KARABAGH

LERNAYIN GHARABAGH
HANRAYIN HERUSTARADIOYIN KERUTYUN
(Public Radio & TV Co. of Mountainous Karabagh)
📧 Tigran Mets St. 23a, Stepanakert, Mountainous Karabagh (mail: via Armenia) ☎ +374 47 945261 **W:** artsakh.tv
L.P: Chmn: Norek A. Gasparyan
Run by the administration of the "Nagorno-Karabagh Republic".
FM: Stepanakert 102.3MHz. **D.Prgr:** in Armenian.

OTHER STATIONS ¦) time-shared

SW	kHz	kW	Location	Station
1)	¦ 9677±	5	Stepanakert	Ädalätin Säsi
9)	¦ 9677±	5	Stepanakert	Tolisstoni Sädo

FM	MHz	kW	Location	Station
6)	101.8	-	Stepanakert	Ekho Moskvy
4)	103.0	-	Stepanakert	Star FM
3)	104.3	-	Stepanakert	R. Pace
5)	105.0	-	Stepanakert	Mix FM
2)	105.5	-	Stepanakert	R. Hay
A)	106.0	-	Stepanakert	R. Sputnik relay
8)	106.6	-	Stepanakert	Avtoradio
7)	107.5	-	Stepanakert	R. Sevan

Addresses & other information:
1) Tigran Mets St. 23a, Stepanakert. In Azeri: Wed/Sat 0600-0630, Tue/Fri 1400-1430. – **2)** Azatamartikneri St. 18a, Stepanakert. Rel. Hay FM (Armenia) – **3)** Vazgen Sarkisyan St. 25, Stepanakert **E:** pace@nk.am – **4)** A.Akopyan 30, Stepanakert. In Russian – **5)** Azatamartikneri St. 18a, Stepanakert **E:** radio@mix.am – **6)** Stepanakert. Rel. Ekho Moskvy (Russia) – **7)** Stepanakert. Rel. R. Sevan (Lebanon). – **8)** Stepanakert. Rel. Avtoradio (Russia). – **9)** c/o Modus Vivendi Center, Agatangeghos St. 2, 0010 Yerevan, Armenia **E:** tolishstonisado@gmail.com; info@modusvivendicenter.org. MF in Talysh, Azeri: 0900-1000, 1200-1300, 1500-1600. Times may vary. – **A)** Rel. R. Sputnik (Russia).

NB: Radio stns in Mountainous Karabagh are de facto subject to authorisation by the administration of the soi-disant "Nagorno-Karabagh Republic".

AZORES (Portugal)

L.T: UTC -1h (27 Mar-30 Oct: UTC) — **Pop:** 245,000 — **Pr.L:** Portuguese — **E.C:** 50Hz, 220/380V — **ITU:** AZR

ANACOM-Autoridade Nacional de Comunicações, Delegação dos Açores
📧 Rua dos Valados 18, 9500-652 Relva (São Miguel)
☎ +351 296 30 20 40 🖹 +351 291 30 20 41

RÁDIO E TELEVISÃO DE PORTUGAL, S.A. (RTP) - Centro Regional da RDP-Açores
📧 Rua de Castelo Branco, 9500-761 Ponta Delgada ☎ +351 296 201100 🖹 +351 296 201120 **E:** rdp.acores@rtp.pt **W:** rtp.pt
L.P: Maria do Carmo Figueiredo

RDP Antena 1 Açores

MW	kHz	kW	Island
Santa Bárbara	693	*10	Terceira
Monte das Cruzes	828	1	Flores

* = r. currently running at 3kW

FM (MHz)	Ant. 1	Ant. 2	Ant. 3	kW
Arrife	94.5	97.5		0.3
Cabeço Gordo	88.9	105.8		9.1
Cabeço Verde	98.1	92.9		1
Cascalho Negro	92.2	103.3	104.2	1
Espalamaca	93.8	101.4	102.7	0.03/0.5/1
Fajãzinha	100.4	103.7		1
Furnas	93.6			0.5
Lajes das Flores	102.6	97.0		0.2/0.5
Lajes do Pico	96.5	93.5	98.6	1

FM (MHz)	Ant. 1	Ant. 2	Ant. 3	kW
Macela	87.6	93.2		1
Monte das Cruzes	99.8	97.4	102.0	1
Morro Alto	93.5	91.9	95.6	1
Mosteiros	95.1	105.2	107.0	0.1
Nordeste	104.6			0.1
Nordestinho	103.7	91.8		1
Pico Alto Santa Maria	96.7			10
Pico Bartolomeu	92.7	89.9	99.1	0.5/1
Pico da Barrosa	97.9	101.7	87.7	33/33/30
Pico das Éguas	89.5			10
Pico do Geraldo	103.7	107.5		1
Pico do Jardim	97.0			0.9
Pico São Mateus	103.4			0.1
Ponta Delgada	94.1	100.8		0.3/1.3
Ponta Ruiva	87.6			1
Povoação	102.8	97.2	94.2	0.5
Santa Bárbara	90.5	98.9	103.0	35/35/30
Serra do Cume	99.7	89.2	103.9	0.9

D.Prgrs: all networks 24h
V: by QSL card via RDP in Lisboa
Prgr: RDP Antena 1 Açores carries its own prgrs M-F 0730-0200, Sat. 0700-0200, Sun. 0800-0200 LT; Antena 2 & Antena 3 relay Lisboa 24h

DAB: RDP halted T-DAB broadcasts in June 2011. There are no current plans to reactivate this service, which does not mean that it will not be restored in future.

COMMERCIAL STATIONS:
RÁDIO RENASCENÇA – Emissora Católica Portuguesa (Rlg/Comm)
☐ (see Portugal) - **FM:** Pico da Barrosa 95.2MHz 50kW (RR), 100.0MHz 50kW (RFM)

Private stations
RÁDIO CLUBE DE ANGRA – "A VOZ DA TERCEIRA" (Comm.)
☐ Av. Tenente Coronel José Agostinho, 4, 9700-108 Angra do Heroísmo ☎+351 295 21 31 01 ☐ +351 295 21 31 02 **E:** administrativo@rcangra.com direccao@rcangra.com **W:** rcangra.com
FM: Santa Bárbara 101.1MHz 0.4kW, Serra do Cume 94.7MHz 0.05kW & Pico Matias Simão 89.6 MHz 0.05 kW (all in Terceira island)

ESTAÇÃO EMISSORA DO CLUBE ASAS DO ATLÂNTICO (Comm.)
☐ Aeroporto de Santa Maria, Apartado 545, 9580-908 Vila do Porto ☎+351 296 820 720/1/2 ☐+351 296 82 07 25 **E:** geral@asasdoatlantico.pt, radio@asasdoatlantico.pt **W:** asasdoatlantico.pt
FM: Pico Alto, 103.2MHz, 2kW **D.Prgr:** 24h

NB: R. Clube de Angra & R. Clube Asas do Atlântico own also MW licenses although they have been broadcasting only on VHF-FM.

Private stations only owning FM licenses:
CANAL FM (Comm.)
☐Rua Manuel Augusto Amaral 1-D 2-Direito, 9500-222 Ponta Delgada ☎+351 296 307 470 ☐+351 296 307 479 **E:** radio@canal.fm, info@canal.fm **W:** canal.fm
FM: S. Miguel island: 91.0 MHz 0.5 kW Pico da Barrosa, 94,5 & 95.8 Povoação (both 0.05 kW); S. Jorge island: 100.5 MHz 0.5 kW Calheta (Macelinha); Pico island: 92.7 MHz 0.05 kW Madalena; Flores Island: 104.5 MHz 0.5 kW Santa Cruz das Flores

TOP FM (Comm.)
☐ Caminho do Meio, n.º 51, 9700-222 Angra do Heroísmo ☎295 216 011/13 ☐295 216 015 **E:** geral@mytop.fm **W:** mytop.fm
FM: S. Miguel island: tx at Pico da Barrosa (Ponta Delgada, São Miguel island) 102.4 MHz 0.5 kW; Terceira island: Santa Bárbara (Praia da Vitória) 106.6 MHz 1 kW & Serra do Cume (Praia da Vitória) 92.4 MHz 0.050 kW

Other Stations

FM	Island	MHz	kW	Station, location
7)	São Miguel	88.5	3	R. Atlântida, Ponta Delgada
6)	São Miguel	90.2	0.5	R80 R., Nordeste
2)	Faial	91.3	0.5	Antena Nove, Horta
8)	São Miguel	99.4	3	R. Comercial dos Açores/TSF, Ponta Delgada
5)	Pico	100.2	0.5	R. Pico, Madalena do Pico
1)	Terceira	104.4	1	R. Horizonte Açores, Angra do Heroísmo
3)	Pico	104.7	0.5	R. Clube das Lajes do Pico, "A Voz da Montanha", Lajes do Pico
13)	São Miguel	105.0	0.5	105 FM, Pico da Barrosa
9)	São Miguel	105.5	2	R. Nova Cidade,Ribeira Grande
1)	Pico	106.1	0.5	Rádio Cais, São Roque do Pico
12)	São Jorge	107.1	0.5	R. Lumena, Pico Rebineu
4)	São Miguel	107.2	1	R. Insular, Lagoa
10)	Graciosa	107.9	0.5	R. Graciosa, Serra Branca

+ 12 relays of 50W used by 9 stns
Addresses & other information (add +351 to tel/fax nos):
1) Caminho do Meio, nº 51, S. Carlos, 9700 Angra do Heroísmo ☎295-216011/2/3/4 ☐295- 216015 **E:** comercial@horizonteacores. com **W:** horizonteacores.com – **2)** Rua de São João, 38-B, 9900-129 Horta ☎292-29 33 90, ☐ 292-39 16 02 **E:** antenanove@iol.pt **W:** antenanove.com – **3)** R. S. Pedro, 9, 9930-129 Lajes do Pico ☎292-672299 ☐292 - 672950 **E:** radiomontanha@iol.pt **W:** radiomontanha. pt.to– **4)** (relays R. Horizonte Açores 104.4) ☎296- 653 911/2/3/4 ☐ 296- 653 910 **E:** horizonte2@horizonteacores.com **W:** horizonteacores. com – **5)** Avenida Machado Serpa nº 57, 9950-321 Madalena do Pico ☎292- 622 727 ☐292- 622 874 **E:** geral@radiopico.com **W:** radiopico. com – **6)** Rua Bento José Morais, 23 - 5º Esqº, 9500-772 Ponta Delgada ☎296- 201 919 **E:** r80.superonda@gmail.com **W:** r80.ph – **7)** Rua Bento José Morais 23 - 5º Sul, 9500-772 Ponta Delgada ☎296 201 910 ☐296 629 856 **E:** webmaster@radioatlantida.net, director@ radioatlantida.net **W:** radioatlantida.net – **8)** (relays TSF Lisboa) Rua Dr. Bruno Tavares Carreiro, 34-2.º, 9500-055 Ponta Delgada (296 202 800 2 296 202 825 **E:** radioacores@acorianooriental.pt **W:** acorianooriental. pt/noticias/tsf – **9)** R. Adolfo Coutinho de Medeiros, 24 (Apartado 007), 9600-516 Ribeira Grande☎296 472738/296 472802 ☐296 472654 **E:** radionovacidade@gmail.com **W:** radionovacidade.pt – **10)** R. do Corpo Santo, 37, 9880-368 Santa Cruz da Graciosa ☎295-732536 ☐295 712768 **E:** radiograciosa@sapo.pt **W:** rgraciosa.blogspot.com – **11)** Largo do Museu da Indústria da Baleia, 9940-000 São Roque do Pico ☎292642930 ☐ 292 642 934 – **12)** Rua Cunha da Silveira, 25, Apartado 8, 9800-531 Velas ☎295 412575/295 412819 ☐295 412810 **E:** radiolumena@iol.pt, josemachado.1@iol.pt **W:** radiolumena.com – **13)** Av. Infante D. Henrique, 71 - 1º Piso, Loja 129, 9504-529 Ponta Delgada ☎296 654 112 /277 **E:** clubedamusica@105fmazores.com **W:** podcast105fm.com

Military Stations:
RÁDIO LAJES – A VOZ DA FAP-FORÇA AÉREA PORTUGUESA (The Voice of the Portuguese Air Force)
☐ Comando da Zona Aérea dos Açores, 9760-290 Lajes, Terceira ☎+351 295 540891/2/3 ☐ +351 295 540791 **E:** fap.radiolajes@emfa. pt **W:** radiolajes.pt **LP:** Dir.: Major Paulo Roda
MW to be reactivated on the new freq. of 1530kHz (ex-648) 1kW
FM 93.5MHz 150W **F.PI.:** 500W 24h

UNITED STATES AFRTS
☐ Lajes, Terceira, 9760 Praia da Vitoria ☎+351 295 57 34 97 **W:** lajes.af.mil
MW 1503kHz 100W (1kW nominal). **FM** 96.1MHz 150W
D.Prgr: Locally produced & relays of AFRTS

BAHAMAS

L.T: UTC -5h (13 Mar–6 Nov: -4h) — **Pop:** 368,000 — **Pr.L:** English — **E.C:** 60Hz, 120/220V — **ITU:** BAH

ZNS – THE BROADCASTING CORPORATION OF THE BAHAMAS (Comm., Gov.)
☐ Harcourt 'Rusty' Bethel Drive, Third Terrace, Centreville, PO Box N-1347, Nassau ☎ +1 242 502 3800 ☐ +1 242 322 6598 **W:** znsbahamas.com **E:** info@znsbahamas.com
L.P: GM: Diana Swann. CEN: Keith Gomez.
MW: ZNS-1 National Voice of Bahamas: Nassau: 1540kHz 50kW ZNS-3 Gospel: Freeport 810kHz 10kW
FM: ZNS-1 National Voice of Bahamas: Nassau: 104.5MHz 5 kW ZNS-2: Alice Town 107.1MHz 0.3kW & Nassau 107.9MHz 10kW ZNS-Power FM: Freeport 104.5MHz 10kW All four channels are on the air 24h.

TRIBUNE MEDIA GROUP (Comm.)
☐ Radio House, PO Box N-3207, Nassau ☎ +1 242 328 0950 ☐ +1 242 356 5343 **W:** 100jamz.com **LP:** PD Eric Ward
Stations: COOL 96 FM: Yellow Pine Street, PO Box F-40773, Freeport ☎ +1 242 352 7440 ☐ +1 242 352 8709 **W:** cool96fm.com L.P: GM: Andrea Gottlieb. FM: 96.1MHz – **100 JAMZ** FM: Nassau 100.3, Freeport 100.3, Abaco: 100.1 and Coopers Town: 100.5MHz – **JOY FM**, PO Box N-1807, Nassau +1 242 356 5110. L.P.: Steven Haughey. FM: Nassau 101.9MHz – **Y98.7. FM:** Nassau 98.7MHz – **CLASSICAL 98.1:** FM Nassau 98.1

THE NASSAU GUARDIAN (Comm.)
☐ Carter St, PO Box N-3011, Nassau ☎ +1 242 302 2300/328 6868

📠 +1 242 328 5311 **W:** guardiantalkradio.com & hot917fm.com & star106fm.com
Stations: GUARDIAN RADIO: FM 96.9MHz – **HOT 91.7:** FM 91.7MHz – **STAR 106.5:** FM 106.5MHz

OTHER STATIONS:
BBN BIBLE BASED NETWORK, PO Box N-8993 Nassau ☎ +1 242 322 6273 **W:** tprb1023fm.com. FM: Nassau: 102.3MHz – **BREEZE FM**, Farmers Hill Settlement, PO Box EE-17095, Exuma ☎ +1 242 358 7201. L.P.: CEO Dwight Hart. FM: 98.3MHz – **COAST 106.1**, Russel St, GPO, Matthew Town, Inagua ☎ +1 242 225 3389. FM: Inagua 106.1MHz – **DOVE 103**, PO Box F-44008, Freeport, Grand Bahama ☎ +1 242 351 3683. **W:** dove103fm.com. FM: Freeport 103.7MHz – **GEMS RADIO**, Mt. Rose Ave, Sears Hill, PO Box SS-6094, Nassau ☎ +1 242 326 4381 📠 +1 242 326 4371 **W:** gemsnewmediabah.com L.P.: CEO Deborah Bartlett. SM: Mickél Bethel. FM: Nassau: 105.9MHz – **GLOBAL 99.5 FM**, Christie St., Nassau ☎ +1 242 326 0270. FM: Nassau: 99.5MHz – **ISLAND FM**, Center Marketing, Edmark House, Dowdeswell St, PO Box N-1807, Nassau ☎ +1 242 332 8826. **W:** islandfmonline.com. FM: Nassau 102.9MHz – **LOVE-97 FM**, East St North, PO Box N-3909, Nassau ☎ +1 242 356 2555 📠 +1 242 356 7256. FM: Nassau 97.5MHz – **LYFE 90.9 JAZZ FM**, Nassau. FM: Nassau 90.9MHz – **MIX 102.1**, 31 Bishops Place, PO Box F-44008, Freeport ☎ +1 242 373 2275 📠 +1 242 373 2271 L.P: GM: Don Martin. FM: Freeport 102.1MHz 5kW – **MORE 94 FM**, Carmiohael Rd, PO Box CR54245, Nassau ☎ +1 242 361 2447 📠 +1 242 361 2448. **W:** more94fm.com FM: Nassau 94.9MHz – **PEACE 107**, McKinney Broadcasting Network, Gibbs Lane 6, Fort Charlotte, PO Box N-1220, Nassau ☎ +1 242 320 0235. FM: Nassau 107.5MHz – **SPLASH FM SPIRIT GOSPEL**, #12 St., PO Box EL-27495, Spanish Wells, Eleuthera ☎ +1 242 333 4638 📠 +1 242 333 4693. **W:** splash899fm.com and spgospel.com. L.P.: Chris Forsythe. FM: Eleuthera: 89.9MHz, Nassau: 92.5MHz (Spirit Gospel, PO Box CR 54245, Nassau), Abaco 95.5MHz and South Eleuthera 98.5MHz – **SPORTSRADIO 103**, ZSR Media, 2A Dewgard Plaza, Madera St, PO Box N-296, Palmdale, Nassau ☎ +1 242 676 4205 📠 +1 242 676 4199. **W:** bahamassportsradio.com FM: Nassau 103.5MHz

BAHRAIN

L.T: UTC +3h — **Pop:** 700,000 — **Pr.L:** Arabic — **E.C:** 50Hz, 230V(60/110 at Awala) — **ITU:** BHR

INFORMATION AFFAIRS AUTHORITY (IAA)
✉ P.O. Box 33766, Al Esteglal Highway, Manama ☎+973 17 684222 📠 +973 17 781400 **W:** iaa.bh **E:** info@iaa.gov.bh **L.P:** Dir. Tech Affairs: Abdulla Ahmed Al-Balooshi.

BAHRAIN RADIO & TV CORPORATION (BRTC, Gov.)
✉ P.O.Box 33766, Manama ☎+973 17 686000 📠 +973 17 687567 **W:** radiobahrain.fm **E:** btw@brtc.gov.bh **L.P:** CEO: Ahmed Najim. Dir. of Bc: Hamad Al-Manai.
General Prgr. in Arabic: 24h on **MW:** 801kHz 100kW. **FM:** 90.9MHz 3kW – **2nd Prgr. in Arabic** : 24h. **MW:** 1521kHz 10kW, **FM:** 93.3MHz 3kW – **Quran Prgr. in Arabic:** Quran recitation & religious affairs 0300-2100 on **MW:** 612kHz 100kW. **FM:** 106.1MHz. – **Prgr. for the Indian community:** 24h on **FM:** 104.2MHz – **English Sce (R. Bahrain):** 0300-2100 on **MW:** 1584kHz 1kW, **FM:** 96.5MHz 2.5kW. 1600-2100 on 99.5MHz 0.5kW – **Shabab FM**(Youth prgr.): Manama 98.4MHz.
Ann: A: "Idha'atul-Bahrain". E: "Radio Bahrain".
IS: Local composition on guitar and violin.
Relays for abroad on shortwave: see International Radio section.

Other stations:
Sowt al-Khaleej, Manama: 94.4MHz. See Qatar for main entry.
Sawt el-Ghad, Manama: 94.8MHz. **W:** sawtelghad.com
Voice FM, Manama: 104.2MHz. **W:** radiovoice.bh
Emarat FM, Manama: 92.3MHz. See main entry under UAE.
Panorama FM, Manama 103.0MHz. See main entry under UAE.
BBC World Sce, Manama: English 101.0MHz, Arabic 103.8MHz.
Deutsche Welle/Monte Carlo Doualiya, Manama: 90.9MHz 1kW.
R. Sawa, Manama 89.2MHz 1kW. 24h in Arabic

BANGLADESH

L.T: UTC +6h — **Pop:** 157 million — **Pr.L:** Bengali — **E.C:** 50Hz, 220/440V — **ITU:** BGD

BANGLADESH BETAR (Gov.)
✉ National Broadcasting Authority, NBA House, 121 Kazi Nazrul Islam Ave, Dhaka-1000 ☎ +880 2 ,8625538 8625904 📠 +880 2 8612021 **E:** rrc@dhaka.net **W:** betar.gov.bd

L.P: DG: Kazi Akhter Uddin Ahmed DDG (News): Narayan Chandra Sheel : Chief Engr: Ahmed Kamruzzaman Sr. Engr.: Md. Nazrul Islam Sr. Engr (Research): Zia Hassan Dy. Stn. Engr.: Muzibur Rahman Asst. Radio Engr: A. T. M. Mehedi Kamal

MW	kHz	kW	Times
Khulna	558	100	0030-0400, 0600-1710
Dhaka-B	630	100	0000-0145, 0300-1710, 1800-2100
Dhaka-A	693	1000	0030-0610, 0830-1730
Rajshahi	846	100	0030-0400, 0600-1710
Chittagong	873	100	0030-0400, 0600-1710
Sylhet	963	20	0030-0400, 0800-1710
Thakurgaon	999	10	0950-1710
Rangpur	1053	10	0030-0400, 0800-1710
Rajshahi	1080	10	0030-0400 0600-1710
Rangamati	1161	10	0530-1030
Dhaka-C	1170	20	0900-1100
Barishal	1287	10	0445-1115
Cox's Bazar	1314	10	0545-1045
Comilla	1413	10	1000-1710
Bandorban	1431	10	0530-1030
SW	**kHz**	**kW**	**Times**
Shavar	4750	100	0600-1715

NB: Rel. Dhaka A prog. Sign on/off varies due to special prgr rel.

FM	MHz	kW	Rel	Times
Chittagong	105.4	5	c	0030-0400, 1300-1710
Chittagong	88.8	10	j, b	0000-0400 1145-1710
Chittagong	90.0	5	c	0000-1800
Comilla	101.2	2	j	1500-1545
Comilla	103.6	10	b	0030-0200 1200-1710
Dhaka	97.6	5		0030-0600 0800-1730
Dhaka	104.0	10	j	1500-1545
Dhaka	90.0	5		0100-0400
Dhaka	103.2	5		1330-1600
Dhaka	102.0	10	c	0000-1830
Dhaka	100.0	3	b	0000-0600, 0700-0900 1100-1700
Dhaka	106.0	10		0300-0600 1200-1730
Khulna	102.0	1		0000-0400, 1300-1710
Khulna	88.8	10	j, b	0030-0400 1300-1710
Khulna	90.0	5		0600-0700
Rajshahi	104.0	5		0030-0400
Rajshahi	88.8	10	j, b	0030-0400 1300-1710
Rajshahi	90.0	5		0400-0500
Rajshahi	105.0	1		Test trs
Rangpur	105.4	1	j	1110-1235 1500-1545
Rangpur	88.8	10	b	0030-0400 0800-1710
Rangpur	90.0	5		Test trs
Sylhet	105.0	1	j	1100-1710
Sylhet	88.8	10	b	0030-0400 1000-1710
Sylhet	90.0	5		Test trs
Thakurgaon	92.0	5	b	0030-0200 1330-1700
Traffic Channel	88.8	10		0100-1500
Barisal	105.0	10	b	0030-0200 0445-1115 1330-1700
Coxsbazar	100.8	10	b	0030-0200 0645-1045 1330-1700
Rangamati	103.2	10		0830-1030
Bandorban	104.0	10		0830-1030
Nowapara	100.8	10		Test trs

b) Rel. BBC World Service Dhaka 100 MHz 0000-0600, 1100-1700 Other cities 0030-0100 0130-0200, 1330-1400, 1630-1700 j) Radio Japan 1500-1545 c) China R Int. 1300-1400
N. in English: 0200, 1100, 1530, 1805. **N. in Bengali:** 0100, 0300, 0400, 0500, 0600, , 0900, 1000, 1200, 1430, 1600, 1700 **SAARC N. in Bengali:** 1235 **SAARC N. in Bengali:** 1250 Every Mon
F.PI: Establishment of new FM stations located in Gopalganj & Mymensingh, 100kW tx at Chittagong to be replaced. Replacement of 100kW tx at Dhaka B. One standby 100kW tx for Dhaka B. Introduction of new MW frequency 819 kHz

EXTERNAL SERVICE: BANGLADESH BETAR
See International Radio section.

OTHER STATIONS:
RADIO TODAY
✉ Radio Broadcasting FM (Bangladesh) Co. Ltd Awal Centre (13th & 19th floor), Kamal Atraturk Avenue, Banani, Dhaka 1213 ☎ +880 2 982 0370 - 4 📠 +880 2 9821486
E: wm@radiotodaybd.fm **W:** radiotodaybd.fm
FM: 89.6MHz 10kW Dhaka Khulna Chittagong Coxsbazar Sylhet Rajshahi Barishal Mymensingh

RADIO FOORTI
✉ Radio Foorti Limited Landmark (8th flr), 12-14 Gulshan-2 North C/A, Dhaka 1212 ☎ +880 2 8835747 8835748 **E:** info@radiofoorti. fm **W:** radiofoorti.fm **FM:** 88.0MHz 20kW Dhaka Chittagong, Sylhet, Mymensingh, Rajshahi, Barishal, Khulna, Cox's Bazar

UNIWAVE BROADCASTING COMPANY LTD
⌨ Uniwave Broadcasting Company Limited, Silver Tower (12th Floor), 52, Gulshan Avenue, Gulshan- 1, Dhaka- 1212 ☎ +880 2 9886800, 9861133, 8832989 **E:** info@radioaamar.com **W:** radioaamar.com **LP:** CEO: Zulfiker Ahmed **FM:** Radio Aamar 24h 88.4 MHz Dhaka

AYENA BROADCASTING CORPORATION
⌨ Dhaka Trade Centre, 99 Kazi Nazrul Islam Avenue, Kawran Bazar, Dhaka 1215 ☎ +880 2 8142038 8189307 ▤ +880 2 9128141 **E:** program@abcradiobd.fm **W:** abcradiobd.fm
LP: Man. Dir.: Matiur Rahman Choudhury. **FM:** 89.2MHz 24h in Dhaka Chittagong Coxsbazar

DHAKA FM
⌨ Navana Tower (15th floor), Navana Tower (15th Floor) 45, Gulshan South, Circle-1 Dhaka-1212, ☎ +880 2 8811720-21 ▤ +880 2 8811722 **E:** admin90.4@dhakafm904.com **W:** dhakafm904.com
FM: 90.4 MHz 10 kW 24h Dhaka Rajshahi Bogra Barishal Chittagong Coxsbazar Sylhet Khulna Rangpur Mymensignh

PEOPLES RADIO
⌨ 41, Samsuddin Mashon, 5th floor, Gulshan-2 Dhaka 1212 ☎ +880 2 9890952-3 ▤ +880 2 9570757 **E:** hello@peoplesradio.fm **W:** peoplesradio.fm - **FM:** Dhaka 91.6MHz

RADIO SHADHIN
⌨ Asiatic Centre, House 63, Block H, Road 7B, Banani, Dhaka 1213 ☎+880 9666924924 **E:** sales@radioshadhin.fm **W:** radioshadhin.fm - **FM** Dhaka 92.4 MHz

RADIO BHUMI
⌨ 40, Shahid Tajuddin Ahmed Sarani Tejgaon, Dhaka – 1208 ☎ +880 1191928928 **E:** info@radiobhumi.fm **W:** radiobhumi.fm - **FM** Dhaka 92.8 MHz 24h

CITY FM
⌨ Hasan Holdings Building, 14th floor, New Eskaton Road, Banglamotor, Dhaka -1000,☎ +880 2 9341828-9, **W:** cityfm.com - **FM:** Dhaka, 96 MHz 24h 5kW

ASIAN RADIO
⌨ Ka-34 Chowdhury Bari, South Badda Gulshan, Dhaka -1212 ☎ +880 2 9854475-78 **E:** info@asianradiofm.com **W:** asianradiofm.com - **LP:** Chrmn.: Alhaj Harun Ur Rashid **FM:** Dhaka 90.8 MHz 24h

COLOURS FM
⌨ 67/4, Pioneer Road, Kakrail, Dhaka-1000, Dhaka, Bangladesh **W:** colours.fm - **FM:** Dhaka 101.6MHz 24h

JAGO FM
⌨ Pran RFL Centre, 105 Middle Badda, Dhaka 1212 ☎ +880 2 9881792 **E:** info@jago.fm **W:** jago.fm - **FM:** Dhaka 90.4MHz

RADIO EDGE
⌨ 7th Floor, 84 Skylark Mark, Road-11, Dhaka ☎ +880 2 9820971 **W:** radioedge.fm - **FM:** Dhaka 95.6MHz

RADIO CAPITAL
⌨ 371/A, Block-D, Bashundhara R/A, 1229 Dhaka ☎ +880 2 8402047 **E:** info@radiocapital.fm **W:** radiocapital.fm - **FM:** Dhaka 94.8MHz

Community Stations
R. Chilmari, Kurigram - **FM:** 99.2MHz – R. Mukti, Bogra - **FM:** 99.2MHz – Barendra R., Naogaon - **FM:** 99.2MHz – R. Mahananda, Chapai Nawabganj - **FM:** 98.8MHz – R. Padma, Rajshahi - **FM:** 99.2MHz – R. Jhenuk, Jhenidah - **FM:** 99.2MHz – R. Nalta, Satkhira - **FM:** 99.2MHz – R. Sundarban, Khulna - **FM:** 98.8MHz – Loko Betar, Barguna - **FM:** 99.2MHz – Krishi R., Barguna - **FM:** 98.8MHz – R. Naf, Cox's Bazar - **FM:** 99.2MHz – R. SagorGiri, Chittagong - **FM:** 99.2MHz – R. Bikrampur, Munsiganj - **FM:** 99.2MHz – R. Pallikantho, Moulavi Bazar - **FM:** 99.2MHz
F.PI: License to be issued for one community station in each district.

BARBADOS

L.T: UTC -4h — **Pop:** 285,000 — **Pr.L:** English — **E.C:** 50Hz 110V — **ITU:** BRB

CARIBBEAN BROADCASTING CORP. (Gov. Comm.)
⌨ The Pine, Wildey, St.Michael ☎ +1 246 467 5400 ▤ +1 246 429 4795 **W:** cbc.bb **LP:** Chrmn: Michael Worrell. **GM:** Rodwell London. Head of Radio: Pearson Bowen
MW: FM 94.7: 900kHz 5kW: 24h (// 94.7)
FM: FM 94.7: 94.7MHz 5kW: 24h – **98.1 FM The One:** 98.1MHz

5kW: 24h – **Quality/Q. FM 100.7** 100.7MHz 5kW – **Government Emergency Broadcast Station:** 91.1MHz 1kW

BARBADOS BROADCASTING SERVICE (Comm.)
⌨ Astoria, St George ☎ +1 246 437 9550 ▤ +1 246 437 9203
L.P: MD: Anthony T. Brian. GM: Shery Anne Padmore
FM: BBS-FM 90.7MHz 5kW: 24h – **Faith FM** (Rlg.) 102.1MHz 1kW: 24h

STARCOM NETWORK INC. (Comm.)
⌨ River Road, PO Box 1267, Bridgetown ☎ +1 246 430 7300 ▤ +1 246 426 5377 **W:** starcomnetwork.net & vob929.com
L.P: CEO: Victor Fernandez. Mgr Ops: Lennox Edwards. PM (Radio): Patrick Gollop
FM: Life 97.5: 97.5MHz 1kW – **VOB Voice of Barbados:** 92.9MHz 5kW – **Hott 95.3 FM:** 95.3MHz 3kW – **The Beat 104.1 FM:** 104.1MHz 5kW

HABMAR INVESTMENTS INC. (Comm.)
⌨ Haggatt Hall, Bridgetown ☎ +1 246 434 1011 ▤ +1 246 437 7526 **W:** slam101fm.com & y103fm.com.
FM: Slam FM: 101.1MHz 5kW – **Y103:** 103.3MHz 5kW

Other Stations:
BBC: FM 92.1MHz 5kW. 24h relay of BBC World Service – **CHRIST IS THE ANSWER RADIO** (Rlg.): ⌨ Bishop's Court Hill, BB46307, St. Michael ☎ +1 246 430 3599 **W:** citaradio.com. **FM:** 90.1MHz 5kW – **MIX 96.9** (Comm.) ⌨ Garden House, Upper Bay St., St. Michael ☎ +1 246 228 4183 ▤ +1 246 228 3550 **W:** mix969fm.com/new/privacy. cfm **LP:** MD: Scott Weatherhead. **FM:** 96.9MHz 4kW – **RADIO GED** (Educ.) ⌨ Barbados Community College, General Education Dept., Eyrie Howells Cross Road, St. Michael ☎ +1 246 426 3312 ▤ +1 246 429 5935. **FM:** 106.1MHz 0.1kW. D.Prgr: 1500-1900MF during school terms only.
F.pl: Due on the air March 2016: 99.3MHz Pulse FM, 104.7MHz: Nothing But God and 105.3MHz: Power Radio (HeartBeat Ministries)

BELARUS

L.T: UTC +3h — **Pop:** 9.5 million — **Pr.L:** Belarusian, Russian — **E.C:** 50Hz, 220V — **ITU:** BLR

MINISTERSTVA KULTURY (Ministry of Culture)
⌨ pr. Peramozcaú 11, 220004 Minsk ☎ +375 17 2037574 **E:** ministerstvo@kultura.by **W:** kultura.gov.by **L.P:** Minister: Barys Sviatloú
NB: The Ministry of Culture is issuing broadcasting licenses.

NACYJANALNAJA DZIARZAÚNAJA TELERADYJO-KAMPANIJA RESPUBLIKI BELARUS (BELTELE-RADYJOKAMPANIJA) (Gov)
(State TV & Radio Co. of Belarus)
⌨ vul. Makaionka 9, 220807 Minsk ☎ +375 17 3896352 ▤ +375 17 2678182 **E:** pr@tvr.by **W:** tvr.by
⌨ **Radio studios:** vul. Cyrvonaja 4, 220807 Minsk; exc. **Radyus FM:** vul. Cyhunacnaja 27/2, 220014 Minsk.
L.P: Chmn: Henadz Davydzka

LW	kHz	kW	Prgr	MW	kHz	kW	Prgr
Sasnovy	279	500	1	Sasnovy	1170	800	F, 1

F=International Service

SW relay for listeners in Russia & Ukraine (Radyjo 1): see Int. Radio section

FM (MHz)	*1	2	*1	2	3	4	kW
Asipovicy	67.46d	71.69	91.0d	107.7	72.47	104.9	2x4/1/3x2
Asveja	-	-	103.5e	106.0	-	-	4
Babrujsk	71.45d	68.96	101.6d	106.0	73.01	104.1	2x4/2x2/4/2
Berazino	70.79	-	94.7	104.7	67.07	100.7	3x1/0.25/1
Brahin	67.37b	68.30	103.3b	105.8	69.11	100.8	2x4/2/2x4/2
Braslaú	69.08e	71.99	105.7e	107.7	73.49	102.3	2x4/2/2x4/2
Brest	70.91a	71.69	100.0a	88.5	72.47	103.7	2x4/2x1/2x4
Drahicyn	72.14a	-	101.8a	-	69.80	102.4	0.5/1/0.5/1
Heraniony	72.32c	68.39	105.8c	102.2	69.26	103.3	2x4/2/1/4/2
Homiel	67.76b	69.26	105.1b	91.5	66.20	100.1	2x2/2x1/21
Hrodna	66.98c	66.20	103.0c	95.0	68.90	100.5	3x4/1/4/2
Kapyl	-	70.97	102.3	101.6	73.22	103.9	01/4/05/01/05
Kasciukovicy	66.47d	68.03	104.7d	107.2	69.38	102.2	2x4/2/1/4/2
Krupki	-	-	103.8	106.3	-	-	4
Luki	-	-	90.6c	94.7	-	104.3	1
Mahilioú	72.74d	71.96	105.9d	99.1	71.18	100.9	2x4/2/1/4/1
Miadziel	68.69	70.31	106.4	104.9	66.86	103.9	2x4/2x2/2x4
Minsk	71.33	70.43	106.2	102.9	105.1	103.7	2x4/2/1/1/4
Minsk	-	-	-	-	72.89	72.11	4
Mscislaúl	66.89d	-	106.7d	101.7	73.73	102.9	3x1/0.25/1

FM (MHz)	*1	2	*1	2	3	4	kW
Pinsk	66.32a	67.10	104.5a	106.8	67.88	102.0	2x4/2/3x4
Salihorsk	70.22	72.23	100.3	106.7	68.57	102.8	2x1/4/2/1/4
Slonim	66.56c	67.34	106.5c	97.3	-	104.0	3x4/1/4
Smarhon	67.97c	70.13	103.6c		- 66.38	101.4	2x2/3x1
Smiatanicy	67.22b	68.00	106.3b	104.6	70.28	103.8	4
Staryja Darohi	-		100.6	103.1	-		1
Svislac	-	66.08	105.9c	98.9	68.72	96.7	2x4/0.5/4/0.1
Trokeniki	-	70.76	104.5c		-		0.5/1
Ušacy	72.65e	66.74	106.7e	101.7	70.94	102.7	3x4/1/2x4
Vasilievicy	-		102.0b	106.5	73.19		1
Viciebsk	70.67e	69.92	100.5e	99.3	72.26	105.5	2x4/2x2/2x4
Vorša	67.85e	69.14	107.0e	105.0	73.02	100.2	2/4/3x1/2
Zlobin	69.68b	71.03	105.5b	101.0	71.81	100.5	3x2/1/2x2

NB: Sites with only txs below 1kW not listed. *) incl. reg. prgrs

D.Prgr: Prgr 1 (Radyjo 1): 24h in Belarusian, Russian. Most FM txs are shared with regional broadcasting stations (see below). Txs that do not carry reg. prgrs, relay instead R. Stalica at 0340-0400 (W), 1500-1600 (W). – **Prgr 2 (Kanal Kultura):** 24h in Belarusian, Russian. – **Prgr 3 (Radyjo Stalica):** 24h in Belarusian, Russian. – **Prgr 4 (Radyus FM):** 0400-2100 in Russian.

International Service (R. Belarus): see Int. Radio section. On FM: Brest 96.4 (0.5kW), Hrodna 96.9 (1kW), Heraniony 99.9 (1kW), Svislac 100.8 (1kW), Miadziel 102.0 (4kW), Braslaú 106.6 (1kW).

Belteleradyjokampanija Regional Stations
D.Prgr: In addition to the services shown below, all stns broadcast reg. prgrs via Radyjo 1 txs (see FM table above) at 0340-0400 (W), 1500-1600 (W). All stns broadcast in Belarusian and Russian. TRK = teleradyjokampanija. **a) TRK "Brest"**, vul. Kujbyšava 64, 224030 Brest. E: radiobrestgosti@tut.by. "R. Brest" 24h on (MHz) 69.08 (Pinsk 4kW), 69.44 (Slonim 4kW), 69.68 (Brest 4kW), 94.6 (Pinsk 1kW), 101.1 (Baranavicy 0.5kW), 102.5 (Stolin 0.5kW), 104.2 (Drahicyn 2kW), 104.8 (Brest 2kW), 105.6 (Pruzany 0.1kW). – **b) TRK "Homiel"**, E: radio@tvrgomel.by. Prgr 1 ("Homiel FM") 24h on (MHz) 66.44 (Smiatanicy 4kW), 66.98 (Homiel 2kW), 68.45 (Zlobin 2kW), 69.92 (Brahin 4kW), 101.3 (Homiel 1kW), 103.0 (Zlobin 2kW), 103.3 (Smiatanicy 2kW), 105.3 (Brahin 1kW), 105.4 (Mazyr 0.5kW), 107.8 (Vasilievicy 1kW). Prgr 2 ("Homiel Plus"): 24h on Homiel 103.7MHz (0.5kW). – **c) TRK "Hrodna"**, vul. Horkaha 85, 230015 Hrodna. E: radio@tvr.grodno.by. "R. Hrodna" 24h on (MHz) 67.76 (Hrodna 4kW), 68.12 (Slonim 4kW), 68.48 (Masty 0.5kW), 71.54 (Heraniony 4kW), 72.80 (Trokeniki 0.5kW), 101.2 (Hrodna 1kW), 101.8 (Luki 1kW), 102.5 (Slonim 1kW), 102.8 (Smarhon 1kW), 104.4 (Svislac 4kW), 107.8 (Heraniony 1kW). – **d) TRK "Mahilioú"**, vul. Peršamajskaja 83, 212030 Mahilioú. E: radiomogilev@tut.by. "R. Mahilioú" 0340-1900 on (MHz) 66.02 (Babrujsk 4kW), 67.25 (Kasciukovicy 4kW), 70.10 (Mahilioú 4kW), 70.91 (Asipovicy 2kW), 96.4 (Mahilioú 1kW), 99.4 (Kasciukovicy 1kW), 100.0 (Krycaú 0.5kW), 100.4 (Mscislaúl 0.25kW), 102.3 (Asipovicy 1kW), 102.7 (Slavharad 0.25kW), 106.6 (Babrujsk 1kW), 106.8 (Techtin 0.25kW). – **e) TRK "Viciebsk"**, vul. Kamunistycnaja 8, 210602 Viciebsk. E: info@radio.vitebsk.by. "R. Viciebsk" 24h on (MHz) 67.64 (Miadziel 4kW), 68.30 (Ušacy 4kW), 71.48 (Viciebsk 4kW), 91.2 (Viciebsk 2kW), 100.6 (Hara 1kW), 102.0 (Asveja 1kW), 102.4 (Vorša 2kW), 104.0 (Bycycha 0.5kW), 104.6 (Braslaú 1kW), 105.2 (Sianno 1kW), 107.8 (Ušacy 4kW).

OTHER REGIONAL STATIONS (Gov)
Minskaya volna: vul. Ckalova 5, 220039 Minsk. "MV-Radyjo" in Russian, Belarusian 0400-2200 on (MHz) 97.4 (Minsk 2kW), 102.4 (Miadziel 1kW), 102.6 (Krupki 0.5kW), 104.2 (Barysaú 0.5kW), 104.8 (Kapyl 1kW), 105.3 (Salihorsk 2kW), 105.5 (Berazino 1kW), 105.6 (Staryja Darohi 1kW), 107.4 (Maladzecna 2kW).

OTHER STATIONS

FM	MHz	kW	Location	Station
18)	88.2	1	Hrodna	Dushevnoye R.
1A)	91.0	1	Homiel	R. BA
5)	92.2	1	Viciebsk	Pilot FM
15)	92.4	2	Minsk	R. Minsk
4)	93.2	1	Mahilioú	Pilot FM
20)	93.7	2	Minsk	Yumor FM
1A)	95.7	1	Hrodna	R. BA
1B)	96.2	1	Minsk	Melodii veka
7)	97.8	1	Viciebsk	Evropa plus Vitebsk
9)	98.4	1	Minsk	Novoye R.
11)	98.6	1	Mahilioú	Russkoye R. Mahilioú
9A)	98.7	1	Viciebsk	Novoye R.
3)	98.9	2	Minsk	Russkoye R.
6)	99.5	2	Minsk	R. Unistar
19)	100.0	1	Baranavicy	Baranavicy FM
13)	100.4	1.5	Minsk	Hit R.
4)	100.8	2	Brest	Alfa-Radio

FM	MHz	kW	Location	Station
2)	101.2	1	Brest	R. ROKS
5)	101.2	2	Minsk	Pilot FM
1A)	101.5	1	Slonim	R. BA
14)	101.7	2	Minsk	R. ONT
8)	101.8	1	Viciebsk	R. Mir Belarus
5)	102.1	1	Hrodna	Pilot FM
2)	102.1	1	Minsk	R. ROKS
6)	102.3	1	Brest	R. Unistar
9B)	102.5	1	Minsk	Narodnoye R.
2)	102.6	1	Homiel	R. ROKS
5)	102.9	1	Brest	Pilot FM
2)	103.0	1	Viciebsk	R. ROKS
2)	103.4	1	Mahilioú	R. ROKS
8)	103.6	1	Babrujsk	R. Mir Belarus
8)	104.3	2	Salihorsk	R. Mir Belarus
1A)	104.5	1	Mahilioú	R. BA
1A)	104.6	4	Minsk	R. BA
12)	104.6	1	Viciebsk	Retro FM
12)	104.7	1	Palack	Retro FM
16)	105.0	1	Hrodna	MFM
18)	105.7	2	Minsk	Dushevnoye R.
18)	106.0	1	Homiel	Dushevnoye R.
10)	106.1	1	Pinsk	Svaje R.
1A)	106.2	4	Brest	R. BA
15)	106.4	1	Viciebsk	R. Minsk
8)	106.6	1	Brest	R. Mir Belarus
9A)	106.7	1	Homiel	Novoye R.
2)	106.9	1	Hrodna	R. ROKS
8)	107.1	4	Minsk	R. Mir Belarus
17)	107.4	1	Homiel	Gomelskoye R.
4)	107.6	1	Viciebsk	Alfa-Radio
17)	107.6	1	Zlobin	Gomelskoye R.
8)	107.8	1	Mahilioú	R. Mir Belarus
4)	107.9	2	Minsk	Alfa-Radio

NB: Txs below 1kW not listed.
Addresses & other information:
1A,B) vul. Surhanova 26, 220010 Minsk E: radioba@list.ru – **2)** vul. Starazoúskaja 8a, 220002 Minsk E: info@roks.com. In Russian. – **3)** vul. Starazoúskaja 8a, 220002 Minsk E: info@rusradio.by. In Russian. – **4)** pr. Nezaleznasci 181, 220125 Minsk E: alpha@alpha.by. In Russian. – **5)** vul. K.Marksa 40, 220030 Minsk E: pilot-fm@mail.ru – **6)** pr. Nezaleznasci 4, 220050 Minsk E: radio@unistar.by. In Russian. – **7)** Maskaúski pr. 10, 210015 Viciebsk. In Russian. – **8)** vul. Kamunistycny 17, 220029 Minsk E: info@radiomir.by. In Russian. – **9A.B)** pr. Puškina 39, 220092 Minsk E: 9A) reklama@novoeradio.by, 9B) reklama@narodnoeradio.by. In Russian. – **10)** vul. Karasiova 6, 225710 Pinsk E: v_vizit@varjag.net. In Russian. – **11)** vul. Caljuskincaú 105, 212003 Mahilioú – **12)** vul. Hoholia 11, 210601 Viciebsk. Rel. Retro FM (Russia). – **13)** vul. Kamunistycny 6a, 220029 Minsk. Rel. Hit FM (Russia). – **14)** vul. Kamunistycny 6, 220029 Minsk E: fm@ont.by – **15)** zav. Kalininradski 20a, 220012 Minsk E: radio924fm@gmail.com. In Russian. – **16)** pr. Saveckaja 6, 230025 Hrodna E: grodnoplustv@gmail.com – **17)** vul. Šasiejnaja 41 , 246004 Homiel E: news@gomelradio.by – **18)** vul. K.Marksa 40, 220030 Minsk E: program@dushevnoeradio.by. In Russian. – **19)** vul. Haharina 40, 225409 Baranavicy E: pr@100fm.by. In Russian. – **20)** vul. Uschodnjaja 131, 220113 Minsk.

Radio via DTT: see National TV section

BELGIUM

L.T: UTC +1h (27 Mar-30 Oct: +2h) — **Pop:** 11.2 million — **Pr.L:** Flemish, French, German — **E.C:** 50Hz, 230V — **ITU:** BEL

FLANDERS Pop: 6.4 million — **Pr.L:** Flemish

VLAAMSE RADIO EN TELEVISIEOMROEP (VRT) (Pub) Flemish (Dutch) Language Network
Public Sce. grants by Flemish government.
✉ VRT, August Reyerslaan 52, B-1043 Brussels ☎+32 2 741 3111 🖷 +32 2 734 9351 **W:** vrt.be **E:** info@vrt.be
L.P: General Director Media: Peter Claes; Radiomanager: Els Van de Sijpe
Regional Centres Radio 2:
Antwerpen: Jan Van Rijswijcklaan 157, 2018 Antwerpen ☎+32 3 2479111 🖷 +32 3 2378282 **E:** redactieantwerpen@radio2.be
Vlaams-Brabant: Dikke Lindelaan 2, 1020 Brussels ☎+32 2 7414111 🖷 +32 2 4780800 **E:** redactievlaamsbrabant@radio2.be
Oost-Vlaanderen: Martelaarslaan 232, 9000 Gent ☎+32 9 2247256 🖷 +32 9 2254903 **E:** redactieoostvlaanderen@radio2.be

West-Vlaanderen: Doorniksesteenweg 241B, 8500 Kortrijk ☎+32 56 247311 ▤ +32 56 221358 **E:** redactiewestvlaanderen@radio2.be
Limburg: Via Media 2, 3500 Hasselt ☎+32 11 249611 ▤ +32 11 242436 **E:** redactielimburg@radio2.be

FM (MHz)	R1	R2	RK	SB	M	kW
Antwerpen	-	-	92.0	-	-	1
Brussegem	-	90.7	-	-	-	2
Brussels	-	-	-	88.3	1
Diest	-	92.4	-	-	-	1
Egem O.+W.-Vl.	95.7	-	90.4	102.1	101.5	50/50/50/40
Egem O.-Vl	-	98.6	-	-	-	50
Egem W.-Vl.	-	-	-	100.1	-	50
Genk	99.9	97.9	89.9	101.4	102.0	20/20/20/40/40
	-	-	-	-	93.0	3
Gent	-	-	-	94.5	-	0.5
Leuven	98.5	-	-	88.0	-	0.5/0.5
N'kerken Waas	-	89.8	-	-	-	1
Schoten	94.2	97.5	96.4	100.9	89.0	20/20/3/40/20
St-Pieters-Leeuw	91.7	93.7	89.5	100.6	97.0	50/50/50/50/2
Veltem	-	88.7	-	-	94.8	1/1

+3 txs under 1kW

R1=Radio Een (information and music), **R2**=Radio Twee (light & popular music), **RK**=Radio Klara (classical music), **SB**=Studio Brussel (youth stn), **M**=MNM (hit music stn)
Radio 2 Regional prgrs: 0500-0700 (M-F), 1100-1200 (M-F), 1500-1700 (daily) on FM
Sporza: replaces normal R.1 prgrs during sports events **W:** sporza.be
D.Prgr: Night prgr on all frequencies.
DAB: 223.936MHz all services plus Sporza, MNM hits, Klara continuo, and nieuws+.
Ann: R1:"Radio Een", R2: "Radio Twee", RK: "Klara", SB: "Studio Brussel", M: "MNM"

COMMERCIAL NETWORKS:
NB: For further information on all radio stns in Flanders visit **W:** radioinvlaanderen.info

FM	Mhz	kW	Location	Station
1)	87.6	3	Oostende	Nostalgie
1)	88.0	2	Kortrijk	Nostalgie
1)	88.1	1	Brugge	Nostalgie
2)	88.3	1	Oost-Vleteren	QMusic
2)	88.6	3	Gent	QMusic
4)	88.9	1	Diksmuide	Club FM
3)	89.1	1	Tongeren	Joe FM
5)	89.6	2	Brugge	VBRO
3)	90.6	5	Turnhout	Joe FM
6)	91.3	3	Brugge	Topradio
3)	92.2	3	Dendermonde	Joe FM
2)	92.2	2	Herentals	Qmusic
7)	92.7	2	Kortrijk	R. Maria
3)	92.8	1	Gent	Joe FM
1)	92.8	1	Beringen	Nostalgie
3)	93.5	2	Sint-Niklaas	Joe FM
3)	93.5	2	Geel	Joe FM
3)	93.5	1	Bree	Joe FM
4)	93.6	5	Egem	Club FM
13)	95.1	1	Turnhout	Family R.
3)	95.5	1	StPietersLeeuw	Joe FM
3)	95.6	1	Brussegem	Joe FM
2)	95.8	1	Veltem	Qmusic
7)	96.3	2	Gent	R. Maria
3)	96.7	2	Mechelen	Joe FM
1)	96.9	1	Sint-Truiden	Nostalgie
9)	98.0	1	Antwerpen	Minerva
1)	98.1	10	Brussel	Nostalgie
1)	98.2	1	Egem	Nostalgie
10)	98.8	3	Brussel	FM Brussel
11)	99.0	1	Mechelen	Randstad
2)	99.2	10	Antwerpen	Qmusic
13)	99.3	1	Bree	Family R.
6)	99.4	4	Gent	Topradio
3)	99.7	1	Leuven	Joe FM
2)	100.0	1	Wuustwezel	Qmusic
8)	100.2	2	Antwerpen	FG DJ R.
1)	101.0	20	Oost-Vleteren	Nostalgie
2)	102.5	1	Brussel	QMusic
2)	102.5	50	Genk	Qmusic
12)	102.6	2	Leuven	Hit FM
13)	102.6	1	Eeklo	Family R.
14)	102.7	3	Aalst	City Music
15)	102.7	2	Brugge	Exclusief
4)	102.8	1	Brussel	Club FM

FM	Mhz	kW	Location	Station
16)	102.8	1	Gent	Zen FM
1)	102.9	50	Schoten	Nostalgie
2)	103.0	20	Egem	Qmusic
1)	103.0	1	Bree	Nostalgie
2)	103.1	50	StPietersLeeuw	Qmusic
3)	103.3	1	Diest	Joe FM
2)	103.3	1	Brugge	Qmusic
3)	103.4	10	Brussel	Joe FM
3)	103.4	5	Antwerpen	Joe FM
3)	103.4	20	Genk	Joe FM
1)	103.5	20	Gent	Nostalgie
4)	103.6	1	Oostende	Club FM
3)	103.7	1	Wuustwezel	Joe FM
3)	103.7	3	Lommel	Joe FM
1)	103.7	2	Sint-Niklaas	Nostalgie
1)	103.7	3	Leuven	Nostalgie
14)	103.8	2	Gent	City Music
13)	103.8	1	Geel	Family R.
13)	103.8	1	Hasselt	Family R.
3)	104.1	50	Egem	Joe FM
4)	104.1	2	Hasselt	Club FM
7)	104.2	5	Leuven	R. Maria
3)	104.2	1	Aalst	Joe FM
17)	104.2	2	Antwerpen	Crooze FM
1)	104.2	1	Overpelt	Nostalgie
5)	104.5	2	Oostende	VBRO
6)	104.5	1	Poperinge	Topradio
1)	104.5	1	Mechelen	Nostalgie
1)	104.5	1	Turnhout	Nostalgie
1)	104.6	2	Geel	Nostalgie
7)	104.6	2	Antwerpen	R. Maria
6)	104.7	1	Hasselt	Topradio
1)	104.8	3	Aalst	Nostalgie

+ 273 stns below 1kW

Addresses and other information
1) Katwilgweg 2, 2050 Antwerpen **W:** nostalgie.eu – **2)** Medialaan 1, 1800 Vilvoorde **W:** qmusic.be – **3)** Medialaan 1, 1800 Vilvoorde **W:** joe.be – **4)** Stationsstraat 68, 9900 Eeklo **W:** clubfm.be – **5)** Jan Miraelstraat 24, 8000 Brugge **W:** vbro.be – **6)** Nekkerputstraat 150, 9000 Gent **W:** topradio.be – **7)** Postbus 5045, 5201 GA 's-Hertogenbosch, Netherlands **W:** radiomaria.be – **8)** Koningin Astridplein 38 bus 3 - 2000 Antwerpen **W:** radiofg.com – **9)** Wandeldijk 20, 2050 Antwerpen **W:** radio-minerva.be – **10)** Eugène Flageyplein 18 bus 18, 1050 Elsene **W:** fmbrussel.be – **11)** Hogeweg 211 2800 Mechelen **W:** randstad.fm – **12)** KAAI.16, Scheepvaartkaai 16 A bus 8, 3500 Hasselt **W:** hitfm.be – **13)** Leopoldlaan 98c, 9900 Eeklo **W:** familyradio.be – **14)** Geraardsbergsestraat 21, 9300 Aalst **W:** city-music.be – **15)** Emile Bethunelaan 5, 8200 Brugge – **16)** Einde Were 150, 9000 Gent **W:** zenfm.be – **17)** Diksmuidelaan 173, 2600 Berchem **W:** crooze.fm

WALLONIA Pop: 4.1 million — **Pr.L.:** French, German

RADIO-TÉLÉVISION BELGE DE LA COMMUNAUTE FRANCAISE (R.T.B.F.) (Pub.)
French Language Network
Public sce. Grants by French Parliament.
▤ Cité de la Radio-Television, B-1044 Brussels ☎+32 2 737 2111 ▤ +32 2 737 4357 **W:** rtbf.be
L.P: Admin. Gen: Jean-Paul Philippot. Dir. Radio: Francis Goffin
Regional & Local Centres: Bruxelles: Reyerslaan 52, 1044 Brussel **Charleroi:** Passage de la Bourse, 6000 Charleroi **Liège:** Palais des congrès, 4020 Liège **Hainaut:** Rue du gouvernement 15, 7000 Mons **Namur-Brabant-Wallon:** Av. Golenvaux 8, 5000 Namur **Verviers:** Rue de Verviers 203, 4821 Andrimont **Luxembourg:** Parc des Expositions, 6700 Arlon

MW	kHz	kW	Prgr	MW	kHz	kW	Prgr
Wavre	621	300	Ext.Svce	Houdeng	1125	9	2

FM (MHz)	1	2	3	4	5	kW
Anderlues	93.4	92.3		99.1	96.6	0.6/40/40/40
Bruxelles		99.3	91.2	93.2	88.8	3/40/1/?
Léglise	96.4	91.5	94.1	87.6		10/10/10/10
Liège	96.4	90.5	99.5	95.6	92.5	5/40/40/13/0.1
Malmédy	89.2	91.6				1/0.1
Marche	93.3	95.2				0.5/4
Profondeville	102.7		92.8	90.8		25/10/10
Tournai	106.0	101.8	102.6	104.6	90.6	25/30/30/30/?
Verviers	91.3	103.0			87.9	1/3/0.1
Wavre	96.1	97.3			101.1	10/35/50

+ many txs under 1kW

Network 1 (Première – information & musique)
Network 2 (Vivacité – light music)
Reg. Prgrs: W 0530-0800, 1200-1300, 1600-1800; Fri 1800-2100 – R. Hainaut (Mons) on 92.3/101.8MHz – R. Liège 90.5/103.0/94.6/89.1/89.4MHz – R. Namur on 97.3/92.8/89.3/91.5/89.4/90.2MHz – R. Bruxelles on 93.2MHz
Local Prgrs: R. Verviers (Radiolène) on 103.0MHz
Network 3 (Musique 3 – classical music)
Network 4 (Classic 21 – oldies & rock classics)
Network 5 (Pure FM – youth stn)
DAB: 225.648MHz
Ann: "Vous écoutez La Première, Vivacité, Musique trois, Radio 21, Pure FM, Classic 21"

EXTERNAL SERVICE: RTBFi
See International Broadcasting section

BELGISCHES RUNDFUNK-UND FERNSEHZENTRUM DER DEUTSCHSPRACHIGEN GEMEINSCHAFT (BRF)
German Language Network (Pub)
Grants by RDG-Rat (German speaking community council)
✉ Kehrweg 11, B-4700 Eupen ☎+32 87 59 1111 🖷+32 87 591199
W: brf.be **E:** info@brf.be
Regional: ✉ Blvd. Reyers 52, B-1044 Brussels – Malmedyer Str. 25, B-4780 St. Vith **LP:** Dir.: Toni Wimmer

FM	MHz	kW	Ch.	FM	MHz	kW	Ch.
Lüttich	88.5	50	1	Eupen	94.9	0.05	1
Lüttich	91.0	0.5	2	Brussel*	95.2	2	1
Auel	92.2	0.16	1	Eupen	98.4	1	2
Lontzen	93.2	5	2	Recht	104.1	20	2
Recht	94.9	5	1	Raeren	105.9	0.1	2

*: broadcasts joined prgrs of Deutschlandfunk and BRF
Ann: "Hier ist der Belgischer Rundfunk"

COMMERCIAL NETWORKS:
NB: For further information on all radio stations in Wallonia visit **W:** tuner.be/#cat-3

FM	Mhz	kW	Location	Station
14)	87.6	1	Ath	Sud R.
14)	88.2	1	Charleroi	Sud R.
11)	88.3	5	Bouillon	NRJ
11)	88.7	1	Arsimont	NRJ
1)	88.9	1	Fauquez	Bel RTL
10)	89.2	1	La Louvière	R. Nostalgie
14)	90.0	1	Tournai	Sud R
10)	92.3	1	Verviers	R. Nostalgie
11)	92.7	1	Malmédy	NRJ
7)	92.9	1	Bastogne	Fun R.
2)	94.4	1	Bütgenbach	100.5 Das Hitradio
9)	94.7	5	Bouillon	Must FM
10)	95.0	1	Liège	R. Nostalgie
15)	95.6	1	Houdeng	Twizz
12)	97.1	4	Bouillon	R. Contact
14)	97.6	1	Braine-le-cte	Sud R.
12)	98.0	2	Bütgenbach	R. Contact (DE)
1)	99.0	2	Bouillon	Bel RTL
7)	99.0	1	Liège	Fun R.
10)	100.0	5	Brussel	R. Nostalgie
4)	100.1	1	Liège	Equinoxe FM
1)	100.2	1	Limal	Bel RTL
10)	100.4	4	Namur	R. Nostalgie
2)	100.5	20	Eupen	100.5 Das Hitradio
10)	100.5	2	Couvin	R. Nostalgie
10)	100.7	2	Dinant	R. Nostalgie
8)	100.9	2	Liège	Maximum FM
12)	101.6	5	Marche	R. Contact
12)	101.6	1	Verviers	R. Contact
1)	101.7	2	Namur	Bel RTL
1)	101.7	1	Couvin	Bel RTL
1)	101.8	50	Meix Le Tige	Bel RTL
1)	101.9	1	Dinant	Bel RTL
14)	102.0	2	Mons	Sud R
12)	102.2	10	Brussel	R. Contact
12)	102.2	5	Charleroi	R. Contact
12)	102.2	1	Liège	R. Contact
12)	102.3	5	Mons	R. Contact
10)	102.4	1	Arlon	R. Nostalgie
12)	102.5	1	Houffalize	R. Contact
11)	103.2	10	Vlessart	NRJ
15)	103.2	2	Liège	Twizz
1)	103.4	5	Mons	Bel RTL
7)	103.5	1	Charleroi	Fun R.
1)	103.6	1	Ath	Bel RTL
1)	103.6	50	Liège	Bel RTL
11)	103.7	1	Brussel	NRJ
6)	104.0	1	Brussel	Foo Rire
1)	104.0	2	Charleroi	Bel RTL
10)	104.1	1	Huy	R. Nostalgie
1)	104.3	15	Brussel	Bel RTL
11)	104.3	5	Namur	NRJ
12)	104.5	1	Wavre	R. Contact
12)	104.6	1	Marche	R. Contact
7)	104.7	1	Brussel	Fun R.
12)	104.7	2	Malmédy	R. Contact
12)	104.7	5	Namur	R. Contact
2)	104.8	3	Sankt Vith	100.5 Das Hitradio
12)	104.8	1	Virton	R. Contact
7)	105.5	1	Louvain-L-N	Fun R.
12)	106.2	1	Florzé	R. Ourthe Amblève
3)	106.3	2	Tubize	R. Antipode
11)	106.7	1	Bastogne	NRJ
5)	106.8	1	Malmédy	Est FM
8)	106.9	1	Aywaille	Maximum FM
10)	100.2	50	Saint-Hubert	Radio Nostalgie
11)	104.5	5	Liège	NRJ
12)	107.0	1	Eupen	R. Contact (DE)
7)	107.5	1	Arlon	Fun R.
2)	107.6	1	Honsfeld	100.5 Das Hitradio
10)	107.6	5	Bouillon	R. Nostalgie
11)	107.7	1	Tournai	NRJ
12)	107.8	1	Libramont	R. Contact

+ many stns below 1kW
Addresses:
1) Avenue Georgin 2, 1030 Bruxelles 02-3376911 **W:** belrtl.be – **2)** Kehrweg 11, B-4700 Eupen ☎+32 87 591259 🖷 +32 87 591249 **W:** hitradioworld.fm – **3)** Boîte postale 2, 1348 Louvain-La-Neuve ☎ 010-451110 🖷 010-451717 **W:** antipode.be – **4)** Rue Montagne St Walburge, 261, 4000 Liège **W:** equinoxefm.be – **5)** Malmédy – **6)** Avenue d'Hougoumont, 2, 1180 Bruxelles **W:** foorirefm.be – **7)** Av. Telemaque 33, 1190 Bruxelles ☎ 02-3457575 **W:** funradio.be – **8)** 22 Rue de la Chaudronnerie, 4030 Grivegnée **W:** maximumfm.be – **9)** BP20, 1360 Perwez ☎ 081-655469 **W:** mustfm.be – **10)** Quai au Foin 55, 1010 Bruxelles ☎ 02-2270450 🖷 02-2231455 **W:** nostalgie.eu – **11)** Chaussée de Louvain 467, 1030 Bruxelles ☎ 02-5137575 🖷 02-5114859 **W:** nrj.be – **12)** Avenue des Croix de Guerre 94, 1120 Bruxelles 02-2442711 🖷 02-2442710 **W:** radiocontact.be and derbestemix.be (DE) – **13)** Rue Armand Binet 35B, 4140 Rouvreux (Sprimont) – **14)** 42, rue de la chaussée de Mons, 7000 Mons ☎ 065-401010 🖷 065-401011 **W:** sudradio.net – **15)** Rue des Francs, 79, 1040 Bruxelles **W:** twizz.be

Military Stations:
AMERICAN FORCES NETWORK, SHAPE
✉ Box 7, 7010 SHAPE. (APO AE 09700) ☎+32 65 44 41 21
L.P: Officer-in-charge: Cpt. G. Martel. Broadc. Superv: SFC C. Kubicek. Chief Eng: René Libre
Stations: Kleine Breugel 106.2MHz 0.1kW, Brussels 101.7MHz 0.9kW, SHAPE 104.2/106.5MHz 4kW, Florennes 107.7MHz 0.1kW, Chievres 107.9.
D.Prgr: 24h on 101.7/104.2/107.7MHz. Own prgrs Mon-Fri 0500-0800, 1400-1700; Sat 0800-1200. Other times rel. AFN Europe.
AFN-2: 24h easy listening stereo prgr on 106.5MHz

BRITISH FORCES BROADCASTING SERVICE
Stations: BFBS 1 Casteau 107.6MHz 0.05kW, SHAPE 107.7MHz
✉ Wentworth B., Listnstr., D-32049 Herford, Germany
D.Prgr: rel. BFBS Germany

BELIZE

L.T: UTC -6h — **Pop:** 301,000 — **Pr.L:** English, Spanish — **E.C:** 60Hz, 110/220V — **ITU:** BLZ

PUBLIC UTILITIES COMMISSION (PUC)
✉ PO Box 300, 41 Gabourel Lane, Belize City ☎+501 2234938 🖷 +501 2236818 **W:** puc.bz **E:** info@puc.bz **LP:** Chairman: John Avery. Dir. Telecomm: Kingsley Smith.

FM	MHz	kW	Name and loc. (Hrs of tr usually 24h)
5)	88.9	40	Love FM, Ladyville
1)	90.5	0.25	Positive Vibes R, Belize City
6)	91.1	13	Krem FM, Ladyville
2)	92.3		Reef R, San Pedro
8)	93.7	0.5	My Refuge Christian R, Roaring Creek

FM	MHz	kW	Name and loc. (Hrs of tr usually 24h)
3)	94.3		Our Lady of Mount Carmel R, Benque Viejo
4)	94.5		People's R. (Da Beat), Belize City
5)	95.1		Love FM, Belize City
5)	95.9		Estéreo Amor, Belize City
6)	96.5	6	Krem FM, Belize/Carmelita/Cattle Landing
7)	97.1		Integrity R., Belize City
5)	97.5		Estéreo Amor, Belize City
5)	99.5		More FM, Belize City
8)	100.5	0.2	My Refuge Christian R, Belize City
6)	101.1	1	Krem FM, Dangriga
9)	101.3		R. Emanuel, San Pedro
1)	102.9		Positive Vibes R, Belmopan
10)	103.1		Suga City R.
11)	104.5		Faith FM, Pine Ridge
11)	104.5		Faith FM, Punta Gorda
12)	105.9		Wave 105.9, Belmopan
5)	107.1		More FM, Belmopan

+ several other local FM stns

Addresses and other information:
1) Belize City. **E:** vibesradiogm@gmail.com – **2)** San Pedro **W:** threee-fradio.com – **3)** Our Lady of Mount Carmel High School, Benque Viejo del Carmen. **W:** carmelradio.org **F.PI:** 1 kW FM transmitter at Pine Ridge – **4)** 3321 Central American Boulevard, Belize City **E:** modula-tion945@yahoo.com – **5)** 7145 Slaughterhouse Road, PO Box 1865, Belize City. **FM:** Belize City 95.1MHz + 9 FM repeaters. **W:** lovefm.com – **6)** 3304 Partridge Str, c/o P.O. Box 15, Belize City. **W:** krembz.com – **8)** P. O. Box 275, Belmopan. **W:** myrefugebelize.org – **9)** San Pedro, Ambergris Caye – **10)** 30 Stadium St, Orange Walk Town **W:** scrs.bz – **11)** PO Box 145, Santa Elena, Cayo District. **W:** faithfmbelize.com – **12)** Belmopan **E:** waveradio105_9@yahoo.com

BENIN

L.T: UTC +1h — **Pop:** 9 million — **Pr.L:** French + 18 ethnic — **E.C:** 50Hz, 220V — **ITU:** BEN

HAUTE AUTORITÉ DE L'AUDIOVISUEL ET DE LA COMMUNICATION (HAAC)
BP 3567, Ave. de la Marina, Face Hôtel du Port, 01 Cotonou ☎+229 21311743 ▤ +229 21311742 **W:** haacbenin.org

OFFICE DE RADIODIFFUSION ET TÉLÉVISION DU BÉNIN (ORTB, Gov.)
01 B.P. 366, Cotonou ☎+229 21360047 **W:** ortb.bj **E:** ortb@intnet.bj **L.P:** DG: Hamado Ouangraoua. Chief Tech. Sces: Anastase Adjoko.
Regional ▤ B.P. 128, Parakou ☎+229 23611096
FM: Cotonou 94.7 10kW, Parakou 89.4/92.5MHz 2kW.
Radio Nationale: from Cotonou in French/ethnic.
N. in French: 0615MF, 0800SS, 1200SS, 1215MF, 1930, 2115.
R. Regionale Parakou: in French/ethnic.
(Cotonou & Parakou carry the same programme between 1900-2000).
Atlantic FM, Cotonou: 0700-2300 on 92.2MHz.
Ann: "Ici R. Bénin, Office de Radiodiffusion et Télévision du Bénin, émettant de Cotonou". "Ici Parakou, Office de Radiodiffusion et Télévision du Bénin, station regionale" **IS:** Bénin Tam-Tam

Other stations:
R. Adja Ouèrè FM, Cotonou: 92.6/100/100.6/107.6MHz – **R. Afrique Espoir,** Porto-Novo: 99.1MHz – **Benin Culture,** Porto-Novo: 98.4MHz – **CAPP FM,** Cotonou: 99.6MHz – **R. Carrefour,** Cotonou: 90.4MHz – **Cité Savalou Culture FM,** Cotonou: 87.8MHz – **Deeman R,** Parakou: 90.2MHz – **FM Ahémé,** Possotome: 99.6MHz – **FM Alakétou,** Value: 95.8MHz – **FM Monts Kouffé,** Bassila: 103MHz – **FM Noon Sina,** Bembereke: 90.8MHz – **FM Oré Ofé,** Tchetti: 102.1MHz – **Gerddes FM,** Cotonou: 89.5 MHz – **Golfe FM,** Cotonou: 105.7MHz **W:** eit.to/golfefm.htm – **La Voix de la Lama,** Porto-Novo: 103.8MHz – **La Voix de l'Islam,** Cotonou: 91.2MHz – **R. Immaculee Conception** (Rlg.): Djougou 89.1MHz, Natitingou 93.1MHz, Parakou 93.3MHz, Cotonou 98.7MHz, Bembèrèkè 100.8MHz, Bohicon 100.9MHz, Allada 101.3MHz, Dassa-Zoumey 107.3MHz – **R. Liéma,** Cotonou: 104MHz – **R. Planète,** Cotonou: 95.7MHz – **R. Maranatha,** Cotonou: 103.1MHz **W:** eit.to/RadioMaranatha.htm – **R. Allodalome,** Cotonou: 97.4MHz – **R. Star,** Cotonou: 94.3/96.3MHz – **R. Tokpa,** Cotonou: 104.3MHz – **R. Tonassé,** Covè: 107.6MHz – **R. Wekè,** Cotonou: 107MHz – **R. Rurale** stns in Tanguiéta 90, Ouessè 97.7, Dogbo 100, Ouaké 101 & Banikoara 104.2MHz – **BBC African Service:** Cotonou 101.7MHz – **RFI Afrique:** Cotonou 90.0MHz, Parakou 106.1MHz.
Trans World R, Parakou: 1566kHz 100kW 0315-0545, 1725-2230. **W:** twrbenin.com (For details see International Radio section)

BERMUDA (UK)

L.T: UTC -4h (13 Mar-6 Nov: -3h) — **Pop:** 64,000 — **Pr.L:** English — **E.C:** 60Hz, 115/230V — **ITU:** BER

BERMUDA BROADCASTING CO. LTD. (Comm.)
4 Fort Hill Road, Prospect, Devonshire DV 02, PO Box HM 452, Hamilton HM BX ☎ +1 441 295 2828 ▤ +1 441 295 4282 **W:** bermudabroadcasting.com **L.P:** Owner: Chris Perry. Acting CEO: David Hills, News Dir.: Gary Moreno. News Producer: Gary Foster Skelton, CEN: Earlston Chapman.
FM: Ocean 89: 89.1MHz 1kW – **Power 95 FM:** 94.9MHz 2kW – **Moody Radio (Rlg.):** 105.1MHz 2kW – **Gov. Emergency Broadc. Stn:** 100.1MHz

DEFONTES BROADCASTING CO. LTD. (Comm.)
P.O. Box HM 1450 (**studios:** 94 Reid Str.) Hamilton HM FX ☎ +1 441 292 0050 ▤ +1 441 295 1658 **E:** info@vsb.bm **W:** vsb.bm **L.P:** Op. mgr.: Lynn Jefferson. Op. consult.: Kenneth De Fontes.
MW: BBN Bible Broadcasting Network 1280kHz 1kW 24h (rlg.). (May move to FM early 2016)
FM: Mix 106 FM: 106.1MHz 2.5kW: 24h (CHR)
F.PI: The planned take-over of Defontes late 2015 by KG2 Ltd. was cancelled. The former '1450 AM Gold' may be relaunched on FM. The company is expected to be renamed in 2017.

INTER-ISLAND COMMUNICATIONS (Comm.)
49 Union Square Mall, Hamilton ☎ +1 441 297 1076 ▤ +1 441 296 7680 **E:** feedback@hott1075bermuda.bm **W:** hott1075bermuda.bm and magic1027bermuda.com. **L.P:** CEO: Glenn Blakeney. **FM: Magic 102.7:** 102.7MHz – **Hott 107.5** 107.5MHz

LTT BROADCASTING LTD. (Comm.)
P.O. Box 1564 HMGX, Hamilton HMEX ☎ +1 441 700 9810 ▤ +1 441 292 1593 **E:** iriebermuda@gmail.com **L.P:** Leo Trott
FM: Irie FM: 98.3MHz

HARPER DIGITAL ENTERTAINMENT LTD. (Comm.)
12 Whale Bay Rd, Southhampton SB03 ☎ +1 441 232 0699 **E:** info@vibe103.com **W:** vibe103.com
FM: Vibe 103 FM: 103.3MHz

BHUTAN

L.T: UTC +6h — **Pop:** 2 million — **Pr.L:** Dzongha, Sharchhop, Lhotsam(Nepali), English — **E.C:** 50Hz, 220V — **ITU:** BTN

BHUTAN BROADCASTING SERVICE (Corp.)
P.O. Box 101, Thimphu ☎ +975 2 322866/322533/323071 2 +975 2 323073 **W:** bbs.bt **E:** request@bbs.com.bt
L.P: Exec. Dir: Sonam Tshong.Tech. MD: Pema Choden, Dir: Dorji Wangchuk. Prgr. Dir: Tashi Dhendup. News Dir: Thinley Tobgye
SW: 6035kHz 100/50kW

FM(MHz)	Main	R.Dz	FM(MHz)	Main	R.Dz
Bangtar	90.0	96.0	Samtse-Saurani	98.0	96.0
Bumthang	90.0	92.0	Samtse-Tendu	93.0	90.0
Chukha-Dala	98.0	96.0	Sarpang	98.0	96.0
Chukha-Pachu	90.0	93.0	Thimphu	88.1	90.0
Dagana	90.0	88.1	Thimphu	96.0	98.0
Haa	98.0	90.0	Thonphu	96.0	98.0
Lamsorong	90.0	93.0	Trashigang	90.0	88.1
Mongar	90.0	88.1	Trongsa	93.0	96.0
Ngalamdung	98.0	90.0	Tsirang	92.0	88.1
Panbang	90.0	93.0	Wangdue	98.0	96.0
Paro	92.0	93.0	Zhemgang	88.1	90.0
Phuentsholing	92.0		Zorchen Tranhiyangtse	98.0	96.0

NB: R.Dz = R. Dzongkha 24h on FM only.

Main D.Prgr: on SW: 0000-1300(s/on & s/off varies), **on FM** 24h
English: Daily 0800-1200. 1800-2100 English Music/Repeat broadcast **N:** Daily: 0800, 0900,1000, 1100; **English Request Show:**Sun 0915;**UN Radio Prgr:** Thurs 0815; **Sharchhop:** 0000-0400,1200-1400 (N:0100,0200,0300,1200,1300), 2100-2400 Music/Repeat broadcast; **Lhotsam** (Nepali): Daily 0400-0800, 1400-1600 (N:0400,0500,0600,07 00,1400,1500), 1600-1800 Music/Repeat broadcast.
V. by QSL card. 15 min prgr details req. Rp. (2 IRCs)

Other FM Stations
Kuzoo FM, + P.O. Box 419, Thimphu **W:** kuzoo.net **DPrgr:** 24h in English on 104.0MHz and Dzongkha on 105.0MHz – **Radio Valley,**

+ P.O. Box 224/225, Thimphu **W:** radiovalley.bt **DPrgr:** 0200-1630 in E on 99.9MHz – **Sherubtse FM** 94.7MHz (including College Campus at 1300-1500)– **Centennial Radio** Thimphu 101.0 MHz – **Radio High** Thimphu 92.7 MHz (alliance with India's Big FM netw.) – **Radio Waves** Thimpu 88.8 MHz (Music Stn)

BOLIVIA

L.T: UTC -4h — **Pop:** 10.1 million — **Pr.L:** Spanish, Quechua, Aymara — **E.C:** 50Hz, La Paz 110/220V, Santa Cruz 220/380V — **ITU:** BOL — **Int. dialling code:** +591

AUTORIDAD DE FISCALIZACIÓN Y CONTROL SOCIAL DE TELECOMUNICACIONES Y TRANSPORTES (ATT)
Dirección Oficina Central: ✉Calle 13 Calacote No. 8260 La Paz ☎2 2772266 🖷2 2772299 **E:** informaciones@att.gov.bo **W:**att.gob.bo **LP:** Superintendente: Lic. Jóse Antonio Morales
Office in Santa Cruz: Calle Prolongación No 29, Edifico Bicenteario Tercer Piso, Santa Cruz de la Sierra ☎3 120587 🖷3 1220978
Office in Cochabamba: Av. Ayacucho No 460, enter Calama y Jordan, edifico Santa Isabel Piso 3, Cochabamba ☎4 458182
Office in Tarija: Calle General Trigo No 474, Edifico Colonial Center Piso 1, Of. 7-8-9, Tarija ☎4 4666484
NB: ‡ = inactive, ± = varying freq., † = irregular, RPO – Radioemisoras de los Pueblos Originarios, RCB – Radio Comunitarias de Bolivia

MW	kHz	kW	Station, location, h of tr
LP77)	540		Radiodifusora Victoria, La Paz
LP03)	‡560	15	R. El Mundo, La Paz
LP01)	580	10	R. Panamericana, La Paz: 1000-0300 (Sun 1100-0100)
CH01)	600	10	R. ACLO, Sucre: 0800-0200
LP35)	600	1	Radioemisoras del Recobro, La Paz
SC55)	600		R.Familiar, Santa Cruz
LP02)	620	10	R. San Gabriel, El Alto
TA12)	640		R. ALCO, Tarija: 0850-0130
LP11)	650	15	R. Dif. Integración, El Alto: 0930-0200
LP150)	660		R. Taller de Historia Oral Andina, La Paz
SC10)	660	1	R. ABC, Santa Cruz: 0900-0100
LP147)	670		R. Comunitaria Cadena Provincial, Jihuacuta
PO28)	680		R. ACLO, Potosí: 0850-0130
LP27)	680	5	R. Andina, La Paz: 0900-0300
LP155)	680	10	R.Jallalla Coca, Chulumani
LP116)	700		R. Pacha Kamasa, El Alto (RCB): 0955-0100 (Sat -1805, Sun -1615)
PO40)	710	10	R. Pío XII, Siglo Veinte: 0830-0230
LP06)	720	10	R. La Cruz del Sur, La Paz: Sat 1300(Sun 1200)-2100
LP05)	730	2.5	R. Yungas, Chulumani: 0900-1700, 2000-0100
LP151)	740		R. Pueblo de Dios, La Paz
LP07)	760	50	R. Fides, La Paz: 1045-0100
CO02)	770	5	R. Cosmos, Cochabamba: 1100-0300
SC44)	780		R. Sol, Santa Cruz: 24h
LP08)	800	5	R. Play, La Paz
LP10)	820	10	R. Altiplano Advenir, La Paz: 24h
LP75)	840	3	R. Atipiri, El Alto: 1045-0030 (Sun: 2300)
SC03)	850	5	R. María, Montero: 0900-0100
LP12)	860	10	R. Nueva America, La Paz
CO86)	860		R. FM Colores, Cochabamba
LP42)	880		R. Nueva Jacha, El Alto: -0200
SC39)	880		Rdif. Oriente, Santa Cruz
CH31)	900		R. Tomina la Frontera, Villa Tomina
TA01)	900	0.25	R. LV Nacional, Tarija: 0100-2300
LP36)	900	5/0.1	La Popular, La Paz: 1000-0100
PO39)	900		R. Dios es Amor Universal, Potosi
CO33)	‡902	1	R. Central Misionera, Cochabamba:1100-0100
CO85)	920		R. Dios es Amor Universal, Cochabamba
CH11)	920	3	R. Encuentro, Sucre: 0900-0100, Sat: 2300-0200, Sun: 1000-2200
LP65)	920	1	R. San Andres de Topohoco, Topohoco: 0900-0330
LP88)	920		R. Bartolina Sisa, El Alto
SC46)	920		R. El Mana, Santa Cruz
CH13)	940	1	R. Chuquisaca XXI, Sucre
LP13)	940		R. Metropolitana, La Paz: 0930-0430, Sat: 1100-0530 Sun: 1000-0400
SC53)	940		R. Pan de de Vida, Santa Cruz
PO02)	960	1	R. Kollasuyo, Potosí: 1000-0400(Sun -0200)
SC04)	960	10	R. Santa Cruz, Santa Cruz
LP43)	960	1	R. Huayna Potosí, Milluni
CO04)	980	3	R. Esperanza, Cochabamba: 0900-0100(Fri -0400), Sat 1000-0300(Sun -2230)
LP14)	980	2.5	R. Mar, La Paz: 1000-0200
OR41)	980		R.dif. Concordia, Oruro

MW	kHz	kW	Station, location, h of tr
CH26)	980		R. La Bohemia, Sucre
PO30)	990		R. Municipal de Colcha "K"
CO84)	1000		FM Unica, Cochabamba
SC33)	1000	1	Rdif. del Oriente, Santa Cruz: 0930-0400, Sat: 0900-0330, Sun: 1130-0430
OR03)	1000	10	R. Bahá'í de Bolivia, Oruro
LP115)	1000		R. LV del Arrebatamiento, Guaqui
LP44)	1000	1	R. Taypi, La Paz: 1000-0400
LP15)	1020	10	R. Illimani - R.Patria Nueva, La Paz: 0900-0400
CO57)	1020		R. Illimani - R.Patria Nueva, Cochabamba
CO59)	1020		R. Illimani - R.Patria Nueva, Valle Alto
CO60)	1020		R. Illimani - R.Patria Nueva, Tarata
CO61)	1020		R. Illimani - R.Patria Nueva, Chapare
CO70)	1020		R. Illimani - R.Patria Nueva, Colomi
BE21)	1020		R. Illimani - R.Patria Nueva, Trinidad
BE22)	1020		R. Illimani - R.Patria Nueva, San Borja
BE24)	1020		R. Illimani - R.Patria Nueva, Riberalta
PA10)	1020		R. Illimani - R.Patria Nueva, Cobija
PO07)	1020		R. Illimani - R.Patria Nueva, Potosi
PO08	1020		R. Illimani - R.Patria Nueva, Catavi
PO32)	1020		R. Illimani - R.Patria Nueva, Unica
PO33)	1020		R. Illimani - R.Patria Nueva, Villazon
PO34)	1020		R. Illimani - R.Patria Nueva, Llica
PO35)	1020		R. Illimani - R.Patria Nueva, Tupiza
PO35)	1020		R. Illimani - R.Patria Nueva, Uyuni
SC40)	1020		R. Illimani - R.Patria Nueva, Santa Cruz
SC41)	1020		R. Illimani - R.Patria Nueva, Vallegrande
SC42)	1020		R. Illimani - R.Patria Nueva, Camiri
SC43)	1020		R. Illimani - R.Patria Nueva, Yapacani
CO62)	1020		R. Illimani - R.Patria Nueva, Kami
CO68)	1020		R. Illimani - R.Patria Nueva, Independencia
CH21)	1020		R. Illimani - R.Patria Nueva, Sucre
CH32)	1020		R. Illimani - R.Patria Nueva, Sopachuy
CH35)	1020		R. Illimani - R.Patria Nueva, Azurduy
CH36)	1020		R. Illimani - R.Patria Nueva, Machareti
TA13)	1020		R. Illimani - R.Patria Nueva, Tarija
TA14)	1020		R. Illimani - R.Patria Nueva, Bermejo
TA16)	1020		R. Illimani - R.Patria Nueva, Villamontes
TA18)	1020		R. Illimani - R.Patria Nueva, Yacuiba
TA19)	1020		R. Illimani - R.Patria Nueva, Entre Rios
OR29)	1020		R. Illimani - R.Patria Nueva, Oruro
OR36)	1020		R. Illimani - R.Patria Nueva, Caracolla
OR37)	1020		R. Illimani - R.Patria Nueva, Huanuni
LP89)	1020		R. Illimani - R.Patria Nueva, Achacachi
LP90)	1020		R. Illimani - R.Patria Nueva, Carabuco
LP91)	1020		R. Illimani - R.Patria Nueva, Copacabana
LP92)	1020		R. Illimani - R.Patria Nueva, Caranavi
LP93)	1020		R. Illimani - R.Patria Nueva, Chulumani
LP94)	1020		R. Illimani - R.Patria Nueva, Guaqui
LP124)	1020		R. Illimani - R.Patria Nueva, Huarina
LP126)	1020		R. Illimani - R.Patria Nueva, Topohoco
LP127)	1020		R. Illimani - R.Patria Nueva, Vilaque
LP128)	1020		R. Illimani - R.Patria Nueva, Taraco
LP129)	1020		R. Illimani - R.Patria Nueva, Tapichullo
LP130)	1020		R. Illimani - R.Patria Nueva, Tiawanaku
LP132)	1020		R. Illimani - R.Patria Nueva, Qhurpa
LP133)	1020		R. Illimani - R.Patria Nueva, Asunta
LP135)	1020		R. Illimani - R.Patria Nueva, Escoma
LP136)	1020		R. Illimani - R.Patria Nueva, Desaguadero
LP140)	1020		R. Illimani - R.Patria Nueva, Corocoro
CH19)	1030		R. Mojocoya AM (RCB), Mojocoya:1000-0200
OR26)	1030	3	R. de los Pueblos Originarios (RCB) , Orinaca
CO48)	1030	3	R. Independencia (RCB), Independencia
CO51)	1030		R. 24 de Junio (RCB) Totora
BE20)	1030	3	R. Comunitaria Riberalte (RCB), Riberalta
CH18	1040		R. 12 de Marzo (RCB), Tarabuco
CO20)	1040	0.25	R. Sipe Sipe, Quillacollo
OR42)	1040		R. Qaqachaca (RCB), Qaqachaca
TA11)	1040		R. Comunitaria Libertad (RCB), Villamontes
SC37)	1040		R. Nanduti (RCB), Camiri
SC30)	1040		R. San José (RCB), San José de Chiquitos
SC38)	1040		R. San Julián (RCB), San Julián
LP45)	1040	1	R. Bolivianíssima, La Paz
OR14)	1040	0.25	R. Atlántida, Oruro: 1100-2400
CH33)	1050		R. Comunitaria, Villa Huaca
OR27)	1050	3	R. Sabaya (RCB) Sabaya
PO26)	1050		R. Caiza D (RCB), Caiza D
PO27)	1050		R. Colquechaca (RBC), Colquechaca
LP95)	1050		R.Qhana Amazonía, Caranavi
OR01)	1060	1.5	R. Noticias, Oruro: 1000-2200, 0200-0600
CH02)	1060	1	R. Dif. Colosal, Sucre: 0900-0300
LP38)	1060	10	R. Presencia de Dios, La Paz:

MW	kHz	kW	Station, location, h of tr
CH30)	1080		R. Comunitaria, Sopachuy
CH34)	1080		R. Comunitaria, Juana Azurduy
CH40)	1080		R. Comunitaria, Carama
CO83)	1080		R. Cultura, Cochabamba
LP76)	1080		LV de la Mayoria (RCB), Caranavi
CO63)	1090		R. Cultura , Cliza
LP110)	1090		R. Comunitaria Pachakuti
CO76)	1100		R. Raqaypampa (RPO), Raqaypampa
OR06)	1100	1	R. Universidad de Oruro: 1100(Sun 1200)-2300
LP29)	1100		R. Cultural Chaka, Pucarani: 0900-1300, 2030-0130
LP153)	1100		Universal Radio Conciencia, El Alto
CO53)	1120		R. El Porvenir, Tiquipaya
LP96)	1120		R. Celestial, El Alto
LP97)	1120		R. Wiñay Khantatt, Tiawuanaku
CO69)	1140		R. San Isidro, Colomi
CO82)	1140		FM Fiesta, Cochabamba
LP98)	1140		R. Sol Poder de Dios, La Paz: 0930-0300
LP99)	1140		R. Sol Poder de Dios, Huanca: 0930-0300
LP50)	1150	0.3	R. Guaqui, Puerto de Guaqui
SC11)	1160	5	R. Centenario "La Nueva", Sta. Cruz
CO08)	1160	3/1	R. RTC Deportiva, Cochabamba: 10454-2330
CH03)	1160	1	R. Nuevo Mundo, Sucre: 1000-0300
LP33)	1160	10	R. Continental, La Paz: 0930-2400
LP18)	1180	1	R. Ingavi, Viacha: 1000-0200 (Sun 1100-2400)
CO09)	1180	1	R. Independencia, Quillacollo
OR40)	1180		R. Sajama Estero, Oruro
LP122)	1190		R. Comunitara, Guaqui
LP100)	1200		Cuarzo Comunicaciones, La Paz
LP115)	1200		R. Carlos Palenque, La Paz
LP117)	1200		R. Maria de la Candelaria, Copacabana
SC12)	1200	5	R. Oriental, Santa Cruz
CO10)	1200	0.25	R. 24 de Noviembre, Arani
CO81)	1200		R. San Simón, Cochabamba
OR31)	1200		R. Capital, Oruro
CO80)	1220		R. Progreso La Luz del Alba, Cochabamba
LP19)	1220	1	R. Nueva Splendid, La Paz: 0800-0200
LP134)	1220		R. La Asunta, Asunta
LP143)	1220		R. La Voz Cristiana, Achacachi
OR09)	1220	1	R. Batallión Topátar, Oruro 1055-0100
PO29)	1240		R. Indoamerica, Potosi
TA03)	1240	2	R. Los Andes, Tarija: 1000-2200
LP51)	1240		Rdif. Achocalla, Achocalla
LP131)	1240		R. Nueva Generación, Qhurpa
LP154)	1240		R, Zaráte Willka, La Paz
PA01)	1250	0.1	R. Frontera, Cobija: 1000-1800
CH04)	1250	2.5	R. La Plata, Sucre: 1000-0200
LP146)	1250		R. Comunitaria Compi, Capilaya
CO54)	1260		R. LV de la Esperanza, Quillacollo
LP137)	1260		R. SERVIR, Caranavi
OR20)	1260	10	R. Nacional de Huanuni, Hunanuni: 0930-0200, Sat 1100-1800(Sun -1600)
SC52)	1260		R. Amboro, Santa Cruz
SC54)	1260		R. Sararenda, Camiri
TA21)	1260		R. Dios es Amor Universal, Tarija
LP125)	1270		R. Comunitaria Norte, Puerto Acosta
CO65)	1280		R. Comunitaria del Sur, Cochabamba
LP68)	1280		R. Comunitaria Ondas del Titicaca, Huarina
LP142)	1280		R. Altar de Dios, Achacachi
TA17)	1280		R. Fronera, Yacuiba
LP148)	1290		R. Comunitaria Alaxpacha, Canaviri
OR12)	1290	1	Radiodifusoras Minería, Oruro
PO31)	1290		R. Tomas Katari de America, Ocuri
CH05)	1300	2.5	R. Loyola, Sucre: 1000-2400, Sun 1015-0200
CO72)	1300		R. San Simón, Cochabamba
SC16)	1300	1	R. Fuerzas Armadas, Sta. Cruz
LP23)	1300	15/6	R. Sol Poder de Diós, El Alto: 0930-0300
BE18)	1300	5	R. Bandera Beniana, Trinidad
OR39)	1300		Sistem de Comuncacion "Perez", Oruro
PO38)	1300		R. Fides, Potosi
CO14)	1310	10	R. San Rafael, Cochabamba: 0900-0200
CH25)	1320		R. Sucre, Sucre
LP53)	1320		R. Comunitaria Tawantinsuyo, Taraco
LP111)	1320		R. Em. Septima Voz, Achocalla
LP121)	1320		R. Comunitaria La Lumberia, La Paz
CO79)	1340		TV Sist. de Comunicacione Mundial, Cochabama
SC17)	±1340	1	R. Grigotá, Santa Cruz
LP39)	1340	0.5	R. Copacabana, Copacabana: 1000(Sun 1100)-0200
LP40)	1340	0.5	R. Jach'a Suyu, Corocoro: 1000-1630, 2000-0100
LP145)	1340		R. Comunitaria La Voz de Valle, Sococoni
LP152)	1340		R. La Mision, La Paz
CH06)	1350		R. America, Sucre: 1000-0400
CO05)	1350	2.5	R. Cochabamba "CBA", Cochabamba: 1030-0200
LP113)	1350		R. Comunitario Inti, Contorno/Viacha
LP123)	1350		R. Llacxa, Achocalla
CO15)	±1355	0.25	R. Armonía, Cliza (n.f.: 1350)
LP16)	1360	5	R.Cordiale, El Alto: 0800-0100
LP103)	1360		R. Em. Tunupa, Tiawuanaku
OR32)	1360		Cadena Coral, Oruro
PO37)	1360		R. La Cruz del Sur, Potosi
SC47)	1360		R. 24 de Septiembre, Santa Cruz
SC49)	1360		R. TV Salesiana, Yapacani
CO16)	1370	0.15	R. Libertad, Cliza
CH22)	1380		R. Global, Sucre
LP104)	1380		R. Maria, La Paz
LP141)	1380		R. TV Minera Matilde, Carabuco
SC51)	1380		R. Maria, Santa Cruz
CO34)	1380	1.5	R. Bandera Tricolor, Cochabamba: 1100-0300
OR33)	1380		R. Horizontes, Huanuni
TA06)	1380	0.5	R. Luis de Fuentes, Tarija: 0930-0400
CO50)	1390		R. Andina (RCB), Pongo Khasa
CH20)	1400		R. Antena 2000, Sucre
CO71)	1400		R. Tricolor, Villa Tunari
LP25)	‡1400	5	R. Nacional de Bolivia, La Paz: 0900-0200
OR38)	1400	0.25	R. Atlantida, Oruro
LP105)	1420		R. Omasuyos Andina, Achacachi
LP114)	1420		R. Creo en Milagros, Murillo
TA05)	1420	1.5	R. Guadalquivir, Tarija: 0900-0100
CO18)	1420	1	R. Centro, Cochabamba: 1030-2300 (Sun 1100-0000)
CH15)	1420	1	R. Real Audiencia, Sucre: 0900-0200
SC50)	1420		R. Comunitaria, José Ballivian
CH39)	1440		Sistema de Comunicaciones Horizontes, Sucre
LP26)	1440	1	R. Batallón Colorados, La Paz: 1100-0100(Sun -2400)
LP139)	1440		R. Comunitaria Eco Saywani, Carabuco
SC21)	1440	2/1	R. Yaguary, Vallegrande: 1000- 0200
CO42)	‡1440	0.25	R. Bolivia, Cochabamba
CO74)	1440		LV de Juno (RCB), Tiraque
BE02)	1440		R. Dif. Tropico, Trinidad
OR13)	1440	1	R. Em. Bolivia, Oruro
CO39)	1450	0.5	R. Magnal, Capinota
LP106)	1460		R. Plenitud de Vida, El Alto
LP138)	1460		R. Jiwasa, Carabuco
CO78)	1460		R. Canal de Television Quillacollo
CH29)	1470	1	R. Integración, Padilla
CO44)	1470		R. Morochata (RCB), Morochata
LP109)	1470		R. Em. Ayni, Corapata
CH24)	1480		R. Charcas-Mundial, Sucre
LP108)	1480		LV de los Andes, Carabuco
PO12)	1480	0.1	R. Cadena Sur, Potosi
CO32)	1480	1/0.8	R. Chiwalaqui, Vacas: 0900-1400, 2100-0100
CO40)	1480		R. Domingo Savio, Independencia
CO66)	1480		R. Bendita Trinidad y Espirito Santo, Cochabamba
PA09)	1480		R. Bendita Trinidad y Espirito Santo, Cobija
SC48)	1480		R. Bendita Trinidad y Espirito Santo, Santa Cruz
LP58)	1480		R. Amor de Diós, El Alto
LP107)	1480		R. Comunitaria Waley, Deaguadero
OR15)	1480	1	R. San José, Oruro
LP144)	1490		R. Wiñay Jatha, El Alto
CO77)	1500		R. Litoral, Cochabamba
OR43)	1500		R. Jacinto Rodriguez, Ciudad
SC25)	1500	1	R. Sagrado Corazón, Mineros
TA15)	1500		R. Universidad Juan Misael Saracho, Villamontes
LP31)	‡1500	5/1	R. Chuquisaca, El Alto
CH38)	1520		R. Universidad Juan Misael Saracho, Sucre
CO64)	1520	1	R. la Chiwana, Cochabamba
CO67)	1520		R. Salesiana, Kami
CO73)	1520		R. Rural, Tarata
LP59)	1520		R. La Luz del Tiempo, El Alto
LP120)	1520		R. San Pedro, Tiawuanaku
PO10)	1520	0.25	R. Litoral, Llica
CH38)	1520		R. Universidad Juan Misael Saracho, Sucre
BE07)	1530	0.5	R. Em. Ballivián, San Borja
CH37)	1540		R. Comunitaria Rio Chico, Sucre
LP34)	1540	0.8	R. Sariri, Escoma: 1000-1300, 2200-0200
LP112)	1540		R. Comunitario Tutuka, Vilaque
LP67)	1540		R. Bendita Trinidad y Espirito Santo, El Alto
LP28)	1550	10	R. Caranavi, Caranavi: 0930-1800, 2200-0200
LP149)	1560	5	R. Luz del Mundo, La Paz
OR19)	1560	1	R. Occidental, Oruro
CO27)	1560	0.5	R. Urkupiña, Quillacollo: 1000-2400
BE23)	1570		R. Pedro Ignacio Muiba
LP101)	1570		R. Comunitaria Tawantinsuyo, Taraco
CH28)	1580		R. Contacto, Sucre: 0830-2300, Sat/Sun.: 1800
CO75)	1580		LV del Valle, Valle Alto
OR35)	1580		R. Comunitaria Jacinto Rodrìguez, Caracolla

MW	kHz	kW	Station, location, h of tr
SC29)	1580	1	R. Adonai, Santa Cruz: 1000-0300
LP62)	1580		R. El Fuego del Espíritu Santo, El Alto: 1000-2400
TA07)	1580	3	R. Bermejo, Bermejo
TA20)	1580		R. Magazine Tarija, Tarija
CO24)	1590	1	R. Wayana Songo, Pongo K´asa
LP61)	1590		R. Kollasuyo Marka, Tiawanaku
CO28)	1600	0.5	R. P.C.A., Punata
LP63)	1600	1	R. LV del Espíritu Santo, El Alto

SW	kHz	kW	Station, location, h of tr
CO29)	3310	10	R. Mosoj Chaski, Cochabamba: 0900-1300, 2100-0100
CH08)	3390	1	R. Em. Camargo "LV del Valle Cinteño", Camargo
BE10)	4409	0.5	R. Eco, Reyes
BE04)	4451	1	R. Santa Ana, Santa Ana del Yacuma:
BE08)	±4699		R. San Miguel, Riberalta: 1030-0330
PO15)	±4717	1	R. Yatun Ayllu Yura, Yura (n. 4715)
LP74)	4782		R. Tacana, Tumupasa
PO19)	±4796		R. Lípez, Uyuni: 1000-2330
SC36)	4865	5	R. Logos, Santa Cruz
BE02)	†4958		R. Tropico, Trinidad: 1030-0300
SC30)	† 5580	0.25	R. San José, San José de Chiquitos: 1100-1700, 2100-0200±
PO40)	±5952	5	R. Pío XII, Siglo Veinte: (n. 5955)
LP15)	6025	10	Rede Illimani - R. Patria Nueva, La Paz: 0930-0300
SC02)	±6054	3	R. Cultural Juan XXIII, San Ignacio de Velasco: 1030-2300 (n. 6055)
LP07)	6055	10	R. Fides, La Paz
LP01)	±6105	10	R. Panamericana, La Paz
SC04)	6135	10	R. Santa Cruz, Santa Cruz: 1100-0200
LP07)	9625	15	R. Fides, La Paz

Addresses and other information

NB: Whenever listed, Casilla addresses should preferably be used for mailing purposes.

ERBOL (Educación Radiofónica de Bolivia), Calle Ballivián 1323, 4° piso (Cas. 5946), La Paz ☎ 2 2324606, 232 4768 🖹 2 2391985 **W:** erbol.combo – Pte.: Jorge Trias S.J. Secr. Ejecutivo: Jorge Aliaga Murillo

UNESBO (Unión de Emisoras Sindicales de Bolivia), Yanacocha 689, La Paz ☎1 2341881 Pte: Jorge Bustillo Burgos

BE00 (BENI)
BE02) Avenida Panamericana Carretera a Santa Crtuz km 2½ - EPARU, Trinidad ☎3 4635300 **W:** Facebook: Radio Tropico **E:** radiodifusorastropico@yahoo.com – **FM:** 92.2 MHz – **BE04)** Calle Sucre 250, Santa Ana de Yacuma – **BE06)** Sucre 320, Guayaramerín – **BE07)** Oruro 52, San Borja ☎3 8483020 – **BE08)** Calle Tomás Daney s/n, Barrio San José, Riberalta ☎3 9523363 🖹3 8523268 - **FM:** 99.1MHz "Centenario" – **BE09)** Av Selim Majuli (Correo Central), San Borja, Pcia BalliviáN – **BE10)** Reyes, Pcia Ballivián **E:** gonzaloeco@hotmail.com – **BE12)** Calle Nicanor Gonzalo Salvatierra 249, Riberalta - **FM:** 91.1MHz – **BE13)** Ballivián s/n, San Ignacio de Moxos – **BE14)** Cas 395, Guayaramerín – **BE15)** Calle Beni s/n, Guayaramerín – **BE16)** Plaza Fr Martín Baltasar de Espinosa, Santa Ana del Yacuma – **BE18)** Calle Santa Cruz esq Mamoré s/n, Trinidad – **BE19)** Avenida Primero de Mayo esquina Loreto, Guayaramerin **E:** ninafelima@hotmail.com – **BE20)** Riberalta, Prov Vaca Diez – **BE21)** Trinidad – **BE22)** San Borja – **BE23)** Calle Isiboro esquina Machupo, Trinidad **W:** apcbolivia.org/Medios/muiba.aspx - **FM:** 89.5 MHz – **BE24)** Riberalta

CH00 (CHUQUISACA)
CH01) Guillermo Loayza N° 274 esq Vicente Donso (Zona Mercado Campesino), (Cas 538), Sucre ☎4 6441665 Prgrs in **Quechua** except **Spanish** 1330-2030 0900-0200 **W:** aclo.org.bo **E:** aclo@aclo.org.bo – **FM:** 101.5 MHz – **CH02)** Calle San Alberto N° 19 (Cas 335), Sucre ☎4 6442888 🖹4 6444433 **W:** colosal.com.bo **E:** fundacionradiotv@colosal.com.bo – **FM:** 90.7MHz – **CH03)** Junin N° 841 (Cas 25), Sucre – **CH04)** Abaroa 422, Cas 276, Sucre ☎4 6453231 **W:** facebook.com – Radio La Plata Sucre - **FM:** 92.1MHz – **CH05)** Calle Ayacucho 161, Sucre ☎4 6453677 🖹4 6442555 **E:** loyola@radiofides.com - **FM:** 98.3MHz "Onda Joven" – **CH06)** Calle Guillermo Loayza 377, Mercado Campesino, Sucre ☎4 46446574 🖹4 46444445 – **W:** radioamericatk.com.bo **E:** info@radioamericatk.com.bo – **FM:** 97.5 MHz – **CH08)** Cas 09, Camargo, Pcia Nor Cinti **W:** radiocamargo.cjb.net – **FM:** 100.0MHz – **CH09)** Alcaldía Municipal, Padilla **CH11)** Calle Loa No 41, Sucre ☎6 441300 **W:** encuentroradio.com – **FM:** 95.9MHz – **CH13)** Calle Kantuta 3 Ed. Canal 15, Barrio Ferroviario, Zona San Matias, Sucre ☎6 461157 🖹6 458321 **E:** pulsartv@bolivia.com– **CH15)** Calle Avarioa 537, Sucre – **CH16)** Sucre – **CH17)** Sucre – **CH18)** Comunidad de Tarabco, Prov Yamparáez – **CH19)** Comunida de Mojocoya, Prov Zudáñez – **CH20)** Calle Lima Pampa 72, Esq. Elidora Ayllón, Sucre ☎6 440 606 **E:** contacto@radioantena2000.com – **FM:** 89.1 MHz – **CH21)** Sucre – **CH22)** Barrio Petrolero, Sucre ☎6 442900 **W:** radioglobalbolivia.com – **FM:** 106.7 MHz – **CH23)** Calle Eduardo Berdecio

568, Sucre. **W:** radiohorizonte.boliviastreaming.com – **FM:** 91.1 MHz – **CH24)** Calle Eduardo Berdecio N° 522, Sucre ☎6 461 112 **W:** facebook.com – Radio Charcas-Mundial **E:** radiocharcasam1480@hotmail.com - **FM:** 96.4 MHz – **CH25)** Sucre **W:** radiosucre1320.com – **FM:** 105.9 MHz – **CH26)** Sucre – **CH28)** Calle Bustillos N° 322, Sucre ☎4 6435205 **W:** radiocontactosucre.com **E:** direccion@radiocontactosucre.com – **CH29)** Padilla – **FM:** 98.5 MHz – **CH30)** Sopachuy – **CH31)** Villa Tomina – **CH32)** Sopachuy – **CO33)** Huacaya – **CH34)** Azurduy – **CH35)** Azurduy – **CH36)** Machareti – **CH37)** Sucre – **CH38)** Sucre – **CH39)** Sucre – **CH40)** Sucre

CO00 (COCHABAMBA)
CO02) Av Heroinas O-0467, Centro Nor Oeste, (Cas 1092), Cochabamba ☎4 4250422 🖹4 4251173 **Quechua:** 0930-1030, 0000-0200 1100-0300 - **FM:** 95.1MHz "Fides" – **CO04)** Calle Loa Final s/n, Ivirganzama, (Cas 5716), Cochabamba. ☎4 4343085 **W:** Facebook: R.Esperanza **Quechua:** 8 hours daily - **FM:** 100.3MHz – **CO05)** Calle 25 de Mayo 230 entre Bolívar y Sucre (Cas 5500), Cochabamba ☎4 4251504 🖹4 4251561 **E:** ragarobol@yahoo.es - **FM:** 104.3MHz "Gaviota" – **CO07)** Cochabamba – **CO08)** Lanza esq Ecuador N-0261 (Cas 846), Cochabamba ☎4 4257289 🖹4 4241414 **W:** web.supernet.com.bo/radiortc **E:** radiortc@yahoo.com – **CO09)** Cochabamba esq Heroes del Chaco, Quillacollo (or Cas 108), Cochabamba – **CO10)** Arani – **CO14)** Calle Calama E- 0315 (Cas 546), Cochabamba ☎4 4256563 🖹4 250 522 **Quechua/Aymara:** 0900-0200 - **FM:** 92.1MHz – **CO15)** Calle 6 de Agosto 11, Cliza – **CO16)** Calle Santa Cruz 4, Cliza – **CO18)** Calle Ecuador casi Avenida Ayaccucho No 115 (Cas 839), Cochabamba ☎4 4251434 **W:** grupocentro.com.bo **E:** contactos@grupocentro.com.bo - **FM:** 96.3 & 106.7 MHz – **CO20)** Plaza de Granos 44, Quillacollo - **FM:** 99.1MHz – **CO24)** Cas 1151, Cochabamba ☎4 8119295 **W:** sdb.bo **E:** japaricio@sdb.bo – **CO27)** A. Suarez Miranda final s/n, Zona Norte, Cochabamba ☎4 260 661 **E:** radioam1560@hotmail.com – **CO28)** Ayacucho 138, Punata – **CO29)** Calle Abaroa S-0254 (Cas 4493), Cochabamba **E:** rmchaski@bo.net ☎4 4220651 🖹4 4251041 – **CO32)** Misuk'ani (Cas 80), Vacas ☎4 223089 🖹4 255390 **E:** chiwalak@entelnet.bo Prgrs mainly in **Quechua** 0900-1400, 2100-0100 – **CO33)** Av Petrolera Km 0.5, Cochabamba – **CO34)** Av. Oquendo No 560 entre Paccieri y Federeico Blanco (Cas 3655), Zona Muyurina, Cochabamba ☎4 520202 **E:** latripple999@yahoo.com **Quechua:** 1000-1200 - **FM:** 99.9MHz "La Triple" – **CO39)** Augusto Larrain, Capinota. – **CO40)** Independencia, Prov. Ayopaya (Av. Papa Paulo No 0982, Muyurina, Cochabamba) **W:** radiosavio.galeon.com **E:** radiosavio@hotmail.com – **FM:** 98.1 MHz – **CO42)** Calle Calama 0-0135, Cochabamba – **CO43)** Calle Junín 309, Tiraque, Prov Arani – **CO44)** Calle Tumusla esquina Ecuador No 310, Plazuela Cobija, area Oeste (Cas 1986) Cochabamba ☎4 589366 🖹4 589377 **W:** ceprabolivia.org **E:** cepra@supernet.– **CO48)** Independencia – **CO50)** Calle Tumusla esquina Ecuador No 310, Plazuela Cobija, area Oeste (Cas. 1986) Cochabamba ☎4 589366 🖹4 589377 **W:** ceprabolivia.org **E:** cepra@supernet.com.bo - **FM:** 101.1 MHz – **CO51)** Totora, Prov Carrasco – **CO53)** Calle Pablo Jaimes 188, Tiquipaya, Prov Quillacollo – **FM:** 90.5MHz – **CO54)** Calle Montenegro N° 234 Zona: Villa Paraiso, Cochabamba ☎4 448647– **CO57)** Cochabamba – **CO59)** Valle Alto – **CO60)** Tarata – **CO61)** Chapare – **CO62)** Kami – **CO63)** Cliza – **CO64)** Junin casi Aroma, Edif. De la Federacion de Campesinos - 5° piso, Cochabamba ☎4 4584389 **W:** radiolachiwana.org **E:** radiolachiwana@gmail.com - **FM:** 107.9 MHz – **CO65)** Heroinas esquina 16 de Julio, Cochabamba ☎4 661203 **W:** http//radiocomunitariadelsur.com **E:** info@radiocomunitariadelsur.com – **CO66)** Av. Circunbalacion, Calle Atahuallpa, Cochabamba **W:** facebook.com – Radio Bendita Trinidad Bolivia – **CO67)** Kami – **CO68)** Independencia – **CO69)** Colomi – **CO70)** Colomi – **CO71)** Villa Tunari – **CO72)** Campus Universitaria, Prolongaión Jordán s/n, Cochabamba – **FM:** 104.7 MHz – **CO73)** Tarata – **CO74)** Tiraque – **CO75)** Valle Alto – **CO76)** Raqay Pampa – **CO77)** Cochabamba – **CO78)** Cochabamba – **CO79)** Cochabamba – **CO80)** Cochabamba – **CO81)** Campus Universitario. Prolongación Jordán s/n, Cochabamba – **CO82)** Cochabamba – **CO83)** Cochabamba – **CO84)** Cochabamba – **CO85)** Cochabamba – **CO86)** Cochabamba

LP00 (LA PAZ)
LP01) Edificio 16 de Julio, P.9, Of 902, El Prado, La Paz **W:** panamericana-bolivia.com **E:** pana@panamericana.bo ☎2 2334271 **N:** «El Panamericano» relayed by many stns – **LP02)** Pza de la Cruz N° 100 – Av.Bolivia, Comunidad Charapaqui Colpani Villa Adela, (C.P. 4792) El Alto ☎2 2832544 **W:** radiosangabriel.org.bo **E:** info@radiosangabriel.org.bo Prgrs in **Aymara** exc Sp & Quechua 1400-1430, Sat 2100-2130 – **LP03)** Av. La Bandera No 1462, V.Pabón, La Paz – **LP05)** Calle Nuñez del Prado s/n, Chulumani (Cas 4535, La Paz) ☎2 2203672 **Aymara. E:** radioyungas@qhana.org.bo – **FM:** 92.1MHz – **LP06)** Calle Nicaragua 1759(Cas 1408), La Paz ☎2 220541 🖹2 243337 **W:** radiocruzdelsur.com **E:** contactos@radiocruzdelsur.com – **LP07)** Calle Jenaro Sanjinés 799, Centro (Cas 9143), La Paz ☎2 406363 🖹2 406332 **W:** radiofides.com **E:** sistemas@radiofides.com - **N:** «La hora del país», relayed by many stns, at 1100, 1630, 2230, 0130 – **LP08)** Calle 24 de Calacoto, Edif.

TorreCesur, Piso 4 Of 402,La Paz ☎ 2 790743 🖹 2 770292 **W:** radioplay-bolibvia.com **E:** info@radioplaybolivia.com – **LP10)** Calle Abdon Saavedra N° 2110 casi esquina Fernando Guachalla, (Cas 8631), Sopocachi) La Paz ☎2 426742 redadvento.org/proyectos/radio-altiplano – **LP11)** Calle 2 No 95 P.3 entre Av. 6 de Marzo y Jorge Carrasco, Ceja – El Alto (Cas. 312472, La Paz) ☎2 810048 🖹2 810048 **W:** radio-integracion.com **E:** integracionam@yahoo.es **Aymara:** 0830-1200 0900-0130 – **LP12)** Calle Abdón Saavedra 1990 (or Cas 2431), La Paz ☎ 2356622 – **LP13)** Juan de la Riva 1527 (Cas 8704), Zona Central, La Paz ☎2 203339 **W:** rtpbolivia.com **E:** contactosrtp@rtpbolivia.com – **LP14)** Calle Jenaro Sanjinés 799 esqquina Calle Sucre, Centro, La Paz ☎2 406 590 🖹2 406740 **E:** editor@radiofides.com – **LP15)** Av Camacho 1485, Edificio Ministerio Informaciones P 6, La Paz ☎2 2200282 🖹2 200390 **W:** patrianueva.bo **E:** radio@patrianueva.bo – **LP16)** Av Panamericana 93, Zona Alpacoma, El Alto (Cas 6412, La Paz) ☎2 310796 – **LP18)** Calle General Lanza 93, Viacha, Provincia Ingavi – **LP19)** Calle Máx paredes, Zona Garita de Lima N° 408. 1er Piso, La Paz. ☎2 2452422 Prgr. in Aymara 0800-0200 **W:** cercacomuni-caciones.com **E:** radiosplendid@ cercacomunicaciones.com **LP23)** Calle Calama s/n entre Humahuaca y Montenegro, Zona Norte, La Paz ☎2 286983 **W:** poderdedios.com – **FM:** 90.1 MHz – **LP25)** Av. Tumusla No 639, 2° piso (or Cas 2532), Zona 14 de Septiembre, La Paz ☎2 453945 🖹2 434 211 **W:** lafolklorisima1035.com.ar – **FM:** 103.5/107.7 MHz – **LP26)** Av. Saavedra del Ejército, Zona Miraflores, La Paz ☎2 149439 **Aymara:** 1100-1200 – **LP27)** Calle Francisco de Chirino No 1080, Miraflores (Cas. 12413), La Paz– **LP28)** Liga de Oración en medio Mundial, Av Civica S/N, Caranavi, (Cas. 266, La Paz) 🖹2 823 2239 **W:** Facebook: Radio Television Caranavi **E:** rtc@hotmail.com – **FM:** 92.1 MHz – **LP29)** Casilla 204, Colegio Don Bosco, Pucarani Prgrs mainly in **Aymara**, but also in Spanish 0900-1300, 2030-0130 – **LP31)** Ave. Saavedra No 1145, Edif. Holanda P10 Of. 1002, Zona Miraflores (Cas 3123), La Paz ☎2 246158 – **LP33)** Av República 870 Esq. Quintanilla Zuazo, Zona Pura Pura, La Paz ☎2 463470 – **LP34)** Colegio Don Bosco, Parroquia Escoma, Escoma (Cas 204, La Paz) **E:** escoma@caoba.entelnet.bo ☎🖹2 135336 – **FM:** 104.7MHz – **LP35)** Calle Murillo 1379, La Paz ☎2 350588 – **LP36)** Calle Panama N° 1153 Shopping Miraflores Pido 4 Oficina 1, Zona Miraflores sobre la Plaza Uyuni, La Paz ☎2 222368 **W:** radiogentebolivia.com **E:** sistemapopular@hotmail.com – **FM:** 88.9 MHz – **LP38)** Plaza Alonso de Mendoza 500 5° piso del Edificio Santa Anita, Ofic 501 (or Cas 4973), La Paz ☎2 390542 **W:** loyolas.edu.bo/univ/index.php **E:** radioeco@loyola.edu.bo – **LP39)** Ca Gral. Hugo Ballivián No 11 Copacabana, Prov. Manco Capac La Paz ☎2 341920 **W:** apcbolivia.org/Medios/copacabana.aspx – **FM:** 95.7 MHz – **LP40)** Plaza 15 de Agosto, Corocoro, Prov Pacajes **E:** tricolor-jachasuyu@hotmail.com ☎2 830192 Prgr In **Aymara & Sp** 1000-1630, 2000-0100 – **LP42)** Av Buenos Aires 712, 1er Piso Oficina 1, El Alto ☎2 2454618 **W:** Facebook: Radio Jacka 800 AM **E:** radiiojacha@hotmail.com – **LP43)** Avenida del Ejercito No 30, Viacha ☎2 800208 – **FM:** 101.9 MHz– **LP44)** Ca Policarpio Eyzaguirre N° 1156 entre Padre L. Bertonio y Calatayod, Zona Callampaya (Cementerio), La Paz ☎2 2461224 🖹2455319 **W:** radiotaypi.com **E:** radio-taypi@hotmail.com – **LP45)** Calle Viacha # 360 e/ Avenida Manco Kapac y Av. América, Barrio Churubamba , La Paz – **LP46)** Comunidad Contorno Letania, Camino a Collana 30, Letania, Prov Ingavl – **LP47)** Av Manco Kapac 50, Tiawanaku, Prov Ingavi – **LP50)** Calle Costa Rica No 1229, Miraflores, La Paz ☎2 220401 – **LP51)** Av. Franco Valle No 87, Achocalla, Prov. de Murillo – **LP53)** Plaza 16 de Julio s/n, Cantón Taraco, Taraco ☎8 114157 – **FM:** 105.3 MHz – **LP54)** Calle Noel Kempf 140, El Alto, La Paz – **LP55)** Tiawanaku, Prov Ingavi – **LP56)** Calle Yanacocha 70, Achacachi – **LP57)** Plaza 4 de Octubre, Rosario, Corapata, Prov Los Andes – **LP58)** Calle Noaviri 2105, Zona Amor de Dios, El Alto ☎2 223916 – **LP59)** Raúl Salmón 92 entre Calle 4 y 5, Zona Ceja, El Alto (Cas. 8631, Murillo, La Paz) ☎2 2825169 **E:** radiomisionglobal@yahoo.es– **LP60)** Plaza Principal, Cantón Villa Iquiaca, Vilaque, Prov Los Andes – **LP61)** Calle C No 57, Zona V. Tejda, El Alto ☎2 822470 – **LP62)** Avenida Panoramica No. 5018, Zona Faro Murillo , El Alto ☎2 2813504 **W:** cesi.pastoralcl – **LP63)** El Alto – **LP64)** Calle Topater 830, La Paz – **LP65)** Plaza Principal, Topohoco, Prov. Pacajes – **LP66)** Ca Jotan Save 3132 entre Bluniel, Zona 16 de Julio, La Paz – **LP67)** Calle Pascoe N° 2614-B, Zona 16 de Julio, La Paz ☎78937570 **W:** Facebook: Radio Bendita Trinidad Bolivia – **LP68)** Ca Batalla de Huarina No 255, Huarina ☎71977644 – **LP74)** Tumupasa, Prov de Iturralde – **LP75)** Av. Grigota N° 1514, Urb. Atipiris 8 Sector Ex-Tranca Senkata, La Paz ☎2 2882066 **W:** cecopi.org/atipiri.php **E:** info@cecopi.org – **LP76)** Caranavi, Prov Caranavi – Prgr. in Aymara – **LP77)** Calle 11 de Calacote No 7837, La Paz.– **LP88)** Calle S.Rodriguez No 1155, Zona 16 de Febrero, Distrito 4 Carretera a Laja antes del Puente Seke, Zona 16 de Febrero ☎73700079 **E:** barto-linasisa920am@gmail.com – **LP89)** Achacachi – **LP90)** Carabuco – **LP91)** Copacabana – **LP92)** Caranavi – **LP93)** Chulumani – **LP94)** Guaqui – **LP95)** Av Ciivica frente Estadio Orlando Quiroga, Caranavi ☎2 8243810 **W:** qhana.org.bo **E:** rqamazonia@qhana.org.bo **LP96)** Pza. Ballivian No 525, 16 de Julio, El Alto ☎2 844344 – **LP97)** Av. Manco Kapaca No 50, Tiawanacu ☎2 597 357 – **LP98)** Calle Calama,

entre Humahuca y Montenegro, Zona Norte, La Paz ☎2 286983 **W:** poderdedios.com **E:** radiosol@poderdedios.com – **FM:** 90.5 MHz – **LP99)** Chulumani - Huancane **W:** poderdedios.com **E:** radiosol@poderdedios.com **LP100)** Calle Topáter # 830, Zona Norte, La Paz – **LP101)** Laja, Prov. de Los Andes – **LP103)** Av. Manco Kapac, Tiawuanaku ☎2 898541 – **LP104)** Lanza N° 844, Cochabamba ☎4 520313 **W:** radiomaria.org.bo **E.** info.bol@radiomaria.org – **LP105)** Calle Bolivar No 249, Achacachi – **LP106)** Av. Chacaltaya, calle Tiquina N° 6580 Alto Lima primera sección (Cas.8628), El Alto ☎🖹2 2842492 **W:** plenituddevida.net **E:** info@plenituddevida.net – **LP107)** Ave. Cornelio Saavedra No 2875 esq. Kantuta, Desaguadero ☎2 730 628 - – **LP108)** Batallas, ☎71580034 – **LP109)** Corapata, Prov. De Los Andes– **LP110)** Letania, Prov. de Ingavi – **LP111)** Achocalla, Prov. de Murillo ☎ – **LP112)** Villa Iquiaca, Prov. de Los Andes – **LP113)** Contorno/Viacha, Prov. de Ingavi – **LP114)** Av.Eduardo 1168, Zona Los Andes, Murillo ☎2 2458567 **E:** jorgetito@redcotel.bo – **LP115)** Av. Illimani No 1938, Miraflores, La Paz. ☎2 240 420 🖹2 222413 **W:** redpalenque.com **E:** palenque_radiotv@gmail.com – **LP116)** Plaza Avaroa N° 105, Carr. Viacha, El Alto. ☎2 825504 🖹2 821007 **E:** pachaqamasa700@yahoo.es – **LP120)** Unidad Académica Campesina de Tiahuanacu, Tiawuanaku ☎2 898542 – **LP121)** Iglesia Bautista la Lumbrera, Av. Mecapaca No 6735, Zona Obrajes, La Paz ☎2 786947 – **LP122)** Ca Cochabamba N° 102, Puerto de Guaqui ☎77592170 **W:** http//1190adioguaqui.blogspot.no **E:** radio1190guaqui@hotmail.com – **LP123)** Achocalla – **LP124)** Huarina – **LP125)** Puerto Acosta – **LP126)** Topohoco – **LP127)** Vilaque – **LP128)** Taraco – **LP129)** Tapichullo – **LP130)** Tiawanaku – **LP131)** Qhurpa – **LP132)** Qhurpa – **LP133)** Asunta – **LP134)** Asunta – **LP135)** Escoma – **LP136)** Desaguadero – **LP137)** Caranavi – **LP138)** Carabuco – **LP139)** Corocoro – **LP140)** Carabuco – **LP141)** Carabuco – **LP142)** Achacachi – **LP143)** Achacachi – **LP144)** El Alto – **LP145)** Sococoni – **LP146)** Capilaya – **LP147)** Jihuacuta – **LP148)** Canaviri – **LP149)** Calle Jorge Carrasco N°12 entre calle 1 y calle 2 - Zona 12 de Octubre, El Alto ☎22 821473 **W:** radioluzdelmundobolivia.com **E:** luzdelmundo.bolivia@hotmail.com – **LP150)** León M. Loza No. 1199, Esquina Ascencio Padilla Alto San Pedro, La Paz ☎2-483395 – **LP151)** Ca 140 N° 140, Zona Villa Avaros, El Alto ☎2 115472 – **LP152)** La Paz – **LP153)** 3er piso, Edifico Las Delicias, frente a la linea roja del Teleférico, Av. Panorámica, El Alto – **LP154)** La Paz – **LP155)** Chulumani **W:** Facebook: Radio Jallalla Coca - **FM:** 100.1MHz

OR00 (ORURO)
OR01) Calle Ayacucho 785 (Alto) (Cas 670), Oruro ☎2 5253500 🖹2 5252500 **E:** cpi@coteor.net.bo **Aymara & Quechua:** 1130, 0230 – 1000-2200, 0200-0600 – **OR03)** Cas 1019, Oruro ☎2 5112259 **W:** bahai.org.bo **E:** servicio@bahai.org.bo **Aymara & Quechua:** 11 hours daily – **OR05)** Oruro – **OR06)** Calle Cochabamba esquina 6 de Octubre (Cas 49), Oruro ☎2 525 0004 🖹2 524 2215 – **OR09)** Calle Junín y 6 de Agosto, Oruro ☎2 5260200 **W:** radiobatallonlopater.com **Aymara & Quechua:** 1000-1100 – **FM:** 98.2MHz – **OR12)** San Felipe 493 entre Tarapacá y Tejerina (Cas 247), Oruro **Aymara:** 2200-2400 - **FM:** 107.7MHz – **OR13)** Av Velasco Galvarro entre León y Rodriguez 1551, Oruro - **FM:** 105.1MHz – **OR14)** Linares 1160 entre Cochabamba y Caro, Oruro – **OR15)** Caro 235 entre Pagador y Av Velasco Galvarro, Oruro – **OR19)** Av Bakovic 1027 entre Caro y Montecinos, (Cas 326), Oruro **Aymara & Quechua:** 0930-1030 - **FM:** 93.1MHz **OR20)** Calle Sucre, Huanuni (Cas 681), Oruro ☎2 5520421 **W:** nacionaldehuanuni.com **E:** nacionaldehuanuni@gmail.com – **OR24)** Calle Adolfo Mier 1231, Oruro – **OR25)** Huanuni – **OR26)** Orinoca, Prov Sud Carangas – **OR27)** Sabaya, Prov Sabaya – **OR29)** Oruro – **OR31)** Calle 6 de Octubre # 6160, Oruro ☎5 275344 **E:** radiocapitaloruro@hotmail.com – **FM:** 102.7 MHz – **OR32)** Avenida 6 de Octubre y Montecinos 1042, Oruro ☎5 25143 🖹5 276 645 – **FM:** 97.1 MHz **E:** Davidglg@hotmail.com – **OR33)** Centro de Apoyo a la Educación Popular (CAEP), Huanuni – **OR34)** Oruro – **OR35)** Caracollo – **OR36)** Caracolla – **OR37)** Huanuni – **OR38)** Oruro – **OR39)** Oruro – **OR40)** Oruro – **OR41)** Oruro – **FM:** 98.7 MHz – **OR42)** Qaqachaca – **OR43)** Ciudad - **FM:** 107.9 MHz

PA00 (PANDO)
PA09) Barrio Paraiso, Calle Margarita, Esquina Jazmin, Cobija **W:** facebook.com – Radio Bendita Trinidad Bolivia – **PA10)** Cobija

P000 (POTOSI)
PO02) Calle Cobija 15, Zona Central, Potosí ☎6 222680 🖹6 226210 **W:** radiokollasuyo.net – **FM:** 105.1MHz – **PO07)** Potosi – **PO08)** Catavi – **PO10)** Llica, Pcia Daniel Campos – **PO12)** Potosi - **FM.** 107.5 MHz – **PO14)** Campamento Minero Tazna, Pcia Nor Chichas – **PO15)** Cas 139, Uyuni, Prov Antonio Quijarro **E:** radioyura@hotmail.com – **PO16)** Dtto Minero de Animas, Uyuni – **PO19)** Calle Final Uruguay s/n (Cas 16), Uyuni, Prov Antonio Quijarro ☎2 693 2145 **E:** max_nelson_t@hotmail.com – **PO26)** Comunidad de Caiza, Prov Chayanta – **PO27)** Comunidad de Colquechaca, Prov de José María Linares – **PO28)** Av. Civica 739 (Cas. 538), Potosi ☎6 22236660 **W:** aclo.org.bo/bolivia **E:** aclopotosi@aclo.org.bo– **FM:** 106.7 MHz – **PO29)** Calle Matos No 107 (Cas.472), Potosi. ☎6 223 936 **W:** indoamericafm.com/ **E:** info@indoamericafm.com – **PO30)** Colcha "K" – **PO31)** Ocuri – **PO32)** Unica – **PO33)** Villazon – **PO34)** Llica – **PO35)** Tupiza – **PU36)** Uyuni

– **PO37)** Potosi **W:** radiocruzdelsur.com **E:** contactos@radiocruzdelsur.com – **PO38)** Potosi **W:** radiofides.com **E:** sistemas@radiofides.com – **PO39)** Potosi – **PO40)** Campamento Siglo XX, Llallagua (or Cas ´434, Oruro) **W:** radiopio12.com.bo **E:** rpiodoce@entelnet.bo – ☎2 5820250 ⓵2 5820554 **Aymara** & **Quechua** 6 hrs daily - **FM:** 99.9MHz

SC00 (SANTA CRUZ)

SC02) Plaza 31 de Julio, San Ignacio de Velasco ☎3 962 2188 **W:** sanignacio-diocesis.com/ **E:** radiojuan@hotmail.com – **FM:** 100.3MHz – **SC03)** Calle Potosí s/n entre calles German Bush y Rafael Terrazas, Barrio la Floresta (or Cas 38), Montero ☎3 9220237 **W:** radiomariaaux-iliadora.sdb.bo **E:** ramacon@cotas.com.br - **FM:** 105.5MHz "Concierto" – **SC04)** Calle Mario Flores esquina Güendá No 20 Cas 672 or 3213), Santa Cruz **W:** Facebook **E:** radiosantacruzbolivia@gmail.com ☎3 3531817 **Guarani:** 1830-1900 - **FM:** 92.3MHz – **SC10)** Warnes 334 (Cas 629), Santa Cruz ☎3 3363990 ⓵3 3363992 - **FM:** 92.7MHz – **SC11)** Av. Grigota s/n, B.Matpetrol (2Cdra. Antes del 4to Anillo) Cas 818), Santa Cruz ☎3 3529265 ⓵3 3524747 **E:** mision.eplabol@scbbs-bo.com **Quechua & Guarani:** 0900-0945 - **FM:** 90.7MHz "R Super Color" – **SC12)** Independencia 372 (Cas 186), Santa Cruz ☎3 3337194 ⓵3 3335778 - **FM:** 96.3MHz – **SC16)** Av Charcas 1051 lado octava División del Ejército, Santa Cruz ☎3 3360447 ⓵3 3372242 - **FM:** 98.1MHz – **SC17)** Calle Colón 58, piso 5 Of 501-2, Cas 1399, Santa Cruz ☎3 3322142 **E:** grigotafm@hotmail.com **FM:** 90.3MHz – **SC21)** Florida esq Montes Claros 143, Vallegrande ☎3 9422033 – **SC25)** Cas 507, Santa Cruz - **FM:** 89.5MHz. Prgrs also in **Quechua** – **SC29)** Calle España 572, 2°piso, Santa Cruz - **FM:** 97.9MHz – **SC30)** Cas 15, Santa Cruz de Chiquitos – **SC33)** Cas 1766, Santa Cruz **W:** difusorasdeloriente.galeon.com **E:** verdeyblanco5@hotmail.com – **SC35)** Calle Quijarro 74 esq Av Uruguay, Santa Cruz - **FM:** 105.5MHz –**SC37)** Comunidad de Camiri, Prov Cordillera **SC38)** Comunidad de San Julián, Prov Nuflo de Chávez – **SC39)** Santa Cruz – **SC40)** Santa Cruz – **SC41)** Vallegrande – **SC42)** Camiri – **SC43)** Yapacani – **SC44)** Santa Cruz **W:** poderdedios.net **E:** radiosol@poderdedios.com - **FM:** 105.5 MHz – **SC45)** Calle Lanza No 84 entre La Paz y Oruro, Santa Cruz ☎4 4526100 ⓵4 4681178 **W:** radiomaria.org.bo **E:** info.bol@radiomaria.org.bo – **SC46)** Santa Cruz – **SC47)** Santa Cruz – **SC48)** Zona Plan 3000 Av. Paurito Frente al Mercado Guapurú, Santa Cruz ☎3 3318829 **W:** facebook.com/Radio.Bendita.Trinidad.Bolivia.OFFICIAL – **SC49)** Yapacani – **SC50)** José Ballivian – **SC51)** Calle Lanza 844 (entre C La Paz y C Oruro) Santa Cruz **W:** radiomaria.org.bo **E:** web@radiomaria.org.bo – **FM:** 97.5 MHz – **SC52)** Santa Cruz ☎3 33346299 **W:** facebook.com- Radio Amboro - **FM:** 97.5 MHz – **SC53)** Santa Cruz – **SC54)** Camiri – **SC55)** Santa Cruz **W:** Facebook: Radio Familiar 92.5 MHz y 600 khz AM – **FM:** 92.5 MHz

TA00 (TARIJA) TA01) Calle Virginio Lema 788 (Cas 404), Tarija ☎4 6643890 – **TA03)** Av Las Américas 9630, Edif Radiofónico Los Andes (Cas 344), Tarija ☎6 642800 - **FM:** 103.1MHz – **TA05)** Calle Bolivar esq. Méndez N° 327 piso 1 Tarija ☎4 6634444 ⓵4 6635555 **W:** facebook.com – Radio Guadalquivir **E:** radioguadalquivir@entelnet.com.bo - **FM:** 91.5MHz – **TA06)** Bolívar 376, Edificio Borda (Cas 125), Tarija - **FM:** 93.1MHz – **TA07)** Av Barrientos esq Ameller, Bermejo ☎4 6961584 - **FM:** 99.1MHz – **TA10)** Av Bolívar 608, Bermejo – **TA11)** Comunidad de Villamontes, Prov Gran Chaco **TA12)** Calle Oruro E-1458 Esq. España (Cas. 1003), Tarija ☎4 6643425 **W:** aclo.org.bo/bolivia **E:** aclotarija@aclo.org.bo – **FM:** 101.5 MHz – **TA13)** Tarija – **TA14)** Bermejo – **TA15)** Villamontes – **TA16)** Villamontes – **TA17)** Yacuiba – **TA18)** Ycuiba – **TA19)** Entre Rios – **TA20)** Ca Cochabamba N° 1403, Tarija ☎4 6664141 – **FM:** 101.5 MHz – **TA21)** Tarija

FM in La Paz (MHz): 87.7 87.7 FM –88.5 Doble 8 Latina – 88.9 Gente – 89.3 Sistema Cristiano de Comunicaciones – 89.7 Salesiana – **LP23)** 90.1 R.Sol Poder de Dios – 90.5 Panamericana Classica – 90.9 PCM – 91.3 Ciudad – 91.7 El Comercio – 92.1 Estudio 92 FM – 92.5 Estelar – 92.9 Galáctica – 93.3 Melodia – 93.7 Chacaltaya – 94.1 R La Voz de Bolivia – 94.5 Red Nuevo Tiempo – 94.9 Gigante – **LP06)** 95.3 – 95.7 Digital Star – 96.1 – 96.5 R.Panamericana – 96.9 Diferente – 97.3 Stereo 97 – 97.7 – 98.1 Láser – 98.5 Andina – 98.9 Restauración – 99.3 Melodía – 99.7 Cristo Viene – 100.1 FM Cien – 100.5 Constelación – 100.9 R. Color – **LP07)** 101.3 – 101.7 Graffitti – 102.1 RRB – 102.5 Sintonia – 102.9 Cristal – 103.3 R. Deseo – **LP25)** 103.5 - 103.7 San Francisco de Asis – 104.1 Cadena CNT – 104.5 RCN – **LP26)** 104,8 - 104.9 Fantástica – 105.3 Nuevo Amanacer – 105.7 Majestad – 106.1 Pachamama – 106.5 – 106.9 Paris-La Paz – 107.3 Nueva Cosmos – **LP08)** 107.5 R.Play – 107.7 Central FM

BONAIRE (Netherlands

L.T: UTC -4h — **Pop:** 18,500 — **Pr.L:** Dutch (official), Papiamentu, English — **E.C:** 50Hz, 127/220V — **ITU:** BES

BUREAU TELECOMMUNICATIE EN POST
✉ Kaya Grandi 69, P.O. Box 791, Bonaire ☎ + 599 717 3140 ⓵ +599 717 3554 **W:** BTnP.org **E:** gen.affairs@burtel.an

MW	Call	kHz	kW	Station, location
1)	PJB	800	100	Trans World R., Kralendijk

FM	MHz	kW	Station, location
1)	89.5		Trans World R., Kralendijk
5)	91.1		R. Digital FM, Kralendijk
2)	93.1	0.5	Alpha FM 93.1, Kralendijk
2)	94.7	0.5	Voz di Bonaire, Kralendijk
3)	97.1	5	R. Energia Boneiru, Kralendijk
4)	97.5		Dolfijn FM, Kralendijk
8)	99.9		Live 99.9 FM, Kralendijk
6)	101.1	0.5	Mega Hit FM, Kralendijk
6)	102.7		Bon FM, Kralendijk
7)	107.7		Rumbera Network, Kralendijk

Addresses and other information
1) Kaya Gobernador N. Debrot 64, Kralendijk, Bonaire ☎ +599 717 8800 ⓵ +599 717 8808 Dir: Mr. Dick Veldman; 800 khz: 00.30-07.00 Spanish, 07.00-09.00 Portuguese, 09.00-12.30 Spanish, 21.30-23.00 Spanish, 23.00-00.30 English. 89.5 MHz 24 h mostly music with occasional Bible based prgrs in English, Spanish, Dutch and Papiamentu **W:** twrbonaire.com **E:** 800am@twr.org, 895fm@twr.org – **2)** Radiodifucion Boneriano NV, Kaya Gobernador N. Debrot 2, Kralendijk, ☎ +599 717 5947 ⓵ +599 717 8820, Dir: Feliciano da Silva Piloto **W:** vozdibonaire.com **E:** vozdibonaire@gmail.com **Voz di Bonaire:** Papiamentu and Dutch, music and information 24 hrs **Mega Hit FM:** Dutch and English, music and information 24 hrs **Alpha FM**:Spanish , music and information 24 hrs – **3)** Kaya Grandi 8, Bonaire ☎ +599 717 0971 **W:** circuitoenergia.com– **4)** Mambo Beach Blvd, Willemstad, Curacao ☎ +599 9 465 9975 ⓵ 599 9 461 9975 Dir. Egon Sybrandy **DPrgr.** 24h in Dutch **E:** info@digital911fm.net **W:** dolfijnfm.com – **5)** Kaya Dialma1 , Kralendijk, Bonaire Station Manager : Zamir Ayubi ☎ +599 717 9911 **W:** radiodigital911fm.net **E:** richtraveling@gmail.com – **6)** Kaya Irlanda 11, Kralendijk ☎ +599 717 2102 ⓵ +599 717 2002 GM: Carmo R. Cecilia. 24h in Papiamentu **W:** bonfm.com **E:** bonfm@hotmail.com – **7)** Caracasbaaiweg 194, Willemstad, Curaçao ☎ +599 9 465 9580 ⓵ +599 9 461 5028 **W:** rumberanetwork.com **E:** contacto@rumberanetwork.com.ve – **8)** Kralendijk ☎+599 717 9999 **W:** live99fm.com **E:** info@live99fm.com

TRANS WORLD RADIO (Rlg. Cult. Educ.)
see International Broadcasting section

BOSNIA & HERZEGOVINA

L.T: UTC +1h (27 Mar-30 Oct: +2h) — **Pop:** 3.8 million — **Pr.L:** Bosnian, Croatian, Serbian — **E.C:** 50Hz, 220V — **ITU:** BIH

REGULATORNA AGENCIJA ZA KOMUNIKACIJE BIH (RAK) (Communications Regulatory Agency BH)
✉ Mehmeda Spahe 1, 71000 Sarajevo ☎ +387 33 250600 ⓵ +387 33 713080 **E:** info@rak.ba **W:** rak.ba **L.P:** DG: Jasenko Lasta

RADIO-TELEVIZIJA BOSNE I HERCEGOVINE (BHRT) (Pub)
✉ Bulevar Meše Selimovica 12, 71000 Sarajevo ☎ +387 33 461101 ⓵ +387 33 464061 **E:** smaila.resic@bhrt.ba **W:** bhrt.ba **L.P:** DG: Belmin Karamehmedovic

FM	MHz	kW	FM	MHz	kW
Tušnica	88.1	30	Vlašic	97.0	100
V. Gomila	88.8	30	Lisin	100.3	30
Lipik	93.7	30	Hum	100.7	10
Leotar	94.1	30	Kozara	103.1	30
Drvar	94.7	5	Trebevic	103.7	10

NB: Txs below 1kW not listed.
D.Prgr: BHR1 in Bosnian, Croatian, Serbian: 24h.

FEDERACIJA BOSNE I HERCEGOVINE

RADIO-TELEVIZIJA FEDERACIJE BOSNE I HERCEGOVINE (RTV FBiH) (Pub)
✉ Bulevar Meše Selimovica 12, 71000 Sarajevo ☎ +387 33 461539 ⓵ +387 33 461539 **E:** press@rtvfbih.ba **W:** rtvfbih.ba **L.P:** DG: Dzemal Šabic

FM	MHz	kW	FM	MHz	kW
Tuzla	88.5	10	V. Gomila	95.7	30
Vlašic	89.3	100	Hum	95.7	10
Fortica	91.7	30	Lipik	98.9	30
Tušnica	92.5	30	Hadzica Brdo	99.5	5
Lisin	94.5	30	Gradacac	103.5	5

NB: Txs below 1kW not listed.
D.Prgr: Radio FBiH in Bosnian, Croatian: 24h.

OTHER STATIONS

MW	kHz	kW	Location	Station
38)	792	1	Banovici	R. Banovici
39)	1503	1	Zavidovici	R. 1503 Zavidovici
40)	1584	1	Bos. Petrovac	R. Bosanski Petrovac

FM	MHz	kW	Location	Station
4)	88.6	1	Mostar	Omladinski R. X
15)	88.7	1	Doboj*	R. Antena
26)	88.8	1	Makljen	R. Rama
33)	89.5	2	Drvar	R. Drvar
37)	89.9	1	Cazin	R. Cazin
23)	90.3	1	Radovan	R. Plus
14)	90.5	1	Sarajevo	R. Postaja Vrhbosna
5)	90.9	1	Sarajevo	Antena Sarajevo
22)	91.5	1	Sarajevo	R. Kalman
7)	91.5	5	Bos. Grahovo	R. Livno
2)	93.1	5	Grude	R. Široki Brijeg
19)	93.7	1	Bos. Grahovo	Obiteljski R. Valentino
19)	94.3	2.5	Lipik	Obiteljski R. Valentino
18)	94.7	1	Bihac	R. Bihac
25)	94.8	1	Brcko	R. Brcko
35)	95.0	1	Konjic	R. Konjic
32)	95.2	1	Sarajevo	Studenski eFM R.
6A)	95.6	5	Gradacac	R. Kameleon
30)	95.9	1	Duvno	R. Tomislavgrad
11)	96.2	1	Mostar	R. Dobre Vibracija
1)	96.2	5	Brekovica	RTV USK
20)	96.5	5	Sarajevo	R. BIR
13)	97.5	5	Zenica	RSG R.
28)	97.6	1	Livno	R. Studio N
9)	97.9	5	Mostar	R. Mostar
8)	98.7	1	Sarajevo	R. M
3)	99.3	5	Zenica	BM R.
1)	99.5	1.5	Sanski Most	RTV USK
7)	100.9	1	Livno	R. Livno
6B)	101.2	1	Sarajevo	City Kameleon R.
16)	101.5	1.2	Gorazde	R. Gorazde
27)	101.7	1	Mostar	R. Stari Most
17)	101.8	1	Bugojno	R. Mir Medjugorje
24)	102.9	1	Radovan	R. Posušje
29)	103.4	5	Mostar	R. Oscar - C
10)	103.7	2	Lokveni Vrh*	R. Sana
8)	104.2	1	Banja Luka*	R. M
13)	104.3	30	Bjelašnica	RSG R.
17)	104.7	1	Prozor	R. Mir Medjugorje
12)	105.0	1	Kmur	R. Istocno Sarajevo
1)	105.1	30	Licka Plješivica**	RTV USK
34)	105.2	1	Kruščica	Soundset R. Q
12)	105.6	1	Sarajevo	R. Istocno Sarajevo
30)	105.8	5	Bos. Grahovo	R. Tomislavgrad
21)	106.6	10	Lisac	R. Zenica
19)	106.7	1.2	Drvar	Obiteljski R. Valentino
17)	106.7	3	Kozara*	R. Mir Medjugorje
31)	107.0	5	Pecigrad	R. Velkaton
36)	107.4	5	Bihac	Otvorena Mreza
17)	107.8	50	Licka Plješivica**	R. Mir Medjugorje

NB: Txs below 1kW not listed.
*) Located in Republika Srpska **) Located in Croatia

Addresses & other information:
1) Kulturni centar bb, 77000 Bihac – 2) Trg Gojka Šuška 5c, 88220 Široki Brijeg – 3) Talica brdo 11, 72000 Zenica – 4) Rade Bitange 13, 88104 Mostar – 5) Urijan Dedina 7, 71000 Sarajevo – 6A) Dr. Milana Jovanovica 6, 75000 Tuzla. 6B) Zmaja od Bosne 52a, 71000 Sarajevo – 7) Kneza Mutimira 29, 80101 Livno – 8) Fra Andjela Zvizdovica 1, 71000 Sarajevo – 9) Lacina bb, 88000 Mostar – 10) Banjalucka 2, 75260 Sanski Most – 11) Kralja Petra Kresimira IV bb, 88000 Mostar – 12) Stefana Nemanje 8, 71123 Istocno Sarajevo – 13) Urijan Dedina 7, 71000 Sarajevo – 14) Maršala Tita 56/1, 71000 Sarajevo – 15) Titova bb, 74264 Jelah – 16) Marka Oreškovica 42, 80260 Drvar – 17) Gospin Trg 1, 88266 Medjugorje – 18) Krupska bb, 77000 Bihac – 19) Kolodvorska 108a, 76204 Bijela – 20) Reisa Dzemaludina Causevica 2, 71000 Sarajevo – 21) Bulevar Kralja Tvrtka I bb, 72000 Zenica – 22) Varazdinska 18, 71000 Sarajevo – 23) Fra Grge Martica bb, 88240 Posušje – 24) Kraljice Jelene 2, 88240 Posušje – 25) Klosterska br. 20, 76100 Brcko – 26) Kralja Tomislava bb, 88440 Prozor-Rama – 27) Jusovina 19, 88000 Mostar – 28) Splitska bb, 80101 Livno – 29) Smrcenjaci bb, 88000 Mostar – 30) Mijata Tomica bb, 80240 Tomislavgrad – 31) Kulište 2, 77230 Velika Kladuša – 32) Zmaja od Bosne 8, 71000 Sarajevo – 33) Marka Oreškovica 42, 80260 Drvar – 34) Školska 10, 72 000 Zenica – 35) Trg Državnosti - Alija Izetbegovic 1, 88400 Konjic – 36) Hamdije Cemerlica 21, 71000 Sarajevo – 37) Cazinskih brigada 12, 77220 Cazin – 38) 7. novembra 4, 75290 Banovici E: radiobanovici@yahoo.com – 39) Maršala Tita 3, 72220 Zavidovici

E: dadozavi@zona.ba – 40) Bosanska bb, 77250 Bosanski Petrovac E: centarzakulturubp@gmail.com.

REPUBLIKA SRPSKA

RADIO TELEVIZIJA REPUBLIKE SRPSKE (RTRS) (Pub)
✆ Trg Republike Srpske 9, 78000 Banja Luka ☎ +387 51 339900 🖷 +387 51 301922 E: radiodesk@rtrs.tv W: rtrs.tv
L.P: DG: Draško Milinovic

FM	MHz	kW	FM	MHz	kW
Kmur*	87.8	1	Djuga Niva	90.7	10
Trebevic*	88.7	10	Kozara	92.7	30
Udrigovo*	89.9	30	Leotar	92.8	30
Veliki Zep*	90.3	30			

NB: Txs below 1kW not listed. *) Located in Federacije Bosne i Herc.
D.Prgr: Radio RS in Serbian: 24h.

OTHER STATIONS

FM	MHz	kW	Location	Station
9)	87.7	5	Hum*	Nes R.
9)	88.4	1	Banja Luka	Nes R.
5)	88.4	6	Ugljevik	R. Slobomir
11)	88.9	1	Kmur*	Bobar R.
7)	88.9	1	Modrica	R. Ljubic
17)	89.5	1	Udrigovo	R. HIT
6)	89.9	2	Kozarska Dubica	Vikom R.
16)	90.0	1	Gacko	R. Gacko
12B)	91.5	1	Banja Luka	BiG 2
8)	92.5	1	Kmur*	R. Foca
12A)	93.6	1	Banja Luka	BiG 1
3)	94.7	2	Bosanska Dubica	R. Feniks
11)	95.3	23	Kozara	Bobar R.
1)	95.9	1	Banja Luka	Balkan R
10)	95.9	1	Trebinje	R. Trebinje
2)	96.3	2	Doboj	R. Doboj
12C)	96.5	1	Banja Luka	BiG 3
15)	96.7	1	Kozarska Dubica	Dub R.
14)	97.6	1	Banja Luka	Nes Castra R.
13)	99.1	1	Kljuc	R. Kljuc
4)	99.9	9	Banja Luka	BN R.
11)	100.9	30	Duga Njiva	Bobar R.
11)	100.9	10	Busija	Bobar R.
18)	102.7	2.2	Banja Luka	Hard Rock R.
11)	102.8	8	Trebevic*	Bobar R.
19)	104.0	1	Višegrad	R. Višegrad
11)	104.7	30	Vlasic*	Bobar R.
20)	105.3	3	Banja Luka	Plavi R.
11)	105.5	22	Leotar	Bobar R.
21)	105.7	1	Kozara	Free R.
11)	105.9	40	Hrgud	Bobar R.
9)	106.4	22.5	Kozara	Nes R.
22)	107.5	1	Banja Luka	Uno R.

NB: Txs below 1kW not listed. *) Located in Federacije Bosne i Herc.
Addresses & other information:
1) Kralja Petra I Karadordevica 113-115, 78000 Banja Luka – 2) Kneza Lazara 8, 74000 Doboj – 3) Svetosavska bb, 79240 Kozarska Dubica – 4) Laze Kostica 146, 76320 Bijeljina – 5) Trzni centar bb, 76300 Bijeljina – 6) Srpska 2/II, 78000 Banja Luka – 7) Trg Srpskih Boraca bb, 78430 Prnjavor – 8) Njegoševa 1, 73300 Foca – 9) Brace Pišteljic 1, 78000 Banja Luka – 10) Svetosavska 21, 79240 Kozarska Dubica – 11) Filipa Višnjica 211, 76320 Bijeljina – 12A-C) Vuka Karadzica 6, 78000 Banja Luka – 13) Branilaca BiH bb., 79280 Kljuc – 14) Brace Pišteljica 1, 78000 Banja Luka – 15) Svetosavska 21, 79240 Kozarska Dubica – 16) Solunskih Dobrovoljaca 2, 89240 Gacko – 17) Miroslava Krleze 48, 76100 Brcko – 18) 78000 Banja Luka – 19) Vuka Karadzica bb, 73240 Višegrad – 20) Branka Popovica 92a, 78000 Banjaluka – 21) Zarka Zgonjanjina 15, 79101 Prijedor – 22) Veselina Masleše br. 1/12, 78000 Banja Luka

BOTSWANA

L.T: UTC +2h — **Pop:** 2 million — **Pr.L:** Setswana, English — **E.C:** 50Hz, 220V — **ITU:** BOT

NATIONAL BROADCASTING BOARD (NBB)
✆ 206/207 Independence Ave, Private Bag 00495, Gaborone ☎+267 3957755 🖷 +267 3957976 W: bta.org.bw/nbb.htm E: info@bta.org.bw
L.P: Chairman: Dr. Masego Mpotokwane.

RADIO BOTSWANA (Pub, Comm.)
✆ Private Bag 0060, Gaborone ☎+267 3653000 W: radiobotswana. gov.bw dib.gov.bw E: Rbeng@info.bw L.P: Dir. Broadc. Sces: Habuji Sosome. Chief Broadc. Officer: Mrs Banyana Segwe. CE: Kingsley Reetsang. Mgr RB: Margaret Modise.

MW	kHz	kW	MW	kHz	kW
Maun	531	50	Mmathethe	945	25
Muchenje	558	50	Takotokwane	972	
Selebi-Phikwe	621	100	Jwaneng	1071	25
Mopipi	648	50	Mahalapye	1215	50
Shakawe	693	25	Tshabong	1350	50
Gantsi	873	50	‡inactive		

FM(MHz)	RB1	RB2	kW	FM(MHz)	RB1	RB2	kW
Bobonong	95.9	102.7	0.5	Mabule	92.3	105.9	
Charleshill	93.5	103.5		Mabutsane	94.2	104.6	
Francistown	103.6	90.5	3	Mahalapye	96.6	107.0	2.5
Gaborone	89.9	103.0	5	Maun	94.2	104.6	0.5
Gantsi	94.0	100.8	0.1	Olifant's Drift	88.0	104.7	
Good Hope	94.6	101.6	0.5	Orapa	89.9	98.6	0.1
Hukuntsi	89.9	96.2	0.5	Palapye	91.5	101.5	0.5
Jwaneng	92.2	106.3	0.5	Sekakangwe Hill	91.9	101.9	2
Kanye	89.0	95.3	0.5	Selebi-Phikwe	94.2	104.6	0.1
Kang	89.3	98.9		Serowe	99.4	92.9	1
Kasane	94.4	104.8	0.5	Sojwe	87.7	90.7	
Lobatse	98.6	105.7	1	Tsabong	96.6	107.0	0.5

National Sce. (RB1) in Setswana/English on MW/FM: 24h.
N. in English: on the hour exc. **in Setswana:** 1100, 1600, 1900.
Commercial Sce. (RB2): 24h. **N:** rel. RB1.
Ann: E: "This is R. Botswana broadcasting from Gaborone", "RB", "RB1", "RB2". Setswana: "Se Ke Seromamowa Sa Botswana mo Gaborone".
IS: RB1: Bird chirps and first bars of the National Anthem.

Other stations (all MHz):
Duma FM: Gaborone 93.0, Francistown 93.6 – **Gabz FM,** Private Bag BO 319, 2nd Floor, Beta House, Plot 17954, Old Lobatse Rd, Gaborone. **W:** gabzfm.com **FM:** Maun/Selebi-Phikwe 91.0, Mahalapye 93.4, Lobatse 94.1, Palapye 94.7, Serowe 96.1, Gaborone 96.2, Francistown 96.8 – **Yarona FM:** Francistown 100.1, Gaborone: 106.6. **W:** yaronafm.co.bw
Voice of America relay station (MW):
Selebi-Phikwe, Moepeng Hill: 909kHz 600kW 0300-0700 ,1600-2200 & SW. For further details see International Radio section (USA)

BRAZIL

L.T: PE (Fernando de Noronha only): UTC -2h. AL, AP, BA, CE, DF*, ES*, GO*, MA, MG*, PA, PB, PE, PI, PR*, RJ*, RN, RS*, SC*, SP*, TO: UTC -3h (*=DST: -2h). AC, AM, MS*, MT*, RO, RR: UTC -4h (*=DST: -3h). *) DST: 18 Oct 15-20 Feb 16, 16 Oct 16-19 Feb 17 — **Pop:** 202.8 million — **Pr.L:** Portuguese — **E.C:** 60Hz, 110V and 220V — **ITU:** B — **Int. dialling code:** +55

AGÊNCIA NACIONAL DE COMUNICAÇÕES (ANATEL)
🖃 SAS Quadra 06 Bloco H, Ed. Ministro Sérgio Motta, 2° andar, 70313-900 Brasília, DF **W:** anatel.gov.br
LP: Dir. Gen. Dr. Rubens Bussacos. Dir. of Radio: Roberto Blois Montes de Souza. Dir. Dept. of Authorizations: Domingo Poty Chabalgoity

ASSOCIAÇÃO BRASILEIRA DE EMISSORAS DE RADIO E TELEVISÃO (ABERT)
🖃 SCN Quadra 4 Bloco B-100, sala 501, Centro Empresarial Varig, 70714-900 Brasília, DF (C.P. 08780, 70312-970)
☎ 61 2104 4600 📠 61 2104 4626 **W:** abert.org.br
LP: Pres.: Paulo Machado de Carvalho Neto. Exec. Dir: Antonio Abelin

Callsign For the full callsign add ZY to the front of the calls shown. The letters preceding the stn number indicate the state or territory. ‡ = inactive † = varying freq † = irregular
N.B: all stns carry «A Voz do Brasil» (official prgr.). Main tr. M-F 2200-2300 but stns may also transmit at other times during the day.

MW	Call	kHz	kW	Station, location, h. of tr.
BA01)	H481	540	1/0.25	R. Regional, Irecê: 24h
CE01)	H610	540	1/0.25	R. Jornal, Canindé
GO01)	H755	540	10/1	R. Riviera, Goiânia
MA01)	H894	540	1/0.25	R. Guajajara, Barra do Corda
MG151)	L331	540	1/0.5	R. Ipanema, Ipanema
PI31)	I914	540	1/0.25	R. Primeiro de Julho, Agua Branca
PR110)	J322	540	1/0.25	R. Nova Era, Borrazópolis
RJ01)	J450	540	10/2.5	R. Fluminense, Niterói
RS01)	K226	540	1/0.5	R. Real, Canoas: 0900-0200
RS02)	K322	540	10/1	R. Sepé, Santo Ângelo: 24h
SC01)	J778	540	10/1	R. Mirador, Rio do Sul: 0800-0300
SE01)	J924	540	10/2.5	R. Jornal AM, Aracaju: 24h
SP01)	K697	540	1/0.25	R. Globo, Bauru
SP02)	K734	540	1/0.25	R. Nova Sumaré, Sumaré: 24h
CE59)	H644	550	1/0.25	R. Vale do Quincoê, Acopiara: 1400-

MW	Call	kHz	kW	Station, location, h. of tr.
				2100 Sun 1600-2100
MG01)	L225	550	5/0.5	R. Cataguases, Cataguases
MG02)	L263	550	20/5	R. Soc. Norte de Minas (RBV), M. Claros: 24h
MT29)	I429	550	10/5	R. Mais, Sinop
PE01)	I796	550	5/1	R. Meridional, Garanhuns
PI01)	I902	550	1/0.25	R. Serra da Capivara, São Raimundo Nonato
PI22)	I907	550	10/0.5	R. Globo, Parnaíba: 24h
PR139)	J331	550	10/0.5	R. Banda B, Curitiba: 24h
RS03)	K287	550	2.5/0.25	R. Sta. Cruz do Sul, Sta. Cruz do Sul: 0800-0230
SP03)	K578	550	5/0.5	R. Mantiqueira, Cruzeiro: 0800-0300
SP04)	K700	550	5/0.5	R. Boa Vontade, Sertãozinho: 24h
AM09)	H289	560	1/0.25	R. Coari, Coari
BA02)	H456	560	5/1	R. Jornal, Itabuna: 0700-0100(SS-2200)
CE41)	H604	560	5/0.25	R. Educ. Jaguaribana, Limoeiro do Nte.
GO25)	H769	560	5/0.25	R. Sul Goiana, Quirinópolis: 24h
MA02)	H887	560	25/5	R. Educadora do Maranhão, São Luís: 0800-0300 SS 24h
MG05)	L277	560	5/0.5	R. Dif., Patrocínio
MT01)	I395	560	10/2.5	R. Aruanã, Pontal do Aragua
MT24)	I419	560	10/1	R. Pioneira, Tangará da Serra
PB16)	I695	560	1/0.25	R. Maná, Mamanguape
PR01)	J214	560	1/0.5	R. Londrina Londrina
PR02)	J281	560	2.5/0.25	R. Cultura, Guarapuava: 24h
RJ02)	J496	560	5/0.25	R. Costa do Sol, Araruama:24h
RS04)	K231	560	5/1	R. São Francisco Sat, Caxias do Sul: 24h
SP213)	K761	560	35/1	R. Paulista, Santa Isabel: 24h
AL01)	H244	570	5/1	R. Novo Nordeste, Arapiraca: 24h
CE02)	H613	570	5/0.25	R. Verde Vale, Juazeiro do Norte
CE03)	H614	570	1/0.25	R. Uirapuru, Itapipoca: 0800-0100
GO02)	H750	570	2.5/0.5	R. Cultura, Catalão
MA03)	H890	570	10/1	R. Cidade Esperança, Imperatriz
MA42)	H898	570	2.5	R.Timon, Timon
MG03)	L261	570	25/5	R. Capital, Belo Horizonte: 24h
MT30)	N407	570	1/0.25	R. Jornal, São José dos Quatro Marcos: 0900-0000
PR146)	J349	570	1/0.5	R. Continental, Palotina
RS05)	K267	570	1/0.5	R. Diário da Manhã, Passo Fundo: 24h
SC02)	J735	570	5/0.5	R. Eldorado, Criciúma: 24h
SC99)	J794	570	1/0.25	R. Fronteira, Dionísio Cerqueira: 0800-0100, Sun 1000-0000
SP05)	K595	570	1/0.25	R. Clube Gospel, Itapeva
SP06)	K672	570	5/1	R. Dif., Taubaté
SP195)	K698	570	1/0.25	R. Jornal, Nhandeara
SP150)	K717	570	1/0.25	Bariri R. Clube, Bariri
BA03)	H477	580	1/0.25	R. Dif., Teixeira de Freitas: 0630-0300
GO44)	H799	580	10/1	R. Serra Azul, Caiapônia
MG04)	L328	580	7/0.5	R. América, Uberlândia: 24h
MS01)	I387	580	25/1	R. Imaculada Conceicao, Campo Grande: 24h
PE02)	I776	580	20/10	R. Boas Novas, Recife: 24h
PI12)	I905	580	5/1	R. Itamaraty, Piripiri
PR105)	J327	580	2/0.25	R. Pitanga, Pitanga: 24h
PR03)	J330	580	25/5	R. Grande Lago, Santa Helena
RJ03)	J465	580	50/5	R. Relogio, Sao Gonçalo: 0900-0300
RS06)	K299	580	2/0.5	R. São Gabriel, São Gabriel: 0900-0300
RS07)	K318	580	10/5	R. Fátima, Vacaria: 24h
SP07)	K540	580	1/0.25	R. Você, Americana
SP08)	K274	580	1/0.25	R. Regional, Palmital: 0800-0200
TO01)	H785	580	10/2	R. Tocantins, Porto Nacional
BA04)	H445	590	10/5	R. Cruzeiro da Bahia, Salvador: 24h
CE04)	H627	590	5/0.25	R. Poty, Crateús: 0730(SS 0800) 24h
ES01)	I213	590	10/5	R. Tribuna, Vitória
GO03)	H798	590	10/1	R. Manchester, Anápolis
MG93)	L249	590	10/0.5	R. Cultura, João Monlevade
MT03)	I420	590	10/1	CBN Cuiabá, Cuiabá: 24h
PB25)	I692	590	5/0.25	R. Serrana, Araruna: 0800-0100
PR04)	J234	590	10/5	R. Difusora AM 590, Curitiba: 24h
PR38)	J240	590	2.7/0.75	R. Dif. Regional, Cruzeiro do Oeste
RR01)	O700	590	10	R. Dif. de Roraima, Boa Vista: 0800-0300 SS 0900-0230
RS08)	K210	590	5/0.5	R. Alegrete, Alegrete: 0830-0230
SC03)	J901	590	2/1	R. Progresso, Descanso: 24h
SP09)	K534	590	10/1	R. Atlântica, Santos: 24h
SP10)	K612	590	1/0.25	R. Clube, Mirandópolis: 0800-2300 Sat -1530 Sun 0900-1200
SP11)	K643	590	5/1	R. 79, Ribeirão Preto
AM02)	H287	600	10	R. Municipal, São Gabriel da Cachoeira: 24h
BA05)	H486	600	10/1	R. Vale do Rio Grande, Barreiras: 1100-000 Sun 1000-1500

MW	Call	kHz	kW	Station, location, h. of tr.
BA64)	H...	600	1/0.25	R. Dif.de Rio Real, Rio Real: 0900-0100 Sat -2200 Sun -0000
CE38)	H627	600	1/0.25	R. Cultura, Aracati
MA38)	H920	600	10/1	R. Mirante, São Luís: 24h
PE03)	I789	600	1/0.25	R. Cardeal Arcoverde, Arcoverde
RS09)	K278	600	100	R. Gaúcha, Porto Alegre:24h
AL10)	H249	610	10/2	R. Imperial, Marechal Deodoro
AM18)	H321	610	10	Super R.Boa Vontade, Iranduba: 24h
GO10)	H786	610	25/0.5	R. Mega, Luziânia
MG06)	L268	610	100/25	R. Itatiaia, Belo Horizonte: 24h
MT04)	I425	610	10/5	R. Celeste, Sinop
PB01)	I678	610	1/0.25	R. Progresso, Sousa
PI02)	I899	‡610	10/1	R. Poty, Teresina
SC04)	J746	610	10/0.5	R. Super Condá, Chapecó
SP12)	K532	‡610	1/0.25	CBN, Mogi Mirim
SP13)	K577	610	1/0.25	R. Globo, Catanduva: 24h
SP14)	K589	610	1/0.25	Super R. Piratininga, Guaratinguetá
SP15)	K726	610	1/0.25	R. Paranapanema, Piraju: 0800-0100
SP113)	K502	610	1/0.25	R. Presidente Venceslau, Pres. Venceslau: 0900-0200 (Sun silent)
CE05)	H590	620	10	R. Assunção CearenseFortaleza: 24h
PR05)	J332	620	2.5/0.25	R. Jandaia, Jandaia do Sul: 0800(Sun 1030)-0100
RS10)	K270	620	10/1	R. Pelotense, Pelotas: 24h
RS11)	K315	620	10/1	R. Municipal, Tenente Portela
SC05)	J779	620	5/0.25	Super-Radio Dif., Rio do Sul: 24h
SP16)	K521	620	50/10	R. Jovem Pan, São Paulo: 24h
AP01)	H422	630	25/10	R. Dif. de Macapá, Macapá: 24h
CE58)	H636	630	1/0.5	R. Cidade, Campos Sales: 24h
GO04)	H777	630	10/0.5	R. Gospel 630 AM, Pires do Rio
MA16)	H924	630	10/0.5	R. Macaru, Viana
MG07)	L299	630	1/0.5	R. Jornal da Manhã, Uberaba
MS32)	N603	630	10/1	R. Novo Tempo, Campo Grande: 24h
MT05)	I384	630	10/5	R. Dif. Bom Jesús, Cuiabá
PI03)	I904	630	1/0.5	R. Dif., Barras
PR06)	J284	630	10/0.5	R. Educativa, Curitiba: 24h
PR07)	J300	630	5/0.25	R. Educadora, Marechal Cândido Rondón
RJ04)	J466	630	25/10	R. Roquete Pinto, Rio de Janeiro: 24h
RS12)	K259	630	1/0.5	R. Cacique, Lagoa Vermelha: 24h
RS13)	K289	630	1/0.25	R. Santamariense, Santa Maria
SC06)	J800	630	1/0.25	R. Doze de Maio, São Lourenço d'Oeste: 0800-0200
SE02)	J920	630	10/5	R. Aperipe, Aracaju: 24h
SP17)	K613	630	1/0.25	R. Dif. Mirassol: 0800-0300, Sun 1000-2330
SP18)	K635	‡630	5/0.25	R. Cidade, Presidente Prudente
BA12)	H458	640	10/0.5	R. Dif. Sul da Bahia, Itabuna: 0700-0300
ES02)	I204	640	10/0.5	R. Vitória, Vitória: 24h
GO05)	H757	640	50/5	R. Dif. Goiânia, Goiânia
MG08)	L308	640	3/0.25	R. Santa Cruz, Pará de Minas: 24h
MG125)	L320	640	10/0.25	R. Educadora, Porteirinha: 24h
MT06)	I406	640	10/5	R. Progresso, Alta Floresta: 0800-0200, Sun 0900-0100
MT18)	I424	640	10/1	R. Tangará, Tangará da Serra
PI28)	I924	640	1/0.25	R. Cruzeiro, Pedro II: 0800-0000, SS 0900-2300)
PR08)	J262	640	20/1	Super R. Deus é Amor, Londrina: 24h
RJ05)	J489	640	5/1	R. Agulhas Negras, Resende
RN01)	J590	640	10/5	R. Globo, Natal: 24h
RS14)	K277	640	50/10	R. Bandeirantes, Porto Alegre: 24h
SP19)	K547	640	5/1	R. Morada do Sol, Araraquara: 24h
BA06)	H462	650	5/0.5	R. Clube, Valença: 24h
GO06)	H790	650	1/0.25	R. Cultural do Araguaia, Jussara
MG09)	L200	650	10/0.5	R. Vitoriosa, Lagoa Formosa
MG85)	L309	650	5/0.5	R. Globo, Unaí: 24h
MG142)	L372	650	10/1	R. Itatiaia AM Vale do Aço, Timóteo
MT19)	I414	650	5	R. Educadora, Colider: 0800-0300
PA20)	I540	650	10/1	R. Tropical, Santarém
PB02)	I672	650	5/0.5	R. Alto Piranhas, Cajazeiras
PI26)	I925	650	1/0.25	R. Tapuio, Miguel Alves
PR09)	J202	650	1/0.5	R. Banda B Norte Pioneiro, Cambará: 24h
PR91)	J250	650	8/1	R. Colméia, Cascavel
RS15)	K238	650	1/0.25	Radiodif. Sul Riograndense, Erechim
SP20)	K508	650	1/0.25	R. Andradina, Andradina
SP22)	K518	650	5/1	R. Terra, Praia Grande
SP21)	K524	650	1/0.25	R. Dif., Piracicaba: 24h
BA07)	H465	660	5/0.25	R. Nova Jornal, Itapetinga: 0800-2300
BA36)	H480	660	10/0.25	R. Bom Jesus, Bom Jesus da Lapa: 0800-0300(Sun -0000)
BA65)	H518	660	1/0.25	R. Planalto, Euclides da Cunha
CE06)	H619	660	1/0.25	R. Rio das Garças, Itarema (Acaraú)
GO07)	H778	660	5/0.25	R. Primavera, Itapuranga: 0800-0300
GO51)	H794	660	1/0.25	R. Alvorada, Quirinópolis
MG11)	L206	660	10/0.25	R. Clube, Curvelo:24h Sun 1000-0300
MT07)	I401	660	10/0.5	R. Amorim Juventude, Rondonópolis
PA21)	I552	660	10/0.25	R. Xinguara, Xinguara: 0800(SS 0900)-0100
PE04)	I787	660	5/1	R. Jornal, Limoeiro
PE05)	I795	660	1/0.25	R. Grande Serra, Araripina
PI34)	I925	660	1/0.25	R. Tacarijus, São Miguel do Tapuio
RJ06)	J472	660	5/1	R. Friburgo, Nova Friburgo: 24h
R001)	J673	660	10/5	R. Boas Novas AM, Porto Velho
RS16)	K286	660	1/0.25	R. Marajá, Rosário do Sul: 0815-0255, Sat 0830-0200, Sun 0900-0255
RS17)	K319	660	1/0.25	R. Esmeralda, Vacaria: 24h
SP23)	K639	660	10/0.5	R. Clube, Ribeirão Preto
SP112)	K777	660	20/0.5	R. Mundial, São Paulo
AC11)	H208	670	0.25	R. Dif., Sena Madureira: 0900-0400
AM04)	H288	670	1	R. Nac. do Alto Solimões, Tabatinga: 24h
AM03)	H297	670	1/0.25	R. Vale do Rio Madeira R-VRM, Humaitá: 0900-0200, Sun 1000-2100
AP02)	H420	670	10/1	R. Globo - Equatorial, Macapá: 24h
CE07)	H606	670	1/0.25	R. Cultura, Várzea Alegre: 0800-0100
GO08)	H747	670	10/1	R. São Francisco, Anápolis
MG12)	L310	670	10/2.5	R. Educadora, Montes Claros: 0800-0300
MG126)	L347	670	1/0.25	R. Montanhesa, Ponte Nova: 24h
MG123)	L361	670	5/0.25	R. Vitoriosa, Uberaba
MG135)	N202	670	1/0.25	R. Cidade, Bambuí: 0800-0300(Sat -0000)
MS23)	I408	670	1/0.25	R. Patriarca, Cassilândia
MS28)	N600	670	10	Super R. Fronteira, Ponta Porã
MT16)	I422	670	6/1	R. Transpantaneira, Poconé
MT44)	I436	670	1	R. Atitude, Lucas do Rio Verde
PA02)	I537	670	5/0.25	R. Rural, Altamira: 0730-0100
PA22)	I539	670	5/0.25	R. Atalaia, Óbidos
PA27)	I546	670	1/0.25	R. Tropical, Paragominas
PI32)	I927	670	1/0.25	R. Livramento, José de Freitas
PR10)	J231	670	3/0.25	R. Canção Nova Esperança, Nova Esperança: 24h
PR11)	J248	670	10/2	R. Globo, Curitiba:24h
RS18)	K296	670	2.5/0.25	R. Cult. Jaguarão, Santa. Vitória do Palmar
RS19)	K370	670	1/0.25	R. Gazeta, Carazinho: 24h
SE03)	J921	670	10/5	R. Cultura de Sergipe, Aracaju: 24h
SP24)	K574	670	1/0.5	R. Oceânica, Caraguatatuba: 0900-2200 (SS silent)
SP25)	K585	670	1/0.25	R. Centro Oeste, Garça
SP26)	K598	670	1/0.5	R. Convenção, Itu: 24h
BA08)	H471	680	10/2	R. Clube, Sto. Antônio de Jesús: 24h
GO09)	H765	680	10/0.5	R. Difusora, Jataí
GO49)	H787	680	5/1	R. Mantiqueira, Niquelândia: 0800-0100, (Sat -2200, Sun 1100-)
MA03)	H885	680	20	R. Dif. do Maranhão, São Luís: 24h
MG173)	L270	680	2/0.25	R. Difusora, Ouro Fino: 24h
MG13)	L326	680	1/0.25	R. União, João Pinheiro
MG71)	L296	680	5/0.25	R. Novo Tempo, Governador Valadares
MG196)	L348	680	1/0.25	R. Futura, Ibiá
MS02)	I389	680	10/1	R. Cultura, Campo Grande: 0830-0500, Sun 1000-0400
PB26)	I683	680	2.5/0.25	R. Integração do Brejo, Bananeiras: 24h
PE06)	I793	680	10/1	R. Grande Rio, Petrolina
PR155)	J362	680	5/0.25	R. Poema, Pitanga: 24h
RJ07)	J452	680	20/5	R. Copacabana, Rio de Janeiro
RS69)	K275	680	50	R. Farroupilha, Porto Alegre: 24h
SP27)	K576	680	1/0.25	R. Dif.680 AM, Catanduva
SP28)	K628	680	2/0.25	R. Piratininga, Piraju
BA96)	H453	690	10/1	R. Cultura, Ilhéus: 24h
CE08)	H587	690	25/10	R. Shalom, Fortaleza: 24h
ES10)	I201	690	10/1	R. America, Vitoria: 24h, SS 1000-2200
GO48)	H780	690	50/1	R. Sociedade Ceres, Ceres
MG14)	L228	690	50/5	R. Mineira, Belo Horizonte: 1200-0245
MS03)	I402	690	5/0.25	R. Cultura, Naviraí: 0800-0300, Sun 1100-0100
MT31)	I451	690	5/1	R. Parecis, Diamantino
PA03)	I532	690	20/5	R. Clube do Pará, Belém: 24h
PR13)	I229	690	5/1	R. Dif. de Londrina, Londrina
PR14)	J252	690	1/0.25	R. Dif., Ponta Grossa
PR143)	J360	690	5/0.25	R. Voz do Sudoeste, Coronel Vivida: 24h
RS21)	K252	690	5/0.5	R. Progresso, Ijuí: 0800-0400 SS -0300
SC07)	J772	690	5/1	R. Clube, Lages: 24h
SP29)	K561	690	1/0.25	R. Bebedouro, Bebedouro: 0800-0100
SP30)	K588	690	1/0.25	R. Clube, Guaratinguetá
SP31)	K625	690	1/0.25	R. Cidade, Pereira Barreto: 0800-2300
SP220)	K646	690	1/0.25	R. Brasil, Santa Bárbara d'Oeste: 24h
TO12)	N661	690	25/1.5	R. Liberdade, Palmas: 24h
BA10)	H500	700	25/1	R. Cultura, Feira de Santana: 24h
GO47)	H801	700	25/0.5	R. Pouso Alto, Piracanjuba

MW	Call	kHz	kW	Station, location, h. of tr.
MT21)	I428	700	20/1	R. Sorriso, Sorriso
PI04)	I890	700	10/5	R. Globo, Teresina: 24h
PR92)	J225	700	10/0.25	R. Capital do Papel, Telêmaco Borba
RJ56)	J507	700	5/0.4	R. Aliança, Italva
RS123)	K247	700	1/0.25	R. Sideral, Getúlio Vargas: 24h
RS22)	K356	700	1/0.25	R. Batovi, São Gabriel
SP32)	K686	700	50	R. Estadão, São Paulo
AL02)	H240	710	5/1	R. Jornal, Maceió
BA46)	H490	710	10/0.25	R. 21 News, Eunápolis
CE09)	H628	710	1/0.25	R. Asa Branca, Boa Viagem: 0800-2300
DF07)	H710	710	10/2.5	R. Aliança, Brasília: 24h
MA12)	H891	710	1	R. Verdes Campos, Pinheiro: 0800-0100
MA27)	H910	710	1/0.5	R. Verdes Vales, Grajaú
MG79)	L219	710	1/0.25	R. Cancella, Ituiutaba: 0800-0200
MG15)	L258	710	20/0.5	R. Manhuaçu, Manhuaçu: 24h
MG80)	L319	710	2/0.25	R. Planeta, Carmo do Paranaíba: 24h
MG16)	L333	710	2/0.25	R. Dif., Pouso Alegre: 24h
MT08)	I386	710	5/0.5	R. Cultura, Cuiabá
MT23)	I436	710	5/1	R. Nova Xavantina, Nova Xavantina
PA04)	I534	710	25/5	R. Rural, Santarém: 0700-0300
PB03)	I685	710	5/0.25	R. Educadora, Conceição: 24h
PI19)	I901	‡710	1/0.25	R. Alvorada do Sertão, São João do Piauí
PI23)	I933	710	1/0.5	R. Clube, Barras
PR141)	J328	710	1/0.25	R. Alternativa, Cândido de Abreu: 0800-0100(Sun -1000)
RJ09)	J451	710	10	R. Sucesso AM, Rio de Janeiro:24h
SC08)	J793	710	1/0.25	R. Fraiburgo, Fraiburgo: 0800-0300
SP33)	K559	710	10/0.25	R. 710, Bauru
AC01)	H202	720	10	R. Integração, Cruzeiro do Sul: 0900-0300
AM05)	H281	720	1	CBN, Itacoatiara: 24h
MG28)	L330	720	2.5/0.5	R. Divinópolis, Divinópolis: 24h
MS04)	I390	720	5/1	R. Clube, Dourados
MT20)	I411	720	5/1	R. Difusora, Barra do Garças
PE07)	I770	720	100	R. Globo, Recife: 24h
RS23)	K276	720	100	R. Guaíba, Porto Alegre: 24h
SP34)	K575	720	1/0.25	R. Difusora, Casa Branca
SP35)	K701	720	1/0.25	R. Sentinela, Ourinhos: 24h
SP36)	K718	720	1/0.25	R. RC Vale, Cruzeiro
SP37)	K722	720	1/0.25	R. Espaço Livre, Olímpia: 24h
CE45)	H640	730	1/0.25	R. Sinal, Aracati
ES16)	I217	730	10/0.5	R. Novo Tempo, Vitória
GO31)	H759	730	50/5	R. 730 do Brasil, Goiânia
MA04)	H896	730	1/0.25	R. Eldorado, Codó
MG17)	L287	730	5/1	R. JM 730, Uberaba
MG18)	L297	730	10/1	R. Manchester, Juiz de Fora
MS38)	I452	730	1/0.5	R. Princesa do Vale, Camapuã
MT09)	I410	730	10/2.5	R. Jornal, Cáceres
PE08)	I780	730	10/5	Em. Rural, A Voz do São Francisco, Petrolina
PR15)	J208	730	7/0.6	R. Marumby, Curitiba
PR16)	J323	730	1/0.25	R. Objetiva, Campo Mourão
PR147)	J353	730	5/0.25	R. Integração Metropolitana, Corbélia
RS24)	K268	730	5/1	R. Planalto, Passo Fundo: 24h
SC09)	J787	730	5/1	R. Tubá, Tubarão: 0800-0100
SP38)	K523	730	10/0.25	R. Cidade, Jundiaí
SP39)	K610	730	10/1	R. Dirceu, Marília
AC02)	H206	740	20/10	CBN Amazonia, Rio Branco:24h
BA11)	H446	740	100	R. Soc. da Bahia, Salvador: 24h
MT25)	N403	740	1/0.5	R. Cidade, Alto Araguaia
PR17)	J259	740	1/0.25	R. Goioerê, Goioerê: 0800-0100(Sun -2100)
PR135)	J354	740	1/0.25	R. Placar, Ortigueira: 0800-2200(Sun -1800)
RS25)	K265	740	2.5/0.25	R. Palmeira, Palmeira das Missões: 0900-0300
RS26)	K283	740	5/0.25	R. Cultura Riograndina, Rio Grande: 24h
SC10)	J753	740	10/1	CBN, Florianópolis: 24h
SP93)	K519	740	10/1	R. Assunção, Jales
SP40)	K553	740	1/0.25	R. Cultura, Bariri: 0730-0200(Sat-0100), Sun 1000-2300
SP41)	K650	740	25/0.5	R. Trianon, São Paulo
DF01)	H709	750	50/25	R. Jovem Pan, Brasília: 24h
MG19)	L213	750	100/5	R. América, Belo Horizonte
PA28)	I541	750	1/0.25	R. Ximango, Alenquer
PB04)	I682	750	1/0.25	R. Panati, Patos
PI05)	I897	750	1/0.25	R. Liberdade, Campo Maior
RS27)	K264	750	5/0.25	R. Osório, Osório: 0900-0200 Sun -2300
SC11)	J815	750	5/0.25	R. Aliança, Concórdia: 0730-0300
SE04)	J927	750	10/0.25	R. Progresso, Lagarto: 0800-0300
SP42)	K516	750	1/0.25	R. Clube, Osvaldo Cruz: 1000-2200, Sat 1200-1800, Sun 0900-1700
SP43)	K642	750	12/0.5	R. CMN, Ribeirão Preto
SP44)	K661	750	1.5/0.25	R. Super Piratininga, São José dos Campos
SP283)	K696	750	5/0.5	R. Atual, Registro
TO03)	H792	750	1/0.25	R. Tocantins, Tocantinópolis
AL12)	H252	760	1/0.25	R.Delmiro, Delmiro Gouveia: 0900-2400
AP03)	H424	760	5	Rede Amapaense de Rdif., Macapá
BA44)	H461	760	5/0.5	R. Cidade, Vitória da Conquista (fpl 1550)
CE10)	H588	760	25/10	R. Uirapuru, Fortaleza
GO43)	H775	760	5/0.5	R. Rio Claro, Iporã: 0800-2300
GO11)	H783	760	10/0.5	R. Pousada do Rio Quente, Caldas Novas: 0800-0300 SS -2200
MG83)	L257	760	2.5/0.25	R. Difusora, Machado
MG137)	L360	760	10/5	R. Terra, Monte Claros
MT32)	N408	760	10/5	R. Natureza, Chapada dos Guimarães: 24h
PR12)	J343	760	10/0.25	R. Cacique, Guarapuava
RJ11)	J478	760	25/1	R. Manchete AM, Niterói: 24h
RS28)	K222	760	1/0.25	R. Princesa do Jacuí, Candelária
RS29)	K351	760	2.5/0.25	R. Ametista, Planalto: 0800-0200
SC12)	J742	760	25/2	R. Nereu Ramos, Blumenau: 0730-0100
SP149)	K541	760	1/0.25	R. Urubupungá, Andradina
SP45)	K560	760	10/0.5	R. Auri-Verde, Bauru
BA51)	H491	770	1/0.25	R. Rio Corrente, Santa Maria da Vitória
CE11)	H609	770	10/0.25	R. Vale do Salgado, Lavras da Mangabeira: 0800-2300, SS 0900-2200
ES03)	I211	770	5/0.25	R. Globo AM, Cachoeiro de Itapemirim
GO12)	H745	770	5/1	R. A Voz do Coração Imaculado, Anápolis: 24h
MA28)	H922	770	1/0.25	R. Vitória, Coelho Neto
MA41)	H902	770	10	R. Boa Noticia, Balsas
MG20)	L209	770	2.5/0.25	R. Cultura d'Oeste, Lavras: 0800-0200
MG21)	L302	770	10/0.5	R. Clube de Patos, Patos de Minas: 0700-0200(SS. 0900-0300)
MG108)	L315	770	5/0.5	R. Pontal do Triangulo, Iturama
MG22)	L337	770	1/0.25	R. Itabira, Itabira
MS11)	I412	770	5/0.5	R. Caiuás, Dourados
MT28)	N404	770	1	R. Cidade de Matupá, Matupá: 0900-0300
MT45)	I434	770	5/1	R. Xavantes, Jaciara: 0900-0030, (Sun 1000-2200)
PA29)	I560	770	10/0.25	R. Clube, Marabá
PR131)	J344	770	5/0.25	R. Cidade, Cambé
SE05)	J922	770	10/5	R. Atalaia de Sergipe, Aracaju
SP46)	K506	770	5/0.5	R. Mix, Limeira: 0700-0000 SS -0100
CE55)	H657	780	10/1	R. Seara, Nova Russas: 24h
GO13)	H789	780	10/1	R. Soc. Vera Cruz, Goianésia: 0700-2300
MA24)	H919	780	10/5	R. Alvorada, Zé Doca
MG23)	L246	780	1	R. Educadora Jovem Pan, Uberlândia
MG103)	L259	780	10/1	R. Manhumirim, Manhumirim: 0800-0100(Sat -0300, Sun -0000)
PE09)	I771	780	30/10	R. Jornal do Comércio, Recife: 24h
PR18)	J247	780	1/0.25	R. Porta Voz, Cianorte: 24h
PR19)	J305	780	5/0.25	R. Chopinzinho, Chopinzinho: 24h
RS30)	K229	780	5/2	R. Diário da Manhã, Carazinho:24h
RS31)	K279	780	25	R. Caicara, Porto Alegre: 24h
SC13)	J788	780	2.5	R. Marconi, Urussanga: 0900-0200, Sun 1000-2230
SC54)	J751	780	0.5	R. Brasil Novo, Jaraguá do Sul: 24h
SP161)	K619	780	1/0.25	R. Dif., Monte Aprazível: 0800-0100
SP47)	K695	780	50/10	CBN, São Paulo: 24h
BA13)	H484	790	10/1	R. Barreiras "RB 790", Barreiras: 0800-0500(SS -0300)
BA14)	H505	790	1/0.25	R. Regional, Serrinha
CE12)	H629	790	1/0.25	R. Jornal Centro Sul, Iguatu
GO28)	H761	790	5/0.5	R. Xavantes, Ipameri
GO14)	H771	790	1/0.25	R. Eldorado, Mineiros
MA29)	H904	790	1/0.25	R. Rio Turiaçu, Santa Helena
MA20)	H915	790	1/0.25	R. Cultura, Açailândia
MA30)	H899	790	1/0.25	R. Rio Flores, Tuntum: 24h
MG24)	L299	790	5/0.25	R. Soc. Ponte Nova, Ponte Nova: 0800-0200
MG25)	L311	790	1/0.25	R. Treze de Junho, Mantena
MG26)	L314	790	5/1	R. Tropical, Lagoa da Prata: 24h
MT22)	I456	790	1	R. Regional, Nortelândia
PB05)	I679	790	2.5/1	R. Cultura 790, Guarabira: 0700-0300
PI36)	I931	790	1/0.25	R. Mafrense, Simplício Mendes
PR130)	J316	790	2.5/0.25	R. Clube, Faxinal
PR20)	J337	790	10/0.25	R. RCC, Curitiba: 24h
RS32)	K285	790	1/0.25	R. Rio Pardo, Rio Pardo
SC14)	J789	790	1/0.25	R. Videira, Videira: 0830-0300
SP48)	K538	790	1/0.25	R. Brasil, Adamantina: 24h
SP49)	K546	790	5/0.5	R. Cultura, Araraquara: 24h
SP162)	K674	790	1/0.25	R. Cultura, Taubaté
AL17)	H256	800	10	R. Palmares, Maceió
DF02)	H705	800	10/1	R. MEC, Brasília: 24h
PI08)	I921	800	10	R. Antares, Teresina: 0930-0100
RJ12)	J457	800	100	R. MEC, Rio de Janeiro: 24h
RS33)	K292	800	10	R. Universidade, Santa Maria: 24h
BA54)	H528	810	10/0.25	R. Nossa Senhora de Guadalupe,

MW	Call	kHz	kW	Station, location, h. of tr.
				Riacho de Santana
CE13)	H589	810	50/5	R. Verdes Mares, Fortaleza: 24h
GO15)	H767	810	5/0.5	R. Alvorada, Rialma: 0830-0100
MG27)	L202	810	1	R. Aimorés, Aimorés
MG92)	L252	810	1/0.25	R. Educadora, Ubá: 24h
MG76)	L266	810	2/0.25	R. Clube, Nepomuceno
MG138)	L354	810	1/0.25	R. Cidade, Capinópolis
MG156)	L366	810	5/0.5	R. Rainha de Paz, Patrocínio: 24h
MT33)	N402	810	1/0.25	R. Floresta, São José do Rio Claro: 0900-0200
MT34)	N406	810	1/0.25	R. Floresta AM, Alta Floresta: 0900-0200
PR49)	J261	810	2/0.25	Rede Terra Nativa, Cornélio Procópio
PR111)	J336	810	5/0.5	R. Esperança, Prudentópolis
RS136)	K324	810	1.9/0.25	R. Cinderela, Campo Bom
SP50)	K604	810	1/0.25	R. Dif. Jundiaiense, Jundiaí
SP89)	K655	810	1/0.5	R. Universal, Santos
SP51)	K732	810	5/0.5	R. Cancao Nova São José do Rio Preto
AC03)	H...	820	1/0.25	R. Educ. 6 de Agosto, Xapuri: 1000-0100
AC12)	H207	820	0.25	R. Dif. de Tarauacá, Tarauacá
AM06)	H294	820	1/0.25	R. Princesa, Manacapuru: 24h
BA15)	H534	820	20/1	R. Cultura, Utinga: 0830-0100
CE14)	H624	820	1/0.25	R. União, Camocim
CE60)	H655	‡820	1/0.25	R. Sul Cearense, Brejo Santo
ES04)	I212	820	10/2.5	R. Gazeta, Vitória
GO16)	H752	820	50/5	R. Bandeirantes, Goiânia
MG29)	L255	820	1/0.25	R. Globo, Barbacena: 24h
MG167)	L373	820	3/0.25	R. Bom Sucesso, Minas Movas
MG30)	L291	820	1/0.25	R. da Familia, São Sebastião do Paraíso: 24h
MT10)	I400	820	10/1	R. Dif., Cáceres: 0800-0130
PA05)	I543	820	1	R. Regional, Conceição do Araguaia: 0900-2300
PE10)	I775	820	5/1	R. Universitária, Recife
PI06)	I912	820	5/0.25	R. Cacique Bruenque, Regeneração
PR21)	J238	820	10/5	R. Cultura, Foz do Iguaçu
PR150)	J357	820	1/0.25	R. Princesa, Roncador: 0830-0030
RJ13)	J477	820	5/0.25	R. Globo, Macaé: 24h
RS34)	K241	820	5/1	R. do Vale, Estrela: 0900-0200
SC15)	J738	820	10/5	R. Globo, Vale do Itajai: 24h
SP52)	K542	820	1/0.25	R. Aparecida, Aparecida
SP53)	K602	820	1/0.25	R. Jauense, Jaú: 0700-0300, Sun 0800-2200
SP54)	K622	820	0.5/0.25	R. Clube, Ourinhos
SP55)	K624	820	1/0.25	R. Difusora, Penápolis
BA67)	H506	830	5/0.25	R. Extremo Sul da Bahia, Itamaraju: 0700-0100 Sun: -0000
CE65)	H659	830	1/0.25	R. Pioneira, Forquilha: 0800-0230, Sat 1000(Sun 0800)-0100
GO50)	H805	830	1/0.25	R. Sempre, Goiatuba: 24h
MA26)	H905	830	10/1	R. Mirante do Maranhão, Imperatriz
MA21)	H925	830	1/0.25	R. Boa Esperança, Esperantinópolis
MG31)	L244	830	15/5	R. Gerais, Belo Horizonte
MS07)	I396	830	5/0.5	R. Cidade Maracaju, Maracaju: 0900-0300
MT26)	N401	830	1/0.25	R. Educadora, Juina
PA24)	I556	830	10/1	R. Guarany de Marajó, Soure
PI07)	I906	830	1/0.25	R. Primeira Capital, Oeiras
PI37)	I934	830	1/0.25	R. União, União
PR22)	J224	830	7.5/0.75	R. Iguassu, Araucária: 24h
PR24)	J266	830	10/0.5	CBN, Londrina: 24h
PR23)	J311	830	1/0.25	R. Progresso, Clevelândia
RJ30)	J488	830	10/0.5	R. Tropical Solimões, Rio de Janeiro: 24h
RN02)	J595	830	1/0.25	R. Rural do Caicó, Caicó
RS35)	K332	830	5/0.25	R. Independente, Cruz Alta
RS232)	K346	830	5/0.6	R. Cassino, Rio Grande: M-F 0900-2300
RS200)	K346	830	5	R. Cassino, Rio Grande: 0900-2300
SC16)	J773	830	1/0.25	R. Cruz de Malta, Lauro Müller
SE06)	J926	830	20/1	R. Princesa da Serra, Itabaiana: 24h
SP56)	K681	830	10/1	R. Lider, Votuporanga: 24h
SP227)	K746	830	5/1	R. Novo Tempo, Nova Odessa: 24h
AL13)	H253	840	10/0.25	R. Canavieiro, Coruripe dos Palmares
AM07)	H298	840	25/5	R. Rio Madeira, Manicoré
BA16)	H447	840	25/5	R. Excelsior da Bahia, Salvador: 24h
CE51)	H648	840	1/0.5	R. Campo Maior, Quixeramobim: 0800-2000 Sat -2200 Sun -2300
PI38)	I930	840	1/0.25	R. Ribeirão, Demerval Lobão
PI39)	I937	‡840	1/0.25	R. Vitória, Batalha
PR75)	J320	840	10/1.2	R. Inconfidência, Umuarama: 24h
RS36)	K248	840	10/1	R. Capital, Porto Alegre
SC17)	J750	840	10/1	R. Rural, Concórdia: 24h
SP57)	K687	840	100/50	R. Bandeirantes, São Paulo: 24h
BA17)	H474	850	5/0.25	R. Caraiba, Senhor do Bonfim
CE15)	H599	850	1	R. Iracema, Juazeiro do Nte

MW	Call	kHz	kW	Station, location, h. of tr.
GO17)	H776	850	5/1	R. Tropical, Porangatu: 0900-0300
MA31)	H923	850	10/0.5	R. Cidade, Vitória do Mearim: 0900-2200
MG32)	L233	850	1/0.25	R. Difusora Formiguense, Formiga
MG33)	L254	850	10/0.5	R. Por um Mundo Melhor, Governador Valadares: 24h
MG34)	L295	850	5/0.25	R. Tupaciguara, Tupaciguara: 0900-0300
MS30)	I438	850	1/0.25	R. Difusora Nor'estado, São Gabriel
MT02)	I416	850	10/2	R. Sulmatogrossense, Poxoréo: 24h, Sat -1900, Sun 0800-1700
PA17)	I538	850	10/1	R. Itacaíunas, Marabá
PA06)	I555	850	1/0.25	R. Tocantins, Cametá
PA18)	I557	850	5/1	R. Itaituba, Itaituba
PB22)	I693	850	5/1	R. Rural, Guarabira
PI30)	I909	850	1/0.25	R. Grande Picos, Picos
PR50)	J254	850	5/0.25	R. Dif. Colméia, Campo Mourão
PR86)	J291	850	2/0.25	R. Alvorada do Sul, Rebouças
RJ31)	J470	850	10/0.5	R. Campos Dif., Campos dos Goytacazes: 24h
RO03)	J675	‡850	5/1	R. Ariquemes, Ariquemes
SC20)	J808	850	2.5/0.25	R. Cidade, Brusque
SC102)	J807	850	1/0.25	R. Atalaia, Campo Erê
SP59)	K563	850	2.5/0.5	R. Nova Clube, Biriguí
SP58)	K644	850	2.5/0.25	R. Jornal, Rio Claro
CE16)	H592	860	25/10	R. Cidade de Fortaleza, Maracanaú
RJ14)	J459	860	100	R. CBN, Rio de Janeiro
RS37)	K288	860	10/1	R. Guarathan, Santa Maria: 0800-0300
AL03)	H245	870	5/1	R. Educ. Sampaio, Palmeira dos Indios: 0800-0300
AM19)	H322	870	1/0.25	R. Cidade, Manacapuru: 1000-0200
BA18)	H457	870	12/0.25	R. Nacional, Itabuna
BA84)	H499	870	5/1	R. Cidade, Juazeiro: 24h, Sun 1000-2200
CE17)	H591	870	1/0.25	R. Liberdade, Iguatu
CE66)	H658	870	1/0.25	R. Tabajara, São Benedito
ES20)	ZYI213	870	5/0.25	R. Globo. Linhares: 24h
GO18)	H749	870	5/0.5	R. Lago Dourado, Uruaçu
GO32)	H754	870	1/0.25	R. Universitária, Goiânia:24h
MA05)	H906	870	10/0.5	R. Mirante, Codó: 24h
MG78)	L350	870	10/0.5	R. Juriti, Januária
MG38)	L318	870	1/0.5	R. Cultura, Diamantina
MG66)	L324	870	5/0.25	R. Sacramento, Sacramento: 0800-2300, Sat 1200-2200)
MG128)	L349	870	5/0.25	R. Atividade Muriaé
MG127)	L350	870	5/0.25	R. Voz, Januária: 24h
MT35)	N409	870	1/0.5	R. Garça Branca, Guiratinga
PA11)	I547	870	1/0.25	R. Marajó, Breves
PR25)	J243	870	5/0.25	R. Nova Ingá, Maringá: 1000-0100
SC96)	J784	870	12/0.25	R. São Francisco, São Francisco do Sul: 24h
SP60)	K620	870	1/0.25	R. Novo Horizonte, Novo Horizonte
SP61)	K705	870	5/1	R. Central, Campinas: 24h
TO04)	H762	870	1/0.25	R. Anhanguera, Araguaína
MG35)	L235	880	100	R. Inconfidência, Belo Horizonte: 24h
PB18)	I680	880	1/0.25	R. Maringá, Pombal
RS38)	K249	880	25/2.5	R. Itaí, Porto Alegre: 24h
RS87)	K317	880	2.5/0.25	R. São Miguel, Uruguaiana
RS20)	K363	880	8/0.25	R. Seberi, Seberi: 24h
CE46)	H642	890	1/0.25	R. Itatiaia, Santa Quitéria: 0800-0100 (Sun 0900-)
DF03)	H706	890	50/2.5	R. Clube AM 890, Brasília: 24h
MG36)	L250	890	10/1	R. Santa Cruz, Almenara: 0900-2300(Sun -1500)
MG154)	L370	890	5/0.25	R. Clube, Inhapim
MS33)	L453	890	10/0.5	R. Guaicurus, Fátima do Sul: 1000-0000 (Sat -1900), Sun 0800-1700
PA13)	I536	890	5/1	R. Ponta Negra, Santarém
PE11)	I772	890	20/10	R. Tamandaré, Olinda: 24h
PR117)	J287	890	2.5/0.25	R. Ubá, Ivaiporã: 0800-0100
PR26)	J334	890	5/0.25	R. Itapuã, Pato Branco24h
RJ59)	J499	890	10/0.5	R. Musical, Cantagalo
RS39)	K215	890	5/0.25	R. Difusora, Bento Gonçalves
RS40)	K295	890	1/0.5	R. Noroeste, Santa Rosa
SC52)	J745	890	1/0.25	R. Clube, Canoinhas: 24h
SC18)	J755	890	1/0.25	R. Santa Catarina, Florianópolis
SP62)	K690	890	50/10	R. Gazeta, São Paulo
SP127)	K703	890	2.5/0.25	R. Cidade, Matão: 24h
SP178)	K562	890	1/0.25	R. Imaculada Conceicao, Bilac
BA19)	H488	900	1	R. Sisal, Conceição do Coité: 0800-0100(SS -2300)
GO41)	H768	900	10/1	R. Rio Verde AM, Rio Verde
MG86)	L207	900	5/0.25	R. Imbiara, Araxá: 24h
MG148)	L311	900	2.5/0.25	Rede Gerais, Carangola: 24h
MG124)	L338	900	5/0.25	R. Vinícola, Andradas
MT36)	I455	900	10/2.5	R. Dif. Arco-Iris, Araputanga: 0900-0030

MW	Call	kHz	kW	Station, location, h. of tr.
MT41)	I431	900	5/1	R. Integração, Primavera do Leste
PA10)	I533	900	25/5	R. Liberal, Belém: 24h
PR27)	J272	900	5/0.25	R. Sant'Ana, Ponta Grossa: 0800-0300
PR28)	J295	900	5/0.25	R. União, Toledo: 0800-0300, Sun 0900-2300
RJ15)	J454	900	50/10	R. Tamoio, Rio de Janeiro: 24h
RN03)	J591	900	10	R. Nordeste Evangélica, Natal: 24h
RO04)	J672	900	5/1	R. Alvorada de Rondônia, Ji-Paraná: 0800-0400
RS41)	K211	900	2.5/0.5	R. Aratiba, Aratiba: 24h
RS179)	K263	900	5/0.5	R. ABC 900, Nôvo Hamburgo: 24h
RS164)	K301	900	1/0.25	R. Municipal, São Pedro do Sul: 24h
SP63)	K511	900	5/0.25	R. Difusora, Presidente Prudente
SP64)	K664	900	10/0.8	R. Jovem Pan, São José do Rio Preto
SP65)	K742	900	1/0.25	R. Globo, Itapetininga
CE61)	H645	910	4/0.25	R. Caiçari, Sobral
GO20)	H763	910	5/0.25	R. Paranaíba, Itumbiara: 0800-0300
GO23)	H804	910	10/0.5	R. Cidade, Jaraguá: 0800-0300
MG37)	L292	910	1/0.25	R. Teófilo Otoni, Teófilo Otoni: 24h
MG132)	L346	910	1/0.25	R. Gospel CRN, Nova Serrana
MG149)	N206	910	5/1	R. Globo, Juiz de Fora: 24h
PE12)	I785	910	5/1	R. Super Liberdade, Caruaru: 24h
PI41)	I935	910	10/1	CBN, Teresina: 24h
PR29)	J207	910	1/0.25	R. Nova AM, Apucarana: 0800-0000
RS43)	K320	910	5/0.5	R. Venâncio Aires, Venâncio Aires:
SC19)	J811	910	4/0.5	R. Difusora, Içara: 24h
SC90)	J824	910	1/0.25	R. Rainha das Quedas, Abelardo Luz
SP66)	K536	910	7.5/0.25	R. Onda Livre, Piracicaba: 24h
SP228)	K763	910	1/0.25	R. Princesa, Monte Azul Paulista
BA42)	H476	920	5/0.25	R. Educ. Santana de Caetité, Caetité: 24h
BA57)	H519	920	25/2	R. Novo Tempo, Salvador
ES05)	I207	920	10/5	R. Cultura, Linhares
GO33)	H788	920	5/1	R.. Vale da Serra, São Luís de Monte Belos: 0800-2300
MG39)	L271	920	5/0.5	R. Cultura, Visconde do Rio Branco: 0800-0200, Sun 0900-2100
PB31)	I697	‡920	5/0.5	R. CBN, João Pessoa
PI09)	I895	920	1/0.25	R. Dif. Grande, Picos
PI11)	I893	920	10/0.5	R. Educadora, Parnaíba
RJ41)	J494	920	10/0.5	R. Sociedade, Volta Redonda
RN04)	J600	920	1/0.25	R. Currais Novos, Currais Novos
RS44)	K348	920	20/2	R.Tramandaí, Tramandaí
SP67)	K584	920	10/0.25	R. Imperador, Franca
SP222)	K769	920	1/0.25	R. Bandeirantes, Penápolis: 24h
SP221)	K775	920	40/1	R. Nacional Gospel, Cotia
AM16)	H296	930	10	R. Boas Novas, Manaus: 24h
CE18)	H605	930	1/0.25	R. Cetama, Barbalha
CE52)	H646	930	7/0.25	R. Metropolitana, Caucaia
MG41)	L220	930	2.5/0.25	R. Clube, Campo Belo: 0900-0100 (SS -2100)
MG42)	L229	930	10/5	R. Vitoriosa, Araguari
MG87)	L237	930	20/1	R. Globo, Governador Valadares: 24h
MS05)	I454	930	10/0.25	R. Capital, Campo Grande
MT12)	I423	930	10/0.5	R. Clube, Rondonópolis: 0900-0200 (Sat -2200, Sun -0000)
MT37)	N400	930	10/0.25	R. Jornal, Pontes e Lacerda: 0900-0100
PR30)	J227	930	1/0.25	R. Cultura, Rolândia
PR31)	J232	930	10/1	R. Cultura, Curitiba
PR69)	J235	930	10/1	R. Princesa, Francisco Beltrão: 0845-0200, Sun 0955-0100
RS45)	K230	930	20/2.5	R. Caxias, Caxias do Sul:24h
RS46)	K298	930	10/0.5	R. Santo Angelo, Santo Angelo: 0800-0300
SE07)	J923	930	20/5	R. 930AM - Liberdade AM, Aracaju
SP71)	K500	930	1/0.25	R. Dinâmica , Santa. Fé do Sul: 0900-0100 (Sun -0000)
SP68)	K503	930	1/0.25	R. Clube, Itapira
SP69)	K652	930	10/1	R. Cultura, Santos: 24h
SP70)	K713	930	5/1	R. Canção Nova, Agudos
SP214)	K747	930	1/0.25	R. Jóia, Adamantina: 0900-0100
AC04)	H204	940	10/1	R. Verdes Florestas, Cruzeiro do Sul: 0930-0200 Sun 1000-0040
PI25)	I911	940	10/0.25	R. AM 7 Cidades, Piracuruca
RJ16)	J453	940	100	Super RBV, Rio de Janeiro
BA50)	H489	950	1/0.25	R. Bahia Noroeste, Paulo Afonso
CE19)	H593	950	10/1	R. Educadora do Nordeste, Sobral: 0800-0130
GO21)	H764	950	5/0.25	R. Dif., Itumbiara: 0800-0300(Sun -1000)
MA17)	H916	950	10/0.25	R. Dif. Karajás, João Lisboa
MG43)	L212	950	25/10	R. Atalaia, Belo Horizonte
MG44)	L281	950	7/0.5	R. Indy, Bueno Brandão: 0800-2200
MT17)	I439	950	5/1	R. Tucunaré, Juara: 24h
PB17)	I681	950	1/0.25	R. Jornal, Sousa

MW	Call	kHz	kW	Station, location, h. of tr.
PE13)	I782	950	25/5	R. Planalto, Carpina: 24h
PI20)	I932	950	10/0.25	R. São José dos Altos, Altos
PI42)	I923	950	1/0.25	R. Boa Esperança, Padre Marcos
PR114)	J239	950	5/0.25	R. Difusora, Irati: 24h
RS47)	K260	950	10/0.25	R. Independente, Lajeado: 24h
SC21)	J736	950	1/0.25	R. Vale, Tijucas: 24h
SP72)	K510	950	5/0.25	R. 950, Vera Cruz
AL04)	H241	960	10	R. Difusora de Alagôas, Maceió: 24h
CE37)	H618	960	1/0.25	R. Cultura dos Inhamuns, Tauá
ES15)	I216	960	25/0.25	R. Diocesana, Cachoeiro de Itapemirim: 24h, Sat 0700-1510
GO45)	H802	960	50/1	R. Caraíba, Aparecida de Goiânia: 0500-0100
MS61)	N609	960	5	R. Fronteira, Corumbá
PA26)	I551	960	1/0.25	R. Clube, Itaituba
PR109)	J217	960	2.5/0.25	R. Legendária, Lapa: 0830-0300
PR32)	J257	960	1/0.25	R. Globo, Maringá: 24h
RS48)	K291	960	10/1	R. Imembuí, Santa Maria: 24h
SC22)	J733	960	5/0.25	R. Guarujá, Orleans: 0800-0100(Sun -0000)
SC23)	J813	960	8/0.25	R. Super Difusora, Xanxerê
SP73)	K689	960	50/10	R. São Paulo, São Paulo
TO09)	H793	960	25/5	R. Jovem Palmas, Palmas
BA20)	H451	970	10/5	R. Sociedade, Feira de Santana: 0700-0100
CE20)	H612	970	5/0.25	R. Monólitos, Quixadá
MG45)	L243	970	5/0.25	R. Caratinga, Caratinga
MG46)	L285	970	2.5/0.25	R. São João Del Rey, São João Del Rey: 24h
MG47)	L321	970	1/0.25	R. Central, Monte Alegre de Minas: 0900-2300
MS18)	I399	970	5/0.5	R. Vale do Taquari, Coxim: 1000-0500, Sun 24h
PB06)	I684	970	1/0.25	R. Princesa Isabel, Princesa Isabel: 0830-2300
PI43)	I910	970	3/0.5	R. Vale do Parnaíba, Luzilândia: 0940-2100 Sat 1500-2100 Sun 1430-1700
PR33)	J260	970	7.5/1	R. Alvorada, Londrina
PR34)	J277	970	10/0.25	R. Difusora do Paraná, Marechal Cândido Rondón: 0800-0300
RS49)	K201	970	50/10	R. Pampa, Porto Alegre: 24h
RS50)	K349	970	10/0.5	R. Alto Uruguai, Humaitá: 0800-0200 (Sat -2200), Sun 0900-0100
SC24)	J730	970	5/0.25	R. Araguaia, Brusque: 24h
SP74)	K505	970	5/0.25	R. Super Dif., Itapetininga: 24h, Sun 1400-0300
SP75)	K529	970	1/0.25	R. Piratininga, São João da Boa Vista
SP76)	K684	970	5/0.25	R. Hertz, Franca: 24h
SP215)	K744	970	5/0.25	R. Alvorada, Estrela d'Oeste: 24h
DF04)	H707	980	50/300	R. Nacional, Brasília: 24h
AM23)	H299	990	1	R. Independência, Maués: 0900-0200
BA21)	H483	990	1/0.25	R. Alvorada Gospel, Teixeira de Freitas
PI44)	I922	990	1/0.25	R. Vale do Canindé, Oeiras
PR128)	J293	990	5/0.25	R. Najuá, Irati: 24h
PR121)	J321	990	5/0.25	R. Capital, Cianorte: 24h
RJ53)	J461	990	100/10	R. Record, Rio de Janeiro: 24h
RN05)	J596	990	10/1	R. Rural, Mossoró: 24h
RS51)	K314	990	2/0.5	R. Tupã, Tupanciretã: 24h
RS52)	K335	990	2.5/0.25	R. Sananduva, Sananduva: 0900-0100
RS154)	K360	990	1/0.25	R. Clube, Pedro Osório
SC25)	J763	990	20/0.25	R. Itapiranga, Itapiranga: 0800-0300
SP239)	K579	990	10/0.25	R. Cultura Regional, Dois Córregos
PB30)	I698	1000	2.5/0.5	R. Oeste da Paraíba, Cajazeiras
PE14)	I791	1000	1/0.25	R. Princesa Serrana, Timbaúba: 0800-0100(SS -2230)
SP77)	K522	1000	200	R. Record, São Paulo: 24h
BA22)	H448	1010	25/5	R. Bahia, Salvador
CE21)	H625	1010	12.5/2.5	R. O'Povo, Fortaleza
GO39)	H772	1010	10/0.25	R. Santelenense, Sta. Helena de Goiás
MG50)	L230	1010	10/1	R. Educadora, Coronel Fabriciano
MG48)	L264	1010	10/0.5	CBN, Juiz de Fora: 24h
MG49)	L325	1010	5/0.25	R. Estância, Jacutinga: 0800-2300(SS -0230)
MT13)	I421	1010	5/1	R. Dif., Mirassol d'Oeste: 0900-0200
PR35)	J263	1010	25/5	R. Celinauta, Pato Branco
RS53)	K232	1010	7/0.75	R. 1010, Caxias do Sul: 24h
RS54)	K344	1010	3/1	R. Missionária, São Luíz Gonzaga: 0800(Sun 0900)-0200
SC71)	J764	1010	10/0.3	R. Jaraguá, Jaraguá do Sul: 24h
SC75)	J758	1010	10/1	R. Bandeirantes, Imbituba
SP151)	K507	1010	5/0.5	R. Dif., Lençóis Paulista: 0700-0300
SP78)	K556	1010	5/0.5	R. Independente, Barretos
SP79)	K611	1010	5/0.25	R. Diario, Martinópolis
AL05)	H247	1020	25/1	R. Jovem Pan, Rio Largo
AP04)	H423	1020	1/0.25	R. Porto, Santana
CE22)	H600	1020	5/1	R. Educadora Cariri, Crato: 24h

MW	Call	kHz	kW	Station, location, h. of tr.
CE79)	H664	1020	1/0.25	R. Macambira, Ipueiras: 0800-0000 (Sat -2230), Sun 0700-2130
ES06)	I205	1020	10/0.4	R. Difusora, Colatina: 0800-0300
GO52)	H781	1020	10/0.5	R. Boas Novas, Firminópolis
MG55)	L224	1020	10/1	R. Congonhas, Congonhas: 0800-0100
MG51)	L260	1020	10/0.25	R. Globo, Uberlândia
MS06)	I381	1020	10/0.25	R. Independente, Aquidauana
PB19)	I686	1020	1/0.25	R. Cenecista, Picuí: 0800(SS 1000)-2300
PR36)	J244	1020	10/0.25	R. Super Colombo, Curitiba:24h
PR37)	J307	1020	1/0.25	R. Independência, Medianeira: 0800-0100
PR142)	J359	1020	1/0.25	R. Campo Aberto, Laranjeiras do Sul: 0800-0000
RJ42)	J484	1020	5/0.25	R. Canção Nova, Campos dos Goytacazes: 24h
RO02)	J680	1020	5/1	R. Educadora, Rolim de Moura
RR04)	J702	1020	10/5	R. Folha, Boa Vista: 0800-0200(Sun -2300)
RS102)	K202	1020	25/5	R. Grenal, Porto Alegre: 24h
SC27)	J805	1020	2.5/0.25	R. Continental, Coronel Freitas: 0500-0100, SS silent
SP80)	K513	1020	10/0.25	R. Canção Nova, Cachoeira Paulista
SP81)	K515	1020	5/0.25	R. Cultura, Assis
SP82)	K531	1020	2.5/0.5	R. Educadora, Limeira:24h
SP83)	K600	1020	1.6/0.25	R. Cultura, Jales
BA40)	H475	1030	10/1	R. Bahiana, Itaberaba
GO22)	H746	1030	10/1	R. Imprensa, Anápolis: 0800-0300
MA07)	H892	1030	10/1	R. Jainara, Bacabal
PE15)	I777	1030	20/5	R. Olinda, Olinda: 24h
PR39)	J271	1030	5/0.25	R. Atalaia, Londrina
PR120)	J312	1030	2.5/0.25	R. Clube, Realeza: 0830-0300
PR40)	J329	1030	1/0.25	R. Dif. do Xisto, São Mateus do Sul: 0800-0300
RJ18)	J467	1030	100/5	R. Capital, Rio de Janeiro: 24h
RN31)	J612	1030	1/0.25	R. Vale do Apodi, Apodi: 0800-0200
RO10)	J683	1030	5/1	R. Rondônia, Ariquemes
RS129)	K224	1030	10/0.5	R. Cultura, Cangucu: 0900-0000
RS55)	K253	1030	10/0.5	R. Repórter, Ijuí
SC28)	J771	1030	2/0.5	R. Princesa, Lages
SP84)	K525	1030	5/0.25	R. Difusora, Franca
SP85)	K554	1030	1/0.25	R. Emissora da Barra, Barra Bonita
SP86)	K606	1030	1/0.25	Lins Rádio Clube, Lins
T005)	H791	1030	1/0.25	R. Colinas, Colinas do Tocantins
SP87)	K537	1040	200/100	R. Capital, São Paulo: 24h
BA47)	H494	1050	25/0.75	R. Noticias, Camaçari: 24h
CE54)	H647	1050	1/0.25	R. Primeira Capital, Aquiraz
ES07)	I203	1050	100/1	R. Capixaba, Vitória
GO40)	H760	1050	1/0.25	R. Jornal, Inhumas
MG52)	L236	1050	1/0.25	R. Rural, Tupaciguara: 0900-2200, Sun 0800-1900
MS20)	I391	1050	10/0.5	R. Dif. Paranaibense, Paranaíba: 24h
PB07)	I676	1050	5/1	R. Caturité, Campina Grande: 24h
PR66)	J226	1050	1/0.25	R. Dif. Platinense, Sto. Antônio da Platine
PR99)	J286	1050	5/0.25	R. Cl. AM, Palmas: 24h
RJ19)	J497	1050	10/0.5	R. Angra, Angra dos Reis
SC26)	J867	1050	7/0.25	R. Verde Vale, Braço do Norte: 0715-0300
SP160)	K601	1050	10/0.5	R. Show Jardinópolis
BA23)	H460	1060	5/1	R. Cl. de Conquista, Vitória da Conquista
BA68)	H520	1060	2.5/0.25	R. Cl., Itapicuru: 0800-0200
GO54)	H807	1060	5	R. Serra Dourada, Minacu: 24h
MG53)	L278	1060	25	R. Grande, Belo Horizonte
MG54)	L306	1060	1/0.25	R. Itajubá, Itajubá: 24h
MS39)	N604	1060	5/1	R. Imaculada Conceição, Dourados: 24h
PR42)	J246	1060	10/0.5	R. Evangelizar, Curitiba: 24h
PR43)	J298	1060	1/0.25	R. Colorado, Colorado: 0830-2200 (Sat -2345)
PR44)	J306	1060	10/0.5	R. Educadora, Francisco Beltrão
RJ20)	J495	1060	30/1	R. Canção Nova, Nova Iguaçu
RN06)	J597	1060	5	R. Tapuyo, Mossoró (RPC)
RS56)	K220	1060	1/0.25	R. Camaquense, Camaquã
RS57)	K302	1060	2/0.25	R. São Luís, São Luís Gonzaga: 24h
RS81)	K307	1060	2/0.5	R. Cristal, Soledade: 24h
SC103)	J830	1060	2/0.4	R. Mais Alegria, Florianópolis
SP88)	K533	1060	5/0.25	R. Educadora, Piracicaba: 24h
SP229)	K765	1060	5/0.25	R. Universitária, Garça
BA48)	H492	1070	5/0.5	R. Rural "R. Tropical", Ipiaú
MG56)	L316	1070	1/0.25	R. do Povo, Muzambinho
MG150)	L355	1070	10/0.25	Super Radio Patos, Patos de Minas
MT14)	I427	1070	10/2.5	R. Industrial, Várzea Grande: 24h
PB08)	I673	1070	20/2.5	R. Dif. Cajazeiras, Cajazeiras: 0730-0300
PR45)	J203	1070	1/0.25	R. Dif. União, União da Vitória
PR46)	J319	1070	1/0.25	Super RG, Guaraniaçu: 0830-0300, Sun 1000-0200
RJ21)	J483	1070	10/0.25	R. Cultura Fluminense, Campos dos Goitacazes
RS58)	K218	1070	2/0.25	R. Caçapava, Caçapava do Sul
RS59)	K343	1070	1/0.25	R. Metrópole, Crissiumal: 0830-2200, Sun 0900-0000
RS60)	K357	1070	2/0.25	R. Viva, Bento Gonçalves
SC91)	J747	1070	1/0.25	R. Gralha Azul, Urubici: 0930(Sat 1100)-0200, Sun 1300-1440
SP91)	K603	1070	1/0.25	R. Nova Piratininga, Jaú: 24h
SP145)	K615	1070	10/0.25	R. Metropolitana, Mogi das Cruzes: 24h
SP92)	K633	1070	10/1	R. Presidente Prudente, P. Prudente: 24h
SP212)	K758	1070	1/0.25	R. Jornal, Barretos: 24h
BA24)	H470	1080	10/0.5	R. Subaé, Feira de Santana:24h
BA25)	H485	1080	1/0.25	R. Fascinação, Itapetinga: 0800-0230
CE82)	H670	1080	2.5/0.25	R. Cultura, Quixadá: 0800-2300(SS-0030)
DF05)	H708	1080	25/5	R. Capital, Brasília
MG109)	L232	1080	2.5/0.5	R. Cultura, Dores do Indaiá
MG57)	L261	1080	25/0.7	R. Capital, Juiz de Fora
MT27)	I437	1080	1/0.25	R. Difusora, Itiquira: 24h
PA32)	I540	1080	15/5	R. Novo Tempo, Belém: 24h
PE16)	I784	1080	10/0.5	R. Jornal do Comercio, Caruaru: 24h
PE33)	I824	1080	1/0.25	R. Voluntários da Pátria, Ouricuri
PR47)	J201	1080	2.5/0.5	R. Cl Pontagrossense, Ponta Grossa: 24h
PR48)	J245	1080	1/0.25	R. Cultura do Norte, Paranavaí: 24h
RS61)	K254	1080	3/0.25	R. Marabá, Iraí: 0830-0130
RS62)	K280	1080	10	R. da Universidade, Porto Alegre: 24h
SC29)	J759	1080	2/1	R. Clube, Indaial: 0400-000
SP94)	K557	1080	5/1	R. Difusora, Batatais: 24h
SP95)	K607	1080	1/0.25	R. Alvorada, Lins
SP96)	K669	1080	10/1	R. Boa Nova, Sorocaba
SP97)	K704	1080	1/0.25	R. Monumental, Aparecida: 24h
SP190)	K710	1080	1/0.25	R. Alvorada, Cardoso: 0900-0100
AL15)	H254	1090	5/0.5	R. Gazeta, Pão de Açucar
BA26)	H455	1090	1/0.25	R. Santa Cruz, Ilhéus: 24h
GO24)	H758	1090	25/1	R. 1090, Aparecida de Goiânia: 24h
MA08)	H893	1090	10	R. Rio Balsas, Balsas
MG145)	L357	1090	5/0.25	R. Catuaí, Manhuaçu
PR51)	J283	1090	2.5/0.25	R. Vicente Palotti, Coronel Vivida: 0800-0200(SS -0100)
PR171)	J345	1090	1/0.25	R. Banda 1, Sarandi: 0800-0330
RJ22)	J468	1090	50/5	R. Metropolitana, Rio de Janeiro: 24h
RN07)	J592	1090	10/5	R. Rural, Natal
RS63)	K216	1090	5/0.25	R. Cachoeira, Cachoeira do Sul
RS64)	K262	1090	1/0.25	R. Salette, Marcelino Ramos: 0900-0100
RS65)	K341	1090	1/0.25	R. Giruá, Giruá: 0800-0300
SC30)	J732	1090	1/0.25	R. Colón, Joinville
SC31)	J786	1090	5/0.5	R. Bandeirantes, Tubarão
SP98)	K609	1090	3/0.5	R. Clube, Marília: 24h
SP99)	K618	1090	3/0.25	R. Cultura, Monte Alto: 0830-0100
SP233)	K768	1090	1/0.25	R. Canção Nova, Paulina
CE67)	H638	1100	1/0.25	R. Dif. dos Inhamuns, Tauá: 0730 (Sun 0800)-0030
CE73)	H668	1100	1/0.25	R. Difusora do Vale Acaraú, Acaraú
RN18)	J607	1100	1/0.25	R. Seridó, Caicó
SP100)	K694	1100	150/50	R. Globo, São Paulo: 24h
CE32)	H620	1110	5/0.25	R. Litoral, Cascavel: Tu 0800-2100, Sat 0800-2300, Sun 0900-0300
GO46)	H782	1110	25/2	R. Redentor, Sto. Antônio do Descoberto: 24h
MG58)	L205	1110	1/0.25	R. Planalto, Araguari: 24h
MG59)	L267	1110	1	R. Aurilândia, Nova Lima
MS08)	I392	1110	1	R. Transamérica, Ponta Porã
PB09)	I689	1110	20/10	R. Tabajara, João Pessoa
PR52)	J241	1110	10/1	R. Paiquerê, Londrina: 24h, Sat 0900-0300
PR151)	J356	1110	1/0.5	R. Clube, Ubiratã
RJ23)	J471	1110	50/5	R. Record, Campos dos Goitacazes: 24h
RS66)	K257	1110	2.5/0.25	R. Cultura Jaguarão, Jaguarão: 24h
RS67)	K306	1110	2/0.25	R. Sobradinho, Sobradinho
RS68)	K325	1110	2.5/0.25	R. Cruzeiro do Sul, Itaqui: 0830-0200
RS152)	K364	1110	1/0,25	R. Solaris, Antônio Prado: 24h
SC74)	J743	1110	1/0.25	R. Caçanjure, Caçador: 0900-0300
SC32)	J752	1110	1/0.5	R. Cultura, Florianópolis: 24h
SC33)	J812	1110	2.5	R. São Carlos, São Carlos
SP101)	K544	1110	1/0.25	R. Jovem Luz, Araçatuba: 1000-0000
SP102)	K592	1110	3/0.25	R. Ibitinga, Ibitinga
SP103)	K617	1110	1/0.25	Transamerica Hits, Mogi Mirim
BA72)	H513	1120	5/0.5	R. Belo Campo, Belo Campo
BA79)	H511	1120	0.3	R. Jornal, Souto Soares: 0830-2200, Sun 0800-0100
BA98)	H257	1120	10	R. Estrela, Valenta: 0900-2200(Sun -1500)
CE23)	H598	1120	5/1	R. Tupinambá, Sobral
ES14)	I215	1120	10/1	R. Cricare, São Mateus
MG10)	L272	1120	10/0.5	R. Itatiaia, Ouro Preto

MW	Call	kHz	kW	Station, location, h. of tr.
MG60)	L301	1120	2.5	R. Sete Colinas, Uberaba: 24h
MG61)	L332	1120	1/0.25	R. Serra AM, Boa Esperança: 24h
MS40)	N606	1120	25/1	R. Concordia, Campo Grande
PB10)	I687	1120	1/0.25	R. Independência, Catolé do Rocha: 0800-0100
PE17)	I778	1120	5/1	R. Relógio, Paulista: 24h
PR53)	J253	1120	25/1	R. Mais, São José dos Pinhais: 24h
PR85)	J285	1120	5/0.5	R. Educadora, Laranjeiras do Sul: 0800-0200(Sun -0100)
RS191)	K274	1120	50	R. Rural, Porto Alegre
RS156)	K367	1120	10/0.6	R. Querência, Santo Augusto: 0800-0300
SP104)	K631	1120	1/0.25	R. Nova Porto, Porto Feliz: 24h
SP105)	K660	1120	10/1	R. Cidade, São José dos Campos: 24h
SP106)	K671	1120	1/0.25	R. Clube Imperial, Taquaritinga: 24h
CE72)	H667	1130	10/0.25	R. Patu, Senador Pompeu: 1700-2200 (Sun -1800)
PA08)	I531	1130	10	R. Marajoara, Belém: 24h
PE18)	I783	1130	5/1	R. Cultura do Nordeste, Caruaru: 24h
PR55)	J220	1130	1/0.25	R. Castro, Castro: 24h
PR54)	J333	1130	5/0.25	R. Ingamar, Marialva
RJ17)	J460	1130	100/50	R. Nacional, Rio de Janeiro: 24h
RO06)	J677	1130	5/0.25	R. Ji-Parana, Ji-Paraná
RS70)	K290	1130	5/1	R. Medianeira, Santa Maria
SC34)	J790	1130	5/1	R. Princesa d'Oeste, Xanxerê: 24h
SP107)	K676	1130	2.5/0.25	R. Tupã, Tupã
BA81)	H449	1140	10	R. Cultura da Bahia, Salvador: 24h
CE24)	H607	1140	10/1	R. Progresso, Russas
GO26)	H751	1140	5/0.25	R. Formosa, Formosa: 0800-2300, Sat 1200-2200, Sun silent
MG62)	L204	1140	5/0.25	R. Minas, Divinópolis
MG63)	L248	1140	1/0.25	R. Doicesana, Campanha: 1100-0300, SS 24h
MG64)	L253	1140	8/0.5	R. Muriaé, Muriaé: 0800-0300
MG129)	L362	1140	10/0.5	R. Clube, Bocaiuva: 0800-0300
MS22)	I398	1140	10/0.5	R. Globo, Dif. do Sul: 24h
MT47)	I435	1140	1/0.25	R. Dif. Juara, Juara
PR144)	J352	1140	1/0.25	R. Dif. America, Chopinzinho: 24h
RS71)	K228	1140	2/0.25	R. Cruz Alta, Cruz Alta
RS72)	K316	1140	5/0.7	R. Charrua, Uruguaiana: 0900-2200
RS73)	K330	1140	2/0.5	R. Jornal Sobral, Butiá: 1000-2200
SC35)	J748	1140	10/0.5	R. Coroado, Curitibanos: 24h
SP108)	K550	1140	10/0.5	R. Difusora, Assis
SP109)	K555	1140	2/0.5	R. Barretos, Barretos
SP110)	K645	1140	1/0.25	R. Educação e Cultura, Rio Claro
SP111)	K709	1140	5/0.25	R. Costa Azul, Ubatuba
SP273)	K708	1140	1/0.25	R. Nova Regional, Registro: 24h
AL11)	K250	1150	20/1	R. Cultura, Arapiraca
CE47)	H643	1150	5/0.5	R. Cultura - Rede Imaculada, Paracuru: 24h
MG65)	L283	1150	50/10	R. Globo, Belo Horizonte: 24h
PI10)	I891	1150	10/5	R. Pioneira, Teresina: 24h
RJ24)	J456	1150	10/0.5	R. Três Rios, Três Rios
RN25)	J617	1150	5/0.5	R. Cabugi do Seridó, Jardim do Seridó: 0800-0100, Sat 1700-0000
SP232)	K656	1150	100/50	Super R. AM, São Paulo: 24h
AM24)	H323	1160	1/0.25	R. Soc. TV Manauara, Boca do Acre
BA94)	H...	1160	5/0.25	R. São José Canção Nova, Itabuna
CE62)	H652	1160	1/0.25	R. Vale do Coreaú, Granja
CE80)	H660	1160	1/0.25	R. Montevidéo, Cedro: 0800-0100 (Sun -2330)
DF09)	H714	1160	30/0.5	R. Globo, Brasilia: 24h
ES08)	I202	1160	50/10	R. Espírito Santo, Vitória
GO42)	H784	1160	1/0.5	R. Silvestre, Itaberaí
MT15)	I385	1160	10/5	R. A. Voz d'Oeste, Cuiabá
PA30)	I558	1160	5/1	R. Guamá, São Miguel do Guamá: 0800-0300
PB11)	I674	1160	1	R. Cariri, Campina Grande: 0700-0200, SS 0900-0100
PR56)	J258	1160	10/1	R. Globo, Londrina: 24h
RS74)	K242	1160	9/1	R. Miriam, Farroupilha: 0830-2100
RS75)	K245	1160	5/1	R. Luz e Alegria, Frederico Westphalen
RS76)	K256	1160	2.5/0.5	R. Jaguari, Jaguari
RS77)	K273	1160	2.5/1	R. Universidade Católica, Pelotas: 24h
SC36)	J741	1160	9/0.7	R. Itaberá, Blumenau: 24h
SC37)	J767	1160	1/0.25	R. Dif. Laguna
SP114)	K517	1160	5/0.5	R. Cacique, Sorocaba
SP124)	K558	1160	2.5/1	R. Bandeirantes, Bauru: 24h
SP115)	K582	1160	5/0.25	R. Difusora, Fernandópolis
SP237)	K673	1160	4/0.25	R. Cacique, Taubaté
SP116)	K685	1160	1/0.25	R. Boa Nova, Mococa: 24h
AC15)	H205	1170	1/0.25	R. Dif. de Feijó, Feijó
AM08)	H284	1170	5/2.5	R. Guaranópolis, Maués
BA27)	H473	1170	5/0.25	R. Jornal, Eunápolis
MG152)	L234	1170	1/0.25	R. Clube Fronteira
MG104)	L269	1170	5/0.25	R. Sociedade, Oliveira
MG75)	L327	1170	10/0.25	R. Vanguarda, Ipatinga
MG67)	L336	1170	5/0.25	R. Cidade, Araxá: 0800-0000
PR57)	J273	1170	20/10	R. Atalaia, Curitiba
PR90)	J334	1170	2.5/0.45	R. Entre Rios, Sto. Antônio do Sudoeste: 0800-020000 SS -2200
PR154)	J363	1170	8/1	R. Colméia, Mandaguaçu: 24h
RJ49)	J498	1170	5/0.25	R. Bom Jesus, Bom Jesus de Itabapoana: 24h
RN08)	J598	1170	10/1	R. Difusora, Mossoró
RS78)	K207	1170	1/0.25	R. Itapuí, Santo Antônio da Patrulha: 0900-0300
RS79)	K213	1170	5/1	R. Difusora, Bagé: 0900-0230
RS80)	K359	1170	5/0.6	R. Uirapuru, Passo Fundo: 24h
RS155)	K380	1170	1.5	R. Pitangueira, Itaqui:24h
SP117)	K569	1170	10/5	R. Bandeirantes, Campinas: 24h
AL06)	H248	1180	1/0.25	R. Correio do Sertão, Santana do Ipanema
AM20)	H280	1180	10/2.5	R. Dif. do Amazonas, Manaus: 24h
MA09)	H889	1180	10/5	R. Capital, São Luís
MG118)	L203	1180	10/0.25	R. Cultura, Alfenas: 24h
MS34)	N602	1180	10	R. Ativa, Campo Grande
MT38)	N405	1180	1/0.25	R. Enauan, Garantã do Norte
PB20)	I690	1180	1/0.25	R. Bonsucesso, Pombal: 0830-0100 SS -2100
PE19)	I797	1180	1/0.25	R. Jornal, Vitória de Sto. Antão
PR126)	J223	1180	2.5/0.5	R. Atalaia, Guarapuava
PR58)	J237	1180	10/0.5	R. Guaçu, Toledo: 0800-0000
PR81)	J314	1180	2.5/0.25	R. Educadora, São João do Ivaí: 24h
RJ25)	J463	1180	50/10	R. Mundial, Rio de Janeiro: 24h
RS128)	K340	1180	10/0.5	R. Gazeta, Santa Cruz do Sul: 24h
SC39)	J737	1180	5/0.25	R. Integração d'Oeste, São José do Cedro: 0830-0100
SC72)	J770	1180	1/0.5	R. Guri, Lages
SP260)	K567	1180	1/0.25	R. Brotense, Brotas:24h
SP179)	K647	1180	2/0.5	R. Super Nova Difusora, Santa Cruz do Rio Pardo: 0800-0100
SP217)	K749	1180	5/0.25	R. Nova, Bebedouro
BA28)	H459	1190	10/1	R. Juazeiro, Juazeiro: 0800-2300 (Sat -1930, Sun -1800)
CE68)	H663	1190	1/0.25	R. Guaraciaba, Guaraciaba do Norte: 24h
GO35)	H800	1190	10/0.25	R. Rio Vermelho, Silvânia: 0800-0300 (SS -0200)
MG68)	L221	1190	50/1	R. Guarani, Belo Horizonte
MG40)	L276	1190	10/0.25	R. Mineira do Sul, Passa Quatro: 0800-0100, SS 24h
PR59)	J309	1190	1/0.25	R. Pontal, Nova Londrina: 0800-2300
PR136)	J355	1190	5/0.4	R. Cidade, Palmital: 0830-0100
RN09)	J594	1190	10/1	CBN, Natal: 24h
RS82)	K234	1190	5/0.5	R. Cerro Azul, Cerro Largo
RS102)	K301	1190	2.5/0.25	R. São Lourenço, São Lourenço do Sul: 0900-0300, Sun 1000-0200
RS83)	K354	1190	2.5/1	R. Rosário, Serafina Corrêa
SC40)	J783	1190	10/0.25	R. Clube, São João Batista: 24h
SC87)	J817	1190	1/0.25	R. Planalto, Major Vieira: 24h
SC41)	J820	1190	2.5/0.25	R. Clube, São Domingos
SP199)	K512	1190	5/0.25	R. Marconi, Paraguaçu Paulista: 0800-0100
SP118)	K700	1190	5/0.25	R. Cidade, Votuporanga: 0900-0300
SP119)	K729	1190	10/0.25	R. 31 de Março, Sta. Cruz das Palmeiras
SP120)	K741	1190	1/0.5	R. Regional, Taquarituba: 0800-0200, Sun Silent
AL14)	H251	1200	50/1	R. Correio, Pilar
BA29)	H482	1200	10/0.5	R. Clube Rio do Ouro, Jacobina: 24h
CE26)	H585	1200	10	R. Clube, Fortaleza: 24h
RS84)	K239	1200	5/1	R. Erechim, Erechim: 0800(SS 0900)-0300
RS85)	K342	1200	1/0.5	R. Fundação Cotrisel, São Sepé: 0800-0200(SS -0100)
SP121)	K520	1200	100/20	R. Cultura Brasil, São Paulo
BA30)	H452	1210	10/1	R. Povo, Feira de Santana
BA58)	H498	1210	5/0.25	R. Canção Nova, Vitória da Conquista
CE50)	H637	1210	5/0.25	R. Príncipe Imperial, Crateús
CE48)	H641	1210	5/0.25	R. Boa Esperança, Barro
DF08)	H711	1210	50/2.5	Super R. Brasília (RBV), Brasília: 24h
ES09)	I200	1210	25/1	R. Sim Cachoeiro, Cachoeiro de Itapemirim: 24h
MG69)	L238	1210	10/0.5	R. Clube, Varginha: 24h
PE20)	I786	1210	10/1	R. Jornal, Garanhuns: 24h
PR60)	J219	1210	25/5	Super Rádio Deus é Amor, Curitiba: 24h
PR140)	J325	1210	5/5	R. Brotense, Porecatu: 24h
RN29)	J620	1210	5/0.5	R. Potengi, São Paulo do Potengi: 0800-0300, Sun 1000-1500
RS86)	K240	1210	10/5	R. Catedral, Porto Alegre

MW	Call	kHz	kW	Station, location, h. of tr.
RS88)	K353	1210	1/0.5	R. Blau Nunes, Santa Bárbara do Sul
SC42)	J785	1210	10/0.5	R. Super Santa, Tubarão: 0800-0200 (Sun -2300)
SP122)	K509	1210	10/1	R. Vida Nova, Jaboticabal
SP123)	K545	1210	5/0.25	R. Bandeirantes, Araçatuba
SP125)	K668	1210	5/0.25	R. Vanguarda, Sorocaba: 24h
RJ61)	J458	1220	150	R. Globo, Rio de Janeiro: 24h
BA59)	H532	1230	1/0.25	R. Povo, Ubatã
GO27)	H756	1230	10/2.5	R. Daqui, Goiânia
MA23)	H....	1230	1/0.25	R. Veneza, Caxias
MG105)	L208	1230	5/0.25	R. Correio da Serra, Barbacena
MG102)	L216	1230	2.5/0.25	R. Passos, Passos:24h
MG176)	N203	1230	10/0.7	R. Estrela de Ibiúna, Campina Verde
PB12)	I670	1230	10/1	R. Correio Jovem Pan, João Pessoa
PR170)	J350	1230	1/0.25	R. Nova Mensagem, Telêmaco Borba: 1200(Sat 1000)-0300, Sun 1300-1900
RS146)	K297	1230	4/0.25	R. Santiago, Santiago: 0800-0300, Sun 0900-0200
RS89)	K326	1230	2/0.25	R. Clube Nonoai, Nonoai
RS90)	K333	1230	2.3/0.35	R. Prata, Nova Prata: 0800-0100 SS -2200
RS91)	K352	1230	5/0.25	R. Encruzilhadense, Encruzilhada do Sul
SC38)	J776	1230	5/0.65	R. Dif. Colméia, Porto União: 0800(Sun 0900)-0300
SC88)	J816	1230	10/1	R. Guararema, São José: 24h
SP126)	K573	1230	1/0.25	R. Cacique, Capão Bonito: 24h
SP258)	K637	1230	10/0.25	R. Difusora, Rancharia
SP128)	K716	1230	5/0.5	R. Jequitibá, Campinas
SP266)	R699	1230	50/10	Super R. Boa Vontade, São Paulo
BA31)	H463	1240	10/0.5	R. Nova AM 1240, Alagoinhas: 0900-0200 Sat-1900 Sun 1000-2200
CE49)	H654	1240	1/0.25	R. São Francisco, Canindé
MG97)	L294	1240	5/0.25	R. Três Pontas, Três Pontas
MG84)	L298	1240	1/0.25	R. Ubaense, Ubá: 24h
MG72)	L303	1240	10/0.35	R. Globo, Ituiutaba: 24h
MG116)	L317	1240	5/0.25	R. Pirapora AM, Pirapora: 24h
MS09)	I388	1240	5/1	R. Dif. Pantanal, Campo Grande: 24h
PE21)	I774	1240	5	R. Capibaribe, Recife: 0900-0300
PR112)	J215	1240	1/0.25	R. Arapongas, Arapongas: 24h
PR61)	J280	1240	2/0.25	R. Matelândia, Matelândia: 0800-0100
RS92)	K200	1240	1/0.25	R. Aparados da Serra, Bom Jesus: 0830-0300 Sat 1030-0230 Sun 1000-0300
RS93)	K251	1240	1/0.25	R. Ibirubá, Ibirubá: 0800-0100(SS -2300)
RS94)	K355	1240	5/0.25	R. São Jerônimo, São Jerônimo
SC43)	J774	1240	5/0.5	R. São José, Mafra: 24h
SC44)	J810	1240	2.2	R. Iracema, Cunhae Porã
SP129)	K565	1240	10/0.25	R. Municipalista, Botucatu
SP130)	K621	1240	5/0.25	Orlândia R. Clube, Orlândia: 24h
SP131)	K653	1240	10/2.5	R. Clube, Santos
SP132)	K711	1240	1/0.25	R. Vale do Tietê, José Bonifácio: 24h
CE27)	H594	1250	1	R. Educadora, Crateús
CE69)	H669	1250	1	R. Liberdade, Itarema
ES18)	I218	1250	10/1	R. Nova Estação, Vitória
GO29)	H748	1250	1/0.25	R. Coração Fiel, Ceres
MG73)	L282	1250	5	R. Difusora, Poços de Caldas: 24h
MG153)	L367	1250	50	R. Metropolitana, Vespasiano
MS10)	I394	1250	1/0.25	R. Difusora, Três Lagoas: 0900-0300, Sun 1000-0200
MS11)	I412	1250	5/0.5	R. Caiuás, Dourados
PB27)	I701	1250	1/0.25	R. Sociedade de Soledade, Soledade
PI47)	I915	1250	1/0.25	R. João de Paiva, Altos
PR62)	J211	1250	10/0.5	R. Difusora, Guarapuava
PR63)	J233	1250	5/0.4	R. Paranavaí, Paranavaí
PR64)	J313	1250	2.5/0.25	R. Danúbio Azul, Sta. Isabel do Oeste: 24h
RJ50)	J500	1250	15/0.5	R. Litoral, Casimiro de Abreu
RS95)	K233	1250	15/0.5	R. Dif. Caxiense, Caxias do Sul
RS96)	K272	1250	1	R. Tupanci, Pelotas: 0800-0200, Sun 0900-0000
RS142)	K361	1250	5/0.6	R. Aguas Claras, Catuípe: 0800-0200 (Sat -0100), Sun 1000-2200
SC45)	J766	1250	5/0.25	R. Cultura, Joinville: 24h
SE08)	J925	1250	10/1	R. Esperança, Estância
SP133)	K702	1250	5/0.5	R. Canção Nova, Caçapava
AL07)	H242	1260	50/5	R. Gazeta de Alagoas, Maceió: 24h
CE28)	H596	1260	1/0.25	R. Vale do Jaguaribe, Limoeiro do Nte: 0730-0100
RO09)	J670	1260	5	R. Educação, Guajará Mirim: 0900-0300
RS97)	K204	1260	1/0.25	R. Cultura, São Borja: 0500-2400
RS98)	K327	1260	5/0.25	R. Fandango, Cachoeira do Sul: 0830-0100
RS99)	K345	1260	1/0.25	R. Gaurama, Gaurama
SC46)	J740	1260	10/0.5	R. Arca da Aliança, Blumenau
SP257)	K629	1260	1/0.25	Pirajau R. Clube, Pirajuí: 24h

MW	Call	kHz	kW	Station, location, h. of tr.
SP134)	K688	1260	100/40	R. Morada do Sol, São Paulo: 24h
AM10)	H271	1270	5	R. Educação Rural, Tefé: 1000-0200
GO30)	H753	1270	100/10	R. Brasil Central, Goiânia
MG74)	L227	1270	5/1	R. Carijós, Conselheiro Lafaiete
MG107)	L300	1270	2.5/0.5	R. Estância, São Lourenço
MG155)	L240	1270	5/1	R. Globo, Ipatinga: 24h
PA09)	I530	1270	10/2.5	R. Boas Novas, Belém: 24h
PB28)	I696	1270	5/0.25	R. Cidade, Sumé: 1100-0300,
PR65)	J222	1270	5/0.5	R. Guairacá, Mandaguari: 0800-0100, SS 0800-0000
PR67)	J236	1270	10/1	R. Continental, Curitiba: 24h
PR68)	J289	1270	5/0.5	R. Globo, Cascavel: 24h
RJ26)	J474	1270	5/0.5	R. Continental, Campos dos Goitacazes: 0800-0230
RN10)	J593	1270	5/0.5	R. Clube AM 1270, Natal: 24h
RS131)	K206	1270	5/0.5	R. América, Montenegro: 24h
RS101)	K250	1270	5/0.5	R. Vera Cruz, Horizontina: 0800-0300
SC47)	J765	1270	12/0.25	R. Catarinense, Joaçaba
SC48)	J768	1270	1/0.25	R. Garibaldi, Laguna: 09000-0200, Sun 1045-2200
SP136)	K678	1270	5/0.5	R. Brasil, Campinas: 24h
SP274)	K640	1270	2/0.5	R. Bandeirantes, Ribeirao Preto
PB21)	I688	1280	10/5	R. Sanhauá, Bayeux: 0800-0300(SS -2300)
RJ27)	J455	1280	100	R. Tupi, Rio de Janeiro
AM11)	H286	1290	10/2.5	R. Rio Mar, Manaus: 0900-0300
BA32)	H450	1290	10/1	R. Metropole, Salvador
ES24)		1290	1	R. Sim, Vila Velha
MA10)	H888	1290	10/5	R. Timbira, São Luís: 0800(Sun 1000)-0300
MG77)	L273	1290	10/5	R. Uberlandia, Uberlandia
MG164)	L345	1290	5/0.25	R. Cidade, Arcos
PR73)	J310	1290	25/0.5	R. Brasil Sul, Londrina: 24h
RN26)	J619	1290	5/0.25	R. Caicó, Caicó
RS103)	K331	1290	5/2	R. Planetário, Espumoso: 0800-0100 (Sun -2300)
SC81)	J734	1290	5/1	R. Araranguá, Araranguá: 0800-0100 (Sun -0900)
SC49)	J804	1290	5/1	R. Camboriú, Balneário Camboriú
SP240)	K662	1290	5/0.5	R. Difusora, São José do Rio Pardo
SP137)	K663	1290	5/1	R. Novo Tempo, São José do Rio Preto:24h
SP216)	K745	1290	1/0.5	R. Estadão, São José dos Campos: 24h
CE29)	H586	1300	10	R. Iracema, Fortaleza:24h
ES11)	I210	1300	5/0.25	R. Novo Tempo, Afonso Cláudio
MG143)	L339	1300	5/1	R. Eldorado, Sete Lagoas: 24h
PE22)	I799	1300	1/0.25	R. Guarany, Camaragibe
PR71)	J278	1300	1/0.25	CBN, Ponta Grossa: 24h
PR127)	J288	1300	5/0.25	R. Educadora, Dois Vizinhos: 0800-0300
RS104)	K203	1300	80/13	Super R. Boa Vontade, Porto Alegre: 24h
RS105)	K337	1300	1/0.25	R. Regional, Santo Cristo
RS106)	K347	1300	5/0.5	R. Maratan, Santana do Livramento: 24h
SC89)	J819	1300	1/0.25	R. Alvorada, Santa Cecília
SP138)	K535	1300	50/1	R. Universo, São Paulo: 24h
SP252)	K649	1300	30/0,25	R. Onda Viva, Santo Anastácio
SP226)	K742	1300	2/0.25	R. Realidade, São Carlos
AP05)	H422	1310	1/0.25	R. Nova Mazagão, Mazagão
BA33)	H454	1310	1/0.25	R. Bahiana, Ilhéus: 0800-0300
BA63)	H501	1310	5/0.25	R. Jaraguar, Jacobina: 0800-0200, Sat 0900-0000 Sun: 1100-1400
CE30)	H602	1310	1	R. Progresso de Juazeiro, Juazeiro do Nte.
CE63)	H656	1310	1/0.25	R. Liberdade, Boa Viagem: 0800-2300
MG144)	L359	1310	1/0.25	R. Montanheza, Vazante
MG168)	L351	1310	10/0.25	R. Difusora, Salinas
MS31)	I426	1310	5/1	R. Pindorama, Sidrolândia
PB23)	I691	1310	10/0.5	R. Cidade Esperança, Esperança
PR70)	J274	1310	10/0.5	R. Atalaia, Maringá
RJ28)	J504	1310	1/0.25	R. Coroados, São Fidélis: 0800-0100 (SS -2100)
RO17)	J684	1310	10/5	R. Globo, Porto Velho: 24h
RS107)	K305	1310	10/1	R. Sarandi, Sarandi: 24h
RS124)	K329	1310	5/0.45	R. Integração, Restinga Seca: 0830-0200 (Sat -2300), Sun 0900-2300
RS160)	K371	1310	5/0.5	R. Horizonte, Capão da Canoa
SC85)	J801	1310	10/0.5	R. Sintonia, Ituporanga
SP141)	K566	1310	5/0.25	R. Bragança, Bragança Paulista
SP139)	K596	1310	2/1	R. Difusora, Itápolis
AL08)	H243	1320	10/0.25	R. Imaculada Conceição, Maceió: 24h
BA69)	H503	1320	5/0.25	R. Regional, Cícero Dantas: 0900-2300
CE31)	H597	±1320	1	R. Regional, Sobral
CE70)	H672	1320	1/0.5	R. Moriá, Aracati
MG136)	L322	1320	5/0.25	R. Mucuri, Teófilo Otoni: 24h, Sun silent
PE31)	I823	1320	1/0.25	R. Cultura, São José do Egito
PR72)	J255	1320	12/0.5	R. Tropical, Curitiba: 24h

MW	Call	kHz	kW	Station, location, h. of tr.
PR145)	J351	1320	5/0.5	CBN, Foz do Iguaçu: 24h
RJ29)	J475	1320	50/5	R. Boas Novas, Petropôlis: 24h
RS108)	K223	1320	1/0.25	R. Clube, Canela
RS109)	K266	1320	3/0.25	R. Sulbrasileira, Panambi
RS110)	K271	1320	5/1	R. Cultura, Pelotas: 24h
SC68)	J762	1320	9	R. Litoral, Imaruí: 24h
SC104)		1320	5/0.45	R. Vitôria, Videira
SP140)	K630	1320	1/0.25	R. Difusora, Pirassununga: 24h
SP241)	K675	1320	0.5	R. Clube, Tupã
BA34)	H468	1330	1	R. Continental, Serrinha
MS54	N610	1330	1/0,25	R. Pantanal, Coxim
PA07)	I600	†1330	5/1	R. Liberal, Castanhal
PR74)	J264	1330	10/0.5	R. Jaguariaíva, Jaguariaíva
RN27)	J621	1330	10/0.5	R. Eldorado, Natal
RS111)	K236	1330	1/0.25	R. Upacaraí, Dom Pedrito: 0900-0200
RS112)	K323	1330	2.5/0.5	R. Diplomata, São Marcos: 0800-0200 Sun 0800-0100
SC50)	J739	1330	10/0.5	R. Clube, Blumenau: 0800(Sun 0900)-0100
SC51)	J749	1330	5/1	R. Chapecó, Chapecó
SP142)	K638	1330	30/0.25	R. Paulista, Regente Feijó
SP143)	K641	1330	5/1	R. Cultura, Ribeirão Preto
SP187)	K736	1330	50/10	R. Terra, Osasco: 24h
CE71)	H661	1340	2.5/0.25	R. Pitaguary, Maracanaú: 0800-0300 (Sun -1900)
MA11)	H886	1340	10/2	R. São Luís, São Luís: 24h
MG81)	L241	1340	10/5	R. Cultura, Itabirito: 24h
MG139)	L352	1340	5/0.5	R. Globo, Passos: 24h
MS12)	I380	1340	3/0.25	R. Dif. 1340, Aquidauana: 0900-0300 (SS -0020)
PB13)	I671	1340	5/1	R. Correio, João Pessoa
PR76)	J205	1340	2.5/0.25	R. Difusora, Rio Negro
PR77)	J249	1340	5/0.25	R. Cultura, Arapongas
PR41)	J368	1340	20/0.25	CBN, Cascavel: 24h
RJ40)	J490	1340	5/0.5	R. 1340, Rio Bonito
RS113)	K227	1340	25/4	CBN, Porto Alegre: 24h
RS173)	K374	1340	10/4	R. Journal da Manhã, Ijui: 24h
SP144)	K543	1340	5/1	R. Cultura, Araçatuba
SP203)	K571	1340	5/0.25	R. Em. Campos do Jordão, Campos do Jordão: 24h
SP146)	K738	1340	1/0.25	R. Nova Canoa Grande, Igaraçu do Tietê
AC05)	H201	1350	50/5	R. Capital (RBV), Rio Branco
BA70)	H520	1350	50/10	Super R. Cristal, Salvador: 24h
CE56)	H662	1350	1/0.25	R. Liberal Jagoaribana, Morada Nova
MG82)	L214	1350	10/5	R. Cultura, Poços de Caldas:0800-0300, SS 1100-1500
PB14)	I675	1350	5/0.5	R. Clube AM 1350, Campina Grande: 24h
RS114)	K205	1350	2.5/0.25	R. Aurora, Guaporé
RS115)	K313	1350	5/1	R. Difusora, Três Passos
RS116)	K336	1350	2.5/0.25	R. Agudo, Agudo
SC53)	J760	1350	1/0.25	R. Bandeirantes, Itajaí
SP265)	K692	1350	50/0.25	R. Excelsior, Ibiúna: 24h
BA35)	H469	1360	10/1	R. Cultura, Paulo Afonso: 24h
CE57)	H650	1360	5/0.25	R. Iracema, Ipu: 0900-0200, SS 0800 -2100
MS64)	I383	1360	2	R. Difusora, Corumbá
PR165)	J265	1360	10/0.25	R. Cidade, Pato Branco: 24h
PR78)	J268	1360	1/0.25	Rede Terra Nativa, Assaí: 24h
RJ30)	J464	1360	50/10	R. Bandeirantes, Rio de Janeiro: 24h
RN11)	J605	1360	1/0.5	R. Ouro Branco, Currais Novos
RS117)	K261	1360	5/0.5	R. Alvorada, Marau:24h
RS151)	K281	1360	3/0.25	R. Navegantes, Porto Lucena: 0800-0300
SC69)	J757	1360	25/0.4	R. Belos Vales, Ibirama: 0800-0100
SP147)	K581	1360	5/1	R. Aguas Quentes, Fernandópolis: 24h
SP148)	K739	1360	1/0.25	R. Regional, Dracena: 24h
SP235)	K759	1360	1/0.25	R. Luzes da Ribalta, Santa Bárbara d'Oeste
BA82)	H555	1370	0.25	R. Jornal Grande, Monte Santo: 0800-0300
CE81)	H628	1370	1/0.25	R. Vanguarda, Caridade
PE34)	I800	1370	1/0.25	R. Vale do Capibaribe, Sta. Cruz do Capibaribe
PI13)	I892	1370	2.5	R. Difusora, Teresina
PR80)	J267	1370	50/7	R. Canção Nova, Curitiba: 1000-0200
RN28)	J618	1370	2.5/0.25	R. Dif.,São Miguel: 0930-2100, Sun silent
RS118)	K243	1370	25/0.5	R. Mãe de Deus, Flores da Cunha: 24h
RS119)	K334	1370	1/0.25	R. Gazeta, Alegrete: 0900-0200(Sun -0000)
SC55)	J782	1370	10/0.5	R. Peperí AM, São Miguel do Oeste: 0800-0300
SE09)	J929	1370	5/0.5	R. Cultura do Agreste, Itabaiana: 0700(Sun 0800)-0300
SP223)	K766	1370	100/20	Rede Apolo de Radio, São Paulo: 24h
AM12)	H283	1380	5/1	R. Alvorada, Parintins: 0900-0200
BA83)	H495	†1380	5/0.25	R. União, Gandu
ES21)	I...	1380	10/1	R. Itaí de Rio Claro, Iúna
MA40)	H909	1380	1/0.25	R. Tropical, Caixas
MG172)	L218	1380	1/0.25	Rede Gerais, Brasópolis
MG120)	L284	1380	5/0.25	R. Paranaíba, Rio Paranaíba
MG130)	L323	1380	1/0.25	R. Gorutubana, Janaúba
PE23)	I773	1380	10/5	R. Novas de Paz, Recife
PR122)	J276	1380	2/0.25	R. Bom Jesus, Siqueira Campos: 24h
PR152)	J367	1380	1/0.25	R. Integração, Toledo: 0800-0100
RS120)	K293	1380	1/0.25	R. Cultura, Santana do Livramento
RS134)	K311	1380	3/0.25	R. Maristela, Torres: 24h
RS121)	K350	1380	6/0.25	R. Cultura, Tapera: 0830-0100(SS -2300)
RS165)	K372	1380	6/0.25	R. Chiru, Palmitinho: 24h SS Silent
SC56)	J821	1380	6/0.25	R. Cidade, Itaiópolis: 0900(Sun 1200)-0100
SC93)	J827	1380	6/0.25	R. Barriga Verde, Capinzal: 0830-2000
SC105)	J831	1380	1/0.25	R. Freguencia, Garopaba
SP152)	K616	1380	1/0.5	R. Difusora, Mogi Guaçu
SP247)	K623	1380	1/0.25	R. Cultura, Pederneiras: 24h
SP224)	K751	1380	5/0.25	R. Globo, Presidente Prudente: 24h
SP234)	K772	1380	1/0.25	R. República, Morro Agudo: 24h
ES13)	I209	1390	5/0.25	R. Educadora, Afonso Cláudio: 0700-0100
MG157)	L358	1390	2.5/0.25	R. Ouro Verde, São Sebastião do Paraíso: 0800-0300
MG178)	L305	1390	10/0.5	R. Vitoriosa, Uberlândia
PA12)	I535	1390	10/1	R. Educadora, Bragança: 0830-0100
PE24)	I788	1390	5/1	R. Jornal, Pesqueira
PR82)	J242	1390	10/1	R. Cultura, Maringá
PR83)	J335	1390	1/0.25	R. Independência, Salto do Lontra: 0830-0005(SS -0130)
RJ32)	J473	1390	5/0.5	R. Sul Fluminense, Barra Mansa
RN32)	J599	1390	5/0.5	R. Farol, Touros: 1000-2200
RO18)	J687	±1390	5/1	R. Planalto, Ji-Paraná
RR02)	0701	1390	10/5	R. Roraima, Caracaraí
RS122)	K209	1390	25	R. Esperança, Porto Alegre: 24h
RS166)	K368	1390	8/0.25	R. Atlântica, Constantina: 0900-0100
SC57)	J769	1390	7.5/0.65	R. CBN, Lages
SP153)	K570	1390	25	R. Globo, Campinas: 24h
SP154)	K636	1390	1/0.25	R. Cultura, Promissão
SP2859	K594	1390	2.5	R. Anchieta, Itanhaém
AC06)	H200	1400	10/1	R. Dif. Acreana, Rio Branco: 0900-0400
BA71)	H529	1400	1/0.25	R. Vaza-Barris, Jeremoabo
PB15)	I677	1400	5/1	R. Espinharas, Patos
PI27)	I926	1400	1/0.25	R. Cantagalo, Jaicós
PR84)	J256	1400	5/0.25	R. Globo, Londrina: 24h
PR87)	J299	1400	1/0.25	R. Fronteira d'Oeste, Terra Roxa
PR119)	J339	1400	10/1	R. Ágape, Balsa Nova: 0800-0100
PR148)	J346	1400	2/0.45	R. Jornal São Miguel, São Miguel do Iguaçu: 0900-0200
RJ33)	J462	1400	50/5	R. Rio de Janeiro, Rio de Janeiro: 24h
RS192)	J376	1400	1/0,4	R. Educadora, São João da Urtiga: 0800-0130 SS 0900-0100
SC58)	J775	1400	5/0.35	R. Entre Rios, Palmitos: 0000-0200
SP155)	K527	1400	1/0.25	R. Difusora, Lucélia
SP156)	K658	1400	5/0.25	R. Cl., São Carlos: 0900(Sun 1100)-0300
SP157)	K682	1400	5/0.25	R. Metrópole, São José do Rio Preto
TO08)	N660	1400	1	Radiodifusão Guaraí, Guaraí
BA37)	H467	1410	10/0.5	R. Planeta, São Gonçalo dos Campos: 0800-2000 SS -0000
CE25)	H639	1410	10/1	R. Boa Nova, Pacajus
GO19)	H803	1410	30/0.85	R. Bandeirantes, Santo Antônio do Descoberto
MS14)	I382	1410	5/1	Nova R. Clube, Corumbá: 0700-2200 (Sat -0100); Sun Silent
RJ34)	J486	1410	10/0.5	R. Itaperuna, Itaperuna: 0800-0300
RN21)	J614	1410	5/0.5	R. Santa Cruz, Santa Cruz: 0800-0200, Sun 0900-0100
RS137)	K246	1410	5/1	R. Garibaldi, Garibaldi: 24h
RS125)	K284	1410	1/0.25	R. Minuano, Rio Grande: 24h
RS126)	K294	1410	5	R. Santa Rosa, Santa Rosa
SC100)	J799	1410	2/0.5	R. Nambá, Ponte Serrada
SC84)	J818	1410	1/0.25	R. Pomerode, Pomerode
SP158)	K691	1410	50/25	R. América, São Paulo: 24h
SP264	K683	1410	1/0.25	R. Excelsior, Rio Claro
BA60)	H504	1420	1/0.25	R. Cidade, Irecê: 24h
MG88)	L286	1420	1/0.25	R. Difusora, São João Nepomuceno: 24h, Sun 0800-0200
MG89)	L288	1420	5/1	R. Cultura, Sete Lagoas
MG90)	L313	1420	1/0.25	R. Montanhês Botelhos, Botelhos
MS16)	I397	1420	1/0.25	R. Difusora Cacique, Nova Andradina
PR88)	J269	1420	5/0.25	R. Cult. Umuarama: 0900-2105(Sun -1000)
PR89)	J282	1420	1/0.25	R. Educadora, Jacarezinho: 24h
RN12)	J609	1420	1/0.25	R. Farol, Alexandria
RS149)	K258	1420	5/0.25	R. 14 de Julho, Júlio de Castilhos
RS171)	K308	1420	3	R. Tapense, Tapes: 0900-0130(Sun -2300)

MW	Call	kHz	kW	Station, location, h. of tr.
SC60)	J744	1420	6/0.5	R. Cultura, Campos Novos: 0830-0100
SC59)	J754	1420	10/2.5	R. Guarujá, Florianópolis
SP159)	K597	1420	2.5/0.5	C.R.N., Itatiba: 24h
SP163)	K733	1420	1/0.25	R. Nova São Manuel, São Manuel: 0800-0300
MG91)	L239	1430	1/0.25	R. Clube, Guaxupé
MG158)	L371	1430	2.5/0.25	R. Globo, Perdizes
PE32)	I826	1430	5/0.25	R. Independência, Goiana
PR134)	J200	1430	50/10	R. RB2, Curitiba: 24h
RN13)	J604	1430	10/0.5	R. Libertadora , Mossoró
RO11)	J671	1430	10	R. Caiari, Porto Velho: 24h
RS167)	K366	1430	1/0.25	R. Guarita, Coronel Bicaco: 0900-0100
RS198)	K379	1430	1	R. AM 1430, Portão: 0900-0130
SP164)	K666	1430	1/0.25	R. Serra Negra, Serra Negra
SP275)	K707	1430	25/0.25	R. Imaculada Conceição, São Roque
AM13)	H285	1440	10	R. Amazonas FM, Manaus: 24h
BA38)	H466	1440	50/1	R. Independência, Santo Amaro
CE33)	H603	1440	10/1	R. Canaã Araripe, Crato
MG159)	L365	1440	1/0.25	R. Som 2000, Santa Vitória: 0900-0200
MS41)	I407	1440	1/0.25	R. Bela Vista, Bela Vista: 24h
RJ35)	J469	1440	20/5	R. Livre, Rio de Janeiro: 24h
RS168)	K221	1440	2.5/0.5	R. Ceres, Naõ Me Toque: 24h
RS130)	K328	1440	5/0.3	R. Excelsior, Gramado: 0900-0300
RS153)	K362	1440	2.5/0.25	R. Caibaté, Caibaté: 0830-0200
SC61)	J792	1440	2.5/0.25	R. Difusora, Maravilha: 24h
SC82)	J797	1440	10/0.35	R. Educadora, Taió: 1000-0300 SS 24
SE11)	J930	1440	5/0.25	R. Educadora, Frei Paulo: 0700-0300
SP253)	K568	1440	1/0.25	R. Eldorado Centro Norte Paulista, Cajuru
SP165)	K634	1440	10/0,25	R. Comercial, Presidente Prudente: 24h
SP218)	K752	1440	1/0.25	R. Azul Celeste, Americana: 24h
SP284)		1440	2.5/0.5	R. Clarim de Palmas, Itai
BA73)	H531	1450	1/0.25	R. Ipirá, Ipirá
CE34)	H601	1450	1/0.25	R. Difusora Cristal, Quixeramobim
CE35)	H623	1450	1/0.25	R. Pinto Martins, Camocim
CE99)		1450		R. Carinhosa, Acopiara: 0800-0100 (SS -2300)
ES12)	I208	1450	1/0.5	R. Sim, Guarapari
MA32)	H900	1450	1/0.25	R. Boa Esperança, São João dos Patos
MA13)	H901	1450	1/0.25	R. Cultura, Pedreiras
MG94)	L312	1450	3/0.25	R. Diamante, Coromandel
MS13)	I417	1450	1/0.25	R. Difusora, Rio Brilhante: 0900-0200
MS63)		1450	1	R. Portal, Bataguassu: 24h Sun Silent
PA33)	I559	1450	1/0.25	R. Juruá, São Felix do Xingu
PA56)	I56I	1450	1	R. Paraense, Castanhal
PB29)	I699	1450	1/0.25	R. Certao, Patos: 0700-0300
PE25)	I794	1450	1/0.25	R. Cultura, Palmares: 24h
PI21)	I908	1450	1/0.25	R. Cultura do Gurguéia, Bom Jesus
PI35)	I917	1450	1/0.25	R. Confederação Valenciana, Valença do Piauí
PR93)	J279	1450	1/0.25	R. Cabiúna, Bandeirantes
PR95)	J317	1450	1/0.25	R. Rainha de Altônia, Altônia: 24h
PR162)	J364	1450	1/0.25	R. Clube, Mallet
PR179)	J301	1450	1/0.25	R. Dif. Ubiratanense, Ubiratã: 0800-2300
PR188)	J279	1450	1/0.25	R. Cabiúna, Bandeirantes: 0800-0200
RJ36)	J480	1450	5/0.25	R. Comércio, Barra Mansa: 24h
RJ37)	J503	1450	1/0.25	R. Felíz, Santo Antônio de Pádua: 0800-0100
RO12)	J674	1450	1/0.25	R. Vilhena, Vilhena: 0800-0400(SS -2000)
RR03)	O701	1450	1/0.25	R. Transamérca Hits, Alto Alegre
RS177)	K338	1450	1/0.25	R. Cultura, Arvorezinha
SC62)	J802	1450	1/0.25	R. São Bento, São Bento do Sul: 0800-0200
SC63)	J822	1450	10/0.25	R. Hulha Negra, Criciúma: 24h
SC97)	J828	1450	2.5/0.25	R. Belos Montes, Seara: 0800-0300 (SS -0200)
SP238)	K526	1450	2.5/0.25	R. Cultura, Ituverava: 24h
SP166)	K587	1450	1/0.25	R. Dif., Guararapes: 0900-0300
SP167)	K591	1450	50/5	R. Boa Nova, Guarulhos: 24h
SP168)	K657	1450	1/0.25	R. São Carlos, São Carlos do Pinhal: 24h
AM17)	H300	1460	5	R. Clube, Parintins
BA39)	H472	1460	1	R. Povo, Jequié
BA85)	H523	1460	1/0.25	R. Ferro Doido, Morro do Chapéu
BA74)	H536	1460	1/0.25	R. Alvorada, Cruz das Almas
CE53)	H595	1460	1/0.25	R. Ressurreição, Massapé
CE36)	H616	1460	1/0.25	R. Uirapuru, Morada Nova
GO34)	H766	1460	1/0.25	R. Morrinhos, Morrinhos
MA33)	H917	1460	1/0.25	R. Vanguarda, Santa Luzia
MG95)	L201	1460	1/0.25	R. Cul. do Porto Novo, Além Paraíba
MG161)	L356	1460	1/0.25	R. Buritis, Buritis
MG131)	L363	1460	1/0.25	R. Gerais AM, Raul Soares: 24h
MS56)	I....	1460	1/0.25	R. Globo, Costa Rica
PI14)	I903	1460	1/0.25	R. Cultura, Amarante
PR96)	J204	1460	2/0.25	R. Difusora, Paranaguá
PR97)	J228	1460	1/0.25	R. Central do Paraná, Ponta Grossa: 24h
PR98)	J251	1460	1/0.25	R. Cultura, Apucarana
PR100)	J297	1460	1/0.25	R. Guaíra, Guaíra: 24h
PR101)	J308	1460	5/0.25	R. Ampere, Ampere: 0830-0100
PR102)	J318	1460	1/0.25	R. Guadalupe AM, Loanda: 24h
RN20)	J615	1460	10/0,25	R. Agreste, Santo Antônio
RS133)	K214	1460	1/0.25	R. Cultura, Bagé
RS135)	K312	1460	1/0.25	R. Colonial, Três de Maio: 0800-0300
RS175)	K373	1460	1/0.25	R. Campinas, Campinas do Sul
RS176)	K378	1460	0.25	R. Mostardas, Mostardas: 24h
RS199)	K......	1460	1	R. Litoral, Imbé: 24h
SC64)	J756	1460	2.5	R. Sentinela do Vale, Gaspar
SE12)	J932	1460	1/0.25	R. Abais, Estância: 0900-2300(SS -1700)
SP242)	K548	1460	5/0.5	R. Clube Ararense, Araras: 24h
SP170)	K608	1460	1/0.25	R. Cultura, Lorena: 24h
TO02)	H774	1460	1/0.25	R. Independência do Tocantins, Paraíso do Tocantins
BA86)	H509	1470	0.25	R. Morro Verde, Mairi
CE64)	H665	1470	1/0.25	R. Guanancés de Itapajé, Itapajé:
ES17)	I214	1470	1/0.25	R. Globo, Barra de São Francisco: 24h
GO36)	H773	1470	10/0.25	R. Dif. Serra dos Cristais, Cristalina
GO37)	H779	1470	1/0.25	R. Cidade, Goiás
MA34)	H908	1470	1/0.25	R. Paranoá, Presidente Dutra
MA39)	H901	1470	1/0.25	R. Urbano Santos,Urbano Santos
MA43)		1470	1	R. Cidade, Turiaçu
MG96)	L247	1470	1/0,25	R. Dif., Ituiutaba: 24h
MS29)	I413	1470	1/0.25	R. Alvorada, Itaporã
PA25)	I548	1470	1/0.25	R. Moreno Braga, Vigia
PE35)	I822	1470	1/0.25	R. Educadora, Belém de São Francisco: 0900-0300, Sat 1100-0100, Sun 1700-2000
PE37)	I827	1470	1/0.25	R. Papacaça, Bom Conselho: 0700-0300, Sun 0800-0100
PI15)	I900	1470	1/0.25	R. Difusora Vale do Uruçuí, Uruçuí
PI24)	I913	1470	1/0.25	R. Ingazeira, Paulistana
PI33)	I928	1470	1/0.25	R. Cidade, Castelo do Piauí
PR103)	J294	1470	1/0.25	R. Educadora, Ibaiti: 24h
PR104)	J304	1470	5/0.25	R. Jornal, Assis Chateaubriand
PR172)	J...	1470	1/0.25	R. Panorama, Itapejara d'Oeste
PR173)	J...	1470	3/0.25	R. Tradição, Rio Branco do Sul: 24h
RJ08)	J476	1470	1/0.25	R. Absoluta, Campos dos Goytacazes
RJ38)	J481	1470	5/0.25	R. Barra do Pirai, Barra do Piraí: 0900-0300
RN23)	J616	1470	1/0.25	R. Rural de Parelhas, Parelhas
RO05)	J676	1470	1/0.25	R. Rondônia, Cacoal
RS169)	K219	1470	0.25	R. Cultura, Cacequi
SC65)	J781	‡1470	10/1	R. Record, São José
SC66)	J798	1470	3/0.25	R. Nova Líder, Herval d'Oeste
SP172)	K586	1470	1/0.25	R. Cultura, Guaíra
SP173)	K599	1470	5/0.25	R. Mensagem, Jacareí: 24h
SP174)	K632	1470	1/0.25	R. Primavera, Porto Ferreira
SP175)	K712	1470	1/0.25	R. Jornal, Indaiatuba: 24h
SP243)	K771	1470	1/0.25	R. Bastos AM, Bastos
BA61)	H508	1480	5/1	R. Alvorada, Guanambi. 0800-0200
BA66)	H510	1480	1/0.25	R. Tribuna do Vale do São Francisco, Xique-Xique
BA75)	H524	1480	1/0.25	R. Santana, Santana
CE74)	H671	1480	1/0.25	R. Princesa do Norte, Morrinhos. 0800-2000, Sat 1400-1500
MA14)	H897	1480	10	R. Itapecuru, Colinas
MG98)	L235	1480	1/0.25	R. Nova Frutal AM, Frutal
MG99)	L265	1480	1/0.25	R. Difusora, Nanuque
MG100)	L307	1480	2.5/0.25	R. Emboabas, Tiradentes: 24h
MS17)	I393	1480	1/0.25	R. Caçula, Três Lagoas: 24h
PE26)	I790	1480	1/0.25	R. A Voz do Sertão, Serra Talhada: 0900-0100, Sat 0800-2200
PE36)	I825	1480	5/0.25	R. Canção Nova, Gravatá: 24h
PI29)	I929	1480	1/0.25	R. Vale do Coroatá, Elesbão Veloso
PR79)	J302	1480	1/0.25	R. Cultura, Iporã
PR153)	J221	1480	1/0.25	R. Brotas, Piraí do Sul
PR106)	J230	1480	1/0.25	R. Astorga, Astorga
PR107)	J270	1480	5/0.25	R. Educadora, União da Vitória
PR174)	J370	1480	1/0.25	R. Pérola, Pérola d'Oeste
RJ55)	J485	1480	10/0.5	R. Popular, Duque de Caxias
RN14)	J601	1480	1/0.25	R. Princesa do Vale, Açu: 0700-2333, Sat 0915-1500 Sun 1100-0100
RO15)	J681	1480	1/0.25	R. Rondônia, Pimenta Bueno
RS100)	K244	1480	2.5/0.25	R. São Roque, Faxinal do Soturno
RS127)	K321	1480	5/0.25	R. Veranense, Veranópolis: 24h
RS178)	K255	1480	0.5/0.25	R. Guaramano, Guarani das Missões: 0800-0200(Sun -0100)
SC67)	J731	1480	1/0.25	R. Arca da Aliança, Joinville
SC94)	J826	1480	2.5/0.25	R. Caibi, Caibi
SE10)	J928	1480	1/0.25	R. Nova Cidade, Simão Dias: 24h

MW	Call	kHz	kW	Station, location, h. of tr.
SP176)	K539	1480	1/0.25	R. Cl. Regional., Altinópolis: 0900-2110 (Sun -0100)
SP177)	K551	1480	1/0.25	R. Atibaia, Atibaia
SP255)	K767	1480	0.5	R. Nova America, Boituva
TO06)	H795	1480	1/0.25	R. Cultura, Miracema do Tocantins: 24h
AL09)	H246	1490	5/1	Em. Rio São Francisco, Penedo
BA41)	H478	1490	1/0.25	R. Educadora, Ipiaú: 0800-0300
BA77)	H507	1490	1/0.25	R. Rio São Francisco, Bom Jesus da Lapa
BA87)	H512	1490	0.25	R. Planalto d'Oeste, Correntina: 0800-0100
MG162)	L231	1490	0.25	R. Onda Viva, Araguari
MG163)	L274	1490	1/0.25	R. Paraisópolis, Paraisópolis
MG165)	L353	1490	1/0.25	R. Pirapetinga, Pirapetinga: 0800-0100(Sun -2300)
MS19)	I404	1490	1/0.25	R. Nova Paiaguás, Glória de Dourados
MT53)		1490	1/0.25	R. Continental, Vila Rica: 0900-0400
PR108)	J210	1490	1/0.25	R. Cornélio, Cornélio Procópio
PR149)	J347	1490	1/0.25	R. Dif., São Jorge do Oeste: 0900-0100
RS138)	K208	1490	25/0.25	R. Assisense, São Francisco de Assis
RS140)	K309	1490	3/0.25	R. Taquara, Taquara: 0830-0200
SC70)	J791	1490	2.5/0.25	R. Cultura, Xaxim
SP180)	K530	1490	1/0.25	R. Difusora, Olímpia: 24h
SP181)	K580	1490	1/0.25	R. Globo, Dracena: 24h
SP182)	K583	1490	1/0.25	R. Educadora, Fernandópolis: 24h
SP244)	K680	1490	1/0.25	R. Cult., Vargem Grande do Sul: 0900-0100
SP183)	K764	1490	25/0.5	R. Imaculada Conceição, Mauá
BA49)	H487	1500	0.5	R. Jacuípe, Riachão do Jacuípe
CE39)	H615	1500	2.5/0.25	R. Macico, Baturité
MG101)	L215	1500	5/0.25	R. Montanhea, Viçosa
MG140)	L340	1500	1/0.25	R. Aparecida do Sul, Ilicínea: 0900-2200
PA19)	I542	1500	1/0.25	R. Floresta, Tucuruí
PE27)	I779	1500	1/0.25	R. Pajeu, Afogados da Ingazeira: 0700(SS 0800)-0300
PI46)	I919	1500	1/0.25	R. Voz da Longa, Esperantina
PR163)	J366	1500	2.5/0.25	R. Aracauria, Mangueirinha
RS139)	K225	1500	4/0.25	R. Liberdade, Canguçu: 0900-0100
RS161)	K365	1500	3/0.25	R. Simpatia, Chapada: 0900-0100
SC106)	J......	1500	1/0.25	R. Catolica, Balneário Camboriú
SP184)	K549	1500	2.5/0.25	R. Fraternidade, Araras
SP185)	K626	1500	1/0.25	R. Difusora, Pindamonhangaba
SP186)	K706	1500	1/0.25	R. Vale do Rio Grande, Miguelópolis
SP211)	K773	1500	1/0.25	R. Cumbica, Guarulhos: 24h
SP236)	K776	1500	1/0.25	R. Cidade, Apiaí: 24h
BA52)	H493	1510	5/0.5	R. Dif. do Descobrimento, Porto Seguro
CE40)	H608	1510	1/0.25	R. Nova Plan, São Benedito: 24h
CE84)	H630	1510	0.25	R. Trapiá, Pedra Branca
GO38)	H770	1510	1/0.25	R. Goiatuba, Goiatuba
MS62)	N613	1510	1/0.25	R. Maria, Mundo Novo
PA01)	I544	‡1510	10/0.25	R. Oriente de Redenção, Redenção
PI16)	I894	1510	1/0.25	R. Difusora, Floriano
PI17)	I896	‡1510	1/0.25	R. Progresso, Corrente
PI49)	I936	1510	1/0.25	R. Nordeste, Picos
PR113)	J216	1510	1/0.25	R. Educadora, Wenceslau Bráz: 24h
PR115)	J326	1510	1/0.25	R. União, Céu Azul
RJ43)	J492	1510	1/0.25	R. Teresópolis, Teresópolis: 0900-0300
RN15)	J602	1510	1/0.25	R. Centenário, Caraúbas: 0700-0100 (SS -2300)
SC73)	J795	1510	1/0.25	R. Centro Oeste, Pinhalzinho: 0800-0200 (Sun -0100)
SP188)	K654	1510	10/1	R. Cacique, Santos
SP189)	K665	1510	1/0.25	R. Cl. Regional, São Manuel: 0700-2300
SP256)	K770	1510	0.5/0.25	R. Vale do Tietê, Salto
SP230)	K...	1510	1/0.25	R. Rural, Rinópolis
SP269)	K719	1510	1/0.25	R. Athenas Paulista, Jaboticabal
BA78)	H530	1520	5/1	R. Povo, Poções
CE75)	H635	1520	1/0.25	R. Regional, Ipu: 0800-0300
CE83)	H653	1520	1/0.25	R. Cachoeira, Solonópole
GO53)	H806	1520	1/0.25	R. Nova RCB, Campos Belos: 24h
MA15)	H899	1520	1/0.25	R. Mirante, Pindaré-Mirim
MA35)	H928	1520	1/0.25	R. Mirante AM, Chapadinha
MG174)	L223	1520	0.25	R. Cultura, Cássia
MG106)	L245	1520	2.5/0.25	R. Clube, Itaúna
MS21)	I405	1520	1/0.25	R. Globo, Amambaí: 24h
MS42)	N605	1520	1/0.25	R. Campo Alegre, Rio Verde de Mato Grosso
PE28)	I801	1520	1/0.25	R. Surubim, Surubim: 0800-0100 (Sat -1700), Sun silent
PR116)	J218	1520	2.5/0.25	R. Serra do Mar, Antonina: 24h
PR118)	J292	1520	1/0.25	R. Nova Cultura, Palotina
PR132)	J340	1520	1/0.25	R. Internacional, Quedas do Iguaçu: 0830-0100, SS: 0900-0000
PR156)	J358	1520	1/0.25	R. Guairacá, Terra Rica: 24h
RJ44)	J491	1520	10/0.5	R. Continental, São João do Meriti: 24h
RN22)	J610	1520	1/0.25	R. Salinas, Macau
RS141)	K217	1520	1/0.25	R. Vale do Jacui, Cachoeira do Sul: 0830-0100
SC76)	J806	1520	2.5/0.25	R. Cultura, Timbó
SE13)	J931	1520	10/0.5	R. Ilha AM, Tobias Barreto
SP191)	K614	1520	10/1	Rede Apolo de R., Mogi das Cruzes: 24h
SP192)	K627	1520	1/0.25	Pinhal R. Cl., Espírito Sto. do Pinhal
SP225)	K760	1520	1/0.25	R. Manchester, Sorocaba
SP270)	K...	1520	1/0.25	Dif. Torre Forte, Buritama
SP286)	K....	1520	0.25	R. Legal, Viradouro: 24h
TO07)	H797	1520	1/0.25	R. Cristal, Cristalândia
BA43)	H479	1530	10/0.5	R. Cultura, Guanambi
BA99)	H533	1530	0.25	R. Progresso, Capim Grosso
CE76)	H666	1530	1/0.25	R. Tres Fronteiras, Campos Sales: 0800-2300
MG175)	L262	1530	0.25	R. Progresso, Monte Santo de Minas
MG110)	L280	1530	1/0.25	R. Clube, Pouso Alegre
MT42)	I432	1530	1/0.25	R. Amiga, Peixoto de Azevedo
MT64)		1530	1/0.25	R. Parecis. Campo Novo de Parecis
PE29)	I781	1530	1/0.25	R. Bitury, Belo Jardim
PR157)	J348	1530	2.5/0.25	R. Vale do Iguaçu, Verê: 0800-0100
RJ57)	J482	1530	1/0.25	R. Búzios, Cabo Frio
RJ45)	J502	1530	1/0.25	R. Princesinha do Norte, Miracema: 0800-0100(Sat -2030, Sun -1700)
RN16)	J603	1530	1/0.25	R. Curimataú, Nova Cruz
RO16)	J685	1530	5/1	R. Planalto, Vilhena: 0900-0330
RS143)	K235	1530	1/0.25	R. Sulina, Dom Pedrito: 0800-0030
RS144)	K300	1530	5/0.25	R. Progresso, São Leopoldo: 1000-0100
RS145)	K304	1530	4/0.25	R. Tapejara, Tapejara: 24h
SC77)	J761	1530	1/0.25	R. Dif., Itajaí: 0800-0300, Sun 1000-0200
SC78)	J780	1530	2.5/0.25	R. Difusora, São Joaquim: 0900-0200
SC79)	J796	1530	2.5	R. Porto Feliz, Mondaí
SP193)	K677	1530	1/0.25	R. Difusora Digital, Tupi Paulista
SP194)	K714	1530	1/0.25	R. Noticias, Tatuí: 24h
SP231)	K755	1530	1/0.25	R. Universal, Teodoro Sampaio
BA89)	H...	1540	0.25	R. Sociedade, Itiruçu
CE42)	H611	1540	1/0.5	R. Sant'Ana, Tianguá: 0830-0100, SS 0900-2300
CE77)	H631	1540	1/0.25	R. Sertões, Mombaça
MA36)	H921	1540	1/0.25	R. Santa Maura, Lago da Pedra
MG111)	L217	1540	1/0.25	R. Bomdespachense, Bom Despacho
MG112)	L226	1540	1/0.25	R. Globo, Conselheiro Lafaiete
MG113)	L293	1540	2/0.25	R. Tropical, Três Corações: 24h
MS35)	N601	1540	1/0.5	R. Nova Piravevê, Ivinhema
MT65)	I442	1540	1/0.25	R. Ativa, Barra do Burges: 0830-0200 Sun: silent
PA14)	I545	1540	1/0.25	R. Boa Vista, São Sebastião da Boa Vista
PB24)	I694	1540	1/0.5	R. Santa Maria, Monteiro
PR168)	J206	1540	1/0.25	R. Litorânea, Guaratuba: 24h
RJ54)	J508	1540	1/0.25	R. Clube, Paraíba do Sul: 0900-0300
RN30)	J611	‡1540	1/0.25	R. Baixa Verde, João Câmara: 0900-0000
RS157)	K282	1540	1/0.25	R. Quaraí, Quaraí
SC80)	J803	1540	5/0.25	R. Capinzal, Capinzal: 0800-0200 Sun 24h
SP245)	K514	1540	1/0.25	R. Cultura, Leme
SP196)	K564	1540	2/0.5	R. Em. Botucatu, Botucatu: 0800-0300
SP197)	K723	1540	50/1	R. Nova Difusora, Osasco: 0900-0100
SP246)	K737	1540	0.5/0.25	R. Central, Campéia
SP288)		1540		R. Novo Milenio, Ribeirao Preto (IPDA)
BA80)	H518	1550	5/0.25	R. Independencia do São Francisco, Juazeiro
MA37)	H926	1550	10/1	Sist. Janaina de Rdif, Vargem Grande
MG114)	L211	1550	1/0.25	R. Cultura, Monte Carmelo: 24h
MG169)	L222	1550	1/0.25	R. Difusora, Carmo do Rio Claro
MG115)	L289	1550	1/0.25	R. Difusora Santarritense, Santa Rita do Sapucaí: 0800-0200
MG195)	N211	1550	1/0.25	R. Cidade, Guanhães: 24h
PA34)	I550	1550	1/0.25	R. Cabano, Maracanã
PB32)	I700	1550	10/0.25	R. Jardim da Borborema, Areia: 0800-0200
PR133)	J213	1550	1/0.25	R. Ipiranga, Palmeira
PR123)	J303	1550	1/0.25	R. Pioneira, Formosa do Oeste: 1000-2200, Sun silent
PR124)	J315	1550	2.5/0.25	R. Cristal, Marmeleiro: 24h
PR169)	J217	1550	1/0.25	R. Itay, Lapa: 0900-2200
PR185)	J371	1550	1	R. Globo, Jacarezinho: 24h
RJ46)	J479	1550	1/0.25	R. Imperial, Petrópolis: 0900-0300
RN19)	J606	1550	1/0.25	R. Ivipanin, Areia Branca (RPC)
RO23)	J...	1550	0.25	R. Suprema, Cacoal: 24h
RS162)	K377	1550	1/0.25	R. Opinião Gospel, Capão do Leão
RS159)	K375	1550	1/0.25	R. Soledad, Soledade: 0800(Sun 0900)-0300
SC92)	J814	1550	5/0.25	R. Imigrantes, Turvo: 0800-0100
SP198)	K501	1550	1/0.25	R. Clube, Itararé

MW	Call	kHz	kW	Station, location, h. of tr.
SP259)	K528	1550	1/0.25	R. Tambaú, Tambaú: 0900-0300
SP200)	K572	1550	1/0.25	R. Cacique, Capivari
SP201)	K590	1550	10/1	R. Guarujá AM, Guarujá: 24h
SP202)	K659	1550	1/0.5	R. São Joaquim, São Joaquim da Barra
SP219)	K740	1550	1/0.25	R. Nova Difusora, Auriflama
AL16)	H257	1560	1/0.25	R. Princesa das Matas, Viçosa: 0830-0200, SS 24h
BA90)	H526	1560	0.25	R. Povo Pombal, Ribeira do Pombal
CE43)	H622	1560	1/0.25	R. Difusora Vale de Curu, Pentecoste
MA18)	H903	1560	1/0.25	R. Agua Branca, Vitorino Freire
MG117)	L256	1560	1/0.25	R. Jornal, Leopoldina: 0800-0500
MT56)	I…	1560	1/0.25	R. Paranaita. Paranaita
PR125)	J275	1560	1/0.25	R. Capanema, Capanema: 24h
PR161)	J361	1560	0.25	R. Cultura Serpin, Ribeirão do Pinhal: 0800-0200(Sun -2100)
PR184)		1560	10/0.25	R. Barigui, Almirante Tamandaré: 24h
RJ47)	J501	1560	5/0.25	R. Grande Rio, Itaguaí: 24h
RN17)	J608	1560	1/0.25	R. Cultura do Oeste, Pau dos Ferros: 0800-0100
RS158)	K310	1560	2.5/0.25	R. Açoriana, Taquari: 1000-0100(Sun -2200)
RS172)	K369	1560	5/0.25	R. Poatã, São José do Ouro: 0900-0100
SC95)	J825	1560	1/0.25	R. Cidade, São Miguel d'Oeste
SP261)	K593	1560	1/0.25	R. Show, Igarapava: 24h
SP248)	K679	1560	0.25	R. Valparaíso, Valparaíso: 24h
SP249)	K725	‡1560	0.25	R. Cidade, Pedreira
SP250)	K778	1560	1/0.25	R. Vale do Rio Paraná, Presidente Epitácio
BA56)	H496	1570	1/0.25	R. Povo, Jaguaquara
CE44)	H621	1570	1/0.25	R. Sertão Central,Senador Pompeu
MA22)	H907	1570	10/0.5	R. Cultura do Rio Jordão, Coroatá
MG146)	L242	1570	0.25	R. Unifei, Itajubá
MG141)	L344	1570	1/0.25	R. Cidade, Corinto
MG170)	L364	1570	10/0.25	R. Difusora, Piranga
MS24)	I409	1570	1/0.25	R. Nova Difusora, Caarapó
MS55)	I418	1570	1/0.25	R. Cidade, Aparecida do Taboado
PE30)	I798	1570	5/1	R. Asa Branca, Salgueiro
PR158)	J324	1570	0.25	R. Nova Brasileira, Bela Vista do Paraíso
PR137)	J341	1570	1/0.25	R. Club, Nova Aurora: 24h
PR159)	J365	1570	1/0.25	R. Globo, Arapoti
PR166)	J209	1570	0.25	R. Terra Nativa, Paranaguá
RJ48)	J493	1570	1/0.25	R. Cultura, Valença: 24h
RO19)	J678	1570	5/0.25	R. Soc. Espigão, Espigão d'Oeste
RS147)	K358	1570	5/0.25	R. Metrópole, Gravataí: 24h
SC83)	J777	1570	1/0.25	R. Rio Negrinho, Rio Negrinho
SC98)	J829	1570	1/0.25	R. Modelo, Modelo: 0800(SS 0900)-0100
SC107)	J…	1570	1/0.25	R. Tangrá, Tangará
SP204)	K552	1570	1/0.25	R. Avaré, Avaré
SP205)	K605	1570	1/0.25	R. Junqueirópolis, Junqueirópolis: 0900-2300
SP262)	K648	1570	1/0.25	R. Zequinha de Abreu, Santa Rita do Passa Quatro: 0800-2300
SP206)	K651	1570	10/0.25	R. ABC, Santo André: 24h
SP207)	K667	1570	1/0.25	R. Socorro, Socorro
SP208)	K670	1570	1/0.25	R. Clube, Tanabi: 24h
TO10)	N665	1570	1/0.25	R. Nossa R., Gurupi: 0900-0300 Sat -2100 Sun 1100-1500
BA53)	H497	1580	2.5/0.25	R. Barra de Mendes, Barra de Mendes
BA62)	H502	1580	1/0.25	R. Atalaia, Canavieiras
MG119)	L210	1580	1/0.25	R. Liberdade, Itapecirica
MG121)	L290	1580	1/0.25	R. Cultura, Santos Dumont
MG122)	L329	1580	1/0.25	R. Educadora, Espinosa
MG133)	L335	1580	1/0.25	R. Nova Guaranésia, Guaranésia
MS25)	I415	1580	1/0.25	R. Laguna, Amambaí: 0900-0200
MS43)	N611	1580	1/0.25	R. Difusora, Ivinhema
PI18)	I898	1580	1/0.25	R. Santa Clara, Floriano: 0800-0030, Sun 1000-1500
PR164)	J342	1580	2.5/0.25	R. São João do Sudoeste, São João: 24h
PR186)		1580	0.25	R. Terra Nativa, Cambé
RJ51)	J487	1580	1/0.5	R. Popular Fluminense, Conceição de Macabu: 24h
RJ52)	J506	1580	5/0.25	R. Resende AM, Resende: 0800-0100, SS 1000-0100
RJ58)	J505	1580	0.25	R. Geração 2000, Teresópolis
RN24)	J613	1580	1/0.25	R. Novos Tempos, Ceará Mirim
RS148)	K237	1580	9/0.25	R. Encantado AM, Encantado
RS150)	K339	1580	0.25	R. Dif. Fronteira, Arroio Grande: 24h
SP251)	K504	1580	1/0.25	R. Difusora, Amparo: 24h
SP209)	K743	1580	0.25	R. Pedra Bonita, Itaporanga
SP289)		1580	0.25	R. Grande Vale, Paraíbuna
BA55)	H…	1590	0.3	R. Vale do Jiquiriçá, Jiquiriça
CE100)	H…	1590	1	R. Veneza, Eusébio
ES22)	I…	1590	1/0.25	R. Sim Tupi, Cachoeiro de Itapemirim
MG171)	L368	1590	1/0.25	R. Cidade Carinho, Ubá

MW	Call	kHz	kW	Station, location, h. of tr.
MG134)	L369	1590	10/1	R. Guaicuí, Várzea da Palma
MG193)	N207	1590	0,25	R. Globo, Lambari
MS26)	I403	1590	1/0.25	R. Independência, Eldorado
PB34)	I703	1590	1/0.25	R. Correio do Vale, Itaporanga
PE41)	ZYI802	1590	1	R. Restauração, Bezerros:24h
PR129)	J290	1590	1/0.25	R. Super Cultura, Andirá
PR160)	J296	1590	1/0.25	R. Hawaí, Capitão Leônidas Marques
RS174)	K212	1590	0.25	R. Clube, Bagé: 0900-0300
SC101)	J823	1590	10/0.5	R. Clube, Joinville
SP254)	K774	1590	10/0.5	R. Japi, Cabreúva
BA45)	H464	1600	10/1	R. Nova Voz, Muritiba
SP263)	K779	1600	100/20	R. Nove de Julho, São Paulo: 24h
SW	**Call**	**kHz**	**kW**	**Station, location, h. of tr.**
SP82)	G852	2380	0.25	R. Educadora, Limeira
SP49)	G855	3365	1	R. Cultura, Araraquara
AM02)	F276	3375	1	R. Municipal, São Gabriel da Cachoeira
MS01)	F904	‡4765	10	R. Imaculada Conceição, Campo Grande
AC01)	H202	4765	10	R. Integração, Cruzeiro do Sul: 0900-0300
PA04)	G363	‡4765	5	R. Rural, Santarem
MG55)	G207	4775	1	R. Congonhas, Congonhas: 0800-0100
RO11)	G790	4785	10	R. Caiari, Porto Velho: 0900-1400, 1900-0300
AM20)	F273	4805	10/5	R. Dif. do Amazonas, Manaus
PR13)	G640	4815	10	R. Difusora, Londrina
SP80)	G868	4825	10	R. Canção Nova, Cachoeira Paulista
PA12)	G364	‡4825	5	R. Educadora, Bragança: 0830-0300
SP287)	G869	4845	1	R. Meteorologia Paulista, Ibitinga: (r. R. Ternura FM)
AM14)	F278	4845	10	R. Cultura, Manaus: 1000-0200
AC04)	F203	4865	5	R. Verdes Florestas, Cruzeiro do Sul: 0930-0200 Sun.: 1000-0040
PR33)	G641	4865	5	R. Alvorada, Londrina
RR01)	G810	4876	10	R. Roraima, Boa Vista: 0800-0300
AC06)	F201	‡4885	10	R. Dif. Acreana, Rio Branco: 0900-0400
PA03)	G362	‡4885	10	R. Clube do Pará, Belém: 24h
MS32)	R200	4895	5	R. Novo Tempo, Campo Grande
TO04)	F693	‡4905	1	R. Anhanguera, Araguaína
RJ03)	G683	4905	5	R. Relogio Federal, São Gonçalo
AP01)	F360	4915	25	R. Dif. Macapá, Macapá: 24h
GO27)	F691	4915	10	R. Daqui, Goiânia
AM10)	F282	4925	5	R. Educação Rural, Tefé: 1000-1600, 2000-0200
AM12)	ZYF275	4965	5	R. Alvorada, Parintins: 2200- 0200
SP223)	G865	‡4975	1	Rede Apoo de Radio, São Paulo
GO30)	F690	4985	10	R. Brasil Central, Goiânia
MT08)	F903	5015		R. Cultura, Cuiabá
SP52)	G853	5035	10	R. Aparecida, Aparecida
AM09)	F272	‡5035	5	R. Educação Rural, Coari
SC86)		5940	10	R. Voz Missionária, Camboriú
SP280)	E858	5965	7.5	R. Trans Mundial, Santa Maria
MG06)	E523	‡5970	10	R. Itatiaia, Belo Horizonte
RS23)	E852	6000	10	R. Guaiba, Porto Alegre
MG35)	E521	6010	5	R. Inconfidência, Belo Horizonte
RS09)	E850	6020	10	R. Gaucha, Porto Alegre
PR134)	E275	6040	7.5	R.RB2, Curitiba
PR60)	E726	6060	10	Super Rádio Deus é Amor, Curitiba
PR15)	E726	6080	10	R. Marumby, Curitiba
GO27)	E441	‡6080	6	R. Daqui, Goiânia
SP57)	E956	6090	10	R. Bandeirantes, São Paulo
PR138)	E728	6105	10	R. Cultura Filadélfia, Foz do Iguaçu: 24h
SP80)	E971	‡6105	5	R. Canção Nova, Cachoeira Paulista
PR60)	E968	6120	10	Super Rádio Deus é Amor, Sao Paulo
SP52)	E954	6135	25	R. Aparecida, Aparecida
SP77)	E950	6150	7.5	R. Record, São Paulo
AM11)	E245	‡6160	7.5	R. Rio Mar, Manau
RS104)	E854	6160	1	Super Rede Boa Vontade, Porto Alegre
DF06)	E365	6180	250	R. Nal. da Amazônia, Brasília: 0900-0400
PR15)	E726	9515	10	R. Marumby, Curitiba
SP280)	E858	9530	7.5	R. Trans Mundial, Santa Maria
RS104)	E855	9550	10	Super Rede Boa Vontade, Porto Alegre
PR60)	E727	9565	20	Super Rádio Deus é Amor, Curitiba (r)
PR60)	E969	9585	10	Super Rádio Deus é Amor, Sao Paulo
SP52)	E954	9630	10	R. Aparecida, Aparecida.
SP57)	E957	9645	7.5	R. Bandeirantes, São Paulo
SC86)	E890	9665	10	R. Voz Missionária, Camboriú
AM11)	E245	9695	7.5	R. Rio Mar, Manaus: 1000-2100
PR134)	E725	9725	7.5	R.RB2, Curitiba
SP263)	E971	9820	10	R. Nove de Julho, São Paulo: 24h
SP280)	E858	11735	50	R. Trans Mundial, Santa Maria
PR60)	E726	11765	20	Super Rádio Deus é Amor, Curitiba
DF06)	E365	11780	250	R. Nal. da Amazônia, Brasília
GO30)	E440	11815	7.5	R. Brasil Central, Goiânia

SW	Call	kHz	kW	Station, location, h. of tr.
GO27)	E441	‡11830	10	R. Daqui, Goiânia
SP52)	E954	11855	1	R. Aparecida, Aparecida
RS104)	E856	‡11895	10	Super Rede Boa Vontade, Porto Alegre
RS09)	E851	11915	10	R. Gaucha, Porto Alegre
SP57)	E958	11925	10	R. Bandeirantes, São Paulo
PR134	E725	‡11935	7.5	R.RB2, Curitiba
MG35)	E622	‡15190	5	R. Inconfidência, Belo Horizonte

RADIO NETWORKS
There are several radio networks. Below are listed just some of them. The affiliated outlets are often subject to alteration.

CENTRAL BRASILEIRA DE NOTICIAS – CBN: W: radioclick.globo. com/cbn
EMPRESA BRASIL DE COMUNIÇÃCAO – EBC: W: facebook. com/ebcnarede/info
IGREJA PENTECOSTAL DEUS È AMOR: W: ipda.com.br
IGREJA UNIVERSAL DO REINO DE DEUS: W: igrejauniversal. org.br
Rede JOVEM PAN ☞ Av. Paulista 807, 24° andar, 01311-915 São Paulo, SP **W:** jovempan.uol.com.br
RADIO BANDEIRANTES W: radiobandeirantes com.br
RADIO GLOBO: W: radioclick.globo com
REDE BOA VONTADE - LBV ☞ Legião da Boa Vontade, Rua Doraci 90, Bairro Bom Retiro, 01134-020 São Paulo, SP **W:** redeboavontada.com
REDE BOAS NOVAS – RBN: W: rbn.org.br
REDE CANÇÃO NOVA DE RÁDIO ☞ Rua João Paulo II s/, Alto da Bela Vista, 12630-000 Cachoeira Paulista, SP **W:** cancaonova.com **E:** radio@cancaonova.com
REDE CATÓLICA DE RÁDIO - RCR: ☞ União de Radiodifusão Católica, Rua Vergueiro 3086, Conj. 91, Vila Mariana, 04102-001 São Paulo, SP **W:** rcrunda.com **E:** rcr@rcrunda.com
REDE DO ESTADO DE SÃO PAULO: W: redecbs.com.br
REDE GAÚCHA SAT ☞ Av. Erico Veríssimo 400, Edifício Maurício Sirotsky Sobrinho, 90169-900 Porto Alegre, RS **W:** rbs.clicrbs.com.br
REDE ESPERANCA: W: redeesperança.com
REDE ITATIAIA: W: itatiaia.com.br/rede
REDE MILICIA SAT: W: milicia.org.br
REDE MINERIA DE RADIO: W: redemineiraderadio.com.br
REDE NOVO TEMPO: W: novotempo.org.br
REDE PAULUS SAT: ☞ Rua Doutor Pinto Ferraz 183, Vila Mariana, 04117-900 São Paulo, SP **W:** radioamericasp.com.br/paulussat.htm
REDE POTGUAR DE COMUNICAÇÃO (RPC): W: redepotiguar.com
REDE SUL DE RÁDIO: W: saofrancisco.am.br
REDE TRANSAMÉRICA DE RÁDIO: W: transanet.uol.com.br
SISTEMA GLOBO DE RÁDIO: W: radioclick.globo.com/globobrasil
SISTEMA GUAÍBA SAT: ☞ Rua Caldas Jr. 219, 2° andar, 90019-900 Porto Alegre, RS **W:** guaiba.com.br
REDE SOMZOOM SAT: ☞ Av. Herois do Acre 590, Passaré, 60743-760 Fortaleza, CE **W:** somzoom.com.br **E:** somzoomsat@somzoom. com.br

AC00) ACRE
AC01) Rua de Alagoas, 270 - Colégio, 69980-000 Cruzeiro do Sul ☎68 3322 4637 **W:** radioetvintegracao.com.br **E:** radiointegracao@ hotmail.com - **FM:** 99.9MHz – **AC02)** Rua Marechal Deodoro, 197 sala 210/211, 69900-066 Rio Branco ☎68 3223 2239 **W:** cbnamazonia. com.br – **AC03)** Rua Coronel Brandão, 1665 - Bairro Aeroporto, 69930-000 Xapuri ☎68 3542 2830 **E:** raimari.cardoso@gmail.com – **AC04)** Travessa Mário Lobão 81, 69980-000 Cruzeiro do Sul ☎68 3322 3309 ☐68 3322 2634 **W:** diocesecruzeirodosul.org/index.php?s=radio-verdes-florestas **E:** verdesflorestas@yahoo.com.br – **AC05)** Rua Epaminondas Jacome, 3121 - Base, 69900-28 Rio Branco ☎68 3224 0505 – **AC06)** Rua Benjamin Constant 1232, 69900-161 Rio Branco ☎68 3223 9696 **W:** difusora.ac.gov.br **E:** comercial.difusora@ac.gov. br – **AC11)** Rua Maria Glória Farias, 1 qd 3 c 4 - Cannisio Brasil, 69940-000 Sena Madureira ☎68 3612 3733 **E:** rivaldosevero@hotmail.com - **FM:** 105.9MHz – **AC12)** Rua Nilo Freire de Albuquerqe, s/n - Novo, 69970-000 Tarauacá ☎68 3462 1416 **E:** railtonrodrigues@ac.gov.br – **AC15)** Travasse Posto, 168 - Cidade Novo, 69960-000 Feijo ☎68 3463 3310 **E:** jocivaldogomes@bol.com.br

AL00) ALAGOAS
AL01) Av. Deputada Cecj Cunha, 6 - Brásilia, 57313-085 Arapiraca ☎82 3522 085 **W:** novonordeste.am.br **E:** am@novonordeste.com.br – **AL02)** Av Siqueira 494, Prado, 57010-000 Maceió ☎82 3223 1710 **W:** Facebook: Rádio-Jornal **E:** comercial@jornalam710.com.br – **AL03)** Rua José e Maria Passos, 25 - Centro, 57600-030 Palmeiras dos Indios ☎82 3421 2289 **W:** radiosampaio.com.br **E:** estudio@radiosampaio.com.br - **FM:**

92.5MHz – **AL04)** Av Fernandes Lima,1047 - Farol, 57050-000 Maceió ☎82 3315 9927 **W:** izp.al.gov.br **E:** ascom@izp.al.gov.ar – **AL05)** Rua Miguel Palmeira 1513, 7° andar, Farol, 57055-330 Maceió ☎82 3241 2284 **W:** jovempanam1020.com.br – **AL06)** Praça Senador Eneas Araújo 61, 57500-000 Santana do Ipanema **W:** radiocorreiodosertao. com.br – **AL07)** Av Aristeu Andrade, 355 - Farol, 57051-090 Maceió ☎82 3336 1260 **W:** gazetaweb.globo.com - **FM:** 94.1MHz – **AL08)** Rua Vila Kennedy, 45 - Ponta Grosse, 57014-630 Maceió ☎82 3362 1320 **W:** miliciaimaculada.rcr.org.br **E:** 1320am@miliciadaimaculada. org.br – **AL09)** Cj São José s/n, gdC, Dom Constantino, 57200-000 Penedo ☎82 3551 2215 – **AL10)** Loteamento Cidade Imperia,l 4 lt 3 - Pedras, 57160-000 Taperagua ☎82 3263 7298 **W:** jovempanam1020. com.br/afiliadas.html – **AL11)** Rua Miguel Palmeira, 1513 7° andar - Farol, 57055-330 Maceió – **W:** jovempanam1020.com.br/afiliadas. html – **AL12)** Praça Manoel Monteiro 72, 57480-000 Delmiro Gouveia - ☎82 3641 2007 ☐82 3641 4047 **W:** radiomar.com.br **E:** radiodelmiro@gclnet.com.br - **FM:** 89.9MHz – **AL13)** BR-104 Km 36, Roberto Correia de Arajuó, 57800-000 União dos Palmares **AL14)** Rua Pedro Oliverio Rocha 784, 3 AND SL 01, Farol, 57075-560 Maceió ☎82 4009 0009 **W:** radiocorreio.com.br - **FM:** 91.7 MHz – **AL15)** Rua Aristeu de Andrade, 355 - Farol, 57021-050 Maceio ☎82 3624 1157 – **AL16)**Rua Frederico Maia, s/n - Centro , 57700-000 Viçosa ☎82 3283 1842 **W:** princesadasmatas.com **E:** contato@princesadasmatas.com – **AL17)** Rua Coronel Francisco Silva, 97 - Pitanguinha, 57052-190 Maceió ☎82 3356 8019 **W:** Facebook: PalmaresAM

AM00) AMAZONAS
AM02) Av Alvaro Maia s/n, 69750-000 São Gabriel da Cachoeira ☎97 3471 1109 – **AM03)** Rua Júlio de Oliveira, 1323 – São Pedro, 69800-000 Humaitá ☎97 3373 3946 **W:** radiovrm.com **E:** radiovrm@bol.com.br – **AM04)** A/C Prefeitura Municipal de Tabatinga (✉C.P 31), 69640-000 Tabatinga ☎97 3412 2829 **W:** radios.ebc. com.br/nacionalaltosolimo **E:** altossolimoes@ebc.com.br– **FM:** 96.1 MHz – **AM05)** Rua Solimões, 809 - Centro, 69100-000 Itacoatiara ☎92 3521 1635 **W:** facebook.com/cbnitacoatiara **E:** radiodifusora_ita@hotmail.com - **FM:** 94.5MHz– **AM06)** Rua Joana D'Angelo, s/n - Biri Biri, 69400-000 Manacapuru ☎92 3361 2042– **AM07)** Av Major Santana 2502, 69280-000 Manicoré – **AM08)** Rua Guaranópolis 533, 69190-000 Maués.☎92 3542 1254 **E:** radioguaranopolis@hotmail. com – **AM09)** Praça São Sebastião 263, 69460-000 Coari ☎97 3561 2383 **W:** radiocoariamot.blogspot.no **E:** radiocoari@hotmail. com – **AM10)** Praça Santa Tereza, 283 (✉ C.P. 21), 69470-000 Tefé ☎97 3343 3017 **W:** radiorualtefe.com.br **E:** radioruralam1270@ hotmail.com – **AM11)** Rua José Clemente, 500 - Centro, 69010-070 Manaus ☎92 3633 2295 **W:** rederiomar.com.br **E:** contato@rede-riomar.com.br - **FM:** 103.3 MHz – **AM12)** Rua Governador Leopoldo Neves (✉ C.P. 004),503 – Centro, 69151-460 Parintins ☎92 3533 3097 **W:** alvoradaparintins.com.br **E:** contato@alvoradaparintins. com.br - **FM:** 100.1MHz – **AM13)** Av André Araújo, 1555 – Aleixo, 69060-000 Manaus ☎92 3216 5536 **W:** http://amamazonia. com/radar10/amazonas-fm/ **E:** yara.malcher@redeamazonica.com. br – **FM:** 101.5 MHz– **AM14)** Rua Barcelos, s/n - Praça 14, 69020-200 Manaus ☎92 3215 4743 ☐92 3215 4759 **W:** tvcultura.am.gov. br **E:** radiocultura@tvcultura.am.gov.br or radiocultura@hotmail.com – **AM16)** Av General Rodrigo Jordão Ramos, 1655 Anexo 3 - Japiim, 69077-000 Manaus ☎92 3614 0007 **W:** ipda.com.br/radio/amazonas/index.htmk - **FM:** 107.9 MHz – **AM17)** Estrada Odvaldo Novo, s/n Km 1 - Parintins/AM, 69152-470 Parintins ☎92 3533 1564 **W:** radioclubeparintinsam.com.br **E:** contato@radioclubeparintinsam. com.br – **AM18)** Rodovia Manoel Urbano, km 2, 69405-000 Iranduba **W:** boavontade.com/radio– **AM19)** Boulevard Pedro Rate, 176 - São José, 69400-000 Manacapuru.☎ 92 3361 2192 ☐ 92 3361 2453 – **AM20)** Av Eduardo Ribeiro, 639 - Centro, 69010-001 Manaus ☎92 3633 1009 **W:** difusora24h.com **E:** comercial@difusora24h.com - **FM:** 96.9MHz – **AM23)** Rua Coronel João Vercosa, 47 - Centro, 69190-000 Maués ☎92 3542 1897 **W:** facebook.com - Rádio-Independência – **AM24)** Av Eduardo Ribeiro 520, 2 andar sala 201/215, 69010-690 Manaus ☎92 3633 2345

AP00) AMAPÁ
AP01) Av. Padre Júlio Maria Lombeard, 1614 - Santa Rita, 68901-283 Macapá ☎96 3312 1000 **W:** difusora.ap.gov.br **E:** rdm@rdm.ap.gov.br – **AP02)** Rua Eliezer Levy 684, 68900-140 Macapá ☎96 3222 3111 **W:** zsistemaequatorial.com.br– **AP03)** Av Nações Unidas 256, 68906-100 Macapá – **AP04)** Av. Rio Branco 3748, Fonte Nova, 68925-000 Santana ☎96 3281 5649 **W:** radioporto.xpg.com.br – **AP05)** Rua Hildemar Maia 1000, 68940-000 Mazagão ☎96 3271 1227 **W:** facebook.com/radionova.mazagao

BA00) BAHIA
BA01) Praça Mario Dourado, 78-A - Centro, 44900-000 Irecê ☎74 3641 3717 **W:** regionalam.com.br **E:** comercial@redecaraibes.com.br – **BA02)** Av. Itajuipe, 1789 - Santo Antonio, 45602-380 Itabuna. ☎73 3211 2385 **W:** radiojornaldeitabuna.com.br **E:** radiojornaldeitabuna@

hotmail.com – **BA03)** Praça da Independência 244, 45995-000 Teixeira de Freitas **W:** radiodifusoraam580.com.br – **BA04)** Rua Lord Cochrane, 66 - Barra, 40140-070 Salvador ☎71 3264 1244 **W:** sistemacruzeiro.com.br **E.** cruzeiro@veloxmail.com.br – **BA05)** Rua Dom Pedro II, 306 2° andar - Primavera, 47804-510 Barreiras ☎77 3611 3570 **W:** radiovale.com.br **E:** radiovale@radiovale.com.br – **BA06)** R Jorge Antonio Menezes Silva, 220 - Dendezeiros, 45400-000 Valença ☎75 3641 0660 **W:** radioclubedevalenca.com.br – **BA07)** Alamaeda Rui Barbosa, 42 - Centro, 45700-000 Itapetinga ☎77 3261 1010 **W:** novajornal. net– **BA08)** Rua Monsenhor Francisco Manoel da Silva, 46 - Centro , 44571-022 Santo Antônio de Jesus ☎75 3631 5680 **W:** radioclube680. com.br **E:** clubeam@hotmail.com – **BA10)** Rua Castro Alves, 868 - Centro, 44001-592 Feira de Santana ☎75 3223 0700 **W:** radiocultura-feiradesantana.com.br **E:** radioculturadefeiradesantana@hotmail.com **BA11)** Rua Jardim Federação, 81 - Federação, 40231-901 Salvador ☎71 3486 3201 ☎71 3486 3214 **W:** radiosociedadeam.com.br **E:** comercial@radiosociedadeam.com.br – **BA12)** Rua Cinquenteário, 1429 - Centro, 45600-006 Itabuna ☎73 3215 2271 **W:** difusorabahia.com.br – **BA13)** Rua Guadaljara, 389 - Vila Dulca, 47800-000 Barreiras ☎77 3611 4545 **W:** rb.am.br **E:** comercialfmrb@hotmail.com – **BA14)** Praça Luiz Nogueira 385, 48700-000 Serrinha **W:** grupoolmos.com.br **E:** grupolomes@grupolomes.com.br – **BA15)** Rua Antonio Neto, 27 - Centro, 46810-000 Utinga ☎75 3337 1011 **W:** radiocultura820.com.br **E:** comercial@radiocultura820.com.br – **BA16)** Fundação Dom Avelar Brandão, Rua Martin Afonso de Souza, 270 - Garcia, 40100-050 Salvador ☎71 3114 5088 ▤71 3114 3319 **W:** am840.com.br **E:** excelsiorcomercial@gmail.com – **BA17)** Av Visconde do Rio Branco. 68 - Centro, 48970-000 Senhor do Bonfim ☎74 3541 4617 **W:** radiocaraiba.com.br – **BA18)** Travessa da Catedral s/n, 45600-000 Itabuna ☎73 3215 0909 – **BA19)** Rua Wercelêncio da Mota, 81 - Centro, 48730-000 Conceição do Coité ☎75 3262 1010 **W:** radiosisal.com **E:** comercial@radiosisal.com **BA20)** Rua Frei Hermenegildo, 300 – Capuchinos (C.P. 1525), 44050-000 Feira de Santana ☎75 2101 9700 **W:** sociadadedefeiraam.com.br **E:** comercialsociedade@princesafm.com.br – **FM:** 96.9MHz – **BA21)** Gleba Fazenda Ouro Verde, 45900-000 Caravelas ☎73 3011 1299 **W:** Facebook – R.Alvorado Gospel – **BA22)** Rua Gabriel Soares, 23 - Ladeira dos Aflitos, 40060-040 Salvador – **BA23)** Praça Barão do Rio Branco 42, 45100-000 Vitória da Conquista **W:** radioclubeconquista.com.br **BA24)** Av Maria Quitéria, 223 - Serraria Brasil, 44062-630 Feira de Santana ☎75 3623 8927 ▤75 3623 2851 **W:** radiosubaeam.com – **FM:** 95.3MHz Nordeste FM **BA25)** Rua José Bonifacio, 17 2° andar - Centro, 45700-000 Itapetinga ☎77 3261 2610 **W:** radiofascinacao.com.br **E:** comercial@radiofascinacao.com.br – **BA26)** Rua Marquês de Paranagua, 259 – Centro 45660-000 ☎73 3231 3612 **W:** santacruzam.com.br **E:** – **BA27)** Av. Dq de Caxias, 491 S 301 – Centro (C.P 29), 45820-000 Eunápolis ☎73 3281 5370 – **BA28)** Rua Cel. Aprigio Duarte N, 05 - Centro, 48903-410 Juazeiro ☎76 3611 7211 **W:** radiojuazeiro.com.br **E:** contato@radiojuazeiro.com.br – **BA29)** Rua Senador Pedro Lago, 54 - Centro, 44700-000 Jacobina ☎74 3621 3636 **W:** radiocluberiodooruro.com.br **E:** radio@radiocluberiodoouro.com.br **BA30)** Rua Monte Castelo,45 - Sobradinha, 44018-210 Feira de Santana ☎75 3623 0717 **W:** radiopovo.com.br – **BA31)** Rua Dom Pedro II 98, 48100-000 Alagoinhas ☎75 3423 4366 **W:** novaam1240.com.br – **BA32)** Rua Conde Pereire Carneiro, 226 -Pernambúes, 41100-010 Salvador ☎71 3460 8500 **W:** radiometropole.com.br – **FM:** 101.3MHz **BA33)** Av. Itabuna, 63 – Centro, 45663-160 Ilhéus ☎73 3231 5462 **W:** radionovabahianaam1310.blogspot.com.br **E:** clinton.alves@hotmail.com – **BA34)** Praça Luiz Nogueira, 99 1° andar - Centro, 48700-000 Serrinha **W:** continentalam.com.br – **BA35)** Rua São Francisco 159-163A, 48601-070 Paulo Afonso ☎75 3281 5588 **W:** redecultura.com.br **E:** redecultura@redecultura.com.br – **FM:** 92.7MHz – **BA36)** Praça da Bandeira, s/n - Centro, 47600-000 Bom Jesus da Lapa ☎77 3481 4329 **W:** radiobomjesusam.com.br – **BA37)** Av Getúlio Vargas 394, 44330-000 São Gonçalo dos Campos – ☎77 3481 6161 **W:** planeta1410.com.br **BA38)** Av Barros Reis 295, 40353-100 Salvador ☎71 3383 5283 **W:** radioindependenciabahia.com.br – **BA39)** Rua 1 - Lotm Jardim Amaralina s/n 45204-010, 45204-010Jequié ☎73 3527 4114 **W:** radiopovo.com.br/jequie **E:** radiopovojequie@gmail.com – **BA40)** Rodovia BR 242, s/n km 98 - Zona Rural , 46880-000 Itaberaba ☎75 3252 1184 – **FM:** 95.5 MHz – **BA41)** Praça Virgilio Damasio, 140b 1° andar – Centro, 45570-000 Ipiaú ☎73 3531 3441 ▤73 3531 3419 **W:** radioeducadoradeipiau.com.br **E:** – **BA42)** Av. Dom Manuel Raimundo de Mello, 607 - São José, 46400-000 Caetité ☎77 3454 1819 **W:** educadorasantana.com.br **E:** educadora920@yahoo.com.br – **BA43)** Rua Otavio Mangabeira 1026, Bela Vista, 46880-000 Guanambi ☎77 3451 1348 **W:** radioculturabgi.com.br **E:** radioculturagbi@radioculturagbi.com.br – **BA44)** Av Ascendino Melo 297, 267 – Sis 106/107, Shopping Itatiaia, Recreio, 45020-908 Vitória da Conquista ☎77 3472 0760 **W:** clubenet.com.br **E:** radiocidade@clubenet.com.br – **BA45)** Tv Virgillo Gonzalves Pereira, 196 - Centro, 44340-000 Muritiba ☎73 3424 2048 – **BA46)** Av Porto Seguro, 718, 1° andar - Centro, 45820-006 Eunápolis.

☎73 3281 5594 **W:** facebook.com/radio21news – **BA47)** Rua da Bandeira 27, 42800-000 Camaçari – **BA49)** Rua Padre Argemiro Guimarães, 32 - Centro, 44640-000 Riachão do Jacuípe ☎73 3264 2189 **W:** radiojacuipe.com.br – **BA50)** Av Getúlio Vargas 43, 48601-000 Paulo Afonso ☎75 3281 3009 **W:** radiobahianordeste.com.br – **BA51)** Rua Rio Corrente s/n, 47640-000 Santa Maria da Vitória – **BA52)** Rua Saldanha Marinho, 30 Sala 23/24, Mesmo, 45810-000 Porto Seguro ☎73 3288 2136 **E:** radioguadalupeam@yahoo.com.br – **BA53)** Rua Alvaro Campos 83, 44990-000 Barra do Mendes **W:** facebook.com: Radio Barra do Mendes– **BA54)** Av Dom Avelar Brandão Vilella, s/n - Sítio São Félix, 46470-970 Riacho de Santana ☎77 3457 2104 **E:** radioguadalupeam@yahoo.com.br – **BA55)** Rua Coronel Vicente s/n, 45470-000 Jiquiriça – **BA56)** Loteamento Nova Jaguaquara s/n, Casca, 45345-000 Jaguaquara ☎73 3534 1422 **W:** radiopovo.com.br/povojaguaquara **E:** educadoraam1570@hotmail.com – **BA57)** Rua Gamboa de Cima 18, Campo Grande, 40060-008 Salvador ☎71 3337 3216 **W:** novotemposalvador.com.br – **BA58)** Av Regis Pacheco, 534 - Centro, 45100-000 Vitória da Conquista **W:** blog.cancaonova.com/conquista **E:** radioconquista@cancaonova.com.br – **BA59)** Rua Lauro de Freitas, 1176 - Alto da Bela Vista, 45550-000 Ubatã ☎73 3245 1233 **W:** radiopovo.com.br **E:** admpovoubata@gmail.com – **BA60)** Rua Antônio Otaviano Dourado, 91 - Centro, 44900-000 Irecê ☎74 3641 3111 **W:** programacao10cidade.com.br **E:** – **BA61)** Av Tiradentes, 1340 - Villa Nova, 46430-000 Guanambi ☎77 3451 2626 **W:** alvoradaam.com.br **E:** alvorada@alvoradaam.com.br **W:** alvoradaam.com.br – **BA62)** Rua Virgilio Brasil, 175 - Cidade Nova, 45860-000 Canavieiras ☎73 9823 0453 **W:** atalaiaamba.web-node.pt **E:** radioatalaia_am@hotmail.com – **BA63)** Rua Mario Luis Vieira, 100 - Centro, 44700-000 Jacobina ☎74 3621 7474 **W:** radioraguar.com.br **E:** jaraguar.am@gmail.com – **BA64)** Rua Farias Goes 164, 48330-000 Rio Real **W:** radiodifusora600.com.br – **BA65)** Rua Manoel Conselho Campos, 135 - Centro, 48500-000 Euclides da Cunha ☎75 3271 1652 – **BA66)** Rua Rui Barbosa, 119 - Centro, 47400-000 Xique-Xique – **BA67)** Rua Jose de Anchita, 128 - 2° andar - Centro, 45836-000 Itamaraju. ☎73 3294 5455 **W:** extremosulam.com.br – **BA68)** Av José Candido dos Santos, 20 - Centro, Lagos Redonda, 49300-000 Itapicuru ☎79 3541 1067 **W:** radioclube1060.combr **E:** radioclube.ba@bol.com.br **BA69)** Rua Frei Apolônio de Tody,10 - Centro, 48410-000 Cícero Dantas ☎75 3278 2298 ☎75 3278 2252 **W:** radioregionalam.com.br **E:** radioregional@tadioregionalam.com.br – **BA70)** Terreiro de Jesus 13, Centro Histórico, Pelourino, 40025-010 Salvador ☎71 3421 6300 ▤71 3234 9324 **W:** radio.boavontade.com.br **E:** radiocristal@uol.com.br – **BA71)** Rua Vicente Paula Costa 16, 48540-000 Jeremoabo ☎75 3203 2358 – **BA72)** Rua 2 de Julho, s/n - Centro, 45160-000 Belo Campo ☎77 3437 2122 – **BA73)** Praça Sao José 279 44600-000 Ipirá. – **BA74)** Rua Desidério Brandão, 15 – Centro, 44380-000 Cruz das Almas ☎ 75 3621 2716 **W:** radioalvoradaam1460.com.br **E:** alvoradaamcomercial@hotmail.com – **BA75)** Rua Teixeira de Freitas s/n, 47700-000 Santana – **BA77)** Rua Barão do Rio Branco s/n, 47600-000 Bom Jesus da Lapa **BA78)** Rua Dulce Pazzi, 6 - Alto da Bela Vista, 45260-000 Poções ☎77 3431 1135 **W:** radiopovo.com.br **E:** povopocoes@hotmail.com – **BA79)** Av Luis Eduardo Magalhães, s/n - Centro, 46990-000 Souto Soares ☎75 3339 2328 **W:** radiojornal1120. com.br **E:** radiojornal@bol.com.br – **BA80)** Rua Jvencio Alves, 01, 1 andar - Centro, 48930-480 Juazeiro – **BA81)** Rua Carlos Gomes, 980 - Centro, 40285-280 Salvador ☎71 3329 7463 – **BA82)** Rua Élcio Cardoso de Matos, s/n - Centro, 48800-000 Monte Santo ☎75 3275 1212 – **BA83)** Praça Simões Filho 54, 45450-000 Gandu – **BA84)** Praça Sta Terezinha, 3 - Piranga, 44900-130 Juazeiro ☎74 3611 5533 **W:** radiocidadeam870.com.br **E:** cidade870@yahoo.com.br – **BA85)** Rua Coronel Dias Coelho 249, 44850-000 Morro do Chapéu – **BA86)** Travessa Juracy Magalhães 4, 2° andar, 44630-000 Mairi – **BA87)** Praça Raimundo Sales, 94 - centro - 1° andar, 47650-000 Correntina ☎77 3488 2827 **W:** radioplanaltodooeste.com.br **E:** radioplanaltoba@yahoo.com.br – **BA90)** Rua: Ferreira Brito, 26 - Centro, 48400-000 Ribeira do Pombal ☎75 3276 1164 **W:** radiopovo.com.br/povopombal **E:** educadorapombalgerencia@hotmail.com – **BA94)** Rua Dr Gil Nunes Maia, 373 - Centro, 45600-000 Itabuna ☎73 3043 6026 **W:** blog.cancaonova.com/itabuna/radio-am-1160-khz **E:** radioitabuna@cancaonova.com – **BA96)** Rua Juana Angélica, 125 – Conquista, 45650-023 Iléhus ☎73 3634 7020 **W:** radioculturadeilheus.com.br **E:** radiocultura@radioculturadeilheus.com.br – **FM:** 97.9 MHz – **BA98)** Rua Padroeira de Brasil, 100 - Centro, 48790 Valente ☎71 8727 8216 **W:** radioestreladovale.com **E** radioestreladoval@hotmail.com – **BA99)** Av. ACM, 228 Centro, 44695-000 Campim Gross ☎74 3651 0800 **W:** grupolomesderadidifusao.com.br

CE00) CEARA

CE01) Rua Romeu Martins, Centro S/N, Ed 29 de Julho, 62700-000 Canindé ☎85 3343 2233 **W:** radiojornal540.com.br **E:** radiojornal540@hotmail.com – **CE02)** Rua Monsenhor Lima, 227 - Lagoa Seca, 63050-020 Juazeiro do Norte ☎88 3512 5557 **W:** radioverdevale570.com.br**E:** contato@radioverdevale570.com.br – **CE03)** Av Monsenhor

Tabosa, 2514 – Centro, 62500-000 Itapipoca ☎88 3631 2173 **W:** radiouirapurudeitapipoca.com.br **E:** ribamar.p@bol.com.br – **CE04)** Rodovia BR 226, s/n - Zona Rural, 63700-000 Crateús ☎88 3691 0355 **W:** radiopoty.com.br **E:** radiopoty@bol.com.br – **CE05)** Av.Rui Barbosa, 1901 - Aldeota, 60115-221 Fortaleza ☎88 3264 5500 **W:** 620am.com. br – **CE06)** Praça da Matriz s/n, 62590-000 Itarema – **CE07)** Rua Dep. Luiz Otacílio Correia, 221 - Centro, 63540-000 Várzea Alegre ☎88 3541 1055 **W:** radiocultura670.com **E:** culturaam670@hotmail.com – **CE08)** Shalom da Paz, Rua Maria Tomásia, 72 – Aldeota, 60150-170 Fortaleza ☎85 3261 4444 **W:** shalom690.com**E:** benfeitordapaz@comshalom. org **FM:** 89.1 MHz – **CE09)** Praca Monsenhor José Cândido, 91 - Centro, 63870-000 Boa Viagem ☎88 3427 1104 **W:** radioasabranca. com.br – **CE10)** Rua Uirapuru, 500 - Jardim Cearence, 60711-790 Fortaleza ☎88 3298 2655 Facebook: Rádio Uirapuru de Fortaleza **CE11)** Rua Hilda Augusto 201, 63300-000 Lavras da Mangabeira ☎88 3536 1257 **W:** radiovaledosalgado.com.br **E:** radiovaledosalgado@ gmail.com– **CE12)** Rua Deocleciano Bezerra, 649 - Cento, 63500-000 Iguatu ☎88 3581 1403 🖵88 3581 0828 **W:** jornalam.com.br **E:** conta-to@jornalam.com.br – **CE13)** Av. Desembargador Moreira, 2430 - Dionísio Torres, 60170-002 Fortaleza ☎85 3261 2323 **W:** verdinha. com.br **E:** radios@verdesmares.com.br – **CE14)** Rua Dr João Thomé, 16 - Centro, 62400-000 Camocim ☎88 3621 0370 **W:** radiouniaodecamo-cim.blogspot.no – **CE15)** Rua Padre Cicero 1045, Salesiano, 63010-020 Juazeiro do Norte ☎88 3512 3581 – **CE16)** Av Desembargo Moreira, 2565 - Dionísio Torres, 60170-002 Fortaleza ☎85 3261 7000 **W:** cida-deam860.com.br **E:** comercial860@yahoo.com.br – **CE17)** Rua Floriano Peixoto 358, 63500-000 Iguatu **W:** radioliberdadeam.com – **CE18)** Rua Totonho Figueiras 244, 63180-000 Barbalha ☎88 3532 3020 **W:** radio-cetama.com.br – **CE19)** Praça Quirino Rodrigues 76/3, 62011-260 Sobral ☎88 3611 2496 🖵88 3611 1550 **W:** radioeducadora950.com.br **E:** radioeducadora@gmail.com – **CE20)** Rua Tabelião Enéas, 495 - 2° Andar – Centro, (✉ C.P. 87, 63901-970) 63900-000 Quixadá ☎88 3414 5970 🖵88 3412 0554 **W:** sistemamonolitos.com.br/radiomonolitosam **E:** contato@sistemamonolitos.com.br – **FM:** 105.9 MHz – **CE21)** Av. Aguanambi, 282 - José Bonifácio, 60060-200 Fortaleza ☎85 3066 4000 **W:** radios.opovo.com.br/opovocbn – **FM:** 95.5 MHz CBN – **CE22)** Rua Coronel Antônio Luiz, 1068 - Pimenta, 63100-000 Crato ☎88 3523 3198 **W:** radioeducadora1020.com.br **E:** comercial@radioeducadora1020. com.br – **CE23)** Travessa Crateús, 46 - Centro, 62010-560 Sobral ☎88 3614 8282 **W:** radiotupinamba.com **E:** radiotupinambaam@bol.com.br – **CE24)** Av Francisco R Oliveira, 643 - Alto Bela Vista, 62900-000 Russas ☎88 3411 0320 **W:** radioprogresso1140.com.br – **CE25)** Rodovia BR 116 s/n km 54/Fazende Guarani, Zona Rural 62870-000 Pacajús ☎85 3348 0725 **W:** comshalom.org/radio **E:** radioboano-va1410@hotmail.com – **CE26)** Av Senador Virgilio Távora, 2279 - Dionisio Torres, 60170-251 Fortaleza ☎85 3264 2944 **W:** radioclubece. com.br **E:** fransilveira@gmail.com – **CE27)** Rua Coronel Zezé 1158, 63700-000 Crateús – **CE28)** Rua Luis Vicente Ferreira Lima, 222 - José Brito, 62930-000 Limoeiro do Norte – **W:**🖵88 3423 2400 **W:** radiovale-dojaguaribeam.com.br/site**E:** radiovale1260@gmail.com – **CE29)** Av General Osóri Paiva, 7235 – Canindezinho, 60731-335 Fortaleza ☎ 85 3498 4796 **W:** ipda.com.br/nova/vozlibertacao/nr/iracema.html – **CE30)** Rua Sáo Francisco 374, 63010-210 Juazeiro do Norte ☎88 3511 2404 **W:** radioprogressoam.com.br – **CE31)** Rua Cel Joaquim Ribeiro, 405 sala 04 - Centro, 62011-020 Sobral ☎88 3611 7888 – **CE32)** Av Dr Pedro de Queiroz Ferreira 2129, 62850-000 Cascavel **W:** litoralam.com.br – **CE33)** Rua São Francisco, 139 - Villa Lobo, 63100-000 Crato **W:** rcnesportes.com.br – **CE34)** Rua Monsenhor Salviano Pinto, 71 - Centro, 63800-000 Quixeramobim ☎88 3441 1516 **W:** difusoracristal. com.br **E:** contato@difusoracristal.com.br – **CE35)** Praça Pinto Martins 260, 62400-000 Camocim – **CE36)** Av Manoel Castro 815, 62940-000 Morada Nova ☎88 3422 1198 – **CE37)** Av. Moacir Pereira Gondim, 333 - Planalto dos Colibris, 63660-000 Tauá 🖵88 3437 1345 **W:** cultura-960am.com.br **E:** cultura960am@hotmail.com – **CE38)** Travessa São Pedro, 62800-000 Aracati ☎88 3421 1805 – **CE39)** Rua Hildo Furtado, s/n - Centro, 62760-000 Baturité ☎88 3347 1117 – **CE40)** Rua José Armando Rodrigues, 311 - Centro,, 62370-000 São Benedito ☎88 3626 2142 **W:** novaplan.am.br – **CE41)** Rua Coronel Antônio Joaquim 2143, 62930-000 Limoeiro do Norte ☎88 3423 4225 **W:** radioeducadora.com. br **E:** educadora560@yahoo.com.br – **CE42)** Av. Pref. Jaques Nunes, 648 - Centro, 62320-000 Tianguá ☎88 3671 1322 **W:**santana1540. com.br – **CE43)** Rua João Verçosa s/n, 62640-000 Pentecoste ☎85 3352 2554 **W:** difusoravaledocuru.com.br – **CE44)** Av Francisco Franca, 414 - Centro, 63600-000 Senador Pompeu ☎88 3449 0206 **W:** radio-sertaocentralam.com.br **E:** radiosertaocentral@hotmail.com – **CE45)** Praça Adolfo Caminha, 247 - Centro, 62800-000 Aracati ☎88 3421 4567– **CE46)** Rua Doutor Otávio Lobo, 198 - Santa Quitéria, 62280-000 Santa Quitéria ☎88 3628 0033 **W:** itataia890.com.br – **CE47)** Rua Coronel Austragésilo, s/n - Centro, 62680-000 Paracuru ☎85 3344 1111 **W:** redeimaculada.org.br **E:** pr.francisco.oliveira@hotmail.com – **CE48)** Rua Justino Alves Feitosa, 364 - Centro, 63380-000 Barro ☎88

3554 1166 – **CE49)** Rua Simão Barbosa,1209 – São Mateus, 62700-000 Canindé ☎ 85 3343 1597 **W:** sistemadecomunicacao.net – **CE50)** Rua Coronel Lucio 489, 63700-000 Crateús ☎88 3691 5155 – **CE51)** Rua Monsenhor Salviano Pinto 507, 63800-000 Quixeramobim ☎88 3441 0263 🖵88 3441 1209 **W:** sistemamaior.com.br/radio_campomaior **E:** contatomaior@sistemamaior.com.br – **CE52)** Rua Engenheiro João Alfredo, 1554 - Centro, 61600-050 Caucaia ☎85 3342 3677 **W:** tvcau-caia.org **E:** comercial.metropolitana@hotmail.com – **CE53)** Av da Ressurreiçao, 926 - Pe Ibiapina, 62000-000 Sobral ☎88 3111 3121 **W:** radioressurreicao.com.br– **CE54)** Rua Tibúrcio Targino 155, 61700-000 Aquiraz ☎85 3361 1285 – **CE55)** Rua Dr Almir Farias, 446 - Timbauba, 62200-000 Nova Russas ☎88 3672 1050 **W:** radioseara.com.br – **FM:** 103.3 MHz– **CE56)** Rua Raimundo Nonato, 81 – Centro, 62940-000 Morada Nova ☎88 3422 2561– **CE57)** Rua Dr Chagas Pinto, 351 - Centro, 62250-000 Ipu ☎88 3683 2186 **W:** radioiracemadeipu.com.br **E:** recados1360@hotmail.com– **CE58)** Rua Francisco Gomes de Souza, 198 - Centro, 63150-000 Campos Sales. ☎88 3533 1188 **W:** cidade-am630.com.br –**CE59)** Av Cazuzinha Marques, 87 - Centro, 63560-000 Acopiara ☎88 3565 0063 **W:** radiovaleacopiara.am.br **E:** radiovaleaco-piara@gmail.com – **CE60)** Rua Manoel Inacio de Lucena, 249 an 2 - Centro, 63260-000 Brejo Santo ☎88 3531 1093 **W:** radiosulcearense. com.br – **CE61)** Av. Mons Aloísio Pinto, 100 - Dom Expedito, 62050-100 Sobral ☎88 3614 4043 **W:** radiocaicara.com **E:** radio@radiocaicara. com – **CE62)** Av. Senador Esmerino Arruda s/n, 62430-000 Granja ☎88 3624 1106 **W:** Facebook:Rádio Vale do Coreaú Am **E:** radiovaleam@ hotmail.com – **CE63)** Rua Antônio Queiroz, 343 - Centro, 63870-000 Boa Viagem ☎88 3427 1064 **W:** radioamliberdade.blogspot.no**E:** deadator@gmail.com – **CE64)** Rua Major Barreto, 3000 - Centro, 62600-000 Itapajé ☎🖵85 9104 5447 **W:** radioguanaces.com.br **E:** kekpubli@hotmail.com – **CE65)** Rua Padre Fialho 265, Centro 62010-970 Sobral ☎88 3613 2749 **W:** pioneiraam830.com.br **E:** gerardone-to@pioneiraam830.com.br – **CE66)** Rua Capitão Carapeba, 67 - Centro, 62370-000 São Benedito ☎88 3611280 **W:** tabajara.am.br **E:** radio-tabajara1@hotmail.com – **CE67)** Rua Monsenhor Jovinano Baretto 22, 2° andar- Centro, 63660-000 Tauá ☎88 3437 1509 **W:** difusorataua. com.br **E:** contato@difusorataua.com.br – **CE68)** Rua Monsenhor Furtado, 149 - Centro, 62380-000 Guaraciaba do Norte ☎88 3652 2112 **W:** somzoom.com.br/guaraciaba-am-1190 **E:** somzoom@hotmail.com – **CE69)** Rua Mangel Sales Pereira, 273 - Centro, 62590-000 Itarema ☎88 3667 1212 **W:** Facebook: R.Liberdade de Itarema AM 1250 – **CE70)** Av Coronel Alexanzito 369, 62800-000 Aracati ☎88 3421 3033 **W:** Facebook: R.Moria– **CE71)** Av.7 N 260 Altos Conj. Jereissati - Maracanau, 61900-320 Maracanaú ☎85 3382 2222 **W:** radiopi-taguaryam.com **E:** radiopitaguary@ibest.com.br – **CE72)** Rodovia BR-226 km 20, Distrito de Bonfim, 63600-000 Senador Pompeu **W:** face-book.com/AMPATU1130 – **CE73)** Avenida José Júlio Lousada, 312 - Centro, 62680-000 Acaraú ☎88 36611280 **W:** difusoraacarau.com **E:** rdifusoraacarau@hotmail.com – **CE74)** Avenida Alcides Rocha, s/n - São Luis, 62500-000 Morrinhos ☎88 3665 1422 **W:** princesaam.com **E:** princesaam@outlook.com – **CE75)** Rua Cel. José Lourenço, 97 – Altos, (C.P. 063) 62250-000 Ipu ☎88 3683 1204 **W:** radioregionaldeipu.com.br **E:** radioregional1520am@hotmail.com – **CE76)** Rua Joaquim Tavora, 333 - Centro, 63150-000 Campos Sales ☎88 3533 1530 **W:** tresfron-teirasam.com.br **E:** tresfrontelrasam@gmail.com – **CE77)** Rua Manoel Alencar 35, 63610-000 Mombaça – **CE79)** Rua Raul Catunda Fontenele, 61 - Centro, 62230-000 Ipueiras ☎88 3685 1368 **W:** radiomacambira. com.br – **CE80)** Rua Raimundo Guedes Martins, 25 - Centro,, 63400-000 Cedro ☎88 3564 1075 **W:** radiomontevideoam.com.br – **CE81)** Ro BR 020, s/n - Zona Rural, 62730-000 Caridade ☎85 3324 1292 – **CE82)** Rua Francisco Brasileiro, 213 - Centro, 63900-000 Quixadá ☎88 3412 3047 **W:** am1080.com.br – **CE83)** Av. Rabelo, s/n – Alto Vistoso, 63620- 000 Solonópole ☎88 3518 1520 **W:** radiocachoeiraam.com.br MSN: radio.cachoeira.am@hotmail.com – **CE84)** Rua Augusto Vieira, 32 - Centro, 63630-000 Pedro Branca ☎88 3515 2121 **W:** Facebook: R. Trapiá AM 1510 kHz **E:** contato@ amtrapia1510.com.br – **CE99)** Rua Afonso Pena 109, 63560-000 Acopiara ☎88 3565 0214 **W:** carinhosaam.com.br **E:** contato@carino-hsaam.com.br – **CE100)** Rua Mário Perdigão 130, 61760-000 Eusébio ☎85 3361 2755

DF00) DISTRITO FEDERAL
DF01) SRTS, Qd 701, Ed Assis Chateaubriand, Bl 2, salas 701 a 716, 70340-906 Brasília ☎61 3039 8771 **W:** brasilia.jovempanfm.virgula. uol.com.br **E:** jovempan@jovempadf.com.br – **FM:** 107.9 MHz – **DF02)** SCS Q.08 – Bloco B-60 - 1° Subsolo – Ed. Venâncio, 70333-900 Brasília ☎61 3799 5700 **W:** radiomec.com.br – **DF03)** Sig Quadra.02 Lt 340 Bl.02, 1°. andar,(✉ C.P. 8042, 70673-1080) 70610-901 Brasília ☎61 3342 1050 **W:** clube.fm **E:** contato@clube.fm – **DF04)** SCRN 702/03, B1 «B», Edifício Radiobrás, (CP 259) 70710-750 Brasília ☎61 3799 5474 **W:** radios.ebc.com.br/nacionalbrasiliaam **E:** centraldoouvinte@ebc. com.br – **DF05)** SRTV/Sul, Q-701, bloco E, Térreo, 70340-000 Brasília – **DF06)** C.P. 259, 70710-750 Brasília **W:** radios.ebc.com.br/nacionalama-

zonia **E:** amazoniabrasileira@ebc.com.br – **DF07)** SGAS 601 Módulos 3/4, Av L2 Sul, 70340-902 Brasília ☎61 2103 0710 **W:** novaalianca. org.br **E:** contato@novaallanca.org.br – **FM:** 103.3MHz – **DF08)** SGAS 915 lt 75, 70390-150 Asa Sul ☎61 3114 1010 **W:** redeboavontade. com.br **E:** superrbv@boavontade.com – **DF09)** C - 01, Lotes 1/12 – Ed. Taguatinga Trade Center, Sala 1025, 72010-010 Taguatinga ☎61 3451 3700 – **DF10)** Senado Federal, Praça dos Tres Poderes, Anexo II, Bloco B - Térreo, 70165-900 Brasília ☎61 3303 4691 **W:** senado.gov.br/radio **E:** radio@senado.gov.br

ES00) ESPÍRITO SANTO
ES01) Rua Joaquim Plácido da Silva, 225 - Ihla de Santa Maria, 29051-070 Vitória ☎27 3331 9000 **W:** redetribuna.com.br/radio/am **E:** diretoriatvradios@redetribuna.com.br – **FM:** 99.1MHz – **ES02)** Av. Presidente Florentino Avidos, 350, 29018-190 Vitória ☎27 3322 0640 **W:** radiovitoriaes.com.br **E:** janandaCS@radiovitoriaes.com.br – **ES03)** Praça Hilda Calazans dos Santos, 4 - Gilberto Machada, 29303-275 Cacheiro de Itapemirim ☎28 3511 0770 – **ES04)** Rua Chafic Murad, 902 - Ilha de Monte Belo, 29050-901 Vitória **W:** Facebook: R.Gazeta AM - FM: 92.5MHz «Antena Um», 102.3MHz «Litoral FM» – **ES05)** Av. Prefeito Samuel Batista Cruz 4530, 29904-000 Linhares ☎27 3373 2000 **W:** radioculturadelinhares.com.br **E:** contato@radioculturadelinhares. com.br - **FM:** 98.7MHz –**ES06)** Rua Geraldo Pereira, 194 - Centro, 29700-971 Colatina ☎27 3721 1506 **W:** difusoracolatina.com.br **E:** radio@difusoracolatina.com.br – **ES07)** Av Santo Antônio, 366 al Caratoira, 29025-645 Vitória ☎27 3222 4376 ☎27 3222 7747 **W:** radiocapixaba.com.br **E:** Santa Luzia, 29045-403 Vitória ☎27 3137 2900 **W:** rtv.es.gov.br – **ES09)** Rua Walter de Oliveira, 05 - Gilbertao Mchado, 29303-292 Cacheiro de Itapemirim ☎28 3521 6640 **W:** simnoticias.com.br **E:** sbcachoeiro@gmail.com - **FM:** 107.7 MHz – **ES10)** Rua Alberto de Oliveira Santos 42, Edifico Ames 19° andar, salas 1916-1920, Centro, 29010-901 Vitória ☎27 3198 0850 ☎27 3222 4960 **W:** redeamericaes.com.br - **FM:** 101.5MHz "Cidade" – **ES11)** Rua José Cupertino 120, 29600-000 Afonso Cláudio **W:** novotempo.com/radio **E:** contatornt@novotempo.org.br – **ES12)** Rua da Matriz 85, 29200-000 Guarapari **W:** simnoticias.com.br – **ES13)** Av Presidente Vargas, 449 - Centro, 29600-000 Afonso Cláudio ☎27 3735 1120 **W:** educadoraafonsoclaudio.com.br – **ES14)** Rua Doutor Ademar Oliveira Neves, 826 - Sernamby, 29930-670 São Mateus ☎27 3773 3604 – **ES15)** Rua Costa Pereira, 37 - Centro, 29300-090 Cachoeiro de Itapemirim ☎28 3521 1960 – **W:** radiodiocesana.com.br **E:** radio@radiodiocesana.com.br – **ES16)** Rua Graciano Neves 250, 29156-050 Cariacica ☎27 3331 8300 **W:** novotemponet.com.br **E:** recepcaonovotempo@gmail.com - **FM:** 95.9 MHz – **ES17)** Rua Astrogildo Romão dos Anjos, 277 - Centro, 29800-000 Barra de São Francisco ☎27 3765 2779 **W:** radiosaofranciscoam.com **E:** couvinte@gmail.com – **ES18)** Av Marechal Campos, 310 pa 2 - Horto29050-135 Vitória ☎27 3322 1250 – **ES20)** Rua Governador Avidos, 33 – Conceição, 29900-490 Linhares ☎22 3372 3100 **W:** globolinhares.com.br **E:** diretoria@globolinhares. com.br – **ES21)** Rodovia Mickel Chequer, s/n - Zona Rural, 293900-000 Iúna ☎28 3545 1205 – **ES22)** 29300-000 Cachoeiro de Itapemirim **W:** Facebook: R.Tupi AM 1590 Cachoeiro – **ES24)** Rua Dr Moacir Veloso, 63 – Gloria, 29122-610 Vila Velha ☎27 3434 5700 **W:** simnoticias. com.br

G000) GOIÁS
GO01) Av. Goiás Q 10, 1449 - Centro, 74010-010 Goiânia ☎62 3212 0735 **W:** radioriviera.webnode.com **E:** radioam.riviera@gmail.com – **GO02)** Av. João XXIII 381, S Central - Centro, 75703-902 Catalão ☎64 3441 3206 **W:** radiocuturaonline.com.br – **GO03)** Rua Rui Barbosa, 420 – Central, 75025-060 Anápolis **W:** radiomanchester.com. br **E:** fm@radiomanchester.com.br – **FM:** 93.3 MHz – **GO04)** Av Egídio Francisco Rodrigues, 54 - Centro, 75200-000 Pires do Rio ☎64 3461 7346 **W:** Facebook: Gospel AM 630 kHz **E:** am630gospel@hotmail. com – **GO05)** Av 24 de Outubro, 1854 - Campinas, 74505-011 Goiânia ☎62 3233 4000 **W:** difusoragoiania.com.br **E:** difusora@netgo.com. br – **GO06)** Av Marechal Rondón, 1088 - Central, 76270-000 Jussara ☎62 3373 1621 – **GO07)** Rua 48, 1254 - Joaquim da Silva Moreira, 76680-000 Itapuranga ☎62 3312 1546 **W:** radioprimaveraam.com.br **E:** comercial@radioprimaveraam.com.br – **GO08)** Av 1° de Maio, 30 - Centro, 75020 050 Anápolis ☎62 3315 6927 **W:** radiosaochico.com.br - **FM:** 96.3MHz –**GO09)** Rua José de Carvalho, 542 - Centro, 75800-447 Jataí ☎64 3631 1245 **W:** difusoraonline.com.br **E:** contato@difusora-online.com.br – **GO10)** Rua Evangelino Meireles, 26 - Centro, 72800-680 Luziânia ☎61 3621 4700 - **FM:** 90.9 MHz – **GO11)** Rua Coronel Gonzaga, 540 - Central, 75030-090 Rio Verde ☎64 3435 1100 **W:** radiopousada.com.br – **GO12)** Chacara Miranapolis br 153 km 1209 (C.P. 354) 75024-970 Anápolis ☎62 3098 3977 **W:** radiovozdocoracaoimaculado.com **E:** radiovozdocoracaoimaculado@gmail.com –**GO13)** Rua 29, 234 - Carrilho, 76380-000 Goianésia ☎62 3353 3355 **W:** rvc780.com.br – **GO14)** Praca Carrijo, 30 - Centro, 75830-000 Mineiros ☎62 3661 1353 **W:** eldorado790.com.br **E:** radioeldorado@gmail. com –**GO15)** Rua José Rêgo, 45 - Centro, 76310-000 Rialma

☎62 3397 1181 **W:** radioalvorada810.com.br – **GO16)** Rua Teixeira de Freitas Qd. 04 Lt 26, Setor Serrinha 74463-300 Goiânia ☎62 3945 3820 **W:** 820am.com.br – **GO17)** Av Belém Brasilia Q5 10 lt 4, S Central, 76550-000 Porangatu ☎62 3362 4085 **W:** radiotropical850am.com.br – **GO18)** Av Tocantins N° 65 1° andar, Centro, 76400-000 Uruaçu ☎62 3357 6626 **W:** radiolagodourado.com.br **E:** contato@radiolagodourado. com.br – **GO19)** SBS Qd 2, s/n Bl Q lt 03 Ed João Carlos Saad. Asa Sul, 70070-120 Brasilia ☎61 3325 1499 **W:** radiobandeirantes.band. uol.com.br **GO20)** Rua Minas Gerais, 135 - Central, – ☎64 3431 8888 **W:** radioparanaiba.com.br - **FM:** 92.3MHz – **GO21)** Rua Uberaba 9, 75510-140 Itumbiara ☎64 3431 7400 **W:** difusoraitumbiara.com. br – **GO22)** Av. Tiradentes, 1.402–Sl. 04 - Centro, 75040-010 Anápolis ☎66 3327 0000 **W:** radioimprensa.am.br **E:** diretoria@radioimprensa. am.br – **GO23)** Rua Diógenes de Castro Ribeirao, 223 - Central, 76330-000 Jaraguá ☎62 3361 4020 **W:** portal910.com.br – **GO24)** Rua F-52 Qd. 164 Lt 5/18 No 120, Faiçalville IV, 74350-450 Goiânia ☎62 8401 0508 **W:** redefonte.com **E:** portalredefonte@gmail.com – **GO25)** Rua Freio João Batista, 76 - Centro, 75860-000 Quirinópolis. ☎64 3651 1452 **W:** sulgoiana.com.br **E:** quirinopolis@hotmail.com – **GO26)** Praça Rui Barbosa, 276 - Centro, 73800-000 Formosa ☎61 3642 1140 **W:** radioformosaam.com.br – **GO27)** Rua Thomaz Edson Qd 07, St. Serrinha, 74835-130 Goiânia ☎62 3250 1455 **W:** facebook. com – Radio Daqui **E:** jornaldaqui@jdaqui.com.br – **GO28)** Av. Br. Rio Branco, 1 – S. Central, (✉C.P 34, 75781-970) 75780-000 Ipameri ☎64 3491 1314 **W:** xavantes.net **E:** radio_xavantes@hotmail.com – **GO29)** Rua Coração Fiel 50, Rialma II,76310-000 Rialma ☎62 3397 2175 **W:** coracaofiel.com.br **E:** radio@coracaofiel.com.br – **GO30)** Agencia Goiania de Comunicaço, Rua SC-01, 299 - Parque Santa Cruz, 74860-270 Goiânia ☎62 3201 7600 **W:** radiobrasilcentral.com. br **E:** rbc@agecom.go.gov.br – **GO31)** Av Goiás 174, Ed.São Judas Tadeu, 16° andar, Centro 74010-010 Goiânia ☎62 3216 0730 **W:** portal730.com.br – **GO32)** Av jornalismo@radio730.com.br – **GO32)** Alameda das Rosas, 2.200 - Setor Oeste, 74126-010 Goiânia ☎62 3521 0600 **W:** radio.ufg.br **E:** radioufg870@gmail.com – **GO33)** Av Amazonas, 356 - Central, 76100-000 São Luís de Montes Belos ☎64 3671 1621 **W:** redediocesanaderadio.com **E:** radiovaleamfm@hotmail.com – **GO34)** Rua Barão Rio Branco Qd 40, 989 lt 7 - Central, 75650-000 Morrinhos ☎64 3416 2416 Facebook: R.Morrinhos **E:** 1460am@morrinhosam. com.br – **GO35)** Praca Rui Barbosa, 471 - Centro, 75180-000 Silvânia ☎62 3332 1155 **W:** radioriovermelho.com.br **E:** comercial@radio-riovermelho.com.br– **GO36)** Rua Tapajós, 137 - St Oeste, 73850-000 Cristalina ☎61 3612 2929 **W:** radioserradoscristais.com.br – **GO37)** Rua 15 Novembro Q ,1 36 lt 1, Central, 76600-000 Goiás ☎62 3371 1575 – **GO38)** Rua Sao Paulo, 557 - Centro, 75600-000 Goiatuba ☎64 3495 1802 – **GO39)** Praça Pres Médici, s/n - Central, 75920-000 Santa Helena de Goiás ☎63 3641 1555 **W:** radiosantelenense.com.br **E:** radiosantelenense@globo.com – **GO40)** Rua Dr Antonio Balduino,1260 - Centro, 75400-000 Inhumas ☎62 3511 2040 **W:** radiojornaldeinhumas.com.br **E:** rjiamcom@gmail.com – **GO41)** Av. Pauzanes Carvalho Q 25,s/n lt 7/9, S.Pauzanes (✉ C.P 131, 75901-970) 75930-000 Rio Verde – ☎64 3621 4433 **W:** rioverdeam.com.br – **GO42)** Rua Benedito Lemes, 45 – Centro, 76630-000 Itaberaí. ☎62 3375 2901– **GO43)** Av Pará, 541 - Central, 76200-000 Iporá ☎64 3674 1153 **W:** rededioce-sanaderadio.com – **GO44)** Rua 23 Q 1 s/n lt 3, Andrade, 75850-000 Caiapônia ☎64 3363 1219 – **GO45)** Rua Lazer Q82, s/n lt 2 - Res Village Garavelo, 74900-000 Aparecida de Goiânia ☎62 3283 1040 **W:** radiocaraiba.com.br **E:** caraiba@radiocaraiba.com.br – **GO46)** QS 03 lotes 3,5,7 e 9 salas 1513/1515, Ed. Pátio Capital. Aguas Claros, 71953-000 Brasilia DF (C.P 06-799, 71701-970 Brasília, DF) ☎61 3039 1162 **W:** radioredentor.com.br **E:** contato@radioredentor.com. br – **GO47)** Rua 22, 150 – St.Aeroporto, 75640-000 Piracanjuba ☎64 3405 1919 **W:** radiopousalto.com.br – **GO48)** Rua 49, Q 53 218 - Nova Vila, 76300-000 Ceres ☎62 3307 3042 – **GO49)** Praça Silva Junior, 184 - Centro76420-000 Niquelândia ☎62 3354 1430 **W:** radiomantiquei-raam.com.br **E:** radiomantiqueira@uol.com.br – **GO50)** Rua Maranhão 1355, 75600-000 Goiatuba ☎64 3495 7556 **W:** radiosempre.com.br **E:** contato@radiosempre.com.br – **GO51)** Rua Francisco Corra Neves, 100 – 2° andar - Central, 75860-000 Quirinópolis ☎☎ 64 3651 2106 **W:** radioalvoradaam.com **E:** radioalvorada@cultura.com.br – **GO52)** Av Joaquim David Ferreira, 1390 - Central, 76105-000 Firminópolis ☎64 3681 1217 **W:** radioboasnovas1020am.com.br – **GO53)** Av Santana, Qd 55, lote 01 - Sector Vila Baiana, 73840-000 Campas Belos ☎62 3451 1209 **W:** novarcbam.websom.net – **GO54)** Rua 73, 349-Bloco A Térreo – Jardim Goiás, 74810-370 Minacu ☎62 8401 0530 **W:** reedeserradourada.com.br/emissora/minacu

MA00) MARANHÃO
MA01) Av Eliézer Moreira, s/n - Centro, 65950-000 Barra do Corda – **MA02)** Rua Frei Querubim, 57 – Apicum – Centro, 65025-420 São Luís ☎98 3878 5709 **W:** educadora560.com.br – **MA03)** Av Camboa do Mato, 120 - Camboa, 65020-260 São Luís – ☎98 3214 3094 **W:** difusora94fm.com.br - **FM:** 94.3MHz – **MA04)** Pc Pallmeiro Cantanhede

1524, 65400-000 Codó ☎99 3661 1944 **W:** eldoradoam.com.br **E:** radioeldoradoam@hotmail.com – **MA05)** Av São Benedito, 1075 - Bairro São Benedito, 65400-000 Codó – **MA06)** Rua Gonçalves Dias, 565 - Centro, 65900-450 Imperatriz **W:** apazdosenhor.org.br – **MA07)** Rua Manoel Alves de Abreu, 373 - Centro, 65700-000 Bacabal ☎99 3621 1510 **W:** Facebook: R.Jainari – **MA08)** Av Coronel Fonseca, 200 - Centro, 65800-000 Balsas ☎99 3541 2458 – **MA09)** Av Cel Colares Moreira, 1000 sala 12- Marcus Center - Sao francisco, 65075-440 São Luís ☎98 3235 7676 **W:** http//radio.capital118+.com.brt **E:** radio@capital1180.com.br – **MA10)** Rua Beira Mar, 276 - Centro, 65010-400 Sao Luis - ☎98 2108 6329 **W:** ma.gov.br/timbira **E:** timbira@secom.ma.gov.br – **MA11)** Av President Media, 77 - Areinha, 65032-075 São Luís ☎98 2109 7777 **W:** grupozildenifalcao.com.br **E:** edjandejesus@yahoo.com.br – **MA12)** Rua 30 de Março, 627 - Centro, 65200-000 Pinheiro ☎98 3381 3215 **W:** sistemapericuma.com.br – **MA13)** Av Rio Branco, 670, 65725-000 Pedreiras – **MA14)** Av Kennedy, 353 - Centro, 65690-000 Colinas ☎99 3552 1411 – **MA15)** Av. Ana Jansen 200, 65076-902 São Luis ☎98 3235 3013 – **MA16)** Rua Antônio Lopes, 971 - Centro, 65215-000 Viana ☎98 3351 1353 – **MA17)** Rua Guarani, s/n QD 03 LOTE 09 - Caicara, 65922-000 João Lisboa – **MA18)** Rua João Castelo, s/n - Centro, 65320-000 Vitorino Freire ☎98 3655 1240 **W:** sistemaaguabranca.com – **MA20)** Rua Piauí 895, 65930-000 Açailândia – **MA21)** Rua Cláudio Carneiro, 177 - Centro, 65750-000 Esperantinópolis ☎99 3645 1403 – **MA22)** Alexandre Trovao 338, 338 - Centro, 65415-000 Coroatá ☎99 3641 0931 – **MA23)** Rua Aarão Reis, 1963 - Morro Alecrim, 65604-060 Caxias ☎93 3521 0047 – **MA24)** Rua Tiradente, 134 - Centro, 65365-000 Zê Doca ☎98 3655 3972 – **MA26)** Rua Alagoas 497, 65900-450 Imperatriz ☎99 3524 6611 **W:** imirante.globo.com**E:** imirante@mirante.com.br- **FM:** 96.1 MHz – **MA27)** Av Amaral Raposo, s/n - Centro, 65940-000 Grajaú ☎99 3532 6165 – **MA28)** Rua Rui Barbosa s/n, 65620-000 Coelho Neto – **MA29)** Rua Dr Paulo Ramos, 495 - Centro, 65208-000 Santa Helena ☎98 3382 1196 **W:** radiorioturiacuam.com.br **E:** contato@radiorioturiacuam.com.br – **MA30)** Rua Frederico Coelho esquina com Av Frei Aniceto, 65763-000 Tuntum **W:** imirante.globo.com **E:** imirante@mirante.com.br – **MA31)** Praca Rio Branco, 5 - Centro, 65350-000 Vitória do Mearim ☎98 3352 1108 **W:** radiocidadedevitoria.com.br – **MA32)** Parque da Bandeira, 222, Edificio Ariana - Centro, 65660-000 São João dos Patos ☎95 3551 2418 – **MA33)** Praça do Guarim s/n, 65390-000 Santa Luzia – **MA34)** Rua Terra esquina com Rua Jupiter s/n, 65760-000 Presidente Dutra – **MA35)** Praça Coronel Luis Vieira, 26 - Centro, 65500-000 Chapadinha ☎98 3471 1337 **W:** imirante.globo.com **E:** imirante@mirante.com.br – **MA36)** Rua Senador Vitorino Freira, 85 - Centro, 65715-000 Lago da Pedra ☎99 3644 1220 **W:** radiosantamaura.com.br – **MA37)** Rua Hemeterio Leitão 103, 65430-00 Vargem Grande – **MA38)** Av Ana Jansen 200, 65076-902 São Luís ☎98 3230 3013 **W:** imirante.globo.com – **MA39)** Rua Monsenhor Gentil, s/n - Centro, 65530-000 Urbano Santos – **MA40)** Rua Bela Vista 1894, Castelo Branco, 65604-160 Caxias ☎99 3521 013 – **MA41)** Praça Roosevelt Moreira, s/n – Centro, 65800-000 Balsas ☎99 3541 2999 🖹99 3541 7308 **W:** radioboanoticia.com.br **E:**radio@radioboanoticia.com.br – **MA42)** Belo Horizonte, s/n - Formosa, 65634-080 Timon ☎89 2107 3000 – **MA43)** Rua Principal, Turiaçu

MG00) MINAS GERAIS

MG01) Rua Rabelo Horta, 39 - Centro, 36770-064 Cataguases ☎32 3422 1724 **W:** radiocataguases.com **E:** contato@radiocataguases.com- **FM:** 89.5MHz –**MG02)** Rua General Carneiro 10, Edificio Milinardo, s 200 à 305 - Centro, 39400-095 Montes Claros – **MG03)** Rua Serrinha, 1200 - Vale do Jacobá, 30668-250 Belo Horizonte ☎31 3322 1945 – **MG04)** Praça Nossa Senhora Aparecida, 134 - Aparecida, 38400-726 Uberlândia ☎34 3292 0401 **W:** radioamerica.com.br **E:** america@radioamerica.com.br – **MG05)** Av Padre Matias, 1089 - Marciano Pires, 38740-000 Patrocínio ☎34 3839 9980 **W:** sistemadifusoraderadio.com.br - **FM:** 98.9MHz –**MG06)** Rua Itatiaia, 117 - Bonfim, 31210-170 Belo Horizonte ☎31 2105 3588 🖹31 2105 3613 **W:** www itatiaia.com.br **E:** itatiaia@itatiaia.com.br – **FM:** 95.7MHz – **MG07)** Av. Dr. Fidélis Reis, 820 - Centro, 38010-030 Uberaba. ☎34 3331 7900 🖹34 3321 8200 **W:** jmonline.com.br **E:** jmonlin@emonline.com.br – **MG08)** Av Presidente Vargas, 272 - Centro, 37640-000 Pará de Minas ☎37 3232 1588 **W:** santacruzam.com.br **E:** comercial@santacruzam.com.br – **FM:** 101.7 MHz – **MG09)** Rua Euripides Ribeiro, 739 - Centro, 38720-000 Lagoa Formosa ☎34 3824 9980 **W:** radiovitoriosa.com.br – **MG10)** Rua Xavier de Veiga 85, 35400-000 Ouro Preto ☎31 3551 2166 **W:** itatiaia.com.br/ouropreto/ **E:** ouropreto@itatiaia.com.br – **MG11)** Avenida Juscelino Kubitschek, 30 - Passaginha, 35790-000 Curvelo ☎38 3721 2300 **W:** radioclubecurvelo.com.br - **FM:** 95.5 MHz – **MG12)** Rua Lincoln Alves Santos, 20 - Distrito Industrial Montes Claros ☎38 3216 6045 **W:** educadoraam670.com.br **E:** contatoradioouvinte@gmail.com – **MG13)** Rua Geraldo Rios, 98 - Centro, 38770-000 João Pinheiro ☎38 3561 1381 – **MG14)** Rua Entre Rios, 33 - Carlos Prates, 30710-080 Belo Horizonte ☎31 8406 0673 **W:** radiomineiro.

com **E:** radiomineiro@radiominerio.com – **MG15)** Praça 15 de Novembro, 339 - 5° andar - Centro, 36900-000 Manhuaçu ☎33 3332 4080 **W:** radiomanhuacu.com.br **E:** contato@radiomanhuacu.com.br - **FM:** 88 MHz – **MG16)** Rua Cel. José Inácio, 96 - Centro, 37550-000 Pouso Alegre ☎35 3423 1488 **W:** difusora710am.com.br **E:** difusora@difusora710am.com.br – **MG17)** Av Dr Fidélis Reis, 810 - Centro, 38010-030 Uberaba ☎34 3331 7999 **W:** radiojm730.com.br – **MG18)** Av Barão do Rio Branco, 3231 Sl 1004 - Centro, 36010-012 Juiz de Fora ☎32 3231 1388 – **MG19)** Av Itaú, 515 Sl 1013 - Dom Bosco, 30850-035 Belo Horizonte **W:** americabh.com.br **E:** radioamerica-diretoria@pucminas.br ☎31 3336 2600 – **MG20)** Praça Leonardo Venerando Pereira, 200 - Centro, 37200-000 Lavras ☎35 3822 5000 **W:** radiocultura770.com.br – **MG21)** Avenida Getúlio Vargas, 142 - Centro, 38700 128 Patos de Minas ☎34 3818 1770 **W:** clubeam.com **E:** clubeam@clubeam.com – **MG22)** Rua dos Cravos, 467 – Bairro São Pedro, 35900-125 Itabira ☎31 3831 2928 **W:** radioitabira.com.br **E:** euclideseder@yahoo.com.br – **MG23)** Av Prof José Ignácio de Souza 2710 - Umuarama, 38405-330 Uberlândia ☎34 3222 0780 **W:** educadorajp.com.br – **MG24)** Rua Reporter Luiz Quirino 190, 35430-017 Ponte Nova ☎31 3817 1025 **W:** radiopontenova.com.br **E:**diretoria@radiopontenova.com.br – **MG25)** Rua Margarida Monteiro, 125 - Centro, 35500-000 Mantena ☎33 3241 3000 **W:** radio13dejunho.com.br **E:** radio13dejunho@ralnet.com.br – **MG26)** Rua Luz, 235 -Américo Silva, (CP 34) 35590-000 Lagoa da Prata. ☎37 3261 4500 **W:** tropical790.com.br **E:** tropical@tropical790.com – **MG27)** Rua Profesora Esposalina Leal, 141 - Centro, 35200-000 Aimorés ☎33 3267 1021 **W:** radioam810.org.br – **MG28)** Rua Maranhao, 400 - Centro, 35500-066 Divinópolis ☎37 3222 7070 **W:**divinopolisam.com.br **E:** contato@divinopolisam.com.br - **FM:**100.5MHz – **MG29)** Praça Dom Pedro Teixeira, 49 - 5° andar - Centro, 36200-001 Barbacena ☎32 3331 8788 **E:** radioglobo@barbacena.com.br – **MG30)** Rua Dos Antunes, 1175, Ed São Sebastião - Centro, 37950-000 São Sebastião do Paraíso ☎35 3531 2396 **W:** radiodafamilia.com.br **E:** contato@radiofamilia.com.br – **MG31)** Rua Rio Mantiqueira, 769 – Novo Riacho, 30130-003 Contagem ☎31 3565 6289 **W:** redegeraisderadio.com.br/am830.php **E:** contato@redegeraisradio.com.br – **MG32)** Rua Barão de Piunhi, 247 - Centro, 35500-000 Formiga ☎37 3322 2565 **W:** difusoraformiga.com.br – **FM.** 93 MHz – **MG33)** Av Brasil, 2770 2° andar - Centro, 35020-070 Governador Valadares. ☎33 3271 7322 **W:** radiomundomelhor.com.br **E:** contato@radiomundomelhor.com.br - **FM:** 97.7MHz – **MG34)** Rua José Bueno Azerdo, 89 sl 1 - Tiradentes, 38430-000 Tupaciguara ☎34 3281 4050 **W:** radiotupaciguara.com.br **E:** radiotupaciguara@– **MG35)** Av Raja Gabáglia, 1666 – Gutierrez, 30441-194 Belo Horizonte ☎31 3298 3401 🖹31 3298 3400 **W:** inconfidencia.com.br **E:** inconfidencia@inconfidencia.com.br – **FM:** 100.9 MHz – **MG36)** Rua Dr Olinto Martins 207, 39960-000 Jequitinhonha ☎33 3741 1521 **W:** santacruz890.com.br – **MG37)** Av Getúlio Vargas, 420 - Centro, 39800-015 Teófilo Otoni ☎33 3522 3635 **W:** radioteofilotoni.com.br **E:** vanessa@radioteofilotoni.com.br – **MG38)** Largo Dom João, 122 - Centro, 39100-000 Diamantina ☎38 3531 1408 – **MG39)** Praça 28 de Setembro, 95 - Centro, 36520-000 Visconde do Rio Branco ☎32 3551 1877 **W:** radioculturariobranco.com.br **E:** radiocultauravrb@gmail.com or radiocultura920@hotmail.com – **MG40)** Rua Brandão Carneiro, 33- Centro, 37460-000 Passa Quatro ☎35 3371 3301 **W:** mineiradosul.com **E:** radio@mineiradosul.com.br – **MG41)** Av Afonso Pena, 795 2° andar - Centro, (CP 586) 37270-000 Campo Belo ☎35 3832 2700 **W:** radioclubecampobelo. com br **E:** radioclube10@gmail.com – **MG42)** Av Minas Gerais 3399, Bosque, 38440-000 Araguari ☎34 3512 0291 **W:** radiovitoriosa.com.br – **MG43)** Rua Santa Catarina, 610 3° andar - Lourdes, 30170-081 Belo Horizonte ☎31 3349 7308 **W:** radioatalaiabh.com.br – **MG44)** Av Bom Jesus, 330 - Centro, (CP 10) 37578-000 Bueno Brandão ☎35 3463 1006 **W:** radioindy.com.br **E:** indyamcomercial@gmail.com – **MG45)** Rua Radialista Hamilton Macedo, 204 - Limoeiro, 35300-121 Caratinga ☎33 3321 2800 – **MG46)** Rua Santa Teresa 97, Centro, 36300-114 São João del Rei ☎32 3371 7777 **W:** radiosaojoaodelrei.am.br **E:** radiosaojoaodelrei@hotmail.com – **MG47)** Rua Rio Barbosa 259, 38420-000 Monte Alegre de Minas ☎34 3283 2595 **W:** radiocentralmontealegre.com.br **E:** radiocentralam970@terra.com.br – **MG48)** Rua Espírito Santo, 95 – Poco Rico, 36020-000 Juiz de Fora ☎32 3215 2120 **W:** radiosolaram.com.br **E:** comercial@radiosolar.com.br – **MG49)** Rua Afonso Pena, 340 - Centro, 37590-000 Jacutinga ☎35 3443 2121 **W:** radiojacutinga.com.br **E:** radioestanciajacutinga@hotmail.com – **MG50)** Rua Manoel Joaquim Pires, 63 - Centro, 35170-082 Coronel Fabriciano ☎31 3842 1400 **W:** educadoramg.com.br - **FM:** 107.1MHz –**MG51)** Rua Rio Grande do Norte, 1096 - Umuarama, 38402-016 Uberlândia ☎34 3291 5566 **W:** culturaam.net - **FM:** 95.1MHz –**MG52)** Rua Duque de Caxias 258, Primavera, 38430-000 Tupaciguara ☎34 3281 5800 **W:** rural1050.com –**MG53)** Av. Alvares Cabral, 1030 s 206 - Lourdes, 30170.001 Belo Horizonte ☎31 3453 3989 **W:** ipda.com.br **E:** – **MG54)** Rua Olegário Maciel, 200 - Avenida, 37500-000 Itajubá ☎35 3623 2471 **W:** radiotajuba-.com.br – **MG55)** Praça da Basílica, 130 - Barrio Basilica, (🖂CP

05) 36415-000 Congonhas ☎31 3731 8308 📠31 3731 8313 **W:** radio-congonhas.com.br **E:** gerencia@radiocongonhas.com.br – **MG56)** Av Dr Américo Luz, 153, Sala 105 - Centro, 37890-000 Muzambinho ☎35 3571 1145 **W:** radiodopovo.com.br **E:** radiodopovoam@yahoo.com.br – **MG57)** Rua Halfeld, 744 Sl 401 - Centro,36010-003 Juiz de Fora ☎32 3215 4477 – **MG58)** Av Bahia, 720 - Centro, 38440-000 Araguari ☎34 3241 3131 **W:** radioplanaltoaraguari.com.br **E:** ouvintes@radioplanaltoa-raguari.com – **MG59)** Rua Areião do Matadouro, 1281 - Matadouro, 34000-000 Nova Lima ☎31 3541 1823 – **MG60)** Rua França, 506 – Boa Vista, 38070-474 Uberaba ☎34 3326 7777 **W:** setecolinas.com.br **E:** contato@setecolinas.com.br – **FM:** 98.1MHz – **MG61)** Rua Governador Valadares, 80, Sala 112 Ed. José Mateiro -Centro, 37170-000 Boa Esperança ☎35 3851 1000 📠35 3851 1475 **W:** radioserraam.com.br **E:** radioserra@yahoo.com.br – **MG62)** Av Antonio Olímpio de Morais, 545 - Centro, 35500-005 Divinópolis ☎37 3222 0001 **W:** radiominasam.com.br ☎37 3222 0001 – **MG63)** Rua João Bressane, 1 - Centro, 37400-000 Campanha ☎35 3261 1229 **W:** radiodiocesana-am.com.br **E:** radiocesana@yahoo.com.br – **MG64)** Av Constantino Pinto, 90 - Centro, 36880-000 Muriaé ☎32 3729 2929 **W:** radiomuriae.com.br **E:** diretoria@radiomuriae.com.br – **MG65)** Av Raja Gabáglia, 3502, 4° andar - São Bento, 30350-540 Belo Horizonte ☎31 3293 0102 – **MG66)** Rua do Rádio, 60 - Pepétuo Socorro, 38190-000 Sacramento ☎34 3351 1735 **W:** radiosacramento.net **E:** contato@radiosacramen-to.net – **MG67)** Rua Cassiano Lemos, 87 - Centro, 38183-036 Araxá ☎34 3612 3000 **W:** cidadeamfm.com.br **E:** cidade@radiocidadedeara-xa.com.br – **FM:** 94.5 MHz – **MG68)** Av Assis Chateaubriand, 499 - Floresta, 30150-101 Belo Horizonte ☎31 3237 6000 **W:** guarani.com.br **E:** guarani@guarani.com– **FM:** 96.5 MHz – **MG69)** Praça Cleber de Holanda, 111 - Alton Sion, 37048-000 Varginha ☎35 3222 8288 **W:** sistemaclube.com.br **E:** sac@sistemaclube.com.br – **FM:** 99.3MHz – **MG71)** Rua Afonso Pena, 3402 - Centro, 35010-001 Governador Valadares ☎33 3271 4000 **W:** novotempo.com/gv/ **E:** radio@novotempo.com – **MG72)** Av. Treze, 658 6° andar, Edifico Ituiutaba, 38300-140 Ituiutaba ☎34 3271 7400 **W:** radiogloboituiutaba.com.br – **FM:** 97.3 MHz – **MG73)** Rua Rio Grande do Sul, 629 - Centro, 37701-001 Poços de Caldas ☎35 3722 1530 **W:** difusorapocos.com.br **E:** conta-to@difusorapocos.com.br - **FM:**104.1MHz– **MG74)** Pc. Getúlio Vargas, 81 - Centro, 36400-000 Conselheiro Lafaiete ☎31 3763 1470 **W:** radiocarijos.com.br – **FM:** 89.9MHz – **MG75)** Rua Itajubá, 62 - Centro, 35160-035 Ipatinga ☎31 3801 4300 **W:** vanguardaam.com.br **E:** comercial@radio95fm.com.br – **FM:** 95 MHz – **MG76)** Rua Ernane Vilela Lima, Apart 114-A 1° andar, Centro, 37250-000 Nepomuceno ☎35 3861 1278 **W:** radioam810.com.br **E:** radionep@hotmail.com – **MG77)** Rua Duque de Caxias, 450, 16° andar, Edificio Chams - Erlan, 38400-066 Uberlândia ☎34 3219 4707 – **MG78)** Rua Alexandre Silva, 295 - Centro, 38600-000 Paracatu ☎ 38 3671 3047 **W:** radiojuriti.com.br **E:** contato@radiojuriti.com – **MG79)** Av Treze, 658, 6° andar, Edifício Ituiutaba 6° andar Centro, 38300-140 Ituiutaba ☎34 3271 7400 **W:** cancelaam.com - **FM:** 97.3MHz – **MG80)** Av Costa Junior, 467 - Centro, 38840-000 Carmo do Paranaíba ☎34 3851 2066 **W:** sistemaplaneta.net **E:** rplaneta@sistemaplaneta.net – **MG81)** Rua Mariana, 178 -Monte Sinai, 35450-000 Itabirito ☎31 3561 3499 **W:** redegeraisderadio.com.br/am1340.php **E:** rgr1340amitabirito@redegeraisderadio.com.br – **MG82)** Av João Pinheiro 596, 1° andar (C.P 143), 37701-386 Poços de Caldas **W:** radioculturapocos.com.br **E:** radio@radioculturapocos.com ☎35 3722 1687 📠35 3722 2687 – **MG83)** Rua Col José Paulino, 261 - Centro, 37750-000 Machado ☎35 3295 1361 **W:** difusoramachado.com.br **E:** gilson0408@gmail.com – **MG84)** Peixoto Filho 112 s 310, 36500-000 Ubá ☎32 3532 2934 **W:** ubaensam.com.br **E:** gleidsone-tkd@gmail.com – **MG85)** Rua Calixto Martins de Melo,391 - Centro, 38610-000 Unaí ☎38 3676 1490 **W:** radioveredas.com.br **E:** contato@radioveredas.com.br - **FM:** 98.0MHz – **MG86)** Av Geraldo Porofirio Bothelo, 2265 - Fertiza, 38180-000 Araxá ☎34 3661 2300 **W:** radiom-biara.com.br **E:** rjornalismo@terra.com.br – **FM:** 100.9 MHz – **MG87)** Rua Antônio Dias Adorno. 1290 – Vila Rica, 35045-040 Governador Valadares ☎33 3275 0930 **W:** radioglobogv.com.br **E:** comercial@radioglobogv.com.br – **FM:** 100.1MHz – **MG88)** Praça Dr Carlos Alves, Edifico No 1 Sala 204, Centro, 36680-000 São João Nepomuceno ☎32 3261 1344 **W:** difusorasjn.com.br **E:** contato@difusorasjn.com.br – **MG89)** Rua Niquel, 457 - Industrial, 35701-107 Sete Lagoas ☎31 3773 3694 **W:** culturasl.com.br – **FM:** 92.1MHz «Musirama» – **MG90)** Av Major Antônio Alberto Fernandes, 178 - Centro, 37720-000 Botelhos ☎35 3741 1277 – **MG91)** Av Conde Ribeirão do Vale 661, 37800-000 Guaxupé ☎35 3551 1245 **W:** amclube.com.br **E:** amclube@amclube.com.br – **MG92)** Rua XV de Novembro 62, 36500-000 Ubá ☎32 3531 1830 **W:** educadora.com.br – **FM:** 94.5MHz – **MG93)** Praça Minas Gerais, 50 - Satélite, 35930-259 João Monlevade ☎31 3851 6001 **W:** cultura590.com.br – **MG94)** Av Governador Israel Pinheiro, 651 - Centro, 38550-000 Coromandel ☎34 8855 2288 **W:** Facebook: R.Diamante **E:** locutoresdiamanteam@gmail.com – **MG95)** Rua Juliano Marques Duarte, 110 - Iha Gama Cerqueira, 36660-000 Além Paraíba

☎32 3462 7400 **W:** Facebook: R.Cultura de Porto Novo **E:** sistemahf@gmail.com – **MG96)** Av 15 895, 10° andar Sala 1002 e 1005 - Centro, Edifico Executivo, 38300-000 Ituiutaba ☎34 3261 7118 **W:** difusorai-tuiutaba.com.br **E:** administracao@difusoraituiutaba.com.br – **MG97)** Av. Iparanga, 198 - Centro, 37190-000 Três Pontas ☎35 3265 2252 – **MG98)** Rua Bias Fortes 597, 38200-000 Frutal ☎34 3421 7075 – **MG99)** Av Belo Horizonte 108, 39860-000 Nanuque – **MG100)** Praça Dr. Antônio das Chagas Viegas, 130 2° andar - Centro, 36300-060 São João del Rei ☎32 3371 8025 **W:** emboabasfm.com.br **E:** administrati-vo@emboabas.com - **FM:** 96.9 MHz – **MG101)** Rua Floriano Peixoto, 31 - Centro, 36570-000 Viçosa ☎31 3891 1242 **W:** montanhesa.am.br **E:** montanhesavicosa@montanhesa.am.br - **FM:** 97.9MHz – **MG102)** Rua Doutor Bernardino Vieira, 41 an 2 sl 7 - Centro, 37900-060 Passos ☎35 3521 7416 **W:** radiopassos.com.br **E:** radiopassos@passos.com.br – **MG103)** Rua Nunes Roas, 70 - Centro , 36970-000 Manhumirim ☎33 3341 1491 **W:** radiomanhumirim.com.br **E:** radiomanhumirimfinan-ceiro@gmail.com – **MG104)** Rua Dr Coelho de Moura, 158 - Centro, 35540-000 Oliveira ☎37 3331 1170 **W:** radiosociedade.com.br **E:** geral@radiosociedade.com.br – **MG105)** Rua João Ribeiro Navarro 285, 36200-000 Barbacena ☎32 3331 7988 **W:** correiosat.com.br – **FM:** 100.3 MHZ – **MG106)** Praça Dr Augusto Gonçalves, 146, salas 411/412 - Centro, 35680-054 Itaúna ☎37 3242 1910 **W:** clubeamfm.com.br **E:** comercial@clubeamfm.com.br – **FM:** 93.5 MHz – **MG107)** Alameda Monteiro Lobato, Solar dos Lagos, 37470-000 São Lourenço ☎35 3332 4333 **W:** radioestancia.com.br **E:** estancia@radioestancia.com.br - **FM:** 94.3MHz – **MG108)** Av Juscelino Kubtschek, 1016 – Boa Vista, 38280-000 Iturama ☎34 3411 0055 **W:** centralcomunicacao.com.br – **MG109)** Av Magalhães Pinto, 829 - São Sebastião, 35610-000 Dores do Indaiá ☎37 3551 1402 – **MG110)** Rua Cel Otávio Meyer, 150 s 507 - Centro, 37550-000 Pouso Alegre ☎35 3423 6566 **W:** radioclu-bepousoalegre.com.br **E:** radioclube@tcnet.com.br – **MG111)** Rua Dr José Gonçalves, 17 sl 17 - Centro, 35600-000 Bom Despacho ☎37 3522 4111 – **MG112)** Praça Getúlio Vargas, 81,1° andar - Centro, (C.P 123) 36400-000 Conselheiro Lafaiete ☎31 3763 2466 – **MG113)** Rua Casemiro Avelar Filho, 143 - Centro, 37410-000 Três Corações ☎35 231 1000 **W:** radiotropical.net - **FM:** 95.7MHz – **MG114)** Praça Nossa Senhora do Carmo 224, 38500-000 Monte Carmelo ☎34 3842 4969 – **MG115)** Rua Sancho Viderla, 19 - Radio, 37540-000 Santa Rita de Sapucaí ☎35 3473 4400 **W:** difusora1550.com.br **E:** comercial@difu-sora1550.com.br - **FM:** 95.3MHz – **MG116)** Av Brasil, 508 - Centro, 39270-000 Pirapora ☎38 3741 1400 **W:** facebook.com/radiopirapora **E:** radiopirapora@hotmail.com – **MG117)** Praça João XXIII 15, salas 303/307/308, 36700-000 Leopoldina ☎32 3441 4260 **W:** radiojorna-lam.net **E:** radiojornalam1560@hotmail.com – **MG118)** Rua Bias Fortes, 191 - Centro, 37130-000 Alfenas ☎35 3299 3886 **W:** radiocul-turaalfenas.com.br **E:** radiocultura@unifenas.br – **MG119)** Av JK 108, 35500-000 Itapecerica ☎37 3341 8533 **FM:** 101.3MHz – **MG120)** Rua Anastácio José Gonçalves, 139 - Centro, 38810-000 Rio Paranaíba ☎38 3855 1433 **W:** paranaibamaximus.com.br **E:** contato@paranaibamaximus.com - **FM:** 101.5 MHz – **MG121)** Rua Sérgio Neves, 63/Sala 103 – Centro, 36240-000 Santos Dumont ☎32 3251 6534 **W:** radioculturasd.com – **MG122)** Av Minas Gerais 584, 39510-000 Espinosa ☎38 3812 1299 – **MG123)** Rua Pepino Laterza, 920 - Independência, 38304-216 Uberaba ☎34 3269 0255 📠34 3269 0244 **W:** redevitoriosa.com.br **E:** comercial@redevitoriosa.com.br – **MG124)** Av Hermenegildo Donatti, 199 - Jd. Nova Andradas, 37795-000 Andradas ☎35 3731 2291 **W:** radiovinicola.com.br **E:** vinicola@andra-das-net.com.br - **FM:** 94.9MHz – **MG125)** Praça Coronel Odilon Coelho 123, 39520-000 Porteirinha. ☎38 3831 1228 **W:** educadoraam640.com.br – **MG126)** Av. Dr. Otávo Soares 108, Palmeiras, 35430-229 Ponte Nova ☎31 3881 6700 **W:** montanhesa.am.br/pontenova/ **E:** montanhesapontenova@montanhesa.am.br – **MG127)** Travessa Dona Santinha, 20 - Centro, 39480-000 Januária ☎38 3621 1856 **W:** alter-nativafm.com.br **E:** comercialalternativa@gmail.com – **FM:** 90.7MHz – **MG128)** Rua Benedito Valadares433, Barra, 36880-000 Muriaé ☎32 3729 4800 **W:** redeatividade.com/radioam – **FM:** 94.7MHz – **MG129)** Rua Padre Pedro, 53 - Bonfim, 39390-000 Bocaiúva ☎38 3251 1995 **W:** radioclubebocaiuva.com.br – **MG130)** Rua José Teotônio 87-b,, 39440-000 Janaúba ☎38 3821 2000 📠38 3821 2263 **W:** radiogorutubanaam.com **E:** radiogorutubanaam@gmail.com – **MG131)** Av Afonso Pena, 726, Conj. 1000 10° andar - Centro, 30130-003 Belo Horizonte **W:** redegeraisderadio.com.br/am1460.php **E:** contato@redegeraisderadio.com.br – **MG132)** Rua Eli Correie de Lacerda, Apt. 119 - São Marcos, 35519-000 Nova Serrana – ☎37 9199 4681 **W:** radioclickgospel.blogspot.no **E:** dercysat@hotmail.com – **MG133)** Av. Deputada Humborta de Almeida, 60 - Centro, 37810-000 Guaranésia ☎35 3555 1350 **W:** radioam1580guaranesia.com.br **E:** radioam1580@guaranesia.com.br – **MG134)** BR-496 Km 33, 39260-000 Várzea da Palma – **MG135)** Rua Expedicionário, 68 an 2 - Centro, 38900-000 Bambuí ☎37 3431 3290 **W:** cidadeambambui.com – **MG136)** Rua Jair Werneck, 330 - Cidade Alta, 39800-000 Teófilo Otoni ☎33 3522 2000 **W:** radiomucuri.com.br

– **MG137)** Rua Major Honor Sarmento, 393 - São João, 39400-533 Montes Claros ☎38 3223 5666 📠38 3221 5590 **W:** radioterraam.com. br – **MG138)** Av 119 Nº 122, Brasilia, 38360-000 Capinópolis ☎34 3263 1095 – **MG139)** Avenida Dr. Breno Soares Maia, 493 - Centro, 37900-110 Passos ☎35 3521 4070 **W:** globopassos.com.br **E:** conta-to@globopassos.com.br – **MG140)** Rua Tiradentes, 784 - Nova Horizonte, 37175-000 Ilicínea ☎35 3854 1342 **W:** radioaparecidadosu-lam.com **E:** apdosulam@gmail.com – **MG141)** Rua Astor Goulart de Moura, 51 - Vila Virgilio, 39200-000 Corinto ☎38 3751 1858 **W:** radio-cidadecorinto.com.br **E:** radiocidadadecorinto@futuretec.com.br – **MG142)** Rodovia, BR-381 Km 195 - Cachoeira, 35180-001 Timóteo ☎31 3849 4000 **W:** classificadositatiaiavale.com.br **E:** contato@clas-sificadositatiaiavale.com.br **- FM:** 95.7MHz – **MG143)** Rua Dr Pena, 35 - Centro, 35700-032 Sete Lagoas ☎31 3772 0244 **W:** eldorado1300. com.br **E:** contato@eldorado1300.com.br – **MG144)** Av Paracatu, 778 - Centro, 38780-000 Vazante ☎34 3813 1113 **W:** montanheza.com.br **E:** radio@montanheza.com.br – **MG145)** Pc Cordovil Pinto Coelho, 165, Sala 1003 - Centro, 36900-000 Manhuaçu – **MG146)** Av BPS, 1303 - Pinheirinho,, 37500-000 Itajubá ☎35 3622 1008 **W:** unifei.edu.br/radio **E:** radiounifei@unifei.edu.br – **MG148)** Praça Getúlio Vargas, 108 – Centro, 36800-000 Carangola ☎32 3741 1770 **W:** redegeraisderadio. com.br/am900.php br **E:** rgr900amcarangola@redegeraisderadio. br **- FM:** 102.7MHz «Caparaó» – **MG149)** Rua Oscar Vidal, 416 - Centro, 36016-290 Juiz de Fora ☎32 2102 9500 **W:** radioglobojf.com.br **E:** atendimento@radioglobojf.com.br – **MG150)** Rua Ceara, 833 - Cristo Redentor, 38700-208 Patos de Minas ☎34 3823 1070 **W:** radiopatos. com.br **E:** radiopatos@radiopatos.com.br – **MG151)** Av 7 de Setembro 55-A, 36950-000 Ipanema **W:** radioipanemaam.com – **MG152)** Rua Julio Cosi, 5 - Centro, 38230-000 Fronteira ☎34 3428 2099 – **MG153)** Av Francisco Epifâno Fagundes,161 - Fagundes, 33200-000 Vespasiano ☎31 3621 3811 – **MG154)** Rua Padre Vigilato, 230 - Centro, 35330-000 Inhapim ☎33 3315 1299 **W:** Facebook: Radio Clube de Inhapim – **MG155)** Rua Buritis, 105 - Horto, 35160-300 Ipatinga ☎31 3824 7700 **W:** radiogloboipatinga.com.br – **MG156)** Rua Nonato Matias, 524 - Mathina, 38740-000 Patrocínio ☎34 3831 7244 **W:** radiorainhadapaz. com.br **E:** contato@radiorainhadapaz.com.br – **MG157)** Av. Zezé Amaral, 180 - Cristo Rei, 37950-000 São Sebastião do Paraiso ☎35 3531 7461 **W:** facebook.com/ouroverdeam – **MG158)** Praça Governador Valadares, 255 - Perdizes, 38400-000 Perdizes ☎34 3663 1309 **W:** planaltoam.com.br – **MG159)** Av Joaquim Ribeiro de Gouveia,1651 - Centro, 38320-000 Santa Vitória ☎34 3251 2000 **W:** radiosom2000. com.br – **MG161)** Rua –Ceara 677, 38660-000 Buritis ☎38 3662 1492 **W:** Fcebook: R.Buritis **E:** radioburitis@hotmail.com – **MG162)** Rua Silvino Brandão, 164 – Aeroporto, 38440-170 Araguari ☎34 3246 0103 **W:** ondaviaaraguari.com.br **E:** comercialmaisfm@yahoo.com.br **– FM:** 93.5 MHz – **MG163)** Travessa Cônego Benedito Profício, 95 - Centro, 37660-000 Paraisópolis ☎35 3651 1119 **W:** paraisopolisam.com.br – **MG164)** Av Progresso, 177 - Olaria, 35588-000 Arcos ☎37 3351 2100 **E:** radiocidadeam@gmail.com – **MG165)** Rua Antônio Ribeiro da Costa Junior 16, 36730-000 Pirapetinga ☎32 3465 1233 **W:** radiopirapetinga. com.br – **MG167)** Praça Dr Badaró, 112 - Centro, 39650-000 Minas Novas ☎33 3764 1185 **W:** radiobomsucesso.com.br **E:** lalado@radio-bomsucesso.com.br – **MG168)** Rua Marcos Vinícius Ferreira, 226 - São Miguel, 39560-000 Salinas ☎38 341 1060 **W:** radiodifusoradesalinas. com.br **E:** programacao@radiodifusoradesalinas.com.br – **MG169)** Av Rondón Pacheco, 450 – Santo Antônio, 37150-000 Carmo do Rio Claro ☎35 3561 1967 – **MG170)** Rua Vereador Maria Anselmo, 33 - Centro, 36480-000 Piranga ☎31 3746 1322 – **MG171)** Rua Coronel Carlos Brandão 98, sala 07/08, 36500-000 Ubá ☎32 3532 3122 – **MG172)** Av Dr Pedro Rosa s/n, 37530-000 Brasópolis ☎35 3641 1317 **W:** redege-raisderadio.com.br/am1380.php **E:** contato@redegeaisderadio.com.br – **MG173)** Rua Silviano Brandão, 795 - Centro, (✉ C.P 100) 37570-000 Ouro Fino ☎35 3441 1433 **W:** difusoraourofino.com.br **E:** radio@difu-soraourofino.com.br – **MG174)** Praça Vital Brasil 56, 37980-000 Cássia ☎35 3541 5100 **W:** cassia.mg.gov./radio_cultura_am.php **E:** radiocul-tura@cassia.mg.gov.br – **MG175)** Praça Coronel Silverio de Melo 172, 37958-000 Monte Santo de Minas **W:** radioprogresoam.zip.net – **MG176)** Rua 18, 1974 - Industrial, 38270-000 Campina Verde ☎34 3412 1504 – **MG178)** Av Bernardo Guimarães, - Centro, 38440-198 Uberlândia ☎34 3293 1300 **W:** radiovitoriosa.com.br **E:** comercial@ redevitoriosa.com.br – **MG193)** Rua Coronel Ferraz 135, 37470-000 São Lourejo ☎35 3332 6646 **W:** radioglobolambari.blogspot.com.br – **MG195)** Av. Gov. Milton Campos, 2232 sl 201 - Centro, 39740 000 Guanhães ☎33 3421 3503 **W:** cidadeam.com.br **E:** cidadeam@hot-mail.com – **MG196)** Rua 20, 2080 - Santa Cruz,38950-000 Ibiá ☎34 9981 7016 **W:** maximafm.com.br **E:** futura@ibiamg.com.br **- FM:** 87.9 MHz

MS00) MATO GROSSO DO SUL

MS01) Av Mato Grosso, 530 - Centro, 79002-233 Campo Grande **W:** miliciadaimaculada.org.br/v2/Rural580.asp **E:** 580am@miliciadai-maculada.org.br – **MS02)** Av Senador Felinto Müller 59, 79004-383

Campo Grande ☎67 3323 6500 **W:** culturaam680.com.br – **MS03)** Rua Jamil Selem 27(✉C.P 104 79951-970) 79950-000 Naviraí **W:** cultura690.com.br **E:** culturanav@terra.com.br – **MS04)** Rua Ciro Melo, 2045 - Centro, 79805-000 Dourados ☎67 3421 1540 – **MS05)** Rua Anchieta, 871 - Parati, 79081-180 Campo Grande ☎67 3346 2686 **W:** amcapital.com.br – **MS06)** Rua 15 de Agosto, 98 - Alto, 79200-000 Aquidauana ☎67 3241 2902 **W:** pantanalnews.com.br/radioindepen-dente – **MS07)** Rua Melanio Garcia Barbosa, 749 - Centro, 79150-000 Maracaju ☎67 3454 1181 **W:** rcmdigital.com.br **E:** rcmdigital@terra. com.br – **MS08)** Rua Jorge Roberto Salomão, 1301 - Vila Industrial, 79904-170 Ponta Porã – **MS09)** Rua Marrey Junior, 448 - Tiradentes, 79042-150 Campo Grande ☎67 3341 1240 **W:** difusorapantanal.com. br **E:** contato@difusorapantanal.com.br – **MS10)** Rua Tiburcia Queiroz Monteiro, 850 - Jardim das Oliveiras 79630-212 Três Lagoas ☎67 3524 2129 **W:** radiodifusora1250.com.br **E:** contato@radiodifuso-ra1250.com.br – **MS11)** Av Marcelino Pires, 1404 - Centro, 79801-002 Dourados ☎67 3423 0498 – **MS12)** Rua Marechal Deodoro, 504 - Guanandy, 27000-000 Aquidauana ☎67 3241 3957 **W:** difusora1340. com.br **E:** difusora@difusora1340.com.br – **MS13)** Rua Antônio Lino Barbosa 961, 79130-970 Rio Brilhante ☎67 3452 7451 **W:** difusorarb. com.br– **MS14)** Rua Dom Pedro II, 26 - Previsul, 79300-000 Corumbá ☎67 3231 7397 **W:** novaclubeam.com **E:** novaclube1410am@gmail. com – **MS16)** Av –Ivinhema. 1493 - Vila Operária, 79750-000 Nova Andradina ☎67 3441 1420 **W:** radiocacique.com **E:** radiocacique@ hotmail.com – **MS17)** Av Aldair Rosa de Oliveira, 1045 - Circular da Lagoa, 79640-100 Três Lagoas ☎67 3521 2305 **E:** radiocacula.com.br – **MS18)** Rua Ferreira, 69 B - Cidade Piracema, 79400-000 Coxim ☎67 3291 1124 **W:** radiovaledotaquari.com.br – **MS19)** Rua Angélica 455 - Centro, 79730-000 Glória de Dourados ☎63 3466 1128 **W:** paiaguas. grupofeitosa.com.br – **MS20)** Rua Visconde de Taunay, 895 - Centro, 79500-000 Paranaíba ☎67 3668 2080 **W:** radiodifusoraam.com.br **E:** radiodifusoraparanaibenseltda@yahoo.com.br – **MS21)** Rua General Câmara, 888 1° andar - Centro, 79990-000 Amambaí ☎67 3481 1391 **W:** radiogloboamambai.com.br **E:** radiojornaldeamambai@gmail. com **- FM:** 102.5MHz – **MS22)** Rua Severino Araújo, 1375 - Centro, 79700-000 Fátima do Sul ☎67 3467 1833 – **MS23)** Rua Joaquim Balduina Souza. 646 - Centro, ☎79540-000 Cassilândia **W:** Facebook: R.Patriarca – **MS24)** Av Presidente Vargas, 669 - Centro, 79940-000 Caarapó ☎67 3453 1810 – **MS25)** Rua/Av.Ra 7 de Setembro,704 - Centro, 79240-000 Jardim ☎67 3251 1531 **W:** radiolaguna.com. br – **MS26)** Rua Ponta Porã, s/n - Jardim das Grevileas, 79970-000 Eldorado ☎67 3473 2022 – **MS28)** Rua 7 de Setembre, 575 - Centro, 79900-00 Ponta Porã – **MS29)** Pedro Celestino C Costa, 687 - Centro, 79890-000 Itapora ☎67 3421 1104 **W:** radioalvorada1470.com.br – **MS30)** Rua São Paulo 1359, 79490-000 São Gabriel d'Oeste ☎67 3295 1816 **W:** difusora850.com.br – **MS31)** Rua Thomás Cáceres, 349 - São Bento, 79170-000 Sidrolândia ☎67 3272 1543 – **MS32)** 135 Rua Amando de Oliveria, 135 - Amambai, 79005-370 Campo Grande ☎67 3383 6300 **W:** novotempo.com/campogrande/ br – **MS33)** Rua Severino de Araujo Ferreira, 1375 - Marta Rocha, 79700-000 Fátima do Sul ☎67 3467 1833 **W:** radioguaicurus.com.br – **MS34)** Rua 26 de Agosto, 384 an7 - Centro, 79002-081 Campo Grande ☎67 3384 6647 **- FM:** 102.7 MHz – **MS35)** Rua Joao Ferreira Borges, 369 - Piravevé, 79740-000 Ivinhema ☎67 3442 4052 – **MS38)** Rua Candido Severino 462, 79420-000 Camapuã ☎67 3286 1366 – **MS39)** Rua Ipiranga, 566 - Jardim Itaipu, 79824-190 Dourados ☎67 3426 9261 **W:** miliciadai-maculada.org.br **E:** 1060am@miliciadaimaculada.org.br – **MS40)** Av Aracruz, 21 - Parque dos Novas Estados, 79034-450 Campo Grande ☎67 3354 2222 **W:** ipda.com.br – **MS41)** Rua Antônio Maria Coelho, 480 - Centro, 79260-000 Bela Vista ☎67 3439 1243 **W:** radiobela-vista.com.br **E:** contato@radiobelavista.com.br – **MS42)** Rua Santos Dumont, 880 - Centro, 79480-000 Rio Verde de Mato Grosso ☎67 3292 1561 **W:** radiocampoalegre.com.br **E:** rcams@brturbo.com.br – **MS43)** Av Reinaldo Massi, 2144 - Centro, 79740-000 Ivinhema – **MS54)** Rua Viriato Bandeira, Centro, 79400-000 Coxim ☎67 3291 4455 – **MS55)** Av.Joao Pedro Pedrossian, 4058 - Centro, 79570-000 Aperecida do Taboado 67 3565 1075 – **MS56)** Av José Ferreira da Costa, 771, 79550-000 Costa Rica ☎67 3247 1090 **W:** radiocostarica.com.br **E:** contato@ radiocostarica.com.br – **MS61)** Rua 15 de Novembro, 564 - Sala 2, 79300-000 Corumbá ☎67 3232 8080 **W:** radiofronteiraam960.com.br **E:** radiofronteira@terra.com.br – **MS62)** QE 13 Conjunto C casa 02, Guará II, 71050-030 Brasilia **W:** radiomaria.net.br **E:** imprensa@radiomaria. org.br – **MS63)** Rua Ribas de Rio Pardo, 263 – Centro, 79780-000 Bataguassu ☎67 3541 1630 **W:**radiortal.omegasistemas.com.br – **MS64)** Rua 15 de Novembro, 564 - Centro, 79330-000 Corumbá ☎67 3231 1059

MT00) MATO GROSSO

MT01) Rua Boróros, 673 - Centro, 78600-000 Barra do Garças ☎66 3401 1345 **W:** radioaruana.com.br **E:** radioaruana@gmail.com – **MT02)** Av Brasil, 55 - Centro, 78600-000 Poxoréo ☎66 3436 1080 **W:** rsm850. com.br/novo/ – **MT03)** Professora Tereza Lobo, 30 - Concil, 78048-700

Cuiabá ☎65 3612 6500 **W:** cbncuiaba.com.br **E:** equipedeouro@
gazetadigital.com.br – **MT04)** Rua das Primaveras, 3971 - St Res Norte,
78550-000 Sinop ☎66 3531 5477 – **MT05)** Praça do Seminário, 239
- Centro, 78015-140 Cuiabá ☎65 3046 7900 **W:** blog.cancaonova.
com/radiodifusora/sobre **E:** radiocuiaba@cancaonova.com – **MT06)**
Av Ludovico de Riva Netto, 3224 - Centro, 78580-000 Alta Floresta
☎66 3521 3501 **W:** radioprogresso640.com.br **E:** ouvinte@radiopro-
gresso640.com.br – **MT07)** Rua Joao Pessao, 453 - Centro (C.P 401,
78700-970) 78700-082 Rondonópolis ☎66 3423 1226 – **MT08)** Rua
Joaquim Murtinho,1456 - Centro Sul - Porto, 78025-000 Cuiabá ☎65
3321 6198 **W:** radioculturadecuiaba.com.br – **MT09)** Rua São Pedro
806, 78200-000 Cáceres – **MT10)** Rua Tiradentes, 979 - Centro, 78200-
000 Cáceres ☎65 3223 3830 **W:** difusoracaceres.com.br **E:** difuso-
ra102@difusoracaceres.com.br - **FM:** 102.3MHz – **MT12)** Av Cuiabá
829, Edifício Mikerinos, 12° andar, 78700-090 Rondonópolis ☎66
3425 1070 **W:** radioclubemt.com.br – **MT13)** Rua 28 de Outobro 3391,
78280-000 Mirassol d'Oeste ☎65 3241 1288 **W:** difusoramirassol.
com.br **E:** contato@difusoramirassol.com.br – **MT14)** Av. Governador
Júlio Campos, 3111 - Jardim Glória, 78140-400 Várzea Grande ☎65
3682 2525 **W:** industrial1070.com.br **E:** radioindustrial@industrial1070.
com.br – **MT15)** Rua Zulmira Canavarros 285, 78005-390 Cuiabá
– **MT16)** Rua 2 No 32, 78175-000 Poconé – **MT17)** Rua aracuai, 1105
- Centro, 78575-000 Juara ☎66 3556 1316 **W:** radiotucunare.com.br
E: radio@radiotucunare.com.br – **MT18** Rua João do Padro Arantes,
95S - Centro, 78300-000 Tangará da Serra ☎65 3326 2080 **W:** radio-
tangara.com.br– **MT19)** Av T Neves, 1682 - Centro 78500-000 Colíder
☎66 3541 1233 **W:** radioeducadoracolider.com.br **E:** educadoralider@
hotmail.com – **MT20)** Travessa Pref Alexandrina Gomes, 87 - Centro,
78600-000 Barra do Garças ☎65 3401 6155 **W:** difusora720.com.br –
MT21) Rua Criciúma, 165 - Centro, 78890-000 Sorriso ☎66 3544 2595
W: radiosorriso.com.br **E:** radiosorriso@radiosorriso.com.br – **MT22)**
Praça Edgar de Araujo, Centro, (✉ CP40) 78430-000 Nortelândia
☎65 3346 1729 – **MT23)** Av Mato Grosso 133, 78690-000 Nova
Xavantina ☎65 3438 1218 **W:** Facebook: R.Nova Xavantina – **MT24)**
Rua 6 No - Manoel D Sobrino 498, 78300-000 Tangará da Serra ☎65
3326 3131 **W:** radiopioneira.com.br – **MT25)** Rua Benjamin Constant
s/n, 78780-000 Alto Araguaia – **MT26)** Av Holmis Ioris, 429 - Modulo
I, 78320-000 Juina ☎66 3566 1228 – **MT27)** Av Mario Correa 350,
78790-000 Itiquira ☎65 3491 1070 **W:** radiodifusora1080.com.br **E:**
contato@radiodifusora1080.com.br – **MT28)** Rua 01, 600 - Bairro
ZH3-00|, 78525-000 Matupá ☎66 3595 1144 **W:** cidade770.com.br **E:**
radiocidade@vsp.com.br – **MT29)** Rua das Gravioøas, 52 - Centro, (✉
C.P. 509) 78550-116 Sinop ☎66 3517 3550 **W:** rtvmais.com.br – **MT30)**
Avenida Luiz Barbosa esq. c/ Sete de Setembro No 477, 78285-000
São José dos Quatro Marcos ☎65 3251 1062 **W:** radiojornalam570.
com.br – **MT31)** Rua 6, s/n - Jardim Eldorado, 78400-000 Diamantino
☎65 3366 1000 **W:** radioparecis690am.com.br **E:** contato@radiopa-
recis690am.com.br – **MT32)** Rua Cipriano Curvo, s/n - Centro, (✉
CP 29), 78195-000 Chapada dos Guimarães ☎65 3301 2525 **W:** natu-
rezaam.com.br **E:** contato@naturezaam.com.br – **MT33)** Av Roberto
Valdecir Briante, 99 - Centro, 78435-000 São José do Rio Claro ☎66
3386 2216 **W:** sj.radiofloresta.com.br **E:** contato@radiofloresta.com.
br – **MT34)** Rua U-2, s/n – Canteiro Central, 78580-000 Alta Floresta
W: af.radiofloresta.com.br **E:** contato@radiofloresta.com.br – **MT35)**
Rua Jovino Lopes, 1292, 2° andar - Santa Maria Bertila, 78760-000
Guiratinga ☎66 3431 2002 **W:** radiorgbam.com **E:** Rua Joaquim
Nabuco, 450 - Centro, 78260-000 Araputanga ☎65 3261 1460 **W:**
radioarcoiris.com.br **E:** arcoir@terra.com.br – **MT37)** Av São Paulo
1440, 78250-000 Pontes e Lacerda ☎65 3266 1809 **W:** radiojornal930.
com.br – **MT38)** Rua do Burtis, s/n - Centro, 78520-000 Guarantã do
Norte ☎66 3552 1114 **W:** Facebook: Radio Enauan – **MT41)** Rua do
Comercio, 1155 - Castelândia, 78850-000 Primavera do Leste ☎66
3496 1414 – **MT42)** Rua Filinto Muller, 1804 - Morada do Sol, 78043-
500 Cuiaba ☎66 3575 2842 **W:** anoticiadigital.com.br – **MT44)** Av
Mato Grosso, 1196S - Alvorado, 78455-000 Lucas do Rio Verde ☎65
3549 5443 **W:** atitudeam.com.br **E:** atendimento@atitudeam.com.br
– **MT45)** Rua Potiguares, 809 – Centro Edifico Santa Fé - 2° andar, (✉
C.P. 227), 78820-000 Jaciara ☎66 3461 1966 **W:** radioxavantes.com.
br **E:** radioxavantes@gmail.com – **MT47)** Rua Araçuai, 1105 - Centro,
78575-000 Juara ☎66 3556 1478 **W:** difusorajuara.com.br **E:** difuso-
raaovivo@hotmail.com – **MT53)** Rua São Salvador, 1 - Inconfidencia,
78645-000 Vila Rica ☎66 3554-2266 **W:** redecontinental.com.br/amvi-
larica – **MT64)** Campo Novo de Parecis **W:** radioparecisam.com.br
– **MT65)** Av Catselo Branco 341, 78390-000 Barra do Bugres ☎65
9978 5368 **W:** radioativaam.com **E:** ativaam@gmail.com

PA00) PARÁ

PA01) Av Araguaia 247, 68551-000 Redenção – **PA02)** Manoel
Umbuzeiro, 1456 -Altos Centro, 68371-180 Altamira ☎93 9171 0908
W: radioruralaltamira.no.comunidades.net **E:** radioruralaltamira@
hotmail.com – **PA03)** Av Almirante Barroso, 2190 3° andar - Marco,
66095-000 Belém ☎91 3084 0112 **W:** radioclubedopara.com.br **E:**

timaocampeao@radioclubedopara.com.br – **PA04)** Av São Sebastião,
622-A Bloco A - Centro, 68005-090 Santarém ☎93 3523 1066 ▤93
3523 2685 **W:** radioruraldesantarem.com.br **E:** edilrural@gmail.com.br
– **PA05)** Av. Juscalino Kubitschek Oliveira, 3975 - Centro, 68540-000
Conceição do Araguaia ☎94 3421 1576 **W:** radioregionaldoaraguaia.
com.br – **PA06)** Praça dos Notáveis 1006, 68400-000 Cametá ☎91
3781 1495 – **PA07)** Rodovia BR-316 Km 58, 68742-190 Castanhal
Grande – **PA08)** Travessa Campos Sales 370, 66015-080 Belém ☎91
4005 4400 **W:** supermarajoara.com **E:** contato@supermarajoara.
com.br - **FM:** 100.9MHz – **PA09)** Travessa Vileta 2193, 66093-380
Belém ☎91 3344 4718 **W:** boasnovas.net **E:** marketing@boasnovas.
net – **PA10)** Av Brás de Aguiar, 351 - Nazaré, 66035-395 Belém ☎91
3213 1540 **W:** radioliberal.com.br – **PA11)** Tv. Cap, 75 - Centro, 68801-
970 Breves ☎91 3783 1269 – **PA12)** Rua 13 de Mayo, s/n - Centro,
68600-000 Bragança ☎91 3425 1774 **W:** fundacaoeducadora.com.
br - **FM:** 106.7MHz – **PA13)** Av Mendonça Furtado, 1481 - Santa
Clara, 68005-100 Santarém **W:** rtvpontanegra.com.br **E:** am890@
rtvpontanegra.com.br ☎93 3523 3348 – **PA14)** Av Coronel Monfredo
42, 68820-000 São Sebastião da Boa Vista – **PA16)** Av Almirante
Barroso 735, 66093-020 Belém ☎91 4005 7700 **W:** portalcultura.com.
br - **FM:** 93.7MHz – **PA17)** Rod. Transamazonica Km, 4 Rua das TV´s,
Folha Industrial Qd. 05 Lt 06, 68507-765 Marabá ☎94 3322 2200
– **PA18)** Rodovia Transamazonica Km 01, 68180-010 Itaituba – **PA19)**
Rua Lauro Sodré, 730 - Centro, 68456-000 Tucuruí ☎94 3787 1288 **W:**
sistemafloresta.com.br – **PA20)** Av Afonso Pena, 25 - Aeroporto Velho,
68005-390 Santarém ☎93 3523 5114 **E:** tvsantarem@hotmail.com
– **PA21)** Av Xingu, s/n - Centro, 68555-010 Xinguara ☎94 3426 1008
W: radioxinguaraam.com.br **E:** radioxinguara@hotmail.com – **PA22)**
Travessa Dom Floriano 330, 68250-000 Óbidos ☎93 3547 1966
– **PA24)** Travessa 18 No 1863, entre 4 e 5 ruas, 68870-000 Soure ☎91
3741 1248 **W:** Facebook: R.Guarany do Marajó – **PA25)** Av Marcionilo
Alves, 537 - Centro, 68780-000 Vigia ☎91 3731 1015 **W:** radiomoreno-
braga.com.br – **PA26)** Av.Fernando Guilhon, 358 Bela Vista, 68180-000
Itaituba ☎93 3518 4169 **W:** radioclubedeitaituba.com.br **E:** radioclu-
be@hotmail.com – **PA27)** Rua Rui Barbosa, 153 - Centro, 68625-000
Paragominas ☎91 3729 3333 – **PA28)** Travessa sete de setembro
com a Rua Visconde do Rio Branco, 68200-000 Alenquer ☎93 9175
6458 **W:** radioximango.com.br **E:** radioximango@hotmail.com – **PA29)**
Rodovia Transamazônica s/n Km 04, 68502-290 Marabá ☎94 3322
4838 **W:** radioclubemaraba.com.br – **PA30)** Rodovia BR-010 Km 1409,
Industrial, 68660-000 São Miguel do Guamá ☎91 8022 0000 **W:** http//
radioguama.com **E:** direcao.radioguama@gmail.com – **PA32)** Rodovia
BR-316 KM 11 3528, São João, 67200-000 Marituba ☎91 3323 3059
W: novotempobelem.org.br **E:** belemnovotempo@hotmail.com – **PA33)**
Av Antonio Marques Ribeiro 242, 68380-000 São Felix do Xingu ☎91
4351 1243 – **PA34)** Av Bertoldo Costa, 68710-000 Maracanã – **PA56)**
Rua do Contorno s/n, 68746-475 Castanhal ☎91 3711 0053 **W:** radio-
paranaense.com.br **E:** contato@radioparaense.com.br

PB00) PARAÍBA

PB01) Rua Pres. João Pessoa 07,Centro, 58800-000 Sousa ☎83 3521
2197 **W:** portalprogresso.com – **PB02)** Rua Justino Bezerra 41, Centro,
58900-000 Cajazeiras ☎83 3531 1236 **W:** radioaltopiranhas.com.br **E:**
altopiranhas@uol.com.br – **PB03)** Rua Padre Manoel Otaviano 340,
Centro, 58970-000 Conceição ☎83 3453 2656 **W:** radioeducadorade-
conceicao.com **E:** radioeducadoradeconceicao@hotmail.com – **PB04)**
Rua Presidente Epitácio Pessoa 242, Centro, 58700-020 Patos ☎83
3421 3884 **W:** radiopanati.com.br - **FM:** 93.9 MHz – **PB05)** Rod PB 075
s/n km 1,25, Zona Rural 58200-000 Guarabira **W:** Facebook: R.Cultra
AM 790 - **PB06)** Praça Pres Epitácio Pessoa 167, Centro, 58755-000
Princesa Isabel ☎83 3457 2183 **W:** radioprincesa970.com **E:** radio-
princesaisabel@bol.com.br – **PB07)** Rua João Pessoa 313 1° andar,
Centro, Campina Grande ☎83 3349 2101▤83 3341 3613 **W:** radiocatu-
rite.com.br **E:** radiocaturite@radiocaturite.com.br –**PB08)** Rua Coronel
Juvêncio Cameiro, 160 - Centro, (CP 20) 58900-000 Cajazeiras ☎88
3531 4530 **W:** radioscajazeiras.com.br **E:** radiocajazeiras@hotmail.com
- **FM:** 94.5 MHz – **PB09)** Av D.Pedro II s/n, Torre, (C.P 1089, 58001-970)
58040-440 João Pessoa ☎83 3218 7900 **W:** radiotabajara.pb.gov.br **E:**
redacaotabajara@gmail.com - **FM:** 105.5 MHz – **PB10)** Rua Manoel
Pedro 304, 1° andar, Centro, 58884-000 Catolé do Rocha ☎83 3441
2013 **W:** radioindependencia1120.com.br **E:** independenciaamcato-
le@hotmail.com or independenciaamcatole@gmail.com – **PB11)** Rua
XV de Novembro 162, Palmeira, 58101-200 Campina Grande ☎83
3343 0589 **W:** radiocariri.com – **PB12)** Av Pedro II 523, Centro, 58013-
420 João Pessoa ☎83 3216 5044 **W:** correiosat.com.br – **PB13)** Rua
das Trincheiras 198, Centro, 58011-000 João Pessoa ☎83 3216 5015
W: diariosassociados.com.br – **PB14)** Rua Venâncio Neiva 287, Centro, 58400-000 Campina Grande
☎83 3349 2910 **W:** http://diariosassociados.com.br/home/veiculos.
php?co_veiculo=43 – **PB15)** Rua Rui Barbosa, 53 – Centro 58700-060
Patos ☎83 3421 3791 **W:** radioespinharas.com.br **E:**radioespinhares@
uol.com.br – **PB16)** Rua Antônio Fernandes 25, Centro, Mamanguape
☎83 3292 2645 **W:** http//manaam560.blogspot.com.br **E:** blogradioma-

na@gmail.com – **PB17)** Rua Dr Carlos Pires 17, São José, 58804-200 Sousa ☎83 3522 1796 **W:** Facebook: R.Jornal 950 AM Sousa **E:** – **PB18)** Rua Monsenhor Valeriano s/n, 58840-000 Pombal ☎83 3431 2277 **W:** maringa98fm@hotmail.com **E:** maringa98fm@hotmail.com – **FM:** 98.7 MHz – **PB19)** Rua Antônio Firmino 344, Centro, 58187-000 Picuí ☎83 3371 2217 **W:** radiocenecistapicui.com.br – **PB20)** Rua Coronel Jose Fernandes, Centro, 58840-000 Pombal ☎83 3431 3558 **W:** bonsucessoam.com.br **E:** contactos@bonsucessoam.com.br – **PB21)** Rua Conselheiro Henrique, 17 – Centro, 58000-000 João Pessoa ☎83 3249 2020 **W:** portalsanhaua.com.br **E:** radioshanua@hotmail.com – **PB22)** Rua Epitácio Pessoa, 8 - Centro, 58200-000 Guarabira ☎83 3271 1000 **W:** radioruralam850.com.br **E:** contato@radiororuralam850.com.br – **PB23)** Rua Monsenhor Palmeira 471, Centro, 58135-000 Esperança ☎83 3361 2452**W:** redeesperanca.com.br – **PB24)** Rua Getúlio Vargas 129, 58500-000 Monteiro ☎83 3351 2612 **W:** correiosat.com. br/?radio=9 **E:** elson@sistemacorreio.com.br – **PB25)** Rua Coronel Pedro Targino s/n, Centro, 58233-000 Araruna ☎83 3373 1102 **W:** radioserranadeararuna.com.br/ **E:**radioserrana@gmail.com or radioserranaam@hotmail.com – **PB26)** Rod. PB 105, km 33, Anel do Brejo, 58220-000 Bananeiras ☎83 3363 2488 **W:**radiointegracaodobrejo.com.br **E:**radioinetgracao@hotmail.com – **PB27)** Rua Gouveia Nobrega 34, 58155-000 Soledade ☎83 3383 1229 – **PB28)** Rua João Sabiá 56, Centro, 58540-000 Sumé ☎83 3372 1089 **W:** radiocidadesume.com **E:** contato@radiocidadedesume.com.br – **FM:** 89 MHz – **PB29)** Praça Frei Martinho s/n, 1° andar - Centro, 58700-100 Patos ☎83 3421 3704 **W:** radiosertaoam.com.br **E:** marketing@radiosertaoam.com.br - **FM:** 102.9MHz – **PB30)** Rua Cel Guimarães, 56 - Centro, 58900-000 Cajazeiras ☎83 3531 3715 **W:** oeste1000.com.br **E:** radiooesteam@hotmail.com – **PB31)** Joao Pessoa– **PB32)** Rua Epitácio Pessoa, 184 - Centro, 58397-000 Areia ☎63 3362 2423 **W:** Facebook: Radio Jardim Da Borborema Am **E:** germanosoaresbrasil@hotmail.com – **PB34)** Av Ananias Conserva 18, 58780-000 Itaporanga ☎83 3451 3879 **W:** correiosat.com.br

PE00) PERNAMBUCO
PE01) Lotm Bela Vista, s/n - Heliopolis, ☎87 3762 2211 55290-000 Garanhuns – **PE02)** Rua Caramuru, 72 – Santo Amaro, 81 3221-000 Recife ☎81 3221 6767 **W:** rbc1.com.br **E:** comercial@rbc1.com.br – **PE03)** Av Joaquim Nabuco, 322 - São Crístovão,56503-150 Arcoverde ☎87 3821 0664 **MSN:** cardealam@hotmail.com – **PE04)** Rua Vigário Joaquim Pinto, 721 al 12 - Centro, 55700-000 Limoeiro ☎81 3628 9733 **W:** radiojornal.com.br **E:** programacao@radiojornal.com.br – **PE05)** Vila Conceição BR 317km 21.7, 56280-000 Araripina ☎87 3873 1366 **W:** radiograndeserra.com.br/am/ **FM:** 87.9 & 94MHz – **PE06)** Av Sete de Setembro, s/n - Km 02, 56302-060 Petrolina ☎87 3864 4744 **W:** granderioam.com.br **E:** granderioam@uol.com.br – **PE07)** Rua do Veiga, 600 - Santo Amaro, 50040-915 Recife ☎81 3412 4432 **W:** radioclubeam.com.br – **PE08)** Praça Maria Auxiliadora, 205 - Centro, 56302-335 Petrolina ☎87 3862 1522 **W:** am730.com.br – **PE09)** Rua Capitão Lima, 250 - Santo Amaro, 50040-080 Recife ☎81 3413 6110 **W:** radiojornal.com.br **E:** programacao@radiojornal.com.br – **PE10)** Av.Norte, 68 – Santo Amaro, 50040-200 Recife ☎81 3423 4000 ▤81 3423 8533 **W:** tvu.ufpe.br – **PE11)** Av Pres Kennedy, 3092 - Peixinhos, 53260-640 Olinda ☎81 3423 0033 **W:** radiotamandare.com.br **E:** pastores@radiotamandares.com.br – **PE12)** Rua da Conceição, 16/22, 2° andar - Centro, 55000-000 Caruaru ☎81 2103 1170 **W:** liberdade.com. br **E:** programacaoam@liberdade.com.br – **FM:** 94.7MHz – **PE13)** Av Padre Rocha, s/n - Centro, 55810-000 Carpina – **PE14)** Av Maria Emília Cavalcanti, 570 - Barro, 55870-000 Timbaúba ☎81 3631 2229 **W:** princesaserrana.com.br **E:** contato@princesaserrana.com.br – **PE15)** Rua Duarte Coelho, 240 – Santa Tereza, 53010-010 Olinda ☎81 3444 7855 **W:**radiolindaam.com.br **E:** comercial@radiolindaam.com.br – **PE16)** C.P 88, 55001-970 Caruaru **W:** radiojornal.com **E:** programacao@radiojornal.com.br – **PE17)** Av Presidente Kennedy, 3092 - Peixinhos, 53260-640 Olinda ☎81 3444 9499 **W:** radiorelogio1120am.com.br **E:** contato@radiorelogio1120am.com.br – **PE18)** Rua Rádio Cultura Nordeste. 1130 - Indianópolis, 55026-690 Caruaru ☎81 37211130 **W:** radiocultura1130.com.br **E:** jornalismo@radiocultura1130.com.br – **PE19)** Rua Prefeito José Joaquim Silva, 50 an 2 - Livramento, 55602-150 Vitória de Santo Antão ☎81 3523 2003 – **PE20)** Av. Rui Barbosa, 1236 - Heliopólis 55293-300 Garanhuns ☎87 3762 7244 **W:** radiojornal.ne10.uol.com.br – **PE21)** Rua Coronel Urbano Ribeiro de Sena, 956 - Água Fria, 52221-000 Recife ☎55 3444 2562 **W:** radiocapibaribe.com. br **E:** contato@radiocapibaribe.com.br – **PE22)** –Rua Radio Guarany, Nova Tiúma, 54727-160 Sao Lourenço da Mata ☎81 3485 1322 **W:** radioguarany.com.br **E:** falecom@radioguarany.com.br – **PE23)** Rua Pajussara, 225 - Tejipio, 50920-120 Recife ☎81 3252 5868 **W:** radionovasdepaz.com.br/novasdepaz – **PE24)** Av F Pessoa de Queiróz s/n, 55200-000 Pesqueira **W:** radiojornal.com.br – **PE25)** Rodovia BR101 Sul, s/n km 117 - Newton Carneiro, 55540-000 Palmares ☎81 3662 1288 **W:**rcpalmares.com.br **E:** rcpalmares@yahoo.com.br – **PE26)** Rua Inocôncio Gomes Andrade, 619 – Nossa Sra de Penha, 56912 440 Serra

Talhada ☎87 3831 1700 **W:** radioavozdosertao.com.br – **PE27)** Rua 3 de Maio, s/n - Centro, 56800-000 Afogados da Ingazeira ☎87 3838 1213 **W:** radiopajeu.com.br **E:** radiopajeu@radiopajeu.com.br – **PE28)** Rua Agamenom Magalhães 271, 55750-000 Surubim ☎81 3634 1448 **W:** radiosurubimam.com.br – **PE29)** Rua Siquira Campos, 1 2° andar - Centro, 55150-000 Belo Jardim ☎81 3726 1489 **W:** bituryam.com.br **E:** bituryam@hotmail.com – **PE30)** Rua Antônio F Soares, s/n – Nossa Sra de Fátima 56000-000 Salgueiro ☎87 3871 0471 **W:** asabrancaam.com – **PE31)** Tv José Paulo, 16 - Centro, 56700-999 São José do Egito ☎87 3844 1081 **W:** radiocultura1320.com.br**E;** radiocultura1320@yahoo. com.br – **PE32)** Praça Duque de Caxias 818, 55900-000 Goiana – **PE33)** Av Fernando Bezerra, 1123 - Centro, 56200-000 Ouricuri ☎87 3874 1559 **W:** voluntariosdapatriaam.com.br – **PE34)** Rua Maria Santina, 200 - Bela Vista, 55190-000 Santa Cruz do Capibaribe ☎81 3731 4033 **W:** radiovaleam.com **E:** radio.vale.am@hotmail.com – **PE35)** Av Coronel Trapia, s/n – Centro, 56440-000 Belém de São Francisco ☎87 3876 1105 **W:** radioeducadoradebelem.com.br **E:** educadoradebelem@ yahoo.com.br – **PE36)** Rd Luis Gonzaga, km 81 s/n - Centro, 55640-000 Gravatá (C.P 64, 55641-970) ☎81 3533 4709 **W:** cancaonova.com or blog.cancaonova.com/gravata **E:** radiogravata@cancaonova.com – **PE37)** Rodovia PE 218 km 46, 654 - Lagoa do Jacu, 55330-000 Bom Conselho ☎87 3771 1231 ▤87 3771 1262 **W:** radiopapacaca.com.br **E:** atendimentopapacaca@gmail.com – **PE41)** Comunidade Restauração Casa-Mae, 55000-000 Caruaru ☎81 3728 8255 **W:** comunidadecr. blogspot.no **E:** radiorestauracao_am1590@hotmail.com

PI00) PIAUÍ
PI01) Av Professor João Menezea, Centro, 64770-000 São Raimundo Nonato ☎89 3582 1497 ▤89 3582 1649 **W:** radioserradacapivara. com.br **E:** capivara550@yahoo.com.br – **PI02)** Rua Alvaro Mendes 972, 64000-060 Teresina – **PI03)** Rua Taumaturgo de Azevedo 995, 64100-000 Barras – **PI04)** Av Valter Alencar, 2120 - Monte Castelo, 64076-410 Teresina ☎86 2107 6640 – **PI07)** Praça Coronel Orlando Carvalho, 400 - Centro, 64500-000 Oeiras 89 3462 1200 – **PI08)** Av Valter Alencar, 2021 - Monte Castelo, 64019-625 Teresina ☎86 3216 5056 **W:** fundacaoantares.org **E:** antres@fundacaoantares.org – **PI09)** Rua Coronel Joaquim Balduino, 40 – Bomba, 64600-000 Picos ☎89 3422 1989 – **PI10)** Rua 24 de Janeiro Sul, 150 - Centro, 64001-230 Teresina ☎86 2107 8121 **W:** radiopioneira.am.br **E:** jornalismopioneira@gmail.com – **PI12)** Rua Profesor Bem, 712 - Centro, 64260-000 Piripiri ☎86 3276 1734 **W:** itamaratyam.com.br – **PI13)** Rua Professor Magalhães, 4190 - Recanto das Palmares, 64045-750 Teresina ☎86 3232 5411 **W:** portaldifusora.com – **PI14)** Av Mathias Olimpico, s/n - Centro, 64400-000 Amarante ☎86 3292 1129 – **PI15)** Rua Barão Rio Branco, 314 - Centro64860-000 Uruçuí ☎89 3544 1328 – **PI16)** Rua Clementino Ribeiro, 56 2° andar - Centro, 64800-000 Floriano ☎89 3522 1207 **W:**difusorafloriano.com.br – **PI17)** Av Des Amaral. 2616, 64980-000 Corrente – **PI18)** Rua Clementino Ribeiro, 187 – Sambaida Veklha, 64800-000 Floriano ☎89 3522 1504 **W:** radiosantaclara. br **E:** radiosantaclara@veloxmail.com – **PI19)** Rua Sabino Paulo, 696 - Centro, 64760-000 São João do Piauí ☎89 3483 1317 – **PI20)** Pc Independencia, 1 – Centro, 64290-000 Altos ☎86 3262 1212 – **PI21)** Rua Arcenio Santos, 555 - Centro, 64900-000 Bom Jesus ☎89 3562 1525 – **PI22)** Praca Sto. Antônio, 1019 - ap 101 - Centero, 64200-361 Parnaíba ☎86 3322 3550 **W:** Facebook: R,Globo Parnaiba – AM 550 – **PI23)** Rua Leonidas Melo, 867 - Centro, 64100-000 Barras ☎86 3242 1590 – **PI24)** Pc Presidente Castelo Branco, 161 - Cetro, 64750-000 Paulistana ☎89 3487 1373 **W:** http//radioingazeira.com.br – **PI25)** Av. São Vicente Paula, s/n – Centro, 64240-000 Piracuruca ☎86 3343 1107 **W:** amsetecidades940.blogspot.no – **PI26)** Av José de Deus Lacerda 584, 64130-000 Miguel Alves – **PI27)** Tv Benedito da C Alencar, 78 - Centro, 64575-000 Jaicós ☎89 3457 1610 – **PI28)** Rua Corinto Andrade, 460 - Centro, 64255-000 Pedro II ☎86 3271 1186 **W:** radiocruzeiroam.com.br **E:** radiocruzeiroam@hotmail.com – **PI29)** Praça da Independência 69 - Centro, 64325-000 Elesbão Veloso ☎86 3285 1276 – **PI30)** Rua Joaquim Baldoíno, 48 - Bomba, 64600-000 Picos ☎89 3422 2512 – **PI31)** Av João Ferreira 199, 64460-000 Agua Branca ☎86 3282 1344 **W:** radio1dejulho.blogspot.com.br **E:** radio1dejulho@hotmail.com – **PI32)** Rua Hugo Napoleão, 940 - Centro, 64110-000 José de Freitas ☎86 3264 1407 – **PI33)** Av Antonio Freire, 606 - Centro, 64340-000 Castelo do Piauí ☎86 3274 1106 – **PI34)** Rua Pedro II, 249, 64330-000 São Miguel do Tapuio ☎86 3249 1101 – **PI35)** Rua Coronel Anibal Martins, 481 - Centro, 64300-000 Valença do Piauí ☎89 3465 1244 – **PI36)** Rua Matias Gomes, 510 – Centro, 64700-000 Simplício Mendes ☎89 3482 1105 – **PI37)** Rua Coronel Narciso, 728 - Centro, 64120-000 União ☎86 3265 1411 – **PI38)** Av Padre Joaquim Nonato, 517 - Centro, 64390-000 Demerval Lobão ☎86 3260 1158 – **PI39)** Rua Coronel Messeas Melo, 430 - Centro, 64190-000 Batalha ☎86 3347 1314 – **PI41)** Av Deputado Paulo Ferraz, 1940 2° andar – Beira Rio, 64075-535 Teresina ☎86 3194 3034 **W:** cbnteresina.com.br **E:** redacao@cbnteresina.com.br – **PI42)** Rua Joaquim Rodrigues Macedo, 245 - Centro, 64680-000 Padre Marcos ☎89 3431 1137 – **PI43)** Rua

Sete de Setembro, 471 - Centro, 64160-000 Luzilândia ☎86 3393 1429 **W:** radiovaledoparnaiba.com.br **E:** radiorvpam@hotmail.com – **PI44)** Praça da Bandeira, 91 - Centro, 64500-000 Oeiras ☎89 3462 1482 – **PI46)** Rua Coronel José Fortes, 549 - Centro, 64180-000 Esperantina ☎86 3383 1245 – **PI47)** Rodovia BR-343 s/n, 64290-000 Altos ☎86 3262 1234 – **PI49)** Rua Padre Madeira. 191 - Centro 64600-000 Picos ☎89 3422 1900

PR00) PARANÁ
PR01) Rua Quintino Bocaiuva, 41 - Centro, 86020-100 Londrina ☎43 3344 2038 **W:** radiolondrina.com.br **E:** radiolondrina@onda.com.br – **PR02)** Rua XV do Novembro, 7466 -Centro, 85010-000 Guarapuava ☎42 3623 6423 ▤42 3723 7269 **W:** centralcultura.com.br - **FM:** 93.7MHz – **PR03)** Av Brasil, 1720(▨C.P 10, 85892-970), 85892-000 Santa Helena ☎45 3268 1212 **W:** radiograndelago.com.br **E:** grandelago@rgl.com.br – **PR04)** Rua Humberto de Alencar Castelo Branco, 590 - Cristo Rei, 82530-195 Curitiba ☎41 3268 6550 **W:** difusora-am590.com.br – **PR05)** Praça de Café Nº 1100, 86900-000 Jandaia do Sul ☎43 3432 9797 **W:** radiojandaia.com.br **FM:** 103.3MHz – **PR06)** Rua Julio Perneta, 695 - Mercês, 80810-110 Curitiba ☎41 3331 7400 **W:** e-parana.pr.gov.br – **FM:** 97.1 MHz – **PR07)** Rua 7 de Setembro, 520 - Centro, 85960-000 Marechal Cândido Rondón ☎45 3284 1212 **W:** radioeducadora.com **E:** educadora@rondonet.com.br – **PR08)** Rod João Carlos Strass, s/n - Heimtal, 86084-610 Londrina ☎43 3339 6244 **W:** superradiodeuseamor.com.br – **PR09)** Rua António Costa, 529 - Bela Vista Alegre, 80820-020 ☎41 3240 7500 **W:** radiobandab.com.br **E:** portal@radiobandab.com.br – **PR10)** Rua Lord Lovat, 497 - Centro, 87600-000 Nova Esperança ☎44 3252 4533 **W:** cancaonova.com **E:** rede@cancaonova.com – **PR11)** Rua Oyapock, 649 - Cristo Rei, 80050-450 Curitiba ☎41 3218 5800 **W:** radioglobocuritiba.com.br **E:** conta-to@radioglobocuritiba.com.br – **PR12)** Rua Saldanha Marinho, 1581 Apto B - Ventro, 85010-290 Guarapuava ☎42 3035 7010 **W:** radiocaciqueam.com **E:** contat@radiocaciqueam.com – **PR13)** Rua Sergipe, 843 - sala 05, 86010-360 Londrina ☎43 3306 1105 **W:** radiodifusoradelondrina.com.br **E:** contato@radiodifusoralondrina.com.br – **PR14)** Rua Quinze de Novembro, 433 - Centro, 84010-020 Ponta Grossa. ☎42 3027 7090 **W:** difusora690.com **Email.** difusorapg@yahoo.com.br – **PR15)** Av Paraná, 1885 - Boa Vista, 82510-000 Curitiba ☎41 3251 2410 **W:**radioevangelismo.com.br **E:** marumby@terra.com.br – **PR16)** Av. Capitão Índio Bandeira, 1400 5º Andar – Centro Empresarial Antares, 87300-005 Campo Mourão ☎44 3017 0013 **W:** Facebook: R.Objetiva – **PR17)** Av 19 de Agosto, 522 1° andar - Centro, 87360-000 Goioerê ☎44 3522 7777 ▤44 3522 1162 **W:** radiogoioere.com **E:** rgam@goioere.com.br – **PR18)** Av. Maranhão 62, Shopping Urbano 2º Andar – Sala 21 - Centro, 87200-000 Cianorte ☎▤44 3629 1514 **W:** radiportavoz.com.br **E:** radioportavoz@irapida.com.br **PR19)** Rua Frei Everaldo, 3835 - Centro, 85560-000 Chopinzinho ☎46 3242 1495 **W:** radiochopinzinho.com.br **E:** radio@radiochopinzino.com.br – **PR20)** Av D.Pedro I, 1596 - Jardim São Silvestre, 86300-000 Cornélia Procópio ☎43 3524 1266 **W:** redecartani.com.br – **PR21)** Rua Francisco Rosa e Silva, 28 - Parque Presidente, 85852-250 Foz do Iguaçu ☎45 3026 8020 **W:** radioculturafoz.com.br **E:** jornalismocultura@foz.net – **PR22)** Rodovia do Xisto BR 476 Km 20 No 2018, Centro, 83700-000 Araucária ☎41 3642 1010 **W:** radioiguassu.com.br **E:** radioiguassu@radioiguassu.com.br – **PR23)** Rua Coronel Manoel Ferreira Bello, 64 - Centro, 85530-000 Clevelândia ☎46 3252 1286 **W:** rdprogresso.com.br **E:** redacao@rdprogresso.com.br – **PR24)** Rua Mchado de Assis, 25 - Jd. Shangri-lá, 86070-620 Londrina ☎43 3032 1500 **W:** cbnlondrina.com. br **E:** cbnlondrina@cbnlondrina.com.br – **FM:** 93.5MHz – **PR25)** Av. Euclides Cunha 455, Zona 04, 87015-180 Maringá ☎44 3225 8050 **W:** novainga.com.br **E:**comercial@pingafogo.com.br – **PR26)** Guerra Comunicações - Rua Ibiporã, 1004 – Centro, 85501-010 Pato Branco ☎46 3220 0890 **W:** oalvo.com.br – **PR27)** Praça Marechal Floriano Peixoto 581 - 3° andar, (C.P 090 84001-970) 84010-910 Ponta Grossa ☎42 3028 0042 ▤42 3222 3566 **W:** radiosantana.com.br **E:** adm@radiosantana.com.br – **PR28)** Av Largo São Vicente de Paulo 1085, 85900-215 Toledo ☎45 3055 2841 **W:** radiouniaodetoledo.com.br **E:** contato@radiouniaodetoledo.com.br – **PR29)** Rua Sao Paulo, 910 - Centro, 86808-070 Apucarana ☎43 3423 1100 **W:** novaam.com.br **E:** novaam@uol.com.br – **PR30)** Av Aylton Rodrigues Alves 1189, 86600-000 43 3255 2276 Rolândia **W:** Facebook: R.Cultura de Rolândia **E:** radioculturaderolandia@gmail – **PR31)** Rua Robero Vichinheski, 242 - Pilarzinh, 82530-130 Curitiba ☎41 3013 3280 **W:** Facebook: R.Cultura AM 930 – **PR32)** Av XV de Novembro, 462–Sala 05 – Zona 01, 87013-230 Maringá ☎44 3041 4960 **W:** radioglobomaringa.com.br **E:** radioglobo@radioglobomaringa.com.br – **PR33)** Rua Dom Bosco, 145 – Jd Dom Bosco, 86060-340 Londrina ☎ **W:** alvoradalondrina.rcr.org.br **E:** radioalvoradalondrina@gmail.com ☎43 3347 0303 – **PR34)** Rua Santa Catarina 970, 85960-000 Marechal Cândido Rondón ☎45 3284 8080 **W:** radiodifusora.com.br **E:** comercial@radiodifusora.net - **FM:** 95.1 MHz – **PR35)** Rua Araribóia, 1909 - Parque Santa Clara,(CP 540) 85505-030 Pato Branco ☎46 2101 2244 **W:** radiocelinauta.com.br **E:** comer-

cial@redecelinauta.com.br – **PR36)** Praça Generoso Marques 90, Galeria Andrade, Ed Claudia 1° andar, Centro, 80020-230 Curitiba ☎41 3322 8483 **W:** radiocolombo.com.br **E:** comercial@radiocolombo.com. br – **PR37)** Av Pedro Soccol, 542 - Centro, 85884-000 Medianeira ☎45 3264 1713 **W:** independenciaam.com.br – **PR38)** Rua Paraná, 650 - Centro, 874-000 Cruzeiro do Oeste ☎44 3676 1184 **W:** difusoraregional.com.br – **PR39)** Rua Visconde de Mauá, 123 - Jardim Shangrilá, 86070-540 Londrina ☎43 3328 1030 – **PR40)** Rua Ulisses Faria 1077, 83900-000 São Mateus do Sul ☎42 3532 1644 **W:** difusoradoxisto. com.br – **PR41)** Rua Maranhão, 2955 – Alto Alegre, 85805-220 Cascavel ☎45 3321 7000 ▤45 3226 5565 **W:** cbncascavel.com.br **E:** cantini@cbncascavel.com.br – **PR42)** Praça Senador Corrêa 128 (▨ CP 20548, 81810-980 Curitiba), 80230-130 Curitiba ☎41 3221 6070 **W:** padrereginaldomanzotti.org.br **E:** sas@evangelizarepreciso.com.br– **PR43)** Rua Bahia, 667 - Centro, 86690-000 Colorado ☎44 3323 1003 **W:** coloradoam.com.br –**PR44)** Rua Porto Alegre 21, Edifico Scala - 1° andar - Centro, 85601-480 Francisco Beltrão ☎46 3055 2255**W:** radioeducadorafb.com.br **E:** contato@radioeducadorefb.com.br – **PR45)** Rua Dario Antônio Bordin, 313 - Centro, 84600-000 União da Vitória ☎42 3521 2050 **W:** vvale.com.br/radiouniaoam/ **E:** gerente@radiouniaoam. com.br – **PR46)** Av Ivan Ferreira do Amaral, 331 - Centro,85400-000 Guaraniaçu ☎45 3232 1129 **W:** superrg.com.br **E:** comercial@superrg. com.br – **PR47)** Rua 15 de Novembro, 344 - Centro, 84010-020 Ponta Grossa ☎42 3225 2288 **W:** prj2.com.br – **PR48)** Rua Edson Martins, 1935 Esquina c/Avenida Parigot de Souza - Centro, 87703-420 Paranavaí ☎44 3423 6565 **W:** culturaparanavai.com.br **E:** am@culturaparanavai. com.br – **PR49)** Rua João Carlos Farias, 85 - Centro, 86300-000 Cornélio Procópio ☎43 3524 2333 **W:** terranativaam.com.br – **PR50)** Av Capitão Índio Bandeira, 1400 s 509 - Centro, 87300-005 Campo Mourão ☎44 3525 1413 **W:** radiocolmeiaam.com.br – **PR51)** Rua das Américas, 255 - Centro, 85550-000 Coronel Vivida ☎46 3232 1142 **W:** portalrvp.com.br **E:** atendimento@radiovicentepallotti.com.br – **PR52)** Av Higienópolis 2100, 86015-905 Londrina ☎43 3325 2555 **W:** paiquere.com.br **E:** paiquere@paiquere.com.br – **PR53)** Rua Quince de Novembro 2175 - 8° andar, 83005-000 São José dos Pinhais ☎41 3058 1120 **W:** radiomaisam1120.com.br **E:** radio@radiomais.am.br – **PR54)** Av Cristóvão Colombo 1055, 86990-000 Marialva ☎44 3232 1115 – **PR55)** Praça Manoel Ribas, 112 - Centro, 84165-510 Castro ☎42 3232 0556 **W:** radiocastro.com.br – **PR56)** Rua Machado de Assis, 25 – Centro, 86070-620 Londrina ☎43 3032 1500 **E:** radioglobolondrina. com.br – **FM:** 90.1 MHz – **PR57)** Av. Sete de Setembro, 3341 - Cristo Rei, 80050-315 Curitiba ☎41 3025 5770 **W:** radioatalaiacuritiba.com. br – **PR58)** Rua Raimundo Leonardi, 1301 - Centro, 85900-110 Toledo ☎45 3378 3161 **W:** radioguacu.com.br **E:** radioguacu@uol.com.br – **PR59)** Rua Valdir Santin, 309 - Centro, 87970-000 Nova Londrina ☎44 3432 1540 **W:** pontalweb.com.br **E:** contato@pontalweb.com.br – **PR60)** Rua João Negrão, 595 - Centro, 80010-200 Curitiba ☎41 3324 3849 **W:** superradiodeuseamor.com.br – **PR61)** Av Paraná, 596 - Centro, 85887-000 Matelândia ☎45 3262 1140 **W:** radiomatelandia. com.br **E:** radiomatelandia@matelnet.com.br – **PR62)** Rua Afonso Alves de Camargo 1175. Alta da XV, 85010-320 Guarapuava ☎42 3035 8000 **W:** difusoraguarapuava.com.br **E:** difusora@mattosleao.com.br – **PR63)** Av Paeaná, 271 an 1, 87704-100 Paranavaí ☎44 3422 3322 **W:** radioparanavai.com.br **E:** contato@radioparanavai.com.br – **PR64)** Rua Cedro 418, 85650-000 Santa Isabel do Oeste ☎46 3542 1239 **W:** radiodanubioazul.com.br **E:** radio@radiodanubioazul.com.br – **PR65)** Rua José Ferreira "Nhô Belo", 262- Centro, 86975-000 Mandaguari ☎44 3233 1180 **W:** radioguairaca.com.br **E:** guairaca@bwnet.com.br – **PR66)** Rua Marchal Deodora, 1272 - Centro, 86430-000 Santo Antônio da Platina ☎43 3534 4321 **W:** difusoraplatinense.com.br **E:** radiofmvaledosol@bol.com.br – **FM.:** 100.5MHz – **PR67)** Rua Pedro Eloy de Souza, 51 - Alto, 82820-130 Curitiba ☎41 3367 3663 **W:** grp-com.com.br/continental – **PR68)** Rua Rio Grande do Sul 1110, 85806-010 Cascavel ☎45 3224 2717 **W:** radioglobocascavel.com.br **E:** radio-cidade@certto.com.br – **PR69)** Rua Ponta Grossa 1682 1° Andar (▨ C.P. 71), 85601-600 Francisco Beltrão ☎46 3524 2676 **W:** seleski.com. br **E:** seleski@seleski.com.br – **PR70)** Av Pedro Taques, 1864 - Jd Alvorada 87033-000 Maringá ☎44 3267 3000 **W:** radioatalaia.com.br **E:** radioatalaiamaringa@hotmail.com – **PR71)** Rua XV de Novembro, 591 - Centro, 84010-020 Ponta Grossa ☎42 3028 1300 **W:** cbnpg.com. br **E:** cbnpg@cbnpg.com.br – **PR72)** Rua Ana Berta Rosekamp, 940 – Jardim Rosekamp, 81530-250 Curitiba ☎41 3266 1320 **W:** radiotropicalgospel.com.br **E:** comercial@radiobrasilsul.com.br – **PR73)** Rua Ébio Ferraz de Carvalho, 699 – Jardim Montecatine, 86031-720 Londrina ☎43 3378 2100 **W:** radiobrasilsul. com.br **E:** comercial@radiobrasilsul.com.br – **PR74)** Rua TV Silvério Carneiro, 3 - Centro, 84220-000 Cidade Sengés ☎43 3535 1144 – **PR75)** Rua Doutor Camargo 5152, 87502-010 Umuarama ☎44 3622 5033 **W:** radioinconfidenciaam.com.br **E:** nova@radioinconfidenciaam. com.br – **PR76)** Rua Exp Adir Jorge, 511 - Centro, 83880-000 Rio Negro ☎47 3642 3969 – **PR77)** Rua Flamingos 357, 86701-390 Arapongas ☎42 3252 0570 **W:** cultura1340.com.br– **PR78)** Av Paul Harris, 50 –

Conjunto Paraiso, 86220-000 Assaí ☎43 3262 1367 **W:** redeterranati-va.com **E:** radiolideram@hotmail.com.br – **PR79)** Rua Pedro Alvares Cabral 1574, 87560-000 Iporã ☎44 3652 1582 – **PR80)** Av. Marechal Floriano Peixa, 4809 - Vila Hauer, 81610-150 Curitiba ☎41 3091 1370 **W:** blog.cancaonova.com/curitiba **E:** radiocuritiba@cancaonova.com – **PR81)** Rua Paraíba, 168 - Centro, 86930-000 São João do Ivaí ☎43 3477 1117 **E:** radioeducadora1180@gmail.com – **PR82)** Av.Mauá, 1988 - Vila Operária, 87050-020 Maringa ☎44 3220 8061 – **FM:** 102.5MHz – **PR83)** Av Bertino Warmling, 1110 sala 02 - Centro, 85670-000 Salto do Lontra ☎46 3538 1320 **W:** rinet.com.br **E:** ricliente@slnet.com.br – **PR84)** Rua Pref Hugo Cabral, 192 - Centro, 86020-110 Londrina ☎43 3373 5500 **W:** radioglobolondrina.com.br **E:** radioglobolondrina@radioglobolondrina.com.br – **PR85)** Av Dep Ivan Ferreira do Amaral Filho, 86 - Centro, 85301-070 Laranjeiras do Sul ☎42 3635 1120 **W:** radioeducadora1120.com.br **E:** comercial@radioeducadora1120.com.br – **PR86)** Rua Simão Domingues, 26 - Centro, 84550-000 Rebouças ☎42 3457 1150 **W:** alvoradanoar.com.br **E:** comercial@alvoradanoar.com.br – **PR87)** Rua Azauri Guedez Pereira 1351, 85990-000 Terra Roxa ☎44 3645 1135 **E:** radiofronteiraam@hotmail.com – **PR88)** Rua Nicanor dos Santos Silva 4465, 87501-120 Umuarama ☎44 3624 4664 **W:** culturaumuarama.com.br – **PR89)** Rua Antônio Lemos, 807 - Centro, 86400-000 Jacarezinho ☎43 3525 0773 **W:** educadora1420.com.br **E:** radio1420@uol.com.br – **PR90)** Rua Dom Pedro I 420, 85710-000 Santo Antônio do Sudoeste ☎46 3563 1541 **W:** radioentrerios1170.com.br **E:** contato@radioentrerios1170.com.br – **PR91)** Rua Mato Grosso, 2229 - Centro, 85812-020 Cascavel ☎45 3220 1717 **W:** radiocolmeia.com.br **E:** radiocolmeia@brturbo.com – **PR92)** Rua V Pref V Pref Reginaldo G Nocera, 335 - Centro, 84261-020 Telêmaco Borba ☎42 3272 9000 **W:** radiocapitaldopapel.com.br – **PR93)** Rua Vicente Inácio Filho 241, 86360-000 Bandeirantes ☎43 3542 3233 **W:** radiocabiuna.com.br – **PR95)** Rua Mal Deodoro da Fonseca 717, 87550-000 Altônia ☎44 3659 3444 **W:** radiorainha.com.br – **PR96)** Rua Prof Cleto, 281 - Centro, 83203-070 Paranaguá ☎41 3423 4322 **W:** difusoraam1460.com.br **E:** administracao@difusoraam1460.com.br – **PR97)** Rua Coronel Dulcido 1101, 84010-908 Ponta Grossa ☎42 3225 2144 📠3222 7115 **W:** centraldoparana.com.br **E:** central@centraldoparana.com.br – **PR98)** Rua Doutor Munhoz da Rocha, 1601 - Centro, 86800-010 Apucarana ☎43 3023 2055 **W:** radioculturaapucarana.com.br **E:** contato@radiocultura-apucarana.com.br or amcultura@net21.com.br – **PR99)** Rua Jesuino Alves da Rocha Loures, 1764 - Centro, 85555-000 Palmas ☎46 3263 9000 **W:** clubam.com.br/ **E:** comercial@radioclubeamfm.com.br – **PR100)** Rua Acácio Nunes 1065, 85980-000 Guaíra ☎44 3642 2068 **W:** radioguaira.com.br **E:** radioguaira@gmail.com – **PR101)** Rua dos Andradas, 249 - Centro, 85640-000 Ampére ☎46 3547 1236 **W:** radio-ampere.com.br **E:** radioampere@ampernet.com.br – **PR102)** Av. Belo Horizonte 497, 87900-00 Loanda ☎44 3425 5252 **W:** guadalupeam.com.br **E:** guadelupeam@guadelupeam.com.br – **PR103)** Rua Nilo Sampaio, 531 - Centro, 84900-000 Ibaiti ☎43 3546 1291 **W:** radioeducadora1470.com **E:** contato@radioeducadora1470.com – **PR104)** Praça Nossa Senhora do Carmo, 99 - Centro, 85935-000 Assis Chateaubriand ☎44 3528 4477 **W:** radiojornalam.com.br **E:** atendimento@radiojornalam.com.br – **PR105)** Rua Ebano Pereira 157, 85200-000 Pitanga ☎43 3641 1739 **W:** radiopitanga.com.br **E:** radiopitanga@radiopitanga.com.br – **PR106)** Av. Interventor Mnoel Ribas, 115 - Centro,, 86730-000 Astorga ☎44 3234 3211 **W:** fmturquesa.com.br – **FM:** 93.9 MHz – **PR107)** Rua Ipiranga 91, 84600-000 União da Vitória ☎42 3522 1098 **W:** educadora1480.com.br **E:** contato@educadora1480.com.br – **PR108)** Rua João Carlos Farias, 85 - Centro, 86300-000 Cornélio Procópio ☎43 3524 2333 **W:** rc1490.com/ **E:** radiocornelio@uol.com.br – **PR109)** Rua 7 de Setembro, 42 - Centro, 83750-000 Lapa ☎41 3622 1918 📠41 3622 1918 **W:** legendaria.am.br – **PR110)** Avenida Paraná,540, 86925-000 Borrazópolis ☎43 3425 1233 **W:** radionovaera.com.br – **PR111)** Av, São João No. 1952 (✉C.P 121, 84400-970) 84400-000 Prudentópolis ☎42 3446 1547 **W:** radioesperancaam.com.br **E:** radioesperanca810@hotmail.yahoo.com – **PR112)** Rua Rouxinol 752, 86703-150 Arapongas ☎43 3055 2133 **W:** radioarapongas.com.br **E:** radioarapongas@uol.com.br – **PR113)** Rua João Ramos Piedad 120, 84950-000 Wenceslau Brás ☎43 3528 1105 **W:** educado-rawb.com.br **E:** contato@educadoraweb.com.br – **FM:**95.7MHz – **PR114)** Rua Dr Correis, 289 - Centro, 84500-000 Irati ☎42 3423 2533 **W:** difusoradeirati.com.br **E:** difusoraam@hotmail.com – **PR115)** Rua Florianópolis 1636, 85840-000 Céu Azul ☎45 3266 1489 **W:** uniaoam.com.br – **PR116)** Praça Cel. Macado, 10 - Centro, (✉ CP 55) 83370-000 Antonina ☎41 3432 1362 **W:** serradomaram1520.com **E:** radioserra-domar@yahoo.com.br – **PR117)** Av Souza Naves 890, 86870-000 Ivaiporã ☎43 3472 4366 **W:** radiouba.com.br – **PR118)** Rua 1° DE Maio 694, 85950-000 Palotina ☎44 3694 5266 **W:** vivaoeste.com.br **E:** vivaoeste@novaradiocultura.co.br – **PR119)** Rua Dom Pedro II, 1889 - Vila Dom Pedro II, 834608-380 Campo Largo ☎41 3392 1111 **W:** radioagapeam.com.br **E:**radioagapeam@brturbo.com.br – **PR120)** Rua Mauá, 2518 - Centro, 85770-000 Realeza ☎46 3543 1030 **W:** radioclu-

berza.com **E:** radioclube@wln.com.br – **PR121)** Rua Florianópolis, 1813 - Zona 02, 87200-000 Cianorte ☎44 3629 1317 **W:** radiocapital990.com.br **E:** radiocapitalam@hotmail.com – **PR122)** Praça Alfredo João Lazzarotto 100, 89490-000 Siqueira Campos ☎43 3571 1588 **W:** radio-bomjesus.com.br **E:** bomjesus@hotmail.com – **PR123)** Av. Redife, 434, 85830-970 Formosa do Oeste ☎41 3243 0950 **W:** pioneiraam.com.br **E:** radio@pioneiraam.com.br – **PR124)** Av Dambros e Piva, 946 85615-000 Marmeleiro ☎46 3525 1183 **W:** cristal.seleski.com.br **E:** radiocristal@wln.com.br – **PR125)** Av Brasil, 502 - Centro, 85760-000 Capanema ☎46 3552 1584 📠46 3552 1336 **W:** radiocapanema.com.br **E:** radio@radiocapanema.com.br – **PR126)** Rua Senador Pinheiro Machado, 1536 - Centro, 85010-100 Guarapuava ☎42 3035 8000 **E:** atalaia@mattos-leao.com.br – **PR127)** Rua do Comércio, 654 - Centro, 85660-000 Dois Vizinhos ☎46 3536 3131 **W:** educadoradv.com.br **E:** radio@educado-radv.com.br – **PR128)** Rua Benjamin Constant, 440 - Centro, 84500-000 Irati ☎42 9840 0002 **W:** radionajua.com.br **E:** radionajua@radionajua.com.br **FM:** 106.9MHz – **PR129)** Rua Sao Paulo 180, 86380-000 Andirá ☎43 3538 3522 **W:** culturaandira.com.br **E:** comercial@culturaandira.com.br – **PR130)** Rua São Paulo, 489 - Centro, 86840-000 Faxinal ☎📠43 3461 1291 **W:** radioclubedefaxinal.com.br – **PR131)** Rua Noruega, 98 - Centro, 86182-000 Cambé ☎43 3154 1772 **W:** cidadeam770.com.br – **PR132)** Rua Jacaranda, 498 - Centro, 85460-000 Quedas do Iguaçu ☎46 3532 1416 **W:** radiointernacional.com.br **E:** radiointernacionalam@hotmail.com – **PR133)** Praça Marechal Floriano Peixito 108, 84130-000 Palmeira ☎42 3252 3669 **W:** radioipiranga.com.br **E:** radioipiranga@br10.com.br – **PR134)** Rua Ivo Leão, 220 - Alto da Glória, 80030-180 Curitiba ☎41 3041 0743 **W:** radiorb2.com.br **E:** rb2@radiorb2.com.br - **FM:** 101.5MHz – **PR135)** Av Brasil, 740 - Centro, 84350-000 Ortigueira ☎42 3277 1366 **W:** radioplacar.com – **PR136)** Av Maximiliano Vicentin 240, 85270-000 Palmital ☎42 3657 1442 **W:** radiocidadepalmital.com.br **E:** radiopalmital@bol.com.br – **PR137)** Rua Melissa, 520 - Centro, 85410-000 Nova Aurora ☎45 3243 1233 **W:** clubamnovaaurora.com.br **E:** comercial@clubamnovaaurora.com.br – **PR138)** Avenida Brasil, 531 - Centro, 85851-000 Foz do Iguaçu ☎45 3572 2410 **W:** radiofiladelfia.com.br **E:** radioculturamorenafiladelfia@gmail.com – **PR139)** Rua Antônio Costa, 529 - Vista Alegere das Mercês, 80820-020 Curitiba ☎41 3240 7000 **W:** radiobandab.com.br **E:** bandad@radiobandab.com.br – **PR140)** Rua Urbano Lunardelli 875, 86160-000 Porecatu ☎43 3623 1050 **W:** radiobrotense.com.br **E:** ouvinte@radiobrotense.com.br – **PR141)** Av Paraná, 220 - Centro, 84470-000 Cândido de Abreu ☎43 3476 1244 **W:** alternativa710.com.br **E:** ralternativa@onda.com.br – **PR142)** Av Santos Dumont, 2505 - Centro, 85301-040 Laranjeiras do Sul ☎42 3635 1755 **W:** radiocampoaberto.com.br **E:** rca@radiocampoaberto.com.br – **PR143)** Av Genoroso Marques, 599, 2° andar, 85550-000 Coronel Vivida ☎46 3232 1564 **W:** radiovozdosudoeste.com.br/2011 – **PR144)** Rua Cet San Tiago Dantas, 159 - Centro, 85560-000 Chopinzinho ☎46 3242 1435 **W:** radiodifusoraamerica.com.br – **PR145)** Av Paraná, 201 – Jardim Itajubá, 85857-970 Foz do Iguaçu ☎45 3523 2211 **W:** cbnfoz.com.br **E:** administrativo@cbnfoz.com.br – **PR146)** Av Presidente Kennedy, 170 - Norte, 85950-000 Palotina ☎44 3649 0570 **W:** Facebook: R.Continental Palotina **E:** radiocontinentalam@hotmail.com – **PR147)** Av. Minas Gerais, 31- Centro, 85420-000 Corbélia ☎45 3242 1799 **W:** radiointegracao.net – **PR148)** Rua Farroupilha 80, 2° andar, 85877-000 São Miguel do Iguaçu ☎43 3565 1033 **W:** radiojornalsao-miguel.com.br **E:** rjcomercial@brturbo.com.br – **PR149)** Av Iguaçu, 288 - Centro, 85575-000 São Jorge d'Oeste ☎46 3534 1184 **W:** difusora-saojorge.com.br **E:** radiodifusora1490@hotmail.com – **PR150)** Av Sao Paulo, 440 - Centro, 87320-000 Roncador ☎44 3575 1341 **W:** prince-sa820.com.br – **FM:** 87.9 MHz – **PR151)** Av Nilza de Oliveira Pipino 4444, 87350-000 Ubiratã ☎44 3543 1133 – **PR152)** Rua Dom Pedro II, 1581 – Centro, 85901-270 Toledo. ☎45 3055 2240 **W:** radiointegraca-oam.com.br **E:** radiointegracao@uol.com.br – **PR153)** Rua Perfeito Pedro Rolim de Moura 104, 84240-000 Piraí do Sul ☎📠42 3237 1174 **W:** radiobrotas.net.br – **PR154)** Rua Sao Vicente, 83 – Alto da Gloria, (C.P 20) 87160-000 Mandaguaçu ☎44 3245 3265 **W:** colmeia1170am.com **E:** radio@colmeia1170am.com – **PR155)** Rua Rosalvo Petrechem, 551 - Centro, 85200-000 Pitanga ☎42 3646 3366.**W:** radiopoema.com.br **E:** radiopoema@radiopoema.com.br – **PR156)** Av Euclides da Cunha s/n, 87890-000 Terra Rica ☎44 3441 1991 **W:** brasilam.com.br **E:** radioguairaca@hotmail.com – **PR157)** Av Iguaçu 858, Ed Fabiane, 85585-000 Verê **W:** radiovaledoiguacu.com.br– **PR158)** Av Paraná, s/n - Centro, 86130-000 Bela Vista do Paraíso ☎43 3242 1818 **W:** nrbr.com.br **E:** br1570@hotmail.com – **PR159)** Rua Telêmaco Carneiro 1060 Ed. Moreira I - sala 4, 84990-000 Arapoti ☎43 3557 2055 **W:** radioara-potiam.com.br **E:** radioarapoti@yahoo.com.br – **PR160)** Av Iguaçu, 366 - Centro, 85790-000 Capitão Leônidas Marques ☎📠43 3286 1314 **W:** radiohawai.com.br – **PR161)** Rua Antonio Rosa 1170, 86490-000 Ribeirão do Pinhal ☎43 3551 1438 **W:** culturapinhal.com **E:** contat@culturapinhal.com – **PR162)** Rua Vicente Machado, 385 - Centro, 84570-000 Mallet ☎42 3542 2004 – **PR163)** Rua Marechal Deodoro,

22 - Centro, 85540-000 Mangueirinha ☎46 3243 1541 **W:** radioaraucaria.com.br – **PR164)** Rua São Miguel, 577 - Centro, 85570-000 São João ☎46 3533 1474 **W:** radiosaojoao.com.br **E:** radiosj@sudonet.com.br– **PR165)** Rua Guarani, 829 - Centro, 85501-050 Pato Branco ☎46 3225 4000 **W:** radiopatobranco.com.br **E:** ouvinte@radiopatobranco.com.br – **PR166)** Rua Pres Getúlio Vargas 807, Raia, 83206-020 Paranaguá ☎41 3424 2408 **W:** terranativasul.com.br **E:** falecom@terranativasul.com.br – **PR168)** Rua Octaviano Henrique de Carvalho, 2920 - Chopar, 83280-000 Guaratuba ☎41 3472 3275 ▤41 3472 3019 **W:** radiolitoranea.com.br **E:** radiolitoranea@gmail.com – **PR169)** Rua Ana Beje, 84300-000 Tibagi – ☎42 3275 3247 **W:** radioitay.com.br **E:** radioitay@radioitay.com.br – **PR170)** Av Vice-Prefeito Reginaldo Guedes Nocera, 84260-000 Telêmaco Borba ☎42 3910 1230 **W:** radionovamensagem.com.br – **PR171)** Av Londrina, 523 - Centro, 87111-220 Sarandi ☎44 3042 1090 **W:** banda1am.com.br – **PR172)** Rua José M.Soares 104, 85580-000 Itapejara d'Oeste ☎46 3526 1926 **W:** panoramaam.com.br **E:** radiopanorama@brturbo.com.br **PR173)** Rua Paraná 21, 83540-000 Rio Branco do Sul ☎41 3652 7070 **W:** radiotradicaoam.com.br **E:** comercial@radiotradicaoam.com.br– **PR174)** Rua Parigot de Souza, 47 - Centro, 86740 Pérola d'Oeste ☎46 3556 1048 **W:** radioperola.com.br **E:** contato@radioperola.com.br – **PR179)** Rua Pedro de Oliveira 938, 85440-000 Ubiratã ☎▤44 3543 1717 **W:** radiodifusoraubirata.com.br **E:** rdifusora@gmail.com –**PR184)** Rua José Carlos Colodel, 306 cj 5 - Vila Santa Terezina, 83501-140 Almirante Tamandaré ☎41 3699 6622 **W:** radiobarigui.com.br– **PR185)** Rua Santos Dumont, 268 – Centro, 86400-000 Jacarezinho/ PR ☎43 3525 0877 **W:** radioglobo1550.com.br **E:** contato@radioglobo1550.com.br – **PR186)** Rua Esado Unidas, 1768-A – Centro, 86181-100 Cambé ☎43 3154 1580 **W:** terranativacambe.com.br **E.** radioterranativacambe@gmail.com – **PR188)** Rua Vicente Inácio Filho, 241 – Altos da Vila Maria, (✉ CP 111) 86360-000 Bandeirantes ☎43 3542 3233 ▤43 3542 4730 **W:** radiocabiuna.com.br

RJ00) RIO DE JANEIRO

RJ01) Rua Visconde Itaboraí, 184 - Guaratiba, 23032-500 Niterói ☎21 2556 8131 **W:** ofluminense.com.br – **RJ02)** Rua Costa Rica, 151 - Parque Hotel, 28970-000 Araruama ☎22 2665 4119 **W:** radiocostadosol.com.br **E:** contato@radiocostadosol.com.br – **RJ03)** Estrada dos Bandeirantes, 1000 – Taquara, 22710-112 Rio de Janeiro ☎21 3412 1175 **W:** radiorelogiofederal.blogspot.no **E:** nossaradiorio@gmail.com – **RJ04)** Av.Erasmo Brage, 118, 11°andar – Centro 20020-000 Rio de Janeiro ☎21 2333 2094 **E:** faleconosco@94fm.rj.gov.br – **FM:** 94.1 MHz – **RJ05)** Av. Dr Jefferson Geraldo Bruno, s/n - Paraiso, 27365-015 Resende ☎24 3358 1600 **W:** radioagulhasnegras.com.br – **RJ06)** Praça Demerval Barbosa Moreira, 28 - Centro, 28610-160 Nova Friburgo ☎22 2523 3034 **W:** radiofriburgoam.com.br **E:** contato@novafriburgoam.com.br – **RJ07)** Rua General Gustavo Cordeiro de Farias, 84 - Benfica, 20910-220 Rio de Janeiro ☎21 2567 2000 – **RJ08)** Rua Vinte e Um de Abril, 272 An 4 Sl 413 - Centro, 28010-170 Campos dos Goytacazes – ☎22 2723 8080 **W:** radioabsoluta.com.br – **RJ09)** Rua México 111 slj, Centro, 20031-145 Rio de Janeiro ☎21 2220 3656 **W:** redesucesso.com **RJ11)** Rua de Assembléia, 10/3401 - Centro, 20011-001 Rio de Janeiro ☎21 3572 0760 ▤21 3572 0770 **W:** radiomanchete.com.br **E:** comercial@radiomanchete.com.br – **RJ12)** Rua da Relação, 18 – 12° andar - Centro, 20231-110 Rio de Janeiro ☎21 2117-6202 ▤21 2117 6235 **W:** radios.ebc.com.br – **RJ13)** Av Rui Barbosa, 749 - 3°andar - Centro, 27910-361 Macaé ☎22 3311 3145 **W:** radioglobomacae.com.br **E:** comercial@radioglobomacae.com.br – **RJ14)** Rua do Russel, 434 - Glória, 22210-010 Rio de Janeiro ☎21 2555 8282 – **FM:** 92.5 MHz **W:** RJ15) Rua Prof Eurico Rabelo, s/n - Maracanã", 20271-150 Rio de Janeiro ☎21 4002 4190 **W:** radiotamoio.com.br – **RJ16)** Av. Marchal Floriano, 114 - Centro, 20080-002 Rio de Janeiro **W:** boavontade.com.br **E:** superrbv@boavontade.com – **RJ17)** Rua de Relação, 18 – 12° andar - Centro, 20231 110 Rio de Janeiro ☎21 2117 6202 **W:** radios.ebc.com.br/nacionalrioam – **RJ18)** Rua Senador Pompeu, 27 - Centro, 20008-010 Rio de Janeiro ☎21 2263 7521 **W:** radiocapitalrio.com.br – **RJ19)** Travessa Santa Luiza 91, 23900-900 Angra dos Reis ☎24 3365 1352 – **RJ20)** Rua Buenos Aires, 68 - 19° andar - Centro, 20070-020 Rio de Janeiro ☎21 3171 1060 **W:** blog.cancaonova.com/riodejaneiro **E:** radioespiritosanto@cancaonova.com – **RJ21)** Av Deputada Alair Ferreira, 201 - Parque Turf Club, 28024-600 Campos dos Goitacazes ☎22 2723 8989 – **RJ22)** Estrada Adhemar Bebiano (ex-Estr. Velha da Pavuna), 3517 - Inhaúma, 20765-170 Rio de Janeiro ☎21 2176 8276 **W:** metropolitana1090.com **E:** contato@metropolitana1090.com.br –**RJ23)** Av Alair Ferreira, 201 - Turf-Club, 28015-020 Campos dos Goitacazes ☎22 2728 1110 **W:** radiorecord1110.weebly.com **E:** producaoradiorecordcampos@gmail.com – **RJ24)** Rua Presidente Vargas, 541 - Centro, 25802-220 Três Rios ☎24 2252 0720 **W:** Facebook: Radio 3 Rios **E:** rtr@radiotresrios.com.br – **FM:** 89.7MHz – **RJ25)** Rua da Assembléia, 10–Sala 1201 – Centro,20011-901 Rio de Janeiro ☎21 3799 1180 **W:** mundial1180.com.br – **RJ26)** Rua dos

Andrades, 109 - 3°andar - Centro, 28010-300 Campos dos Goitacazes ☎22 2733 1270 **W:** radiocontinentalam.com.br **E:** continental1270@yahoo.com.br **RJ27)** Rua do Livramento, 189 8°andar - Gamboa, 20221-194 Rio de Janeiro ☎21 2126 2421 **W:** tupi.am – **FM:** 96.5 MHz – **RJ28)** Rua Alberto Torres, 410 an3°- Centro, 28400-000 São Fidelis ☎22 2758 1275 **W:** radiocoroadosam.com **E:** radiocoroadosam1310@hotmail.com – **RJ29)** Av 28 de Setembro, 258–Loja 01 - Vila Isabel, 20551-031 Rio de Janeiro ☎21 2576 9737 **W:** radioboasnovas.com.br **E:** comercial@radioboasnovas.com.br – **RJ30)** Rua Alvaro Ramos, 350 - Botafogo, 22280-110 Rio de Janeiro ☎21 2543 1360 – **RJ31)** Rua Carlos de Lacerda, 52 –an 2°- Centro, 28010-242 Campos de Goytacazes ☎22 3055 0091 **W:** radiocamposdifusora.com **E:** angeladifusora@yahoo.com.br – **RJ32)** Av.Joaquim Leite, 465 – ap 101 - Centro, 27345-391 Barra Mansa ☎24 3323 3300 ▤24 3323 1152 **W:** sulfluminense.com.br **E:** comrcial@sulfluminense.com.br- **FM:** 96.1MHz – **RJ33)** Estrada do Dendê, 659-Tauá - Ilha do Governador, 21920-000 Rio de Janeiro ☎21 3386 1400 **W:** radioriodejaneiro.am.br **E:** marketing@radioriodejaneiro.am.br – **RJ34)** Av Cardoso Moreira, 422-Sobrado - Centro, 28300-000 Itaperuna ☎24 3824 1410 **W:** radioitaperuna1410.blogspot.no **E:** radioitaperunaam@gmail.com – **RJ35)** Rua do Mercado, 34-Sala 802, Centro - 20010-120 Rio de Janeiro ☎21 2233 8822 **W:** radiolivream.com.br **E:** falecom@radiolivream.com.br – **RJ36)** Av Joaquim Leite, 279 - Centro, 27330-042 Barra Mansa **W:** radiodocomercio.com.br **E:** atendimento@radiodocomercio.com.br ☎24 3323 3848 – **RJ37)** Rua Dr Temistocles de Almeida, 97 – Centro, 28470-000 Santo Antônio de Pádua ☎22 3853 3173 **W:** radiofeliz.com.br – **RJ38)** Rua Ana Nery, 120 9° andar - Centro, 27123-150 Barra do Piraí ☎24 2443 1470 ▤24 2401 8367 **W:** gruporbp.com **E:** radiobpfm@gmail.com - **FM:** 89.9MHz – **RJ39)** Rua Senador Dantas 117, cob 02, Nova Iguaçú ☎21 2767 3333 **W:** tropical830am.com.br **E:** tropical@tropical830am.com.br – **RJ40)** Av Sete de Maio, 702 sala 301 - Centro, 28800-000 Rio Bonito ☎21 2734 1693 **W:** radio1340.com.br – **RJ41)** Rua Lúcio Bittencourt, 107 an 2 – Vila Santa Cecilia, 27260-119 Volta Redonda ☎24 3348 9533 **W:** Facebook: R.Soc. de Volta Redonda – **FM:** 101.5 MHz – **RJ42)** Rua Cardoso 357, 28013-460 Campos dos Goytacazes ☎22 2733 9072 **W:** cancaonova.com/campos – **RJ43)** Rua Rui Barbosa, 184 loja1 - Várzea, 25963-090 Teresópolis ☎21 2643 5555 **W:** radioteresopolis.com.br **E:** radioteresopolisam@gmail.com – **RJ44)** Rua Carvalho de Souza, 20 an 3° - Madureira, 21350-180 Rio de Janeiro ☎21 3390 1422 **W:** continental1520.com.br **E:** contato@continental1520.com.br – **RJ45)** Rua Paulino Padilha, 80 - Centro, 28460-000 Miracema ☎22 3852 0899 **W:** princesinhaam.com.br **E:** radioprincesinha@yahoo.com.br – **RJ46)** Rua Marechal Deodoro, 46 an 9°salas 905, 25620-150 Petrópolis ☎24 2237 6161 ▤24 2237 6161 **W:** http//radioimperiala.com.br **E:** imperialam@compuland.com.br – **RJ47)** Rua Francisco Belisário, 439 – Santa Cruz, 23570-510 Rio de Janeiro ☎21 3395 1560 **W:** granderioam.com **E:** dmxrio@yahoo.com.br – **RJ48)** Rua Carneiro de Mendonça. 29-A - Centro, 27600-000 Valença ☎24 2453 4418 **W:** radioculturadovale.com.br – **RJ49)** Rua Tenente José Teixeira, 147-an 1° - Centro, 28360-000 Bom Jesus do Itabapoana ☎22 3831 1570 **W:** bomjesusam.com.br – **RJ50)** Rodovia Barão 101, s/n Km 206 - Centro, 28860-000 Casimiro de Abreu ☎22 2778 5101 – **RJ51)** Rua Frei Valerio, 58 - Centro, 28740-00 Conceição de Macabu ☎22 2779 2100 **W:** popularfluminens.com **E:** frpfluminense@yahoo.com.br – **RJ52)** Av Nilo Peçanha, 320 an 3° - Campos Eliseos, 27542-210 Resende ☎24 3354 7532 **W:** rlr2.com.br **FM:** 90.5 MHz – **RJ53)** Rua Gal.Gustavo C.Farias, 84 - Benfica, 20910-220 Rio de Janeiro ☎21 2582 0990 **W:** radiorecordrj.com.br **E:** aovivo@radiorecordrj.com – **RJ54)** Rua Barão Piabanha, 107 Anexo 1 Mini Shopping - Centro, 25850-000 Paraíba do Sul ☎24 2263 2343 **W:** radioclube1540.br **E:** radioclube1540@hotmail.com – **RJ55)** Rua Gal Dionísio, 327 - Guaratiba, 23025-330 Duque de Caxias ☎21 3652 1480 – **RJ56)** Rua Berlindo Figueira de Barros 100, 28250-000 Italva ☎22 2783 1777 **W:** aliancaam.com.br **E:** superaliancaam@yahoo.com.br – **RJ57)** Praça Porto Rocha, 56, Apt 102 - Centro, 28905-250 Cabo Frio ☎22 2645 4000 **W:** radiocabofrio.com.br **E:** contato@radiocabofrio.com.br **RJ58)** Rua Coronel Santiago, 250 - Agriões, 25963-220 Teresópolis ☎21 2642 2000 **W:** radiogeracao2000.com.br – **RJ59)** Av.Djalma Beda Combe, 719 – Centro, 28500-000 Cantagalo ☎22 2555 4455 – **RJ61)** Rua do Russel, 434 – Gloria, 22210-010 Rio de Janeiro ☎21 2461 1220 **W:** globoradio.com.br **E:** minhaglobo@radioglobo.com.br - **FM:** 98.1 MHz

RN00) RIO GRANDE DO NORTE

RN01) Av Duque de Caxias, 106 - Ribeira, 59010-200 Natal ☎84 4006 6100 **W:** radioglobonatal.com.br **E:** comercial@radioglobonatal.com.br – **RN02)** Praça Dom José Delgado, s/n , 59300-000 Caicó ☎84 3471 2401 **W:** radiorural.com **E:** comercial@radiorural.com - **FM:** 95.0 MHz – **RN03)** Rua Luiz XV, 10 - Nordeste, 59042-070 Natal ☎84 3653 3780 **W:** nordesteevangelica.com.br **E:** nordeste@nordesteevangelica.com.br – **RN04)** Rua João Pessoa, 22, 1° andar - Centro, 59380-000 Currais

Novos ☎84 3431 1720 **W:** radiocurraisnovosam.com **E:** radiocurrais-novosam@hotmail.com – **RN05)** Praça Vigário Antonio Joaquim, 39 - Centro, 59600-520 Mossoró ☎84 8723 7993 **W:** ruraldemossoro.com.br **E:** gerencial@ruraldemossoro.com.br – **RN06)** Rua Augusto da Escossia Nogueira Neto, 2141,, 59625-750 Mossoró ☎84 3312 4618 **W:** redepotiguar.com.br – **RN07)** Rua Açú, 335 - Tirol, 59020-110 Natal ☎84 3201 1690 **W:** blog.cancaonova.com/natal **E:** radionatal@cancaonova.com – **RN08)** Av Dr Cunha Mota, s/n - Pereiros, 59600-160 Mossoró ☎📠84 3317 6167 **W:** portaldifusoramossoro.com**E:** difusora@difusoramossore.com.br – **RN09)** Rua Romualdo Galvão, 973 - Lagoa Seca, 59056-100 Natal ☎84 3211 6400 **W:** cbnnatal.com.br – **E:** cbn@redetropical.com.br – **RN10)** Av Deodoro, 245, 59012-600 Natal **W:** redeclubebrasil.blogspot.no – **RN11)** Praça Desembargador Tomáz Salustino, 42 - Centro, 59380-000 Currais Novos ☎84 3431 1266 – **RN12)** Rua Francisca Delfina, 30 - Centro, 59860-620 Alexandria ☎84 3381 2321 **W:** redepotiguar.com.br **E:** comercial@rederpc.com.br – **RN13)** Pc Bento Praxedes, 104 – Centro, 59600-182 Mossoró ☎84 3321 3133 **W:** libertadoraevangelica.com.br **E:** radio.libertadora@gmail.com – **RN14)** Rua Otávio Amorim, 643 - Centro, 59650-000 Açu ☎84 3331 1223 **W:** radioprincesadovale.com.br **E;** contato@radioprincesadovale.com.br **RN15)** Rua Nero Nazareno Fernandes, 250 – Alto de Liberdade, 59780-0100 Caraúbas ☎📠84 3337 2297 **W:** rpccentenario.com.br/ **E:** rpccentenario@hotmail.com – **RN16)** Rua Frei Alberto Cabral, 08 - Centro, 59215-000 Nova Cruz ☎📠 84 3281 2123 – **RN17)** Rua Getúlio Vargas, 1296-Centro, 59900-000 Pau dos Ferros ☎📠84 3351 2388 **W:** culturadooeste.com.br – **RN18)** Rua Major Lula, Centro, 59300-000 Caicó ☎84 3421 2500 **W:** radioserido.com.br **E:** daguisoares@hotmail.com – **RN19)** Rua Avinida Rio Branco, 173 - Centro, 59655-000 Areia Branca ☎📠84 3312 4618 **W:** redepotiguar.com.br **E:** comecial@rederpc.com.br – **RN20)** Rua Ana de Pontes, 419, 59255-000 Santo Antônio ☎84 3282 2347 – **RN21)** Rua Odorico Férreira de Souza, 70 - Bairro DNER, 59200-000 Santa Cruz ☎84 3291 2300 **W:** radiosantacruzam.com.br **E:** radiosantacruzam@yahoo.com.br – **RN22)** Rua Experidião Coimbra, 22 - Centro, 59500-000 Macau ☎84 3521 1765 **W:** redetropical.com.br – **RN23)** Rua Cícero Tomáz de Azevedo, 1052 - Cruz do Monte, 59360-000 Parelhas ☎84 3471 2401 **W:** ruralam.com.br **E:** ruraldeparelhas@hotmail.com – **RN24)** Rua Heráclito Vilar, Centro, 59570-000 Ceará Mirim ☎84 3274 2794 – **RN25)** Rua Sebastião Guilherme Caldas, s/n – Baixa da Beleza, 59343-000 Jardim do Seridó ☎📠84 3472 2587 **W:** radiocabugidoserido.com **E:** cabugidoserido@yahoo.com.br – **RN26)** A. Cel Martiniano, 1077 - Centro, 59300-000 Caicó ☎84 3421 4181 **W:** radiocaico.com.br **E:** gizeldaa@hotmail.com – **RN27)** Rua Presidente Quaresma, 708 – Alecrim, 59031-150 Natal ☎84 3213 8911 – **RN28)** Rua Deputado Hésiquio Fernandes, Centro, 59930-000 São Miguel ☎84 3353 2112 **W:** radiodifusoradesaomiguel.blogspot.com.br – **RN29)** Av Ouro Branco, 430 - Centro, 59460-000 São Paulo do Potengi 84 3251 2381**W:** radiopotengi.com.br – **RN30)** Av 21 de Abril 460, BR-460, 59550-000 João Câmara ☎ 📠84 3262 2189 – **RN31)** Rua Joel do Amaral Gurgel, 2512 - Cohab, 59700-000 Apodi ☎84 3333 2512 **W:** radiovaledoapodi.com.br – **RN32)** Rua do Chafariz 1390, Bairro Novo Horizonte, 59584-000 Touros ☎84 3263 2121 **W:** R.Farol AM 1390 **E:** radiofarolgerencia@hotmail.com

RO00) RONDÔNIA
RO01) Rua José Bonifácio, 787 – Olaria, 78902-280 Porto Velho ☎69 3224 1887 **W:** rbn-pvh.com.br – **RO02)** Av Dr Miguel Vieira Pereira, 5927 – Cidade Alta, 78987-000 Rolim de Moura ☎69 3442 1122 – **RO03)** Av Jamari, 4218, 78932-000 Ariquemes ☎69 3536 3385 **W:** radioariquemes.com **E:** amauri@ariquemes.com.br – **RO04)** Rua Capitão Silvio, 145 - Centro, 76900-117 Ji-Paraná ☎69 3421 5233 **W:** radioalvoradajp.com.br **E:** contato@radioalvorada.com.br – **RO05)** Rua Rui Barbosa, 3375 - Floresta, 76965-736 Cacoal ☎69 3441 2122 **W:** portalradiorondonia.com.br – **RO06)** Rua Feijo, 2930 - Cafézinho, 76913-152 Ji-Paraná ☎69 3424 0432 **W:** radiojiparana.com.br **E:** radiojiparana@uol.com.br – **RO09)** Praça Mário Correa, 90 - Cristo Rei, 76850-000 Guajará Mirim ☎69 3541 2670 **W:** radioeducadoraam.com **E:** radio2@dariodamanha.net – **RO10)** Rua Dourados 4, Setor Industriales, 78930-000 Ariquemes ☎69 3535 3000 **W:** portalradiorondonia.com – **RO11)** Av. Nações Unidas,605 - Nossa Senhora das Graças, 76804-175 Porto Velho ☎69 3210 3621 **W:** radiocaiari.com **E:** radiocaiari@gmail.com – **RO12)** Rua Princesa Isabel, 128, 78995-000 Vilhena ☎69 3321 3309 **W:** radiovilhena.com.br **E:** radiovilhena@brturbo.com.br – **RO15)** Rua Carlos Doneje 1304, Ctg, 78984-000 Pimenta Bueno ☎69 3222 5308 **W:** radiorondonia.com.br **E:** comercialpb@radiorondonia.com.br – **RO16)** Rua 1005, 1522 - Setor Pioneira (✉ C.P. 105), 76980-000 Vilhena ☎69 3322 2589 **W:** plansol.com.br **E:** plansol@hotmail.com – **RO17)** Av. Calama esquina com Rafael Vaz e Silva, 2666 – Liberdade, 76803-884 Porto Velho ☎69 2182 0300 **W:** radiogloboro.com.br **E:** radiogloboro@hotmail.com – **RO18)** Rua 6 de Maio,1811 - Casa Preta (✉ C.P. 163), 76980-000 Ji-Paraná ☎69 3421 1390 **W:** plansol.com.br – **RO19)** Rua Sergipe, 1766 - Morada do Sol, 78983-000 Espigão d'Oeste ☎69 3481

3348 **W:** radiosociedadeespigao.com.br **E:** contate@radiosociedade-espigao.com.br – **RO23)** Rua Anel Viario, 1782, Parque Brizon, 78975-000 Cacoal ☎69 3443 2928 **W:** radiosuprema.com.br **E:** estudio@radiosuprema.com.br

RR00) RORAIMA
RR01) Av Capitão Ene Garcez, 888 - São Francisco, 69304-000 Boa Vista ☎95 3224 1651 **W:** radiororaima.com.br – **RR02)** Rua Sebastião Diniz, 363 - Centro, 69360-000 Caracaraí – **RR03)** 69350-000 Alto Alegre – **RR04)** Rua Lobo D´Almada, 43 - Sao Francisco, 69035-050 Boa Vista ☎95 3623 8801 📠95 3623 8801 **W:** folhabv.com **E:** radiofolha@folhabv.com.br

RS00) RIO GRANDE DO SUL
RS01) Av Víctor Barreto, 3056 Conj 207 - Centro, 92010-000 Canoas ☎51 3059 5677 **W:** radiorealam.com.br **E:** bruno@radiorealam.com.br – **RS02)** Rua Antunes Ribas, 1535-an 3° - Centro, 98801-630 Santo Angelo ☎55 3313 3666 **W:** radiosepe.com.br **E:** contato@radiosepe.com.br – **RS03)** Rua Marechal Deodoro, 1157 - Centro, 96810-110 Santa Cruz ☎51 3715 5958 **W:** radiosantacruz.com.br **E:** gerencia@radiosantacruz.com.br – **RS04)** Rua General Sampaio, 161 - Rio Branco, 95097-000 Caxias do Sul ☎54 3220 9400 📠54 2101 5236 **W:** redesul.am.br/Sao-Francisco **E:** redsul@saofrancisco.am.br - **FM:** 98.5MHz – **RS05)** Av. Sete de Setembro 509, 99010-121 Passo Fundo ☎54 3316 4800 **W:** diarioam570.com.br **E:** diretoria@diariodamanha.net – **FM:** 98.7 MHz – **RS06)** Av Mascarenhas de Morães, 586 - Centro, 97300-000 São Gabriel ☎55 3232 6336 **W:** redetche.com.br – **RS07)** Avenida Moreira Paz, 726 (✉ C.P. 67), 95200-000 Vacaria ☎54 3231 7500 **W:** redesul.am.br/Fatima-AM **E:** gerente@fatima.am.br – **RS08)** Praça Oswaldo Aranha, 39 - Centro, 97541-540 Alegrete ☎55 3422 1600 **W:** redetche.com.br/alegrete **E:** joaoulisses@radioalegrete.com.br – **RS09)** Av Ipiranga, 1075-an3° - Azenha, 90160-093 Porto Alegre ☎51 3218 6600 **W:** clicrbs.com.br **E:** gaucha@rdgaucha.com.br – **RS10)** Rua Andrade Neves, 2316-Centro 96020-080 Pelotas ☎53 3222 7407 **W:** radiopelotense.com.br **E:** radiopelot@terra.com.br – **RS11)** Rua Suécia, 255 - Centro, 98500-000 Tenente Portela ☎55 3551 1395 **W:** radiomunicipalam.com **E:** sec@radiomunicipalam.com – **RS12)** Rua 14 de Julho, 588 – Centro, 95300-000 Lagoa Vermelha ☎📠54 3358 6900 **W:** redesul.am.br/Cacique-AM **E:** cacique@cacique.am.br – **RS13)** Rua Paul Harris, 02 - Centro, 97015-480 Santa Maria ☎55 3220 2131 **W:** radiosantamariense.com.br **E:** radiosantamariense@terra.com.br – **RS14)** Rua Delfino Riet, 183 - Santo Antonio, 90660-120 Porto Alegre ☎51 3218 2100 **W:** band.com.br/rs – **RS15)** Av Mauricio Cardoso, 88 1° andar - Centro, 99700-000 Erechim ☎54 3321 2243 **W:** radiodifusoasul.com.br - **FM:** 94.9 MHz – **RS16)** Rua Voluntários da Patria, 1432 - Centro, 97590-000 Rosário do Sul ☎55 3231 2533 **W:** radiomaraja.com **E:** contacto@radiomaraja.com – **RS17)** Rua Farroupilha, 110 - Centro, 95200-000 Vacaria ☎54 3231 2828 **W:** radioesmeralda.com.br **E:** comercial@radioesmeralda.com.br - **FM:** 93.1MHz – **RS18)** Rua Neita Ramos, 217 - Centro, 96230-000 Santa Vitória do Palmar ☎53 3263 1660 **W:** redemeridional.com/sta.html **E:** culturasantavitoria@redemeridional.com – **RS19)** Rua Domingos Secchi, 35 - Boa Vista, 99500-000 Carazinho **W:** gazeta670.com.br **E:** comercial@gazeta670.com.br ☎54 3330 3143 – **RS20)** Travessa 4 de Junho, 84 - Centro, 98380-000 Seberi ☎55 3746 1040 📠55 3746 1033 **W:** seberiam.com **E:** diretor@seberiam.com.br – **RS21)** Rua 15 de Novembro, 275, 9° andar - Centro 98700-000 Ijuí ☎55 3332 9999 **W:** radioprogresso.com.br **E:** contato@radioprogresso.com.br – **RS22)** Rua Mascarenhas de Morães, 298 - Centro, 97300-000 São Gabriel ☎55 3232 2244 **W:** radiobatovi.com.br **E:** radiobatovi@terra.com.br – **RS23)** Rua Caldas Jr., 219 - Centro, 90019-900 Porto Alegre ☎51 3215 6320 **W:** radioguaiba.com.br **E:** guaibeiro@radioguaiba.com.br - **FM:** 101.3MHz – **RS24)** Rua Coronel Chicuta, 436 5° andar - Centro, 99010-051 Passo Fundo ☎54 3045 3088 **W:** rdplanalto.com **E:** am@rdplanalto.com - **FM:** 105.9MHz – **RS25)** Av Júlio de Castilhos, 435 - Vila Vista Alegre, 98300-000 Palmeira das Missões **W:** radiopalmeira.com.br **E:** am740@radiopalmeira.com.br ☎55 3742 2255 - **FM:** 101.7MHz – **RS26)** República do Libano, 240 - Centro, 96200-340 Rio Grande ☎53 3232 2303 **W:** radioculturariograndina.com.br **E:** radioculturariograndina@vetorial.net – **RS27)** Av Marechal Floriano, 920-Sala 301 - Centro, 95520-000 Osório ☎51 3663 3435 **W:** radioosorio.com.br **E:** radioosori@hotmail.com – **RS28)** Rua Botucaraí, 911 - Centro, 96930-000 Candelária ☎51 3743 1900 **W:** princesacandelaria.com.br – **RS29)** Av Gal Daltro Filho, 1000 - Centro, 98470-000 Planalto ☎55 3794 1025 **W:** radioametista.com.br **E:** contato@radioametista.com.br – **RS30)** Rua Pedro Vargas, 846 - Centro, 99500-000 Carazinho ☎54 3331 5250 **W:** diarioam780.com.br **E:** radio2@dariodamanha.net – **RS31)** Rua Orfanatrófio, 711 – Alto Teresópolis , 90840-440 Porto Alegre ☎51 3218 2620 **W:** pampa.com.br/caicara **E:** ouvintrcaicara@pampa.com.br – **RS32)** Rua Senhor dos Passos, 34, 96640-000 Rio Pardo ☎51 3731 3790 **W:** Facebook: R.Rio Pardo AM **E:** radioriopardo@hotmaul.com – **RS33)** Av Roraima, 1000-Cidade Universitária - Camboi, 97105-900 Santa Maria ☎51 3220 8550 **W:** coral.ufsm.br/radio/ **E:** radio800am@

ufsn.br – **RS34)** Rua Max Henrique Erichsen, 38 sala 101 - Oriental, 95880-000 Estrela – ☎51 3712 1259 **W:** 820dovale.com.br **E:** ouvinte@820dovale.com.br – **RS35)** Av Presidente Vargas, 892 - Centro, 98005-160 Cruz Alta ☎55 3322 1803 **W:** radioindependente.am.br – **RS36)** Av Julio de Castilhos, 607 – Centro Historico,, 90030-131 Porto Alegre ☎51 3284 0772 **W:** radiocapital.net **E:** contato@radiocapital.net – **RS37)** Caladão Salvador Isaia, 1330 - 3° andar, 97010-902 Santa Maria ☎55 3025 5757 **W:** guarathan.com.br **E:** guarathan@terra.com.br– **RS38)** Rua Álvaro Guaspari, 80 – Marcilio Dias, 90035-020 Porto Alegre ☎51 3024 7421 **W:** radioitai.com.br **E:** radioitairs@gmail.com – **RS39)** Rua Osvaldo Aranha, 808 Sala 102B – Juventud, 95700-000 Bento Gonçalves ☎54 3452 7777 **W:** difusora890.com.br **E:** contato@difusora890.com.br – **RS40)** Praça da Bandeira, 36 - Centro, 98900-000 Santa Rosa ☎55 3512 5757 **W:** jornalnoroeste.com **E:** faleconosco@jornalnoroeste.com.br– **FM:** 97.7 Guaíra – **RS41)** Rua XV de Novembro, 336, 99770-000 Aratiba ☎54 3376 1138 **W:** radioaratiba.com.br am.900@hotmail.com – **RS43)** Rua 7 de Setembro, 1441 - Centro, 95800-000 Venâncio Aires ☎51 3741 2000 **W:** radiovenancioaires.com.br **E:** rva@radiovenancioaires.com.br**RS44)** Av.Fernandes Bastos, 1683–Sobreloja - Centro, 95590-000 Tramandaí ☎51 3661 5657 **W:** Facebook: Radio Tramandaí AM 920 **E:** radiotramandai@hotmail.com **W:** 97.1 MHz – **RS45)** Rua Garibaldi, 789-21° andar, Ed. Estrela - Centro, 95084-900 Caxias do Sul ☎54 3289 3000 **W:** radiocaxias.am.br **E:** radiocaxias@radiocaxias.am.br – **FM:** 93.5 MHz –**RS46)** Av. Brasil, 523 - Centro, 98801-590 Santo Ângelo ☎55 3313 2440 **W:** radiosantoangelo.com.br **E:** radiosan@radiosantoangelo.com.br – **RS47)** Av Alberto Müller, 242 – Alto do Parque, 95900-000 Lajeado ☎51 3710 4900 **W:** independente.com.br **E:** recepcao@independente.com.br – **RS48)** Av. Walter Jobim, 222 s 106 – Patronato, 97020-425 Santa Maria ☎55 3212 6060 **W:** imembui.com.br –**RS49)** Rua Orfanatrófio, 711 - Teresópolis, 90840-440 Canoas ☎51 3233 8899 **W:** radiopampa.com.br/pampa/ **E:** pampa@pampa.com.br – **RS50)** Av Getúlio Vargas, 412 - Centro, 98670-670 Humaitá ☎55 3525 1212 **W:** radioaltouruguai.com.br **E:** 970am@radioaltouruguai.com.br – **FM:** 92.5 MHz – **RS51)** Rua Otacílio Tupanciretã de Azevedo, 2 - Centro, 98170-970 Tupanciretã ☎55 3272 1763 **W:** tupa.am.br **E:** contato@tupa.am.br –**RS52)** Rua Fiorentino Bachi, 791 - Centro, 99840-000 Sananduva ☎54 3343 1438 **W:** radiosananduva.com.br **E:** contato@radiosananduva.com.br – **FM:** 97.7MHz –**RS53)** Rua Garibaldi, 789 21° andar - Centro, 95084-900 Caxias do Sul ☎54 3289 3000 **W:** radio1010.am.br –**RS54)** Rua Julio de Castilhos, 2236 - Centro, 97800-000 São Luís Gonzaga ☎55 3352 4141 **W:** radiomissioneira.com **E:** atendimento@radiomissioneira.com – **RS55)** Av David José Martins, 1206 - Centro, 98700-000 Iraí ☎55 3332 8000 **W:** radioreporter.com.br **E:** atendimento@grupooreporter.com.br – **FM:** 101.5MHz «Iguatemi» – **RS56)** Rua General Zeca Netto, 1396 - Centro, 96180-000 Camaquã ☎51 3671 0962 **W:** redemeridional.com **E:** radiocamaquense@redemeridional.com – **RS57)** Rua São João, 1894- Centro, 97800-000 São Luís Gonzaga ☎55 3352 4444 **W:** radiosaoluiz.com **E:** redacao@radiosaoluiz.com **RS58)** Rua General Osório, 625 - Centro, 96570-000 Caçapava do Sul ☎55 3281 1495 **W:** redemeridional.com/cacapava.html **E:** radiocacapava@redemeridional.com –**RS59)** Rua Tucunduva, 758 - Centro, 98640-000 Crissiumal ☎55 3524 1212 **W:** metropole1070.com.br – **RS60)** Rua Marechal Deodoro, 101 7° andar - Centro, 95700-000 Bento Gonçalves **W:** radioviva.com.br **E:** geral1070@radioviva.com.br ☎54 3455 3999 – **RS61)** Rua João Carlos Machado, 645 - Centro, 98460-000 Iraí ☎55 3745 1444 **W:** radiomaraba.com.br **E:** maraba@speedrs.com.br – **RS62)** Rua Sarmento Leite, 426 - Centro, 90046-900 Porto Alegre ☎51 3316 3435 ☎51 3308 3017 **W:** ufrgs.br/radio **E:** radiodir@ufrgs.br – **RS63)** Rua Ramiro Barcelos, 2092 - Augusta, 96508-070 Cachoeira do Sul ☎51 3722 4022 **W:** radiocachoeira.com.br **E:** radiocachoeira@radiocachoeira.com.br – **RS64)** Praça Padre Basso, 95, 99800-000 Marcelino Ramos ☎54 3372 1389 **W:** radiosalette.com.br **E:** radiosalette@terra.com.br – **RS65)** Av Bento Gonçalves, 733 - Centro, 98870-000 Giruá ☎55 3361 2020 **W:** radiogirua.com **E:** radiogirua@terra.com.br – **RS66)** Av Odilo Gonçalves, 633 – Centro, 96300-000 Jaguarão ☎53 3261 2933 **W:** redemeridional.com/jaguarao.html **E:** culturajaguarao@redemeridional.com – **RS67)** Rua Padre Oswaldo Stracke, 56 - Centro, 96900-000 Sobradinho ☎51 3742 1089 **W:** radiosobradinho.com.br **E:** recepcao@radiosobradinho.com.br – **FM:** 97.3MHz "R.Jacuí" – **RS68)** Rua Borges do Canto, 1056, 97650-000 Itaqui ☎55 3433 8181 **W:** radiocruzeirodosul.com.br **E:** radiocruzeirodosul@terra.com.br – **RS69)** Rua Corrêa Lima, 1960 – Morro Santa Tereza, 90850-250 Porto Alegre ☎51 3218 5781 🖷51 3218 5789 **W:** radiofarroupilha.com.br **E:** farroupilha@rdfarroupilha.com.br – **RS70)** Av Rio Branco, 809 - Centro, 97010-423 Santa Maria ☎55 3222 9500 🖷55 3228 9500 **W:** radiomedianeiraam.com.br **E:** radiomed@terra.com.br – **RS71)** Rua Gel. João Manoel, 341 - Centro, 98005-170 Cruz Alta ☎55 3322 7222 **W:** radiocruzalta.com.br **E:** eduardo@radiocruzalta.com.br – **FM:** 105.1MHz –**RS72)** Rua Domingos de Almeida, 2194 - Centro, 97501-690 Uruguaiana ☎55 3412 1731 **W:**

radiocharruaamfm.com.br **E:** amfm@radiocharrua.com.br - **FM:** 97.7MHz – **RS73)** Travess Victor Hugo Demaman Tomé, 02 – Centro, 96750-000 Butiá, **W:** radiojornalsobral.com.br **E:** radiosob@terra.com.br ☎51 3652 1140 – **RS74)** Rua Rui Barbosa 96 - Centro, 95180-000 Farroupilha ☎54 3261 2121 **W:** radiomiriam.com.br **E:** radiomiriam@radiomiriam.com.br– **RS75)** Rua Tenente Lira, 950 - Centro (C.P. 74), 98400-000 Frederico Westphalen ☎55 3744 3500 **W:** luzealegria.com.br **E:** direcao@luzealegria.com.br – **FM:** 95.9MHz –**RS76)** Rua General Osório, 1160 - Centro, 97760-000 Jaguari ☎55 3255 1474 **W:** radiojaguari.com.br **E:** radiojaguari@brturbo.com.br – **RS77)** Rua Félix da Cunha, 412, 96010-000 Pelotas ☎53 3225 1160 **W:** radiouniversidadeam.com.br – **RS78)** Av Coronel Victor Villa Verde, 491 - Pitangueiras, 95500-000 Santo Antônio da Patrulha ☎51 3662 1255 **W:** radioitapui.com.br **E:** itapui@radioitapui.com.br – **RS79)** Av 7 de Setembro, 1115, 96400-000 Bagé ☎53 3242 5211 **W:** difusorabage.com **E:** difusora@difusorabage.com.br – **FM:** 99.7 FM Delta – **RS80)** Av 7 de Setembro, 160 – Integração,99034-297 Passo Fundo ☎54 2104 1600 🖷54 2104 1612 **W:** radiouirapuru.com.br **E:** uirapuru@rduirapuru.com.br – **FM:** 90.1 MHz– **RS81)** Av Maurício Cardoso, 697, 99300-000 Soledade ☎54 3381 9100 **W:** redesul.am.br/index.php?emissora=24**E:** gerente@cristal.am.br – **RS82)** Rua Anunciação, 480 - Morro do Convento, 97900-000 Cerro Largo – ☎55 3359 2022 **W:** radiocerroazul.com.br **E:** radiocerroazul@via-rs.net – **FM:** 105.9MHz «Shamballa» –**RS83)** Plaza San Marco, s/n - Centro, 99250-000 Serafina Corrêa ☎54 3444 1212 **W:** redesul.am.br/Rosario-AME: rdrosario@net11.com.br – **RS84)** Av Cmdt Kraemer, 96 2° andar - Centro, 99700-000 Erechim ☎54 3522 1389 **W:** redetche.com.br **E:** administracao@radioerechim.com.br – **RS85)** BR 392 - Km 232(🖂 C.P. 130), 97340-000 São Sepé ☎55 3233 1113 🖷55 3233 1163 **W:** radiocotrisel.com.br **E:** radiocotrisel@radiocotirsel.com.br – **RS86)** Av Júlio de Castilho, 607 - Centro, 90030-131 Porto Alegre ☎51 3284 0778 **W:** radiotranscontinental.net **E:** radiorec@terra.com.br – **RS87)** Rua General Canabarro, 1450 - Francisca Tarragaô, 97503-384 Uruguaiana ☎55 3412 1217 **W:** radiosaomiguel.com.br **E:** contato@radiosaomiguel.com.br – **RS88)** Rua Coronel Vitor Dumoncel, 1756 - Centro, 98240-000 Santa Bárbara do Sul ☎55 3372 2503 **W:** radioblaununes.com.br **E:** radioblaununes@radioblaununes.br**RS89)** Rua Rui Barbosa, 373 - Centro, 99600-000 Nonoai ☎54 3362 1384 **W:** cluberadio.com.br – **FM:** 89.7 MHz – **RS90)** Av Adolfo Schneider,85 - 2° andar - Centro, 95320-000 Nova Prata ☎54 3242 1648 **W:** radioprata.com.br **E:** radioprata@radioprata.com.br – **RS91)** Praça Silvestre Corréa, 77 - Centro, 96610-000 Encruzilhada do Sul ☎51 3733 1157**W:** radioencruzilhadense.com.br – **RS92)** Rua Júlio de Castilhos, 605 2° andar - Centro, 95290-000 Bom Jesus ☎54 3237 1247 **W:** bomjesus.rs.gov.br/radio_aparados.php **E:** radioaparados@bomjesus.rs.gov.br– **RS93)** Rua General Osório, 1134 – Centro, 98200-000 Ibirubá ☎54 3324 1758 **W:** sistemaepu.com.br **E:** atendimento@sistemaepu.com.br – **FM:** 96.6MHz – **RS94)** Rua Ponciano Ramos, 74, 96700-000 São Jerônimo ☎51 3651 1113 **W:** radiosaojeronimo.com.br **E:** am.1240@hotmail.com – **RS95)** Av Júlio de Castilhos, 1511-8° andar, salas 81/84 - Centro, 95010-003 Caxias do Sul ☎54 3221 7653 **W:** radiodifusoracaxiense.com.br **E:** radio@radiodifusoracaxiense.com.br – **RS96)** Rua 15 de Novembro, 717 - Centro, 96015-000 Pelotas ☎53 3222 7263 **E:** tupanci@terra.com.br –**RS97)** Rua Riachuelo, 928 - Centro, 97670-000 São Borja ☎55 3431 2244 **W:** radioculturaam1260.com.br **E:** radio@gps-net.com.br **RS98)** Rua 15 de Noviembre, 884 Ed Cecilia Germano - Centro, 96508-750 Cachoeira do Sul ☎51 3722 3033 🖷51 3722 3622 **W:** radiofandango.com.br **E:** radiofandango@radiofandango.com.br **RS99)** Rua José Sponchiado, 418 - Centro, 99830-000 Gaurama ☎🖷54 3391 1134 **E:** radiogaurama@awo.com.br – **RS100)** Rua Benjamim Santo Zago, 601 - Centro, 97220-000 Faxinal do Soturno ☎55 3263 1021 **W:** redejauru.com **E:** falecom@radiosaoroque.com.br – **RS101)** Rua Baldulno Schneider, 254-Centro, 98920-000 Horizontina ☎🖷55 3537 1212 **W:** radioveracruz.com.br **E:** recepcao@radioveracruz.com.br – **RS102)** Rua Dr Pio Ferreira, 453 - Centro, 96170-000 São Lourenço do Sul ☎53 3251 1303 **W:** radiosaolourenco.com.br **E:** radio.sls@vetorial.net – **RS103)** Av Angelo Macalós, 246, 99400-000 Espumoso ☎54 3383 3600 **W:** radioplanetario.com **E:** contato@radioplanetario.com – **FM:** 95.3MHz –**RS104)** Av São Paulo, 722, 3° andar - São Geraldo, 90230-160 Porto Alegre **W:** boavontade.com/radio/ **E:** superrbv@bosvontade.com ☎51 3325 7000 – **RS105)** Rua 25 de Julho, 39 - Centro, 98960-000 Santo Cristo ☎55 3541 1188 **W:** radioregional1300.com.br – **RS106)** Rua dos Andrades, 663 - Centro, 97573-000 Santana do Livramento ☎55 3244 2444 **W:** facebook.com – Radio Maratan Am **E:** radiomaratan1300@gmail.com – **RS107)** Av Duque de Caxias, 1320, 99560-000 Sarandi ☎54 3361 1777 **W:** redesul.am.br/sarandi-am **E:** midia1310@gmail.com – **RS108)** Av Júlio de Castilhos, 232 - Centro, 95680-000 Canela ☎54 3282 8822 **W:** radioclubedecanela.com.br **E:** radioclube@pdh.com.br – **FM:** 88.5MHz **RS109)** Rua General Osório, 1276, 98280-000 Panambi ☎55 3375 8200 **W:** grupopilau.com.br **E:** panambi@grupopilau.com.br – **RS110)** Av Bento Goncalves, 3361 –

Centro, 96015-145 Pelotas ☎53 3027 2175 **W:** radioculturapelotas. com.br **E:** estudio@radioculturapelotas.com.br – **RS111)** Av Rio Branco 401, 96450-000 Dom Pedrito ☎53 3243 4000 **W:** radioupacarai. com.br **E:** comercial.upacarai@hotmail.com – **RS112)** Rua Pe Feijo, 833 Sala 42 - Centro, 95190-000 São Marcos ☎54 3291 2422 **W:** radiodiplomata.am.br **E:** diplomata@radiodiplomata.am.br – **FM:** 99.7 – **RS113)** Av. Ipiranga, 1075 - Azena, 90160-093 Porto Alegre ☎51 3218 6754 **W:** cbn.com.br **E:** cbn@rbsradios.com.br – **RS114)** Av Scalabrini, 777, 99200-000 Guaporé ☎54 3443 4488 **W:** redesul.am.br/Aurora-AME: radioaurora@tl.com.br – **RS115)** Av Santos Dumont, 240 - Centro, 98600-000 Três Passos ☎55 3522 1011 **W:** rd3.net.br **E:** radiodifusoratrespassos@yahoo.com – **RS116)** Av Concordia, 1480 - Centro, 96540-970 Agudo ☎55 3265 1112 **W:** radioagudo.com.br **E:** radioagudo@terra.com.br – **RS117)** Rua Lauro R.Bortolon, 402 - Centro, 99150-970 Marau ☎54 3342 3300 **W:** redesul.am.br/Alvorada-AME: gerencia@alvorada.am.br – **RS118)** Rua John Kennedy, 2220 sala 18 - Centro, 95270-000 Flores da Cunha ☎54 3028 3888 **W:** http://comunidadeoasis.org.br **E:** oasis@comunidadeoasis.org.br – **FM:** 107.9 MHz – **RS119)** Rua Gaspar Martins 55-3° andar - Centro, 97542-000 Alegrete ☎55 3422 1236 **W:** gazetadealegrete.comE: rgta@ig.com.br – **RS120)** Rua Conde de Porto Alegre, 521 - Centro, 97573-581 Sant´Ana do Livramento ☎55 3242 5021 **W:** culturalivramento.am.br **E:** culturalivramento@brturbo.com.br – **RS121)** Rua Presidente Getúlio Vargas, 153 – Centro, 99490-000 Tapera ☎54 3385 1166 **W:** sistemaepu.com.br **E:** cultura@sistemaepu.com.br – **RS122)** Rua Chaves Barcellos, 36, conj 1205 - Centro Historico, 90030-120 Porto Alegre ☎51 3228-903 **W:** radioesperanca.com.br **E:** adm@radioesperanca. com.br – **RS123)** Rua Pedro Toniollo, 529 - Centro, 99900-000 Getúlio Vargas **W:** radiosideral.com.br **E:** sideral@radiosideral.com.br ☎54 3341 1555 – **FM:** 98.1 MHz – **RS124)** Rua Augusto Rossi, 316 - Centro, 97200-970 Restinga Sêca **W:** radiojornalintegracao.com.br **E:** radio@integracao-rs.com.br ☎📠55 3261 1030 – **RS125)** Rua Marechal Floriano, 373 - Cassino, 96205-190 Rio Grande ☎53 3035 3141 **W:** radiominuano.com.br **E:** minuano@radiominuano.com.br – **RS126)** Rua São Francisco, 246 - Centro, 98900-970 Santa Rosa ☎55 3312 4060 **W:** radiosantarosa.com.br – **RS127)** Rua 24 de Maio, 671, 95330-000 Veranópolis ☎53 3441 3200 **W:** veranense.am.br – **RS128)** Rua Ramiro Barcelos, 1206 - Centro, 96810-900 Santa Cruz do Sul ☎51 3715 7831 **W:** grupogaz.com.br **E:**radio@gazetaam.com. br - **FM:** 101.7MHz – **RS129)** Rua Teófilo Conrado de Matos, 135 - Centro, 96600-000 Canguçu ☎53 3252 1144 **W:** radiocultura-1030am.com.br **E:** cultura1030@brturbo.com.br – **RS130)** Av das Hortencias, 78 - Centro, 95670-000 Gramado ☎54 3286 2323 **W:** radioexcelsior.com.br **E:** excelsioram@serragaucha.com.br – **RS131)** Rua São João, 1637 - Centro, 95780-000 Montenegro ☎51 3632 1799 **W:** radioamerica1270.radiosom2.com.br/portal – **RS132)** Rua Republica de Líbano, 135 - Centro, 96200-360 Rio Grande ☎53 3035 3060 **W:** radiocassino.com.br **E:** diretor@radiocassino.com.br – **RS133)** Av Sete de Setembro, 672 - Centro, 96400-003 Bagé ☎53 3242 1471 **W:** radioculturabage.com.br **E:** radioculturabage@hotmail.com – **RS134)** Rua Borges de Medeiros, 401, 95560-000 Torres ☎51 3664 1110 **W:** redesul.am.br/maristela-am **E:** administracao@radiomaristela.com.br – **RS135)** Rua Dr Bruno Dockhorn, 18 - Centro, 98910-000 Três de Maio ☎📠55 3535 1022 **W:** radiocolonial.com.br **E:** colonialam@gmail.com – **RS136)** Rua Santos Inacio de Loiola, 253, sl 203 - Centro, 93700-000 Campo Bom ☎51 3585 1470 **E:** radiocinderela@gmail.com – **RS137)** Rua Julio de Castilhos, 325 - Centro, 95720-000 Garibaldi ☎54 3464 7500 **W:** redesul.am.br/Garibaldi-AM/ **E:** jornalismo@garibaldi.am.br – **RS138)** Rua Gabriel Machado, 1590, 3° andar, 97610-000 São Francisco de Assis **E:** radiodifusao@terra.com.br ☎55 3252 1166 – **RS139)** Rua General Osorio, 943 - Centro, 96600-000 Canguçu ☎53 3252 1515 **W:** radioliberdadeam.com.br **E:** atendimento@radioliberdadeam.com.br – **RS140)** Rua Rio Branco, 1006 - Centro, 95600-000 Taquara **W:** jornalpanorama.com.br **E:** radiotaquara@faccat.br ☎51 3542 2288 – **RS141)** Rua São Vicente, 345 - Gonçalves, 96501-180 Cachoeira do Sul ☎51 3723 6151 **W:** radiovale1520am.blogspot.no **E:** radiovaledopjacui@gmail.com – **RS142)** Av Rio Branco, 616 - Centro, 98770-000 Catuípe ☎55 3336 1328 **W:** radioaguasclaras.com.br **E:** contato@radioaguasclaras.com.br – **RS143)** Rua José Bonafácio, 1128 - Centro, (✉ C.P. 144) 96450-970 Dom Pedrito ☎53 3243 1434 **W:** modulosite.tecnologia.ws/modulo-am/SULINA **E:** **radio**sulina@hotmail.com – **RS144)** –Rua Quitino Bocaiuva 100, 93135-030 São Leopoldo ☎51 3554 2894 **W:** redetche.com.br – **RS145)** Rua Cel Amâncio Cardoso, 596, 99950-000 Tapejara ☎54 3344 1185 **W:** radiotapejara.com.br **E:** contato@radiotapejara.com.br – **RS146)** Trav Jaime Pinto, 136 - Centro, 97700-000 Santiago ☎55 3251 2211 **W:** radiosantiago.com.br **E:** zyk297@radiosantiago.com.br – **RS147)** Av Flores da Cunha, 4283 - Centro, 949150-004 Cachoeirinha ☎53 3421 1922 **W:** radiometropoleam.com.br **E:** radiometropoleam@terra.com.br – **RS148)** Rua 7 de Setembro, 792 - Centro, 95960-970 Encantado ☎51 3751 1580 **W:** rdencantado.com.br **E:** radio@encanto-

am.com.br - **FM:** 97.7 MHz – **RS149)** Av Assis Brasil, 263 - Centro, 98130-970 Júlio de Castilhos ☎55 3271 1414 **W:** radio14dejulho.com. br **E:** comercial@radio14dejulho.com.br – **RS150)** Rua José Bonifácio 41, 96330-970 Arroio Grande ☎53 3262 1008 **W:** difusora1580.com.br **E:** radiodifusoraam@terra.com.br– **RS151)** Rua Paraguai 42, 98980-000 Porto Lucena **W:** radionavegantes.com.br **E:** radionavegantes@san.psi.br ☎📠55 3565 1200 – **RS152)** Av Valdomiro Bocchese, 872 - Centro, 95250-970 Antônio Prado ☎54 3293 1110 ☎54 3293 1733 **W:** radiosolaris.com.br **E:** radiosolaris@radiosolaris.com.br – **FM:** 97.3 MHz – **RS153)** Av Santa Lúcia, 1401 - Centro, 97930-000 Caibaté **W:** radiocaibate.com.br **E:** radiocaibate@radiocaibate.com.br ☎55 3355 1335 – **RS154)** Rua Tiradentes, 2839 Sala 5 – Centro,, 96360-970 Pedro Osório ☎53 3254 1239 **W:** radioclube990.com.br **E:** comercial@radioclube990.com.br – **RS155)** Av Borges de Medeiros, 1462 - Chacara, 97650-000 Itaqui ☎56 3433 2301 **W:** radiopitangueira.com.br **E:** radio@pintagueira.com.br – **FM:** 94.5 MHz – **RS156)** Rua. Padre Roque Gonzáles, 08 - Centro, 98590-000 Santo Augusto ☎55 3781 1255 **W:** radioquerenciaonline.com **E:** radio@querenciaonline.com – **RS157)** Rua Baltazar Brum, 343, 97560-000 Quaraí ☎55 3423 1065 –**RS158)** Rua Sete de Setembro, 1835 - Centro, 95860-000 Taquari ☎51 3653 4033 **W:** jornaloacoriano.com **E:** contato@jornaloacoriano.com– **RS159)** Av Maurício Cardoso, 761 - Centro 99300-000 Soledade ☎54 3381 1550 **W:** radiosoledadeam.com.br **E:** radiosoledade@terra.com.br – **RS160)** Rua Dom Luiz Guanella, 2313 - Centro, 95555-970 Capão da Canoa ☎51 3625 2300 **W:** radiohorizonte.com.br **E:** radiohorizonte@radiohorizonte.com.br– **RS161)** Rua da República, 220 - Centro, 99530-000 Chapada ☎54 3333 1338 **W:** radiosimpatia.com.br **E:** simpatia@radiosimpatia.com.br– **RS162)** Av. Narciso Silva 1791, Centro, 96160-000 Capão do Leão ☎53 3227 4252 **W:** opiniaogospel.com.br **E:** opiniaogoslpel1550@hotmail.com – **RS164)** Rua Floriano Peixoto 222, 97400-000 São Pedro do Sul ☎55 3276 1311 **W:** radiomunicipalsaopedrense.com.br **E:** contato@radiomunicipalsaopedrense.com.br – **RS165)** Rua Duque de Caxias 375 – Sala 302 - Centro, 98430-000 Palmitinho ☎55 3791 1175 **W:** radiochiru.com **E:** radiochiru@radiochiru.com.br – **FM:** 107.9 MHz – **RS166)** Rua João Maffesoni, 10 - Centro, 99680-000 Constantina ☎54 3363 1330 **W:** radioatlantica.net.br **E:** radio.atlantica@hotmail.com – **RS167)** Rua Francisco Gobbi, 545 - Centro, 98580-970 Coronel Bicaco ☎55 3557 1195 📠55 3557 1220 **W:** radioguarita.com.br **E:** radioguarita@yahoo.com.br – **RS168)** Av Alto Jacuí, 435 - Centro, 99470-000 Não Me Toque ☎54 3332 1488 **W:** radioceres.com.br **E:** radioceres@radioceres.com.br – **RS169)** Rua Brasil, 806 - Centro, 97450-000 Cacequi ☎55 3254 1366 **E:** radioculturacacequi@yahoo.com.br – **RS171)** Rua Luiz Vieira, 525 - Centro, 96760-970 Tapes ☎51 3672 1031 **W:** radiotapense.com **E:** rt@conect-sul.com.br –**RS172)** Av Antônio Finco 700 (C.P 19), 99870-000 São José do Ouro ☎54 3352 1108 **W:** radiopoata.com.br **E:** radiopoata@radiopoata.com.br – **RS173)** Rua Albino Brendler, 122 – Centro, 98700-000 Ijuí ☎55 3332 7090 **W:** jmijui.com.br **E:** radiojmijui@gmail.com – **RS174)** Rua Consórcio, s/n Conj 09 - Centro, 96400-097 Bagé ☎53 3242 4668 **W:** radioclubebage.com.br **E:** radioclubebage@radioclube-bage.com.br – **RS175)** Rua Pedro Alvares Cabral, 164 - Centro, 99660-000 Campinas do Sul ☎51 3366 1266 **W:** radiocampinasdosul.com.br **E:** radiocampinas@tolrs.com.br – **RS176)** Rua 15 de Novembro, 690 - Centro, 96270-000 Mostardas ☎51 3673 2062 **W:** radiomostardas. com.br **E:** radiomostardas@hotmail.com – **RS177)** Av Barão do Triunfo, 584 2 andar - Centro, 95995-000 Arvorezinha ☎51 3772 2443 **W:** redeculturaderadio.com.br **E:** admcultura@msbnet.com.br – **FM:** 92.3MHz – **RS178)** Av. Castelo Branco, 1053 - Centro, 97950-000 Guarani das Missões **W:** grupoguaramano.com.br **E:** radioguaramano@brturbo.com.br ☎53 3353 1721 – **FM:** 91.1 – **RS179)** Rua Jornal NH, 99 - Ideal, 93334-350 Novo Hamburgo ☎51 3593 9000 **W:** radiobc900.com.br **E:** diretorabc@gruposinos.com.br – **RS191)** Rua –Correia Lima, 1960 - Santa Tereza, 90850-250 Porto Alegre ☎51 3218 5693 **W:** clickrbs.com.br **E:** radiorural.am1120@rdrural.com.br – **RS192)** Rua Sananduva, 178-Centro, 99855-970 São João da Urtiga ☎54 3532 1247 **W:** redeeducadoraurtiga.com.br **E:** rdeducadora@brturbo.com.br – **RS198)** Av. Brasil, 385 – sala 202 – Centro, 93180-000 Portão ☎55 3562 6161 **W:** estacaoportao.com.br – **RS199)** Av. Paraguassu, 180/05, 95625-000 Ivlmê ☎51 3627 1988 **W:** radiolitoraljp.com.br **E:** contato@radiolitoraljp.com.br – **RS201)** Rua Orfanotrófio, 711 – Santa Tereza, 90840-440 Porto Alegre ☎51 3218 2525 **W:** redepampa.com.br/rdgenral **E:** grenal@rdgrenal.com.br – **FM:** 95.9 MHz

SC00) SANTA CATARINA

SC01) Almeda Aristiliano Ramos 36 , 89160-149 Rio do Sul **W:** radiomirador.com.br **E:** am540@radiomirador.com.br ☎47 3531 2100 📠47 3531 2102 – **SC02)** Av Centenario, 6050 - Próspera, 88815-000 Criciuma ☎48 3461 5700 **W:**radioeldorado.net **E:** eldoradoam@radioeldorado.net – **FM:** 89.5 MHz – **SC03)** Av Martin Piaseski, 25 - Centro, 89910-970 Descano. ☎49 3623 0307 **W:**progresso.am.br **E:** comerical@progresso.am.br – **SC04)** Rua Benjamin Constant, 286-D 3 e 4 andares - Centro, 89801-970 Chapecó ☎49 3323 5177 📠49 3323 0526

W: superconda.com.br **E:** jornalismoconda@zipway.com.br – **SC05)** Rua Carlos Gomes 12, Centro, 89160-051 Rio do Sul ☎47 3521 1155 **W:** superdifusora.am.br/?pg=2Vale **E:** difusora@superdifusora.am.br - **FM**: 94.9 «Amanda FM» – **SC06)** Rua João Beux Sobredinho, 350 - Centro, 89990-000 São Lourenço d'Oeste **W:** radiodoze.com.br **E:** contato@radiodoze.com.br ☎49 3344 1544 – **SC07)** Rua Carlos Jofre do Amaral, 67 - Centro, 88501-015 Lages ☎49 3221 3147 **W:** radioclube-delages.com.br – **SC08)** Av Sete de Setembro, 109 - Centro, 89580-000 Fraiburgo ☎49 3246 2507 **W:** radiofraiburgo.am.br **E:** comercial@radiofraiburgo.am.br – **SC09)** Rua Gustavo Richard, 90 - Centro, 88701-220 Tubarão ☎48 3626 4633 **W:** radiotuba.com.br **E:** radiotuba@radiotuba.com – **SC10)** Rua General Vieira da Rosa, 1570 – Centro, 88020-420 Florianópolis ☎48 3216 2540 **W:** cbndiario.com.br **E:** cbn-diario@rbsradios.com.br – **SC11)** Rua Guilherme Helmut Arent, 277 - Centro, 89700-970 Concórdia ☎49 3441 2800 **W:** radioalianca.com.br – **SC12)** Rua Buenos Aires, 145 - Ponta Agude, 89051-050 Blumenau ☎47 3222 9004 **W:** radionereuramos.com.br – **SC13)** Rua da Criança, 75 - Centro, 88840-970 Urussanga ☎48 3465 1055 **W:** radiomarconi.net **E:** gerencia@radiomarconi.net – **SC14)** Rua Veneriano dos Passos, 385 - Centro, 89560-000 Videira ☎49 3533 4000 **W:** radiovideira.com.br – **SC15)** Rua Ângelo Dias 207, Cj 61/62/63 - Centro, 89010-020 Blumenau ☎47 3041 9699 – **SC16)** Rua Alexandre Doneda, 215 - Centro, 88880-970 Lauro Müller ☎48 3464 3762 **W:** radiocruzdemalta.com.br **E:** radiocruzdemalta@netlm.com.br – **SC17)** Rua João Suzin Marini, 64 – Centro, 89700-000 Concórdia ☎49 3441 3838 **W:** radioural.com.br – **SC18)** Av do Adão 1784, Morro da Cruz, 88025-150 Florianópolis **W:** ipda.com.br/radio/santacatarina/index.html – **SC19)** Rua Rodovia SC, 445 - km3 - Centro, 88820-000 Içara ☎48 3461 0700 ☐48 3461 0711 **W:** difusora910.com.br **E:** atendimento@difusora910.com.br – **SC20)** Rua Conselheiro Rui Barbosa, 50 1° andar - Centro, 88350-320 Brusque ☎47 3351 4611 **W:** radiocidadeam.com.br **E:** diretoria@radiocidadeam.com.br – **SC21)** Rua Santa Catarina, 93 Sala 2 - Centro, 88200-000 Tijucas ☎48 3263 0303 **W:** radiovaletj.com.br **E:** contato@radiovaletj.com.br – **SC22)** Rua João Ramiro Machado, 321 Edificio Cidade das Colinas - Centro, 88870-000 Orleãns ☎48 3466 0533 **W:** guarujaam.com.br **E:** guarujadirecao@terra.com.br – **SC23)** Av Brasil, 260 Centro Comercial Tiradentes-3° andar - Centro, 89820-970 Xanxerê ☎49 3433 0171 **W:** superdifusora.com.br **E:** difusora@superdifusora.com.br – **SC24)** Centro Comercial Geschäfthaus, sala 20/21, 88353-120 Brusque ☎47 3351 1744 **W:** araguaia970am.com.br **E:** fale@araguaia970am.com.br – **SC25)** Rua São Bonifacio, 280 – Centro, 89896-000 Itapiranga ☎49 3677 0362 **W:** peperi.com.br – **SC26)** Rua Severiano Francisco Sombrio, 684 - Centro (✉C.P 67), 88750-000 Braço do Norte ☎48 3658 2178 **W:** verdevaleam.com.br – **SC27)** Rua Pernambuco, 72 - Centro, 89840-000 Coronel Freitas ☎49 3347 0131 **W:** continentalam1020.com.br – **SC28)** Rua Otacilio Vieira da Costa, 40 - Centro, 88501-050 Lages ☎49 3222 3011 **W:** radioprincesalages.com – **SC29)** Rua Manoel Simão, 177-Salas 24 e 25 - Nações, 89130-970 Indaial ☎☐47 3333 0499 **W:** radioclubeindaial.com.br **E:** falecom@radioclubeindaial.com.br – **SC30)** Alameda Rolf Colin, 80 - America, 89204-070 Joinville ☎47 3422 2325 **W:**radiocolon.com.br – **SC31)** Rua Vidal Ramos 519, 88701-160 Tubarão ☎48 3632 9009 **W:** bandeirantes1090.com.br – **SC32)** Rua Pe. Schrader, 01 – Agronômica, 88025-090 Florianópolis ☎48 3224 6470 **W:** radioculturafloripa.blogspot.com.br **E** radio@radiocultura1110am.com.br – **SC33)** Av Santa Catarina 828, Edifico Dona Olivia-2° andar - Centro, 89885-000 São Carlos ☎49 3325 4355 ☐49 3325 4483 **W:** radiosaocarlos.com.br – **SC34)** Travessa João Winkler, 15 - Centro, 89820-000 Xanxerê ☎49 3433 1110 **W:** redeprincesa.com.br **E:** ademir@redeprincesa.com.br - **FM:** 101.3 MHz – **SC35)** Rua Cel. Vidal Ramos, 861 - Centro, 89520-000 Curitibanos ☎49 3241 1140 **W:**coroado.am.br **E:** coroado@coroado.am.br – **SC36)** Rua 15 de Novembro, 600-sala 401, Edifico Visconde de Mauá - Centro, 89010-000 Blumenau ☎47 3322 9773 **W:** radioitabera.com.br **E:** contato@radioitabera.com – **SC37)** Rua Conselheiro Jeronimo Coelho, 48 - Centro, 88790-000 Laguna ☎48 3644 0025 **W:** difusoralaguna.com.br **E:** radio_difusora@yahoo.com.br – **SC38)** Rua Siqueira Campos 33, 89400-970 Porto União ☎42 3522 2245 **W:** colmeia.am.br **E:** colmeia@colmeia.am.br – **SC39)** Rua Padre Aurélio, 240 - Centro, 89930-970 São José do Cedro ☎49 3643 0211 **W:** radiointegracaoam1180.com.br **E:** comercial@radiointegracaoam1180.com.br – **SC40)** Rua Otavianpo Dadam, 355-Centro, 88240-000 São João Batista ☎48 3265 0222 **W:** http//clubei.com **E:** redacao@rclubei.com – **SC41)** Rua São Cristóvão 393 (C.P 59, 89835-970), 89835-000 São Domingos ☎49 3443 6190 **W:** clubesd.com.br **E:** contato@clubesd.com.br – **SC42)** Bruno Pedro dal Toe 303, Humaitá de Cima, 88708-197 Tubarão ☎48 3628 0658 ☐48 3628 1356 **W:** radiosc.com.br **E:** radiosc@radiosc.com.br – **SC43)** Rua Tenente Ary Rauen, 1361 - Centro, 89300-970 Mafra ☎47 3642 3955 **W:** radiosc.com.br **E:** radionovaera@netuno.com.br - **FM:** 104.5MHz «Nova Era» – **SC44)** Av Canal, 130 – Centro, 89890-000 Cunha Porã ☎49 3646 0157 **W:** http// iracema.radio.br – **SC45)** Rua Nove de Março, 737-Ed.Turim 8° andar

- Centro, 89201-400 Joinville ☎47 3026 1000 **W:** http//radiocultura-joinville.blogspot.com **E:** jornalismo@jovempanjoinville.com.br – **FM:** 91.1 MHz **SC46)** Rua Dr. Amadeu da Luz, 31-sala 03 - Centro, 89010-160 Bluemau ☎47 3340 1260 **W:** arcadaalianca.com.br **E:** fale@radioblumenau.com.br – **SC47)** Av XV de Novembro, 608-Centro, 89600-000 Joaçaba **W:** radiocatarinense.com.br **E:** radiocatarinense@radiocatarinense.com.br ☎49 3551 2424 ☐49 3551 2426 – **FM:** 97.3MHz – **SC48)** Rua Osvaldo Cabral 68-1° andar - Centro, 88790-000 Laguna, ☎48 3646 0337. **W:** garibaldilaguna.com.br **E:** radiogaribaldi@brturbo.com.br – **SC49)** Av Alvin Bauer, 585 - Centro, 88330-643 Balneário Camboriú ☎47 3405 1644 ☎47 3405 1609 **W:** radiocamboriu.com.br **E:** radiocamboriu@radiocamboriu.com.br – **SC50)** Rua Buenos Aires, 145 - Ponta Aguda, 89051-050 Blumenau ☎47 3222 9070 **W:** radioclubeblumenau.com.br – **SC51)** Rua Marechal Floriano Peixoto, 161 - Centro, 89802-010 Chapecó ☎49 3322 0688 **W:** radiochapeco.com.br **E:** comercial@radiochapeco.com.br - **FM:** 107.1MHz – **SC52)** Rua Vereador Guilherme Prust, 311 - Campo d'Água Verde, 89460-000 Canoinhas ☎47 3622 7000 **W:** radioclubedecanoinhas.com.br – **SC53)** Rua Imbituba, 190 – Dom Bosco, 88303-570 Itajaí ☎47 3241 0092 **W:** bandamitajai.com.br**E:** contato@bandamitajai.com.br – **SC54)** Rua Olivio D Brugnago, 181 - Vila Nova, 89259-260 Jaraguá do Sul ☎47 3274 5555 **W:** radiobrasilnovo.com.br **E:** radiobrasilnovo.com.br – **SC55)** Rua Duque de Caxias, 1302-2° andar - Centro, 89900-970 São Miguel do Oeste **W:** peperi.com.br **E:** rede@peperi.com.br ☎49 3622 1964 – **SC56)** Rua José Gonçalves, 333 - Centro, 89340-970 Itaiópolis ☎ ☐47 3652 2279 **W:** cidade1380.am.br **E:** comercial@cidade1380.am.br – **SC57)** Rua Carlos Jofre do Amaral, 67 - CentroCentro, 88501-015 Lages ☎49 3221 3110 **W:**cbnlages.com.br **E:** cbnlages@scc.com.br – **SC58)** Rua Visconde do Rio Branco, 1028 - Centro, 89887-000 Palmitos ☎49 3647 0292 **W:** radioentrerios.com.br **E:** entrerios@futurasc.net – **SC59)** Rua Nunes Machado, 94, Edifico Tiradentes-10° andar - Centro, 88010-460 Florianópolis ☎☐48 2108 5555 **W:**radioguaruja.com.br - **FM:** 92.1 MHz – **SC60)** Rua Marechal Deodoro, 298-Ed Pe Quintilio Costini - Centro, 89620-000 Campos Novos ☎☐49 3541 0391 **W:** rsradios.com.br/cultura-am/ **E:** cultura-am@rsradios.com.br – **SC61)** Rua 7 de Setembro, 341 - Centro, 89874-000 Maravilha ☎49 3664 0029 **W:** difusoramaravilha.com.br **E:** atendimento@difusoramaravilha.com.br – **SC62)** Rua Carlos Fürst, 37 - Serra Alta, 89291-697 São Bento do Sul ☎47 3633 0572 **W:** radiosaobento.com **E:** programacao@radiosaobento.com – **SC63)** Av Centenario, 6050 - Santa Barbara, 88804-972 Criciúma ☎48 3431 5190 **W:** hulha-net.com.br – **SC64)** Rua São Pedro, 245 - Centro, 89110-000 Gaspar ☎47 3332 0783 **W:** sentineladovale.com.br **E:** radiosentinela@terra.com.br – **SC65)** Av do Antão, 1762 – Morro da Cruz, 88025-163 Florianopolis ☎49 3251 1470 **W:** ricmais.com.br/sc/radiorecord **E:** redacao@radiorecordsc.com.br – **SC66)** Rua Santos Dumont, 204 - Centro, 89610-000 Herval d'Oeste ☎49 3527 9013 **W:** radiolider.am.br **E:** gerencia@radiolider.am.br – **SC67)** Av Coronel Procópio Gomes, 1155 - Bucarein, 89202-300 Joinville ☎47 3026 1480 **W:** arcadaalianca.com.br **E:** contato@radioarcadaalianca.com.br – **SC68)** Rua Antônio Bittencourt Capanama, 260 – Centro, 88770-000 Imaruí ☎48 3643 0000 **W:** litoralam.com.br – **SC69)** Rua Tiradentes, 283- Edifico D. Martha sala 21 - Centro, 89140-000 Ibirama – ☎47 3357 2236 **W:** belosvales.com.br – **SC70)** Av Plínio Arlindo de Nes, 476 - Centro, 89825-000 Xaxim ☎49 3353 2425 **W:** radioculturaxaxim.com.br **E:** cultura@radioculturaxaxim.com.br – **SC71)** Rua Max Wilhelm, 373 - Baependi, 89256-000 Jaraguá do Sul ☎47 3371 1010 **W:** jaraguaam.com.br **E:** jaraguaam@jaraguaam.com.br – **SC72)** Av Luis de Camões, 1370 - Coral, 88523-000 Lages ☎43 3222 8222 **W:** radioguri.com.br **E:** comercial@radioguri.com.br – **SC73)** Av Belém, 500 - Centro, 89870-000 Pinhalzinho ☎49 3366 1111 **W:** rco.com.br **E:** rco@rco.com.br – **SC74)** Rua Altamiro Guimarães, 480 - Centro, 89500-000 Caçador ☎49 3536 2211 **W:** am1110.com.br – **SC75)** Av. Dr. João Rinsa, 1002 - Centro, 88780-000 Imbituba ☎48 3255 3787 **W:** bandeirantes1010.com.br – **SC76)** Rua Equador, 245 - Centro, 89120-970 Timbó ☎47 3382 3888 **W:** radiocultumam.com.br **E:** radiocultura@radiocultumam.com.br – **SC77)** Rua Manoel Vieira Garcao 3-Edif. Catarinense 15 andar - Centro , 88301-425 Itajaí 47 3348 2992 **W:** difusoraitajai.com.br – **SC78)** Rua Boanerges Pereira de Medeiros, 205-Ed. Santa Rosa 2° e 3° andares, 88600-000 São Joaquim ☎49 3233 0021 **W:** difusora1530.com **E:** difusora@iscc.com.br – **SC79)** Av Porto Feliz, 151 - Centro, 89893-000 Mondaí ☎49 3674 0122 **W:** portofeliz.am.br **E:** jornalismo2@portofeliz.am.br – **SC80)** Rua Carmello Zocolli, 205 - Centro, 89600-000 Capinzal ☎49 3555 1333 ☐49 3555 1333 **W:** radiocapinzal.am.br **E:** contato@radiocapinzal.am.br – **SC81)** Av Getúlio Vargas, 429 - Centro, 88900-000 Araranguá ☎48 3524 0137 **W:** radioararangua.com.br **E:** radioararangua@radioararangua.com.br - **FM:** 92.5MHz – **SC82)**Rodovia SC,422 km 3, 89190-000 Taió ☎47 3562 1440 **W:** educadora.am.br **E:** comercial@educadora.com.br – **SC83)** Rua Carlos Weber, 228 - Centro, 89295-000 Rio Negrinho 47 3644 2900 – **SC84)** Av 21 de Janeiro, 1410 - Centro, 89107-000 Pomerode ☎47 3395 1410 **W:**

radiopomerode.com.br **E:** pomerodam@radiopomerode.com.br – **SC85)** Rua João Steffens, 260 – Centro, (C.P 100) 88400-000 Ituporanga ☎47 3533 8310 **W:** sintonia.am.br **E:** radio@sintonia.am.br – **SC86)** Rua Joaquim Nuns, 244 - Centro, (C.P. 2008) 888340-000 Camboriú ☎47 3404 8700 **W:** gideoes.com.br**E:** contato@gideoes.com.br – **SC87)** Rua João Florentino de Souza, 700 - Centro, 89480-000 Major Vieira ☎47 3655 1177 **W:** radioplanaltodemajorvieira.com.br – **SC88)** Rua Renato Ramos da Silva, 239 - Barreiros, 88110-015 São José ☎48 3381 3500 **W:** radioguararema.com.br – **FM:** 103.5/107.7MHz – **SC89)** Rua Sargento Juvenil, 476 - Centro, 89540-000 Santa Cecília ☎49 3244 2188 **W:** radioalvorada1300.com – **SC90)** Av Getúlio Vargas, 860 - Centro, 89830-000 Abelardo Luz ☎49 3445 4297 **W:**rainhadasquedas. com.br – **SC91)** Rua Ricardo Kruger, 140-sala 02 - Centro, 88650-970 Urubici ☎49 3278 5095 **W:** radiogralhaazul.com.br – **SC92)** Rua Rui Barbosa, 1321 - Centro, 88930-000 Turvo ☎48 3525 0321 **W:** radioimigrantes.com.br **E:** imigrantes@radioimigrantes.com.br – **SC93)** Rua AV XV de Novembro, 6-sala 2 - Centro, 89665-000 Capinzal ☎49 3555 1799 **W:** radiobarrigaverde.am.br – **SC94)** Av Progresso, 569 - Centro, 89888-000 Caibi ☎49 3648 0233 **W:** nossaradio.net.br/caibi – **SC95)** Rua Duque de Caxias, 1302-2° andar - Centro, 89900-000 São Miguel d'Oeste **W:** peperi.com.br ☎49 3622 1717 – **SC96)** Rua Rafael Pardinho, 249 - Centro, 89240-000 São Francisco do Sul ☎47 3444 2733 ☐47 3444 0450 **W:** radiosaofranciscosc.com.br **E:** ouvintes@ radiosaofranciscosc.com.br – **SC97)** Rua do Comercio, 215 - Centro, 89770-000 Seara ☎49 3452 8500 **W:** radiobelosmontes.com.br **E:** contato@seara.psi.br – **SC98)** Rua do Comércio, Centro, 89872-000 Modelo ☎49 3365 3294 **W:** Facebook: Radio Modelo **E:** radiomodelo@ mhnet.com.br – **SC99)** Rua 7 de Setembro, 496 - Centro, 89950-000 Dionísio Cerqueira ☎49 3644 1042 **W:** radiofronteira.com.br – **FM:** 94.3 – **SC100)** Rua Marechal Floriano, 505 – Ponte Serrada, 89683-000 Ponte Serrada ☎49 3435 0171 **W:** radionamba.com.br **E:** atendimen-to@radionamba.com.br – **SC101)** Av Dr Albano Schultz, 925 - 2° andar Centro, 89201-220 Joinville ☎47 3481 3030 **W:** radioclubejoinville. com.br **E:** jornalismo@radioclubejoinville.com.br – **FM:** 103.1MHz – **SC102)** Rua Maranhão 700, sala 02, 89980-000 Campo Erê **W:** peperi. com.br – **SC103)** Rua Pref.Dib Cherem 3440 Salas 02/03, Capoeiras, 88090-001 Florianopolsi ☎48 3028 1240 **W:** radiomaisalegria.com.br - **FM:** 106.5 MHz – **SC104)** Rua XV de Novembro 495, 89560-000 Videira ☎49 3650 2500 **W:** vitoriaam.com.br **E:** adm@vitoriaam.com. br – **SC105)** Rua João Lino da Silva Neto 621, 88495-000 Garopaba ☎48 3254 3055 **W:** radiofrequencia.net **E:** frequencia@radiofrequen-cia.net – **SC106)** 88330-000 Balneário Cambouri ☎47 3360 2344 **W:** radiocatolica1500am.blogspot.no **E:** radiocatolicaam1500@gmail.com – **SC107)** 89642-000

SE00) SERGIPE
SE01) Rua Claudio Batista, 334 - Santo Antônio, 49060-100 Aracaju ☎79 3234 3232 **W:** radiojornal540.com.br **E:** jornal@radiojornal540. com.br – **SE02)** Rua Laranjeiras, 1837 - Getúlio Vargas, 49055-380 Aracaju ☎79 3198 2700 **W:** aperipe.com.br – **FM:** 104.9MHz – **SE03)** Rua Simão Dias, 643 - Centro, 49010-430 Aracaju ☎79 3226 8710 **W:** cultura670.com.br **E:** cultura@cultura670.com.br – **SE04)** Rua São José, s/n – Cidade Nova, 49400-000 Lagarto ☎79 3631 1866 **W:** radioprogressoam.com **E:** recepcao.aparecidafm@hotmail.com - **FM:** 87.5 MHz – **SE05)** Av Bastos Coelho, 1704 - Indusrtrial, 49060-514 Aracaju ☎79 3215 5792**W:** amatalaia.com.br – **SE06)** Rua 13 de Maio, 119 - Centro, 49500-000 Itabaiana ☎79 3431 1762 **W:** radio-princesadaserra.com.br ☎79 3431 5036 – **SE07)** Rua Pacatuba, 254 - Centro, 49010-150 Aracaju ☎79 3213 1174 **W:** 930am.com.br **E:** jornalismo@930am.com.br – **SE08)** Praça Coronel Gonçalo Prado, s/n - Centro, 49200-000 Estância ☎79 3522 1411**W.** radioesperancaes-tancia.com.br **E:** radioesperancaestancia@gmail.com – **SE09)** Av Dr Luíz Magalhães, 346 - Centro, 49500-970 Itabaiana ☎☐79 3431 1117 **W:** capitaloagreste.com.br **E:** comercial@capitaloagreste.com.br – **SE10)** Rodovia Lourival Batista, 2153 - Centro, 49480-000 Simão Dias ☎79 3611 1488 **W:** novacidadeam.com.br **E:** novacidadeam@hotmail. com – **SE11)** Av. Napoleão Emifio Costa, 1052 – Centro, 49514-000 Frei Paulo ☎79 3447 1745 **W:** radioeducadoradefreipaulo.com.br **E:** radioe-ducadorafreipaulo@yahoo.com.br – **SE12)** Av Raimundo Silveira, 3996- 01 Andar Sala 02 – Alagoas, 49200-000 Estância ☎79 3522 4804 **W:** radioabaisam.com.br **E:** radioabaisamcomercial@hotmail.com – **SE13)** Travessa Santa Luzia, 69 - Centro, 49300-000 Tobias Barreto ☎79 3541 1548 **W:** redeilha.com.br **E:** am1520@redeilha.com

SP00) SÃO PAULO
SP01) Av Nove de Julho 2875, 16204-050 Biriguí ☎18 3642 3500 **W:** radioglobobirigui.com.br – **SP02)** Rua Antônio do Vale Mello, 807, 13170-011 Sumaré ☎19 3873 2972 **W:** radionovasumare.com.br **E:** rns@rns.com.br – **SP03)** Rua Dom Bosco, 573, 12700-000 Cruzeiro ☎12 3144 1364 **W:** radiomantiqueira.com.br **E:** atendimento@mantiquei-ra.com **FM:** 100.7MHz – **SP04)** Rua José Bonini, 1415, 14160-000 Sertãozinho **W:** http://boavontade.com/radio/?cdgEms=6 **E:** superrbv@ boavontade.com – **SP05)** Prefeito João Benedito Barbosa,161 - Vila

Nova, 18400-000 Itapeva ☎15 3522 2000 **W:** radioclubegospel.com.br - **FM:** 93.5MHz «Cristal» – **SP06)** Rua Dr Sousa Alves, 960 - Centro, 12020-030 Taubaté ☎12 3632 8122 **W:** rededifusora.com.br **E:** mkt@ rededifusora.com.br – **SP07)** Rua Tamoio, 875 – Vila Santa Catarina, 13465-250 Americana ☎19 3475 8001 **W:** radiovoce.com.br **E:** radio-voce@radiovoce.com.br – **SP08)** Av Rotary, 85 - Centro, 19970-000 Palmital ☎18 3351 2601 **W:** radioregionalpalmital.com.br – **SP09)** Rua Pedro Lessa 1640, sala 809 – Embaré, 11025-002 Santos ☎13 3273 6900 **W:** radioatlantica.com.br **E:** radioatlantica@radioatlantica.com.br – **SP10)** Rua das Nações Unidas, 127 - Centro, 16800-000 Mirandópolis ☎18 3701 4084 **W:** clubeam590.com.br – **SP11)** Av Maurilio Biagi, 2103 - Ribeirânia, 14096-170 Ribeirão Preto ☎16 3968 7000 **W:** radio79.com.br **E:** natocampos@thathi.com.br – **SP12)** Mogi Mirim – **SP13)** Rua Pará, 147 - Centro, 15800-040 Catanduva ☎17 3531 1000 **W:** amglobo.com.br **E:** minhaglobo@globonoroestepaulista.com.br – **SP14)** Praça Conselheiro Rodrigues Alves, 104-3° andar - Centro, 12560-020 Guaratinguetá ☎12 3122 3155 **W:**superradiopiratininga. com.br **E:** jornalismo@superradiopiratininga.com.br – **SP15)** Av. Dr. Domingos Teodoro Galla, 528 – Centro, 18800-000 Piraju ☎14 3351 1066 **W:** paranapanema.com.br **E:** atendimento610@paranapanema. com.br – **SP16)** Av Paulista, 807-24° andar – Bela Vista, 01311-941 São Paulo ☎11 2870 9700 **E:** info@jovempan.com.br **W:** jovempan. com.br **E:** jovempanonline@jovempan.com.br – **SP17)** Rua Capitão Neves, 1840 - Centro, 15130-000 Mirassol ☎17 3242 2101 **W:** wwwdifusora630.com **E:** comercial@difuasora630.com – **SP18)** Rua Casemiro Dias, 785 – Vila Ocidental, 19015-250 Presidente Prudente – **SP19)** Av. Bento de Abreu 889 – Jardim Mirmavera 14802-386 Araraquara ☎16 3303 3622 **W:** radiomorada.com.br **E:** radiomorada@ uol.com.br - **FM:** 98.1MHz – **SP20)** Rua Homero Rodrigues Silva, 1072 - Centro, 16901-025 Andradina ☎18 3722 2352 – **SP21)** Praça José Bonifácio, 815 - Centro, 13400-340 Piracicaba ☎19 2105 6622 **W:** portaldifusora.com.br **E:** atendimento@portaldifusora.com.br - **FM:** 102.3MHz – **SP22)** Rua Tolentino Figueiras, 119 7° andar - cj 71/72 - Gonzaga, 11060-471 Santos ☎13 3289 4727 **W:** radioterralitoral.com - **FM:** 105.5MHz – **SP23)** Av Nove de Julho, 600 – Jardim Sumaré, 14025-000 Ribeirão Preto ☎16 2101 3500 **W:** clubeam.com.br - **FM:** 100.5MHz – **SP24)** Rua Teotonio Tibiriçá Pimenta, 380 - Centro, 11660-230 Caraguatatuba ☎12 3882 5000 **W:** radiooceanicaam.com.br – **SP25)** Rua Prefeito Salviano, 20 - Centro, 17400-000 Garça ☎14 3471 2241 **W:** 670am.com.br **E:** estudio@670am.com.br – **SP26)** Rua Quintino Bocaiúva, 37 - Centro, 13300-135 Itu.– ☐11 4023 2363 **W:** radioconvencao.com.br **E:** radioconvencao@hotmail.com – **SP27)** Rua 13 de Maio, 720 - Centro, 15800-010 Catanduva ☎17 3522 2228 **W:** difusora680.com.br – **SP28)** Av Vereador Eduardo Cassanho, 317 - Centro, 18800-970 Piraju ☎14 3351 1680 **W:** piratiningapiraju.com.br **E:** contato@piratiningapiraju.com.br – **SP29)** Rua Prudente Moraes, 325 sl 2 - Centro, 14700-000 Bebedouro ☎17 3342 2484 **W:** radiobe-bedouro.com.br **E:** gerencia.rb@mdbrasil.com.br – **SP30)** Praça Conselheiro Rodrigues Alves, 170 - Centro, 12500-020 Guaratinguetá ☎12 9138 1622 **W:** clubeam690.com.br **E:** cesarcornetti@hotmail.com - **FM:** 97.1MHz – **SP31)** Av Humberto Liedtke, 1936 - Centro, 15370-970 Pereira Barreto ☎18 3704 2121 **W:** radiocidadeam690.com.br **E:** con-tato@radiocidadeam690.com.br **MSN:** radiocidadeampb@hotmail. com – **SP32)** Av.Eng Caetano Alvares, 55 – Limão, 02598-900 Sao Paulo ☎11 2108 6700 **W:** radio.estado.com.br - **FM:** 92.9MHz – **SP33)** Rua 1 de Agosto 927, 17010-011 Bauru – **SP34)** Rua dos Pelegrinis 11 - Desterro, 13700-000 Casa Branca ☎19 3671 2101 **W:** radiodifusora-casabranca.com.br **E:** contato@radiodifusoracasabranca.com.br – **SP35)** Rua Antonio Carlos Mori, 288 - Centro, 19900 080 Ourinhos ☎14 3322 5758 **W:** sentinelaam.com.br – **SP36)** Rua Dr Carlos Varela, 104 - Centro, Cruzeiro ☎12 3143 6894 **W:** rcvale.com.br – **SP37)** Rua Washington Luis, 576 - Centro, 15400-000 Olímpia ☎17 3281 3044 **W:** espaciolivream.com.br **E:** adm@espaciolivream.com.br – **SP38)** Rua Siqueira de Morães, 578 10° andar - Centro, 13201-803 Jundiaí ☎11 4586 0969 ☐11 4586 4188 **W:** cidadeam.com **E:** radio@cidadeam.com – **SP39)** Rua Coronel Galdino de Almeida, 55 – Centro, 17500-100 Marília ☎14 3402 5128 **W:** dirceu.am.br - **SP40)** Av. João Lemos. 578 – Centro, 17250-970 Bariri ☎14 3662 1276 **W:** radioculturadebariri. com.br – **SP41)** Av Paulista, 900 – Bela Vista, 01310-100 São Paulo ☎11 3289 3755 ☐11 3280 3768 **W:** new.radiotrianon.com.br **E:** conta-to@radiotrianon.com.br – **SP42)** Rua Itapura, 6 - Centro, 17700-970 Osvaldo Cruz ☎18 3528 1089 **W:** radiosvaldocruz.com.br **E:** contato@ radioosvaldocruz.com.br - **FM:** 97.3MHz «California FM» – **SP43)** Rua Ramos de Azevedo, 622 – Jardim Paulista, 14090-180 Ribeirão Preto ☎16 3624 2622 **W:** radiocmn.com.br – **SP44)** Rua Euclides Miragaia 394 – 18° andar, 12245-820 São José dos Campos ☎12 3909 8000 **W:** radiopiratininga.com.br **E:** jornalismo@radiopiratininga.com. br - **FM:** 99.7MHz **SP45)** Rua Virgilio Malta, 6-78 - Centro, 17015-220 Bauru ☎14 3104 0760 **W:** auriverde.am.br **E:** jornalismo@auriverde. am.br – **SP46)** Av Dr Lauro Correa da Silva, 3230 – Jardim do Lago, 13480-041 Limeira ☎19 3404 4000 **W:** mixam.com.br **E:** manoelmixregional@gmail.com – **SP47)** Rua das Palmeiras, 315 - Vila Buarque, 01226-901 São Paulo ☎11 3824 3200 **W:** cbn.globoradio.globo.com – **FM:** 90.5 MHz – **SP48)** Alameda Dr Armando de Salles Oliveira, 575 – Centro, 17800-000 Adamantina ☎18 3521 1242 **W:** radiobrasilam. com.br **E:** contato@radiobrasilam.com.br – **SP49)** Av Bento de Abreu, 889 – Jardim Primavera, 14802-3986 Araraquara ☎16 3303 3622 **W:** radiocultura.net **E:** comercial@radiocultura.net- **FM:** 97.3MHz – **SP50)** Rua Barão de Jundiaí, 1041-9° andar - Centro, 13201-906 Jundiaí ☎11 4586 2020 **W:** radiodifusorajundiai.com.br **E:** radio@radiodifusorajundiai.com.br – **SP51)** Rua Quince de Novembro, 3131 - Centro, 15015-110 São José do Rio Preto ☎17 3233 4600**W:** blog.cancaonova.com/ riopreto **E:** radioriopreto@cancaonova.com.br – **SP52)** Av Julio Prestes, s/n - Centro, 12570-000 Aparecida ☎12 3104 2590 **W:** a12.com/radio-aparecida **E:** contato@a12.com **DX-prgrm:** Encontro DX, Saturdays at 22.30 UTC - **FM:** 90.9MHz – **SP53)** Rua Tenente Lopes, 191-Centro, (C.P.3) 17201-460 Jaú ☎14 3622 2800 ☎14 3622 4376 **W:** radiojauense@netsite.com.br - **FM:** 101.1MHz – **SP54)** Rua José Galvão, 359 – Vila Moraes, (C.P 94) 19900-260 Ourinhos ☎14 3322 2997 ☎14 3322 6255 **W:** radioclube820.com.br – **SP55)** Av. Antonieta Vilela Ferreira 900 - Vilage, 16300-000 Penápolis ☎18 3654 2250 **W:** difusoradepenapolis.com.br **E:** difusora@difusoradepenapolis.com.br – **SP56)** Rua Pernambuco, 4006 – Jardim Eldorado, 15500-006 Votuporanga ☎17 3422 3301 **W:** lider830.com.br – **SP57)** Rua Radiantes, 13 – Jardim Leonor, 05614-900 São Paulo **W:** radiobandeirantes.band.uol.com.br**E:** rbnoar@band.com.br - **FM:** 90.9MHz – **SP58)** Avenida 2, 1420 - Jardim Claret, 13502-240 Rio Claro ☎19 3533 2307 **W:** radioclubeam.am.br **E:** comercial@radioclubefm.fm.br – **FM:** 94.3 MHz – **SP59)** Av Nove de Julho, 2875 – Novo Jardim Stábile, 16204-050 Birigui ☎18 3642 2240 **W:** tropicalbirigui.com **E:** clubeam@tropicalbirigui.com.br – **SP60)** Rua Prudente de Morães 418, 14960-000 Novo Horizonte **W:** radio870.com.br – **SP61)** Rua Romualdo Andreazzi, 516 - Jd Leonor, 13041-030 Campinas ☎19 3772 1750 ☎19 3772 1766 **W:** radiocentral.am.br **E:** radiocentral@radiocentral.com.br – **SP62)** Av. Paulista, 900 4° andar - Bela Vista, 01310-940 Sao Paulo ☎11 3170 5757 ☎11 3170 5630 **W:** gazetaam.com.br **E:** hrocha@radiogazeta.com.br – **FM:** 88.1 MHz – **SP63)** Rua Rui Barbosa 723 - Centro, 19015-000 Presidente Prudente ☎18 222 2500 – **SP64)** Rua Siqueira Campos, 3223 - Centro, 15010-040 São José do Rio Preto - **FM:** 102.1MHz «R Onda Nova FM» – **SP65)** Rua Miguel Janez, 19 – Vila Arlindo Luz, 18212-480 Itapetininga ☎15 3373 7301 **E:** radioglobo90@bol.com.br – **SP66)** Av Limeira, 222 – Vila Areão,, 13414-018 Piracicaba ☎19 3436 6300 **W:** ondalivream.com.br **E:** comercial@ondalivre.com.br - **FM:** 105.3 – **SP67)** Rua Monsenhor Rosa, 1561 - Centro, 14400-670 Franca ☎16 3713 3977 **W:** radioimperador.com.br **E:** contato@radio-imperador.com.br – **SP68)** Av Brasil, 31 – Parque de Felicidade, 13973-255 Itapira ☎19 3863 0138 **W:** radioclubeitapira.com.br **E:** radioclube@dglnet.com.br – **SP69)** Av Ana Costa 532 - 5° andar, Gonzaga, 11060-002 Santos ☎13 3289 5757 **W:** radiocultura.br **E:** cultura@radiocultura.com.br – **SP70)** rRua Rio Branco, 9-70 - Centro, 17015-310 Bauru ☎14 3243 4104 **W:** cancaonova.com.br **E:** davibauru@cancaonova.com – **SP71)** Rua Doce, 303 - Centro, 15775-000 Santa Fé do Sul ☎17 3631 4859 **W:** radiosantafe.com.br **E:** comercial@radiosantafe.com.br - **FM:** 104.7MHz – **SP72)** Av Sampaio Vidal, 185 - Barbosa, 17500-441 Marília ☎14 3401 4341 **W:** radio950.com.br – **SP73)** Av João Dias, 1800 - Santo Amaro, 04724-002 São Paulo ☎11 3442 2660 – **SP74)** Rua Quintino Bocaiuva, 330 - Centro 18200-014 Itapetininga 15 3271 2000 **W:** radiosuperdifusora.com.br – **SP75)** Rua Floriano Peixoto, 64 - Centro, 13870-060 São João da Boa Vista ☎19 3631 5853 **W:** piratininga970am.com.br **E:** radio970@dglnet.com.br – **SP76)** Rua Luis Pires, 250 – Jardim Redentor, 14409-283 Franca – ☎16 3704 7733 **W:** radiohertz.com.br - **FM:** 96.5MHz – **SP77)** Rua da Várzea, 240 – Várzea da Brra Funda, 01140-080 São Paulo ☎11 3661 6727 **W:** radiosetvs.com/radiorecord_sp **E:** radiorecordamsp@r7.com – **SP78)** Av. Zero Nove, 1 - Centro, 14781-574 Barretos ☎17 3321 7070 **W:** odiarioonline.com.br – **SP79)** Rua Kametaro Morishita, 95–3°andar – Universitaria, 19050-700 Presidente Prudente – **SP80)** Rua João Paulo II, s/n - Centro, (C.P 57), 12630-000 Cachoeira Paulista ☎12 3186 2600 **W:** cancaonova.com.br **E:** radio@cancaonova. com – **SP81)** Rua Benjamin Constant, 33, 10° andar - Centro, 19806-130 Assis ☎18 3322 8811 **W:** culturadeassis.com.br **E:** cultura@culturadeassis.com.br – **SP82)** Rua Profa Aparecida M.Faveri, 988 – Parque Egisto Ragazzo, 13485-316 Limeira ☎19 3441 3760 **W:** educadoraam.com.br **E:** radio@educadoraam.com.br - **SP83)** Rua 24, 2442 - Centro, 15040-040 São José do Rio Preto ☎17 3622 5508 **W:** radioculturadejales.com. br – **SP84)** Av Eliz Verzola Gosuen, 3103 – Jardim Angela Rosa, , 14403-605 Franca ☎16 3713 8899 **W:** difusora **E:** difusora@gcn.net.br – **SP85)** Av Industrial José E Ortigosa, 570 an 1 – Dis Industrial 1 - Centro, 17340-970 Barra Bonita ☎14 3641 0131 – **SP86)** Rua Luiz Gama, 378 an 8 - Centro, 16400-080 Lins 14 3532 7000 – **SP87)** Praça Rodrigues de Abreu, 228 - Paraiso, 04040-080 São Paulo ☎11 3053 1040 **W:** radiocapital-1040.com.br **E:** faleconosco@radioca-

pital.am.br – **SP88)** Rua Boa Morte, 1122 - Centro, 13400-140 Piracicaba ☎19 3422 1060 **W:** educadora1060.com.br **E:** ouvinte@educadora1060.com.br – **SP89)** Av Rangel Pestana, 147 – Vila Matias, 11031-551 Santos ☎13 3224 3098 – **SP91)** Rua Marechal Bitencourt, 346 - Centro, 17201-430 Jaú **W:** radiopiratiningajau.com **E:** contato@radiopiratiningajau.com – **SP92)** Av Washington Luiz, 1250 - Centro, 19015-150 Presidente Prudente ☎81 3916 1578 **W:** prudente.am.br – **FM** 101.1MHz – **SP93)** Rua 20, 3011 – Jardim Pegolo, 15700-000 Jales ☎17 3622 5505 **W:** radioassuncao.com.br **E:** comercial@regionalfm.com.br – **SP94)** Rua Santos Dumont, 239 - Centro, 14300-000 Batatais **W:** difusoraam.com.br **E:** diretoria@difusoraam.com.br ☎16 3761 3600 – **SP95)** Rua Olavo Bilac, 693 - Centro, 16400-000 Lins ☎☐14 3522 4644 **W:** radioalvoradadelins.com.br **E:** alvorada@superig.com.br – **SP96)** Av André Luiz, 723 - Picanco, 07082-050 Sorocaba ☎11 2457 7000 **W:** radioboanova.com.br **E:** rede@radioboanova.com.br – **SP97)** Av Zezé Valadão, 359 – Centro, 12570-970 Aparecida ☎12 3105 0754 **W:** radiomonumental.com.br **E:** radio_monumental@hotmail.com – **SP98)** Av Carlos Artêncio, 117 - Centro, 17519-255 Marília ☎14 3402 3077 **W:** radioclubemarilia.com.br **E:** clubeam@terra.com.br – **SP99)** Av 15 de Maio, 455, 15910-970 Monte Alto ☎16 3242 5231 **W:** radioculturamontealto.com.br **E:** contato@radioculturamontealto.com.br – **SP100)** Rua das Palmeiras 315, 01221-010 São Paulo **W:**radioglobo.com.br **E:** midiassociais@radioglobo.com.br – **SP101)** Rua Marechal Deodoro da Fonseca, 675 - Centro, 16011-000 Araçatuba ☎18 3305 9852 **E:** radioluz@terra.com.br – **SP102)** Rua Gabriel Hadad, 283 – Centro,14940-970 Ibatinga ☎16 3341 9900 **W:** radioibitinga.com.br **E:** radio.ibatinga@ibinet.com.br - **FM:** 99.3MHz «Ternura FM» – **SP103)** Av Luíz Gonzaga de Amoêdo Campos, 28 – Vila Áurea, 13800-908 Mogi Mirim ☎19 3814 1234 **W:** hitstransamerica.com.br - **FM:** 91.1MHz – **SP104)** Rua Bandeirantes, 104 – Centro, 18540-970 Porto Feliz ☎15 3261 5003 **W:** radionovaporto.com.br **E:** jornalismo@radionovaporto.com.br – **SP105)** Rua Euclides Miragaia, 548 - Centro, 12245-820 São José dos Campos ☎12 3941 4108 **W:** cidadeam1120.com.br **E:** radio@cidadeam1120.com.br – **SP106)** Rua Duque de Caxias, 260 cj 22 an 2 - Centro, 15900-970 Taquaritinga ☎16 3252 2999 **W:** radioimperial.com.br – **SP107)** Rua Cherentes, 250–13° andar – Centro, 17600-090 Tupã ☎14 3404 3255 **W:** Facebook:Rádio Tupã AM/FM - **FM:** 97.7MHz – **SP108)** Rua Gonçalves Dias, 208 - Centro, 19800-110 Assis ☎18 3322 3833 **W:** difusoraassis.com.br **E:** difusora@difusoraassis.com.br – **SP109)** Praça Joel Waldo Dal Moro 1, Centro, 14781-574 Barretos ☎17 3321 7070 **W:** odiarioonline.com.br **E:** contato@grupomonteirasdebarros.com.br – **SP110)** Av. 2, 1420 – Jardim Claret, 13503-240 Rio Claro ☎19 3534 0555 – **SP111)** Rua Dr. Esteves da Silva, 100 – Centro, 11680-000 Ubatuba ☎12 3832 2993 **W:** radiocostaazul.com.br **E:** comercial@radiocostaazul.com.br – **SP112)** Av Paulista, 2200Cerquira Cesar, 01310-300, Sao Paulo ☎11 3016 5999 **W:** radiomundial.com.br - **FM:** 95.7MHz – **SP113)** Rua Almirante Barroso, 456 - Centro, 19400-970 Presidente Venceslau ☎18 3271 1386 **W:** www venceslauam.com.br **E:** comercial@venceslauam.com.br - **FM:** 95.1MHz «R Jovem Som» – **SP114)** Rua Saldanha de Gama, 184 - Centro, 18035-040 Sorocaba ☎15 3232 3207 **W:** radiocacique.com.br **E:** contato@radiocacique.com.br - **FM:** 96.5MHz – **SP115)** Av. Manoel Marques Rosa, 1075-Ed. Atlântis - Centro, 15600-000 Fernandópolis ☎17 3442 2666 **W:** radiodifusorafernandopolis.com.br – **FM:** 99.0MHz – **SP116)** Rua Barão de Monte Santo, 1211-3° andar - Centro, 13730-060 Mococa ☎19 3656 6534 **W:** radioboanova.com.br **E:** rede@radioboanova.com.br – **SP117)** Av Eng Antonio Francisco de Paula Souz, 2799 – Vila Georgina, 13044-370 Campinas ☎19 3779 7500 **W:** rb1170.com.br **E:** jornalcps@band.com.br – **SP118)** Rua Barão do Rio Branco, 4454 – Vila Paes, 15500-055 Votuporanga ☎17 3421 2113 **W:** radiocidade1190.com.br **E:** contato@radiocidade1190.com.br – **SP119)** Av XV de Novembro, 715 - Centro, 13650-000 Santa Cruz das Palmeiras ☎19 3672 6976 – **SP120)** Rodovia Taquarituba Avare, s/n km 384, 18740-000 Taquarituba ☎14 3762 1487 **W:** radioregional1190.com.br **E:** regionalam@yahoo.com.br – **SP121)** Rua Vladimir Herzog, 75 - Agua Branca, 05036-900 São Paulo **W:** culturabrasil.com.br ☎11 2182 3080 – **SP122)** Rua Rui Barbosa, 546-4° andar - Centro, 14870-300 Jaboticabal ☎16 3202 0266 **W:** radiovidanova.com.br **E:** falecom@diovidanovaam.com.br – **SP123)** Rua Tupinambás, 115 – São João, 16025-065 Araçatuba – **SP124)** Av Dr Nunu de Assis 5050 – Jardim Bela Vista, 17010-120 Bauru ☎14 3232 3571 **W:** radiobandeirantesbauru.com.br – **SP125)** Av. Roberto Simonsen, 280 - Jd. Santa Rosalia,18090-000 Sorocaba ☎15 3224 5300 **W:** radiovanguarda.com.br **E:** comercial@radiovanguarda.com.br - **FM:** 94.9MHz – **SP126)** Rua Rafael Machado Neto, 101 – Vila Nova Capão Bonita, 18304-130 Capão Bonito ☎15 3542 1593 **W:** siteadministravel.com.br – **SP127)** Av. Tiradentes, 312 – Nova Mateo, 15990-607 Matão. ☎16 3384 6417 **W:** radiocidade890.com.br **E:** financeiro@radiocidade890.am.br – **SP128)** Rua Dr Miguel Penteado 585, Jardim Chapadão, 13073-180 Santos – **SP129)** Praça Emilio Peduti, 28 - Centro, 18600-410 Botucatu ☎14 3882 0236 **W:** radiomunicipalista.com.br – **SP130)** Rua 8, 472 -

Centro, 14620-000 Orlândia ☎16 3826 3000 📠16 3826 3006 **W:** orc.com.br **E:** orc@orc.com.br – **SP131)** Rua Julia Conceição,510 - Encruzilhada 11055-320 Santos **W:** Facebook: Rádio Clube de Santos 1240AM – **SP132)** Av Nove de Julho, 265 - Centro, 15200-000 José Bonifácio ☎17 3245 1621 **W:** radiovaledotiete.com.br **E:** contato@radiovaledotiete.com.br – **SP133)** Rua Vilaa, 195-Sala 23 - Centro, 12210-000 São Jose dos Campos ☎12 3923 7000 **W:** blog.cancaonova.com/saojosedoscampos **E:** radiosjc@cancaonova.com – **SP134)** Av Bento Abreu, 889 – Centro, 1408-396 Araraquara ☎16 3303 3622 **W:** radiomorada.com.br **E:** radiomorada@uol.com.br – **SP136)** Rua Irmã Serafina, 88 – Bosque, 13026-066 Campinas ☎19 3231 7860 **W:** brasilcampinas.com.br **E:** radio@brasilcampinas.com.br – **SP137)** Rua dos Radialistas Riopretense, 895 – Nova Redentora, 15090-070 São José do Rio Preto ☎17 3233 3322 **W:** novotempoam.com **E:**comercial@novotempoam.com.br – **SP138)** Av do Estado, 4568 – Cambuchi, 01516-901 Sao Paulo **W:** ipda.com.br **E:** webmaster@ipda.com.br – **SP139)** Rua Barao do Rio Branco 559, 14900-000 Itápolis ☎16 3262 3063 – **SP140)** Rua Antônio Gambagote, 27-esquina com Av. Newton Prado – Centro, 13631-096 Pirassununga ☎19 3561 2200 **W:** difusorapirassununga.com.br – **SP141)** Rua Coronel Osório, 84 - Centro, 12900-150 Bragança Paulista ☎11 4034 0442 **W:** radiobraganca.com.br **E:** radiobraganca@radiobraganca.com.br – **SP142)** Rua Siqueira Campos, 633 - Centro, Centro, 19010-061 Presidente Prudente ☎18 3222 6021 **W:** radiopaulista1330.com.br **E:** contato@radiopaulista1330.com.br – **SP143)** –Rua Batatais, 36-Jardim Paulista, 14090-160 Ribeirão Preto ☎16 3967 6002 –**SP144)** Rua Osvaldo Cruz, 67 - Centro, 16010-040 Araçatuba. ☎18 3623 8726 **W:** culturaam1340.com.br **FM:** 95.5MHz – **SP145)** Rua Barão de Jaceguai, 468 - Centro, 08710-905 Mogi das Cruzes ☎11 4799 2888 **W:** redemetropolitana.com.br – **SP146)** Rua Hipólito Lopes, 13 - Centro, 17350-000 Igaraçu do Tietê ☎14 3644 1122 **W:** novacanoa.com.br – **SP147)** Rua Sao Paulo, 1726 – Centro, 15600-000 Fernandópolis ☎17 3442 6639 **W:** aguasquentes1360.com.br – **SP148)** Av Orlando Fruchi, 97 - Distrito Industrial, 17900-000 Dracena ☎18 3821 2593 **W:** radioregionaljp.com.br **E:** contato@radioregionaljp.com – **SP149)** Rua Cuiabá, 361 - Centro, 16901-200 Andradina ☎18 3722 2729 – **SP150)** Av João Lemos, 578 - Centro, 17250-000 Bariri ☎14 3662 4000 **W:** baririradioclube.com.br **E:** contato@baririradioclube.com.br – **SP151)** Rua Pedro Natália Lorenzetti, 172 - Centro, 18680-110 Lençóis Paulista ☎14 3264 8100 **W:** difusora1010.com.br **E:** administracao@difusora1010.com.br – **SP152)** Rua Vereador Eugênio Mazon, Jardim Centenário, 13845-197 Mogi Guaçu ☎19 3861 0098 – **SP153)** Av. Benjamin Constant, 1214-3° andar - Centro, 13010-141 Campinas ☎19 3731 5100 **W:** globocampinas.com.br **E:** contato@globocampinas.com.br – **SP154)** Rua Dr Erico de Abreu Sodré, 542 - Centro, 16370-000 Promissão ☎14 3541 0508 **W:** radioculturapromissao.com **E:** radioculturaam@yahoo.com.br – **SP155)** Av Brasil, 1119 – Zana Sul, 17780-000 Lucélia ☎18 3551 1831 – **SP156)** Rua Salomao Shevs, 670 – Jardim Cruzeiro do Sul, 13572-083 São Carlos ☎16 3375 3046 **W:** clube.com.br **E:** info@clube.com.br – **FM:** 104.7MHz –**SP157)** Rua –Voluntários de Sao Paulo. 3066-10 andar conjunto 1003 - Centro, 15015-200 São José do Rio Preto ☎17 3212 7012 **W:** radiometropole-1400am.blogspot.com.br **E:** metropoleam@terra.com.br – **SP158)** Av Brigadeiro Luiz Antonio, 3175 – Jardim Paulista , 01401-001 São Paulo ☎11 2039 1410 **W:** blog.america.cancaonova.com **E:** americawebcn@gmail.com – **SP159)** Ladeira Prof Irineu Lopes de Lima, 418 - Centro, 13250-241 Itatiba ☎11 4524 0003 **W:** crnitatiba.com.br **E:** crnitatiba@terra.com.br – **SP160)** Rua Cerqueira Cesar 481, 14010-130 Ribeirão Preto – **SP161)** Rua Mato Grosso, 37 - Vila Aparecida, 15150-000 Monte Aprazível ☎17 3275 1772 **W:** difusoraaparecida.com.br **E:** difusoraaparecida@bol.com.br – **SP162)** Praça Barão do Rio Branco 30, 12010-090 Taubaté ☎12 3622 1866 **W:** dt7.com.br/radio **E:** radiocultura790.com.br – **SP163)** Av Doutor Júlio Faria, 828 - Centro , 18650-970 São Manuel ☎14 3841 3590 **W:** novasaomanuel.com.br – **SP164)** Rua Juca Cintra, 85 - Centro, 13930-000 Serra Negra ☎19 389 1125 **W:** Facebook: Rádio Serra Negra AM 1430 **E:** radio.serranegra@terra.com.br – **SP165)** Av Manoel Goulart, 291 1° andar - Centro, 19010-270 Presidente Prudente ☎18 3221 2900 **W:** comercialam.com.br – **SP166)** Rua Dom Pedro I, 556 – Centro, 16700-000 Guararapes ☎18 3406 3886 **W:** rdgguararapes.com.br – **SP167)** Av André Luís, 723 - Picanço, 07082-050 Guarulhos. ☎11 2457 7000 **W:** radioboanova.com.br **E:** rede@radioboanova.com.br – **SP168)** Rua 9 de Julho, 1801 - Centro, 13560-042 Sao Carlos do Pinhal ☎16 3371 3724 **W:** saocarlosam.com.br **E:** comercial@saocarlosam.com.br – **SP170)** Rua Duque de Caixas, 53 2° andar - Centro, 12600-040 Lorena ☎12 3157 7032 **W:** radiocultura1460.com.br **E:** radiocultura@provale.com.br – **SP172)** Av 15, 225 - Centro, 14790-000 Guaíra 17 3331 1177 **W:** radioculturaguaira.com.br **FM:** 90.1 MHz – **SP173)** Av Rui Barbosa, 229,- Centro, 12308-520 Jacareí ☎12 3954 3000 📠12 3954 3009 **W:** radiomensagem.am.br **E:** mensagem@radiomensagem.am.br – **SP174)** Rua Sao Sebastiao, 33 - Centro, 13660-000 Porto Ferreira ☎13 3581 1552 – **SP175)** Rua 13 de Maio, 2680 – Vila Georgina, 13333-080

Indaiatuba ☎19 3875 9141 **W:** radiojornalindaiatuba.com.br **E:** contato@radiojornalindaiatuba.com.br – **SP176)** Rua Renato Jardim, 511 - Centro, 14350-970 Altinópolis **W:** clubregionalam.com.br – **SP177)** Av Brigadeiro José Vicente Faria Lima, 54 - Centro, 12940-284 Atibaia ☎11 4411 8773 – **SP178)** Rua Conceiçao, 596 - Centro, 16210-000 Bilac ☎18 3659 1854 **W:** miliciadaimaculada.org.br **E:** 890am@miliciadaimaculada.org.br – **SP179)** Rua Conselheiro Dantas, 30 - Centro, 18900-000 Santa Cruz do Rio Pardo ☎14 3372 1763 **W:** difusorasantacruz.com.br **E:** contato@difusorasantacruz.com.br – **SP180)** Av Governador Ademar Pereira de Barros, 134 – Lotamente Canterville, 15400-000 Olímpia ☎17 3281 1097 **W:** difusoraolimpia.com.br – **SP181)** Rua Monte Castelo. 941 - Centro, 17900-000 Dracena ☎18 3821 8132 **W:** radioglobodracena.com.br – **SP182)** Av Brasil, 1712, 15600-970 Fernandópolis ☎17 3462 1112 **W:** educadorafernandopolis.com.br **E:** ouvinteeducadora@terra.com.br – **SP183)** Rua Padre Moro Grande, 870 - Dos Finco, 09831-250 São Bernardo do Campo ☎11 4397 6500 **W:** miliciadaimaculada.org.br **E:** sam@miliciadaimaculada.org.br – **SP184)** Av Guerino Turatti, 200 - DistritoIndustrial 381, 13602-900 Araras ☎📠19 3543 7990 **W:** fraternidade.com.br **E:** contato@fraternidadefm.com.br – **FM:** 97.9MHz – **SP185)** Rua Rubião Júnior, 192 - Centro, 12400-450 Pindamonhangaba ☎12 3643 1566 **W:** rededifusora.com.br/am1500/index.htm **E:** mkt@rededifusora.com.br – **SP186)** Av Leopoldo Carlos de Oliveira, 1038 - Centro, 14530-000 Miguelópolis ☎16 3835 1500 **W:** radiofmvale.com.br – **FM:** 87.9 MHz – **SP187)** Av.Paulista, 2200 13° andar - Cerqueira Cesar, 01310-300 Osasco ☎11 3266 6880 **W:** radioterra.am.br – **SP188)** Rua Silva Jardim, 480 - Macuco, 11015-020 Santos ☎13 3221 9500 📠13 3327 7643 **W:** radiocacique1510.com.br **E:** radio.cacique@hotmail.com – **SP189)** Rua Coronel Rodrigues Simôs, 69 – Centro, 18650-000 São Manuel ☎14 3841 2555 **W:** cluberegional.com.br **E:** jornalismo@cluberegional.com.br – **SP190)** Av Romeu Viana Romaneli, 1510 - Centro, 15570-970 Cardoso ☎17 3453 1376 **W:** radioalvoradacardoso.com **E:** radioalvoradacardoso@gmail.com – **SP191)** Rua Princesa Isabel de Bragança, 235 - Centro, 08710-460 Mogi das Cruzes ☎11 4796 1478 **W:** radioiguatemi.com.br – **SP192)** Rua Vereador Rosas, 171 - Centro, 13990-000 Espírito Santo do Pinhal ☎19 3651 1755 **W:** pinhalradioclube.com.br **E:** radiopinhal@dglnet.com.br – **FM:** 102.7MHz – **SP193)** Rua Marchal Deodora, 519 - Centro, 17930-970 Tupi Paulista – **SP194)** Rua Capitão Lisboa, 1080 - Centro, 18270-000 Tatuí ☎15 3251 3840 **W:** radionoticias.com.br – **SP195)** Rua Benedito Carlos dos Reis, 700 - Centro, 15190-970 Nhandeara ☎17 3472 1668 – **SP196)** Rua Marechal Deodoro, 320 - Centro, 18600-320 Botucatu ☎14 3882 1535 **W:** radiof8.com.br **E:** gravadorf8@hotmail.com – **SP197)** Av Diogo Antonio Feijo, 1184 – Jardim das Flores , 06114-029 Osasco ☎11 3681 1134 **W:** novadifusora.com.br **E:** faleconosco@novadifusora.com.br – **SP198)** Rua Dom José Carlos Aguirre, 567, 18460-000 Itararé ☎15 3532 4055 **W:** radioclube.cjb.net **E:** falecom@radioclubeam.net – **SP199)** Rua Pedro de Toledo, 205 - Centro, 19700-000 Paraguaçu Paulista ☎18 3361 1203 📠18 3362 2306 **W:** radiomarconi.com.br **E:** marconi@radiomarconi.com.br – **SP200)** Rua Lino Dorelli, 120 – Centro, 13360-000 Capivari ☎19 3492 1550 **W:** caciqueam.com.br **E:** matheus@caciqueam.com.br – **SP201)** Rua José Vaz de Porto, 175 - Vila Santa Rosa, 11431-190 Guarujá ☎13 3269 1010 **W:** radioguarujaam.com.br **E:** radioguarujaam@radioguarujaam.com.br – **FM:** 104.5MHz –**SP202)** Rua Minas Gerais, 1225 - Centro , 124600-970 São Joaquim da Barra ☎16 3818 1324 **W:** radiosaojoaquim.com.br – **SP203)** Av Dr Januario Miraglia. 650, Vila Abernessia, 12460-970 Campos do Jordão ☎12 3662 1906 **W:** hcamposdojordao1340.com.br **E:** emisora1340am@hotmail.com – **SP204)** Rua Rio Grande do Sul, 2165 – Braz I 18701-190 Avaré ☎14 3732 1564 **W:** radioavare.com.br **E:** radioavare@yahoo.com.br– **SP205)** Rua Belo Horizonte Nº930 17890-000 Junqueirópolis ☎18 3841 1465 **W:** radiojunqueiropolis.com.br **E:** contato@radiojunqueiropolis.com – **SP206)** Av Pereira Barreto, 1200 - Vila Gilda, 09190-210 Santo André ☎11 4435 9000 📠11 4435 9001 **W:** radioabc.com.br – **E:** faleconosco@radioabc.com.br – **SP207)** Rua Dr Vicente D´Anna, 473 - Centro, 13960-970 Socorro ☎19 3895 1444 **W:** radiosocorro.com.br **E:** comercial@radiosocrro.com.br – **SP208)** Rodovia Dep. Bady Bassit, km 15 – Jardim Covizzi, 15170-000 Tanabi ☎17 3272 2967 **W:** radioclubetanabi.com.br **E:** contato@radioclubetanabi.com.br – **SP209)** Rua Dr Felipe Vita, 1616 - Centro, 18480-000 Itaporanga ☎15 9753 6358 – **SP211)** Rua Joaquim Moreira, 12 - Parque São Miguel, 07260-220 Guarulhos ☎11 2496 1542 **W:** radiocumbica.com.br **E:** moacyrcustodio@radiocumbica.com.br – **SP212)** Av 17, 560 - Centro, 14780-000 Barretos ☎17 3324 1000 **W:** radiojornalbarretos.com.br **E:** radiojornal@jornalbarretos.com.br – **FM:** 101.1 MHz – **SP213)** Av Paulista 2202, 8° andar, Conj 81/82, 01310-300 São Paulo ☎11 5543 0762 – **SP214)** Av Capitão José Antônio de Oliveira, 544 - Centro, 17800-000 Adamantina ☎18 3521 3547 **W:** radiojoia.com.br **E:** contato@radiojoia.com.br – **FM:** 93.7MHz «Antena 1» – **SP215)** Rua Rio Grande do Sul, 1215 - Centro, 15600-000 Fernandopolis ☎17 3442 3192 **W:** alvorada970.com.br **E:** jornalismoalvorada970@hotmail.com – **SP216)** Rua Rubião

Junior, 84 sl.89–Shopping Centro - Centro, 12210-180 São José dos Campos ☎12 33221290 **W:** am1290.com.br – **SP217)** Rua Coronel João Manoel, 604 sl - Centro, 14700-000 Bebedouro ☎17 3343 6528 **W:** radionovaamaovivo.com.br – **SP218)** Rua Antônio Lobo, 237 1° andar - Centro, 13465-005 Americana ☎19 3462 3992 **W:** azulceleste.com.br **E:** azulceleste@azulceleste.com.br – **SP219)** Rua João Pacheco de Lima, 56-89 - Centro, 15350-000 Auriflama ☎17 3482 2068 **W:** radioauriflama.com.br **E:** radioauriflama@hotmail.com – **SP220)** A Monte Castelo, 225 - Centro, 13450-285 Santa Bárbara d'Oeste ☎19 3463 5255 **W:** radiobrasilsbo.com.br **E:** radiobrasil@radibrasilsbo.com.br – **SP221)** Rua Maximo Ribeiro Nunes, 75 – Jardim Peri Peri, 05535-000 Sao Paulo ☎11 3723 7575 **W:** nacionalgospel.com.br **E:** radio@nacionalgospel.com.br - **FM:** 100.5 MHz – **SP222)** Av Antonieta Vilela Ferreira, 900 - Vilage, 16300-000 Penápolis ☎☎18 3654 2250 **W:** banddepenapolis.com.br **E:** bandpenapolis@banddepenapolis.com.br – **SP223)** Av Paulista, 2200-10°andar – Cerqueira Cesar, 01310-300 São Paulo ☎11 3016 5999 http://radioapolo.com.br– **SP224)** Rua Kametaro Morishita, 95 - Cidade Universitária, 19050-700 Presidente Prudente ☎18 3299 0300 **W:** radioglobopp.com.br - **FM:** 106.7MHz – **SP225)** Rua Imperatriz Leopoldina, 41 – Vila Delgado Romano, 18044-010 Sorocaba ☎15 3222 5740 – **SP226)** Rua Bento Carlos, 61 - Centro, 13560-660 São Carlos ☎16 3362 3322 **W:** portalrealidade.com.br – **SP227)** Rua Duque de Caxias, 33 - Centro, 13460-000 Nova Odessa ☎19 3466 5026 **W:** novotempocampinas.com.br **E:** comercial@novotempocampinas.com.br – **SP228)** Rua Américo Vespúcio, 20 - Centro, 14730-000 Monte Azul Paulista ☎17 3361 2215 **W:** radioprincesaam.com.br **E:** radioprincesamonteazulpaulista@hotmail.com.br – **SP229)** Av Dr Labiano da Costa Machado, 1735 – Hilmar Machado, 17400-000 Garça ☎14 3471 0700 **W:** unimidianet.com.br – **SP231)** Francisco Troani, 1211 - Centro, 19280-000 Teodoro Sampaio ☎18 3282 1534 – **SP232)** Av Paulista, 2200-17 andar – Bela Vista, 01310-300 São Paulo ☎11 5081 579 – **SP233)** Av 9 de Julho, 304 - Nova Paulina, 13150-000 Paulínia ☎19 3844 8300 **W:** blog.cancaonova.com/paulinia **E:** cpaulinia@cancaonova.com – **SP234)** Rua Carlos Gomes, 534 - Centro, 14640-000 Morro Agudo ☎16 3851 2414 **W:** radiorepublica.com.br **E:** republica@com4.com.br – **SP235)** Rua Joaquim de Oliveira, 586 - Centro, 13450-038 Santa Bárbara d'Oeste ☎19 3464 1300 **W:** radioluzes.com.br **E:** radioluzes@uol.com.br – **SP236)** Av Izodoro Alpheu Santiago 126 – Santa Bárbara,18320-970 Apiaí ☎15 3552 4088 **W:** radiocidadeapiai.com.br – **SP237)** Rua Marechal Rondon, 170 - Alto São Pedro, 12082-420 Taubaté ☎12 3632 0555 – **SP238)** Av Dr Soares de Oliveira, 2070 - Centro, 14500-970 Ituverava ☎16 3839 7739 **W:** radiocultura1450.com.br **E:** radiocultura@netsite.com.br – **SP239)** Av Frederico Ozanan, 554, 17300-000 Dois Córregos ☎14 3652 2949 **W:** radioculturaregional.com.br – **SP240)** Av Olinda Ralston, 411B - Centro, 13720-000 São José do Rio Pardo **W** amdifusora.com.br – **SP241)** Rua Tocantins, 425 – Vila Espanha, 17607-070 Tupã ☎14 3496 1756 – **SP242)** Av Washington Luíz, 214 - Centro, 13600-720 Araras ☎19 3541 3714 **W:** radioclube.com.br **E:** radioclube@radioclube.com.br – **SP243)** Rua Dom Pedro I, 65 – Centro, 17690-970 Bastos ☎14 3478 2525 – **SP244)** Rua Santana, 440 - Centro, 13880-000 Vargem Grande do Sul ☎19 3641 5646 **W:** http//radioculturaam.com **E:** r.cultura@itelefonica.com.br – **SP245)** R. Rafael de Barros, 126 - Centro, 13610-120 Lemé ☎19 3571 4288 **W:** radioculturadeleme.com.br **E:** ouvinte@radioculturadeleme.com.br – **SP246)** Rua Francisco Geraldino 71 - Centro, 17580-970 Pompéia ☎14 3452 3900 **W:** radiojovemcentral.com.br – **SP247)** Rua 7 de Setembro, 73 - Centro, 17280-000 Pederneiras 14 3248 1989 **W:** amcultura.net – **FM:** 88.3MHz – **SP248)** Rua Tenente Adolfo Padilha, 157 - Centro, 16880-000 Valparaíso 18 3401 1130 **W:** radiovalparaiso.com.br **E:** radiovalparaise@globo.com – **SP249)** Rua 15 de Novembro 52, 13920-000 Pedreira – **SP250)** Av Presidente Vargas, 244 - Centro, 19470-000 Presidente Epitácio ☎18 3281 2577 **W:** facebook.rádio.vela.do.rio.paraná – **SP251)** Rua Comendador Guimarães, 25 sl 402 - Centro, 13900-470 Amparo ☎19 3807 2237 **W:** difusoradeamparo.com.br radio@difusoradeamparo.com.br – **SP252)** Rua Padre João Goetz, 370 - Jardim Esplanada, 19061-460 Presidete Prudente ☎☎18 3918 5300 **W:** ondaviva.com.br **E:** radioondaviva@stetnet.com.br – **SP253)** Rua 7 de Setembro 911, 14240-000 Cajuru – **SP254)** Av São Paulo, 100 - Jacaré, 13318-000 Cabreúva **W:** radiojapi.radio.br – **SP255)** Alameda dos Lírios, 111 - Centro, 18550-000 Boituva ☎15 3363 7352 **W:** radioamerica1480.com.br **E:** radionovamerica@fasternet.com.br – **SP256)** Rua José Revel, 477 - Centro, 13320-020 Salto ☎11 4029 0198 **W:** radiovaledotiete.com.br – **SP257)** Rua 9 de Julho, 666 - Centro, 16600-000 Pirajuí ☎14 3572 1352 **W:** pirajuiradioclube.net.br **E:** contato@pirajuiradioclube.net.br – **SP258)** Rua dos Operários, 1441 - Vila Rigueti, 19600-000 Rancharia ☎18 3265 1528 – **SP259)** Rua Antônio João de Carvalho, 39 1° andar - Centro, 13710-000 Tambaú ☎19 3673 1729 **W:** radiotambauam.com.br **E:** leandro@radiotambauam.com.br – **SP260)** Av. Professor Jesuíno, 352 - Centro, 17380-000 Brotas ☎14 3653 1306 **W:** radiobrotense.com.br **E:** ouvinte@radiobrotense.com.br

– **SP261)** Rua Nicalau Nassif, 523 – Jardim Imperial, 14540-000 Igarapava ☎16 3172 2570 **W:** radioshowam.blogspot.no/ **E:** radioshowigarapava@gmail.com – **SP262)** Rua Inácio Ribeiro, 592 - Centro, 13670-000 Santa Rita do Passa Quatro ☎☎19 3582 1278 **W:** radiozequinhadeabreu.com.br **E:** contato@radiozequinhadeabreu.com.br – **SP263)** Rua Manoel de Arzão, 85 - Vila Albertina, 02730-030 São Paulo ☎11 3932 3393 **W:** radio9deljulho.com.br **E:** radio@radio9dejulho.com.br – **SP264)** Av 04, 882 - Centro, 13500-030 Rio Claro ☎19 3526 1055 **W:** jornalcidade.net –**E:** radio@jcrioclaro.com.br – **SP265)** Av São Sebastião, 162, 3° piso, sala 1 - Centro, 18150-000 Ibiúna ☎15 3241 5679 **W:** radioexcelsiorad.com.br **E:**radioad1350@hotmail.com – **SP266)** Legião da Boa Vontade (LBV), Rua Doraci, 90 – Bom Retiro, 01134-050 Sao Paulo **W:** redeboavontade.com.br **E:** superrbv@boavontade.com – **SP269)** Rua 24 de Maio, 690 - Centro, 14870-350 Jaboticabal ☎16 3203 5355 **W:** radioathenas.com.br **E:** adm@radioathenas.com – **SP270)** Rua Dos Pereiras, 1197 - Centro, 15290-970 Buritama ☎18 3691 3279 **W:** torreforteam.radioamiga.com.br**E:** torreforteam@uol.com.br – **SP273)** Av Clara Gianotti de Suza, 1124 - Centro, 11900-970 Registro ☎13 3821 1606 **W:** radionovaregionalam.blogspot.com.br **E:** radionovaregionalam1140@gmail.com – **SP274)** Rdv. Anel Viário Contorno Sul, 99 - City, 14021-800 Ribeirao Preto ☎16 3621 2337 **W:** radiobandeirantes.com.br – **SP275)** Rua Honório Mendes de Moraes, 23 - Esplanada Mendes Moares, 18130-760 São Roque ☎11 4712 4976 **W:** miliciadaimaculada.org.br **E:** 1430am@miliciadaiimaculada.org.bra – **SP280)** Rua Épiró, 110 - Vila Alexandria, (C.P 80761, 04646-970) 04635-030 São Paulo **W:** transmundial.org.br **E:** rtm@transmundial.org.br – Recepcion Reports to: qsl@transmundial.com.br – **SP283)** Praca Osvaldo Cruz, 124 – Conjuto 116, 11900-000 Registro –**SP284)** Rua Aristides Pires, 1397 - Centro, 18370-970 Itaí ☎14 3761 2753 –**SP285)** Rua Luiza Bechelli, 284 – Jardim Sabaúna, 11740-000 Itanhaém ☎13 3422 1177 **W:** Facebook: Rádio Anchiete AM 1390 kHz – **SP286)** Rua Tiradentes,31 – Centro,14740-000 Viradouro ☎17 3392 3008 **W:** cliqueradiolegal.com **E:** contato@ cliqueradiolegal.com.br – **SP287)** Rua Gabriel Hadad, 283 – Centro,14940-970 Ibatinga ☎16 3341 9900 **W:** radioibitinga.com.br **E:** radio.ibatinga@ibinet.com.br - **FM:** 99.3MHz «Ternura FM» - **SP288)** IPDA, Rua Saldanha Marinho 740, Ribeirao Preto ☎16 3636 6111 – **SP289)** Rua Coronel Nabor Nogueira Santos 258 – 3° andar, 12260-000 Paraibuna **W:** radiograndevale.com.br **E.** ouvinte@radiograndevale.com.br

T000) TOCANTINS

T001) Av Joaquim Aires 2393, 77500-000 Porto Nacional ☎63 3363 1608 – **T002)** Praça José Tôrres 3, 77600-000 Paraíso do Tocantins ☎63 3602 1135 – **T003)** Av Nossa Senhora de Fátima 894, 77900-000 Tocantinópolis ☎63 3471 1572– **T004)** BR-157 Km 1103, Zona Rural, 77804-970 Araguaína - **FM:** 99.7MHz «Araguaia» – **T005)** Rua Raul do Espírito Santo 1334,77760-000 Colinas do Tocantins ☎63 3476 1180 – **T006)** Rua Justianio Borpa, Q.3 – Setor Santa Filomena, 77650-000 Miracema do Tocantins ☎63 3366 1264 **W:** radioojornal.com.br **E:** radiocultura1480@hotmail.com – **T007)** Almeda João Pires Querido 827, 77490-000 Cristalândia ☎63 3354 1600 – **T008)** Av Bernardo Sayão 2201, 77700-000 Guaraí **W:** Facebook: Rádio Guaraí Am 1400 kHz **E:** gersonnk@hotmail.com – **T009)** Rua Ns B Q Cj2, 0-Lt2 – Acsu Ne 10, 77000-000 Palmas – **T010)** Av Piaui, entre Ruas 3 e 4, Centro, 77402-970 Gurupi **W:** nossaradioto.com.br **E:** nossaradioto@outlook.com – **T012)** 306 Sul Almeda 2, Plano Diretor Sul, 77021-048 Palmas ☎63 3218 8585 **W:** liberdadeam.com.br **E:** financeiro@liberdadeam.com.br

BRITISH INDIAN OCEAN TERRITORY

L.T: UTC + 6h — **Pr.L:** English — **Pop:** variable (US & British military personnel). Original population of c. 3000 was removed to Mauritius — **E.C:** 60Hz, 110/220V – **ITU:** BIO **Diego Garcia ITU:** DGA

ARMED FORCES RADIO AND TELEVISION SCE (U.S. Mil.)
🖳 Naval Media Center Detachment-Diego Garcia, PSC 466 Box 14, FPO, AP 96595-0014. ☎+246 370 3680/3685 🖷+246 370 3681 **E:** dgar@mediacen.navy.mil
SW: AFN – see International section (USA) for details.
FM: Power 99, 99.1MHz 0.25kW, weekdays 0600-1400, rock & roll, live DJ. **Island Variety,** 109.9MHz 200W, mixture of rock, alternative, urban & country.
D.Prgr: 24h **V.** by letter.

BRITISH FORCES BROADCASTING SERVICE
FM: Diego Garcia 90.7MHz

BRUNEI DARUSSALAM

L.T: UTC +8h — **Pop:** 440,000 — **Pr.L:** Malay, English, Chinese, Gurkha — **E.C:** 50Hz, 240V — **ITU:** BRU

AUTHORITY FOR INFO-COMMUNICATIONS TECHNOLOGY INDUSTRY OF BRUNEI DARUSSALAM - AITI (Regulatory Body)
✉ Block B14, Simpang 32-5, Kampung Anggerek Desa, Jalan Berakas BB3713 ☎ +673 2323232 🖷 +673 2382447 **E:** info@aiti.gov.bn
W: aiti.gov.bn
LP: Chmn: Dato Paduka Hj Alaihuddin bin POKDG Haji Mohd Taha

RADIO TELEVISION BRUNEI - RTB (Gov.)
✉ Jalan Elizabeth II, Bandar Seri Begawan BS8610 ☎ +673 2243111
🖷 +673 2241882 **E:** rtbipro@brunet.bn **W:** rtb.gov.bn
LP: Acting Dir: Haji Idris bin Haji Md. Ali. Acting Dep. Dir: Pg. Hj. Mahari Pg Hj Abd Rajak. Head R. Prgrs Div: Hajah Zalinar binti Haji Abdullah. Sup. Engng: Madam Lim Soh Kwang

FM (MHz)	RN	RPi	RPe	RH	NI	kW
1) Andulau	93.8	96.9	91.0	97.7	94.9	5
2) Bukit Subok	92.3	95.9	91.4	94.1	93.3	5/0.5

DAB: on 225.648MHz
1) Kuala Belait & Tutong areas. **2)** Bandar Seri Begawan (BSB) area. RN = Rangkaian Nasional FM in Malay: 24h RPi = R. Pilihan. English: 0300-0800 (Sat 0300-0700), 1200-0100. Chinese: 0100-0300, 0800-1100. Gurkha: daily 1100-1200, Sat 0700-0800. RPe = Rangkaian Pelangi (Pelangi FM, prgrs for young people): 24h Additional FM freqs: 88.5MHz in BSB area, 96.3MHz in Kuala Belait area. RH = Rangkaian Harmoni (music sce.): 24h NI = Rangkaian Nur Islam (rlg. talk channel): 24h Ann: (RN in Malay) "Nasional FM, Radio Brunei"

KRISTAL MEDIA SDN. BHD. (subsidiary of DST Group, DataStream Technology Sdn Bhd) (Comm.)
✉ Unit 1-345, 1st Fl., Gadong Properties Centre, Gadong BE 4119 11 ☎ +673 2456828 🖷 +673 2420682 **W:** kristal.fm **E:** kristalfm@dst-group.com

FM (MHz)	KFM	RQ
1) Andulau	98.7	99.7
2) Bukit Subok	90.7	89.1

KFM=Kristal FM. RQ=Recital of Al-Quran. 1), 2) as above
D.Prgr: Kristal FM: 24h in English/Malay. RQ: 24h in Arabic
N: (Kristal FM) rel. RTB (0500, 0930, 1200, 1300, 2300) and BBC WS (0600, 1100)

BRITISH FORCES BROADCASTING SERVICE
✉ BFBS Brunei, BFPO 11 ☎ +673 3223424 🖷 +673 3224113 **E:** bfbsbrunei@bfbs.com **W:** bfbs-radio.com/ 24h in English on 101.7MHz 0.25kW, in Nepali (Gurkha) on 89.5MHz 0.25kW. Location: Brunei Garrison HQ, Tuker Lines, Seria, Belait District

BULGARIA

LT: UTC +2h (27 Mar-30 Oct: +3h) — **Pop:** 7.4 million — **Pr.L:** Bulgarian, Turkish — **E.C:** 50Hz, 220V — **ITU:** BUL

SAVET ZA ELEKTRONNI MEDII
(Council for Electronic Media)
✉ bul. Shipchenski prohod 69, 1574 Sofiya ☎ +359 29708810 🖷+359 29733769 **E:** office@cem.bg **W:** cem.bg
LP: Chmn: Georgi Lozanov
NB: The Council is the regulatory authority for broadcasting.

BALGARSKO NATSIONALNO RADIO (BNR) (Pub)
✉ bul. Dragan Tsankov 4, 1040 Sofiya ☎ +359 29336330 **E:** bnr@bnr.bg **W:** bnr.bg **LP:** DG: Radoslav Yankulov

MW	kHz	kW	Prgr
Vidin	576	400	1+P+T

FM(MHz)	1	2	kW	FM	1	2	kW
Babyak	87.6	-	1	Momchilgrad	105.0	99.2	10/1
Belogradchik	102.3	88.2	10/1	Momchilgrad	*90.0	-	1
Berkovitsa	101.4	99.5	10/7	Montana	100.4	-	1
Bistritsa	91.8	-	1	Nesebar	102.5	99.3	10
Botev vrah	100.9	92.2	10	Nikopol	96.4	98.2	0.1/1
Burgas	90.2	96.1	1	Oryahovo	99.8	101.7	1
Dobrich	104.3	102.3	3/1	Pleven	102.7	100.2	1
Dupnitsa	104.1	87.8	1	Plovdiv	88.1	91.7	1
Dzhebel	102.1	88.4	1	Popovo	103.5	95.7	0.5/1
G.Delchev	100.3	98.5	10/1	Provadiya	88.9	102.9	3
Gabrovo	103.2	95.4	1	Razgrad	103.5	99.4	1
Ivailovgrad	91.6	96.4	0.1/1	Roman	94.7	-	1
Karnobat	103.2	95.0	1	Ruse	103.0	95.7	10/1
Kavarna	88.1	90.1	10/1	Shumen	102.0	100.4	10/1
Kresna	88.8	89.7	1	Shumen	*90.1	-	1
Kyustendil	102.1	99.3	10	Silistra	103.3	107.2	3/1
M. Tarnovo	90.2	106.1	1	Sliven	87.8	98.7	1

FM(MHz)	1	2	kW	FM	1	2	kW
Smolyan	101.6	96.0	5/1	Tsarevo	102.2	90.8	1
Sofiya	103.0	92.9	10	V.Tarnovo	96.0	99.6	1
St.Zagora	-	98.3	1	Varna	100.9	104.8	5/1
Svilengrad	99.7	94.9	3	Vratsa	103.4	97.81/0.45	
Targovishte	92.8	95.4	1/0.5	Yablanitsa	89.2	95.0	1
Tran	97.6	90.0	1				

NB: Sites with only txs below 1kW not listed. *) incl. P+T
D.Prgr: Prgr 1 (Horizont): 24h. – **Prgr 2 (Hristo Botev):** 24h. – **Parlamentaren kanal (P):** broadcasts from parliament Wed-Fri 0700-1200. – **Service for Turkish ethnic minority (T):** 0600-0630 (SS 0700), 1300-1400, 1830-1930 in Turkish.

BNR Regional Stations
D.Prgr: all stns: 24h. – **BNR R. Blagoevgrad:** ul. Ivan Mihaylov 56, 2700 Blagoevgrad **E:** koordinacia.blg@bnr.bg. On (MHz) 90.9 (Yakoruda 0.1kW), 102.3 (Gotse Delchev 1kW), 103.2 (Blagoevgrad 0.25kW), 105.2 (Kresna 1kW), 106.6 (Kyustendil 1kW), Dubnitsa 107.4. – **BNR R. Burgas:** ul. Filip Kutev 2, 8000 Burgas **E:** radioburgas@bnr.bg. On (MHz) 90.2 (M.Tarnovo 1kW), 91.7 (Tsarevo 1kW), 91.9 (Yambol 1kW), 92.5 (Burgas 1kW), 106.0 (Elhovo 0.5kW): own prgrs 0400-1900 (Sat 1600, Sun 1700); rel. BNR Prg.1 (Horizont) at other times. (*) – **BNR R. Kardzhali (to start in January 2016):** 6600 Kardzhali. On 90.0MHz (Momchilgrad 1kW) in Bulgarian, Turkish. – **BNR R. Plovdiv:** ul. Dondukov korsakov 2, 4000 Plovdiv **E:** director@radioplovdiv.bg. On (MHz) 88.3 (Panagyurishte 0.25kW), 94.0 (Plovdiv 1kW), 100.1 (Velingrad 0.1kW), 100.6 (Dospat 0.2kW), 103.1 (Smolyan 1kW). – **BNR R. Sofiya:** bul. Dragan Tsankov 4, 1040 Sofiya **E:** sofia@bnr.bg. On (MHz) 90.4 (Svoge 0.15kW), 94.5 (Sofiya 1kW), 100.0 (Samokov 0.2kW), 104.6 (Ihtiman 0.3kW). – **BNR R. Stara Zagora:** ul. Knyaz Boris 75, 6000 Stara Zagora **E:** rsz@radio-sz.net. On (MHz) 88.3 (Stara Zagora 1kW), 97.2 (Sliven 1kW), 107.8 (Svilengrad 1kW). – **BNR R. Shumen:** ul. Dobro Voynikov 7, 9700 Shumen **E:** admin@radioshumen.net. On (MHz) 87.6 (Shumen 10kW), 90.3 (Silistra 3kW), 93.4 (Shumen/City 1kW), 94.0 (Targovishte 0.5kW), 97.0 (Razgrad 0.5kW), 96.8 (Ruse 1kW), 104.5 (Isperih). – **BNR R. Varna:** bul. Primorski 22, 9000 Varna **E:** bnr@radiovarna.com. On (MHz) 88.5 (Nesebar 1kW), 88.7 (Dobrich 1kW), 98.2 (Kavarna 0.5kW), 103.4 (Varna 1kW), 105.3 (Provadiya 1kW). (*) – **BNR R. Vidin:** ul. Gradinska 1, 3700 Vidin **E:** office@radiovidin.com. On (MHz) 94.4 (Vratsa 0.3kW), 97.1 (Vidin 0.25kW), 103.9 (Berkovitsa 1.5kW), 106.8 (Belogradchik 1kW). (*) These outlets also carry N. in English & Russian for holidaymakers during July/August, produced by BNR's "R.Bulgaria" service.

OTHER STATIONS
FM	MHz	kW	Location	Station
2)	87.6	1	Nesebar	R. N-Joy
1)	87.9	1	Sandanski	Darik R.
5C)	88.2	1	Sofiya	The Voice
7)	89.5	1	Varna	R. Fokus
1)	89.7	2	Samokov	Darik R.
10)	90.2	1	Petrich	R. Bella
4)	90.6	1	Belogradchik	R. NRJ
5B)	90.9	1	Smolyan	R. Vitosha
1)	91.0	1	Belogradchik	Darik R.
8)	91.1	1	Burgas	Power FM
1)	91.5	1	Shumen	Darik R.
3A)	91.9	1	Petrich	R. Vega+
1)	93.2	1	Momchilgrad	Darik R.
6)	94.1	1	Burgas	R. FM+
5A)	94.3	1	Smolyan	R. Veselina
5A)	94.8	1	Burgas	R. Veselina
4)	95.5	1	Kozloduy	R. NRJ
9)	95.7	1	Burgas	BG R.
2)	96.0	1	Tutrakan	R. N-Joy
1)	96.7	1	Yablanitsa	Darik R.
5B)	96.7	1	Burgas	R. Vitosha
11)	97.3	1	Sandanski	R. Gea
12)	98.3	1	Burgas	Glast na Burgas
1)	99.3	1	Varna	R. NRJ
4)	99.9	1	Burgas	R. NRJ
1)	100.6	1	Kyustendil	Darik R.
1)	100.6	1	Primorsko	R. N-Joy
1)	100.7	1	Silistra	Darik R.
2)	101.2	1	Sliven	R. N-Joy
2)	101.8	1	Burgas	R. N-Joy
5A)	102.4	1	Vidin	R. Veselina
3B)	103.4	1	Sandanski	R. Ultra
1)	104.0	1	Svilengrad	Darik R.
1)	104.5	2	Burgas	Darik R.
2)	105.0	2	Sofiya	R. N-Joy
1)	105.2	3	Plovdiv	Darik R.
5A)	105.7	1	Sandanski	R. Veselina

FM	MHz	kW	Location	Station
1)	106.2	1	Gotse Delchev	Darik R.
1)	106.6	1	V.Tarnovo	Darik R.
1)	106.8	1	Kavarna	Darik R.
1)	107.0	1	Smolyan	Darik R.
1)	107.2	1	Blageovgrad	Darik R.
1)	107.7	1	Dobrich	Darik R.
7)	107.7	1	Vidin	R. Fokus

NB: Txs below 1kW not listed.
Addresses & other information:
1) bul. Knyaz A.Dondukov 82, 1504 Sofija **E:** reklama@darik.net – **2)** ul. Panayot Volov 3, 1504 Sofija **E:** njoy@njoybg.com – **3A,B)** ul. Todor Aleksandrov 3, 2700 Blagoevgrad **E:** 3A) vega_plus@abv.bg, 3B) radio_ultra@abv.bg – **4)** bul. Tsar Boris III 23, 1612 Sofija **E:** reklama@nrj.bg – **5A-C)** ul. Srebarna 21, 1407 Sofija **E:** office@bssmedia.bg – **6)** bul. Erusalim 51, Zhilishen Kompleks Mladost 1, 1784 Sofija **E:** fmplus@fmplus.net – **7)** ul. Filip Stanislavov 6, 1505 Sofija **E:** focus@focus-news.net – **8)** ul. A.Bogoridi 16, 8000 Burgas **E:** office@powerfm.bg – **9)** ul. Sofiyski geroy 3a, 1612 Sofiya **E:** office@bgradio.net – **10)** pl. Makedoniya10, 2850 Petrich **E:** office@radiobella.com – **11)** bul. Svoboda 13, 2800 Sandanski **E:** gea@sani.net – **12)** ul Aleksandrovska 26, 8000 Burgas **E:** office@radioburgas.net.

Radio via DTT: see National TV section

BURKINA FASO

L.T: UTC — **Pop:** 15 million — **Pr.L:** French + 16 ethnic — **E.C:** 50Hz, 220V — **ITU:** BFA

CONSEIL SUPÉRIEUR DE LA COMMUNICATION (CSC)
☐ 01 BP 6437, Ouagadougou ☎+226 50301124 🖷 +226 50301133 **W:** csc.bf **E:** infos@csc.bf **L.P:** Dir: Luc Adolphe Diao.

RADIODIFFUSION TÉLÉVISION DU BURKINA (Gov.)
☐ BP 7029, Ouagadougou 01 ☎+226 50324302 🖷 +226 50310441 **W:** rtb.bf **E:** radio@rtb.bf **L.P:** MD: Marcel Toe. Head of Tr. Centre: Marcel Teho. Prgr.Dir: Pascal Goba.
FM: 88.5/92.0/99.9MHz 0.02kW
D.Prgr in French/Ethnic: 24h. **N. in French:** 0630MF, 1000SS + Thurs, 1245 (regional), 1300, 1900, 2200. **N. in English:** W1920 (approx). **Ann:** "RTV Burkina", "RTB". **IS:** Balafon.
Canal Arc-en-Ciel, 03 BP 7045, Ouagadougou. **L.P:** Alphousseini Bassolet. **FM:** Ouagadougou 96.6MHz, Bobo-Dioulasso 89.8MHz.

REGIONAL STATIONS:
Radio Bobo, BP 392, Bobo-Dioulasso. **FM:** 92.0MHz 0.02kW. **D.Prgr:** MF 0600-0800, 1200-1400, 1600-2400, SS 0800-2400 – **R. Gaoua,** Gaoua. **FM:** 90.1MHz – **R. Rurale:** FM txs in Diapaga, Djibasso, Gassan, Kongoussi, Orodara & Poura.

Other Stations (all MHz):
Al Houda FM, Ouagadougou: 98.5 – **Bankuy FM,** Dédougou: 107.7 – **Horizon FM:** Tenkodogo 97.6, Banfora 98, Koudougou 98.7, Ouayigouya 100.4, Dédougou 102.7, Ouagadougou 104.4, Dori 104.6 **W:** facebook.com/Horizonfm.bf?fref=ts – **Ouaga FM:** Bobo-Dioulasso 101.1, Ouagadougou 105.2 **W:** ouagafm-bf.com – **R. Ahmadiya,** Dori: 104.6 – **R. de l'Alliance Chrétienne,** Bobo-Dioulasso: 95.9 – **R. Balafon,** Bobo-Dioulasso: 102.7 – **R. Buayaba,** Diapaga 96.2MHz – **R. FM Boulgou,** Garango: 101.1 – **R. Cascade,** Banfora: 98 – **R. Catholique Teriya,** Banfora 94.7 – **R. Djawoampo,** Bogandé 98.0 – **R. Djongo,** Pô: 106.4 – **Echo des Cotonniers,** Solenzo: 95.1 – **R. Djibasso:** 94.6 – **R. Énergie:** Kaya 92.2, Yako 94.9, Fada N'Gourma 98.8 – **R. de l'Espoir,** Réo: 102.8 – **R. Évangile Développement:** Ouagadougou 93.4, Houndé 95.5, Léo 97.8, Koudougou 101.0, Ouahigouya 104.0, Yako 105.3, Bobo-Dioulasso 106.3. **W:** red-burkina.org – **R. Evangile du Sud-Ouest,** Gaoua: 99.7 – **R. Eveil,** Bogandé 101.0 – **R. Fréquence Espoir:** Dédougou 96.8 1kW, Tougan 101.4 0.1kW – **R. Frontière,** Tenkodogo: 97.6 – **R. Gambidi,** Ouagadougou: 97.7 – **R. Gassan:** 105.5 – **R. Gayeri:** 91.8 – **R. Goulou,** Po 99.5 – **R. du Grand Nord,** Dori: 97.5 – **R. Kadoadb,** Ziniare: 107.7 – **R. Kantigya,** Nouna 88.8 – **R. Kongoussi:** 93.2 – **R. Kouritta,** Koupela: 93.7 – **R. La Voix des Bales,** Boromo 103.6 – **R. La Voix du Soum,** Djibo 92.1 – **R. Lotamu,** Solenzo 101.9 – **R. LCD,** Djibo 98.6 – **R. Loudon,** Sapouy 104.9 – **R. Lumière:** Ouagoudougou: 98.1 – **R. Manegda,** Kaya: 99.4 – **R. Maria:** Ouagadougou 91.6 1kW, Kaya 99.4, Koupéla 96.9 1kW. **W:** radiomaria.org – **Media Star,** Bobo-Dioulasso: 96.7 – **R. Munyu FM,** Banfora: 94.7 – **R. Naboswende,** Pouytenga: 103.7 – **R. Natigmeb Zanga,** Yako: 98.2 – **R. Nemaro,** Cassou 94.2 – **R. Nerwaya,** Kongoussi 99.7 – **R. Notre Dame de la Réconciliation,** Koudougou 105.8 – **R. Nostalgie,** Ouagadougou, 94.4 – **R. Notre Dame:** Kaya 102.9, Kouhoudan 105.8, Ouahigouya

102.6 – **R. Omega:** Ouagadougou 103.9, Bobo-Dioulasso 104.7 **W:** omegabf.net – **R. Paglayiri,** Zabré 94.3 – **R. Palabre,** B.P. 196, Kougougou: 92.2 – **R. Pog-Neere,** Pouytenga 100.2MHz – **R. Poura:** 98.2 – **R. Pulsar,** Ouagadougou: 94.8 0.4kW – **R. Salaki,** Dedougou 101.1 – **R. Salankoloto,** Ouagadougou: 97.3 – **R. Sanmentenga,** Kaya: 96.1 – **R. Tin-Taani,** Kantchari 100.0 – **La Voix du Sud-Ouest,** Diébougou: 101.5 – **R. Taanba,** Fada N'Gourma: 98.8 1kW **W:** radioafricanetwork.org.za/RadioTaanba.html – **R. Tapao,** Diapaga: 95.8 – **R. Unitas,** Diébougou: 94.7 – **R. Vive le Paysan,** Saponé: 107.0 – **R. la Voix du Passoré,** Yako: 105.3 – **R. la Voix du Paysan,** Ouahigouya: 97.0 – **R. La Voix du Verger,** Orodara: 91.2 – **R. Zoodo,** Ouahigouya: 100.4 **R. Savane,** Ouagadougou: 103.4 **W:** savanefm.bf
BBC African Sce: Ouagadougou 99.2 4kW.
RFI Afrique: Banfora 91.5, Koudougou 93.0, Ouagadougou 94.0, Ouahigouya 94.3, Bobo-Dioulasso 99.4.
Voice of America: Ouagadougou 102.4

BURUNDI

L.T: UTC +2h — **Pop:** 9 million — **Pr.L:** Kirundi, Swahili, French, English — **E.C:** 50Hz, 220V — **ITU:** BDI

CONSEIL NATIONAL DE LA COMMUNICATION (CNC)
☎+257 22223742 🖷 +257 22226547 **W:** burundi.gov.bi
L.P: Chairman: Vestine Nahimana.

RADIO-TÉLÉVISION NATIONALE DU BURUNDI (RTNB, Gov.)
☐ B.P. 1900, Bujumbura ☎+257 22223742 🖷 +257 22226547 **W:** rtnb.bi **E:** rtnb@cbinf.com **L.P:** D.G.: Innocent Muhozi

FM(MHz)	RTNB1	RTNB2	FM(MHz)	RTNB1	RTNB2
Birime	94.2	98.9	Kaberenge	94.7	98.0
Bujumbura	102.9	92.9	Manga	95.6	98.9
Inanzerwe	88.4	91.4	Mutumba	88.8	91.9

D.Prgr: W 0300-0700 & 0900-2100, Sun 0300-2100. (RTNB1 in Kirundi, RTNB2 in French/Swahili/English). **N.** in French: 0530, 1200, 1500, 1900. **N.** in Swahili: 0630, 1245, 1800. **N.** in Kirundi: 0500, 0700, 1130, 1800, 2000. **N.** in English: 0445, 1230, 1600, 1845.
Ann: "Ici Bujumbura, Radio-Télévision Nationale du Burundi". **IS:** Drums.

Other stations (FM MHz):
Bonesha FM: Manga 87.7 20kW, Bujumbura 96.8, Jenda 102.4 **W:** bonesha.bi – **R. CCIB FM,** Bujumbura: 99.4, nationwide 102.4 – **R. Culture,** Bujumbura: 88.2/99.9 – **R. Isanganiro:** Bujumbura 89.7, Bururi 93.3/95.1, Kirundo 90.6, Ruyigi 90.7, Manga 101.0. **W:** web-africa.org/isanganiro – **R. Ivyizigiro,** Bujumbura: 90.9/104.8 – **R. Public Africaine,** Bugesera 89.4, Birime 92.6, Bujumbura 93.7, Manga 107.1 **W:** rpa.bi – **R. Renaissance,** Bujumbura 101.4 – **R. Scolaire Nderagakura,** Bujumbura 87.9 – **Rema FM,** Bujumbura: 88.6/103.6/107.5. **W:** remafm.com.
RFI Afrique: Manga 103.7 in F/E/Swahili.
BBC African Sce: Bujumbura 90.2, Manga 105.6

CAMBODIA

L.T: UTC +7h — **Pop:** 15.7 million — **Pr.L:** Khmer (Cambodian) — **E.C:** 50Hz, 230V — **ITU:** CBG

NATIONAL RADIO OF KAMPUCHEA (RNK)
☐ No 6 Street 19 (Corner Street 102), Sangkat Wat Phnom, Khan Daun Penh, Phnom Penh 12202 ☎ +855 23 725522 🖷 +855 23 427319 **W:** rnk.gov.kh
L.P: Dir. Gen: HE Tan Yan. Dir. R. Prgr: Mr Bou Vannarith. Dir. R. Tech: Oum Phin. Dep. Dir. Gen. FM 96: Touch Sareth
Wat Phnom FM: Phnom Penh 105.7MHz 10kW
FM-96 (comm.): ☐ Steung Meanchey, Phnom Penh 12352 **FM:** 96.0MHz 20kW
Cambodia-China Friendship Radio (joint service with China Radio International): 2300-1700 in Chaozhou, English, Khmer and Mandarin **FM:** Phnom Penh 96.5MHz 10kW, Siem Reap 105.0MHz
Provincial sces: Battambang (R. Chamka Chek) 92.7MHz 2kW, Kampot (R. 9 Makhara) 99.7MHz 2kW, Kampong Thom 98.3MHz, Kratie 98.5MHz 2kW, Pailin 90.5MHz 2kW. Pursat 98.5MHz 2kW, Siem Reap 102.9MHz 2kW, Sihanoukville 93.0MHz 2kW, Svay Rieng 98.7MHz, Takeo (R. Kork Thlok) 98.5MHz 2kW
Ann (Khmer): "Thini Sathani Vithayu Cheat Kampuchea"

PHNOM PENH MUNICIPAL RADIO STATION
☐ No 29, Street 335 / 1005 National Road 2, Phnom Penh 12312 ☎ +855 23 982265

Sweet FM: Phnom Penh 88.0MHz. **Sweet FM stations in provinces:** Battambang 103.25MHz, Kampong Cham 100.5MHz, Kampong Chhnang 104.7MHz, Kampong Thom 103.5MHz, Kampot 93.25MHz, Preah Vihear 99.5MHz, Kampong Thom 103.5MHz, Siem Reap 100.5MHz, Sihanoukville 100.5MHz, Sisophon 103.5MHz, Stung Treng 100.5MHz, Svay Rieng 103.75MHz

Love FM: Phnom Penh 97.5MHz, Siem Reap (relay) 97.5MHz in English and Khmer

Municipality R.: Phnom Penh 103.0MHz, 10kW

RADIO BAYON FM

Russei Sros Village, Sangkat Niroth, Khan Meanchey, Phnom Penh 12410 ☎ +855 23 333795

FM: Kandal (Phnom Penh area) 95.0MHz 24kW. Rel. stns: Banteay Meanchay 97.5MHz 5kW, Battambang 104.0MHz 2kW, Kampong Cham 91.5MHz 10kW, Kampong Thom 91.0MHz 2kW, Kampot 91.0MHz 2kW, Koh Kong 95.5MHz 2kW, Kratie 91.0MHz 2kW, Mondulkiri 95.0MHz 2kW, Oddar Meanchey 94.0MHz 2kW, Preah Vihear 95.0MHz 2.5kW, Pursat 91.5MHz 2kW, Ratanakiri 94.0MHz 1kW, Siem Reap 93.0MHz 10kW, Sihanoukville 92.0MHz 3kW, Stung Treng 92.0MHz 2kW, Svay Rieng 95.5MHz 2kW

Other stations

FM	Location	MHz	kW	Station
1)	Battambang	87.5		VO Koh Santepheap
2)	Phnom Penh	87.5		Daun Penh EFM
2)	Kampong Cham	87.75	1	Daun Penh FM
1)	Phnom Penh	87.75		VO Koh Santepheap
2)	Siem Reap	87.75	1	Daun Penh FM
3)	Battambang	88.0		Vayo FM
3)	Siem Reap	88.0		Vayo FM
4)	Kampot	88.25		South East Asia FM
5)	Phnom Penh	88.3		R. Meanchey FM
6)	Siem Reap	88.3	2	R. Mahanakor Khemara
7)	Battambang	88.5		Kolyanmet R.
8)	Kompong Thom	88.5	1	Steung Sen R.
9)	Sihanoukville	88.5		Vitthayu Yeung (Our R.)
10)	Kampong Cham	88.7		Mongkulsavann FM
11)	Kampot	88.7		Voice of Khmer (VOK)
12)	Siem Reap	88.7		Friend R.
13)	Phnom Penh	88.9		NRG 89 FM
14)	Phnom Penh	89.3		Samphos FM
15)	Battambang	89.5		ABC Cambodia R.
16)	Phnom Penh	89.5	10	VO New Life R. (Samlang Chivit Thmey)
17)	Ratanakiri	89.5	2	Provincial R.
15)	Siem Reap	89.5		ABC Cambodia R. (R. Krong Angkor)
18)	Phnom Penh	89.7		Wellness FM
19)	Battambang	89.8		Voice of Health
20)	Phnom Penh	90.0	10	R. Khlaing Meoung (FM90)
21)	Poipet	90.0		My FM
22)	Sisophon	90.0		Angel FM
20)	Battambang	90.3	1	R. Khlaing Meoung
23)	Siem Reap	90.3		Voice of Entrak Tevy
24)	Phnom Penh	90.5	5	Ta Phrom Radio
25)	Phnom Penh	90.7		FM 90.75
26)	Siem Reap	90.7		Town FM
4)	Pursat	90.75		South East Asia FM
4)	Sisophon	90.75		South East Asia FM
27)	Battambang	91.0	5	R. FM Khemara
28)	Phnom Penh	91.0		R. New Phnom Penh (Phnom Penh Thmey)
29)	Pursat	91.2		Voice of Friendship
22)	Battambang	91.3		Angel FM
30)	Phnom Penh	91.3		Sleuk Mas FM
17)	Oddar Meanchey	91.5	2	Provincial R.
31)	Phnom Penh	91.5		VOY FM (Voice of Youth)
32)	Phnom Penh	91.7		Green FM (Bai Thong)
10)	Sispohon	91.7		Mongkulsavann FM
31)	Battambang	92.0		VOY FM (Voice of Youth)
31)	Kampong Thom	92.0		VOY FM (Voice of Youth)
31)	Tbong Kmoum	92.0		VOY FM (Voice of Youth)
33)	Battambang	92.3		Nature FM (Thommocheat)
16)	Kampong Chhnang	92.3		VO New Life R. (Samlang Chivit Thmey)
34)	Phnom Penh	92.3	5	Top FM
15)	Kampot	92.5		ABC Cambodia R.
15)	Pursat	92.5		ABC Cambodia R.
22)	Sihanoukville	92.5		Angel FM
35)	Phnom Penh	92.7		AEC Teen FM
36)	Siem Reap	92.75		Khmer Soren
21)	Battambang	93.2		My FM
37)	Phnom Penh	93.25		Friend R.
38)	Poipet	93.3		Seven FM
39)	Soung	93.3		Peanichakam FM
10)	Batttambang	93.5		Mongkulsavann FM
40)	Phnom Penh	93.5	10	Mahanakor (Metropolitan FM)

FM	Location	MHz	kW	Station
41)	Siem Reap	93.5		Mongkul Thmey
42)	Svay Rieng	93.75	1	R. WMC
43)	Phnom Penh	93.8		DAP Radio (Doem Ampil)
31)	Siem Reap	94.0		VOY FM (Voice of Youth)
31)	Sihanoukville	94.0		VOY FM (Voice of Youth)
44)	Takeo	94.3		Bayong FM
45)	Phnom Penh	94.5		ABC Traffic Radio
46)	Svay Rieng	95.3		R. Mohachun
47)	Battambang	95.3		R. Bopha
46)	Phnom Penh	95.3		R. Mohachun
48)	Poipet	95.5		Music FM (Dontreay)
49)	Siem Reap	95.5	10	R. Angkor Ratha (R. Sarika Angkor)
26)	Battambang	95.7		Town FM
50)	Phnom Penh	95.7	5	Reasmey Hang Meas FM
17)	Sisopohon	96.5	10	Banteay Meanchey Provincial R.
51)	Kampong Cham	96.7		Kong Meas
52)	Pursat	96.7		R. Bopha
53)	Mondulkiri	96.75		Sok San Monorom
54)	Phnom Penh	97.0	10	R Apsara
55)	Kompong Cham	97.3		New Style
56)	Pailin	97.5		R O Torng Pailin
52)	Ratanakiri	97.5		R. Bopha
54)	Svay Rieng	97.75		R Apsara
58)	Phnom Penh	98.0	10	FM98 (Armed Forces R., Khemark Phomin)
58)	Siem Reap	98.0	5	FM98 (Armed Forces R.)
59)	Phnom Penh	98.3		Farmers R. (Kasekor FM)
60)	Poipet	98.3		FM98.3
61)	Phnom Penh	98.5		J R.
58)	Sihanoukville	98.5	1	FM98.5 (Armed Forces R.)
15)	Sisophon	98.5		ABC Cambodia R.
62)	Battambang	98.7		Voice of Steung Khiev (VSK)
63)	Kampong Cham	98.7		Tonle Omm
4)	Kampong Thom	98.75		South East Asia FM
64)	Phnom Penh	99.0	10	FM99
65)	Sisophon	99.0	2	Meanchey FM
66)	Koh Kong	99.5	1	FM 99.5
52)	Kratie	99.5		R. Bopha
21)	Sisophon	99.5	1	My FM
67)	Phnom Penh	99.5	10	KRUSA FM (FEBC/Family FM)
39)	Kampong Cham	99.7		Peanichakam FM
68)	Koh Kong	99.7		Koh Kong FM
39)	Moung Roussei	99.7		R. WMC (Strey FM)
69)	Phnom Penh	99.75		DP FM
70)	Battambang	100.0		VO Dombang Kronhoung (VOD FM)
71)	Battambang	100.3		People R. (Pracheachon)
42)	Kratie	100.0	1	R. WMC (Kratie FM)
21)	Phnom Penh	100.5		My FM
72)	Phnom Penh	100.7		Cool FM
58)	Battambang	101.0	1	FM 101.0 (Armed Forces R.)
73)	Phnom Penh	101.0		Nokorwat FM
74)	Phnom Penh	101.3		Our Motherland R. (Meatophum Yoeng)
75)	Kampong Cham	101.7		Neak Phoun
10)	Pursat	101.7		Mongkulsavann FM
42)	Phnom Penh	102.0	10	R. WMC
76)	Battambang	102.3		Star FM
26)	Phnom Penh	102.3	5	Town FM
77)	Phnom Penh	102.5	2	R. Tonle FM (River FM)
78)	Siem Reap	102.5	1	Sathani Vithayu Krom Siem Reap (Siem Reap City R. Stn)
3)	Sihanoukville	102.5		Vayo FM
79)	Sisophon	103.5	2.5	Sweet FM
80)	Phnom Penh	103.7		Radio One
76)	Siem Reap	103.7		Star FM
81)	Phnom Penh	104.0	10	R. Sovann Phum
82)	Sihanoukville	104.0	2	Sung Meas FM
83)	Siem Reap	104.25		R. Phnom Pemh International
42)	Kompong Thom	104.3	1	R. WMC
84)	Battambang	104.5		Mohasal FM (Sangke FM)
85)	Phnom Penh	104.5	5	R. Hang Meas FM
86)	Preah Vihear	104.5		Krong Preah Vihear
87)	Phnom Penh	105.0	10	Sombok Ka Mum (R. Beehive)
88)	Kampong Thom	105.3		Music FM (Dontreay)
3)	Phnom Penh	105.5		Vayo FM
10)	Siem Reap	105.5		Mongkulsavann FM
4)	Phnom Penh	106.0	10	South East Asia FM
89)	Battambang	106.0		Sovann Angkor FM
90)	Siem Reap	106.25	5	R. For Buddhism (r. inactive)
91)	Phnom Penh	106.3		Vong Kamha Slek Meas
92)	Kampong Thom	106.5		R. Bopha
93)	Phnom Penh	106.5	10	R. Sarika FM (V of Democracy)
94)	Sisophon	106.5	1	U FM
46)	Battambang	106.7		R. Mohachun

FM	Location	MHz	kW	Station
95)	Phnom Penh	106.7		Wonderful FM
96)	Siem Reap	106.75		Mekea
97)	Phnom Penh	107.0	10	Khmer FM (Smile R.)
4)	Sihanoukville	107.25		South East Asia FM
98)	Battambang	107.3		Voice of the Blind (VOB)
15)	Kampong Cham	107.3		ABC Cambodia R.
15)	Kampong Thom	107.5		ABC Cambodia R.
15)	Kampot	107.5		ABC Cambodia R.
15)	Phnom Penh	107.5	5	ABC Cambodia R.
99)	Siem Reap	107.5		Krong Kampuchea
15)	Sihanoukville	107.5		ABC Cambodia R.
84)	Kampong Cham	107.7		Mohasal FM
100)	Phnom Penh	107.75		Sky FM
22)	Kampot	107.8		Angel FM
101)	Phnom Penh	108.0	10	R. Solida (Soft FM)

Addresses and other information

1) No 240, Street 271, Phnom Penh 12351 – **2)** No 25B, Street 320, Phnom Penh 12304 – **3)** No 13B Street 70, Phnom Penh **W:** vayofm. com – **4)** Sleng Roleung Village, Khan Sen Sok, Phnom Penh – **5)** Thmey Village, Chamkardong, Phnom Penh 12410 – **6)**.National Rd 6, Borey Seang Nam, Khnar Thmey Village, Siem Reap – **7)** Phum Wattamem, Khum O Dombong I, Sangke District, Battambang Province – **8)**.Slaket Village, Prey Tahou Commune, Steung Sen District, Kompong Thom – **10)**.National Highway 6, Ta Tean Village, Sala Kamkreuk, Siem Reap – **11)**.Treay Koh, Kampot – **12)** No. 627, Street 99, Sala Kanseng Village, Sangkat Svay Dangkum, Siem Reap – **13)** No 131B, Street 271, Boeung Salang, Toul Kork, Phnom Penh – **15)** 50A Russian Boulevard, Sangkat Tektla, Khan Rusey Keo, Phnom Penh **W:** abccambodia.com – **16)** PO Box 1426 Phnom Penh. Operated by Final Frontiers Foundation – **18)** Street 24BT, Phnom Penh 12351 – **20)** Chamkadong, Phnom Penh 12401 – **21)** Romchek 3 Village, Sangkat Rattanak, Battambang. Kampong Svay Village, Sisophon, Banteay Meanchey Province – **22)** Romchek 4 Village, Sangkat Rattanak, Battambang – **24)** No 27B Street 472, Phnom Penh 12312. Owned by Funcinpec Party – **26)** No 44A, Street 592, Phnom Penh 12152 – **27)** Prek Mohatep Village, Sangkat Svay Por, Battambang – **30)** No. 227C, Trasak Paem (Street 63), Phnom Penh 12302 – **31)** Thmey Village, Sangkat Dangkor, Phnom Penh 12401 – **32)** Phnom Penh 12401 – **34)** Lot 35 Street 1709, Sangkat Kilomet 6, Khan Orsey Koe, Phnom Penh – **36)** Psa Ler, Tavean Village, Sangkat Sala Kamroeuk, Siem Reap – **37)** No 246AEo Street 63, Sangkat Boeung Keng Khan I, Phnom Penh – **40)** Cheung Ek Village, Phnom Penh 12415 – **42)** Women's Media Center of Cambodia, 30 Street 488, Sangkat Phsar Demthkov, Khan Chamcar Morn, Phnom Penh 12307. **W:** wmc.org.kh **49)** Group 10, Chong Kaosou Village, Siem Reap – **50)** No 33 Street 115, Phnom Penh 12258 – **52)** No 8, Street 12, Kampong Thom – **54)** No 69, Street No 57 (Corner Street No 370), Phnom Penh – **56)** Chamkar Cafe Village, Pailin – **58)** Street 169, Borei Keila, Phnom Penh 12253. – Module 3 Slorkram Village, Siem Reap. – **60)** Km 4, Poipet, Banteay Meanchey Province – **61)** No 7, Monireth (Street 217), Phnom Penh 12352 – **64)** No 69, No Street No 360, Phnom Penh 12302 – **65)** Sangkat O'Ambel, Sispohon – **67)** No 8D Street 355, Phnom Penh 12105 – **70)** Wat Leap, Wat Leap Village, Battambang **W:** vodfm.com – **72)** Nr Cambodian Red Cross, Street 271, Phnom Penh 12401 – **73)** No. 147-153, Preah Monivong (Street 93), corner of Kampuchea Krom (Street 128), BS Office Center Phnom Penh 12208 – **74)** Preah Monivong (corner Kampuchea Krom), Phnom Penh – **76)** Romchek IV Village, Sangkat Ratana, Battambang Chong Kaosou Village, Siem Reap – **77)** as stn 72) – **78)** No. 627, Street 99, Sala Kanseng Village, Sangkat Svay Dangkum, Siem Reap – **79)** West of Sispohon Market, Village 3, Sangkat Preah Ponlea, Sisophon, Banteay Meanchey Province – **80)** Cheung Ek, Phnom Penh – **84)** Romchek 4 Village, Sangkat Rattanak, Battambang. Village 6, Sangkat Veal Vong, Kompong Cham – **87)** No 33, Street 26BT, Thnort Chrum Village, Sangkat Boeng Thumpon, Phnom Penh 12351 **W:** sbk.com.kh – **89)** Romchek IV Village, Sangkat Ratana, Battambang **W:** sovannangkorfm106.com – **90)** Wat Bo, Sangkat Sala Kamroek, Siem Reap – **93)** No 14A, Street 392, Boeung Keng Kang 1, Khan Chamkarmorn, Phnom Penh 12302 (operated by Cambodian Center for Independent Media, CCIM) – **95)** No 208, Street 358, Tuol Svay Prey, Phnom Penh 12308 – **97)** No 18, Rd. 562, Phnom Penh 12151 – **101)** 375 Thmey Village, Phnom Penh 12401.

Relays of International Broadcasters

BBC World Service: Phnom Penh 100.0MHz, Siem Reap (r. inactive) 99.25MHz in English.
Radio Australia: Phnom Penh 101.5MHz, Siem Reap 101.5MHz, Sihanoukville 101.5MHz in English
Radio France Internationale (RFI): Battambang 94.5MHz, Kampong Cham 92.0MHz, Phnom Penh 92.0MHz, Siem Reap 92.0MHz, Sihanoukville 94.5MHz in French and Khmer.

L.T: UTC +1h — **Pop:** 19 million — **Pr.L:** French, English, ethnic — **E.C:** 50Hz, 220V — **ITU:** CME

NATIONAL COMMUNICATIONS COUNCIL (CNC)

✉ Siège CNC Yaoundé, Quartier Bastos, B.P. 12 535, Yaoundé Centre 237 ☎+237 22 210309 📠 +237 22 210308 **W:** cnc.gov.cm **E:** contact@cnc.gov.cm **L.P:** Prof. Laurent Charles Boyomo.

CAMEROON RADIO TELEVISION (CRTV, Gov.)

✉ B.P. 1634, Yaoundé +237 22214077 📠 +237 22204340 **W:** crtv.cm **E:** infos@crtv.cm **L.P:** DG: Amadou Vamoulke. Deputy DG: Francis Wete. Dir of Inf. Radio: Michel Ndjock Abanda.
FM (MHz):
CRTV R. Nationale: Yaoundé 88.8 10kW, Douala 89.2 10kW, Bertoua 89.8 10kW, Bafoussam 91.1 10kW, Ngaoundéré 92.5. Buéa 98.6.
Regional stations:
CRTV Yaoundé FM: 94.0, **CRTV Centre,** Yaoundé: 101.9 – **CRTV Littoral,** B.P. 986, Douala: 91.3, **Suelaba FM:** 104.9 10kW – **CRTV Sud-Ouest,** Buea 94.5, **CRTV Mont Cameroun,** Buea 98.0 – **CRTV Nord,** B.P. 103, Garoua: 101.2 10kW – **CRTV Est,** B.P. 230, Bertoua: 92.9 10kW – **CRTV Ouest,** B.P. 970, Bafoussam: 93.5 10kW, Pouala FM 104.5 – **CRTV Nord-Ouest,** B.P. 4049, Bamenda: 93.5 10kW – **CRTV Sud,** Ebolowa 97.6 10kW, **Kaze FM** 91.1 – **CRTV Adamaoua,** Ngaoundéré: 102.5 10kW – **CRTV Extrême-Nord,** Maroua 94.8, Kousseri 95.5.

Other FM stations (MHz):
Dynamic FM, Douala: 103.9 – **Magic FM,** Yaoundé: 100.1 – **R. Bon Berger,** Kaélé 99.0 – **R. Bonne Nouvelle:** Yaoundé 97.7, Ngaoundére 98.5, Douala 102.5, Ebolowa 102.7 – **R. Campus,** Ngaoundéré: 99.0 – **R. Environnement,** Yaoundé: 107.7 – **R. Equinoxe,** Douala: 93 **W:** lanouvelleexpression.net – **R. Le Lauréat,** Douala: 90.5 – **R. Lumière,** Yaoundé: 91.9 – **R. Noor,** Ngaoundéré: 106.1 – **R. Nostalgie,** Douala: 96 – **R. Reine:** Yaoundé 103.7 1kW, Buéa 97.7 1kW – **R. Salaaman,** Garoua: 89.0 – **R. Sawtu Linjiila,** Ngaoundéré: 95.7 1kW (SW relays see Target Broadcasts Section) – **R. Siantou,** Yaoundé: 90.5 – **R. Venus,** Yaoundé: 95.4 – **R. Veritas,** Douala: 96.8 – **R. Vie Nouvelle,** Douala: 100.5 – **Real Time Music,** Douala: 103.5, Yaoundé 106.0 – **Sky One R,** Yaoundé: 104.5, Douala 100.1. **W:** skyonecameroun.com – **Sweet FM,** Douala: 88.7 – **TBC FM,** Yaoundé: 93.0.
BBC African Sce: Garoua 94.4, Bamenda 95.7, Yaoundé 98.4, Douala 101.3.
RFI Afrique: Yaoundé 105.5, Douala 97.8, Bafoussam 101.1

L.T: See World Time Table (DST where applicable 13 Mar-6 Nov) — **Pop:** 35.6 million — **Pr.L:** English, French — **E.C:** 60Hz, 120V — **ITU:** CAN

CANADIAN RADIO-TELEVISION AND TELECOMMUNICATIONS COMMISSION - CRTC

✉ Ottawa, ON K1A 0N2 ☎+1 819 997 0313 📠+1 819 994 0218 **W:** crtc.gc.ca **L.P:** Chair and CEO: Jean-Pierre Blais. Exec. Dir., Broadcasting: Scott Hutton
The CRTC is an independent public organization that regulates and supervises Canadian broadcasting and telecommunications systems.

Provinces & Terrritories: AB=Alberta, BC=British Columbia, MB=Manitoba, NB=New Brunswick, NL=Newfoundland & Labrador, NS=Nova Scotia, NT=North West Territories, NU=Nunavut, ON=Ontario, PE=Prince Edward Island, QC=Québec, SK=Saskatchewan, YT=Yukon

CBC/RADIO-CANADA (Pub)

✉ Box 3220 Stn C, Ottawa ON K1Y 1E4 ☎+1 613 288 6033 **W:** cbc.radio-canada.ca **L.P:** Chair, Board of Dir: Rémi Racine. Pres. and CEO: Hubert T. Lacroix. Exec. VP, Media Technology and Infrastructure Sces: Steven Guiton. VP, Legal Sces. General Counsel and Corp. Secretary: Sylvie Gadoury. VP and CFO: Judith Purves. VP, People and Culture: Roula Zaarour. VP, Strategy and Public Affairs: Marco Dubé. Exec. Dir. Corp. Comms: Martine Ménard
English Networks: ✉ Box 500 Stn A, Toronto ON M5W 1E6 **W:** cbc.ca **L.P:** Exec. VP, English Sces: Heather Conway. GM and Ed. in Chief, CBC News, English Sces: Jennifer McGuire. Exec. Dir. Marketing Comms, English Sces: Bonnie Brownlee
French Networks: ✉ Box 6000, Montréal PQ H3C 3A8 +1 514 597 6000 **W:** ici.radio-canada.ca **L.P:** Exec. VP, French Sces: Louis Lalande. Exec. Dir. News and Current Affairs, French Sces: Michel Cormier. Exec. Dir. Comm. and Branding: Guylaine Bergeron

English Radio
CBC Radio One: *=also on SW

MW	Location	Prov.	kHz	kW	N	Call
1)	Grand Falls	NL	540	10		CBT
2)	Watrous	SK	540	50		CBK
3)	Dawson	YT	560	0.4		CBDN
15)	St. Anthony	NL	600	10		CBNA
4)	St. John's	NL	640	10		CBN
5)	Vancouver	BC	690	50	*	CBU
7)	Edmonton	AB	740	50		CBX
24)	Bonavista Bay	NL	750	10		CBGY
10)	Prince Rupert	BC	860	10/2.5		CFPR
11)	Inuvik	NT	860	1		CHAK
15)	Winnipeg	MB	990	50/46		CBW
16)	Corner Brook	NL	990	10		CBY
3)	Watson Lake	YT	990	.4/.17		CBDB
17)	Calgary	AB	1010	50		CBR
19)	Sydney	NS	1140	10		CBI
15)	Churchill	MB	1230	0.25		CHFC
21)	Iqaluit	NU	1230	1		CFFB
24)	Gander	NL	1400	4		CBG

SW	Location	Prov.	kHz	kW	Call	Relays
5)	Vancouver	BC	6160	0.5	CKZU	CBU
22)	St. John's	NL	6160	1	CKZN	CFGB-FM

FM	Location	Prov.	MHz	kW	N	Call
17)	Calgary	AB	99.1	7		CBR-1-FM
7)	Edmonton	AB	93.9	3.9		CBX-2-FM
7)	Grand Prairie	AB	102.5	100		CBXP-FM
17)	Lethbridge	AB	100.1	100		CBRL-FM
28)	Kamloops	BC	94.1	4.8		CBYK-FM
30)	Kelowna	BC	88.9	5.2		CBTK-FM
33)	Prince George	BC	91.5	100		CBYG-FM
5)	Vancouver	BC	88.1	97.6	*	CBU-2-FM
31)	Victoria	BC	90.5	6.3		CBCV-FM
16)	Brandon	MB	97.9	90		CBWV-FM
16)	Dauphin/Baldy Mtn.	MB	105.3	95		CBWW-FM
16)	Winnipeg	MB	89.3	2.8		CBW-1-FM
18)	Allardville	NB	97.9	50		CBAA-FM
14)	Fredericton	NB	99.5	3.2		CBZF-FM
18)	Moncton	NB	106.1	69.5		CBAM-FM
32)	Saint John	NB	91.3	80		CBD-FM
22)	Goose Bay	NL	89.5	4.5	*	CFGB-FM
4)	Marystown	NL	90.3	100		CBNM-FM
9)	Halifax	NS	90.5	91		CBHA-FM
9)	Middleton	NS	106.5	93.4		CBHM-FM
9)	Mulgrave	NS	106.7	100		CBHB-FM
9)	Yarmouth	NS	92.1	94.3		CBHY-FM
11)	Yellowknife	NT	98.9	4.1		CFYK-FM
21)	Iqaluit	NU	91.1	0.8		CFFB-FM-3
6)	Huntsville	ON	94.3	70		CBLU-FM
6)	Kingston	ON	107.5	100		CBCK-FM
34)	Kitchener/Waterloo	ON	89.1	10.4		CBLA-FM-2
6)	London	ON	93.5	100		CBCL-FM
20)	North Bay	ON	96.1	100		CBCN-FM
12)	Ottawa	ON	91.5	84		CBO-FM
6)	Owen Sound	ON	98.7	100		CBCB-FM
12)	Pembroke	ON	92.5	100		CBCD-FM
6)	Peterborough	ON	98.7	19.2		CBCP-FM
20)	Sault Ste. Marie	ON	89.5	46		CBSM-FM
20)	Sudbury	ON	99.9	50		CBCS-FM
8)	Thunder Bay	ON	88.3	23.7		CBQT-FM
6)	Toronto	ON	99.1	98		CBLA-FM
25)	Windsor	ON	97.5	19		CBEW-FM
23)	Charlottetown	PE	96.1	100		CBCT-FM
29)	Chicoutimi	QC	102.7	30		CBJE-FM
13)	Montréal	QC	88.5	25		CBME-FM
13)	Québec	QC	104.7	65.8		CBVE-FM
13)	Sherbrooke	QC	91.7	15.9		CBMB-FM
2)	Regina	SK	102.5	2.7		CBKR-FM
35)	Saskatoon	SK	94.1	4.1		CBK-1-FM
5)	Whitehorse	YT	94.5	6.3		CFWH-FM

+approx 375 relay txs **NB:** calls not announced

CBC Radio Two:

FM	Location	Prov.	MHz	kW	Call
17)	Calgary	AB	102.1	100	CBR-FM
7)	Edmonton	AB	90.9	100	CBX-FM
17)	Lethbridge	AB	91.7	100	CBBC-FM
17)	Red Deer	AB	99.9	71.5	CBR-FM-1
5)	Kamloops	BC	105.3	4.8	CBU-FM-4
5)	Kelowna	BC	89.7	5	CBU-FM-3
5)	Vancouver	BC	105.7	50	CBU-FM
31)	Victoria	BC	92.1	87	CBU-FM-1
16)	Brandon	MB	92.7	90	CBWS-FM

FM	Location	Prov.	MHz	kW	Call
16)	Winnipeg	MB	98.3	160	CBW-FM
32)	Fredericton/St.John	NB	101.5	81	CBZ-FM
18)	Moncton	NB	95.5	77	CBA-FM
4)	Baie Verte	NL	95.5	49	CBN-FM-6
15)	Corner Brook	NL	91.1	3	CBN-FM-2
1)	Grand Falls	NL	90.7	100	CBN-FM-1
4)	Marystown	NL	91.7	100	CBN-FM-5
4)	St. John's	NL	106.9	100	CBN-FM
9)	Halifax	NS	102.7	92	CBH-FM
9)	Middleton	NS	93.3	16.6	CBH-FM-1
9)	Mulgrave	NS	103.1	81.7	CBH-FM-2
19)	Sydney	NS	105.1	100	CBI-FM
11)	Yellowknife	NT	95.3	0.1	CFYK-FM
6)	Huntsville	ON	106.9	70	CBL-FM-1
6)	Kingston	ON	92.9	1.6	CBBK-FM
6)	Kitchener/Waterloo	ON	90.7	8.2	CBL-FM-2
6)	London	ON	100.5	22.5	CBBL-FM
12)	Ottawa	ON	103.3	84	CBOQ-FM
6)	Peterborough	ON	103.9	26	CBBP-FM
20)	Sudbury	ON	90.1	50	CBBS-FM
8)	Thunder Bay	ON	101.7	25	CBQ-FM
6)	Toronto	ON	94.1	38	CBL-FM
25)	Windsor	ON	89.9	100	CBE-FM
23)	Charlottetown	PE	104.7	100	CBCH-FM
13)	Montréal	QC	93.5	100	CBM-FM
13)	Québec	QC	96.1	0.8	CBM-FM-2
13)	Sherbrooke	QC	89.7	16.9	CBM-FM-1
2)	Regina	SK	96.9	100	CBK-FM
2)	Saskatoon	SK	105.5	98	CBKS-FM
2)	Warmley	SK	101.5	100	CBK-FM-2
2)	Yorkton	SK	91.7	57	CBK-FM-3
3)	Whitehorse	YT	104.5	0.5	CBU-FM-8

+approx 13 relay txs **NB:** calls not announced
NB: Full list of CBC English freqs at **W:** cbc.ca/frequency

French Radio – Ici Radio Canada
IRC Première:

MW	Location	Prov.	kHz	kW	N	Call
2)	Gravelbourg	SK	690	5		CBKF-1
6)	Toronto	ON	860	50		CJBC
2)	Saskatoon	SK	860	10		CBKF-2
25)	Windsor	ON	1550	10		CBEF

FM	Location	Prov.	MHz	kW	Call
7)	Calgary	AB	103.9	22	CBRF-FM
7)	Edmonton	AB	90.1	100	CHFA-10-FM
5)	Vancouver	BC	97.7	100	CBUF-FM
5)	Victoria	BC	99.7	1.2	CBUF-FM-9
16)	Winnipeg	MB	88.1	100	CKSB-10-FM
18)	Allardville	NB	105.7	50	CBAF-FM-2
18)	Fredericton/St.John	NB	102.3	84	CBAF-FM-1
18)	Moncton	NB	88.5	50	CBAF-FM
4)	St. John's	NL	105.9	45.6	CBAF-FM-17
9)	Halifax	NS	92.3	91	CBAF-FM-5
9)	Mulgrave	NS	107.5	93.4	CBAF-FM-11
9)	Sydney	NS	95.9	100	CBAF-FM-14
20)	North Bay	ON	95.1	100	CBON-FM-17
12)	Ottawa	ON	90.7	84	CBOF-FM
20)	Sudbury	ON	98.1	50	CBON-FM
25)	Windsor	ON	105.5	2.4	CBEF-2-FM
9)	Charlottetown	PE	88.1	94.2	CBAF-FM-15
36)	Amos/Val-d'or	QC	91.5	100	CHLM-FM-1
29)	Chicoutimi	QC	93.7	50	CBJ-FM
26)	Gaspe	QC	89.3	4.3	CBGA-10-FM
26)	Harve St-Pierre	QC	92.5	50	CBSI-FM-7
26)	Matane	QC	102.1	42.9	CBGA-FM
13)	Mont-Laurier	QC	91.9	38	CBF-FM-9
13)	Montréal	QC	95.1	100	CBF-FM
27)	Québec	QC	106.3	52.5	CBV-FM
26)	Rimouski	QC	89.1	38.8	CJBR-FM
26)	Rivière-du-Loup	QC	89.5	100	CJBR-FM-1
26)	Rouyn-Noranda	QC	90.7	25	CHLM-FM
26)	Sept îles	QC	98.1	96.8	CBSI-FM
38)	Sherbrooke	QC	101.1	31.4	CBF-FM-10
37)	Trois-Rivières	QC	96.5	100	CBF-FM-8
36)	Ville-Marie	QC	89.1	66.4	CBFY-FM
2)	Regina	SK	97.7	22.3	CBKF-FM

+approx 151 relay txs

Ici musique:

FM	Location	Prov.	MHz	kW	Call
7)	Calgary	AB	89.7	10	CBCX-FM
7)	Edmonton	AB	101.1	3.9	CBCX-FM-1
5)	Vancouver	BC	90.9	2.8	CBUX-FM
16)	Winnipeg	MB	89.9	61	CKSB-FM

FM	Location	Prov.	MHz	kW	Call
18)	Allardville	NB	101.9	25	CBAL-FM-1
18)	Edmundston	NB	94.3	100	CBAL-FM-5
18)	Fredericton/St.John	NB	88.1	78.5	CBAL-FM-4
18)	Moncton	NB	98.3	77	CBAL-FM
9)	St. John's	NL	101.9	90.2	CBAX-FM-2
9)	Halifax	NS	91.5	77.5	CBAX-FM
12)	Ottawa	ON	102.5	84	CBOX-FM
20)	Sudbury	ON	90.9	50	CBBX-FM
6)	Toronto	ON	90.3	10	CJBC-FM
9)	Charlottetown	PE	88.9	88	CBAX-FM-1
36)	Amos/Val-d'or	QC	88.3	100	CBFX-FM-3
26)	Chicoutimi	QC	100.9	50	CBJX-FM
26)	Gaspe	QC	90.1	6.2	CBFX-FM-5
26)	Matane	QC	107.5	31.7	CBRX-FM-1
13)	Mont-Laurier	QC	91.1	72	CBFX-FM-6
13)	Montréal	QC	100.7	100	CBFX-FM
27)	Québec	QC	95.3	64.6	CBVX-FM
26)	Rimouski	QC	101.5	100	CBRX-FM
26)	Rivière-du-Loup	QC	90.7	100	CBRX-FM-3
36)	Rouyn-Noranda	QC	89.9	26.7	CBFX-FM-4
26)	Sept îles	QC	96.1	84.8	CBRX-FM-2
38)	Sherbrooke	QC	90.7	33.2	CBFX-FM-2
37)	Trois-Rivières	QC	104.3	100	CBFX-FM-1
2)	Regina	SK	88.9	96.4	CKSB-FM-1
2)	Saskatoon	SK	88.7	100	CKSB-FM-2

+approx 10 relay txs
NB: Full list of French freqs at **W:** ici.radio-canada.ca/radio/frequences

Addresses:
1) 4 Harris Ave, Grand Falls-Windsor NL A2A 2Y2 **W:** cbc.ca/centralmorning – **2)** 2440 Broad St, Regina SK S4P 4A1 **W:** cbc.ca/news/canada/saskatchewan **W:** (F): ici.radio-canada.ca/saskatchewan – **3)** 3103 3rd Ave, Whitehorse YT Y1A 1E5 **W:** cbc.ca/news/canada/north – **4)** Box 12010 Stn A, St. John's NL A1B 3T8 **W:** cbc.ca/news/canada/newfoundland-labrador – **5)** Box 4600, Vancouver BC V6B 4A2 **W:** cbc.ca/news/canada/british-columbia **W:** (F): ici.radio-canada.ca/colombie-britannique-et-yukon – **6)** Box 500 Stn A, Toronto ON M5W 1E6 **W:** cbc.ca/news/canada/toronto **W:** (F): ici.radio-canada.ca/ontario – **7)** 123 Edmonton City Centre 10062-102 Ave, Edmonton AB T5J 2Y8 **W:** cbc.ca/news/canada/edmonton **W:** (F): ici.radio-canada.ca/alberta – **8)** 213 Miles St E, Thunder Bay ON P7C 1J5 **W:** cbc.ca/news/canada/thunder-bay – **9)** 7067 Chebucto Rd Suite 100, Halifax NS B3L 4R5 **W:** cbc.ca/news/canada/nova-scotia **W:** (F): ici.radio-canada.ca/acadie – **10)** Unit 1 222 3rd Ave W, Prince Rupert BC V8J 1L1 **W:** cbc.ca/daybreaknorth – **11)** Box 160, Yellowknife NT X1A 2N2 **W:** cbc.ca/news/canada/north – **12)** Box 3220 Stn C, Ottawa ON K1Y 1E4 **W:** cbc.ca/news/canada/ottawa **W:** (F): ici.radio-canada.ca/ottawa-gatineau – **13)** Box 6000, Montréal QC H3C 3A8 **W:** cbc.ca/news/canada/montreal **W:** (F): ici.radio-canada.ca/grandmontreal – **14)** Box 2200, Fredericton NB E3B 5G4 **W:** cbc.ca/informationmorningfredericton – **15)** 541 Portage Ave, Winnipeg MB R3B 2G1 **W:** cbc.ca/news/canada/manitoba **W:** (F): ici.radio-canada.ca/manitoba – **16)** address as 4) **W:** cbc.ca/thecornerbrookmorningshow – **17)** Box 2640, Calgary AB T2P 2M7 **W:** cbc.ca/news/canada/calgary – **18)** Box 950, Moncton NB E1C 8N8 **W:** cbc.ca/informationmorningmoncton **W:** (F): ici.radio-canada.ca/acadie – **19)** 500 George St, Sydney NS B1P 1K6 **W:** cbc.ca/informationmorningcb – **20)** 15 MacKenzie St, Sudbury ON P3C 4Y1 **W:** cbc.ca/news/canada/sudbury – **21)** Box 490, Iqaluit NU X0A 0H0 **W:** cbc.ca/news/canada/north – **22)** Box 1029 Stn C, Happy Valley-Goose Bay NL A0P 1C0 **W:** cbc.ca/labradormorning – **23)** Box 2230, Charlottetown PE C1A 8B9 **W:** cbc.ca/news/canada/prince-edward-island – **24)** address as 1) **W:** cbc.ca/centralmorning – **25)** 825 Riverside Dr W, Windsor ON N9A 5K9 **W:** cbc.ca/news/canada/windsor – **26)** 185 boul René-Lepage Est, Rimouski QC G5L 1P2 **W:** (F): ici.radio-canada.ca/est-du-quebec – **27)** 888 rue Saint-Jean, Québec QC G1R 5H6 **W:** ici.radio-canada.ca/quebec – **28)** 218 Victoria St, Kamloops BC V2C 2A2 **W:** cbc.ca/news/canada/kamloops – **29)** 500 rue des Sagenéens, Chicoutimi QC G7H 6N4 **W:** (F): ici.radio-canada.ca/saguenay-lac-saint-jean – **30)** 243 Lawrence Ave, Kelowna BC V1Y 6L2 **W:** cbc.ca/daybreaksouth – **31)** 780 Kings Rd, Victoria BC V8T 5A2 **W:** cbc.ca/ontheisland – **32)** Box 2358, Saint John NB E2L 3V6 **W:** cbc.ca/informationmorningsaintjohn – **33)** Unit 1 890 Victoria St, Prince George BC V2L 5P1 **W:** cbc.ca/daybreaknorth – **34)** 117 King St W, Kitchener ON N2G 1A7 **W:** cbc.ca/news/canada/kitchener-waterloo – **35)** 100 128 4th Ave S, Saskatoon SK S7K 1M8 **W:** cbc.ca/news/canada/saskatoon – **36)** 70 avenue Principale, Rouyn-Noranda QC J9X 4P2 **W:** (F): ici.radio-canada.ca/abitibi-temiscamingue – **37)** 225 des Forges suite 101, Trois-Rivières QC G9A 2G7 **W:** (F): ici.radio-canada.ca/mauricie – **38)** 1335 rue King Ouest, Sherbrooke QC J1J 2B8 **W:** (F): ici.radio-canada.ca/estrie

PRIVATE STATIONS c=moving to FM F=French m=ethnic/multilingual r=relay *=also on SW
NB: Txs 100W and higher

MW	kHz	Call	kW	N	Location, Prov.
705)	530	CIAO	1/0.25	m	Brampton, ON
701)	560	CFOS	7.5/1		Owen Sound, ON
204)	570	CKWL	1		Williams Lake, BC
500)	570	CFCB	10/1		Corner Brook, NL
702)	570	CKGL	10		Kitchener, ON
912)	570	CKSW	10		Swift Current, SK
703)	580	CFRA	50/30		Ottawa, ON
706)	580	CKWW	0.5		Windsor, ON
207)	590	CFTK	1		Terrace. BC
302)	590	CFAR	10/1		Flin Flon, MB
402)	590	CJCW	1/0.25		Sussex, NB
501)	590	VOCM	20		St. John's, NL
707)	590	CJCL	50		Toronto, ON
708)	600	CKAT	10/5		North Bay, ON
900)	600	CJWW	25/8		Saskatoon, SK
101)	610	CKYL	10		Peace River, AB
209)	610	CHNL	25/5		Kamloops, BC
303)	610	CHTM	1		Thompson, MB
709)	610	CKTB	10/5		St. Catharines, ON
950)	610	CKRW	1		Whitehorse, YT
501b)	620	CKCM	10		Grand Falls-Windsor, NL
901)	620	CKRM	10		Regina, SK
102)	630	CHED	50		Edmonton, AB
711)	630	CFCO	10/6		Chatham-Kent, ON
712)	640	CFMJ	50		Toronto, ON
238)	650	CISL	20/4		Richmond/Vancouver, BC
501d)	650	CKGA	5		Gander, NL
908)	650	CKOM	10		Saskatoon, SK
108)	660	CFFR	50		Calgary, AB
305)	680	CJOB	50		Winnipeg, MB
707)	680	CFTR	50		Toronto, ON
819)	690	CKGM	50		Montréal, QC
105)	700	CJLI	50/20		Calgary, AB
501e)	710	CKVO	10		Clarenville, NL
213)	730	CHMJ	50		Vancouver, BC
306)	730	CKDM	10/5		Dauphin, MB
804)	730	CKAC	50	F	Montréal, QC
501a)	740	CHCM	10		Marystown, NL
717)	740	CFZM	50		Toronto, ON
911)	750	CKJH	25		Melfort, SK
224a)	760	CFLD	1	r	Burns Lake, BC
103)	770	CHQR	50		Calgary, AB
206)	800	CKOR	10/0.5		Penticton, BC
502)	800	VOWR	10/2.5		St. John's, NL
704)	800	CJBQ	10		Belleville, ON
706)	800	CKLW	50		Windsor, ON
810)	800	CJAD	50/10		Montréal, QC
902)	800	CHAB	10		Moose Jaw, SK
307)	810	CKJS	10	m	Winnipeg, MB
403)	810	CJVA	10	c F	Caraquet, NB
724)	820	CHAM	50/10		Hamilton, ON
104)	840	CFCW	50/40		Camrose, AB
204a)	840	CKBX	1/0.5		100 Mile House, BC
206c)	870	CKIR	1/0.25	r	Invermere, BC
224)	870	CFBV	1/0.5		Smithers, BC
500a)	870	CFSX	0.5	r	Stephenville, NL
102)	880	CHQT	10		Edmonton, AB
312)	880	CKLQ	10		Brandon, MB
230)	890	CJDC	10		Dawson Creek, BC
725)	900	CHML	50		Hamilton, ON
903)	900	CKBI	10/2.8		Prince Albert, SK
106)	910	CKDQ	50		Drumheller, AB
308)	920	CFRY	25/15		Portage la Prairie, MB
728)	920	CKNX	10/1		Wingham, ON
107)	930	CJCA	50		Edmonton, AB
405)	930	CFBC	50		St. John, NB
501)	930	CJYQ	25/3.5		St. John's, NL
904)	940	CJGX	50/10		Yorkton, SK
309)	950	CFAM	10		Altona, MB
406)	950	CKNB	10/1		Campbellton, NB
108)	960	CFAC	50		Calgary, AB
213)	980	CKNW	50		Vancouver, BC
731)	980	CFPL	10/5		London, ON
806)	980	CHRF	50/10	F	Montréal, QC
905)	980	CJME	10/5		Regina, SK
733)	1010	CFRB	50	*	Toronto, ON
215)	1040	CKST	50		Vancouver, BC
820)	1040	CJMS	10/5	F	Saint-Constant, QC
733)	1050	CHUM	50		Toronto, ON

MW	kHz	Call	kW	N	Location, Prov.
906)	1050	CJNB	10		North Battleford, SK
111)	1060	CKMX	50	*	Calgary, AB
220)	1070	CFAX	10		Victoria, BC
736)	1070	CHOK	10		Sarnia, ON
221)	1130	CKWX	50		Vancouver, BC
122)	1140	CHRB	50/46		High River, AB
222)	1150	CKFR	10		Kelowna, BC
724)	1150	CKOC	50/20		Hamilton, ON
909)	1150	CJSL	10		Estevan, SK
907)	1190	CFSL	10/5		Weyburn, SK
225)	1200	CJRJ	25	m	Vancouver, BC
703)	1200	CFGO	50		Ottawa, ON
505)	1210	VOAR	10		St. John's, NL
910a)	1210	CFYM	1/0.25		Kindersley, SK
309a)	1220	CJRB	10		Boissevain, MB
209c)	1230	CJNL	1	r	Merritt, BC
500b)	1230	CFGN	0.25	r	Ch.-Port aux Basques, NL
223)	1240	CKMK	1	r	Mackenzie, BC
206b)	1240	CJOR	1		Osoyoos, BC
233)	1240	CFNI	1		Port Hardy , BC
302a)	1240	CJAR	1		The Pas, MB
501c)	1240	CKIM	1	r	Baie Verte, NL
747)	1240	CJCS	1	c	Stratford, ON
309b)	1250	CHSM	10		Steinbach, MB
721)	1250	CJYE	10		Oakville, ON
119)	1260	CFRN	50		Edmonton, AB
410)	1260	CKHJ	10		Fredericton, NB
605)	1270	CJCB	10		Sydney, NS
833)	1280	CFMB	50	m	Montréal, QC
311)	1290	CFRW	10		Winnipeg, MB
751)	1290	CJBK	10		London, ON
753)	1310	CIWW	50		Ottawa, ON
229)	1320	CHMB	10	m	Vancouver, BC
721)	1320	CJMR	10	m	Oakville, ON
910)	1330	CJYM	10		Rosetown, SK
209a)	1340	CINL	1	r	Ashcroft, BC
210)	1340	CFKC	0.25	r	Creston, BC
211)	1340	CIVH	1		Vanderhoof, BC
507)	1340	CKHV	1		Happy Valley, NL
612)	1350	CKAD	1		Middleton, NS
758)	1380	CKPC	25		Brantford, ON
209b)	1400	CHNL-1	1	r	Clearwater, BC
206a)	1400	CIOR	1	r	Princeton, BC
215)	1410	CFTE	50		Vancouver, BC
751)	1410	CKSL	10		London, ON
836)	1410	CJWI	10	m	Montréal, QC
606)	1420	CKDY	1		Digby, NS
764)	1430	CHKT	50	m	Toronto, ON
121)	1440	CKJR	10		Wetaskiwin, AB
607)	1450	CFAB	1		Windsor, NS
834)	1450	CHOU	2/1	m	Montréal, QC
768)	1460	CJOY	1		Guelph, ON
234)	1470	CJVB	50	m	Vancouver, BC
912a)	1490	CJSN	1		Shaunavon, SK
773)	1540	CHIN	50/30	m	Toronto, ON
835)	1570	CJLV	10	F	Laval/Montréal, QC
756)	1580	CKDO	10		Oshawa, ON
774)	1610	CHHA	6.25	m	Toronto, ON
729)	1650	CINA	5/0.68	m	Mississauga, ON
837)	1650	CJRS	1	m	Montréal, QC
823)	1670	CJEU	1	F	Gatineau, QC
720)	1690	CHTO	6/1	m	Toronto, ON
831)	1690	CJLO	1		Montréal, QC

SW	kHz	Call	kW	Location	Relays
111)	6030	CFVP	0.1	Calgary, AB	CKMX
733)	6070	CFRX	1	Toronto, ON	CFRB

NB: Affiliates of stns that broadcast a common prgr during part of the day have a letter as part of the reference no.

Alberta
101) Box 300, Peace River AB T8S 1T5 – 102) 5204 84th St NW, Edmonton AB T6E 5N8 – 103) Shaw Court, 105 630 - 3rd Ave SW, Calgary AB T2P 4L4 – 104) 5708-48 Ave, Camrose AB T4V 0K1 – 105) 4510 MacLeod Trail S, Calgary AB T2G 0A4 – 106) Box 1480, Drumheller AB T0J 0Y0 – 107) 5316 Calgary Trail NW, Edmonton AB T6H 4J8 – 108) 2723 37th Ave NE #240, Calgary AB T1Y 5R8 –111) 300-1110 Centre St NE, Calgary AB T2E 2R2. Rpt: **E:** qslcalgary@gmail.com – 119) 100-18520 Stony Plain Rd NW, Edmonton AB T5S 2E2 – 121) 5214A-50th Ave, Wetaskiwin AB T9A 0S8 – 122) 11-5th Ave SE, High River AB T1V 1G2
British Columbia
204) 83 First Ave S, Williams Lake BC V2G 1H4 – 204a) Box 1834, 100 Mile House BC V0K 2E0 – 206) 33 Carmi Ave, Penticton BC V2A 3G4 – 206a) Box 1400, Princeton BC V0X 1W0 – 206b) 203 – 8309 Main St, Osoyoos BC V0H 1V0 – 206c) Box 1403, Golden BC V0A 1H0 (Lic to Invermere) – 207) 4625 Lazelle Ave, Terrace BC V8G 1S4 – 209) 611 Lansdowne St, Kamloops BC V2C 1Y6 – 209a) Ashcroft BC – 209b) Clearwater BC – 209c) Box 1630 Stn Main, Merritt BC V1K 1B8 – 210) Box 310, Creston BC V1R 1M4. Rel: CJAT-FM – 211) Box 1370, Vanderhoof BC V0J 3A0 – 213) 2000-700 W Georgia St, Vancouver BC V7Y 1K9 – 215) 500-969 Robson St, Vancouver BC V6Z 1X5 – 220) 1420 Broad St, Victoria BC V8W 2B1 – 221) 2440 Ash St, Vancouver BC V5Z 4J6 – 222) 300-435 Bernard Ave, Kelowna BC V1Y 6N8 – 223) 2nd flr – 1810 3rd Ave, Prince George BC V2M 1G4. Rel: CKDV-FM – 224) Box 335, Smithers BC V0J 2N0 – 224a) Burns Lake BC – 225) 110-3060 Norland Ave, Burnaby BC V5B 3A6 (Lic to Vancouver) – 229) 100-1200 73rd Ave W, Vancouver BC V6P 6G5. Mostly Chinese – 230) 901 102nd Ave, Dawson Creek BC V1G 2B6 – 233) 7035A Market St, Port Hardy BC V0N 2P0 – 234) 2090 Aberdeen Centre 4151 Hazelbridge Way, Richmond BC V6X 4J7 (Lic to Vancouver). Mostly langs – 238) #20-11151 Horseshoe Way, Richmond BC V7A 4S5
Manitoba
302) Box 430 Stn Main, Flin Flon MB R8A 1N3 – 302a) Box 2980 Stn Main, The Pas MB R9A 1R7 – 303) 103 Cree Rd, Thompson MB R8N 0B9 – 305) 200-1440 Jack Blick Ave, Winnipeg MB R3G 0L4 – 306) 27 3rd Ave NE, Dauphin MB R7N 0Y5 – 307) 520 Corydon Ave, Winnipeg MB R3L 0P1 – 308) 350 River Rd, Portage la Prairie MB R1N 3V6 – 309) Box 950, Altona MB R0G 0B0 – 309a) Boissevain MB – 309b) 105-32 Brandt St, Steinbach MB R5G 2J7 – 311) 1445 Pembina Hwy, Winnipeg MB R3T 5C2 – 312) Box 880, Brandon MB R7A 6N6
New Brunswick
402) Box 5900 Stn Main, Sussex NB E4E 5M2 – 403) 195 rue Main 2nd flr, Bathurst NB E2A 1A7. Rel: CKLE-FM – 405) Box 930 Stn Main, St. John NB E2L 1B1 – 406) 74 Water St, Campbellton NB E3N 1B1 – 410) 206 Rookwood Ave, Fredericton NB E3B 2M2
Newfoundland & Labrador
500) Box 570 Stn Main, Corner Brook NL A2H 6H5 – 500a) 60 West St, Stephenville NL A2N 1C6 – 500b) Gen. Delivery, Ch.-Port aux Basques NL A0M 1C0 – 501) Box 8590 Stn A, St. John's NL A1B 3P5 – 501a) Box 560, Marystown NL A0E 2M0 – 501b) Box 620 Stn Main, Grand Falls-Windsor NL A2A 2K2 – 501c) Baie Verte NL – 501d) Box 650 Stn Main, Gander NL A1V 1X2 – 501e) Gen. Delivery, Clarenville NL A5A 2C1 – 502) Box 7430 Stn C, St. John's NL A1E 3Y5 – 505) 1041 Topsail Rd, Mt. Pearl NL A1N 5E9 (Lic to St. John's) – 507) Box 160, Nain NL A0P 1L0 (Lic to Happy Valley)
Nova Scotia
605) Box 1270 Stn A, Sydney NS B1P 1C8 – 606) Box 1420, Digby NS B0V 1A0 – 607) 169-A Water St, Windsor NS B0N 2T0 – 612) Box 550, Middleton NS B0S 1P0
Ontario
701) Box 280 Stn Main, Owen Sound ON N4K 5P5 – 702) 305 King St W #1101, Kitchener ON N2G 4E4 – 703) 87 George St, Ottawa ON K1N 9H7 – 704) Box 488 Stn Main, Belleville ON K8N 5B2 – 705) 5312 Dundas St W, Toronto ON M9B 1B3 (Lic to Brampton). Mostly langs – 706) 1640 Ouellette Ave, Windsor ON N8X 1L1 – 707) 777 Jarvis St, Toronto ON M4Y 3B7 – 708) Box 3000, North Bay ON P1B 8K8 – 709) Box 977 Stn Main, St. Catharines ON L2R 6J4 – 711) Box 100 Stn Main, Chatham-Kent ON N7M 5K1 – 712) Corus Quay 25 Dockside Dr, Toronto ON M5A 0B5 (Lic to Richmond Hill) – 717) 70 Jefferson Ave, Toronto ON M6K 1Y4 – 720) 437 Danforth Ave Suite 204, Toronto ON M4K 1P1. Mostly Greek – 721) 284 Church St, Oakville ON L6J 7N2 – 724) 883 Upper Wentworth St Suite 401, Hamilton ON L9A 4Y6 – 725) 875 Main St W #900, Hamilton ON L8S 4R1 – 728) 215 Carling Terrace, Wingham ON N0G 2W0 – 729) 1515 Britannia Rd Suite 315, Mississauga ON L4W 4K1. Mostly langs – 731) Box 2580 Stn B, London ON N6A 4H3 – 733) 250 Richmond St W, Toronto ON M5V 1W4. CFRB/CFRX Rpt: W: odxa.org/cfrbcfrx-qsl – 736) 1415 London Rd, Sarnia ON N7S 1P6 – 747) 376 Romeo St S, Stratford ON N5A 4T9 – 751) 743 Wellington Rd S, London ON N6C 4R5 – 753) 2001 Thurston Dr, Ottawa ON K1G 6C9 – 756) 207-1200 Airport Blvd, Oshawa ON L1J 8P5 – 758) 571 West St, Brantford ON N3T 5P8 – 764) 8-135 East Beaver Creek Rd, Richmond Hill ON L4B 1E2 (Lic to Toronto). Mostly Chinese – 768) 75 Speedvale Ave E, Guelph ON N1E 6M3 – 773) 622 College St, Toronto ON M6G 1B6. Mostly Italian – 774) 22 Wenderly Dr, Toronto ON M6B 2N9. Mostly Spanish
Québec
804) 800 rue de la Gauchetière Ouest Bureau 1100, Montréal QC H5A 1M1 – 806) 5877 ave Papineau, Montréal QC H2G 2W3 – 810) 50-1717 boulevard René-Lévesque Est, Montréal QC H2L 4T9 – 819) 300 - 1310 Greene Ave, Westmount QC H3Z 2B5 (Lic to Montréal) – 823) 14 rue Saint-Pierre, Saint-Constant QC J5A 2G9 – 823) 855 boul. de Gappe pièce 310, Gatineau QC J8T 8H9 – 831) 7141 Sherbrooke St Ouest Room CC430, Montréal QC H4B 1R6 – 833) 35 rue York, Westmount QC

H3Z 2Z5 (Lic to Montréal). Mostly langs – **834)** 11876 rue demeulles, Montréal QC H4J 2E6. Mostly langs – **835)** 2040 Autoroute Laval, Laval QC H7S 2M9 – **836)** 3733 rue Jarry E 2e etage, Montréal QC H1Z 2G1 (Lic to St. Constant) – **837)** 4835 Côte St. Catherine Rd #2, Montréal QC H3W 1M4. Mostly langs

Saskatchewan

900) 366 3rd Ave S, Saskatoon SK S7K 1M5 – **901)** 1900 Rose St, Regina SK S4P 0A9 – **902)** Box 800 Stn Main, Moose Jaw SK S6H 4P5 – **903)** Box 900 Stn Main, Prince Albert SK S6V 7R4 – **904)** Broadc Place 120 Smith St E, Yorkton SK S3N 3V3 – **905)** 210-2401 Saskatchewan Dr, Regina SK S4P 4H8 – **906)** Box 1460 Stn Main, North Battleford SK S9A 2Z5 – **907)** Box 340 Stn Main, Weyburn SK S4H 2K2 – **908)** 715 Saskatchewan Cres W, Saskatoon SK S7M 5V7 – **909)** Box 1280 Stn Main, Estevan SK S4A 2H8 – **910)** Box 490, Rosetown SK S0L 2V0 – **910a)** Box 1330, Kindersley SK S0L 1S1 – **911)** Box 750, Melfort SK S0E 1A0 – **912)** 134 Central Ave N, Swift Current SK S9H 0L1 – **912a)** Box 1176, Shaunavon SK S0N 2M0

Yukon Territory

950) 203-4103 4th Ave, Whitehorse YT Y1A 1H6

NB: Txs 3kW and higher

FM	Prov.	MHz	kW	N	Call
Airdrie	AB	106.1	100		CFIT-FM
Athabasca	AB	94.1	7.2		CKBA-FM
Bonnyville	AB	98.7	12.3	F	CHFB-FM
Bonnyville	AB	99.7	50		CFNA-FM
Bonnyville	AB	101.3	27		CJEG-FM
Brooks	AB	101.1	8.6		CIXF-FM
Brooks	AB	105.7	14		CIBQ-FM
Calgary	AB	88.1	27	m	CKAV-FM-3
Calgary	AB	88.9	100		CJSI-FM
Calgary	AB	90.3	100		CKMP-FM
Calgary	AB	90.9	18		CJSW-FM
Calgary	AB	92.1	100		CJAY-FM
Calgary	AB	92.9	100		CFEX-FM
Calgary	AB	93.7	100		CKUA-FM-1
Calgary	AB	94.7	53		CHKF-FM
Calgary	AB	95.3	100		CHPK-FM
Calgary	AB	95.9	100		CHFM-FM
Calgary	AB	96.9	100		CJAQ-FM
Calgary	AB	97.7	100		CHUP-FM
Calgary	AB	98.5	100		CIBK-FM
Calgary	AB	101.5	100		CKCE-FM
Calgary	AB	103.1	100		CFXL-FM
Calgary	AB	105.1	100		CKRY-FM
Calgary	AB	106.7	8	m	CKYR-FM
Calgary	AB	107.3	100		CFGQ-FM
Camrose	AB	98.1	50		CFCW-FM
Cold Lake	AB	95.3	100		CJXK-FM
Drayton Valley	AB	92.9	50		CIBW-FM
Drumheller	AB	91.3	22		CKUA-FM-13
Edmonton	AB	91.7	96		CHBN-FM
Edmonton	AB	92.5	97		CKNG-FM
Edmonton	AB	94.9	100		CKUA-FM
Edmonton	AB	95.7	100		CKEA-FM
Edmonton	AB	96.3	100		CKRA-FM
Edmonton	AB	97.3	100		CIRK-FM
Edmonton	AB	98.5	100	m	CFWE-FM-4
Edmonton	AB	99.3	100		CIUP-FM
Edmonton	AB	100.3	97		CFBR-FM
Edmonton	AB	101.7	100	m	CKER-FM
Edmonton	AB	102.3	100		CKNO-FM
Edmonton	AB	102.9	100		CHDI-FM
Edmonton	AB	103.9	98		CISN-FM
Edmonton	AB	104.9	100		CFMG-FM
Edmonton	AB	105.9	100		CJRY-FM
Edmonton	AB	107.1	40		CJNW-FM
Edson	AB	94.3	20		CFXE-FM
Fort McMurray	AB	93.3	43.5		CJOK-FM
Fort McMurray	AB	94.5	23.5	m	CFWE-FM-5
Fort McMurray	AB	97.9	43.5		CKYX-FM
Fort McMurray	AB	100.5	50		CHFT-FM
Fort McMurray	AB	103.7	50		CFVR-FM
Fort Saskatchewan	AB	107.9	20		CKFT-FM
Grande Prairie	AB	93.1	100		CJXX-FM
Grande Prairie	AB	96.3	70		CJGY-FM
Grande Prairie	AB	97.7	100		CFGP-FM
Grande Prairie	AB	98.9	100		CIKT-FM
Grande Prairie	AB	100.9	100		CKUA-FM-4
Grande Prairie	AB	104.7	100		CFRI-FM
High Level	AB	102.1	34		CKHL-FM
High Level	AB	106.1	34		CFKX-FM
High Prairie	AB	93.5	29		CKVH-FM

FM	Prov.	MHz	kW	N	Call
High River/Okotoks	AB	99.7	16		CFXO-FM
High River/Okotoks	AB	100.9	100		CKUV-FM
Joussard	AB	91.7	4.2	m	CFWE-FM-1
Lac La Biche	AB	90.5	19.6	m	CFWE-FM-6
Lacombe	AB	94.1	55		CJUV-FM
Lethbridge	AB	94.1	100		CJOC-FM
Lethbridge	AB	95.5	100		CHLB-FM
Lethbridge	AB	98.1	20		CKBD-FM
Lethbridge	AB	99.3	100		CKUA-FM-2
Lethbridge/Taber	AB	106.7	100		CJRX-FM
Lethbridge	AB	107.7	100		CFRV-FM
Lloydminster	AB	95.9	100		CKSA-FM
Lloydminster	AB	106.1	100		CKLM-FM
Medicine Hat	AB	94.5	100		CHAT-FM
Medicine Hat	AB	96.1	100		CFMY-FM
Medicine Hat	AB	97.3	100		CKUA-FM-3
Medicine Hat	AB	102.1	40		CJCY-FM
Medicine Hat	AB	105.3	100		CKMH-FM
Moose Hills	AB	96.7	100	m	CFWE-FM-3
Olds	AB	96.5	35		CKLJ-FM
Olds	AB	104.5	35		CKJX-FM
Peace River	AB	96.9	22		CKUA-FM-5
Peigan/Blood River	AB	89.3	10.2	m	CFWE-FM-2
Pincher Creek	AB	92.7	6		CJPV-FM
Red Deer	AB	90.5	38		CKRD-FM
Red Deer	AB	95.5	100		CKGY-FM
Red Deer	AB	98.9	100		CIZZ-FM
Red Deer	AB	100.7	100		CKRI-FM
Red Deer	AB	101.3	50		CKIK-FM
Red Deer	AB	105.5	100		CHUB-FM
Red Deer	AB	106.7	100		CFDV-FM
Red Deer	AB	107.7	100		CKUA-FM-6
Slave Lake	AB	92.7	5		CHSL-FM
St. Paul	AB	97.7	45		CHSP-FM
Stettler	AB	93.3	23		CKSQ-FM
Suffield	AB	104.1	4.3		CKBF-FM
Taber	AB	93.3	100		CJBZ-FM
Vegreville	AB	106.5	13		CKVG-FM
Wabasca	AB	94.3	6		CHSL-FM-1
Wainwright	AB	93.7	50		CKWY-FM
Wainwright	AB	101.9	50		CKKY-FM
Westlock	AB	97.9	48		CKWB-FM
Wetaskiwin	AB	93.5	5.1		CIHS-FM
Whitecourt	AB	96.7	9		CFXW-FM
Whitecourt	AB	105.3	42.3		CIXM-FM
Campbell River	BC	99.7	6		CIQC-FM
Chilliwack	BC	98.3	5		CKSR-FM
Courtenay	BC	97.3	11.6		CKLR-FM
Courtenay	BC	98.9	5		CFCP-FM
Duncan	BC	89.7	3.5		CJSU-FM
Fort St. John	BC	98.5	50		CHRX-FM
Fort St. John	BC	101.5	40		CKNL-FM
Gibsons	BC	107.5	4.6		CISC-FM
Houston	BC	105.5	3.5		CJFW-FM-7
Kamloops	BC	97.5	4.3		CKRV-FM
Kamloops	BC	98.3	4.3		CIFM-FM
Kamloops	BC	100.1	3.5		CKBZ-FM
Kamloops	BC	103.1	5		CJKC-FM
Kelowna	BC	96.3	31		CKKO-FM
Kelowna	BC	99.9	35		CHSU-FM
Kelowna	BC	101.5	33.3		CILK-FM
Kelowna	BC	103.1	35		CKQQ-FM
Kelowna	BC	103.9	36.8		CJUI-FM
Kelowna	BC	104.7	36		CKLZ-FM
Nanaimo	BC	101.7	3		CHLY-FM
Nanaimo	BC	102.3	3		CKWV-FM
Nanaimo	BC	106.9	3		CHWF-FM
Penticton	BC	100.7	14.1		CIGV-FM
Port Alberni	BC	93.3	6		CJAV-FM
Powell River	BC	95.7	5.8		CFPW-FM
Prince George	BC	94.3	11.5		CIRX-FM
Prince George	BC	97.3	12		CJCI-FM
Prince George	BC	99.3	9.3		CKDV-FM
Prince George	BC	101.3	9.1		CKKN-FM
Squamish	BC	107.1	30		CISQ-FM
Terrace	BC	103.1	3.2		CJFW-FM
Trail	BC	95.7	14		CJAT-FM
Vancouver	BC	93.1	8	m	CKYE-FM
Vancouver	BC	93.7	70		CJJR-FM
Vancouver	BC	94.5	90		CFBT-FM
Vancouver	BC	95.3	57		CKZZ-FM
Vancouver	BC	96.1	100	m	CHKG-FM

FM	Prov.	MHz	kW	N	Call	FM	Prov.	MHz	kW	N	Call
Vancouver	BC	96.9	70		CJAX-FM	Grand Falls	NL	102.3	36		CKXG-FM
Vancouver	BC	99.3	100		CFOX-FM	Marystown	NL	96.3	27		CIOZ-FM
Vancouver	BC	100.5	11		CFRO-FM	Port au Choix	NL	96.7	4.3		CFNW-FM
Vancouver	BC	101.1	100		CFMI-FM	St. John's	NL	94.7	100		CHOZ-FM
Vancouver	BC	102.7	95		CKPK-FM	St. John's	NL	97.5	100		VOCM-FM
Vancouver	BC	103.5	100		CHQM-FM	St. John's	NL	99.1	100		CKIX-FM
Vancouver	BC	104.3	9.1		CHLG-FM	St. John's	NL	101.1	20		CKSJ-FM
Vancouver	BC	104.9	31		CKKS-FM-2	Stephenville	NL	98.5	3		CIOS-FM
Vernon	BC	105.7	100		CICF-FM	Amherst	NS	101.7	50		CKDH-FM
Vernon	BC	107.5	100		CKIZ-FM	Amherst	NS	107.9	6.5		CFTA-FM
Victoria	BC	91.3	3.5		CJZN-FM	Antigonish	NS	98.9	75.4		CJFX-FM
Victoria	BC	98.5	100		CIOC-FM	Barrington	NS	96.3	5.5		CJLS-FM-2
Victoria	BC	100.3	100		CKKQ-FM	Bridgewater	NS	98.1	32		CKBW-FM
Victoria	BC	103.1	20		CHTT-FM	Bridgewater	NS	100.7	10		CJHK-FM
Victoria	BC	107.3	20		CHBE-FM	Cheticamp	NS	106.1	3	F	CKJM-FM
Brandon	MB	91.5	100		CIWM-FM	Glace Bay	NS	89.7	6		CKOA-FM
Brandon	MB	94.7	100		CKLF-FM	Halifax	NS	89.9	100		CHNS-FM
Brandon	MB	96.1	100		CKX-FM	Halifax/Dartmouth	NS	92.9	100		CFLT-FM
Brandon	MB	101.1	100		CKXA-FM	Halifax/Dartmouth	NS	93.9	3.1		CJLU-FM
Nepawa	MB	97.1	3.2		CJBP-FM	Halifax	NS	95.7	65		CJNI-FM
Portage La Prairie	MB	93.1	27		CHPO-FM	Halifax	NS	96.5	100		CKUL-FM
Portage La Prairie	MB	96.5	24		CJPG-FM	Halifax	NS	100.1	100		CIOO-FM
Steinbach	MB	96.7	100		CILT-FM	Halifax	NS	101.3	100		CJCH-FM
Steinbach	MB	107.7	30		CJXR-FM	Halifax	NS	101.9	91		CHFX-FM
Swan Lake	MB	90.5	3.7		CISF-FM	Halifax	NS	103.5	100		CKHZ-FM
Winkler	MB	88.9	100		CKMW-FM	Halifax/Dartmouth	NS	104.3	100		CFRQ-FM
Winkler/Morden	MB	93.5	100		CJEL-FM	Halifax	NS	105.1	100		CKHY-FM
Winnipeg/St. Boniface	MB	91.1	61	F	CKXL-FM	Inverness	NS	102.5	10		CJFX-FM-1
Winnipeg	MB	92.1	140		CITI-FM	Kentville	NS	89.3	30		CIJK-FM
Winnipeg	MB	94.3	100		CHIQ-FM	Kentville	NS	94.9	100		CKWM-FM
Winnipeg	MB	95.1	100		CHVN-FM	Kentville	NS	97.7	18		CKEN-FM
Winnipeg	MB	97.5	310		CJKR-FM	Liverpool	NS	94.5	8.7		CKBW-1-FM
Winnipeg	MB	99.1	100		CJGV-FM	New Glasgow	NS	94.1	80		CKEC-FM
Winnipeg	MB	99.9	100		CFWM-FM	New Tusket	NS	93.5	3		CJLS-FM-1
Winnipeg	MB	100.5	100		CFJL-FM	Petit-de-Grat	NS	104.1	5.8	F	CITU-FM
Winnipeg	MB	102.3	100		CKY-FM	Pictou	NS	97.9	100		CKEZ-FM
Winnipeg	MB	103.1	100		CKMM-FM	Port Hawkesbury	NS	101.5	38.1		CIGO-FM
Winnipeg/Selkirk	MB	104.1	100		CFQX-FM	Shelburne	NS	93.1	8.6		CKBW-2-FM
Winnipeg	MB	104.7	3		CIUR-FM	Sydney	NS	94.9	61		CKPE-FM
Winnipeg/Selkirk	MB	105.5	100		CICY-FM	Sydney	NS	98.3	100		CHER-FM
Winnipeg	MB	106.1	40		CHWE-FM	Sydney	NS	101.9	58		CHRK-FM
Winnipeg	MB	107.1	100		CKCL-FM	Sydney	NS	103.5	26.5		CKCH-FM
Bathurst	NB	92.9	100	F	CKLE-FM	Truro	NS	99.5	16.8		CKTY-FM
Bathurst	NB	104.9	33.5		CKBC-FM	Truro	NS	100.9	50		CKTO-FM
Campbellton	NB	103.9	15	F	CIMS-FM	Weymouth	NS	103.3	3		CKDY-1-FM
Edmundston	NB	92.7	40.8	F	CJEM-FM	Yarmouth	NS	95.5	18		CJLS-FM
Fredericton	NB	92.3	100		CFRK-FM	Yarmouth	NS	104.1	39.3	F	CIFA-FM
Fredericton	NB	93.1	100		CIHI-FM	Ajax	ON	95.9	50		CJKX-FM
Fredericton	NB	105.3	78		CFXY-FM	Alliston	ON	92.1	3.8		CIMA-FM
Fredericton	NB	106.9	78		CIBX-FM	Bancroft	ON	97.7	50		CHMS-FM
Grand Falls	NB	93.5	5.3		CIKX-FM	Barrie	ON	93.1	100		CHAY-FM
Grand-Sault	NB	105.1	3	F	CFAI-FM-1	Barrie	ON	95.7	100		CFJB-FM
Inkerman/Pokemouche	NB	97.1	44.4	F	CKRO-FM	Barrie	ON	100.3	32.8		CJLF-FM
Kedgwick	NB	90.1	3	F	CFJU-FM	Barrie	ON	101.1	7.5		CIQB-FM
Miramichi	NB	93.7	11	F	CKMA-FM	Barrie	ON	107.5	50		CKMB-FM
Miramichi	NB	95.9	25		CHHI-FM	Barry's Bay	ON	106.5	12		CHBY-FM
Miramichi	NB	99.3	17.8		CFAN-FM	Belleville	ON	91.3	3.2		CJLX-FM
Moncton	NB	90.7	30	F	CFBO-FM	Belleville	ON	95.5	64		CJOJ-FM
Moncton	NB	91.9	70		CKNI-FM	Belleville	ON	97.1	50		CIGL-FM
Moncton	NB	94.5	19		CKCW-FM	Belleville	ON	100.1	32		CHCQ-FM
Moncton	NB	96.9	100		CJXL-FM	Belleville	ON	102.3	15		CKJJ-FM
Moncton	NB	99.9	9.5	F	CHOY-FM	Bluewater	ON	91.7	6		CIBU-FM-1
Moncton	NB	103.1	46.8		CJMO-FM	Bracebridge	ON	99.5	12		CFBG-FM
Moncton	NB	103.9	70		CFQM-FM	Brantford	ON	92.1	80		CKPC-FM
Saint John	NB	88.9	25		CHNI-FM	Brockville	ON	103.7	100		CJPT-FM
Saint John	NB	94.1	100		CHSJ-FM	Brockville	ON	104.9	7.7		CFJR-FM
Saint John	NB	97.3	100		CHWV-FM	Cambridge	ON	107.5	6		CJDV-FM
Saint John	NB	98.9	12		CJYC-FM	Chatham	ON	89.3	18.7		CKGW-FM
Saint John	NB	100.5	100		CIOK-FM	Chatham	ON	94.3	50		CKSY-FM
Shediac	NB	89.5	38	F	CJSE-FM	Chatham	ON	95.1	42		CKUE-FM
St. Stephen	NB	98.1	40		CHTD-FM	Cobourg	ON	93.3	15.5		CKSG-FM
Woodstock	NB	104.1	10		CJCJ-FM	Cobourg	ON	103.1	86.7		CFMX-FM
Argentia	NL	100.3	3.7		CFOZ-FM	Cobourg	ON	107.9	20		CHUC-FM
Bonavista	NL	92.1	6.7		CJOZ-FM	Collingwood	ON	102.9	23		CFMO-FM
Carbonear	NL	103.9	30		CHVO-FM	Cornwall	ON	92.1	60	F	CHOD-FM
Clarenville	NL	100.7	4.1		VOCM-FM-1	Cornwall	ON	101.9	3.2		CJSS-FM
Clarenville	NL	105.3	4.7		CJMY-FM	Cornwall	ON	104.5	28.2		CFLG-FM
Clarenville	NL	107.5	25.5		CKSJ-FM-1	Dryden	ON	92.7	39		CKDR-FM
Corner Brook	NL	92.3	7.7		CKOZ-FM	Elliot Lake	ON	94.1	90		CKNR-FM
Corner Brook	NL	103.9	40		CKXX-FM	Fort Erie	ON	101.1	50		CFLZ-FM
Gander	NL	98.7	6		CKXD-FM	Fort Frances	ON	93.1	21		CFOB-FM
Grand Falls/Windsor	NL	95.9	47		CKMY-FM	Gananoque	ON	99.9	4.5		CJGM-FM

FM	Prov.	MHz	kW	N	Call	FM	Prov.	MHz	kW	N	Call
Goderich	ON	104.9	12.6		CHWC-FM	Port Elgin	ON	90.9	3.1		CIYN-FM-2
Guelph	ON	106.1	50		CIMJ-FM	Port Elgin	ON	97.9	9		CFPS-FM
Haldimand	ON	92.9	10		CKJN-FM	Prescott	ON	107.9	4.2		CKPP-FM
Haliburton	ON	93.5	6		CFZN-FM	Prince Edward County	ON	99.3	3		CJPE-FM
Haliburton	ON	100.9	3.4		CKHA-FM	Renfrew	ON	96.1	7.1		CHMY-FM
Hamilton/Burlington	ON	94.7	100		CHKX-FM	Renfrew	ON	98.7	20		CJHR-FM
Hamilton	ON	95.3	100		CING-FM	Sarnia	ON	99.9	50		CFGX-FM
Hamilton	ON	102.9	40.3		CKLH-FM	Sarnia	ON	103.3	6		CKCI-FM
Hamilton/Burlington	ON	107.9	26.1		CJXY-FM	Sarnia	ON	106.3	50		CHKS-FM
Hearst	ON	91.1	28	F	CINN-FM	Sault Ste. Marie	ON	100.5	13.9		CHAS-FM
Huntsville	ON	88.7	5.7		CKAR-FM	Sault Ste. Marie	ON	104.3	100		CJQM-FM
Huntsville	ON	105.5	43.4		CFBK-FM	Shelburne	ON	104.9	50		CFDC-FM
Kapuskasing	ON	89.7	3	F	CKGN-FM	Simcoe	ON	98.9	50		CHCD-FM
Kapuskasing	ON	93.7	3.4	F	CHYX-FM	Smiths Falls	ON	92.3	17		CJET-FM
Kapuskasing	ON	100.9	12		CKAP-FM	Smiths Falls	ON	101.1	100		CKBY-FM
Kenora	ON	89.5	50		CJRL-FM	St. Catharines	ON	97.7	50		CHTZ-FM
Kincardine	ON	95.5	5.7		CIYN-FM	St. Catharines	ON	105.7	50		CHRE-FM
Kingston	ON	93.5	7.5		CKXC-FM	St. Thomas	ON	94.1	4.4		CKZM-FM
Kingston	ON	96.3	28		CFMK-FM	St. Thomas	ON	103.1	60		CFHK-FM
Kingston	ON	98.3	95.5		CFLY-FM	Stratford	ON	107.7	6		CHGK-FM
Kingston	ON	98.9	15		CKLC-FM	Sturgeon Falls	ON	97.1	6.5	F	CHYQ-FM
Kingston	ON	101.9	3		CFRC-FM	Sudbury	ON	91.7	50		CICS-FM
Kingston	ON	104.3	8		CKWS-FM	Sudbury	ON	92.7	100		CJRQ-FM
Kingston	ON	105.7	50		CIKR-FM	Sudbury	ON	93.5	100		CIGM-FM
Kirkland Lake	ON	101.5	23		CJKL-FM	Sudbury	ON	95.5	8.1		CJTK-FM
Kitchener/Waterloo	ON	91.5	10		CKBT-FM	Sudbury	ON	98.9	3.8	F	CHYC-FM
Kitchener	ON	96.7	80		CHYM-FM	Sudbury	ON	103.9	100		CHNO-FM
Kitchener/Waterloo	ON	98.5	27		CKWR-FM	Sudbury	ON	105.3	100		CJMX-FM
Kitchener	ON	99.5	4.3		CKKW-FM	Sunderland	ON	89.9	5		CJKX-FM-1
Kitchener	ON	105.3	100		CFCA-FM	Thunder Bay	ON	91.5	100		CKPR-FM
Kitchener/Waterloo	ON	106.7	5		CIKZ-FM	Thunder Bay	ON	94.3	93		CJSD-FM
Leamington	ON	92.7	4		CJSP-FM	Thunder Bay	ON	105.3	100		CKTG-FM
Leamington	ON	96.7	27		CHYR-FM	Tillsonburg	ON	101.3	26		CKOT-FM
Lindsay	ON	91.9	11.4		CKLY-FM	Tillsonburg	ON	107.3	7.8		CJDL-FM
Little Current	ON	100.7	27.5		CFRM-FM	Timmins	ON	92.1	40		CJQQ-FM
London	ON	92.7	50		CJBX-FM	Timmins	ON	93.1	16.4		CHMT-FM
London	ON	94.9	6		CHRW-FM	Timmins	ON	99.3	40		CKGB-FM
London	ON	95.9	300		CFPL-FM	Timmins	ON	104.1	3.5	F	CHYK-FM
London	ON	97.5	50		CIQM-FM	Toronto	ON	88.1	4		CIND-FM
London	ON	98.1	40		CKLO-FM	Toronto	ON	88.9	4.2	m	CIRV-FM
London	ON	102.3	100		CHST-FM	Toronto	ON	89.5	15		CIUT-FM
London	ON	106.9	3		CIXX-FM	Toronto	ON	91.1	40		CJRT-FM
Marathon	ON	93.1	50		CFNO-FM	Toronto	ON	91.9	5	m	CHIN-1-FM
Midland	ON	104.1	20		CICZ-FM	Toronto	ON	92.5	13		CKIS-FM
Napanee	ON	88.7	11.1		CKYM-FM	Toronto	ON	93.5	3.7		CFXJ-FM
New Liskeard	ON	104.5	10		CJTT-FM	Toronto	ON	96.3	60		CFMZ-FM
Newmarket	ON	88.5	30		CKDX-FM	Toronto	ON	97.3	28.9		CHBM-FM
Niagara Falls	ON	105.1	15		CJED-FM	Toronto	ON	98.1	44		CHFI-FM
North Bay	ON	100.5	100		CHUR-FM	Toronto	ON	99.9	40		CKFM-FM
North Bay	ON	101.9	100		CKFX-FM	Toronto	ON	100.7	8.5	m	CHIN-FM
North Bay	ON	106.3	10		CFXN-FM	Toronto	ON	102.1	35.4		CFNY-FM
Orangeville	ON	103.5	30.7		CIDC-FM	Toronto	ON	104.5	40		CHUM-FM
Orillia	ON	105.9	20		CICX-FM	Toronto	ON	107.1	40		CILQ-FM
Oshawa	ON	94.9	50		CKGE-FM	Trenton	ON	107.1	15		CJTN-FM
Ottawa	ON	88.5	90		CILV-FM	Wallaceburg	ON	99.1	3		CKXS-FM
Ottawa	ON	89.1	18.1		CHUO-FM	Welland	ON	89.1	3.1		CKYY-FM
Ottawa	ON	89.9	27		CIHT-FM	Welland	ON	91.7	50		CIXL-FM
Ottawa	ON	93.1	12		CKCU-FM	Windsor	ON	88.7	100		CIMX-FM
Ottawa	ON	93.9	95		CKKL-FM	Windsor	ON	93.9	100		CIDR-FM
Ottawa	ON	97.9	6.8	m	CJLL-FM	Windsor	ON	95.9	11.8		CJWF-FM
Ottawa	ON	99.1	66		CHRI-FM	Windsor	ON	100.7	9		CKUE-FM-1
Ottawa	ON	99.7	100		CJOT-FM	Windsor	ON	102.3	5	m	CINA-FM
Ottawa	ON	100.3	100		CJMJ-FM	Wingham	ON	94.5	75		CIBU-FM
Ottawa	ON	101.9	5.5		CIDG-FM	Wingham	ON	101.7	100		CKNX-FM
Ottawa	ON	105.3	84		CISS-FM	Woodstock	ON	103.9	51		CKDK-FM
Ottawa	ON	106.1	100		CHEZ-FM	Woodstock	ON	104.7	20		CIHR-FM
Ottawa	ON	106.9	84		CKQB-FM	Charlottetown	PE	93.1	75		CHLQ-FM
Owen Sound	ON	92.3	9.4		CJOS-FM	Charlottetown	PE	95.1	100		CFCY-FM
Owen Sound	ON	93.7	22		CKYC-FM	Charlottetown	PE	100.3	88		CHTN-FM
Owen Sound	ON	106.5	28		CIXK-FM	Charlottetown	PE	105.5	88		CKQK-FM
Paris	ON	88.3	8.2		CJIQ-FM	Elmira	PE	99.9	3.4		CHTN-FM-1
Parry Sound	ON	103.3	46.6		CKLP-FM	Elmira	PE	103.7	3.4		CKQK-FM-1
Pembroke	ON	96.7	100		CHVR-FM	St. Edward	PE	89.9	5		CHTN-FM-2
Pembroke	ON	99.9	7.5		CKQB-FM-1	St. Edward	PE	91.1	5		CKQK-FM-2
Pembroke	ON	104.9	31.6		CIMY-FM	Summerside	PE	102.1	50		CJRW-FM
Penetanguishene	ON	88.1	40	F	CFRH-FM	Alma	QC	95.7	100	F	CKYK-FM
Perth	ON	88.1	5.4		CHLK-FM	Alma	QC	104.5	20	F	CFGT-FM
Peterborough	ON	96.7	7		CJWV-FM	Amos/Val d'Or	QC	103.5	100	F	CHOA-FM-1
Peterborough	ON	99.7	11		CKPT-FM	Amos/Val d'Or	QC	104.3	100	F	CHGO-FM
Peterborough	ON	100.5	15		CKRU-FM	Amos	QC	105.3	32.2	F	CHOW-FM
Peterborough	ON	101.5	15.2		CKWF-FM	Amqui	QC	99.9	23.8	F	CFVM-FM
Peterborough	ON	105.1	7.5		CKQM-FM	Asbestos	QC	99.3	11.1	F	CJAN-FM

FM	Prov.	MHz	kW	N	Call	FM	Prov.	MHz	kW	N	Call
Baie-Comeau	QC	97.1	4.2	F	CHLC-FM	Sherbrooke	QC	102.7	92	F	CITE-FM-1
Bécancour-Nicolet	QC	90.5	60	F	CKBN-FM	Sherbrooke	QC	107.7	25	F	CKOY-FM
Cabano	QC	98.3	3	F	CIEL-FM-3	Sorel	QC	101.7	3	F	CJSO-FM
Cap-aux-Meules	QC	92.7	6.3	F	CFIM-FM	Ste-Marie-De-Beauce	QC	101.5	72	F	CHEQ-FM
Carleton	QC	94.9	37.6	F	CIEU-FM	St-Gabriel-De-Brandon	QC	99.1	9.8	F	CFNJ-FM
Chandler	QC	96.3	22.9	F	CFMV-FM	St-Georges-De-Beauce	QC	99.7	100	F	CHJM-FM
Chibougamau	QC	93.5	56.2	F	CKXO-FM	St-Georges-De-Beauce	QC	103.5	15	F	CKRB-FM
Chicoutimi	QC	94.5	100	F	CJAB-FM	Thetford Mines	QC	97.3	100	F	CFJO-FM
Chicoutimi	QC	96.9	100	F	CFIX-FM	Thetford Mines	QC	105.5	6	F	CKLD-FM
Chicoutimi	QC	98.3	100	F	CILM-FM	Trois-Rivières	QC	89.1	3	F	CFOU-FM
Chicoutimi	QC	106.7	46.2	F	CION-FM-2	Trois-Rivières	QC	89.9	3.2	F	CIRA-FM-2
Chisasibi	QC	101.1	3	F	CHFG-FM	Trois-Rivières	QC	94.7	100	F	CHEY-FM
Dégelis	QC	95.5	12.5	F	CFVD-FM	Trois-Rivières	QC	100.1	64.1	F	CJEB-FM
Dolbeau	QC	100.3	50	F	CHVD-FM	Trois-Rivières	QC	102.3	5.8	F	CIGB-FM
Drummondville	QC	92.1	3	F	CJDM-FM	Trois-Rivières	QC	106.9	100	F	CKOB-FM
Drummondville	QC	105.3	5.3	F	CHRD-FM	Val-d'Or	QC	102.7	96	F	CJMV-FM
Forestville	QC	100.5	6	F	CFRP-FM	Ville-Marie	QC	93.1	34	F	CKVM-FM
Fort Coulonge	QC	101.7	11.9	F	CHIP-FM	Waskaganish	QC	92.5	38	m	CJRH-FM
Gaspé	QC	94.5	6	F	CJRG-FM	Waswanipi	QC	93.9	6.2	m	CFNE-FM
Gatineau	QC	94.9	84	F	CIMF-FM	Wemindji	QC	99.7	24.7	m	CHPH-FM
Gatineau	QC	97.1	11.2	F	CHLX-FM	Dafoe	SK	100.3	100		CJVR-FM-1
Gatineau	QC	104.1	19	F	CKTF-FM	Estevan	SK	102.3	100		CHSN-FM
Gatineau	QC	104.7	100	F	CKOF-FM	Estevan	SK	106.1	100		CKSE-FM
Granby	QC	104.9	4.3	F	CFXM-FM	Gravelbourg	SK	107.1	97		CJME-2-FM
Joliette	QC	103.5	4.5	F	CJLM-FM	Humboldt	SK	107.5	100		CHBO-FM
La Baie	QC	105.5	6	F	CKGS-FM	Meadow Lake	SK	102.3	45		CJNS-FM
La Pocatière	QC	97.5	25.2	F	CHOX-FM	Meadow Lake	SK	104.5	45		CJCQ-FM-1
La Sarre	QC	102.1	4.1	F	CJGO-FM	Melfort	SK	105.1	100		CJVR-FM
La Tuque	QC	97.1	28.4	F	CFLM-FM	Moose Jaw	SK	100.7	100		CILG-FM
Lac-Etchemin	QC	100.5	9.6	F	CFIN-FM	Moose Jaw	SK	103.9	100		CJAW-FM
Lachute	QC	104.9	3	F	CJLA-FM	Nipawin	SK	94.7	14.8		CJNE-FM
Lac-Mégantic	QC	106.7	4.3	F	CJIT-FM	North Battleford	SK	93.3	100		CJHD-FM
Les Escoumins	QC	94.9	4.7	F	CHME-FM	North Battleford	SK	95.5	28	m	CJLR-FM-6
Louisville	QC	103.1	4.2	F	CHHO-FM	North Battleford	SK	97.9	100		CJCQ-FM
Matane	QC	95.3	14.6	F	CHOE-FM	Okanese First Nation	SK	95.3	50		CHXL-FM
Matane	QC	105.3	30	F	CHRM-FM	Prince Albert	SK	88.1	49	m	CJLR-FM-3
Mistissini	QC	95.3	50		CINI-FM	Prince Albert	SK	90.1	3	F	CKSF-FM
Mont-Laurier	QC	104.7	16.9	F	CFLO-FM	Prince Albert	SK	99.1	100		CFMM-FM
Montmagny	QC	90.3	40.7	F	CIQI-FM	Prince Albert	SK	101.5	100		CHQX-FM
Montréal	QC	89.3	10	F	CISM-FM	Regina	SK	90.3	43	m	CJLR-FM-4
Montréal	QC	90.3	5		CKUT-FM	Regina	SK	92.1	100		CHMX-FM
Montréal	QC	91.3	36.2	F	CIRA-FM	Regina	SK	92.7	100		CHBD-FM
Montréal	QC	91.9	4.7	F	CKLX-FM	Regina	SK	94.5	100		CKCK-FM
Montréal	QC	92.5	100	F	CKBE-FM	Regina	SK	98.9	100		CIZL-FM
Montréal	QC	94.3	41.4	F	CKMF-FM	Regina	SK	104.9	100		CFWF-FM
Montréal	QC	95.9	41.2		CJFM-FM	Saskatoon	SK	92.9	100		CKBL-FM
Montréal	QC	96.9	307	F	CKOI-FM	Saskatoon	SK	95.1	100		CFMC-FM
Montréal	QC	97.7	41.2		CHOM-FM	Saskatoon	SK	96.3	100		CFWD-FM
Montréal	QC	98.5	100	F	CHMP-FM	Saskatoon	SK	98.3	100		CJMK-FM
Montréal	QC	99.5	8.7	F	CJPX-FM	Saskatoon	SK	102.1	100		CJDJ-FM
Montréal/Laval	QC	105.7	41	F	CFGL-FM	Swift Current	SK	94.1	100		CIMG-FM
Montréal	QC	107.3	42.9	F	CITE-FM	Swift Current	SK	97.1	100		CKFI-FM
Natashquan	QC	104.1	6.6	F	CKNA-FM	Swift Current	SK	101.7	100		CJME-1-FM
New Carlisle	QC	107.1	5.4	F	CHNC-FM	Wapella	SK	102.9	14		CFGW-FM-2
Pikogan	QC	100.1	3.7	m	CKAG-FM	Warmley	SK	107.3	87		CJME-3-FM
Port-Cartier	QC	99.1	45	F	CIPC-FM	Waskesiu Lake	SK	106.3	11		CJVR-FM-2
Québec	QC	90.9	5.7	F	CION-FM	Weyburn	SK	103.5	100		CKRC-FM
Québec	QC	91.9	31	F	CJEC-FM	Weyburn	SK	106.7	100		CHWY-FM
Québec	QC	93.3	33	F	CJMF-FM	Yorkton	SK	94.1	100		CFGW-FM
Québec	QC	98.1	40	F	CHOI-FM	Yorkton	SK	98.5	50		CJJC-FM
Québec	QC	98.9	41	F	CHIK-FM	Whitehorse	YT	98.1	4.3		CHON-FM
Québec/Lévis	QC	102.1	33.9	F	CFEL-FM						
Québec/Lévis	QC	102.9	32.8	F	CFOM-FM						
Québec	QC	107.5	37	F	CITF-FM						
Rimouski	QC	96.5	5.8	F	CKMN-FM						
Rimouski	QC	98.7	100	F	CIKI-FM						
Rimouski	QC	102.9	33.6	F	CJOI-FM						
Rivière-du-Loup	QC	103.7	60	F	CIEL-FM						
Rivière-du-Loup	QC	107.1	100	F	CIBM-FM						
Roberval	QC	99.5	50	F	CHRL-FM						
Rouyn-Noranda	QC	88.7	3.4	F	CHIC-FM						
Rouyn-Noranda	QC	95.7	44	F	CJGO-FM-1						
Rouyn-Noranda	QC	96.5	61.1	F	CHOA-FM						
Rouyn-Noranda	QC	98.3	3.4	F	CHUN-FM						
Rouyn	QC	99.1	3	F	CJMM-FM						
Saguenay	QC	92.5	14.2	F	CKAJ-FM						
Sainte-Foy	QC	94.3	6	F	CHYZ-FM						
Saint-Hyacinthe	QC	106.5	3	F	CFEI-FM						
Saint-Jérôme	QC	103.9	39.3	F	CIME-FM						
Salaberry-de-Valleyfield	QC	103.1	3	F	CKOD-FM						
Sept-îles	QC	94.1	11.3	F	CKCN-FM						
Sherbrooke	QC	93.7	25.5	F	CFGE-FM						

NB: Most stns identify using a name rather than calls. Industry Canada stn list database **W:** ic.gc.ca/eic/site/smt-gst.nsf/eng/h_sf01842.html Stn history & info **W:** broadcasting-history.ca

BRITISH FORCES BROADC. SCE. Suffield AB
☎ +1 403 544 4104 **W:** bfbs.com **BFBS 1: FM:** 98.1, 104.1MHz

CANARY ISLANDS (Spain)

L.T: UTC (27 Mar-30 Oct: +1h) — **Pop:** 2.1 million — **Pr.L:** Spanish — **E.C:** 50Hz, 220V — **ITU:** CNR

MW	kHz	kW	Net	Location	Island
1)	576	20	RNE-1	Las Palmas	GC
2)	621	300	RNE-1	Santa Cruz	TF
2)	720	10	RNE-5	Santa Cruz	TF
1)	747	25	RNE-5	Las Palmas	GC
5)	1008	10	Grupo R.	Las Palmas	GC
6)	1179	25	SER	R. Clube Tenerife	TF

Addresses and other information

Abbreviations: GC=Gran Canaria, GCF=Fuerteventura, GCL=Lanzarote, TF=Tenerife, TFP=Isla de la Palma, TFG=Isla de la Gomera, TFH=Hierro. (For network abbreviations refer to Spain)

1) R. Nacional de España, Av.1 de Mayo 21, 35002 Las Palmas de Gran Canaria ☎ +34 928 364 088 ≣ +34 928 362 754 – **2)** R. Nacional de España, San Martín 1, 38001 Sta. Cruz de Tenerife ☎ +34 (922) 288400 ≣ +34 922 283363 **R.1:** 24h on 621kHz **N:** On the h. **R.2:** (classical music) 24h. **R.3:** 24h. **R.5:** 24h – **3)** R. Popular de Las Palmas, Av. Escaleritas 60-1°, Las Palmas 35011 ☎ +34 928 286970 **E:** direccion. laspalmas@cadenacope.net Dir: Antonio Miguel Díaz **D.Prgr:** 24h. **FM** :90.1MHz – **4)** R. Popular de Tenerife, Darias y Padron, 1-2°-38003 Santa Cruz de Tenerife ☎ +34 922 236900/05/09 ≣ +34 922 2369121 **E:** tenerife@cadenacope.net Dir: José Carlos Marrero Gonzales. **D.Prgr:** 24h FM only – **5)** GRUPO Radio Las Palmas, C/ Profesor Lozano 5, 2°, Urb. Industrial El Sebadal, 35008 Las Palmas de Gran Canaria **W:** radiolaspalmas.com **FM** :100.3MHz **E:** informacion@radiolaspalmas. com ☎ +34 928 462052 ≣ +34 928 462057 Dir: María Enma Hernández Martín. **D.Prgr:** 24h – **6)** R. Club Tenerife, Av. de Anaga 35, Santa Cruz de Tenerife 38001 ☎ +34 922 270400 ≣ +34 922 281043 **E:** radioclub-tenerife@unionradio.es Dir: Juan Ramon Hernandez. **FM** 101.1MHz – **7)** Av. Escaleritas 64 1°, 35011 Las Palmas de Gran Canaria **W:** radioecca.org **E:** info@radioecca.org **FM:** 99.5MHz

Dial FM Networks:

Gran Canaria Las Palmas (MHz): R.T.I. Insular 87.7 – R. Maria 87.9 – R. Marca 88.2 – RNE1 88.5 – RNE5 INF.88.6 – Hit FM 88.9 –FUN R 89.9 – ECCA 90.4 – R.ECCA 90.7– COPE 91.0 – esRadio 91.2 – Canaras R. 91.4 – C100 91.8 – R. Top 21 92.0 –RNE1 92.8 – Aire Radio 93.4– R. Juventud 94.1 – Los 40 94.4 – RNE2 95.1 – Inolvidable FM 95.8 – Tamaran FM Formula Hits 96.2 – R.Las Palmas 97.3 – Europa FM 98.0 – RNE3 98.5 – COPE FM 99.1 – Infierno FM 99.5 – SER Las Palmas 100.3 – Global FM 100.6 – Canarias R. 100.8 – Gestiona R. 101.1 – Cadena Dial 101.7 – Maxima FM 102.7 – Radio Canarias 103.0 – UD Radio 103.4 – R.Univerdance 103.8 – R. Faycan 104.2 – M80 105.4 – R. Guiniguada 105.9 – OCR 106.8

Gran Canaria Maspalomas Playa del Ingles (MHz): 9 Radio 87.9 – R.Arguineguin 89.4 – 7,7 Radio 89.6 – COPE FM 90.7 – ECCA Sur 91.4 – R.TOP 21 92.0 – R.Faro 92.5 – Onda Islena 93.8 – R.Sol 94.8 – esRadio 95.3 – R.Faro Sur 97.2 – R.Rondo 98.2 – SER Maspalomas 99.6 – R.Maria 102.7 – R.Abrisajac 103.5 – RNE5 INF. 106.5 – R.Dunas 107.6

Fuerteventura (MHz): RNE2 87.7 – R.Sintonia 88.2 – Nueve R. OCR 90.7 – COPE 91.2 – COPE 91.6 – R.Maxorata 92.1 – ECCA 93.0 – Atlantica FM 94.2 – Dunas FM 94.4 – RNE1 94.6 – Europa FM 95.6 – Canarias R. 96.9 – Nueve R. 97.7 – Q FM Corralejo 98.0 – R.Agua Cabra 99.6 Morro Jable – Canarias R. 104.4 – RNE5 INF. 104.8 – R.Archipielago 105.0 – C.100 Puerto del Rosario 105.3 – MCM Mision Cristiana Moderna Radio 106.9

Lanzarote (MHz): O2 Radio 88.5 – SER 89.7 – Alo FM 90.1 – OCR 90.7 – OCR 91.1 – R.Cristal 92.0 – RNE1 92.5 – ECCA 93.0 – R.Marca 93.6 – R.Maria 93.9 – RNE2 94.9 – O2 Radio 96.4 – R.Insular 96.7 – COPE 98.3 – R. Las Arenas 98.6 – Onda Conejera 99.1 – RNE5 INF. 100.2 – Guapa FM 100.9 – Canarias R. 101.2 – RNE3 102.8 – Mi Tierra FM 103.1 – Los 40 104.0 – Cronicas R. 105.5 – Europa FM 106.5 – Latina Stereo 107.7

Tenerife Norte (MHz): R.Decibelios FM 87.5 – Cadena Dial 87.8 – MM Radio La Laguna 88.1 – Onda CIT 88.5 – RNE5 INF. 88.8 – Cadena Dial Sur 88.9 – ROCK FM 89.1 – C100 89.4 – ECCA La Laguna 89.6 – Marcha FM 89.8 – RNE3 90.0 – onda 7 90.2 – R.El Dia La Laguna 90.8 – Maxima FM 91.1 – R.Marca Tenerife 91.5 – R.Atlantida 91.9 – RNE1 92.3 — Los 40 Tenerife 93.2 – Antena de Canarias 93.5 – Marcha FM La Laguna 93.8 – Teide OCR 94.0 R.Marca La Laguna 94.5 – RNE1 94.8 – Onda CIT R. Turismo La Laguna 95.2 – Gente R. 95.6 –Fun FM La Laguna 95.8 – RNE2 96.2 – Inter Magica FM 96.8 – COPE La Laguna 97.1 – R.Maria 97.5 – R.Marca 97.7 – Onda 7 La Laguna 97.9 – RNE5 INF. 98.1 – Onda Tenerife 98.5 – Canal 4 98.8 – Los 40 99.1 – Kiss FM 99.4 – SER R.Club Norte 99.8 – M80 100.1 – R.Pimienta La Orotava 100.3 – Orquestras del Atlantico La Laguna R. 100.5 – R.Taoro 100.7 – SER R.Clube Tenerife101.1 – COPE 101.4 – R.Majuelos La Laguna 101.7 – RNE2 102.1 – esRadio 102.3 – Kiss FM 102.5 – R.Maria La Laguna 103.2 – R.ECCA Los Cristianos 103.4 – RKM R. 103.8 – RNE5 INF.104.0 – Canarias R. 104.2 – La Mega Latina La Laguna 104.5 – Canal R. 104.7 – esRadio 104.9 – R.Union Tenerife 105.3 – RNE3 105.7 – Canal 4 R. 106.1 – ECCA 106.6 – Exito R. 107.0 – R.La Guancha 107.2 – R.Realejos Los Realejos 107.9

Tenerife Sur (MHz): R. Gigante 87.7 – El Faro FM 87.9 – Canarias R. 88.1 – Cadena Dial Playa de las Americas 88.9 – R.ECCA 90.4 – Inter Magica FM 91.1 – RNE 2 92.6 – Los 40 Playa de las Americas 93.3 – R.Costa 93.8 – Canal 4 R. 94.8 – RNE3 95.4 – SER R.Club Sur Playa de las Americas 95.9 – Fun R. 96.2 – Fun Radio 96.8 – Atlantico FM

97.1 – R.Marca 97.7 – Onda Nueva 99.7 – Onda Tenerife Arona 100.1 – Astrovision Magica FM 101.9 – Bomba FM R. 102.4 – Hit R. S.Miguel de Abona 103.0 – RNE1 105.6 – Teide OCR S.Miguel de Abona 106.3 – R.Decibelios FM Arona 107.5

Isla de la Palma (MHz): RNE5 INF. 89.6 – RNE1 90.8 – R.Murion 91.0 – R.Isla Bonita OCR 92.7 – Canarias R. 93.0 – COPE 95.1 – C100 95.6 – RNE2 96.7 – Los 40 97.4 – Canarias R. 97.5 – R.21 Musica 98.0 – RNE5 INF.98.4 – ECCA 99.5 – Canarias R. 100.5 – SER R.La Palma 101.6 – RNE1 102.7 – R.Maria 103.1 – Cadena Dial 104.1 – RNE2 104.5 – RNE3 106.1 – R.Isla Bonita OCR 106.4 – Radio LUZ Garafia 107.0 Onda Taburiente El Paso 107.0

La Gomera (MHz): Intersur R. 88.0 – Onda Tagoror Gomera R. 88.5 – R.CLM 90.2 – RNE5 91.7 – R.Insular de la Gomera 92.2 – R.Insular de la Gomera 92.2 – RNE1 94.3 – R.Cantera 94.7 – R.Atlantico Sur 95.6 – Canarias R. 96.7 – SER R.Garoè 98.8 – RNE2 101.8 – R.Gigante 102.2 – R.Garajonay 102.6 – ECCA 103.4 – Formula Hit 103.7 – RNE3 105.2 – R.Insular de la Gomera 105.9 – R.Vallehermoso 107.4 – R.Agulo 107.6 – R.Ipalan 107.7

El Hierro (MHz): RNE5 89.8 – ECCA Valverde 90.6 – SER R.Garoè La Frontera 92.0 – RNE1 92.5 – RNE2 93.9 – RNE3 96.4 – RNE2 97.0 – RNE5 98.2 – Onda Herrena Valverde100.8 – RNE1 101.2 – Canarias R. Frontera 102.3 – Canarias R. Valverde 103.2 – RNE3 104.9 – R.Tajaraste Valverde 105.2 – Onda Herrena Frontera 107.0

NB: For LPFM stns on all islands: **W:** lalistadelafm.com/canarias.htm

Tourist Radio FM Stations

These stns broadcast in German, English and other languages to tourists visiting the Canary Islands. Most operate 24h

Atlantis FM (GCF) 98.0 (GCL) 101.7MHz **W:** atlantisfm.de – **Buzz FM** (GCL) 88.6, 88.8MHz **W:** buzzfm.tm – **Coast FM** (TF) 89.9, 106.6MHz **W:** coastfmtenerife.com –**Energy FM** (TFG) 89.2, 95.7MHz **W:** dancemusicradio.net **Express FM** (TFG) 105.3, 94.6MHz **W:** express-fm.net – **Hola FM** (GCF) 95.1MHz **W:** holafm.de – **Holiday FM** (GC, TF) 95.3, 98.2, 99.0, 100.0MHz **W:** holidayfm.com – **Holland FM** (GC) 90.7MHz **W:** hollandfm906.nl – **Horizon FM** (TFG) 89.9, 104.5MHz **W:** horizon. fm – **Mix 101 FM Radio** (GC) 101.0, 104.8MHz **W:** mix-radio.net – **Oasis FM** (TFG) 101.0, 101.2 (TF) 91.3, 98.1MHz **W:** oasisfm.com – **On Life FM** (TF) ,90-5,99.7 **W:** onlifefm.tenerife.com – **QFM** (TF) 94.3MHz **W:** qmusica.com – **R. Europa FM (TF)** 100.6 (GCL) 102.5 **W:** radio-europa.fm **R. Mega Welle** (TF) 88.3, 102.0, 104.7MHz (GC) 88.3, 102.0MHz **W:** megawelle.radio.de – **Russkoe R.** 105 FM (TF) 105.0MHz **W:** russkoe-105fm.ru **Spectrum FM** (TF) 105.3MHz **W:** canaries.spectrumfm.net – **R. Syd** (TF) 90.0, 100.6MHz **W:** radiosyd. net – **UK Away FM** (GCL) 99.4, 99.9MHz **W:** ukawayfm.uk – **Vaughan Radio** (GC) 96.7 **W:** vaughanradio.com – **Volna FM** (TF) 102.9MHz **W:** volnafm.ru – **Yumbo FM** (GC) 105.1MHz **W:** yumbofm.com

L.T: UTC -1h – **Pop:** 400,000 – **Pr.L:** Portuguese, Crioulo – **E.C:** 50Hz, 220V – **ITU:** CPV.

AGENCIA NACIONAL DAS COMUNICAÇÕES (ANAC)

⌂ C.P. 892, Edifício MIT, Ponta Belém, Praia ☎+238 2604400 ≣ +238 2613069 **W:** anac.cv **E:** info@anac.cv

RÁDIOTELEVISÃO DE CABO VERDE (RCV, Gov.)

⌂ Rua 13 de Janeiro 1-A, Achada de Santo António, Praia ⌂C.P. 29, Av. Marginal, Mindelo, São Vicente ⌂ C.P. 40, Espargos, Ilha do Sal ☎≣+238 2411444 **W:** rtc.cv **E:** rtc@cvtelecom.cv
L.P: Dir: Marcos Oliveira. PD: Giordano Custodio. Dir. Inf: Mario Almeida. Dir. Tec: Francisco Lopes Monteiro.
FM: Monte Verde 87.6MHz 1kW, Morro Curral 89.7MHz 0.25kW, Monte Tchota 91.6MHz 1kW, Mindelo 95.6MHz 0.5kW, Praia 98.1MHz 0.1kW + 12 relays below 0.1kW. **D.Prgr:** 24h.

Other stations:

R. Nova, C.P. 426, Mindelo, São Vicente. **E:** radionova@cvtelecom. cv **FM (MHz):** Pinhão 91.8, Monte Vermelho 94.1, Cachaço 95.1, Sal Rei 97.0, Monte Tropetona 99.1, Pedra Rachada 99.9, M. Tchota 101.6 0.25kW, Mindelo 102.3, M. Verde 104.3 0.5kW, Morro do Curral 106.4 – **R. Comercial**: Santiago 92.9 1kW, Ponta Rachada 96.1MHz, Praia/M. Verde 99.9MHz – **R. Crioula**: M. Tchota 88.5MHz, M. Barro/M. Verde 89.6MHz, Praia 94.9MHz, Morro Curral 98.9Mhz – **R. Educativa**: Monte Verde 101.5MHz, M. Tchota 102.3MHz, Praia & 4 sites 103.1MHz – **Mosteiros FM**: M. Chota 96.1MHz, São Filipe/Mosteiros 97.3MHz
RDP África: Monte Verde 93.9MHz 3kW, Monte Tchota/Pedra Rachada 105.2MHz 3/1kW, Pedra Rachada 105.2MHz 1kW + 4 trs under 1kW.

RFI Afrique, Praia/Santo Antão 99.3MHz 1kW, Fogo/Mindelo/Sal 100.7MHz 0.25kW in French and Portuguese

CAYMAN ISLANDS (UK)

L.T: UTC -5h (13Mar – 6Nov: -4) — **Pop:** 55,500 — **Pr.L:** English — **E.C:** 60Hz, 110V — **ITU:** CYM

RADIO CAYMAN (Gov. Comm.)
✉ 71B Elgin Av, PO Box 1110, George Town, Grand Cayman KY1-1102 ☎ +1 345 949 7799 🖷 +1 345 949 6536 **W:** radiocayman.gov.ky **L.P:** Dir: Norma McField. Dep. Dir: Paulette Conolly-Bailey
FM: R. Cayman One: Grand Cayman 89.9MHz 5kW Cayman Brac: 93.9MHz 0.3kW music, current affairs, news: 24h Relays BBCWS 0500-1100 – **Breeze FM:** Grand Cayman 105.3MHz 5kW Cayman Brac: 91.9MHz 0.3kW music and news

CAYMAN ISLANDS WEATHER SERVICE (Gov.)
✉ Ministry of District Adm, Works, Lands & Agriculture, Gov't Adm Bldg, George Town, Grand Cayman KY1-9000
FM: Cayman Weather Radio/Sunny: 107.9MHz 1kW

HURLEYS ENTERTAINMENT CORPORATION (Comm.)
✉ Grand Harbour, Suite 21-22, Shamrock Rd, PO Box 30110, KY1 1201 Red Bay, Grand Cayman ☎ +1 345 945 1166 🖷 +1 345 945 1006 **E:** info@z99.ky **W:** z99.ky and rooster101.ky
L.P: Pres. & GM: Randy Merren. PD: Jason Howard.
FM: Z99: George Town 99.9MHz 5kW CHR – **Rooster 101.9:** 101.9MHz 5kW Cayman Brac 101.9MHz 1kW: Country

PARAMOUNT MEDIA SERVICES (Comm.)
✉ Rankin's Plaza, 21 Eclipse Drive, PO Box 10734, George Town, Grand Cayman KY1-1002 ☎ +1 345 949 8423 🖷 +1 345 946 9867 **E:** info@paramountmedia.ky **W:** spinfm.ky and vibefm.ky
FM: Spin FM: George Town 94.9MHz 1kW dance music – **Vibe 98.9:** George Town 98.9MHz 2kW Cayman Brac 98.9MHz 0.3kW urban Caribbean

ICCI-FM (Educ.)
✉ International College of the Cayman Islands, Newlands, 595 Hirst Rd, PO Box 136, Grand Cayman KY1-1501. College ☎ +1 345 947 1100 🖷 +1 809 947 1230 **W:** icci.edu.ky/icci-fm-radio/. **L.P:** College Pres.: David Marshall. **FM:** 101.1MHz 0.5kW **D.Prgr:** 24h Locally prod. prgrs for residents, or continuous jazz, classical and easy listening music, acc. to availability of student volunteers.

DMS BROADCASTING LTD. (Comm.)
✉ 38 Godfrey Nixon Way, PO Box 31910, Grand Cayman KY1-1208 ☎ + 1 345 943 1367 🖷 +1 345 943 1368 **E:** dms@dmsbroadcasting.ky **W:** dmsbroadcasting.ky **L.P:** MD: Don Seymour. GM: Dan Charleston.
FM: CayRock George Town: 96.5MHz (1kW) Cayman Brac: 96.5MHz (0.3kW) – **HOT FM** George Town: 104.1MHz – **KISS FM** George Town 106.1MHz – **X 107.1** George Town 107.1MHz

PRAISE 87.9 RADIO (Rlg.)
✉ 209 Walkers Rd, PO Box 515, George Town, Grand Cayman KY1-1106 ☎ + 1 345 640 2647 **W:** caymanadventist.org **FM:** 87.9MHz Adventist

CAYMAN BROADCASTING LTD. (Rlg.)
✉ 125 Eastern Av., PO Box 1336, George Town, Grand Cayman KY1-1010 **E:** info@lovefm.ky **W:** lovefm.ky **Love FM:** 103.1MHz 2kW Format: Gospel

INTERACTIVE BROADCASTING & MEDIA LTD. (Comm.)
✉ 42 Edward St., Unit #2, PO Box 976, George Town KY-1102 ☎ + 1 345 943 3600 **W:** star927cayman.ky **L.P:** John Watler. **FM: Star FM** 92.7MHz 2.5kW Urban

BIG FISH (Rlg.)
✉ PO Box 1408, Prospect KY-1501 **E:** pam@bigfish955.ky **W:** bigfish955.ky **L.P:** Pamela Norton. **FM:** 95.5MHz 3kW Contemp. Christian

CENTRAL AFRICAN REPUBLIC

L.T: UTC +1h — **Pop:** 4.5 million — **Pr.L:** French, Sango — **E.C:** 50Hz, 220V — **ITU:** CAF.

MINISTÈRE DE LA COMMUNICATION
✉ B.P. 940, Bangui ☎+236 21610437. **L.P:** Minister: Abdou Karim Meckassolia

RADIO CENTRAFRIQUE (Gov.)
✉ B.P. 940, Bangui ☎+236 75503632. **W:** facebook.com/pages/RADIO-CENTRAFRIQUE/128958907146671 **E:** radio.centrafrique@yahoo.fr **L.P:** DG: Aimé-Christian Ndotah. PD: Mrs. Pauline Gbianza.
FM: Bangui 106.9MHz 1kW 24h.
F.PI: during 2016 reactivation of both MW & SW operation on 1440kHz & 5035/7220kHz, both 10kW.
D.Prgr in French/Sango: 24h. **N. in French:** 0600, 0700, 1300, 1800. **Ann:** F: "Ici Bangui, Radio Centreafricaine". **IS:** Repeated piano chord. Opens and closes with National Anthem.

RADIO ICDI (Integrated Community Development Int., Rlg)
✉ B.P. 362, Bangui **W:** icdinternational.org/radio **E:** radioicdi@gmail.com **L.P:** CPO: Richard Klopp, Coordinator: Mr. Farel Ndango
SW: Boali 6030 1kW. **D.Prgr.** in French, Sango, Bayaka and Fulfulde: Mon-Sat 0600-1100, daily 1400-1700 on 6030kHz. **Ann:** "C'est la Radio ICDI qui émet depuis Boali sur 6030 kHz".

RADIO NDEKE LUKA
(joint initiative between the UN Development Programme, CAF government and Hirondelle Foundation)
✉ c/o PNUD, Av. de l'Indépendance, B.P. 872, Bangui ☎+236 72295252. **W:** radiondekeluka.org **L.P:** Dir: Martin Faye.
FM: Bambari/Bangui/Bouar 100.9MHz 1kW. **D.Prgr:** 24h in Sango/French. Also relayed by R. ICDI, Boali on 6030 kHz between 1700-1900. Hirondelle-aided community radios (MHz):
R. Barangbaké, Bria: 100.1 – **R. Be Oko,** Bambari: 103.5 – **R. Kuli Ndounga,** Nola: 98.0 – **R. Linga,** Bangui: 96.5 – **R. Magbadja,** Alindao – **R. Maïgaro,** Bouar: 108.0 – **R. Voix de la Pende,** Paoua: 102.6 – **R. Zoukpana,** Berbérati: 105.9 – **Voix de l'Ouham,** Bossangoa: 99.7.

Other stations (MHz):
R. Anidussa, M'Boki: 100.5 – **R. ESCA La Voix de la Grâce,** Bangui: 98.5 **E:** radiovoixdelagrace@yahoo.fr – **R. Notre Dame,** Bangui: 103.3 1kW **W:** radionotredame.org – **R. Siriri,** Bouar: 103.6 **W:** facebook.com/RadioSiriri – **R. Zereda,** Obo: 100.6 **W:** facebook.com/pages/Radio-Zereda/453484071414186?fref=ts – **R. Yemusse,** Djéma: 103.5.
BBC African Sce, Bangui: 90.2MHz.
RFI Afrique, Bangui: 99.8MHz.
Voice of America, Bangui: 107.1MHz

CHAD

L.T: UTC +1h — **Pop:** 10 million — **Pr.L:** French, Arabic, 8 ethnic — **E.C:** 50Hz, 220V — **ITU:** TCD

HAUT CONSEIL DE LA COMMUNICATION (HCC)
✉ N'Djamena. **L.P:** Moussa Mahamat Dago, president.

OFFICE NATIONAL DE RADIO ET TÉLÉVISION DU TCHAD (ONRTV, Gov.)
✉ B.P. 892, Av. Mobotu, N'Djamena. ☎+235 22521513 🖷 +235 22521517 **W:** onrtv.td **L.P:** Dir: Nguérébaye Adoum Saleh.
Station: N'Djamena-Gredia.
MW: 840kHz 20kW (inactive). **SW:** 6165kHz 250kW (inactive).
FM: 94.5MHz 0.1kW. **D.Prgr:** in French/Arabic/others:24h. Local prgr. for N'djamena on 92.5MHz. **Ann:** "Ici N'Djamena, Office National de Radio et Télévision du Tchad".

REGIONAL FM STATIONS
R. Moundou, B.P. 122, Moundou: 94.05/98.3MHz 200/450W – **R. Sarh,** B.P. 270, Sarh: 94MHz – **R. Abéché,** B.P. 105, Abéché: 101MHz – **R. Faya-Largeau:** 99.1MHz.
F.PI: 13 more regional stations.

Other stations:
Al-Bayan FM, N'Djamena: 93.7MHz – **Al-Nasr,** N'Djamena: 102.1MHz – **Dja FM,** N'Djamena: 96.9MHz 0.5kW – **R. Al-Quran,** N'Djamena: 91.0MHz – **R. Arc en Ciel,** N'Djamena: 90.7MHz – **R. Duji Lokar,** Mondou: 101.8MHz 0.5kW – **R. Effata,** Lai: 98.0MHz **W:** dioceselai.org – **R. Évangile Développement,** Pala: 88.5MHz – **FM Liberté,** N'Djamena: 105.1MHz – **R. Harmonie FM,** N'Djamena: 106.3MHz 0.5kW – **R. Lotiko:** Koumra 100.1MHz, Sarh 97.6MHz 0.5kW **W:** sarh.info/membres/nangadoumbaye/Lotiko Radio.html – **R. Terre Nouvelle,** Bangor 99.4MHz 1.1kW – **La Voix du Paysan,** Doba: 96.2MHz 1kW.
BBC African Sce: N'Djamena 90.6MHz
RFI Afrique: N'Djamena/Abéché/Moundou/Sarh 100.2MHz

CHILE

L.T: UTC -4h — **Pop:** 17.7 million — **Pr.L:** Spanish — **E.C:** 50Hz, 220V — **ITU:** CHL — **Int. dialling code:** +56

SUBSECRETARIA DE TELECOMUNICACIONES
Offices: Amunátegui 139, Santiago ✉ Clasificador 120, Correo 21, Santiago ☎ 2 24213500 📠 2 26995138 **W:** subtel.cl

ASOCIACION DE RADIODIFUSORES DE CHILE - ARCI
✉Pasaje Matte 966, Piso 8. Of. 801 Santiago ☎2 28898900 📠2 26394205 **W:** archi.cl
STATIONS: MW: Call letters CA, CB, CC and CD indicate: A=No. Zone, B=Central Zone, C=So. Zone and D=Antarctic Zone. The figures indicate the freq. in kHz minus one cipher, f. inst. CB82 = Central Zone 820kHz. SW: Call letters CE are used for all zones.° = on-air stn name not confirmed ‡ = inactive ± = varying freq.

MW	Call	kHz	kW	Station, location, h of tr
MS01)	CB54	540	1	R. Ignacio Serrano, Melipilla
BB01)	CC55	550	2	R. Corporación, Concepción
AR02)	CC55	550	1	R. Voz de la Tierra, Angol:1000-0200
BB26)	CC59	590	1	CARACOL 590, Concepción: 24h
MC01)	CD59	590	10	R. Pingüino, Punta Arenas
MS03)	CB60	600	10	R. Vida Nueva, Santiago: 1100-0500
CO01)	CA62	620	1	R. Norte Verde, Ovalle
BB03)	CC62	620	10	R. Bío-Bío, Concepción: 24h
VA01)	CB63	630	10	R. Stela Maris, Valparaíso: 1200-0600
AR03)	CD64	640	1	R. Cooperativa AM, Temuco: 24h
MA13)	CC64	640	0.25	R. Portales, Curico
MS26)	CB66	660	50	R. UC, Santiago
BB04)	CC68	680	10	R. Cooperativa, Concepción: 24h
MS05)	CB69	690	10	R. Santiago, Santiago
LL02)	CD69	‡690	10	R. Estrella del Mar (R.Maria), Ancud: 24h
LR01)	CD70	700	1	Nueva R. Valdivia, Valdivia
MC02)	CD70A	700	5	R. Magallanes, Punta Arenas: 24h
TA09)	CA72	720	1	R. Portales, Iquique
VA02)	CB73	730	10	R. Cooperativa AM, Valparaíso: 24h
BB19)	CD73	730	1	R. Angelina, Los Angeles
MS06)	CB76	760	50	R. Cooperativa, Santiago: 24h
AR10)	CD127	770	1	R. Agricultura, Temuco: 24h
LL04)	CD77	770	1	R. Cooperativa, Castro: 24h
LL05)	CD78	780	10	R. Sago, Osorno
VA03)	CB80	800	5/1	R. Maria, Viña del Mar: 24h
CO02)	CA82B	820	10/1	R. Portales Corporacion, La Serena
MS07)	CB82	820	10/5	R. Carabineros, Santiago
BB05)	CC82	‡820	1	R.UCSC, Concepción
LR02)	CD82	820	1	R. Concordia, La Unión: 24h
VA04)	CB84	‡840	10	R. Portales, Valparaíso
AS03)	CD84	840	10	R. Santa María, Coyhaique
BB06)	CC86	860	10	R. Inés de Suárez, Concepción: 24h
MS08)	CB88	880	10	R. Colo Colo, Santiago: 24h
BB07)	CC89	890	1	R. Interamericana, Concepción
MC03)	CD89	890	20	R. Nacional., Punta Arenas
VA05)	CB90	‡900	1	Viña del Mar
BB08)	CC90	‡900	1	R. Nuble, Chillán: 1100-0400
LL07)	CD90	900	1	R. LV de la Costa, Osorno:0930-0300
MA14)	CC91	910	1	R. Tropical Latina (RTL), Talca
AR04)	CD92	‡920	1	R. 920, Temuco: 1000-0300
MS09)	CB93	930	10	R. Nuevo Mundo, Santiago: 24h
LL08)	CD93	930	10	R. Reloncaví, Puerto Montt
VA06)	CB94	‡940	10	R. Valentín Letelier, Valparaíso
MS10)	CB96	960	10	R. Carrera, Santiago
MC04)	CD96	960	10	R. Polar, Punta Arenas
MA01)	CC97	970	10	R. Lautaro, Talca: 1000-0500
AS04)	CD97A	970	1	R. Patagonia Chilena, Coyhaique
LR03)	CD97	970	1	R. Austral, Valdivia
CO11)	CA98	980	1	La Serena
VA07)	CB98	‡980	5	Valparaíso
MS11)	CB100	1000	10	BBN Radio, Santiago
AR22)	CD101	‡1010	10	Temuco
MA02)	CC102	‡1020	5	Talca
BB25)	CB103	1030	10	R. Chilena, Concepción: 1000-0300
MS12)	CB103	1030	1	R. Progreso, Talagante
LL10)	CD103	1030	1	R. Chiloé, Castro:1100-0330
MC05)	CD103A	1030	1	R. Payne AM, Puerto Natales
LL11)	CD105	‡1050	1	Osorno
MS13)	CB106	1060	100	R. Maria, Santiago
CO03)	CA108	‡1080	2	Vicuña
AR07)	CD108	1080	1	R. Los Confines, Angol

MW	Call	kHz	kW	Station, location, h of tr
LL23)	CD109	1090	5	Castro
MA11)	CC109	1090	5/1	R. Chilena del Maule, Talca: 1000-0300
VA08	CB110	1100	10	BBN R., Viña del Mar
AR08)	CD111	1110	10	R. La Frontera, Temuco: 0900-0400
MS14)	CB114	1140	100	R. Nal., Santiago
MA04)	CC116	‡1160	1	R. Ancoa, Linares
CO10)	CB116	1160	1	R. America, La Serena
AR01)	CD116A	1160	1	R. Baha'i, Temuco: 0930-0130
MC06)	CD117	1170	5	R. Natales, Puerto Natales: 1200-0400
MS15)	CB118	±1180	50	R. Portales, Santiago: 24h
BB20)	CD120	1200	10	R. Agricultura, Los Angeles
LL12)	CD121	‡1210	1	Puerto Montt
MA05)	CC121	1210	1	R. Universidad de Talca, Talca: 24h
VA20)	CB121	‡1210		R. Valparaiso, Valparaiso
AR09)	CD122	1220	10	R. Maria, Temuco
MS16)	CB124	1240	25	R. Universidad de Santiago, Santiago
LR04)	CD125	1250	10	R. Pilmaiquen, Valdivia: 24h
AP02)	CA126	‡1260	10	R. Nacional, Arica
MA06)	CC126	1260	1	R. Condell, Curicó
MC07)	CD126	‡1260	10	R. Maria, Punta Arenas
VA09)	CB127	±1270	5	R. Festival, Viña del Mar: 0900-0300
LL14)	CD128	1280	1	R. la Palabra, Osorno
AN07)	CA129	‡1290	0.25	R. Coya, Los Angeles
MS25)	CB130	1300	5	R. Conexiones, Santiago: 1200-0300
BB21)	CD132	‡1320	1	R. Lincoyan, Mulchén
MS17)	CB133	1330	3	R. La Perla del Dial, Santiago: 24h
LL16)	CD133	‡1330	3/15	Puerto Montt
VA10)	CD134	1340	10	R. Colo Colo, Valparaíso: 24h
BB11)	CC134	‡1340	1	R. La Discusión, Chillán: 24h
LR06)	CD134	1340	1	R. Vida Nueva, Panguipulli
CO06)	CA135	1350	1	R. Riquelme, Coquimbo: 1030-0430
LL24)	CD135	‡1350	0.02	Puerto Montt
BB12)	CC136	1360	5	R. Universidad Bio Bio, Concepcion: 24h
AR11)	CD137	1370	1	R. Emaus, Temuco: 1100-0500
MS18)	CB138	1380	50	R. Corporación, Santiago: 24h
BB22)	CD140	1400	5	R. La Amistad, Los Angeles
LL18)	CD140A	1400	1	R. Maria, Puerto Montt
VA11)	CB141	‡1410	5	Valparaíso
AR12)	CD141	1410	1	R. Loncoche, Loncoche
MS19)	CB142	‡1420	1	R. Panamericana, Santiago
GB06)	CC143	‡1430	1	Rancagua
BB13)	CC144	1440	1	R. El Sembrador, Chillán: 1000-0230
CO07)	C144A	1440	1	R. Agricultura, La Serene: 24h
VA12)	CB145	1450	1	R. Universidad Técnica "Federico Santa María, Valparaíso
MA08)	CC145	1450	4	R. Tropical Latina – RTL, Curicó: 24h
MS20)	CB146	1460	1	R. Palabra Viva, Santiago
BB14)	CC146	1460	1	R. Armonía, Talcahuano
VA13)	CB147	1470	1	R. Sargento Aldea, San Antonio
BB15)	CC148	1480	1	R. La Amistad de Tomé, Tomé
CO08)	CA148	1480	1	R. Comunicativa, Ovalle
AT06)	CA149	‡1490	1	R. Alicanto, El Salvador
MS21)	CB149	1490	0.25	El Canelo, San Bernardo:
AR13)	CD149	1490	5	R. Malleco, Victoria
MA09)	CC150	‡1500	1	R. Centenario
MC08)	CD150	1500	1	R. Tierra del Fuego, Porvenir
VA14)	CB150	1500	1	R. Trasandina, Los Andes: 24h Sun.: 2000-2200
CO09)	CA151	1510	1/0.5	R. Luís Alvarez Sierra, Illapel: 1000-0100 Sat: -0400 Sun: 1100-0100
GB02)	CC151	1510	1	R. Poder Pentecostal, Rancagua: 24h
AR20)	CD151	1510	0.05	R. Loncoche, Loncoche
MA10)	CC152	1520	1	R. Soberanía, Linares:0930-0005
VA15)	CB152	‡1520	1	R. Integración, San Antonio
AT05)	CA153	1530	1	R. Vida Nueva, Copiapó: 1100-0500
VA16)	CB153	1530	1	R. Parque, Quillota: 1000-0300
LL21)	CD153	‡1530	0.25	Puerto Montt
MS22)	CB154	‡1540	1	R. Sudamérica, Santiago
BB17)	CC154	‡1540	1	Chillán
LR05)	CC154	‡1540	1	R. San José de Alcudia, Río Bueno:
VA17)	CB155	1550	1	R. Provincial AM, Putaendo
GB03)	CC155	‡1550	1	R. Manuel Rodríguez, San Fernando:
AP01)	CA156	1560	5/3	R. Parinacota, Putre: 24h
MS23)	CB156	1560	1	R. Manantial, Talagante: 1000-0300 Sat: -0500
AR16)	CD156	1560	1	R. Parque, Villarrica
GB04)	CC157	±1570	1	R. Cristo Llama Al Pecador, Rancagua: 24h
MA11)	CC157A	1570	1	R. Familia del Maule, Talca: 1000-0300
GB05)	CC158	1580	1	R. Colchagua, Santa Cruz
VA18)	CB159	±1590	1	R. Aconcagua, San Felipe: 1000-2300
MA15)	CC159A	‡1590	0.1	Parral
MS24)	CB160	1600	0.25	R. Nuevo Tiempo, Santiago: 24h

MW	Call	kHz	kW	Station, location, h of tr
VA19)	CB160A	‡1600	0.25	R. Positiva, Viña del Mar
BB18)	CC160	±1600	0.25	R. Llacolén, Concepción
AR23)	CD160	1600	0.25	R. Alternativa, Temuco: 1000-0100

SW	Call	kHz	kW	Station, location, h of tr
AR19)	CE609	‡6090	10	R. Esperanza, Temuco: 24h

Addresses and other information

AN00 (ANTOFAGASTA – Region II):
AN07) Av Ignacio Carrera Pinto No 401-A, María Elena ☎55 641176 **E:** contacto@radiocoya.cl – **FM:** 92.5 MHz

AP00 (ARICA Y PARINACOTA – Region XV):
AP01) Calle José Miguel Carrera 350 esquina Av. Circulación O'Higgins, Putre ☎58 2252803 **W:** imputre.cl **E:** prensaputre@hotmail.com – **FM:** 94.5MHz – **AP02)** Arica –

AR00 (ARAUCANIA – Region IX):
AR01) Cl 1Norte 0684, Labranza, Temuco ☎45 2375142 **W:** radio.bahai.cl – **AR02)** Av. Bernardo O'Higgins 297, piso 2, Angol ☎45 2712331 **W:** Facebook: Radio Voz de la Tierra **E:** radiovozdelatierra@gmail.com – **AR03)** Temuco **W:** cooperativa.cl **E:** internet@cooperativa.cl – **FM:** 103.1 MHz – **AR04)** Portales 527, Temuco ☎45 2277148 **W:** radionueveveinte.com **E:** radionueveveinte@gmail.com – **AR07)** Lautaro 124 Piso 2, Angol ☎45 2413647 **W:** losconfines.cl – **FM:** 94.9MHz – **AR08)** Av Caupolicián 110 Of 2003 Piso 20, Temuco ☎45 2213166 ☎45 2210309 **W:** araucanayfrontera.cl **E:** contacto@araucanayfrontera.cl – **FM:** 95.9MHz «La Araucana» – **AR09)** Temuco **W:** radiomaria.cl **E:** contacto@radiomaria.cl – **AR10)** Lynch 6464, Temuco ☎45 213854 **W:** radioagricultura.cl – **AR11)** Av. Maquehue 1115 – Padre las Casas, Temuco ☎452 734948 **W:** radioemaustemuco.cl – **AR12)** Ignacio Serrano 264, Loncoche ☎45 2471052 **W:** radioloncoche.cl **E:** radiocd141@gmail.com – **FM:** 105.9MHz «Vibración» – **AR13)** Pisagua 1133, Victoria ☎45 2841322 **E:** radiomalleco@yahoo.es – **AR16)** Vicente Reyes 528, Villarrica ☎45 411567 **W:** radioparque.cl **E:** radiopnacional@gmail.com – **AR19)** Luis Durand 3057, Temuco ☎45 2367070 ☎45 2213790. - **English:** 0800-0830. **German:** Sun 1230-1300 - **FM:** 101.3MHz – **AR20)** Sector Elecoyan, Loncoche ☎45 2471052 **W:** radioloncoche.cl – **AR22)** Temuco. – **AR23)** Manuel Montt 381-C, Temuco ☎45 2483356 **W:** radioalternativa.cl

AS00 (AISÉN – Region XI)
AS03) Francisco Bilbao 691, Coyhaique ☎67 2232398 ☐67 2231306 **W:** radiosantamaria.cl **E:** contacto@radiosantamaria.cl – **FM:** 102.3MHz – **AS04)** Av Francisco Bilboa 457 ☎67 245632 **W:** radiopatagoniachilena.cl **E:** radiopatagoniachilena@gmail.com – **FM:** 99.3MHz «Acro Iris»

AT00 (ATACAMA – Region III):
AT05) Colipi 371, Copiapo ☎52 212031 **W:** radiovidanuevaencristojesus.com – **AT06)** Av. El Tofo 535, Diego de Almagro ☎52 2475023

BB00 (BIO BIO – Region VIII):
BB01) Angol 648, 2° piso, Concepción ☎41 2738650 **W:** radio-corporacion.cl **E:** contacto@radio-corporacion.cl – **BB03)** O'Higgins 680, Piso 3, Concepción ☎41 2620620 **W:** radiobiobio.cl **E:** biobio@laradio.cl – **FM:** 98.1MHz – **BB04)** Paicavi 119, 2° piso, (Plaza Peru) (or Cas. 2337), Concepción **W:** cooperativa.cl **E:** internet@cooperativa.cl – **FM:** 93.3 MHz– **BB05)** Campus San Andres, Alonso de Ribera 2850, Concepción ☎41 2345000 ☎41 2345001W: ucsc.cl/ucsc-radio – **BB06)** Castellón 477, 3° piso, Concepción ☎41 246 0486 **W:** radioinesdesuarez.cl – **BB07)** Calle Barros Arana 871, 5° piso, Of. 51, Concepción ☎41 2214450 **W:** radiointeramericana.cl **E:** contacto@radiointeramericana.cl – **BB08)** 5 de Abril 655, Chillán ☎42 2215530 **W:** radionuble.cl/ **E:** radiocontigo@gmail.com – **FM:** 89.7MHz "R.Nuble" – **BB11)** 18 de Septiembre 721, Chillán ☎42 2211667**W:** ladiscusion.cl **E:** radiotv@ladiscusion.cl – **FM:** 94.7MHz – **BB12)** Avd Collao 1202, Casilla 5-C, Concepción ☎41 3111 1040 **W:** radioubb.cl **E:** ubb@ubiobio.cl – **BB13)** Arauco 447, Chillán ☎42 2224603 **W:** radioelsembrador.cl **E:** administracion@radioelsembrador.cl – **FM:** 104.7MHz «Aurora FM» – **BB14)** Av.Los Carrera N° 464, Concepcion ☎41 2854594 **W:** concepcion@armonia.cl – **FM:** 99.5 MHz – **BB15)** Sotomayor 1184 2° piso of 203, Tomé ☎41 2650657 **W:** radiolaamistaddetome.cl **E:** contacto@radiolaamistaddetome.cl – **B17)** Chillán – **BB18)** Calle Barros Arana, Concepción ☎41 2440201 **W:** radiollacolen.cl **E:** radiollacolen@gmail.com – **BB19)** Colo-Colo 451 Of. 120, Nivel 2, Los Angeles ☎43 2349920 **E:** contacto@radiocamila.cl – **FM:** 98.3 MHz – **BB20)** Calle Janequeo 615, Los Angeles ☎43 324212 **W:** radioagricultura.cl – **BB21)** Mulchén – **BB22)** Lautaro 279, Departemento 301, Los Angeles ☎43 2329834 **W:** radiolaamistad.cl **E:** radiolaamistad@gmail.com – **BB25)** Arzobispado de la Santísima Concepción, Barros Arana 544, 3° piso, Concepción ☎41 2626167 **W:** radiochilenaconcepcion.cl **E:** contacto@radiochilenaconcepcion.cl – **BB26)** Castellón 746, 2° piso, Concepcion ☎41 2460193 **W:** radiocaracol590.cl

CO00 (COQUIMBO – Region IV):
CO01) Ca Santiago355, Ovalle ☎53 2620359 **W:** radionorteverde.cl/ – **CO02)** Los Carrera 525, 3° piso, Departamento C, La Serena **W:** Facebook: Radio Portales Corporacion – **CO03)** Vicuña – **CO06)** Aldunate 1619, Coquimbo ☎51 2321051 **W:** radioriquelme.cl – **CO07)** Cas 536, La Serena ☎51 240291 **W:** radioagricultura.cl – **CO08)** Pedro Montt 181, Ovalle **W:** radiocomunicativa.cl **E:** radiocomunicativa@gmail.com - **FM:** 93.7 MHz – **CO09)** Independencia 175, Illapel ☎☐53 2522831**W:** las.co.cl/Radio.htm **E:** direccionlas@entelchile.net – **FM:** 100.9MHz – **CO10)** O'Higgins No 519, Piso 2, Oficina 09, La Serena ☎6 1999542 **E:** radiosamericachile@yahoo.cl – **CO11)** Benavente 1141, La Serena

GB00 (O'HIGGINS – Region VI):
GB02) Santa María n° 61, Rancagua – ☎72 2229586 **W:** poderpentecostal.org **E:** pastorclaudioespinoza@hotmail.com – **GB03)** Altos Mercado, calle Chacabuco esq. España, San Fernando ☎☐72 714267 **E:** cc155laradio@hotmail.com – **GB04)** Ca Santa Maria 126, Rancagua ☎72 242741 **W:** contacto@radio-corporacion.cl – **GB05)** Rafael Casanova 146, Santa Cruz ☎☐72 2822193 – **FM:** 105.5MHz «Ensueño» – **GB06)** Rancagua

LL00 (LOS LAGOS – Region X):
LL02) Elutero Ramírez 207, Ancud ☎56 6562 2722 – **W:** radioestrelladelmar.cl/ – **LL04)** Thompson 255 (Cas. 174), Castro **W:** cooperativa.cl **E:** internet@cooperativa.cl – **LL05)** Juan Mckenna 904, Osorno ☎64 2321601 **W:** radiosago.cl **E:** mcifuentes@radiosago.cl – **FM:** 94.5 MHz – **LL07)** Cochrane 746, Osorno ☎64 312525 **W:** radiovozdelacosta.cl – **LL08)** Egana 29, Puerto Montt ☎65 2252234 **W:** radioreloncavi.cl – **LL10)** Bernardo O'Higgins 486 (Cas. 106), Castro ☎2 632260 **W:** radiochiloe.cl **E:** prensa@radiochiloe.cl – **FM:** 90.1MHz «Martin Ruiz de Gamboa» –**LL11)** Edifico Gran Hotel O´Higgins No 615, Of 426 4° Piso, Osorno ☎64 643651 **W:** armonia.cl **E:** osorno@armonia.cl – **FM:** 98.7 MHz – **LL12)** Av Presidente Ibañez No 872 Piso 2, Puerto Montt ☎65 383290 **W.** armonia.cl **E:** puertomontt@armonia.cl – **LL14)** Eleuterio Ramírez 1050 Dpto.41,, Osorno ☎64 2237440 **W:** radiolapalabra.cl **E:** tuprogramas@radiolapalabra.cl – **FM:** 101.5MHz «La Palabra» – **LL16)** Puerto Montt – **LL18)** Puerto Montt **W:** radiomaria.cl **E:** contacto@radiomaria.cl – **FM:** 103.5 MHz – **LL21)** Puerto Montt – **LL22)** Pedro Lagos 295, Río Bueno ☎64 2341531 **W:** radiosanjosedealcudia.cl **E:** radio@radiosanjosedealcudia.cl – **LL23)** Castro –**LL24)** Puerto Montt

LR00 (LOS RIOS – Region XIV)
LR01) Arauco 340 Piso 3 Of. 307, Valdivia **W:** Facebook: Radio Nueva Valdivia – **LR02)** Arturo Prat 466, La Unión ☎64 2322275 **W:** radioconcordia.cl – **LR03)** Arauco 363 3° piso, Valdivia ☎63 2202642 **W:** radioaustralvaldivia.cl – **LR04)** Arauco No 340 4 Piso, Valdiva ☎63 2202642 **W:** radiopilmaiquen.cl – **FM:** 98.9 MHz – **LR05)** Pedro Lagos 295, Río Bueno ☎64 2341531 **W:** radiosanjosedealcudia.cl **E:** radio@radiosanjosedealcudia.cl – **LR06)** Bernard O'Higgins 793, Panguipulli. ☎63 2310796 **W:** radiovidanuevaencristojesus.com

MA00 (MAULE – Region VII):
MA01) Tres Sur 767 1 Ote y Pte., Talca ☎71 2970758 **W:** Facebook.com/RadioLautaro **E:** radiolautaro@gmail.com – **MA02)** Talca – **MA04)** Independencia 631, Linares ☎76 2612320**W:** radioancoa.cl – **FM:** 103.5MHz – **MA05)** Casa 2 Norte 685, Talca ☎71 200160 **W:** radioemisoras.utalca.cl **E:** storres@utalca.cl - **FM:** 102., 93.7MHz – **MA06)** Carmen 714, Curicó. ☎75 2543520 **W:** radiocondell.cl **E:** direccion@radiocondell.cl - **FM:** 92.7MHz – **MA08)** 157 Manuel Montt, Curicó ☎75 2328021 **W:** radiortl.cl – **FM:** 95.5MHz – **MA09)** San Javier – **MA10)** Diputado Dario Dueñas 777, Linares ☎73 2210277 **W:** radiosoberania.es.tl **E:** soberania@hotmail.com – **MA11)** 5 Poniente No 1150, Talca **W:** radiofamiliachilena.cl **E:** info@radiofamiliachilena.cl ☎71 613756 – **MA13)** Villouta N° 558, Curico **W:** radiocorporacioncurico.cl – **MA14)** Manuel Montt 198, Curico ☎75 328021 **W:** radiortl.cl –**MA15)** Parral

MC00 (MAGALLANES Y DE LA ANTARCTICA CHILENA – Region XII):
MC01) Av España 959, 6200 623 Punta Arenas ☎61 2292900 **W:** elpinguino.com **E:** secretaria@elpinguino.com – **FM:** 95.3MHz – **MC02)** José Nogueira 1370, Punta Arenas ☎61 2243551 **W:** radiomagallanes.cl **E:** prensa@radiomagallanes.cl – **MC03)** Ignacio Carrera Pinto 718, Piso 2, Punto Arenas ☎61 2617115 **W:** nacionaldechile.cl – **MC04)** Bories 871 Piso 2, Punta Arenas ☎61 2241417 **W:** radiopolar.com **E:** radiopolar.com - **FM:** 96.5-98.5-105.7MHz «Finísima» – **MC05)** Cl Bulnes 819, Puerto Natales ☎61 2411450 **E:** famm1605@hotmail.com – **FM:** 89.5 MHz – **MC06)** Eberhard 212, Puerto Natales ☎61 2410157 ☐61 2414746 – **MC07)** Punta Arenas **W:** radiomaria.cl **E:** - **FM:** 88.9 MHz – **MC08)** Bulnes 449, Porvenir ☎61 2580100 **W:** radiotierradelfuego.cl **E:** director@radiotierradelfuego.cl

MS00 (METROPOLITANA DE SANTIAGO – Region RM):
MS01) Cla Ortuzar 935 , Melipilla ☎28323440 **W:** http://radioprensa.
cl **E:** cgp.medios@gmail.com - **FM:** 104.5MHz R.Carica – **MS03)** Av.
Condell 910, Santiago ☎2 2224500 **W:** radiovidanuevaencristojesus.
com – FM: 104,5 MHz – **MS05)** Triana 868, Providencia, Santiago. ☎2
2236 0096 **W:** radiosantiago.cl **E:** gerenciageneral@radiosantiago.cl
– **MS06)** Maipú 525, Santiago 8350372 **W:** cooperativa.cl **E:** internet@
cooperativa.cl ☎2 3264 8000 📠2 2236 0535 – **MS07)** Av Presidente
Bulnes 80, Of. 127, Santiago **E:** radioemisora@carabineros.cl – **FM:**
98.1 MHz – **MS08)** Av Libertador Bernardo O'Higgins 4623, Estación
Central Santiago **W:** Facebook: R.Colo Colo ☎21 2776 4830 – **MS09)**
San Pablo 2271, Santiago ☎2 2688 3175 **W:** radionuevomundo.cl
E: info@radionuevomundo.cl –**MS10)** Eleodoro Flores 2475, Nunoa,
Santiago ☎2 2361 1894 **W:** radiocarrera.com – **MS11)** Paseo
Bulnes 120, Oficina 72, Santiago Centro a metros de la Alameda ☎2
2671 8602 **W:** bbnradio.org **E:** red@bbnmedia.org – **MS12)** Enrique
Alcalde 1081, Talagante ☎2 815 3279 **W:** radioprogresoycontacto.
cl **E:** ventas@radioprogresoycontacto.cl - **FM:** 103.9MHz «Contacto»
– **MS13)** Santiago ☎22 225 8544 **W:** radiomaria.cl **E:** contacto@
radiomaria.cl **FM:** 89.3 MHz – **MS14)** Dardignac 196 Oficina 22,
Bellavista-Patronato, Santiago ☎2 1737 0101 **W:** nacionaldechile.cl
F. radio@nacionaldechile.cl – **MS15)** Fanor Velasco 11, Santiago ☎2
2671 5002 – **W:** radioportales.cl **E:** administracion@radioportales.cl.
– **MS16)** Alameda 3363, Estación Central, Santiago ☎2 7181722 **W:**
radiousach.cl **E:** radio@usach.cl – **MS17)** Los Leones 668, Providencia,
Santiago ☎2 25836602 **W:** 3radio.cl **E:** santiago@laperladeldial.
cl – **MS18)** Av Salvador Allende 92, Santiago ☎2 25529266 **W:**
radiocorporacion.cl – **MS19)** Gran Avenida Jose Miguel Carrera 5848,
4° piso, Santiago ☎2 2416 0725 **W:** Facebook: Radio Panamericana
– **MS20)** Ubicado en Carmen No 1436, Santiago Central ☎2 25511378
W: radiopalabraviva.cl – **MS21)** Av. Portales 3020, San Bernardo ☎2
2841 4135 **W:** Facebook: Radio Canelo **E:** caneloradio@gmail.com
– **MS22)** Av Ossa No 0106, Santiago ☎2 2527 3999 **W:** radiosuda-
merica.cl **E:** scptelecomunicaciones@gmail.com – **MS23)** Av. Lib.
Bdo. O'Higginsa 854, Talagante ☎2 28151374 **W:** radiomanantial.cl
E: radiomanantial@tie.cl – **FM:** 102.9MHz «Embrujo FM» – **MS24)** Los
Cerezos No 6251, Peñalolén, Santiago ☎2 22844921 **W:** nuevotiempo.
cl **E:** contactos@nuevotiempo.cl – **MS25)** Purisima 251, Recoleta,
Santiago ☎2 2735 1790 **W:** radioconexiones.cl - **MS26)** Casa Central
de la Universidad Católica, Alameda 340, Santiago ☎2 2354 2320 📠2
2354 2054 **W:** radiouc.cl **E:** radio@uc.cl

TA00 (TARAPACA – Region I):
TA09) Iquique **W:** radioportales.cl
VA00 (VALPARAISO – Region V):
VA01) Pedro Montt 1766 (Cas. 3304), Valparaíso ☎32 274 5537 **W:**
radiostellamaris.cl **E:** contacto@radiostellamaris.cl – **VA02)** Morris No
106, Depto. 155, Piso 15, Valparaiso – **W:** cooperativa.cl **E:** internet@
cooperativa.cl – **VA03)** Viña del Mar **W:** cooperativa.cl – **VA04)**
radiomaria.cl **E:** Condell 1190 Of 21, Valparaíso ☎32 2214115
– **W:** radioportalesvalparaiso.cl **E:** radioportalesgerencia@gmail.com
- **FM:** 89.5MHz – **VA05)** Valparaíso – **VA06)** Av. Errazuriz 2120,
Valparaíso ☎32 2507657 **W:** rvl.uv.cl **E:** radio@uv.cl - **FM:** 97.3MHz
– **VA07)** Valparaíso – **VA08)** Paseo Bulnes 120, Oficina 72 , Santiago
Centro a metros de la Alameda ☎32 2885524 **W:** bbnradio.org **E:**
red@bbnmedia.org – **VA09)** Ca Quinta 124 Segundo Nivel Oficina A,
Viña del Mar ☎32 2684251 **W:** radiofestival.cl **E:** servicios@festival.
cl – **VA10)** Plaza de la Justicia 45, Piso 7 Of. 704, Valparaíso ☎32
2566664 **W:** radiocolocolovalparaiso.cl – **VA11)** Valparaíso – **VA12)**
Av. España 1680, Valparaíso ☎📠32 2797511 **W:** radio.utfsm.cl - **FM:**
99.7MHz – **VA13)** Av. Barros Luco 1678 (✉ Cas. 68,Correo 2) San
Antonio ☎35 211321 – **FM:** 90.9 MHz – **VA14)** Papudo 155, Los Andes
☎34 2421425 **W:** radiotrasandina1500.cl **E:** transdinaradioam@
gmail.com – **VA15)** San Antonio – **VA16)** Blanco 185, Quillota ☎33
2268001 **W:** radiolibra.cl **E:** lpardo@radiolibra.cl – **FM:** 104.7MHz
«Libra Stereo FM» – **VA17)** Arturo Prat Poniente no 565, Of 5 Piso
2, Putaendo ☎34 502762 **W:** radioprovincialdeputaendo.cl – **VA18)**
Santo Domingo 99 – oficina 4, San Felipe ☎34 2510198 **W:** radioacon-
cagua.cl **E:** ecornejo@radioaconcagua.cl - **FM:** 91.7MHz – **VA19)** Viña
del Mar – **VA20)** Eusebio Lillo 520, local 12, edifico Torre Valparaiso,
Valparaiso ☎32 3148080 **W:** radiovalparaiso.cl **E:** prensa@radioval-
paraiso.cl – **FM:** 97.7 & 102.5 MHz

FM in Santiago (all MHz) Power 1-10kW **Slogans:** Name + «FM»:
MS26) 88.1 Aurora – 88.5 Concierto – MS14) 88.9 R. Futuro –
MS13) 89.3 R.Maria – MS26) 89.7 Duna – 90.5 Pudahuel – 91.3 El
Conquistador – 91.7 Amistad – 92.5 Radioactiva – 92.9 Romance
– 93.3 La Cooperativa – 93.7 Universo – VA02) 94.1 Rock & Pop – 95.3
40 principales – MS25) 95.9 Tiempo – 96.5 Beethoven – 97.1 Caracol
– 97.7 Zero – 98.5 FM 2 – MS08) 99.3 Carolina – 99.7 Bío Bío – MS25)
100.1 Infinita – MS26) 100.9 – 101.3 Corazón – 101.7 FM Hit – 102.1
Oasis – 102.5 Univ. de Chile – 103.3 Horizonte – 103.9 Maria – 104.1

Romantica – MS03) 104.5 Monumental – 104.9 Nina – 105.7 Para ti
– 106.3 Armonía – MS11) 106.9 Sintonia – 107.5 Fantasía

CHINA (People's Rep. of)

L.T: UTC +8h — **Pop:** 1,366 million — **Pr.L:** Mandarin, Amoy,
Cantonese, Chaozhou, Hakka, Kazakh, Korean, Mongolian, Tibetan,
Uighur, Zhuang, a.o. — **E.C:** 50Hz, 220V — **ITU:** CHN

**MINISTRY OF INDUSTRY AND INFORMATION
TECHNOLOGY**
⌨ 13 Xi Chang'an Jie, Beijing 100804 **W:** miit.gov.cn **L.P:** Minister:
Miao Wei

**THE STATE ADMINISTRATION OF PRESS,
PUBLICATION, RADIO, FILM AND TELEVISION
(SAPPRFT) (Gov.)**
⌨ 2 Fuxingmenwai Dajie, Beijing 100866 or P.O.Box 4501, Beijing ☎
+86 10 6809 2707 📠 +86 10 6851 2174
W: sarft.gov.cn **L.P:** Dir: Cai Fuchao

Official P.R.C Abbreviations: The 31 regions of the People's Republic
of China, with their abbreviations and names in Pinyin (Chinese
Phonetic Alphabet) version followed by the old spelling in brackets):
AH: Anhui (Anhwei) – BJ: Beijing M. (Peking) – CQ: Chongqing M.
(Chungking) – FJ: Fujian (Fukien) – GD: Guangdong (Kwangtung)
– GS: Gansu (Kansu) – GX: Guangxi Zhuang A.R. (Kwangsi) – GZ:
Guizhou (Kweichow) – HAN: Hainan (Hainan) – HB: Hubei (Hupeh)
– HEB: Hebei (Hopeh) – HEN: Henan (Honan) – HL: Heilongjiang
(Heilungkiang) – HN: Hunan (Hunan) – JL: Jilin (Kirin) – JS: Jiangsu
(Kiangsu) – JX: Jiangxi (Kiangsi) – LN: Liaoning (Liaoning) – NM:
Nei Menggu A.R. (Inner Mongolia) – NX: Ningxia Hui A.R. (Ningxia)
– QH: Qinghai (Tsinghai) – SC: Sichuan (Szechwan) – SD: Shandong
(Shantung) – SH: Shanghai M. (Shanghai) – SN: Shaanxi (Shensi)
– SX: Shanxi (Shansi) – TJ: Tianjin M. (Tientsin) – XJ: Xinjiang Uighur
A.R. (Sinkiang) – XZ: Xizang A.R.(Tibet) – YN: Yunnan (Yunnan) – ZJ:
Zhejiang (Chekiang).

Regional Services: Add "Renmin Guangbo Diantai" (People's
Broadcasting Station) to the stn name shown in the table below to
obtain the full name in Standard Chinese.
Abbreviations: 1 = 1st prgr, 2 = 2nd prgr, 3 = 3rd prgr; EBS =
Economic Broadcasting Station.
Languages: Standard Chinese (Putonghua), based on the Beijing
dialect, is used in broadcasts throughout China. Various dialects and
minority languages are included in the relevant regional services and
in broadcasts to Taiwan.
Abbreviations: Ch = Standard Chinese, Kg = Kirghiz, Ko = Korean, Kz
= Kazakh, Mo = Mongolian, Tb = Tibetan, Ug = Uighur.

MW	kHz	kW	Station	Tx Location
ZJ1)	531	10	Zhejiang	Jinhua
1)	540	50	CNR 1	Shenyang/Hefei
NM1)	540	1	Nei Menggu	Wuhai
NM18)	540		Genhe	
QH4)	540	10	Haixi	Da Qaidam
1)	549	1200	CNR 5	Putian, FJ
EN2)	549	25	Zhengzhou	
NM12)	549	10	Alxa	Bayanhot
NM5)	549	10	Chifeng	
EB1)	558	3	Hebei	Shijiazhuang
FJ1)	558	50	Fujian	Jianyang
FJ1)	558	10	Fujian	Pingtan/Longyan
NM17)	558	1	Zalantun	
NM3)	558	10	Baotou	
XJ1)	558	120	Xinjiang	Hutubi
YN16)	558	10	Nujiang	Lushui
1)	567	10	CNR 1	Lianyungang, JS
EN17)	567	10	Zhoukou	
TJ1)	567	20	Tianjin	
EN4)	576	10	Luoyang	
FJ5)	576	3	Quanzhou	
YN1)	576	200	Yunnan	Kunming
ZJ1)	±576	1	Zhejiang	Linhai
14)	585	200	Southeast BC	Fuzhou, FJ
EB11)	585	10	Langfang	
EN14)	585	10	Nanyang	
GS3)	585	3	Jinchang	
HB8)	585	10	Jingzhou	
HL3)	585	10	Qiqihar	
JL2)	585	10	Changchun	
JL10)	585	1	Yanbian	Hunchun

MW	kHz	kW	Station	Tx Location	MW	kHz	kW	Station	Tx Location
JS1)	585	50	Jiangsu	Nanjing	YN12)	675	1	Gejiu	
JX5)	585	10	Xinyu		YN15)	675	10	Diqing	Shangri-la
LN1)	585		Liaoning	Suizhong	ZJ9)	675	1	Jinhua	
LN16)	585	1	Chaoyang	Beipiao	1)	684	1200	CNR 6	Putian, FJ
SX6)	585	10	Jincheng		AH1)	684		Anhui	Xuancheng
SD1)	594	50	Shandong	Jinan/Yantai	AH13)	684		Suzhou	
XZ1)	594	300	Xizang	Lhasa	EB8)	684	10	Tangshan	
13)	603	10	VO Pujiang	SH	GS1)	684	200	Gansu	Lanzhou
AH1)	603	10	Anhui	Hefei	HB2)	684	10	Hubei	Jingmen
BJ1)	603	25	Beijing		HB2)	684		Hubei Chutian	Huangshi
EB1)	603	1	Hebei	Shijiazhuang	HL9)	684	50	Mudanjiang	
EB6)	603		Zhangjiakou		LN5)	684	10	Fushun	
EN13)	603	10	Sanmenxia		XJ1)	684	3	Xinjiang	Hotan
EN1A)	603	100	Henan	Zhengzhou	ZJ11)	684	10	Zhoushan	
GD1)	603	10	Guangdong	Guangzhou	HL3)	693	10	Qiqihar	
GZ1)	603	10	Guizhou	Guiyang	SN1)	693	300	Shaanxi	Xianyang
HB3)	603	10	Wuhan		2)	702		CRI DS	Zhuhai, GD
HL5)	603		Shuangyashan		JL3)	702	10	Jilin-shi	
JL1)	603		Jilin	Songyuan	JS1)	702	200	Jiangsu	Nanjing
JL10)	603		Yanbian	Dunhua	LN16)	702	3	Chaoyang	Lingyuan
JL3A)	603		Jilin-shi EBS		NM15)	702	1	Manzhouli	
JS1)	603		Jiangsu	Yangzhou	NM5)	702	10	Tongliao	
JS12)	603		VO Jiangnan		NM6)	702	10	Ulanqab	Jining
JS16)	603	5	Suzhou		SC11)	702	1	Neijiang	
JS9)	603	5	Nantong		XJ1)	702	10	Xinjiang	Urumqi
JX9)	603	10	Ji'an		YN5)	702	10	Honghe	Gejiu
LN1)	603		Liaoning		AH12)	711	3	Fuyang	
LN10)	603		Yingkou		AH16)	711	1	Lu'an	
LN7)	603	10	Dandong		EN2)	711	10	Zhengzhou	
NM1)	603	1	Nei Menggu	Chifeng	QH1)	711	10	Qinghai	Golmud
NM10)	603	10	Ordos BS		GZ3)	711	1	Liupanshui	
NM19)	603		Morin Dawa		SC5)	711	1	Panzhihua	
NM8)	603	50	Hulun Buir	Hailar	SC8)	711	1	Mianyang	
SD1)	603	1	Shandong	Zibo	ZJ10)	711	3	Quzhou	
SD3)	603	10	Qingdao		ZJ12)	711	1	Lishui	
SD10)	603	10	Jining		1)	720	50	CNR 2	Xiamen, FJ
SD5)	603	10	Zaozhuang		1)	720	10	CNR 13	Yining/Kashi, XJ
SH1)	603	10	Shanghai		1)	720	200	CNR 16	BJ
SN1)	603	25	Shaanxi	Xi'an	AH1)	720	10	Anhui	Chaohu/Chuzhou
SN7)	603		Yan'an		SC7)	720	1	Deyang	
SX1)	603	50	Shanxi	Taiyuan	EN16)	729	10	Shangqiu	
SX4)	603	1	Yangquan		JX1)	729	200	Jiangxi	Nanchang
XJ10)	603	1	Shihezi		EB12)	738	10	Hengshui	
XJ9)	603	1	Ili	Yining	EN1)	738		Henan	Anyang
YN1)	603	1	Yunnan	Zhaotong/Gejiu	HN1)	738	200	Hunan	Changsha
ZJ1)	603	1	Zhejiang	Hangzhou/Wenzhou	JL1)	738	150	Jilin	Changchun
ZJ4)	603	10	Ningbo		XJ1)	738	120	Xinjiang	Hutubi
FJ1)	612	10	Fujian	Ningde	ZJ8)	738	5	Shaoxing	
LN1)	612	10	Liaoning	Chaoyang/Dandong	1)	747	10	CNR 12	BJ
SC1)	612	10	Sichuan	Neijiang/Yibin	AH2)	747	1	Hefei	
SD13)	612	10	Linyi		EB5)	747	10	Baoding	
HB9)	621	10	Yichang		EN1)	747	20	Henan	Nanyang/Xichuan
HL1)	621	200	Heilongjiang	Harbin	EN5)	747	10	Pingdingshan	
QH4)	621	20	Haixi	Da Qaidam	FJ6)	747		Longyan	
SC9)	621	3	Guangyuan		GD14)	747		Zhongshan	
SD1)	621	10	Shandong	Liaocheng	HB1)	747	30	Hubei	Qichun
1)	630	200	CNR 2	Nanchang, JX	JS11)	747	3	Changzhou	
1)	630	100	CNR 2	Yingyang, HEN	JS6)	747		Yancheng	
1)	639	200	CNR 1	BJ	JX8)	747		Ganzhou	
1)	639	100	CNR 1	Chengdu, SC	LN1)	747		Liaoning	Dandong
AH3)	648	1	Huainan		LN10)	747		Yingkou	
GD1)	648	150	Guangdong	Guangzhou	LN12)	747		Fuxin	
LN16)	648	3	Chaoyang		LN16)	747	3	Chaoyang	Jianping
SH1)	648	10	Shanghai		LN5)	747		Fushun	
XJ7)	648		Kashi		NM1)	747	1	Nei Menggu	Erenhot
EN1)	657	300	Henan	Zhengzhou	NM4)	747	1	Wuhai	
JL7)	657	1	Baishan		NX1)	747	10	Ningxia	Yinchuan
ZJ6)	657		Jiaxing		SC1)	747	200	Sichuan	Chengdu
11)	666	600	VO Strait	Fuzhou, FJ	SC13)	747	1	Nanchong	
AH2)	666	10	Hefei		SD11)	747	10	Rizhao	
GZ5)	666	1	Anshun		SD13)	747	10	Linyi	
HL10)	666	10	Jiamusi		SN1)	747	50	Shaanxi	Xianyang
JL4)	666	10	Siping		SN6)	747	1	Weinan	
LN8)	666	2	Jinzhou		SX1)	747	10	Shanxi	Luliang
NM1)	666	10	Nei Menggu	Hailar/Xilinhot	TJ1)	747	50	Tianjin	
QH1)	666	200	Qinghai	Xining	YN6)	747	100	Xishuangbanna	Jinghong
SD10)	666	1	Jining		ZJ11)	747		Zhoushan	
TJ1)	666	50	Tianjin		ZJ4)	747		Ningbo	
YN10)	666	1	Dongchuan		SX8)	750	1	Xinzhou	
ZJ5)	666	10	Wenzhou		1)	756	150	CNR 1	Harbin, HL
NM1)	675	200	Nei Menggu	Hohhot	1)	765	600	CNR 5	Fuzhou, FJ
XJ1)	675	1	Xinjiang	Altay	AH7)	765	1	Bengbu	

MW	kHz	kW	Station	Tx Location
EN23)	765	10	Gongyi	
GD8)	765	10	Shaoguan	
GZ1)	765	10	Guizhou	Zunyi
NM1)	765	10	Nei Menggu	Baotou/Xilinhot
BJ1)	774	10	Beijing	
HB1)	774	200	Hubei	Wuhan
LN8)	774	2	Jinzhou	
SX2)	774		Taiyuan	
XJ6)	774	10	Hotan	
11)	783	600	VO Strait	Zhangpu, FJ
EB1)	783	100	Hebei	Baoding
EB1)	783	10	Hebei	Chengde
EB1)	783		Hebei	Langfang/Handan
GD10)	783	20	Meizhou	
EN2)	792	1	Zhengzhou	
GS5)	792	1	Jiayuguan	
GX1)	792	200	Guangxi	Nanning
LN2)	792	10	Shenyang	
NM10)	792		Ordos BS	Otog
SC3)	792	10	Chengdu	
SH1)	792	50	Shanghai	
XJ2)	792		Urumqi	
AH1)	801	10	Anhui	Hefei
AH12)	801	3	Fuyang	
AH15)	801	1	Chizhou	
EB10)	801	25	Cangzhou	
EB8)	801	10	Tangshan	
EN8)	801		Xinxiang	
FJ3)	801		Xiamen	
GD2)	801	50	Zhujiang EBS	Maoming
GS1)	801		Gansu	Lanzhou
HB1)	801	10	Hubei	Jingmen/Macheng
HB2)	801	10	Hubei	Chongyang
JS1)	801	1	Jiangsu	Zhenjiang
JS3)	801		Xuzhou	
JS5)	801	10	Huai'an	
JS7)	801		Yangzhou	
LN1)	801		Liaoning	Dandong/Gaizhou
LN16)	801	1	Chaoyang	Lingyuan
NX2)	801	10	Yinchuan	
SD10)	801	10	Jining	
SD14)	801	10	Liaocheng	
SD4)	801	10	Zibo	
SD8)	801	10	Yantai	
SN1)	801	1	Shaanxi	Weinan
SN2)	801		Xi'an	
XJ7)	801	1	Kashi	
ZJ5)	801	10	Wenzhou	
EN18)	810	25	Zhumadian	
JL5)	810	10	Liaoyuan	
LN1)	810	5	Liaoning	Panjin
LN15)	810		Tieling	
LN16)	810	10	Chaoyang	
SN2)	810	50	Xi'an	
ZJ1)	810	200	Zhejiang	Hangzhou
SD3)	819		Qingdao	
SX1)	819	200	Shanxi	Yuci
XJ11)	819	1	Kuytun	
XJ12)	819		Bayingolin	Korla
BJ1)	828	50	Beijing	
EN1)	828	10	Henan	
EN17)	±828	10	Zhoukou	
EN6)	828	10	Jiaozuo	
GD1)	828	50	Guangdong	Heyuan
HB23)	±828	1	Xiantao	
HB8)	828	10	Jingzhou	
1)	837	1000	CNR 5	Quanzhou, FJ
AH1)	837		Anhui	Bengbu
EN15)	837	25	Xinyang	
FJ1)	837	3	Fujian	Fuding
FJ1)	837		Fujian	Pucheng
HL2)	837	50	Harbin	
LN14)	837	10	Liaoyang	
XJ1)	837	10	Xinjiang	Urumqi
2)	846	10	CRI DS 4	BJ
AH1)	846	10	Anhui	Suzhou
AH2)	846	1	Hefei	Chaohu
EB1)	846		Hebei	Hengshui/Tangshan
EB10)	846	10	Cangzhou	
EB11)	846	10	Langfang	
EB3)	846		Handan	
EN1)	846	50	Henan	Zhengzhou

MW	kHz	kW	Station	Tx Location
EN5)	846	3	Pingdingshan	
EN7)	846		Hebi	
GD1)	846		Guangdong	Zhaoqing
GX1)	846	10	Guangxi	Qinzhou
HB1)	846	30	Hubei	Qichun
HB2)	846	10	Hubei	Xianning/Yichang
JL1)	846	10	Jilin	Changchun
JS1)	846	5	Jiangsu	Nanjing
JS11)	846	10	Changzhou	
JS13)	846	5	Suzhou	
LN13)	846	10	Fuxin Mo BS	
LN8)	846		Jinzhou	
SD15)	846	10	Binzhou	
SD2)	846	10	Jinan	
SD7)	846	5	Weifang	
SD9)	846	10	Weihai	
SX1)	846	20	Shanxi	Changzhi
XJ1)	846	3	Xinjiang	Hotan
XZ1)	846	10	Xizang	Lhasa
YN1)	846		Yunnan	Longchuan/Gejiu
YN11)	846	1	Zhaotong	
1)	855	50	CNR 2	Anning, YN
1)	855	10	CNR 13	Urumqi
NM1)	855		Nei Menggu	Alxa Zuoqi
AH1)	864	50	Anhui	Hefei
EB20)	864		Renqiu	
EN19)	864		Qinyang	
SD15)	864	10	Binzhou	
ZJ1)	864		Zhejiang	Ninghai
ZJ15)	864	1	Jiangshan	
15)	873	200	China Huayi BC	Xiamen, FJ
EB13)	±873		Xinji	
EN3)	±873	10	Kaifeng	
GS1)	873	50	Gansu	Linxia
HB3)	873	50	Wuhan	
HL1)	873	100	Heilongjiang	Harbin
SD13)	873	10	Linyi	
XJ8)	873		Changji	
ZJ7)	873		Huzhou	
EB2)	882	20	Shijiazhuang	
EN22)	882		Ruzhou	
EN9)	882		Anyang	
FJ1)	882	200	Fujian	Fuzhou
FJ1)	882	10	Fujian	Fu'an/Sanming
GZ6)	882	1	Qiannan	Duyun
LN1)	882	10	Liaoning	Shenyang
LN3)	882	50	Dalian	
NM2)	882	10	Hohhot	
QH3)	882	10	Yushu	
XJ4)	882		Karamay	
XJ9)	882	1	Ili	Yining
LN7)	891	10	Dandong	
NM13)	891	10	Hinggan	Ulanhot
NX1)	891	200	Ningxia	Yinchuan
SD1)	891	10	Shandong	Dongying
XJ10)	891	10	Shihezi	
1)	900	10	CNR 2	Golmud, QH
2)	900		CRI DS 5	BJ
AH1)	900		Anhui	Lu'an/Bengbu/Haungshan
EB1)	900		Hebei	Shijiazhuang
EB6)	900	10	Zhangjiakou	
EB7)	900	1	Chengde	
EB8)	900		Tangshan	
EB9)	900		Qinhuangdao	
EN1)	900	100	Henan	Zhengzhou
EN1)	900	25	Henan	Zhoukou/Yima
EN12A)	900		Luohe EBS	
FJ1)	900	1	Fujian	Yongding
GD5)	900	1	Shenzhen	
GD6)	900		Zhuhai	
HB1)	900	10	Hubei	Enshi
HB2)	900	10	Hubei	Xiangyang
HL1)	900	50	Heilongjiang	Bei'an/Jiamusi
HN1)	900		Hunan	Changsha
JL16)	900	1	Yanji	
JL2)	900	10	Changchun	
JL4)	900	1	Siping	
JS10)	900	1	Zhenjiang	
JS12)	900		Wuxi	
JS2)	900	10	Nanjing	
JS4)	900	10	Lianyungang	

MW	kHz	kW	Station	Tx Location
JS6)	900		Yancheng	
LN1)	900		Liaoning	Chaoyang/Huludao
LN12)	900		Fuxin	
LN19)	900	1	Haicheng	
LN6)	900	1	Benxi	
NM1)	900	10	Nei Menggu	Ulanqab
NM5)	900	10	Chifeng	
SD3)	900	10	Qingdao	
SN1)	900	30	Shaanxi	Xi'an
SN4)	900	1	Baoji	
SX1)	900	10	Shanxi	Jincheng
SX3)	900	10	Datong	
YN9)	900	100	Dehong	Luxi
ZJ11)	900		Zhoushan	
1)	909	300	CNR 6	Quanzhou, FJ
HL8)	909	7.5	Yichun	
JL6)	909	10	Tonghua	
QH1)	909	10	Qinghai	Xining
SC1)	909	100	Sichuan	Fuling
TJ1)	909	50	Tianjin	
XJ1)	909	10	Xinjiang	Bortala
SD1)	918	200	Shandong	Jinan
1)	927	100	CNR 6	Xiamen, FJ
BJ1)	927	50	Beijing	
EB4)	927	12.5	Xingtai	
EN11)	927		Xuchang	
EN14)	927	10	Nanyang	
EN16)	927	10	Shangqiu	
GD1)	927	10	Guangdong	Guangzhou
GZ1)	927	200	Guizhou	Kaili
HB1)	927	10	Hubei	Xianning
HB10)	927		Jingmen	
HB12)	927	3	Xiaogan	
HB2)	927	10	Hubei	Suizhou
HL1)	927	10	Heilongjiang	Shuangyashan
HL2)	927	1	Harbin	Hulan
JL19)	927	1	Hunchun	
JL3)	927	10	Jilin-shi	
JS11)	927	3	Changzhou	
JS16)	927	1	Changshu	
JS8)	927		Taizhou	
JX1)	927	10	Jiangxi	Nanchang
LN1)	927	50	Liaoning	Shenyang
NM7)	927	10	Xilingol	Xilinhot
SH1)	927	1	Shanghai	
XJ2)	927		Urumqi	
YN1)	927		Yunnan	Kaiyuan
YN17)	927	1	Lufeng	
ZJ7)	927		Huzhou	
ZJ1)	930		Zhejiang	
AH1)	936	200	Anhui	Hefei
NM10)	936	10	Ordos BS	
1)	945	400	CNR 1	Jiaohe, JL
1)	945	10	CNR 13	Hami/Kuqa, XJ
HB2)	945	10	Hubei	Qichun
HB2)	945	10	Hubei	Jingzhou
HL1)	945	50	Heilongjiang	Harbin/Fujin
EB12)	954	10	Hengshui	
GS2)	954	10	Lanzhou	
HA1)	954	30	Hainan	Haikou
LN4)	954	10	Anshan	
NM8)	954	50	Hulun Buir	Hailar
SC1)	954	10	Sichuan	Chengdu
SC6)	954	1	Luzhou	
ZJ2)	954	25	Hangzhou	
EB3)	963	10	Handan	
HB5)	963	10	Huangshi	
LN1)	963	50	Liaoning	Dalian
XJ1)	963	10	Xinjiang	Qoqek/Gulja
ZJ1)	963	10	Zhejiang	
EN1)	972	150	Henan	Xingyang
HL2)	972	10	Harbin	
XJ1)	972		Xinjiang	Altay
1)	981	200	CNR 1	Changchun, JL
1)	981	200	CNR 1	Nanchang, JX
SD7)	981	5	Weifang	
EB9)	990	1	Qinhuangdao	
NM1)	990	10	Nei Menggu	Hohhot/Chifeng
SH1)	990	100	Shanghai	
YN1)	990	20	Yunnan	Hekou
AH19)	999	1	Bozhou	
GD1)	999	10	Guangdong	Guangzhou

MW	kHz	kW	Station	Tx Location
GZ2)	999	10	Guiyang	
HL15)	999		Aihui	
LN1)	999	200	Liaoning	Shenyang
NM1)	999	1	Nei Menggu	Ulanhot
SD1)	999	10	Shandong	Jining
XJ1)	999	10	Xinjiang	Hami/Bortala
XZ1)	999	10	Xizang	Lhasa
1)	1008	200	CNR 1	Anning, YN
2)	1008		CNR DS 3	BJ
2)	1008	3	CNR DS	Urumqi, XJ
AH1)	1008	10	Anhui	Hefei/Wuhu
EB11)	1008		Langfang	
EB3)	1008	10	Handan	
EN13)	1008		Sanmenxia	
EN2)	1008	25	Zhengzhou	
FJ1)	1008	1	Fujian	Zhangping
FJ3)	1008	10	Xiamen	
GD1)	1008		Guangdong	Guangzhou
GD22)	1008		Chenghai	
HB2)	1008	50	Hubei	Jingmen
HB22)	1008	10	Suizhou	
HN7)	±1008	1	Yueyang	
JS12)	1008		Wuxi	
JS2)	1008	10	Nanjing	
NX1)	1008	1	Ningxia	Guyuan
SD12)	1008	10	Dezhou	
SD3)	1008	10	Qingdao	
SN1)	1008	10	Shaanxi	Hanzhong/Yan'an
SN1)	1008		Shannxi	Xi'an
SX1)	1008		Shanxi	Xinzhou
TJ1)	1008	50	Tianjin	
1)	1017		CNR 1	Dongtou, ZJ
1)	1017	600	CNR 8	Changchun, JL
EB5)	1017	10	Baoding	
GD1)	1017	50	Guangdong	Shaoguan
BJ1)	1026	50	Beijing	
GZ1)	1026	200	Guizhou	Guiyang
JS14)	1026	1	Yizheng	
JS6)	1026	10	Yancheng	
LN10)	1026	2	Yingkou	
XJ6)	1026	10	Hotan	
1)	1035	50	CNR 1	Dalian/Wuhan
XJ1)	1044	10	Xinjiang	Urumqi/Korla
YN8)	1044	1	Dali	
ZJ1)	1050		Zhejiang	
1)	1053	10	CNR 10	BJ
AH2)	1053	1	Hefei	
EB10)	1053	10	Cangzhou	
EB15)	1053	1	Shahe	
EB17)	1053	1	Zhuozhou	
EN18)	1053	10	Zhumadian	
EN3)	1053	10	Kaifeng	
EN4)	1053	10	Luoyang	
HB1)	1053	50	Hubei	Qianjiang
HN7)	1053		Yueyang	
HN9)	1053		Yiyang	
JL10)	1053	20	Yanbian	Yanji
JS1)	1053	10	Jiangsu	Nanjing
LN1)	1053	50	Liaoning	Shenyang
SD2)	1053	10	Jinan	
YN1)	1053		Yunnan	Zhaotong
YN4)	1053	50	Wenshan	
GD2)	1062	150	Zhujiang EBS	Guangzhou
HL11)	1062	1	Qitaihe	
FJ1)	±1071		Fujian	
GX1)	1071	10	Guangxi	Ningming
HN5)	1071	10	Hengyang	
LN4)	1071	2	Anshan	
SD16)	1071	10	Heze	
SN4)	1071	10	Baoji	
TJ1)	1071	50	Tianjin	
XJ3)	1071	100	Urumqi	
ZJ1)	1071	10	Zhejiang	Hangzhou
GD7)	1080	5	Shantou	
HL7)	1080	1	Daqing	
HL12)	1080	1	Suihua	
JS13)	1080	10	Suzhou	
YN1)	1080		Yunnan	
ZJ1)	±1080	1	Zhejiang	Xiangshan
1)	1089	600	CNR 6	Fuzhou, FJ
HN3)	1089		Zhuzhou	
LN1)	1089	200	Liaoning	Shenyang

MW	kHz	kW	Station	Tx Location	MW	kHz	kW	Station	Tx Location
1)	1098	1000	CNR 1/11	Golmud, QH	YN1)	1143		Yunnan	Gejiu
AH1)	1098		Anhui	Hefei/Wuhu	ZJ1)	1143	1	Zhejiang	Yuhuan
AH18)	1098		Dangtu Xian		HN1)	1152	150	Hunan	Changde
AH7)	±1098	1	Bengbu		LN3)	1152	10	Dalian	
EB1)	1098	1	Hebei	Zhangjiakou	NM11)	1152	10	Bayannur	Linhe
EB12)	1098		Hengshui		NM13)	1152	10	Hinggan	Ulanhot
EN1)	1098		Henan	Zhoukou	1)	1161		CNR 1	
EN5)	1098		Pingdingshan		GD2)	1161	1	Zhujiang EBS	Taishan
GD11)	1098	1	Huizhou		GX1)	1161	7.5	Guangxi	Beihai
GD19)	1098	5	Maoming		HB10)	1161	10	Jingmen	
GD4)	1098		Guangzhou		JS12)	1161	10	Wuxi	
HB1)	1098	10	Hubei	Jingzhou/Suizhou	SD7)	1161	10	Weifang	
HB8)	1098	10	Xiangyang		1)	1170	600	CNR 1	Ji'an, JX
JS1)	1098	1	Jiangsu	Zhenjiang	AH16)	1170	1	Lu'an	
JS17)	1098	10	Zhangjiagang		AH17)	1170	3	Xuancheng	
JS3)	1098		Xuzhou		AH2)	1170	10	Hefei	
LN8)	1098		Jinzhou		GD3)	1170	10	Guangzhou	
LN12)	1098		Fuxin		GS1)	1170	10	Gansu	Zhangye
NM1)	1098	10	Nei Menggu		JS2)	1170	10	Nanjing	
SD12)	1098	10	Dezhou		JS9)	1170	10	Nantong	
SX1)	1098		Shanxi	Yangzhou/Changzhi	SD15)	1170	10	Binzhou	
TJ1)	1098	50	Tianjin		SD5)	1170	10	Zaozhuang	
XJ5)	1098	1	Hami		HB2)	1179	100	Hubei	Wuhan
YN1)	1098	1	Yunnan	Kaiyuan	HL5)	1179	10	Shuangyashan	
ZJ11)	1098	10	Zhoushan		JS7)	1179	10	Yangzhou	
AH6)	1107	3	Tongling		XJ4)	1179	10	Karamay	
EN7)	1107	10	Hebi		EB19)	1188	10	Botou	
FJ3)	1107	10	Xiamen		EB4)	1188	10	Xingtai	
HA1)	1107	10	Hainan	Tongshi	JL10)	1188		Yanbian	Longjing
JL1)	1107	10	Jilin	Yushu/Hunchun	FJ5)	1197		Quanzhou	
JX4)	1107	1	Pingxiang		HL3)	1197	10	Qiqihar	
XJ1)	1107	120	Xinjiang	Hutubi	SD16)	1197	10	Heze	
ZJ6)	1107	10	Jiaxing		SH1)	1197	10	Shanghai	
1)	1116	120	CNR 2	Harbin, HL	YN1)	1197		Yunnan	
1)	1116	600	CNR 5	Shaowu, FJ	EB10)	1206	25	Cangzhou	
AH12)	1116	10	Fuyang		EB3)	1206	10	Handan	
HA1)	1116	30	Hainan	Ledong	EN20)	1206	1	Huixian	
SC1)	1116	200	Sichuan	Chengdu	GD1)	1206	1	Guangdong	Shenzhen/Zhaoqing
SD10)	1116	1	Jining		HN1)	1206	10	Hubei	Xiangyang
EB1)	1125	10	Hebei	Shijiazhuang	JL10)	1206	200	Yanbian	Longjing
HB2)	1125		Hubei	Xiantao	JS1)	1206	1	Jiangsu	Nanjing
HB3)	1125	50	Wuhan		NX1)	1206	1	Ningxia	Zhongning
GD18)	1134	10	Zhanjiang		SD9)	1206	10	Weihai	
GS9)	1134	1	Yumen		SX1)	1206	10	Shanxi	Shuozhou
SN3)	1134	10	Tongchuan		1)	1215	20	CNR 2	Shenyang, LN
XJ9)	1134	1	Ili	Yining	1)	1215	50	CNR 7	Zhuhai, GD
ZJ1)	1134	1	Zhejiang	Wenzhou/Zhoushan	HB1)	1215	10	Hubei	Yichang
1)	1143	10	CNR 8	BJ	HL14)	1215	50	Heihe	
EB18)	1143	1	Dingzhou		XJ1)	1215	10	Xinjiang	Urumqi
EB8)	1143		Tangshan		1)	1224	100	CNR 6	Xiamen, FJ
EN1)	1143	50	Henan	Zhengzhou	GX1)	1224	100	Guangxi	Nanning
EN5)	1143	3	Pingdingshan		JS10)	1224	10	Zhenjiang	
GD1)	1143		Guangdong	Zhanjiang	NM1)	1224	10	Nei Menggu	Ulanqab
GS4)	1143	10	Tianshui		HN1)	1233	10	Hunan	Yueyang/Shaoyang
GZ5)	1143		Anshun		JS9)	1233	25	Nantong	
HA1)	1143		Hainan	Haikou	XJ1)	1233	120	Xinjiang	Hutubi
HB1)	1143	10	Hubei	Shiyan	XJ1)	1233	10	Xinjiang	Bortala
HB2)	1143		Hubei	Chanchun	AH16)	1242		Lu'an	
HL10)	1143	1	Jiamusi		HB20)	1242	1	Macheng	
JL1)	1143	1	Jilin	Liaoyuan	HB24)	1242	1	Qianjiang	
JL17)	1143	1	Tumen		JX9)	1242		Ji'an	
JL3)	1143	10	Jilin-shi		LN9)	1242	1	Huludao	
JL8)	1143		Songyuan		YN1)	1242	100	Yunnan	Kunming
JS11)	1143	3	Changzhou		ZJ10)	1250	1	Quzhou	
JS9)	1143		Nantong		2)	1251		CRI DS 1	BJ
LN10)	1143		Yingkou		AH13)	1251	1	Suzhou	
LN14)	1143	1	Liaoyang		EB1)	1251		Hebei	Qinhuangdao
LN5)	1143		Fushun		EB2)	1251	25	Shijiazhuang	
NM1)	1143		Nei Menggu	Ulanqab	EN10)	1251	10	Puyang	
NM1)	1143		Nei Menggu	Horqin	EN12)	1251	10	Luohe	
NM5)	1143		Chifeng		EN21)	1251	1	Yima	
NM16)	1143	1	Yakeshi		EN6)	1251		Jiaozuo	
QH1)	1143		Qinghai	Xining	EN9)	±1251		Anyang	
SC11)	1143		Neijiang		HB1)	1251	5	Hubei	Jingmen
SC15)	1143	1	Dazhou		JL3A)	1251		Jilin-shi EBS	
SC9)	1143		Guangyuan		JS12)	1251	10	Wuxi	
SD13)	1143	10	Linyi		JS2)	1251		Nanjing	
SD14)	1143	10	Liaocheng		JS4)	1251		Lianyungang	
SD4)	1143	10	Zibo		JS5)	1251	10	Huai'an	
SN1)	1143	1	Shaanxi	Baoji/Weinan	LN4)	1251		Anshan	
SN9)	1143	1	Yulin		QH1)	1251	200	Qinghai	Xining
XJ1)	1143	10	Xinjiang	Altay					

MW	kHz	kW	Station	Tx Location	MW	kHz	kW	Station	Tx Location
SD1)	1251	10	Shandong	Jinan/Zibo	1)	1377	600	CNR 1	Yingyang, HEN
SD13)	1251	10	Linyi		AH11)	1377	1	Chuzhou	
SD18)	1251		Longkou		FJ1)	1377		Fujian	Nanping
SD3)	1251	10	Qingdao		NX5)	1377	1	Qingtongxia	
SD7)	1251		Weifang		QH1)	1377		Qinghai	Xining
SN8)	1251	10	Hanzhong		SD3)	1377	10	Qingdao	
YN1)	1251	1	Yunnan	Kaiyuan	XZ1)	1377	100	Xizang	Lhasa
YN14)	1251		Yuxi		FJ1)	1386		Fujian	Quanzhou
ZJ1)	1251	1	Zhejiang	Jinhua	GX3)	1386	5	Liuzhou	
ZJ4)	1251		Ningbo		HB11)	1386	1	Ezhou	
ZJ7)	1251		Huzhou		HB17)	1386	1	Shishou	
HN8)	1260	1	Changde		JS15)	1386	1	Jiangyin	
LN1)	1260	10	Liaoning	Fengcheng	SD10)	1386	1	Jining	
XZ3)	1260	1	Shannan	Nedong	TJ1)	1386	50	Tianjin	
JL18)	1269	1	Dunhua		AH1)	1395	50	Anhui	Hefei
JS3)	1269	10	Xuzhou		AH1)	1395	10	Anhui	Fuyang/Chizhou
SX1)	1269	10	Shanxi	Taiyuan/Xinzhou	FJ1)	1395		Fujian	Hui'an/Yongchun
EB1)	1278	100	Hebei	Shijiazhuang/Tangshan	NM1)	1395		Nei Menggu	
					NM7)	1395	10	Xilingol	Xilinhot
FJ3)	1278	10	Xiamen		YN1)	1395		Yunnan	Pu'er
HL13)	1278	7.5	Daxing'anling	Jagdaqi	FJ1)	1404	50	Fujian EBS	Fuzhou
JX2)	1278	10	Nanchang		FJ1)	1404	3	Fujian	Fuqing
1)	1287	10	CNR 1	Ningde, FJ	HB1)	1404	50	Hubei	Jingzhou
EB20)	1287	1	Renqiu		HB1)	1404	10	Hubei	Suizhou/Chongyang
EN11)	1287	1	Xuchang		LN7)	1404	10	Dandong	
GD5)	1287	25	Shenzhen		ZJ1)	1404		Zhejiang	Wenling
JS12)	1287		Wuxi		HL4)	1413	1	Hegang	
LN12)	1287	20	Fuxin		JS1)	1413	10	Jiangsu	Yancheng
NX1)	1287	10	Ningxia	Guyuan	LN15)	1413	1	Tieling	
SD7)	1287	5	Weifang		NM1)	1413	10	Nei Menggu	Tongliao/Ordos
YN7)	1287	10	Chuxiong		NX4)	1413	1	Wuzhong	
ZJ1)	1287	1	Zhejiang	Dongtou	XJ1)	1413	10	Xinjiang	Hami/Bortala
EB16)	1296	1	Qinghe		1)	1422	600	CNR 1/8/13	Kashi, XJ
LN20)	1296	1	Xingcheng		13)	1422	20	VO Pujiang	SH
LN6)	1296	20	Benxi		SC4)	1422	10	Zigong	
SC10)	1296	1	Suining		SH2)	1422	20	Dongfang	
SH1)	1296	25	Shanghai		SX1)	1422	10	Shanxi	Linfen
SN5)	1296	10	Xianyang		SX2)	1422	10	Taiyuan	
1)	1305	10	CNR 2	Xining, QH	AH10)	1431	2	Huangshan	
NM1)	1305		Nei Menggu	Ulanhot	AH4)	1431	10	Huaibei	
SD2)	1305	10	Jinan		EB2)	1431	10	Shijiazhuang	
CQ1)	1314	50	Chongqing		HB16)	1431	1	Danjiangkou	
HB14)	1314	3	Xianning		HN10)	1431	1	Jinshi	
HB6)	1314	10	Xiangyang		JL8)	1431	2	Songyuan	
JS1)	1314	10	Jiangsu	Suzhou/Huai'an	NM14)	1431	1	Fengzhen	
SD8)	1314	10	Yantai		GX1)	1440	50	Guangxi	Bose
ZJ1)	1314		Zhejiang		LN18)	1440	10	Zhuanghe	
1)	1323	200	CNR 2	Shuangyashan, HL	NM12)	1440	10	Alxa	Bayanhot
HN2)	1323	10	Changsha		NM5)	1440	50	Chifeng	
JL9)	1323	10	Baicheng		FJ1)	1449	3	Fujian	Dongshan
LN17)	1323	1	Wafangdian		JX1)	1449	20	Jiangxi	
SD16A)	1323	10	Mudan	Heze	SD11)	1449	10	Rizhao	
SN1)	1323	10	Shaanxi	Xi'an	SD6)	1449	10	Dongying	
ZJ4)	1323	10	Ningbo		EN2)	1458	5	Zhengzhou	
EN1)	1332	10	Henan	Zhengzhou	JS4)	1458	10	Lianyungang	
EN1)	1332	10	Henan	Hebi/Luoyang	LN4)	1458		Anshan	
EN1)	1332		Henan	Anyang	NM1)	1458	200	Nei Menggu	Hohhot
FJ1)	1332	10	Fujian	Yunxiao	EB5)	1467	10	Baoding	
FJ2)	1332	10	Fuzhou		JX3)	1467	7.5	Jingdezhen	
GS6)	1332	10	Gannan	Hezuo	SD1)	1467	5	Shandong	Dezhou
JL2)	1332	10	Changchun		HB15)	1467	1	Laohekou	
1)	1341	100	CNR 1	GD	HL1)	1476	50	Heilongjiang	Qiqihar/Fujin
HB19)	1341	1	Yingcheng		HL9)	1476		Mudanjiang	
HB21)	1341	1	Chibi		JL14)	1476	1	Qian Gorlos	
HL1)	1341	100	Heilongjiang	Heihe	LN7)	1476		Dandong	
JS8)	1341	10	Taizhou		QH2)	1476	10	Xining	
LN1)	1341	10	Liaoning	Shenyang	SC12)	1476	1	Leshan	
SD12)	1341	1	Dezhou		SD4)	1476	10	Zibo	
SD19)	1341	1	Qufu		ZJ1)	1476		Zhejiang	Leqing
JX1)	1350	50	Jiangxi	Ji'an	GS1)	1485		Gansu	
JX1)	1350	10	Jiangxi	Shangrao/Yichun	GX1)	1485	1	Guangxi	Lingshan
JX1)	1350	1	Jiangxi	Jiujiang	GX4)	1485	1	Guilin	
LN19)	1350		Haicheng		GX5)	1485	3	Wuzhou	
NM9)	1350	50	Tongliao		HB7)	1485	10	Shiyan	
YN2)	1350	50	Kunming		HL6)	1485	1	Jixi	
1)	1359		CNR 1		JL11)	1485	1	Gongzhuling	
YN1)	1359	1	Yunnan	Hekou	JX6)	1485	1	Jiujiang	
YN1)	1359	1	Yunnan	Baoshan/Yuxi	LN11)	1485	1	Panjin	
FJ1)	±1368	1	Fujian	Changding	SC3)	1485	1	Chengdu	
HB8)	1368		Jingzhou		SD1)	1485	1	Shandong	Weihai/Liaocheng
HB18)	1368	1	Guangshui		SX10)	1485	1	Shuozhou	
HL6)	1368	10	Jixi		XJ12)	1485	1	Kuytun	

MW	kHz	kW	Station	Tx Location
XJ5)	1485	1	Hami	
YN13)	1485	1	Chuxiong	
YN5)	1485	1	Honghe	Jinping
AH5)	1494	1	Wuhu	
FJ1)	1494	1	Fujian	Lianjiang/Fu'an
NM1)	1494	1	Nei Menggu	Erenhot
NM1)	1494	1	Nei Menggu	Hailar
XJ1)	1494	1	Xinjiang	Yiwu
XJ11)	1494		Korla	
AH12)	1503	1	Fuyang	
HN4)	1503	10	Xiangtan	
SX1)	1503	10	Shanxi	Datong/Jincheng
ZJ1)	1503	1	Zhejiang	Xinchang
GS7)	1512	10	Linxia	
NM5)	1512	1	Chifeng	Lindong
SD2)	1512	10	Jinan	
EB1)	1521		Hebei	Xingtai
EB11)	1521	25	Langfang	
EN1)	1521		Henan	Zhengzhou
EN5)	1521	3	Pingdingshan	
EN8)	1521	10	Xinxiang	
FJ3)	1521	3	Xiamen	
GD20)	1521	1	Zhaoqing	
GZ5)	1521		Anshun	
HB25)	1521	10	Xiangzhou	
HL1)	1521	1	Heilongjiang	Jingbohu
JL1)	1521	1	Jilin	Taonan
JS11)	1521	3	Changzhou	
JS12)	1521		Wuxi	
JS13)	1521	5	Suzhou	
JS17)	1521		Zhangjiagang	
JS5)	1521	10	Huai'an	
JS7)	1521		Yangzhou	
NM1)	1521		Nei Menggu	Ordos
NM6)	1521	10	Ulanqab	Jining
SD2)	1521		Jinan	
SN1)	1521	1	Shaanxi	Shangluo
SX5)	1521	1	Changzhi	Qinxian
YN3)	1521	1	Qujing	
YN5)	1521	1	Honghe	Gejiu
ZJ1)	1521	1	Zhejiang	
ZJ7)	1521		Huzhou	
JL1)	1530	10	Jilin	Yanji/Fuyuan
SX7)	1530	1	Jinzhong	
ZJ1)	1530	50	Zhejiang	Hangzhou
1)	1539	100	CNR 1	Golmud, QH
SD1)	1548	200	Shandong	Linyi
EB10)	1557	25	Cangzhou	
EB14)	1557	1	Nangong	
EB6)	1566	10	Zhangjiakou	
JL10)	1566	1	Yanbian	Longjing
GS8)	1566	1	Pingliang	
HB1)	1566	10	Hubei	Jingmen
SD14)	1566	1	Liaocheng	
SX9)	1566	1	Yuncheng	
GX1)	1575		Guangxi	Yulin
JL12)	1575		Lishu	
LN3)	1575	2	Dalian	
AH8)	1584	1	Ma'anshan	
AH9)	1584	1	Anqing	
EB7)	1584	1	Chengde	
GZ4)	1584	1	Zunyi	
JL13)	1584	1	Meihekou	
NM1)	1584	1	Nei Menggu	Tongliao
NM1)	1584		Nei Menggu	Zalantun
SX1)	1584		Shanxi	Taiyuan
SX3)	1584		Datong	
SX5)	1584	10	Changzhi	
ZJ14)	1584	1	Rui'an	
1)	1593	600	CNR 1	Changzhou, JS
HL1)	1593	10	Heilongjiang	
HL12)	1593	1	Suihua	
XJ1)	1593	10	Xinjiang	Korla
JS1)	1602	1	Jiangsu	Hongze

SW	kHz	kW	Station	Tx Loc.	Times
NM8)	3900	10	Hulun Buir	Hailar	as 603kHz
XJ1)	‡3950	100	Xinjiang	Urumqi	Nov-Apr only
1)	3985	100	CNR 2	Golmud	1200-1605
GS6)	3990	15	Gannan	Hezuo	2250-0100, 1020-1230
XJ1)	‡3990	50	Xinjiang	Urumqi	Nov-Apr only
XJ1)	‡4500	50	Xinjiang	Urumqi	Nov-Apr only

SW	kHz	kW	Station	Tx Loc.	Times
1)	4750	10	CNR 1	Hailar	2025-1805
1)	4800	100	CNR 1	Golmud	2025-1805
XZ1)	4820	100	Xizang	Lhasa	2000-1800
XJ1)	‡4850	100	Xinjiang	Urumqi	Nov-Apr only
11)	‡4900	50	VO Strait	Fuzhou	Winter only
XZ1)	4905	50	Xizang	Lhasa	2050-1805
XZ1)	‡4920	50	Xizang	Lhasa	Nov-Apr only
11)	4940	50	VO Strait	Fuzhou	2230-0400, 0940-1600
XJ1)	‡4980	50	Xinjiang	Urumqi	Nov-Apr only
HN1)	4990	10		Hunan	Changsha
11)	‡5050	50	VO Strait	Fuzhou	Winter only
XJ1)	‡5060	50	Xinjiang	Urumqi	Nov-Apr only
1)	5925	100	CNR 5	Beijing	2055-2400, 1000-1705
XZ1)	‡5935	100	Xizang	Lhasa	Nov-Apr only
1)	5945	100	CNR 1	Beijing	2025-2200, 1300-1805
1)	5955	100	CNR 8	Beijing	0800-0900, 2055-2300
XJ1)	5960	50	Xinjiang	Urumqi	2300-0300, 1200-1800
GS6)	5970	15	Gannan	Hezuo	2250-0100, 1020-1410
1)	5975	100	CNR 8	Beijing	0600-1505
QH1)	5990	50	Qinghai	Xining	2250-1600
1)	6000	100	CNR 1	Beijing	2025-2330, 1100-1805
1)	6010	100	CNR 11	Baoji-Sif.	2155-2400, 1300-1605
XJ1)	6015	100	Xinjiang	Urumqi	2300-0345, 1150-1800
XZ1)	‡6025	100	Xizang	Lhasa	Nov-Apr only
1)	6030	100	CNR 1	Beijing	2025-1805
1)	6040	150	CNR 2	Beijing	2055-2300
NM1)	6040	50	Nei Menggu	Hohhot	2150-1605
XZ1)	6050	100	Xizang	Lhasa	2000-1800
SC1)	6060	50	Sichuan	Xichang	2155-1515
1)	6065	150	CNR 2	Beijing	2055-2230, 1200-1605
1)	6075		CNR1		2300-0300, 1000-1500
1)	6080	100	CNR 1	Golmud	2025-2400, 1100-1805
NM8)	6080	10	Hulun Buir	Hailar	as 954kHz
1)	6090	100	CNR 2	Golmud	2055-0100, 1000-1605
XZ1)	‡6110	100	Xizang	Lhasa	Nov-Apr only
11)	6115	50	VO Strait	Fuzhou	0940-1600
XJ1)	6120	50	Xinjiang	Urumqi	2300-0300, 1200-1800
1)	6125	100	CNR 1	Beijing	2025-2300, 1000-1805
1)	6125	100	CNR 1	Shijiazhuang	2025-2300, 1100-1805
XZ1)	6130	100	Xizang	Lhasa	2050-1805
QH1)	6145	50	Qinghai	Xining	2200-1600
1)	6155	150	CNR 2	Beijing	2055-2300, 1000-1605
1)	6165	100	CNR 6	Beijing	2155-0100, 0900-1605
1)	6175	100	CNR 1	Beijing	2025-2400, 0900-1805
15)	6185	15	China Huayi BC	Fuzhou	0955-1600
1)	6190	100	CNR 2	Golmud	2055-2400
XZ1)	‡6200	100	Xizang	Lhasa	Nov-Apr only
12)	6200	50	VO Jinling	Nanjing	1240-1500
XJ1)	7205	50	Xinjiang	Urumqi	2300-0130, 1400-1800
YN1)	7210	20	Yunnan	Kunming	0630-0830, 1100-1500, 2255-0300
1)	7215	100	CNR 1	Shijiazhuang	2025-2400
1)	7220	100	CNR 2	Golmud	0000-1200
SC1)	7225	50	Sichuan	Xichang	2155-0135, 1000-1515
1)	7230	150	CNR 1	Xianyang	2025-1805
XJ1)	7230	50	Xinjiang	Urumqi	2300-0330, 0510-1030, 1150-1800
XZ1)	7240	100	Xizang	Lhasa	2000-0200, 0900-1800
1)	7245	150	CNR 2	Beijing	2055-2300, 1300-1605
1)	7255	100	CNR 2	Baoji-Sif	2055-0100
XZ1)	7255	100	Xizang	Lhasa	2050-0200, 1300-1805
XJ1)	7260	100	Xinjiang	Urumqi	2300-1800
1)	7265	100	CNR 2	Baoji-Sif	1230-1605
NM1)	7270	50	Nei Menggu	Hohhot	2150-1605
1)	7275	100	CNR 1	Beijing	2025-2300, 1100-1805
XJ1)	7275	100	Xinjiang	Urumqi	2300-1800
1)	7290	100	CNR 1	Beijing	2025-2300, 1100-1805
XJ1)	7295	50	Xinjiang	Urumqi	Nov.-Apr.only
1)	7305	100	CNR 1	Shijiazhuang	2025-2200, 1000-1805
XJ1)	7310	50	Xinjiang	Urumqi	2300-0200, 1200-1800
1)	‡7315	150	CNR 2	Xianyang	2055-0100, 1100-1605
1)	7335	100	CNR 2	Baoji-Sif.	2055-0030, 1300-1605
XJ1)	7340	100	Xinjiang	Urumqi	2300-1800
1)	7345	100	CNR 1	Beijing	2025-2400, 1100-1805
1)	7350	100	CNR 11	Baoji-Sif.	1300-1605
1)	7360	100	CNR 11	Baoji-Sif.	2155-2400
1)	7365	100	CNR 1	Shijiazhuang	1200-1805
1)	7370	150	CNR 1	Beijing	2055-2300, 1300-1605
1)	7375	100	CNR 2	Beijing	1200-1605
XZ1)	7385	100	Xizang	Lhasa	2050-0200, 1100-1800
1)	‡7395	150	CNR 2	Xianyang	2055-2400

SW	kHz	kW	Station	Tx Loc.	Times
1)	7410	100	CNR 5	Beijing	0900-1705
1)	7415	100	CNR 5	Beijing	2055-2300
NM1)	7420	50	Nei Menggu	Hohhot	2150-1605
1)	‡7425	150	CNR 2	Xianyang	1300-1605
XZ1)	7450	100	Xizang	Lhasa	2000-0200, 0900-1800
1)	9410	100	CNR 5	Beijing	1000-1705
1)	9420	50	CNR 6	Beijing	2155-0100, 0900-1605
1)	9420	100	CNR 13	Lingshi	1100-1805
1)	9470	100	CNR 1	Beijing	2025-2300
XJ1)	9470	100	Xinjiang	Urumqi	0345-1150
1)	9480	100	CNR 11	Baoji-Sif.	2155-2400, 1100-1605
XZ1)	9490	100	Xizang	Lhasa	0100-1000
1)	9500	100	CNR 1	Shijiazhuang	2025-1805
XZ1)	9500	100	Xizang	Lhasa	2050-0200, 1300-1805
XJ1)	9510	100	Xinjiang	Urumqi	0510-1030
1)	9515	100	CNR 2	Beijing	2055-2400, 0900-1605
NM1)	9520	50	Nei Menggu	Hohhot	2150-1605
1)	9530	100	CNR 11	Baoji-Sif.	0000-1300
XJ1)	9560	50	Xinjiang	Urumqi	0245-1200
1)	9570	100	CNR 2	Golmud	0100-1150
XZ1)	9580	100	Xizang	Lhasa	0200-1100
XZ1)	9590	100	Xizang	Lhasa	2050-0100, 1100-1805
XJ1)	9600	50	Xinjiang	Urumqi	0200-1200
1)	9610	100	CNR 8	Beijing	2055-0600
1)	9620	150	CNR 2	Beijing	2300-1300
1)	9630	100	CNR 1	Golmud	0000-1100
1)	9630	100	CNR 17	Lingshi	1200-1805
1)	9645	100	CNR 1	Beijing	2330-1100
1)	9665	50	CNR 5	Beijing	2055-2400
1)	9675	100	CNR 1	Beijing	2300-0600, 0900-1000
1)	9685	50	CNR 5	Beijing	0000-1100
XJ1)	9705	50	Xinjiang	Urumqi	0305-0530, 1005-1230
1)	9710	100	CNR 1	Shijiazhuang	2025-2330, 1100-1805
1)	9720	150	CNR 2	Baoji-Xinjie	0000-1000
NM1)	9750	50	Nei Menggu	Hohhot	2150-1605
1)	9755	100	CNR 2	Baoji-Sif.	2055-2400, 1000-1605
1)	9775	150	CNR 2	Beijing	2055-0100, 0900-1605
QH1)	9780	50	Qinghai	Xining	2200-1600
1)	9785	100	CNR 8	Beijing	0600-1505
1)	9810	100	CNR 1	Nanning	2025-2300, 1300-1805
1)	9810	100	CNR 2	Baoji-Sif.	0100-1230
1)	‡9820	150	CNR 2	Xianyang	2055-2400, 1100-1605
1)	9830	100	CNR 1	Beijing	2025-0100, 0730-1805
XJ1)	9835	100	Xinjiang	Urumqi	0300-1200
1)	9845	100	CNR 1	Beijing	2025-2400, 1200-1805
QH1)	9850	15	Qinghai	Xining	2250-1600
1)	9860	100	CNR 1	Beijing	1200-1805
1)	9890	100	CNR 13	Lingshi	1400-1805
1)	11610	150	CNR 2	Beijing	2300-1300
1)	11620	50	CNR 5	Beijing	0000-1000
1)	11630	100	CNR 17	Lingshi	2355-1805
1)	‡11660	150	CNR 2	Xianyang	0100-1100
1)	11670	100	CNR 2	Beijing	2230-1200
1)	11685	100	CNR 11	Baoji-Sif.	0000-1300
1)	11710	100	CNR 1	Beijing	2025-0030, 1000-1805
1)	11720	100	CNR 1	Shijiazhuang	2330-1100
1)	11740	100	CNR 2	Lingshi	2055-0100, 1100-1605
1)	11750	100	CNR 1	Shijiazhuang	2200-1000
1)	11760	100	CNR 1	Shijiazhuang	0000-1200
XJ1)	11770	50	Xinjiang	Urumqi	2300-1800
1)	11800	150	CNR 2	Beijing	2300-1200
1)	11810	100	CNR 2	Beijing	2055-0600
1)	‡11835	150	CNR 2	Xianyang	0000-1300
1)	‡11845	150	CNR 2	Xainyang	0000-1100
XZ1)	11860	100	Xizang	Lhasa	0300-0900
XJ1)	11885	50	Xinjiang	Urumqi	2300-1800
1)	11905	100	CNR 6	Beijing	0100-0900
1)	11915	100	CNR 2	Baoji-Sif.	0030-1300
1)	11925	100	CNR 1	Lingshi	2025-2330, 1200-1805
1)	11935	100	CNR 5	Beijing	2300-0900
XZ1)	11935	100	Xizang	Lhasa	0200-1300
XZ1)	11950	100	Xizang	Lhasa	0200-0900
1)	11960	100	CNR 1	Beijing	0000-0900
XJ1)	11975	50	Xinjiang	Urumqi	0305-0530, 1005-1230
1)	12045	100	CNR 1	Beijing	2300-1200
1)	12055	100	CNR 17	Lingshi	2355-1200
1)	12080	100	CNR 2	Baoji-Sif.	0000-1000
1)	13610	150	CNR 1	Nanning	2300-1300
XJ1)	13670	50	Xinjiang	Urumqi	0130-1400
1)	13700	100	CNR 13	Lingshi	2355-1400
XZ1)	13710	100	Xizang	Lhasa	0100-1100
1)	15270	150	CNR 2	Beijing	0100-0900

SW	kHz	kW	Station	Tx Loc.	Times
1)	15370	100	CNR 1	Shijiazhuang	0100-1100
1)	15380	100	CNR 1	Beijing	2300-1100
1)	15390	100	CNR 13	Lingshi	2355-1100
1)	15480	100	CNR 1	Beijing	2200-1300
1)	15500	150	CNR 2	Beijing	2300-1000
1)	15540	100	CNR 2	Lingshi	0100-1100
1)	15550	100	CNR 1	Beijing	0000-1100
1)	15570	100	CNR 11	Baoji-Sif.	0000-1100
1)	15710	50	CNR 6	Beijing	0100-0900
1)	17550	100	CNR 1	Beijing	0000-1200
1)	17565	100	CNR 1	Beijing	0100-0730
1)	17580	100	CNR 1	Lingshi	2330-1200
1)	17595	100	CNR 1	Shijiazhuang	2300-1100
1)	17605	100	CNR 1	Beijing	0030-1000
1)	17625	150	CNR 2	Beijing	0000-0900
1)	17890	100	CNR 1	Beijing	2300-1100

NB: Baoji-Sif. = Baoji-Sifangshan. ‡=inactive, .±=variable

FM(MHz)	CNR 1	CNR 2	CNR 3	Prov.T	Prov.M	City.T	City.M
Anshan	101.0	105.1	98.3	97.5	-	99.5	93.6
Baoding	98.3	89.7	90.0	99.2	106.4	104.8	105.8
Baotou	96.9	99.3	-	95.7	107.4	89.2	100.1
Beihai	102.5	-	97.1	100.3	95.5	99.1	-
Beijing	106.1	96.6	90.0	-	-	103.9	97.4
Benxi	94.8	100.3	-	97.5	98.6	107.4	-
Changchun	99.1	104.7	94.3	103.8	92.7	96.8	106.3
Changde	94.7	102.9	-	89.5	102.1	97.1	98.5
Changsha	95.0	87.6	107.7	91.8	89.3	106.1a	102.2
Chengdu	103.7	-	107.6	101.7	95.5	91.4	105.6
Chifeng	101.2	107.1	88.5	105.6	94.5	101.8	-
Chongqing	102.9	100.0	90.6	-	-	95.5	88.1
Dalian	89.1	104.3	107.8	97.5	-	100.8	106.7
Daqing	97.3	-	102.3	99.8	102.9	95.0	106.0
Fuzhou	93.5	-	92.6	100.7	91.3	87.6	89.3
Guangzhou	89.3	106.6	87.4	105.2	99.3	106.1	102.7
Guilin	89.8	94.1	-	100.3	95.0	88.3a	-
Guiyang	93.6	105.6	107.3	95.2	91.6	102.7	90.9
Haikou	105.8	87.8	89.8	100.0	94.5	-	91.6
Handan	88.7	-	93.9	99.2	102.4	106.8	102.8
Hangzhou	90.2	97.9	103.2	93.0	96.8	91.8	105.4
Harbin	89.9	88.1	100.9	99.8	95.8	92.5	90.9
Hefei	93.5	104.7	94.3	90.8	89.5	102.6	87.6
Hengyang	95.0	105.9	-	100.3	96.9	101.8	-
Hohhot	97.1	-	99.1	105.6	93.6	107.3	-
Jiamusi	94.4	-	-	99.8	105.8	98.0	-
Jilin-shi	98.0	-	104.5	103.8	93.4	105.3	91.3
Jinan	89.8	96.5	95.5	101.1	99.1	103.1	88.7
Jinzhou	104.9	101.2	106.0	97.5	-	100.3	-
Jiujiang	102.4	-	-	105.4	107.9	88.4	91.6
Kaifeng	106.3	100.8	-	104.1	88.1	105.1	-
Kunming	96.0	-	93.0	91.8	97.0	-	-
Lanzhou	94.8	90.3	88.3	103.5	-	-	99.5
Lhasa	89.2	104.3	96.1	-	-	-	-
Lianyungang	93.6	97.2	-	101.1	-	102.1	-
Lijiang	95.1	-	107.2	93.1	100.7	-	-
Nanchang	89.1	93.8	87.2	105.4	103.4	95.1	90.6
Nanjing	95.8	107.5	98.9	101.1	89.7	102.4	105.8
Nanning	106.2	93.6	99.0	100.3	95.0	107.4a	-
Ningbo	95.7	101.2	107.7	93.0	103.2	97.4	93.9
Qingdao	96.7	104.1	98.0	106.0	106.6	89.7	91.5
Qinhuangdao	96.5	-	-	99.2	106.4	100.4	97.3
Qiqihar	97.7	101.8	-	99.8	90.4	94.1	-
Quanzhou	96.9	98.3	102.5	100.7	-	90.4	92.3
Rizhao	89.4	106.9	-	106.0	-	88.1	-
Shanghai	99.0	91.4	107.7	-	-	105.7	101.7
Shenyang	94.8	93.5	99.8	97.5	98.6	-	-
Shenzhen	95.8	-	101.2	105.2	93.9	106.2	97.1
Shijiazhuang	95.6	97.2	105.1	90.2	102.4	94.6	106.7
Suzhou	100.0	98.7	-	101.1	89.7	104.8	94.8
Taiyuan	97.0	99.0	89.3	88.0	94.0	107.0	102.6
Tangshan	93.2	107.4	-	99.3	89.5	96.8	94.0
Tianjin	102.9	98.0	92.5	-	-	106.8	99.0
Urumqi	88.7	90.6	-	94.9	103.9	97.4	106.5
Weifang	96.7	-	-	106.0	106.6	95.9	88.7
Wenzhou	103.1	-	92.1	93.0	104.7	103.9	100.3
Wuhan	95.6	97.8	90.7	92.7	105.8	89.6	101.8
Wuhu	103.8	-	-	90.8	91.8	96.3	98.2
Wuxi	89.4	98.7	-	101.1	89.7	106.9	91.4
Xiamen	102.6	87.5	105.2	100.7	-	107.0	90.9
Xi'an	96.4	103.0	95.5	91.6	98.8	104.3	93.1
Xining	91.6	105.6	100.6	97.2a	-	-	104.3
Yantai	98.8	98.1	-	106.9	107.8	103.0	91.2

FM(MHz)	CNR 1	CNR 2	CNR 3	Prov.T	Prov.M	City.T	City.M
Yinchuan	96.4	107.8	99.7	98.4	-	100.6a	-
Yueyang	103.2	87.6	107.7	91.8	-	104.1	106.1
Zhangjiakou	88.9	-	-	101.6	93.9	-	98.6
Zhangzhou	102.6	98.3	100.2	100.7	-	96.6	99.1
Zhengzhou	101.2	96.7	100.2	104.1	88.1	-	94.4
Zhuhai	99.1	--	101.2	105.2	93.9	87.5a	

Prov.T=Provincial traffic stn **Prov.M**=Provincial music stn **City.T**=City traffic stn **City.M**=City music stn a) Traffic music stn
Official FM band 87.0-108.0MHz. Low power college stns exist 60-87MHz, some spread over 50-108MHz

Addresses and other information:
1) CHINA NATIONAL RADIO (CNR)
✉ 2 Fuxingmenwai Dajie, Xicheng Qu, Beijing 100866 ☎ +86 10 8609 2636 **W:** cnr.cn
L.P: Gen. Dir: Yan Xiaoming. CE: Qian Yuelin
V.O. China (1st Prgr "News Radio"): 24h on MW/SW(exc. Tues 0600-0850)/FM. **V.O. the Economy (2nd Prgr "China Business Radio"):** 24h on MW/SW(exc. Wed 0600-0900)/FM. **V.O. the Music (3rd Prgr "Music Radio"):** 2155-1605 (exc. Tues 0605-0855) on FM. **V.O. the City (4th Prgr "Metro Radio" "Top FM"):** Sun-Thu 2200-1700 (exc. Tues 0505-0835) Fri & Sat 2300-1600 on 101.8MHz **V.O. Zhonghua (5th Prgr "Zhonghua News Radio"):** 0055-0615, 0955-0005 on MW/SW/102.3/94.9MHz(Fuzhou/Xiamen). **V.O. Shenzhou (6th Prgr "Shenzhou Easy Radio")** in Ch, Amoy and Hakka: 2055-0105, 0355-1805 on MW/SW/106.2/107.9MHz(Fuzhou/Xiamen). **V.O. Huaxia (7th Prgr "Huaxia Radio")** for the Zhujiang Delta: Ch. on 1215kHz/87.8/92.3/104.9MHz 2055-1805 (exc. Tues 0600-0855), Bilingual Ch. on 1215kHz/104.9MHz 2055-1805 in Ch and Cantonese. **V.O. the Literary (9th Prgr "Story Radio"):** 2100-1800 (exc. Tues 0500-0900) on 106.6MHz. **V.O. Old Age (10th Prgr. "Senior Citizen Radio"):** 1955-1735 (exc. Tues 0605-0855) on 1053kHz. **V.O. the Entertainment (12th Prgr "Happy Radio"):** 2055-1805 (exc. Tues 0505-0855) on 747kHz. **V.O. Hong Kong (14th Prgr)** for Hong Kong Special Administrative Region: on DAB 24h (exc. Mon 1605-2055) in Ch and Cantonese. **China Highway Traffic Sce.** (15th Prgr): on 99.6MHz(Beijing) 24h (exc. Tues, Sat and Sun). **V.O. China Country (16th Prgr):** on 720kHz(Beijing) 24h (exc. Mon 1605-2055)

V.O. Minorities (8th Prgr "Ethnic Minority Radio"): 2055-1500 (exc. Wed 0600-0900)on MW/SW/104.5MHz (Hohhot) – +) relayed by regional stns
Korean
0600-1000		9785, 5975
1000-1100+	JL	9785, 5975, 1143, 1017
1100-1505		9785, 5975
Mongolian
2055-0600	11810, 9610, 1143

11th Prgr. Tibetan Service 2155-1605 on MW/SW (exc. Wed 0600-0855)/105.7MHz (Lhasa)
Tibetan
2155-2400	9480, 7360, 6010, 1098
0000-0100	11685, 9530, 9480, 1098
0100-0900	15570, 11685, 9530, 1098
0900-1100	15570, 9530, 7350, 1098
1100-1300	9530, 9480, 7350, 1098
1300-1605	9480, 7350, 6010, 1098
13th Prgr. Uighur Service 2355-1805 on MW/SW (exc. Tues 0600-0855) /FM
Uighur
2355-0600		15390, 13700, 945, 855, 720
0600-0630+	XJ	15390, 13700, 945, 855, 720
0630-1100		15390, 13700, 945, 855, 720
1100-1400		13700, 9420, 945, 855, 720
1400-1700		9890, 9420, 945, 855, 720
1700-1730+	XJ	9890, 9420, 945, 855, 720
1730-1805		9890, 9420, 945, 855, 720
17th Prgr.Kazakh Service 2355-1805 on SW (exc. Tues 0600-0855)
Kazakh
2355-1200	12055,11630
1200-1805	9630,6180

2) CHINA RADIO INTERNATIONAL (CRI)
(Zhongguo Guoji Guangbo Diantai)
✉ Jia 16, Shijingshan Lu, Shijingshan Qu, Beijing 100040 ☎ +86 10 6889 1001 **W:** cri.cn **L.P:** Gen. Dir: Wang Gengnian
Domestic Sce:
Beijing 1 "Easy FM" (1251kHz/91.5MHz): 24h in English – **Beijing 2 "Hit FM"** (88.7MHz): 24h in English – **Beijing 3 "Round the Clock"** (1008kHz): 24h in English – **Beijing 4 "News Plus"** (846kHz) 24h in English – **Beijing 5 "News Radio"** (900kHz/90.5MHz): 24h in Chinese – **Tianjin "News Radio"** (105.4MHz): 24h in Chinese – **Shijiazhuang "News Radio"** (92.2MHz): 24h – **Shanghai 1 "Hit FM"** (87.9MHz): 2200-2400, 0300-1730 – **Shanghai 2 "Easy FM"** (100.1MHz): 24h – **Shanghai 3 "News Radio"** (102.5MHz): 24h – **Hefei 1 "Easy FM"** (92.4MHz): 2200-1700 – **Hefei 2 "News Radio"** (90.1MHz): 2200-1700 – **Wuhu "News Radio"** (89.4MHz): 2200-1700 – **Xiamen 1 "Easy FM"** (95.8MHz): 2200-1700 – **Xiamen 2 "News Radio"** (90.1MHz): 24h – **Yantai "News Radio"** (88.4MHz): 2300-2400, 0400-0430, 0900-1000 – **Wuhan "News Radio"** (90.0MHz): 24h – **Changsha "News Radio"** (99.5MHz): 24h – **Guangzhou 1 "Hit FM"** (88.5MHz): 24h – **Guangzhou 2 "News Radio"** (702kHz/107.1MHz): 24h – **Haikou "News Radio"** (104.4MHz): 24h – **Chongqing 1 "Easy FM"** (89.8MHz): 2200-1600 – **Chongqing 2 "News Radio"** (91.7MHz): 24h – **Lhasa "Easy FM"** (100.0MHz): 1930-1600 – **Guiyang "News Radio"** (102.1MHz): 24h – **Lanzhou "Easy FM"** (98.5MHz): 2200-1600 – **Urumqi "News Radio"** (1008kHz): 24h

DAB: China Digital Multimedia Broadcasting (CDMB), Beijing on 208.720, 210.432, 212.144, 213.856MHz 2200-1600 (exc. Tues 0400-1000). Each freq. contains 5 audio ch and 3 video ch at maximum. Currently there are only one regular regional mux, one trial regional mux and four regular local mux on air.

EXTERNAL SERVICES: China Radio International, Voice of Beibu Bay Radio, Yunnan Broadcasting Station
See International Broadcasting section

BROADCASTS TO TAIWAN
11) Voice of the Strait (Haixia zhi Sheng), Xindian, Fuzhou or P.O.Box 187, Fuzhou, Fujian 350012. Operated by the People's Liberation Army of China **W:** vos.com.cn News Sce. on 666/4940/9505kHz 2230-1600 (exc. Wed 0400-0955) in Ch. English Prgr. "Focus on China": Sun1500-1505 - Automobile Life Sce. on 90.6MHz 24h (exc. Wed 0400-0955) in Ch - Dialect Sce. on 783/4900/6115kHz 2230-1600 (exc. Wed 0400-0953) in Amoy - City Sunshine FM on 99.6MHz 24h – **12)** Voice of Jinling (Jinling zhi Sheng), P.O.Box 268, Nanjing, Jiangsu 210002. On 6200kHz 1240-1500 - Automobile FM 99.7MHz 24h – **13)** Voice of Pujiang (Pujiang zhi Sheng), 1376 Hongqiao Lu, Shanghai or P.O.Box 518, Shanghai 200051 **W:** yicai.com/showtopic/642116. On 1422kHz 2200-1600 **NB:** All SW and FM services have closed since 1 May, 2013 – **14)** Southeast Broadcasting Company, 2 Gutian Lu, Fuzhou, Fujian 350001 **W:** sebc.com.cn On 585kHz/97.6/106.2MHz 2255-1700 in Ch and Amoy – **15)** China Huayi Broadcasting Corporation, P.O.Box 251, Fuzhou, Fujian 350001 **W:** chbcnet.com On 873/6185kHz/107.1MHz for Taiwan, Hong Kong, Macao and Southeast Asia. 24h (exc. Wed 0400-0953)

ANHUI PROVINCE
AH1) Anhui Radio and TV St, 355 Tongcheng Nanlu, Hefei, Anhui 230065 **W:** ahradio.com.cn News General Sce. "V.O. Anhui": on 936/846kHz/103.6MHz 2000-1800(Tues 1500) - Economic Sce. on 864kHz/97.1MHz 24h (exc. Mon 1500-2100) - Travel Sce. Fortune FM on 98.1MHz - Travel Sce. on 1098/837/900kHz/96.1/106.5MHz 2130-1700(Tues 1500) - Traffic Sce. "Automobile 908": on 90.8MHz 24h (exc. Tues 1500-2150) - Life Sce. on 603kHz/105.5MHz 2100-1800 (exc. Mon 1500-1800) - V.O. City and Country: on 720/1008kHz/95.5MHz on 2000-1600(Mon 1500) - Music Sce. "Changxiang 895": on 89.5MHz 24h - Novel and Storytelling Sce. on 1395kHz/102.9/107.4MHz 2000-1800(Tues 1500) - Chinese Opera Sce. on 801kHz/99.5MHz 24h (exc. Tues 1500-2000) "Hefei My FM": on 96.1MHz 24h – **AH2)** Hefei Radio and TV St, 558 Tian'ehu Lu, Hefei, Anhui 230011. News General Sce. on 666kHz/91.5MHz 2050-1700 - Traffic Sce. on 1053kHz/102.6MHz 24h (exc. Tues 0600-0850) - Automobile Music Sce. "Hot FM": on 747kHz/87.6MHz 2200-1700 - Story Sce. on 1170kHz/98.8MHz 2100-1700 - Hui Merchant Sce. on 100.3MHz 2200-1800 - Xincheng Information Sce. on 846kHz/88.1MHz 2125-1500 - Xincheng Traffic and Music Sce. on 93.8MHz 2200-1600 – **AH2A)** 327 Jinzhai Lu, Luyang Qu, Hefei, Anhui 230061. Charm Music Sce. on 88.6MHz 24h – **AH3)** 11 Dongshan Zhonglu, Huainan, Anhui 232001. News General Sce. on 648kHz/103.7MHz 2125-1500 - Traffic and Literary Sce. on 97.9MHz 2140-1500 - Music and Story Sce. on 104.3MHz 24h(exc. Tues 0600-0900) – **AH4)** Huaibei Radio and TV St, 336 Huaihai Donglu, Xiangshan Qu, Huaibei, Anhui 235000. News Sce. on 1431kHz/94.9MHz 2155-1600 - Traffic Sce. on 100.4MHz 2150-1600 (exc. Tues 0630-0900) - Music Sce. on 89.3MHz 2150-1600 – **AH5)** 197 Beijing Donglu, Wuhu, Anhui 241000. News General Sce. on 100.4MHz 2100-1600 - Life Sce. on 1494kHz - Traffic and Economic Sce. on 96.3MHz 2128-1630 (Sun -1600) - Music and Story Sce. on 98.2MHz 2200-1600 – **AH6)**

Tongling Radio and TV St, Yi'an Beilu, Tongling, Anhui 244000. News General Sce. on 1107kHz/95.9MHz 2155-1505 - Traffic and Life Sce. on 88.7MHz 2230-1500 - Music and Story Sce. on 92.4MHz 2225-1505 – **AH7)** Bengbu Radio and TV St, Xuehua Shan, Shengli Donglu, Bengbu, Anhui 233000. News General Sce. on 765kHz/107.9MHz 2200-1400 - Economic Sce. on 1098kHz/104.2MHz 2150-1430 - Traffic and Literary Sce. on 98.4MHz 2200-1500 – **AH8)** Ma'anshan Radio and TV St, 46 Yushan Zhonglu, Ma'anshan, Anhui 243011. News Sce. on 1584kHz/105.1MHz 2150-1500 (exc. Tues 0600-0850) - Traffic Sce. on 92.8MHz 2130-1500 (exc. Tues 0600-0850) - Music FM "Xindong (Heart) 954": on 95.4MHz 2130-1500 – **AH9)** Anqing Radio and TV St, 23 Guanyue Miao, Anqing, Anhui 246004. News General Sce. on 1584kHz/90.3MHz 2200-1500 - Traffic and Music Sce. on 97.7MHz 2200-1500 (exc. Tues 0600-0925) - Story Sce. on 93.7MHz 2200-1500 (exc. Tues 0600-0925) – **AH10)** Huangshan Radio and TV St, 9 Tiandu Dadao, Tunxi Qu, Huangshan, Anhui 245000. News General Sce. on 1431kHz/93.3MHz 2200-1500 - Traffic and Travel Sce. on 100.4MHz 2200-1500 – **AH11)** 225 Langxie Lu, Chuzhou, Anhui 239000. News General Sce. on 95.0/97.3MHz 2125-1440 (exc. Tues 0500-0930) - Traffic and Music Sce. on 105.4MHz 2125-1530 - Literary and Story Sce. on 1377kHz/97.0MHz 2100-1500 – **AH12)** Nan 2 Huan Lu, Fuyang, Anhui 236034. News Sce. on 1116kHz/91.6MHz 2130-1610 - Economic Sce. on 711/801/1503kHz 2145-1550 (exc. Tues 0700-0830) - Traffic Sce. on 90.0/103.5MHz 2130-1530 - Story Sce. on 94.1MHz 2120-1530 – **AH13)** Suzhou Radio and TV St, Baihuiyuan, Huaihai Lu, Suzhou, Anhui 234000. News General Sce. on 1251kHz/100.8/100.2MHz 2155-1450 (exc. Tues 0600-0850) - Traffic Sce. on 96.1MHz/95.1MHz 24h - City Music Sce. on 97.1/107.3MHz 2130-1600 - Story Sce. on 102.3MHz 2200-1600 – **AH15)** Changjiang Nanlu, Guichi Qu, Chizhou, Anhui 247100. News General Sce. on 801kHz/98.1MHz 2200-1500 - Traffic and Travel Sce. on 96.6MHz – **AH16)** Meishan Nanlu, Lu'an, Anhui 237001. News General Sce. on 711/1242kHz/102.1MHz 2155-1505 - Traffic Sce. on 1170kHz/96.4MHz 2155-1505 - Music Ch. on 92.4MHz – **AH17)** 10 Zhuangyuan Lu, Xuancheng, Anhui 242000. News General Sce. on 1170kHz/100.6MHz 2155-1500 - Traffic and Literary Sce. on 106.1MHz 2155-1500 – **AH18)** 8 Chengguan Ximen, Dangtu Xian, Anhui 243100. Automobile Music BS: on 1098kHz/90.1MHz 2155-1400 (exc. Wed 0600-0900) – **AH19)** 62 Renmin Zhonglu, Bozhou, Anhui 236800 - News General Sce. on 999kHz/88.2MHz 2130-1530 - Traffic and Music Sce. on 107.2MHz 2130-1530

BEIJING MUNICIPALITY
BJ1) 14 Jianguomenwai Dajie, Chaoyang Qu, Beijing 100022 **W:** rbc.cn/ News Sce. on 828kHz/100.6MHz 24h (exc. Mon 1630-2100, Thurs 0700-0800). - Public Service Sce. on 1026kHz/107.3MHz 2100-1600 (exc. Mon 1630-2130) - Sports Sce. on 102.5MHz 24h (exc. Mon 1600-2100) - Traffic Sce. on 103.9MHz 24h (exc. Mon 1600-2130) - Story Sce. on 603kHz/89.1MHz 2100-1730(Mon 1630) (exc. Thurs 0700-0800) - Foreign Language Sce. "Radio 774": on 774kHz 2200-1600 (exc. Thurs 0700-0800) - Literary Sce. on 87.6MHz 24h (exc. Mon 1600-2130) - Music Sce. on 97.4MHz 24h (exc. Mon 1600-2100) – "i Home Radio": on 927kHz 2130-1600 (exc. Thurs 0700-0800) — Youth Sce."Metro Radio": on 94.5MHz 24h

CHONGQING MUNICIPALITY
CQ1) 159 Zhongshan 3 Lu, Yuzhong Qu, Chongqing 400015 **W:** fm968.cbg.cn News Sce. on 1314kHz/96.8MHz 24h - Economic Sce. on 101.5/107.7MHz 24h - Traffic Sce. on 95.5/88.9/92.7MHz 24h - City Sce. on 93.8MHz 2130-1800 - Music Sce. on 88.1MHz 24h – **CQ2)** V.O. Jialing, 6 Nanjing Lu, Beibei Qu, Chongqing 400700. On 97.4/102.1MHz 2255-1600

HEBEI PROVINCE
EB1) 63 Yuhua Donglu, Shijiazhuang, Hebei 050012 **W:** hebradio.com News Sce. on 1278/783kHz 2030-1700; on 104.3MHz/FM 24h - Economic Sce. on 846/1125/1521kHz/FM 24h - Life Sce. on 783kHz/89.0/91.0MHz 24h (exc. Tues 1700-2030) - Traffic Sce. on 99.2/101.6MHz 24h - Literary Sce. "Private Car 907": on 900kHz/90.7/94.8MHz 24h - Music Sce. on 102.4MHz/FM 24h (exc. Tues 1700-2015) - Farmer Sce. on 558/1251kHz/98.1/88.3MHz 24h (exc. Tues 1700-2030) - Travel Culture Sce. "Top Radio": on 603/1521kHz/100.3/88.1MHz 24h " Shijiazhuang My FM": on 102.9MHz 24h – **EB2)** 302 Tiyu Nan Dajie, Shijiazhuang, Hebei 050021. News Sce. on 882kHz/88.2MHz 2125-1700 - Economic Sce. "V.O. the City": on 1431kHz/100.9MHz 2125-1600 (exc. Tues 0600-0825) - Farm Sce. on 1251kHz/96.1MHz 2100-1600 - Traffic Sce. on 94.6MHz 2130-1700 - Taxi Sce. on 92.2MHz 2230-1600 - Music Sce. "NuStar Radio": on 106.7MHz 24h - Pinwei (Taste) Music on 87.6MHz 24h – **EB3)** 246 Renmin Lu, Handan, Hebei 056002. News General Sce. on 963kHz/96.4MHz 2100-1600 - Life Sce. on 1206kHz 2100-1600 - Traffic Sce. on 1008kHz/106.8MHz 2100-1600 - Music Sce. on 102.8MHz 2100-1600 - Chinese Opera and Storytelling Sce. on 846kHz/104.8MHz 2100-1600 – **EB4)** 15 Yejin Lu, Xingtai, Hebei 054000. News General Sce. on 1188kHz/89.6/90.3MHz 2125-1600 (exc. Tues 0530-0930) - Economic Life Sce. on 927kHz/

102.0MHz 2120-1500 (exc. Tues 0530-0930) - Traffic and Music Sce. on 91.8/101.2MHz 2225-1500 (exc. Tues 0630-0930) - Kuaile (Happy) Sce. on 96.8MHz – **EB5)** 1620 Yangguang Bei Dajie, Baoding, Hebei 071051. News Sce. on 1467kHz/90.9/93.7MHz 24h (exc. Tues 0600-0855) - Economic Sce. on 1017kHz/99.7MHz 2145-1600 (exc. Tues 0600-0930) - Traffic Sce. on 747kHz/104.8MHz 1850-1600 (exc. Tues 0600-0900) - City Service Sce. on 101.6MHz 2200-1400 - City and Country Alliance Sce. on 101.3/103.2/105.6MHz - Traffic and Music Ch. on 105.8MHz 2200-1630 – **EB6)** 17 Jianguo Lu, Qiaodong Qu, Zhangjiakou, Hebei 075000. News General Sce. on 1566kHz/101.0/107.4MHz 2155-1505 - Traffic Sce. on 900kHz/100.0MHz 2130-1600 - Private Car Sce. on 603kHz/104.3MHz 2130-1300 (exc. Tues 0500-0900) - Pinwei (Taste) Music Sce. on 98.6MHz 2130-1530 (exc. Tues 0600-0900) – **EB7)** 120 Guangdian Lu, Shuangqiao Qu, Chengde, Hebei 067000. News General Ch. on 1584kHz/89.1MHz 2155-0540, 0950-1400 - Traffic and Literary Ch. on 900kHz/97.6MHz 2155-1600 (exc. Tues 0600-0900) - Travel Life Ch. on 100.6MHz 2225-1600 – **EB8)** 1 Guangda Jie, Wenhua Lu, Tangshan, Hebei 063000. News General Sce. on 684kHz/91.7MHz 2030-1605 (exc. Tues 0705-0855) - Economic Life Sce. on 801kHz/95.5MHz 2130-1530 (exc. Tues 0700-0830) - Traffic and Literary Sce. on 1143kHz/96.8MHz 2135-1505 - Music Sce. "NuStar Radio": on 94.0MHz 2200-1600 (exc. Tues 0700-0900) - "V.O. Cao Jidian" Novel Sce. on 900kHz 2200-1600 (exc. Tues 0630-0900) - Cultural and Entertainment Sce. on 105.9MHz – **EB9)** 9 Yingbin Lu, Haigang Qu, Qinhuangdao, Hebei 066000. News General Sce. on 990kHz/89.1MHz 24h - Private Car Sce. on 900kHz/103.8MHz 24h - Traffic Sce. on 100.4MHz 24h (exc. Tues 0500-0800) - Sports and Music Sce. on 97.3MHz 24h - Farm Sce. "Huanle (Joy) FM": on 92.4/89.9MHz 24h – **EB10)** 12 Jiefang Xilu, Cangzhou, Hebei 061001. News General Sce. on 1557kHz/97.0MHz 2057-1500 - Agricultural Economic Sce. on 1053kHz/91.7MHz - Traffic and Music Sce. on 1206kHz/93.8MHz 2200-1600 - Automobile Music Sce. on 105.8MHz 24h - Music Sce. on 846kHz/103.6MHz 2200-1500 - Storytelling Sce. on 801kHz 2200-1500 – **EB11)** 8 Yongfeng Dao, Langfang, Hebei 065000. News General Sce. on 1008/846kHz/95.1MHz 2055-1700 - Storytelling Sce. on 585kHz/100.3MHz 24h - Chinese Opera Sce. on 1521kHz/105.0MHz 2055-1700 – **EB12)** 693 Hongqi Dajie, Taocheng Qu, Hengshui, Hebei 053000. News General Sce. on 954kHz/101.9MHz 2225-0535, 0825-1630 - Traffic Sce. on 1098kHz/105.3MHz 2125-1500 - Literary Sce. on 738kHz/96.1MHz 2230-1400 – **EB13)** 167, Bei Duan, Xinghua Lu, Xinji, Hebei 052360. 2225-2355, 0225-0500, 1025-1250 – **EB14)** Xitou, Shengli Dajie, Nangong, Hebei 055750. 2225-0045, 1005-1400 – **EB15)** 36 Yingxin Dajie, Shahe, Hebei 054100. 2200-1600 – **EB16)** Sanyang Dongjie, Qinghe Xian, Hebei 054800. 2210-0330, 0910-1230 – **EB17)** Beiguan, Zhuozhou, Hebei 072750 – **EB18)** Zhongshan Xilu, Dingzhou, Hebei 073000. 2200-1500 – **EB19)** 393 Xiguan Xijie, Botou, Hebei 062150. 2225-2355, 0345-0450, 1025-1230 – **EB20)** 12-1 Xihuan Lu, Renqiu, Hebei 062550. General Ch. on 1287kHz/92.8MHz 2225-1600 - Storytelling Ch. on 864kHz 2255-1400

HENAN PROVINCE
EN1) 2 Jing 5 Lu, 18 Zhenghua Lu, Zhengzhou, Henan 450003 **W:** radiohenan.com News Sce. on 657kHz/95.4MHz/FM. 24h - Economic Sce. on 738/972/846kHz/103.2MHz 24h - Traffic Sce. on 900kHz/104.1MHz 2200-1500 - Farm Sce. "Manshenghuo (Slow Living)": on 846/107.4MHz 24h - Private Car Sce. on 99.9MHz 24h - Music Sce. "Meili (charm) 881": on 88.1MHz/FM 24h - Visual Sce. "My Radio": on 1521kHz/90.0MHz 24h - Chinese Opera Sce. "Entertainment 976": on 1143kHz/97.6MHz 24h - V.O. the City"City FM 1066": on 1332kHz/106.6MHz 24h –Information Sce. on 603/1098kHz/105.6/FMMHz 24h – **EN2)** 17 Shangwu Neihuan Lu, Zhengzhou, Henan 450018. News Sce. on 549kHz/98.6MHz 24h (exc. Tues 0600-1000, Thurs 1600-2200) - Economic Sce. "Chedao (Lane) 931": on 711kHz/93.1MHz 24h - "FM889": on 1008/792kHz/88.9MHz 24h - City Sce. "Automobile 912": on 91.2MHz 24h - Music Sce. "Huoli (Vitality) 944": on 94.4MHz 24h - Private Car Sce. on 1458kHz/91.8MHz 24h - "Classic 1079": on 107.9MHz 24h – **EN3)** 78 Songcheng Lu, Kaifeng, Henan 475004. General Sce. on 873kHz/98.6MHz 24h - News Sce. on 101.4MHz 2200-1530 - Economic Sce. on 100.2MHz 2155-1530 - Traffic Sce. on 105.1MHz - New Farm Sce. on 1053kHz/96.6MHz 2200-1530 (exc. Tues 0630-0955) – **EN4)** 67, Jiudu Lu, Luoyang, Henan 471009. News Sce. "V.O. Heluo": on 576kHz/88.1MHz 2150-1600 - Economic Sce. on 1053kHz/106.5MHz 2150-1600 - Traffic Sce. on 92.7MHz 2155-1600 - Private Car Sce. on 102.1MHz 2200-1600 – **EN5)** Zhong Duan, Jianshe Lu, Pingdingshan, Henan 467000. News Ch. on 747kHz/98.9MHz 2055-1500 - Economic Ch. on 1143kHz 2155-1600 - Literary Ch. on 846kHz 2200-1600, on 99.6MHz 24h - Traffic Sce. on 1521kHz/96.4MHz 24h – **EN6)** 217 Jiefang Zhonglu, Jiaozuo, Henan 454002. News General Sce. on 828kHz/103.0MHz 2200-1700 - Traffic and Travel Sce. on 99.5MHz - Life and Literary Sce. on 1251kHz/89.4MHz 2200-1700 (exc. Tues 0600-0955) – **EN7)** Zhong Duan, Huashan Lu, Hebi, Henan 458030. On 1107kHz/100.3MHz 2155-0535, 0955-1430 - Economic

Ch. on 846kHz 2155-0535, 0955-1330 – **EN8)** 173 Renmin Lu, Weibin Qu, Xinxiang, Henan 453000. News General Sce. on 801kHz/92.9MHz 2125-1600 (exc. Tues 0530-0955) - Traffic Sce. on 1521kHz/99.1MHz 2155-1500 (exc. Tues 0500-0955) - Music Sce. on 89.2MHz 24h - Private Car Sce. on 90.3MHz 2200-1600 – **EN9)** Zhong Duan, Wenfeng Dadao, Anyang, Henan 455000. News Sce. on 882kHz/94.2MHz 2155-1530 - Traffic Sce. on 1251kHz/89.0MHz 2200-1400. - Automobile Music Sce. "i Radio": on 100.8MHz 2155-1600 – **EN10)** Puyang Radio and TV St, 379 Zhongyuan Lu, Puyang, Henan 457000. News General Sce. on 1251kHz/100.1MHz 2130-1535 (exc. Tues 0600-0900) - Economic Life Sce. on 91.0MHz 2130-1530 - Traffic Sce. on 89.5MHz 2100-1600 – **EN11)** 72 Balong Lu, Xiao Nanhai, Xuchang, Henan 461000. News Sce. on 1287kHz/102.0MHz 2200-1500 - Traffic Sce. on 92.6MHz 2130-1800 - Farm Sce. on 927kHz 2150-1500 - Automobile Music Sce. on 93.8MHz 2130-1800 – **EN12)** 152 Daxue Lu, Luohe, Henan 462000. News Sce. on 1251kHz/89.0MHz 2050-1520 - Traffic and Music Sce. on 106.7MHz 2155-1600 - City Sce. "Car Radio": on 98.1MHz 2155-1600 – **EN12A)** 243 Haihe Lu, Luohe, Henan 462000 – **EN12B)** Luohe FM BS, 215 Shuanghui Lu, Luohe, Henan 462000. Life and Literary Sce. on 93.6MHz 2230-1400 - Story Sce. on 87.5MHz 2155-1430 – **EN13)** Zhong Duan, Jianshe Lu, Sanmenxia, Henan 472000. News General Ch. on 603kHz/90.8MHz 2155-1605 (exc. Tues 0530-0955) - Literary and Traffic Ch. on 1008kHz/104.0MHz 2255-1500 (exc. Tues 0530-1000) - Story Sce. on 100.0MHz 24h - New Farm Sce. on 98.9MHz – **EN14)** Zhong Duan, Funiu Lu, Nanyang, Henan 473000. News Sce. on 104.2MHz 2130-1605 - General Sce. on 585kHz/93.6MHz 2130-1605 - Literary Sce. on 927kHz/106.0MHz 2130-1605 - Traffic Sce. on 97.7/101.0MHz 2155-1605 - Story Sce. on 106.0MHz 2130-1605 – **EN15)** Xinyang Radio and TV St, 19 Dongfanghong Dadao, Xinyang, Henan 464000. General Sce. on 837kHz 2155-1500 - News Sce. on 99.8MHz 2155-1600 - Economic Sce. on 106.8MHz 2155-1600 - Traffic Sce. on 94.8MHz 2155-1600 - Automobile Sce. on 105.8MHz 2300-1600 - Music Sce. on 88.8MHz – **EN16)** 35 Xinjian Nanlu, Shangqiu, Henan 476000. News Sce. on 729kHz/89.0MHz 2100-1500 - City Sce. on 927kHz/100.7MHz 2155-1605 - Traffic Sce. on 94.5MHz 2200-1700 - Music Sce. on 91.4MHz – **EN17)** 10, Dong Duan, Jianshe Lu, Zhoukou, Henan 466000. News Sce. on 828kHz 2050-1515 - Economic Life Sce. on 567kHz 2050-1600 - Traffic Sce. on 89.3MHz - Music Sce. on 96.0MHz – **EN18)** 209 Wenhua Lu, Zhumadian, Henan 463000. News Sce. on 810kHz 2125-? - Traffic and Travel Sce. on 102.4MHz 2200-1600 - City Sce. on 97.2MHz - Literary Sce. on 1053kHz – **EN19)** Lianmeng Xiaoqu, Chengguan Zhen, Qinyang, Henan 454550 – **EN20)** 25 Xi Dajie, Huixian, Henan 453600 – **EN21)** 10 Qianqiu Lu, Yima, Henan 472300 – **EN22)** 30 Guangyu Lu, Ruzhou 467500 – **EN23)** Dufu Lu. Gongyi, Henan 451200. On 765kHz/98.2MHz 2155-1600 - Sunshine Ch. on 107.5MHz 2155-1530

FUJIAN PROVINCE

FJ1) 2 Gutian Lu, Fuzhou, Fujian 350001 **W:** fjgb.com News General Sce. on 558/612/837/882/900/1008/1368/1377/1386/1395/1404/1449/1494/5040kHz/94.4/103.6MHz 24h (exc. Tues 0630-0855) in Ch and Amoy - Private Car Sce. on 98.7/101.5MHz 24h - Traffic Sce. on 87.6/100.7MHz 24h (exc. Tues 0600-0850) - Automobile Music FM on 91.3MHz 24h (exc. Tues 0600-0900) - Fujian EBS "Caijing 961": on 1404kHz/96.1/98.6/103.1MHz 2200-1600 in Ch and Amoy – **FJ2)** Fuzhou Radio and TV St, 1 Yuanyang Lu, Fuzhou, Fujian 350004. News Sce. on 1332kHz/94.4MHz 24h (exc. Wed 0605-0925) in Ch and Fuzhou dialect - Anchorwomen BS: on 89.3MHz 24h (exc. Thurs 0600-0900) - V.O. the Traffic: on 87.6MHz 24h - V.O. Zuohai: on 90.1MHz 24h in Fuzhou dialect – **FJ3)** 123 Hubin Beilu, Xiamen, Fujian 361012. News Sce. on 1107kHz/99.6MHz 2130-1700 (exc. Tues 0600-0900) in Ch and Amoy - Economic and Traffic Sce. on 1278kHz/107.0MHz 2200-1700 (exc. Tues 0600-0900) - V.O. Minnan: on 801kHz/101.2MHz 2200-1600 in Amoy - Music Sce. on 90.9MHz 24h (exc. Tues 0600-0830) - Travel Sce. on 1008kHz/94.0MHz 2200-1600 – **FJ4)** Putian PBS, 416 Puyang Lu, Chengxiang Qu, Putian, Fujian 351100. News General Sce. on 93.7MHz 2130-1800 in Ch and Puxian dialect - Music and Traffic Sce. on 103.0MHz 2130-1800 – **FJ5)** Quanzhou Radio and TV St, 1 Guangdian Lu, Quanzhou, Fujian 362000. News Sce. on 576kHz/88.9MHz 24h - Private Car and Music Sce. on 92.3MHz 24h - V.O. the Traffic: on 90.4MHz 24h (exc. Tues 0500-0900) - V.O. the Music: on 88.1MHz 24h - V.O. Citong: on 105.9MHz 24h in Quanzhou dialect - V.O. Qiaoxiang (Hometown): on 91.4MHz 24h in Ch and Quanzhou dialect – **FJ6)** Longyan PBS, Longyan Dadao, Longyan, Fujian 364000. News General Ch. on 92.5/106.0MHz 2158-1650 (exc. Tues 0630-0900) - V.O. the Travel: on 104.8MHz 2158-1600 (exc. Tues 0600-0900) – **FJ7)** Zhangzhou PBS, Shengli Donglu, Zhangzhou, Fujian 363000. News General Sce. on 89.6/96.2MHz 2200-1700 in Ch and Amoy - Traffic Sce. on 96.6/92.7MHz 2200-1700 (exc. Tues 0600-1000) - Music Sce. on 99.1MHz – **FJ8)** Sanming PBS, 32 Zhuang, Liedong Shuangyuan Xincun, Sanming, Fujian 365000. News General Ch. on 87.6/103.4MHz - City Life Ch. on 97.5MHz

GUANGDONG PROVINCE

GD1) 686 Renmin Beilu, Guangzhou, Guangdong 510012 **W:** rgd.com. cn Satellite Sce. (News Ch.) on 648/828/846/1017/1143/1206kHz/91.4MHz 24h - V.O. the City: on 103.6/90.0MHz 24h - Yangcheng Traffic St. on 105.2MHz 24h in Ch and Cantonese - Southern Life Sce. on 999kHz/93.6MHz 24h (exc. Mon 0400-1000) - Stock Sce. "Caijing 927": on 927kHz/95.3MHz 24h - V.O. the Music: on 1008kHz/99.3/93.9/96.8MHz 24h - Phoenix U Radio Automobile Sce. on 105.7MHz 24h - Literary and Sports Sce. on 603kHz/107.7MHz 24h – **GD2)** Zhujiang EBS, 686 Renmin Beilu, Guangzhou, Guangdong 510012. **W:** e974.com On 1062/801/1161kHz/97.4MHz 24h in Cantonese – **GD4)** 231 Huanshi Zhonglu, Guangzhou, Guangdong 510010. News Information Sce. "Fengyun 962": on 96.2MHz 24h (exc. Sun 1700-2200) in Cantonese. English Prgr: Fri 1300-1400 - Golden Hit Sce. "Jinqu 1027": on 102.7MHz 24h (exc. Sun 1600-2100) in Cantonese - Traffic Sce. "Jiaotong 1061": on 1098kHz/106.1MHz 2200-1600 (exc. Mon 1600-2200) - Youth Sce. "Guangzhou My FM":on 1170kHz/88.0MHz 24h (exc. Mon 1600-2100) – **GD5)** 1 Pengcheng 1 Lu, Futian Qu, Shenzhen, Guangdong 518026. News Ch. on 900kHz/89.8MHz 24h (exc. Tues 0530-0930) in Ch and Cantonese - Private Car Sce. on 94.2MHz 24h in Ch and Cantonese - "Feiyang 971": on 97.1MHz 24h in Ch and Cantonese - Traffic Ch. on 106.2MHz 2230-1800 - V.O. Lingnan on 1287kHz 24h – **GD6)** 1129 Dong, Jiuzhou Dadao, Xiangzhou Qu, Zhuhai, Guangdong 519015. "Xianfeng 951": on 95.1MHz 24h in Ch and Cantonese - Traffic Sce. "Jiaotong 875" on 900kHz/87.5MHz 24h in Ch and Cantonese - V.O. Baidao "Huoli (Vitality) 915": on 91.5MHz 24h – **GD7)** Shantou Radio and TV St, Chaoshan Lu, Shantou, Guangdong 515021. V.O. News Information: on 1080kHz/99.3MHz 24h in Ch and Chaozhou dialect - V.O. the Music: on 102.5MHz 24h - V.O. the Traffic: on 107.2MHz 24h (exc. Wed 0600-0900) – **GD8)** 51 Huimin Beilu, Shaoguan, Guangdong 512026. General Sce. on 105.7MHz 2225-1700 in Ch - Traffic and Travel Sce. on 97.5MHz 2225-1600 in Ch and Cantonese – **GD9)** Heyuan PBS, 1 Xingyuan Donglu, Yuancheng Qu, Heyuan, Guangdong 517000. General Sce. on 91.1MHz in Ch and Cantonese - Travel and Traffic Sce. on 97.8MHz – **GD10)** 42 Dong Jiaochang Bei, Meizhou, Guangdong 514011. News St. on 94.8/97.8MHz 2200-1600 in Ch and Hakka - Traffic St. on 105.8MHz 2200-1600 – **GD11)** Huizhou Radio and TV St, 13 Nantan Beilu, Huicheng Qu, Huizhou, Guangdong 516001. General Sce. "Sunshine 100": on 100.0/88.3MHz 2230-1630 (exc. Tues 0030-0830) in Ch and Cantonese - Traffic and Economic Environment Sce. on 1098kHz/98.8MHz 2230-1600 - Music Sce. "Zui'ai 907": on 90.7MHz 2230-1730 – **GD12)** Shanwei PBS, Zhong Duan, Shanwei Dadao, Shanwei, Guangdong 516600. News General Sce. on 103.5MHz 2200-1700 in Ch and Hakka - Farm Sce. on 91.3MHz – **GD13)** Dongguan PBS, 35 Xizheng Lu, Cheng Qu, Dongguan, Guangdong 523000. News General Ch. on 100.8MHz 24h in Cantonese - Traffic and Music Ch. on 107.5MHz 24h in Cantonese – **GD14)** Zhongshan PBS, 4 Xingzhong Dao, Dong Qu, Zhongshan, Guangdong 528403. General Sce. on 96.7MHz 2200-1800 in Cantonese - Environment and Travel Sce. on 747kHz/88.8MHz 2200-1800 in Ch and Cantonese – **GD15)** Jiangmen PBS, 178 Fazhan Dadao, Jiangmen, Guangdong 529000. News General St. on 100.2MHz 2300-1630 in Cantonese - Travel and Music Sce. on 93.3MHz 2200-1500 in Ch and Cantonese – **GD16)** Foshan PBS, Jihua 6 Lu, Chancheng Qu, Foshan, Guangdong 528000. General Sce. on 94.6MHz 24h in Cantonese - Music Sce. on 98.5MHz 24h in Cantonese - Nanhai Sce. on 92.4MHz 24h - Sanshui Sce. on 90.6MHz 24h - Shunde Sce. on 90.1MHz 2225-1600 - Gaoming Sce. on 88.3MHz 2225-1400 – **GD17)** Yangjiang PBS, 114 Mojiang Lu, Jiangcheng Qu, Yangjiang, Guangdong 529500. V.O. the City: on 95.6MHz in Ch and Cantonese – **GD18)** 93 Yuejin Lu, Chikan Qu, Zhanjiang, Guangdong 524038. News Sce. on 1134kHz/95.1MHz 2220-1700 in Ch, Cantonese and Leizhou dialect Economic Sce. on 98.1MHz 2220-1700 - Traffic and Music Sce. on 102.1MHz 2300-1600 – **GD19)** 13 Gaoliang Zhonglu, Hedong Qu, Maoming, Guangdong 525000. News St. on 106.1MHz 2230-1500 in Ch and Cantonese - Music Sce. on 1098kHz/97.6MHz 2230-1700 – **GD20)** Xinghu Dadao, Zhaoqing, Guangdong 526060. Information Sce. on 1521kHz/92.9MHz 2200-1600 in Ch and Cantonese - Music Sce. on 90.9MHz 2200-1600 in Ch and Cantonese – **GD21)** Qingyuan PBS, 18 Xincheng, Yinquan Lu, Qingyuan, Guangdong 511515. on 88.7/97.8MHz 2225-1600 in Ch and Cantonese – **GD22)** Wenci Donglu, Chenghai Qu, Shantou, Guangdong 515800. 2250-1600 in Ch and Chaoshan dialect – **GD23)** Jieyang PBS, Jinxianmen Dadao, Jieyang, Guangdong 522000. V.O. News and Life: on 103.9MHz 2230-1700 - V.O. Chinese Opera and Music: on 106.5MHz 2330-1600 in Jieyang dialect - V.O. the Traffic and Travel: on 95.2MHz – **GD24)** Jiedong PBS, Zhongxin Dadao, Jiedong, Guangdong 515500. On 100.2MHz 2220-1700

GANSU PROVINCE

GS1) 561 Zhangsutan, Chengguan Qu, Lanzhou, Gansu 730010. **W:** gstv.com.cn News Sce. on 684/873kHz/FM 2150-1605 (exc. Tues 0600-0850) - City FM on 106.6MHz 24h – Scripture Music Sce."City FM Scripture 102.2" on 102.2MHz 2200-1700 - Economic Sce.

"V.O. Yellow River": on 801kHz/93.4MHz 2255-1700 - Traffic Sce. on 103.5/104.8MHz 2150-1800 (exc. Tues 0600-0855) - Youth FM: on 104.8MHz 2250-1600 - Farm Sce. "Voice of Country" on 1170kHz/92.2MHz 2225-1700 (exc. Tues 0600-0850) – **GS2)** 92 Qingyang Lu, Lanzhou, Gansu 730030. News Sce. on 954kHz/97.3MHz 2125-1700 - Traffic and Music Sce. on 99.5MHz 2200-1900 (exc. Mon 0600-1000) - Private Car Sce. "Happy FM 1008" on 100.8MHz 2055-1630 – **GS3)** 6 Yan'an Xilu, Jinchang, Gansu 737100. News General Sce. on 585kHz/101.4MHz 2150-1600 - Traffic and Literary Sce. on 103.8MHz – **GS4)** Tianshui Radio and TV St, 11-5 Huancheng Zhonglu, Qincheng Qu, Tianshui, Gansu 741000. News General Sce. on 1143kHz/98.2MHz 2220-1600 - Music and Literary Sce. on 93.7MHz 2225-1600 – **GS5)** 10 Fuqiang Xilu, Jiayuguan, Gansu 735100 – **GS6)** Gannan Radio and TV St, 49 Xi 2 Lu, Hezuo, Gansu 747000. On 1332/3990/5970kHz/97.2MHz 2250-0100, 1020-1410 in Ch and Tb – **GS7)** 45 Tuanjie Lu, Linxia, Gansu 731100. 2255-0130(Sun 0230) – **GS8)** 45 Hongqi Jie, Kongtong Qu, Pingliang, Gansu 744000. 2200-1500 – **GS9)** Gongyuan Lu, Zhongping Qu, Yumen, Gansu 735200

GUANGXI ZHUANG AUTONOMOUS REGION

GX1) 75 Minzu Dadao, Nanning, Guangxi 530022. **W:** gxradio.com Satellite Sce. on 792/1071/1440/1485/1575/7275kHz/FM. 24h (exc. Tues 0500-0930) - Anchorwomen BS "Hostess Radio" on 846/1161/1224kHz/FM 24h (exc. Tues 0500-0830) in Ch and Guangxi dialect - Private Car 930: on 93.0/88.5/90.1/92.3/96.9MHz 2200-1700 (exc. Tues 0500-0930) in Ch and Zhuang - Traffic St. on 100.3/89.5/106.3MHz 2200-1700 (exc. Tues 0500-0930) - Literary Sce. on 95.0/105.0MHz 24h (exc. Tues 0500-0930) – **GX2)** Nanning PBS, 25 Gecun Lu, Nanning, Guangxi 530012. News General Ch. on 101.4MHz 2055-1700 in Ch and Guangxi dialect - ScriptureSce. on 104.9MHz 24h - Traffic and Music Sce. on 107.4MHz 2240-1600 - Story Sce. "Success 895" on 89.5MHz 24h – **GX3)** 1 Guizhong Dadao, Liuzhou, Guangxi 545006. News Sce. on 1386kHz/102.9MHz 2200-1700 in Ch and Liuzhou dialect - Traffic Sce. "Love Radio" on: 99.1MHz 2200-1700 - Country Life Sce. on 105.9MHz 2200-1700 – **GX4)** 1 Anxin Beilu, Xiangshan Qu, Guilin, Guangxi 541002." V.O. the City" on 1485kHz/97.7MHz 2200-1600, - "Take off FM" on 88.3MHz 2200-1600 – **GX5)** 69 Xinxing 3 Lu, Wuzhou, Guangxi 543002. News Sce. on 1485kHz/100.8MHz 2200-1630 in Ch and Guangxi dialect - V.O. the Music and Traffic: on 107.5MHz 2200-1300 (exc. Mon) – **GX6)** Beihai PBS, 36 Guizhou Nanlu, Beihai, Guangxi 536000. News General Sce. on 93.5/88.4MHz 2200-1700 (exc. Tues 0500-0930) in Ch and Guangxi dialect - Economic Music and Traffic Sce. on 99.1MHz 2200-1700 (exc. Tues 0500-0930) – **GX7)** Qinzhou PBS, 18 Liqiao Jie, Qinzhou, Guangxi 535000. News General Sce. on 98.6MHz 2220-1645 (exc. Tues 0500-0930) - Music Sce. on 88.9MHz 2200-1645 (exc. Tues 0500-0930) – **GX8)** Yulin PBS, 1 Guangdian Lu, Yulin, Guangxi 537000. News Sce. on 97.8MHz 2200-1700 (exc. Tues 0600-0900) - Traffic and Music St. on 99.2MHz 2200-1700

GUIZHOU PROVINCE

GZ1) Guizhou Radio and TV St, 302 Qingyun Lu, Guiyang, Guizhou 550002 **W:** gzstv.com General Sce. on 765/927/1026/7275kHz/94.6MHz/FM 24h (exc. Tues 0600-0900) - Economic Sce. on 603kHz/98.9MHz 24h (exc. Tues 0700-1000) - Travel Sce. on 97.2MHz 24h - Traffic Sce. on 95.2MHz 24h - Automobile Sce. on 106.2MHz 24h (exc. Tues 0700-1000) - Music Sce. on 91.6MHz 24h (exc. Tues 0600-0900) - Chinese Intellectual Sce. on 90.0MHz 24h – **GZ2)** 15 Zunyi Lu, Guiyang, Guizhou 550002. News General Sce. on 999kHz/88.9MHz 24h - City Female Sce. on 104.0MHz 24h - Traffic Sce. on 102.7MHz 24h - Travel and Life Sce. "Dynamic 909" on 90.9MHz 24h – **GZ3)** 31 Minghu Lu, Zhongshan Qu, Liupanshui, Guizhou 553001. News General Ch. on 711kHz/99.8MHz 2225-1800 - Traffic Ch. on 93.8MHz - Music Ch. on 102.1MHz 2225-1800 – **GZ4)** 11 Daxing Lu, Honghuagang Qu, Zunyi, Guizhou 563000. General Sce. on 1584kHz/98.2MHz 2227-1600 - Traffic and Literary Sce. on 94.1MHz 2225-1805 - Travel Life Sce. on 88.0MHz 2230-1800 – **GZ5)** 34 Guihuang Xilu, Anshun, Guizhou 561000. News General Sce. on 666kHz/105.9MHz - Traffic Sce. on 102.9MHz – **GZ6)** Qiannan PBS, 267 Huandong Zhonglu, Duyun, Guizhou 558000. News General Ch. on 882kHz/98.0MHz 2200-1530 - Traffic and Travel Ch. on 93.3/92.2MHz 2225-1800 – **GZ7)** Qiandongnan PBS, 34 Beijing Donglu, Kaili, Guizhou 556000, On 104.9MHz/FM 2230-1600 – **GZ8)** Qianxinan PBS, Xingyi Guangchang Pang, Xingyi, Guizhou 562400. News General Sce. on 107.9MHz 2225-1700(Sun 1600) in Ch, Buyi and Miao - Traffic and Travel Sce. on 88.3MHz 2225-1700(Sun 1600)

HAINAN PROVINCE

HA1) Hainan Radio and TV Headquarters, 61 Nansha Lu, Haikou, Hainan 570206. **W:** channel bluehn.com News Sce. on 954/1107/1116kHz/88.6MHz/FM 24h in Ch and Hainan dialect - V.O. International Tour Island: on 103.8/95.0/99.0/106.8MHz 2200-1700 - Traffic Sce. on 1143kHz/102.0/89.3MHz 2255-1805 - Music Sce. "Dongting 945": on 94.5/91.3/91.6MHz 2200-1700 - People Life Sce. on 101.0MHz 2200-1700 in Ch and Hainan dialect – **HA2)** Haikou Radio and TV St, 15

Zhongsha Lu, Haikou, Hainan 570206. News General Sce. on 101.8MHz 2155-1800 in Ch and hainan dialect - City and Country Sce. on 95.4MHz - Music Sce. "Simul Radio" : on 91.6MHz 2155-1800 – **HA3)** Sanya Radio and TV St, Jiefang 4 Lu, Sanya, Hainan 572000. V.O. Tianya: on 104.6MHz 2200-1700 - Traffic Ch. on 100.3MHz

HUBEI PROVINCE

HB1) 1237 Jiefang Dadao, Hankou, Wuhan, Hubei 430022 **W:** hbtv.com.cn News General Sce. "V.O. Hubei": on 774/1404/1566kHz/104.6MHz/FM 2000-1735 (exc. Tues 0700-0850) - Information Sce. on 1179/927/945/1008kHz 1955-1700 (exc. Tues 0630-0855) - Economic Sce. on 1053/1251kHz/99.8MHz/FM 1940-1800 - Life Sce. on 801/846/900/927/1098/1143/1215kHz/96.6MHz 24h - Farm Sce. on 684/801/846/900/945/1125/1143kHz/91.2MHz/FM 24h (exc. Tues 0630-0855) - Private Car (Sports and Travel) Sce. on 107.8/88.0/90.4MHz 24h - Fashion and Women Sce. on 747/1206kHz/97.1/102.6MHz 2000-1700 - Classic Music Sce. on 103.8MHz 24h - Chutian Traffic Sce. on 92.7MHz 24h (exc. Tues 0630-0855) - Chutian Music Sce. on 684kHz/105.8MHz/FM 24h (exc. Tues 0630-0855).– **HB3)** 620 Jianshe Dadao, Hankou, Wuhan, Hubei 430015. **W:** whtv.com.cn/audio/ General Sce. on 873kHz/88.4MHz 2030-1700 - Changjiang Economic Sce. on 1125kHz/100.6MHz 2030-1700 - Traffic Sce. on 603kHz/89.6MHz 2100-1700 - Music Sce. on 101.8MHz 2100-1700 - Children Sce. "Pinwei 936" "i Radio" on 93.6MHz 2100-1600 – **HB5)** Guanghui Lu, Huangshi, Hubei 435000. News Sce. on 963kHz/101.2MHz 2200-1600 - Traffic Sce. on 103.3MHz 2200-1600 - Automobile Sce. on 106.8MHz 2000-1800 – **HB6)** 200 Tanxi Lu, Fancheng Qu, Xiangyang, Hubei 441021. V.O. Xiangyang (News Sce.): on 1098kHz/104.0MHz 2120-1635 (exc. Tues 0700-0830) - Economic Sce. on 1314kHz/90.9MHz 2120-1635 (exc. Tues 0700-0830). - Automobile Sce. on 105.3MHz 2155-1635 (exc. Tues 0700-0830) - Traffic Sce. "Dongli (Power) 890": on 89.0MHz 2155-1635 (exc. Tues 0700-0830) – **HB7)** 4 Renmin Beilu, Shiyan, Hubei 442000. News St. on 1485kHz/106.2/107.3MHz 2100-1600 - V.O. Checheng (Mobile City): on 99.1MHz 2200-1600 - Music and Traffic Sce. on 101.9MHz 2200-1700 (exc. Tues 0600-1000) – **HB8)** 266 Jiangjin Xilu, Shashi Qu, Jingzhou, Hubei 434000. V.O. Jingzhou: on 585kHz/97.2MHz 2200-1600 - General Sce. on 828/1368kHz/98.4MHz 2030-1630 - 963 Beauty Music Sce. on 96.3MHz 2200-1700 (exc. Tues 0700-0900) - 901 Automobile Sce. on 90.1MHz 2130-1600. – **HB9)** 2 Guoyuan 1 Lu, Yichang, Hubei 443000. News General Sce. on 621kHz/95.6MHz 2100-1615 (exc. Tues 0600-0700) - Automobile St. on 100.6MHz 2130-1600 (exc. Tues 0600-0700) - Traffic and Music St. on 105.9MHz 2225-1645 (exc. Tues 0600-0700) – **HB10)** 100 Xiangshan Dadao, Dongbao Qu, Jingmen, Hubei 448000. News General Sce. on 927kHz/96.6MHz 2150-1500 (exc. Tues 0600-1000) - City Life Sce. on 1161kHz/89.7MHz 2130-1600 (exc. Tues 0600-1000) - Traffic and Music Sce. on 99.3MHz 2200-1500 (exc. Tues 0600-1000) – **HB11)** 157 Binhu Lu, Ezhou, Hubei 436000. 2100-1600 – **HB12)** 116 Changzheng Lu, Xiaogan, Hubei 432100. News General Ch. on 927kHz/91.2MHz 2155-1530 (exc. Tues 0500-1000) - Traffic and Music Sce. on 87.7MHz 2255-1505 – **HB13)** Huanggan PBS, 169 Dongmen Lu, Huangzhou Qu, Huanggang, Hubei 438000. News St. on 91.4MHz 2220-1600 - Traffic Sce. on 107.6MHz 2220-1530 – **HB14)** 38 Wenquan Lu, Xianning, Hubei 437100. News Sce. on 1314kHz/88.1MHz 2150-1505 (exc. Tues 0705-0905) - Traffic Sce. on 95.9MHz 2220-1505 (exc. Tues 0705-0905) – **HB15)** 32 Xuefu Lu, Laohekou, Hubei 441800. 2220-0500, 0800-1400 – **HB16)** 4 Renmin Lu, Danjiangkou, Hubei 441900. News General Ch. on 1431kHz 2220-1600 – **HB17)** 2 Shannan Xiaoqu, Shishou, Hubei 434400. 2200-0005, 0955-1235 – **HB18)** 56 Guangan Lu, Yingshan Zhen, Guangshui, Hubei 432700. 2155-0115, 0955-1305 – **HB19)** 146 Puyang Dadao, Yingcheng, Hubei 432400. 2200-0600, 0900-1305 – **HB20)** 199 Nanhuan Lu, Macheng, Hubei 436100. Educational and Music St. on 1242kHz/92.5/105.0MHz 2155-1430 – **HB21)** 50 Chunchuan Daqiao Lu, Chibi, Hubei 437300. 0950-1340 – **HB22)** 359 Lieshan Dadao, Suizhou, Hubei 441300. News St. on 1008kHz 2150-1600 - Traffic and Economic St. on 96.2MHz 2150-1600 – **HB23)** 117 Mianyang Dadao, Xiantao, Hubei 433000. 2130-1600 – **HB24)** 42 Zhanghua Nanlu, Yuanlin Zhen, Qianjiang, Hubei 433100. On 1242kHz/100.0MHz 2205-0445, 0930-1600 – **HB25)** 201 Hangkong Lu, Xiangzhou Qu, Xiangyang, Hubei 441104. On 1521kHz/96.5MHz 2155-1600

HEILONGJIANG PROVINCE

HL1) 333 Hanshui Lu, Nangang Qu, Harbin, Heilongjiang 150090 **W:** hljradio.com News Sce. on 621/900/927/1341/94.6MHz 2055-1800 - Private Car Ch. (Life Sce.) on 104.5MHz/FM 24h (exc. Tues 1600-2100) - Traffic Sce. on 99.8MHz/FM 2030-1700 - City Women Sce. on 102.1MHz 24h - Favorite Home Ch. (Children Sce.) on 97.0MHz/FM 24h - Music Sce. on 95.8MHz 24h (exc. Tues 1600-2100) - Country Sce. on 945kHz/94.3MHz/FM 24h - University St. "Radio Young" on 99.3MHz/FM 2200-1600 - "873 Story Hour" on 873/1476kHz/FM 0900-1300 - Korean Sce. on 873/1476kHz/FM 2100-2400, 1300-1500 in Ko - V.O. Beidahuang (Great Northern Wilderness): on 1476kHz/FM 2055-1600 – **HL2)** Harbin Radio and TV St, 1 Huashan Lu, Xiangyang Qu,

Harbin, Heilongjiang 150036. News Sce. on 837kHz/94.1/105.6MHz 24h - Literary Sce. on 98.4/97.8MHz 24h - Economic Sce. on 972kHz. 24h (exc. Tues 0500-0900) - Traffic Sce. on 92.5/95.3MHz 24h - Music Sce. on 927kHz/90.9/103.0MHz 24h - Automobile FM "Kuaile (Happy) 973": on 97.3/88.8MHz 24h — **HL3)** 99 Yong'an Dajie, Longsha Qu, Qiqihar, Heilongjiang 161005. News Sce. on 1197kHz/87.8MHz 2000-1600(Tues 1405) - Life and Literary Sce. on 693kHz/89.4/90.0MHz 2020-1505 - Traffic Sce. on 94.1/98.0MHz 2050-1605 - Country Sce. on 585kHz/103.4/87.5MHz — **HL4)** Jiuma Lu, Xiangyang Qu, Hegang, Heilongjiang 154100. News Sce. on 1413kHz/97.2/101.4/107.6MHz 2055-1400 - Traffic and Literary Sce. on 106.1MHz 2145-1400 - Life Sce. on 93.3MHz — **HL5)** Shuangyashan Radio and TV St, 240 Xinxing Dajie, Jianshan Qu, Shuangyashan, Heilongjiang 155100. News Sce. on 1179kHz/103.2/101.5MHz 2120-1230 - Traffic and Literary Sce. on 99.5/98.1MHz - Country Life Sce. on 98.6/104.2MHz - Storytelling Sce. on 603kHz/88.6/94.6MHz — **HL6)** 11 Diantai Lu, Jiguan Qu, Jixi, Heilongjiang 158100. News General Sce. on 1368kHz/94.5MHz 2130-0600, 0850-1350 - Traffic Sce. on 1485kHz/95.9MHz - Literary and Life Sce. on 1143kHz/98.6MHz - Storytelling Sce. on 103.9MHz 2055-1500 — **HL7)** Jia 1, Dongfeng Lu, Sa'ertu Qu, Daqing, Heilongjiang 163311. General Sce. on 1080kHz/96.7/97.5MHz 24h - Traffic Sce. on 95.0MHz 24h - Music Sce. on 106.0MHz 1955-1600.- Storytelling Sce. on 90.9MHz 24h - V.O. Baihu on 91.9MHz 2000-1600 — **HL8)** 16 Linshan Lu, Yichun Qu, Yichun, Heilongjiang 153000. News General Sce. on 909kHz/92.4/102.1MHz 2130-0810 (exc. Mon 0725-1000) - Traffic and Life Sce. on 98.5MHz 2200-1400 — **HL9)** 138 Taiping Lu, Mudanjiang, Heilongjiang 157000. News Sce. on 684kHz/87.9MHz 2105-1400 (exc. Tues 0800-0855) - Life and Story Sce. on 1476kHz/91.6MHz 2200-1530 - Traffic and Literary Sce. on 98.2MHz 2300-1300 — **HL10)** 35 Shunhe Lu, Jiamusi, Heilongjiang 154002. News General Sce. on 666kHz/ 101.7MHz 2055-0530, 0855-1400 - Economic Sce. on 1143kHz/95.0MHz 2055-1600 - Traffic and Literary Sce. on 98.0/93.8MHz 2225-1600 — **HL11)** 2 Shanhu Dajie, Taoshan Qu, Qitaihe, Heilongjiang 154600. News General Sce. on 1062kHz/98.8MHz 2300-1545 - Traffic Ch. on 89.1MHz — **HL12)** 255 Huanghe Beilu, Suihua, Heilongjiang 152054, Traffic Sce. on 90.7MHz 2155-1400 - Farm Sce. on 101.1MHz 2150-? - Music Sce. on 1080kHz/97.4MHz - Storytelling Sce. on 107.0MHz — **HL13)** 2 Xing'an Dajie, Jagdaqi Zhen, Heilongjiang 165000. Peoples Sce. on 1278kHz/100.1MHz 2125-1400 (exc. Tues 0600-0955) — **HL14)** 310 Shengdao, Aihui Qu, Heihe, Heilongjiang 164300. General Sce. on 1215kHz/103.8/107.3MHz 2100-1400 — **HL15)** 89 Xing'an Jie, Aihui Qu, Heihe, Heilongjiang 164300. V.O.Ai-Guang: on 999kHz/91.2MHz 2220-1500 (exc. Tues 0600-0850)

HUNAN PROVINCE

HN1) 167 Yuhua Lu, Changsha, Hunan 410007 **W:** hnradio.com News Ch. on 738/1152/1233/4990kHz/FM 2100-1700 (exc. Tues 0500-0900) - V.O. Xiaoxiang "News 938": on 900kHz/93.8/100.7MHz 24h - Economic Sce. "Meili (Charm) 901": on FM 2130-1700 (exc. Tues 0500-0900) - Literary Ch. "Qingchun 975": on 97.5/87.5/90.6/90.8/96.9MHz 24h (exc. Tues 0500-0900) - Traffic Ch. on 91.8MHz/FM 24h - Automobile Music BS: on 89.3/102.1MHz 24h - Travel Ch. on 106.9MHz 2200-1600 **HN1A)** 77 Huangxing Zhonglu, Changsha, Hunan 410005. Jinying (Golden Hawk) 955 BS."Big Eye BS": on 95.5/91.3/100.6MHz/FM 24h — **HN2)** 237 Laodong Xilu, Changsha, Hunan 410015. News Sce. on 1323kHz/105.0MHz 24h (exc. Tues 0600-0900). - Economic Sce. "Kuaile (Happy) 886": on 88.6MHz 24h - Traffic and Music Sce. "i Radio": on 106.1MHz 24h - Sound of City on 101.7MHz 24h - Pinwei (Taste) Music Sce. on 102.2MHz 24h — **HN3)** Zhuzhou Radio and TV St, 658 Taishan Lu, Tianyuan Qu, Zhuzhou, Hunan 412000. News Ch. on 1089kHz/101.2MHz 24h - Traffic Ch. on 98.4MHz 24h — **HN4)** Xiangtan Radio and TV St, Donghu Lu, Xiangtan, Hunan 411104. Mango Radio "V.O. Xiangtan": on 1503kHz/98.6MHz 24h - Traffic Ch. on 104.2MHz 2200-1600 - Da Yanjing (Big Eye) BS: on 106.5MHz 24h - Le Shenghuo (Happy Life) FM on 97.8MHz — **HN5)** 114 Xianfeng Lu, Hengyang, Hunan 421001. News Ch. on 1071kHz/98.9MHz 24h - Traffic Ch. on 101.8MHz 24h — **HN6)** Shaoyang Radio and TV St, 373 Zhangshulong, Baoqing Xilu, Daxiang Qu, Shaoyang, Hunan 422000. Traffic Ch. on 95.4/87.7MHz 2200-1700 - Music Ch. "Feiyang 928": on 92.8MHz 2300-1700 — **HN7)** Yueyang Radio and TV St, 421 Nanhu Dadao, Yueyang, Hunan 414000. News and Traffic Ch. on 1053kHz/104.1MHz 2155-1700 - Music and Business Ch. on 1008kHz/106.1/104.5MHz 2155-1700 — **HN8)** Changde Radio and TV St, 267 Wuling Dadao, Changde, Hunan 415000. News Ch. on 1260kHz/106.7MHz 2225-1705 - Traffic Ch. on 97.1MHz 2200-1600 - City Traffic and Music Sce. on 98.5MHz — **HN9)** Chaoyang Lu, Yiyang, Hunan 413000. Mango Radio "V.O. Yiyang": on 1053kHz/99.7MHz 2200-1600 (exc. Wed 0800-1000) - Traffic Ch. on 88.1MHz 2200-1600 — **HN10)** 51 Renmin Lu, Jinshi, Hunan 415400 — **HN11)** Chenzhou PBS, 7 Li Dadao, Chenzhou, Hunan 423000. Politics and General Ch. on 99.2/89.9MHz 2200-1700 - Music and Traffic Ch. on 102.8MHz 2225-1700 - Mango Radio "V.O. Chenzhou": on 88.3MHz — **HN12)** Huaihua PBS, Tianxing Lu, Huaihua, Hunan 418000. City

Control Sce. on 97.2/107.6MHz 2230-1600 (exc. Tues 0400-0900) - Traffic Ch. on 103.8MHz 2220-1600

JILIN PROVINCE

JL1) 2066 Weixing Lu, Changchun, Jilin 130033 **W:** jlradio.cn News General Sce. on 738/1107/1521/1530kHz/91.6MHz 24h (exc. Tues 0500-0900) - Economic Sce. on 603/846/1143kHz/93.3MHz 24h - Health and Entertainment Sce. on 101.9MHz 24h (exc Tues 1500-1800) - Traffic Sce. on 103.8MHz 24h - Information Sce. on 100.1MHz 24h (exc. Tues 1500-1800) - Music Sce. on 92.7MHz 24h (exc Tues 1500-1800) - Country Sce. on 97.6MHz/FM 24h - Travel Sce. on 103.3/94.7/107.7MHz 24h - Educational Sce. "Gushi (Story) 963": on 96.3MHz 24h — **JL2)** 149 Baicao Lu, Chaoyang Qu, Changchun, Jilin 130061. News Sce. on 900kHz/88.9MHz 24h - Life and Story Sce. on 1332kHz/90.0MHz 24h "Changchung My FM": on 88.0MHz 24h (exc. SS1600-2200) - V.O. the Traffic: on 96.8/100.6MHz 24h - City Music Sce. "Private Car Radio": on 106.3MHz 24h - City Elite Sce. "Top Radio": on 585kHz/99.6MHz 24h — **JL3)** Nanjing Lu, Chuanying Qu, Jilin-shi, Jilin 132011. News Ch. on 927kHz/102.6MHz 24h - V.O. Old Age: on 702kHz/97.0MHz 24h - Traffic Ch. on 105.3MHz 24h - Music and Story St. on 1143kHz/94.0MHz 24h - Automobile Life St. on 88.3MHz 24h — **JL3A)** Jilin-shi EBS, 2 Nanjing Lu, Chuanying Qu, Jilin-shi, Jilin 132011. Dushi (city) 110: on 1494kHz/90.3MHz 24h - V.O. the Health: on 603kHz/92.6MHz 24h - City Life Sce. on 89.3MHz 2030-1700 - V.O. Jiangcheng Music: on 1251kHz/91.3MHz 24h — **JL4)** 39 Nan Xinhua Dajie, Siping, Jilin 136000. News General Ch. on 666kHz/93.9MHz 2100-1600 - Traffic and Literary St. on 99.5MHz 24h - Public Storytelling St. on 900kHz/90.5MHz 2100-1500 — **JL5)** Liaoyuan Radio and TV St, 20 Hebin Lu, Longshan Qu, Liaoyuan, Jilin 136200. General Ch. on 810kHz/99.2MHz - Traffic and Literary Sce. on 96.2MHz 2125-1500 — **JL6)** 199 Cuiquan Lu, Longquan Jie, Tonghua, Jilin 134001. News Sce. on 909kHz/102.8MHz 2100-1500 (exc. Tues 0705-0855) - City Sce. on 90.9MHz 2200-1400 - Traffic Sce. on 93.8MHz 2140-1700 - Life Sce. on 97.9MHz 2150-1400 — **JL7)** 36 Hunjiang Dajie, Badaojiang Qu, Baishan, Jilin 134302. News General Sce. on 657kHz/107.7/95.8MHz 2100-1530 - Traffic Sce. on 98.4MHz 2100-1500 — **JL8)** 1295 Linjiang Donglu, Ningjiang Qu, Songyuan, Jilin 138000. News General Sce. on 1431kHz/ 89.9MHz 2100-1500 - Traffic and Literary Sce. on 1143kHz/100.0MHz 24h - Public Life Sce. on 96.8/96.8MHz 24h - Story Sce. on 102.5MHz 24h — **JL9)** Baicheng Radio and TV St, 86 Xingfu Nan Dajie, Baicheng, Jilin 137000. News General Sce. on 1323kHz/103.0MHz 24h (exc. Tues 0630-0940) - Traffic Sce. on 96.5MHz - Literary Sce. on 105.8MHz - Storytelling Sce. on 98.5MHz — **JL10)** 166 Juzi Jie, Yanji, Jilin 133000. Ch Satellite Sce. on 1053/603/1566kHz/FM 2130-1630 - Ch News Sce. on 88.2/91.7/92.2/98.3MHz - Ko News General Sce. on 1206kHz 2040-1600 (exc. Tues 0540-0900) - Ko Cultural Life Sce. on 585/1188kHz/FM 2130-1510 - Traffic and Literary Sce. on 105.9MHz 2130-1600 in Ch — **JL11)** 45 Dong Huancheng Lu, Gongzhuling, Jilin 136100. V.O. the Public: on 1485kHz 2050-1420 - V.O. the Traffic: on 101.3MHz — **JL12)** 18 Nan Dalu, Lishu Xian, Jilin 136500. V.O. the Northern Traffic: on 1575kHz/102.4MHz — **JL13)** 70 Henan Jie, Meihekou, Jilin 135000. V.O. the Traffic: on 1584kHz/95.7MHz 2155-1130 — **JL14)** 628 Qingzhen Jie, Qian Gorlos, Jilin 131100. On 1476kHz/91.0MHz 2125-2330, 0325-0500, 0955-1230 in Ch and Mo — **JL15)** Taonan PBS, 298 Tuanjie Xilu, Taonan, Jilin 137100 On 104.6MHz 2055-1500 — **JL16)** 7 Yongle Jie, Yanji, Jilin 133000. Ch Prgr. on 900kHz. 24h - Ko Prgr. "Arirang Radio": on 88.0MHz 2100-1700 - Yanji V.O. the Traffic BS: on 93.5MHz — **JL17)** 12 Xiangshang Jie, Tumen, Jilin 133100. 2155-2400, 0330-0500, 0855-1230 in Ch and Ko — **JL18)** 1-8 Xinhua Xilu, Dunhua, Jilin 133700. 2130-1500 in Ch and Ko — **JL19)** Jinghe Jie, Hunchun, Jilin 133300. Storytelling St. on 927kHz 2030-1530 in Ch and Ko - North East Asia V.O. Hunchun on 101.0MHz

JIANGSU PROVINCE

JS1) Jiangsu Prov. Radio and TV Headquarters, 132 Zhongshan Donglu, Nanjing, Jiangsu 210002 **W:** jsbc.com News General Ch. on 702/801 /1314/1413/1602kHz 2000-1700 (exc. Tues/Thurs 0600-0850) - News Sce. on 93.7MHz/FM 2100-1600 - Home Sce. on 107.1MHz 24h (exc. Tues 0600-0900, Wed 1700-2100) - Health Sce. on 846/603/1098kHz/ 87.7/88.5MHz 24h (exc. Tues 0600-0900) - Financial and Economic Sce. on 585kHz/95.2MHz 2000-1800 - Traffic Sce. on 101.1MHz 24h (exc. Tues 1800-2000) - Story Sce. on 1206kHz 24h - Music St. "Meili (Charm) 897": on 89.7/107.8MHz 24h (exc. Tues 0600-0900) - Classic Music St. on 97.5MHz 24h - Chinese Opera Sce. on 1053kHz 2100-1600 — **JS2)** Nanjing Radio and TV Group, 358 Baixia Lu, Nanjing, Jiangsu 210001. News Sce. on 1008kHz/106.9/88.8MHz 1900-1700 (exc. Tues 0600-0800) - Economic Sce. on 900kHz/98.1MHz 24h - City Control Sce. on 1170kHz/96.6MHz 2200-1600 - Traffic Sce. on 102.4MHz 24h - Music Sce. on 105.8MHz 24h - Sports Sce. on 1251kHz/104.3MHz 24h - Private Car Sce. on 98.1MHz 24h — **JS2A)** 359 Hongwu Lu, Baixia Qu, Nanjing, Jiangsu 210002. "Nanjing My FM": on 103.5MHz 24h — **JS3)** 223 Zhongshan Nanlu, Xuzhou, Jiangsu 221003. News Sce. on 1269kHz/93.0/89.3MHz 2000-1730 - Life Sce. on 801kHz/91.6MHz

2025-1730 - Traffic Sce. on 103.3MHz 2030-1700 - Literary Sce.on 1098kHz/89.6MHz 2015-1600 - Music Sce. on 99.6MHz 24h – **JS4)** 221 Jiefang Xilu, Xinpu Qu, Lianyungang, Jiangsu 222003. News Sce. on 1458kHz/93.6/98.3MHz 2100-1600 (exc. Tues 0600-0855) - Economic Sce. on 1251kHz/90.7MHz 2045-1600 - Traffic Sce. on 92.7/96.0MHz 2155-1600 - V.O. the Music: on 90.2MHz 2050-1600 - Story Sce. on 900kHz/104.8MHz 2200-1600 – **JS5)** 6 Dazhi Lu, Huai'an, Jiangsu 223001. News General Sce. on 801kHz/94.1MHz 2000-1600 (exc. Tues 0600-0900) - Economic Life Sce. on 1251kHz/105.0MHz 2000-1600 (exc. Tues 0600-0840) - Traffic and Literary Sce. on 1521kHz/94.9MHz 2100-1600 - Public (Chengshi Guanli) Sce. on 106.7MHz 2055-1600 - Automobile Music Sce. on 104.2MHz 2100-1600 – **JS6)** Yancheng Radio and TV St, 4 Shengyuan Lu, Yancheng, Jiangsu 224001. News Sce. on 1026kHz/91.5MHz 2100-1600 - Traffic Sce. on 747kHz/105.3MHz 2200-1700 - Private Car Sce. on 900kHz/88.2MHz 2100-1600 - V.O. the Music "Hi FM": on 98.0MHz – **JS7)** Yangzhou Radio and TV Media Group, 168 Weiyang Lu, Yangzhou, Jiangsu 225009. News Sce. on 98.5/105.5MHz 2120-1800 (exc. Tues 0600-0930) - Traffic Sce. on 103.5MHz 2120-1800 - Music Sce. "Yes FM": on 94.9MHz 2100-1600 (exc. Tues 0645-0800) - Health Life Sce. on 1179kHz/96.7MHz 2100-1600 - Classic Music Sce. on 801/1521kHz – **JS8)** 20 Qingnian Lu, Taizhou, Jiangsu 225300. News Sce. on 1341kHz/103.7/106.2MHz 2120-1525 (exc. Tues 0530-0855) - Music Sce. on 927kHz/97.3MHz 2145-1600 - Traffic Sce. on 92.1MHz 2200-1600 – **JS9)** 100 Renmin Zhonglu, Nantong, Jiangsu 226001. News Sce. on 1233kHz/97.0MHz 2130-1600 - Financial and Economic Sce. on 603kHz/103.0/102.6MHz 2130-1600 - Traffic Sce. on 1170kHz/92.9MHz 2200-1600 - Xingfu (Happy) Sce. on 88.5/88.3MHz 2130-1600 - Music Sce. on 91.8MHz 2130-1600 – **JS10)** 94 Zhongshan Xilu, Zhenjiang, Jiangsu 212004. News Sce. on 104.0MHz 2055-1600. - Health Life Ch. on 1224kHz/94.0MHz 2000-1800 - Traffic Sce. on 88.8MHz 2130-1600 - Music Sce. "V.O. Jinshan Lake Music": on 96.3MHz 2100-1800 - City Sce. on 90.5MHz 2030-1800 - Private Car BS "Donggan (Dynamic) 102.7": on 900kHz/102.7MHz 2130-1600 – **JS11)** Changzhou Radio and TV St, 10 Xiheng Jie, Changzhou, Jiangsu 213003. News General Sce. on 846kHz 24h (exc. Tues 0600-0850) - News Sce. on 103.4MHz 24h - Xi Opera Sce. on 1143kHz 24h - Fortune Life Sce. on 105.2MHz 24h - Traffic Sce. on 90.0MHz 24h - Chinese Opera Sce. on 747kHz 24h (exc. Tues 0600-0900) - Music Sce. "Aiting 935": on 93.5MHz 24h - Classic Music Sce. on 927kHz 24h - Literary St. (First Popular Ch): on 1521kHz/100.1MHz 2100-1600 – **JS12)** Wuxi Radio and TV Group, 4 Hubin Lu, Wuxi, Jiangsu 214061. News General Sce. on 1161kHz/89.4MHz 2020-1600 (exc. Tues 0500-0900) - News Sce. on 93.7MHz 2020-1600 - Economic Sce. on 1251kHz/104.0MHz 2020-1600 - Story and Chinese Opera Sce. on 1008kHz 24h - Traffic Sce. on 106.9MHz 24h - Automobile Music Sce. on 900kHz/91.4MHz 2130-1600 - City Life Sce. on 1521kHz/98.7/88.1MHz 2130-1600 - V.O. Liangxi: on 603kHz/92.6MHz 2100-1600 – **JS13)** Suzhou Radio and TV Headquarters, 4 Gongyuan Lu, Suzhou, Jiangsu 215006. News General Sce. on 1080kHz 2030-1600 (exc. Tues 0600-0730) in Ch and Suzhou dialect - V.O. the City "My Radio": on 91.1MHz 2030-1630 - Traffic Sce. on 1521kHz/104.8MHz 2130-1600 - V.O. Old Age: on 603kHz - Life Sce. on 96.5MHz 2130-1600(Tues 1525) - Music Sce. "Dongting 948": on 94.8MHz 24h (exc. Tues 0600-1000) - Chinese Opera Sce. on 846kHz - Automobile Sce. on 102.8MHz 2200-1600 – **JS14)** 43 Gongnong Lu, Yizheng, Jiangsu 211400. on 1026kHz/94.3MHz 2155-0535, 0725-1350 – **JS15)** 79 Zhongshan Nanlu, Jiangyin, Jiangsu 214400. Happy Life Ch. on 1386kHz/106.0MHz 2200-1530 - T Automobile Ch. on 90.7MHz 2200-1500 – **JS16)** 29 Haiyu Beilu, Changshu, Jiangsu 215500. News Sce. on 1116kHz/99.6MHz 2130-1405 - Qinchuan Music Sce. on 927kHz 2155-1400 (exc. Sat 0630-0830) - Traffic Sce. on 747kHz/100.8MHz 2130-1405 (exc. Sat 0600-0800) – **JS17)** Zhangjiagang Radio and TV St, Chenjiachang Nong, Yangshe Zhen, Zhangjiagang, Jiangsu 215600. News Sce. on 1098kHz 2140-1455 (exc. Wed 0600-0830) - Traffic Sce. on 102.0MHz 2155-1500 (exc. Wed 0530-0955) - Music Sce. on 1521kHz 2155-1500 – **JS18)** 7 Fazhan Dadao, Sucheng Qu, Suqian, Jiangsu 223800. News Sce. on 92.1MHz 2110-1600 - Traffic Sce. on 101.9MHz 2150-1700 - Aixin Netw. "Love Radio": on 106.3MHz

JIANGXI PROVINCE

JX1) 207 Hongdu Zhong Dadao, Nanchang, Jiangxi 330046 **W:** radio.jxntv.cn News Sce. on 729/1350/1449kHz/104.4MHz/FM 2000-1700 (exc. Tues 0600-0855) - V.O. the City: on 927kHz/106.5MHz/FM 2100-1800 (exc. Tues 0600-0900) - Financial and Economic Sce. "Chenggong (Success) 992": on 99.2MHz 2200-1600 - People Life Sce. on 101.9MHz/FM 2100-1800 - Farm Sce. "V.O. Green": on 1350kHz/98.5MHz/FM 2200-1600 (exc. Tues 0600-0900) - Traffic Sce. on 105.4MHz 24h (exc. Tues 1730-2030) - Music Sce. "i Radio": on 103.4MHz/FM 24h - Travel Sce. on 97.4MHz 2200-1600 -"Nanchang My FM":on 96.9MHz 24h– **JX2)** 241 Ruzi Lu, Nanchang, Jiangxi 330009. News General Ch. on 1278kHz/91.7MHz 24h (exc. Tues 0500-0900) - Traffic Sce. "Hi Radio": on 95.1MHz 24h (exc. Tues 0500-

0900) - "Big Eye 897": on 89.7MHz 24h - Music and Story Sce. "Xinyi 906": on 90.6MHz 2130-1600 - "Phoenix 879": on 87.9MHz 24h - V.O. Qingshan Lake on 93.4MHz – **JX3)** 1073 Cidu Dadao, Jingdezhen, Jiangxi 333000. News General Sce. on 1467kHz/96.5/107.3MHz 2200-1600 – **JX4)** Jiangwan Li, Binhe Xilu, Pingxiang, Jiangxi 337005. News General Ch. on 1107kHz/96.8/106.8MHz 2155-1500 - Traffic and Literary Ch. on 88.8MHz 24h – **JX5)** 49 Xianlai Zhong Dadao, Xinyu, Jiangxi 338000. News Sce. on 585kHz/94.0MHz 2130-1800 - Traffic Sce. on 96.2MHz 2200-1800 – **JX6)** 84 Changhong Dadao, Jiujiang, Jiangxi 332000. News Sce. on 1485kHz/90.0MHz 2155-1600 - Traffic Sce. on 88.4/88.9MHz 2255-1500 (exc. Tues 0530-0855) - Automobile Music Sce. on 91.6MHz 2155-1600 - V.O. Ganbei: on 94.1MHz 2200-1600 – **JX7)** Yingtan PBS, 3 Jianshe Lu, Yingtan, Jiangxi 335200. V.O. Xinjiang (Xin River): on 103.2MHz 2200-1605 - V.O. the Traffic and Music: on 95.6MHz 2200-1800 – **JX8)** Zhong Duan, Ganjiang Yuan Dadao, Ganzhou, Jiangxi 341000. News Sce. on 747kHz/93.7MHz 2200-1700 (exc. Tues 0600-0830) in Ch and Hakka - Music Sce. on 94.5/103.4MHz 2200-1700 - Traffic Sce. on 99.2/97.5MHz 2200-1700 – **JX9)** Ji'an Radio and TV St, 19 Beimen Jie, Ji'an, Jiangxi 343000. News Sce. on 603/1242kHz/95.6/102.1MHz 2125-1430 - Traffic Sce. on 100.6/94.3MHz 2200-1600 – **JX10)** Shangrao PBS, 51 Qingfeng Lu, Shangrao, Jiangxi 334000. News General Ch. on 93.4MHz 2200-1630 - Traffic and Music Ch. on 96.6/95.9MHz 2200-1630

LIAONING PROVINCE

LN1) Liaoning Radio and TV St, 10 Guangrong Jie, Heping Qu, Shenyang, Liaoning 110003 **W:** lntv.com.cn or lntv.cn General Sce. on 603/612/963/1089/1260kHz/102.9MHz 24h (exc. Tues 0605-0855). - Economic Sce. on 999/585/801/900kHz/88.8MHz/FM 24h (exc. Tues 0540-0855) - Country Sce. on 927kHz/96.9/103.4/107.1MHz 24h (exc. Tues 0500-0800) - Traffic Sce. on 97.5MHz 24h (exc. Tues 0540-0850) - Literary Sce. on 1053/747/801/810kHz/95.9/99.5/101.8MHz 24h (exc. Tues 0540-0900). - Life Sce. on 882kHz/103.4/90.4MHz 24h (exc. Tues 0500-0855) - City Sce. on 1341kHz/92.1MHz 24h - Music Sce. on 98.6MHz 24h (exc. Thurs 0500-0855) - Information Sce. (Dalian Blanch): on 90.6/90.4MHz 24h – **LN2)** Shenyang Radio and TV St, 89 Sanhao Jie, Heping Qu, Shenyang, Liaoning 110004. News Sce. on 792kHz/104.5/107.0MHz 24h – **LN3)** Dalian Radio and TV St, 162 Minquan Jie, Shahekou Qu, Dalian, Liaoning 116022. News Sce. on 882kHz/103.3MHz 1955-1605 (exc. Tues 0600-0800) - Financial Sce. on 1152kHz/93.1MHz 24h (exc. Tues 0630-0800) - Automobile Sce. "V.O. the City": on 99.1MHz 2025-1605 (exc. Tues 0630-0800) - Traffic Sce. on 100.8MHz 24h (exc. Tues 0600-0800) - Sports Sce. on 105.7MHz 2025-1605 (exc. Tues 0600-0800) - New City and Country Sce. "Xingfu (Happy) 956": on 1575kHz/95.6MHz 2025-1600 (exc. Tues 0600-0800) - Music Sce. on 106.7MHz 24h (exc. Tues 0600-0800) – **LN4)** Anshan Radio and TV St, 3, 219 Lu, Tiedong Qu, Anshan, Liaoning 114002. News Sce. on 954kHz/95.3MHz 24h - Economic Sce. on 89.7MHz 24h - Old Age Sce. on 1071kHz/88.5MHz - Traffic Sce. on 1458kHz/99.5MHz 24h - Music Sce. on 93.8MHz 2100-1600 - Storytelling Sce. on 1251kHz/87.9MHz – **LN5)** Fushun Radio and TV St, 2 Hunhe Beilu, Shuncheng Qu, Fushun, Liaoning 113006. News Sce. on 684kHz/93.0/93.8MHz 2000-1500 - Traffic Sce. "i Radio": on 747kHz/106.1MHz 24h - Music Sce. "U Radio": on 100.6MHz 2030-1600 - Storytelling Sce. on 1143kHz/88.2MHz – **LN6)** 15 Tiyu Lu, Mingshan Qu, Benxi, Liaoning 117000. News General St. on 1296kHz/94.0MHz 2030-1605 - Traffic and Economic St. on 900kHz/107.4MHz 24h (exc. Tues 0700-0900) - Life St. on 98.0MHz 2000-1600 - Storytelling St. on 104.1MHz 2055-1505 – **LN7)** Dandong Radio and TV St, 111 Shanshang Jie, Zhenxing Qu, Dandong, Liaoning 118000. News Sce. on 1404kHz/103.6MHz 24h - Traffic Sce. on 891kHz/101.7MHz 2030-1600 - City Sce. on 1476kHz/104.3MHz 2000-1500 in Ch and Korean - Entertainment Sce. (Private Car Music FM): on 603kHz/88.0MHz 2000-1600 – **LN8)** 3, 4 Duan, Beijing Lu, Jinzhou, Liaoning 121000. News Sce. Shiyuan (World Park) Ch. on 666kHz/92.7MHz 2125-1500 (exc. Tues 0530-0855) - Economic Sce. on 774kHz/96.6MHz 2125-1500 (exc. Tues 0530-0855) - People Life Sce. on 1098kHz/90.9/97.7MHz 2125-1500 (exc. Tues 0530-0855) - Traffic Sce. on 846kHz/100.3MHz 2125-1500 (exc. Tues 0530-0855) – **LN9)** Huludao Radio and TV St, 23 Haixing Lu, Longwan Dajie, Huludao, Liaoning 125000. News General Sce. on 1242kHz/93.1/95.2MHz 2130-1535 - Traffic and Literary Sce. on 87.8MHz 2150-1330 (exc. Tues 0540-0955) – **LN10)** Yingkou Radio and TV St, 10, Dong, Bohai Dajie, Zhanqian Qu, Yingkou, Liaoning 115000. News General Sce. on 1026kHz/88.4/106.2MHz 2055-1500 - Economic Life Sce. on 747kHz/89.0/92.8MHz 2100-1500 - Traffic and Literary Sce. on 1143kHz/95.1MHz 2130-1600 - Storytelling and Entertainment Sce. on 603kHz/94.1MHz 2125-1500 – **LN11)** Panjin Radio and TV St, 7 Shifu Dajie, Xinglongtai Qu, Panjin, Liaoning 124010. News General Sce. on 1485kHz/104.2MHz 2100-1600 - Traffic and Literary Sce. on 90.1MHz 2100-1500 - Economic Life Sce. on 97.1MHz 2100-1600 - Storytelling and Chinese Opera Sce. on 101.8MHz 2100-1550 - Music Sce. "V.O. Hexiang": on 95.3MHz – **LN12)** 61 Zhonghua Lu, Haizhou Qu,

Fuxin, Liaoning 123000. News General Sce. on 1287kHz/89.3MHz 2100-1510 - Economic and Storytelling Sce. on 747kHz 2100-1600 - Literary Sce. on 900kHz/105.3MHz 24h - Traffic Sce. on 1098kHz/88.7MHz 2100-1600 – **LN13)** Fuxin Mongolian BS, 84 Shanbei Jie, Haizhou Qu, Fuxin, Liaoning 123000. 2155-0610, 1040-1300 in Mo – **LN14)** Liaoyang Radio and TV St, 59 Qingnian Dajie, Taizihe Qu, Liaoyang, Liaoning 111000. News General Sce. on 837kHz/106.0MHz 2030-1530 (exc. Tues 0600-0800) - Economic Sce. on 1143kHz/102.0MHz 2025-1530 – **LN15)** Tieling Radio and TV St, 45 Gongren Jie, Yinzhou Qu, Tieling, Liaoning 112000. V.O. Tieling: on 1413kHz/101.2MHz 2150-1300 - Traffic Sce. on 102.8MHz 2200-1300 - Country Sce. on 810kHz/90.8MHz 2130-1430 - Literary Sce. on 95.9MHz – **LN16)** Chaoyang Radio and TV St, 88, 1 Duan, Xinhua Lu, Shuangta Qu, Chaoyang, Liaoning 122000. News General Sce. on 585kHz/96.1/106.0MHz 2125-1600 - New Farm Sce. on 810/702/747kHz/99.5MHz 1955-1600 (exc. Tues 0600-0900) - Traffic and Entertainment Sce. on 93.8/103.1MHz 1955-1600 (exc. Tues 0600-0900) - Feiyang FM on 648/801kHz/106.5MHz 1955-1600 – **LN17)** 67 Jinluan Lu, Wafangdian, Liaoning 116300. News General Sce. on 1323kHz/89.8/106.2MHz 2125-1345 – **LN18)** 385, 1 Duan, Huanghai Dajie, Zhuanghe, Liaoning 116400. 2100-0100, 0855-1200 – **LN19)** Haicheng Radio and TV St, 14 Huancheng Xilu, Haicheng, Liaoning 114200. News General Sce. on 900kHz/90.4MHz 2135-1500 - Traffic and Entertainment Sce. on 1350kHz/106.9MHz 2135-1500 – **LN20)** 18, 2 Duan, Xinghai Beilu, Xingcheng, Liaoning 121600 – **LN21)** 6 Qingnian Lu, Nanshan Jie, Beipiao, Liaoning 122100. V.O. Beipiao: on 91.2MHz 2125-1500 (exc. Tues 0500-0930)

NEI MENGGU AUTONOMOUS REGION

NM1) Nei Menggu PBS "V.O. Chinese Grassland", 55 Xinhua Dajie, Hohhot, Nei Menggu 010058 **W:** nmrb.com.cn Chinese News General Sce. on 675/540/603/747/765/ 855/900/999/1143/1494/1521/1584/7420/9520kHz/89.0MHz 2150-1605 (exc. Tues 0600-0950) - Ch News Sce. on 95.0MHz/FM 2150-1605 - Mongolian News General Sce. on 1458/1098/1143/1395/6040/7270/9750kHz/FM 2150-1605 (exc. Tues 0600-0950) - Economic Life Sce. on 101.4/103.8MHz 2100-1700 - V.O. the Traffic: on 89.6MHz/FM 24h - V.O. the Music: on 93.6MHz/FM 2150-1600 - Storytelling and Folk Art Sce. on 102.8MHz 24h - Farm and Pastoral Sce. "V.O. the Green Field": on 990/666/1224/1305/1413/1584kHz/FM 2150-1605 (exc. Tues 0600-0950) – **NM2)** 159 Gongyuan Xilu, Hohhot, Nei Menggu 010035. News General Sce. on 882kHz/92.9MHz 2120-1700 - Traffic Sce. on 107.4MHz 2250-1600 - City Life Sce. on 90.1MHz 24h - Literary Sce. on 99.8MHz 24h - Favorite Car Information Sce. "Happy Radio": on 103.9/98.5MHz 24h – **NM3)** 12 Gangtie Dajie, Hondlon Qu, Baotou, Nei Menggu 014030. General Sce. on 558kHz/94.9MHz 2025-1600 (exc. Tues 0600-0955) - Mongolian Sce. on 105.9MHz 1955-1605 (exc. Tues 0600-0915) - Traffic Sce. on 89.2MHz 24h (exc. Tues 0600-0950) - Urban and Rural Sce. "Automobile Music 100.1": on 100.1MHz 24h (exc. Tues 0730-0930) - Literary Sce. on 98.1MHz 2000-1800 – **NM4)** 17 Ordos Dongjie, Haibowan Qu, Wuhai, Nei Menggu 016000. W2225-0025, Sun0025-0515, W0325-0520, D1025-1305(SS 1405) – **NM5)** Chifeng Radio and TV St, 12, Xi Duan, Gangtie Xijie, Hongshan Qu, Chifeng, Nei Menggu 024001. Ch General Sce. on 1143/549/1512kHz/96.0MHz 2030-1600 - Mo General Sce. on 1440kHz/89.4MHz 24h (exc. Tues 0600-1000) - Traffic Sce. on 101.8MHz 24h (exc. Tues 0700-1000) - Farm and Pastoral Area Sce. on 900kHz/102.4MHz 2100-1600 – **NM6)** 86 Qiaoxi Shahe Lu, Jining Qu, Ulanqab, Nei Menggu 012000. Ch News General Sce. on 702kHz/93.3/98.7MHz 2200-1600 - Mo Sce. on 1521kHz/105.3MHz 2230-1210 - Traffic Sce. on 92.3MHz in Ch 2155-1700 - Literary Sce. on 94.3MHz in Ch 2155-1600 – **NM7)** 89 Xilin Dajie, Xilinhot, Nei Menggu 026000. Ch General Sce. on 1395kHz/99.4MHz 2225-1455 - Mo General Sce. on 927kHz/107.6MHz 2220-1505 - General Literary Sce. on 106.9MHz 2255-1505 - Traffic and Literary Sce. on 97.5MHz 2225-1455 – **NM8)** 43 Manzhouli Lu, Hailar Qu, Hulun Buir, Nei Menggu 021008. Ch News General Ch. on 603/3900kHz/99.9MHz 2130-0700, 0900-1440 (exc. Tues 0210-0700) - Mo News General Ch. on 954/6080kHz/97.3MHz 2150-0530, 0935-1440 - City Sce. on 104.6MHz 2200-1600 (exc. Tues 0100-0830) – **NM9)** Tongliao Radio and TV St, 29 Heping Lu, Horqin Qu, Tongliao, Nei Menggu 028001. V.O. Tongliao: on 702kHz/97.2/87.8MHz 2110-1730 (exc. Tues ?-0855) - Traffic and Literary Sce. on 1233kHz/91.3MHz 2110-1530 (exc. Tues 0600-0855) - Mo Prgr. "V.O. Horqin": on 1350kHz/93.7/94.4/100.3MHz 2110-1730 – **NM10)** Ordos BS, Manduhai Xiang, Dongsheng Qu, Ordos, Nei Menggu 017000. Ch News General Sce. on 936/792kHz/89.6MHz 2115-1600 - Mo News General Sce. on 603kHz/93.5/97.7MHz 2220-1430 - Traffic Literary and Sports Sce. on 100.8/107.1MHz 2130-1600 - Variety Sce. on 97.3MHz 2155-1600 – **NM11)** 26 Xinhua Xijie, Linhe Qu, Bayannur, Nei Menggu 015000. News General Sce. (V.O. Hetao): on 1152kHz/107.0MHz 2000-1600 - Traffic and Literary Sce. (V.O. the Yellow River): on 97.7MHz 2200-1600 - V.O. the Traffic: on 95.8MHz 2200-1600 – **NM12)** 1 Elute Donglu, Bayanhot Zhen, Alxa Zuoqi, Nei Menggu 750306. Ch Prgr. on 549/6025kHz 2230-1600 - Mo Prgr.

on 1440kHz 2230-1600 – **NM13)** 73 Hinggan Bei Dalu, Ulanhot, Nei Menggu 137400. V.O. Hinggan: on 891kHz/89.1MHz 2125-1430 in Ch - V.O. Alateng Hinggan: on 1152kHz/94.7/96.4/96.6/97.7/103.3/107.0MHz 2200-1600 in Ch (0600-0655 in Mo) - V.O. the Traffic: on 99.0MHz 2125-1500 (exc. Tues 0600-0800) - V.O. the City: on 106.8MHz 2200-1500 – **NM14)** Xuegang Shan, Xinchengwan Xiang, Fengzhen, Nei Menggu 012100. 2225-0020, 0355-0505, 0955-1215 – **NM15)** 1 Dianshi Jie, Manzhouli, Nei Menggu 021400. On 702kHz/94.9MHz 2225-1600 in Ch, Mo and Russian – **NM16)** 1 Xing'an Dongjie, Yakeshi, Nei Menggu 022150 – **NM17)** 3 Shengli Lu, Shiqiao Jie, Zalantun, Nei Menggu 162650. On 558kHz/98.6/102.7MHz 2155-1400 – **NM18)** Zhongyang Dajie, Genhe, Nei Menggu 022350. 2130-0700, 0900-1430 – **NM19)** 129 Nawenxi Dajie, Nirji Zhen, Morin Dawa, Nei Menggu 162850

NINGXIA HUI AUTONOMOUS REGION

NX1) 66 Beijing Zhonglu, Jinfeng Qu, Yinchuan, Ningxia 750001 **W:** nxtv.cn/radio/ News Sce. on 891/1206/1287kHz/FM 2100-1700 (exc. Tues 0600-0955) - Economic Sce. on 747kHz/92.8MHz 24h - City Sce. on 103.7MHz 2215-1605 - Traffic Sce. on 98.4MHz 24h (exc. Tues 0600-0950) – **NX2)** Yinchuan Radio and TV St, 11 Zhongshan Beijie, Xingqing Qu, Yinchuan, Ningxia 750004. News General Ch. on 801kHz/90.5MHz 2300-1600 - City Economy Sce. "Pinwei 950": on 95.0MHz 24h - Traffic and Music Sce. on 100.6MHz 2200-1800 - Automobile Life Sce. "Rolling Radio": on 90.5MHz 24h – **NX3)** Shizuishan PBS, 363 Youyi Xijie, Dawukou Qu, Shizuishan, Ningxia 753000 – **NX4)** 54 Yumin Dongjie, Litong Qu, Wuzhong, Ningxia 751100. On 1413kHz/89.3MHz 2230-1600 – **NX5)** Wenhua Jie, Xiaoba Zhen, Qingtongxia, Ningxia 751600

QINGHAI PROVINCE

QH1) Qinghai Radio and TV St, 81 Xiguan Dajie, Xining, Qinghai 810008 **W:** qhradio.com News General Ch. (Satellite Sce.) on 666/711/909/4750/6145/9780kHz/91.6MHz 2200-1600 (exc. Tues 0600-0900) - Tibetan Sce. on 1251/4220/5990/9850kHz/98.3MHz 2250-1600 - Economic Sce. on 1143kHz/107.5MHz 2255-1600 (exc. Tues 0600-0855) - Traffic and Music Sce. on 1377kHz/97.2MHz 2255-1600 - Life Sce. on 90.3MHz in Ch and Qinghai dialect – **QH2)** 43 Nanguan Jie, Xining, Qinghai 810000. News General Sce. on 1476kHz/95.6MHz 2200-1630 - Traffic and Literary Sce. on 104.3MHz 2230-1905 - City Life Sce. "Easy FM": on 101.3MHz - City Service and Control Sce. "Sunshine FM": on 102.7MHz – **QH3)** 139 Hongwei Lu, Jiegu Zhen, Yushu Xian, Qinghai 815000. On 882kHz 2255-0100, 1025-1230 in Ch and Tb. Rel. CNR 1: 1135-1230 – **QH4)** Haixi PBS, 7 Changjiang Lu, Delingha, Qinghai 817000. Ch Prgr. on 621kHz - Mo/Tb Prgr. on 540kHz

SHANDONG PROVINCE

SD1) Shandong Radio and TV St, 81 Jing 10 Lu, Lixia Qu, Jinan, Shandong 250062 **W:** v.iqilu.com General Sce. on 603/891/918/1467/1485/1548kHz/95.0MHz/FM 1940-1700 (exc. Tues 0530-0900) - Economic Sce. on 594kHz/98.6MHz/FM 24h - Economic Ch. "FM96" on 96.0MHz 24h - Life Information Sce. on 105.0/88.6/104.7/104.9/107.8MHz 24h - Traffic Sce. on 101.1/106.0/106.9MHz 24h - Anchorwomen BS "i Radio" on 97.5MHz/FM 24h (exc. Tues 0500-0900) - Country Sce. on 1251/621/999kHz/91.9MHz/FM 24h - Music Sce. "City FM" on 99.1/92.9/96.9/106.6/107.8MHz 24h - Sports and Leasure Sce. on 102.1MHz 24h – **SD2)** Jinan Radio and TV St, 32 Jing 11 Lu, Lixia Qu, Jinan, Shandong 250014. News Sce. on 1053kHz/90.9MHz 24h (exc. Tues 0410-0850) - Economic Sce. on 846kHz/90.9/95.7MHz 24h - Traffic Sce. on 103.1/91.2MHz 24h (exc. Tues 0400-0850) - Music Sce. on 88.7/105.8MHz 24h - Literary Sce. "Xingfu (Happy) FM": on 1305kHz/100.5MHz 24h (exc. Tues 0400-0900) - Story Sce. on 1512kHz/104.3/87.8MHz 24h - Private Car Sce. on 93.6MHz 24h – **SD3)** 200 Ningxia Lu, Qingdao, Shandong 266071. **W:** guangdian.qtv.com.cn/ News Sce. on 1377kHz/107.6MHz 1950-1600 – News & Life Sce. 819, 97.3MHz Economic Sce. Automobile Life Ch. on 1251kHz/102.9MHz 24h - Economic Sce. Storytelling Ch. "Happy 603": on 603kHz/100.7MHz 24h - Traffic Sce. on 900kHz/89.7MHz 24h - Private Car BS: on 1008kHz/96.4MHz 24h - Music and Sports Sce. "Simul Radio": on 91.5MHz 24h - Story Sce. on 95.2MHz 24h – **SD4)** Zibo Radio and TV Headquarters, 52 Huaguang Lu, Zhangdian Qu, Zibo, Shandong 255047. News Sce. on 89.0MHz 2155-1700 - News Story Ch. on 1143kHz - Economy Sce. on 801kHz 2155-1700 - Traffic and Literary Sce. on 1476kHz/100.0MHz 2145-1700 (exc. Tues 0500-0900) - Music Sce. "i Radio":on 92.6MHz 2145-1700 - Private Car Sce. "Yuedong 106.7" on 106.7MHz 2045-1700 – **SD5)** Zaozhuang Radio and TV St, 88 Guangming Xilu, Zaozhuang, Shandong 277102. News Sce. on 1170kHz/99.0MHz 2155-1600 - Life and Entertainment Sce. on 603kHz/101.4MHz 2200-1600 - Traffic and Literary Sce. on 105.2MHz 2200-1600 - Music Sce. on 100.6MHz 2200-1600 – **SD6)** 1229 Dongcheng Nan 1 Lu, Dongying, Shandong 257091. News Sce. on 1449kHz/91.0MHz 2155-1430 - General Sce. on 105.3MHz 2150-1435 - Traffic and Music Sce. on 88.1/98.4MHz 2150-1435 – **SD7)** Weifang Radio and TV St, 85 Shengli Dongjie, Kuiwen Qu, Weifang, Shandong 261061. News Sce. on 1161kHz/100.2/88.1MHz 2055-1600 - Private

Car Sce. on 1287kHz/93.3MHz 2100-1700 - Traffic and Music Sce. on 846kHz/95.9MHz 24h - City Sce. on 98.3MHz 2055-1700 - Music Sce. on 90.8MHz 24h - Story Sce. on 981kHz/107.1MHz 2055-1700 - Huanle (Joy) FM "New Radio": on 89.9MHz 2200-1300 - Music Sce. "Simul Radio": on 88.7MHz 24h – **SD8)** Yantai Radio and TV St, 32 Wenhua Xiang, Zhifu Qu, Yantai, Shandong 264000. News Sce. on 1314kHz/101.0/94.3/98.6MHz 2055-1600 - Economic Sce. on 801kHz/105.9/92.8/102.7MHz 2055-1600 - Traffic Sce. on 103.0/89.0/95.3MHz 2055-1600 - Music Sce. "i Radio": on 91.2/90.5MHz 24h Global Sce. on 88.4/96.6/102.4MHz 24h. Rel. CRI "News Radio": 2300-2400, 0400-0430, 0900-1000 – **SD9)** 66 Wenhua Zhonglu, Weihai, Shandong 264200. News General Ch. on 1206kHz/99.6/105.1MHz 2100-1600 (exc. Tues 0600-0825). Ko Prgr: 0530-0600, 1430-1500 - Traffic and Literary Ch. on 846kHz/95.0/102.2MHz 2125-1500 (exc. Tues 0600-0855) - Story Ch. on 96.1MHz 2100-1600 - Music Fashion Sce. on 90.7MHz – **SD10)** 11 Hongxing Zhonglu, Jining, Shandong 272037. News Sce. on 666kHz/104.2MHz 2200-1700 - Life Sce. on 1116kHz/107.0MHz 2200-1700 - Traffic and Literary Sce. on 801kHz/101.8MHz 2200-1700 - Music and Entertainment Sce. on 1386kHz/103.1MHz 2200-1700 – **SD11)** Rizhao Radio and TV St, Beishou, Yantai Lu, Rizhao, Shandong 276826. News General Ch. on 1449kHz/95.0MHz 2130-1600 (exc. Tues ?-0945) - Traffic and Life Ch. on 747kHz/88.1MHz 2130-1530 - Music Ch. on 104.0MHz 2130-1530 - City Ch. on 103.5MHz 2130-1530 – **SD12)** Dezhou Radio and TV St, 1288 Dongfanghong Xilu, Dezhou, Shandong 253012. News Sce. on 1098kHz/104.1MHz 2150-1600 - Traffic and Music Sce. on 1341kHz/94.1MHz 2150-1600 - Literary and Life Sce. on 1008kHz/92.9MHz 2150-1600 - Private Car Sce. on 98.9MHz 2150-1600 - Music FM on 97.9MHz – **SD13)** Linyi Radio and TV St, 21 Jinqueshan Lu, Lanshan Qu, Linyi, Shandong 276004. News General Sce. on 873kHz/97.6MHz 2125-1600 (exc. Tues 0530-1020) - Private Car Sce. "Fortune 932": on 1143kHz/93.2MHz 2125-1600 - V.O. the City: on 747kHz/101.0MHz 2125-1600 - Traffic Sce. on 612kHz/89.9MHz 2155-1600 (exc. Tues 0600-0950) - Music Sce. on 1251kHz/104.5MHz 2155-1600 – **SD14)** Liaocheng Radio and TV Headquaters, 41 Liuyuan Beilu, Liaocheng, Shandong 252000. News Sce. on 1143kHz/96.8MHz 2125-1600 - Traffic Sce. on 1566kHz/98.9MHz 2200-1600 - Music Sce. "I Music": on 801kHz/92.4MHz 2300-1600 – **SD15)** Binzhou Radio and TV St, 358 Huanghe 5 Lu, Binzhou, Shandong 256603. News Sce. on 864kHz/107.6MHz 2155-1600 - Life Sce. on 1170kHz/99.4MHz 2155-1530 - Traffic Sce. on 93.1MHz 2150-1600 - Music Sce. on 87.8MHz 2200-1400 – **SD16)** 28 Zhonghua Donglu, Heze, Shandong 274033. News Ch. on 1197kHz/92.7MHz 2055-1600 - Traffic Ch. on 94.8MHz 2055-1600 - Chinese Opera Ch. on 1071kHz/96.8MHz 2055-1500 – **SD16A)** Mudan PBS, 2093 Changjiang Lu, Heze, Shandong 274000. V.O. Heze on 1323kHz/97.2MHz 2155-1700 - Heze V.O. the City: on 104.0MHz 2155-1700 - Story Sce. on 88.0MHz 2300-1800 – **SD17)** Qingzhou PBS, 21 Fangongting Xilu, Qingzhou, Shandong 262500. On 95.4MHz 2125-1600 – **SD18)** Huangcheng Xihuan Lu, Longkou, Shandong 265701. On 101.6MHz - Yantai Longkou Economic and Literary BS: on 1251kHz 2228-0200, 0500-0700 – **SD19)** 4 Gulou Beijie, Qufu, Shandong 273100. On 1341kHz/98.4MHz 2155-0510(SS0450), 0955-1430(SS1410) – **SD20)** Tai'an PBS, 200 Yingxuan Dajie, Taishan Qu, Tai'an, Shandong 271000. News Sce. on 93.2MHz 2125-1600 - Economic Sce. on 90.1MHz 2130-1600 (exc. Tues 0600-1000) - Story Sce. on 91.6MHz 2130-1600 - Traffic Information Sce. on 106.2MHz 2125-1600 (exc. Tues 0600-1000) - V.O. City Music: on 104.4MHz

SHANGHAI MUNICIPALITY

SH1) Shanghai Radio and TV St (SMG), 1376 Hongqiao Lu, Shanghai 200051 **W:** smg.cn, eastradio.com News Sce. on 990kHz/93.4MHz 24h (exc. Thurs 1600-2050) - Traffic Sce. on 648kHz/105.7MHz 24h (exc. Fri 1700-2100) - Chinese Opera and Folk Art Sce. on 1197kHz/97.2MHz 2150-1600 (exc. Wed 0530-0830) in Ch and Shanghai dialect - Story Sce. on 927kHz/107.2MHz 2200-1600 (exc. Wed 0530-0830) – Wuxing (Five Stars) Sports Sce. on 94.0MHz 2155-1600 - Dong-Guang News St. on 1296kHz/90.9MHz 24h (exc. Thurs 1600-2100) - Dongfang (Eastern) City Sce. on 792kHz/89.9MHz 24h (exc. Thurs 1600-2100) - First Financial and Ecomonic Sce. on 603kHz/97.7MHz 2130-1600 - Popular Music Ch. "Donggan (Dynamic) 101": on 101.7MHz 2200-1800 (exc. Fri 0600-0800) - Popular Music Ch. "Love Radio": on 103.7MHz 24h (exc. Thurs 1600-2200) - Classical Music Ch. on 94.7MHz 2200-1700

SHAANXI PROVINCE

SN1) 336 Chang'an Nanlu, Xi'an, Shaanxi 710061 **W:** sxtvs.com News Sce. on 693/1008/1143/1521/6176kHz/106.6MHz/FM 24h (exc. Tues 0600-0900) - News Prgr. (City Sce.) on 1008kHz/101.8MHz 2058-1630 - Automobile FM on 89.6MHz 24h - Traffic Sce. on 801/1323kHz/91.6MHz 24h - Farm Sce. on 900kHz 24h - Youth Sce. "Xi'an My FM": on 105.5MHz 24h - Chinese Opera Sce. on 747kHz/107.8MHz 24h - Music Sce. on 98.8/94.8/97.5MHz 24h - Story Sce. on 603kHz 24h (exc. Tues 1700-2000) - Qin Melody Sce. on 101.1MHz 2300-1600 - City Express Sce. 99.9MHz 24h – **SN2)** 100, Zhenxing Lu, Xi'an, Shaanxi 710068. News Sce. on 810kHz/90.4MHz 2055-1700 - Information Sce.

on 106.1MHz 24h - Traffic and Travel Sce. on 104.3MHz 24h - Music Sce. on "i Radio":801kHz/93.1MHz 24h - Variety Sce. on 102.4MHz 2155-1710 – **SN3)** Miaopu Lu, Hongqi Jie, Tongchuan, Shaanxi 727000. News General Sce. on 1134kHz/103.7MHz 2210-0015, 0330-0515, 0915-1405 – **SN4)** 47 Hongqi Lu, Baoji, Shaanxi 721000. News Sce. on 1071kHz 2055-1700 - Music Sce. on 105.3MHz 2155-1700 - Economic Sce. on 900kHz/102.8MHz 2155-1700 - Traffic and Travel Sce. on 99.7MHz 2230-1400 – **SN5)** Nan Duan, Fu'an Lu, Xianyang, Shaanxi 712000. News General Sce. on 1296kHz/100.7/107.6MHz 2150-1740 - City Music Sce. on 99.9MHz 2200-1740 – **SN6)** Xi Duan, Dongfeng Jie, Weinan, Shaanxi 714000. News Sce. on 747kHz/101.3/102.6MHz 2100-1600 (exc. Tues 0430-0700) - Life Sce. on 96.4MHz 2250-1400 (exc. Tues 0500-0850) - Traffic Sce. on 90.9MHz 2157-1600 – **SN7)** Dongguan Jie, Yan'an, Shaanxi 716000. News Sce. on 603kHz/100.1/104.6MHz 2210-1500 (exc. Wed 0630-0910) - Traffic Sce. on 98.7MHz – **SN8)** 14 Dong Jianshe Xiang, Hanzhong, Shaanxi 723000. News Sce. on 1251kHz/95.6MHz 2130-1620 - Music Sce. on 97.1/99.5MHz 24h (exc. Wed 0700-0930) - Traffic and Travel Sce. on 93.0/94.3/101.8MHz – **SN9)** 7 Zhonglou Xiang, Yulin, Shaanxi 719000. News Sce. on 1143kHz/99.4MHz - Traffic and Literary Sce. on 95.9MHz – **SN10)** Ankang PBS, 113 Bashan Zhonglu, Ankang, Shaanxi 725000. News Sce. on 89.7MHz - Traffic Travel and Music Sce. on 95.9MHz 2155-1600

SHANXI PROVINCE

SX1) Shanxi Radio and TV Headquarters, 318 Yingze Dajie, Taiyuan, Shanxi 030001 **W:** sxrtv.com General Sce. on 819/846/900/1269kHz/FM 2100-1600 (exc. Tues 0600-0900) - Economic Sce. on 95.8MHz 24h (exc. Tues 0600-0900) - V.O. the Health: on 1584kHz/105.9MHz 24h (exc. Mon 0600-0900) - Traffic Sce. on 88.0MHz 24h - Farm Sce. on 603/747/1008/1098/1206/1422/1503kHz 2100-1600 - Music Sce. on 94.0MHz 24h – **SX2)** Taiyuan Radio and TV St, 2 Yifen Jie, Taiyuan, Shanxi 030024. News Sce. on 91.2MHz 24h - V.O. Old Age: on 1422kHz/97.5MHz 2155-1600 - Private Car Sce. on 774kHz/104.4MHz 24h - Traffic Sce. on 107.0MHz 24h - Music Sce. "i Radio": on 102.6MHz 24h – **SX3)** Datong Radio and TV St, 178 Yingbin Xilu, Datong, Shanxi 037006. News General Sce. on 1584kHz/103.5MHz 2200-1805 - Music Sce. on 91.1MHz 2200-1605 - Traffic Sce. on 99.6MHz 2200-1805 - Variety Sce. 900kHz/88.5MHz 24h – **SX4)** Yangquan Radio and TV St, Ningbo Lu, Yangquan, Shanxi 045000. News General Sce. on 603kHz/102.7MHz 2150-1355 - Traffic Sce. on 90.1MHz 2200-1600 – **SX5)** 87 Yingxiong Zhonglu, Changzhi, Shanxi 046000. News General Sce. on 1584kHz/98.8MHz 2120-0600, 0915-1530 - Traffic Sce. on 94.9/101.3MHz 2225-1600 (exc. Tues 0500-0900) – **SX6)** Fengtai Xijie, Jincheng, Shanxi 048000. News General Sce. on 585kHz/89.8MHz 2155-1600 - Traffic Sce. on 93.5MHz 2155-1600 – **SX7)** 3 Xiaoyuan Lu, Yuci Qu, Jinzhong, Shanxi 030600. News General Sce. on 1530kHz/103.4MHz 2200-1600 - Traffic and Literary Sce. on 92.1MHz 2300-1500 – **SX8)** Cangcheng Xijie, Xinzhou, Shanxi 034000 – **SX9)** 233 Hongqi Dongjie, Yuncheng, Shanxi 044000. News General Sce. on 1566kHz/93.2MHz 2200-1600 - Traffic and Literary Sce. on 101.9MHz 2200-1600 – **SX10)** Shuozhou Radio and TV St, 1 Minfu Xijie, Shuozhou, Shanxi 036002. News General Sce. on 1485kHz/100.9MHz - Traffic and Literary Sce. on 93.7MHz – **SX11)** Linfen Radio and TV St, 10 Guangxuan Jie, Linfen, Shanxi 041000. News General Sce. on 95.1MHz 2200-1600 - Traffic and Literary Sce. on 88.9MHz 2200-1600

SICHUAN PROVINCE

SC1) Sichuan Radio and TV St, 119-1 Hongxing Zhonglu, Chengdu, Sichuan 610017 **W:** sctv.com News Ch. "News FM": on 612/909/1116kHz/98.1/90.0/93.7/95.7/103.9/106.6MHz 24h - News Information Sce. on 106.1MHz 24h - Economic Ch. Fortune Sce. on 88.4/94.0MHz 2200-1700 - Economic Ch. People Life Sce. on 101.7MHz 24h - Traffic Sce. on 101.7MHz 2300-1600 - Travel Life Sce. "i Radio": on 97.0MHz 2200-1700 - Private Car Sce. "Auto Radio": on 92.5MHz 2300-1700 - Minority Sce. on 954/6060/7225kHz 2155-0135, 1000-1515 in Ch, Tb, Kham (Tb dialect) and Yi -Pleasure Sce. : on 747kHz/90.0MHz 24h - Minjiang Music Sce. "i Radio": on 95.5MHz 24h (exc. Tues 0700-1000) - Sound of City "City FM": on 102.6MHz 24h –**SC3)** 99 Shuanglin Lu, Chengdu, Sichuan 610021. News Sce. on 792kHz/99.8MHz 2130-1700 - Traffic Sce. on 1485kHz/91.4MHz 2200-1700 (exc. Tues 0500-0800) - Economic Sce. "Excellence 1056": on 105.6MHz24h - Cultural and Leisure Sce. "Scripture 946": on 94.6MHz 24h – Unique Music Sce. "Only Radio " : on 103.2MHz 24h – Private Car Music Sce. on 105.1MHz 2200-1700 - V.O.Global: on 96.3MHz 2155-1605 – Story Sce. "Happy Radio": on 88.2MHz 2100-1700 – **SC4)** Zigong Radio and TV St, 122 Dangui Dajie, Huidong Xinqu, Zigong, Sichuan 643000. News Sce. on 1422kHz/97.7MHz 2100-1500 - Cultural and Travel Sce. on 90.8MHz 2300-1700 – **SC5)** Panzhihua Radio and TV St, 43, Zhong Duan, Jinshajiang Dadao, Dong Qu, Panzhihua, Sichuan 617000. Gerenal Sce. on 711kHz/88.5MHz 2120-1700 - Farm Sce. (Automobile St) on 91.0MHz 2230-1700 – **SC6)** Datong Lu, Chengbei Xinqu, Luzhou, Sichuan 646000. News General Sce. on 954kHz/89.8/97.0MHz 2155-1600 - Traffic and Music Sce. on 96.0/100.6MHz 2155-1600 – **SC7)**

63, 1 Duan, Taishan Nanlu, Deyang, Sichuan 618000. News Sce. on 720kHz/95.9MHz 2200-1600 - Music and Traffic Sce. on 107.8MHz 2300-1600 – **SC8)** Mianyang Radio and TV St, 232, Nan Duan, 1 Huan Lu, Fucheng Qu, Mianyang, Sichuan 621000. News Sce. "V.O. Fujiang": on 711kHz/96.7/102.0MHz 2200-1600 - Traffic Sce. on 103.3MHz 2200-1600 - Music Sce. on 91.2/92.6MHz 2200-1600 – **SC9)** 585, Xi Duan, Hezhou Donglu, Guangyuan, Sichuan 628017. News General Ch. on 621/1143kHz/102.7MHz 2200-1700 - City and Country Ch. on 104.8MHz 2220-1600 – **SC10)** Suining Radio and TV St, 686 Suizhou Zhonglu, Chuanshan Qu, Suining, Sichuan 629000. News and Story Sce. on 1260kHz/99.7MHz 2150-1800 - Traffic and Music Sce. on 87.8MHz 2150-1800 – **SC11)** 33, 1 Xiang, Xianglong Lu, Neijiang, Sichuan 641000. Economic Sce. on 1143kHz/101.4MHz – **SC12)** 639, Nan Duan, Chunhua Lu, Shizhong Qu, Leshan, Sichuan 614000. News General Ch. on 1476kHz/102.8MHz 2225-1600 - Music and Traffic Ch. "Big Eye": on 100.5MHz 2300(SS 2330)-1700 – **SC13)** 12 Sichou Lu, Nanchong, Sichuan 637000. News Information Sce. on 747kHz/100.4/97.5MHz 2130-1630 - Traffic and Music Sce. on 91.5MHz 2330-1630 – **SC14)** Yibin Radio and TV St, 7, Zhong Duan, Nan'an Changjiang Dadao, Cuiping Qu, Yibin, Sichuan 644000. News Sce. on 92.8/97.0/101.4MHz 2200-1700 - Traffic Sce. on 94.2/105.9MHz 2200-1700 - Jiudu (Wine City) Music Sce. on 104.2MHz 2100-1600 – **SC15)** 92 Zhangjiawan, Tongchuan Qu, Dazhou, Sichuan 635000. News General Ch. on 1143kHz 2200-1600

TIANJIN MUNICIPALITY
TJ1) 143 Weijin Lu, Heping Qu, Tianjin 300070 **W:** radiotj.com News FM Sce. on 97.2MHz 2055-1800(Tues 1600) - News MW Sce. on 909kHz 2055-1800(Tues 1600) - Economic Sce. on 1071kHz/101.4MHz 2055-1800(Tues 1600) - Economic Sce. "V.O. Hangu": on 101.8MHz - Traffic Sce. "Chinese Comic Dialogue": on 567kHz 2155-1800(Tues 1600) - Traffic Sce. on 106.8MHz 24h (exc. Tues 1600-2100) - Life Sce. on 1386kHz/91.1MHz 2055-1800(Tues 1600) - Literary Sce. on 1098kHz/104.6MHz 2155-1800(Tues 1600) - Music Sce. "Nice Radio": on 99.0MHz 24h (exc. Tues 1600-2055) - Music MW Sce. on 1008kHz 2055-1800(Tues 1600) - Binhai Sce. on 747kHz/92.0MHz 2055-1800(Tues 1600) - Entertainment Sce. on 87.8MHz 2155-1800(Tues 1600) - Novel Sce. on 666kHz 2200-1800(Tues 1600) "Tianjin My FM": on 100.5MHz 24h

XINJIANG UIGHUR AUTONOMOUS REGION
XJ1) 830 Tuanjie Lu, Urumqi, Xinjiang 830044 **W:** xjbs.com.cn Chinese General Sce. on 702/738/999/ 1494/5960/7260/ 7310/9600/ 9835/11770kHz 2300-1800 (exc. Tues 0800-1100) - Uighur General Sce. on 558/855/1044/ 1413/6120/7205/ 7275/9560/11885/ 13670kHz 2300-1800 (exc. Tues 0800-1100) - Kz Prgr. on 963/1233/1107/ 6015/7340/9470kHz 2300-1800 (exc. Tues 0800-1100) - Mo Prgr. on 909/1233/1593/ 6190/7230/9510kHz 2300-0330, 0510-1030(Tues 0800), 1150-1800 - Kirghiz Prgr. on 1233/6190/7230/9705/11975kHz 0305-0530, 1005(Tues/Thurs 1100)-1230 - Ch News Sce. on 96.1MHz 2300-1800 (exc. Tues 0800-1100) - City Sce. on 837/1215kHz/92.9MHz 2300-1800 (exc. Tues 0800-1100) - Traffic Sce. on 94.9/101.8MHz 2330-1800 (exc. Tues 0800-1100) - Music Sce. "Urumqi My FM": on 103.9MHz 2300-1800 - Ug Literary Sce. on 101.7MHz 2300-1800 (exc. Tues 0800-1100) - Story Sce. on 102.8MHz 2300-1800 (exc. Tues 0800-1100) – **XJ2)** 28 Xinmin Lu, Urumqi, Xinjiang 830002. **W:** wlmqradio. com News Sce. on 100.7MHz 2300-1800 - Economic Sce. on 927kHz 2300-1700 - General Sce.: on 792kHz 2300-1700 - Traffic Sce. on 97.4MHz 2300-1800 - Taste (Travel and Music) Sce. on 106.5MHz 24h - Ug General Sce. on 1071kHz/104.6MHz 2300-1700. – **XJ4)** 100 Tianshan Lu, Karamay, Xinjiang 834000. Ch News General Sce. on 1179kHz 2355-1800 (exc. Tues 0800-0930) - Ug Sce. on 882kHz 2355-1800 - City Sce. on 92.6MHz 2355-1800 (exc. Tues 0830-0930) – **XJ5)** 2 Hongxing Xilu, Hami, Xinjiang 839000. Ch News and Traffic Sce. "V.O. Hami": on 1485kHz/103.5MHz 2300-1800 - Ug FM on 1098kHz/107.9MHz 2300-1600 - V.O. Tianmi (Honey): on 98.1MHz 2300-1800 - Legend Story Sce. "Green Ch": on 91.1MHz 2255-1800 - Music Sce. "Touch Radio": on 99.9MHz 24h – **XJ6)** 13 Urumqi Nanlu, Hotan, Xinjiang 848000. Ch Prgr. on 1026kHz - Ug Prgr. on 774kHz/92.2MHz 2300-1800 – **XJ7)** Tiyu Lu, Kashi, Xinjiang 844000. Ch Sce. on 648kHz/101.2MHz 2355-0215, 0455-0710, ?-1335 - Ug Sce. on 801kHz/ 103.0MHz 2355-? – **XJ8)** 66 Shangcheng Lu, Changji, Xinjiang 831100. General Sce. on 873kHz 2300-1700 - Traffic Sce. on 96.9MHz - Story Sce. on 107.4MHz 2330-1800 - Legal Sce. on 105.3MHz - Music Sce. on 103.3MHz – **XJ9)** Ili PBS, 1 Hongqi Lu, Yining, Xinjiang 835000. News General Sce. on 1134kHz/96.3/105.9/107.4MHz2255-1805 – Economic Sce. on 90.5MHz 2325-1835 - Traffic and Music Sce. on 100.8MHz - Ug Prgr. on 882kHz/88.4MHz 2350-0200, 0550-0700, 1150-1600 - Kz Prgr. on 603kHz/93.4MHz 2350-0200, 0550-0700, 1220-1500 – **XJ10)** 184 Bei 2 Lu, Shihezi, Xinjiang 832000. News Ch. on 891kHz/103.5MHz 0030-0730, 1130-1600 - Literary Ch. on 603kHz/89.3MHz – **XJ11)** 8 Kashi Xilu, Kuytun, Xinjiang 833200. Ch Prgr. on 1485kHz W2355-0230, Sun0025-0335, Sun0528-0720, W0558-0740, D1123-1425 - Kz Prgr.

on 819kHz – **XJ12)** Bayingolin PBS, 1 Jianguo Nanlu, Korla, Xinjiang 841000. Music Sce. on 92.2MHz 2300-1800 - Story Sce. on 89.5MHz - Mo Sce. on 104.7MHz

XIZANG AUTONOMOUS REGION
XZ1) 41 Beijing Zhonglu, Lhasa, Xizang 850000 **W:** tibetradio.cn Chinese Sce. on 999/1377/4820/5935/6050/7240/7450/11860/11950kHz/ 93.3MHz 2000(Tues 2100)-1800 (exc. Tues 0600-1000) - Tibetan Sce. on 594/846/4905/4920/6025/6110/6130/6200/7255/7385/949 0/ 9580kHz/101.6MHz 2050(Tues 2100)-1805 (exc. Tues 0600-1000). English Prgr. "Holy Tibet": 0700-0730, 1600-1630 - Kham (Tibetan dialect) General Sce. on 594kHz/91.4MHz 2200-1605 (exc. Tues 0600-1000) - City Life Ch. on 98.0MHz 2300-1700 (exc. Tues 0600-1000) – **XZ2)** Lhasa PBS, Lhasa, Xizang 850000. General Ch. on 91.4MHz 2350-1410 in Tb and Ch – **XZ3)** 25 Nedong Lu, Zetang Zhen, Nedong, Xizang 856000. 2335-0135, 0405-0535, 1005-1340 in Ch and Tb

YUNNAN PROVINCE
YN1) 182 Renmin Xilu, Kunming, Yunnan 650031. News Sce. on 576/846/972/ 990/1080/1197/ 1359/1395kHz/94.4/105.8MHz 2200-1600 - "Shangri-La 99": on 99.0MHz 2230-1430 - Economic Sce. on 1143/88.7MHz 24h. Rel. CRI English prgr: 1300-1500 - Minority Sce. on 7210kHz 2255-0300, 0630-0830, 1100-1500 in Lahu, Jingpo, Lisu, Dehong Dai, Xishuangbanna Dai etc - V.O. the Traffic: on 603/1098kHz/ 91.8MHz 2300-1700. - Music Sce. "Binfen 97": on 846/1053/1251kHz/ 97.0MHz 2300-1600 (exc. Tues 0600-0900) - Knowledge Person Sce. "Xinzhi 100": on 100.0MHz 2245-1700 - Children Sce. on 101.7MHz 2250-1700 - Farm Sce. on 1242kHz 2300-1600 (exc. Tues 0600-0800) - Int Sce. see International Broadcasting section – **YN2)** 198 Danxia Lu, Kunming, Yunnan 650118. City News Sce. "Sunlight Ch." on 1350kHz/100.8MHz 24h (exc. Tues 0400-0800) - New FM on 102.8MHz 24h - Automobile Sce. "954 Car Netw.": on 95.4MHz 24h - Knowledge Person Sce. on 105.0MHz 24h – **YN3)** 225 Qilin Xilu, Qilin Qu, Qujing, Yunnan 655000. V.O. Zhujiang Yuan: on 1521kHz/104.0MHz 2225-1600 - V.O. the Traffic: on 91.0MHz 2250-1600 – **YN4)** 32 Xinwen Lu, Wenshan, Yunnan 663000. Minority Language Ch. on 1053kHz/105.3MHz 2225-0030, 0355-0530, 0955-1400 in Ch, Zhuang, Miao and Yao - News General Ch. on 103.0/102.2MHz 2220-1500 - Qihua FM on 97.3MHz 2220-1600 – **YN5)** Honghe PBS, Jinhua Lu, Gejiu, Yunnan 661000. News Sce. on 1521/1485kHz/101.4MHz 2200-1700 - Traffic Sce. on 99.7MHz 2200-1730 - Minorities Sce. on 702kHz/97.5MHz 2225-1830 in Ch, Hani and Yi – **YN6)** Xishuangbanna PBS, 4 Guangdian Lu, Jinghong, Yunnan 666100. Ch Prgr. on 98.9MHz 2225-1620 - Minority Language Prgr. on 747kHz/90.6MHz 2225-1625 in Ch, Xishuangbanna Dai and Hani – **YN7)** Chuxiong Autonomous Prefecture PBS, 144 Lucheng Donglu, Chuxiong, Yunnan 675000. General Sce. on 1287kHz/106.1MHz 2225-1605 in Ch and Yi - Music Sce. on 90.6/96.3MHz 2225-1605 – **YN8)** Wanhua Lu, Xiaguan Zhen, Dali, Yunnan 671000. News General Sce. on 1044kHz/102.7MHz 2230-1500 - Traffic Sce. on 99.9MHz 2230-1600 - Cang'er FM on 105.5MHz 2200-1600 – **YN9)** Dehong Radio and TV St, 51 Nanbeng Lu, Mang Shi, Yunnan 678400. Minority Language Sce. on 900kHz/106.1MHz 2230-0110, 0330-0700, 1030-1530 in Ch, Dehong Dai, Jingpo and Zaiwa - General Sce. on 104.3MHz 2215-1600 – **YN10)** Donghuan Lu, Dongchuan Qu, Kunming, Yunnan 654100 – **YN11)** 6 Longquan Lu, Zhaotong, Yunnan 657000. News General Sce. "V.O. Wumeng": on 846kHz/97.5MHz 2225-1600 (exc. Tues 0710-0900) - Traffic and Travel Sce. "V.O. Hedu (Crane City)": 2225-1600 – **YN12)** Baohua Lu, Gejiu, Yunnan 661400. V.O. Jinhu (Golden Lake): on 675kHz/102.7MHz – **YN13)** 38 Xueqiao Jie, Chuxiong, Yunnan 675000. W2225-2400, Sun2325-0200, D0325-0600, D0955-1405 – **YN14)** 29 Guihua Lu, Yuxi, Yunnan 653100. Green FM on 1251kHz/102.4MHz 2225-1600 – **YN15)** Diqing PBS, 67 Changzheng Dadao, Jiantang Zhen, Shangri-la Xian, Yunnan 674400. On 675kHz/104.7MHz in Ch and Tb – **YN16)** Nujiang Radio and TV St, 5 Weiyuan Xiang, Liuku Zhen, Lushui Xian, Yunnan 673100. On 558kHz/105.6MHz in Ch and Lisu – **YN17)** Longcheng Lu, Jinshan Zhen, Lufeng Xian, Yunnan 651200. 2225-1230

ZHEJIANG PROVINCE
ZJ1) 111 Moganshan Lu, Hangzhou, Zhejiang 310005 **W:** tv.cztv.com V.O. Zhejiang: on 810kHz/88.0/101.6MHz 24h (exc. Tues 0600-0800) - News Sce. "Xinrui 988": on 1530kHz/98.8MHz 24h - Economic Sce. on 95.0MHz 24h - Private Car First Sce. "V.O. the City": on 107.0MHz 24h - V.O. the Traffic: on 93.0/93.6MHz 24h - Music FM "Dongting (Moving) 968": on 1071kHz/96.8MHz/FM 24h (exc. Tues 0600-0800) - "WiFi Radio": on 930/1050/1314kHz/99.6MHz 24h - Anchorwomen BS: on 603/1251/1521kHz/104.5MHz 24h – **ZJ2)** 888 Zhijiang Lu, Hangzhou, Zhejiang 310016. **W:** radiohz.com "AM 954" (News General Ch): on 954kHz/69.0MHz 2000-1600 - V.O. Hangzhou "News 89": on 89.0MHz 24h – **ZJ2A)** Hangzhou Traffic and Economic Sce, 5 Qingchun Donglu, Hangzhou, Zhejiang 310016. On 91.8MHz 24h – **ZJ3)** City Music "V.O. Xihu", 86 Moganshan Lu, Hangzhou, Zhejiang 310005. On 105.4MHz 24h in Ch and Hangzhou dialect – **ZJ4)** Ningbo Radio and TV Group, 109 Heyi Lu, Ningbo, Zhejiang 315000. News Sce. "V.O. Ningbo": on

1323kHz/92.0MHz 2055-1610. English N: D1600-1610 - "Yangguang (Sunshine) 904": on 1251kHz/90.4MHz 2155-1605 - Economic Sce. "i Radio": on 747kHz/102.9MHz 2100-1600 (exc. Tues 0600-0730) - Traffic Sce. on 603kHz/93.9MHz 24h - Music Sce. "Private Car 986": on 98.6MHz 2300-1600 – **ZJ4A)** 36 Nan Dajie, Zhenhai Qu, Ningbo, Zhejiang 315200. Ningbo Private Car Music St. on 104.7MHz 24h (exc. Mon 0500-0830) - V.O. Yong River: on 100.1MHz – **ZJ5)** Wenzhou Radio and TV Media Group, Xincheng Dadao, Lucheng Qu, Wenzhou, Zhejiang 325027. News Sce. "V.O. Wenzhou": on 666kHz/94.9/102.6MHz 24h (exc. Tues 0600-0900) in Ch and Wenzhou dialect - Economic Life Sce. "Xingyun (Fortunate) 888": on 801kHz/88.8MHz 24h - Traffic Sce. "Automobile FM": on 97.2/103.9MHz 24h - Private Car Music Sce. "i Radio":on 100.3MHz 24h (exc. Tues 0600-0900) - V.O. Green: on 93.8MHz 24h – **ZJ6)** Jiaxing Radio and TV Group, 6 Dongsheng Lu, Jiaxing, Zhejiang 314001. News Sce. on 1107kHz/104.1MHz 2125-1505 - Traffic Sce. on 657kHz/92.2MHz 2130-1505 (exc. Tues 0530-0700) - Life Sce. "Kuaile (Happy) 882" on 88.2MHz 2130-1500 (exc. Tues 0500-0700) – **ZJ7)** Huzhou Radio and TV Headquarters, 628 Xinhua Lu, Huzhou, Zhejiang 313000. News Sce. on 873kHz/105.0MHz 2155-1600 (exc. Tues 0600-0730) - Traffic Sce. on 927/1521kHz/103.5MHz 2155-1600 - Music Sce. on 1251kHz/98.5MHz 2200-1600 – **ZJ8)** Shaoxing Radio and TV Headquarters, 508 Yan'an Donglu, Shaoxing, Zhejiang 312000. News General Sce. on 738kHz/93.6MHz 2100-1600 - Traffic Sce. on 94.1MHz 2130-1600 (exc. Tues 0600-0830) - Chinese Opera Sce. on 102.5MHz 2130-0300 - Music Sce. "i Music": on 103.5MHz 2100-1500 (exc. Tues 0600-0900) – **ZJ9)** 238 Renmin Xilu, Jinhua, Zhejiang 321000. News Sce. on 675kHz/104.4MHz 2100-1600 (exc. Tues 0600-0900) - Economic Sce. "Private Car 101": on 101.4MHz 2200-1700 - Traffic Sce. on 94.2MHz 24h – **ZJ10)** Quzhou Radio and TV Headquarters, 35 Nanjie, Quzhou, Zhejiang 324000. News Sce. "V.O. Quzhou": on 711kHz/105.3MHz 2155-1600 (exc. Tues 0500-0725) - Traffic and Music Sce. on 1250kHz/97.5MHz 2200-1700 – **ZJ11)** Zhoushan Radio and TV Headquarters, 137 Changguo Lu, Dinghai Qu, Zhoushan, Zhejiang 316000. News General Ch. "V.O. Dinghai": on 684kHz/99.8MHz 2130-1500 (exc. Tues 0530-0855) - Traffic and Economic Sce. on 1098kHz/97.0MHz 2155-1500 (exc. Tues 0500-0900) - Automobile Music FM "V.O. the City": on 900kHz/91.0/102.6MHz 2155-1500 (exc. Tues 0530-0855) – **ZJ12)** Lishui Radio and TV Headquarters, 2 Huayuan Lu, Liandu Qu, Lishui, Zhejiang 323000. News General Ch. on 711kHz/90.4/96.4MHz 2155-1600 - Traffic and Music Ch. on 106.9MHz 2155-1600 - New Farm Sce. on 88.3MHz 24h – **ZJ13)** Xiaoshan PBS, Nanduan, Yucai Lu, Xiaoshan Qu, Hangzhou, Zhejiang 311200. On 107.9MHz 2155-1400 – **ZJ14)** Xishan, Chengguan, Rui'an, Zhejiang 325200. On 1584kHz/91.0MHz ?-1305 – **ZJ15)** 121 Zhongshan Lu, Jiangshan, Zhejiang 324100 – **ZJ16)** Taizhou PBS, 355 Donghuan Dadao, Jiaojiang Qu, Taizhou, Zhejiang 318000. News Sce. "987 Ch.": on 98.7/87.5MHz 24h - Traffic Sce. on 102.7MHz 24h - Music St. "Easy Radio" on 100.1/104.9MHz 2200-1600

CHRISTMAS ISLAND (Australia)

L.T: UTC +7h — **Pop:** 1,402 — **Pr.L:** English, Malay, Cantonese, Hokkien, Mandarin — **E.C:** 50Hz, 240V — **ITU:** CHR

AUSTRALIAN BROADCASTING CORP. (ABC)
See Australia for details. 24h satellite relay

MW	kHz	Call	kW	Network
	1422	6ABCRN	0.5	R. National
FM	MHz	Call	kW	Network
	97.3	6ABCRN	0.02	R. National
	100.5	6JJJ	0.02	Triple J

Other Stations

FM	MHz	Call	kW	
1)	98.9	6FMS	0.02	Red FM
2)	102.1	6RCI	0.02	R. Christmas Island
2)	105.3	6RCI	0.02	R. Christmas Island
1)	106.9	6FMS	0.04	Red FM

Addresses & other information
1) 24h satellite relay RedFM, Perth WA **W:** redfm.com.au – **2)** Broadcast House, Nursery Road, Drumsite (PO Box 474) Christmas Island WA 6798 ☎ +61 8 9164 8613 📠 +61 9 9164 8615 **E:** 6rci@pulau.cx **W:** facebook.com/6rciradio Local community stn.

COCOS (KEELING) ISLANDS (Australia)

L.T: UTC +6½h — **Pop:** 596 — **Pr.L:** English, Cocos Malay — **E.C:** 50Hz, 220V — **ITU:** ICO

AUSTRALIAN BROADCASTING CORP. (ABC)
See Australia for details. 24h satellite relay

FM	MHz	Call	kW	Network
	102.3	6ABCRR	0.1	ABC Local R. Kimberley

Other Stations

FM	MHz	Call	kW	
1)	96.0	6CKI	0.1	Voice of the Cocos Islands
2)	100.5	6FMS	0.1	Red FM
1)	102.7	6CKI	0.2	Voice of the Cocos Islands

Addresses & other information
1) PO Box 1093, Cocos (Keeling) Islands WA 6799 ☎ +61 8 9162 6700 **E:** 6cki@cki.cc **W:** facebook.com/6cki-voice-of-the-cocos-keeling-islands **Prgr:** 24h with local news 0700 UTC M-F local community stn – **2)** 24h satellite relay from Perth WA **W:** redfm.com.au

COLOMBIA

L.T: UTC -5h — **Pop:** 45 million — **Pr.L:** Spanish — **E.C:** 60Hz, 110V — **ITU:** CLM

MINISTERIO DE TECNOLOGIAS DE LA INFORMACION Y LAS COMUNICACIONES (MINTIC)
✉ Edificio Murillo Toro, Cra 8a entre Calles 12 y 13, Bogotá, DC ☎ +57 1 344 3460 **W:** mintic.gov.co

Call HJ-, ° also on shortwave, ‡ = inactive, rel. = relay, ± = varying freq. The letters preceding the stn number indicate the departamento. Addresses are listed by departamento in alphabetical order. Hr of tr. usually 24h – see address section for variations.

	MW	Call	kHz	kW	Station, location
DC01)	KA	540	10	R. Auténtica Básica, Bogotá
DC02)	HF	550	50	R. Nac. de Colombia, Medellín (Marinilla)
VP01)	R36	550	30	Vida, Mitú (r. 1130)
DC02)	GS	560	10	R. Nac. de Colombia, Tunja
GU01)	PF	560	25/10	LV de la Pampa, Maicao
DC02)	ND	570	100	R. Nac. de Colombia, Bogotá (El Rosal)
VI01)	C61	570	30	Vida, Puerto Carreño
DC02)	HP	580	50/10	R. Nac. de Colombia, Cali
AN01)	CR	590	50	W Radio, Medellín
AT01)	HJ	600	50	R. Libertad, Barranquilla
NA13)	Z95	600	1	LV de los Awas, Ricaurte el Diviso
DC02)	D90	610	50	R. Nac. de Colombia, Riohacha
DC03)	KL	610	30	La Cariñosa, Bogotá
BO01)	VP	620	10	Colmundo, Cartagena
VA01)	EL	620	50/20	Colmundo, Cali
CL01)	FD	630	10	R. Manizales, Manizales
GN01)	E69	‡630	10	LV del Guainía, Puerto Inírida
MA01)	BJ	640	10	RCN, Santa Marta
DC03)	KH	650	50	RCN Antena 2, Bogotá
NS01)	QS	660	25	Colmundo, Cúcuta
VA02)	EZ	660	10	R. Auténtica, Cali
AN02)	PL	670	50	RCN Antena 2, Medellín
SS28)	R33	670	10	R. U.I.S - Universidad Industrial de Santander, Bucaramanga
DC02)	ZO	680	50	R. Nac. de Colombia, Barranquilla
AN56)	Z73	690	1	Emisora Embera Chami y Zenu de la Palma, Apartado
DC04)	CZ	690	35	W Radio, Bogotá (r. 99.9)
VA03)	CX	700	30	W Radio, Cali
AN03)	NX	710	10	R. Red RCN, Medellín
BY14)	YD	710	1	R. La Paz, Paipa
AT01)	AN	720	30	Emisoras Unidas, Barranquilla
QU01)	VO	720	25	Transmisora Quindío, Armenia
CO03)	TJ	730	15	R. Uno, Montería
DC05)	CU	730	10	Melodía Estéreo, Bogotá
CE01)	NS	740	50	R. Guatapurí, Valledupar
NA01)	HB	740	10	Ecos de Pasto, Pasto
AN01)	DK	750	50	Caracol R, Medellín
CS01)	LH	750	5	LV de Yopal, Yopal
AT02)	AJ	760	25	RCN La Radio, Barranquilla
DC03)	JX	770	100	RCN La Radio, Bogotá (r. 93.9)
GU02)	ZW	‡780	30	R. Almirante, Riohacha
NA15)	FV	780	5	R. Viva, Pasto
SS30)	C21	780	10	Antena del Río, Barrancabermeja
VA04)	ZG	780	10	LV del Valle, Cali
AN01)	DC	790	15	Múnera Eastman R, Medellín
T003)	NC	790	1	Ecos del Combeima, Ibagué
QU06)	JH	‡800	1	R. Ciudad Milagro, Armenia
SS01)	BW	800	100	RCN, Bucaramanga
DC04)	CY	810	60	Caracol R, Bogotá (r. 100.9)
B002)	AD	820	10	R. Vigía, Cartagena
VA03)	ED	820	50	Caracol R, Cali
AN01)	DM	830	10	Q'hubo Radio, Medellín
HU01)	KK	840	30	HJKK Sistema INRAI, Neiva

MW	Call	kHz	kW	Station, location	MW	Call	kHz	kW	Station, location
MA02)	BI	840	10	Ondas del Caribe, Santa Marta	DC11)	CG	1070	30	Q'hubo R./R. Santa Fe, Bogotá
VA24)	NA	840	5	R. Robledo, Cartago (r. still on 1580kHz)	AN01)	AX	1080	10	LV de la Nostalgia, Medellín
DC04)	KC	850	35	Candela AM, Bogotá	CL03)	JS	1080	15	R. Uno, La Dorada
CE02)	NJ	860	50	W Radio, Valledupar	C004)	AW	1080	10	LV de Montería, Montería
VA05)	DV	860	10	Voces de Occidente, Buga	ME03)	KT	1080	10	R. Autentica, Villavicencio
AN09)	ZH	870	5	Vida, Medellín	SS06)	MH	1080	10	R. Melodía, Bucaramanga
BY16)	GD	870	1	Em. Reina de Colombia, Chiquinquirá	VA04)	JF	1080	10	R. Eco, Cali
T001)	LA	870	10	Bésame, Ibagué	BO05)	OM	1090	5	Bluradio, Cartagena
CL04)	FH	880	10	R. Regional Independiente, Anserma	BY03)	IH	1090	8	Caracol R, Sogamoso
SS02)	GE	880	20	Caracol R, Bucaramanga	CA02)	IG	1090	10	R. Autentica, Florencia
AT13)	HKO93	890	0.25	R. Ecos de Soledad, Soledad	CL01)	IA	1090	10	W Radio, Manizales (r. 101.7)
DC06)	CE	890	10	R. Continental, Bogotá	NS06)	BC	1090	15	Caracol R, Cúcuta
MA03)	PM	890	20	R. Galeón, Santa Marta	T005)	JB	1090	10	HJKK Sistema INRAI, El Guamo
NS02)	DD	900	10	RCN Fiesta, Cúcuta	AN06)	GQ	1100	5	Transmisora Surandes, Andes
VA04)	EY	900	10	LV de Cali, Cali	AT04)	AT	1100	15	Caracol R, Barranquilla
AN04)	DO	900	10	LV del Rio Grande, Medellín	C005)	MK	1100	5	Emisora Ideal, Planeta Rica
BY12)	TT	910	1	Ondas del Porvenir, Samacá	DC27)	CN	1100	10	BBN R, Bogotá
DC24)	S52	910	15	Colombia Estereo, Florencia	HU04)	YZ	1100	15	La FM, Neiva
GU02)	C84	910	20	Vida, Puerto Inírida	SS07)	GI	1100	1	LV de Colombia, Socorro
IS01)	MY	910	30	RCN, San Andrés (rel. 770 Bogotá)	AN07)	DI	1110	9	R. Bolivariana, Medellín
BO03)	AA	920	10	Em. Fuentes, Cartagena	AR02)	GP	1110	5	LV del Río Arauca, Arauca
NA02)	JN	920	10	Ondas del Mayo, Pasto	IS02)	PA	‡1110	1	LV de las Islas, San Andrés
TO02)	SJ	920	10	Colmundo, Ibagué	ME04)	JP	1110	10	RCN, Villavicencio
DC07)	CS	930	10	LV de Bogotá, Bogotá	SU02)	ZE	1110	15	R. Piragua, Sincelejo
AN59)	A76	940	5	Frecuencia U, Medellín	VA03)	EW	1110	10	Q'hubo Radio, Cali
NS03)	TL	940	25	RCN, Cúcuta	BY04)	KQ	1120	10	Caracol, Tunja
VA04)	GB	940	10	R. Calima, Cali	DC24)	Q92	1120	5	Colombia Mía, Yopal, CS
BY18)	UJ	950	5	Armonias Boyacenses, Tunja	NS01)	TI	1120	10	Vox Dei, Cúcuta
RI01)	FN	950	15	Caracol R, Pereira	RI03)	JC	1120	5	Vida, Pereira
BO08)	HN	960	10	Caracol R, Magangué	SS02)	GH	1120	15	Q'hubo R, Bucaramanga
IS05)	R31	960	15	Candela, San Andrés: (r. 101.9 Bogotá)	AT07)	AC	1130	10	Em. Riomar, Barranquilla
SS23)	HX	960	5	Bluradio, Bogotá	BO06)	NN	‡1130	1	Ondas del Río, Magangué
CA01)	VK	970	10	Armonias del Caquetá, Florencia	DC09)	VA	1130	15	Vida, Bogotá
DC08)	CI	970	10	R. Red RCN, Bogotá	NA05)	QQ	1130	10	Oxígeno, Pasto
GU03)	ME	‡970	10	RCN Guajira, Maicao	AN02)	DL	1140	10	R. Paisa/La Cariñosa, Medellín
QU09)	HKX59	970	1	Ecos del Cacique, Calarca	BO07)	KO	1140	10	R. Esperanza, Cartagena
NS04)	JV	980	15	Oxígeno, Cúcuta (r. 89.7)	CC12)		1140		R. Piendamo, Piendamo
VA06)	ES	980	100	RCN, Cali	CU01)	CL	1140	10	R. Panamericana, Girardot
AN02)	CH	990	50	RCN, Medellín	ME05)	E67	1140	10	Caracol R, Villavicencio
BY07)	HI	990	5	LV de Garagoa, Garagoa	SS08)	RN	1140	10	RCN, Barbosa
BO04)	AQ	1000	15	RCN, Cartagena	BY05)	GJ	1150	10	W Radio, Duitama
DC02)	JG	1000	10	R. Nac. de Colombia, Manizales	CH01)	TE	‡1150	1	LV del Chocó, Quibdó
GV01)	Q98	1000	20	Vida, San José del Guaviare (r. 1130)	HU05)	FP	1150	10	RCN, Neiva
AT04)	OP	1010	10	W Radio, Barranquilla (r. 97.6)	NS07)	BT	1150	10	R. Catatumbo, Ocaña
C001)	ZD	1010	15	R. Zenzú, Montería	QU03)	FI	1150	15	Caracol R, Armenia
DC04)	CC	1010	10	Acuario Estéreo, Bogotá	AT01)	BL	1160	10	R. Aeropuerto, Barranquilla
HU02)	JR	1010	15	Caracol R, Neiva	CA03)	AU	1160	15	Ondas del Orteguaza, Florencia
NA03)	BN	1010	10/5	LV del Galeras, Pasto	C006)	AZ	1160	5	Frecuencia Bolivariana, Montería
SS03)	IX	1010	10	R. Yarima, Barrancabermeja	DC13)	OC	1160	10	Fuego AM, Bogotá
AN04)	DQ	1020	10	Emisora Claridad, Medellín	NA06)	ZV	1160	5	RCN R. Las Lajas, Ipiales
ME01)	KS	1020	10	LV del Llano, Villavicencio	NS08)	EC	1160	10	R. San José de Cúcuta, Cúcuta
RI02)	FQ	1020	10	RCN, Pereira	SS09)	S31	1160	10	Colombia Mía, Barrancabermeja
SS04)	DZ	1020	15	R. Primavera, Bucaramanga	VA04)	EV	1160	10	R. Unica, Cali
T003)	FT	1020	10	La FM, Ibagué	AN04)	FW	1170	10	R. Nutibara, Medellín
BY01)	DJ	1030	10	La Cariñosa/Antena 2, Duitama	AR04)	E74	1170	10	Meridiano 70, Arauca
CE03)	RF	1030	10	Ondas del Cesar, Aguachica	BO08)	NW	1170	10	Caracol R, Cartagena
C002)	GX	1030	1	CARACOL, Lorica	BY04)	GA	1170	10	Vida, Tunja
VA06)	DT	1030	30	RCN Antena 2, Cali	CE06)	PB	‡1170	10	Ondas de Macondo, Valledupar
VP02)		1030	5	Ondas del Vaupés, Mitú	ME01)	BX	1170	10	Ondas del Meta, Villavicencio
AT01)	AI	1040	15	R. Tropical, Barranquilla	VA08)	JE	1170	1	RCN, Tuluá
CC02)	SY	1040	10	R. 1040/La Caucana 10-40, Popayán	AN08)		1180		Em. Coorpurabá, Apartadó
DC10)	CJ	1040	15	Colmundo, Bogotá	CL05)	FX	1180	15	Caracol R, Manizales
NA04)	UB	1040	15	Colmundo, Pasto	GV02)	WA	°1180	10	LV del Guaviare, San José del Guaviare
NS05)	BF	1040	15	LV del Norte, Cúcuta	SS10)	GK	1180	20	R. Santander 2, Bucaramanga
QU02)	FM	1040	15	LV de Armenia, Armenia	T006)	JT	1180	10/5	RCN, Ibagué
AN04)	DR	1050	10	R. Unica, Medellín	AT05)	CT	1190	10	LV de la Costa, Barranquilla
AR01)	E73	1050	10	LV del Cinaruco/Caracol, Arauca	DC07)	CV	1190	10	R. Cordillera, Bogotá
CE04)	BB	1050	10	Caracol R, Valledupar	NA07)	KG	1190	10	R. Mira, Tumaco
C004)	AW	1050	10	RCN La Radio, Montería	VA09)	EO	‡1190	15	Ondas del Valle, Cartago
CS03)	S62	1050	15	Cusiana R., Yopal	GU05)		1195		Ondas del Ranchería, Barrancas
ME02)	IO	1050	5	LV de la Conquista, Granada	AN49)	IJ	1200	10	R. 1200 "LV de la Raza", Medellín
SS05)	GU	1050	10	R. Bucarica, Bucaramanga	BO17)	BV	‡1200	10	R. Príncipe, Cartagena
T004)	FZ	1050	10	La Cariñosa/Centro, Antena 2, Espinal	BY06)	GC	1200	10	RCN La Radio, Sogamoso
VA07)	NG	1050	5	R. Palmira, Palmira	CU02)	CD	1200	10	Em. Nueva Epoca, Fusagasugá
AN05)	MG	1060	1	R. Litoral, Turbo	GU06)	BZ	1200	10	Ondas del Riohacha, Riohacha
BY02)	MV	1060	10	R. Furatena, Chiquinquirá	VA10)	NF	1200	10	R. Red RCN, Cali
CL02)	FJ	1060	15	RCN Caldas, Manizales	HU02)	FR	1210	10	Oxígeno, Neiva
GU04)	LY	1060	10	R. Delfín, Riohacha	NS03)	E65	1210	10	La Cariñosa, Antena 2, Cúcuta
HU03)	OV	1060	15	R. Surcolombiana, Neiva	RI02)	BQ	1210	10	La Cariñosa, Pereira
SU11)	YX	1060	1	R. Caracolí, Sincelejo	AT01)		1220		Emisora 1220, Barranquilla
AT06)	AH	1070	20	Em. Atlántico, Barranquilla	C007)	AV	1220	10	R. Uno, Montería
CC03)	VR	1070	15	Nueva R. Super, Popayán	DC22)	KR	1220	10	R. María, Bogotá

MW	Call	kHz	kW	Station, location
NA08)	NM	1220	10	R. Viva Cultural Bolívar, Ipiales
SS11)	MT	1220	10	RCN La Radio, San Gil
AN10)	IL	1230	10	Minuto de Dios, Medellín
BY04)	BR	1230	6	Oxígeno, Tunja
CU03)	TP	1230	1	R. Colina, Girardot
GU03)	MJ	‡1230	1	RCN Antena 2, Maicao
SS12)	EH	1230	15	Colmundo, Bucaramanga
VA06)	LK	1230	10	R. Calidad "La Cariñosa", Cali
AR03)	GO	‡1240	1	R. Caribabare, Saravena
QU04)	FG	1240	10	RCN, Calarcá
SS13)	GN	1240	5	R. Barrancabermeja, Barrancabermeja
VA11)	JA	1240	3	R. Buenaventura, Buenaventura
AT07)	OK	1250	10	Em. ABC, Barranquilla
DC14)	CA	1250	10	Capital Radio, Bogotá
NS06)	HS	1250	15	W Radio, Cúcuta (r. 99.9)
SU03)	EM	1250	1	LV de Corozal, Corozal
AM01)	OU	1260	2	Ondas del Amazonas, Leticia
AN11)	DA	1260	5	R. Auténtica, Medellín
BY05)	NO	1260	5	Oxígeno, Duitama
CE08)	OH	1260	5	RCN Cesar, Valledupar
IS03)	HU	1260	1	Caracol R, San Andrés (rel 810 Bogotá)
ME06)	LX	1260	5	Minuto de Dios Eco Llanero, Villavicencio
NS10)	TM	1260	5	R. Sonar, Ocaña
TO07)	CO	1260	5	Caracol R, Ibagué
VA28)	ET	1260	5	R. María, Cali
BO04)	AR	1270	2	La Cariñosa, Cartagena
CE05)	KJ	1270	1.5	LV de Curumaní, Curumaní
CU04)	XQ	1270	1	Vida, Ubaté
DC24)	Q99	1270	5	Colombia Mía, San José del Guaviare
PU01)	SV	1270	1	LV de Orito, Orito
RI05)	IM	1270	1	Colmundo, Pereira
SS02)	TX	1270	5	Bésame, Bucaramanga
TO12)	BM	1270	5	R. Internacional, Honda
AN12)	MB	1280	5	R. Suroeste, Concordia
AT01)	SO	1280	5	R. Playa Mendoza, Barranquilla
DC07)	KN	1280	5	R. Única, Bogotá
GU07)	HO	1280	5	Impacto Popular, San Juan del Cesar
HU06)	CM	1280	5	HJKK Sistema INRAI, Pitalito
NA05)	LR	1280	5	Caracol R, Pasto
NS11)	RP	1280	5	Ecos de Tibú, Tibú
SS14)	NQ	1280	1	LV del Río Saravena, Barbosa
VA12)	TK	‡1280	5	R. Ciudad Centinela, Caicedonia
AN13)	TH	1290	5	LV de las Estrellas, Medellín
DC24)	SZ	1290	5	Colombia Mía, Saravena, AR
CU05)	KY	1290	5	RCN, Girardot
MA04)	EB	1290	5	LV del Turismo, Santa Marta
ME07)	NE	1290	5	LV del Ariari, Granada
SU04)	OI	1290	5	R. Chacurí, Sampués
VA13)	MC	1290	5	R. Viva 12-90, Cali
BO10)	OG	1300	5	LV de las Antillas, Cartagena
BY08)	RB	1300	5	CRB Cadena Radial Boyacense, Tunja
CC04)	IN	1300	5	R. Eucha, Belalcázar
PU02)	UA	1300	5	R. Sindamanoy, Mocoa
RI01)	LD	1300	5	Q'hubo Radio, Pereira
SS02)	NB	1300	5	Onda 5, Bucaramanga
TO08)	EA	1300	5	R. Lumbí, Mariquita
AN14)	LM	1310	5	R. Santa Bárbara
AN15)	IR	1310	5	RCN Urabá, Apartadó
AT08)	AK	1310	5	LV de la Patria Celestial, Barranquilla
CO08)	DG	1310	5	Caracol R, Montería
DC20)	JZ	1310	5	Aviva 2, Bogotá
HU07)	WD	1310	5	Micrófono Cívico, Palermo
NS12)	TQ	1310	5	G12 Radio, Cúcuta (r. 1550)
AN16)	TA	1320	5	R. María, Medellín
BY09)	HT	1320	5	R. Guateque, Guateque
CU06)	NV	1320	5	La Cariñosa, Girardot
IS04)	QI	‡1320	10	R. Leda Int., San Andrés
MA05)	LV	1320	5	R. Onda Fantastica, Fundación
SS15)	MS	1320	5	RCN La Radio, Barrancabermeja
VA14)	NK	1320	1	R. Luna, Palmira
AN17)	RD	1330	1	R. Fénix de Oriente 1330 AM, El Peñol
BO02)	AP	1330	5	R. Auténtica, Cartagena
CE09)	MP	1330	1	LV de Aguachica, Aguachica (nighttime rel. R. María)
CC05)	LS	1330	5	Caracol R, Popayán
CL17)	HKR33	1330	0.25	Alcaldía de Salamina, Salamina
RI02)	FE	1330	1	Antena 2, Pereira
SS16)	NR	1330	5	La Caliente 13-30, San Gil
AN18)	NP	1340	1	R. Comunal, Nariño
AT03)	FA	1340	5	R. Alegre, Barranquilla
DC03)	FB	1340	5	Amor Estereo, Bogotá (r. 96.3)
HU05)	KD	1340	5	La Cariñosa/Antena 2, Neiva

MW	Call	kHz	kW	Station, location
NA10)	HA	1340	5	RCN Nariño, Pasto
NS04)	PY	1340	5	R. Lemas, Cúcuta
NS13)	VL	1340	0.5	Brisas del Catatumbo, Tibú
SS05)	NY	1340	4	R. Unica, Bucaramanga
SU05)	HY	1340	5	RCN Sucre, Sincelejo
VA15)	IS	1340	5	R. El Sol, Buenaventura
AN19)	DS	1350	5	Ondas de la Montaña, Medellín
AN20)	LO	1350	5	RCN Antena 2/La Cariñosa, Caucasia
BY10)	HW	‡1350	1	Em. Ecos del Río, Puerto Boyacá
CE10)	MN	1350	1	R. Perijá, Codazzi
MA01)	OA	1350	5	R. Uno, Santa Marta
TO09)	HL	1350	5	Oxígeno, Ibagué
VA16)	EN	1350	5	R. Armonía, Cali
AN21)	PK	1360	10/5	LV de Abejorral, Abejorral
AN22)		1360	0.5	R. Segovia, Segovia
BO08)	UO	1360	5	Oxígeno, Cartagena
RI06)	RA	1360	5	Ecos 13-60 Radio, Pereira
SS17)	KV	1360	1	R. Láser, Zapatoca
TO18)	MI	1360	5	R. Auténtica, Melgar
AN23)	NU	1370	2.5	RCN, Rionegro
AT09)	BO	1370	5	Minuto de Dios, Barranquilla
CC06)	EQ	1370	5	RCN Cauca, Popayán: 24h
DC01)	KI	1370	5	R. Mundial, Bogotá
NS15)	BD	1370	1	R. Guaimaral, Cúcuta
SU14)	NI	1370	1	R. Sabana, Sincelejo
VA17)	JQ	‡1370	1	RCN Antena 2, Zarzal
AN57)	JD	1380	3	NSE Radio, Medellín
BY11)	EE	1380	5	RCN, Tunja
CE13)	MM	1380	5	Vida, Valledupar
CE06)	LG	1380	3	LV de La Dorada, La Dorada
HU08)	ID	1380	5	R. Potencia Latina, La Plata
VA18)	EJ	1380	1	Armonías del Palmar, Palmira
CL07)	FO	1390	1	Red de los Andes, La Voz de Siempre, Manizales
CU07)	YW	1390	5	R. Auténtica, Pacho
SS18)	ZY	1390	1	La Primera, Bucaramanga (nights r. R. María)
TO10)	FY	1390	5	Oxígeno R. Avendia, Espinal
AN26)	LL	1400	1	RCN Antena 2, Santa Bárbara
AT02)	AS	1400	1	RCN Antena 2, Barranquilla
CC07)	WY	1400	1	LV de los Samanes: Quilichao
CC13)		1400	0.45	R. Cañaveral, Morales
CH02)	ER	1400	1	Ecos del Atrato, Quibdó
CO09)		1400	0.25	Brisas del Sinú, Tierralta
CO10)	DF	‡1400	5	LV de Niquel, Montelíbano
DC16)	KM	1400	5	Em. Mariana, Bogotá
NA11)	JJ	1400	1	R. Ipiales, Ipiales
NA12)		1400	1.5	LV de Samaniego, Samaniego
NS16)	BK	1400	1	LV de la Gran Colombia, Cúcuta
QU04)	HM	1400	5	La Cariñosa de Armenia, Calarcá
SS19)	D31	1400	1	LV de Cimitarra, Cimitarra
SU12)	HKZ25	1400	0.25	Alcaldía de Ovejas, Ovejas
SU13)	HKZ22	1400	0.25	Alcaldía de Majagual, Majagual
AN27)	DU	1410	5	Em. Cultural Univ. de Antioquia, Medellín
BY17)	HKP79	1410	1	R. Universidad, Tunja
BY21)	HKP86	1410	0.25	Alcaldía de Chiquinquira, Chiquinquira
GU08)	P79	1410	2	R. Evangélica, Uribia
SS20)	TY	1410	1	LV del Carare, Vélez
TO11)	FS	‡1410	5	RCN, Honda
VA19)	EI	1410	5	R. Guadalajara, Buga
AN28)	D23	1420	1	Ecos de Frontino, Frontino
CL05)	HK	1420	5	Vida, Manizales
MA06)	BH	1420	5	R. Magdalena, Santa Marta
SS21)	SN	1420	2	R. Lenguerque, Zapatoca
TO06)	LE	1420	1	La Cariñosa, Antena 2, Ibagué
AN29)	CK	1430	1	R. Sensación, Yarumal
AN30)	MF	1430	5	La Ribereña, Puerto Berrío
AN47)	G42	1430	0.5	R. Alejandría, Alejandría
AT10)	PW	1430	5	Colmundo, Barranquilla
CC08)	EG	‡1430	1	LV de Belalcázar, Popayán
CL08)	IU	‡1430	1	Armonías del Ingrumá, Riosucio
DC17)	KU	1430	5	Uniminuto R., Bogotá
NS17)	BP	1430	2	R. Cariongo, Pamplona
PU03)	HKK38	1430	0.5	R. Manantial, Sibundoy
QU08)	X61	1430	0.25	L U FM Estéreo, Armenia
RI08)	HKX73	1430	1	R. Ciudad de Pereira, Pereira
SU07)	QX	1430	5	R. Majagual, Sincelejo
AN46)	NZ	1440	5	Colmundo, Medellín
BY06)	GM	1440	5	RCN Fiesta, Sogamoso
CA04)	IB	1440	5	R. Uno, Florencia
CU19)	HKT58	1440	0.25	Alcaldía de Ubala, Ubala
VA20)	EK	‡1440	5	Caracol R, Tuluá
AN31)	E20	1450	1	R. María, Urrao

MW	Call	kHz	kW	Station, location
BO11)	MX	‡1450	1	R. Mancomoján, Carmen de Bolívar
CC09)		1450	0.5	LV del Cauca, El Bordo
CL02)	NL	1450	5	La Cariñosa, Manizales
SS22)	HH	1450	5	R. Católica Metropolitana, Bucaramanga
TO13)	BY	1450	5	Olímpica, Flandes
AN33)	TN	1450	5	R. María, Turbo
AN34)	MU	1460	1	LV de Amalfi "La Primera", Amalfi
AN45)	E26	1460	1	R. Capiro, La Ceja
AT02)	VH	1460	5	R. Uno, Barranquilla
CL18)	HKR44	1460	1	Alcaldía de Victoria, Victoria
DC18)	JW	1460	5	Em. Nuevo Continente, Bogotá
HU09)	FL	1460	1	Agustiniana Minuto de Dios, San Agustín
NA10)	ZU	1460	5	La Cariñosa, Pasto
NS18)	IW	1460	1	R. Monumental, Cúcuta
SS29)	HKY73	‡1460	0.25	Alcaldía de San Andrés, San Andrés
SU08)	AL	1460	1	R. Sincelejo, Sincelejo
AN04)	Il	1470	5	R. Popular, Medellín
AT14)	HKO96	1470	1	Alcaldía de Baranoa, Baranoa
BO12)	PX	1470	5	Colmundo, Cartagena
BY13)	HJB63	1470	1	R. Uno, Iza
CU09)	HQ	1470	5	R. Futurama, Pacho
PU04)	JIF	‡1470	1	R. Tres Fronteras, Puerto Asís
TO14)	TB	1470	5	Ondas de Ibagué, Ibagué
TO21)	JS20	1470	0.25	Ecos de Palo Cabildo, Palo Cabildo
VA26)	NT	1470	1	R. Huellas, Cali
AN35)	TC	1480	1	R. Sonsón, Sonsón (n.f.1490)
MA07)	OD	1480	5	R. Rodadero, Santa Marta
RI03)	FC	1480	5	R. Matecaña/R. Única, Pereira
SS10)	TZ	1480	1	RCN Antena 2, Bucaramanga
AT11)	AY	1490	5	R. Vida Nueva "Te acerca a Dios", Barranquilla
BO14)	J76	1490	0.2	Alcaldía de El Peñon, El Peñon
DC19)	BS	1490	4	Em. Punto Cinco, Bogotá
HU10)	E62	±1490	1	R. Garzón, Garzón
NA18)	HKW24	1490	0.2	Alcaldía de Guaitarilla, Guaitarilla
SU09)	JO	1490	1	LV de San Marcos, San Marcos
VA21)	ZB	1490	5	Robles 14-90, La Nueva, Tuluá
CL09)	UW	1500	5	R. María, Manizales
CU10)	TW	1500	5	Kirios R, Fusagasugá
CU16)	HKT71	1500	1	Macheta
VA22)	IJ	1500	5	Sonora, La Voz de la Red, Cali
AN37)	D24	1510	5	LV de La Unión, La Unión
BY15)	A22	1510	1	LV de San Luis, San Luis de Gaceno
DC24)	HKY41	1510	1	Colombia Mía, Barrancabermeja, SS
QU07)	ZA	1510	1	R. Cristal, Armenia
SS23)	HX	1510	1	Candela AM, Bucaramanga
VA29)	HKZ94	1510	1	Alcaldía de Buenaventura, Buenaventura
VA30)	HKZ93	1510	1	Alcaldía de Versalles, Versalles
AN38)		1520	0.3	Brisas del Palmar, Caucasia
AN39)	MA	1520	1	LV de Suroeste, Jericó
AT03)	LQ	1520	5	R. Minuto, Barranquilla
CC11)	HKS24	1520	0.5	R. Cristalares Timbío, Timbío
CL10)		1520		Sonoradio 1520 AM, Viterbo
CO12)	HKT20	1520	5	Alcaldía de Montería, Montería
DC09)	LI	1520	5	Libertad, Bogotá
DC24)	T21	1520	0.25	Colombia Mía, Tierralta, CO
NA16)	HKW37	1520	1	R. Universidad, Pasto
NA19)	HKW43	1520	0.1	Alcaldía de Tangua, Tangua
NS19)	J98	1520	1	Em. Una Voz de la Frontera, Puerto Santander
RI07)	RL	1520	1	Antena de los Andes, Santa Rosa de Cabal
SU10)	MZ	1520	1	Ecos de la Sierra Flor, Sincelejo
TO17)	AM	±1520	1	R. Altamizal, Dolores
AN58)	DN	1530	5	Yeshu'a LV de Jesucristo, Medellín
AN50)	HKN57	1530	0.25	Alcaldía de San Juan de Uraba, San Juan de Uraba
AN53)	HKN85	1530	0.25	Alcaldía de Anza, Anza
AN55)	HKN79	1530	0.25	Alcaldía de Uramita, Uramita
CE11)	HKS56	1530		Fascinación AM, Becerril
CE15)	HKS58	1530	0.1	Alcaldía de El Copey, El Copey
CC14)		1530		R. Integración, Morales
DC24)	HKN65	1530	0.25	Colombia Mía, Caucasia, AN
GU09)	OZ	1530	5	LV de la Prov. de Padilla, San Juan del Cesar
ME10)	HKV82°	1530	1	Alcaraván Radio, Puerto Lleras
VA23)	EU	1530	1	Caracol Sevilla, Sevilla
VA25)	HKR73	1530	1	Ecos del Pacífico, Guapí
AN41)	A26	1540	1	Em. Brisas del Río Chico, Belmira
BO15)	HKP50	1540	0.25	Alcaldía de Arjona, Arjona
CL11)	ZF	1540	5	R. Cóndor, Manizales
CS02)	HKR80	1540	0.15	Alcaldía de Sacama, Sacama
DC24)	HKZ52	1540	1	Colombia Mía, Chaparral, TO
NA09)	RQ	1540	2	R. Austral, Túquerres

MW	Call	kHz	kW	Station, location
SS25)	HD	1540	1	LV del Petróleo, Barrancabermeja
AT02)	CB	1550	5	R. El Sol "La Cariñosa", Barranquilla
CL16)	UN	‡1550	5	LV del Río Arma, Aguadas
DC21)	ZI	1550	5	G12 Radio, Bogotá
DC24)	HKV38	1550	1	Colombia Mía, Pitalito, HU
DC24)	HKX29	1550	5	Colombia Mía, Tibú, NS
NA20)	HKW53	1550	0.1	Alcaldía de El Tablón, El Tablón
NA21)	HKW55	1550	0.1	Alcaldía de Guachucal, Guachucal
NA22)	HKW50	1550	0.25	Alcaldía de Mallama, Mallama
QU03)	QD	1550	5	Vida, Calarcá
VA31)	LT	1550	5	Em. Revivir en Cristo, Cali
AN52)	XZ	1560	5	Santa María de la Paz R., Medellín
AN54)	HKO35	1560	0.25	Alcaldía de Cañasgordas, Cañasgordas
CE07)	HKS65	1560	0.5	R. Tamalameque, Tamalameque
CE14)	PZ	‡1560	1	R. Codazzi, Codazzi
CU11)	CP	‡1560	5	RCN Antena 2, Arbelaez
ME11)	HKV90	1560	0.25	Alcaldía de Villavicencio, Villavicencio
SS26)	HE	1560	1	Voces Rovirenses, Málaga
VA08)	LP	1560	5	La Cariñosa, Antena 2, Tuluá
AN43)	HK022	1570	1	R. Ciudad Dabeiba, Dabeiba
BO16)	HKP58	1570	0.25	Alcaldía de Sta Rosa Sur, Sta Rosa Sur
BY22)	HKO83	1570	0.25	Alcaldía de Maripi, Maripi
BY23)	HKO82	1570	0.25	Alcaldía de Sta María, Sta María
CA05)	HKR66	1570	0.2	R. Universidad de la Amazonia, Florencia
CA26)	HJR66	1570	0.5	Timbiquí Estéreo, Timbiquí
CL12)	E70	1570	1	R. Auténtica, Manizales
CU18)	HKU42	1570	0.15	Alcaldía de Cajica, Cajica
DC22)	TG	1570	1	R. María, Machetá
DC24)	E96	1570	1	Colombia Mía, Palmira, VA
DC24)	HKX52	1570	2	Arc. Armada de Colombia, Pto Leguizamo
RI09)	HKX80	1570	0.1	R. Marsella, Marsella
RI11)	HKX78	1570	0.25	Alcaldía de Balboa, Balboa
AT12)	QZ	1580	5	R. María, Barranquilla
CC16)	HKS46	1580	0.15	R. Alcaldía de Padilla, Padilla
CO11)	HKT34	1580	0.25	Alcaldía de San Antero, San Antero
CU17)	HKU42	1580	0.25	Alcaldía de Cajica, Cajica
DC25)	QT	1580	5	Verdad R, Bogotá
HU11)		1580		Alcaldía de Yaguará, Yaguará
MA08)	LC	1580	1	LV del Banco, El Banco
NA23)	HKW74	1580	0.1	Alcaldía de Pupiales, Pupiales
NS20)	KB	‡1580	1	R. Zulima, Villa del Rosario
SU01)	RM	1580	5	Caracol R, Sincelejo
TO19)	E66	1580	1	Celestial 15-80, Rovira
AN44)	IP	1590	5	BBN 15-90 R., Envigado
CE16)	HKS72	1590		Alcaldía de La Gloria, La Gloria
CL13)	QM	‡1590	1	Ecos de la Miel, Samaná
SS27)	WB	1590	5	Em Nuestra Sra del Socorro, Socorro
AN51)	HKO63	1600	0.25	Alcaldía de Jardín, Jardín
CL15)	HKR52	1600	0.25	LV de Colina, Risaralda
CO13)	HKT39	1600	0.25	Alcaldía de Valencia, Valencia
CU13)	HV	1600	5	Emisora Armoniaz, Zipaquirá
DC24)	HJO72	‡1600	5	Colombia Mía, Carepa, AN
RI12)	HKX83	1600	0.25	Alcaldía de La Celia, Celia
TO20)	HKZ79	1600	0.15	Alcaldía de Cajamarca, Cajamarca
TO22)	HKZ77	1600	0.15	Alcaldía de Venadillo, Venadillo
VA27)	F33	1600	0.25	R. Restauración, Cali

SW	Call	kHz	kW	Name and h of tr
DC26)	DH	†5910	5	Alcaraván R, Pto Lleras: 2300-1000 (r. 1530)
DC26)	DH	6010	5	LV de tu Conciencia, Pto Lleras: 2300-1000
GV02)	OY	‡6035	5	LV del Guaviare,S. José del G: 1000-0300

Major Networks:

RADIO NACIONAL DE COLOMBIA (Pub.)
✉ Av. El Dorado Cr. 45 # 26 - 33 Bogotá, D.C. ☎ +571 2200727 🖷 +571 2200700/230 **W:** radionacional.co **E:** info@rtvc.gov.co

CARACOL (Primera Cadena Radial Colombiana)
✉ Calle 67 N° 7-37, Bogotá, DC ☎ +57 1 348 7600 🖷 +57 1 337 7126
W: caracol.com.co **E:** caracolcolombia@caracol.com.co

RCN (Radio Cadena Nacional)
✉ Cra. 13A N° 37-32, Bogotá, DC ☎ +57 1 314 7070 🖷 +57 1 314 7070 **W:** rcnmundo.com
All "La Cariñosa" stations relay sport trs regularly from Antena 2.

TODELAR (Circuito Todelar de Colombia)
✉ Ap. 27344 (Av. Cra 20, N° 83-64), Bogotá, DC ☎ +57 1 621 6621 🖷 +57 1 616 0056 **W:** todelar.com **E:** todelar@telesat.com.co

COLMUNDO
✉ Diagonal 58 N° 26A-29, Bogotá, DC ☎ +57 1 217 8911 🖷 +57 1 348 2746 **W:** colmundoradio.com.co **E:** correo@colmundoradio.com

SISTEMA VIDA INTERNACIONAL (Rlg.)
✉ Avenida Calle 13 No 79-70, Bogotá, DC ☎ +57 1 294 8300
W: sistemavida.net

CADENA RADIAL AUTENTICA DE COLOMBIA (Rlg.)
✉ Ap. 18350, (Calle 32 N° 16-12), Bogotá, DC. Carrera 38D # 1-52, Barrio Santa Isabel, Cali ☎ +57 1 285 3360 🖷 +57 1 285 2505 **W:** cmbflorestacali.org

State abbreviations: (Departamentos) AM = Amazonas, AN = Antioquia, AR = Arauca, AT = Atlántico, BO = Bolívar, BY = Boyacá, CA = Caquetá, CC = Cauca, CE = Cesar, CH = Chocó, CL = Caldas, CO = Córdoba, CS = Casanare, CU = Cundinamarca, DC = Distrito Capital, GN = Guainía, GU = Guajira, GV = Guaviare, HU = Huila, IS = Islas San Andrés y Providencia, MA = Magdalena, ME = Meta, NA = Nariño, NS = Norte de Santander, PU = Putumayo, QU = Quindío, RI = Risaralda, SS = Santander del Sur, SU = Sucre, TO = Todelar, VA = Valle del Cauca, VI = Vichada, VP = Vaupés.
N.B: These abbreviations are not officially recognized by the Colombian Post Office. Letters should therefore carry full name.

Addresses and other information:
AM00) AMAZONAS
AM01) Cra. 6A N° 10-104 (or Ap. 236), Leticia 1100-0500.
AN00) ANTIOQUIA
AN01) Cra. 79A No. 39-63, Medellín. **W:** radiomunera.com qhuboradio. com – **AN02)** Edificio Coltejer, Calle 52 #47-42, Medellín - 1100-0500 **W:** rcnmundo.com/radiopaisa – **AN03)** Calle 50 Colomb N° 67-141, Medellín **W:** radiored.com.co – **AN04)** Av.13 N° 84-42 (or Ap. 1431), Medellín – **AN05)** Cra. 19 N° 20-66, Turbo – **AN06)** Ap. 1431, Andes - 1000-0200 – **AN07)** Circular 1a N° 70-01, Bloque 6, P7 U.P.B. Laureles, Medellín. **W:** radiobolivarianavirtual.com - **FM:** 92.4MHz – **AN08)** Apartadó. – **AN09)** Cra. 77B N° 48-144, Medellín **W:** vidaam.comco – **AN10)** Calle 56 N° 41-57, Medellín. **W:** rccradio.fm/minutodedios – **AN11)** Calle 41 N° 80B-46, P2, Medellín – **AN12)** Cra. 3 Calles 2 y 3, Concordia – **AN13)** Ap. 4300, Medellín – **AN14)** Cra. 51 N° 51-38 (or Ap. 3854) , Medellín - 1000-0500 – **AN15)** Calle 94 N° 99-51, Apartadó – **AN16)** Calle 50 N° 67-141 (or Ap. 65103), Medellín – **AN17)** Centro Cooperativo, Parque Principal, El Peñol – **AN18)** Cra. 11 N° 10-34, Nariño - 1100-0100 – **AN19)** Calle 44 N° 94-15, P3, Medellín. **W:** ondasdelamontana.net – **AN20)** Cra. 2 N° 21-54, Caucasia – **AN21)** Cra. 51 N° 50-09, Abejorral - 0900-0500 – **AN22)** Segovia - 1100-0300 – **AN23)** Cra. 51 N° 49-09, Rionegro – **AN24)** Calle 48B N° 79-38, Medellín – **AN26)** Cra. Bolívar, Calle López, Santa Bárbara – **AN27)** Ap. 1226 (or Cra. 44 N° 48-72), Medellín - 1100-0500 **W:** emisora.udea.edu. co - **FM:** 101.9MHz – **AN28)** Cra. 32 N° 30-05, Frontino – **AN29)** Cra. 20 N° 20-21, Yarumal – **AN30)** Calle 6 N° 1-23, Puerto Berrio – **AN31)** Urrao - 0900-0300 – **AN33)** Ap. 1289, Medellín - 1000-0400 – **AN34)** Cra. 19 Restrepo N° 19-61, Amalfi - 1000-0300 **W:** lavozdeamalfi.com - **FM:** 103.9MHz – **AN35)** Calle 8 N° 6-60, Sonsón – **AN37)** Calle 10 N° 9-37, La Unión (or Ap. 4897, Medellín) - 1000-0200 **E:** emivozunion@ epm.net.co – **AN38)** Batallón de Infantería N° 29 "Rifles", Barrio El Palmar, Caucasia - 1130-0400 – **AN39)** Calle 7, Cras. 3 y 4, Jericó - 1000-0500 – **AN41)** Cra. 20 N° 20-14, Belmira – **AN43)** Edif.Restrepo, P3, Plaza Principal, Dabeiba - 0900-0300 – **AN44)** Ap. 81095 (or Cra. 44A N° 31 Sur-16,Barrio San Marcos, Medellín), Envigado – **AN45)** Calle 20 N° 27-20, La Ceja - 1100-0300 (Sun -0100) **W:** radiocapiro. jimdo.com – **AN46)** Cra. 80 N° 46-74, Medellín. **E:** mpecolmundo@ gmail.com - 1100-0600 – **AN47)** Junta de Acción, Comunal Central, Alejandría – **AN49)** Cra.73 N° 47-35, Medellín – **AN50)** Palacio Municipal de San Juan de Uraba, San Juan de Uraba – **AN51)** Palacio Municipal de Jardín, Jardín – **AN52)** Calle 10 N° 42-22, Medellín **W:** santamariadelapaz.org – **AN53)** Palacio Municipal de Anza, Anza – **AN54)** Palacio Municipal de Cañasgordas – **AN55)** Palacio Municipal de Uramita, Uramita – **AN56)** Calle 105F No. 51-16, Barrio 20 de Enero, Apartadó – **AN57)** Calle 43 No. 67a-16, Barrio San Joaquín, Medellín. **W:** nseradio.com – **AN58)** Cra 81A No. 48-B – 71, Barrio Calasanz, Medellín – **AN59)** Cra 87 No. 65, Univ. de Medellín, Medellín. **W:** webapps.udem.edu.co/FrecuenciaU
AR00) ARAUCA
AR01) Calle 19 N° 19-62 P2, Arauca – **AR02)** Cra. 20 N° 19-09, P5, Arauca (or Ap. 16555, Bogotá) – **AR03)** Calle 20, Cra. 27 (or Ap. 6558), Saravena – **AR04)** Cra 20 N° 17-57, P3, Arauca **W:** meridiano70.net
AT00) ATLÁNTICO
AT01) Cra. 53 N° 55-166,Edificio Diario La Libertad, Barranquilla. **W:** cadenaradiallibertad.com.co – **AT02)** Cr 52 84-78 Alto Prado, Barranquilla **W:** radiouno.com.co - 1000-0300 – **AT03)** Calle 82 N° 42H-54, 2do piso, Barranquilla - 1000-0400 **W:** radiominuto.org – **AT04)** Ap. 1688, Barranquilla **W:** wradio.com.co – **AT05)** Cra. 53 N° 82-132, Barranquilla 1030-0200 **W:** emisoralavozdelacosta.net – **AT06)** Organización Radial Olímpica, Calle 72 No 48-37, Barranquilla - 1000-0500 – **AT07)** Cra. 48 N° 72-25, Ofc. 306, (or Ap. 2010), Barranquilla - 0930-0500 – **AT08)** Cra. 45 No. 76-125, Barranquilla - 0900-0500 **W:** vozdelapatriacelestial1310.com – **AT09)** Calle 53 N° 50-11, P2, Barranquilla **W:** minutodedios.com – **AT10)** Cra. 44 N° 70-61, Barranquilla – **AT11)** Cra. 26, No 75B-07, Barranquilla - 1100-0500 **W:** radiovidanueva.net – **AT12)** Calle 60 N° 47-70, Centro Cultural Santa

Catalina, Barranquilla - 0930-0130 – **AT13)** Palacio Municipal, Soledad – **AT14)** Palacio Municipal, Baranoa.
BO00) BOLÍVAR
BO01) Av. Venezuela, Edif. Banco Internacional, La Matuna 8B-05, Cartagena – **BO02)** Calle Real 20-217, Cartagena - 1000-0500 – **BO03)** Calle Mayor N° 6-34 (or Ap. 1771), Cartagena **W:** cadenaradiallibertad. com.co - 1000-0420 – **BO04)** Ap. 246, Cartagena **W:** lacariñosa.com – **BO05)** **W:** bluradio.com – **BO06)** Ap. 180, Magangué – **BO07)** Calle Sta Fe, N° 13-113, Torices, Cartagena. **W:** radioesperanza1140.net – **BO08)** Matuna, Calle 32 No. 8-21, Of. 1106, Edificio Banco Popular, Cartagena – **BO09)** Av. 3 N° 21-62, La Manga, Cartagena – **BO10)** Cra. 21 N° 29B-10, Cartagena – **BO11)** Calle 56 N° 26-01, Carmen de Bolívar - 1030-0400 – **BO12)** Av. Venezuela, Edif. Suramericana, Of. 801, Cartagena – **BO14)** Palacio Municipal, El Peñon – **BO15)** Palacio Municipal, Arjona – **BO16)** Palacio Municipal, Sta Rosa Sur – **BO17)** Manzana H, Lote 20, La Consolata, Cartagena.
BY00) BOYACÁ
BY01) Calle 16 N° 15-21, P8, Edif.Camara de Comercio, Duitama **W:** lacarinosa.com – **BY02)** Cra. 10 N° 16-36, Chiquinquirá - 0900-0600 – **BY03)** Ap. 282, Sogamoso - **FM:** 88.5MHz, 107.3MHz – **BY04)** Edif. Camol, Piso 11, Cra. 10 Nfby18o. 21-15, Tunja **W:** caracol.com.co cadenaradialvida.com oxigeno.fm – **BY05)** Cra. 15 N° 14-47, Duitama. **W:** wradio.com.co oxigeno.fm – **BY06)** Ap. 019, Sogamoso **W:** rcnmundo. com - 1100-0500 - **FM:** 106.1MHz – **BY07)** Cra. 9 No. 8-65, Garagoa - 1000-0330 – **BY08)** Calle 20 N° 10-64, Tunja – **BY09)** Cra. 7 N° 9-57, Guateque (or Ap. 17387, Bogotá) - 1000-0300 – **BY10)** Cra. 3 N° 13-74, P2, Puerto Boyacá - 0900-0400 – **BY11)** Cra. 10 N° 17-50, P5, Tunja – **BY12)** Calle 5,N° 5-25, P2, Parque Santander, Samacá. **W:** ondasdelporvenir.com 0900-0300 – **BY13)** Iza (or Cra. 7 N° 17-51, Of. 610, Bogotá) – **BY14)** Cra. 6 N° 6-93, Paipa - 1000-0400 – **BY15)** Calle 6 N° 5-42, San Luis de Gaceno - 0900-0300 – **BY16)** Calle 18 N° 12-81, P2, Chiquinquirá - **FM:** 92.6MHz – **BY17)** Universidad Pedagogica y Técnico de Colombia, Tunja – **BY18)** Calle 20 N° 10-64, Ofc.307, Tunja **W:** armoniasboyacenses.com – **BY21)** Palacio Municipal, Chiquinquira – **BY22)** Palacio Municipal, Maripi – **BY23)** Palacio Municipal, Santa María
CA00) CAQUETÁ
CA01) Cra.14 N° 12-129, Casa Episcopal, P2 (Ap. 285), Florencia - 1000-0300 – **CA02)** Ap. 465, Florencia. – **CA03)** Calle 17 N° 10-40, P2, (Ap. 209), Florencia - 1030-0300 – **CA04)** Ap. 150, Florencia **W:** radiouno.com.co – **CA05)** Ap. 192, Florencia **W:** uniamazonia.edu.co - **FM:** 98.1MHz – **CA06)** Timbiquí.
CC00) CAUCA
CC02) Cra 8 N° 3-17 (or Ap. 1321), Popayán - 1000-0400 **W:** caucana1040am.com – **CC03)** Cra. 8 N° 5-41, Popayán **W:** radiosuperpopayan.com – **CC04)** Casa Cural, Parque Principal, Belalcázar – **CC06)** Ap. 535, Popayán – **CC07)** Cra. 13 N° 9-20, Santander de Quilichao - 1100-2400 – **CC08)** Calle 2a N° 1-06 (or Ap. 759), Popayán - 0930-0400 – **CC09)** Batallón José Hilario López, Bordo – **CC11)** Calle 15 Cra. 17 Esq. Casa de la Cultura, Timbío (or Calle 12B N° 13B-22, Popayán) - 1200-2400 – **CC12)** Cra. 4 N° 9-42, Piendamo – **CC13)** Barrio Sagrada Familia, Cra. 3 esq., Morales - 1130-1700, 1900-2200 – **CC14)** Casa de la Cultura, Morales – **CC16)** Palacio Municipal, Padilla
CE00) CESAR
CE01) Calle 17 N° 15-67, Valledupar - 0900-0300 **W:** radioguatapuri. com – **CE02)** Cra. 5 N° 13-52, Valledupar. W. wradio.com.co – **CE03)** Calle 5 N° 1-76, Local 210, Aguachica - 1000-0200 **W:** caracol.com. co – **CE04)** Cl. 15 # 11A-56,, Valledupar - 0900-0500 – **CE05)** Calle 6 N° 19-66, Curumaní - 1000-0100 - **FM:** 95. 7MHz – **CE06)** Calle 16B N° 13-74, Valledupar – **CE07)** Casa de la Cultura, Tamalameque – **CE08)** Ap. 250, Valledupar **CE09)** Cra. 10a N° 4-38, P2, Aguachica – **CE10)** Cra. 16 N° 11-102, Codazzi – **CE11)** Becerril – **CE13)** Cra. 9 N° 5-02, Valledupar **W:** cadenaradialvida.com – **CE14)** Calle 12 N° 15-08, Codazzi – **CE15)** Palacio Municipal de El Copey, El Copey – **CE16)** Palacio Municipal, La Gloria.
CH00) CHOCO
CH01) Calle 28 N° 1-04, P2 (or Ap. 482), Quibdó – **CH02)** Cra. 4 N° 25-18, P2, (or Ap. 196), Quibdó - 1000-0400 – **CH03)** Choco.
CL00) CALDAS
CL01) Ap. 67, Manizales **W:** wradio.com.co – **CL02)** Ap. 244, Manizales **W:** lacariñosa.com - 1000-0500 – **CL03)** Cra. 2 N° 13-31, P3, La Dorada **W:** radiouno.com.co - 1000-0500 – **CL04)** Cra. 4 N° 8-58, P3, Anserma - 0900-0300 – **CL05)** Ap. 2000, Manizales. – **CL06)** Calle 11 N° 3-58 (or Ap. 34), La Dorada – **CL07)** Calle 22 N° 21-40, Plaza Bolívar, Manizales **W:** reddelosandes1390am.com – **CL08)** Cra. 5 N° 11-102, Av. Los Fundadores, Riosucio - 1100-0300 – **CL09)** Cra. 23 N° 71-03 (or Ap. 990), Manizales 1015-0500 – **CL10)** Viterbo – **CL11)** Antigua Estación del Ferrocarril, Manizales - 1200-0400 **W:** radiocondor. fundeca.org.co – **CL12)** Cra. 23 N° 71-03, Av.Sant, Manizales – **CL13)** C. A. M, Samaná - 1100-0100 – **CL15)** Av. Joaquín 1-09, Salida a San

José, Risaralda – **CL16)** Cra. 3 N° 7-31, Aguadas - 1000-0300 – **CL17)** Palacio Municipal, Salamina – **CL18)** Palacio Municipal, Victoria.

CO00) CÓRDOBA
CO01) Cra. 3A N° 30-12, P2, Montería - 1000-0400 – **CO02)** Av. Olaya Herrera, Edif. Jatin, Lorica - 1000-0400 – **CO03)** Calle 23 N° 1-53, Montería – **CO04)** Cra 2 N° 28-53, P2, (or Ap. 497), Montería **W:** rcn-radio.com - 1000-0300 – **CO05)** Cra. 8 N° 17-56, Planeta Rica – **CO06)** Ap. 148, Montería – **CO07)** Calle 27 N° 8-25, Montería **W:** radiouno.com.co – **CO08)** Ap. 364, Montería – **CO09)** Brigada N° 11, Tierralta – **CO10)** Cra. 5 N° 14-85, Montelibano – **CO11)** Palacio Municipal, San Antero – **CO12)** Palacio Municipal, Montería – **CO13)** Palacio Municipal, Valencia.

CS00) CASANARE
CS01) Calle 9 N° 22-63, Edif. Cine Casanare, P2, Yopal - 1000-0500.
FM: 97.7MHz – **CS02)** Palacio Municipal, Sacama – **CS03)** Yopal.

CU00) CUNDINAMARCA
CU01) Calle 14 N° 11-23, P2, Ofc.202, Girardot – **CU02)** Av. Las Palmas N° 5-08, P5, Fusagasugá - 0900-0400 – **CU03)** Terminal de Transportes, Girardot. **W:** radiocolina.com – **CU04)** Cra. 6 N° 6-38, Ubaté **W:** cadenaradioalvida.com – **CU05)** Ap. 416, Girardot – **CU06)** Calle 16 N° 10-38, P3, Girardot. **W:** lacarinosa.com 1030-0300 – **CU07)** Calle 7 N° 14-83, Pacho – **CU09)** Calle 3 N° 16-39, Pacho - 0930-0400 – **CU10)** Calle 8 N° 5-59, Fasagasugá **W:** kiriosradio.com - 0900-0300 – **CU11)** Cra. 3 N° 2-36, Arbeláez (or Av. 37 N° 75-84, Bogotá) – **CU13)** Calle 3 N° 7-56, Zipaquirá. **W:** armoniaz.webcindario.com/html/somos.html – **CU16)** Macheta – **CU17)** Palacio Municipal, Cajica – **CU18)** Palacio Municipal, Cajica – **CU19)** Palacio Municipal, Ubala.

DC00) DISTRITO CAPITAL
DC01) Calle 32 N° 16-12, Bogotá – **DC02)** Cra. 45 No. 26-33, Bogotá **W:** senalradiodecolombia.gov.co – **DC03)** Cra. 13A N° 37-32, Bogotá **W:** amores.com.co – **DC04)** Calle 67 No. 7-37, Bogotá **W:** wradio.com.co radiopolis.fm – **DC05)** Calle 45 N° 13-70 , Ap. 19823, Bogotá. **W:** cadenamelodia.com – **DC06)** Calle 48 N° 18-77, Bogotá – **DC07)** Av. 13 N° 84-42, Bogotá – **DC08)** Calle 39A N° 18-12, Bogotá **W:** radiored.com.co – **DC09)** Avenida Calle 13 N° 79-70, Bogotá, DC - 1100-0300 **W:** vidaam.com.co libertad.com.co – **DC10)** Diagonal 58 N° 26A-29, Bogotá – **DC11)** Calle 57 N° 17-48, Bogotá **W:** qhuboradio.com radiosantafe.com – **DC12)** Cra. 16 N° 43-09, Bogotá. **W:** mci12.com/noticias/108-g12-radio – **DC13)** Calle 25ª No. 32, 46 Barrio Gran América, Ap. 2086350, Bogotá D.C. **W:** fuegoam.com.co – **DC14)** Cra. 30 N° 91-84 (or Ap. 250649), Bogotá – **DC15)** Ap. 9291, Bogotá – **DC16)** Calle 6 N° 7-22, (or Ap. 3201), Bogotá. (alt.address: Calle 385 N° 75-31, Cd. Kennedy, Bogotá) - 1100-0130 **W:** emisoramariana.org – **DC17)** Calle 81B N° 72 B - 70, Barrio Minuto de Dios, Bogotá **W:** radio.uniminuto.edu – **DC18)** Cra. 27 N° 49-48, Bogotá **W:** nuevocontinente.org – **DC19)** Av. 15 N° 123-61, Of. 408, Bogotá - 1100-2300 – **DC20)** **W:** avivamiento.com – **DC21)** Calle 22C N° 31-01, Bogotá – **DC22)** Carrera 21A, No. 151-23, Bogotá **W:** radiomariacol.org – **DC24)** Escuela de Cadetes José María Cordoba, Calle 80 N° 38-00, Bogotá – **DC25)** Diagonal 46A Sur 51-40, Centro Comercial Venecia Plaza 2do piso, Bogotá **W:** palabradevidavenecia.org – **DC26)** Librería Colombia para Cristo, Calle 46 N° 13-56, Blg C, Ap.to 215, (or Apartado Aéreo 67751) Bogotá. (Reports c/o Rafael Rodríguez R., Apartado Aéreo 67751, (oficina Red 4-72 Unicentro), Bogotá, DC. Return postage required for QSL reply) **W:** facebook.com/Fuerza-de-Paz-106687386081261/timeline **E:** 6010lavozdetuconciencia@gmail.com or (for reports) rafaelcoldx@yahoo.com – **DC27)** Av. Boyacá 48 A 11, Edificio Castillo Dorado, Of. 301, Bogotá. **W:** bbnradio.org

GN00) GUAINÍA
GN01) Casa Cultura, Calle 6 con Cra. 3, Puerto Inírida - **FM:** 88.9MHz Super Estación – **GN02)** Inírida **W:** manantialvida.org

GU00) GUAJIRA
GU01) Cra. 9 N° 12-31, Maicao - 0900-0300 – **GU02)** Cra. 8 N° 3-27, Riohacha - 1000-0300 – **GU03)** Ap. 125 & 256, Maicao – **GU04)** Calle 15, Salida a Maicao, Riohacha - 0930-0400 – **GU05)** Barrancas – **GU06)** Cra 8A N° 3-27 (or Ap. 3), Riohacha – **GU07)** Cra. 6 N° 6-60, San Juan del César – **GU08)** Cra. 18 N° 13-54, Uribia – **GU09)** Calle 1 N° 5-63, San Juan del Cesar **W:** vozdelaprovinciadepadilla.blogspot.com - 1000-0400

GV00) GUAVIARE
GV01) San José del Guaviare – **GV02)** Cra 22 con Calle 9, San José del Guaviare. **E:** mercorio@col3.telecom.com.co

HU00) HUILA
HU01) Calle 7 N° 10-36, Neiva - 1000-0300 **W:** sistemainrai.net/hjkk840 – **HU02)** Ap. 150, Neiva. **W:** oxigeno.fm – **HU03)** Ap. 496 (or Cra. 7, Calles 21 y 22), Neiva - 1000-0530 – **HU04)** Cra. 13 N° 3A-24, Neiva. **W:** lafm.com.co – **HU05)** Cra. 4 N° 2-21, Of. 501-502, Neiva. – **HU06)** Calle 6 N° 1A-31, Pitalito - 0900-0400 **W:** sistemainrai.net/hjkk1280 – **HU07)** Cra 8 N° 8-60, P2, Palermo - 0900-0300 – **HU08)** Calle 4a N° 5-59, La Plata - 1000-0100 – **HU09)** Cra. 14 N° 2-47, San Agustín – **HU10)** Cra. 7 N° 7-05, Garzón - 1000-0300 – **HU11)** Palacio Municipal, Yaguará.

IS00) ISLAS SAN ANDRÉS Y PROVIDENCIA
IS01) Ap. 354, San Andrés Isla – **IS02)** Avenida Los Libertadores No 3a – 73, Oficina 204, San Andrés Isla 1030-0300 – **IS03)** Edif. Bermuda, P2, Av. de las Américas, San Andrés Isla – **IS04)** Av. Providencia N° 1A-48, (or Ap. 665), San Andrés Isla - 1100-0500 – **IS5)** San Andrés Isla.

MA00) MAGDALENA
MA01) Av. Libertadores 27-101, Santa Marta. **W:** radio1.com.co – **MA02)** Cra. 5 N° 18-32 (or Ap. 757), Santa Marta 0945-0500 – **MA03)** Calle 17 N° 5-83 (or Ap. 103), Santa Marta **W:** radiogaleon.com.co – **MA04)** Calle 18 N° 5-58, Santa Marta - 1000-0200 – **MA05)** Cra. 9 N° 14-13, Fundación – **MA06)** Ap. 1240, Santa Marta **W:** radio-magdalena1420am.com – **MA07)** Calle 11 C N° 18a-34, Santa Marta - 1100-0300 – **MA08)** Ap. 45, El Banco - 1000-0400

ME00) META
ME01) Calle 41B N° 30-11, Barrio La Grama, Villavicencio **W:** ondasdelmeta.com – **ME02)** Cra. 13 N° 15-52, Granada – **ME03)** Calle 38 N° 32-41, P7, Edif. Prollano, Ofc 702, Villavicencio **W:** autenticavillavicencio.com – **ME04)** Cra. 30 N° 36-14, P4, Villavicencio – **ME05)** Cra. 31 N° 37-71, Of.1001, (Ap. 2472), Villavicencio - 0900-0500 – **ME06)** Cra. 40 N° 34-34, Baltazar Alto, Villavicencio – **ME07)** Calle 13 N° 28-05 (Ap. 001), Granada – **ME10)** (See DC26). **W:** fuerzadepaz.com - **FM:** 88.8MHz Marfil Stereo. – **ME11)** Palacio Municipal, Villavicencio.

NA00) NARIÑO
NA01) Cra. 29 N° 17-30 (or Ap. 375), Pasto - 1000-0200 – **NA02)** Cra.20A N° 16-73, P2, Pasto - 1000-0100 – **NA03)** Ap. 454, Pasto. – **NA04)** Calle 20 N° 24-73, Of 603, P6, Pasto - 0900-0500 – **NA05)** Cra. 27 N° 19-30, Pasto. **W:** oxigeno.fm – **NA06)** Ap. 1005, Ipiales - 1100-0200 – **NA07)** Parque Colón (or Ap. 165), Tumaco - 1100-0400 – **NA08)** Cra. 8 N° 4-48, Ipiales - 1100-0200 – **NA09)** Calle 20 N° 15-13, Túquerres - 0900-0400 – **NA10)** Ap. 516, Pasto **W:** lacarinosa.com – **NA11)** Cra. 6A N° 9-14, P2, Ipiales – **NA12)** Cra. 5 N° 3-15, Samaniego – **NA13)** Fundación Tomás Cipriano de Mosquera, Ricaurte el Diviso 1300-2300 – **NA14)** Nevado Cumbal – **NA15)** Calle 15 N° 14-24 , Pasto - 1100-0500 W. radioviva.com.co – **NA16)** Universidad de Nariño, Cra. 25 N° 19-12, Pasto – **NA17)** Cra. 1 N° 21-36, Pasto – **NA18)** Palacio Municipal, Guaitarilla. – **NA19)** Palacio Municipal, Tangua. – **NA20)** Palacio Municipal, El Tablón. – **NA21)** Palacio Municipal Guachucal. – **NA22)** Palacio Municipal, Mallama. – **NA23)** Palacio Municipal, Pupiales.

NS00) NORTE DE SANTANDER
NS01) Calle 5 N° 3-26 (or Ap. 1650), Cúcuta – **NS02)** Centro Comercial Bolívar, Local E4 y E5, Cúcuta **W:** rcnmundo.com - 1000-0400 – **NS03)** Ap. 400, Cúcuta.– **NS04)** Calle 5A N° 0-45, Cúcuta. **W:** wradio.com.co – **NS05)** Av. O. N° 10-54, P2 (or Ap. 624), Cúcuta – **NS06)** Ap. 519, Cúcuta. **W:** oxigeno.fm – **NS07)** Cra. 13 N° 9-10, P7, Ocaña –**NS08)** Calle 7N N° 4-117 (or Ap. 2284), Cúcuta – **NS10)** Calle 11 N° 15-24, Ocaña - 1030-0300 – **NS11)** Calle 7 N° 4-50, Tibú - 1000-2400 – **NS12)** Calle 17N No. 5-101, Cúcuta **W:** mci12.com – **NS13)** Base Militar "San Jorge", Tibú - 1030-1700, 2100-0200 – **NS15)** Calle 12 N° 4-19, Ofc. 214, (or Ap. 2582), Cúcuta - 1000-0500 – **NS16)** Av. OA N° 12-75, Ofc. 101 (or Ap. 1303), Cúcuta – **NS17)** Cra. 6 N° 4-59, P3 (or Ap. 1074), Pamplona - 0900-0300 – **NS18)** Av. 4 N° 11-17, Ofc. 303, Cúcuta - 1000-0400 – **NS19)** Cra. 2 N° 1-10, Puerto Santander - 1000-2200 – **NS20)** Av. 5 N° 9-58, P2, Edif. Mut.Aux (or Ap. 151), Villa del Rosario.

PU00) PUTUMAYO
PU01) Calle Principal, Orito - 1100-2300 – **PU02)** Calle 10 N° 6-01 (or Ap. 011), Mocoa - 0900-0300 – **PU03)** 19A Barrio Oriental, Sibundoy - 1300-2300 - **FM:** 107.3MHz – **PU04)** Calle 11 N° 17-18 (or Ap. 9), Puerto Asís - 1100-0200

QU00) QUINDÍO
QU01) Cra 16 N° 19-23, P10, Armenia – **QU02)** Calle 9 N° 13-50 (or Ap. 2361), Armenia – **QU03)** Ap. 2481, Armenia – **QU04)** Ap. 556, Calarcá – **QU06)** Cra. 14 N° 21-26, P2, (or km 2 via al Aeropuerto), Armenia - 1000-0500 - **FM:** 104.7MHz Robles FM Stereo – **QU07)** Calle 21 N° 16-31, Ofc 702, (or Ap. 617), Armenia – **QU08)** Universidad del Quindío, Av.Bolívar Cra.15 Calle 12 Norte, Armenia **W:** uniquindio.edu.co/uniquindio/laufm - **FM:** 102.1MHz – **QU09)** Cra.24 N° 39-52, Calarcá. – **QU10)** Palacio Municipal, Armenia.

RI00) RISARALDA
RI01) Ap. 354, Pereira **W:** qhuboradio.com – **RI02)** Ap. 045, Pereira – **RI03)** Ap. 221, Pereira **W:** vidaam.com.co – **RI05)** Crra. 7a N° 18-80, Of. 705, Edificio Centro Financiero, Pereira - 0930-0515 – **RI06)** Cra. 7 N° 15-10, P3 (or Ap. 1262), Pereira **W:** ecos1360.com – **RI07)** Cra. 15 N° 11-80, Santa Rosa de Cabal (or Calle 19 N° 8-74, Pereira) - 1000-0300 – **RI08)** Palacio Municipal, Pereira – **RI09)** Calle 17 N° 9-10, Marsella – **RI11)** Palacio Municipal, Balboa. – **RI12)** Palacio Municipal, La Ceila

SS00) SANTANDER
SS01) Ap. 915, Bucaramanga – **SS02)** Ap. 223, Bucaramanga. **W:**

caracol.com.co qhuboradio.com besame.fm – **SS03)** Calle 50 N° 17-71, P3, Barrancabermeja – **SS04)** Cra. 27 N° 45-80, Bucaramanga - 0900-0400 – **SS05)** Ap. 007, Bucaramanga - 1000-0200. – **SS06)** Calle 36 N° 14, 58 Piso 7, Bucaramanga **W:** melodiaenlinea.com – **SS07)** Calle 16 N° 15-01, Esquina, Socorro - 0930-0300 – **SS08)** Transv. 6 N° 9-56, Barbosa – **SS09)** Batallón de Artillería de Defensa Aerea N° 2 "Nueva Granada" (or Ap. 036), Barrancabermeja – **SS10)** Ap. 1100, Bucaramanga – **SS11)** Calle 11 N° 9-80, p. 3, San Gil – **SS12)** Calle 48 N° 35A-25, Bucaramanga – **SS13)** Edif.Súper Estrellas, Ofc.409 (or Ap. 23), Barrancabermeja - 1000-0300 – **SS14)** Calle 7 N° 17-44, Barbosa 0730-2330 – **SS15)** Ap. 578, Barrancabermeja. **W:** rcn.com. co 0900-0400 – **SS16)** Calle 12 N° 10-30, Centro, San Gil - 0900-0300 **W:** lacaliente1330.com – **SS17)** Calle 16 N° 4-47, Zapatoca – **SS18)** Calle 35 N° 20-39 (or Ap. 3104), Bucaramanga – **SS19)** Cra. 4 N° 4-118, P2, Cimitarra - 0900-0300 – **SS20)** Calle 9 N° 3-21 2° Piso, Vélez **W:** lavozdelcarare.com – **SS21)** Calle 20 N° 6-36, Zapatoca – **SS22)** Av. 36, No. 19-76, Piso 9, Bucaramanga. **W:** rcm1450.com – **SS23)** Calle 41 N° 19-87, Bucaramanga **W:** bluradio.com – **SS25)** Calle 12 N° 17-10, Ofc.302 (or Ap. 250), Barrancabermeja - 1000-0400 – **SS26)** Calle 11 N° 6A-11, Edif. San Gabriel, P2, Málaga - 1000-0200 – **SS27)** Diócesis del Socorro y San Gil, Cra. 13 N° 34, Esquina Socorro - 0500-2300 – **SS28)** Cra.27, Calle 9, Televis, Barrancabermeja – **SS29)** Palacio Municipal, San Andrés – **SS30)** Diócesis de Barrancabermeja, Calle Octava, entre Carreras 15 y 16, Barrancabermeja.

SU00) SUCRE
SU01) Ap. 167, Sincelejo - 1000-0430 – **SU02)** Cra. 18 N° 20-48 (or Ap. 448), Sincelejo – **SU03)** Cra. 24 N° 29-50 (or Ap. 100), Corozal - 1100-0500 – **SU04)** Cra. 20 N° 16-40 (or Ap. 191), Sincelejo - 1100-0300 **W:** radiochacuri.com – **SU05)** Calle 20 N° 24-93, Av. las Penitas, Sincelejo – **SU07)** Cra. 20 N° 25-92 piso 2, Sincelejo – **SU08)** Cra. 20 N° 21-46 (or Ap. 303), Sincelejo - 1000-0400 – **SU09)** Cra. 28 Calle 18, San Marcos – **SU10)** Calle 25A N° 18, Sincelejo - 1030-0430 – **SU11)** Cra. 20 N° 25-92, P2, Sincelejo - 1030-0200 **W:** radiocaracoli.com – **SU12)** Palacio Municipal, Ovejas – **SU13)** Palacio Munivipal, Majagual – **SU14)** Calle 24 No 18-31, Sincelejo.

T000) TOLIMA
T001) Calle 12 N° 1-17, P5, Ibagué **W:** vozdeltolima.blogspot.com besame.fm – **T002)** Calle 14 N° 2A-14, P2, Ibagué **W:** besame.fm – **T003)** Parque Murillo Toro N° 3-29, P4, Ibagué **W:** lafm.com.co - 1000-0400 – **T004)** Cra 7 con Calle 10, Espinal – **T005)** Calle 11 N° 12-51, El Guamo - 1100-2400. **W:** sistemainrai.net/hjkk1090 – **T006)** Ap. 2419, Ibagué – **T007)** Ap. 1094, Ibagué **FM:** 93.9MHz – **T008)** Calle 5 N° 6-25, Mariquita – **T009)** Calle 9 N° 1-124, P3, Ibagué. **W:** oxigeno.fm – **T010)** Calle 11 N° 4-26 (or Ap. 64), Espinal **W:** olimpicastereo.com. co – **T011)** Ap. 536, Honda – **T012)** Ap. 509, Honda - 1000-0300 – **T013)** Cra. 2 N° 11-27, Flandes **W:** olimpicastereo.com.co – **T014)** Cra 3 N° 12-76, Ofc.801 (or Ap. 589), Ibagué - 1000-0400 – **T017)** Cra. 7a N° 5-36, Dolores - 0945-0300 – **To 18)** Calle 7a No. 20-70, Melgar - 0900-0500 – **T019)** Cra. 2 N° 3-74, Rovira **W:** celestial1580am.com – **T020)** Palacio Municipal, Cajamarca. – **T021)** Palacio Municipal, Palo Cabildo. – **T022)** Palacio Municipal, Venadillo.

VA00) VALLE DEL CAUCA
VA01) Cra. 26 N° 5C-25, San Fernando, Cali - 1100-0300 – **VA02)** Cra. 38D Diagonal 37A-52B/Santa Isabel, Cali – **VA03)** Ap. 1941, Cali **W:** qhuboradio.com **VA04)** Ap. 4666, Cali **E:** radiounicacali@todelar.com - 1100-0400 – **VA05)** Cra. 14 N° 2-25, P2 (or Ap. 96), Buga - 1100-0500 – **VA06)** Av. 5B Norte N° 21-02, Cali – **VA07)** Cra. 33 N° 28-51 (Ap. 280), Palmira - 1000-0500. **W:** radiopalmira.com – **VA08)** Ap. 126, Tuluá - 1000-0300 – **VA09)** Cra. 4A N° 10-75 (or Ap. 145), Cartago – **VA11)** Calle 21 Nte N° 3N-49, P5, Cali **W:** radiored.com.co – **VA11)** Calle 12-39, Ofc 301, Edif.R.Buenaventura (Ap 383), Buenaventura 1030-0500. Rel. R. Maria 0200-1000. **W:** radiobuenaventura.com – **VA12)** Cra. 16 N° 6-22, P2, Caicedonia **W:** radiociudadcentinela.com – **VA13)** Cra 19 N° 2N-29, Ofc 21B, Cali – **VA14)** San N° 29-09, Palmira - 1000-0400 – **VA15)** Cra 6 N° 54-08, Av. Simon Bolívar, Buenaventura – **VA16)** Carrera 66B, No. 6-68, Barrio El Limonar, Cali – **VA17)** Cra. 11 N° 11-43, P2, Zarzal – **VA18)** Cra. 9 N° 32-88/90 (or Ap. 201), Palmira - 1130-0300 – **VA19)** Cra. 14 N° 5-77, Buga – **VA20)** Cra. 26 N° 28-72, Tuluá. **W:** caracol.com.co – **VA21)** Calle 27 N° 33-35, Tuluá - 1100-0500 – **VA22)** Av. Roosevelt N° 34-37, Cali **W:** sonora1500am. com – **VA23)** Cra. 51 N° 49-21, Sevilla – **VA24)** Calle 10 N° 6-87, P3, Cartago - 1100-0500 – **VA26)** Calle 13, No. 19-59, Barrio Guayaquil, Cali. **W:** sistemahuellasinternacional.com 1100-0500 – **VA27)** Cra. 13 N° 10-58, Cali – **VA28)** Av.Roosevelt N° 28, Cali. (Or: Transversal 34 N° 149-23, Cedro Golf, Bogotá) – **VA29)** Palacio Municipal, Buenaventura. – **VA30)** Palacio Municipal, Versalles. – **VA31)** Cra. 13 N° 10-62, Cali. **W:** sistemahuellasinternacional.com 1100-0400.

VI00) VICHADA
VI01) Puerto Çarreño **W:** manantialvida.org
VP00) VAUPÉS
VP01) Mitú – **VP02)** Mitú.

FM in Bogotá (MHz): 88.9 R. Uno (RCN) – 89.9 40 Principales (Caracol) – 90.4 La UD (University) – 90.9 La Mega (RCN) – 91.9 Javeriana Estereo (University) – 92.4 Policía Nacional (Police) – 92.9 El Sonido de la Ciudad (Todelar) – 93.4 Colombia Estéreo (Colombian Army) – 93.9 RCN La Radio (rel. 770) – 94.9 La FM (RCN) – 95.9 R. Nac. de Colombia – 96.9 Blu R. – 97.4 La Vallenata (Caracol) – 97.9 Radioactiva (Caracol) – 98.5 Universidad Nacional (University) – 99.1 Radionica (RTVC) – 99.9 W Radio (Caracol) – 100.4 Oxígeno (Caracol) – 100.9 Caracol R (rel. 810kHz) – 101.9 Candela Esteréo – 102.9 Tropicana (Caracol) – 103.9 La X (Todelar) – 104.4 Fantástica – 104.9 Vibra Bogotá (W Radio) – 105.4 Rumba Stereo (RCN) – 105.9 Olímpica – 106.9 Universidad Jorge Tadeo Lozano (University) – 107.9 Minuto de Dios (Rlg)

COMOROS

L.T: UTC +3h — **Pop:** 700,000 — **Pr.L:** French, Comorian, Arabic — **E.C:** 50Hz, 220V — **ITU:** COM

OFFICE DE RADIO TÉLÉVISION DES COMORES (ORTC, Gov.)
✉ BP 452, Moroni, Grand Comoro ☎+269 7732531 📠 +269 7730303 **W:** radiocomores.km **LP:** Tech. Dir: Abdulkader Radjab.
FM: Moroni, R.Studio 1 101.2MHz. Nkazi, R.Nkazi 107.0MHz. 6 x 1kW, 3 x 0.5kW txs. **D.Prgr:** 0300-1900. **Ann:** F: "Ici Radio Comoro".

Other stations:
R. Dziyalandze, Anjouan: 90.0MHz (rel. RFI 1700-1030).
R. Ocean Indien, Ngazidja: 100.5MHz. **W:** radioceanindien.km

CONGO (Dem. Rep.)

L.T: Kinshasa & western part: UTC +1h, eastern part: UTC +2h — **Pop:** 67 million — **Pr.L:** French, Lingala, Swahili, Tshiluba, Kikongo — **E.C:** 50Hz, 220V — **ITU:** COD

CONSEIL SUPÉRIEUR DE L'AUDIOVISUEL ET DE LA COMMUNICATION (CSAC)
✉ Kinshasa **LP:** President: Jean Bosco Bahala.

RADIO-TÉLÉVISION NATIONALE CONGOLAISE (RTNC, Gov.)
✉ B.P. 3164, Kinshasa-Gombe ☎+243 81 9970699 📠+243 81 123 7691 **W:** rtnc-rdc.com **E:** info@rtnc-rdc.com **LP:** DG: Mr. E. Kipolongwa Mukambilwa, Dep. DG: M. Makuala
FM: Kinshasa: **National channel:** 100.0MHz, **Kinshasa channel:** 91.8MHz, **Channel for national languages:** 97.0MHz.
D.Prgr: 24h in French/Swahili/Lingala/Tshiluba/Kikongo. Also relayed by other stns. **Ann:** "RTNC, Radio-Télévision Nationale Congolaise, émettant de Kinshasa".

Provincial Stations:
FM (MHz): 2) 94.5 3kW – **3)** 88.9/92.0 1.5kW – **4)** 93.3 1.5kW/90.0 0.05kW – **5)** 93.5/98.5 – **6)** 89.1 50kW – **7)** 90.0 – **8)** 92.5 1kW – **9)** 94.8 – **10)** 90.1 – **11)** 93.7
Addresses: 2) B.P. 7296, Lubumbashi – **3)** RTNC Kivu, B.P. 475, Bukavu – **4)** B.P. 1061, Mbandaka – **5)** B.P. 1232, Mbuji-Mayi – **6)** B.P. 708, Kananga, Western Kasai – **7)** B.P. 704, Matadi – **8)** B.P. 1745, Kisangani – **9)** Butembo, Nord-Kivu – **10)** Goma, Nord-Kivu. **E:** rtnc-nordkivu@yahoo.fr – **11)** Ulvira, Sud-Kivu.

RADIO TÉLÉ CANDIP
✉ B.P. 373, Bunia ☎+243 81 7363753 **E:** radiotelecandipisp@gmail. com **LP:** Dir: Michel Angaika Bhaba.
SW: Bunia 5066v kHz 1kW. **FM:** 98.0MHz 1kW.
D.Prgr in French/Ethnic: 0250v-0700, 1300-1900v.

RADIO KAHUZI (Rlg.)
✉ 2 Ave. Masikita/Muhumba Ave, Bukavu or B.P. 42, Cyangugu, Rwanda. **W:** radiokahuzi.com **E:** radiokahuzi@gmail.com **LP:** Dir: Richard McDonald, St. Mgr: Barbara Smith.
SW: Bukavu 6210kHz 0.8kW. **FM:** 91.1/102.1MHz 0.2kW. (relocated, inactive).
D.Prgr: 0700-1500 in French, English, Kikongo, Kinyarwanda, Lingala, Mashi, Swahili and Tshiluba.

RADIO OKAPI
(joint initiative between the UN Mission in the DRC [MONUC] and Hirondelle Foundation)
✉ QG Monuc, 12 Av. des Aviateurs, Kinshasa-Gombe ☎+243-81-890-6747 **W:** radiookapi.net **E:** info@hirondelle.org
LP: Dir: Yves Laplume.

FM (MHz): (powers 1-5kW): Isiro 90.1, Beni 92.0, Butembo 92.9, Gbadolite/Kananga/Lisala 93.0, Mbuji-Mayi 93.8, Kisangani 94.8, Bukavu 95.3, Gemena 95.4, Lubumbashi 95.8, Kanyabayonga/Mahagi 96.0, Aru 98.0, Bundundu 99.0, Matadi 102.0, Baraka/Kindu/Mbandaka 103.0, Kikwit/Kinshasa/Mbuji Mayi 103.5, Kamina 104.3, Manono 104.5, Bunia/Walikale 104.9, Kalemie 105.0, Goma/Uvira 105.2, Shabunda 105.4, Tshomo Ini 106.5.
D.Prgr: 0430-2200 in French/Lingala/Swahili/Tshiluba.

Other stations (all MHz):
Business R. Africa, Kinshasa: 98.6. **W:** brt-africa.com – **Canal Congo pour Christ,** Bukavu: 97.3 – **Canal Futur,** Kinshasa-Gombe: 107.4 – **CEBS,** Kinshasa: 93.7 – **RATELKI,** Kinshasa: 90.2 – **R. Artemis,** Bunia: 90.2 – **R. Boboto,** Isiro: 100.6 100W – **R. Butembo:** 100 – **R. Canal CVV,** Kinshasa: 102.3 – **R. Canal Révélation,** Bunia: 100.7 0.3kW – **R. Congo FM,** Kinshasa: 96.4 – **R. ECC,** Kinshasa: 104.0 – **R. Elikya,** Kinshasa: 97.5 – **R. Lwenge,** Baraki-Fizi: 88.9 150W – **R. Liberté Kinshasa (RALIK),** 96.8 – **R. Maendeleo:** Bukavu 88.7 1kW, Chomuhini 103.3 1kW – **R. Malebo Broadcast Channel (MBC),** Kinshasa: 98.3 – **R. Maria Malkia wa Amani** (Rlg.): Bukavu 94.0 & 97.0. **W:** pamojanakakaluigi.org/radio_maria.htm – **R. Méthodiste Lokole,** Kinshasa-Gombe: 100.8 – **R. Moto** (Rlg.): Kivu 103 1.2kW, Butembo 106.0 – **R. Neno la Uzima,** Bukavu: 100.2 – **R. Parole Eternelle,** Kinshasa: 103.8 – **R. Raga FM:** Kinshasa-Binza 90.5 4kW. **W:** raga.cd – **R. Rehema:** Chamuhini 89.5 0.25kW, Bukavu 99.7 1kW – **R. Réveil FM,** Kinshasa-Gombe: 105.4 **W:** reveilfm.itgo.com – **R. Sango Malamu:** Boma 102.5, Kinshasa 104.5 – **R. Tangazeni Kristo** (Rlg.): Bunia 88.6, Aru/Kwandruma 90.0 **E:** buero@diguna.de – **R. Télé Armée de l'Eternel,** Kinshasa: 94.5 – **R. Télé Amani,** Kisangani; 100.1 25W, 103.1 0.5kW. – **R. Télé Boma** (RTB), Boma: 98.0 – **R. Télé Graben,** Beni/Butembo 98 – **R. Télé Groupe l'Avenir (RTGA),** Kinshasa 88.1 – **R. Télé Kin Malebo** (RTKM): Kinshasa 95.1, Kananga 97.5 – **R. Télé Kintuadi** (RTK): Boma 91.1, Kinshasa 97.1, Mbanza Ngungu 103.4, Matadi 107.5 – **R. Télé Message de Vie,** Kinshasa: 88.7 – **R. Télé Mosaïque,** Likasi: 88.5 – **R. Télé Puissance,** Kinshasa 101.0 – **RTV Bukavu Liberté,** Ibanda 107.3 – **RTV Mulangane,** Bukavu: 100.1 0.25kW – **R. Sentinelle,** Kinshasa: 97.1 – **R. Tomisa,** Kikwit: 97.5 0.5kW – **R. Veritas** (Rlg.), Kabinda: 105.0 – **R. Vuvu Kietu,** Mbanza Ngungu: 101.0 – **RCLS,** Kirumba: 91.0 – **REB,** Butembo: 90.7 – **RTIV,** Kisangani: 89.4 0.5kW – **Sauti ya Mkaaji,** Makongo: 87.85 – **Top Congo,** Kinshasa: 88.4.
BBC African Sce Kinshasa 92.7, Kisangani/Lubumbashi 92.0, Goma 93.3, Bukavu 102.2
RFI Afrique: Bunia 90.2, Bukavu/Kisangani/Lubumbashi/Matadi 98.0, Kinshasa 105.0
RTBFi (Belgium), Kinshasa: 99.2MHz

CONGO (Rep.)

L.T: UTC +1h — **Pop:** 4 million — **Pr.L:** French, Lingala, Kikongo — **E.C:** 50Hz, 230V — **ITU:** COG

CONSEIL SUPÉRIEUR DE LA LIBERTÉ DE LA COMMUNICATION (CSLC)
🖃 Brazzaville **W:** cslc.congo.org **L.P:** Pres.: Jacques Banangadzala.

TELEDIFFUSION DU CONGO - RADIO CONGO (Gov.)
🖃 Direction Générale, B.P. 2241, Brazzaville ☎+242 22 2810608
L.P: DG: Jean Médard Bokatola. Dir. Prgr: Jean de Dieu Oko.
SW: Brazzaville 6115kHz 50kW 0600-1900 (irreg.)
FM: 90.1/94/96.4MHz
National Network: 0420-2300 in French & ethnic. **N. in English:** 1900 (approx.) **Ann:** "Radio Congo, Chaîne Nationale".
IS: Zansi solo. Opens and closes with National Anthem.

Other stations:
Digital R. N° 1, Brazzaville: 92.2MHz – **R. Brazzaville:** 98.0MHz – **R. Mucodec,** Brazzaville: 88.4MHz. **W:** mucodec.com – **R. Rurale Congolaise,** Brazzaville: 99.3MHz – **R. Liberté,** Brazzaville 106.0MHz.
BBC African Service: 103.8MHz.
RFI Afrique: Brazzaville/Pointe-Noire 93.2MHz

COOK ISLANDS

L.T: UTC-10h — **Pop**-11,124 — **PrL:** English, Cook Island Maori — **E.C:** 50Hz, 220V — **ITU:**CKH

MW	kHz	kW	Station	Location
1)	630	2.5	R. Cook Islands AM	Rarotonga
FM	**MHz**	**kW**	**Station**	**Location**
2)	88.1		88 FM Boom Boom R	Rarotonga

FM	MHz	kW	Station	Location
1)	89.0		R. Cook Islands	Mitiaro
1)	89.0		R. Cook Islands	Pukapuka
1)	89.9		R. Cook Islands AM	Rarotonga
1)	90.6		R. Cook Islands	Mangaia
1)	90.6		R. Cook Islands	Rakahanga
1)	90.6		R. Cook Islands	Palmerston
8)	91.8		Araura FM	Aitutaki
4)	91.9		Matariki FM	Rarotonga
1)	92.2		R. Cook Islands	Atiu
1)	92.2		R. Cook Islands	Penrhyn
3)	93.0		R. Australia	Rarotonga
1)	93.8		R. Cook Islands	Mauke
1)	93.8		R. Cook Islands	Nassau
1)	95.4		R. Cook Islands	Aitutaki
1)	95.4		R. Cook Islands	Manihiki
4)	96.7		Matariki FM	Rarotonga
9)	97.9		Marantha FM	Rarotonga
5)	98.7		Adventist Radio TK3ANA	Rarotonga
4)	99.9		Matariki FM	Rarotonga
1)	100.0		R. Cook Islands	Aitutaki
1)	101.1		Ocean & Earth HITZ FM	Rarotonga
6)	103.3	1	R. Ikurangi KCFM	Rarotonga

Addresses & other information
1) The Voice of the Nation, Elijah Communications, PO Box 126, Avarua, Rarotonga ☎+682 29460 🖷+682 21907 **W:** radio.co.ck and facebook.com/radio-cook-islands-the-voice-of-the-nation **E:** tunein@radio.co.ck **R. Cook Islands AM,** M-F 1600-0900 [Fri 1000] Sat 1600-1000 Su 1700-0900 **N:** Local news hourly M-F 1700-0200 **RNZI** 1600, 1700, 1800 M-F **Prgr:** Talkback, news, rlg srvcs and music in English and Cook Isl Maori. **Ocean & Earth HITZ FM** 24h **Prgr:** contemporary hit music (r.inactive). **Outer Island Network:** Txs outside Rarotonga are owned by the Cook Islands gvmt and relay R. Cook Islands AM and in some cases also originate prgrs as local community stns (many are r.temp inactive) – **2)** The Digital Factory, Avarua, Rarotonga ☎+682 22836/54188/ 55007 **W:** facebook.com/88fmradio/info **E:** 88fmradio@gmail.com **L.P:** Nicholas Henry **Prgr:** 24h – **3)** 24h English for the Pacific satellite rel. – **4)** Matariki FM Ltd, PO Box 511, Avarua, Rarotonga ☎ +682 25997 **W:** matarikifm.co.ck and streaming also at matarikifm.radio.net **E:** onair@matarikifm.co.ck **L.P:** William Framheim **Format:** local Polynesian music **Associated local community station:** R.Enua Manu, Enuamanu School, Mapumai, Atiu **Format:** local talkback, community affairs, music and school news – **5)** PO Box 31, Avarua, Rarotonga ☎+682 22851 **E:** office@adventist.org.ck **Prgr:** Rlg (r. temp inactive) – **6)** Kia Orana Country R., PO Box 521, Avarua, Rarotonga ☎+682 23203 (r. temp. inactive) – **8)** Aitutaki. **ID:** '88FM Aitutaki's Hottest Hits' 24h. Same family ownership as #2 with joint marketing and sales with the Rarotonga stn – **9)** Rarotonga. **Prgr:** Religious

COSTA RICA

L.T: UTC -6h — **Pop:** 4.2 million — **Pr.L:** Spanish — **E.C:** 60Hz, 120V — **ITU:** CTR

CAMARA NACIONAL DE RADIO (CANARA)
🖃 Ap.1583, 1002 San José ☎ +506 2256 2338 🖷 +506 2255 4483
W: canara.org **E:** info@canara.org

MW	Call	kHz	kW	Station, location and h. of tr
1)	CAL	530		R. La Negrita, Cartago: 1200-0400
2)	SCL	550	5	R. Santa Clara, Cd. Quesada: 1100-0130
3)	ELR	570	5	R. Libertad, San José: 1200-0400
4)	ALY	640	20	R. Rica, San José: 1130-0400
5)	TNT	670	10	R. Managua, San José
6)	JC	700	10	R. Sonora, San José
7)		730	1	R. Pacífico, Puntarenas: 1400-0200
8)	LX	760	5	R. Columbia, San José
9)	RA	780	10	R. América, San José
10)	SD	800	3	R. Gigante, San José
11)	GC	820	2.5	8-20, San José: 1130-0600
12)	RDR	850	2	R. Cartago, Cartago: 1100-0400
13)	UCR	870	10	R. 870 UCR, San Pedro Montes de Oca
14)	BAS	890	10	R. Heredia, Heredia
15)	UM	910	10	BBN, San José/San Carlos
16)	RCR	930	5	R. Costa Rica, Guadalupe
17)		1040		R. Pilarcita, La Garita
18)	HG	1040	2	R. Nosara, Hojancha: 1100-1400, 2100-2300
8)	LX	1060	1	R. Columbia, San Isidro del General (r 760)
19)	FC	1080	1	Faro del Caribe, San José
20)	SCR	1100	5	R. Chorotega, Santa Cruz: 1315-0000

MW Call	kHz	kW	Station, location and h. of tr
21) ACE	1120	1	R. Alajuela, Alajuela: 1100-0300
22) DKN	1140	5	R. Nueva, Guápiles
8) CA	1160	1	R. Columbia, Puntarenas (r. 760)
23) PJ	1180	5	R. Victoria, Heredia: 1100-0400
24) TQ	1200	5	R. Cucú, San José: 1000-0600
25) Q	1220	1	R. Fe y Poder, Limón
26) WC	1240	1	R. Corobicí, Cañas
27) DIO	1260	5	R. Emaús, San Vito de Coto Brus: 1100-0300
28)	1280		R. Visión, San José
29) GL	1300	1	R. La Fuente Musical, Cartago
8) LX	1320	1	R. Columbia, San Carlos (r. 760)
30) HR	1340	5	R. Sideral, San Ramón: 1000-0400
31) MS	1380	1	R. Guanacaste, Liberia: 1000-0500
32) RPN	1420	1	R. Pampa, Liberia: 1100-0100
33) RDVC	1430	3	R. San Carlos, Cd. Quesada: 1100-0300
8) LX	1460	1	R. Columbia, Ciudad Quesada (r. 760)
8) LX	1520	1	R. Columbia, Cartago: (r. 760)
34) OAR	1560	5	R. Nicoya, Nicoya: 1000-0300
35) RCLS	1580	0.25	R. Cultural Los Santos
36)	1580	0.25	R. Cultural de Pérez Zeledón
37) RCLC	1580	0.25	R. Cultural de La Cruz
38) RSCM	1580	0.25	R. Cultural Maleku
39) RCL	1580	5	R. Cultural de Los Chiles
40)	1580		R. Cultural de Tilarán
41) RCVT	1580	0.25	R. Cultural de Talamanca
42) RCS	1580	0.5	R. Cultural de Puriscal
50) LGJ	1590	1.5	R. 16, Grecia: 1100-0400
43)	1600	0.25	R. Cultural de Pital
44) RSCN	1600	0.25	R. Cultural Nicoyano, Nicoya
45) RCT	1600	0.25	R. Cultural de Turrialba
46) RCBA	1600	0.25	R. Cultural de Buenos Aires
47) RCU	1600	0.25	R. Cultural de Upala
51) RPQ	1600	0.5	R. Quepos, Pto Quepos
52) CC	1600	2.5	R. Buenísima, Puerto Golfito
53) MQ	1600	1.5	R. Pococí, Guápiles: 1100-0400

Hrs of tr. 24h except where shown. Add TI– in front of the calls.
‡ = inactive, (r) = repeater, ± = varying fq.

Addresses and other information:
1) 200 m norte de la catedral nuestra señora del Carmen, Cartago **W:** radiocatolicalanegrita.com – **2)** Ap. 221, 4400 Cd. Quesada **W:** radiosantaclara.org – **3)** Cadena Radial Costarricense, 100m oeste de Taca, La Uruca, 1000 San José or Ap. 301-2400 Desamparados **W:** libertad570am.com – **4)** Ap. 1695, 1000 San José **W:** radiorica640.net – **5)** Ap. 800-1000 (or Costado Oeste del Puente Juan Pablo II), 1000 San José. **W:** facebook.com/pages/Radio-Managua-AM/145937732087541 – **6) W:** radiosonorac.com – **7)** Puntarenas **W:** facebook.com/pages/RADIO-PACÍFICO-730-AM/128062147247000 – **8)** Ap. 708, 1000 San José **W:** columbia.co.cr – **9)** Edificio de la Prensa Libre, Calle 4, Avenida 4 (or Ap. 177-1009) San José **W:** 780america.com – **10)** Calles 15-13, Av. 11, Barrio Aranjuez (or Ap. 1735) 1000 San José **W:** radiolagigante800am.com – **11)** Ap. 6133, 1000 San José **W:** radiotigrecr.com – **12)** Altos de Apolo, frente al Palacio Municipal, Cartago **W:** radiocartago.org – **13)** Cd. Universitaria Rodrigo Facio, San Pedro Montes de Oca, 2060-1000 San José **W:** radiosucr.com – **14)** Heredia **W:** radioheredia.com – **15)** De la Municipalidad de Tibas 100 mtrs al Norte y 75 metros al Oeste, casa blanca a mano derecha (Ap. 2006), 1100 San José **W:** bbnradio.org – **16)** Barrio Córdoba, Autos Bohío 100 sur y 100 este, 894-2200 Coronado. **W:** radiocr.net – **17)** Ap. 943-4050, La Garita, Alajuela **W:** radiopilarcita.com – **18)** Casa Cultural de Hojancha, Hojancha, Guanacaste **W:** radionosara.com – **19)** Ap. 2710, 1000 San José. **W:** farodelcaribe.org – **20)** 700 mts este de Almacén Jiménez y Chaverrí, (or Ap. 92), 5175 Santa Cruz **W:** radiochorotega1100am.com – **21)** 300 metros Norte y 50 Oeste del Antiguo Hospital de Alajuela, Alajuela (or Ap. 233-4060, Moll International, Alajuela) **W:** radioalajuela.com – **22)** Ap. 1312, Limon San José **W:** radionueva1140am.com – **23)** Ap. 298, 3000 Heredia **W:** radiovictoria.co.cr – **24)** Ap. 1128, 1000 San José **W:** radiocucu.com – **25)** Iglesia Maranatha, 7300 Puerto Limón **W:** feypoderradio.com – **26)** Frente a la Central de Hielo Frío, Cañas, Guanacaste – **27)** Ap.262, 8257 San Vito de Coto Brus **W:** facebook.com/pages/Radio-Ema%C3%BAs-1260-AM/109844075737548 – **28) W:** estereovision.com – **29)** 1 km este de la Basílica de los Ángeles, Carr. a Paraíso, 7050 Cartago **W:** facebook.com/lafuentemusical – **30)** Ap. 73, 4250 San Ramón **E:** radiosideral.com – **31)** Residencial Las Brisas, Casa #11A, Buscando la quebrada (Ap. 27), 5600 Liberia, (or Ap. 6462, 1000 San José) **W:** radioguanacasteccom – **32)** Ap. 248, 5000 Liberia **W:** radiopampa.com – **33)** 500 Sur 25 Este del Parque de Ciudad Quesada (Ap. 25), 4400 Cd. Quesada **W:** radiosancarlos.co.cr – **34)** Ap. 50, 5200 Nicoya **E:** radionicoya.com **35-46)** Stns are affiliated to Instituto Costarricense

de Enseñanza Radiofónica, Ap.132, 2050 San Pedro Montes de Oca (Ministerio de Educación Pública) **W:** icer.co.cr – **35)** Edificio Municipal, Barrio de las Tres Marías, San Marcos de Tarrazú **W:** radiolossantos.com – **36)** San Isidro de El General **W:** radiopz.com – **37)** Costado sur del Comando Norte, La Cruz, Guanacaste – **38)** Palenque Tonjibe, frente a la plaza de fútbol, Tonjibe, San Rafael de Guatuso, Prov. de Alajuela – **39)** Costado Oeste de Edificio Municipal, Los Chiles, Prov. de Alajuela – **40)** Centro pastoral diocesano de Tilarán, del Restaurante Aromático en la entrada a Tilarán 250 mts al norte carretera a Nuevo Arenal – **41)** Frente de la Plaza de Futbol de Amubri, Talamanca – **42)** Puriscal, San José – **43)** Edificio de la asociación de Desarrollo, Pital, Alajuela – **44)** De la esquina noreste de la Iglesia Nueva, 200m Norte, B:o Santa Lucia, Nicoya, Prov. de Guanacaste – **45)** culturalnicoya.com – **45)** Palacio Municipal, 132-2050 Turrialba, Prov. de Cartago – **46)** 300 metros al Norte del Cuerpo de Bomberos, Buenos Aires de Puntarenas – **47)** Frente a la Sucursal Banco Nacional de Costa Rica, Upala, Prov. de Alajuela – **50)** Centro Comercial San Francisco, Loc. 5 y 6, (or Ap. 16), 4100 Grecia **W:** radio16.com – **51)** 300 metros oeste del Parque de Santa María de Dota, 2541-1707 Quepos **W:** radioquepos.com – **52)** Barrio El Invú, La Rotonda, Pto. Golfito – **53)** Costado Oeste del Estadio de Guápiles (or Ap. 160), 7210 Guápiles **W:** radiopococi.com

FM in San José and vicinity (MHz): 88.7 Lira – 89.1 La Super Estación – 89.9 R. 899 – 89.5 Life FM Una Senda de Vida – 90.3 Sinfonola – 90.7 R. Ritmo 90.7 – 91.1 911 La Radio – 91.5 R. 915 – 91.9 Puntarenas – 92.3 Onda Radial – 92.7 Columbia Stereo – 93.1 R. Fides – 93.5 Monumental – 93.9 Sonido Latino – 94.3 Reloj – 94.7 R. 947 – 95.1 Z-FM – 95.5 R. 95 Cinco Jazz – 95.9 R. Romance – 96.3 Centro – 96.7 Universidad – 97.1 Faro del Caribe – 97.5 R. Musical – 97.9 R. 979 – 98.3 Stéreo Visión – 98.7 Columbia – 99.1 La Mejor FM – 99.5 R. Dos – 99.9 R. Azul – 100.3 FM Globo – 100.7 R. María – 101.1 R. Disney – 101.5 R. Nacional FM – 101.9 "U" – 102.3 La Super – 102.7 Exa FM – 103.1 Cientotres – 103.5 Best FM – 103.9 Sinai – 104.3 Oxígeno – 104.7 R. Hit – 105.1 Omega – 105.5 Ten Fifty-Five/Omega – 105.9 Beatz 106 – 106.3 R. Peninsular – 106.7 Premium – 107.1 R. Actual FM – 107.5 R. 107.5 Real Rock

CROATIA

L.T: UTC +2h (27 Mar-30 Oct: +3h) — **Pop:** 4.3 million — **Pr.L:** Croatian — **E.C:** 50Hz, 230V — **ITU:** HRV

HRVATSKA REGULATORNA AGENCIJA ZA MREZNE DJELATNOSTI (HAKOM)
Roberta Frangeša Mihanovica 9, 10010 Zagreb ☎ +385 1 7007007
🖷 +385 1 7007070 **W:** hakom.hr **LP:** Dir: Mario Weber
NB: HAKOM is the regulatory authority for broadcasting.

HRVATSKA RADIOTELEVIZIJA (HRT) (Pub)
Prisavlje 3, 10000 Zagreb ☎ +385 1 6342634 🖷 +385 1 6343712 **E:** hrt@hrt.hr **W:** hrt.hr **LP:** DG: Goran Radman

FM (MHz)	HR1	HR2	HR3	kW
Belje	93.3	98.1	-	50
Biokovo	89.7	98.9	-	80
Borinci	88.3	96.1	-	3
Brac	99.8	-	88.8	3
Buje	91.3	103.7	93.2	1
Celavac	95.1	98.1	-	80
Drenovci	92.1	104.4	-	3
Gruda	101.7	106.1	-	2
Ivanšcica	102.4	106.4	96.1	2x15/30
Kalnik	90.8	105.8	107.8	15
Labinštica	91.3	96.1	100.4	30
Licka Plješivica	87.7	90.5	100.3	50
Limski kanal	90.2	102.6	-	1
Mirkovica	91.3	93.3	-	30
Murter	92.7	99.4	104.1	1
Pag	98.5	103.4	-	3
Papuk	94.9	106.8	97.7	10
Psunj	97.3	99.7	-	80
Pula	91.4	94.4	102.1	5
Slavonski Brod	91.3	105.1	107.9	15
Sljeme	92.1	98.5	-	120
Srdj	88.9	98.5	-	30
Stipanov Gric	102.3	97.5	89.7	15
Šubicevac	94.0	90.0	102.3	1
Ucka	99.3	105.3	100.5	80
Uglian	91.6	87.6	-	5
Uljenje	95.1	89.3	105.6	3

NB: Txs below 1kW not listed.
D.Prgr: Prgr 1 (Prvi program): 24h. – **Prgr 2 (Drugi program):** 24h. – **Prgr 3 (Treci program):** 24h.

Hrvatski Radio (HR) Regional Stations

D.Prgr: all stns 24h (incl. rel. of HR1). **HR R. Dubrovnik:** Branitelja Dubrovnika 21, 20000 Dubrovnik. **E:** radiodubrovnik@hrt.hr. On (MHz) 88.2 (Rota 1.7kW), 89.5 (Ilija), 97.2 (Blato), 101.1 (Vela Luka), 103.7 (Slano 0.05kW), 103.8 (Korcula 0.2kW), 105.0 (Srdj 30kW), 106.2 (Lastovo & Ston 0.05kW), 106.5 (Lopud 0.03kW). – **HR R. Knin:** Krešimirova 30, 23300 Knin. **E:** radio.knin@hrt.hr. On (MHz) 88.1 (Šubicevac), 90.2 (Knin 0.6kW), 94.4 (Promina 5kW). – **HR R. Osijek:** Šamacka 13, 31000 Osijek. **E:** radioosijek@hrt.hr. On (MHz) 99.3 (Drenovci 3kW), 102.0 (Psunj 80kW), 102.4 (Osijek), 102.8 (Beli Manastir 50kW), 105.3 (Borinci 3kW), 105.6 (Zlatarevac), 105.8 (Ilok). For ethnic minorities: Hungarian ("Eszéki Rádió"): 1805-1830. – **HR R. Pula:** Riva 10, 52100 Pula. **E:** radiopula@hrt.hr. On (MHz) 93.8 (Novigrad 0.15kW), 93.9 (Limski kanal 1kW), 94.2 (Vrsar 0.16kW), 96.3 (Koromacno 0.3kW), 96.4 (Buje 1kW), 100.0 (Pula 5kW), 101.3 (Ucka 80kW), 103.8 (Raša 0.1kW). For ethnic minorities: Italian ("R. Pola"): MF 1000-1003, 1300-1303, 1530-1555 (Sun 1645). – **HR R. Rijeka:** Korzo 24, 51000 Rijeka. **E:** redakcija@radio-rijeka.com. On (MHz) 94.5 (Brgud), 95.1 (Pulac 0.5kW), 97.9 (Cres 0.3kW), 98.1 (Kupjacki Vrh), 101.7 (Prezid), 102.7 (Mirkovica 3kW), 104.0 (Fuzine 0.3kW), 104.7 (Ucka 80kW), 107.4 (Mali Lošinj 0.1kW), 107.5 (Mrkopalj 0.03kW). For ethnic minorities: Italian ("R. Fiume"): W 0930-0935, W 1130-1135, W 1330-1335, W 1500-1510. – **HR R. Sljeme:** Prisavlje 3, 10000 Zagreb. **E:** radio_sljeme@hrt.hr. On 88.1MHz (Sljeme 5kW). – **HR R. Split:** Mazuranicevo šetalište 24a, 21000 Split. **E:** radio.split@hrt.hr. On (MHz) 88.4 (Komiza), 100.2 (Hvar 0.05kW), 101.0 (Labinštica 30kW), 102.0 (Biokovo 80kW), 104.5 (Brac 3kW), 105.3 (Orlovaca), 105.8 (Vrlika). – **HR R. Zadar:** Poljana Šime Budinica 3, 23000 Zadar. **E:** radio_zadar@hrt.hr. On (MHz) 101.8 (Ugljan 5kW), 103.0 (Celevac 80kW), 105.9 (Pag).

OTHER STATIONS

	FM MHz	kW	Location	Station
13)	87.8	10	Brac	R. Dalmacija
7)	88.0	3	Beli Monastir	R. Baranja
21)	88.3	3	Virotivica	R. Marija
13)	88.5	2	Čelevac	R. Dalmacija
38)	88.6	1	Šibenik	R. Šibenik
26)	88.6	5	Slavonski Brod	R. Slavonija
26)	89.1	2	Nova Gradiška	R. Slavonija
30)	89.3	3	Ugljan	Novi R.
6)	89.4	2	Sisak	Totalni FM Sisak
11)	89.6	7	Porec	R. Centar Porec
5)	89.7	4.7	Sljeme	Antena Zagreb
42)	90.1	3	Martinšcak	Hrvatski Radio Karlovac (HRK)
28)	90.2	1	Pozega	R. Vallis Aurea (RVA)
34)	90.2	1	Vinkovci	Radiopostaja Vincovci
1)	90.4	1	Slatina	Narodni R.
41)	90.5	1	Komiza	Nautic R. Vis
2)	90.8	1	Šibenik	Otvoreni R.
35)	91.0	1	Djakovo	Slavonski R.
2)	91.1	1	Moslavacka Gora	Otvoreni R.
31)	91.6	5	Vinkovci	R. Pannonia
19)	91.7	5	Koprivnica	R. Koprivnica (RKC)
1)	92.0	5	Celevac	Narodni R.
4)	92.4	2	Alaginci	Soundset
2)	92.6	1	Zagreb	Otvoreni R.
32)	92.9	1.9	Virovitica	R. Virovitica
37)	93.0	1	Samobor	R. Samobor
2)	93.2	1.7	Gruda	Otvoreni R.
41)	93.4	1.5	Vis	Nautic R. Vis
12)	93.6	1	Sveta Nedelja	Prvi R.
11)	93.6	7	Rusnjak	R. Centar Porec
32)	93.7	1	Slatina	R. Virovitica
18)	93.8	1	Jastrebarsko	R. Jaska
10)	93.9	3	Bjelovar	R. Terezija
26)	94.3	1	Luzani	R. Slavonija
1)	94.5	3	Rijeka	Narodni R.
6)	94.9	5	Velika Gorica	Totalni FM Velika Gorica
1)	95.3	3	Osijek	Narodni R.
45)	95.4	5	Drenovci	Hrvatski R. Vukovar (HRV)
23)	95.4	1	Duga Resa	R. Mreznica
3)	95.5	1	Ugljan	Hrvatski Katolicki R.
27)	95.6	2	Donja Stubica	R. Stubica
1)	95.9	1	Pula	Narodni R.
32)	96.3	1	Pitomaca	R. Virovitica
21)	96.4	1	Zagreb	R. Marija
36)	96.5	1	Varazdin Breg	Kult R.
6)	96.5	1	Rijeka	Totalni FM Rijeka
17)	96.9	80	Ucka	R. Istra
16)	97.1	4	Gospic	R. Gospic
2)	97.3	1	Pula	Otvoreni R.
20)	97.6	4	Bogomolje	R. Makarska Rivijera (RMR)
2)	97.7	3	Pag	Otvoreni R.

	FM MHz	kW	Location	Station
47)	98.0	1.5	Cakovec	Hrvatski R. Cakovec
17)	98.0	5	Pula	R. Istra
4)	98.0	5	Zagreb	Soundset
43)	98.1	1	Nova Gradiška	R. Nova Gradiška
3)	98.6	1	Osijek	Hrvatski Katolicki R.
40)	99.1	1	Osijek	Gradski R. Osijek
15)	99.3	1	Maruševec	R. Max
33)	99.5	1	Zaprešic	R. Zaprešic
3)	100.0	15	Promina	Hrvatski Katolicki R.
39)	100.1	5	Moslavacka Gora	Bjelovarsko-Bilogorski R. (BBR)
38)	100.7	3	Zirje	R. Šibenik
44)	101.0	120	Sljeme	R. 101
1)	101.2	3	Metkovic	Narodni R.
4)	101.3	1	Slavonski Brod	Soundset
46)	101.4	1.5	Kutina	R. Moslavina
19)	101.5	5	Djurdjevac	R. Koprivnica (RKC)
25)	101.7	5	Buje	R. Eurostar
22)	101.8	1	Zagreb	R. Martin
29)	102.1	6	Lovic	Trend R.
2)	102.6	1.5	Mali Lošinj	Otvoreni R.
9)	102.7	1	Brac	R. Brac
2)	103.3	13	Otocac	Otvoreni R.
3)	103.5	120	Sljeme	Hrvatski Katolicki R.
1)	103.5	30	Labinštica	Narodni R.
3)	103.9	80	Psunj	Hrvatski Katolicki R.
3)	104.1	50	Licka Plješivica	Hrvatski Katolicki R.
45)	104.1	5	Zupanja	Hrvatski R. Vukovar (HRV)
2)	104.2	1	Komor	Otvoreni R.
2)	104.4	10	Papuk	Otvoreni R.
12)	104.5	1	Zagreb	Prvi R.
24)	104.9	1	Vidovec	R. Megaton
38)	104.9	5	Šibenik	R. Šibenik
8)	105.5	1	Okucani	R. Bljesak
2)	105.6	2	Zagreb	Otvoreni R.
14)	105.6	1.5	Cakovec	R. 1
16)	105.7	1.5	Stipanov Gric	R. Gospic
1)	106.1	30	Mirkovica	Narodni R.
35)	106.2	50	Beli Manastir	Slavonski R.
2)	106.5	3	Vidova Gora	Otvoreni R.
3)	106.7	80	Ucka	Hrvatski Katolicki R.
13)	106.9	4	Labinštica	R. Dalmacija
27)	106.9	2	Oštri Hum	R. Stubica
29)	106.9	2	Martinšcak	Trend R.
45)	107.2	5	Vinkovci	Hrvatski R. Vukovar (HRV)
1)	107.3	1	Kutina	Narodni R.
2)	107.3	80	Celevac	Otvoreni R.
13)	107.3	1	Komiza	R. Dalmacija
1)	107.5	2	Zagreb	Narodni R.
3)	107.9	80	Biokovo	Hrvatski Katolicki R.
3)	107.9	1	Slatina	Hrvatski Katolicki R.
1)	107.9	3	Pag	Narodni R.

NB: Txs below 1kW not listed.

Addresses & other information:

1) Avenija Veceslava Holjevca 29, 10000 Zagreb. – **2)** Cebini 28/III, 10000 Zagreb – **3)** Vocarska c. 106, 10000 Zagreb – **4)** Slavonska avenija 2, 10000 Zagreb – **5)** Avenija Veceslava Holjevca 29, 10000 Zagreb – **6)** Avenija Veceslava Holjevca 29, 10000 Zagreb – **7)** Trg slobode 32/3, 31300 Beli Manastir – **8)** Blazenog kardinala A. Stepinca 24, 35430 Okucani – **9)** Mladena Vodanovica 3, 21400 Supetar – **10)** Jurja Haulika 23, 43000 Bjelovar – **11)** Vitomira Širole Paje 18, 52440 Porec – **12)** Palmoticeva 7/I, 10000 Zagreb – **13)** Kralja Zvonimira 14/2, 21000 Split – **14)** Nova ulica 7, 40305 Nedeliše – **15)** Cerje Nebojse 151, 42243 Maruševec – **16)** Budacka 12, 53000 Gospic – **17)** Jurja Dobrile 6, 52000 Pazin – **18)** Trg Strossmayerov 5, 10450 Jastrebarsko – **19)** Zagrebacka b.b., 48000 Koprivnica – **20)** Don Mihovila Pavlinovica 1, 21300 Makarska – **21)** Jordanovac 110, 10000 Zagreb – **22)** Bjelovarska 62, 10360 Zagreb – **23)** Jozefinska c. 8, 47250 Duga Resa – **24)** Varazdinska 49/a, 42205 Vidovec – **25)** Rozag 23, 52470 Umag – **26)** Mile Budaka 1, 35000 Slavonski Brod – **27)** Toplicka 2, 49240 Donja Stubica – **28)** Cehovska 8/1, 34000 Pozega – **29)** Trg J. Broza 2, 47000 Karlovac – **30)** Zrinsko Frankopanska 13, 23000 Zadar – **31)** Trg Dr. Franje Tudjmana 2, 32100 Vinkovci – **32)** F. Rusana 1/9, 33000 Virovitica – **33)** Trg zrtava fašizma 6, 10290 Zapresic – **34)** Jurja Dalmatinca 29, 32100 Vinkovci – **35)** Hrvatske Republike 20, 31000 Osijek – **36)** Zagrebacka 94, 42000 Varazdin – **37)** Djure Basaricekove 4, 10432 Bregana – **38)** Bozidara Petranovica 3, 22000 Šibenik – **39)** Trg E. Kvaternika 3, 43000 Bjelovar – **40)** Trg Ante Starcevica 7, 31000 Gospic – **41)** V. Nazora 19, 21480 Vis – **42)** Ambroza Vraniczanya 2, 47000 Karlovac – **43)** Gunduliceva 7, 35400 Nova Gradiška – **44)** Gajeva 10, 10000 Zagreb – **45)** Dr. Franje Tudjmana 13, 32000 Vukovar – **46)** Ivana Gorana Kovacica 25, 44320 Kutina – **47)** Trg republike 5, 40000 Cakovec

CUBA

LT: UTC -5h (13 Mar-6 Nov: -4h) — **Pop:** 11.4 million — **Pr. L:** Spanish — **E.C:** 60Hz, 110/120V — **ITU:** CUB

MINISTERIO DE COMUNICACIONES (MC)
Dirección General de Telecomunicaciones
✉ Plaza de la Revolución, Ciudad de la Habana

INSTITUTO CUBANO DE RADIO Y TELEVISION (ICRT)
✉ Edif.Radiocentro, Av. 23 N° 258, Vedado, Habana 4 ☎ +53 7 8324648. Radio Cubana has links to most national and local stns: **W:** radiocubana.cu
Hrs of tr. usually 24h – see address section for variations. Call CM—

MW	Call	kHz	kW	Primary network, location
N1)	BA	530	1	R. Rebelde, Guantánamo (Antiguo), GU
N1)	BA	530		R. Rebelde, Caribe, IJ
N5)	BQ	530	10	R. Enciclopedia, HA
N1)	BA	540	10	R. Rebelde, Maisí, GU
N1)	BA	540	1	R. Rebelde, Sancti Spíritus, SS
N1)	BA	550	12	R. Rebelde, Pinar del Río, PR
N1)	BA	560	10	R. Rebelde, Ciego de Avila, CA
N1)	BA	570	1	R. Rebelde, Pilón, GR
N2)	BD	570	25	R. Reloj, Santa Clara, VC
N1)	BA	580	2.5	R. Rebelde, Mabujabo, GU
N1)	BA	590	10	R. Rebelde, Guantánamo (Burene), GU
N3)	BF	590	25	R. Musical Nacional, La Julia, MB
N1)	BA	600	50	R. Rebelde, San Germán, HO
N4)	BC	600	5	R. Progreso, Santiago de Cuba, SC
N1)	BA	610	1	R. Rebelde, Cienfuegos, CI
N1)	BA	610	10	R. Rebelde, Bueycito, GR
N1)	BA	610	10	R. Rebelde, Guane, PR
N2)	BD	610	1	R. Reloj, Trinidad, SS
N1)	BA	620	25	R. Rebelde, Colón, MA
N4)	BC	630	5	R. Progreso, Camagüey(Isábel Hortensia), CM
N4)	BC	640	50	R. Progreso, Guanabacoa, CH
N4)	BC	640	10	R. Progreso, Las Tunas, LT
N4)	BC	650	10	R. Progreso, Ciego de Avila, CA
N1)	BA	650	5	R. Rebelde, Santiago de Cuba, SC
N4)	BC	660	12	R. Progreso, Jovellanos, MA
N1)	BA	670	10	R. Rebelde, C. Brasil, CM
N1)	BA	670	10	R. Rebelde, Camagüey (Villa Rosita), CM
N1)	BA	670	50	R. Rebelde, Arroyo Arenas, CH
N1)	BA	670	5	R. Rebelde, Ciego de Avila, CA
N1)	BA	670	10	R. Rebelde, El Coco, HO
N1)	BA	670		R. Rebelde, Mayarí, HO
N1)	BA	670		R. Rebelde, Caribe, IJ
N1)	BA	670	10	R. Rebelde, Victoria de LT, LT
N5)	BQ	670	1	R. Enciclopedia, Cárdenas, MA
N1)	BA	670	5	R. Rebelde, Circunvalación, MA
N1)	BA	670	5	R. Rebelde, Bahía Honda, PR
N1)	BA	670	1	R. Rebelde, Los Palacios, PR
N1)	BA	670	1	R. Rebelde, Pinar del Río, PR
N1)	BA	670	1	R. Rebelde, Santa Lucía, PR
N1)	BA	670	50	R. Rebelde, Santa Clara, VC
N4)	BC	690	5	R. Progreso, Santiago de Cuba, SC
N4)	BC	690	10	R. Progreso, Santa Clara, VC
N1)	BA	710	25	R. Rebelde, Camagüey (Tagarro), CM
N1)	BA	710	200	R. Rebelde, Chambas, CA
N1)	BA	710	50	R. Rebelde, Cacocúm, HO
N1)	BA	710	50	R. Rebelde, Martí, MA
N1)	BA	710	50	R. Rebelde, La Julia, MB
PR01)	AM	710	10	R. Guamá, La Palma, PR
N1)	BA	710	1	R. Rebelde, Yaguajay, SS
N1)	BA	710	50	R. Rebelde, Santa Clara, VC
N1)	BC	720	2.5	R. Progreso, Mabujabo, GU
N4)	BC	730	10	R. Progreso, La Fe, IJ
HO01)	KO	740	10	R. Angulo, Sagua de Tanamo, HO
N4)	BC	750	10	R. Progreso, Palmira, CI
N4)	BC	760	10	R. Progreso, Guane, PR
N4)	BC	760		R. Progreso, Mayarí Arriba, SC
N1)	BA	770	10	R. Rebelde, Victoria de LT, LT
N2)	BD	790	10	R. Reloj, Holguín, HO
N2)	BD	790	25	R. Reloj, Pinar del Río, PR
N4)	BC	810	10	R. Progreso, Guantánamo, GU
N4)	IB	820	10	R. Progreso, Ciego de Avila, CA
CH01)	BU	820	10	R. Ciudad de la Habana, Arroyo Arenas, CH
N4)	BC	820	10	R. Progreso, Ciego de Avila, CA
N4)	BC	820	1	R. Progreso, Moa, HO
N2)	BD	830		R. Reloj, Mayarí Arriba, SC
SC01)	KC	840	1	R. Revolución, Palma Soriano, SC
VC01)	E	840	10	R. CMHW, Santa Clara, VC

MW	Call	kHz	kW	Primary network, location
N2)	BD	850	1	R. Reloj, Nueva Gerona, IJ
N4)	BC	850	1	R. Progreso, Trinidad, SS
N2)	BD	860		R. Reloj, Bolondrón, MA
N2)	BD	860	5	R. Reloj, Jovellanos, MA
N2)	BD	870	10	R. Reloj, Bueycito, GR
N2)	BD	870	10	R. Reloj, Baracoa, GU
N2)	BD	870	1	R. Reloj, Sancti Spíritus, SS
N4)	BC	880	12	R. Progreso, Mantua, PR
N2)	BD	880		R. Reloj, Mayarí Arriba, SC
N4)	BC	890	200	R. Progreso, Chambas, CA
SC01)	KC	890		R. Revolución, Santiago de Cuba, SC
N4)	BC	900	50	R. Progreso, San Germán, HO
CM01)	HA	910	25	R. Cadena Agramonte, Camagüey, CM
CH02)	BL	910	5	R. Metropolitana, V. María, CH
N2)	BD	910	5	R. Reloj, Bolondron, MA
N4)	BC	920	1	R. Progreso, Pilón, GR
CA01)	IP	930	10	R. Surco, Ciego de Ávila, CA
N2)	BD	930	1	R. Reloj, Cienfuegos, CI
N2)	BD	930	1	R. Reloj, La Jaiba, MA
N2)	BD	930	1	R. Reloj, Stgo de Cuba, SC
N4)	BC	940	1	R. Progreso, Sancti Spíritus, SS
N2)	BD	950	10	R. Reloj, Camagüey, CM
N2)	BD	950	10	R. Reloj, Arroyo Arenas, HA
SC01)	KC	950	1	R. R. Revolución, Mayarí Arriba, SC
N2)	BD	960	10	R. Reloj, Guantánamo (La Piña), GU
PR01)	AM	970	5	R. Guamá, Los Palacios, PR
N1)	BA	970	1	R. Rebelde, Trinidad, SS
CH03)	B	980	2.5	R. COCO, El Sapo, CH
N2)	BD	980	1	R. Reloj, Moa, HO
PR01)	AM	990	25	R. Guamá, Pinar del Río, PR
AR01)	SW	1000	10	R. Artemisa, Artemisa, AR
GR02)	NM	1000	5	R. Granma, Media Luna, GR
PR01)	AM	1000	25	R. Guamá, Pinjar del Río, PR
N2)	BD	1010	10	R. Reloj, Victoria de Las Tunas, LT
AR01)	AM	1020		R. Artemisa, AR
GU01)	M	1020	10	R. Guantánamo, Baracoa, GU
PR01)	AM	1020	10	R. Guamá, Bahía Honda, PR
MB01)	CL	1040	10	R. Mayabeque, Güines, MB
LT01)	LL	1050	10	R. Victoria, Victoria de Las Tunas, LT
PR01)	AM	1050	1	R. Guamá, Santa Lucía, PR
MA01)	DL	1060	25	R. 26, Jovellanos, MA
GU01)	M	1070	10	R. Guantánamo, Guantánamo, GU
PR01)	AM	1070	10	R. Guamá, Guane, PR
HA01)	CH	1080	5	R. Cadena Habana, V. María, CH
LT01)	LL	1090	1	R. Victoria, Amancio, LT
HO01)	KO	1100	1	R. Angulo, Mayarí, HO
HO01)	KO	1110	10	R. Angulo, Holguín, HO
N1)	BA	1130		R. Rebelde, Imías, GU
CA01)		1140		R. Surco, Morón, CA
CI01)		1140		R. Ciudad del Mar, Cienfuegos, CI
CM02)	BQ	1140	1	R. Camagüey, Camagüey (Isábel Hortensia),CM
GR01)	NL	1140	1	R. Bayamo, Media Luna, GR
MA02)	DP	1140	1	R. Ciudad Bandera, Cárdenas, MA
MB01)	CL	1140	25	R. Mayabeque, La Salud, MB
N1)	BA	1140	10	R. Rebelde, Aguada, CI
N1)	BA	1140		R. Rebelde, Guantánamo (La Piña), GU
N1)	BA	1140		R. Rebelde, Caribe, IJ
N1)	BA	1140	5	R. Rebelde, Circunvalación, MA
N1)	BA	1140	25	R. Rebelde, Morón, CA
N3)	BF	1140	10	R. Musical Nacional, Santa Clara, VC
GR01)	NL	1150	10	R. Bayamo, Entronque Bueycito, GR
GR01)	NL	1160	1	R. Bayamo, Pilón, GR
GU01)	M	1170	10	R. Guantánamo, Maisí, GU
N1)	BA	1180	10	R. Rebelde, Artemisa, AR
N1)	BA	1180	1	R. Rebelde, San Cristóbal, AR
N1)	BA	1180	10	R. Rebelde, C. Brasil, CM
N1)	BA	1180	50	R. Rebelde, Camagüey, CM
N1)	BA	1180	50	R. Rebelde, Guáimaro, CM
N1)	BA	1180	10	R. Rebelde, Arroyo Arenas, CH
N1)	BA	1180	50	R. Rebelde, Guanabacoa, CH
N1)	BA	1180	1	R. Rebelde, Ciego de Avila, CA
N1)	BA	1180	50	R. Rebelde, Chambas, CA
N1)	BA	1180	1	R. Rebelde, Cienfuegos, CI
N1)	BA	1180	5	R. Rebelde, Tulipán, CI
N1)	BA	1180	1	R. Rebelde, Guantánamo, GU
GU02)	DX	1180	1	R. Baracoa CMDX "LV del Toa", Mabujabo, GU
N1)	BA	1180	1	R. Rebelde, Banes, HO
N1)	BA	1180	50	R. Rebelde, Cacocúm, HO
N1)	BA	1180	1	R. Rebelde, Moa, HO
N1)	BA	1180	5	R. Rebelde, Sagua de Tánamo, HO
N1)	BA	1180	5	R. Rebelde, Nueva Gerona, IJ
N1)	BA	1180	1	R. Rebelde, Puerto Padre, LT

MW	Call	kHz	kW	Primary network, location
N1)	BA	1180	10	R. Rebelde, Victoria de LT, LT
N1)	BA	1180		R. Rebelde, Bolondrón, MA
N1)	BA	1180	5	R. Rebelde, Cárdenas, MA
N1)	BA	1180	25	R. Rebelde, Colón, MA
N1)	BA	1180	5	R. Rebelde, Ja Jaiba, MA
N1)	BA	1180	200	R. Rebelde, Martí, MA
N1)	BA	1180	10	R. Rebelde, Güines, MB
N1)	BA	1180		R. Rebelde, Hectómetro, MB
N1)	BA	1180	10	R. Rebelde, Sta Cruz del Norte, MB
N1)	BA	1180	5	R. Rebelde, Bahía Honda, PR
N1)	BA	1180	10	R. Rebelde, La Palma, PR
N1)	BA	1180	10	R. Rebelde, Los Palacios, PR
N1)	BA	1180	10	R. Rebelde, Pinar del Río, PR
N1)	BA	1180	10	R. Rebelde, Pinar del Río (III), PR
N1)	BA	1180	1	R. Rebelde, Santa Lucía, SS
N1)	BA	1180	1	R. Rebelde, Sancti Spíritus, SS
N1)	BA	1180		R. Rebelde, Corralillo, SC
N1)	BA	1180	1	R. Rebelde, Mayarí Arriba, SC
N1)	BA	1180	1	R. Taíno, Mayarí Arriba, SC
N5)	BQ	1180		R. Enciclopedia, Santiago de Cuba, SC
N1)	BA	1180	10	R. Rebelde, Santa Clara, VC
SC04)	JD	1190	10	R. Coral/R. Revolución, Chivirico, SC
SS01)	GL	1190	1	R. Sancti Spíritus, Trinidad, SS
SS01)	GL	1200	1	R. Sancti Spíritus, Yaguajay, SS
N1)		1210		R. Rebelde, Jobabo, LT
SS01)	GL	1210	10	R. Sancti Spíritus, Sancti Spíritus, SS
IJ01)	BY	1220	10	R. Caribe, La Fe, IJ
N4)	BC	1230		R. Progreso, Bayamo, GR
N4)	BC	1230		R. Progreso, La Palma, PR
GU03)	M	1250	1	R. Playita, Imías, GU
N4)	BC	1260	2.5	R. Progreso, Media Luna, GR
N5)	BQ	1280		R. Enciclopedia, Varadero, MA
SC02)	JN	1280	1	R. Mambí, Santiago de Cuba, SC
SS02)		1280	10	R. Trinidad Digital, Trinidad, SS
HO01)	KO	1300	1	R. Angulo, Banes, HO
N5)	BQ	1310	1	R. Enciclopedia, Nueva Gerona, IJ
N1)	BA	1320	1	R. Rebelde, San Cristóbal, AR
HO02)		1320		Ecos de Sagua, Sagua de Tánamo, HO
MA01)	DL	1320	1	R. 26, La Jaiba, MA
CI01)	FL	1340	10	R. Ciudad del Mar, Palmira, CI
CI01)	FL	1350	10	R. Ciudad del Mar, Aguada, CI
LT03)	LM	1350	1	R. Libertad, Puerto Padre, LT
GU01)		1370	1	R. Guantánamo, Imías, GU
VC02)		1400	1	R. Sagua, Sagua La Grande, VC
LT02)	LN	1450	1	R. Maboas, Amancio Rodríguez, LT
MB01)	CL	1450	1	R. Mayabeque, Santa Cruz del Norte, MB
SC04)		1460		R. 8SF, Mayarí Arriba, SC
LT03)	LM	1470	1	R. Chaparra, Puerto Padre, LT
HO03)	KN	1490	1	R. Mayarí, Mayarí, HO
SC05)	KZ	1520	1	R. Baraguá "LV del Cauto", Palma Soriano, SC
N1)	BA	1550	1	R. Rebelde, San Cristóbal, AR
N1)	BA	1550	5	R. Rebelde, Tulipán, CI
N1)	BA	1550	1	R. Rebelde, Guáimaro, CM
N1)	BA	1550	1	R. Rebelde, Jayama, CM
N1)	BA	1550	1	R. Rebelde, Guantánamo, GU
N1)	BA	1550	5	R. Rebelde, Cárdenas, MA
N1)	BA	1550	5	R. Rebelde, Circunvalación, MA
N1)	BA	1550		R. Rebelde, Hectómetro, MB
N4)	BC	1550		R. Progreso, La Palma, PR
N1)	BA	1550		R. Rebelde, Trinidad, SC
N1)	BA	1550	1	R. Rebelde, Yaguajay, SS
N1)	BA	1550		R. Rebelde, Corralillo, SC
N1)	BA	1550	1	R. Rebelde, Sagua La Grande, VC
N1)	BA	1550	10	R. Rebelde, Santa Clara, VC
N1)	BA	1620		R. Rebelde, El Sapo, CH
N1)	BA	1620	5	R. Rebelde, Guanabacoa, CH
N1)	BA	1620		R. Rebelde, Guantánamo, GU
GR01)	NL	1620		R. Bayamo, Bayamo GR

SW	Call	kHz	kW	Primary network, location
N4)		4765	50	R. Progreso, La Habana: 0030-0400
N1)	BA	5025	50	R. Rebelde, La Habana

Provinces: AR=Artemisa CA=Ciego de Avila CH=Ciudad Habana CI=Cienfuegos CM=Camagüey GR=Granma GU=Guantánamo HA=Habana HO=Holguín IJ=Isla de laJuventud LT=Las Tunas MA=Matanzas MB=Mayabeque PR=Pinar del Río SC=Santiago de Cuba SS=Sancti Spíritus VC=Villa Clara

N.B.: Esp. at night stations relay an upper level station, i.e. municipal station relays the respective provinvial station and provincial station relays a nationwide station. Amount of own programming for the smallest stations can be only a few hours per day. R. Rebelde carries sports events which are relayed by many other stations and also other

relays may occur. Most transmitters operate 24h.

FM in La Habana (MHz): 90.3 R. Progreso – 91.7 CMCK R. COCO – 93.3 R. Taíno – 94.1 R. Enciclopedia – 94.9 R.Ciudad de la Habana – 96.7 R. Rebelde – 98.3 Metropolitana – 99.1 R. Musical Nacional – 99.9 R. Cadena Habana – 100.9 Habana FM –101.5 R. Reloj – 102.5 R. Habana Cuba – 104.7 R. Rebelde – 106.3 R. Progreso – 106.9 Habana R – 107.9 R. Rebelde.

National networks: N1) R. Rebelde, Ap. 6277, La Habana 10600 (or Edif. Del ICRT, Av. 23 N° 258, Vedado, La Habana 10400) **W:** radiorebelde.cu – **N2)** R. Reloj, Ap. 6277, Ciudad de La Habana (or Ed. Radiocentro, Calle 23 No. 258, (8avo piso), entre Ly M, Vedado, La Habana 10400 **W:** radioreloj.cu – **N3)** R. Musical Nacional, Edificio N, Calle N, entre 23 y 21, Vedado La Habana 10400 **W:** cmbfradio.cu – **N4)** R. Progreso, Ap. 4042, La Habana 10300 (or Infanta 105, Esq. A 25, Centro Habnana) **W:** radioprogreso.cu – **N5)** R. Enciclopedia, Edificio N, Calle N. N° 266 (bajos), entre 21 y 23, Vedado, La Habana 10400 **W:** radioenciclopedia. cu – **N6)** R. Taíno, Ap. 6277, La Habana 10400 (or Av. 23 N° 258, Vedado, La Habana 10400) - FM only

Provincial and municipal stations

Artemisa AR01) Calle 50 No. 2310, entre 23 y 25, Artemisa 33800 **W:** artemisaradioweb.cu

Ciego de Ávila CA01) Ap. 183 (or Chicho Valdés 66), Ciego de Ávila 65100 **W:** radiosurco.cu

Ciudad de La Habana CH01) Ap. 6599, La Habana 10600 (or Calle N No. 266 (5to piso), entre 21 y 23, Vedadado, Plaza de la Revolución, La Habana 10400) **W:** radiociudadhabana.icrt.cu – **CH02)** Ed. Focsa, Calle N No. 301 (1er piso), esq. A 17, Vedado, Plaza de la Revolución, La Habana 10400 **W:** radiometropolitana.cu – **CH03)** Ed. Focsa, Calle N No. 301, esq. A 17, Vedado, Plaza de la Revolución, La Habana 10400 **W:** radiococo.icrt.cu

Cienfuegos CI01) Calle 37 No. 3602, entre 36 y 38, Cienfuegos 55100 **W:** rcm.cu

Camagüey CM01) Calle Cisneros # 310 entre Ignacio Agramonte y General Gómez, Camagüey 70100 **W:** cadenagramonte.cu – **CM02)** **W:** radiocamaguey.wordpress.com Camagüey 1200-1800, Cadena Agramonte 1800-1200

Granma GR01) Ap. 74 (or Calle General Calixto García 156, entre Figueredo y Luz Vásquez 74) Bayamo 85100 **W:** radiobayamo.icrt.cu – **GR02)** Ap. 220 (or Calle Martí 341, entre Quintin Banderas y León), Manzanillo 87510 **W:** radiogranma.co.cu

Guantánamo GU01) "Trinchera Antiimperialista", Ap. 96 (or Donato Mármol 409, entre José Martí y Prado y Martí, Guantánamo 95100 **W:** radioguantanamo.icrt.cu – **GU02)** Calle Martí #122, % Frank País y Maraví, Baracoa 97310. H of tr: 1000-0200 **W:** radiobaracoa.icrt.cu – **GU03)** Calle B No. 2050, Imías 97500. facebook.com/Emisora-Radio-Playita-683062335045536

La Habana HA01) Calle 15, esq. a A, No. 210, Vedado, Plaza de la Revolución, La Habana 10400 **W:** cadenahabana.cu

Holguín HO01) Ap. 14 (or Calle Máximo Gómez 298 (3er piso) entre Frexes y Martí), Holguín 80100 **W:** radioangulo.cu – **HO02)** Sagua de Tánamo 83200 – **HO03)** Calle Martí 46, Mayarí 83000 **W:** radiocaribe.icrt.cu

Isla de la Juventud IJ01) Calle 26, entre 41 y 43, Nueva Gerona 25100 **W:** radiocaribe.icrt.cu

Las Tunas LT01) Ap. 211 (or Calle Colón 157, entre Julián Santana y Francisco Vega), Las Tunas 75100 **W:** tiempo21.cu – **LT02)** Avenida Sergio Reynó 19, Amancio Rodriguez 77700 **W:** radiomaboas.cu – **LT03)** Ap. 45 (or Avenida de La Libertad 95), Puerto Padre 77200. Chaparra 16-21, Libertad 21-04, Victoria 04-16. **W:** radiolibertad.cu

Matanzas MA01) Ap. 51 (or Milanés final, esq. a Guachinango), Matanzas 40100 **W:** radio26.icrt.cu – **MA02)** Calzada, esq. a Calvo, Cárdenas 42100 **W:** radiociudadbandera.wordpress.com **FM:** 99.7MHz.

Mayabeque MB01) Calle 76 No. 7707, entre 77 y 81, Güines 33900. 1100-0500 exc. 24h in July/August. **W:** radiomayabeque.icrt.cu

Pinar del Río PR01) Calle Colón 14, entre Adela Azcuy y Juan Gualberto Gómez, Pinar del Río 20100 **W:** rguama.icrt.cu

Santiago de Cuba SC01) Ap. 232 (or Aguilera 554, entre San Augustín y Barnada), Santiago de Cuba 90100 **W:** cmkc.cu – **SC02)** Calle 8 No. 56, entre A e Independencia, Reparto Sueño, Santiago de Cuba 90900 **W:** radiomambi.icrt.cu – **SC03)** R. Coral, Calle C No. 64, Chivirico, Guamá 92800 – **SC04)** R. radio8sf.icrt.cu – **SC05)** R. radiobaragua.cu

Sancti Spíritus SS01) Circunvalación s/n, Los Olivos 1, Sancti Spíritus 60100. **W:** radiosanctispiritus.cu – **SS02)** Antonio Guiteras #226, Trinidad. **W:** radiotrinidad.cu

Villa Clara VC01) Ap. 376 (or Parque Leoncio Vidal 4, entre Martha Abreu y Pao Chao), Santa Clara 50100 **W:** cmhw.cu – **VC02)** Libertadores 100, esq. a Carmen Ribalta, Sagua la grande, Villa Clara 52310 **W:** radiosagua.icrt.cu

Guantánamo Bay (leased to USA)

AFRTS (US Navy)
✉ Naval Media Center Broadcasting Detatchment, Guantánamo Bay, Cuba, PSC 1005, Box 22, FPO AE 09593, USA **E:** gitmo@mediacen.navy.mil
MW: Guantánamo Bay: 1340kHz 0.25kW
FM: 102.1MHz 0.5kW (stereo), 103.1MHz 0.5kW – **D.Prgr:** "R. GTMO" 24h on 1340kHz/102.1MHz. Rel AFRTS satellite sce on 103.1MHz

CURAÇAO (Netherlands)

L.T: UTC -4h — **Pop:** 150,560 — **Pr.L:** Dutch (official), Papiamentu, English, Spanish — **E.C:** 50Hz, 127/220V — **ITU:** CUW

Bureau Telecommunicatie en Post
✉ Beatrixlaan 9, Emmastad; P.O. Box 2047, Curaçao ☎ +599 9 463 1700 🖷 +599 9 736 5265 **W:** btnp.com **E:** gen.affairs@burtel.cw

MW Call	kHz	kW	Station, location
1) PJZ-86	860	10	Z-86 R. Curom, Willemstad

FM	MHz	kW	Station, location
1)	88.3		Rockorsou, Willemstad
12)	89.7		R. Krioyo, Willemstad
1)	91.5		Z-86 FM , Willemstad
11)	92.1		Direct Life 92.1 FM, Willemstad
9)	92.7		R. Edukativo, Deltha 92, Willemstad
20)	93.3	0.5	Tele curaçao FM, Willemstad
3)	93.9	20	R. Korsou FM, Willemstad
19)	94.5	0.5	Voz di Bonaire, Willemstad
8)	95.1	0.5	Clazz FM, Willemstad
1)	95.7	4	Mi 95, Willemstad
13)	96.5	0.5	New Song, Willemstad
10)	97.3	1	Dolfijn FM, Willemstad
8)	97.9	0.5	Easy 97.9 FM, Willemstad
4)	98.5	2.5	R. Semiya, Willemstad
21)	99.1	0.5	Radio Lighthouse, Willemstad
15)	99.7		R. MAS, Santa Maria
7)	100.3		Hit 100.3, Willemstad
3)	101.1	5	Laser 101, Willemstad
2)	101.9	2,5	R. Hoyer 1, Willemstad
5)	103.1		Paradise FM, Willemstad
8)	103.9	0.5	R. One FM, Willemstad
14)	104.5	1	R. Active FM, Willemstad
2)	105.1	2,5	R. Hoyer 2, Willemstad
16)	106.3		Fiesta FM, Willemstad
11)	107.1		R. Direct, Willemstad
6)	107.9	1	Rumbera Network, Willemstad

Addresses and other information
1) Roodeweg 64, Willemstad, Curaçao ☎ +599 9 462 2020 🖷 +599 9 462 5796 **W:** 88rockorsou.fm**E:** sales86@radioz86.com **E:** mi95@curom.com – **2)** Plasa Horacio Hoyer 21, Willemstad, Curaçao ☎ +599 9 461 1678 🖷 +599 9 461 6528 **E:** sales@radiohoyer.com **W:** radiohoyer.com MD: Mrs. Helen Hoyer. R. Hoyer 1 in Papiamentu 0930-0400, R. Hoyer 2 in Dutch 1000-0400 – **3)** Bataljonweg 7, Willemstad, Curaçao ☎ +599 9 737 3012 🖷 +599 9 737 2888. 24h. **E:** studio@korsou.com Separate prgrs ("Laser 101") on 101.1MHz ☎ +599 9 738 5670 **W:** laser-101.com – **4)** Parmantierweg 2, Willemstad, Curaçao ☎ +599 9 462 4000, +599 9 462 4002, +599 462 4005 🖷 +599 9 462 4004. Dir: Ferris Thode. Rlg 24h programs in English and Papiamentu **E:** info@radiosemiyafm.net **W:** radiosemiyafm.net – **5)** Fokkerweg 26, Willemstad or PO Box 6103, Willemstad ☎ +599 9 462 8103 🖷 +599 9 462 9103 **W:** paradisefmcuracao.com **E:** info@paradisefm.cw Dutch with every h and half h Dutch news. Owner: Cees Baas – **6)** Caracasbaaiweg 194, Willemstad ☎ +599 9 465 9580 🖷 +599 9 461 5028 **W:** rumberanetwork.com **E:** contacto@rumberanetwork.com.ve – **7)** Compleho Deportivo Casa Grandi Z/N Willemstad ☎ +599 9 747 3333 🖷 +599 9 747 1003 Manager: Elmer Cijntje. 24h Prgrs in Papiamentu, Spanish, Creole and English– **8)** Arikokweg 19A, Willemstad ☎ +599 9 462 3162 and +599 9 462 2664 🖷 +599 9 462 8712. GM: Quintus Fliervoet ClazzFM **E:** info@clazzfm.com **W:** clazzfm.com 24h light music & jazz in E, Papiamentu & Dutch, R. One FM 24h dance & Top 40 music in E, & Dutch. Easy FM **W:** easyfm.com **E:** radio@easyfm.com – **9)** Suffisantweg 18, Willemstad ☎ +599 9 868 8892🖷 +599 9 888 5260 and + 599 9 869 3878 **W:** radiodeltha927.com **E:** info@radiodeltha927.com – **10)** Mambo Beach Blvd, Willemstad ☎ +599 9 465 9975 🖷 599 9 461 9975 Dir. Egon Sybrandy **D.Prgr.** 24 hours in Dutch **E:** info@dolfijnfm.com **W:** dolfijnfm.com – **11)** F.D Rooseveltlaan 214, Tesoro Shopping Center, Willemstad Dir. Mrs. Jachmin Pinedo R. Direct: in Papiamentu and Spanish 1000-0400, other times music ☎ +599 9 888 5107 🖷 +599 9 888 8407 **E:** studio@direct107.com **W:** direct107.com Direct Life 92.1FM in Papiamentu and Dutch, interviews

also in Dutch, English and Spanish 1030-1300 and 1800-2400 , other times music ☎ +599 9 888 4107 🖷 +599 9 888 8407 **E:** 921local@gmail.com **W:** direct92.com – **12)** Gosieweg 133,Willemstad ☎ +599 9 736 4915 🖷 +599 9 736 4914 **E:** radiokrioyo@live.com– **13)** New Song Building, Muizenberg z/n ☎ +599 9 868 0965 🖷 +599 9 868 4343 **Dir.** Welton F.A. Esprit ; Christian prgrs 24 h in English, French, Papiamentu, Dutch, Spanish, **E:** info@newsong-curacao.com **W:** newsongcuracao.com – **14)** Kaya Simon Pieters Kwiers 67, Willemstad, Curaçao ☎+599 9 560 3302 Dir. Arthur Zimmerman 24h in Papiamentu **W:** active.fm **E:** info@active.fm – **15)** Fosfaatweg 8, Sta. Maria ☎+599 9 888 3997 🖷 +599 9 888 6997 **W:** mas99.com **E** administratie@mas99.com– **16)** Fatimaweg 2, Suffisant, Willemstad ☎+599 9 869 6606 🖷 +599 9 869 6613 Dir. Carlos S. de Abreu Ribeiro **E:** fiesta@fiesta.fm **W:** fiesta.fm – **19)** Arikokweg 30, Charo Dir: Feliciano da Silva Piloto ☎+599 717 5947 🖷 +599 717 8220 **W:** vozdibonaire.com **E:** vozdibonaire@gmail.com Music and information, 24 hrs – **20)** Berg Arafat z/n, Willemstad , GMr: Hugo Lew Jen Tai ☎+599 9 777 1688 🖷 +599 9 461 4138 and +599 9 777 1650 **W:** telecuracao.fm **E:** 93.3@telecuracao.fm – **21)** Totonakenweg z/n, Groot Kwartier ☎+599 9 973 64805 Dir. Robert Braumuller **W:** radiolighthousefm.com **E:** radiolh01@gmail.com **D.Prgr.** 24h in Dutch, Papiamentu, English and Spanish

CYPRUS

L.T: UTC +2h (27 Mar-30 Oct: +3h) — **Pop:** 800,000 — **Pr.L:** Greek, Turkish, Armenian — **E.C:** 50Hz, 240V — **ITU:** CYP

CYPRUS RADIO-TELEVISION AUTHORITY
✉ 32 Nikis Ave, P.O.Box 23377, 1682 Nicosia ☎+357 22 512468 🖷 F+357 22 512473 **W:** crta.org.cy **E:** crtauthority@cytanet.com.cy

CYPRUS BROADCASTING CORPORATION (semi-gov)
✉ CyBC Street, Athalassa, P.O. Bxo 24824, CY-1397 Nicosia ☎+357 22 862000 🖷 +357 22 314050 **W:** riknews.com.cy **E:** rik@cybc.com.cy
L.P: DG: Themis Themistocleous. Deputy DG: Michael Stylianou.

MW	kHz	kW	Ch.		MW	kHz	kW	Ch.
Nicosia	603	100	3		Nicosia	963	100	1

FM (MHz)	Ch. 1	Ch. 2	Ch. 3	Ch.4	kW
Armenochori	105.0	93.1	106.7	90.5	2
Mt. Olympos	97.2	91.1	94.8	88.2	30
Paphos	92.4	97.9	94.0	90.2	7
Paralimni	91.4	94.2	96.0	100.9	4

Ch. 1 (Proto) in Greek: 24h – **Ch. 2 (Deutero)** Multilingual: 24h. Prgrs in English 1030-1400, 1500-0300; Turkish 0300-1400; Armenian 1400-1500 – **Ch. 3 (Trito)** in Greek: 24h – **Ch. 4 (R. Love)** in Greek: 24h.
Ann: Greek: "Radiofonikon Idryma Kyprou". Turkish: "Burasi Kibris Radyo Yayin Korporasyonu". **IS:** "Avkoritssa" (guitar).

Other Stations (all MHz):
ANT1 FM: Larnaca 102.7, Paphos 103.7. **W:** ant1iwo.com/fm – **Dromos FM:** Larnaca 100.5, Limassol 100.3, Nicosia 106.7. **W:** facebook.com/dromosfmcy – **Kanali 6:** Limassol 98.6, Nicosia 106.0, Mount Phanos 107.0 **W:** kanali6.com.cy – **Kanali 7:** Nicosia 98.4, Limassol 102.1 **W:** kanali7.com – **Kiss FM:** Limassol 88.5, Nicosia 89.0. **W:** kissfm.com.cy – **Klik FM:** Limassol 89.6, Larnaca 98.2, Nicosia 105.5 **W:** klikfm.com.cy – **Logos R:** Mount Olympos 101.1, Larnaca 101.6 **W:** logosradio.com.cy – **Mix FM:** Limassol 90.8, Larnaca 102.2, Nicosia 102.3 **W:** mixfmradio.com – **R. Astra:** Mount Olympos 92.8, Larnaca 105.3 **W:** astra.com.cy – **R. Athina:** Limassol 88.7, Nicosia 100.7 **W:** radioathina.com – **R. Proto:** Agia Napa 87.9, Larnaca 89.4, Mount Olympos 99.3 **W:** radioproto.com.cy – **R. Sfera:** Paphos 96.8, Limassol 106.4 **W:** radiosfera.com.cy – **Rock FM:** Limassol 89.2, Paphos 98.5, Latchi 106.7 **W:** rockfmcyprus.com – **Russian Wave:** Larnaca 98.6, Limassol 105.6 **W:** russianwave.com – **Super FM:** Larnaca 95.7, Paphos 103.4, Mount Olympos 104.8 **W:** superfmradio.com – **Super Sport FM:** Limassol 100.3, Larnaca 103.0, Nicosia 106.7 **W:** sport-fm.com.cy
BBC World Sce: MW: 1323kHz English 0200-2300
Monte Carlo Doualiya & **Trans World R.** rel. on **MW:** 1233kHz 0200-2115.
R. Sawa: MW: 990kHz 24h.
For further details on these stns see International Radio section.

NORTHERN CYPRUS

SUPREME BROADCASTING BOARD (YYK)
✉ Memduh Asaf St. 9, Kösklüçiftlik, Lefkosa, Northern Cyprus ☎+90 392 228 1368 🖷+90 392 228 1272 **W:** kktcyyk.com **E:** info@kktcyyk.org

BAYRAK RADYO TELEVIZYON KURUMU (BRTK, Gov.)
✉ BRT Sitesi, Dr. Fasil Küçük Bulvari, Lefkosa, Northern Cyprus, via

Mersin 10, Turkey ☎ +90 392 225 5555 🖷 +90 392 225 4991
W: brtk.net **E:** brt@brtk.net
L.P: DG: Mete Tümerkan. Head Tr. Dept: Mustafa Tosun.

FM	R.1	B.FM	B.Int.	R.Klasik	BTM	BRH	kW
Kantara	90.6	98.1	87.8	93.4			10/1
Selvilitepe	102.0	92.1/88.8	105.0	88.4/102.5	94.6	100.1	20/1
Lefkosa	89.6	94.2					0.3/10

Radyo 1 in Turkish: 24h – **Bayrak FM** in Turkish: 24h – **Bayrak International in** English: 24h – **Radyo Klasik:** 24h – **Bayrak Türk Müzigi:** 24h – **Bayrak Radyo Haber** (news in Turkish/English/Greek/German/Russian/French/Arabic): 24h.

OTHER STATIONS FM (MHz):

	Station	W	E	kW	Location
1)	R. Odtü	103.1		1	Kalkanli
2)	Cool FM	92.6	97.5	1	Magosa
3)	As FM	97.7	95.2	1	Lefkosa
4)	Sim FM	98.6	89.5	2.5/0.3	Lefkosa
5)	Süper FM	98.9		1	Lefkosa
6)	Metro FM	104.0		1	Lefkosa
7)	Kral FM	107.0		1	Lefkosa
8)	Kibris FM	103.4	100.2	5/2.5	Lefkosa
9)	First FM	90.0	96.6	1/0.3	Lefkosa
10)	Akdeniz FM	88.6		1	Lefkosa
11)	R. Vatan Türkü	104.5	94.4	5/1	Lefkosa
12)	R. Vatan Nihavent	100.4	89.8	5/3	Lefkosa
13)	Dance FM	95.5	95.1	1	Lefkosa
14)	Radyo T	96.6		1	Lefkosa
15)	R. Güven	90.4/89.2	90.8	5/2/5	Lefkosa
16)	R. Plus	106.2	105.8	1	Magosa
17)	Laü FM	97.4		1	Lefke
18)	Mayis FM	96.0	101.3	1	Lefkosa
19)	Gaü FM	105.8		1	Gime
20)	Ciu FM	107.2		1	Lefkosa
21)	Daü FM		106.5	2	Magosa
22)	R. Enerji	93.1	100.0	1	Lefkosa
23)	R. Havadis	107.8		2	Lefkosa
24)	Ada FM	96.2	93.8	1	Lefkosa
25)	Capital R.	93.8	99.4	1	Lefkosa
26)	R. Vatan	87.5	104.3	5	Lefkosa
27)	Ydü FM	88.0		1	Lefkosa
28)	R. Juke	90.9	99.8	2.5/1	Lefkosa
29)	Dream Live FM	104.2	102.8	2	Lefkosa
30)	TRT FM	101.3		5	Lefkosa
31)	R. Play FM	102.9	107.2	2/1	Lefkosa

Tx sites: W (west) = Selvilitepe, E (east)= Kantara-Sinan Dagi. All stns 24h. **1)** radyoodtu.com.tr – **5)** superfm.gen.tr – **7)** kralfm.com.tr – **9)** kibrisfirstfm. net – **13)** dancefm.com.tr – **15)** radyoguven.com – **17)** radyo.eul.edu.tr – **18)** radyomayis.com – **20)** ciu.edu.tr/ciu-fm-2 – **21)** dautv.emu.edu.tr – **22)** radyoenerji.com – **23)** radyohavadis.com – **24)** adafmkibris.com – **25)** capitalcyprus.com – **27)** neu.edu.tr – **28)** radyoujuke.com – **29)** dreamflivecyprus.com – **31)** playfm.com.tr

AKROTIRI & DHEKELIA (UK)

Pop: 15,700 — **Pr.L:** English, Greek — **E.C:** 50Hz, 240V — **ITU:** CYP

BFBS RADIO, CYPRUS (Mil.)

🖃 BFBS Akrotiri, BFPO 57, UK ☎ +357 2527 8518 🖷 +357 2527 8580
W: ssvc.com/bfbs/radio/cyprus **E:** cyprus@bfbs.com
L.P: GM: Tess Turner; Eng Mgr: J. Dunlop

FM (MHz)	BFBS1	BFBS2	kW
Akrotiri	89.9	92.1	25
Ayios Nikolaos	107.5	89.7	
Dhekelia	99.6	95.3	25
Nicosia	91.7	89.7	1.5

D.Prgr: 24h. **Ann:** "This is BFBS Radio"

Other stations:
BBC World Sce: MW: Zakaki 639 & 720kHz: Arabic 0300-2200

CZECH REPUBLIC

L.T: UTC +1h (27 Mar-30 Oct: +2h) — **Pop:** 10.5 million — **Pr.L:** Czech — **E.C:** 50Hz, 230V — **ITU:** CZE

CESKÉ RADIOKOMUNIKACE, a.s.

🖃 U nákladového nádrazí 4, 130 00 Praha 3 ☎ +420 267 005 111 **E:** info@radiokomunikace.cz **W:** radiokomunikace.cz
Operates the TV and radio transmission facilities.

CESKY ROZHLAS (CZECH RADIO)

🖃 Vinohradská 12, 120 99 Praha 2 ☎ +420 221 551 111 🖷 +420 221

551 300 **E:** info@rozhlas.cz **W:** rozhlas.cz
L.P: DG: Peter Duhan PD: René Zavoral TD: Karel Zyka

LW & MW:	kHz	kW	Prgr.
Uherské Hradište	270	50	CRo 1
Praha (Liblice)	639	750	CRo 2 + CRo Plus
Ostrava-Svinov	639	30	CRo 2 + CRo Plus
Brno (Dobrochov)	954	200	CRo 2 + CRo Plus
Ceské Budejovice	954	30	CRo 2 + CRo Plus
Karlovy Vary	954	20	CRo 2 + CRo Plus
Moravské Budejovice	1332	50	CRo 2 + CRo Plus

	FM (MHz)	CRo 1	CRo 2	CRo 3	CRo 5	CRoPlus	kW
9)	As	107.9			96.7		0.1/0.2
1)	Benešov				99.0		1(5)
6)	Brno	95.1	102.0			106.5	72/91/72
6)	Brno (city)			90.4	93.1	92.6	6/6/2
2)	C. Budejovice	91.1	103.7	96.1	106.4		80/1/40/80
9)	Cheb		88.2	106.2	100.8	89.5	1
4)	Chomutov	98.9	94.2	96.3	103.1		10
3)	Domazlice	98.0			105.3		10
13)	Frydlant				97.4		0.2
6)	Hodonín	106.2	107.8	100.4	93.6		9/3/9
5)	Hradec Králové				95.3		1
11)	Hradec Králové				104.7		10
9)	Hulín				101.6		1
9)	Jáchymov				103.4		1
8)	Jeseník	91.3	88.7	98.2	106.8		20/0.2/20/20
	Jicin		106.9				1
10)	Jihlava	90.7	107.1	88.4	87.9	95.4	20/10/20/10
	Kaplice			105.9			0.2
9)	Karlovy Vary	102.6		105.7	91.0	97.8	0.1/0.2/1
	Kašperské Hory			107.2			0.5
1)	Kladno				100.5		0.2
3)	Klatovy	99.8	90.3	88.6	102.4		10
1)	Kutná Hora		102.2		100.5		1/3
13)	Liberec	95.9	89.9	103.9	102.3		20/20/20/1
13)	Liberec					91.3	0.5
8)	Lipník n.Becvou				88.7		0.1
9)	Marián.Lázne	97.6			100.3		1
1)	Mladá Boleslav				100.3		0.5
	Nové Hrady		102.2				1
8)	Olomouc				92.8	107.2	1
7)	Opava		101.7		102.6		1/0.5
7)	Ostrava	101.4	101.9	104.8	107.3		43/0.5/43/3
11)	Pardubice	89.7	100.1	102.7	101.0		90/90/90/1
	Písek	97.0	98.9	105.2			1
	Plzen (North)	89.1	107.1	95.6			80
3)	Plzen (East)	99.2			106.7	93.3	10
3)	Plzen (city)				91.0		1
1)	Praha				100.7		50
	Praha (city)	94.6	91.2	105.0		92.6	5/3/5/7
1)	Príbram	102.2	107.0		100.0	103.6	0.4/1/1
13)	Prosec n.N.				102.3		1
1)	Rakovník				100.4		1
5)	Rychnov n.K.				96.5		1
3)	Slavonice		103.3		88.2		1
3)	Sokolov	94.3			98.2		0.4
	Sušice	90.6					1
11)	Svitavy				102.4		1
3)	Tachov				106.3		0.4
10)	Trebíc				90.1		0.2
7)	Trinec	92.1			90.1		1
5)	Trutnov	88.5	93.4		90.5	101.9	10/10/20
10)	Uher. Hradište				99.1		0.2
6)	Uhersky Brod	93.0			107.3		1
12)	Uhersky Brod				107.3		1
4)	Ústí nad Labem	90.9		104.5	88.8		80
	Ústí n.L. (city)		98.6				1
11)	Ústí n. Orlicí				98.6		1
7)	Val. Mezirící	92.5	89.9	96.8	99.0		7/1/7/7
4)	Varnsdorf			88.4	98.5		0.2
	Votice						95
3)	Vratislavice	93.1	103.2		91.3		0.5
7)	Vrbno pod Prad.		103.6		95.5		1
7)	Vsetín	92.1	102.9	98.3	89.5		0.1
12	Vsetín				89.5		0.1
	Zelezná Ruda				95.8		0.2
6)	Zlín	99.5	107.7	94.8	97.5		6
12)	Zlín				97.5		6
6)	Znojmo	101.2	89.6	99.2	97.3		1/3/3/1

CRo 1 (Radiozurnál): 24h (LW: Mon-Sat 0400-2300, Sun 0500-2300).
N: on the h – **CRo 2 (Dvoyka):** 24h (MW: Mon-Fri 0300-1500, Sat+Sun 0400-1500) – **CRo 3 (Vltava):** 24h – **CRo 4 (Radio Wave):** 24h (on internet only **W:** rozhlas.cz/radiowave/portal) – **CRo 5 REGIONAL

STATIONS: 24h own prgrs and relays of other regional stations (esp. in the night) – **CRo Plus:** 24h (MW: 1500-2300), **N:** on the h
Addresses:
CRo Regina Praha, Hybešova 10, 186 72 Praha 8 **W:** rozhlas.cz/regina (On DAB+ only) – **1)** CRo Region - Strední Cechy, Hybešova 10, 186 72 Praha 8 **W:** rozhlas.cz/strednicechy – **2)** CRo Ceské Budejovice, U Trí lvu 1, 370 29 Ceské Budejovice **W:** rozhlas.cz/cb – **3)** CRo Plzen, Nám. Míru 10, 320 70 Plzen **W:** rozhlas.cz/plzen – **4)** CRo Sever (=North), Na schodech 10, 400 91 Ústí nad Labem **W:** rozhlas.cz/sever – **5)** CRo Hradec Králové, Havlíckova 292, 501 01 Hradec Králové **W:** rozhlas.cz/hradec – **6)** CRo Brno, Beethovenova 4, 657 42 Brno **W:** rozhlas.cz/brno – **7)** CRo Ostrava, Dr. Šmerala 2, 729 91 Ostrava (Polish: Mon-Fri 1804-1830) **W:** rozhlas. cz/ostrava – **8)** CRo Olomouc, Horní námestí 21, 771 06 Olomouc **W:** rozhlas.cz/ol – **9)** CRo Karlovy Vary, Zítkova 3, 360 00 Karlovy Vary: Mon-Fri 1400-1640, otherwise CRo Plzen **W:** rozhlas.cz/plzen – **10)** CRo Region - Vysocina, Masarykovo nám 42, 586 01 Jihlava **W:** rozhlas. cz/vysocina – **11)** CRo Pardubice, Sv. Anežky Ceské 29, 530 02 Pardubice **W:** rozhlas.cz/pardubice – **12)** CRo Zlín, Osvoboditelu 187, 760 01 Zlín **W:** rozhlas.cz/brno – **13)** CRo Liberec, Modrá 1048, 460 06 Liberec **W:** rozhlas.cz/liberec/portal

EXTERNAL SERVICE: Radio Prague
See International Broadcasting section.
MAJOR PRIVATE STATIONS/NETWORKS:
RADIO IMPULS (Comm.)
✉ Ortenovo nám. 15a, 170 00 Praha 7 ☎ +420 255 700 700 🖷 +420 255 700 727 **E:** impuls@radioimpuls.cz **W:** radioimpuls.cz
FM: see list below **D.Prgr:** 24h
RADIO FREKVENCE 1 (Comm.)
✉ Wenzigova 4, 120 00 Praha 2 ☎ +420 257 001 111 🖷 +420 257 314 183 **E:** frekvence1@frekvence1.cz **W:** frekvence1.cz
FM: see list below **D.Prgr:** 24h
EVROPA 2 (Comm.)
✉ Wenzigova 4, 120 00 Praha 2 ☎ +420 257 001 111 🖷 +420 257 001 807 **E:** info@evropa2.cz **W:** evropa2.cz
FM: see list below **D.Prgr:** 24h
RADIO KISS FM (Comm.)
✉ Rícanská 3, 101 00 Praha 10-Vinohrady ☎ +420 267 009 800 🖷 +420 267 009 811 **E:** radio@kiss.cz **W:** kiss.cz
Regional branches: R. KISS 98 FM, ✉ Rícanská 3, 101 00 Praha 10-Vinohrady ☎ +420 267 009 800 🖷 +420 267 009 811 **W:** kiss98.cz – **R. KISS Hády,** ✉ Stefánikova 38, 612 00 Brno 12 ☎ +420 541 221 143 🖷 +420 541 211 117 **W:** kisshady.cz – **R. KISS Jizní Cechy** ✉ U Vystaviste 15A, 370 05 Ceské Budejovice ☎ +420 385 510 888 🖷 +420 385 510 990 **W:** kissjiznicechy.cz – **R. KISS Morava** ✉ Starobelská 13, 700 30 Ostrava-Zábreh ☎ +420 596 708 401 🖷 +420 596 708 400 **W:** kissmorava.cz – **R. KISS ProTon** ✉ Husova 58, 301 24 Plzen 1 ☎ +420 377 235 808 🖷 +420 377 235 810 **W:** kissproton.cz – **R. KISS Publikum** ✉ Bartošova 45, 760 01 Zlín ☎ +420 577 009 036 🖷 +420 577 009 033 **W:** kisspublikum.cz – **R. KISS Delta** ✉ Jana Palacha 1025, 293 01 Mladá Boleslav 1 ☎ +420 326 720 000 🖷 +420 326 721 342 **W:** kissdelta.cz
RADIO PROGLAS (Relg)
✉ Barvicova 85, 602 00 Brno ☎ +420 543 217 241-3 🖷 +420 543 217 245 **E:** radio@proglas.cz **W:** proglas.cz
FM: see list below **D.Prgr:** 24h
COUNTRY RADIO (Comm.)
✉ Rícanská 3, 101 00 Praha 10-Vinohrady ☎ +420 251 024 111 🖷 +420 251 024 224 **E:** info@countryradio.cz **W:** countryradio.cz
MW: Praha 1062kHz 20kW (0500-1800), 1kW (1800-0500) **FM:** see list below **D.Prgr:** 24h
RADIO DECHOVKA (Comm.)
✉ U Prutníku 232, 250 72 Predboj ☎ +420 311 280 281 **E:** pusova@radiodechovka.cz **W:** radiodechovka.cz

MW:	kHz	kW
Líbeznice	1233	10
Brno/Dobrochov	1233	5
Ceské Budejovice	1233	2
Ostrava-Svinov	1233	2
Brno-Reckovice	1233	0.5

FM: see list below **D.Prgr:** 24h
RADIO CESKY IMPULS (Comm.)
✉ Ortenovo nám. 15a, 170 00 Praha 7 ☎ (studio) +420 255 700 701 **E:** moderator@ceskyimpuls.cz **W:** ceskyimpuls.cz
MW: Praha (Líbeznice-Boranovice) 981kHz 10kW, Moravské Budejovice (Domamil) 981kHz 5kW, Litomysl 981kHz (F.PI.), Hradec Králové 981kHz (F.PI.). **D.Prgr:** 24h
RADIO ZET (Comm.)
✉ Wenzigova 4, 120 00 Praha 2 ☎ +420 257 001 240 **E:** info@zet.cz **W:** zet.cz

FM: see list below **D.Prgr:** 24h. Own program in Czech: Mon-Fri 0500-1800, Sat+Sun 0600-1700; BBC WS relay in English: Mon-Thu 1800-0500, Fri 1800-0600, Sat 1700-0600, Sun 1700-0500.

Commercial FM Stations:

MHz	kW	Station	Location
87.6	70	R. Impuls	Brno
87.8	1	R. Blaník	Praha
87.8	1	R. Cerná hora	Králíky
88.1	1	R. Evropa 2	Liberec
88.1	10	Hitrádio Orion	Jeseník
88.2	5	R. Evropa 2	Praha
88.3	10	R. Kiss Hády 88 FM	Brno
88.4	1	R. Blaník - JC	Ceské Budejovice
88.7	1	R. Proglas	Tábor
88.9	10	R. Jih	Breclav
89.0	1	R. Práchen	Písek
89.0	45	R. Impuls	Ostrava
89.3	5	R. Sázava	Benešov/Lbosín
89.5	1	R. Cas	Trinec
89.5	5	Country R.	Praha
89.6	1	R. Frekvence 1	Plzen
89.6	7	Rock Max	Zlín
89.8	1	R. Zet	Ceské Budejovice
90.0	1	Hitrádio Dragon	Cheb
90.0	1	R. Rubi	Sumperk
90.0	10	R. Kiss ProTon	Plzen
90.2	1	R. Kiss Delta	Kutná Hora
90.3	5	Expres FM	Praha
90.3	3	R. Kiss Publikum	Zlín
90.5	1.6	R. Evropa 2	Ceské Budejovice
90.6	4	Hitrádio FM Most	Chomutov
90.6	1	R. Proglas	Bystrice pod Hostynem
91.0	70	R. Frekvence 1	Ostrava
91.0	1	R. Evropa 2	Mariánské Lázne
91.1	2	R. Kiss Delta	Pardubice
91.4	66	R. Impuls	Plzen
91.6	1	R. Blanik - SevC	Decín
91.6	5	Fajn rádio Life	Opatovice
91.7	4	R. Zlín	Zlín
91.9	1	R. 1	Praha
92.1	10	R. Impuls	Trutnov
92.3	1	R. Relax	Kladno
92.3	5	R. Haná	Pohorany
92.5	5	R. Egrensis	Mariánské Lázne
92.8	5	R. Cas	Ostrava
92.8	1	Hitradio Magic	Náchod
92.9	1	R. Kiss Delta	Mladá Boleslav
93.2	1	R. Egrensis	Cheb
93.3	20	R. Proglas	Jeseník
93.4	20	R. Frekvence 1	Jihlava
93.5	50	R. Frekvence 1	Ustí nad Labem
93.6	1	Hitrádio Faktor	Písek
93.7	5	R. City	Praha
93.7	45	R. Hellax	Ostrava
93.8	1	R. Evropa 2	Karlovy Vary
93.9	80	R. Blaník V.Cechy	Pardubice
94.0	10	R. Impuls	Klatovy
94.1	10	R. Frekvence 1	Valašské Merizící
94.1	50	R. Frekvence 1	Ceské Budejovice
94.3	10	Hitrádio Vysocina	Jihlava
94.7	1	Country R.Mor.Sev.	Ostrava
95.0	95	R. Blaník	Votice
95.2	5	Fajn North Music	Ustí nad Labem
95.2	1	R. Sumava	Klatovy
95.3	2.5	R. Beat	Praha
95.5	0.4	R. Dechovka	Cesnovice
95.7	2	Signál R. Praha	Praha
95.8	1	Hitrádio Vysocina	Trebíc
96.2	1	R. Spin	Praha
96.2	1	R. Zlín	Uherský Brod
96.4	4	Hitrádio Orion	Ostrava
96.5	1	R. Kiss Morava	Sumperk
96.6	5	R. Impuls	Praha
96.7	5	R. Zet	Jihlava
96.8	1	Country R.Mor.Jih	Brno
96.9	1	Country R.Vychod	Pardubice
97.1	5	R. Rubi	Pohorany
97.1	1	Country R.Sever	Liberec
97.2	5	Fajn rádio	Praha
97.4	50	R. Frekvence 1	Pardubice
97.7	50	R. Kiss Jizní Cechy	Votice
97.7	1	Evropa 2	Ostrava
97.9	20	R. Proglas	Liberec
98.1	1	Fajn rádio Agara	Chomutov
98.1	2	R. Kiss 98 FM	Praha

MHz	kW	Station	Location
98.1	1	R. Orchidej	Brno
98.3	1	R. Cas	Trinec
98.4	20	R. Frekvence 1	Trutnov
98.4	5	R. Impuls	Kašperské Hory
98.6	1	R. Zet	Plzen
98.7	1	Hitrádio Orion	Trinec
98.7	5	R. Classic FM	Praha
99.0	1	Hitradio Brno	Brno
99.1	1	R. Zet	Pardubice
99.2	1	R. Zet	Liberec
99.3	1	Kiss Jizní Cechy	Cesky Krumlov
99.3	10	R. Evropa 2	Jeseník
99.3	1	R.France Int./Fr. Mus.	Praha
99.5	1	R. Evropa 2	Pardubice
99.7	1	Hitradio Dragon	Karlovy Vary
99.7	1	R. Gold	Ceské Budejovice
99.7	5	R. Bonton	Praha
99.8	5	Hitradio Apollo	Valašské Mezirící
99.9	1	Hitrádio Crystal	Ceská Lípa
100.3	20	R. Impuls	Jihlava
100.5	7	R. Impuls	Valašské Mezirící
100.6	2	R. Blaník Sever	Teplice
100.8	1	R. Beat	Slavonice
100.9	20	R. Impuls	Jeseník
101.1	1	R. Kiss Morava	Frydek-Místek
101.1	0.4	R. Dechovka	Strakonice
101.1	3	R. Zet	Praha
101.3	10	R. Evropa 2	Plzen
101.4	20	R. Contact (RCL)	Liberec
101.8	1	Country R.	Tábor
102.0	50	R. Impuls	Ustí nad Labem
102.5	5	R. Frekvence 1	Praha
102.8	5	Hitradio Dragon	Mariánské Lázne
102.8	1	Hitrádio FM Labe	Ustí nad Labem
102.9	50	R. Impuls	Ceské Budejovice
103.0	10	R. Krokodyl	Brno
103.4	1	R. Blaník V. Cechy	Hradec Králové
103.4	5	R. Petrov	Brno
103.6	1	Country R.Vychod	Chotebor
103.7	1	Oldies R. Olympic	Praha
103.8	10	R. Frekvence 1	Klatovy
103.9	7	Hitrádio Orion	Valašské Mezirící
104.1	50	R. Frekvence 1	Plzen
104.2	1	R. Blanik - Jiz. Morava	Znojmo
104.3	20	R. Frekvence 1	Jeseník
104.3	32	Hitrádio Faktor	Ceské Budejovice
104.5	50	R. Frekvence 1	Brno
104.7	10	R. Blanik - Západ	Plzen
105.0	10	R. Frekvence 1	Zlín
105.3	3	R. Cerná hora	Trutnov
105.4	1	R. Rubi	Vrbno pod Pradedem
105.5	95	R. Evropa 2	Votice
105.5	1.5	R. Evropa 2	Brno
105.7	1	Signál Rádio	Mladá Boleslav
105.8	8	Hitrádio FM Plus	Klatovy
105.8	1	R. Zet	Ustí nad Labem
105.9	1	R. Cas	Frenštát p. Radh.
106.0	50	R. Impuls	Pardubice
106.1	3	Hitrádio FM Plus	Plzen
106.3	1	R. Zet	Ostrava
106.4	1	R. Evropa 2	Vrchlabí
106.5	10	R. Blaník - Sever	Chomutov
106.6	1	Fajn rádio	Kutná Hora
106.7	1	R. Evropa 2	Znojmo
107.2	1	R. Evropa 2	Ustí nad Labem
107.4	1	Hitrádio FM Plus	Jáchymov
107.5	3	R. Proglas	Brno
107.5	2	R. Proglas	Nové Hrady

+ more than 70 txs below 1kW

DENMARK

L.T: UTC +1h (27 Mar-30 Oct: +2h) — **Pop:** 5,7 million — **Pr.L:** Danish — **EC:** 50Hz, 230/380V — **ITU:** DNK

TERACOM A/S
✆ Banestrøget 19-21, 2630 Taastrup ☎+45 70118011 📠+45 43711143. Teracom is responsible for the operation of txs carrying prgrs of DR and TV 2.

DR RADIO (Pub.)
✆ DR Byen, Emil Holms Kanal 20, DK-0999 Copenhagen C ☎+45 35203040 **W:** dr.dk **LP:** Chairman: Michael Christiansen. DG: Maria Rørbye Rønn. Media Dir.: Gitte Rabøl. News Dir.: Ulrik Haagerup

LW: Kalundborg 243kHz 50kW

FM	P1/P2	P3	P4	kW
Bornholm	96.2	90.0	99.3	30
Copenhagen	90.8	93.9	96.5	60
Funen	89.0	92.6	96.8	60
Holstebro	90.2	92.9	98.5	60
Nakskov	89.4	94.1	92.2	30
Næstved	94.8	99.6	97.5	100
Skamlebæk	88.4	94.3	92.0	3
So. Jutland	95.1	97.2	99.9	60
Thisted	91.4	99.2	95.6	2
Tolne, N.Jutland	91.0	96.6	94.4	8
Varde	-	-	99.0	8
Vejle	95.5	90.7	94.0	10
Ølgod	88.7	92.3	97.7	10
Aalborg	93.3	89.7	98.1	60
Aarhus	88.1	91.7	95.9	60

+ 18 FM txs below 1kW. A full list is available at dr.dk/OmDR/ Modtagelse/Radio/FM/20091028120111

DAB: DAB1: ch.12C (227.360MHz). DAB2: ch.11C (220.352MHz) on Sealand & Funen, ch. 8B (197.648 MHz) in southern Jutland and ch.13B (232.496MHz) in northern Jutland. DAB3 (due on the air late 2015 and 2016 in DAB+): ch. 6D (187.072MHz) in Western Jutland, ch. 8C (199.360MHz) in Horsens/Vejle/Kolding, ch.11A (216.928MHz) in Esbjerg, ch. 11A (216.928MHz) in Southern Sealand and Lolland/Falster, ch. 11B (218.640MHz) in Northern Jutland, ch. 11B (218.640MHz) on Western Sealand, ch. 11D (222.064MHz) in Copenhagen and Bornholm, ch. 11D (222.064MHz) in Viborg/Skive, ch. 12A (223.936MHz) on Funen, ch. 12B (225.648MHz) in Southern Jutland, ch. 12B (225.648MHz) in Thy and on Mors and ch. 12D (229.072MHz) in Eastern Jutland.
P1 on FM (MF 0500-1700, Sat 0700-1700, Sun 0854-1700) + DAB1 (24h). **N:** on the h (except Su 0900 & 1000). N in Danish from KNR, Greenland: MF 1755-1800 – **P2** on FM (MF 1700-0500, Sat 1700-0700, Sun 1700-0854) + DAB1 (24h): Classical music – **P3** on FM (24h) + DAB1 (24h): Popular music, news and sport. N: on the h + MF: 0530, 0630, 0730 – **P4** on FM + DAB2 (in DAB+). News, entertainment and regional prgrs. N: national news on the h except regional news on the half h – **P5** on DAB1. Music etc. for +60, at times relays P4 – **P6 Beat** on DAB1. Indie/alternative music – **P7 Mix** on DAB1. A/C chart hits – **P8 Jazz** on DAB1. Jazz – **DR Nyhedskanalen** on DAB1. News and sports – **DR Langbølge** on LW 243kHz. 0445-0505, 0700-0805, 1045-1135, 1645-1710. Special prgrs.: Wrp.: 0445-0500, 0745-0800, 1045-1100 & 1645-1700 & navigational warnings: 1703-1710. Also news from P4 or P1 at 0500-0505, 0700-0705, 0800-0805, 1100-1120MF/1100-1115SS & 1700-1703

Regional stations:
MF: 0505-0600, 0605-0700, 0705-0800, 0805-0900, 1130-1133, 1406-1500, 1510-1550 & 1610-1700. Sat 0603-0700, 0707-0800, 0807-0900 & 1130-1132. Sun: 0603-0700, 0703-0800, 0807-0900 & 1130-1132. P4 Trekanten and P4 Esbjerg are on the air at a reduced schedule. At other times national P4 prgrs are carried.
DR Nordjylland, Frederik Bajers Vej 9, 9220 Aalborg: on 89.1/94.4/ 96.7/98.1MHz – **DR Midt- & Vest,** Vestergade 1, 7500 Holstebro: on 95.6/ 97.7/98.5/102.2MHz – **DR Østjylland,** Olof Palmes Alle 10-12, 8200 Aarhus N: on 88.9/95.9/96.4/102.0MHz – **DR Trekanten,** Den Hvide Facet 1, 4., 7100 Vejle: on 94.0MHz – **DR Syd,** H.P. Hansensgade 11, 6220 Aabenraa: on 94.0/96.6/99.0/99.9/103.7MHz – **DR Esbjerg,** Torvegade 8, 6700 Esbjerg: on 99.0/103.7MHz – **DR Fyn,** Lille Tornbjergvej 10, 5220 Odense SØ: on 96.4/96.8MHz – **DR Sjælland,** Vestegade 1, 4700 Næstved: on 92.0/92.2/97.5MHz – **DR København,** Emil Holms Kanal 20, 0999 Copenhagen: on 96.5MHz – **DR Bornholm,** Aakirkebyvej 52, 3700 Rønne: on 93.7/93.8MHz
All prgrs from DR are available on the internet. P1, P2, P3 & P4 København are also available via satellite. **Ann:** FM: "Du lytter til P et/to/tre/fire" (1st, 2nd, 3rd & 4th prgr.) etc. LW: "Du lytter til DRs langbølgesender på 243 kHz"

RADIO 24SYV (Pub.)
✆ Vester Farimagsgade 41, DK-1606 Copenhagen V ☎ +45 31 247 247 **E:** kontakt@radio24syv.dk **W:** radio24syv.dk
L.P: Dir: Jørgen Ramskov
FM (all MHz): Nakskov 98.8 30kW, Holstebro 100.3 60kW, Funen 100.5 60kW, Tolne N. Jutland 100.7 10kW, Vejle 100.9 10kW, Skamlebæk 101.1 5kW, Thisted 101.3 3kW, Næstved 101.6 100kW, So.Jutland 102.1 60kW, Copenhagen 102.3 60kW, Varde 102.5 10kW, Aalborg 102.7 60kW, Aarhus 103.0 60kW, Bornholm 103.5 30kW + 4 FM tx below 1 kW. Also nationwide on DAB2
Format: News/talk

SBS DISCOVERY RADIO (Comm.)

HC Andersens Blvd 1, DK-1553 Copenhagen ☎ +45 33376666
+45 33930807 **W:** sbsradio.com/da
L.P: MD: Jim Receveur. CEN: Jan Andersen
NOVA: AC. Varde 87.8MHz 10kW, So. Jutland 89.3MHz 3kW, Copenhagen 91.4MHz 12kW, Bornholm 92.2MHz 1kW, Funen 93.4MHz 1kW, Vejle 99.3MHz 1kW, Tolne N. Jutland 102.4MHz 1kW, Holstebro 103.4MHz 60kW, Næstved 103.9MHz 100kW, Aalborg 106.0MHz 6kW + 18 stns below 1kW. Also nationwide on DAB2
THE VOICE: CHR. On 24 low power FM txs + nationwide on DAB2
POP FM: Classic hits. Copenhagen 100.0MHz 75kW, Randers 99.9MHz 0.5kW + nationwide on DAB2
RADIO 100: Hot AC. On 21 low power FM txs + nationwide on DAB2
RADIO SOFT: A/C Soft non-stop. On 5 low power FM txs
MYROCK: Rock. On 14 low power FM txs + nationwide on DAB2 + nationwide on DAB2.

DIN RADIO (Comm.)

Langebrogade 5, 1141 Copenhagen K. ☎ +45 38168200 **W:** dinradio.dk. On 7 low power txs in Copenhagen, Odense and Jutland.

RADIO UPDATE

E: red@radioupdate.dk **W:** radioupdate.dk. On 8 low power txs in Copenhagen, No. Sealand and Fredericia.

Private Stations (all MHz):

Approx. 200 organizations are operating low-powered FM txs. (0.16kW-0.5kW at 40m. height). Approx. 500 txs are on the air. Frequency lists by region: dkradio.dk. Major stns in the main cities are as follows (only main frequency/frequencies mentioned):
Aabenraa: Skala FM: 102.6/104.5 – Globus Guld: 106.7 – Radio Alfa: 92.0/104.0
Aalborg: ANR, Langagervej 1, 9220 Aalborg Ø: 87.6/103.2/103.8 – Radio Aura, Langagervej 1, 9220 Aalborg Ø: 105.4/106.9 – The Voice: 100.2 – Radio Nord, Sigsgaardsvej 16, 9490 Pandrup: 95.1/98.9/102.2 – Grassroots/community stns: 92.2 &101.7
Aarhus: Radio go!FM, Jens Baggesens Vej 90K, 8200 Aarhus N: 92.2/94.6/106.5 – The Voice: 93.1/93.7 – Radio 100: 87.6/98.3 – MyRock: 90.9/106.2 – Øst FM/Radio Hinnerup: 95.0/105.1 – Radio ABC: 105.7/107.0 – Radio Alfa: 102.4/104.5 – Din Radio: 105.6/107.6 – Grassroots/community stns: 98.7
Copenhagen: The Voice: 96.1/104.9/105.4 – Din Radio: 88.6/107.1 – Radio 100: 97.2/103.6/104.1 – Radio Soft: 90.4/95.0 – MyRock: 89.4/92.7/104.4 – Grassroots/community stns: 87.6,89.6,90.2, 90.4,92 .9,94.5,95.2,95.5,97.7,98.9,100.9,102.9,103.4,105.9,106.3,107.4
Esbjerg: Radio Victoria, Borgergade 66, 6700 Esbjerg: 106.3 – Skala FM: 101.7/106.8 – Globus Guld: 101.3 – VLR: 95.3 – Rlg. stations: 93.5
Frederikshavn: Vendsyssel FM, Sønderjyllands Allé 35, 9900 Frederikshavn: 106.6 – ANR: 107.5 – Radio Aura: 89.0 – Radio Nord: 96.1 – Radio 100: 90.1 – MyRock: 99.6 – TheVoice: 101.4
Haderslev: Skala FM: 95.8/107.4 – Norea Radio, Porsevej 6, 6100 Haderslev: 96.6 – Radio 100: 90.7 – Radio Globus: 104.9
Herning: Radio M, Østergade 21, 7400 Herning: 99.7/105.8 – Radio Alfa, Østergade 21, 7400 Herning: 89.5/107.4 – Radio Classic, Gl. Kirkevej 33, 7400 Herning: 96.2
Hjørring/Hirtshals: Skaga FM, Jørgen Fibigers Gade 20, 9850 Hirtshals: 105.6/106.7 – ANR: 104.7 – Radio Aura: 89.0 – Nova 107.0
Holstebro: Pulz FM, Lægårdvej 86, 7500 Holstebro: 105.1/106.2 – Radio Holstebro, Gl. Struervej 36, 7500 Holstebro: 97.4
Horsens: Radio VLR Horsens, Nørregade 42, 8700 Horsens: 91.1 – Horsens Classic: 105.3 – The Voice: 106.9 – MyRock: 105.0 – Nova 103.6
Kolding: Skala FM, Dalbygade 40, 6000 Kolding: 87.6/94.4/105.2/106.3 – VLR: 103.2/106.1 – Radio Globus: 92.3 – Globus Guld: 102.7 – The Voice: 90.0
Køge: Radio Køge, Astersvej 23B, 4600 Køge: 98.2/106.2/106.8 – The Voice: 93.6
Nykøbing F: Radio Sydhavsøerne, Tværgade 18, 4800 Nykøbing Falster: 87.8
Nykøbing M/Thisted: Radio Limfjord, Gasværksvej 10, 7900 Nykøbing Mors: 104.7/106.9/107.3/107.8 – Limfjord Plus: 94.7 – ANR: 97.4 – Radio Aura: 106.7 – Radio Nord: 92.1 – Nova 87.9 – Radio 100: 96.5 – The Voice 106.2
Næstved/Ringsted/Slagelse: Radio SLR, Dania 38, 4700 Næstved: 91.6/100.7/101.0/106.5 – The Voice: 93.6/99.1/107.5 – MyRock: 93.0 – Radio 100: 95.6
Odense: Skala FM: 91.1/99.1 – The Voice: 98.0/105.1/107.6 – Din Radio 103.5 – Radio 100: 101.2 – MyRock: 90.6/100.1/106.7 – VLR: 98.4 – Radio Soft: 104.2 – Grassroots/community stations: 87.9 & 107.1
Randers: Radio ABC, Brotoften 10, 8940 Randers SV: 95.3/105.7 – Radio Alfa, Brotoften 10, 8940 Randers SV: 91.3/102.4 – Radio ABC Solo FM: 93.5/96.4 – Radio Randers, Garnisionsvej 17, 8930

Randers : 104.9 – The Voice: 101.8 – Radio 100: 99.1 – Nova: 92.5 – Pop FM: 99.9
Roskilde: The Voice: 104.3/106.6 – Radio 100: 95.6/103.6 – MyRock: 93.0 – Radio Soft: 107.7 – Roskilde Dampradio, Møllehusvej 22, 4000 Roskilde: 97.8
Rødding: Radio Globus, Herredfogedvej 2, 6630 Rødding: 104.4 – Globus Guld, Herredfogedvej 2, 6630 Rødding: 90.1/93.0 – Skala FM: 107.5
Silkeborg: Radio Silkeborg, Papirfabrikken 18, 8600 Silkeborg: 101.2/107.7 – Din Radio 8600, Østergade 13, 8600 Silkeborg: 103.8 – Radio Alfa: 94.5 – Radio 100: 96.9 – Nova: 97.8 – The Voice: 100.1 – My Rock: 107.1
Skive: Radio Skive, Nordbanevej 1A, 7800 Skive: 104.0 – Radio Alfa, Nordbanevej 1A, 7800 Skive: 101.8
Skjern: Radio Max, Bækgårdsvej 35C, 6900 Skjern: 105.0 – Skala FM: 107.5 – Grassrot stns: 96.4
Svendborg: Radio Diablo, Voldgade 9,1., 5700 Svendborg: 107.7 – Radio Alfa Sydfyn: 106.5
Sønderborg: Radio Als, Peblingestien 1, 6430 Nordborg: 88.0 – Globus Guld: 95.4 – Skala FM: 104.4
Vejle: VLR, Bugattivej 8, 7100 Vejle: 98.8/101.3/101.7 – The Voice: 105.9 – MyRock: 107.0.
Viborg: Radio Viborg, Vesterbrogade 8, 8800 Viborg: 105.0 – Viborg Favorit FM: 93.8

L.T: UTC +3h — **Pop:** 500,000 — **Pr.L:** Arabic, French (official), Somali, Afar — **E.C:** 50Hz, 220V — **ITU:** DJI

MINISTÈRE DE LA COMMUNICATION CHARGÉ DES POSTES ET DE TÉLÉCOMMUNICATIONS (MCPT)

B.P. 32, 1 Rue de Moscou, Djibouti ☎+253 21 353928 +253 21 353957 **W:** mccpt.dj **E:** mccpt@intnet.dj **L.P:** Minister: Ali Hassan Bahdon.

RADIODIFFUSION TÉLÉVISION DE DJIBOUTI (Gov.)

B.P. 97, 1 Rue St. Laurent du Var, Djibouti ☎+253 21 352294 +253 21 356502 **W:** rtd.dj **E:** rtd@intnet.dj
L.P: DG: Abdoulkader Ahmed Idriss. Dir. Tech: Mohamed Moussed Yaya. PD: Adoyata Daoud. Dir. Inf: Mr. Dini Aleo.

Djibouti (Dorale) **MW:** 1116kHz & 1539kHz **SW:** 4780kHz 50kW. (all inactive, but expected to return from the new site near Arta).

FM (MHz)	1	2	Q	kW
Ali Sabieh	90.3	94.2	103.0	0.5/0.25
Arta	93.5	89.5	104.0	5/3
Ballembaley	95.3	91.3		1/0.1
Dikhil	96.6	98.8	104.0	0.5/0.25
Djibouti	91.3	95.3		1/1

Channel 1 in Arabic/Somali: 24h on 4780kHz + FM.
Channel 2 in Afar/French: 0300-2100 on FM. French: 0700-1100 & 1400-1800. **Q**=Quran prgr. **Ann:** "Radio Djibouti".

Other stations:
BBC African Sce: Djibouti 99.2MHz 1kW.
Monte-Carlo Doualiya: Arta 97.2MHz 5kW.
R. Sawa: MW: Djibouti (Pk 12) 1431kHz 600kW 1600-0400, **FM:** Arta 100.8MHz 5kW 24h.
Voice of America: Djibouti 102.0MHz 1kW

L.T: UTC -4h — **Pop:** 71,500 — **Pr.L:** English, Creole — **E.C:** 50Hz, 240V — **ITU:** DMA

DOMINICA BROADCASTING CORP. (Gov. Comm.)

Victoria Str, PO Box 148, Roseau ☎ +1 767 448 3282/3 +1 767 448 2918 **W:** dbcradio.net
L.P: Chairman: Bennette Thomas. GM: Cecil Joseph. CEN: Kurt Matthew
DBS Radio: Eggleston Roseau 88.1MHz 1kW, Marigot 103.5MHz 0.3kW, Petite Soufriere 103.1MHz 0.1kW, Grand Bay 103.5MHz 0.1kW, Portsmouth 104.1MHz. Own prgrs: 0900-0300. Creole: 1800-2000MF. BBC relay: 1200-1205 & 0300-0900.
DBS Music Station: Roseau: 89.5MHz. Portsmouth: 104.7. Format: Easy listening

Other stations:
DOMINICA CATHOLIC RADIO, Turkey Lane, Roseau ☎ +1 767

440 7985 **W:** dominicacatholicradio.org FM: 96.1MHz. Format: Rlg. – **KAIRI FM**, 42 Independence St., PO Box 931, Roseau ☎ +1 767 448 7330 🖳 +1 767 448 7332 **W:** kairifm.com L.P: CEO: Frankie Bellot. PD: Steve Vidal. FM: **Kairi FM:** 88.7/93.1/107.9MHz **Hot FM:** 91.1MHz – **POSSIE VIBRATIONS - FRESH 88.5**, Bay St., Portsmouth ☎ +1 767 616 1512 **W:** possievibrations.org FM: 88.5. Format: Community – **RADIO EN BA MANGO**, Grand Bay ☎ +1 767 446 3207 **W:** south-cityagain.webs.com FM: 93.5/96.9MHz D.Prgr: Fr-Mo 2200-0300. Format: Community – **Q95**, 10 Hanover Str., PO Box 861, Roseau ☎ +1 767 448 5822 🖳 +1 767 448 5828 **W:** q95da.com L.P: CEO: Sheridan G. Gregoire FM: 90.5/92.3/95.1/95.7/97.5/98.3/105.7MHz – **VIBES RADIO**, 36 Great George St., 2ⁿᵈ floor, Roseau ☎ +1 767 440 8152 🖳 +1 767 448 7376 **W:** vibesradio.dm L.P: Dir: Lennox Lawrence. FM: 93.9 & 99.5MHz (different music formats) – **VOICE OF LIFE RADIO-ZGBC RADIO**, PO Box 205, Madrelle, Loubiere, Roseau ☎ +1 767 448 7017 🖳 +1 767 440 0551 **E:** volradio@cwdom.dm **W:** voiceofliferadio.dm L.P: GM: Clementina Munro. CEN: Kurt Matthew. FM: 24h Portsmouth 90.7MHz Roseau 102.1MHz Marigot 106.1MHz Format: Rlg.

DOMINICAN REPUBLIC

L.T: UTC -4h — **Pop:** 9.5 million — **Pr.L:** Spanish — **E.C:** 60Hz, 110V — **ITU:** DOM

INDOTEL - INSTITUTO DOMINICANO DE LAS TELECOMUNICACIONES
🖃 Abrahan Lincoln N° 962, Edif. Osiris 1, Planta, 10148 Santo Domingo ☎ +1 829 732 5555 🖳 +1 809 732 3904 **W:** indotel.gob.do **E:** info@indotel.gob.do **L.P:** DG: Lic. Gedeón Santos.

ASOCIACIÓN DOMINICANA DE RADIODIFUSORAS (ADORA)
🖃 Calle Paul Harris No 3, Centro de Los Héroes, Santo Domingo. Hrs of tr. 24h unless otherwise stated. Call HI—

	Call	kHz	kW	Station, location and hr of tr.
1)	B20	540	5	R. ABC, Sto Domingo: 0900-0400
52)	B22	570	10/5	R. Cristal, Sto Domingo
71)	B23	‡580	5	R. Montecristi, Montecristi
4)	B24	590	10/5	R. Santa María, La Vega: 0900-0300
7)	B25	600		R. Santo Domingo, El Seybo (r. 620)
118)	C85	600		Celestial 600, Santo Domingo
60)	B21	610	5	R. Amanecer, Santiago (r. 1580)
7)	B28	620	10	R. Santo Domingo, Sto Domingo: 0900-0400
9)	B31	650	15/5	R. Universal, Sto Domingo
62)	B32	660	3	R. Visión Cristiana, Santiago
59)	B33	670	5	R. Dial, San Pedro de Macorís
11)	B38	680	3	R. Zamba, San Ignacio de Sabaneta: 0930-0300
12)	B39	690	10	R. Guarachita "La Poderosa", Sto Domingo: 0900-0400
13)	B40	700	0.5	R. Mao, Valverde Mao
119)		710		Red Nacional Cristiana, Santo Domingo
104)	B41	710		Ondas del Caribe, San Cristóbal
14)	B42	720	1.5	R. Norte, Santiago: 0900-0500
87)	B48	720	5	R. Cayacoa, Higüey: 0900-0400
15)	B43	730	10	R. HIZ (r. TV channel 45 audio), Sto Domingo: 1100-0500
16)	B44	750	5	R. Jesús AM, Santiago
17)	B45	760	5	Global AM, Santo Domingo
18)	B46	770	5	R. Aguila, Santiago:
19)	B47	780	0.5	R. Constanza, Constanza: 1100-0200
20)	B49	‡790	5	R. Millón, Sto Domingo
70)	B50	800	1	R. Bonao, Bonao: 1000-0400
24)	B52	810	5	R. Salvación Internacional, Baní: 1100-0300
21)	B53	820	1	R. Vida, Santiago
22)	B54	830	10	HIJB Radio, Sto Domingo: 1100-0300
72)	B57	850	5	R. Guarocuya, Barahona: 1000-0400
5)	B58	‡860	10	R. Clarín, Sto Domingo
25)	B59	870	4	R. La Vega, La Vega: 1000-0300
26)		890	3	B-90/La Consentida, Valverde: 1000-0400
28)	B63	‡900	5/1	R. Puerto Plata, Puerto Plata: 0900-0400
60)	B62	900		R. Amanecer, Neyba (r. 1580)
29)	B64	910	3	Tiempo 910, Bonao: 0930-0300
9)	B65	‡920	10	R. 9-20 AM-Stereo "Power", Sto Domingo
32)	B68	950	10	R. Popular, Sto Domingo
33)	B70	960	5/1	LV del Atlántico, Puerto Plata: 1000-0500
50C)	B72	970	5/1	R. Barahona, Barahona
25)	B71	970	6	R. Olímpica, La Vega
36)	B74	990	1	R. Cibao, Santiago (irr, also r. 1510 R. Pueblo)
113)	C84	990	5/1	R. Eternidad, Sto Domingo: 1100-2400
38)	B76	‡1010	10	R. Comercial, Sto Domingo: 1100-0600
39)	B78	1030	5	R. Novedades, La Vega
23)	B79	1040	10	CDN AM, Sto Domingo
14)	B80	1050	1.5	R. Hispaniola, Mao

	Call	kHz	kW	Station, location and hr of tr.
60)	B81	1060		R. Amanecer, San Pedro de Macorís (r. 1580)
42)	B82	1060	1	R. Azua, Azua: 1000-0200
44)	B83	1070	5/1	HIBI R. 1070, San Francisco de Macorís: 0900-0400
45)	B84	1080	1	R. RPQ Sport, Sto Domingo
46)	B85	1090	2.5	R. Amistad, Santiago
50A	B88	1100	1	R. Jimaní, Jimaní
47)	B86	1100	1	R. Oriente, San Pedro de Macorís: 0900-0400
48)	B87	1100	1	R. Ocoa, San José de Ocoa: 1200-0200
49)	B89	1100	1	R. Comercial, Nagua: 0900-0200
51)	B90	1110	2.5	R. Jarabacoa, Jarabacoa: 1000-0400
95)	B91	1110	1/0.5	R. Marién, Dajabón: 0930-0200
52)	B92	1120	10	R. Metro Hit, Sto Domingo
52)	C86	1120		R. Metro Hit, Samaná (r. 1120): 1000-0400
109)	B93	1120		R. Antillas, Barahona
40)	B94	1130	10/1	CDN AM, Santiago (r. 1040)
54)	B95	1140	5	R. Anacaona, San Juan de la Maguana: 1100-0400
55)	B96	1150	5	Onda Musical HIAS, Sto Domingo: 1100-0500
56)	B97	1160	5	Radiolandia, Santiago (Occ r. 1180kHz): 0900-0400
110)	B98	1170		Cadena Espacial, Azua
57)	B99	‡1180	10	R. Mil, Sto Domingo: 1000-0500
50B)	C21	1200	1	R. Caracol, Azua
98)	C23	1200		R. VEN - Voz Evangélica Nacional, Sto Domingo
61)		1210	5	R. Merengue, San Francisco de Macorís
100)	C24	‡1220		R. HIN, Sto Domingo (r. La Z 101)
53)	C26	1240	1	R. María, Santo Domingo
66)	C28	1250	5	LV del Progreso, San Francisco de Macorís: 1000-0400
67)	C29	1250	5	R. Juventud, La Romana: 0930-0430
52)	C31	1270	1.2	R. Metro-Hit 12-70, Santiago
69)	C32	1270	1	R. Ambiente, Baní: 1000-0400
75)	C36	1310	1	R. Real, La Vega: 1100-0400
76)	C37	1320	1/0.5	R. Centro, San Juan de la Maguana
62)	C38	1330	3	R. Visión Cristiana, Sto Domingo
77)	C42	1350	1	R. Rutas Musical, La Romana: 1000-0400
102)	C41	1350	1	Ondas del Yuna, Bonao
108)	C43	1360		R. Tropical, Sto Domingo
79)	C45	1370	5	R. Seybo, El Seybo
80)	C47	1380	1	R. Nacional, Santiago: 1000-0300
81)	C48	1390	1	R. San Cristóbal: 1100-0300
82)	C49	1400	1	Ondas del Valle, La Vega: 1100-0200
65)	C50	1410	1	R. Tricolor, Sto Domingo
85)	C52	1410	1/0.5	R. Grí-Grí, Río San Juan: 1000-0300
50D)		1410	3/0.5	R. 14-10 Cristiana, Barahona
86)	C53	1420	1.5	R. Oro, Cotuí
34)	C54	1430	5	R. Emanuel, Santiago
89)	C56	1440	5	R. San Juan, San Juan de la Maguana: 1000-0300
90)	C55	1440	5	R. Impactante, Sto Domingo
91)	M20	1450	10	R. Util, Salcedo: 0900-0400
92)	C59	1460	0.5	R. Renacimiento, Hato Mayor del Rey
93)	C60	1470	1	LV de la Alabanza, S.Francisco de Macorís: 10-04
50C)	C61	1470		R. Vibra "La Deportiva", Barahona
50D)		1470		R. Barahona, Provincia Independencia (r: R. Barahona 970)
68)	C63	1480	5	R. Villa, Sto Domingo: 1000-0400 (Sun 1100-2300)
97)	C65	1500	5	R. Higüey, Higüey: 0900-0400
111)		1500	3	R. Juan Pablo Duarte, Elías Piña
98)	C67	1510	10/3	R. Pueblo, Sto Domingo: 1000-0400 (Sun 1100-2300)
99)	C68	1520	1	R. Samaná "R. 15-20", Samaná: 0930-0400
112)	C69	1530	0.5	R. 15-30 (irr. TV channel 25 audio), Santiago
41)	C71	1540	1	LV de la Romana, La Romana: 0930-0400
50E)	C74	1560	1/0.5	R. Pedernales, Pedernales
101)	C73	1560	1	R. Única, Santiago
60)	C75	1580	10	R. Amanecer, Sto Domingo: 1000-0300
50F)	C76	1580	1	R. Neyba, Neyba: 0900-0400
101)	C73	1590	1	R. Libertad, Santiago
65)	C78	1600	5	R. Revelación en América, Sto Domingo: 1200-0200
103)	C79	1620		R. Taina/Planeta, San Pedro de Macorís
10)	C80	1640	1/0.5	R. Juventus Don Bosco, Sto Domingo
115)	C81	1670	3	LV del Yuna, Bonao
114)	C82	1680	1.5	R. Senda 1680 AM, San Pedro de Macorís

‡ = inactive, (r) = repeater, ± = varying fq.

Addresses and other information
1) Av Rómulo Betancourt N° 2078, (or Ap 517), Sto Domingo **W:** radio-abc.org – **2)** Calle Félix María Ruiz N° 6, La Trinitaria (or Ap 581), Santiago **FM:** 95.5MHz **W:** digital95fm.com – **4)** Avenida Pedro A Rivera km 1.5 (or Ap 55), La Vega **W:** rsantamaria.com – **FM:** 97.9MHz – **5)** Av Prolongación México, esquina Clarín,Sto Domingo – **7)** Ap 869 (or Dr.Tejada Florentino N° 8), Sto Domingo **W:** certvdominicana. com **E:** certvdominicana@gmail.com – **9)** Av 27 de Febrero, Edificio Kira, Sto Domingo **W:** radiouniversalfm.com – **FM:** 98.1MHz – **10)** Calle Juan Evangelista Jiménez # 49, Barrio María Auxiliadora, (or Apartado Postal 4848), Sto Domingo **W:** radiojuventusdonbosco.com – **11)** Calle Restauración N° 60 (or: Ap 2), San Ignacio de Sabaneta

E: t.sabaneta@verizon.net.do **FM:** 92.3MHz – **12)** Calle Palo Hincado 302, Sto Domingo – **13)** Calle Duarte N° 49 (or Ap 20), Valverde Mao (or Ap. 789, Santiago). few hours on weekends – **14)** Urb Las Hortensias (or Ap 454), Santiago – **W:** norte720.com **W:** radiohispaniola.com **FM:** 103.5MHz – **15)** Calle El Conde Esq Sánchez, Edif Copelic (or Ap 68), Sto Domingo – **W:** zulurd.com – **16)** Calle Sánchez Esq Pedro F Bonó, Santiago **W:** radiojesus750am.org **17)** Calle 1, Esq. Isabel Aguiar N° 1A, Sto Domingo **W:** global760am.com – **18)** Calle El Sol 51, 3a Planta, Edif Lamarche Alvarez (or Ap 1636), Santiago. **FM:** 97.1MHz – **19)** Calle V.M de Robiou N° 18, Constanza – **20)** Abraham Lincoln N° 58 (or Ap 335) , Sto Domingo – **21)** Av Estrella Sadhalá N° 3, Plaza Alejo, 3er piso (or Ap 282), Santiago - **FM:** 99.1MHz **W:** radiosantiago820am.com – **22)** Edif Teleantillas, Carr Duarte km 7.5, Sto Domingo **W:** facebook. com/pages/Emisora-HIJB-830-AM/173438096006789 – **FM:** 95.7MHz – **24)** Calle Mella esquina Calle 27 de Febrero, Baní **W:** radiosalvacion. com FM **– 25)** Av Pedro A Rivera, KM 0, Grupo Medrano (or Ap 203), La Vega **W:** radiolavega.com **W:** olimpica970.com - **FM:** 104.9MHz – **26)** Calle 27 de Febrero Esq Agustin Cabral (or Ap 80), Valverde - **FM:** 106.7MHz – **28)** Av 26 de Agosto N° 38,, Puerto Plata - **FM:** 99.7MHz – **29)** Calle Mella 50, Bonao **W:** radio91am.com – **32)** Av Charles Summer N° 33, Los Prados (or Ap 928), Sto Domingo - **FM:** 97.3MHz – **33)** Av John F Kennedy N° (altos) Puerto Plata - **FM:** 97.3MHz – **34)** Calle Cuba No. 46, 3ra planta, Los Pepines, (or Apartado Postal 897) Santiago **W:** radioemanuel.org - **FM:** 89.1MHz – **36)** Av Imbert, Gurabito (or Ap 141), Santiago - **FM:** 95.1MHz – **38)** E A Morel 27 (or Ap 1322), Sto Domingo **W:** radiocomercial1010.com - **FM:** 106.5MHz – **39)** Av Estrella Sadhalá, Plaza Alejo (3era planta) , Santiago - **FM:** 92.7MHz **W:** radionovedades.net – **40)**Calle Dr Delfillo N° 4, Los Prados, Sto Domingo **W:** elcaribecdn.com – **41)** Av Gregforio Luperón N° 10-A, (or Ap 213), La Romana – **42)** Calle Emilio Prud'homme 17A, Azua - **FM:** 97.1MHz – **44)** Av 27 de Febrero N° 51 (orAp 201), San Francisco de Macorís **W:** hibiradioam.com - **FM:** 102.3MHz – **45)** Edif Jaar, Calle El Conde esq Espaillat, Sto Domingo – **46)** Av Texas Esq Calle 12, Jardines Metropolitanos (or Ap 561), Santiago **W:** amistad1090.com - **FM:** 101.9MHz – **47)** Calle Mariano Soler Merino N° 19 (altos) (or Ap 64), San Pedro de Macorís – **48)** Calle Canada, San José de Ocoa **W:** radioocoa.com – **49)** Calle Narciso Minaya N° 36, Nagua – **50A-F)** Empresas Radiofónicas SA, Ap 20339, Sto Domingo **W:** suprafm.com/ informativo.htm 50A) 27 de Febrero 1, Jimaní; 50B Félix del Rosario 1, Azua;50C-D) Edificio Rodolfo Lama, Calle María Montés #24 (Ap 20339), Barahona; 50E) Duarte 1, Pedernales; 50F) Cambronal 8, Neiba – **51)** Calle Domingo Sabio N° 1 (or Ap 10), Jarabacoa - **FM:** 98.7MHz – **52)** Urbanización Las Hortensias, Santiago **W:** microondasnacionales. com - **FM:** 98.3MHz – **53)** Ave 27 de Febrero # 238, Edificio Rodríguez Sandoval, 5to piso, Santo Domingo **W:** radiomariadominicana.org – **54)** Calle Club de Leones N° 175 (or Ap 37), San Juan de la Maguana – **55)** Calle Pajo Incado N° 161, Sto Domingo **W:** ondamusical1150.com – **56)** Calle Sánchez N° 64 (or Ap 187), Santiago - **FM:** 93.1MHz – **57)** Av Máximo Gómez N° 65 (or Ap 1372), Sto Domingo - **FM:** 103.3MHz – **59)** Av. Independencia No. 169, San Pedro de Macorís - **FM:** 90.7MHz Sultana + 98.7 Estéreo 98 **W:** radiodial670am.com.do – **60)** Juan Sánchez Ramírez #40, Gazcue (or Ap 4680), Sto Domingo (Owned and operated by the Seventh Day Adventist Church) **W:** ra.do – **61)** Calle 27 de Febrero N° (or Ap 57), San Francisco de Macorís **W:** circuito-merengue.com - **FM:** 94.7MHz– **62)** Calle Sabana Larga #64, Santiago / Calle César Dargán #26, El Vergel (Frente a la Plaza Criolla), Sto Domingo (or P.O. Box 2908, Paterson, NJ 07509-2908, USA) **W:** radiovision.net **Local prgr**: Mon-Fri 2000-2300 – **65)** Av 25 de Febrero 144, Ensanche Las Américas, P3 Hotel Hostal Puerto Rico, Sto Domingo **W:** radiorevelacionenamerica.org.do – **66)** Ap 264 (or Calle San Francisco 50), San Francisco de Macorís – **67)** Calle Santa Rosa N° 18 (orAp 151), La Romana - **FM:** 107.5MHz – **69)** Sánchez esq Mella, Baní - **FM:** 96.7MHz – **70)** Calle Libertad N° 15, , Bonao - **FM:** 88.7MHz Latina 88 – **71)** C/ Proecto No 11, Las Colinas, Montecristi **W:** radiomontecristi. com – **72)** Padre Billini esq Jaime Mota, Barahona – **75)** Juan Rodríguez 76-A, La Vega **W:** radioreal.net – **76)** Av Anacaona N° 52 (or Ap 65), San Juan de la Maguana **W:** Radiocentroam.8k.com – **FM:** 100.1MHz Santome FM – **77)** Calle Santa Rosa N° 25 (or Ap 207), La Romana - **FM:** 94.5MHz – **79)** Ap 266 (or Libertad 9), El Seybo **W:** radioseibo.org - **FM:** 93.7MHz – **80)** Las Carreras, Esq Mella (4ta Planta), Santiago **W:** radionacional.net - **FM:** 106.1MHz – **81)** Calle Socorro Sánchez N° 103, San Cristóbal – **82)** Restauración 64, La Vega – **84)** C/ Duarte Esq Mella, Edi Fantino 2da Pta., Santiago – **85)** Calle Sánchez N° 45 (or Ap 003), Río San Juan - **FM:** 105.9MHz – **86)** Calle Sánchez N° 48 , Cotuí - **FM:** 97.3MHz – **87)** Diócesis de la Alta Gracia, Calle General Santana 65, Higüey **W:** lavozdelaaltagracia.com – **88)** Av 27 de Febrero No 265, Suite 202, Piantini, Santo Domingo – **89)** Calle Santomé N° 27 (or Ap 88), San Juan de la Maguana – **FM:** 90.3MHz – **90)** Ave Sarasota esquina Winston Churchill, Plaza Universitaria, Local 9B, Sto Domingo **W:** radioimpacto.org – **91)** Calle Mella N° 90 (altos) (or Ap 2), Salcedo **W:** radioutilfm.com – **FM:** 106.5MHz – **92)** Calle Felipe de Castro Esq

Santana N° 4, Hato Mayor del Rey – **93)** Carr.salida a Nagua al lado del Hospital del Seguro Social, San Francisco de Macorís – **95)** Pres Henriquez 53, Dajabón - **FM:** 105.1MHz – **97)** Calle Altagracia N° 70, Higüey – **98)** Ap 2217 (or Avenida Leopoldo Navarro No 34 Rsq. Juan E. Dunant), Sto Domingo **W:** radioven.com – **99)** Av Malecón, Samaná – **100)** Sto Domingo – **101)** Ap 1091, Santiago – **102)** Calle Duarte Esq Mella, Edif Fantino (2da planta), Bonao – **103)** Circuito Telesonido, Mella N° 177, San Pedro de Macorís – **104)** San Cristóbal – **107)** Calle Proyecto, Neiba – **108)** C/Paseo de Los Periodistas N° 52, Sto Domingo – **109)** Barahona – **110)** Av Pasteur N° 204, Sto Domingo – **111)** C/La Lira N° 18, Ens.Vergel, Elias Piña – **112)** Calle General López Esq 16 de Agosto, Santiago - **FM:** 91.3MHz – **113)** Luís Amiama Tió # 105, Arroyo Hondo, Santo Domingo **W:** radioeternidad.org – **114)** Calle René del Risco Bermúdez No.17, Villa Progreso, San Pedro de Macorís **W:** radiosenda.net – **115)** 16 de Agosto esq. Luperón, Bonao **W:** lavozdelyuna.org – **118)** Avenida Las Américas Esquina España, Santo Domingo. – **119)** Avenida Lope de Vega, Santo Domingo **W:** rednacionalcristiana.net

FM in Sto Domingo (MHz):

88.1 Primera FM – 88.5 Zulu R. – 88.9 Escape – 89.3 Neon – 89.7 Renuevo FM – 90.1 Fuego 90 – 90.5 Estrella 90 – 90.9 Alianza Francesa - 91.3 La 91 FM – 91.7 La Roka FM – 92.1 Hits 92 – 92.5 CDN R. - 92.9 Pura Vida 92.9 – 93.3 Independencia FM – 93.7 Latidos FM – 94.1 Fidelity – 94.5 KQ-94 – 94.9 Kiss 95 – 95.3 Ministerio de Educación – 95.7 La Nota Diferente – 96.1 Quisqueya FM (CERTV) – 96.5 Ritmo 96 – 96.9 Exa FM – 97.3 R. Disney – 97.7 Estación 97.7 – 98.1 Universal – 98.5 Rumba FM – 98.9 Dominicana FM (CERTV) – 99.3 Sonido Suave – 99.7 Listín – 100.1 Antena 100 – 100.9 Super Q – 101.3 Z-101 – 101.7 Supra FM – 102.1 La X 102 – 102.5 Escándalo FM – 102.5 Vaughan Radio – 102.9 Raíces FM - 103.3 Los 40 Principales – 103.7 Power FM – 104.1 R. Caliente – 104.5 ESPN R. – 104.9 Mortal FM – 105.3 ABC – 105.7 La Bakana FM – 106.1 Disco – 106.5 Zol FM – 106.9 LV Cultural de las FF AA – 107.3 Cadena Espacial – 107.7 R. Millón

FM in Santiago (MHz):

88.1 Primera FM – 88.5 Comando FM – 88.9 Disco – 89.3 R. Disney – 89.7 CDN R. – 90.1 Primor FM – 90.5 Fuego 90 – 90.9 R. Amanecer – 91.3 La 91 FM (relay) – 91.7 Contacto FM – 92.1 ZOL FM (relay) – 92.7 Lider FM – 93.1 Concierto FM – 93.7 R. Luz – 94.1 Full FM – 94.7 KV 94 – 95.1 Raices – 95.5 Digital FM – 95.9 Clave FM – 96.3 La Kalle – 97.1 Caliente – 97.5 La Ley – 98.3 Turbo 98 – 99.1 Mortal FM (relay) – 100.3 Monumental FM – 101.1 Premium – 101.5 Z-101 (relay) – 101.9 Amistad FM – 103.1 Super 103 – 103.5 La N – 103.9 Super Regional – 104.3 Sonido HD – 104.7 Matrix – 105.5 Ke Buena – 105.9 La Bakana FM – 106.1 Criolla 106 – 106.5 RADECO – 106.9 La Nueva 107 – 107.3 Suave 107 – 107.9 Mix 107.9

EASTER ISLAND (Chile)

L.T: UTC -6h — **Pop:** 5,034 — **Pr.L:** Spanish, Rapanui — **E.C:** 50Hz, 220V — **ITU:** PAQ

FM	MHz	kW	Station	FM	MHz	kW	Station
1)	88.3	-	ADN R.	3)	104.3	-	Los 40 Principales
2)	88.9	1	R. Manukena	4)	107.3	-	R. Nuevo Tiempo
5)	99.9		R.Maria				

Addresses and other information

1) 24h satellite relay from Santiago **W:** adnradio.cl – **2)** La Misma Municipalidad de Isla de Pascua, Calle Atamu Tekena, Hangaroa. Correo Isla de Pascua, Chile ☎+56 32 2255 1245 **W:** portalrapanui. cl/rapanui/radiomanukena & facebook.com/oficial-radio-manukena **LP:** Dir: Juan Herrera Torres. Community radio stn **Prgr:** 24h – **3)** 24h satellite relay from Santiago. **W:** los40.cl – **4)** 24h satellite relay from Santiago **W:** nuevotiempo.org – **5)** 24h satellite relay from Santiago **W:** radiomaria.cl

ECUADOR

L.T: UTC -5h — **Pop:** 13.9 million — **Pr.L:** Spanish, Quichua — **E.C:** 60Hz, 110/127 V — **ITU:** EQA

AGENCIA DE REGULACIÓN Y CONTROL DE LAS TELECOMUNICACIONES (ARCOTEL)

✉ Av. Diego de Almagro N31-95 entre Whymper y Alpallana, Quito ☎+593 2 294 6400 **W:** arcotel.gob.ec **E:** comunicacion@arcotel. gob.ec

Hrs of tr. 24h unless stated below. Call HC—

MW	Call	kHz	kW	Station, location, hr. of tr.
GU01	FA2	540	25	R. Santiago, Guayaquil: 1100-0600

MW	Call	kHz	kW	Station, location, hr. of tr.
GU02)	RN2	560	25	C. R. E. Satelital, Guayaquil
PI03)	CE1	570	10	R. El Sol, Quito
GU03)	PC2	580	10	R. Uno, Guayaquil
PI04)	SP1	590	10	Super K 800, Quito
GU04)	XY2	600	50	R. Ciudadana, Guayaquil: 1100-0400
PI05)	MJ1	610	10	R. Caravana, Quito
LO01)	XY3	620	50	R. Ciudadana, Loja: 1100-0400
LR01)	HA2	‡620	10	Ondas Quevedeñas, Quevedo
GU05)	X	640		R. Morena, Guayaquil
PI06)	XY1	640	50	R. Ciudadana, Quito: 1100-0400
MA01)	FD4	650	5	R. Visión, Manta: 0900-0500
PI07)	FF1	670	12/5	R. Jesus del Gran Poder, Quito: 0945-0500
GU06)	VP2	680	25/12	R. Atalaya, Guayaquil
PI08)	JB1	°690	50d	LV de los Andes, Quito: 1030-0500
GU07)	RS2	700	50	R. Sucre, Guayaquil
CR01)	ER5	710	8	Escuelas Radiofónicas Populares, Riobamba
EO01)	UE3	720	10	R. Única, Machala
MA03)	GB4	720	10	LV de Portoviejo, Portoviejo: 1030-0500
PI09)	IC1	720	5	R. Municipal, Quito
MA04)	SE4	‡740	10	R. Libertad, Chone: 1100-0600
PI15)	GC1	740	10	R. Melodía "Canal 7-40", Quito: 1100-0400
GU09)	RC2	750	30	R. Caravana, Guayaquil
PI10)	QR1	760	25	R. Quito "LV de la Capital", Quito
GU10)	MF2	770	25/12	R. Revolución, Guayaquil
PI20)	CM1	‡780	10/2	R. Colón AM, Quito
IM01)		‡790		Su Radio 790 AM, Otavalo
GU08)	ML2	800	25	Super K 800, Guayaquil
PI13)	FB1	‡800	5	R. Sensación 800, Quito: 1000-0300
GU11)	VT2	810	5	R. Atalaya, Milagro: 2300-0300
CA01)	VI5	820	5	R. LV de Ingapirca, Cañar: 0900-0330
PI54)	UP1	‡820	25	R. Unión, Quito: 1100-0100
GU12)	RM2	830	25	R. Huancavilca, Guayaquil
MA07)	EM4	‡840	1	R. Costa Azul, Portoviejo
PI16)	PN1	840	50	R. Vigía "LV de la Policía Nacional", Quito
GU13)	VS2	850	20/12	R. San Francisco, Guayaquil
PI17)	PC1	860	10	R. Positiva AM, Quito: 1015-0400
GU14)	NY2	870	20	R. Cristal "RCQ", Guayaquil: 1000-0600
TU02)	GS6	870	1	R. Pillaro, Píllaro: 1100-0400
PI18)	RP1	880	50/40	R. Católica Nacional, Quito: 1000-0200
EO02)	RS3	‡890	25/20	R. Superior, Machala: 0900-0500
PI19)	VA1	900	10	R. Sucre, Quito: 1100-0400
CR04)	GE5	910	5	R. Mundial, Riobamba: 1000-0400
GU15)	BO2	910	2	Futbol FM, Guayaquil
EO03)	RU3	920	10	CRO - Compañía Radiofónica Orense, Machala
PI40)	AB1	920	1	R. Democracia, Quito
TU03)	BA6	930	5	R. Ambato, Ambato
AZ21)		‡940		R. Austral del Ecuador, Cuenca
PI21)	BZ1	940	5	Rdif Casa de la Cultura Ecuatoriana, Quito
CR05)	UE5	950	3	LV de AlIECH, Colta
GU17)	DE2	‡950	10	GRD R. Internacional, Guayaquil
IM02)		950		R. Chaskis del Norte, Ibarra
AZ02)	SA5	960	1	R. Sonoonda Internacional, Cuenca
TU04)	JX6	960	1	R. LV del Santuario, Baños: 1000-0300
IM03)	MB1	970	1	R. Imperio, Ibarra: 1030-0300
CR06)	JI5	980	1	R. El Prado, Riobamba
LO11)	CL3	‡980	5	R. Cariamanga, Cariamanga: 1000-0400
PI24)	GH1	990	25	R. Tarquí, Quito: 1015-0400
AZ04)	RV5	1010	2.5	R. Visión AM, Cuenca
GU20)	RZ2	1010	3	R. Sport, Guayaquil
TU05)	NR6	1010	15	TSB R. Líder, Ambato: 0930-0300
BO01)	CR6	‡1020	5/3	R. Surcos, Guaranda: 1030-0100
PI26)	HR1	1020	5	RTU Radio, Quito
GU21)	RF2	1030	5	R. Ecuantena, Guayaquil: 1100-0500
AZ05)	EV5	1040	10/5	R. Splendid, Cuenca
PI27)	CW1	‡1040	3	LV del Valle, Machachi: 1130-0100
TU06)	GB6	1040	3	R. Colosal, Ambato: 0930-0500
GU49)	RQ2	1050	5	R. Águila, Guayaquil: 1030-0400
IM04)	IM1	1050	5/3	LV de Imbabura, Ibarra: 1000-0400
CP01)	MG6	1060	5	R. Ecos del Pueblo, Saquisilí: 1045-0330
EO19)		1060		R. Fiesta, Machala
LR02)		1060		R. Richi, El Empalme
AZ06)	CJ5	1070	5	LV del Tomebamba, Cuenca: 1000-0500
PI28)	VP1	‡1070	1	R. Libertad, Quito
CP02)	BH6	1080	10	R. Latacunga AM, Latacunga: 0900-0230
GU22)	KD2	1080	10	Sistema 2, Guayaquil
MA11)	AB4	1080	1	R. Contacto, Manta: 0900-0300
PI30)	VI1	1090	5	R. Irfeyal "Fe y Alegría", Quito
CP03)	RV6	1100	5/2	Solo Deportes R. Novedades, Latacunga
NA02)	LE7	1100	1.5	R. Oriental, Tena: 0900-0400
AZ07)	JC5	1110	5	R. Ondas Azuayas, Cuenca: 1100-0200
PI31)	JR1	1110	10	R. Arpeggio, Quito
EO20)		1130		R. Romántica, Machala
LR03)		1130		R. Sibimbe AM, Ventanas
TU08)	PV6	1130	5	R. Centro, Ambato
AZ08)	AZ5	1140	1	R. Alpha Musical, Cuenca: 1100-0600
PI33)	IR1	1140	5	R. Raíz, Quito: 1130-0400
CR07)	GB5	1150	10	LV de Riobamba, Riobamba
LO06)	AV3	‡1150	10	R. Luz y Vida, Loja
CA02)		1160		LV del Pueblo, Azoguez
CP04)	UR6	1160	1	R. Runatacuyaj, Latacunga
EO05)	VR3	1160	2	R. Vía, Machala
PI34)	CP1	‡1160	5	Super Auténtica, Quito
GU26)	RV2	1170	5	R. Filadelfia, Guayaquil
AZ09)	DP5	1180	4	R. Cuenca "LV de los 4 Ríos", Cuenca
MA26)		‡1180		LV del Volante, Portoviejo
PI35)	LR1	1180	12.5	Nueva Em. Central, Quito: 1100-0400
CP05)	RF6	‡1190	5	R. El Sol, Pujilí: 1100-0200
GU24)	DE2	1190	2	UCSG Radio, Guayaquil: 1100-0500
AZ10)	RM5	1200	5	R. El Mercurio, Cuenca: 0900-0500
LR04)	RE2	1200	5	LV del Trópico, Quevedo: 1000-0400
PI36)	CS1	1200	5	R. Super K, Sangolquí: 1000-0100
GU27)	BJ2	1210	20	R. El Mundo, Guayaquil
LO07)	VC3	1210	10	R. Centinela del Sur "CDS", Loja: 1100-0300
TU09)	JM6	1210	3	R. Sira, Ambato: 1000-0700
PI32)	AP1	1220	10	R. Marañón, Quito: 1300-0200
AZ11)	MV5	‡1230	3	R. Popular, Cuenca: 1045-0500
CP06)	RL6	1230	1	LV de Saquisilí, Saquisilí: 1045-0300
GU48)	FV2	1230	15	R. Galáctica, Guayaquil: 1000-0400
IM06)	RI1	1230	3	CRI-Centro Radiofónico de Imbabura, Ibarra: 1100-0400
EO08)	RF3	‡1240	5	R. Fenix, Zaruma: 1000-0100
PI37)	PA1	1240	1	R. Metropolitana, Yaraquí: 1200-0300
CC03)	EM1	1250	10	Ondas Carchenses, Tulcán: 1000-0400
AZ12)	PB5	1260	2	R. Contacto XG, Cuenca: 1100-0300
EO09)	RB3	‡1260	1	R. Benemérita, Sta Rosa: 1030-0100
PI39)	MO1	1260	10	LV del Santuario del Quinche, Quito
TU10)	RO6	1260	3	R. Calidad, Ambato: 0930-0600
GU23)	UM2	1270	15	R. Universal, Guayaquil
MA15)	LD4	1270	3	R. Junín, Junín: 1100-0500
PI61)		1280		R. Universitaria, Quito
AZ13)	JA5	1290	3	LV del Río Tarqui, Cuenca: 0900-0200
IM07)	NS1	1290	1	R. Popular, Atuntaqui: 1100-0300
BO04)		1300		R. La Paz, Guaranda
GU30)	DC2	‡1300	5	R. Cenit, Guayaquil: 1200-0400
SD04)	RV1	1300	5	R. Festival, Sto Domingo de los Colorados
SU02)	RS7	‡1300	2/1	R. Sucumbios, Nueva Loja: 1100-2400
CA03)	CI5	1310	5	R. Internacional TVO, Biblián
CR20)	AI5	1310	0.5	Eco de los Andes, Cumandá: 1000-0200
EO11)	CP3	1310	1	LV de El Oro, Pasaje
PI58)	GB1	‡1310	20	R. Nal. Espejo, Quito
LR05)	FR2	1320	3	R. Guayaquil, Babahoyo: 1030-0300
MA24)	VO4	1320	1	R. Carrizal, Calceta: 1130-0300
TU11)	JD6	1320	10	R. Continental, Ambato: 0930-0300
AZ14)	LW5	1330	2	R. Visión Cristiana, Cuenca
PI42)		1330	3	R. Visión Cristiana, Quito
EO12)	RV3	1330	5	Nacional El Oro, Machala: 1000-0600
ES03)		1340		LV de su Amigo, Esmeraldas
LO08)		1340	1	Ondas de Esperanza, Loja: 1100-0300
TU12)	RT6	1340	5	R. Paz y Bien, Ambato: 0930-0130
AZ15)	SF5	‡1350	2/1	LV de San Fernando, San Fernando
GU47)	VP2	1350	3	Teleradio 13-50 AM Digital , Guayaquil
EO13)	HG3	1360	5	R. Jerusalem AM, Machala
PI44)	MT	1360	3	R. Oyambaro, Tumbaco: 1000-0300
CA04)	AO5	1370	12	R. El Rocio, Biblián
GU32)	VO2	1370	5	LV de Milagro, Milagro
IM08)	JS1	‡1370	2	Ecos Andinos, Pimampiro
EO14)	OA3	1380	1	R. Estelar La Mejor, Balsas
PI45)	CV1	1380	5	R. Cristal "RCQ", Quito: 0830-0300
TU13)		1380	5	R. Mera, Ambato
AZ16)	EA5	1390	5	R. Tropicana, Cuenca: 1200-0300
GU16)	FL2	1400	5	R. Z Uno, Guayaquil
AZ17)	GC5	1400	1	R. Centro Gualaceo, Gualaceo
CR14)		‡1410	1	Ondas Cisnerinas, Riobamba
ES05)	FR4	1410	1	LV de Quinindé, Quinindé
GU33)	CQ2	1410	1	R. Net AM, Milagro
PI59)	EC1	1410	1	R. El Tiempo "Emisora del Amor", Quito
EO15)		1420		Corazón AM, Machala
NA06)	VN7	1420		R. del Napo, Tena
GU34)	MB2	‡1430	10	R. Federal, Virgen de Fátima
PI46)	GF1	1430	3.5	R. Futura, Quito: 1300-0200
CA05)	OV5	1440	2.8	Ondas del Volante, Azogues: 1000-0400
IM11)	DF1	1440	5	R. Panorama, Ibarra: 1030-0400
SE01)	SE2	1450	1	R. Santa Elena, Santa Elena: 2200-0200
PI47)	SC1	1450	1	AS La Radio, Tabacundo

MW	Call	kHz	kW	Station, location, hr. of tr.
CP12)	IC6	1460	5	R. Nuevos Horizontes, Latacunga: 1000-0200
GU37)	LD2	1470	1.5	R. Ecos de Naranjito, Naranjito
PI48)	JC1	1470	5	Rdif. Ecos de Cayambe, Cayambe
CP13)		1480	5	R. Popular de la Maná, La Maná
MA20)	JV4	1480	3	R. LV de Jipijapa, Jipijapa: 1100-0400
CA06)	SM5	1490	5	R. Santa María, Azogues: 0930-0330
ES07)	AE4	‡1490	2.5	R. Unión, Esmeraldas: 1000-0300
GU38)	VY2	1490	1	R. Dinámica, Guayaquil
PI60)		1490		R. La Poderosa, Quito
IM13)	RO1	‡1500	1	R. Otavalo, Otavalo: 1200-0300
BO07)	RY6	1510	1	R. Runacunapac Yachana, Simiátug
CA07)	RC5	1510	2	LV de la Juventud, Cañar
GU39)	HD2	1510	0.5	R. Naval, Guayaquil
PI56)		1510	5	R. Monumental, Quito: 1300-0400
CR18)	RI5	1520	2.5	LV de Guamote, Guamote
GU40)	RN2	‡1520	1	LV de Naranjal, El Naranjal
IM14)	TI1	1520	1	R. Ibarra, Ibarra: 1000-0400
CA08)	CC5	1530	5	Ondas Cañaris, R. Universitaria Católica, Azogues
CR19)	VP5	1530	3	R. LV de Pallatanga, Pallatanga: 1100-0300
SE02)	MP2	‡1530	5	R. LV de la Península, La Libertad: 1100-0400
TU15)	MZ6	1530	1	R. Dorado Deportes, Pelileo: 1130-0230
LR10)	FM2	1540	3	R. Cristal de Ventanas, Babahoyo
MS05)	VB7	‡1540	0.25	R. LV del Upano, Macas
PI49)	DP1	1540	1	R. Caracol, Quito: 1000-0400
AZ18)	AD5	1550	5	R. LV de Chaguarurco, Santa Isabel
GU42)	AD2	1550	2	LV del Triunfo, El Triunfo: 1100-0400
IM15)	ZD1	1560	1.5	Ecos Culturales de Urcuquí, Urcuquí
MA23)		‡1570	1	R. LV Espíritu Santo de Dios, Manta
AZ19)	TP5	‡1580	3	Ecos del Portete, Girón: 1200-0330
PI52)	LF1	1580	1	R. Orellana, Machachi: 1030-0230
PI53)	RZ1	1590	1	R. Mensaje, Cayambe
TU17)	QT6	1590	1	R. Panamericana, Quero

° = also on SW, ‡ = inactive, (r) = repeater, ± = varying fq.

SW	Call	kHz	kW	Station, location, h of tr
NA06)	VN7	‡3280	2.5	LV del Napo, Tena: 0900-0300
NA02)	LE7	‡4782	3	R. Oriental, Tena: 1030-2400
PI08)		6050	8	HCJB, Quito: 0830-1500, 1900-0503

Province-abbreviations: AZ=Azuay BO=Bolívar CA=Cañar CC=Carchi CP=Cotopaxi CR=Chimborazo EO=El Oro ES=Esmeraldas GU=Guayas IM=Imbabura LO=Loja LR=Los Ríos MA=Manabí MS=Morona Santiago,NA=Napo PA=Pastaza PI=Pichincha SD=Santo Domingo de los Tsáchilas SE=Santa Elena SU=Sucumbíos TU=Tungurahua ZC=Zamora Chinchipe **N.B.:** These abbreviations are not recognized by the Ecuadorian Post Office. Letters should carry the full name.

Addresses and other information:

AZ00) AZUAY
AZ02) Av.Remigio Crespo y Calle La Libertad, Cuenca **W:** sonoondainternacional.com – **AZ04)** Cas 198, Cuenca **W:** cadenaradialvision. com – **AZ05)** Cas 01-01-1352, Cuenca **W:** radiosplendid.com.ec - **FM:** 90.5MHz 92.5MHz – **AZ06)** Cas 01-01-0493, Cuenca **W:** lavozdeltombamba.com – **AZ07)** Cas 01-01-4980 (or Av Héroes de Verdeloma 9-15), Cuenca **W:** ondasazuayas.ec - **FM:** 93.7MHz Sunny – **AZ08)** Simon Bolívar 226, Cuenca **W:** facebook.com/RadioAlphaMusical1140Am – **AZ09)** Bomboiza 1-83, entre Loja-Pastaza, Cuenca **W:** radiocuenca.com – **AZ10)** Av.de las Américas, Edif.Mercurio, Cuenca **W:** radioelmercurio.com.ec – **AZ11)** La Gloria de Nanuncay, Av.Loja 2408, Cuenca – **AZ12)** J Dávila y C Merchán, Cuenca **W:** contactoxg.webpin.com – **AZ13)** Manuel Vega 653 y Presidente Córdoba, Cuenca **W:** lavozdelriotarqui. com – **AZ14)** Gran Colombia 7-39 y Presidente Borrero, 4to. piso Oficina E, Cuenca **W:** radiovisioncristiana.ec – **AZ15)** Av José María Quito y Santiago de San Fernando, San Fernando **W:** nuestrosanfernando.com – **AZ16)** Cas 830 (or Pumapungo 5-50), Cuenca **W:** radiotropicana1390. com – **AZ17)** Gran Colombia y 9 de Octubre 3102, Frente al Parque Central, Gualaceo **W:** radiocentrogualaceo.com – **AZ18)** Cas 01-01-46 (or Calle Bolívar 7-64), Aperado (or Calle 24 de Mayo y Abdon Calderón, Cuenca) **W:** radiochaguarurco.blogspot.com – **AZ19)** Antonio Flor 6-57, Girón – **AZ21)** J Roldos 480, Edif El Consorcio, Cuenca.

BO00) BOLÍVAR
BO01) Johnson City 204 y Sucre, Parraquia San Vicente, Guaranda **W:** radiosurcosfm.com - **FM:** 97.5MHz – **BO03)** 10 de Agosto 612, Guaranda - **FM:** 93.9MHz – **BO04)** G Moreno y 7 de Mayo, Guaranda **W:** radiolapazguaranda.com – **BO07)** Simiátug **W:** radiorunacunapac. blogspot.com

CA00) CAÑAR
CA01) Av Ingapirca, Cdla El Vergel, Cañar (or Cas 01-01-0447, Cuenca) **Quichua:** 0900-1300 - **FM:** 94.5MHz **W:** radioingapirca.com. ec – **CA02)** General Vintimilla 1-10 y Oriente, Azogues **W:** radiolavozdelpueblo.com – **CA03)** Mariscal Sucre 722 y B Ochoa, Biblián (or Cas 729, Azogues) **W:** radiointernacionalec.com – **CA04)** Calle Mariscal

Sucre 202 y Tarquí, Biblián. **W:** radioelrocio1370.com – **CA05)** Bolívar y Azuay, Azogues **W:** ondasdelvolante.com.ec – **CA06)** Cas 03-01-730, Azogues **W:** radiosantamaria.com.ec – **CA07)** Bolívar y Borrero (Junto Parque Central), Cañar – **CA08)** Calle Rivera 613, Azogues **W:** ondascanaris.com.ec

CC00) CARCHI
CC03) Olmedo 52-025 y Ayacucho (or Cas 30), Tulcán **W:** ondascarchenses.com

CP00) COTOPAXI
CP01) Imbabura 2333 y 9 de Octubre, Saquisilí **W:** facebook.com/radioecosdelpueblo – **CP02)** Cas 05-01-392 (or Calle Quito 14-56, Pasaje La Catedral), Latacunga **W:** radiolatacunga.com - **FM:** 97.1MHz +102.1MHz – **CP03)** 2 de Mayo 438, entre Tarquí y General Maldonado, Latacunga **W:** facebook.com/SoloDeportesRadioNovedadesAm1100khz – **CP04)** Bel.Quevedo Caserio Illuchi, Latacunga – **CP05)** B Quevedo 555, Pujilí – **CP06)** Av.24 de Mayo 669, Saquisilí – **CP12)** Faustino Sarmiento 5046 y Vela, Latacunga **W:** rnh146.wix.com/rnh146 – **CP13)** Enrique Gallo 164 y Av 19 de Mayo, La Maná

CR00) CHIMBORAZO
CR01) Cas 06-01-693 (or Juan de Velasco N° 20-60 y Guayaquil), Riobamba **W:** erpe.org.ec - **FM:** 91.7MHz – **CR04)** Cas 06-01-572 (or Av.Daniel León Borja 30-44), Riobamba **W:** radio-mundial.com – **CR05)** Cas.87A, Majipamba, Colta **W:** lavozdeaiiech.org.ec Prgrs in Quichua only – **CR06)** Francia 1857 y Villaroel, Riobamba **W:** radioelprado.blogsport.com – **CR07)** Cardondelet 2952 y J.Montalvo, Riobamba **W:** radiolavozderiobamba.com.ec – **CR14)** Cas 334 (or La Paz y México Esq.), Riobamba **W:** facebook.com/ondas.cisnerinas – **CR18)** Comunidad Sta Cruz, Guamote **W:** lavozdeguamote.com – **CR19)** Panamericana y Eloy Alfaro, Pallatanga **W:** radiolavozdepallatanga.jimdo.com – **CR20)** 1 Constituyente y G Rendon, Cumanda.

EO00) EL ORO
EO01) Bolívar Madero 1313, via Pto Bolívar, Machala – **EO02)** Cas 221, Machala **W:** superiorfm.com – **EO03)** Bolívar 601, Edif. Encasa, Machala **W:** radiocro920am.com – **EO05)** Cas 07-01-0086, Machala (or 9 de Octubre y Paéz), Machala **W:** radiovia.com.ec – **EO08)** San Francisco 114 y Sucre, Zaruma – **EO09)** El Oro y Cuenca, Sta Rosa **W:** radiobenemerita.com – **EO11)** San Martín 720, Entre Municipalidad y Och, Pasaje **W:** lavozdeeloro.com – **EO12)** 9 de Octubre y Sta Rosa, Machala facebook.com/pages/Radio-Nacional-El-ORO/570938789584764– **EO13)** Calle Pasaje s/n y Costa Oeste, Machala – **EO14)** Av 10 de Agosto 1303 y 23 de Febrero, Balsas **W:** facebook.com/pages/Radio-y-Tv-La-Mejor/135117216566168?fref=ts – **EO15)** Av Buena Vista 742 y 4ta Norte, Machala – **EO19)** Av 9 de Octubre y 23 de Abril, Machala **W:** radiofiestamachala.com – **EO20)** Av 12va Norte y Buena Vista, Machala **W:** radioromanticamachala. blogspot.com

ES00) ESMERALDAS
ES03) Manuela Cañizares y Olmedo, Esmeraldas **W:** vozdesuamigo. com - **FM:** 96.3MHz – **ES05)** Simon Plata Torres y Maclovio Velazco, Quinindé

GU00) GUAYAS
GU01) Cdla. Bolivariana, Avda. del Libertador Mz K Villa 8, Guayaquil **W:** radiosantiago.com.ec – **GU02)** Boyacá 642 y Padre Solano, Edificio El Torreón, 8vo. piso, Guayaquil **W:** cre.com.ec – **GU03)** Cas 2119, Guayaquil (or Amazonas 743 y Veintemilla, P8, Quito) **W:** radiouno580am.com – **GU04)** Quisquis 316 y Garaicoa, Edif Huancavelica, Guayaquil **W:** laciudadana.gob.ec – **GU05)** Av. Quito 1200 y Aguirre, Guayaquil **W:** radiomorena640.com – **GU06)** Rumichaca 934 y Velez, Guayaquil **W:** radioatalaya.net – **GU07)** Cas 11714 (or Av.Francisco de Orellana y Juan Tanca Marengo), Guayaquil **W:** radiosucre.com. ec – **GU08)** Av. Americas y Av. Constitución, dentro de TC Televisión, Guayaquil **W:** superk800.com – **GU09)** Cas 716, (or Av Juan Tanga Marengo km 3), Guayaquil **W:** radiocaravana.com/reproductores.php – **GU10)** Cas 09-01-4203 (or Colón 548 y Boyacá, P7), Guayaquil – **GU11)** Juan Montalvo 1042, Milagro **W:** facebook.com/pages/Radio-Atalaya-Milagro/317106658330550 – **GU12)** Cas 856 (or Av. Guillermo Pareja Rolando, (Principal de la Alborada) y la novena (esquina), Cdla. IETEI, Mz 2, solar 7), Guayaquil **W:** radiohuancavilca.com.ec – **GU13)** Cas 09-01-5762, Guayaquil **W:** radiosanfrancisco850.blogspot.com – **GU14)** Cas 5062 (or Laque 1407 y Antepara), Guayaquil **E:** radiocristal.com.ec – **GU15)** Malecón 206 entre Juan Montalvo y Loja, Guayaquil - **W:** futbolfm.ec – **GU16)** radioz1.ec – **GU17)** García Moreno y Hurtavbo, en los Altos, Ofc.Delgado Travel P3, Guayaquil – **GU18)** 10 de Agosto 504 y Chimborazo, P3), Guayaquil **E:** servidor1000@hotmail. com – **GU19)** José de Antepara 4415 y Nicolas González, Guayaquil **W:** radiosport.com.ec – **GU21)** Los Ríos 609, Cond Orellana, P4, Ofc 2, Guayaquil **W:** radioecuantena.com.ec – **GU22)** Ciudadela Albatros Calle Fragata # 203, atrás de la Sociedad Italiana Garibaldi, Avenida de las Américas, Guayaquil **W:** radiosistema2.com Also r. R. Sucre 700kHz – **GU23)** Chimborazo 3407 Y El Oro, Guayaquil **W:** radiouniversalgye. com – **GU24)** Universidad Católica de Santiago de Guayaquil, Av.

Carlos Julio Arosemena Km. 1 1/2 Vía Daule, Guayaquil **W:** ucsgrtv.com **GU26)** Veléz 905, Edif.Forum, P16 (or Cas 8729), Guayaquil **W:** radiofiladelfiamundial.com **GU27)** Jiguas 500 y V.Emilio Estrada, Guayaquil – **GU30)** Luis Urdaneta 202 y Cordoba, Guayaquil – **GU32)** Av. 17 de Septiembre y Azogues, esq. Edif. Radio, Milagro **W:** radi-olavozdemilagro.com – **GU33)** Calle García Moreno y Bolívar 1013, Milagro – **GU34)** Km 26.5 vía Duran-Tambo, Virgen de Fátima **W:** face-book.com/pages/Radio-Federal-1430-am/172937509393959 – **GU37)** Av 5 de Octubre 150, Naranjito **W:** radioecosdenaranjito.com – **GU38)** Av 25 de Julio cdla 7 Lagos C, Guayaquil **W:** radiodinamica.com – **GU39)** Cas 5940, Guayaquil **W:** inocar.mil.ec/web/index.php/bole-tines/avisos-navegantes/27-radio-naval/117-radio-naval-on-line **FM:** Esmeraldas 100.3MHz – **GU40)** Pastaza y 15 de Octubre, El Naranjal **E:** davidtoa_2011@hotmail.com – **GU42)** Jaime Roldos 700 y Av.8 de Abril, El Triunfo – **W:** lavozdeltriunfo.com **GU43)** Cdla.Belén Piedrahita y 1era, Daule – **GU47)** 9 de Octubre y Baquerizo Moreno, Edif.Plaza, P1, Guayaquil – **GU48)** Edif El Forum, P5, Ofic 508, Guayaquil **W:** radiogalactica1230am.jimdo.com – **GU49)** Eloy Alfaro Duran en la Av. Samuel Cisneros, via al Secap, Guayaquil **W:** radioaguila1050am.com

IM00) IMBABURA
IM01) Morales 408 y Sucre, Otavalo **W:** gruporadialimbabura.com – **IM02)** Celiano Aguinaga y Panamericana Sur, Atuntaqui, Ibarra – **IM03)** Cas 413 (or Olmedo 1178 y Av.Peréz Guerrero), Ibarra **W:** radio-imperio970.com – **IM04)** Cas 10-01-0179 (or Bolívar y García Moreno), Ibarra **W:** facebook.com/ROMANTICA899 - **FM:** 89.9MHz – **IM06)** Río Chinchipe 397 y Río Daule, Ibarra – **IM07)** Cas 3, Atuntaqui – **IM08)** Bolívar 10020 y Espejo, Pimapiro – **IM11)** Juan José Flores 11-26 y Jaime Rivadeneira, Ibarra **W:** radiopanorama1440.com - **FM:** 93.7MHz – **IM13)** Rocafuerte 1-10 y Guayaquil, Otavalo – **IM14)** Calle Oviedo y Bolívar, Edif Way, P2, Ibarra **W:** radioibarra.webs.com – **IM15)** Antonio Ante s/n, Urcuquí **W:** radioecosculturales.com – **IM16)** Jirón Roldos Aguilera y Panamericana Norte, Otavalo **E:** radiochaskis@hotmail.com

LO00) LOJA
LO01) Av.J.A Eguuigurren y Bolívar, Loja **W:** laciudadana.gob.ec – **LO03)** 24 de Mayo y Eloy Alfaro, Catamayo - **FM:** 93.7MHz – **LO06)** Cas 11-01-222, Loja **W:** radioluzyvidafm.com - **FM:** 88.1MHz – **LO07)** Cas 196 (or Olmedo 11-56 y Mercadillo), Loja - **FM:** 88.9MHz – **LO08)** Olmedo 1146 entre Azuay y Mercadillo, Loja **W:** esperanzaparaloja.org – **LO11)** Sector Colinas de San Juan, Cariamanga **FM:** 104.5 **W:** radiocariamanga.com.ec – **LO15)** Asociación Cristiana de Indigenas Saraguros, Saraguro - **FM:** 93.1MHz

LR00) LOS RÍOS
LR01) 12 Calle N° 207 y 7 de Octubre, Quevedo – **LR02)** Av Manabí y Juan León Mera, El Empalme, Quevedo – **LR03)** Av Velasco Ibarra 1012, Ventanas **W:** facebook.com/pages/Radio-Sibimbe/260566980680351?fref=ts – **LR04)** Av.7 de Octubre 727, Quevedo **W:** rvtradio.com – **LR05)** Cdla El Mamey, Babahoyo **W:** facebook.com/RadioGuayaquil1320Am – **LR10)** 28 de Mayo 1412 y 6 de Octubre, Babahoyo **W:** radiocristal.com.ec

MA00) MANABÍ
MA01) Av.10ma y Calle 17, P2, Manta **W:** radiovisionmanta.com.ec – **MA03)** Ricaurte y P. Moreira, Portoviejo **W:** malluryconsulting.com/index.php/medios-mallury-consulting/item/radio-voz-de-portoviejo-720-am – **MA04)** Av Lascano, Chone – **MA07)** Colón 180, Portoviejo **W:** costazulradio.com **FM:** 89.3MHz – **MA11)** 9 y Malecón, Edif "Jacob Vera", P1 Ofc 7, Manta – **MA15)** 10 de Agosto 180 y Eloy Alfaro, Junín **W:** radiojunin1270.com – **MA20)** Noboa y Colón, Jipijapa – **MA23)** 306 Entre Las Avenidas 204 y 205, Manta **W:** diosvenami@hotmail.com – **MA24)** Flavio Alfaro 718 Ciudadela San Bartolo, Calceta **W:** radiocarrizal.blogspot.com – **MA25)** Cas 13-02-0629 (or Montufar N° 1014 y Aguilera), Bahía de Caráquez - **FM:** 95.3 – **MA26)** Morales 109 y Colón, Ed Sind Choferes Man, Portoviejo

MS00) MORONA SANTIAGO
MS05) Misión Salesiana de Oriente, Calle 10 de Agosto s/n, Macas **W:** radioupano.com.ec - **FM:** 90.5MHz – **MS06)** Federación de Centros Shuar, Domingo Comín 17-38, Sucúa (or Cas 17-01-4122, Quito).

NA00) NAPO
NA02) Cas 260 (or Av.Jumandy 536, Barrio 2 Rios), Tena **W:** facebook.com/radiooriental - **FM:** 89.7MHz – **NA06)** Misión Josefina, Juan Montalvo s/n y P Central, Tena **W:** lavozdelnapo.com

PI00) PICHINCHA
PI03) 18 de Septiembre y Ulpiano Páez, Quito **W:** radioelsol.net – **PI04)** see GU05) – **PI05)** see GU09) – **PI06)** Cas 60 (or Mariano Echeverria y Brasil), Quito **W:** laciudadana.gob.ec – **PI07)** Cuenca 477 y Sucre (El convento de San Francisco), Quito 7 **W:** radiojesusdelgranpoder.com – **PI08)** Cas 17-17-691(or Villalengua 884 y Av.10 de Agosto), Quito. Shortwave: See Int. broadcasting section **W:** radiohcjb.org – **PI09)** García Moreno 751 entre Sucre y Bolívar, P3, Quito **W:** radiomunicipal.gob.ec – **PI10)** Cas 17-21-1971 (or La Coruña 2104 y Whimper, Edif. Aragones) Quito **W:** ecuadoradio.ec – **PI13)** Amazonas 1638 y La Pinta, Quito – **PI15)** Panamericana Sur km 14.5, Quito – **PI16)** Ramírez Dávalos 612 y 10 de Agosto, Quito **W:** vigiaradio.ecuadormedios.com – **PI17)** Av.Amazonas y Colón, Edif.España, P4, Ofc.42, Quito **W:** radiopositiva.com.ec – **PI18)** Cas 17-03-540 (or Av.América 1830 y Mercadillo),Quito **W:** radiocatolica.org.ec – **PI19)** Palacio 303 y Av La Gasca, Quito (see also GU07) – **PI20)** Avellanas E5-107 y Av.Eloy Alfaro, Quito – **PI21)** Cas 17-01-67, Quito **W:** casadelacultura.gob.ec/?ar_id=6&ge_id=17 – **PI24)** García Moreno 1315 y Olmedo, Quito **W:** radiotarqui.com – **PI26)** Edif Sevilla, P9, J L Mera 565 y Carrión, Quito **W:** rtunoticias.com – **PI27)** García Moreno 446, Machachi – **PI28)** Tarquí 785 y Estrada,Edif.de Cosi, P2, Quito **W:** libertadquito.blogspot.com **PI30)** Cas 17-03-31 (or Carrión 1288 y Av 10 de Agosto), Quito **W:** irfeyal.org – **PI31)** Av.América 4829 y Naciones Unidas, Quito – **PI32)** Cas 17-11-2263 (or Bolivar 359 entre García Moreno y Venezuela), Quito **W:** radiomq.jimdo.com – **PI33)** Cas 17-01-638 (or Av Amazonas N35-89 y Corea, P4), Quito **W:** radioraiz.com – **PI34)** Marquesa de Solanda 722, Quito – **PI35)** Central Roca 331 y Av 6 de Diciembre, Quito **W:** nuevaemisoracentral.com.ec – **PI36)** Cas 17-23-47 (or Av General Enriquez N° 29-35 y Río Chinchipe), Sangolquí **W:** radiosuperk1200.com – **PI37)** 12 de Octubre 227, Quito **W:** face-book.com/pages/Radio-Metropolitana-1240-AM/1545443142394044 – **PI39)** Cas 17-01-3386 (or García Moreno N 11-184 y Carchi), Quito **W:** facebook.com/cesar.paredes.9883739 – **PI40)** Edif Doral Mariscal, Of 86, Páez y Mercadillo, Quito **W:** radiogenial.com – **PI42)** Reina Victoria 447 y Ramón Roca, Quito **W:** radiovision.net – **PI44)** Carvajal e Interoceania, Barrio Sta Rosa, Tumbaco - **FM:** 104.1MHz – **PI45)** Av. de la Prensa N°60-22 y Av.de la Prensa, Quito **W:** facebook.com/Rarr50 – **PI46)** Av.Amazonas 3911 y Corea, Unicormio 2, P10, Ofc.1008, Quito **W:** radiofuturaecuador.com.ec – **PI47)** Calle Bolívar y Alfredo Boada (sobre el Banco del Pichincha), Tabacundo **W:** facebook.com/Aslaradio1450am – **PI48)** Cas 17-25-5 (or Terán 409 y Av 10 de Agosto, Cayambe **W:** radioecosdecayambe.com – **PI49)** Venezuela 701 y Espejo, Quito – **PI52)** Luis Cordero 557 y J.Mejia, Machachi **W:** radioorellana.es.tl – **PI53)** Av.Natalia Jarrín 2-77 y Vívar, Cayambe **W:** radiomensaje.blogspot.com – **PI54)** Iñaquito 133-E2 y Unión Nacional de Periodistas, Quito **W:** unionnacionaldeperiodistas.com – **PI56)** Manuel Cajias E 14-09 y Toribio Hidalgo, Quito **W:** radiomonumenta-l1510am.com – **PI58)** Panamericana Sur km 14.5 (teléfono 2 245 300), Quito – **PI59)** Gonzalo Díaz de Pineda 290 y Pedro del Alfaro, Quito **W:** radioeltiempo.com – **PI60)** Av Colón OE3-331 y Versalles, Edificio Villarre, Quito **W:** lapoderosaecuador.com – **PI61)** Universidad Central del Ecuador, Avenida América, Ciudadela Universitaria, Quito **W:** uce.edu.ec/web/comunicacion-social/radio-universitaria

SD00) SANTO DOMINGO DE LAS TSÁCHILAS
SD04) Quito e Ibarra, Santo Domingo de los Colorados **W:** radiofes-tivalfm.com

SE00) SANTA ELENA
SE01) Guayaquil s/n y 9 de Octubre, Santa Elena **W:** rse1450am.blogspot.com – **SE02)** 4a Av 619 y Robles, La Libertad **W:** vozpeninsula.com – **W:** 93.3MHz

SU00) SUCUMBIOS
SU02) Cas 21-01-14 (or Venezuela y Progreso), Nueva Loja **W:** radio-sucumbios.com.ec - **FM:** 105.3

TU00) TUNGURAHUA
TU02) Bolívar 537 y Fund.del Canton, Píllaro (or Cas 18-01-244, Ambato) **W:** facebook.com/pages/Radio-Pillaro/202664373117501 – **TU03)** Cas 18-01-181 (or Sucre 09-42 y Quito), Ambato **W:** radio-ambato.com.ec - **FM:** 96.7MHz R. Amor – **TU04)** 12 de Noviembre y Ambato, Edif.El Pelegrino, Baños **W:** radiosantuario.com – **TU05)** Cas 18-01-0674 (or Av.Cevallos 15-57 y Mera, P10, Ofc 1001), Ambato **W:** radioliderambato.com – **TU06)** Bolívar y Martinez, Ambato **W:** radioco-losal.com – **TU08)** Cas 18-01-0574 (or Castillo entre 12 de Noviembre y Olmedo, Edif.R.Centro), Ambato **W:** radiocentroambato.com - **FM:** 91.7MHz – **TU09)** Cevallos 1624 y Maldonado, Ambato **W:** radiosira.com – **TU10)** Cevallos 754 y Martinez (or Cas 18-01-0198), Ambato **W:** radiocalidadambato.com – **TU11)** Cotacachi 176 e Iliniza, Ambato **W:** gruporadialcontinental.com – **TU12)** Cas 18-01-115 (or Fray Fausto Suárez, Francisco Vior 321), Ambato **W:** radiospazybien.com - **FM:** 92.9MHz 104.5MHz 106.9MHz – **TU13)** Cas 618 (or Calle Ayllón 1753 y Darquea), Ambato **W:** radiomera.com – **TU15)** Av Padre Chancon s/n y Juan Velasco, Pelileo **W:** radiodoradodeportes.com – **TU17)** Montalvo 106, Quero **W:** radiopanamericana.com.ec

FM in Quito (MHz): 88.1 Latina FM – 88.5 Metro – PI08) 89.3 HCJB – 89.7 Majestad – 90.1 Tropicalida – 90.5 Disney – 90.9 Platinum – 91.3 Sabormix – PI17) 91.7 Visión – 92.1 Contacto Nuevo Tiempo – 92.5 Genial Exa FM – 92.9 Música y Sonido – PI33) 93.3 Eres 93.3 – 93.7 Galaxia – PI18) 94.1 Católica Nacional FM – 94.5 Rumba – 94.9 La Gitana – 95.3 Universal – 95.7 R. Legislativa – 96.1 Joya – 96.5 BBN - 96.9 Armónica FM – PI31) 97.3 La Otra FM – 97.7 Centro – 98.1 Proyección – 98.5 Alfa – 98.9 Colón – 99.3 La Luna – 99.7 Añoranza La

Rumbera – 100.1 María – Pl23) 100.5 Stereo Zaracay – 100.9 Nacional del Ecuador – R. Pública – 101.3 Onda Azul – 101.7 Sucesos – 102.1 R.La Red – Pl07) 102.5 Francisco Estéreo – 102.9 Distrito FM – 103.3 Onda Cero FM - 103.7 Sonorama – 104.1 Cobertura - 104.5 América – 104.9 Ecuashyri – 105.3 Kiss – 105.7 CRE – 106.1 Hot 106 R. Fuego – 106.5 Canela – 106.9 R. Genial – 107.3 JC – 107.7 Más Candela

FM in Guayaquil (MHz): 88.1 María – 88.5 Galaxia Stereo – 88.9 Di Blu – 89.3 R. City – 89.7 Punto Rojo FM – 90.1 Romance FM – 90.5 Canela – 90.9 Kiss – 91.3 Tropicalida Stereo – 91.7 Antena Tres – 92.1 Estrella – 92.5 Forever Music FM – 92.9 Colón FM – 93.3 Majestad – 93.7 Disney – 94.1 Onda Positiva – 94.5 Platinum FM – 94.9 La Otra FM – 95.3 Cupido – 95.7 Metro Stereo – 96.1 Onda Cero FM – 96.5 Pasión – 96.9 Más Candela – 97.3 Nuevo Tiempo – 98.1 Morena – 98.5 J C R. – 98.9 Impacto FM – 99.3 Sabormix FM – 99.7 Elite – 100.1 R. La Prensa – 100.5 RSN FM Stereo – 100.9 Mundial – 101.3 La Estación Musical – 101.7 Telequil R. Stereo – 102.1 WQ Dos – 102.5 HCJB – 102.9 Armonía Musical – 103.3 Joya Stereo – 103.7 Sonorama FM – 104.1 Alfa Stereo – 104.5 Corazón – 104.9 Once Q FM – 105.3 Nacional del Ecuador, R. Pública – 105.7 Fabustereo – 106.1 BBN – 106.5 Fuego – 106.9 Francisco Stereo – 107.3 Rumba – 107.7 Visión FM

EGYPT

L.T: UTC +2h — **Pop:** 82 million — **Pr.L:** Arabic — **E.C:** 50Hz, 220V — **ITU:** EGY

EGYPTIAN RADIO & TV UNION (Gov)
P.O. Box 1186, Cairo 11511 (Street: Radio & TV Building, Cornish El Nil, Cairo) ☎ +20 2 25757715, 25789145 🖷 +20 2 25789461 **E:** freqmeg@yahoo.com **W:** ertu.org (Arabic), egradio.eg (live audio) **L.P:** Pres: Essam El Amir, Head Eng. Sector: Amgad Baligh, Head Broadc. Sector: Nadya Mabrook

MW	kHz	kW	P	Times
Cairo	558	100	2j	1200-2400
Sohag	603	50	4	0200-2200
Batra	621	1000	6a	24h
Asswan	702	10	2e	0400-2000
		10	4	0200-0400, 2000-2200
El Kharga	702	10	2h	0400-1000, 1130-2000 (Fri 0400-2000)
		10	4	2000-2200
		10	10	1000-1130 (not Fri)
Tanta	711	100	10	24h
Qena	756	10	2e	0400-2000
		10	4	0200-0400, 2000-2200
Abis	774	500	5	24h
Batra	819	1000	1a	24h
Santah	864	500	4	24h
Matruh	882	10	1a	1100-0700 (Fri 24h)
Bawti	918	10	1a	24h
Cairo	936	50	11	1500-2000
Salum	936	10	1a	24h
Abu Simbel	981	1	1a	24h
Assiut	981	10	2d	0400-2000
		10	4	0200-0400, 2000-2200
Baris	981	1	1a	0300-2400
El Arish	1008	100	6b	0600-1500
El Arish	1008	100	7	1500-2200
El Fayoum	1008	10	2d	0400-2000
Cairo	1071	100	1b	0300-1500
El Minya	1080	10	1a	0300-2400
Luxor	1080	10	1a	0300-2400
Tanta	1161	100	2b	0300-2400
Qena	1179	10	1a	0300-2400
Asswan	1278	10	1a	0300-2400
Assiut	1305	10	1a	0300-2400
Abu Simbel	1314	1	2e	0400-2000
			4	0200-0400, 2000-2200
Nag Hamadi	1314	1	1a	0300-2400
Cairo	1341	100	3c	1700-0100
		100	8a	0500-1700
Bawiti	1341	10	2j	1300-2000
		10	4	0200-0500, 2000-2200
		10	10	0500-1300
Idfu	1341	10	1a	0300-2400
Siwa	1341	10	1a	24h
Quseir	1350	10	1a	0300-2400
El Kharga	1368	10	1a	0300-2400
Luxor	1386	10	2e	0400-2000
		10	4	0200-0400, 2000-2200

MW	kHz	kW	P	Times
Salum	1422	10	2i	0400-2000
		10	4	0200-0400, 2000-2200
El Minya	1476	10	2d	0400-2000
		10	4	0200-0400, 2000-2200
El Arish	1503	25	2f	0400-2200
Quseir	1575	10	2j	1300-2000
		10	4	0200-0500, 2000-2200
		10	10	0500-1300
Baris	1584	1	2h	0400-1000, 1130-2000 (Fri 0400-2000)
		1	4	2000-2200
		1	10	1000-1130 (not Fri)
Idfu	1584	10	2e	0400-2000
		10	4	0200-0400, 2000-2200
Matruh	1593	10	2i	0400-2000
		10	4	0200-0400, 2000-2200
Nag Hamadi	1602	10	2e	0400-2000
		1	4	0200-0400, 2000-2200
Siwa	1602	10	2i	0400-2000
		10	4	0200-0400, 2000-2200

MW Prgrs: 1a=General Prgr, 1b=Adults Prgr, 2=Local Prgrs (2b=Mid Delta, 2d=North Upper Egypt, 2e=South Upper Egypt, 2f=North Sinai, 2h=El Wady El Gadid, 2i=Matruh, 2j=Educational), 3c=Cultural Prgr, 4=Holy Koran Prgr, 5=Middle East Comm. Prgr, 6a=Voice of the Arabs, 6b=Palestine Prgr, 7=Hebrew Prgr, 8a=Nile R. Netw. Songs Prgr, 10=Youth & Sports Prgr, 11=Om Kalthoum Prgr.

FM (MHz):

Site	D	E	G	K	M	N	R	S	Y
Abu			90.6						
Abh						95.7			
Ala				88.7					
Alx	94.3	104.7	90.1	88.0	88.7	101.1	97.6		
Al F	87.6		94.9	98.2		88.6	91.7		87.6
Asy	104.0		104.0	95.3	89.0	88.7		102.0	104.0
Asw	98.6		98.6	95.3	89.0	92.1			98.6
Baris				88.8					
Bawiti				87.6		88.7			
Ben						88.7	101.4		
Cairo[a]		95.4	107.4	98.2	98.8	88.7	102.2	105.8	108.0
Dahab			98.5	92.0					
Dum				93.8		88.7			
El A	87.8	94.1		87.8	90.9		97.4		87.8
El D			91.1	88.0			94.3		
El F				89.8					
El K				88.4					
El M	91.0	94.2	91.0	97.5	101.0	87.9		104.6	91.0
El Tur	89.4		95.7	89.4	92.5		99.0		89.4
El Z				88.4					
Hal				96.7			100.0		
Ham						88.7			
Hga[c]	101.7	94.9	105.3	101.7		88.6		98.2	101.7
Idfu				101.7					98.2
Ism				93.5	90.4	96.7			
Isna				90.3					
Kat			90.0	87.6					
Kom				92.8					
Lux	93.1		93.1	103.1	90.0	96.3			93.1
Mah				99.6	93.1	89.8		89.2	
Man				96.3					
Mat				99.1		95.8	102.6	92.6	
Nag			90.9	87.8				94.1	
Nat						88.7			
Nuw	99.1			92.6	99.1	89.5		95.8	99.1
Pt S		98.0				101.5	88.4	91.5	
Qena	100.1		100.1	90.5		93.6		96.8	100.1
Qus				97.2		88.7			
Rafah				103.9					
Ras	97.3		90.8	94.0		87.7			97.3
Saf			96.1	92.9			89.8		
Salum				89.1		89.1			
SeS[b]	97.6		91.1	97.6	88.0		94.3		97.6
Sha			103.5	93.5					
Sid				101.2					
Siwa			96.9	90.6		93.7			
Soh	99.3		96.0	89.7		88.7	102.5	92.8	99.3
Suez				94.4	91.2	88.1	97.7		

[a]=Also Cultural Prgr on 91.5MHz 11.9kW, Middle East Prgr on 89.5MHz 100kW and Voice of the Arabs on 106.3MHz 11.9kW, [b]=Koran Prgr also on 101.1MHz 0.3kW, [c]=Koran Prgr also on 91.7MHz 7.96kW

FM Prgrs: D=Educational Prgr, E=European Prgr, G=General Prgr, K=Koran Prgr, M=Musical Prgr, N=Radio Misr Prgr, R=Regional Prgr, S=Songs Prgr, Y=Youth & Sport

Stations & powers: Abu=Abu Simbel 0.3kW, Abh=Abu Homus 4kW, Ala=Alamain 11.9kW, Alx=Alexandria 58.6kW/N 11.9kW, Al F=Al Farfra 10kW/ Y,D 0.3kW, Asy=Assyout 11.2kW/N 11.9kW Asw=Aswan 11.9kW, Baris 0.3kW, Bawiti 0.3kW, Ben=Beni Suef 10kW/N 0.3kW, Cairo 100kW, Dahab 0.3kW, Dum=Dumyat 0.3kW, El A=El Arish 54.5kW, El D=El Dakhla 4kW/K 0.3kW, El F=El Fayoum 10kW, El K=El Kharga 0.3kW, El M=El Minyah 18kW/K 10kW/S 4kW, El Tur 11.9kW, El Z=El Zayat 0.3kW, Hal=Halayeb 4kW/K 0.3kW, Ham=Hammam 11.9kW, Hga=Hurghada 28.3kW/E,N 7.96kW/G 10kW, Idfu 0.3kW, Ism=Ismailia 61.5kW, Isna 0.3kW, Kat=Katherina 0.3kW, Kom=Kom Ombo 0.3kW, Lux=Luxor 11.7kW, Mah=Mahalla 155kW/N 10kW, Man=Managem Bahariya 0.3kW, Mat=Matruh 9.77kW, Nag=Naga Hamadi 10kW, Nat=Natron 11.9kW, Nuw=Nuweiba 9.53kW, Pt S=Port Said 10kW, Qena 28.6kW, Qus=Quseir 10kW/K 4kW, Rafah 0.3kW, Ras=Ras Gharb 10kW, Saf=Safaga 10kW, Salum 10kW, SeS=Sharm El Sheikh 7.41kW, Sha=Shalatin 0.3kW, Soh=Sohag 38kW/R 4kW/N 0.3kW, Sid=Sidi Barani 10kW, Siwa 10kW/R 0.3kW, Suez 8.71kW

Ann: General Prgr: "Idha'atu jumhuriya misr al'arabbiya min al-qahira". Voice of the Arabs: "Saut al-'arab, min al-qahira". Holy Koran prgr: "Idha'atu-I-Quran min al-qahira"

Other FM Stations:
Nogoom FM, Cairo 100.6MHz 100kW. Arabic music, 24h
Nile FM, Cairo 104.2MHz 100kW. Mainly English pop & rock, 24h
W: nilefmonline.com
Radio Hits, Cairo 88.2MHz 11.9kW
Mega FM, Cairo, 92.7MHz 11.9kW
Nagham FM, Cairo 105.3MHz 11.9kW
Radio FM 9090, Cairo 90.9MHz 11.9kW
NB: R7 & R8 broadc. R. Misr Prgr on 88.7MHz 11.9kW (unk. loc.)

EXTERNAL SERVICES: Radio Cairo
see International Broadcasting Section.

Other Stations:
AFRTS Low-power broadcasts of NPR and AFN to US contingent of UN MFO in Sinai rep. on wide range of freqs from 92.7 to 106.1. Also 107.0 at Gebel Musa.

EL SALVADOR

L.T: UTC -6h — **Pop:** 7.1 million — **Pr.L:** Spanish — **E.C:** 60Hz, 115V — **ITU:** SLV

SUPERINTENDENCIA GENERAL DE ENERGÍA Y TELECOMUNICACIONES (SIGET)
Sexta Décima Calle Poniente y 3°Av.Sur N° 2001, Colonía Flor Blanca, San Salvador ☎ +503 2257-4438 **W:** siget.gob.sv **E:** info@siget.gob.sv

ASOCIACION SALVADORENA DE RADIODIFUSION (ASDER) Calle La Ceiba # 261, Col. Escalon, San Salvador **W:** asder.com.sv

MW	Call	kHz	kW	Station, location
1)	HV	540	5	La Estación de la Palabra, San Salvador
2)	FG	550	2	R. Cristo Te Llama, Sonsonate (r:900)
3)	NK	600	3	R. Cristo Viene, San Salvador
4)	LN	630	10	R. Santa Sion, San Salvador
5)	UES	660	10	R. Universitaria, San Salvador (irr.)
6)	JW	700	12	R. Mi Gente, San Salvador: 1200-0400
6)	JW	700	12	R. Mi Gente, San Miguel
7)	RA	720	1	Qué Buena, San Salvador (r:88.9)
8)	KL	760	5	YSKL La Poderosa, San Miguel
8)	KL	760	1	YSKL La Poderosa, San Salvador (r:770)
8)	KL	760		YSKL La Poderosa, Zacateluca (r:770)
8)	KL	770	10	YSKL La Poderosa, San Salvador: 1030-0530
8)	KL	780	1	YSKL La Poderosa, Usulután (r:770)
8)	KL	780	1	YSKL La Poderosa, Sta Ana (r:770)
10)	AX	800	12	R. María El Salvador, San Salvador: 1230-0600
11)	FA	810	2	R. Lorenzana, San Vicente
12)	DA	810	1.5	R. Imperial, Sonsonate: 1100-0300
13)	FB	840	10	R. Santa Biblia, San Salvador: 1030-0300
14)	CD	880	1	R. Ritmo, Stgo de María
15)	LA	890	3	R. Renacimiento, Sta Ana: 1000-0500

MW	Call	kHz	kW	Station, location
2)	QJ	900	2	R. Cristo Te Llama, San Salvador
16)		930		R. San José, San Salvador
17)	HG	950	1	R. Chaparrastique, San Miguel
18)	CA	1020	5	R. Int. /La Máxima, San Salvador: 1100-0300
19)	RM	1030	1	R. Frontera, Ahuachapán: 1200-0400
20)	ME	1080	6	R. CRET, San Salvador
20)		1090	1	R. CRET, Sta Ana
21)	MG	1090	3	R. 1090, Atiquizaya
22)	LR	1120	3	R. Elohim, San Salvador: 1045-0500
23)	AJ	1130	1	R. Moderna, Sta Ana: 1200-0400
10)	CF	1150	1	R. María Zona Oriental, San Miguel (r: 800)
24)	CB	1170	0.5	R. Pentecostés, Sonsonate
25)	VG	1180	5	R. VEA–Voz Evangélica de América, San Salvador: 1200-2400
26)	CG	1210	1	R. América/R. La Paz, Zacatecoluca
27)	MT	1240	0.5	R. Metapán, Metapán
28)	QN	1240	1	R. Norteña, San Miguel
29)	AA	1260	12	R. Abba, San Salvador
30)	MQ	1280	1	R. Emaús, San Vicente
31)	MA	1290	1	R. Chalatenango, Chalatenango: 1000-0300
32)	LV	1300	6	W-LV de la Habana
33)	KG	1300		R. Llanera "La Campechana", San Miguel
34)	RV	1310	5	R. Veritas, Stgo de María
35)	KO	1370	1	R. Lluvias de Bendición, San Miguel: 1100-0300
36)	JU	1390	1	R. Getsemani, La Unión
37)		1390		R. Fraternidad de Jesucristo, Chalchuapa
38)	JS	1390	1	Sinaí R, LV del Rey de Gloria, Soyapango
39)	JI	1400	1	LV del Litoral, Usulután: 1100-0400
40)	KR	1450	1	R. Restauración, San Miguel: 1000-0400
41)	CS	1500	1	R. Pentecostal Bethel, Usulután
42)		1550	5	R. Sanidad Divina, San Salvador: 1000-0600
43)	MV	1600		R. Maya Visión, San Salvador

Call YS–, ‡ = inactive, (r) = repeater, ± = varying fq

Addresses and other information:
1) Ap.2854 (or Calle al Matazano N° 1, Final Col.Sta Lucía, Ilopango), San Salvador. **W:** elim.org.sv — **2)** Colonia San Miguel, Cl Principal Pasaje Castillo, San Ramón Mejicanos, San Salvador. **W:** cristotellama.org.sv — **3)** Edif. Antiguo Cine Apolo, 2ª. Av. Sur y 9ª Calle Oriente, San Salvador **W:** radiocristoviene600am.com — **4)** 75 Av Norte, Prolongación Juan Pablo II, Col Jardines de Escalón, final Pasaje KL, San Salvador **W:** radiosantasion.org — **5)** Ciudad Universitaria, San Salvador **W:** ues.edu.sv/YSUES_Radio — **6)** 14 Calle Poniente, entre 43 y 45, Avenida Sur No. 2309, Col. Flor Blanca, San Salvador. **W:** radiocadenamigente.blogspot.com — **7)** Ap.720, San Salvador — **8)** 65 Av S y Av.Olipica, 192 Edif.Corporación YSKL, San Salvador **W:** radioyskl.com — **9) W:** corporacionyskl.com — **10)** Urb.General Escalon, Pasaje Beethoven 8/E, San Salvador **W:** radiomaria.org.sv — **11)** Carretera a Tecoluca, Col. Najarro, San Vicente — **12)** Ap.56, Sonsonate — **13)** Iglesia San Pablo, Final 5a Calle Poniente, Colonia Escalón, San Salvador — **14)** 2a Av.Norte 24, Stgo de María, Usulután — **15)** 4a Av.Sur, Entre 7a y 9a Calle Poniente, Edif.Plaza de Vidrio, Sta Ana — **16)** 1er Calle Josniente, San Salvador 503 **W:** radiosanjose.org — **17)** 4a Av.Sur 303 bis, San Miguel — **18)** Av.España y 23 Calle Oriente, Ex Cine Fausto, San Salvador — **19)** Av.2 de Abril y 8a Calle Poniente, Ahuachapán — **20)** Barrio La Cruz, 10 Av Norte N° 203-Bis, San Miguel **W:** radiocret.net — **21)** 5ª Calle Oriente 3-204, Atiquizaya — **22)** 8a Av. Norte #225, atrás de la Despensa Familiar, por el parque San José, San Salvador **W:** radioelohim.net — **23)** 8a Calle Poniente 11A, Sta Ana — **24)** Colonia Monte Carmelo, Calle a Los Naranjos, Frente Antena de la YSU, Sonsonate — **25)** Calle 5 de Noviembre y final 6 Av. Norte, Frente a Banco de Famila, San Martín, San Salvador. **W:** lacapilla.org.sv — **26)** 2a Calle Poniente 22, Zacatecoluca — **27)** Calle Principal, Costado Norte Centro Judical, Col Lomas de Montecristo, Metapán, Sta Ana — **28)** Col.Hirleman 14 C P Block 14 N° 9, San Miguel — **29)** Antigua Calle Ferrocarril, #2106, Colonia 3 de Mayo, San Salvador **W:** radioabba.org — **30)** 2 Av N N° 10, San Vicente — **31)** Calle a San Francisco Lempa, Col. Veracruz, Chalatenango. **W:** radiochalatenango.com.sv — **32)** 17 Calle Oriente 143, Barrio San Miguelito, San Salvador — **33)** Col. Hirleman, 14 Calle Poniente, Bloque 6, N° 9, San Miguel — **34)** Bo El Centro, C.Bolivar y 4 Av S, Stgo de María, Usulután — **35)** Carr. Panamericana, Crio El Alto, 300 mts al Norte, El Jalacatal, San Miguel. **W:** radiolluviasdebendicion.com.sv — **36)** Col. La Paz, La Unión (part of Radio CRET Network) — **37)** Calle al trapiche, Chalchuapa, Santa Ana — **38)** Carretera al Plan del Pino. Una cuadra antes de la Ciudadela Don Bosco, Soyapango, San Salvador **W:** radioelreydegloria.com — **39)** 12 Av.Sur y final 5a Calle Oriente, Col.Sta Rosa, Usulután. **W:** lavozdellitoral.com - **FM:** 90.1MHz — **40)** Ap.210, San Miguel — **41)** Kilómetro 112½, Carretera El Litoral, Frente a Desvío El Mora, Usulután — **42)** Calle 25 de Abril Poniente, Barrio San José # 22B, San Marcos, San

Salvador. **W:** radiosanidaddivina.com **– 43) W:** radiomayavision.net

FM in San Salvador (MHz): 87.75 Canal 6 – 88.1 AL Radio – 88.5 Paz – 88.9 Qué Buena – (9) 89.3 Cool – 89.7 Bautista – 90.1 Láser (Spanish) – 90.5 Progreso – 90.9 UPA – 91.3 Exa – 91.7 YSUCA – 92.1 La Klave – 92.5 Club – 92.9 Láser (English) – 93.3 Globo – 93.7 El Mundo – 94.1 Super Estrella – 94.5 Vox – 94.9 Astral – (9) 95.3 R. Eco – 95.7 Verdad – 96.1 Scan – 96.5 R. Adventista – 96.9 R. Nacional **W**: turadioelsalvador.com – 97.3 Corazón – 97.7 Luz – 98.1 Gospel FM – 98.5 Cuscatlán – 98.9 La Mejor FM – 99.3 Mesías – 99.7 Full FM – 100.1 ABC – 100.5 Restauración – 100.9 La Chévere – (9) 101.3 Monumental – 101.7 Mil 80 –102.1 102 Uno –102.5 Femenina – 102.9 102 Nueve – 103.3 Clásica – 103.7 Cadena Central – (8) 104.1 YSKL La Poderosa – 104.5 Sonora – 104.9 Fiesta – 105.3 Punto 105 – 105.7 YXY – 106.1 El Camino – 106.5 Ranchera – 106.9 R. Maya Visión – 107.3 R. María – 107.7 Fuego.

FM in San Miguel (MHz): 90.1 Stereo Caliente - 90.5 Siglo 21– 90.9 Popular – 91.7 YSUCA – 92.5 Monseñor Romero – 94.1 Cadena Central – 96.5 Agape R. – 97.3 Carnaval – 98.1 La Pantera – 99.7 Mi Consentida - 102.9 102 Nueve – 104.1 YSKL La Poderosa – 106.1 La Grande – 107.3 R. María.

FM in Santa Ana (MHz): 90.5 Supra Stereo – 91.7 YSUCA - 92.1 Fe y Alegría – (9) 92.5 R. Doremix – 93.3 Shabach – 95.3 Amor – 97.3 La Campirana – 97.9 Real FM – 99.7 Doble H - 102.9 102 Nueve – 104.1 YSKL La Poderosa – 105.3 Soda Stereo – 106.1 Bautista

EQUATORIAL GUINEA

L.T: UTC +1h — **Pop:** 600,000 — **Pr.L:** Spanish, French, ethnic — **E.C:** 50Hz, 220V — **ITU:** GNE

MINISTERIO DE INFORMACIÓN, TURISMO Y CULTURA
✉ Barrio Nzalang (antiguo África 2000), Malabo. ☎+240 333 078221 📠 +240 333 072444. **L.P:** Minister: Purificación Opo Barila. Dir R & TV: Hermenesildo Moliko Djele.

RADIO TELEVISIÓN DE GUINEA ECUATORIAL(RTVGE,Gov.)
✉ Ap. 749, Bata ☎+240 333 082592 📠 +240 333 082093 ✉ Av. 3 de Agosto 90, Ap. 195, Malabo ☎+240 333 072260 📠 +240 333 072097 **W:** rtvge.com **L.P:** Dir. Tech: Barila Sota.

SW	kHz	kW	Times
Bata	5005	50	0430-2300v (highly irregular)
Malabo(Semu)	6250	20	0530-1830 (inactive)

FM: Bata 98/99.9MHz 1kW, Malabo 90.9MHz 12kW.
D.Prgr: in Spanish/ethnic.
Rural radio: La Voz de Kie-Ntem at Ebibeyín, Ecos de Wele Nzás at Mongomo and La Voz de Centro Sur at Evinayong.

Other Stations:
R. Asonga, Malabo 90.0/107.0MHz. **W:** radio.asonga.com
BBC World Sce: Malabo 92.5MHz in English/French.
RFI Afrique: Malabo 97.5/100.0MHz in French/Spanish.

ERITREA

L.T: UTC +3h — **Pop:** 6 million — **Pr.L:** Afar, Amharic, Arabic, Tigrinya, Tigre, others — **E.C:** 50Hz, 230V — **ITU:** ERI.

MINISTRY OF INFORMATION
✉ P.O. Box 872, Asmara ☎+291 1 120478/201820 📠 +291 1 126747 **W:** shabait.com **E:** nesredin@tse.com.er

VOICE OF THE BROAD MASSES OF ERITREA (Gov.)
✉ P.O. Box 242, Asmara ☎+291 1 117111/118711 📠 +291 1 124847 **L.P:** DG: Ghirmay Berhe. TD: Mehreteab Tesfagiorgis. PD: Abdu Heji. Dir. Radio Eng.: Berhane Gerezgiher.
Station: Asmara (Selai Dairo).
MW: 837kHz 100kW (Prgr. 2), 945kHz 100kW (Prgr. 1).
SW: 7200 kHz 100kW (Prgr. 1), 7175 kHz 100kW (Prgr.2). SW frequencies operate irregularly and with reduced times.
Prgr. 1 in Tigrinya/Tigre/Kunama: 0300-1000, 1300-2000 – **Prgr. 2** in Arabic/Afar/Amharic/Oromo/Saho/Bilen: 0300-1000, 1430-2000.
Zara FM: 100MHz + others. **Numa FM:** freq. not known.
Ann: Amharic:"Yeh be Asmera ketema yemigegne yesifiw Yeritsea hezeb demts yeamarigna agelgilot new". Arabic: "Huna Asmara, Idha'at Sawt al-Jamahir al-Iritriyyah". Tigrigna: "Ezi kab Asmara Zemehalalef Medeber Radio Demtsi Hafash Eritrea Eyu".
R. Sawa, west Eritrea: **FM** (fq. not known). Op. by Sawa National Youth Training Centre

ESTONIA

L.T: UTC +2h (27 Mar-30 Oct: +3h) — **Pop:** 1.3 million — **Pr.L:** Estonian, Russian — **E.C:** 50Hz, 230V — **ITU:** EST
KULTUURIMINISTEERIUM (Ministry of Culture)
✉ Suur-Karja 23, 15076 Tallinn ☎ +372 6282222 📠 +372 6282200
E: min@kul.ee **W:** kul.ee **L.P:** Minister: Indrek Saar
NB: The Ministry of Culture issues broadcasting licenses.

EESTI RAHVUSRINGHÄÄLING (ERR) (Pub)
✉ Gonsiori 27, 15029 Tallinn ☎ +372 6284100 📠 +372 6284155
E: err@err.ee **W:** err.ee **L.P:** Chmn: Margus Allikmaa
✉Studios (exc. Prgr 2): Kreutzwaldi 14, 10124 Tallinn; Prgr 2: Gonsiori 21, 15029 Tallinn.

FM (MHz)	1	2	3	4	kW
Koeru	105.1	102.6	107.6	93.4	3x30/7.8
Kohtla-Nõmme	105.4	102.9	90.4	95.3	11.2
Kuressaare	105.6	103.1	107.0	-	1
Kõrgessaare	91.2	99.1	94.9	-	1
Möksi	-	-	-	99.9	3
Orissaare	105.9	103.4	107.8	-	20/2x10
Pärnu	104.8	102.3	107.3	94.8	10
Tallinn	104.1	101.6	106.6	94.5	30
Valga	-	-	-	92.5	1.8
Valgjärve	106.1	103.6	105.7	-	2x40/12.5
Viiratsi	105.8	103.3	107.0	95.5	1

NB: Sites with only txs below 1kW not listed.
D.Prgr: Prgr 1 (Vikerraadio): 24h. – **Prgr 2 (Raadio 2):** 24h. – **Prgr 3 (Klassikaraadio):** 24h. – **Prgr 4 (Raadio 4/Radio 4)** for ethnic minorities (Russian): 24h. – **ERR Raadio Tallinn** 103.5MHz (1kW): 24h. Own prgrs 0500-2000; relays: 0300-0500 & 2000-2300 BBCWS (UK), 2300-0300 RFI (France).

OTHER STATIONS

MW	kHz	kW	Location	Station
6B)	1035	*100	Tartu (Kavastu)	R. Eli
FM	**MHz**	**kW**	**Location**	**Station**
2B)	87.7	1	Kehtna	Sky Plus
3A)	88.1	2	Paide	Star FM
2C)	88.2	1	Kõmsi	Retro FM
1D)	88.3	2	Tallinn	Hit FM
4)	88.6	3	Pärnu	Raadio 7
2F)	88.8	1	Tallinn	R. Mania
6A)	89.0	2.4	Vanamõisa	Pereraadio
6A)	89.0	3	Tartu	Pereraadio
6A)	89.4	1	Kõnnu	Pereraadio
6A)	89.6	3	Tallinn	Pereraadio
1C)	89.8	1.1	Vinni	Raadio Uuno
1A)	89.9	1	Pärnu	Raadio Kuku
9)	90.1	1	Kärdla	Raadio Kadi
9)	90.5	1	Aste	Raadio Kadi
1C)	91.0	3	Pärnu	Raadio Uuno
1B)	91.2	6.5	Valgjärve	Raadio Elmar
8)	91.3	1	Raikküla	Tre Raadio
1B)	91.5	1.5	Tallinn	Raadio Elmar
1B)	91.5	1	Kuressaare	Raadio Elmar
1B)	91.7	7.5	Koeru	Raadio Elmar
1B)	92.2	1	Haapsalu	Raadio Elmar
3A)	92.2	2.9	Padaorg	Star FM
1C)	92.3	1	Parksepa	Raadio Uuno
3B)	92.5	1	Rakvere	Power Hit R.
3A)	92.9	3	Linnamäe	Star FM
2E)	93.2	1.5	Tallinn	Energy FM
3A)	93.3	2.2	Kuressaare	Star FM
2B)	93.8	3	Holsta	Sky Plus
2B)	95.2	1	Tartu	Sky Plus
2B)	95.4	2	Tallinn	Sky Plus
2C)	95.4	1	Aste	Retro FM
4)	96.1	3	Tamsalu	Raadio 7
2B)	96.3	1.9	Vätta	Sky Plus
3A)	96.6	1.5	Maardu	Star FM
7)	96.6	1	Sangaste	Ruut FM
2B)	96.8	1.6	Pärnu	Sky Plus
2B)	96.9	1.5	Palade	Sky Plus
1C)	97.2	2	Tallinn	Raadio Uuno
1C)	97.2	1	Tartu	Raadio Uuno
1C)	97.4	3	Kuressaare	Raadio Uuno
1C)	97.4	2.5	Koeru	Raadio Uuno
2B)	97.6	1	Rohuküla	Sky Plus
2C)	97.8	2	Tallinn	Retro FM
2C)	97.9	1	Viljandi	Retro FM

FM	MHz	kW	Location	Station
2C)	98.3	1.2	Pärnu	Retro FM
2A)	98.4	3	Tallinn	Sky Radio
2C)	98.6	2.5	Tartu	Retro FM
1B)	99.0	3	Pärnu	Raadio Elmar
3A)	99.4	2	Tartu	Star FM
1A)	99.6	3.2	Padaorg	Raadio Kuku
2B)	99.7	1	Viljandi	Sky Plus
1C)	99.8	1	Haapsalu	Raadio Uuno
1E)	100.0	1	Narva	Narodnoe R.
1A)	100.2	2	Tartu	Raadio Kuku
3A)	100.3	2	Pärnu	Star FM
1A)	100.4	1	Kärdla	Raadio Kuku
1A)	100.5	2.2	Paide	Raadio Kuku
1A)	100.6	3	Kuressaare	Raadio Kuku
1A)	100.7	1.9	Tallinn	Raadio Kuku
1A)	100.8	1.5	Viljandi	Raadio Kuku
1A)	100.9	1	Haapsalu	Raadio Kuku
5)	101.0	3	Paide	Kuma Raadio
2D)	101.2	1.3	Tartu	Russkoe R.
2B)	101.3	1	Assamalla	Sky Plus
10)	101.7	1	Mõksi	Ring FM
3B)	102.1	1.5	Maardu	Power Hit R.
3A)	102.8	1	Valga	Star FM
1D)	103.0	1	Tartu	Hit FM
3A)	103.2	3	Parksepa	Star FM
2B)	103.3	1	Maidla	Sky Plus
1C)	104.5	1	Liiva	Raadio Uuno
10)	104.7	1	Tartu	Ring FM
2B)	106.8	1	Kullamaa	Sky Plus

NB: Txs below 1kW not listed. *) 200kW during TWR relays (see International Radio section)
Addresses & other information:
1A-E) Veerenni 58a, 11314 Tallinn, exc. 1B) Õpetaja 9a, 51003 Tartu. 1E) in Russian. **E:** 1A) kuku@kuku.ee, 1B) elmar@elmar.ee, 1C) uuno@uuno. ee, 1D) info@hitfm.ee, 1E) nr@narodnoeradio.ee – **2A-F)** Pärnu mnt. 139f, 11317 Tallinn. 2A,C,D) in Russian. **E:** 2A) skyradio@sky.ee, 2B) info@ skyplus.fm, 2C) info@retrofm.ee, 2D) info@russkoeradio.fm, 2E) info@ energyfm.ee, 2F) radio@mania.ee – **3A,B)** Peterburi 81, 11415 Tallinn **E:** 3A) starfm@starfm.ee, 3B) info@power.ee – **4)** Välja 18, 10616 Tallinn **E:** raadio7@raadio7.ee – **5)** Pärnu 57, 72712 Paide **E:** kuma@kuma.ee – **6A)** Annemõisa 8, 50708 Tartu **E:** pereraadio@pereraadio.ee; **6B)** Vestervalli 20, 20306 Narva. In Russian (incl. TWR relays). **E:** am1035@bk.ru – **7)** Pikk 3a, 68206 Valga **E:** ruutfm@ruutfm.ee – **8)** Asula 4c 11315 Tallinn **E:** info@trreraadio.ee – **9)** Kuressaare **E:** kadi@kadi.ee – **10)** Peterburi 49, 11415 Tallinn **E:** info@ringfm.ee

ETHIOPIA

L.T: UTC +3h — **Pop:** 83 million — **Pr.L:** Amharic, Oromo, Sidamo, Somali, Tigrinya — **E.C:** 50Hz, 220V — **ITU:** ETH

ETHIOPIAN BROADCASTING AUTHORITY (EBA)
P.O. Box 43142, Hailalem Bldg. Kazanchis, Addis Ababa ☎+251 11 5538755 ✆ +251 11 5536767
W: eba.gov.et **E:** e.b.a1@ethionet.et

ETHIOPIA BROADCASTING CORPORATION - RADIO ETHIOPIA (Gov.)
P.O. Box 1020, Addis Ababa ☎+251 11 5516977
W: ebc.et **E:** info@erta.gov.et **L.P:** GM: Ato Solomon Tesfaye. SM: Kasa Miloko. CE: Kebede Gobena. Head of English Prgrs: Melesse Edea Beyi.

MW	kHz	kW	MW	kHz	kW
Bahir Dar	†594	100	Dese	891	100
Metu	684	100	Robe (Bale)	972	100
Arba Minch	828	100	Addis Ababa	‡989	1
Harar	855	100	Mekele	1044	200
Addis Ababa	873	100	Negele Borana	1485	10

SW: Addis Ababa (Geja): 9705kHz 100kW (inactive).
FM(MHz): Addis Ababa 93.2 2.5kW, 94.5, 96.3 3.5kW, 97.1, 97.6.
National Sce. in Amharic/Others: 0300-2100. **In English:** Mon-Fri 1200-1300. **Reg. prgrs** and **BBC relays** at times. External Sce. relay on 989kHz 1200-1830. **FM Addis** in Amharic on 97.1MHz. **EBC R. 97.6** in English on 97.6MHz.
EXTERNAL SERVICE: see International Radio section.

FANA BROADCASTING CORPORATION - RADIO FANA (Priv.)
P.O.Box 30702, near Black Lion Hospital, in front of Sweden Embassy, Addis Ababa. **W:** fanabc.com **E:** fanabc@fanabc.com

L.P: GM: Woldu Yemessel. Tech. Dir: Mulugeta Mehari.
MW: Addis Ababa (Repi) 1080kHz 3kW.
SW: Addis Ababa (Geja) 6110kHz 100kW. 7210kHz inactive.
FM (MHz): Haromaya/Mekele 94.8, Dese 96.0, Nekemit 96.1, Addis Ababa/Gonder/Jimma 98.1, Wolayita 99.9, Shashemenie 103.4.
D.Prgr. in Afar/Amharic/Oromo/Somali/Tigrinya: 0300-2100. FM transmitters carry separate programming to MW and SW.

Regional government stations:
RADIO OROMIYA (Oromiya Radio & TV Organisation, ORTO)
P.O. Box 2919, Adama. **W:** orto.gov.et **L.P:** Mr. Abarra Hailu, Mgr. Mr. Habtamu Dargie Gudeta, Head Eng. Dept.
MW: Robe (Bale) 837kHz 100kW, Adama (Nazret) 1035kHz 10kW, Nekemte 1053kHz 100kW.
SW: Addis Ababa (Geja): 6030kHz 100kW.
FM: Addis Ababa (Intoto) 92.3MHz.
D.Prgr. in Oromo (some Amhara&English): Mon-Fri 0300-0600, 0900-1100, 1530-2000, SS 0300-1900. **Ann:** Oromo: "Kun Radio Oromiya".

VOICE OF TIGRAY REVOLUTION (Gov.)
P.O.Box 450, Mekele, Tigray ☎+251 34 4410544/5 **W:** dimtsiwoyane.com **E:** webmaster@dimtsiwoyane.com **L.P:** Dir: Abera Tesfay.
MW: Mekele 1359kHz 100kW.
SW: Addis Ababa 5950kHz 100kW.
FM: DWET FM: Mekele 102.2MHz 3kW.
D.Prgr in Tigrinya/Afar: MF 0300-2000, SS 0300-1730 (DWET FM 0300-2100). **Ann:** Tigrinya: "Dimtsi Woyane Tigray". **IS:** Melody played on washint (Ethiopian flute).

AMHARA STATE RADIO (Gov.)
Amhara Mass Media Agency, P.O. Box 955, Bahir Dar. **L.P:** Dir: Chalacew Achamyehe. **W:** amma.gov.et **E:** ammawebmaster@yahoo.com
MW: Bahir Dar 801kHz 100kW. **SW:** Addis Ababa 6090kHz 100kW.
D. Prgr in Amhara/Awinya/Himtinya/Oromo: 0300-0600, 0900-1100, 1400-1900. **Ann:** Amhara: "Yeh ye Amhara Killil Radio".

SOUTH FM(Gov.)
Southern Nations & Nationalities Mass Media Agency, P.O. Box 1080, Awasa.
FM: Awasa 96.9MHz, Arba Minch 90.9, Bensa 92.3, Bonga 97.4, Dire Dawa 106.1 2kW, Gedio 99.4, Jinka 87.8, Mizan 104.5, Waka 94.1, Wolkitie 89.2MHz.

Other governmental stations:
Addis Ababa R: 96.3MHz 4kW — **Bahir Dar FM:** 96.9MHz — **Debub FM,** Awasa: 100.6MHz — **Dire Dawa FM:** 106.1MHz 2kW — **Finfine FM:** Adama 92.3MHz — **Harari FM:** Harar: 101.4MHz — **Mekele FM:** 104.4MHz — **Somali FM,** Jigjiga 99.1MHz.

Other stations:
Afro FM, Addis Ababa: 105.3MHz 2.5kW. **W:** afro105fm.com – **Ravos FM,** Awasa: 100.9MHz – **R. Sidama,** c/o Furra Institute of Development Studies, P.O. Box 69, Yirgalem: **MW:** 954kHz 2.5kW; MF 0500-1400, SS 0400-1700 – **Sheger FM,** Addis Ababa: 102.1MHz. **W:** shegerfm.com – **Zami R,** Addis Ababa: 90.7MHz 2kW. **W:** zami.com.et
Community Radio: Korie 92.3MHz, Argoba 98.6MHz, Jimma 102.0MHz, Keffa 102.5, Kombolcha 104.8, Kembata 105.8MHz

FALKLAND ISLANDS (UK)

L.T: UTC -4h (DST: -3h, continuous DST is currently in effect) — **Pop:** 3,100 (excl. military personnel) — **Pr.L:** English — **E.C:** 50Hz, 240V — **ITU:** FLK

FALKLAND ISLANDS RADIO SERVICE (FIRS) (Pub)
John Street, Stanley FIQQ 1ZZ. ☎+500 27277. ✆ +500 27279. **W:** firs.co.fk **E:** cgoss@firs.co.fk **L.P:** Stn Man.: Corina Goss, Prgr Contr.: Elizabeth Elliot, Senior Reporter: Liz Roberts
MW: 530kHz 15kW. **FM**(MHz): Sapper Hill 96.5 2kW, Sussex Mt 97.2 30W, Byron Heights 97.4 300W, Mt Alice 97.6 300W, Mt William 97.8 1kW. **NB:** Rel. BBC World Service when FIRS off air

BRITISH FORCES BROADCASTING SERVICE
Rockhopper Road, RAF Mount Pleasant. BFPO 655. ☎+500 73003. ✆ +500 32193. **E:** falklands@bfbs.com **L.P:** SM: Anthony Ballard. Eng. Mgr: Callum Pilkington.
BFBS Radio 1: FM(MHz): Mt Pleasant 98.5 2kW, Sapper Hill 91.1 300W, Byron Heights/Mt Alice/Mt Kent/ 102.4 10W
BFBS Radio 2: FM(MHz): Mt Sussex 88.2, Mt William 88.8, Mt

Pleasant 93.8 2kW, 300W, Sapper Hill 94.5 300W, Port Howard 100.4, Byron Heights/Mt Alice/Mt Kent 104.2 10W
BFBS Falkland Radio: FM(MHz): Mt Sussex 106.2, Mt William 106.8, Port Howard 101.6
BFBS Gurkha Radio: FM(MHz): Mt Pleasant 96.0 2kW, Byron Heights/Mt Alice/Mt Kent 106.0 10W
D.Prgr: 24h **N:** Every hour from BFBS Radio UK News by satellite from London. **Ann:** "This is BFBS in the Falklands". **V.** by QSL-card. Rp.

KTV RADIO
KTV Ltd, 68 Dean St., Stanley. ☎+500 22349 ⊟ +500 21049 **E:** kmzb@horizon.co.fk **W:** ktv.co.fk
MW: 530kHz **FM:** 106.5MHz (rel. BBC World Service)

Deutsche Welle rel.: 101.1MHz

FAROE ISLANDS (Denmark)

L.T: UTC (27 Mar-30 Oct: +1h) — **Pop:** 49,000 — **Pr.L:** Faroese — **E.C:** 50Hz, 220/380V — **ITU:** FRO

KRINGVARP FØROYA ÚTVARPIÐ (Pub.)
Norðari Ringvegur 20, POBox 1299, FO 100 Tórshavn ☎ +298 347500 ⊟ +298 347501 **E:** netvarp@kvf.fo **W:** kvf.fo
L.P: SM: Dia Midjord. Head of admin: Jákupe Mikkelsen. Head of news: Liljan Weihe. TD: Hjallgrím P. Hentze.
MW: Akraberg 531kHz 10kW
FM (MHz): Tórshavn 89.9 (31kW), Klaksvík 94.3 (41kW), Hesturin Suðurðy 97.5 (27kW), Støðlafjall 100.0 (3kW) + 15 lp stns
D.Prgr: 24h. All prgrs are in Faroese. **Ann:** 'Útvarpið'

MIÐLAR (Comm.)
Grønlandsvegur 38, FO 100 Tórshavn ☎ +298 223910 **E:** midlar@midlar.fo **W:** midlar.fo. **L.P:** Háldan Haldansen.
Rás 2: Tórshavn 98.7, Klaksvík: 88.7, Streymoy 95.9 **D.Prgr:** 24h
VoxPop: Tórshavn 104.1, Klaksvík 90.7, Streymoy 104.8. **D.Prgr:** 24h

R2NET (Comm.)
Søldarfjarðarvegur 11, FO 660 Søldarfjørður ☎ +298 559997 **E:** r2net@r2net.fo **W:** r2net.fo **L.P:** Petur Jacobsen. **R7:** Tórshavn 102.0, Suðuroy 102.6, Streymoy 106.0, Klaksvík: 107.0 + 10 LPFM stns.

LINDIN KRISTILIGT KRINGVARP (Rlg.)
Bøkjaragøta 9, POBox 2063, FO 165 Argir (Tórshavn) ☎ +298 321377 ⊟ +298 321379 **E:** lindin@lindin.fo **W:** lindin.fo
L.P: Chairman: Preben Hansen
FM (MHz): Tórshavn 101.0, Klaksvík: 103.0 + 11 lp stns. **D.Prgr:** 24h

Local stations:
KROSSFELTIÐ, Undir Gørðum 5, FO 625 Glyvrar: FM 95.0MHz – **STAÐIÐ FM,** Ungdómshúsið, FO 350 Vestmanna. Su&Th 2100. FM: 101.0 – **STREAM 98.7,** Skáltavehur 29, PO Box 242, FO 700 Klaksvík. **W:** stream.fo. **L.P.:** Johnny Olsen. **FM:** 98.7MHz

FIJI

L.T: UTC +12h (1 Nov 15-17 Jan 16, 6 Nov 16-15 Jan 17: +13h) — **Pop:** 944,720 — **Pr.L:** English, Fijian, Hindi — **E.C:** 50Hz, 240V — **ITU:** FJI

DEPARTMENT OF COMMUNICATIONS
1st Floor, Credit Corporation Building, Suva ☎ +679 330 0766 ⊟ +679 331 5167 **L.P:** Dep. Secretary: Josua Turaganivalu

TELECOMMUNICATIONS AUTHORITY OF FIJI
76 Gordon Street, GPO Box 13413, Suva. ☎+679 3310101 ⊟+679 3310110 **W:** taf.org.fj **E:** contact@taf.org.fj
Regulator of radio broadcasting in Fiji

FIJI BROADCASTING CORPORATION LTD (Pub)
PO Box 334, Suva ☎ +679 331 4333 ⊟ +679 330 1643 **W:** fbc.com.fj **E:** infocenter@fbc.com.fj **L.P:** CEO: Riyaz Saiyed Khaiyum C.E: Apisai Bakani
Netw.: RF1 (R.Fiji One Na Domoiviti) Fijian ☎ +679 330 2588 **W:** rf1.fbc.com.fj & facebook.com/radio-fiji-one-domoiviti — **RF2 (R.Fiji Two Desh ki Dhadkan)** Hindi ☎ +679 330 2588 **W:** rf2.fbc.com.fj & facebook.com/radio-fiji-two — **R.Mirchi** Hindi ☎ +679 330 2588 **W:** mirchifm@fbc.com.fj & facebook.com/mirchifm — **RFGold (R.Fiji Gold)** English ☎ +679 330 4500 **W:** goldfm@fbc.com.fj & facebook.com/goldfmfiji — **Bula FM** Fijian ☎ +679 331 4211 **W:** bulafm@fbc.com.fj & facebook.com/bula-fm — **2dayFM** English ☎ +679 331 6415 **W:** 2dayfm@fbc.com.fj & facebook.com/2dayfm-fiji **Prgr:** All 24/7 audio streaming via individual station websites

MW	kHz	kW	Netw.
Suva	558	10	RF1
-	*990		

* planned late 2015 [both 558/990 are funded by a Japanese aid program for cyclone warnings, tsunami alerts and other national emergency events]

FM	RF1	RF2	Bula FM	R.Mirchi	RFGOLD	2dayFM
1)	93.0	105.0	102.6	97.8	100.2	95.4
2)	92.8	104.8	102.4	97.6	100.0	95.2
3)	93.2	105.4	102.8	98.0	100.4	95.6
4)	93.4	105.4	103.0	98.2	100.6	95.8

1) Deuba, Navua, Lami, Suva, Nausori, Korovou, Nadi, Lautoka, Yasawas, Mamanuca, Savusavu, Tavenui – **2)** Coral Coast, Nabau, Serua, Ba – **3)** Tavua – **4)** Rakiraki

Private commercial network
COMMUNICATIONS FIJI LTD
231 Waimanu Road [Private Mail Bag], Suva ☎ +679 331 4766 ⊟ +679 330 3748 **W:** fijivillage.com [audio streaming needs registration and annual fee] **E:** info@fm96.com.fj **L.P:** Man.Dir: William Parkinson, GM Fiji: Ian Jackson **E:** ian@fm96.com.fj **CE:** Philip Wilikibau **E:** philip@fm96.com.fj
Netw.: FM96 (English) PD: Tony Rahiman **E:** tony@fm96.com.fj – **Legend FM** (English) PD: Alex Elbourne **E:** alex@fm96.com.fj – **Viti FM** (Fijian) PD: Malakai Veisamasama **E:** mala@fm96.com.fj – **Navtarang** (Hindi) PD: Satya Nand **E:** satya@fm96.com.fj – **R. Sargam** (Hindi) PD: Roneel Narayan **E:** roneel@sargam.com.fj **Prgr:** All 24/7

FM	FM96	Navtarang	Viti FM	Legend FM	R.Sargam
1)	96.2	101.0	92.2	98.6	103.4
2)	96.0	100.8	92.0	98.4	103.2
3)	96.6	101.4	92.6	99.0	103.8

1) Suva, Nausori, Central Division, Nadi, Lautoka, Labassa – **2)** Sigatoka, Coral Coast, Ba, Tavua, Vatukoula – **3)** Rakiraki

Other Stations:

FM	MHz	Station	Location
1)	88.2	BBC	Suva
2)	88.8	R.Pasifik Triple 8	Suva
3)	89.2	fem'TALK 89.2	Suva
3)	89.2	fem'TALK 89.2	Sigatoka
8)	89.8	Harvest R.	Suva
4)	91.8	R. France Int.	Suva
5)	93.6	MIX 94FM	Sigatoka
5)	93.8	MIX 94FM	Suva/Lautoka/Nadi/ Mamanucas/Yasawas
5)	94.2	MIX 94FM	Ba.Tavua/Ra
6)	94.6	R. Naya Jiwan	Suva
6)	103.4	Nai Talai FM	Suva
6)	104.0	R.Light	
6)	104.2	R.Light	Suva
10)	106.4	R. Australia	Ba
10)	106.6	R. Australia	Suva/Nadi/Labassa
9)	107.0	Hope FM	Suva
9)	107.4	Hope FM	Ba/Tavua/Vatukaola

Addresses and other information
1) 24/7 Pacific stream via satellite from London – **2)** School of Law, Arts & Media, University of the South Pacific, Private Mail Bag, Laucala, Suva ☎ +679 3232797 ⊟+679 3231500 **L.P:** SM: Semi Francis, Co-Ord: Shirley Tagi **W:** usp.ac.fj **D.Prgr:** 24h includes prgrs in English,French,Hindi, Fijian and Mandarin – **3)** Community Media Center, 54 Ratu Sukuna Road, Suva ☎ + 679 3318160/3310307 ⊟ +679 33077207 **W:** femlinkpacific.org.fj **L.P:** Exec.Dir Sharon Bhagwan Rolls. Stations: Suva **Prgr:** 24/7 Labassa : **Prgr:** 2200-0200 M-F Mobile: Also operates a mobile community radio stn studio for women on Viti Levu – **4)** 24/7 English language stream via satellite from Paris – **5)** 11 Nasoki St, Lautoka ☎ +679 666 8900 **W:** facebook.com/mix-fm94 audio streaming http://live.mix94fm **E:** info@mix94.fm **ID:** "Fiji's Best Mix" 24h/7 – **6)** Pacific Islands Christian Network [PICN], Evangelical Bible Missions Trust Board. Studio:15 Tower Street, Suva. PO Box 2525, Gov.Bldgs, Suva. Stations: **R.Light** (English) **W:** facebook.com/pacific-islands-christian-network & radio-light.org **E:** radiolight@connect.com.fj ☎ +679 331 9956, **R. Naya Jiwan** (Hindi) **W:** http://nayajiwan.radio12345.com [audio streaming] ☎ +679 331 9535 **R. Nai Talai** (Fijian) **W:** http://naitalai.listen2myradio.com [audio streaming] **E:** revival@naitalai.org currently inactive on FM – **8)** Christian Mission Fellowship International, Cnr Kings Rd & Khalsa Rd, Kinoya, Suva. PO Box 1499, Nabua, Suva ☎ +679 3398902 **W:** facebook.com/cmfinternationalfiji & cmfi. info/livestream [audio streaming] **L.P:** Mktg Mgr: Rajiv Puran **D.Prgr:** 24/7 rlg **F.PI:** Sigatoka authorised – **9)** Seventh Day Adventist Church Mission, PO Box 297, Suva ☎ +679 336 1022 ⊟ +679 336 1446

W: facebook.com/hopefm107 & http://hopefm-fijiradio.net [audio streaming] – **10)** 24/7 Pacific stream via satellite from Melbourne .

FINLAND

LT: UTC +2h (27 Mar-30 Oct: +3h) — **Pop:** 5.5 million — **Pr.L:** Finnish, Swedish — **E.C:** 50Hz, 230V — **ITU:** FIN

VIESTINTÄVIRASTO
(FICORA, Finnish Communications Regulatory Authority)
✉ PL 313, FI-00181 Helsinki ☎+358 9 69661 🖷 +358 9 6966410
W: ficora.fi **E:** info@ficora.fi **LP:** DG: Rauni Hagman. Dir. of Radio Adm.: Kari Koho.

DIGITA OY (programme distributor)
✉ Jämsänk. 2, FI-00520 Helsinki ☎+358 20411711 🖷 +358 204117234 **W:** digita.fi **E:** info@digita.fi
LP: DG: Sirpa Ojala. Vice Pres, Netw. & Site Sces: Ilari Anttila.
YLEISRADIO (YLE, Pub.)
✉ FI-00024 Yleisradio ☎+358 9 14801 🖷 +358 9 14803216 **W:** yle.fi
E: fbc@yle.fi **LP:** DG: Lauri Kivinen.

FM (MHz)	1	2	3	4	5	6	7	kW
Aavasaksa	87.9	89.8	94.7					3
Ahvenanmaa			100.3		104.9	93.1		10/3
Anjalankoski	88.5	92.8	96.9	91.4	99.5b			30
Enontekiö	88.5	91.4	98.7	104.6			101.2	5
Espoo	87.9	91.9	94.0	103.7	98.9	101.1		60
Eurajoki	87.7	103.5	94.8	92.0	99.4	103.0		30
Fiskars	90.9	93.1	97.0	105.0	102.5	99.7		3
Haapavesi	89.0	96.1	98.4	101.9				30
Hämeenlinna			99.2					1
Iisalmi	87.7	92.8	96.5	107.9				2
Ilomantsi				106.1				1
Inari	88.4	92.8	98.8	105.3			101.9	50/30
Joensuu			106.9					1
Joutseno	88.0	90.9	98.5	100.7				30
Jyväskylä	89.9	87.6	99.3	92.5	103.5			3/30
Karigasniemi	89.5	93.4	96.8	103.7			100.8	2
Kerimäki	90.5	95.8	99.1	103.2				30
			97.7	103.2				6/3
Kiihtelysvaara	88.4	94.9	97.2	100.4				5
Koli	90.2	93.4	99.6	106.4	102.4b			30/5
Kruunupuy	91.4	94.0	97.6	88.8	99.7	102.7		60/3
Kuopio	91.6	93.9	98.1	88.1	100.2b			50
Kuttanen	94.1	97.2	99.6	105.6			102.2	3
Lahti	93.2	95.5	97.9	90.5	100.6b			50/0.2
Lapua	88.2	90.1	93.1	97.5	95.2	101.5		60/2
Lohja			96.1	105.0				3
Mikkeli	88.9	92.1	94.6	101.8				30
Nuorgam	88.6	93.9	97.7	107.8			101.2	3
Oulu	90.4	93.2	97.3	107.7	100.3b			50/5
Parikkala			95.1					1
Pello	90.2	97.0	99.7	103.4				3
Perho			95.9					3
Pernaja	89.5	92.3	95.0	96.4	102.2	98.3		3/1
Pieksämäki	89.4	95.3	97.4	104.9				2/0.5
Pihtipudas	88.6	91.1	97.0	94.7	100.8b			50/2.5
Posio	87.6	91.5	98.6	104.0				30/3
Pyhätunturi	91.0	97.6	99.9	102.4				50
Pyhävuori	88.9	91.0	94.2/97.2	96.1	98.6	102.6		3/10
Rovaniemi	88.2	94.0	96.7	106.8			103.0	30/10
Ruka	90.7	92.8	95.1	104.3				3/2
Sievi			90.3					1
Sodankylä	87.8	90.1	94.3	106.5		101.3		3
Taivalkoski	89.2	91.9	99.2/103.6	106.5				60
Tammela	89.2	91.3	96.0	105.4				5
Tampere	90.7	93.7	99.9	88.3	102.1b			60/6
Tenola(NOR)	89.0	94.1	95.8			100.5		0.02
Tervola	88.6	92.6	95.6	101.6				30
Turku	89.8	92.6	94.3	96.7	98.2	101.4		60/6
Utsjoki	90.7	93.1	99.4	107.1			102.6	2/5
Vaasa	87.8	89.6	94.8	105.2	97.3	101.0		1
Vuokatti	92.3	94.3	98.9	101.2				60
Ylläs	92.2	95.3	98.1	100.7		103.8		50
Ähtäri	91.9	94.6	96.6	102.9				3

+about 30 transmitters under 1kW not mentioned.
b = "FSR Mix", mixture of FM5 & FM6.
D.Prgr: FM1 "YLE Radio 1" (classical music, culture, actualities): 24h. **N:** 0400, 0500, 0600, 0900, 1100, 1400, 1600, 1700, 2000, 2200.
N. in English: 1525. **N. in Russian:** 2055. **N. in Latin:** Fri 0755, Sat

1055 – **FM2 "YleX"** (rock & pop culture for youth): 24h (r. FM1 W00-04). **N:** on the h – **FM3 "Radio Suomi"** (news, sports, popular music and regional prgrs): 24h. **N:** on the h – **FM4 "YLE Puhe"** (news & talk prgr.): 24h. – **FM5 "Radio Extrem"** (Swedish language prgr for young people). 24h (simultaneous night prgr. with R Vega) – **FM6 "Radio Vega"** (Swedish language prgr for elderly people and regional prgrs). 24h – **"FSR Mix"** carries R. eXtrem MF 0400-0650, 1415-1700, 2000-2200 Sat 1500-0000 Sun 1500-2200. At other times R. Vega – **FM7 "Sámiradio"** (Sámi language network). 24h. Carries YLE, SR & NRK Sámiradio: MF: 0515-0830, 1100-1130, 1300-1630 Sat 1700-1800 Sun 1700-1830, at other times FM3 – **"YLE Mondo"** (digital network carried also via Espoo 97.5MHz 5kW): 24h.

Regional & local prgrs:
In Finnish on FM3: MF 0430-1600 excl. nationwide news on the h. (combined prgr. in June-July exc. regional news at half hour) – **Ylen aikainen,** Helsinki: 94.0MHz – **R. Itä-Uusimaa,** Porvoo: 90.3/95.0MHz. (also r. 94.0MHz) – **Ylen läntinen,** Lohja: 97.0/105.0MHz. (also r. 94.0MHz) – **Tampereen R,** Tampere: 99.9MHz – **Lahden R,** Lahti: 97.9MHz – **R. Häme,** Hämeenlinna: 96.0/97.3/99.2/107.1MHz – **Turun R,** Turku: 94.3/100.3/107.1MHz – **Satakunnan R,** Pori: 94.8/97.2MHz – **R. Keski-Suomi,** Jyväskylä: 87.6/97.0/99.3MHz – **Kymenlaakson R,** Kouvola: 96.9MHz – **Etelä-Karjalan R,** Lappeenranta: 89.1/95.1/97.2/98.5/103.2MHz – **Pohjois-Karjalan R,** Joensuu: 97.2/97.7/99.6/106.9MHz – **Savon R,** Mikkeli: 94.6/97.4/99.1MHz – **R. Savo,** Kuopio: 96.5/98.1MHz – **Pohjanmaan R,** Vaasa: 93.1/94.2/94.8/96.6MHz – **R. Keski-Pohjanmaa,** Kokkola: 90.3/95.9/97.6MHz – **Oulu-R,** Oulu: 95.1/97 .3/98.4/99.2/102.5MHz – **Kainuun R,** Kajaani: 98.9/103.6MHz – **R. Perämeri,** Kemi: 94.7/95.6MHz – **Lapin R,** Rovaniemi: 96.7MHz + 15 more freqs.
In Swedish on FM6: MF 0430-1000, 1330 &. 1430. **R. Vega Mellannyland,** Helsingfors: 101.1MHz. – **R. Vega Östnyland,** Borgå: 91.4/98.3MHz. – **R. Vega Västnyland,** Ekenäs: 99.7/101.9MHz. – **R. Vega Åboland,** Åbo: 93.1/101.4/103.0MHz. – **R. Vega Österbotten,** Vasa: 101.0/101.5/102.6/102.7MHz.

Digital: YLE's digital radio broadcasts are carried on Digital Video Broadcasting (DVB) network within the digital TV multiplexes. They include Ylen 1, Ylen klassinen, YleX, R. Extrem, YLE Puhe, R. Suomi, R. Vega, YLE World, YLE Mondo, YLE Multifoorumi, YLE FSR+ and commercial channels The Voice, Iskelmä and Harju ja Pöntinen.

Other stations; main nationwide networks:

FM (MHz)	1)	2)	3)	4)	5)	6)	7)	8)	9)
Alajärvi		104.3				102.2			
Anjalankoski	105.7		102.7	90.0	89.3		104.9	96.2	
Espoo	106.2					92.5			100.0
Eurajoki		90.4	105.1	104.5	96.5	106.0	101.7	95.7	
Forssa			98.5	103.6	107.5	103.3	90.1		
Haapavesi	104.1	100.1	96.8		105.6	93.4	106.1		99.5
Hanko		107.5	96.2		104.5	95.7	95.3		
Harjavalta					93.9				
Heinola		87.6							
Helsinki		96.2	104.6	94.9	98.1	96.8	90.0	89.0	105.5
Huittinen		93.0							
Hyvinkää			95.7		104.0				
Hämeenlinna	100.2	101.7	106.5	92.3		97.3		105.9	88.5
Iisalmi		89.5	103.1	104.7	89.1		95.6		
Ikaalinen		99.0							
Imatra	105.3				101.5	102.5			
Inari				104.1					
Inkoo					105.5				
Joensuu		92.8	87.9	103.7	102.9	96.4	101.9		
Joutseno	103.8		94.2				96.0		
Juuka		103.3							
Jyväskylä	105.8	107.1	101.6	97.7	104.9	97.3	101.0	94.1	90.9
Jämsä		100.3	94.4			88.8	89.6		
Järvenpää						101.8			
Kajaani		102.8	107.0	96.3	93.7	94.8			
Kalajoki			104.6						
Kemi		105.2	98.8						
Kemijärvi	104.7								
Kerimäki	107.7					91.3			
Kitee		102.2							
Kokkola		99.1	106.3		99.1				
Koli	104.3		95.7		94.7		107.4		
Kotka		87.7				101.5		89.0	
Kouvola		100.1			93.8	107.7	96.2	101.3	
Kristiinankaup.	105.1	93.4							
Kruunupyy	98.8		107.2		105.3	104.9		104.3	

FM (MHz)	1)	2)	3)	4)	5)	6)	7)	8)	9)
Kuopio	106.7	96.7	93.0	100.9	107.3	101.6	89.1	106.1	89.7
Kurikka		92.3			100.1				
Köyliö						107.9			
Lahti	102.4	103.0	105.0	89.7	104.4	96.6	94.2	106.4	87.6
Lappeenranta		93.5			94.8	96.5	100.2	96.0	89.5
Lapua	106.5	96.9	105.4	100.4				89.4	
Lempäälä						102.8			
Lohja		96.5		104.8		88.8		107.2	100.5
Loimaa		98.5							
Loviisa						104.6	105.2		
Luumäki								96.0	
Mikkeli	106.9	89.7	100.5	93.0	104.8	106.3	100.9	87.8	
Mäntyharju					93.0				
Nilsiä						97.5			
Orivesi		103.8	101.2	89.3					
Oulu	104.8	89.4	101.4	95.8	96.4	99.1	106.2	106.9	94.3
Outokumpu		101.7							
Padasjoki	87.8								
Parkano		99.0			100.2				
Pieksämäki		102.2	101.3		103.0	96.5			
Pihtipudas	105.1	107.0	98.5		104.5	101.7	102.3		
Pohja		95.1							
Pori	91.6	100.4	104.5	96.5	90.4	98.7		95.7	89.9
Porvoo		99.8	107.9			93.5			88.4
Pyhätunturi	105.8					106.2			
Pyhävuori	107.6								
Raahe		92.5	107.0	89.9	105.8	87.7			
Rauma		105.1	103.6			93.9			
Riihimäki			99.6				94.7		
Rovaniemi	105.5	89.3	102.0	107.0	103.3	101.1		93.4	
Ruka	100.8					96.3			
Ruovesi		103.8							
Salo			99.1				107.7		97.3
Savonlinna		96.7	104.2		101.4	105.2		91.3	
Seinäjoki		96.9		100.4	103.3	91.2		89.4	
Sievi		107.7							
Siilinjärvi		102.0							
Sonkajärvi		107.1							
Suomussalmi					88.8	104.5			
Sysmä	90.2	106.8	101.3	93.5		96.1	89.1		
Taivalkoski	106.5					94.6			
Tammisaari		95.1	100.2	91.4	103.2		107.0		
Tampere	104.7	100.9	89.6	104.2	91.6	90.0	105.6	98.8	92.7
Tervola	107.5				96.2	100.1			
Tornio					92.0		98.3		
Turku	103.9	100.1	98.7	97.6	103.4	104.6	102.4	107.3	100.5
Uusikaupunki		96.2	91.1						
Vaasa			104.4	91.6	102.0	93.9			98.4
Valkeakoski		95.0	94.4						
Vammala		101.2	97.7		88.0				
Varkaus		92.7				91.0	105.5	102.8	
Vihti		105.6							
Vilppula		95.4							
Vuokatti	105.7					88.8			
Ylivieska			88.3						
Ylläs	107.9					91.6			
Ähtäri		97.8	102.9		104.9	98.4	105.5		

Addresses:
1) Nova, Ilmalank. 2C, PL 123, 00241 Helsinki **W:** radionova.fi Powers 1-60kW – **2) Iskelmä,** Kehräsaari B5. 33200 Tampere. **W:** iskelma.fi Powers 0.1-3kW – **3) The Voice,** Tallbergink. 1C 7. krs, 00180 Helsinki **W:** voice.fi Powers 0.1-60kW – **4) R. Rock,** PL 350, Tehtaankatu 27-29 A, 00151 Helsinki **W:** radiorock.fi Powers 0.1-4kW – **5) R. Suomipop,** Lintulahdenk. 10, 00500 Helsinki **W:** radiosuomipop.fi Powers 0.1-3kW – **6) R. NRJ (Energy),** Kiviaidankatu 2 i, 00210 Helsinki **W:** nrj.fi Powers 0.1-30kW – **7) R. Aalto,** PL 350, Tehtaankatu 27-29 A, 00151 Helsinki. **W:** radioaalto.fi Powers 0.1-10kW – **8) R. Dei** (Rlg.), Ilmankuja 2 i, 00240 Helsinki. **W:** radiodei.fi Powers 0.2-5kW – **9) R. Nostalgia,** Kiviaidankatu 2 i, 00210 Helsinki **W:** radionostalgia.fi Powers 0.2-2kW.
About 50 more stations are in operation.

ÅLAND (autonomous province)

SVERIGES RADIO cf. Sweden

FM (MHz)	P1	P2	P3	P4	kW
Mariehamn	95.0	97.1	88.6	102.3	10

Steel FM, Mariehamn: 95.9MHz 0.2kW. **W:** steelfm.net – **Rix FM** (cf. Sweden), Mariehamn: 101.8MHz 3kW – **R. Harmonica,** Mariehamn: 102.8MHz 1kW – **Soft FM,** Mariehamn: 107.2MHz 0.2kW. **W:** softfm.

net – **Ålands R.,** Mariehamn: 91.3MHz 10kW. **W:** radiotv.aland.fi

L.T: UTC +1h (27 Mar-30 Oct: +2h) — **Pop:** 64 million — **Pr.L:** French — **E.C:** 50Hz, 220V — **ITU:** F

CONSEIL SUPÉRIEUR DE L'AUDIOVISUEL (CSA)
✉ 39/43 quai André Citroën, 75739 Paris cedex 15 ☎ +33 1 40583800 🖳 +33 1 45790006 **W:** csa.fr **LP:** Pres: Olivier Schrameck
The CSA regulates TV and radio, and issues broadcast licences

TDF
✉ 106 avenue Marx Dormoy, 92541 Montrouge cedex ☎ +33 1 55951000 🖳 +33 1 55952000 **W:** tdf.fr **LP:** Pres & DG: Olivier Huart
TDF operates the majority of radio and TV txs

TOWERCAST
✉ 46/50 avenue Théophile Gautier, 75016 Paris ☎ +33 1 40714071 **W:** towercast.fr **LP:** Pres: Jacques Roques
Towercast operates radio and TV txs

ITAS TIM
✉ 1 rue Royale, 92213 Saint-Cloud Cedex ☎ +33 1 41122700 **W:** itastim.com **LP:** Pres: Gilles Bastard.
Itas Tim operates FM and TV txs

OUTRE-MER 1ère (Pub)
✉ 35/37 rue Danton, 92240 Malakoff ☎ +33 1 55227100 **W:** la1ere.fr **LP:** Dir.: Michel Kops.
Outre-Mer 1ère is a part of France Télévisions and produces public service prgrs (radio & TV) in the French overseas territories

RADIO FRANCE (Pub)
✉ 116 Av. du Président Kennedy, 75220 Paris cedex 16 ☎ +33 1 56402222 **W:** radiofrance.fr **LP:** Pres. & DG: Mathieu Gallet

HOME SERVICES:

LW & MW	N	kHz	kW	MW	N	kHz	kW
Allouis	A	*162	*2000	Ajaccio	B+L	1404	20
Lyon	I	603	300	Brest	I	1404	20
Rennes	I	711	300	Dijon	I	1404	5
Paris	B+L	s864	300	Grenoble	I	1404	20
Bordeaux	I	1206	300	Bastia	B+L	1494	20
Marseille	I	1242	150	Clermont-Fd	I	1494	20
Strasbourg	B+L	1278	300	Nice	I	1557	300
Lille	I	1377	300				

NB: Radio France has scheduled the end of all MW trs on 31 December 2015
N=Networks: A=France Inter, B=France Bleu, F=FIP, I= France Info, L=rel. local stns at certain times. s=AM stereo C-QUAM. *=run at 1000kW 1700-0500 (Wi. time) 1900-0400 (Su. time)

FM: Station (MHz)	C	D	E	F	kW
Abbeville	93.1	97.4	89.8		2.5
Ajaccio	92.4	97.6	88.0		10
Ajaccio (La Punta)	88.6	103.9		105.6	4
Albi				105.5	1
Alençon	93.0	88.0	91.0		13
Ales	87.6	96.1	98.6	105.1	1
Amiens (St Just)	95.4	102.5	99.4		20
Amiens (Dury)	92.6	89.9	89.3	105.5	2
Angers	93.2	91.4	97.4		10
Angers (La Ballue)				105.5	1
Angoulême	92.4	87.6	95.1	105.5	2
Arcachon	88.3	97.0	91.0	105.5	1.2
Argenton sur Creuse	101.9	89.8	97.2		5
Arles				105.0	1
Arnay le Duc	94.6	90.3	100.3	105.5	3
Aurillac	94.5	98.0	91.9		7
Autun	88.1	97.3	94.1		10
Auxerre	99.5	89.5	92.8		5
Auxerre (Venoy)				105.5	1
Avallon				105.6	1
Avignon	97.4	90.7	93.2		4
Avignon (Sorgues)				105.2	2
Bar le Duc	90.9	88.4	92.7	104.5	10
Bastia	95.9	89.2	93.9	105.5	10
Bayonne	89.0	96.1	92.7	105.5	16
Beaucaire				105.2	1
Beauvais				105.5	1
Bergerac	92.3	94.0	97.1		26
Besançon (Montfaucon)	98.7	89.3	95.0		10

FM: Station	C	D	E	F	kW
Besançon (Lomont)	90.0	97.7	92.9		18
Beziers				105.1	1
Bordeaux	89.7	97.7	93.5	105.5	6
Boulogne sur Mer	103.3	99.9	89.4	106.5	1
Bourges	94.9	88.5	91.8		74
Bourges (town)				105.5	1
Brest	95.4	97.8	89.4		200
Brest (town)				105.5	3
Briançon	91.5	97.8	89.5	105.4	1
Brignoles	106.7	104.0	105.5		1.5
Caen	99.6	91.5	95.6		100
Caen (town)				105.5	1
Calais	104.7			105.6	1
Cannes				105.9	1
Carcassone	88.3	96.5	90.9		80
Castres				105.5	2
Chambéry	93.5	90.5	98.6		8
Chambéry (town)				105.1	1
Champagnole	88.5	91.7	98.3		1
Charleville-Mézières	95.8	90.1	93.5	105.9	10
Chartres	94.6	98.1	89.7		32
Chartres (town)				105.7	4
Chateaubriant				105.5	1
Châteauroux				105.5	1
Chaumont	96.5	90.4	93.3		15
Chaumont (town)				105.5	1
Cherbourg-Octeville	94.1	89.2	92.3	105.6	1
Cholet				105.9	1
Clermont-Fd	90.4	98.4	95.5	105.5	35
Compiègne				105.3	1
Corse (East)	968	92.3	99.8		17
Corte	98.2	91.0	94.8	105.5	1.3
Cosne Cours s.Loire				105.3	1
Creil	87.6	93.3	91.9	105.6	1
Dijon	95.9	93.7	99.2		25
Dunkerque				106.5	1
Epinal	98.6	92.4	89.4	106.5	10
Evreux	88.5	98.9	97.3	105.5	1
Falaise				105.3	1
Fontainebleau				105.5	2
Gap	98.3	88.5	95.3	105.5	5
Gex	94.4	96.7	89.6	101.1	25
Grenoble (Chamrousse)	99.4	88.2	91.8		1
Grenoble (T. s. Venin)	89.9	92.8	107.3	105.1	1
Guéret	100.7	98.8	90.8	105.5	12
Hirson	94.4	99.7	97.2		5
Hyères	91.6	97.5	94.5	107.1	1.5
Laon				105.3	1
Laval	95.1	88.3	92.1	105.5	5
La Rochelle				105.5	1
Le Havre	88.9	93.3	98.5	105.5	1
Le Mans	92.6	89.0	97.0	105.5	128
Le Puy	99.3	89.3	92.8		10
Lesparre	92.4	90.3	95.1		1.6
Lille (Bouvigny)	103.7	98.0	88.7	105.2	125
Limoges	93.0	89.5	97.5		150
Limoges (town)				105.5	2
Longwy	98.1	88.3	91.0	104.3	5
Lourdes				105.3	3.5
Lyon (Mont Pilat)	99.8	88.8	92.4	103.4	150
Lyon (Town)	101.1	94.1	98.0	105.4	2
Mantes la Jolie	95.0	92.4	97.1		5
Marseille	91.3	99.0	94.2		400
Marseille				105.3	13
Marseille (town)	91.7	98.6	94.7		1
Maubeuge				106.2	2
Melun				105.7	1
Mende	90.1	96.9	93.7		10
Menton	97.0	89.6	91.7	105.5	5
Metz	99.8	94.5	89.7	106.8	145
Millau	94.9	99.2	88.9		6
Mont de Marsan				105.5	6
Montargis	102.9	98.8	94.1	105.5	1
Montauban				105.7	1
Montereau				105.7	1
Montlieu la Garde	88.3	104.4	98.8		3.5
Montluçon				105.5	1
Montpellier	89.4	97.8	92.9		18
Montpellier (Town)	89.1		96.4	105.1	1
Morosaglia	97.1	88.8	93.4		1
Mulhouse	95.7	88.6	91.6	105.5	100
Nancy	96.9	88.7	91.7	105.9	5

FM: Station	C	D	E	F	kW
Nantes	90.6	94.2	98.9	105.5	125
Neufchateau	96.3	100.3	91.5		1
Neufchatel-en-Bray	92.7	96.0	90.2		5
Nevers				105.5	1
Nice	100.2	101.9	92.2	105.7	100
Nimes				105.1	1/5
Niort	99.4	96.4	91.1		190
Niort (town)				105.5	1
Orléans	99.2	95.8	90.7		4
Orléans (town)				105.5	1
Paris	87.8	93.5	91.7	105.5	10
Parthenay	93.8	87.9	98.5	105.5	12
Pau				105.5	1
Perpignan	92.1	99.8	97.2	105.1	10
Poitiers	97.7	92.3	95.5	105.5	1
Porto Vecchio (Col de Mela)	96.8	90.8	98.9		1.5
Porto Vecchio (Punto di a Varra)	92.6	87.9	94.6	100.4	1
Privas	89.8	96.5	94.7	105.2	1
Redon				95.8	1
Reims	96.8	98.8	89.2	105.5	135
Rennes	93.5	98.3	89.9		100
Rennes (town)				105.5	1
Roanne				105.5	1
Rochefort				105.3	1
Rouen	96.5	94.0	92.0		100
Rouen (town)				105.7	2.7
Ruffec				105.2	1
Saint Brieuc				105.5	1
Saint Etienne	99.5	89.1	92.7	105.6	2
Saint-Nazaire	95.2	92.2	102.6	105.5	1.5
Saint-Quentin				105.6	1
Saint-Raphaël	96.3	88.7	99.6		40
Saint-Raphaël (town)				106.0	1
Sainte Foy la Grande				105.5	1
Sarrebourg	93.1	99.4	90.3		10
Sens	96.3	98.5	93.8		10
Sens (town)				105.7	1.3
Soissons				105.7	1
Strasbourg	97.3	87.7	95.0	104.4	48
Toulon	92.0	97.1	94.9	105.8	5
Toulouse (town)	88.1	96.3	91.1	105.5	2
Toulouse (Pic du Midi)	87.9	95.7	91.5		72
Tours	99.9	97.8	92.2		8
Tours (town)				105.5	1
Troyes	95.3	97.9	91.4		50
Troyes (town)				105.5	1
Ussel	96.0	88.2	99.7		10
Valence				105.4	3
Vannes	88.6	96.0	91.8	105.5	20
Verdun	92.1	99.3	97.4	106.3	6
Villebon sur Yvette	95.4	98.0	97.1		1
Villers-Cotterets	91.1	89.6	92.9		13
Vittel	98.2	89.0	94.0		8
Voiron	91.5	89.2	107.2	105.4	1

+ 1490 stns under 1kW

C=France Inter (stereo), D=France-Culture (stereo), E=France-Musique (stereo), F=France Info (mono). RDS on all txs.

France Inter Network A on **LW** Allouis 162kHz, C on **FM** : **D.Prgrs**:24h exc. Tues 0005-0358. FM txs: 24h **N**: Hourly, plus 0430, 0530, 0630 — **France Culture** (Network D) (stereo) **D.Prgrs**:24h **N**: 0530, 0600, 0630, 0700, 0800, 1100, 1130, 1700, 1800, 2100 — **France Musique** (Network E) (stereo): **D.Prgrs**:24h **N**: 0600, 0730, 0800, 1200, 1800 — **France Info** (Network I on MW, F on FM) News and informations **D.Prgrs**:24h

Mouv'

Station	MHz	kW	Station	MHz	kW
Ajaccio	92.0	4	Limoges	107.6	2
Amiens	91.0	1	Lorient	103.3	0.5
Angers	96.0	1	Lyon	87.8	4
Annecy	99.4	1	Marseille	96.8	2.5
Besançon	93.5	1	Marseille (town)	96.4	1
Bordeaux	87.7	1	Mende	107.2	0.2
Brest	94.0	3	Montpellier	102.7	3
Caen	87.8	1	Nantes	96.1	3
Cannes	101.0	0.2	Nice	101.0	2.5
Carcassonne	90.0	1	Paris	92.1	8
Clermont-Fd	97.5	2	Reims	101.1	0.5
Dijon	88.9	1	Rennes	107.3	2
Grenoble	95.5	1	Rouen	95.8	1
Lille	91.0	2	St Etienne	88.0	2

Station	MHz	kW	Station	MHz	kW
Toulouse	95.2	5	Valence	100.7	0.5
Tours	94.1	2			

D.Prgrs: 24h RDS on all txs (stereo)

Local Stations "FIP"

FIP Bordeaux, 12 allée Serr, 33100 Bordeaux ☎ +33 5 56241515 - Bordeaux 96.7MHz 2.5kW, Arcachon 96.5 0.5 kW
FIP Nantes, 2 bis quai François Mitterrand, 44100 Nantes ☎ +33 2 40444555 - Nantes 95.7MHz 2.5kW, St Nazaire 97.2MHz 1.5kW
FIP Paris, 116 avenue du Président Kennedy, 75220 Paris Cedex 16 ☎ +33 1 42201234 - 105.1MHz 10kW
FIP Strasbourg, 4 rue Joseph Massol, 67080 Strasbourg Cedex ☎ +33 3 88352400 - 92.3MHz 4kW
Sts without local news: Marseille 90.9MHz 4kW, Montpellier 99.7MHz 1kW, Rennes 101.2MHz 1kW, Toulouse 103.5MHz 2kW
RDS on all txs **D.Prgrs:** 24h Prgrs consist of music and news

France Bleu

✉ 116 av. du Président Kennedy, 75220 Paris Cedex 16
D.Prgrs: 24h uninterrupted music 2100-0400 (can vary on each France Bleu stn)
Stations: MW: Network B + **FM**
France Bleu Local Stations (F.B = France Bleu) - At certain times, local stns relay national France Bleu prgrs.
F.B 107.1, 116 av du Président Kennedy, 75220 Paris Cedex 16 ☎ +33 1 56402222: **FM:** Paris 107.1MHz 10kW, Chartres 97.3MHz 4kW, **MW:** Paris 864kHz 300kW (C-QUAM stereo)
F.B Alsace, 4 rue Joseph Massol, 67000 Strasbourg ☎ +33 3 88762000 **FM:** Strasbourg 101.4MHz 48kW, Mulhouse 102.6MHz 100kW, **MW:** 1278kHz 300kW
F.B Armorique, 14 av Jean Janvier, 35031 Rennes Cedex ☎ +33 2 99674321 **FM:** Vannes 101.3MHz 20kW, Rennes 103.1MHz 100kW
F.B Auxerre, 12 place Saint Amâtre, B.P 101, 89002 Auxerre Cedex ☎ +33 3 86723456 **FM:** Sens 100.5MHz 10kW, Auxerre 101.3MHz 5kW, Nevers 104.0MHz 1kW
F.B Azur, 2 place Grimaldi, 06012 Nice Cedex 1 ☎ +33 4 97033636 **FM:** Nice 103.8MHz 100kW, Menton 94.8MHz 5kW, Saint Raphaël 100.7MHz 1kW
F.B Basse Normandie, 75 rue Basse, 14053 Caen Cedex ☎ +33 2 31471414 **FM:** Le Havre 102.2MHz 2.5kW, Caen 102.6MHz 100kW
F.B Béarn, 5 place Clémenceau, 64000 Pau ☎ +33 5 59983030 **FM:** Oloron Sainte Marie 93.2MHz 1.5kW, Pau 102.5MHz 10kW
F.B Belfort Montbéliard, 10 rue des Capucins, 90000 Belfort ☎ +33 3 84579090 **FM:** Belfort 106.8MHz 2kW
F.B Berry, 10/12 rue de la République, 36000 Châteauroux ☎ +33 2 54606060 **FM:** Argenton 93.5MHz 5kW, Bourges 103.2MHz 19kW
F.B Besançon, 2 Place Granvelle, BP 591, 25027 Besançon Cedex ☎ +33 3 81212525 **FM:** Besançon 101.4MHz 18kW + 102.8MHz 10kW
F.B Bourgogne, 29 rue Guillaume Tell, 21888 21018 Dijon Cedex ☎ +33 3 80592121 **FM:** Troyes 87.8 60kW, Arnay le Duc 103.4MHz 3kW, Dijon 103.7MHz 25kW
F.B Breizh Izel, 12 esplanade François Mitterrand, 29000 Quimper ☎ +33 2 98552929 **FM:** Brest 93.0MHz 20kW
F.B Champagne-Ardenne, 28 bd du Maréchal Joffre, BP 1094, 51054 Reims Cedex ☎ +33 3 26845151 **FM:** Charleville-Mézières 100.9MHz 10kW, Reims 95.1MHz 2kW, Châlons en Champagne 94.8MHz 1kW, Troyes 100.8MHz 1kW
F.B Cotentin, Hôtel Atlantique, impasse Piedagnel, 50100 Cherbourg-Octeville ☎ +33 2 33885050 **FM:** Cherbourg-Octeville 100.7MHz 4kW
F.B Creuse, 7 avenue de la République, 23000 Guéret ☎ +33 5 55612323 **FM:** Guéret 94.3MHz 12kW
F.B Drôme Ardèche, 70 avenue de Romans, 26000 Valence Cedex ☎ +33 4 75813333 **FM:** Valence 87.9MHz 10kW, Privas 98.4MHz 1.5kW, Vals les Bains 103.8MHz 1kW
F.B Gard Lozère, 10 bd des Arènes, 30020 Nîmes Cedex 1 ☎ +33 4 66363030 **FM:** Nîmes 90.2MHz 1kW, Alès 91.6MHz 2kW, Mende 104.9MHz 10kW
F.B Gascogne, 13 place Jean Jaurès, 40000 Mont de Marsan ☎ +33 5 58465050 **FM:** Mont de Marsan 98.8MHz 20kW, Bayonne 100.5MHz 26kW, Mimizan 103.4MHz 20kW
F.B Gironde, 91 rue Nuyens, CS 91882, 33072 Bordeaux Cedex ☎ +33 5 57812020 **FM:** Bordeaux 100.1MHz 6kW, Lesparre 101.6MHz 1.6kW
F.B Haute Normandie, Hangar A, quai Boisguilbert, 76000 Rouen ☎ +33 2 35073107 **FM:** Le Havre 95.1MHz 1kW, Rouen 100.1MHz 100kW, Neufchâtel en Bray 101.6MHz 5kW, Evreux 89.5MHz 1kW
F.B Hérault, 374 allée Henri II de Montmorency, 34000 Montpellier ☎ +33 4 67066565 **FM:** Montpellier 101.1MHz 18kW + 100.6MHz 1kW
F.B Isère, 27 av Félix Viallet, 38000 Grenoble ☎ +33 4 76503838 **FM:** Chambéry 99.1MHz 5kW, Lyon 101.8MHz 25kW, Grenoble 102.8MHz

1kW + 98.2MHz 1.2kW
F.B La Rochelle, 5 av Michel Crépeau, 17000 La Rochelle ☎ +33 5 46351717 **FM:** Royan 103.6MHz 1kW, Saintes 103.9MHz 60kW, Angoulême 101.5MHz 2kW, La Rochelle 98,2MHz 1kW
F.B Limousin, 23 bd Gambetta87000 Limoges ☎ +33 5 55113811 **FM:** Chateauponsac 92.5MHz 1kW, Ussel 101.4MHz 10kW, Limoges 103.5MHz 150kW
F.B Loire Océan, 2 bis quai François Mitterrand, 44200 Nantes ☎ +33 2 40444546 **FM:** Saint Nazaire 88.1MHz 1.5kW, Nantes 101.8MHz 200kW, Angers 88.5MHz 1k W
F.B Lorraine Nord, 5, rue d'Austrasie, B.P 50071, 57003 Metz cedex 01 ☎ +33 3 87682222 **FM:** Metz 98.5MHz 1kW, Sarreguemines 104 MHz 1kW
F.B. Maine, 17 avenue Pierre Mendès France, 72000 Le Mans ☎ +33 2 43297272 **FM:** La Flèche 91.7MHz 1kW, Le Mans 96MHz 2.5 kW, Sablé sur Sarthe 105.7MHz 1kW
F.B Mayenne, 41 av Robert Buron, 53000 Laval ☎ +33 2 43495050 **FM:** Laval 96.6MHz 5kW
F.B Nord, 507 avenue du Président Hoover, 59000 Lille ☎ +33 3 20135962 **FM:** Lille (town) 87.8MHz 1kW, Lille (Bouvigny) 94.7MHz 125kW, Boulogne sur Mer 95.5MHz 1kW, Le Touquet 97.8MHz 2kW, Calais 106.2MHz 1kW
F.B Orléans, 3/5 place du Châtelet, 45000 Orléans ☎ +33 2 38714545 **FM:** Blois 93.9MHz 1kW, Orléans 100.9MHz 4kW, Montargis 106.8MHz 1kW
F.B Pays Basque, 46 allées Marines, 64116 Bayonne Cedex ☎ +33 5 59466464 **FM:** Bayonne 101.3MHz 15kW
F.B Pays d'Auvergne, 80 bd François Mitterand, 63000 Clermont-Fd ☎+33 4 73346363 **FM:** Clermont-Fd 102.5MHz 37kW, Aurillac 100.2MHz 1kW, Montluçon 96.7MHz 1kW
F.B Pays de Savoie, 256 rue de la République, 73000 Chambéry ☎ +33 4 79707374 **FM:** Annecy 95.2MHz 1kW, Chambéry 103.9MHz 8kW, Gex 106.1MHz 20kW
F.B Périgord, 1 cours Saint Georges, BP 3033, 24003 Périgueux Cedex ☎ +33 5 53062000 **FM:** Limoges 91.7MHz 100kW, Bergerac 99.0MHz 26kW
F.B Picardie, 2 rue du Maréchal de Lattre de Tassigny, 80000 Amiens ☎ +33 3 22711515 **FM:** Amiens 100.6MHz 2kW, Abbeville 100.6MHz 5kW, Hirson 101.3MHz 1kW, Sailly Saillisel 102.8MHz 15kW
F.B Poitou, 27, bd de Solférino, 86000 Poitiers ☎ +33 5 49605000 **FM:** Parthenay 106.4MHz 12kW, Niort 101.0MHz 1kW
F.B Provence, 560 av Mozart, 13617 Aix en Provence.Cedex 01 ☎ +33 4 42991313 **FM:** Brignoles 102.1MHz 1.5kW, Hyères 102.5MHz 1.5kW, Toulon 102.9MHz 5kW, Marseille 103.6MHz 200kW
F.B RCFM, 4 rue Favalelli, BP 130, 20292 Bastia Cedex ☎ +33 4 95329532 **FM:** Corse (east) 88.2MHz 17kW, Ajaccio 100.5MHz 10kW, + 97.0MHz 4kW + 1404kHz 20kW, Canavaggia 101.7MHz 1kW, Corte 100.0MHz 1.33kW, Bastia 101.7MHz 10kW + 1494kHz 20kW, Porto Vecchio 101.8MHz 1.5kW + 105.4MHz 1kW, Morosaglia 104.6MHz 1kW
F.B Roussillon, 24 av du Général Leclerc, 66000 Perpignan ☎ +33 4 68519000 **FM:** Perpignan 101.6MHz 10kW
F.B. Saint-Étienne Loire, 5 rue Pablo Picasso, BP 10091, 42003 Saint-Étienne Cedex 1 ☎ +33 4 77520808 **FM:** Saint-Étienne 97.1MHz 2kW
F.B Sud Lorraine, 21/23 bd du Recteur Senn, CS 94206, 54042 Nancy Cedex ☎ +33 3 83195488 **FM:** Epinal 100.0MHz 1kW, Nancy 100.5MHz 5kW, Vittel 102.6MHz 1kW, Neufchateau 103.0MHz 1kW
F.B. Toulouse, 78 allée Jean Jaurès, BP 50901, 31009 Toulouse ☎ +33 5 34417000 **FM:** Toulouse 90.5MHz 2kW
F.B Touraine, place Gaston Pailhou, BP 3231, 37032 Tours Cedex 1 ☎ +33 2 47363737 **FM:** Tours 105.0MHz 8kW +98.7MHz 1kW
F.B Vaucluse, 25 rue de la République, 84000 Avignon Cedex ☎ +33 4 90141312 **FM:** Avignon 100.4MHz 2kW
+ 329 txs less than 1kW not mentioned. Stereo and RDS on all txs

Special Programmes (MW)

Lyon 603kHz (Rlg) Sun 1700-1800. ✉ Foyer Notre Dame des Ondes, 24 rue Paul Sisley, 69003 Lyon – **Strasbourg** 1278kHz (Rlg) Sun 0800-1100. First Sun 1207-1300 prgr in cooperation with SWR (Freiburg), Studio Karlsruhe and Radio DRS (Basel). F.B. Elsass Prgr in Alsatian language 0700-1100 + 1230-1530 ✉ See under F.B. Alsace
F.PI. Radio France has scheduled the end of all MW txs on 31 December 2015

RADIO FRANCE INTERNATIONALE (Pub)

✉ 80 rue Camille Desmoulins, 92130 Issy les Moulineaux ☎ +33 1 84228484 **W:** rfi.fr **LP:** Marie-Christine Saragosse
RFI1 (French service): Paris **FM** 89MHz 10kW (stereo)

EXTERNAL SERVICE see International Broadcasting section

PRIVATE MW STATION

BRETAGNE 5 ✉ Le Pôle, Parc d'activités de l'Espérance Ouest, 10 rue de la Doucine, 22120 QUESSOY ☎ +33 2 96330504 **W:** bretagne5.fr. **MW:** Saint Guéno 1593kHz 10 kW 0800-1600, 5 kW 1600-0800. **D.Prgrs:**24h

PRIVATE FM STATIONS:

FM Station	MHz	kW
25) Auxerre	87.6	1
23) Bayonne	87.6	3
20) Bernay	87.6	1
17) Besançon	87.6	1
23) Castres	87.6	1
26) Laval	87.6	1
20) Le Havre	87.6	1
26) Le Mans	87.6	1
22) Niort	87.6	1
7) Orléans	87.6	1
17) Romilly sur Seine	87.6	1
22) Vannes	87.6	1
8) Yssingeaux	87.6	1
23) Bourges	87.7	1
13) Clermont Ferrand	87.7	1
7) Corte	87.7	1
5) Figeac	87.7	1
19) Nice	87.7	2
21) Saint Omer	87.7	1
9) Tours	87.7	2
19) La Flèche	87.8	1
5) Le Blanc	87.8	1
19) Mayenne	87.8	1
23) Mazamet	87.8	1
7) Montluçon	87.8	1
14) Nantes	87.8	1
6) Verdun	87.8	1
6) Dijon	87.9	1
21) Menton	87.9	1
6) Montreuil	87.9	1
17) Reims	87.9	2
5) Saint Raphaël	87.9	1
2) Toulon	87.9	1
7) Yvetot	87.9	1
10) Calais	88.0	1
17) Châteauroux	88.0	1
23) Colmar	88.0	1
17) St Gilles Croix de Vie	88.0	1
7) Vesoul	88.0	1
3) Villefranche /Saône	88.0	1
9) Vitry le François	88.0	1
17) Angers	88.1	1
3) Avignon	88.1	1
3) Brive la Gaillarde	88.1	1
18) Châtellerault	88.1	1
23) Dole	88.1	1
6) Nice	88.1	5
17) Rouen	88.1	1
6) Soissons	88.1	1
3) Fontenay le Comte	88.2	1
17) Le Havre	88.2	1
10) Lille	88.2	1
10) Metz	88.2	1
10) Nancy	88.2	1
6) Saint Quentin	88.2	1
9) Strasbourg	88.2	4
22) Tours	88.2	2
13) Bonifacio	88.3	1
3) Brioude	88.3	1
17) Dijon	88.3	1
9) L'Île Rousse	88.3	1
18) Lorient	88.3	1
9) Moulins	88.3	1
17) Roanne	88.3	1
17) Saint Flour	88.3	1
14) Amiens	88.4	1
4) Laon	88.4	1
9) Luxeuil les Bains	88.4	1
17) Lyon	88.4	4
6) Mont de Marsan	88.4	1
19) Nantes	88.4	2
21) Sarrebourg	88.4	1
21) Sarreguemines	88.4	1
6) Thouars	88.4	1
8) Bordeaux	88.5	4
10) Compiègne	88.5	1
6) Nogent le Rotrou	88.5	1

FM Station	MHz	kW
20) Quimper	88.5	1
17) Annecy	88.6	1
17) Châlons en Champ.	88.6	1
6) Châteaubriant	88.6	1
8) Chaumont	88.6	1
19) Confolens	88.6	1
16) Paris	88.6	4
23) Porto Vecchio	88.6	1
18) Vichy	88.6	1
10) Alençon	88.7	1
7) Avallon	88.7	1
25) Bastia	88.7	1
8) Caen	88.7	2
19) Chartres	88.7	1
18) Châteauroux	88.7	1
19) Étampes	88.7	1
25) Ghisonaccia	88.7	4
3) Gray	88.7	1
18) Saint Flour	88.7	1
13) Saintes	88.7	1
22) Toulouse	88.7	5
6) Bonnières sur Seine	88.8	2
12) Clermont Ferrand	88.8	1
4) Laval	88.8	1
8) Nantes	88.8	3
6) Reims	88.8	2
17) Saint Dizier	88.8	1
4) Bagnères de Bigorre	88.9	1
17) Bordeaux	88.9	1
13) Montluçon	88.9	1
23) Rennes	88.9	1
6) Aurillac	89.0	1
6) Avignon	89.0	1
6) Avranches	89.0	1
17) Brest	89.0	3
17) Clamecy	89.0	1
13) Moulins	89.0	1
23) Bernay	89.1	1
1) Bourges	89.1	1
5) Gien	89.1	1
18) Perpignan	89.1	3
8) Saint Nazaire	89.1	1
22) Saint Quentin	89.1	1
22) Valenciennes	89.1	1
19) Brive la Gaillarde	89.2	1
23) Châteaubriant	89.2	1
23) Châtellerault	89.2	1
22) Lille	89.2	2
18) Marseille	89.2	10
13) Montbard	89.2	1
17) Nevers	89.2	1
23) Ussel	89.2	1
17) Vichy	89.2	1
17) Castres	89.3	1
17) Cholet	89.3	1
13) Longwy	89.3	1
4) Niort	89.3	1
9) Nogaro	89.3	1
23) Rouen	89.3	2
25) Arras	89.4	1
17) Aurillac	89.4	1
18) Bayeux	89.4	1
18) Bayonne	89.4	2
6) Chambéry	89.4	1
23) Marmande	89.4	1
6) Roanne	89.4	1
8) Saint Dizier	89.4	1
15) Toulon	89.4	2
5) Saintes	89.4	1
23) Chaumont	89.5	1
3) Strasbourg	89.5	1
18) Ajaccio	89.6	8
14) Angers	89.6	2
4) Auch	89.6	1
6) Clermont Ferrand	89.6	2
10) La Rochelle	89.6	1
23) Le Havre	89.6	1

FM Station	MHz	kW
4) Marseille	89.6	4
21) Mende	89.6	1
7) Vierzon	89.6	1
5) Aubusson	89.7	1
23) Bastia	89.7	1
13) Nevers	89.7	1
10) Nîmes	89.7	1
23) Perpignan	89.7	3
18) Saint Nazaire	89.7	1
2) Tours	89.7	2
6) Troyes	89.7	1
6) Agen	89.8	1
6) Brioude	89.8	1
23) Corte	89.8	1
3) Gray	89.8	1
18) Quimper	89.8	1
6) Sablé sur Sarthe	89.8	1
18) Toulon	89.8	4
19) Alès	89.9	1
17) Cognac	89.9	1
18) Douai	89.9	1
10) Épinal	89.9	1
19) Montpellier	89.9	3
20) Nancy	89.9	1
28) Paris	89.9	10
7) Périgueux	89.9	1
6) Saint Dizier	89.9	1
20) Saint Girons	89.9	1
18) Saint Raphaël	89.9	1
20) Bagnères de Bigorre	90.0	1
17) Bayeux	90.0	1
22) Brest	90.0	3
13) Cosne Cours/Loire	90.0	1
23) Marseille	90.0	10
21) Quimperlé	90.0	1
9) Royan	90.0	1
3) Vichy	90.0	1
6) Béthune	90.1	1
22) Évreux	90.1	1
18) Nantes	90.1	3
5) Neufchâteau	90.1	1
19) Perpignan	90.1	3
5) Poligny	90.1	1
9) Toul	90.1	1
23) Bar le Duc	90.2	1
3) Bergerac	90.2	1
9) La Ferté s/Jouarre	90.2	1
13) Melun	90.2	1
18) Mimizan	90.2	1
28) Nevers	90.2	1
14) Pau	90.2	1
20) Porto Vecchio	90.2	1
9) Thionville	90.2	1
17) Vannes	90.2	2
5) Bastia	90.3	4
13) Compiègne	90.3	1
18) Decazeville	90.3	1
17) Montargis	90.3	1
4) Montmorillon	90.3	1
24) Pamiers	90.3	1
3) Saumur	90.3	1
19) Valence	90.3	1
20) Abbeville	90.4	1
6) Auch	90.4	1
13) Beauvais	90.4	1
5) Bourg en Bresse	90.4	1
10) Caen	90.4	2
5) Calvi	90.4	1
13) Châteaudun	90.4	1
22) Dinan	90.4	1
21) Longwy	90.4	1
13) Paris	90.4	10
23) Sablé sur Sarthe	90.4	1
19) Alès	90.5	1
8) Bourges	90.5	1
26) Brest	90.5	1
13) Chartres	90.5	1
23) Le Mans	90.5	2
24) Limoges	90.5	1
5) Mont de Marsan	90.5	1
6) Narbonne	90.5	1
13) Rodez	90.5	1
23) Tours	90.5	2
4) Lourdes	90.6	1

FM Station	MHz	kW
7) Maubeuge	90.6	1
20) Melun	90.6	1
8) Millau	90.6	1
26) Creil	90.7	2
7) Dijon	90.7	1
18) Figeac	90.7	1
4) Laon	90.7	1
9) Laval	90.7	1
21) Périgueux	90.7	1
6) Soustons	90.7	1
13) Troyes	90.7	1
6) Avallon	90.8	1
1) Bastia	90.8	1
9) Château Thierry	90.8	1
9) La Flèche	90.8	1
3) Vannes	90.8	1
23) Vesoul	90.8	1
7) Annonay	90.9	1
19) Brest	90.9	3
6) Brive la Gaillarde	90.9	1
13) Montreuil	90.9	1
14) Poitiers	90.9	1
17) Segré	90.9	1
7) Villefranche /Saône	90.9	1
5) Ajaccio	91.0	8
19) Besançon	91.0	1
6) Bourges	91.0	1
10) Chambéry	91.0	1
9) Colmar	91.0	1
13) Fleurance	91.0	1
24) Le Puy en Velay	91.0	1
4) Sarrebourg	91.0	1
2) Sens	91.0	1
10) Vichy	91.0	1
5) Boulogne sur Mer	91.1	1
20) Dunkerque	91.1	1
19) Malataverne	91.1	1
8) Metz	91.1	1
19) Montélimar	91.1	1
8) Nancy	91.1	1
19) Orange	91.1	1
23) Pau	91.1	1
3) Villeneuve sur Lot	91.1	1
7) Aubusson	91.2	1
8) Épinal	91.2	1
6) Grenoble	91.2	1
9) Laval	91.2	1
22) Mulhouse	91.2	1
17) Orléans	91.2	2
6) Saint Tropez	91.2	1
19) Agen	91.3	1
19) Cahors	91.3	1
22) Cambrai	91.3	1
5) Dinan	91.3	1
3) Paris	91.3	10
27) Reims	91.3	1
19) Amiens	91.4	1
13) Bastia	91.4	4
10) Béziers	91.4	1
17) Brive la Gaillarde	91.4	1
18) Jonzac	91.4	1
21) Morlaix	91.4	1
7) Beaune	91.5	1
3) Blois	91.5	1
6) Boulogne sur Mer	91.5	1
22) Le Puy en Velay	91.5	1
26) Roanne	91.5	1
17) Clermont Ferrand	91.6	1
9) Corte	91.6	1
5) Dunkerque	91.6	1
17) Épernay	91.6	1
17) La Châtre	91.6	1
5) Lens	91.6	1
5) Perpignan	91.6	3
13) Royan	91.6	1
3) Tours	91.6	2
19) Agen	91.7	1
18) Bourgoin Jallieu	91.7	1
23) Cholet	91.7	1
17) Mortagne au Perche	91.7	1
14) Saint Étienne	91.7	2
17) Villefranche/Saône	91.7	1
7) Amiens	91.8	1
7) Bordeaux	91.8	5
8) Brioude	91.8	1

FM	Station	MHz	kW
3)	Castres	91.8	1
18)	La Rochelle	91.8	1
21)	Montélimar	91.8	1
7)	Montpellier	91.8	3
7)	Saint Dizier	91.8	1
7)	Saint Malo	91.8	1
7)	Saint Quentin	91.8	1
2)	Vichy	91.8	1
7)	Bressuire	91.9	1
9)	Chalon sur Saône	91.9	1
19)	Chaumont	91.9	1
4)	Civray	91.9	1
9)	Épinal	91.9	1
7)	Le Puy en Velay	91.9	1
7)	Lessay	91.9	1
9)	Porto Vecchio	91.9	1
8)	Salon de Provence	91.9	1
8)	Aix en Provence	92.0	1
8)	Albi	92.0	1
7)	Arcachon	92.0	1
23)	Auxerre	92.0	1
6)	Lille	92.0	2
23)	Montargis	92.0	1
13)	Pamiers	92.0	1
8)	Saint Affrique	92.0	1
7)	Saint Brieuc	92.0	1
10)	Saintes	92.0	1
19)	Soissons	92.0	1
3)	Brive la Gaillarde	92.1	1
21)	Cambrai	92.1	1
6)	Menton	92.1	1
18)	Nontron	92.1	1
19)	Troyes	92.1	1
13)	Amiens	92.2	1
22)	Béthune	92.2	1
10)	Bordeaux	92.2	1
7)	Colmar	92.2	1
7)	Dunkerque	92.2	1
4)	Lannemezan	92.2	1
7)	Laon	92.2	1
7)	Limoges	92.2 2	2.2
22)	Metz	92.2	1
22)	Mont de Marsan	92.2	1
5)	Montélimar	92.2	1
7)	Mulhouse	92.2	1
18)	Carcassonne	92.3	1
7)	Mimizan	92.3	1
10)	Rennes	92.3	1
13)	Vitry le François	92.3	1
23)	Albi	92.4	1
20)	Brest	92.4	1
14)	Montpellier	92.4	3
22)	Romilly sur Seine	92.4	1
5)	Saint Quentin	92.4	1
6)	Vannes	92.4	1
23)	Avignon	92.5	1
3)	Brive la Gaillarde	92.5	1
4)	Cahors	92.5	1
17)	Fontenay le Comte	92.5	1
17)	Issoudun	92.5	1
9)	Le Havre	92.5	1
5)	Lille	92.5	2
7)	Lourdes	92.5	3
19)	Rodez	92.5	1
1)	Aix en Provence	92.6	1
3)	Calvi	92.6	1
3)	Charolles	92.6	1
10)	Clermont Ferrand	92.6	1
3)	Corte	92.6	1
5)	Cosne Cours/Loire	92.6	1
23)	Nîmes	92.6	1
17)	Quimper	92.6	1
7)	Saint Raphaël	92.6	1
3)	Bastia	92.7	4
23)	Boulogne sur Mer	92.7	1
1)	Dreux	92.7	1
26)	Lorient	92.7	1
13)	Montélimar	92.7	1
22)	Rennes	92.7	1
9)	Béthune	92.8	1
10)	Blois	92.8	1
3)	Castres	92.8	1
22)	Grenoble	92.8	1
8)	Châteauroux	92.8	1
25)	Marseille	92.8	4
22)	Nice	92.8	5
23)	Vannes	92.8	1
3)	Cambrai	92.9	1
20)	Château Gontier	92.9	1
26)	Colmar	92.9	1
13)	Lyon	92.9	10
22)	Menton	92.9	1
7)	Montauban	92.9	3
10)	Orléans	92.9	2
25)	Roanne	92.9	1
7)	Rochefort	92.9	1
5)	St Amand Montrond	92.9	1
13)	Ajaccio	93.0	8
22)	Bonifacio	93.0	1
5)	Cosne Cours/Loire	93.0	1
5)	Courtenay	93.0	1
18)	Hirson	93.0	1
21)	Lille	93.0	2
9)	Lourdes	93.0	3
22)	Saint Raphaël	93.0	1
17)	Verdun	93.0	1
13)	Annecy	93.1	1
13)	Arcachon	93.1	1
6)	Bayeux	93.1	1
13)	Bourg en Bresse	93.1	1
21)	Châlons en Champ.	93.1	1
6)	Châteaudun	93.1	1
5)	Coutances	93.1	1
13)	Dole	93.1	1
8)	Ernée	93.1	1
23)	Fontenay le Comte	93.1	1
13)	La Tour du Pin	93.1	1
20)	Mulhouse	93.1	1
23)	Royan	93.1	1
13)	Saint Étienne	93.1	2
7)	Toulon	93.1	4
19)	Avallon	93.2	1
6)	Bergerac	93.2	1
9)	Commercy	93.2	1
5)	Evreux	93.2	1
8)	Guéret	93.2	1
23)	Nevers	93.2	1
21)	Provins	93.2	1
21)	Romilly sur Seine	93.2	1
22)	Saint Tropez	93.2	1
5)	Ussel	93.2	1
13)	Arras	93.3	1
5)	Dreux	93.3	1
13)	Grenoble	93.3	1
7)	Lyon	93.3	1
6)	Marmande	93.3	1
23)	Meaux	93.3	3
4)	Montauban	93.3	3
8)	Montluçon	93.3	1
18)	Orléans	93.3	2
5)	Pamiers	93.3	1
3)	Poitiers	93.3	1
15)	Paris	93.3	1
17)	Argentan	93.4	1
25)	Bourges	93.4	1
21)	Épernay	93.4	1
6)	Le Chambon s/Lignon	93.4	1
13)	Lille	93.4	1
8)	Marseille	93.4	4
7)	Moulins	93.4	1
10)	Narbonne	93.4	1
23)	Quimper	93.4	1
6)	Vic Fezensac	93.4	1
22)	Ajaccio	93.5	8
13)	Béthune	93.5	1
18)	Dax	93.5	1
14)	Metz	93.5	1
20)	Neufchâteau	93.5	1
10)	Amiens	93.6	1
10)	Angers	93.6	1
8)	Brest	93.6	1
4)	Calvi	93.6	1
18)	Evreux	93.6	1
13)	La Roche sur Yon	93.6	1
19)	Laon	93.6	1
17)	Mazamet	93.6	1
6)	Montbard	93.6	1
9)	Pau	93.6	1
8)	Saint Gaudens	93.6	1
22)	Grenoble	93.7	1
10)	Le Havre	93.7	1
8)	Lyon	93.7	1
17)	Nancy	93.7	1
13)	Orléans	93.7	2
25)	Reims	93.7	1
20)	Saint Nazaire	93.7	1
6)	Saintes	93.7	1
13)	Toulon	93.7	4
17)	Alençon	93.8	1
6)	Chaumont	93.8	1
27)	Marseille	93.8	4
18)	Montauban	93.8	3
7)	Orange	93.8	1
21)	Avallon	93.9	1
7)	Bar le Duc	93.9	1
17)	Bourg en Bresse	93.9	1
19)	Bourges	93.9	1
7)	Carcassonne	93.9	1
13)	Château Gontier	93.9	1
20)	Condom	93.9	1
9)	Épernay	93.9	1
18)	Guéret	93.9	1
20)	Jonzac	93.9	1
3)	Lille	93.9	1
25)	Nogent le Rotrou	93.9	1
13)	Saint Brieuc	93.9	1
20)	Vannes	93.9	1
13)	Verdun	93.9	1
7)	Avignon	94.0	1
6)	Pau	94.0	1
9)	Rochefort	94.0	1
22)	Saint Flour	94.0	1
4)	Thionville	94.0	1
1)	Troyes	94.0	1
21)	Ussel	94.0	1
6)	Arcachon	94.1	1
25)	Chartres	94.1	1
13)	Creil	94.1	2
19)	Decazeville	94.1	1
12)	Dijon	94.1	1
18)	Grenoble	94.1	1
8)	Mayenne	94.1	1
24)	Mont de Marsan	94.1	1
13)	Montmorillon	94.1	1
5)	Narbonne	94.1	1
4)	Saint Gaudens	94.1	1
13)	Soissons	94.1	1
13)	Châlons en Champ.	94.2	1
3)	Chaumont	94.2	1
5)	Saint Omer	94.2	1
13)	Tarbes	94.2	1
6)	Bordeaux	94.3	5
21)	Cosne Cours/Loire	94.3	1
18)	La Côte Saint André	94.3	1
18)	Le Mans	94.3	2
23)	Lille	94.3	1
23)	Lorient	94.3	1
15)	Paris	94.3	4
23)	Saint Dizier	94.3	1
1)	Saint Étienne	94.3	2
10)	Saint Raphaël	94.3	1
21)	Sens	94.3	1
8)	Clermont Ferrand	94.4	1
8)	Le Puy en Velay	94.4	1
22)	Loches	94.4	1
19)	Orléans	94.4	1
4)	Parthenay	94.4	1
18)	Pau	94.4	1
5)	St Gilles Croix de Vie	94.4	1
9)	Saintes	94.4	1
19)	Toulouse	94.4	1
5)	Creil	94.5	2
5)	Gournay en Bray	94.5	1
9)	La Rochelle	94.5	1
9)	Laval	94.5	1
9)	Mazamet	94.5	1
9)	Montmorillon	94.5	1
9)	Nevers	94.5	1
7)	Rennes	94.5	2
17)	Arcachon	94.6	1
13)	Chambéry	94.6	1
5)	Colmar	94.6	1
18)	Lannemezan	94.6	1
6)	Perpignan	94.6	3
13)	Pouzauges	94.6	1
6)	Reims	94.6	1
23)	Romilly sur Seine	94.6	1
7)	Saint Lô	94.6	1
5)	Béziers	94.7	1
18)	Fougères	94.7	1
18)	La Ferté Macé	94.7	1
13)	Le Havre	94.7	1
2)	Limoges	94.7	2
7)	Mende	94.7	1
6)	Nantes	94.7	3
4)	Poitiers	94.7	1
8)	Quimper	94.7	1
17)	Saint Étienne	94.7	2
22)	Sarrebourg	94.7	1
3)	Vesoul	94.7	1
6)	Angers	94.8	2
23)	Annecy	94.8	1
20)	Chalon sur Saône	94.8	1
9)	Chaumont	94.8	1
22)	Forbach	94.8	1
6)	Longwy	94.8	1
5)	Mulhouse	94.8	1
22)	Nancy	94.8	1
5)	Nîmes	94.8	1
20)	Riscle	94.8	1
5)	Avignon	94.9	1
12)	Bastia	94.9	1
14)	Bordeaux	94.9	1
7)	Caen	94.9	1
13)	Hirson	94.9	1
9)	La Roche sur Yon	94.9	1
13)	Le Puy en Velay	94.9	1
19)	Lyon	94.9	1
5)	Montpellier	94.9	3
8)	Rennes	94.9	1
24)	Alès	95.0	1
21)	Autun	95.0	1
7)	Chambéry	95.0	1
6)	Cholet	95.0	1
19)	Clermont Ferrand	95.0	1
9)	Dinan	95.0	1
19)	Grenoble	95.0	1
10)	Lorient	95.0	1
13)	Mimizan	95.0	1
9)	Montauban	95.0	3
7)	Nice	95.0	5
9)	Niort	95.0	1
13)	Porto Vecchio	95.0	1
3)	Aubusson	95.1	1
17)	Douai	95.1	1
23)	Épinal	95.1	1
13)	Mâcon	95.1	1
24)	Marseille	95.1	4
17)	Pithiviers	95.1	1
10)	Saint Étienne	95.1	2
9)	Saint Raphaël	95.1	1
3)	Ussel	95.1	1
3)	Béziers	95.2	1
21)	Dunkerque	95.2	1
21)	Fontenay le Comte	95.2	1
5)	Jussey	95.2	1
5)	Périgueux	95.2	1
24)	Tarascon	95.2	1
21)	Argentan	95.3	1
3)	Bordeaux	95.3	5
20)	Chartres	95.3	1
20)	Château Thierry	95.3	1
7)	Dax	95.3	1
21)	Evreux	95.3	1
10)	Le Puy en Velay	95.3	1
21)	Lisieux	95.3	1
2)	Lyon	95.3	10
3)	Mirande	95.3	1
13)	Montélimar	95.3	1
13)	Nancy	95.3	1
3)	Tarbes	95.3	1
4)	Toulon	95.3	4
18)	Cahors	95.4	1
13)	Chambéry	95.4	1
13)	Commercy	95.4	1
19)	Le Mans	95.4	2
23)	Orléans	95.4	2
17)	Pouzauges	95.4	1
17)	Ruffec	95.4	1
8)	Angers	95.5	1
5)	Annonay	95.5	1
24)	Bergerac	95.5	1
23)	Besançon	95.5	1
13)	Calvi	95.5	1
5)	Corte	95.5	1

FM Station	MHz	kW	FM Station	MHz	kW	FM Station	MHz	kW	FM Station	MHz	kW
17) La Rochelle	95.5	1	13) Granville	96.4	1	23) Carmaux	97.5	1	18) Mazamet	98.4	1
6) Mâcon	95.5	1	2) Lille	96.4	2	13) Corte	97.5	1	5) Mirande	98.4	1
19) Marseille	95.5	10	10) Lorient	96.4	1	13) Dijon	97.5	1	8) Royan	98.4	1
9) Millau	95.5	1	13) Mont de Marsan	96.4	1	7) Mayenne	97.5	1	18) Agen	98.5	1
19) Nogent le Rotrou	95.5	1	2) Paris	96.4	4	21) Neufchâteau	97.5	1	3) Alençon	98.5	1
6) Niort	95.6	1	9) Saint Quentin	96.4	1	3) Nogent le Rotrou	97.5	1	18) Bastia	98.5	1
11) Paris	95.6	4	19) Sarrebourg	96.4	1	3) Rouen	97.5	2	8) Beauvais	98.5	1
9) Saint Tropez	95.6	1	20) Bourges	96.5	1	7) Alès	97.6	1	17) Béziers	98.5	1
19) Vannes	95.6	1	6) Brest	96.5	3	18) Avallon	97.6	1	28) Bourg en Bresse	98.5	1
23) Le Puy en Velay	95.7	1	6) Colmar	96.5	1	23) Caen	97.6	2	21) Hirson	98.5	1
19) Lorient	95.7	1	10) Lyon	96.5	4	5) Chambéry	97.6	1	3) Laval	98.5	1
22) Lyon	95.7	4	20) Marmande	96.5	1	22) Fontenay le Comte	97.6	1	5) Albi	98.6	1
23) Metz	95.7	1	23) Saint Flour	96.5	1	3) Le Mans	97.6	2	22) Bergerac	98.6	1
23) Nancy	95.7	1	23) Saint Nazaire	96.5	1	7) L'Île Rousse	97.6	1	9) Cognac	98.6	1
23) Perpignan	95.7	3	23) Saint Omer	96.5	1	18) Menton	97.6	1	20) Dax	98.6	1
17) St Amand Montrond	95.7	1	5) Auxerre	96.6	1	6) Metz	97.6	1	18) La Roche sur Yon	98.6	1
13) Angoulême	95.8	1	6) Châteauroux	96.6	1	13) Montauban	97.6	3	18) Vannes	98.6	1
22) Chambéry	95.8	1	7) Clermont Ferrand	96.6	2	7) Pamiers	97.6	1	7) Auch	98.7	1
6) Montpellier	95.8	3	3) Nîmes	96.6	1	3) Perpignan	97.6	1	12) Caen	98.7	1
3) Nice	95.8	5	9) Toulon	96.6	4	13) Rennes	97.6	3	10) Chartres	98.7	1
21) Saint Brieuc	95.8	1	6) Yssingeaux	96.6	1	6) Bayonne	97.7	5	13) La Rochelle	98.7	1
23) Thionville	95.8	1	23) Abbeville	96.7	1	9) Castres	97.7	1	9) Le Puy en Velay	98.7	1
6) Toulon	95.8	4	23) Limoges	96.7	2	7) Compiègne	97.7	1	6) Niederbronn l. Bains	98.7	1
23) Beauvais	95.9	1	13) Montargis	96.7	1	2) Dreux	97.7	1	5) Argentan	98.8	1
18) Béthune	95.9	1	17) Saint Lô	96.7	1	4) Figeac	97.7	1	20) Cannes	98.8	1
6) Bourges	95.9	1	22) Thionville	96.7	1	28) Laval	97.7	1	21) Castres	98.8	1
13) Brioude	95.9	1	19) Angoulême	96.8	1	5) Maubeuge	97.7	1	7) Grenoble	98.8	1
18) Cavaillon	95.9	1	23) Brive la Gaillarde	96.8	1	6) Montargis	97.7	1	20) Lorient	98.8	1
18) Commercy	95.9	1	6) Caen	96.8	2	22) Nantes	97.7	3	20) Nice	98.8	1
17) La Tour du Pin	95.9	1	6) Cahors	96.8	1	2) Ussel	97.7	1	19) Toulon	98.8	4
10) Limoges	95.9	2	17) Cannes	96.8	1	15) Vienne	97.7	1	7) Valence	98.8	1
22) Mazamet	95.9	1	20) Châtellerault	96.8	1	24) Brive la Gaillarde	97.8	1	3) Arcachon	98.9	1
23) Montélimar	95.9	1	14) Dreux	96.8	1	6) Chalon sur Saône	97.8	1	6) Auxerre	98.9	1
3) Saint Étienne	95.9	2	7) Lille	96.8	1	1) Grenoble	97.8	1	7) Brest	98.9	3
3) Annecy	96.0	1	18) Mont de Marsan	96.8	1	17) Porto Vecchio	97.8	1	6) Le Creusot	98.9	1
9) Brignoles	96.0	1	13) Nantes	96.8	3	2) Reims	97.8	2	3) Lyon	98.9	1
23) Châteaudun	96.0	1	13) Redon	96.8	1	6) Saint Étienne	97.8	2	3) Mende	98.9	1
13) Châtillon sur Seine	96.0	1	13) Roanne	96.8	1	4) Bastia	97.9	1	3) Montauban	98.9	3
3) Cognac	96.0	1	13) Rochefort	96.8	1	13) Parthenay	97.9	1	21) Nemours	98.9	1
23) Grenoble	96.0	1	13) Valence	96.8	1	4) Toulouse	97.9	5	6) Sens	98.9	1
18) Lille	96.0	2	7) Arras	96.9	1	9) Angers	98.0	1	3) Vierzon	98.9	1
6) Lisieux	96.0	1	13) Guéret	96.9	1	18) Mirande	98.0	1	9) Amiens	99.0	1
13) Marseille	96.0	4	7) Montbard	96.9	1	6) Montélimar	98.0	1	22) Bayonne	99.0	2
23) Paris	96.0	10	3) Montpellier	96.9	3	23) Montluçon	98.0	1	10) Boulogne sur Mer	99.0	1
23) Valence	96.0	2	17) Moulins	96.9	1	23) Moulins	98.0	1	22) Carcassonne	99.0	1
22) Auxerre	96.1	1	18) Rennes	96.9	1	9) Vannes	98.0	1	5) La Ferté Macé	99.0	1
22) Béziers	96.1	2	1) Toulouse	96.9	1	23) Ajaccio	98.1	8	18) Metz	99.0	1
23) Chartres	96.1	1	21) Chambéry	97.0	1	18) Besançon	98.1	1	22) Poitiers	99.0	1
8) Decazeville	96.1	1	9) Condom	97.0	1	9) Dax	98.1	1	8) Royan	99.0	1
6) Le Puy en Velay	96.1	1	3) Mazamet	97.0	1	28) Nice	98.1	5	17) Saint Raphaël	99.0	1
23) Lyon	96.1	4	7) Albi	97.1	1	9) Périgueux	98.1	1	6) Ussel	99.0	1
23) Montauban	96.1	3	8) Bar le Duc	97.1	1	9) Saint Flour	98.1	2	3) Aurillac	99.1	1
19) Moulins	96.1	1	21) La Ferté s/Jouarre	97.1	1	20) Saintes	98.1	1	9) Cervione	99.1	2
6) Nancy	96.1	1	26) Montélimar	97.1	1	23) Samatan	98.1	1	3) Châteauroux	99.1	1
13) Saint Dizier	96.1	1	6) Montluçon	97.1	1	13) Sens	98.1	1	5) Châtillon sur Seine	99.1	1
6) Tours	96.1	2	6) Pouzauges	97.1	1	12) Strasbourg	98.1	1	9) Limoges	99.1	2
17) Vire	96.1	1	7) Bagnères de Bigorre	97.2	1	5) Annonay	98.2	1	20) Provins	99.1	1
25) Aix en Provence	96.2	1	10) Bourg en Bresse	97.2	1	13) Auxerre	98.2	1	18) Toulouse	99.1	5
19) Alençon	96.2	1	18) Chaumont	97.2	1	9) Avignon	98.2	1	3) Abbeville	99.2	1
6) Bar le Duc	96.2	1	19) Épinal	97.2	1	22) Bernay	98.2	1	25) Alençon	99.2	1
18) Brive la Gaillarde	96.2	1	7) Pithiviers	97.2	1	19) Bordeaux	98.2	1	23) Aubusson	99.2	1
22) Châteauroux	96.2	1	21) Propriano	97.2	1	22) Bourges	98.2	1	7) Bourges	99.2	1
23) Clermont Ferrand	96.2	1	18) Saint Omer	97.2	1	7) Compiègne	98.2	1	13) Brive la Gaillarde	99.2	1
23) Compiègne	96.2	1	20) Alençon	97.3	1	19) Limoges	98.2	2	22) Calais	99.2	1
6) Douai	96.2	1	21) Auch	97.3	1	6) Lourdes	98.2	3	4) Châtellerault	99.2	1
6) Dunkerque	96.2	1	19) Beauvais	97.3	1	23) Mâcon	98.2	1	7) Condom	99.2	1
23) Montbard	96.2	1	23) Bordeaux	97.3	5	17) Narbonne	98.2	1	7) Mont de Marsan	99.2	1
6) Saint Brieuc	96.2	1	22) Le Havre	97.3	1	22) Nevers	98.2	1	20) Narbonne	99.2	1
13) Sedan	96.2	1	25) Lyon	97.3	1	23) Niort	98.2	1	5) Nice	99.2	5
12) Amiens	96.3	1	7) Poitiers	97.3	1	12) Paris	98.2	4	25) Saint Lô	99.2	1
23) Annonay	96.3	1	8) Rodez	97.3	1	2) Quimperlé	98.2	1	23) Vichy	99.3	1
6) Bourg en Bresse	96.3	1	6) Vire	97.3	1	3) Sablé sur Sarthe	98.2	1	3) Argentan	99.3	1
6) Caen	96.3	2	21) Agen	97.4	1	12) Toulon	98.2	1	22) Cambrai	99.3	1
7) L'Aigle	96.3	1	22) Bayeux	97.4	1	13) Tours	98.2	2	13) L'Aigle	99.3	1
6) Montluçon	96.3	1	13) Brest	97.4	3	13) Aix en Provence	98.3	1	14) Laval	99.3	1
6) Morlaix	96.3	1	21) Grenoble	97.4	1	7) Bar le Duc	98.3	1	18) Montpellier	99.3	3
7) Nogent le Rotrou	96.3	1	23) Mont de Marsan	97.4	1	9) Gien	98.3	1	6) Saint Nazaire	99.3	1
17) Rennes	96.3	1	4) Morhange	97.4	1	17) Montpellier	98.3	3	10) Avignon	99.4	1
9) Rodez	96.3	1	21) Nice	97.4	5	3) Rouen	98.3	1	7) Bastia	99.4	4
7) Saint Étienne	96.3	2	19) Paris	97.4	4	21) Saint Affrique	98.3	1	3) Calvi	99.4	1
2) Annecy	96.4	1	18) Saint Malo	97.4	1	23) Saint Quentin	98.3	1	5) Charolles	99.4	1
22) Bastia	96.4	4	3) Toulouse	97.4	2	20) Sarrebourg	98.3	1	25) Clermont Ferrand	99.4	1
17) Blois	96.4	1	23) Argentan	97.5	1	23) Amiens	98.4	1	5) Fontainebleau	99.4	2
22) Calvi	96.4	1.3	18) Béziers	97.5	1	13) Chaumont	98.4	1	3) Mâcon	99.4	1
20) Cosne Cours/Loire	96.4	1				21) Falaise	98.4	1	7) Mazamet	99.4	1
7) Épernay	96.4	1				3) La Flèche	98.4	1			

FM	Station	MHz	kW
27)	Metz	99.4	1
13)	Mulhouse	99.4	1
5)	Saint Malo	99.4	1
3)	Châteaudun	99.5	1
13)	Eauze	99.5	1
27)	Paris	99.5	4
13)	Toulouse	99.5	1
6)	Abbeville	99.6	1
25)	Aurillac	99.6	1
18)	Bordeaux	99.6	5
6)	Bourges	99.6	1
3)	Carcassonne	99.6	1
17)	Carmaux	99.6	1
22)	Cholet	99.6	1
18)	Dijon	99.6	1
5)	Ile de Ré	99.6	1
17)	Limoges	99.6	2
5)	Porto Vecchio	99.6	1
17)	Quimperlé	99.6	1
7)	Salon de Provence	99.6	1
9)	Vichy	99.6	1
6)	Bagnères de Bigorre	99.7	1
7)	Brest	99.7	3
13)	La Flèche	99.7	1
7)	Marseille	99.7	4
22)	Montauban	99.7	3
6)	Nevers	99.7	1
6)	Orléans	99.7	1
3)	Troyes	99.7	1
3)	Ajaccio	99.8	8
21)	Chartres	99.8	1
9)	Guéret	99.8	1
17)	Lavaur	99.8	1
9)	Menton	99.8	1
18)	Montargis	99.8	1
6)	Mulhouse	99.8	1
21)	Noyon	99.8	1
21)	Parthenay	99.8	1
19)	Argentan	99.9	1
9)	Mimizan	99.9	1
7)	Nîmes	99.9	1
24)	Paris	99.9	4
9)	Quimper	99.9	1
7)	Belfort	100.0	1
23)	Béziers	100.0	1
9)	Fontenay le Comte	100.0	1
2)	Laval	100.0	1
3)	L'Île Rousse	100.0	1
13)	Limoges	100.0	2
9)	Montélimar	100.0	1
9)	Pithiviers	100.0	1
9)	Poitiers	100.0	1
22)	Porto Vecchio	100.0	1
3)	Rodez	100.0	1
13)	Romilly sur Seine	100.0	2
23)	Toulouse	100.0	2
18)	Angers	100.1	1
6)	Bagnères de Bigorre	100.1	1
3)	Bayonne	100.1	3
9)	Carcassonne	100.1	1
13)	Châteauroux	100.1	1
3)	Marseille	100.1	4
3)	Meaux	100.1	3
9)	Melun	100.1	1
22)	Reims	100.1	2
20)	Saint Brieuc	100.1	1
9)	Sens	100.1	1
23)	Alès	100.2	1
14)	Brest	100.2	1
7)	Chinon	100.2	1
5)	Coutances	100.2	1
13)	Gien	100.2	1
6)	Guéret	100.2	1
9)	La Rochelle	100.2	1
23)	Montpellier	100.2	3
3)	Orthez	100.2	1
9)	Troyes	100.2	1
9)	Valence	100.2	2
14)	Agen	100.3	1
6)	Angoulême	100.3	1
7)	Le Mans	100.3	2
6)	Lyon	100.3	4
13)	Mende	100.3	1
3)	Mont de Marsan	100.3	1
3)	Narbonne	100.3	1
9)	Paris	100.3	10

FM	Station	MHz	kW
19)	St Gilles Croix de Vie	100.3	1
9)	Soissons	100.3	1
24)	Arcachon	100.4	1
6)	Besançon	100.4	1
21)	Bourges	100.4	1
9)	Chartres	100.4	1
22)	Chaumont	100.4	1
4)	Corte	100.4	1
13)	Lens	100.4	1
6)	Limoges	100.4	2.2
9)	Niort	100.4	1
22)	Royan	100.4	1
21)	Toulon	100.4	4
9)	Toulouse	100.4	5
17)	Tours	100.4	1
9)	Alençon	100.5	1
9)	Annecy	100.5	1
9)	Argentan	100.5	1
21)	Brive la Gaillarde	100.5	1
9)	Château Gontier	100.5	1
6)	Compiègne	100.5	1
3)	La Tour du Pin	100.5	1
12)	Marseille	100.5	2
23)	Mulhouse	100.5	1
9)	Nogent le Rotrou	100.5	1
18)	Rodez	100.5	1
9)	Rouen	100.5	2
18)	Ruffec	100.5	1
22)	Saint Étienne	100.5	2
9)	Saint Nazaire	100.5	1
9)	Albi	100.6	1
9)	Avallon	100.6	1
7)	Blois	100.6	1
6)	Bourg en Bresse	100.6	1
3)	Brioude	100.6	1
9)	Carcassonne	100.6	1
3)	Dijon	100.6	1
3)	Douarnenez	100.6	1
9)	Ghisonaccia	100.6	4
5)	Parthenay	100.6	1
17)	Reims	100.6	2
20)	Villeneuve sur Lot	100.6	1
13)	Béziers	100.7	1
6)	Decazeville	100.7	1
13)	Laon	100.7	1
13)	Laval	100.7	1
13)	Le Mans	100.7	2
13)	Le Puy en Velay	100.7	1
4)	Paris	100.7	10
9)	Bastia	100.8	4
9)	Calvi	100.8	1
20)	Castres	100.8	1
23)	Chambéry	100.8	1
3)	Clermont Ferrand	100.8	1
2)	Grenoble	100.8	1
5)	Lisieux	100.8	1
4)	Nîmes	100.8	1
12)	Perpignan	100.8	1
7)	Saint Gaudens	100.8	1
8)	Thouars	100.8	1
20)	Vire	100.8	1
6)	Alençon	100.9	1
9)	Bayonne	100.9	5
9)	Besançon	100.9	1
10)	Marseille	100.9	10
9)	Nancy	100.9	1
22)	Rodez	100.9	1
3)	Amiens	101.0	1
24)	Aurillac	101.0	1
14)	Avignon	101.0	1
23)	Bergerac	101.0	1
13)	Château Thierry	101.0	1
5)	L'Aigle	101.0	1
5)	Lourdes	101.0	3
6)	Quimper	101.0	1
9)	Agen	101.1	1
9)	Aubusson	101.1	1
17)	Bar le Duc	101.1	1
10)	Beauvais	101.1	1
9)	Châteauroux	101.1	1
4)	Ghisonaccia	101.1	1
6)	La Roche sur Yon	101.1	1
10)	Laval	101.1	1
11)	Le Havre	101.1	1

FM	Station	MHz	kW
13)	Metz	101.1	1
10)	Paris	101.1	10
23)	Poitiers	101.1	1
9)	Saint Malo	101.1	1
9)	Ajaccio	101.2	8
24)	Albi	101.2	1
9)	Arras	101.2	1
13)	Blois	101.2	1
21)	Chaumont	101.2	1
9)	Clermont Ferrand	101.2	1
7)	Épinal	101.2	1
3)	Chambéry	101.3	1
21)	Châtellerault	101.3	1
22)	Dreux	101.3	1
9)	Dunkerque	101.3	1
4)	Forbach	101.3	1
6)	Jonzac	101.3	1
22)	La Rochelle	101.3	1
7)	La Tour du Pin	101.3	1
21)	Le Blanc	101.3	1
9)	Lille	101.3	2
5)	Menton	101.3	1
20)	Orange	101.3	1
19)	Saint Étienne	101.3	2
9)	Sarlat la Canéda	101.3	1
10)	Amiens	101.4	1
9)	Caen	101.4	2
17)	Longwy	101.4	1
21)	Marseille	101.4	10
5)	Nice	101.4	5
21)	St Gilles Croix de Vie	101.4	1
24)	Toulouse	101.4	1
9)	Vic Fezensac	101.4	1
18)	Alès	101.5	1
9)	Cahors	101.5	1
14)	Évreux	101.5	1
5)	Montbard	101.5	1
18)	Nevers	101.5	1
14)	Paris	101.5	10
13)	Poitiers	101.5	1
21)	Redon	101.5	1
21)	Rodez	101.5	1
17)	Valence	101.5	1
19)	Vendôme	101.5	1
18)	Cambrai	101.6	1
5)	Chaumont	101.6	1
18)	Issoudun	101.6	1
10)	Le Mans	101.6	2
5)	Mâcon	101.6	1
20)	Montargis	101.6	1
23)	Périgueux	101.6	1
10)	Quimper	101.6	1
21)	Saint Malo	101.6	1
13)	Valence	101.6	1
21)	Albi	101.7	1
6)	Bayeux	101.7	1
5)	Bayonne	101.7	5
18)	Compiègne	101.7	1
17)	Cosne Cours/Loire	101.7	1
17)	Le Puy en Velay	101.7	1
22)	Limoges	101.7	2.2
21)	Mazamet	101.7	1
18)	Montluçon	101.7	1
22)	Montpellier	101.7	1
23)	Morlaix	101.7	1
9)	Provins	101.7	1
7)	Reims	101.7	2
13)	Romilly sur Seine	101.7	1
22)	Tarascon	101.7	1
6)	Aubusson	101.8	1
6)	Auxerre	101.8	1
9)	Bergerac	101.8	1
23)	Brest	101.8	3
21)	Laon	101.8	1
6)	Le Havre	101.8	1
4)	Aix en Provence	101.9	1
3)	Cahors	101.9	1
9)	Châtillon sur Seine	101.9	1
6)	Cognac	101.9	1
9)	Coutances	101.9	1
7)	Évreux	101.9	1
4)	Martigues	101.9	1
9)	Mayenne	101.9	1
18)	Moulins	101.9	1
7)	Paris	101.9	10
9)	Tonnerre	101.9	1

FM	Station	MHz	kW
17)	Vendôme	101.9	1
7)	Abbeville	102.0	1
6)	Bar le Duc	102.0	1
17)	Beaune	102.0	1
5)	Épinal	102.0	1
6)	Falaise	102.0	1
23)	La Rochelle	102.0	1
4)	Metz	102.0	1
6)	Neufchâteau	102.0	1
22)	Quimper	102.0	1
6)	Rennes	102.0	3
21)	Saint Quentin	102.0	1
24)	Toulouse	102.0	60
7)	Annecy	102.1	1
20)	Avallon	102.1	1
20)	Calvi	102.1	1
9)	Charolles	102.1	1
18)	Limoges	102.1	2.2
26)	Melun	102.1	1
9)	Mulhouse	102.1	1
6)	Nîmes	102.1	1
7)	St Amand Montrond	102.1	1
18)	Strasbourg	102.1	4
9)	Arcachon	102.2	1
9)	Blois	102.2	1
21)	Dole	102.2	1
17)	La Ferté Macé	102.2	1
7)	Montargis	102.2	1
9)	Thouars	102.2	1
7)	Troyes	102.2	1
9)	Avranches	102.3	1
13)	Cahors	102.3	1
17)	Chambéry	102.3	1
9)	Forbach	102.3	1
21)	Le Puy en Velay	102.3	1
9)	Marseille	102.3	10
9)	Montbard	102.3	1
9)	Nancy	102.3	1
21)	Nevers	102.3	1
26)	Paris	102.3	4
3)	Quimperlé	102.3	1
9)	Saint Brieuc	102.3	1
9)	Saint Omer	102.3	1
10)	Tours	102.3	2
7)	Auxerre	102.4	1
9)	Bordeaux	102.4	5
9)	Brest	102.4	1
9)	Castres	102.4	1
3)	Chalon sur Saône	102.4	1
20)	Chaumont	102.4	1
9)	Decazeville	102.4	1
10)	Grenoble	102.4	1
6)	Haguenau	102.4	1
5)	Montmorillon	102.4	1
9)	Nantes	102.4	3
9)	Perpignan	102.4	3
2)	Rennes	102.4	1
9)	Romorantin Lanthen.	102.4	1
6)	Thionville	102.4	1
6)	Toulouse	102.4	5
2)	Vienne	102.4	1
22)	Angers	102.5	1
9)	Calais	102.5	1
24)	Carmaux	102.5	1
5)	Chartres	102.5	1
6)	Commercy	102.5	1
3)	Dijon	102.5	1
18)	Gourdon	102.5	1
5)	Melun	102.5	1
9)	Niort	102.5	1
18)	Angoulême	102.6	1
13)	Bergerac	102.6	1
21)	Montauban	102.6	3
27)	Orléans	102.6	1
3)	Quimper	102.6	1
9)	Saint Gaudens	102.6	1
20)	Troyes	102.6	1
22)	Abbeville	102.7	1
22)	Avallon	102.7	1
9)	Limoges	102.7	2
5)	Morlaix	102.7	1
9)	Nérac	102.7	1
8)	Paris	102.7	10
20)	Rochefort	102.7	1
9)	Saint Dizier	102.7	1

FM	Station	MHz	kW
5)	Saint Flour	102.7	1
18)	Valence	102.7	1
13)	Alès	102.8	1
9)	Annecy	102.8	1
18)	Annonay	102.8	1
13)	Avignon	102.8	1
23)	Bordeaux	102.8	5
9)	Bourg en Bresse	102.8	1
22)	Brive la Gaillarde	102.8	1
21)	Dax	102.8	1
17)	Lorient	102.8	1
20)	Parthenay	102.8	1
9)	Saint Étienne	102.8	2
2)	Saint Raphaël	102.8	3
7)	Tours	102.8	2
9)	Vitré	102.8	1
13)	Charolles	102.9	1
14)	Clermont Ferrand	102.9	1
21)	Confolens	102.9	1
5)	Guéret	102.9	1
1)	Le Mans	102.9	2
21)	Lourdes	102.9	3
9)	Lunéville	102.9	1
23)	Nantes	102.9	3
9)	Saint Lô	102.9	1
24)	Villeneuve sur Lot	102.9	1
17)	Carcassonne	103.0	1
9)	Chambéry	103.0	1
9)	Châteaudun	103.0	1
13)	Colmar	103.0	1
6)	Condom	103.0	1
18)	Le Puy en Velay	103.0	1
9)	Lyon	103.0	10
3)	Metz	103.0	1
21)	Moulins	103.0	1
17)	Neufchâtel en Bray	103.0	1
12)	Poitiers	103.0	1
7)	Tonnerre	103.0	1
23)	Angoulême	103.1	1
21)	Arcachon	103.1	1
3)	Bar le Duc	103.1	1
20)	Bergerac	103.1	1
17)	Charensat	103.1	1
2)	Marseille	103.1	4
20)	Mont de Marsan	103.1	1
20)	Paris	103.1	10
5)	Roanne	103.1	1
24)	Saint Affrique	103.1	1
3)	Saint Dizier	103.1	1
13)	Saint Flour	103.1	1
10)	Toulouse	103.1	5
22)	Amiens	103.2	1
21)	Belfort	103.2	1
21)	Cervione	103.2	1
17)	Dole	103.2	1
6)	Douarnenez	103.2	1
9)	Grenoble	103.2	1
9)	Mirande	103.2	1
20)	Montmorillon	103.2	1
19)	Niort	103.2	1
20)	Nogent le Rotrou	103.2	1
24)	Perpignan	103.2	10
20)	Albi	103.3	1
21)	Aurillac	103.3	1
21)	Avesnes sur Helpe	103.3	1
6)	Carpentras	103.3	1
6)	Chartres	103.3	1
11)	Compiègne	103.3	1
20)	La Rochelle	103.3	1
20)	Lille	103.3	2
7)	Nancy	103.3	1
7)	Nérac	103.3	1
20)	Orthez	103.3	1
21)	Rouen	103.3	2
20)	Sarlat la Canéda	103.3	1
5)	Strasbourg	103.3	4
10)	Toulon	103.3	1
7)	Vichy	103.3	1
2)	Bastia	103.4	1
25)	Cahors	103.4	1
13)	Carcassonne	103.4	1
7)	Metz	103.4	1
7)	Nantes	103.4	3
12)	Orléans	103.4	1
20)	Rodez	103.4	1
5)	Saint Lô	103.4	1
25)	Tours	103.4	2
6)	Beauvais	103.5	1
7)	Dinan	103.5	1
6)	Épinal	103.5	1
19)	Le Havre	103.5	1
6)	Le Mans	103.5	1
9)	Morlaix	103.5	1
6)	Paris	103.5	10
9)	Saint Affrique	103.5	1
23)	Angers	103.6	2
21)	Blois	103.6	1
7)	Longwy	103.6	1
5)	Montluçon	103.6	1
20)	Saint Gaudens	103.6	1
7)	Saint Nazaire	103.6	1
23)	Alençon	103.7	1
6)	Creil	103.7	2
6)	Fontainebleau	103.7	2
17)	Grenoble	103.7	1
23)	Laval	103.7	1
6)	Meaux	103.7	3
20)	Mirande	103.7	1
18)	Niort	103.7	1
21)	Bastia	103.8	4
21)	Bergerac	103.8	1
17)	Chinon	103.8	1
24)	Figeac	103.8	1
22)	Lorient	103.8	1
20)	Lourdes	103.8	3
4)	Nantes	103.8	2
5)	Saint Brieuc	103.8	2
18)	Troyes	103.8	1
9)	Ussel	103.8	1
24)	Bayonne	103.9	5
18)	Beauvais	103.9	1
21)	Calvi	103.9	1
18)	Épinal	103.9	1
18)	Le Havre	103.9	1
20)	Le Mans	103.9	2
21)	Montpellier	103.9	2
9)	Rennes	103.9	3
21)	Saint Dizier	103.9	1
19)	Saint Flour	103.9	1
5)	Saint Lô	103.9	1
3)	Saint Quentin	103.9	1
21)	Toulouse	103.9	5
21)	Vierzon	103.9	1
17)	Avignon	104.0	1
21)	Besançon	104.0	1
3)	Cervione	104.0	1
2)	Mauriac	104.0	1
2)	Metz	104.0	1
21)	Millau	104.0	1
21)	Romorantin Lanthen.	104.0	1
18)	St Gilles Croix de Vie	104.0	1
21)	Tours	104.0	2
24)	Villefranche Rouerg.	104.0	1
21)	Abbeville	104.1	1
21)	Alençon	104.1	1
9)	Bressuire	104.1	1
18)	Chartres	104.1	1
20)	Compiègne	104.1	1
17)	Confolens	104.1	1
21)	Laval	104.1	1
20)	Mâcon	104.1	1
24)	Mazamet	104.1	1
20)	Melun	104.1	1
8)	Menton	104.1	1
20)	Montauban	104.1	3
20)	Montélimar	104.1	1
21)	Montluçon	104.1	1
2)	Nancy	104.1	1
6)	Rouen	104.1	1
20)	Annecy	104.2	1
20)	Bordeaux	104.2	5
21)	Dijon	104.2	1
20)	Grenoble	104.2	1
20)	Lyon	104.2	4
21)	Mende	104.2	1
4)	Mirande	104.2	1
21)	Nogent le Rotrou	104.2	1
20)	Troyes	104.2	1
20)	Ajaccio	104.3	8
21)	Amiens	104.3	1
21)	Angers	104.3	1
20)	Bastia	104.3	4
20)	Bayonne	104.3	5
20)	Béziers	104.3	1
20)	Bonifacio	104.3	1
21)	Brest	104.3	3
21)	Clermont Ferrand	104.3	2
21)	Épinal	104.3	1
21)	La Ferté Macé	104.3	1
21)	La Rochelle	104.3	1
21)	Le Havre	104.3	1
21)	Le Mans	104.3	2
21)	Limoges	104.3	2.2
21)	Lorient	104.3	1
20)	Marseille	104.3	10
17)	Montbard	104.3	1
20)	Montpellier	104.3	3
21)	Nantes	104.3	3
13)	Neufchâteau	104.3	1
20)	Nîmes	104.3	1
21)	Orléans	104.3	2
21)	Paris	104.3	10
20)	Pau	104.3	1
21)	Péronne	104.3	1
21)	Perpignan	104.3	3
21)	Poitiers	104.3	1
21)	Quimper	104.3	1
21)	Rennes	104.3	3
20)	Saint Affrique	104.3	1
21)	St Amand Montrond	104.3	1
21)	Saint Nazaire	104.3	1
21)	Soissons	104.3	1
20)	Toulon	104.3	4
20)	Toulouse	104.3	5
21)	Valence	104.3	1
21)	Vannes	104.3	1
21)	Aubusson	104.4	1
21)	Auxerre	104.4	1
7)	Bourg en Bresse	104.4	1
21)	Jonzac	104.4	1
20)	Le Puy en Velay	104.4	1
19)	Montargis	104.4	1
2)	Nice	104.4	5
21)	Reims	104.4	2
24)	Rodez	104.4	1
18)	Romorantin Lanthen.	104.4	1
13)	Ruffec	104.4	1
20)	Saint Étienne	104.4	1
20)	Agen	104.5	1
5)	Alençon	104.5	1
20)	Arles	104.5	1
20)	Avignon	104.5	1
7)	Baccarat	104.5	1
20)	Chambéry	104.5	1
21)	Compiègne	104.5	1
19)	Forbach	104.5	1
17)	La Roche sur Yon	104.5	1
5)	Laval	104.5	1
9)	Le Creusot	104.5	1
5)	Melun	104.5	1
17)	Redon	104.5	1
21)	Rouen	104.5	2
5)	Tours	104.5	2
1)	Alès	104.6	1
3)	Avallon	104.6	1
5)	Bayeux	104.6	1
5)	Bordeaux	104.6	5
5)	Grenoble	104.6	1
5)	L'Aigle	104.6	1
5)	Lyon	104.6	4
5)	Nevers	104.6	1
5)	Nogent le Rotrou	104.6	1
5)	Propriano	104.6	1
20)	Saint Flour	104.6	1
21)	Saint Raphaël	104.6	1
22)	Zonza	104.6	1
5)	Amiens	104.7	1
5)	Angers	104.7	1
5)	Beauvais	104.7	1
5)	Brest	104.7	3
24)	Carcassonne	104.7	80
5)	Cholet	104.7	1
5)	Clermont Ferrand	104.7	2
5)	Dijon	104.7	1
22)	Ghisonaccia	104.7	2
5)	La Rochelle	104.7	1
5)	Le Mans	104.7	2
5)	Limoges	104.7	2.2
5)	Lorient	104.7	1
24)	Montpellier	104.7	1
5)	Nantes	104.7	3
5)	Orléans	104.7	2
5)	Paris	104.7	10
5)	Poitiers	104.7	1
5)	Quimper	104.7	1
5)	Rennes	104.7	2
5)	Saint Nazaire	104.7	1
5)	Soissons	104.7	1
5)	Toulon	104.7	4
5)	Troyes	104.7	1
5)	Vannes	104.7	1
5)	Annecy	104.8	1
5)	Arcachon	104.8	1
3)	Argentan	104.8	1
20)	Aubusson	104.8	1
20)	Auxerre	104.8	1
5)	Bernay	104.8	1
5)	Cambrai	104.8	1
5)	Châlons en Champ.	104.8	1
4)	Gourdon	104.8	1
5)	La Tour du Pin	104.8	1
5)	Marseille	104.8	10
21)	Metz	104.8	1
18)	Neufchâteau	104.8	1
13)	St Amand Montrond	104.8	1
5)	Saint Étienne	104.8	2
18)	Saint Lô	104.8	1
5)	Valence	104.8	1
5)	Abbeville	104.9	1
5)	Agen	104.9	1
5)	Besançon	104.9	1
7)	Chartres	104.9	1
5)	Compiègne	104.9	1
7)	La Roche sur Yon	104.9	1
22)	Laval	104.9	1
5)	Mont de Marsan	104.9	1
7)	Montereau F/Yonne	104.9	1
5)	Moulins	104.9	1
5)	Parthenay	104.9	1
24)	Périgueux	104.9	1
5)	Rouen	104.9	2
21)	Royan	104.9	1
20)	Angoulême	105.0	1
20)	Auch	105.0	1
21)	Bar le Duc	105.0	1
21)	Caen	105.0	2
24)	Cahors	105.0	1
21)	L'Aigle	105.0	1
13)	Luxeuil les Bains	105.0	1
21)	Lyon	105.0	4
7)	Morlaix	105.0	1
23)	Reims	105.0	2
22)	Alençon	105.1	1
3)	Angers	105.1	2
21)	Bayonne	105.1	5
9)	Bonifacio	105.1	1
21)	Bordeaux	105.1	5
21)	Charolles	105.1	1
20)	Clermont Ferrand	105.1	1
9)	Dinan	105.1	1
25)	Le Puy en Velay	105.1	1
20)	Limoges	105.1	1
21)	Nancy	105.1	1
20)	Niort	105.1	1
17)	Toulon	105.1	4
7)	Ajaccio	105.2	8
20)	Brive la Gaillarde	105.2	1
21)	Épinal	105.2	1
9)	Issoudun	105.2	1
3)	Lons le Saunier	105.2	1
5)	Montauban	105.2	3
21)	Saint Étienne	105.2	2
13)	Saint Lô	105.2	1
21)	Vitré	105.2	1
3)	Chartres	105.3	1
19)	Cholet	105.3	1
5)	Metz	105.3	1
13)	Rouen	105.3	1
22)	Sens	105.3	1
13)	Strasbourg	105.3	4

FM Station	MHz	kW	FM Station	MHz	kW	FM Station	MHz	kW	FM Station	MHz	kW
18) Dole	105.4	1	5) Castres	106.3	1	19) Châteauroux	106.9	1	2) Angers	107.2	1
5) Nancy	105.5	1	25) Dijon	106.3	1	22) Compiègne	106.9	1	21) Avignon	107.2	1
12) Lens	105.6	1	5) Ghisonaccia	106.3	1	8) Grenoble	106.9	1	6) Bastia	107.2	1
9) Béziers	105.7	1	6) Laon	106.3	1	8) La Roche sur Yon	106.9	1	20) Blois	107.2	1
23) Bonifacio	105.7	1	20) Moulins	106.3	1	7) Le Havre	106.9	1	21) Figeac	107.2	1
7) Lannemezan	105.7	1	21) Pau	106.3	1	8) Le Mans	106.9	2	14) Limoges	107.2	2
21) Le Creusot	105.7	1	13) Quimper	106.3	1	7) Lorient	106.9	1	19) Mâcon	107.2	1
20) Lesparre Médoc	105.7	1	22) Saint Brieuc	106.3	1	9) Mantes la Jolie	106.9	2	2) Nantes	107.2	3
17) Loches	105.7	1	5) Sarlat la Canéda	106.3	1	5) Mazamet	106.9	1	10) Pau	107.2	1
14) Marseille	105.7	1	5) Toulouse	106.3	5	23) Melun	106.9	1	2) Rochefort	107.2	1
7) Neufchâteau	105.7	1	13) Tours	106.3	2	3) Mers les Bains	106.9	1	7) Soissons	107.2	1
9) Redon	105.7	1	8) Vannes	106.3	1	21) Montpellier	106.9	3	2) Toulouse	107.2	1
3) Saint Flour	105.7	2	5) Avallon	106.4	1	8) Périgueux	106.9	1	20) Tours	107.2	2
19) Sancerre	105.7	1	15) Bordeaux	106.4	5	18) Poligny	106.9	1	24) Ussel	107.2	1
21) Strasbourg	105.7	4	8) Caen	106.4	2	5) Propriano	106.9	1	7) Arnay le Duc	107.3	1
13) Vesoul	105.7	1	8) Chambéry	106.4	1	5) Provins	106.9	1	3) Arras	107.3	1
17) Argenton sur Creuse	105.8	1	18) Clermont Ferrand	106.4	1	5) Romilly sur Seine	106.9	1.2	10) Auxerre	107.3	1
4) Carcassonne	105.8	1	5) Marseille	106.4	10	26) Saint Lô	106.9	1	2) Bordeaux	107.3	1
10) Dijon	105.8	1	5) Montargis	106.4	1	2) Strasbourg	106.9	1	2) Brest	107.3	3.2
3) Grenoble	105.8	1	10) Troyes	106.4	1	5) Bar le Duc	107.0	1	10) Brive la Gaillarde	107.3	1
9) Nîmes	105.8	1	10) Valence	106.4	1	8) Bressuire	107.0	1	1) Carcassonne	107.3	1
23) Segré	105.8	1	7) Agen	106.5	1	8) Cahors	107.0	1	10) Chantilly	107.3	4
5) Bourges	105.9	1	5) Aurillac	106.5	1	2) Château Thierry	107.0	1	3) Châteauroux	107.3	1
18) Brest	105.9	3	5) Blois	106.5	1	2) Clermont Ferrand	107.0	1	21) Colmar	107.3	1
5) Caen	105.9	2	5) Châteauroux	106.5	1	23) La Ferté Macé	107.0	1	9) Dax	107.3	1
22) Clermont Ferrand	105.9	1	15) Évreux	106.5	1	6) L'Aigle	107.0	1	23) Évreux	107.3	1
21) Corte	105.9	1	9) Fougères	106.5	1	5) Le Puy en Velay	107.0	1	3) Lens	107.3	1
9) Ghisonaccia	105.9	2	17) Lons le Saunier	106.5	1	23) Mont de Marsan	107.0	1	18) Lorient	107.3	1
9) Le Mans	105.9	1	22) Lourdes	106.5	1	8) Montauban	107.0	1	8) Lyon	107.3	2
9) Mende	105.9	1	13) Nogent le Rotrou	106.5	1	17) Montluçon	107.0	1	5) Mazamet	107.3	1
22) Paris	105.9	10	22) Périgueux	106.5	1	23) Nice	107.0	5	2) Menton	107.3	1
7) Pau	105.9	1	5) Reims	106.5	2	21) Nîmes	107.0	1	9) Metz	107.3	1
20) Périgueux	105.9	1	23) Saint Étienne	106.5	2	22) Porto Vecchio	107.0	1	5) Millau	107.3	1
9) Perpignan	105.9	1	17) Yvetot	106.5	1	7) Rouen	107.0	1	10) Montpellier	107.3	3
13) Saint Nazaire	105.9	1	22) Albi	106.6	1	8) Saint Quentin	107.0	1	20) Orléans	107.3	1
21) Saintes	105.9	1	10) Brest	106.6	3	1) Valence	107.0	1	2) Parthenay	107.3	1
7) Toulouse	105.9	5	20) Cahors	106.6	1	19) Abbeville	107.1	1	21) Perpignan	107.3	3
23) Troyes	105.9	1	5) Châtellerault	106.6	1	10) Arcachon	107.1	1	23) Saint Brieuc	107.3	1
21) Valence	105.9	1	17) Châtillon sur Seine	106.6	1	5) Bourges	107.1	1	23) Saint Raphaël	107.3	1
7) Ajaccio	106.0	8	21) Commercy	106.6	1	2) Caen	107.1	2	9) Verdun	107.3	1
22) Besançon	106.0	1	15) Dreux	106.6	1	21) Carmaux	107.1	1	23) Dreux	107.4	1
22) Blois	106.0	1	9) Gournay en Bray	106.6	1	23) Dijon	107.1	1	5) Granville	107.4	1
24) Bordeaux	106.0	5	18) La Flèche	106.6	1	8) Laval	107.1	1	7) Lisieux	107.4	1
7) Cahors	106.0	1	6) La Rochelle	106.6	1	21) Mulhouse	107.1	1	5) Nevers	107.4	1
5) Forbach	106.0	1	5) Le Puy en Velay	106.6	1	5) Nancy	107.1	1	18) Provins	107.4	1
17) L'Aigle	106.0	1	25) Montélimar	106.6	1	10) Poitiers	107.1	1	4) Château Gontier	107.5	1
8) Limoges	106.0	2	20) Montluçon	106.6	1	7) Quimper	107.1	1	20) Châteaudun	107.5	1
9) Lorient	106.0	1	23) Quimperlé	106.6	1	18) Saint Étienne	107.1	2	21) Cherbourg Octeville	107.5	1
3) Martigues	106.0	1	13) Saint Malo	106.6	1	21) Saint Flour	107.1	1	20) Saint Dizier	107.5	1
20) Mauriac	106.0	1	8) Toulon	106.6	1	5) Saint Méen le Grand	107.1	1	20) La Ferté Macé	107.9	1
21) Mayenne	106.0	1	9) Vire	106.6	1	21) Alès	107.2	1	20) L'Aigle	107.9	1
21) Montargis	106.0	1	5) Alençon	106.7	1						
21) Niort	106.0	1	18) Bourges	106.7	1						
20) Rennes	106.0	3	5) Calvi	106.7	1						
9) Roanne	106.0	1	10) Carcassonne	106.7	1						
13) St Gilles Croix de Vie	106.0	1	5) Chalon sur Saône	106.7	1						
23) Agen	106.1	1	5) Condom	106.7	1						
3) Albi	106.1	1	18) Laval	106.7	1						
27) Amiens	106.1	1	25) Lisieux	106.7	1						
21) Angers	106.1	2	15) Lyon	106.7	1						
8) Aubusson	106.1	1	5) Mende	106.7	1						
19) Bastia	106.1	4	10) Nantes	106.7	4						
19) Brive la Gaillarde	106.1	1	1) Paris	106.7	4						
19) Calvi	106.1	1	5) Roanne	106.7	1						
22) Chartres	106.1	1	5) Royan	106.7	1						
5) Commercy	106.1	1	5) Saint Gaudens	106.7	1						
22) Melun	106.1	1	20) Ussel	106.7	1						
21) Montpellier	106.1	3	6) Vitry le François	106.7	1						
10) Rouen	106.1	1	4) Alès	106.8	1						
5) Saint Dizier	106.1	1	8) Avallon	106.8	1						
5) Sarrebourg	106.1	1	22) Bordeaux	106.8	5						
13) Tarbes	106.1	1	20) Brioude	106.8	1						
21) Angoulême	106.2	1	4) Chartres	106.8	1						
7) Argentan	106.2	1	13) Château Renault	106.8	1						
19) Avignon	106.2	1	20) Grasse	106.8	1						
5) Bergerac	106.2	1	17) La Côte Saint André	106.8	1						
18) Étampes	106.2	1	22) Marseille	106.8	4						
12) Laval	106.2	1	5) Niort	106.8	1						
13) Morlaix	106.2	1	5) Pau	106.8	1						
3) Nantes	106.2	2	13) Perpignan	106.8	1						
6) Neufchâteau	106.2	1	3) Rennes	106.8	3						
18) Tonnerre	106.2	1	5) Rethel	106.8	1						
22) Toulon	106.2	1	18) Saint Affrique	106.8	1						
13) Vendôme	106.2	1	23) Béthune	106.9	1						
21) Arras	106.3	1	21) Bourg en Bresse	106.9	1						
13) Bourges	106.3	1										

NB: Stns under 1kW not mentioned.

As of August 2015, 5188 licenses (txs) were allocated to private commercial and non-commercial FM stns. Approx. 3540 stns are affiliated to one of the following private commercial national networks.

Addresses:
1) **Beur FM** ✉ 2 rue du Nouveau Bercy, 94220 Charenton le Pont ☎ +33 1 53483030 **W:** beurfm.net + 4 tx less than 1kW – 2) **BFM Business** ✉ 12 rue d'Oradour sur Glane, 75740 Paris Cedex 15 ☎ +33 1 71191181 **W:** bfmbusiness.bfmtv.com + 6 txs less than 1kW – 3) **Chérie FM** ✉ 22 rue Boileau, 75016 Paris ☎ +33 1 40714000 ▤ +33 1 40714040 **W:** cheriefm.fr+ 62 txs less than 1kW – 4) **COFRAC-Radio Notre Dame** ✉ 6 bd Edgard Quinet, 75014 Paris ☎ +33 1 56564444 **W:** cofrac-media.com + 17 txs less than 1kW – 5) **Europe 1** ✉ 28 rue François 1er, 75008 Paris ☎ +33 1 44319000 ▤ +33 1 47231900 **W:** europe1.fr **LW:** 183kHz 2000kW see Germany. + 153 txs less than 1kW – 6) **Virgin Radio** ✉ 28 rue François 1er, 75008 Paris ☎ +33 1 47231000 **W:** virginradio.fr + 100 txs less than 1kW– 7) **Fun Radio** ✉ 22 rue Bayard, 75008 Paris ☎ +33 1 40704848. **W:** funradio.fr + 106 txs less than 1kW – 8) **MFM Radio** ✉ 50 avenue Daumesnil, 75012 Paris ☎ +33 1 43416380 **W:** mfmradio.fr + 35 txs less than 1kW – 9) **NRJ** ✉ 22 rue Boileau, 75016 Paris ☎ +33 1 40714000 ▤ +33 1 40714040 **W:** nrj.fr + 146 txs less than 1kW – 10) **Radio Classique** ✉ 12 bis place Henri Bergson, 75382 Paris. Cedex 08 ☎ +33 1 40085000 ▤ +33 1 40085080 **W:** radioclassique.fr + 24 txs less than 1kW – 11) **Radio Courtoisie** ✉ 61 bd Murat 75016 Paris ☎ +33 1 46510085 ▤ +33 1 46512182 **W:** radiocourtoisie.fr + 3 txs less than 1kW – 12) **Radio FG** ✉ 51 rue de Rivoli, 75001 Paris ☎ +33 1 40137351 **W:** radiofg.com + 9 txs less than 1kW – 13) **Nostalgie** ✉ 22 rue Boileau, 75016 Paris ☎ +33 1 40714000. ▤ +33 1 40714040 **W:** nostalgie.fr + 115 txs less than 1kW – 14) **Radio**

Nova ⊟ 127 avenue Ledru Rollin, 75011 Paris ☎ +33 1 53333300 **W:** novaplanet.com + 6 txs less than 1kW – **15) Radio Orient** ⊟ 98 bd Victor Hugo, 92110 Clichy ☎ +33 1 41061600 ≣ +33 1 41061619 **W:** radioorient.com + 4 tx less than 1kW – **16) Radio Soleil** ⊟ 57 rue Avron, 75020 Paris ☎ +33 1 43488974 ≣ +33 1 43485558 **W:** radio-soleil.com + 2 txs less than 1kW – **17) RCF** ⊟ 7 place Saint Irénée, 69321 Lyon Cedex 05 ☎ +33 4 72382022. ≣ +33 4 72382057 **W:** rcf.fr + 121 txs less than 1kW – **18) RFM** ⊟ 28 rue François 1er, 75008 Paris ☎ +33 1 42322000 **W:** rfm.fr + 90 txs less than 1kW – **19) Rire et Chansons** ⊟ 22 rue Boileau, 75016 Paris ☎ +33 1 40714000 ≣ +33 1 40714040 **W:** rireetchansons.fr + 48 txs less than 1kW – **20) RMC** ⊟ 12 rue d'Oradour sur Glane, 75740 Paris Cedex 15 ☎ +33 1 71191191 ≣ +33 01 71191190 **W:** rmc.bfmtv.com **LW:** Roumoules 216kHz 1400kW See Monaco. + 144 txs less than 1kW – **21) RTL** ⊟ 22 rue Bayard, 75008 Paris. ☎ +33 1 40704070 **W:** rtl. fr **LW:** 234kHz 2000kW see Luxembourg. + 122 txs less than 1kW – **22) RTL 2** ⊟ 22 rue Bayard, 75008 Paris ☎ +33 1 40704000 **W:** rtl2.fr + 70 txs less than 1kW – **23) Skyrock** ⊟ 37 bis rue Greneta, 75002 Paris ☎ +33 1 44888200 **W:** skyrock.fm + 106 txs less than 1kW – **24) Sud Radio** ⊟ 93 rue du Lac, 31670 Labège ☎ +33 5 61632020 **W:** sudradio.fr + 29 txs less than 1kW – **25) Jazz Radio** ⊟ 40 quai Rambaud, 69002 Lyon ☎ +33 4 72101535 **W:** jazzradio.fr + 20 txs less than 1 kW – **26) Ouï FM** ⊟ 2 rue de la Roquette, 75011 Paris ☎ +33 1 55281414 **W:** ouifm.fr + 1 txs less than 1 kW – **27) France Maghreb 2** ⊟ 84 rue des Couronnes, 75020 Paris ☎ +33 1 40339081 **W:** francemaghreb2.fr + 3 txs less than 1kW – **28) TSF Jazz** ⊟ 127 avenue Ledru Rollin, 75011 Paris ☎ +33 1 53332280 **W:** tsfjazz.com + 6 txs less than 1kW

DAB+: Marseille: 7A, 8A, 8C, 8D. Nice: 7B, 11A, 11C.Paris:6A, 6D, 9A, 9B, 11A, 11D, Toulouse LF
Tests (DMB & DAB+): Lyon: 7D, 11B. Nantes: 9A. Rambouillet: 5C

FRENCH GUIANA

L.T: UTC -3h — **Pop:** 240,000 — **Pr.L:** French — **E.C:** 50Hz, 127/220V — **ITU:** GUF — **Int. dialling code:** +594

Guyane Première
⊟ B.P. 7013, 97305 Cayenne ☎ 594 301500 ≣ 594 302649 **W:** http://guyane.la1ere.fr **L.P:** Dir: Anastasie Bourquin. Dir. Tec: Serge Sulpice-Timothe. PD: Jean-Pierre Karam
FM: Cacao, Ouanary 90.0MHz – Sinnamary Corossony, Saint Lauren, Grand Saint, Maripasoula 91.0MHz – Cayenne, Iracubo 92.0MHz – Mana, Kourou Saint-Georges, Apatou, Kourou 94.0MHz – Papaichton, Camopi - 95.0MHz **D.Prgr:** 24h **Ann:** "Ici Cayenne, RFO Guyane" **IS:** "Nos richesses" on guitar. **V.** by QSL-folder. Rec. acc.

Other stations in Cayenne: R. Mosaique 88.1MHz – Ouest FM 89.4MHz – R. Metis 90.6MHz – R. Jam 96.2MHz – R. 2000 96.9MHz – NRJ, 97.3MHz – RVLD 98.3MHz – Nostalgie Guyane 99.6MHz – Vinyl R. 102.9MHz – RTM 103.3MHz – Trace 104.3MHz – Chéri 104.7MHz – R. RMP 105.9MHz

RADIO FRANCE INTERNATIONALE RELAY STATION
⊟ TDF Montsinery, B.P. 97307, Cayenne Cedex
FM: Cayenne 98.7MHz, 102.0MHz. Sinnamary 104.0MHz

FRENCH POLYNESIA

L.T: Tahiti: UTC-10h, **Marquesas Is:** -9½h **Gambier Is:** -9h — **Pop:** 294,935 — **Pr.L:** French, Tahitian — **E.C:** 60Hz, 220V — **ITU:** OCE

CONSEIL SUPERIOR DE L'AUDIOVISUEL
Regulator of broadcasting for French Polynesia.
Comite territorial de l'audiovisuel de Polynesie francaise
⊟ Immeuble Charles Levy, B.P. 20659, boulevard Pomare, 98713, Papeete-Tahiti ☎+689 689548888 **W:** csa.fr **E:** cta-papeete.csa@mail.pf

Iles du Vent

MW kHz	Location	kW	Station
4) 738	Mahina, Tahiti	20	R.Polynesie 1ere

FM MHz	Location	kW	Station
1) 87.6	Pueu, Tahiti	1	R.Maria no Te Hau
2) 88.2	Mont Marau	3	R.Maohi
3) 88.6	Moorea	4	R.NRJ Polynesie
4) 89.0	Moorea	-	R.Polynesie 1ere
4) 89.6	Moorea	-	R.Polynesie 1ere
4) 90.5	Papeete, Tahiti	-	R.Polynesie 1ere
4) 90.5	Tiarei, Tahiti	-	R.Polynesie 1ere
4) 90.9	Afaahiti, Tahiti	1	R.1
6) 91.4	Mont Marau, Tahiti	3	R.Te Vevo o Te Tiaturiraa
4) 91.8	Mont Marau, Tahiti	-	R.Polynesie 1ere
2) 92.3	Moorea	3.6	R.Maohi
7) 93.2	Papara, Tahiti	1.3	HITI FM
4) 94.3	Papeete, Tahiti	-	R.Polynesie 1ere
2) 94.8	Pueu, Tahiti	1	R.Maohi
4) 95.2	Mahaena, Tahiti	-	R.Polynesie 1ere
4) 95.2	Papara, Tahiti	-	R.Polynesie 1ere
4) 95.2	Pic Rouge, Tahiti	-	R.Polynesie 1ere
8) 95.6	Mont Marau, Tahiti	3	R.La Voix de l'Esperance
1) 96.4	Mont Marau, Tahiti	3	R.Maria no Te Hau
9) 97.4	Maatea, Moorea	3	R. Te Reo o Tefana
10) 97.8	Moorea	12	R.Faa'a Taui FM
5) 98.3	Afaahiti, Tahiti	1	R.Tiare FM
4) 99.0	Papeete, Tahiti	-	R.Polynesie 1ere
4) 99.0	Pueu, Tahiti	-	R.Polynesie 1ere
8) 99.5	Moorea	3	R.La Voix de l'Esperance
5) 100.0	Moorea	3	R.1
11) 100.8	Pueu, Tahiti	-	Rire et Chansons Tahiti
11) 101.0	Moorea	-	Rire et Chansons Tahiti
1) 101.5	Moorea	2	R.Maria no Te Hau
11) 102.6	Mont Marau, Tahiti	-	Rire et Chansons Tahiti
3) 103.0	Mont Marau, Tahiti	3	R.NRJ Polynesie
5) 103.8	Mont Marau, Tahiti	3	R.Tiare FM
12) 104.7	Moorea	3	R.Paofai
5) 105.5	Moorea	3	R.Tiare FM
10) 107.3	Mont Marau, Tahiti	1	R.Faa'a Taui FM

+ 20 stations less than 1kW

Iles Sous le Vent

FM MHz	Location	kW	Station
4) 94.0	Raiatea	-	R.Polynesie 1ere
8) 96.2	Raiatea	2	R.La Voix de l'Esperance
4) 96.6	Bora Bora	-	R.Polynesie 1ere
1) 105.4	Bora Bora	1	R.Maria no Te Hau

+ 14 stations less than 1kW

Archipel des Australes

FM MHz	Location	kW	Station
4) 89.6	Raivavae/Rurutu	-	R.Polynesie 1ere
4) 99.4	Rapa/ Rimatara/Tubuai-R.Polynesie 1ere		

+ 4 stations less than 1kW

Les Isles Marquises

FM MHz	Location	kW	Station
4) 88.2	Hiva Oa	-	R.Polynesie 1ere
4) 89.0	Nuku Hiva	-	R.Polynesie 1ere
4) 89.5	Hiva Oa	-	R.Polynesie 1ere
4) 90.5	Nuku Hiva	-	R.Polynesie 1ere
4) 91.5	Ua Huka	-	R.Polynesie 1ere
6) 93.5	Nuku Hiva	1	R.Te Vevo o Te Tiaturiraa

+ 10 stations less than 1kW

Iles des Tuamotu Gambier

FM MHz	Location	kW	Station
4) 90.5	Arutua	-	R.Polynesie 1ere
4) 93.6	Ahe/Hao/Kaukura/Mataiva/Napuka/Takaroa		
		-	R.Polynesie 1ere
4) 94.0	Faaite/Makemo//Mangareva/Nukutavake/Puka Puka/Rangiroa		
		-	R.Polynesie 1ere
4) 94.4	Fakahina/FakaravaHikueru/Manihi/Mururoa/Reau		
4) 94.8	Anaa/Fangatau/Takapoto/Tatakoto/Tikehau/Tureia		
		-	R.Polynesie 1ere
4) 95.2	Apataki/Pukarua	-	R.Polynesie 1ere
13) 96.0	Marutea Sud	1	R.Marutea Sud
1) 98.0	Rangiroa	1	R.Maria no Te Hau
14) 101.0	Rangiroa	1	R.Te Reo Tuamotu

+ 5 stations less than 1kW

Addresses & other information
1) BP 94-98713 Papeete ☎ +689 689420011 ≣ +689 689420635 **E:** contactmnth@radiomarianotehau.com **W:** radiomarianotehau.com & facebook.com/radiomarianotehau – **2)** BP 5038-98716 Pirae ☎ +689 689501616 **E:** courier@radiomaohi.pf **W:** radiomaohi.pf – **3)** BP 50-98713 Papeete ☎ +689 689421042 ≣ +689 689464346 **E:** nrj@mail.pf **W:** nrj.pf – **4) POLYNESIE LA PREMIÈRE (Gov)** ⊟ Centre Pamatai, FAAA BP 60125-98702, Papeete-Tahiti ☎ +689 689861616 ≣ +689 689861616 **W:** polynesie1ere.fr **E:** premiere@mail.pf **Prgr:** 24h **LP:** Jean-Phiippe Pascal Dir.Regional [most FM relays are of unknown low power – **5)** BP 3601-98713 Papeete ☎ +689 689 434100/436100 ≣ +689 689 422421 [R.1] +689 689 423406 [R.Tiare FM] **E:** contact@aline. pf **Brands: Radio 1 W:** radio1.pf **Radio Tiare: W:** tiare.pf & facebook. com/pages/tiarefm – **6)** BP 1817-98713 Papeete, 51, rue Dumont D'Urville, Orovini, Papeete ☎ +689 689412341 **F:** +689 689412322 **E:** contacts@mail.pf – **7)** Punaauia, ☎ +689 689877725444 **W:** facebook. com/hiti-fm-tahiti media partner & tahitinews.co – **8)** BP 95-97813 Papeete ☎ +689 689508259 ≣ +689 689464346 **E:** lvdl@mail.pf – **9)** BP 6295-98703 Faa, ☎ +689 689819797 ≣ +689 689825493 **E:** tereo@ mail.pf **W:** facebook.com/tereootefana – **10)** BP 60076 Faa'a-Centre, Papeete, ☎ +689 689854747 ≣: +689 689412555 **E:** tauifm@mail.pf

W: tauifm.net – **11)** SARL Pac FM ☎ +689 68940421414 **E:** commu-nity-rpp@rpp.pf **W:** facebook.com/rire.et.chansons – **12)** BP 113-98713 Papeete, ☎ +689 689460624/689460606 🖷 +689 689419357 **E:** radio-paofai@epm.pf **W:** radio.radiopaofai.org – **13)** ☎ +689 689416151 (atoll r. has no permanent population] – **14)** Cultural Association Iva Manu-Manu Arii, Avatoru, Rangiroa, Tuamotu-Gambier [r.silent]

FRENCH SOUTHERN & ANTARCTIC LANDS

L.T: UTC+5h — **Pop:** 150 (wi), 310 (su) — **Pr.L:** French — **E.C:** 50Hz, 220V — **ITU:** none (**WRTH:** FSA); Isles Kerguelen: ITU: KER

FM	MHz	Station	FM	MHz	Station
1)	98.0	Radio Ker	3)	100.0	RTL
2)	100.0	France Inter			

Addresses & other information:
1) Port-aux-Francais, District de Kerguelen, Terres Australes & Antarctiques Francaises [via Reunion, Indian Ocean]. 24h community station. – **2)** 24h satellite relay from Paris, Mon-Fri. – **3)** 24h satellite relay from Paris, weekends

GABON

L.T: UTC +1h — **Pop:** 1.5 million — **Pr.L:** French, Fang, Bopounou, Obamba, Djebi — **E.C:** 50Hz, 220V — **ITU:** GAB

CONCEIL NATIONAL DE LA COMMUNICATION(CNC)
🖃 B.P. 6437, Libreville ☎+241 1762796 **L.P:** Pres: Pierre-Marie Dong.

RADIODIFFUSION-TÉLÉVISION GABONAISE(RTG,Gov.)
🖃 B.P. 10150, Libreville ☎+241 1732459 🖷 +241 1739775.
L.P: DG RTG-1: Willy Kombény. DG RTG-2: Jules Legnongo. Asst. DGs: Radio: Gilles Terence Nzoghe. Tech: Claude Nganga. Provincial Stns: Robert Aloli.
MW **kHz** **kW N** **Times**
Oyem 549 20 2 0430-0630, 1030-1430, 1600-2230
SW relays via Moyabi on 4777/7270kHz not heard recently., irr.
FM(MHz): Libreville 87.7/96.54 (**1**), 92.5 (2), Franceville 87.86 (**2**), Makokou 100.5 (**2**), Oyem 87.94 (**2**), Pt. Gentil 88.03 (2), Tchibanga 91.04 (2).
1 = **RTG Chaîne 1** in French **2** = **RTG Chaîne 2** (provincial netw.) in French & ethnic languages. **FM Prgr:** 0500-2305 on FM only.
Ann: 1: "Ici Libreville, vouz écoutez Radio Gabon, chaîne 1".
IS: Indigenous instruments. Opens and closes with National Anthem.

Other stations:
R. Émergence, B.P. 06, Libreville: 91.6MHz 30W **W:** f-i-a.org/emer-gence – **R. Génération Nouvelle**, B.P. 727, Libreville: 97.4MHz – **R. Mandarine**, B.P. 511, Libreville: 106.6MHz – **R. Nostalgie**, B.P. 13050, Libreville: 93.0MHz – **R. Notre-Dame de Sainte-Marie**, B.P 20348, Libreville: 99MHz – **R. Soleil FM**, B.P. 5420, Libreville: 107.7MHz – **Top FM**, B.P. 6554, Libreville: 105.5MHz (also rel. VOA) – **R. Unité**, B.P. 2676, Libreville: 100.5MHz.
Medi 1 Afrique, Libreville: 100.5MHz (see main entry under Morocco).
RFI Afrique in Franceville, Libreville & Port-Gentil on 104MHz

GALAPAGOS ISLANDS (Ecuador)

L.T: UTC -6h — **Pop:** 25,000 — **Pr.L:** Spanish — **E.C:** 60Hz 110/220V — **ITU:** EQA (**WRTH:** GAL)

LA VOZ DE GALAPAGOS (RIg)
Prefectura Apostólica de Galápagos, Puerto Baquerizo Moreno
☎ +593 5 459435 **W:** lavozdegalapagos.net
FM: Galápagos Stereo 97.1MHz.
FM in Pto Baquerizo Moreno (MHz): 91.1 R. Pública/Nacional del Ecuador – 94.7 R. Mar – 97.1 LV de Galápagos FM – 100.7 R. María – 101.9 Encantada FM – 104.3 Telegalápagos FM
FM in Pto Ayora (MHz): 88.7 R. Santa Cruz – 89.9 Caravana AM – 93.5 Pacífica FM - 94.7 R. Mar – 95.9 Antena 9 FM – 98.3 Stereo Zaracay – 101.9 Encantada FM

GAMBIA

L.T: UTC — **Pop:** 1.8 million — **Pr.L:** English, Mandinka, Fula, Wolof, Jola, Serahuleh, Manjago, Aku — **E.C:** 50Hz, 230V — **ITU:** GMB

PUBLIC UTILITIES REGULATORY AUTHORITY (PURA)
🖃 94 Kairaba Ave, Bakau, KSMD, Banjul ☎220 4399601 🖷 +220 4399905 **W:** pura.gm **E:** info@pura.gm

GAMBIA RADIO AND TELEVISION SERVICE (GRTS)
🖃 Mile 7 Studios, P.O. Box 387, Banjul ☎+220 4495101/4497419 🖷 +220 4495102 **W:** grts.gm **L.P:** DG: Mr. Modou Sanyang. Deputy DG: Mr. Alhaji Modou Joof.
FM: Serrekunda 96.0MHz, Banjul 98.6MHz, Bonto 102.6MHz.
D.Prgr: in E/local langs: 0600-2400. N. in E: 0700, 1300, 1800, 2200.
Ann: "GRTS Radio". **IS:** Cora (harp).

Other stations (all MHz**):**
Capital FM, Banjul: 100.4 **W:** capitalfm.gm – **City Limits R,** Serrekunda: 93.6 0.25kW – **Hill Top R,** Serrekunda: 104.7 100W – **Kora FM,** Banjul: 103.9 **W:** korafm.gm – **Paradise FM,** Farafenni/ Serrekunda: 105.5 1kW. **W:** paradisefm.gm – **R. KWT** (Kids With Talent), Banjul: 107.6 – **Unique FM,** Banjul/Basse: 100.7 **W:** uniq-uefm.gm Also r. VOA – **West Coast R,** Serrekunda: 92.1 & 95.3 (different prgr.) **W:** westcoast.gm – **Vibes FM,** Banjul: 106.1 **W:** vibesfm.gm

RFI Afrique: Banjul 89.0MHz

GEORGIA

L.T: UTC +4h; Abkhazia and South Ossetia (de facto): UTC +3h — **Pop:** 5 million — **Pr.L:** Georgian, Abkhaz, Ossetic — **E.C:** 50Hz, 220V — **ITU:** GEO

GEORGIAN NATIONAL COMMUNICATIONS COMMISSION (GNCC)
🖃 Ave. Ketevan Tsamebuli/Bochorma St. 50/18, 0144 Tbilisi ☎ +995 32 2921667 🖷 +995 32 2921625 **E:** post@gncc.ge **W:** gncc.ge **L.P:** Chmn: Vakhtang Abashidze
NB: GNCC is the regulatory authority for broadcasting.

SAKARTVELOS SAZOGADOEBRIVI MAUTS'Q'EBELI (Georgian Public Broadcaster)
🖃 M.Kostava St. 68, 0171 Tbilisi ☎ +995 32 2409477 🖷 +995 32 2409477 **E:** info@gbp.ge **W:** gpb.ge
L.P: DG: George Baratashvili
FM (MHz)	R.1	R.2	kW	FM	R.1	R.2	kW
Akhaltsikhe	102.4	-	1	Tbilisi	102.4	100.9	10/5
Batumi*	102.4	-	1	Telavi	100.6	-	1
Qutaisi	100.3	-	2	Zugdidi	101.3	-	1
NB: Sites with only txs below 1kW not listed. *) Located in Ajara (autonomous republic)
D.Prgr: Radio 1: 24h. – **Radio 2:** 0400-2200. – **Regional Branch** in Ajara: see below.

OTHER STATIONS
FM	MHz	kW	Location	Station
14)	93.9	1	Tbilisi	Star FM
15)	94.3	1	Tbilisi	R. GIPA
22)	94.7	1	Tbilisi	R. Maestro
5E)	95.1	1	Tbilisi	Avtoradio
3)	95.5	1	Tbilisi	R. Komersant
6)	95.9	1	Tbilisi	R. Muza
17)	96.3	5	Tbilisi	R. Jako
5C)	96.7	1	Tbilisi	R. Ar Daidardo
18)	97.1	1	Tbilisi	Dardimandi FM
10)	98.0	1	Tbilisi	R. Utsnobi
21)	98.5	1	Tbilisi	Tskeli Shokoladi
5D)	99.7	1	Tbilisi	R. Vinil
9)	100.0	1	Gori	R. Imedi
9)	100.2	1	Telavi	R. Imedi
5E)	100.2	1	Dmasisi	Avtoradio
7)	100.3	1	Tbilisi	Med FM
12)	100.6	1	Dedoplistskaro	R. Mtsvane talga
9)	100.9	2.5	Qutaisi	R. Imedi
12)	101.0	1	Dmanisi	R. Mtsvane talga
9)	101.2	1	Akhalkalaki	R. Imedi
2)	101.4	5	Tbilisi	R. Monte-Karlo
12)	101.5	1	Gori	R. Mtsvane talga
19)	101.9	1	Tbilisi	R. Kalaki
5E)	102.3	1	Kutaisi	Avtoradio
5C)	102.7	2.5	Qutaisi	R. Ar Daidardo
5B)	103.4	1	Tbilisi	R. Fortuna+
5B)	103.4	5	Gori	R. Fortuna+
5B)	103.4	1	Qutaisi	R. Fortuna+
12)	103.6	1	Zugdidi	R. Mtsvane talga
23)	103.9	1	Tbilisi	R. Palitra
9)	104.2	1	Zugdidi	R. Imedi
4)	104.3	1	Tbilisi	Positive FM
9)	104.7	1	Dedoplistskaro	R. Imedi

FM	MHz	kW	Location	Station
16)	104.8	1	Gori	R. Trialeti
20)	105.0	1	Qutaisi	White FM
8)	105.0	1	Tbilisi	R. 105
1)	105.4	1	Qutaisi	R. Iveria
1)	105.4	1	Tbilisi	R. Iveria
9)	105.9	1	Tbilisi	R. Imedi
11)	106.4	10	Tbilisi	Pirveli R.
11)	106.4	1	Gori	Pirveli R.
11)	106.4	1	Senaki	Pirveli R.
5A)	106.9	1	Tbilisi	R. Fortuna
5A)	106.9	1	Gori	R. Fortuna
5E)	107.3	1	Kvareli	Avtoradio
12)	107.4	10	Tbilisi	R. Mtsvane talga
12)	107.4	2	Qutaisi	R. Mtsvane talga
13)	107.9	1	Tbilisi	R. Saqartvelos khma

NB: Txs below 1kW not listed.

Addresses & other information:
1) Erekle II square 1, 0105 Tbilisi **E:** iveria105.4@yahoo.com – **2)** M.Kostava St. 14, 0169 Tbilisi. In Russian. – **3)** Nadiradze St. 8, 0102 Tbilisi. **E:** info@commersant.ge – **4)** Chubinashvili St. 55, 0132 Tbilisi. **E:** info@positivefm.ge – **5A-D)** Marshal Gelovani St. 2, 0179 Tbilisi **E:** marketing@fortuna.ge – **6)** Zandukeli St. 12, 0108 Tbilisi **E:** info@radio-muza.ge. In Georgian & English. – **7)** Akaki Beliashvili St. 8, 0159 Tbilisi – **8)** Agladze St. 31, 0119 Tbilisi **E:** n1001@geo.net.ge – **9)** Lubliana St. 5, 0159 Tbilisi **E:** info@radio-imedi.ge – **10)** M.Kostava St. 68, 0171 Tbilisi **E:** radio@ucnobifm.ge – **11)** Aleksidze St. 1, 0193 Tbilisi **E:** 106.4@radioone.ge – **12)** Vazha-Pshavela Ave. 45, 0177 Tbilisi **E:** pd@grn.ge – **13)** Tashkenti St. 51, 0160 Tbilisi – **14)** Vazha-Pshavela Ave. 16, 0160 Tbilisi **E:** marketing@stargroup.ge – **15)** Marie Brosset St. 2, 0108 Tbilisi – **16)** Chavchavadze St. 45, 1400 Gori **E:** contact@trialeti.ge – **17)** Tbilisi – **18)** Kindzmarauli St. 15, 0168 Tbilisi – **19)** Melikishvili St. 1, 0179 Tbilisi **E:** info@radiokalaki.ge – **20)** Tamar Mepe Ave. 56, 4600 Qutaisi – **21)** Tbilisi – **22)** Akaki Beliashvili St. 8, 0159 Tbilisi – **23)** Iosebidze St. 49, 0160 Tbilisi **E:** info@radiopalitra.ge

ABKHAZIA

APSNYTWI AXWYNTKARRATW TELERADIOEILAXWYRA (Abkhaz State Radio & TV Co.)
✉ Lasuria St. 16, Sokhumi, Abkhazia (mail: via Russia) ☎ +7 840 2264867 🖷 +7 840 2266144 **E:** apsua.radio@gmail.com **W:** apsua.tv
L.P: Dir: Alxas Colokwua
Run by the administration of the "Republic of Abkhazia".

MW	kHz	kW	SW	kHz	kW
Sokhumi	1350	30	Sokhumi	†9535	5
FM	**MHz**	**kW**	**FM**	**MHz**	**kW**
Sokhumi	68.80	-	Sokhumi	103.7	-
Tkvarcheli	102.2	-	Gagra	107.1	-
Ochamchire	104.0	-		†) irreg.	

D.Prgr: Apsua R. with own prgrs in Abkhaz, Russian. Outside of own prgrs, various other stns may be relayed (e.g. Avtoradio). On MW/SW: limited schedule, changing frequently.

OTHER STATIONS

FM	MHz	kW	Location	Station
1)	91.2	-	Ochamchire	R. Soma
A)	100.7	-	Ochamchire	R. Sputnik relay
3)	101.1	-	Sokhumi	R. Xara Xradio
3)	101.7	-	Gagra	R. Xara Xradio
4)	101.9	-	Sokhumi	R. Rio Rita
A)	102.5	-	Gagra	R. Sputnik relay
2)	103.6	-	Gagra	Pervoye R.
A)	104.4	-	Sokhumi	R. Sputnik relay
2)	104.8	-	Gagra	Pervoye R.
5)	105.1	-	Sokhumi	Serebryanyy dozhd
6)	105.6	-	Sokhumi	R. Shanson
1)	106.1	-	Tkvarcheli	R. Soma
1)	107.9	1.5	Sokhumi	R. Soma

Addresses & other information:
1) Zvanba St. 9, Sokhumi **E:** info@radiosoma.com Incl. rel. R. Sputnik* – **2)** Sokhumi – **3)** pr. Leona 17, Sokhumi **E:** reklama.sukhum@gmail.com – **4)** Sokhumi – **5)** Rel. Serebryanyy dozhd* – **6)** Rel. R. Shanson* – **A)** Rel. R. Sputnik* (*= Relays from Russia)

AJARA

AJARA RADIO & TV (Pub)
✉ Memed Abashidze Ave. 41, 6010 Batumi ☎ +995 422 274370 🖷 +995 422 274384 **E:** info@radioajara.ge **W:** radioajara.ge; ajaratv.ge
L.P: Dir: Soso Sturua

FM: Batumi 104.5MHz (0.5kW)
D.Prgr: R. Ajara 24h.
NB: Ajara Radio & TV is a branch of Georgian Public Broadcaster.

OTHER STATIONS

FM	MHz	kW	Location	Station
9)	100.1	1	Batumi	R. Imedi
5B)	103.4	5	Batumi	R. Fortuna+
1)	105.4	5	Batumi	R. Iveria
5A)	106.9	1	Batumi	R. Fortuna

NB: Txs below 1kW not listed.
Addresses & other information: see main tx table.

SOUTH OSSETIA

GTRK "IR" (Gov)
✉ Geroev St. 37, Tskhinvali, South Ossetia (mail: via Russia) ☎ +7 929 8066070 **E:** radio-ir@yandex.ru **W:** 102-3fm.ru
L.P: Dir (Radio): Kosta Kochiyev
Run by the administration of the "Republic of South Ossetia".
FM: Tskhinvali 102.3MHz.
D.Prgr: R. Ir FM in Russian, Ossetic: 24h.

OTHER STATIONS

FM	MHz	kW	Location	Station
3)	104.1	-	Tskhinvali	R. City
A)	104.5	-	Tskhinvali	Vesti FM relay
1)	105.9	-	Tskhinvali	Volna FM
B)	106.3	-	Tskhinvali	R. Mayak relay
2)	107.3	-	Tskhinvali	R. Yuzhnyy gorod

Addresses & other information:
1) Tskhinvali – **2)** Geroev St. 1, Tskhinvali **E:** info@yugfm.ru – **2)** Tskhinvali. Incl. rel. R. Sputnik* – **A)** Rel. Vesti FM* – **B)** Rel. Mayak* (*= Relays from Russia)

NB: Radio stns in Abkhazia and South Ossetia are de facto subject to authorisation by the administrations of the soi-disant "Republic of Abkhazia" resp. "Republic of South Ossetia"

GERMANY

L.T: UTC +1h (27 Mar-30 Oct: +2h) — **Pop:** 81 million — **Pr.L:** German — **E.C:** 50Hz, 230V — **ITU:** D

BUNDESNETZAGENTUR
✉ Postfach 8001, 53105 Bonn (office location: Tulpenfeld 4) ☎ +49 (228) 14 0 🖷 + 49 228 14 8872 **W:** bnetza.de

NB: Broadcasting regulation, except aspects of spectrum use/transmitter operations regulated by Bundesnetzagentur, is in Germany the sole responsibility of the federal states. Some of the public broadcasting institutions shown in section I are common operations by various states. Some states have also agreed a common regulation of the private sector as shown in section II.

I. PUBLIC STATIONS

ARBEITSGEMEINSCHAFT DER ÖFFENTLICH-RECHTLICHEN RUNDFUNKANSTALTEN DEUTSCHLANDS (ARD)
Formalised co-operation of institutions B)-J), Deutschlandradio and Deutsche Welle (see International Broadcasting section) are associated members.
Radio operations under ARD umbrella: Common overnight prgr. ARD-Hitnacht (2205-0500, oldies, produced by SR 3), ARD-Popnacht (2305-0400, AC, produced by SWR 3), ARD-Nachtkonzert (2305-0500, classical, produced by BR Klassik), ARD-Infonacht (2200-0500, news, produced by MDR Info). Common summertime evening prgr. ARD-Radiofestival mid July to mid September daily 1900-2300
Satellite radio: Most radio stations of member institutions B)-J) are carried on Astra 1M, 12.266 GHz

A) DEUTSCHLANDRADIO
Common operation of all federal states
Cologne seat: ✉ Raderberggürtel 40, 50968 Köln ☎ +49 221 345 0 2 +49 221 345 4803
Berlin seat: ✉ Hans-Rosenthal-Platz, 10825 Berlin ☎ +49 30 8503 0 🖷 +49 30 8503 6168 **W:** deutschlandradio.de
LW/MW: 153/207kHz closed in 2014, 549/756/1269/1422kHz close on 31 December 2015. 177kHz: See section III.

FM (MHz)	DLF	DK	kW
Baden-Württemberg			
Baden-Baden	-	107.9	0.1
Biberach	100.5	-	0.5
Blauen	105.1	-	10
Esslingen	96.7	-	0.1
Freiburg	-	90.6	0.2
Geislingen	-	87.7	0.2
Göppingen	99.8	-	0.1
Heidelberg	106.5	-	0.4
Heidenheim	94.0	100.8	0.1
Heilbronn	91.3	97.3	0.1
Hornisgrinde	106.3	-	80
Kirchheim	91.3	-	0.1
Konstanz	-	94.5	0.2
Lörrach	-	95.0	0.1
Ludwigsburg	94.1	97.3	0.5/0.1
Pforzheim	89.2	95.2	0.1/0.5
Rottweil	106.0	-	0.1
Schwäb. Hall	95.8	-	0.1
Schw. Gmünd	-	95.9	0.2
Stuttgart	96.0	87.9	0.5/1
Tübingen	93.9	99.4	0.5/1
Ulm	103.5	91.5	0.5/1
Witthoh	100.6	-	40
Wörth	-	96.6	0.2
Bayern			
Amberg	-	107.9	0.1
Ansbach	92.7	102.7	0.2
Aschaffenbg.	-	94.8	0.1
Augsburg	97.8	100.0	0.3/15
B. Reichenhall	-	92.6	0.1
Bad Tölz	87.8	93.2	0.1
Berchtesgd.	91.6	103.4	0.1
Brotjacklrieg.	100.1	-	100
Burgbernhm.	106.3	94.3	0.2/0.3
Burglengenf.	-	107.3	0.1
Cham	-	101.4	0.1
Freilassing	100.3	-	15
Füssen	87.6	103.4	0.1
Hof Waldst.	-	89.3	20
Hohe Linie	-	101.3	0.2
Hohenpeißbg.	94.7	-	0.1
Ingolstadt	107.0	88.6	0.5
Kaufbeuren	-	107.3	0.1
Kempten	89.3	89.8	0.1
Landsberg	90.3	107.9	0.1
Landshut	95.9	100.5	0.2
Mittenwald	91.9	105.2	0.1
München	101.7	96.8	0.3
Nürnberg	90.1	105.6	0.1
Oberstdorf	92.0	96.5	0.1
Ochsenkopf	100.3	-	100
Passau	-	97.7	0.5
Pfronten	96.5	-	0.02
Regensburg	95.5	101.3	0.2
Rhön	103.3	-	100
Rosenheim	97.2	96.2	0.1
Rosenh.-D'bg.	97.7	-	0.1
Starnberg	87.9	94.7	0.1
Straubing	-	88.7	0.4
Traunstein	-	88.3	0.1
Weiden	-	103.7	0.1
Weilheim	94.7	-	0.05
Würzburg	100.3	101.3	0.1
Berlin & Brandenburg			
Berlin A'platz	97.7	89.6	100
Calau	-	90.8	20
Casekow	105.2	-	6
Cottbus	88.6	-	3
Eisenhütt.st.	100.2	-	1
Frankfurt (Bo.)	97.3	92.7	0.5/5
Herzberg/Els.	94.5	-	0.3
Rhinow	-	103.7	0.2
Bremen			
Bremen	107.1	100.3	100/1
Bremerhaven	103.4	106.2	0.5/5
Hamburg			
Hamburg	88.7	89.1	3/0.1
Hessen			
Alsfeld	104.0	-	0.1
Bad Camberg	99.8	-	0.2
Bad Hersfeld	102.9	-	0.3

FM (MHz)	DLF	DK	kW
Darmstadt	102.0	98.2	0.3
Eschwege	100.6	-	0.5
Frankfurt/M.	97.6	91.2	0.3
Friedberg	89.9	-	0.3
Fritzlar	-	96.0	0.1
Fulda	-	90.7	0.3
Gelnhausen	93.9	-	0.2
Gießen	103.1	107.5	0.6/0.3
Hanau	92.4	107.7	0.3
Heusenstamm	-	99.8	0.2
Hofgeismar	106.9	-	0.3
Kassel	92.7	-	0.1
Korbach	92.8	-	0.1
Limburg	103.3	105.1	0.3
Mainz-Kastel	-	107.2	0.4
Marburg	103.5	93.3	0.5/0.1
Michelstadt	105.7	107.2	0.2
Oberursel	103.5	101.8	0.1
Rimberg	91.3	-	50
Wetzlar	103.7	97.3	0.5/0.3
Wiesbaden	103.7	-	0.5
Mecklenburg-Vorpommern			
Anklam	107.4	-	1
Barth	100.3	-	0.1
Dargun	89.8	-	0.5
Demmin	89.8	106.2	1/0.5
Greifswald	104.3	96.9	0.2
Güstrow	106.0	-	0.8
Helpterberg	96.5	97.1	10/30
Heringsdorf	98.4	107.1	0.5
Neukloster	90.6	-	0.3
Neustrelitz	97.9	-	1
Ribn.-Damg.	102.1	-	0.2
Röbel	102.4	90.0	3
Rostock	97.3	96.7	5/40
Sassnitz	104.0	101.4	8
Schwerin	106.3	95.3	2/100
Stralsund	89.3	92.1	0.4
Waren/Mü.	91.3	-	0.2
Niedersachsen			
Aurich	101.8	106.9	100/1
Cloppenbg.	-	95.5	0.1
Cuxhaven	101.6	107.7	2/20
Damme	95.4	97.5	0.3
Emden	-	93.4	1
Göttingen	101.0	-	0.1
Hannover	94.0	-	0.1
Hann. Münd.	98.5	-	0.5
Höhbeck	102.2	-	100
Jever	-	89.0	0.5
Leer	-	91.5	0.5
Lingen	102.0	-	25
		91.6*	0.4
		102.9*	0.3
Lübbecke	-	97.7	0.2
Lüneburg	-	97.9	0.5
Meppen	-	100.7	0.3
Norden	-	105.3	0.3
Nordhorn	-	97.1	0.2
Oldenburg	-	102.8	1
Osnabrück	101.8	-	0.5
Seesen	88.0	-	0.1
Soltau	89.3	-	0.1
Stadthagen	106.1	-	1
Tecklenburg	-	101.1	0.5
Torfh./Harz	103.5	-	100
Uelzen	107.5	97.1	0.5/0.2
Visselhövede	-	88.8	1
Warendorf	107.2	-	1
Nordrhein-Westfalen			
Aachen	102.7	-	0.5
B. Oeynhsn.	93.9	-	0.1
Beckum	91.5	-	0.2
Bielefeld	95.5	106.2	0.1
Bonn	89.1	98.9	5/0.1
Eifel-Bärbelk.	-	106.1	20
Gronau	-	94.6	0.2
Kleve	-	90.1	1
Köln	91.3	-	0.1
Langenberg	-	96.5	35
Lemgo	92.2	88.9	0.3
Lennestadt	-	96.9	0.1

FM (MHz)	DLF	DK	kW
Lübbecke	-	97.7	0.2
Münster	104.5	97.5	0.3/0.1
Nordhelle	102.7	-	20
Olpe	-	96.3	0.1
Olsberg	-	106.1	10
Paderborn	94.5	-	0.2
Schwerte	104.4	-	0.2
Siegen	94.2	100.2	0.1
Stadthagen	106.1	-	1
Steinfurt	-	91.0	0.2
Tecklenburg	-	101.1	0.5
Warendorf	107.2	-	1
Warburg	106.6	-	0.2
Wesel	102.8	-	50
Wuppertal	91.0	-	0.3
Rheinland-Pfalz			
B. Kreuznach	106.5	-	0.1
Bingen	-	106.3	0.2
Bitburg	-	95.3	0.1
Boppard	90.5	88.9	0.1
Idar-Oberst.	89.5	94.7	0.2
Kaiserslaut.	105.1	98.1	0.2
Koblenz	99.8	105.3	0.5
Limburg	103.3	105.1	0.3
Linz	-	98.3	0.1
Lorch	88.1	-	0.1
Ludwigshafen	-	97.3	0.1
Mayen	100.8	-	0.2
Pirmasens	106.1	94.4	0.4
Prüm	95.4	-	0.1
Saarburg	104.6	105.3	20/0.1
Traben-Trarb.	88.7	106.2	0.3
Trier	-	94.3	0.2
Wörth	-	96.6	0.2
Saarland			
Lebach	-	107.9	0.1
Neunkirchen	-	105.0	5
Oberperl	-	106.2	5
Saarbrücken	90.1	107.5	1/0.4
Saarlouis	-	96.3	0.1
Völklingen	-	88.6	0.1
Sachsen			
Bad Düben	-	99.4	0.2
Bärenstein	-	104.3	1
Belgern	-	101.1	1
Chemnitz	-	106.3	0.5
Collmberg	-	96.1	0.3
Döbeln	-	101.3	1
Dresden	97.3	93.2	100/1
Eilenburg	-	92.0	0.2
Freiberg	-	100.7	1
Geyer (Erzg.)	97.0	-	100

*) directional with different beams
F.PI.: See section III.
DAB: See section II.
Satellite: Astra 1N, 11.954GHz h (operated by ZDF, see TV section).
D.Prgr: Deutschlandfunk from Köln studios, full sce. with strong emphasis on information – **Deutschlandradio Kultur** from Berlin studios, culture, during daytime music format Alternative – **DRadio Wissen**, from Köln studios, for young audiences – **Dokumente & Debatten**, parliament coverage, audio of TV talkshows and other special prgrs.

B) BAYERISCHER RUNDFUNK (BR)
Public broadcasting institution of Bayern

Bayerischer Rundfunk, 80300 München (location of radio operations: Rundfunkplatz 1) ☎ +49 89 5900 01 🖷 +49 89 5900 2375 **W:** br-online.de

MW: Closed down in 2015

FM (MHz)	DLF	DK	kW
Grimma	-	91.6	0.1
Hoyerswerda	-	89.7	0.5
Leipzig-Holzh.	-	100.4	2
Löbau	99.5	103.0	5/2
Pulsnitz	-	106.7	0.5
Schöneck	94.5	-	3
Weißwasser	-	97.7	2
Wiederau	96.6	-	100
Zwickau	-	104.6	0.2
Sachsen-Anhalt			
Brocken/Harz	-	97.4	100
Dessau	107.1	-	0.3
Dequede	-	96.9	7
Eisleben	103.8	-	0.5
Schönebeck	102.0	-	20
Wittenberg	89.3	107.7	1/0.5
Zeitz	-	91.8	0.5
Schleswig-Holstein			
Bungsberg	101.9	103.1	95/0.2
Flensburg	103.3	92.1	20/0.2
Garding	102.3	101.7	0.5
Güby	-	105.0	0.2
Heide	104.4	92.2	1/0.1
Helgoland	107.4	103.0	0.1
Husum	-	101.0	0.1
Itzehoe	102.2	97.5	0.4/0.1
Kaltenkirchen	-	105.5	0.1
Kiel	-	104.7	0.3
Lauenburg	-	95.8	0.1
Neumünster	-	107.8	0.5
Niebüll	-	104.2	0.3
Rendsburg	-	95.2	0.3
Schleswig	-	105.0	0.2
Sylt	90.3	103.9	0.2
Thüringen			
Altenburg	-	97.3	0.4
Bleßberg	-	94.2	100
Eisenach	106.5	-	0.5
Erfurt	103.1	-	2
Gera	94.3	93.6	0.3
Gotha	94.0	-	0.1
Ilmenau	99.9	-	0.1
Inselsberg	-	97.2	100
Jena	104.5	98.2	0.3
Mühlhausen	107.0	-	1
Nordhausen	96.4	-	0.1
Pößneck	89.2	-	0.1
Saalfeld	98.7	-	0.1
Sondershaus.	101.9	-	0.1
Suhl	98.8	-	0.1
Weimar	89.7	-	0.5

FM (MHz)	B1	B2	B3	BR K	B5	kW
Augsburg	-	-	-	-	105.3	0.5
Bad Reichenhall	91.8	89.9	96.7	98.3	105.0	0.3
Bamberg	94.8N	98.6	99.8	102.9	97.4	25/5
Berchtesgaden	90.4	96.9	96.9	94.2	106.4	0.3/0.1
Brotjacklriegel	92.1R	96.5	94.4	100.9	106.9	100/50
Büttelberg	91.4M	88.2	99.3	95.5	104.0	25/10
Coburg	93.5N	88.3	99.2	97.7	92.8	5/0.3
Dillberg	88.9N	92.3	97.9	87.6	102.0	25
	104.5R					5
Eichstätt	101.6	90.5	97.6	89.0	106.1	25/10
Garmisch-Partenk.	89.2	93.5	97.7	95.9	104.9	0.1

FM (MHz)	B1	B2	B3	BR K	B5	kW
Grünten (Allgäu)	90.7U	88.7	95.8	101.0	106.9	50/100
Herzogstand	88.1	97.0	91.0	–	106.7	0.1
Hochberg-Traunst.	98.0	91.5	95.9	97.0	107.1	5/0.5
Hohenpeißenberg	92.8	94.2	99.2	100.4	–	25
Hoher Bogen	96.8R	91.6	94.7	88.3	104.4	50/5
Hühnerberg	91.9U	96.1	99.5	93.1	107.6	25/11
Kreuzberg (Rhön)	98.3W	93.1	96.3	107.9	105.3	100/50
Landshut	90.2R	97.8	95.3	93.2	106.6	0.1
Lindau	88.1U	92.0	94.0	87.6	100.4	0.5/0.1
München-Ismaning	91.3	88.4	97.3	103.2	90.0	25
Ochsenkopf	90.7N	96.0	99.4	102.3	107.1	100/50
	91.2R					20
Passau	87.7R	93.2	90.4	95.6	105.9	0.5/0.3
Pfaffenberg	95.6W	88.4	93.4	98.0	106.4	25/1
Regensburg	95.0R	93.0	99.6	97.0	105.0	25/5
Untersb. Geiereck*)	87.8	92.9	96.1	100.7	–	0.1
Wallberg	94.0	87.7	99.7	97.9	101.8	0.1
Wendelstein	93.7	89.5	98.5	102.3	105.7	100
Würzburg	90.9W	90.0	97.6	89.0	105.7	5/0.2

*) Site in Austria.

F.Pl.: Using FM network of BR Klassik for Puls instead as of 2018, subject of legal action at time of editing.
DAB: 40 txs on ch. 11D (222MHz): All prgr., with all Bayern 1 regional versions separately. Rel. via ch. 10D/11C/12D muxes see L).
D.Prgr: Bayern 1, oldies, rel. ARD-Hitnacht, Mon-Fri 1105-1200 and 1805-1855 regional prgr. from Nürnberg (N), Regensburg (R), Würzburg (W) and Ulm (U) – **Bayern 2**, various prgr., rel. ARD-Nachtkonzert – **Bayern 3**, AC, 24h – **BR Klassik**, classical music, 24h – **B5 aktuell**, news, on FM txs mono signal, rel. ARD-Infonacht – **Bayern Plus**, German light music, 24h – **BR Heimat**, German/Bavarian folk music, 24h – **Puls**, for young listeners, 24h – **B5 Plus**, coverage of parliament, sports and other special prgr. – **BR Verkehr**, traffic announcements

C) HESSISCHER RUNDFUNK (HR)

Public broadcasting institution of Hessen
✉ 60222 Frankfurt am Main (office and studio location: Bertramstraße 8) ☎ +49 69 155 1 📠 +49 69 155 2900 W: hr-online.de

FM (MHz)	hr1	hr2	hr3	hr4	kW
Alsfeld-Homberg	–	–	105.6	–	0.1
Bad Hersfeld	88.9	–	102.9	–	0.3
Bingen	–	–	91.1	–	0.3
Feldberg (Taunus)	94.4	96.7	89.3	102.5R	100
Frankfurt (HR headq.)	–	87.9	–	–	0.1
Fulda	–	106.6	88.5	103.9N	0.3
Habichtswald	–	–	101.2	103.2N	20
Hardberg (Odenw.)	90.6	–	92.7	101.6R	50
Heidelstein (Rhön)	104.8	–	106.2	107.3N	50
Hoher Meißner	99.0	95.5	89.5	101.7N	100
Kassel	94.3	93.7	–	–	0.5
Limburg	–	100.8	–	97.1M	0.3/0.2
Marburg	–	–	–	102.8M	1
Rimberg	–	–	–	91.9N	50/20
Rotenburg	–	–	105.7	–	0.3
Sackpfeife	91.0	–	87.6	104.3M	100
Schlüchtern	–	–	88.9	–	0.3
Weilburg	–	–	–	97.9M	0.1
Wetzlar	–	–	–	90.5M	0.3
Wiesbaden	98.3	93.1	–	–	0.1
Würzburg (Odenw.)	88.1	97.4	89.7	103.8R	5

FM (MHz)	You FM	hr-info	kW
Alsfeld	–	104.0	0.1
Bad Hersfeld	–	106.9	0.3
Bad Nauheim	–	88.9	0.3
Bad Orb	–	89.8	0.3
Bensheim	90.2	91.2	0.2/0.1
Bingen	92.3	–	0.3
Darmstadt	104.3	107.0	0.8/5
Eltville	96.2	–	0.5
Eschwege	106.6	–	0.1
Frankfurt/Main	90.4	103.9	0.5
Friedberg	94.0	92.1	0.3
Fritzlar	–	106.6	0.1
Fulda	93.6	89.7	0.3/0.2
Gelnhausen	99.4	–	0.3
Gießen	97.9	99.2	0.5/0.3
Hardberg	95.3	–	50
Herborn	103.4	–	0.5
Kassel-Wilhelmsh.	100.1	107.5	0.5/1
Korbach	91.6	102.6	0.5/1
Limburg	90.7	99.2	0.2/0.3

FM (MHz)	You FM	hr-info	kW
Marburg	93.9	98.5	1/0.3
Michelstadt	91.0	–	0.2
Reinhardshain	–	92.9	0.2
Rimberg	97.7	95.0	50
Rotenburg	–	96.8	0.3
Sackpfeife	102.3	99.6	10/100
Schlüchtern	88.2	91.5	0.3
Seeheim	–	88.2	0.1
Sontra	–	90.8	0.1
Wetzlar	105.5	93.2	0.3
Wiesbaden	99.7	97.2	0.2/0.1
Witzenhausen	91.1	–	0.3

DAB: 5 txs on ch. 7B (191MHz).
D.Prgr: hr1, oldies, rel. ARD-Popnacht – **hr2**, culture and classical music, rel. ARD-Nachtkonzert, ARD-Radiofestival – **hr3**, AC, rel. ARD-Popnacht – **hr4**, produced at Kassel (Wilhelmshöher Allee 347, 34131 Kassel), light music format, rel. ARD-Hitnacht, regional news Nordhessen (N; Kassel/Fulda), Mittelhessen (M; Gießen) and Rhein-Main (R; Frankfurt/Darmstadt) – **You FM**, CHR, 24h – **hr-info**, news, rel. ARD-Infonacht with own insertions.

D) MITTELDEUTSCHER RUNDFUNK (MDR)

Public broadcasting institution of Sachsen, Sachsen-Anhalt and Thüringen . ✉ Kantstraße 71-73, 04360 Leipzig (TV and administration) **W:** mdr.de
✉ Gerberstraße 2, 06110 Halle/Saale ☎ +49 345 300 0 📠 +49 345 300 5544 (radio, except MDR 1 stns, see below)

FM (MHz)	MDR 1	Jump	Figaro	Info	Sputnik	kW
Txs in Sachsen:						
Altenburg	–	–	–	101.5	–	1
Annaberg-Buchholz	–	–	–	91.2	–	0.2
Aue	–	–	–	95.1	–	1
Auerbach	–	–	–	101.7	–	0.4
Bautzen	–	98.8	–	87.9	–	0.2/0.1
Chemnitz-Reichenh.	–	–	–	94.7	–	0.5
Collmberg	101.8L	103.7	98.9	105.9	–	2x5/0.5/30
Döbeln-Mockritz	–	–	–	99.6	–	0.1
Dresden-Wachwitz	92.2	90.1	95.4	106.1	–	3x100/0.5
Eilenburg	–	–	–	92.4	–	0.2
Freiberg	99.1C	–	–	93.7	–	1/0.2
Freital	–	–	–	95.9	–	0.2
Geyer (Erzgebirge)	92.8C	89.8	87.7	–	–	100
Grimma-Hohnstädt	–	–	–	100.6	–	0.2
Görlitz	–	–	–	106.9	–	1
Hoyerswerda	93.0B	89.0	94.7	94.2	–	1/0.5/1
	100.4					30
Kamenz	–	–	–	93.9	–	1
Klingenthal	93.7C	–	98.4	–	–	0.2
Leipzig city	–	–	–	95.6	–	0.5
Löbau	98.2B	91.8	96.2	–	–	5
Markneukirchen	104.8C	–	106.4	–	–	0.5
Meißen-Korbitz	–	–	–	94.9	–	1
Neustadt	–	–	–	89.6	–	0.3
Plauen	–	–	–	102.0	–	1
Raschau	–	–	–	91.6	–	0.2
Seifhennersdorf	94.5B	96.9	103.4	–	–	0.25/0.1
Schöneck	88.7C	101.2	98.7	–	–	3/30/3
Stollberg	–	–	–	89.3	–	0.1
Torgau	88.9L	–	93.0	–	–	0.5/0.2
Weißwasser	–	–	–	90.5	–	1
Wiederau (Leipzig)	93.9L	90.4	88.4	–	–	100
	106.5H					*30
Zittau	87.7B	107.1	95.4	106.4	–	0.2/0.5
Zschopau	–	–	–	99.5	–	0.2
Zwickau	–	–	–	91.4	–	1
Txs in Sachsen-Anhalt:						
Aschersleben	–	–	–	102.8	–	1
Brocken	94.6	91.5	107.8	–	–	60/100/10
Burg	–	–	–	89.6	–	1
Dequede	94.9St	98.9	89.4	–	–	10
Dessau-Mildensee	–	–	–	90.0	–	0.3
Fleetmark	–	–	–	90.1	105.0	2/1
Gernrode	–	–	–	91.0	–	0.1
Haidberg	–	–	–	–	100.7	5
Haldensleben	–	–	–	99.1	–	1
Halle Petersberg	100.8H	–	95.3	104.4		5/2/10
Halle city	–	89.6	107.3	–	–	1
Hergisdorf	92.9H	–	–	–	–	1
Jerichow	–	–	–	–	90.5	1
Jessen	–	–	87.6	–	–	1
Klötze	–	–	–	–	100.7	5

FM (MHz)	MDR 1	Jump	Figaro	Info	Sputnik	kW
Köthen	–	–	–	106.4	–	0.3
Magdeburg	96.1	–	107.4	–	–	10/30
Naumburg	92.3H	–	–	–	93.1	1/0.5
Sangerhausen	101.1H	–	–	99.9	–	0.1/1
Schneidlingen	–	–	–	106.7	–	0.5
Schönebeck	–	–	–	91.1	105.2	2/1.5
Stendal-Borstel	–	–	–	87.8	104.8	1
Weißenfels	–	–	–	88.8	–	1
Wernigerode	–	–	–	98.6	–	1
Wittenberg	88.1D	101.6	104.0	–	–	30/2x55
Zeitz-Hainichen	–	–	–	–	89.4	0.5
Txs in Thüringen:						
Apolda	–	–	–	91.2	–	1
Arnstadt	–	–	–	106.1	–	0.5
Bad Salzungen	–	–	–	94.0	–	0.1
Bleßberg	91.7S	96.9	–	–	–	100/20
Eisenach	–	–	–	100.0	–	0.2
Erfurt	94.4	–	–	97.8	–	2/1
Gera	–	–	–	91.1	–	1
Gotha	–	–	–	88.8	–	0.1
Greiz	–	–	–	93.3	–	0.2
Heiligenstadt	93.6He	–	–	90.5	–	0.1
Ilmenau	–	–	–	93.0	–	0.1
Inselsberg	92.5	90.2	87.9	–	–	100/100/60
Jena-Oßmaritz	88.2G	101.9	96.4	89.5	–	1/0.2
Keula	98.5He	–	–	–	–	20
Lobenstein	95.5G	–	–	101.8	–	2/0.5
Magdala	92.9	–	–	99.2	–	0.01/0.05
Meiningen	–	–	–	94.7	–	0.2
Mühlhausen	–	–	–	105.8	–	0.1
Nordhausen	88.3He	–	–	93.7	–	0.1
Pößneck	–	–	–	101.6	–	0.2
Remda	103.6	105.6	100.7	–	–	60
Ronneburg	97.8G	100.9	103.9	–	–	10/30/30
Saalfeld	–	–	–	104.6	–	0.1
Schleiz	–	–	–	105.1	–	0.2
Schmalkalden	–	–	–	100.0	–	0.1
Schmölln	–	–	–	107.9	–	0.2
Sondershausen	100.1He	–	–	95.1	–	0.05/0.1
Sonneberg	–	–	–	105.8	–	0.1
Suhl Erleshügel	93.7S	91.1	89.8	97.5	–	1/0.1/0.2/5
Weimar Ettersberg	93.3	–	–	–	–	5
Weimar Belvedere	–	–	–	102.6	–	2

*) Directional, to north and west only

DAB: 6 txs in Sachsen-Anhalt on ch. 6B (184MHz), 7 txs in Thüringen on ch. 8B (198MHz), 7 txs in Sachsen on ch. 9A (203MHz). Carry central prgr. plus respective MDR 1 stn. in all regional versions.

D.Prgr: MDR 1 Radio Sachsen, Königsbrücker Str. 88, 01099 Dresden, regional prgr. from studios Bautzen (freq. marked (B), Chemnitz (C) and Leipzig (L); **MDR Sachsen-Anhalt**, Stadtparkstr. 8, 39114 Magdeburg, regional prgr. Dessau (D), Halle (H) and Stendal (St); **MDR Thüringen**, Gothaer Str. 36, 99094 Erfurt; regional prgr. Gera (G), Heiligenstadt (He) and Suhl (S). 2200-0400 on all MDR 1 stns common prgr. – **MDR Jump**, AC – **MDR Figaro**, culture, rel. ARD-Nachtkonzert, ARD-Radiofestival – **MDR Info**, news – **MDR Sputnik**, CHR – **MDR Klassik**, classical music, at times rel. MDR Figaro – **Serbske Rozhlas**, Am Postplatz 2, 02607 Bautzen. Prgr. in Upper Sorbian on 100.4MHz Mon-Fri 0405-0700, Sat 0505-0800, Sun 1000-1130. Radio Satkula for young listeners Mon 1900-2100. Also rel. Bramborske Serbske Radio, see G).

E) NORDDEUTSCHER RUNDFUNK (NDR)

Public broadcasting institution of Hamburg, Mecklenburg-Vorpommern, Niedersachsen and Schleswig-Holstein

✉ Rothenbaumchaussee 132, 20149 Hamburg ☎ +49 40 4156 0 📠 +49 40 447 602 **W:** ndr.de

MW: Closed down in 2015

FM (MHz)	NDR 1	NDR 2	NDR-K	Info	N-Joy	kW
Txs in Hamburg:						
Moorfleet	90.3	87.6	99.2	92.3	94.2	80/5/1
	89.5No					10
Txs in Mecklenburg-Vorpommern:						
Anklam	94.6Gr	–	–	–	103.0	6.3/1.25
Bad Doberan	94.3R	–	–	–	103.7	0.2/5
Barth	87.6Gr	–	–	–	95.0	0.4/0.3
Demmin	97.6N	92.5	91.8	101.5	95.1	0.1/1
Dömitz	88.3	–	–	–	–	1
Garz/Rügen	102.5Gr	99.8	91.5	88.6	95.5	50/10
Greifswald	101.0Gr	–	–	–	–	0.16
Grevesmühlen	100.7W	–	–	–	103.4	0.5/5
Güstrow-Strentz	92.5R	–	–	–	104.4	1.25/0.63
Helptberg	90.5N	99.1	96.0	101.8	103.2	100/1.25

FM (MHz)	NDR 1	NDR 2	NDR-K	Info	N-Joy	kW
		94.2Gr				6.3
Heringsdorf	97.6Gr	94.0	102.7	100.5	92.3	1
Malchin	–	–	–	103.5	94.4	1
Neubrandenburg	–	–	–	–	89.5	1
Pasewalk	93.7Gr	–	–	–	94.8	2.5/1.25
Ribnitz-Damgarten	–	–	–	–	99.4	0.3
Röbel	88.5N	107.0	94.7	100.4	97.4	10/60/4
Rostock	91.0R	93.5	88.2	102.8	88.9	160/40/5
Schwerin	92.8	98.5	89.2	105.3	99.5	30/100/2
Stralsund	92.1Gr	–	–	–	–	0.4
Ueckermünde	90.1Gr	–	–	–	104.1	4/1.5
Wismar	96.2W	–	–	–	–	0.2
Wolgast-Moeckow	89.0Gr	–	–	–	93.2	0.4/0.3
Txs in and for Niedersachsen:						
Alfeld	87.8B	93.6	96.5	91.1	92.9	0.05
Aurich-Popens	95.8Ol	98.1	90.0	96.4	92.7	25/10/1
Bad Pyrmont	88.6	92.6	95.7	98.5		0.05
Bad Rothenfelde	–	–	–	97.9	91.2	0.2/0.1
Braunlage	–	–	–	–	96.1	0.02
Braunschweig	–	–	–	–	100.3	15
Bremen-Walle	–	–	–	95.0	–	1
Bremerhaven	–	–	–	98.9	92.8	0.5/0.05
Cloppenburg	–	–	–	103.7	93.5	1
Cuxhaven	105.4Ol	97.9	94.6	93.1	91.6	20/10/1/10
	98.4					1
Damme	–	–	–	106.5	105.0	0.5/1
Dannenberg	91.2L	96.4	93.3	90.7	94.0	25/10/3/1
Goslar	88.2B	93.7	95.1	96.0	96.5	0.1
Göttingen	88.5B	94.1	96.8	99.9	95.9	5/0.5/5/0.5
Hann. Münden	88.2B	96.1	90.8	92.9	94.8	0.05
Hannover-Hemm.	90.9	96.2	98.7	88.6	92.6	
15/5/15/0.5/2.5						
Hildesheim	–	–	–	–	95.7	0.5
Holzminden	92.7B	96.0	98.4	88.6	99.7	0.5/0.1
Jever	–	–	–	–	97.3	0.3
Königslutter-Elm	–	–	88.7	–	–	0.2
Lingen	92.8O	97.8	90.2	88.9	96.6	15/0.2/0.5
Meppen	–	–	–	–	93.3	0.05
Osnabrück	92.4O	89.2	98.8	87.6	96.4	8/2x0.2
Rinteln	–	–	–	95.3	105.2	0.1/0.04
Rosengarten	103.2L	–	–	–	91.4	20/0.3
Seesen	–	–	–	90.4	96.6	0.2/0.05
Stadthagen	100.8	102.6	104.4	98.2	91.3	25/1
Steinkimmen	91.10l	99.8	94.4	98.6	92.9	100/3/1
Torfhaus	98.0B	92.1	89.9	99.5	–	100/50
Visselhövede	91.8L	95.9	87.8	98.4	97.6	5/2/5/1/30
Wedel	–	–	–	–	95.6	0.2
Wolfsburg	–	–	–	88.2	–	0.1
Txs in Schleswig-Holstein:						
Bungsberg	97.8Lb	91.9	89.9	96.6	99.0	50/1/0.5
Flensburg	89.6F	93.2	96.1	87.7	91.0	25/10/0.5
Garding-Katingsiel	–	–	–	–	88.8	0.5
Heide-Welmbüttel	90.5H	96.3	99.4	87.9	94.9	15/0.5
Helgoland island	88.9H	93.4	97.0	92.5	91.7	0.01
Husum	–	–	–	–	93.7	0.05
Kiel-Kronshagen	91.3	98.3	95.7	99.7	94.5	15/1/0.4/15
Lauenburg	94.7Lb	–	–	96.8	99.8	0.3
Lübeck	93.1Lb	90.7	88.0	95.9	94.0	0.5/0.1/0.5
Mölln	104.5Lb	–	–	–	90.9	20/0.5
Neumünster	106.4No	–	–	90.8	98.7	20/1/0.5
Niebüll-Süderlügum	–	–	–	–	91.5	0.2
Sylt	90.9F	98.7	94.3	92.7	95.6	5
Wedel	–	–	–	–	95.6	0.2

DAB: Visselhövede tx on ch. 6A (182MHz), Hannover tx on ch. 6D (187MHz), Hamburg txs on ch. 7A (189MHz), Kiel tx on ch. 9C (206MHz), Braunschweig tx on ch. 11B (219MHz), Steinkimmen tx on ch. 12A (224MHz), Schwerin tx on ch. 12B (226MHz)

D.Prgr: NDR 90,3 from Hamburg studios, on 90.3/98.4MHz – **NDR 1 Radio MV**, Schloßgartenallee 61, 19061 Schwerin; via txs in Mecklenburg-Vorpommern, regional prgr. Greifswald (Gr), Neubrandenburg (N), Rostock (R) and Wismar (W, from Schwerin studios) – **NDR 1 Niedersachsen**, Rudolf-von-Bennigsen-Ufer 22, 30169 Hannover; via txs in Niedersachsen, regional prgr. Braunschweig (B), Göttingen (G), Lüneburg area (L, from Hannover studios), Oldenburg (Ol) and Osnabrück (O) – **NDR 1 Welle Nord**, Postfach 34 80, 24033 Kiel (studio location: Eggerstr. 16); via txs in Schleswig-Holstein and 89.5MHz; regional prgr. Flensburg (F), Heide (H), Lübeck (Lb) and Norderstedt (No). 2110-0430 common prgr. on all NDR 1 stns – **NDR 2**, AC – **NDR Kultur**, classical music, rel. ARD-Nachtkonzert, ARD-Radiofestival – **NDR Info**, Mon-Fri 0500-1850 and Sat 0500-1700 news format, other times diverse prgr., at night music specials – **NDR Info Spezial**, special prgr. rel. ARD-Infonacht, Mon-Fri 1500-2000

Funkhaus Europa (see J), Sun 0500-0700 NDR 90,3 (for Hamburger Hafenkonzert prgr., broadcast since 1929). Sea weather forecasts at 2305 (also via NDR Info FM txs in Mecklenburg-Vorpommern), 0730 and 2105 – **N-Joy**, CHR – **NDR Blue**, alternative – **NDR Traffic**, traffic announcements

F) RADIO BREMEN (RB)
Public broadcasting institution of Bremen
✉ Diepenau 10, 28195 Bremen ☎ +49 421 246 0 🖷 +49 421 246 1010 **W:** radiobremen.de

FM (MHz)	Eins	NWRadio	Vier	Europa	kW
Bremen-Walle	93.8	88.3	101.2	96.7	100/50
Bremerhaven	93.4	95.4	100.8	92.1	25

DAB: Bremen-Walle tx on ch. 7B (191MHz), rel. also Kiraka, see J).
D.Prgr: Bremen Eins, oldies, rel. 2305-0400 (Sun to 0500) SWR1 – **Nordwestradio**, culture, in cooperation with NDR. Rel. ARD-Nachtkonzert, ARD-Radiofestival – **Bremen Vier**, AC, rel. ARD-Popnacht – **Funkhaus Europa** see J).

G) RUNDFUNK BERLIN-BRANDENBURG (RBB)
Public broadcasting institution of Berlin and Brandenburg, operating from two main seats:
Potsdam: ✉ Marlene-Dietrich-Allee 20, 14482 Potsdam-Babelsberg ☎ +49 331 731 0 🖷 +49 331 731 3571
Berlin: ✉ 14046 Berlin (studio/office location: Masurenallee 8-14) ☎ +49 30 3031 0 🖷 +49 30)3015 062 **W:** rbb-online.de
Txs in Berlin:

MHz	kW	Site	Program
88.8	80	Scholzplatz	R. Berlin
92.4	80	Scholzplatz	Kulturradio
93.1	25	Scholzplatz	Inforadio
95.8	100	Alexanderplatz	radioeins
96.3	80	Scholzplatz	Funkhaus Europa
99.7	100	Alexanderplatz	Antenne Brandenburg
102.6	20	Alexanderplatz	Fritz

Txs in Brandenburg:

FM (MHz)	Ant.B.	Eins	Fritz	Kultur	Info	kW
Belzig-Lütte	106.2	99.3	91.9	100.2	–	100/10
Booßen	87.6F	89.1F	101.5	96.8	102.0	5/30/1.5
Calau	98.6C	95.1C	103.2	104.4	93.4+	100/30
Casekow	91.1Pr	106.1	100.1	104.4	–	60/10
Cottbus	–	–	–	–	99.9	1
Guben	100.9C	–	–	–	–	6
Lübben	–	–	–	–	92.4	0.4
Perleberg	–	–	–	–	92.3	1
Prenzlau	99.4Pr	–	–	–	98.6	0.5
Pritzwalk	106.6Pe	99.9	103.1	91.7	–	100/10
Wittstock	–	–	–	–	97.7	1.3
Zehlendorf	90.8F	–	–	–	–	1.3

+) Bramborske Serbske Radio
DAB: Berlin txs on ch. 7D (194MHz), also rel. Bayern 2, BR Klassik (see B), MDR Jump (see D), SWR3 (see I), WDR 2 (see J).
D.Prgr from Berlin studios: Radio Berlin, Berlin city prgr., rel. ARD-Popnacht – **Inforadio**, news, rel. ARD-Infonacht with local insertions – **Kulturradio**, classical music, rel. ARD-Nachtkonzert, ARD-Radiofestival
D.Prgr from Potsdam studios: Antenne Brandenburg, light music, regional prgr. from studios Perleberg (Pe), Prenzlau (Pr), Frankfurt/Oder (F) and Cottbus (C), 2100-2305 common prgr. with Radio Berlin, rel. ARD-Nachtexpress – **radioeins**, progressive-style rock/pop and information, regional prgr. from Frankfurt/Oder and Cottbus – **Fritz**, youth
Funkhaus Europa: See J).
Bramborske Serbske Radio: RBB, Studio Cottbus, Berliner Straße 155, 03046 Cottbus. Prgr. in Lower Sorbian Mon-Fri 1100-1200 and repeat at 1800-1900, Sundays and holidays 1130-1300. 93.4MHz otherwise rel. Inforadio and Serbske Rozhlas (see D)

H) SAARLÄNDISCHER RUNDFUNK (SR)
Public broadcasting institution of Saarland
✉ Funkhaus Halberg, 66100 Saarbrücken ☎ +49 681 602 0 🖷 +49 681 602 3874 **W:** sr-online.de
MW: 1179kHz closes by 31 December 2015

FM (MHz)	SR 1	SR 2	SR 3	UnserDing	kW
Bliestal-Webenheim	92.3	–	89.1	98.0	5
Göttelborner Höhe	88.0	91.3	95.5	–	100
Homburg	–	98.6	–	–	0.2
Merzig-Hilbringen	89.3	92.1	98.0	–	0.1
Neunkirchen	–	–	–	–	5
Oberperl	91.9	88.6	96.1	–	5
Saarbr. Schocksberg	–	–	–	103.7	100
Sankt Wendel	–	–	–	90.3	0.1

DAB: 5 txs on ch. 9A (203MHz), also rel. Kiraka (see J), R. Salü (see U)
D.Prgr: SR 1 Europawelle Saar, AC, rel. ARD-Popnacht – **SR 2 KulturRadio**, culture, rel. ARD-Nachtkonzert, ARD-Radiofestival – **SR 3 Saarlandwelle**, light music, news in French at 0805 – **Unser Ding**, CHR, at times rel. Das Ding (SWR) – **Antenne Saar**, rel. of SR 2, SWR Info and Radio France Internationale

I) SÜDWESTRUNDFUNK (SWR)
Public broadc.institution of Baden-Württemberg and Rheinland-Pfalz
✉ 76522 Baden-Baden (Location: Hans-Bredow-Straße) ☎ +49 7221 929 0 🖷 +49 7221 929 2010
Broadcasting house Mainz: ✉ Postfach 3740, 55122 Mainz (Location: Am Fort Gonsenheim 39) ☎ +49 6131 929 0
Broadcasting house Stuttgart: ✉ Postfach 106040, 70049 Stuttgart (Location: Neckarstraße 230) ☎ +49 711 929 0 **W:** swr.de

FM (MHz)	SWR1	SWR2	SWR3	SWR4	DasDing	–	kW
Txs in and for Baden-Württemberg:							
Aalen Braunenberg	95.1	91.1	98.1	96.9U	–		50/5
Albstadt-Mahlesfeld	–	–	–	99.5Tü	87.8		0.1/0.3
Bad Bellingen	–	–	–	96.6F	–		0.1
Bad Mergentheim	87.8	93.2	99.7	105.5H	100.5		10/0.1
Baden-Baden	90.9	98.9	99.6	88.5Ka	91.7		0.8/0.4
Baiersbronn	–	–	–	87.9O	–		0.1
Basel St. Crischona*	87.9	92.0	98.3	89.5L	–		5
Blauen-Hochblauen	89.2	92.6	97.0	–	–		8.4
Buchen	91.9	97.1	94.1	107.5M	100.6		0.1/25
Elzach Hörnleberg	–	–	–	101.8F	–		0.1
Feldberg	89.8	97.9	93.8	104.0F	–		5
Freiburg-Lehen	107.0	91.1	99.2	100.7F	–		0.1/1
Freudenberg	90.3	97.2	94.9	91.6H	–		0.01
Geislingen	93.0	88.5	95.5	107.9	–		0.5/0.1
Grünten*	98.7	–	103.0	–	–		30
Hausach Brandenkopf	95.4	–	99.7	97.6O	–		0.5/0.1
Heidelberg Königstuhl	97.8	88.8	99.9	104.1M	–		100
Heilbronn	–	–	–	99.5H	–		2
Hornisgrinde	93.5	96.2	98.4	94.00	–		80/5
Karlsruhe-Ettlingen	–	–	–	97.0Ka	–		20
Klettgau	95.1	92.8	98.5	87.7L6	–		2.6
Lichtenstein	99.1	–	–	89.0Tü	–		0.1
Mannheim	–	–	–	–	91.5		4
Mötzingen	–	–	97.2	87.6Tü	90.5		1
Mühlacker	–	–	–	95.7B	–		2
Pforzheim	92.9	88.1	99.3	87.6Ka	–		– 5/0.2/0.5
Raichberg	88.3	91.8	94.3	107.3Tü	–		40/25
Ravensburg	99.0	–	87.9	–	107.2		0.1
Reutlingen	–	–	–	–	97.7		2
Schiltach-Simonsberg	90.8	–	94.5	99.20	–		0.1
Schwäbisch Gmünd	–	–	–	100.9U	–		0.1
Sigmaringen	–	–	–	101.2Fr	–		0.1
Strasbourg*	–	–	–	88.90	–		1
Stuttgart-Degerloch	94.7	105.7	92.2	90.1	90.8		100/2
Stuttgart (town)	99.6	93.1	–	–	–		0.5/0.2
					†91.5		0.3
Tübingen	–	–	–	–	97.3		2
Ulm Kuhberg	92.6	89.2	97.4	94.5U	98.9		10/1
Vaihingen	–	98.6	–	–	–		0.1
Villingen-Schwenningen	–	–	–	91.1F	–		1
Waldenburg	98.8	93.8	96.5	106.6H	–		100/50
Waldburg	–	94.9	–	99.5H	–		60
				91.2Fr	–		25
Weinheim	97.1	–	99.5	100.7M	–		0.04/0.1
Wertheim	96.9	91.8	94.6	101.2H	–		0.1
Witthoh	92.4	90.4	97.1	89.0Fr	–		40/5
Zell Hohe Möhr	87.6	–	96.8	100.2F	–		0.1
Zwiefalten	93.7	–	92.8	87.6Fr	–		0.1

†) SWR Info. *Basel site in Switzerland, Strasbourg site in France, Grünten site in Bayern

FM (MHz)	SWR1	SWR2	SWR3	SWR4	DasDing	kW
Txs in and for Rheinland-Pfalz:						
Bad Kreuznach	–	–	–	–	90.9	0.1
Bleialf-Buchet	88.3	99.7	98.9	94.6T	–	0.1
Daun	91.1	–	98.5	93.6T	–	8
Diez-Geisenberg	88.4	93.4	98.2	87.9K	–	0.01/0.1
Donnersberg	99.1	92.0	101.1	105.6KI	–	60
Haardtkopf	97.7	93.0	90.0	107.1T	–	50/25
Hohe Wurzel	–	–	–	107.9M	–	6.2
Idar-Oberstein	88.5	95.1	98.1	106.4T	–	0.01/1
Kaisersl. Bornberg	90.8	93.9	97.5	99.6KI	92.5	25/0.3
Koblenz-Waldesch	96.1	94.0	91.6	107.4K	99.4	10/40/0.2
Kreuzweiler	–	–	–	97.3T	–	0.3
Linz	92.4	–	94.8	97.4K	–	50
Mainz-Kastel*	87.7	103.2	93.7	91.4M	105.2	1
Mainz-Wolfsheim	–	–	–	94.9M	–	5

FM (MHz)	SWR1	SWR2	SWR3	SWR4	DasDing	kW
Marienberger Höhe	89.8	95.4	92.8	106.3K	91.3	25/0.1
Nierstein-Oppenheim*	–	–	–	92.9M	98.4	0.1/0.3
Pirmasens Kettrichhof	100.8	–	107.2	104.2KI	–	5
Rüdesheim*	–	99.4	93.3	88.6M	–	0.1/0.5
Saarburg	99.2	93.8	90.6	101.2T	–	5
Trier	94.9	89.4	98.2	98.8T	91.7	0.1/0.3
Tübingen Herrenberg	–	–	97.2	87.6Tü	90.5	1
Weinbiet	89.9	102.2	–	95.9L	–	25
Zweibrücken	–	–	–	90.5KI	–	0.2

*) Site in Hessen. +20 stns below 0.1kW

DAB: 9 txs on ch. 8D (201MHz), 10 txs on ch. 9D (208MHz), 9 txs on ch. 11A (217MHz). Only ch. 11A txs also rel. Big FM World Beats

D.Prgr. from Stuttgart studios, via txs in Baden-Württemberg: **SWR1 Baden-Württemberg**, oldies, at night common SWR1 prgrs from Baden-Baden; **SWR4 Baden-Württemberg**, light music, with local prgr. from Freiburg (F), Friedrichshafen (F), Heilbronn (H), Karlsruhe (Ka), Lörrach (Lö), Mannheim (M), Offenburg (O), Tübingen (T) and Ulm (U), rel. ARD-Hitnacht

D.Prgr. from Mainz studios, via txs in Rheinland-Pfalz: **SWR1 Rheinland-Pfalz**, oldies, at night common SWR1 prgrs from Baden-Baden; **SWR4 Rheinland-Pfalz**, light music, with local prgrs from Kaiserslautern (KI), Koblenz (K), Ludwigshafen (L) and Trier (T), rel. ARD-Hitnacht

D.Prgr. from Baden-Baden studios: SWR2, culture, 1740-1800 prgr. from Mainz/Stuttgart, at night rel. ARD-Nachtkonzert; **SWR3**, AC; **Das Ding**, youth; **SWR Info**, news, rel. ARD-Infonacht

J) WESTDEUTSCHER RUNDFUNK (WDR)

Public broadcasting institution of Nordrhein-Westfalen

✉ 50600 Köln (location: Appellhofplatz 1) ☎ +49 221 220 1 🖷 +49 221 220 4800 **W:** wdr.de

MW: Closed down in 2015

FM (MHz)	ELive	WDR 2	WDR 3	WDR4	WDR5	kW
Aachen-Stolberg	106.4	100.8A	95.9	93.9	101.9	20
Arnsberg	96.0	99.4S	97.5	91.7	88.5	0.1
Bad Oeynhausen	107.7	99.1B	92.7	90.1	87.7	0.1
Bergheim	–	88.4K	–	–	–	0.5
Bonn Venusberg	102.4	100.4K	93.1	90.7	88.0	50
Dortmund	–	87.8D	–	–	–	2
Ederkopf	107.2	101.8S	–	100.7	95.8	15/20
Eifel-Bärbelkreuz	105.5	101.0	96.3	104.4	89.6	20/10/20/10
Gummersbach	–	91.8W	–	–	–	10
Hallenberg	105.7	–	–	96.1	88.3	0.1
Höxter Hasselberg	107.3	96.4B	95.2	87.8	93.9	0.5
Ibbenbüren	102.5	96.0M	97.3	99.5	88.5	0.5
Klever Berg	103.7	93.3Dü	97.3	101.7	99.7	2
Köln	87.6	98.6K	–	–	–	0.3/0.5
Langenberg	106.7	99.2Dü	95.1	101.3	88.8	100
					103.3+	100
Lübbecke	93.6	96.0B	91.7	99.6	88.6	0.1
Münster-Baumberge	107.9	94.1M	89.7	100.0	92.0	25
Nordhelle	104.7	93.5S	98.1	103.8	90.3	35
Olsberg	107.0	102.1S	–	104.1	98.6	10
Remscheid	–	95.7W	–	–	–	1
Schmallenberg	100.1	93.8S	97.8	101.1	90.0	0.1
Siegen	107.5	97.1S	98.4	101.2	97.6	0.5/1/0.5/1
Teutoburger Wald	105.5	93.2B	97.0	100.5	90.6	100
Warburg	98.2	91.8B	94.3	104.5	88.4	0.5
Wittgenstein	–	92.3S	88.7	–	–	15
Wuppertal	–	99.8W	–	–	–	1

*) Funkhaus Europa

DAB: 23 txs on ch. 11D (222MHz), also rel. Domradio (see S)

D.Prgr: 1 Live, CHR – **WDR 2**, AC, incl. local news from Aachen (A), Bielefeld (B), Köln (K), Dortmund (D), Düsseldorf (Dü), Münster (M), Siegen (S), Wuppertal (W); at night rel. NDR 2 – **WDR 3**, culture, rel. ARD-Nachtkonzert, ARD-Radiofestival – **WDR 4**, light music, rel. ARD-Hitnacht – **WDR 5**, information, repeats overnight – **Funkhaus Europa**, multicultural, also via RBB and RB txs (see F/G) and with some prgrs from their Bremen/Berlin studios. Existing contracts with RBB and RB have been terminated effective year end 2015, continuation of this cooperation uncertain at time of editing – **VERA**, continuous traffic jam information – **WDR Event**, live coverage of various events, otherwise silent – **1 Live Diggi**, continuous CHR music – **Kiraka**, for childrens

II. COMMERCIAL AND OTHER STATIONS

K) BADEN-WÜRTTEMBERG

Media institution: Landesanstalt für Kommunikation (LfK) ✉ Postfach 102927, 70025 Stuttgart (office location: Reinsburgstraße 27 ☎ +49 711 669910 🖷 +49 711 6699111 **W:** lfk.de

Commercial stations:

FM	MHz	kW	Site	Station
2)	87.8	1	Mannheim	big FM
6)	88.6	2	Langenburg	R. Ton
3)	89.1	0.5	Heilbronn	Hit-R. Antenne 1
3)	89.3	0.1	Bad Urach	Hit-R. Antenne 1
2)	89.5	10	Stuttgart Frauenkopf	big FM
3)	89.5	0.1	Wertheim	Hit-R. Antenne 1
2)	89.7	1	Tübingen	big FM
11)	90.4	2	Karlsruhe	Klassik R.
9)	90.5	2	Achern	Hitradio Ohr
2)	90.9	0.1	Heidelberg city	big FM
15)	91.4	3	Lützenhardt	R. TV R.
7)	91.4	0.5	Pforzheim	die neue welle
18)	92.4	1	Hockenheimring	Rennradio
2)	92.7	1	Horb	big FM
9)	93.0	0.1	Haslach	Schwarzwald R.
16)	93.1	1	Rottweil-Zimmern	R. Neckarburg
15)	94.7	0.5	Freiburg-Lehen	baden.fm
17)	95.4	0.1	Stuttgart SWR bldg.	Metropol FM
6)	95.6	1	Balingen	R. Ton*)
6)	96.0	0.1	Künzelsau	R. Ton
10)	96.4	1	Überlingen	R. Seefunk
6)	96.8	0.3	Eppingen	R. Ton
4)	96.9	0.1	Schussental	R. 7
12)	97.2	1	Stuttgart-Münster	egoFM
2)	97.2	0.5	Sinsheim-Dühren	big FM
13)	97.5	0.5	Esslingen	Die Neue 107.7
8)	97.6	0.3	Rudersberg	Energy Stuttgart
2)	99.0	0.5	Rottweil	big FM
6)	99.0	0.1	Bad Urach	R. Ton*)
15)	99.2	0.2	Herrenberg	R. TV R.
9)	99.2	0.1	Oberkirch	Hitradio Ohr
10)	99.3	5	Friedrichshafen	R. Seefunk
2)	99.7	1	Ulm	big FM
3)	100.1	50	Schwäbisch Hall	Hit-R. Antenne 1
6)	100.1	0.1	Hechingen	R. Ton
10)	100.3	5	Geislingen	big FM
1)	100.4	80	Hornisgrinde	R. Regenbogen
8)	100.7	20	Güglingen	Energy Stuttgart
6)	100.9	1	Tübingen	R. Ton*)
7)	100.9	0.8	Baden-Baden	die neue welle
1)	101.1	8.4	Blauen-Müllheim	R. Regenbogen
4)	101.2	0.1	Villingen-Schwenningen	R. 7
3)	101.3	75	Stuttgart Frauenkopf	Hit-R. Antenne 1
9)	101.6	0.5	Brandenkopf	Hit-R. Ohr
7)	101.8	25	Karlsruhe	die neue welle
4)	101.8	10	Ulm-Ermingen	R. 7
10)	101.8	10	Konstanz	R. Seefunk
8)	101.8	1	Backnang	Energy Stuttgart
10)	101.9	0.1	Schopfheim	R. Seefunk
16)	102.0	3	Villingen-Schwenningen	R. Neckarburg
12)	102.1	25	Mudau	sunshine live
10)	102.4	0.2	Laufenburg [Switzerl.]	R. Seefunk
4)	102.5	40	Witthoh-Tuttlingen	R. 7
6)	102.6	0.5	Schwäbisch Hall	R. Ton
10)	102.6	0.3	Ravensburg	R. Seefunk
8)	102.6	0.1	Bad Wildbad	die neue welle
6)	102.7	0.1	Nagold	die neue welle
1)	102.8	50	Heidelberg.Königstuhl	R. Regenbogen
2)	102.8	0.5	Freiburg	big FM
11)	103.0	1	Göppingen	Klassik R.
8)	103.0	0.3	Calw	die neue welle
10)	103.1	5	Rheinfelden	R. Seefunk
3)	103.1	0.1	Reutlingen	Hit-R. Antenne 1
6)	103.2	25	Heilbronn	R. Ton
3)	103.4	50	Raichberg	Hit-R. Antenne 1
6)	103.5	20	Bad Mergentheim	R. Ton
4)	103.7	50	Aalen	R. 7
16)	103.7	0.1	Schramberg	R. Neckarburg
2)	103.8	2	Baden-Baden	big FM
10)	103.9	10	Iberger Kugel	R. Seefunk
11)	103.9	2	Stuttgart-Münster	Klassik R.
10)	104.2	3	Sigmaringen	R. Seefunk
6)	104.2	0.1	Heidenheim	R. Ton
8)	104.3	2	Sindelfingen	Energy Stuttgart
8)	104.3	0.1	Lörrach	Energy Stuttgart
8)	104.5	2	Waiblingen	Energy Stuttgart
8)	104.5	0.1	Winnenden	Energy Stuttgart
16)	104.6	1	Oberndorf	R. Neckarburg
14)	104.6	0.3	Biberach	Donau 3 FM
1)	104.6	0.1	Buchen	R. Regenbogen
2)	104.7	0.2	Heilbronn	big FM

FM	MHz	kW	Site	Station
6)	104.7	0.1	Wertheim	R. Ton
13)	104.7	0.1	Geislingen	Die Neue 107.7
6)	104.8	1	Reutlingen	R. Ton*)
9)	104.9	5	Offenburg-Ohlsbach	Hit-R. Ohr
5)	104.9	1	Stuttgart-Münster	sunshine live
4)	105.0	50	Grünenbach	R. 7
2)	105.1	0.2	Aalen	big FM
2)	105.2	20	Pforzheim	big FM
10)	105.3	0.5	Singen	R. Seefunk
3)	105.4	1	Geislingen	Hit-R. Antenne 1
3)	105.4	0.3	Balingen	Hit-R. Antenne 1
10)	105.4	0.1	Waldshut-Tiengen	R. Seefunk
9)	105.5	0.5	Bühl	Hit-R. Ohr
14)	105.9	5	Ulm-Ermingen	Donau 3 FM
15)	106.0	8.4	Blauen-Müllheim	baden.fm
3)	106.0	0.1	Bad Mergentheim	Hit-R. Antenne 1
5)	106.1	1	Heidelberg-Königstuhl	sunshine live
13)	106.1	1	Göppingen	Die Neue 107.7
14)	106.2	0.5	Riedlingen	Donau 3 FM
13)	106.5	0.1	Kirchheim	Die Neue 107.7
15)	106.6	0.1	Titisee-Neustadt	baden.fm
13)	106.8	1	Nürtingen	Die Neue 107.7
3)	106.9	0.1	Leonberg	Hit-R. Antenne 1
10)	107.0	5	Wannenberg-Klettgau	R. Seefunk
3)	107.0	1	Pforzheim	Hit-R. Antenne 1
6)	107.1	20	Aalen	R. Ton
5)	107.1	0.1	Wiesloch	sunshine live
7)	107.3	0.1	Bruchsal	die neue welle
9)	107.4	5	Lahr	Hit-R. Ohr
13)	107.4	0.1	Gosbach	Die Neue 107.7
13)	107.7	4	Stuttgart Frauenkopf	Die Neue 107.7
15)	107.7	0.5	Freiburg-Littenweiler	baden.fm
5)	107.7	0.1	Weinheim	sunshine live
6)	107.9	1	Sickingen	R. Ton*)
5)	107.9	0.1	Mosbach	sunshine live
7)	107.9	0.1	Bretten	die neue welle

*) Will rel. a new station called Radio RN1 as of 1 Jan 2016

Addresses and other information:
1) P.O.-Box 10 26 55, 68026 Mannheim (studio location: Dudenstr. 12-26); **W:** regenbogenweb.de AC – **2)** Kronenstr. 24, 70173 Stuttgart; **W:** bigfm.de CHR, further txs see T), U) – **3)** Plieningerstr. 150, 70567 Stuttgart; **W:** antenne1.de AC – **4)** Gaisenbergstr. 29, 89073 Ulm; **W:** radio7.de AC – **5)** Hafenstr. 68-72, 68159 Mannheim; **W:** sunshine-live.de Techno, also via Astra 1N, 12.148GHz – **6)** Allee 2, 74072 Heilbronn; **W:** radio-ton.de AC – **7)** Albert-Nestler-Str. 26, 76131 Karlsruhe; **W:** meine-neue-welle.de AC – **8)** Anton-Schmidt-Str. 36, 71332 Waiblingen; **W:** energy-stuttgart.de CHR – **9)** Postfach 20 80, 77610 Offenburg (studio location: Hauptstr. 83a); **W:** hitradio-ohr.de schwarzwaldradio.com AC – **10)** Konzilstr. 1, 78462 Konstanz; **W:** radio-seefunk.de AC – **11)** see O) – **12)** see L). Rel. will start on 1 Jan 2016 – **13)** Königstr. 2, 70173 Stuttgart; **W:** dieneue1077.de Rock – **14)** Basteistr. 37, 89073 Ulm; **W:** donau3fm.de AC – **15)** Munzingerstr. 1, 79111 Freiburg; **W:** baden.fm AC – **16)** August-Schuhmacher-Str. 10, 78664 Eschbronn-Mariazell; **W:** radio-neckarburg.de – **17)** see M), stn. 15 – 18) during Hockenheimring races only

Non-commercial stations:

FM	MHz	kW	Site	Station
10)	88.4	0.3	Freiburg univ.	echo-fm
6)	88.6	1	Stuttgart-Münster	Hochschulr. Stuttg.
9)	89.2	0.1	Horb	Freies R. Freudens.
1)	89.6	0.1	Mannheim	bermuda.funk
4)	91.2	0.1	Bruchsal	LernR.
8)	96.6	1	Tübingen	Wüste Welle
2)	97.5	0.1	Schwäbisch Hall	R. StHörfunk
5)	99.2	0.3	Stuttgart-Münster	Freies R. f. Stuttg.
9)	100.0	0.5	Freudenstadt	Freies R. Freudens.
10)	102.3	1	Freiburg Vogtsberg	R. Dreyeckland
7)	102.6	1	Ulm-Ermingen	R. FreeFM
9)	104.1	0.1	Baiersbronn	Freies R. Freudens.
12)	104.5	0.5	Hohe Möhr	R. Kanal Ratte
3)	104.8	1	Karlsruhe	Querfunk
2)	104.8	0.1	Crailsheim	R. StHörfunk
1)	105.4	0.1	Heidelberg Königstuhl	bermuda.funk

Addresses and other information:
1) Brückenstr. 2-4, 68167 Mannheim; **W:** bermudafunk.org. Also rel. R. Aktiv (Universität Mannheim, Postfach 144, 68131 Mannheim); **W:** radioaktiv-online.de; Mon-Wed 0600-1000 and 1700-1900, Thu-Fri 2300-1000 and 1700-1900, Sun 1900-2100 – **2)** Haalstr. 9, 74523 Schwäbisch Hall; **W:** sthoerfunk.de – **3)** Steinstr. 23, 76133 Karlsruhe; **W:** querfunk.de, rel. Mon-Fri 0600-1100 and Mon-Thu 1600-2100 stn. 4) – **4)** Hochschule für Musik, Postfach 6040, 76040 Karlsruhe (studio

location: Wolfartsweierer Str. 7a); **W:** lernradio.de – **5)** Freies R. für Stuttgart, Rieckestr. 24, 70190 Stuttgart; **W:** freies-radio.de – **6)** Hochschulradio Stuttgart, Nobelstr. 10, 70569 Stuttgart; **W:** horads.de – **7)** Söflinger Str. 206, 89077 Ulm; **W:** freefm.de – **8)** Hechinger Str. 203, 72072 Tübingen; **W:** wueste-welle.de Rel. Tue-Thu 0700-0800 Helle Welle (religious). Tübingen university prgr. ceased in 2015 – **9)** Freies R. Freudenstadt, Forststr. 23, 72250 Freudenstadt; **W:** radio-fds. de – **10)** Adlerstr. 12, 79098 Freiburg; **W:** rdl.de – **11)** Georges-Köhler-Allee Geb. 076, 79110 Freiburg; **W:** echo-fm.uni-freiburg.de – **12)** Bahnhofstr. 3, 79650 Schopfheim; **W:** kanalrattefm.de
DAB: 8 txs on ch. 5C (178MHz) Deutschlandfunk, Deutschlandradio Kultur, DRadio Wissen, Dokumente & Debatten, Absolut Relax, Energy, ERF, Klassik Radio, Radio Bob, Radio Horeb, Schlagerparadies, Sunshine Live – 11 txs on ch. 11B (219MHz) Big FM World Beats, mixed prgr. of non-commercial stns and rel. of 12 commercial FM stns

L) BAYERN

Media institution: Bayerische Landeszentrale für Neue Medien (BLM) ✉ Heinrich-Lübke-Straße 27, 81737 München ☎ +49 89 638 080 📠 +49 89 63808140; **W:** blm.de
FM networks:

Location	Ant.B.	Rock.	Klass	egoFM	Galaxy	kW
Amberg	–	–	–	–	105.5	0.1
Ansbach	–	–	–	–	105.8	0.1
Aschaffenburg	103.0	–	–	–	91.6	25/0.1
Augsburg	104.2	87.9	92.2	94.8	–	0.1/0.3
Bad Reichenhall	103.7	–	–	–	–	0.3
Bamberg	101.1	–	–	–	104.7	25/0.5
Bayreuth	–	–	–	–	92.7	0.1
Bayrischzell	106.7	–	–	–	–	0.1
Berchtesgaden	107.9	–	–	–	–	0.3
Breithart	101.5	–	–	–	–	25
Brotjacklriegel	103.5	–	–	–	–	100
Coburg	103.8	–	–	–	90.4	5/0.2
Dillberg	100.6	–	–	–	–	25
Eichstätt	100.2	–	–	–	–	25
Enterbach	101.1	–	–	–	–	0.5
Fürth	–	–	–	91.0	–	0.2
Grünten	104.4	–	–	–	–	50
Heidelstein	101.9	–	–	–	–	100
Herzogstand	102.0	–	–	–	–	0.1
Hochries	107.7	–	–	–	–	50
Hof	–	–	–	–	94.0	0.2
Högl-Freilassing	105.3	–	–	–	–	1
Hohenpeißenb.	103.8	–	–	–	–	25
Hoher Bogen	101.9	–	–	–	–	50
Ingolstadt	–	–	–	–	107.9	0.1
Kempten	–	–	–	–	88.1	0.3
Konradsreuth	–	–	–	–	98.1	0.1
Landshut	99.3	–	–	–	99.8	0.2
Lindau	99.0	–	–	–	–	0.5
Münchberg	–	–	–	–	98.1	0.1
München	101.3	–	107.2	100.8	–	0.3/1/0.3
Naila	–	–	–	–	96.5	0.1
Nördlingen	103.3	–	–	–	–	25
Nürnberg	–	–	105.1	103.6	–	0.5/0.3
Oberaudorf	94.6	–	–	–	–	0.3
Ochsenkopf	103.2	–	–	–	–	100
Passau	102.1	–	–	–	91.7	1/0.2
Pfaffenhofen	92.6	–	–	–	–	0.5
Regensburg	103.0	–	91.1	107.5	–	–25/0.3/0.3
Reit im Winkel	101.6	–	–	–	–	0.1
Rosenheim	–	–	–	–	106.6	0.1
Selb	–	–	–	–	93.4	0.1
Sonthofen	93.6	–	–	–	–	0.1
Traunstein	103.7	–	–	–	–	5
Ulm	104.8	–	–	–	–	0.1
Weiden	–	–	–	–	89.8	0.1
Weiler Simm.	106.0	–	–	–	–	0.1
Wunsiedel	–	–	–	–	97.3	0.1
Würzburg	104.4	–	92.1	95.8	–	5/0.3
Zugspitze	102.7	–	–	–	–	2

Addresses and other information:
Antenne Bayern (AC), **Rockantenne** (rock): Münchener Straße 101c, 85737 Ismaning; also via Astra 1N, 12.148GHz h; **W:** antenne. de rockantenne.de – **Klassik R.:** see O) – **egoFM:** Leopoldstraße 254, 80807 München; also via Astra 1M, 12.460GHz; **W:** egofm.de Alternative – **R. Galaxy:** Lilienthalstraße 3c, 93049 Regensburg. **W:** radiogalaxy.de CHR. Mon-Fri 1400-1800 local prgr. produced by stns 17), 26), 29), 30/31), 32), 33), 35) (R. Euroherz), 36), 41), 42), 43) and 48) listed below

Local stations:

FM	MHz	kW	Site	Station
39)	87.9	0.3	Straubing Bogenberg	R. AWN
44)	87.9	0.1	Erding	Hitwelle Erding
35)	88.0	5	Großer Waldstein	extra~rad. / Euroherz
19)	88.1	0.1	Krumbach-Kirchberg	R. Prima 1
18)	88.2	0.2	Kaufbeuren	R. Ostallgäu
51)	88.2	0.1	Bad Reichenhall	R. Untersberg
32)	88.5	0.5	Bamberg Rothof	R. Bamberg
36)	88.5	0.1	Tirschenreuth	R. Ramasuri
27)	88.6	0.1	Karlstadt	R. Charivari
5)	89.0	0.3	München Olympiaturm	2DAY/Neues Europa
42)	89.0	0.1	Dingolfing	R. Trausnitz
51)	89.0	0.1	Högl-Freilassing	R. Untersberg
26)	89.1	0.1	Wassertrüdingen	R. 8
31)	89.2	0.5	Coburg Eckardtsberg	R. EINS
17)	89.3	0.1	Oberstdorf-Steinach	RSA R.
40)	89.3	0.2	Regen Geiskopf	Unser R. Deggendorf
26)	89.4	0.3	Ansbach Ludwigshöhe	R. 8
24)	89.7	0.1	Dillingen	RT.1 Nordschwaben
38)	89.7	0.3	Regensburg Ziegetsberg	gong fm
41)	89.7	0.3	Bad Griesbach	Unser R. Passau
26)	89.8	0.1	Dinkelsbühl	R. 8
45)	89.8	0.1	Landsberg-Stoffen	R. 106.4
31)	90.0	0.1	Kronach-Neuses	R. EINS
19)	90.2	0.32	Bad Grönenbach	R. Prima 1
26)	90.2	0.1	Gunzenhausen	R. 8
47)	90.2	0.1	Miesbach-Bergham	R. Alpenwelle
21)	90.3	0.1	Günzburg	Hitradio X
26)	90.4	0.2	Neuastadt / Aisch	R. 8
27)	90.4	0.1	Gemünden / Lohr	R. Charivari
49)	90.4	0.1	Mühldorf	Inn-Salzach-Welle
30)	90.5	0.1	Bad Kissingen	R. PrimaTon
29)	90.8	0.2	Alzenau	R. Primavera
47)	91.7	0.1	Holzkirchen Jasberg	R. Alpenwelle
42)	91.8	0.2	Pfeffenhausen-Stollnried	R. Trausnitz
47)	92.0	0.1	Wolfratshausen	R. Alpenwelle
6)	92.4	0.3	München Olympiaturm	(shared freq.)
16)	92.7	0.1	Weiler Simmerberg	Welle Bodensee
37)	92.7	0.4	Hoher Bogen	Charivari Regensbg.
49)	92.7	0.3	Reichertsheim	Inn-Salzach-Welle
13)	92.9	0.3	Nürnberg	Hi R. N1
17)	93.0	0.1	Immenstadt	RSA R.
49)	93.1	0.1	Burgkirchen-Gendorf	Inn-Salzach-Welle
2)	93.3	0.1	München Olympiaturm	Energy 93.3
33)	93.3	0.1	Pegnitz	R. Mainwelle
23)	93.4	0.3	Augsburg	R. Fantasy
9)	93.6	0.3	Erlangen	Energy Nürnberg
36)	93.6	0.1	Waidhaus Fischerberg	R. Ramasuri
19)	93.9	0.3	Mindelheim-Altensteig	R. Prima 1
41)	93.9	0.3	Vilshofen-Otterkirchen	Unser R. Passau
30)	94.0	0.1	Bad Brückenau	R. PrimaTon
37)	94.0	1	Seubersdorf Göschberg	Charivari Regensbg.
7)	94.5	0.1	München Blutenburgstr.	M 94,5
11)	94.5	0.3	Nürnberg	R. F / Jazztime
43)	94.6	0.1	Schrobenhausen	R. IN / R. ND1
47)	95.0	0.2	Bad Tölz	R. Alpenwelle
35)	95.1	0.1	Marktredwitz	extra~r. / Euroherz
36)	95.3	1	Hirschberg Rothbühl	R. Ramasuri
31)	95.4	0.3	Lichtenfels	R. EINS
43)	95.4	0.1	Ingolstadt	R. IN
3)	95.5	0.3	München Olympiaturm	Charivari 95.5
24)	95.6	1	Harburg Hühnerberg	RT.1 Nordschwaben
30)	95.7	0.1	Haßfurt/Main	R. PrimaTon
39)	95.7	0.1	Mallersdorf-Hofkirchen	R. AWN
14)	95.8	0.3	Nürnberg	R. Z
4)	96.3	0.3	München Olympiaturm	R. Gong 96,3
38)	96.3	0.32	Burglengenfeld	gong fm
25)	96.4	1	Fürth	star fm
32)	96.6	0.1	Forchheim Pinzberg	R. Bamberg
45)	96.6	0.1	Starnberg	R. 106.4
17)	96.7	0.1	Kempten town	RSA R.
22)	96.7	0.3	Augsburg	Kit R. RT.1
48)	96.7	0.3	Flintsbach Dandlberg	Charivari Rosenheim
12)	97.1	0.1	Nürnberg	Gong 97.1
24)	97.1	0.1	Donauwörth	RT.1 Nordschwaben
41)	97.2	0.1	Grafenau Liebersberg	Unser R. Passau
26)	97.3	0.3	Feuchtwangen	R. 8
38)	97.3	0.1	Schwandorf Weinberg	gong fm
46)	97.5	0.1	Weilheim	R. Oberland
17)	97.6	1	Kempten Blender	RSA R.
18)	98.0	0.1	Füssen	R. Ostallgäu
51)	98.1	0.1	Berchtesgaden	R. Untersberg

FM	MHz	kW	Site	Station
37)	98.2	0.3	Regensburg Ziegetsberg	Charivari Regensb.
41)	98.3	0.2	Passau-Haidenhof	Unser R. Passau
40)	98.6	0.3	Nürnberg	Charivari 98.6
40)	98.7	0.1	Deggendorf-Hochobernd.	Unser R. Deggendorf
37)	98.8	0.5	Burglengenfeld	Charivari Regensbg.
34)	98.9	0.1	Stadtsteinach	R. Plassenburg
25)	99.0	0.2	Lauf Moritzberg	star fm
27)	99.0	0.1	Marktheidenfeld	R. Charivari
43)	99.1	0.1	Eichstätt-Seuversholz	R. IN
50)	99.4	0.3	Haslach-Einham	R. Chiemgau
36)	99.9	0.2	Weiden Fischerberg	R. Ramasuri
47)	99.9	0.1	Herzogstand	R. Alpenwelle
29)	100.4	1	Aschaffenburg	R. Primavera
30)	100.5	0.5	Schweinfurth	R. PrimaTon
26)	100.8	0.1	Burgbernheim	R. 8
43)	101.2	0.2	Neuburg/Donau	R. IN / R. ND1
46)	101.2	0.1	Oberammergau	R. Oberland
46)	101.4	0.3	Sindelsdorf	R. Oberland
30)	101.5	1	Bad Neustadt-Unsleben	R. PrimaTon
41)	101.5	0.1	Freyung Geyersberg	Unser R. Passau
50)	101.5	0.3	Trostberg	R. Chiemgau
34)	101.6	5	Kulmbach Rehberg	R. Plassenburg
27)	102.4	0.3	Würzburg	R. Charivari
37)	102.6	0.32	Waldmünchen Perlhütte	Charivari Regensbg.
16)	103.6	0.5	Lindau Hoyerberg	Welle Bodensee
36)	103.9	0.1	Amberg Eisberg	R. Ramasuri
37)	103.9	0.5	Kelheim Leitenberg	Charivari Regensbg.
1)	104.0	0.1	München Blutenburgstr.	R. Arabella
42)	104.1	1	Landshut	R. Trausnitz
48)	104.2	0.3	Oberaudorf-Hölzelsau	Charivari Rosenheim
33)	104.3	10	Oschenberg	R. Mainwelle
47)	104.3	0.5	Enterbach-Ringberg	R. Alpenwelle
46)	104.6	0.1	Herzogstand	R. Oberland
43)	104.8	0.2	Pfaffenhofen Wolfsberg	R. IN
36)	105.1	0.5	Wiesau-Fuchsmühle	R. Ramasuri
1)	105.2	25	München-Isen	R. Arabella
18)	105.2	0.1	Obergünzburg	R. Ostallgäu
43)	105.4	0.1	Beilngries	R. IN
37)	105.5	0.3	Lam-Koppenhof	Charivari Regensbg.
42)	105.5	0.32	Landau	R. Trausnitz
20)	105.9	5	Ulm-Ermingen	R. Donau 1
37)	105.9	0.32	Nabburg Galgenberg	Charivari Regensbg.
32)	106.1	0.1	Burglesau Reisberg	R. Bamberg
8)	106.2	0.2	Erlangen	afk max
46)	106.2	0.3	Garmisch-Partenkirchen	R. Oberland
47)	106.2	0.1	Schliersbergalm	R. Alpenwelle
18)	106.3	0.5	Eisenberg Schloßberg	R. Ostallgäu
36)	106.4	0.1	Königstein Gr. Ossinger	R. Ramasuri
45)	106.4	2	Fürstenfeldbruck	R. 106.4
49)	106.4	0.3	Lohkirchen	Inn-Salzach-Welle
8)	106.5	0.1	Nürnberg	afk max
28)	106.9	5	Würzburg	R. Gong 106,9
9)	106.9	0.3	Nürnberg	Energy Nürnberg
42)	107.4	1	Pfarrkirchen-Postm.	R. Trausnitz
25)	107.8	0.2	Schwabach Heidenberg	star fm
40)	107.9	0.2	Brotjacklriegel	Unser R. Deggendorf

+ 28 txs less than 0.1kW

Addresses and other information:
Dienstleistungsgesellschaft für Bayerische Lokal-Radioprogramme (BLR) ✉ Rosenheimer Straße 145c, 81671 München **W:** blr.de. Provides network prgr. and other content for many of the above listed stns
1) Paul-Heyse-Str. 2-4, 80336 München, **W:** radioarabella.de – **2)** Pestalozzistr. 15-19, 80469 München, **W:** energy.de/muenchen – **3)** Postfach 20 16 09, 80016 München (studio location as stn. 1), **W:** charivari.de – **4)** Franz-Joseph-Str. 14, 80801 München, **W:** radiogong.de – **5)** Schneemanstr. 25, 81369 München, **W:** radio2-day.de Rel. Sat 2300-Mon 0500 R. Neues Europa: Konviktstr. 1, 85049 Ingolstadt – **6)** Radio Horeb, Postfach 1165, 87501 Immenstadt, **W:** radiohoreb.de Religious. Also via Astra 1L, 12.604GHz h. On 92.4MHz Mon-Fri 2300-1500, Sat/Sun 2300-0500, Sun 0900-1200 and 1300-2000. Christliches Radio München, Postfach 310201, 80102 München; **W:** christliches-radiomuenchen.de Religious. Mon-Fri 1500-1600, Sun 0800-0900 and 1200-1300. Lora München, Gravelottestr. 6, 81667 München, **W:** lora924.de Non-commercial. Mon-Fri 1600-2300. Feierwerk München, Hansastr. 39, 81373 München; **W:** feierwerk.de Non-commercial. Sat 0500-2300, Sun 0600-0800 and 2000-2200 – **7)** Schwere-Reiter-Str. 35, 80797 München, 80538 München, **W:** m945.afk.de Journalist training stn. – **8)** Führer Str. 212, 90429 Nürnberg, **W:** afkmax.de Journalist training stn. – **9)** Ostendstr. 100, 90482 Nürnberg, **W:** energy.de/nuernberg – **10),11),12),13)** Funkhaus Nürnberg, Senefelder

Str. 7, 90409 Nürnberg, **W:** funkhaus.de 92,0MHz also rel. Camillo 92.9 (Mon, Tue, Sun 2000-2200), R. AREF (Sun 0900-1100), Pray 92.9 (Sun 1100-1200), R. Meilensteine (Sun 0800-0900), 94.5MHz also rel. Jazztime Nürnberg (Mon 2100-2200, Thu 2000-2100). – **14)** Kopernikusplatz 12, 90459 Nürnberg, **W:** radio-z.net. 1300-0100 only, other times rel. stn. 25) – **15)** Vilradio closed down in 2015 – **16) W:** welle-bodensee.de – **17)** Rottachstr. 17, 87439 Kempten, **W:** allgaeuseite.de/rsa_radio – **18) W:** roal.de – **19)** Hirschgasse 1, 87700 Memmingen, **W:** prima1.de – **20)** Leipzigstr. 26, 88400 Biberach, **W:** radiodonau1.de – **21)** Augsburger Str. 112, 89312 Günzburg, **W:** hitradiox.de – **22)** Curt-Frenzel-Str. 4, 86167 Augsburg, **W:** radio-rt1.de – **23)** Ludwigstr. 1, 86150 Augsburg, **W:** fantasy.de Rel. Mon 2100-2400 Kanal C (university stn.): Eichleitnerstr. 30, 86159 Augsburg, **W:** kanal-c.de – **24)** Artur-Proeller-Str. 1, 86609 Donauwörth, **W:** rt1-nordschwaben.de – **25)** O´Brien Str. 2, 91126 Schwabach; **W:** rocksender.de/rocksender_nuernberg – **26)** Postfach 8, 91510 Ansbach (studio location: Schalkhäuser Landstr. 5), **W:** radio8.de – **27), 28)** Semmelstr. 15, 97070 Würzburg, **W:** charivari.fm and gong.fm Also rel. Radio Opera – **29)** Am Funkhaus 1, 63743 Aschaffenburg, **W:** radio-primavera.de – **30), 31)** Seifartshofstr. 21, 96450 Coburg, **W:** radioeins.com – **32)** Gutenbergstr. 5, 96050 Bamberg, **W:** radio-bamberg.de – **33)** Postfach 10 11 61, 95411 Bayreuth (studio location: Richard-Wagner-Str. 33), **W:** mainwelle.de – **34)** E.C.-Baumann-Str. 5, 95326 Kulmbach, **W:** radio-plassenburg.de – **35)** 0900-1000, 1200-1300 and 1800-2000 extra~radio, Postfach 1745, 95016 Hof (studio location: Kreuzsteinstr. 2-6), **W:** extra-radio.de; otherwise: R. Euroherz, Pfarr 1, 95028 Hof, **W:** euroherz.de – **36)** Unterer Markt 35, 92637 Weiden, **W:** ramasuri.de – **37), 38)** Lilienthalstr. 3c, 93049 Regensburg, **W:** radiocharivari.de and gongfm.de – **39), 40)** Bahnhofstr. 28, 94469 Deggendorf, **W:** unserradio.de – **41)** Medienstr. 5, 94036 Passau, **W:** as stn. 40) – **42)** Altstadt 361, 84028 Landshut, **W:** radio-trausnitz.de – **43)** Donaustr. 11, 85049 Ingolstadt, **W:** radio-in.de, tel. 0500-0900 on 94.6/101.2MHz R. ND1 – **44)** Postfach 1155, 84420 Isen, **W:** hitwelle.de – **45)** Schöngeisingerstr. 18, 82256 Fürstenfeldbruck, **W:** radio1064.de – **46)** Postfach 1752, 82467 Garmisch-Partenkirchen (studio location: Marienplatz 17), **W:** radio-oberland.de – **47) W:** radio-alpenwelle.de – **48)** Hafnerstr. 5-7, 83022 Rosenheim, **W:** radio-charivari.de – **49)** Mozartstr. 3a, 84508 Burgkirchen/Alz, **W:** inn-salzach-welle.de – **50)** Rupertistr. 40-42, 83278 Traunstein, **W:** radio-chiemgau.de – **51)** untersberg.de **N.B** stns 49), 50), 51) also rel. prgr. of independent producers
DAB: 8 txs on 178MHz (ch. 5C), use see K) – Erlangen tx on ch. 6A 182MHz) Bit Xpress – Augsburg tx on ch. 9C (206MHz) 12 stns – 25 txs on ch. 10D (215MHz) Bayern 1, Bayern 2, B5 plus, Antenne Bayern, Rockantenne, R. Galaxy, Absolut Hot, Kultradio – Nürnberg txs on ch. 10C (213MHz) 11 stns – Ingolstadt txs on ch. 11A (217MHz) 11 stns – München txs on ch. 11C (220MHz) 15 stns – München tx on ch. 12A (224MHz) engineering tests

M) BERLIN & BRANDENBURG
Media institution: Medienanstalt Berlin-Brandenburg (MABB) ✉ Kleine Präsidentenstraße 1, 10178 Berlin (+49 30 264 9670 2 +49 30 264 96730 **W:** mabb.de

Berlin FM txs:

FM	MHz	kW	Site	Station
14)	87.9	1	Alexanderplatz	Star FM
16)	88.4	0.5	Hallesches Ufer	88vier
24)	89.2	*0.5	Schäferberg	R. Potsdam
19)	90.2	16	Alexanderplatz	R. Teddy
16)	90.7	0.1	Schäferberg	88vier
2)	91.4	100	Alexanderplatz	Berliner Rundfunk
10)	93.6	3	Alexanderplatz	JAM FM
3)	94.3	20	Alexanderplatz	rs2
12)	94.8	4	Schäferberg	BBC WS
17)	96.7	0.5	Hallesches Ufer	RFI
13)	97.2	0.1	Hallesches Ufer	R. Russkij
9)	98.2	8	Scholzplatz	R. Paradiso
11)	98.8	1	Alexanderplatz	KISS FM
4)	100.6	13	Alexanderplatz	Flux FM
8)	101.3	5	Alexanderplatz	Klassik R.
15)	101.9	0.5	Alexanderplatz	Metropol FM
5)	103.4	10	Alexanderplatz	Energy Berlin
18)	104.1	0.2	Hallesches Ufer	NPR FM Berlin
6)	104.6	10	Alexanderplatz	104.6 RTL
7)	105.5	5	Alexanderplatz	Spreeradio
21)	106.0	1	Alexanderplatz	R. B2
12)	106.8	2	Scholzplatz	Jazz R.
1)	107.5	13	Schäferberg	BB R.

*) directional towards Potsdam
F.PI.: Closure of Schäferberg and Hallesches Ufer facilities, to be replaced by other tx sites

Brandenburg FM txs:

FM	MHz	kW	Site	Station
8)	87.6	–	Brandenburg/Havel	(closed down)
5)	87.6	0.2	Prenzlau	Energy Berlin
6)	88.0	1	Crinitz	104.6 RTL
20)	88.3	0.5	Neuruppin	Power R.
6)	89.5	0.5	Elsterwerda-Hohenl.	104.6 RTL
23)	90.3	0.5	Spremberg	R. Cottbus
9)	90.4	0.2	Guben-Reichenbach	R. Paradiso
1)	90.9	0.8	Rhinow	BB R.
8)	91.0	–	Booßen (Frankf./O.)	(closed down)
3)	91.3	1	Lauchhammer West	rs2
5)	91.6	1.3	Casekow	Energy Berlin
21)	91.6	0.5	Cottbus-Klein Oßnig	R. B2
5)	91.7	0.1	Herzberg/Elster	Energy Berlin
20)	91.8	1.3	Zehlendorf	Power R.
23)	92.1	1	Guben-Reichenbach	R. Cottbus
20)	93.3	0.5	Schwedt	Power R.
22)	93.9	3	Fürstenwalde	HitRadio SKW
20)	94.4	1.3	Perleberg	Power R.
23)	94.5	0.3	Cottbus-Madlow	R. Cottbus
3)	94.7	3	Booßen (Frankf./O.)	rs2
20)	95.2	0.4	Belzig-Lütte	Power R.
20)	95.3	0.1	Fürstenwalde	Power R.
25)	95.3	0.6	Potsdam	BHeins
1)	95.4	1.3	Zehlendorf	BB R.
9)	95.5	0.2	Eisenhüttenstadt	R. Paradiso
3)	95.6	1.3	Cottbus-Klein Oßnig	rs2
5)	96.6	0.5	Wittstock	Energy Berlin
3)	96.7	1	Crinitz	rs2
6)	96.9	1	Luckenwalde	104.6 RTL
21)	97.0	0.6	Potsdam	R. B2
20)	97.0	0.3	Erkner	Power R.
22)	99.1	–	Lübben	(closed down)
23)	99.3	0.8	Booßen (Frankf./O.)	R. Frankfurt/O.
3)	100.1	3	Lübben	rs2
2)	100.9	5	Casekow	Berliner Rundfunk
1)	102.1	20	Casekow	BB-R.
20)	102.1	1	Potsdam	Power R.
2)	102.2	3	Cottbus-Klein Oßnig	Berliner Rundfunk
23)	102.7	0.5	Forst	R. Cottbus
1)	103.7	0.6	Eisenhüttenstadt	BB R.
26)	103.8	1.5	Großräschen	Elsterwelle
3)	103.9	6	Forst	rs2
2)	104.2	20	Booßen (Frankf./O.)	Berliner Rundfunk
1)	104.3	100	Pritzwalk-Buchholz	BB R.
21)	104.9	1.3	Zehlendorf	R. B2
1)	105.0	3	Brandenburg-Krahne	BB R.
22)	105.1	0.8	Königs Wusterh.	HitRadio SKW
9)	105.9	1.6	Booßen (Frankf./O.)	R. Paradiso
3)	106.3	4	Spremberg	rs2
3)	107.2	100	Calau	BB R.
3)	107.3	12	Casekow	rs2
1)	107.8	30	Booßen (Frankf./O.)	BB R.
1)	107.9	5	Zehlendorf	BB R.

Addresses and other information:
1) Großbeerenstr. 185, 14482 Potsdam; **W:** bbradio.de. AC, with short local insertions (different ones on both Zehlendorf freq.) – **2)** Grunewaldstr. 3, 12165 Berlin; **W:** berliner-rundfunk.de Oldies – **3)** as stn. 2); **W:** rs2.de. AC – **4)** Pfuelstr. 5, 10997 Berlin; **W:** fluxfm.de. Alternative – **5)** Hardenbergstr. 4-5, 10623 Berlin; **W:** energy.de/berlin. CHR – **6), 7)** Kurfürstendamm 207-208, 10719 Berlin; **W:** 104.6rtl.com (CHR), spreeradio.de (oldies) – **8)** see O) – **9)** Am Kleinen Wannsee 5, 14109 Berlin; **W:** paradiso.de. Soft AC. Run by Protestant church – **10)** as stn. 9); **W:** jamfm.de. Black, also via Astra 1M, 12.460GHz – **11)** as stn. 2); **W:** kissfm.de. CHR – **12)** See International Broadcasting section under UK – **13)** Kochstr. 54, 10969 Berlin; **W:** radio-rb.de. In Russian – **14)** Dircksenstr. 48, 10178 Berlin; **W:** starfm.de. Rock – **15)** Markgrafenstr. 11, 10969 Berlin; **W:** metropolfm.de; prgr. in Turkish. Further txs see K) and T) – **16)** c/o ALEX, Voltastr. 5, 13355 Berlin; **W:** alex-berlin.de. Run by MABB, citizen radio and prgr. from various small ventures, on FM in mono – **17)** See International Broadcasting section under France – **18)** See National Public Radio under USA; **W:** nprberlin.de – **19)** August-Bebel-Str. 26-53, 14482 Potsdam; **W:** radioteddy.de; childrens prgr., also via Astra 2C, 12.148GHz h. Further txs see P), Q), T) – **20)** Potsdamer Str. 131, 10783 Berlin; **W:** powerradio918.de. Oldies – **21)** Pfalzburger Str. 43-44, 10717 Berlin; **W:** radiob2.de – **22)** Karl-Marx-Str. 116, 15745 Wildau; **W:** hitradio-skw.de. Oldies – **23)** Schloßkirchplatz 3, 03046 Cottbus; **W:** radiocottbus.de and radiofrankfurt.de. AC – **24)** Brandenburger Str. 48, 14467 Potsdam; **W:** radio-potsdam.de – **25)** August-Bebel-Str. 26-53, Fach 43, 14482 Potsdam; **W:** bheins.de – **26)** see V), stn. 8)

F.Pl.: Branch of stns 23/24 at Brandenburg/Havel. Plans to put R. Paloma on FM are given up.
DAB: Alexanderplatz/Scholzplatz txs on ch. 5C (178MHz) see K) – Alexanderplatz tx on ch. 7B (191MHz) Bayern Plus, SWR Info, Mega R. SNA (rel. R. Sputnik, see International Broadcasting section under Russia), BHeins, Mauma, R. B2, R. Paradiso, R. Paloma, Pure FM, ERF Pop, FG DJ R., Schlagerparadies, R. Gold, Deluxe Music, Jack FM, Starsat R.

N) BREMEN
Media institution: Bremische Landesmedienanstalt (Brema) + Grünenweg 26, 28215 Bremen (✆49 421 334940 🖷 +49 421 323533 **W:** bremische-landesmedienanstalt.de

FM	MHz	kW	Site	Station
1)	89.8	1	Bremen-Walle	Energy Bremen
4)	90.7	0.2	Bremerhaven	R. Wester TV
4)	92.5	0.2	Bremen Neuenstr.	R. Weser TV
3)	97.2	–	Bremen-Walle	(to be allocated)
1)	104.3	8	Bremerhaven	Energy Bremen
2)	104.8	0.1	Bremen-Walle	R. Teddy
5)	107.6	0.2	Bremen-Walle	R. 21
2)	107.9	0.3	Bremerhaven	R. Teddy

Addresses and other information:
1) Erste Schlachtpforte, 28195 Bremen; **W:** energy.de/bremen CHR – **2)** see M), stn. 19 – **3)** Rel. of Flux FM ceased in 2015 – **4)** Richtweg 14, 28195 Bremen; **W:** radioweser.tv Citizen radio – **5)** see R)
DAB: Bremen-Walle tx on ch. 5C (178MHz) see K)

O) HAMBURG & SCHLESWIG-HOLSTEIN
Media institution: Medienanstalt Hamburg / Schleswig-Holstein (MA HSH) ☛ Rathausallee 72-76, 22846 Norderstedt ☎ +49 40 3690050 🖷 +49 40 36900555 **W:** ma-hsh.de

FM	R.SH	delta	Nora	Klass.	kW
Ahrensburg	–	96.5	–	–	2
Bredstedt	–	–	98.1	–	0.1
Bungsberg (Eutin)	100.2	104.1	106.2	97.2	2x50/0.2
Flensburg-Freienwill	101.4	105.6	–	–	20
Flensburg-Harrislee	–	–	88.5	106.5	0.5
Garding	–	–	94.1	91.7	0.5
Hamburg-Bergedorf	102.0	107.7	93.7	–	0.1
Hamburg Hertz-T.	100.0	93.4	–	98.1	2x2/0.1
Heide-Welmbüttel	103.8	100.4	–	–	15
Heide (town)	–	–	96.9	–	0.3
Helgoland (island)	100.0	103.5	101.6	89.8	0.1
Husum	–	–	92.0	–	0.1
Itzehoe	–	–	104.9	92.7	1/0.5
Kaltenkirchen	102.9	107.4	101.1	–	20
Kiel	102.4	105.9	97.0	97.4	2x15/0.3
Lauenburg	102.5	105.6	97.4	–	1/1/0.3
Lübeck	–	–	91.5	–	0.3
Mölln-Berkenthin	101.5	107.9	91.5	93.6	2x20/0.3
Neumünster	–	–	88.9	–	0.5
Niebüll	–	–	107.2	94.7	0.2
Rendsburg	–	–	93.6	92.9	0.5
Schleswig (town)	–	–	92.4	100.8	1/0.5
Schleswig-Borgwedel	–	–	–	93.9	0.5
Westerland (Sylt)	102.8	104.8	89.1	89.8	5/5/1/0.5

Addresses and other information:
R.SH (AC), **delta radio** (CHR), **R. Nora** (oldies): Wittland 3, 24109 Kiel; **W:** rsh.de deltaradio.de radionora.de – **Klassik R.:** Postfach 57 03 60, 22772 Hamburg (studio location: Planckstr. 15); **W:** klassikradio. de Light classical and lounge music. Further txs see K), L), M), P), R) (parts of the FM network have been closed in 2015). Also via Astra 1M, 12.460GHz

Hamburg area only:

FM	MHz	kW	Site	Station
1)	88.1	0.1	Bergedorf	Hamburg Zwei
1)	88.5	2	Otterndorf*)	R. Hamburg
2)	91.7	0.1	H.-Hertz-Turm	917xfm
2)	93.6	2	Otterndorf*)	Alsterradio
1)	95.0	0.1	H.-Hertz-Turm	Hamburg Zwei
3)	97.1	0.1	H.-Hertz-Turm	Energy Hamburg
3)	100.9	0.1	Bergedorf	Energy Hamburg
3)	101.6	0.1	Wedel	Energy Hamburg
1)	103.6	80	Moorfleet	R. Hamburg
1)	104.0	0.2	H.-Hertz-Turm	R. Hamburg
1)	105.8	0.5	Ahrensburg	Hamburg Zwei
2)	106.8	40	Rahlstedt	106!8 rock'n pop

*) tx in Niedersachsen, serving Neuwerk and Scharhörn islands (belonging to Hamburg)

Addresses and other information:
1) Postfach 10 01 23, 20001 Hamburg (studio location: Spitalerstraße 10); **W:** radiohamburg.de (AC), hamburg-zwei.de (former Oldie 95, relaunched in 2014) – **2)** Messberg 4, 20095 Hamburg; **W:** 106acht. de (AC), 917xfm.de (alternative) – **3)** Winterhuder Marktplatz 6, 22299 Hamburg; **W:** energy.de/hamburg CHR

Non-commercial stations:

FM	MHz	kW	Site	Station
1)	93.0	0.1	Hamburg Hertz-Turm	Freies Sender Kombinat
2)	96.0	0.1	Hamburg Hertz-Turm	TIDE 96.0 / HLR
4)	97.6	0.5	Garding	OK Westküste
5)	98.8	0.5	Lübeck-Stockelsdorf	OK Lübeck
4)	98.8	0.1	Husum	OK Westküste
3)	101.2	0.1	Kiel	Kiel FM
5)	105.2	0.1	Heide	OK Westküste

Addresses and other information:
1) Schulterblatt 23c, 20357 Hamburg; **W:** fsk-hh.org – **2)** TIDE **96.0**, Uferstraße 2, 22081 Hamburg; **W:** tidenet.de Run by Hamburg Media School. Mon 0500-2300 and thorough Tue 0500 til Sun 0500. **Hamburger Lokalradio**, Kulturzentrum LOLA, Lohbrügger Landstraße 8, 21031 Hamburg; **W:** hhlr.de On 96.0MHz Sun 0500 til Mon 0500 and night Mon/Tue 2300-0500 – **3)** Hamburger Chaussee 36, 24113 Kiel; **W:** kielfm.de – **4)** Landvogt-Johannsen-Str. 11, 25746 Heide; **W:** okwestkueste.de – **5)** Kanalstr. 42-48, 23554 Lübeck; **W:** ok-luebeck.de
DAB: Hamburg/Kiel txs on ch. 5C (178MHz) see K) – Hamburg tx on ch. 11C (220MHz) FSK, HLR, R. Paradiso, Mega R. (rel. R. Sputnik), Mauma FM, Pure FM, 80s80s.

P) HESSEN
Media institution: Hessische Landesanstalt für Privaten Rundfunk (LPR) ☛ Wilhelmshöher Allee 262, 34131 Kassel ☎ +49 561 935860 🖷 +49 561 9358630; **W:** lpr-hessen.de

FM	FFH	plan.	Kla.	Bob	Ant	harm	kW
Alsfeld	88.1	–	–	101.5	–	94.1	4/0.1
Bad Camberg	–	–	–	–	–	105.4	0.2
Bad Hersfeld	95.9	–	*)	99.8	–	88.4	0.1/0.3
Bad Nauheim	–	104.6	–	106.6	–	100.4	0.5/1
Bensheim	–	–	–	103.3	–	107.5	0.2
Bingen	106.9	–	*)	–	–	101.8	0.2/0.3
Butzbach	–	–	*)	–	–	–	0.1
Darmstadt	–	–	–	92.4	100.8	–	0.2/0.5
Dieburg	–	90.1	–	99.5	–	104.7	1/0.2
Dillenburg	100.0	–	–	–	–	–	30
Driedorf	106.8	–	–	–	–	–	30
Eisenberg	–	100.3	–	–	–	–	50
Eltville	90.3	–	–	–	–	–	0.2
Eschwege	–	104.6	–	103.0	–	88.3	0.5/0.3
Feldberg	105.9	–	–	–	–	–	100
Frankfurt	–	100.2	107.5	101.4	95.1	105.4	1/0.1
	–	–	–	–	–	97.1	0.2
Fritzlar	–	–	–	88.4	–	–	0.1
Fulda	–	99.9	102.8	105.7	–	95.7	0.2/0.3
Gießen	–	93.7	88.0	92.6	105.2	102.0	0.5/0.1
Glashütten	–	–	–	–	–	93.2	0.5
Habichtsw.	103.7	–	–	–	–	–	20
Hanau	–	–	–	97.3	106.8	–	0.5
Heidelstein*	100.9	–	–	–	–	–	50
Hofgeismar	–	–	–	88.8	–	–	0.1
Hoherodskopf	–	–	–	94.7	–	–	0.1
Homberg	–	–	–	99.3	–	–	0.1
H. Meißner	105.1	–	–	–	–	–	100
Idstein	–	–	–	–	–	93.2	0.5
Kassel	–	104.6	104.1	99.4	–	96.6	0.5/0.2
Krehberg	105.0	–	–	–	–	–	20
Korbach	107.7	94.0	–	96.5	–	107.4	20/0.2
Limburg	–	97.6	*)	90.2	–	92.1	0.5/0.2
Marburg	–	101.0	104.9	103.9	–	96.2	0.3/0.1
Michelstadt	96.1	–	–	98.5	–	104.6	0.1/1
Offenbach	–	–	–	–	–	99.3	0.3
Rimberg	–	–	–	90.5	–	–	0.1
Rotenburg	–	–	–	93.5	104.5	–	0.1
Schlüchtern	–	–	–	101.3	–	–	0.2
Schotten	–	–	–	94.7	–	–	0.1
Vogelsberg	–	–	–	94.7	–	–	0.1
Wetzlar	–	–	*)	88.2	105.0	101.3	0.3/0.5
Wiesbaden	102.0	90.1	–	101.4	95.1	88.2	0.1/0.5

*) Closed down in 2015, to be reallocated.

Addresses and other information:
Hit-R. FFH (AC), **Planet R.** (black/CHR), **harmony.fm** (oldies): FFH-

Platz 1, 61111 Bad Vilbel; **W:** ffh.de, planet-radio.de, harmonyfm.de; also via Astra 1L, 12.633GHz (harmony.fm using two freq. at Frankfurt due to interference situation) – **Klassik R.** see O) – **R. Bob**, Friedrich-Ebert-Str. 2, 34117 Kassel; **W:** radiobob.de. Rock – **Antenne Frankfurt**, Rüsselsheimer Str. 22, 60326 Frankfurt am Main; **W:** antenne-frankfurt.de

Other stations:

FM	MHz	kW	Site	Station
5)	90.1	0.1	Marburg-Lahnberge	R. Unerhört
3)	90.9	0.3	Rüsselsheim	R. Rüsselsheim
8)	91.7	0.2	Kassel Tannenwäldchen	R. Teddy
1)	91.8	0.1	Frankfurt-Ginnheim	R. X
2)	92.5	0.1	Wiesbaden	R. RheinWelle 92,5
7)	96.5	0.3	Witzenhausen	RundFunk Meißner
9)	99.2	0.3	Fulda	Domradio
7)	99.4	0.1	Sontra	RundFunk Meißner
7)	99.7	0.5	Eschwege	RundFunk Meißner
7)	102.6	0.3	Hessisch Lichtenau	RundFunk Meißner
4)	103.4	0.3	Darmstadt	R. Darmstadt
6)	105.8	0.5	Kassel Tannenwäldchen	Freies R. Kassel

Addresses and other information:
1) Schützenstr. 12, 60311 Frankfurt; **W:** radiox.de – **2)** Postfach 49 20, 65039 Wiesbaden; **W:** rheinwelle.de – **3)** Ludwigstr. 13-15, 65428 Rüsselsheim; **W:** radiok2r.de – **4)** Steubenplatz 12, 64293 Darmstadt; **W:** radiodarmstadt.de – **5)** Rudolf-Bultmann-Str. 2b, 35039 Marburg, **W:** radio-rum.de – **6), 7)** Niederhoner Str. 1, 37269 Eschwege, **W:** eschwege.de/rfm – **8)** see M) – **9)** see S)
DAB: 7 txs on ch. 5C (178MHz) see K) – Feldberg/Frankfurt/Mainz txs on ch. 11C (220MHz) FFH, Harmony FM, Planet R., Absolut Hot, R. Teddy, Mega R. (rel. R. Sputnik)

Q) MECKLENBURG-VORPOMMERN

Media institution: Landesrundfunkzentrale Mecklenburg-Vorpommern, ✉ Bleicheufer 1, 19053 Schwerin ☎ +49 385 5588 10 🖹 +49 385 5588 130 **W:** lrz-mv.de

Location	A.MV	Osts	Klass	Tedd	Jazz	kW
Ahrenshoop	–	–	103.3	–	–	0.6
Demmin	–	107.9	–	–	–	0.2
Garz (Rügen)	105.1	107.6	–	–	–	50
Grevesmühlen	105.8	94.7	–	–	–	0.2/0.1
Güstrow	107.7	98.0	–	–	–	1/0.4
Helpterberg	103.8	105.8	–	–	–	100
Heringsdorf	105.4	103.3	–	–	–	10/2
Röbel	93.8	92.2	–	–	–	50/0.1
Rostock	100.8	104.8	89.7	95.8	105.6	130/0.1
Schwerin	101.3	107.3	103.9	102.9	–	100/0.2
Stralsund	–	–	(F.Pl.)	–	–	0.4
Waren	98.3	93.0	–	–	–	0.2/0.1
Wismar	88.7	93.7	–	–	–	0.2/0.1
Wolgast	–	100.0	–	–	–	0.5

NB. Klassik Radio txs on 90.1/97.0/97.3/98.9MHz closed down in 2015, freq. to be reallocated
Addresses and other information:
Antenne MV, Am Bahnhof 4, 19086 Plate; **W:** antennemv.de. AC – **Ostseewelle**, Warnowufer 59a, 18057 Rostock; **W:** ostseewelle. de. CHR – **Radio Paradiso, Radio Teddy, Jazz Radio** see M)

Local stations:

FM	MHz	kW	Site	Station
1)	88.0	0.8	Neubrandenburg	NB-Radiotreff
3)	90.2	0.1	Rostock	LOHRO
2)	98.1	0.2	Greifswald	R. 98eins
1)	98.7	0.1	Malchin	NB-Radiotreff

NB. Ahrenshoop local stn. closed down
Addresses and other information:
1) Treptower Str. 9, 17033 Neubrandenburg; **W:** nb-radiotreff.de; run by Landesrundfunkzentrale, also prgr. from Malchin studio – **2)** Domstr. 12, 17489 Greifswald; **W:** 98eins.de; run by university, Mon-Fri 1800-2200 only, otherwise rel. stn. 1) – **3)** Margaretenstr. 43, 18057 Rostock; **W:** lohro.de; non-commercial
DAB: Schwerin tx on ch. 5C (178MHz) see K)

R) NIEDERSACHSEN

Media institution: Niedersächsische Landesmedienanstalt für privaten Rundfunk (NLM), ✉ Seelhorststraße 18, 30175 Hannover ☎ +49 511 28477 0 🖹 +49 511 28477 36 **W:** nlm.de

FM	ffn	Ant.	R. 21	Klass	kW
Aurich	103.1	104.9	100.6	–	2x25/1
Bad Rehburg	–	–	89.4	–	0.5
Barsinghausen	101.9	103.8	–	–	25
Braunschw.-Broitzem	103.1	106.9	104.1	–	15/13/1
Buxtehude	–	–	106.0	–	1
Celle	–	–	93.5	–	0.2
Cuxhaven	–	–	106.6	–	0.6
Cuxhaven-Otterndorf	102.6	104.6	–	–	20
Dannenberg-Zernien	102.7	106.1	–	–	25
Delmenhorst	–	–	107.6	–	0.1
Goslar	–	–	87.7	–	0.5
Göttingen	102.8	106.0	93.4	–	2x5/1
Hannoversch Münden	100.7	106.7	–	–	0.5
Hannover	–	–	104.9	107.4	0.5/0.2
Helmstedt	–	–	94.1	–	0.5
Hildesheim	–	–	105.8	–	1
Holzminden	102.2	105.7	–	–	0.5
Leer-Nüttermoor	–	–	104.5	–	0.3
Lingen-Damaschke	101.5	104.3	106.9	–	2x15/0.5
Lüneburg	–	–	91.9	–	0.1
Oldenburg	–	–	104.1	–	0.2
Osnabrück	103.4	105.9	95.3	–	2x10/0.1
Rosengarten	100.6	105.1	–	–	20
Seesen	–	100.9	–	–	0.1
Stade	–	–	97.3	–	0.2
Steinkimmen	102.3	105.7	–	–	100
Torfhaus (Harz)	102.4	106.3	–	–	100
Uelzen	–	–	99.7	–	0.5
Visselhövede	101.7	104.2	90.1	–	2x10/1
Wilhelmshaven	–	–	99.1	–	0.3
Wolfsburg	–	–	95.1	–	0.1

NB. Bremen txs on Hit-R. Antenne and R. 21 see N). R. Hamburg / 106!8 rock'n pop txs at Cuxhaven see O)
Addresses and other information:
R. ffn, Stiftstraße 8, 30159 Hannover; **W:** ffn.de AC – **Hit-R. Antenne**, Goseriede 9, 30159 Hannover; **W:** antenne.com. AC – **R. 21**, An der Feuerwache 3-5, 30823 Garbsen; **W:** radio21.de Rock, cooperates with Rockland Radio, see T) – **Klassik R.** see O)

Local stations:

FM	MHz	kW	Site	Station
13)	87.6	0.1	Hannover Telemax	R. Hannover
4)	87.7	0.2	Emden	R. Ostfriesland
3)	87.8	1	Wilhelmshaven	R. Jade
1)	88.0	1	Uelzen	R. ZuSa
1)	89.7	0.5	Dannenberg-Zernien	R. ZuSa
4)	94.0	1	Aurich-Haxtum	R. Ostfriesland
8)	94.8	0.1	Bad Pyrmont	R. Aktiv
5)	95.2	0.2	Nordhorn	Ems-Vechte-Welle
1)	95.5	1	Lüneburg	R. ZuSa
5)	95.6	1	Lingen-Schepsdorf	Ems-Vechte-Welle
14)	98.2	0.3	Osnabrück	R. Osnabrück
5)	99.3	1	Molbergen-Cloppenburg	Ems-Vechte-Welle
8)	100.0	0.3	Hameln	R. Aktiv
12)	100.0	0.1	Hannover Bettfedernf.	R. Flora
4)	103.9	0.2	Leer	R. Ostfriesland
10)	104.6	0.5	Braunschweig-Broitzem	R. Okerwelle
6)	104.8	1	Osnabrück	OS R. 104,8
11)	105.3	1	Hildesheim	R. Tonkuhle
2)	106.5	1	Oldenburg-Wahnbek	Oldenburg Eins
7)	106.5	0.3	Hannover Telemaxx tower	Leinehertz
9)	107.1	1	Göttingen	StadtR. Gött.

Adresses and other information:
1) Ilmenauufer 47, 29525 Uelzen and Scharnhorststr. 1, 21335 Lüneburg; **W:** zusa.de – **2)** Bahnhofstr. 11, 26122 Oldenburg; **W:** uni-oldenburg. de/ok_ol/ – **3)** Kieler Str. 31, 26382 Wilhelmshaven; **W:** radio-jade. de – **4)** VHS Emden, An der Berufsschule 3, 26721 Emden; **W:** radio-ostfriesland.net – **5)** Halle IV, Kaiserstr. 10a, 49809 Lingen; **W:** emsvechtewelle.de – **6)** Lohstr. 45a, 49074 Osnabrück; **W:** os-radio. de – **7)** Hildesheimer Str. 29, 30169 Hannover; **W:** leinehertz.de – **8)** Hefehof 23, 31785 Hameln; **W:** radio-aktiv.de – **9)** Groner Str. 2, 37073 Göttingen; **W:** stadtradio-goettingen.de – **10)** Rebenring 18, 38106 Braunschweig; **W:** okerwelle.de – **11)** Andreas-Passage 1, 31134 Hildesheim; **W:** tonkuhle.de – **12)** Zur Bettfedernfabrik 3, 30451 Hannover; **W:** radioflora.de; on 100.0MHz during special events, otherwise via webstream only – **13)** Münzstr. 3, 30159 Hannover; **W:** radio-hannover.de – **14)** Jürgensort 10, 49074 Osnabrück; **W:** radioosnabrueck.com
Permanent special stns: R. SWS (**W:** radio-sws.de), Norderney 104.0MHz; **R. S.A.S.** (**W:** radio-sas.de), Stadthagen 94.5MHz; **Lamberti-Kirchenfunk** (**W:** soerenkoenig.com/Radlam) Aurich 106.0MHz; **Kirchenfunk Esterwegen**, 106.6MHz; **Kirchenfunk Lorup**, 107.6MHz; **Kirchenfunk Herzlake**, 106.1MHz; **Pfarrfunk Breitenberg**, 98.4MHz; **Kirchenfunk Meppen**, 95.0MHz; **Pfarrradio Warsingsfehn**, Moormerland 95.2MHz
DAB: 6 txs on ch. 5C (178MHz) see K)

S) NORDRHEIN-WESTFALEN

Media institution: Landesanstalt für Medien Nordrhein-Westfalen (LFM) ✉ Postfach 10 34 43, 40025 Düsseldorf (office location: Zollhof 2) ☎ +49 211 77 007 0 📠 +49 211 727 170 **W:** lfm-nrw.de

R. NRW, Essener Str. 55, 46047 Oberhausen; **W:** radionrw.de The following stns are affiliates with some hours of own prgrs per day, other times rel. R. NRW with local IDs inserted automatically.

FM	MHz	kW	Site	Station
5)	87.7	0.2	Krefeld-Oppum	Welle Niederrhein
26)	88.1	4	Eggegebirge	R. Hochstift
19)	88.2	0.5	Lüdinghausen	R. Kiepenkerl
37)	88.2	0.5	Siegen	R. Siegen
35)	88.3	0.1	Meinerzhagen	R. MK
16)	88.4	1	Bocholt	Westmünsterlandw.
36)	89.1	0.2	Schmallenberg	R. Sauerland
7)	89.4	1	Düsseldorf Rheinturm	NE-WS 89.4
6)	90.1	0.3	Mönchengladbach	R. 90,1
31)	90.8	0.1	Herne	Herne 90acht
30)	91.2	0.2	Dortmund	R. 91.2
39)	91.2	0.2	Siegburg	R. Bonn/Rhein-Sieg
42)	91.4	0.1	Bergheim	R. Erft
35)	91.5	0.1	Altena	R. MK
33)	91.5	0.1	Hattingen-Schierken	R. en
3)	91.7	0.1	Moers-Meerbeck	R. K.W.
23)	91.7	0.1	Vlotho	R. Herford
4)	92.2	0.1	Duisburg	R. Duisburg
35)	92.5	0.3	Iserlohn	R. MK
20)	92.6	1	Sendenhorst	R. WAF
43)	92.7	0.5	Düren-Hürtgenwald	R. Rur
13)	92.9	0.5	Mülheim-Saarn	R. Mülheim
29)	92.9	0.1	Selm	antenne unna
16)	93.0	0.5	Ahaus	Westmünsterlandw.
26)	93.7	0.1	Paderborn	R. Hochstift
39)	94.2	0.1	Much-Wersch	R.Bonn/Rhein-Sieg
9)	94.3	0.2	Solingen	R. RSG
15)	94.6	0.1	Recklinghausen	Hit R. Vest
20)	94.7	0.2	Warendorf	R. WAF
36)	94.8	0.1	Marsberg	R. Sauerland
23)	94.9	0.5	Herford	R. Herford
24)	95.1	0.1	Rahden	R. Westfalica
18)	95.4	0.2	Münster	Antenne Münster
15)	95.6	0.1	Berghaltern	Hit R. Vest
24)	95.7	0.5	Minden Jakobsberg	R. Westfalica
20)	95.7	0.3	Beckum	R. WAF
14)	96.1	0.1	Gelsenkirchen	REL
36)	96.2	0.4	Olsberg-Antfeld	R. Sauerland
20)	96.3	0.3	Oelde	R. WAF
38)	96.9	0.5	Leverkusen-Opladen	R. Berg
1)	97.2	0.1	Simmerath	Antenne AC
35)	97.2	0.1	Werdohl	R. MK
37)	97.3	0.1	Bad Laasphe	R. Siegen
29)	97.4	0.5	Lünen	Antenne Unna
11)	97.6	4	Langenberg	R. Neandertal
16)	97.6	1	Borken	Westmünsterlandw.
22)	97.6	0.4	Friedrichsdorf	R. Bielefeld
39)	97.8	0.5	Bonn Venusberg	R. Bonn/Rhein-Sieg
2)	98.0	1	Kleve	Antenne Niederrhein
22)	98.3	0.1	Bielefeld	R. Bielefeld
32)	98.5	0.5	Bochum	R. 98.5
14)	98.7	0.5	Bottrop	REL
37)	98.9	0.1	Neunkirchen	R. Siegen
35)	99.5	0.1	Plettenberg	R. MK
44)	99.7	0.1	Euskirchen	R. Euskirchen
38)	99.7	0.5	Gremberg	R. Berg
39)	99.9	0.5	Bonn-Königswinter	R. Bonn/Rhein-Sieg
1)	100.1	0.4	Aachen Karlshöhe	Antenne AC
35)	100.2	0.5	Lüdenscheid	R. MK
5)	100.6	1	Viersen	Welle Niederrhein
27)	100.9	1	Soest-Möhnesee	Hellweg R.
25)	101.0	0.5	Schieder-Schwalenbg.	R. Lippe
7)	102.1	0.3	Grevenbroich	NE-WS 89.4
12)	102.2	0.3	Essen-Werden	R. Essen
29)	102.3	1	Schwerte Sommerberg	Antenne Unna
5)	102.5	0.3	Viersen Süchtelner Höhe	Welle Niederrhein
16)	103.6	0.1	Gronau	Westmünsterlandw.
27)	103.6	0.1	Lippstadt	Hellweg R.
17)	104.0	1	Tecklenburg	R. RST
8)	104.2	1	Düsseldorf	Antenne Düsseldorf
33)	104.2	0.1	Witten-Stockum	R. en
26)	104.8	0.5	Neuhaus-Hasselberg	R. Hochstift
26)	104.8	0.1	Büren	R. Hochstift
36)	104.9	0.1	Meschede	R. Sauerland
1)	105.0	0.1	Monschau	Antenne AC

FM	MHz	kW	Site	Station
12)	105.0	0.1	Essen-Holsterhausen	R. Essen
28)	105.0	0.2	Hamm	R. Lippewelle
38)	105.2	4	Lindlar	R. Berg
17)	105.2	4	Schöppingen	R. RST
15)	105.2	0.1	Dorsten	Hit Radio Vest
37)	105.4	4	Aue-Kirchhundem	R. Siegen
38)	105.7	1	Waldbröl	R. Berg
2)	105.7	0.5	Geldern	Antenne Niederrhein
33)	105.7	0.1	Gevelsberg	R. en
42)	105.8	1	Köln-Ehrenfeld	R. Erft
13)	106.2	0.1	Oberhausen	R. Oberhausen
19)	106.3	0.2	Dülmen	R. Kiepenkerl
36)	106.5	0.5	Hallenberg	R. Sauerland
36)	106.5	0.3	Arnsberg	R. Sauerland
25)	106.6	1	Lemgo	R. Lippe
24)	106.6	0.1	Lübbecke	R. Westfalica
21)	106.8	0.4	Borgholzhausen	R. Gütersloh
45)	106.9	4	Schleiden (Eifel)	R. Euskirchen
41)	107.1	0.5	Köln Neumarkt	R. Köln
33)	107.2	0.1	Herdecke	R. en
27)	107.3	0.2	Wickede	Hellweg R.
19)	107.4	1	Coesfeld	R. Kiepenkerl
25)	107.4	1	Linderhofe-Dörenberg	R. Lippe
10)	107.4	0.5	Wuppertal	R. Wuppertal
44)	107.4	0.1	Bad Münstereifel	R. Euskirchen
21)	107.5	1	Oelde	R. Gütersloh
43)	107.5	0.1	Linnich	R. Rur
36)	107.6	0.1	Sundern	R. Sauerland
3)	107.6	0.2	Wesel-Büderich	R. K.W.
40)	107.6	0.1	Leverkusen-Wiesdorf	R. Leverkusen
27)	107.7	0.2	Belecke-Sennhöfe	Hellweg R.
34)	107.7	0.2	Hagen	R. Hagen
1)	107.8	0.4	Aachen Stolberg	Antenne AC
39)	107.9	0.1	Herchen-Rosbach	R. Bonn/Rhein-Sieg
9)	107.9	0.1	Remscheid	R. RSG

Addresses and other information:
1) Merzbrück 214, 52146 Würselen, **W:** antenne-ac.de – **2)** Stechbahn 2-8, 47533 Kleve, **W:** antenneniederrhein.de – **3)** Rheinstr. 24-26, 47495 Rheinberg, **W:** radiokw.de – **4)** Ruhrorter Str. 187, 47119 Duisburg, **W:** medien.freepage.de/guidojansen – **5)** Uerdinger Str. 543, 47800 Krefeld, **W:** welleniederrhein.de – **6)** Lüpertzender Str. 159, 41061 Mönchengladbach, **W:** radio901.de – **7)** Moselstr. 16, 41464 Neuss, **W:** news894.de – **8)** Kaistr. 7, 40221 Düsseldorf, **W:** antenneduesseldorf.de – **9)** Postfach, 42621 Solingen (studio location: Alleestr. 1) **W:** radiorsg.de – **10)** Friedrich-Engels-Allee 426, 42283 Wupperta, **W:** radiowuppertal.de – **11)** Elberfelder Str. 81, 40804 Mettmann, **W:** radioneandertal.de – **12)** Sachsenstr. 36, 45128 Essen, **W:** radio-essen.de – **13)** Essener Str. 99, 46047 Oberhausen, **W:** 106.2.radiooberhausen.de and 92.9.radiomuelheim.de – **14)** Hochstr. 68, 45894 Gelsenkirchen, **W:** radio-emscher-lippe.de – **15)** Schaumburgstr. 14, 45657 Recklinghausen **W:** hitradiovest.de – **16)** Heinrich-Hertz-Str. 6, 46325 Borken **W:** radiowmw.de – **17)** Postnstr. 3, 48431 Rheine, **W:** radiorst.de – **18)** Nevinghoff 14/16, 48147 Münster, **W:** antennemuenster.de – **19)** Tiberstr. 21, 48249 Dülmen, **W:** radio-kiepenkerl.de – **20)** Am Schweinemarkt 8, 48231 Warendorf, **W:** radiowaf.de – **21)** Feldstr. 14, 33330 Gütersloh **W:** radioguetersloh.de – **22)** Niederstr. 21-27, 33602 Bielefeld **W:** radio-bielefeld.de – **23)** Berliner Str. 30, 32052 Herford **W:** radioherford.de – **24)** Johanniskirchhof 2, 32423 Minden **W:** radiowestfalica.de – **25)** Lagesche Str. 17, 32756 Detmold **W:** radiolippe.de – **26)** Frankfurter Weg 22, 33106 Paderborn **W:** radiohochstift.de – **27)** Jakobistr. 46, 59494 Soest **W:** hellwegradio.de – **28)** Königstr. 39, 59065 Hamm **W:** lippewelle.de – **30)** Karl-Zahn-Str. 11, 44141 Dortmund **W:** radio912.de – **31)** Bahnhofstr. 45, 44623 Herne **W:** radio-herne.de – **32)** Westring 26, 44787 Bochum, **W:** ruhrwelle-bochum.de – **33)** Mühlenstr. 25, 58285 Gevelsberg **W:** radio-en.de – **34)** Rathausstr. 23, 58095 Hagen, **W:** radio-hagen.de – **35)** Vinckestr. 9-13, 58636 Iserlohn, **W:** radio-mk.de – **36)** Steinstr. 32, 59872 Meschede, **W:** radio-sauerland.de – **37)** Postfach 10 02 42, 57002 Siegen (studio location: Obergraben 33), **W:** radio-siegen.de – **38)** Friedrich-Ebert-Str., 51429 Bergisch Gladbach, **W:** radioberg.de – **39)** Kennedybrücke 4, 53225 Bonn, **W:** radio-bonn.de – **40)** Bismarckstr. 71, 51373 Leverkusen, **W:** radioleverkusen.de – **41)** Stolberger Str. 374, 50933 Köln, **W:** radiokoeln.de – **42)** Hürth Park, 50354 Hürth, **W:** radioerft.de – **44)** August-Klotz-Str. 21, 52349 Düren, **W:** radiorur.de – **45)** Rheinstr. 55, 53881 Euskirchen, **W:** radioeuskirchen.de

Stns not affiliated to Radio NRW:

FM	MHz	kW	Site	Station
12)	87.9	0.05	Bielefeld	Hertz 87.9
13)	89.4	0.03	Paderborn	L'Unico
9)	90.0	0.3	Bochum	CT das radio

FM	MHz	kW	Site	Station
11)	90.9	0.05	Münster university	R. Q
1)	92.0	0.05	Pulheim	Domradio
2)	92.1	0.03	Siegen university	Radius 92,1
8)	93.0	0.05	Dortmund university	Eldoradio
3)	94.3	0.05	Bielefeld-Bethel	Antenne Bethel
14)	94.7	0.05	Meschede	R. FH
7)	96.8	0.5	Bonn	(shared freq.)
6)	97.1	0.04	Düsseldorf-Bilk	Hochschulr. Düsseld.
15)	89.4	0.03	Paderborn university	L'Unico FM
4)	99.1	0.1	Aachen	Hochschulr. Aachen
5)	100.0	0.1	Köln Sternengasse	Kölncampus
1)	101.7	0.03	Köln Sternengasse	Domradio
11)	103.9	0.5	Steinfurt college	R. Q
10)	104.5	0.2	Essen university	Campus FM
10)	105.6	0.05	Essen university	Campus FM

Addresses and other information:
1) Domkloster 3, 50667 Köln; **W:** domradio.de; further txs see P) and T), also via Astra 1L, 12.460GHz h. Run by Catholic church – **2)** Hölderlinstr. 3, 57068 Siegen; **W:** radius921.de – **3)** Quellenhofweg 25, 33617 Bielefeld-Bethel; **W:** antenne-bethel.de Run by diacony – **4)** Wüllnerstr. 5, 52056 Aachen; **W:** hochschulradio-aachen.de – **5)** Albertus-Magnus-Platz, 50923 Köln; **W:** koelncampus.com – **6)** Universitätsstr. 1, 40225 Düsseldorf; **W:** hochschulradio.uni-duesseldorf.de – **7)** shared by six groups – **8)** Vogelpothsweg 74, 44227 Dortmund; **W:** eldoradio.de – **9)** 44780 Bochum (studio location: Ruhr university, room 04/452); **W:** radioct.de – **10)** Universitätsstr. 2, 45141 Essen; **W:** campusfm.info – **11)** Bismarckallee 3, 48151 Münster; **W:** radioq.de – **12)** Universitätsstr. 25, 33615 Bielefeld; **W:** radiohertz.de – **13)** Warburger Str. 100, 33098 Paderborn; **W:** l-unico.de – **14)** Jahnstr. 23, 59872 Meschede; **W:** radiofh.de – **15)** Warburger Str. 100, 33098 Paderborn; **W:** l-unico.de – **16)** Radio Triquency, Liebigstr. 87, 32657 Lemgo; **W:** triquency.de Via lp. txs on 95.9/96.1/99.4MHz **N.B** Stns 2) and 4)-16) university/college
F.PI.: Metropol FM (see M), stn. 15) on Essen 88.3MHz, Olpe 89.0MHz, Bochum 89.3MHz, Hagen 89.4MHz, Köln 89.9MHz, Krefeld 90.5MHz, Mülheim 93.7MHz, Dorsten 97.0MHz, Lennestadt 98.9MHz, Herdecke 107.2MHz, Attendorn 107.8MHz. Allocation was subject of legal action at time of editing.
DAB: 7 txs on ch. 5C (178MHz) see K). Domradio rel. by J)

T) RHEINLAND-PFALZ
Media institution: Landesanstalt für Medien und Kommunikation (LMK) ✉ Postfach 21 73 63, 67072 Ludwigshafen (office loc.: Turmstraße 8) ☎ +49 621 5252 0 🖷 +49 621 5252 152 **W:** lmk-online.de

FM	RPR 1	bigFM	Rockl.	Metrop	kW
Bad Bergzabern	103.3	–	–	–	0.3
Bad Dürkheim	98.1	96.4	–	–	0.1
Bad Kreuznach	89.7	104.8	–	–	0.1/0.2
Bad Marienberg	102.9	–	–	–	25
Bernkastel-Kues	–	100.5	–	–	0.1
Betzdorf	–	107.7	–	–	0.5
Bitburg	–	–	107.9	–	0.1
Bornberg-Eßweiler	103.1	107.6	–	–	25
Daun (Eifel)	102.1	106.6	–	–	20
Diezer Hain	101.2	100.4	–	–	0.1
Grünstadt/Mertesh.	103.3	–	–	–	0.1
Haardtkopf	100.1	–	–	–	50
Heckenbach	103.5	104.9	–	–	30
Hohe Wurzel	–	–	107.9	–	6
Idar-Oberstein	100.3	101.9	–	–	1
Kalmit	103.6	106.7	–	–	25
Kirchheimbolanden	–	–	97.1	–	0.2
Kleinkarlbach	91.1	–	–	–	0.1
Koblenz Kühkopf	101.5	104.0	–	–	40
Koblenz-Bendorf	–	–	88.3	107.8	0.3
Linz	–	–	96.9	–	0.2
Ludwigshafen	–	–	–	88.4	0.1
Mainz Ober-Olm	100.6	104.5	–	–	20
Mainz (city)	98.1	106.6	–	96.0	0.2/0.4
Mannheim	–	–	93.2	–	1
Pirmas. Kettrichhof	104.7	–	–	–	5
Pirmasens (town)	–	96.7	–	–	0.4
Rivenich	–	95.8	–	–	0.2
Saarburg	102.6	96.5	–	–	20
Trier Petrisberg	102.9	106.4	105.8	–	0.1/0.5
Zweibrücken	103.3	106.6	–	–	2/0.1

Addresses and other information:
RPR 1, Turmstr. 8, 67059 Ludwigshafen; **W:** rpr1.de – **bigFM:** see K), stn.2); rel. of adopted version in responsibility of RPR – **Rockland R.**, Wallstr. 1-5, 55122 Mainz; **W:** rockland.de; cooperates with R. 21, see R) – **Metropol FM** see M), stn 15

Local stations:

FM	MHz	kW	Site	Station
3)	87.6	0.2	Idar-Oberstein	R. Idar-Oberstein
7)	87.8	0.1	Welschbillig	Cityradio Trier
10)	87.9	0.1	Bretzenheim (church)	Studio Nahe
2)	88.3	0.1	Bad Kreuznach	Antenne Bad Kreuznach
7)	88.4	0.5	Trier Petrisberg	Cityradio Trier
6)	88.4	0.3	Pirmasens	R. Pirmasens
8)	94.1	0.3	Mommenhein	Antenne Mainz
5)	94.2	1	Neustadt/Weinstr.	Antenne Pfalz
9)	94.7	0.2	Wittlich	R. Wittlich
7)	94.7	0.1	Trierweiler	Cityradio Trier
5)	94.8	0.1	Landau	Antenne Landau
4)	96.9	0.5	Kaiserslautern	Antenne Kaiserslautern
8)	97.1	0.1	Bodenheim	Antenne Mainz
11)	87.8	0.1	Koblenz	R. Teddy
1)	98.0	1	Koblenz Moselw. Str.	Antenne Koblenz
1)	98.0	1	Neuwied	Antenne Koblenz
1)	98.9	1	Koblenz-Bendorf	Antenne Koblenz
8)	106.6	0.1	Mainz	Antenne Mainz

Addresses and other information:
1) Friedrich-Ebert-Ring 54, 56068 Koblenz; **W:** akoblenz.de – **2)** Kreuzstr. 31-33, 55543 Bad Kreuznach; **W:** antenne-kh.de – **3)** Auf der Idar 2a, 55743 Idar-Oberstein; **W:** radio-io.de – **4)** Am Altenhof 11-13, 67655 Kaiserslautern; **W:** antenne-kl.de – **5)** Europastr. 3, 67433 Neustadt/Wstr.; **W:** antenne-landau.de antenne-pfalz.de – **6)** Schloßstr. 44, 66953 Pirmasens; **W:** radio-pirmasens.de – **7)** Paulinstr. 1, 54292 Trier; **W:** cityradio-trier.de – **8)** Hechtsheimer Str. 35, 55131 Mainz; **W:** antenne-mainz.de – **9)** Schloßstr. 7a, 54516 Wittlich; **W:** radio-wittlich.de – **10)** Obere Grabenstr. 29, 55450 Langenlonsheim; **W:** studio-nahe.de Run by Catholic church, mostly rel. Domradio, see S) – **11)** See M), stn. 19)
DAB: Koblenz/Scharteberg txs on ch. 5C (178MHz) see K). Rel. of Big FM World Beats see I)

U) SAARLAND
Media institution: Landesmedienanstalt Saar (LMS) ✉ Postfach 11 01 64, 66070 Saarbrücken (office location: Nell-Breuning-Allee 6) ☎ +49 681 389880; 🖷 +49 681 3898820; **W:** lmsaar.de

LW	kHz	kW	Prgr.
Saarlouis (Felsberg)	183	2000	Europe 1

NB. See under France. Power may be lower after tx reconfiguration now. Usually off 0000-0300

FM	Salü	C.Ro.	bigFM	Saar.	kW
Homburg	–	–	–	89.6	1
Lebach-Hoxberg	–	100.9	–	–	1
Merzig	103.0	–	92.6	105.1	0.1/0.5
Mettlach	104.2	–	–	106.1	0.1
Neunkirchen	–	99.3	–	94.6	1/0.6
Oberperl	100.3	–	–	–	1
Saarbr. Schoksbg.	101.7	–	–	–	100
Saarbr. Halberg	–	–	94.2	–	1
Saarbr. Winterberg	–	92.9	–	–	1
Saarbr. Schwarzenbg.	–	–	–	99.6	1
Saarlouis	–	102.8	99.5	–	1
St. Ingbert	–	100.6	–	–	0.1
Sulzbach	–	–	96.8	–	0.1
Webenheim	100.0	–	–	–	5

Addresses and other information:
R. Salü, Classic Rock R.: Postfach 10 08 44, 66008 Saarbrücken (studio location: Richard-Wagner-Str. 58-60); **W:** salue.de, classic-rock-radio.de – **bigFM Saarland:** Gutenbergstr. 11-23, 66103 Saarbrücken; **W:** bigfm-saarland.de; mostly rel. Stuttgart prgr. (see K), stn. 2) – **R. Saarbrücken, R. Merzig, R. Neunkirchen, R. Homburg:** Nell-Breuning-Allee 6, 66115 Saarbrücken; **W:** radio-sb.de, radiomerzig.de, antenneneunkirchen.de, radio-homburg.de
DAB: Schoksberg tx on ch. 5C (178MHz) see K). Rel. of R. Salü see H)

V) SACHSEN
Media institution: Sächsische Landesanstalt für privaten Rundfunk und neue Medien (SLM) ✉ Postfach 10 16 62, 04016 Leipzig ☎ +49 341 22 59 0 🖷 +49 341 22 59 199; **W:** slm-online.de; office location: Ferdinand-Lassalle-Straße 21

FM	PSR	R.SA	RTL	Radio	Energ.	kW
Annaberg-Buchholz	–	104.8	–	–	–	0.5
Auerbach	–	107.9	–	–	–	0.1
Bärenstein	–	–	–	107.2E	–	0.2
Beilrode	–	99.6	–	–	–	1
Borna	–	–	–	99.5L	–	0.1
Chemnitz-Reichenh.	–	91.0	–	102.1C	97.5	3
Collmberg	98.0	–	104.7	–	–	5/10
Döbeln	–	107.9	–	–	98.3	1/0.2

FM	PSR	R.SA	RTL	Radio	Energ.	kW
Dresden-Gompitz	–	–	–	91.1D	–	1
Dresden-Wachwitz 102.4	89.2	105.2	103.5D	100.2	100/2
Ebersbach	–	106.1	–	–	–	0.5
Elsterberg	–	99.7	–	–	–	0.2
Flöha	–	98.4	–	99.0C	–	0.1
Freiberg	–	90.6	–	104.2D	96.4	0.2/0.5
Freital	–	88.3	–	107.0D	–	0.2
Geyer (Erzgebirge) 100.0	–	105.4	–	–	100
Görlitz	–	105.1	–	–	–	1
Grimma	–	107.4	–	90.9L	93.3	2/0.3
Hoyerswerda-Zeißig	–	96.9	–	–	87.6	0.2/0.3
Kamenz	–	106.2	–	–	–	0.2
Leipzig-Holzhausen	–	–	–	91.3L	99.8	4
Leipzig-Reudnitz	–	98.2	–	–	–	1
Leisnig	–	100.5	–	–	–	0.2
Limbach-Oberfrohna	–	–	–	107.3C	–	0.1
Löbau Schafberg 101.0	–	105.6	107.6G	–	30
Löbau town	–	87.6	–	–	–	0.5
Markneukirchen	–	89.6	–	–	–	1
Meerane	–	–	–	89.2Z	–	0.1
Meißen-Korbitz	–	–	–	107.5D	–	0.2
Mittelherwigsdorf	–	100.0	–	94.3G	–	0.5/0.3
Mügeln	–	91.2	–	–	–	0.5
Neukirchen	–	–	–	95.8C	–	1
Niederschöna	–	94.4	–	–	–	0.5
Niesky	–	95.0	–	–	–	0.2
Nossen	–	91.4	–	–	–	0.5
Oelsnitz (Vogtland)	–	91.5	–	–	–	0.1
Olbernhau	–	101.0	–	–	–	0.5
Oschatz	–	89.1	–	–	–	0.3
Pirna	–	–	–	96.4D	–	0.1
Plauen	–	93.5	–	–	–	1
Reichenbach/Vogtl.	–	92.4	–	–	–	0.2
Riesa	–	106.4	–	–	91.7	2/1
Rothenburg	–	100.0	–	–	–	0.2
Schöneck	92.0	–	106.0	–	–	10/30
Sohland	–	107.0	–	–	–	0.2
Stollberg	–	93.4	–	–	–	1
Torgau	–	91.1	–	–	–	0.2
Weißwasser	–	101.9	–	–	–	0.5
Werdau	–	–	–	90.9Z	–	0.3
Wiederau (Leipzig) 102.9	–	106.9	–	–	100
Wilkau-Haßlau	–	92.3	–	103.4Z	–	0.5
Wilthen	–	106.5	–	–	104.9	1/0.5
Wurzen	–	95.0	–	–	–	0.4
Zittau	–	100.0	–	–	–	0.5
Zschopau	–	–	–	91.7C	–	0.3
Zwickau-Ebersbrunn	–	–	–	96.2Z	98.2	0.5/0.3
Zwickau-Planitz	–	95.5	–	–	–	0.5

Addresses and other information:
R. PSR (AC), **R.SA** (oldie-based, specifically aiming at GDR-socialized audiences), **Energy Sachsen** (CHR): Thomasgasse 2, 04102 Leipzig; **W:** radiopsr.de rsa-sachsen.de nrj.de – **Hitradio RTL** (AC), **R. Chemnitz / Dresden / Erzgebirge / Lausitz / Leipzig / Zwickau** (AC, on freq. marked C, D, E, G, L, Z, with some content from local studios): Ammonstr. 35, 01067 Dresden; **W:** bcs-sachsen.de

Other stations:

FM	MHz	kW	Site	Station
7)	88.2	0.4	Auerbach	Vogtland R.
9)	88.2	1	Weißig (Bernsdorf)	Elsterwelle
1)	88.9	1	Chemnitz-Reichenhain	Apollo R.
10)	89.2	1	Weißwasser	R. WSW
2)	89.2	0.1	Leipzig-Reudnitz	R. Blau
2)	94.4	0.3	Leipzig-Stahmeln	R. Blau
10)	94.9	0.2	Wilthen	R. WSW
7)	95.4	2	Plauen	Vogtland R.
5)	97.6	4	Leipzig-Holzhausen	mephisto 97.6
3)	98.4	0.1	Dresden-Gompitz	coloRadio
2)	99.2	0.5	Leipzig-Connewitz	R. Blau
3)	99.3	0.1	Freital (Dresden)	coloRadio
6)	99.3	0.1	Mittweida	R. Mittweida
7)	100.5	1	Reichenbach/Vogtland	Vogtland R.
4)	102.7	1	Chemnitz-Reichenhain	R. T
9)	102.8	0.5	Hoyerswerda-Zeißig	Elsterwelle
7)	103.8	0.5	Markneukirchen	Vogtland R.
8)	107.7	2	Fichtelberg	R. Erzgebirge

Adresses and other information:
1) As Hitradio RTL; **W:** apolloradio.de; classical music and jazz, also Mon-Fri 2200-1700, Sat-Sun 2300-1100 via txs of stns 2), 3), 4) – **2)** Paul-Gruner-Str. 62, 04107 Leipzig; **W:** radioblau.de – **3)** Jordanstr. 5, 01099 Dresden; **W:** coloradio.org – **4)** Karl-Liebknecht-Str. 19, 09111 Chemnitz; **W:** radiot.de; rel. 1700-1800 Chemnitz university prgr. – **5)**

Ritterstr. 9-13, 04109 Leipzig; **W:** mephisto976.uni-leipzig.de; run by Leipzig university; Mon-Fri 0900-1100 and 1700-1900, other times rel. R.SA – **6)** Leisniger Str. 9, 09648 Mittweida; **W:** radio-mittweida.de; run by Mittweida college – **7)** Haselbrunner Str. 114, 08225 Plauen; **W:** vogtlandradio.de – **8)** Vierenstr. 11, 09484 Oberwiesenthal; **W:** radioerzgebirge-online.de – **9)** Walther-Rathenau-Str. 27, 02977 Hoyerswerda; **W:** elsterwelle.de, 103.8MHz tx see M) – **10)** Werner-Seelenbinder-Str. 54a, 02943 Weißwasser; **W:** radiowsw.de
DAB: 5 txs on ch. 5C (178MHz) see K)

W) SACHSEN-ANHALT
Media institution: Medienanstalt Sachsen-Anhalt (MSA) ☑ Reichardtstraße 9, 06114 Halle/Saale ☎ +49 345 52550 🖷 +49 345 5255 121 **W:** msa-online.de

FM	R Bro	RTL	SAW	Rock	kW
Bernburg	–	–	–	95.0	1
Blankenburg	99.9	–	95.7	–	0.3/0.1
Brocken	–	89.0	101.4	–	60/100
Dequede	101.0	–	95.6	–	60/1
Dessau-Mildensee	90.6	–	92.6	94.1	0.8/2/0.3
Eisleben	93.7	–	–	–	1
Fleetmark-Lüge	–	–	103.9	–	5
Halle Petersberg	93.5	–	103.3	–	5
Halle city	–	–	–	98.3	0.5
Hergisdorf-Wolferode	93.7	–	–	–	1
Köthen	–	–	–	97.1	1
Magdeburg-Buckau	–	–	–	98.7	0.2
Naumburg	98.8	–	95.1	99.6	10/0.5/1
Sangerhausen	107.1	–	99.4	–	0.1
Schneidlingen	–	–	–	107.2	2.5
Schönebeck	105.7	–	100.1	–	15/20
Stendal Tucholsky-Str.	–	–	100.5	–	0.5
Weißenfels	–	–	–	88.0	1
Wernigerode	105.4	–	90.8	–	0.5/1
Wiederau (Leipzig)	–	–	104.9	–	*90
Wittenberg-Gallun	102.3	–	98.4	–	4/5
Zeitz-Hainichen	99.1	–	–	–	0.5
Ziesar	–	–	102.8	–	2

*) tx in Sachsen, sharply directional towards Sachsen-Anhalt
Addresses and other information:
R. Brocken (oldie-based AC), **89.0 RTL** (CHR): Große Ulrichstr. 60D, 06108 Halle; **W:** brocken.de, 89.0rtl.de – **R. SAW** (AC), **Rockland Sachsen-Anhalt:** Hansapark 1, 39116 Magdeburg; **W:** radiosaw.de rockland-digital.de

Non-commercial stations:

FM	MHz	kW	Site	Station
2)	92.5	1	Aschersleben	R. hbw
1)	95.9	0.6	Halle Petersberg	R. Corax

Adresses and other information:
1) Unterberg 11, 06108 Halle; **W:** radiocorax.de – **2)** Herrenbreite 9, 06449 Aschersleben; **W:** radio-hbw.de
DAB: 4 txs on ch. 5C (178MHz) see K) – 4 txs on ch. 11C (220MHz) and 3 txs on ch. 12C (227MHz) R. Brocken, 89.0 RTL, SAW, Rockland

X) THÜRINGEN
Media institution: Thüringer Landesmedienanstalt (TLM) ☑ P.O.-Box 90 03 61 (office location: Steigerstraße 10), 99096 Erfurt ☎ +49 361 211770 🖷 +49 361 2117755 **W:** tlm.de

FM	Ant.T	LW	Top 40	Klass	kW
Altenburg	–	–	98.4	(107.5)	0.5
Bleßberg	102.7	106.7	–	–	60
Dingelstädt	103.9	–	–	–	5
Eisenach	–	–	93.5	(90.9)	0.2
Erfurt-Windischh.	100.2	99.7	–	–	3/0.5
Erfurt-Hochheim	–	–	88.6	–	0.5
Gera	98.3	105.8	95.3	(104.5)	0.2/1
Gotha	–	–	90.8	(99.3)	0.1/0.2
Heiligenstadt	–	88.7	–	–	0.1
Ilmenau	–	–	94.8	–	0.1
Inselsberg	102.2	104.2	–	–	100
Jena-Oßmaritz	90.9	106.1	–	–	1
Jena Kernberge	–	–	94.8	–	0.2
Keula	–	104.5	–	–	10
Kulpenberg	104.7	96.8	–	–	3
Lobenstein	93.2	98.5	–	–	1/2
Meiningen	–	–	99.5	–	0.2
Mühlhausen	–	–	93.8	–	0.2
Nordhausen	106.8	105.8	103.0	(107.4)	0.1/0.2
Pößneck	–	–	98.9	–	0.2
Remda Kalmberg	107.6	95.7	–	–	60/10
Ronneburg	102.5	94.9	–	–	30/3
Saalfeld	–	–	97.6	–	0.1

FM	Ant.T	LW	Top 40	Klass	kW
Sömmerda	–	–	91.0	–	0.1
Sondershausen	–	–	90.7	–	0.2
Sonneberg	–	–	88.8	–	0.1
Suhl	101.3	88.6	92.1	–	2x1/0.1
Weimar Ettersberg	107.2	89.2	–	–	0.25
Weimar Belvedere	–	–	97.9	(88.7)	0.1

*) Network abandoned by Klassik R. in 2015. No decision about further use of txs at time of editing.

Addresses and other information:
Antenne Thüringen (AC), **Top 40** (rock): Belvederer Allee 25, 99425 Weimar; **W:** antennethueringen.de radiotop40.de; Top 40 also via Astra 1H, 12.633GHz – **LandesWelle Thüringen** (AC): Mehringstr. 5, 99086 Erfurt; **W:** landeswelle.de

Non-commercial and other stations:

FM	MHz	kW	Site	Station
1)	96.2	0.6	Erfurt-Hochheim	Funkwerk, F.R.E.I.
4)	96.5	0.2	Eisenach	Wartburg-R.
3)	98.1	0.1	Ilmenau	hsf Studentenradio
6)	100.4	0.1	Nordhausen	Offener Kanal Nordh.
7)	101.4	0.1	Saalfeld	SRB
5)	103.4	0.3	Jena-Oßmaritz	R. OKJ
2)	106.6	2	Weimar Belvedere	Funkwerk, Lotte, b11

Addresses and other information:
1) Funkwerk, Juri-Gagarin-Ring 96, 99084 Erfurt; **W:** funkwerk.de Mon-Fri 1200-2000, Fri 2300- Sat 2300. **F.R.E.I.**, Gotthardstr. 21, 99084 Erfurt; **W:** radio-frei.de Mon-Thu 0600-1200 and 2000-2400, Fri 0600-1200 and 2000-2300, Sat 2300- Sun 2400 – **2) R. Lotte**, Herderplatz 14, 99423 Weimar; **W:** radiolotte.de Mon 0600-1200 and 2300-2400, Tue-Thu 0600-1200 and 2000-2400, Fri 0600-1200 and 2000-2300, Sat 2300- Sun 2400. **studio b11**, Bauhaus-Universität, Bauhausstr. 11, 99421 Weimar; **W:** radiostudio.org. Mon 1900-2300 only. Also rel. Funkwerk from Erfurt – **3)** Postfach 100 565, 98684 Ilmenau; **W:** hsf.tu-ilmenau.de – **4)** Georgenstr. 43, 99817 Eisenach; **W:** wartburgradio.com – **5)** Helmboldstr. 1, 07749 Jena; **W:** radio-okj.de – **6)** August-Bebel-Platz 6, 99734 Nordhausen; **W:** ok-nordhausen.de – **7)** Tiefer Weg 7, 07318 Saalfeld; **W:** srb.fm
DAB: 5 txs on ch. 5C (178MHz) see K)

III. ARMED FORCES STATIONS

LW & MW	kHz	kW	Site	Prgr.
1)	177	150	Zehlendorf	(encrypted DRM)
3)	1107	10	Vilseck	AFN Bavaria
7)	1143	1	Mönchengladbach	AFN Benelux
1)	(SW)	90	Nauen	(encrypted DRM)

NB. Spangdahlem MW tx and all 1485kHz txs closed down in 2015. 1107/1143kHz slated for closure in 2016

FM	MHz	kW	Site	Prgr.
Baden-Württemberg				
2)	102.3	100	Stuttgart	AFN Stuttgart
Bayern				
3)	89.4	0.2	Hohenfels	AFN Bavaria
3)	90.0	0.2	Amberg	AFN Bavaria
3)	90.3	0.1	Garmisch-Partenk.	AFN Bavaria
3)	98.5	0.1	Grafenwöhr	AFN Bavaria
3)	101.4	0.2	Grafenwöhr	AFN Bavaria
3)	104.9	0.4	Illesheim	AFN Bavaria
3)	107.3	1	Ansbach	AFN Bavaria
3)	107.6	0.2	Vilseck	AFN Bavaria
Hessen				
4)	98.7	50	Feldberg	AFN Wiesbaden

F.PI.: Freq. swap with Deutschlandfunk, AFN to use Wiesbaden 103.7MHz in future

FM	MHz	kW	Site	Prgr.
Niedersachsen				
8)	93.0	40	Braunschweig	BFBS Germany
8)	95.2	0.1	Bad Fallingbostel	BFBS R. 2
8)	95.4	0.2	Celle	BFBS R. 2
8)	99.3	0.1	Hameln	BFBS Germany
8)	100.1	0.1	Bad Fallingbostel	BFBS Germany
8)	104.7	0.2	Bergen-Hohne	BFBS R. 2
8)	106.7	0.2	Bergen-Hohne	BFBS R. 2
8)	106.8	0.1	Hameln	BFBS R. 2
Nordrhein-Westfalen				
8)	91.3	0.1	Rheindahlen	BFBS Germany
8)	91.7	0.3	Gütersloh	BFBS R. 2
8)	92.5	0.8	Dülmen	BFBS R. 2
8)	101.6	0.3	Bielefeld	BFBS R. 2
8)	101.9	7	Wulfen	BFBS Germany
8)	102.2	0.3	Münster	BFBS R. 2
8)	103.0	70	Bielefeld	BFBS Germany
8)	104.0	2.4	Niederkrüchten	BFBS Germany

FM	MHz	kW	Site	Prgr.
8)	104.3	0.3	Rheindahlen	BFBS R. 2
8)	105.0	0.3	Paderborn	BFBS R. 2
8)	105.1	0.5	Rheinberg	BFBS Germany
8)	106.0	3	Dortmund	BFBS Germany

NB. Geilenkirchen Air Base served by AFN and BFBS txs at Brunssum, see under Netherlands

Rheinland-Pfalz				
5)	100.2	1	Kaiserslautern	AFN Kaiserslautern
5)	103.0	0.4	Pirmasens	AFN Kaiserslautern
6)	105.1	1	Spangdahlem	AFN Spangdahlem
5)	106.1	0.1	Baumholder	AFN Kaiserslautern
Schleswig-Holstein				
8)	88.4	0.1	Kiel-Holtenau	BFBS Germany

Addresses and other information:
1) Bundeswehr, Zentrum Operative Information, Kürrenberger Steig 34, 56727 Mayen; **W:** radio-andernach.de. Prgr. for Bundeswehr operations abroad presented as **Radio Andernach**, distributed via local FM txs, during maritime operations also as encrypted DRM signal via 177kHz and unpublicized shortwave freq. – **2) AFN Stuttgart**, Robinson Barracks, 70376 Stuttgart; **W:** stuttgart.afneurope.net Own prgr. Mon-Fri 0400-0800 and 1400-1700 – **3) AFN Bavaria**, Rose Barracks, 92249 Vilseck; **W:** bavaria.afneurope.net Own prgr. Mon-Fri 0500-0800 and 1400-1700 – **4) AFN Wiesbaden**, Würgelstr. 1217, Flugplatz Erbenheim, 65205 Wiesbaden; **W:** wiesbaden.afneurope.net. Own prgr. Mon-Fri 0500-0900 and 1300-1700 – **5) AFN Kaiserslautern**, Vogelweh, Bldg. 2058, 67661 Kaiserslautern; **W:** kaiserslautern.afneurope.net Own prgr. Mon-Fri 0500-1700, Sat 0700-1100. **F.PI.:** Replacing 100.2MHz by another freq. – **6) AFN Spangdahlem**, Spangdahlem Air Base, 54529 Spangdahlem; **W:** spangdahlem.afneurope.net Own prgr. Mon-Fri 0500-0900 and 1300-1600, Sat 0800-1100 – **7)** see under Belgium – **8) BFBS Germany**, Marienfelder Str. 1, 33330 Gütersloh; **W:** bfbs-radio.com. Also via Eutelsat 10A, 11.221GHz v. Slated to close altogether in 2019, individual txs may close at any moment – **AFN Europe**, Sembach Kaserne, building 166, 67681 Sembach-Heuberg; **W:** afneurope.net. Produces network prgr., rel. by local AFN stns in Germany, Belgium and Italy

L.T: UTC — **Pop:** 23 million — **Pr.L:** English, Akan, Dagbani, Ga, Ewe, Hausa, Nzema, others — **E.C:** 50Hz, 230V — **ITU:** GHA

NATIONAL COMMUNICATIONS AUTHORITY (NCA)
P.O. Box CT 1568, 1st Rangoon Close, Switchback Rd, Cantonments, Accra ☎+233 30 2776621 🖷 +233 30 2763449 **W:** nca.org.gh **E:** info@nca.org.gh **L:P:** Acting DG: Major J. R. K. Tandoh.

GHANA BROADCASTING CORPORATION (GBC, Pub.)
P.O. Box 1633, Broadcasting House, Ring Road Central, Kanda, Accra ☎+233 30 2786567 🖷 +233 30 2773247
W: gbcghana.com **E:** info@gbcghana.com **L:P:** DG: Albert Don Chebe. Dir. Radio: Theo Agbam. Dir. Eng: Mrs. Sarah Boye.
Network N. in E (rel. by all GBC stations): 0600, 0700, 0900, 1100SS, 1300, 1400, 1800, 2000, 2200, 2345.

GBC Regional & partnership stations:

FM	MHz	Name	Web/Addr./Area
Bolgatanga	89.5	URA R.	Upper East
Han	90.1	Upper West R.	Upper West
Tamale	91.2	R.Savannah	North
Ho	91.5	Volta Star R.	Volta
Kumasi	92.1	Garden City R.	Ashanti
Cape Coast	92.5	R.Central	Central
Accra	93.7	R. Ada	P.O. Box 9482, K.I.A
Wa	93.9	Upper West R.	Upper West
Sunyani	94.7	R. Bar	Brong Ahafo
Sekondi-Takoradi	94.7	Twin City R.	West
Dormaa-Ahenkro	94.9	R. Dormaa	Brong Ahafo
Accra	95.7	Uniiq FM	Greater Accra
Accra	96.5	Obonu FM	Greater Accra
Apam	96.5	Apam R.	Central
Swedru	98.6	Swedru R.	Central
Kumasi	99.5	Luv FM	P.O. Box 17207, Accra
Accra	99.7	Joy FM	myjoyonline.com
Koforidua	106.7	Sunrise FM	East

Other FM stations in Accra:
Asempa FM, P.O. Box 17013, Accra-North: 94.7MHz – **Atlantis R,** P.O. Box 14629, Accra: 87.9MHz 5kW – **Channel R,** P.O. Box AN 8135, Accra-North: 92.7MHz – **Choice FM,** Accra: 102.3MHz. **W:** choicefmghana.com – **Citi FM,** P.O. Box 30211, K.I.A, Accra: 97.3MHz – **Happy FM,** P.O.

Box 1538, Dansoman, Accra: 98.9MHz – **Hot FM**, P.O. Box KD594, Kanda, Accra: 93.9MHz – **Peace FM**, Accra: 104.3MHz 5kW. **W:** peacefmonline. com – **R. Gold FM**, P.O. Box 17298, Accra: 90.5MHz – **R. Hit**, P.O. Box 17013, Accra-North: 103.7MHz – **R. Universe**, P.O. Box 25, Legon: 105.7MHz – **Sunny FM**, Box CT 3850, Cantonments, Accra: 88.7MHz – **Top R**, P.O. Box CT 4748, Cantonments, Accra: 103.1MHz – **Vibe FM**, Priv. Mailbag CT 183, Accra 91.9MHz.
+ 75 more stations elsewhere.
BBC World Sce: Accra 101.3MHz, Sekondi-Takoradi 104.7MHz.
RFI Afrique: Accra 89.5MHz, Kumasi 92.9Mhz in French/English.
VOA Africa: Accra 98.1MHz

GIBRALTAR (UK)

L.T: UTC +1h (27 Mar-30 Oct: +2h) — **Pop:** 30,000 — **Pr.L:** English, Spanish — **E.C:** 50Hz, 240V — **ITU:** GIB

GIBRALTAR BROADCASTING CORP. - Radio Gibraltar
Broadcasting House, 18 South Barrack Rd, Gibraltar GX11 1AA
☎ +350 200 79760 +350 200 76432 **W:** gbc.gi **E:** radiogibraltar@gbc.gi
L.P: CEO: Gerard Teuma, Head of Radio & Online: James Neish, Head of Eng.: John Tewkesbury
MW: 1458kHz 4kW
FM: 91.3MHz 0.2kW, 92.6MHz 1.0kW, 100.5MHz 1.0kW
D. Prgr: 24h **Radio Gibraltar Plus** opt out in Spanish M-F 1300-1500 on 100.5 MHz and 1458 kHz **Ann:** "Radio Gibraltar"
DAB: DAB+ Mux on 225.648MHz and 227.360MHz with 4 GBC ch.

BRITISH FORCES BROADCASTING SCE. GIBRALTAR
BFBS Gibraltar, BFPO 52, Rooke, Queensway, Gibraltar ☎ +350 200 55389 +350 200 55528 **W:** bfbs.com/radio **E:** gib@bfbs.com
FM: BFBS Gibraltar: North Mole 93.5MHz 0.2kW; O'Hara's Battery 97.8MHz 1kW (Relays BFBS UK when not carrying local prgs.)
BFBS Radio 2: North Mole 89.4MHz 0.2 kW; O'Hara's Battery 99.5MHz 0.25kW. **D. Prgr:** 24h

GREECE

L.T: UTC +2h (27 Mar-30 Oct: +3h) — **Pop:** 11 million — **Pr.L:** Greek — **E.C:** 50Hz, 220V — **ITU:** GRC

ETHNIKO SIMVOULIO RADIOTILEORASIS (ESR, National Council for Radio & Television)
Panepistimiou & Amerikis 5, 10564 Athina ☎ +30 213 1502300
+30 210 3319881 **W:** esr.gr **E:** ncrtv@otenet.gr
L.P: President: Orsalia Alexiou.

ELLINIKI RADIOFONIA (ERA, Greek Public Radio)
Leof. Mesogeion 432, 15342 Agia Paraskevi, Athina ☎ +30 210 6066000 +30 210 6002941 **W:** ert.gr **E:** info@ert.gr ertopen@gmail. com **L.P:** Dir: Dionysis Tsaknis. CEO: Lambis Tagmatarchis. Tech. Dir: Aris Kondizas.
MW: Athina (Bogiati) 729 kHz 100kW, Rhodes 1260 kHz 100kW*, Florina 1278 kHz 10kW*, Tripoli 1314 kHz 10kW, Komotini 1404 kHz 100kW, Volos 1485 kHz 1kW*, Hania 1512 kHz 100kW.

FM(MHz)	NET	ERA2	ERA3	ERASp	Reg.	ERP
17)Agios Ioannis					96.4	1
5) Ahentrias	94.4*	96.4			105.6	3/10
3) Ainos	96.9	98.9	104.2*	106.8	93.2	100/35/10
2) Akarnanika	88.9	97.3	102.5	91.3*	100.3*	10/35
9) Assea	88.3	103.5	90.3	95.3		10/35
Borsa	90.5			106.6		1
1) Bournias		104.8		106.8	89.7	3
8) Devas	93.5	95.2		91.1*		6
Didima	101.2	99.4		103.2		6
9) Doliana					101.5	35
4) Dovroutsi					98.3	35
12)Erateini		96.5	94.5		89.9	35
Finiki	91.0	96.2	93.0	104.8		1
Geraneia	97.9	99.9		105.0*		100/35
Hamezi	91.9*		89.0*		89.9*	6/3
Hlomo		101.5		107.4		6
Hortiatis	88.0	90.0	92.0	93.9		100
1) Ikaria					89.1	3
Imittos	105.8	103.7	90.9	101.8		100/6
12) Kalavrita					93.9	35
Kallithea	101.4*			101.1*		1
1) Karfas	102.1				100.1	1
19) Kastania	103.6	88.2*	105.6		100.2	35/2
Katsikas		107.0				35

FM(MHz)	NET	ERA2	ERA3	ERASp	Reg.	ERP
14) Kefalas		92.5*			103.8*	1
17) Kefalohori					101.5	35
Lefkes		98.9*		102.7		35
1) Lepetimnos					99.4	1
Lidoriki		99.5			90.4	1
2) Ligiades	106.1	99.8	97.8	102.1	88.2	6/35
Lihada	88.7	104.2				35
Makrovouni	99.4			97.4		10
15) Malaxa					100.6	6
14) Monte Smith					93.1	3
1) Olympos	92.3	94.3	106.4		104.4	35
Paggaio	89.2	91.2	97.5	107.3		35
12) Panahaiko		104.3	102.3	87.9	92.5	35/20
6) Pantokratoras	91.8	93.8	89.8	101.1	99.3	35
Parnitha	91.6	102.9	95.6	100.9		100
16)Petalidi	92.2	94.2	89.3	100.4	107.2	35/10
13)Pilio	92.8*	94.8	96.8	107.1	101.2	100/35
1) Pithio	98.9	88.1*	93.8*	89.4	101.0	35/6
1) Platanos		87.7			91.7*	6/3
11) Plaka	103.5	90.7			98.1	4/2
7) Plaka					101.0	2
1) Plomari					105.9	1
7) Prof. Ilias (L)			97.2		103.0	6/1
14)Prof. Ilias (R)	88.4	90.4	103.4	101.4	92.7	35
5) Rogdia	104.8	99.2	91.3*	93.9	97.5	3
15)Skloka	92.9	94.9	106.0	90.1*	104.0*	35
3) Skopos					95.2	6
10)Smerna					102.4	35
13) Soros					100.7	6
8) Stavros (Fl.)					99.1	1
5) Stavros (Las.)					105.3*	1
14) Sympetro	107.9*	100.3*		94.1*	98.4	3
1) Thanos					96.5	1
18)Thasos	95.1	96.3	100.8	104.7		35
1) Tholo Potami					95.2	3
Tsotili	89.1					1
Vasilaki	106.7					1
Vasiliko	92.1	94.2		101.7		3
1) Vathi					89.7	3
8) Vitsi	88.6	90.6	103.1	105.1	96.6*	100/35
19) Vitsi					89.1	6

+14 stations under 1 kW.
D.Prgr: All 24h. **ERA1:** News, talk, current affairs, sports. **ERA2:** Greek music and culture. **ERA3:** Classical music, arts. **ERA Sport:** sports.
*) Currently off air.

Other ERT Stations:
Kosmos Radio: Parnitha 93.6 100kW, Imittos 107.0 6kW, Didima 97.4 6kW.

Regional station addresses:
1) Northern Aegean: E. Bostani 69, GR-81100 Mitilini **2) Ioannina:** N. Papadopoulou 2, GR-45444 Ioannina **3) Zakynthos:** Ampelokipoi, GR-201 00 Zakynthos **4) Larissa:** Iroon Politehniou 1, 1h Stratia, GR-412 22 Larissa **5) Heraklion:** Maxis Kritis 161, GR-71303 Iraklio **6) Kerkira:** Ethniki Lefkimis, GR-49100 Kerkira **7) Orestiada:** Euripidou 15, GR-68200 Orestiada **8) Florina:** Megarovou 20, GR-53100 Florina **9) Tripoli:** Erithrou Staurou 1, 221 00 Tripoli **10) Pirgos:** Olympion 70, GR-27100 Pirgos **11) Komotini:** P.O. Box 5, Kosmiou Terma, GR-69100 Komotini **12) Patra:** Riga Feraiou 104, GR-26221 Patra **13) Volos:** Pl. Agiou Konstantinou, GR-32222 Volos **14) Southern Aegean:** 30 km. Leof. Kallitheas, GR-85100 Rhodes **15) Chania:** Ellis 40, GR-73200 Chania **16) Kalamata:** Anataliko Kentro 10-11, GR-24100 Kalamata **17) Serres:** P.O. Box 91, Stratopedou Kolokotroni, GR-62100 Serres **18) Kavala:** Sof. Venizelou & Iokastis, Ag. Paraskevi., GR-65100 Kavala **19) Kozani:** I. Tranta 19, GR-50100 Kozani. **W:** webradio.ert.gr/periferia
IS: The opening notes of the Greek folk song "Tsopanakos Imouna" (Once I Was A Shepherd Boy) played on flute and sheep bells.

EXTERNAL SERVICE: see International Radio section.

RADIOFONIKOS STATHMOS MAKEDONIAS (Gov.)
Aggelaki 14, 546 36 Thessaloniki ☎ +30 2310 299600 +30 2310 299451 **W:** ert.gr **E:** makedonia@ert.gr
Makedonia 1: FM: FM: Hortiatis 102.0MHz 100kW, 24h., Agios Ioannis (Serres) 89.6MHz 2kW*, Metaxas (Kozani) 89.1MHz 2kW*, Vitsi (Kastoria) 100.6MHz 10kW.*
Makedonia 2: FM: Hortiatis 95.8MHz 100kW, 24h.
ANN: "Elliniki Radiophonia, Radiofonikos Stathmos Makedonias"
F.PI.: Shutdown of Makedonia 2.

ERT OPEN - ELLINIKI RADIOFONIA & TILEORASIS (ERA, Greek Public Radio)

Leof. Mesogeion 463, 15343 Agia Paraskevi, Athina ☎+30 210 6002909-10 📠 +30 210 6002941 **W:** ertopen.com
FM: Parnitha 106.7MHz, Lefkes (Paros) 98.9MHz.
NB: Operated by former ERT employees who lost their jobs when ERT was shut down on 11 June 2013 and who were not rehired when ERT was officially reestablished on 11 June 2015.

ILIDA RADIO (RADIOFONIKOS STATHMOS AMALIADAS, Comm.)

Ag. Trifonos 5, 27200 Amaliada. **W:** ilida911.gr **E:** info@ilida911.gr **D.Prgr:** 24h.
MW: Kastro 1584kHz 1kW. **FM:** Kastro 92.7MHz 4kW, Frangapidima 91.1MHz 2kW.

1431 AM (Educ.)

Aristotle University of Thessaloniki. 1os Orofos Ptergas THMMHY, Politehniki Sholi, 54124 Thessaloniki. **W:** 1431am.org **D.Prgr:** 24h.
MW: Thessaloniki 1431kHz 350W.

PRIVATE FM STATIONS in Athina, Thessaloniki and Patra

Athina

FM	MHz	Station	kW	FM	MHz	Station	kW
1)	87.5	Kriti FM	2	28)	96.6	Pepper 96,6	10
2)	87.7	En Lefko	10	29)	96.9	Rock 969	10
3)	88.0	Menta 88	10	30)	97.2	Easy 97.2	10
4)	88.3	R. Penies	2	31)	97.5	Love R.	10
5)	88.6	Up Radio	10	32)	97.8	Real FM	10
6)	88.9	Hit 88,9	14	33)	98.0	Free FM	1
7)	89.2	Music 89,2	10	34)	98.3	Athena 9,84	10
8)	89.5	Ekklesia Ell.	19	35)	98.6	Derti 98,6	10
9)	89.8	Dromos 89,8	10	36)	98.9	Alpha 989	10
10)	90.1	Parapolitika FM	10	37)	99.2	Melodia 99,2	10
11)	90.4	Kanali 1	10	38)	99.5	Vima FM	10
12)	90.6	Art FM	4	39)	99.8	99,8 FM	5
13)	91.2	Peiraiki Ekkl.	10	40)	100.3	Skai 100,3	12
14)	91.4	Kritiki Radiof.	2	41)	100.5	Top FM	10
15)	92.0	Galaxy 92	10	42)	101.3	Diesi 101,3	10
16)	92.3	Lampsi 92,3	10	43)	101.6	Paradise R.	5
17)	92.6	Best 926	10	44)	102.2	Sfera 102,2.	10
18)	92.9	Kiss FM	14	45)	102.4	Nitro R.	10
19)	93.2	Ellinikos 93,2	10	46)	102.7	Palmos FM	5
20)	93.8	93,8 FM	1	47)	103.1	R. Blackman.	5
21)	94.0	R. Epikoinonia	5	48)	103.3	Sport 24 R.	10
22)	94.3	Dirla FM	2	49)	104.0	104 FM	10
23)	94.6	Spor FM	10	50)	104.3	Minore FM	10
24)	94.9	Rythmos 949	10	51)	104.6	Hot FM	10
25)	95.2	Athens Deejay	10	52)	104.9	Styl FM	10
26)	96.0	Flash 96	10	53)	105.2	Atlantis FM	10
27)	96.3	Red 96,3	10	54)	105.5	Sto Kokkino	10
55)	106.2	Mad R.	10	58)	107.7	Star FM	10
56)	106.4	R. Argosaronikos	5	59)	108.0	Fresh FM	10
57)	107.4	R. Mythos	5				

Thessaloniki

FM	MHz	Station	kW	FM	MHz	Station	kW
60)	87.6	Laikos FM	5	87)	98.7	Classic 98,7	5
61)	88.5	88miso	5	88)	99.0	R. Ena	20
62)	89.0	89 Rainbow	15	89)	99.4	Flash 99,4	5
63)	89.4	Arena FM	10	90)	99.8	Radio Ekrixi	5
64)	89.7	Imagine 89,7	3	91)	100.0	FM 100	20
65)	90.4	904 Aristera	30	92)	100.3	Republic 100,3	15
66)	90.8	Zoo R.	5	93)	100.6	FM 100,6	20
67)	91.1	VFM 91,1	5	94)	101.0	FM 101	20
68)	91.4	Ola FM	15	95)	101.3	POPS 101,3	5
69)	91.7	RSO 91,7	5	96)	101.7	Kalamaria FM	25
70)	92.4	R. Ekfrasi	5	97)	102.3	R. Akrites	10
71)	92.8	Yellow R.	15	98)	102.6	Plus R.	10
72)	93.1	Ble FM	5	99)	103.0	More R.	5
73)	93.4	Sto Kokkino	3	100)	103.6	Focus FM	5
74)	93.7	R. Gnomi	2	101)	104.0	Rythmos 104	20
75)	94.2	R. Lydia	18	102)	104.4	Radiokymata	5
76)	94.5	R. Thessaloniki	5	103)	104.7	Rock R.	10
77)	94.8	Eroticos FM	5	104)	104.9	Praktoreio FM	15
78)	95.1	Cosmoradio	20	105)	105.2	Live 105,2	5
79)	95.5	Metropolis FM	5	106)	105.5	1055 Rock	5
80)	96.1	Next 96,1	10	107)	105.8	Hroma FM	2
81)	96.5	Alpha 96,5	5	108)	106.1	City International	2
82)	96.8	Velvet 96,8	5	109)	106.5	Rockxtreme	5
83)	97.1	R. Almopia	5	110)	106.8	Iera Mt. Langada	1
84)	97.5	Easy 97,5	25	111)	107.1	Real FM	3
85)	98.0	R. North	20	112)	107.4	Libero 107,4	5
86)	98.4	Panorama 9,84	20	113)	107.7	Sunshine FM	5

Patra FM (MHz): Like R. 88.2 – Iera Mitropoli Patras 88.5 – Melody FM 88.8 – ‡Politia FM 89.1 – Skai Patras 89.4 –Parapolitika Patras 90.0 – Imera FM 90.4 – Mythos FM 90.7/104.8 – Yes R. 91.2 – Radio 91,5 91.5 – R. Enter 91.7 – Kiss FM 92.2 – Top FM 93.0 – Max FM 93.4 – R. Gamma 94.0 – Alpha Patras 94.4 – Rythmos 94.9 – Oxygen 95.3 – Spor FM Patras 96.3 – Sfera Patras 96.6 – Wave R. 97.4 – R. Messatida 98.0 – Flash Patras 98.7 – R. Aigio 99.2 – Fasma FM 99.7 – You FM 100.1 – Melodia Patras 100.4 – Smart FM 100.7 – Free 101.1 – Hroma 102.1 – Loux FM 102.7 – Mousiki Lampsi 103.3 – Palmos FM 103.7 –Sport24 Patras 104.1 – Antenna Patras 105.3 – Derti 105.7 – Galaxy FM 106.1 – R. Patra 106.5 – Sto Kokkino 107.7. Powers 1–5kW.
+ approx 1100 additional private stns nationwide.
‡ inactive
NB: no official information available about powers of most Athina stations and Thessaloniki powers are mostly based on estimates.

Addresses & other information:
1) Peloponissou 42, 18121 Koridallos **W:** kritifm.com – **2)** Fraggoklisias 8, 15125 Maroussi **W:** enlefko.fm – **3)** Mesogeion 174, 15125 Maroussi **W:** menta88.gr – **4)** Athina – **5)** Mesogeion 174, 15125 Maroussi **W:** 886upradio.com – **6)** Fraggoklisias 8, 15125 Maroussi **W:** hit889.gr – **7)** Apostolou Pavlou 7, 15125 Maroussi **W:** music892.gr – **8)** Iasiou 1, 11526 Athina **W:** ecclesia.gr/greek/ecclesiaradio/index.asp – **9)** Viltanioti 36, 14564 Kato Kifisia **W:** dromosfm.gr – **10)** Iasonos 2, 18537 Piraeus **W:** parapolitika.gr – **11)** Evripidou 79, 18532 Piraeus **W:** e-kanaliena.gr – **12)** Praxitelous 58, 17674 Kallithea **W:** arttv.info – **13)** Deligiorgi 47, 18535 Piraeus **W:** pe912fm.com – **14)** Athina **W:** radiocreta.gr – **15)** Pirronos 12, 16346 Ilioupoli **W:** galaxy92.gr – **16)** Viltanioti 36, 14564 Kato Kifisia **W:** lampsifm.com – **17)** Perikleous 49, 15451 Neo Psyhiko – **18)** Vas. Sofias 85, 15124 Maroussi **W:** kiss.gr – **19)** Dimitros 31, 17778 Tavros – **20)** **W:** radio98fm.org – **21)** S. Karagiorgi 2 & M. Antypa, 14121 Iraklio **W:** 94fm.gr – **22)** Athina. **W:** dirla.gr 23) Davaki 58, 17672 Kallithea **W:** sport-fm.gr – **24)** Theotokopoulou 4 & Astronafton, 15124 Maroussi **W:** rythmosfm.gr – **25)** Viltanioti 36, 14564 Kato Kifisia **W:** athensdeejay.gr – **26)** Agiou Filippou 7, 10555 Athina **W:** radio96fm.blogspot.com – **27)** Fraggoklisias 8, 15125 Maroussi **W:** redfm.gr – **28)** Mesogeion 174, 15125 Maroussi **W:** pepper966.gr – **29)** Viltanioti 36, 14564 Kato Kifisia **W:** rockfm.gr – **30)** Leof. Kifisias 10-12, 15125 Maroussi **W:** easy972.gr – **31)** Dimitros 31, 17778 Tavros **W:** loveradio.gr – **32)** Leof. Kifisias 197, 15124 Maroussi **W:** realfm.gr – **33)** Athina – **34)** Leof. Peiraios 100, 11854 Athina **W:** athina984.gr – **35)** Agias Annis 1 & Palaiologou, 15232 Halandri **W:** derti.gr – **36)** 40o km. Attikis Odou, SEA Mesogeion, Ktirio 6, 19002 Paiania **W:** alpha989.com – **37)** Eth. Makariou/Delta Falireos 2, 18547 Neo Faliro **W:** melodia.gr – **38)** Mihalakopoulou 80, 11528 Athina **W:** vimafm995.gr – **39)** Athina **W:** astrofm.gr – **40)** Eth. Makariou/Delta Falireos 2, 18547 Neo Faliro **W:** skai.gr/1003 – **41)** Athina – **42)** Viltanioti 36, 14564 Kato Kifisia **W:** diesi.gr – **43)** Askeli Porou 18020 **W:** paradiseradio.gr **44)** Agias Annis 1 & Palaiologou, 15232 Halandri **W:** sfera.gr – **45)** Beaki Aimiliou 58, 12134 Peristeri **W:** athensnitroradio.gr – **46)** 18020 Poros **W:** palmosradio.gr – **47)** Papanastasiou 25, 18755 Keratsini **W:** mariosblackman.gr – **48)** Leof. Syggrou 166, 17671 Kallithea **W:** sport24radio.gr – **49)** Athina – **50)** Athina **W:** minorefm.gr – **51)** Vas. Sofias 85, 15124 Maroussi **W:** hotfm.gr – **52)** Athina **W:** stylfm.gr – **53)** Ag. Konstantinou 11, 18544 Piraeus. **W:** atlantisfm.gr – **54)** Sarri 19, 10554 Athina **W:** stokokkino.gr – **55)** Eth. Antistaseos 253, 15351 Pallini **W:** madradio.gr – **56)** Dritseika Methanon, 18030 Methana **W:** radioargosaronikos.gr – **57)** Athina. – **58)** Athina. **W:** athenshits.blogspot.com – **59)** Athina. **W:** freshradio.gr – **60)** G. Kranidioti 2, 57001 Pylaia Thessaloniki. **W:** laikos.gr – **61)** Armenopoulou 9, 54635 Thessaloniki **W:** 88miso.gr – **62)** Harisi 63, 54639 Thessaloniki **W:** 89rainbow.gr – **63)** Tompazi 15, 55535 Thessaloniki **W:** arenafm.gr – **64)** Adrianoupoleos 20A, 55133 Kalamaria Thessaloniki **W:** imagine897.gr – **65)** Egnatias 69, 54631 Thessaloniki **W:** 902.gr – **66)** Aristotelous 3, 54624 Thessaloniki **W:** zooradio.gr – **67)** Psaron 21, 54642 Thessaloniki **W:** 911.gr – **68)** 1o km. Filirou-Langada, 57010 Filiro Thessaloniki **W:** olafm.gr – **69)** 1o km. Filirou-Langada, 57010 Filiro Thessaloniki **W:** rso.gr – **70)** Fanariou 13 & Mouson, 56429 Stavroupoli Thessaloniki **W:** fm-ekfrasi.gr – **71)** Nea Egnatia 171, 54249 Thessaloniki **W:** yellowradio.gr – **72)** 4hs Avgoustou 6, 57003 Agios Athanasios Thessaloniki – **73)** Karolou Diel 22, 54623 Thessaloniki **W:** stokokkino.gr/kokkino-thes.php – **74)** Ag. Sofias 43, 54623 Thessaloniki **W:** gnominet.gr – **75)** Eleftherias 15, 56123 Ambelokipi Thessaloniki **W:** radiolydia.gr – **76)** 17o km. Moudianon, Kombos Risiou, 57001 Thermi Thessaloniki **W:** rthess.gr – **77)** 17o km. Moudianon, Kombos Risiou, 57001 Thermi Thessaloniki – **78)** **W:** eroticos.gr – **78)** 1os Orofos, 54623 Thessaloniki **W:** cosmoradio.gr – **79)** K. Palama 6A, 54352 Pylaia Thessaloniki. **W:** metropolisradio.gr – **80)** 17o km. Moudianon, Kombos Risiou, 57001 Thermi Thessaloniki **W:** nextfm.gr – **81)** K. Kristalli 4, 54630 Thessaloniki **W:** alpha965.gr – **82)** K. Palama 6G, 54630 Thessaloniki **W:** velvet968.gr

– **83)** Lohagou N. Papadopoulou 17, 58400 Aridaia **W:** aridaia-gego-nota.blogspot.com – **84)** 26hs Oktovriou 90, 54627 Thessaloniki **85)** Mitropoleos 34, 54623 Thessaloniki **W:** radionorth.gr – **86)** Mitropoleos 34, 54623 Thessaloniki **W:** panorama984.gr – **87)** Valaoritou 4, 54626 Thessaloniki – **88)** K. Karamanli 175, 54249 Thessaloniki **W:** 99fm.gr – **89)** 26hs Oktovriou 46, 54627 Thessaloniki **W:** flash994.gr – **90)** Melenikou 31A, 56224 Evosmos Thessaloniki **W:** ekrixifm.gr – **91)** N. Germanou 1, 54645 Thessaloniki **W:** fm100.gr – **92)** Aristotelous 7, 54624 Thessaloniki **W:** republicradio.gr – **93)** N. Germanou 1, 54645 Thessaloniki **W:** fm100.gr – **94)** N. Germanou 1, 54645 Thessaloniki. **W:** fm100.gr – **95)** Isminis 46, 54633 Thessaloniki – **96)** Andrianoupoleos 8 & Epanomis 26, 55133 Kalamaria Thessaloniki **W:** kalamariafm.gr – **97)** Vas. Othonos 12, 54629 Stavroupoli, Thessaloniki **W:** radioakri-tes.gr – **98)** Aristotelous 7, 54624 Thessaloniki **W:** plusradio.gr – **99)** Aristotelous 7, 54624 Thessaloniki **W:** moreradio.gr – **100)** Politehniou 21, 54623 Thessaloniki **W:** focusfm.gr – **101)** 26hs Oktovriou 90, 54627 Thessaloniki **W:** rythmosfm.gr – **102)** A. Papandreou 27, 56334 Kordelio Thessaloniki **W:** radiokymata.gr – **103)** Kouskoura 5, 54625 Thessaloniki **W:** rockradio.gr – **104)** Salaminos 5, 54625 Thessaloniki **W:** amna.gr/praktoreioFM/ – **105)** Promitheos 33 & Afroditis 12, 54630 Thessaloniki – **106)** Aggelaki 31, 54621 Thessaloniki **W:** 1055rock.gr – **107)** Kromnis 10, 54453 Toumpa Thessaloniki **W:** hroma.gr/1058 – **108)** Karatassou 31, 55132 Kalamaria Thessaloniki **W:** cityinternatio-nal.gr – **109)** Aggelaki 31, 54621 Thessaloniki **W:** 1055rock.gr – **110)** 57200 Langadas Thessaloniki **W:** imlagada.gr/default.aspx?catid=89 – **111)** Aristotelous 5, 54624 Thessaloniki **W:** realfm.gr – **112)** Leontos Sofou 18, 54625 Thessaloniki **W:** libero.fm – **113)** Makedonikis Aminis 1, 54631 Thessaloniki. **W:** sunshinefm.gr

AMERICAN FORCES RADIO & TV SERVICE (Mil.)
W: soudabay.afneurope.net **FM:** "107.3 The Odyssey": Souda Bay 107.3MHz 0.5kW

GREENLAND (Denmark)

L.T: UTC -3h (DST*: -2h). Qaanaaq & Thule Air Base: UTC -4h (DST*: -3h; not Thule AB), Ittoqqortoormiit: UTC -1h (DST*: UTC), Danmarkshavn: UTC. *) 27 Mar-30 Oct — **Pop:** 56,000 — **Pr.L:** Greenlandic, Danish — **E.C:** 50Hz, 220V — **ITU:** GRL

KALAALLIT NUNAATA RADIOA – KNR (Pub. Comm.)
✉ Issortarfimmut 1A, PO Box 1007, DK-3900 Nuuk ☎ +299 361500 🖷 +299 361502 **W:** knr.gl **E:** info@knr.gl
L.P: Chrmn: Nukaaraq Eugenius. Acting MD: Jan Berg Hd of Radio: Masaana Egede

MW	kHz	kW			
Nuuk	570	5			
Oeqertarsuaq	650	5			
Simiutaq	720	10			
FM	**MHz**	**kW**	**FM**	**MHz**	**kW**
Nuuk	90.5	0.5	Ilulissat	96.0	0.1
Sisimiut	95.0	0.1	Tasillaq	96.0	0.08
Uummannaq	95.0	0.05	Sanderson Hope	96.0	0.1
Upernavik	95.0	0.05	Aasiaat	96.5	0.1
Qaqortoq	95.5	0.1	Manitsoq	97.0	0.08
Kangerlussuaq	96.0	0.08	Dye Four	98.7	0.08

+ 62 additional stns 0.1kW or less. On 88.1-99MHz. Most txs use 94.0, 95.0, 95.4, 95.5, 96.0 or 97MHz **KNR:** 24h in Greenlandic (approx. 90%) and in Danish. N on the h in Greenlandic and Danish. Main N in Greenlandic: 1500, 2100. Danish: 1515, 2115
Ann: "Kallaallit-Nunaata Radioa", "Grønlands Radio" **IS:** "Sunnia Kalippoq" (The Whaleboat "Sonja" drags whale) played on celeste

DR P1, Denmark. Satellite relay 24h Nuuk 98.0MHz 0.1kW
RÚV Rás 2, Iceland. Satellite relay 24h Narsaq 88.0MHz (0.01kW)

INUUNERUP NIPAA (Rlg)
✉ Ilivinnguaq 1, PO Box 67, DK-3900 Nuuk ☎ +299 321382 🖷 +299 321226 **W:** ino.nuuk@greennet.gl
L.P: Chrmn: John Østergaard Nielsen. Hd of Prgr.: Jan Berthelsen
FM: 88.5MHz (all tx's are 0.05kW) in Aasiaat, Ilulissat, Kullorsuaq, Maniitsoq, Nanortalik, Nuuk, Qaanaaq, Qaqortoq, Sisimiut, Tasiilaq, Upernavik and Uummannaq
D.Prgr: 1030-1430, 1600-1930 and 2200-0230. Most prgrs in Greenlandic

PRIVATE STATIONS (local radio):
Ice FM, Industrivej 18, Box 1082, 3900 Nuuk **W:** 93.5MHz (0.1 kW) **W:** icefm.gl – **Nipi FM**, Box 279, 3921 Maniitsoq: 90.5 and 93.0MHz (Maniitsoq) and 99.0MHz (Kangaamiut) **W:** nipifm.gl – **Nuuk FM**, Nuukullak 32-B, Box 1462, 3900 Nuuk: 93.0MHz (0.1kW) **W:** nuukfm.

gl – **Radio 5OZ20 - Thule Radio**, Community Centret bygn. 362, Box 1, Thule Air Base, 3970 Pituffik: 97.1MHz (0.1kW) – **Radio Narsaq**, Josifip aqq. 543, 3961 Narsaq: 93.0MHz (0.025kW). W: radionarsaq.gl – **Radio Upernavik**, Box 244, 3962 Upernavik: 93.0MHz – **Seekon Radio**, Box 361, 3920 Qaqortoq: 93.0MHz – **Sisimiut Tusaataat**, Box 312, 3911 Sisimiut: Sisimiut: 93.0MHz (0.05kW), Kangerlussuaq 93.0MHz (0.02kW), Itilleq 91.5MHz (0.02kW) and Sarfannguit 98.5MHz (0.02kW) – **Tusaat Aasiaat 93 MHz**, Aqqusinersuaq 5, Box 20, 3950 Aasiaat: 93.0MHz (0.1kW)

GRENADA

L.T: UTC -4h — **Pop:** 103,000 — **Pr.L:** English — **E.C:** 50Hz, 230/400V — **ITU:** GRD

GRENADA BROADCASTING NETWORK – G.B.N. Radio (Gov, Comm.)
✉ Observatory Road, PO. Box 535, St. George's ☎ +1 473 440 3033 🖷 +1 473 444 4180 **W:** gbn.gd **E:** gbn@spiceisle.com
L.P: GM: Odetta Campbell. CEN: Kennedy Bowen
FM: HOTT FM: 98.5/98.7MHz 1000-0300 – **K105:** 105.5(South) /105.9(North)MHz

HARBOUR LIGHT OF THE WINDWARDS (Rlg.)
✉ Harbour Light Way, Hillsborough Post Office, Tarleton Point, Carriacou ☎ +1 473 443 7628 🖷 +1 473 443 7628 **W:** harbourlightra-dio.org **E:** harbourlight@spiceisle.com **L.P:** SM: Randy Cornelius
MW: 1400kHz 5kW **FM:** 92.3MHz 0.25kW, 94.5MHz 0.25kW
D.Prgr: MW: 0953-0245. FM: 24h. **N:** rel. BBC
Ann: "This is the Harbour Light of the Windwards broadcasting from beautiful and friendly Carriacou"

PRIVATE STATIONS:
Boss FM, Sauteurs, St Patricks ☎+1 473 442 1177 **W:** bossfmgre-nada.com. FM: 104.1/104.9MHz – **Chime FM**, PO Box 553, Tanteen, St George's ☎+1 473 440 7746. FM: 100.9MHz – **City Sound**, River Road, St George's ☎+1 473 440 9616 🖷+1 473 440 7838 **W:** citysoundfm. com. FM: 96.5/97.5MHz – **CRFM Community Radio**, Morne Jaloux, St George's ☎+1 473 440 4848 🖷+1 473 440 4991. FM: 89.5MHz – **Fresh FM**, Bruce St Mall, St George's. FM: 90.9/102.7MHz – **GFN – Grenada Family Network**, PO Box 2747, St George's ☎+1 473 435 4297. FM: 91.3/100.3MHz. Format: Rlg. (Adventist) – **GNCN - Good News Catholic Radio**, Church St., Box 224, St George's ☎+1 473 435 0143. FM: 99.5MHz. Format: Rlg – **Greenz FM**, Mt.Craven, St Patrick's ☎+1 473 405 7030. FM: 103.1MHz – **GTC Radio**, Morne Rouge, Grand Anse, St George's ☎+1 473 439 9700 **E:** gtc@gtcfm.com **W:** gtcfm. com FM: 89.9/90.5MHz – **Kyak 106 FM**, Church Street, Hillsborough, Carriacou ☎+1 473 443 6262 **W:** kyak106.com FM: 106.3MHz – **Live Wire HD**, Ross Point, PO Box 90, St George's ☎/🖷+1 473 435 3563. **W:** livewirehd.com FM: 90.1MHz. Evenings: Community Heartbeat Radio, St. John's – **Magic 103**, Moving Target Co., Lagoon Road, St George's ☎+1 473 440 8171 🖷 +1 473 440 8505. **W:** magic103fm. com & vogfm.com FM: 88.9/95.7/103.3MHz – **Real FM Grenada**, High Street, St. Patrick ☎+1 473 442 0975. **W:** realfmgrenada.com FM: 91.5/91.9MHz – **SGU 107.5**, Office of University Communications, 2nd floor, Chancellery, St George's University, St George's ☎+1 473 444 4175 ext. 2191 🖷+1 473 444 3153 **W:** sgu.edu FM: 107.5MHz. Format: Non-comm. community radio – **Sister Isle Radio**, Fort Hill, Hillsborough, Carriacou ☎+1 473 443 8141/8142. **W:** sisterislesradio. com FM: 92.9MHz – **Vibes 101.3**, Church St, Hillsborough, Carriacou ☎+1 473 443 7733 🖷+1 473 443 8212 **W:** kimsplaza.net/vibes-101.3.html. FM: 101.3MHz – **Wee FM**, Grenada Wireless Comm Network, Cross St, PO Box 555, Gouyave, St John's ☎+1 473 440 4933 🖷+1 473 440 8724 **W:** weefmgrenada.com FM: 93.3/93.9MHz

GUADELOUPE (France)

L.T: UTC -4h — **Pop:** 394,000 — **Pr.L:** French, Créole Patois — **E.C:** 50Hz, 230V — **ITU:** GLP

GUADELOUPE PREMIÈRE (Pub)
✉ Morne Bernard-Destrellan, B.P. 180, F-97122 Baie-Mahault. ☎+590 590939696. 🖷+590 590939682 **W:** guadeloupe.la1ere.fr **L.P:** Dir: R.Surjus. Editor-in-Chief: Philippe Goudé. PD: L.Francil. Head Comms Dept: Sonia Gémieux
MW: Point-à-Pitre 640kHz 40kW
FM: Point-à-Pitre 88.9MHz 1kW, Haut du Morne des Pères 89.1MHz 1kW, Deshaies 96.8MHz 0.1kW, Basse-Terre 97.0MHz 3kW, Pointe-Noire 97.4MHz 16kW
D.Prgr: 24h. **N:** 1100, 1700, 2230, plus relays of France-Inter.
Ann: "Ici Point-à-Pitre, La Première Guadeloupe".
IS: "Biguin" (guitar) **V.** by QSL-card. Rp.

RADIO CARAÏBES INTERNATIONAL (Comm.)
📧 **RCI Guadeloupe**, B.P. 1309, F-97187 Point-à-Pitre Cédex. ☎ +590 590839696 📠 +590 590839697
FM: Basse-Terre 98.6MHz 1kW, Deshaies 98.6MHz 0.3kW, Morne-à-Louis 100.2MHz 2kW, Point-à-Pitre 106.6MHz 1kW, Haut du Morne 106.6MHz 0.05kW. **D.Prgr:** 24h.

RADIO BASSES INTERNATIONALE (Comm)
📧 Stations de radio, Lieu-dit les Basses, 97112 Grand Bourg ☎ +590 590977088 📠 +590 590978062
FM: Haut du Morne des Pères 88.7MHz 1kW, Grand-Bourg 90.4MHz 1kW, Morne-à-Louis 98.2MHz 2kW, Basse-Terre 102.2MHz 1kW

RADIO MASSABIELLE (RCF) (Rlg)
📧 B.P. 607, 97168 Point-à-Pitre ☎+590 590 832521 📠 +590 590 834861. **L.P:** Pres: José Colat-Jolivière, Dir: Père Silvère Numa **W:** radiomassabielle.fr **E:** contact@radiomassabielle.fr
FM: Point-à-Pitre 97.8MHz 0.6kW, Pointe-Noire 101.8MHz 1kW

RADIO SAPHIR FM
📧 rue Bel Air Bourg, 97170 Petit-Bourg ☎+590 690 352274
E: saphirfm@live.fr **W:** radiosaphirfm.com
FM: Point-à-Pitre 89.4MHz 1kW

Other stations (all MHz):
France Inter, Pointe-à-Pitre 91.2 1kW, Haut du Morne des Pères 91.7 1kW, Morne-à-Louis 95.0 16kW, Basse-Terre 95.4 3kW – **NRJ Guadeloupe**, Pointe-à-Pitre, 100.6 1kW, Basse-Terre 102.6 1kW, Morne-à-Louis 107.2 2kW – **Antilles Infos**, 105.8 2kW, 106.5 1kW – **Bel'Radio**, Morne-à-Louis 106.9 1kW – **Fréquence Alizée**, 96.6 1kW, 103.4 2kW – **R. Éclair**, 96.0 1kW, 101.0 2kW – **R. Gaïac FM**, 99.8 1kW, 104.7 1kW – **R. Haute Tensi**, 99.8 1kW, 90.8 1kW – **R. Karata**, 90.6 1kW, 106.5 1kW – **Radio Madras FM**, 92.5 2kW, 92.9 1kW – **Radio Nostalgie**, 105.4 1kW, 107.6 2kW – **Trace FM**, 92.1 2kW, 94.1 1kW. **NB:** +11 other stations

GUAM (USA)

L.T: UTC +10h — **Pop:** 172,600 — **Pr.L:** English, Chamorro, Filipino — **E.C:** 60Hz, 110/220V — **ITU:** GUM

FEDERAL COMMUNICATIONS COMMISSION (FCC)
see USA for details

		kHz	kW			kHz	kW
1)	KGUM	567	10.0	12)	KUSG	1350	0.3
2)	KUAM	630	10	13)	KVOG	1530	0.25
3)	KTWG	801	10.0				

SW: AFN: see International section (USA) for details

		MHz	kW			MHz	kW
4)	KHMG	88.1	8	1)	KZGZ	97.5	40
5)	KPRG	89.3	9.2	9)	KOKU	100.3	50
15)	KKGU	90.1	4	11)	KNUT	101.1	8
6)	KOLG	90.9	5.7	10)	KTKB-FM	101.9	46
7)	KSDA-FM	91.9	3.8	8)	KISH	102.9	25
9)	KMOY	92.7	42	11)	KIJI	104.3	12.5
12)	KUSG-FM	92.9	0.01	1)	KGUM-FM	105.1	12
2)	KUAM-FM	93.9	5.2	14)	KGCA-LP	106.9	0.07
8)	KSTO	95.5	2	14)	KGCA-LP	107.9	0.023

Addresses and other information
1) Sorensen Pacific Broadcasting Inc 111 Chalan Santa Papa, Suite 800; Hagatna, GU 96910-5193 ☎+1 671 477-5700, +1 808 524-6495, 📠+1 671 477-3982 **Brands:** KGUM-AM Talk, news **W:** k57.com; KZGZ Power98 CHR **W:** power98guam.com [KZGU 99.5 currently licenced to Garapan-Saipan, N Marianas but serves Guam as 'The Shark'] **W:** guamshark.com KGUM-FM 'The Kat' **W:** facebook.com/105thekat – **2) Pacific Telestations LLC** 600 Harmon Loop Road, Suite 102; Dededo, GU 96929-6536 ☎+1 671 637-KUAM (637-5826) 📠+1 671 637-9865 **W:** kuam.com **Brands:** KUAM: Isla63 'Island Pride' contemporary island music; KUAM-FM: i94 Champion Radio CHR – **3) Edward H Poppe Jr & Frances W Poppe**, Cornerstone 800AM, 1868 Halsey Drive; Asan, GU 96910-1505 ☎+1 671 477-5894 📠+1 671 477-6411 **W:** ktwg.com **E:** am800guam@gmail.com Format: Protestant Christian talk and instruction, gospel music **NB:** Korean Mon & Fri 0800-0830, Tagalog Wed 0800-0830, Chamorro Thu 0800-0815 & Sun 0700-0730, Japanese Thu 0815-0830 – **4) Harvest Christian Academy**, Harvest Family Radio, PO Box 23189 Barrigada, GU 96921 ☎ +1 671 477 6341📠+1 671 477 7136 **W:** hbcguam.net **E:** khmg@hbcguam.net **L.P:** GM: John Collier **Prgr:** 24h religious– **5) Guam Educational Radio Foundation** c/o University of Guam, 303

University Drive; UOG Station; Mangilao, GU 96923-1871 **NB:** BBCWS Daily 0700-0800, Sun 1900-2100, Mon 1900-2000, Tue 1400-2000, Wed & Thu 1400-1800 & 1900-2000, Fri 1400-1800, Sat 1700-2000 **W:** kprgfm.com **STA** 4.6kw because of typhoon damage and need to relocate tower – **6) Catholic Educational Radio**, Chalan Santo Papa; P.O. 23006, Guam Mail Facility, Barrigada, GU 96921-3006 **W:** kolg.com **L.P:** GM: Deacon Frank Tenorio, Dir. Prgr: Chuck White **Prgr:** 24h relig – **7) Good News Broadcasting Corp**, Joy FM, 290 Chalan Palasyo, Hagatna Heights, GU 96910-6405 ☎ +1 671 472 1111, 📠+1 671 477 4678 **W:** joyfmguam.com **L.P:** GM: Matthew Dodd **Prgr:** 24h religious **Languages:** English, Chinese, Chuukese, Japanese, Korean, Tagalog – **8) Inter-Island Communications Inc**, Nimitz Hill, 1868 Halsey Drive, Piti, GU 96910-1505 – **9) Moy Communications**, Guam Hit Radio 100, 107 Julale Center, 424 West O'Brien Drive, Hagatna, GU 96910-5078 **W:** hitradio100.com **E:** marketing@hitradio100.com **KOKU:** "Guam's #1 Hit Music Station" CHR **KMOY** – **10) KM Broadcasting of Guam LLC**, 177-B Ilipog Drive, Suite 203; Tamuning, GU 96913-4107 **E:** rolly@ktkb.com **W:** ktkb.com **Brand:** Megamixx 101.9 Format: OPM Origil Pilipino Music **Prgr Language:** Tagalog – **11) Choice Broadcasting Company** 543A Top-Plaza Building, N Marine Dr, Tamuning, GU 96913-4217☎+1 671 478-0104 📠+1 671 647-7480 **KNUT** Fun 101 FM "Guam's Hottest OPM & US Hit Station" **Prgr:** Filippino **W:** facebook.com/fun101Guam **KIJI** 3F La Casa de Colina Building, Tamuning GU 96913 "The Boss 104.3FM" **Prgr:** Classic Rock **L.P:** SM: Rich de Vera **W:** kijifm104.com **E:** rich@kijifm104.com **Other:** sister company to iConnect – **13) MCS LLC**, 125 Tun Jesus, Crisotomo Street #308, Tamuning GU 96913 ☎+1 671 648-4262 – **13) Guam Power II Inc**, 1100 Alakea #1800, Honolulu HI 96813-2839 ☎+1 808 521-4711 – **14) KGCA Inc**, Melodies of Prayer Inc, 154 Calachucha Ave, Barrigada GU 96913 ☎+1 671 637 5975 **W:** melodiesofprayer.com **E:** mail@melodiesofprayer.com **L.P:** Chair: Edwin Supit **Prgr:** 24h religious – **15) Hurao Inc**, 264 Calle de los Marteres St, Agat GU 96935 ☎ +1 671 482-4630

ADVENTIST WORLD RADIO - ASIA (Rlg.) and TRANS WORLD RADIO - ASIA (Rlg.): See International Radio section

GUATEMALA

L.T: UTC -6h — **Pop:** 13 million — **Pr.L:** Spanish — **E.C:** 60Hz, 120V — **ITU:** GTM

SUPERINTENDENCIA DE TELECOMUNICACIONES
📧 4a Avenida N° 15-51, Z-10, Guatemala ☎+502 2321100 ext. 101 **W:** sit.gob.gt

CÁMARA DE RADIODIFUSION DE GUATEMALA
📧 12 Calle 1-25, Zona 10, Edificio Geminis 10, Torre Norte, Of. 812, Guatemala ☎+502 23353077 **W:** camaraderadiodifusiongt.com
Call TG—, ‡ = inactive, (r) = repeater, ± = varying fq.

MW Call		kHz	kW	Station, location, h. of tr.
S003)		540	0.02	R. Amistad, San Pedro de Laguna
SM01)		560	1	R. Quetzal, Malacatán
ES01)	PA	570	1	R. Palmeras, Escuintla
GU02)	Y	580	5	R. Progreso, Guatemala: 1300-0100
QU01)	RQ	590	5	R. Quiché, Sta Cruz del Quiché: 1100-0400
GU03)	GA	610	5	R. Alianza, Guatemala: 1000-0500
TO01)	PQ	620	5	R. 6-20, San Cristóbal: 1200-0400
PE01)	EL	630		R. Cultural Porvenir, Sta Elena: (r. 730)
QE01)	Q	640	3	LV de Quetzaltenango: 1100-0400
AV02)	VP	680	10	R. Norte, Cobán: 1000-0500
JU01)	VB	690	1	R. Tamazulapa, Jutiapa
ES03)	AJ	700	1	R. Inspiración, Escuintla
GU06)	HR	700	15	R. Mundial, Guatemala
QE02)	XL	710	1	R. Tecún Umán, Quetzaltenango (r. 730)
GU07)	N	730	10	R. Cultural, Guatemala
ZA01)	CK	780	1	Sultana La Cristiana, Zacapa
PE02)		810		R. Moapán, Sta Elena
SA01)		810		R. Circuito San Juan, San Juan
SM06)	END	810	1	R. Constelación, San Marcos: 1200-0200
GU10)	TO	‡820	10	R. Kyrios/R. Internacional, Guatemala:1000-0600
SU01)	AV	830	5	R. Satélite, Mazatenango: 1100-0400
AV06)		840	2.5	R. Luz, San Pedro Carchá
JU04)		840		R. Idea 840, Jutiapa
SU02)	L	870	0.5	R. Victoria, Mazatenango
ES04)	HU	890	1	R. Escuintla, Escuintla
IZ02)	MA	900	1	R. Amatique, Puerto Barrios
GU30)	KL	910	10	R. Fe y Esperanza, Guatemala: 1130-0600
ES05)	RS	920	0.2	R. Cultural, Escuintla (r. 730)
GU13)	TL	940	10	Eventos Católicos R., San Pedro Sacatepéquez, Guatemala: 1200-0500
SU03)	AF	950	1	R. Indiana, Mazatenango

MW Call	kHz	kW	Station, location, h. of tr.
GU14) AX	970	5	R. Continental, Guatemala: 1200-0430
CH01) AL	990	1	R. Perla de Oriente, Chiquimula
CM02)	1000		R. Cultural y Educativa, Patzún
GU32)	1000		R. Revelación y Verdad, Guatemala: 1055-0500
IZ06)	1010	1	R. Caribe, Izabal
QU03) XI	1010	1	R. Ixil, Nebaj: 1100-0200
SM05) CM	1020	5	R. Frontera, Pajapita: 1100-0400
GU15) UX	1030	10	R. Panamericana, Guatemala: 1400-0100
JA01) JP	1040	1	R. Oriental, Jalapa
HU01) SL	1050	5/1	LV de los Cuchumatanes, Huehuetenango: 1100-0600
QE04) D	1070	3/2	LV de Occidente, Quetzaltenango: 1200-0400
ZA02) LU	1080	1	R. Novedad, Zacapa
QE05) SR	1100	1	R. Superior, Coatepeque
AV04) MK	1110	1	R. Verapaz, Cobán
GU17) C	1120	0.5	R. Poderosa "La Voz de la Liberación", Guatemala: 1100-0600
RE01) VR	1130	1	Em. Unidas LV de la Costa Sur, Retalhuleu
GU17) T	1150	10	R. Sonora, Guatemala: 1100-0600
IZ03) RI	1160	1	R. Izabal, Morales (r: 730): 1300-0300
QE06) RL	1170	5	R. Cadena Landívar, Quetzaltenango: 0900-0300
JU02) RJ	1200	12	R. Unción, Jutiapa
GU19) MX	1210	10/5	R. Miel, Guatemala
IZ04) AT	1230	1	R. Atlántida, Puerto Barrios: 1130-0500
SU04)	1230		R. América, Cuyotenango
GU20) K	1240	5	R. Luz, Guatemala
CH02) PY	1250	1	R. Payakí, Esquipulas: 1100-0300
TO04)	1250		LV Cristiana, Totonicapán
GU21) CQ	1270	2.5	R. Exclusiva, Guatemala
ZA03)	1290		R. Miramundo "LV del Ejercito", Zacapa
QE07) AN	1310	1	R. LV de los Altos, Quetzaltenango: 1100-0700
JU03) ME	1320	0.5	R. Quezada, Jutiapa
GU22) MU	1330	5	Unión R, Guatemala: 1100-2330
AV05) MC	1350	1	R. Monja Blanca, Cobán
GU15) LK	1360	10	R. Tic Tac "LV del Evangelio", Guatemala
QE09) AC	1370	1	LV de Colomba, Colomba
TO03) EB	1380	0.5	R. Momostenango Educativa, Momost.:1100-0300
QE10) GH	1410	5	Nueva R. Xelajú, Quetzaltenango: 1200-0600
HU02) AG	1430	1.2	LV de Huehuetenango: 1100-0400
SU05) MS	1440	0.5	R. Nacional, Mazatenango: 0000-0400
GU06) LG	1450	1	R. Hosanna, Guatemala: 1000-0600
PE04) RN	1460	2.5	R. Petén, Flores: 1100-0500
GU25) HB	1480	5	R. Horizontes, Guatemala: 1030-0200
RE02) RE	1490	1	R. Modelo, Retalhuleu
PE05)	1520		R. Taysal, Sta Elena de la Cruz
QE11)	1560		R. Inspiración, Quetzaltenango
GU27) VE	1570	10	VEA-Voz Evangélica de América, Guatemala: 1030-0600
CM01) XC	1590	1	R. Triunfadora, Chimaltenango
SWCall	**kHz**	**kW**	**Station, location & h. of tr**
CH04) AV	4055	0.7	R. Verdad, Chiquimula: 0910-0600

State abbreviations: (Departamentos) AV = Alta Verapaz, BV = Baja Verapaz, CH = Chiquimula, CM = Chimaltenango, ES = Escuintla, GU = Guatemala, HU = Huehuetenango, IZ = Izabal, JA = Jalapa, JU = Jutiapa, PE = Petén, QE = Quetzaltenango, QU = Quiché, RE = Retalhuleu, SA = Sacatepéquez, SR = Santa Rosa, SM = San Marcos, SO = Sololá, SU = Suchitepéquez, TO = Totonicapán, ZA = Zacapa. **N.B:** These abbreviations are not recognized by the Post Office. Letters should therefore carry the full name.

Addresses and other information:
AV00) ALTA VERAPAZ
AV01) 5 Calle 1-06, Z-3, 16001 Cobán – **AV02)** 2 Calle 5-57, Z-3, 16001 Cobán – **AV04)** 2 Calle 5-57, Z-3, 16001 Cobán – **AV05)** Edif Municipalidad, 5a Calle 1-06, 16001 Cobán – **AV06)** 11 Av Zona 1, Colonia Cuatro Caminos, San Pedro Carchá (or Apartado Postal 14, 16001 Cobán) - 1100-0400.
BV00) BAJA VERAPAZ
BV01) Inst de Educación Básica, Barrio Abajo San Jerónimo, 15001 Salamá. Prgrs. in Spanish, Achi and Q'eqchí
CH00) CHIQUIMULA
CH01) 7 Calle Av 4-00, Z-1, 20001 Chiquimula (or 6 Av 0-60, Z-4, Torre Prof II, Of 904, 01004 Guatemala) – **CH02)** 5 Av 6-37, Z-1, 20007 Esquipulas - **FM:** 91.5MHz – **CH04)** Estación Educativa Evangélica, Ap. 5, 20901 Chiquimula. **W:** radioverdad.org
CM00) CHIMALTENANGO
CM01) 2 Calle 3-33, Z-3, 04001 Chimaltenango – **CM02)** 6ta Calle 3-88, Zona 5, Patzún 050, Chimaltenango.
ES00) ESCUINTLA
ES01) 15 Calle 2-48, Z-3, 05001 Escuintla – **ES02)** Col 15 de Junio,

Z-3, Tiquisate, 05001 Escuintla - **FM:** 92.3MHz – **ES03)** 4 Av 12-27, Z-1, 05001 Escuintla. **E:** radioinspiracion@gmail.com – **ES04)** 4 Av 11-38, Z-1, 05001 Escuintla – **ES05)** Central American Benevolent Association, 05001 Escuintla – **FM:** 96.3MHz
GU00) GUATEMALA
GU02) 9 Av 0-32, Z-2, 01002 Guatemala. **W:** radioprogresoguatemala.com – **GU03)** 34 Av "A" 7-60 Tikal 2, Z-7, 01007 Guatemala. **W:** radioalianza.org – **GU04)** 18 Calle 6-72, Z-1, 01001 Guatemala – **GU06)** 8 C 10-54, Zona 11, Col. Roosevelt, 01011 Guatemala. **W:** radiomundial.com.gt – **GU07)** Ap 601 (or 4 Av 30-09, Z-3), 01901 Guatemala - **English:** 0300-0430 on 730 kHz. **W:** radiocultural.net – **GU08)** 30 Av 3-86, Z-11, Utatlán II, 01011 Guatemala – **GU09)** 11 Calle 2-43, Z-1, 01001 Guatemala – **GU10)** 25 Calle 4-91, Zona 12, Barrio La Reformita, 01012 Guatemala – **GU11)** Calzada San Juan 7-90, Edif.Acuario, Z-7, 01007 Guatemala – **GU12)** 6a Av 0-60, Zona 4, Torre Profesional 1, Niv. 9, Of. 911, 01004 Guatemala – **GU13)** 10a Avenida "A" 2-43 Zona 1, 01001 Guatemala **W:** eventoscatolicos.com.gt – **GU14)** 15 Calle 3-45, Z-1, 01001 Guatemala – **GU15)** 1 Av 35-48, Z-7, Col Toledo, 01017 Guatemala. **W:** panamericanadeguatemala.net radiotictaclavozdelevangelio.blogspot.com – **GU16)** 10 Calle 5-20, Z-1, 01001 Guatemala – **GU17)** 2 Calle 18-07, Zona 15, Vista Hermosa 1, 01015 Guatemala. **W:** sonora.com.gt – **GU19)** 4 Av 1-14, Z-1, 01001 Guatemala. **W:** centralpalabramiel.org – **GU20)** Ap 281, 01901 Guatemala – **GU21)** 7 Av. 15-13, Zona 1, Edificio Ejecutivo, Niv. 8, 01001 Guatemala. **W:** radioexclusiva.org – **GU22)** Ap 51-C, 01015 Guatemala. **W:** unionradiogt.org – **GU24)** 4 Av 0-60, Z-4, 01004 Guatemala. **W:** radiocapital1420am.com.gt – **GU25)** 17 Av.21, Cnt. Com Las Pergolas, Z-11, 01011 Guatemala – **GU27)** Ap 1213, (or 30 Av "A" 7-33, Z-7, Col Tikal, 01007 Guatemala), 01901 Guatemala. **W:** radiovea.org – **GU29)** Guatemala – **GU30)** 10a Avenida 0-61, Z-19, Colonia La Florida, 01019 Guatemala – **GU32)** 17 Av. 5-47, Zona 11, Col. Miraflores, 01011 Guatemala
HU00) HUEHUETENANGO
HU01) 2 Calle 4-42, Z-1, 13001 Huehuetenango – **HU02)** Ap 13, 13901 Huehuetenango – **HU03)** lavozdehuehue.comlu.com – **HU04)** 13025 San Sebastián Coatán Programming in Spanish & Chuj Coatán. **FM:** 92.5MHz – **HU05)** 13020 San Sebastián H, Huehuetenango. **W:** tgmi-radiobuenasnuevas.com
IZ00) IZABAL
IZ01) Calle Principal, Morales – **IZ02)** Ruta Atlántico km 291, 18001 Puerto Barrios – **IZ03)** Barrio El Carrizal, Morales – **IZ04)** Ap 425, 18901Puerto Barrios – **IZ05)** 8 Av 15 y 16 Calle, 18001 Puerto Barrios – **IZ06)** Izabal
JA00) JALAPA
JA01) Barrio San Francisco, Una Cuadra Abajo de Incav, Jalapa **W:** facebook.com/pages/Radio-Oriental-Jalapa-Guatemala/234662116555928
JU00) JUTIAPA
JU01) 4 Avenida 4-79, Zona 1, Colonia El Latino, 22001 Jutiapa – **JU02)** Carr Interamericana km 117, 22001 Jutiapa. **W:** radiouncionjutiapa.com – **JU03)** Quezada – **JU04)** 6ta Calle 5-00, Zona 3, a un costado del puente del Incienso, 22001 Jutiapa
PE00) PETÉN
PE01) Sta Elena de la Cruz **FM:** 96.9MHz – **PE02)** Sta Elena de la Cruz – **PE04)** Isleta Sta Bárbara, 17001 Flores (or 1 Av 1-22, Z-1, Guatemala) **W:** radiopeten.com.gt - **FM:** 105.3MHz– **PE05)** Ministerio de la Defensa Nacional, Sta Elena de la Cruz
QE00) QUETZALTENANGO
QE01) Ap 113 (or 13 Av 8-19, Z-1), 09901 Quetzaltenango – **QE02)** 6 Av 6-41, Z-1, 09001 Quetzaltenango – **QE03)** 5 C 13-56, Zona 3, Xelajú (Ap 90), 09901 Quetzaltenango - **FM:** 99.1MHz– **QE04)** 7 Av 0-26, Z-2, 09002 Quetzaltenango. **W:** radiotgd.com – **QE05)** 3 Calle 3-38, Z-1, Coatepeque – **QE06)** 14 Av "A" 0-78, Z-1, 09002 Quetzaltenango – **QE07)** Ap 107, 09901 Quetzaltenango – **QE09)** Calle Principal, Z-2, Colomba. - **FM:** 99.1MHz – **QE10)** 4 Calle 15A-62, Z-1, 09002 Quetzaltenango. **W:** nuevaradioxelaju.com – **QE11)** 3 Calle 3-38, Z-1, Coatepeque, Retalhuleu – **QE12)** Km 211, Aldea Duraznales, Concepción, Chiquirichapa, Quetzaltenango.
QU00) QUICHÉ
QU01) 7 Calle 3-67, Z-5, 14001 Sta Cruz del Quiché **W:** radioscatolicasdequiche.com - **FM:** 90.7 MHz – **QU03)** 5 Av 1-32, Canton Batzbaca, 14013 Nebaj
RE00) RETALHULEU
RE01) Ap 84, 11901Retalhuleu – **RE02)** 7 Av 6-72, 11001 Retalhuleu (or Ap 183-A, Guatemala): 0900-0300
SA00) SACATEPÉQUEZ
SA01) San Juan Sacatepéquez. **W:** radiocircuitosanjuan.com
SR00) SANTA ROSA
SR01) Edif Municipal, Chiquimulilla
SM00) SAN MARCOS
SM01) 4 Avenida 4-32, Z-1, Malacatán – **SM04)** 5 Calle 8-21, Z-1,

San Pedro – **SM05)** Pajapita, 12001 San Marcos – **SM06)** 12001 San Marcos
SO00) SOLOLA
SO03) Iglesia Bautista Getsemani, San Pedro La Laguna (or International Mission Board, SBC, Ap 25, Bulevares, MX 53140, México) - **FM:** 97.6MHz
SU00) SUCHITEPEQUEZ
SU01) 10001 Mazatenango - 1100-0400 – **SU02)** La Libertad 9-91, Z-1, 10001 Mazatenango – **SU03)** 6 Av 10-54, Z-1, 10001 Mazatenango – **SU04)** 13 Av 23-60, Z-12, 10012 Coyotenango – **SU05)** Calle 30 de Junio 1a y 2a, Z-5, 10001 Mazatenango
TO00) TOTONICAPAN
TO01) Barrio La Cienaga, 08002 San Cristóbal Totonicapán – **TO03)** Momostenango, 08001 Totonicapán – **TO04)** Totonicapán
ZA00) ZACAPA
ZA01) 4 Calle 12-54, Z-1, 19001 Zacapa – **ZA02)** 4 Calle 10-34, Z-1, 19001 Zacapa – **ZA03)** Zona Militar N° 7, 19001 Zacapa

FM in Guatemala City (MHz): 88.1 Fabuestereo - 88.5 Galaxia La Picosa – 88.9 Fabulosa 88.9 – 89.3 Estrella – 89.7 Em.Unidas – 90.1 Yo Sí Sideral – 90.5 Punto – 90.9 Exitos – 91.3 Furia Musical – 91.7 Fiesta – 92.1 Universidad – 92.5 40 Principales – 92.9 Disney – 93.3 FM Joya – 93.7 Mía – 94.1 94 FM – 94.5 La Sabrosita – 94.9 Nueve Cuatro Nueve – 95.3 Kyrios – 95.7 Ranchero – 96.1 Nuevo Mundo – 96.5 Atmósfera - 96.9 Sonora – 97.3 Alfa – 97.7 Kiss FM - 98.1 Doble S – 98.9 Globo – 99.3 La Grande - 99.7 Conga - 100.1 Infinita – 100.5 Cultural – 100.9 La Hit FM – 101.3 R. Extrema – 101.7 R. Activa – 102.1 Stereo 102 – 102.5 FM Fama – 102.9 Caliente – 103.3 R. María – 103.7 R. Fiesta – 104.1 Stereo Visión – 104.5 TGRF R. Faro Cultural – 104.9 Tropicálida – 105.3 Celebra FM – 105.7 Union – 106.1 Red Deportiva – 106.5 Clásica – 106.9 ¡UyUyUy! – GU04) 107.3 TGW LV de Guatemala – 107.7 Mega

FM in Quetzaltenango (MHz): 87.5 Estéreo Bendición – 88.1 Dinámica – 88.5 La Consentida – 89.5 Emisoras Unidas – 89.9 Prisima FM – 90.3 Tropicálida – 90.7 María – 91.1 La Nueva Mega – 91.7 La Rubia – 92.3 R. Cadena Sonora – 92.7 Cadena Caliente – 93.1 Nahual Estereo – 93.7 Fiesta – 94.3 Diamante – 94.7 Punto – 95.1 Ke Buena – 95.5 Evolución – 95.9 FM Globo – 96.3 FM Intima – 97.1 Exa FM – 97.5 Gaviota FM – 98.3 La Grande – 98.7 Yo Sí Sideral – 99.1 RTVA Arqueocesana – 99.5 Génesis – 99.9 Galaxia – La Picosa – 100.3 Stereo Cien – 100.7 R. Culturas – 101.1 R. Estéreo Tulán – 101.5 Estéreo Alegre – 102.3 Precencias R. – 102.9 Cristal – 103.3 La Voz de Dios – 104.3 Emisoras Unidas – 104.7 Razón – 105.3 La Voz del Evangelio – 105.9 FM Luna – 106.3 La Visión F – 106.7 Alfa – 107.1 R. Exitos – 107.5 TGQ La Voz de Quetzaltenango – 107.9 R. Estéreo Vida

GUINEA

L.T: UTC — **Pop:** 10 million — **Pr.L:** French, Fulah, Maninké, Soussou — **E.C:** 50Hz, 220V — **ITU:** GUI

CONSEIL NATIONAL DE LA COMMUNICATION (CNC)
✉ Conakry **W:** guinee.gov.gn **L.P:** Chmn: Mounir Camar.

RADIO TÉLÉVISION GUINÉE (RTG, Gov.)
✉ B. P. 391, Conakry ☎+224 30 41 55 19. **W:** rtg- conakry.com **L.P:** DG: Alpha Kabinet Keita. Dir. Tech: Aladji Touré.
SW: Conakry (Sonfonia): 7125kHz 50kW (inactive).
FM: Conakry 88.5/91.7MHz. **R. Kaloum Stereo:** 94.9MHz.
D.Prgr. in French/Others: W 0555-2400, Sun 0800-2400. **N: French:** 0645, 0915Sun, 1200Sun, 1245W, 1300Sun, 1615W, 1945W, 2000Sun, 2200, 2350. **English:** 1845 (irr.)
Ann: F: "R. Conakry", "R. Guineé". **IS:** Guitar.

RADIO RURALE (RTG rural stations):
Basse Guinée, Kindia: 98.7/99.2/99.3MHz – **Beyla:** 94.4/98.2MHz – **Bissikirima:** 91.0MHz – **Boké:** 95.3MHz – **Dinguiraye:** 98.6MHz – **Faranah:** 88.2MHz – **Gaoual:** 98.6MHz – **Guinée Forestiere,** N´zérékoré: 89.0MHz – **Haute Guinée:** Mandiana 88.2MHz, Kankan 92.1MHz, Dabadou 93.0MHz, Siguiri 97.0MHz, Douabou 99.0MHz – **Kérouané:** 92.2MHz – **Kindia:** 88.3MHz, Kakoulima 98.7MHz, Koliadi 99.9MHz – **Kissidougou:** 95.4/98.1MHz – **Koundara:** 98.6MHz – **Macenta:** 88.6/98.2MHz – **Mali:** 101.6MHz – **Mamou:** 91.1/101.1MHz – **Moyenne Guinée,** Pita: 87.6MHz – **Siguiri:** 94.4MHz – **Télimélé:** 97.7MHz – **Tougué:** 98.3MHz.

RADIO RENAISSANCE (Rlg, operated by Actualité Féminine en Guinée, former Familia FM)
✉ Conakry **L.P:** DG: Mrs. Colette Baudais.

SW: Timbi-Madina 4900kHz 1kW. (inactive). **FM:** Conakry 95.9MHz. **D.Prgr.** in French/Susu/Kpèlè/Pular/Maninka: FM: 0600-2400.

Private stations:
Atlantic FM: Conakry 96.5MHz – **Bambou FM:** Coyah/Faranah 89.3MHz – **Cherie FM:** Conakry 104.1MHz **W:** cheriefmguinee.com – **Djiguii FM,** Conakry: 105.7/107.7MHz. **W:** djiguii.com – **Djoliba FM:** Conakry/Siguiri 95.6MHz – **Espace FM:** Conakry 99.6MHz, Labé 99.7MHz **W:** espacefmguinee.info – **Gangan FM:** Conakry 101.1MHz – **Horizon FM:** Conakry/Kankan 103.4MHz – **R. Liberté FM:** Conakry/N'zérékoré 101.7MHz **W:** radiolibertefm.com – **R. Maria,** Conakry: 100.8MHz **W:** radiomaria.org – **R. Milo,** Kankan/Siguiri: 99.5MHz **W:** milo-fm.com – **R. Nostalgie Guinée:** Conakry 98.2MHz 1kW **W:** nostalgieguinee.net – **Sabari FM:** Conakry 97.3MHz 1kW. **W:** sabarifm.com – **Soleil FM:** Conakry 101.7MHz – **Swet FM:** Conakry 102.2MHz.
BBC World Sce: Conakry/Labé 93.9MHz.
R. France Int: Conakry/Kankan/Labé 89.9MHz

GUINEA-BISSAU

L.T: UTC — **Pop:** 1.5 million — **Pr.L:** Portuguese, Crioulo, others — **E.C:** 50Hz, 220V — **ITU:** GNB

INSTITUTO DAS COMUNICAÇÕES DA GUINÉ-BISSAU(ICGB)
✉ Av. Domingos Ramos 53, C.P. 1372, Bissau ☎+245 3204873/74 🖷 +245 3204876 **E:** icgb@mail.bissau.net

RADIODIFUSÃO NACIONAL (RDN, Gov.)
✉ C.P. 191, Bissau ☎+245 3212426 **L.P:** DG: Hipolito José Mendes.
FM: 88/91.5/93.7/98MHz. **D.Prgr:** 0600-2400.
Ann: "Escutam a Radiodifusão Nacional da República da Guiné-Bissau"

Other stations:
R. Bombolom, Bissau: 106.2MHz. Also rel. BBC & DW – **R. Jovem,** Bissau: 102.8MHz **W:** radiojovem.info – **R. Luz,** Bissau: 97.7MHz **W:** radioluzafrica.com – **R. Mavegro,** Bissau: 100.0MHz. Also rel. BBC – **R. Nossa** (Rlg.), Bissau: 98.9MHz – **R. Pindjiguiti,** Bissau: 95.0MHz. Also rel. VOA – **R. Sol Mansi** (Rlg.) Mansoa: 90.0MHz 4kW, Bissau/Bafatá 101.8MHz 1kW. 0630-2300. Also rel. Vatican R. and UN prgrs.
RFI Afrique: Bissau 94.7MHz in French/Portuguese.
RDP Africa: Nhacra 88.4MHz 25kW, Gabú 100MHz 1kW +1tx under 1kW. +20 community radio stations

GUYANA

L.T: UTC -4h — **Pop:** 790,000 — **Pr.L:** Creole, English, Hindi, Urdu, Amerindian dialects — **E.C:** 50Hz, 240V — **ITU:** GUY

PUBLIC UTILITIES COMMISSION
✉ Parliament Buildings, Brickdam, Georgetown ☎ +592 227 3293 🖷+592 227 3534

NATIONAL COMMUNICATIONS NETWORK INC. (ex. GUYANA BROADCASTING CORP)
✉ Broadcasting House, P.O. Box 10760, Georgetown ☎+592 223 6049, +592 223 1566/1577 🖷+592 226 2253 **W:** ncnguyana.com **E:** feedback@ncnguyana.com
L.P: SEO: Mohammed Sattaur GM: Mazrul Bacchus Prod. Mgr: Martin Goolsarran
MW: Georgetown 560/‡760kHz 10kW, Linden 700kHz 1kW **NB:** 760kHz is inactive
SW: Georgetown 3290/5950kHz 10kW
FM: Georgetown 100.1/102.5MHz, Linden 106.5MHz
R. Roraima: 0800-0200 on (760kHz‡) + 100.1MHz **N:** 0900, 1000, 1100, 1330, 1500, 1900, 2100, 2230 (W), 0100
Voice of Guyana: 24h on 560kHz 2200-0900 on 3290kHz **N:** as R. Roraima. **V.** by letter
Other FM stations: Megajams, Georgetown 87.7MHz – R. Guyana Incorporated, Georgetown 89.5MHz, Essequibo 89.3MHz, Berbice 89.3MHz **W:** radioguyanafm89.com

HAITI

L.T: UTC -5h; (13 Mar-6 Nov: -4h) — **Pop:** 8.9 million — **Pr.L:** Creole, French — **E.C:** 50+60Hz, 110V — **ITU:** HTI

CONSEIL NATIONAL DES TELECOMMUNICATIONS (CONATEL)
✉ B.P.2002 (or Cité de l'Exposition 16), Port-au-Prince ☎ +509

25163325 📠+509 22239229 **W:** conatel.gouv.ht **E:** info@conatel.
gouv.ht

MW	kHz	kW	Station, location
1)	‡660	5	R. Lumière, Port-au-Prince
1)	720	1	R. Lumière, Petite Riviere
1)	740	1	R. Lumière, Pignon
1)	760	2	R. Lumière, Les Cayes
11)	840	10	R. 4VEH, Cap Haitien

FM	MHz	kW	Station, location
1)	88.1		R. Lumière, Gonaives
3)	88.5		Caraibes FM, Cap-Haitien
6)	88.5		R. Kiskeya, Port-au-Prince
6)	88.9		R. Kiskeya, Camp-Perrin
34)	89.7		Voix de l'Espérance, Port-au-Prince
10)	88.9		R. Parole de Vie, Fort-Liberté
14)	88.9		R. Télé Express Continental, Jacmel
9)	90.3		R. Timoun, Jacmel
9)	90.5		R. Timoun, Cap-Haitien
40)	90.5		Signal FM, Port-au-Prince
9)	90.7		R. Timoun, Les Cayes
5)	90.9		R. Vision 2000, Jacmel
9)	90.9		R. Timoun, Port-au-Prince
9)	91.5		R. Timoun, Hinche/Port-de-Paix
10)	91.7		R. Ephphatha, Jacmel
9)	91.9		R. Timoun, Jérémie
1)	92.1		R. Lumière Stereo 92, Port-au-Prince
2)	92.1		R. Ginen, Cap-Haitien
5)	92.5		R. Vision 2000, Port-de-Paix
21)	92.5		R. Commerciale d'Haiti, Port-au-Prince
2)	92.9		R. Télé Ginen, Port-au-Prince + 4 sites
11)	93.3		R. 4VEH, Pignon
19)	93.3		Canal du Christ, Port-au-Prince
41)	93.7		R. Vasco, Port-au-Prince
11)	94.1		R. 4VEH, Cap-Haitien
29)	94.1		R. Nouvelle Génération, Port-au-Prince
3)	94.5	3	Caraibes FM, Port-au-Prince
10)	94.7		R. Voix de la Paix, Port-de-Paix
4)	94.9		R. Metropole, Jacmel
9)	94.9		R. MBC, Port-au-Prince
27)	95.3		La Voix de l'Evangile, Port-au-Prince
10)	95.5		R. Men Kontre, Les Cayes
15)	95.7		R. Horizon 2000, Port-au-Prince
1)	95.9		R. Lumière, Les Cayes/Jérémie
20)	95.9		R. Boukman, Port-au-Prince
36)	96.1		RCH 2000, Port-au-Prince
30)	96.5		Sky FM, Port-au-Prince
11)	96.7		R. 4VEH, Mirelabais
19)	96.9		R. Tele Antilles Internationale, Port-au-Prince
16)	97.3		R. Télémegastar, Port-au-Prince
1)	97.9		R. Lumière, Dame Marie
5)	98.1		R. Vision 2000, Gonaives
28)	98.1		Maxima FM, Port-au-Prince
9)	98.5		R. Timoun, Gonaives
10)	98.5		R. Voix Ave Maria, Cap-Haitien
26)	98.5		R. Ibo, Port-au-Prince
10)	98.7		R. Christ Roi, Gonaives
13)	98.9		Alleluia FM, Port-au-Prince
5)	99.3		R. Vision 2000, Port-au-Prince
2)	99.5		R. Ginen, Miragoâne
32)	99.7		Sweet FM, Port-au-Prince
5)	99.9		R. Vision 2000, Saint-Marc
4)	100.1	2	R. Metropole, Port-au-Prince
11)	100.3		R. 4VEH, Ile de la Tortue
23)	100.5		R. Eclair, Port-au-Prince
2)	100.7		R. Ginen, Miragoâne
12)	100.9		Magik 9, Port-au-Prince
4)	101.3		R. Metropole, Saint-Marc
33)	101.3		Univers FM, Port-au-Prince
22)	101.3		R. Télé Digital, Port-au-Prince
5)	101.7		R. Vision 2000, Les Cayes
24)	101.7		Energie FM, Port-au-Prince
7)	102.1		R. Nationale d'Haiti, Port-au-Prince
3)	102.5		Caraibes FM, Port-de-Paix
4)	102.5		R. Metropole, Les Cayes
35)	102.5		R. Télé Zenith, Port-au-Prince
6)	102.9		R. Kiskeya, Saint-Marc
31)	102.9		R. Super Star, Port-au-Prince
4)	103.3		R. Metropole, Gonaives
17)	103.3		R. Melodie, Port-au-Prince
10)	103.5		R. de l'Immaculée Conception, Hinche
39)	103.7		Shalom, Port-au-Prince
25)	104.5		R. Galaxie, Port-au-Prince

FM	MHz	kW	Station, location
37)	104.9		RFM, Port-au-Prince
7)	105.1		R. Nationale d'Haiti, Cap-Haitien
7)	105.3		R. Nationale d'Haiti, Port-au-Prince
5)	105.7		R. Vision 2000, Cap-Haitien
10)	105.7		R. Soleil, Port-au-Prince
10)	105.9		R. Tet Ansamn, Jérémie
7)	106.3		R. Nationale d'Haiti, Cap-Haitien
18)	106.5		Planet Kreyol, Port-au-Prince
6)	106.9		R. Kiskeya, Sans Souci
42)	107.3		R. Solidarité, Port-au-Prince
38)	107.7		Scoop FM, Port-au-Prince

Addresses and other information:
1) Côte Plage 16, Carrefour, B.P .1050, Port-au-Prince **W:** radiolumiere.
org – **2)** #28, Delmas 31, Port-au-Prince **W:** rtghaiti.com/radioginen
– **3)** 45 Rue Chavannes, Port-au-Prince **W:** radiotelevisioncaraibes.com
– **4)** 8, Delmas 52, B.P. 62, Port-au-Prince **W:** metropolehaiti.com – **5)**
184, Av. John Brown, Lalue, Port-au-Prince **W:** radiovision2000haiti.net
– **6)** 42, Rue Villemenay, Bois Verna, Port-au-Prince **W:** radiokiskeya.
com – **7)** Delmas 65, Impasse Orchidée, B.P. 1143, Port-au-Prince – **8)**
11, Rue Rigaud, P.V, Port-au-Prince **W:** freewebs.com/radiombc – **9)** **W:**
radiotimoun.com – **10)** 14, Rue Pinchinat, Pétionville, Port-au-Prince **W:**
radiosoleil.org radiovoixavemaria.com – **11)** Route Nationale 1, Morne
Rouge, B.P. 1, Cap-Haitien **W:** radio4veh.org – **12)** **W:** magik9haiti.
com – **13)** **W:** alleluiafmhaiti.com – **14)** #35, Rue de l'Eglise, Jacmel
W: radioteleexpress.com – **15)** Rue Butte # 2, Bourdon, Port-au-Prince
6111 **W:** radiohorizon2000endirect.com – **16)** **W:** radiotelemegastar.
com – **17)** **W:** radiomelodiehaiti.com – **18)** Delmas 48 #34, Port-au-
Prince **W:** planetkreyol.com – **19)** 77 Rue Metellus, Bas de la Montagne
Noire, Pétionville, Port-au-Prince 6140 **W:** radioteleantilleshaiti.com
– **20)** **W:** facebook.com/pages/Radio-Boukman/157901850906631
– **21)** 39 Blvd. 15 Octobre, Tabarre, Port-au-Prince **W:** radiocommer-
cialedhaiti.com – **22)** **W:** radioteledigital.fr.ht – **23)** **W:** radioeclairhaiti.
com – **24)** **W:** energiefm.com – **25)** **W:** radiogalaxiehaiti.com – **26)**
W: radioibo.net – **27)** **W:** rvehaiti.org – **28)** facebook.com/maximafm.
haiti – **29)** Delmas 64, No. 6, Port-au-Prince **W:** palimpalem.com/6/
radionouvellegeneration – **30)** **W:** haitiskyfm.com – **31)** Delmas 68,
Angle rues Safran et C. Henri, Pétionville, Haïti **W:** superstarhaiti.com
– **32)** Rue Dr Coles #8, Résidences du soleil, Delmas 25, Port-au-Prince
W: sweetfmhaiti.com – **33)** Rue Villate, Pétionville, Port-au-Prince
W: universfm.ht – **34)** Diquini 63, Campus de l'Université Adventiste
d'Haiti, B.P. 1339, Port-au-Prince **W:** 4vve.org – **35)** 33, Bon Repos,
Route nationale #1,Port-Au-Prince **W:** radiotelezenith.net – **36)** **W:**
rch2000.net – **37)** **W:** rfmhaiti.net – **38)** 93 Rue Vilatte, Pétionville,
Port-au-Prince **W:** scoopfmhaiti.com – **39)** radioshalomhaiti.com
40) #127 Rue Louverture, Pétionville, Port-au-Prince **W:** signalfmhaiti.
com – **41)** **W:** radiovascohaiti.com – **42)** 6 Rue Fernand, Canape Vert,
Port-au-Prince **W:** radiosolidaritehaiti.com

RADIO FRANCE INTERNATIONALE
FM: Port-au-Prince 89.3MHz, Cap Haïtien 100.5MHz

HAWAII (USA)

L.T: UTC -10h — **Pop:** 1.42 million — **Pr.L:** English, Japanese, Filipino
— **E.C:** 60Hz, 120V — **ITU:** HWA

FEDERAL COMMUNICATIONS COMMISSION (FCC)
see USA for details

THE HAWAII ASSOCIATION OF BROADCASTERS, INC.
✉ P.O. Box 61562, Honolulu HI 96839 **W:** hawaiibroadcasters com
E: jamie.hartnett@gmail.com **L.P:** Pres: Chris Leonard, Exec. Dir:
Jamie Hartnett

MW	kHz	kW	Call	Location
1)	550	5	KNUI	Kahului, Maui
37)	570	1	KUAI	Eleele, Kauai
3)	590	7.5	KSSK	Honolulu, Oahu
4)	620	5	KHNU	Hilo, Hawaii
4)	620	10	KHNU	Kalaoa, Hawaii
4)	620	5	KHNU	Naalehu, Hawaii
43)	650	10	KPRP	Honolulu, Oahu
6)	670	5	KPUA	Hilo, Hawaii
7)	690	10	KHNR	Honolulu, Oahu
37)	720	5	KQNG	Kekaha, Kauai
35)	740	5	KCIK	Kihei, Maui
7)	760	10	KGU	Honolulu, Oahu
7)	790	5	KKON	Kealakekua, Hawaii
3)	830	10	KHVH	Honolulu, Oahu
1)	850	5	KHLO	Hilo, Hawaii
8)	880	2	KHCM	Honolulu, Oahu
1)	900	5	KNUI	Kahului, Maui

MW	kHz	kW	Call	Location
5)	940	10	KKNE	Honolulu, Oahu
3)	990	5	KIKI	Honolulu, Oahu
9)	1040	10	KLHT	Honolulu, Oahu
30)	1060	5	KIPA	Hilo, Hawaii*
11)	1080	5	KWAI	Honolulu, Oahu
2)	1110	5	KAOI	Kihei, Maui
12)	1130	1	KPHI	Honolulu, Oahu
13)	1210	1	KZOO	Honolulu, Oahu
14)	1270	5	KNDI	Honolulu, Oahu
16)	1370	6.2	KUPA	Pearl City, Oahu
17)	1420	5	KKEA	Honolulu, Oahu
18)	1460	5	KHRA	Honolulu, Oahu
17)	1500	10	KHKA	Honolulu, Oahu
19)	1540	5	KREA	Honolulu, Oahu
20)	1570	15	KUAU	Haiku, Maui

FM	MHz	kW	Call	Location
21)	88.1	39	KHPR	Honolulu, Oahu
21)	88.1	4	KHPR-FM1	Makaha, Hawaii
21)	88.1	3	KHPR-FM3	Kailua, Hawaii
21)	88.7	6.5	KHPH	Kailua, Hawaii
9A)	88.9	2.5	KHJC	Lihue, Kauai
21)	89.1	12	KANO	Hilo, Hawaii (CP)
21)	89.3	38.5	KIPO-FM	Honolulu, Oahu
21)	89.3	4	KIPO-FM1	Makaha, Hawaii
21)	89.7	62	KIPM	Waikapu, Maui
38)	89.9	1	KIPL	Lihue, Kauai
22)	90.1	7	KTUH	Honolulu, Oahu (CP)
22)	90.3	3	KTUH	Honolulu, Oahu
23)	90.3	5	KCIF	Hilo, Hawaii
21)	90.7	56	KKUA	Wailuku, Maui
26)	90.9	0.9	KKCR	Hanalei, Kauai
21)	91.1	30	KANO	Hilo, Hawaii
21)	91.3	12	KAHU	Pahala, Hawaii (CP)
9)	91.5	100	KLHT-FM	Honolulu, Oahu (CP)
44)	91.7	1.2	KMNO	Wailuku, Maui
26)	91.9	6	KAQA	Kilauea, Kauai
30)	92.1	4.5	KHWI	Holualea, Hawaii
3)	92.3	100	KSSK-FM	Waipahu, Oahu
1)	92.5	1.7	KLHI-FM	Kahului, Maui
30)	92.7	7.5	KHBC	Hilo, Hawaii
37)	93.1	100	KQMQ-FM	Honolulu, Oahu
6)	93.1	10	KMWB	Captain Cook, Hawaii
1)	93.5	72	KPOA	Lahaina, Maui
37)	93.5	51	KQNG-FM	Lihue, Kauai
3)	93.9	100	KHJZ	Honolulu, Oahu
1)	93.9	7.3	KLUA	Kailua-Kona, Hawaii
2)	94.3	2	KDLX	Makawao, Maui
39)	94.3	100	KZZV	Hanapepe, Kauai (CP)
37)	94.7	100	KUMU-FM	Honolulu, Oahu
6)	94.7	51	KWXX-FM	Hilo, Hawaii
2)	95.1	3.5	KAOI-FM	Wailuku, Maui
1)	95.5	100	KAIM-FM	Honolulu, Oahu
1)	95.9	39	KPVS	Hilo, Hawaii
37)	95.9	51	KSRF	Poipu, Kauai
5)	96.3	75	KRTR-FM	Kailua, Oahu
29)	96.9	100	KFMN	Lihue, Kauai
6)	97.1	38	KNWB	Hilo, Hawaii
12)	97.3	1.5	KRKH	Wailea-Makena, Maui
7)	97.5	80	KHCM-FM	Honolulu, Oahu
1)	97.9	51	KKBG	Hilo, Hawaii
12)	98.1	51	KJMQ	Lihue, Kauai
1)	98.3	9.4	KJMD	Pukalani, Maui
3)	98.5	51	KDNN	Honolulu, Oahu
12)	98.9	51	KITH	Kapaa, Kauai
1)	99.1	7.3	KAGB	Waimea-Kamuela, Hawaii
7)	99.5	100	KGU-FM	Honolulu, Oahu
1)	99.9	72	KJKS	Kahului, Maui
12)	99.9	51	KTOH	Kalaheo, Kauai
1)	100.3	35	KAPA	Hilo, Hawaii
1)	100.3	7.1	KAPA-FM1	Puueo, Hawaii
5)	100.3	100	KCCN-FM	Honolulu, Oahu
40)	100.7	2.2	KQMY	Kihei, Maui
12)	101.1	100	KORL-FM	Waianae, Oahu
12)	101.1	0.98	KORL-FM	Lahaina, Maui
6)	101.1	6.5	KAOY	Kealakekua, Hawaii
3)	101.9	100	KUCD	Pearl City, Oahu
45)	102.3	1.9	KNIT	Kaunakakai, Molokai
37)	102.7	61	KDDB	Waipahu, Oahu
30)	102.1	50	KTBH-FM	Kurtistown, Hawaii
30)	102.9	1.5	KMKV	Paia, Maui
2)	103.3	51	KSHK	Hanamaulu, Kauai
31)	103.5	100	KLUU	Wahiawa, Oahu

FM	MHz	kW	Call	Location
2)	103.9	100	KNUQ	Paauilo, Maui
5)	104.3	75	KPHW	Kaneohe, Oahu
12)	104.7	72	KONI	Lanai City, Maui
5)	105.1	100	KINE-FM	Honolulu, Oahu
4)	105.3	28	KBGX	Keaau, Hawaii
4)	105.3	1	KBGX-FM5	Naalehu, Hawaii
32)	105.5	21	KPMW	Haliimaile, Maui
37)	105.9	100	KPOI-FM	Honolulu, Oahu
1)	106.1	7.3	KLEO	Kahaluu-Kona, Hawaii
12)	106.5	72	KRYL	Haiku, Maui
33)	106.7	25	KNAN	Nanakali, Oahu
34)	106.9	5.5	KWYI	Kawaihae, Hawaii
4)	107.7	28	KKOA	Volcano, Hawaii
4)	107.7	1	KKOA-FM1	Hilo, Hawaii
4)	107.7	1	KKOA-FM5	Naalehu, Hawaii
7)	107.9	100	KKOL	Aiea, Oahu

Txs on air or CP less than 1kW not mentioned. *) currently silent

Addresses and other information:
Addresses: Add state abbreviation HI between location and zip code as appropriate. **Prgr:** All stns 24h unless otherwise stated
1) Pacific Radio Group, Maui: KMVI **W:** espnmaui.com KNUI **W:** knuimaui.com KLHI-FM **W:** x925.fm KPOA **W:** kpoa.com KJMD **W:** dajam983.com KJKS **W:** kiss99fm.com ☞ 311 Ano Street, Kahului, 96732-1304; **Hawaii:** KKON **W:** espnhawaii.com KHLO **W:** espn-hawaii.com KLUA **W:** nativefm.com KPVS **W:** nativefm.com KKBG **W:** kbigfm.com KAGB **W:** kaparadio.com KAPA **W:** kaparadio.com KLEO **W:** kbigfm.com ☞ 913 Kanoelehua Ave, Hilo 96720-5116 – **2) Visionary Related Entertainment LLC, Molokai:** KMKK-FM ☞ 130 Kamehameha V Highway, Kaunakaka 96748; **Maui:** KAOI **W:** kaoi1110.com KAOI-FM **W:** kaoifm.com KNUQ **W:** q103maui.com KDLX **W:** kdlx943.com ☞ 1900 Main Street, Wailuku 96793-1900 – **3) Capstar TX Ltd Partnership, Oahu:** KSSK **W:** ksskradio.com KHVH **W:** khvhradio.com KHBZ **W:** khbz.com KSSK-FM KHJZ 939jamz. com KDNN **W:** island985.com KUCD **W:** star1019.com ☞ 650 Iwilei Rd #400, Honolulu 96817-5319 – **4) Mahalo Broadcasting LLC, Hawaii:** KHNU **W:** honu62.com KBGX **W:** lava1053.com KKOA ☞ 74-5605 Luhia St #B-7, Kailua-Kona 96740-1678 -**5) Summit Media Corporation, Oahu:** KKNE **W:** am940hawaii.com KRTR-FM **W:** krater96.com KCCN-FM **W:** kccnfm100.com KPHW **W:** power1043. com KINE **W:** hawaiian105.com F.P.L 50kW **W:** 900 Fort St Mall #700, Honolulu 96813-3797 **L.P:** Patti Milburn VP & CEO, TJ Malievsky President [KHPW] – **6) New West Broadcasting Corporation, Hawaii:** KPUA **W:** kpua.net KWXX-FM **W:** kwxx.com KNWB **W:** b97hawaii.com KMWB **W:** b97hawaii.com KAOY **W:** kwxx.com ☞ 1145 Kilauea Ave, Hilo 96720-4203 – **7) Salem Media of Hawaii Inc, Oahu:** KHNR **W:** khnrtownhall.com KGU-FM **W:** kguradio.com KGU-FM **W:** 995kgufm.com KHCM **Prgr:** 24h. China R. International relay in English, Chinese, Korean & Japanese KAIM-FM **W:** thefishhawaii. com KHCM **W:** 975countrykhcm.com KKOL **W:** oldies1079honolulu. com ☞ 1160 N King St #200, Honolulu 96817-330 – **9) Calvary Chapel of Honolulu Inc, Oahu:** KLHT **W:** klight.org KLHT-FM (91.5) CP 98-106 Komo Mai Drive, Aiea 96701-1901 **-9A) Calvary Chapel of Twin Falls Inc:** KHJC **W:** csnradio.com/stations/studiowaivered/khjc. php ☞: 2970 Kele St #117, Lihue 96766-1803 – **11) Radio Hawaii Inc, Oahu:** KWAI **W:** kwai1080am.com ☞ 100 N Beretania St #401, Honolulu 968174724 – **12) Hochman-McCann Hawaii Inc, Oahu:** KPHI **W:** pinoypowerkphiradio.com **Prgr:** Filipino "Today's Filipino Mix" KORL-FM **W:** korl1011.com KORL-FM HD2 **W:** korl1015.com KORL-FM HD3 **W:** korl971.com **Prgr:** Korean KORL-FM HD4 **W:** korl1075.com **Prgr:** Japanese ☞ 900 Fort St Mall #450, Honolulu 96813-3713; **Maui:** KRKH **W:** krock973.com KONI **W:** koni1047.com KRYL **W:** kryl1065.com ☞ 300 Ohukai Road #C-318, Kihei 96753-7050; **Kauai:** KJMQ **W:** 981jamz.com KITH **W:** islandradio989.com KTOH **W:** roostercountry. com ☞ 4334 Rice St #204-B, Lihue 96766-1801 **W:** hhawaiimedia.net – **13) Polynesian Broadcasting Inc, Oahu:** KZOO **W:** kzoohawaii. com **Prgr:** Japanese. ☞ 2752 Woodlawn Drive #5-204, Honolulu 96822-1855 – **14) Broadcast House of the Pacific Inc, Oahu:** KNDI **W:** kndi.com **Prgr:** multicultural, religious. ☞ 1734 S King St, Honolulu 96826-2042 – **16) Broadcasting Corporation of America, Oahu:** KUPA: 4766 Holladay Blvd, Holladay UT 84117 – **17) Blow Up LLC, Oahu:** KKEA **W:** sportsradio1420.com KHKA **Format:** NBC Sports Radio Network ☞ 1088 Bishop St #112, Honolulu 96813-3113 – **18) RK Media Group, Oahu:** KHRA **W:** radiokoreahawaiii.com **Prgr:** Korean. ☞ 1311 Kapiolani Blvd #204, Honolulu 96814-4513 – **19) JMK Communications Inc, Oahu:** KREA **W:** radiokrea.com **Prgr:** Korean. ☞ 1839 S King St #203, Honolulu 96814-2137 – **20) First Assembly King's Cathedral & Chapel, Maui:** KUAU **W:** kingscathedral.com ☞ 777 Mokulele Hwy, Kahului 96732 – **21) Hawaii Public Radio Inc, Oahu:** KHPR **W:** hawaiipublicradio.org] KIPO [includes BBC relay] ☞ 738 Kaheka St

#101, Honolulu 96814-3726; **Simulcast: Maui:** KKUA **F.PL:** KIPM [KIPO relay] **Hawaii:** KANO **F.PL:** KIPH (KIPO relay) – **22) The University of Hawaii, Oahu:** KTUH **W:** ktuh.org ✉ 202 Hemenway Hall, University of Hawaii, 2445 Campus Road, Honolulu 96822-2216 – **23) Hilo Christian Broadcasting Corporation, Hawaii:** KCIF **W:** kcifhawaii.org ✉ 180 Kinoole St, Hilo 96720-2827 – **26) Kekahu Foundation Inc, Kauai:** KKCR **W:** kkcr.org KAQA **W:** kkcr.com **F.PL:** 6kW] ✉ 4520-D Hanalei Plantation Road, PO Box 825, Hanalei 96714-0825 – **29) FM97 Associates, Kauai:** KFMN **W:** kfmn97.com ✉ 1860 Leleiona Road, Lihue 96766-9000 – **30) Resonate Hawaii LLC, Hawaii:** KIPA KHBC **W:** khbcradio.com KHWI **W:** hawaiiswave.com KTBH-FM **W:** 1027thebeach.fm 74-5605 Luhia St #B-7, Kailua-Kona 96740 – **31) Educational Media Foundation, Oahu:** KLUU **W:** air1.com **Maui:** KMKV **W:** mauifm.com 5700 W Oaks Blvd, Rocklin CA 96765 – **32) Rey-Cel Broadcasting Inc, Maui:** KPMW **W:** mix1055.fm **Prgr:** Filipino ✉ 230 Hana Hwy, Kahului 96732 – **33) Big D Consulting Ltd, Oahu:** KNAN: 3800 Howard Hughes Parkway 17th Floor, Las Vegas NV 89109 – **34) Colin H Naito, Hawaii:** KWYI ✉ 64-1040 Mamalahoa Hwy #4, Kamuela 96743-6540 – **35) IHR Educational Broadcasters, Maui:** KCIK PO Box 180, Tahoma CA 96142 – **37) Ohana Broadcast Company LLC, Kauai:** KQNG KQNG-FM **W:** kongradio.com KUAI KSRF **W:** surf959fm.com KSHK **W:** shaka103.com 4271 Halenani St, Lihue 96766-1312 **Oahu:** KQMQ-FM **W:** 931thezone.net KUMU-FM **W:** kumu.com KDDB **W:** 1027dabomb.net KPOI-FM **W:** kpoifm.com 765 Amana St #206, Honolulu 96814-3248 – **39) Virtues Communications Network, LLC: Kauai:** KZZV PO Box 215, Kings Park NY 11754 – **40) Future Modulation Broadcasting, LLC: Maui:** KQMY 4700 Allan Road, Cheyenne WY 82009 – **43) SM-KRTR-AM LLC, Oahu:** KPRP [LMA]: Pinoy Power Media, Pioneer Plaza, 900 Fort Street Mall, 7th Floor, Honolulu 96813-3797 **W:** kprpam650.com **L.P:** Founder & CEO Imelda Ortega Anderson **Format:** Filipino – **44) Maui Media Initiative, Inc:** Maui KMNO 72 Kono Pl, Kahului 96732-1326 – **45) Kona Coast Radio LLC, Molokai:** KNIT 130 Kamehameha V Highway, Kaunakakai 96748 [associated with #37]

HONDURAS

L.T: UTC -6h — **Pop:** 7.6 million — **Pr.L:** Spanish — **E.C:** 60Hz, 110V — **ITU:** HND

COMISIÓN NACIONAL DE TELECOMUNICACIONES (CONATEL)
✉ Ap. 15012, Edificio CONATEL, Colonia Modelo, Sexta Avenida Suroeste Contigua a Hondutel, Tegucigalpa ☎ +504 2552 7484 🖷 +504 2236 8611 **W:** conatel.gob.hn **E:** transparencia@conatel.gob.hn Hrs of tr 24h unless otherwise stated.
Call HR—, ‡ = inactive, † =irregular

MW	Call	kHz	kW	Station, location
155)	XT	550	1	ABC Radio, Tegucigalpa
2)	XD	†550	0.5	R. Manantial, San Marcos: 1115-0300
3)	RZ	†560	1	VRZ R. Juticalpa, Juticalpa: 1100-0400
4)	KL	560	1	R. Reloj, San Pedro Sula
6)	ZQ	580	3	R. Cadena Voces, Tegucigalpa
112)	EO	580	3	Super Estrella de Occidente, Sta Rosa de Copán
5)	LP3	590	10	R. América, San Pedro Sula
5)	LP3	590	1	R. América, Tela
5)		610	1	R. América, Gracias
5)	LD	610	10	R. América, Tegucigalpa: 1030-0400
5)	LP	610	3	R. América, Santa Rosa de Copán
5)	LP	620	1	R. América, Juticalpa
5)		620	10	R. América, Siguatepeque
28)	LP17	620	1	R. Continental, San Pedro Sula
5)	LP	630	3.5	R. América, Danlí
5)	LP7	630	5	R. América, La Ceiba
7)	UP	640	1	R. Centro, Tegucigalpa: 1045-0500
5)	LP	650	1	R. América, Danlí
5)		650	2.5	R. América, Olanchito
5)		650	1	R. América, Tocoa
198)	VS	650	2.5	R. Católica de Olancho, Juticalpa
241)	VS	650	25	R. Nuestra Señora de la Esperanza, S. P. S.
8)	NN8	660	3	LV de Honduras, La Ceiba
8)	N	670	10	LV de Honduras, Tegucigalpa
8)	NN20	670	1	LV de Honduras, Sta Rosa de Copán
8)	NN8	680	10	LV de Honduras, San Pedro Sula
8)	NN2	680	10	LV de Honduras, Siguatepeque
8)	NN7	680	1	LV de Honduras, Danlí
8)	NN10	680	1	LV de Honduras, Juticalpa
8)	NN3	690	1	LV de Honduras, Choluteca
27)	KL	700	5	Cadena Radial Reloj, Tegucigalpa
11)	SG	710	2.5	R. LV de la Libertad, Catacamas
79)	NN3	720	1	R. Caribe, La Ceiba

MW	Call	kHz	kW	Station, location
10)	NN4	730	1	R. Exitos, Tegucigalpa
12)	QQ	740	1	R. Intibucá, La Esperanza: 1100-0100
13)	IH	740	1	La Super Grande, Juticalpa: 1200-0400
9)	TG2	740	1	R. Satélite, San Pedro Sula: 1100-0600
90)	VC	†740	2.5	LV Evangélica, Olanchito
16)	XW	760	2.5	R. Comayagüela, Tegucigalpa
14)	NN21	770	10	R. Norte, San Pedro Sula
135)	RD	770	1	R. Majestad "LV del Guayape", Juticalpa
163)	SE	780	1	Alabanza Estéreo, Choluteca
9)	TG	790	3	R. Satélite, Tegucigalpa
21)	DL	800	1	R. Corporación, Comayagua: 1100-0400
17)	MA	800	3	R. Moderna, San Pedro Sula
90)	VC	810	6	LV Evangélica, La Ceiba
25)	LP24	810	3	R. Valle, Choluteca: 1000-0400
17)	LP16	820	5	R. Moderna, Tegucigalpa
84)	KW	820	7/3	R. Sultana, Sta Rosa de Copán: 1100-0400
24)	RU	830	1	R. Uno, San Pedro Sula
26)	JB	830	1	Cadena Radial Impacto, Comayagua
90)		840	3	LV Evangélica, Tela
19)		†860	0.5	R. Río de Dios, Olanchito
110)	LS	860	0.5	R. Dinorama, La Paz
225)	BV	860	1.5	R. Piedra Blanca, Catacamas
1)	H	880	10	R. Nacional de Honduras, Tegucigalpa
9)	UP6	900	1	R. Satélite, La Ceiba
7)	UP	900	1	R. Centro, Choluteca
29)	VS	910	10	R. Católica "LV de Suyapa", Tegucigalpa
21)	RM	920	1	R. Sistema, Comayagua
31)	ZV	920	1	Voz Que Clama en el Desierto, S. P. Sula
32)	SK	920	5	R. Catacamas, Catacamas: 1200-0400
91)	CQ	930	3	Cadena R. Samaritano, La Ceiba
237)	LD	†930	2.5	R. Estéreo Leed, Nacaome
18)	CR	940	1	Dif. Cristiana de R. (DCR), Tegucigalpa
34)	QL	950	1	R. Centro de Honduras, Siguatepeque
36)	YF	†960	1	R. Fergusón, Choluteca
38)	LY	970	2	R. Millenium, Tegucigalpa
41)	AO	†980	1	R. Tocoa, Tocoa
39)	ZC	980	2	R. Rhema, San Pedro Sula
90)	VC	980	5	LV Evangélica, Comayagua
140)	PR	990	3.5	R. Paz, Choluteca: 1100-0200
30)	CY	†1000	3	R. Congolón, Gracias: 1100-0500
44)	XZ	1000	1	HCH Radio, Tegucigalpa
89)	CD	1010	1	R. Constelación. Juticalpa: 1200-0400
255)	LL	1010	1	R. Visión Cristiana, Tocoa
236)	PN	†1020	3	R. Visión Cristiana Internacional, Marcovia
152)	RJ	1030	1	R. Ticante, Ocotepeque: 1200-0400
90)	VC	1040	5	LV Evangélica, Juticalpa
90)	VC	1040	5	LV Evangélica, Danlí
53)	LE	1070	1	R. Unica AM, San Pedro Sula
180)	BB	1070	3	R. Unidad Evangélica, Catacamas
235)	IE	1080	3	R. Senda de Vida, Nacaome: 1100-2300
91)	CQ	1090	1	Cadena Radial Samaritano, Tegucigalpa
58)	ND	1100	1	R. Esperanza, La Esperanza: 1100-0300
59)	VA	1100	1	R. Tiempo, San Pedro Sula
222)	AJ	‡1100	5	R. Antena 5, Catacamas
38)	TL	†1120	2	R. Fiesta, Tegucigalpa
61)	PL	‡1130	5	R. Progreso, El Progreso
99)	HP	1130	1	R. Pinares, Siguatepeque
65)	UL	1140	1	R. Pico Bonito, La Ceiba
90)	VC	1140	3	LV Evangélica, Choluteca
5)	LP12	1150	1	R. Universal, Tegucigalpa
66)	AV	‡1150	5	Ondas del Ulúa, Sta Bárbara: 0900-0400
35)	VZ	1160	1	R. Juan Pablo II, Siguatepeque
204)	FJ	‡1160	5	R. País, Progreso
212)	HZ	‡1160	1	R. Liberación, Tocoa
45)	AF	1170	2	R. Campeonísima, Choluteca
19)		†1180	1	R. Río de Dios, Belén
188)	AZ	†1180	1	R. El Tigre, Tegucigalpa
6)	VW3	1190	5	R. Cadena Voces, El Progreso
72)	SI	1200	1	R. Impacto, Tela: 1200-0400
90)	VC	1210	2	LV Evangélica, Danlí
74)	OP	1220	1	R. Costeña Ebenezer, San Pedro Sula: 1100-0600
75)	YS	1220	1	R. Suari, Marcala
148)	SD	‡1220	3	R. Destellos de Luz, Sabá
91)	CQ	1230	0.25	Cad. R. Samaritano, San Marcos de Colón
133)	ZC	1240	1	R. Vanguardia, Tegucigalpa
37)		1250	1	R. Garzel, Juticalpa
51)	YF	1250	1	R. Renacimiento, Comayagua
115)	DG	‡1250	1	R. Cadena Oriental, Danlí
77)	FP	1260	1	R. Amistad, San Marcos de Colón
107)	BN	1280	1	R. San Miguel, Marcala: 1000-0400
251)	OW	1280	1	R. LV de la Victoria, Juticalpa
81)	NN26	‡1290	1	R. Choluteca, Choluteca: 1050-0400

MW	Call	kHz	kW	Station, location
82)	LR	1300	5	R. Santa Rosa, Sta Rosa de Copán
83)	IV	1300	5	CCI Radio, Tegucigalpa
90)	VC	1310	2.5	LV Evangélica, San Pedro Sula
103)	RL	‡1310	1	R. Libertad, Marcala, La Paz: 1200-0500
258)	CM	1310	5	R. Universidad de Agricultura, Catacamas
119)	MG	†1320	1	R. Bahía "La Super Grande", La Ceiba
262)		1330	1	R. Emisora Evangélica, Tegucigalpa
153)	TQ	1340	10	Ebenezer 1340, San Pedro Sula
91)	CQ	1340	1	Cadena Radial Samaritano, Comayagua
193)	EL	†1350	1	R. Estelar, La Ceiba
28)	BS	1360	1	R. San Pedro, Tegucigalpa: 1100-0600
197)	BH	‡1360	5	R. Sta Bárbara, Sta Bárbara
175)	SQ	1370	1	R. El Shaddai R., Siguatepeque
220)	UN	1370	5	LV de Catacamas, Catacamas
127)	AH	1380	0.5	R. Redención, Jutiapa: 1200-0600
90)	VC	1390	10/5	LV Evangélica, Tegucigalpa
90)	VC	1390	1	LV Evangélica, Sta Rosa de Copán
80)	YT	1400	1	R. Estrella de Oro, San Pedro Sula
90)	FO	1430	1	LV Evangélica, Puerto Cortés
97)	VM	1430	1	R. Maranatha, La Paz
211)	QV	‡1430	1	R. Futura "La Nueva Potencia", Olanchito
98)	RD	1440	1	R. Belén, La Ceiba
202)	GC	1460	2.5	R. Reino, San Pedro Sula
122)	CX	‡1460	0.5	LV de Patuca, Catacamas: 1000-0400
102)	EZ	‡1480	1	LV de Misiones "R. MI", Comayagüela
264)	HY	1490	1	R. Boquerón, Juticalpa
124)	PG	‡1510	1	R. Gualcho, Tegucigalpa
106)	EM	‡1510	1	R. Emanuel, Ocotepeque: 1100-2330
183)	DF	1520	1	Estéreo Kabod, Siguatepeque
192)	MQ	1520	5	R. Manantial de Vida Eterna, Juticalpa
247)		1530	2.5	R. La Guarachera, Choluteca
194)	VK	‡1540	2.5	R. Nuevo Mundo, Tegucigalpa
40)		1550	1	R. Miel, Saba
57)	RF	‡1570	2.5	R. Cadena Nac. de Noticias, Tegucigalpa
181)	BX	1590	5	R. Perla, El Progreso
111)	PC	‡1600	1	R. Luz y Vida, San Luís: 1100-0400

Addresses and other information:

1) Ap 403 (or Bulevar Supaya, contiguo a televicentro, Tegucigalpa **W:** radiohrn.hn - **FM:** 92.9MHz – **2)** San Marcos, Ocotepeque **W:** manantial550.radio12345.com – **3)** Ap 3, Barrio de Jésus, 4ta Avenida, 5ta Calle, Juticalpa, Olancho **W:** radiojuticalpa.net - **FM:** 97.9MHz – **4)** Ap 24, San Pedro Sula – **5)** Edif Audio Video, Ap 259, Tegucigalpa **W:** americamultimedios.com – **6)** Blvd Morazán, Edificio Classic, 2ndo piso, Frente a Banco Ficohsa, Tegucigalpa **W:** radiocadenavoceshn.com – **7)** Emisoras Unidas, Col Florencia, Blv Suyapa (or Ap 642), Tegucigalpa **W:** radiocentro.hn – **8)** Emisoras Unidas, Col Florencia, Blv Suyapa (or Ap 642), Tegucigalpa **W:** radiohrn.hn – **9)** Emisoras Unidas, Col Florencia, Blv Suyapa (or Ap 642), Tegucigalpa **W:** radiosatelite.hn – **10) W:** stereoexitos.hn – **11) W:** radiolavozdelalibertad.com – **12)** Barrio El Way, Calle Principal, La Esperanza, Intibucá **W:** radiointibuca.webs.com – **13)** Ap 9, Barrio de Jésus, 4ta y 5ta Ave, 6ta Calle, Juticalpa **W:** grupocnc.net/radio740.html – **14)** Emisoras Unidas, Col Florencia, Blv Suyapa (or Ap 642), Tegucigalpa **W:** radionorte.hn – **15)** Atras de Gasolinera Shell, La Entrada, Copán **-16) W:** radiocomayaguela.com – **17)** Edif Audio Video, Ap 259, Tegucigalpa **W:** radiomoderna.net – **18)** Ap 3448 (or Iglesia Amor Viviente, Col Godoy frente a F.H.I.S.), Tegucigalpa **W:** dcr940.net – **19) W:** radioriodedios.org – **21)** Barrio San Francisco, Fte Parque, Comayagua - **FM:** 99.9MHz – **22)** Danlí, El Paraíso – **24)** Edif.Maranata, Calle 8 y 9, San Pedro Sula **W:** radiouno830.com – **25)** Ap 29, Choluteca **W:** radiovalle.net - **FM:** 90.7MHz – **26)** Ap 33, Comayagua **W:** grupoimpactohn.net - **FM** 93.9MHz – **27) W:** cadenaradialreloj.hn – **28)** Ap 364 (or Av.New Orleans), San Pedro Sula **W:** radiosanpedrohn.net - **FM:** San Pedro Sula 88.9MHz – **29)** Ap 480 (or Edif Radio Católica, Av Paz Barahona, Casa 1119, atrás del Palacio Arzobispal), Tegucigalpa **W:** fundacioncatolica.org/lavozdesuyapa.html – **30)** Frente al Parque "Lempira", Gracias, Lempira (or Ap.1579, Tegucigalpa) - **FM:** 95.1MHz R Galaxia 21 FM Stereo – **W:** lacentro.com/radiocongolon – **31)** Ap 2918 (or 5 Calle, 10 y 11 Av S.O 91), San Pedro Sula **W:** unavozqueclamaenhonduras.org **FM:** 102.1MHz Radio Fabulosa – **32)** Ap 50, Catacamas **W:** catacamas.net – **33)** Ap 10, 12101 Comayagua 1100-2400 - **FM:** 89.1MHz R.Vida – **34)** Barrio Abajo, 2 Ave, 2da. y 3era. Cll S. E, Siguatepeque **W:** lacentro.centroradialreloj.hn - **FM:** 96.3MHz – **35)** Barrio Juan pabloii.caster.fm – **36)** Calle Vicente Williams, Edif Fergusón, Choluteca **W:** facebook.com/radioferguson - **FM:** 103.3MHz – **37)** Juticalpa, Olancho **W:** radiogarzel.com – **38)** Ap 2821, Col. ave Guanacaste #1511, Tegucigalpa **W:** circuitopop.com – **39)** Ap 996 (or 9 Calle, S.O 44, Entre 8 y 9 Av), San Pedro Sula **W:** ebenezer.hn/?page_id=825 - **FM:** 98.5MHz Estéreo Mass – **40)** Barrio el Chorro, 2da. Avenida, entre 7 y 8 calle, Saba, Colón **W:** radiomielsaba.com – **41)** Tocoa, Colón **W:** 980am.mex.tl – **44)** Ap

614 (or Lomas del Mayab, calle San Marcos esquina a Novel Center, Casa # 1647), Tegucigalpa **W:** hchradio.hn – **45)** Ap 78, Choluteca **W:** emisorasaliadashn.com/html/la-campeonisima.html - **FM:** 105.1MHz – **51)** Barrio Cabañas 2 cuadras al Norte de la Planta de la ENEE, Comayagua **W:** facebook.com/Radio-Renacimiento-374089842665596 – **53)** 9 Av 4 Calle, Edif Las Fuentes, San Pedro Sula **W:** radiounicahn.com - **FM:** 88.3MHz – **57)** Ap 2250, Tegucigalpa – **58)** Ap 25, La Esperanza, Intibucá **W:** radioesperanza.com – **59)** Ap 906, Bo. Lempira, 10 Calle, 8-9 Ave., S.O, San Pedro Sula **W:** radiotiempohn.com - **FM:** Stero Fama 97.9MHz – **61)** Ap 20, El Progreso, Yoro **W:** radioprogresohn.net - **FM:** 103.3MHz – **65)** Barrio La Isla, La Ceiba **W:** facebook.com/RADIO-PICO-BONITO-1140-am-165026650238268 – **66)** Ap 004, Sta Bárbara **W:** sbmultimedios.com/radioondasdelulua - **FM:** 97.5MHz – **72)** Calle José Trinidad Cabañas, Edif Hotel Presidente, Tela - **FM:** 89.9 – **74)** Iglesia de Cristo, Ministerio Ebenezer, 14 Calle A, Costado Sur de Wendy's Circunvalación (or Ap 34-76), San Pedro Sula **W:** ebenezer.hn - **FM:** 91.9MHz +93.7MHz – **75)** Calle Principal, Marcala, La Paz – **77)** Barrio Fátima, San Marcos de Colón, Choluteca **W:** facebook.com/Radio-Amistad-259775717401282 – **79)** Emisoras Unidas, Solares Nuevos, Av República, La Ceiba **W:** radiocaribe.hn - **FM:** 93.1MHz – **80)** Ap 303, Barrio los Andes 9 calle B, 15 Avenida circunvalación, San Pedro Sula **W:** radioestrelladeoro.org - **FM:** 97.3MHz – **81)** Barrio Campo Luna, Choluteca **W:** emisorasunidas.net - **FM:** 88.7MHz – **82)** Ap 203, Av 7 NO, Santa Rosa de Copán 41101, Sta Rosa de Copán **W:** radiosantarosa.net - **FM:** 94.5MHz – **83)** Ap 955, Residencial El Trapiche, Colonia Florencia Sur, Tegucigalpa **W:** cciradio.org – **84)** Ap 204, Sta Rosa de Copán **W:** radiosultana.net - **FM:** 90.3MHz – **89)** Barrio Las Flores, Avenida La Trinidad, Casa O54, Juticalpa **W:** radioconstelacion.net - **FM:** 101.9MHz – **90)** Ap 3252, Tegucigalpa – (Owned and operated by Conservative Baptist Home Mission Society, Box 828, Wheaton, IL 60187, USA) **W:** hrvc.org – **91)** Colonia Payaqui, bulevar San Juan Bosco, frente al segundo porton del instituto San Miguel, Casa 3658, 504, Tegucigalpa **W:** radiosamaritano.net 1100-0500 – **95)** 12 Calle 2a Ave 206, Barrio La Curva, Puerto Cortés – **97)** Santiago de la Paz, La Paz (or Col.21 de Octubre, Sector 3, Bloque 2, Casa 5, Tegucigalpa) **W:** facebook.com/MaranathaHonduras – **98)** Ap. 614, Av San Isidro, Entre Calles 9 y 10, La Ceiba – **99)** Casa 269, Barrio Abajo, Siguatepeque 1155 **W:** radio.centroradialhn.net - **FM:** 91.5MHz – **102)** Ap. 20583, Comayagüela (or IMF World Missions, 3068 2nd St, Norco, CA 92860, USA) - 1100-0300 **W:** radiomi.com **FM:** 99.3MHz – **103)** Barrio San Miguel, Calle Principal, Marcala, La Paz **W:** radiolibertadhn.blogspot.com - **FM:** 90.7MHz – **106)** Barrio San Andrés, Ocotepeque **W:** facebook.com/Radio-Emmanuel-1510-AM-160416914020684 – **107)** Barrio Concepción, Marcala, La Paz (or Palacio Arzobispal, Av. Cervantes, Barrio El Centro, Tegucigalpa) **W:** radiosanmiguelhn.blogspot.com – **110)** Parque Central, La Paz – **111)** Barrio Luz y Vida, San Luis, Sta Bárbara (or Ap 303, San Pedro Sula) **W:** radioluzyvida.com – **112)** Sta Rosa de Copán **W:** superestrella.org - **FM:** 93.1MHz – **115)** Danlí, El Paraíso **W:** radioorientalhonduras.es.tl - **FM:** 105.9MHz – **119)** Barrio La Isla 4C. Ave. Juan Ramon Molina, La Ceiba – **122)** Barrio La Mora, Catacamas, Olancho - **FM:** 99.1MHz – **124)** Col 21 de Octubre, Sector 3, Bl 1, Casa 4, Tegucigalpa **W:** hondurasunidaporunaconstituyente.blogspot.hn/p/radio-y-chat-de-la-gualcho.html – **127)** Edif. R. Redención, Barrio Lempira, Jutiapa, Atlántida **W:** radioredencionhonduras.org - **FM:** 95.7 – **128)** Radio Ensenanzas Evangelicas, Puerto Lempira – **133)** Ap 914, Tegucigalpa – **135)** Ap 15, 16101 Juticalpa - **FM:** 106.3MHz Prgrs in Sp and E – **140)** Ap 40, B. El Hospital Edificio Obispado, frente a oficinas del sanaa, Choluteca **W:** radiopazhn.org - **FM:** 95 5MHz – **147)** Ap 888, (or Centro Comercial San José), La Ceiba **W:** applegatefellowship.org/missions/honduras.asp **E:** radiolitoral@psinet.hn – **148)** Barrio La Pava, Sabá, Colón **W:** radiodestellosdeluz.org – **152)** Media Cuadra Al Norte del ParWque, B:o El Centro, Ocotepeque **FM:** 92.1MHz – **153)** Ap 210 (or 5 Calle, 10 y 11 Av S.O, Barrio Beuque), San Pedro Sula **W:** 1340am.org - **FM:** 90.7MHz – **155)** Col Miraflores, Tegucigalpa **W:** abcradio.hn –**163)** Barrio La Esperanza 4A N° 142, Choluteca **FM:** 98.5MHz – **175)** Barrio El Centro, Siguatepeque – **180)** Barrio La Cruz, Contiguo a la Iglesia el Encuentro, Catacamas, Olancho **W:** facebook.com/unidad.evangelica – **181)** 4 y 5 Ave, 3 Calle 442, Barrio Las Delicias, El Progreso, Yoro **W:** radioperla.com – **183)** Barrio El Centro, Valle del Boulevard, Contiguo a la Iglesia Adventista, Siguatepeque **W:** facebook.com/estereokabod – **188)** Tegucigalpa **W:** radioeltigre.hn - **W:** 91.5MHz – **192)** Barrio de Jesús, Casa 7, Calle Principal, Juticalpa **W:** facebook.com/pages/Radio-Manantial-de-Vida-Eterna-1520-AM/1728150261057037?ref=ts – **193)** Col.Irias, Primera Calle, 5 Casas a Mano Izquierda, La Ceiba – **194)** Aretista Principal a Col. San Miguel, Sector Industrial, Tegucigalpa – **197)** Apartado 004, Barrio El Centro, Av. La Libertad, Santa Bárbara **W:** sbmultimedios.com/sbstereo - **FM:** 102.3/102.7MHz – **198)** Juticalpa, Olancho **W:** rcolancho.org – **202)** Misión Cristiana Internacional El Shaddai, San Pedro Sula **W:** elshaddaihn.com/index.php/radio-reino –

204) Progreso, Yoro **W:** facebook.com/Radio-Pais-1160-AM-342357765898331 – **205)** Puerto Lempira, Gracias a Dios **211)** Olanchito, Yoro **W:** radiofuturafm.net – **212)** Tocoa, Colón facebook.com/radioliberacionhd - **FM:** 89.7MHz – **220)** Barrio La Cruz, cuadra y media al Este de la Municipalidad de Catacamas, Olancho **W:** lavozde-catacamas.com – **222)** Av. Independencia, Edificio Moradel Muñoz, 504 Catacamas, Olancho **W:** facebook.com/Radio-Antena-5-Catacamas-166356130054679 - **FM:** 89.5MHz – **224)** San Esteban, Olancho – **225)** Barrio de Jésus, Catacamas, Olancho **W:** radiopiedrablancahn.com – **235)** Nacaome, Choluteca **W:** radiosendadevida.net – **236)** Marcovia, Choluteca **W:** rvci.net - **FM:** 93.7MHz – **237)** Barrio La Cruz, Primera Calle, Contiguo a Deposito de la Cervecería, Valle **W:** estereoleed.com – **241)** Avenida N.O. No.1. Apartado 207, C.P. 21105, San Pedro Sula **W:** diocesissps.org – **247)** Choluteca **W:** laguaracherahn.com – **251)** Juticalpa, Olancho **W:** radiolavozdelavictoria.com – **254)** Sonaguera, Colón – **255)** Tocoa, Colón **W:** facebook.com/Radio-Visión-Cristiana-130896803597583 – **257)** Puerto Cortés, Cortés – **258)** Kilometro 9 en la Carretera que conduce al Municipio Dulce Nombre de Culmi, Catacamas, Olancho **W:** unag.edu.hn/producion – **262)** Asociación de Iglesias Evangélicas Centroamericanas, Tegucigalpa **W:** reecaasiecah.blogspot.com – **264)** Juticalpa, Olancho 16101 **W:** radioboqueron.net

FM in Tegucigalpa (MHz): 88.1 Stereo Exitos – 88.7 Globo Grupera – 88.9 RDS R. – 89.3 Power – 89.9 R. Red de Radiodifusión Bíblica – 90.5 R. Corazón 90.5 – 91.1 R. Kairos FM – 91.7 R. Buenísima – 92.3 Rock n' Pop – 92.9 R. HRN – 93.3 Cadena Voces – 93.5 R. Notícias STC – 94.1 FM 94 – 94.7 América – 94.9 HCH Radio – 95.3 Digital – 95.9 R. Panamericana – 96.5 R. Estéreo Fiel – 97.1 EstéreoTic Tac – 97.7 Azul – 98.3 Estéreo Concierto – 98.9 Estéreo Fe – 99.5 Suprema – 100.1 Super 100 – 100.7 R. Exa FM – 101.3 R. Nacional de Honduras – 101.9 Vox – 102.5 Suave FM – 103.1 FM 103.1 – 103.7 Luz – 104.3 Momentos FM – 104.9 Estéreo Amor – 105.5 Musiquera – 106.1 Romántica – 106.7 Stereo Rumba – 107.3 W107 Energía Estéreo – 107.9 Top Music con La Onda del Nuevo Mundo.

AFRTS (Air Force)
✉ JTF-B, APO AA 34042, USA **E:** PAO@jtfb-emh1.army.mil
FM: 106.5MHz Soto Cano Air Base, 0.25kW **D.Prgr:** 24h

HONG KONG (China, SAR)

L.T: UTC +8h — **Pop:** 7.2 million — **Pr.L:** Cantonese, English — **E.C** 50Hz, 200/220V — **ITU:** HKG

RADIO TELEVISION HONG KONG (Gov.)
✉ Broadcasting House, 30 Broadcast Drive, Kowloon, Hong Kong ☎ +852 2272 0000 📠 +852 2336 9314 **E:** ccu@rthk.org.hk **W:** rthk.org.hk
L.P: Dir. of Broadc:Roy Tang, Asst. Dir. of Broadc. (Radio & Corporate Programming): Lisa Liu

MW (kHz)	Network	Location	kW
567	R. 3	Golden Hill	20
621	P. Ch	Golden Hill	20
675	R. 6	Peng Chau	10
783	R. 5	Golden Hill	20
1584	R. 3	Chung Hom Kok	0.1

P. Ch = Putonghua Channel

FM(MHz)	Network	kW	Tx Location	Target Div.
92.3	R. 5	0.025	Tin Shui Wai	
92.6	R. 1	3	Mt. Gough	Kowloon
92.9	R. 1	0.1	Golden Hill	Tsuen Wan
93.2	R. 1	0.5	Cloudy Hill	Fan Ling
93.4	R. 1	0.7	Castle Peak	Tuen Mun
93.5	R. 1	0.15	Beacon Hill	Sha Tin
93.6	R. 1	0.05	Hill 374	
94.4	R. 1	1	Kowloon Peak	HK Isl. north, Sai Kung
94.8	R. 2	3	Mt. Gough	Kowloon
95.2	R. 5	0.02	Mt. Nicholson	Jardine's Lookout
95.3	R. 2	0.5	Cloudy Hill	Fan Ling
95.6	R. 2	0.05	Hill 374	
96.0	R. 2	0.5	Lamma Isl.	HK Isl. south
96.3	R. 2	0.15	Beacon Hill	Sha Tin
96.4	R. 2	0.7	Castle Peak	Tuen Mun,
96.9	R. 2	1	Kowloon Peak	HK Isl. north, Sai Kung
97.6	R. 4	3	Mt. Gough	Kowloon
97.8	R. 4	0.5	Cloudy Hill	Fan Ling
97.9	R. 3	0.02	Mt. Nicholson	Jardine's Lookout
98.1	R. 4	0.15	Beacon Hill	Sha Tin
98.2	R. 4	0.5	Lamma Isl.	HK Isl. south
98.2	R. 4	0.05	Hill 374	
98.4	R. 4	0.1	Golden Hill	Tsuen Wan
98.7	R. 4	0.7	Castle Peak	Tuen Mun,
98.9	R. 4	1	Kowloon Peak	HK Isl. north, Sai Kung
99.4	R. 5	0.015	Tseung Kwan O	Jank Bay
100.9	P. Ch	0.01	Tai Hang Road	
100.9	P. Ch	0.003	Castle Peak	Tuen Mun
103.3	P. Ch	0.015	Tseung Kwan O	Jank Bay
103.3	P. Ch	0.025	Tin Shui Wai	
106.8	R. 5	0.03	Castle Peak	Tuen Mun
106.8	R. 3	0.15	Chung Hom Kok	HK Isl. south
107.8	R. 3	0.015	Tseung Kwan O	Jank Bay
107.8	R. 3	0.025	Tin Shui Wai	

RTHK Radio 1 in Cantonese/Chinese: 24h – **RTHK Radio 2** in Cantonese: 24h – **RTHK Radio 3** in English: 24h – **RTHK Radio 4** in English/Cantonese: 24h – **RTHK Radio 5** in Cantonese/Chinese: 24h – **RTHK Radio 6** Relay BBCWS English: 24h – **RTHK Putonghua Channel** in Chinese: 24h
Ann: Cantonese: "Heunggong dintoi dai (number) toi"

HONG KONG COMMERCIAL BROADC. CO. LTD
✉ 3 Broadcast Drive, Kowloon, Hong Kong ☎ +852 2336 5111 📠+852 2338 0021 **E:** cs@881903.com **W:** 881903.com

MW(kHz)	kW	Location	Prgr.
864	10	Peng Chau	24h music

FM(MHz)	Network	kW	Tx Location	Target Div.
88.1	CR1	3	Mt.Gough	Kowloon
88.3	CR1	0.5	Cloudy Hill	Fan Ling
88.6	CR1	0.7	Castle Peak	Tuen Mun
88.9	CR1	0.1	Golden Hill	Tsuen Wan
89.1	CR1	0.5	Lamma Isl.	HK Isl. south
89.2	CR1	0.15	Beacon Hill	Sha Tin
89.5	CR1	1	Kowloon Peak	HK Isl. north, Sai Kung
90.3	CR2	3	Mt.Gough	Kowloon
90.7	CR2	0.5	Cloudy Hill	Fan Ling
90.9	CR2	0.1	Golden Hill	Tsuen Wan
91.1	CR2	0.15	Beacon Hill	Sha Tin
91.2	CR2	0.7	Castle Peak	Tuen Mun
91.6	CR2	0.5	Lamma Isl.	HK Isl. south
92.1	CR2	1	Kowloon Peak	HK Isl. north, Sai Kung

HKCR CR1 (Supercharged 881) in Cantonese. 24h **N:** half-hourly **HKCR CR2** (Ultimate 903) in Cantonese 24h **N:** hourly **Ann:** "Chikja gaulingsaam"
HKCR AM864 in English, partly Filipino on Fri and Sat 1300-1500. 24h **N:**On the h from 2300-1500

METRO BROADCAST CORPORATION LTD.
✉ Basement 2, Site 6, Whampoa Gardens Hunghom, Kowloon, Hong Kong ☎ +852 3698 8000 📠+852 2123 9889 **E:** prenquiry@metroradio.com.hk **W:** metroradio.com.hk

MW(kHz)	Network	kW	Location
1044	Metro Plus	5	Peng Chau

FM(MHz)	Network	kW	Tx Location	Target Div.
99.7	Metro Info	3	Mt.Gough	Kowloon
100.0	Metro info	0.5	Cloudy Hill	Fan Ling
100.4	Metro info	0.7	Castle Peak	Tuen Mun
100.5	Metro Info	0.15	Beacon Hill	Sha Tin
101.0	Metro Info	0.01	Stanley	
101.6	Metro Info	0.1	Golden Hill	Tsuen Wan
101.8	Metro Info	1	Kowloon Peak	HK Isl. north
102.1	Metro info	0.5	Lamma Isl.	HK Isl. south
102.4	Metro Finance	0.15	Beacon Hill	Sha Tin
102.5	Metro Finance	0.7	Castle Peak	Tuen Mun
102.6	Metro Finance	0.01	Stanley	
104.0	Metro Finance	3	Mt.Gough	Kowloon
104.5	Metro Finance	0.5	Lamma Isl.	HK Isl. south
104.7	Metro Finance	0.5	Cloudy Hill	Fan Ling
105.5	Metro Finance	0.1	Golden Hill	Tsuen Wan
106.3	Metro Finance	1	Kowloon Peak	HK Isl. north

Metro Plus in English (Partly Cantonese, Mandarin, Filipino and Indonesian) 24h music, news and information **Metro Info** in Cantonese. 24h **Ann:** "Sansing jiseung toi" **Metro Finance** in Cantonese 24h

DIGITAL RADIO (DAB)
Three broadcasters share 16 channels of one frequency – DAB+ Ch 11C (220.352MHz): 5 channels by Radio Television Hong Kong, 3channels by Metro Broadcast Corporaion Ltd., 7 channels by Digital Broadcasting Corporation Hong Kong Ltd. ✉ Unit 302, Level 3, IT Street, Cyberport 3, 100 Cyberport Road, Hong Kong **W:** dbc.hk 2 channels by Phoenix U Radio Ltd. ✉ No. 2-6 Dai King Street, Tai Po Industral Estate, Tai Po, N.T., Hong Kong **W:** uradiohk.com Channels

of Radio Television Hong Kong includes BBC and Voice of Hong Kong, the 14th Prgr of China National Radio (CNR)

HUNGARY

L.T: UTC +1h (27 Mar-30 Oct: UTC +2h) — **Pop**: 9.85 million — **Pr.L**: Hungarian — **E.C**: 50Hz, 230V — **ITU**: HNG

MAGYAR RÁDIÓ
⌨ 1016 Budapest, Naphegy tér 8 ☎ +36 1 3287000 2 36 1 3287447 **W**: radio.hu **E**: info@radio.hu **L.P**: CEO: István Jónás
Kossuth Rádió ☎ +36 1 3287945 **W**: mediaklikk.hu/kossuth **Petöfi Rádió** ☎ +36 1 3288555 **W**: mediaklikk.hu/petofi **Bartók Rádió** ☎ +36 1 3288772 **W**: mediaklikk.hu/bartok

MW	kHz	kW	Prg	MW	kHz	kW	Prg
Solt	540	1000	1	Marcali	1188	300	4
Lakihegy	873	20	4	Szolnok	1188	100	4
Pécs	873	20	4	Szombathely	1251	25	D
Miskolc	1116	15	D	Nyíregyháza	1251	25	D
Mosonmagyaróvár	1116	5	D	Györ	1350	5	4

FM (MHz):	MR1	MR2	MR3	Dankó	kW(erp)
Aggtelek	94.6				2.3
Balassagyarmat		93.7			3
Barcs	89.5				2
Budapest	107.8	94.8	105.3	100.8	83/77/81/79
Cegléd	93.0				1.1
Csávoly	96.7	89.4			6.1/6.3
Debrecen	99.7	89.0	106.6	91.4	1.4/1/1/1.2
Dombóvár				100.2	1
Fehérgyarmat	105.9				5.6
Gerecse	105.6				10
Györ	87.6	93.1	106.8	106.4	7.6/7.5/7.4/0.8
Kabhegy	107.2	93.9	105.0	102.3	87/65/69/5.4
Kaposvár	96.7				3.5
Karcag	97.9				10
Kecskemét	104.9				1.1
Kékestetö	95.5	102.7	90.7	99.8	20/30/28/0.3
Kiskörös	88.4	95.1	105.9		2/1.7/3
Komádi	103.0	96.7	105.1	89.9	39/37/30/5
Miskolc	97.1		107.5	102.3	5.6/1.4/1.4
Mosonmagyaróvár	95.0				0.8
Nagykanizsa	90.2	94.3	104.7	106.7	8.3/12/20/5
Nyíregyháza				107.4	1
Pécs	95.9	103.7	104.6		25/49/10/5.6
Rábaszentandrás				105.2	4.9
Sátoraljaújhely	91.9				0.5
Siófok				93.6	3
Sopron	96.8	99.5	107.9	101.6	9.3/9/7/5.1
Szeged	90.3	104.6	105.7	93.1	0.6/5/2.2/1
Szekszárd	99.0				1.1
Szentes	100.4	98.8	107.3	91.6	34/32/34/2
Szolnok	94.3			101.2	6.3/2
Telkibánya	90.2				3.6
Tokaj	97.5	92.7	105.5	88.3	50/50/50/6
Úzd	101.5	90.3	106.9		3/3/3
Vasvár	91.6	98.2	106.9	103.6	6.8/7.5/3/3

+ 16 Kossuth txs & + 13 Dankó txs below 1kW

Programmes: P1= **Kossuth R.** (news-talk) P2= **Petöfi R.** (pop) P3= **Bartók R.** (classical) P4= **Nemzetiségi adások** (Ethnic broadcasts), P5= **Parlamenti adások** (Parliamentary broadcasts, internet/satellite only), P6= **Duna World Rádió** (internet/satellite only) D= **Dankó Rádió** (folk+operetta)
Daily pr: 24h exc. **P1** MW: Mo-Fr 0330-2130, Sa-Su: 0400-2130 & **P4** MW: 0700-1900
ANN: **P1**: "Kossuth Rádió, otthon a világban" **P2**: "Petöfi Rádió, nagyon zene" **P3**: "Bartók Rádió, több, mint klasszikus"
P4: Nemzetiségi (Ethnic pr): ☎ +36 (1) 328-8672 🖷 +36 (1) 328-8682. **W**: mediaklikk.hu/nemzetisegiadasok/ **Daily**: Croatian: 0700-0900, German: 0900-1100, Serbian: 1300-1500, Romanian: 1500-1700, Slovak: 1700-1900; **Mo-Fr**: Roma/Gipsy: 1103-1200; Ethnic music: 1230-1300; **Weekly at 1200-1230**: Mo: Slovenian, Tu: Rusyn/Ruthenian, We: Greek, Th: Bulgarian, Fr: Ukrainian, Sa: Armenian; Sa-Su: Ethnic music (1103-1200), Sa: Polish 1230-1300; Su: Hungarian "In One Home" (1200-1255)
Dankó Rádió: ⌨ Kunigunda útja 64, 1037 Budapest ☎ +36 1 7596071 **W**: mediaklikk.hu/danko/ **E**: dankoradio@mtva.hu
Daily pr: 24h on FM; **Mo-Fr**: 0330-2005, **Sa-Su**: 0400-2005 on MW;
Ann: "Dankó Rádió, csendül a nóta, száll a muzsika"

National Media and Communications Authority (NMHH)
⌨ 1015 Budapest, Ostrom utca 23-25 ☎+36 1 4577100 🖷+36 1 3565520 **W**: nmhh.hu **E**: info@nmhh.hu
Media Council
⌨ 1088 Budapest, Reviczky u. 5 ☎ +36 1 4298600, 2672590 🖷 +36 1 2672612 **W**: mediatanacs.hu **E**: kapcsolat@mtmi.hu
Antenna Hungária Broadc. & Radiocommunications Ltd (AH Zrt.)
⌨ 1119 Budapest, Petzvál József u. 31-33 ☎ +36 1 4642464 🖷 +36 1 4642525 **W**: ahrt.hu **E**: antennah@ahrt.hu
National Association of Local Radios (HEROE)
⌨ 8000 Székesfehérvár, Donát u. 92 ☎ +36 22 505310 🖷 +36 22 505312 **W**: heroe.hu **E**: heroeelnok@lakihegyradio.hu
⌨ 6800 Hódmezövásárhely, Szabadság tér 71. **E**: heroe1@radio7.hu
DX data: radiosite.hu, frekvencia.hu

National network
CLASS FM (National, Comm.)
⌨ 1089 Budapest, Üllöi út 102 ☎ +36 1 5555500 **W**: classfm.hu **E**: classfm@classfm.hu

Location	MHz	kW	Location	MHz	kW
Budapest	103.3	81	Miskolc	98.3	5.6
Debrecen	101.1	1	Nagykanizsa	93.6	0.25
Györ	101.4	7.6	Pécs	105.5	50
Kabhegy	100.5	67.6	Sopron	102.0	22
Kaposvár	89.0	0.05	Szeged	94.9	0.6
Kékes	104.7	27	Szekszárd	98.4	1
Komádi	101.6	22	Tokaj	103.5	50

Other Stations

FM	MHz	kW	Location	Station
20)	87.9	1	Szeged	Európa R.
9)	88.1	1	Budapest	InfoRádió (news)
2)	88.3	1	Komárom	Mária R. (rlg)
2)	88.3	1	Cegléd	Mária R. (rlg)
1)	89.5	77	Budapest	Music FM
5)	90.3	0.4	Budapest	Tilos R. (community)
11)	90.5	1	Komárom	Forrás R.
7)	90.6	1	Sátoraljaújh.	Szent István R. (rlg)
26)	90.9	2	Budapest	Jazzy (smooth jazz)
14)	91.7	1.2	Kiskörös	Magyar Katolikus R. (rlg)
7)	91.8	0.46	Eger	Szent István R. (rlg)
28)	92.1	1	Budapest	Klasszik R. (classical)
14)	92.5	0.43	Esztergom	Magyar Katolikus R. (rlg)
4)	92.6	1	Siófok	Part FM
24)	92.9	2.6	Budapest	Klubrádió (talk)
14)	92.9	1	Zalaegerszeg	Magyar Katolikus R. (rlg)
23)	93.4	1	Dabas	R. Dabas
25)	93.6	0.85	Nagykörös	Gong R.
18)	94.2	1	Budapest	Gazdasági R.
20)	94.4	1	Debrecen	Európa R.
7)	95.1	1	Miskolc	Szent István R. (rlg)
29)	95.1	1	Zalaegerszeg	R. Pont 1
7)	95.4	1	Encs	Szent István R. (rlg)
14)	96.1	0.1	Székesfehérv.	Magyar Katolikus R. (rlg)
27)	96.3	5	Miskolc	Ozone FM
25)	96.5	1	Kecskemét	Gong R.
16)	97.1	2	Szombathely	Lánchíd R. (newstalk)
32)	97.7	1	Szombathely	Frissz FM
11)	97.8	0.8	Tatabánya	Forrás R.
12)	98.0	0.14	Budapest	Civil R. (community)
16)	98.9	1	Szigetvár	Lánchíd R. (newstalk)
13)	99.5	5	Budapest	R. Q
10)	100.0	0.5	Kalocsa	Koronafm100
33)	100.1	1	Györ	Györ+ R.
16)	100.3	1	Budapest	Lánchíd R. (newstalk)
20)	100.5	1	Nyíregyháza	Európa Rádió
2)	100.6	3	Telkibánya	Mária R. (rlg)
37)	100.7	1	FM7	Eger
14)	101.2	2	Pécs	Magyar Katolikus R. (rlg)
8)	101.3	1	Eger	Rádió Eger
21)	101.6	1	Miskolc	R. M (CHR)
31)	101.9	1	Tamási	Tamási R.
14)	102.1	0.74	Budapest	Magyar Katolikus R. (rlg)
30)	102.4	0.8	Szolnok	Amadeus R.
14)	102.5	0.5	Szekszárd	Magyar Katolikus R. (rlg)
34)	102.7	0.95	Barcs	Aqua R.
27)	103.1	0.1	Györ	Ozone FM
6)	103.8	0.8	Székesfehérv.	Kék Duna R.
22)	103.9	1	Nyíregyháza	Retro R.
3)	103.9	5	Budapest	Juventus R. (AC)
17)	104.0	1	Békéscsaba	Csaba R.

FM	MHz	kW	Location	Station
35)	104.6	0.8	Debrecen	Best FM
14)	104.6	1	Sopron	Magyar Katolikus R. (rlg)
2)	104.9	0.8	Dömös	Mária R. (rlg)
36)	105.1	0.74	Szekszárd	R. Antritt
16)	107.0	1	Tatabánya	Lánchíd R. (newstalk)
15)	107.0	0.8	Kistelek	R. 7
19)	107.0	0.76	Szigetsz.mikl.	Lakihegy R.
14)	107.4	0.5	Szombathely	Magyar Katolikus R. (rlg)

+ approximately 170 additional FM txs from 50W to 1kW

Addresses and other information

1) ⌨ 1138 Budapest, Népfürdö utca 22. B torony V. em. ☎+36 1 7998895 **W:** musicfm.hu **E:** info@musicfm.hu – **2)** ⌨ 1142 Budapest, Szönyi út 16 ☎+36 1 3730701 **W:** mariaradio.hu **E:** info@mariaradio.hu **NB:** total 19 txs – **3)** ⌨ 1134 Budapest, Róbert Károly körút 82-84 ☎+36 1 2375300 **W:** juventus.hu **E:** musicradio@juventus.hu – **4)** ⌨ 8600 Siófok, Budai Nagy Antal u. 1-3 ☎ +36 84 310168 **W:** partfm.hu **E:** info@partfm.hu – **5)** ⌨ 1085 Budapest, Üllöi út 32. ☎ +36 1 4768491 **W:** tilos.hu **E:** radio@tilos.hu **NB:** Some English px – **6)** ⌨ 2501 Esztergom, P.F: 400 ☎ +36 30 2107777 **W:** kekduna.hu **E:** szekesfehervar@kekduna.hu mosonmagyarovar@kekduna.hu **NB:** total 2 txs – **7)** ⌨ 3300 Eger, Széchenyi utca 5. ☎ +36 36 510-610 **W:** szentistvanradio.hu **E:** info@szentistvanradio.hu **NB:** total 8 txs – **8)** ⌨ 3300 Eger, Trinitárius út 1. ☎ +36 36 410450 **W:** radioeger.hu **E:** info@radioeger.hu – **9)** ⌨ 1033 Budapest, Polgár u. 8-10 ☎ +36 1 4832950 **W:** inforadio.hu **E:** info@inforadio.hu – **10)** ⌨ 6300 Kalocsa, Szent István kir. út 34, ☎+36 78 567662 **W:** koronaradio.hu **E:** info@koronaradio.hu – **11)** ⌨ 2800 Tatabánya, Stúdium tér 1. ☎ +36 34 310021 **W:** forrasradio.hu **E:** forras@forrasradio.hu **NB:** total 2 txs – **12)** ⌨ 1116 Budapest, Sztregova utca 3 ☎ +36 1 489-0997 **W:** civilradio.hu **E:** civilradio@civilradio.hu – **13)** ⌨ 1119 Budapest, Keveháza u. 1-3 ☎+36 1 3539453 **W:** radioq.hu **E:** bognar.eva@radioq.hu – **14)** ⌨ 1062 Budapest, Délibáb u. 15-17 ☎ +36 1 255-3366 **W:** katolikusradio.hu **E:** info@katradio.hu **NB:** total 18 txs – **15)** ⌨ 6800 Hódmezövásárhely, Szabadság tér 71. ☎ +36 62 533777 **W:** http://promenad.hu/radio-7/musorok **E:** radio7@radio7.hu **NB:** total 3 txs – **16)** ⌨ 1089 Budapest, Üllöi út 102 ☎ +36 1 8148730 **W:** mno.hu/lanchidradio **E:** info@lanchidradio.hu **NB:** total 14 txs – **17)** ⌨ 5600 Békéscsaba, Bartók Béla út 7. ☎ +36 66 441111 🖷 +36 66 441112 **W:** csabaradio.hu **E:** info@csabaradio.hu – **18)** ⌨ 1133 Budapest, Váci út 78/B ☎ +36 1 8881500 **W:** gazdasagiradio.hu **E:** info@gazdasagiradio.hu – **19)** ⌨ 2310 Szigetszentmiklós, Csepeli út 15. ☎+36 20 2754003 **W:** lakihegyradio.hu **E:** info@lakihegyradio.hu – **20)** ⌨ 3530 Miskolc, Toronyalja utca 13. ☎+36 46 509904 **W:** refradio.eu/radio/euradio **E:** euradio@euradio.hu, euradiodebrecen@gmail.com, nyiregyhaza@euradio.hu **NB:** total 4 txs – **21)** ⌨ 3525 Miskolc, Széchenyi István út 46. I. em. 5. ☎🖷 +36 46 320075 **W:** fmradiom.com **E:** hir@fmradiom.hu **NB:** total 4 txs – **22)** ⌨ 4400 Nyíregyháza, Eötvös utca 9/A ☎🖷+36 42 401035 **W:** retrofm.hu **E:** info@retrofm.hu – **23)** ⌨ 2370 Dabas, Szent István tér 1/b ☎+36 29 562562 **W:** radiodabas.hu **E:** info@radiodabas.hu – **24)** ⌨ 1037 Budapest, Bokor u 1-3-5 ☎ +36 1 2406953 **W:** klubradio.hu **E:** info@klubradio.hu – **25)** ⌨ 6000 Kecskemét, Petöfi Sándor u 1/b ☎+36 76 414020 **W:** gongradio.hu **E:** gongradio@gongradio.hu **NB:** total 7 txs – **26)** ⌨ 1022 Budapest Detrekö u. 12. ☎+36 1 7876992 **W:** jazzy.hu **E:** jazzy@jazzy.hu – **27)** ⌨ 9023 Györ, Magyar u. 9. ☎+36 30 7474777 **W:** o3.hu/ **E:** info@ozonefm.hu **NB:** total 9 txs – **28)** ⌨ 1022 Budapest, Detrekö u. 12 ☎+36 1 7866464 **W:** klasszikradio.hu **E:** info@klasszikradio.hu – **29)** ⌨ 8900 Zalaegerszeg, Tompa utca 1-3 ☎+36 92 707951 🖷+36 1 4732610 – **30)** ⌨ 5000 Szolnok, Baross út 3. ☎+36 56 221024 **W:** amadeusradio.hu **E:** amadeus@amadeusradio.hu – **31)** ⌨ 7090 Tamási, Szabadság utca 54. ☎ +36 74 570260 **W:** tamasiradio.tamasinet.hu **E:** tamasiradio@tamasinet.hu – **32)** ⌨ 9700 Szombathely, Dolgozók útja 1/A ☎+36 94 506977 **W:** frisss.hu **E:** info@frisss.hu – **33)** ⌨ 9023 Györ, Magyar u. 9. ☎ +36 96 444222 **W:** radio.gyorplusz.hu **E:** radio@gyorplusz.hu – **34)** ⌨ 7570 Barcs, Köztársaság u. 2/1 ☎+36 82 565266 **W:** barcsmedia.hu **E:** aquaradio@t-online.hu – **35)** ⌨ 4026 Debrecen, Darabos u. 35. ☎ +36 52 450900 **W:** bestfm.hu **E:** info@bestfm.hu – **36)** ⌨ 7100 Szekszárd, Wesselényi u. 16. ☎+36 74 444444 **W:** radioantritt.hu **E:** szerk@radioantritt.hu – **37)** ⌨ 3300 Eger, Csákány u. 1. ☎+36 36 787808 **W:** fm7.hu/ **E:** info@fm7.hu

Kisközösségi rádió (lowpower community radio)
Non-profit low-power stns (0.1–10W) had been granted licences in cities and country villages. In the recent years the number of these stns drastically decreased, mainly due to financial reasons. Currently only 27 such stns are operating in the whole country. See **W:** frekvencia.hu/kiskozossegi.htm

DAB+: Budapest – Hármashatár-hegy, Budapest – Széchenyi-hegy, Budapest – Száva utca, MR1-3, Dankó Rádió, Magyar Katolikus R., InfoRádió, Klubrádió, Lánchíd R. on 222.064 MHz (ch 11D) 3 x 250W

L.T: UTC — **Pop:** 325,000 — **Pr.L:** Icelandic — **E.C:** 50Hz, 230V — **ITU:** ISL

FJÖLMIÐLANEFND (The Media Commission)
⌨ Borgartúni 21, 105 Reykjavík ☎ +354 4150415 🖷 +354 4150410 **E:** postur@fjolmidlanefnd.is **W:** fjolmidlanefnd.is
L.P: Dir: Elfa Ýr Gylfadóttir
NB. Fjölmiðlanefnd issues broadcasting licenses.

RÍKISÚTVARPIÐ (RÚV) (Pub)
⌨ Efstaleiti 1, 150 Reykjavík ☎ +354 5153000 🖷 +354 5153010 **E:** frettir@ruv.is **W:** ruv.is **L.P:** DG: Magnús Geir Þórðarsson

LW	kHz	kW	Prgr	LW	kHz	kW	Prgr
Gufuskálar	189	300	Rás 1/2	Eiðar	207	100	Rás 1/2

FM (MHz)	Rás 1	Rás 2	Rondó	kW
Almannaskarð	90.3	104.8	-	1
Auðsholt	91.3	95.3	-	2.5
Gagnheiði	99.8	87.7	-	5
Girðisholt	92.9	-	-	3.5
Háfell	93.8	98.7	-	14/34
Hegranes	90.6	98.8	-	3.1/5
Hnjúkar	89.1	95.5	-	6/6.2
Reykjavík	93.5	90.1	87.7	3.4/2/2
Skálafell	92.4	99.9	-	24
Stykkishólmur	88.0	96.3	-	3/3.5
Vaðlaheiði	91.6	96.5	-	9.3
Vestmannaeyar	97.1	88.1	-	17/24
Viðarfjall	88.1	96.1	-	3.3

NB: Sites with only txs below 1kW not listed.
D.Prgr: Rás 1: 24h. – **Rás 2**: 24h. – **Rondó**: 24h.

On LW: 0000-0625 Rás 2, 0625-0900 Rás 1+2 (joint tr), 0900-1000 Rás 2, 1000-1400 (Tue/Wed) Rás 1, 1000-1017 (exc. Tue/Wed) Rás 1, 1017-1220 (exc. Tue/Wed) Rás 2, 1220-1400 (Mon/Thu/Fri) Rás 1, 1220-1300 (Sat/Sun) Rás 1, 1400 (Sat/Sun 1300)-1800 Rás 2, 1800-1900 Rás 1, 1900-2200 Rás 2, 2200-2220 Rás 1, 2220-2400 Rás 2.

OTHER STATIONS

FM	MHz	kW	Location	Station
5)	88.5	1	Reykjavík	XA Radíó
1E)	90.4	2	Vestmannaeyjar	X-997
1C)	90.9	2	Ulfarsfell	GullBylgjan
1A)	92.7	2	Vaðlaheiði	Bylgjan
4)	92.9	1	Vestmannaeyjar	Suðurland FM
1A)	94.5	2	Háfell	Bylgjan
1B)	94.7	1	Egilsstaðir	FM957
1B)	95.1	1	Hegranes	FM957
1B)	95.7	2	Reykjavík	FM957
4)	96.3	1	Selfoss	Suðurland FM
1D)	96.7	2	Ulfarsfell	LéttBylgjan
1E)	97.7	2	Ulfarsfell	X-997
1A)	97.9	1	Hegranes	Bylgjan
1A)	98.9	2	Reykjavík	Bylgjan
1A)	98.9	2	Hnjúkar	Bylgjan
2)	100.5	1	Bláfjöll	K 100.5
1A)	100.9	2	Vestmannaeyjar	Bylgjan
1B)	101.7	2	Vestmannaeyjar	FM957
1B)	102.5	1	Skáneyjarbunga	FM957
3)	102.9	2	Reykjavík	Lindin
1B)	103.2	1	Selfoss	FM957
1A)	103.3	1	Skáneyjarbunga	Bylgjan
A)	103.5	1	Ulfarsfell	BBCWS relay
1F)	103.9	1	Reykjavík	FMX Klassík
1A)	104.5	2	Grenjadalsfell	Bylgjan

NB: Txs below 1kW not listed.
Addresses & other information:
1A-1F) Skaftahlíð 24, 105 Reykjavík – **2)** Skipholti 31, 105 Reykjavík – **3)** Krókhálsi 4a, 110 Reykjavík **E:** lindin@lindin.is – **4)** Hrísmýri 6, 800 Selfoss **E:** 963@963.is – **5)** Brávallagötu 18, 101 Reykjavík. Mainly in English. – **A)** Rel. BBCWS (UK)

L.T: UTC +5½h — **Pop:** 1.28 million — **Pr.L:** Assamese, Bangla, Bodo, Dogri, English, Gujarati, Hindi, Kannada, Kashmiri, Maithili, Marathi, Malayalam, Nepali, Odia, Punjabi, Santhali, Sindhi, Tamil, Telugu & Urdu — **E.C:** 50Hz 220/400V — **ITU:** IND

MINISTRY OF INFORMATION & BROADCASTING
Main Secretariat: ⌨ A-Wing, Shastri Bhawan, New Delhi-110001 **W:** mib.nic.in

L.P: Minister for Info. & Broadcasting: Arun Jaitley. Minister of State for Information & Broadcasting: Col. Rajyavardhan Rathore

PRASAR BHARATI (BROADCASTING CORPORATION OF INDIA) (Public Corporation)

2nd Floor, PTI Building, Parliament Street, New Delhi-110001 ☎ +91 11 23382094/5/7/8/9 ✉ +91 11 23386507 **L.P:** Chairman: Dr.A.Surya Prakash ☎+91 11 23737687, 23737589 23352549 **E:** chairman@prasarbharati.org **W:** prasarbharati.gov.in
CEO: Jawhar Sircar ☎ 91 11 23737603, 23352558 ✉ 91 11 23352549 **E:** ceo@prasarbharati.org

AKASHVANI – ALL INDIA RADIO

Administration/Engineering: Directorate General, All India Radio, Akashvani Bhavan, Parliament Street, New Delhi-110001
☎ +91 11 23421006 and 23715413 ✉ +91 11 23711956
E: airlive@air.org.in **W:** allindiaradio.gov.in
L.P: DG: F.Sheheryar ☎ +91 11 23421300 ✉ 91 11 23421956
E: dgair@air.org.in Eng. in Chief: Animesh Chakrborty ☎+91 11 23421058 ✉ +91 11 23421459 **E:** einc@air.org.in
Spectrum Management & Synergy: Room No.204, All India Radio, Akashvani Bhavan, Parliament Street, New Delhi-110001 **L.P:** Dy. Dir. Gen.: Sunil Bhatia, Dy. Dir. (Engg) : K.C.Sharma ☎ +91 11 23421062, 23421145 **E:** spectrum-manager@air.org.in
Programming: New Broadcasting House, 27 Mahadev Road, New Delhi-110 001 ☎ +91 (11) 23421218
Akashvani Bhavan, Parliament Street, New Delhi-110001 ☎ +91 11 23715411
News Services Division: New Broadcasting House, 27 Mahadev Road, New Delhi-110 001 Newsroom ☎ +91 11 23421100 ✉+91 11 23421219 **E:** nbhnews@air.org.in **W:** newsonair.nic.in **L.P:** Dir.Gen. (News): Sitanshu Kar **E:** dgn.nsd@gmail.com News on phone: English ☎ +91 11 2332-4343/1259, Hindi +91 11 2332-4242/1258
Commercial Service (Vividh Bharati): All India Radio, Gorai Road, Borivli West, Mumbai-400 091, Maharashtra ☎ +91 22 28692698 **E:** vbsmumbai@gmail.com
National Channel: All India Radio, Todapur, New Delhi 110012 ☎ +91 11 25843207 **E:** delhi.nationalchannel@air.org.in
Research & Development: Office of the Addl. Director General, R & D, All India Radio, 14-B, Indra Prashta Estate, Ring Road, New Delhi-110002 ☎ +91 11 23379329, 23379255, **E:** researchdelhi@yahoo.co.in
Monitoring: International Monitoring Stn., All India Radio, Dr. K.S. Krishnan Rd, Todapur, New Delhi-110012 ☎ +91 11 25842939 **E.**delhi.todapur@air.org.in Central Monitoring Stn, All India Radio, Ayanagar, New Delhi-110047 **E:**delhi.ayanagarcms@air.org.in
Audience Research: Audience Research Unit, AIR, Akashwani Bhavan, Parliament Street, New Delhi 110001 ☎ +91 11 23421022
Live streaming: W: http://allindiaradio.gov.in/Default.aspx

Regional Headquarters: (Office of the Additional Director General)
North Zone: AIR, Jamnagar House, Shahjahan Road, New Delhi-110011 ☎ +91 11 23382519
East Zone: AIR, 4th Floor, Akashvani Bhavan, Eden Garden, Kolkata-700001 ☎ +91 33 22480158
North-East Zone: AIR, Doordarshan Complex, KG Baruah Road, P.O. Zoo Road, Guwahati – 781024, Assam ☎ +91 361 2200326
West Zone: AIR, 101 M.K.Road, Mumbai-400020, Maharashtra ☎ +91 22 22014287
South Zone: AIR, Swami Sivanada Salai, Chepauk, Chennai-600005 ☎ +91 44 25383253

NB: Thiruvananthapuram is given in all cases as Trivandrum.
MW: c) Vividh Bharati, e) ext.sce., n) national channel, r) relay stn

KHz	Station	kW	reg	KHz	Station	kW	reg
531	Jodhpur A	300	N	666	New Delhi B	100	N
540	Aizawl	20	NE	675	Bhadravathi	20	S
549	Ranchi A	100	E	675	Chhatarpur	20	W
558	Mumbai B	100	W	675	Itanagar	100	NE
567	Dibrugarh	300	NE	684	KozhikodeA	100	S
576	Alappuzha	200	S, r	684	Port Blair	100	S
585	Nagpur A	300	W	684	Kargil A	200	N
594	Chinsurah	1000	E, er	702	Jalandhar A	200	N, e
603	Ajmer	200	N, r	711	Siliguri	200	E
612	BengaluruA	200	S	720	Chennai A	200	S
621	Patna A	100	E	729	Guwahati A	100	NE
630	Thrissur	100	S	738	Hyderabad A	200	S
639	Kohima	100	NE	747	Lucknow A	300	N
648	Indore A	200	W	756	Jagdalpur	100	W
657	Kolkata A	200	E	765	Dharwad A	200	S

KHz	Station	kW	reg	KHz	Station	kW	reg
774	Shimla	100	N	1269	Agartala	20	NE
783	Chennai C	20	S, c	1269	Madurai	20	S
792	Pune A	100	W	1278	Lucknow C	10	N, c
801	Jabalpur	200	W	1287	Panaji A	100	W
810	Rajkot A	300	W	1296	Darbhanga	10	E
819	New Delhi A	200	N	1305	Parbhani	20	W
828	Panaji B	20	W, c	1314	Bhuj	20	W
828	Silchar	20	NE	1314	Cuttack B	1	E, c
837	Vijayawada A	100	S	1323	Kolkata C	20	E, c
846	Ahmedabad A	200	W	1332	Tezu	10	NE
864	Shillong	100	NE	1341	Kohima	1	NE
873	Jalandhar B	300	N	1350	Jalandhar C	1	N, c
882	Imphal	300	NE	1350	Kupwara	1	N, r
891	Rampur	20	N	1377	Hyderabad B	20	S
900	Kadapa	100	S	1386	Gwalior	20	W
909	Gorakhpur	100	N	1395	Bikaner	20	N
918	Suratgarh	300	N	1404	Gangtok	20	NE
927	Visakhapatnam	100	S	1413	Kota	20	N
936	Tiruchirapalli A	100	S	1440	Kurseong	1	E
945	Sambalpur	100	E	1458	Barmer	20	N
954	Najibabad	200	N	1458	Bhagalpur	20	E
963	Jalgaon	20	W	1467	Jeypore	100	E
972	Cuttack A	300	E	1476	Jaipur A	1	W
981	Raipur	100	W	1485	Adilabad	1	S
990	Jammu A	100	N	1485	Ahwa	1	W
999	Almora	1	N	1485	Chamoli	1	N
999	Coimbatore	20	S	1485	Drass	1	N, cr
1008	Kolkata B	100	E	1485	Dunagrpur	1	W
1017	Chennai B	20	S	1485	Joranda	1	E
1017	New Delhi	10	N	1485	Khaltsi	1	N, cr
1026	Allahabad A	20	N	1485	Nongstoin	1	NE
1035	Guwahati B	20	NE	1485	Nyoma	1	N, cr
1044	Mumbai A	100	W	1485	Pithoragarh	1	N, r
1053	Leh	20	N	1485	Soro	1	E
1053	Tuticorin	200	S, e	1512	Kokrajhar	20	NE
1062	Passighat	100	NE	1521	Tawang	20	NE
1071	Rajkot	870	W, e	1530	Agra	20	N
1089	Udipi	20	S, r	1566	Nagpur	1000	W, nr
1089	Naushera	20	N, r	1584	Dharmanagar	1	NE
1107	Gulbarga	20	S	1584	Diphu	1	NE
1116	Srinagar A	300	N	1584	Himmat Nagar	1	W
1125	Tezpur	20	NE	1584	Jamshedpur	1	E
1125	Udaipur	20	N	1584	Kalpa	1	N, r
1134	Chinsurah	1000	E, ner	1584	Kargil B	1	N
1143	Ratnagiri	20	W	1584	Kavaratti	1	S
1143	Rohtak	20	N	1584	Keonjhar	1	E
1152	Kavaratti	10	S	1584	Kota	1	N
1161	Trivandrum	20	S	1584	Mathura	1	N
1170	Hyderabad (St'by)	1	S	1584	Mon	1	NE
1179	Rewa	20	W	1584	Padam	1	N,c
1188	Mumbai C	50	W,c	1593	Bhopal A	10	W
1197	Shillong (St'by)	1	NE	1602	Diskit	1	N cr
1197	Tirunelveli	20	S	1602	Pauri	1	N
1206	Bhawanipatna	200	E	1602	Saiha	1	NE
1215	New Delhi	20	N, n	1602	Tiesuru	1	N,cr
1215	Pudducherri	20	S	1602	Tuensang	1	NE
1224	Srinagar C	10	N	1602	Udagamangalam	1	S
1233	Tura	20	NE	1602	Uttarkashi	1	N
1242	Varanasi	100	W	1602	Varanasi B	1	N, c
1251	Sangli	20	W	1602	William Nagar	1	NE
1260	Ambikapur	20	W	1602	Ziro	1	NE

DRM frequencies on MW

KHz	Station	kW	reg	KHz	Station	kW	reg
558	Ranchi	100	E	856	Ahmedabad	200	W
568	Mumbai B	100	W	883	Jalandhar	300	N
577	Dibrugarh	300	NE	928	Suratgarh	300	N
604	Chinsurah	1000	E	946	Tiruchirapalli	100	S
613	Ajmer	200	N	1000	Jammu	300	N
621	Bengaluru	200	S	1018	Kolkata	100	E
631	Patna	100	E	1045	Guwahati B	20	NE
667	Kolkata	200	E	1054	Mumbai	100	W
685	Itanagar	200	NE	1072	Passighat	100	NE
721	Siliguri	200	E	1081	Rajkot	1000	W
729	Chennai A	200	S	1144	Chinsurah	1000	E
757	Lucknow	300	N	1252	Varanasi	100	N
775	Dharwad	200	S	1297	Panaji	100	W
792	Chennai	20	S	1368	New Delhi	20	N
802	Pune	20	S	1405	Bikaner	20	N
811	Jabalpur	200	W	1468	Barmer	20	N
820	Rajkot	200	W	1531	Tawang	20	NE
829	New Delhi	200	N				
847	Vijayawada	100	S				

D.Prgr: Varies from stn to stn. Some stns have only 1 or 2 transmissions while others have 3. Extended coverage during sports or special events. **National Ch.:** 1325-0043 on 1215, 1566, 6156, 9380, 9425 kHz
F.PI: More DRM transmitters under installation **Replacement: 1kW MW to 1kW FM:** Almora, Joranda, Kalpa, Kota, Soro **1kW MW to 10kW FM:** Jaipur, Jamshedpur, Kurseong, Mathura, **Udagamangalam 100kW to 200kW:** Itanagar

Addresses of MW stations (See also SW stn addresses):
1000kW MW stations:
1) AIR, Super Power Transmitter, Chinsurah-712102, Paschim Banga –
2) AIR, National Channel, Seminary Hills, Nagpur-440006, Maharashtra
– **3)** AIR, Super Power Transmitter, Radio Colony, Jamnagar Road, Rajkot -360006, Gujarat

Other MW stations:
Adilabad-504002, Telengana – Palace Compound, North Gate – **Agarthala**-799001, Tripura – Vivbhav Nagar, **Agra**-282001, Uttar Pradesh – Ashram Rd, Navarangpura, **Ahmedabad**-380009, Gujarat – **Ahwa**-394710, Dangs Dist., Gujarat – 21/10 Vaishali Nagar, **Ajmer**-305001, Rajasthan – Pathirapally, **Alappuzha**-688521, Kerala – Z-9 Dayanand Marg, **Allahabad**-211001, Uttar Pradesh – **Almora**-263601, Kumaon Dist., Uttarakhand – Kumar Palace, **Ambikapur**-497001, Surguja Dist., Chhatisgarh –Raj Bhavan Rd, **Bengaluru**-560001, Karnataka – Laxmi Nagar, **Barmer**-344001, Rajasthan – J.P.S.Colony, Paper Tower, **Bhadravati**-577302, Karnataka – Port Campus, **Bhagalpur**-812001, Bihar – **Bhawanipatna**-766001, Nektiguda, Kalahandi Dist., Odisha – **Bhuj**-370001, Kutch Dist., Gujarat – **Bikaner**-334001, Rajasthan – **Chamoli**-246424, Gopeshwar, Uttarakhand – 7, Kamarajar Salai, Mylapore, **Chennai**-600004, Tamilnadu – **Chhatarpur**-471001, Madhya Pradesh – Trichy Rd, Ramanathapuram, **Coimbatore**-641045, Tamilnadu – Madhupur House, Bakshi Bazar, Cantonment Rd, **Cuttack**-753001, Odisha – **Darbhanga**-846004, Bihar – **Dharmanagar**-799250, Tripura – Saptapur, **Dharwad**-580008, Karnataka – Malakhubasa, **Dibrugarh**-786001, Assam – **Diphu**-782460, Kabri Anglong Dist., Assam – **Diskit**-194401, Leh Dist., Jammu & Kashmir – **Drass**-194102, Kargil, Jammu & Kashmir – Dungarpur-314001, Rajasthan – Aiwan-e-Shahi, Municipal Garden, **Gulbarga**-585103, Karnataka – Town Hall, **Gorakhpur**-273001, Uttar Pradesh – Chandmari, **Guwahati**-781003 Assam – Gandhi Rd, **Gwalior**-474002, Madhya Pradesh – **Himmat Nagar** – 383001, Gujarat – Malwa House, Residency Area, **Indore**-452001, Madhya Pradesh – 373 Napier Town, **Jabalpur**-482001, Madhya Pradesh – Collectorate Rd, **Jagdalpur**-494 001, Bastar Dist., Chhattisgarh – **Jalandhar**-144001, Punjab – Jilhapet, **Jalgaon**-425001, Maharashtra – R. Kashmir, Begum Haveli, Old Palace Road, **Jammu**-180001, Jammu & Kashmir – Adityapur, Gamharia Rd, **Jamshedpur**-831013, Jharkhand – Paoata 'C' Road, **Jodhpur**-342006, Rajasthan – **Joranda**-759014, Dhenkanal Dist., Odisha – Cooperative Colony, **Kadapa**-516001, YSR Dist., Andhra Pradesh – **Kalpa**-172108, Kinnaur Dist., Himachal Pradesh– **Kargil**-194103, Jammu & Kashmir – **Kavaratti**-682555, Lakshadeep – **Khaltsi**-194106, Leh, Jammu & Kashmir –**Kokrajhar**-783370, Assam – Jawahar Rd, **Kota**-324001, Rajasthan – Beach Rd, **Kozhikode**-673001, Kerala – **Kupwara** – 193222, Jammu & Kashmir –Lady Doak College Rd, Chokkikulam, **Madurai**-625002, Tamilnadu – Vrindavan Rd, Gayatri Tapobhumi, **Mathura**-281003, Uttar Pradesh – **Mon**-798621, Nagaland – Broadcasting House, Backbay Reclamation, Mumbai-400020, Maharashtra – Civil Lines, Palam Rd, **Nagpur**-440001, Maharashtra – Kotwali Rd, **Najibabad**-246763, Bijnor Dist., Uttar Pradesh – **Naushera**–193105, Jammu & Kashmir – **Nongstoin**-793119, West Khasi Hills, Meghalaya – **Nyoma**-194101, Leh Dist, Jammu & Kashmir – **Obra**-231219, Uttar Pradesh – **Padam**, Jammu & Kashmir - Altinho, **Panaji**-403001, Goa – Jamakar Colony, Nawa Mondha, **Parbhani**-431401, Maharashtra – **Pasighat**-791102, East Siang Dist., Arunachal Pradesh – Frazer Road, Chhaju Bagh, **Patna**-800001, Bihar – **Pauri**-246001, Uttarakhand – **Pithorgarh**-262501, Uttarakhand – Indira Nagar, Gorimedu, **Puducherri**-605006 – University Rd, Shivaji Nagar, **Pune**-411005, Maharashtra – Sitaram Pandit Marg, **Rajkot**-360001, Gujarat – **Rampur**-244901, Uttar Pradesh – 6 Ratu Rd, **Ranchi**-834001, Jharkhand – Thiba Palace Rd, **Ratnagiri**-415612, Maharashtra – 6 Civil Lines, **Rewa**-486001, Madhya Pradesh – Subhash Rd, **Rohtak**-124001, Haryana – **Saiha**-796901, Chhimtuipui Dist., Mizoram – 3, Kuchery Rd, **Sambalpur**-768001, Odisha – Market Yard, Kolhapur Rd, **Sangli**-416416, Maharashtra – **Silchar**-788001, Cachar Dist., Assam – 2 Mile Sevoke Rd, **Siliguri**-734401, Darjeeling Dist., Paschim Banga –**Soro**-756045 , Balasore Dist, Odisha – **Suratgarh**-335804, Srigangasagar Dist., Rajasthan – **Tawang**-790104, Arunachal Pradesh – **Tezpur**-784001, Sonitpur Dist., Assam – **Tezu**-792001, Lohit Dist., Arunachal Pradesh – Ramavarmapuram, **Thrissur**-680631, Kerala – **Tiesuru,**

Jammu & Kashmir, 28-3 Promenade Rd, **Tiruchirapalli**-620001, Tamilnadu – Sarojini Park, Palayamkottai, **Tirunelveli**-627006, Tamilnadu – **Tuensang**-798612, Nagaland – Lower Chandmari, **Tura**-794001, Meghalaya – Millerpuram, Playamkottai Road, **Tuticorin**-628008, Tamilnadu – Chetak Circle, **Udagamangalam**-643001, Nilgris, Tamilnadu – **Udaipur**-313001, Rajasthan – Brahmavar, **Udipi**-576213, Dakshina Kanara Dist., Karnataka – **Uttar Kashi**-249193, Uttarakhand –Mahmoorganj, **Varanasi**-221010, Uttar Pradesh – Bandar Rd, Punnammathota, **Vijayawada**-520010, Andhra Pradesh – Siripuram, **Visakhapatnam**-530003, Andhra Pradesh – **William Nagar**, Meghalaya – **Ziro**-791120, Lower Subansiri Dist., Arunachal Pradesh

Web addresses of AIR stns: Bengaluru: airbengaluru.com **Bhawanipatna:** airbpn.org **Cuttack:** aircuttack.com, cbscuttack.com **Guwahati:** airguwahati.gov.in **Jamshedpur:** airjamshedpur.in **New Delhi (Khampur):** hptkhampur.wix.com/airkhampur **Kota:** airkota. com **Panaji:** airpanaji.gov.in **Shillong:** airshillong.org **Shimla:** air-shimla.com **Siliguri:** airsiliguri.in **Thiruvanathapuram:** airtvm.com **Email:** ID of AIR stns is normally location followed by @air.org.in e.g.: hyderabad@air.org.in:

Regional Domestic SW stations:

kHz	kW	Station	H. of tr.
4760	10	Leh	s0130/w0213-0430, 1130-1630
4760	4	Port Blair	2355-0300, 1030-1700(Sat, Sun -1730)
4775†	50	Imphal	s0000/w0030-0215, 1030-1700/1730
4800	50	Hyderabad	0020-0215, 1130-1744
4810	50	Bhopal	0025-0215 1130-1741
4820	50	Kolkata	0025-0410 1130-1745
4835	10	Gangtok	0100-0500 1030-1600
4850†	50	Kohima	0000-0415 1000-1600/1630/1700
4860†	50	Shimla	0025-0200 1300-1741
4870#	100	Delhi (Kingsway)	0230-0330 1430-1530 (R. Sadaye Kashmir)
4880	50	Lucknow	0025-0430 (Sun 0415), 1215-1741
4895	50	Kurseong	0055-0430 1130-1700
4910	50	Jaipur	0025-0430, 1130-1741
4920	50	Chennai	0015-0245 1200-1739
4950†	50	Srinagar	s0030/w0120-0215 1120-1740 (2145v-2245v during Ramadan)
4970	50	Shillong	0025-0400 1056-1630
4990†	50	Itanagar	0020-0400 1000-1630
5010	50	Trivandrum	0020-0215 1130-1745
5040	50	Jeypore	0025-0445, 1130-1741
5050	10	Aizawl	0025-0400 1130-1630
6000	10	Leh	0700(Sun 0630)-0930
6020†	50	Shimla	0215-0410, 0700-0930 (Sun 0415-1030),1130-1230
6030	250	Delhi (Khampur)	0200-0230, 1215-1430
6040†	50	Jeypore	0446-0915
6065†	50	Kohima	0430-0510 0700-0900
6085	10	Gangtok	For special broadcasts in day time
6100	250	Delhi (Khampur)	0730-0830 (Radio Sadaye Kashmir)
6100	50	Delhi (Khampur)	0900-1200 (DRM)
6110†	50	Srinagar	0225-1115
6150†	50	Itanagar	0700-0900
6155	250	Delhi (Khampur)	1320-0043 (Nat. Ch.: ex 9425)
7210	50	Kolkata	0230-0400
7230	50	Kurseong	0620-1030
7250#	100	Delhi (Kingsway)	1130-1140
7270#	100	Chennai	0130-0430 (FM Gold)
7290	50	Trivandrum	0230-0930 (Sat , Sun 1030)
7295	10	Aizawl	0700-1000
7315	50	Shillong	0656-0931
7325	50	Jaipur	0630-0931
7335†	50	Imphal	0225-0400 (Sun 0430), 0630-1000
7340#	†100	Mumbai	1130-1140
7380	50	Chennai	0300-0930 (Sun 1130)
7390	4	Port Blair	0315-0400(SS -0500), 0700-0931(Sun -1000)
7420	50	Hyderabad	0225-0930 (Sun 1030)
7420#	100	Delhi (Kingsway)	1515-1600, 1730-1740
7430	50	Bhopal	0225-0932
7440	50	Lucknow	0700(Sun 0430)-1000
7505#	100	Delhi (Kingsway)	0230-0300: (ex 7520)
9380	250	Aligarh	0100-0430 0900-1200 (Vividh Bharati), 1320-0043 (National Channel)
9870	500	Benguluru	0025-0435, 0900-1200, 1245-1740 (Vividh Bharati)
9940	100	Delhi (Kingsway)	1130-1140
11620#	250	Delhi (Khampur)	1130-1140
15185	100	Delhi (Kinsway)	1130-1140

s = summer, w = winter, v = timing/frequency varies. † = irregular/off air, #= frequency also used by External Services at other times

N in English originating in New Delhi and relayed by most stns: 0035-0040, 0245-0300, 0630-0635, 0730-0735, 0830-0845, 0935-0940, 1030-1035, 1135-1140, 1230-1235, 1430-1435, 1435-1440(Sports), 1530-1545, 1730-1735. Extended broadc. for special events, important Parliament sessions, sports and on January 26 (Republic Day) and August 15 (Independence Day)
V. by QSL-card. Reception Reports to: ✉ Dy. Director General (Spectrum Management & Synergy), All India Radio, Room No.204, Akashvani Bhavan, New Delhi-110001 ☎ 91-11-23421062, 23421145 **E:** spectrum-manager@air.org.in . Local stns also verify directly in many cases by letter or email. No return postage necessary.

Addresses of SW stations (Reception reports may be addressed to the Station Engineer):
1) Aizawl: R. Tila, Tuikhuahtlang, Box 13, Aizawl-796001 ☎+91 389 2322415 **E:** aizawl@air.org.in – **2) Aligarh**: Anoopshahar Road, Aligarh-202001, Uttar Pradesh ☎+91 571 2700972 **E:** aligarh@air.org.in – **3) Bengaluru**: Super Power Transmitters, Yelahanka New Town, Bengaluru-560064, Karnataka ☎+91 80 27601149 **E:** sptair-ynk@rediffmail.com – **4) Bhopal**: Shyamla Hills, Bhopal-462002, Madhya Pradesh ☎+91 755 2660088 **E:** bhopal@air.org.in – **5) Chennai**: S.M.Nagar PO, Avadi, Chennai-600062, Tamilnadu. Tel. 91 44 26383204. email : Chennai.avadi@air.org.in – **6) Gangtok**: Old MLA Hostel, Gangtok-737101, Sikkim ☎+91 3592 202636 **E:** gangtok@air.org.in – **7) Hyderabad**: Rocklands, Saifabad, Hyderabad-500004, Telangana ☎+91 40 23234904. **E:** airhyderabad@rediffmail.com – **8) Imphal**: Palace Compound Imphal-795001, Manipur ☎+91 385 2450534 **E:** imphal@air.org.in – **9) Itanagar**: 'C' Sector, Itanagar-791111, Arunachal Pradesh ☎+91 360 2213007 **E:** itanagar@air.org.in – **10) Jaipur**: 5 Park House, Mirza Ismail Road, Jaipur-302001, Rajasthan ☎.91 141 2366263 **E:** jaipur@air.org.in – **11) Jeypore**:764005, Odisha ☎+91 6854 232524 **E:** jeypore@air.org.in – **12) Kohima**:797001, Nagaland ☎+91 370 2245556 **E:** kohima@air.org.in – **13) Kolkata**: Eden Gardens, Kolkata-700001, Paschim Banga ☎+91 33 22481705 **E:** kolkata@air.org.in – **14) Kurseong**: Mehta Club Bldg, Kurseong-734203, Darjeeling Dist., Paschim Banga ☎+91 354 2344350 **E:** kurseong@air.org.in – **15) Leh**: Leh-194101, Ladakh Dist., Jammu & Kashmir ☎+91 1982 252063 **E:** leh@air.org.in – **16) Lucknow**:18 Vidhan Sabha Marg, Lucknow-226001, Uttar Pradesh ☎+91 522 2237476 **E:** lucknow@air.org.in – **17) Mumbai**: Marve Road, Malwani, Malad West, Mumbai 400095, Maharashtra. ☎+91 22 28882867. **E:** mumbai.malad@air.org.in – **18A) New Delhi**: High Power Transmitters, Khampur, New Delhi -110036 ☎+91 11 27831474 **E:** hptkhampur@gmail.com **W:** wix.com/hptkhampur/airkhampur – **18B)** High Power Transmitters, Kingsway, New Delhi-110009 ☎+91 11 27606661 **E:** delhi.kingsway@air.org.in – **19) Panaji**: Goa University PO, Panaji-403206 ☎+91 832 2459096 **E:** panaji.spt@air.org.in – **20) Port Blair**: Haddo Post, Dilanipur, Port Blair-744102, Andaman & Nicobar Islands ☎+91 3192 230682 **E:** airportblair@rediffmail.com – **21) Shillong**: North Eastern Service, Pomdngiem, Opposite GPO, Shillong-793001, Meghalaya ☎ +91 364 2224443 **W:** airshillong.org **E:** shillong@air.org.in – **22) Shimla**: Choura Maidan, Shimla-171004, Himachal Pradesh ☎+91 177 2811355 **W:** airshimla.com **E:** shimla@air.org.in – **23) Srinagar**: R. Kashmir, Sherwani Rd, Srinagar-190001, Jammu & Kashmir ☎+91 194 2452100 **E:** srinagar@air.org.in – **24) Thiruvanathapuram**: Bhakti Vilas, Vazuthacaud, Thiruvanathapuram-695014, Kerala ☎+91 471 2325009 **W:** airtvm.com **E:** thiruvananthapuram@air.org.in

FM: b) FM Rainbow c) Vividh Bharati g) FM Gold r) relay stn

MHz	location	kW	reg	MHz	location	kW	reg
93.9	Vadodara	10	W, c	100.3	Jaipur B	6	N, c
96.7	Ahmedabad	10	W, c	100.3	Jammu A	3	N
100.1	Ahmednagar	6	W	100.3	Karaikal	6	S
100.1	Bengaluru	3	S	100.3	Mangalore	10	S
100.1	Dehradun	10	N	100.4	Bareilly	6	N
100.1	Gorakhpur	10	N, c	100.4	Cuttack	6	E, c
100.1	Keonjhar	10	E	100.4	Mandla	1	W, c
100.1	Kothagudem	6	S	100.5	Chennai	10	S, c
100.1	New Delhi	10	N, c	100.5	Dhule	6	W
100.2	Adilabad	10	S	100.5	Hospet	10	S
100.2	Darjeeling	10	E	100.5	Kodaikanal	10	S, b
100.2	Haflong	6	NE	100.6	Berhampur	6	E
100.2	Kolkata	20	E, g	100.6	Jalandhar	6	N, c
100.2	Patiala	6	N	100.6	Mysore	6	S
100.2	Shivpuri	6	W	100.6	Nagpur	10	W, c
100.3	Allahabad	10	N, c	100.6	Sangli	1	W
100.3	Asansol	6	E, r	100.6	Varanasi	10	N,c

MHz	location	kW	reg	MHz	location	kW	reg
100.7	Aizawl	6	NE	102.3	Kochi A	10	S
100.7	Churu	6	N	102.3	Kurseong	5	E, b
100.7	Lucknow	10	N, b	102.3	Lakhimpur Kheri	10	N, b
100.7	Mumbai	20	W, g	102.4	Akola	6	W
100.7	Poonch	6	N	102.4	Kurnool	6	S
100.7	Raigarh	6	W, c	102.4	Rajkot	10	W, c
100.7	Rajgarh	3	W	102.4	Tezpur	1	NE
100.8	Guwahati	10	NE, c	102.5	Dharmapuri	10	S
100.8	Jamshedpur	6	E, c	102.5	Kullu	6	N, r
100.9	Chandigarh	10	N	102.5	Mumbai	5	W, c
100.9	Mokokchung	6	NE	102.5	Patna	10	E, c
100.9	Port Blair	10	S, c	102.5	Ujjain	5	W, c
101.0	Bhaderwah	6	N	102.6	Chitradurga	6	S
101.0	Nagercoil	10	S	102.6	New Delhi	20	N, b
101.0	Pune	10	W, c	102.6	Rourkela	6	E
101.0	Suryapet	1	S, r	102.6	Sagar	5	W
101.1	Bathinda	6	N	102.6	Srinagar	10	N, c
101.1	Jowai	6	NE	102.7	Tirunelveli	10	S
101.1	Nanded	6	W	102.7	Jalandhar	10	N,b
101.1	Surat	10	W, c	102.7	Kolhapur	6	W
101.1	Thrissur	1	S	102.7	Manjeri	10	S, b
101.1	Tuticorin	1	S	102.7	Nagaon	6	NE
101.2	Banda	10	N	102.7	Obra	6	N
101.2	Jaipur	10	N	102.7	Srikakulam	1	S
101.2	Khandwa	6	W	102.7	Yavatmal	6	W
101.2	Mahabubnagar	10	S, r	102.8	Hyderabad	10	S, c
101.3	Aligarh	6	N, br	102.8	Puducherry	10	S,b
101.3	Balaghat	6	W	102.8	Rae Bareilly	5	N, b
101.3	Banswara	10	N	102.8	Saraipalli	1	W, c
101.3	Bengaluru	10	S, b	102.9	Baripada	6	E
101.3	Cuttack	6	E, b	102.9	Beed	6	W
101.3	Dibrugarh	1	NE	102.9	Bengaluru	10	S, c
101.3	Osmanabad	6	W	102.9	Chittorgarh	10	N
101.4	Chennai	10	S, b	102.9	Jabalpur	10	W
101.4	Churachandpur	6	NE	102.9	Rampur	1	N, c
101.4	Devikulam	6	S	103.0	Chandrapur	6	W
101.4	Kurukshetra	10	N	103.0	Coimbatore	10	S, b,c
101.4	Nashik	6	W	103.0	Daltonganj	6	E
101.4	Siliguri	10	E, c	103.0	Dharwad	10	S, c
101.5	Amravati	10	W,cr	103.0	Gangtok	10	NE
101.5	Kannur	6	S	103.0	Jhansi	10	N
101.5	Markapur	6	S	103.0	Kohima	10	NE
101.5	Ratnagiri	1	W	103.1	Alwar	10	N
101.5	Sawai Madhopur	6	N	103.1	Amethi	5	N, b
101.6	Agartala	10	NE, c	103.1	Betul	6	W
101.6	Indore	10	W, c	103.1	Chandigarh	6	N, c
101.6	Lucknow	10	N, c	103.1	Itanagar	10	NE
101.6	Raipur	10	W	103.1	Macherla	3	S
101.7	Anantapur	6	S	103.1	Madikeri	6	S
101.7	Aurangabad	10	W, c	103.1	Satara	6	W
101.7	Chaibasa	6	E	103.1	Shanthi Nikethan	3	E
101.7	Junagadh	10	W	103.2	Bilaspur	6	W
101.7	Udaipur	10	N, c	103.2	Jhalawar	6	N
101.8	Bijapur	6	S	103.2	Kailashahar	6	NE
101.8	Hamirpur	6	N	103.2	Nizamabad	6	S
101.8	Jaisalmer	10	N	103.2	Tirupati-I	10	S
101.8	Kolkata	10	E, c	103.3	Bellary	10	S
101.9	Bolangir	6	E	103.3	Dhubri	6	NE, r
101.9	Faizabad	6	N	103.3	Madurai	10	S
101.9	Hyderabad	10	S, b	103.3	Ranchi	10	E, c
101.9	Lungleh	6	NE	103.4	Dharamsala	10	N
101.9	Rajouri	10	N, r	103.4	Jorhat	10	NE
101.9	Trivandrum	10	S, c	103.4	Puri	3	E
102.0	Rairangpur	1	E	103.4	Sasaram	6	E
102.0	Parbhani	1	W	103.4	Solapur	6	W
102.0	Shahdol	6	W	103.4	Vijayawada	1	S, b
102.0	Visakhapatnam	10	S, b	103.5	Bhadravathi	1	S
102.1	Hazaribagh	6	E	103.5	Bhopal	5	W, c
102.1	Jodhpur	10	N, c	103.5	Chennai	10	S, c
102.1	Mussoorie	10	N, br	103.5	Imphal	10	NE c
102.1	Raichur	6	S	103.5	Mount Abu	6	N
102.1	Tiruchirapalli	10	S, b,c	103.5	Rohtak	10	N, c
102.2	Chindwara	6	W	103.5	Srinagar	10	N
102.2	Godhra	6	W	103.5	Warangal	10	S
102.2	Hassan	6	S	103.6	Jeypore	1	E
102.2	Kathua	10	N	103.6	Kozhikode	10	S, c
102.2	Maunath Bhanjan	10	N	103.6	Kadapa	10	S
102.2	Murshidabad	6	E	103.6	Oros	6	W
102.2	Vijayawada	10	S, c	103.6	Shillong	10	NE, b
102.3	Chennai	20	S, g	103.6	Belonia	10	NE
102.3	Daman	3	W	103.7	Gulbarga	6	S,c
102.3	Guna	6	W	103.7	Kanpur	10	N
102.3	Hissar	6	N	103.7	Nagaur	10	N
102.3	Karimnagar	5	S	103.7	Purnea	10	E
102.3	Karwar	3	S	103.7	Shimla	10	N, c

MHz	location	kW	reg	MHz	location	kW	reg
104.5	Jammu B	10	N, c	107.1	Mumbai	20	W, b
105.4	Panaji	6	W, b	107.2	Kasauli	10	N, bar
106.4	New Delhi	20	N, g	107.5	Kochi B	10	S, c
106.6	Bikaner	10	N	107.5	Tirupati II	3	S
107.0	Kolkata	20	E, b				

+ about 200 relay stns of 100W operating mostly on 100.1 MHz

NB: AWR, FEBA, R. Atmeeya Yatra, TWR etc. also broadcasting via AIR stns on MW, SW & FM.

F.PI: 1kW: Relay stations in 100 locations, Bomdila, Champai, Changlang, Cherapunjee, Daporijo, Gairsen, Goalpara, Karimganj, Khonsa, Kolasib, Lumding, New Tehri, Nutan Bazar, Phek, Roing, Tamenglong, Tuipang, Udaipur (Tripura), Ukhrul, Wokha, Zunheboto. **5kW:** Agra, Ajmer, Alappuzha, Amethi, Almora, Ambikapur, Bageshwar, Bhawanipatna, Bhuj, Chhatarpur, Gwalior, Jalgaon, Kurseong, Longtherai, Rewa, Sambalpur, Silchar, Tura. **6kW:** Replacement of 6kW txs at many locations. **10kW:** Bankatwa, Balurghat, Bardhaman, Champawat, Coochbehar, Etawah, Dhanbad, Forbesganj, Green Ridge, Haldwani, Himbotingla, Jayanagar, Kakinada, Kanpur, Kolkata, Krishna Nagar, Ludhiana, Meerut, Muzzafarpur, Naushera, Panaji, Patni Top, Ratlam, Raxaul, Suryapet & replacement of 10kW txs at many locations. **20kW:** Amritsar, Chautan Hill, Chennai, Fazilka, Kolkata, Mumbai, New Delhi, Rai Bareilly.

Addresses of FM stations (See also SW & MW stn addresses): **Adilabad**-504002, Telangana – **Ahmednagar**-414001, Maharashtra – **Akola**-444001, Maharashtra – Scheme No 6, Mangal Vihar, **Alwar**-301001, Rajasthan – **Amethi**, Uttar Pradesh – Tapovan Gate, Camp, **Amravati**-444602, Maharashtra – Near Collectorate, **Anantapur**-515001, Andhra Pradesh – **Asansol**-713301, Burdwan Dist., Paschim Banga – Jalna Rd, **Aurangabad**-431005, Maharashtra – **Aurangabad**-842101, Bihar – **Balaghat**-481001, Madhya Pradesh – **Banda**-210001, Uttar Pradesh – **Banswara**-327001, Rajasthan – No 15, Lal Phatak, Badaun Road, **Bareilly**-243004, Uttar Pradesh – **Baripada**-757001, Mayurbhanj Dist., Odisha – **Beed**-431122, Maharashtra – **Bellary**-583101, Karnataka – **Belonia**-799155, Tripura – **Berhampur**-760001, Ganjam Dist., Odisha – **Betul**-460001, Madhya Pradesh – **Bathinda**-151005, Punjab – **Bhaderwah**-182222, Doda Dist., Jammu & Kashmir – **Bijapur**-586101, Karnataka – Nutan Colony, **Bilaspur**-495001, Chhattisgarh – **Bolangir**-767001, Odisha – Tungri Maidan, **Chaibasa**-833201, Singhbhum Dist., Jharkhand – **Chandrapur**-442401, Maharashtra – Sector-19B, **Chandigarh**-160019 – **Chindwara**-480001, Madhya Pradesh – **Chitradurga**-577501, Karnataka – Sector 4, Gandhi Nagar, **Chittorgarh**-312001, Rajasthan – **Churu**-331001, Rajasthan – **Churachandpur**- 795128, Manipur – **Daltonganj**-822101, Jharkhand – Opp. Varkunt, Mota Fliya, **Daman**-396210, Daman & Diu – **Darjeeling**-734101, Paschim Banga – **Dehradun** 248001, Uttarakhand – **Devikulam**-685613, Idukki Dist., Kerala – **Dharmapuri**-636701, Tamilnadu – **Dharmasala**-176215, Kangra Dist., Himachal Pradesh – **Dhubri**-783301, Assam – **Dhule**-424001, Maharashtra – Begumganj Garahiya, **Faizabad**-224001, Uttar Pradesh – **Godhra**-389001, Gujarat – **Guna**-473001, Madhya Pradesh – Haflong-788819, Assam – Salagame Road, **Hassan**-573201, Karnataka – Jail Road, **Hazaribagh**-825301, Jharkhand – **Hissar**-125001, Haryana – **Hospet**-583201, Karnataka – Vyas Colony, **Jaisalmer**-345001, Rajasthan – Jungle Road, **Jhalawar**-326001, Rajasthan – Kanpur Road, **Jhansi**-284128, Uttar Pradesh – **Jorhat**-785001, Assam – **Jowai**-793150, Jaintia Hills, Meghalaya – **Junagadh**, Gujarat – **Kailashahar**-799277, Tripura – **Kannur**-670101, Kerala – Radio Avenue, Nehru Ngr., **Karaikal**-609606, Puducherri – **Kanpur**-208001, Uttar Pradesh – **Karimnagar**-505001, Telangana – **Karwar**-581301, Karnataka – **Kasauli**-173204, Solan Dist., Himachal Pradesh – **Kathua**-184104, Jammu & Kashmir – **Keonjhar**-758001, Odisha – **Khandwa**-450001, Nimar Dist., Madhya Pradesh – BMC PO, **Kochi**-682021, Ernakulam Dist., Kerala – Anandagiri, **Kodaikanal**-624101, Tamilnadu – Sardar Cly, Taravai Park, **Kolhapur**-416003, Maharashtra – Ramavaram, **Kothagudam**-507118, Khammam Dist., Telangana – **Kulu**-175101, Himachal Pradesh – Bellary Road, **Kurnool**-518003, Andhra Pradesh – **Kurushetra**-132118, Haryana – **Lakhimpur Kheri**-262701, Uttar Pradesh – **Lunglei**-796701, Mizoram – **Macherla**-522426, Guntur Dist, Andhra Pradesh – **Madikeri**-571201, Kodagu Dist., Karnataka – **Mahabubnagar**-509001, Telangana – Kadri Hills, **Mangalore**-575004, Dakshin Kanara Dist., Karnataka – **Manjeri**-676121, Kerala – **Mandla**-481661, Madhya Pradesh – **Markapur**-523316, Prakasam Dist., Andhra Pradesh – **Maunath Bhanjan**-275101, Mau Dist. Uttar Pradesh – **Mokokchung**-798601, Nagaland – **Mount Abu**-307501, Sirohi Dist., Rajasthan – **Murshidabad**-742101, Paschim Banga

– **Mussoorie**-248179, Dehradun Dist., Uttarakhand – Yadavagiri, Mysore-570020, Karnataka – **Nagaon**-782002, Assam – Basni Rd, **Nagaur**-341001, Rajasthan – Konam, **Nagercoil**-629001, Kanya Kumari Dist., Tamilnadu – Vasrania, **Nanded**-431601, Maharashtra – **Nashik**-422001, Maharashtra – **Nizamabad**-503012, Telangana – Tambri Vibhag, **Oros**-416812, Sindhudurg Dist, Maharashtra – **Osmanabad**-413501, Maharashtra – Phase-I, Urban Estate, Rajpura Rd, **Patiala**-147002, Punjab – **Poonch**-185101, Jammu & Kashmir – **Puri**-751001, Odisha – **Purnea**-854302, Bihar – **Rae Bareilly**-229001, Uttar Pradesh – **Raichur**-584101, Karnataka – Chote Atarmude, **Raigarh**-496001, Chhattisgarh – Kamla Nehru Marg, Civil Lines, **Raipur**-492001, Chhattisgarh – **Rairangpur**-757043, Mayurbhanj Dist., Odisha – **Rajgarh**-465661, Madhya Pradesh – **Rajouri**-185131, Jammu & Kashmir – **Rourkela**-769001, Odisha – **Sagar**-470001, Madhya Pradesh – **Saraipalli**-493558, Raipur, Chhattisgarh – **Sasaram**-821115, Rohtas Dist., Bihar – **Satara**-415001, Maharashtra – Pali Road, **Shahdol**-484001, Madhya Pradesh – **Shanthi Nikethan**, Paschim Banga – Physical College, **Shivpuri**-473551, Madhya Pradesh – **Solapur**-413006, Maharashtra – **Srikakulam**-532001, Andhra Pradesh – **Surat**-395001, Gujarat – **Suryapet**-508213, Nalgonda Dist., Telangana – **Swai Madhopur**-322001, Rajasthan – **Tirupati**-517501, Andhra Pradesh – **Ujjain**-456001, Madhya Pradesh – Makarpura Rd, **Vadadora**-390009, Gujarat – **Warangal**-506002, Telangana – **Yavatmal**-445001, Maharashtra.

EXTERNAL SERVICES: All India Radio
see International Broadcasting section

Private FM Stations:

Location	MHz	Station	Location	MHz	Station
Agartala	91.9	R.Ooo La La	Coimbatore	106.4	R. Hello 106.4 FM
Agra	91.9	R. Mantra	Cuttack	92.7	Big 92.7 FM
Agra	92.7	Big 92.7 FM	Cuttack	93.5	Red FM
Ahmedabad	91.1	R. City	Cuttack	104.0	R. Choklate
Ahmedabad	93.5	Red FM	Dhule	106.4	Dhamaal 24
Ahmedabad	94.3	My FM	Gangtok	91.9	Nine FM
Ahmedabad	98.3	R.Mirchi	Gangtok	93.5	Red FM
Ahmedabad	95.0	R. One	Gangtok	95.0	R. Misty
Ahmednagar	91.1	R. City	Gorakhpur	91.9	R. Mantra
Ahmednagar	106.4	Dhamaal 24	Gulbarga	93.5	Red FM
Aizawl	93.5	Red FM	Guwahati	91.9	R. Ooo La La
Ajmer	91.1	R. City	Guwahati	92.7	Big 92.7 FM
Ajmer	92.7	Big 92.7 FM	Guwahati	93.5	Red FM
Ajmer	94.3	My FM	Guwahati	94.3	Gup Shup
Akola	91.1	R. City	Gwalior	91.9	Suno Lemon
Aligarh	92.7	Big 92.7 FM	Gwalior	92.7	Big 92.7 FM
Allahabad	92.7	Big 92.7 FM	Gwalior	94.3	My FM
Allahabad	93.5	Red FM	Gwalior	95.0	Tadka 95 FM
Amritsar	92.7	Big 92.7 FM	Hissar	91.9	R. Mantra
Amritsar	94.3	My FM	Hissar	92.7	Big 92.7 FM
Amritsar	104.8	Oye FM	Hissar	104.0	R. Tarang
Asansol	92.7	Big 92.7 FM	Hissar	106.4	Dhamaal 24
Asansol	93.5	Red FM	Hyderabad	91.1	R. City
Aurangabad	93.5	Red FM	Hyderabad	92.7	Big 92.7 FM
Aurangabad	98.3	R. Mirchi	Hyderabad	93.5	Red FM
Bareilly	91.9	R. Mantra	Hyderabad	98.3	R. Mirchi
Bareilly	92.7	Big 92.7 FM	Indore	92.7	Big 92.7 FM
Bengaluru	91.1	R. City	Indore	93.5	Red FM
Bengaluru	91.9	R. Indigo	Indore	94.3	My FM
Bengaluru	92.7	Big 92.7 FM	Indore	98.3	R. Mirchi
Bengaluru	93.5	Red FM	Itanagar	91.9	R. Ooo La La
Bengaluru	94.3	R. One	Jabalpur	93.5	Red FM
Bengaluru	98.3	R. Mirchi	Jabalpur	94.3	My FM
Bengaluru	104.0	Fever FM	Jabalpur	98.3	R. Mirchi
Bhopal	92.7	Big 92.7 FM	Jabalpur	106.4	Dhamaal 24
Bhopal	93.5	Red FM	Jaipur	91.1	R. City
Bhopal	94.3	My FM	Jaipur	93.5	Red FM
Bhopal	98.3	R. Mirchi	Jaipur	94.3	My FM
Bikaner	92.7	Big 92.7 FM	Jaipur	95.0	Tadka 95 FM
Bilaspur	94.3	My FM	Jaipur	98.3	R. Mirchi
Chandigarh	92.7	Big 92.7 FM	Jalandhar	91.9	R. Mantra
Chandigarh	94.3	My FM	Jalandhar	92.7	Big 92.7 FM
Chennai	91.1	R. City	Jalandhar	94.3	My FM
Chennai	91.9	Aahaa FM	Jalandhar	98.3	R. Mirchi
Chennai	92.7	Big 92.7 FM	Jalgaon	91.1	R. City
Chennai	93.5	Suryan FM	Jalgaon	106.4	Dhamaal 24
Chennai	94.3	R. One	Jammu	92.7	Big 92.7 FM
Chennai	98.3	R. Mirchi	Jamshedpur	92.7	Big 92.7 FM
Chennai	104.8	Chennai Live	Jamshedpur	93.5	Red FM
Chennai	106.4	R. Hello 106.4 FM	Jamshedpur	104.8	R. Dhoom
Coimbatore	91.1	R. City	Jhansi	92.7	Big 92.7 FM
Coimbatore	93.5	Suryan FM	Jodhpur	92.7	Big 92.7 FM
Coimbatore	98.3	R. Mirchi	Jodhpur	94.3	My FM

Location	MHz	Station	Location	MHz	Station
Jodhpur	104.8	Oye FM	Puducherry	92.7	Big 92.7 FM
Kannur	91.9	R. Mango	Puducherry	93.5	Suryan FM
Kannur	93.5	Red FM	Puducherry	106.4	R. Hello 106.4 FM
Kannur	94.3	Club FM	Pune	91.1	R. City
Kannur	95.0	Best FM 95	Pune	93.5	Red FM
Kanpur	92.7	Big 92.7 FM	Pune	94.3	R. One
Kanpur	93.5	Red FM	Pune	98.3	R. Mirchi
Kanpur	98.3	R. Mirchi	Raipur	94.3	My FM
Karnal	91.9	R. Mantra	Raipur	95.0	Tadka 95 FM
Karnal	106.4	Dhamaal 24	Raipur	98.3	R. Mirchi
Kochi	91.9	R. Mango	Raipur	104.8	Rangila FM
Kochi	93.5	Red FM	Rajahmundry	93.5	Red FM
Kochi	94.3	Club FM	Rajkot	92.7	Big 92.7 FM
Kolhapur	94.3	Tomato FM	Rajkot	93.5	Red FM
Kolhapur	98.3	R. Mirchi	Rajkot	98.3	R. Mirchi
Kolkata	91.9	Friends FM	Ranchi	91.9	R. Mantra
Kolkata	92.7	Big 92.7 FM	Ranchi	92.7	Big 92.7 FM
Kolkata	93.5	Red FM	Ranchi	104.0	R. Tarang
Kolkata	94.3	R. One	Ranchi	104.8	R. Dhoom
Kolkata	98.3	R. Mirchi	Ranchi	106.4	Dhamaal 24
Kolkata	104.0	Fever FM	Rourkela	92.7	Big 92.7 FM
Kolkata	104.8	Oye FM	Rourkela	104.0	R. Choklate
Kolkata	106.2	Amar FM	Sangli	91.1	R. City
Kolkata	107.8	Power FM	Shillong	91.9	R. Ooo La La
Kota	92.7	Big 92.7 FM	Shillong	93.5	Red FM
Kota	94.3	My FM	Shimla	95.0	Big FM
Kota	95.0	Tadka 95 FM	Shimla	104.8	Oye FM
Kozhikode	91.9	R. Mango	Shimla	106.4	Dhamaal 24
Kozhikode	93.5	Red FM	Siliguri	92.7	High 92.7 FM
Lucknow	91.1	R. City	Siliguri	93.5	Red FM
Lucknow	92.7	Big 92.7 FM	Siliguri	94.3	R. Misty
Lucknow	93.5	Red FM	Solapur	91.1	R. City
Lucknow	98.3	R. Mirchi	Solapur	92.7	Big 92.7 FM
Madurai	93.5	Suryan FM	Srinagar	92.7	Big 92.7 FM
Madurai	98.3	R. Mirchi	Surat	91.1	R. City
Madurai	106.4	R. Hello 106.4 FM	Surat	92.7	Big 92.7 FM
Mangalore	92.7	Big 92.7 FM	Surat	94.3	My FM
Mangalore	93.5	Red FM	Surat	98.3	R. Mirchi
Mangalore	98.3	R. Mirchi	Trivandrum	92.7	Big 92.7 FM
Mumbai	91.1	R. City	Trivandrum	93.5	Red FM
Mumbai	92.7	Big 92.7 FM	Trivandrum	94.3	Club FM
Mumbai	93.5	Red FM	Trivandrum	98.3	R. Mirchi
Mumbai	94.3	R. One	Thrissur	91.1	Red FM
Mumbai	98.3	R. Mirchi	Thrissur	91.9	R. Mango
Mumbai	104.0	Fever FM	Thrissur	95.0	Best FM 95
Mumbai	104.8	Oye FM	Thrissur	104.8	Club FM
Muzzafarpur	106.4	Dhamaal 24	Tiruchirapalli	93.5	Suryan FM
Mysore	92.7	Big 92.7 FM	Tiruchirapalli	106.4	R. Hello 106.4 FM
Mysore	93.5	Red FM	Tirunelveli	93.5	Suryan FM
Nagpur	91.1	R. City	Tirunelveli	106.4	R. Hello 106.4 FM
Nagpur	93.5	Red FM	Tirupati	92.7	Big 92.7 FM
Nagpur	94.3	My FM	Tirupati	93.5	Red FM
Nagpur	98.3	R. Mirchi	Tuticorin	93.5	Suryan FM
Nanded	91.1	R. City	Tuticorin	106.4	R. Hello 106.4 FM
Nashik	93.5	Red FM	Udaipur	92.7	Big 92.7 FM
Nashik	98.3	R. Mirchi	Udaipur	94.3	My FM
New Delhi	91.1	R. City	Udaipur	95.0	Tadka 95 FM
New Delhi	92.7	Big 92.7 FM	Vadodara	91.1	R. City
New Delhi	93.5	Red FM	Vadodara	92.7	Big 92.7 FM
New Delhi	94.3	R. One	Vadodara	93.5	Red FM
New Delhi	95.0	Hit FM	Vadodara	98.3	R. Mirchi
New Delhi	98.3	R. Mirchi	Varanasi	91.9	R. Mantra
New Delhi	104.0	Fever FM	Varanasi	93.5	Red FM
New Delhi	104.8	Oye FM	Varanasi	98.3	R. Mirchi
Panaji	91.9	R. Indigo	Vijayawada	93.5	Red FM
Panaji	92.7	Big 92.7 FM	Vijayawada	98.3	R. Mirchi
Panaji	98.3	R. Mirchi	Visakhapatnam	91.1	R. City
Patiala	92.7	Big 92.7 FM	Visakhapatnam	92.7	Big 92.7 FM
Patiala	104.8	Oye FM	Visakhapatnam	93.5	Red FM
Patiala	106.4	Dhamaal 24	Visakhapatnam	98.3	R. Mirchi
Patna	98.3	R. Mirchi	Warangal	93.5	Red FM

F.PI: 839 New stns in 294 new cities

Web addresses: Aahaa FM: aahaafm.com **Big FM:** big927fm.com **Chennai Live:** chennailive.fm **Club FM:** clubfm.in **Dhamaal 24:** dhamaal24.com **Fever FM:** fever.fm **Friends FM:** 919friendsfm.blogspot.in **Hello 106.4 FM:** hello.fm **My FM:** myfmindia.com **Oye FM:** oyefm.in **Power FM:** power1078fm.com **R. Chaska:** radio-chaska.com **R. Choklate:** radiochoklate.com **R.City:** planetradiocity.com **Radio High:** radiohigh927fm.com/ **R. Indigo:** radioindigo.in **R. Mango:** radiomango.co.in **R.Manthra:** radiomanthra.co.in **R. Mirchi:** radiomirchi.com **R. One:** radioone.in **Radio Ooolala:** radio-ooolala.com **Red FM:** redfm.in **Suno Lemon:** sunolemonfm.com **Suryan**

FM: suryanfm.in

The following new Private FM stns will be on air in 2016:

Location	MHz	Station	Location	MHz	Station
Agartala	92.7	Big FM	Jodhpur	93.5	
Agra	93.7	Fever FM	Kanpur	91.9	Radio Mirchi
Agra	94.5	Tadka FM	Kanpur	95.0	Fever FM
Ahmedabad	94.0	Radio Mirchi	Kanpur	104.8	Radio City
Ahmednagar	104.0		Karnal	94.5	
Ahmednagar	92.7	Big FM	Kochi	104.0	Radio Mirchi
Aizawl	92.7	Big FM	Kolhapur	95.0	Radio City
Ajmer	104.8	Radio City	Kolhapur	92.7	Big FM
Ajmer	106.4	Tadka FM	Kota	91.1	Radio City
Akola	91.9		Kozhikode	92.7	Radio Mirchi
Akola	94.3		Kozhikode	104.8	Club FM
Aligarh	94.9	Fever FM	Lucknow	107.2	Radio Mirchi
Aligarh	104.6	Tadka FM	Lucknow	104.0	Fever FM
Aligarh	94.1		Lucknow	92.7	Big FM
Allahabad	94.3	Fever FM	Madurai	91.9	Radio City
Allahabad	106.4	Tadka FM	Mumbai	106.4	
Aurangabad	94.3		Mumbai	91.9	Fever FM
Aurangabad	92.7	Big FM	Muzzafarpur	94.3	
Bareilly	94.3	Fever FM	Muzzafarpur	91.9	Tadka FM
Bareilly	91.1	Tadka FM	Muzzafarpur	92.7	Big FM
Bengaluru	95.0	Radio Mirchi	Nagpur	91.9	Radio Mirchi
Bhubaneswar	91.9		Nagpur	92.7	Big FM
Bikaner	94.3		Nanded	94.3	
Bikaner	91.1	Radio City	Nashik	104.2	
Bikaner	95.0	Tadka FM	Nashik	95.0	Radio City
Bilaspur	91.9		New Delhi	107.2	Fever FM
Bilaspur	92.7		Patiala	107.2	Radio City
Bilaspur	91.1	Tadka FM	Patna	91.1	Radio City
Chandigarh	98.3	Radio Mirchi	Patna	95.0	Big FM
Dhule	95.0		Pune	104.2	Radio Mirchi
Gorkahpur	94.3	Fever FM	Pune	95.0	Big FM
Gorkahpur	91.1	Tadka FM	Rajkot	94.3	
Gorkahpur	92.7	Big FM	Rourkela	98.3	
Guwahati	95.0	Radio Mirchi	Rourkela	91.9	
Hisar	94.5		Sangli	104.0	
Hyderabad	95.0	Radio Mirchi	Shillong	91.1	Radio Mirchi
Hyderabad	104.0	Radio Mirchi	Shillong	98.3	Big FM
Hyderabad	94.3	Fever FM	Solapur	95.0	
Itanagar	92.7	Big FM	Solapur	104.8	Tadka FM
Jaipur	104.0	Radio Mirchi	Srinagar	93.5	
Jalgaon	94.3		Srinagar	98.3	Radio Mirchi
Jalgaon	98.3	Tadka FM	Srinagar	95.0	Tadka FM
Jammu	98.3	Radio Mirchi	Surat	91.9	Radio Mirchi
Jammu	95.0	Tadka FM	Udaipur	91.9	Radio City
Jamshedpur	91.1	Radio City	Varanasi	95.0	Big FM
Jhansi	91.1	Tadka FM			

Gyan Vani (Educational FM Channel)

Electronic Media Production Centre, Sanchar Kendra, Indira Gandhi National Open University (IGNOU), Maidan Garhi, New Delhi110068 ☎ 911129533079, 911129534299 **E:** gyandarshan@ignou.ac.in **W:** www.ignou.ac.in/ignou/aboutignou/broadcast/schedule/schedule

Location	MHz	kW	Location	MHz	kW
Agra	105.6	10	Lucknow	105.6	10
Ahmedabad	105.6	6	Madurai	105.6	10
Allahabad	107.4	10	Mumbai	105.6	10
Aurangabad	105.6	10	Mysore	105.6	10
Bengaluru	106.4	10	Nagpur	105.6	10
Bhopal	105.0	10	New Delhi	105.6	10
Chandigarh	105.6	10	Panaji	107.8	10
Chennai	105.6	10	Patna	105.6	10
Coimbatore	91.9	10	Pune	105.6	10
Cuttack	105.6	10	Raipur	105.6	10
Hyderabad	105.6	10	Rajkot	105.6	10
Indore	105.6	10	Shillong	103.6	10
Guwahati	107.8	10	Srinagar	107.8	10
Jabalpur	105.6	10	Trivandrum	105.6	10
Jaipur	105.6	10	Tiruchirapalli	104.8	10
Jalandhar	105.6	10	Tirunelveli	105.6	10
Kanpur	106.4	10	Varanasi	105.6	10
Kochi	105.6	10	Visakhapatnam	106.4	10
Kolkata	105.4	10			

NB: Txs located at and maintained by AIR.

Community FM Radio Stations: Over 184 stns run by Educational Institutions, NGOs and others with 50W on **FM (MHz):** 90.4, 90.8, 91.2, 96.9, 106.8, 107.2, 107.4 and 107.8. **F.PI.** More community stns by different institutions.

INDONESIA

LT: We. Indonesia (Java, Sumatra, We. & Ce. Kalimantan): UTC +7h; Ce. Indonesia (So. & Ea. Kalimantan, Sulawesi, Bali, Nusa Tenggara): UTC +8h; Ea. Indonesia (Maluku, Papua): UTC +9h — **Pr.L**: Bahasa Indonesia (Indonesian), Javanese, Sundanese and over 700 others — **Pop**: 253.3 million — **E.C**: 50 Hz, 230V — **ITU**: INS

DIRECTORATE GENERAL OF POSTS & TELECOMMUNICATIONS (Direktorat Jenderal Pos dan Telekomunikasi)
✉ Gedung Sapta Pesona, Medan Merdeka Barat 17, Jakarta 10110 ☎ +62 21 3835955 🖷 +62 21 3860754 **W**: postel.go.id **E**: admin@postel.go.id

INDONESIAN BROADCASTING COMMISSION (Komisi Penyiaran Indonesia, KPI)
✉ Gedung Sekretariat Negara Lt VI, Jl. Gajah Mada 8, Jakarta 10120 ☎ +62 21 6340713 🖷 +62 21 6340667 **W**: kpi.go.id
LP: Head: Mr Judhariksawan. Dep. Head: Mr Idy Muzayyad

RADIO REPUBLIK INDONESIA (RRI) (Gov.)
National Station: RRI, Jakarta ✉ Jl. Medan Merdeka Barat 4-5, Jakarta 10110, or Tromolpos 1157 (or Kotak Pos 356), Jakarta 10001 ☎ +62 21 3842083 🖷 +62 21 3457132 **W**: rri.co.id **E**: info@rri.co.id
LP: Man. Dir.: Ms Rosarita Niken Widiastuti, Dir. of Tech. & New Media: Mr Muhammad Rohanudin
Pro 1 (Prosatu): Information and entertainment on 91.2MHz **Pro 2 (Produa)**: Prgrs for young people on 105.0MHz **Pro 3 (Protiga)**: National news network on 999kHz, 88.8MHz 24h, also relayed in full on FM by most regional stns. N: on the h. Sports N. (Berita Olahraga): 0400, 0800. **Pro 4 (Proempat)**: Educational and cultural prgrs on 1332kHz, 92.8MHz 24h. Relays Pro 3 1700-2200
Local Stations: Pro 1 (music and information), Pro 2 (for young people), Pro 3 (relay of Pro 3 Jakarta), Pro 4 (education and culture). MW and SW freqs below carry the local Pro 1 sce except where marked "3" or "4". **H** of tr: Pro 3 24h, others usually 0430/0500-2400 local time

MW	kHz	kW	Station		MW	kHz	kW	Station
JB01)	540	10	Bandung 4		SH01)	1035		Palu
JT01)	585	50	Surabaya 4		PA04)	1044	2	Biak
SL01)	630	50	Makassar		ST02)	1044	10	Tahuna
PB01)	702	10	Manokwari		SU02)	1044	10	Sibolga
MA01)	720	10	Ambon		PA01)	1053	10	Jayapura
PA06)	729	10	Nabire		BA02)	1080	10	Singaraja
BE01)	747	10	Bengkulu		JA01)	1098	10	Jambi
JH03)	756	10	Purwokerto		JT05)	1098	10	Sumenep
MA02)	765	1	Tual		NT01)	1107	5	Kupang
PB02)	774		Fak-Fak		YG01)	1107	10	Yogyakarta 4
NT02)	783	10	Ende		KS01)	‡1134	25	Banjarmasin 4
JH01)	801	10	Semarang		SB01)	1179	10	Padang
SU01)	801	50	Medan 4		ST01)	1188	10	Manado 4
PA02)	810	7.5	Merauke		KH01)	1197	10	Palangkaraya
NB01)	855	10	Mataram		JB01)	1215		Bandung 3
JB03)	864	10	Cirebon		KT01)	1215	10	Samarinda
JT02)	‡891	10	Malang		KB01)	1233	5	Pontianak
MU01)	891	10	Ternate		JB02)	1242	10	Bogor
PB03)	909	10	Sorong		AC01)	1251	10	Banda Aceh
RI01)	927	25	Pekanbaru 4		SS01)	1287	25	Palembang
SG01)	954	10	Kendari		JK01)	1332	10	Jakarta 4
JT03)	963	10	Jember		KR01)	1341	5	Tanjung Pinang
JH02)	972	50	Surakarta		KU01)	1350	10	Tarakan
JK01)	999	150	Jakarta 3		SH02)	1377	10	Tolitoli
G001)	1008	10	Gorontalo		PA05)	1395	1	Wamena
JT04)	1008	10	Madiun		BB01)	1413	5	Sungai Liat
PA03)	1026	5	Serui		SB02)	1512	10	Bukittinggi
LA01)	1035	5	Bandar Lampung					

SW	kHz	kW	Station, h. of tr.
KH01)	3325	10	Palangkaraya: 2200-0100, 0900-1700
MU01)	‡v3345	10	Ternate irr.
PA02)	3905		Merauke
SH01)	‡v3960		Palu: 2000-2400, 0900-1600 irr.
SL01)	4750	20	Makassar 4: 2100-0200, 0800-1600
PB02)	‡4790		Fak-Fak irr.
PA05)	4870		Wamena: 2000-2315, 0800-1500
PA06)	‡6125		Nabire
PA06)	v7290		Nabire: 2200-2300, 0500-0830v
JK01)	‡9680	250	Jakarta 4 (Cimanggis): 2200-1500v

NB: ‡ = r. inactive at editorial deadline. During the Muslim fasting month of Ramadan several stns begin morning transmissions as early as 1800.

Addresses (Jl = Jalan). All **FM**: in MHz. FM freqs are listed in order of prgr (Pro 1, Pro 2, Pro 3, Pro4) exc. where noted. Local FM relays are marked after + and generally carry Pro-1.
AC01) Jl Sultan Iskandar Muda 13, P.O. Box 112, Banda Aceh 23423, Nanggroe Aceh Darussalam – **FM**: 97.7/92.6/87.8/88.6 + 90.5 Tapaktuan, 91.9 Langsa, 92.0 Sinabang, 92.3 Kutacane, 93.0 Subulussalam, 95.1 Lamno, 97.3 Jantho, 97.5 Calang, 99.7 Beuneuruan – **AC02)** Jl Peutua Ibrahim 75, Teumpok Teungoh, Lhokseumawe 24352, Nanggroe Aceh Darussalam – **FM**: 89.3/100.9/95.2 – **AC03)** RRI Sabang, Jl Yos Sudarso 65, Cot Bak U, Kecamatan Sukajaya, Sabang, Nanggroe Aceh Darussalam – **FM**: 94.0 – **AC04)** RRI Takengon, Jl Lembaga Kemili, Takengon, Aceh Tengah, Nanggroe Aceh Darussalam – **FM**: 93.0 – **AC05)** RRI Meulaboh, Meulaboh, Nanggroe Aceh Darussalam – **FM**: 97.0 (Pro 1)/88.7 (Pro 3) – **AC06)** RRI Singkil, Singkil, Nanggroe Aceh Darussalam – **FM**: 92.2
BA01) Jl Hayam Wuruk 70, Keladis, Denpasar 80233 (Kotak Pos 31, Denpasar 80001), Bali - **FM**: 88.6/95.3/93.0/100.0 + 99.5 Tamblingan, 100.9 Karangasem – **BA02)** Jl Gajah Mada 144, Tromolpos 153, Singaraja 81113, Bali - **FM**: 97.9/103.7/102.0
BB01) Jl Jend Ahmad Yani, Sungai Liat 33211, Bangka, Bangka Belitung - **FM**: 96.4/101.4/97.2 + 90.4 Toboali, 95.4 Mentok, 95.5 Tanjung Pandan, 99.8 Pangkalpinang
BE01) Jl Let Jend S Parman 25, Kotak Pos 13, Bengkulu 38227, Bengkulu - **FM**: 92.5/105.1/90.9 + 95.4 Muko-Muko, 97.0 Bintuhan, 98.0 Curup, 101.3 Ipuh
BN01) RRI Banten, Kompleks Pendopo Gubernur Banten, Serang, Banten - **FM**: 94.9
G001) Jl Jenderal Sudirman 30, Gorontalo 96128, Gorontalo - **FM**: 101.8/92.4/96.7 + 92.5 Baroko, 94.9 Paguyaman, 97.0 Marisa **JA01)** Jl Jendral A Yani 5, Telanaipura, Jambi 36122, Jambi - **FM**: 88.5/90.9/94.4 + 95.8 Bangko, 99.0 Kualatungkal, 99.0 Sarolangun, 99.8 Sungai Penuh, 99.8 Tungkal Ilir, 101.0 Muara Bungo – **JA02)** RRI Sungai Penuh, Sungai Penuh, Jambi – **FM**: 97.1/101.0
JB01) Jl Diponegoro 61, Bandung 40122 (Kotak Pos 1055, Bandung 40001), Jawa Barat – **FM**: 97.6/96.0 + 95.0 Gunung Malang, 97.0 Purwakarta/Subang, 97.8 Tasikmalaya, 98.0 Bayah, 98.2 Puncak Surangga, 98.9 Saketi, 102.5 Cikuray, 103.3 Garut – **JB02)** Jl Pangrango 30, P.O Box 232, Bogor 16161, Jawa Barat – **FM**: 93.7/106.8 – **JB03)** Jl Brigjen Dharsono/By Pass, Cirebon 45132, Jawa Barat - **FM**: 93.7/94.8/97.5
JH01) Jl Ahmad Yani 144-146, Kotak Pos 1307, Semarang 50241, Jawa Tengah - **FM**: 89.0/95.3/88.2/91.4 + 94.2 Colo, 96.7 Batang, 97.7 Gunung Gantungan) 99.4 Gunung Depok, 99.5 Gunung Perikisa – **JH02)** Jl Abdul Rahman Saleh 51, Kotak Pos 40, Surakarta 57133, Jawa Tengah - **FM**: 105.5/97.0/95.1 + 96.3/102.0 Tawangmangu – **JH03)** Jl Jendral Sudirman 427, Kotak Pos 5, Purwokerto 53116, Jawa Tengah - **FM**: 93.1/99.0/107.3
JK01) Jl Medan Merdeka Barat 4-5, Jakarta 10110 (Tromolpos 1157, Jakarta 10001).
JT01) Jl Pemuda 82-90, Kotak Pos 239, Surabaya 60271, Jawa Timur - **FM**: 99.2/95.2/106.3/96.8 + 91.1 Cemoro Lawang, 97.9 Pacitan, 99.2 Alas Malang, 99.2 Pare, 102.3 Pulau Bawean; Studio 5 (additional music sce for Surabaya area): 91.7MHz – **JT02)** Jl Candi Panggung 58, Kotak Pos 78, Mojolangu, Malang 65142, Jawa Timur - **FM**: 91.5/87.9/94.6/105.3 – **JT03)** Jl D.I Panjaitan 61, Jember 68110 (Kotak Pos 166, Jember 68101), Jawa Timur - **FM**: 95.4/89.5/87.9 – **JT04)** Jl Mayjen Panjaitan 10-12, Madiun 63133, Jawa Timur - **FM**: 99.7/97.7/104.0 + 96.3 Kemiri – **JT05)** Jl Urip Sumoharjo 26, Sumenep 69411, Madura, Jawa Timur - **FM**: 98.5/101.3/103.0 – **JT06)** RRI Sampang, Jl Peliang Km 2, Torjun, Sampang, Madura, Jawa Timur - **FM**: 93.1 – **JT06)** RRI Kediri, Pare – Kediri, Jawa Timur - **FM**: 100.2
KB01) Jl Jendral Sudirman 7, Kotak Pos 6, Pontianak 78111, Kalimantan Barat - **FM**: 104.2/101.8/90.3 + 95.0 Nanggamerakai, 96.8 Ketapang, 97.0 Sanggau) 97.7 Sambas, 97.7 Singkawang, 98.0 Kendawangan, 98.2 Semitau, 99.3 Sanggau Ledo, 100.2 Balaikarangan – **KB02)** RRI Sintang, Jl Oevang Oeraya, Baning, Sintang, Kalimantan Barat - **FM**: 96.6/90.7/102.5 – **KB03)** RRI Entikong, Jl Lintas Negara Indonesia-Malaysia, Entikong – Sanggau, Kalimantan Barat - **FM**: 100.2
KH01) Jl M Husni Thamrin 1, Palangkaraya 73112, Kalimantan Tengah - **FM**: 89.2/92.4/95.9 + 93.6 Kuala Kapuas, 93.6 Sampit, 96.0 Muara Teweh, 97.1 Pulang Pisau, 97.3 Buntok, 99.2 Pangkalan Bun
KR01) Jl Ahmad Yani KM 5, Kotak Pos 8, Tanjung Pinang 29133, Bintan, Kepulauan Riau - **FM**: 98.3/92.1/101.3 + 96.6 Karimun, 99.6 Terempa – **KR02)** RRI Ranai, Jl Sepempang, Ranai, Pulau Natuna Besar /29183, Kepulauan Riau - **FM**: 90.0/105.9/104.0 – **KR03)** RRI Batam, Komplek Politeknik Batam, Batam Centre, Batam, Kepulauan Riau - **FM**: 105.1/105.5/90.9
KS01) Jl Jenderal A. Yani Km 3.5 No 234, Kotak Pos 117, Banjarmasin

70234, Kalimantan Selatan - **FM**: 97.6/95.2/92.5/87.7 + 89.4 Batu Licin, 90.2 Kotabaru, 90.7 Amuntai, 99.6 Banjarbaru,105.7 Kandangan
KT01) Jl Moh Yamin 8, P.O Box 45, Samarinda 75110, Kalimantan Timur - **FM**: 97.6/88.5/98.4 + 95.5 Pulau Sebatik, 96.0 Penajam, 96.7 Berau, 96.8 Tanah Grogot, 97.0 Balikpapan, 97.4 Melak, 97.4 Bontang/ Sangata, 99.0 Tenggarong – **KT02)** RRI Sendawar, Jl D.I. Panjaitan 61, Dusun Busur, Kampung Barong Tongkok, Sendawar, Kutai Barat, Kalimantan Timur - **FM**: 103.3 – **KT03)** RRI Long Bagun, Mahakam Hulu, Kalimantan Timur **FM**: freq. not yet conf.
KU01) Jl Sungai Mahakam 10, Kampung Empat, Tarakan Timur 77125, Kalimantan Utara - **FM**: 97.9/101.9/88.8 – **KU02)** Jl Pelajar Perumda II, Malinau, Kalimantan Utara - **FM**: 95.5 – **KU03)** Jl TVRI 77, Nunukan, Kalimantan Utara - **FM**: 97.1
LA01) Jl Gatot Subroto 26, Kotak Pos 24, Pahoman, Bandar Lampung 35213, Lampung - **FM**: 90.9/92.5/87.7 + 95.8 Kotabumi, 97.0 Kota Agung, 99.0 Simpang Pematang, 99.4 Liwa, 99.7 Padang Cermin, 100.2 Tulungbawang – **LA02)** Way Kanan, Lampung- FM: 103.6
MA01) Jl Jendral Akhmad Yani 1, Ambon 97124; Maluku - **FM**: 95.4/98.4/102.0 + 92.0 Amahai/Masohi, 94.3 Saumlaki – **MA02)** Jl Sukarno-Hatta, Kec Wat Deh, Tual 97661, Pulau Kai, Maluku - **FM**: 93.2/97.6/103.6 – **MA03)** RRI Bula, Seram Bagian Timur, Maluku **FM**: freq. not yet conf.
MU01) Jl Sultan Khairun 2, Kedaton, Ternate 97720, Maluku Utara - **FM**: 101.8/96.7/104.1 + 92.8 Pulau Morotai, 93.7 Soasiu
NB01) Komplek Perumahan RRI Mataram, Jl Majapahit, P.O Box 2, Mataram, Lombok, Nusa Tenggara Barat - **FM**: 89.2/104.2/94.3 + 89.1 Dompu, 89.3 Sumbawa Besar, 92.7 Kuripan, 96.3 Aik Bukak, 97.9 Lombok Timur
NT01) Jl Tompello 8, Kupang 85225, Timor, Nusa Tenggara Timur - **FM**: 94.4/90.0/101.9 + 88.8 Soe, 90.7 Kefamenanu – **NT02)** Jl Durian, Ende 86317, Flores, Nusa Tenggara Timur - **FM**: 100.5/104.8/92.2 – **NT03)** RRI Rote Ndao, Baa, Rote 85371, Nusa Tenggara Timur - **FM**: 93.3 – **NT04)** RRI Atambua, Komplek Kantor Bupati Belu, Jl Eltari 1, Atambua, Timor, Nusa Tenggara Timur - **FM**: 91.5
PA01) Jl Tasangkapura 23, Kotak Pos 1077, Jayapura 99200, Papua - **FM**: 96.0/90.1/105.9/89.3 + 93.5 Sentani, 94.5 Timika, 96.5 Sarmi, 96.7 Sorendiweri, 100.0 Genyem – **PA02)** Jl Jendral Ahmad Yani 11, Mopa Baru, Merauke 99611 (Kotak Pos 111, Merauke 99601), Papua - **FM**: 90.0&95.4 (Pro-1)/98.1/105.0 – **PA03)** Jl Pattimura, Serui 98213, Papua - **FM**: 96.4/101.5/94.5 – **PA04)** Jl Majapahit, Kotak Pos 505, Biak 98117, Papua - **FM**: 96.9/95.3/95.8 + 96.3/97.6 Numfor – **PA05)** Jl Jendral A Yani 64, Wamena 99511 (Kotak Pos 10, Wamena 99501), Papua - **FM**: 97.1/96.3/94.7 – **PA06)** Jl Merdeka 74, Nabire 98811 (Kotak Pos 110, Nabire 98801), Papua - **FM**: 97.6/90.1/94.4 – **PA07)** RRI Boven Digul, Jl Trans Papua 17, Tanah Merah, Papua – **FM**: 93.6 – **PA08)** RRI Oksibil, Jl. Perbukitan Okpol, Oksibil, Papua - **FM**: 90.0 – **PA09)** RRI Skow, Jl RRI Stasiun Perbatasan, Skow, Papua - **FM**: 98.3
PB01) Jl Merdeka 68, Manokwari 98311, Papua Barat - **FM**: 94.3/97.8/95.1 – **PB02)** Jl Kapt P Tendean, Kotak Pos 154, Fak-Fak 98612, Papua Barat - **FM**: 97.2/99.0/93.15 + 98.1 Kokas – **PB03)** Jl Sam Ratulangi 4, Kotak Pos 146, Sorong 98414, Papua Barat - **FM**: 102.6/95.9/95.1 + 95.9 Bintuni, 96.3 Teminabuan – **PB04)** Jl Air Merah, Kaimana, Papua Barat - **FM**: 96.3
RI01) Jl Jend Sudirman 440, Kotak Pos 51, Pekanbaru 28115, Riau - **FM**: 99.1/88.4/89.2/95.9 + 92.6 Pasir Pangaraian, 93.0 Dumai, 94.7 Selat Panjang, 96.5 Sei Pakning, 98.5 Baserah, 99.3 Tembilahan, 99.9 Siak – **RI02)** Bengkalis, Riau - **FM**: 90.6 (Pro-1)/89.8 (Pro-3)
SB01) Jl Jendral Sudirman 12, Kotak Pos 77, Padang 25124, Sumatera Barat - **FM**: 97.5/90.8/88.4 + 88.4 Pandai Sikek Padang Pariaman, 89.5 Bukit Gompong Solok, 92.0 Bungkit Palakat, 96.0 Lubuk Sikaping, 96.8 Pasaman Barat, 97.9 Bukit Langkisau Painan, 97.9 Dharma Seraya, 98.5 Mentawai – **SB02)** Jl.Prof Muhammad Yamin 199, Kotak Pos 3, Aurkuning, Bukittinggi 26131, Sumatera Barat - **FM**: 94.8/97.2/90.5 – **SB03)** Jl Diponegoro 48, Pariaman, Sumatera Barat - **FM**: 97.1
SG01) Jl Laute Mandonga 44, Kotak Pos 7, Kendari 93111, Sulawesi Tenggara - **FM**: 96.7/90.8/91.6 + 93.5 Boepinang, 97.0 Raha, 99.5 Lasolo – **SG02)** Bau-Bau, Sulawesi Tenggara - FM: 99.4
SH01) Jl R.A Kartini 39, Palu 94112, Sulawesi Tengah - **FM**: 90.8/105.0/92.4 + 95.4 Ampana, 95.5 Tanjung Santigi, 96.0 Banggai, 96.2 Poso, 97.1 Toboli, 99.2 Luwuk – **SH02)** Jl Jenderal Sudirman, Tolitoli 94514, Sulawesi Tengah - **FM**: 102.0/90.2/94.5 – **SH03)** RRI Ampana, Jl Tanjungulu Tojo Una-Una, Ampana, Sulawesi Tengah - **FM**: 93.0
SL01) Jl Riburane 3, Kotak Pos 103, Makassar 90111, Sulawesi Selatan - **FM**: 94.4/96.8/106.3/92.9 + 90.6 Bontu Tabang, 94.0 Baraka, 99.0 Parepare, 99.0 Bantaeng – **SL02)** RRI Bone, Jl Ahmad Yani, Watampone, Sulawesi Selatan - **FM**: 97.7
SR01) Jl H. Abdul Malik Pattana Endeng, Mamuju, Sulawesi Barat - **FM**: 96.0
SS01) Jl Radio 2 Km 4, Palembang 30128, Sumatera Selatan - **FM**: 92.4/91.6/97.1/88.4 + 90.3 Sekayu, 90.5 Baturaja, 90.5 Pagar Alam,

95.1 Lubuklinggau, 97.7 Prabumulih, 99.9 Muara Enim
ST01) Jl Radio 1, Kotak Pos 1110, Tikala Ares, Manado 95124, Sulawesi Utara - **FM**: 94.5/97.7/104.4/99.9 + 92.0 Lirung, 92.5 Buroko, 98.1 Tondano, 99.5 Melonguane (Pro-3) – **ST02)** Jl Tona, Tahuna, Sangihe, Sulawesi Utara - **FM**: 98.7/92.0/105.4 – **ST03)** RRI Talaud **FM**: 101.2
SU01) Jl Jend Gatot Subroto Km 5.6, Medan 20123, Sumatera Utara - **FM**: 94.3/92.4/88.8/88.4 + 90.0 Natal, 90.6 Rantau Prapat, 91.9 Kotanopan, 92.0 Prapat, 92.0 Sidikalang, 94.5 Simar Jarunjung, 96.1 Pematang Siantar, 96.3 Tarutung, 99.1 Sibuhan, 99.3 Pulau Raja – **SU02)** Jl Ade Irma Suryani Nasution 11, Sibolga 22513, Sumatera Utara - **FM**: 97.2/94.8/103.1 + 99.9 Padangsidempuan – **SU03)** RRI Gunungsitoli, Desa Iraonogeba, Gunungsitoli, Nias, Sumatera Utara - **FM**: 96.2/101.3/90.3– **SU04)** RRI Nias Selatan, Teluk Dalam, Nias Selatan, Sumatera Utara - **FM**: 93.1
YG01) Jl Ahmad Jazuli 4, Tromolpos 18, Kotabaru, Yogyakarta 55224, Daerah Istimewa Yogyakarta - **FM**: 91.1/102.5/102.9/106.6

EXTERNAL SERVICES: The Voice of Indonesia
see International Broadcasting section.

FEDERATION OF INDONESIAN NATIONAL COMMERCIAL BROADCASTERS (Persatuan Radio Siaran Swasta Nasional Indonesia)
Komplek Rukan Fatmawati Mas Blok I/105 Lantai IV, Jl RS Fatmawati 20, Cilandak, Jakarta 12430 ☎ +62 21 75903438 📠 +62 21 75903417 **W**: radioprssni.com/prssninew/ **E**: radioprssni@radio-prssni.com or ppjkt@indosat.net.id **LP**: Chmn: Rohmad Hadiwojoyo. Commercial station permitted power: up to 1kW (MW) and 10kW (FM).

LOCAL PUBLIC BROADCASTING STATIONS (Lembaga Penyiaran Publik Lokal)
Local government stations have made the transition to local government owned but autonomous public broadcasters. As a result, the names of former local government radio stations (Radio Siaran Pemerintah Daerah) have been changed. Where occasionally still referred to, these station headings apply: **RKPD**: Radio Khusus Pemerintah Daerah – **RPD**: Radio Pemerintah Daerah – **RPD Kotamadya**: Radio Pemerintah Daerah Kotamadya (only intended for particular cities) – **RPK**: Radio Pemerintah Kabupaten – **RSPD**: Radio Siaran Pemerintah Daerah – **RSPK**: Radio Siaran Pemerintah Kabupaten.

INDONESIAN COMMUNITY RADIO NETWORK (Jaringan Radio Komunitas Indonesia)
Sekretariat, Jaringan Radio Komunitas Indonesia, Jl Dwi Sri 10, Bandung, Jawa Barat ☎ +62 22 5224205 **W**: jrki.wordpress.com **E**: suara.jrki@gmail.com or jrk_kongres04@yahoo.com
LP: Chrmn: Bowo Usodo
The majority of community stns operate from 107.7 to 108.0 MHz. Maximum permitted power is 50W

MW	kHz	kW	Station, location
BN02)	531		R. Palanta, Tangerang
JB04)	549		Inyong R., Depok
BN03)	±576		R. Hutama Buana Suara (HBS), Ciledug
JK02)	594		R. AM 594, Jakarta
KB04)	621		R. Kijang Berantai (Kiber) Perkasa, Sambas
JK03)	630	1	R. Samhan, Jakarta
JK04)	648		R. Rahmat Emmanuel Ministries (REM), Jakarta
YG02)	648		R. Unisia Media Umat, Sleman
JH05)	666		R. Rama Solo, Surakarta
JH06)	666		R. Tunggul Suara Dirgantara, Purbalingga
JK05)	666		R. AM Stereo 666
JK06)	693		R. Musik Asik Nusantara (R. Muara), Jakarta
PA10)	702		R. Suara Kasih Agung, Jayapura
YG03)	711		R. Suara Konco Tani, Sidokarto
JB05)	720		R. Silaturahim, Cibubur
JH07)	720	0.25	R. Lusiana Namberwan (R. Silaturahim), Semarang
BN04)	738		R. Bharata Bhakti Nusa (Jakarta Music & News R.), Tangerang
KB05)	738		R. Swara Pinohperkasa, Sintang
JA03)	740		RSPD Batanghari, Muarabulian
JB06)	756		R. Rodja, Cileungsi - Bogor
SB04)	774	0.35	RSPD Kotamadya Payakumbuh
KS02)	±783		R. Dakwah Masjid Raya Sabilal Muhtadin Banjarmasin
YG04)	783		R. Swara Kenanga, Yogyakarta
JT07)	±790	0.5	R. Suara Jombang (Jombang FM), Jombang
JB07)	792		R. Swara Citra Cianjur Mandiri, Cianjur

MW	kHz	kW	Station, location
JH08)	792		R. Bayu Sakti, Kroya
JK07)	792	1	R. As Syafi'iyah, Jakarta
JB08)	810		RSPD Kabupaten Bandung (R. Kandaga)
JH09)	810		R. Suara Maung Sakti, Banjarnegara
JH10)	819		R. Pancabayu Madugondo (Suara R.P.M.), Sukoharjo
JB09)	828	0.25	R. Leidya Swara Utama (R. Kharisma), Bandung
JB10)	828		R. Adhika Pariwara, Pelabuhanratu
JK08)	828		R. Berita Klasik (RBK), Jakarta
SL03)	828		R. Swara Christy Ria, Makassar
YG05)	±828		R. Suara Parangtritis, Parangtritis
JA04)	837		R. Kelapa Indah (R. KIN), Tanjung Jabung Barat
JH11)	846		R. Swara Anggada Senatama, Purbalingga
JT08)	846		R. Suara Al Iman, Surabaya
JT09)	‡846	0.5	RKPD Ponorogo (R. Suara Ponorogo)
JB11)	855		R. Kabar Empat, Bekasi
YG06)	±855		R. Gemma Satunama, Gunung Kidul
JK09)	‡864		R. Hana Citra Swara Jakarta (Suara Jakarta), Jakarta
JT10)	864		R. Menara Tiga, Surabaya
JT11)	864		R. Menara Tiga
JH12)	873	0.5	R. Buana Asri (R. Publik Kabupaten Sragen), Sragen
JB12)	882		R. Suara Anggada Senatama (S.A.S.), Banjarsari
JK10)	882		R. Pelangi Nusantara, Jakarta
JH13)	882		R. Swara Kranggan Persada, Temanggung
JA05)	900	0.25	R. Gema Nugraha, Sungai Penuh
JH14)	900		R. Suara Sendang Mas, Banyumas
JH15)	900		R. Darussalaf, Sukoharjo
JK11)	±900		R. Sindajaya, Jakarta
KB06)	900		R. Aries Sanggau Perkasa, Sanggau
SU05)	±900		R. Aksi Bethany, Medan
JB13)	909		R. Mustaqbal, Bekasi
JB14)	918		R. Siaran Gema Nury (R. Elnury), Bogor
JH16)	918		R. Suara Selomanik (R.S.S.), Banjarnegara
JK12)	936	0.25	R. Puspa Dwi Swara Cipta (P2SC), Jakarta
JB15)	936		R. Samhan Mulya, Sumedang
JH17)	945		R. Swara Buana Asri, Wonosobo
BN05)	±954		R. Benda Baru (RBB), Pamulang, Tangerang
JT12)	954	0.25	R. El Bayu, Gresik
SS02)	954	0.15	R. Garuda Kenten Jaya (Bazz R., Islamic R. Palembang), Palembang
SL04)	954		R. Wadhatama Nusantara (Makkah AM), Makassar
JK13)	963		R. Prestasi FM, Jakarta
BN06)	972		R. Pusako Minangkabau, Tangerang
KS03)	990		R. Bahana Al-Mursyidul Amin, Martapura
KB07)	1008		R. Suara Pemangkat, Pemangkat
SL05)	1008		R. Suara Adyafiri, Watansoppeng
BN07)	±1017		R. Swara Angkasa Semesta (RASS), Teluknada, Tangerang
JK14)	1026		R. Suara Khatulistiwa (SK), Jakarta
SS03)	1026		R. Suara Enim Jaya Perkasa (En-J), Muara Enim
JB16)	1029	0.5	RPK Ciamis
JB17)	1044		R. Duta Angkasa, Pangandaran
JH18)	1062		R. P.T.D.I. Unisa 205, Semarang
JK15)	±1062	0.25	R. Cendrawasih Pusat, Jakarta
JT13)	1062	1	R. Sangkakala, Surabaya
PA11)	±1062		R. Swara Lembah Baliem, Wamena
SU06)	1062		R. Tembang Perbaungan Indah, Perbaungan
JT14)	1071		RKPD Pacitan (Suara Pacitan)
SL06)	1080		R. Suara Viktori, Makassar
JK16)	1098		Perkumpulan R. Siaran Pendidikan Tinggi Universitas Tarumanegara (VOMS)
JB18)	±1116		R. Adhika Swara (R. Alawiyah), Bekasi
JB19)	1116	1	R. Barani, Bandung
JT15)	±1117	0.25	R. Carolina Arjuno, Surabaya
JK17)	1134	2	R. Swara Mega Asri (R. Safari), Jakarta
JH19)	±1143		R. Swara Delanggu (Swadesi), Delanggu
JK18)	1152		R. Ikadi, Jakarta
JT16)	1152		R. Yasmara, Surabaya
JB20)	±1170		R. Dios (R. Paksi), Bandung
PA12)	1170		R. Suara Nusa Bahagia, Jayapura
JH20)	±1180	0.5	RSPD Wonogiri
JT17)	1188		R. Swara Perak Jaya P.T.D.I., Surabaya
BN08)	1197		R. Swara Mitra, Tangerang
BN09)	1206		GES Radio, Tangerang
SB05)	1206		R. Suara Diraksa Bawana (Dirgan Bravo), Padang
JH21)	1224		R. Angkasa Bahana Citra (A.B.C.), Surakarta
JH22)	1224		R. Suara Sendang Mas (RSPD Banyumas), Purwokerto
YG07)	1251		R. Edukasi, Yogyakarta
JB21)	1260		R. Suara Pekerja (SP), Bekasi
PA13)	1278		R. Pikonane, Yahukimo
JH23)	1287		Java Radio Station, Semarang
JB22)	1314		R. Mutiara, Bandung
JH24)	1314		Suara Sion Perdana, Karanganyar
YG08)	1323		R. Kartini Indah Swara, Yogyakarta
JT18)	±1350		R. Gelora Surabaya (RGS)
BN10)	±1440		R. Edukasi, Tangerang
SH04)	1440		R. Setia Nada, Luwuk
JT19)	±1449	0.7	R. Pertanian Wonocolo, Surabaya
JB23)	1458		R. Fajri, Bandung
SH05)	1458	1	R. Kareme Nuvula (RPK Parigi Moutong), Parigi
JB24)	1475		RKDT Karawang (Studio Radio Daerah Pangkal Perjuangan)
JB25)	1476		R. Rodja Bandung, Bandung
PA14)	1476		R. Wagadei, Paniai
ST04)	1494		R. Swara Kasih, Tahuna
KT04)	1512	0.25	R. Swara Mitra Dirgantara (Rasmira), Balikpapan
JB26)	±1523		R. Swara Primadona Mahardika, Cikampek
JK19)	1530		R. Mesjid Sunda Kelapa, Jakarta

NB: ‡ = r. inactive ± = variable. A number of unlicensed stations operating in the Tangerang area, Banten province, are not included in the list above.

Addresses (JI = Jalan)

BN00) BANTEN
BN02) Jl Gatot Subroto Km 8, Jatake, Tangerang – **BN03)** Jl Radeh Fatah, Perum Lembang Baru I/3, Ciledug, Tangerang 15151 – **BN04)** as stn BN03) – **BN05)** Benda Baru, Pamulang, Tangerang – **BN06)** Jl KH. Hasyim Ashari, Gedung Berkah Motor Lt 3, Cipondoh, Tangerang – **BN07)** Jl Kampung Melayu Barat, Teluknaga, Tangerang – **BN08)** Jl Komplek Peruri, Ciledug, Tangerang – **BN09)** Tangerang **BN10)** Pusat Teknologi Informasi dan Komunikasi (PUSTEKKOM), Departemen Pendidikan Nasional (DEPDIKNAS), Ciputat, Tangerang.

JA00) JAMBI
JA03) Jl.Gajah Mada, Muarabulian 36610 – **JA04)** Jl Panglima H Saman 297B, Kuala Tungkal, Tanjung Jabung Barat 36513 – **JA05)** Jl Yos Sudarso 55, Sungai Penuh, Kerinci.

JB00) JAWA BARAT (West Java)
JB04) Jl Perintis I, Kalimulya, Depok – **JB05)** Jl Masjid Silaturahim 36, Kalimanggis, Cibubur, Bekasi – **JB06)** Masjid Al Barkah, Jl Pahlawan kp Tengah, Cileungsi - Bogor – **JB07)** Cianjur – **JB08)** Jl Adikusumah, Bale Endah, Dayeuh Kolot, Bandung – **JB09)** Jl Siliwangi 5, Bandung 40132 – **JB10)** Jl Siliwangi 103, Pelabuhanratu, Sukabumi 43164 – **JB11)** Jl Kain Raya 3, Rawa Lumbu, Bekasi – **JB12)** Jl Raya Barat 98, Banjarsari, Ciamis 46383 – **JB13)** Kompleks Pondok Pesantren Al Binaa IBS, Jl Raya Pebayuran, Kertasari, Pebayuran, Bekasi 17710 – **JB14)** Jl Raya Kedunghalang 2, Warung Jambu, Bogor 16155 – **JB15)** Jalan Raya Jatinagor 138, Sumedang 45363 – **JB16)** Jl Ir H Juanda 128, Ciamis 46211 – **JB17)** Jl Pramuka 653, Pangandaran, Ciamis – **JB18)** Jl Raya Jatiwaringin 50, Bekasi 17411– **JB19)** Jl Raya Cinunuk 84, Cileunyi, Bandung 40393 – **JB20)** ITC Kosambi Blok G-16 Lt I, Jl Baranangsiang, Bandung 40112 – **JB21)** Jl Ahmad Yani 1, Bekasi – **JB22)** Jl Cikamiri 7, Cisadea, Bandung – **JB23)** Jl Nagrak Cangkuang RT 02/10, Soreang, Bandung – **JB24)** Jl Siswa 56, Cikampek, Karawang 41373 – **JB25)** Jl Masjid Umar Ibnul Khatab, Desa Selacau RT 02/05, Lembur Tengah, Batujajar, Bandung Barat 40561 – **JB26)** Jalan Brigpol Nasuha 2, Karawang.

JH00) JAWA TENGAH (Central Java)
JH05) Jl Purworejo VI/10, Surakarta – **JH06)** Jl Mayjen Sungkono 89, Purbalingga – **JH07)** Jl Raung 7, Candi Baru, Semarang – **JH08)** Jl Kendeng (Pesayangan) 55, Kroya, Cilacap – **JH09)** Jl Letjend S Parman 28, Banjarnegara – **JH10)** Jl Madugondo 15, Grogol, Sukoharjo 57552 – **JH11)** Jl Raya Barat 99, Banjarsari, Purbalingga – **JH12)** Jl Veteran 21, Sragen 57211 – **JH13)** Jl Kanjengan C-308, Kranggan, Temanggung 56271 – **JH14)** Jl Kompleks Kawedanan Lama 296, Banyumas 53192 – **JH15)** Cemani, Sukoharjo – **JH16)** Jl D.I Panjaitan 3, Banjarnegara 53415 – **JH17)** Jl Raya Kertek-Kalikajar 33, Wonosobo 56311 – **JH18)** Yayasan Badan Wakaf Sultan Agung (YBWSA), Universitas Islam Sultan Agung, Jl Raya Kaligawe Km 4, Semarang 50012 – **JH19)** Jl Raya Delanggu Utara 53, Delanggu, Klaten 57471 – **JH20)** Komplek Perluasan Kota, Jl Plongkowati, Wonogiri – **JH21)** Jl Kapt Mulyadi 117, Surakarta 57113 – **JH22)** Jl Komplek Kewedanan Lama 296, Purwokerto 53192 – **JH23)** Semarang – **JH24)** Jl Dr Muwardi 47, Badranasri, Karanganyar.

JK00) JAKARTA
JK02) Jl Matraman 39, Jakarta – **JK03)** Jl Swadaya Raya 26/143, Raden Inten, Jakarta – **JK04)** Apartemen Robinson Lt 6, Jembatan Dua Raya 2, Jakarta – **JK05)** Jl Abdurahman II no 31, Kebayoran Lama

Utara, Jakarta 12230 – **JK06)** Jl Cipinang Timur 15, Rawamangun, Jakarta 13240 – **JK07)** Jl Masjid Al Barkah 17, Tebet, Jakarta Selatan – **JK08)** Jl Danau Agung II/5-7, Sunter Agung, Podomoro, Jakarta Utara 14350 – **JK09)** Gedung AKA, Jl Bangka Raya 2, Kebayoran Baru, Jakarta Selatan 12720 – **JK10)** Gedung Sasana Kriya TMII Lantai 2, Jl Pondok Gede Arena Taman Mini Indonesia Indah, Jakarta Timur – **JK11)** Kampung Beting, Jakarta Utara – **JK12)** Jl Dakota V/1, Kemayoran, Jakarta 10630 – **JK13)** Perkantoran Plaza Pasifik Blok B3 64, Kelapa Gading Permai, Jakarta Utara – **JK14)** Jl Tipar Cakung 9, Cilincing, Jakarta Utara – **JK15)** Jl Batu Ceper V/52, Jakarta Pusat 10120 – **JK16)** Kampus II Universitas Tarumanegara, Jl. Tanjung Duren Utara no 1 Blok D, Tanjung Duren, Jakarta 11470.– **JK17)** Gedung AKA, Jl Bangka Raya 2, Kebayoran Baru, Jakarta Selatan 12720 – **JK18)** Ikatan Da'i Indonesia, Jl Bambu Apus Raya 62, Jakarta Timur 13890 – **JK19)** Menteng, Jakarta.

JT00) JAWA TIMUR (East Java)
JT07) Jl K.H. Wakhid Hasyim 133, Jombang 61419 – **JT08)** Komplek STAI Ali Bin Abi Thalib, Jl Sitopo Kidul 51, Surabaya – **JT09)** Jl Alun-Alun Utara 3, Ponorogo 63413 – **JT10)** Komplek STAI Ali Bin Abi Thalin, Jl Sidotopo Kidul 51, Surabaya 60152 – **JT11)** Jl Simolawang I/96, Surabaya 60144 – **JT12)** Jl Aipda Karel Sasuit Tubun 15, Gresik 61114 – **JT13)** Kompleks Manyar Indah Plaza, Jl Ngagel Jaya Selatan, Surabaya – **JT14)** Jl Jaksa Agung Suprapto 8, Pacitan 63512 – **JT15)** Jl Ngagel Jaya Utara IV/21, Surabaya 60283 – **JT16)** Jl Amir Hamzah 18, Surabaya 60241 – **JT17)** Jl Teluk Aru 68, Surabaya 60165 – **JT18)** Humas Gelora 10 Nopember, Jl Tambaksari, Surabaya 60136 – **JT19)** Jl Ahmad Yani 112, Wonokromo, Surabaya.

KB00) KALIMANTAN BARAT (West Kalimantan)
KB04) Jl Raya Sambas Bukitluwing 1, Sambas 79162 – **KB05)** Jl Kelam Akcaya I/18, Sintang 78611 – **KB06)** Jl Kom Yos Sudarso 9, Sanggau 78582 – **KB07)** Jl Pembangunan RT 003/XIV, Desa Harapan, Pemangkat 79153.
KS00) KALIMANTAN SELATAN (South Kalimantan)
KS02) Jl Jend. Sudirman 1, Banjarmasin 70114 – **KS03)** Jl Barintik 35, P.O. Box 48, Martapura 70613
KT00) KALIMANTAN TIMUR (East Kalimantan)
KT04) Jl A Yani 50, Balikpapan 76123.
PA00) PAPUA (formerly Irian Jaya)
PA10) Jl Trikora 30 Lantai 2, Dok V, Jayapura – **PA11)** Jl Bhayangkara, Wamena – **PA12)** Jl Skyline, Jayapura – **PA13)** Anyelma, Kurima, Yahukimo – **PA14)** Enarotali, Paniai.
SB00) SUMATERA BARAT (West Sumatra)
SB04) Jl Jend Sudirman 18, Payakumbuh 26211 – **SB05)** Jl W.R Mongonsidi 4B, Lantai 2, Padang.
SH00) SULAWESI TENGAH (Central Celebes)
SH04) Jl Jenderal Sudirman 128, Luwuk 94715, Banggai – **SH05)** Jl Toraraga 234, Parigi 94371.
SL00) SULAWESI SELATAN (South Celebes)
SL03) Jl Manggis 16, Makassar 90112 – **SL04)** Masjid Wihdatul Ummah, Jl Abdullah Daeng Sirua 52J, Makassar – **SL05)** Jl Poros Cabenge 1, Watansoppeng – **SL06)** Kompleks Ruko Somba Opu Blok B/19, Tanjung Bunga - Makassar
SS00) SUMATERA SELATAN (South Sumatra)
SS02) Jl Dr M Isa 38, 8 Ilir, Palembang 30114 – **SS03)** Jl Pramuka I/15, Muara Enim.
ST00) SULAWESI UTARA (North Celebes)
ST04) Manente, Tahuna, Kepulauan Sangihe.
SU00) SUMATERA UTARA (North Sumatra)
SU05) Jl Pabrik Tenun 102, Medan – **SU06)** Jl Deli Gg Kereta Api 6, Perbaungan, Deli Serdang 20586.
YG00) DAERAH ISTIMEWA YOGYAKARTA (Yogyakarta Special Reg.)
YG02) Universitas Islam Indonesia, Jl Demanangbaru 24, Sleman – **YG03)** Jl Godean Km 9, Dukuh Sidokarto Godean, Sleman – **YG04)** Jl Panti Wreda 5, Giwangan, Umbulharjo, Yogyakarta 55163 – **YG05)** Jl Parangtritis 22, Tegalsari RT46, Donotirto Kretek, Parangtritis 55772, Bantul – **YG06)** USC Satunama, Wiladeg, Gunung Kidul – **YG07)** Balai Pengembangan Media Radio, Pusat Teknologi Informasi dan Komunikasi Pendidikan, Departemen Pendidikan Nasional, Jl Sorowajan Baru 367, Banguntapan, Yogyakarta 55198 – **YG08)** Bantul, Yogyakarta.

FM: A large number of RRI stns operate throughout the country. See RRI address list for RRI FM freqs.
Jakarta area FM (MHz): 87.6 Antarnusa Jaya (Hard Rock) – 87.8 Bogor Swaratama (Sheba), Bogor – 88.0 Mustang Utama – 88.2 M2, Bekasi – 88.4 Arief Rahman Hakim (ARH/Global R.) – 89.2 Metro Jaya Kartika (R. 68H/Green R.) – 89.4 Sipatahunan (RSPK Bogor), Bogor – 89.6 Mustika Abadi (I R.) – 90.0 Elshinta – 90.2 Harmoni FM, Bekasi – 90.4 Muara Abdi Nusa (Cosmopolitan) – 90.6 RH56, Bekasi – 90.8 Suara Gema Pembangunan Utama (Oz R. Jakarta) – 91.0 Cherry Black R., Bogor – 91.6 Indika Millenia – 92.0 Sonora – 92.2 Radiotemen

Nagaswara, Bogor – 92.4 Primaswara Adi Spirit Semesta (PAS/R. Bisnis Jakarta) – 93.0 Teman, Bogor – 93.2 Merpati Dharmawangsa (MD R.) – 93.4 Kancah Irama Suara Indonesia (KISI), Bogor – 93.6 Gema Wargakarya Satnawa (Gaya), Bekasi – 93.9 Swara Mersidiona (Mersi), Tangerang – 94.3 Gardia Asia Bumi (Woman) – 94.5 Ganadas, Bogor – 94.7 Agustina Yunior (U) – 95.1 Kirana Indah Suara (KIS) – 95.3 Pertanian Ciawi, Bogor – 95.5 Siaran Alaikassalam Sejahtera (RAS) – 95.7 Win FM, Bogor – 95.9 Smart Media Utama – 96.3 Pelita Kasih (RPK) – 96.7 Swara Rhadana Dunia (Hitz FM) – 97.1 Suara Monalisa (Dangdut Indonesia) – 97.5 Safari Bina Budaya (Motion) – 97.9 Bahana Sanada Dunia (Female), Tangerang – 98.1 One Center, Bekasi – 98.3 Cakrawala Gita Swara – 98.5 Islamic Centre Dakwah Al-Awwabin (Rida) , Depok– 98.7 Attahiriyah (Gen) – 99.1 Delta Insani – 99.3 Fajri, Bogor – 99.5 Kayumanis (Urban RKM) – 99.7 Bahana Suara Alam (WADI), Bogor – 99.9 Draba (Sys NS)– 100.1 Lesmana, Bogor – 100.3 Elgangga, Bekasi – 100.6 Jati Yaski Mandiri (Heartline), Tangerang – 100.8 Megaswara, Bogor – 101.0 Suara Irama Indah (Jak) – 101.4 Suara Kejayaan (Trax) – 101.8 Terik Matahari Bahana Pembangunan – 102.2 Prambors – 102.4 Media Akbar Zhapin (ZFM), Depok – 102.6 Camajaya Surya Nada – 102.8 Gema Annisa Persada, Cikarang-Bekasi – 103.0 Irnusa Ria, Depok – 103.2 Duta Swara Parahyangan, Bekasi – 103.4 Taman Mini (DFM) – 103.6 Swara Irama Kusuma Sena (Elpas), Bogor – 103.8 Pesona Gita Anindita (Brava) – 104.0 Forum 77 (8EH), Bekasi – 104.2 Media Suara Trisakti (MS-Tri) – 104.4 Swara Widya Sari (Puncak), Bogor – 104.6 Trijaya Sakti (Sindo Trijaya R.) – 105.4 Niaga Chakti Bhudi Bhakti (CBB) – 105.6 Suara Pendidikan Al-Ihya dan Insan Kamil, Bogor – 105.6 Gema Annisa, Cikarang-Bekasi – 105.8 Ramako Jaya Raya (Lite) – 106.0 Siaran Gema Nury (Elnury), Bogor – 106.2 Bergaya Nyanyian Irama Sejati, Tangerang (Bens) – 106.4 R. Attaqwa FM, Bekasi – 106.6 Sabda Sosok Sohor (V Radio) – 107.0 Nada Komunikasi Utama (Dakta), Bekasi – 107.2 Cemerlang, Depok – 107.3 Suara Tunggal Angkasa Raya (Star), Tangerang – 107.5 Mitra Carita Enambelas (Music City / MC), Depok – 107.7 Prestasi – 107.7 Islamic R. – 107.7 Sahabat Pramuka (Scout R.), Cibubur – 107.7 UG, Depok – 107.7 Komunitas Institut Pertanian Bogor (Agri), Bogor – 107.9 Suara Sorak Kemenangan – 107.9 Telekomunikasi Cipta (UI FM), Depok – 107.9 Jalesviva Jayamahe (Suara Samudera).

Bandung FM (MHz): 87.7 Ekacita Swara Buana (Hard Rock FM) – 88.1 Swara Emas (SE) – 88.5 Mora Purna Karsa – 88.9 Hasil Era Reformasi (Auto Radio) – 89.3 Cipta Swara Global (Elshinta) – 89.7 Media Wisata Sariasih (Global R.) – 90.1 Karang Tumaritis (Zora) – 90.5 Cakra – 90.9 Lita Sari – 91.3 Manca Suara (Sindo R.) – 91.7 Citra Bahana Limbangan (INB) – 92.1 Bandung Suara Indah (Mei Sheng) – 92.5 Madah Ekaristi Swaratronika (Maestro) – 92.9 Arus Rizki (ARFM), Cimahi– 93.3 Ganesha Nada (Walagri) – 93.7 Paramuda – 94.1 Sanndy Qyu, Soreang – 94.4 Bandung Cipta Perdana (Delta FM) – 94.8 Galang Wahana Raya (Radio ON) – 95.2 Swara Pandawa Lima Shakti (Bandung R.) – 95.6 Suara Burinyay (B Radio) – 96.4 Swaratama Cicalengka (Bobotoh) – 96.8 Nada Kencana Agung – 97.2 Shinta Buana – 98.0 Maya Nada – 98.4 Suara Sembilan Delapan Lima (Prambors) – 98.8 Candrika Widya Swara (Sonora) – 99.2 Manggala Gemini Bandung (Kids FM) – 99.6 Thomson – 100.0 Swara Milliard Artha (Ninety-Niners) – 100.4 Ilnafir Karanglayung Citra Budaya Suara (KLCBS) – 100.7 RSPD Kabupaten Bandung (R. Kandaga), Bale Endah – 101.1 Swakarsa Megantara (MGT) – 101.5 Dahlia Flora – 101.9 Putramas Mulia Rahayu (Cosmo) – 102.3 Tiara Rase Perdana – 102.7 Madinatussalam Bandung (MQ) – 103.1 Mitragamma Swara (Oz FM) – 103.5 Citrahutama Eltravidya (Chevy) – 103.9 Antassalam Bagja (Hits) – 104.3 Generasi Muda (U FM) – 104.7 Salam Rama Dwihasta – 105.1 Loma Dwipa (I R.) – 105.5 Garuda Tunggal Angkasa – 105.9 Ardan Swaratama – 106.3 Bhakti Musik Wastukencana (Urban R) – 106.7 Mara Ghita – 107.1 Lintas Kontinental (K-Lite) – 107.5 Mustika Parahyangan (PR FM) – 107.9 Jabar One

Batam FM (MHz): 87.6 Discovery Minang – 91.7 Aljabar Serumpun – 100.7 Ramako Batam (Batam FM) – 101.6 Matra Komersial Batam (Zoo FM) – 102.3 Kencana Ria Indah Suara (Kei FM) – 104.3 Lintas Sei Ladi (Seila) – 104.7 Batam Indah Gelora Suara (BiGSFM) – 106.0 Media Hang Batam (Hang FM) – 106.5 Suara Marga Semesta (Sing FM) – 107.0 Be FM – 107.7 R. Alfa Omega – 107.9 R. Komunitas Hang Tuah

Denpasar (Bali) FM (MHz): 87.8 Baturiti Menara Swara (Hard Rock) – 89.4 Gema Sunari Indah – 89.8 Organik Lestari Sejahtera (Pak Oles), Tabanan – 90.2 Suara Yudha – 90.6 Gema Megantara Pratama (Megantara Bali), Tabanan – 91.0 Gita Bakti Persada (Phoenix) – 91.4 Beat – 91.8 Flamboyant Bali Indah (FBI) – 92.2 Gema Megantara Pesona (Heartline) – 92.6 RPKD Denpasar – 93.3 Berita Bagus Sejati (Bali News R.), Kuta – 94.5 Citra Dharma Bali Satya (CDBS) – 94.9 Click Gita Saraswati, Bangli – 96.1 Genta Suara Bali – 96.5 Swara

Kinijani (Global), Tabanan – 96.9 Elang Kosa Gagana (Elkoga) – 97.3 Sonata Indah (Soni) – 97.7 Gema Merdeka – 98.1 Gia, Gianyar – 98.5 Plus – 98.9 Bali Perkasa (Bali FM), Gianyar – 99.3 Duta Dewata (Duta Female) – 99.7 Srinadi FM, Klungkung – 100.5 Dunia Bokashi Raya, Klungkung – 101.2 Bali Swara Mitragama (D'Oz R. Bali), Kuta – 102.0 Suara Denpasar Chakti (Cassanova) – 102.8 Menara – 103.2 Mega Nada, Tabanan – 103.6 Pinguin – 104.0 Pelangi FM, Tabanan – 104.4 Aneka Rama (AR) – 104.8 R. Gelora Gianyar – 105.2 Surya Permai (Storm FM) – 105.6 Bali Mandala Perkasa, Gianyar – 106.0 Swara Kreasi Utama (Kuta R.), Kuta – 106.9 Swara Bukit Bali Indah (BBI), Kuta – 107.7 Komunitas Dwijendra

Medan FM (MHz): 87.6 DASS FM, Lubuk Pakam – 88.0 Cikal Anugrah Fiesta (La Femme) – 89.2 RPDK Deli Serdang, Lubuk Pakam – 89.6 Visi Orang Medan Sumatera – 90.0 Gebyar Nada Satuwarna (Hot 90 FM), Deli Serdang – 90.4 Swara Teladan Anugrah – 90.8 Garuda Pentasindo Hutama (Mix FM) – 91.2 RPD2, Lubuk Pakam – 91.6 Surya Damusu (Umsu FM) – 92.4 Suara Dirgantara (Lite FM), Namorambe – 92.8 Berita Jaringan Global (Elshinta) – 94.7 Bonita Jaya (Suara Medan) – 95.1 Prapanca Buana Suara (Sindo Trijaya R.) – 95.5 Citra Buana Indah (CB) – 95.9 Mutiara Mandiri Buana Swara (City R.) – 96.3 Rhodesa (Medan FM) – 96.7 Citra Ayu Senada (Dangdut Indonesia) – 97.1 Sikamoni (Narwastu FM) – 97.5 Swara Kencana Yuda (Prambors) – 97.9 Tuah Singalorlau (Narwastu FM) – 98.3 Komersil Siaran Nusantara (I Radio) – 99.1 Khamasutra (Moze FM) – 99.5/106.2 Kardopa – 101.0 Suara Binuang (Joy FM) – 101.8 Radio Media Indah Suara Handalan (Smart FM) – 102.2 Bonsita – 102.6 Alnora (Star News FM) – 103.4 Simponi – 103.8 Gitasukma Bahana (A R.) – 104.2 Mitramedia Dirgantara (R. Maria Indonesia) – 104.6 Anugrah Pradana Muda (Star FM), Deli Serdang – 105.0 Kindung Indah Seleras Suara (KISS FM) – 105.4 Pesona Ciptaswara (RPC), Binjai – 105.8 Medan Cipta Perdana (Delta FM) – 106.6 Sonya Portibi – 107.3 Lips FM

Surabaya FM (MHz): 87.7 R. Zodiac (Colors) – 88.1 Kota Buaya Mandiri – 88.5 Metro Gema Mega – 88.9 JT-FM (Smart FM)– 89.3 Surabaya Pesona Femina (Prambors) – 89.7 Hafini Jaya Mandiri (Hard Rock FM.) – 90.1 Media Caraka Angkasa – 90.5 Ampel Denta – 90.9 Global Nada Prima – 91.3 Suzana Suara Bhakti – 92.5 Kreasi Indah Dunia Swara (Kosmonita) – 92.9 BFM – 93.3 Eka Laras Vicaksana Torya (El Victor) – 93.8 Shamsindo Indonusa (Sham FM) – 94.4 Suara Digital Indonesia (My Radio) – 94.8 Devina Jelita (DJ FM) – 96.0 Mercury Masa Depan Sukses – 96.4 Bahtera Yudha – 97.1 Suara Masa Depan Cerah (Life R.) – 97.6 Shinta Warga Gemilang (Elshinta) – 98.0 Salvatore Surabaya (Sonora) – 98.4 Giri Swara Indah Sakti (Swara Giri FM), Gresik – 98.8 Kartika Bahari Dirgantara (M R.) – 99.6 Gitaya Gegana (She R.) – 100.0 Fiskaria Jaya Suara Surabaya – 100.5 Delta FM – 101.1 Laras Pancar Istana Suara (Istara) – 101.5 Cakrawala Bhakti – 101.9 Stratosfir (Strato) – 102.7 Suara Mahasiswa Turun Bekerja (MTB) – 103.1 Camar (Gen FM) – 103.5 Wijaya – 103.8 Rajawali Megah (Primaradio) – 104.3 Bisnis Surabaya (PAS FM) – 104.7 Cakra Awigra (Sindo Trijaya R.) – 105.1 Wahana Informasi Gemilang (JJ R.) – 105.5 Star Wibawa Anugrah, Pandaan – 105.9 Era Bimasakti Selaras (EBS) – 106.7 Merdeka Lokatama – 107.3 Suara Dering Edukasi – 107.5 Media Assalam Surabaya (SAS FM) – 107.7 TOC FM (R. Spirit) – 107.9 Suara An-Nida

IRAN

L.T: UTC +3½h (21 Mar–21 Sept: +4½h) — **Pop:** 77 million — **Pr.L:** Farsi (Persian) — **E.C:** 50Hz, 230V — **ITU:** IRN

ISLAMIC REPUBLIC OF IRAN BROADCASTING (Gov.)
✉ P O. Box 19395-333, Tehran ☎ +98 21 2204 1093 📠 +98 21 2222 1508 **W:** radio.ir **E:** radio@irib.ir
L.P: President: Ezatollah Zarghami. DG: Gholamali Ramezani.

MW:

Prov & Location	kHz	kW	N	Prov & Location	kHz	kW	N
3 Azarshahr	531	500	I	11 Bandar Abbas	621	50	R
24 Iranshahr	531	600	I	30 Birjand (Bojd)	621	200	R
29 Mashhad	540	200	I	3 Bonab	639	400	E
13 Sirjan	549	400	I	5 Sefiddasht	648	50	I
21 Gheslagh	558	1000	F	8 Kiashahr	657	100	R
2 Maku	576	50	R	24 Zahedan	657	100	R
15 Mahshahr	576	600	E	12 Shushtar	666	50	I
25 Tehran	585	600	Q	10 Hamadan	675	50	R
24 Zahedan	594	50	I	29 Mashhad	684	100	R
7 Shiraz (Dehnow)	603	400	R	11 Bandar Lengeh	693	100	R
29 Bajgiran	603	10	R	8 Kiashahr	702	50	E
14 Qasr-e Shirin	612	600	R	15 Ahvaz	711	400	R

Prov & Location	kHz	kW	N	Prov & Location	kHz	kW	N
14 Mahidasht	720	750	I	30 Nehbandan	1206	10	R
29 Taybad	720	400	R/E	20 Chalus	1215	60	R
4 Dayyer	738	50	R	13 Kerman	1224	50	I
9 Gonbad	747	600	I	11 Kish Island	1224	400	E
13 Sirjan	747	150	R	7 Abadeh	1233	50	R
24 Chabahar	765	600	R/E	27 Zanjan	1242	50	I
5 Shahr-e-Kord	765	50	R	8 Kiashahr	1251	100	I
19 Arak	774	100	R	6 Khur	1260	10	R
24 Iranshahr	783	150	R	1 Khalkhal	1269	50	R
27 Sohravard (Zanjan)	792	50	R	14 Kermanshah	1278	300	R
29 Kashmar	801	50	R	7 Darab	1359	60	R
18 Khorramabad	810	100	R	7 Lar	1287	50	R
20 Sari	819	30	R	7 Lamerd	1287	50	R
30 Tabas	828	50	R	24 Zabol	1296	50	R
6 Habibabad	837	300	R	4 Busherhr	1305	50	R
3 Mianeh	846	50	R	1 Ardabil	1314	50	I
14 Qasr-e Shirin	864	50	R	unk. location	1314		I
28 Bojnurd	873	50	R	3 Jolfa	1323	50	E/R
32 Mahabad	882	60	R	25 Tehran	1332	300	T
16 Dehdasht	891	50	R	13 Bam	1341	20	R
25 Tehran	900	600	I	9 Gonbad	1368	150	R
unk. location	900		I	24 Chabahar	1377	50	R
13 Jiroft	918	50	R	14 Paveh	1377	50	I
18 Dorud	927	50	R	11 Hajiabad	1395	50	I
2 Miandoab	936	300	R	9 unk. location	1395		E
2 Urmia	936	50	R	7 Dasht-e Qir	1404	10	I
17 Dehgolan	945	100	R	7 Estahban	1413	10	R
30 Birjand	963	200	I	6 Habibabad	1431	200	I
12 Ilam	972	100	R	9 Bandar Torkaman	1449	400	E
10 Hamadan	981	100	I	30 Ghayen	1458	10	R
7 Shiraz (Dehnow)	990	400	I	22 Alborz (Qom)	1467	100	R
7 Baneh	999	50	R	17 Marivan	1476	50	R
23 Semnan	1008	100	I	2 Khoy	1485	10	R
11 Bandar Abbas	1017	50	I	7 Jahrom	1485	10	R
3 Azarshahr	1026	200	R	33 Jamshidabad	1485	100	R
26 Yazd	1035	100	R	23 Damghan	1485	1	I
12 Dehloran	1044	50	R	29 Taybad	1494	10	R
18 Khorramabad	1053	100	I	4 Bushehr	1503	200	I
24 Saravan	1053	30	I	1 Ardabil	1512	50	R
13 Kerman	1062	200	R	26 Yazd	1530	50	I
22 Alborz (Qom)	1071	100	M	9 Derazno	1539	50	R
15 Mahshahr	1080	600	E	23 Garmsar	1539	10	R
23 Shahrud	1089	50	R	16 Gachsaran	1548	15	R
24 Zabol	1098	200	E	17 Sanandaj	1548	10	I
29 Sabzevar	1107	50	R	20 Larijan	1548	10	R
26 Ardekan	1116	200	I	22 Eshtehard	1548	50	I
21 Qazvin	1125	50	R	30 Ferdows	1548	10	R
3 Kalibar	1134	10	R	24 Zabol	1557	50	I
28 Bojnurd	1134	50	I	11 Bandar Abbas	1566	100	I
16 Yasuj	1143	50	I	15 Abadan	1575	800	I
14 Qasr-e-Shirin	1161	600	E	23 Semnan	1584	50	R
33 Abadan	1170	50	I	5 Kazerun	1602	10	R
9 Gorgan	1179	50	I	15 Dezful	1602	10	R
24 Chabahar	1179	50	I	26 Bahabad	1602	10	I
25 Tehran	1188	300	P	23 Damghan	1602	10	R
1 Moghan	1197	50	R	23 Garmsar	1602	10	R
7 Dasht-e Qir	1197	50	R				

FM:

Pr. Location	I	R	Q	P	M	J	F	V/Tj
1 Ardabil	88.8	101.6	94.8	100.9	98.3	102.4	89.3	105.2
1 Khalkhal		94.4	99.2	90.1		103.9	95.8	94.0
1 Parsabad		92.4	92.8	106.5	98.0		99.3	
2 Khoy			95.0	93.8	98.2		101.8	
2 Maku	100.0	102.6		92.2	104.9			
2 Urmia	106.5	91.1	106.1	95.8		92.6	102.6	99.1
3 Maragheh			94.7	95.3	101.5		98.0	
3 Tabriz	98.7	96.3	90.7	102.9	96.1	93.9	94.2	99.4
4 Bushehr	94.2	92.2	90.0	104.4	96.2		94.2	106.6
5 Ardal		106.9	99.8	93.2	90.2	96.5	103.2	
5 Ben				94.4	97.7	91.2		
5 Borujen		92.0	106.7	96.2	103.1	99.6	93.1	90.0
5 Farsan		99.5	94.5	98.5	100.5	106.5		92.5
5 Lordegan	90.8		100.0	95.8	102.6	91.2		95.8
5 Saman		98.8		89.3	95.5	92.3	102.3	105.9
5 Shahr-e-Kord	97.1		90.0	96.0	104.3	93.6	98.0	87.6
5 Shalamzar		88.2		97.8	101.3	94.5	91.3	104.9
6 Fereydunshahr	101.8	108.0			96.6		93.3	103.3
6 Golpayegan	106.0			93.8			97.0	107.2
6 Isfahan	88.1	96.8	107.2	88.5	96.8		98.6	

Pr.	Location	I	R	Q	P	M	J	F	V/Tj
6	Kashan	98.0	101.1	102.8		105.5		96.8	
6	Khonsar			99.3	107.3	102.8		106.0	
6	Nain	98.1			93.3	92.8		91.1	
6	Semirom	99.0	105.6		90.8	102.0		93.8	
7	Marvdasht			96.2		93.0		99.5	107.3
7	Shiraz	88.3	94.7	95.6	93.7	107.3	96.0	91.6	96.5
8	Rasht	98.5	92.5	101.3	104.9	104.1	91.3	106.0	107.7
8	Rudbar	91.8		97.6	108.0	91.8			
9	Gorgan		97.5	96.8	91.0	101.0	103.6	97.5	94.2
10	Hamadan	96.0	101.4	91.4	97.8	103.7	90.0	106.1	88.4
10	Malayer			96.1	96.3	93.1			96.0
10	Nahavand			94.2	94.7	101.0		101.7	
11	Bandar e Jask		105.0	100.7		94.6	88.3	91.4	97.9
11	Bandar Abbas	93.4	96.2	90.1	99.7	95.2	94.2	104.6	105.6
11	Hajiabad		96.2	98.0	101.5	105.1	94.7	88.4	91.5
11	Kish Island	103.9	99.2			89.9			107.1
11	Parsian		96.2	96.3	104.6	107.8	94.3		
12	Dehloran	100.7	102.9			94.7		101.4	
12	Ilam	92.1	106.1	105.0	93.3	100.0	93.5	98.6	102.1
12	Malekshahy	98.6	104.3	95.7	96.8	92.5			
13	Jiroft			103.2	96.4	99.7		94.5	
13	Kerman	92.8	90.2	90.2	93.3	96.5	93.9	95.1	99.8
13	Sirjan			90.7	100.7	104.3		97.2	
13	Zarand			103.5	93.3	93.5		101.1	
14	Kermanshah			106.9	93.3	90.2	93.0	99.8	103.3
15	Abadan	89.7	98.8	107.6	87.6	104.5		104.4	93.8
15	Ahvaz	106.0	93.3	103.0	93.7	97.9	90.0	99.6	107.4
15	Dezful			104.2	103.0	107.3		93.7	
15	Masjed Soleiman			105.4	97.5	104.5		99.3	
16	Yasuj	97.7	100.0	106.5	96.1	89.8	99.4	92.9	102.9
17	Baneh	107.0		93.2	99.7		96.4	103.2	
17	Bijar			100.2	90.6	103.7	96.9	107.3	93.7
17	Dehgolan			95.2			100.0	102.0	98.5
17	Divandareh	90.0		93.5	103.5		96.7	100.0	
17	Kamyaran	87.5		93.0	99.5		96.2	103.0	
17	Marivan	93.5		95.7	102.5		99.0		92.5
17	Qorveh			102.8		96.0	92.8	99.3	
17	Sanandaj	89.4	97.1	95.7	92.5		102.5	99.0	106.1
17	Saqez	106.1		92.5	99.2		95.7	102.5	
17	Sarvabad			92.9	106.5		100.2	99.4	88.8
18	Borujerd	89.3	92.9	94.9	89.0	98.2		93.6	
18	Khorramabad			93.2	91.0	101.0	100.1	94.2	
18	Kuhdasht			106.2	94.6	102.6		92.4	
19	Arak	90.1	88.5	99.7	105.8	93.2		106.8	96.4
19	Ashtian	101.0		97.5	87.9	91.0	94.2	97.3	104.6
19	Delijan	95.7	96.0	102.5	92.5	99.0	89.4	100.6	106.1
19	Komejan	91.0		94.2	97.5	104.6	101.0		87.9
19	Khomein	87.7		97.3	94.0	90.8	103.8	100.8	104.4
19	Khondab	106.6		91.4	97.8	102.0	104.0	101.4	103.0
19	Mahallat	94.9		88.6	101.7	91.7	98.2	107.6	105.3
19	Saveh	90.7		101.2	94.4	97.2	107.0	87.8	103.4
19	Shazand	93.6		90.5	96.8	100.1	103.6	107.2	89.4
19	Tafresh	91.0	89.1	101.0	100.0	97.5	92.2	103.2	94.2
20	Behshahr			96.8	87.7	96.2		93.0	
20	Chalus	97.5		98.2		88.6		91.7	
20	Sari	101.1	96.5	94.2	98.6	96.2	105.7	102.1	92.1
21	Abgarm			90.9	87.8	94.1	100.9	97.4	
21	Moallem Kalayeh		92.0	102.0	95.2	88.9	98.5		105.6
21	Ghazvin	94.3	100.1	107.2	103.7	93.6	96.8	91.1	97.6
22	Qom			96.5		94.5			
23	Biarjmand			95.9	98.5	98.5		88.9	
23	Semnan	92.7	94.5	94.0	89.6	102.7		101.5	99.2
23	Shahrud	90.8		97.3	100.8		104.4	90.8	94.0
24	Saravan	95.5	92.2	95.4		92.2			
24	Zabol	92.0	96.0	87.9	97.5	91.0		94.2	
24	Zahedan	93.7	90.5	93.7	90.5	100.1	100.1	103.3	107.3
25	Tehran			91.3	104.7	99.6	88.1	106.7	102.5
26	Ardakan	100.0		99.4	92.2	102.9	101.5	92.9	92.7
26	Bafgh			90.8	95.7	99.0		92.5	
26	Tabas	101.0	100.0		102.7	102.4		98.9	
26	Yazd	101.5	97.1	99.6	94.4	96.3	94.7	93.1	103.1
27	Mahnshan	92.3			102.0	94.1			99.8
27	Zanjan	99.7	93.2	105.4	96.4	103.2	90.1	93.2	106.8
28	Bojnurd	88.1	101.0	103.0		93.5	90.1	95.0	
29	Dorud	94.5		104.8	102.9	101.2		98.6	
29	Ferdows	89.0		94.3	96.0	96.7		93.6	
29	Torbat	94.0	100.9	92.6				98.0	
29	Mashhad	94.8	98.1	95.2	101.6	105.8	98.7	102.2	91.6
29	Sabzevar	92.9		96.0	96.4			91.1	
30	Birjand	90.0	94.0	100.0	104.0	96.0	88.0	106.0	92.0
32	Mahabad	91.1		97.0	92.2				93.4

NB: Iran has not provided comprehensive update information regarding their transmitter network in recent years and all information is based on various web sources and monitoring observations.

Provinces & regional centres: 1) Ardabil **2)** West Azerbajan **E:** 162-waz@irib.ir **3)** East Azerbayjan **E:** tabriz@irib.ir **4)** Bushehr **E:** prbushehr@irib.ir **5)** Chaharmahal & Bakhtiari: R. Jahanbin **6)** Isfahan **E:** isfahan@irib.ir **7)** Fars **E:** fars162@irib.ir **8)** Gilan **E:** gilan@irib.ir **9)** Golestan **10)** Hamadan **11)** Hormozgan: R. Khalij & Fars: **W:** khalijefars.irib.ir R. Kish: info@kish.irib.ir **12)** Ilam **13)** Kerman **E:** web@kerman.irib.ir **14)** Kermanshah **15)** Ahvaz (also Arabic) **16)** Kohgiluyeh & Boyerahmad: R. Dena **17)** Kurdistan **18)** Lorestan **19)** Markazi **20)** Mazandaran: R. Tabaristan **E:** 162-mzn@irib.ir **21)** Qazvin **22)** Qom **E:** info@qom.irib.ir **23)** Semnan **E:** semnan@irib.ir **24)** Systan & Baluchestan **E:** zahedan@irib.ir **25)** Tehran **26)** Yazd **E:** taban@yazd.irib.ir **27)** Zanjan **28)** North Khorasan (R. Bojnurd) **E:** kh-shomali@irib.ir **29)** Razavi Khorasan: R. Mashhad **E:** infoplanning-ksnr@irib.ir **30)** South Khorasan: (R. Birjand) **E:** birjand@irib.ir **31)** Alborz **32)** Mahabad **33)** Abadan **E:** prabadan@irib.ir

Access to regional web pages also via **W:** dpp.irib.ir

Networks:

I=Radio Iran: 24h, but hrs. of operation vary by station. Frequencies for R. Iran and provincial prgrs at the same transmitter site may be swapped. **N:** on the half hour – **R=Regional (Provincial)** network. Studios in 32 centres producing prgrs in Farsi and local langs, including some locally produced Ext. Sce. prgrs. Regional prgrs are usually between 0230-1630, in some cases 24h, and they may r. R. Iran network 1630-2030 or overnight. Most provincials stations also carry "Shabhaye Iran" (Iran Nights) between 2030-2230, produced in turn by each studio. – **Q=R. Quran**(rlg.): 24h on MW 585kHz and FM – **P=R. Payam** ("Message", music, traffic, news): 24h on MW 1188kHz + FM. – **M=R. Ma'aref** ("Presentation", rlg.): 24h on MW 1071kHz & FM **English: Call of Islam R.** on satellite and Internet: mms://62.220.122.10/maarefeng – **J=R. Javan** (Youth): 24h on MW 1206kHz and FM – **F=R. Farhang** (cultural): 24h on MW 558kHz & FM – **V=R. Varzesh** (sports) and **Tj=R. Tejarat** (R. Trade) on FM. Partly sharing their frequencies – **T=Tehran City Prgr.** 24h on MW 1332kHz & FM 95.0MHz. – **R. Salamat** (Health R): 0230-1430 in Tehran on 103.9MHz – **R Ava/Nava,** Tehran: 24h on 107.2MHz. – **R. Goftegoo,** Tehran: 0230-2030 on 103.9MHz.

Foreign Language prgrs in Tehran: 100.7MHz: various 24h. On 106.7MHz: **English:** 2130-2230, 2030-2130. **Russian:** 1930-2030.

Ann: S: "Inja Tehran ast, Sedaye Jomhuriye Islamiye Iran, Radyoe Iran". Farhang: "Inja Tehran ast, Sedaye Jomhuriye Islamiye Iran, shabakeye Farhang". M: "Inja Qom ast, shabakeye Ma'aref, Sedaye Jomhuriye Islamiye Iran". Q: "Radyoe Qur'an". R: "Inja (capital) ast, Sedaye Jomhuriye Islamiye Iran, shabakeye/markazye (province)."

EXTERNAL SERVICE: Voice of the Islamic Republic of Iran
see International Radio section

IRAQ

LT: UTC +3h — **Pop:** 28 million — **Pr.L:** Arabic, Kurdish, Assyrian, Turkoman — **E.C:** 50Hz, 230V — **ITU:** IRQ

COMMUNICATIONS AND MEDIA COMMISSION (CMC) ✉ P.O. Box 2044, District 929, Street 32, Building 18 , Jadreiah, Baghdad ☎+964 1 7180009 ▤ +964 1 719 5839 **W:** cmc.iq **E:** enquiries@cmc.iq **L.P:** Deputy Dir: Ali Nasir.

IRAQI MEDIA NET - REPUBLIC OF IRAQ RADIO (Gov) ✉ near Al-Mansoor Melia Hotel, Salihiya, Baghdad **W:** center-im.net **E:** info@imn.iq **L.P:** DG: Hassan Al-Musawi. Dir. Eng: Emad Aziz.

MW	kHz	kW	Prgr.
Baghdad	792		Main

FM	MHz	kW	Prgr.	FM	MHz	kW	Prgr.
Diwaniya	88.1		Provincial	Baquba	94.8	10	Provincial
Mosul	88.7		Main/Provincial	Ali Al-Garbi	95.0		Main
Ninewa	88.7		Main	Basra	96.0	1	Quran
Sinjar	90.5		Main	Diyala	96.0		Main
Ramadi	90.8		Main	Tikrit	96.1		Main
Kirkuk	91.5		Main	Najaf	96.5	5	Quran
Hit	92.0		Main	Baghdad	98.3	1	Main
Karbala	92.2	1	Main	Kut	98.5	1	Main
Muthanna	92.7		Main	Qaim	98.5		Main
Karbala	93.3		Provincial	Babylon	99.0		Provincial
Shomali	94.2	10	Main	Hadiha	99.0		Main

FM	MHz	kW	Prgr.	FM	MHz	kW	Prgr.
Rutba	99.0		Main	Mosul	103.4		Main/Provincial
Nasiriya	99.0		Quran	Amara	104.1		Quran
Falluja	99.9	1	Main	Baghdad	105.0		Al Jel
Basra	100.0	5	Main	Amara	106.0		Main
Najaf	101.0	5	Provincial				

Main Prgr (Republic of Iraq R.): 24h in Arabic on on MW and FM except for Provincial programmes on some transmitters during the day. **Quran prgr:** 24h. **R. Al Jel** (for youth). **R. Nineva:** daytime on Mosul trs. **R. Babil:** on 1071kHz and FM. **Ann:** Main prgr: "Idha'at Jumhuriyah al-Iraq min Baghdad".

Other stations:

MW	kHz	kW	Location	Station	H of tr
10)	756	3	Basra	R. Dar as-Salam	0400-2100
8)	810	5/3	Baghdad	R. Om al-Qura	0400-1830
3)	819	10	Basra	R. Al-Amal	0400-1830
10)	882	5	Mosul	R. Dar as-Salam	0400-2100
18)	936	20	Basra	R. as-Safir	
5)	999	20	Baghdad	R. Bilad	0240-1810
6)	1008	20	Najaf	Sowt al-Fadhila	
	1017	10	Karbala	R. Karbala	
7)	1053	3	Baghdad	R. As-Salam	0300-2100
10)	1116	20	Baghdad	R. Dar as-Salam	0400-2100
11)	1179	30	Baghdad	R. Voice of Iraq	0400-1800
10)	1197	1	Kirkuk	R. Dar as-Salam	0400-2100
4)	1404		Maysan	R. Kull al-Iraq	

FM	MHz	kW	Location	Station	H of tr
14)	87.5		Penjwin	R. Garmiyan (Yekgirtu R.)	
48)	87.5		Kirkuk	R. Vision	
21)	87.7	1	Baghdad	Monte-Carlo Doualiya	24h
9)	87.8		Kirkuk	Vo Kurdistan	0300-2000
10)	88.0		Kirkuk	R. Dar as-Salam	0400-2100
19)	88.0	2	Basra	BBC English	24h
20)	88.0		Sulaimaniya	R. Sawa	24h
21)	88.1	1	Mosul	Monte-Carlo Doualiya	24h
43)	88.2		Baghdad	R. Dijla	0500-0100
22)	88.3	1	Sulaimaniya	R. Nawxo	
1)	88.4		Karbala	Imam Hussein FM	0200-1900
22)	88.4		Erbil	R. Nawxo	
43)	88.4		Basra	R. Dijla	0500-0100
46)	88.5		Mosul	R. Nawa (Arabic)	
23)	88.6	1	Baghdad	Panorama FM	24h
38)	88.6	1	Halabja	R. Dênge Nwe	0500-1700
47)	88.9		Erbil	R. Duhok	0400-2300
19)	89.0	2	Baghdad +2 stns	BBC Arabic	24h
39)	89.0		Kirkuk	R. Ashur	
47)	89.0		Amediye	R. Duhok	0400-2300
46)	89.1		Penjwin	R. Nawa (Kurdish)	
14)	89.1		Kalar	R. Garmiyan (Yekgirtu R.)	
3)	89.1		Basra	R. Al-Amal	
46)	89.3		Saidsadeq	R. Nawa (Kurdish)	
45)	89.3		Amara	Al-Mirbad R.	24h
46)	89.3		Halabja	R. Nawa (Kurdish)	
10)	89.4		Mosul	R. Dar as-Salam	0500-2100
18)	89.4		Basra	R. As-Safir	
	89.4			R. Melbend	
46)	89.5		Kirkuk	R. Nawa (Kurdish)	
47)	89.5		Duhok	R. Duhok	0400-2300
	89.6			VO Islam (Kurdish)	
31)	89.7		Karbala	Al-Huda Islamic R.	24h
46)	89.9		Baghdad	R. Nawa (Kurdish)	
19)	90.0	1	Basra/Shumali	BBC Arabic	
24)	90.0		Kirkuk	Turkoman FM	0510-2200
39)	90.0		Mosul	R, Ashur	
27)	90.3		Baghdad	R. Al-Noor	(inactive)
20)	90.4	1	Hilla	R. Sawa	24h
26)	90.4		Baghdad	R. Al-Yauwm	-1500
4)	90.6	0.2	Basra	R. Shanasheel	0400-2300
17)	90.6	0.1	Kirkuk	R. Lawani Kurdistan	
46)	90.6		Sulaimaniya	R. Nawa (Arabic)	
10)	91.0	1	Baghdad/Tikrit	R. Dar as-Salam	0500-2100
39)	91.1		Nineva	R. Ashur	
3)	91.3		Najaf	R. Al-Amal	
9)	91.4		Salah al Din	Vo Kurdistan	0300-2000
28)	91.5	5	Baghdad	Al-Rasheed R.	0300-2300
9)	91.5		Erbil	VO Kurdistan	0300-2000
47)	91.5		Zakho	R. Duhok	0400-2300
28)	91.6	5	Basra	Al-Rasheed R.	0300-2300
34)	91.7		Sulaimaniya	Zed R.	
40)	91.8		Basra	Sumer FM	24h

	FM	MHz	kW	Location	Station	H of tr
7)		91.9	0.3	Baghdad	R. As-Salam	0700-2100
21)		92.0		Basra	Monte-Carlo Doualiya	24h
17)		92.0	0.1	Ranye	R. Lawani Kurdistan	
46)		92.0		5 locations	R. Nawa (Kurdish)	
46)		92.0		Basra	R. Nawa (Arabic)	
28)		92.1		Kirkuk	Al-Rasheed R.	0300-2300
34)		92.3		Erbil/Duhok	Zed R.	
2)		92.4		Basra	Sawt al-Khaleej	
34)		92.5		Kirkuk	Zed R.	
19)		92.5	2	Sulaimaniya	BBC Arabic	24h
46)		92.6		Erbil	R. Nawa (Arabic)	
46)		92.7		Duhok	R. Nawa (Kurdish)	
1)		92.7		Najaf/Wasit	Imam Hussein FM	0200-1900
32)		92.8	0.6	Basra	Al-Nakhil R.	0300-2100
40)		92.8		Sulaimaniya	Sumer FM	24h
19)		92.9	2	Kirkuk	BBC Arabic	24h
43)		93.0		Sulaimaniya	R. Dijla	0500-0100
45)		93.3		Basra	Al-Mirbad R.	24h
9)		93.3		Dohuk	Vo Kurdistan	0300-2000
5)		93.5		Baghdad	R. Bilad	0400-1700
1)		93.7		Baghdad	Imam Hussein FM	0200-1900
43)		94.0		Mosul	R. Dijla	0500-0100
8)		94.5	5	Baghdad	R. Om Al-Qura	0400-1830
46)		94.6		Kirkuk	R. Nawa (Arabic)	
4)		94.6		Basra	R. Nahrain	
2)		95.0		Baghdad	Sawt al-Khaleej	
28)		95.5		Mosul	Al-Rasheed R	0300-2300
12)		95.5		Kirkuk	VO People Kurdistan	0500-2100
16)		95.5	2	Erbil	R. Al-Salam	
20)		95.6	10	Samawa	R. Sawa	24h
19)		96.0	2	Mosul	BBC Arabic	24h
		96.1		Najaf	Al-Ghadeer R.	
20)		96.1		Amarah	R. Sawa	24h
30)		96.1		Babylon	R. Al-Hilla	
33)		96.1	5	Baghdad	R. Al-Mahaba	
35)		96.3		No. Iraq	Guven R.	
46)		96.5		Koya/Qaladezi	R. Nawa (Kurdish)	
1)		96.6	5	Baghdad	R. Al-Nas	0400-1500
19)		96.9	2	Baghdad	BBC English	24h
20)		97.1	1	Tikrit	R. Sawa	24h
46)		97.1		Ranya/Sara	R. Nawa (Kurdish)	
37)		97.3		Baghdad	Sowt al-Jam'ah	
20)		97.5		Baquba	R. Sawa	24h
46)		97.5		Darbandekhan	R. Nawa (Kurdish)	
12)		97.9		Baghdad	Al-Hurriyah R.	0500-2100
24)		98.0	0.1	Erbil	Turkoman FM	0510-2200
46)		98.0		Zakho	R. Nawa (Kurdish)	
40)		98.2		Erbil	Sumer FM	24h
46)		98.5		Zakho	R. Nawa (Arabic)	
2)		98.7		Mosul	Sawt al-Khaleej	
43)		98.8		Erbil	R. Dijla	0500-0100
36)		98.8	5	Baghdad	Ur FM	24h
20)		98.8	1	Kirkuk	R. Sawa	24h
		98.8		Babylon	University R.	
25)		99.1		Karbala	Karbala FM	0300-1500
15)		99.3	3	Bahrez	Ind. RTV Netw.	0500-2100
39)		99.4		Baghdad	R. Ashur	0600-1700
20)		99.6		Ramadi	R. Sawa	24h
22)		99.9		Kirkuk	R. Nawxo	
40)		99.9	5	Baghdad	Sumer FM	24h
40)		99.9		Dohuk	Sumer FM	24h
19)		100.0	2	Nasiriya	BBC Arabic	24h
14)		100.2		Tawella	R. Garmiyan (Yekgirtu R.)	
4)		100.4		Basra	R. Nahrain	
20)		100.5	10	Baghdad	R. Sawa	24h
42)		101.0		Baghdad	R. Al-Ahd	
45)		101.4		Nasiriya	Al-Mirbad R.	24h
17)		101.5		Baghdad	VO Iraqi National Congress	
41)		102.0	3	Baghdad	R. Shafaq	0300-2300
21)		103.0		Erbil	Monte-Carlo Doualiya	24h
29)		103.3		Erbil	R. Runaky	
49)		103.3		Kirkuk	R. Justice	
14)		103.4		Kifri	R. Garmiyan (Yekgirtu R.)	
12)		104.0		Kirkuk	R. Kirkuk	
14)		105.4		Darbandikhan	R. Garmiyan (Yekgirtu R.)	
20)		105.8	1	Najaf	R. Sawa	24h
40)		105.8		Diwaniya	Sumer FM	24h
21)		106.3		Tikrit	Monte-Carlo Doualiya	24h
44)		106.0	1	Baghdad	As-Salam 106 FM	24h
20)		106.6	5	Erbil/Mosul	R. Sawa	24h

FM	MHz	kW	Location	Station	H of tr
20)	107.0	10	Basra	R. Sawa	24h
	107.7		Zakho	R. Hizal	

Addresses and other information:
1) W: imamhussain-fm.com – 2) See main entry under Qatar – 3) ("Hope"). W: alamel.org – 4) R. Kull al-Iraq ("All of Iraq"), Maysan – 5) R. Bilad ("Lands"). Operated by the Islamic Virtue Party. W: albilad.org E: albilad@albilad.org – 6) Sowt al- Fadhila ("Voice of Virtue"), Najaf – 7) R. As-Salam ("Peace") E: mail@tvalsalam.tv – 8) W: heyetnet.org – 9) Operated by the Kurdistan Democratic Party W: kurdistanradio. net E: info@kurdistanradio.net Prgrs in Sorani Kurdish/Arabic – 10) R. Dar As-Salam ("Haven of Peace"), The Voice of the Iraqi Islamic Party. W: darusalam.net – 11) Operated by Imam Al-Shirazi International Association. W: voiraq.com E: voiceiraq@yahoo.com Prgrs in Arabic/ English/Turkmen – 12) Operated by the Patriotic Union of Kurdistan W: hurriya.net E: hurriyanet@yahoo.com . In Sorani Kurdish/Arabic – 13) Operated by the Kurdistan Islamic Group. W: komalnews.net . Prgrs in Arabic/Kurdish/Turkish – 14) W: radiogarmyan.net – 15) E: kahoofy2005@yahoo.com – 16) W: facebook.com/RadioAlSalam – 17) Kurdistan Youth R. W: mosy-krg.org – 18) Basra. W: aliraqnews. com – 19) BBC Arabic Service W: arabicservice@bbc.co.uk – 20) R. Sawa ("Together"). Also on MW via Kuwait 1593kHz 150kW 24h. For more details see International Radio section (USA) – 21) R. France Internationale & Monte-Carlo Doualiya. prgrs in Arabic/French. For details see International radio section (France) –22) facebook. com/Radiorunaky.tk?fref=nf – 23) See MBC entry under UAE – 24) W: kerkuk.net Prgrs in Turkoman/Arabic – 25) Shammasyia St. 29, Quarter 318, Line 55, House 31, Adhadmyia, Baghdad – 26) R. Al-Yauwm ("Today Radio") – 27) R. Al-Noor ("Light"). E: alnoor903fm@ yahoo.com – 28) W: alrasheedmedia.com E: alrasheedfm@yahoo. com . Different prgr. to each region – 29) facebook.com/Radiorunaky. tk?fref=nf – 31) W: al-hodaonline.com/radio E: alhodaonline@gmail. com – 32) Operated by the Islamic Supreme Council of Iraq. W: almej-lis.org E: info@almejlis.org – 33) R. Al-Mahaba ("Friendship"), Voice of Iraqi Women. Supported by the United Nations Development Fund for Women (UNIFEM). W: okiinc.org/vow_radio.html – 34) W: zagrostv. com – 35) Operated by the Turkish army – 36) W: radiourfm.com E: info@radiourfm.com – 38) Sawt al-Jam'ah ("Voice of the University") – 38) R. Dênge Nwe ("New Voice"). W: halabja.info/Radio halabja.htm E: dangynwe@yahoo.com – 39) Operated by the Assyrian Democratic Movement (ADM/ZOWAA) W: zowaa.org E: info@zowaa.org .In Assyrian/Arabic – 40) W: sumerfm.com – 41) R. Shafaq ("Twilight"). W: shafaaq.com . In Kurdish/Arabic – 42) R. Al-Ahd (Oath), Baghdad – 43) R. Dijla (Tigris). W: radiodijla.com – 44) As-Salam (Peace) 106 FM. W: peace106fm.com E-mail: peace106fm@yahoo.com – 45) W: almirbad.com E: info@almirbad.com – 46) W: radionawa.com E: info@ radionawa.com – 47) duhokradio.org – 48) Operated by the Iraqi Turkmen Brotherhood Party – 49) Operated by the Iraqi Turkmen Justice Party – 50) W: uobabylon.edu.iq

IRELAND

L.T: UTC (27 Mar-30 Oct: +1h) — **Pop:** 4.6 million — **Pr.L:** Irish Gaelic, English — **E.C:** 50Hz, 230V — **ITU:** IRL

RAIDIÓ TEILIFÍS EIREANN (Statutory Corporation)
Donnybrook, Dublin 4 ☎ +353 1 208 3111 📠 +353 1 208 3080 E: info@rte.ie W: rte.ie
L.P: DG: Noel Curran; Ch. Fin. Offr.: Breda O'Keeffe. MD TV: Glen Killane. MD Radio: Jim Jennings; MD Corp.Dev.: Brian Dalton, Ch. Tech. Offr: Richard Waghorn, MD News: Kevin Bakhurst
Raidió Na Gaeltachta: Casla, Conamara, Co Galway ☎ +353 91 506677 📠 +353 91 506666 E: rnag@rte.ie W: rte.ie/rnag
Lyric FM: Cornmarket Square, Limerick ☎ +353 61 410222 📠 +353 61 310223 E: lyric@rte.ie W: rte.ie/lyricfm Pub.: RTE Guide
Networks:1=R1, 2=2FM, 3=Raidió Na Gaeltachta, 4=Lyric FM

LW	kHz		kW	Prg.
Summerhill	252		150/300	1

FM (MHz)	1	2	3	4	kW
Achill	89.9	92.1	94.3	99.5	3
Aranmore	89.6	91.8	94.0	99.2	3
Ballybofey	89.7	91.9	94.1	99.3	0.5
Bantry	88.7	90.9	93.1	98.3	1
Cahirciveen	89.5	91.7	93.9	99.1	3
Cairn Hl (Longford)	89.8	-	-	-	20
Casla	88.4	90.6	92.8	98.0	2
Castlebar	89.3	91.5	93.7	98.9	3
Castletownbere	88.3	90.5	92.7	97.9	3
Clermont Carn	87.8	97.0	102.7	95.2	40
Clifden	89.5	91.7	93.9	99.1	3

FM (MHz)	1	2	3	4	kW
Clonmel	88.3	90.5	92.7	97.9	1
Cnoc an Oir	89.2	91.4	93.6	98.7	1
Cork (Spur Hill)	89.2	91.4	93.6	98.8	5
Crosshaven	88.2	90.4	92.6	97.8	3
Dungarvan	88.5	90.7	92.9	98.1	3
Fanad	89.8	92.0	94.2	99.4	4
Greystones	89.5	91.7	93.9	99.1	1
Holywell Hill	89.2	91.4	93.6	98.8	6
Kilduff	90.2	-	-	-	3
Kippure	89.1	91.3	93.5	98.7	50
Knockmoyle	88.4	90.6	92.8	98.0	1
Limerick City	89.4	91.6	93.8	99.0	2.5
Maghera	88.8	91.0	93.2	98.4	160
Malin	88.9	91.1	93.3	98.5	2
Monaghan	88.9	91.1	93.3	98.5	2.5
Moville	88.3	90.5	92.7	97.9	1
Mt. Leinster	89.6	91.8	94.0	99.2	200
Mullaghanish	90.0	92.2	94.4	99.6	160
Suir Valley	89.0	91.2	93.4	98.6	3
Three Rock	88.5	90.7	92.9	96.7	10
Truskmore	88.2	90.4	92.6	97.8	120

+ 10 relays below 0.5kW

1) RTE R. 1: 24h in English & Irish on LW, FM, satellite and internet. **N. in English:** on the h **N. in Irish Gaelic:** 2150 – 2) **2FM:** 24h in English on FM, satellite and internet. – 3) **Raidió Na Gaeltachta:** 24h in Irish Gaelic on FM, satellite and internet – 4) **Lyric FM:** 24h on FM, satellite and internet

EXTERNAL SERVICE (RTE Radio Worldwide): see Int. section

DIGITAL RADIO (DAB): DAB trs are on Band 3. **RTE national multi-plex** Block 12C 227.360 MHz trs. in Dublin, NE Ireland, Cork, Limerick carrying RTE services: R1, 2FM, Lyric FM, R Na Gaeltachta, 2XM, Chill, Junior, Gold, R1 Extra, Pulse
Independent test multiplexes: DB Digital Broadcasting Block 12A 223.936 MHz trs, in Dublin, Cork, Limerick carrying Amazing R., Amazing+, R. Ri-Ra, R. Ri-Ra+, Sunshine, UCB R., UCB+, Zenith, Zenith+. Further information: **W:** dbdb.ie
2RN (formerly RTE Network)
Block B, Cookstown Court, Old Belgard Road, Dublin 24 ☎ +353 1 208 2259 E: 2rntech@2rn.ie W: 2rn.ie
Distributes RTE radio and TV, Today FM and some local and regional broadcasters

BROADCASTING AUTHORITY OF IRELAND (BAI)
2-5 Warrington Place, Dublin D02 XP29 ☎ +353 1 644 1200 📠 +353 1 644 1299 E: info@bai.ie W: bai.ie L.P: Chief Exec: Michael O'Keeffe.
Responsible for regulation of commercial broadcasting in the Irish Republic. Full list of licensed stns can be found on BAI website

TODAY FM (Comm.)
Marconi House, Digges Lane, Dublin 2 ☎ +353 1 804 9000 W: todayfm.com

FM	MHz	kW	FM	MHz	kW
Crosshaven	100.0	6	Knockanore	101.0	2
Truskmore	100.0	250	Castlebar	101.1	6
Moville	100.1	2	Woodcock Hill	101.2	5
Clonmel	100.1	2	Greystones	101.3	1
Knockmoyle	100.2	2	Clifden	101.3	6
Dungarvan	100.3	6	Kilkeaveragh	101.3	4
Maghera	100.6	320	Mt. Leinster	101.4	400
Monaghan	100.7	5	Fanad	101.6	8
Suir Valley	100.8	6	Achill	101.7	6
Kippure	100.9	100	Mullaghanish	101.8	320
Holywell Hill	101.0	12	Three Rock	101.8	2
Spur Hill, Cork	101.0	10	Clermont Carn	105.5	80

+ 5 trs.under 1kW
D.Prgr: 24h **N:** on the h, also on the half h at peak times

NEWSTALK (Comm.)
Marconi House, Digges Lane, Dublin 2 ☎ + 353 1 644 5100 📠 + 353 1 644 5101 W: newstalk.com E: info@newstalk.com
L.P: CE: Gerard Whelan

FM	MHz	kW	FM	MHz	kW
Monaghan	103.3	2.5	Ballyguile	107.0	2
Capard	105.8	4	Clifden	107.0	4
Three Rock	106.0	10	Kilitimagh	107.2	6
Holywell Hill	106.9	12	Mt Leinster	107.2	4
Longford	106.9	5	Knockmoyle	107.2	4
Limerick City	107.0	2	Mullaghanish	107.4	80.0
Nagles	107.0	0.5	Truskmore	107.4	80.0

FM	MHz	kW	FM	MHz	kW
Mohercrom	107.4	10.0	Achill	107.6	1.3
Waterford	107.4	2.0	Cork City	107.8	10.0
Maghera	107.6	32.0	Cahirciveen	107.8	4.0
Saggart	107.6	2.0	Kilduff	107.8	2.0
Dungarvan	107.6	5.0	Gorey	107.8	1.0
+6 trs. under 1 kW					

SPIRIT RADIO (Rlg.)

✉ Radio Centre, Killarney Rd., Bray, Co Wicklow ☎ + 353 1 272 4760
W: spiritradio.ie E: info@spiritradio.ie

MW	kHz	kW
Carrickroe	549	25

FM	MHz	kW	FM	MHz	kW
Limerick	89.8	0.4	Dundalk	90.4	0.1
Dublin	89.9	0.4	Cork	90.9	0.5
Waterford	90.1	0.2	Galway	91.7	0.4
Bray	90.1	0.2	Naas/Newbridge	92.2	-

D.Prgr: 24h

Local Stations:

FM	MHz	kW	Station, tx location
31)	87.8	1	Connemara Community R
30)	94.6	1	Classic Hits 4FM, Saggart
32)	94.7	5	Spin South West, Clifden
18)	94.8	4	Northern Sound, Slieve Glah
30)	94.8	3	Classic Hits 4FM, Churchfield (Mallow)
1)	94.9	9	East Coast FM, Avoca
30)	94.9	3	Classic Hits 4FM, Nowen Hill
2)	95.0	10	Limerick's Live 95 FM, Woodcock Hill
16)	95.1	10	WLR FM, Faha, Dungarvan
10)	95.2	2	Highland R, Aran Mor
30)	95.4	9	Classic Hits 4FM, Nowen Hill
7)	95.5	2	Clare FM, Kilrush
17)	95.6	1	Cork's 96 FM, Kilworth,NE Cork
3)	95.6	4	South East R, Mt.Leinster
4)	95.8	10	LM FM, Mt. Oriel
17)	95.8	10	Cork's 96 FM, Nowen Hill
7)	95.9	2	Clare FM, Woodcock Hill
8)	96.0	1	KCLR, Corbally Wood
6)	96.1	10	MWR FM, Kiltimagh
17)	96.1	1	Cork's 96 FM, Mount Hillary
20)	96.2	6	R. Kerry, Cahirciveen
1)	96.2	10	East Coast FM, Bray
18)	96.3	10	Northern Sound, Monaghan
7)	96.4	10	Clare FM, Maghera
17)	96.4	10	Cork's 96 FM, Holly Hill
8)	96.6	10	KCLR , Johns Well
8)	96.8	10	Galway Bay FM, Knockroe
8)	96.9	4	KCLR, Rossmore
34)	96.9	9	iRadio, Scalp Mountain
20)	97.0	40	R. Kerry, Mullaghanish
11)	97.1	10	Tipp FM, Scrouthea
5)	97.1	3	MWR FM, Achill
12)	97.3	5	KFM, Rossmore
30)	97.4	4	Classic Hits 4FM, Bweeng Mountain
9)	97.4	2	Galway Bay FM, Redmount Hl
16)	97.5	10	WLR FM, East Waterford
20)	97.6	2	R. Kerry, Knockanore
12)	97.6	4	KFM, Slieve Thuile
13)	98.1	5	98 FM, Three Rock
1)	99.9	9	East Coast FM, Saggart Hill
33)	100.1	-	R, Nova, Balbriggan
33)	100.3	12	R. Nova, Three Rock
24)	102.0	13	Beat 102-103 FM, Mount Leinster
34)	102.1	9	iRadio, South Galway
10)	102.1	1.3	Highland R., Feirn Hill
24)	102.2	6	Beat 102-103 FM, West Waterford
26)	102.2	5	Q 102, Three Rock
32)	102.3	1	Spin South West, Ennistynmon
24)	102.4	10	Beat 102-103 FM, Clonmel
21)	102.5	4	Ocean FM, Truskmore
32	102.5	5	Spin South West, Knockmoyle
17a)	102.6	10	C103, Cork City
32)	102.7	9	Spin South West, Maghera
24)	102.8	10	Beat 102-103 FM, East Waterford
1)	102.9	16	East Coast FM, Ballyguille
1)	102.9	2	East Coast FM, Baltinglass
17)	102.9	1	C103, NE Cork
32)	102.9	9	Spin South West, Cahirciveen
32)	103.0	2.5	Spin South West, Woodcock Hill

FM	MHz	kW	Station, tx location
34)	103.1	9	iRadio, Longford
34)	103.1	3	i102-104, Achill
34)	103.1	1	iRadio, Senafaistin
22)	103.2	0.5	Dublin City FM, Three Rock
10)	103.3	10	Highland R, Scalp Mountain
17a)	103.3	10	C103, Nowen Hill
34)	103.3	4	iRadio, Clifden
6)	103.5	2.5	Midlands 103, Sliabh Bloom
32)	103.5	1	Spin South West, Knockanore
17a)	103.7	5	C103, Mt. Hillary
34)	103.7	9	iRadio, Castlebar
25)	103.8	5	Spin 103.8, Three Rock
11)	103.9	3.2	Tipp FM, Kilduff
34)	104.0	2	iRadio, Aranmore
14)	104.1	2.5	Shannonside 104FM, Sliabh Bawn
30)	104.2	9	Classic Hits 4FM, Limerick
15)	104.4	5	FM 104, Three Rock
34)	104.4	9	iRadio, Sligo (Truskmore)
28)	104.5	10	Red FM, W. Cork (Nowen Hill)
10)	104.5	2	Highland R., Back Mountain
30)	104.6	9	Classic Hits 4FM, Maghera,Co Clare
34)	104.7	1	iRadio, Saggart
19)	104.8	10	Tipperary Mid-West R, Dangandargan
34)	104.8	2.5	iRadio, Cavan (Sliabh Giah)
30)	104.9	9	Classic Hits 4FM, Galway City
21)	105.0	10	Ocean FM, Mt.Charles
34)	105.0	5	iRadio, Mt Oriel (Louth)
29)	105.2	4	TX FM, Three Rock
28)	105.7	5	Red FM, North Cork (Nagles)
28)	106.1	10	Red FM, Churchfield, Cork
34)	106.2	5	iRadio, Capard
23)	106.4	2	Raidió Na Life, Three Rock
34)	106.7	10	iRadio, Monaghan
27)	106.8	4	Sunshine 106.8, Three Rock
+ approx 110 additional txs of less than 1kW			

Addresses and other information:

1) Radio Centre, Killarney Rd, Bray, Co Wicklow A98 R6F6 E: reception@eastcoast.fm W: eastcoast.fm – 2) Radio House, Richard Court, Dock Rd, Limerick V94 HG51 E: info@live95fm.ie W: live95fm.ie – 3) Custom House Quay, Wexford Town E: info@southeastradio.ie W: southeastradio.ie – 4) Broadcasting House, Rathmullen Rd, Drogheda, Co Louth E: info@lmfm.ie W: lmfm.ie – 5) Clare Str, Ballyhaunis, Co Mayo W: midwestradio.ie – 6) Tindle House, Axis Business Park, Tullamore, Co Offaly E: info@midlandsradio.fm W: midlandsradio. fm – 7) Abbeyfield Centre, Francis Str, Ennis, Co Clare W: clare.fm – 8) Leggetsrath Business Park, Carlow Rd, Kilkenny E: info@kclr96fm. com W: kclr96fm.com – 9) Unit 13, Sandy Rd, Galway E: info@ galwaybayfm.ie W: galwaybayfm.ie – 10) Pine Hill, Letterkenny, Co Donegal E: enquries@highlandradio.com W: highlandradio.com – 11) Broadcast Centre, 4A Gurtnafleur Business Park, Clonmel, Co Tipperary E: reception@tippfm.com W: tippfm.com – 12) KFM Broadcast Centre, M7 Business Park, Newhall, Naas, Co Kildare E: info@kfmradio.com W: kfmradio.com – 13) Level 3, South Block, The Malt House, Grand Canal Quay, Dublin 2 E: website@98fm.com W: 98fm.com – 14) Unit 1E Master Tech Business Park, Athlone Rd, Longford W: shannonside. ie – 15) Macken House, Mayor Str Upper, Dublin 1 E: sales@fm104.ie W: fm104.ie – 16) Broadcast Centre, Ardkeen, Dunmore Rd, Waterford E: reception@wlrfm.com W: wlrfm.com – 17) Broadcasting House, Patrick's Place, Cork E: info@96fm.ie W: 96fm.ie – 17a) Weir Str., Bandon, Co. Cork E: info@c103.ie W: c103.ie – 18) Unit 3 Milltown Business Park, Monaghan & Thomas Ashe St.,Cavan E: info@northernsound.ie W: northernsound.ie – 19) St Michael Str, Tipperary W: tippmidwestradio.com – 20) Maine Str., Tralee, Co Kerry E: info@ radiokerry.ie W: radiokerry.ie – 21) Ocean FM Broadcasting Centre, North West Business Park, Collooney, Co Sligo E: sales@oceanfm.ie W: oceanfm.ie – 22) Docklands Innovation Park, Unit 6, 128-130 East Wall Rd, Dublin 3 E: admin@dublincityfm.ie W: dublincityfm.ie – 23) 7 Merrion Square, Dublin 2 E: eolas@raidionalife.ie W: raidionalife. ie (Irish language stn) – 24) Broadcast Centre, Ardkeen, Dunmore Rd, Waterford E: promo@beat102103.com W: beat102103.com – 25) Level 3, South Block, Malt House, Grand Canal Quay, Dublin 2 E: info@ spin1038.com W: spin1038.com – 26) Macken House, 39-40 Upper Mayor Str, Dublin 1 E: info@q102.ie W: q102.ie – 27) 73 North Wall Quay, Dublin 1 E: mail@sunshineradio.ie W: sunshine1068.com – 28) 1 University Technology Centre, Curraheen Rd., Bishopstown, Cork E: info@redfm.ie W: redfm.ie – 29) Marconi House, Digges Lane, Dublin 2 E: info@txfm.ie W: txfm.ie – 30) Ground Floor, Castleforbes House, Castleforbes Rd., Dublin 1. E: info@classichits.ie W: classichits.ie – 31) Connemara West Centre, Letterfrack, Co Galway E: info@conne-

marafm.com **W:** connemarafm.com – **32)** 2nd Floor Landmark Building, Raheen, Limerick **E:** info@spinsouthwest.com **W:** spinsouthwest.com – **33)** 1st Floor, Castleforbes House, Castleforbes Rd, Dublin 1 **E:** info@ nova.ie **W:** nova.ie – **34)** iRadio, Level 3, Unit C, Monksland Business Park, Athlone. **E:** info@iradio.ie **W:** iradio.ie

ZENITH CLASSIC ROCK
◻ Total Broadcast Consultants Ltd, Unit 25, Waterford Business Park, Cork Road, Waterford ☎ + 353 51 845422 ◲ + 353 51 845414 **W:** zenithclassicrock.com **E:** info@totalbroadcast.net
D.Prgr: 24h online & DAB only.

Unofficial MW stations:
kHz	kW	Station, tx location
846	1	R. North, Redcastle, Co Donegal
981	1	R. Star Country, Emyvale, Co Monaghan
1539	0.4	Energy, Dublin: (Weekends - alt. freq 1395)

Community/special interest stns: 23 stns in operation at October 2015. **Hospital/Institutions:** 6 stns. **Temporary/Special Event services:** see BAI **W:** bai.ie. **Wireless Public Address System (WPAS):** religious and other sces broadc. to househound via CB radio 26.7–27.99MHz

ISRAEL

L.T: UTC +2h (25 Mar-30 Oct: +3h) — **Pop:** 7.7 million — **Pr.L:** Hebrew, Arabic — **E.C:** 50Hz, 230V — **ITU:** ISR

ISRAEL BROADCASTING AUTHORITY (IBA)
◻ 161 Jaffa Road, P.O. Box 28080, Jerusalem 91280 ☎+972 2 5015555 ◲ +972 2 5015504 **W:** iba.org.il **E:** webmaster@iba.org.il
L.P: Chairman: Amir Gilat. DG: Moti Sklar. Transmission Mgr: David Gombosh.

KOL ISRAEL (Pub.)
◻ Heleni Hamalka 21, P.O. Box 1082, Jerusalem 91010 ☎+972 3 6944777 & inside Israel 1599 509510 **W:** iba.org.il/world **E:** reception@iba.org.il **L.P:** Dir. & PD (Radio): Michael Miro. Dir. of Eng: Efraim Porat. Dir. Liaison & Coordination: Raphael Kochanowski.

MW	kHz	kW	Prgr.	MW	kHz	kW	Prgr.
Yavne	531	50	A	Yavne	1080	50	D
Yavne	657	100	B	Akko (Acre)	1206	50	B
Akko (Acre)	738	10	B	Eilat	1458	10	A
She'ar Yashuv	882	10	B	She'ar Yashuv	1458	10	A

FM (MHz)	A	B	C	D	M	X	R	kW
Akko (Acre)							101.3	40
Ariel	105.3	95.2			97.5	88.2		4
Atara	105.3	95.2	97.5	93.7	103.7	88.2	100.5	16/40
Beersheba	100.7	94.4	105.5	92.4	98.4	88.5	101.8	4/80
Efrat	105.3	95.2	97.5	93.7		88.2		8
Eilat		94.5	105.5	92.3	98.4	88.5		4
Ein Yahav		95.2	97.5					4
Eitanim	105.1	95.5	97.8	88.8	91.3	87.6	100.3	160/100
Grofit		95.0	98.9		92.4	87.6		16
Haifa		94.5	105.5	92.4	98.5			80
	104.8	95.0		88.8		88.0		2
Heletz	104.8							20
Jerusalem	104.8	95.0	89.7	99.3		88.0	101.3	8/2
Kalya		95.5	97.8	88.8	91.3			8/0.5
Katzir		95.2		93.7				40
Kohav Hayarden	104.8	95.0	89.7		97.2		101.3	40
Menara	104.8	95.0	89.7		97.2		101.3	2
Mitzpe Ramon		95.0	89.7		97.2			20
Netanya							100.5	8
Safed	105.1	95.5	97.8	88.8	91.3	87.6	100.3	40
Sha'ar HaNegev		95.0		99.3				4
Tel Aviv	104.8	95.0	89.7		97.2	88.0	101.3	10/4/2

Prgrs (in Hebrew if not mentioned otherwise):
A: "Reshet Alef": Talk & cultural programming 24h excl. times listed in Reshet Moreshet below. **N.** in Hebrew: rel. Prgr. B. – **B:** "Reshet Bet":** 24h. News, current affairs & sports. **N:** on the h. – **C:** "Reshet Gimel":** 24h Israeli popular music. **N:** rel. Prgr. B. – **D:** "Reshet Dalet"** (Arabic). 24h. Ann: "Sowt Israel" – **X:** "88 FM":** 24h. **N:** rel. Prgr. B. Light music, traffic reports – **R: REQA** (Reshet Qlitat Aliya): immigrants network, 24h in Russian, Amharic, French, Yiddish, Ladino, Romanian, Spanish, Moghrabi, Bukharian, Georgian, Hungarian and English 0430-0445, 1030-1045 & 1830-1845 – **M: "Kol Ha Musica"** (VO Music): 24h, classical music and drama. – **"Reshet Moreshet"** (Heritage Network). Religious programming on Reshet Alef. Sun-Thurs

1400-2200, Fri 0600-1500, Sat 1900-2200 – **Educational radio** "Kol HaCampus" is operating on 106.0MHz with 1kW in Holon, Tiberias, Beersheba, Haifa, Bet El and other trs in colleges around Israel. **W:** 106fm.co.il

GALEI TZAHAL (Israel Defence Forces R, Mil.)
◻ 1 Dror St, corner of Yehuda Hayamit St, Tel Aviv. Military ◻ MPO Box 01005 Jaffa ☎+972 3 5126666 **W:** glz.co.il **E:** glz@galatz.co.il
L.P: Commander: Yaron Dekel.

FM (MHz)	Main	kW	GalGalatz	kW
Beersheba	102.3	10	99.8	10
Beit She'an	104.0	5	91.8	5
Eilat	104.0	1	107.0	1
Grofit	96.6	10	93.5	10
Haifa	102.3	10	107.0	10
Jerusalem	104.0	1	107.1	1
Kalya	104.0	2	99.8	2
Kiryat Shmona	104.0	1	107.0	1
Ma'ale Adumim	104.0	0.3	-	
Ma'ale Efraim	96.6	1	107.0	1
Mitzpe Ramon	104.0	5	107.0	5
Ramla	96.6	20	91.8	10
Safed	96.6	5	93.5	5
Sapir	102.3	2	91.8	2
Tel Aviv	104.0	2	93.5	2
Wadi Ara	104.0	5	99.8	5

Main Prgr: 24h. (news, talk show, music). **N:** on the h.
GalGalatz (traffic reports and music): 24h.
Ann: Main Prgr: "Galei Tzahal, Shidure Tsva Hagana Le'Yisrael".

SECOND AUTHORITY FOR TELEVISION & RADIO
◻ 20 Beit Hadfus St, P.O.Box 3445, Jerusalem ☎+972 2 6556222 **W:** rashut2.org.il **E:** rashut@rashut2.org.il

Regional commercial FM radio (all in Hebrew except as noted):
ECO99fm, Hertzliyah: 99.0MHz **W:** echo99.fm – **Galey Israel:** Benjamin area 89.3MHz, Central Israel 94.0MHz, South 102.5MHz, Dan area 106.5 MHz. **W:** srugim.co.il/galeyisrael – **Pervoye R,** Rishon Le'Zion. In Russian: Ashdod 89.1MHz. **W:** 891fm.co.il – **R. A'shams** (The Sun) in Arabic at Nazareth-Ein Hahoresh area. 98.1 & 101.1MHz. **W:** ashams.com – **R. Darom** (Southern R.): Beersheba 97.0MHz, Kiryat Gat, Ashkelon. Arava & Dead Sea settlements: 95.8MHz. **W:** radiodarom.co.il **R. Darom** (Southern R.) :101.5MHz. **W:** radiodarom.co.il/?page_id=2880 – **R. Haifa,** Haifa: 95.9, 107.5MHz. **W:** radiohaifa.mediacast.co.il – **R. Jerusalem:** Jerusalem 101.0MHz, Bet Shemesh 89.5MHz. **W:** tapuz.co.il/minisites/radiojerusalem – **R. Kol Barama,** Tel Aviv 92.1MHz, Beersheva 104.3MHz, Jerusalem 105.7MHz. **W:** kol-barama.co.il – **R. Kol Chai:** Bene Brak 92.8, Jerusalem 93.0MHz. **W:** 93fm.co.il – **R. Kol Rega:** Galilee 96.0MHz, Tiberias 91.5MHz. **W:** 96fm.co.il – **R. Lev Ha Medina:** Shfela 91.0MHz, Beersheba 93.3MHz. **W:** 91fm.co.il – **Kol Ha Yam Ha Adom** (VO the Red Sea): 101.1, 102.0MHz 1kW. **W:** fm102.co.il – **R. L'Lo Hafsaka** (Nonstop): Upper Galilee 101.5MHz, Ramat Gan 103.0MHz, Lower Galilee 104.5MHz. **W:** 103.fm – **R. Tel Aviv:** 102.0MHz. **W:** tapuz.co.il/minisites/102fm – **R. Tishim,** (90), Tel Aviv: 90.0, 94.7MHz. **W:** 90fm.co.il – **Radius 100 FM,** Tel Aviv: 100.0MHz. **W:** 100fm.co.il

WEST BANK & GAZA STRIP
(Palestinian territories)
L.T: UTC +2h (26 Mar-21 Oct: +3h; suspended during month of Ramadan; dates subject to confirmation) — **Pop:** 4 million — **Pr.L:** Arabic — **E.C:** 50Hz, 230V — **ITU:** XWB (West Bank), XGZ (Gaza)

PALESTINIAN BROADCASTING CORPORATION (Gov)
◻ P.O. Box 984, Al-Bireh, Ramallah, West Bank ☎+970 2 2988888 **W:** pbc.ps **E:** info@pbc.ps
FM: Jenin & Ramallah 90.7MHz, Gaza 99.4MHz, Jenin 102.2MHz.
D.Prgr. in Arabic: 0400-2300 **Ann:** "Sawt Filastin".

Private FM stations:
Al-Balad R, Jenin: 104.8/105.8MHz. **W:** albaladfm.com – **Al-Horya R,** Ramallah: 104.5MHz. **W:** alhorya.com – **Al-Manar R,** Gaza: 92.0MHz. **W:** manarfm.com – **Al-Qamar R,** Jericho: 89.4MHz. **W:** maannet.org – **Ajyal R** Ramallah 103.4MHz, Hebron 107.1MHz. **W:** arn.ps – **Amwaj R.,** Ramallah 91.5MHz, south 99.4MHz, north 104.8MHz. **W:** amwaj.ps – **Angham R.,** Ramallah: 92.3MHz. **W:** radioangham.com – **Cool FM:** 104.0MHz, all English. **W:** coolfm.ps – **Gaza FM:** 100.9MHz. **W:** gazafm.net – **Hala FM:** 94.3MHz. See main entry under Jordan – **Hebron R:** 90.4MHz. **W:** hebronradio.com – **Holy Quran R,** Jerusalem 88.4MHz, Nablus 96.9MHz. **W:** quran-

radio.com — **Iman R,** Gaza: 96.2MHz **W:** imanradio.com — **Kul Al-Nas R,** Tulkarem: 107.3MHz **W:** najah. **Najah FM,** Nablus: 88.4MHz. **W:** najah. edu/fm — **Quds R,** Gaza: 102.7MHz. **W:** qudsradio.ps — **R. Al-Shamal,** Qalqiliya: 96.6MHz. **W:** alshamal.net — **R. All for Peace,** Ramallah: 107.2MHz (Hebrew), 89.8MHz (Arabic). **W:** allforpeace.org Also rel. VOR R. Japan and Polish R. — **R. Bethlehem 2000**, Bethlehem: 89.6/106.4MHz 5kW. **W:** radiobethlehem2000.net Also rel. BBC&DW — **R. Isis,** Bethlehem: 87.5MHz. **W:** radioisis.net — **R. Marah,** Hebron: 100.4MHz. **W:** marah-fm.ps — **R. Mawwal,** Bethlehem: 101.7MHz. **W:** mawwal.ps — **R. Minbar Al-Hurriya,** Hebron: 92.7MHz **W:** hr.ps — **R. Nagham,** Qalqiliya: 99.6MHz. **W:** radionagham.com — **R. Nisaa,** Ramallah: 96.0MHz, Gaza 96.2MHz. **W:** radionisaa.net — **R. Ray,** Gaza: 98.0MHz **W:** alrayradio.ps — **R. Tariq al-Mahabeh,** Nablus: 97.7/108.0MHz. **W:** tmfm.net — **Sawt al-Aqsa,** Gaza: 106.7MHz. **W:** alaqsavoice.ps— **Sawt al-Asra,** Gaza: 107.9MHz. **W:** asravoice.ps — **Sirajj R,** Hebron: 105.7MHz. **W:** sirajfm.com — **VO Love and Peace,** Ramallah: freq. not known **W:** volpfm.com
Monte-Carlo Doualiya: Ramallah 94.6MHz, Nablus 97.3MHz, Hebron 99.7MHz.
R. Sawa: Jenin 93.5MHz, Bethlehem 94.2MHz, Nablus 94.5MHz, Hebron 100.2MHz

ITALY

L.T: UTC +1h (27 Mar-30 Oct: +2h) — **Pop:** 60.8 million — **Pr.L:** Italian — **E.C:** 50Hz, 220V — **ITU:** I

RAI-RADIOTELEVISIONE ITALIANA (Pub.)
⌨ Via Asiago 10, 00195 Roma ☎ +39 06 38781 📠 +39 06 3622621 ⌨ (Listeners) Centro Corrispondenza, C.P. 320, 00100 Roma ☎ +39 06 3317 2591 📠 +39 06 3317 1895 **E:** service@rai.it **W:** rai.it Tech. Dept: Rai Teche: Via Cernaia 33, 10121 Torino, **Dir.;** Barbara Scaramucci **W:** teche.rai.it **E:** teche@rai.it Rai Way:Centro Ascolto e Qualità Controllo Servizio RAI Monza, Via Parco Mirabellino 1, 20900 Monza **L.P:** Pres.: Roberto Sergio **W:** raiway.rai.it **E:** raiway@rai.it **V:** QSL-card. No Rp. **W:** contattalarai.rai.it/dl/rai/contattalarai.html Sedi Regionali: sediregionali.rai.it **E:** sedi.regionali@rai.it **W:** raiway.rai.it/index.php?lang=IT&&cat=71
L.P: Pres.: Monica Maggioni, GM: Luigi Gubitosi, Dir.Reg.Radio: Alessandro Zucca i, Dir.Rai Italia:Piero Badaloni
Regional Centres ⌨ **1** Abruzzo: Viale di Amicis 27, 65123 Pescara — **2** Alto Adige: Piazza Mazzini 23, 39100 Bolzano/Bozen — **3** Basilicata: Via dell'Edilizia 2, 85100 Potenza — **4** Calabria: Viale G. Marconi 1, 87100 Cosenza — **5** Campania: Via Marconi 11, 80125 Napoli — **6** Emilia-Romagna: Viale della Fiera 13, 40127 Bologna — **7** Friuli-Venezia-Giulia: Via Fabio Severo 7, 34133 Trieste — **8** Lazio: Largo Villy de Luca 4, 00188 Roma — **9** Liguria: Corso Europa 125, 16132 Genova — **10** Lombardia: Corso Sempione 27, 20145 Milano — **11** Marche: Piazza della Repubblica 8, 60121 Ancona — **12** Molise: Viale Principe di Piemonte 59, 86100 Campobasso — **13** Piemonte: Via G.Verdi 16, 10121 Torino — **14** Puglia: Via Dalmazia 104, 70121 Bari — **15** Sardegna: Via Barone Rossi 27, 09125 Cagliari — **16** Sicilia: Viale Strasburgo 19, 90146 Palermo — **17** Toscana: Largo Alcide de Gasperi 1, 50136 Firenze — **18** Trentino: Via Fratelli Perini 141, 38122 Trento — **19** Umbria: Via L. Masi 2, 06124 Perugia — **20** Valle d'Aosta: Loc.Grande Charriere 70, 11020 Saint Cristophe — **21** Veneto: Palazzo Labia, Campo S. Geremia,Sestiere Cannaregio 275, 30121 Venezia

MW Station		kHz	kW	Prg
17)	Pisa (Coltano)	657	100	R1
10)	Milano (Siziano)	900	100/50	R1
21)	Venezia (Campalto)	936	10/5	R1 (+a)
7)	Trieste(Monte Radio)	981	20/10	S
13)	Torino (Volpiano)	999	50/10	R1
11)	Ancona (Montagnolo)	1062	10/6	R1
15)	Cagliari (Decimoputzu)	1062	60/10	Rp (d)
16)	Catania (Barriera del B)	1062	20/2	R1 (c)
8)	Roma (Monte Ciocci)	1107	10	R1
16)	Palermo(MtePellegrino)	1116	10	R1 (c)
14)	Foggia	1431	5/2	R1
21)	Belluno Cortina	1449	2	R1 (+a)
9)	Genova (Portofino)	1575	50/30	R1

FM (MHz)		R1	R2	R3	R4	GRP	kW
6)	Bertinoro	90.8	93.4	99.6	-	89.7	30
6)	Bologna	89.5	91.7	93.9	-	93.6	60
2)	Bolzano	91.5	93.7	97.1	99.6	95.1	14
6)	Ca' del Vento	92.1	96.5	98.5	-	90.6	40
8)	Canepina-PNibbio	93.7	99.4	-	-	-	12
4)	Capo Spartivento	95.6	97.6	99.7	-	104.2	10
21)	Col Visentin	91.1	93.1	95.5	-	-	30

FM (MHz)		R1	R2	R3	R4	GRP	kW
4)	Crotone	94.9	97.9	99.9	-	97.4	10
17)	Firenze	87.8	91.1	98.4	-	88.0	10
7)	Friscano	88.4	90.5	94.1	-	-	10
4)	Gambarie	95.3	97.3	99.3	-	-	40
		-	103.9			-	40
9)	Genova	89.5	91.9	95.1	-	104.5	80
5)	Golfo di Policastro	88.5	90.5	92.5	-	-	10
5)	Golfo di Salerno	95.1	97.1	99.1	-	-	20
7)	Gorizia	89.5	92.3	94.6	98.3	106.8	10
14)	Martina Franca	89.1	91.1	93.1	-	90.3	100
10)	Milano	90.6	93.7	99.4	102.2	88.3	60
17)	Monte Argentario	90.1	92.1	94.3	-	99.6	70
		-	89.0			-	16
9)	Monte Beigua	91.5	94.6	98.9	-	100.5	40
14)	Monte Caccia	94.6	96.7	98.9	-	98.2	100
16)	Monte Cammarata	91.1	95.9	99.9	-	98.3	100
6)	Monte Canate	-	95.9	-	-	-	24
8)	Monte Cavo	87.6	91.2	98.4	-	99.3	40
11)	Monte Conero	88.3	90.3	92.3	-	105.2	100
5)	Monte Faito	94.1	96.1	98.1	-	91.0	100
16)	Monte Lauro	94.7	96.7	98.7	-	89.0	100
15)	Monte Limbara	88.9	95.3	99.3	-	-	60
17)	Monte Luco	88.1	92.5	96.2	-	103.2	30
17)	Monte Nerone	94.7	96.6	98.7	-	88.1	100
19)	Monte Miranda	95.7	97.7	99.7	-	102.1	60
		-	88.3			-	30
10)	Monte Penice	94.2	97.4	99.9	-	88.2	120
		-	103.0			-	120
3)	Monte Pierfaone	88.1	90.1	92.1	-	91.2	45
19)	Monte Sambuco	88.6	90.7	93.5	-	-	100
		-	100.7			-	100
4)	Monte Scuro	88.5	90.5	92.5	-	98.4	30
15)	Monte Serpeddi	90.7	92.7	96.3	-	106.5	70
17)	Monte Serra	88.5	90.5	92.9	-	88.2	70
16)	Monte Soro	89.9	91.9	93.9	-	104.2	30
19)	Monte Subasio	89.3	91.4	93.5	-	104.6	30
21)	Monte Venda	88.1	89.0	89.9	-	-	160
5)	Monte Vergine (AV)	87.9	90.3	92.3	-	93.0	20
5)	Napoli Camaldoli	89.3	91.3	93.3	103.9	101.0	12
3)	Nova Siri	-	-	89.5	-	-	10
16)	PalermoMtePellegri	94.9	96.9	98.9	-	90.3	40
1)	Pescara S. Silvestro	89.2	94.3	96.4	-	102.0	70
3)	Pomarico	88.7	92.7	95.7	-	-	10
15)	Punta Badde Urbara	91.3	93.3	97.3	-	-	70
8)	Roma M. Mario	89.7	91.7	93.7	-	100.3	100
4)	Roseto Capo Spulico	94.4	96.5	98.5	-	-	10
14)	Salento Turrisi	90.7	95.5	97.5	-	91.0	60
16)	San Cerbone	95.3	97.3	99.3	-	-	12
21)	SanZenodiMontagna	93.2	96.5	98.5	-	89.5	10
10)	Selva Piana	88.4	90.3	92.4	-	-	10
13)	Torino Eremo	92.1	95.6	98.2	101.8	88.2	100
16)	Trapani Erice	88.4	90.5	92.5	-	90.8	60
7)	TriesteMteBelvedere	91.5	93.6	95.8	103.9	106.7	10
7)	Udine	94.9	97.2	99.8	-	-	60
21)	Velletri	88.7	90.3	92.7	-	-	15

+ over 6000 stns below 1kW not mentioned
D.Prgr: All stns transmit from 0500 to 2300, except for Milano 900kHz, Roma 1107kHz 24h **R1**=Radiouno, **R2FM**=Radiodue, **R3FM**=Radiotre, **S**=Special Prgrs.

Regional Prgrs: 0618 -0628 Mon/Sat RAI1; 1110-1127 Mon Sat.. 1730-1735 Mon-Fri, , Sun : 1115-1126
(a) Friuli: 0618 -0657 Mon-Sat RAI1, 1003-1157 Mon-Sat RAI1, 1130-1157 Sun RAI 1,1300-1415 Mon-Fri RAI1, 1330-1400 Sat RAI1, 1730-1756 Mon/Fri RAI1, 1715-1756 Sat RAI1, 0740-0910, 1108-1157, 1730-1756 Sun sport RAI1; (+a): "L'ora della Venezia Giulia" 1345-1445 Mon/Sat RAI1, 1330-1400 Sun RAI1. – **(b) Sicilia:** 1230-1245, Mon/Sat RAI1 Arabic sce only on FM stns. – **(c) Sicilia:** 0630-0657,1110-1127,1315-1400, 1730-1756 Mon/Sat; RAI1 1140-1157,1730-1756 Sun sport RAI1. – **(d) Sardegna:** 0630-0657,1315-1400, 1730-1756 Mon/Sat RAI1; 1730-1756 Sun sport RAI1. – **(f) Valle D'Aosta:** 1315-1400 Mo/Sat, 1730-1756 Sun sport RAI1(Bilingual). – **(e) Alto Adige** 0630-0657, 1315-1400, 1730-1756 Mon/Sat; 1730-1756 Sun sport RAI1
NB: All 1h earlier in summertime

SPECIAL PRGRS
ISO Radio: 24h sce for motorway users on 103.3MHz FM (220 txs of 5kW or less);103.2MHz Milano,Como,Lecco area; 103.5MHz, Rome area **E:** isoradio@rai.it **W:** isoradio.it **Dir. :** Daniele Scarrone
GR Parlamento: 24h sce Italian Parliament channel. FM (150 txs of 5kW or less) **W:** grparlamento.rai.it **Dir.;**Flavio Mucciante . **Sender Bozen (Bolzano):** Prgrs in German on FM (46 txs of 1kW or less) **DPrgr:** 0500 (Sun 0600)-2300. N. 0615 (W), 0800 (Sun), 1000 (W), 1100, 1200, 1300, 1700 (W), 1930 **E:** kontakt@rai.it **W:** senderbozen.rai.it
Regional Prgr. in Slovene: Trieste 981kHz 20 kW + 103.9MHz 20kW (and 22 additional FM-txs). **D. Prgr:** 0500 (Sun 0600)-1900. **N:** W 0500, 0700, 0900, 1200, 1300, 1600, 1800; Sun 0700, 1200, 1300, 1800. Dir. : Guido Corso. **N.** in German: 0900 (W). Night : Relay V channel Filodiffusione or RAI programmen 1900-0500. **Ann:** Home Sce: "RAI Radiouno", "RAI Radiodue", "RAI Radiotre" as appropriate. Night Prgr: "RAI-Radiotelevisione Italiana stazioni a onda media di Milano kHz 900, di Roma kHz 1107"

R.A.S.
✉ Europaallee 164/A, 39100 Bozen ☎ +39 0471 546666 🖷 +39 0471 200378 **E:** info@ras.bz.it **W:** ras.bz.it
L.P: Pres: . Rudi Gamper MD: Georg Plattner, Dir. Tec: Dr .Johann Silbernagl
RAS is a public body of the autonomous Region of Southern Tyrol whose purpose is to relay TV and radio from Germany, Austria and Switzerland to the German-speaking population.

FM (MHz)	RAS 1	RAS 2	RAS 3	kW
Kronplatz	100.7	103.0	104.7	2
Meransen	101.3	103.9	107.3	1
Obervinschgau	100.5	103.0	106.1	0.6
Penegal	103.3	100.3	104.7	2
Perdonig	101.8	104.0	106.0	1
Plose	99.8	102.0	105.6	1
Vinschgau	101.1	102.9	105.0	2

+ 880 low power stns
RAS 1: rel. OE-3 (Austria) - **RAS-2:** rel. OE-R (Austria) - **RAS-3:** rel. OE-1 (Austria)

DAB: RAI & RAS on Blocks 12A-12DA, 223.936MHz - 229.072MHz Consorzio DAB Italia on block 9D. 208.064MHz **W:** dab.it

PRIVATE STATIONS
Only stns with MW/SW broadcasts and FM networks are listed. A number of other stns are heard irr. There are approx. 600 FM stns

	MW kHz	kW	Station, location and h of tr.
1)	567	1	Challenger R, Villa Estense (Test)
1)	846	1	Challenger R. Villa Estense (Test)
6)	1017	1	Media Veneta Broadcast, Piove di Sacco †
7)	1350	5	R. I AM, norh Milano TEST irr. Fri/Sun*
8)	1323	1	R. Base 101, Vigonza di Padova †
1)	1368	10	Challenger R., Villa Estense: rel VOA Europe, IRRS-Nexus.
3)	1476	5	R. Treviso 1476 (Test)
2)	1584	12	R. Studio X, M omigno: 24h
5)	±1404	1	Gruppo R. Luna 106, Chiozza di Scandiano: 0600-1900

* **Prgr:** Studio DX Sat/Sun 2100-2130 **E:** info@studiodx.net
Addresses and other information:
1) Via Legnaro 6, 35040 Villa Estense (PD) 🖷 +39 0429 662280 **W:** challenger.it **E:** challenger@challenger.it **V.** by letter Rp. SM: Maurizio Anselmo – 2) Via Mammianese 687, 51030 Momigno (PT) **W:** radiostudiox.it **E:** info@radiostudiox.it **SM:** Luca Betti.i- **FM:** 87,30MHz 5kW **V.** by letter Rp – 3) **E: radiotreviso@libero.it** – 5) Via Brolo Sotto 52, 42019 Chiozza di Scandiano (RE) ☎ +39 0522 856598 🖷+39 0522 5263255 **W:** radio106.it **E:** info@radioluna.com - **FM:** 104.4,105.9MHz 5kW **SM:** Battista Francia – 6) Media Veneta Broadcast, **E:** media-venetabroadcast@libero.it – 7) **E: report@iamradio.am** – 8) Via

Germania 15, 35010 Peraga di Vigonza (PD). ☎ +39 049 8936870 **W:** radiobase101.it **E:** info@radiobase.it

FM NETWORKS IN MAJOR CITIES (MHz):

	Network	To	Mi	Ve	Bo	Ge
1)	Circuito Margherita	91.8	89.5	-	-	90.1
2)	Kiss Kiss	92.4	97.6	-	101.8	104.9
3)	InBlu R.	89.0	95.3	94.6	97.0	88.8
4)	Latte Miele	88.5	-	107.6	-	-
5)	m2o	93.0	91.0	87.8	89.0	88.6
6)	Popolare Network	97.6	107.6	97.3	96.2	-
7)	R. Capital	90.3	90.1	98.5	99.4	93.9
8)	R. 105	99.6	99.1	98.9	103.5	99.5
9)	R. 101	101.0	100.9	107.3	96.0	-
10)	R. Classica	98.7	94.0	-	-	101.1
11)	R. Cuore	92.7	92.6	-	-	-
12)	R. Deejay	106.9	99.7	94.8	99.7	96.9
13)	R. RDS	96.4	94.4	99.8	104.2	95.7
14)	R. Italia Anni 60	103.7	106.3	101.7	102.1	91.3
15)	R. Italia	106.6	98.4	98.1	100.6	103.5
16)	R. Maria	107.5	107.9	106.5	90.5	106.6
17)	R. Mater	105.7	95.3	100.1	-	-
18)	R. Padania Libera	106.0	103.5	93.8	106.2	96.0
20)	R. Radicale	102.8	96.8	104.7	92.0	95.4
21)	R. RMC 1	105.5	105.3	100.4	101.3	104.2
23)	R. 24	105.0	104.8	106.8	107.0	97.2
24)	RTL 102.5	102.5	102.5	102.5	101.6	102.4
25)	Virgin R.	90.9	104.5	93.1	106.5	105.5
26)	R. Sportiva	101.5	95.8	-	87.7	105.8
	Network	**Fi**	**Rm**	**Na**	**Ba**	**Pa**
1)	Circuito Margherita	96.7	96.4	100.7	95.2	95.2
2)	Kiss Kiss	92.8	97.2	89.0	100.8	103.0
3)	InBlu R.	93.9	96.3	93,45	100.0	88.0
4)	Latte Miele	91.4	93.1	101.2	-	94.6
5)	m2o	105.8	97.0	98.3	88.5	107.8
6)	Popolare Network	93.6	103.3	-	97.3	-
7)	R. Capital	97.6	95.5	104.6	88.5	92.9
8)	R. 105	105.0	96.1	99.7	87.9	105.1
9)	R. 101	94.9	100.0	93.0	107.3	97.2
10)	R. Classica	99.4	89.5	-	105.0	99.5
11)	R. Cuore	100.2	-	-	-	89.1
12)	R. Deejay	100.6	101.0	92.3	93.2	107.5
13)	R. RDS	101. 8	103.0	107.5	89.1	106.6
14)	R. Italia Anni 60	-	-	104.1	89.6	95.8
15)	R. Italia	107.6	104.2	96.8	103.5	104.8
16)	R. Maria	88.8	95.1	98.8	102.0	89.4
17)	R. Mater	93.9	93.5	-	95.4	-
18)	R. Norba	-	-	92.7	105.5	-
19)	R. Padania Libera	-	-	-	-	-
20)	R. Radicale	97.0	88.6	101.6	89.3	92.0
21)	R. RMC	106.6	106.3	91.6	92.0	90.0
22)	R. Subasio	94.5	94.5	106.5	-	-
23)	R. 24	103.8	107.9	103.5	88.2	104.5
24)	RTL 102.5	100.9	102.1	102.6	102.5	102.3
25)	Virgin R.	107.2	98.7	93.5	106.6	93.2
26)	R. Sportiva	94.2	88.3	105 3	100.2	100.5

To=Torino Mi=Milano Ve=Venezia Bo=Bologna Ge=Genova Fi=Firenze Rm=Roma Na=Napoli Ba=Bari Pa=Palermo
Reference to Italian frequencies on **W:** frndx.altervista.org

Addresses and other information
1) Via Marchese di Villabianca 82, 90143 Palermo (PA) ☎ +39 091 302712 🖷 +39 091 8724835 **W:** radiomargherita.com **E:** info@radiomargherita.com SM: Giuseppe Orobello **V.** by letter. Rp. – **2)** Via Sgambati 61, 80131 Napoli (NA) ☎ +39 081 5461212 🖷 +39 081 5467789 **W:** kisskiss.it **E:** info@kisskiss.it, ufficiotecnico@kisskiss.it SM: Lucia Niespolo TM: Ugo Lombardi **V.** by letter. Rp. – 3) Via Aurelia 796, 00165 Roma (RM) ☎ +39 06 6650851 🖷+39 06 66508516 **W:** radioinblu.it **E:** info@radioinblu.it TM: Paolo Ruffini . **V.** by letter. Rp – 4) Via Andrea Costa 10, 40013 Castelmaggiore (BO) ☎ +39 051 70928 🖷 +39 051 6325710 **W:** lattemiele.com **E:** info@lattemiele.com SM: Franco Mignani – 5) Piazza della Repubblica 23/c, 00185 Roma (RM) ☎ +39 06 492311 🖷 +39 06 4453758 **W:** m2o.it **E:** contatti@m2o.it PM: Fabrizio Tamburini **V.** by letter. Rp – 6) Via U.Olleare 5, 20155 Milano (MI) ☎ +39 02 392411 🖷 +39 02 39273125 **W:** radiopopolare.it **E:** Radiopop@radiopopolare.it SM: Massimo Bacchetta **V.** by QSL-card. Rp – 7) Via C. Colombo 90, 00147 Roma (RM) ☎ +39 06 494321 🖷 +39 06 44702290 **W:** capital.it **E:** infoline@capital.it SM: Vittorio Zucconi. **V.** by QSL-card. Rp – 8) Largo G. Donegani 1, 20121 Milano (MI) ☎ +39 02 6596116 🖷 +39 02 6592272 **W:** 105.net **E:** diretta@105.net, altafrequenza@radioengineering.net SM: Alberto Hazan **V.** QSL-Card.

Rp. – **9)** Via Giovanni Ventura 3, 20134 , Milano (MI) ☎ +39 02 210831 🖹 +39 02 21083210 **W:** r101.it **E:** infor101@r101.it SM: Mirko Lagonegro. **V.** by QSL-card. Rp. – **10)** Via M.Burigozzo 5, 20122 Milano (MI) ☎+39 02 58219600 🖹 +39 02 58219407 **W:** radioclassica.fm **E:** radioclassica@class.it SM: Carla Signorile **V.** by letter. Rp. – **11)** Via Giovanni da Verrazzano 16, Localita Le Melorie, 56038 Ponsacco (PI) ☎ +39 0587 2861 🖹 +39 0587 733861 **W:** mediahit.it **E:** info@mediahit. it SM: Italo Bessi **V.** by letter. Rp – **12)** Via Massena 2, 20154 Milano (MI) ☎ +39 02 342522 🖹 +39 02 342888 **W:** deejay.it **E:** segnalazioni@ deejay.it SM: Linus **V.** by QSL-card. Rp.– **13)** Via Pier Ruggero Piccio 55, 00136 Roma (RM) ☎ +39 06 37704242 🖹 +39 06 37704250 **W:** rds.it **E:** ufficiotecnico@rds.it SM: Stefano Montefusco **V.** by letter. Rp. **W** : rds.it/frequenze/ – **14)** Via Zambra 11, 38121 Trento (TN) ☎ +39 0461 828990 🖹 +39 0461 428960 **W:** radioitaliaanni60.it **E:** info@ radioitaliaanni60.it SM: Franco Nisi **V.** by letter. Rp. – **15)** Viale Europa 49, 20093 Cologno Monzese (MI) ☎ +39 02 25441 🖹 +39 02 25444220 **W:** radioitalia.it **E:** info@radioitalia.it SM: Mario Volanti **V.** by letter. Rp.– **16)** Via Milano 12 , 22036 Erba (CO) ☎ +39 031 610600 🖹 +39 031 611288 **W:** radiomaria.it **E:** info@radiomaria.org SM: Don Livio Fanzaga **V.** by QSL-card. Rp. Rpt requested to **E:** QSL@radiomaria.org QSL Mgr. Giampiero Bernardini, St Eng, Claudio Re. – **17)** Via XXV Aprile 1, 22031 Albavilla (CO) ☎ +39 031 645214 🖹 +39 031 6490527 **W:** radiomater.com **E:** info@radiomater.it SM: Don Mario Galbiati **V.** by letter. Rp. – **18)** Via Foggia 29, 70014 Conversano (BA) ☎ +39 80 4951229 🖹 +39 80 4953079 **W:** radionorba.it **E:** radionorba@radionor-ba.it SM: Annamaria Fantasia **V.** by letter. Rp. – **19)** Via C.Bellerio 41, 20161 Milano (MI) ☎ +39 02 66203529 🖹 +39 02 66220964 **W:** radio-padania.net **E:** direzione@radiopadania.net **SM:** Cesare Bossetti **V.** by letter. Rp – **20)** Centro di Produzione, Via Principe Amedeo 2, 00185 Roma (RM) ☎ +39 06 488781 🖹 +39 06 4880196 **W:** radioradicale. it **E:** ioascolto@radioradicale.it SM: Alessio Falconio **V.** by letter. Rp. – **21)** Via Principe Amedeo 2, 20121 Milano (MI) ☎ +39 02 29001636 🖹 +39 02 6591451 **W:** radiomontecarlo.net **E:** rmc@radiomontecarlo. net, altafrequenza@radioengineering.net SM: Paolo Del Forno **V.** by QSL-card.Rp. – **22)** Localita Colle de Bensi, 06081 Assisi (PG) ☎ +39 075 8060 🖹 +39 075 8065419 **W:** radiosubasio.it **E:** subasio@ radiosubasio.it SM: Rita Settimi **V.** by letter. Rp. – **23)** Via Monte Rosa 91, 20149 Milano (MI) ☎ +39 02 30221 🖹 +39 02 30224462 **W:** radio24.it **E:** info@radio24.it SM: Roberto Napoletano **V.** Dario Arbulla (Ufficio Tecnico) by letter. Rp – **24)** Viale Piemonte 61/63, 20093 Cologno Monzese (MI) ☎ +39 02 251515 🖹 +39 02 25096201 **W:** rtl. it **E:** qualita@rtl.it QSL Manager Armando Finocchi (Chief Eng.) SM: Luigi Tornari **V.** QSL-card. Rp. – **25)** Largo Donegani 1, 20121 Milano (MI) ☎ +39 02 6596116 🖹 +39 02 62537460 **W:** virginradio.it **E:** guastivirgin@virginradio.it altafrequenza@radioengineering.net SM: Francesco Migliozzi **V.** QSL-Card. Rp. – **26)** Via Giovanni da Verrazzano 16, Localita Le Melorie, 56038 Ponsacco (PI) ☎ +39 0587 2861 🖹 +39 0587 733861 **W:** radiosportiva.it **E:**redazione@radiosportiva.it SM: Italo Bessi **V.** by letter. Rp

EXTERNAL SERVICES:
NEXUS - INTERNATIONAL BROADCASTING ASSOCIATION
See International Broadcasting section

AMERICAN FORCES NETWORK EUROPE (U.S. Mil.)
W: afneurope.net **E:** harringtonj@afns.vicenza.army.mil
1st Prgr. The Eagle on 106.0MHz Key stns: Vicenza (10kW) AFN,C/o Caserma Ederle,Via della Pace 100, 36100 Vicenza (VI) **W:** vicenza. afneurope.net ☎+039 0444 397111 **V.** by letter. No Rp. Livorno (10kW) AFN Livorno,UNIT 31301,Box 64,APO AE,09613,USA. Other stns:, Napoli "LAVA 106" (10kW), PSC 817,Box 31,FPO AE 09622,USA **W:** naples.afneurope.net **E:** ask.nsa@nsa.naples.navy.mil ☎+039 081 811 424

IVORY COAST

L.T: UTC — **Pop:** 21 million — **Pr.L:** French, Diola, 12 ethnic — **E.C:** 50Hz, 220V — **ITU:** CTI

HAUTE AUTORITÉ DE LA COMMUNICATION AUDIOVISUELLE (HACA)
✉ 2 Plateaux Vallons, Rue J93, lot n°2460, B.P. V56, Abidjan ☎+225 22 419658 🖹 +225 22 411455 **W:** haca.ci **E:** infos@haca.ci **L.P:** Chmn: Ibrahim Sy Savane.

RADIODIFFUSION-TÉLÉVISION IVOIRIENNE(RTI, Gov.)
✉ B.P. 191, Abidjan ☎+225 20 214800 🖹 +225 20 215038
W: rti.ci **L.P:** Acting DG: Lazare Saye Aka. Deputy DG for Radio: Jean-Claude Bayala.

FM (MHz)	1	2	kW	FM (MHz)	1	2	kW
Abobo-Abidjan	90.0	92.0	5	Bouaflé	99.0	102.6	-

FM (MHz)	1	2	kW	FM (MHz)	1	2	kW
Dabakala	91.0	101.0	-	Naingbo	93.0	103.0	-
Dimbokro	99.0	102.9	-	Niangue	93.0	95.9	-
Divo	88.0	90.8	10	Séguéla	89.0	95.0	-
Grabo	88.0	91.0	0.5	Tengréla	96.3	99.6	-
Kouakoussikro	89.3	92.4	-	Tiémé	88.0	91.0	5/1
Koun Fao	94.2	101.0	-	Touba	94.7	101.5	-
Man	96.9	100.2	-				

R. Côte d'Ivoire (1): 0500-2400. **Fréquence Deux (2):** 24h.
Ann: "R. Côte d'Ivoire" or "Fréquence Deux". **IS:** s/on with clock chimes.

Other stations:
City FM, Abidjan: 106.1MHz – **Cocody FM**, Abidjan: 98.5MHz 1kW. **W:** radiococodyfm.com – **Fréquence Vie**, Abidjan: 89.4MHz 1kW. **W:** frequencevie.com – **Ivoire FM**, Abidjan: 103.4MHz **W:** ivoirefm.ci – **N'Gowa FM**, Abidjan: 89.7MHz – **La Voix de l'Esperance**, Abidjan: 101.6MHz **W:** lavoixdelesperance.org – **R. Al Bayane**, Gagnoa 88.6, Seguela 89.6, Yamoussoukro 91.2, Abidjan 95.7, Bouna 96.0, Korhogo 102.2, Daloa 102.6, San-Pédro 102.7MHz. **W:** radio-albayane.com – **R. Arc-en-ciel**, Abidjan: 102.0MHz – **R. Jam:** Yamoussokro 88.1 1kW, Korhogo 92.2, San-Pédro 94.0, Man 95.5, Abengourou 96.9, Abidjan 99.3 3kW, Bouaké 104.3, Gagnoa 105.3MHz **W:** radiojam. ci – **R. Nationale Catolique:** Aboisso 89.2, Man 96.7, Abengourou 99.0, San-Pédro 99.2, Yamoussoukro 101.2, Abidjan 102.5/102.8, Gagnoa 104.7, Daloa 105.0, Bondoukou 107.2MHz **W:** rnc-ci.net – **R. Nostalgie**, Abidjan: 101.1MHz. **W:** nostalgie.ci – **Onuci FM:** Yamoussoukro 94.4MHz, Abidjan 96.0MHz & 16 other sites **W:** onucifm.net – **Zenith FM**, Abidjan: 92.8MHz
BBC African Sce = Bouaké 93.9, Abidjan 94.3, Yamoussoukro 97.7.
RFI Afrique: Abidjan/Bouaké/Korogho on 97.6MHz.
Voice of America, Abidjan: 99.0MHz

JAMAICA

L.T: UTC -5h — **Pop:** 2.7 million — **Pr.L:** English — **E.C:** 50Hz, 110/220V — **ITU:** JMC

RJR COMMUNICATIONS GROUP
RADIO JAMAICA LTD (Comm.)
✉ 32 Lyndhurst Road, Kingston 5 ☎ +1 876 926 1100 🖹 +1 876 929 7467 **E:** webmaster@radiojamaica.com
W: radiojamaica.com
L.P: Chmn. J.A. Lester Spaulding. MD: Gary Allen. GM Radio: Francois St.Juste.
FM (MHz): RJR94 94.1/94.3/94.5/94.7/94.9 – **Fame95:** 95.1/95.3/95.5/95.7/95.9 – **Hitz92:** 92.1/92.3/92.5/92.2/92.9

Other Stations:
BBC FM: 104.1/104.3/104.5/104.7/104.9MHz D.Prgr: 24h relay of the BBC World Service – **Bess FM**, 4 East Bloomsbury Rd, Kingston 10 ☎ +1 876 754 1898 🖹 +1 876 920 4749 **w:** bessfm.com FM: 100.1/100.3/100.5/100.7/100.9MHz – **Free FM**, General Penitentiary, South Camp Rd, Kingston. FM: Kingston 88.9MHz Prison Community Radio – **Fyah 105**, 40-41 Beechwood Ave, Kingston 5 ☎ +1 876 754 4182 🖹 +1 876 920 1440 **W:** fyah105.com FM: 105.3/105.5/105.7MHz – **Gospel JA**, 38 Cassia Park Rd, Kingston 10 ☎ +1 876 755 3105 **W:** gospelja.com FM: 91.7/91.9MHz – **Hot 102FM**, 69 Constant Spring Rd, Kingston 10 ☎ +1 876 969 9445 **W:** hot102.com.fm FM: 102.1/102.3/102.5/102.7/102.9MHz. Format: Talk & hit radio – **Irie FM,** P.O Box 282, Coconut Grove, Ocho Rios ☎ +1 876 974 5051/968 5023 🖹 +1 876 974 5943 **E:** info@iriefm.net **W:** iriefm.net **L.P.:** MD Debbian Dewar. FM: 107.1/107.3/107.5/107.7/107.9MHz. Format: Reggae – **Jet FM,** Jeffrey Town, Hills of St Mary. FM: 88.7. Format: Community radio operated by Jeffrey Town Farmers Association Ltd. – **Klas FM**, 17 Haining Rd, Kingston 5 ☎ +1 876 929 1344 🖹 +1 876 906 0572 **W:** klassportsradio.com FM: 89.1/89.3/89.5/89.9MHz Format: Sport – **Kool 97 FM**, 1 Braemar Ave, Kingston 10 ☎ +1 876 818 7620 **W:** kool97fm.com FM: 97.1/97.3/97.5/97.7/97.9MHz – **Linkz FM**, 8 Beckford St., Savanna-la-mar ☎ +1 876 955 9523 🖹 +1 876 955 9523 **W:** linkzfm.com FM: 96.5/96.7/96.9MHz – **Love FM,** 81 Hagley Pk Rd, Kingston 11 ☎ +1 876 968 9596 **W:** love101. org FM: 101.3/101.5/101.7/101.9MHz Format: Rlg. – **Mega Jamz**, 20 Ballater Av., Kingston 10 ☎ +1 876 631 5269 🖹 +1 876 929 9566 **W:** megajamz98fm.com L.P: MD Lorraine Vonstrolley. FM: 98.1/98.3/98.5/98.7/98.9MHz. Format: Oldies – **Mello FM**, 63 Barnett St, Montego Bay ☎ +1 876 971 4163 **W:** mellofmjamaica.com L.P.: CEO Al Robinson. Ops Mgr Edwin George. FM: 88.3/88.5MHz – **Music 99,** 6 Bradley Av, Kingston 10 ☎ +1 876 968 4880 🖹 +1 876 968 9165. FM: 99.1/99.3/99.5/99.7/99.9MHz – **Nationwide News Network**, Bradley Av, Kingston ☎ +1 876 630 1210 **W:** nationwideradiojm.com FM: 90.3/90.5/90.7MHz – **NCU 91 FM,** Northern Caribbean University,

East Campus, Manchester Rd, Mandeville ☎ +1 876 963 7711 **W:** ncumediagroup.com FM: 91.1/91.3/91.5MHz. Format: Rlg. (Adventist) – **Newstalk 93FM**, Universal Media Company, 18 Ring Rd., Mona, Kingston 7 ☎ +1 876 970 2345 🗎 +1 876 970 2472 **W:** newstalk93fm.com FM: 93.1/93.3/93.5/93.7/93.9MHz – **Power 106 FM**, 7 North St, Kingston ☎ +1 876 968 4880 🗎 +1 876 968 9165 **E:** power106@cwjamaica.com **W:** go-jamaica.com/power FM: 106.1/106.3/106.5/106.7/106.9MHz – **Radio France Internationale:** FM: 96.5MHz – **Roots FM**, 1 Mahoe Drive, Kingston 11 ☎ +1 876 923 6488 🗎 +1 876 923 6000. FM: Kingston 96.1MHz – **Stylz FM**, 4 Boundbrooke Ave, Port Antonio P.O., Portland ☎ +1 876 453 1444 **W:** stylzfm.com FM: 96.1/96.3/96.7MHz – **SunCity Radio**, Shop #30-32, Portmore Pines Plaza, Portmore, St. Catherine ☎ +1 876 989 3318 **W:** suncityradio.fm FM: 104.9MHz – **TBC FM (The Breath of Change)**, 51 Molynes Rd, Kingston 10 ☎ +1 876 754 5120 🗎 +1 876 968 9159 **W:** tbcradio.org FM: Kingston 88.5MHz. Format: Rlg (Baptist) – **Vybz FM**, 98 Great George Street, Savanna-la-Mar, Westmoreland ☎ +1 876 918 2521 🗎 +1 876 918 2394. FM: Westmoreland 96.3MHz – **Zip 103**, 1B Courtney Walsh Drive, Kingston 10 ☎ +1 876 929 6233 🗎 +1 876 960 0523 **W:** zipfm.net L.P: MD Debbian Dewar. FM: 103.1/103.3/103.5/103.7/103.9 MHz. Format: Techo/dance/alternative.

JAPAN

L.T: UTC +9h — **Pop:** 126.8 million — **Pr.L:** Japanese — **EC:** 50 & 60Hz, 100V — **ITU:** J

INFORMATION AND COMMUNICATIONS BUREAU, MINISTRY OF INTERNAL AFFAIRS AND COMMUNICATIONS (SOUMU SHO)
🖃 1-2, Kasumigaseki 2-chome, Chiyoda-ku, Tokyo 100-8926 ☎ +81 3 5253 5111 **W:** soumu.go.jp **L.P:** Minister: S. Takaichi

NIPPON HOSO KYOKAI (NHK)
(The Japan Broadcasting Corporation)
🖃 2-1, Jinnan 2-chome, Shibuya-ku, Tokyo 150-8001 ☎ +81 3 3465 1111 **W:** nhk.or.jp
L.P: Chmn. (Board of Governors): K.Hamada. Pres: K.Momii. Exec. Vice-Pres: H.Doumoto. Gen. MD's: H.Tsukada, K.Yoshikuni, Y.Itano, T.Fukui. MD & Exec. Dir. Gen: Y.Hamada. MD's: K.Morinaga, T.Inoue, J.Imai, T.Sakamoto, H.Anzai. **Pub:** NHK Nenkan (Japanese), NHK Update (English)

MW Loc. & Prgr	Call	kHz	kW	MW Loc. & Prgr	Call	kHz	kW
E2) Nago 1		531	1	G4) Enbetsu 1		792	1
F2) Morioka 1	QG	531	10.0	A2) Nagano 1	NK	819	5
A2) Matsumoto 1		540	1	B1) Osaka 1	BB	828	300
C2) Nanao 1		540	1.0	A3) Niigata 1	QK	837	10
E2) Ishigaki 1		540	1	G4) Nayoro 1		837	1
E3) Miyazaki 1	MG	540	5	E8) Hitoyoshi 1		846	1
E4) Kitakyushu 1	SK	540	1	F5) Koriyama 1		846	5
F3) Yamagata 1	JG	540	5	H1) Uwajima 1		846	1
E2) Okinawa 1	AP	549	10	E8) Kumamoto 2	GB	873	500
G1) Sapporo 1	IK	567	100	C3) Shizuoka 1	PK	882	10
C3) Hamamatsu 1	DG	576	1	F1) Sendai 1	HK	891	20
E5) Kagoshima 1	HG	576	10	C1) Nagoya 1	CB	909	10
G2) Kushiro 1	PG	585	10	A4) Kofu 1	KG	927	5
A1) Tokyo 1	AK	594	300	C6) Fukui 1	FG	927	5
D2) Okayama 1	KK	603	5	D2) Tsuyama 1		927	1
G3) Obihiro 1	OG	603	10	G4) Wakkanai 1		927	1
E1) Fukuoka 1	LK	612	100	B3) Hikone 1	QP*	945	1
A2) Iida 1		621	1	E7) Fukue 1		945	1
E3) Nobeoka 1		621	1	G7) Muroran 1	IQ	945	3
G4) Asahikawa 1	CG	621	3	H2) Tokushima 1	XK	945	5
C3) Shizuoka 2	PB	639	10	D3) Hagi 1		963	1
E6) Oita 1	IP	639	5	D4) Yonago 1		963	1
C4) Toyama 1	IG	648	5	E9) Saga 1	SP	963	1
B1) Osaka 1	BK	666	100	F6) Aomori 1	TG	963	5
D3) Yamaguchi 1	UG	675	5	H1) Matsuyama 1	ZK	963	5
G5) Hakodate 1	VK	675	10	A2) Kisofukushima 1		981	1
E7) Nagasaki 1	AG	684	5	E7) Sasebo 1		981	1
A1) Tokyo 2	AB	693	500	H3) Kochi 1	RK	990	10
D1) Hiroshima 2	FB	702	10	D1) Fukuyama 1		999	1
G6) Kitami 2	KD	702	10	F6) Hachinohe 1		999	1
C1) Nagoya 1	CK	729	50	H3) Nakamura 1		999	1
G1) Sapporo 2	IB	747	500	E1) Fukuoka 2	LB	1017	50
E8) Kumamoto 1	GK	756	10	C4) Toyama 2	IC	1035	1
F4) Akita 2	UB	774	500	F3) Tsuruoka 2		1035	1
A3) Takada 1		792	1	H4) Takamatsu 1	HD	1035	1
C5) Takayama 1		792	1	D1) Hiroshima 1	FK	1071	20
E5) Naze 1		792	1	F1) Sendai 2	HB	1089	10

MW Loc. & Prgr	Call	kHz	kW	MW Loc. & Prgr	Call	kHz	kW
C5) Takayama 2		1125	1	E6) Oita 2	ID	1467	1
D3) Hagi 2		1125	1	G4) Wakkanai 2		1467	1
D4) Tottori 2	LC	1125	1	G5) Hakodate 2	VB	1467	1
E2) Okinawa 2	AD	1125	10	A2) Iida 2		1476	1
G3) Obihiro 2	OC	1125	1	E8) Aso 1		1503	1
G4) Nayoro 2		1125	1	F4) Akita 1	UK	1503	10
G7) Muroran 2	IZ	1125	1	A2) Matsumoto 2		1512	1
G2) Kushiro 2	PC	1152	1	F5) Koriyama 2		1512	1
H3) Kochi 2	RB	1152	10	H1) Matsuyama 2	ZB	1512	5
G6) Kitami 1	KP	1188	10	D3) Hamamatsu 2	DC	1521	1
C2) Kanazawa 1	JK	1224	10	C6) Fukui 2	FC	1521	1
D5) Matsue 1	TK	1296	10	D4) Yonago 2		1521	1
F2) Yamada 1		1323	1	E2) Ishigaki 2		1521	1
F5) Fukushima 1	FP	1323	1	F3) Yamagata 2	JC	1521	1
E8) Minamata 1		1341	1	F6) Aomori 2	TC	1521	1
F5) Iwaki 1		1341	1	H3) Nakamura 2		1521	1
D4) Tottori 1	LG	1368	1	A3) Niigata 2	QB	1593	10
F3) Tsuruoka 1		1368	1	D5) Matsue 2	TB	1593	10
H4) Takamatsu 1	HP	1368	5	A4) Kofu 2	KC	1602	1
D3) Yamaguchi 2	UC	1377	5	D1) Fukuyama 2		1602	1
E7) Nagasaki 2	AC	1377	1	E3) Nobeoka 2		1602	1
F6) Hachinohe 2		1377		E4) Kitakyushu 2	SB	1602	1
C2) Kanazawa 2	JB	1386	10	E5) Naze 2		1602	1
D2) Okayama 2	KB	1386	10	E8) Hitoyoshi 2		1602	1
E5) Kagoshima 2	HC	1386	10	F5) Fukushima 2	FD	1602	1
F2) Morioka 2	QC	1386	10	G4) Asahikawa 2	CC	1602	1
A2) Nagano 2	NB	1467	1	G4) Enbetsu 2		1602	1
E3) Miyazaki 2	MC	1467	1	H1) Uwajima 2		1602	1

+ approx 240 stns below 1kW
1: NHK Radio One, **2:** NHK Radio Two. **Call:** JO(call). *stn announces its callsign as "JOBK"

FM Location	Call	MHz	kW	FM Location	Call	MHz	kW
A5) Utsunomiya	BP	80.3	1	E1) Fukuoka	LK	84.8	3
A6) Chiba	MP	80.7	5.0	E2) Miyakojima		85.0	1
C4) Toyama	IG	81.5	1	A10) Saitama	LP	85.1	5
A7) Maebashi	TP	81.6	1.0	G1) Sapporo	IK	85.2	5
C7) Tsu	NP	81.8	3.0	F5) Fukushima	FP	85.3	1
A8) Yokohama	GP	81.9	5	E8) Kumamoto	GK	85.4	1
F3) Yamagata	JG	82.1	1	A4) Kofu	KG	85.6	1
C2) Kanazawa	JK	82.2	1	E5) Kagoshima	HG	85.6	1
A3) Niigata	QK	82.3	1	D5) Hamada		85.8	1
A1) Tokyo	AK	82.5	10	F6) Aomori	TG	86.0	3
C1) Nagoya	CK	82.5	10	H4) Takamatsu	HP	86.0	1
F1) Sendai	HK	82.5	5	F4) Akita	UK	86.7	3
B2) Kyoto	OK	82.8	1	H1) Matsuyama	ZK	87.7	1
F2) Morioka	QG	83.1	5	B1) Osaka	BK	88.1	10
A9) Mito	EP	83.2	1	E2) Okinawa	AP	88.1	1
C6) Fukui	FG	83.4	1	G4) Nayoro		88.2	1
H2) Tokushima	XK	83.4	1	D1) Hiroshima	FK	88.3	1
A3) Yamato		83.5	1	D2) Okayama	KK	88.7	1
C5) Gifu	OP	83.6	1	C3) Shizuoka	PK	88.8	1
B3) Otsu	QP	84.0	1	E6) Oita	IP	88.9	1
B4) Himeji		84.2	1	G4) Chikoma		89.1	1
E5) Tanegashima		84.4	1	G2) Nakashibetsu		89.9	1

+ approx 481 stns below 1kW **Call:** JO(call)-FM

Addresses of regional HQs:
A) Kanto-Koshinetsu area = Tokyo A1): same as NHK general HQ address. **B)** Kinki area = Osaka B1): 1-20, Otemae 4-chome, Chuo-ku, Osaka 540-8501. **C)** Tokai-Hokuriku area = Nagoya C1): 13-3, Higashisakura 1-chome, Higashi-ku, Nagoya 461-8725. **D)** Chugoku area = Hiroshima D1): 11-10, Otemachi 2-chome, Naka-ku, Hiroshima 730-8672. **E)** Kyushu area = Fukuoka E1): 1-10, Ropponmatsu 1-chome, Chuo-ku, Fukuoka 810-8577. **F)** Tohoku area = Sendai F1): 11-1, Nishiki-machi 1-chome, Aoba-ku, Sendai 980-8435. **G)** Hokkaido area = Sapporo G1): 1, Odori Nishi 1-chome, Chuo-ku, Sapporo 060-8703 **H)** Shikoku area = Matsuyama H1): 5, Horinouchi, Matsuyama 790-8501

NHK R. One (General prgr): 24h **N:** every h(exc Sun 0000). Also at 2140(exc Sat), 1130(exc Sat&Sun). **Regional and local prgrs** (the amount of local prgrs varies between stns) 2055wrp, 2125N/wrp/inf, 2155 wrp/inf, 2220(Fri&Sat 2215)N/wrp, 2240(Sat 2255)N/wrp, 2355N/wrp/inf, 0055(exc Sun)N/wrp/inf, 0155N/wrp/inf, 0250wrp/inf, 0315(Sat & Sun 0310)N/wrp, 0355(exc Sun)wrp/inf, 0455N/wrp/inf, 0555N/wrp/inf, 0655N/wrp/inf, 0755N/wrp/inf, 0855N/wrp/inf, 0950N/wrp/inf, 1015(Sat & Sun)N/wrp, 1045(exc. Sat &Sun)N/wrp/inf, 1055(Sat)wrp/inf, 1155(exc. Sat & Sun)N/wrp/inf, 1255N/wrp/inf, 1405(Sat & Sun 1410)N/wrp. **IS:** Original music played by Celesta. **Ann:** "JO(call), NHK (location) Daiichi Hoso desu". Local ID's with call letters, network & location given by studio stns just before: 2000, 0300, 1000

NHK R. Two (Educational prgr): 2100-1540(Sun 1520). No regular regional and local prgrs. **Foreign language N** (rel. NHK World - R. Japan): **Chinese:** 0900-0915(Sat&Sun 0910). **Korean:** 0915-0930(Sat&Sun 0910-0920). **English:** 0500- 0530(Sat&Sun 0510). **Portuguese:** 0930-0945(Sat&Sun 0920-0930). **Spanish:** 0400-0415(Sat&Sun 0410). Weather map: 0700-0720. **IS:** Original music played by Celesta. Nat. Anthem at s/on on national holidays & s/off. **Ann:** "JO(call), NHK (location) Daini Hoso desu". Local IDs on certain stns (as 1st Netw) just before 2100, 0720 and sign off.

NHK FM Netw: 24h. 1600-2000 relays R. One, **N:** 2200, 0300, 0950(local), 1000. **Ann:** "JO(call)-FM, NHK (location) FM Hoso desu". Local IDs just before 2000, 0300, 1000

V: NHK officially has no organised QSL sce. However, many local stns verify by QSL card or letter for DX reports.

EXTERNAL SERVICES:
RADIO JAPAN, NHK WORLD NETWORK
See International Broadcasting section

THE JAPAN COMMERCIAL BROADCASTERS ASSOCIATION (NIPPON MINKAN HOSO RENMEI)
✉ 3-23, Kioi-cho, Chiyoda-ku, Tokyo 102-8577 ☎ +81 3 5213 7711 🖷 +81 3 5213 7703 **W:** j-ba.or.jp
LP: Pres: H.Inoue. Vice-Presidents: M.Toizumi, S.Takeda, Y.Okubo, H. Hayakawa, C.Kameyama, Y.Takahashi, T.Yamamoto, S.Fukui. Exec. Dir: S.Kimura. **Pub:** Nippon Minkan Hoso Nenkan, Gekkan Minpo, Minkan Hoso (all Japanese) and NAB Handbook (English) etc.

MW	Call	kHz	kW	ID	Station, location & h of tr
1)	CR	558	20	CRK	R. Kansai, Kobe
2)	WN	639	5	STV	STV R., Hakodate
3)	DF	684	5	IBC	Iwate Hoso, Morioka
3)	LO	684	1	IBC	Iwate Hoso, Ofunato
4)	IL	720	1	KBC	Kyushu Asahi Hoso, Kitakyushu
5)	LR	738	5	KNB	Kita Nihon Hoso, Toyama
5)		738	1	KNB	Kita Nihon Hoso, Takaoka
6)	RR	738	10	RBC	Ryukyu Hoso, Naha
7)	JF	765	5	YBS	Yamanashi Hoso, Kofu
8)	PF	765	5	KRY	Yamaguchi Hoso, Shunan
9)	XR	864	10	ROK	R. Okinawa, Naha: 2000-1800(Sun1530)
10)	SO	864	1	SBC	Shin'etsu Hoso, Matsumoto
11)	HE	864	3	HBC	Hokkaido Hoso, Asahikawa
11)	QF	864	3	HBC	Hokkaido Hoso, Muroran
11)		864	1	HBC	Hokkaido Hoso, Enbetsu
12)	PR	864	5	FBC	Fukui Hoso, Fukui
13)	XN	864	1	CRT	Tochigi Hoso, Nasu
2)	WS	882	5	STV	STV R., Kushiro
2)		882	1	STV	STV R., Esashi
11)	HO	900	5	HBC	Hokkaido Hoso, Hakodate
14)	HF	900	5	BSS	San'in Hoso, Yonago: (off air Sat1800-1955, Sun1500-1855)
15)	ZR	900	5	RKC	Kochi Hoso, Kochi
2)	VX	909	5	STV	STV R., Abashiri
16)	EF	918	5	YBC	Yamagata Hoso, Yamagata
16)		918	1	YBC	Yamagata Hoso, Tsuruoka
16)		918	1	YBC	Yamagata Hoso, Yonezawa
16)		918	1	YBC	Yamagata Hoso, Shinjo
8)	PM	918	1	KRY	Yamaguchi Hoso, Shimonoseki
8)	PN	918	1	KRY	Yamaguchi Hoso, Iwakuni
17)	TR	936	5	ABS	Akita Hoso, Akita
18)	NF	936	5	MRT	Miyazaki Hoso, Miyazaki
18)		936	1	MRT	Miyazaki Hoso, Nobeoka
18)		936	1	MRT	Miyazaki Hoso, Nichinan
18)		936	1	MRT	Miyazaki Hoso, Kobayashi
18)		936	1	MRT	Miyazaki Hoso, Takachiho
19)	KR	954	100	TBS	TBS R., Tokyo
20)	NR	1008	50	ABC	Asahi Hoso, Osaka
21)	AR	1053	50	CBC	Chubu Nippon Hoso, Nagoya: (S)
2)	WM	1071	5	STV	STV R., Obihiro
10)	SR	1098	5	SBC	Shin'etsu Hoso, Nagano
10)	SW	1098	1	SBC	Shin'etsu Hoso, Iida
22)	MF	1098	1	NBC	Nagasaki Hoso, Sasebo
23)	GF	1098	5	OBS	Oita Hoso, Oita
24)	WO	1098	5	RFC	R. Fukushima, Koriyama
25)	CF	1107	20	MBC	Minami Nihon Hoso, Kagoshima
25)		1107	1	MBC	Minami Nihon Hoso, Akune
25)		1107	1	MBC	Minami Nihon Hoso, Oguchi
25)		1107	1	MBC	Minami Nihon Hoso, Sendai
26)	MR	1107	5	MRO	Hokuriku Hoso, Kanazawa

MW	Call	kHz	kW	ID	Station, location & h of tr
26)		1107	1	MRO	Hokuriku Hoso, Nanao
27)	AF	1116	5	RNB	Nankai Hoso, Matsuyama
27)	AL	1116	1	RNB	Nankai Hoso, Niihama
27)	AM	1116	1	RNB	Nankai Hoso, Uwajima
28)	DR	1116	5	BSN	Niigata Hoso, Niigata
29)	QR	1134	100	NCB	Bunka Hoso, Tokyo
30)	BR	1143	20	KBS	KBS Kyoto, Kyoto
31)	OR	1179	50	MBS	Mainichi Hoso, Osaka
15)		1197	1	RKC	Kochi Hoso, Nakamura
32)	FO	1197	1	RKB	RKB Mainichi Hoso, Kitakyushu
33)	BF	1197	10	RKK	Kumamoto Hoso, Kumamoto
33)		1197	1	RKK	Kumamoto Hoso, Hitoyoshi
33)		1197	1	RKK	Kumamoto Hoso, Aso
33)		1197	1	RKK	Kumamoto Hoso, Goshoura
34)	YF	1197	5	IBS	Ibaraki Hoso, Mito: 2050 (Fri,Sat 2100)-2000 (Sun 1500)
2)	WL	1197	3	STV	STV R., Asahikawa
2)		1197	1	STV	STV R., Wakkanai
2)		1197	1	STV	STV R., Nayoro
2)		1197	1	STV	STV R., Enbetsu
30)	BO	1215	2	KBS	KBS Kyoto, Maizuru
30a)	BW	1215	1	KBS	KBS Shiga, Hikone
22)	UR	1233	5	NBC	Nagasaki Hoso, Nagasaki
35)	GR	1233	5	RAB	Aomori Hoso, Aomori
36)	LF	1242	100	NBS	Nippon Hoso, Tokyo: (S)
37)	IR	1260	20	TBC	Tohoku Hoso, Sendai
11)	HW	1269	5	HBC	Hokkaido Hoso, Obihiro
11)	FM	1269	1	HBC	Hokkaido Hoso, Esashi
38)	JR	1269	5	JRT	Shikoku Hoso, Tokushima
38)		1269	1	JRT	Shikoku Hoso, Ikeda
32)	FR	1278	50	RKB	RKB Mainichi Hoso, Fukuoka
11)	HR	1287	50	HBC	Hokkaido Hoso, Sapporo
39)	UF	1314	50	OBC	R. Osaka, Osaka: (S)
40)	SF	1332	50	Tokai	R. Tokai, Nagoya
41)	ER	1350	20	RCC	Chugoku Hoso, Hiroshima
11)	TS	1368	1	HBC	Hokkaido Hoso, Wakkanai
1)	CE	1395	1	CRK	R. Kansai, Toyooka
24)	WE	1395	1	RFC	R. Fukushima, Wakamatsu
11)	QL	1404	5	HBC	Hokkaido Hoso, Kushiro
42)	VR	1404	10	SBS	Shizuoka Hoso, Shizuoka
42)	VO	1404	1	SBS	Shizuoka Hoso, Hamamatsu
4)	IF	1413	50	KBC	Kyushu Asahi Hoso, Fukuoka
43)	RF	1422	50	RF	RF R. Nippon, Yokohama
14)	HL	1431	1	BSS	San'in Hoso, Tottori: (as 900kHz)
14)		1431	1	BSS	San'in Hoso, Izumo: (as 900kHz)
22)		1431	1	NBC	Nagasaki Hoso, Fukue
24)	WW	1431	1	RFC	R. Fukushima, Iwaki
44)	VF	1431	5	WBS	Wakayama Hoso, Wakayama: (S)
45)	ZF	1431	5	GBS	Gifu Hoso, Gifu: 2100-1600
2)	WF	1440	50	STV	STV R., Sapporo
2)		1440	3	STV	STV R., Muroran
2)		1440	1	STV	STV R., Tomakomai
11)	QM	1449	5	HBC	Hokkaido Hoso, Abashiri
46)	KF	1449	5	RNC	Nishi Nippon Hoso, Takamatsu
46)		1449	1	RNC	Nishi Nippon Hoso, Marugame
22a)	UO	1458	1	NBC	Nagasaki Hoso, Saga
24)	WR	1458	1	RFC	R. Fukushima, Fukushima
34)	YL	1458	1	IBS	Ibaraki Hoso, Tsuchiura
34)		1458	1	IBS	Ibaraki Hoso, Sekijo
41)		1458	1	RCC	Chugoku Hoso, Shobara
8)	PL	1485	1	KRY	Yamaguchi Hoso, Hagi
35)	GO	1485	1	RAB	Aomori Hoso, Hachinohe
11)	TL	1494	1	HBC	Hokkaido Hoso, Nayoro
47)	YR	1494	10	RSK	Sanyo Hoso, Okayama
47)		1494	1	RSK	Sanyo Hoso, Takahashi
47)		1494	1	RSK	Sanyo Hoso, Tsuyama
47)		1494	1	RSK	Sanyo Hoso, Niimi
47)		1494	1	RSK	Sanyo Hoso, Bizen
47)		1494	1	RSK	Sanyo Hoso, Ochiai
28)	DO	1530	1	BSN	Niigata Hoso, Joetsu
13)	XF	1530	5	CRT	Tochigi Hoso, Utsunomiya
41)	EO	1530	1	RCC	Chugoku Hoso, Fukuyama
41)		1530	1	RCC	Chugoku Hoso, Mihara

Relay stns below 1kW (approx 125 stns) not included.

Simultaneous FM broadcasts of MW stns

FM	MHz	kW	Stn, loc	FM	MHz	kW	Stn, loc
17)	90.1	1	ABS, Akita	45)	90.4		GBS, Gifu
5)	90.2	1	KNB, Toyama		90.4		Sapporo
	90.2		Fukuoka	19)	90.5	7	TBS, Tokyo
46)	90.3		RNC, Takamatsu	3)	90.6		IBC, Morioka
18)	90.4		ABS, Akita	31)	90.6	7	MBS, Osaka

FM	MHz	kW	Stn, loc	FM	MHz	kW	Stn, loc
15)	90.8		RKC, Kochi	28)	92.7	1	BSN, Niigata
24)	90.8		RFC, Fukushima	25)	92.8	1	MBC, Kagoshima
7)	90.9		YBS, Kofu	40)	92.9	7	Tokai R, Nagoya
	91.0		Fukuoka	36)	93.0	7	NBS, Tokyo
1)	91.1		CRK, Kobe		93.0		JRT, Tokushima
33)	91.4		RKK, Kumamoto		93.1		,Naha
47)	91.4		RSK, Okayama	20)	93.3	7	ABC, Osaka
	91.5		Sapporo	23)	93.3		OBS, Oita
	91.5		Naha	37)	93.5		TBC, Sendai
29)	91.6	7	NCR, Tokyo	21)	93.7	7	CBC, Nagoya
27)	91.7	1	RNB, Matsuyama	42)	93.9		SBS, Shizuoka
35)	91.7		RAB, Aomori	26)	94.0		MRO, Kanazawa
39)	91.9	7	OBC, Osaka	13)	94.1		CRT, Utsunomiya
10)	92.2		SBC, Nagano	44)	94.2		WBS, Wakayama
14)	92.2		BSS, Matsue	12)	94.6		FBC, Fukui
8)	92.3	1	KRY, Shunan	34)	94.6	1	IBS, Mito
16)	92.4		YBC, Yamagata	41)	94.6	1	RCC, Hiroshima
43)	92.4		RF, Yokohama	30)	94.9		KBS, Kyoto
22)	92.6	1	NBC, Nagasaki				

Relay stns below 1kW not included. Brank Power stns F.Pl.

Call: JO(call). (S): AM Stereo (C-QUAM System). **Schedule:** 24h unless otherwise indicated above. Most 24h stns are off the air for 1 to 5 hours until 1900 or 2000 on Sun unless mentioned. All other days a network prgr is aired 1600 or 1800 to 2000 on most stns. Network prgrs may also be broadcast at other times of day. **ID:** Company initials are usually used as stn identification.

Addresses and other information:

1) R Kansai Co., Ltd., 5-7, Higashi Kawasaki-cho 1-chome, Chuo-ku, Kobe 650-8580 **W:** jocr.jp – **2)** The STVradio Broadcasting Co., Ltd, 1-1, Nishi 8-chome, Kita 1-jo, Chuo-ku, Sapporo 060-8705 **W:** stv.ne.jp – **3)** Iwate Broadc Co., Ltd., 6-1, Shike-cho, Morioka 020-8566 **W:** ibc.co.jp – **4)** Kyushu Asahi Broadc Co., Ltd, 1-1, Nagahama 1-chome, Chuo-ku, Fukuoka 810-8571 **W:** kbc.co.jp – **5)** Kita-nihon Broadc Co., Ltd.,10-18, Ushijima-machi, Toyama 930-8585 **W:** knb.ne.jp – **6)** Ryukyu Broadc Corp., 3-1, Kumoji 2-chome, Naha 900-8711 **W:** rbc.co.jp – **7)** Yamanashi Broadc Co., Ltd., 6-10, Kitaguchi 2-chome, Kofu 400-8525 **W:** ybs.jp – **8)** Yamaguchi Broadc Co., Ltd., Koen-ku, Shunan 745-8686 **W:** kry.co.jp – **9)** R Okinawa Corp., 4-8, Nishi 1-chome, Naha 900-8604 **W:** rokinawa.co.jp – **10)** Shinetsu Broadc Co., Ltd., 1200, Toigoshomachi, Nagano 380-8521 **W:** sbc21.co.jp – **11)** Hokkaido Broadc Co., Ltd., 2, Nishi 5-chome, kita 1-jo, Chuo-ku, Sapporo 060-8501 **W:** hbc.co.jp – **12)** Fukui Broadc Corp., 510, Owada 2-chome, Fukui 910-8588 **W:** fbc.jp –**13)** Tochigi Broadc Co., Ltd., 12-11, Honcho, Utsunomiya 320-8601 **W:** crt-radio.co.jp – **14)** Broadc System of San-in, 1-71, Nishi-Fukubara 1-chome, Yonago 683-8670 **W:** bss.jp – **15)** Kochi Broadc Co., Ltd., 2-15, Honmachi 3-chome, Kochi 780-8550 **W:** rkc-kochi.co.jp – **16)** Yamagata Broadc Co., Ltd., 5-12, Hatago-machi 2-chome, Yamagata 990-8555 **W:** ybc.co.jp – **17)** Akita Broadc System, 9-42, Sanno 7-chome, Akita 010-8611 **W:** akita-abs.co.jp – **18)** Miyazaki Broadc Co., Ltd., 6-7, Tachibanadori-nishi 4-chome, Miyazaki 880-8639 **W:** mrt.jp – **19)** TBS Radio & Communications, Inc., 3-6, Akasaka 5-chome, Minato-ku, Tokyo 107-8006 **W:** tbs.co.jp/radio – **20)** Asahi Broadc Corp., 1-30, Fukushima 1-chome, Fukushima-ku, Osaka 553-8503 **W:** asahi.co.jp – **21)** CBCradio Co., Ltd., 2-8, Shinsakae 1-chome, Naka-ku, Nagoya 460-8405 **W:** hicbc.com/radio – **22)** Nagasaki Broadc Co., Ltd., 1-35, Uwa-machi, Nagasaki 850-8650 **W:** nbc-nagasaki.co.jp – **22a)** Nagasaki Broadc Co., Ltd Saga station, 1249, Honjo-machi, Saga 840-0027 **W:** nbc-saga.jp – **23)** Oita Broadc System, 1-1, Imazuru 3-chome, Oita 870-8620 **W:** e-obs.com – **24)** R Fukushima Broadc Co., Ltd., 8, Shimoarako, Fukushima 960-8655 **W:** rfc.jp – **25)** Minaminihon Broadc Co., Ltd., 5-25, Korai-cho, Kagoshima 890-8570 **W:** mbc.co.jp – **26)** Hokuriku Broadc Co., Ltd., 2-1, Honda-machi 3-chome, Kanazawa 920-8560 **W:** mro.co.jp – **27)** Nankai Broadc Co., Ltd., 1-1, Honmachi 1-chome, Matsuyama 790-8510 **W:** rnb.co.jp – **28)** Broadc System of Niigata, Inc., 18, Kawagishi-cho 3-chome, Chuo-ku, Niigata 951-8655 **W:** ohbsn.com – **29)** Nippon Cultural Broadc., Inc.,31, Hamamatsucho 1-chome, Minato-ku, Tokyo 105-8002 **W:** joqr.co.jp – **30)** Kyoto Broadc System Co., Ltd., Kamichojamachi, Karasumadori, Kamigyo-ku, Kyoto 602-8588 **W:** kbs-kyoto.co.jp – **30a)** KBS Shiga Station, 6-19, Tachibana-cho, Hikone 522-0062 – **31)** Mainichi Broadc System, Inc., 17-1, Chayamachi, Kita-ku, Osaka 530-8304 **W:** mbs.jp – **32)** RKB Mainichi Broadc Corp., 3-8, Momochihama 2-chome, Sawara-ku, Fukuoka 814-8585 **W:** rkb.jp – **33)** Kumamoto Broadc Co., Ltd., 30, Yamasaki-machi, Kumamoto 860-8611 **W:** rkk.jp – **34)** Ibaraki Broadc System, 2084-2, Senba-cho, Mito 310-8505 **W:** ibs-radio.com – **35)** Aomori Broadc Corp., 8-1, Matsumori 1-chome, Aomori 030-8655 **W:** rab.co.jp – **36)** Nippon Broadc System, Inc., 9-3, Yurakucho 1-chome, Chiyoda-ku, Tokyo 100-8439 **W:** 1242.com – **37)** Tohoku Broadc Co., Ltd., 26-1, Kasumi-cho, Yagiyama, Taihaku-ku, Sendai 980-8668 **W:** tbc-sendai.co.jp – **38)** Shikoku Broadc Co., Ltd., 5-2, Nakatokushima-cho 2-chome, Tokushima 770-8573 **W:** jrt.co.jp – **39)** Osaka Broadc Corp., 2-4, Benten 1-chome, Minato-ku, Osaka 552-8501 **W:** obc1314.co.jp – **40)** Tokai Radio Broadc Co., Ltd., 14-27, Higashisakura 1-chome, Higashi-ku, Nagoya 461-8503 **W:** tokairadio.co.jp – **41)** RCC Broadc Co., Ltd., 21-3, Moto-machi, Naka-ku, Hiroshima 730-8504 **W:** rcc.net – **42)** Shizuoka Broadc System, 1-1, Toro 3-chome, Suruga-ku, Shizuoka 422-8680 **W:** at-s.com – **43)** RF Radio Nippon Co., Ltd., 85, Choja-machi 5-chome, Naka-ku, Yokohama 231-8611 **W:** jorf.co.jp – **44)** Wakayama Broadc System, 3, Minato-honmachi 3-chome, Wakayama 640-8577 **W:** wbs.co.jp – **45)** Gifu Broadc System, 52, Hashimoto 2-chome, Gifu 500-8588 **W:** zf-web.com – **46)** Nishinippon Broadc Co., Ltd., 8-15, Marunouchi, Takamatsu 760-8575 **W:** rnc.co.jp – **47)** Sanyo Broadc Co., Ltd., 1-3, Marunouchi 2-chome, Okayama 700-8580 **W:** rsk.co.jp.

V: Most stns verify by QSL-card. Rec acc. Rp

NIKKEI RADIO BROADCASTING CORPORATION (RADIO NIKKEI)

2-8, Toranomon 1-chome, Minato-ku, Tokyo 105-8565 ☎ +81 3 6205 7810 📠 +81 3 6205 7809 **W:** radionikkei.jp

SW	kHz	kW	Prgr	SW	kHz	kW	Prgr
JOZ	3925	50	1	JOZ6	6115	50	2
JOZ4	*3925	10	1	JOZ3	9595	50	1
JOZ5	3945	10	2	JOZ7	9760	50	2
JOZ2	6055	50	1				

*) Nemuro; others Nagara (Chiba)

1st Prgr: 2155-1500 on 3925/ 6055/9595kHz; as above except 2300-0750 on 3925kHz (Nagara)
2nd Prgr: Sun-Thu 2300-1400, Fri & Sat 2300- 0900 (9760kHz: 0800)
IS: Slow tempo chime with Japanese instrument "Koto" at sign on and sign off - **V.** by QSL card. Rp.

COMMERCIAL FM STATIONS:

FM	Call	MHz	kW	Station, location & h of tr
1)	QU	76.1	1	FM Iwate, Morioka
2)	LU	76.1	1	FM Fukui, Fukui
3)	FW	76.1	1	Love FM, Fukuoka
4)	SV	76.4	1	R. Berry, Utsunomiya
5)	AW	76.5	10	FM COCOLO, Osaka
6)	VV	76.8	1	FM Okayama, Okayama
7)	UV	77.0	1	E-R., Otsu
8)	JU	77.1	5	Date FM, Sendai
9)	SU	77.4	1	FM Kumamoto, Kumamoto
10)	VU	77.4	0.5	V-air, Matsue
11)	XU	77.5	1	FM Niigata, Niigata
12)		77.6	1	Kiss-FM, Himeji
13)	QV	77.8	10	ZIP FM, Nagoya
14)	NV	77.9	0.5	FM Saga, Saga
15)	GV	78.0	5	bayfm, Chiba
16)	GU	78.2	1	Hiroshima FM, Hiroshima
17)	YU	78.6	1	FM Kagawa, Takamatsuh
18)	FV	78.7	3	CROSS FM, Kitakyushu (Fukuoka)
19)	NU	78.9	3	Radio Cube, Tsu
20)	WV	79.0	1	FM Port, Niigata: (off air SS 1600-2053)
21)	KU	79.2	1	K-MIX, Hamamatsu (Shizuoka)
22)	UU	79.2	1	FM Yamaguchi, Yamaguchi
23)	NU	79.5	1	FM Nagasaki, Nagasaki
52a)	CW	79.5	1	Inter FM Nagoya, Nagoya
24)	DV	79.5	5	NACK 5, Saitama
25)	EU	79.7	1	FM Ehime, Matsuyama: 2057-1803 (†)
26)	ZU	79.7	1	FM Nagano, Matsumoto (Nagano)
27)	OV	79.8	1	μ FM, Kagoshima
28)	WU	80.0	1	FM Aomori, Aomori
29)	AU	80.0	10	Tokyo FM, Tokyo
30)	XV	80.0	1	Radio 80, Ogaki (Gifu)
31)	FV	80.2	10	FM 802, Osaka
32)	FU	80.4	5	AIR-G', Sapporo
33)	EV	80.4	1	Rhythm Station, Yamagata
34)	HV	80.5	1	FM Ishikawa, Kanazawa
35)	CU	80.7	10	FM Aichi, Nagoya
36)	MV	80.7	1	FM Tokushima, Tokushima
37)	DU	80.7	3	FM Fukuoka, Fukuoka
38)	AV	81.3	7	J-WAVE, Tokyo
39)	LV	81.6	0.5	Hi-six, Kochi
40)	TV	81.8	1	Fukushima FM, Koriyama(Fukushima)
41)	PV	82.5	5	FM North Wave, Sapporo
42)	OU	82.7	1	FM Toyama, Toyama
43)	PU	82.8	3	FM Akita, Akita
44)	CV	83.0	1	FM Fuji, Kofu: 1950-1800(variable)
45)	MU	83.2	1	Joy FM, Miyazaki

FM	Call	MHz	kW	Station, location & h of tr
46)	TU	84.7	5	FM Yokohama, Yokohama
47)	BU	85.1	10	FM Osaka, Osaka
48)	RU	86.3	1	FM Gunma, Maebashi
11)		86.5	1	FM Niigata, Yamato
10)		86.6	1	V-air, Hamada
49)	IU	87.3	1	FM Okinawa, Naha
50)	JV	88.0	1	FM Oita, Oita
51)	KV	89.4	3	Alpha-Station, Kyoto
52)	DW	89.7	10	Inter FM, Tokyo
12)	IV	89.9	1	Kiss-FM, Kobe

NB: Relay stns below 1kW and community stns are not included.
Call: JO(call)-FM. **Schedule:** 24h unless otherwise indicated above. Most 24h stns are off the air for 2 to 5 hours until 1900, 2000 or 2100 on Sun.

Addresses and other information:
1) FM Iwate Broadc Co., 2-10, Uchimaru, Morioka 020-8512 **W:** fmii. co.jp – **2)** Fukui FM Broadc Co., Ltd., 1-1, Miyuki 1-chome, Fukui 910-8553 **W:** fmfukui.jp – **3)** LOVE FM International Broadc Co., Ltd., 1F, Soralia Plaza, 2-43, Tenjin 2-chome, Chuo-ku, Fukuoka 810-0001 Prgr in English, Chinese and Korean etc **W:** lovefm.co.jp – **4)** FM Tochigi Brordc co.,ltd., 2-1, Chuo 1-chome, Utsunomiya 320-8550 **W:** berry. co.jp – **5)** FM 802 Co., Ltd., (See 32). Foreign language prgr in English, Chinese, Korean, etc. Since April 2012, the business has been transfered from Kansai Intermedia Corp. to FM 802 Co. Ltd. **W:** cocolo.jp – **6)** Okayama FM Broadc Co., Ltd., 1-8-45, Nakasange, Okayama 700-0821 **W:** fm-okayama.co.jp – **7)** FM Shiga Co., Ltd., 19-10, Nishinosho, Otsu 520-0818 **W:** e-radio.co.jp – **98)** Sendai FM Broadc., Inc., 10-28, Honcho 2-chome, Aoba-ku, Sendai 980-8420 **W:** datefm.co.jp – **9)** FM Kumamoto Broadc Co., Ltd., 5-50, Chibajomachi, Kumamoto 860-0001 **W:** fmk.fm – **10)** FM San-in Co., Ltd., 383, Tono-machi, Matsue 690-8508 **W:** fm-sanin.co.jp – **11)** FM Radio Niigata Co., Ltd., 3-5, Saiwainishi 4-chome, Chuo-ku, Niigata 950-8581 **W:** fmniigata.com – **12)** Kiss-FM KOBE Inc., 5-4 Hatoba-cho, Chuo-ku, Kobe 650-8589 **W:** kiss-fm.co.jp – **13)** ZIP-FM Inc., 20-17, Marunouchi 3-chome, Naka-ku, Nagoya 460-8578 **W:** zip-fm.co.jp – **14)** FM Saga Co., Ltd., 286-5, Fukuro, Honjo-machi, Saga 840-0023 **W:** fmsaga.co.jp – **15)** bayfm78 Co., Ltd., 6-1, Nakase 2-chome, Mihama-ku, Chiba 261-7127 **W:** bayfm.co.jp – **16)** Hiroshima FM Broadc Co., Ltd., 8-2, Minamimachi 1-chome, Minami-ku, Hiroshima 734-8511 **W:** hfm.jp – **17)** FM Kagawa Broadc Co., Ltd., 4-23, Saiho-cho 1-chome, Takamatsu 760-8584 **W:** fmkagawa.co.jp – **18)** Cross FM Co., Ltd, 1-1, Kyomachi 3-chome, Kokurakita-ku, Kitakyushu 802-8570 **W:** crossfm.co.jp – **19)** Mie FM Broadc co., Ltd., 1043-1, Kannonji-cho, Tsu 514-8505 **W:** fmmie. jp – **20)** Niigata Kenmin FM Broadcast Co., Ltd., 1-1, Bandai 2-chome, Chuo-ku, Niigata 950-8579 **W:** fmport.com – **21)** Shizuoka FM Broadc Co., Ltd, 133-24, Tokiwa-cho, Naka-ku, Hamamatsu 430-8575 **W:** k-mix.co.jp – **22)** FM Yamaguchi Co., Ltd., 3-31, Midori-cho, Yamaguchi 753-8521 **W:** fmy.co.jp – **23)** FM Nagasaki Co., Ltd., 5-5, Sakae-machi, Nagasaki 850-8550 **W:** fmnagasaki.co.jp – **24)** FM Nack 5 Co Ltd., 682-2, Nishiki-cho, Omiya-ku, Saitama 330-8579 **W:** nack5.co.jp – **25)** FM Ehime Broadc Co., 10-7, Takewara-machi 1-chome, Matsuyama 790-8565 **W:** joeufm.co.jp – **26)** Nagano FM Broadc Co., Ltd, 13-5, Honjo 1-chome, Matsumoto 390-8520 **W:** fmnagano.co.jp – **27)** FM Kagoshima Co., Ltd., 1-38, Higashisengoku-cho, Kagoshima 892-8579 **W:** myufm.jp – **28)** Aomori FM Broadc Co., Ltd., 7-19, Tsutsumi-machi 1-chome, Aomori 030-0812 **W:** afb.co.jp – **29)** Tokyo FM Broadc Co., Ltd., 7, Kojimachi 1-chome, Chiyoda-ku, Tokyo 102-8080 **W:** tfm.co.jp – **30)** Gifu FM Broadc Co., Ltd., 35-10, Kono 4-chome, Gifu 500-8580 **W:** radio-80.com – **31)** FM 802 Co., Ltd., Kita 2-6, Tenjinbashi 2-chome, Kita-ku, Osaka 530-8580 **W:** funky802.com – **32)** FM Hokkaido Broadc Co., Ltd., 1, Nishi 2-chome, kita 1-jo, Chuo-ku, Sapporo 060-8532 **W:** air-g.co.jp – **33)** FM Yamagata Co., Ltd., 14-69, Matsuyama 3-chome, Yamagata 990-9543 **W:** rfm.co.jp – **34)** FM Ishikawa Broadc Co., Ltd., 1-45, Hikoso-machi 2-chome, Kanazawa 920-8605 **W:** hellofive.jp – **35)** FM Aichi Broadc Co., Ltd., 15-18, Chiyoda 2-chome, Naka-ku, Nagoya 460-8388 **W:** fma.co.jp – **36)** FM Tokushima Broadc Co., 6, Saiwai-cho 1-chome, Tokushima 770-8567 **W:** fm807.jp – **37)** Fukuoka FM Broadc Co., Ltd., 9-19, Kiyokawa 1-chome, Chuo-ku, Fukuoka, 810-8575 **W:** fmfukuoka.co.jp – **38)** J-WAVE Inc., Roppongi Hills Mori Tower 33F, 10-1, Roppongi 6-chome,, Minato-ku, Tokyo 106-6188 **W:** j-wave.co.jp – **39)** FM Kochi Broadc Co., Ltd., 1-5, Takashocho 2-chome, Kochi 780-8532 **W:** fmkochi.com – **40)** FM Fukushima Inc., 4-4 Shinmei-cho, Koriyama, 960-8013 **W:** fmf.co.jp – **41)** FM North Wave Co., Ltd., 3-1, Nishi 4-chome, Kita 7-jo, Kita-ku, Sapporo 060-8557 **W:** fmnorth.co.jp – **42)** Toyama FM Broadc Co., Ltd., 2-11, Okuda-machi, Toyama 930-8567 **W:** fmtoyama. co.jp – **43)** FM Akita Broadc Co.,Ltd., 7-10, Yabase-Honcho 3-chome, Akita 010-0973 **W:** fm-akita.co.jp – **44)** FM Fuji Co Ltd., Aria 105, Kawadamachi, Kofu 400-8550 **W:** fmfuji.jp – **45)** Miyazaki FM Broadc

Co., Ltd., 78, Gion 2-chome, Miyazaki 880-8583 **W:** joyfm.co.jp – **46)** Yokohama FM Broadc Co., Ltd., 2-1, Minato-Mirai 2-chome, Nishi-ku, Yokohama 220-8110 **W:** fmyokohama.co.jp – **47)** FM Osaka Co., Ltd., 3-1, Minatomachi 1-chome, Naniwa-ku, Osaka 556-8510 **W:** fmosaka. net – **48)** FM Gunma Broadc Co., Ltd., 4-8, Wakamiyacho 1-chome, Maebashi 371-8533 **W:** fmgunma.com – **49)** FM Okinawa Broadc Corp., 40, Kowan, Urasoe, Okinawa 901-2525 **W:** fc.fmokinawa.co.jp – **50)** FM Oita Broadc., Co., Ltd., 3-8-8, funai-machi, Oita 870-8558 **W:** fmoita.co.jp – **51)** FM Kyoto, Inc., CoCon Karasuma 8F, 620, Suiginyacho, Karasuma-dori Shijo-sagaru, Shimogyo-ku, Kyoto 600-8566 **W:** fm-kyoto.jp – **52)** Inter FM Co., Ltd., 3-3, Higashi-shinagawa 1-chome, Shinagawa-ku, Tokyo 140-0002 - Prgr in English & foreign languages **W:** interfm.co.jp – **52a)** Inter FM Nagoya, 1-33-2, Kitaharacho, Mizuho-ku, Nagoya 467-0811
V. Most stns verify by QSL card. Rec acc. Rp.

THE OPEN UNIVERSITY OF JAPAN (HOSO DAIGAKU)
✉ Hoso Daigaku, 2-11, Wakaba, Mihama-ku, Chiba 261-8586 ☎ +81 43 276 5111 **W:** ouj.ac.jp
FM: JOUD-FM 77.1MHz 10kW, Tokyo. 78.8MHz 1kW, Maebashi **D. Prgr:** 2100-1500 **V.** by QSL card. Rp.

AMERICAN FORCES NETWORK (AFN) (U.S. Mil.)
The network serves the members of the US forces. The stns in Japan broadcast by authority of Commander, US Forces, Japan, in cooperation with the Information and Communications Policy Bureau in Japan. Stns are linked by land line and microwave.
✉ **AFN Tokyo,** Det 10, Unit 5091 Bldg 3266, Yokota Air Base, Fussa, Tokyo 197-0001 or Det 10, Unit 5091 Bldg 3266, APO/AP 96328-5091 ☎ +81 42 552 2511 ext 52374 🖷 +81 42 552 2511 ext 52386 **E:** AFN. Eagle810@yokota.af.mil **W:** afnpacific.net/LocalStations/Tokyo

Other stns: AFN Okinawa: Okinawa **E:** AFNRadio@us.kadena.af.mil **W:** afnpacific.net/LocalStations/Okinawa – **AFN Misawa:** Misawa, Aomori **E:** afn@misawa.af.mil **W:** afnpacific.net/LocalStations/ Misawa **AFN Iwakuni:** Iwakuni, Yamaguchi **W:** afnpacific.net/ LocalStations/Iwakuni – **AFN Sasebo:** Sasebo, Nagasaki **W:** afnpacific.net/LocalStations/Sasebo

MW	kHz	kW	MW	kHz	kW
Okinawa	648	10	Misawa	1575	0.6
Tokyo	810	50	Sasebo	1575	0.25
Iwakuni	1575	1			

FM: Okinawa 89.1MHz 20kW
D. Prgr: 24h **N:** on the h. **Ann:** "This is the American Forces Network" **V.** by QSL card or letter

LT: UTC +2h (1 Apr-28 Oct: +3h; dates subject to confirmation) — **Pop:** 6.4 million — **Pr.L:** Arabic — **E.C:** 50Hz, 230V — **ITU:** JOR

AUDIOVISUAL COMMISSION (AVC)
✉ P.O.Box 142515, Amman 11814 ☎+ 962 6 5549720 🖷 + 962 6 5535093 **W:** avc.gov.jo **E:** avc.inv@nic.jo **LP:** Dir: Hussein Bani Bani.

JORDAN RADIO & TELEVISION CORP. (JRTV, Gov.)
✉ Al-Shara Al-Musharrafah St, P.O.Box 909, JO-11118 Amman ☎+962 6 4773111 🖷 +962 6 4778 578 **W:** jrtv.gov.jo **E:** rj@jrtv.gov.jo **LP:** CEO: Mohammad Al-Tarawnah. Dir. Radio: Naser Anani. Dir. Eng: Khalaf Khawaldah. CE: Lana A. Elsheikh.

MW	kHz	kW	Prgr.	Times
Shobak	612	100	Main	24h
Amman	855	10	Quran	24h
Amman	1035	20	Main	24h

FM	Main	Amman FM	English	Quran	Hadaf	kW
Ajlun	95.8	-	90.9			10/5
Amman	90.0/106.7	99.0	96.3	93.1	88.0	5/10
Aqaba	101.5	105.6/98.1	99.7	91.5		5/1
Irbid	103.6			98.7		1
Kerak	103.6			98.7		1
Salt		105.0				1
Tafeleh	90.8					1

Main Arabic sce: 24h. Jordan Armed Forces R: 1400-1600. **Amman FM** in Arabic: 0430-2000 (Irbid with some local prgr). **English prgr:** 0300-2400. **French:** 1500-1800 on English prgr fqs. **Quran Prgr:** 24h on FM & MW 855kHz. **Hadaf** (sports prgr.): 24h.
Ann: Arabic: "Huna Amman, Idha'atu-l-Mamlaka al-Urdoniya al-Hashemiya". Armed forces R: "Idha'at Al-Quwaat Al-Musala al-Urdoniya, al-Gayish al-Arabi". E: "This is R. Jordan broadcasting from Amman".

Other stations (FM MHz):
Amen FM: Amman/Aqaba 89.5, Irbid 89.7. **W:** amenfm.jo – **Ayyam**

FM: Amman 91.5, Irbid 91.9, Petra 92.1. **W:**ayaamfm.jo – **Beat FM,** Amman: 102.5. English. **W:** mybeat.fm – **Energy FM,** Amman: 97.7. English. **W:** energyradio.jo – **Hala FM:** Aqaba 91.1, Irbid/Ruweished 91.3, Al-Karak 94.3, Al-Salt/Tafilaq 94.7, Ajlun 94.3, Amman 102.1, Petra 105.4. **W:** hala.jo – **Hawa FM,** Amman: 105.9MHz. **W:** amman-city.gov.jo – **Hayat FM:** Irbid 94.7, Amman 104.7, Azraq 105.4. **W:** hayat.fm – **Mazaj FM:** Amman 95.3, Irbid 101.7. **W:** mazajfm.com – **Melody FM:** Amman 91.1, Zarqa 105.5. – **Mood FM,** Amman: 92.0. English. **W:** mood.fm – **Play FM:** Amman 99.6, Irbid 105.3. English. **W:** play.jo – **R. Al-Balad,** Amman: 92.4 **W:** balad.fm – **R. Fann:** Aqaba 91.1, Irbid/Ruweished 91.3, Ajlun/Karak 94.3, Salt/Tafileh 94.7, Amman 102.1/104.2, Petra/Azraq 105.4. **W:** radiofann.com – **R. Farah Al-Nas,** Amman: 98.5. **W:** farahalnas.jo – **Rotana R:** Irbid 90.5, Amman 99.9. **W:** rotana.net – **Sawt Al-Janoub,** Ma'an: 90.5 – **Sawt al-Madina:** Amman: 88.7. **W:** sawtalmadenah.net – **Sawt el-Ghad:** Amman 101.5. **W:** sawtelghad.com – **Spin Jordan:** Irbid 88.3, Ma'an 88.5, Amman 94.1, Aqaba 103.5. English. **W:** spin.jo – **Sunny,** Amman: 105.1. English. **W:** sunny.jo – **Virgin R. Jordan,** Amman: 105.7. **W:** virginradiojordan.com – **Yarmouk FM,** Irbid: 105.7. **W:** yu.edu.jo

BBC Arabic Sce: Amman 103.1 5kW, Ajlun 89.1 10kW.
China R. Int: Amman 94.5 2kW.
Monte Carlo Doualiya/DW: Amman 97.4, Ajlun 106.2.
R. Sawa: Amman 98.1 10kW, Ajlun 107.4

KAZAKHSTAN

L.T: UTC +6h (Western Kazakhstan: +5h) — **Pop:** 17.8 million — **Pr.L:** Kazakh, Russian — **E.C:** 50Hz, 220V — **ITU:** KAZ

**MÄDENÏET JÄNE SPORT MÏNÏSTRLIGI
(Ministry of Culture and Sport)**
House of Ministries, 010000 Astana ☎ +7 7172 740251 **W:** mks.gov.kz **L.P:** Minister: Muxamedïuli Aristanbek
NB. The ministry issues broadcasting licenses.

**"QAZAQSTAN" RESPWBLÏKALIQ TELERADÏO-
KORPORACÏYASI ("QAZAQSTAN" RTRK) (Gov)
(Republican Broadcasting Corp. "Qazaqstan")**
Qonaev k. 4, 010000 Astana ☎ +7 7172 553335 **E:** info@kaztrk.kz **W:** kaztrk.kz **L.P:** Chair: Nurjan Muxamedjanova

MW	kHz	kW	Prgr	MW	kHz	kW	Prgr
Aqtaw	1341	25	QR	Lepsi.	1557		QR
FM (MHz)	**QR***	**SR**	**FM**		**QR***	**SR**	
Almati	101.0a	106.5	Petropavl		106.8n	104.7	
Aqtaw	100.1g	102.1	Qaragandi		103.4j	102.3	
Aqtöbe	102.2c	105.7	Qizilorda		102.0l	101.0	
Astana	106.8	100.4	Qostanay		105.4k	107.4	
Atiraw	100.1d	102.8	Semey		100.1m	104.4	
Köksetaw	101.0b	103.7	Simkent		100.0h	102.7	
Oral	101.2e	103.2	Taraz		100.8f	102.6	
Öskemen	104.0o	105.6	Türkistan		101.0a	-	
Pavlodar	101.0i	103.0	Ülken Sagan		101.0f	-	
+ translators. *) incl. reg. prgrs a-o (see below)							

D.Prgrs: Qazaq radïosi (QR) in Kazakh, Russian: 24h. For ethnic minorities ("Dostiq"): W 1505-1530 (Mon German, Tue Uighur, Wed Korean, Thur Russian, Fri Tatar, Sat Azeri) in Kazakh: 0000-1800. – **Salqar radïosi (SR)** in Kazakh: 0000-1800. – **Local stations: Astana radïosi** on Astana 101.4MHz (1kW) in Kazakh, Russian: 24h. **Classic FM** on Almati 102.8MHz (1kW): 24h.

"QAZAQSTAN" RTRK Regional Services
All regional branches (fïlïali) of "Qazaqstan" RTRK broadcast at various times via txs of QR. In addition, some branches are also broadcasting on own FM frequencies in Kazakh and languages of ethnic minorities.
a) Almati qalaliq fïlïali: Jeltoqsan k. 177, 050013 Almati. **E:** kzcont@kaztv.kz – **b) Aqmola oblistiq fïlïali:** Kwybisev k. 19, 020000 Köksetaw. **E:** kokshetv@mail.ru – **c) Aqtöbe oblistiq fïlïali:** Axtanov k. 54, 030002 Aqtöbe. **E:** atrk@aktobe.kazakstan.kz – **d) Atiraw oblistiq fïlïali:** Moldagalïev k. 29, 060005 Atiraw. **E:** atyrautv@kazakstan.kz On Atyrau 102.0MHz + translators. – **e) Batis Qazaqstan oblistiq fïlïali:** Amanjolov k. 104, 090000 Oral. **E:** zapad_tv@mail.kz – **f) Jambil oblistiq fïlïali:** Süleymenov k. 6, 080000 Taraz. **E:** jotrk@mail.ru – **g) Mangistaw oblistiq fïlïali:** 24 sagin awdan, 130000 Aqtaw. **E:** kazakhstan-aktau@bk.ru – **h) Oñtüstik Qazaqstan oblistiq fïlïali:** Qazibek bï k. 20, 160000 Simkent. **E:** uktv_aha@mail.ru – **i) Pavlodar oblistiq fïlïali:** Derïbas k. 21, 140000 Pavlodar. **E:** director@pavlodar.kazakstan.kz. On Pavlodar 100.5MHz + translators. – **j) Qaragandi oblistiq fïlïali:** Jawinger-

ïnternacïonalïster k. 14, 100000 Qaragandi. **E:** karrtrk@mail.ru – **k) Qostanay oblistiq fïlïali:** Äl-Farabï dangili 126, 110033 Qostanay. **E:** office@kostanai.kazakstan.k – **l) Qizilorda oblistiq fïlïali:** Jeltoqsan k. 11, 120014 Qizilorda. **E:** baiimbet@mail.ru – **m) Semey oblistiq fïlïali:** Sugaev k. 157, 071403 Semey. **E:** semey-tv@kazakstan.kz On Semey 106.9MHz (R.7). **E:** semey-tv@kazakstan.kz – **n) Soltüstik Qazaqstan oblistiq fïlïali:** Brwsïlovskïy k. 1, 150000 Petropavl. **E:** info@petropavl.kazakstan.kz – **o) Sigis Qazaqstan oblistiq fïlïali:** Staxanovskaya k. 70, 070010 Öskemen. **E:** vktrk@inbox.ru.

OTHER STATIONS

FM	MHz	kW	Location	Station
4B)	100.4	1	Taldiqorgan	Jüldiz FM
4A)	100.5	1	Qaragandi	Tengri FM
4B)	100.8	1	Astana	Jüldiz FM
5)	101.2	1	Simkent	Love R.
4A)	101.4	1	Aqtaw	Tengri FM
4A)	101.4	1	Semey	Tengri FM
4B)	101.4	1	Almati	Jüldiz FM
2A)	101.4	1	Taldiqorgan	Avtoradio
2B)	101.8	1	Almati	R. Rekord
4B)	101.8	1	Astana	Jüldiz FM
4B)	102.0	1	Qizilorda	Jüldiz FM
4A)	102.7	1	Aqtöbe	Tengri FM
4B)	102.9	1	Öskemen	Jüldiz FM
6)	103.2	1	Astana	Orda FM
3)	103.5	2	Almati	Love R.
4A)	103.5	1	Öskemen	Tengri FM
2A)	103.8	1	Qostanay	Avtoradio
1)	104.0	1	Qaragandi	Retro FM
4A)	104.5	1	Astana	Tengri FM
2A)	104.6	1	Qizilorda	Avtoradio
4A)	104.7	1	Simkent	Tengri FM
1)	105.0	1	Astana	Retro FM
2A)	105.2	1	Aqtöbe	Avtoradio
2A)	105.2	1	Simkent	Avtoradio
2A)	105.4	1	Almati	Avtoradio
2A)	105.6	1	Pavlodar	Avtoradio
4A)	105.8	1	Oral	Tengri FM
4B)	106.1	1	Köksetaw	Jüldiz FM
2A)	106.2	1	Jezqazgan	Avtoradio
2A)	106.3	1	Qaragandi	Avtoradio
4B)	106.3	1	Petropavl	Jüldiz FM
2A)	106.4	1	Astana	Avtoradio
4B)	106.5	1	Semey	Jüldiz FM
4B)	106.7	1	Taraz	Jüldiz FM
4A)	106.7	1	Sagan	Tengri FM
8)	106.8	1	Taraz	Jüldiz FM
1)	107.0	1	Almati	Retro FM
4A)	107.5	1	Almati	Tengri FM
4A)	107.6	1	Köksetaw	Tengri FM
4A)	107.7	1	Taraz	Tengri FM
2A)	107.7	1	Atiraw	Avtoradio
7)	107.9	1	Öskemen	R. Miks

NB: Txs below 1kW not listed.
Addresses & other information:
1) Respwblïk alana 13, 050013 Almati **E:** radio@retrofm.kz – **2A,B)** Satlaev k. 30a, 050057 Almati **E:** info@avtoradio.kz – **3)** Minbaev k. 53, 050057 Almati **E:** radio@loveradio.kz – **4A,B)** Begalïn k. 148, 050051 Almati – **5)** Simkent – **6)** Jeltoqsan k. 49, 010000 Astana **E:** radio@astv.kz – **7)** Gagarïn k. 11, 070000 Öskemen

KENYA

L.T: UTC +3h — **Pop:** 38 million — **Pr.L:** English, Swahili, Kikuyu, Luhya, Luo, Kalenjin, Somali, others — **E.C:** 50Hz, 240V — **ITU:** KEN

COMMUNICATIONS AUTHORITY OF KENYA
P.O. Box 14448, Nairobi 00800 ☎+254 20 4242000 **W:** ca.go.ke **E:** info@ca.go.ke

KENYA BROADCASTING CORPORATION (KBC, Pub.)
P.O. Box 30456, Nairobi 00100 ☎+254 20 2766000 📠 +254 20 2220675 **W:** kbc.co.ke **E:** md@kbc.co.ke **L.P:** Chmn: Charles Musyoki Muoki. MD: Waithaka Waihenya.

MW	kHz	kW	Netw.	MW	kHz	kW	Netw.
Kapsimotwa#	558	25	W	Ngong§	747	100	C
Garissa	567	50	S	Maralal	1107	100	S
Ngong§	612	100	S	Wajir	1152	50	S
Garissa	639	50	I	Marsabit	1233	50	I
Marsabit	675	50	S	Wajir	1305	50	E/N

MW	kHz	kW	Netw.
Maralal	1386	100	E/N

#) near Kisumu, §) near Nairobi.

FM	S	E	Co	Pw	Mi	Ki	Ma	Mw	I
Limuru*	92.9	95.6	99.5	-	-	98.0	-	-	101.9
Malindi	96.5	93.3	-	93.7	-	-	-	-	-
Meru**	90.4	103.5	-	-	-	-	-	100.3	-
Nyeri	87.6	100.7	102.3	-	-	-	-	-	-
Mombasa	100.7	103.1	-	104.7	-	-	-	-	-
Timboroa	88.6	91.5	-	-	-	-	-	-	-
Nakuru	104.1	96.5	-	-	-	-	-	-	-
Eldoret	-	-	-	-	-	92.9	-	-	-
Kapsimotwa	-	-	-	-	-	-	-	-	-
Kisumu	88.6	91.5	-	-	-	-	93.5	-	-
Kisii	103.3	-	-	101.7	-	-	-	-	-
Nyadundo	-	99.7	-	-	-	-	-	-	-

*Limuru txs serve Greater Nairobi. **) also called Nyambene.

Networks (from Nairobi studios unless stated):
S=Swahili Sce "Radio Taifa": 0200-2110 on MW, 24h on FM. Also rel. China R. Int. 1905-2000 – **E=English Sce**: 0200-2105 (on FM non-stop music 2105-0200). Includes relays of CRI 1700-1800 & BBC. MW freqs carry N sce at times – **N= (North)Eastern Sce**: MF variable between 0900-1900: Turkana on 1386kHz, Borana, Burji & Rendille on 1233kHz – **C=**relays of Mwatu FM and Nosim FM: Mon-Sat 0200-2010 – **I=**Iftiin FM in Somali on 639/1305kHz and 101.9MHz – **W=Western Sce.** from Kisumu studios in local langs Mon-Fri 0300-1905 on 558kHz – **Co=Coro FM** in Kikuyu – **Pw=Pwani FM** from Mombasa studios – **Mi=Minto FM** (from Keroka studios in Kisii) – **Ki=Kitwek FM** in Kalenjin – **Ma=Mayienga FM** (from Kisumu studios in Luo) – **Mw=Mwago FM** in Meru – **Ingo FM**: western Kenya on 100.5MHz in Luhya – **Mwatu FM**: Kibwezi 93.1MHz in Kamba – **Nosim FM**: Narok 90.5MHz in Masai.
Ann: E: "This is KBC English Service". **IS:** Flute & drum melody in some services.

ROYAL MEDIA SERVICES LTD. (RMS)
P.O. Box 7468, Nairobi 00300 ☎+254 20 2721415/6 ▤ +254 20 2724211 **W:** royalmediaservices.co.ke **E:** info@royalmedia.co.ke **L.P:** Owner: Samuel K. Macharia. MD: Wachira Waruru.
FM(MHz): **R. Citizen** in Swahili/Eng: Eldoret 90.4, Voi 91.8, Chuka 93.1, Machakos 94.2, Meru 94.3, Kibwezi 95.4, Narok 95.5, Garissa 95.7, Maralal 95.9, Kapenguria 96.1, Kanyenyeini 96.5, Wajir 97.0, Mombasa 97.3, Malindi 97.4, Nakuru 98.5, Marsabit 98.0, Kitui 98.6, Nakuru 100.5, Nyadundo 103.6, Nyeri 104.3, Homa Bay 105.2, Nairobi/Namanga 106.7, Kisii nic known. – **Hot 96 FM** in Eng/Sheng/Swahili: Nairobi 96.0, Eldoret 87.6, Kisumu 103.1, Mombasa 90.4, Nakuru 102.5, Nyeri 88.6.
RMS also operates the following stns for specific lang. communities:
FM (MHz): Bahari FM (in Swahili & coastal langs): Mombasa 94.2 – **Chamgei FM** (in Kalenjin): 90.4, Nakuru 95.0, Eldoret 97.5 – **Egesa FM** (in Kisii): Kisii 94.6, Nairobi 103.2 – **Inooro FM** (in Kikuyu): Nyadundo 88.9, Nakuru 89.8, Meru 95.1, Muranga 96.9, Nyeri 97.8, Nairobi 98.9, Mombasa 99.2, Chuka 102.0, Eldoret 107.0 – **Mulembe FM** (in Luhya): Webuye 89.6, Rift Valley 94.0, Eldoret 95.8, Nairobi 97.9 – **Musyi FM** (in Kamba): Nairobi 102.2, Kitui 103.6 – **Muuga FM** (in Meru): Meru 88.9 – **Ramogi FM** (in Luo): Nakuru 95.4, Mombasa 96.0, Homa Bay 97.0, Siaya 98.4, Nairobi 107.1, Kisumu 107.6 – **Wimwaro FM** (in Embu): Embu 93.0 – **Vuuka FM** (in Maragoli): Kisumu 100.4.

RADIO AFRICA LTD.
P.O. Box 74497, Nairobi ☎+254 20 4244000 ▤ +254 20 4447410 **W:** kissfm.co.ke **E:** info@kissfm.co.ke **L.P:** MD: Patrick Quarcoo.
FM(MHz): **Kiss 100** in Eng/Swahili: Nairobi 100.3, Eldoret 89.1, Kisumu 92.5, Meru 93.5 , Mombasa 88.7, Nakuru 98.1, Nyeri 100.1, Webuye 104.7 – **Classic 105 FM** in Eng/Swahili: Nakuru 95.7, Nairobi 105.2, Mombasa 107.5 – **East FM** (Asian): Nairobi 106.3, Mombasa 89.5 – **Jambo FM** (sports): Kisii 89.3, Mombasa 92.3, Meru 92.7, Webuye 95.3, Nakuru 96.9, Maralal/Narok/Nyahururu 97.3, Nairobi 97.5, Malindi 98.1, Nyeri 99.3, Eldoret 99.5, Kapenguria 99.7, Kisumu 100.1, Garissa 104.3, Kibwezi/Lamu 104.7, Kitui 104.9, Voi 105.7 – **X FM** (rock music): Nairobi 105.5 – **Relax FM** (R&B music): Nairobi 103.5.

NATION MEDIA GROUP LTD.
P.O. Box 49010, Nairobi 00100 ☎+254 20 3288000 **W:** nationmedia.com **L.P:** Chmn: Wilfred Kiboro. CEO: Linus Gitahi. Managing Ed. Broadc. Div: Linus Kaikai.
FM(MHz): **Nation** in Eng/Swahili: Nairobi 96.3, Eldoret 102.7, Kisumu 102.1, Meru 93.9, Mombasa 101.5, Nakuru 97.7, Nyeri 104.9 – **QFM** in Swahili: Nairobi 94.4, Eldoret 96.7, Meru 107.1, Mombasa 87.9, Nakuru 103.3, Nyeri 90.9.

OTHER FM STNS IN NAIROBI (including relays elsewhere; freqs are in Nairobi unless stated, & in MHz): **1 FM** (ex Countryside FM): 97.1, Meru 99.1, Nyeri 106.1, Nakuru 106.5, Mombasa 107.3 – **Biblia Husema Broadcasting** (Christian): 96.7, Eldoret 96.3, Lokichokio 102.5, Nakuru 102.9, Machakos 96.7, Timboroa 101.5 – **Capital FM** (in Eng): 98.4, Garissa 102.7, Kitui 106.5, Malindi 104.5, Meru 103.9, Mombasa 98.4, Nakuru 98.5, Nyeri 98.5, Timboroa 93.0, Voi 104.9 – **East Africa R.** (in Eng/Swahili - relay of Tanzanian stn): 94.7 – **ECN FM** (Kenya Institute of Mass Communication): 104.7 – **R. 316** (Christian, formerly Family FM): 103.9, Kisumu 96.5, Mombasa 97.9, Nakuru 102.1 – **Ghetto R.** (in Sheng): 89.5 – **Homeboyz R.:** 103.5 – **Hope FM** (Pentecostal Church): 93.3, Mombasa 101.9, Timboroa 93.9 – **Iqra FM** (Islamic): 95.1 – **Kameme FM** (mainly in Kikuyu): 101.1, Eldoret 101.9, Nakuru 99.3, Nyeri 92.3, Meru 88.3. Also rel. BBC – **Kass FM** (in Kalenjin): 89.1, Eldoret 90.0, Kisumu 91.0, Nakuru 92.5, Kisii 99.3, Mombasa 102.7 – **Milele FM** (in Swahili): 93.6, Kapenguria 88.3, Taita-Taveta (Voi) 89.7, Nakuru/Nyahururu 90.2, Kitui/Lamu 91.3, Nyeri 91.7, Webuye 92.7, Kisii 95.1, Mombasa 96.7, Maralal/Narok 98.7, Kisumu 99.7, Garissa 99.9, Malindi 101.3, Meru 101.5, Eldoret 103.1, Kibwezi 104.3 – **R. Maisha** 102.7, Nakuru 104.5, Mombasa/Meru 105.1, Kisumu 105.3, Nyeri 105.7 – **R. Nam Lolwe:** 101.5, Kisumu 97.3, Mombasa 94.7, Nakuru 87.7 – **Sound Asia:** 88.0, Mombasa 89.9 – **Star FM** (in Somali/Swahili/Eng): 105.9, Dadaab/Garissa 97.1, Wajir 97.3, Mandera 97.5. Also rel. BBC. **W:** starfm.co.ke – **Truth FM:** 90.7 – **Uptown Radio:** 91.1 – **R. Waumini:** 88.3. **W:** catholicchurch.or.ke

NB: 99.9MHz is assigned for use in Nairobi by several very low-powered community stns. There are many private FM stns outside Nairobi. **Relays of international stations (FM, MHz): BBC WS** (E/Swahili): Nairobi 93.9, Mombasa 93.9, Kisumu 88.1 – **VOA** (E/Swahili): Nairobi 107.5 – **RFI Afrique** (F/E/Swahili): Nairobi 89.9, Mombasa 105.5 – **China R. Int.** (E/Swahili/Chinese): Nairobi 91.9, Mombasa 103.9

KIRIBATI

L.T: UTC +12h – **Pop:** 100,743 – **Pr.L:** I-Kiribati, English, Gilbertese – **E.C:** 50Hz, 240V – **ITU:** KIR

COMMUNICATIONS COMMISSION OF KIRIBATI
PO Box 529, Betio, Tarawa ☎ +686 25431/25488 **W:** cck.ki **E:** enquiry@cck.ki
Regulator of broadcasting in Kiribati [including Kiritimati Island]

MW	kHz	kW	Station
1) Bairiki	1440	10	R. Kiribati

FM	MHz	kW	Station
1) Bairiki	88.0	0.1	R. Kiribati 88 FM
2) Betio	89.0	-	Newair FM
3) Bairiki	90.0	-	R. Australia
1) Ronton	93.5	0.5	R. Kiribati Kiritimati FM
4) Bairiki	95.0	-	BBC
4) Tarawa	100.0	-	BBC
2) Bairiki	101.0	-	Newair FM

Addresses and other information
1) BROADCASTING & PUBLICATIONS AUTHORITY – RADIO KIRIBATI PO Box 78, Bairiki, Tarawa **LP:** CEO Teannaki Tongaua [**E:** ceo@bpa.org.ki] Mgr Program & Publications Mrs Reita Andrew [**E:** program-publications@bpa.org.ki] Engineering Netw. Mgr Babera Marewenimakin [**E:** engineering-network@bpa.org.ki] ☎ +686 21457 ▤ +686 21096. **E:** radio.kiribati@gmail.com **W:** bpa.org.ki Audio streaming at Icecast 202.6.120.13:8000 **MW:** Bairiki 1440kHz 10kW **FM:** 88.0MHz 0.1kW [relays MW] **D.Prgr:** I-Kiribati (90%) English (10%): 1855-2030, 0000-0130, 0500-1000 **N. in English:** 2000, 0100, 1800 (RNZI) followed by local news bulletin [r.relaying other RNZI programs irregularly]. Incl. sponsored programs from government agencies, international agencies on AM, with spot advertising only on FM. **Ann:** "This is Radio Kiribati, the national broadcasting service of Kiribati in the Central Pacific" "Aio bwanaan Kiribati te botaki ni kanako bwanaa I bukin Kiribati I nukan te Betebeke".

RADIO KIRIBATI KIRITIMATI FM Ronton, Kiritimati Island, Kiribati, Central Pacific **FM:** Ronton (London) 93.5MHz 0.5kW **Prgr:** Satellite feed from R. Kiribati 88.0 FM and local originated prgrs for Kiritimati (Christmas) Island in the Line Islands [Responsibility of Kiritimati Branch Broadcasting Services via Enginnering Netw Mgr]. – **2)** PO Box 204, Bairiki, Tarawa. **LP:** Sir Ieremia Tabai. **D.Prgr:** Local commercial prgrs in English & I-Kiribati ☎ +686 21671 **E:** newairfm89kiribati@gmail.com – **3)** 24/7 Pacific stream in English via satellite from Melbourne – **4)** 24/7 Pacific stream in English via satellite from London

KOREA (North, DPR)

L.T: UTC +8½h — **Pop:** 25 million — **Pr.L:** Korean — **E.C:** 60Hz, 100/200/220V — **ITU:** KRE

THE RADIO AND TELEVISION BROADCASTING COMMITEE OF THE DEMOCRATIC PEOPLE'S REPUBLIC OF KOREA
✉ Jonsung-dong, Moranbong District, Pyongyang ☎ +850 2 816035

KOREAN CENTRAL BROADCASTING STATION
(Joson Jung-ang Pangsong)
✉ Jonsung-dong, Moranbong District, Pyongyang ☎ +850 2 812301

MW	kHz	kW	Prgr	MW	kHz	kW	Prgr
Chongjin	702	50	C/R	Sinuiju	873	250	C/R
Wiwon*	720	500	C/R	Wonsan	882	250	C/R
Hyesan	765	50	C/R	Hwangju+	927	50	C/R
Kaesong	810	50	C/R	Hamhung	999	250	C/R
Pyongyang	819	500	C	Pyongyang	1368	2	E

SW	kHz	Prgr	SW	kHz	Prgr
Sariwon	2350	C/R	Wonsan	v3968	C/R
Pyongyang	2850	C	Chongjin	v3980	C/R
Hamhung	3220	C/R	Kanggye	6100	C
Pyongsong	#3350	C/R	Pyongyang	9665	C
Hyesan	#3920	C/R	Kanggye	11680	C
Kanggye	3959	C/R			

*= Kanggye, += Sariwon, #=inactive, v= variable, C = Central Broadcast from Pyongyang, R = Regional Sce, E = rel. Ext. Sce.
NB: all freqs variable **FM:** Kaesong 102.3MHz
D.Prgr. in Korean: 2030-1830 on all freqs exc. 6100 (2030-0900 & 1330-1830). **N:** 2130, 2230, 0130, 0330, 0630, 0830, 1130, 1230, 1330. Regional Prgrs: W0530-0630. Rel. Pyongyang Broadc. St: 1530-1830 on 702/720/864kHz 1530-2030 on 102.3MHz 1830-2030 on 3220kHz. **Ann:** "Joson Jung-ang Pangsong-imnida". Reg. Prgrs: "(location) Pangsong-imnida". **IS:** Song of General Kim Il Sung. Opening & closing music: Nat. Anthem. **V:** not verified
EXTERNAL SERVICES: Voice of Korea, Pyongyang Broadcasting Station, Echo of Unification– See International Broadcasting section

PYONGYANG FM BROADCASTING STATION
(Pyongyang FM Pangsong)

FM	MHz	kW	FM	MHz	kW
Pyongsong	90.1	2	Sariwon	103.0	2
Kaesong	92.5	2	Haeju	103.7	10
Kanggye	93.3	5	Pyongyang	105.2	20
Hyesan	93.8	2	Chongjin	105.5	10
Wonsan	95.1	5	Hamhung	106.1	20
Sinuiju	101.3	5	Nampo	107.2	2
Komdok	102.1	1			

D.Prgr: 0730-2030, 2130-0030 (National holidays: 2130-2100) (music, drama and news)
Ann: "Pyongyang FM Pangsong-imnida". **IS:** Song of General Kim Jong Il. Opening music: Pyongyang Is My Heart

FRONTLINE SOLDIERS RADIO
(Jonyon Chobyongdurul Wihan Pangsong)
MW: ±1610kHz (irr.), **SW:** 3025kHz (inactive) **D.Prgr in Korean:** 2100-2300 and 0800-1130. Almost relay of Korean Central Broadcasting Station. Times and freqs are variable.
Ann: "Jonyon Chobyongdurul Wihan Pangsong-imnida"

KOREAN PEOPLE'S ARMY FM BROADCASTING STATION
(Josong Inmingun FM Pangsong)
FM: 95.5MHz **Ann:** "Josong Inmingun FM Pangsong-imnida"

KOREA (South, Rep.)

L.T: UTC +9h — **Pop:** 50 million — **Pr.L:** Korean — **E.C:** 60Hz, 110/220V — **ITU:** KOR

KOREAN BROADCASTING SYSTEM (KBS)
(Hanguk Bangsong Gongsa) (Public Corporation)
✉13, Yeouidaebang-ro, Yeongdeungpo-gu, Seoul 07235 ☎ +82 2 781 1000 🖷 +82 2 761 2499 **W:** kbs.co.kr
L.P: Pres & CEO: Cho Dae-hyun. Auditor Gen.: Kim Seung-Jong. Exec. Vice Pres: Keum Dong-Soo, Exec. Man. Dirs: Kwon Soon-Woo (Prgr), Kang Sun-Kyu (N & Sports), Lee Eung-Jin (TV), Kim Seok-Doo (New Media & Tech), Kim Seong-O (Audience Rel.), Suh Jae-Suhk (Policy

Planning). Dir. Int. Rel. Div:Hong Seung-Joo

MW	Location	Call	kHz	kW	MW	Location	Call	kHz	kW
8)	Hongseong	-	540	10	18)	Geochang	-	1026	1
10)	Jangheung	-	540	1	3)	Hwacheon	-	1026	1
9)	Jangsu	-	540	1	15)	Pohang+	CP	1035	10
13)	Jeomchon	-	540	1	7)	Jecheon	-	1044	10
13)	Daegu+2	QH	558	250	4)	Samcheok	-	1044	10
9)	Jeonju*	KF	567	100	6)	Cheongju+	KQ	1062	50
12)	Suncheon 3		576	1	7)	Chungju+	CH	1089	10
14)	Yeongju	-	594	10	18)	Jinju+	CJ	1098	20
N2)	Namyang*	SA	603	500	N3)	Hwaseong*	KC	1134	500
19)	Seogwipo	-	621	10	5)	Wonju+	CW	1152	10
4)	Taebaek	-	621	10	K2E)	Gimje*	SR	1170	500
6)	Yeongdong	-	621	1	14)	Cheongsong	-	1206	1
3)	Inje	-	630	5	5)	Jeongseon	-	1206	1
12)	Yeosu	-	630	10	10)	Gwangju 3	-	1224	20
10)	Boseong	-	648	1	5)	Pyeongchang	-	1233	1
3)	Chuncheon+	KM	657	50	9)	Namwon	-	1260	10
9)	Jeonju 3	-	675	10	9)	Gurye	-	1269	1
N1)	Sorae*	KA	711	500	N1)	Yangju	-	1269	10
13)	Daegu+	KG	738	100	16)	Hapcheon	-	1278	1
10)	Gwangju+	KH	747	100	15)	Uljin	-	1305	10
N1)	Yeoju*	-	756	100	15)	Ulleung	-	1323	1
5)	Yeongwol	-	783	10	10)	Yeonggwang	-	1323	1
3)	Yanggu	-	846	5	9)	Muju	-	1368	1
4)	Gangneung+	KR	864	100	N1)	Cheorwon*	-	1395	10
8)	Daejeon+	KI	882	20	17)	Ulsan+	QB	1449	10
2)	Busan+	KB	891	250	14)	Bonghwa	-	1458	1
13)	Gumi	-	909	10	18)	Hamyang	-	1458	1
N1)	Yeoncheon*	-	918	50	11)	Mokpo+	KN	1467	50
8)	Buyeo	-	927	10	12)	Goheung	-	1485	1
18)	Hadong	-	927	1	8)	Gongju	-	1485	1
5)	Hongcheon	-	927	1	13)	Gimcheon	-	1503	1
16)	Changwon 3	-	936	10	19)	Gosan	-	1539	1
6)	Boeun	-	945	10	7)	Danyang	-	1584	1
14)	Andong+	-	963	10	8)	Geumsan	-	1584	1
19)	Jeju+	KS	963	10	18)	Sancheong	-	1584	1
K1)	Dangjin*	CA	972	1500	5)	Sabuk	-	1602	1
4)	Gangneung 3	-	1008	50					

MW: N1 = KBS R. One, N2 = KBS R. Two, N3 = KBS R. Three, K1 = Global Korean Network 1, K2 = Global Korean Network 2, E = also used for Ext. sce., KBS WORLD R, N = Netw. or local stn. area, *) Key stn, +) = Regional key St, 2 = rel N2 exc. for local prgrs, 3 = rel N3 (other local st take N1), Call: HL(call)
NB: Global Korean Network stns and FM-stns do not use call letters (even if assigned). Other stns without call letters use the calls from their regional key stns.

FM	Location	I	II	III	kW
1)	Namsan		93.1	89.1a	-/10/10
1)	Gwanaksan	97.3*		106.1b	10/-/10
1)	Gwanaksan			104.9c	-/-/2
1)	Yongmunsan	90.3*			1
2)	Hwangnyeongsan	103.7	92.7	97.1b	3/5/3
3)	Hwaaksan	99.5*	91.1	98.7b	5/5/3
4)	Gwaebangsan	98.9*	89.1	102.1b	1/5/5
5)	Baegunsan	97.1	89.5		1/5/3
5)	Taegisan	95.5*			1
4)	Hambaeksan	93.7*	97.3		1/5/3
6)	Sikchangsan		102.1		-/3
8)	Sikchangsan			100.9b	-/-/3
6)	Heukseongsan	89.9*			1
6)	Uamsan	89.3	94.1	90.9b	1/1/3
7)	Gayeopsan	92.1*	100.3		1/3
8)	Gyeryongsan	94.7*	98.5		1/5
8)	Moaksan	96.9*	100.7	92.9b	5/5/?
9)	Nogodan	88.3*	104.5		1/3
10)	Mudeungsan	90.5*	92.3	95.5b	5/5/3
11)	Yangulsan		98.3		-/1
11)	Daedeoksan	105.9			2
12)	Namsan			102.7b	-/-/3
12)	Mangunsan	95.7*	94.5		1/3
13)	Palgongsan	101.3*	89.7	102.3b	5/5/3
14)	Ilwolsan	90.5*			1
14)	Hakkasan		88.1		-/3
15)	Johangsan	95.9*	93.5		1/3
16)	Bulmosan	91.7*	93.9	106.1b	1/1/3
17)	Muryongsan	90.7*	101.9		1/3
18)	Gamaksan		92.1		-/3
18)	Mangjinsan	90.3	89.3		1/1
19)	Gyeonwolak	99.1*	96.3	91.9b	5/3/3
19)	Sammaebong	95.3	99.9	89.7b	3/3/3

+ low power relay stn

Reg = region in MW section. I-Standard FM (R. One); II-KBS FM One; III
a = KBS FM Two, b = R. Two, c=R. Three. *) also SCA (R. Three)

KBS R. One (KBS Je-il Radio, HLKA): 24h Non-commercial nationwide news sce. Key freqs 711/756kHz, 90.3/97.3MHz. Also rel. by
Standard FM stns and most reg. stns. Reg. stns may broadcast local
prgrs at designated times. **N:** hourly 2000-1600 except 1100(W). Local
N: 2205(Sun), 2210(W), 0000(Sun), 0005(w), 0310(Sun), 0315(W),
0605, 0805(Mon-Fri), 0900(Sun), 0905(W)
KBS R. Two (KBS Je-i Radio, Happy FM, HLSA): 2000-1800 (558kHz
to 1500). Commercial. Key freq's 603kHz/106.1MHz. Reg. stns may
broadcast local prgrs at designated times. **N:** hourly 2000-1200. Local
N: 2300, 0400, 0700, 1200. Global Korean Network prgr 1700-1800
KBS R. Three (KBS Je-sam Radio, Sarang-ui Sori Bangsong,
HLKC): 2100-1800. Non-comm. sce. **N:** 0000(W), 0100(W), 0300(W),
0800(Mon-Fri)
KBS FM One (KBS Je-il FM Bangsong, Classic FM, HLKA-FM): 24h.
Mainly Korean traditional and western classical music
KBS FM Two (KBS Je-i FM Bangsong, Cool FM, HLKC-FM): 24h.
Mainly Korean and western popular and light classical music
NB: Regional FM One stns relay FM Two 2100-2200

Ann: N1: "AM Chilbaek-sib-il(711)kHz, FM Gusib-chil-jeom-
sam(97.3)MHz, Je-il Radiomnida. HLKA". **N2:** "KBS Je-i Radiomnida".
N3: "KBS Je-sam Radio, Sarang-ui Sori Bangsong-imnida. HLKC".

Addresses of regional key stations:
2) 429, Suyeong-ro, Suyeong-gu, Busan 48316 – **3)** 109, Bangsong-gil,
Chuncheon-si, Gangwon-do 24363 – **4)** 13, Imyeong-ro 131beon-gil,
Gangneung-si, Gangwon-do 255340 – **5)** 37, Wonil-ro, Wonju-si,
Gangwon-do 26432 – **6)** 1428, Seobu-ro, Heungdeok-gu, Cheongju-si,
Chungcheongbuk-do 28637 – **7)** 3448, Jungwon-daero, Chungju-si,
Chungcheongbuk-do 27428 – **8)** 128, Dunsan-daero 117beon-gil, Seo-
gu, Daejeon 35203 – **9)** 30, Majeonjungang-ro, Wansan-gu, Jeonju-si,
Jeollabuk-do 54962 –**10)** 287, Uncheon-ro, Seo-gu, Gwangju 61946
– **11)** 221, Yangeul-ro, Mokpo-si, Jeollanam-do 58613 – **12)** 250,
Jungang-ro, Suncheon-si, Jeollanam-do 57938 – **13)** 30, Dalgubeol-
daero 496-gil, Suseong-gu, Daegu 42095 – **14)** 27, Gamnamu 3-gil,
Andong-si, Gyeongsangbuk-do 36647 – **15)** 72, Jungseom-ro, Nam-
gu, Pohang-si, Gyeongsangbuk-do 37771 – **16)** 178, Jungang-daero,
Changwon-si, Gyeongsangnam-do 51444 – **17)** 212, Beonyeong-ro,
Nam-gu, Ulsan 44702 – **18)** 85, Sinan-ro, Jinju-si, Gyeongsangnam-do
52695 – **19)** 668, Donam-dong, Jeju-si, Jeju 63124
Local identifications: Within local prgrs. **N1:** just before the h. at
2000, 2200(Sun), 2300, 0000(W), 0200, 0300, 0500, 0700(Mon-Fri),
0800, 0900(Sun), 1000(W), 1100(Sun), 1300, 1400, 1500(Sun), 1600.
N2: just before the h. 2000-1700. **N3:** just before the h. 2100-1700. **FM
One:** just before the h. at 2000-2200, 0000, 0200, 0300, 0500, 0700-
0900, 1100, 1300, 1500, 1600, 1800. **FM Two:** just before the h

Digital services: 19 DMB and 2 DAB sces. Seoul chs: 181.280MHz,
183.008MHz, 184.736MHz, 205.280MHz, 207.008MHz, 208.736MHz.
National chs: 183.008MHz (Seogwipo), 201.008MHz (Cheongju),
207.008MHz (Busan/Ulsan/Jeonju), 213.008MHz (Chuncheon/Jeju
City)

**EXTERNAL SERVICES: KBS WORLD RADIO, KBS Global Korean
Network (Hanminjok Bangsong)** See International Radio section

KOREA EDUCATIONAL BROADCASTING SYSTEM (EBS)
(Gyoyuk Bangsong) (Pub.)
35, Baumoe-ro 1-gil, Seocho-gu, Seoul 006762 ☎ +82 2 526 2000
+82 2 526 2419 **W:** ebs.co.kr
Call letters HLQL used for all the stns.

FM	Tx location	MHz	kW
Chungju	Gayeopsan	104.1	3
Changwon	Bulmosan	104.3	3
Seoul	Gwanaksan	104.5	10
Jinju	Gamaksan	104.7	3
Gangneung	Gwaebangsan	104.9	3
Wonju	Baegunsan	104.9	3
Seogwipo	Sammaebang	104.9	3
Daegu	Palgongsan	105.1	3
Gwangju	Mudeungsan	105.3	3
Daejeon	Gyeryongsan	105.7	5
Ulsan	Muryongsan	105.9	3
Yeosu	Mangunsan	106.3	3
Chuncheon	Hwaaksan	106.5	5
Pohang	Johangsan	106.7	3
Jeonju	Moaksan	106.9	5
Taebaek	Hambaeksan	107.1	3

FM	Tx location	MHz	kW
Jeju	Gyeonwolak	107.3	3
Namwom	Nogodan	107.5	3
Daegu	Ilwolsan	107.7	3
Andong	Hakkasan	107.7	3
Busan	Hwangnyeongsan	107.7	3
Cheongju	Sikjangsan	107.9	3
+ low power relay stns
D.Prgr: 2000-1700 **Ann:** "EBS, Gyoyuk Bangsong-imnida"

GUGAK FM BROADCASTING SYSTEM
(Gugak Bangsong) (Pub.)
DMS Bldg., 12, World Cup Buk-ro 54-gil, Mapo-gu, Seoul 03925
☎ +82 2 300 9990 +82 2 300 9959
W: gugakfm.co.kr
Stations: Seoul HLQA-FM 99.1MHz 5kW: 24h, Namwon 95.9MHz
1kW: 24h, Namdo 94.7MHz 0.5kW: 24h, Gyeongju/Pohang 107.9MHz
3kW: 24h, Jeonju 95.3MHz 1kW: 24h, Busan 98.5MHz 1kW: 24h,
Gangneung 103.3MHz 1kW: 24h, Daegu 107.5MHz 1kW: 24h, Gwangju
99.3MHz 1kw: 24h
Ann: "Gugak Bangsong-imnida"

MUNHWA BROADCASTING CORP. (MBC)
(Munhwa Bangsong) Nationwide comm. netw.
267, Seongam-ro, Mapo-gu, Seoul 03925 ☎ +82 2 789 0011 **W:**
imbc.com

	Call	kHz	kW	Station		Call	kHz	kW	Station
1)	CQ	765	10	Daejeon MBC	11)	AT	1080	10	Yeosu MBC
2)	AJ	774	10	Jeju MBC	12)	AV	1107	10	Pohang MBC
3)	AN	774	10	Chuncheon MBC	13)	KI	1161	20	Busan MBC
4)	CT	810	10	Daegu MBC	14)	AK	1215	10	Jinju MBC
5)	CN	819	20	Gwangju MBC	15)	SB	1242	10	Wonju MBC
6)	AU	846	10	Ulsan MBC	16)	AF	1287	10	Gangneung MBC
7)	CX	855	10	Jeonju MBC	17)	AX	1287	10	Cheongju MBC
8)	KV	900	50	Seoul MBC	18)	AO	1332	10	Chungju MBC
9)	AP	990	10	Changwon MBC	19)	AQ	1350	10	Samcheok MBC
10)	AW	1017	10	Andong MBC	20)	AM	1386	10	Mokpo MBC

D.Prgr: All 24h

FM	Location	Music FM MHz	kW	Standard FM MHz	kW
8)	Seoul	91.9	10	95.9	10
13)	Busan	88.9	5	95.9	3
4)	Daegu	95.3	5	96.5	5
5)	Gwangju	91.5	5	93.9	5
	Gwangju	95.1	3	-	
1)	Daejeon	97.5	5	92.5	3
7)	Jeonju	99.1	5	94.3	2
	Jeonju (Namwon)	-		101.7	3
9)	Changwon	100.5	1	98.9	3
3)	Chuncheon	94.5	3	92.3	3
17)	Cheongju	99.7	1	107.1	1
2)	Jeju	90.1	3	97.9	1
	Jeju(Seogwipo)	102.9	3	97.1	1
6)	Ulsan	98.7	3	97.5	1
16)	Gangneung	94.3	5	96.3	3
14)	Jinju	97.7	1	91.1	3
	Jinju	96.1	3	93.5	1
20)	Mokpo	102.3	1	89.1	2
11)	Yeosu	98.3	2	100.3	1
10)	Andong	91.3	3	100.1	3
15)	Wonju	98.9	3	92.7	1
	Wonju			102.5	1
18)	Chungju	88.7	3	96.1	1
19)	Samcheok	98.1	3	101.5	1
	Samcheok	99.9	1	93.1	3
12)	Pohang	97.9	3	100.7	3
	Pohang(Uljin)	94.9	1	102.7	1

+low power rel. stns
NB: Standard FM stns simulcast with the MW stn in the same city.
A separate sce. is provided to the Music FM stns. All regional stns
broadcast a combination of a feed from Seoul and their own local prgrs.
Standard FM stns follow the same schedule as their corresponding
MW outlet. Music FM of Seoul MBC sched: 24h
Ann: "(freq. and location) Munhwa Bangsong-imnida. (Call)" or "Munhwa
Bangsong-imnida" or "MBC". Seoul: "Jungpa Gubaek (900)kHz, Pyojun
FM Gushib-o-jeom-gu 95.9MHz Munhwa Bangsong-imnida"

Addresses and other information
NB: Add "(location) Munhwa Broadc. Corp." to addr.
1) 161, EXPO-ro, Yuseong-gu, Daejeon 34125 **W:** tjmbc.co.kr – **2)** 35,
Munyeon-ro, Jeju-si, Jeju Special Self-do 63120 **W:** jejumbc.co.kr – **3)**
54, Subyengongwon-gil, Chuncheon-si, Gangwon-do 24239 **W:** chmbc.

co.kr – **4)** 400, Dongdaegu-ro, Suseong-gu, Daegu 42020 **W:** tgmbc.
co.kr – **5)** 17, Wolsan-ro 116byeon-gil, Nam-gu, Gwangju 61629 **W:**
kjmbc.co.kr – **6)** 65, Seowon 3-gil, Jung-gu, Ulsan 44512 **W:** ulsanmbc.
co.kr – **7)** 50, Sanneomeo 1-gil, Wansan-gu, Jeonju-si, Jeollabuk-do
54986 **W:** jmbc.co.kr – **8)** National addr. – **9)** 11-11, Yangdeokseo 9-
gil, Masan Hoewon-gu, Changwon-si, Gyeongsangnam-do 51322 **W:**
changwonmbc.co.kr – **10)** 20, Dangwon-ro, Andong-si, Gyeongsangbuk-
do 36645 **W:** andongmbc.co.kr – **11)** 135, Munsu-ro, Yeosu-si,
Jeollanam-do 59700 **W:** ysmbc.co.kr – **12)** 421, Saecheingnyeng-
ro, Pohang-si, Gyeongsangbuk-do 37685 **W:** phmbc.co.kr – **13)** 69,
Gamporo 8beon-gil, Suyeong-gu. Busan 48276 **W:** busanmbc.co.kr
– **14)** 13, Gaho-ro, Jinju-si, Gyeongsangnam-do 52817 **W:** jinjumbc.
co.kr – **15)** 67, Hakseong-gil, Wonju-si, Gangwon-do 26412 **W:** wjmbc.
co.kr – **16)** 267, Gajak-ro, Gangneung-si, Gangwon-do 25477 **W:**
gnmbc.co.kr – **17)** 1322, 2 Sunhwan-ro, Heungdeok-gu, Cheongju-si,
Chungcheongbuk-do 28382 **W:** mbccj.co.kr – **18)** 3250, Jungwon-
daero, Chungju-si, Chungcheongbuk-do 27480 **W:** cjmbc.co.kr – **19)**
629-59, Saecheongnyeon-doro, Samcheok-si, Gangwon-do 25909 **W:**
scmbc.co.kr – **20)** 334, Yeongsan-ro, Mokpo-si, Jeollanam-do 58700
W: mokpombc.co.kr

CHRISTIAN BROADCASTING SYSTEM (CBS)
(Gidokkyo Bangsong)

	MW Call	kHz	kW	Station and h.of tr.
1)	KY	837	50	CBS Seoul: 24h
2)	CL	999	10	CBS Gwangju: 2000-1600
4)	KT	1251	10	CBS Daegu: 2000-1600
5)	CM	1314	10	CBS Jeonbuk: 2000-1600
6)	KP	1404	10	CBS Busan: 2000-1600

	CBS FM	Call	MHz	kW	h. of tr.
1)	CBS-FM Seoul FM)	HLKY-FM	93.9	7	24h (Music
1)	CBS Seoul	HLKY-SFM	98.1	10	24h
2)	CBS Gwangju	HLCL-SFM	103.1	5	2000-1600
3)	CBS Jeonnam	HLCL-FM	102.1	1	2000-1600
4)	CBS Daegu	HLKT-SFM	103.1	5	2000-1600
5)	CBS Jeonbuk	HLCM-SFM	103.7	5	2000-1600
6)	CBS Busan	HLKP-SFM	102.9	5	2000-1600
6)	CBS-FM Busan	HLKP-FM	102.1	1	24h
7)	CBS Cheongju	HLAC-FM	91.5	3	2000-1600
8)	CBS Gangwon	HLDC-FM	93.7	3	2000-1600
8)	CBS Gangwon	(W)	94.9	1	2000-1600
9)	CBS Daejeon	HLDX-FM	91.7	5	2000-1600
10)	CBS Pohang	HLCB-FM	91.5	3	2000-1600
11)	CBS Gyeongnam	HLCC-FM	106.9	5	2000-1600
12)	CBS Jeju	HLKO-FM	93.3	3	2000-1600
12)	CBS Jeju	(S)	90.9	1	2000-1600
13)	CBS Yeongdong	HLCO-FM	91.5	3	2000-1600
14)	CBS Ulsan	HLKP-FM	100.3	1	2000-1600

+low power relay stns. (W)=Wonju relay st. (S)= Seogwipo relay st

Addresses and other information:

1) 159-1, Mokdongseo-ro, Yangcheon-gu, Seoul 07997 ☎ +82 2 2650
7000 **W:** cbs.co.kr **Ann:** "Jeongjikhan Sesang-eul Gakkuneun AM
Palbaek-samsip-chil(837)kHz, Pyojun FM Gusip-pal-jeom-il(98.1)MHz,
CBS-mnida. HLKY." – **2)** 89, Uncheon-ro, Seo-gu, Gwangju 62002 ☎
+82 62 376 8500 – **3)** 166, Jungang-ro, Suncheon-si, Jeollanam-do
57939 ☎ +82 61 902 1000 – **4)** 612, Jungang-daero, Buk-ku, Daegu
41561 ☎ +82 53 426 8001 – **5)** 453, Beonyeong-ro, Deokjin-gu,
Jeonju-si, Jeollabuk-do 54806 ☎ +82 63 256 1000 – **6)** 141, Sinam-
ro, Busanjin-gu, Busan 47344 ☎ +82 51 636 0050 – **7)** 17, Sujuk-ro
5beon-gil, Seowon-gu, Cheongju-si, Chungcheongbuk-do 28697 ☎
+82 43 292 4100 – **8)** 120, Geumgang-ro, Chuncheon-si, Gangwon-
do 24335 ☎ +82 33 255 2001 – **9)** 1712, Gyebaek-ro, Jung-gu,
Daejeon 34956 ☎ +82 42 259 8888 – **10)** 10, Sanggong-ro, Nam-gu,
Pohang-si, Gyeongsangbuk-do 37831 ☎ +82 54 277 5500 – **11)** 84,
Heodang-ro, Masan Happo-gu, Changwon-si, Gyeongsangnam-do
51723 ☎ +82 55 224 5600 – **12)** 15, Singgwang-ro, Jeju-si, Jeju
Teukbyeol Jachido 63125 ☎ +82 64 744 0933 – **13)** 32, Won-daero
26-gil, Gangneung-si, Gangwon-do 25506 ☎ +82 33 642 9131 - **14)**
216, Jungang-ro, Nam-gu, Ulsan44690 ☎ +82 52 256 3333
Ann: stns 2)-8): "Jeongjikhan Sesang-eul Gakkuneun (freq.), CBS (loca-
tion) Bangsong-imnida (call)" or "Maeumgwa Maeumi Mannaneun
Bangsong (freq.), CBS (location) Bangsong-imnida (call)"
F.PI: Relay stns in Chungju, Wonju, Jinju, Gongju, Seosan. Music
FM in Daejeon, Gwangju, Jeju, Ulsan, Jeonbuk (Jeonju), Gyeongnam
(Changwon), Busan, Daegu

SEOUL BROADCASTING SYSTEM (SBS)

✉ 161, Mok-dong Seo-ro, Yangcheon-gu, Seoul 07996 ☎ +82 2 2061
0006 🖷 +82 2 2113 3169 **W:** sbs.co.kr
MW: HLSQ Goyang (near Seoul) 792kHz 50kW **D.Prgr:** 24h

Standard FM (Love FM): 103.5MHz HLSQ-SFM 10kW: 24h
Music FM (Power FM): 107.7MHz HLSQ-FM 10kW: 24h + low power
relay stn.
Ann: "AM Chilbaek-gusib-I 792kHz, FM Baek-sam-jeom-o 103.5MHz,
SBS Love FM-imnida. HLSQ", "FM Baek-chil-jeom-chil 107.7MHz,
Yeoreobune SBS Power FM-imnida. HLSQ"

FAR EAST BROADCASTING CO., KOREA (Rlg.)

	MW	kHz	kW	Station, location
1)		1188	100	HLKX, Seoul
2)		1566	250	HLAZ, Jeju
	FM	**MHz**	**kW**	**Station, location**
1)		106.9	5	HLKX-SFM, Seoul
2)		101.1	1	HLAZ-SFM, Jeju(Sammaebong)
3)		93.3	5	HLAD-FM, Daejeon
4)		98.1	5	HLDD-FM, Changwon
5)		90.1	3	HLDY-FM, Yeongdong
6)		100.5	1	HLKW-FM, Mokpo
7)		90.3	3	HLDZ-FM, Pohang
8)		107.3	3	HLQR-FM, Ulsan
9)		93.3	1	HLQQ-FM, Busan
10)		91.9	1	HLCU-FM, Daegu
11)		93.1	1	HLED-FM Gwangju

+ low power relay stns

Addresses and other information

1) Far East Broadc. Co.(Geukdong Bangsong), 56, Wausan-ro, Mapo-gu,
Seoul 04067 ☎ +82 2 320 0114 🖷 +82 2 320 0229 **W:** febc.net **D.Prgr:**
24h. Korean: 1900-1100, 1600-1700 (Stangdard FM: 1900-1700)
English: 1100-1200(1188kHz) **Chinese:** 1500-1600(1188kHz). **VOA
Relay in Korean:** 1200-1500(1188kHz). **RFA Relay in Korean:** 1500-
1900(1188kHz). **Ann:** Korean "Jungpa Cheonbaek-palsip-pal(1188)kHz,
Pyojun FM Paeng-nyuk-jeom-gu(106.9)MHz, Areumdaun Chanyanggwa
Gibbeoun Sosigeul Jeonhaneun Geukdong Bangsong-imnida.". English:
"This is HLKX Radio broadcasting with 100,000 watts of power on
1188kHz" **FI:** by contributions & free will offerings – **2)** Jeju Geukdong
Bangsong, 67, Gamundongsan 4-gil, Aewol-up, Jeju-si, Jeju Teukbyel
Jachido 63050 ☎ +82 64 799 8100 **D.Prgr:** 24h. **Korean:** 1900-1100.
Chinese: 1100-1230, 1345-1730, 1730-1830. **Japanese:** 1230-1345.
Russian: 1830-1900 – **3)** Daejeon Geukdong Bangsong, 38-8, Jijok-ro
364-gil, Yuseong-gu, Daejeon 34076 ☎ +82 42 828 9330. **D.Prgr:** 24h
– **4)** Changwon Geukdong Bangsong, 147, Du-daero, Seongsan-gu,
Changwon-si, Gyeongsang-nam-do 51519 ☎ +82 55 269 9810 **D.Prgr:**
24h – **5)** Yeongdong Geukdong Bangsong, 465 Jungang-ro, Sokcho-si,
Sokcho-si, Gangwon-do 24803 ☎ +82 33 638 9000 **D.Prgr:** 1900-1700
– **6)** Mokpo Geukdong Bangsong, 61, Bipa-ro, Mokpo-si, Jeollanam-do
58690 ☎ +82 61 284 9000 **D.Prgr:** 1900-1700 – **7)** Pohang Geukdong
Bangson, 164, Yongnam-ro, Buk-gu, Pohang-si, Gyeongsangnam-
do 58690 ☎ +82 54 256 3000 **D.Prgr:** 24h – **8)** Ulsan Geukdong
Bangsong, 145, Beonyeong-ro, Nam-gu, Ulsan-si 44695 ☎ +82 52
256 2000 **D.Prgr:** 24h – **9)** Busan Geukdong Bangsong, 105, Senteom
Jungang-ro, Haeundae-gu, Busan 48058 ☎ +82 51 759 6000 **D.Prgr:**
24h – **10)** Daegu Geukdong Bangsong, 90, Hwarang-ro, Suseong-
gu, Daegu 42037 ☎ +82 53 770 3000 **D.Prgr:** 24h – **11)** Gwangju
Geukdong Bangsong, 73, Sangmubeonyeong-ro, Seo-gu, Gwangju
61946 ☎ +82 62 373 1000 **D.Prgr:** 24h. **F.PI:** Regional stns in Yeosu.
Relay stn in Taebaek

PYEONGHWA BROADCASTING CORP. (PBC)
(Pyeonghwa Bangsong) Endowment by the Catholic Church.
Stations:
1) Seoul HLQP-FM 105.3MHz 5kW: 1957-1702 – **2)** Gwangju HLDL-FM
99.9MHz 5kW, 99.5MHz 1kW(rel. stn in Yeosu): 1957-1702 – **3)** Deagu
HLDK-FM 93.1MHz 3kW, 96.9MHz 0.5kW(rel. st. in Pohang), 100.7MHz
(rel. stn in Andong): 1957-1702 – **4)** Busan HLDW-FM 101.1MHz 3kW,
94.3MHz 0.5kW(rel. st in Ulsan), 105.5MHz(rel. stn in Changwon): 1957-
1702 – **5)** Daejeon HLQO-FM 106.3MHz 3kW: 1957-1702.
Addresses:
1) 330, Samil-daero, Jung-gu, Seoul 04552 ☎ +82 2 2270 2114
🖷 +82 2 2270 2210 **W:** pbc.co.kr **Ann:** "Saengmyeong Sarang, FM
Baeg-o-jeom-sam(105.3)MHz, Gibbeun Sosik, Balgeun Sesang, PBC
Pyeonghwa Bangsong-imnida. HLQP." – **2)** 75, Sangmusimin-ro, Seo-
gu, Gwangju 61951 – **3)** 20, Seoseong-ro, Jung-gu, Daegu 41933 – **4)**
71, Jungnyang-ro, Jung-gu, Busan 48968 – **5)** 471, Daejong-ro, Jung-gu,
Daejeon 34915 ☎ +82 42 250 3200

BUDDHIST BROADCASTING SYSTEM (BBS)
(Bulgyo Bangsong) Owned and operated by the Buddhistns.
Stations:
1) Seoul HLSG-FM 101.9MHz 5kW: 2000-1700 – **2)** Gwangju HLDB-FM
89.7MHz 3kW, 105.7MHz 0.5kW(rel. stn in Gwnagyang): 2000-1700 – **3)**

Busan HLDA-FM 89.9MHz 5kW, 89.5MHz 0.5kW (rel. stn in Changwon): 2000-1700 – **4)** Daegu HLDI-FM 94.5MHz 3kW, 105.5MHz 0.5kW (rel. stn in Pohang), 97.7MHz 0.5kW (rel. stn in Andong): 2000-1700 – **5)** Cheongju HLDJ-FM 96.7MHz 3kW: 2000-1700 – **6)** Chuncheon HLQM-FM 100.1MHz 3kW, 104.3MHz 0.1kW(rel. stn in Gangneung): 2000-1700 – **7)** Ulsan HLQU-FM 88.3MHz 1kW: 2000-1700 +low Power rel. stns

Addresses:
1) Dabo Building;20, Mapo-daero, Mapo-gu, Seoul 04175 ☎ +82 2 705 5114 📠 +82 2 705 5229 **W:** bbsfm.co.kr – **2)** Dongyang Bldg, 9, Sangmu Jungang-ro, Seo-gu, Gwangju 61962 ☎ +82 62 520 1114 – **3)** Boseong Bldg, 201, Beomil-ro, Dong-gu, Busan 48738 ☎ +82 51 520 5114 – **4)** Jingak Bldg, 261, Myeongdeok-ro, Jung-gu, Daegu 41956 ☎ +82 53 427 5114 – **5)** 1239, 1sunhwan-ro, Sangdang-gu, Cheongju-si, Chungcheongbuk-do 28776 ☎ +82 43 294 5114 – **6)** 10, Jungang-ro, Chuncheon-si, Gangwon-do 24270 ☎ +82 33 250 2114 – **7)** 201, Samsan-ro, Nam-gu, Ulsan 44703 ☎ +82 52 279 8114
Ann: 1) "FM Baeg-il-jeom-gu (101.9)MHz, BBS Bulgyo Bangsong-imnida. HLSG."

SEOUL TRAFFIC BROADCASTING SYSTEM (TBS)
(Gyotong Bangsong)
Municipal Station. This stn is operated by the Seoul Municipal Traffic Broadcast Headquarters to provide traffic information and education to the citizens of Seoul and surroundings.
✉ 36, Toegye-ro 26-gil, Jung-gu, Seoul 100-250 ☎ +82 2 311 5114 📠 +82 2 311 5219 **W:** tbs.seoul.kr
Station: HLST-FM(Live FM) 95.1MHz 5kW: 24h in Korean. HLSW-FM(Soul FM) 101.3MHz 1kW: 2000-1700 in English.
Ann: "FM Gusib-o-jeom-il(95.1)MHz, TBS Gyotong Bangsong-imnida","You're listening to 101.3 tbs-eFM"

TRAFFIC BROADCASTING NETWORK (TBN)
(Hanguk Gyotong Bangsong)
✉ 407, Wangsimni-ro, Jung-gu, Seoul 04580 ☎ +82 2 2230 6114 📠 +82 2 2230 6269 **W:** tbn.or.kr
Stations:
1) Busan 94.9MHz HLDN-FM 3kW: 24h – **2)** Gwangju 97.3MHz HLDM-FM 3kW, 103.5MHz 1kW (rel. st. in Gwangyang): 24h – **3)** Daejeon 102.9MHz HLDT-FM 3kW: 24h – **4)** Daegu 103.9MHz HLDU-FM 3kW: 24h – **5)** Incheon 100.5MHz HLSU-FM 1kW: 24h – **6)** Gangwon(Wonju) 105.9MHz HLSV-FM 3kW: 24h, Gangwon(Chuncheon) 103.7MHz 3kW: 24h , Gangwon(Gangneung) 105.5MHz 1kW: 24h – **7)** Jeonju 102.5MHz HLCM-FM 3kW: 24h – **8)** Ulsan 104.1MHz HLCV-FM 1kW: 24h+ low power relay stns– **9)** Changwon 95.5MHz HLEE-FM 1kW: 24h, Changwon(Jinju) 100.1MHz 1kW: 24h – **10)** Gyeobuk(Gyeongju) 103.5MHz HLEF-FM 1kW: 24h, Gyeongbuk(Uljin) 103.7MHz 1kW: 24h
Addresses and other information
1) 68, Yongso-ro, Nam-gu, Busan 48501 ☎ +82 51 6105 114 **Ann:** "FM Gusib-sa-jeom-gu(94.9)MHz, Busan Gyotong Bangsong-imnida. HLDN-FM" – **2)** 40, Cheomdanjungang-ro 182-gil, Gwangsan-gu, Gwangju 62274 ☎ +82 62 9701 114 **Ann:** "FM Gusib-chil-jeom-sam(97.3)MHz, Gwangju Gyotong Bangsong-imnida. HLDM" – **3)** 17, Singalma-ro, Seo-gu, Daejeon 35280 ☎ +82 42 6001 114 **Ann:** "FM Baeg-i-jeom-gu(102.9)MHz, Dallineun Radio Daejeon Gyotong Bangsong-imnida." – **4)** 120, Hyeonchug-ro, Nam-gu, Daegu 42420 ☎ +82 53 6060 114 **Ann:** "FM Baek-sam-jeom-gu(103.9)MHz, Daegu Gyotong Bangsong-imnida. HLDU-FM" – **5)** 251, Maesohol-ro, Nam-gu, Incheon 22201 ☎ +82 32 4531 114 **Ann:** "FM Baek-jeom-o(100.5)MHz, TBN Incheon Gyotong Bangsong-imnida. HLSU" – **6)** 183, Dongbusunhwan-ro, Wonju-si, Gangwon-do 26457 ☎ +82 33 7490 114 **Ann:** "Haengbogui Giljabi, Ggumi Inneun Bangsong, FM Baeg-o-jeom-gu(105.9)MHz, Gangwon Gyotong Bangsong-imnida." – **7)** 1097-10, Jeogyeorip-ro, Deokjin-gu, Jeonju54859. ☎ +82 63 2593 114 **Ann:** "FM Baeg-i-jeom-chil(102.7)MHz, TBN Jeonju Gyotong Bangsong-imnida. HLCM" – **8)** 11, Hamwol 7-gil, Jung-gu, Ulsan 44426. ☎ +82 52 290 8514 – **9)** 82-4, Changwoncheon-ro 94-gil, Uichang-gu, Changwon-si 51409. ☎ +82 55 272 6114 – **10)** 95, Samheung-ro, Buk-gu, Pohang-si 37613. ☎ +82 54 240 6214
F.PI: Regional stns in Jeju, Chungbuk

KOREA NEW NETWORK CORP. (KNN)
✉ 30, Senteomseo-ro, Haeundae-gu, Busan 48058 ☎ +82 51 850 9000 **W:** knn.co.kr **Station:** HLDG-FM 99.9MHz 3kW, 102.5MHz 1kw(rel. stn in Changwon), 105.5MHz 1kW(rel. stn in Jinju): 24h **Ann:** "Guship-gu-jeom-gu (99.9), KNN Radiomnida.HLDG"

TAEGU BROADCASTING CORPORATION (TBC)
(Daegu Bangsong)
✉ 23, Dongdaegu-ro, Susong-gu, Daegu 42175 ☎ +82 53 760 1900 **W:** tbc.co.kr
Station: HLDE-FM(Dream FM) 99.3MHz 5kW: 24h. Relay stn: Pohang

99.7MHz 1kW, Andong 106.5MHz 0.5kW. **Ann:** "HLDE-FM TBC Dream FM-imnida"

KWANGJU BROADCASTING CO., LTD. (KBC) (Gwangju Bangsong)
✉ 87, Jungang-ro, Nam-gu, Gwangju 61637 ☎ +82 62 650 3114 **W:** ikbc.co.kr **Station:** HLDH-FM(MY FM) 101.1MHz 5kW: 24h. Relay stn: Yeosu 96.7MHz 1kW. **Ann:** "HLDH, FM 101.1MHz, 96.7MHz, Yeollin Sesang, Joheun Chingu, KBC MY FM"

TAEJON BROADCASTING CO., LTD. (TJB)
(Daejeon Bangsong)
✉ 131, EXPO-ro, Yuseong-gu, Daejeon 34125 ☎ +82 42 281 1101 **W:** tjb.co.kr
Station: HLDF-FM(Power FM) 95.7MHz 5kW: 24h Relay stn: Seosan 96.5MHz 0.5kW. **Ann:** "Gusib-o-jeom-chil(95.7), Gusim-nyuk-jeom-o(96.5)MHz, TJB Power FM-imnida. HLDF"

JEONJU TELEVISION CORPORATION (JTV)
(Jeonju Bangsong)
✉ 1083, Jeongyeorip-ro, Deokjin-gu, Jeonju-si, Jeollabuk-do 54859 ☎ +82 63 250 5200 **W:** jtv.co.kr
Station: HLDQ-FM(Magic FM) 90.1MHz 5kW: 24h
Ann: "FM Gusib-jeom-il(90.1)MHz, JTV Magic FM-imnida. HLDQ"

CHEONGJU BROADCASTING CORPORATION (CJB)
(Cheongju Bangsong)
✉ 59-1, Saun-ro, Seowon-gu, Cheongju-si, Chungcheongbuk-do 28654 ☎ +82 43 265 7000 **W:** cjb.co.kr
Station: HLDI-FM(Joy FM) 101.5MHz 5kW, 97.9MHz 2kW(rel. stn in Eumseong): 24h
Ann: "FM Baeg-il-jeom-o(101.5)MHz, CJB Joy FM-imnida. HLDI"

ULSAN BROADCASTING CORPORATION (UBC)
(Jeonju Bangsong)
✉ 41, Gugyo-ro, Jung-gu, Ulsan 44520 ☎ +82 52 228 6000 **W:** ubc.co.kr **Station:** HLDP-FM(Green FM) 92.3MHz 3kW: 24h
Ann: "Gusib-i-jeom-sam(92.3)MHz, UBC Green FM Bangsong-imnida. HLDP"

JEJU FREE INTERNATIONAL CITY BROADCASTING SYSTEM (JIBS) (Jeju Gukje Jayu Dosi Bangsong)
✉ 95, Yeonsam-ro, Jeju-si, Jeju Teukbyeol Jachido 63148 ☎ +82 64 740 7800 **W:** jibstv.com
Station: HLQC-FM(Power FM) 101.5MHz 3kW: 24h. Relay stn: Seogwipo 98.5MHz 1kW
Ann: "JIBS New Power FM Bangsong-imnida"

GANGWON TELEVISION BROADCASTING CO., LTD (GTB)
(Gangwon Minbang)
✉ G1, 274, Soyanggang-ro, Dong-myeon, Chuncheon-si, Gangwon-do 24210 ☎ +82 33 248 5000 **W:** igtb.co.kr
Station: HLCG-FM(Fresh FM) 105.1MHz 3kW: 24h. Relay stn: Gangneung 106.1MHz 1kW, Wongju 103.1MHz 0.5kW
Ann: "Chuncheon Baeg-o-jeom-il(105.1)MHz, Gangneung Baeng-ryuk-jeom-il(106.1)MHz, GTB Fresh FM, HLCG"

KYONGGI BROADCASTING CO. (KFM) (Gyeonggi Bangsong)
✉ 111, Maeyeong-ro 345-gil, Yeongtong-gu, Suwon-si, Gyeonggi-do 16703 ☎ +82 31 210 0999 **W:** kfm.co.kr
Station: HLDS-FM 99.9MHz 5kW: 24h
Ann: "FM Gusib-gu-jeom-gu(99.9)MHz, Gyeonggi Bangsong-imnida. HLDS"

Kyung-In Broadcasting SUNNY FM
✉ 7, Aam-daero 287beon-gil, Nam-gu, Incheon 22196 ☎ +82 32 830 1000 **W:** sunnyfm.co.kr
Station: HLDO-FM 90.7MHz 5kW: 24h **Ann:** "Gusib-jeom-chil(90.7)MHz, Gyeong-In Bangsong, Sunny FM-imnida"

YTN RADIO(YTN FM)
✉ 76, Sangamsan-ro, Mapo-gu, Seoul 03926 ☎ +82 2 398 8000 **W:** ytnfm.co.kr
Station: HLQV-FM 94.5MHz 3kW: 24h **Ann:** "FM Gusib-sa-jeom-o(94.5)MHz, YTN FM-imnida. HLQV"

WON-BUDDHISM BROADCASTING SYSTEM (WBS) (Woneum Bangsong)
✉ **1)** 75, Hyeonchung-ro, Dongjak-gu, Seoul 06904 ☎ +82 2 2102 7700 **W:** wbsfm.com – **2)** 10, Gwangbokjungang-ro 33beon-gil, Jung-gu, Busan 48947 ☎ +82 51 247 3844 – **3)** 501, Iksan-daero, Iksan-si, Jeollabuk-do 54536 ☎ +82 63 837 0979 – **4)** 31, Sangmuowol-ro Seo-gu, Gwanju 61966 – **5)** 42, Jungang-daero 66-gil, Jung-gu, Daegu 41961 ☎ +82 53 425 0983.
Stations: 1) Seoul HLQK-FM 89.7MHz 1kW: 24h – **2)** Busan HLQJ-FM

104.9MHz 3kW: 24h – **3)** Jeonbuk(Iksan) HLDV-FM 97.9MHz 3kW: 24h – **4)** Gwangju HLQN-FM 107.9MHz 1kW: 24h – **5)** Daegu HLCS-FM 98.3MHz 1kW: 24h.
Ann: 1) FM Palsip-gu-jeom-chil(89.7)MHz, WBS Woneum Bangsong-imnida. HLQK" – **2)** "FM Baek-sa-jeom-gu(104.9)MHz, WBS Busan Woneum Bangsong-imnida. HLQJ" – **3)** "FM Gusip-chil-jeom-gu(97.9)MHz, WBS Jeonbuk Woneum Bangsong-imnida. HLDV" – **4)** "FM Baek-chil-jeom-gu(107.9)MHz, WBS Gwangju Woneum Bangsong-imnida. HLQN" – **5)** "FM Gusip-pal-jeom-sam(98.3)MHz, WBS Daegu Woneum Bangsong-imnida. HLCS"

KOREA INTERNATIONAL BROADCASTING FOUNDATION (Arirang Radio)
⌨ Arirang Tower, 2351, Nambusunhwan-ro, Seocho-gu, Seoul 06713 ☎ +82 2 3475 5000 **W:** arirang.co.kr
Station: Jeju HLSE-FM 88.7MHz 3kW: 24h in English. Relay stn: Seogwipo 88.1MHz 1kW. **Ann:** "You're listening to Arirang Radio"

GFN FOUNDATION
⌨ 17, Sajik-ro, Nam-gu, Gwangju 61640 ☎ +82 62 460 0987 **W:** gfn.or.kr
Station: HLSY-FM 98.7MHz 1kW, 93.7MHz 1kW(rel. stn in Yeosu): 2000-1700 in English. **Ann:** "Listen more Feel more! GFN 98.7 FM"

BUSAN e-FM
⌨ Centum venture town 4F, 41, Centum dong-ro, Haeundae-gu, Busan 48059 ☎ +82 51 861 8601 **W:** befm.or.kr
Station: HLSX-FM 90.5MHz 1kW: 2000-1700 in English. **Ann:** "Now you're listening to Busan e-FM 90.5"

KOREAN FORCES NETWORK (Friends FM) (Gukkun Bangsong)
⌨ 54-99, Duteopbawi-ro, Yongsan-gu, Seoul 04353 **W:** dema.mil.kr/web/fm.do
Stations: FM (operated by KBS): Namsan HLSF-FM 96.7MHz 2kW, Hwaaksan 96.7MHz 5kW, Yongmunsan 101.1MHz 3kW, Gwaebangsan 92.5MHz 3kW , Jeju 94.1MHz 3kW + 7 lp stns
D.Prgr: 24h. Own prgrs 2100-1500, other times relay KBS R. One (HLKA). prgrs for soldiers located near the demilitarized zone. Also 0805-0900(Sun) via KBS R. One network.
Ann: "Hamggehaeyo Seonjin Ganggun, Silcheonhaeyo Noksaek Seongjang, Friends FM Gukkun Bangsong Radio"

AMERICAN FORCES NETWORK KOREA (AFN)
⌨ As below ☎ +82 2 7914 6495/6 **W:** afnkorea.com

MW & FM Stations	kHz	kW	MHz	kW
1) Seoul/Yongsan	1530	5	102.7	5
2) Munsan/Western Corridor	576	5		
3) Daegu/Camp Walker			88.5	1
4) Busan/Camp Hialeah	+1260	5		
Chuncheon/Camp Page	1044	1	88.5	0.1
Uijeongbu/Camp Red Cloud	1161	0.25	88.5	0.3
5) Dongducheon/Camp Casey	+1197	1	88.3	0.3
Chuncheon/Camp Page (F.PI)	1260	1		
6) Songtan/Osan Air Base	-		88.5	0.05
7) Pyeongtaek/Camp Humphroys	+1440	1	88.3	0.05
8) Gunsan/Gunsan Air Base	1440	1	88.5	0.25
Wonju/Camp Long	1440	0.25		
Waegwan/Camp Carrol	1440	5		
2) Munsan/Western Corridor (F.PI)	1440	5	88.5	0.05
Pohang/Camp Libby	1512	0.25		
Jinhae/Naval St.	1512	1	88.5	0.1
Yongsan	1530	5		

Lp: 1512kHz (Sangdong, Jeju Teukbyel Jachido); 88.5MHz Gwangju Air Base. += local prgrs 2005-0000 Mon-Fri; otherwise rel.1)
D.Prgr: 24h (MW/FM sep. prgrs). N. on the h Formal sign on at 1505
Ann: AM: "American Forces Network Korea", FM (Seoul): "This is Eagle FM"
Addresses
1) Headquarters, American Forces Network Korea, Unit #15324, APO AP 96205-0097, USA (+82(2) 7914 6495. Commanding Officer: LTC Chad C. Starr – **2)** Unit #15325, APO AP 96250-0098, USA – **3)** Unit #15029, APO AP 96218-0186, USA – **4)** Unit #15184. APO AP 96259-0274, USA – **5)** Unit #15116, APO AP 96224-0380, USA – **6)** Unit #2034. APO AP 96278-5000, USA – **7)** Unit #15473. APO AP 96271-0543, USA – **8)** Unit #2011, APO AP 96264-5000, USA

KOSOVO

LT: UTC +1h (27 Mar-30 Oct: +2h) — **Pop:** 1.7 million — **Pr.L:** Albanian, Serbian — **E.C:** 50Hz, 220V — **ITU:** pending (**WRTH:** RKS)

KOMISIONI I PAVARUR PËR MEDIA (KPM) (Independent Media Commission)
⌨ Rr. "Perandori Justinian" nr. 14, Qyteza Pejton, 10000 Prishtinë ☎ +381 38 245031 🖷 +381 38 245034 **E:** info@kpm-ks.org **W:** kpm-ks.org
L.P: Chmn: Adnan Merovci
NB. KPM is the licensing body for broadcasting.

RADIOTELEVIZIONI I KOSOVËS (RTK) (Pub)
⌨ Rr. "Xhemail Prishtina" nr. 12, 10000 Prishtinë ☎+381 38 230102 🖷 +381 38 235336 **E:** post@rtklive.com **W:** rtklive.com
L.P: Chmn: Ismet Bexheti

FM (MHz)	1	2	kW	FM	1	2	kW
Cërnusha	87.6	91.5	0.4	Prishtinë	91.9	93.3	0.5
Maja e Gjelbërt	88.5	90.5	1	Prishtinë	-	99.2	0.5
Golesh	95.7	97.7	30	Zatriq	88.9	92.4	2.5
Leposaviq*	-	97.3	0.3	*) KFOR Camp Nothing Hill			

D.Prgr: Prgr 1 (R. Kosova 1): 24h in Albanian. N. English: MF 1400-1403. – **Prgr 2 (R. Kosova 2):** 0600-2400 in Albanian; exc. 1300-1500 Serbian, 1500-1600 Turkish, 1700-1900 Bosnian, 1900-2000 Romany.

OTHER STATIONS

FM	MHz	kW	Location	Station
23)	88.1	1	Podujevë	R. Vizioni
12)	89.1	1	Zubin Potok	R. Kolasin
4)	89.4	1	Ljubinjë e Epërme	R. Astra
25)	90.2	2	Golesh	R. K4 (Albanian)
11)	92.2	1	Mitrovicë	R. Kiss
6)	92.6	1	Ferizaj	R. Ferizaj
2)	92.7	1	Maja e Gjelbërt	R. Djukagjini
15)	92.9	1	Leposaviq	R. Mir
3)	94.0	1	Kamenicë	R. 24
2)	94.5	2.5	Zariq	R. Djukagjini
1)	94.8	1	Maja e Gjelbërt	R. 21
24)	94.9	1	Mitrovicë	R. Ylberi
9)	95.4	1	Kaçanik	R. Kaçaniku
4)	96.2	1	Prishtinë	RFE-RL/VOA Relay
18)	96.4	1	Dragash	R. Sharri
20)	96.4	1	Gjilan	R. Star
25)	96.6	2	Golesh	R. K4 (Serbian)
22)	97.9	1	Gjilan	R. Victoria
17)	98.4	1	Gjilan	R. Rinia
B)	98.6	1	Golesh	BBCWS relay
10)	98.8	1	Kamenicë	R. Kamenica
16)	99.0	1	Mitrovicë	R. Mitrovica
2)	99.7	30	Golesh	R. Djukagjini
8)	100.3	1	Leposaviq	R. Impuls
19)	100.9	1	Gjilan	R. Mega Vox
C)	101.2	1	Prishtinë	RFI Relay
13)	101.9	1	Mitrovicë	R. Kontakt Plus
14)	102.4	1	Shillovë	R. Max
1)	102.8	30	Golesh	R. 21
5)	103.3	1	Gjilan	R. Energji
1)	103.9	2.5	Zatriq	R. 21
7)	104.1	1	Viti	R. Iliria
21)	105.7	1	Vushtrri	R. Vicianum

NB: Txs below 1kW not listed.
Addresses & other information:
1) Pallati i mediave, aneks II, 10000 Prishtinë. **E:** radio21@rtv21.tv – **2)** Rr. "Ismail Qemajli" nr. 7, 30000 Pejë. **E:** info@dukagjini.com – **3)** 70000 Lagjja Liria **E:** radio_24@hotmail.com – **4)** 20000 Ljubinjë e Epërme **E:** radioastra@gmail.com. In Bosnian. – **5)** Rr. "Abdullah Presheva" nr. 63, 60000 Gjilan **E:** energji102@yahoo.com – **6)** Rr. "Dëshmoret e Kombit", 70000 Ferizaj **E:** radioferizaj@hotmail.com – **7)** Rr. "Hoxhë Jonuzi" p.n., 61000 Viti **E:** rtv_iliriaviti@gmail.com – **8)** Rr. "24 November" p.n., 40000 Leposaviq **E:** radioimpuls@gmail.com. In Serbian. – **9)** Rr. "Vellezerit Çaka" p.n., 71000 Kaçanik **E:** radiokacanik@yahoo.com – **10)** Shtëpia e Kultures, 62000 Kamenicë. **E:** radiokamenica@hotmail.com – **11)** Rr. "Kralj Petar I" p.n., 40000 Mitrovicë **E:** rtvkisskm@gmail.com – **12)** Rr. "Arsenija Carnojevca" nr. 48, 40650 Zubin Potok **E:** radio_kolasin@yahoo.com – **13)** Rr. "Lole Ribara" nr. 58, 40000 Mitrovicë **E:** radiokontaktplus@yahoo.com – **14)** 60000 Shillovë **E:** maxradio102_4@yahoo.com. In Serbian. – **15)** Rr. "Viskse Jugoslavije" nr. 26, 40000 Leposaviq **E:** rtvmir@gmail.com. In Serbian. – **16)** Sheshi "Jasharaj", 40000 Mitrovicë **E:** r_mitrovica@yahoo.com – **17)** Rr. "Skenderbeu"13, 60000 Gjilan **E:** radiorinia@hotmail.com – **18)** Rr. "Rruga e Dëshmorve", 22000 Dragash **E:** beqir.beqaj@radio-sharri.info – **19)** Rr. "Abdullah Presheva" nr. 63, 60000 Gjilan **E:** radiomegavox@hotmail.com – **20)** Rr. "Lagja Dardania" 1, 60000 Gjilan **E:** radiostargjilan@yahoo.com – **21)** Rr. "Faruk Beqiri" p.n., 40000 Vushtrri **E:** radiostar_gjilan@gmail.com – **22)** Rr. "Dardania I" nr. 12/9, 60000 Gjilan **E:** radiovictoria_2001@yahoo.com – **23)** Rr. "Zahir Pajaziti" p.n., 11000 Podujevë **E:** vizioni@hotmail.com – **24)** Sheshi "Agim Hajrizi" p.n., 40000 Mitrovicë **E:** radioylberi@hotmail.com – **25)** HQ KFOR, Film City, 10000

Prishtinë **E:** info@radiokfor.com — **A)** Rel. RFE-RL & VOA (USA) — **B)** Rel. BBCWS (UK) – **C)** Rel. RFI (France)

KUWAIT

L.T: UTC +3h — **Pop:** 2.7 million — **Pr.L:** Arabic — **E.C:** 50Hz, 240V — **ITU:** KWT

MINISTRY OF INFORMATION
⌨ P.O. Box 193, 13002 Safat ☎+965 22415301 🖷 +965 22434511

RADIO OF THE STATE OF KUWAIT
⌨ P.O. Box 967, 13010 Safat ☎+965 22436193 🖷 +965 22417830 **W:** media.gov.kw **E:** kwtfreq@media.gov.kw
L.P: Mr. Hani Al-Naqi, Dir. Freq. Mgmt.

MW(kHz)	kW	Prgr.	Times
540	600	Main Arabic	24h
630	10	Quran prgr.	24h
963	20	Main Arabic	1200-1600, 2100-0500
		Multilingual	0500-1200, 1600-2100
1134	100	Main Arabic &Sports	24h
1269	100	Classical Arab Music	24h
1341	100	Quran prgr.	2100-0700
		2nd Arabic	0700-2100

FM(MHz)	kW	Prgr.	Times
87.9	20	Classical Arab Music	24h
89.5	20	Main Arabic	24h
90.4		"Huna al-Kuwait"	24
92.5	5	Easy FM	24h
93.3	20	Multilingual	0600-2100
94.9	20	Folklore prgr.	24h
96.3	20	Main & Easy FM	24h (Main 21-05, 12-16)
97.5	20	Quran & 2nd Arabic	24h (2nd Ar. 0700-1900)
98.9	20	Quran prgr.	24h
99.7	20	Super Station	24h
100.5	3	TV sound (Prgr. 1)	24h
103.7	20	Modern Arab Music	24h

Main Arabic prgr: 24h. **N:** 0300, 0500, 1000, 1700, 2100 – **2nd Arabic prgr:** 0700-1700 – **Classical Arab Music prgr:** 24h – **Modern Arab Music prgr:** 24h – **Multilingual prgr:** English 0500-0800, 1800-2100, Persian 0800-1000, Filipino 1000-1200, Urdu 1600-1800 – **Quran prgr:** 24h – **"Easy FM" in English:** 24h – **"FM Super Station"** in English: 24h. **N:** on the hour.
Ann: "Idha'at al-Dawlat Al Kuwait".
External service on shortwave: see International Radio section.

Other Stations:
Marina FM, 88.8MHz. **W:** marinafm.com
U FM, 98.4MHz. **W:** ufm4u.com
AFN: Al-Jabber/Camp Doha 101.5/107.9MHz 50W/5kW.
BBC World Sce in Kuwait City: Arabic 90.1MHz, English 100.1MHz.
Panorama FM: 91.4MHz. See main entry under UAE.
Monte Carlo Doualiya: 107.3MHz 1kW. **RfI:** 106.3MHz.
R. Sawa: 1548kHz 600kW, 1593kHz 150kW, 95.7MHz 5kW, all 24h.
VOA: 96.9MHz 1kW

KYRGYZSTAN

L.T: UTC +6h — **Pop:** 5.7 million — **Pr.L:** Kyrgyz, Russian, Uzbek — **E.C:** 50Hz, 220V — **ITU:** KGZ

MADANIYAT, MAALYMAT JANA TURIZM MINISTRILIGI (Ministry of Culture, Information and Tourism)
⌨ Pushkin St. 78, 720040 Bishkek ☎ +996 312 620482 🖷 +996 312 623589 **E:** minculture.kg@gmail.com **W:** minculture.gov.kg
L.P: Minister: Altynbek Maksutov
NB. The Ministry is responsible for issuing broadcasting licenses.

KOOMDUK TELERADIOBERÜÜ KORPORATSIYASY (KTRK) (Public Radio Corp.)
⌨ Jash Gvardiya blvd. 59, 720010 Bishkek ☎ +996 312 392059
E: public@ktrk.kg **W:** ktrk.kg **L.P:** DG: Ilim Karypbekov

MW	kHz	kW	Net	MW	kHz	kW	Net
Bishkek (a)	612	150	1	Dödömöl	1404	20	1
Naryn	1404	7	1	Orgochor	1404	-	1
Cholponata	1404	1	1	Jalalabat	1431	40	1
Aydarken	1404	7	1				

SW	kHz	kW	Net	SW	kHz	kW	Net
Bishkek (a)	4010	100	1	Bishkek (a)	4820	15	1

FM (MHz)	1	2	3	FM	1	2	3
Batken	104.2	-	102.2	Bishkek	104.1	106.9	103.7
Jalalabat	104.7	105.9	106.3	Osh	100.7	-	-
Karakol	102.4	106.0		Talas	102.0	107.6	-
Naryn	100.5	103.2	107.7				

+ translators (a) Krasnaya Rechka

D.Prgr: Net 1 (Birinchi radio/Baldar FM): Birinchi radio: 0000-0500, 0900-1800 in Kyrgyz, Russian; **Baldar FM:** 0500-0900 – **Net 2 (Kyrgyz radiosu/Dostuk radiosu): Kyrgyz radiosu:** 0000-1800; **Dostuk radiosu:** 1800-2300. – **Net 3 (Ming kyyal FM)** 24h in Kyrgyz.

OTHER STATIONS

MW	kHz	kW	Location	Station
C)	1287	150	Bishkek (a)	TWR relay

FM	MHz	kW	Location	Station
A)	66.26	4	Karakol	R. Rossii relay
A)	67.94	4	Bishkek	R. Rossii relay
A)	68.66	4	Karaköl	R. Rossii relay
A)	69.92	4	Osh	R. Rossii relay
A)	69.95	4	Kazarman	R. Rossii relay
A)	70.07	4	Arstanbap	R. Rossii relay
A)	70.40	4	Sülüktü	R. Rossii relay
A)	70.82	4	Naryn	R. Rossii relay
A)	72.20	4	Jalalabat	R. Rossii relay
A)	72.44	4	Sülüktü	R. Rossii relay
6)	87.5	1	Bishkek	R. Mir
B)	88.0	1	Bishkek	R. Mayak relay
4)	89.0	1	Bishkek	R. Rekord
10)	90.2	1	Bishkek	R. Parlament
9)	101.4	1	Cholponata	Hit FM
7A)	101.7	1	Bishkek	Evropa Plus
5)	102.9	1	Bishkek	R. Manas FM
1)	103.2	1	Cholponata	Russkoye R.
7B)	104.5	1	Bishkek	Russkaya volna
3)	105.0	1	Bishkek	Russkoye R.
8)	106.3	1	Karabalta	R. Tatina
11)	107.4	2	Bishkek	Sanjyra R.

NB: Txs below 1kW not listed. (a) Krasnaya Rechka
Addresses & other information:
1) Almaty St. 4b, 720082 Bishkek **E:** rusradio@europa.kg – **2)** Bishkek **3)** Jantoshev St. 70, 720005 Bishkek **E:** pyramid@mail.elcat.kg – **4)** Ibraimov St. 24, 720031 Bishkek **E:** office@loveradio.kg – **5)** Mir pr. 56, 720044 Bishkek **E:** manasfm@manas.kg – **6)** Bishkek – **7A,B)** Bishkek – **8)** Gvardeyskaya St. 18, 722030 Karabalta **E:** tatina@infotel.kg – **9)** Bishkek – **10)** Bishkek – **11)** Tokombaev St. 46a, 720000 Bishkek– **A)** Rel. R. Rossii (Russia) –**B)** Rel. Mayak (Russia) – **C)** Rel. TWR (USA).

Radio via DTT: see National TV section.

Int. relays on MW: (txs operated by Kyrgyztelecom) Bishkek (Krasnaya Rechka) 1287kHz 150kW; operated on behalf of TWR: 1467kHz 500kW. See International Radio section

LAOS

L.T: UTC +7h — **Pop:** 7.2 million — **Pr.L:** Lao (Lao Soung, Lao Theung dialects), Hmong, Khmu — **E.C:** 50Hz, 230V — **ITU:** LAO

LAO NATIONAL RADIO – LNR (Gov.)
⌨ PO Box 310, Vientiane; Phaynam Rd, Ban Sisakhet, Chantabouly District, Vientiane ☎ +856 21 243250 🖷 +856 21 212430 **W:** laonationalradio.com **L.P:** DG: Mr Sipha Nonglath
City and Provincial sces: These are operated by the local governments + Sisavangvong Rd, Ban Pakhame, Luang Prabang – Km 2 Route 13 South, Oudomsavane Village, Pakse, Champassak Province - Manthatulat Road, Vientiane – Houamouangtai Village, Savannakhet, Khantabouly – Nongbouakham Village, Tha Khek, Khammouane

MW	kHz	kW	S	H of tr
Vientiane*	567	200	N	2200-0230, 0430-0800, 0900-1600
Khantabouly, Sa	585	20	P	2230-1300
Luang Prabang	705	10	P	2200-0800, 1025-1500

SW	kHz	kW	S	H of tr
Vientiane	6130	50	N	2200-0230, 0430-0800, 0900-1600

S=Sce., **N**=National, **P**=Provincial, **Sa**=Savannakhet prov.
*) Tx loc.: Kilometre 49 (GC: 18N20 102E27)
Reg. stns generally rel. national news at 0000, 0500, 1200
National Sce in Lao: 2300-0230, 0430-0600, 0900-1330; **Hmong:** 2200-2300, 0600-0700; **Khmu:** 2230-2300, 0700-0800; **Thai:** 1330-1400; **English:** 1400-1430; **French:** 1430-1500; **Vietnamese:** 1500-1530; **Khmer:** 1530-1600. **N:** 2300, 0000, 0500, 0800, 1200

Ann: LNR: "Thini Sathani Vitthayou Krachaisiang Hengsat"
IS: Music on Khéne (mouth organ) & Solo (bamboo instrument)

LNR FM (MHz): Vientiane FM 103.7 20kW: 2300-1600 – VIP Radio 97.3 20kW: 2200-1700 – Phoenix Radio 95.0: 2230-1700
Vientiane City FM (MHz): Vientiane 105.5 1kW: 2330-1700 – Vientiane 98.8 10kW: operated by Butterfly Media Co. Ltd
Provincial FM (MHz): Attapeu: 95.0 10kW – Paksan, Bolikhamsay Prov: 101.5 5kW – Houai Xay, Bokeo Prov: 102.75 1kW – Khantabouly, S: 100.75 1kW Luang – Namtha Prov: 98.0 1kW Luang Prabang: 103.5MHz 0.3kW. Muang Hay, Oudomxay Prov: 100MHz 0.1kW – Pakse, Champassak Prov: 103.7 1kW – Phonsavan, Xieng Khuang Prov: 97.5 5kW – Phongsali Prov: 102 100W – Sam Neua, Houa Phan Prov: 102.0 10kW – Saravane: 101.2 0.3kW – Saiyabouly: 96.5 5kW – Saysomboun Special Reg.: 100 5kW – Sekong: 102.7 1kW – Siphandon, Champassak Prov: 97.3 0.33kW – Tha Khek, Khammouane Prov: 95.5 0.1kW

LAO PEOPLE'S ARMY BROADCASTING (Mil.)
✉ Phonkheng Village, Vientiane
FM: Vientiane 99.7MHz 10kW. Rel. on 99.7MHz: Attapeu, Bolikhamsay, Houai Xay, Houai Xe, Luang Prabang, Nam Bak, Pak Lay, Paksan, Pakse, Paksong, Phonsavan, Saiyabouly, Saravane, Savannakhet, Sekong, Siphandon. Tha Khek, Viengxay.

PUBLIC SECURITY RADIO STATION (Gov.)
✉ Public Security Ministry, Sengsavang Village, Saysettha District, Vientiane.
FM: Vientiane 101.5MHz 10kW
OTHER STATIONS:
China R. International: Vientiane 93.0MHz 10kW D.Prgr: 0300-1530 rel. CRI from Beijing in Chinese, English & Lao
R. Australia: Vientiane 96.0 MHz 5kW D.Prgr: 24h in English
R. France Internationale: Vientiane 100.5 MHz 5kW D.Prgr: 24h rel. RFI from Paris in French

LATVIA

L.T: UTC +2h (27 Mar-30 Oct: +3h) — **Pop:** 2 million — **Pr.L:** Latvian, Russian — **E.C:** 50Hz, 220V — **ITU:** LVA

NACIONALA ELEKTRONISKO PLAŠSAZINAS LIDZEKLU PADOME (NEPLP)
(National Council for Electronic Media)
✉ Doma laukums 8A, LV-1939 Riga ☎ +371 67221848 🖷 +371 67220448 **E:** neplpadome@neplpadome.lv **W:** neplpadome.lv
L.P: Chairperson (acting): Aija Dulevska
NB: NEPLP is the licensing body for broadcasting.

LATVIJAS RADIO (Pub)
✉ Doma laukums 8, LV-1505 Riga ☎ +371 67206722 🖷 +371 67206709 **E:** radio@latvijasradio.lv **W:** latvijasradio.lv
L.P: DG: Aldis Pauliņš

FM (MHz)	1	2	3	4	5	kW
Aluksne	106.8	104.3	-	100.5	-	3.5
Auce	99.6	-	-	-	-	1
Cesvaine	102.5	105.0	103.5	-	-	2x20/4.5
Dagda	102.6	-	-	99.1	-	1.7/0.9
Daugavpils	90.6	100.7	88.1	88.7	104.0	4/7.9/1.3/6.3/3.2
Dundaga	91.1	106.7	-	-	-	4
Kuldiga	95.9	101.3	92.0	-	-	10/16.6/3.3
Liepaja	107.1	101.0	104.6	97.9	102.1	2x12.6/3.2/6.3/0.2
Limbazi	105.5	-	-	-	-	5.6
Piedruja	-	-	-	94.5	-	1.6
Rezekne	107.5	101.0	101.8	104.2	103.8	2x20/5/20/0.4
Riga	90.7	91.5	103.7	107.7	93.1	2x35/9.5/6.6/8.9
Valmiera	104.0	101.5	87.6	-	89.5	2x20/2x2.4
Ventspils	99.2	103.0	89.8	95.3	96.5	3x0.3/1/0.2
Viesite	107.6	104.7	102.2	91.1	-	3x5/1.6
Vilaka	-	-	-	100.0	-	1.7

D.Prgr: Prgr 1 (Latvijas R.1): 24h. – **Prgr 2 (Latvijas R.2):** 24h. – **Prgr 3 (Latvijas R.3 - Klasika):** 24h. – **Prgr 4 (Latvijas R.4 - Doma laukums/Domskaya ploshchad)** for ethnic minorities: 24h in Russian (exc. Mon-Wed 1715-1800 for other ethnic communities, rotating each day/week: Armenian, Azeri, Bashkir, Belarusian, Estonian, Lithuanian, Georgian, German, Polish, Russian for the Jewish community, Tatar, Ukrainian). – **Prgr 5 (Latvijas R.5 - Pieci.lv):** 24h. At night incl. rel. R. NABA (see Prgr 6) – **Prgr 6:** 24h on Riga 95.8MHz (0.7kW). This outlet provides a relay of the Latvijas Universitate student radio station R. NABA (✉ Aspazijas blvd. 5, LV-1050 Riga **E:** naba@radionaba.lv) and live broadcasts from parliament (Saeima).

OTHER STATIONS

MW	kHz	kW	Location	Station
22)	1485	1.25	Riga	R. Merkurs
22)	+(SW)	0.5	Riga	R. Merkurs (F. pl)

+) Local DRM tests planned (26MHz band)

FM	MHz	kW	Location	Station
3C)	87.7	1.6	Liepaja	Krievijas Hiti
2)	87.9	2.5	Madona	Star FM
3B)	88.4	1	Gulbene	European Hit R.
9)	88.4	1.3	Liepaja	Kurzemes R.
4C)	88.6	1	Riga	Jumor FM
1C)	89.2	4	Riga	R. SWH Rock
1A)	89.3	1	Dundaga	R. SWH
18)	89.5	1.1	Aizpute	R. Tev
19)	90.1	3.2	Daugavpils	Divu Krastu R.
3A)	90.3	1	Matisi	Super FM
5)	90.8	1	Ventspils	Kristigais R.
3A)	90.9	3	Madona	Super FM
2)	91.0	1.9	Liepaja	Star FM
2)	91.9	1.5	Rezekne	Star FM
8)	91.9	2	Iecava	Top R.
2)	92.0	1	Vilkene	Star FM
17)	92.3	1	Liepaja	City R.
9)	92.4	1.3	Tukums	Kurzemes R.
3B)	92.9	2	Daugavpils	European Hit R.
16)	93.5	1.8	Liepaja	1.Biznesa R.
4D)	93.9	2.8	Riga	R. Baltkom
18)	94.0	1	Valka	R. Tev
1D)	94.1	1.1	Jekabpils	R. SWH Gold
3A)	94.3	1.6	Talsi	Super FM
6B)	94.6	1	Valka	R. Skonto Vidzeme
1A)	94.7	1	Broceni	R. SWH
7)	94.9	1.3	Riga	Capital FM
18)	95.0	2.5	Dundaga	R. Tev
20)	95.2	6.3	Daugavpils	Latgolys Radeja
3A)	95.2	1.6	Liepaja	Super FM
8)	95.4	1	Riteri	Top R.
20)	95.8	1	Jekabpils	Latgolys Radeja
7)	95.9	1	Valmiera	Capital FM
21)	96.1	2.1	Kraslava	Autoradio (R. Kraslavas Pluss)
3B)	96.1	1.6	Liepaja	European Hit R.
3C)	96.2	2	Riga	Krievijas Hiti
3A)	96.8	1	Riga	Super FM
6B)	97.0	1	Valmiera	R. Skonto Vidzeme
10)	97.3	2.6	Riga	NRJ
6A)	97.5	3.2	Liepaja	R. Skonto Kurzeme
2)	97.7	1.1	Pure	Star FM
8)	97.7	1	Livani	Top R.
18)	98.1	1	Valmiera	R. Tev
8)	98.3	2.3	Riga	Top R.
5)	98.5	3.3	Kuldiga	Kristigais R.
13)	99.0	1	Jurmala	R. Jurmala
21)	99.4	1.6	Daugavpils	Autoradio
20)	99.5	2	Balvi	Latgolys Radeja
4B)	99.5	2.8	Riga	R.99.5 FM
6B)	99.8	2	Cesvaine	R. Skonto Vidzeme
5)	99.9	2	Daugavpils	Kristigais R.
15)	100.0	2.5	Riga	R. PIK
1A)	100.1	1.9	Kuldiga	R. SWH
5)	100.1	1	Valmiera	Kristigais R.
6A)	100.5	1	Ventspils	R. Skonto Kurzeme
A)	100.5	1.3	Riga	BBCWS relay
5)	100.6	1.6	Liepaja	Kristigais R.
3B)	100.8	1	Talsi	European Hit R.
16)	101.0	2.6	Riga	1. Biznesa R.
1A)	101.2	2.5	Jekabpils	R. SWH
5)	101.3	1.1	Kraslava	Kristigais R.
14)	101.6	3.2	Daugavpils	Alise Plus
5)	101.8	5.6	Riga	Kristigais R.
3B)	101.9	1	Ventspils	European Hit R.
2)	102.0	2.3	Broceni	Star FM
1A)	102.2	4	Talsi	R. SWH
4A)	102.7	2.8	Riga	Mix FM
5)	102.8	1	Jekabpils	Kristigais R.
20)	103.0	1.8	Rezekne	Latgolys Radeja
2)	103.2	5	Svente	Star FM
3A)	103.2	1	Kuldiga	Super FM
2)	103.8	1.3	Kuldiga	Star FM
3B)	104.3	4.8	Riga	European Hit R.
16)	104.7	1.1	Cesis	1.Biznesa R.
2)	105.0	1.6	Pope	Star FM
1A)	105.1	1	Liepaja	R. SWH
3C)	105.1	1.3	Rezekne	Krievijas Hiti (R. Rezekne)

FM	MHz	kW	Location	Station
1A)	105.2	3.2	Daugavpils	R. SWH
1A)	105.2	13.2	Riga	R. SWH
1A)	105.4	1	Ventspils	R. SWH
21)	105.5	2	Rezekne	Autoradio
1B)	105.7	4.1	Riga	R. SWH+
11)	105.8	1.6	Liepaja	Rietumu R.
5)	105.9	3.5	Cesvaine	Kristigais R.
2)	106.2	10	Riga	Star FM
9)	106.4	11.5	Kuldiga	Kurzemes R.
1A)	106.5	4	Rezekne	R. SWH
1A)	106.5	5	Valmiera	R. SWH
2)	106.6	1	Bauska	Star FM
12)	107.0	1	Jekabpils	R. 1
1B)	107.2	6.2	Daugavpils	R. SWH+
6)	107.2	4	Riga	R. Skonto
2)	107.4	2	Valmiera	Star FM
3B)	107.4	1.3	Kuldiga	European Hit R.
8)	107.6	1.6	Liepaja	Top R.
1A)	107.9	5	Cesvaine	R. SWH
9)	107.9	1	Ventspils	Kurzemes R.

NB: Txs below 1kW not listed.
Addresses & other information:
1A-D) Ganibu dambis 24D, LV-1005 Riga. 1B) in Russian. **E:** 1A) radio@radioswh.lv, 1B) plus@radioswh.lv, 1C) rock@radioswh.lv, 1D) gold@radioswh.lv – **2)** Dzelzavas iela 120G, LV-1021 Riga. **E:** info@starfm.lv – **3A-C)** Elijas iela 17, LV-1050 Riga. 3C) In Russian. **E:** 3A) birojs@superfm.lv, 3B) radio@europeanhitradio.com, 3C) radio@hitirossii.com – **4A-D)** Kr.Valdemara iela 8, LV-1010 Riga. In Russian, incl. rebroadcasts* of prgrs from Russia: 4B) Europa+, 4C) Yumor FM, 4D) Ekho Moskvy. **E:** 4A) radio@mixfm.lv, 4C) radio@jumorfm.lv, 4D) radio@radiobaltkom.lv – **5)** Lacpleša iela 37, LV-1011 Riga. **E:** lkr@lkr.lv – **6)** Kr.Valdemara iela 100, LV-1013 Riga **E:** studija@radioskonto.lv. Reg. stns: **6A)** Graudu iela 27/29, LV-3401 Liepaja. **E:** kurzeme@radioskonto.lv; **6B)** Rigas iela 13, LV-4201 Valmiera **E:** vidzeme@radioskonto.lv – **7)** L.Nometnu iela 62, LV-1002 Riga **E:** radio@capitalfm.lv – **8)** Terbatas iela 83B, LV-1001 Riga. In Russian **E:** topradio@inbox.lv – **9)** Pilsetas laukums 4, LV-3301 Kuldiga **E:** studija@kurzemesradio.lv – **10)** Jaunmoku iela 34, LV-1046 Riga **E:** studija@energyfm.lv – **11)** Zivju iela 2A, LV-3401 Liepaja **E:** info@rietumuradio.lv – **12)** Brivibas iela 116, LV-5201 Jekabpils **E:** info@radio1.lv – **13)** Brivibas bulv. 30, LV-1050 Riga **E:** info@radiojurmala.lv – **14)** Raina iela 28, LV-5401 Daugavpils. In Russian. **E:** radio@aliseplus.lv – **15)** Brivibas bulv. 30, LV-1050 Riga. In Russian, incl. rebroadcasts* of R. Sputnik (Russia). **E:** info@pik.lv – **16)** Elizabetes iela 55, LV-1010 Riga **E:** radio@1br.lv – **17)** Zivju iela 3, LV-3401 Liepaja **E:** radio@cityradio.lv – **18)** Rigas iela 13, LV-4201 Valmiera **E:** studija@radiotev.lv – **19)** Atbrivosanas aleja 98, LV-4601 Rezekne **E:** info@dkradio.lv – **20)** Atbrivosanas aleja 81/5, LV-4601 Rezekne. In Latgalian. **E:** radeja@lr.lv – **21)** Zakusalas krastmala 5, LV-1050 Riga. In Russian, incl. rebroadcasts* of prgrs from Russia: Avtoradio (daytime), R. Sputnik (nighttime). Local branches also carry local prgrs. **E:** info@avtoradio.lv – **22)** P.O.Box 371, LV-1010 Riga. **E:** rni@apollo.lv – **A)** Rel. BBCWS (UK). (*= Pre-recorded)

LEBANON

LT: UTC +2h (27 Mar–30 Oct: +3h) — **Pop:** 4 million — **Pr.L:** Arabic, French, English, Armenian — **E.C:** 50Hz, 110/220V — **ITU:** LBN

MINISTRY OF INFORMATION
✉ Hamra, Beirut ☎+961 1 754400 **W:** ministryinfo.gov.lb

RADIO LEBANON (Gov.)
✉ Rue Lyon, Sanayeh, P.O. Box 4848, Beirut ☎+961 1 743531 **W:** 96-2.com **E:** mykee@cyberia.net.lb
LP: Dir: Fuad Hamdan. Tech. Dir: Nazih Chahine. Chief, Prgr. Dept: Waheed Jalal. Chief, Public Rel: Faouzi Fehmy.
1st Prgr. in Arabic: 0330-2330 on 98.1/98.5MHz. **2nd Prgr. in French/ English/Armenian:** 24h on 96.2MHz. **Rel. R. France Int:** 13h daily. **Ann:** A: "Iza'at Loubnan min Beirut". F: "Ici Radio Liban émettant de Beyrouth" **IS:** Opening notes from the Lebanese National anthem played on guitar.

OTHER STATIONS:

FM	MHz	Name	FM	MHz	Name
40)	87.7	R. Sawa	32)	89.5	Virgin R.
20)	88.1	R. Nostalgie	16)	89.9	Cedars R - VOL Plus
4)	88.5	R. Orient	16)	90.1	Sawt al Hurriya
13)	89.1	Holy Quran R.	12)	90.3	Sawt al-Jadeed
7)	89.3	Risala R.	17)	90.5	R. Light FM

FM	MHz	Name	FM	MHz	Name
31)	90.8	R. Sevan	1)	100.3	Voice of Lebanon
8)	91.3	Nidaa al-Maarifa	37)	100.7	R. Al-Fajir
3)	91.9	R. Al-Nour	25)	101.1	R. Jaras Scoop
28)	92.7	Sawt el-Mada	31)	101.5	R. Sevan
23)	93.3	Voice of Lebanon	22)	101.8	R. Delta
13)	94.1	Holy Quran R	9)	102.4	R. Free Lebanon
38)	94.5	R.Al-Tawhid Al-Islami	21)	103.1	Pax R.
33)	94.5	Voice of Gospel	29)	103.3	Monte-Carlo Doualiya
10)	94.9	Voice of Van	38)	103.5	R. Al-Tawhid Al-Islamiy
34)	95.5	Voice of Faith	23)	103.7	Voice of the People
30)	95.9	Sawt el-Noujoum	39)	104.1	R. Mazzika
35)	96.5	Sawt Beirut	19)	104.6	Mix FM
11)	96.9	Sawt el-Ghad	37)	104.9	R. Al-Fajir
26)	97.5	R. Strike	6)	105.3	R. One
40)	98.0	R. Sawa	14)	106.1	Voice of Charity
36)	98.9	R. Aghani Aghani	27)	106.7	Al-Balad R. Station
5)	99.0	NRJ	37)	107.3	R. MBS
38)	99.3	R. Al-Tawhid Al-Islami	37)	107.7	R. Al-Fajir
15)	99.7	Fame FM	30)	107.8	Sawt el-Noujoum
24)	100.0	R. Scope, Zahle			

NB: the stns have been allocated 400kHz frequency range, of which mostly the centre freq. is listed above. In many cases the trs from various sites are placed on both upper and lower limits of the range.
Addresses & other information:
1) P.O. Box 165271, Ashrafieh, Bachir el Gemayel Ave, Beirut **W:** sawtlebnan.com – **2)** Jabal el Arab St, Wata el Mousaitbeh, P.O.Box 14/5425, Beirut **W:** sawtachaab.com – **3)** Al-Nour Bldg, Abdel Nour St, Haret Hreïk, P.O.Box 25-197, Ghbeiry, Beirut **W:** alnour.com.lb . Also relayed via Tartus, Syria on 1071 kHz – **4)** Annajah Centre, Mar Elias St, Karakol Druz, P.O. Box 11-6362, Beirut. **W:** radioorient.com.lb – **5)** Studiovision Bldg, Naccache, Metn, Beirut. **W:** nrjlebanon.com 24h in English. – **6)** Zakhem Bldg, Beit Meri El Metn, Beirut **W:** radioone.fm 24h in English – **7)** Fraiha Bld. 3rd Floor, Barbour Beirut. **W:** risalation.com – **8)** Shaykh Ahmad Iskandarani Centre, Bourj Abi Haidar, Beirut. **W:** nidaa.fm – **9)** Kebbe Bldg, Adonis, Zouk Mosbeh, P.O.Box 110, Zouk Mekhael, Jounieh **W:** rll.com.lb – **10)** 2nd floor, Shaghzoyan Centre, Borj Hammoud, P.O. Box 80-860, Beirut. **W:** voiceofvan.net 24h in Armenian & Arabic – **11)** Jal el Dib, Beirut 60073 **W:** sawtelghad.com – **12)** Watta al-Museitbeh, Ghbeiri, Beirut **W:** aljadeed.tv – **13)** Dar al Fatwa, P.O. Box 14-5380, Al Mazraa-Beirut – **14)** Couvent St. Jean, Fouad Chehab St, P.O. Box 850, Jounieh. **W:** voiceofcharity.org 24h in Arabic/French/others – **15)** 3rd floor, La Perla Centre, Sabra Highway, Jounieh. **W:** famefm.com – **16)** Achrafieh, Kobayate St, Tutunji Center 7th floor, Beirut 1100 **W:** cedarsradio.com sawtelhouria.com – **17)** cityarama, delcawaneh, sin el fil the private club, 3rd floor, Beirut **W:** radiolightfm.com 0500-2200 in English/French – **18)** 1st floor, Pères Paulistes building, Off Highway, Haret Sakhre, Kesrouane **W:** facebook.com/RadioMBS – **19)** Alfred Naccache Ave, P.O. Box 166-815, Achrafieh, Beirut. **W:** mixfm.com.lb 24h in English – **20)** Mont Liban Bldg, Ave. Fouad Chehab, Fassouh, P.O.Box 16-6000, Achrafieh, Beirut. **W:** nostalgie.com.lb 24h in French – **21)** P.O. Box 116-5104, Achrafieh. Beirut. 24h in English. **W:** paxradio.net – **22)** Kahalé Bldg, Old St, P.O.Box 1306, Beit Meri el Metn. **W:** radiodelta.fm – **23)** c/o Modern Media Company, Dbayeh, Beirut. **W:** vdl.com.lb – **24)** facing Tal-Shiha Hospital, Tal-Shiha, Zahlé – **25)** 4th Floor, Hawa Chicken Building, Damascus Highway, Hazmiyé **W:** jarasfm.com – **26)** Sin El Fil, Saydeh Str, Facing Saydeh Church ,Beirut **W:** radiostrike.com – **27)** Centre Nasrallah, Rue Al-Anwar, Jdeideh, P.O. Box 90-1119, Beirut. **W:** albaladradiostation.com – **28)** Mirna el Chalouhi Centre 2nd floor, Sin el-Fil, Beirut. **W:** sawtlemada.com – **29)** txs in Beirut/Tripoli/Tyros/Sidon. For details see IntRad under France – **30)** Kreshet Bldg. 7th floor, Suyoufi St, Algazlep, Achrafieh, Beirut. **W:** sawtelnoujoum.com – **31)** Khatchadurian Street, Khederlarian Building, Ground Floor, Beirut **W:** radiosevan.com – **32)** Jal al-Dib highway, Beirut **W:** virginradiolebanon.com – **33)** Sawt al-Injil, Maronite Archdiocese of Beirut **W:** voiceofgospel.com – **34)** Sawt el-Bachaer, Beirut **W:** albachaer.com – **35)** Beirut **W:** sawtbeirut.com – **36)** Beirut Media Zone, Studiovision Bldg #1, Naccache, Beirut **W:** aghaniaghani.com – **37)** Beirut **W:** fajrradio.com – **38)** Beirut **W:** radiotawhid.com – **39)** **W:** mazzikagroup.net – **40)** Beirut/Tripoli/West Bekaa 87.7, Zahle 98.3 (for details see Int. section under USA)

LESOTHO

LT: UTC +2h — **Pop:** 2.2 million — **Pr.L:** Sesotho, English — **E.C:** 50Hz, 220V — **ITU:** LSO

LESOTHO COMMUNICATIONS AUTHORITY (LCA)
✉ P.O. Box 15896, 6th Floor, Moposo House, Kingsway Road, Maseru ☎+266 22224300 🖷 +266 22310984 **W:** lca.org.ls **E:** lca@lca.org.ls

LESOTHO NATIONAL BROADCASTING SERVICES (LNBS, Pub.)

P. O. Box 552, Lerotholi St, Opposite Royal Palace, Maseru 100 ☎+266 22321460 ▤ +266 22313980 **W:** lnbs.org.ls **LP:** D.G. Broadc: Mr. Lebohang Dada Mokasa. CE: Mr. Motlatsi Monyane.Sr. Tr. Eng MW: Mr. Khoabane Qhobela. Sr. Tr. Eng. FM&TV: Mr. Ncheme Sekhoane & Mr. Ntima Molete. CE: Mr. Motlatsi Monyane.
MW: Maseru (Lancer's Gap): 639kHz 100kW, 891kHz 50kW, 1197kHz 50kW.

FM	MHzkW(TRP)	FM	MHzkW(TRP)
Katse	90.8 0.3	Maseru (Berea)	99.8 5
Ha-Sottho	92.6 0.25	Thaba-Putsoa	100.2 1
Lebelonyane	93.2 1	Sheep Stud Hill	102.4 1
Maseru (Berea)	93.3 5	Popa	103.6 1
Chafo	96.0 1	Souru	105.4 1
Matshoana	96.8 1	Sehong-hon	106.1 0.25
Likhoele	97.2 1		

R. Lesotho in Sesotho/English: 24h on 639kHz & FM excl 99.8MHz.
Ultimate FM in English: 891 & 1197kHz and 99.8MHz 24h.
Ann: E: "This is Radio Lesotho" or "This is the Lesotho National Broadcasting Service, Maseru". Sesotho: "Se-ea-le-moea sa Lesotho, Maseru". **IS:** native horn instruments.

OTHER STATIONS:
Catholic R. FM: Qoatsaneng, Maseru 103.3MHz – **Dope FM,** Maseru: 103.6 MHz – **Fill the Gap (Jesu ke Karabo):** Mafeteng 87.6MHz, Leribe 102.8MHz, Lancer's Gap 105.3MHz – **Harvest FM:** Lancer's Gap, Maseru 98.9MHz – **Joy FM,** Private Bag A68, Maseru 100: 106.9MHz 1kW **W:** joyfm.co.ls Also rel. VOA. F.PI: trs in Mafeteng and Maputsoe – **LM R:** Maseru 104.0MHz **W:** lmradio.net – **Lesotho Evangelical Church R,** Lancer's Gap, Maseru: 102.4MHz – **MoAfrika FM:** Leribe 89.7MHz, Mafeteng 90.7MHz, Lancer's Gap 99.3MHz. **W:** moafrika.co.ls – **People's Choice FM,** Development House, Block D, Floor 9, Kingsway Str, Maseru: 95.6MHz. **W:** pcfm.co.ls – **Thaha-Khube FM,** Ha Ts'osane, Maseru: 97.6MHz – **Tšenolo FM,** Khubetsoana: 91.3MHz.
BBC African Sce, Maseru (Berea): 90.2MHz.
RFI Afrique, Maseru (Berea): 96.5MHz in French/English

LIBERIA

L.T: UTC — **Pop:** 3.5 million — **Pr.L:** English, 18 ethnic — **E.C:** 60Hz, 120V — **ITU:** LBR

LIBERIA TELECOMMUNICATIONS AUTHORITY (LTA)
National Investment Commission Annex, 12th Street, Sinkor, Tubman Boulevard, Monrovia ☎+231 770 54054 ▤ +231 770 00825 **W:** lta.gov.lr **E:** info@lta.gov.lr

LIBERIA BROADCASTING SYSTEM (LBS, Pub.)
P.O. Box 594, Paynesville **W:** elbcradio.com **E:** lbs@yahoo.com **LP:** DG: Darryl Ambrose Nmah, Sr. Deputy DG: Ledgerhood Rennie.
FM: ELBC Radio 99.9MHz 10kW **D.Prgr:** 0530-2400.

RADIO ELWA (Rlg.)
P.O. Box 192, Monrovia **W:** elwaministries.org **E:** elwaradio@yahoo.com **LP:** GM: Moses T. Nyantee.
SW: Monrovia 4760 & 6050kHz 1kW (4760 kHz inactive).
FM: Monrovia 94.5MHz 2kW.
D.Prgr in English/local lang's: 0530-1000, 1700-2400 (SS -2230).

UNMIL RADIO (United Nations Mission in Liberia)
UNMIL Force HQ, Star Building, Monrovia **W:** unmilradio.org **E:** webmaster@unmil.org **LP:** Dir: Joseph Roberts-Mensah.
FM: Gbarnga 90.5MHz, Harper/Monrovia/Zwedru 91.5MHz, Sanniquellie 95.1MHz. Greenville/Voinjama 97.1MHz (Harper/Sanniquelle 1kW, others 5kW). **D.Prgr:** 24h in English/local langs

Other stations:
ABCU R, Yekepa: 95.7MHz 0.6kW. **W:** africanbiblecolleges.org/abcu_liberia.php — **City FM,** Monrovia: 90.2MHz — **Crystal FM,** Monrovia: 95.5MHz — **DC 101.1 FM,** Monrovia: 101.1MHz. Also rel. BBC African Sce. – **King's FM,** Monrovia: 88.5MHz. Also rel. VOA. – **Liberian Christian Broadcasting Network,** Monrovia: 102.3MHz — **Love FM,** Monrovia: 105.5MHz — **Power FM,** Monrovia: 93.3MHz — **Magic FM,** Monrovia: 99.2MHz — **R. Monrovia:** 92.1MHz. **W:** radiomonrovia247.com — **Sky FM,** Monrovia: 107.0MHz. **E:** skyliberia@yahoo.com — **Truth FM,** Monrovia 96.1MHz. **W:** truthfm.com.lr — **United Metodist Church R,** Monrovia: 98.7MHz 0.3kW.
BBC African Sce, Monrovia: 103.0MHz
China R. Int: Tubmanburg/Zwedru 91.7, Monrovia/Voinjama 104.7,

Buchanan 105.6MHz.
RFI Afrique: Monrovia 106.0MHz in French/English.
About 35 community radio stations are in operation

LIBYA

L.T: UTC +2h — **Pop:** 6.5 million — **Pr.L:** Arabic — **E.C:** 50Hz, 127/230V — **ITU:** LBY

LIBYAN RADIO & TELEVISION NETWORK (Gov)
El Fath Rd, P.O. Box 80237, Tripoli ☎+218 21 4442252 ▤ +218 21 3403458.

MW	kHz	kW	Prgr.
Benghazi	‡675	100	R. Free Libya (0500v-2300v)
Tripoli	1053	100	VO Homeland (0500v-2100v)
El Beida	‡1126	500	R. Free Libya
Tripoli	‡1251	200	R. Libya

FM: El Beida 87.9MHz, Tripoli 88.8MHz (youth channel), Tripoli 90.3MHz (with 1251kHz), Sabha 92.9MHz, Sabha 93.4MHz (with 1053kHz), Misrata 95.5MHz (Koran), Sabha 96.1MHz, Tripoli 96.6MHz (with 1053kHz), El Beida 98.1MHz, Benghazi 98.3MHz (with 675kHz), Benghazi 98.9MHz, Tripoli 99.9MHz (Al Iman), Al-Zawiyah 101.3MHz., Tobruk 102.6MHz, Sabha 102.9MHz, Tripoli 103.4/105.3 (city council).
Ann: "Shabakat Radio wa Television Libya: Radio Libya min Tarablus al-assema".

Other Stations:

FM	MHz	Station, Prgr & other info:
Tripoli	87.7	Tripolitana
Benghazi	88.1	R. Sawa
Benghazi	88.5	Libya FM
Tripoli	88.8	Al-Shababiya: (Youth R. of 17th February)
Misrata	88.9	R. Ram
Derna	89.3	R. Free Derna
Misrata	90.0	Al Aan TV sound relay
Misrata	90.5	Al-Furqan R.
Tripoli	91.1	BBC WS: (in Arabic/English)
Benghazi	91.2	Minhaj
Benghazi	91.5	BBC WS (in Arabic/English)
Misrata	91.5	BBC WS (in Arabic/English)
Ajdabiya	92.4	Al Jazeera (Arabic sce. TV sound relay)
Benghazi	92.4	Tribute FM (W: tributefm.com, in English)
Tripoli	92.5	Libya FM
Misrata	92.5	Flash FM
Tripoli	93.4	Lebda FM
Benghazi	95.5	Al-Manarah
Benghazi	95.5	Al Jazeera (Arabic sce. TV sound relay)
Misrata	96.5	Tubaktes FM Koran prgr.
Misrata	97.5	Tubaktes FM
Al-Khums	97.9	Libya FM
Tripoli	98.1	Tribute FM (W: tributefm.com, in English)
Nalut	98.2	R. Free Nalut (in Tamazight)
4 sites	98.7	Al-Wasat R. (live.alwasat.ly)
Misrata	99.1	R. Sawa
Benghazi	99.9	Al Jazeera (Arabic sce TV sound relay)
Tripoli	100.7	R. Zone (W: radiozone.ly)
Benghazi	101.1	Shabab FM
Benghazi	102.4	Koran al-Karim
Tripoli	102.5	Tripoli FM
Ajdabiya	103.0	Libya Free TV sound (W: libya.tv)
Misrata	104.0	Medina FM
Benghazi	105.3	Al Aan TV sound relay
Tripoli	106.6	R. Sawa: 2kW
Tripoli	107.7	Al-Jawhara FM

LIECHTENSTEIN

L.T: UTC +1h (27 Mar-30 Oct: +2h) — **Pop:** 36,000 — **Pr.L:** German, Alemannic German — **E.C:** 50Hz, 230V — **ITU:** LIE

LIECHTENSTEINISCHER RUNDFUNK (Pub)
Dorfstr. 24, 9495 Triesen, Fürstentum Liechtenstein ☎+423 3991313 ▤ +423 3991366 **E:** admin@radio.li **W:** radio.li
LP: DG: Alois Ospelt
FM (MHz): Balzers 88.8 (0.05kW), Buchs* 89.2 (0.5kW), Steg 96.6 (0.25kW), Vaduz 96.9 (0.1kW), Nendeln 100.2 (0.05kW), Vilters* 103.4 (0.1kW), Thal* 105.9 (0.2kW), Rüthi* 106.1 (1kW). *) Located in Switzerland. Also on DAB Block 9D (208.064MHz) via txs in Eastern Switzerland (see Switzerland entry).
D.Prgr: Radio L 24h

LITHUANIA

L.T: UTC +2h (27 Mar-30 Oct: +3h) — **Pop:** 3 million — **Pr.L:** Lithuanian, Polish, Russian — **E.C:** 50Hz, 230V — **ITU:** LTU

LIETUVOS RADIJO IR TELEVIZIJOS KOMISIJA (LRTK)
✉ Šeimyniškiu g. 3a, 09312 Vilnius ☎ +370 5 2330660 📠 +370 5 2647125 **E:** lrtk@rtk.lt **W:** rtk.lt
LP: Chmn: Edmundas Vaitekunas
NB. LRTK is the regulatory authority for broadcasting.

LIETUVOS NACIONALINIS RADIJAS IR TELEVIZIJA (LRT) (Pub)
✉ S.Konarskio g. 49, 03123 Vilnius ☎ +370 5 2363209 📠 +370 5 2363208 **E:** lrt@lrt.lt **W:** lrt.lt **LP:** DG: Audrius Siaurusevicius

FM (MHz)	1	2	3	kW
Birzai	100.8	87.5	-	5/1.3
Bubiai	100.9	103.4	90.5	2x20/0.8
Druskininkai	102.3	103.7	-	8.2/5
Giruliai	102.8	105.3	91.9	27.5/29/0.5
Juragiai	102.1	96.2	98.0	2x10/1.9
Kalvarija	104.8	-	-	1
Mazeikiai	93.3	101.8	-	2
Pazagieniai	107.5	105.3	93.7	2x1.5/1.7
Plunge	88.0	105.0	-	1/0.7
Skuodas	99.3	103.5	-	0.7/2
Taurage	98.8	107.4	104.2	13/2/1
Viešintos	101.9	104.4	106.5	17.4/18/0.9
Vilnius	89.0	105.1	98.3	20/6.5/3.5
Visaginas	102.9	100.4	-	10

NB: Sites with only txs below 1kW not listed.
D.Prgr: Prgr 1 (LRT radijas): 24h. For ethnic minorities: 1430-1500 Russian. — **Prgr 2 (LRT Klasika):** 0400-2200. For ethnic minorities: 1300-1330 Belarusian (Tue), Russian (Wed-Sun); 1330-1400 Polish. — **Prgr 3 (LRT Opus):** 24h.

OTHER STATIONS

FM	MHz	kW	Location	Station
B)	68.24	6.3	Visaginas	Euroradio relay
2D)	87.8	5.3	Vilnius	Classic Rock FM
2B)	88.2	3.2	Bubiai	ZIP FM
16)	88.3	1	Utena	Relax FM
19)	88.5	5	Vilnius	Extra FM
19)	89.1	1	Marijampole	Extra FM
2A)	89.6	3	Vilnius	Radiocentras
3B)	90.1	2	Perkunai	Pukas 2
2D)	90.3	20	Juragiai	Classic Rock FM
2C)	90.6	2.3	Giruliai	Russkoje R. Baltija
2A)	91.2	4	Tryškiai	Radiocentras
22)	91.4	3.2	Klaipeda	XFM
7)	91.4	2.1	Marijampole	Marijos radijas
2B)	91.6	2	Skuodas	ZIP FM
7)	91.8	2	Bubiai	Marijos radijas
2A)	92.2	3.5	Bubiai	Radiocentras
4A)	92.3	1	Utena	Ziniu radijas
3B)	92.4	3.2	Kaunas	Pukas 2
2B)	92.5	4.5	Giruliai	ZIP FM
2B)	92.7	2.1	Mazeikiai	ZIP FM
1A)	92.8	11.7	Krakes	M-1
7)	93.1	1.3	Vilnius	Marijos radijas
4A)	93.4	1	Marijampole	Ziniu radijas
3A)	94.0	2.5	Lelionys	Pukas
3A)	94.2	4.8	Liktenai	Pukas
3A)	94.6	2	Ukmerge	Pukas
3A)	94.8	2.5	Daukšiai	Pukas
15A)	94.9	3.2	Giruliai	Laluna
7)	95.0	4	Viešintos	Marijos radijas
3B)	95.4	4	Liepkalnis	Pukas 2
A)	95.5	3.2	Vilnius	BBCWS relay
3A)	95.7	2	Šiauliai	Pukas
4)	96.4	1.8	Mazeikiai	Ziniu radijas
11)	96.4	1.4	Vilnius	A2
10)	96.6	1	Panevezys	Pulsas
9)	96.7	2.3	Giruliai	Power Hit R.
3B)	97.4	1	Šiauliai	Pukas 2
1B)	97.6	4	Juragiai	M-1 Plius
21)	97.8	1.6	Šiauliai	Antroji radijo stotis
7)	98.2	1.9	Birzai	Marijos radijas
1B)	98.3	3.4	Giruliai	M-1 Plius
1B)	98.7	1.6	Utena	M-1 Plius
12)	99.0	3.2	Alytus	FM 99

FM	MHz	kW	Location	Station
13)	99.7	1	Vilnius	European Hit R.
6)	99.8	2	Giruliai	Kelyje
2A)	99.9	2	Raseiniai	Radiocentras
2B)	100.1	4	Vilnius	ZIP FM
1B)	100.2	5	Pazagieniai	M-1 Plius
19)	100.2	1	Klaipeda	Extra FM
8)	100.4	4	Mazeikiai	Mazeikiu aidas
2C)	100.4	2.4	Kaunas	Russkoje R. Baltija
1B)	100.5	3	Bubiai	M-1 Plius
15B)	100.8	1.3	Klaipeda	Raduga
3B)	100.9	1.1	Vilnius	Pukas 2
2A)	101.1	1.4	Alytus	Radiocentras
2A)	101.4	3.8	Pazagieniai	Radiocentras
2A)	101.5	2	Giruliai	Radiocentras
4B)	101.5	2.3	Vilnius	Easy FM
3A)	101.6	1.7	Taurage	Pukas
2A)	101.6	1.9	Druskininkai	Radiocentras
16)	101.7	1.6	Bubiai	Relax FM
2A)	101.8	2	Marijampole	Radiocentras
3A)	102.0	1	Karlai	Pukas
4A)	102.2	1.6	Giruliai	Ziniu radijas
17)	102.5	3.4	Bubiai	Saules radijas
3A)	102.6	1	Skuodas	Pukas
5)	102.6	5.8	Vilnius	Laisvoji banga
2A)	102.7	1.5	Taurage	Radiocentras
18)	102.9	4	Kaunas	Tau
1C)	103.0	2.2	Pazagieniai	Lietus
1C)	103.1	1.1	Tryškiai	Lietus
1C)	103.1	2.5	Vilnius	Lietus
1C)	103.1	1.7	Taurage	Lietus
1C)	103.3	1	Birzai	Lietus
1C)	103.4	1.1	Utena	Lietus
1C)	103.5	4.2	Juragiai	Lietus
1C)	103.7	1.6	Giruliai	Lietus
4A)	103.7	1.1	Visaginas	Ziniu radijas
20)	103.8	1.9	Vilnius	Znad Wilii
1C)	103.9	3.7	Bubiai	Lietus
5)	104.1	4	Giruliai	Laisvoji banga
2B)	104.1	20	Juragiai	ZIP FM
1B)	104.3	2	Marijampole	M-1 Plius
5)	104.3	1.2	Šiauliai	Laisvoji banga
5)	104.5	4	Kaunas	Laisvoji banga
23)	104.7	1	Vilnius	Lietuvos ryto radijas
5)	104.8	1.2	Pazagieniai	Laisvoji banga
4A)	104.8	2.2	Taurage	Ziniu radijas
4A)	104.9	1	Juragiai	Ziniu radijas
2B)	105.0	1	Utena	ZIP FM
2B)	105.2	1.3	Raseiniai	ZIP FM
14)	105.2	3.9	Kaunas	Hot FM
2B)	105.4	10	Visaginas	ZIP FM
2A)	105.5	1.7	Birzai	Radiocentras
2C)	105.6	2.2	Vilnius	Russkoje R. Baltija
2B)	105.7	2	Taurage	ZIP FM
2C)	105.8	4.2	Bubiai	Russkoje R. Baltija
1A)	105.9	3.2	Ignalina	M-1
6)	105.9	1	Kaunas	Kelyje
1A)	106.0	2.2	Pazagieniai	M-1
1A)	106.0	2	Tryškiai	M-1
1A)	106.2	1.5	Taurage	M-1
1B)	106.2	4	Vilnius	M-1 Plius
1A)	106.3	3.9	Marijampole	M-1
1A)	106.3	2.5	Bubiai	M-1
1A)	106.3	2	Utena	M-1
1A)	106.4	2	Raseiniai	M-1
1A)	106.5	3	Giruliai	M-1
1A)	106.6	4	Juragiai	M-1
2B)	106.7	2	Laukuva	ZIP FM
1A)	106.8	1	Vilnius	M-1
2A)	107.1	3.9	Juragiai	Radiocentras
3A)	107.3	2	Vilnius	Pukas
10)	107.3	3.2	Birzai	Pulsas
3A)	107.6	3.7	Kaunas	Pukas
3A)	107.8	4.5	Perkunai	Pukas
4A)	107.9	1	Pazagenai	Ziniu radijas

NB: Txs below 1kW not listed.
Addresses & other information:
1A-C) Laisves pr. 60, 05120 Vilnius **E:** 1A) m-1@m-1.fm, 1B) pliusas@pliusas.fm, 1C) lietus@lietus.fm — **2A-D)** Laisves pr. 60, 05120 Vilnius. 2C) in Russian. **E:** 2A) programa@rc.lt; 2B) info@zipfm.lt; 2C) rusradio@rc.lt; 2D) info@rock.lt — **3A,B)** Šaldytuvu g. 25, 45123 Kaunas **E:** radio@pukas.lt — **4A,B)** A.Smetonos g. 6, 01115 Vilnius **E:** biuras@ziniuradijas.lt — **5)** Gedimino pr. 50/2, 01110 Vilnius **E:** info@laisvojibanga.lt — 6)

Savanoriu pr. 151, 50174 Kaunas **E:** buhalterija@radijaskelyje.lt – **7)** M.Daukšos g. 21, 44282 Kaunas **E:** direktorius@marijosradijas.lt – **8)** Sodu g. 13-93, 89116 Mazeikiai **E:** info@mazeikiuaidas.lt – **9)** Kalvariju g. 143, 08221 Vilnius **E:** info@powerhitradio.lt – **10)** Respublikos g. 28, 35174 Panevezys **E:** reklama@pulsas.lt – **11)** Laisves pr. 3, 04215 Vilnius **E:** a2@a2.lt – **12)** Rotušes a. 2a, 62141 Alytus **E:** fm99@fm99.lt – **13)** Odminiu g. 8, LT-01112 Vilnius **E:** info@ehr.lt – **14)** Simno g. 35a, 46372 Kaunas **E:** info@hotfm.lt – **15A,B)** Taikos pr. 81, 94114 Klaipeda. 15B) in Russian. **E:** 15A) laluna@laluna.lt; 15B) info@raduga.lt – **16)** Laisves pr. 60, 05120 Vilnius **E:** info@relaxfm.lt – **17)** Aušros al. 64, 76240 Šiauliai **E:** info@saulesradijas.lt – **18)** Draugystes g. 19, 51230 Kaunas **E:** info@tau.lt – **19)** Konstitucijos pr. 7, 09308 Vilnius **E:** info@extrafm.lt – **20)** Laisves pr. 60, 05120 Vilnius **E:** info@zw.lt. In Polish. – **21)** Varpo g. 22, 76297 Šiauliai **E:** admin@2ra.lt – **22)** Pylimo g. 20-10, 01118 Vilnius **E:** reklama@xfm.lt – **23)** Gedimino pr. 12a, 01103 Vilnius – **A)** Rel. BBCWS (UK).– **B)** Rel. Euroradio (Poland). In Belarusian. Provided by R. Baltic Waves International: Algirdo g. 13-9, 03219 Vilnius **E:** riplei@takas.lt.

Int. relays on MW: (provided by R. Baltic Waves International; tx leased from Lietuvos radijo ir televizijos centras) Kaunas (Sitkunai) 1386kHz 75/150kW. See International Radio section.

LORD HOWE ISLAND (Australia)

L.T: UTC +10½ (4 Oct 15-3 Apr 16, 2 Oct 16-2 Apr 17: +11h) — **Pop:** 347 — **Pr.L:** English — **E.C:** 50Hz, 240V. — **ITU:** AUS (**WRTH:** LHW)

AUSTRALIAN BROADCASTING CORP. [ABC]

FM(MHz)	Call	kW	Station
104.1	2ABCFM	0.02	ABC Classic FM
105.3	2JJJ	0.02	Triple J
106.1	2ABCFM	0.02	ABC Classic FM

NB: all ABC stns r.inactive with reception via satellite only

LORD HOWE ISLAND RADIO
🖳 The Shack, New Jetty Complex, Lagoon Road [PO Box 52], Lord Howe Island NSW 2898 ☎+61 2 6563 2123 🖷 +61 2 6563 2127 **FM:** 100.1MHz, 40W **Prgr:** Irr. Local prgr. Wed midday, and Thurs night 2130-0230. Local community stn

LUXEMBOURG

L.T: UTC +1h (27 Mar-30 Oct: +2h) — **Pop:** 514,862 — **Pr.L:** Luxembourgish, French, German — **E.C:** 50Hz, 110/220V — **ITU:** LUX

RTL (Comm.)
🖳 45 blvd. Pierre Frieden, L-1543 Luxembourg ☎ +352 4214 22175 🖷 +352 4214 22756 **W:** radio.rtl.lu **L.P:** Pres: Jacques Santer.
Luxembourg Sce: RTL Radio Lëtzebuerg: ☎ +352 4214 23 🖷 +352 4214 22737 **W:** rtl.lu
German Sce: RTL Radio – die Grössten Oldies: ☎ +352 4214 23500 🖷 +352 4214 22738 **W:** rtlradio.de **L.P:** PD: Holger Richter

FM(MHz)	Station	Location	kW
88.9	R. Lëtzebuerg	Dudelange	100
92.5	R. Lëtzebuerg	Hosingen	50
93.3	R. die Grössten Oldies	Dudelange	100
97.0	R. die Grössten Oldies	Hosingen	100
100.7	R. Socioculturelle	Dudelange	100

Also FM relays in France & Germany.
RTL Radio Lëtzebuerg in English/German/Luxembourgish: 24h on 92.5MHz (2000-0500 rel. German Sce.)

OTHER STATIONS (all MHz)
R. City FM - FM: 100.2 – **R. Honnert.7**, b.p. 1833, 1018 Luxembourg **W:** 100komma7.lu - **FM:** 100.7 – **RTL2 - W:** rtl2.fr - **FM:** 102.9/104.2/107.7 – **R. Latina**, 2 rue Astrid, 1143 Luxembourg **W:** radiolatina.lu - **FM:** 101.2/103.1 – **R. Ara**, 2 rue de la Boucherie, 1247 Luxembourg **W:** ara.lu - **FM:** 103.3/105.2 – **R. Eldoradio**, B.P. 1344, 1013 Luxembourg **W:** eldoradio.lu - **FM:** 105.0/107.2 – **R. Challenger - FM:** 102.2 – **R. Lora**, 32 Av. de la Gare, 9233 Diekirch - **FM:** 102.2 – **R. LNW**, 27, rue Général Patton, 9551 Wiltz **W:** radiolnw.eu - **FM:** 102.2 – **R. Diddeleng**, Place de l'hôtel de ville, 3590 Dudelange **W:** dudelangefm.lu - **FM:** 103.6 – **R. LRB**, B.P. 8, 3201 Bettembourg **W:** lrb.lu - **FM:** 103.9/105.7 – **R. Interculturelle**, 4 rue principale, 9370 Gilsdorf; **FM:** 103.9 – **R. Gudd Laun**, B.P.24, 4001 Esch/Alzette **W:** rgl.lu - **FM:** 106.1 – **R. Amizade**, 10 Rue du Parc, 3872 Schifflange - **FM:** 106.1 – **R. Classique vu Bergem - FM:** 106.1 – **R. Aktiv**, Rue du pont, 6471 Echternach **W:** radioaktiv106-5.org - **FM:** 106.5 – **R. Sympa**, 15 Rue René de Geysen, 4971 Dippach - **FM:** 106.5 – **ROM - Lokalradio vu Miedernach**, 28 rue Savelborn, 7660 Medernach **W:** rom.lu - **FM:** 106.5 – **R. Belle Vallée**, 312 Route d'Esch, 4451 Belvaux - **FM:** 107.0

MACAU (China, SAR)

L.T: UTC +8h — **Pop:**610,000 — **Pr.L:** Portuguese, Cantonese — **E.C:** 50Hz, 220V — **ITU:** MAC

TELEDIFUSÃO DE MACAU, SARL (Priv. Comm.)
🖳 Avenida Dr. Rodrigo Rodrigues, No. 223-225, Edificio Nam Kwong 7°Andar, Macau ☎ +853 28713025 🖷 +853 28717194 **E:** rmacau@tdm.com.mo **W:** tdm.com.mo
FM: 98.0MHz 2.5kW **D.Prgr:** Portuguese Sun-Thu 2300-1200, Fri & Sat 2400-1200, 100.7MHz 2.5kW **D.Prgr:** Cantonese and Chinese 24h

RÁDIO VILA VERDE LDA (Priv. Comm.)
🖳 Hipódromo da Taipa, Macau ☎ +853 28820338 🖷 +853 28820337 **E:** am738@am738.com **W:** am738.com
MW: 99.5MHz, suspended **D.Prgr:** Cantonese 24h

MACEDONIA

L.T: UTC +1h (27 Mar-30 Oct: +2h) — **Pop:** 2.1 million — **Pr.L:** Macedonian, Albanian — **E.C:** 50Hz, 220V — **ITU:** MKD

AGENCIJA ZA AUDIO I AUDIOVIZUELNI MEDIUMSKI USLUGI (AVMU) (Agency for Audio and Audiovisual Media Services)
🖳 bul. VMRO 3, 1000 Skopje ☎ +389 2 3103400 🖷 +389 2 3103401 **E:** contact@avmu.mk **W:** avmu.mk **L.P:** Dir: Zoran Trajcevski
NB: AVMU is the regulatory authority for broadcasting.

MAKEDONSKO RADIO TELEVIZIJA (MRT) (Pub)
🖳 bul. Goce Delcev bb, 1000 Skopje ☎ +389 2 519900 **E:** mrtvweb@gmail.com **W:** mrt.com.mk **L.P:** DG: Marjan Cvetkovski

MW	kHz	kW	Prgr	
Sveti Nikole	810	100	1, International Service	
FM (MHz)	1	2	3	kW
Belasica	91.5	97.8	106.8	10
Boskija	95.3	98.1	105.4	10
Bukovic	89.2	95.9	104.3	1
Cocon	88.8	93.8	98.1	1
Crn Vrv	97.3	94.1	101.3	100
Gevgelija	99.2	102.4	96.5	10
Golak	94.5	97.0	107.7	10
Mali Vlaj	93.3	97.7	91.0	10
Pelister	92.3	96.1	102.6	20
Popova Šapka	88.8	96.3	98.3	5
Stogovo	95.3	101.0	91.3	3
Tepavci	94.9	103.4	91.5	1
Turtel	93.3	90.5	99.7	50
Vodno	98.9	92.4	87.8	10

NB: Txs below 1kW not listed.
D.Prgr: Prgr 1 (R. Skopje): 24h. – **Prgr 2 (R. 2):** 24h – **Prgr 3 (R. Shkupi):** 24h in Albanian & other ethnic minority languages (Bosnian, Romany, Serbian, Turkish, Vlakh).
International Service (R. Makedonija): see Int. Radio section.

OTHER STATIONS

FM	MHz	kW	Location	Station
2)	89.7	1	Vodno	Kanal 77
A)	91.3	1	Skopje	RFI relay
1)	92.9	1	Pelister	Antena 5
1)	95.5	1	Vodno	Antena 5
1)	104.8	1	Turtel	Antena 5
1)	106.3	1	Boskija	Antena 5

NB: Txs below 1kW not listed.
Addresses & other information:
1) ul. Tetovska 35, 1000 Skopje. **E:** mail@antenna5.com.mk – **2)** ul. Josif Kovacev 18, 2000 Štip. **E:** kanal77@kanal77.com.mk – **A)** Rel. RFI (France)

MADAGASCAR

L.T: UTC +3h — **Pop:** 22 million — **Pr.L:** Malagasy, French — **E.C:** 50Hz, 220V — **ITU:** MDG

RADIO MADAGASIKARA - RADIO NATIONALE MALA-GASY (RNM, Pub.)
🖳 BP 4422, Anosy, 101 Antananarivo **W:** facebook.com/radio.mada-gasikara (stream on anio-info.com) **E:** r.radiomadagaskara@yahoo.fr ☎+261 20 2221745 🖷 +261 20 2232715 **L.P:** Dir: Johary Ravoa-janarahy.

MW	kHz	kW	H of tr
Fenoarivo	630	50	0300-1900

SW	kHz	kW	H of tr
Ambohidrano	v5010	10	0300-0500, 1500-1900
Ambohidrano	6135	30	0500-1500

All transmitters operate irregularly.
FM: Antananarivo 99.2MHz (0.5kW) & relay txs.
D.Prgr: 0300-1900 (SS 2200) in Malagasy & French.
Ann: Malagasy: "R. Madagasikara"; F: "R. Madagascar".

OTHER STATIONS

FM	MHz	kW	Location	Station
2)	88.6		Antananarivo	R. Fahazavana
	89.2		Antananarivo	BBCWS relay
3)	92.0		Antananarivo	Alliance FM (also r. RFI)
4)	93.4		Antananarivo	R. Don Bosco
5A)	94.4		Antananarivo	R. Tana
	96.0		Antananarivo	RFI
6)	96.6		Antananarivo	R. Des Jeunes
7)	97.6		Antananarivo	R. Antsiva
8)	98.2		Toamasina	R. Voanio
5B)	102.0		Antananarivo	R. 102
1)	105.0	0.75	Ambositra	R. Maria
9)	105.2		Antananarivo	Ma FM
10)	106.0		Antananarivo	R. Lazan larivo
11)	107.4		Antananarivo	R. FMFOI

NB: Unlicensed stns are operating in many parts of the country.
Addresses & other information:
1) W: radiomaria.org – **2)** BP 623, Lot II J 11, Faravohitra, Rue Joël Rakotomalala, 101 Antananarivo. **W:** radiofahazavana.agilityhoster. com – **3)** Enceinte Maison Laborde, Andohalo, 101 Antananarivo. **W:** alliancefr.mg/institution/part_dg.htm#alliance92 – **4)** BP 60, Maison Don Bosco, Ivato Airport, 105 Antananarivo. **W:** radiodonbosco.mg – **5A-B)** Enceinte Sitram, Ankorondrano, 101 Antananarivo. **W:** rta. mg . A) in Malagasy, B) in French –**6)** BP 4370, Immeuble Vitasoa, Analakely, 101 Antananarivo. **W:** rdeejay.net – **7)** BP 12170, Zone Zital Ankorondrano, Enceinte RTA, 101 Antananarivo. **W:** radio-antsiva. com –**8)** BP 489, 11 Rue Grandidier, 501 Toamasina. **W:** voanio.com – **9)** BP 1414, Ankorondrano, 101 Antananarivo. **W:** matv.mg – **10)** BP 6319, V.A 49 Andafiavaratra, 101 Antananarivo. **W:** rli106fm.com – **11)** Rue Docteur Ralarosy V W01, Ambohipotsy, 101 Antananarivo. **W:** fmfoi.ifrance.com

MADEIRA (Portugal)

L.T: UTC (27 Mar-30 Oct: +1h) — **Pop:** 300,000 — **Pr.L:** Portuguese — **E.C:** 50Hz, 220/380V —**ITU:** MDR

ANACOM-Autoridade Nacional de Comunicações, Delegação da Madeira
⌨ Rua do Vale das Neves, 19, São Gonçalo, 9050-332 Funchal
☎ +351 291 79 02 00 🖷+351 291 79 02 01

RÁDIO E TELEVISÃO DE PORTUGAL, S.A. (RTP)
Centro Regional da RTP-Madeira (radio & TV)
⌨ Caminho de Santo António, n.º 145 , 9020-002 Funchal ☎ +351 291 20 20 00 🖷 +351 291 23 07 53 **W:** rtp.pt **E:** rdpmadeira@rtp.pt
LP: Dir: Martim Santos

FM(MHz)	Ant. 1	Ant.2	Ant. 3	kW
Achada da Cruz	104.3		105.0	0.8
Cabo Girão	96.7	99.4	94.8	1/3/1
Calheta	105.4		107.5	0.1
Caniço	101.6	99.0	89.3	0.5
Encumeada	93.1		90.8	0.06
Gaula	98.5	106.3	91.3	1/0.7/1
Maçapez	92.0		95.7	0.1
Monte	104.6	102.4	89.8	1/1/0.7
Paúl da Serra	101.9		93.3	1
Pico do Areeiro	95.5		94.1	13/15
Pico do Facho	93.1		90.8	0.03
Ponta do Pargo	90.2		94.6	1
Porto Santo	100.5	103.3	96.5	10
Ribeira Brava	105.6		103.1	1
Santa Clara	104.6	102.4	89.8	1

D.Prgr: all networks 24h. Antena 1 of RDP Madeira provides regional prgrs M-F 0700-2000, Sat 0700-1800, Sun 0900-1800 LT; Antena 2 relays Lisboa 24h; Antena 3 Madeira carries own prgrs. M-F 0700-2400, Sat 0000-0300 & 0600-2400, Sun 0800-2400 LT. Technical info may be obtained from **W:** gabinete.tecnologias@rtp.pt
V. by QSL-card via RDP Lisboa

RÁDIO RENASCENÇA – Em. Católica Portuguesa (Rlg/Comm)
⌨ (see Portugal) - **FM:** Pico do Silva 88.0MHz 44kW (RR), 93.6MHz 44kW (RFM)

PEF – Posto Emissor de Radiodifusão do Funchal (Priv., comm.)
⌨ Rua Ponte de São Lázaro 3, 9000-027 Funchal ☎ +351 291 23 03 93 🖷 +351 291 22 17 97 **E:** pef@netmadeira.com **W:** pef.pt
MW: Funchal 1530kHz 3kW (nominal power: 10kW)
FM: Funchal 92.0MHz 2kW **D.Prgr:** 24h Relays R. Renascença, Lisboa, at certain times **Ann:** "PEF - a sua rádio regional"

Local FM stations:

FM	Island	Station & location	MHz	kW
4)	Madeira	R. Jornal da Madeira, Funchal	88.8	1
13)	Madeira	R. São Vicente, São Vicente	89.2	0.5
6)	Madeira	R. Zarco, Machico	89.6	1
9)	Pto Santo	R. Praia, Pto Santo	91.6	0.5
12)	Madeira	Santana FM, Santana	92.5	0.5
11)	Madeira	R. Palmeira, Santa Cruz	96.1	0.5
10)	Madeira	R. Festival, Ribeira Brava	98.4	0.5
1)	Madeira	R. Calheta, Calheta	98.8	0.5
5)	Madeira	R. Notícias/TSF, Funchal	100.0	2
2)	Madeira	R. Popular da Madeira, Câm. de Lobos	101.0	2
8)	Madeira	R. Porto Moniz, Porto Moniz	102.9	0.5
7)	Madeira	R. Sol, Ponta do Sol	103.7	0.5
3)	Madeira	R.Clube da Madeira, Funchal	106.8	0.4

+ five 50W repeaters used by three stns
Addresses and other information (add +351 to tel/fax nos):
1) & 12) Edifício Ondaparque, Av.ª D. Manuel I, 9370-133 Calheta ☎ 291 82 01 32/6, 🖷 291 82 01 38 **E:** radiocalheta@gmail.com, santana-fm@gmail.com **W:** radiocalheta.pt, santanafm.com.pt – **2), 3) & 10)** Rua Estados Unidos da América 147 a 150, Bairro da Nazaré, 9000-090 Funchal ☎ 291 766 101/ 291 761 068/ 291 762 984🖷 291 20 23 86 **E:** ssfranco75@gmail.com & radiofestival98.4@gmail.com **W:** radioclube. pt & radiosmadeira.net – **4)** Rua Dr. Fernão de Ornelas, 35-r/c, 9054-528 Funchal ☎ 291 210 42/448 🖷291 231 028 **E:** radio@jornaldama-deira.pt **W:** radio.jornaldamadeira.pt – **5)** Rua Fernão de Ornelas, 56-3°, 9050-021 Funchal ☎ 291 20 23 94/5/6 🖷 291 20 23 87; relays TSF Lisboa **E:** rmoliveira@dnoticias.pt **W:** dnoticias.pt/tsfmadeira – **6) & 11)** Conjunto Habitacional da Bemposta, Bloco 1, Água de Pena, 9200-012 Machico ☎ 291 526 896 & 291 526 961 **E:** radiozarcomachico@gmail.com & radiopalmeira96.1@gmail.com **W:** radiosmadeira.net –**7)** Estrada da Igreja da Piedade, 36, Canhas, 9360-301 Ponta do Sol☎ 291 982 782 **E:** radiopontadosol@gmail.com **W:** radiosmadeira.net – **8)** Bombeiros Voluntários de S. Vicente e Porto Moniz, Vila de S. Vicente, 9240 São Vicente ☎ 291 842 135 🖷 291 842 666 – **9)** Hotel Praia Dourada, Rua Dr. Estêvão Alencastre ☎ 291 98 01 30 🖷 291 980 137 **E:** radiopraia91.6fm@gmail.com **W:** radiopraia.com – **10)** (see 7) – **11)** (see 6) – **12)** Rua da Igreja, 8-3°, 9325-031 Estreito de Câmara de Lobos ☎ 291 573 830 🖷 291 573 833 **E:** santanafm@gmail.com noticiasra-dios@gmail.com **W:** santanafm.com.pt – **13)** Bombeiros Voluntários de São Vicente e Porto Moniz, Sítio do Pé do Passo, 9240-225 São Vicente ☎ 291 84 26 94 & 291 84 26 61 🖷 291 84 23 93

MALAWI

L.T: UTC +2h — **Pop:** 14 million — **Pr.L:** English, Chichewa, Tumbuka, Lomwe, Sena, Yao, Nkhonde, Tonga — **E.C:** 50Hz, 230V — **ITU:** MWI

MALAWI COMMUNICATIONS REGULATORY AUTHORITY (MACRA)
⌨ Salmon Amour Rd, Private Bag 261, Blantyre ☎+265 1 623611 🖷 +265 1 623890 **LP:** DG: Allexon Chiwaya. Dir of Broadc: Fegus Lipenga. **W:** macra.org.mw **E:** info@macra.org.mw

MALAWI BROADCASTING CORPORATION (MBC, Pub.)
⌨ P.O. Box 30133, Chichiri, Blantyre 3 ☎+265 1 871461 **W:** mbc.mw **E:** dgmbc@mbc.mw **LP:** DG: Dr. Benson Tembo. Ag. Dir. Prgr. & News: Hamilton Chimala. Dir. of Signal Distr. &Projects: Joseph Chikagwa.

MW	kHz	kW	MW	kHz	kW
Mangochi	540	10	Blantyre	756	10
Karonga	558	10	Bangula	‡810	10
Lilongwe	594	30	Chitipa	1404	10
Ekwendeni	675	50	Matiya	1422	10

FM	R1	R2FM	kW	FM	R1	R2FM	kW
Bangula	104.5	88.1	1.0	Ekwendeni	92.2	100.5	1
Chikangawa	105.9	103.0	1.0	Kanengo	94.7	91.5	5/1
Chitipa	90.7	100.5	1.0	Karonga	95.5	98.7	2
Dedza	90.1	104.5	1.0	Kasungu	94.5	96.2	1
Dwangwa	103.6	93.6	1	Mangochi	98.3	91.8	1

FM	R1	R2FM	kW	FM	R1	R2FM	kW
Mchinji	88.0	95.4	1	Ntchisi	100.5	92.4	2
Mpingwe	95.4	92.2	1/5	Salima	105.9	100.0	1
Nkhotakota	95.6	-	1	Zomba	94.1	96.8	2/5
Nsanje	95.5	94.4	0.05				

Radio 1 in English/Chichewa/Others on MW/FM: 24h.
Radio 2FM in English/Chichewa on FM: 24h.
Ann: E: R1: "Radio 1", R2: "Radio 2FM". Chichewa: "Kuno ndi ku Radio ya MBC".

Other stations (FM MHz):
R. Alinafe, Lilongwe: 97.1. **E:** radioalinafe@sdnp.org.mw — **Calvary Family Church R,** Blantyre 3: 105.8 0.25kW. **E:** calvaryministries@hot-mail.com — **Capital R:** Blantyre/Mzuzu 102.5, Dedza 105.2, Lilongwe 102.8, Zomba 96.1, all 1kW. **W:** capitalradiomalawi.com — **Channel For All Nations,** Lilongwe: 101.5 – **FM 101 Power:** (all txs 0.5/1kW): Ntcheu 88.1, Livingstonia 93.2, Chintheche 98.6, Mzuzu 99.0, Nkhoma 100.3, Blantyre/Lilongwe/Nkhota-kota 101, Dedza 103.9, Ntchisi 104, Dwangwa 107.2. **W:** fm101.malawi.net – **Joy R,** Blantyre: 89.6 – **MIJ FM:** Blantyre/Lilongwe/Mzuzu: 90.3 **W:** mijmw.net – **R. Islam:** Blantyre 97.6, Dedza 105.7, Dowa 89.7, Karonga 97.6, Lilongwe 97.6, Mtengo Wa Ung'ono 99.7, Mangochi 101.8, Mzuzu 97.0, Namwera 97.4, Zomba 102.9, all 1kW **W:** radioislam.org.mw – **R. Maria Malawi:** Mangochi 88.5 1kW, Dowa 94.0 1kW, Blantyre 99.2 1kW, Zomba 99.4 2kW, Dedza 99.7 2kW. **W:** radiomaria.mw – **Star FM,** Blantyre: 89.0 – **Trans World Radio Malawi:** Blantyre 89.1, Ntchis 90.7, Mvera 91.1, Dedza 96.4, Yawo 106.2, Chikangawa/Zomba 106.4, Lilongwe 106.5, Thyolo 107.1, all 2kW. **W:** twrmalawi.wordpress.com – **Ufulu FM:** Blantyre 92.5MHz **W:** ufulufm.com — **YONECO FM:** Lilongwe 90.0, Blantyre 101.9, Zomba 101.9, Mzuzu 104.0 **W:** yoneco. org – **Zodiak BS:** Chitipa 89.5, Dedza 89.0, Dowa 92.9, Karonga 93.7, Lilongwe 95.1, Livingstonia 95.0, Mpingwe 97.0, Mzuzu 95.1, Namwera 103.3, Zomba 89.3. **W:** zbsmw.com
BBC African Sce: Mzuzu 87.9, Lilongwe 98.0, Blantyre 98.1

MALAYSIA

L.T: UTC +8h — **Pop:** 30.3 million — **Pr.L:** Bahasa Malaysia (Malay), English, Chinese. In West Malaysia also Tamil and various Orang Asli languages, East Malaysia also 12 local languages or dialects — **E.C:** 50Hz, 240V — **ITU:** UTC.

MALAYSIAN COMMUNICATIONS AND MULTIMEDIA COMMISSION (MCMC) (Suruhan Komunikasi dan Multimedia Malaysia, SKMM)
Regulatory body for the communications & multimedia industries.
✉ 63000 Cyberjaya, Selangor ☎ +60 3 8688 8000 🖷 +60 3 8688 1000 **W:** skmm.gov.my **L.P:** Chairman: YBhg. Dato' Mohamed Sharil Mohamed Tarmizi

JABATAN PENYIARAN MALAYSIA (Dept of Broadcasting of Malaysia) (Gov.)
Parent body of RTM ✉ Angkasapuri, 50614 Kuala Lumpur ☎ +60 3 2282 5333 🖷 +60 3 2282 5103

RADIO TELEVISION MALAYSIA - RTM (Gov.)
✉ Dept. of Broadcasting, Angkasapuri, Bukit Putra, 50614 Kuala Lumpur ☎ +60 3 2282 5333 🖷 +60 3 2282 4735 **W:** rtm.gov.my **E:** teknikalradio@rtm.net.my
L.P: DG: Datuk Norhyati Ismail. Prgr Dir (Radio): Dr Nawiyah Che Lah. Dir. Tech. Sces: Hj Ab. Wahid Bin Ab. Hamid
SW: Kajang:

kHz	kW	Sce.	H of tr	kHz	kW	Sce.	H of tr
5965†	100	1	24h	7295	100	4	24h
6050†	50	1	24h				

† = Rel. Asyik FM 0000-1500, rel. Salam FM 1500-2400. ±) variable.
5965 & 7295kHz inactive at editorial deadline.

FM (MHz)	Site	1	2	4	5	6	kW
Alor Setar	a	94.9	100.5	98.7	101.3	96.7	5
Balik Pulau	b	99.5	93.9	88.5	92.1	98.9	0.1
Baling	c	88.7	89.7	91.7	92.5	93.3	1
Besut	d	94.3	98.8	97.0	97.8	95.3	0.1
Cameron	e	89.1	93.1	101.1	103.5	104.3	0.1
Dungun	f	95.9	96.9	98.9	99.7	100.7	1
Gerik	g	97.8	95.4	98.4	100.8	100.0	0.1
Ipoh	h	88.3	90.9	90.1	92.1	98.9	1
Jeli	i	88.4	89.2	90.8	91.6	92.4	0.1
Jerantut	j	88.1	93.5	89.9	90.7	91.9	0.1
Johor Bahru	k	106.7	105.7	102.9	104.9	101.1	5
Kota Bharu	l	101.1	101.9	104.7	105.7	106.7	5

FM (MHz)	Site	1	2	4	5	6	kW
Kuala Lumpur	m	87.7	88.5	90.3	89.3	92.3	1
KL2		98.3	95.3	100.1	106.7	96.3	1
KT	o	92.5	91.7	89.7	90.5	87.9	1
Kuantan	p	107.9	107.1	105.3	106.1	103.3	1
Machang	q	95.5	96.5	98.5	99.3	100.9	2
Maran	r	87.9	91.2	94.7	89.6	90.4	
Melaka	s	93.6	96.6	97.4	100.4	103.3	0.5
Mersing	t	90.1	90.9	92.9	89.1	88.3	1
Seremban	u	87.9	91.7	88.7	89.7	90.5	0.1
Sik	w	99.5	102.7	105.9	106.7	107.5	1
Taiping	x	103.3	107.1	105.3	106.1	107.9	0.5
Tapah		88.7	-	-	-	-	0.5
U. Tembeling	z	90.1	88.5	-	87.5	-	0.1

National networks 1-6: see below. KL2=KL/Selangor/Pahang (West). KT=Kuala Terengganu.
Sites: a) Gunung Jerai, b) Bukit Genting (Penang) c) Bukit Palong, d) Bukit Bintang, e) Gunung Berinchang, f) Bukit Bauk, g) RTM Gerik h) Bukit Keledang, i) Bukit Tangki Air, j) Bukit Istana, k) Gunung Pulai, l) Telipot, m) Menara KL (Bukit Nanas), n) Gunung Ulu Kali, o) Bukit Besar, p) Bukit Pelindung, q) Bukit Bakar, r) Gunung Ledang (Mt Ophir), s) Bukit Tinggi, t) Bukit Telapa Burok, u) RTM Seremban, v) Bukit Dedap, w) Bukit Larut (Maxwell Hill) x) Changkat Rembian, z) Kampung Bantal, Ulu Tembeling

Asyik FM/Salam FM: Cameron Highlands 105.1MHz, Gunung Ledang 95.6MHz, Gunung Ulu Kali 102.5MHz, Kuala Lumpur 91.1MHz, Ulu Tembeling 89.3MHz, RTM Gerik 96.7MHz

NB: All **FM** powers throughout are TRP

RTM national services
(1) Klasik Nasional FM (R. Klasik): 24h news, information & Malay oldies presented in Malay. **(2) Nasional FM:** 24h General sce presented in Malay. **(4) Traxx FM:** 24h News, music and travel sce in English. **(5) Ai FM:** 24h General Sce in Chinese (Mandarin exc. news at 0200 in Hakka, 0500 Cantonese, 0700 Hakka & 1300 Chaozhou). **(6) Minnal FM:** 24h General sce in Tamil. **Asyik FM:** 0000-1500 for Orang Asli in Jakun, Malay, Semai, Temiar & Temuan. **Salam FM:** Rlg. prgrs in Malay from Jabatan Kemajuan Islam Malaysia 1500-2400 **V.** occasionally by letter or Email. **Ann:** names of networks and regional sces are sometimes preceded by the words "Radio Malaysia".

RTM regional services in West Malaysia:
Most sces. operate 24h in Malay. Exceptions include Langkawi, which carries local & tourist information in English and Malay. Some sces relay RTM Klasik Nasional overnight. Refer to above lists for tx sites and powers for frequencies marked a-y
Johor: Johor FM (JFM), Karung Berkunci 716, 80990 Johor Bahru, Johor. On 92.1MHz t, 101.9MHz k, 105.3MHz s – **Kedah:** Kedah FM, Kompleks Penerangan dan Penyiaran Sultan Abdul Halim, KM 3, Jalan Kuala Kedah, 05400 Alor Setar, Kedah. On 88.5MHz Selama-Bandar Baharu (site Bukit Sungai Kecil Hilir) 0.25kW, 90.5MHz b, 97.5MHz a, 105.1MHz w, 105.7MHz Gunung Raya 1kW, 107.0MHz Kuah – **Kelantan:** Kelantan FM, Peti Surat 143, 15720 Kota Bharu, Kelantan. On 88.1MHz FELDA Paloh 1kW, 97.3MHz q 102.9MHz l, 92.0MHz Gua Musang 0.1kW, 90.0MHz i, 88.9MHz Taman Wangi 0.1kW, 107.1MHz d – **Kuala Lumpur:** KL.fm On 97.2MHz m – **Langkawi (Kedah):** Langkawi FM, Tingkat 2, Bangunan Tabung Haji, Jalan Padang Mat Sirat, 07000 Kuah, Langkawi. On 87.5MHz Kuah 0.1kW, 104.8MHz Gunung Raya 1kW **English:** 0100-0400, 0700-1000 Malay/English 1300-1600 – **Melaka:** Melaka FM (MFM), Jalan Taming Sari, 75614 Melaka. On 102.3MHz s – **Negeri Sembilan:** Negeri FM, Jalan Raja Ali, 71000 Seremban, Negeri Sembilan. On 92.5MHz u, 95.7MHz Gunung Tampin 0.1kW, 107.7MHz s – **Pahang:** Pahang FM, Peti Surat 152, 25710 Kuantan, Pahang. On 104.1MHz p, 107.5MHz n, 100.3MHz e, 92.7MHz j, 88.0MHz Bandar Muadzam Shah (Bukit Sembilan), 92.0MHz r 0.25kW, 91.9MHz Rompin 0.25kW – **Perak:** Perak FM, Jalan Dairy, 31400 Ipoh, Perak. On 89.6MHz Bukit Asa, 94.2MHz Lenggong (Bukit Ladang Teh) 0.025kW, 94.7MHz e, 96.2MHz g, 95.6MHz h, 97.3MHz Changkat Rembian 0.5kW, 104.1MHz x – **Perlis:** Perlis FM, Tingkat 6, Bangunan WSP, Jalan Bukit Lagi, 01000 Kangar, Perlis. On 102.9MHz Pauh 2kW – **Pulau Pinang (Penang):** Mutiara FM, Jalan Burmah, Peti Surat 433, 10350 Pulau Pinang. On 90.9MHz b, 93.9MHz a, 95.7MHz Bukit Penara 1kW – **Selangor:** Selangor FM Bangunan Sultan Salehudin Abdul Aziz Shah, 40000 Shah Alam, Selangor. On 100.9MHz n – **Terengganu:** Terengganu FM, Peti Surat 63, 20914 Kuala Terengganu, Terengganu. On 88.7MHz o, 96.2MHz c, 97.7MHz f, 90.0MHz FELDA Cerul

RADIO TELEVISION MALAYSIA SABAH (Gov)
✉ 2.4km, Tuaran Road, Beg Berkunci 2022, 88614 Kota Kinabalu ☎ +60 88 213444 🖷 +60 88 223493

Addresses of local stns: ✉ Tingkat 6, Wisma Persekutuan, W.D.T. 52, 90500 Sandakan - Peti Surat 606, 91008 Tawau - Aras Bawah Rumah Persekutuan Keningau, Peti Surat 424, 89008 Keningau
LP: Dir. Broadcasting: Encik Zubad Ibrahim. Dir. Tech. (R.): Abdul Jalani bin Mahmud. Dep. Dir. (R. Prgr): Tuan Haji Hashim Jaffrey

RADIO TELEVISION MALAYSIA LABUAN (Gov)
✉ 5004 Tanjung Taras, Peti Surat 299, 87008 WP Labuan ☎ +60 87 415677 🖷 +60 87 416658

MW	kHz	kW	Netw.	H of tr			
Kudat	801	10	SF	2130-0800			

FM (MHz)	Tx	SF	SV	1	2	4	5	kW
FELDA S		104.1	106.7	99.9	102.9	104.9	105.7	0.1
Gadong	b	89.3	92.6	88.0	88.9	90.7	91.6	0.1
Kota Belud	c	101.5	104.1	99.9	100.7	102.5	103.3	0.1
K. Kinabalu	d	89.9	92.7	88.1	88.9	90.7	91.9	1
Kudat	e	95.9	98.9	94.1	94.9	96.7	98.1	1
Labuan	f	-	93.3	87.6	88.5	90.3	92.3	0.1
Lahad Datu	g	89.7	92.6	87.9	88.7	90.5	91.7	1
Langkon		97.1	91.1	101.6	90.1	89.0	87.7	0.1
Layang-L.	h	104.5	107.1	99.9	100.3	105.3	106.3	1
Luasong		-	-	87.7	88.5	89.3	90.1	0.1
Sandakan	j	92.9	96.1	91.1	92.1	94.3	95.1	1
Sipitang	k	97.9	102.9	95.5	96.5	99.1	99.9	1
Tawau	l	95.7	99.3	93.9	94.7	97.1	98.1	1
Tenom	m	90.3	93.1	88.5	89.3	91.7	92.3	1

Sites: , a) FELDA Sahabat, b) Bukit Gadong, c) Bukit Pompoda d) Kota Kinabalu (Bukit Lawa Mandau) e) Bukit Kelapa, f) Bukit Timbalai, g) Gunung Silam, h) Layang-Layang (Mount Kinabalu) j) Bukit Trig, k) Bukit Tampulagus, l) Gunung Andrassy, m) Bukit Sigapon
National networks: 1-5: see RTM national sces above
State networks: SF= Sabah FM in Malay 24h. **Reg. N:** 2200, 2330, 0400, 0530, 0830, 1400. **SV=** Sabah V FM in **English** 0400-0700 & 1800-2000, Mandarin 0100-0400 inc. news in Hakka at 0100, Bajau 0700-1100 & 2000-2300, Dusun 1300-1700, Kadazan 2030-0100 & 0600-0830, Murut 1100-1300 & 1700-1800. **N.** (English): 0500
Local Sces: Labuan FM on 89.4MHz 0.1kW (Bukit Timbalai) & 103.7MHz 0.1kW (RTM Labuan): 2145-1200 inc. English 0100-0300 – Tawau FM on 93.6MHz 1 kW (Guning Silam), 99.1MHz 0.1kW (FELDA Sahabat), 100.1MHz 1kW (Gunung Andrassy): 2245-1100 in Malay – Sandakan FM on 90.1MHz 1kW (Bukit Trig): 2150-1000 – Keningau FM on 94.7 (Tenom), 98.1MHz (Keningau): 2300-0900 in Malay, Dusun and Murut

RADIO TELEVISION MALAYSIA SARAWAK (Gov.)
✉ Broadcasting House, Jalan P. Ramlee, 93614 Kuching ☎ +60 82 248422 🖷 +60 82 246523
LP: Dir. Broadcasting:Tuan Haji Monshi Abdullah
Addresses of local stns: Bangunan Penyiaran, 98700 Limbang – Bangunan Penyiaran, Jalan Brighton, 98000 Miri – Bangunan Penyiaran, 96009 Sibu – Bangunan Penyiaran, 95000 Sri Aman– Bangunan Penyiaran, Jalan Sommerville, Bintulu

Stations: Kajang (near Kuala Lumpur).

SW	kHz	kW	Netw.	SW	kHz	kW	Netw.
Kajang	9835	100	SF	Kajang	11665	100	W

FM (MHz)	Tx	SF	Red	1	2	4	5	kW
Belaga		105.4	107.8	103.8	104.6	106.2	107.0	0.1
Betong	a	94.4	97.8	92.8	93.6	95.2	96.0	0.1
Bintulu	b	93.7	100.5	87.9	90.3	98.5	99.3	1
Bintulu	c	94.7	96.7	-	-	-	-	1
Dalat		-	96.9					0.1
Kapit	d	92.7	89.9	90.7	91.9	88.1	88.9	0.1
Kuching	e	88.9	91.9	92.9	88.1	89.9	90.7	10
Lambir Hills	f	88.1	90.7	91.9	92.7	88.9	89.9	1
Lawas	g	97.5	100.5	94.7	96.7	98.5	99.3	0.1
Limbang	h	101.5	104.1	97.1	98.1	102.3	103.3	1
Limbang	j	100.0	107.7	95.3	99.2	106.0	106.8	0.1
Marudi	k	-	-	102.9	-	-	-	1
Miri	l	100.3	106.3	107.1	99.3	104.5	105.3	0.1
Mukah		89.3	92.3	88.3	89.1	90.7	91.5	0.5
Sarikei	m	91.5	89.2	87.9	90.3	92.3	93.6	10
Serian	n	94.8	97.2	98.0	94.0	95.6	96.4	0.5
Sibu	o	101.5	104.1	95.5	98.5	102.5	103.3	0.1
Song	p	95.7	99.0	-	-	-	-	1
Sri Aman	q	100.3	106.3	107.3	98.9	92.3	105.3	1
Stapong	r	95.1	101.1	93.3	94.1	95.9	97.1	1

SF=Sarawak FM, W=Wai FM, Red=Red FM L=Limbang FM S=Sibu
National networks: 1, 2, 4, 5: see RTM national sces
SW: 9835kHz: 2200-1600 (rel. Sarawak FM), 11665kHz: 2200-1600 (rel. Wai FM)
FM: Additional local sce. freqs: Gunung Serapi (Kuching) 101.3MHz

10kW (Wai FM Iban) & 106.1MHz (Wai FM Bidayuh / Kayan-Kenyah), Bukit Ampangan 101.7MHz 0.5kW (Wai FM Bidayuh / Kayan-Kenyah) & 106.9MHz 0.5kW (Wai FM Iban)
Sites: a) Off. Spaoh b) Bukit Setiam c) Bukit Nyabau d) Bukit Kapit e) Gunung Serapi f) Bukit Lambir g) Bukit Tiong h) Bukit Mas j) Bukit Sagan Rudang, k) Bukit Kayu Malam, l) RTM Miri, m) Bukit Dabei, n) Bukit Ampangan o) Bukit Lima p) Bukit Song q) Bukit Temunduk r) Bukit Singgalang.
State networks: Sarawak FM in Malay 24h. **N.** (Kuching): 2200, 0400, 1000, 1400. **Red FM** 2200-1600, in Chinese: 2200-0200, 0700-1300; English: 0200-0700, 1300-1600. Educational prgs during school terms: MF 0100-0300. **N.** (Kuching): English 0400, 0700, 1300; Chinese 0000, 0801, 1000, 1245; Hakka 1030; Hokkien 1045. **Wai FM:** 2200-1600 in Iban. Relays Limbang FM Mon/Thurs 1300-1400. **Wai FM:** 2200-1600, in Bidayuh 2200-0400 & 1000-1600; Kayan/Kenyah: 0400-1000. FM txs of all state networks relay Sarawak FM 1600-2200
Local sces: Bintulu FM: 0100-1100 in Malay and Iban. Bukit Nyabau 97.5MHz 1kW. **Limbang FM:** in Malay 0100-0400, 1000-1300; Lun Bawang (Murut) 0400-0700, also relayed via Kuching 7270kHz; Bisaya 0700-1000; Iban 1300-1400 also relayed by Wai FM Iban Mon/Thurs. Bukit Mas 104.9MHz 1kW, Bukit Tiong 101.1MHz 0.1kW, Bukit Sagan Rudang 94.5MHz 0.1kW. **Miri FM:** in Malay 0000-0300, 1000-1300, Chinese 0700-1000, Iban 0400-0700, Kenyah 0300-0400. Lambir Hills 95.7MHz 1kW, Miri (RTM Miri) 98.0MHz 0.1kW. **Sibu FM:** in Malay 0100-0400, 1000-1300, Chinese 0700-1000, Iban 0400-0700. Bukit Lima 87.6MHz 0.1kW, Bukit Kayu Malam 94.6MHz 1kW, Bukit Song 99.8MHz, Bukit Kapit 94.3MHz 0.1kW, Belaga 103.0MHz 0.1kW, Bukit Singgalang 102.1MHz 1kW, Mukah 98.7MHz 0.5kW. **Sri Aman (RaSa FM):** in Malay, Iban, Chinese. Bukit Temunduk 89.5MHz 1kW. **NB** Local sces relay Wai FM Iban 2200-0100 and from close of local prgrs until 1600, and relay Sarawak FM 1600-2200
IS: A musical phrase (played on a native instrument, the Sape), alternating between A and F

ASTRO RADIO SDN. BHD. (Comm.)
✉ All Asia Broadcast Centre, Technology Park Malaysia, Bukit Jalil, 57000 Kuala Lumpur **W:** astroradio.com.my
LP: CEO: Mr Jake Abdullah

FM(MHz)	Tx	MY	ERA	Lite	Mix	Hitz	Sin	Mel	THR
Alor Setar	a	99.7	103.6	104.4	91.0	92.3	97.1	106.5	102.4
Ipoh	b	100.6	103.7	101.5	94.3	92.7	96.9	98.5	102.7
Johor Bahru	c	95.4	104.5	94.6	99.1	97.6	87.8	98.4	103.7
Johor Bahru	d							103.3	
Kota Bharu	e	102.3	103.3	104.3	94.6	92.8	93.8	99.8	88.1+
KK	f	104.0	102.4	103.2	101.6	100.8	104.9	98.6	-
KT	g	101.2	102.8	105.9	98.3	94.8	97.5	104.0	100.2+
KL/Selangor	h	101.8	103.3	105.7	94.5	92.9	96.7	103.0	99.3
Kuantan	i	101.1	98.0	104.7	94.1	93.2	97.2	100.0	88.8+
Kuching	j	96.9	96.1	100.1	97.7	95.3	102.1	103.7	-
Langkawi	k	100.1	90.7	-	-	92.4	100.9	-	101.9
Melaka	l	106.4	90.3	92.2	91.1	93.0	96.0	107.3	99.7
Miri	m	103.2	101.3	-	-	105.8	87.7	102.4	-
Penang								-	99.3
Sandakan	no	100.6	103.0	-	102.2		99.8	104.6	-
Seremban	o	100.6	103.6	104.6	94.3	95.0	96.9	97.9	101.5
Taiping	1q	100.2	95.2	89.3	91.3	93.6	96.4	109.9	102.1
Tapah	r	-	102.0	-					

Prgrs: MY FM: Music channel in Mandarin & Cantonese. **ERA:** Contemporary Malaysian music channel in Malay. **Lite FM:** Easy listening music in English. **Mix FM:** Music and variety in English. **Hitz. fm:** Top 40 presented in English. **Sinar FM:** Malay oldies. **Melody FM:** Programming in Chinese. **THR Raaga:**Music and traffic information presented in Tamil: 24h. **THR Gegar:** Separate prgrs in Malay for East Coast on freqs marked +
Sites: a) Gunung Jerai b) Bukit Keledang c) Gunung Pulai d) Metropolis Tower, JB e) Bukit Panau f) Kota Panau (Bukit Kokol) g) Kuala Terengganu (Bukit Jerung) h) Gunung Ulu Kali i) Bukit Pelindong j) Bukit Djin k) Gunung Raya l) Gunung Ledang m) Tanjong Lobang n) Bukit Penara o) Bukit Trig p) Telapa Barok q) Bukit Larut r) Changkat Rembian.
TRP: generally 2kW, exc. Sinar FM at sites e, f, j, k and l: 0.25kW, THR 1kW exc 0.5kW at sites b, n and q.

BFM MEDIA (Comm.)
✉ 5.01 Wisma BU8, 11 Lebuh Bandar Utama, 47800 Petaling Jaya ☎ +60 3 7629 7112 **W:** bfm.my **LP:** Exec. Dir: Malek Ali
BFM: Kuala Lumpur/Klang Valley (Gunung Ulu Kali) 89.9MHz, 24h business prgrs and music in E and Malay

DIGITAL MEDIA BROADCASTING SDN. BHD. (Bernama News Agency) (Gov.)
✉ 15th Fl, Wisma Bernama, 28 Jalan 1/65A, off Jalan Tun Razak,

53300 Kuala Lumpur ☎+60 3 2692 7939 🖷 +60 3 2692 8939
W: radio24.com.my
Bernama Radio24: Kuala Lumpur/Klang Valley (Bukit Nanas), 93.9MHz 1kW & Johor Bahru (Gunung Pulai) 107.5MHz 1kW, 24h in E and Malay

GENMEDIA SDN. BHD.
(1Malaysia for Youth) (Comm.)
🖃 Unit C-06-11, Block C, Plaza Mont Kiara, 55100 Kuala Lumpur ☎ +60 3 6206 4848 **W:** 1m4youth.my
1M4U FM: Kuala Lumpur/Klang Valley (Bukit Sungai Besi) 107.9MHz, 24h prgr. for young people and volunteers in E and Malay.

HUSA NETWORK SDN. BHD. (Comm.)
🖃 Tingkat 2&3, Bangunan Epic Pavilion, Jalan Pejabat, 20200 Kuala Terangganu ☎ +60 9 6262255 🖷 +60 9 6262266
W: manis.fm
Manis FM: Kota Bharu (Bangunan Billion) 90.6MHz, Kuantan (Bukit Pelindong) 95.1MHz, Kuala Terengganu (Bukit Jerung) 102.0MHz. Prgrs in Malay. **TRP:** all sites 2kW

INSTITUT KEFAHAMAN ISLAM MALAYSIA (Institute of Islamic Understanding) (Gov., Rlg.)
🖃 No 2, Langgak Tunku, Off Jalan Duta, 50480 Kuala Lumpur ☎+60 3 62046273 🖷 +60 3 620462779 **W:** ikimfm.my
L.P: Dir. of R.: Nik Roskiman bin Abdul Samad

FM	Tx	MHz	FM	Tx	MHz
Alor Setar	a	89.0	Kuching	h	93.6
Ipoh	b	102.7	Lahad Datu		107.3
Johor Bahru	c	106.2	Melaka	j	89.5
Kota Bharu	d	89.9	Miri		104.0
Kota Kinabalu	e	90.3	Negeri Sembilan	k	102.7
Kuala Lumpur	i	91.5	Penang (Balik Pulau)	l	102.7
Kuala Terengganu	f	100.2	Tawau		100.7
Kuantan	g	89.5			

Radio Ikim (IKIM.FM): 24h in Malay with limited Arabic and English. **Sites:** a) Gunung Jerai, b) Bukit Keledang, c) Gunung Pulai, d) Bukit Panau, e) Bukit Kokol, f) Bukit Besar, g) Bukit Pelindong 2, h) Pending, i) Bukit Cincin, j) Gunung Ledang, k) Gunung Telapa Burok l) Bukit Genting. **TRP:** sites a-k: 2kW

KRISTAL HARTA SDN. BHD. (CATS RADIO) (Comm.)
🖃 Lot 287, Jalan Bako, Petra Jaya, 93050 Kuching, Sarawak ☎ +60 82 311799 🖷 +60 82 254993 **W:** catsfm.my **L.P:** Chmn: Tan Sri Datuk Amar Haji Bujang Mohd Nor. GM: Haji Mohd Iskandar Hajni Mohd Nawawi

FM	Tx location	MHz	FM	Tx location	MHz
Bintulu	Bukit Setiam	88.3	Sarikei	Bt. K. Malam	96.7
Kuching	Gunung Serapi	99.3	Sibu	Bukit Lima	88.4
Limbang	Bukit Mas	88.7	Sibu	Bt. Singgalang	99.9
Miri	Lambir Hills	93.3	Sri Aman	Bt. Temudok	88.7
Mukah	Mukah	97.9			

Prgr: 24h in Malay, E and Iban. **TRP:** all sites 1kW

LAUREATE SDN. BHD.
Ultra FM: Kuala Lumpur/Klang Valley (Bukit Sungai Besi) 101.3MHz, 24h in Malay.
Pi Mai FM: Penang (Bukit Penara) 90.2MHz, 24h in Malay.

MEDIA PRIMA BHD. (Comm.)
🖃 Tingkat 2, South Wing, Sri Pentas, Persiaran Bandar Utama, 47800 Petaling Jaya, Selangor Darul Ehsan ☎ +60 3 77105022 🖷 +60 3 77107098 **W:** hotfm.com.my or flyfm.com.my or onefm.com.my
L.P: Head of Radio Ntwks: Ahmad Izham Omar

FM(MHz)	Tx	Hot	Fly	One	FM(MHz)	Tx	Hot	Fly	One
Alor Setar	a	88.2	99.1	87.8	Kuantan	h	92.4	87.6	100.4
Ipoh	b	104.5	87.9	87.6	Kuching	i	94.3	-	98.3
Johor Bahru	c	90.1	102.5	105.3	Melaka	j	104.3	94.0	88.1
Kota Bharu	d	105.1	107.4	-	Penang	k	-	89.9	-
Kota Kinabalu	e	87.7	-	95.7	Seremban	l	99.5	98.6	88.3
KL/Selangor	f	97.6	95.8	88.1	Taiping	m	90.5	-	-
KT	g	105.0	107.5	-					

Hot FM: 24h in Malay. Hot FM freqs are licensed to Synchrosound Studios Sdn Bhd. **Fly FM:** 24h in English/Malay. FlyFM freqs are licensed to Malaysian Airports (Sepang) Sdn. Bhd. **One FM:** 24h in Mandarin and Cantonese.
Sites: a) Gunung Jerai exc. 99.1MHz: Wisma PKNK, Alor Setar b) Bukit Keledang c) Gunung Pulai exc. 105.3MHz: Taman Sentosa, JB d)

Peringat e) Hot FM: Bukit Kokol, One FM: Bukit Karatong f) Gunung Ulu Kali g) Kuala Terengganu h) Bukit Pelindung i) Hot FM: Gunung Serapi, One FM: Bukit Djin j) Gunung Ledang k) Bukit Penara l) Bukit Telapa Burok exc. One FM: Bukit Gan m) Bukit Larut. **TRP:** Fly FM 0.25kW exc. Bukit Cincin: 2kW

RIMAKMUR SDN. BHD. (Comm.)
🖃 Tropicana City Office Towers, Level 2.01, No. 3, Jalan SS 20/27, 47400 Petaling Jaya, Selangor Darul Ehsan ☎ +60 3 78851188 🖷 +60 3 78851099 **W:** suriafm.com.my **L.P:** COO: Engku Emran Engku Zainal Abidin

FM	Tx	MHz	FM	Tx	MHz
Alor Setar	a	106.9	Kuala Terengganu	g	102.4
Ipoh	b	96.0	Kuantan	h	96.1
Johor Bahru	c	101.4	Melaka	i	88.5
Klang Valley (KL)	d	105.3	Seremban	j	107.0
Kota Bharu	e	106.1	Taiping	k	91.7
Kota Kinabalu	f	105.9			

Suria FM: 24h in Malay. **Sites:** a) Gunung Jerai b) Bukit Keledang c) Gunung Pulai d) Gunung Ulu Kali e) Bukit Panau f) Bukit Kokol g) Bukit Besar h) Bukit Pelindong 2 i) Gunung Ledang j) Gunung Telapa Burok k) Bukit Larut. Kota Kinabalu 105.9MHz carries local prgrs at times.

SENANDUNG SONIK SDN. BHD. (Comm.)
Tea FM: Kota Kinabalu (Bukit Keratong) 102.8MHz, Kuching (Bukit Antu) 102.7MHz. 24h in Chinese.

STAR MEDIA GROUP (Comm.)
🖃 Concorde Hotel, Jalan Sultan Ismail, Kuala Lumpur **W:** capitalfm.com.my
Capital FM: Kuala Lumpur/Klang Valley (Gunung Ulu Kali) 88.9MHz, Penang (Bukit Penara) 107.6MHz: 24h in E and Malay

STAR RFM SDN. BHD. (Comm.)
🖃 Tropicana City Office Towers Level 2.01 No 3, Jalan SS20/27, 47400 Petaling Jaya, Selangor Darul Ehsan ☎ +60 3 78851188 🖷 +60 3 78851099 **W:** 988.com.my or red.fm **E:** info@starrfm.com.my or rfm988@silicon.net.my

FM(MHz)	Tx	Red	988	FM(MHz)	Tx	Red	988
Alor Setar	a	98.1	96.1	Kuantan	e	91.6	90.4
Ipoh	b	106.4	99.8	Melaka	f	98.9	98.2
Johor Bahru	c	92.8	99.9	Penang	g	-	94.5
KL/Selangor	d	104.9	98.8	Seremban	h	-	93.3

Red FM: 24h in English & Malay. **988** (jiu ba ba): 24h in Mandarin & Chinese dialects. **Sites:** a) Gunung Jerai b) Gunung Keledang c) Gunung Pulai d) Gunung Ulu Kali e) Bukit Pelindong f) Gunung Ledang g) Bukit Penara h) Bkt Telapa Burok i) Bukit Larut

SUARA JOHOR (Comm.)
🖃 Bukit Pelangi, Jalan Pasir Pelangi, 80050 Johor Bahru, Johor ☎ +60 7 3314104 🖷 +60 7 3351104 **L.P:** CEO: Haji Bakhtiar Haji Arshad
BEST 104: Melaka & Segamat (Gunung Ledang) 94.8MHz, Johor Bahru (Gunung Pulai) 104.1MHz 10kW TRP, Kuala Lumpur/Selangor (Gunung Ulu Kali) 104.1MHz, Mersing (Bukit Tinggi) 102.5MHz
D.Prgr: 24h (Malay & E music)

University stations:
Putra FM, 🖃 Tingkat 2 Jabatan Komunikasi, Fakulti Bahasa Moden dan Komunikasi, Universiti Putra Malaysia, 43400 UPM Serdang, Selangor **W:** putrafm.upm.edu.my
Station: 90.7MHz 1kW: Mon-Fri 0200-1600 in Malay & E
Radio UiTM (UFM), 🖃 Level 13, Menara Ilmu Universiti Teknologi MARA, 40450 Bandaraya Shah Alam, Selangor **W:** uitm.edu.my/ufm
Station: 93.6MHz 1kW
KK FM, 🖃 University Malaysia Sabah (UMS), Jalan UMS, 88400 Kota Kinabalu, Sabah **W:** kkfm.my **Station:** 91.1MHz

MALDIVES

LT: UTC +5h — **Pop:** 400,000 — **Pr.L:** Dhivehi (Maldivian) — **E.C:** 50Hz, 230V — **ITU:** MLD

MALDIVES BROADCASTING CORPORATION (MBC, Pub.)
🖃 M Radio Bldg, Buruzu, Magu, Male ☎+960 3000200 🖷 +960 3317273 **W:** mbc.mv **E:** info@mbc.mv **L.P:** MD: Ibrahim Khaleel. Asst. Eng: Mohammed Hashim.
MW: 1449kHz 10kW. **"Dhivehi Raajjeyge Adu"** (Vo Maldives) 1449kHz in Dhivehi: 24h. English: 1300-1315.
FM: Male 91.0MHz 1kW, 103.8MHz 20W, Addu 90.0MHz 500W, Foahmula 89.0MHz 0.5kW. **"Rajjee FM"** (music channel) on 91.0MHz.

R. Eke (music, sports & entertainment) on 103.8MHz: 1745-0020.
Ann: MW: "Mee Dhivehi Raajjeyge Adu".

Other stations:
Capital R, Male: 95.6MHz 1 kW – **Dhi FM,** Male: 95.2MHz. **W:** dhifm.mv – **Faraway FM,** Male: 96.9MHz – **H FM,** Male: 92.6MHz. **W:** hfm.com.mv

MALI

L.T: UTC — **Pop:** 13 million — **Pr.L:** French, Bambara, Peuls, Sonrhai, Sarakolé, Bobo, others — **E.C:** 50Hz, 220V — **ITU:** MLI

CONSEIL SUPÉRIEUR DE LA COMMUNICATION (CSC)
✉ B.P. 116, Bamako ☎+223 20232101

OFFICE DE RADIODIFFUSION TÉLÉVISION DU MALI (ORTM, Gov.)
✉ B.P. 171, Rue del Marne 287, Bamako ☎+223 20212019 🖷 +223 20214205 **W:** ortm.ml **E:** info@ortm.info
L.P: DG: Baba Dagamaissa. Dir. Nat. Radio: Oumar Sangare. Dir. Rural Radio: Mamadou Niama Diarra. Dir. Transm. Netw.: Soumailou Aboubacrine Dicko.
SW: Bamako (Kati) 50/100kW

kHz	Times	kHz	Times
5995	0555-0800, 1800-2400	9635	0800-1800

FM:
National R. Bamako: 92.0MHz 1 kW + 47 txs of 0.5/0.25kW
Regional R. (Channel 2)

Location	MHz	kW	Location	MHz	kW
Mopti	94.4	10	Ségou	96.8	1
Bamako	95.2	1	Sikasso	98.3	1
Kayes	95.4	10			

National R. (Radio Mali) in French/Arabic/English/Bambara/others: SW & FM. **D.Prgr:** 0555-2400. **N. in English:** Sat 1905-1920.
Regional R. (Channel 2) on FM only: **D.Prgr:** 0800-1945.
Ann: "Vous écoutez l'office de Radiodiffusion-Télévision Malienne émettant de Bamako". **E:** "This is Bamako, Mali Radio Telecommunications". **IS:** Guitar.
R. Rurale on FM in Kayes 89.1MHz, Kolondieba 93.7Mhz, Koutiala and Macina.

Other stations in Bamako:
R. Patriote FM 88.1MHz – **R. Canal 2000:** 90.7MHz. **W:** membres.lycos.fr/canal2000 – **R. Mirador** 91.1MHz – **La Voix de la Verité** 91.5MHz – **Fréquence 3** 93.8MHz – **R. Tabalé** 94.3MHz – **R. Guintan** 94.7MHz – **R. Benkan** 97.1MHz – **R.Liberté** 97.7MHz **W:** comfm/live/radio/radioliberte **E:** liberte@mtelecom-mali.net – **R. Bamankan** 100.3MHz – **R. Klédu** FM 101.2MHz – **R Jakafo** 100.7MHz – **R. Kayira FM** 104.4MHz – **R. Voix de l'Islam** 107.4MHz.
RFI Afrique: Bamako 98.5MHz. Gao 92.1MHz, Kayes 102.2MHz, Mopti 97.7MHz, Segou 93.6MHz, Sikasso 95.0MHz.
BBC African Service: Bamako 88.9MHz.
China R Int.: Bamako 92.7MHz.
VOA: Bamako 102.0MHz.
China R. Int relay station: see International Radio section

MALTA

L.T: UTC +1h (27 Mar-30 Oct: +2h) — **Pop:** 430,000 — **Pr.L:** English, Maltese — **E.C:** 50Hz, 240V — **ITU:** MLT

MALTA BROADCASTING AUTHORITY (Regulatory Authority)
✉ 7 Mile-end Rd, Hamrun HMR1719 ☎ +356 21221281, 21247908 🖷 +356 21240855 **E:** info.ba@ba.org.mt **W:** ba-malta.org **L.P:** Chrmn: Mr. Anthony J. Tabone, Chief Exec: Dr. Pierre Cassar

PUBLIC BROADCASTING SERVICES LTD
✉ 75, St. Luke's Road, Gwardamangia MSD 09 ☎ +356 21225051 🖷 +356 21244601 **E:** info@tvm.com.mt **W:** tvm.com.mt/radio
L.P: Head of News: Reno Bugeja. Chief Exec.: Anton Attard, Consultant Manager: Costantino Abela

RADIO MALTA: MW: Bizbizia 999kHz 5kW
FM: Bizbizia 93.7MHz 8kW, 107.5MHz 0.025kW
D.Prgr: 24h. **N:** D.Prgr: 24h. N: 0700 - 0800 - 1000 - 1200 - 1600 - 1800 - 2230. BBC News 0900 - 1100. Radio France International News 1400
RADJU MALTA 2: FM: 105.9MHz 8kW
MAGIC MALTA: FM: 91.7MHz 8kW, 24h.

DIGI B NETWORK LTD: ✉ 136, Alwetta Street, Mosta MST4508 ☎ +356 27420570 **E:** info@digibnetwork.com **W:** digibnetwork. com **LP:** Man. Dir: Sergio D'Amico. **DAB+:** 6A, 6C, 12A, LP. Bouquet includes local, gov., and international stations

COMMERCIAL STATIONS:
89.7 BAY, Eden Place, St. George's Bay, St. Julian's STJ3310 ☎ +356 23710800 🖷 +356 23710845 **E:** 897@bay.com.mt **W:** bay. com.mt - **FM:** 89.7MHz 8kW. **LP:** Stn Mngr: Kevin DeCesare Jnr – **CALYPSO 101.8,** 28 New Street in Valletta Road, Luqa ☎ +356 21578022 - 52102055 🖷 +356 21578026 **E:** calypsoradio1@gmail.com **W:** calypsoradio.com - **FM:** 101.8MHz 8kW. **LP:** Dir.: Frank Camilleri – **CAMPUS FM,** University Broadcasting Services, Old Humanities Building, University of Malta, Tal-Qroqq Msida MSD 06 ☎ +356 21333313 🖷 +356 21314485 **E:** campusfm@um.edu.mt **W:** campusfm. um.edu.mt - **FM:** 103.7MHz 8kW. **LP:** Stn Mngr: Rev. Joseph Borg. Also relay of BBC WS – **ONE R.,** A28B, Industrial Estate, Marsa, LQA 06 ☎ +35625682568 🖷 +35621248420 **E:** onenews@one.com.mt **W:** one.com.mt - **FM:** 92.7MHz 8kW, 88.2MHz 200W, 88.0MHz 25W. **LP:** Man. Dir.: Dr. Michael Vella-Haber, Senior Manager Broadcasting: Ms. Ruth Vella Micallef, Manager Radio: Clint Bajada. (Operated by Maltese Labour Party) – **R. 101,** 2 Triq Herbert Ganado, Pieta' PTA1450 ☎ +356 25965407 🖷 +356 21240261 **E:** news@media.link. com.mt. **W:** radio101.com.mt - **FM:** 101.0MHz 8kW, 95.5MHz 300W. (Operated by Maltese Nationalist Partys) – **R. MARIJA,** Kunvent Patrijiet Dumnikani, Misrah San Duminku, Rabat RBT 2521 ☎ +356 21453105 - 21453106 🖷 +356 21453103 **E:** info.mal@radiomaria.org **W:** radjumarija.org - **FM:** 102.3MHz 8kW, 107.8MHz 200W. **LP:** Dir: Fr. Charles Fenech – **RTK, MEDIA CENTRE,** Archdiocese of Malta and Diocese of Ghawdex, Triq Nazzjonali, Blata-Badja HMR02 ☎ +356 2569 9400, +356 2124 6714-5 🖷 +356 2569 9151, +356 2569 9160 **E:** info@rtk.org.mt **W:** rtk.org.mt - **FM:** 103.0MHz 8kW, Ghawdex 97.8MHz 400W, Malta 97.6MHz 250W. **LP:** Head of Radio: Karl Wright (kwright@rtk.com.mt). Program Manager: Tonio Bonello (tbonello@rtk.com.mt). Technical Manager: George Pollacco (studios@rtk.com. mt). Head of News: Josianne Camilleri (josianne@newsbook.com.mt) – **SMASH R.,** 4 Thistle Lane, Paola PLA 19 ☎ +356 21667777 🖷 +356 21697830 **E:** info@smash.com.mt **W:** smash.com.mt - **FM:** 104.6MHz 8kW. – **VIBE FM,** Triq Tas-Sliema, Kappara, San Gwann, SGN4411 ☎ +356 21385887 🖷 +356 21383826 **E:** info@vibefm.com.mt **W:** vibefm. com.mt - **FM:** 88.7MHz 8kW. **LP:** Head: Justin Chircop – **XFM 100.2,** 15, Naxxar Road, Birkirkara, BKR 9043 ☎ +356 21378871 **E:** info@xfm.com.mt **W:** xfm.com.mt - **FM:** 100.2MHz 8kW
Established Community Stations (all MHz):
Bastjanizi FM: 95.0, Big FM: 107.1, BKR Radio 94.5FM: 94.5, Deejays Radio 95.6FM: 95.6, Energy FM: 96.4, 96.5, Hearth 94.3 FM: 94.3, Kottoner 98 FM: 98.0, La Salle FM: 99.4, Lehen il-Belt Gorgjana: 105.6, Lehen il-Belt Victoria: 104.0, Pure Gold Christian Radio: 97.8, Radio City 107.6FM: 107.6, Radio Galaxy Network: 105.0, Radju Bambina: 98.3, Radju Elenjani 95.8FM: 95.8, Radju Hompesch: 90.0, Radju Katidral: 90.9, Radju Lehen il-Qala: 106.3, Radju Luminarja: 106.9, Radju Prekursur: 99.3, Radju Sacro Cuor: 105.2, Radju Santa Katarina: 90.6, Radju Sokkors: 95.1, Radju Vilhena: 106.0, Radju Vizitazzjoni: 92.4, Radju Xeb-er-ras: 90.8, South End FM: 91.0, Trinitarji FM: 89.3, Y4J Radio: 105.4
Temporary Community Stations (all MHz):
Temporary licences for up to 2 years and powers of 0.25-1W: Circuit Assembly of Jehovah's Witnesses: 108.0, Gozeppini 891FM: 89.1, International Bible Students Association: 108.0, Lehen il-Karmelitani: 101.4, MMG FM: 97.5, Radio 12th May: 96.5, Radio Leonardo: 105.2, Radju 15 t'Awwissu: 98.3, Radju Banda Fgura: 93.1, Radju al Tarxien: 99.0, Radju Kazin Banda San Filep: 106.3, Radju Lauretana: 89.3, Radju Margerita: 96.1, Radju Maria Bambina 90.2FM: 90.2, Radju Marija Assunta: 98.9, Radju Sant'Andrija: 88.4, Tal-Gilju FM 95.4: 95.4

MARSHALL IS (USA associated)

L.T: UTC +12h — **Pop:** 64,522 — **Pr.L:** English, Kajin Majol— **E.C:** 60Hz, 110/220V — **ITU:** MHL

RADIO MARSHALLS (Gov/Comm)
✉ PO Box 19, Majuro 96960 ☎+692 625 8413. Studio ☎ + 692 625 8411 **E:** v7ab@ntamar.net
W: http://radiov7abmajuro.listen2myradio.com audio streaming
L.P: GM: Antari Elbon, PD: Nixon Elisha, CE: Jambre Ralpho
MW: V7AB 1098kHz 25kW (r. reduced power 0.7kW) **FM:** 97.9MHz
D.Prgr: 1830 (Sun 1900)-1130 **News:** Local bulletins and BBC hourly.
Other Stations:

MW	kHz	kW	Station
7) Majuro	1170	5	Eagle Christian R.

FM	MHz	kW	Station	FM	MHz	kW	Station
2) Majuro	95.5		V7MI	1) Kwajalein	102.1		AFN
6) Majuro	96.5	0.03	WSO-FM	4) Majuro	102.5		V7DJ
1) Kwajalein	99.9	1	AFN	3) Majuro	104.1		V7AA
7) Majuro	99.9		Eagle Christ. R	8) Majuro	105.0		V7WU
1) Kwajalein	99.9	1	AFN				

Addresses and other information:
1) Armed Forces Network, Box 23 APO San Francisco CA 96555 **FM:** Country Music (99.9), Active Rock Music (101.1) Hot AC Music (102.1) via satellite from AFRS. **D.Prgr:** 24h Local studio facilities are available, local breakfast show on 101.1 FM – **2)** Pacific Media Services, Majuro 96960 ☎+692 625 2911 **E:** v7emon@ntamar.net **LP:** Mgr: Fred Pedro, CE: Benitito Kom **ID:** "V7Emon" [= 'V7Good'] **Format:** music, local/international news, talkback – **3)** Majuro Independent Baptist Church, PO Drawer H, Majuro 96960-1008 ☎+692 625 3141 🖃+692 625 3141 **E:** v7aafm@ntamar.net **ID:** "The Change 104.1 FM" – **4)** Ace Broadcasting, Majuro 96960 **LP:** Mgr: Harry Doulatram ☎+692 247 8735 [reported silent] – **6)** National Weather Radio, Majuro 96960. Live and recorded local weather and emergency information for the Majuro atoll area, 24h – **7)** Bukot Nan Jesus Church [Assembly of God Part Two], Majuro 96960 ☎+692 625 7914 **E:** eagle1@ntamar.net **W:** facebook.com/1st-bnj-international-eagle-christian-radio-999fm-1170am **LP:** Pastor Paul & Laura Hensene **D.Prgr:** 1800-1200 **ID:** 'V7Eagle' – **8)** WUTMI-FM, Women United Together Marshall Islands, PO Box 105, Majuro 96960 **W:** wutmirmi.com **Prgr:** women's prgrs 10.5 hours daily **FPL:** AM coverage beyond Majuro [reported silent]

MARTINIQUE (France)

L.T: UTC -4h — **Pop:** 381,000 — **Pr.L:** French, Creole — **E.C:** 50Hz, 220V — **ITU:** MRT

MARTINIQUE PREMIÈRE (groupe France Télévision)
🖃 La Clairière, BP 662, 97263 Fort-de-France Cédex ☎+596 596595200
🖃 +596 596595226 **W:** martinique.la1ere.fr/radio
LP: Dir. Régional: Jean-Philippe Pascal, CE: Charles Diony
MW: Lamentin 1310kHz 5kW (inactive)
FM: 92.0/93.0/93.2/94.3/98.9/100.9MHz
D.Prgr: 24h. **Main N:** 1000, 1100, 1200, 1700, 2000. Rel. France-Inter & France Info

RADIO CARAÏBES INTERNATIONAL MARTINIQUE (Comm)
🖃 2 Boulevard de la Marne, 97200 Fort-de-France ☎+596 596639870
🖃 +596 596632659 **W:** rcimartinique.fm **LP:** Dir: José Anelka. Ed.-in-Chief: Jean Philippe Ludon CE: Guy Lenormand
FM: 91.2/92.6/98.7/103.0/104.6MHz
D.Prgr: 24h. **N:** on the h. (rel. Europe 1). **Ann.:** RCI

Other FM stations in Fort-de-France (in MHz):
88.1 Radio Liberté – 88.9 FM Plus – 89.3 Radio Sud-Est – 89.7 ICS – 90.1 Radio Intertropicale – 90.9 France Inter – 91.6 Radio Esperance – 92.4 Radio Transat – 92.8 Radio Actif – 93.6 RFA Radio Frequence Atlantique – 94.0 Radio Bel'Age – 94.9 Radio APAL – 95.3 Radio Fusion FM – 95.8 France Inter – 96.2 Radio Imagine – 96.7 Nostalgie – 97.1 Trace FM – 97.5 RLDM Radio Lévé Doubout Matinik – 98.1 Super Radio – 99.1 REM Radio Evangile Martinique – 99.5 Radio Saint Louis – 100.6 Radio Canal Antilles & Radio France Internationale – 101.6 Chérie FM – 102.0 Ekla FM – 103.4 RBR Radio Banlieue Relax – 103.9 Radio Liberté – 104.4 NRJ – 104.8 Radio Mouv' Martinique – 105.5 Campus FM – 105.7 Super Radio – 106.2 Radio AS & Radio France Internationale – 107.3 RMC Radio Maxxi – 107.6 Nostalgie

MAURITANIA

L.T: UTC — **Pop:** 3.3 million — **Pr.L:** Arabic, French, Poular, Soninké, Wolof — **E.C:** 50Hz, 220V — **ITU:** MTN

HAUTE AUTORITÉ DE LA PRESSE ET DE L'AUDIOVISUEL (HAPA)
🖃 BP 3192, Ilot C Lot 406, Tevragh Zeina, Nouakchott ☎+222 45241088 🖃 +222 45241051 **W:** hapa.mr **LP:** Dir: M. Imam Cheikh Ould Ely.

RADIO MAURITANIE (RM, Gov.)
🖃 Av. Gamal Abdel Nasser 387, BP 200, Nost Ksar, Nouakchott ☎+222 45253 266 🖃 +222 4525 4069 **W:** radiomauritanie.mr radiocoran.mr radiochabab.mr radioculturelle.com **E:** rm@radiomauritanie.mr **LP:** DG: Yeslem Ben Abdem.
MW: Nouakchott 783kHz 50kW.
FM (MHz, 2nd frequency for Quran prgr.): Aïoun 94.7/88.1, Akjoujt 90.4/98.7, Aleg 94.0/87.7 1kW + 90.8 1kW (local stn), Atar 98.0/90.2, Barkéol 100.0, Boghe 88.1/90.2, Boutilimit 92.2/95.4, Chinguitti 102.0, Guerou 99.3/103.8, Kaedi 97.2/89.0, Kiffa 91.4/96.7, Magta Lahjar 89.0/94.0, M'Bout 98.4/93.2, Néma 98.5/90.1, Nouadhibou 94.7/91.5, Nouakchott 93.3 2kW, Ouadane 98.6, Oualata 98.0, Rosso 98.0/94.0, Sélibabi 97.7/92.4, Tembedra 96.9/107.3, Tichit 98.0, Tidjikja 98.5/90.2, Tintane 94.8/98.2 Zouérate 97.5/93.3.
NB: Where no power is shown, stns are 0.1kW.
Youth R: Nouakchott 98.0MHz.
D.Prgr. in Arabic/French/others: 24h. N: Arabic: 0700, 1100(not Fri), 1200, 1300, 1500(not Fri), 1600(Fri), 2200, 2400. French: 1330(Fri), 1430, 1800v. **Quran prgr.** 24h. **Ann:** A: "Huna Nouakchott, Idha'at al-Gumhuriyati al-Islamiyya al-Mauritaniya". F: "Ici Nouakckott, R. Mauritanie". **IS:** Mauritanian guitar.

Other Stations:
R. Koubeni: Nouakchott 94.2MHz **W:** koubeni.net
R. Nouakchott: 92.0/99.5MHz **W:** facebook.com/Radionoukchote
R. Sahara FM: Nouakchott 92.8MHz **W:** saharamedias.net
BBC Arabic Sce: Nouakchott 106.9MHz, Nouadhibou 102.4MHz – **China R. Int:** Nouakchott 95.7MHz – **DW/Monte-Carlo Doualiya,** Nouakchott: 90.2MHz 1kW – **RFI Afrique:** Nouakchott 88.0MHz – **Monte-Carlo Doualiya:** Nouakchott 90.2MHz – **R. Sawa:** Nouakchott 93.8MHz

MAURITIUS

L.T: UTC +4h — **Pop:** 1.3 million — **Pr.L:** English, French, 6 Indian langs, Chinese — **E.C:** 50Hz, 240V — **ITU:** MAU (Rodrigues: ROD)

INDEPENDENT BROADCASTING AUTHORITY
🖃 5 De Courson Str, Curepipe Rd, Forest Side **W:** iba.gov.mu
E: iba@intnet.mu

MAURITIUS BROADCASTING CORPORATION (MBC, Pub)
🖃 1 Louis Pasteur Str, Forest Side ☎+230 6021200 🖃 +230 6757332 **W:** mbc.intnet.mu **E:** mbc@mbc.intnet.mu **LP:** DG: Dhanjay Callikan. Ag. CE: Cyril Nankoo.
MW: RM1, R.Maurice, Malherbes: 684kHz 10kW **D.Prgr:** 24h in French. Relay of KOOL FM during daytime and VOA English during local nighttime. **N** on the h. **English:** 0500-0515.
RM2, R.Mauritius, Malherbes: 819kHz 10kW. **D.Prgr:** 24h in Indian languages.
R. Rodrigues, Citronelle: 1206kHz 1kW **Prgr:** Relay of RM1. Local prgr. 1400-1415. **FM**(MHz): 97.3 0.5kW 24h.

MBC FM	Location	MHz	kW
Kool FM	Signal Mt.	91.7	0.5
Kool FM	Plaine Wilhelms	97.3	1.0
Kool FM	Jurançon	89.3	0.5
Taal FM	Signal Mt.	98.2	0.5
Taal FM	Plaine Wilhelms	94.0	1
Taal FM	Jurançon	95.6	0.5
One World FM	Signal Mt.	94.9	0.5
One World FM	Plaine Wilhelms	90.8	1
One World FM	Jurançon	92.4	0.5

Other stations:
R. Plus, Labourdonnais Str, Port Louis. **FM**(MHz): Centre 87.7, North 88.6, South 98.9 – **R. One,** Brown Sequard Str, Port Louis. **FM**(MHz): Centre 100.8, North 101.7, South 102.4 – **Top FM Skywave:** **FM**(MHz): Centre 104.4, North 105.7, South 106.0.
BBC World Sce: Bigara 1575kHz 2kW. 24h.
RFI Afrique: Port-Louis 100.8MHz, Rodrigues 93.2MHz

MAYOTTE (France)

L.T: UTC +3h — **Pop:** 200,000 — **Pr.L:** French, Mahorian — **E.C:** 50Hz, 220V — **ITU:** MYT

MAYOTTE PREMIÈRE
🖃 B.P. 103, Rue de jardins, 97610 Dzaoudzi ☎+262 269601017 🖃 +262 269601852 **W:** mayotte.la1ere.fr **LP:** DG: Georges Chow-Toun.
MW: Pamanzi 1458kHz 5kW.
FM: Dzaoudzi 91.0MHz 0.1kW, M'lima Combani 92.0MHz 0.5kW, Kanikeli-Choungui 101.3MHz 0.5kW, Mtsanboro-Madjabalini 103.2MHz 0.5kW.
D.Prgr in French/Mahorian: Local prgr. Mon-Sat 0000-1900, Sun 0145-1830. Relays RFI overnight.
Ann: "Vous êtes à l'écoute de Mayotte Première".
IS: Melody on guitar.

Europe 2: Boueni 90.2MHz, Mamoudzou 99.1MHz, Pamandzi 97.7MHz
France-Inter: Dzaoudzi 101.0MHz 24h

MEXICO

L.T: UTC -6h (DST*: -5h). QR: UTC -5h. BS, CH, NA, SN, SO: UTC -7h (DST* exc. SO: -6h); BC: UTC -8h (DST**: -7h) *) 3 Apr-30 Oct **) 13 Mar-6 Nov (NB: the latter DST period also applies to certain towns/areas along the border with the USA) — **Pop:** 110 million — **Pr.L:** Spanish — **E.C:** 60Hz, 127V — **ITU:** MEX

INSTITUTO FEDERAL DE TELECOMUNICACIONES(IFT)
Unidad de Sistemas de Radio y Televisión
✉ Insurgentes Sur #1143, Col. Noche Buena, Delegación Benito Juárez, CP 03720, México D.F. **W:** ift.org.mx **E:** quejas@ift.org.mx ☎ +52 55 50154000.

DIRECCION DE RADIO
Departamento de Asignación de Frecuencias
✉ Eugenia 197, Col.Narvarte, 03020 Delg. Benito Juárez México, D.F ☎ +52 55 5015 4785.

Call XE–,° = also on SW, ‡= inactive, (r) = repeater, v = varying fq, d = daytime operation. The letters preceding the stn number indicate the state. Addresses are listed by state in alphabetical order. Hrs of tr usually 24h – see address section for variations.
N.B: most stations carry "La Hora Nacional" (official prgr.) Mon. 0400-0500 (Sun. local time), first half hour nationwide prgr, second regional programming.

MW	Call	kHz	kW	Station, location
BC01)	SURF	540	0.1	R. Zion, Tijuana
CH15)	TX	540	4/1	La TX/La Ranchera de Paquimé, Nuevo Casas Grandes (r. XHTX 90.5)
CS01)	MIT	540	5/1	R. IMER, Comitán (r. XHEIMT 107.9)
ME01)	WF	540	20/2.5	La Bestia Grupera, Tlalmanalco
NL01)	WA	540	1.5/1	Los 40 Principales, Monterrey
SL01)	WA	540	150	Los 40 Principales, S.L. Potosí (r. XHEWA 103.9)
SN01)	HS	540	5/2.5	La Mejor, Los Mochis (r. XHHS 90.9)
CH01)	PL	550	5/0.15	La Super Estación, Cd. Cuauhtémoc
JL01)	ZK	550	2.5/1	Poder 55, Tepatitlán (r. XHZK 96.7)
NA01)	TNC	550	2.5/0.15	R. Aztlán, "La Señal de la Gente", Tepic
OX01)	HLL	550	1.5/0.25	Los 40 Principales, Salina Cruz (r. XHHLL 97.1)
CO01)	GIK	560	1.4/0.25	La Acerera, Monclova (r. XHGIK 106.3)
DF01)	OC	560	0.75/0.15	R. Chapultepec, México
DG01)	SRD	560	10/1	La Tremenda, Santiago Papasquiaro (r. XHSRD 89.3)
CL01)	MZA	560	10/1	Sol FM, Manzanillo (Cihuatlán JL) (r. XHMZA 89.7)
QR01)	QAA	560	5/1	La Poderosa, Chetumal (r. XHQAA 99.3)
SO01)	YO	560	1/0.5	R. Lobo, Huatabampo
ZC01)	XZ	560	5/1	Lupe, Zacatecas (r. XHEXZ 93.3)
DG02)	TJ	570	1	Los 40 Principales, Gómez Palacio(r. XHTJ 94.7)
MI01)	LQ	570	2/1.7	Candela, Morelia (r. XHLQ 90.1)
NA02)	TD	570	5/1	R. Red, Tecuala (r. XHETD 92.5)
NL02)	BJB	570	5/0.5	Nueva Vida, Monterrey
OX02)	UA	570	5/2.5	La Mexicana, Oaxaca (r. XHEQA 94.9)
PU01)	VJP	570	0.5	R. Xicotepec, Xicotepec de Juárez
SO02)	UK	570	0.5/0.25	La UK, Caborca
CH08)	FI	580	5/0.7	R. Mexicana, Chihuahua
CO02)	MU	580	5/2.5	La Rancherita del Aire, Piedras Negras (r. XHEMU 103.7)
JL02)	AV	580	10/1	Canal 58, Guadalajara
QE01)	UAQ	580	0.25	R. UAQ 89.5, Querétaro (r. XHUAQ 89.5)
QR02)	YI	580	1/0.25	Mix FM, Cancún (incl. XHYI 93.1)
SO03)	HO	580	5/0.5	Máxima, Cd. Obregón (r. XHHO 97.7)
TM01)	HP	580	1	La Más Prendida, Cd.Victoria (r. XHHP 97.5)
VE02)	DZ	580	1	Imagen R, Córdoba
CS04)	ZZZ	590	5/1	Los 40 Principales, Tapachula (r. XHEZZZ 99.5)
DF02)	PH	590	25/10	Sabrosita 590, México
DG03)	E	590	1	R. Fórmula Durango, Durango (r. XHE 105.3)
GJ01)	GTO	590	10/0.25	Tu Recuerdo, León (r XHGTO 95.9)
JL03)	CJU	590	10/5	La Explosiva 590, Puerto Vallarta
SO04)	BH	590	1	La Mejor, Hermosillo (r. XHBH 98.5)
TM02)	FD	590	5/0.5	La Mejor, Reynosa
CS05)	OCH	600	10/0.5	K'in Radio, Ococingo
DG02)	DN	600	1/0.5	Ke Buena, Gómez Palacio (r. XHDN 101.1)
GR02)	BB	600	5/1	La 101.5, La Comadre, Puros Éxitos, Acapulco (r. XHBB 101.5)
JL04)	LAZ	600	5/0.5	La Mejor, Cd. Guzmán (r. XHLAZ 93.5)
MI02)	TA	600	1	600 Solo Hits, Zitácuaro
NL03)	MN	600	1/0.5	La Regiomontana, Monterrey

MW	Call	kHz	kW	Station, location
SL02)	CV	600	5/1	La Gran Compañía, Cd.Valles
SN02)	HW	600	5/1	La Mejor, Rosario (r. XHHW 102.7)
YU03)	Z	600	5/1	R. Fórmula, Segunda Cadena, Mérida (r. XHZ 105.1)
CO03)	BX	610	5/0.5	BX La Primera, Sabinas (r. XHBX 105.9)
CO04)	SAC	610	1/0.9	R. Lobo, Saltillo (r. XHSAC 99.3)
MI03)	UF	610	5/1	La Mexicana, Uruapan (r. XHUF 100.5)
OX03)	KZ	610	1/0.5	La Poderosa, Tehuantepec (r. XHKZ 98.1)
SL03)	GS	610	6/1	La GS, Guasave (r. XHGS 106.1)
YU04)	UM	610	10/0.2	Candela FM, Valladolid (r. XHUM 92.7)
BC02)	SS	620	5	ESPN Deportes, Ensenada
CH36)	BU	620	5/1	La Norteñita, Chihuahua
DF03)	NK	620	50/5	R. 6-20, México (Ecatepec ME)
DG04)	CK	620	1/0.5	+Pop FM, Durango (r. XHCK 95.7)
NA03)	OO	620	5/1	Los 40 Principales, Tepic (r. XHEOO 96.1)
SL03)	WZ	620	2.5/0.5	R. Novedades, S. L. Potosí (r. XHWZ 90.9)
TM03)	GH	620	1/0.25	La Lupe, Reynosa (r. XHCAO 89.1)
GR04)	JR	630	5/2.5	Coral 630, Zihuatanejo (r. XHJR 95.3)
JL05)	JB	630	10/0.5	C7 Radio, Guadalajara (r. XEJB 96.3)
NL03)	FB	630	10	La FB 630, "La FB del Fútbol", Monterrey
QR03)	CCQ	630	0.5	La Z, Cancún (r. XHCCQ 91.5)
SN04)	OPE	630	14/0.25	Exa FM, Mazatlán (r. XHOPE 89.7)
SO05)	FX	630	1/0.25	Amor 101, Guaymas (r. XHFX 101.3)
TM04)	ERO	630	1/0.15	R. Tamaulipas, Esteros
VE03)	FU	630	10/0.75	La Nueva Voz, Cosamaloapan (r. XHFU 103.3)
CH27)	JUA	640	5	BM R. 6-40, Cd.Juárez
CH06)	HHI	640	10/1	Los 40 Principales, Hidalgo del Parral (r. XHHHI 99.3)
HG01)	NQ	640	50/25	La NQ, Tulancingo (r. XHNQ 90.1)
OX04)	HDL	640	1d	O AM, Huajuapan de León
TM05)	TAM	640	5/1	Ke Buena, Cd.Victoria (r. XHTAM 96.1)
ZC01)	YQ	640	5/1	La Tremenda, Fresnillo (r. XHYQ 98.5)
CO05)	RCG	650	1	D-Rock, Cd. Acuña (r. XHRCG 105.1)
GR05)	CHH	650	5/0.25	Capital Máxima, Chilpancingo (r. XHCHH 97.1)
JL06)	EJ	650	10	La Patrona, Puerto Vallarta (r. XHEJ 93.5)
MI04)	ZM	650	5/1	La Zamorana, Zamora (r. XHEZM 103.9)
OX05)	PX	650	5/0.2	LV de Ángel, Puerto Ángel
SN05)	TNT	650	5/1	R. 65 FM, Los Mochis (r. XHTNT 106.5)
SO06)	VSS	650	1/0.25	Romántica, Hermosillo (r. XHVSS 101.1)
TB03)	VILL	650	1/0.5	Notícias, Villahermosa (r. XHVILL 103.3)
YU03)	VG	650	2.5/0.02	R. Fórmula, Primera Cad, Mérida (r. XHVG 94.5)
AG01)	EY	660	50/10	La Kaliente, Aguascalientes(r. XHEY 102.9)
BS06)	SJC	660	2.5/0.25	KVOZ, San José del Cabo
CH04)	ACB	660	5	R. 6-60/La Tremenda N:o Uno, Cd. Delicias
DF04)	DTL	660	50	R. Ciudadana, México
DG05)	WX	660	1/0.5	Ke Buena, Durango (r. XHWX 98.1)
NL02)	FZ	660	10/1	ABC R., Monterrey
OX06)	YG	660	1/0.5	La Consentida, Matías Romero(r. XHYG 90.5)
QR04)	CPR	660	30d	R. Chan Santa Cruz, Felipe Carrillo Puerto
TM06)	AR	660	5	La Mexicana, Tampico (Pueblo Viejo VE) (r. XHAR 101.7)
CO06)	TOR	670	1/0.25	R. Ranchito, Torreón (r. XHETOR 107.5)
JL07)	IS	670	5/1	La Rancherita Consentida, Cd. Guzmán (r. XHIS 106.3)
CH08)	FO	680	1/0.25	Éxtasis Digital, Chihuahua
CS08)	KQ	680	5/3	Fiesta Mexicana, Tapachula (r. XHKQ 93.1)
GR06)	CHG	680	5/2.5	W Radio, Chilpancingo (r. XHCHG 107.1)
OX04)	OAX	680	1	O AM, Oaxaca
PU02)	FJ	680	1/0.1	La FJ, R. Teziutlán, Teziutlán (r. XHFJ 95.1)
SN06)	ORO	680	1/0.5	La Mera Jefa, Guasave (r. XHEORO 93.7)
SO06)	SON	680	1	Éxtasis, Hermosillo (r. XHESON 88.9)
BC03)	WW	690	78/50	W R. América, Tijuana
CL02)	CS	690	5/1	La Mejor, Manzanillo (r. XHECS 96.1)
DF05)	N	690	50/5	La 69, México
MI05)	XL	690	2.5	La Ley, Pátzcuaro (r. XHEXL 94.9)
NL04)	RG	690	10/1	RG La Deportiva, Monterrey (r. XHFMTU 103.7 HD2)
SN07)	ST	690	2/0.25	Romántica, Mazatlán (r. XHST 94.7)
ZC03)	MA	690	50/2	La Mejor Zacatecas, Fresnillo (r.XHEMA 107.9)
CA09)	XPUJ	700	5	LV del Corazón de la Selva, X'pujil
CH25)	GD	700	5/0.25	La Poderosa, Hidalgo del Parral
JL08)	DKR	700	10/0.15	R. Red, Guadalajara
MI02)	LX	700	5	La Ke Buena, Zitácuaro
SO07)	ETCH	700	5d	LV de los Tres Ríos, Etchoja
VE14)	VC	700	2.5/0.1	La Más Buena, Córdoba (r. XHEVC 104.5)
CH05)	DP	710	7/0.1	La Ranchera de Cuauhtémoc, Cd.Cuauhtémoc
CL03)	RL	710	1	La RL, Colima (r. XHERL 98.9)
CO06)	LZ	710	1/0.25	RCG R, Torreón (r. XHLZ 103.5)
DF04)	MP	710	10	La Nueva 710, Mexico
GR02)	MAR	710	1	R. Disney, Acapulco (r. XHMAR 98.5)
NA05)	RK	710	1	Fusión FM, Tepic (r. XHERK 104.9)
OX07)	RPO	710	5d	La Z, Oaxaca (r. XHRPO 97.7)

MW Call	kHz	kW	Station, location
SN08) BL	710	5/0.25	La Ke Buena, Culiacán (r. XHBL 91.9)
SO08) PS	710	1/0.25	La Super Grupera, Guaymas (r. XHEPS 102.1)
TM07)OLA	710	1	Huasteca, Tampico (r. XHOLA 107.9)
CH30) JCC	720	1	Extremo 7-20, Cd. Juárez
CO07) DE	720	8/0.25	La Kaliente, Saltillo
JL09) QZ	720	1/0.4	Ritmo 720, San Juan de los Lagos (r. XHQZ 94.9)
MI06) KN	720	5d	La Z, Huetamo (r. XHKN 95.5)
SN07) VU	720	1/0.5	Éxtasis Digital, Mazatlán (r. XHVU 97.1)
BC04) EBC	730	1/0.25	Ke Buena, Ensenada (r. XHEBC 97.9)
BS07) LBC	730	10/1	R. La Giganta 730 AM, Loreto (r. XHLBC 95.7)
CH07) HB	730	50/1	Ke Buena, Hidalgo del Parral
CO08) PQ	730	5/1	La 73/La Sabrosita, Cd.Muzquiz(r. XHEPQ 106.7)
DF06) X	730	100	TDW R., México
JL10) GDL	730	5/1	La Explosiva, Guadalajara
SO39) SOS	730	2/0.3	La Ranchera, Agua Prieta (r. XHSOS 97.3)
YU07) PET	730	10d	LV de los Mayas, Peto
CO09) QN	740	10/1	R. Fórmula, Torreón (r. XHQN 105.9)
GJ03) OF	740	5/1	Hit 101.9, Celaya (r. XHEOF 101.9)
JL11) VAY	740	1	Amor, Puerto Vallarta (r. XHVAY 92.7)
OX08) POR	740	5/1	T-Prende, Putla de Guerrero(r. XHPOR 98.7)
QR06) CAQ	740	20/10	R. Fórmula QR Cancún, Cancún (r. XHCAQ 92.3)
SN09) CW	740	5/1	R. Variedades, Los Mochis (r. XHCW 96.5)
CH21) OH	750	1/0.75	La Pantera, Camargo
CS22) MG	750	1/0.25	La Ke Buena, Arriaga
GR03) KOK	750	5/0.25	Éxtasis Digital, Acapulco (r. XHKOK 107.5)
MI07) URM	750	10/0.5	Los 40 Principales, Uruapan (r. XHURM 102.1)
NA06) JMN	750	10d	LV de los Cuatro Pueblos, Jesús María
OX09) CORO	750	1/0.1	Ke Buena, Loma Bonita (r. XHCORO 98.7)
SL06) RASA	750	1/0.1	Candela 750, Pura Pasión Grupera, San Luis Potosí (r. XHRASA 94.1)
SN08) CSI	750	5/0.25	Éxtasis Digital, Culiacán (r. XHCSI 89.5)
VE31) TI	750	10/0.25	La Huasteca, Tempoal (r. XHTI 90.5)
CH03) ES	760	10	Antena Musical 7-60, Chihuahua
CS11) RA	760	5/0.5	R. Uno, San Cristóbal las Casas
DF07) ABC	760	70/10	ABC Radio, México (La Paz ME) (r. 101.5)
DG06) DGO	760	5/0.5	La Mejor, Durango (r. XHDGO 103.7)
JL12) ZZ	760	5/1	R. Gallito, Guadalajara
SO10) EB	760	5/1	Preciosa, Cd.Obregón (r. XHEB 98.5)
SO11) NY	760	5/0.1	R. Xeny, Nogales
GR07) SUR	770	5/1	Tu Ritmo Musical, Chilapa
MI08) ML	770	5/1.5	La Ranchera, Apatzingán (r. XHEML 98.3)
NL05) ACH	770	25/1	R. Fórmula Monterrey, Monterrey
OX04) MRO	770	1d	OAM, Matías Romero
OX04) HUA	770	1d	OAM, Santa Cruz Huatulco
SL07) ANT	770	10	LV de las Huastecas, Tancanhuitz de Santos
SN05) REV	770	5/0.1	Los 40 Principales, Los Mochis (r. XHREV 104.3)
CO10) WGR	780	10/0.25	Exa FM, Monclova (r. XHWGR 101.1)
CS04) TS	780	5/0.5	Ke Buena, Tapachula (r. XHETS 94.7)
GJ03) ZN	780	5/1	EXA FM, Celaya (r. XHZN 104.5)
GR08) XY	780	2.5/1	LV del Balsas, Cd.Altamirano
JL13) LD	780	5/0.5	R. Costa, Autlán (r. XHLD 103.9)
OX10) GLO	780	10d	LV de la Sierra Juárez, Guelatao de Juárez
TM09)SFT	780	1	La Poderosa, San Fernando(r.XHSFT 103.7)
AG02) BI	‡790	10/5	R. B-I, Aguascalientes
BC05) SU	790	1/0.25	La Dinámica, Mexicali (r. XHSU 105.9)
BS01) NT	790	5/0.75	R. La Paz/R. Fórmula, La Paz
CH02) RPC	790	5/0.4	R. Ranchito, Chihuahua
CO11) GZ	790	1	Milenio R, Torreón (r. XHGZ 99.5)
DF05) RC	790	50/1	Formato 21, México
JL14) GAJ	790	0.25	R. Fórmula, Primera Cadena, Guadalajara
TM10) FE	790	1/0.5	La Pegajosa, Nuevo Laredo
BC06) SPN	800	0.5/0.25	Cadena 800 AM, Tijuana
CH12) ROK	800	50	R. Cañón, Cd.Juárez
CO12) ZR	800	2	La Traviesa de Coahuila, Zaragoza(r. XHZR 97.3)
GJ04) GX	800	5/1	Fiesta Mexicana, S. L. de la Paz (r. XHGX 92.5)
GR09) ZV	800	5d	LV de la Montaña, Tlapa de Comonfort
JL15) AN	800	5/2.5	La Ribereña, Ocotlán (r. XHAN 91.1)
NL06) DD	800	10/2.5	Delta FM, Montemorelos (r. XHDD 92.9)
VE09) QT	800	1	La Poderosa, Veracruz (r. XHQT 106.9)
CA12) IC	810	0.1	R. I-C, Campeche
CH07) SB	810	1	R. Mexicana/La S B, Santa Bárbara
CL04) MAX	810	1/0.25	R. Max, Tecomán (r. XHEMAX 106.1)
CO04) IM	810	1/0.5	La Vecina, Saltillo (r. XHEIM 91.3)
GJ05) EMM	810	1/0.5	La Salmantina, Salamanca
GR10) AGR	810	7/0.6	R. Fórmula, Acapulco (r. XHAGR 105.5)
NA07) UX	810	10/0.25	Capital FM, Tepic (r. XHUX 92.1)
QR07) RB	810	2.5/0.25	Sol Estéreo, Cozumel (r. XHRB 89.9)
SO12) RSV	810	5d	Tribuna R., Cd. Obregón
TM11)RI	810	1/0.1	R. Rey, Reynosa
TX01) HT	810	1	R. Huamantla, Huamantla (r. XHHT 106.9)
ZC04) ZC	810	5/1	La Grande, Río Grande (r. XHZC 97.1)
BC07) ABCA	820	3.5/0.5	R. Frontera, Mexicali

MW Call	kHz	kW	Station, location
DG05) DRD	820	10/0.5	W R., Durango (r. XHDRD 106.1)
GR11) GRC	820	1d	RTG R, Coyuca de Catalán
JL12) BA	820	10/1	La Consentida, Guadalajara
OX02) YN	820	1/0.5	Los 40 Principales, Oaxaca (r. XHYN 102.9)
SL05) BM	820	10/1	La Mera Mera, San Luis Potosí(r. XHBM 105.7)
SN10) UDO	820	1/0.25	R. Universidad de Occidente, Los Mochis (r. XHUDO 89.3)
VE14) KG	820	2.5/0.1	La Dorada, Córdoba (r. XHKG 107.5)
DF08) ITE	830	10/5	R. Capital, México
MI09) PUR	830	8d	LV de los P'urhepechas, Cheran
NL07) LN	830	5/0.25	La Caliente, Linares (r. XHLN 105.7)
OX11) TLX	830	1/0.5	La Poderosa, Tlaxiaco (r. XHTLX 100.5)
SN11) VQ	830	5/1	Amor, Culiacán (r. XHVQ 96.9)
SO08) DR	830	2.5d	Digital 99.5, Guaymas (r. XHDR 99.5)
VE26) DQ	830	1	Amor, San Andrés Tuxtla (r. XHDQ 103.9)
ZC01) LK	830	10/0.5	Digital, Zacatecas (r. XHLK 106.5)
GJ03) FG	840	5/0.5	La Mejor, Celaya (r. XHEFG 89.1)
JL16) XXX	840	5/1	Fiesta Mexicana, Tamazula(r. XHXXX 97.5)
NA03) TEY	840	1/0.25	R. Sensación, Tepic (r. XHTEY 93.7)
TM13)MY	840	1d	La Jefa, Cd.Mante (r. XHEMY 98.7)
VE11) PV	840	2.5/0.1	La Fiera Grupera, Papantla (r. XHPV 97.3)
BC05) ZF	850	0.25d	Ke Buena, Mexicali
CH03) M	850	5/1	Renacimiento 850 , Chihuahua
JL17) MIA	850	3/1	La 850 AM, Guadalajara
MI10) ZI	850	1d	Maxistar, Zacapu (r. XHZI 98.5)
QE03) JAQ	850	1/0.1	La Jefa, Jalpan (r. XHJAQ 107.1)
SO13) US	850	1/0.2	R. Univ. de Sonora, Hermosillo (r. XHUSH 107.5)
AG03) PLA	‡860	2.5	La Mexicana, Aguascalientes (r. XHPLA 91.3)
BC08) MO	860	10/7.5	8-60 La Poderosa, Tijuana
CH33) ZOL	860	1/0.5	R. Noticias 860, Cd.Juárez
CL05) AL	860	5/0.1	R. Fórmula, Manzanillo
CS13) DB	860	5/0.25	Extremo Grupero, Tonalá (r. XHDB 101.5)
DF09) UN	860	45/10	R. UNAM, México
DG06) DU	860	1/0.5	XEDU, la que le gusta a Usted, Durango (r. XHDU 98.9)
NL04) NL	860	5/1.5	R. Recuerdo, Monterrey
QR08) CTL	860	10/1	R. Chetumal, Chetumal
QR09) CCN	860	5d	R. Caribe, Cancún (r. XHCBJ 106.7)
SN12) NW	860	1/0.25	Máxima 103, Culiacán (r. XHNW 103.3)
SO14) HX	860	5/0.8	La Mía, Cd.Obregón (r. XHHX 107.1)
TM12)TW	860	1/0.25	R. Latina, Tampico (r. XHTW 107.1)
CH18) TAR	870	10d	LV de la Sierra Tarahumara, Guachochi
GJ05) AMO	870	1/0.5	Éxitos 98.9, Irapuato (r. XHAMO 98.9)
GR12) GRO	870	1	RTG R, Chilpancingo (r. XHGRC 97.7)
MI01) LY	870	1/0.1	Candela, Morelia (r. XHLY 92.3)
OX12) ACC	870	10/0.25	LV del Puerto, Puerto Escondido
PU03) NG	870	1/0.1	Canal 87, Huauchinango
SN07) FIL	870	1/0.25	La Sinaloense, Mazatlán (r. XHFIL 88.9)
CH14) V	880	5/0.25	R. Fórmula, Chihuahua (r. XHV 101.7)
CO14) TC	880	10/1	Kiuu, Torreón (r. XHTC 91.1)
JL18) AAA	880	20/1	ESNE R, Guadalajara
PU04) RTP	880	1	La Poderosa, S. M. Texmelucan (r. XHRTP 90.7)
SL04) EM	880	5/1	La M Mexicana, Río Verde (r. XHEEM 94.5)
SN09) PNK	880	10/2	Planeta, Los Mochis: (r. XHPNK 103.5)
CS14) FRT	890	10/1	R. Frontera, Comitán (r. XHFRT 92.5)
GJ06) AK	890	5/0.5	R. Consentida, Acámbaro
NA03) PNA	890	1/0.25	Romántica, Tepic (r. XHPNA 101.9)
SN13) NZ	890	10/0.5	La Sinaloense, Culiacán (r. XHENZ 92.9)
VE24) BY	890	1/0.3	Éxtasis Digital, Tuxpan (r. XHBY 96.7)
ZC06) PC	890	5/1	Sonido Estrella, Zacatecas (r. XHEPC 89.9)
CH31) DT	900	5/1	Hits FM, Cuauhtémoc (r. 98.3)
DF06) W	900	250	W R., México (r. XEW 96.9)
JL19) ED	900	1	La Líder, Ameca (r. XHED 99.1)
VE05) WB	900	50/10	Los 40 Principales, Veracruz (r. XHBW 98.9)
NL08) OK	900	10/2.5	OK Noticias, Monterrey
BC05) AO	910	0.25	R. Mexicana, Mexicali
JL20) NAY	910	10/1	Los 40 Principales, Puerto Vallarta (Bulcerías NA) (r. XHNY 105.1)
PU05) OL	910	10/2.5	R. Impacto, Teziutlán (r. XHOL 99.7)
CA11) TEB	910	1.5/0.5	Voces, Campeche
CH36) QD	920	1/0.25	R. Noticias 920, Chihuahua
CO06) RCA	920	5/0.2	Planeta Rojo, Torreón (Gómez Palacio DG) (r. XHRCA 102.7)
CO15) MJ	920	1/0.25	FM Globo, Piedras Negras (r. XHMJ 97.9)
GJ08) RE	920	5/1	La Comadre, Puros Éxitos, Celaya (r. XHRE 88.1)
JL21) LT	920	10/1	R. María, Tlaquepaque
MI11) LCM	920	5/2.5	R. Mexicana, Cd.Lázaro Cárdenas
OX13) PNX	920	1/0.125	R. Costa, Pinotepa Nacional(r. XHPNX 98.1)
PU06) ZAR	920	1	Éxtasis Digital, Puebla
SN14) CQ	920	5/0.5	La Nueva Nueva Ranchera, Culiacán (r. XHECQ 104.1)
SO04) HQ	920	5/1	R. Capital, Hermosillo (r. XHHQ 97.1)

MW Call	kHz	kW	Station, location
TM14) LE	920	10	La Preferida, Tampico
CL06) TTT	930	1	Capital FM, Colima (r. XHTTT 104.5)
CO16) SHT	930	1/0.25	La Más Buena, Saltillo (r. XHSHT 102.5)
CS15) MK	930	5/2.5	La Mexicana, Huixtla (r. XHMK 104.3)
HG02) CY	930	2/1	Banda 930, Huejutla
MI12) ZU	930	1	Candela, Zacapu (r. XHZU 97.7)
OX17) TLA	930	5d	LV de la Mixteca, Tlaxiaco
ZC03) QS	930	10/3	Romántica, Fresnillo (r. XHQS 90.3)
BC07) MMM	940	1/0.1	940 AM Oldies, Mexicali
BS08) RLA	940	10/1	R. Santa Rosalía, Santa Rosalía
CO17) YJ	940	10/0.1	La Fiera Musical, Nueva Rosita(r. XHYJ 105.1)
DF06) Q	940	50	Ke Buena 9-40, México
JL22) HE	940	1	La Voz, Atotonilco
TM15) RKS	940	1d	Romántica 9-40, Reynosa
BC09) KAM	950	20/5	R. Fórmula Californias, Tijuana
CA02) MAB	950	3/0.9	La Poderosa, Cd. del Carmen (r. XHMAB 101.7)
CH02) FA	950	1/0.5	La Poderosa, Chihuahua (r. XHFA 89.3)
GJ09) CEL	950	10/1	Él y Ella, Celaya (r. XHCEL103.7)
GR10) ACA	950	5/1	R. Fórmula, Acapulco (r. XHACA 106.3)
JL23) MEX	950	5/0.5	La Mexicana, Cd.Guzmán (r. XHMEX 104.9)
NA08) ZE	950	2.5/1	La Poderosa, Santiago Ixcuintla(r. XHZE 92.9)
NL09) RN	950	5/1	R. Naranjera, Monterrey (r. XHERN 100.9)
OX15) OJN	950	10d	LV de la Chinantla, San Lucas Ojitlán
SN09) ORF	950	4/0.5	Los Mochis: (r. XHORF 99.7)
SO15) PB	950	10/0.1	Grupera 93.1, Hermosillo
TM06) TO	950	5/2	Romántica, Tampico (r. XHETO 98.5)
CH20) FAMA	960	1/0.5	R. Fama, Cd.Camargo (r. XHFAMA 97.5)
CO18) KS	960	0.5/0.1	Super KS, Saltillo (r. XHKS 104.9)
DG09) TPH	960	5d	Las Tres Voces de Durango, Santa María Ocotán
GR14) UQ	960	1/0.5	La Poderosa, Zihuatanejo (r. XHUQ 101.9)
GR15) XC	960	1.5/1	ABC R. 960, Taxco (r. XHXC 96.1)
JL24) HK	960	10/2.5	LV de Guadalajara, Guadalajara
MI13) MM	960	1	Mix, Morelia (r. XHEMM 101.7)
SL08) CZ	960	1	ABC R., San Luis Potosí
SO16) IQ	960	1/0.5	Futura R, Cd.Obregón (r. XHIQ 102.5)
TM16) K	960	5/1	La Estación Grande, Nuevo Laredo
VE08) OZ	960	1/0.25	Amor, Xalapa (r. XHOZ 91.7)
CH22) SW	970	1/0.5	R. Madera/La Mera Mera, Cd. Madera
CH30) J	970	10/5	La J Mexicana, Cd.Juárez
CO10) MF	970	1/0.5	La Mejor, Monclova (r. XHEMF 96.3)
DF10) RFR	970	50/4	R. Fórmula, Primera Cadena, México
GJ10) UG	970	1	R. Universidad de Guanajuato, Guanajuato
MI14) CJ	970	1/0.25	R. Apatzingán, Apatzingán (r. XHCJ 94.3)
SN15) VOX	970	5/0.4	Fiesta Mexicana, Mazatlán (r. XHVOX 98.7)
SO02) EZ	970	5/0.25	La Mejor, Caborca (r. XHEZ 90.7)
TM01) BJ	970	1	Di Hit All, Cd. Victoria (r. XHBJ 107.1)
TM17) O	970	1	NotiGape 970 AM, Matamoros
YU05) MH	970	5/0.5	Candela FM, Mérida (r. XHMH 95.3)
ZC01) ZAZ	970	5/0.5	Amor, Zacatecas (r. XHZAZ 99.3)
CH24) JK	980	1	La Poderosa, Cd.Delicias
CO19) NR	980	5/0.5	La Que Gusta Más, Nueva Rosita(r. XHENR 89.1)
MI15) LC	980	5/0.2	Dual Stereo, La Piedad (r. XELC FM 92.7)
NA09) XT	980	1	La Caliente, Tepic (r. XHTX 107.3)
PU07) FS	980	5	La Mexicana, Izúcar de Matamoros (r. XHFS 91.1)
SO17) FQ	980	2.5/0.5	La FQ, Cananea ((r. XHFQ 103.1)
SO18) KE	980	1/0.25	KE, Navojoa (r. XHKE 104.5)
TM18) TU	980	10/1	Tu Recuerdo, Tampico (Pueblo Viejo VE) (r. XHTU 99.3)
BC05) CL	990	1.4/3	Rockola 990, Mexicali
BS02) HZ	990	5/0.25	HZ La Pura Sabrosura, La Paz
CH13) ER	990	5/0.25	R. Lobo, Cd.Cuauhtémoc
CS09) TG	990	20/1	Extremo, Tuxtla Gutiérrez (r. XHTG 90.3)
GR06) PI	990	20/5	Ke Buena, Chilpancingo (r. XHEPI 99.7)
JL07) BC	990	1/0.1	La Buena Onda, Cd.Guzmán (r. XHBC 95.1)
MI16) ATM	990	1	R. Fórmula, Morelia (r. XHATM 105.1)
NL04) T	990	50	La T Grande, Monterrey
OX16) IU	990	2.5/1	Amor, Oaxaca (r. XHIU 105.7)
ZC06) FP	990	10/3	R. Alegría, Xalpa
CH33) FV	1000	1	La Rancherita, Cd.Juárez
CH29) HPC	1000	1/0.5	R. Mil/R. Fórmula, Hidalgo del Parral
CS02) TAC	1000	10/1	Exa FM, Tapachula (r. XHTAC 91.5)
DF02) OY	1000	50/20	R. Mil, México
GJ01) RZ	1000	1/0.5	W R., León (r. XHRZ 93.1)
MI17) GQ	1000	3.5d	La Reyna, León (r. XHGQ 92.5)
SN16) MIL	1000	1/0.25	Romántica, Los Mochis (r. XHMIL 90.1)
SN07) MMS	1000	1	La Ke Buena, Mazatlán (r. XHMMS 97.9)
TM19) NLT	1000	1/0.1	R. Fórmula Nuevo Laredo, Nuevo Laredo
VE30) CSV	1000	1	Máxima FM, Coatzacoalcos (r. XHCSV 93.1)
YU01) MYL	1000	5/0.35	Los 40 Principales, Mérida (r. XHMYL 92.1)
BC11) DX	1010	2/0.5	Cadena 1010 AM, Ensenada(r. XHDX 100.3)
CH25) LO	1010	5/0.5	Exa FM, Chihuahua (r. XHLO 100.9)
CO05) KD	1010	0.5/0.25	Digital, Cd.Acuña (r. XHKD 103.1)
DG02) VK	1010	5/1	Tu Recuerdo, Gómez Palacio (r. XHVK 106.7)
HG03) HGO	1010	1d	Hidalgo R, Huejutla
JL12) HL	1010	50/5	TDW, Guadalajara
MI18) TUMI	1010	5d	LV de la Sierra Oriente, Tuxpan
PU08) PA	1010	20/2	Ke Buena, Puebla
SN08) WS	1010	5/1	Romántica, Culiacán (r. XHWS 102.5)
SO19) XN	1010	0.5/0.2	R. Ures, Ures
VE09) FM	1010	5/0.5	Romántica, Veracruz (r. XHFM 94.9)
CL07) VE	1020	1	La Mexicana, Colima (r. XHEVE 93.3)
NA03) PIC	1020	1	Éxtasis Digital, Tepic (r. XHEPIC 98.5)
OX17) OU	1020	5/1	La Mejor FM, Huajuapan de León(r. XHOU 105.3)
QE04) KH	1020	5	Top Music, Querétaro (r. XHKH 91.7)
QR11) WO	1020	1/0.25	97.7, Chetumal (r. XHWO 97.7)
VE11) PR	1020	5/0.5	Los 40 Principales, Poza Rica (r. XEPR 102.7)
BC02) SDD	1030	5	La Tremenda, Ensenada
CA06) BCC	1030	1/0.25	La Mejor, Cd. del Carmen (r. XHBCC 100.5)
CH26) YC	1030	5/0.5	R. Fórmula, Cd.Juárez
CS18) VFS	1030	10/0.25	LV de la Frontera Sur, Las Margaritas
DF05) QR	1030	50/5	R. Centro, México
GR01) VP	1030	1/0.5	La Mexicana, Acapulco (r. XHEVP 95.3)
JL25) LJ	1030	20/2	Ke Buena, Lagos de Moreno (r. XHLJ 105.7)
OX18) TEKA	1030	0.5/0.2	Ke Buena, Juchitán (r. XHTEKA 91.7)
QR12) NKA‡	1030	5d	LV del Gran Pueblo, Felipe Carillo Puerto
SL09) IE	1030	5/1	Stereo 1030, Matehuala (r. XHIE 106.3)
SN01) MPM	1030	10/1	Exa FM, Los Mochis (r. XHMPM 98.9)
TM18) PAV	1030	1/0.5	La Picuda, Tampico (r. XHPAV 91.7)
CH08) HES	1040	5/0.25	Radiorama Siglo XXI, Chihuahua
CS19) PLE	1040	5/0.5	R. Palanque, Palenque
GJ09) SAG	1040	5/0.5	R. Lobo Bajío, Irapuato
JL18) BBB	1040	10/1	R. Mujer, Guadalajara
ME02) CH	1040	5/0.75	R. Capital 1040, Toluca
SO20) GYS	1040	5/0.25	Radiovisa, Guaymas (r. XHGYS 90.1)
AG01) DC	1050	1	Amor, Aguascalientes (r. XHDC 104.5)
BC05) D	1050	10d	La Gran D, Mexicali
BS05) BCS	1050	10/1	La Radio de Sudcalifornia, La Paz
GR16) ZUM	1050	15	ABC R., Chilpancingo (r. XHEZUM 105.1)
MI07) IP	1050	1	La Poderosa, Uruapán (r. XHIP 89.7)
NA10) RIO	1050	5d	La Nayarita, Ixtlán del Río (r. XHERIO 106.9)
NL10) Q	1050	100	La Ranchera 1050, Monterrey
QR13) OOO	1050	35/2.5	Imagen, Cancún (r. XHQOO 90.7)
VE25) JF	1050	5d	R. Max, Tierra Blanca
DF11) EP	°1060	100/20	R. Educación, México
TM30) RDO	1060	7/2.5	La Raza 1060, Reynosa
CA05) IT	1070	1/0.25	Exa FM, Cd. del Carmen (r. XHIT 99.7)
GR02) AGS	1070	1/0.2	Amor, Acapulco (r. XHAGS 101.3)
JL26) SP	1070	10/1	R. Notícias 10-70, Guadalajara
PU09) GY	1070	1/0.25	La Mejor, Huauchinango (r. XHGY 100.7)
SO16) OBS	1070	1/0.25	Xtasis, Cd.Obregón (r. XHOBS 92.1)
BS09) PAB	1080	0.5/0.25	R. Celebridad, La Paz
CL08) UU	1080	1/0.13	La Mejor, Colima (r. XHUU 92.5)
GJ05) CN	1080	1/0.5	Los 40 Principales, Irapuato (r. XHCN 88.5)
JL27) JLV	1080	5d	C7 Radio, Puerto Vallarta (r. XHVJL 91.9)
ME03) TUL	1080	5/0.25	R. Mexiquense Valle de México, Tultitlán
OX19) AX	1080	5/0.5	R. Fórmula Oaxaca, Oaxaca (r. XHAX 93.7)
SO21) OO	1080	1/0.25	Río Digital, San Luis Río Colorado(r. XHDY 107.1)
BC12) PRS	1090	50	XX Sports 1090 AM/Mighty 1090, Rosarito
JL28) LB	1090	5/1	Candela, La Barca (r. XHLB 104.7)
NL04) AU	1090	5/0.5	Milenio R, Monterrey (r. XHFMTU 103.7)
PU10) HR	1090	1	La HR, Puebla
QE05) XE	1090	2.5/1	Íntegra 2 siete, Querétaro (r. XHXE 92.7)
TM20) WL	1090	1d	La Romántica, Nuevo Laredo
VE50) MCA	1090	10	La Grande de las Huastecas, Pánuco
VE13) IL	1090	1/0.5	La Nueva Mix, Veracruz (r. XHIL 88.5)
BS10) BAC	1100	1	R. Asunción/R. Sur California, Bahía Asunción
GJ11) BV	1100	5	R. Alegría, Moroleón (r. XHBV 95.7)
GR17) GRM	1100	1d	RTG R, Ometepec
SL05) PO	1100	1/0.25	Imagen, San Luis Potosí (r. XHEPO 103.1)
SO22) NAS	1100	1/0.5	95.5 Sin Límites, Navojoa (r. XHNAS 95.5)
ZC07) TGO	1100	5/0.5	R. Cañón, Tlaltenango (r. XHTGO 90.1)
CH33) WR	1110	1/0.5	Cristo Rey Radio, Ciudad Juarez
CO20) PU	1110	0.25	La P-U, Monclova
DF05) RED	1110	100	R. Red, México (Tlalnepantla ME)
GJ12) LEO	1110	5/1	La Rancherita, León (r. XHLEO 105.1)
JL20) PVJ	1110	1/0.2	Ke Buena, Puerto Vallarta (r. XHPVJ 94.3)
OX04) TEO	1110	0.4	O AM, Teotitlán de Flores Magon
OX04) TUX	1110	0.5	O AM, Tuxtepec
SO23) VS	1110	1/0.25	Maxima 96-3, Hermosillo (r. XHVS 96.3)
TM21) OQ	1110	1	Notigape 11-10/R. Fórmula, Reynosa
VE51) HTY	1110	10	La Mejor, Tlapacayan (r. XHHTY 107.1)
BC13) MX	1120	0.4/0.1	MIC R., Mexicali
JL29) UNO	1120	0.5	R. Uno La Popular , Guadalajara

MW Call	kHz	kW	Station, location
PU10) POP	1120	5	Fórmula 11-20 AM, Puebla
QE06) GV	1120	1/0.5	La Nueva Mix, Querétaro (r. XHGV 106.5)
SL10) TR	1120	1	R. Panorámica, Cd.Valles (r. XHETR 99.7)
TB14) TQE	1120	5/0.5	La R. de Tabasco, Tenosique(r. XETVH 1230kHz)
YU09) RUY	1120	1d	R. Universidad, Mérida (r. XHRUY 103.9)
AG02) YZ	1130	10/2.5	La Poderosa, Aguascalientes (r. XHYZ 107.7)
ME04) TOL	1130	10/5	La Comadre, Toluca (r. XHTOL 102.9)
MI19) FN	1130	1/0.1	Moderna R, Uruapan (r. XHFN 91.1)
NA11) LUP	1130	1/0.5	R. Lupita, Las Varas (r. XHLUP 89.1)
SN16) MOS	1130	1/0.25	Éxtasis Digital, Los Mochis (r. XHEMOS 94.1)
SO24) HN	1130	1	Toño, Nogales
CS20) TEC	1140	1/0.5	R. Tecpatán, Tecpatán
HG04) PEC	1140	1	Hidalgo R., San Bartolo Tutotepec
MI20) LIA	1140	5/0.5	Grupera 93.1, Morelia (r. XHLIA 93.1)
NL02) MR	1140	50	R. Esperanza, Monterrey
PU11) TE	1140	5	Ella, Tehuacán (r. XHETE 106.3)
BC14) RM	1150	1	R. Fórmula, Mexicali
CH16) JS	1150	1/0.5	R. Exitos/JS Digital, Hidalgo del Parral
CO21) BF	1150	2.5/1	La Poderosa, San Pedro (r. XHBF 98.3)
DF05) JP	1150	50/10	El Fonógrafo, México
JL10) AD	1150	50/1	R. Metrópoli, Guadalajara
OX20) XP	1150	10/1	La Mejor, Tuxtepec (r. XHESO 104.9)
SL14) WU	1150	0.25	La Poderosa, Matehuala (r. XHWU 96.9)
SN17) UAS	1150	10/0.15	R. UAS, Culiacán (r. XHUAS 96.1)
SO16) SO	1150	5/0.3	Fiesta Mexicana, Cd.Obregón(r. XHESO 104.9)
VE24) TVR	1150	1.5/0.5	La Nueva Azul, Tuxpan (r. XETVR 106.9)
ZC08) XM	1150	5/1	R. Jerez, Jerez de García Salinas(r. XHXM 89.1)
BC15) QIN	1160	10	LV del Valle, San Quintín
GJ06) VW	1160	2.5/0.5	Stereo Sensación, Acámbaro(r. XHVW 90.5)
MI21) IW	1160	1/0.1	Canal Stereo Juvenil, Uruapan (r. XHIW 101.3)
SL11) GI	1160	1/0.1	R. Reyna - "La Gigante del Cuadrante", Tamazunchale (r. XHGI 97.3)
AG02) UVA	‡1170	10/2.5	UVA, Aguascalientes (r. XHUVA 90.5)
CO20) MDA	1170	1/0.5	La Mera Ley, Monclova (r. XHMDA 104.9)
JL30) JTF	1170	1/0.1	La Tremenda, Zacoalco de Torres (r. XHJTF 103.1)
ME05) RLK	1170	1/0.25	Super Stereo Miled, Atlacomulco (r. XHRLK 104.7)
PU06) CD	1170	10/2.5	Ciudad W, Puebla
SO25) IB	1170	1d	Radiovisa, Caborca (r. XHIB 89.9)
SO26) FEM	1170	5/0.1	R. Disney, Hermosillo (r. XHFEM 99.5)
TM15) RT	1170	5d	Ke Buena, Reynosa
VE46) JS	1170	2.5/1	R. Hit, Coatzacoalcos (r. XHZS 92.3)
BS05) UBS	1180	10	R. Universidad Autonoma de Baja California Sur, La Paz
CH35) DCH	1180	5/1.5	Ke Buena, Cd. Delicias
DF12) FR	1180	10/5	R. Felicidad, México
GJ05) YA	1180	1/0.8	La Picosa, Irapuato (r. XHYA 91.9)
OX18) AH	1180	0.5	Hits, Juchitán (r. XHAH 90.1)
BC16) MBC	1190	0.25/0.1	Cadena 1190 AM, Mexicali
CH30) PZ	1190	5/0.1	R. Norteña, Cd.Juárez
JL12) WK	1190	50/10	W R./W Guadalajara, Guadalajara
MI22) SOL	1190	5/2.5	R. Sol, la pura ley, Cd.Hidalgo
M001) JPA	1190	5	La Mexicana, Cuernavaca (r. XHJPA 90.3)
NL10) CT	1190	10/0.1	Contacto 11-90, Monterrey
SL12) XQ	1190	25/1	R. Universidad, San Luís Potosí
TM22) TOT	1190	8/0.125	ABC R., Tampico (r. XHTOT 89.3)
VE32) PP	1190	5	La Comadre, Orizaba (r. XHPP 100.3)
BS11) PAS	1200	1	R. Punta Abreojos, Punta Abreojos
ME06) QY	1200	2.5	La Bestia Grupera, Toluca
QE07) QJAL	1200	5	R. y Televisión Querétaro, Jalpan
SN08) WT	1200	1/0.25	W R., Culiacán (r. XHWT 97.7)
SO27) YF	1200	1/0.25	R. Fórmula, Hermosillo (r. XHYF 91.5)
CS21) COPA	1210	5d	LV de los Vientos, Copainalá
GJ14) ITC	1210	1	R. Tecnológico, Celaya (r. XHITC 89.9)
PU10) PUE	1210	5/1	Méxicana 12-10 AM, Puebla
CO22) SAL	1220	4.5d	R. Universidad Agraria, Saltillo
DF04) B	1220	100	La B Grande, México
JL14) DKN	1230	1/0.25	R. Fórmula, Segunda Cadena, Guadalajara
MI15) LP	1230	1	R. Pía, La Piedad (r. XHLP 89.9)
NL05) IZ	1230	10/1	R. Fórmula, Tercera Cadena, Monterrey
PU12) TCP	1230	1	Los 40 Principales, Tehuacán(r. XHTCP 90.7)
SN18) EX	1230	10/2	R. Fórmula, Culiacán (r. XHEX 88.7)
TB14) TVH	1230	20/1	La Radio de Tabasco, Villahermosa
CH12) WG	1240	1	Cambio 1240, Cd.Juárez
CH17) BN	1240	1	Radiola, Cd.Delicias
CO13) VM	1240	1	La 100.9 FM, Piedras Negras (r. XHVM 100.9)
HG05) RD	1240	1	La Comadre, Pachuca (r. XHRD 104.5)
MI23) RPA	1240	25/2	R. Ranchito, Morelia (r. XHRPA 102.5)
NA12) SI	1240	1	La Mejor, Santiago Ixcuintla (r. XHSI 94.5)
OX21) CE	1240	2.5/1	Ke Buena, Oaxaca (r. XHCE 95.7)
SO24) CG	1240	1	Romántica, Nogales
SO28) BQ	1240	1	FM 105, Guaymas (r. XHBQ 105.3)
TM23) S	1240	1/0.25	R. Unción, Tampico (r. XHS 100.9)
CH29) AT	1250	5/0.25	La Caliente, Hidalgo del Parral(r. XEAT 102.5)
CO03) SC	1250	1/0.5	La 97.7, Sabinas (r. XHESC 97.7)
CO16) SJ	1250	5/0.5	SJ, Saltillo (r. XHSJ 103.3)
JL24) DK	1250	10/1	DK 12-50, Guadalajara
ME07) TEJ	1250	1/0.5	R. Mexiquense, Tejupilco
PU13) ZT	1250	5/0.5	La Mejor 12-50 AM, Puebla
SO29) DL	1250	1/0.5	Activa R, Hermosillo (r. XHEDL 1290kHz)
VE49) TF	1250	10	R. Fórmula Segunda Cadena, Veracruz
CH20) OG	1260	5/0.5	R. Ranchito, Ojinaga
DF12) L	1260	20/10	La Comadre, México
GJ15) ZH	1260	1/0.25	La Estación que se Escucha, Salamanca
JL31) JY	1260	5/1	La Mejor, Autlán (r. XHJY 101.5)
MI04) QL	1260	1	Catedral de la Música, Zamora (r. XHQL 91.7)
NL11) R	1260	1/0.25	Hits FM, Linares (r. XHR 104.9)
OX22) JAM	1260	10d	LV de la Costa Chica, Santiago Jamiltepec
SL02) XR	1260	5/1	R. Mensajera, Cd.Valles
SN19) SA	1260	5/0.5	Exa FM, Culiacán (r. XHESA 101.7)
SO30) MW	1260	1/0.25	Dimensión 1260, San Luis Río Colorado
VE22) MTV	1260	1	R. Lobo de Mina, Minatitlán (r. XHMTV 100.9)
VE48) TBV	1260	1	Ke Buena, Tierra Blanca (r. XHTBV 100.9)
BC17) AZ	1270	0.5	La Z, Tijuana
CO06) WN	1270	0.5/0.15	El Fonógrafo, Torreón (Gómez Palacio DG)
DG07) HD	1270	1.5/0.4	R. Universidad, Durango (r. XHHD 100.5)
GJ16) RPL	1270	10/1	La Poderosa RPL, León (r. XHRPL 93.9)
SO31) GL	1270	1	R. XEGL, Navojoa
TM07) RRT	1270	2/0.5	Voz, Cd.Madero (r.k XHRRT 92.5)
VE11) RRR	1270	1/0.25	Romántica, Papantla
CA03) CAM	1280	2.5/1	Kiss FM, Campeche (r. XHCAM 101.9)
CH36) BW	1280	1	Palabra Viva, Chihuahua
GJ17) SQ	1280	2.5/1	R. San Miguel, S. M. de Allende (r. XHSQ 103.3)
JL14) BON	1280	5/0.25	R. Fórmula, Tercera Cadena, Guadalajara
NL04) AW	1280	10/1	AW, Involvidable, Monterrey
PU14) EG	1280	1/0.25	ABC Radio, Puebla
TM24) TUT	1280	1d	R. Tamaulipas, Tula
DF13) DA	‡1290	20/5	R. Trece, México
GJ18) FAC	1290	5/0.25	La Poderosa, Salvatierra (r. XHFAC 92.9)
MI18) IX	1290	1/0.25	La Pantera, Sahuayo
SN15) NX	1290	10/1	R. Mujer, Mazatlán (r. XHENX 104.3)
SO16) AP	1290	1/0.25	Romántica, Cd.Obregón (r. XHAP 96.9)
CH30) P	1300	38/0.2	R. 13/R. Centro, Cd.Juárez
GJ19) XV	1300	10/0.75	La Z, León (r. XHXV 88.9)
HG07) AWL	1300	1	R. Jacala/Hidalgo R.,Jacala
MI25) KW	1300	1	Kiss FM, Morelia (r. XHKW 89.3)
SN20) JL	1300	1/0.25	La 130, Guamuchil (r. XHJL 99.3)
SO24) XW	1300	1/0.1	Ke Buena, Nogales
BC18) C	1310	1	R. Enciso, Tijuana
BS12) BTS	1310	1d	R. Bahía de Tortugas, Bahía de Tortugas
BS13) LPZ	1310	1d	R. La Paz, La Paz
GR18) GRT	1310	1d	RTG R, Taxco
JL10) TIA	1310	10/1	R. Vital, Guadalajara
NL02) VB	1310	5/0.25	Mujer 1310.com, Monterrey
PU15) HIT	1310	1d	R. Felicidad, Puebla
SO32) FH	1310	1d	R. Plan, Agua Prieta (r. XHFH 107.9)
TM25) AM	1310	1/0.25	La Mandona, Matamoros
AG04) NM	1320	1/0.25	Romance, Aguascalientes (r. XHNM 98.1)
BS03) SR	1320	0.5/0.25	R. Cachanía, Santa Rosalia
CH06) JZ	1320	2.5/0.25	La Campera/R. Fórmula, Cd.Jimenez:
CO24) CPN	1320	10/0.1	La Poderosa, Piedras Negras (r. XHCPN 101.7)
MI07) NI	1320	10/1	Stereo Vida, Uruapán (r. XHNI 93.7)
OX20) UH	1320	10/2	Ke Buena, Tuxtepec (r. XHUH 96.9)
SN04) RJ	1320	1/0.25	La Nueva RJ, Mazatlán (r. XHERJ 107.5)
CL09) MAC	1330	10	La Poderosa, Manzanillo (r. XHMAC 95.3)
CO25) WQ	1330	4/0.25	La Super Estación, Monclova(r. XHWQ 103.1)
CO26) AJ	1330	5/0.9	La Primera, Saltillo (r. XHAJ 88.9)
GJ20) BO	1330	5/1	R. Variedades, Irapuato
PU14) EV	1330	0.5d	R. Capital, Izúcar de Matamoros
TM07) RP	1330	1/0.1	Boom FM, Cd.Madero (r. XHERP 104.7)
BC19) AA	1340	1	13-40 AM, Mexicali
CH34) RCH	1340	1/0.5	Estéreo Romance, Ojinaga (r. XHRCH 100.1)
CO05) DH	1340	1	Exa FM, Cd.Acuña (r. XHDH 91.5)
GR03) CI	1340	1	Hit FM, Acapulco (r. XHCI 104.7)
HG08) QB	1340	1	La Divertida, Tulancingo (r. XHQB 97.1)
JL24) DKT	1340	5/1	R. Ranchito, Guadalajara
MI08) APM	1340	1	Candela, Apatzingán (r. XHAPM 95.1)
MI26) CR	1340	1	La Zeta, Morelia (r. XHCR 96.3)
M001) ASM	1340	5	Éxtasis Digital, Cuernavaca (r. XHASM 107.7)
NL02) NV	1340	1	Romántica 1340, Monterrey (r. XHXL 91.7)
PU17) LU	1340	10/5	Ke Buena Puebla, Cd. Serdán (r. XHLU 93.5)
SN21) QE	1340	1	La Kañona, Escuinapa (r. XHQE 94.3)
SO14) OS	1340	1/0.64	R. Mujer, Cd.Obregón (r. XHOS 105.7)
TM01) RPV	1340	1	LV de Victoria, Cd.Victoria (r. XHRPV 104.1)

MW Call	kHz	kW	Station, location
TM25) MT	1340	0.6	Nostalgia, Matamoros
TM26) BK	1340	1	La Raza, Nuevo Laredo (r. XHBK 95.7)
CO06) TB	1350	5/0.5	R. Laguna, Torreón
CS23) CAH	1350	5/1	La Popular, LV de Soconusco, Cacahoatán (r. XHCAH 89.1)
DF04) QK	1350	5/1	Tropicalísima 13-50, México
PU18) CTZ	1350	10d	LV de la Sierra Norte, Cuetzalán
SO30) LBL	1350	8d	R. Centro, San Luis Río Colorado
TM27)ZD	1350	0.25	La Incondicional, Camargo
CH02) DI	1360	1/0.4	La Nueva, Chihuahua (r. XHDI 88.5)
GJ21) Y	1360	1/0.25	Los 40 Principales, Celaya (r. XHY 96.7)
GR19) KF	1360	1	La Z, Iguala (r. XHKF 90.5)
VE42) ZON	1360	10d	LV de la Sierra, Zongolica
BC05) HG	1370	0.5	Super, Mexicali
DG08) RPU	1370	1/0.25	La Z, Durango (r. XHRPU 102.9)
JL24) PJ	1370	10/1	Frecuencia Deportiva, Guadalajara
MI27) SV	1370	5/1	R. Nicolaita, Morelia
NL05) MON	1370	10/0.4	R. Fórmula, Segunda Cadena, Monterrey
SO33) HF	1370	5	R. Fórmula, Nogales
TM20)GNK	1370	5/1	Fiesta Mexicana, Nuevo Laredo
CO27) VD	1380	1/0.1	R. Sensaciónal Digital, Allende(r. XHVD 93.9)
DF14) CO	1380	50/5	Romántica AM Digital, México
DG02) RS	1380	1/0.5	Éxtasis Digital, Gómes Palacio (r. XHERS 104.3)
TM01)GW	1380	5/1	Imagen, Cd.Victoria (r. XHGW 99.3)
VE27) TP	1380	1/0.1	Sensación FM, Xalapa (r. XHTP 95.5)
BC20) KT	1390	5/0.1	La Súper KT, Tecate (r. XHKT 88.5)
CL10) TY	1390	10/2.5	Los 40 Principales, Tecomán (r. XHTY 91.3)
GJ07) RW	1390	10/0.25	R Fórmula, León (r. XHERW 101.1)
MO02) CTA	1390	1	Visión 90.9, Cuautla (r. XHYTE 90.9)
SO34) QC	1390	1/0.5	La Reyna del Mar, Puerto Peñasco
TM13)XO	1390	5/0.1	La Super Buena, Cd.Mante (r. XHXO 95.7)
TM21)OR	1390	1	NotiGape 1390 AM, Reynosa
VE54) TL	1390	5/1	R. Ola, Tuxpan (r. XHTL 91.5)
AG03) AC	1400	1	Ke Buena, Aguascalientes (r. XHAC 106.9)
BC04) PF	1400	1	Vida, Ensenada (r. XHEPF 89.1)
GR01) KJ	1400	1	Vida, Acapulco (r. XHKJ 89.7)
ME08)XI	1400	2.5/1	Capital Máxima, Ixtapan de la Sal
MI28) QUI	1400	1	R. Horizonte/R. Fórmula, Cd.Lázaro Cárdenas
MI20) I	1400	5/1	Máxima 100.9, Morelia (r. XHI 100.9)
NL11) SH	1400	51	R. Sabinas, Cd.Sabinas
OX23) UBJ	1400	1	R. Universidad, Oaxaca
QE09) VI	1400	1	EXA FM 99.1, San Juan del Río (r. XHVI 99.1)
SO35) AB	1400	0.25	R. Santa Ana, Santa Ana
CA13) CUA	1400	1/0.25	R. Universidad, Campeche
DF02) BS	1400	25/1	Perrona 14-10, México
GR20) ZHO	1410	2/1	Aquamarina R., Zihuatanejo
JL32) KB	1410	25/10	La 1410, Guadalajara
SL15) IR	1410	5/0.5	Stereo Bit, Cd.Valles (r. XHIR 106.1)
SN01) CF	1410	10/0.5	La Mexicana, Los Mochis (r. XHCF 93.3)
TM16)AS	1410	1/0.25	Ke Buena, Nuevo Laredo (r. XHAS 101.5)
BC21) XX	1420	10/2	Vida, Tijuana
CH33) F	1420	5/0.5	R. Activa, Cd.Juárez
GJ05) WE	1420	10/1	La Estación Familiar, Irapuato (r.XHWE 107.9)
NL03) H	1420	5/0.4	La H, Antología Vallenata, Monterrey
TM21)EW	1420	1	W1420/LV del Bajo Bravo, Matamoros
CL11) COC	1430	1	Amor, Colima (r. XHCOC 99.7)
SO14) OX	1430	5/0.5	Exa FM, Cd.Obregón (r. XHOX 106.5)
TM29)WD	1430	5/0.15	La Grande, Cd. Miguel Alemán
TX02) TT	1430	5/1	R. Tlaxcala, La Doble TTlaxcala
DF15) EST	1440	25/5	Quiéreme 14-40, México
JL33) ABCJ	1440	10/1	La Estrella del Caribe, Guadalajara
CH26) ARE	1440	1/0.25	R. Pegüis/R. Lobo, Ojinaga
DG02) BP	1450	1	La Más Buena, Gómez Palacio
GR21) RY	1450	2/1	La Poderosa LV del Sur, Arcelia
MI24) RNB	1450	1	R. Impacto, Sahuayo y Jiquilpan
NL04) JM	1450	5/1	La Caliente, Monterrey (r. XET 94.1)
OX04) PNO	1450	0.4d	O AM, Santiago Pinotepa Nacional
SN09) CU	1450	10/1	La Z, Los Mochis (r. XHECU 91.7)
TM13)CM	1450	1	Bonita, Cd.Mante
OX07) KC	1460	5/0.5	Planeta, Oaxaca (r. XHKC 100.9)
SO30) CB	1460	10/0.25	R. Ranchito, San Luis Río Colorado
VE51) JH	1460	1/0.1	ABC R., Xalapa (r. XHJH 92.9)
BC08) RCN	1460	10/5	Uniradio 14-70, Tijuana (r. CRI 12h)
CA11) BAL	1470	2.5/0.5	R. Voz Maya de México, Bécal
DF10) AI	1470	50/5	Fórmula Femenina, México
DG06) CAV	1470	5/1	Exa FM, Durango (r. XHCAV 101.3)
GJ01) IRG	1470	1	La Campirana, Irapuato (r. XHIRG 102.7)
HG10) IND	1470	1/0.5	LV Sierra Hidalguense, Tlanchinol (occ. r. XHBCD 98.1 Hidalgo R.)
SN22) ACE	1470	1/0.1	R. Fórmula Mazatlán, Mazatlán (r. XHACE 91.3)

MW Call	kHz	kW	Station, location
TM31)HI	1470	10/0.25	La Consentida, Ciudad Miguel Alemán
CH36) HM	1480	1/0.5	La Caliente, Cd.Delicias (r. XHHM 90.5)
CO29) XU	1480	1/0.1	La Poderosa, Cd.Frontera (f. XHXU 94.7)
HG11) CARH	1480	5	LV del Pueblo Hña-hñu, Cárdonal (r. XHCARH 89.1)
JL24) ZJ	1480	20/1	Ciudad 14-80, Guadalajara
NL04) TKR	1480	10/1	La TKR, Rancherita y Regional, Monterrey
SO18) NS	1480	1/0.25	Z107.1, Navojoa (r. XHENS 107.1)
TM32)VIC	1480	5/0.15	R. Tamaulipas, Cd.Victoria
CH37) CJC	1490	1	R. Net, Cd.Juárez
MI04) GT	1490	5/1	W R., Zamora (r. XHGT 94.1)
NA13) SK	1490	1/0.25	La Super K/La Costeñita, Cd.Ruiz
SL14) FF	1490	1/0.25	R. Norteña, Matehuala (r. XHFF 89.3)
SO37) AQ	1490	0.25	La Caliente, Agua Prieta (r. XHAQ 106.9)
TM33)MS	1490	1	R. Mexicana, Matamoros
VE28) YT	1490	1	R. Teocelo, Teocelo
CO30) JQ	1500	0.4d	La Explosiva, Parras (r. XHJQ 89.9)
DF10) DF	1500	50/10	R. Fórmula 1500, Segunda Cadena, México
GJ23) FL	1500	1/0.5	R. Santa Fe, Guanajuato (r. XHFL 90.7)
HG09) HUI	1510	0.25	R. Huichapán, Huichapán (occ. r.XHBCD 98.1)
NL12) QI	1510	10d	La Nueva Radio, Monterrey
CO31) VUC	1510	1d	La Norteñita, Allende (r. XHVUC 95.9)
ME07)ATL	1520	1/0.25	R. Mexiquense, Atlacomulco
MO03)ART	1520	2	Señal 152, Jojutla (r. XHART 89.3)
SO38) EH	1520	1d	La Primera, San Luis Río Colorado
TM13)YP	1520	1/0.5	Imagen, Cd. Mante
VE35) VO	1520	1d	La Furia, San Rafael
DF14) UR	1530	50/1	Éxtasis Digital, México
GJ01) SD	1530	10/0.1	Arroba FM, Silao (r. XHSD 99.3)
GJ21) NC	1540	1/0.25	Fiesta Mexicana, Celaya (r. XHNC 102.9)
NL13) STN	1540	5/0.5	R. Red, Monterrey (r. XERED 1110kHz)
SO39) HOS	1540	5	La Invasora, Hermosillo
BC06) BG	1550	1	Cadena 1550 AM, Tijuana
MI29) REL	1550	1	R. Michoacán, Morelia (r. XHREL 106.9)
TM20)NU	1550	5/0.25	La Rancherita, Nuevo Laredo
VE36) RUV	1550	10	R. Universidad Veracruzana, Xalapa
CH33) JPV	1560	1d	R. Viva, Cd. Juárez
CS24) CHZ	1560	20/0.15	R. Lagarto/LV Viva de Chiapas, Chiapa de Corzo (r. XHCHZ 107.9)
DF05) INFO	1560	50/10	15-60 AM, México (Tlalnepantla ME)
GJ15) MAS	1560	1/0.25	WE, Salamanca
MI30) LAC	1560	5/1	R. Azul/LV del Balsas, Cd.Lázaro Cárdenas
CO32) RF	1570	100	La Poderosa, Cd.Acuña (r. XHRF 103.9)
GJ21) AF	1580	1/0.5	Éxtasis Digital, Celaya (r. XHAF 99.5)
GR06) LI	1580	1/0.25	Super 94.7, Chilpancingo (r. XHLI 94.7)
ME09)VAB	1580	20	Super Stereo Miled, Valle del Bravo (r. XHEVAB 93.5)
SO26) DM	1580	10	Mix, Hermosillo (r. XHDN 102.7)
BC04) HC	1590	1	La Bestia Grupera, Ensenada (r. XHHC 92.1)
CH24) BZ	1590	1/0.25	Extasis Digital, Cd.Delicias
DF14) VOZ	1590	20/10	R. Mexicana, México (La Paz ME)
GR22) TPA	1600	1d	RTG R, Tlapa de Comonfort
ME07)GEM	1600	5	R. Mexiquense, Metepec
ME07)UACH	1610	5	R. Chapingo, Chapingo
BC22) UT	1630	10/1	UABC R, Mexicali
DF16) ARZ	1650	5	ZER R. 16-50, México
ME11)ANAH	1670	1	R. Anáhuac, Huixquilucan
BC12) PE	1700	10	ESPN R., Tecate
YU10) FCSM	1700	50/1	XEFCSM (test tr.)
SW Call	**kHz**	**kW**	**Station, location & h of tr**
DF11) PPM	6185	10	R. Educación, México: 24h

Stns with (‡) are reported to be inactive.

State abbreviations: AG = Aguascalientes; BC = Baja California; BS = Baja California Sur; CA = Campeche; CH = Chihuahua; CL = Colima; CO = Coahuila; CS = Chiapas; DF = Distrito Federal; DG = Durango; GJ = Guanajuato; GR = Guerrero; HG = Hidalgo; ME = Estado de México; MI = Michoacán; MO = Morelos; NA = Nayarit; NL = Nuevo León; OX = Oaxaca; PU = Puebla; QE = Querétaro; QR = Quintana Roo; SL = San Luis Potosí; SN = Sinaloa; SO = Sonora; TB = Tabasco; TM = Tamaulipas; TX = Tlaxcala; VE = Veracruz; YU = Yucatán; ZC = Zacatecas.

N.B: These abbreviations are not officially recognized by the Mexican Post Office. Letters should therefore carry the abbreviations in brackets or full state name.

Addresses and other information:
AG00) AGUASCALIENTES (Ags.)
AG01) Grupo Radiofónico Zer, San Miguel 117-A, Col. Salud, 20240 Aguascalientes **W:** grupozer.net – **AG02)** Morelos 222, Col. Centro, 20000 Aguascalientes **W:** radiogrupo.com.mx – **AG03)** Madero 333,

1er piso, Col. Centro, 20000 Aguascalientes **W:** radiouniversal.com. mx – **AG04)** Av. 28 de Agosto s/n, 2020259 Aguascalientes **W:** aguascalientes.gob.mx/ryta/default.aspx - 1200-0600.

BC00) BAJA CALIFORNIA (B.C.)
BC01) Calle Iluvia 2554, Fracc. Playas de Tijuana 22500, Tijuana (or: P.O. Box 40231 Downey, CA. 90239 USA) **W:** radiozion.net – **BC02)** Av. General Ferreira 3250, Col. Madero Sur, Tijuana. **W:** espn620am.com latremenda1030.com – **BC03)** Carr. Libre Tijuana- Ensenada No. 3100, 22710 Playas de Rosarito. (or: 3500 W. Olive Ave. Suite 250 Burbank, CA 91505 USA) **W:** wradio690.com – **BC04)** Audiorama Ensenada, Calle 16, N° 159, Centro, 22800 Ensenada. **W:** radioramaensenada. com – **BC05)** Radiorama Mexicali, Pasaje Vallarta 1128, Centro Cívico, 21000 Mexicali. **W:** radioramamexicali.com – 1400-0300 – **BC06)** Grupo Cadena, Av.de los Olivos 3401, Fracc. Cubillas, 22410 Tijuana. **W:** cadenanoticias.mx – **BC07)** Grupo ABC Radio, Ave. Francisco I. Madero 1345, Col. Nueva, 21100 Mexicali. **W:** radiofrontera820am. com 940oldies.com - **BC08)** Uniradio, Gral. Manuel Márquez de León 950, Zona Urbana Río, 22010 Tijuana (or: 5030 Camino de la Siesta, Suite 403, San Diego, CA 92108, USA) **W:** uniradio.com – **BC09)** Radio Fórmula Tijuana, Blvd. Agua Caliente 8710. local 17 y 18. Plaza Pío Pico, Centro, 22000 Tijuana – **BC10)** Radiorama Mexicali, Av. Calafia 519, Centro Cívico, 21000 Mexicali – **BC11)** Av. Juárez 539, Centro, 22800 Ensenada. **W:** cadenanoticias.mx – **BC12)** Blvd. Agua Caliente 10535-506, Fracc. Chapultepec, 22420 Tijuana (or: 6160 Cornerstone Court, East, Suite 100, San Diego, CA 92121, USA) **W:** mighty1090.com espnradio1700.com sandiego1700.com Prgrs in E – **BC13)** Francisco L. Montejano 2200, Fracc. Fovisste, 21030 Mexicali (or: P.O.Box 872125, Calexico, CA 92232) – **BC14)** Pasaje Cozumel 1140, Centro Cívico, 21000 Mexicali. – **BC15)** Calle Octava n° 139, Fracc. Cd San Quintín, 22930 San Quintín - 1200-0200 (Sun – 2200) Prgrs in Sp., Mixteco, Triqui and Zapateco – **BC16)** Grupo Cadena, Prolongación Alfareros No. 253 Centro Cívico, 21000 Mexicali. – **BC17)** Baja California 1310, Zona Norte, 22100 Tijuana (or: Box 430233, San Ysidro, CA 92073, USA) – **BC18)** Blvd. Agua Caliente esq.-Blvd. Cuauhtémoc 2513-6, 22400 Tijuana (or P.O.Box 430521, San Ysidro, CA 92143 USA) – **BC19)** Boulevard Benito Juárez No 1990, Local 12, Plaza Fimbres, Col Jardines del Valle, 21270 Mexicali – **BC20)** Av. Lázaro Cárdenas 13-6A, 21400 Tecate. **W:** xekt.com.mx – **BC21)** Carlos Robirosa 3110, Fracc. Aviación, 22420 Tijuana **W:** radiorama.com.mx – **BC22)** Edif. Rectoría, Av. Álvaro Obregón y Calle Julián Carrillo s/n, Col. Nueva, 21100 Mexicali (or: UABC Radio, 233 Paulin Avenue, P O Box MSC 5163, Calexico, CA 92231-2646, USA) – 1400-0800. **W:** uabcradio.mx.

BS00) BAJA CALIFORNIA SUR (B.C.S.)
BS01) Ap.105, 23010 La Paz - 1300-0700 – **BS02)** Hidalgo 314-B, Centro, 23000 La Paz – **BS03)** Av.Las Flores 1, 23920 Santa Rosalía - 1200-0600 – **BS05)** Ap.19-B, 23010 La Paz - 1300-0500 – **BS06)** Blvd. Mauricio Castro, Dorada's Plaza 4, 23400 San José del Cabo - 1200-0700 – **BS07)** 23880 Loreto – **BS08)** Av de Las Flores 1, 23920 Santa Rosalía – **BS09)** 23010 La Paz – **BS10)** 23960 Bahía Asunción – **BS11)** 23970 Punta Abreojos – **BS12)** 23950 Bahía de Tortugas – **BS13)** 23010 La Paz.

CA00) CAMPECHE (Camp.)
CA02) Calle 22 N° 131, 24100 Cd.del Carmen - 1200-0400 – **CA03)** Av.Luis Álvarez Barret 11, 24000 Campeche 1155-0500 – **CA05)** Calle 32 N° 23-2 P.B., Centro, 24100 Cd.del Carmen - 1200-0600 – **CA06)** Tamaulipas 15, Col.Santa Ana, 24050 Campeche - 1200-0600 – **CA07)** Tamaulipas 15, Col.Santa Ana, 24050 Campeche - 1200-2400 – **CA08)** Ap.1, 24930 Bécal - 1200-0600 – **CA09)** Domicilio Conocido, 24640 X'pujil - 1100-1600, 2000-0000 - Prgrs in Sp., Maya and Chol – **CA10)** 24000 Campeche – **CA11)** Prol.Calle 53, Esq.Av.16 de Septiembre s/n, 24000 Campeche - 1200-0600 – **CA12)** NCS, Calle 30 No. 23, 24400 Champotón - 1200-2400. – **CA13)** Universidad Autónoma de Campeche, Orquidea y Narcisos s/n, Col Jardines, 24000 Campeche - 1200-0200.

CH00) CHIHUAHUA (Chih.)
CH01) Calle Agustín Melgar 473, 31500 Cd.Cuauhtémoc **W:** xepl. com.mx – **CH02)** Julián Carrillo No 701, 31000 Chihuahua – **CH03)** Boulevard Ortíz Mena No 3406, Col Lomas del Santuario 2ª Etapa, 31240 Chihuahua - 1300-0500 – **CH04)** Calle 4a Poniente 436, 33000 Cd.Delicias - 1200-0600 – **CH05)** Calle 2A N° 437 (or Ap.271), 31500 Cd.Cuauhtémoc - 2300-0700 – **CH06)** Allende 613, 33980 Cd.Jiménez - 1300-0200 – **CH07)** Boulevard Ortíz Mena 54, 3er. piso, Col. Centro, 33800 Hidalgo del Parral – **CH08)** Julián Carrillo 705-A, 31000 Chihuahua **W:** radiorama.com.mx/secciones.php?sec_id=32 – **CH09)** Coronado 71, 33580 Santa Bárbara – **CH10)** José Borunda 1178 Oriente, 32030 Cd.Juárez **W:** radionet1490.com – **CH11)** Gonzáles Ortega 1130, Centro, 33700 Cd.Camargo – **CH12)** Av.Insurgentes 2127, Col.Ex-Hipódromo, 32330 Cd Juárez **E:** radiocanon800@lat-inmail.com – **CH13)** Ap.1771, 31500 Cd.Cuauhtémoc - 1300-0600 – **CH14)** Cuauhtémoc 2000, Col.Centro, 31020 Chihuahua - 1200-0600 – **CH15)** Jesús Urueta 504, 31700 Nuevo Casas Grandes - 1200-0400

W: radiocasasgrandes.com.mx – **CH16)** Ap.125, 33800 Hidalgo del Parral - 1245-0500 – **CH17)** Ap.222, 33000 Cd.Delicias - 1300-0400 – **CH18)** Grupo Radio Divertida, Agustín Melgar 602, Centro, 31500 Cuauhtémoc. **W:** lareina900.com – **CH19)** Ap.122, 33800 Hidalgo del Parral - 1200-0500 – **CH20)** Calle de la Paz 602, 32880 Ojinaga - 1200-0400 – **CH21)** Av.Mariano Negrete 8, Fracc Los Pinos, 33700 Cd.Camargo – **CH22)** Calle.3a N° 1204, 31940 Cd.Madero - 1300-0400 – **CH24)** Ap.250, 33000 Cd.Delicias - 1300-0500 – **CH25)** Ap.190, 33800 Hidalgo del Parral - 1200-0600 – **CH26)** Juárez y 2a 201, 32881 Ojinaga (or Box 276, Presido, TX 79845, USA) - 1200-0500 – **CH27)** Avenida Tecnológico 1770, Colonia Fuentes del Valle, Galería C, Local D-07, 32000 Cd.Juárez - 1200-0700 – **CH28)** Av.del Parque Sur 6, 33000 Cd.Delicias - 1300-0300 – **CH29)** Blvd.Ortíz Mena 54, P3, 33800 Hidalgo del Parral **W:** los40.com.mx – **CH30)** Av Vicente Guerrero 2329, Col. Partido Romero, 32280 Cd.Juárez - 1200-0500 – **CH31)** Agustín Melgar 602, Niños Heroes, 31500 Cuauhtémoc. **W:** mmradio.com/hitsfm – **CH32)** José Borunda 1178, Col.Partido Romero, 32030 Cd.Juárez – **CH33)** Mega Radio, Av. Chapultepec 316, Col Cuauhtémoc, Edificio NAFTA Center, 32000 Cd.Juárez **W:** megaradio.mx 860noticias.mx larancherita1000.com.mx cristoreyradio.com activa1420.mx radioviva. mx – **CH35)** Calle 2a Norte N° 309, Interior 107, Col.Centro, 33000 Cd.Delicias - 1200-0600 – **CH36)** Ignacio Allende No 2211, Colonia Zarco, 31020 Chihuahua - 1200-0700.

CL00 COLIMA (Col.)
CL01) Grupo Radiofónico ZER, Blvd. Costero Miguel de la Madrid 505, Col. Playa Azul, 28218 Manzanillo **E:**xemza@hotmail.com **W:**solfm-manzanillo.com – **CL02)** Carretera Manzanillo-Minatitlán, Km 0.2, 28200 Manzanillo **W:** lamejor.com.mx/#!/manzanillo/home – **CL03)** Radio Levy, Calzada la Armonía 270, Col. La Armonía, 28020 Colima **W:** angelguardian.mx/beta/seccion/xerl **E:**redaccion@radiolevy.com – **CL04)** Radio Levy, Allende 408-102, Centro, 28100 Tecomán - 1100-0400 **W:** angelguardian.mx/beta/xhemax – **CL05)** Blvd. Costera Miguel de la Madrid 801-3, Col. Las Brisas, 28200 Manzanillo - 1100-0700 – **CL06)** Grupo MAC Multimedia, Tercer Anillo Periférico 147 Residencial Santa Bárbara. 28017 Colima **W:** gruporadiocapital.com. mx/index.php/capital-fm/colima-colima – **CL07)** Radiorama Colima, Av. Anastasio Brizuela No. 83 - 4, Col. Albarrada, 28078 Colima – **CL08)** Ignacio Sandoval 13, Centro, 28000 Colima - 1200-0600 **W:** lamejor.com. mx/#!/colima/home – **CL09)** Radiorama Manzanillo, Av. Audiencia 48, Local A 57, Col. Península de Santiago Manzanillo, 28860, Manzanillo **W:** radiorama.com.mx/secciones.php?sec_id=33&ent_id=54 – **CL10)** Radiorama Tecomán, Av. Antonio Leaño del Castillo 663, Col. Ponciano Arriaga, 28160 Tecomán - 1100-0300 – **CL11)** Av. Felipe Sevilla del Río 585, Col. Jardines Vista Hermosa, 28017 Colima - 1200-0400.

C000) COAHUILA (Coah.)
C001) De la Fuente 223 Pte., Col. Los Telefonistas, 25700 Monclova **W:** portal.laacerera.com – **C002)** San Juan 819, Fracc. San José, 26014 Piedras Negras **W:** larancherita.com.mx – **C003)** GRD Radio, Emilio Carranza 124, Centro, 26700 Sabinas **W:** radioxebx.com, la97.com.mx – **C004)** Radiorama Saltillo, Chihuahua 151, P1, Col. República, 25280 Saltillo – **C005)** RCG Radio y Televisión, Madero 274 Pte. (Ap.10), 26200 Cd. Acuña **W:** drock1051.com – **C006)** Grupo Radio México, Priv. Eulogio Ortiz y Jesús Pamanes, Col. Ampl. Los Ángeles, 27140 Torreón. **W:** grmtorreon.webs.com/radioranchito.htm, planetaradio. com.mx/torreon– **C007)** Av. Universidad No 1035, Col Universidad, 25260 Saltillo – **C008)** Carr. Múzquiz Rosita s/n. Col. Infonavit, 26342 Cd. Múzquiz - 1200-0400 – **C009)** Grupo Radio Fórmula, Independencia 706, Mza 29, Col. Los Ángeles, 27140 Torreón y – **C010)** Puebla y Washington s/n, Guadalupe, 25750 Monclova **W:** nrtmexico. com – **C011)** Multimedias Laguna, Treviño 50, Centro, 27000 Torreón – **C012)** Zaragoza Radio, Zaragoza 505 Sur Altos, 26850, 26450 Zaragoza - 1200-0400 **W:** zaragozaradio.com – **C013)** Radio Zócalo, Col. Vista Hermosa, 26060 Piedras Negras **W:** radiozocalo.com.mx/estaciones – **C014)** Grupo Stereo Mayran, Acuña 276 Sur, P2, 27000 Torreón **W:** kiuu.gremradio.com.mx – **C015)** Grupo Radio Grande, Blvd. República 200, Col. Tecnológico, 26080 Piedras Negras **W:** fmglobo.com/piedrasnegras – **C016)** Allende Norte 202, Edificio Castilla Sales, Centro, 25022 Saltillo **W:** mmradio.com – **C017)** Radio Televisión Norteña, América 9, Centro, 26800 Nueva Rosita – **C018)** Gral. Manuel Pérez Treviño 839, Pte. Interior, Centro, 25000 Saltillo **W:** xeks.com.mx/portal – **C019)** Presidente Carranza 1000, Col. Comercial, 26850 Nueva Rosita **W:** xenrnuevarosita.com – **C020)** GRM Radio, Venustiano Carranza 612-2 Ote., 25700 Monclova - **W:** grmradio.com – **C021)** Radiorama San Pedro, Pedro G Garza s/n, Col Magisterial, 35000 San Pedro – **C022)** Universidad Autónoma Agraria, "Antonio Narro", Periférico Luis Echeverría S/N, Lourdes, 25070 Saltillo **W:** radionarro.com – **C023)** RCG Radio, América Latina y Alaska, Col. Virreyes Residencial, (Ap.27), 25230 Saltillo – **C024)** Radiorama Piedras Negras, Lerdo 1612, Col. Nísperos, 26020 Piedras Negras **W:** radioramapn.com – **C025)** De la Fuente 304 Ote., 25700 Monclova **W:** wqlasuper.com.mx – **C026)** Av. Universidad 1035, Col.

Universidad, 25260 Saltillo **W:** eldiariodecoahuila.com.mx/primera.asp – **CO27)** Juárez 1400 Sur, 26530 Allende - 1200-0400 **W:** radioxevd. com – **CO29)** Emiliano Zapata 1, Col. Elsa Hernández, 25626 Frontera - 1200-0600 **W:** xexupoderosa.com **E:** xexupoderosa@yahoo.com.mx – **CO30)** Fco. I. Madero 501 Pte., 27980 Parras - 1100-0100 **W:** xejq. mashter.com/page1.html – **CO31)** Boulevard Leónides Guadarrama No 890 Norte, Centro, 26170 Nava – **CO32)** Madero 600, Centro, 26200 Cd. Acuña **W:** lapoderosa.imer.com.mx

CS00 CHIAPAS (Chis.)

CS01) Instituto Mexicano de la Radio, Av. Chichimá 405, (or A. P. 16) 30000 Comitán - 1100-0700 **W:** radioimer.imer.gob.mx – **CS02)** Radio Núcleo, Carretera Panamericana Km. 1006, Santo Domingo, Cintalapa **W:** cintalapa.radionucleo.com – **CS04)** Radio Núcleo, Séptima Avenida Norte No. 2 Parvial, Centro, 30700 Tapachula - 1100-0500 **W:** radio-nucleo.com/tapachula – **CS05)** Radio Chiapas, Segunda Sur Oriente 132, 29950 Ocosingo **W:** radiotvycine.chiapas.gob.mx **E:** xeoch@radiotvycine.chiapas.gob.mx – **CS08)** Radiorama Chiapas, Primera Avenida Sur Galeana 2, Parque Bicentenario, 30700, Tapachula – **CS09)** Grupo Radio Digital, Av. Central Pte. 554-4, 29000 Tuxtla Gutiérrez - 1200-0600 **W:** gruporadiodigital.com.mx – **CS11)** Radio Chiapas, Avenida Benito Juárez 48, Interior Altos, 29200 San Cristóbal las Casas **E:** xera@radiotvycine.chiapas.gob.mx – **CS13)** Radio Núcleo, Carr. Tonalá-Arriaga Km. 2, Col. del Valle, 30500 Tonalá **W:** radionucleo.com/tonala – **CS14)** Primera Calle Norte Pte 7, 30000 Comitán - 1100-0500 – **CS15)** Radiorama Huixtla, Av. Central Norte 8, Centro, 30640 Huixtla - 1100-0300 – **CS17)** Segunda Calle Poniente No 4, Centro, 30700 Tapachula - 1100-0500 **W:** exatapachula.com – **CS18)** 14a Sur-Poniente s/n, Barrio San Sebastián, 30180 Las Margaritas - 1200-0030 (SS – 2400) Prgrs in Sp., Tojobal, Mame, Tzeltal and Tzotzil – **CS19)** Radio Chiapas, Av. 5 de Mayo entre Aldama y Allende s/n, Centro, 29960 Palenque 1000-0400 **W:** radiotvycine.chiapas.gob.mx – **CS20)** Radio Chiapas, 2ª Sur y 1ª s/n, 29610 Tecpatan **W:** radiotvycine.chiapas.gob.mx – **CS21)** Primera Oriente s/n, Barrio Siete Huesos, 29620 Copainalá 1230-2230 Prg in Sp., Zoque and Tzotzil – **CS22)** Radio Núcleo, Cuarta Avenida Ote. 4, (or Ap.28), Centro, 30450 Arriaga - 1200-0400 – **CS23)** Instituto Mexicano de la Radio, Km. 1.5 Carr. Cacahoatán-Unión Juárez, Ejido Rosario Ixtal, 30890 Cacahoatán **W:** lapopular.imer.gob.mx – **CS24)** Instituto Mexicano de la Radio, Km. 14 Libramiento Norte, 29160 Chiapa de Corzo **W:** imer.mx/radiolagarto

DF00) DISTRITO FEDERAL (D.F.)

DF01) Grupo Radio Digital, Av. Chapultepec 473 P.7, Col. Juárez, 06600 México. 1100-0700. **W:** radiochapultepec.mx **E:** contacto@radiochapultepec.mx – **DF02)** NRM Comunicaciones, Prolongación Paseo de la Reforma 115, Col. Paseo de las Lomas, 01330 México. **W:** nrm.com.mx – R. Mil: Ap.21-1000, 04021 México **W:** radiomil.com.mx – **DF03)** Radiodifusoras Asociadas, Durango 341, Planta Baja, Col. Roma, 06700 México **W:** 620.com.mx – **DF04)** Instituto Mexicano de la Radio, Real de Mayorazgo 83, Barrio Xoco, 03330 México. **W:** imer.mx – **DF05)** Grupo R. Centro, Av. Constituyentes 1154, Col. Lomas Altas, 11950 México. **W:** radiocentro.mx – **DF06)** Televisa Radio, Calzada de Tlalpan 3000, Col. Espartaco, 04870 México. **W:** televisa.com wradio.com.mx los40.com.mx kebuena.com. mx, xeqradio.mx televisadeportes.esmas.com/tdn – **DF07)** Grupo ABC Radio, Basilio Vadillo 29, Col Tabacalera, 06030 México. **W:** abcradio.com.mx – **DF08)** Grupo Radiodifusoras Capital, Montes Urales 425, Col. Lomas de Chapultepec, 11000 México. **W:** gruporadiocapital.com.mx – **DF09)** Universidad Nacional Autónoma de México, Adolfo Prieto 133, Col. del Valle, 03100 México. **W:** radiounam.unam.mx – **DF10)** Grupo R. Fórmula, Av. Universidad 1273, Col. del Valle, 03100 México. **W:** radioformula.com.mx – **DF11)** Radio Educación, Ángel Urraza 622, Col. del Valle 03100 México. **W:** radioeducacion.edu.mx – **DF12)** Grupo ACIR, S.A., Pirineos 770, Lomas de Chapultepec, 11000; **W:** grupoacir.com.mx, 889noticias.com.mx, amorfm.com.mx, digital99. com.mx, mixfm.com.mx, radiofelicidad.com.mx, comadre.mx – **DF13)** Radio S.A., Rodolfo Emerson 412, Col. Chapultepec Morales, 11570 México. **W:** radiotrece.com.mx – **DF14)** Radiorama Valle de México, Paseo de la Reforma 56, P1, Col. Juárez, 06000 México. **W:** radioram-avalledemexico.com.mx – **DF15)** Grupo 7 División Radio, Montecito 59, Col. Nápoles, 03810 México. **W:** gruposiete.com.mx, quiereme1440. mx – **DF16) W:** grupozer.net/estados.php?estado=6 facebook.com/ZerRadio1650 – **DF17)** Imagen Telecomunicaciones, Av. Prol. Prado Sur 150, Col. Lomas de Chapultepec, 11000 México. **W:** imagen.com. mx reporte.com.mx – **DF18)** Universidad Iberoamericana, Av. Prol. Paseo de la Reforma 880, Lomas de Santa Fe, 01219 México. **W:** ibero909.fm – **DF19)** Universidad Autónoma Metropolitana, Prol. Canal de Miramontes 3855, Col. Ex-Hacienda de San Juan de Dios, 14387 México. **W:** uamradio.uam.mx – **DF20)** Instituto Politécnico Nacional, Av. Santa Ana 1000, San Fco. Culhuacán, 04430, México. **W:** radio.ipn. mx – **DF21)** MVS Radio, Mariano Escobedo 532, Col. Anzures, 11300 México. **W:** mvsradio.com

DG00) DURANGO (Dgo.)

DG01) Fco. I. Madero y Heroico Colegio Militar s/n, Col. Altamira, 34600 Santiago Papasquiaro. **W:** latremenda.com.mx – **DG02)** Radiorama Laguna, Blvd. González de la Vega y Piedras Negras s/n, Col. Valle de Nazas, 35070 Gómez Palacio – **DG03)** Jesús Contreras 111, Col. Guillermina, 34279 Durango – **DG04)** Boulevard Guadiana 121, Col. Vista Hermosa del Guadiana, 34116 Durango **W:** ww2.maspopfm. com – **DG05)** Radiorama Durango, Manuel Rangel 100, 1er. Piso, Col. Guillermina, 34270 Durango – **DG06)** Blvd. Fco. Villa 3115, Fracc. Gpe. Victoria INFONAVIT, 34125 Durango **W:** xhdgofm.com,xedu860.com – **DG07)** Universidad Juárez del Estado de Durango, Blvd. Guadiana esquina Av. Veterinaria, Circuito Universitario s/n, 34120 Durango. **W:** radio.ujed.mx – **DG08)** Grupo Radio México, Capitán de Ibarra 1203 Ote., Fracc. del Lago, 34080 Durango. **W:** durango.lazradio.com.mx – **DG09)** DCI, Domicilio conocido, 34985 Santa María Ocotán

GJ00) GUANAJUATO (Gto.)

GJ01) Boulevard Algeciras 1504, Col. Lomas de Arbide, 37368, León **W:** radioramabajio.com arroba.fm facebook.com/arrobafmleon – **GJ03)** Blvd.López Mateos Ote 1117, 38070 Celaya. **W:** tvrcomunicaciones.com.mx - 1200-0600 – **GJ04)** Niños Héroes 254, Centro, 37900 San Luis de la Paz **W:** fiestamexicanaradio.net – **GJ05)** Morelos 110, 36500 Irapuato **W:** radioirapuato.com - 1200-0600 – **GJ06)** Allende 17, 38600 Acámbaro. **W:** radioconsentida.com.mx - 1200-0400 – **GJ07)** Rossini 318 Col. León Moderno,37480 León **W:** globalmedia. mx/guanajuato – **GJ08)** Corporación ACIR Celaya, Guanajuato 106, Col Alameda, 38090 Celaya – **GJ09)** Corporación Bajío Comunicaciones, Av.Guerrero y Francisco Sarabia, Centro Plaza Magna, Locales 1,2 y 3 C, 36500 Irapuato **W:** elyella.mx radiolobobajio.mx – **GJ10)** Palacio Federal, Casa de Moneda, Sopeña 1, P2, 36000 Guanajuato **W:** radiouniversidad.ugto.mx - 1300-0500 – **GJ11)** Elodia Ledezma 658, Fracc. Las Flores, 38890 Moroleón **W:** radiomoroleon.mx - 1200-0600 – **GJ12)** Grupo Promomedios, Paseo de los Insurgentes 1703, Col. Jardines del Moral, 37160 León **W:** promomediosleon.com.mx – **GJ14)** Av Tecnológico y García Cubas s/n, 38110 Celaya **E:** xeite@ite.mx - 1200-0600 – **GJ15)** Juárez 100 Altos (or Ap.24), 36700 Salamanca - 1300-0500 **W:** radioirapuato.com/estaciones/wesalamanca – **GJ16)** Cañada 310, Esq.Roca, Col Jardines de Moral, 37160 León **W:** lapoderosa.com.mx – **GJ17)** Calle Solano 4, 37700 San Miguel de Allende **W:** xesqradiosanmiguelallende.com - 1200-0400 – **GJ18)** Morelos 704, Centro, 38900 Salvatierra - 1230-0130 – **GJ19)** 10 de Mayo No. 126, Centro, 37000 León **W:** lazradio.com.mx - 1200-2400 – **GJ20)** Morelos 135, Esq. 5 de Mayo, 36500 Irapuato - 1030-0600 – **GJ21)** Radiorama Bajío, Adolfo Lopez Mateos 932 Pte. Centro, 38090 Celaya – **GJ23)** Municipio Libre 8, 36080 Guanajuato **W:** radiosantafedeguanajuato. mx - 1300-0300.

GR00) GUERRERO (Gro.)

GR01) Radiorama Guerrero, Calle de la Paz 190, P2, Edif. Nick, 39300 Acapulco. **W:** radioramaguerrero.com.mx – **GR02)** Grupo ACIR, Av. La Suiza 19, Fracc. Las Playas, 39390 Acapulco. **W:** comadre1015.mx amor1031.mx – **GR03)** Radiorama Acapulco, Paraíso 10,Fraccionamiento Condesa, 39690 Acapulco. **W:** acapulcoradiorama. com.mx – **GR04)** Paseo de la Boquita No 53, Col Centro, 40880 Zihuatanejo. **W:** coral630.com.mx —**GR05)** Zapata 28, 5to.Piso, esquina Galeana, Centro, 39000 Chilpancingo. **W:** gruporadiocapital.mx/index.php/capital-maxima/chilpancingo-guerrero - 1100-0400 – **GR06)** Radiorama Guerrero, Av. Del Sur 14, Col. Margarita Vigurí, 39060 Chilpancingo. **W:** radioramaguerrero.com.mx – **GR07)** Calle 5 Sur 305, 41100 Chilapa - 1200-0200 – **GR08)** Fray Bautista Moya 410, Centro, 40660 Cd. Altamirano. **W:** radioxexy.com.mx - 1200-0430 – **GR09)** Av. Heroico Colegio Militar No 234, Col Aviación, 41304 Tlapa de Comonfort - 1200-0100 (SS -2000) Prgrs in Sp., Náhuatl, Mixteco and Tlapaneco – **GR10)** Carretera Escénica 109, Col. Villas Guitarrón, Acapulco – **GR11)** Av. Revolución 6, 40700 Coyuca de Catalán. **W:** rtvgro.net – **GR12)** Palacio de la Cultura "Ignacio Manuel Altamirano", tercer piso, Plaza Cívica 1er Congreso de Anáhuac, Col Centro, 39900 Chilpancingo. **W:** rtvgro.net - 1200-0700 – **GR14)** Paseo de Zihuatanejo Pte. No 143, Col. Limón, 40880 Zihuatanejo. **W:** radioramaixtapa.com - 1200-0300 – **GR15)** Cerro de la Bermeja s/n, Col. Bermeja, Taxco de Juan Ruíz de Alarcón, 40200 Taxco. **W:** taxco.abcradiogro.com.mx - 1200-0300 – **GR16)** Zapata 28, 2do piso, Col. Centro, 39000 Chilpancingo. **W:** chilpancingo.abcradiogro.com.mx - 1200-0400 – **GR17)** Benito Juárez 19-A, Barrio del Carmen, 41700 Omotepec. **W:** rtvgro.net – **GR18)** Hacienda del Cernillo, Casa Gallos s/n, 40200 Taxco. **W:** rtvgro.net - 1200-0400 – **GR19)** Grupo Radio México, Juan N. Álvarez 1, Desp. 3, 40900 Iguala. **W:** gradiomex. com - 1155-0500 – **GR20)** Avenida Benito Juárez No 21-A, Col Centro, 40880 Zihuatanejo – **GR21)** Avenida Lázaro Cárdenas 54, Col Héroes Surianos, 40500 Arcelia. **W:** radioarcelia.com - 1200-0300 – **GR22)** 41300 Tlapa de Comonfort **W:** rtvgro.net

HG00 HIDALGO (Hgo.)

HG01) Plaza de la Constitución y Manuel F Soto (or Ap.96), 43600 Tulancingo **W:** nqradio.com - 1200-0600 – **HG02)** AMorelos 27 (or

Ap.35), Zona Centro, 43000 Huejutla **W:** telecomunicacionesdela-huasteca.com - 1100-0200 – **HG03)** R. y Televisión de Hidalgo, Blvd. Adolfo López Mateos s/n, Col. Aviación Civil, 43000 Huejutla - 1100-0300 – **HG04)** Radio y Televisión de Hidalgo, Nicolás Bravo 3, Centro, 43440 San Bartolo Tutotepec - 1200-0100 – **HG05)** Plaza Juárez 103 (or Ap.123), 42000 Pachuca **W:** comadre.mx/index.php/comadre-nacional/pachuca - 1200-0600 – **HG07)** Radio y Televisión de Hidalgo, Calle de la Radio s/n, Barrio Cuartel Guerrero, 42200 Jacala - 1200-0300 – **HG08)** Hidalgo Ote.209, Col. Centro, 43600 Tulancingo **W:** ladivertida.com - 1200-0600 – **HG10)** 43150 Tlanchinol - 1200-0200 – **HG11)** Domicilio Conocido, Col Buenos Aires, 42370 Cárdonal - 1300-2300 Prgrs in Sp., Otomí and Náhuatl – **HG12)** Chávez Macotela 8, 42400 Huichapan
JL00) JALISCO (Jal.)
JL01) Organización Radio Alteña, Antonio Rojas 80-A, Col. El Cerrito, 47610, Tepatitlán - 1200-0300 **W:** radiotepatitlan.com – **JL02)** México Radio, Calzada Independencia Sur 324, Col. Centro, 44100 Guadalajara **W:** canal58.com.mx – **JL03)** Blvd. Francisco Medina Asencio km. 7.5, Plaza Marina Local 101, Col. Marina Vallarta, 48300 Puerto Vallarta **W:** laexplosiva.com – **JL04)** Radiorama de Occidente, Moctezuma 68, Centro, 49000 Cd. Guzmán - 1200-0600 – **JL05)** C7 Jalisco, Francisco Rojas González 155, Col. Ladrón de Guevara, 44600 Guadalajara. **W:** c7jalisco.com – **JL06)** Av. Francisco Villa 549, Col. Versalles, 48310 Puerto Vallarta – **JL07)** Hidalgo 158, Centro, 49000 Cd. Guzmán - 1200-0600 – **JL08)** Lorenzana 884, Col. Chapalita, 45040 Guadalajara – **JL09)** Deportes 109, La Martinica, 47020 San Juan de los Lagos - 1300-0300 **W:** radiotepatitlan.com – **JL10)** Notisistema, Av. México 3150 Fracc. Moraz, 44670 Guadalajara. **W:** notisistema.com – **JL11)** Grupo ACIR, Paseo de Las Gaviotas 198, Col. Las Gaviotas, 48351 Puerto Vallarta – **JL12)** Televisa Radio, Rubén Darío 158, Circunvalación Vallarta, 44680 Guadalajara **W:** Av. Hidalgo 111, Centro, 48900 Autlán. **W:** radiocosta.com.mx – **JL14)** Av. México 3370, Plaza Bonita, Local Subanda P, 45120 Guadalajara - 1300-0700 – **JL15)** Zaragoza 215, Centro, 47820 Ocotlán - 1200-0400 **W:** radioramadeoccidente.com – **JL16)** Promomedios, Portal Hidalgo 13, Int.10, Centro, 49650 Tamazula - 1200-0600 – **JL17)** Grupo ACIR, Av. Lázaro Cárdenas 2820, Jardines del Bosque, 44520 Guadalajara - 1200-0600 – **JL19)** Ramón Corona 204, Centro, 46600 Ameca. 1200-0400 **W:** radioameca.com.mx – **JL20)** Radiorama Puerto Vallarta, Honduras 309, Int. 161, Col.5 de Diciembre, 48350 Puerto Vallarta – **JL21)** San Juan Bosco 3623, Fracc. Jardines de San Ignacio, 45050 Zapopan. **W:** radiomariamexico.com – **JL22)** Av. Independencia 750, Local 17 (Plaza del Valle), 44750 Atotonilco el Alto – **JL23)** Primero de Mayo 126-8, 49000 Cd. Guzmán - 1200-0600 **W:** lamexicana.com.mx – **JL24)** Radiorama de Occidente, Av. Niños Héroes 1555, 6to. Piso, Col. Moderna, 44190 Guadalajara. **W:** radioramadeoccidente.com – **JL25)** Constituyentes 262, Centro, 47400 Lagos de Moreno. **W:** kebuenaradio.com.mx – **JL26)** Mega Radio, Av. Pablo Casals 567, Col. Prados Providencia, 44670 Guadalajara. **W:** megaradio.mx 1070noticias.com.mx – **JL27)** Océano Pacífico 201, Palmar de Aramara, 48300 Puerto Vallarta – **JL28)** RASA, Pasaje Juárez 20 Int. 6, Centro, 47910 La Barca – **JL29)** Hidalgo 2055 Esq. Tomas de Gómez, Col Arcos Sur, 44500 Guadalajara – **JL30)** Fco. I. Madero 77, 45750 Zacoalco de Torres - 1300-0100 – **JL31)** Hidalgo 122, 1er. piso, Centro, 48900 Autlan – **JL32)** Av. Francia 1783, Col. Moderna, Sector Juárez, 44190 Guadalajara - 1200-0600 – **JL33)** c/o El Periódico el Occidental, Calzada Independencia Sur 324, Col Centro, 44100 Guadalajara
ME00) ESTADO DE MÉXICO (Edo.Méx.)
ME01) Audiorama del Valle de México, Paseo de la Reforma 56, P1, Col.Juárez, 06000 México, D.F. **W:** radiorama.com.mx – 1200-0600 – **ME02)** Grupo R. Capital, Allende Sur 209, Col. Centro, 50000 Toluca. **W:** gruporadiocapital.mx - 1100-0600 – **ME03)** Sistema de R. y Televisión Mexiquense, Av. Quintana Roo 44, Col. Prado Sur, Tultitlan **W:** radioytvmexiquense.mx – **ME04)** Grupo ACIR Toluca, Paseo Tollocan Poniente 300, Col. Universidad, 50130 Toluca – **ME05)** Grupo Corporativo Miled México, Carretera Panamericana km 24, 50450 Atlacomulco. **W:** miled.com/radio/radio.php – **ME06)** Radiorama Toluca, Av. José María Morelos 903, esq. con Quintana Roo, Col. La Merced (Alameda), 50080 Toluca. **W:** radiorama.com.mx – **ME07)** Sistema de R. y TV Mexiquense, Av. Estado de México km 1, Col. La Virgen, 52140 Metepec **W:** radioytvmexiquense.mx - 1200-0600 – **ME08)** José María Morelos 948, Esq. Carretera a Tonatico, 51900 Ixtapan de la Sal. **W:** gruporadiocapital.mx/index.php/capital-maxima/ixtapan-de-la-sal - 1200-0600 – **ME09)** Grupo Corporativo Miled México, Independencia 506, 51200 Valle del Bravo **W:** miled.com/radio/radio.php - 1300-0400 – **ME10)** Universidad Autónoma de Chapingo, Carr. México-Texcoco km 38.5, 56235 Chapingo **W:** chapingo.mx/cultura/radio.php - 1800-0200 – **ME11)** Cabina 5, Edificio CAD, Escuela de Comunicación, Av. Universidad Anáhuac 46, Col. Lomas Anáhuac, Huixquilucan. **W:** anahuac.mx/radio
MI00) MICHOACÁN (Mich.)
MI01) Aqua 78, Col.Prados del Campestre, 58297 Morelia **W:** cande-

lamorelia.mx - 1200-0300 – **MI02)** Av. Revolución Sur 66 (or Ap.50), 61500 Zitácuaro **W:** radiozitacuaro.com - 1200-0600 (SS -0400) – **MI03)** Privada de Diligencias 53, Int. 1, Fraccionamiento El Mirador (or Ap.61), 60100 Uruapan **W:** exafm.com/#!/uruapan/home – **MI04)** Av.5 de Mayo 501 Sur, Jardines de Catedral, 59670 Zamora **W:** radiozamora.com.mx - 1200-0600 – **MI05)** Camécuaro S/N, Col. Morelo, 61609 Pátzcuaro **W:** radiomejor.com - 1200-0600 – **MI06)** Madero Norte 15, 61940 Huetamo **W:** lazeta.com.mx – **MI07)** Macarena 32, Inhuambo, 60130 Uruapan **W:** radioramamichoacan.com – **MI08)** Av.Constitución de 1814 Norte 2 Altos, 60600 Apatzingan **W:** gruporadioapatzingan.com.mx - 1200-0500 – **MI09)** Domicilio Conocido, Predio INI, 60270 Cheran **W:** ecos.cdi.gob.mx/xepur.html - 1300-0020 Prgrs in Sp and Purépecha – **MI10)** Avenida Morelos No 529, Plaza Ruíz, Centro, (Ap.65), 58600 Zacapu **W:** maxistarxezi.com - 1200-0200 – **MI11)** Carr. Lázaro Cárdenas-La Mira, 5 de Mayo, 60990 Lázaro Cárdenas – **MI12)** Ap.50, 58600 Zacapu – **MI13)** Laguna de Parras 630, Col.Ventura Puente, 58020 Morelia – **MI14)** Av.Constitución de 1814 Norte 2 Altos, 60600 Apatzingán **W:** xecj.com - 1200-0400 – **MI15)** Madero 116, Col. Centro, 59300 La Piedad – **MI16)** Dulcamara s/n, 58254 Morelia - 1200-0900 – **MI17)** Mariano Jiménez Norte 8-1, Centro, 60300 Los Reyes **W:** grupotremor.es.tl - 1200-0200 – **MI18)** Carretera Federal N° 15 Morelia-Zitácuaro km 125.6, 61420 Tuxpan - 1200-2330 Prgrs in Sp., Mazahua, Otomí & Matlatzinca – **MI19)** Juan Ayala 10, Int 102, Centro, 60000 Uruapan **W:** modernaradio.com – **MI20)** 20 de Noviembre 358, 58000 Morelia **W:** maxima1009.com - 1200-0400 – **MI21)** Mazatlán 30, Col. La Magdalena, 60080 Uruapan – **MI22)** Altos Mercado Emiliano Zapata, 61100 Cd.Hidalgo **W:** radiomejor.com - 1200-0400 – **MI23)** Av. Madero Pte 644, 58000 Morelia **W:** ultra.com.mx/radio/index.php/michoacan.html - 1200-0300 – **MI24)** Av. Díaz Ordaz 225A (Ap.60), 59000 Sahuayo **W:** promoradio.com.mx - 1300-0400 – **MI25)** Artilleros 47 No. 1585 local C, Col Chapultepec Oriente, 58260 Morelia **W:** kissfm.mx – **MI26)** Aquiles Serdán 548 , 58020 Morelia **W:** lazeta.com.mx – **MI27)** Universidad Michoacana de San Nicolás de Hidalgo, Cd. Universitaria, 58000 Morelia **W:** radionic.umich.mx – **MI28)** Av.Río Balsas 7, 60950 Cd. Lázaro Cárdenas - 1200-0400 – **MI29)** Camino de los Gatos 200, 58000 Morelia **W:** smrtv.michoacan.gob.mx – **MI30)** . José María Morelos 14, Segundo Sector del Fidelac, 60950 Lázaro Cárdenas **W:** radioazul.imer.gob.mx - 1100-0600.
MO00) MORELOS (MoR)
MO01) Paseo del Conquistador 55, Col. San Cristóbal, 62230 Cuernavaca **W:** radioramamorelos.com.mx - 1200-0600 – **MO02)** 62746 Cuautla (alt.address: Hidalgo 105, 62220 Ocotepec, Cuernavaca) – **MO03)** Plaza Yuliana, P2, 62900 Jojutla **W:** jojutlaradio.tv - 1200-0100.
NA00) NAYARIT (Nay.)
NA01) Radio Aztlán, Av. Victoria 213 A Pte, 63940 Tepic. **W:** radioaztlan.com.mx – **NA02)** Carretera Tecuala – Acaponeta km. 1, Tecuala (or Ap.7, 63440 Tecuala) - 1200-2400 **W:** radiored925fm.com – **NA03)** Radiorama Nayarit, Puebla 64 Sur, Centro, 63060 Tepic. **E:** radiorama-nayarit@hotmail.com **W:** radioramanayarit.mx – **NA05)** Insurgentes 1046 Pte., Col. El Rodeo, 63060 Tepic. - 1200-0800 **W:** grk.com.mx – **NA06)** Domicilio Conocido, 63530 Jesús María - 1200-2000 Prgrs in Sp., Cora, Huichol, Tepehuáno and Náhuatl – **NA07)** Grupo MAC Multimedia, Atenas 80 Altos, Fracc. Ciudad del Valle, 63157 Tepic. **W:** gruporadiocapital.mx/index.php/capital-fm/tepic-nayarit – **NA08)** Amado Nervo 106-B Ote, (or: Ap.4), 63310 Santiago Ixcuintla - 1200-0300 – **NA09)** Insurgentes 2222, Col. Burócrata Federal, 63180 Tepic - 1300-0700 – **NA10)** Justo Barajas No 50 Norte, Centro, 63940 Ixtlán del Río - 1300-0100 – **NA11)** López Mateos 61, 63715 Las Varas - 1300-0100 – **NA12)** P Sánchez 87 (or: Ap.22), 63310 Santiago Ixcuintla - 1300-0500 – **NA13)** Puebla 3, 63600 Cd. Ruíz - 1200-0300
NL00) NUEVO LEÓN (N.L.)
NL01) Parque Industrial Regiomontano, 64540 Monterrey – **NL02)** Grupo Radio Alegría, Av. Madero Oriente 1110, 64000 Monterrey. **W:** epsilonmedia.mx/?page_id=15313 – **NL03)** Grupo Radio México, Juan Ignacio Ramón 506 Oriente, P20, Edif. Latino, 64000 Monterrey **W:** lareinadelnorte.com fb630.com – **NL04)** Paricutín Sur 316, Col. Roma, (or: Ap.203) 64700 Monterrey - 1200-0700 **W:** mmradio.com/rg690/envivo – **NL05)** Av. Paseo de los Leones 2935, Col. Cumbres 5to. Sector, 64000 Monterrey - 1200-0000 – **NL06)** Capitán Alonso de León s/n o Antigua Carretera Nacional km 904, Barrio Zaragoza, 67500 Montemorelos. **W:** delta929fm.com – **NL07)** Carr. Nacional Km. 856, Col. La Amistad, 67700 Linares (or. Ap.81), 67700 Linares - 1200-0600 – **NL08)** Radio ACIR, Monterrey 698, Esq. Cerralvo, Col. Libertad, 64130 Guadalupe. **W:** radioacir.net – **NL09)** Carr. Nacional Km 208, El Desagüe, 67535 Montemorelos. – **NL10)** NRM Comunicaciones, Av. Cuauhtémoc 725 Nte., Centro, (or Ap.118) 64000 Monterrey. **W:** larancheradementerrey.com.mx contacto1190.com.mx – **NL11)** Grupo Radio Alegría, Reforma s/n, Col. Enrique Lozano, 65290 Cd. Sabinas Hidalgo - 1200-0600 – **NL12)** Av. San Francisco y Loma Grande, Col. Loma Grande, 64000 Monterrey. **W:** radionuevoleon.com.mx – **NL13)** Grupo Radio Centro,

Padre Mier Poniente 439, Centro, 64000 Monterrey

OX00) OAXACA (Oax.)
OX01) Carr. Transístmica Km. 6.5, Co. El Granadillo, 70600 Salina Cruz - 1200-0500 – **OX02)** Radiorama Oaxaca, Macedonio Alcalá 915, Centro, 68000 Oaxaca – **OX03)** Carretera Transístmica s/n, Barrio de Bixama, (or: Ap.21) 70760 Tehuantepec - 1200-0600 – **OX04)** Corporación Oaxaqueña de Radio y Televisión, Madero s/n, Centro Cultural, 68000 Oaxaca. **W:** cortv.com.mx – **OX05)** Ap.35, 70900 Puerto Ángel - 1200-0200 – **OX06)** Aquiles Serdán y Mina 502, Col. Benito Juárez Norte, 70301 Matías Romero - 1200-0100 **W:** facebook.com/xeyg. lakebuena660 – **OX07)** Grupo Radio México, Netzahualcóyotl 216, Col Reforma, 68050 Oaxaca - 1200-0600 – **OX08)** Morelos 6-2, 71000 Putla de Guerrero - 1200-0130 – **OX09)** Carr. Cd. Alemán a Sayula Km 27, 68400 Loma Bonita - 1200-0400 – **OX10)** Lázaro Cárdenas s/n, 68770 Guelatao de Juárez - 1200-0130 Prgrs in Sp., Zapoteco, Mixe and Chinanteco – **OX11)** 5 de Mayo 21-A, Centro, 69800 Tlaxiaco - 1200-0500 **W:** lapoderosatlaxiaco.com – **OX12)** Carr. Puerto Escondido-Pochutla Km. 143, 71980 Puerto Escondido - 1300-0600 – **OX13)** Av. Alfonso Perez Gasca 504, 71600 Pinotepa Nacional - 1200-0600 – **OX14)** Carr. Yucudaa km 54.5, 69899 Tlaxiaco - 1200-2400 Prgrs in Sp., Mixteco and Triqui – **OX15)** Independencia s/n, Sección Segunda, 68470 San Lucas Ojitlán - 1400-2200 Prgrs in Sp., Mazateco, Cuicateco and Chinanteco – **OX16)** Jazmines 907, 68000 Oaxaca - 1200-0600 – **OX17)** Venustiano Carranza 74-A, Col. Altavista de Juárez, (Apartado 48), 69005 Huajuapan de León - 1300-0100 **W:** xeouradio.com – **OX18)** Carr. Juchitán - El Espinal Km. 1, Zona Industrial, 70050 Juchitán **W:** facebook.com/KBjuchitanfans – **OX19)** Gómez Farias 113, Centro, 68000 Oaxaca - 1200-0400 **W:** formulaoaxaca.caster.fm – **OX20)** Abasolo 37, Centro, 68300 Tuxtepec - 1200-0100 **W:** facebook. com/lamejortuxtepec – **OX21)** Valerio Trujano 708, Centro, 68000 Oaxaca - 1130-0600 – **OX22)** Plaza de la Constitución y Negrete s/n, 71700 Santiago Jamiltepec. Prgrs in Sp., Mixteco, Amuzgo and Chatino - 1200-2400 – **OX23)** Universidad Autónoma Benito Juárez, Av. Universidad s/n, Ex-Hacienda de 5 Señores, 68120 Oaxaca. **W:** uabjo.mx/radio.php

PU00) PUEBLA (Pue.)
PU01) Plaza de la Constitución 102, altos 1, 73080 Xicotepec de Juárez **W:** facebook.com/RadioXicotepec – **PU02)** Allende 507, Col. Centro, 73800 Teziutlán **W:** xefj.com.mx - 1200-0400 – **PU03)** Matamoros No. 29-C, Col. Centro, 73160 Huauchinango. **W:** xengradio.com – **PU04)** Edificio Impacto, Tlaxcala 3, Col. La Santísima, (Ap.4), 74000 San Martín Texmelucan - 1200-0600 – **PU05)** Av. Juárez 1002, Col. Centro, 73800 Teziutlán. **W:** xhol.com.mx – **PU06)** Teziutlán Sur 17, Col. La Paz, 72160 Puebla **W:** radiooro.com.mx – **PU07)** Zaragoza 31-A, Centro, 74400 Izúcar de Matamoros **W:** radiorama.com.mx – **PU08)** Blvd. Atlixco 37, Local 218, Plaza JV, Col. San José, 72170 Puebla. **W:** kebuena1010.com.mx – **PU09)** Uno Sur 112, Mezzanine (or Ap.84), 75700 Tehuacán **W:** http://lamejor.com.mx/#!/tehuacan/home exafm. com/#!/tehuacan/home - 1200-0700 – **PU10)** Av. 15 de Mayo 2939, Col. Las Hadas, 72070 Puebla. **W:** cincoradio.com.mx – **PU11)** Cinco Radio, Manuel Pereyra Mejía 417, Col. Ignacio Zaragoza, 75770 Tehuacán. **W:** cincoradio.com.mx - 1300-0100 – **PU12)** 1 Sur 108, Desp. 307, Col. Centro, 75700 Tehuacán. **W:** radiorama.com.mx – **PU13)** Calle Matamoros 77, esq. San Martin Texmelucan, Col. La Paz, 72160 Puebla. **W:** tribunacomunicacion.com – **PU14)** 3 Oriente no, 201, col. Centro Histórico, 72000 Puebla. **W:** abcradiopuebla.com.mx – **PU15)** Av. 15 Pte. 1306, Col. Santiago, 72000 Puebla. **W:** grupoacir.com – **PU16)** Hidalgo 65, Centro, 74400 Izúcar de Matamoros **W:** gruporadiocapital.mx - 1200-0600 – **PU17)** Esmeralda Comunicaciones, Prol. Manuel M. Flores s/n, 75520 Cd. Serdán. **W:** kebuenapuebla.com - 1300-0100 – **PU18)** Priv. Miguel Alvarado s/n, 73560 Cuetzalán. **W:** cdi.gob.mx - 1200-0100 prgrs in Sp, Náhuatl and Totonaco.

QE00) QUERÉTARO (Qro.)
QE01) Universidad Autónoma de Querétaro, Av. Hidalgo s/n 76010 Querétaro **W:** radio.uaq.mx -1200-0600 – **QE03)** Carr. San Juan del Rio-Xilitla km 181, Col. San José, 76340 Jalpan - 1200-0600 – **QE04)** Av. Carrizal 28-F2, Fracc. Ampliación Carrizal, 76030 Querétaro. **W:** respuestaradiofonica.com.mx - 1200-0600 – **QE05)** Av. Tecnológico Sur 2, Local 106, Col. Niños Héroes, 76010 Querétaro **W:** integra927. com – **QE06)** Paseo del Prado 102, Desp 401, Fracc. el Prado, 76030 Querétaro – **QE07)** Camino de Piedras Anchas 100, Cabecera Municipal de Jalpan de Serra, 76000 Jalpan **W:** radioytelevisionquere-taro.mx – **QE09)** Av .Juárez 38 Pte, 76800 San Juan del Río. **W:** exafm. com - 1200-0400

QR00) QUINTANA ROO (Q.Roo.)
QR01) Radiorama Chetumal, Palermo 327, Col. Josefa Ortíz de Domínguez, 77036 Chetumal – **QR02)** Calle 63, Supermanzana 61, Mzna 7, Lote 1, 77500 Cancún - 1100-0600 – **QR03)** Grupo Radio México, Av. López Portillo, Supermanzana 59, Manzana 8 Lote 2, Local 1433-A, Col. Benito Juárez, 77515 Cancún - 1200-0300 **W:** cancun. lazradio.com.mx – **QR04)** Sistema Quintanarroense de Comunicación

Social, Carretera a Tulum, Km. 1.5, 77200 Félipe Carillo Puerto. **W:** sqcs. com.mx – **QR06)** Plaza Hollywood local 86, Supermanzana 35, 77508 Cancún **W:** radioformulaqr.com – **QR07)** 20 Av. Sur 965, Entre 13 y 15, Sur. Col. Andrés Quintana Roo. (or:Ap.299) 77600 Cozumel, **W:** sol899. com – **QR08)** Av. Miguel Hidalgo 201, 77000 Chetumal - 1100-0700 **W:** sqcs.com.mx – **QR09)** Av. Uxmal 30, Supermanzana 62, 77513 Cancún - 1100-0500 **W:** sqcs.com.mx – **QR11)** Prol. Av.Héroes 680, 77000 Chetumal - 1200-0400 **W:** sol899.com – **QR12)** Av. Altamirano 83, Col. Emiliano Zapata, 77229 Félipe Carillo Puerto - 1200-1700 Prgrs in Sp and Maya – **QR13)** Av. Náder 25, SM2 Mzna. 13, Desp.401, 77500 Cancún

SL00) SAN LUIS POTOSÍ (S.L.P.)
SL01) Radiorama San Luis Potosí, Eucaliptos 565, Col. Jardín, 78270 San Luis Potosí **W:** los40sanluis.com.mx romantica931.com – **SL02)** Londres y atenas s/n, Fracc.Lomas, 79090 Cd.Valles **W:** lagrancompa-nia.com radiomensajera.com– **SL03)** Fausto Nieto 220, 78000 San Luis Potosí - 1200-0400 – **SL04)** Hidalgo 7-A, 79600 Río Verde - 1300-0100 – **SL05)** Globalmedia, Av. Dr. Salvador Nava Martínez No 278, Col El Paseo, 78320 San Luis Potosí **W:** globalmedia.mx – **SL06)** Carranza 1408-interior, Col. Tequisquiapan, 78250 San Luis Potosí – **SL07)** Josefa Ortíz de Domínguez s/n, 79800 Tancanhuitz de Santos - 1200-0700. Prgrs in Sp., Náhuatl, Pame and Huasteco – **SL08)** Los Bravo 445 Altos, 78000 San Luis Potosí **W:** abcradio.com.mx/xeabc.asp – **SL09)** Betancourt No 401, Col. Centro, 78700 Matehuala **W:** stereo1030. com - 1155-0405 – **SL10)** Avenida México Laredo No 29, Sur, 79050 Cd.Valles **W:** panoramicaxetr.com – **SL11)** Privada Pemex 3 Barrio San Rafael, 79960 Tamazunchale **W:** radioreyna.com.mx - 1200-0800 – **SL12)** General Mariano Arista 245, Centro Histórico, 78000 San Luis Potosí. **W:** radiouniversidad.uaslp.mx – **SL14)** MG Radio, Capitán Caldera 315, Col. Tequisquiapan, 78250 San Luis Potosí **W:** factor961. fm/laz1021 – **SL15)** Ap.80, 78700 Matehuala - 1200-0400 – **SL16)** Carretera México-Laredo Sur s/n, Lomas Poniente, 79099 Cd. Valles. **W:** xeir.net

SN00) SINALOA (Sin.)
SN01) Aquiles Serdán 860 Pte, Col. Scally, 81200 Los Mochis - 1300-0700 **W:** lamejor.com.mx/#!/losmochis/home exafm.com/#!/losmo-chis/home – **SN02)** RSN, Av. Rafael Buelna 202, Fracc. Hacienda Las Cruces, 82134 Mazatlán **W:** lamejor.com.mx/#!/mazatlan/home – **SN03)** Chávez Radiocast, Ignacio Zaragoza 200, 2do.piso, Centro, 81000 Guasave - 1230-0800 **W:** chavezradiocast.com – **SN04)** Av. Benemérito de las Américas 400, Lomas del Mar, 82010 Mazatlán **W:** exafm.com/mazatlan – **SN05)** Cjon. Sinaloa 442 Pte., Centro, 81200 Los Mochis, **W:** chavezradiocast.com.mx – **SN06)** Megamedios Guasave, Macario Gaxiola 856, Centro, 81000 Guasave - 1200-0600 – **SN07)** Radiorama Mazatlán, Av. Miguel Alemán 619 Ote, Centro, 82000 Mazatlán – **SN08)** Radiorama Culiacán, Av. Álvaro Obregón 424 Sur, Local 53 2do. piso, Plaza Paladio, Centro, 80000, Culiacán – SN09) Grupo Radio México, Hidalgo 755 Pte, 81200 Los Mochis – **SN10)** Universidad de Occidente, Blvd. Macario Gaxiola y Carr. Internacional, 81200 Los Mochis **W:** radiouto.tk – **SN11)** Grupo ACIR, Paseo Niños Héroes 310 Ote., Centro, 80000 Culiacán - 1300-0600 **W:** maxima103.com – **SN13)** Radiorama Navolato, Niños Héroes 143 Ote. Col. Pueblo Nuevo II, 80320 Navolato – **SN14)** Grupo Promomedios, Insurgentes 334 Sur, Centro Sinaloa, 80129 Culiacán – **SN15)** Grupo ABC Radio, Av. Miguel Alemán No 312, Centro (Ap.148), 82006 Mazatlán – **SN16)** Radiorama Los Mochis, Av. Vicente Guerrero 599 Sur, Centro, 81200 Los Mochis – **SN17)** Radio Universidad Autónoma de Sinaloa, Agustina Ramírez 1249, Col. Gabriel Leyva, 80030 Culiacán - 1300-0200 **W:** radiouas.org – **SN18)** Grupo Fórmula, Insurgentes 1225 - 25, Ejidal, 80120 Culiacán - 1300-0200 – **SN19)** RSN, Juan Macedo López 201-1 Desarrollo Urbano Tres Ríos, 80020 Culiacán – **SN20)** Chavez Radiocast, Blvd Antonio Rosales 509 Ote, Col. Morelos, 81460 Guamuchil - 1200-0800 – **SN21)** MegaMedios Sur, 16 de Septiembre 6-B Norte, Centro, 82400 Escuinapa - 1200-0200 **W:** megamediossur. com – **SN22)** Insurgentes 313, Col. Flamingos, 82149 Mazatlán

SO00) SONORA (Son.)
SO01) Av.16 de Septiembre 22, Centro, 85900 Huatabampo - 1300-0700 – **SO02)** Grupo R. Palacios, Álvaro Obregón 184, Centro, 83600 Caborca **W:** gruporadiopalacios.com.mx – **SO03)** Blvd. Rodolfo Elías Calles 252 Ote, Centro, 85000 Cd.Obregón. **W:** maximaobregon.com – **SO04)** Yáñez 5, entre Zacatecas y San Luis Potosí, 83000 Hermosillo - 1200-0700 **W:** lamejor.com.mx/#!/hermosillo/home – **SO05)** Av. Serdán, y Calle 29 N° 415, Centro, (or: Ap.630) 85480 Guaymas – **SO06)** Larsa Comunicaciones, Paseo Río Sonora Sur 205, esquina con Galeana, Col. Proyecto Río, 83270 Hermosillo **W:** http:larsavision. tv – **SO07)** Carr. a Novojoa km 27, 85280 Etchojoa y Pueblo Yaqui in Sp., Mayo, Yaqui and Guarijío – **SO08)** Calle 19 N° 81, entre 15 y 16, Centro, 85400 Guaymas - 1300-0700 **W:** gruporadioguaymas.com – **SO09)** Grupo Radiofónico ZER, Calle Internacional y Av. 5 Int. 8-C, 84200 Agua Prieta. **W:** grupozer.net/estados.php?estado=4 – **SO10)**

Uniradio, Norte 811 Oriente, Centro, 85000 Cd. Obregón. **W:** lapreciosa.com.mx – **S011)** Obregón 38, 1 Altos, Centro, 84000 Nogales (or: Box 1472, Nogales, AZ 85628, USA) **W:** xenygenial.com – **S012)** Durango 901 Sur Altos, Col. Campestre, 85160 Cd. Obregón - 1300-0200 - **S013)** Av. Escobedo S/N. entre Blvd. Luis Encinas Johnson y Blvd. Abelardo Rodríguez, Centro,83000 Hermosillo - 1200-0620 **E:** universidad@radio.uson.mx **W:** radio.uson.mx – **S014)** Radio Grupo García de León, Veracruz 230 Sur Altos, Centro, 85000 Cd. Obregón – **S015)** Radio SA, Nayarit 96, 83000 Hermosillo - 1300-0800 **W:** grupera931.com – **S016)** Larsa Comunicaciones, Sinaloa 408 Sur, Entre Galeana y Zaragoza, 85000 Cd. Obregón– **S017)** IMER, Av. Juárez 9ª Este, 84620 Cananea - 1200-0700 **W:** lafq.imer.gob.mx – **S018)** Uniradio, Juárez 206, Centro, 85800 Navojoa - 1200-0700 **W:** ke980.com – **S019)** Pino Suarez 99, 84900 Ures - 1300-0500 – **S020)** Abelardo Rodríguez 180, Desp.45, Col. Centro, 85400 Guaymas **W:** radiovisa.com.mx/Guaymas – **S021)** Av. Madero 1107, entre las calles 11 y 12, 83449 San Luis Río Colorado - 1200-0700 - (transmitter site: Morelos, B.C.) – **S022)** Larsa Comunicaciones, Blvd. Álvaro Obregón No 216-1, Col Reforma, 85830 Navojoa – **S023)** Heriberto Aja 96 y Nayarit, 83000 Hermosillo – **S024)** Larsa Comunicaciones, Vázquez 127, Col. Fundo Legal, 84000 Nogales - 1200-0200 **W:** kebuena.com.mx – **S025)** Radiovisa, Av.13 de Julio 5-A, Centro, 83600 Caborca – **S026)** Matamoros 1, Edif. Combate, Centro, 83000 Hermosillo – **S027)** Oaxaca 142, Centro, 83000 Hermosillo. **W:** radioformulasonora.com – **S028)** Calle 25 No. 20 Altos, Centro, 85400 Guaymas. **W:** fm105.com.mx – **S029)** Radio SA, Nayarit y Heriberto Aja 96, Centro, 83000 Hermosillo. **W:** activa897.com – **S030)** Ave. Francisco Eusebio Kino y Calle 5 No 470, Barrio Comercial (Ap.44), 83449 San Luis Río Colorado - 1300-0100. **W:** radiogrupooir.com/zeta radiogrupooir.com/centro – **S031)** Av. Morelos y Ramón Corona s/n, Col. Constitución, 83850 Navojoa - 1200-0700 – **S032)** Av. 6 No. 660, Centro, (or Ap.28), 84200 Agua Prieta - 1400-0300 – **S033)** Grupo Radio Fórmula, Váquez 127 Altos, Col. Fundo Legal, 84000 Nogales – **S034)** Blvd. Benito Juárez y Martires de Chicago, Centro, (or Ap.66) 83550 Pto. Peñasco - 1200-0100 **W:** facebook.com/XEQC1390AM – **S035)** Ap.44, 84600 Santa Ana - 1400-0500 – **S037)** Ap.28, 84200 Agua Prieta 1500-0600 – **S038)** Carr. del Valle y Prol. Ave. Madero, 83449 San Luis Río Colorado – **S039)** Uniradio, Blvd Navarrete 38, Local 2, Col. Valle Hermoso, 83209 Hermosillo **W:** uniradionoticias.com/invasora1019

TB00) TABASCO (Tab.)
TB03) Paseo de la Ceiba 102, Piso 3, Col. Primero de Mayo, 86190 Villahermosa – **TB14)** Comisión de Radio y Televisión de Tabasco, Prolongación 27 de Febrero No.1001, 86035 Villahermosa. **W:** corat.mx

TM00) TAMAULIPAS (Tamps.)
TM01) Organización Radiofónica Tamaulipeca, Gaspar de la Garza 170 Sur, 87000 Cd. Victoria - 1200-0600 **W:** ort.com.mx/radio – **TM02)** Blvd. Miguel Hidalgo 200 A, Col. Polanco, 88710 Reynosa - 1300-0100 – **TM03)** BMP Radio, Lázaro Cárdenas 210, Local 19,20 y 21, Col. Centro, 88500 Reynosa – **TM04)** Altamira Calle Principal de Esteros, Carr. Tampico-González, 89600 Altamira - 1200-0400 **W:** radio.tamaulipas.gob.mx – **TM05)** Radiorama Cd. Victoria, Carretera Victoria-Mante Km 2 s/n, Col Las Brisas, 87180 Cd. Victoria – **TM06)** Radiorama Tampico G. AS, Benito Juárez 506-A, Col. Tolteca, 89160 Tampico. **W:** radioramatampico.com – **TM07)** Radiorama Tampico R.G., Valentín Gómez Farías 407, Col. Otomí, 89150 Tampico - 1200-0600 **W:** radioramatampico.com.mx – **TM09)** Zaragoza 85, 87600 San Fernando - 1200-0600 **W:** es-es.facebook.com/pages/La-Poderosa-780-San-Fernando-Tamps/208401075867066 – **TM10)** Grupo Mi Radio, Paseo Colón 3822. 2do. piso, local 16, Plaza Cristal Colonia Jardín. 88060 Nuevo Laredo. **W:** grupomiradio.mx/portal/estaciones/nuevolaredo – **TM11)** Tiburcio Garza Zamora 335, Rodríguez, 88630 Reynosa. **W:** radiorey.com – **TM12)** Colón 207 Norte, Centro, 89000 Tampico. **W:** laestrellafm.com.mx – **TM13)** Av. Juárez 703 Ote., 89800 Cd. Mante - 1200-0100 **W:** ort.com.mx/radio – **TM14)** – Boulevard Adolfo López Mateos 3205, Local 9 y 10, Col. Santo Niño, 89160 Tampico **W:** grupomiradio.mx/portal/estaciones/tampico - 1200-0600 – **TM15)** Radiorama Reynosa, Tiburcio Garza Zamora No 1245, Col Beatty, 88630 Reynosa - 1200-0400 – **TM16)** González 2409 3er. Piso, 88000 Nuevo Laredo – **TM17)** Calle 14 y Abasolo, No 76, 87300 Matamoros - 1200-0600 **W:** notigape.com – **TM18)** Radiorama Tamaulipas, Chairel 2101, Col. Águila, 89230 Tampico – **TM19)** Morelos 2513, Juárez, 88209 Nuevo Laredo - 1200-0600 – **TM20)** Radiorama Nuevo Laredo, Mendoza 747, Centro, 88000 – **TM21)** Blvd. Hidalgo 22 A, Fracc. Polanco, 88710 Reynosa – **TM22)** Altamira No 311, Poniente, Zona Centro, 89000 Tampico – **TM23)** Valentín Gómez Farías, 89150 Tampico - 1200-0600 **W:** radiouncion1009fm.com – **TM24)** Diego Acuña, 87900 Cd. Tula - 1200-0400 – **TM25)** Sexta 75, Centro, (or Ap.540), 87300 Matamoros - 1200-0700 **W:** grupomiradio.mx/portal/estaciones/matamoros – **TM26)** Morelos 2513, Col. Juárez, (or. Ap.232), 88000 Nuevo Laredo - 1155-0600 (Sat –0800, Sun -0200) – **TM27)** Carretera Ribereña KM 62, 88440 Cd. Camargo - 1200-0400 **W:** grupomiradio.mx/portal/estaciones/reynosa – **TM28)** Av. Cuauhtémoc

y Calle 12, Col. San Francisco, 87350 Matamoros - 1155-0600. **W:** w1420.com – **TM29)** Quinta 226, Centro, (or Ap.13), 83000 Cd. Miguel Alemán 1155-0400 – **TM30)** Grupo R. Avanzado, Ignacio Zaragoza 660, Local 4, 88500 Reynosa - 1200-0600. **W:** laraza1060.com – **TM31)** Séptima 233 Altos, Centro, 88300 Ciudad Miguel Alemán - 1155-0200 **W:** grupomiradio.mx/portal/estaciones/miguelaleman – **TM32)** Calle 8 y Cuauhtémoc 125, Col. Pedro Sosa, 87120 Cd Victoria - 1200-0800 **W:** radio.tamaulipas.gob.mx – **TM33)** Sexta y Fuerza Aérea, Edif. María Rebeca, 87300 Matamoros

TX00) TLAXCALA (Tlax.)
TX01) Av.Juárez Norte 203, 90500 Huamantla - 1200-0600 – **TX02)** Calle Uno 420, Col. Xicohtencatl, 90070 Tlaxcala - 1200-0600.

VE00) VERACRUZ (Ver.)
VE02) Av. Tres 425, 94500 Córdoba **W:** imagen.com.mx 1230-0430 – **VE03)** Ruíz Cortines 303, Col. Centro, 95400 Cosamaloapan. **W:** xefuradio.com.mx – **VE05)** Playa Aventura s/n, Col. Playa Linda, 91810 Veracruz **W:** los40.com.mx – **VE08)** Moctezuma 77, Bis Col. Centro, 91000 Xalapa. **W:** gruporadiocapital.mx/xezl – **VE09)** Benjamín Franklin 4, Col. Centro, 91700 Veracruz. **W:** avanradio-radiorama.com – **VE11)** Av. Unión esq. Michoacan 101, Col. Lazaro Cardenas, 93200 Poza Rica. – **VE12)** Ignacio de la Llave 38, 92000 Pánuco – **VE13)** Av.Salvador Díaz Mirón 2625, Esq. Heroico, Col. Militar, 91700 Veracruz. **W:** mix885.mx – **VE14)** Calle 9 y Ave 5 No. 311, Col. Centro, 94500 Cordoba – **VE21)** Bravo 1103 N° 201, 91700 Veracruz **W:** radioramapozarica.com.mx – **VE22)** Eulalio Vela 15, Col. Obrera, 96700 Minatitlán. **W:** gruporadiomina.com – **VE24)** Morelos No. 37 Altos 3er. Piso Frente al Parque Reforma, Col. Centro, 92800 Tuxpan. **W:** radiorama.com.mx – **VE25)** Libertad y Morelos 301, 96100 Tierra Blanca - 1200-0200 – **VE26)** Francisco González Bocanegra No 10-B, Centro, 95700 San Andrés Tuxtla. **W:** grupoacir.com – **VE27)** Plaza Crystal, Local 20, 91150 Xalapa. **W:** olivanoticias.com - 1200-0600 – **VE28)** Bernarda Soto Mercado 2, 91615 Teocelo. **W:** radioteocelo.org - 1100-0200 – **VE30)** R. Mil de Veracruz, Ignacio Zaragoza 519, 96400 Coatzacoales **W:** maxima931.com.mx – **VE31)** Calle Bella Vista 65, Col. Cerro de la Cruz, 92123 Tantoyuca. **W:** radioramatampico.com – **VE32)** Sur 31 N° 336, 94300 Orizaba. **W:** grupoacir.com.mx 1200-0600 – **VE35)** Cra. Nacional 38, 93620 San Rafel - 1300-0100 – **VE36)** Universidad Veracruzana, Francisco de Clavijero 24, 91000 Xalapa. **W:** uv.mx/radio - 1300-0700 – **VE37)** Zamora 364-Altos, Centro, 91700 Veracruz – **VE41)** Fernando Silíceo 801, 91970 Veracruz – **VE42)** Azueta No. 8, Col. Centro, 95000 Zongolica – **VE43)** Banderas 4, 92800 Tuxpam – **VE46)** Av. Guerrero 202 Sur, Zona Centro, 96400 Coatzacoalcos **W:** radiohit.com.mx – **VE48)** Libertad No 315, Altos, entre Juárez y Madero, Centro, 95100 Tierra Blanca. **W:** radiorama.com.mx – **VE49)** 16 de Septiembre 341, 2° Piso esq. Canal, Fracc. Faros, 91700 Veracruz. **W:** radioformula.com.mx – **VE50)** Ignacio de la Llave 36, Centro, 93990 Pánuco. **W:** grupomiradio.mx/portal/estaciones/panuco – **VE51)** **W:** lamejor.com.mx/tlapacoyan – **VE52)** Carretera Xalapa-Veracruz 200; 91190 Xalapa. **W:** abcradio.com.mx – **VE54)** Garizurieta 25, Zona Centro, 92800 Tuxpan. **W:** radioola.com.mx – **VE55)** Pedro Belli 229, Col. Centro, 93600 Martínez de la Torre. **W:** lamejor.com.mx/tlapacoyan

YU00) YUCATÁN (Yuc.)
YU01) Grupo Rivas, Calle 62 N° 465, Entre 53 y 55, Centro, 97000 Mérida - 1130-0100. **W:** gruporivas.com.mx – **YU03)** Calle 33-B No. 513, Col. García Gineres, 97070 Mérida. – **YU04)** Cadena RASA, Km 1 Carr. Valladolid-Carillo Puerto, 97780 Valladolid - 1100-0500 **W:** cadenarasa.com/candela_valladolid – **YU05)** Cadena RASA, Edificio Publicentro, Calle 62, No 508 Altos, (Ap.217), 97001 Mérida - 1200-0600 **W:** cadenarasa.com – **YU07)** Carretera Peto-Tzucacab Km 2, 97930, Peto. - 1100-0100 (Sun - 1300-2200) Prgrs in Sp And Maya – **YU09)** Universidad Autónoma de Yucatán, Calle 60 No. 491-A, Esquina con 57, Centro, 97000 Mérida. - 1200-0600 **W:** radio.uady.mx **E:** radio@uady.mx – **YU10)** Fundación Cultural para la Sociedad Mexicana A.C., 97000 Mérida.

ZC00) ZACATECAS (Zac.)
ZC01) Juan de Tolosa 402, Col. Sierra de Álica, 98000 Zacatecas **W:** grupozer.net - 1100-0800 – **ZC03)** Av. Hidalgo 316, P1, Centro, 99000 Fresnillo **W:** b15.com.mx – **ZC04)** DR Gilberto Delgadillo 18-3, 98400 Río Grande **W:** lagrandederiogrande.com – **ZC05)** Radio S.A.Julián Aguirre 110, Col.Lomas de la Soledad, 98040 Zacatecas **W:** sonidoestrella.com.mx – **ZC06)** Edificio de la Radio, J. Mota Padilla 505, Col. San Antonio, 99601 Xalpa **W:** radioalegria.com.mx – **ZC07)** Josefa Ortiz de Dominguez 51, P3, 99700 Tlaltenango **W:** 1100am.tv - 1200-0600.

FM in México City (MHz): (HD Radio): DF05) 88.1 (HD1: R. Red FM, HD2: XERED 1110 R. Red) – DF12) Siempre 88.9 – DF02) 89.7 Oye 89.7 – DF17) 90.5 (HD1: R. Imagen, HD2: República RMX, HD3: Excélsior TV) – DF18) 90.9 (HD1: Ibero 90.9) – DF05) 91.3 (HD1: Alfa 91.3, HD2: XEN 690 La 69) – DF05) 92.1 Universal – DF06) 92.9 La Ke

Buena – DF05) 93.7 (HD1: Stereo Joya, HD2: XEJP 1150 El fonógrafo) – DF19) 94.1 UAM R. – DF04) 94.5 (HD1: Opus 94, HD2: XEB 1220 La B Grande de México, HD3: Jazz Digital) – DF12) 95.3 La Nueva Amor – DF20) 95.7 El Politécnico en R. – DF09) 96.1 UNAM – DF06) 96.9 W R. – DF05) 97.7 (HD1: Stereo 97-7, HD2: XERC 970 Formato 21) – DF17) 98.5 Reporte 98.5 – DF12) 99.3 R. Disney – DF02) 100.1 Stereo Cien – DF02) 100.9 Beat – DF06) 101.7 Los 40 Principales – DF21) 102.5 MVS R. – DF10) 103.3 (HD1: R. Fórmula FM 103, HD2: XEAI 1470 Fórmula Femenina 14-70, HD3: Fórmula Oldies, HD4:Jazz FM) – DF10) 104.1 (HD1: R. Uno, HD2: XEAI 1470 Fórmula Femenina 14-70, HD3: Fórmula Romántica, HD4: Fórmula Internacional) – DF21) 104.9 Exa FM – DF04) 105.7 (HD1: Reactor 105, HD2: RMI, R. México Internacional, HD3: HD3) – DF12) 106.5 Mix 106 – DF05) 107.3 (HD1: La Z, HD2: XEQR 1030 R. Centro) – DF04) 107.9 (HD1: Horizonte 108, HD2: XEDTL 660 R. Ciudadana, HD3: Música del Mundo)

MICRONESIA (USA associated)

L.T: Chuuk, Yap: UTC +10h; Kosrae, Pohnpei: UTC +11h — **Pop:** 106,836 — **Pr.L:** Yapese, Trukese, Ponapean, Kosraean, English — **E.C:** 60Hz, 110/220V — **ITU:** FSM

FEDERATED STATES OF MICRONESIA BROADCASTING SERVICE (Gov.)
✉ Public Information Office, P.O. Box 34, Palikir Station, Pohnpei State FSM 96941 **L.P:** Chairman, Board of Directors: Shelten G Neth **E:** chairman@mail.fm ☎ +691 320 2548 🖷 +691 320 4356

CHUUK STATE

MW Call	kHz	kW		MW Call	kHz	kW
1) V6A	1350	1		2) V6AK	1593	5
FM Call	**MHz**	**kW**		**FM Call**	**MHz**	**kW**
3) V6BC	88.1	0.1		4) V6CWS	89.5	
5)	89.1	0.2		4) V6CWS	98.5	
2) BWXX	89.5					

Addresses and other information
1) Baptist Mid-Missions P.O. Box 819, Weno, Chuuk State FSM 96942 **L.P:** Pastor Jody J Colson ☎ +691 330 3453 **E:** jtcolson@mail.fm – **2)** FSMBS R. Chuuk, PO Box 189, Weno, Chuuk State FSM 96942 **L.P:** Mgr Ennis Timothy ☎+691 3302374 🖷 +691 3302593 **W:** fm/chuuk/radio **ID:** "Ach nenien appio V6AK ion Chuuk' **D.Prgr:** 1900-2300 daily restricted service because of power disruptions and lack of fuel for generator. BWXX-FM repeater [currently inactive] – **3)** Baptist Church, Weno, Chuuk State FSM 96942 **L.P:** Rev.Tom Phillips **Prgr:** conservative religious music and supplied paid prgrs – **4)** National Weather R. [WSO FM], PO Box A, Weno, Chuuk State, FSM 96942. Live and recorded local weather and emergency information for Chuuk Lagoon area 24h – **5)** New Shine R., New Shine Church, Weno, Chuuk State FSM 96942 [currently inactive].

KOSRAE STATE

MW	Call	kHz	kW
1)	V6AJ	1503	1

Addresses and other information
1) FSMBS R. Kosrae, PO Box 147, Tofol, Kosrae State FSM 96944 **L.P:** Mgr Keitson Jonas ☎ +691 370 3040 🖷 +691 370 3880 **W:** fm/kosrae/radio **E:** v6aj@mail.fm **ID:** "Painge station V6AJ, fwin an Kosrae" **D.Prgr:** 2000-1400, 24h during adverse weather.

POHNPEI STATE

SW	Station	kHz	kW			
4)	V6MP	4755	1			
MW	**Station**	**kHz**	**kW**	**MW**	**Station**	**kHz kW**
1)	V6AF	999	1	2) V6AH		1449 10
FM	**Station**	**MHz**	**kW**	**FM**	**Station**	**MHz kW**
4)	V6MA	88.5	0.3	8) V6AV		101.0
6)	V6WI	89.5		1) V6AF		104.1
7)	Magic FM	100.3				

Addresses and other information
1) Baptist R. Pohnpei, PO Box H, Kolonia, Pohnpei State FSM 96941. ☎+691 3202475 **E:** v6afpohnpei@gmail.com **L.P:** Gabe Eiben **D.Prgr:** 24h – **2)** FSMBS R. Pohnpei, PO Box 1086, Kolonia, Pohnpei State FSM 96941 **L.P:** Commissioner Shelten G Neth ☎+691 320 2296 🖷+691 320 5212 **W:** fm/pohnpei/radio **E:** v6ah_radio@mail.fm **ID:** "Met Station V6AH nan Pohnpei" **D.Prgr:** 2000-1400, 24h during adverse weather – **3)** Bernard's Enterprises, Pohnpei State FSM 96941 ☎+691 320 2441 🖷+691 320 2444 – **4)** the Cross, Pacific Missionary Aviation, Radio Station, PO Box 517, Kolonia, Pohnpei State FSM 96941 ☎ +691 320 1122/2496 **W:** pmapacific.org **E:** radio@pmapacific.org **SW:** Ninseitamw, Kolonia, simulcast of 88.5MHz – **6)** R. Paradise, Paradise Media, PO Box 1748, Kolonia, Pohnpei State FSM 96941 **W:** paradisemediapni.com **E:** paradiseradiopni@gmail.com **L.P:** GM:

William Hoffman **Format:** hiphop & reggae music, community news – **7)** Kolonia, Pohnpei State FSM 96941, joint ownership with KWAW Saipan CNM – **8)** 24h BBC Pacific stream satellite rel from London

YAP STATE

MW	Station	kHz	kW			
2)	V6AG	1260	1			
1)	V6AI	1494	5			
FM	**Station**	**MHz**	**kW**	**FM**	**Station**	**MHz kW**
1)	KUTE FM	88.1		3) V6AA		89.7
2)	V6JY	88.9	0.25	4) YEC-FM		101.1 0.25

Addresses and other information
1) FSMBS R. Yap, PO Box 117, Colonia, Yap State FSM 96943 **L.P:** Mgr Sebastian Tamagken ☎ +691 350 2174 🖷 +691 350 2160 **W:** fm/yap/radio **E:** s_tamagken@yahoo.com **ID:** "Pary e radio station V6AI nu Waab' **D.Prgr:** 2000-1400, 24h during adverse weather. KUTE-FM is repeater – **2)** Joy Family R., Colonia, Yap State FSM 96943 ☎ +691 350 8483 **D.Prgr:** 24h religious – **3)** Voice of Hope, Colonia, Yap State FSM 96943 **Prgr:** religious – **4)** Yap Evangelical Church, Colonia, Yap State FSM 96943 ☎ +691 350 6101 **Prgr:** religious

MOLDOVA

L.T: UTC +2h (27 Mar-30 Oct: +3h) — **Pop:** 3.5 million — **Pr.L:** Romanian, Ukrainian, Russian, Gagauz — **E.C:** 50Hz, 220V — **ITU:** MDA

CONSILIUL COORDONATOR AL AUDIOVIZUALULUI (CCA) (Coordinating Audio-Visual Council)
✉ str. Vlaicu Parcalab 46, 2012 Chisinau ☎ +373 22277551 🖷 +373 22277471 **E:** office@cca.md **W:** cca.md
L.P: Pres: Dino Ciocan
NB: CCA is the licensing authority for broadcasting.

TELERADIO MOLDOVA (Pub)
✉ str. Miorita 1, 2028 Chisinau ☎ +373 22721388 🖷 +373 22723537 **E:** info@trm.md **W:** trm.md **L.P:** Pres: Olga Bordeianu

MW	kHz	kW	Prgr		MW	kHz	kW	Prgr
Chisinau (Codru)	873	50	1		Edinet	1494	20	1
Cahul	1494	20	1					
FM (MHz)	**1**	**2**	**kW**	**FM**		**1**	**2**	**kW**
Balti	-	99.4	4	Mîndrestii Noi		104.9	-	2
Cahul	100.7	-	4	Straseni		100.5	-	5
Causeni	106.8	-	4	Trifesti		103.3	-	4
Cimislia	103.5	-	2	Ungheni		102.0	-	4
Edinet	101.3	-	4					

NB: Sites with only txs below 1kW not listed.
D.Prgr: Prgr 1 (R. Moldova Actualitati) 24h. For ethnic minorities: 0700-0715 (Sun 0710) Russian, 0900-0905 Russian, 1200-1210 (SS 1205) Russian, 1600-1610 Russian; 1815-1835 Romany (Tue), Yiddish (Wed); 1815-1855 Gagauz (Mon), Ukrainian (Thu), Bulgarian (Fri); 1835-1855 Russian (Tue/Wed), MF 1900-1930 (Mon 1945) Russian. – **Prgr 2 (R. Moldova Tineret):** 24h. – **Prgr 3 (R. Moldova Muzical):** 24h via webcasting.

OTHER STATIONS

FM	MHz	kW	Location	Station
B)	68.48	17	Straseni	RFE-RL relay
B)	69.53	17	Ungheni	RFE-RL relay
B)	70.31	17	Edinet	RFE-RL relay
10)	71.57	2.5	Chisinau	Vocea Basarabiei
3)	87.6	1	Chisinau	R. Stil
2)	88.0	1	Chisinau	Muz FM
19)	88.7	4	Edinet	Publika FM
14)	89.1	2	Chisinau	Retro FM
2)	89.5	4	Edinet	Muz FM
17)	89.6	1	Chisinau	R. Chisinau
15)	90.4	1.8	Cahul	Cool R.
2)	90.5	2	Balti	Muz FM
21)	90.7	3.2	Chisinau	Aquarelle FM
20)	91.0	3.2	Balti	Maestro FM
8)	91.2	7.9	Rezina	Jurnal FM
10)	91.9	2	Causeni	Vocea Basarabiei
2)	92.3	1.25	Ungheni	Muz FM
2)	92.6	2	Cahul	Muz FM
2)	94.7	1	Varnita	Muz FM
23)	95.9	1	Proteagailovca	Dialog FM
16)	96.7	2	Chisinau	R. Alla
9)	97.2	3.1	Chisinau	R. Plai
9)	98.8	2.5	Cimislia	R. Plai
6)	99.7	1.4	Chisinau	R. Noroc

FM	MHz	kW	Location	Station
6)	99.9	3.2	Causeni	R. Noroc
18)	99.9	3.2	Glodeni	R. Prim
8)	100.1	3.2	Chisinau	Jurnal FM
9)	100.5	1	Briceni	R. Plai
9)	100.6	1	Stefan Voda	R. Plai
5)	100.7	1.3	Mîndrestii Noi	Micul Samaritean
12)	100.9	2	Chisinau	Kiss FM
6)	100.9	1.6	Iargara	R. Noroc
1)	101.1	1.3	Proteagailovca	Hit FM
22)	101.3	2	Chisinau	R. Sport
23)	101.5	16	Causeni	R. Plai
1)	101.7	1	Chisinau	Hit FM
10)	101.9	5	Taraclia	Vocea Basarabiei
5)	102.0	1	Causeni	Micul Samaritean
10)	102.3	10	Straseni	Vocea Basarabiei
13)	102.7	1	Chisinau	R. 21
23)	102.9	15.8	Mîndrestii Noi	R. Plai
4)	103.0	3.2	Causeni	Russkoye R.
3)	103.5	1.6	Balti	R. Stil
4)	103.7	1.6	Chisinau	Russkoye R.
5)	103.8	10	Edinet	Micul Samaritean
5)	104.2	1	Chisinau	Micul Samaritean
6)	104.3	5	Floresti	R. Noroc
1)	105.2	20	Cahul	Hit FM
5)	105.4	10	Trifesti	Micul Samaritean
11)	105.6	1.6	Balti	Megapolis FM
10)	105.7	5	Nisporeni	Vocea Basarabiei
7)	105.9	5	Chisinau	Fresh FM
17)	106.1	2.5	Proteagailovca	R. Chisinau
9)	106.8	1.6	Floresti	R. Plai
5)	107.0	20	Ungheni	Micul Samaritean
A)	107.3	10	Straseni	RFI relay
1)	107.6	20	Mîndrestii Noi	Hit FM
5)	107.7	20	Cahul	Micul Samaritean
8)	107.9	10	Edinet	Jurnal FM

NB: Txs below 1kW not listed.

Addresses & other information:
1) str. Bucuresti 68, 2012 Chisinau. Rel. Hit FM (Russia) – **2)** str. Veronica Micle 10, 2012 Chisinau – **3)** str. Sciusev 93, 2012 Chisinau. Rel. R. Shanson (Ukraine) – **4)** sos. Hîncesti 59/1, 2028 Chisinau – **5)** str. Bucuresti 68, 2012 Chisinau – **6)** bd. Negruzzi 6, 2001 Chisinau – **7)** str. Bucuresti 68, 2012 Chisinau – **8)** str. Mihai Vitezul 1, 2004 Chisinau – **9)** str. Inculet 105, 2025 Chisinau – **10)** str. A.Puskin 20a, 2012 Chisinau – **11)** str. Alba Iulia 75, 2028 Chisinau – **12)** str. Ismail 33, 2011 Chisinau. Rel. Kiss FM (Romania) – **13)** str. Alecu Russo 1, 2068 Chisinau. Rel. R. 21 (Romania) – **14)** str. Frumusica 1, 2002 Chisinau. Rel. Retro FM (Russia) – **15)** str. Maior Petru 7, 2001 Chisinau – **16)** str. Bucuresti 68, 2012 Chisinau. Rel. R. Alla (Russia) – **17)** str. Bucuresti 42A, ap. 3, 2012 Chisinau. Own prgrs & rel. R.România Actualitati (Romania) – **18)** str. Suveranitati 5, 2901 Glodeni – **19)** str. Ghioceilor 1, 2071 Chisinau – **20)** bd. Moscovei 21, 2068 Chisinau – **21)** str. Puskin 47/1C, 2012 Chisinau – **22)** str. Gradinilor 25-13, 2001 Chisinau – **23)** str. Primar Carol Schmidt 7, 2021 Chisinau – **A)** Rel. RFI (France) – **B)** Rel. RFE-RL (USA).

GAGAUZIA

GAGAUZIYA RADIO TELEVISIONU (GRT) (Pub)
🖃 str. Lenin 164, 3805 Comrat ☎ +373 29823086 🖷 +373 29826934 **E:** gagauztv@gagauztv.md **W:** gagauztv.md
LP: Chmn: Piron Stepan

FM	MHz	kW	FM	MHz	kW
Comrat	102.1	5	Baurci	104.6	1.25
Vulcanesti	103.6	0.2			

D.Prgr: GRT FM in Gagauz, Russian: 0500-2200.

OTHER STATIONS

FM	MHz	kW	Location	Station
19)	98.0	2.5	Comrat	Publika FM
6)	99.5	2.5	Comrat	R. Noroc
23)	100.3	1	Comrat	PRO 100 R.
5)	103.2	1	Ciadîr-Lunga	Micul Samaritean
1)	106.6	5	Comrat	Hit FM
2)	107.5	1	Baurci	Muz FM

NB: Txs below 1kW not listed.
Addresses & other information: see main tx table. **23)** str. Novaia 23, 3801 Comrat.

TRANSNISTRIA

PRIDNESTROVSKAYA GTRK (PGTRK)
🖃 per. Khristoforova 5, 3300 Tiraspol, Transnistria ☎ +373 533 73074

E: radio1@pgtrk.ru **W:** radio.pgtrk.ru **L.P:** Dir: Irina Dementyeva
Run by the administration of the "Pridnestrovian Moldavian Republic"

MW	kHz	kW	Prgr			
Maiac	621	150	1			
FM (MHz)	**1**	**2**	**kW**	**FM**	**1**	**2**	**kW**
Camenca	105.0	-	-	Slobozia	74.00	-	0.1
Camenca II	106.4	-	-	Slobozia	100.7	105.0	1.5
Caterinovca	104.0	-	-	Tiraspol	104.0	105.0	0.2
Dnestrovsc	100.3	-	-	Valea Adinca	100.1	-	-
	-	105.0	-	Voroncovo	106.0	-	1

D.Prgr: Prgr 1 (R. 1): 24h in Russian, Ukrainian, Romanian on FM, and on MW during morning hours – **Prgr 2 (R. Pridnestrovya):** 24h.

OTHER STATIONS

FM	MHz	kW	Location	Station
4)	88.3	-	Tiraspol	Tiraspol FM
3)	88.8	3	Tiraspol[1]	R. Shanson
6)	89.3	-	Varnita	R. Novaya volna
2)	89.6	-	Tiraspol	Hit FM
7)	90.1	-	Slobozia	Retro FM
12)	90.5	-	Tiraspol	R. Rekord
8)	91.2	-	Tiraspol	Klevoye R.
9)	91.5	-	Slobozia	R. Romantika
15)	91.7	-	Dubasari	Dubasari FM
14)	92.5	-	Tiraspol	R. Tochka
13)	93.7	-	Bender	R. Dacha
A)	100.1	-	Tiraspol[1]	R. Sputnik relay
10)	100.3	0.03	Dubasari	Dubossarskoye R.
5)	100.9	-	Voroncovo	Dorozhnoye R.
A)	104.6	-	Ribnita	R. Sputnik relay
11)	104.6	0.1	Slobozia	Ekho Moskvy
5)	105.4	2	Bender	Dorozhnoye R.
A)	106.5	-	Maiac	R. Sputnik relay
16)	107.1	-	Tiraspol	Avtoradio
1)	107.7	1	Tiraspol[1]	R. Inter FM

[1] Synchro-network with txs in several towns
Addresses & other information:
1) ul. K.Libnikhta 1/2, 3300 Tiraspol **E:** reklama@inter-fm.idknet.com – **2)** Rel. Hit FM* – **3)** ul. K.Libnikhta 1/2, 3300 Tiraspol. Rel. R. Shanson* – **4)** 3300 Tiraspol. Rel. Dorozhnoye R.* – **6)** ul. Internatsionalistov 13, Bender **E:** nv893@mail.ru. Rel. Love R.* – **7)** Rel. Retro FM* – **8)** ul. Yunosti 1, 3300 Tiraspol – **9)** Rel. R. Romantika* – **10)** ul. Dzerzhinskogo 4, 4501 Dubasari. Rel. Dorozhnoye R.* – **11)** Rel. Ekho Moskvy* – **12)** Rel. R. Rekord* – **13)** Rel. R. Dacha* – **14)** 3300 Tiraspol – **15)** 4501 Dubasari – **16)** Rel. Avtoradio* – **A)** Rel. R. Sputnik* (*= Relays from Russia)

Int. relays on MW: (operated by Pridnestrovskiy radioteletsentr) Grigoriopol (Maiac) 999/1413kHz 1000kW. See Int. Radio section.

NB: Radio stns in Transnistria are de facto subject to authorisation by the administration of the soi-disant "Pridnestrovian Moldavian Republic"

L.T: UTC +1h (27 Mar-30 Oct: +2h) — **Pop:** 33,000 — **Pr.L:** French — **E.C:** 50Hz, 220V — **ITU:** MCO

MONTE CARLO RADIODIFFUSION (Comm.)
🖃 10 Quai Antoine 1er, MC-98000 Monaco ☎ +377 97974799 🖷 +377 97974707 **W:** mcr.mc **E:** mcradiodiffusion@mcr.mc
L.P: Patrick Jean

MW	kHz	kW	Prgr
Col de la Madone (France)	702	200	(currently inactive)
Roumoules (France)	1467	1000	TWR relay (2045-2315)*
Col de la Madone (France) 1467	40		R. Maria France (0500-1900)**

*mainly Arab & Eng. Prgs,
**R. Maria France, 230 rue Marc Delage F-83430 La Garde, France
W: radiomaria.fr **E:** info@radiomaria.fr **V.** by letter

RMC (Comm.)
🖃 HQ: 12 Rue d'Oradour sur Glane, F-75740 Paris Cedex 15, France ☎ +33 1 71191191 🖷 +331 71191190 **W:** rmc.fr **E:** technique@rmc.fr **L.P:** Pres: Alain Weill, GD: Franck Lanoux **LW:** Roumoules (France) 216kHz 1400kW (reduced to 900kW.), RMC 0358-2308 (Id as "RMC" only) **FM:** Mont Agel 98.5MHz 50kW; Monaco Jardin Exotique 98.8MHz 0.1kW 24h.

RADIO MONACO (Comm.)
🖃 HQ: 7 Rue du Gabian, Gildo Pastor Centre, MC-98000 Monaco

☎ +377 97700700 🖷 +377 97700701 **W**: radio-monaco.com
FM: Monaco Mont Agel 98.2MHz 1kW; Mont Agel 95.4MHz 40kW, Grasse (France) 103.2MHz 0.5kW **E**: info@radio-monaco.com

EXTERNAL SERVICE: see International Radio section for details

NB: News relays via Monaco Radio utility stn for seamen weather forecast in French & English 0530, 1103. 1630 on 8728 kHz SSB News bulletin from Radio Monaco relay over Monaco Radio in French 1100-1103 (M-F) on 4363, 8728, 13246, 17260 SSB

RADIO MONTE CARLO ITALIE (Comm.)
🖳 8 Quai Antoine 1er, MC-98000 Monaco ☎ +377 97976666 🖷 +377 97708661 **W**: radiomontecarlo.net **E**: rmc@radiomontercarlo.net
FM: RMC1 Monaco Mont Agel 106.8MHz 1kW **RMC2** MC2 Monaco **Mont Agel 93.2 MHz 1 kW** Ventimiglia (IM) Italy 101.6 MHz
V.by QSL-card. Rp.

RIVIERA RADIO (Comm)
🖳 10 Quai Antoine 1er, MC-98000 Monaco ☎ +377 97979494 🖷 +377 97979495 **W**: rivieraradio.mc **E**: info@rivieraradio.mc
L.P: MD: Paul Kavanagh. Tech. Manager: Peter Miller
FM: Monaco Jardin Exotique 106.3MHz 1kW; Col de la Madone 106.5MHz 10kW **D.Prgr.** in English: 24h Rel. BBCWS **N** every h.

Other FM stations (all sces. 24h):

FM	MHz	kW	Station, location
-)	88.2	0.1	R. Maria France, Jardin Exotique
-)	90.3	50	MFM, Col de la Madone
6)	90.6	2	Médi 1, Mont Agel
5)	91.4	0.1	Crooner R., Jardin Exotique
7)	92.7	0.1	Sud R., Monaco Port
)	93.2	1	MC 2, Mont Agel (see R. Monte Carlo)
-)	93.5	50	R. Nostalgie, Col de la Madone
-)	93.8	1	R. Nostalgie, Mont Agel
3)	94.5	0.1	Hit R., Morocco,Monaco Port
4)	95.1	0.1	FUN R., Monaco Port
-)	95.7	0.1	Jazz R., Monaco Port
-)	96.1	1	Radio FG, Mont Agel
9)	96.4	0.1	Nice R., Jardin Exotique
)	96.7	0.5	Av. Hector Otto
1)	97.9	2	Chik R., Mont Agel
-)	99.1	0.1	R. 105 Italia, Port
2)	100.9	50	Music100.9, rel. San Remo(IM) Italy
	101.1	0.1	Jardin Exotique
-)	102.1	0.1	RTL 2, Jardin Exotique
-)	102.4	0.1	R. Rire & Chansons, Jardin Exotique
-)	102.7	50	R .Classique, Col de la Madone
-)	103.0	1.5	RFM, Mont Agel
-)	103.3	0.4	RDS Italia, Jardin Exotique
1)	103.6		Chik R., rel. Bordighera/San Remo (IM) Italy
-)	104.5	0.1	Cherie FM, Jardin Exotique
8)	106.0		Plein Sud in French, rel. Bordighera (IM) Italy

Addresses and other information:
1) 10 Quai Antoine 1er, MC-98000 Monaco in Russian language **W:** chikmontecarlo.com **E**: contact@chikradio.com – **2)** in Italian, French, English, German languages **E** info@music1009.com **W:** music1009. com – **3) W**: hitradio.ma – **4) W**: funradiomonaco.com – **5) W**: crooner.fr – **6) W**: medi1.com **7)** studios in Toulouse (F) **W**: sudradio.fr **8) W**: radiopleinsud.it **9) W**: niceradio.fr

Digital Radio DAB+
From Mont Agel on 195.936 MHz with 10 kW on Bloc 8A

Stations:
Ado FM (Fr) – Chik Radio (Ru) – Crooner Radio (Fr) – Latina (Fr) – MC2 (It) – Médi 1 (Fr/Ar) – Radio Ethic (Fr) – Radio Maria France (Fr) – Radio Monaco (Fr) – Riviera Radio (En) – Rete 105 (It) – RMC 1 (It)
Fr: French, Ru: Russian, It: Italian, Ar: Arabic, En: English

MONGOLIA

L.T: UTC +8h (DST*: +9h) (Western Mongolia: +7h; DST*: +8h) *26 Mar-24 Sep — **Pop:** 3 million — **Pr.L:** Mongolian — **E.C:** 50Hz, 230V — **ITU:** MNG

HARILTSAA HOLBOONÏ ZOHITSÜÜLAH HOROO
(Communications Regulatory Commission)
🖳 Sühbaatar district, Metro Business Center, Sühbaatar St. 13, 5th floor, Ulaanbaatar 14201 ☎ +976 11 304257 🖷 +976 11 327720 **E:** info@crc.gov.mn **W:** crc.gov.mn

L.P: Chmn: Balgansuren Batsukh (Mongolian: Batsüh Balgansüren)

MONGOLÏN ÜNDESNIY OLON NIYTIYN RADIO TELEVIZ (MÜONRT) (Pub)
(Mongolian National Broadcaster)
🖳 Bayangol district, 11th subdistrict, Huvisgalïn Rd. 3, Ulaanbaatar ☎ +976 11 325802 🖷 +976 11 328334 **E:** info@mnb.mn **W:** mnb.mn
L.P: DG: Oyundari Tsagaan (Mongolian: Tsagaanï Oyuundari)

LW	kHz	kW	Prgr	LW/MW	kHz	kW	Prgr
Ulaanbaatar (a)	164	500	1	Ölgiy	209	75	1
Choybalsan	209	75	1	Altay	¦ 227	75	1
Dalanzadgad	209	75	1	Mörön	882	75	1

(a) Honhor ¦=Timeshare: tx also carries prgrs of the non-affiliated regional public broadcaster Olon Niytiyn Altay R. (see under "Regional Public Service Stations")

SW	kHz	kW	Prgr	SW	kHz	kW	Prgr
Altay	4830	10	2	Ulaanbaatar (a)	7260	50	1
Mörön	4895	10	2	(a) Honhor			

FM (MHz)	1	2	3	kW
Altay	107.0	-	-	0.05
Choybalsan	101.5	106.7	-	0.05
Dalanzadgad	107.5	-	-	1
Mörön	103.0	103.6	-	0.05
Ölgiy	107.0	-	-	0.05
Saynshand	100.9	-	-	1
Ulaanbaatar	106.0	-	100.9	1
Zamïn-Üüd	105.2	-	-	0.1
+ translators				

D.Prgr: Prgr 1 (Mongolïn R.): 2200-1500 – **Prgr 2 (Altan san R.):** 2300-1500. Incl. prgrs for ethnic minorities in Buryat, Kazakh, Tuvan. Some broadcasts are simulcast with Prgr 1. – **Prgr 3 (R3):** 2300-1500.
Intern. Service (Voice of Mongolia): See Intern. Radio section.

REGIONAL PUBLIC SERVICE STATIONS
Olon Niytiyn Altay R.: Yesönbulag district, Badsuuriyn Rd. On Altay 227kHz (timeshared with Prgr 1 of Mongolian National Broadcaster)
Züün Büsiyn Olon Niytiyn R.: On Choybalsan 106.4MHz.
NB: These stns are not part of or affiliated with Mongolian National Broadcaster.

OTHER STATIONS

FM	MHz	kW	Location	Station
1A)	91.1	1	Ulaanbaatar	Toym R. 91.1
2)	91.7	1	Ulaanbaatar	Evseg Mongol
1B)	92.1	1	Ulaanbaatar	Toym R. 92.1
3)	92.5	1	Ulaanbaatar	92.5 FM
4)	95.1	1	Ulaanbaatar	Hamag Mongol R.
5)	95.7	1	Ulaanbaatar	Arga bilig R.
6)	96.9	1	Ulaanbaatar	Elgen Nutag R.
7)	97.5	1	Ulaanbaatar	Lavayn Egshig R.
8)	98.1	1	Ulaanbaatar	Formula FM
9)	98.5	1	Ulaanbaatar	Best R.
10)	98.9	1	Ulaanbaatar	Royal FM
11)	99.3	1	Ulaanbaatar	Ineemseglel R.
12)	99.7	1	Ulaanbaatar	Ih Mongol
13)	100.1	1	Ulaanbaatar	Kiss FM
14)	100.5	1	Ulaanbaatar	Miniy Mongol FM
15)	101.7	1	Ulaanbaatar	Tergüülegch R.
16)	102.5	1	Ulaanbaatar	R. ÜB
A)	103.1	1	Ulaanbaatar	BBCWS relay
17)	103.6	1	Ulaanbaatar	Tengerleg R.
18)	104.0	1	Ulaanbaatar	Erh chölöö FM
19)	104.5	1	Ulaanbaatar	Ger Büüliyn R.
20)	105.5	1	Ulaanbaatar	Nandin FM
21)	107.5	1	Ulaanbaatar	Shine dolgion R.

NB: Txs below 1kW not listed.
Addresses & other information:
1A,B) Chingeltey district, 2nd subdistrict, Sansar Cable LLC Building, Ulaanbaatar – **2)** Ulaanbaatar – **3)** Ulaanbaatar – **4)** Sühbaatar district, 5th subdistrict, N&N center, 3rd floor, Room 302, Ulaanbaatar 14192 **E:** hamag-mongol@yahoo.com – **5)** Sühbaatar district, 8th subdistrict, Independence Palace, Amar St., 1st floor, Ulaanbaatar 14200 **E:** argabilig_fm@yahoo.com – **6)** Han-Uul district, 15th subdistrict, Narhan hothon 61-r Building, Room 32, Ulaanbaatar 13380 **E:** dnaba_d@yahoo.com – **7)** Chingeltey district, 2nd subdistrict, Hudaldaa St., Javzandamba Center, 3rd floor, Ulaanbaatar **E:** info@lavain-egshig.mn – **8)** Chingeltey district, 5th subdistrict, Narnï Titem Building, 2nd floor, Ulaanbaatar **E:** ubradio@mail.mn – **9)** Chingeltey district, 4th subdistrict, Business Development Centre, Ulaanbaaatar Bank Building, 2nd floor, Ulaanbaatar 15160 **E:** best_985@yahoo.com – **10)** Bayanzürh district, Ih zasag ih surguuliyn St., Royal Academy Building,

1st floor, Room 102, Ulaanbaatar **E:** royalradio989@yahoo.com – **11)** Sühbaatar district, 8th subdistrict, Amar St., CT House, 5th floor, Room 433, Ulaanbaatar 14200 – **12)** Bayangol district, Enhtayvan Ave., Grand Plaza, 14th floor, Room 1404, Ulaanbaatar 16050 **E:** fm_997@yahoo.com – **13)** Chingeltey district, 1st subdistrict, Ulaanbaator Bank bayr, 13th floor, Room 1302, Ulaanbaatar **E:** gerlees2002@yahoo.com – **14)** Sühbaatar district, 8th subdistrict, Amar St., CT House, 12th floor, Room 1208, Ulaanbaatar 14200 – **15)** Chingeltey district, 5th subdistrict, Narnï Titem Building, 2nd floor, Ulaanbaatar **E:** reclam1017@yahoo.com – **16)** Bayangol district, Enhtayvan Ave., Grand Plaza, 14th floor, Room 1108, Ulaanbaatar 16050 **E:** fmub1025@yahoo.com – **17)** Sühbaatar district, 9th subdistrict, Erönhiy sayd Amar St., TV9 Building, 1 floor, Ulaanbaatar **E:** simona_9859@ yahoo.com – **18)** Chingeltey district, 2nd subdistrict, Orange Plaza, Room 707, Ulaanbaatar **E:** freedom_fm104@yahoo.com – **19)** Bayanzürh district, 2nd subdistrict, 15th microdistrict, 10A-r Building, Ulaanbaatar **E:** windfm1045@yahoo.com – **20)** Bayangol district, Enhtayvan Ave., Grand Plaza, 14th floor, Room 1404, Ulaanbaatar 16050 – **21)** Bayanzürh district, 6th subdistrict, 13th microdistrict, Namiyanjugiyn St., Ereliyn 40-r Building, Ulaanbaatar **E:** badam_rose@yahoo.com – **A)** Rel. BBCWS (UK)

MONTENEGRO

L.T: UTC+1h (27 Mar-30 Oct: +2h) — **Pop:** 630,000 — **Pr.L:** Montenegrin, Serbian — **E.C:** 50Hz, 220V — **ITU:** MNE

RADIO TELEVIZIJA CRNE GORE

✉ Bul. Revolucije 19, 81000 Podgorica ☎ +382 20 245595 **W:** rtcg. me **E:** marketing@rtcg.org **L.P:** DG: S. Sestic

MW	kHz	kW	Station			
Podgorica	882	5	R. Pogorica			
FM (MHz)	RCG 1	R. 98	kW	FM (MHz)	RCG 1	R. 98	kW
Bjelasica	92.1	99.3	54	Podgorica	96.5	89.3	10
Durmitor	96.1	91.3	10	Tovic	88.0	98.9	10
Lovcen	94.9	98.0	54	Velji Grad	99.8	89.6	10
Mozura	97.3	93.4	10				

+ 11 txs.less than 1kW

Local/private stations
R. Antena M, Podgorica 87.6MHz + 5 relays – **R. Cetinje** 94.5MHz + 1 relay – **R. Elmag**, Podgorica 96.0MHz + 7 relays – **R. Bar** 91.8MHz + 1 relay – **R. Berane** 88.2MHz + 1 relay – **R Bijelo**, Polje 101.1MHz + 1 relay – **R. Budva** 98.7MHz + 1 relay – **R. Corona**, Bar 88.9MHz +1 relay – **R. D**, Podgorica 88.6MHz + 2 relays – **R. Danilovgrad** 92.9MHz – **R. Fokus**, Bijelo Polje 93.9MHz – **R. Free Montenegro**, Podgorica 103.0.MHz – **R. Glas** Plava, Plav 102.9.MHz – **R. Gorica**, Podgorica 93.3MHz – **R. Herceg** Novi 90.0MHz +1 relay – **R. Jupok**, Rozaje 98.7MHz + 1 relay – **R. Kotor** 95.3MHz + 1 relay – **R. Max**, Danilovgrad 107.5MHz + 1 relay – **R. Mir**, Tuzi 106.1MHz +1 relay – **R. Mojkovac** 92.8MHz – **R. Montena**, Podgorica 105.7MHz + 5 relays – **R. Niksic** 89.8MHz + 2 relays – **R. Ozon**, Kolasin 97.6MHz – **R. Panorama**, Pljevlja 89.2MHz – **R. Pljevlja** 94.8MHz – **R. Rozaje** 104.4MHz – **R. Svetigora**, Cetinje 101.0.MHz – **R. Tivat** 88.5.MHz – **R. Ulcinj** 91.3MHz + 1 relay – **R. Zeta**, Podgorica 93.8.MHz – **R. City**, Podgorica 107.3MHz

MONTSERRAT (UK)

L.T: UTC -4h — **Pop:** 4,900 — **Pr.L:** English — **E.C:** 60Hz, 220V — **ITU:** MSR

RADIO MONTSERRAT (Gov. Comm.)

✉ PO Box 51, Sweeneys ☎ +1 664 491 2885 🖷 +1 664 491 9250 **W:** zjb.gov.ms **E:** zjb@gov.ms **L.P:** SM: Herman Sargeant. Techn: Ivor Greenaway
FM: 88.3MHz, 0.1kW (Isles Bay Hill), 95.5MHz, 5kW (Silver Hills)
D.Prgr: 24h BBC relay at night 0400-0930
Ann: "ZJB Radio Montserrat, the Voice of Montserrat"

Other stations:
ETERNAL LIFE RADIO ✉ Cavalla Hill ☎ +1 664 496 6982. **W:** eternal-liferadio.com FM: 106.1MHz – **CSS CARIBBEAN SUPER STATION - FM:** 93.9MHz (relay Trinidad) – **VIBZ FM - Family Radio Network** ✉ P.O. Box 350, Baker Hill ☎ +1 664 491 7331 **W:** vibzfm. com FM: 89.9MHz (relay Antigua)

MOROCCO

L.T: UTC (27 Mar-30 Oct: +1h; suspended during month of Ramadan) — **Pop:** 35 million — **Pr.L:** Arabic, French, Spanish, English, Berber languages, Hassania — **E.C:** 50Hz, 127/220V — **ITU:** MRC

HAUTE AUTORITÉ DE LA COMMUNICATION AUDIOVISUELLE (HACA)

✉ Espace les Palmiers, Lot 26,Angle Avenues Anakhil et Mehdi Ben Barka, B.P. 20590, Rabat Ryad ☎+212 53 7579600 🖷 +212 53 7714274 **W:** haca.ma **E:** info@haca.ma **L.P:** DG: Ahmed Akhchichine.

SOCIÉTÉ NATIONALE DE RADIODIFFUSION ET DE TÉLÉVISION (SNRT) - RADIO MAROCAINE (Pub.)

✉ 1, Rue El Brihi, B.P. 1042, MA-10000 Rabat ☎+212 53 7700 319 🖷 +212 53 772 2047 **W:** snrt.ma **E:** lemediateur@snrt.ma **Reg.** ✉ B.P. 459, Laayoune. **L.P:** DG: Mohamed Ayad. Dir. Tech: Allal Kacimi.

LW/MW	kHz	kW	N	LW/MW	kHz	kW	N
Azilal	207	400	A	Laâyoune	‡711	300	R
Sidi Bennour	540	600	A/R	Agadir	‡936	100	C/R
Oujda	*595	50	A/R	Sebaa-Aioun	‡1044	300	C
Sebaa-Aioun	612	300	A	*alt. on 594 kHz			

F.PI: two 400 kW MW transmitters in Agadir.

FM (MHz)	A	B	C	O&R	kW
Agadir	91.0	94.2	97.5	87.9	
Beni Mellal	89.8	92.9	96.1		10
Casablanca	96.0	90.0	95.3	98.6	
Dakhla	93.5	91.8		91.8	
El Houceima	105.7	92.1	95.3		8
El Jadida	90.4				
Errachidia	91.3	97.8	94.5		
Essaouira	97.9	91.4			
Fès	88.8	95.1	101.9	98.4	
Figuig	91.9	95.1	98.4		
Ifrane	90.5	93.6	96.8		
Khenifra	91.6	87.9	104.6	94.2	10
Lâayoune	93.9	97.9	91.1	91.0	10
Marrakech	94.9	98.8		91.7	30
Meknès	88.8	95.1	101.9	92.5	10
Nador	87.6	93.9	97.2		
Ouarzazate	90.3	93.4	96.6		
Oujda	89.9	99.4		96.1	10
Oum Dreiga	97.9				
Rabat	91.0	87.9	104.6	94.2	40
Safi	90.9		94.1		
Settat	92.1	89.0			
Tanger	88.7	91.8	95.0 /98.3	88.7	
Tantan	90.3				
Taza	91.7	94.9			10
Tétouan	90.6	100.2		93.7	12

A: National Network in Arabic: 0500-0100. **N:** on the h. — **Netw. B, Chaîne Inter:** 0600-0100. **Spanish:** Sa-Th 1200-1230, **English:** Sa-Th 1230-1300. Other times in French. — **Netw. C in Berber/Arabic dialects:** 1200-2400 (incl. rel. Netw. A 0600-1200). **Netw. O: Quran R. "Mohammed VI":** 24h, MW 1800-0600.
Regional Prgrs (FM on O network). M**W: Agadir**, Avenue Hassan II, Agadir: on 936kHz. **Casablanca**, Ain Chock, Casablanca: **Laâyoune/Dakhla:** on 711kHz. **Marrakech:** 40 Ave. Yugoslavie, Marrakech: on 540kHz. **Fès & Meknès:** on 612kHz (Fès 0600-1200, Meknès 1200-1800). **Oujda**, Avenue Omar Errifi, Oujda: on 594kHz. **Tangier:** 33, Avenue Amir Moulay Abdallah, Tangier: on 540kHz. **Tetouan**, 30, Avenue Mohammed V, Tetouan.
Ann: Arabic: "Huna Ribat, Idha'atu-I-Mamlaka al Maghribiyya" or "Idha'at al-Wataniya". French: "Ici Rabat, Radiodiffusion Télévision Marocaine". Berber: "Dahab Rbad al-idaa al-Amazighia Li Mamlaka L'Maghrib".

RADIO MEDITERRANÉE INTERNATIONALE - MEDI 1 RADIO (Comm, Semi-Gov.)

✉ B.P. 2055, 3/5 rue Emsallah, 90000 Tanger ☎&🖷 +212 539936363 **W:** medi1.com **E:** medi1@medi1.com **L.P:** Dir: Hassan Kiyar.
LW/SW: Nador 171kHz 1600kW & 9575kHz 250kW: **see International Radio section.**
FM (MHz):Agadir 104.6 20kW, Al Hoceima/El Jadida 96.7, Beni Mellal 102.9, Casablanca 99.6 9kW, Dakhla 96.4, Enjil 97.0, Essaouira 94.6 12kW, Fès 101.4 2kW, Laâyoune 101.0 10kW, Marrakech 105.3 1kW, Meknès 105.5 10kW, Merchiche 87.6, Nador 105.3 10kW, Ouarzazate/Zaio 99.9, Oujda 102.9 12kW, Rabat 97.5 20kW, Safi 97.0, Slokia 95.3, Taliouine 92.2, Tanger 101.0 1kW, Tantan 93.4, Taroudante 95.4, Tetouan 103.7 12kW, Zagora 97.0.
D.Prgr. in Arabic/French: 24h. **N. in Arabic:** 0600, 0700, 0800, 1200, 2000, 2300. **N. in French:** 0630, 0730, 0830, 1230, 1700, 1930, 2200.**Ann:** "Médi 1".

Other stations:

FM	1)	2)	3)	4)	5)	6)	7)	8)	9)	10)
Agadir	100.4	93.1	96.5		95.6		89.3	103.7		
Al Hoceima	97.7	93.3		102.1					94.4	
Béni Mellal	94.0				98.1			94.7	91.6	105.1
Boujdour							88.9			
Casablanca	104.3	93.1	88.7		100.3	92.5	88.2	100.8	91.2	102.1
Dakhla	89.7				99.7		88.7	88.0		
El Jadida	95.1	93.1			94.5	97.3	89.3	96.2	91.5	101.3
Errachadia	102.5				104.1		100.5	105.6		
Essaouira	92.8	93.3	99.9		96.1		89.8			
Fès	103.9				94.1	98.8			89.4	103.2
Figuig		93.1		105.5						
Gharb	99.3									
Guelmin					98.5					
Goulmima		93.1					91.0			
Ifrane	103.6									103.2
Khenifra	102.4									
Laâyoune	104.6		107.1		91.6		89.4	98.6		
Larache					92.8					
Marrakech	100.6	93.8	97.7		94.4	90.5	88.6	98.5		
Meknès	99.9	93.7	102.5		97.2				90.7	92.9
Nador	104.3		101.0	90.7					100.7	101.4
Oujda	102.0			92.9	98.5		106.5	97.7	87.8	
Ouarzazate	91.2				92.0		88.9	103.4		
Rabat	95.7	93.5			99.8	106.9	90.2	103.7	96.5	97.0
Safi	103.6						90.3			
Sarsar										90.1
Settat	103.8				98.9	106.4	93.4	97.9	94.7	96.4
Skhour	102.2		102.6		95.8		88.0			
Smara							91.8			
Tafraoute			99.2							
Tamanar			98.4							
Tantan		93.1	99.9				101.3			
Tanger	102.3	93.3		105.4	96.4	103.3			92.3	91.1
Tarfaya							89.6			
Targuist			95.8							
Taroudante	101.3						88.1			
Taza	95.8				98.6		97.8			101.7
Tétouan	105.9	93.9		104.5	97.8					93.0
Tiznit			104.2		91.5		88.4			
Zagora								105.9		

1) Aswat FM: Ghandi Mall, Imm 9, Bd. Ghandi, Casablanca. **W:** aswat.ma – **2) Radio 2M** (Semi-Gov.): Km 7300 route de Rabat Ain Seeba, Casablanca. **W:** 2m.tv/radio2M – **3) MFM Atlas/Oriental/ Sahara/Saïss/Souss & Casa FM**: Groupe New Publicity, 58 Av. des FAR, Tour des Habous, 18ème étage, Casablanca. **W:** mfmradio.ma radiocasafm.ma – **4) Cap Radio**: Zone industrielle, Route de Tétouan, Allée principale lot n°123, Tanger. **W:** capradio.ma – **5) Hit Radio**: 3 rue Assouhaili, Agdal, Rabat. **W:** hitradio.ma – **6) R. Atlantic**: Eco-Médias, 70 Bd. Massira Khadra, Casablanca. **W:** atlanticradio.ma – **7) Med Radio**: 55, intersection Blvd Zerktouni et rue Sebta, 5ème étage n° 20, Casablanca. **W:** medradio.ma – **8) R. Chada FM**: Société R. Kolinass, 42 Bd. Idriss 1er quartier des Hôpitaux, Casablanca. **W:** chadafm.net – **9) R. Mars**: 30 Ave. des Far 13ème étage, Casablanca 20000. **W:** radiomars.ma – **10) Medina FM**: Rue Oued ziz imm 51 appt 4 agdal, Rabat. **W:** medinafm.net

R. Sawa: Meknès 91.9MHz, Fès 97.9MHz 2kW, Tetouan 92.1 20 kW, Rabat/Agadir 101.0MHz 20kW, Casablanca 101.5MHz 10kW, Marrakech 101.7MHz 12kW, Tanger 101.8MHz 20kW.

CEUTA (Spain)
L.T: see Spain — **Pop:** 84,000 — **Pr.L:** Spanish

R. Nacional de España, Real 90, E-51001 Ceuta. **FM:** RNE-1 97.2MHz, R. Clásica 100.8MHz, RNE5TN 101.9MHz, RNE-3 106.8MHz, all 1kW.
SER Radiolé - R. Ceuta, Poblado Marinero, Local 32, E-51001 Ceuta. **MW:** 1584kHz 5kW 24h rel. of Radiolé netw. **FM:** 96.2MHz R. Ceuta
COPE, Sargento Mena 8,1ºizq, E-51001 Ceuta. **FM:** 89.8MHz.
Onda Cero R, Calle Delgado Serrano 1, 1º, E-51001 Ceuta. **FM:** 101.4MHz 3kW.
RTV Ceuta, Paseo Alcalde Sánchez Prado, 3 – 5, 51001 Ceuta. **FM:** 99.0MHz. **W:** rtvce.es

MELILLA (Spain)
L.T: see Spain — **Pop:** 81,000 — **Pr.L:** Spanish

R. Nacional de España, Altos de la Vía 3, E-52004 Melilla. **MW:** RNE1 972kHz 5kW. **FM:** (0.3kW): 97.7MHz (R1), 100.1MHz (RNE5TN), 105.3MHz (R3), 107.6MHz (R. Clásica).

SER R. Melilla, Calle Cardenal Cisneros 8 bajo, E-52001 Melilla. **E:** radiomelilla@unionradio.es .**MW:** 1485kHz 1kW 24h. **FM:** (MHz): 96.3 Cadena 40 Melilla, 101.1 Dial Melilla.
COPE, C/ Pablo Vallescá 6 "Edificio Ánfora"2º - 1, E-52001 Melilla. **W:** copemelilla.com **FM:** 91.3MHz Cadena 100, 98.4MHz COPE Melilla.
Onda Cero R, Calle de Musico Granados 2, E-52004 Melilla. **FM:** (MHz): 89.6MHz.
esRadio, Melilla: 92.2MHz

MOZAMBIQUE

L.T: UTC +2h — **Pop:** 22 million — **Pr.L:** Portuguese, 20 ethnic languages — **E.C:** 50Hz, 220V — **ITU:** MOZ

INSTITUTO NACIONAL DAS COMUNICAÇÕES (INCM)
✉ Av. Eduardo Mondlane, 123/127, PO Box 848, Maputo ☎+258 21 490131 ≣ +258 21 494435. **W:** incm.gov.mz **E:** info@incm.gov.mz

RÁDIO MOÇAMBIQUE (Pub.)
✉ Rua da Rádio n.º 2, C.P. 2000, Maputo ☎+258 21 431687 ≣ +258 21 321816 **W:** rm.co.mz **E:** caprimoe@zebra.uem.mz
L.P: Chmn/CEO: Ricardo Malate. TD: Mr Hermenegildo Basílio Mula. Int. Rel. Dir: Ms. Maria Cremilda Massingue. Fin. Dir: Arlindo Piedade de Sousa.

MW	kHz	kW	N	MW	kHz	kW	N
1) Maputo	‡738	50	N	4) Chimoio	1026	50	EP
3) Nampula	765	50	EP	7) Quelimane	1179	50	EP
10) Xai-Xai	810	50	EP	5) Inhambane	1206	50	EP
2) Beira	873	50	EP	8) Pemba	1224	50	EP
9) Tete	963	50	EP	6) Lichinga	1260	50	EP
1) Maputo	1008	50	EP				

FM	MHz	kW	N	FM	MHz	kW	N
10) Xai-Xai	87.8	-	N	1) Maputo	97.9	5	C
5) Massinga	89.9	0.12	N	9) Tete	100.7	-	EP
9) Tete	90.7	-	N	6) Inhambane	101.6	-	N
10) Xai-Xai	90.9	-	EP	6) Lichinga	101.7	-	N
2) Beira	91.6	-	N	1) Maputo	102.3	-	M
7) Quelimane	92.1	10	N	4) Chimoio	102.5	-	EP
1) Maputo	92.3	10	N	5) Inhambane	105.1	-	EP
1) Maputo	93.1	-	D	2) Beira	105.2	-	C
3) Nampula	95.1	-	N	3) Nampula	105.5	0.25	EP
8) Pemba	95.3	-	N	1) Maputo	105.9	-	E

Antena Nacional (N) in Portuguese: 24h. On MW 0300-2200, night prgr. weekends on 1008/1206/1224/1260kHz.
Cidade FM (C) in Portuguese: 24h. Also rel. BBC.
RM Desporto (D) in Portuguese: 0300-2200.
Emissão Provincial (EP) in Portuguese/ethnic: Provincial prgrs (between 0240-2100) and rel. of Antena Nacional on MW/FM: 24h.
1) EP de Maputo – **2)** EP de Sofala, C.P. 1942, Beira – **3)** EP de Nampula, C.P. 93, Nampula – **4)** EP de Manica, C.P. 390, Chimoio – **5)** EP de Inhambane, C.P. 196, Inhambane – **6)** EP do Niassa, C.P. 45, Lichinga – **7)** EP de Zambézia, C.P. 333, Quelimane – **8)** EP de Cabo Delgado, C.P. 45, Pemba – **9)** EP de Tete, C.P. 384, Tete – **10)** EP de Gaza, C.P. 130, Xai-Xai.
Ann: "Rádio Moçambique, Antena Nacional", EP: "Rádio Moçambique, (province)". **IS:** Mbira (indigenous xylophone). Opens and closes with National Anthem.

Other Stations (FM MHz):
A Voz do Islão, Maputo: 96.3 – **KFM,** Maputo: 88.3 – **Lifetime Music R,** Maputo: 87.8 1kW **W:** lmradio.net – **R. Capital,** Maputo: 90.7 (also rel. TWR) – **R. Haq,** Nampula: 104.4 – **R. Indico:** Maputo 89.5, Inhambane 89.7, Quelimane 88.2, Beira/Chimoio/Lichinga/ Nampula/Pemba/Tete/Xai-Xai 90.0 **W:** teste.radioindico.fm – **R. Maria Moçambique:** Maputo 103.1, Villankulo/Xai Xai 102, Chokwe 101.4, Govure 102.5, Quissico 106.4, Maxixe 104.2, Nova Mambone 104.0 **W:** radiomaria.org.mz – **R. Miramar:** Maputo: 101.4, Beira 98.1, Nampula 98.4 **W:** radiomiramarfm.blogspot.com – **R. N'tyana,** Maputo: 93.5 – **R. Savana,** Maputo: 100.2 **W:** savana.co.mz – **R. SFM,** Maputo: 94.6 – **R. Terra Verde,** Maputo: 98.6 – **99FM:** Maputo 99.3, Beira 89.3, Tete/Xai-Xai 95.0, Inhambane 96.0, Nampula 97.3, Pemba 99.5 **W:**99fm.co.mz – **R. Viva:** Maputo 99.6 1kW, Nampula 90.8 **W:** radio-viva.fm – **Top R,** Maputo: 104.2 **W:** topradiomoz.blogspot.com
BBC African Service: Tete 87.8, Nampula 88.3, Beira 88.5, Quelimane 95.3, Maputo 95.5 1kW, Chimoio 99.0, Xai-Xai 100.9 – **RDP África:** Beira 94.8, Maputo 89.2, Nampula 91.9, Quelimane 89.0 (all 50kW) – **RFI Afrique:** Maputo 105.0 1kW in French/English/Portuguese.
In addition about 100 community radio stations are in operation

MYANMAR

L.T: UTC + 6½h — **Pop:** 54.1 million — **Pr.L:** Burmese (Bamar), English. Major minority languages: Kachin, Kayah, Kayin (Po & Sakaw), Chin, Mon, Rakhine, Shan — **E.C:** 50Hz, 230V — **ITU:** BRM

MINISTRY OF INFORMATION
✉ Yaza Thingaha Rd, Zeya Theiddhi Ward, Naypyidaw ☎+95 67 412323 **W:** moi.gov.mm

MYANMA RADIO AND TELEVISION DEPT, MRTV (Gov.)
MYANMA RADIO
✉ Tatkon Township, Naypyidaw ☎ +95 67 79483 🖷 +95 67 79403
Yangon centre: Pyay Rd, Kamayut-11041, Yangon ☎+95 1 527119
🖷+95 1 534211 **W:** mrtv.gov.mm **E:** mrtv@mptmail.net.mm **L.P:** DG: U Tint Swe, Dir. R.: U Zay Yar. CE: U Myo Win, Dir TV: U Myo Myint Aung

MW (kHz)	kW	Loc	Pr	H. of tr.
576	100	Y	N	2300-1700
594	200	N	N	2300-1700
711	400	N		‡
729	100	Y	Y	2330(SS 2300)-1630
SW (kHz)	**kW**	**Loc**	**Pr**	**H. of tr.**
5915	50	N	Mi	2300-1700
5985	50	Y	N	2300-0130, 1130-1700
7200±	50	Y	Y	2330-1500v
9730	50	Y	N	0130-1130

±) variable ‡) inactive

FM	MHz	kW	Region/State
Yangon	87.6		Yangon Region
Hsipaw	88.0	0.3	Shan State
Nyaunglaybin	88.3	2	Bago Region
Pyin U Lwin	88.3		Mandalay Region
Taungdwingyi	88.3	2	Magwe Region
Theinni	88.3	0.15	Shan State
Ye-U	88.3	2	Sagaing Region
Maungdaw (Buthidaung)	88.9	2	Rakhine State
Taunggyi	88.9		Shan State
Tachilek	89.0		Shan State
Naypyidaw (Tatkon)	89.2	2	Union Territory
Yanbye	89.2	2	Rakhine State
Kanbalu	89.5	0.3	Sagaing Region
Sittwe	89.8	2	Rakhine State
Kennedy Peak	90.4	2	Chin State
Loikaw	90.7	2	Kayah State
Lashio	91.3		Shan State
Mawlamyine	91.3		Mon State
Bago	92.5	2	Bago Region
Minbu	92.5		Magwe Region
Pathein	92.5		Pathein District
Magwe (Popa)	94.3		Magwe Region
Sagaing	94.6		Sagaing Region
Pyinmana	94.9		Union Territory

NB: Other FM freqs are in operation, details not available. FM network carries N prgr, but some FM freqs opt out to carry Mi or Y prgrs in minority languages at times.
Loc=Location: N=Naypyidaw. Y=Yangon. **Pr=Prgr:** N=National prgr in Burmese, English. M=minorities prgrs in Kachin, Shan, Phalan Chin, Mindat Chin, Rakhine, Wa and Kokang. Y=Yangon prgr in Sakaw Kayin, Po Kayin, Mon, Kayah, Gekho and Gebo. E=Educational prgr in Burmese and English. **English** (in N Prgr): 0230-0330, 0700-0730, 1530-1630. **N:** Generally 30 mins past the UTC h on N prgr; in English on N prgr at 0230, 0700, 1530
Ann: E: "This is Myanma R" IS: Myanma Orchestral Music

THAZIN RADIO (Mil.)
✉ Tatmadaw Broadcasting, Thin Village, Pyin U Lwin ☎ +95 33 60165 **W:** thazinfm.com
Operated by the Directorate of Public Relations and Psychological Warfare, Ministry of Defence

MW (kHz)	kW	Pr	H. of tr.			
639	50	M	2330-0200, 0430-0700, 0930-1500			
SW (kHz)	**kW**	**Pr**	**H. of tr.**	**SW (kHz)**	**kW**	**Pr**	**H. of tr.**

SW (kHz)	kW	Pr	H. of tr.	SW (kHz)	kW	Pr	H. of tr.
6030	50	M	2330-0200	9460	50	M	0430-0700
6165	50	Mi	2330-0130	9590	50	Mi	0130-0330, 0430-0830, 0930-1330
6165	50	M	0930-1500				

Thazin FM: 24h in Burmese. Magwe/Naypyidaw/Taunggyi 87.6MHz, Hakha/Lashio/Meikhtila/Myeik/Sagaing/Sittwe 88.6MHz, Myitkyina 89.2MHz, Monywa/Pathein/Pyin U Lwin/Tachilek 89.5MHz, Dawei/Muse 91.0MHz.
Pr=Prgr: M=Main prgr in Burmese, exc.English 0130-0200, 0630-

0700, 1430-1500. Mi=minorities prgr in Chin, Kachin, La, Po, Geba, Kokang, Karen, Shan, Kayah, Gekho and Mon.

Other Stations:
Cherry FM (Comm.) ✉ Mya Yeik Nyo Hotel, Yangon **W:** cherryfmmym.com Operated by Zay Kaba Co. **FM:** Hpa-an/Kawkareik 88.3MHz, Yangon 89.3MHz, Loikaw/Muse 89.5MHz, Hsipaw/Kunlong/Kyaingtong/Lashio/Laukkaing/Pyin U Lwin/Tachilek/Taunggyi 89.8MHz, Pathein 91.3MHz, Sagaing 92.2MHz, Naypyidaw/Pyay 92.5MHz, Popa 93.1MHz – **City FM (FM-89) (Gov.)** ✉ 573 Pyay Rd, Kamayut Township, Yangon ☎ +95 1 536042 **FM:** Yangon 89.0MHz – **FM Bagan (Comm.)** ✉ A-2, Min Dhama Road, Mayangone Township, Yangon ☎ +95 1 655301-3 **W:** fmbagan.org Operated by Htoo Co. **FM:** Popa 88.3MHz, Gangaw/Kennedy Peak 89.2MHz, Hakha/Minhla 89.8MHz, Yangon 89.9MHz, Sagaing 93.4MHz, Pyinmana 93.7MHz – **Mandalay FM (Gov.)** ✉ Mandalay. Yangon office: Rm 1402-3, Olympic Twr, Bo Aung Kyaw St, Yangon **W:** mandalayfm.com Joint venture of Forever Group and Mandalay City Development Committee (MCDC). **FM:** Mandalay (Sagaing Hill)/Taungoo/Yangon 87.9MHz, Naypyidaw 88.3MHz – **Padamyar FM (Comm.) (Ruby FM)** ✉ Shop House 4, 3rd Floor & 4th Floor, Junction Square Compound, Between Kyun Taw Street and Pyay Road, Kamayut Township, Yangon ☎ +95 1 2306011 **W:** padamyarfm.com Operated by Thein Kyaw Kyaw Co. **FM:** Yangon 88.2, Kanbalu/Monywa 88.6MHz, Bhamo/Katha/Myitkyina/Nam Mar/Sagaing 88.9MHz, Naypyidaw 89.5MHz, Popa 90.7MHz, Bago/Pyay 91.3MHz, Taunggyi 92.2MHz, Mawlamyine 92.5MHz – **Pyinsawaddy FM (Comm.)** ✉ Rm 1402-3, Olympic Twr, Bo Aung Kyaw St, Yangon Operated by Forever Group ✉ Sittwe, Rakhine State. **FM:** Pathein/Sittwe/Thandwe 88.9MHz, Yangon 91.0MHz, Kyaungon 100.6MHz – **Shwe FM (Comm.) (Gold FM)** Operated by Shwe Thanlwin Co. ☎ 131/133 Botahtaung Pagoda Road, Yangon ☎ +95 1 9010082 **W:** shwefmradio.com **FM:** Bilin/Nyaunglaybin/Pyay 89.5MHz, Yangon 89.6MHz, Bago/Dawei/Hpa-an/Kawthaung/Kyaikto/Mawlamyine/Myawaddy/Myeik/Taunggyi 89.8MHz, Sagaing/Taunggyi 91.0MHz, Naypyidaw 91.3MHz, Popa 91.9MHz

NAMIBIA

L.T: UTC +1h (6 Sep 15-3 Apr 16, 4 Sep 16-2 Apr 17: +2h) — **Pop:** 2.1 million — **Pr.L:** English, Afrikaans, German, local languages — **E.C:** 50Hz, 220V — **ITU:** NMB

COMMUNICATIONS REGULATORY AUTHORITY OF NAMIBIA (CRAN)
✉ Private Bag 13309, Communication House, 56 Robert Mugabe Ave, Windhoek ☎+264 61 222666 🖷 + 264 61 238646 **W:** ncc.org. na **E:** info@cran.na **L.P:** CEO: Stanley Shanapinda. Head Eng.: Ronel le Grange

NAMIBIAN BROADCASTING CORPORATION (Pub)
✉ P.O. Box 321, Pettenkofer Str, Windhoek West 9000 ☎+264 61 291 9111 🖷 + 264 612 913325 **W:** nbc.na **E:** pr@nbc.com.na **L.P:** Chmn: Mr. Ponhele Ya France. DG: Albertus Aochamub. Tech. Mgr: Ruben Prinz.

FM (MHz)	Afr.	Nat.	Ger.	Ova.	Her.	D/N.	Kav.Lozi	Tsw.	San.
Aminuis	88.9	92.0		95.2				98.5	
Andara		92.5		95.7			106.1	102.5	
Arendsnes	88.7	90.1	91.8	96.4	99.7	106.8	93.2	95.0	98.3	103.2
Aroab	87.9	94.2			104.6				
Aus	92.5		95.8	102.6		160.2			
Aussenkjer	92.5	95.7		98.7		102.5			
Bethanien	88.1	91.2	94.4	97.7	101.2	104.8			
Brukkaros	92.0	96.5			106.9				
Buitepos		95.0		98.3	101.8				105.4
Ekuli		91.5		88.4			94.7	98.0	
Epukiro	91.6	98.1		101.6					105.2
Erongo	90.6	93.7	96.9	100.2	103.7	107.3			
Gam		92.6		102.6	99.1				95.8
Gibeon					100.7				
Gobabis	87.6	90.7	93.9	102.9	100.7	104.3	106.5	92.9	97.2
Gross-Herzog	88.6	91.7	94.9	98.2	101.7	105.3			
Kamanjab	89.7				106.4				
Katima Mulilo	88.2	92.6	90.9	99.1	94.1	106.2	100.9	95.8	87.8
Keetmanshoop	87.6	90.7	93.9	97.2	89.3	104.3			
KL Waterberg	89.6	92.7	95.9	99.2	102.7	106.3			
Koës	88.8	95.1			105.5				
Kongola		88.3		91.4			94.6	97.9	
Lüderitz	89.7	92.8	96.0	99.3	100.2	103.7			
Maltahöhe	88.5		94.8		105.2				

FM (MHz)	Afr.	Nat.	Ger.	Ova.	Her.	D/N.	Kav.Lozi	Tsw.	San.
Mariental	87.7	90.8	94.0	101.8	105.4	104.4			
Nakop	90.6	93.7		100.2		103.7			
Nkurenkuru		90.7		87.6	97.2		105.1 93.9		
Noordoewer	87.7	90.8		97.3		100.8			
Okongo		89.0		92.1		95.3	98.6		
Omega		89.4		92.5			95.5 99.0		
Omuthiya		89.2		98.8	102.3	105.9			
Opuwo		91.1		97.6	101.1				
Oranjemund	90.0	93.1		99.6		106.7			
Oshakati	89.2	87.8	96.4	97.4	98.8	105.9	92.3 90.9	99.7	
Otjimbingwe					102.3	105.9			
Otjinene	90.2	93.5			96.7			103.5	
Paresis	88.7	91.8	95.0	98.3	101.8	105.4			
Renosterkop	87.9	91.0			101.0	104.6			
Rietfontein		92.2		89.1	95.4			98.7	
Rosh Pinah	90.3	93.4		96.6		99.9			
Rössing	89.7	92.8	96.0	99.3	101.1	106.4			
Rundu		89.6					95.9		
Sesfontein		91.6		98.1	101.6	105.2			
Shamvura		91.3		97.8			94.5 104.9		
Signalberg	87.7	90.8	94.0	97.3	100.8	104.4			
Stampriet	89.7	92.8	96.0			106.4			
Terrace Bay		104.3							
Tsumeb	88.6	91.7	94.9	98.2		105.3			
Tsumkwe		90.4		100.0	93.5			103.5	
Ur		89.8	92.9	96.1	99.4	102.9	106.5		
Windhoek		89.5	92.6	95.8			107.1 93.5	90.4	

Afrikaans Sce: MF 0900-1600 & 1700-2000, SS 0600-2000. Relayed on other services overnight. – **National R. in English**: 24hrs – **German Sce:** 24h –**Oshiwambo Sce in Ovambo/Kwanyama:** 0900 (SS 0500)-2200 – **Otjiherero Sce in Herero/Setswana:** MF 0900-1600 & 1700-2000, SS 0500-2000 – **Damara/Nama Sce:** MF 0900-1600 & 1700-2000, SS 0500-2000 – **Rukavango Sce in Kwangali:** 0900 (Sat/Sun 0500)-2000 – **Lozi Sce** – **Tirelo ya Setswana Sce.**

Ann: National Sce: "National Radio". On all NBC trs overnight: "Here is the National Sce. of the NBC Nationwide". G: "Hier ist das Deutsche Hörfunkprogramm der NBC". Damara/Nam: "Nes ge Damara/Nama Gowab loabas NBC's disa". A: "Dit is die Afrikaanse diens van die NBC". Otjiherero: "Indji oradio ja Namibia morupa rueraka Otjiherero".
IS: at s/on: National Anthem with choir/orchestra.

Other Stations (FM MHz):
Base FM, P.O. Box 70448, 17 Clemence Kapuuo Str, Khomasdal. **W:** basefm.com.na . Katatura 106.2 – **E FM**, P.O. Box 11525, 17 Jan Jonker Str, Klein Windhoek. **W:** efm913.blogspot.com . Klein Windhoek 91.3 0.25kW – **Fresh FM**, P.O. Box 40775, 158 Jan Jonker Str, Klein Windhoek. **W:** freshfm.com.na . Windhoek 102.9 – **Hitradio Namibia**, P.O. Box 30765, Windhoek. **W:** hitradio.com.na . In German. Swakopmund 97.5 1kW, Windhoek 99.5 1kW – **Kanaal 7**, P.O. Box 20500, Ara Str, Dorado Park, Windhoek: 102.3 + 18 FM fq's. **W:** k7.com. na – **Kosmos**, P.O. Box 9639, 17 Eros, Windhoek. **W:** kosmos.com.na . Klein Windhoek 94.1 – **Kudu FM**, P.O. Box 5369, 158 Jan Jonker Str, Windhoek. **W:** kudufm.com . In English. Otjiwarongo 90.9 0.1kW, Tsumeb 92.6 0.1kW, Rundu 92.7 0.1kW, Oranjemund 94.0, Swakopmund 94.3 0.5kW, Karibib/Omaruru/Usakos 94.6 0.1kW, Lüderitz 94.7 0.1kW, Walvis Bay 95.1 0.1kW, Grootfontein/Ondangwa/Ongwediva/Oshakati 95.5 1kW, Gobabis/Keetmanshoop 95.6 0.1kW, Mariental 97.3 0.1kW, Rosh Pinah 103.4 0.1kW, Okahandja/Rehoboth/Windhoek 103.5 1kW, Katima Mulilo 107.4 0.1kW – **Live FM**, P.O. Box 3363, 253 Bahnhof Str, Rehoboth. **E:** livefm@iway.na . Rehoboth 90.3 – **R. 99**, P.O. Box 11849, 14 General Muratala Muhammed Ave, Eros, Windhoek. **W:** 99fm.com. na. Walvis Bay & Swakopmund 96.5, Windhoek 99.0, Otjiwarongo 99.9, Tsumeb 101.7, Oshakati & Ondangwa 104.5 – **R. Energy,** P.O. Box 676, 17 Bismarck Str, Windhoek West 9000. **W:** energy100fm.com . Walvis Bay 88.8 0.5kW, Klein Windhoek 100.0 0.5kW, Oshakati 100.9 2kW – **Omulunga R**, P.O. Box 40789, 158 Jan Jonker Str, Windhoek. Prgrs in Oshiwambo. **W:** omulunga.com. Otjiwarongo 87.8 0.1kW, Grootfontein 92 0.1kW, Mariental 95.0 0.1kW, Rundu 99.2 0.1kW, Rehoboth/Windhoek 100.9 1kW, Ongwediva/Oshakati 102.3 1kW, Swakopmund/Walvis Bay 105.5 0.1kW, Keetmanshoop 106 0.1kW, Lüderitz 106,4 0.1kW, Gobabis 107.5 0.1kW – **R. Wave**, P.O. Box 9953, 19 Michael Scott Str, Windhoek. **W:** radiowave.com.na . Otjimbingwe 87.8 1.5kW, Grootfontein 88.9 0.1kW, Lüderitz 90.6 0.1kW, Rossing 91.1 0.25kW, Walvis Bay 91.9 0.1kW, Usakos 92.4 0.1kW, Tsumeb 95.8 0.1kW, Klein Windhoek 96.7 1.5kW, Otjiwarongo 100.9 0.1kW, Katima Mulilo 104.5 0.35kW, Rundu 105.4 0.35kW, Oshakati 106.8 0.35kW– **UNAM R**, Private Box 13301, Windhoek. **W:** unam.na/unam radio/index_unam_radio.html . Windhoek 97.4 0.1kW

– **West Coast FM**, P.O. Box 4420, Swakopmund. **W:** westcoastfmnamibia.com. In Afrikaans/E. Swakopmund 107.7 0.25kW.
R. France Int, Windhoek: 107..9

NAURU

L.T: UTC +12h — **Pop:** 9,322 — **Pr.L:** English, Nauruan — **E.C:** 50Hz, 110/240V — **ITU:** NRU

NAURU BROADCASTING SERVICE (Gov)
Nauru Media Bureau, Home Affairs Department
P O Box 429, Rep. of Nauru, Ce. Pacific ☎ +674 555 6066 📠 +674 4443195 **E:** radionaurufm@hotmail.com **LP:** SM: Dominic Appi, Tech. Mgr: Max Gadaloa
FM: 105.1MHz **D.Prgr:** 1800-1100 now includes local health, sports and education prgrs. Other times carries **Radio Australia** English for the Pacific satellite relay from Melbourne 1100-1800 **N:** hourly on the hour local and R. Australia.

RADIO PASIFIK NAURU Triple 9 FM (Edu)
University of the South Pacific Campus, Private Bag, Nauru PO, Nauru 00674 ☎ +674 4443774 **FM:** 99.9MHz 0.03kW **LP:** Dir.: Alamanda Lauti. **D.Prgr:** Mon-Sat 3 hrs daily [6-9pm] includes local prgrs and lectures & tutorials supplied digitally from USP Suva, Fiji. (current status unknown)

NEPAL

L.T: UTC +5¾h — **Pop:** 25.3 million — **Pr.L:** Nepali, English — **E.C:** 50Hz, 220V — **ITU:** NPL

RADIO NEPAL (Semi-Gov, Comm.)
Radio Broadcasting Service, G.P.O. Box 634, Singha Durbar, Kathmandu ☎+977 1 4231804 📠+977 1 4221952 **W:** radionepal.gov. np **E:** program@radionepal.gov.np **E:** engg@wlink.com.np)(Eng. div: ☎+977 1 4211842
LP: Exec. Dir: Er. R.S. Karki. Dep. Exec. Dirs: Mr Rajendra Prasad Sharma & Mr Sushil Koirala. Chief Eng.: Er. Ramesh Jung Karkee

MW	kHz	kW	MW	kHz	kW
Surkhet	576	100	Kathmandu	792	100
Dhankuta	648	100	Dipayal	810	10
Pokhara	684	100	Bardibas	1143	10

SW: Khumaltar 5005kHz 100kW/5kW (not heard any more)
D.Prgr on MW/SW: 2315-1715 (SW except 0515-0715 m-f). **N.** in **Nepali** at 0015,0115, 0315,0415, 0515, 0615, 0715, 0915, 1015, 1115, 1315, 1515, 1715; **Regional N** at 0325,0825; in **English:** 0215, 0815, 1415; in **Sanskrit** 0010; in **Sherpa** 1020; for **Children** 1110; in **Tamang** 1120; in **Bhojpuri** 1205; in **Urdu** 1210; in **Maithili** 1215; in **Hindi:** 1615; **Variation at Regional Centres:** 0400-0415 & 1215-1300
Ann: Nepali: 'Yo Radio Nepal Ho'; English: 'This is Radio Nepal'
IS: Instruments used are conch shell, violin, piano and jal tarang
V. by QSL-card

FM STATIONS:

FM	MHz Station	FM	MHz Station
Achhaam	88.2 R. Vaijnath FM	Banke	104.8 Nepalgunj FM
Achhaam	92.0 R. Ramaroshan †	Banke	105.4 Bheri FM †
Amargadi	90.8 Seti-Mahakali	Bara	88.8 Sanskar FM
	Ganatantra FM	Bara	106.0 R. Simara
Arghakhanchi	101.0 R. Deurali †	Bardiya	100.6 Fulbari FM
Arghakhanchi	105.8 R. Argakhanchi †	Bardiya	106.0 R. Babai
Attariya	100.4 Ghodaghodi FM	Bardiya	106.4 R. Gurubaga †
Baglung	91.6 Saypatri FM †	Besisahar	95.0 R. Marsyangdi
Baglung	96.4 Baglung FM †	Bhairahawa	98.8 Siddhartha FM
Baglung	98.6 Dhaulagiri FM †	Bhairahawa	102.0 Rupandehi FM †
Baglung	104.1 R. Dhorpatan	Bhaktapur	88.8 NepaliKo R.
Baglung	107.0 R. Baglung	Bhaktapur	105.4 Bhaktapur FM
Baglung	107.4 Sarathi FM	Bharatpur	91.0 Kalika FM 2
Baitadi	103.6 Saugat FM	Bharatpur	91.6 Synergy FM †
Baitadi	106.6 R. Sansher	Bharatpur	94.0 Hamro FM
Bajhang	93.6 Seti FM	Bharatpur	94.6 Chitawan FM †
Bajhang	98.0 R. Nepal	Bharatpur	95.2 Kalika FM †
Bajura	104.0 R. Bajura	Bharatpur	96.1 Narayani FM
Banepa	89.8 R. ABC †	Bharatpur	96.8 V. of Youth FM
Banke	88.4 X-press FM	Bharatpur	97.9 Image FM
Banke	94.0 R. Krishnasar †	Bharatpur	98.6 R. Chomolungma
Banke	96.8 Youth FM	Bhojpur	103.6 R. Bhojpur
Banke	97.9 Image FM	Bhojpur	98.6 R. Chomolungma
Banke	101.2 R. Kohalpur †	Biratnagar	88.2 Kankai Sangeet
Banke	102.4 R. Pratibodh	Biratnagar	
Banke	104.2 Naya Nepal Sanchar	Biratnagar	
Banke	104.5 R. Rubaru †	Biratnagar	91.2 Birat FM

FM	MHz	Station
Biratnagar	94.3	Koshi FM
Biratnagar	105.6	SaptaKoshi FM
Biratnagar	106.7	Sky FM
Birgunj	91.4	Gadimai FM †
Birgunj	92.2	Kalika FM
Birgunj	96.1	Kantipur FM
Birgunj	96.8	V. of Youth FM
Birgunj	97.0	Image FM
Birgunj	97.6	Indreni FM
Birgunj	99.0	Birgunj FM †
Birgunj	100.0	R. Nepal
Birgunj	103.8	Narayani FM †
Birgunj	105.4	Star FM
Birtamod	92.6	Kanchanjunga FM
Birtamod	105.0	Kankai Samaaj
Buditola	100.0	R. Nepal
Butwal	92.2	Kalika FM
Butwal	92.8	R. Namaste
Butwal	93.6	Jagaran R. †
Butwal	94.4	Butwal FM †
Butwal	96.1	Kantipur FM
Butwal	97.9	Image FM
Butwal	98.2	Tinau FM †
Butwal	99.4	R. Jagran
Byash	105.8	Madi Seti FM
Chainpur	100.6	Saipal R. †
Chainpur	105.2	R. Kailash
Chainpur	106.6	Saipal R.
Charpane	105.4	R. Kechana
Chitawan	89.8	R. Dhruvatara
Chitawan	91.0	Kalika FM
Chitawan	96.8	Youth FM
Chitawan	97.9	Image FM
Chitawan	100.6	R. Triveni
Chitawan	103.0	R. Nepal
Chitawan	104.5	R. Arpan
Chitawan	105.2	R. Narayani †
Chitawan	107.6	R. Madi
Dadeldhura	95.0	R. Sudur Aawaj
Dadeldhura	96.0	Paschim Nepal Media
Dadeldhura	97.4	Vikash Nyaya Manch
Dadeldhura	104.8	Aafno FM †
Dailekh	89.8	R. Dhurbatara FM †
Dailekh	104.0	R. Panchakoshi FM†
Damak	91.8	Star FM
Damak	93.6	Pathibhara FM †
Damak	101.6	Saptarangi FM
Daman	97.0	Prathidhwani FM
Damauli	94.2	Damauli FM
Dang	88.0	R. Jharana
Dang	89.0	R. Hamro Pahuch
Dang	92.4	Indreni FM
Dang	93.4	R. Prakriti
Dang	95.1	R. Ganatantra Rapti
Dang	98.0	R. Nepal
Dang	103.5	R. Highway
Dang	104.0	R. Saryu Ganga
Dang	106.4	Super FM
Dang	107.0	Dang FM †
Dang	107.3	R. Naya Yug
Darchula	98.0	R. Nepal
Darchula	102.2	Kalapani FM †
Darchula	104.5	R. Naya Nepal
Daunne	100.0	R. Nepal
Dhading	89.4	R. Loktranta FM †
Dhading	92.1	Rajmarga Sanchar Kendra
Dhading	97.6	Shree Sahid Smriti Sanchar
Dhading	105.0	Krishi R. †
Dhading	105.6	R. Trishuli
Dhading	106.0	R. Dhading †
Dhangadi	89.4	R. Jana Aawaj
Dhangadi	92.4	Khaptad FM
Dhangadi	93.8	Dinesh FM †
Dhangadi	101.8	Kantipur FM
Dhankuta	87.6	Heart FM
Dhankuta	92.2	R. Makalu
Dhankuta	96.8	Youth FM
Dhankuta	97.9	Image FM
Dhankuta	105.2	R. Laliguransh
Dhankuta	106.2	R. Dhankuta †
Dhanusha	93.8	City Sahakari R.
Dhanusha	95.0	Kamalamai FM
Dhanusha	99.4	Mithilanchal FM
Dhanusha	106.6	Mithila Sanchar Samuha
Dharan	95.1	R. Ganatantra †
Dharan	95.6	Star FM
Dharan	106.6	Budasubba FM
Dhulikhel	104.0	Madhyapurwa FM †
Dolakha	103.4	Hamro R. †
Dolakha	104.0	R. Sailung
Dolakha	106.0	Gaurishankar FM
Dolakha	106.4	R. Kalinchowk †
Dolakha	108.8	Chyomongmo Media Pvt. Ltd.
Dolpa	100.0	R. Nepal
Dolpa	106.3	Se Foksundo Sanchar
Doti	94.4	Triveni FM
Doti	105.9	R. Shaileshwari FM
Gaidakot	101.6	Vijay FM
Ghorahi	91.4	R. MadhyaPaschim†
Ghorahi	102.8	R. Swargadwari FM†
Godawari	104.2	ECR FM
Gorkha	102.4	R. Manakamana
Gorkha	103.6	Gorakhkali FM
Gorkha	103.9	R. Manaslu †
Gorkha	104.6	R. Lamjung
Gorkha	105.4	R. Harmi
Gorkha	106.4	Deurali FM
Gorkha	107.2	Mero Saathi
Gulariya	100.6	Phoolbari FM
Gulmi	88.4	R. Sky FM
Gulmi	91.2	R. Gulmi
Gulmi	94.8	Ruru FM
Gulmi	100.0	R. Nepal
Hetauda	90.4	National FM
Hetauda	92.9	Manakamana FM
Hetauda	96.6	Hetauda FM †
Hetauda	103.4	Shakti FM
Humla	94.2	Eklai Vikash Kendra
Humla	96.8	V. of Youth FM
Humla	100.0	R. Nepal
Humla	101.4	Sarkegad FM
Humla	103.4	R. Kailash †
Illam	90.6	R. Fikkal FM
Illam	93.0	Illam FM †
Illam	94.9	R. Nepalbani †
Illam	100.0	R. Nepal
Illam	104.0	Sandakpur FM
Itahari	107.2	Namaste FM
Jajarkot	97.9	Asal Sashan Jilla Samiti
Jajarkot	105.0	R. Paila
Jajarkot	107.6	Khalanga FM
Jalweshwor	106.7	R. Appan Mithila
Janakpur	91.0	R. Today †
Janakpur	97.0	R. Janakpur †
Janakpur	100.8	R. Mithila †
Janakpur	101.8	Janakpur FM †
Janakpur	105.0	Mithilanchal FM
Janakpur	106.0	Janaki FM
Jhapa	88.8	R. Saragam
Jhapa	89.1	Hamro Sanchar Samuha
Jhapa	96.8	FM Mechi Tunes
Jhapa	101.6	Saptarangi FM †
Jhapa	103.9	R. Sandesh
Jhapa	105.8	Birta FM
Jhapa	105.9	R. Sunrise
Jhapa	106.9	Seemana FM
Jhapa	107.5	Nagarik FM
Jomsom	100.0	R. Nepal
Jumla	100.0	R. Nepal
Jumla	100.6	Hamro Aawaj Hamro Sarokar
Jumla	105.2	R. Karnali FM
Kailali	87.9	Godavari FM
Kailali	88.8	Paschim Today FM
Kailali	91.4	Ghodaghodi FM †
Kailali	93.2	Fulbari FM †
Kailali	93.8	Dinesh FM?
Kailali	98.2	Khaptad FM
Kailali	101.0	Tikapur FM?
Kailali	101.8	Kantipur FM
Kailali	103.0	R. Nepal
Kailali	103.7	R. Kailali FM
Kailali	105.3	Sita Sanchar Samuha
Kailali	105.6	Ujvalo Sudur Paschhim
Kailali	107.3	Hamro Fulbari FM
Kalikot	100.0	R. Nepal
Kalikot	101.2	R. Bhek Aawaj †
Kalikot	101.8	R. Chulimalika †
Kalikot	102.8	R. Malika †
Kalyanpur	106.8	Nuwakot FM
Kamalamai	103.6	R. Sindhuligadi
Kanchanpur	104.3	Angel FM
Kapilvastu	89.6	R. Buddha Aawaj
Kapilvastu	104.2	R. Kapilvastu †
Kapilvastu	105.4	R. Samanata
Kapilvastu	106.1	Janakpur Sanchar Samuha
Kapilvastu	107.6	Tilarakot R. FM
Kaski	87.9	R. Chhunumunu
Kaski	90.6	R. Gandaki
Kaski	96.8	Youth FM
Kaski	97.9	Image FM
Kaski	99.6	Annapurna Music FM
Kaski	101.2	Big FM
Kaski	101.8	Kantipur FM
Kaski	102.2	Sunaulo FM
Kaski	103.4	R. Safalta
Kaski	106.0	Gorkhali R.
Kaski	106.6	R. Lekhnath
Kaski	107.6	Tarang Pvt. Ltd
Kathmandu	87.6	R. Upatyaka †
Kathmandu	87.9	R. Masti
Kathmandu	88.8	Nepaliko R.
Kathmandu	89.4	R. Mirmire
Kathmandu	89.8	BF BS FM
Kathmandu	90.6	Times FM
Kathmandu	91.2	Hits FM
Kathmandu	91.8	Nepal FM
Kathmandu	92.4	Capital FM
Kathmandu	93.0	Gorkha FM
Kathmandu	93.5	R. Jana Sandesh
Kathmandu	94.0	HBC FM
Kathmandu	94.6	Metro FM
Kathmandu	95.2	Star FM
Kathmandu	96.8	V. of Youth FM
Kathmandu	97.9	Image FM
Kathmandu	98.3	Keeps Media
Kathmandu	98.8	R. City FM
Kathmandu	99.4	Maitri FM
Kathmandu	100.0	R. Nepal
Kathmandu	100.6	RBC FM
Kathmandu	101.8	GopiKrishna FM
Kathmandu	103.6	R. Bagmati
Kathmandu	104.8	FM Adhyatma Jyoti
Kathmandu	105.1	Good News FM
Kathmandu	106.0	CJMC FM
Kathmandu	106.3	R. Audio
Kathmandu	107.0	TU FM
Kavre	87.9	R. Masti
Kavre	88.4	R. Shepherd
Kavre	104.0	Madhyapurwa FM†
Kavre	104.5	R. Naya Sandesh
Kavre	106.7	R. Namobuddha†
Kavre	107.3	R. Janasanchar
Kavre	107.6	Grace FM
Khalanga	92.0	R. Pyuthan †
Khalanga	101.0	R. Salyan
Khanigau	103.6	R. Parbat
Khotang	102.4	R. Haleshi †
Khotang	105.0	Rupakot R. †
Kirtipur	106.7	Newa FM
Kohalpur	101.2	R. Kohalpur
Lahan	102.6	Samad FM
Lahan	105.4	Fulbari R.
Lalitpur	90.0	Ujyaalo FM
Lalitpur	96.1	Kantipur FM
Lalitpur	97.2	Headlines & Music FM
Lalitpur	100.0	R. Nepal
Lalitpur	100.9	R. Lalitpur
Lalitpur	101.2	Classic FM
Lalitpur	102.4	R. Sagarmatha †
Lalitpur	103.0	BBC FM #
Lalitpur	103.6	Image News
Lalitpur	104.2	Paryawaran Chakra R.
Lalitpur	105.7	BFBS
Lamahi	105.8	R. Deukhuri
Lamjung	88.4	R. Lamjung
Lamjung	95.0	R. Marsyangdi †
Liwang	93.8	R. Rolpa †
Mahend.	90.2	Kanchanpur FM
Mahend.	96.2	R. Mahakali
Mahend.	99.4	Suklafanta FM †
Mahottari	88.4	R. Darpan
Mahottari	90.4	Jaleshwarnath FM†
Mahottari	94.4	R. Appan Mithila†
Mahottari	103.4	R. Rudraksha
Mahottari	103.7	R. Gunjan
Mahottari	107.0	R. Sungava FM†
Makwanpur	88.0	Hetauda Media
Makwanpur	88.5	R. Aakash Ganga
Makwanpur	97.0	R. Pratidhwani
Makwanpur	98.0	R. Nepal
Makwanpur	98.6	R. Thaha Sansar
Makwanpur	101.3	R. Makwanpur
Makwanpur	106.6	R. Asmita
Mechinagar	96.8	FM Mechi Tunes
Morang	87.9	Jagriti FM
Morang	91.2	B FM †
Morang	94.3	Koshi FM
Morang	95.1	Janasanchar Kendra
Morang	101.0	R. Chamatkar
Morang	102.1	R. Makalu
Morang	102.6	R. Sunakhari
Morang	104.4	R. Purwanchal †
Morang	104.8	Sajha R.
Morang	106.3	R. Suseli FM
Morang	106.6	Sky FM
Mugu	100.0	R. Nepal
Mugu	102.2	R. Suryadaya FM
Mugu	104.6	R. Rara
Mugu	106.6	Mugali Chalchitra Vikash Sang
Mugu	107.4	R. Mugu
Musikot	92.8	R. Sisne FM
Mustang	89.0	Gramin Suchana Vikash Kendra
Mustang	96.8	V. of Youth FM
Mustang	103.0	R. Nepal
Myagdi	104.4	R. Myagdi †
Myanglung	104.2	R. Samhaltung
Nawalparasi	90.2	R. Parasi †
Nawalparasi	100.0	R. Nepal
Nawalparasi	101.0	R. Madhyavindu FM†
Nawalparasi	103.4	Daunne FM
Nepalgunj	94.6	R. Bageshwori
Nepalgunj	95.6	R. Bheri Aawaj †
Nepalgunj	96.8	V. of Youth FM
Nepalgunj	97.3	R. Jana Aawaj
Nepalgunj	97.9	Image FM
Nepalgunj	101.8	Kantipur FM
Nepalgunj	104.8	R. Nepalgunj†
Nilkantha	106.0	Dhading FM
Nuwakot	104.5	R. Jalapa
Nuwakot	107.4	R. Abhiyan
Okhaldhunga	100.6	Ramailo Community R.
Okhaldhunga	104.8	Afno FM †
Okhaldhunga	107.6	R. Okhaldhunga
Palpa	103.6	R. Rampur
Palpa	103.9	R. Palpa
Palpa	106.9	R. Madanpokhara†
Palung	107.2	R. Palung FM
Panchthar	97.3	Simhalila FM
Panchthar	99.2	Eagle FM
Panchthar	104.2	Sumhatlung FM†
Parbat	95.2	R. Didi Bahini †
Parbat	100.6	R. Shaligram †
Parsa	92.8	Bhojpuriya FM
Parsa	96.1	R. Kantipur
Parsa	96.8	Youth FM
Parsa	97.6	Indreni FM
Parsa	97.9	Image FM
Parsa	100.0	R. Nepal
Parsa	101.9	Aakas FM
Parsa	105.8	Birgunj Musical FM
Parsa	107.0	R. Tarang
Pokhara	91.0	Machhapuchhre FM †
Pokhara	92.2	Himchuli FM †
Pokhara	93.4	R. Annapurna †
Pokhara	95.8	Pokhara FM
Pokhara	96.8	V. of Youth FM
Pokhara	97.9	Image FM
Pokhara	99.2	R. Barahi FM
Pokhara	106.6	R. Sarangkot
Prithivinarayan	92.8	R. Gorkha †
Putalibazar	90.2	Syangja FM †
Pyuthan	90.0	R. Mahila Aawaj
Pyuthan	97.0	R. Mandhawi †
Pyuthan	103.6	R. Lishne Aawaj
Rajbiraj	105.8	R. Rajbiraj
Ramechhap	88.6	R. Tinlal
Ramechhap	102.1	Hajurko R.
Rasuwa	100.9	Durgam FM
Rasuwa	102.1	Rasuwa FM
Rautahat	89.6	R. Madhes
Rautahat	90.4	R. Jivan Jyoti
Rautahat	90.8	Rautahat FM †

FM	MHz	Station	FM	MHz	Station
Rautahat	93.2	Rajdevi FM †	Siraha	88.1	R. Saugat
Rautahat	98.2	R. Sanskriti	Siraha	88.8	Bhaluwahi Samudaik R.
Rautahat	98.6	Madhesh Jana Aawaj	Siraha	107.8	R. Samagra
Rautahat	102.2	Gaur FM	Solukhumbu	94.6	R. Dudhkoshi
Rautahat	102.6	R. Nunthar FM	Solukhumbu	101.2	Solu FM
Rukum	89.2	R. Sani Bheri	Solukhumbu	105.3	R. Everest
Rukum	92.8	R. Sisne †	Sunsari	88.5	Dantakali FM
Rukum	100.8	R. SanoBheri	Sunsari	89.4	R. Jaya Nepal
Rukum	102.0	Uttarjganga Sanchar Kendra	Sunsari	90.0	Saptakoshi FM †
Rupandehi	88.2	R. Republic	Sunsari	96.1	R. Kantipur
Rupandehi	88.6	R. Malmala	Sunsari	98.8	Vijaypur FM
Rupandehi	92.8	Star FM	Sunsari	99.5	Popular FM †
Rupandehi	95.5	R. Mukti †	Sunsari	103.6	Jana Sanchar
Rupandehi	96.1	R. Kantipur	1		Kendra Nepal
Rupandehi	96.8	R. Lumbini †	Surkhet	90.2	R. Surkhet †
Rupandehi	97.6	Image FM	Surkhet	90.8	Jagaran FM †
Rupandehi	105.0	R. Samabesi	Surkhet	92.6	R. Himal
Rupandehi	106.6	R. Devdaha	Surkhet	98.6	R. Bheri †
Rupandehi	107.2	Aasha ko Sandesh	Surkhet	101.2	R. Bheka Aawaj
Salleri	94.6	R. Dudhkoshi	Surkhet	103.4	Bulbule FM †
Salleri	102.2	Solu FM	Surkhet	106.7	Himal FM
Salyan	101.0	R. Salyan †	Syangja	89.2	R. Waling
Salyan	102.2	R. Sharada FM	Syangja	89.6	R. Syangja †
Salyan	103.8	R. Sahara	Tamghas	106.2	R. Resunga
Salyan	104.8	R. Rapti FM †	Tanahu	88.2	Dhorbarahi FM
Salyan	106.1	R. Kapurkot	Tanahu	88.8	R. Bandipur †
Sankhuwa.	100.8	R. Arun Sandesh	Tanahu	94.2	Damauli FM †
Sankhuwa.	107.5	Gurans FM	Tanahu	97.2	R. Tanahun †
Sankhuwa.	105.8	Khadbari FM †	Tanahu	102.6	R. Devghat
Saptari	91.8	Today FM	Tanahu	104.2	R. Bhanubhakta†
Saptari	92.8	Bhorukawa	Tansen	90.8	Muktinath FM †
Saptari	101.4	R. Chhinnamasta Samuha	Tansen	93.2	Shreenagar FM
Saptari	102.1	Janak Sanchar Samuha	Tansen	99.4	R. Paschimanchal
Saptari	104.6	Appan FM	Taplejung	94.0	R. Taplejung
Sarlahi	89.3	R. Madhes †	Taplejung	102.0	R. Tamor †
Sarlahi	94.6	R. Ekata	Tawlihawa	104.2	R. Kapilbastu
Sarlahi	104.8	Malangwa FM	Thulasen	92.0	R. Ramaroshan †
Sarlahi	105.6	R. Sarlahi †	Tikapur	101.0	Tikapur FM †
Sarlahi	107.4	Mai FM †	Tribhuwan.	92.4	Indreni FM
Siligadi	96.8	V. of Youth FM	Tulsipur	100.2	R. Tulsipur FM †
Simikot	100.0	R. Nepal	Udaypur	91.6	Amurta FM
Sindhuli	92.0	R. Sindhuligadi †	Udaypur	102.4	R. Udayapur †
Sindhuli	104.2	R. Sahara	Udaypur	104.0	R. Triyuga
Sindhup.	89.1	R. Avarv	Udaypur	106.8	UK FM
Sindhup.	96.8	Youth FM	Walling	105.4	R. Aandhikhola †
Sindhup.	102.8	Sindhu FM			
Sindhup.	105.0	R. Sindhu †			

NB: Mahend.=Mahendranagar, Sankhuwa.=Sankhuwasabha, Sindhup.=Sindhupalchok, Tribhuwan.=Tribhuwannagar

† BBC Nepali rel. daily 0130-0145,1500-1530
# BBC WS rel. 24hrs except BBC Nepali Rel. daily 0130-0145,1500-1530(Sun -1600)
BBCWS daily MW relay via R. Nepal Surkhet 576 kHz: 1600-1630 Hindi, 1630-1730 WS in English.
Other Stations:
Guru-Baba FM: Bansgadi, 106.4MHz 0.1kW. Prgrs in Tharu
BFBS: Gurkha R., Kathmandu **FM:** 105.7MHz (Nepali & English)

	FM	NP01	NP02	NP03	NP04	kW
Alphen ad Rijn	96.5	-	-	-	-	0.06
Amsterdam	98.6	92.3	96.5	94.5		0.03/0.03/0.03/0.03
Arnhem	98.6	92.9	96.5	92.1		0.06/0.06/0.06/0.06
Den Haag	105.5	92.9	-	94.1		0.013/0.05/0.008
Emmaberg	105.3	93.4	103.9	98.7		10/10/10/10
Eys	-	97.2	-	-		10
Goes	104.4	94.4	99.8	95.0		40/0.1/10/10
Hoogersmilde	91.8	88.0	88.6	94.8		100/100/40/100
Hoorn	98.6	105.1	96.5	-		0.4/0.01/0.4
Hulst	-	107.1	-	-		0.05
IJsselstein	98.9	92.6	96.8	94.3		70/70/70/50
Jirnsum	104.3	-	-	-		0.07
Loon op Zand	-	-	-	98.2		55
Markelo	98.4	104.6	96.2	91.4		80/80/80/80
Mierlo	104.6	92.3	97.1	-		0.03/0.07/0.07
Roermond	104.8	88.2	90.9	94.5		100/100/100/100
Roosendaal	92.1	95.9	96.5	87.6		0.06/0.02/0.03/0.02
Rotterdam	98.6	92.9	97.1	94.7		0.08/0.08/0.04/13
Rijswijk	-	-	96.5	-		0.003
Wageningen	-	-	-	94.7		0.05
West Terschelling	-	89.9	-	-		0.05
Westdorpe	-	97.8	-	-		100
Wieringerwerf	95.0	92.9	97.1	101.6		15/15/15/35

Ann: "Dit is de VARA", "Dit is de VPRO" etc. **NPO R. 1:** news, sport; **NPO R. 2** and **NPO 3 FM:** music; **R. 4:** classical music

Regional stations:

FM	Mhz	kW	Location	Station
2)	87.6	8	Mierlo	Omroep Brabant
4)	87.9	15	Goes	Omroep Zeeland
9)	88.7	1	Alkmaar	RTV. Noord Holland
9)	88.9	10	Amsterdam	RTV. Noord-Holland
6)	89.1	5	Megen	R. Gelderland
13)	89.3	20	Rotterdam	R West
10)	89.4	10	Hengelo	R. Oost
12)	89.8	25	Lelystad	R. Flevoland
6)	90.4	10	Ruurlo	R. Gelderland
5)	90.8	3	Hoogersmilde	R. Drenthe
6)	91.0	15	Roosendaal	Omroep Brabant
2)	91.9	2	Loon op Zand	Omroep Brabant
3)	92.2	25	Jirnsum	Omrop Fryslân
7)	93.1	4	IJsselstein	R. M Utrecht
11)	93.4	10	Rotterdam	R. Rijnmond
9)	93.9	11	Wieringerwerf	RTV. Noord-Holland
1)	95.3	10	Emmaberg	L1 R.
10)	95.6	5	Markelo	R. Oost
2)	95.8	5	Megen	Omroep Brabant
8)	97.5	20	Groningen	R. Noord
7)	97.9	3	Rhenen	R. M Utrecht
10)	99.4	25	Zwolle	R. Oost
6)	99.6	4	Zaltbommel	R. Gelderland
1)	100.3	100	Roermond	L1 R.
6)	103.5	20	Ugchelen	R. Gelderland

+4 low-power relays

NETHERLANDS

L.T: UTC +1h (27 Mar-30 Oct: +2h) — **Pop:** 16.9 million — **Pr.L:** Dutch — **E.C:** 50Hz, 230V — **ITU:** HOL

NEDERLANDSE OMROEP STICHTING (NOS)
Mediapark, Journaalplein 1, 1217 ZK Hilversum; Postbus 26600, 1202 JT Hilversum ☎ +31 35 6779222
W: nos.nl **E:** publieksvoorlichting@nos.nl

NTR (PUBLIEKE TAAKOMROEP)
Mediapark, Wim T. Schippersplein 5-7, 1217WD Hilversum or P.O. Box 29000, 1202 MA Hilversum ☎ +31 35 677 9333 **W:** ntr.nl **E:** info@ntr.nl

NEDERLANDSE PUBLIEKE OMROEP (NPO)
Bart de Graaffweg 2, 1217ZL Hilversum or P.O. Box 26444, 1202 JJ Hilversum **W:** npo.nl
Representing the following broadcasting organizations: AVROTROS, BNN, BOS, EO, Human, IKON, Joodse Omroep, KRO, KRO-NCRV, MAX, Moslim Omroep, NCRV, OHM, Omrop Fryslan,VARA, VPRO, WNL, ZvK

Dutch national public prgrs are provided by the **NOS**, **NTR** and the broadcasting organisations of the **NPO**.

Addresses:
1) Postbus 31, 6200 AA Maastricht ☎ +31 43 850 60 00 ▤ +31 43 850 61 01 **E:** redactie@L1.nl **W:** l1.nl — **2)** Postbus 108, 5600 AC Eindhoven ☎ +31 40 2949494 ▤ +31 40 2949320 **E:** contact@omroepbrabant. nl **W:** omroepbrabant.nl — **3)** Postbus 7600, 8903 JP Leeuwarden ☎ +31 58 299 7799 ▤ +31 58 2997778 **E:** direksje@omropfryslan.nl **W:** omropfryslan.nl — **4)** Postbus 1090, 4388 ZH Oost-Souburg ☎ +31 118 499900 ▤ +31 118 499929 **E:** nieuws@omroepzeeland.nl **W:** omroep-zeeland.nl — **5)** Postbus 999, 9400 AZ Assen ☎ +31 592 338080 **E:** redactie@rtvdrenthe.nl **W:** rtvdrenthe.nl — **6)** Postbus 747, 6800 AS Arnhem ☎ +31 26 3713713 ▤ +31 26 3713708 **E:** omroep@gld.nl **W:** omroepgelderland.nl — **7)** Postbus 1012, 3500 BA Utrecht ☎ +31 30 8500600 ▤ +31 30 8500601 **E:** vraag@rtvutrecht.nl **W:** rtvutrecht. nl — **8)** Postbus 30101, 9700 RP Groningen ☎ +31 50 3199999 ▤ +31 50 3185147 **E:** redactie@rtvnoord.nl **W:** rtvnoord.nl– **9)** Postbus 9823, 1006AM Amsterdam ☎ +31 88 850 5050 **E:** communicatie@rtvnh. nl **W:** rtvnh.nl — **10)** Postbus 1000, 7550BA Hengelo (Ov) ☎ +31 74 2456456 **E:** info@rtvoost.nl **W:** rtvoost.nl — **11)** Postbus 1515, 3000 BM Rotterdam ☎ +31 10 436 64 36 **E:** help@rijnmond.nl **W:** rijnmond. nl — **12)** Postbus 567, 8200 AN Lelystad ☎ +31 320 285085 **E:** rtv@omroepfleveland.nl **W:** omroepfleveland.nl — **13)** Postbus 24025, 2490 AA Den Haag ☎ +31 70 3078888 ▤ +31 70 3078844 **E:** west@omroepwest.nl **W:** omroepwest.nl

Public local stations in major cities: FM(MHz):
Amsterdam 96.1 FUN X, 99.4 Wereld FM, 105.2 Radio Zuid Oost (RAZO), 106.8 Stads FM, 107.9 Caribbean FM – **Den Haag** 92.0 Den

Haag FM, 98.4 FUN X – **Rotterdam** 91.8 FUN X– **Utrecht** 96.1 FUN X, 105.7 Bingo FM, 107.7 Bingo FM
NB: FUN X is an initiative of SALTO Omroep Amsterdam, Slor Rotterdam, Stadsomroep Den Haag and Omroep RTV Utrecht
Addresses: FUN X Rotterdam, Lloydstraat 21,3024EA Rotterdam ☎ +31 10 22 14 900 🖹 +31 10 22 14 918 – FUN X Amsterdam, Piet Heinkade 181K, 1019HC Amsterdam ☎ +31 20 530 4960 – FUN X Den Haag, Calandstraat 1, 2521AD Den Haag ☎ +31 70 31 317 4900 – FUN X Utrecht, Hengeveldstraat 29, 3572KH Utrecht ☎ +31 30 850 0740 **W:** funx.nl – Wereld Fm, Caribbean FM, Stads FM, RAZO, Piet Heinkade 181ᴱ, 1019HC Amsterdam ☎ +31 20 638 6386 🖹 +31 20 620 4629 **W:**salto.nl/radio/radio.asp – Den Haag FM: Laan van 's-Gravenmade 4, 2495AJ, Den Haag ☎ +31 70 307 8899 **W:** denhaagfm.nl/radio **E:** info@denhaagfm.nl – Bingo FM, postbus 1012, 3500BA Utrecht ☎ +31 30 850 0600 🖹 +31 30 850 0601 **W:** rtvutrecht.nl/bingofm **E:** vraag@rtvutrecht.nl

Digital services DAB+ and DMB on Band III: National DAB+ on 220.352MHz and 227.360MHz. Regional DAB+ on 195.936MHz (West), 208.064MHz (Noordwest), 183.648MHz (Oost) 188.928MHz (Zuid), 208.064MHz (Zuidwest).

OTHER STATIONS

MW	kHz	kW	Location	Station
14)	891	20	Emmaberg	R. 538 (Comm.)
53)	1008	100	Zeewolde	Groot Nieuws R. (Rlg.)
49)	1116	0.5	Bloemendaal	R. Bloemendaal (Rlg.)
60)	1566	1	Den Haag	Vahon Hindustani R.
52)	1584	0.15	Utrecht	R. Paradijs (Comm.)
51)	1602	1	Harlingen	KBC R./R.Seagull

FM	MHz	kW	Location	Station
20)	87.6	1	Enschede	Freez FM
61)	87.6	45	Hoogersmilde	R. 10
61)	87.7	115	Lelystad	R. 10
61)	87.9	8	Den Bosch	R. 10
61)	88.1	4	Hilversum	R. 10
23)	88.2	1	Ugchelen	100%NL
23)	88.3	2	Wieringerwerf	100%NL
9)	88.4	43	Roosendaal	Slam FM
3)	88.6	26	Mierlo	BNR Nieuws R.
57)	88.8	1	Vlissingen	Sublime FM
15)	88.9	1	Den Bosch	R. 8FM
23)	89.0	3	Lochem	100%NL
11)	89.1	2	Groningen	R. NL
20)	89.2	3	Zwolle	Freez FM
62)	89.2	1	Amersfoort	EVA R.
15)	89.2	1	Breda	R. 8FM
15)	89.3	1	Eindhoven	R. 8FM
23)	89.5	10	Alkmaar	100%NL
23)	89.5	5	Utrecht	100%NL
3)	89.6	5	Hoogersmilde	BNR NieuwsR.
30)	89.6	1	Nieuwbergen	Maasland R.
57)	89.7	2.5	Mierlo	Sublime FM
11)	89.9	1	Emmen	R. NL
23)	90.0	3	Breskens	100%NL
23)	90.0	17	Loon op Zand	100%NL
9)	90.1	7	Wieringerwerf	Slam FM
23)	90.2	50	Roosendaal	100%NL
27)	90.3	4	Eindhoven	Puur NL
57)	90.3	10	Groningen	Sublime FM
57)	90.4	25	Hoorn	Sublime FM
57)	90.5	8	Rotterdam	Sublime FM
57)	90.5	15	Hoogersmilde	Sublime FM
27)	90.5	4	Helmond	Puur NL
57)	90.7	100	Ijsselstein	Sublime FM
57)	90.7	10	Enschede	Sublime FM
57)	90.8	2	Terneuzen	Sublime FM
9)	91.0	10	Tjerkgaast	Slam FM
9)	91.1	40	Hilversum	Slam FM
48)	91.1	1	Gemert	Centraal FM
18)	91.3	1	Hoogezand	Simone FM
3)	91.3	70	Rotterdam	BNR Nieuws R.
3)	91.3	1	Tilburg	BNR Nieuws R.
3)	91.5	3	Biervliet	BNR Nieuws R.
3)	91.5	10	Eys	BNR Nieuws R.
19)	91.6	5	Amsterdam	R. Veronica
23)	92.1	10	Emmaberg	100%NL
39)	92.3	1	Rijssen	R. 350
27	92.4	3	Westdorpe	Puur NL
58)	92.4	1	Hoogezand	R. Continu
47)	92.9	1	Wellerooi	Maasland R.
44)	93.0	1	Meppel	Omroep Meppel

FM	MHz	kW	Location	Station
61)	93.0	12	Westdorpe	R. 10
9)	93.1	1	Emmen	Slam FM
26)	93.2	20	Jirnsum	Waterstad FM
11)	93.3	1	Enschede	R. NL
27)	93.3	1	Loon op Zand	Puur NL
61)	93.3	2	Breskens	R. 10
11)	93.5	3	Markelo	R. NL
65)	93.5	1	Cuijk	Rivierstad FM
29)	93.6	1	Amsterdam	Wild FM HitR.
11)	93.6	1	Eindhoven	R. NL
9)	93.6	6	Zwolle	Slam FM
9)	93.7	2	Hoogezand	Slam FM
9)	93.7	2	Hengelo	Slam FM
40)	93.7	2	Leiden	Sleutelstad FM
9)	93.8	17	Megen	Slam FM
23)	93.8	1	Haarlem	100%NL
59)	93.9	5	Rotterdam	Open Rotterdam
15)	93.9	4	Roosendaal	R. 8FM
19)	94.0	1	Emmen	R. Veronica
27)	94.1	1	Den Bosch	Puur NL
11)	94.1	2	Tjerkgaast	R. NL
23)	94.2	1	Hoogersmilde	100%NL
11)	94.5	1	Den Helder	R. NL
23)	94.9	12	Mierlo	100%NL
23)	95.0	2	Amersfoort	100%NL
23)	95.0	2	Nijmegen	100%NL
9)	95.2	25	Alphen aan den Rijn	Slam FM
15)	95.2	1	Weert	R. 8FM
3)	95.3	20	Zwolle	BNR Nieuws R.
43)	95.3	1	Bedum	Regio FM
3)	95.4	1	Emmen	BNR Nieuws R.
3)	95.4	15	Gilze	BNR Nieuws R
3)	95.5	30	Tjerkgaast	BNR Nieuws R.
6)	95.6	1	Rijswijk	Fresh FM
6)	95.7	5	Amsterdam	Fresh FM
11)	95.7	2	Meppel	R. NL
6)	95.9	5	Alphen aan den Rijn	Fresh FM
20)	96.0	2	Wieringerwerf	Freez FM
66)	96.2	1	Zoetermeer	ZFM
29)	96.3	1	Alkmaar	Wild FM Hit R.
19)	96.3	30	Loon op Zand	R. Veronica
64)	96.4	1	Balk	R Spannenburg
19)	96.6	1	Goes	R. Veronica
11)	96.6	1	Leeuwarden	R. NL
11)	97.0	2	Hoogeveen	R. NL
11)	97.1	1	Hoogersmilde	R. NL
19)	97.1	1	Vlissingen	R. Veronica
29)	97.3	2	Haarlem	Wild FM Hit R.
3)	97.6	1	Hengelo	100%NL
63)	97.6	2	Maastricht	Q-Music Limburg
36)	97.6	60	Rotterdam	R. Decibel
19)	97.7	10	Arnhem	R. Veronica
19)	97.7	6	Mierlo	R. Veronica
63)	97.7	15	Landgraaf	Q-Music Limburg
19)	97.8	4	IJsselstein	R. Veronica
58)	97.9	3	Tjerkgaast	R Continu
36)	98.0	12	Amsterdam	R. Decibel
58)	98.0	1	Hengelo,Gld	R. Continu
63)	98.1	2	Eys	Q-Music Limburg
36)	98.3	5	Alkmaar	R. Decibel
20)	98.5	2	Groningen	Freez FM
20)	98.5	1	Tjerkgaast	Freez FM
63)	98.5	1	Weert	Q-Music Limburg
20)	98.7	20	Hoogersmilde	Freez FM
23)	99.1	15	Enschede	100%NL
23)	99.1	3	Hoogezand	100%NL
23)	99.1	3	Tjerkgaast	100%NL
32)	99.1	1	Geleen	Streekomroep START
9)	99.2	25	Breskens	Slam FM
9)	99.4	30	Mierlo	Slam FM
9)	99.4	1	Breda	Slam FM
67)	99.4	2	Den Haag	R. Royaal
9)	99.6	25	Hoorn	Slam FM
9)	99.6	6	Hoogersmilde	Slam FM
3)	99.9	1	Dedemsvaart	BNR Nieuws R.
3)	99.9	3	Ugchelen	BNR Nieuws R.
3)	99.9	27	Wormer	BNR Nieuws R.
3)	100.1	60	IJsselstein	BNR Nieuws R.
3)	100.1	4	Nijmegen	BNR Nieuws R.
3)	100.2	12	Lochem	BNR Nieuws R.
13)	100.4	25	Westdorpe	QMusic
13)	100.4	7	Roosendaal	QMusic

FM	MHz	kW	Location	Station
13)	100.4	3	Rotterdam	QMusic
13)	100.4	95	Hoogersmilde	Qmusic
13)	100.4	10	Doetinchem	QMusic
13)	100.5	5	Wieringerwerf	QMusic
13)	100.5	2	Nijmegen	QMUsic
13)	100.7	25	Breskens	QMusic
13)	100.7	6	Hengelo	QMusic
13)	100.7	68	IJsselstein	QMusic
13)	100.7	10	Lichtenvoorde	Qmusic
24)	101.0	75	Hoogersmilde	Sky R. 101 FM
24)	101.1	5	Nijmegen	Sky R. 101 FM
24)	101.2	13	Hengelo	Sky R. 101 FM
24)	101.2	200	Hilversum	Sky R. 101 FM
24)	101.3	5	Roosendaal	Sky R. 101 FM
24)	101.4	10	Deventer	Sky R. 101 FM
24)	101.5	4	Arnhem	Sky R. 101 FM
24)	101.5	7	Den Bosch	Sky R. 101 FM
24)	101.5	8	Rotterdam	Sky R. 101 FM
24)	101.6	5	Mierlo	Sky R. 101 FM
24)	101.6	3	Roermond	Sky R. 101 FM
24)	101.7	5	Breda	Sky R. 101 FM
18)	101.7	2	Emmen	Simone FM
24)	101.9	8	Tilburg	Sky R. 101 FM
24)	101.9	50	Goes	Sky R. 101 FM
58)	101.9	1	Zieuwent	R. Continu
14)	102.1	100	Hilversum	R. 538
14)	102.2	10	Hoogersmilde	R. 538
14)	102.3	13	Alkmaar	R. 538
14)	102.3	100	De Mortel	R. 538
14)	102.3	15	Lochem	R. 538
14)	102.3	2	Roermond	R. 538
14)	102.4	1	Arnhem	R. 538
14)	102.4	1	Amsterdam	R. 538
14)	102.4	20	Westdorpe	R. 538
14)	102.5	8	Tilburg	R. 538
14)	102.5	100	Tjerkgaast	R. 538
14)	102.5	1	Utrecht	R. 538
14)	102.6	2	Nijmegen	R. 538
14)	102.6	5	Hengelo	R. 538
14)	102.7	10	Emmen	R. 538
14)	102.7	100	Rotterdam	R. 538
14)	102.7	10	Markelo	R. 538
19)	102.8	1	Leusden	R. Veronica
19)	103.0	40	Lelystad	R. Veronica
19)	103.1	20	De Lutte	R. Veronica
19)	103.1	5	Megen	R. Veronica
19)	103.2	40	Rotterdam	R. Veronica
19)	103.2	25	Hoogersmilde	R. Veronica
19)	103.3	6	Terneuzen	R. Veronica
19)	103.4	5	Groningen	R. Veronica
19)	103.5	2	Roosendaal	R. Veronica
61)	103.6	15	Amsterdam	R. 10
15)	103.6	10	Tilburg	R. 8 FM
61)	103.8	15	Emmen	R. 10
61)	103.8	1	Goes	R. 10
61)	103.8	20	Rotterdam	R. 10
61)	103.8	10	Tjerkgaast	R. 10
61)	103.9	1	Enschede	R. 10
61)	104.0	1	Haarlem	R. 10
61)	104.1	100	Arnhem	R. 10
11)	104.2	3	Alkmaar	R. NL
23)	104.4	50	Hilversum	100%NL
26)	104.4	2	Groningen	Joy R.
23)	104.6	87	Rotterdam	100%NL
45)	104.8	1	Zuidwolde	Streek R.
34)	106.7	1	Lochem	Achterhoek FM

+ 448 stns below 1kW

Addresses:
3) Prins Bernhardplein 173 1097BL Amsterdam or Postbus 651, 1000 AR Amsterdam ☎ +31 20 592 8500 ▤ +31 20 592 8800 **E:** operations@bnr.nl **W:** bnr.nl –**6)** Bleiswijkseweg 43/C, 2712PB Zoetermeer or PO Box 92 2260AB Leidschendam ☎ +31 79 343 4491 ▤ +31 79 3434492 **W:** fresh.fm **E:** info@fresh.fm –**9)** Postbus 910 1200AX Hilversum ☎ +31 35 625 27 27 **E:** info@slamfm.nl **W:** slamfm.nl – **11)** Postbus 248, 8600AE Sneek ☎ +31 515 432360 **W:** radionl.fm **E:** info@radionl.fm –**13)** De Kauwgomballenfabriek, Paul van Vlissingenstraat 10D, 1096BK Amsterdam ☎ +31 20 7970 500 **E:** info@q-music.nl **W:** q-music.nl – **14)** Postbus 2538, 1200 CM Hilversum ☎ +31 35 5385538 **W:** radio538.nl –**15)** Postbus 8, 5201 AA Den Bosch ☎ +31 73 6312003 ▤ +31 73 6313311 **W:** radio8fm.nl **E:** info@radio8fm.nl –**18)** Nijbracht 138, 7821CE Emmen ☎ +31 591

652 025 **E:** bert@simonefm.nl **W:** radiosimone.nl – **19)** Postbus 103, 1400 AC Bussum ☎ +31 35 699 01 03 **E:** info@radioveronica.nl **W:** radioveronica.nl – **20)** Koperslagerstraat 26, 8601 WL Sneek ☎ +31 515 432360 **W:** freezfm.nl **E:** info@freezfm.nl 24 h. Commercial Pop Rock –**23)** Postbus 34, 1400AA Bussum **W:** 100p.nl – **24)** Postbus 101, 1400AC Naarden ☎ +31 35 699 01 01 ▤ +31 35 699 10 05 **E** :info@skyradio.nl **W:** skyradio.nl **26)** Postbus 248, 8600AE Sneek ☎ +31 515 432360 ▤ +31 515 432 986 **E:** info@waterstadfm.nl **W:** waterstadfm.nl **E:** info@joyradio.nl **W:**joyradio.nl– **27)** Postbus 8, 5201AA Den Bosch ☎ +31 73 631 2003 ▤ +31 73 631 3311 **E:** info@puurnl.nl **W:** puurnl.fm – **29)** Jan Evertsenstraat 713-715, 1061XZ Amsterdam ☎ +31 20 447 0030 **W:** wildfm.nl **E:** info@wildfm.nl – **30)** Raadhuisstraat 5, 5854AX Nieuwbergen ☎ +31 485 34 1939 **W:** maaslandradio.nl **E:** kantoor@maaslandradio.nl – **32)** Postbus 114, 6160AC Geleen ☎ +31 46 4747555 ▤ +31 4748493 **W:** streekomroepstart.nl **E:** redactie@streekomroepstart.nl – **34)** Postbus 115, 7250AC Vorden ☎ +31 575 556560 ▤ +31 575 556564 **E:** info@achterhoekfm.nl **W:** achterhoekfm.nl – **36)** Wilgenweg 16A, 1031HV Amsterdam ☎ +31 +31 20 47 10 468 **W:** radiodecibel.nl **E:** info@radiodecibel.nl – **39)** Postbus 234, 7460AE Rijssen ☎ +31 548 681 010 **W:** radio350.nl **E:** info@radio350.nl – **40)** Evertsenstraat 69/Y 2315SK Leiden ☎ +31 71 523 5907 **W:** sleutelstad.nl **E:** info@sleutelstad.nl – **43)** Postbus 40, 9628ZG Siddeburen **W:** regiofm.info **E:** info@regiofm.nl – **44)** Kromme Elleboog 11, 7941KC Meppel ☎ +31 522 259319 ▤ +31 522 240674 **W:** rtvmeppel.nl **E:** secretariaat@rtvmeppel.nl – **45)** Postbus 8, 7920AA Zuidwolde ☎ +31 528 373444 **W:** streekradio.com **E:** info@streekradio.com – **47)** Raadhuisstraat 5, 5854AX Nieuw Bergen ☎ +31 485 341234 **W:** maaslandradio.nl **E:** redactie@maaslandradio.nl – **48)** St. Annastraat 60, 5421KC Gemert ☎ +31 492 366833 **W:** omroepcentraal.nl **E:** info@omroepcentraal.nl – **49)** Kerkplein 20, 2061JD Bloemendaal ☎ +31 23 524 9013 **E:** bureau@radiobloemendaal.nl **W:** radiobloemendaal.nl **D.Prgr:** Religious programs on Sun 0800-2000 & Tues 1100-1230 –**51)** Aragonstraat 6, 6718WT Ede ☎ +31 318 552 491 Dir. Eric van Willegen; Dutch 0600-1800 **W:** kbcradio.eu **E:** themightykbc@gmail.com ; receptionreports to themightykbc@gmail.com , also transmissions on shortwave; 1800-0600 Radio Seagull in English , PO Box 24 8860AA Harlingen **W:** radioseagull.com **E:** office@radioseagull.com – **52)** Postbus 11122, 3505 BC Utrecht, Dir. Ruud Poeze ☎ +31 30 244 5580 **W:** radioparadijs.nl **E:** info@radioparadijs.nl **D.Prgr:** 24 hours in Dutch, Music, non stop classic hits; also low power transmitters on 1224 khz (0.01 kW) and 1332 khz (0.0002 kW) – **53)** Einsteinlaan 41b, 3902 HN Veenendaal or Postbus 1027, 3900BA Veenendaal, Manager: Koos Timmer 24h rlg pgr.☎ +31 318 584 384 ▤ +31 318 584 380 **W:** grootnieuwsradio.nl **E:** info@grootnieuwsradio.nl **V:** by letter – **57)** Jaarbeursplein 6, 3521AL Utrecht **W:** sublimefm.nl **E:** info@sublimefm.nl – **58)** Exloërkijl Zuid 38, 9571AC Tweede Exloërmond ☎ +31 599 67 11 01 ▤ +31 599 67 11 02 **W:** radiocontinu.nl **E:** info@radiocontinu.nl and techniek@radiocontinu.nl – **59)** Hoogstraat 110, 3011PV Rotterdam ☎ +31 10 820 1702 **W:** openrotterdam.nl **E:** info@openrotterdam.nl - **60)** Newtonstraat 25, 2562KC Den Haag ☎ +31 70 365 2247 and +31 70 362 2077 24 hours in Sarnami Hindustani and Dutch **W:** vahon.fm **E:** info@vahonfm.nl QSL-manager: Koos Wijnants, qsl.vahon@ziggo.nl– **61)** Postbus 34, 1400AA Bussum ☎ 0909 300 10 10 **W:** radio10.nl **E:** info@radio10.nl– **62)** Van Persijnstraat 19a, 3811LS Amersfoort ☎ +31 33 8893 492 **W:** mediagroep-eva.nl **E:** redactie@mediagroep-eva.nl – **63)** Cannerweg 135, 6213BA Maastricht **W:** q-musiclimburg.nl **E:** directie@radiolimburg.nl – **64)** Dubbelstraat 3, 8561BC Balk ☎ +31 514 602121 **W:** radiospannenburg.nl **E:** info@radiospannenburg.nl – **65)** Molenstraat 47, 5431EA Cuijk ☎ +31 6 205 614 51 **E:** redactie@rivierstad.nl **W:** rivierstad.nl – **66)** Postbus 841, 2700AV Zoetermeer ☎ +31 79 331 7287 ▤ +31 79 343 41 93 **E:** studio@zfmradio.nl **W:** zfmradio.nl – **67)** Giessenweg 3, 3044AK Rotterdam **W:** radioroyaal.nl **E:** info@radioroyaal.nl

Military stations

FM	MHz	kW	Location	Station
2)	87.8	0.05	Maastricht	BFBS 1
1)	89.2	1	Brunssum	AFN Power Netw./The Eagle
2)	90.2	0.05	Brunssum	BFBS 1
1)	107.9	0.1	Zeeland	AFN Power Netw./The Eagle

Addresses and other information:
1) **W:** benelux.afneurope.net **D.Prgr:** 24h relay AFN SHAPE (Belgium) – **2)** **D.Prgr:** Relays BFBS 1 prgrs Germany ☎ +44 1494 874 461 ▤ +44 1494 878 202 **E:** info@bfbs.com **W:** bfbs.com

NEW CALEDONIA (France)

LT: UTC +11h — **Pop:** 256,275 — **Pr.L:** French, Kanak and other Melanesian-Polynesian dialects — **E.C:** 50Hz, 220V — **ITU:** NCL

CONSEIL SUPERIEUR DE L'AUDIOVISUEL
Comite territorial de l'audiovisuel de Nouvelle-Caledonie et des Iles Wallis-et-Futuna
✉ 1, rue du Contre-Amiral Joseph Bouzet-Nouville, B.P. 739-98845, Noumea ☎ +687 687254051 🖷 +687 687254085 **W:** csa.fr **E:** ctr.noumea.csa@lagoon.nc
Regulator of broadcasting for New Caledonia & Wallis and Futuna

MW	kHz	kW	Station
1) Noumea	666	20	NouvelleCaledonie 1ere
1) Touho	729	5	NouvelleCaledonie 1ere

FM	MHz	kW	Station
1) Bouliupari	88.0	2.2	NouvelleCaledonie 1ere
1) Kaaka-Gomen	88.0	1.2	NouvelleCaledonie 1ere
1) Mont Dore	88.0	3	NouvelleCaledonie 1ere
2) Noumea-Mont Coffyn	89.0	2.2	R.O
2) Ponerihouen	89.0	3	R.O
1) Kone	90.0	3.5	NouvelleCaledonie 1ere
1) Noumea-Mont Koghis	90.0	5	NouvelleCaledonie 1ere
1) Lifou	90.5	11	NouvelleCaledonie 1ere
1) Houailou	91.0	2	NouvelleCaledonie 1ere
1) Koumac	91.0	4	NouvelleCaledonie 1ere
1) Noumea	91.5	2.2	NouvelleCaledonie 1ere
3) Bouloupari	92.0	2.2	France Inter
3) Mont Dore	92.0	3	France Inter
3) Ponerihouen	93.0	3	France Inter
3) Noumea-Mont Coffyn	93.0	2.2	France Inter
3) Noumea-Mont Coffyn	93.5	1	NRJ
3) Kone	94.0	3.5	France Inter
3) Noumea-Mont Koghis	94.0	5	France Inter
5) Dumbea [Noumea]	95.0	1	R.Oceane
6) Mont Dore	96.0	2.2	R.Djiido
6) Noumea	94.7	1.5	R.Djiido
7) Dumbea [Noumea]	98.0	5.3	R.Rythme Bleu
7) Kone	98.0	1	R.Rythme Bleu
6) Lifou	98.5	1.5	R.Djiido
7) Koumac	99.0	1.5	R.Rythme Bleu
7) Mont Dore	100.0	2.2	R.Rythme Bleu
7) Noumea	100.4	1.5	R.Rythme Bleu
6) Dumbea [Noumea]	102.0	5.3	R.Djiido
7) Lifou	102.5	1.5	R.Rythme Bleu
6) Koumac	103.0	1.5	R.Djiido

+ 55 stations less than 1kw

Addresses and other information
1) NOUVELLE CALEDONIE PREMIÈRE (Gov) ✉ 1 rue Maréchal Leclerc, Mt Coffyn, B.P. G3 - 98848 Noumea Cedex ☎ +687 687274327 🖷 +687 687281252 **W:** nouvellecaledonie.la1ere.fr (live streaming) **L.P:** Reg. Dir: Benoit Saudeau **D.Prgr:** 24h in French (local and RFO common prgr satellite feed) and Kanak (local) – **2) Radio Ô (Gov)** satellite relay from Paris: **W:** radioo.fr 24h in French – **3) Radio France Inter (Gov):** satellite relay from Paris 24h in French – **4) NRJ**, 41/43 rue Sebastopol, B.P G5 - 98848 Noumea Cedex ☎ +687 687279446 🖷 +687 687279447 **W:** nrj.nc 24h – **5) R. Oceane**, 1, avenue d'Auteuill Lotissement FSH Koutio - 98835. Dumbea ☎ +687 687410095 🖷 +687 687410099 **L.P:** President, Dumbea Communications – Robert Lucas, Dir: Veronique Loisel **E:** oceane.fm@lagoon.nc **W:** oceanefm.nc 24h – **6) R. Djiido**, 29, rue du Marechal Juin, 98880 Noumea ☎ + 687 687253515 🖷 +687 687272187 **W:** radiodjiido.nc **E:** radiodjiido@radiodjiido.nc **L.P:** Thierry Kameremoin 24h – **7) R. Rythme Bleu**, B.P 578 - 98845 Noumea Cedex ☎ +687 687254646 🖷 +687 687284928 **W:** rrb.nc **E:** rrb@lagoon.nc **Prgr:** local + prgrs from Europe 1. 24h

NEW ZEALAND

LT: UTC +12h (27 Sep 15-3 Apr 16, 25 Sep 16-2 Apr 17: +13h) — **Pop:** 4.4 million — **Pr.L:** English, Maori, Samoan — **E.C:** 50Hz, 230V — **ITU:** NZL

RADIO SPECTRUM MANAGEMENT GROUP
Ministry of Business, Innovation & Employment
✉ P.O. Box 2847, Wellington 6140 ☎ +64 4 962 2603 NZ Freephone 0508 776 463 🖷 +64 4 978 3162 **W:** rsm.govt.nz **E:** info@rsm.govt.nz **L.P:** Mgr Policy Planning: Len Starling Mgr Licencing: Jeff Hicks. **RSMG** is the statutory authority responsible for radio spectrum licencing & administration.

BROADCASTING STANDARDS AUTHORITY
✉ P.O. Box 9213, Marion Square, Wellington 6141 ☎ +64 4 382 9508 🖷 +64 4 382 9543 NZ Freephone 0800 366 996 **W:** bsa.govt.nz **E:** info@bsa.govt.nz **L.P:** CE: Karen Scott-Howman The **BSA** statutory authority has codes of broadc. practice, broadc. standards, ethical conduct and has a complaints procedure.

NEW ZEALAND ON AIR
✉ P.O. Box 9744, Marion Square, Wellington 6141 ☎ +64 4 382 9524 🖷 +64 4 382 9546 **W:** nzonair.govt.nz **E:** info@nzonair.govt.nz **L.P:** CE: Jane Wrightson, Mgr Community. Broadc.: Keith Collins **NZOA** is the operational funding agency for R. New Zealand, Community Access R., R. Reading Service, National Pacific R. Trust, Samoan Capital R., [bNet] and TV and New Media.

RADIO NEW ZEALAND (Non-commercial, Pub)
✉ P.O. Box 123, Wellington 6140 ☎ +64 4 474 1999 🖷 +64 4 474 1730 **W:** radionz.co.nz **L.P:** CE: Paul Thompson; Infrastructure Mgr: Matthew Finn; Trs. Mgr: Gary Fowles
Network Stations: RNZ National (**N**), RNZ Concert (**C**), RNZ AM Network (**AM**). For full FM listings see website. **Prgr:** 24h from Wellington studios except for RNZ AM Network which only broadc. when Parliament in session [rel. commercial stn Star at other times]. **N:** RNZ News bulletins

Network Stations MW

MW	kHz	kW	Net	MW	kHz	kW	Net
Wellington	567	50	N	Napier-Hastings	909	5	AM
Napier-Hastings	630	10	N	New Plymouth	918	2.5	N
Alexandra	639	2	N	Timaru	918	2.5	N
Tauranga	657	10	AM	Christchurch	963	10	AM
Wellington	657	50	AM	Kaikohe	981	2	N
Christchurch	675	10	N	Masterton	1071	2.5	N
Invercargill	720	10	N	Nelson	1116	2.5	N
Tokoroa	729	2.5	N	Queenstown	1134	2.0	N
Auckland	756	10	N	Hamilton	1143	2.5	N
Dunedin	810	10	N	Rotorua	1188	0.4	N
Tauranga	819	10	N	Gisborne	1314	2	N
Kaitaia	837	2	N	Invercargill	1314	5	AM
Whangarei	837	2.5	N	Palmerston North	1449	2.5	N
Auckland	882	10	AM	Westport	1458	2.5	N
Dunedin	900	10	AM	Hamilton	1494	2.5	AM

Network Stations FM
Major Radio Market

FM (MHz)	N	C	FM (MHz)	N	C
Auckland	101.4	92.6	Kapiti Coast	101.5	98.3
Christchurch	101.7	89.7/99.7	Napier-Hastings	101.5	91.1
Dunedin	101.4	92.6/99.0/99.4	Nelson	101.6	91.2
Gisborne	101.3	97.3	New Plymouth	101.2	91.6
Hamilton	101.0	91.4	Palmerston N.	101.0	89.0
Invercargill	101.2	90.0	Queenstown	101.6	98.4
Rotorua	101.5	90.3	Timaru	101.0	99.5
Taupo	101.6/104.8	98.4	Wellington	101.3/101.7	92.5/96.1
Tauranga	101.0	91.4	Whangarei	101.2/104.4	100.4/105.2

EXTERNAL SERVICE: Radio New Zealand Int.
- see International broadcasting section

COMMUNITY ACCESS RADIO
12 independent stns affiliated to the **Association of Community Access Broadcasters [ACAB] W:** acab.org.nz **E:** info@acab.org.nz. Each stn serves local urban communities with a variety of ethnic language, cultural and comm. group prgrs. BBC WS is carried overnight on several stns. **H. of tr:** 24h

MW	KHz	kW	Station
1) Wellington	783	10	Wellington Access R
2) Palmerston North	999	1.5	Manawatu Access R.
4) Napier-Hastings	1431	2	R.Kidnappers
5) Dunedin	1575	2.5	OAR 105.4FM

FM	MHz	kW	Station
3) Hamilton	89.0	5	Free FM89
7) Masterton	92.7	0.8	Masterton
8) Christchurch	96.9	3.5	Plains FM
9) Invercargill	96.4	3.2	R.Southland
12) New Plymouth	104.4	5	Access R. Taranaki
10) Auckland	104.6	15.8	Planet FM
4) Napier-Hastings	104.7	4	R.Kidnappers
11) Kapiti Coast	104.7	0.63	Coast Access R,
6) Nelson	104.8	1.6	Fresh FM
5) Dunedin	105.4	8	OAR 105.4FM

Addresses & other information
1) P.O. Box 9073, Marion Square, Wellington 6141 ☎ +64 4 385 7210 🖷 +64 4 385 7212 **W:** accessradio.org.nz **E:** info@accessradio.org.nz – **2)** P.O. Box 4666, Manawatu Mail Centre, Palmerston North 4442 ☎ +64 6 357 9340 🖷 +64 6 357 9345 **W:** accessmanawatu.co.nz **E:** info@accessmanawatu.co.nz **Prgr:** BBC WS 0900-2100 overnight daily – **3)** P.O. Box 110, Waikato Mail Centre, Hamilton 3240 ☎ +64

7 834 2170 🖷 +64 7 834 2174 **W:** freefm.org.nz **E:** info@freefm.org.nz – **4)** P.O. Box 680, Hastings 4156 ☎+64 6 878 8710 🖷 +64 6 871 0590 **W:** radiokidnappers.org.nz **E:** chris@radiokidnappers.org.nz **FM:** 104.7 – **5)** 301 Moray Place, Dunedin ☎ +64 3 471 6161 🖷 +64 3 471 6162 **W:** oar.org.nz **E:** manager@oar.org.nz **Mgr: Prgr:** BBC WS overnight 1200-1800 daily – **6)** c/o NMIT, Private Bag 19, Nelson 7042 ☎+64 3 546 9891 🖷 +64 3 546 9892 **W:** freshfm.net **E:** nelson@freshfm.net **FM Network:** 89.2 Blenheim/95.2 Takaka/104.8 Nelson City-Tasman – **7)** 92 Queen Street, Masterton ☎+64 6 378 0255 **W:** arrowfm.co.nz **E:** quiver@arrowfm.co.nz – **8)** P.O. Box 22297, Christchurch ☎ +64 3 365 7997 🖷 +64 3 340 0967 **W:** plainsfm.org.nz **E:** info@plainsfm.org.nz **Prgr:** BBC WS overnight 1200-1800 daily – **9)** P.O. Box 1, Invercargill ☎ +64 3 218 9891 🖷 +64 3 214 1425 **W:** radiosouthland.org.nz **E:** darren@ radiosouthland.org.nz**Prgr:** BBC WS overnight 1200-1800 daily – **10)** P.O. Box 44215, Pt Chevalier, Auckland 1246 ☎ +64 9 815 8600 🖷 +64 9 815 8620 **W:** planetaudio.org.nz **E:** info@planetaudio.org.nz – **11)** P.O. Box 213, Waikanae ☎/🖷 +64 4 293 4838 **W:** coastaccessradio.org. nz **E:** accessradio.kapiti@xtra.co.nz – **12)** PO Box 445, Taranaki Mail Center, New Plymouth 4340 ☎ 06 751 3720 **W:** accessradiotaranaki. com **E:** dk@accessradiotaranaki.com

COMMUNITY RADIO
Independent unaffiliated community stns.

FM	MHz	kW	Station
1) Kaitaia	97.9	0.25	Far North Community R.
2) Raglan	98.1	0.06	Raglan Community R.
3) Rangiora	104.9	2	Compass FM
4) Lower Hutt	106.1	0.15	Hutt Community R.
5) Eketahuna	106.5	0.5	Eketahuna Community R.

Addresses & other information
1) PO Box 30, Mangonui ☎+64 9 4060644 **W:** farnorthcommunityra-dio.co.nz **E:** info@farnorthcommunityradio.co.nz**Net:** 88.1/107.1 – **2)** Municipal Bldgs, 37 Bow St, Raglan ☎ +64 7 825 2981 **W:** raglanradio. com **E:** manager@raglanradio.com -**3)** P.O. Box 27, Rangiora 7440 ☎ +64 3 313 7101 **W:** compassfm.org.nz **E:** manager@compassfm.org. nz **Ann:** 'The Voices of North Canterbury" – **4)** 11 Hillary Ct, Naenae, Lower Hutt ☎ +64 4 891 0446 **W:** huttradio.co.nz **E:** huttradio@hut-tradio.co.nz **Prgr:** 24h (BBC WS overnight.) - **5)** Main St, Eketahuna**T:** 06 375 8080 **W:** radioeketahuna.co.nz **E:** studio@radioeketahuna. co.nz **Net:** 88.3

TE MANGAI PAHO
🖃 P.O. Box 10004, Wellington 6143 ☎ +64 4 915 0700 🖷 +64 4 915 0701 **W:** tmp.govt.nz **E:** radio@tmp.govt.nz **L:P:** CEO: John Bishara, Mgr Radio Portfolio: Carl Goldsmith. **TMP** is the operational funding agency for the 21 independent commercial Maori Iwi Radio stns that operate 24h and often network prgrs overnight.

MAORI IWI RADIO (Comm.)
All Iwi stns and Maori TV are connected by PungaNet2 a broadband internet system for prgr and data sharing, monitoring and archiving. **W:** irirangi.net

MW	KHz	kW	Station
1) Ruatoria	585	2	R.Ngati Porou
2) Auckland	603	5	R.Waatea
3) Napier-Hastings	765	2.5	R.Kahngungu
4) Wellington	1161	5	Te Upoko o te Ika
5) Tauranga	1440	0.2	Moana AM
FM	**MHz**	**kW**	**Station**
6) Rotorua	88.7	0.8	Ta Arawa FM
7) Palmerston North	89.8	1	Kia Ora FM
8) Christchurch	90.5	15.8	Tahu FM
11) Gisborne	91.7	0.8	Turanga FM
14) New Plymouth	94.8	2	Te Korimako o Taranaki
16) Lower Hutt	94.9	1	Atiawa FM
15) Ngaruwahia	95.4	7.9	R.Tainui
9) Tokoroa	95.7	1	Raukawa FM
13) Kaitaia	97.1	4	Te Hiku o te Ika
10) Mangamuka Br.	97.5	6.3	Tautoko FM
17) Turangi	97.6	4	Tuwharetoa FM
19) Whangarei	99.1	10	Ngati Hine FM
12) Te Kuiti	99.6	0.8	Maniapoto FM
20) Paeroa	99.6	0.1	Ngati Iwi FM
21) Whanganui	100.0	0.8	Awa FM
13) Kaitaia	104.3	4	Sunshine FM
18) Whakatane	106.5	1.6	Sun FM

NB: location shown is central studio location only
Addresses & other information (all MHz):
1)P.O. Box 55, Ruatoria 4043 ☎ +64 6 864 8020 🖷 +64 6 864 8023 **W:** radiongatiporou.co.nz **E:** manager@radiongatiporou.co.nz**FM:** 89. 3/90.5/93.3/98.5/105.3/106.5 – **2)** P.O. Box 43157, Favona, Mangere,

Manukau 2153 ☎ +64 9 275 9070 🖷 +64 9 275 8060 **W:** waatea603am. co.nz **E:** info@waatea603am.co.nz – **3)** P.O. Box 2406, Hastings 4153 ☎ +64 6 872 8943 🖷 +64 6 876 4157 **W:** radiokahungunu.co.nz **E:** pat@ radio-kahungunu.co.nz **FM:** 94.3 – **4)** P.O. Box 11812, Manners Street, Wellington 6142 ☎ +64 4 801 5002 🖷 +64 4 801 5009 **E:** wena@ teupoko.co.nz– **5)** P. O. Box 382, Seventh Avenue, Tauranga 3140 ☎ +64 7 571 0009 🖷 +64 7 571 0007 **W:** moanaradio.co.nz **E:** charlie@ moanaradio.co.nz **FM:** Moana 98.2 FM – **6)** P.O. Box 883, Rotorua 3040 ☎ +64 7 349 2959 **W:** facebook.com/tearawafm **E:** rodger@ tearawa.com – **7)** P.O. Box 1341, Palmerston NorthCentral, Palmerston North 4440 ☎ +64 6 353 1881 🖷 +64 6 353 1880 **W:** kiaorafm898. maori.nz **E:** danielle@rangitaane.co.nz – **8)** P.O. Box 13469, Armagh, Christchurch 8141 ☎ +64 3 371 3905 🖷 +64 3 371 3901 **W:** tahufm.com **E:** blade_jones@ngaitahu.iwi.nz **FM Netw.:** 89.1/90.7/95.0/99.6 – **9)** P.O. Box 842, Tokoroa 3444 ☎ +64 7 886 0127 🖷 +64 7 886 0947 **W:** raukawafm.co.nz **E:** wendy@raukawafm.com **FM Netw.:** 90.6/93.2 – **10)** Mangamuka Bridge RD2, Okaihau 0476 ☎+64 9 401 8991 🖷 +64 9 401 9746 **W:** tautokofm.com **E:** cyrilchapman@clear.net.nz **FM Netw.:** 99.5 – **11)** P.O. Box 1224, Gisborne 4040 ☎ +64 6 868 6821 🖷 +64 6 868 1564 **W:** turangafm.co.nz **E:** fred@turangafm.maori.nz **FM Netw.:** 95.7/98.1 – **12)** P.O. Box 416, Te Kuiti 3941 ☎ +64 7 878 1160 🖷 +64 7 878 3002 **W:** mfmradio.co.nz **E:** info@mfmradio.com **FM Netw.:** 91.8/92.7/106.2 – **13)** P.O. Box 458, Kaitaia 0441 ☎ +64 9 408 3944 🖷 +64 9 408 1061 **E:** wiremu@tehiku.co.nz – **14)** P.O. Box 4232, Taranaki Mail Centre, New Plymouth 4340 ☎+ 64 6 757 9055 🖷+64 6 757 9093 **W:** tekorimako.co.nz **E:** tipene@tekorimako.co.nz – **15)** P.O. Box 208, Ngaruawahia 3742 ☎ +64 7 824 5650 🖷 +64 7 824 5659 **W:** facebook. com/pages/radio-tainui/225921040728 **FM Netw.:** 96.5/106.4 – **16)** P.O. Box 36111, Waiwhetu, Lower Hutt 5043 ☎+64 4 569 7993 🖷 +64 4 560 3278 **W:** atiawatoafn.co.nz **E:** wluke@atiawa.co.nz **FM Netw.:** 100.9 – **17)** 33 Town Centre, Turangi 3533 ☎+64 7 386 0935 🖷 +64 7 386 0994 **W:** facebook.com/tuwharetoafm **E:** katipo@tuwharetoa.co.nz **FM Netw.:** 91.9/92.6/95.1/99.4/100.6 – **18)** P.O. Box 2090, Kopeopeo, Whakatane ☎+64 7 308 0403 🖷 +64 7 308 0150 **W:** sunfm.com – **19)** P.O. Box 1127, Whangarei 0110 ☎ +64 9 438 6115 🖷 +64 9 438 5367 **W:** ngatihinefm.co.nz **E:** mike@ngatihinefm.co.nz**FM Netw.:** 99.6 – **20)** P.O. Box 135, Paeroa 3640 ☎+ 64 7 862 6247 🖷 + 64 7 862 6279 **W:** ngaiwifm.co.nz **E:** nifm@ngaiwifm.co.nz **FM Netw.:** 92.2/92.4 – **21)** P.O. Box 430, Whanganui 4540 ☎+ 64 6 347 1402 🖷+64 6 347 2339 **W:** awafm.co.nz **E:** geoff@awafm.co.nz **FM Netw.:** 91.2/93.5

NATIONAL PACIFIC R. TRUST (PACIFIC MEDIA NETW., Comm)
🖃 P.O. Box 99582, Newmarket, Auckland ☎ +64 9 361 6656 🖷 +64 9 361 3966 **W:** niufm.com **E:** info@niufm.com **LP:** CE in Command Tony Amos CE on Watch Lefoa Henry Jenkins Dep CE Patrick Lino **Stns:** **531PI W** 531pi.com **E:** info@radio531pi.com Market: older Pacific people **NiuFM Auckland 103.8** Market: Pacific youth in Auckland **NiuFM Network** Market: Pacific youth nationwide **Prgr: 531PI** 24/7 English/individual Pacific languages **NiuFM** 24/7pan-Pacific English 1800-0600 daily 10 Pacific languages 0600-1800 daily. **Other:** Pacific R. News **W:** pacificradionews.com Independent charitable trust funded by NZ On Air and Ministry for Culture & Heritage

531PI

MW	Khz	kW
Auckland	531	5

NiuFM Auckland

FM	MHz	kW
Auckland	103.8	15.8

NiuFM Network

FM	MHz	kW	FM	MHz	kW
Whangarei	103.6	0.4	Wellington	103.7	7.9
Hamilton	103.4	79.4	Wellington	104.1	0.8
Rotorua	103.9	0.8	Christchurch	104.1	15.8
Taupo	104.0	1.6	Dunedin	103.8	4
New Plymouth	103.6	5	Invercargill	103.8	4
Napier-Hastings	103.9	6.3			

RADIO BROADCASTERS ASSOCIATION
🖃 P.O. Box 3762, Auckland ☎ +64 9 378 0788 🖷 +64 9 378 8180 **W:** rba.co.nz **E:** bill@rba.co.nz **L:P:** CE: Bill Francis. **RBA** represents NZ commercial radio industry and sponsors NZ Radio Awards.

MAJOR COMMERCIAL NETWORKS
MEDIAWORKS, Level 2, 239 Ponsonby Road, Ponsonby, Auckland 1011. 🖃 P.O. Box 8880, Symonds Street, Auckland 1150 ☎ 64 9 928 9300 🖷 +64 9 373 4000 **W:** mediaworks.co.nz **L:P:** Group CEO Mark Wheldon, CEO MediaWorks Radio: Wendy Palmer.
Prgrs: 24h **Owner:** MediaWorks Holdings Ltd
Netw. Brands P.O. Box 47560, Ponsonby, Auckland 1144 ☎ +64 9 928 9000 🖷 +64 9 361 1677 **Radio LIVE:** P.O. Box 8880, Symonds Street, Auckland 1150 ☎+64 9 928 9270 🖷 +64 9 360 0390. **George**

FM: P.O. Box 47664, Ponsonby, Auckland 1144 ☎ +64 9 928 9150 🖷 +64 9 360 0044. **Prgr:** 24h from Auckland studios. **N:** R.LIVE bulletins.

Netw. Brands: The Edge **W:** theedge.co.nz – R. LIVE **W:** radiolive.co.nz – The Rock **W:** therock.co.nz – The Sound **W:** thesound.co.nz – George FM **W:** georgefm.co.nz – Mai FM **W:** maifm.co.nz – Magic **W:** magic.co.nz Full FM listings at individual netw. websites.

MW	Khz	kW	Station	MW	Khz	kW	Station
Alexandra	531	2	MORE FM L	Wellington	1233	2	R.LIVE	N
Auckland	702	10	Magic	N	Dunedin	1305	2.5	R.Dunedin L
Christchurch	738	5	Magic	N	Queenstown	1359	1	MORE FM L
Wellington	891	5	Magic	N	Napier-			
Rotorua	1107	1	R.LIVE	N	Hastings	1368	1	R.LIVE	N
Tauranga	1107	1	R.LIVE	N				

L = Local N = Network

FM	1	2	3	4	5	6	7
Whangarei	94.0	90.8	-	90.0	107.3	-	98.0
Auckland	94.2	100.6	-	90.2	93.8	96.6	88.6
Hamilton	97.8	100.2	-	93.0	93.8	107.3	105.8
Tauranga	97.8	100.8	88.6	94.2	92.6	107.4	96.6
Rotorua	99.9	95.1	100.7	92.7	91.1	-	105.5
Taupo	88.8	99.2	-	94.4	100.0	-	-
Gisborne	99.7	94.9	-	94.1	96.5	-	89.3
Napier-Hastings	98.3	-	92.7	95.1	91.9	-	105.5
New Plymouth	94.0	89.2	-	95.6	98.0	-	-
Palmerston North	93.0	93.8	-	95.4	94.6	104.2	97.0
Kapiti Coast	97.5	99.1	95.1	91.9	94.3	-	-
Wellington	91.7	98.9	-	96.5	97.3	104.5	100.5
Nelson	88.0	96.0	99.2	94.4	98.4	95.2	-
Christchurch	88.9	99.3	-	93.7	92.9	106.9	88.9
Timaru	95.5	89.9	-	91.5	97.1	-	-
Dunedin	91.8	96.6	99.8	93.4	90.2	100.6	100.6
Queenstown	95.2	91.2	104.0	100.0	97.6	96.8	-
Invercargill	97.2	94.0	106.0	90.8	98.0	-	-

1= The Edge, **2** = R.LIVE, **3**= Magic, **4**= The Rock, **5**= The Sound **6**= George **7** = Mai FM

Local Brands: The Breeze **W:** thebreeze.co.nz – MORE FM **W:** morefm.co.nz – R. Dunedin **W:** radiodunedin.co.nz

Overnight and weekends often networked from Auckland except for R. Dunedin. **Prgr:** 24h **N:** R.LIVE bulletins. For full FM listings see individual local brand websites

FM	Location	1	2	FM	Location	1	2
4)	Northland	-	91.6	15)	Manawatu	98.6	92.2
24)	Auckland	-	88.9	16)	Wairarapa	99.8	89.3/105.5
5)	Auckland	93.4	91.8	17)	Horowhenua	-	104.2
6)	Waikato	99.4	92.2	18)	Kapiti	100.7	90.3
7)	Tauranga	95.8	93.4	2)	Wellington	94.0/98.5	94.7/99.7
8)	Mercury Bay	96.6	-	19)	Nelson	97.6	92.8
9)	Rotorua	91.9	95.9	20)	Marlborough	*96.1	§92.9
10)	Taupo	100.8	93.6	21)	Christchurch	94.5	92.1
11)	Gisborne	-	98.9/90.1	3)	Dunedin	98.2	97.4
12)	Hawkes Bay	97.5	92.1	1)	Central Otago	96.7	90.3/94.3
13)	Taranaki	92.4	93.2	22)	Queenstown	99.2	92.0/99.4
14)	Wanganui	97.6	92.8	23)	Southland	91.6	89.2

1= The Breeze, **2**=MORE FM, *****) also 97.3/98.5, **§** also 94.5/96.3

Addresses & other information
1) P.O. Box 143, Alexandra 9340 ☎ +64 3 901 6200 🖷 +64 3 448 6502 – **2)** P.O. Box 11441, Manners Street, Wellington 6142 ☎+64 4 915 1000 🖷 +64 4 915 1009 – **3)** P.O. Box 1500, Dunedin 9054 **R. Dunedin:** ☎ +64 3 477 6934 **FM:** 107.7MHz **The Breeze/MORE FM:** ☎ +64 3 951 3600 🖷 +64 3 477 6874 – **4)** P.O. Box 100, Whangarei 0140 ☎ +64 9 986 9990 🖷 +64 9 438 2348 – **5) The Breeze/MORE FM:** P.O. Box 8880, Symonds Street, Auckland 1150 ☎+64 9 928 9300 🖷 +64 9 373 4000 **Mai FM:** P.O. Box 68886, Newton, Auckland ☎ +64 9 977 7800 🖷 +64 9 977 7801 – **6)** P.O. Box 19293, Hamilton 3244 ☎ +64 7 958 7050 🖷 +64 7 838 2893 – **7)** Box 13344, Tauranga 3141 ☎ +64 7 928 7300 🖷 +64 7 577 0294 – **8)** P.O. Box 16, Whitianga +64 7 866 5696 🖷 +64 7 866 2553 – **9)** P.O. Box 92, Rotorua 3040 ☎ +64 7 921 7630 🖷 +64 7 348 3830 – **10)** Box 393, Taupo 3351 ☎+64 7 906 7500 🖷 +64 7 378 2701 – **11)** P.O. Box 468, Gisborne 4040 ☎+64 6 986 3700 🖷 +64 6 869 0037 – **12)** P.O. Box 193, Hastings 4156 ☎ +64 6 974 6150 🖷 +64 6 876 5626 – **13)** P.O. Box 869, Taranaki Mail Centre, New Plymouth ☎+64 6 968 6000 🖷 +64 6 757 5020 – **14)** P.O. Box 928, Wanganui 4540 ☎ +64 6 965 6300 🖷 +64 6 345 5592 – **15)** P.O. Box 446, Palmerston North Central, Palmerston North 4440 ☎ +64 6 952 6420 🖷 +64 6 356 1317 – **16)** P.O. Box 881, Masterton ☎+64 6 370 2548 🖷 +64 6 378 8877 – **17)** P.O. Box 603, Levin ☎+64 6 368 2827 🖷 +64 6 368 0415 – **18)** P.O. Box 132, Paraparaumu 5254 ☎ +64 4 903 0400 🖷 +64 4 297 2999 – **19)** P.O. Box 907, Nelson 7040 ☎+64 3 546 9670 🖷 +64 3 546 9427 – **20)** P.O. Box 391, Blenheim ☎+64 3 579 0393 – **21) The Breeze:** Private Bag 4750, Christchurch 8140 ☎

+64 3 961 3102 🖷 +64 3 366 5301 **MORE FM:** P.O. Box 25209, Victoria Street, Christchurch 8144 ☎+64 3 961 3322 🖷 +64 3 377 1993 – **22)** P.O. Box 224, Queenstown ☎ +64 3 901 0810 🖷 +64 3 442 7799 – **23)** P.O. Box 1740, Invercargill ☎ +64 3 948 3900 🖷 +64 3 218 8015 – **24)** The Village, 292 Hibiscus Coast Highway, Orewa 0931 ☎ +64 9 928 9940 🖷 +64 9 427 0251

C) Associated local Radioworks stations
These stns operate as independent local brands. Local mornings but mainly other times networked from MORE FM.**Prgr:** 24h **N:** R.LIVE bulletins
1) Coromandel FM, Paeroa 89.0MHz, **2)** Big River R., Balclutha 92.9MHz

Addresses & Other Information
1) PO Box 962, Thames 3540 ☎+64 7 868 6063 🖷 +64 7 868 6681 **W:** coromandelfm.co.nz/ 89.0/ 89.1/89.9/90.3/93.8/93.9/94.0 /96.2/97.5 – **2)** 1st Fl. PO John Street, Balclutha ☎+64 3 418 1969 **W:** bigriverradio.webs.com **FM Network:** 92.9/93.7

RHEMA BROADCASTING GROUP
🖳 **Corporate:** 53 Upper Queen Street, Auckland. 🖳 **Postal:** Private Bag 92636, Symonds Street, Auckland 1150. ☎ +64 9 307 1251 🖷 +64 9 309 6888 **W:** rbg.co.nz **L.P:** Chief Exec: Mike Brewer **Dir.Prgr-Radio:** Gary Hoogvliet **Other Media:** Shine TV, UCB International **Owner:** NZ charitable organization.
Netw. Stns: Prgr: 24h from Auckland studios. Star also broadc. on RNZ AM Netw. txs when Parliament not in session. An duplicate networkin several markets carries Star 24/7 so that listeners can hear it without interruption when Parliament is in session.**N:** IRN bulletins.
Netw. Brands: Life FM **W:** lifefm.co.nz – Rhema **W:** rhema.co.nz – Star **W:** sstar.co.nz – . Full FM listings at individual netw. brand websites.

Rhema

MW	kHz	kW	MW	KHz	kW
Tauranga	540	5	Gisborne	684	5
New Plymouth	540	3	Nelson	801	2
Christchurch	540	2	Hamilton	855	2
Kaitaia	549	3	Wellington	972	5
Wanganui	594	2	Timaru	981	2.5
Whangarei	621	2	Auckland	1251	5
Dunedin	621	2	Invercargill	1404	5

Star

MW	kHz	kW	MW	KHz	kW
Hamilton	576	2.5	Dunedin	900	*10
Timaru	594	5	Napier-Hastings	909	*5
Nelson	612	1.5	Christchurch	963	*10
Christchurch	612	1.5	Invercargill	1026	2.5
Tauranga	657	10*	Invercargill	1314	*5
Wellington	657	50*	Dunedin	1377	3
Auckland	882	10*	Invercargill	1494	*3

* shares frequency with RNZ AM Network. Duplicate frequencies in same market carry Star 24/7 and when alternate * frequency carrying RNZ AM Network.

FM	1	2	3	FM	1	2	3
Whangarei	-	-	98.8	Palmerston North	91.4	-	96.2
Auckland	-	-	99.8	Kapiti Coast	-	-	96.7
Hamilton	-	-	94.6	Wellington	-	-	98.1
Tauranga	-	-	94.6	Nelson	-	-	93.6
Rotorua	93.5	-	94.6	Christchurch	-	-	106.9
Taupo	95.2	88.3	107.0	Timaru	104.3	-	93.9
Gisborne	103.7	92.5	100.5	Dunedin	-	-	94.2
Napier-Hastings	99.1	-	93.5	Queenstown	94.4	107.0	-
New Plymouth	-	-	99.6	Invercargill	-	-	100.0

1 = Rhema, **2** = Star, **3** = Life FM

NZ MEDIA & ENTERTAINMENT [NZME}
🖳 **NZME Radio Corporate:** 54 Cook Street, Auckland. 🖳 **Postal:** Private Bag 92198, Auckland Mail Centre, Auckland 1142 ☎ +64 9 373 0000 🖷 +64 9 367 4802 **W:** nzme.co.nz **L.P:** CEO APN News & Media: Jane Hastings, Managing Dir: Dean Buchanan Owner: APN News & Media [Australia].
A) Netw. Brands: Prgr: 24h from Auckland studios **N:** NewstalkZB bulletins. **Brands:** Coast **W:** thecoast.net.nz - Flava **W:** flava.co.nz - Radio Hauraki **W:** hauraki.co.nz – Mix **W:** mixonline.co.nz - NewstalkZB **W:** newstalkzb.co.nz - Radio Sport **W:** radiosport.co.nz - ZM **W:** zmonline.com Full FM listings at individual netw. brand websites.

Radio Sport

MW	kHz	kW	MW	KHz	kW
Nelson	549	1	New Plymouth	774	5
Invercargill	558	5	Hamilton	792	5
Dunedin	693	5	Christchurch*	1017	2.5
Ashburton	702	1	Wanganui	1062	1
Whangarei	729	3	Palmerston North	1089	2.5

MW	kHz	kW	MW	KHz	kW
Napier-Hastings	1125	1	Timaru	1494	2.5
Auckland	1332	10	Christchurch	1503	2.5
Rotorua	1350	1	Wellington	1503	5
Levin	1377	2	Tauranga	1521	1

* alternate for 1503, sometimes carries NewstalkZB

NewstalkZB

MW	kHz	kW	MW	KHz	kW
Rotorua	747	0.4	New Plymouth	1053	2
Masterton	846	2	Auckland	1080	10
Invercargill	864	10	Christchurch#	1098	2
Ashburton	873	1	Timaru	1152	2
Palmerston N.	927	2	Wanganui	1197	2
Gisborne	945	2	Kaikohe	1215	2
Tauranga	1008	10	Napier-Hastings	1278	2
Christchurch*	1017	10	Westport	1287	2
Kaitaia	1026	2	Hamilton	1296	2.5
Whangarei	1026	2	Nelson	1341	2
Wellington#	1035	20	Oamaru	1395	2
Dunedin	1044	10	Tokoroa	1413	2

* alternate for 1098, sometimes carries R.Sport

Radio Hauraki

MW	kHz	kW
Dunedin	1125	1

Coast

MW	kHz	kW	MW	KHz	kW
Whangarei	900	2.5	Palmerston North	1548	1
Dunedin	954	1	Napier-Hastings	1584	1
Hawera	1323	3	Christchurch	1593	2.5
New Plymouth	1359	2.5			

FM	1	2	3	4	5	6	7
Whangarei	-	106.0	93.2	-	-	94.8	-
Auckland	105.4	95.8	99.0	89.4	-	91.0	98.2
Hamilton	105.0	-	96.2	97.0	-	89.4	-
Tauranga	97.4	99.0	91.0	90.2	-	89.8	-
Rotorua	96.7	89.5	94.3	-	-	98.3	-
Taupo	-	-	92.8	96.0	107.7	90.4	-
Gisborne	88.3	-	105.3	-	-	107.4	-
Napier-Hastings	-	96.7	99.9	90.3	-	95.9	-
New Plymouth	-	106.0		96.4	-	98.8	-
Palmerston North	-	-	105.8	100.2	-	90.6	-
Kapiti Coast	95.9	-	-	89.5	-	91.1	-
Wellington	95.7	104.5	93.3	89.3	93.7	90.9	-
Nelson	100.8	-	90.4	-	-	96.8	-
Christchurch	90.1-	88.0/ 107.0	106.5/ 89.3	100.1	-	91.3/ 90.9	91.7
Timaru	-	-	-	-	98.7	96.3	-
Dunedin	-	88.6	106.2	-	-	95.8	-
Queenstown	-	-	-	89.6-	-	88.8	-
Invercargill	92.4	-	93.2	-	-	95.8	-

1=Coast, 2=Flava, 3=R.Hauraki, 4=NewstalkZB, 5=R.Sport, 6=ZM 7 = Mix
B) Local Brand: The Hits W: hits.co.nz Full FM lists see local brand websites.

MW	kHz	kW	MW	KHz	kW
1) Takaka	1269	0.4	2) Picton	1539	0.4

FM	MHz	FM	MHz	FM	MHz
23) Dunedin	89.4	18) Greymouth	90.9	2) Blenheim	96.9
11) Hawkes Bay	89.5	18) Greymouth	91.1	3) Northland	97.2
1) Nelson	89.6	20) Ashburton	92.5	18) Greymouth	97.3
13) Wanganui	89.6	16) Kapiti	92.7	4) Auckland	97.4
12) Taranaki	90.0	18) Greymouth	93.1	7) Rotorua	97.5
15) Masterton	90.1	21) Timaru	94.7	3) Northland	97.6
17) Wellington	90.1	6) Tauranga	95.0	19) Christchurch	97.7
24) Central Otago	90.4	3) Northland	95.6	14) Manawatu	97.8
25) Southland	90.4	24) Central Otago	96.2	22) Oamaru	98.4
18) Greymouth	90.5	8) Tokoroa	96.4	5) Waikato	98.6
12) Taranaki	90.7	19) Christchurch	96.5	21) Timaru	98.7
7) Rotorua	90.8	3) Northland	96.8	25) Southland	98.8
10) Gisborne	90.9	9) Taupo	96.8	24) Central Otago	99.9

Addresses & other information
1) P.O. Box 43, Nelson 7043 ☎ +64 3 546 2557 – 2) P.O. Box 225, Blenheim ☎+64 3 578 0129– 3) P. O. Box 845, Whangarei ☎ +64 9 430 4950 – 4) Private Bag 92198, Auckland ☎ +64 9 373 0000 – 5) P.O. Box 489, Hamilton ☎+64 7 858 0700 – 6) P.O. Box 642, Tauranga ☎ +64 7 578 9139 – 7) P.O. Box 1147, Rotorua ☎ +64 7 348 9089 – 8) P.O. Box 272, Tokoroa ☎ +64 7 886 8399 – 9) P.O. Box 967, Taupo ☎ +64 7 376 0550 – 10) P.O. Box 1040, Gisborne ☎+64 6 867 2139 – 11) P.O. Box 241, Napier ☎ +64 6 833 8400 – 12) P.O. Box 141, New Plymouth ☎ +64 6 759 2460 - 13) P.O. Box 632, Wanganui ☎ +64 6 348 1176 – 14) P.O. Box 1045, Palmerston North ☎ +64 6 350 3550 – 15) P.O. Box 220, Masterton ☎+64 6 370 5014 – 16) 39 Kapiti Road, Paraparaumu ☎+64 4 902 9886 – 17) P.O. Box 300, Wellington ☎+64 4 802 4710 #NewstalkZB 1035MW/90.1FM carries local breakfast show – 18) P.O. Box 378, Greymouth ☎+64 3 768 7068 – 19) P.O. Box 1484, Christchurch ☎ +64 3 379 9600 #NewstalkZB 1098MW/89.3FM carries local breakfast show – 20) P.O. Box 465, Ashburton ☎+64 3 307 8927 – 21) P.O. Box 275, Timaru ☎ +64 3 684 8152 – 22) P.O. Box 426, Oamaru ☎ +64 3 433 1090 – 23) P.O. Box 888, Dunedin ☎ +64 3 474 8400 – 24) P.O Box 1769, Queenstown ☎ +64 3 447 3175 – 25) P.O. Box 802, Invercargill ☎+64 3 211 1500

Associated local NZME station

MW	KHz	kw
Hawera	1557	2

Hokonui R. PO Box 292, Gore 9700 ☎+64 3 208 9325 **W:** hokonui.co.nz facebook.com/hokonui **FM Netw:** 88.2/91.3/92.5/94.8/95.2/96.5 **Prgr:** 24/7 breakfast live from local studios in Gore, Balclutha & Ashburton then networked from Dunedin/Gore **N:** NewstalkZB [Hokonui is privately owned but under long term lease to NZME]

TAB TRACKSIDE RADIO
PO Box 38899, Wellington Mail Centre, Lower Hutt 5045 ☎+64 4 576 6999 NZ Freephone 0800 102 106 Freephone from Australia: 0011 800 10 20 30 44 ⮑+64 4 576 6942 **W:** tab.co.nz/help/tv-radio/radio-trackside **E:** helpdesk@tab.co.nz **Other:** Totalisator Agency Board operated betting and race reporting services by NZ Racing Board.
For full FM listing see website.

MW	kHz	kW	MW	kHz	kW
Napier-Hastings	549	1	Dunedin	1206	2
Wellington	711	5	Invercargill	1224	2
Palmerston North	828	2	Timaru	1242	2
Tauranga	873	5	Christchurch	1260	2
Hamilton	954	2	Auckland	1476	5
Nelson	990	1	Gisborne	1485	1
Ashburton	1071	1	Rotorua	1548	0.9

FM	MHz	kW	FM	MHz	kW
Whangarei	92.4	0.16	Kapiti Coast	93.5	0.63
Taupo	91.2	2	Queenstown	93.6	0.8
New Plymouth	97.2	5			

+ 11 other stations in minor markets

STUDENT RADIO (bNet affiliated stations)

FM	MHz	kW	Station
1) Wellington	88.6	0.5	R.Active
2) Dunedin	91.0	2.5	R.One
3) Auckland	95.0	12.6	95bFM
4) Christchurch	98.5	1.6	RDU 98.5FM
5) Palmerston North	99.4	0.16	R.Control

+ 1 other low power FM
1) PO Box 11971 Wellington **W:** radioactive.fm **E:** agency@radioactive.fm – 2) PO Box 1436, Dunedin **W:** r1.co.nz **E:** r1@r1.co.nz – 3) PO Box 4560, Shortland St, Auckland 1001 **W:** 95bfm.com **E:** 95bfm@95bfm.com – 4) PO Box 699, Christchurch Central **W:** rdu.org.nz **E:** james@rdu.org.nz – 5) c/o MUSA, Students Centre Bldg, Massey University, Private Bag 11-222, Palmerston North **W:** radiocontrol.org.nz **E:** manager@radiocontrol.org.nz

INDEPENDENT STATIONS

MW	kHz	kW	Station
1) Ranfurly	729	0.1	Burn729am
2) Palmerston	756	0.8	Puketapu R.
3) Wellington	783	10	Samoan Capital R.
4) Auckland	810	2	BBC World Service NZ
5) Auckland	936	1	New Supremo
6) Auckland	990	1	Apna 990
16) Te Kuiti	1170	1.25	FPL 2016 [irr.tests]
7) Auckland	1179	5	Ake
8) Whakatane	1242	2	One Double X
57) Taupo	1251	6.3	FPL 2016
9) Tauranga	1368	0.8/0.1	Village R.
10) Auckland	1386	10	R Tarana
11) Christchurch	1413	1	R.Ferrymead
17) Napier-Hastings	1530	1	The Wireless Station
5) Wellington	1566	15.8	FPL 2016
13) Auckland	1593	5	R.Samoa
14) Levin	1602	2.5	R.Reading Service

FM	MHz	kW	Station
Northland			
12) Mangawhai	90.4	0.1	The Wireless
60) Dargaville	98.6	0.5	Big River FM
15) Waipu	105.6	0.02	R.Waves
12) Mangawhai	106.4	0.05	Heads FM
Auckland			
18) Auckland	90.6	1.6	Chinese R 90.6FM
19) Station Rock GBI	94.6	1	Aotea FM
5) Auckland	99.4	1.6	Chinese R. FM99.4

FM	MHz	kW	Station
19) Port Fitzroy GBI	104.0	0.1	Aotea FM
5) Auckland	104.2	3	Chinese R. FM104.2
20) Auckland	106.2	15.8	Humm FM
Waikato			
21) Waihi/Tokatea	96.4	0.1/0.1	Gold FM
22) Whangamata	97.9	0.3	Kool FM
23) Pauanui S/			
Whangamata	100.3	0.8/0.1	Sea FM
24) Te Kuiti/			
Mangakino	104.4	0.8/0.1	Cruise FM
24) Tokoroa	105.3	0.3	Cruise FM
25) Taupo	106.4	6	Timeless Taupo
BOP Lakes			
26) Opotiki	91.7	0.1	Sea 92FM
8) Whakatane	92.9	0.16	One Double X
8) E. BOP	93.7	1.6	Bayrock
8) E. BOP	97.7	2	Q97
27) Rotorua	99.1	0.25	The Heat
8) Whakatane	99.3	0.16	Q97
8) Whakatane	100.1	0.1	Bayrock
28) Rotorua	104.7	0.63	Good News Community R
29) Tauranga	105.4	8	Bollypop 105.4FM
HB-East Coast			
30) Napier-Hastings	100.7	4	R.Bay FM
31) Waipukurau-			
Dannevirke	105.2	2	Central FM
31) Waipukurau-			
Waipawa	106.0	2	Central FM
Central North			
32) Taihape	90.0	0.63	Ski FM
32) Taumarunui	91.1	1	Ski FM
33) Wanganui	91.2	0.8	Brian FM
33) Waipuna	91.8	1.6	Ski FM
33) Wanganui	92.0	0.8	Reelworld FM
34) Taumarunui	92.7	1.6	Peak FM
33) Taihape	93.2	0.16	Brian FM
32) Wanganui	93.6	0.16	Ski FM
24) Taumarunui	94.3	1	Cruise FM
34) Waipuna	95.8	1.6	Peak FM
32) Waipuna	96.6	0.8	Ski FM
24) Waipuna	99.0	1.6	Cruise FM
31) Dannevirke	99.4	0.03	Central FM
35) Woodville	99.6	0.05	R.Woodville
34) Taihape	99.6	0.8	Peak FM
34) Taumarunui	99.9	0.16	Peak FM
36) New Plymouth	100.4	1.6	The Most
37) Palmerston North	105.0	0.1	Vision FM
38) New Plymouth	105.2	5	Cruize FM
39) Foxton	105.4	0.16	R.Foxton
24) National Park	105.4	0.8	Cruise FM
40) Wanganui	106.2	0.8	The Avenue
Wellington			
58) Wellington	105.3	2	Wellington 105.3FM
59) Kapiti Coast	106.3	0.63	Beach FM
Nelson			
33) Blenheim	100.9	0.1	Brian FM
33) Seddon	104.3	0.3	Brian FM
33) Picton	105.9	0.16	Brian FM
Canterbury			
41) Tekapo	89.8	0.08	Port FM
42) Akaroa	90.3	0.3	R.Akaroa
43) Reefton	90.3	0.5	Coast FM
41) Omarama	90.9	0.05	Port FM
42) Hilltop	91.1	0.3	R.Akaroa
41) Waimate	93.1	0.8	Port FM
41) Timaru	93.1	0.1	Port FM
44) Mt Hutt Skifield	94.1	0.16	Mt Hutt R. Ski
41) Twizel	94.2	0.5	Port FM
41) Mid-Canterbury	94.9	8	Port FM
41) Fairlie	95.0	1.6	Port FM
45) Twizel	95.8	0.08	R.Twizel
46) Christchurch	96.1	15.8	Chalk 96.1
43) Westport	96.5	1.6	Coast FM
41) Kurow	96.8	0.8	Port FM
41) S. Canterbury	97.9	8	Port FM
43) Greymouth	97.9	0.5	Coast FM
41) Ashburton	98.9	0.16	Port FM
43) Karamea	99.3	1.6	Coast FM
43) Greymouth-			
Hokitika	99.5	1.6	Coast FM
47) Kaikoura	100.3	0.5	Blue FM
48) S.Canterbury	100.3	1	Kiwi Access 100FM
43) Hokitika	100.3	2.5	Coast FM
49) Christchurch	100.9	5	V. of the South Pole
50) Christchurch	105.7	5	Pulzar FM

FM	MHz	kW	Station
41) Ashburton	106.1	0.1	Port FM
Southern Lakes			
51) Glenorchy	89.2	0.3	Glenorchy Country R.
52) Cromwell	91.9	0.1	Local R.Central
52) Alexandra	91.9	0.8	Local R.Central
53) Wanaka	92.2	0.5	R.Wanaka
8) Wanaka	93.0	0.25	Bayrock
52) Roxburgh	94.3	0.02	Local R.Central
53) Wanaka	94.6	0.5	Roy
41) Oamaru	100.0	0.8	Port FM
54) Ranfurly	104.3	0.63	The Hawk
55) Invercargill	105.2	4	Country R.
56) Gore	106.4	0.8	Cave FM

Addresses & other information

1) 10 Pery St, Ranfurly 9332 **E:** burn729am@xtra,co.nz– **2)** 118 Ronaldsay St, Palmerston 9430 **W:** puketapuradio.weebly.com **E:** puketapuradio@xtra.co.nz **Prgr:** Day: local community radio – Night: relay UK based Planet Caroline online stream –**3)** PO Box 6647, Marion Square, Wellington 6141 **W:** samoancapitalradio.co.nz **E:** info@samo-acapitalradio.co.nz **Prgr:** Samoan "Siufofoga O Le Laumua" Mon-Wed 1900-0300 Thu 1900-1230, 0600-1200 Fri 1900-0400 at other times 783 AM is used by Wellington Access R. – **4)** Auckland Radio Trust, PO Box 28622, Remuera, Auckland **W:** worldservice.co.nz **E:** vince@worldser-vice.co.nz **Prgr:** BBC World Service satellite relay from London 24/7, RNZI Dateline Pacific and local advertising & programs achieved by trimming seconds per minute off the satellite feed and 'saving' about 3 minutes per hour – **5)** PO Box 12743, Penrose, Auckland 1642 **W:** chi-nesevoice.co.nz **E:** info@wtv.co.nz **Prgr:** 936AM Mandarin [incl satel-lite services from China & Taiwan], 99.4 FM Cantonese [incl satellite services from Hong Kong], **104.2 FM** Mandarin [12h daily], China R. International English [12h daily] – **6)** Level 3, 362 Great North Rd, Henderson, Waitakere 0612 **W:** apna990.co.nz **E:** info@apna990.com **Prgr:** Hindi – **7)** Te Reo o Ngati Whenua, Te Runanga o Ngati Whatua, PO Box 1784, Whangarei. **W:** ngatiwhatua.iwi.nz/manaakitanga/ake-1179am **E:** ake1179@ngatiwhatua.iwi.nz **Prgr:** Maori reggae favorites, soul, R&B music – **8)** Radio Bay of Plenty Ltd, PO Box 383, Whakatane 3158 **Brands:** 1XX **W:** 1xx.co.nz facebook.com/radio1xx - Bayrock **W:** bayrock.co.nz facebook.com/bayrockonline– Q97 **W:** q97.co.nz & face-book.com/q97hits **E:** reception@1xx.com – **9)** PO Box 841 Seventh Avenue, Tauranga 3140 **W:** villageradio.co.nz **E:** info@villageradio.co.nz **Prgr:** Nostalgia Mon-Fri 2100-0500 Sat-Sun 2100-0500 – **10)** PO Box 5956, Wellesley Street, Auckland 1141 **W:** tarana.co.nz facebook.com/radiotarananz **E:** info@tarana.co.nz **Prgr:** Hindi – **11)** PO Box 19090, Woolston, Christchurch 8241 **W:** radioferrymead.co.nz **Prgr:** Fri 2000-Mon 1200 non-stop including automated prgrs, Statutory Holidays & Christmas New Year period **-12)** Perryscope Productions Ltd, PO Box 180, Mangawhai 0540 **Brands:** Heads FM **W:** facebook.com/heads106.4fm The Wireless **W:** facebook.com/thewirelessfm **E:** mark@perryscope.co.nz – **13)** PO Box 200105, Papatoetoe Central, Manukau 2156 **W:** radiosamoa.co.nz **E:** sales@samoatimes.co.nz **Prgr:** Samoan **Other:** Samoa Times newspaper – **14)** PO Box 360, Levin 5500 **W:** radioreading.org.nz & facebook.com/radioreading **E:** rrsinfo@radioread-ing.org.nz **Prgr:** RNZ National relay Fri 0800-2000 Mon non-stop, all other times own programs **–15)** 88 The Centre, Waipu **W:** facebook.com/radiowaveswaipu **E:** info@radiowaveswaipu.co.nz **Prgr:** Mon-Fri 2100-0530 Sat/Sun 0000-0700 – **16)** Robert Jeffares, 64 Warner Park Ave, Laingholm, Auckland [testing with programs in English/Hindi Oct 2015] – **17)** PO Box 8947, Havelock North **Prgr:** mostly automated standards, rock & roll music, obs. with some live anncrs in primetime. – **18)** 194 Marua Road, Mt Wellington, Auckland 1051 **W:** fm906.co.nz **E:** info@fm906.co.nz **Prgr:** 24/7 Mandarin **Other:** owned by Global CAMG Media Group [includes 3CW 1241/1620 Melbourne] **W:** camg-media.com **–19)** Hector Sanderson Road, Claris, Great Barrier Island **W:** aoteafm.org & facebook.com/aoteafm **E:** aoteafm@xtra.co.nz **Prgr:** 1930-0600 daily – **20)** PO Box 27647, Mt Roskill, Auckland 1440 **W:** hummfm.com & facebook.com/hummfm **E:** connect@hummfm.com **Prgr:** 24/7 Hindi – **21)** PO Box 341, Waihi 3641 **W:** goldfm.co.nz **E:** info@goldfm.co.nz **Other:** 88.0/88.3 **-22)** 500 Tairua Road, Whangamata 3691 **W:** koolfm.biz **E:** studio@koolfm.biz **-23)** Level 1, Ti Rakau Drive, Burswood, Manukau **W:** seafm.co.nz & facebook.com/seafmcoroman-del **E:** contact@seafm.co.nz – **24)** Level 1, 203 Leith Place, Tokoroa **W:** cruisefm.co.nz & facebook.com/cruise-fm **E:** johnnydryden@xtra.co.nz – **25)** Great Lake Taupo R Ltd, 23 Scannell Street, Taupo **W:** time-lesstaupo.co.nz & facebook.com/timeless-taupo-1064.fm **E:** radio@timelesstaupo.co.nz – **26)** 25 Eliott Street, Opotiki **W:** whakaata.wix.com/sea92fm & facebook.com/sea92fm **E:** wwt88.1@xtra.co.nz – **27)** 1478a Hinemoa Street, Rotorua **W:** facebook.com/the heat99.1 – **28)** Rotorua Gospel Broadc. Charitable Trust, 42 Mount View Dr, Mangakakahi, Rotorua 3013 **E:** comrad@xtra.co.nz – **29)** 232a Waihi Road, Judea, Tauranga 3110 **W:** bollypop.co.nz & facebook.com/bolly-pop **E:** studio@bollypop.co.nz **Prgr:** 24/7 Hindi – **30)** PO Box 220,

Hastings **W**: radiobayfm.co.nz & facebook.com/radiobayfm **E**: radio-bayfm@xtra.co.nz – **31)** PO Box 195, 215-217 Ruataniwha Street, Waipukurau **W**: centralfm.co.nz & facebook.com/central.fm.3 **E**: centralfm@xtra.co.nz – **32)** PO Box 661, Taupo **W**: skifmnnetwork.co.nz & facebook.com/skifm **E**: info@skifmnetwork.com **Other**: FPL 1251 MW Taupo also – **33)** 268 Broadway Ave, Palmerston North **Brands**: Brian FM **W**: brianfm.com & facebook.com/brianfm Reelworld FM **E**: brian@brianfm.com studios in Springvale [Wanganui], Blenheim – **34)** PO Box 37, Raetihi **W**: peakfm.nz & facebook.com/peak-fm **E**: geoff@peakfm-ruapehu.co.nz– **35)** 79 Vogel Street, Woodville **W**: radiowoodville.co.nz **E**: station@radiowoodville.co.nz + 88.3 **-36)** 12 Bell Street, New Plymouth 4310 **W**: themostfm.co.nz **E**: mosrfm@mostfm.com – **37)** DX Mail MA75001, DX Mail Sort Centre, Palmerston North **W**: vision100.com – **38)** 38 Liardet Street, New Plymouth **W**: cruizefm.co.nz & facebook.com/cruizefm **E**: info@bigmedia.co.nz **-39)** MAVTECH The National Museum of Audio Visual Technology, Avenue Road, Foxton **W**: mavtech.co.nz & facebook.com/mavtechnz **E**: mavtech@xtra.co.nz – **40)** 180 Upper Roberts Avenue, RD14, Wanganui **W**: theavenue.co.nz – **41)** PO Box 635, Timaru **W**: portfmnz.com & facebook.com/port-fm-music-network **E**: portfmstudio@xtra.co.nz **Other**: commercial affiliation with Radioworks network brands The Edge/The Rock/The Sound in Mid Canterbury, South Canterbury, North Otago and West Coast; studios in Timaru/Ashburton and Oamaru with local breakouts – **42)** 1 Edwards Road, Wainui, Banks Peninsula, Christchurch **W**: akaroaradio.co.nz **E**: dave@akaroaradio.co.nz – **43)** 171 Palmerston Street, Westport **W**: coastfm.net.nz & facebook.com/coast.fm **E**: studio@coastfm.nz **Other**: Westport News newspaper r – **44)** seasonal only station based at Mt Hutt Skifield associated with Radioworks – **45)** Twizel Promotion & Development Assoc. Inc, PO Box 4, Market Place, Twizel **W**: twizel.info **E**: tpda@twizel.info – **46)** NZ Broadcasting School, CPIT Campus, 150 Madras Street, Christchurch **W**: nzbs.co.nz/chalk961 & facebook.com/chalk961 **E**: chalk@chalk961.co.nz **NB**: each year the NZBS operates a different station on 96.1 to give students broadcasting experience. This data is for 2015 but a new brand and format will use the frequency in 2016 – **47)** Scarborough Street, Kaikoura **W**: facebook.com/kkbluefm **E**: bluefm@xtra.co.nz – **48)** James Valentine, 8 Lisava Street, Timaru. Automated music only – **49)** 12 Walters Road, Marshland, Christchurch **W**: tvo.cc **E**: vsp@tvo.cc **Prgr**: 24/7 mainly Chinese including programs from China R.International in various languages on weekends – **50)** PO Box 13209, Christchurch **W**: pulzarfm.co.nz & facebook.com/pulzarfm **E**: info@pulzarfm.co.nz – **51)** PO Box 52, Glenorchy **W**: glenorchycommunity.nz/community-services/glenorchy-country-radio **E**: glenorchycountry@gmail.com – **52)** Alexandra: 2/22 Centennial Ave, Alexandra 9320 Cromwell: 34 Ree Crescent, Cromwell **W**: localradiocentral.nz & facebook.com/localradiocentral facebook.com/localradiocromwell **E**: diack@xtra.co.nz Roxburgh + 88.0 – **53)** PO Box 825, Wanaka **Brands**: R.Wanaka **W**: wanakalive.com & facebook.com/radiowanaka **E**: info@radiowanaka.co.nz Roy **E**: jamie@tadiowanaka.co.nz – **54)** PO Box 18, Omakau 9352 **W**: thehawk.nz & facebook.com/1043-the-hawk **E**: studio@thehawk.nz – **55)** 145 Islington Street, Invercargill **W**: countryradionetwork.com **E**: countryradio@xtra.co.nz + 88.1/87.7 – **56)** 6 North Tce, Gore **W**: caveman4music.vpweb.co.nz & facebook.com/caveman– **57)** associated with Ski FM #32 – **58)** 18 Ashwood Street, Woodridge, Newlands, Wellington **W**: facebook.com/wellington105.3fm **E**: info@wellington105.3fm **Prgr**: 24/7 Hindi – **60)** Lindale Complex, Paraparaumu **W**: beachfm.co.nz & facebook.com/beachfm106.3
NB: Major network stations less than 1kw not included. LPFM [1w or less] stations broadcasting on 87.6-88.3 and 106.7-107.7MHz throughout the country and ALL stations less than 1kw are included in a regularly updated free NZ Radio Guide maintained by the Radio Heritage Foundation **W**: radioheritage.net

NICARAGUA

L.T: UTC -6h — **Pop**: 5.8 million — **Pr.L**: Spanish — **E.C**: 60Hz, 120V — **ITU**: NCG

TELCOR – INSTITUTO NICARAGÜENSE DE TELECOMUNICACIONES Y CORREOS
☑ Ave. Bolívar Esquina Diagonal a la Cancillería, Managua
☎ +505 2222 7350 **W**: telcor.gob.ni

MW Call		kHz	kW	Station, location & h. of tr.
MA01)	A3OW	540	25	R. Corporación, Managua: 0950-0505
CH01)	A2RQ	570	5	R. Veritas 5-70, Chinandega: 1030-0250
MA02)	A3LP	580	10	R. 5-80, Managua: 1030-0000 (Sat 1200-, Sun 1100-)
MA03)	A3MD	600	10	La Nueva R. Ya, Managua: 1000-0600 (SS 24h)
MA04)	N	620	50	R. Nicaragua, Managua: 1000-0400
MA04)	A4LR	640	10	La Mera Mera , Managua

MW Call		kHz	kW	Station, location & h. of tr.
MT01)	A6RS	650	5	R. Muzun, Matagalpa: 1100-0100
GR01)	RD	650	10/8	R. Diriangén "La Super D", Granada: 0950-2300
MA25)		‡660	5	R. Máxima, Managua
ZE01)	RC	‡670		R. Caribe, Pto Cabezas
MA05)	AM	680	10/2	R. La Primerísima, Managua: 1045-0500 (SS -2400)
MT02)	RH	690	10/5	R. Hermanos, Matagalpa: 1000-0400
MA27)	MM	700	30	R. La Poderosa, Managua: 1100-0200, Sat 1100-2400, Sun 1200-2400
MA06)	A3RC	720	25	R. Católica, Managua: 1000-0430
MA07)	A3LS	740	50	R. Sandino "La S Grande", Managua: 1000-0400
MA26)	A3AR	760	10	R. Magic, Managua
MA08)	A3RO	800	50	R. 800, Managua: 0800-0500
MA09)	FAOL	820	20	R. Ondas de Luz, Managua: 1000-0400
MA10)	A3NT	840	5	R. Noticias, Managua: 1030-0200
MA26)	A3CO	860	5	La Gran Cadena, Managua
CT01)	CD	870	10	R. Centro, Juigalpa: 1100-0200
MA11)	A3EP	880	10	R. El Pensamiento, Managua: 1100-0300
MA12)	A3RT	900	5	R. Tiempo, Managua: 1050-0400
JI01)		910	5	R. Jinotega, Jinotega
MA13)	W	920	10	R. Mundial, Managua: 1100-0400
RS01)	ACTH	960	2.5	LV del Trópico Húmedo, San Carlos: 1000-0300
MA13)	A3NO	980	1	R. Redención Internac., Managua
MA15)	FF	1000	10	R. Hosanna R, Managua: 1200-0400
NS02)	FAVP	1010	5	R. LV del Pinar, Ocotal: 1100-0400
JI02)	VJ	1040	2	LV de Jinotega, Jinotega
MS02)	LL	1050	3	R. Masaya, Masaya
ZE03)		‡1060	1	LV del Atlántico, Bluefields
MA16)	A3LC	1080	10	R. 15 de Septiembre, Managua: 1100-0100
ES01)	HAAL	‡1090	5	R. Alma Latina, Estelí: 1100-0400
LE01)	F2MT	‡1110	1	R. Momotombo, La Paz Centro
MA17)	A3CP	1120	5	R. CEPAD "El Arco Iris del Amor", Managua: 1100-0100
NS03)		1130	0.5	Voz Evangélica de Jalapa, Jalapa
ES02)	HM	‡1160	1	R. Satélite, Estelí
CH03)	A6RB	1190	1	R. Bendición, Cayanlipe
MA18)	A3AC	1200		1200 La Radio, Managua
MA19)	A3RA	1220	1	R. América, Managua: 1200-0400
AS01)	MNG	1230	5	R. Manantial, Nueva Guinea: 1000-0300
MA20)	A3RR	1240	5	R. Vida Managua
ES03)	CR	1250	2.5	Cad. Radial Samaritano, Condega: 1000-0400
MT03)	RA	1270	3	R. Amistad, Matagalpa
MA21)	A2CC	1300	1	Canal 130 AM, Managua: 1200-2330
CH02)	SC	1310	10/1	R. San Cristóbal, Chinandega: 1000-0200
MT04)	A6RM	1330	5	R. Matagalpa, Matagalpa: 1100-0500
MA22)	OS	‡1340	1	R. Ondas Sonoras, Managua
MD01)	AARS	‡1370	1	R. Fronteras, Somoto
MA23)	A3MA	‡1400	10	R. María, Managua
LE02)	RA	1410	3/1	La Estación de la Amistad, León: 1000-0200
ES04)	AARL	1430	5	R. Liberación "La Tayacana", Estelí: 1100-0300
MA24)	A3MR	1440	25	R. Maranatha, Managua: 1000-0500
BO01)	RY	1470	1	R. Yarrince, Boaco
MA01)	PT	‡1500	1	R. Minuto, Managua
CA02)	A4TS	1530	0.5	LV de Sta Teresa, Sta Teresa: 1400-2200

Hrs of tr 24h except where shown. Call YN– ‡ = inactive, ± = varying fq

Addresses and other information:
AS00) ATLANTICO SUR
AS01) TELCOR, 1½ c este, Nueva Guinea
B000) BOACO
BO01) Casa del Finquero, 20 vrs al este, Boaco
CA00) CARAZO
CA02) Entrada II Calle, ½ c abajo, Sta Teresa
CH00) CHINANDEGA
CH01) Frente Iglesia de Guadalupe (or Ap. 12), Chinandega – **CH02)** Club Eden, 2½ c. Al Sur, (or Ap. 59), Chinandega – **CH03)** Cayanlipe
CT00) CHONTALES
CT01) Caracoles negros,Juigalpa **W**: radiocentro870.com
ES00) ESTELÍ
ES01) Esquina Norte de Hospital Adb, 2 c al norte, 3½ c este, Estelí– **ES02)** Esquina Sur-Oeste de la Escuela Nexo, 25 vrs al Río, Estelí –**ES03)** Instituto Biblico Samaritado, Calle Principal, Condega – **ES04)** Shell, 1 c al norte, Estelí **W**: radioliberacion.com
GR00) GRANADA
GR01) Cuerpo de Bomberos 1c al N 1c al E No. 110, Granada ☎+505 2552 2040
JI00) JINOTEGA
JI01) Escuela Gabriela Mistral, ½ al Norte, Avenida Ernesto Rosales, Jinotega. **W**: radiojinotega.hostoi.com – **JI02)** Cine Betty, 2½ c al norte, Jinotega

LE00) LEÓN
LE01) Del Pto del Mct, 1 c abajo, ½ c norte, León – **LE02)** Unan 1½ c al norte, León FM 91.9
MA00) MANAGUA
MA01) Cd. Jardín Q-20, Av. Ponciano Lombillo (Apartado Postal 2442), Managua **W:** radio-corporacion.com – **MA02)** Reparto El Carmen,Costado Oeste del Parque, Managua **W:** la580.com – **MA03)** Frente a la Universidad Centroamericana, Managua **W:** nuevaya. com.ni – **MA04)** Villa Fontana, Contiguo a TELCOR, Managua **W:** nicaragua620.com – **MA05)** Apartado Postal 4003 (or Barrio Bolonia, de Tica bus, 100 metros al sur, 100 metros al este), Managua **W:** radiolaprimerisima.com – **MA06)** Altamira D'Este 621, Managua **W:** radiocatolica.org – **MA07)** Paseo Tiscapa (or Ap. 4776), Managua **W:** rsandino.comi – **MA08)** Semaforos de Lozelsa 1c al lago, ½ abajo, Managua **W:** radio800.com – **MA09)** Costado Sur del Hospital Bautista N° 945, Managua – **MA10)** Ciudad Jardín, Casa N-10, Managua – **MA11)** Distribuidora Vicky, 4C Al lago, Casa 73, Managua **W:** radioelpensamiento.com – **MA12)** Los Robles Gimn Atlas, 1c al E. 20 vs Al S N° 217, Managua – **MA13)** Reparto Miraflores, Rest. Munich 4c Al lago 1 c al Oe, Managua – **MA14)** Calle Edgar Lang, Managua – **MA15)** Urb. de Puntaldía, Managua **W:** hosannaradio.info – **MA16)** Altamira de Este contiguo Embajada de Taiwán, Managua **W:** radio15deseptiembre.com – **MA17)** Apartado 3091, Managua– **MA18)** Managua – **MA19)** Foto Castillo 1 c Al sur ½ c, Villa Don Bosco E-182, Managua – **MA20)** Carret. Vieja a León, km 10 ¾, 500 m al N 200 al Oe, Managua **E:** vidaradio1240am.com – **MA21)** Carretera a Masaya, Km 12 ¾, 450 Metros al este, Managua – **MA22)** Bo La Cruz, Cine Blanca, 5c al N, ½ c al E, Casa 1112, Managua – **MA23)** De la Iglesia San Francisco 150 metros al este, Bolonia, Managua **W:** radiomaria.org/ni – **MA24)** Rotonda Metrocentro 1 c al sur, ½ C Abajo, Casa 41, Managua **W:** radiomaranatha.fm – **MA25)** Managua – **MA26)** RATENSA, Mansión Teodolinda, 2c al Oe, Managua – **MA27)** Managua **W:** radiolapoderosa700.com
MD00) MADRIZ
MD01) Somoto
MS00) MASAYA
MS01) Carr. a Managua km 24½, Masaya – **MS02)** Teatro Masaya, 1½ c al Oeste, N° 135, Masaya
MT00) MATAGALPA
MT01) Frente al Catedral, Matagalpa – **MT02)** Bo. Liberación Igl. Catedral. 1c al N 25 vs al Oe, Matagalpa **FM:** 92.3 **W:** radiohermanos. com – **MT03)** Detras de la Iglesia San José, Matagalpa – **MT04)** Rep. Brenes ½c al N, Matagalpa
NS00) NUEVA SEGOVIA
NS02) Perroquita Asunción, 1 cal norte, Ocotal **W:** radiolavozdelpinar. com **FM:** 100.9MHz Stereo Mogotón, 101.7MHz R. Sí. – **NS03)** Jalapa. 102.1MHz
RS00) RIO SAN JUAN
RS01) Costado Norte de la Iglesia Católica, San Carlos
ZE00) ZELAYA
ZE01) Barrio 19 de Julio, Pto Cabezas – **ZE03)** Frente al Palacio Municipal, Barrio Beholdsen, Bluefields

FM in Managua (MHz): 89.1 Exitos – 89.5 R. Visión – 89.9 Tropicálida – 90.5 Nicaragua – 90.9 La Marka –91.3 Futura – 91.7 La Primerísima – 92.1 Estación X – 92.7 Advent Estéreo – 93.1 La Buenísima – 93.5 Alfa Radio – 93.7 La Gran Cadena – 93.9 La Tigre – 94.3 Ondas de Luz – 94.7 Mujer – 95.1 La Pachanguera – 95.5 Amor – 95.9 Estéreo Ritmo – 96.3 La Gran Cadena – 96.7 Furia Magic – 97.1 Estéreo Mía – 97.5 Corporación – 97.9 Salsa 98 – 98.3 R. Viva – 98.7 Romántica – 99.1 R. Ya – 99.5 Universidad – 99.9 María – 100.7 Tuani – 100.7 Disney – 101.1 Güegüense – 101.5 Juvenil – 101.9 R. Clásica – 102.3 Universidad – 102.7 Magic – 103.1 Bautista – 103.5 Maranatha – 103.9 Joya FM – 104.3 Estrella del Mar – 104.7 Hit – 105.1 Mi Preferida – 105.5 Rock FM – 105.9 Rica – 106.3 Galaxia, La Picosa – 106.7 Eco Romántico – 107.1 Sol – 107.5 Sandino – 107.9 Restauración

NIGER

LT: UTC +1h — **Pop:** 14 million — **Pr.L:** French, Hausa, Zarma, Tamashek, Fulfulde, Arabic etc. — **E.C:** 50Hz, 220V — **ITU:** NGR

CONSEIL SUPÉRIEUR DE LA COMMUNICATION (CSC)
⌨ Plateau I, Niamey ☎+227 20 722356 🖷 +227 20 722667 **LP:** Chmn: Daouda Diallo. Vice Chmn: Hamidou Kô.
LA VOIX DU SAHEL – OFFICE DE RADIODIFFUSION-TÉLÉVISION DU NIGER (ORTN, Gov.)
⌨ Maison de la Radio, B.P. 361, Niamey ☎+227 20 722272 🖷 +227 20 722548 **W:** ortn.ne **E:** ortny@ortn-niger.com **LP:** DG: Amadou Harouna Yayé. Dir. Voix du Sahel: Mahaman Chamsou Maïgary. Gen. Secr: Mrs. Diaffra Fadimou Moumouni. Tech. Dir: Maraka Laouali.

MW: Niamey (Goudel) 1125kHz 20kW. (inactive)
SW: Niamey (Goudel) 9705kHz 40kW (inactive).
FM (MHz): Maradi 88.4, Doutchi 89.7, Niamey 91.3, Zinder 91.3 2.5kW, Diffa 92.0, B. Konni 96.2, Madaoua 97.2, Tillaberi 99.0 10kW, Dosso 99.8, Tahoua 100.0, Agadez 106.8. All 1kW if not given otherwise. In addition 16 txs under 1kW.
D.Prgr in French/ethnic: 0500-2300 (Sun -2200). Local prgrs: 0700-1130 & 1500-1700. **N. in French:** 0545, 1200, 1900. **IS:** Local flute.
Ann: F:"Ici la Voix du Sahel", A: "Idha'at al-Jumhuriya al-Niger, Sawt as-Sahel min Niamey".

Other Stations:
Alternative FM: Niamey/Agadez/Zinder: 99.4MHz. **W:** alternativeniger.org – **Anfani FM:** Niamey/Birni Nkonni/Diffa/Maradi/Zinder 100.0MHz 1.5kW. **W:** anfani-info.com – **Dounia FM,** Niamey: 89.0MHz 3kW. **E:** radioteledounianiger@yahoo.fr – **Espoir FM,** Niamey: 101MHz **W:** espoirfm@iniger.com – **La Voix de l'Hemicycle,** Niamey: 95.1MHz – **Radio & Musique (R&M)**: Niamey: 104.5MHz 1kW **E:** retm@intnet.ne – **R. Bonferey,** Niamey: 105.0MHz 1kW **W:** sites. google.com/a/bonferey.com/www – **R. Dounia,** Niamey: 99.0MHz 1kW. **E:** nodiabaoba@yahoo.fr – **R. Saraounia**, Niamey/Birnin Konni/ Madoua/Maradi/Tahoua: 102.1MHz – **Sahara FM,** Agadez: 97.0 **W:** radiosahara.blog.fr – **Tambara FM,** Niamey: 107.0MHz 0.5kW **E:** tambarafm@yahoo.fr – **Ténére FM,** Niamey/Agadez/Diffa/Dosso/ Maradio/Tahoua/Tillaberi/Zinder: 98.0MHz 1kW.
R. Rurale stations on FM in Agadez, Bankilaré, Diffa, Dosso, Gaya, Maradi, Niamey, Tahoua, Tillabéri, Zinder.
BBC African Sce, Niamey: 100.4MHz.
CRI: Niamey 106.0MHz, Agadez/Maradi/Zinder: fq not known.
RFI Afrique: Niamey/Agadez/Diffa/Maradi/Tahoua/Zinder 96.2MHz

NIGERIA

L.T: UTC +1h — **Pop**: 150 million — **Pr.L:** English, Yoruba, Hausa, Igbo — **E.C:** 50Hz, 230V — **ITU**: NIG

NATIONAL BROADCASTING COMMISSION (NBC)
⌨ Road 14, Badagry Rd, Gwarinpa, Abuja ☎+234 1 2647867 **W:** nbc. gov.ng **L.P:** DG: Yomi Bolarinwa **LP:** DG: Mr. Emeka Mba. Dir. Pub. Aff: Malam Awwal Salihu.

FEDERAL RADIO CORPORATION OF NIGERIA (Gov.)
⌨ Radio House, Herbert Macauley Way, Area 10, PMB 452, Garki, Abuja, Federal Capital Territory ☎+234 9 2341103 🖷 +234 9 2346486 **W:** radionigeriaonline.com **E:** kns@radionigeria.net **LP:** DG: Malam Muhammad Ladan Salihu. Dir. Eng. Sces: Ibrahim Abdullahi.
1) FRCN Lagos, Broadcasting House, P.M.B. 12504, Ikoyi, Lagos, Lagos State. ☎+234 1 2690301-5. L.P: Exec. Dir: Prince Atilade Atoyebi. R. One in English. **NB:** Nigerian N. from Lagos or Abuja at 0600, 1500 & 2100 is relayed by all FRCN stations and most state stations. Ann: "This is R. Nigeria, Lagos". Metro FM in English: 0500-2300 on 97.6MHz 20kW. Bond FM in Pidgin/English/Yoruba/Hausa/Igbo on 92.9MHz 20kW: 0430-2300 – **2) FRCN Abuja**, Broadcasting House, Gwangwalada, P.M.B. 71, Abuja, Federal Capital Territory ☎+234 9 88210410 L.P: Exec. Dir: Shuaibu Ibrahim. D.Prgr: 0530-2305 (7275kHz inactive) in English/Hausa/Igbo/Yoruba and others. Local N. in English 0500, 1700. Ann: "This is R. Nigeria, Abuja". – **3) FRCN Enugu**, Broadcasting House, Onitsha Rd, P.M.B. 1051, Enugu, Enugu State ☎+234 42 254400 🖷 + 234 42 254173 L.P: Exec. Dir: Eddy Agwuegbo. 0430-2315 in English/Igbo/Tiv/Efik/Izon – **4) FRCN Ibadan**, Broadcasting House, Oba Adebimpe Rd, P.M.B. 5003, Dugbe, Ibadan, Oyo State ☎+234 2 2414093 🖷 + 234 2 2413930 **W:** radionigeriaibadan.net **E:** info@radionigeriaibadan.net L.P: Exec. Dir: Princess Banke Ademola. D.Prgr: 0430-2305 in English/Yoruba/ Edo/Igala/Urhobo. Ann: "R. Nigeria Ibadan, Station with distinction" – **5) FRCN Kaduna**, No. 7 Yakubu Gowon Way, P.O.Box 250, Kaduna, Kaduna State **W:** radionigeriakaduna.net ☎+234 62 235390 🖷 + 234 62 245392 **L.P:** Ag. Zonal Dir: Alhaji Muhammad Sani Suleiman. Chief Tech. Officer: Shehu A. Muhammad. Ch. 1 in Hausa: 0430-2300 on 594/6090kHz. Ch. 2 in English/Hausa/Fulfulde/Kanuri/Nupe: 0430-2300 on 1107kHz. Supreme FM in English: 0500-2400 on 96.1MHz. Karama FM in Hausa: 92.1MHz. Ann: "This is R. Nigeria, Kaduna".

MW	kHz	kW	MW	kHz	kW
4) Aloho	567	50	3) Enugu	828	100
4) Moniya	576	25	2) Gwagwalada	909	50
5) Jaji	594	200	5) Jaji	1107	25
4) Ibadan	657	100			
SW	kHz	kW			
5) Kaduna	†6090	50			

FM (MHz): **1)** 92.9/97.6 **2)** 93.5 **3)** 92.85 **4)** 93.4 **5)** 92.1/96.1.
Further federal FM stations (MHz): Abakaliki 101.5, Abeokuta

94.5, Akure 102.5, Asaba 104.5, Awka 102.5, Bauchi 98.5, Benin 101.5, Benue (Makurdi)103.5, Bida (Minna) 100.5, Birnin-Kebbi 103.5, Maiduguri (Borno) 102.5, Calabar 99.5, Damaturu 104.5, Dutse 100.5, Ado-Ekiti 100.5, Gombe 103.5, Gusau 102.5, Kano 103.5, Kastina 104.5, Ilesha 95.5, Ilorin 103.3, Jalingo 100.5, Lafia 102.5, Lokoja 101.5, Osogbo 93.5, Owerri 100.5, Port-Harcourt 98.5, Sokoto 101.5, Umuahia103.5, Uyo 104, Yenogoa 101.5, Yola 101.5.
Aso FM: Abuja: 93.5MHz. **W:** asoradioonline.com

STATE RADIO AND OTHER STATIONS:

MW	Location	kHz	kW	MW	Location	kHz	kW
17)	Sokoto	540	50	43)	Yola	917	50
37)	Ado	549	25	10)	Makurdi	918	50
13)	Owerri	567	50	27)	Birnin Kebbi	945	10
9)	Maiduguri	603	50	25)	Katsina	972	25
18)	Abeokuta	603	25	35)	Otite	972	10
16)	Ilorin	612	50	20)	Ikeja	990	10
8)	Katabu	639	50	21)	Bauchi	990	50
14)	Jogana	729	50	12)	Kontagora	1008	10
42)	Kaduna	747	60	34)	Iree	1008	10
15)	Ibadan	756	100	33)	Dutse	1026	25
27)	Zuru	801	1	23)	Ugaga	1134	20
30)	Damaturu	801	20	31)	Jalingo	1269	10

FM (MHz): **6)** 96.1 **7)** 95.8 **8)** 89.9/90.9 **9)** 95.3 **10)** 95.0 **11)** 95.8 **12)** 91.2 **13)** 94.4 **14)** 89.3 **15)** 98.5 **16)** 99.0 **17)** 96.4 **18)** 91.4 **19)** 96.5 **20)** 107.5 **21)** 94.6 **22)** 99.1 **23)** 92.7 **24)** 90.5 **26)** 90.5 **28)** 88.5 **29)** 88.6/97.9 **31)** 90.6 **32)** 88.1 **34)** 89.5 **35)** 94.0 **36)** 97.1 **37)** 91.5 **38)** 97.3 **39)** 96.8 **41)** 98.1

State Radio information:
6) Enugu State Broadc. Sce (ESBS), Broadcasting House, Independence Layout, P.M.B. 01600, Enugu, Enugu State. Prgr 1 on M**W:** 0430-2300 in English/others. Prgr. 2 on FM ("Sunrise 96"): 0500-2100 – **7)** Edo State Broadc. Sce, P.M.B. 1012, Aduwawa, Benin City, Edo State. 0400-2305 in English + 12 local languages – **8)** Kaduna State Media Corp. (KSMC), Wurno/Rabah Road, PMB 2013, Kaduna North, Kaduna State. Kada 1 AM: 0430-2315 in English/Hausa on 639kHz. Kada 2 on 89.9MHz. Capital Sound on 90.9MHz **W:** ksmc.com.ng – **9)** Borno Radio & TV Corp., P.M.B. 1020, Broadcasting House, Along Shehu Laminu Way, Maiduguri, Borno State **E:** brtvnews@yahoo.com 0400-2305 in English/Hausa/Kanuri/Marghi/Suwa/Babur-Bura – **10)** R. Benue, P.M.B. 102202, Makurdi, Benue State. Prgr. 1: 0430-2305 in English/others. Prgr. 2 on FM: 0500-2105. Ann: "This is R. Benue, Makurdi" – **11)** Adamawa Broadc. Corp. (ABC), P.M.B. 2123, Yola, Adamawa State. 0430-2100 in English/Hausa + 6 Nigerian languages. Ann: "This is GBC Yola, your No. 1 Radio Station" – **12)** Niger State Media Corp., Radio House, Ibrahim Babangida St, P.M.B. 88, Minna, Niger State **E:** radioniger@yahoo.com 0430-2130 in English/others – **13)** Imo Broadc. Corp., Ebu Rd, P.O. Box 329, Owerri, Imo State. Prgr. 1: 0425-2305 on MW. Prgr. 2: 0440-2305 on FM. English: 0430-0630, 1100-1830, 2100-2300 (Sat/Sun 0100), other times Igbo – **14)** Kano State BC, 1 Ibrahim Taiwo Rd, Gidan Bello Dandago, P.M.B. 3014, Kano, Kano State. **W:** radiokanoonline.com Prgr. 1 on MW: 0430-2320. Prgr. 2: on FM: 0550-2320 in English/Hausa. Ann: "Radio Kano" – **15)** Broadc. Corp. of Oyo State, P.M.B. 1, Akodi Post Office, Ibadan, Oyo State. Prgr. 1: 0400-2200 in English/Yoruba. Prgr 2: on FM: 0700-2100. Ann: "R. O-y-o" – **16)** Kwara State Broadc. Corp, Akpata Yakuba, P.M.B. 1345, Ilorin, Kwara State. 0400-2305 in English/others – **17)** Sokoto State BC, Moliba Adamawa Rd, Tudua Wada, P.M.B. 2156, Sokoto, Sokoto State. 0430-2305 in English/Hausa. Ann: "Rima Radio" – **18)** Ogun State BC, Ibara Housing Estate, P.M.B. 2084, Abeokuta, Ogun State. OGBC1 on MW, OGBC2 on FM: 0400-2400 in English/Yoruba – **19)** Ondo State Radio Corp, Broadcasting House, Oba-Ile, P.M.B. 709, Akure, Ondo State. 0400-2300 in English/others – **20)** Lagos State Broadc. Corp, Obafemi Awolowo Way, P.M.B. 21035, Ikeja, Lagos State. 0430-0005 in English/Yoruba. Ann: "NBC" – **21)** Bauchi Radio Corp, 18 Ahmadu Bello Way, P.M.B. 0133, Bauchi, Bauchi State. **W:** brcbauchi.info Prgr 1: 0430-2300 on MW, Prgr. 2: 24h on 94.6MHz and 10 other txs. 846 kHz being renovated – **22)** Rivers State Broadc. Corp, 4 Degema St, P.M.B. 5170, Port Harcourt, Rivers State. Prgr. 1: 0450-2310 on MW, Prgr. 2: 0450-2310 on FM in English/others – **23)** Cross River State Broadc. Corp. (CRBC), No. 8 IBB Way, P.M.B. 1035, Calabar, Cross River State **E:** crbc@skannet.com 0430-2315 in English/others – **24)** Plateau Radio & TV Corp. (PRTVC), 5 Joseph Gomwalk Rd, P.M.B. 2043, Jos, Plateau State. Ch. 1 on MW: 0500-2300, Ch. 2 on FM: 0500-2300 in English/others. Ann: "This is Radio Plateau 1 AM", "This is Radio Plateau 2, 90.5 FM Stereo" – **25)** Katsina State Radio & TV Sces (KSRTV), Former SDP State Headquarters, Batsari Rd, P.M.B. 2163, Katsina, Katsina State. 0430-2300 in English/others. Ann: "This is Katsina State R." – **26)** Akwa Ibom Broadc. Corp, 205 Aka Rd, P.M.B. 1122, Uyo, Akwa Ibom State. 0500-2300 in English/others – **27)** R. Kebbi, km 9 Kalgo Rd, Birnin Kebbi, Kebbi State. 0500-2300 in English/others – **28)** Anambra Broadc. Sce (ABS), off Arroma Junction, P.M.B. 5070, Awka, Anambra State. 0500-2300 in English/Igbo – **29)** Delta State Broadc. Sce, Broadc. House P.M.B. 5032, Asaba, Delta State. 0500-2300 in English/others – **30)** Yobe Broadc. Corp, km 6 Gujba Rd, P.M.B. 1044, Damaturu, Yobe State. 0500-2300 in English/others – **31)** Taraba State Broadc. Sces, Broadc. House, adjacent Gen. Sani Abacha State Secretariat, P.M.B. 1038, Jalingo, Taraba State. 0500-2300 in English/others – **32)** Broadc. Corp. of Abia State (BCA), Broadc. House, Government Station Layout, B.M.P. 7276, Umuahia, Abia State. **W:** bcanigeria.com 0500-2300 in English/Igbo – **33)** Jigawa Broadc. Corp., Broadc. House, Kiyawa Rd, P.M.B. 7032, Dutse, Jigawa State. 0500-2205 **W:** facebook.com/pages/Radio-Jigawa/1537960919805870?ref=ts – **34)** Osun State Broadc. Corp, Studio 1, Ita-Akogun St, P.M.B. 4425, Osogbo, Osun State. 0500-2300 in English/others – **35)** Kogi State Broadc. Corp, 1 Danladi Zakari Rd, P.M.B. 1095 GRA, Lokoja, Kogi State. 0500-2300 in English/others. Ann: "R. Kogi" – **36)** Nasawara Broadc. Sce (NBS), Tudun K. Nasarawa auri, Makurdi Rd, P.M.B. 97, Lafia, Nasarawa State. 24h in English/others – **37)** Broadc. Sce of Ekiti State, Old Ado Ekiti Local Government Secretariat, Okeyinmi, P.M.B. 5343, Ado, Ekiti State – **38)** Bayelsa State Broadc. Corp, P.M.B. 56, Ekeki, Yenagoa, Bayelsa State. "Glory FM" in English/others – **39)** Gombe State Broadc. Sce, Buhari Estate Rd, GRA, Gombe, Gombe State. 0500-2300 English/others – **40)** Zamfara State R, Mall. Yahaya Secretariat, Off Zaria Road, P.M.B. 01007, Gusau, Zamfara State – **41)** Ebonyi Broadcasting Service (EBBS), Ministry of Information Building, Government House Annex, Abakaliki, Ebonyi State – **42) Nagarta R**, Nagarta Communications Complex, Katabu, Mararraban, Jos, P.O. Box 574, Kaduna. **W:** nagartaradio.tripod.com **E:** nagartaradio@yahoo.com – **43) R. Gotel**, P.O. Box 5759, Modire (After Yola Bridge), Off Yola-Mubi Expressway, Jimeta-Yola, Adamawa State. **W:** radiogotelyola.com **E:** info@radiogotelyola.com D.Prgr: 0500-2305.

EXTERNAL SCE: Voice of Nigeria: see International Radio section.

Other stations:
Alheri R: Kaduna 97.7MHz **W:** ditvalheriradiokaduna.9f.com – **Brila FM:** Abuja/Lagos/Kaduna/Onitsha 88.9MHz **W:** brilafm.net – **Choice FM:** 103.5MHz – **Cool FM,** 267A, AIM Plaza, Etim Inyang Crescent Victoria Island Annex.P.M.B. 10096, Victoria Island, Lagos: Port Harcourt 95.9, Abuja/Lagos 96.9MHz. **W:** coolfm.us – **Cosmo FM,** Plot 18, Pocket Estate, Independence Layout, Enugu: 105.5MHz – **Defence FM** (Mil), Abuja: 107.7MHz – **Eko-FM,** Lagos: 89.75MHz – **Freedom R:** Kaduna 92.9MHz, Dutse/Kano 99.5MHz **W:** freedomradionig.com – **Independent R,** Benin City: 92.3MHz **W:** itvradionigeria.com – **Liberty R,** Kaduna 91.7MHz – **Naija FM,** Ibadan/Lagos: 102.7MHz **W:** naija102.com – **Ray Power 1:** Lagos/Abuja 100.5MHz. **Ray Power 2:** Lagos/Kano 106.5MHz + rel. in other towns (Incl. rel. of BBC African Sce in English/Hausa) – **Rhythm FM,** 17A Commercial Ave, Yaba, Lagos: 93.7MHz – **Rhythm 94.7,** Hilltop, Karu, Abuja: 94.7MHz – **Space FM,** Ibadan: 90.1MHz **W:** spacefm901.org.ng – **Splash FM,** Ibadan: 105.5MHz **W:** splashfm1055.com – **The Beat:** Ibadan: 97.9MHz. Lagos 99.9MHz **W:** thebeat97.com thebeat99.com – **Wazobia FM:** for addr. see Cool FM above. Port Harcourt 94.1MHz, Lagos 95.1MHz, Abuja 99.5MHz. **W:** wazobiafm.com – **Vo Women:** Lagos 91.7MHz **W:** wfm917.com **F.PI:** transmitters in other states.

NB: 17 community radio stations also in operation

NIUE

L.T: UTC -11h — **Pop:** 1,311 — **Pr.L:** Niuean, English — **E.C:** 50Hz, 230V — **ITU:** NIU

BROADCASTING CORPORATION OF NIUE (BCN)
P.O. Box 68, Alofi, Niue, South Pacific. Studio: Fonuakula, Alofi ☎ +683 4226 ☐ +683 4217 **E:** sunshine@mail.gov.nu
L.P: CEO: Trevor Tiakia
FM: 91.0MHz 0.5kW, 102.0MHz 0.1kW
D.Prgr: Mon-Sat. N: international news bulletins from R. Australia/RNZI 1800, 1900, 0200 **Ann:** "This is Radio Sunshine"

Other Stations:
1) Oka Rock FM, Alofi 107.9MHz , OKA-KOA Multimedia Systems, Commercial Centre, PO Box 5, Alofi, Niue, South Pacific. ☎ +683 4379 **W:** niuemusic.com **E:** sales@niuemusic.com **D.Prgr:** 24/7 incl. **Sunday** gospel music and evening jazz

NORFOLK ISLAND (Australia)

L.T: UTC +11h — **Pop:** 2,169 — **Pr.L:** English, Pitcairn Norfolk — **E.C:** 50Hz, 220V — **ITU:** NFK

AUSTRALIAN BROADCASTING CORP. (ABC)
See Australia. 24h satellite relay.

FM (MHz)	Call	kW	Station
91.9	2ABCRN	0.15	R. National [stereo]
93.9	2ABCFM	0.05	ABC Classic FM [stereo]
95.9	2ABCRR	0.15	ABC Local R (Western Plains, Dubbo, NSW)
98.2	2JJJ	0.25	Triple J [stereo]

Other Stations

AM	kHz	Call	kW	Station
1)	1566	VL2NI	0.1	R. Norfolk

FM	MHz	Call	kW	
1)	89.9	VL2NI	0.25	R. Norfolk [stereo]

Addresses and other information
1) Norfolk Island Broadcasting Sce. (Local Gov.). New Cascade Road (PO Box 456), Norfolk Island 2899, Australia ☎ +6723 22137 **M:** +6723 50806 🖷 +6723 23298 **E:** manager@radio.gov.nf & news@radio.gov.nf **L.P:** Louci Reynolds ASM Gary Summerscales Contract Tech. **D.Prgr:** 1930-0500 M-F, 1930-0030 Sat-Sun **MW:** relay R. New Zealand National rnz.co.nz from Wellington via satellite overnight daily 0500-1930 **FM:** relay MW during the day, pre-programmed music nightly M-F from 0500 but with variety of volunteer anncrs with individual prgrs daily except Wed during the evenings at various times otherwise pre-programmed music. **V:** responds promptly to email reports.

NORTHERN MARIANA ISLANDS (USA Commonwealth)

L.T: UTC +10h — **Pop:** 51,483 — **Pr.L:** English, Chamorro, Carolinian, Filipino — **E.C:** 60Hz, 110V — **ITU:** MRA

FEDERAL COMMUNICATIONS COMMISSION (FCC)
see USA for details

MW	kHz	kW	Station	MW	kHz	kW	Station
1)	1080	5	KCNM	2)	1440	1.1	KKMP
FM	**MHz**	**kW**	**Station**	**FM**	**MHz**	**kW**	**Station**
3)	88.1	1.8	KRNM	4)	97.9	6.5	KPXP
3)	89.1	0.25	KRNM	4)	99.5	6.5	KZGU*
6)	89.9	1.8	KORU	5)	100.3	1.1	KWAW
3)	90.7	0.62	KCKD	1)	103.9	3.2	KZMI
3)	91.5	0.06	KMOP				* serves Guam
2)	92.1	0.01	KKMP				

Addresses and other information:
1) Choice Broadcasting Company LLC, PO Box 500914, Saipan 96950-0914 ☎ +1 671 2347239 🖷 +1 671 2340447 **Format: KCNM:** News/Talk **KZMI:** Adult Contemporary **L.P:** GM Bob Webb **Prgr:** 24h – **2) Blue Continent Communications Inc.** PO Box 500815, Saipan 96950-0815 ☎ +1 670 233 1440 **W:** cnmiradio.com **E:** kkmp670@gmail. com **L.P:** CEO: Rosemond Santos, VP: Gary Sword **Format:** 'Strickly Island' Islands Music – **3) Marianas Educational Media Services Inc** Sunny Plaza, 125 Tun Jesus Crisostomo St #301, Tamuning GU 96913 **E:** darryl@guamtelecom.com **L.P:** CEO: Robert F Kelly, Community Radio Mgr: Darryl Taggerty **Format: KRNM 88.1** Chalan Kanoa simulcast 24h KPRG Guam **KRNM 89.1** Capital Hill simulcast 24h KPRG Guam **Format:** NPR, Public Radio International and BBC World Service **KCKD: Format:** relay WCPE Wake Forest NC **W:** theclassicalstation.org 24h classical music **KMOP: Format:** Melodies of Prayer **W:** melodiesofprayer.com 24h religious – **4) Sorensen Pacific Broadcasting Inc.** PPP415 Box 10000, Saipan 96950 ☎ +1 670 2357996 🖷+1 670 2357998 **W:** sorensenmediagroup.com **L.P:** SM: Tina Palacios **Format: KZGU** 'The Shark' [licenced to Garapan but actually serves Guam and has CP for 17.5kw at Mangilao, Guam] **KPXP:** 'Power99' Top 40/Islands Music [STA 1.5kw because of typhoon damage] **Prgr:** 24h – **5) Magic 100FM.** 1st Fl, Naru Building, Susupe, Saipan 96950 ☎ +1 670 2345929 🖷 +1 670 2342262 **W:** magic100radio.com **E:** kwaw100.3@magic100radio. com **D.Prgr:** 24h – **6) Good News Broadcasting Corp.** 290 Chalan Palasyo, Agana Heights, GU 96910 ☎ +1 671 472 1111 🖷+1 671 4774678 **W:** joyfmguam.com **L.P:** GM: Matthew Dodd **Format:** simulcast 24h KSDA-FM Guam religious Joy FM Family Friendly Radio

NORWAY

L.T: UTC +1h (27 Mar-30 Oct: +2h) — **Pop:** 5.2 million — **Pr.L:** Norwegian — **EC:** 50Hz, 230V — **ITU:** NOR

NORWEGIAN COMMUNICATIONS AUTHORITY
🖃 PB 93, NO-4791 Lillesand ☎+47 22824600 🖷 +47 22824640 **W:** nkom.no

NORKRING (Transmission provider)
🖃 PB 1, NO-1331 Fornebu ☎+47 67892000 🖷 +47 67893611 **W:** norkring.no

NRK - NORSK RIKSKRINGKASTING AS (Pub.)
🖃 NO-0340 Oslo ☎+47 23047000 🖷+47 23047575 **Inf.Dpt:** ☎+47 81565900 **E:** info@nrk.no **W:** nrk.no
L.P: DG: Thor Gjermund Eriksen

LW	kHz	R	kW		
Ingøy	153	b	100		

FM	P1	R	P2	R	P3	kW
Alta	89.7	b	94.6	Þ	91.3	3.5
Bagn	91.7	h	95.3		88.0	35
Bangsberget	90.4	h				4.1
Bergen	89.1	d	94.8		99.0	46
Bjerkreim	94.2	i	98.7		91.8	60
Bokn	93.5	i	97.3		91.1	120
Bremanger	93.6	j	98.1		91.3	46
Dikkevikfjell	87.8	b	93.4	Þ	95.0	1.4
Førde	92.8	j	88.7		97.1	12
Gamlemsvet	91.9	e	96.3		90.0	50
Gausta	89.5	m	96.4		99.7	55
	101.1	a				6.7
Greipstad	88.8	k	92.5		97.0	57.5
Grong	91.9	g	96.6		88.9	95
Gulen	88.0	j	94.5		97.6	39
Hadsel	92.4	f	99.3		94.5	30
Halden	94.8	p	89.1		101.5	72.5
Hammerfest	96.6	b	87.7	Þ	93.6	24
Hasvik	90.1	b	99	Þ	94.9	2
Hemnes	88.5	f	99.8		96.1	36
Hestmannen	97.0	f	90.7		93.5	1.2
Hovdefjell	87.8	k	93.7		95.0	25
Hvitingen	91.7	o				2.76
Iskuras	88.7	b	96.1	Þ	92.0	2.2
Jetta	95.9	h	99.5		91.1	85
Kappfjell	95.5	f	99.4		93.4	1.3
Karasjok	87.9	b	94.7	Þ		1.5
Kautokeino	90.3	b	93.8	Þ	99.2	35
Kistefjell	91.8	n	95.7	Þ	99.8	44
Kongsberg	91.3	a	95.5		§97.8	60/30§
Kongsvinger	89.8	c	93.9		96.1	33
	98.9	q				11
Kopparen	88.1		94.5		96.0	40
Lyngdal	97.6	k	88.3		95.0	50
Lyngen	93.3	n	97.5	Þ		4.2
Lønahorgi	93.3	d	88.3		96.7	48
Melhus	92.4	l	97.2		99.1	60
Mosvik	90.9	g	98.4		93.4	33
Narvik	88.8	f	98.9	Þ	91.1	90
Nordfjordeid	89.4	j	99.3		92.3	12
Nordhue	87.6	c	§97.1		92.5	70/60§
Nordkapp	89.2	b	95.4	Þ	98.2	15
Oslo	88.7	q	100.0		93.5	90
Reinsfjell	89.1	e	95.1		90.7	24
Salten	93.3	f	95.5		89.8	48
Skien	88.2	m	92.3		100.4	80
	90.3	o				7.25
Sogndal	91.5	j	95.1		98.7	25
Sprinklerfjell	94.1	o				84
Steigen	90.3	f	97.8	Þ	93.9	102/106/107
Stord	96.0	d	99.6		92.6	60
Store Jekkir	99.9	b	97.3	Þ	90.9	1.2/1.16/1.13
Tana	92.5	b	97.0	Þ	91.1	24
Trolltind	88.2	n	94.0	Þ	90.5	50
Tron	98.3	c	88.6		94.3	24
Varanger	88.1	b	91.8	Þ	100.2	30
Vega	89.3	f	95.2		98.2	55
Åndalsnes			99.9			2.2

+ more than 1800 lp txs less than 1kW Þ) carries Sámi R.
a-q) refers to reg prgrs listed below

FM	AN	AK	MP3	FM	AN	AK	MP3
Alta	90.8	93.4	96.3	Oslo	93.0	91.9	97.0
Bangsberget	88.4	93.3	93.2	Porsgrunn	95.8	97.4	90.8
Bergen	93.8	98.2	95.4	Stavanger	93.0	99.3	96.6
Bodø	94.8	90.9	97.2	Tromsø	89.8	94.4	96.8
Bokn	95.6	89.4	92.2	Trondheim	94.9	96.3	92.7
Fredrikstad	90.7	-	87.6	Vadsø	90.7	88.8	92.2
Kristiansand	94.0	98.6	95.7				

Transmitter powers 40W-3kW, typically 50-200W

P1:🖃 NO-7005 Trondheim ☎+47 73881400 🖷 +47 73881809 24h on FM and DAB. **N:** MF on the h also 0530, 0630, 0730, 1130,

1530, 1630. Sat on the h also 0630, 1130. Sun on the h also 0430. Regional prgrs: see below

P2: ✉ NO-0340 Oslo ☎+47 23047297 🗎 +47 23047480
24h cultural prgr on FM and DAB. **N:** MF on the h 0500-0000 except 1800, 1900 2000 and 2200. Also 0530, 0630, 0730, 1130, 1630. Sat: on the h. 0500-0000 except 0900, 1200, 1800, 1900, 2000. Also 0630, 1130, 1530. Sun: on the h 0500-2300 except 1200, 1300, 1600, 1800, 1900. Also 1530.

P3: ✉ NO-7005 Trondheim ☎+47 73881600 🗎 +47 73881609
24h youth prgr on FM and DAB. Rly P1 2300-0500. **N:** MF on the h 0500-2300 except 1600, 1800, 2000, 2200, also 0530, 0630, 0730, 0830. Sat: on the h except 1600, 1800, 2000, 2100, 2200. Sun: on the h except 2200

Sámi NRK Sámiradio (special prgrs in Lappish): ✉ PB 183, NO-9730 Karasjok ☎+47 78469200 🗎 +47 78469223

D.Prgr: P1: Sun 2030-2100 (in Norwegian). P2: MF 1230-1300. Additional prgrs on P2 in northern Norway (marked Þ in the frequency table) plus 90.1MHz (122W) in Oslo: MF 0600-0800, 1300-1630, (Fri also1200-1230, 1630-1700), Sat/sun 1700-1800

AK: NRK Alltid Klassisk: ✉ NO-0340 Oslo ☎+47 23047882 🗎 +47 23048575. 24h FM and DAB. Classical music channel. Some rly P2

AN: NRK Alltid Nyheter): ✉ NO-0340 Oslo ☎+47 23047000 🗎 +47 23045141 24h rolling news sce on FM and DAB. Rly BBC World Service most of the day Sat/Sun and 2100-0500 weekdays

MP3: NRK MPETRE: ✉ NO-7005 Trondheim ☎+47 73881600 🗎 +47 73881609. 24h teenager channel based on techno/dance music on FM and DAB. Some rly of P3

NRK REGIONAL SERVICES:

On **P1**. D.Prgr: MF 0503-0530, 0533-0600, 0603-0630, 0640-0700, 0703-0730, 0733-0800, 0903-0905, 1003-1005, 1103-1105, 1203-1205, 1303-1400, 1405-1500, 1503-1600. Sat: 0703-0705, 0803-0805, 0903-0905 **a)** NRK Buskerud, PB 733 Strømsø, NO-3003 Drammen: 91.3/101.1MHz Some shared prgr with Telemark and Vestfold, as NRK Østafjells. – **b)** NRK Finnmark, PB 1333, NO-9506 Alta: **153kHz**, 87.9/88.1/88.7/89.2/89.790.1//90.3/92.5/96.9/99.9MHz Some shared prgr with Troms and Nordland. – **c+h)** NRK Hedmark og Oppland, PB 174, NO-2601 Lillehammer: 90.4/91.7/ 95.9MHz and NO-2418 Elverum: 87.6/89.8/98.3MHz Separate news hrly, remaining prgrs shared – **d)** NRK Hordaland, PB 7777, NO-5020 Bergen: 89.1/93.3/ 96.0MHz – **e)** NRK Møre og Romsdal, PB 1516, NO-6025 Ålesund: 89.1/91.9MHz – **f)** NRK Nordland, PB 1446, NO-8038 Bodø: 88.5/88.8/89.3/90.3/92.4/93.3/95.5/97.0MHz Some shared prgr with Finnmark and Troms.– **g+l)** NRK Trøndelag, PB 2450 Sluppen, NO-7005 Trondheim: 88.3/92.4MHz and Løshalla 15, NO-7712 Steinkjer: 90.9/ 91.9MHz Some separate newsbulletins, remaining prgrs shared – **i)** NRK Rogaland, PB 614, NO-4090 Hafrsfjord: 93.5/94.2MHz – **j)** NRK Sogn og Fjordane, PB 100, NO-6801 Førde: 88.0/89.4/91.5/ 92.8/93.6MHz – **k)** NRK Sørlandet, PB 413, NO-4664 Kristiansand: 87.8/88.8/97.6MHz– **m)** NRK Telemark, PB 284, NO-3901 Porsgrunn: 88.2/89.5MHz Some shared prgr with Buskerud and Vestfold, as NRK Østafjells. – **n)** NRK Troms, PB 6138 Langnes, NO-9291 Tromsø: 88.2/91.8/ 93.3MHz Some shared prgr with Finnmark and Nordland. – **o)** NRK Vestfold, PB 120, NO-3101 Tønsberg: 90.3/91.7/94.1MHz Some shared prgr with Buskerud and Telemark, as NRK Østafjells. – **p)** NRK Østfold, PB 33, NO-1629 Gamle Fredrikstad: 94.8MHz – **q)** NRK Østlandssendingen, PB 4555 Nydalen, NO-0421 Oslo: 88.7/98.9MHz

Ann: 1st Prgr: "P1". 2nd Prgr: "P2". 3rd Prgr: "Petre". Lappish: "Datlae Sámeradio, Kárássjagga"

DAB: One DAB-multiplex (12D) covering parts of Norway. Includes all NRK-channels, P4, and NRK Alltid Folkemusikk. Regional DAB-multiplex (12C) for southeastern Norway. Includes NRK Østfold, Østlandssendinga, Buskerud, Vestfold, Telemark, NRK Stortinget, NRK P1 Oslofjord and Met. Oslofjord. In addition, regional multiplex 12B Rogaland, 12C Trøndelag and 13E Troms.

OTHER STATIONS:
RADIO NORGE (Comm.)
✉ Jernbanetorget 4, NO-0154 Oslo ☎+47 07270 **W:** bauermedia.no / radionorge.no **L.P:** MD: Lasse Kokvik

FM	MHz	kW	FM	MHz	kW
Alta	101.0	3.5	Grong	102.0	9.5
Bagn	102.1	7	Gulen	101.4	7.8
Bergen	102.5	46	Hadsel	101.4	6
Bjerkreim	101.0	6	Hammerfest	102.8	4.2
Bokn	90.3	120	Hemnes	104.2	7.2
Bremanger	103.2	9.2	Hovdefjell	103.6	5
Førde	102.0	2.4	Jetta	101.6	8.5
Gamlemsvet	102.8	50	Kistefjell	103.1	4.4
Gausta	103.1	5.5	Kongsberg	102.5	60
Greipstad	100.1	57.5	Kongsvinger	107.2	6.6

FM	MHz	kW	FM	MHz	kW
Kopparen	102.4	8	Salten	100.4	9.8
Lyngdal	102.0	10	Skien	105.2	80.0
Lønahorgi	100.6	4.8	Sogndal	103.9	2.4
Melhus	101.1	2.4	Steigen	102.1	7.0
Narvik	101.1	9.0	Stord	101.8	6
Nordfjordeid	101.2	2.4	Store Jekkir	103.3	1.2
Nordhue	106.5	70.0	Trolltind	101.7	5
Nordkapp	102.5	3.0	Tron	102.5	4.8
Oslo	103.9	90.0	Varanger	105.8	6
Reinsfjell	100.2	2.4	Vega	102.8	5.5

D.Prgr: 24h **N:** M-F: on the h. 0500-2300, also 0630, 0730, 1430, 1530. Sat: on the h. 0800-2300. Sun: on the h.0800-2300

P4 – RADIO HELE NORGE (Comm.)
✉ PB 817, NO-2626 Lillehammer ☎+47 61248444 🗎 +47 61248445 **W:** p4.no **L.P:** MD: Trygve Rønningen
FM Main freqs (MHz): Bjerkreim: 88.5 1kW, Kistefjell: 89.4 4kW, Steigen: 91.5 10kW, Vega: 94.1 2kW, Ski: 94.5 1kW, Nordhue: 95.0 5kW, Horta: 95.6 1.1kW, Hammerfest: 96.8 7kW, Hadsel: 97.3 5kW, Førde: 98.4 4kW, Hemnes: 98.6 5kW, Sogndal: 99.9 5kW, Varanger: 102.8 8kW, Bokn: 102.8 120kW, Mosvik: 103.8 33kW, Greipstad: 104.9 38kW, Tron: 105.8 6kW, Halden: 106.1 72.5kW + 102 txs below 1kW
D.Prgr: 24h on FM and DAB. **N:** M-F: on the h 0500-2300, also 0530, 0630, 0730, 1430, 1530, 1630. Sat-Sun: on the h 0700-2300

RADIO 1 HITS (Comm.)
✉ PB 1102 Sentrum, NO-0104 Oslo ☎+47 22023300 🗎 +47 22952202 **W:** radio1.no
FM (MHz): Oslo: 103.4, Bergen: 90.4, 97.1, 106.4, 107.1, Stavanger: 107.2, Trondheim: 96.3. All txs below 1 kW

RADIO METRO (Comm.)
✉ Akersgata 45, NO-0158 Oslo ☎+47 21555910 **W:** radiometro.no
FM Main freqs (MHz): Oslo: 106.8, Askim: 105.4, Lillestrøm: 107.9, Drammen: 101.8, Hønefoss: 103.5, Gjøvik: 105.8, Lillehammer: 105.0, Elverum/Hamar: 102,9, Trondheim: 104.2/107.0, Stjørdal: 97.5, Levanger: 99.8, Steinkjer: 95.2. All txs below 1 kW

NRJ NORGE (Comm.)
✉ Akersgata 73, NO-0180 Oslo ☎+47 22797500 🗎 +47 22797501 **W:** nrj.no
FM Main freqs (MHz): Oslo: 90.5, Drammen: 95.3, Kristiansand: 93.2/106.9, Stavanger: 99.3, Bergen: 98.2, Trondheim: 95,5/105.1/106.7
All txs below 1 kW

Internet: Most stns provide webstreams and/or on-demand audio sces.
Satellite: Most NRK-channels, radio and TV (incl NRK regional TV), Radio Norge and P4 are available through satellite.

LOCAL FM STATIONS
Around 300 low power FM commercial stns are in operation, some sharing freqs. Many of them organised through Lokalradioforbundet **W:** lokalradioforbundet.no

AFRTS (U.S. Mil.)
FM: Lifjell 101.5MHz (Stavanger). D.Prgr: 24h rly AFN Europe

SVALBARD (SPITSBERGEN) (Norwegian Territory)
L.T: UTC +1h (27 Mar-30 Oct: UTC +2h) — **Pr.L:** Norwegian — **E.C:** 50Hz, 230V

NRK - NORSK RIKSKRINGKASTING AS (Pub.)
MW: Longyearbyen: 1485kHz 1kW
D.Prgr: 24h relay NRK P1 (incl. regional prgr NRK Troms)

FM	P1	P2	P3	kW
Isfjord R.	89.7	93.6	97.3	0.05
Longyearbyen	88.8	94.5	98.3	0.045
Ny-Ålesund	91.3	94.8		0.12
Svea	89.1	92.0		0.025

RADIO NORGE (Comm.)
FM: Longyearbyen 104.0 0.013kHz

OMAN

L.T: UTC +4h — **Pop:** 3.4 million — **Pr.L:** Arabic — **E.C:** 50Hz, 240V — **ITU:** OMA

MINISTRY OF INFORMATION
✉ Omanet Team, Oman Electronic Network, P.O.Box 600, 113 Mascat ☎+968 24603222 🗎 +968 24693770 **W:** omanet.om **E:** omanet@omantel.net.om **L.P:** Minister: Hamad bin Mohammed Al Rashdi

PUBLIC AUTHORITY FOR RADIO AND TV - RADIO SULTANATE OF OMAN (RSO, Gov.)

✉ P.O. Box 397, 113 Masqat ☎+968 24 601538 🖷+968 24 602831 **W:** part.gov.om **LP:** DG Radio:Nasser Al-Sybani. DG Eng.: Mohd Salim Al Marhouby. Dir. Freq: Salim Al-Nomani. Dir. Trs: Saif Al-Rashedi

MW	kHz	kW	MW	kHz	kW
Bidiya	558	500	Salalah	738	100
Buraimi	639	100	Barka (Seeb)	1242	500
Haima	576	100	Bahla	1278	100

FM	G	Q	Y	E	kW(TRP)
Bahla	107.3	96.5	-	-	1
Barka	101.8	107.3	-	-	5
Batina	-	-	91.7	-	
Buraimi	96.1	93.0	-	-	5
Dhalkut	-	-	94.5	-	
Dhank	-	-	91.2	-	
Haima	-	106.5	98.8	-	
Hasikiya	96.5	-	-	-	1
Dakhiliya	-	-	98.8	-	
Ibra	93.2	-	98.8	-	2
Ibri	99.1	106.9	-	-	5
Jalan Bani Buali	88.1	97.7	-	-	5
Khasab	100.6	-	-	-	1
Madha	97.4	-	-	-	0.1
Masqat	94.4	93.2	100.0	90.4	5
Mazyunah	88.2	88.5	-	-	1
Murbat	-	-	100.0	-	
Nizwa	88.5	100.5	-	-	1
Quriyat	100.4	-	-	-	2.5
Sadah	88.2	-	100.0	-	1
Saham	91.1	93.6	-	-	5
Salalah	-	-	100.0	90.4	
Sayq	89.3	94.0	-	-	5
Sur	97.2	87.6	-	-	2
Taqah	-	-	100.0	-	
Thumrait	-	93.0	100.0	91.3	

G=General Arabic prgr: 24h on MW & FM. **N:** 0300, 0700 (Fri 0830), 1300, 1600, 1700, 1900, 2000. **Q=Quran prgr:** 24h. **Al-Shabab (Youth) channel:** 24h. **R. Oman FM in English:** 24h.
Ann: A: "Idha'atul Saltanat al-Oman min Masqat." E: "This is the English Service of Radio Sultanate of Oman from Masqat".

EXTERNAL SERVICE: See International Broadcasting section.

Other Stations:
Al Wisal FM, Masqat: 96.5MHz. **W:** wisal.fm – **Hala FM,** Masqat: 102.7MHz. **W:** halafm.com – **Hi FM,** Masqat: 95.9MHz. **W:** hifmradio. com – **Merge FM,** Masqat: 104.8MHz. **W:** radiomerge.fm – **Sowt al-Khaleej,** Masqat: 105.2MHz. See Qatar for main entry.
BBC relay station: MW (702kHz 1500-2100 & 1413kHz 0030-0400, 1300-2100) & SW: for details see International Broadcasting section

PAKISTAN

L.T: UTC +5h — **Pop:** 177 million — **Pr.L:** Urdu, Punjabi, Sindhi, Pushto, Balochi, English — **E.C:** 50Hz, 230V — **ITU:** PAK

PAKISTAN ELECTRONIC MEDIA REGULATORY AUTHORITY (PEMRA)

✉ Green Trust Tower, 6th Floor F-6, Jinnah Ave, Blue Area, Islamabad **W:** pemra.gov.pk **E:** info@pemra.gov.pk **LP:** Chairman: Mian Muhammad Javed.

PAKISTAN BROADCASTING CORPORATION (PBC, Gov.) RADIO PAKISTAN

✉ Broadcasting House, Constitution Avenue, Islamabad 44000 ☎+92 51 9214278 🖷 +92 51 9223827 **W:** radio.gov.pk **E:** info@radio. gov.pk **LP:** DG: Mr. Syed Imran Gardezi. Eng. Mgr: Asad Ayub.

MW	kHz	kW	R	MW	kHz	kW	R
Peshawar-I	540	300	K	Turbat	‡981	100	B
Khuzdar	567	300	B	Hyderabad (city)	1008	100	S
Islamabad	585	500	F	Multan	1035	120	P
Lahore-I	630	100	P	Quetta (city)	1134	100	B
Karachi (Landhi)	639	100	S	Rawalpindi	1152	100	P
Dera Ismail Khan	711	100	K	Peshawar-III	1170	100	K
Quetta (Yaru)	756	100	B	Loralai	1251	10	B
Karachi-I	828	100	S	Peshawar-II	1260	400	K
Khairpur	‡927	100	S	Lahore (city)	1332	100	P

MW	kHz	kW	R	MW	kHz	kW	R
Bhawalpur	1341	10	P	Skardu	1557	10	K
Zhob	1449	10	B	Chitral	1584	0	N
Faisalabad	1476	10	P	Sibi	1584	0	B
Gilgit	1512	10	K	Abbotabad	1602	0	K

R=Region: N=North, K=Khyber Pakhtoonkhawa & Northern tribal areas, F=Federal District of Islamabad, P=Punjab, S=Sindh, B=Balochistan.
NCAC: News & Current Affairs Channel on MW: 0200-1810/1900 in Urdu & English. Also regional programmes in other languages. Times vary by frequency. **N. in English:** 0300, 0800, 1100, 1300, 1600, 1700. 585/630/756kHz carry Voice of Quran 0200-0700.
FM93 (community radio stations): on 93.0MHz in Abbottabad, Bannu, Chitral, Dera Ismail Khan, Faisalabad, Gilgit, Gwadar, Hyderabad, Islamabad, Karachi, Kohat, Lahore, Muzaffarabad, Mianwali, Mithi, Multan, Larkana, Quetta, Skardu and Sargodha. Powers 2-5 kW. (Also r. CRI in Urdu & English).
Voice of Quran: 93.5MHz in Islamabad, Karachi, Lahore, Narowal, Peshawar, Quetta. **FPI:** transmitters in 14 more cities.
Varsa FM-94 (in Urdu): Islamabad, Karachi and Lahore on 94.0MHz.
FM101: information and entertainment channel on 101.0MHz in Faisalabad, Hyderabad, Islamabad, Kalarkahar, Karachi, Lahore, Larkana, Multan, Muree, Peshawar, Quetta and Sialkot. Powers 2kW except Karachi 5kW. **W:** fm101.gov.pk
Regional prgr: Khairpur 93.3MHz, Bhit Shah & Rawalpindi 93.5MHz. In tribal areas: R. Paktunhkhwa 92.2MHz. R. Swat 96.0MHz.
D.Prgr: as above in Urdu, English and regional languages. Local IDs are usually heard at sign on/off.
Ann: "This is Radio Pakistan".
F.PI: MW: 1000kW at Lahore. 1000/500kW at Umarkot on 558kHz. 100 kW at Chamar, Gwadar, Hyderabad, Larkana, Multan, Muzaffarabad and Paranichar. 10kW at Abbottabad. **SW:** 1x100kW to be added at Islamabad (Rewat) and Karachi. **FM93:** is being extended to Umerkot, Sukkur, Nawabshah, Jacobabad, Dadu, Badin, Mirpurkhas, Sanghar and Thatta. In total the network will have 47 stns. Prgrs will be 40% English/Urdu and 60% regional.

EXTERNAL SERVICE: See International Broadcasting section.

AZAD KASHMIR RADIO (AKR, Gov.)

✉ Broadcasting House, Muzaffarabad (AJK) 13100, via Pakistan.
LP: Dir: Javed Iqbal.
MW: Muzaffarabad ‡792kHz 150kW, Mirpur 936kHz 100kW.
SW: Islamabad (Rewat) 7265kHz 100kW.
FM: Mirpur/Muzaffarabad 93.0MHz.
NB: 792kHz r. inactive, but expected to return.
D.Prgr: Muzaffarabad channel: 0045-0445 & 1000-1810 on 792kHz Mirpur: 0045-0515 & 1100-1810. Rawalpindi-III channel (from Islamabad 100kW): 7265kHz: 1100-1300 & 1600-1810 (irregular, times variable). Prgrs on all channels also include R. Pakistan NBS relays.
Ann: 792kHz: "Yeh Azad Kashmir Radio Muzaffarabad Hay". 936kHz: "Mediumwave na-sau-chattis (936) kHz par. Yeh Azad Kashmir Radio hay". **SW:** "Yeh Azad Kashmir Radio Trarkhal Hay".
IS: "Azad Kashmir" anthem at open and close.

Other stations (FM MHz. Powers normally in Islamabad/Karachi/ Lahore 2kW, other cities 1kW and univ./public radio 200-500W):
Apna Karachi 107: Karachi 107.0. **W:** apnakarachi107.fm – **City FM 89:** Karachi/Lahore/Islamabad/Faisalabad 89.0 **W:** cityfm89.com – **FM 100 Pakistan:** Abbottabad/Gujrat(Hyderabad/Islamabad/Jhelum/Karachi/ Lahore/Multan/Rahim Yar Khan 100.0 **W:** fm100pakistan.com – **FM Sunrise Pakistan:** Jhelum 95.0, Sardogha/Sahiwal 96.0, Islamabad 97.0 **W:** fmsunrise.com – **Hamara FM Network:** Kharian 97.0, Mandi Bahuddin 98.0 **W:** hamarafm.com.pk – **Hot FM 105,** Karachi & 13 other cities on 105.0MHz **W:** hotfm.com.pk – **Hum FM,** Islamabad & 5 other cities: 106.2 **W:** hum.fm – **Humara FM,** Faisalabad: 90.0 **W:** humara.fm – **Josh FM,** Hyderabad/Karachi/Lahore: 99.0 – **KUST FM 99,** Kohat: 98.0 **W:** radio.kust.edu.pk – **Mast FM 103,** Faisalabad/ Karachi/Lahore/Multan: 103.0 **W:** mastfm103.com.pk – **Power FM,** Abbottabad/Islamabad/Vehari: 99.0 **W:** power99.com.pk – **Punjab Univ. FM,** Lahore: 104.6 0.1kW **W:** pu.edu.pk/news/fm_schedule2007. asp – **Radioactive 96,** Karachi: 96.0 **W:** radioactive96.fm – **R. Awaz:** Gujranwala & 11 other sites in Punjab on 105.0 **W:** radioawaz.com.pk – **R. Buraq:** Abbottabad/Mardan/Peshawar/Sialkot: 104.0 **W:** radio-buraq.com – **R. One,** Gwadar/Islamabad/Karachi/Lahore: 91.0 **W:** fm91.com.pk – **Super FM,** Bahawalnagar: 90.0 **W:** superfmnetwork. com – **VO Kashmir,** Muzaffarabad: 105.0 **W:** vokfm105.com – **Zab FM,** Islamabad/Karachi/Lahore: 106.6 0 **W:** zabfm.org
China R. Int. (Urdu/English): Karachi/Islamabad 98.0, Kohat/Lahore/ Multan 93.0.
VOA R. Aap ki Dunyaa: via Orzu TJK 972kHz 800kW 1400-0200

PALAU (USA associated)

L.T: UTC +9h — **Pop:** 20,956 — **Pr.L:** Palauan, English — **E.C:** 60Hz, 115/230V — **ITU:** PLW

T8AA BROADCASTING STATION (Gov)
Bureau of Domestic Affairs
📧 Box 279, Koror State, Republic of Palau 96940 ☎ +680 4882417
📄 +680 4881932 **L.P:** SM: Ms Eunice Akiwo **E:** ecoparadise@
palaugov.net
MW: Voice of Palau T8AA 1584kHz 5kW: 1900-1300 **N:** includes
R. Australia via satellite **FM:** Eco-Paradise FM 87.9MHz [relay
T8AA programs] **Format:** local news, music and talkback

Other Stations:
FM MHz	kW	Station	FM MHz	kW	Station
1) 88.5		WPRK	2) 98.5	0.5	KDFM Pinoy FM
2) 89.5	0.5	WWFM	3) 102.5	0.75	KRST-FM
4) 89.9	0.6	PWFM			

Addresses & other information
1) Rudimich Enterprises, Sure Save Store, PO Box 2000, Koror 96940
☎+680 4881359 **E:** rudimich@palaunet.com **ID:** "Island Rhythm"
Format: Contemporary Top 40 **D.Prgr:** 24h in English/Palauan – **2)**
Diaz Broadcasting Co, PO Box 1327, Koror 96940 ☎+680 4884848
📄 +688 5874420 **L.P:** GM Alfonzo Diaz, Mgr KDFM: Imelda Aban.
WWFM English & Palaun, KDFM Filipino, classical, jazz, easy listening format **W:** brouhaha.net/palau/wwfm **E:** wwfm@palaunet.com
D.Prgr: 24h – **3)** World Harvest R., PO Box 12, South Bend IN 46614,
USA ☎ (574) 2918200 📄 (574) 2919043 **E:** whr@lesea.com **W:** whr.
org **Prgr:** relays English language relig prgrs from SW stn T8WH – **4)**
1A Building [above Dollar 99 store], Room S, Floor 3, Medalai hamlet,
Koror ☎ +680 4885350, 📄 +680 488 5250 **TXT:** +680 778 5490 US
based message line +1 503 928 7718 **W:** palauwaveradio.com **ID:**
"Palau Wave Radio" **L.P:** Sha Merirei Ongelungel, GM **Format:** social,
cultural & political news, information and music.
NB: Calls beginning with K and W are unofficial as Palau regulates its
own broadc. spectrum. American-style calls are more familiar to locals.

EXTERNAL SERVICES: T8WH (Rlg.) See Int. Broadcasting section

PANAMA

L.T: UTC -5h — **Pop:** 3.4 million — **Pr.L:** Spanish — **E.C:** 60Hz, 110V
— **ITU:** PNR

AUTORIDAD NACIONAL DE SERVICIOS PUBLICOS
📧 Vía España, Edificio Office Park, Ciudad de Panamá (Apartado
Postal 0816-01235, Zona 5, Panamá ☎ + 507-508 4500
W: asep.gob.pa **E:** atencionalusuario@asep.gob.pa

Call HO–, ‡ = inactive, (r) = repeater, ± = varying fq.
Hr of tr 24h unless otherwise stated.

MW	Call	kHz	kW	Station, location, hr. of tr.
PA02)	PU	540	10	R. Líder, Panamá: 1000-0400
PA03)	H2	560	3	RPC Radio, Colón
PA04)	S	570	5	R. Soberana, Panamá: 1000-0300
PA03)	H4	580	10	RPC Radio, David
PA03)	H3	590	10	RPC Radio, Chitré
PA03)	HM	610	10	RPC Radio, Panamá
HE01)	J35	630	2	R. Provincias, Chitré
CN01)	K22	640	2.5	CPR, Colón
PA14)		640	2.5	R. Panamá, La Palma
PA01)	S22	650	5	R. Mía "Cadena Nacional", Panamá
PA03)	H5	660	1	RPC Radio, Bocas del Toro
PA09)		660	5	La Nueva Exitosa, Sabana Grande (r: 930)
PA26)	F32	680	5	Mujer AM, David
DA01)		680	5	Voz Sin Fronteras, Metetí: 1000-2400
PA18)		690	5	R. Evangelio Vivo, Panamá
PA08)	Q51	710	5	KW R. Continente, Panamá
BT01)	B52	710	5	Ondas del Caribe, Bocas del Toro: 1000-0400
HE04)	B50	720	10	R. República, Chitré: 1100-0300
PA37)	R44	740	2.6	La Exitosa de Chorrera, La Chorrera
CH03)	N26	740	5	R. Cristal, David
HE07)		750	5	R. Inolvidable, Chitré: 1000-2300
PA10)	XO	760	5	LV del Istmo, Panamá: 1145-0300
PA07)		780	5	R. Recuerdo, Panamá
PA14)		790	6	R. Panamá, Santiago
CE02)		800	3	Tropical 800, Los Santos: 1030-0300
PA11)	G	810	1	R. 10, Panamá
CH05)	F28	820	5	R. Ritmo Chiriquí, David: 1100-0400
LS01)	R56	830	5	R. Península, Macaracas: 1000-0200

MW	Call	kHz	kW	Station, location, hr. of tr.
PA12)	L80	840	10	R. Nacional, Panamá
PA09)		850	1	La Exitosa, Colón
PA09)	T61	850	5	La Exitosa de Chiriquí, David (r: 930)
HE03)	L55	860	10	R. Reforma, Chitré: 1030-0400
PA13)	HO	870	5.5	R. Libre, Panamá
CN02)	B51	880	1	R. Visión Panamá, Colón
PA14)		880	2.5	R. Panamá, Bocas del Toro
PA14)		880	2.5	R. Panamá, Chiriquí
HE02)	Q62	890	5	R. Ritmo Stereo, Chitré
PA14)	HA	900	10	CD Radio, Panamá
PA01)	S56	920	5	R. Mía, Los Santos
PA09)	R46	930	10	La Nueva Exitosa, Panamá
CH06)	K85	930	2	R. Mi Preferida,Pto Armuelles:1000-0400
PA05)		960	1	R. Capital, Panamá
CH07)	M33	960	1	AM Tropical, David
VE02)	S97	970	3	Ondas Centrales, Santiago: 1000-0300
PA15)		990	5	W Radio, Panamá
CE01)	K36	1000	10	R. Poderosa "La Fuerte", Aguadulce
PA16)		1020	5	R. Ancón, Panamá: 1000-0400
LS02)	J2	1040	2.5	Ondas del Canajagua, Las Tablas
PA39)	J60	1060	3.5	LV de Panamá "La Auténtica", Panamá
CE02)		1070	3	R. Estéreo Mi Favorita, Penonomé
PA07)	J24	1080	5	R. Mundo Internacional, Panamá
PA08)	M92	1100	5	R. Sabrosa, Panamá
PA19)	M21	1120	5	R. Sonora, Panamá: 1030-0300
CE03)	U80	1130	2.5	Vox MN, Aguadulce
PA20)	B49	1140	5	R. Panamericana, Panamá: 1100-0500
PA17)	WK	1160	10	R. Metrópolis, Panamá
CH08)	C20	1160	5	Ondas Chiricanas, David
PA21)		1180	10	R. Chinavisión, Panamá
VE03)	U	1180	10	AM Original, Santiago: 1100-0200
PA11)	E91	1210	1	R. Diez, Panamá
PA17)		1240	1	R. Infantil, Panamá
CH09)	M56	1240	3	Ondas de Vida, David
PA22)	J22	1270	3	R. Tipy Q, Panamá
CH13)		1290	5	R. Única, Panamá
CH13)	S23	1290	3	R. Única, Chiriquí
CH13)		1290	5.5	R. Única, Los Santos
CH10)	I417	1300	5	R. Baha´ís, Boca del Monte
PA25)		1330	5	LV Poderosa, Panamá
LS05)		1340	2.5	R. Tipikal, Las Tablas
PA36)	Z38	1350	5	BBN R., Panamá
PA26)		1380	10	Mujer AM, Panamá: 1130-0400
PA07)		1390	5	R. Mundo Internacional, Colón
PA27)	T40	1400	10	Digital R. Luz, La Chorrera
LS03)	H779	1410	5	R. Mensabé, Las Tablas: 1000-0300
PA28)		1430	7.5	R. Kids, Panamá
PA29)		1450	5	R. Melódica, Panamá: 1000-0330
BT02)	D42	1460	0.5	LV de Almirante, Bocas del Toro: 1400-0400
PA30)		1470	5	La Primerísima, Panamá
PA38)		1490	3	Asamblea Nacional, Cocle
PA31)	A95	1510	5	Hosanna R., Panamá
PA32)		1530	10	R. Avivamiento, Panamá
VE04)		1540	4	Festival AM Digital, Santiago
PA33)		1560	10	R. Adventista, Panamá: 1000-0300
PA34)		1580	1	Hosanna Oeste, Panamá

Province abbreviations: (Provincias) BT = Bocas del Toro, CE =
Coclé, CH = Chiriquí, CN = Colón, DA = Darién, HE = Herrera, LS = Los
Santos, PA = Panamá, VE = Veraguas. **N.B:** These abbreviations are
not recognized by the Post Office. Letters should carry the full name.
Addresses and other information:
BT00) BOCAS DEL TORO
BT01) Finca 13, Empalme, Changuinola - **FM:** 90.1MHz **W:** bocason-
dasdelcaribe.com – **BT02)** Calle 6 y Av. N. Almirante.
CE00) COCLÉ
CE01) Ap. 090 (or Vía al Puerto), Aguadulce **W:** radiopoderosa99.com -
FM: 99.9MHz – **CE02)** Av. Juan Demóstenes Arosemena, Galerías Aro,
Penonomé - **FM:** 91.7MHz – **CE03)** Calle Rodolfo Chiari, Edificio Don
Chopo, planta alta, Aguadulce **W:** voxpanama.com - **FM:** 103.7MHz.
CH00) CHIRIQUÍ
CH03) Ap. 540 (or Av. 8 y Calle A Norte, Barrio Bolívar), David - **FM:**
98.1MHz – **CH05)** Av. D.Noreste, Medio Oeste, David - **FM:** 93.1MHz
– **CH06)** Ap. 44 (or Barriada San José), Puerto Armuelles - **FM:**
105.3MHz – **CH07)** Calle Central, David - **FM:** 107.9MHz – **CH08)**
Ap. 172 (or Calle Elisandro Calvo, Doleguita), David - **FM:** 100.1MHz
– **CH09)** Av.Estudiante, Calle 4 final, Edif.Hermanos Pinzón, David –
CH10) Ap. 1187, David – **CH13)** Zahita SA, Calle 45, Bella Vista, Ed. El
Conquistador, Panamá. **W:** radiometropolis.com.pa/afiliadas/launica
CN00) COLON
CN01) Calle 2da detras de Panamá All Brown, Colón - **FM:** 101.5MHz,
103.5MHz – **CN02)** Calle 1 Paseo Washington, Colón - **FM:** 105.3MHz

DA00) DARIÉN
DA01) Calle Principal de Meteti, Meteti. (or Ap. 87-0871 Panamá 7) **W:** facebook.com/pages/RADIO-VOZ-SIN-FRONTERAS/27403452929 4042 - **FM:** 100.1MHz
HE00) HERRERA
HE01) Ap. 423 (or Urb.Las Mercedes), Chitré **W:** radioprovincias630. com – **HE02)** Paseo Enrique Geenzier, Chitré. **W:** ritmostereo975. com - **FM:** 97.5 – **HE03)** Ap. 194, Chitré - **FM:** 98.5MHz – **HE04)** Ap. 191, Chitré - **FM:** 103.3MHz – **HE07)** Ap. 375 (or Calle Francisco Audia), Chitré.
LS00) LOS SANTOS
LS01) Calle Central, Macaracas - **FM:** 93.7MHz – **LS02)** Ap. 10 (or Av. Belisario Porras, final), Las Tablas **W:** canajaguaamstereo.com – **LS03)** Ap. 20 (or Av. Agustín Cano Castillero), Las Tablas – **LS05)** Los Cerritos, Las Tablas
PA00) PANAMÁ
PA01) Ap. 5117, Panamá 5 **W:** radiomiapanama.com radiomials920am. com – **PA02)** Parque Lefebre, Edif.Sta Elena Torre II, Ofc.11, Panamá – **PA03)** Ap. 0827-00116, Avenida 12 de Octubre, Panamá **W:** rpcradio. com **PA04)** Ap. 6-2323, El Dorado (or Calle 63B, Casa N° 2), Panamá **W:** radio-soberana.com – **PA05)** Edif. Orion, P8, Vía España frente al PIEX, Panamá – **PA07)** Radio Hit SA, Calle 50 y 77 San Francisco 35, (Apartado 0819-0391) Panamá **W:** estereobahia.com – **PA08)** Ap. 87-1324, Panamá 7 (or Vía Argentina, Edif. Carillón, Panamá) **W:** kwcontinente.com **E:** kwcontinente@cableonda.net – **PA09)** Ap. 7462, Panamá 5 **W:** sinfo.net/exitosa – **PA10)** Ap. 6-1192, (or 66 Oeste N° 641) El Dorado, Panamá. **E:** atrd@panama.c-com.net – **PA11)** La Gloria 31-B Bethania, Panamá – **PA13)** Edif. Dorchester, Vía España, Panamá 4 **W:** radiometropolis.com.pa/afiliadas/radiolibre – **PA14)** Calle 54 Obarrio, Edificio Plaza Globus, 2do piso, Panamá **W:** radiopanama. com.pa – **PA15)** **W:** wradio.com.co – **PA16)** Calle Cuba y Calle 37, Panamá – **PA17)** Vía España y Calle 45, Edif. El Conquistador PB, Panamá **W:** radiometropolis.com.pa – **PA18)** Condomino Dorado N° 2, Ofc. 10A, Vía Ricardo J. Alfaro, Panamá – **PA19)** Ap. 87-1165 (or Calle 63 Oeste N° E-21, Urb. Los Angeles), Panamá 7 **W:** sonora1120.com – **PA20)** Ap. 6956 (or Vía José Agustín Arango), Panamá 5 – **PA21)** Sun Tower Mall, Av. Ricardo J.Alfaro, Panamá **W:** chinavision1180am. com – **PA22)** Calle 45, Edif. Conquistador, Bella Vista, P2, Panamá – **PA25)** Iglesia Internacional del Evangélico Cuadrangular, Los Andes N° 2, Panamá – **PA26)** Calle 51 51 Av Manuel María Icaza, Edif. Torre Cosmos, Panamá – **PA27)** Ap. 473, La Chorrera – **PA28)** Río Abajo, Panamá – **PA29)** Ap. 87-3541 (or Vía Fernández de Córdoba, Jardin Cosita Buena), Panamá 7 **E:** lizbethcardenas@hotmail.com – **PA30)** Edif.La Marqueta, Vía Porras, Panamá **W:** laprimerisima-depanama.com **PA31)** Ap. 6-8229 (or Calle Erick del Valle y Vía Argentina, Edif. Vicky 2), El Dorado, Panamá **W:** hosanna.pma.org/sra-dio.htm – **PA32)** Av. Ernesto T. Lefevre, Panamá – **PA33)** Ap. 3244, Panamá 3 (or Carrasquilla, Calle 2da N° 39, Panamá) **W:** cursoslavoz. org/2014/08/25/nuestras-filiales-panama – **PA34)** Sky Phone S.A., Cerro Peñon, Panamá – **PA36)** Ap. 0860-00356, (or Vía Cincuentenario final, a 300 metros del McDonald's de Río Abajo, después del Edificio La Reina) Panamá – **PA37)** Av. Las Américas, La Chorrera. – **PA39)** Vía España y Calle 45, Edif. El Conquistador, PB, Panamá **E:** vozdep-anama@hotmail.com
VE00) VERAGUAS
VE02) Ap. 131, Santiago – **VE03)** Ap. 286 (or Calle 10), Santiago – **VE04)** Calle Calidonia, Ave B Norte, Mercado Público, Santiago **W:** festival1540am.com

FM in Panamá City (MHz): 88.1 Diez – 88.5 85.5 FM Stereo – 88.9 Sol 88.9 – 89.3 Cool FM – 89.9 Estéreo 89 – 90.5 Super Q – 90.9 RPC Radio – 91.3 Los 40 Principales – 91.7 La Nueva 91.7 – 92.1 Power – 92.5 La KY – 92.9 YXY – 93.5 Metrópolis – 93.9 María – 94.5 W Panamá – 94.9 Hosanna Capital 94.9 – 95.3 La Nueva Exitosa – 95.9 KW Continente – 96.3 Stereo Fe – 96.7 TVN R. – 97.1 Caliente Panamá – 97.5 WAO 97½ – 97.9 Mix – 98.3 La Mega – 98.9 Ultra Estéreo – 99.3 La 99 – 99.7 Tropic Q – 100.1 Antena 8 – 100.5 Fabulosa – 101.1 Estéreo Azul – 101.5 Economía – 101.9 Nacional/SERTV – 102.1 Lo Nuestro – 102.5 FM Corazón – 103.1 Blast – 103.5 Quiubo Estéreo – 103.9 Mil – 104.3 KYS FM – 104.7 La Tipik – 105.1 Estéreo Vida – 105.7 La Nueva Bahía – 106.1 Con Sabor a Romance – 106.7 Rock & Pop – 107.5 Omega Stereo

PAPUA NEW GUINEA

L.T: UTC +10h; Bougainville: +11h — **Pop:** 6 million — **Pr.L:** English, Tok Pisin, Motu + 860 ethnic langs — **E.C:** 50Hz, 240V — **ITU:** PNG

NATIONAL INFORMATION & COMMUNICATIONS TECHNOLOGY AUTHORITY (Gov)
✉ P.O Box 8444, Boroko, NCD ☎ +675 3258633 🖷 +675 3256868,

3004829 **W:** nicta.gov.pg **E:** licensing@nicta.gov.pg **L.P:** CEO: Charles Punaha. Regulator of broadc. and communications (2010)

NATIONAL BROADCASTING CORPORATION (Gov)
✉ P.O. Box 1359, Boroko NCD ☎ +675 325 5233 🖷 +675 325 6296 **E:** info@nbc.com.pg **W:** nbc.com.pg **L.P:** MD: Memafu Kapera, Dir. Engineering: Robin Vuvut. **Networks:** **NBC National** (English/Tok Pisin), **NBC Kundu** (Provincial: English/Tok Pisin & local vernaculars), **Tribe FM** (National: English/Tok Pisin)

NBC National (Voice of Papua New Guinea):

SW	KHz	kW	SW	KHz	kW
Pt. Moresby	4890	*25	Pt. Moresby	#6040	10*

#) using NBC Central 3290 tx on NBC Milne Bay 6040 frequency
*used irr. for events of national importance. **F.PL:** new 25kW txs
In 2015, NBC has leased time on SW transmitters located in Victoria and Queensland [Australia] to provide coverage of events of national importance and can be expected to do the same in the future.

MW	kHz	kW
Pt Moresby	585	10

FM	MHz	kW	FM	MHz	kW
Pt Moresby	90.7	1	Rabaul	103.3	0.3

F.PL: FM coverage of NBC National is being expanded nationwide at existing NBC Kundu transmitter sites. A full list of NBC National FM stations is currently still unavailable.
D.Prgr: 1900-1400 daily **N:** on the h 1900-1400 **Format:** National public service prgr. **V:** card or letter
NBC Kundu Network (local provincial stns often funded in partnership with provincial govts):

MW	kHz	kW	Station, slogan, location
4)	675	10	NBC Wewak, "Maus Bilong Sepi", Wewak
6)	675	10	NBC Morobe, "Maus Bilong Kund", Lae
10)	810	2	NBC Rabaul, "Maus Bilong Tavuvu", Rabaul
13)	864	10	NBC Madang, "Maus Bilong Garamut", Madang
2)	900	10	NBC Kimbe, "Singaut Bilong Tavur", Kimbe

SW	kHz	kW	Station, slogan, location
4)	‡2410	10	NBC Enga, Wabag
1)	3205	10	NBC Vanimo, "Maus Bilong Sandaun", Vanimo
10)	3220	10	NBC Morobe, "Maus Bilong Kundu", Lae
2)	‡3235	10	NBC Kimbe, "Singaut Bilong Tavur", Kimbe
7)	‡3245	10	NBC Gulf, "Voice of the Seagull", Kerema
13)	3260	10	NBC Madang, "Maus Bilong Garamut", Madang
17)	3275	10	NBC Southern Highlands, Mendii
5)	3290	10	NBC Central, "Voice of the Conch-Shell", Pt Moresby
18)	3305	10	NBC Western, "Voice of the Sunset", Daru
11)	3315	10	NBC Manus, "Maus Bilong Chauka", Lorengau
19)	3325	10	NBC Buka, "Maus Bilong Sankamap", Buka ARB
14)	‡3335	10	NBC East Sepik, "Maus Bilong Sepik", Wewak
12)	3345	10	NBC Northern, "Voice of the People of Oro", Popondetta
15)	3355	10	NBC Simbu, "Karai Bilong Mumbu", Kundiawa
20)	3365	10	NBC Milne Bay, "Voice of Kula", Alotau
8)	3375	10	NBC Western Highlands, "Eagle FM", Mt Hagen
9)	3385	10	NBC East New Britain, "Maus Bilong Tavuvur", Rabaul
6)	3395	10	NBC Eastern Highlands, "Karai Blong Kumul", Goroka
3)	3905	10	NBC New Ireland, "Singaut Bilong Drongo", Kavieng
8)	*‡5985	10	NBC Western Highlands, "Eagle FM", Mt Hagen
9)	*‡5985	10	NBC East New Britain, "Maus Bilong Tavuvur", Rabaul
19)	*‡6020	10	NBC Buka, "Maus Bilong Sankamap", Buka ARB
20)	*‡6040	10	NBC Milne Bay, "Voice of Kula", Alotau
18)	*‡6080	10	NBC Western, "Voice of the Sunset", Daru
14)	*‡6140	10	NBC East Sepik, "Maus Bilong Sepik", Wewak

NB: Stns may operate irr. schedules or have long periods of silence because of technical, power, funding or other issues reflecting local and provincial government resources and priorites. Broadcasts are sometimes heard during local sports or political events or special anniversaries with little or no advance notice.
‡ Currently inactive on SW but could reactivate without notice.
*‡ Licensed but inactive. May be used irr. for events of nat. importance but not necessarily from the same location because of the lack of reliable SW transmission facilities.

FM	MHz	kW	Station, slogan, location
7)	91.1		NBC Gulf, "Voice of the Seagull", Kerema
6)	91.1		NBC Eastern Highlands, "Kam Gud FM", Kainantu
8)	91.4		NBC Western Highlands, "Eagle FM", Mt Hagen
6)	91.7	3	NBC Eastern Highlands, "Kam Gud FM", Goroka
5)	95.5		NBC Central, "Voice of the Conch Shell", Pt Moresby
19)	100.0		NBC Buka, "Maus Blong Sankamap", Buka ARB
9)	103.3		NBC East New Britain, "Maus Blong Tavuvur", Kenabot
10)	105.1	1	NBC Morobe, "Kundu FM", Morobe

D.Prgr: 2000-2200, 0800-1200v. **Format:** Non-commercial local music

and health, education, public safety and sports prgrs. **N:** NBC National Network. **V:** card or letter, email; send reports direct to stn.
FM: An increasing number of Kundu stns now also broadcast locally on FM from existing transmitter sites. **Note:** A full list of current Kundu FM stns is currently still unavailable.
NBC Tribe FM: Pt Moresby. New youth netw. delivered via satellite. **W:** facebook.com/tribefm **F.PL:** FM coverage is being expanded nationwide with local relay broadcasts from existing Kundu transmitter sites but a list of locations is currently still unavailable.
F.PL: A recent review of provincial stns may result in consolidation of smaller number of NBC stns which is why some SW stns are simply not being repaired or operating as they will not be replaced when equipment fails. Satellite delivery of NBC National and Tribe FM to be expanded via local FM txs and this is currently taking place as resources and funding allows. Local NBC Kundu studio prgrs continue on FM (and SW only as necessary) giving 3 NBC prgr streams (2 national 1 local) at all proposed remaining locations as FM equipment is also installed in association with the national expansion of the Kundu2 TV service. Funding for provincial Kundu stns is allocated at a provincial political level. National NBC services are centrally funded but need provincially funded infrastructure to be available.

Addresses and other information:
Regions: ARB=Autonomous Region of Bougainville, Cen=Central, Chi=Chimbu, EHP=Eastern Highlands, ENB=East New Britain, Eng=Enga, ESP=East Sepik, Gul=Gulf, Mad=Madang, Man=Manus, MBP=Milne Bay, Mor=Morobe, NCD=National Capital District, NIP=New Ireland, Or=Oro, SHP=Southern Highlands, WHP=Western Highlands, WNB=West New Britain, WP=Western, WSP=West Sepik
1) P.O Box 37, Vanimo, WSP ☎ +675 857 1144/1149 🖷 +675 8571305 – **2)** P.O.Box 412, Kimbe, WNB ☎ +675 983 5600/5185/5010 🖷 +675 9835600 – **3)** P.O.Box 477, Kavieng, NIP ☎ +675 9842077 🖷 +675 984 2191 – **4)** P.O.Box 300, Wabag, Eng ☎ +675 5471013 🖷 +675 5471069 – **5)** P.O Box 1359, Boroko NCD ☎ +675 3217155 🖷 +675 3217110. **FM:** 90.7 carries Karai Network including Tribe FM [youth prgr] Sa 2100-0000 local; **SW:** carries FM 95.5 'Radio Gadona' – **6)** P.O Box 311, Goroka, EHP ☎ +675 732 1618/1733/1607 🖷 +675 7321533 – **7)** P.O.Box 36, Kerema, Gul. ☎ +675 6481076 🖷 +675 6481003 – **8)** P.O.Box 311, Mount Hagen WHP ☎ +675 5421000 🖷 +675 5421001 – **9)** P.O.Box 393, Rabaul, ENB ☎ +675 982 8966/67/68/69/70 🖷 +675 9828971 – **10)** P.O.Box 1262, Lae, Mor ☎ +675 472 1311/7520/4209 🖷 +675 4726423 – **11)** P.O Box 505, Lorengau, Man ☎ +675 4709079 🖷 +675 4709079 – **12)** P.O.Box 137, Popondetta, Or ☎ +675 329 7037/38 🖷 +675 3297362 – **13)** P.O Box 2036, Jomba, Mad. ☎ +675 852 2415/2301/2360 🖷 +675 8522360 – **14)** P.O Box 65, Wewak, ESP ☎ +675 856 2316/2398 🖷 +675 8562405 – **15)** P.O.Box 228, Kundiawa, Chi ☎ +675 7351012 🖷 +675 7351012 – **17)** P.O.Box 104, Mendi SHP ☎ +675 549 1017/1020 🖷 +675 5491017 – **18)** P.O.Box 23, Daru WP ☎ +675 645 9234/9151 🖷 +675 6459319 – **19)** P.O.Box 35 Buka, ARB ☎ +675 9739911 🖷 +675 9739912 – **20)** P.O.Box 111, Alotau MBP ☎ +675 641 1028/1334 🖷 +675 6411028

MAJOR COMMERCIAL NETWORKS:
FM 100 Kalang Advertising Ltd (Telikom PNG subsidiary)
🖃 P.O. Box 1534, Boroko, NCD ☎ +675 300 4300 🖷 +675 300 4316 **L.P:** CEO: John Mong, Ops Mgr: Bonner Tito **D.Prgr:** 24h via satellite **F.PL:** Continued FM expansion nationwide
FM(MHz): Brands FM100: W: fm100.com.pg **E:** info@fm100.com **Format:** Contemporary music "PNG's Information & Music Leader" **Sports** relay 2GB Sydney NRL Live Fri/Sat/Sun - 100.1 Kandrian, 100.2 Kavieng/Goroka/Tabubil, 100.3 1kW Pt Moresby/Lorengau/Kimbe/Tabubil/Finschafen/Mendi, 100.4 Mt Hagen, 100.5 Popondetta/Lae/Namatanai/Daru/Tari, 100.6 Pomio/Buka, 100.8 1kW Rabaul/Madang/Wewak, 101.1 Kundiawa, 102.0 Paga Hill, 107.1 Mt Horeatoa/Mt Kainguma, 107.3 Mt Boregoro/Mt Waterholes, 107.7 Mt Dimodimo **Hot FM: W:** facebook.com/hot97fm **E:** sashahot97fm@gmail.com **Format:** youth oriented contemporary music - Port Moresby 97.0 and other locations

PNGFM
🖃 P.O. Box 774, Port Moresby NCD ☎ +675 323 4288 🖷 +675 323 1628 **L.P:** MD: Adrian Au, CE: Clezy Rakole **W:** cfl.com.fj/radiopng **E:** aau@naufm.com.pg **D.Prgr:** 24h via satellite
Netw.: Nau FM PD: Turner Arifeae **Format:** E, urban westernized youth market **Yumi FM** PD: Rosemary Botong **Format:** Tok Pisin, local and adult contemporary music **Legend FM Bikpla 101:** E, Hits of 1970s-2000s. **F.PL:** Continued FM expansion nationwide
FM(MHz): Nau FM: 96.1 1kW Goroka, 96.3 1kW Lae/Madang, 96.5 1kW Kimbe/Port Moresby/Lihir/Rabaul/Lorengau, 96.7 Alotau, 96.9 1kW Mt Hagen. **Yumi FM: W:** facebook.com/pages/93fm-yumi-fm 93.1 1kW Pt Moresby/Lihir, 93.3 Tinputz, 93.5 Mt Hagen, 93.7 1kW

Lae/Madang, 93.9 Rabaul/Goroka, 95.0 Kundiawa, 96.3 Balimo **Legend FM Bikpla: W:** facebook.com/pages/legend-fm-png 101.1 Port Moresby/Lae/Madang/Goroka/Mt Hagen/Rabaul/Kokopo

MAJOR NON-COMMERCIAL NETWORKS:
Wantok Radio Light – PNG Bible Church
🖃 Papua New Guinea Christian Broadcasting Network, P.O. Box 1273, Port Moresby NCD ☎ +675 326 2933 🖷 +675 326 1104 **L.P:** GM: Pawa Warena **W:** wantokradio.org **E:** admin@wantokradio.org **Format:** religious **F.PL:** Continued FM expansion nationwide via satellite **Affiliation:** HCJB/Evangelical Bible Missions through Life Radio Ministries, Griffin GA, USA
SW: ‡7325kHz1kW Pt Moresby NCD **QSL:** r. to **E:** qsl@wantokradio.org
FM(MHz): 93.9 1kW Port Moresby, 105.9 Wewak/Kimbe/Buka/Popondetta/Lae/Kokopo/Kiunga/Goroka/Mt Hagen/Ialibu/Wabag/Alotau/Mendi/Kainantu/Madang

CRN (Catholic Radio Network) – Radio Maria
🖃 Radio Maria PNG Inc, PO Box 8719, Boroko, NCD ☎ +675 325 9178 **L.P:** Father Peter Kote **W:** radiomaria.org **E:** director.pg@radiomaria.org **Format:** religious **D.Prgr:** 24h via satellite **F.PL:** continued FM expansion nationwide via satellite
SW: 4960 KHz 1kW Vanimo WSP **ID:** R.St.Gabriel **Address:** P.O Box 205, Vanimo WSP ☎ +675 857 1305 **Prgr:** local studio and network prgrs from Port Moresby **QSL:** qsl@radiomaria.org
FM(MHz): 88.1/91.3 Rabaul 91.5 Vanimo 92.9 Aitape 98.1 Mt Hagen 101.0 Lihir 103.1 Kimbe/Wabag 103.3 Alotau 103.5 Port Moresby/Wewak/Porgera 103.7 Lae

OTHER STATIONS:

FM	MHz	kW	Location	Station
1)	88.1	0.3	Vunapope ENB	Voice of Blessed Peter Torot
1)	88.5	0.3	Bereina Cen	Voice of Blessed Peter Torot
24)	89.1		Port Moresby NCD	Lalokau FM
2)	89.3	0.3	Moro SHP	CDI FM
3)	89.9	1	Port Moresby NCD	FM Central
4)	90.0		Hela SHP	ECPNG FM
2)	90.9	0.5	Gobe SHP	CDI FM
1)	91.3	0.5	Rabaul ENB	Voice of Blessed Peter Torot
2)	92.3	0.5	Kikori WP	CDI FM
6)	92.5	0.5	Mt Hagen WHP	KBBN
1)	94.3	0.3	Kerema Gul	Voice of Blessed Peter Torot
7)	94.7	1	Lae Mor	FM Morobe
9)	95.3	1	Maprik ESP	FM Sepik Central
23)	95.3		Buka ARB	New Dawn FM
10)	96.0		Mosa WNB	NBPOL FM
1)	97.9	1	Port Moresby NCD	2G 97.9 FM
10)	98.0		Healla WNB	NBPOL FM
10)	98.0		Kapiura WNB	NBPOL FM
12)	98.0	0.02	Lihir NIP	FM Lihir
13)	98.1	0.3	Mt Hagen WHP	Trinity FM
14)	98.3	1	Wewak WSP	Laif FM
15)	98.5	0.02	Port Moresby NCD	Campus FM
16)	98.9	0.02	Misima Mine MBP	FM Misima
17)	99.5	0.5	Port Moresby NCD	Rait FM**
18)	99.5	0.01	Bereina Cen	Waima FM
19)	99.9	0.1	WSP	99.9 FM
19)	99.9	0.1	Kompian Eng	Kom Community R. 99.9 FM
20)	102.1	0.3	Lae Mor	R. Australia
21)	103.3	0.5	Mougolu SHP	Mougolu FM
22)	103.7	0.3	Lae Mor	CDL-103.7
1)	105.1	0.3	Lorengau Man	Voice of Blessed Peter Torot
20)	106.7	0.1	Port Moresby NCD	BBC
20)	106.9	0.1	Lae Mor	BBC
20)	109.9	0.1	Port Moresby NCD	R. Australia

‡ currently reported inactive
** relaunched as new nationwide commercial network
Addresses and other information
1) PO Box 300, Boroko, NCD ☎ +675 3410110. Individually owned and operated by several Catholic Church dioceses **L.P:** Father Mlak Zdzislaw SVD **Slogan:** "Your Daily Spiritual Companion" **W:** catholicpng.org.pg & voiceoftorot.com **E:** admin@voiceoftorot.com – **2)** CDI Foundation Trust Fund, P.O. Box 383, Port Moresby NCD ☎ +675 325 0706/1759 **W:** cdi.org.pg **Prgr:** 24h – **3)** HIRAD Ltd, P.O Box 333, Port Moresby NCD ☎ +675 321 0533 – **4)** Evangelical Church of PNG – **6)** Krai Bilong Baibel [Bible FM], Bible Broadcasting Network, P.O. Box 617, Mt Hagen WHP **L.P:** Brad & Deborah Wells **W:** biblefm.com **E:** bwellspng@yahoo.com **Prgr:** 24h **F.PI:** Bible FM Lae and repeater in WHP – **7)** Intouch Media, P.O. Box 3310, Lae Mor

☎ +675 479 1477 – **9)** Papindo Trading – **10)** NBPOL – **11)** Pacific Adventist University (PAU), PMB, Boroko NCD ☎ +675 328 0400 **W:** pau.ac.pg facebook.com/2g.97.9fm **E:** 2g@pau.ac.pg **ID:** "Exalting God above all the earth. Psalms 97.9" – **12)** Lihir Gold Mine – **13)** Catholic Archdiocese of Mt. Hagen, Mt Hagen WHP **Prgr:** 0600-2000 – **14)** United Christian Broadcasting [UCB Pacific Partners], P.O. Box 556, Wewak ESP ☎ +675 456 1400 **L.P:** Mgr Tony Dua **Affiliation:** UCB International, Auckland NZ – **15)** University of PNG (Physics Dept), P.O. Box 320, University, Port Moresby NCD ☎ +675 326 7191 – **16)** Misima Gold Mines Pty Ltd – **17)** CHM-Rabi FM, P.O. Box 1106, Boroko, NCD ☎ +675 325 6644 🖷 +675 325 0134 **L.P:** MD Raymond Chin, Mgr-Provincial Radio Richard Francisco **W:** chmsupersound.com **Note:** new nationwide FM service launched Sept 2013 with relays in several provincial towns. No further information is still currently available. This will be a new major commercial network. – **18)** Waima Radio Station Assoc, Bereina Cen – **19)** Baptist Union of PNG, PO Box 705, Mt Hagen WHP ☎ 🖷+675 542 3726 **W:** bupng.net **E:** bupng@global.net.pg **L.P:** Dir: John Kaewa **Community Radio:** KOM, Kompiam, Eng 99.9 relay 95.9 Pakau; Tekin CR, Oksaprim, Sanduan 0.1kW – **20)** TEPNG, P.O. Box 1388, Boroko NCD ☎ +675 325 6322 🖷 +675 325 0350 **L.P:** Mgr Ops Wayne Wilson **E:** wwilson@tepng.com **R. Australia:** 24/7 Pacific stream via satellite from Melbourne **BBC:** 24/7 Pacific stream via satellite from London – **21)** Mougolu SHP – **22)** Catholic Diocese of Lae, Lae Mor – **23)** Buka ARB ☎ +675 973 9319 🖷 +675 973 9285 **L.P:** Stn Mgr Aloysius Laukai **W:** bougainville.typepad.com/newdawn **E:** tambolema@daltron.com.pg . – **24)** Port Moresby, NCD ☎ +675 320 1888 **W:** facebook.com/lalokau891 **L.P:** Dir.Prgr Peter Heni

PARAGUAY

L.T: UTC -4h (4 Oct 15-27 Mar 16, 2 Oct 16-26 Mar 17: -3h; dates subject to confirmation) – **Pop:** 6.8 million — **Pr.L:** Spanish, Guaraní — **E.C:** 50Hz, 220V — **ITU:** PRG — **Int. dialling code:** +595

COMISIÓN NACIONAL DE TELECOMUNICACIONES (CONATEL)

🖃 **Offices:** Presidente. Franco N° 780, Esq. Ayolas, Asunción ☎ 21 438 2000 **W:** conatel.gov.py **L.P:** Pres: Dr. Eduardo González
NB: ‡ = inactive, ± = varying freq., † = irregular

MW	Call	kHz	kW	Station, location, h. of tr
AP01)	ZP16	550	20/12	R. Parque, Ciudad del Este: 0800-0100
AM01)	ZP15	570	1	R. LV del Amambay, Pedro Juan Caballero: 0900-0200 Sun 1100-00200
M0I3)	ZP39	570	12	R. San Roque, Ayolas 0930-0100
SP01)	ZP32	590	5	R. Ycuámandyyú, San Pedro: 0900-020
BO01)	ZP30	610	50	LV del Chaco Paraguayo, Filadelfia: 0900-0230 SS 1000-0130
SP02)	ZP40	±620	5	R. Nasaindý, San Estanislao 0900-0300 Sat.: -000 Sun: -2300
CG01)	ZP19	±640	15	R. Caaguazú, Coronel Oviedo : 0900-0500
CA01)	ZP4	650	50	R. Uno, Asunción: 0900-0430 Sat:24h Sun 1000-0300
CO05)	ZP74	660	10	R. Regional, Concepción
AP02)	ZP26	660	5	R. Itapirú, Cd. del Este
CA02)	ZP11	680	50	R. Caritas, Asunción: 24h
NE01)	ZP12	700	12	R. Cachos Antonio López, Pilar; (rel. R. Nal 920): 0800-0300
PH01)	ZP17	720	50	R. Pai Puku, Teniente Irala Fernández 0900-0100 Sun; silent
CA03)	ZP7	730	50	R. Cardinal, Lambaré: 24h
CZ01)	ZP38	740	1/0.5	R. Hechizo, Caazapá
CA04)	ZP42	750	5	R. LV de la Policía, Asunción
IP01)	ZP80	760	25/10	R. Encarnación, Encarnación – irr test
CA05)	ZP70	780	30	R. Primero de Marzo, Asunción: 24h
CN01)	ZP27	800	5/3	R. Mbaracayú, Salto del Guairá: 24h
CA13)	ZP23	800	5	La Union R800, Asunción: 1000-0300 Sat: 1400-2100 Sun: 1100-2000
GU01)	ZP6	840	5	R. Guairá, Villarrica: 0900-2400
CR01)	ZP28	±860	1	LV de la Cordillera, Caacupé: 0900(SS 1000)-0400
CE01)	ZP33	±890	5/0.5	R. Tres de Febrero, Itá (895 at night)
CA06)	ZP1	920	100	R. Nal. del Paraguay, Asunción: 0800-0300
CA07)	ZP9	970	80	R. 9-70 , Asunción: 0800-0400
AM02)	ZP31	980	5	R. Mburucuyá, Pedro Juan Caballero: 0900-0130
CE02)	ZP36	1000	5/0.5	R. Mil, Asunción: 0930-0400
CA08)	ZP14	1020	25	R. Nandutí, Asunción: 24h
MI01)	ZP43	1040	5	R. Arapysandú, San Ignacio: 0900-0200
IP02)	ZP51	1070	3	AM 1070 Radio, Puerto Triunfo
CE03)	ZP25	1080	10	R. Monumental, Luque: 1100(Sun 0900)-2330

MW	Call	kHz	kW	Station, location, h. of tr
AM03)	ZP71	1100	5	R. Nú Verá, Capitán Bado
CE04)	ZP24	1120	10	La Deportiva, Lambaré, San Lorenzo: 0900-0300
CR02)	CP22	1140	5/2	R. Central de Notícias, Atyrá
CA09)	ZP72	1160	10	R. Antena Dos, Asunción
CG02)	ZP52	1180	5/1	R. Coronel Oviedo – RCO-AM, Coronel Oviedo
AP03)	ZP45	1190	5	LV de la Libertad, Henendarias
CE05)	ZP44	1200	10	R. Libre, Fernando de la Mora:0930-0130,
CA10)	ZP3	1250	5	R. Asunción, Asunción
GU03)	ZP34	1260	5	R. Panambi Vera, Villarrica
AP04)	ZP53	1280	10/025	LV del Este, Cd. del Este (F.P.I. to 1310)
CA11)	ZP53	1300	5	R. Fe y Alegria, Villa Hayes
AP04)	ZP53	1310	10/025	LV del Este, Cd. del Este (F.P.I.)
CA12)	ZP13	1330	10	R. Chaco Boreal, Asunción: 24h
C001)	ZP37	1360	1	R. Yby Ya´u, Ybu Ya´u
C002)	ZP8	1380	1	R. Concepción, Concepción
C003)	ZP42	1420	5	R. Güyrá Campana, Horqueta
MI02)	ZP35	1430	2	R. Mangore, S. Juan Bautista: 0900-0200 (Sun -0000)
C004)	ZP29	1450	5	R. Vallemi, Vallemi
AM04)	ZP23	1480	1	R. Dos Fronteras, Bella Vista Norte
CE06)	ZP20	1480	5	R. América, Nemby: 24h

SW	Call	kHz	kW	Name, location and h of tr
BO1)	ZP30	6884	0.1	LV del Chaco Paraguayo, Filadelfia: (USB feed)
PH1)	ZP17	6890	0.1	R. Pa´í Puku, Tte. Irala Fernández: (USB feed)
CA6)	ZPA1‡9735		100	R. Nal. del Paraguay, Asunción

Addresses and other information:

AM00 (AMAMBAY)
AM01) 14 de Mayo 485 esq Cerro León, Pedro Juan Caballero ☎336 272537 **W:** amambay570.com.py **E:** amambay570@gmail.com - **FM:** 100.5MHz – **AM02)** Villa María Victoria, Fracción San Jorge, Pedro Juan Caballero ☎336 272528 **W:** mburucuya.com.py –**AM03)** Estrella c/4 de Enero, Capitán Bado, Amambay ☎337 230262 **W:** capitanba-donoticias.com/radio1100 **E:** radiozp71@gmail.com – **AM04)** Calle Iturbe 146, Bella Vista Norte **W:** amambay570.com.py - **FM:** 100.5MHz
AP00 (ALTO PARANA)
AP01) Km 10 Av San Blas.. Ciudad del Este **W:** Facebook: RadioParqueFm1025 – **FM:** 102.5 MHz – **AP02)** Av Coronel Sánchez 3800, Cd del Este **W:** radioitapiru.com **E:** radioitapiru@hotmail. com - **FM:** 96.1MHz – **AP03)** Juan E.O´Leary 152, 1a piso, Oficina 5, Hernandarias **W:** radiolavozdelalibertad1190.jimdo.com – **AP04)** Avenida San Blás No 353, Ciudad del Este ☎61 512 583 **W:** lavoz.com. py **E:** lavozam@hotmail.com
B000 (BOQUERÓN)
B001) 29 Filadelfia, 9300 Fernheim ☎491 432330 🖷491 432501 **W:** zp30.com.py **E:** info@zp30.com.py
CA00 (CAPITAL)
CA01) Av Mariscal López 2948 c/MacArthur, Asunción ☎ 21 603400 **W:** hoy.com.py/radio-uno **E:** info@radiouno.com.py – **CA02)** Kubischek 661 y Azara, (Cas 1313), Asunción **W:** caritas.com.py **E:** caritas@caritas. com.py ☎21 213570 🖷21 204161 – **CA03)** Calles Comendador Nicolás Bó y Guaranies 1334, Lambaré (Cas 247), Asunción ☎21 303089 **W:** cardinal.com.py **E:** info@cardinal.com.py – **CA04)** Comandancia de la Policia Nacional, El Paraguayo Independiente c/Chile, Asunción ☎ 21 492 515 **W:** fmenvivo.com/la_voz_de_la_policia **E:** rrpnacional@ gmail.com – **CA05)** Av Perón y Concepción Prieto Yegros, Asunción ☎21 300380 **W:** 780am.com.py **E:** administracion@780am.com.py – **CA06)** Av Blas Garay 241e/Yegros e Iturbe, asunción ☎ 21 390 376 🖷21 390 375 **W:** radionacionaldelparaguay.com **E:** contacto@ radionacional.com.py – **CA07)** Av Rodriguez de Francia 34, Asunción ☎21 450 283 **W:** radio970am.com.py **E:** info@radio970am.com.py – **CA08)** Choferes del Chaco 1194, Asunción ☎21 604308 **W:** nanduti. com.py **E:** publicidad@holdingderadio.com.py – **CA09)** Estados Unidos 2019, Asunción ☎21 282 661 – **CA11)** O´Leary 1109 c/ Séptima Proyectada, Asunción ☎21 371659 **W:** radiofeyalegriapy.org **E:** comunicaciones@feyalegria. org.py – **CA12)** Alejo Garcia 2589 con Rio de la Plata, Asuncion ☎ 21 425 589 **W:** chacoboreal.com.py **E:** info@chacoboreal.com.py – **CA13)** Av Republica Argentina 316 (con Souza), Asunción ☎21 611 370 **W:** launionr800.com.py **E:** info@launionr800.com.py
CE00 (CENTRAL)
CE01) Av Enrique Doldán Ibieta y Presidente Franco, Itá ☎24 32543 **Guaraní:** 0900-1000, 1330-1430, 1800-1845 – **CE02)** ☎21 674000 **W:** radio1000.com.py **E:** info@radio1000.com.py – **CE03)** Av General Aquino 9999 y José Bonifacio, Luque ☎21 644330 **W:** monumental. com.py **E:** mensajes@monumental.com.py – **FM:** 91.9 MHz – **CE04)** Av Médicos del Chaco c/Paz del Chaco, Altcenter, Plaza de Negocios, Lambaré ☎21 307101 **W:** ladeportiva.am **E:** info@ladeportiva.am– **CE05)** Av Zavalaa Cué 1620, Fernando de la Mora Zona Sur ☎21

509 087 📄21 509076 **W:** rlibre.wordpress.com/la-fundacion-libre **E:** radiolibre@gmail.com – **CE06)** Cas 2220, Asunción ☎21 964 100 **W:** radioiglesia.com **E:** jglesiaradio@gmail.com
CG00 (CAAGUAZÚ)
CG01) Jóvenes por la democracia c/ Km 131, Coronel Oviedo ☎521 1202251**W:** Facebook - Radio Caaguazú - **FM:** 102.3MHz – **CG02)** Av Mariscal Estigarribia 304 casi Yrendague, Coronel Oviedo ☎521 202579 **W:** Facebook: - Radio Coronel Oviedo **E:** rco1180@hotmail.com - **Guaraní:** 50% of prgr 0900-0100 - **FM:** 91.9MHz FM del Sol
CN00 (CANINDEYÚ)
CN01) Eduardo López Moreira 5155, Salto del Guairá ☎462 42 350
CO00 (CONCEPCIÓN)
CO01) Av San Juan y alas Paraguayo, Ybu Ya'u ☎39 210 263 **W:** Facebook: Radio Yby Yby ZP37 **E:** carlosescobar777@hotmail.es – **CO02)** Panchito López 241 entre Prof.Cabral y Screiber, (Cas 78), Concepción ☎31 242318 📄31 242254 – **CO03)** José Luís Arbues c/Ruta 5, Horqueta ☎32 222364 – **CO04)** Zona Urbana, Vallemi ☎351 230329 – **CO05)** Av Pinedo y Mayor Lorenzo Medina, Concepción ☎331 243589 **W:** Facebook: Radio Regional 660 AM **E:** contacto@radioregional660.com
CZ00 (CAAZAPA)
CZ01) Mariscal Estigarribia esquina Boulevard Villarica,Caazapá ☎542 232607 **E:** causacomunpy@hotmail.com
CR00 (CORDILLERA)
CR01) Dr Venancio Pino y 3ra Proyectada, Caacupé ☎511 423326 **W:** radiozp28.com **E:** cordillera860am@hotmail.com – **CR02)** Atyrá
GU00 (GUAIRA)
GU01) Pte Franco 788 y Alejo Garcia, Villarrica ☎📄 54 142385 **W:** radioguaira.com.py **E:** info@radioguaira.com.py **FM:** 103.5MHz – **GU03)** Angostura y Olimpio, Bo Ybarotu, Villarrica ☎541 42229 **W:** Facebook: Radio Panambivera **E:** panambivera@grupopanambi.com
IP00 (ITAÚA)
IP01) Mcal Estigarribia – casi 14 de Mayo – Centro, Encarnación ☎71 205195 **W:** radioencarnacion.com **E:** gerencia@radioencarnacion.com – **FM:** 95.7 MHz – **IP02)** Puerto Triunfo
MI00 (MISIONES)
MI01) Av Mariscal López y Capitan del Puerto, San Ignacio ☎82 232374 **W:** arapysanduam.blogspot.no **E:** arapysanduam@gmail.com – **MI02)** Coronel Alfredo A Ramos esq San Juan, San Juan Bautista, Misiones ☎81 212 306 **W:** radiomangore.com/index **E:** mangoream@hotmail.es – **MI03)** 7ma. y 2da. Proyectadas. Villa Permanente, Ayolas ☎7222 2433 **W:** .radiosanroque.com **E:** radiosanroque570@gmail.com
NE00 (ÑEEMBUCÚ)
NE01) Alberdi y Av Iralda, Pilar ☎786 232219 **W:** radionacionaldel-paraguay.com.py **E:** zp12pilar@gmail.com
PH00 (PRESIDENTE HAYES)
PH01) Tta. Irala Fernández, Ruta Transchaco km-. 389, Chaco ☎424 270349 (In Asuncion J. Eulogio Estigarribia c/ M. Molas ☎21 605754) **W:** radiopaipuku.org.py **E:** rppuku@tigo.com.py
SP00 (SAN PEDRO)
SP01) Ruta 11 Juana M de Lara, Villa de San Pedro ☎34 2222300 **W:** Facebook: Radio Ycuamandyyu **E:** radioycuamandyyu@gmail.com – **SP02)** Av Cnl. Zoilo González e/ Pedro Juan Caballero y Mauricio José Troche, San Pedro ☎43 4342 2095 📄43 4342 0292 **W:** radio-nasaindy.com.py

FM in Metro Asunción (MHz): 88.3 R. Ñemby – 89.1 R. Conquistador – 90.1 R.Viva – 90.7 Ysapy – 91.1 Estacion 40 – 91.5 R. Top Milenium – 91.9 Hit FM – **CA3:** 92.3 Los 4o Principales – 92.7 R. Fernando de la Mora – 94.7 R. Azul y Oro – **CA6:** 95.1 R.Nacional – 95.5 Rock & Pop – 95.9 R. Amor – 96.5 R. Disney – **CA5:** 97.1 FM Latina – 97.9 R. Nuevo Tiempo – 98.5 Yacyretá – 99.1 R. Corazón – 100.1 Canal 100 – 100.5 Arpa –100.9 Monte Carlo – 101.3 R. Farra – 101.7 FM Puerto Elsa – 102.1 R. Obedira – 102.7 Aspen Classic FM – 103.1 FM Popular – 103.7 R. Lambaré 2000 – 105.1 R. Venus– 106.1 FM Paraguay – 106.9 R. Urbana – 107.3 R. Maria – 25) 107.7 FM Concert

PERU

L.T: UTC -5h — **Pop:** 30.5 million — **Pr.L:** Spanish, Quechua, Aymara — **E.C:** 60Hz, 220V — **ITU:** PRU — **Int. dialling code:** +51

MINISTERIO DE TRANSPORTES, COMUNICACIONES, VIVIENDA Y CONSTRUCCION
Dirección General de Telecomunicaciones
📋 Jr. Zorritos N° 1203, Lima 1 ☎ 1 1 6157800 **W:** mtc.gob.pe **E:** estadistica@mtcgob.pe
L.P: Viseministro de comunicaciones: Raúl Ricardo Pérez – Reyes Espejo

ASOCIACION DE RADIO Y TELEVISION DEL PERU (ARTV)
📋 Av. Manco Capac N° 333, Lima 13 ☎ 1 3321656

‡ = inactive ± = varying freq † = irregular
Aqp = Provincia de Arequipa

	MW Call	kHzkW	Station, location, h of tr.
LM01)	OBX4E	540 10	R. Inca del Perú, Lima: 24h
LL01)	OCX2D	540 1	R. San Antonio, El Porvenir
TC20)	OBU6W	550 1	R.Bacan Sat // 750, Pocollay
JN49)	OBU4M	560 1	R. La Luz, Sicaya
LM02)	OBZ4L	±560 5	R. Oriente, Lima
LB01)	OBX1H	560 5	Radiomar, Chiclayo
IC33)	OAM5I	570 1	R. OAM5I, Salas
LB02)	OAU1M	570 3	R. Univ. Nal. Pedro Ruiz Gallo, Lambayeque
LL51)	OAM2M	570 3	R. Antena 9, Huamachuco
CJ01)	OAX2E	580 10	R. Marañón, Jaén: 24h
LL02)	OCY2L	580 1	R. El Sol, La Esperanza
LM03)	OAX4M	580 12	R. Maria, Lima: 24h
PU58)	OAM7N	580 1	R. Publica, Puno
AQ02)	OCX6V	590	NSE Radio, Arequipa
PI28)	OAM5E	590 1	R. OAM5E, Chincha
LD03)	OBX2B	600 1	R. Ondas de Paz (IPDA), Trujillo: 24h
LM04)	OBZ4W	600 10	R. Cora, Lima: 24h
PI55)	OCU1K	600 1	R. Frias, Frias
CJ32)	OCY2I	610 6	R. Santa Monica, Chota: 1100-0100, Sun 1145-1700
TC19)	OBU6V	610 1	R. OBU6V, Pocollay
AQ53)	OCX6K	620 1	R. Maria, Uchumayo, Aqp
LL04)	OAX2M	620 0.4	R. Chepen, Chepen
LM05)	OBU4B	620 10	R. Ovación, San Isidro
CU72)	OBU7I	630 1	Chaski R., Urubamba: 1000-1500, 1700-0100
PI04)	OBX1U	630 18	R. Cutivalú "LV del Desierto", Castilla: 1000-0100 Sat/Sun 1100
LB03)	OAU1Y	640 3	R. La Luz, José Leonardo Ortiz
LM06)	OAZ4K	640 10	R. Del Pacifico, Lima: 1030-0430
PU01)	OBX7B	640 10	R. Onda Azul, Puno. 0800-0400, S/S -0300
AM11)	OAU9D	†650	R. Kampagkis, Nieva
CJ67)	OBU2P	650 1.5	R. Bendición Cristiana, Huambos: 1000-0400
IC25)	OCU5Q	650 1	R. OCU5Q, Pueblo Nuevo
LL05)	OAX2N	650 1	R. Regional del Norte, Trujillo
PU57)	OBM7C	650 1	R. OBM7C, Sandia
TC24)	OCU6L	650 1	R. OCU6L, Alto de la Alianza
CU35)	OAZ7J	660 3	R. Santa Monica, Wanshaq
LB04)	OCX1U	660 5	R. J.H.C., Chiclayo
LM07)	OCX4R	660 10	R. La Inolvidable, Lima: 1100-0700
PU02)	OAX7H	670 10	R. Nal... del Perú, Puno
CJ03)	OCY2Y	680 5	R. San Luis, Jaén
CU73)	OBU7G	680 1	R. Vida, Cusco
IC01)	OAX5E	680 5	Emisora del Pacifico, Ica: 1100-0600
LL06)	OBX2L	680 0.5	R. Amauta, Chócope
LM08)	OBX4A	680 20	RBC Satelital, San Isidro
PA13)	OAM4B	680 5	R. OAM4B, Chaupimarca
CU74)	OAM7C	690 1	R. Altiva, Yanaoca
CU04)	OBU7K	700 1	R. La Salle, Maras
JN01)	OBU4J	700 3	R. La Luz, El Tambo
LL07)	OBU2T	700 1	R. Sausal Superior, Ascope
LM09)	OBZ4H	700 25	R. R. Integridad, San Miguel
SM15)	OAU9A	700 1	R. Canal Catolica San Gabriel, Moyobamba
AQ04)	OAU6L	710 1	R. Amor, Socabaya, Aqp
IC02)	OBX5Q	710 5	R. Programas del Perú, Ica
MD01)	OCX7I	‡710 10	R. Nacional del Peru, Puerto Maldonado
CU05)	OBU7O	720 3	NSE Radio, Santiago
JN04)	OAU4E	720 10	R. Sideral, La Oroya: 24h
LL08)	OAX2J	‡720 25	R. Nal.. del Perú, Trujillo
LB06)	OAU10	720 0.5	R. Frecuencia Oceánica, San José
PU45)	OCU7J	720 2	R. Noticias, Puno
CJ05)	OBU2Q	730 2.5	R. Maria, Cajamarca
LM10)	OAX4G	730 50	R. Programas del Perú - RPP, San Isidro:24h
PI05)	OAX1D	730 10	R. del Pacifico, Piura: 1100-0500
PU52)	OAM7X	730 1	R. Altura, Macusani: 0900-0100
TC20)	OCU6G	730 1	R. OCU6G, Tacna
AQ05)	OAX6C	740 10	R. Continental, Paucarpat Aqp
CJ38)	OBX2U	740 5	R. Ilucan, Cutervo: 1000-0300
CU06)	OBU7C	740 1	R. La Rompa, Cusco
JN46)	OCU4X	740 1	R. Vision, Huancayo
LL09)	OCX2X	740 1	R. El Puerto, Pascamayo
PU50)	OAM7R	740 1	R. OAM7R, Juliaca
CU75)	OCU7O	750 1	R. OCU7O, Yanaoca
PA01)	OCX4X	750 10	R. Altura, Cerro de Pasco: 1000-0400
IC27)	OAM5D	750 1	R. OAM5D, Chincha
TC14)	OBU6I	750 1	R. Bacan Sat 2, Pocollay
SM19)	OAU9G	750 5	R. OAU9G, Bellavista

MW	Call	kHz	kW	Station, location, h of tr.
AP11)	OBU5B	760	1	R. Municipal, Chincheros
LL10)	OBX2K	760	0.5	R. Andino, Otuzco
LM11)	OCU4G	760	10	R. Mar Plus, Chorillos: 24h
PU59)	OAM7Q	760	1	R. Azángaro, Azángaro
AQ06)	OBX6H	770	2.5	R. La Inolvidable, Caiama, Aqp
CU76)	OCU7K	770	1	R.R. LV Evangelica, Urcos
LB31)	OCX1T	770	3	R. Vision, José Leonardo Ortiz: 24h
PU03)	OAU7D	770	2.5	R. LV del Allinccapac, Macusani
AY31)	OCU5L	780	2	R. OCU5L, Ayacucho
CJ07)	OBU2N	780	1	R. Coremarca, Bambamarca: 1000-0200
LM12)	OAX4X	780	3	R. Victoria,Lima: 24h
PU04)	OAZ7S	780	10	R. Nuevo Tiempo, Juliaca: 24h
TB01)	OAX1K	780	10	R. Nal. del Perú, Tumbes
CU07)	OAZ7H	790	3	R. La Luz, Cusco
LL11)	OAX2I	790	10	R. Programas del Perú - RPP, Trujillo
TC16)	OBU6D	790	2.5	R. Uno, Tacna
AO07)	OBX6A	800	0.3	Contacto Sur, Cerro Colorado, Aqp
CJ71)	OCU2Y	800	3	R. Vision, Cajamarca: 24h
IC03)	OBX5B	‡800	0.5	R. Sur, Ica
JN05)	OBU4D	800	1	R. Vida, Huancayo
LM13)	OAU4H	800	0.5	R. La Luz, Huaral
PI06)	OCX1P	800	1	Telecom del Norte, Piura
AY19)	OBU5E	810	1.5	R. OBU5E, Huamanga
AP19)	OCU5Z	810	3	R.Asociación Cultural Tintaya, Cotabambas
CJ80)	OCU2V	810	1	R. OCU2V, Jaen
CU70)	OAM7E	‡810	5	R. Jerusalen, Cusco
LL12)	OAU2G	810	1	R. Apocali, Trujillo
MQ14)	OCU6Q	810	2	R. OCU6Q, Moquegua
PU05)	OAX7T	810	10	R. Programas del Perú - RPP, Juliaca: 24h
CJ43)	OBX2J	820	0.5	R. Nuevo Continente, Cajamarca
PI54)	OBU1X	820		R. Vision, Piura
LM14)	OAX4O	820	20	R. Libertad, Lima: 1000-0300
CU08)	OAZ7U	830	1	R. Inti Raimi, Santiago: 0900-0100
CJ62)	OCU2M	830	1	R. Ebenezer, Bambamarca
JN06)	OAU4C	830	10	R. Capital, El Tambo
LL52)	OAM2A	830	5	R. Educacion, Trujillo
PU53)	OAM7W	830	1	R. OAM7W, Macusani
TC02)	OAX6D	830	10	R. Nacional del Perú, Tacna
AN01)	OAU3Q	840	1	R. Vision, Casma: 24h
AN25)		840		R. Campesina, Huari: 24h
AP15)	OCU5N	840	1	R. OCU5N, Abancay
AQ01)	OBX6Y	840	1	R. Azul, Cayama Aqp: 24h
CJ08)	OAU2E	840	1	R. Nuevo Continente, San Ignacio
CU58)	OCU7I	840	1	R. Santa Cruz, Kunturkanki
PI50)	OCU1C	840	1	R. Campesina de Ayabaca), Ayabaca
AM12)	OBX9W	850	1	R. OBX9W, Chachapoyas
CU77)	OAM7I	850	5	R. Lorena, San Sebastian
HN19)	OBU3B	850	1	R. OBU3B. Cerro Jactay
LB49)	OCU1Y	850	1	R.OCU1Y, Chiclayo
LM15)	OAX4A	850	40	R. Nal. del Perú, Lima: 24h
PI56)	OBU1M	850	1	R. Nal. del Peru, Ayabaca
TC11)	OAU6S	‡850		R. Nal. del Peru, Tarata
PU35)	OBU7Z	850		R. Pachamama, Puno: 0830-0300
CJ48)	OCY2A	860		R. Norandina, Celendin: 0900-0300
PI08)	OCX1M	860	3	R. Nuevo Norte, Sullana
PU609	OBM7B	860		R. OBM7B, Sandia
AQ52)	OCX6F	870	2.5	R. Impacto Universal, Uchumayo Aqp
CU10)	OCX7R	870	1	R. Mundo, Wanchaq: 24h
JN34)	OCX4D	870	2.5	R. Huancayo, El Tambo: 24h
LB08)	OBX1F	870	10	R. Programas del Perú - RPP, Chiclayo: 24h
PU06)	OAU7O	870	5	R. Libertad, Puno
AY22)	OBU5W	880	1	R. OBU5W,
LL15)	OAX2P	880	2	R. Sintonia, Trujillo
LM16)	OBX4R	880	50	R. Union, Lima: 24h
PU09)	OCU4S	880	5	R. Cumbre, Chaupimarca
AP16)	OCU5J	890	1	R. Cielo, San Pedro de Cachora
CU56)	OCU7C	890	1	R. Laramani, Espinar
IC29)	OCU5W	890	1	R.OCU5W, Ica
PU07)	OBX7S	890	3	R. Bahá'í del Lago Titicaca, Chiucuito: 0900-0200
CJ10)	OAU2N	890	1	R. Panorama, Cajamarca: 1000-0400
AQ11)	OBX6K	900	3	R. Nevada, Uchumayo, Aqp: 24h
HN02)	OAX3E	900		R. Ribereña, Aucaycu
LM17)	OBX4X	‡900	10	R. Felicidad, Lima: 24h
PI52)	OCU1P	900	1	R.Huarmaca, Huarmaca
AY02)	OAU5M	910	1	R. Estacion Wari, Ayacucho
CU40)	OAU7M	910	1	R. Regional – R.Quechua, Sicuani
PU08)	OAU7G	910	1	R. Vision del Altiplano, Juliaca
CJ66)	OAM2G	910	1	R. Vision, Samangay: 24h
CU66)	OAM7H	920	1	CVC La Voz, Cusco
IC04)	OCX5C	920	1	R. Stelar, Chinca Alta
MD07)	OCU7W	920	1	R. OCU7W, Tambopata
LL16)	OBX2S	920	1	R. Ollantay, Virú
PI10)	OBX1J	920	10	R. Programas del Peru - RPP, Piura: 24h
PU42)		920		R. Campesina, Juli: 0900-0300
SM01)	OAX9V	920	1	R. Marginal, Tocache
TC16)	OBU6M	920	2.5	R. Uno, Tacna: 24h
AM13)	OBX9V	930	5	R. OBX9V, Huambo
AQ12)	OBX6T	930	5	R. Yaravi, Cerro Colorado, Aqp.
AY23)	OBU5S	930	1	R. OBU5S, Pucar del Sara Sara
CU67)	OAM7J	930	1	R. Cadena Sur, Espinar
LB40)	OCU1O	930	3	R. Nor Andina, Olmos: 0900-0300
LL17)	OCX2V	930	1	R. Inti, Chepén
LM18)	OAX4E	930	5	R. Moderna - "R. Papa", Lima: 24h
PU09)	OBU7T	930	3	R. Cadena Colca, Juliaca
AQ55)	OBU6G	940	1	R. OBU6G, Cotahuasi
CU13)	OBX9P	940	1.5	R. Las Vegas – W Radio, Wanchaq: 24h
JN08)	OBU4E	940	1	R. Luz, Jauja
PI47)	OBU1Y	940	1	R. Studio Satelite, Tambo Grande
AN02)	OBX3S	950	1	R. Programas del Perú - RPP, Chimbote
AP12)	OBU5R	950	1	R. OBU5R, Cotabambas
AY24)	OBU5N	950	1	R. OBU5N, Paucar del Sara Sara
CJ72)	OAM2H	950	1.5	Onda Popular, Bambamarca
PU46)	OAM7S	950	1	R. OAM7S, Juliaca
TC13)		950		R. Campesina, Tarata
AQ13)	OBX6S	960	18	R. El Pueblo 960, Mariano Melgar, Aqp
CU14)	OBU7P	960	1	R. Concierto Santa Monica, Espinar
JN09)	OCY4V	960	1	R. Manantial, Chilca
LB11)	OBX1Y	±960	3	R. WSP, Chiclayo: (r. on 958): 0900-0400
LM19)	OAX4D	960	10	R. Panamericana, Lima: 24h
CJ13)	OAU2K	970	1	R. Lider del Norte, Cajamarca
CU15)	OAU7A	970	5	R. Tropicana, Wanchaq
IC05)	OBX5A	970	1	R. Comericial Sonora, Ica
PI11)	OBX1V	970	1.5	R. La Capullana, Sullana
PU11)	OBU7B	970	1	R. Union Qollasuyo, Juliaca
AQ14)	OAU6F	980	1.5	R. Universidad, Arequipa: 1000-0100
AM14)		980		R. Comercial Cosmos, La Peca
AY14)	OBU5K	980	1	R. LV de Huamanga, Huamanga
CJ42)	OCX2R	980	1	Andina R., Chota
CU78)	OCU7X	980	1	R. R. Caden Sur, Sicuani
JN10)	OBU4H	980	1	R. OBU4H, Huancayo
LB12)	OAU1N	980	1	R. Primavera, Lambayeque
PI51)	OBU1N	980	1	R. Campesina, Huancabamba
AN04)	OBX3L	990		R. Peruana, Chimbote
CJ14)	OBX2M	990	0.5	R. Contumaza, Contumaza
LM20)	OBX4J	990	12	R. Latina, Miraflores: 24h
PA07)	OCU4A	990		R. Oro, Huayllay
PI57)	OCU1H	990	3	R. Bendicion Cristiana, Piura
PU47)	OCU7T	990	2.5	R. OCU7T, Juliaca
TC04)	OAX6K	‡990	10	R. Continental, Tacna
AQ15)	OBX6R	1000	2.5	R. Edesa, Cerro Colorado, Aqp
CU16)	OAZ7P	‡1000	2	R. Prensa al Dia, Cusco
HV01)	OBX5W	1000	1	R. Lircay, Lircay
HN03)	OBX3V	1000	1	R. Huanuco
JN50)	OBU4Z	1000	1	R. OBU4Z, Pariahuanaca
LB44)	OCU1N	1000	7	R. OCU1N, San José
AM10)	OBX9T	1010	1	R. Fé, Bagua Grande
AQ56)	OBU6L	1010	1	R.Orcopampa, Orcopampa
AP13)	OBU5T	1010	1	R. OBU5T, Cotabambas
CJ15)	OBX2P	‡1010	1.5	R. San Francisco, Cajamarca
LM54)	OAX4U	1010	10	R. Cielo, Lima: 24h
PI13)	OBU1L	1010	1	LV de las Huarinjas, Huancabamba
PU48)	OCU7P	1010	1	R. Nac. del Peru, Juli
TB02)	OBZ1C	1010	1	R. Sonora, Tumbes
AY25)	OBU5M	1020	0.5	R. AM Vida, Huamanga
CJ41)	OAU2P	1020	2	R. Bambamarca, Bambamarca
LB45)	OCU1M	1020	1	R. OCU1M, José Leonardo Ortiz
CU17)	OBU7O	1020	1	R. Informes, Sicuani
CU85)	OAM7Y	1020	5	R.Kinsachata Tintaya, Espinar
JN11)	OBU4F	1020	1	R. Cristo Vive, Huancayo
PI14)	OBU1D	1020	1	R. La Luz, Piura
TC05)	OAU6J	‡1020	1	R. Internacional, Tacna
AQ16)	OCX6L	1030	1	R. Cumbia, Arequipa
CJ73)	OAM2E	1030	5	R. Cajamarca Viva, Cajamarca
CU18)	OCX7O	1030	1	R. HG-AM, Cusco
LL19)	OAU2U	1030	5	R. Los Andes, Huamachuco
PU12)	OAX7N	1030	1	R. LV del Altiplano, Puno
SM16)	OBX9Z	1030	1	R. OBX9Z, San Ramon
AN29)	OAU3P	1040	1	R. Nueva Vida, Chimbote
CJ74)	OAM2L	1040	1	R. OAM2L, Pomahuaca
CU19)	OAU7L	1040	1	R. Los Andes, Espinar
IC06)	OBX5U	1040	1	R. La Luz, Ica
LM21)	OBX4O	1040	10	R. Metropolitana, Miraflores
PI15)	OAZ1D	1040	1	R. Vecinal, Piura
AQ17)	OBX6B	1050	3	Bethel Radio, Uchumayo, Aqp

MW Call	kHz	kW	Station, location, h of tr.
CJ56) OCU2N	1050	1	R. Campesina, Cajamarca
JN12) OBZ4J	1050	1	Bethel Radio, Huancayo
LB42) OCU1E	1050	3	R. Bendición Cristiana, Chiclayo
LL20) OCX2B	1050	1	R. San Sebastian (R. Maria), Chepen
PI58) OAZ1C	1050	1	R. Superior, Chulucanas
PU13) OAZ7Q	1050	1	R. Noticias, Juliaca: 24h
AN27) OAU3S	1060	3	R. R.Cielo, Chimbote
AP14) OBU5Q	1060	2	R. Restauracion, Andahuaylas
AY26) OAU5P	1060	1	Estacion Wari, Huamanga
CJ17) OCY2O	±1060	5	R. Sudamerica, Cutervo
CU20) OAU7U	1060	1	R. Estudio 1060, Cusco
LM22) OCY4D	1060	1	R. Exito, Lima
MD04) OCU7V	1060	1	Tambopata
MQ10) OBU6O	1060	1	R. Municipilidad, Omate
PI41) OBU1F	1060		R. Studio 1060. Piura
AQ18) OAU6K	1070	1	R. Trinidad, Paucarpata, Aqp.: 1000-0200
HN13) OAU3N	1070	1	R. OAU3N, Huánuco
IC07) OAX5A	1070	0.2	R. San Juan, San Juan de Marcona
JN13) OBX4G	1070	1	R. Visión, San Ramón
LB14) OAU1J	1070	1	R. Vida, José Leonardo Ortiz
SM03) OBX9J	1070	3	R. Andes, Tarapoto
CJ18) OAU2L	1080	1	R. Nueva Vida, Cajamarca
CU21) OAX7S	1080	2.2	R. Salkantay, Cusco
JN51) OBU4W	1080	1	R. OBU4W, Huancayo
LM23) OAU4I	1080	10	R. La Luz, Lima: 24h
MQ11) OBU6H	1080	1	R. LV del Sur, Moquegua
PA10) OCU4O	1080	5	R. Mineria, Chaupimarca
PI16) OBX1D	±1080	1.5	R. La Luz, Piura
PU14) OCU7O	1080	1	R. Nacional, Ayaviri
AQ61) OBX6X	1090	1	R. Amistad (IPDA), Arequipa
AY05) OAU5F	1090	1	R. Inti Andina, Aucara
JN14) OCY4G	1090	1	Sonorama R., Huancayo
LB15) OBX1L	1100	1	R. Ondas de Paz (IPDA), Chiclayo
LM64) OAZ4W	1100	1	R. Programas del Peru - RPP, Barranca
LM71) OCU4N	1100	1	R. OCU4N, Cañete
LL46) OCU2E	1100		R. 1000, Julcan
PU15) OBX7Z	1100	1	R. LTC, Juliaca
CJ20) OCX2U	1110	1	R. Jaén, Jaén: 1030-0600
CU22) OCX7T	1110	5	R. Machupicchu, Cusco
HN17) OAU3R	1110	3	R. Cielo, Huánuco
LM24) OAU4J	1110	1	R. Feliz, Lima: 24h
MQ04) OBU6F	1110	1	R. Austral, Ilo
PI17) OCX1R	1110	0.5	R. Centro Popular, La Union
AQ20) OCX6U	1120	1	R. Municipal, Cerro Colorado, Aqp
AY06) OAU5H	1120	1	R. Quispillaccta, Ayacucho: 0900-1400. 2100-0100
CJ61) OAM2F	1120	3	R. Bambamarca – Frecuencia Lider, Chota
HV03) OAU5W	1120	0.5	R. Huayllahuara
JN58)	1120		R. San Bartolome, Junin
LL21) OBX2I	1120	1.5	R. Dinamica, Trujillo
LM67) OCU4E	1120	1	R. Bendición, Barranca
LT05) OAX8A	1120	5	R. Nacional, Iquitos
UC09) OBX8R	1120	1	R. OAX8A, Campoverde
CJ21) OAX2V	1130	1.2	R. Los Andes (RPP), Cjamarca
CU65) OAM7F	1130	5	R. Túpac Amaru, San Sebastian
JN60) OAM4K	1130		R. OAM4K, Junin
LM27) OAX4N	1130	2.6	R. Bacán, Lima: 24h
MQ09) OBU6Q	1130	3	R. OBU6Q, Moquegua
PI53) OCU1R	1130	1	R. OCU1R, (Huarmaca)
PU16) OAU7B	1130	1	R. Onda Popular, Juliaca
AN07) OAU3C	1140	1	R. Bahia, Chimbote: 1000-0200(Sun -2200)
AQ21) OAX6L	1140	1	R. Capital, Cerro Colorado, Aqp: (rel.: R.Capital, Lima)
CJ83) OAM2O	1140	1	R. Maria, Chota
IC08) OAX5W	1140	0.5	R. Chinchaysuyo, Chinca Alta
JN16) OCY4C	1140	1	R. Programas del Perú - RPP, Pilcomayo
LB16) OAU1T	1140	5	R. Fraternal, Ferreñafe
LL48) OCU2D	1140		Chami R., Otuzco
PI18) OBX1W	1140	1.5	R. Piura, Piura
CJ22) OCY2E	1150	0.5	R. Chasquillacta, Pedro Galvez: 1030-2200
CU23) OCX7Q	1150	2.5	R. Universal, Wanchaq: Mon-Sat 0900-1200
PA02) OBU4K	1150	5	R. Mineria, Cerro de Pasco
PU17) OAU7X	1150	2.5	R. La Sureña, Juliaca:
AY07) OBX5O	1160	1	R. Huanta 2000, Huanta : 1030-0130
CJ23) OAU2T	1160	1	R. Siglo 21, Chota
JN52) OCU4V	1160	1	R. Maranatha, Huancayo
LL22) OAX2C	1160	0.3	R. Libertad Mundo, Trujillo: 24h
LB17) OCX1S	1160	1	Radiales Nor Oriental del Marañón, Chiclayo
LM56) OAX4C	1160	1	R. 1160/R.Onda Cero Lima: 24h
MD02) OCX7Z	1160	1	R. del Sur, Tambopata
MQ05) OBX6G	‡1160	1	R. Nac. del Perú, Moquegua
PI59) OCU1Q	41160	1	R. LV Campesino, Huarmaca
AN08) OAZ3K	‡1170	1	R. Nor Peruana Chimbote
AQ22) OBX6L	1170	10	R. Programas del Perú, Uchumayo, Aqp
CJ24) OAU2M	1170	1	R. Layzon, Cajamarca
CU24) OBU7F	1170	1	Bethel Radio, Cusco
HV06) OAM5B	1170	2	R.OAM5B, Acobamba
IC19) OAU4N	1170	1	R. Horizonte La Voz del Agro, Pueblo Nuevo
JN58) OAM4I	1170	1	R. COSAT, Satipo
LM72) OAM7A	1170	1	R. OAM4E, Paramonga
PU18) OCX7Y	1170	0.5	R. Constelación, Puno
CJ25) OAM2K	1180	1	Municipalidad Provincial de Jaen, Jaen
JN18) OCY4Z	1180	1	R. Libertad , Junin
LM62) OCU4K	1180	10	NSE Radio, Lima
PI60) OAZ1H	1180	2.5	R. Vencinal, Piura
TC14) OCU6N	1180	1	R. Bacan Sat 2, Pocollay
AN09) OBX3D	1190	5	R. Ancash, Huaraz
AQ23) OCX6G	1190	1	R. Central de Noticias, Miraflores Aqp
AY27) OBU5U	1190	2	R.OBU5U, Huamanga
LB18) OAX1E	1190	10	Bravasa Radio, Chiclayo
CU25) OAX7B	1190	2	R. Tawantinsuyo, Cusco
MD08) OAM7V	1190	3	R. Cielo, Tambopata
TB08) OCU1S	1190	3	R. Cielo. Tumbes
AP03) OBX5X	1200	1	R. Comercial, Abancay
CJ26) OAU2A	1200	1	LV de Cumbe, Cajamarca: 1000-0200
JN19) OAU4G	1200	3	R. Andes, Huancayo
LM60) OAX4B	1200	3	Cadena R. 1200, Lima
PI61) OCU1A	1200	1	R. Fe, Piura
PU19) OCX7S	1200	1	R. Continental, Juliaca
PU55) OAM7O	1200	1	R.Universidad, Puno
TC06) OAU6P	1200	3	R. La Luz, Tacna
HV05)	1200		R. Master Mix, Huancavelica
AN34) OBU3D	1210	1	R. OBU3D, Chimbote
CJ75) OCU2W	1210	1	R. OCU2W, Querocoto
CU26) OAX7M	1210	1	R. Quillabamba, Quillabamba: 1000-0300
CU55) OCU7B	1210	1	R. Qorilazo, Chumbivilcas
HN12) OBX3X	1210	1	R. Ondas de Paz, Huanuco
JN20) OCY4T	1210	1	R. Galaxia, Satipo
LL24) OAX2Q	1210	1	R. Universo, Trujillo: 24h
AQ24) OAX6X	1220	10	R. Melodia, Hunter, Aqp: 24h
CU02) OAU7N	1220	1	R. Universidad de San Antonio Abad , Cusco: 24h
IC20) OBU5I	1220		R. Amor y Paz, San Clemente
JN53) OCU4W	1220	1.5	R. OCU4W, Huancayo
LB19) OCX1X	1220	3	R. Libertad, Chiclayo: 0900-0400
LM63) OCU4H	1220	1	R. Fe, Lima: 24h
CJ76) OAM2B	1230	1	R. Fé, Cajamarca
JN21) OBZA4Y	1230	1	R. Selecciones,Tarma: 1100-0200(Sun -1800)
LM65) OCU4C	1230		R. La Luz, Huacho
MD06) OAM7T	1230	2.5	R. Tambopata, Tambopata
MQ12) OBU6T	1230	1	R. OBU6T, Moquegua
PA03) OBX4Z	‡1230	1	R. LV de Oxapampa, Oxapampa
PU20) OAU7V	1230	1	R. Surupana, Caminca
AM01) OAU9B	1240	1	R. Bagua Grande, Chachapoyas
AN10) OAU3L	1240	1	R. La Luz, Chimbote
AQ25) OAU6D	1240	15	R. Lider, Socabaya, Aqp
CU27) OCU7Z	1240	1	R. Pachatusán, Sicuani
IC10) OAU5U	1240	1	R. Eco, Ica
JN22) OAU4V	1240	12	R. Maria, Huancayo: 24h
LB21) OAZ1A	1240	1	R. Ferreñafe, Ferrañafe
LL26) OAU2Y	1240	1	R. Nor Andino, Santiago de Chuco
PI69) OCX1C	1240	1	R.Sechura, Sechura
PU44) OCX1C	1240		R. Campesina, Ayaviri
CJ27) OAU2V	1250	1	HGV, Santa Cruz
CU28) OBX7A	1250	1	R. Solar, Cusco: 1000-0500
LM30) OAX4L	1250	5	R. Miraflores, Miraflores: 24h
MQ08) OAU6I	1250	1	R. Campesina, Omate
PI23) OBZ1B	1250	1.5	R. Dif. BNS, Talara Alta
SM07) OAX9C	1250	1	R. Americana, Nueva Cajamarca
UC10) OBX8S	1250	3	R. Cielo, Calleria
AN11) OAU3G	1260	1	R. El Pregonero Cristiano, Chimbote
AQ26) OBX6D	1260	1	R. Manahaim, Uchumayo Aqp
HN04) OAU3F	1260	1	R. La Luz, Huanuco
JN54) OCU4F	1260	1	R. Corazón Andino, El Tambo
LB20) OCX10	1260	1	R. Nova, Chiclayo
LL49) OBX2C	1260		R. Otuzco, Otuzco
LM68) OCU4B	1260	3	R. La Luz, San Vicente de Cañete
AY08) OBX5S	1260	0.3	R. Nac. del Perú, Ayacucho
AQ46) OBU6P	1270	1	R. San Antonio, Callalli
CU30) OAU7S	1270	2	R. Horizonte – LV de Agro, Cusco
CJ50)			R. Ebenezer, Bambamarca
HV07) OAM5A	1270	2	R. OAM5A, Huancavelica
JN23) OBZ4T	1270	0.4	R. La Merced, Chanchamayo
LL28) OCX2Z	1270	1	R. Estacion Latina, Cepén
LM31) OAZ4H	1270	0.4	R. Huacho, Huacho

MW	Call	kHz	kW	Station, location, h of tr.
PI24)	OAU1S	1270	1	R. Nor Peru, Paita
TC21)	OBU6N	1270	3	R. OBU6N, Tacna
AN12)	OBX3C	‡1280	1	R. El Puerto, Chimbote
AQ27)	OBX6P	1280	0.5	R. Fénix, Camaná
CJ28)	OBX2F	1280	1	R. Moderna, Cajamarca: 1000-0400(Sun -0300)
CU61)	OCU7R	1280	1	R. Fé, Sicuani
HN01)	OAX3Y	1280	1	R. La Selva, Rupa-Rupa
IC21)	OBU5J	1280	3	Yeshua Radio, Chinca Alta
LB22)	OAU1R	1280	1	Bethel Radio, San Jose
PA11)		1280		R. Bethel, Chaquimarca
PU49)	OCU7S	1280	2.5	R. Altura, Macusani
AQ28)	OCX6B	1290	5	R. Cielo, Cerro Colorado Aqp
AY20)	OBU5V	1290	1	R. OBU5V, Ayacucho
CJ69)	OAM2C	1290		R. Estelar, Chota: 1000-0200
JN24)	OBU4S	1290	1	R. Exito, La Oroya
LM32)	OBU4Q	1290	1	S & RD, Hualmay
LM69)	OCU4P	1290	1	San Vicente de Cañete
LL53)	OBU2D	1290	1	R. Sonorama, Trujillo
PU21)	OAX7X	1290	0.35	R. Juliaca, Juliaca: 0900-0300 (nf. on 1300)
TB04)	OCX1Q	1290	1	R. Programas del Perú, Tumbes: 24h
AN13)	OAX3O	1300	0.5	R. Huascarán, Independencia: 1100-0300
CJ29)	OAU2I	1300	1	R. Paraiso, Cajabamba
CU31)	OAX7P	‡1300	1	R. Onda Imperial, Cusco: 1200-2130
JN55)	OCU4R	1300	2.5	R. OCU4R, Ahuac
LB23)	OAU1U	1300	1	R. Frecuencia Lider, Morro
LM33)	OAX4S	1300	5	R. Comas, Comas: 24h
PU21)	OAX7X	1300	0.35	R. Juliaca, Juliaca: 0900-0300 (r. 1290)
SM08)	OBX9P	‡1300	1	R. La Luz, Tarapoto
TC18)	OBU6X	1300	3	R.Candarave, Ilabaya
UC03)	OAZ8B	1300	1	R. Nuevo Mundo, Pucallpa
AQ50)	OAU6N	1310	6	R. Libertad, Alto Selva Alegre Aqp
AY21)	OBU5X	1310	3	Ayacucho
CJ30)	OBX2D	1310	1	R. Chota, Chota: 1100-0300
LM34)	OBX4L	1310	1	R. Irvisa, Huacho
HN15)	OAU3T	1310	1	R. OAU3T, Rupa Rupa
LT09)	OBX8L	1310	12	R. Vision Amazonia (R. MIVIA), Iquitos
PI62)	OCU1D	1310	3	Bethel Radio, Piura
AN31)	OAU3W	1320	5	R. OAU3W, La Caleta
AP19)	OCU5V	1320	5	R.Cultural Tintaya, Cotabambas
AQ60)	OBU6B	1320	0.5	R. Majes
IC22)	OBU5L	1320	1	La Luz del Mundo, Pueblo Nuevo
JN26)	OCU4T	1320	2.5	R. Bacan, Huancayo
LB24)	OBU1S	1320	1	R. Frecuencia Popular, Olmos
LM55)	OAX4I	1320		R. La Cronica, Lima
PU22)	OAU7W	1320	3	R.TV Peru, Juliaca: 1000-0300
TC17)	OBU6A	1320	1	R. OBU6A, Tacna
AQ30)	OCX6E	1330	5	R. Frecuencia 1330, Cayma Aqp
AY09)	OBU5P	1330	0.5	Bethel R., Huamanga
CU32)	OCX7K	1330	1	R. San Miguel, Wanchaq
LB25)	OAU1A	1330	1	R. Amistad, Chiclayo
LL54)	OAM2D	1330	1	R. Fé, La Esperanza
PI63)	OCU1J	1330	1	R. Frecuencia Ideal, Frias
SM17)	OBX9Y	1330	1	R.Fé, Tarapoto
AN33)	OBU3C	1340	1	R. OBU3C, Casma
CJ31)	OAU2S	1340	1	R. Shalom, Cajamarca
CU87)		1340		R.Choque, Chumbivilcas
IC11)	OAX5D	1340	0.5	R. Chincha, Chincha Alta
JN27)	OAU4N	1340	1	R. Jauja, Jauja
LM35)	OAU4Q	1340	10	R. Alegria, Pucasana
PI64)	OBX1K	1340	1	R. San Francisco, Piura
PU23)	OBU7V	1340	1	R. Sudamericana, Juliaca
AY18)	OBU5O	1350	1	R. Atlantis, Huamanga
HN16)	OAU3X	1350	1	R. OAU3X, Pillco Marca
LB31)	OAU1H	1350	1	R. Vision, Chiclayo: 24h
LM73)	OAM4H	1350	1	R. Paraiso, Huacho
MO16)	OCU6D	1350	3	R.OCU6D, Ichuña
TB09)	OCU1I	1350	1	R. Fé, Tumbes
UC04)	OBX8D	1350		R. Super, Pucallpa
AN16)	OAU3A	1360	1	R. Intercontinental, Yungay
AQ32)	OCX6T	1360	3	R. Popular, Mariano Melgar
CJ77)	OCU2Z	1360	2	R. OCU2Z, Querocotillo
CU34)	OAX7R	‡1360	2.5	R. Sicuani, Sicuani
IC12)	OBZ5Z	1360	1	R. Cruz del Sur, Palpa
JN28)	OAU4O	1360	1	R. Sudamericana, Tarma
LM58)	OCU4I	1360	10	R. Bienestar, Lima: 24h
PI25)	OBZ1A	1360	2.5	R. del Norte, Sullana
PU24)	OUA7L	1360	2.5	R. Continente, Juliaca
AP05)	OCX5A	1370	1	Inti R., Abancay
AP17)	OCU5Y	1370	3	R. OCU5Y, Chalhuahuacho
AQ62)	OBU6Y	1370	1	R. OBU6Y, Viraco
CU79)	OAM7G	1370	1	R. Qosqo Wayra, Cusco
MQ07)	OAX6T‡	1370		R. Moquegua, Moquegua
SM18)	OAU9E	1370	5	R. OAU9E, Moyobamba
PA01)	OCU4U	1370	10	R. Altura, Cerro de Pasco
AN32)	OAU3U	1380	1	R. R.dif San Juan, Chimbote
AQ33)	OAX6O	1380	3	R. San Martin, Arequipa: 1055-0500
CJ33)	OAX2W	‡1380	1	R. Atahualpa, Cajamarca
JN29)	OBU4L	1380	1	R. Chilca,Chilca
HN06)	OBX3I	‡1380	1	R. Pilco Mozo, Huanuco
IC31)	OAM5E	1380	1	R. OAM5E, Salas
LM38)	OCY4U	1380	1	R. Nuevo Tiempo, Lima: 24h
MD05)	OCU7U	1380	1	R. OCU7U, Tambopata
PI26)	OBZ1D	1380	1	R. Bellavista, Bellavista
AY28)	OCU5C	1390	2.5	R. Cielo, Ayacucho
CJ70)	OBU2U	1390	0.5	Frequencia del Norte, Santa Cruz
CU36)	OAU7T	1390	1	R. Enlace, Kunturkanki
CU69)	OAM7A	1390	3	R. Exitosa, Sicuani: 24h
LL32)	OAU2Z	1390	3	R. La Luz, Trujillo
LB41)	OCU1G	1390		R. Fe, Pimentel
AN35)	OBU3E	1400	1	R. OBU3E, Chimbote
CJ34)	OAU2H	1400	1	R. Nueva Campesina, Cajamarca
CJ37)	OAX7I	1400	1	R. La Hora - IPDA, Cuzco
IC30)	OAM5G	1400	1	R. OAM5G, Ica
JN30)	OBX4H	1400	1	R. Luz, Tarma
LM39)	OBX4W	1400	2.5	R. Callao Super, Lima: 24h
TC22)	OCU6F	1400	1	R. OCU6F, Calano
AY33)	OCU5G	1410	3	R.Genesis, Huanta
CJ64)	OCU2Q	1410	1	R. San Marcos, Pedro Galvez
HN18)	OAU3Y	1410	1	R. Ke Buena, Paucarbambilia
LB29)	OBU1G	1410	1	R. Olmos, Olomos
LM40)	OBZ4V	1410	1	Bethel Radio, Huacho
PU26)	OBU7A	1410	1	R. La Luz, Juliaca
TB05)	OBU1H	1410	3	R. La Luz, Tumbes
CU05)	OBX8I	1410	1	Dif. Comercial, Pucallpa
AQ57)	OBU6C	1420	1	R. Fe, Arequipa
IC23)	OBU5H	1420	0.5	R. la Luz, Salas
CJ85)	OAM2P	1420	5	R. La Positiva, Bambamarca
LM41)	OBZ4G	1420	1	R. San Isidro, Lima
PI65)	OCU1F	1420	2	R. OCU1F, Tambo Grande
AM03)	OBX9H	1430	1	R. Utcubamba, Bagua Grande
AN18)	OAZ3H	‡1430	1	R. Chavin, Chimbote
CJ78)	OCU2U	1430	1	R. OCU2U, Jaen
CU39)	OAZ7M	1430	1	R. OAZ7M, Cusco
JN31)	OAZ4V	1430	0.5	R. Universal, El Tambo: 1100-0500
LM42)	OCU4L	1430	1	Chilca, Cañete
PU27)	OBU7U	1430	3	R. Red Andina, Juliaca
TC08)	OAU6M	‡1430	1	R. Lider, Tacna
AQ19)	OAX6R	1440	2.5	R. Santa Monica, Hunter, Aqp:
AY32)	OCU5K	1440	2.5	R. OCU5K, Ayacucho
CU71)	OAM7L	1440	3	R. Solar, Espinar
CJ35)	OAU2O	1440	2	R. Frecuencia VH, Celendin
IC26)	OCU5P	1440	3	R. Cielo, Ica
CJ80)	OBX1T	1440	2	R. Cooperativa Tumán, , Tumán
LM43)	OAX4K	1440	1	R. Imperial 2, Lima
PI66)	OBU1Z	1440	1	R. OBU1Z, Vice
AO58)	OBU6K	1450	1	R. OBU6K, Chivay
CJ81)	OAU2W	1450		R. Manantial de Vida, Cajamarca:1100-0100 (Sun -1300)
CJ82)		1450		R. Libertad, Bambamarca
JN45)	OBU4Y	1450	1	R. La Nueva Andina (IPDA) Huancayo
LL35)	OCX2J	1450	1	R. San Juan, Trujillo
LM44)	OBX4K	1450	1	R. Fortaleza, Barranca
MO15)	OCU6E	1450	1	R. OCU6E, Ichuña
PA08)	OAM4A	1450	1	R. OAM4A, Tinyahuarco
AN30)	OAU3V	1460	2.5	R. Municipal, Cabana
AQ37)	OBU6R	1460	1	R. Bahia, Mollendo
CU42)	OBU7M	1460		R. OBU7M, Marcapata
IC32)	OAM5C	1460	1	Rdif. Disaga, Pueblo Nuevo
JN32)	OCY4I	1460	0.5	R. Imperial, Junin
JN33)	OAZ4F	1460	1	R. La Oroya, La Oroya: 1000-0500
JN48)	OCU4Y	1460	1	R. Voz Cristiana, Chongo Bajo: 24h (n.f. 1470)
PI29)	OAX1V	1460	1	R. Sullana "LV de Chira", Sullana
PU28)	OAX7W	1460	10	R. Sol de los Andes, Juliaca: 0900-0300
AQ38)	OAU6E	1470	2.5	R. Victoria, Alto Selva Alegre Aqp
CU43)	OAX7G	1470	1	R. Cusco, Cusco
JN48)	OCU4Y	1470	1	R. Voz Cristiana, Chongo Bajo: 24h (r. 1460)
LB46)	OAU1P	1470	1	R. California, Lambayeque
LL37)	OCY2G	1470	1	R. Occidental, Quiruvilca
LM45)	OAU4B	1470	20	R. Capital, Lima
TC09)	OAX6M	‡1470	0.8	R. Tacna, Tacna: 24h
CU44)	OAZ7G	1480	1	R. Espinar, Yauri
CJ44)	OBU2H	1480	0.2	R. Santa Ana, Cutervo: 1000-0100
JN35)	OAU4A	1480	1	R. Mineria, Santa Rosa de Sacco: 1100-2300
LL38)	OCX2C	1480	0.6	R. Comercial San Pedro, Virú

MW	Call	kHzkW	Station, location, h of tr.
LM70)	OAM4F	1480 1	R. OAM4F, Barranca
AQ39)	OAX6Q	1490 1.3	R. Fidelidad, Cerro Colorado, Aqp
AP10)	OBU5C	1490 25	Radiodifusora los Chankas, Andahuaylas
AP18)		1490	R. Patron Santiago, Challhuacho
CU80)	OCU7Y	1490 25	R. Nuevo Tiempo, Cusco
IC15)	OAX5N	1490 1	R. Nazca, Nazca
LB47)	OAX1L	±1490 1	R. Imperio, Chiclayo
LT14)	OAX8F	1490 1	R. Atlántiada, Iquitos
PA15)	OCX4P	1490 0.5	R. La Luz, Cerro de Pasco
PU51)	OAM7P	1490 1	R. OAM7P, Capachica
CJ39)	OBU2J	1500 2	R. San Pablo, San Pablo
CU81)	OAM7B	1500 1	R. TV Cristiana, Sicuani
HN07)	OBX3J	1500 1	R. Luz y Sonido, Huanuco: 0900-0300
JN56)	OAX4Q	1500 1	R. Scala de Oro, Huancayo
LL39)	OBX2X	1500 0.5	R. Comercial, Trujillo
LM47)	OBX4I	±1500 18	R. Santa Rosa, Lima: 24h
TC10)	OAU6B	±1500 1	R. Bulevar, Tacna
AQ40)	OCX6Q	±1510 3	R. Alegria, Mariano Melgar, Aqp
CU82)	OBX7P	1510 1	R. Las Vegas, Wanchaq
JN37)	OCX4J	1510 1	R. Tarma, Tarma: 1000-0200, Sun 1100-2300
LB32)	OBU1B	1510 1	R. Super Real, Olmos
LM66)	OCU4M	1510 1	R. OCU4M, San Vicente de Cañete
TB06)	OCX1V	1510 1	R. Tumbes, Tumbes
UC06)	OBX8K	1510 1	R. Centro de los Medios, Sepahua
AY29)	OCU5F	1520 2	R. OCU5F, Huanta
CU48)	OBU7X	1520 1	R. Voz Evangelica, Espinar
LB26)	OAX1C	1520 1	R. Cristal, Chiclayo
HV04)	OBU5Z	1520 3	R. Municipal, Castrovirreyna
MQ13)	OBU6Z	1520 6	R. OBU6Z, Mascal Nieto
PA12)	OAM4C	1520 1	R. OAM4C, San Juan
PI68)	OCU1T	1520 1	R. LV del Campesino, Ayabacha
PU56)		1520	R Andina, Lampa
CJ06)	OBX2R	1530 3	R. Oriental, Jaén
CJ84)	OAM2Q	1530 1	R. Charles, Bambamarca
CU49)	OAZ7F	1530 0.5	Rdif. Espinar , Yauri
CU50)	OBU7N	1530 1	R. Ondas del Sur Oriente, Quillabamba
IC17)	OAU5R	1530 1	R. Universidad San Juan Bautista, Subtanjalla
JN38)	OAZ4S	1530 1	R. 15-50, Huancayo: 24h
LM49)	OBU4C	1530 10	R. Milenia, Lima
AQ41)	OAU6A	1540 1	R. Milenio Universal, Alto Selva Alegre
CJ63)	OCU2X	1540 5	R.Turbomix, Cajamarca
CU51)	OCX7V	‡1540 1	R. Los Andes, Cusco
LL42)	OBU2A	1540 2	R. Mundial AM, Trujillo
LM74)	OAM4G	1540 1	R. Angie@Net, Barranca
PA05)	OBX4N	1540 0.3	R. Corporacion, Cerro de Pasco: 0900-0500
TB07)	OBX1B	1540 1	R. LV de la Frontera, Tumbes
TC23)	OCU6H	1540 1	R. OCU6H, Pocollay
AN22)	OAU3D	‡1550 1	R. Cruz, Chimbote
AY10)	OBX5J	1550 1	R. Maria, Huamanaga
CU83)	OAM7D	±1550 1	R . San Sebastian, Livitaca
IC24)	OAX5S	1550 3	R. La Luz del Mundo, Subtanjalla
LB48)	OCU1W	1550 1	R. OCU1W, Monsefú
LM51)	OBX4P	1550 5	R. Independencia, Independencia
PI67)	OCU1B	1550 1	R. La Clave, Castilla
AQ42)	OCX6N	1560 1	R. Sabor, Marino Melgar, Aqp
CJ79)	OAM2I	1560 1	R. OAM2I, Cajabamba
CU52)	OAZ7N	1560 1	R. Maria, Wanchaq
JN57)	OCU4Z	1560 2.5	R. OCU4Z, Hualhuas
TC25)	OCU6K	1560 1	R. OCU6K, Alto de la Alianza
AY34)	OCU5O	1570 2.5	R. Musuq Chaski Radio, Huamanga
CJ54)	OBU2L	1570 1	R. Colonial, Contumaza
CU62)	OCU7L	1570 1	R. Vilcanota, Sicuani
HN20)	OBU3A	1570 1	R. OBU3A. Cerro Jactay
IC31)	OAM5H	1570 1	R. OAM5H, Chinca Alta
LM59)	OCU4J	1570 25	Bethel Radio, Lima
LL47)	OCU2C	1570 1	Radiodifusora Julcan, Otuzco
PI32)	OCX1Z	1570 1	R. La Nueva Esperanza, Tambo Grande
PU32)	OAU7Z	1570 1	R. Carraviz, Juliaca
AQ59)	OBU6S	1580 1	R. OBU6S, Orcopampa
HV02)	OAU5J	1580 1	R. Virgen del Carmen, Huancavelica: 24h
JN40)	OAU4P	1580 1	R. San Juan, Tarma
LB36)	OBX1M	1580 1	R. Naylamp, Lambayeque
AQ44)	OCX6S	1590 1	R. Mundo, Arequipa
AY30)	OBU5F	1590 1	R. OBU5F, Lucanas
CJ68)		1590	R. Municipal, San Marcos
LL43)	OBU2C	1590 1	R. Bendicion, Trujillo
LM52)	OAZ4Z	1590 1.5	R. Vida, Lima
PU33)	OAU7C	1590 1	R. Asillo, Azangaro
CU84)		1600	R. Andina, Velille
CU86)	OBM7A	1600 3	R.OBM7A, Wanchaq
JN44)	OBU4R	1600 2.5	R. Nuevo Tiempo, Huancayo: 24h
AQ45)	OAU6O	1610 0.5	R. Flor de los Andes, Paucarpata

MW	Call	kHzkW	Station, location, h of tr.
PU54)		1610	R. Inka, Acora
CU63)		1640	R. Kalikanto, Chamaca

SW	Call	kHzkW	Station, location, h of tr.
HU05)	OAX3Q	±3330 5	R. Ondas del Huallaga, Huánuco
AY07)	OAZ5B	‡4747 0.5	R. Huanta 2000, Huanta: (n.f.: 4755): 1100-0100
JN37)	OCX4E	4775 0.5	R. Tarma, Tarma: 1000-1400 2000-0200
			Sun.: 1100-1400 2000-2300
CU64)	OAW7I	4780	R. OAW7I, Cusco
LB31)	OAW1D	4790 1	R. Vision, Chiclayo: 24h
CU68)	OAW7J	4800 1	R. OAW7J, Cusco
SM14)	OAW9A	4810 1	R. Logos, Chazuta
LT01)	OAX8R	4824 10	LV de la Selva, Iquitos
CU34)	OAX7T	±4826 0.3	R. Sicuani "LV de Canchis", Sicuani:
CU50)		4835 1	R. Ondas del Sur Oriente, Quillabamba
			1000-0300
AY7)	OAW5E	4851 1	R. Genesis, Huanta
LM61)	OAW4Y	‡4880 1	R. JPJ, Lima
HV02)	OAX5X	4887 1	R. Virgen del Carmen, Huancavelica: irr
LL54)	OAW2H	4910 1	R. OAW2H, Santiago de Chuco
UC07)	OAW8A	4940 1	R. San Antonio, Villa Atalaya: 2200-0030†
MD03)	OBX7I	4950 5	R. Madre de Dios, Puerto Maldonado:
			1000(Sun 1100)-0200
AY13)	OAX5S	4955 5	R. Cultural Amauta, Huanta: 1000-1400,
			2100-0100
LM06)	OAZ4X	±4975 5	R. Pacifico, Lima: 2300- 0100
AN09)	OAZ3B	4992 5	R. Ancash, Huaraz: (n.f.: 4990)(irr.)
JN48)	OAW4G	4984	R. Voz Cristiana, Chilca
PA01)	OBZ4B	5014 1	R. Altura, Cerro de Pasco
CU26)	OAX7Q	5025 5	R. Quillabamba, Quillabamba: 1000-0200
JN18)	OCY4Y	5039 1	R. Libertad de Junin, Junín: 1100-1400
PI13)	OAW1B	5060	LV de las Huarinjas, Huancabamba
LL26)		5460	R. LV Bolivar, Bolivar: 2330-0130
AM06)		5487	Reina de la Selva, Chachapoyas
AQ17)	OAX6A	5921 1	Bethel Radio, Achumayo, Aqp (r.)
AQ24)	OBX6I	±5939 1	R. Melodia, Hunter Aqp
CU72)	OBX4M	5980 5	R. Chaski R., Urubamba: 1000-1500, 2200-0100
LM12)	OAX4Q	±6020 3	R. Victoria, Lima
LM47)	OCY4H	±6047 10	R. Santa Rosa, Lima
JN47)	OAD4A	6060	Aroma Cafe R., Pichanaqui
AN36)	OAD3A	6090 1	R. OAD3A, Independencia
CU25)	OAX7C	6174 1	R. Tawantinsuyo, Cusco
LM06)		9675 5	R. Pacifico, Lima: 1300-2300
LM12)	OCX4C	±9722 1	R. Victoria, Lima

NB: ‡ = inactive, ± = varying freq., † = irregular
° = on-air stn name not confirmed,

Addresses and other information:
NB: Names of *departamentos* should be added to addresses.
AMOO (AMAZONAS):
AM01) Jr.Grau N° 617, 01001 Chachapoyas – **AM03)** Jr F Villareal N° 400, 01671 Bagua Grande - **FM:** 96.9MHz – **AM04)** Jr Amazonas N° 1717 (Ap 69), 01001 Chachapoyas ☎41 777793 **W:** horizonteperu. com **E:** rhorizonte@hotmail.com - **FM:** 99.9MHz – **AM06)** Jr Ayacucho N° 936, Plaza Mayor, 01001 Chachapoyas ☎41 477203 **W:** reinad-elaselva.com.pe - **E:** joreno@terra.com.pe - **FM:** 101.5MHz – **AM10)** Calle Higos Urcos 651, 01671 Bagua Grande, Utcubamba – **AM11)** Av.Gonzalo Puerta s/n, 01131 Nieva, Condorcanqui – **FM.** 91.7 MHz – **AM12)** Jr Salamanca N° 1183, 01001 Chachapoyas - **AM13)** Jr Amazonas s/n, Urb. Tupac Amaru, 01321 Huambo - **AM14)** Av La Circunvalacion N° 1249, 01651 La Peca
ANOO (ANCASH):
AN01) Tabon Alta, Fundo El Milagro, 02661 Casma ☎43 711266 **W:** visionradioperu.com - **FM:** 93.7 MHz – **AN02)** Av Francisco Pizzarro, 02741 Chimbote - **FM:** 95.5MHz – **AN04)** Urb. el Trapecio 2da etapa, MZ G, Lote 18, 02741 Chimbote - **FM:** 97.5MHz – **AN07)** Jr Elias Aguirre N° 755 cerca a Panamericana Television, 02741 Chimbote ☎44 272639 – **AN08)** Pasaje Los Jardines N° 129, 02741 Chimbote - **FM:** 104.3MHz – **AN09)** Av Las Americas N° 302, 02001 Huaraz **W:** radioancash.com.pe **E:** radioancash@hotmail.com ☎43 427217 - **FM:** 101.3MHz – **AN10)** Av Enrique Meiggs N° 2013, 02741 Chimbote ☎43 805591 **W:** radioluzca.com **E:** programacion@radioluz.com - **FM:** 89.9MHz – **AN11)** Jr Elias Aguirre N° 549, 2do Piso Oficina 205, 02741 Chimbote – **AN12)** Jr Alfonso Ugarte N° 554, 02741 Chimbote - **FM:** 89.9MHz – **AN13)** Jr San Martin N° 655, 02001 Huaraz - **FM:** 104.5MHz – **AN16)** Casero el Rayan, 02816 Yungay – **AN18)** Urb. San Juan ZN 5, 02741 Chimbote - **FM:** 92.3MHz – **AN22)** Jr Alfonso Ugarte N° 627 4° piso, 02741 Chimbote – **AN25)** Huari **W:** agrorural. gob.pe/pagina/huari-ancash – **AN27)** Av Jorge Chávez N° 364, 02741 Chimbote **W:** radiocielo.pe – **AN29)** Jr John F.Kennedy MZ. 36, Lote 1, Miraflores Alto, 02741 Chimbote – **AN30)** Plaza de Armas N° 106, Cabana– **AN31)** Av Malecón s/n, La Caleta – **AN32)** Av Santa Cruz

397, Chimbote – **AN33)** Av Peru 1263, Casma – **AN34)** Av Jorge Chavez 364, Chimbote – **AN35)** Jr Francisco Pizarro 610, Chimbote - **AN36)** Jr Los Jardines 670, Independencia
AP00 (APURIMAC):
AP03) Av Nuñez 401, 03001 Abancay – **AP05)** Av Seoane 375, Region Inca, 03001 Abancay ☎8 332 4087 **W:** corporacionsolar.com **E:** intiradio@corporacionsolar.com - **FM:** 103.3 Solar FM – **AP10)** Jr. Juan Antonio Trellers N° 278, 03281 Andahuaylas ☎83 721511 – **FM:** 94.9 MHz – **AP11)** Tres Cruces, 03141 Ocobamba – **AP12)** Av Cristo de Los Andes, Barrio El Salvador, 03301 Challhuahuacho, Cotabamba – **AP13)** Barrio Pampaña Calle Apurimac s/n, 03341 Cotabambas – **AP14)** Jr Los Sauces N° 283, U.V. Pochccota, 03281 Andahuaylas **W:** restauracionandahuaylas.com – **AP15)** Jr Manuel Seone 320, Abancay – **AP16)** Comunidad Campesina de Totoray, San Pedro de Cachora **W:** radiocielo.pe – **AP17)** Comunidad de Fuerobamba, Chalhuahuacho – **AP18)** Ca 8 de Agosto, 03301 Challhuahuacho – **AP19)** Comunidad de Fuerabamba, Dist. Callhuahuach, Cotabambas
AQ00 (AREQUIPA):
AQ01) Ca San Juan de Dios N° 210, Zona Alto, 04001 Arequipa ☎54 200982 **W:** radioazularequipaperu.com **E:** radioazulamfm@hotmail.com - **FM:** 89.5MHz – **AQ02)** Ca San Juan de Dios 210, 04001 Arequipa **W:** nseradio.com **E:** nsearequipa@nseradio.com – **AQ04)** Av. Salaverry 103, Socabaya, 04051 Arequipa ☎54 507362 – **AQ05)** Centro Comercial, Av Independencia 600, Of 401-A, Cercado, 04001 Arequipa ☎54 406175 - **FM:** 93.5MHz – **AQ06)** Jr.Palacio Viejo 216, Cayma, 04016 Arequipa - **FM:** 89.5 MHz – **AQ07)** Av Emmel 216, Yanahuara, 04020 Arequipa **E:** radioportena@hotmail.com – **AQ11)** Av Victor A Belaúnde C-8, Umacollo, 04001 Arequipa ☎54 255888 📠54 251822 - **FM:** 97.1MHz – **AQ12)** Ca Los Robles 139, Urb. Orrantia, 04001 Arequipa ☎54 289952 – Quechua: Sat.2h **W:** radioyaravi.org pe **E:** direccion@radioyaravi.org.pe - **FM:** 106.3MHz – **AQ13)** Calle Palacio Viejo 401, 04001 Arequipa **W:** radioelpueblo960. pe - **FM:** 98.5MHz in Majes, 102.1 in Tacna – **AQ14)** Av Independencia s/n 2° piso, Pabellón de la Cultura, Ciudad Universitaria (Cas 23), 04001 Arequipa.☎ 54 287771 **W:** unsa.edu.pe and radiouniversidadaqp. blogspot.no **E:** radiouniversidad@unsa.edu.pe – **AQ15)** At 200 Millas La Pino, 04039 Paucarpata – **AQ16)** Av Independencia 905 - 2do piso, 04001 Arequipa ☎54 204904 - **FM:** 107.7MHz – **AQ17)** Av Union 225, Miraflores, 04009 Arequipa (Also in Lima: LI59) **W:** bethelradio.fm **E:** betheltradio@bethelradio.fm – **AQ18)** Ca La Paz 504, 04001 Arequipa ☎54 204847 **Quechua:** 1000-1200 – **AQ19)** Av Independencia 905 2° piso, Ur. Municipal 04001 Arequipa ☎54 204904 **W:** radiosantamonicaarequipa.com **E:** gerencia@radiosantamonicaarequipa.com – **AQ20)** Calle 28 de Julio N° 129 – La Libertad, Cerro Colorado, 04023 Arequipa – **AQ21)** Av.La Paz 512, Costado Grifo Repsol, 04001 Arequipa ☎54 446053 - **FM:** 95.8MHz – **AQ22)** Av La Paz 511 "A", Of 312 – 3er piso, 04001 Arequipa ☎54 287821 **W:** rpp.com.pe – **AQ23)** Av La Salle 124, Urb. Daniel Alcides Carrión G-14, 04044 José Luis Bustamente y Rivero 04001 Arequipa ☎54 431051 – **AQ24)** Calle San Camilo 501-A Cercado, 04001 Arequipa ☎54 205811 📠54 204420 **W:** radiomelodia. com.pe - **FM:** 104.3MHz – **AQ25)** Av Independencia 1819, 04001 Arequipa ☎54 286438 **E:** lideraqp@gmail.com – **AQ26)** Ca Pierola 209, Of 205, 04001 Arequipa ☎54 284411 – **AQ27)** Esq Av Lima y Calle Bolognesi, 04446 Camaná – **AQ28)** Av. Independencia 600, Edifico C.C. Independencia N° 321D, 04001 Arequipa **W:** radiocielo. pe – rel. of R.Cielo, Lima 24h – **AQ30)** Sebastian Luna 105a, Parque Azángarao 2° Pisa, Miraflores, 04009 Arequipa ☎54 221262 **W:** frecuencia1330arequipa.blogspot.no – **AQ32)** Av.Independencia N° 600, Oficina 302-A, 04001 Arequipa **W:** Facebook: Radio Popular Arequipa – **AQ33)** Calle Deán Valdivia 221, Cercado, 04001 Arequipa **W:** radiosanmartin.pe **E:** director@radiosanmartin.pe - **FM:** 97.7MHz – **AQ37)** C.Baca Flor 410, (Cas 128), 04466 Mollendo ☎54 532521 **W:** radiobahiaperu.es.tl **E:** radiobahiadelvalle@hotmail. com - **FM:** 101.5MHz – **AQ38)** Dean Valdivia 418, Piso 3, Cercado, 04001 Arequipa ☎54 405480 **W:** radiovictoriaperu.com **E:** radiovictoria_aqp@hotmail.com – **AQ39)** Santo Domingo 113 , Galerias Gamesa Of 700, 04001 Arequipa, (Ap 2330) ☎54 214997 **E:** radiominuto@terra. com - **FM:** 99.9MHz – **AQ40)** Centro Comercial Independencia, Av Independencia N° 403-A, Ofic 433, 4° piso, 04001 Arequipa ☎54 287211 - **FM:** 95.1 MHz – **AQ41)** Ca Puente Grau 122, 04001 Arequipa ☎54 507643 **W:** mileniouniversal.com **E:** radiomileniouniversal@hotmail.com – **AQ42)** Cl. Melgar N° 204, Cercado Arequipa, 04001 Arequipa ☎54 330970 **W:** radiolaluz.com **E:** radiolibertadaqp@hotmail.com – **AQ44)** Ca Castilla 39, Urb. Municipal, 04001 Arequipa – **AQ45)** Urb. Mi Peru MZ G Lote 3, 04044 Jose Luis Bustamente y Rivero– **AQ46)** Parroquia San Antonio de Padua, Plaza Principal s/n, 04201 Callalli, Prov de Caylloma **E:** rsan_antonio14@hotmail.com - **FM:** 94.5MHz – **AQ50)** Ca Trabada 105, VI Centenario, 04001 Arequipa ☎54 202022 **W:** radiolibertadaqp.com **E:** radiolibertadaqp@hotmail.com – **AQ52)** Calle Puente Arnao 705, 3 Cdras de la Av. Progreso, 04001 Arequipa – **AQ53)** 04001 Arequipa **W:** radiomariaperu.org – **AQ55)** Casinino Peralta 102, 04101 Cotahuasi,

La Union – **AQ56)** Ca 22 de Octubre s/n, Urb. Los Miradores, 04231 Orcopampa – **AQ57)** Av Del Ejercito 1013, 04001 Arequipa – **AQ58)** Sector Escalera, 04341 Chivay – **AQ59)** Av Buena Ventura s/n, 04231 Orcopampa – **AQ60)** Mz. 3E Lte. 18 Pedregal, 04426 Majes – **AQ61)** Av Independencia 905, 04001 Arequipa ☎54 288787 **W:** ipda.com. pe/radioarequipa.htm – **AQ62)** Plaza de Armas s/n, 04556 Viraco
AY00 (AYACUCHO):
AY02) Ca Nazareno 108H, 05001 Ayacucho **E:** macebu90@hotmail. com - **FM:** 95.3MHz – **AY05)** Plaza Mayor Felipe Guzman Poma, 05411 Aucara, Lucanas **E:** radioia1090@hotmail.com – **AY06)** Jr Chorro 274 – Int "A", 05001 Ayacucho, ☎66 326042 **W:** radioquispillaccta.com Prgr mainly in **Quechua** – **AY07)** Jr Gervasio Santillana 455, 05111 Huanta ☎66 322105 **W:** radiohuanta2000.com/ **E:** webmaster@radiohuanta2000fm.com - **FM:** 92.9MHz – **AY08)** Jr Piura s/n, 05001 Ayacucho - **FM:** 97.9MHz – **AY09)** Jr. Los Girasoles 194, Canan Bajo, 05001 Ayacucho - **FM:** 93.9 MHz – **AY10)** Local de Obispado, 05021 Carmen Alto, **W:** radiomariaperu.org - **FM:**106.7MHz – **AY13)** Jr Cahuide 278, 05111 Huanta (Cas 24) ☎66 322153 **W:** radioamauta.net/ **E:** radioamauta@hotmail.com - **FM:** 99.9MHz – **AY14)** Ca El Nazareno, 2do Pasaje 159, Cercado, 05001 Ayacucho ☎66 528523 **W:** diariolavozdehuamanga.com **E:** diariolavozdehuamanga@yahoo.com.ar - **FM:** 91.1MHz – **AY17)** Jr.Jr Miguel Untiveros 431, 05111 Huanta. – **AY18)** Ca Manco Capac 157, 05001 Ayacucho **W:** Facebook: R.Atlantis – **FM:** 99.3 MHz – **AY19)** Jr Angel del Señor MZ C Lote 1A, Asociacion Los Mecanicos, 05001 Ayacucho – **AY20)** Av Mariscal Cáceres 641, 05001 Ayacucho – **AY21)** Jr Arequipa N° 231, 05001 Ayacucho – **AY22)** Av Mariscal Cáceres 641, 05001 Ayacucho – **AY23)** Jr Bolognes 147-149, Barrio Huánuco, 05571 Pausa, Paúcar del Sara Sara – **AY24)** Av 28 de Julio s/n, 05571 Pausa – **AY25)** Jr Dos de Mayo 610, 05001 Ayacucho **W:** radioamvida1020khz.blogspot.no **E:** radioamvida1020@yahoo.com. pe – **AY26)** Urb. Mariscal Cáceres, Mz. K Lote 12, 05001 Ayacucho ☎966 905992 **W:** Facebook: Estacion Wari 1060 khz A.M.– **AY27)** Jr Primavera 175, Santa Ana, 05001 Ayacucho – **AY28)** Av.Miguel Grau 256, 05001 Ayacucho **W:** radiocielo.pe – **AY29)** Jr Miller 177, 05111 Huanta – **AY30)** Jr Tacna N° 617, 05601 Pucuio – **AY31)** Jr Cesar Vallejo 325 – San Juan Bautista, 05001 Ayacucho – **AY32)** Av. Los Andes 624, 05001 Ayacucho – **AY33)** Jr. Libertad 153, 05111 Huanta – **AY34)** Av. Javier Pérez de Cuellar 546, Urb. José Ortiz Vergara Mx. "S", Ayacucho ☎97 8465290**W:** FB: Musuq Chaski Radio 1570 AM
CJ00(CAJAMARCA)
CJ01) Jr Francisco de Orellana 343 (Apt 50), 06101 Jaén **W:** radiomaranon.org.pe **E:** correo@radiomaranon.org.pe ☎76 431147 - **FM:** 96.1 & 97.5 MHz – **CJ03)** Km 5 Carretera Jaen-San Ignacio, 06101 Jaen - **FM:** 90.9MHz – **CJ05)** Predio Coliga, 06001 Cajamarca **W:** radiomariaperu.org – **CJ06)** Av Mesones Muro 157, 06101 Jaén – **CJ07)** Jr 28 de Julio 712, 06115 Bambamarca ☎76 353462 **W:** radiocoremarca. com **E:** coremarca@radiocoremarca.com – **CJ08)** Jr Villanueva Pinillos N°N330, 06151 San Ignacio – **CJ10)** Jr. Junin 1172 06001 Cajamarca ☎76 362581 – **CJ13)** Jr Huánuco 2361, 06001 Cajamarca ☎76 341347 **W:** Facebook: Radio Líder Cajamarca **E:** radiolider970cajamarca@hotmail.com - **FM:** 90.3MHz – **CJ14)** Jr David León N° 601, 06001 Contumazá – **CJ15)** Jr Dos de Mayo 271, 06001 Cajamarca ☎76 369915 **W:** radiosanfranciscoperu.com **E:** radiosanfrancisco@gmail.com - **FM:** 91.9MHz – **CJ17)** Jr Orozco 320, 06858 Cutervo ☎76 737090 **W:** radiosudamerica.com - **CJ18)** Av Via de Evitamiento Norte 280, 06001 Cajamarca ☎76 343725 **W:** radionuevavidacomunicaciones.com **E:** radiotvnc@radionuevavidacomunicaciones.com or radiotvnvc@hotmail.com – **CJ20)** Jr Mariscal Castilla 439, 06101 Jaén– **CJ21)** Av San Martin De Porres s/n, 06001 Cajamarca ☎76 828566– **CJ22)** Jr Leoncio Prado 330, 06501 San Marcos ☎76 858083 – **CJ23)** Av Inca Garcilazo de la Vega 473, 05301 Chota – **CJ24)** Jr Mariano Melgar 138 , Cajamarca ☎76 368975 **W:** layzonradio.com **E:** radiolayzon@yahoo. com - **FM:** 90.5MHz – **CJ25)** Ca. San Martin 1371, Jaèn ☎76 433414 – **CJ26)** Jr. Huanuco 100, Barrio San Pedro, 06001 Cajamarca ☎76 368952 **W:** radiolavozdelcumbe.net **E:** cia.radioytvlavozdelcumbe@hotmail.com – **CJ27)** Jr Simon Bolivar 280, 06813 Santa Cruz – **CJ28)** Jr. Revilla Peréz 540, Barrio Pueblo Nuevo, 06001 Cajamarca ☎76 344465 **W:** radiomoderna.pe **E:** radio_moderna@yahoo.es - **FM:** 98.1 & 106.5 MHz – **CJ29)** Jr Silva 673, 06001 Cajabamba ☎76 551421 **E:** radioparaiso1300@hotmail.com – **CJ30)** Jr Santa Rosa 674-680, 06301 Chota ☎76 351240 **W:** radiochota.com **E:** radiochota@hotmail. com – **CJ31)** Av La Paz N° Cd Int 11, 06001 Cajamarca ☎76 885580 – **CJ32)** Jr. 27 de Noviembre 557, 06301 Chota **W:** radiosantamonica. org **E:** radiosantamonica@hotmail.com ☎76 351477 📠76 351132 - **FM:** 95.7MHz – **CJ33)** Juan XXIII s/n (Plaza Bolognesi), 06001 Cajamarca - **FM:** 89.9MHz – **CJ34)** Av. Los Héreos 630, 06001 Cajamarca ☎76 341300 **W:** radionuevacampesinadecajamarca.com **E:** campesinaradio@hotmail.com – **CJ35)** Jr. Arica cuadra. 5 s/n, Celendin ☎76 555115 **E:** frecuenciavh_1440@hotmail.com – **CJ36)** Jr. Alfonso Ugarte N° 668, 06001 Cajamarca ☎7655 7075 **W:** facebook. – Radio San Miguel Cajamarca **E:** sanmiguelradioradio@hotmail.com

- **FM:** 101.1MHz – **CJ38)** Jr. Lima 290, 06858 Cutervo ☎76 437010 **W:** radioilucan.com **E:** radioilucan@hotmail.com - **FM:** 96.5MHz – **CJ39)** Av Bolognesi 501, 06652 San Pablo – **FM:** 95.3 MHz – **CJ41)** Jr Jorge Chávez 416, 06115 Bambamarca ☎76 501297 **W:** radiobambamarca. com - **FM:** 101.3 MHz "Stereo Líder" – **CJ42)** Anaximandro Vega 481, Plaza de Armas, 06031 Chota ☎76 351442 📠76 352027 **W:** andina-radio.net **E:** webmaster@andinaradio.net – **CJ43)** Jr Manuel Seoane 285, Cajamarca ☎976 017576 **W:** radiocontinente.pe – **CJ44)** Av San Juan 835, 06858 Cutervo. ☎76 437272 **W:** www.radiosantaana. com **E:** info@radiosantaana.com – **CJ48)** Celendin **W:** radionorandina. com – **FM:** 101.9 MHz – **CJ50)** Los Libertadores 250, Bambamarca – **CJ54)** Jr Jose Galvez 698, 06631 Contumaza – **CJ56)** Av Los Heroes 630, 06001 Cajamarca ☎76 367973 **W:** agrorural.gob.pe/radio-caja-marca.html – **CJ61)** Jr Jorge Chávez 416, 06115 Bambamarca ☎76 501297 **W:** radiobambamarca.com – **FM:** 98.5 MHz – **CJ62)** Jr Los Libertadores 250, 06115 Bambamarca – **CJ63)** Jr Miguel Iglesia 483-489, 06001 Cajamarca ☎76 366985 **W:** turbomix.com.pe - **FM:** 92.5MHz – **CJ64)** Jr Leonico Prado 550, 06501 Pedro Galvez, San Marcos – **CJ66)** 06115 Samangay **W:** visionradioperu.com – **CJ67)** José Osores 331, 06301 Chota ☎97 6163606 **W:** corporacionrbc.org **E:** carranzamori@hotmail.com – **CJ68)** Jr Leoncios Prado 360, 06501 San Marcos ☎76 558338 **W:** munisanmarcos.gob.pe/portal/index. php/radio-tv – **CJ69)** Jr Anaximandro Vega 688, 06301 Chota ☎97 68011212 **W:** radioytvestelar.com **E:** digitelssac@hotmail.com – **CJ70)** Jr Cutervo 543, 06813 Santa Cruz ☎76 844068 **W:** frecuenciadelnorte.globered. com – **CJ71)** Carretera Agocucho s/n, Parimarca Baja, Zona Rural Marcopampa, 06001 Cajamarca **W:** visionradioperu.com – **CJ72)** Jr. San Martin 950 & Av Miguel Carducci 101, 06115 Bambamarca ☎97 6407575**W:** ondapopular.pe/bambamarca **E:** ondapopular.radio@hot-mail.com – **FM:** 96.5 MHz – **CJ73)** Jr Eten 152, 06001 Cajamarca ☎76 343996 **W:** http//radiocajamarcavivi.com **E:** elnoticierodecajamarca@gmail.com – **CJ74)** Cerro Chamusco, 06873 Pomahuaca – **CJ75)** Vista Alegre, Querocoto ista Alegre, 06846 Querocoto – **CJ76)** Av Peru 729, La Esperanza, 06001 Cajamarca – **CJ77)** Prolongacion Arequipa s/s, Barrios Altos,06861 Querocotillo – **CJ78)** Simon Bolivar 1480, 06101 Jaen – **CJ79)** Jr Marañon 345, 06536 Cajabamba – **CJ80)** Ca Lambayeque 156, 06101 Jaen – **CJ81)** Jr. Teresa de Journet 131, Urb. Alameda, 06001 Cajamarca ☎94 2021465 **W:** manantialdevida1450. com **E:** manantialdevidaradio@hotmail.com – **CJ82)** Bambamarca **W:** facebook.com/radiolibertadbambamarca – **CJ83)** Jr.Juan XXIII 287, 06031 Chota – **CJ84)** Jr Alfonso Ugarte 212, Bambamarca ☎76 353642 **W:**.radiocharles.com **E:** radiocharles91.1@hotmail.com – **FM:** 91.1 MHz – **CJ85)** Jr Mariscal Sucre 715, Bambamarca ☎97 58011485 **W:** radiolapositivaperu.com

CU00 (CUSCO):
CU02) Universidad Nacional de San Antonio Abad del Cusco, Av. de la Cultura 733, 08001 Cusco ☎84 786874 **W:** abel-ww.wix.com/radiouni-versidad-unsaac-cusco **E:** radio_universidad@hotmail.com – **CU04)** Av Charcahuaylla s/n, 08028 Maras, Prov Urubamba ☎84 201410 **W:** radiolasalle.com **E:** webmaster@radiolasalle.com.pe - **FM:** 91.7MHz – **CU05)** Prolongacion Av. Grau 30, Huancaro, 08001 Cusco ☎84 221045 **W:** nseradio.com **E:** nsecusco@nseradio.com – **CU06)** Ca Tres Cruces de Oro 430, 3er piso, 08001 Cusco – **CU07)** Ca Puputi K-3B, Cercado de Cusco, 08001 Cusco ☎84 505364 **W:** radioluzcusco. org – **CU08)** Ca Inca 650, Santiago, 08001 Cusco ☎84 228649 **W:** radiointiraymi.com **E:** intiraymiradio@hotmail.com – **Quechua:** 2 hrs: - 1100, 1500 – **CU10)** Ca Daniel A Carrioón 602, Urb. Fideranda, 08006 Wanchaq ☎84 255491 – **CU13)** Av Tupac Amaru, Urb. Progreso 23, 08006 Wanchaq ☎84 504961 **W:** radiolasvegas.pe **E:** administra-cion@grupovegas.com.pe – **FM:** 100.1 MHz – **CU14)** Jr Cusco 805 - Yauri, 08451 Espinar ☎84 773692 **W:** http//radioconciertocusco. galeon.com - **FM:** 103.9MHz – **CU15)** Asoc. Pro-Vivendi el Periodista Lt B-13, 08006 Wanchaq ☎84 261556 **W:** radiotropicanacusco. blogspot.no **E:** RadioTropicanaCusco@gmail.com – **CU16)** Urb. Villa el Periodista Lote E-1, 08001 Cusco ☎84 239514 **W:** cuscoctv47.com **E:** prensaaldiaperu@gmail.com – **CU17)** Ca Sucre 107, 08351 Sicuani – **CU18)** Jr Ricardo Palma M 2, Wanchaq, 08001 Cusco ☎84 246201 - **FM:** 100.7MHz – **CU19)** Ca Anta s/n, Antanampa, 08541 Espinar **W:** radiolosandesdelperu.es.tl - **FM:** 98.9MHz – **CU20)** Jr Juan Espinoza Medrano P-13, Urb Rosas Pata, 08001 Cusco **E:** sernaquem@hotmail. com – **CU21)** Ca Retiro 296-A, 08001 Cusco ☎84 224567 - **FM:** 92.7MHz – **CU22)** Lote E-11, Urb Bancopata, 08001 Cusco **W:** machu-picchuradio.com **E:** machupicchuradio@hotmail.com - **FM:** 100.1MHz – **CU23)** Jr José Santos Chocano, Bloque G-11, Urb. Santa Monica, 08001 Cusco ☎84 226765 📠84 234494 **W:** radiouniversalcusco. com.pe **E:** radiouniversal@speedy.com.pe – Rprts to Carlos Gamarra Moscoso, Av Garcilazo 411, Wanchác **E:** adalidcusco@hotmail.com - **FM:** 103.3MHz – **CU24)** Ca Meloc 417, 08001 Cusco **W:** bethelradio. fm – **CU25)** Av El Sol N° 830, 08001 Cusco ☎84 228411 **W:** radio-tawantinsuyo.com - Rprts to Carlos Gamarra Moscoso, Av Garcilazo

411, Wanchác **E:** adalidcusco@hotmail.com - **FM:** 91.3MHz – **CU26)** Av Martin Pio Concha 339, 08141 Santa Ana **Quechua:** 1300-1430, 2100-0100 ☎84 281002 **W:** facebook.com – Radio Quillabamba - **FM:** 91.1MHz – **CU27)** Jr Bolivar 217, 08351 Sicuani **W:** radiopachatusan. com**E:** pachatusanradio1240@hotmail.com – **CU28)** Pasaje Constancia 102, Of 410, 08006 Wanchaq **W:** solimperiotvradio.blogspot.com – **CU30)** Jr José Olaya Mz H-9, Urb Bancopata, 08009 Santiago ☎84 252591 – **CU31)** Ca Sacsaywaman K-10, Urb. Manuel Prado, 08001 Cusco - **FM:** 104.1MHz – **CU32)** Av. Garcilazo de la Vega 604, 08006 Wanchaq ☎84 226912 – **CU34)** Jr 2 de Mayo 206, 08351 Sicuani ☎84 351136 **W:** radiosicuani.org.pe **E:** radiosicuani@gmail.com - **Quechua:** 0930-1100, 2300-0300 0900-0300 - **FM:** 91.1MHz – **CU35)** Urb. Marcavalle, P-20, 08006 Wanchaq ☎84 226555 **W:** radiotvsanta-monica.com **E:** radiosantamonica@gmail.com - **FM:** 93.9MHz – **CU36)** Plaza de Armas s/n, El Descanso, 08371 Kunturkanki Canas, Prov. de Canas **E:** cpmaldonado@caritas.org.pe – **CU37)** Conjunto Habitacional Pachacútec A-105, 08001 Cusco ☎84 211371 **W:** radiovidacusco.org – **CU39)** Jr Matara 526, 08001 Cusco - **FM:** 106.5MHz – **CU40)** Av Manuel Callo Zevallos 161, 08351 Sicuani ☎84 351700 **W:** radioque-chua.pe **E:** radioquechus@gmail.com - **FM:** 97.7MHz – **CU42)** Plaza de Armas s/n, 08281 Marcapata, Provincia de Quispicanchi – **CU43)** Ca Saphi 601, Cusco ☎84 225851 - **FM:** 90.1MHz – **CU44)** Av El Sol 230, Yauri, 08451 Espinar - **FM:** 103.1MHz – **CU48)** Av Panamericana 105, Yauri, 08451 Espinar – **CU49)** Av Cusco s/n, Yauri, 08451 Espinar – **CU50)** Jr Ricardo Palma 516, 08141 Quillabamba - **FM:** 96.5MHz – **CU51)** Ca Choquechaca 152, 08001 Cusco ☎84 802444 – **CU52)** Ca Heladeros 220, 08006 Wanchaq **W:** radiomariaperu.org - **FM:** 102.1MHz – **CU55)** Comunidad de Usañaje, Ca 28 de Junio 507, 08551 Santo Tomas, Chumbivilcas **W:** radioqorilazo.zragteam.com – **CU56)** Av San Martin 305, Yauri, 08451 Espinar ☎84 301099 **W:** radiolaramani. com **E:** radiolaramani@latinmail.com – **CU58)** Plaza de Armas s/n, El Descanso, 08371 Kunturkanki, Prov de Canas ☎84 812761 **E:** radio-santacruz@peru.com - **FM:** 97.7MHz – **CU61)** Ca Arequipa 590, 08351 Sicuani – **CU62)** Av Arequipa s/n, 08351 Sicuani **W:** radiovilcanota. blogspot.no – **CU63)** Chamaco, Provincia de Chumbivilcas – **CU64)** Ca Monjaspata 745, 08001 Cusco – **CU65)** Prolongación Avenida de la Cultura 1505, 08058 San Sebastian – **CU66)** Puputi 208, Int. N° 01, 08001 Cusco – **CU67)** Av San Martin 311, 08451 Espinar ☎84 250132 **W:** radiocadenasurespinar.blogspot.no **E:** waldervalero@hotmail.com - **FM:** 103.1 MHz – **CU68)** Av Cuzco 117, 08058 San Sebastian – **CU69)** Malecón Sicuani s/n, 08351 Sicuani,**W:** radioexitosa.pe – **CU70)** Av Infancia 551, 08001 Cusco ☎84 784397 – **W:** facebook.com – Radio Jerusalen – **CU71)** Ca Alfonso Ugarte 433, 08451 Espinar ☎984 938 428 **W:** radiosolarespinar.blogspot.no – **CU72)** Ca Belen 600, 08031 Urubamba ☎99 6783273 **W:** radiochaski.org **E:** chaskiradio@hotmail. com - **FM:** 94.9 MHz – **CU73)** Av Ejercito 200, 08001 Cusco ☎84 775511 **W:** radiovidacusco.org – **CU74)** Av Tupac Amaru 535, 08386 Yanaoca **W:** Facebook – Radio Altiva Canas – **CU75)** Av Tupac Amaru s/n, 08386 Yanaoca – **CU76)** Urb. Tambillo L-5, 08086 Urcos – **CU77)** Av de la Cultura 3035 A-1, 08058 San Sebastian – **CU78)** Av Carrion 313, 08351 Sicuani **W:** redinformativadelsur.blogspot.se – **CU79)** Ca Mojospata 745, Cusco ☎98 665 5540 **W:** radiowayraperu.com – **CU80)** Ca Bernardo Tambohuacso 100 Of 31, 08001 Cusco – **CU81)** Esquina Calle Alegria 205 con Av.Arequipa No 119, 08351 Sicuani – **CU82)** Av Tupac Amaru D-3, Urb. Progreso, 08006 Wanchaq ☎84 246832 **W:** radiolasvegas.pe – **CU83)** Ca Concepcion MZ J-4, Lote 4, 08531 Livitica – **CU84)** Velille, Prov. de Chumbivilcas – **CU85)** Yauri, Espinar ☎973 583596 **W:** radiokinsachata.pe **E:** info@radiokinsa-chata.pe – **CU86)** Av. Diagonal (R.Zavaleta) 117 5° piso, Wanchaq – **CU87)** Chumbbivilcas

HN00 (HUANUCO):
HN01) Av Raymondi N° 432, 10221 Rupa-Rupa ☎6256 2024 – **HN02)** Malecón Huallaga 1038, 10261 Aucayacu – **HN03)** Jr Tacna 693, 10001 Huanuco ☎62 517996 **W:** radiohuanuco.com – **HN04)** Jr Hermilio Valdiz 272,10001 Huanuco ☎62 516360 **W:** radiolaluz.com – **HN05)** Jr Leoncio Prado 723 (Cas 343), 10001 Huánuco ☎62 511525 📠62 512428 Prgr in **Sp & Quechua** - **FM:** 88.9MHz – **HN06)** Ruben Dario 128, 10051 Amarilis, 10001 Huánuco ☎62 512428 – **HN07)** Jr Dos de Mayo 1286, Of 208, 10001 Huánuco **E:** luzysonido@hotmail.com ☎62 518500 📠62 511985 **Quechua:** 1000-1200, 2300-0200 - **FM:** 105.7MHz – **HN12)** Jr. Aguilar N° 560, 2do Piso, 10001 Huanuco – **HN13)** Sector San Cristóbal de Huayllabamba, 10066 San Francisco de Cayran – **HN15)** Pasaje Uchiza 170, Int 7, 10221 Rupa-Rupa – **HN16)** Sector Mesepata, 10061 Pilco Marca – **HN17)** Jr Leonicio con Libertad, 10001 Huanuco **W:** radiocielo.pe – **HN18)** Jr. Ambo 112, Amarilis **W:** kebuenaradioytv.com – **FM:** 99.7 – **HN19)** Jr Colonial 312, 10021 Amarilis – **HN20)** Jr Colonial N° 312, 10021 Amarilis

HV00 (HUANCAVELICA):
HV01) Puno 110, 09481 Lircay, Prov de Angaraes – **HV02)** Plaza Bolognesi 142, Cercado,09001 Huancavelica **E:** jlopez_alvarado@hotmail.com ☎67 451257 **FM:** 99.1MHz – **HV03)** Ca Arequipa S/N,

09841 Huayllahuara – **HV04)** Av Los Libertadores s/n, Castrovirreina – **HV05)** Cl Mercurio 101, Urb. Santa Bárbara, Huancavelica ☎67 451376 **W:** radiomastermixfm.com **E:** mastermixfm@hotmail.com – **HV06)** Jr Armado Revorredo 588, Acobamba – **HV07)** Jr Sebastián 353, Huancavelica

IC00 (ICA):
IC01) Conde de Nieva 125, 11001 Ica – **IC02)** Av Ayacucho Esq Grau s/n, 11001 Ica ☎56 231956 - **FM:** 105.3MHz – **IC03)** Av Conde de Nieva, Urb Luren, 11001 Ica - **FM:** 90.7MHz – **IC04)** Av San Martín 305, 2° piso, 11101 Chincha Alta – **IC05)** Ca Cajamarca 195, 11001 Ica - **FM:** 103.3MHz – **IC06)** Av Leon de Bivero 100 2do Piso, 11001 Ica ☎56 237326 **W:** radioluaz.com – **IC07)** Zona M-6, San Juan de Marcona, 111521 Marcona ☎56 525268 – **IC10)** Ca Bolivar 473, 11001 Ica – ☎56 219300 – **IC11)** Calle Grocio Prado 122, 11101 Chincha Alta – **IC12)** Los Portales de Escribanos 167, Plaza de Armas, Palpa **E:** radiocruzdelsur@hotmail.com – **FM:** 99.7 MHz – **IC15)** San Martín 120, Urb Pencal, 11521 Nazca – **IC17)** Km 300, Panamericana Sur, 11011 Subtanjalla **E:** epcc@upsjb.edu.pe – **IC19)** Jr Los Ángeles 296 3er Piso, Publo Nuvo, 11141 Chincha ☎56 263278 – **IC20)** Ca San Francisco 301, 11241 San Clemente ☎56 312416 **W:** facebook.com/carlosalberto.bautistagutierrez – **IC21)** Jr Lima 529,11141 Chincha Alta **W:** yeshuara-diofm.blogspot.se – **FM:** 107.5 MHz – **IC22)** Urb. Fernando de Leon de Vivero R` 1-7, 11146 Pueblo Nuevo – **IC23)** Ca Camino Real s/n, Sector Guadeloupe, 11021 Salas **W:**radioluaz.com – **IC24)** Programa de Vivienda Vallea Hermoso, 11011 Subtanjalla – **IC25)** Jirón Miraflores 342, 4588 Pueblo Nuevo – **IC26)** Av Arenales 685, Ica – **IC27)** Ca San Francisco s/n – Sector Colorado, Chincha – **PI28)** Av.Victor Andrés Belaunde 1328, Distr. Pueblo Nuevo, Chincha – **IC29)** Av Arenales 685, Ica – **IC30)** Av Arenales 685, Ica – **IC31)** Av Progreso 168, Chinca Alta – **IC31)** Prolongación Cañete Mz. D- 1, LT21-A, Salas – **IC32)** Jr. Ica 357, Pueblo Nuevo – **IC33)** Prolongación Cañete s/n, Salas

JN00 (JUNIN):
JN01) Jr Los Manzanos 695, 12009 El Tambo ☎64 789459 **W:** radioluaz.com - **FM:** 101.7MHz – **JN04)** Av Tayacaja 324, Of 202, 12851 La Oroya – **JN05)** Av Jorge Chavez 851, Anexo Zaños Grande, 12009 El Tambo **E:** radiovida@hotmail.com – **JN06)** Ca Ancash 543, Of 208, 12001 Huancayo - **FM:** 103.1MHz – **JN08)** Jr Bolognesi 484 2de Piso, 12741 Jauja **W:** radioluzdetarma.com – **JN09)** Av Calmell del Solar 469-481, Sn Carlos Hye, 12001 Huancayo ☎64 211312 **W:** rmanantial.webcindario.com **E:** manantialradio960@hotmail.com - **FM:** 94.9 MHz – **JN10)** Jr. Huancas 251, a San Carlos, 12001 Huancayo – **JN11)** Esquina Prolongación Pachitea 136 y Pasaje Andaluz 106 4° piso, 12001 Huancayo – **JN12)** Paraje Aliguata, Anexo A Azapampa, 12014 Chilca **W:** bethelradio.fm – **JN13)** Ca Mercado 194, 12321 San Ramón **JN14)** Ca Real 270, El Tambo, 12001 Huancayo ☎64 245396 📄64 253921 - **FM:** 96.7MHz "R Futura" – **JN16)** Paseo La Breña 174 2 piso Of 202, 12001 Huancayo ☎64 219990 – **JN18)** Jr Cerro de Pasco 582, (Ap 2), 12101 Junín ☎64 344029 **W:** rlibertadjunin.com **E:** radiolibertadjunin@yahoo.es - **FM:** 98.9MHz – **JN19)** Av Ayacucho 7300, 12001 Huancayo - **FM:** 105.7MHz – **JN20)** Av Manuel Prado 239,12411 Satipo – **JN21)** Jr Moquegua 648, 12221 Tarma – **JN22)** Prongolacion Ancash No 555, 12014 Chilca **W:** radiomariaperu.org- **FM:** 98.5MHz – **JN23)** Jr Junín 163, 12331 La Merced Chanchamayo – **JN24)** Jr Dario Leon 198, 4° piso, 12851 La Oroya **W:** Facebook **FM:** 91.7 MHz – **JN26)** Ca Real 1453, 12001 Huancayo **W:** radiobacan.com.pe **E:** corplus@radiobacan.com – **JN27)** Jr Junin 843 , 2° piso, 12741 Jauja ☎64 362428 📄64 361850 – **JN28)** Jr Jauja 494, 12221 Tarma – **JN29)** Prolongacion los Proceres s/n, Barrio Las Lomas, 12014 Chilca – **JN30)** Jr Moquegua 642, 12221 Tarma ☎64 321864 **W:** radioluzdetarma.com – **JN31)** Av Jose Carlos Mariátegui 699, Urb Tambo, 12001 Huancayo ☎64 241941 📄64 252840 - **FM:** 102.5MHz – **JN32)** Ca Bolivar 481, 12101 Junin – **JN33)** Marcavelle Block "F" 191,Santa Rosa de Sacco, 12851 La Oroya **W:** Facebook – Radio La Oroya **E:** radio_la_oroya@hotmail.com ☎64 391401 📄64 391748 - **FM:** 100.1MHz – **JN34)** Ca Real 517, Of 403, 12001 Huancayo ☎64 231831 **W:** radiohuancayo.com.pe - **FM:** 104.3MHz – **JN35)** Av Arevaldo 484, Anexo Chuccus, 12841 Santa Rosa de Sacco, Prov de Yauli **W:** mineriaradiotv.com – **JN37)** Jr Molino del Amo 167 (Cas.167), 12221 Tarma ☎64 321510 📄6432 1167 **W:** radiotarma.com **E:** informacion@grupomonteverde.com - **FM:** 99.3 & 101.7MHz "R Tropicana" in La Merced – **JN38)** Av Huancavelica 430, 2° piso (Ap 230), 12001 Huancayo ☎64 233851 **W:** radio1550.com **E:** radio@radio1550.com - **FM:** 88.9MHz – **JN40)** Jr Pasco y Amazonas 420 2 piso Edifico San Juan, 12221 Tarma ☎64 321820 - **FM:** 106.5 MHz – **JN44)** Ca Principal de Lama, Pariahuanca, 12001 Huancayo **W:** nuevotiempo.org.pe – **JN45)** Av.Huancavlica 439 4to pisi, 12001 Huancyo – **JN46)** Prolongacion ICA y la Ca. Real s/n, 12001 Huancayo **W:** visionradioperu.com – **JN47)** Jr Miguel Grau 220, 12471 Pichanaqui, Chanchamayo – **JN48)** Jr Santa Cecilia 107 12014 Chilca ☎64 201011 **W:** radiovozcristianaperu.com **E:** radio-vozcristiana1470am@hotmail.com – **JN49)** Pasaje Omacoto, 12072 Sicaya **W:** radioluaz.com – **JN50)** Ca Principal de Lampa s/n, 12006

Pariahuanca - **JN51)** Jr Ayacucho 297, 12001 Huancayo – **JN52)** Av los Incas 421, Huancán ☎64 248362 **W:** ministerioevangelicoapoc-alipsis.com– **JN53)** Conjunto Habitacional Villa Mercedes – Block 03 – Tiends 1, 12001 Huancayo – **JN54)** Av Deusta 548,12009 El Tambo – **JN55)** Jr La Victoria 322, Costado Colegio Casillo, 12009 El Tambo ☎64 249121 – **JN56)** Jr Cajamarca 178, Huancayo ☎64 215038 **W:** radioscaladeoro.com **E:** escalaradio@hotmail.com – **FM:** 107.1 MHz – **JN57)** Jr Ayacucho 297,12001 Huancayo – **JN58)** Centro Poblado de Tzancuvatziari, Satipo – **JN59)** Junin – **JN60)** Altura de Puente Chacachimpa, Carretera Junin Ondores, JuninJ

LB00 (LAMBAYEQUE):
LB01) Km 4 de la Carretera Pimentel, 14001 Chiclayo - **FM:** 105.1MHz – **LB02)** Ca Juan XXXIII 391 (Ciudad Universitaria), 14601 Lambayeque **W:** unprg.edu.pe **E:** universitariaradio@hotmail.com – **LB03)** Psje. Woyke 179,Oficina Radio, Edifico Angelica, 14011 San José ☎74 237850 **W:** radioluaz.com - **LB04)** Juan Cuglievan 984, 14001 Chiclayo – Quechua: **Sun:** 0600-1100 – **LB06)** Alfonso Ugarte 505, 14011 San José ☎74 608991 – **LB08)** Ca San José 462, Of 207, 14001 Chiclayo ☎74 204786 - **FM:** 96.7MHz – **LB11)** Av Pedro Ruiz 1123, 3° piso, 14001 Chiclayo – **LB12)** Calle 28 de Julio 440, 14041 San Jose ☎74 650332 **W:** radioprimaverachiclayo.com – **LB14)** Colombia 1637, Urb. V.R.Haya de la Torre, 14001 Chiclayo ☎74 208523 – **LB15)** Av Saenz Peña 1046, 14001 Chiclayo ☎74 208872 - **FM:** 98.3MHz – **LB16)** Av Tupac Amaru 532, 14301 Ferreñafe ☎73 286044 **E:** aflff@hotmail.com – **LB17)** Ca San José 1084, 14001 Chiclayo – **LB18)** Av. Lora y Lora 1505, Urb. San Isidro, 14001 Chiclayo ☎74 320616 - **FM:** 94.1MHz – **LB19)** Ca Manuel Seano 918, 14001 Chiclayo ☎74 236363 – **LB20)** Ca Las Violetas s/n, 14001 Chiclayo **W:** radionova.com.pe/nova_chiclayo.html - **FM:** 94.9MHz – **LB21)** Ca Francisco Gonzales Burgán 717, 14301 Ferreñafe ☎74 286351 **E:** radioferrenafe@hotmail.com – **LB22)** Ca 1 de Mayo 278, Urrunaga, 14001 Chiclayo – **LB23)** Caserio Tranca Falupe, 14101 Morrope – **LB24)** Ca San Francisco 1499 – P.J.Cruz de Chalpo, 14161 Olmos – **LB25)** Jr. Juan Cuglievan 984, 14001 Chiclayo ☎98 1877701 **W:** radioamistadperu.net – **LB26)** Empresa Capimag S.R.L., Calle Justicia 102, Urb. Túpac Amaru, 14001 Chiclayo – **LB29)** Ca San Jose 148, 14161 Olmos **E:** clori1009@yahoo.es – **LB30)** Av el Tren s/n, 14001 Chiclayo – **LB31)** Ca Juan Fanning N° 457, 14001 San Juan, 14001 Chiclayo ☎74 239889 **W:** visionradioperu.com **E:** informes@visionradioperu.com – **LB32)** Ca Tarata 931, 14161 Olmos **W:** Facebook – Radio Super Real 1510 – **LB36)** Av Huamaucho 1080, 14601 Lambayeque ☎74 284085 **W:** radionaylamp.com **E:** naylamp@llampallec.rep.net.pe - **FM:** 96.1MHz – **LB40)** Ca Amadeo Ruiz 320, 14161 Olmos **W:** radionorandinaolmos.com – **FM:** 102.7 MHz – **LB41)** Ca Nazca 300, 14021 La Victoria ☎74 232559 **W:** radiofechiclayo.tk **E** jesusmiguela1077@hotmail.com att.: Pastor José Huamán – **LB42)** Ca Vicente de la Vega 873, 14001 Chiclayo ☎74 224287 **W:** corporacionrbc.org **E:** carranzamori@hotmail.com – **LB44)** Av Lora y Lora 399, Urb. Patazca, 14001 Chiclayo – **LB45)** Av Los Andes No 950, 14021 La Victoria – **LB46)** Prolongacion 8 de Octubre No 263, 14601 Lambayeque - **LB47)** Av Pedro Ruiz 1250, 14001 Chiclayo ☎74 229494 – **LB48)** Ca Diego Ferre 637, Monsefú – **LB49)** Av Pacifico 483, Chiclayo

LL00 (LA LIBERTAD):
LL01) Av.Gonzales Prada 695-12, 13001 Trujillo ☎44 436007 – **LL02)** Jr Benito Juarez 1753, 13009 La Esperanza – **LL03)** Ca Opalo 298 2° piso-A, Urb Sta.Ines, 13001 Trujillo ☎44 291058 - **FM:** 98.3MHz – **LL04)** Ca Lima 599, 13171 Chepén – **LL05)** San Martín 472, 13001 Trujillo ☎44 251792 – **LL06)** Av Los Incas s/n, Anexo Facala, Ascope - **LL07)** Ca Junín 23, Sausal, 12651 Ascope – **LL08)** Francisco Pizarro 532, Of 205, 13001 Trujillo – **LL09)** Jr Ayacucho 65, 13111 Pacasmayo ☎44 583042 – **LL10)** Jr San Antonio 880 Piso 2, 13301 Otuzco ☎44 436007 – **LL11)** Jr Marcelo Corne 224, Urb San Andrés, 13001 Trujillo ☎44 294050 - **FM:** 90.9MHz – **LL12)** Av V Belaunde MZ.L lote 15, Urb Santo Dominguito, 13001 Trujillo – **LL15)** Av Gran Chimu 1791 – Esperanza Alta, 13009 La Esperanza – **LL16)** Alfonso Ugarte 222, 13052 Virú – ☎44 371046 **W:** radioollantayperu.com **E:** viru@radioollantayperu.com - **FM:** 102.3MHz – **LL17)** Ca Trujillo 699-A, 13171 Chepén – **LL19)** Psje. Damián Nicolau 108, 13501 Huamachuco. ☎44 441502 **W:** radiolosandesdehuamachuco.com **E:** radiolosandesdireccion@yahoo.es – **LL20)** Psje. Rosa Elvira Farro Solis 3, Urb. Ignacioa Reaño, 13171 Chepen ☎44 561430 **W:** sansebastianradio.com **E:** info@sansebastianradio.com - **FM:** 103.3 MHz – **LL21)** Miguel Grau 439, Of. 213, 13001 Trujillo ☎44 217885 – **LL22)** Zepita 452, 13001 Trujillo ☎44 249326 📄44 252970 **W:** radiolibertadmundo.com **E:** contactanos@radiolibertadmundo.com – **LL24)** Bolívar 780 (Cas 1029), 13001 Trujillo ☎44 233981 – **LL26)** Ca Cáceres 1338, 13761 Santiago de Chuco ☎44 230277 – **LL28)** Jr Progreso 987, 13171 Chepén - **FM:** 98.7MHz – **LL32)** Av. Geronimo La Torre 175, Urb. Las Quintanas, 13001 Trujillo ☎44 803037 **W:** Facebook – Radio La Luz 1390 – **LL35)** Pasaje San Martin 300, Urb Alto Mochica, (Ap 352) 13001 Trujillo ☎44 201606 **W:** sanjuansuperradio.com **E:** radiosanjuan@hotmail.com – **LL37)** Jr Trujillo 281, 13701 Quiruvilca – **LL38)** Av. Virú N° 1205, 13052

Virú – **LL39)** Av. España 1238 – oficina 305, 13001 Trujillo ☎44 210494 – **LL42)** Jr Ayacucho 459, Sto. piso, 13001 Trujillo ☎44 694345 **W:** Facebook – Radio Mundial Trujillo – **FM:** 96.9MHz – **LL43)** Av España 1210, 13001 Trujillo ☎44 295214 **W:** Facebook **E:** pastormamerto@hotmail.com – **LL46)** Ca Victor Julio Rossel 324, 13831 Julcan – **LL47)** Ca Progreso 551, 13301 Otuzco ☎44 220221 – **LL48)** Ca La Libertad 120, 13301 Otuzco ☎44 436565 **W:** chamiradio.org.pe **E:** direccion@chamiradio.org.pe – **LL49)** Ca Progreso 551, 13301 Otuzco **W:** radiootuzco.blogspot.no – **LL51)** Jr Lara 591, 13501 Huamachuco **W:** radioantena9.com – **LL52)** Av America Sur 3145, Urb. Monserrat (Apt. 1075), 13001 Trujillo ☎44 604444 **W:** upao.edu.pe/radio **E:** cceli@upao.edu.pe – **LL53)** Jr Francisco Pizarro 970, 13001 Trujillo – **LL54)** Panamericana Norte Km 570 – El Milagro, 13009 La Esperanza – **LL55)** Ca Simón Bolivar 675, Santiago de Chuco

LM00 (LIMA):
LM01) Juan Vargas 147, Chorrillos, Lima 09 ☎1 4388850 **W:** radioinca.com.pe – **LM02)** Jr Camana 615 of 60, Lima 01 ☎1 4272639 **W:** radiooriente.com **E:** radiooriente@hotmail.es – **LM03)** Av Garzón 2031, Jesús Maria, Lima 11 **W:** radiomariaperu.org **E:** info.per@radiomaria. org ☎1 7001600 ☎1 4333276 – **LM04)** Mz. 11 – Lote 6 – Urb. Mariscal Cáceres – San Juan de Luringancho ☎1 4280938 **W:** radiocora. net – **LM05)** Ca Miguel Dasso 144, Of 2A, San Isidro, Lima 27 ☎1 5922291 **W:** ovacion.com.pe/radio/ **E:** radioovacion@ovacion.com. pe – **LM06)** Av Guzman Blanco 465, 7° piso, (Ap 4236) Lima 01 ☎1 4337879 ☎1 4333276 **W:** pacificoradio.com **E:** informes@pacificoradio. com – **LM07)** Justo Pastor Davila 197, Chorillos, Lima 09 ☎1 6176600 **W:** radiolainolvidable.com.pe **E:**crpradio@crpradio.com.pe – **LM08)** Jr Jose de Sucre 184, Comas, Lima 13 ☎1 4337674 **W:** rbcsatelital.pe **E:** contacto@rbcradio.pe – **LM09)** Jr. Alejandro Tirado 508, Urb. Santa Beatriz, Lima 01 (✉ C.P. 138, La Molina, Lima 12 ☎1 2653291 **W:** redradiointegridad.com **E:** info@redradiointegridad.org – **LM10)** Av Paseo de la República 3866, 2° piso, San Isidro, Lima 27 ☎1 2150200 **W:** rpp.com.pe **E:** info@gruporpp.com.pe – **LM11)** Justo Pastor Dávila 197, Chorillos, Lima 09 ☎1 6176600 ☎1 2513324 **W:** radiomar. pe – **LM12)** Jr. Camana 625-605, Cercado de Lima ☎1 4272639 **W:** radiovictoria.pe or orienteproducciones.com – **LM13)** Prolongación los Angeles 676, Huaral, Lima 18 ☎1 2465296 **W:** Facebook – Radio la Luz Huaral **E:** radiolaluzhuaral@hotmail.com – **FM:** 94.7 MHz – **LM14)** Av Salaverry 1082, Jesús Maria, Lima 11 **W:** radiolibertad.com.pe **E:** info@radiolibertad.com.pe ☎1 2660777 ☎1 4715319 – **LM15)** Av Petit Thouars 447, Santa Beatriz, Lima 01 **W:** radionacional.com. pe ☎1 4338956 – **LM16)** Av José Pardo 138, Of. 1501, Miraflores, Lima 18 ☎1 7120145 **W:** unionlaradio.com **E:** informes@unionlaradio. com – **LM17)** Av Paseo de la Republica 3866, San Isidro Lima 27 ☎1 2210941 **W:** felicidad.com.pe – **LM18)** Av Republica de Chile 295, Of. 1104, Santa Beatriz, Lima 01 ☎1 3327779 **W:** modernaradiopapa. com **E:** correomoderna@hotmail.com – **LM19)** Paseo Parodi 340, San Isidro, Lima 27 **W:** radiopanamericana.com **E:** radio@panamericana. com ☎1 4388585 ☎1 4221223 – **LM20)** Jr Ignacio Merino 230, Santa Cruz, Miraflores, Lima 18 ☎1 4428810 **W:** radiolatina.com.pe **E:** contacto@radiolatina.com.pe – **LM21)** Julio C.Tello 152, Lince, Lima 14 ☎1 4714291 **W:** metropolitanaradioperuana.pe **E:** metropolitanaradioperuana@gmail.com – **LM22)** Julio C.Tello 152, Lince, Lima 14 ☎1 4714291 **W:** radioexitoperu.com **E:** radioexitoperu@gmail.com – **LM23)** Av Alfonso Ugarte 1465, 01 Lima ☎1 3305656 **W:** radiolaluz. com **E:** ministeriolaluz2010@hotmail.com – **LM24)** Gerardo Unger 6347, San Martin de Porres, Lima 31 ☎1 5373204 **W:** radiofelizperu. com – **LM27)** Jr Bernardo Alcedo 375, Lince, Lima 14 ☎1 2652333 **W:** radiobacan.com **E:** corplus@radiobacan.com – **LM30)** Av Manco Cápac 495, 4to Piso, Of 401, Miraflores, Lima 18 **W:** radiomiraflores.net ☎1 4441773 ☎1 4450126 – **LM31)** Jr Echenique 140, 15140 Huacho – **LM32)** Mz L, Lt 7, Urb La Esperanza, 15146 Hualmay – **LM33)** Av Estados Unidos 327, Urb Huaquillay, Comas, Lima 07 **W:** radiocomas. com **E:** comas@radiocomas.com ☎1 5250094 ☎1 5250859 – **LM34)** Ca MCDO Sur 105, 15140 Huacho – **LM35)** Av Alfonso Ugarte 1428 Of 202, Lima ☎1 330-4774 **W:** radioalegria1340peru.com **E:** informacion@radioalegria1340peru.com – **LM37)** Av Comandante Espinar N° 680, Miraflores, Lima 18 ☎1 6107760 ☎1 6107761 **W:** nuevotiempo.org.pe **E:** radio@nuevotiempo.org.pe – **LM39)** Ca Juan de Carpio 140-144 2° piso, San Isidro, Lima 27 ☎1 4422042 ☎1 4421693 **W:** radiocallao.com **E:** radiocallao@gmail.com – **LM40)** Av 28 de Julio 1781, La Victoria. Lima 13 ☎1 6131701 **W:** bethelradio.fm **E:** bethelradio@bethelradio. fm – **LM41)** Av Petit Thouars 1806, Lince, Lima 14 ☎1 4711278 **W:** luisfernando-97.wix.com/radiosanisidro – **LM42)** Mz C, Lte. 5, Asoc. Virgen de la Familia, 15857 Chilca – **LM43)** Av Separadora Industrial s/n, Lote 4, MZ5, M25, Parcela 1, Villa El Salvador, Lima 42 ☎1 2913146 – **LM44)** Alfonso Ugarte 149, 15170 Barranca ☎1 2354238 – **FM:** 101.5 MHz – **LM45)** À.Paseo de la República 3866, San Isidro **W:** capital.com.pe – **LM47)** Jr Camaná 170, (Apt 4451 San Miguel), El Cercado, Lima 01 **W:** radiosantarosa.com.pe **E:** contacto@radiosantarosa.com.pe ☎1 4277488 – **LM49)** Av. Universitaria 4518 of 1202,

Torre D.Villa Sol, Los Olivos ☎1 7153264 ☎1 4617757 **W:** radiomileni-aperu.com – **LM51)** Jr. Yahuar Huaca Piso 3 106, Urb. Tahuantinsuyo, Independencia, Lima 28 ☎1 5260469 **W:** radioindependenciadelperu.com **E:** wbaldeon@radioindependcniadelperu.com – **LM52)** Av Colombia 325, Pueblo Libre, Lima ☎1 4236201 **W:** Facebook: R.Vida – **LM54)** Jr. Almirante Guisse N° 1885, Lince, Lima 14 ☎1 4723110 **W:** radiocielo.pe – **LM55)** Av Petit Thouars 447, Santa Beatriz, Lima 01 **W:** radionacional.com.pe ☎1 4331404 – **LM56)** Av. Paseo Parodi 340, San Isidro, Lima 43 ☎1 4413050 **W:** radio1160.com.pe – **LM58)** CRP – Justo Pastor Davila 197, Chorrillos, Lima 09 ☎1 617 6606 **W:** radiobienestar.pe– **LM59)** Av 28 de Julio 1781, La Victoria. Lima 13 ☎1 6131701 **W:** bethelradio.fm **E:** bethelradio@bethelradio.fm – **LM60)** Jr. Morales Bermúdez 140, Pueblo Libre (Alt. 14 de Av. Brasil), Lima 21 ☎1 4248122 **W:** cadena1200.org **E:** informes@cadena1200.com – **LM61)** Av Los Olivos Parad, 12rb monte los Olivos II etapa, San Martin de Porres, Lima 24 ☎1 4848379 **W:** radiojpj.com **E:** radiojpj@hotmail. com – **LM62)** Av.Salaverry 862, Jesus Maria, Lima 11 **W:** nseradio. com **E:** nselima@nseradio.com ☎1 4714172 – **LM63)** Av.Gerardo Unger 6995, Independencia, Lima 28 ☎1 5331848 **W:** radiofeperu.org **E:** gerencia@radiofeperu.org – **LM64)** KM 193 Panamericana Norte, Barranca, Lima 04 – **LM65)** Urb. Lever Pacocha "D" 13 Av. San Martin 1 Piso, 15140 Huacho ☎1 3045427 **W:** radioaluz.com – **LM66)** Luis Alberto Lizarraga Alva, Cerro Laguna, 15703 San Vicente de Cañete, Provinca de Cañete – **LM67)** Jr Mariano Melgar 235, 15173 Barranca **W:** radiobendicionbarranca.blogspot.no – **LM68)** Mz. E Lt. 1 AAHH Cocharcas Asuncion 8, 15708 Imperial – **LM69)** Ca Tupac Amaru 140, Urb. Casuarina, 15703 San Vicente de Cañete – **LM70)** Jr. Lima 1398, 15173 Barranca – **LM71)** Jr.Cusco s/n, Cuadra 1, Quilmana, 15875 Cañete – **LM72)** Av Miguel Grau s/n, Paramonga – **LM73)** Av Grau 592, Oficina 502, Huacho ☎1 3970739 **W:** radioparaisofm.com – **FM:** 103.5 MHz – **LM74)** Pampa de Lara s/n, Barranca ☎992 619756 **W:** angienetradio.com **E:** alzejara@hotmail.com

LT00 (LORETO):
LT01) Jr Abtao 255, 16001 Iquitos ☎65 265244 **W:** radiolavozdelaselva.org **E:** administracion@radiolavozdelaselva.org – **FM:** 93.9 MHz – **LT05)** Av Antonio Raymondi 331, 16001 Iquitos – **FM:** 101.3MHz – **LT09)** Av Arica 737, 16001 Iquitos – **LT10)** Ca Progreso 112-114, 16421 Yurimaguas, Alto Amazonas **W:** roriente.org **E:** oriente995@yahoo.com ☎65 351611 – **FM:** 99.5MHz – **LT14)** Arica 441, 16001 Iquitos

MD00 (MADRE DE DIOS):
MD01) Jr Guillermo Billingurst 406 PTO, 17001 Puerto Maldonado - **FM:** 101.3MHz – **MD02)** Nueva Plaza de Armas 200, 17001 Puerto Maldonado – **MD03)** Jr Daniel A Carrion 387, 17001 Puerto Maldonado ☎82 571050 - **FM:** 92.5MHz – **MD04)** Av Fitzcarrald 130, 17001 Madre de Dios – **MD05)** Av Andres Avelino Caceres km 4.5, Carreter de Tambopata a Cusco – Zona La Pastora, 17001 Madre de Dios – **MD06)** Jr Apurimac Psj. Tacna Lt.10 Mz.B5, 17001 Tambopata – **MD07)** Sector Triunfo s/n, Tambopata – **MD08)** Jr Lerón 368, Tambopata **W:** radiocielo.pe

MQ00 (MOQUEGUA):
MQ04) PP.JJ. John F. Kennedy, Mz. E Lte. 48, 18311 Ilo – **MQ05)** Jr Tarapaca 260, 18001 Moquegua – **FM:** 101. – **MQ07)** Jr Ayacucho N° 639 (Ap 22), 18001 Moquegua ☎53 461542 - **FM:** 105.3MHz – **MQ08)** Mollejo s/n, 18401 Omate **W:** agrorural.gob.pe/escuchar-radios-campesinas – **MQ09)** Marsical Andrés A.Cáceres 193, 18001 Moquegua – **MQ10)** Ca Grau 101 – Frenta a la Plazade Armas, 18401 Omate – **MQ11)** Ca Libertad 1015, 18001 Cercado Moquegua ☎53 463276 **W:** radiolavozdelsurmoquegua.com **E:** radiolavozdelsur@yahoo.com – **MQ12)** Sector Charsawa-Centro Poblado Menor Los Angeles, 18001 Moquegua – **MQ13)** Pse San Antonio s/n, Mascal Nieto – **MQ14)** Av Ancash 555-2, Moquegua – **MO015)** Anexo Santa Cruz Oyo Oyo, Ichuña, Prov. Sanches Cerro – **MO016)** Plaza de Armas s/n, Prov. Sanches Cerro

PA00 (PASCO):
PA01) Plazuela Gamaniel Blanco, 127- 2°Nivel - Ninguno, 19001 Chaupimarca ☎63 422398 **W:** radioalturatv.com **E:** radioalturatv@hotmail.com – **FM:** 97.7MHz – **PA02)** Jr Puno s/n, 19001 Chaupimarca - **FM:** 102.5MHz – **PA03)** Jr Mullembruck 468, Urb Cercado, 191100Oxapampa **- FM:** 101.5MHz – **PA05)** Jr Huamachuco 214, Cerro de Pasco ☎63 330109 **W:** radiocorporacion. com.pe – **PA07)** Jr Daniel Alcids Carrion 250, 19026 Huayllay – **PA08)** Av Tupac Amaru 1066, Colquijirca, 19016 Tinyahuarco – **PA09)** Jr.Pedro Caballero y Lira s/n, Galeria Mina de Oro, 19001 Chaupimarca **W:** radiocumbre.com.pe - **FM:** 103.1 MHz – **PA10)** Jr.Bolognesi 225, 19001 Chaupimarca **W:** radiomineria.com.pe/radiomineria - **FM:**102.5 MHz – **PA11)** Jr Lima 365, 19001 Chaquimarca – **PA12)** Av Simon Bolivar 410, San Juan, 19151 Yanacancha – **PA13)** Pasaje Jauja 106, Chaupimarca – **PA14)** Oxapampa – **PA15)** Cerro de Pasco

PI00 (PIURA):
PI04) Jr San Ignacio de Loyola 300, 20011 Castilla ☎73 342802 **W:** radiocutivalu.org **E:** cutivalu@radiocutivalu.org - **FM:** 100.5MHz

– **PI05)** Ica 419, Of 206, 20001Piura - **FM:** 92.1MHz – **PI06)** Santa Maria C., 20001 Piura - **FM:** 94.5MHz.– **PI08)** Ugarteche 490, 20201 Sullana - **FM:** 99.3MHz – **PI10)** Ca Tacna 260 4 piso, (frente al banco de la nación), 20001 Piura ☎73 303369 – **PI11)**Ca San Martin 1041, 20201 Sullana ☎73 503071 **W:** Facebook – Radio Capullana **E:** capullanaradio@latinmail.com.pe - **FM:** 95.7MHz – **PI13)** Barrio el Altillo s/n, 20541 Huancabamba ☎73 473259 **W:** lavozdelashuarinjas.com **E:** radio@lavozdehuarinjas.com – **FM:** 103.7 MHz – **PI14)** Av Sánches Cerro 582 2do Piso, 20001 Piura ☎73 304221 **W:** radioluz.com - **FM:** 107.9MHz – **PI15)** Carretera Piura-Chulucanas km 4, 20011 Castilla ☎73 324180 – **PI16)** Av. Sanches Cerro 582 - 2° piso, 20001 Piura ☎73 304221 **W:** radioluz.com - **FM:** 107.9 MHz – **PI17)** Ca Unión 515 – B, Barrio Punta Arena, 20001 Piura ☎73 374106 – **PI18)** Zona Industrial Mz D Km 5, Carretera Piura, 20201 Sullana **E:** piuraradio@terra.com.pe - **FM:** 101.9MHz – **PI23)** Ca 8 s/n, 20131 Talara Alta, ☎383 750 **W:** radiobns.com **E:** radiobns1992@hotmail.com – **PI24)** Mz "E" Lote 8, Urb. Isabel Barreto I Etapa, 20801 Paita ☎73 211885 **W:** radionorperu.blogspot.no - **FM:** 102.9MHz – **PI25)** Jr Leoncio Prado 425, 20001 Piura – **PI26)** Madre de Dios 258, 20201 Sullana ☎73 505026 – **PI32)** Av Grau Cuadra N° 5, Cruceta San Lorenzo, 20701 Tambo Grande – **PI41)** Km 993.8, Carretera Panamericana, Predio Don Bosco, Sector Coscomba, 20001 Piura – **PI47)** Av Principal, Caserio La Peñita, 20701 Tambo Grande –**PI50)** Av.Miguel F. Cerro s/n, AA HH, San Jose, 20046 Vice **W:** agrorural.gob.pe/radio-ayabaca-de-piura.html – **PI51)** Jr 9 de Octubre 110, 20571 Huarmaca **W:** agrorural.gob.pe/radio-huancabamba-de-piura.html – **PI52)** Jr 9 de Octubre 110, 20571 Huarmaca **W:** radiohuarmaca.com **E:** radiohuarmaca@hotmail.com – **FM:** 98.1 MHz – **PI53)** Bolivar 114, 20441 Ayabaca – **PI54)** Km. 248 Panamericana Carretera a Chulucanas, 20011 Castilla **W:** visionaradioperu.com – **PI55)** Ca Piura 508, 20611 Frias ☎73 631459 **W:** Facebook: R.Frias – **FM:** 96.5 MHz– **PI56)** Barrio Santa Rosa s/n, 20441 Ayabaca – **PI57)** Jr Morro Solar, Block F, 20001 Piura **W:** corporacionrbc.org – **PI58)** Jr Pisagua 812, 20601 Chulucanas ☎73 378627 – **PI59)** Esq. Calle Jorge Chavez y 9 de Octubre, 20571 Huarmaca **W:** rvclagrande1160am.es.tl – **PI60)** MZ. H. LT 14 – Urb. San Eduardo, 20001 Piura – **PI61)** Av Circunvalacion Lopez Albujar MZ. B.LT. 8, 20001 Piura – **PI62)** Predio de Mercedec Vite Quezada s/n, San Miguel – Valle Medio, 20001 Piura **W:** bethelradio.fm – **PI63)** Cl. Piura 311, 20611 Frias 944360440 **W:** radiofrecuenciaideal.com **E:** contacto@radiofrecuenciaideal.com – **PI64)** Calle Tacna No 235 – Edif. El Sol – 3er Piso, 20001 Piura – **PI65)** Parcela T15.8 – 42 Sector 7, 20701 Tambo Grande – **PI66)** Calle Alfonso Ugarte 118, 20046 Vice – **PI67)** Av Progreso 101, Castilla ☎73 340301 **W:** laclave.com.pe **E:** laclave100mail.com - **FM:** 104.5 MHz – **PI68)** Ca Bolognesi s/n, 20441 Ayabacha – **PI69)** Tambopata

PU00 (PUNO):
PU01) Jr Conde Lemos 212, 21001 Puno ☎51 351562 **W:** radioondaazul.com **E:** ondazul@radioondaazul.com - Quechua & Aymara: 6h daily - **FM:** 95.7MHz "Stereo Azul" – **PU02)** Jr Arequipa 385, 21001 Puno – **PU03)** Jr Miraflores MZ E-1, Lt-4 – Barrio Jorge Chavez, 21111 Macusani ☎51 51837009 **E:** rvamacusani@terra.com.pe - **FM:** 90.5MHz – **PU04)** Jr Jauregui 966, 21621 Juliaca ☎51 800601 **W:** nuevotiempo.pe **E:** nuevotiempojuliaca@hotmail.com – **PU05)** Ca San Román 116, 21621 Juliaca ☎51 325357 – **PU06)** Simon Bolivar 442, 21001 Puno – **PU07)** "Lugar Denominado ""Barco Chuco""",21061 Chucuito **Aymara & Quechua**: 0900-1400, 1900-0100 – **PU08)** Jr.Huanynacapac T4,Centro Comerical No2, 21621 Juliaca☎51 322313 - **FM:** 107.9MHz – **PU09)** Jr. San Isidro MZ. S, Lote 14.-B, Urb. Señor de Huanca, 21621 Juliaca ☎51 502319 – **PU11)** Jr 2 de Mayo 418 – 4to nivel, 21621 Juliaca **W.** 24horasradionoticias.com **E:** radionoticias24horasamotmail.com – **PU12)** Jr Moquegua 180, 21001 Puno ☎51 351502 **W:** Facebook – Radio La Voz Del Altiplano – **PU13)** Ca Mariano Pandía 166, 2° piso, 21621 Juliaca – **PU14)** Jr.Leonicio Prado, 21001 Puno –**PU15)** Jr Unión 242, 21621 Juliaca **E:** radioltcj@latinmail.com ☎51 322452 ☎51 369450 – **PU16)** Jr Apurimac 638-644, 21621 Juliaca ☎51 325733 - **FM:** 88.9Mhz – **PU17)** Jr Antonio (Sierra) 178, prolongación Ramón Castilla, a dos cuadras del Cuartel Bolognesi, 21621 Juliaca ☎51 793059 **W:** http://radiolasurenajuliaca.blogspot.com – **PU18)** Jr Piura 167, 21001 Puno ☎51 9731663 - **Aymara & Quechua**: 0900-1100 – **PU19)** Jr. Carabaya 998, Juliaca **W:** http://andino.pe/~rtv/ **E:** info@radiotvcontinental.com – **PU20)** Jr Lima s/n, 21666 Caminaca **E:** trebol34@mixmail.com – **PU21)** Ramon Castilla 949, 21621 Juliaca ☎51 321372 **W:** radiojuliaca.com.pe **E:** webmaster@radiojuliaca.com - **FM:** 90.9MHz – **PU22)** Jr Apurimac 644 Cercado, 21621 Juliaca ☎51 641342 **W:** radiotvperu.pe **E:** radiotvperu@hotmail.com - **FM:** 106.7 MHz – **PU23)** Jr 2 de Mayo 790, 21621 Juliaca – **PU24)** Jr Ricardo Palma 111, 21621 Juliaca ☎51 327208 – **PU26)** Urb. Municipal Taparache – w.Amazonas MZ.E-4, Lote 21 y 22, 21621 Juliaca – **PU27)** Jr Chachani 220, Barrioa San Martin de Porr, 21621 Juliaca – ☎51 324846 **E:** radioredandina@hotmail.com – **PU28)** Jr 2 de Mayo 209, Oficina 406, 21621 Juliaca

☎51 321115 **W:** radiosoldelosandes.com - **FM:** 104.5MHz "El Sol de los Andes FM" – **PU32)** Jr 2 de Mayo , 21621 Juliaca **E:** carraviz@gmail.com or carraviz@hotmail.com - Listeners correspondence to: Iván Tito Vizcarra – **PU33)** Azangaro **W:** radioasillo.com – **PU35)** Jr Acora 222, 21001 Puno ☎51 366222 **W:** pachamamaradio.org **E:** info@pachamamaradio.org **PU42)** Túpac Amaru Altura Coliseo Juli s/n, 21401 Juli ☎51 554173 **W:** agrorural.gob.pe/radio-juli-de-puno **E:** radiocampesinajuli@hotmail.com – **PU44)** 21701 Ayaviri **W:** agrorural.gob.pe/radio-ayaviri-de-puno.html– **PU45)** Jr Jose Galvez 542, Urb Bellavista, 21001 Puno ☎51 323546 **W.** 24horasradionoticias.com **E:** radionoticias24horasamotmail.com – **PU46)** Jatun Pampa Chejollani Cupi-Esquen, 21621 Juliaca – **PU47)** Ca s/n – Sector Taparachi Zona Industrial, Urb. La Rinconada 3ra E-17, 21621 Juliaca – **PU48)** Zona Fortaleza Pucara, Sector Chuñawi, 21401 Juli – **PU49)** Jr Ayacucho 679, 21601 Caracoto **E:** radioaltura@hotmail.com – **PU50)** Jatun Pampa Chejollani Cupi-Esquen, 21621 Juliaca – **PU51)** Jr Arequipa 403, 21051 Capachica – **PU52)** Jr. Alfonso Ugarte N° 608 Macusani, Carabaya, 21 111 Macusani ☎950 300420 **W:** radioaltura.com **E:** gerencia@radioaltura.com - **FM:** 100.1MHz – **PU53)** Pasaje Echenique 110, Cercado, 21 111 Macusani – **PU54)** Acora **W:** Facebook: R. Inca-Acora – **PU55)** Jr Lima 317, Puno **W:** Facebook: R.Universidad Puno - **FM:** 92.9 MHz – **PU56)** Jr 2 de Mayo s/n, Lampa ☎950 984 787 **W:** activeweb.es/radioandinalampa – **PU57)** Jr Pedro de Candida s/n, Sandia – **PU58)** Puno **W:** Facebook: R.Publica **E:** radiopublica.580@gmail.com – **PU59)** Azángaro – **PU60)** Cl Sandia s/n, Cuyocuyo, Sandia

SM00 (SAN MARTIN):
SM01) Jr San Martín 257, 22411 Tocache ☎42 551031 – **FM:** 100.1 MHz – **SM03)** Av Compagñión 410, 22221 Tarapoto – **SM07)** Jr Imperio 764, 22056 Nueva Cajamarca– **FM:** 100.3 MHz – **SM08)** Jr Bolognesi 180 Altos, 22221 Tarapoto **W:** radioluz.com – **SM14)** Jr Loreto 300, 22251 Chazuta **W:** ethnicradio.org **E:** agiazo@hotmail.com – **SM15)** Jr Callao 650 (Apt. 133), 22001 Moyobamba ☎42 562353 **W:** facebook.com/canalcatolicosangabriel **E:** canalcatolico@gmail.com – **SM16)** Av Celedin s/n, 22066 San Fernando – **SM17)** Av Alfonso Ugarte Cdra 18, Los Olivos, 22221 Tarapoto – **SM18)** Jr Libertad 157, Moyobamba – **SM19)** Jr Las Dalias s/n Mz 17, Lt E, Bellavista

TC00 (TACNA)
TC02) Prolong Unanue 1041 (Cas 113), 23001 Tacna - **FM:** 99.9MHz – **TC04)** Jr Sir Jones s/n (Cas 281), 23001 Tacna – **TC05)** Arias y Araguez 584, 23001 Tacna – **TC06)** Cl Tarata 665, Urb San José - Bacigalup, 23001 Tacna **W:** radioluz.com – **TC08)** Av Internacional 484, Alto de la Alianza, 23001 Tacna ☎52 804100 – **FM:** 106.7 MHz – **TC09)** Av.Dos de Mayo 2-A 23001 Tacna ☎52 414871 **W:** radiotacna.com.pe **E:** gerencia@radiotacna.com.pe – **FM:** 104.3 & 104.7MHz – **TC10)** Av San Martín de Porras 209, Natividad, 23001 Tacna **E:** radiobulevar@hotmail.com ☎5284 8537 – **TC11)** Jose Olaya s/n 2° piso, 23341 Tarata – **TC13)** 23341 Tarata **W:** agrorural.gob.pe/escuchar-radios-campesinas.html – **TC14)** Villa Universitaria Capannique A 20, 23031 Pocoally **W:** radiobacan.com – **TC16)** Ca 2 de Mayo 263, 23001 Tacna ☎52 428184 **W:** radiouno.pe **E:** prensa@radiouno.pe – **FM:** 93.7 MHz – **TC17)** Ca Progreso 43 – Vigila, 23001 Tacna – **TC18)** Barrio Azul S-27, 23121 Toquepala **W:** Facebook. Radio Candarave – **TC19)** Sector Buganvillas – A 200m. Cruze de Tarapaca con Buganvillas, Distr. de Pocollay, Dept. de Tacna – **TC19)** Villa Universitaria Capanique A-20, Pocollay – **TC20)** Calle Gil de Herrera 186, Tacna – **TC21)** Av El Sol 427, Tacna – **TC22)** Sector Cerro Blanco, Calano – **TC23)** Calle Gil de Herrera 186, Pocoally – **TC24)** Pampa de Layagache – Alt. Km 25 Carretera a Tarata, Alto de la Alianza – **TC26)** Prolongación Hermanos Reynosa s/n, Pocollay

TB00 (TUMBES):
TB01) Pza Alipio Rosales s/n, 24001 Tumbes - **FM:** 99.7MHz – **TB02)** Ca Tarapaca 163, 24001 Tumbes – **TB04)** Panamericana Norte Km 1321, 24001 Tumbes **W:** rpp.com.pe – **FM:** 100.5MHz – **TB05)** Av.Mayor Novoa 814 2° piso, 24001 Tumbes ☎72 527002 – **TB06)** Jr Bolívar 117, 24001 Tumbes ☎72 523003 – **TB07)** Jr Piura 1010, 24001 Tumbes – **TB08)** Av.Mariscal Castilla 432, 24001 Tumbes **W:** radiocielo - **pe** – **TB09)** Paseo Concordia y Bolognesi 2° piso, 24001 Tumbes

UC00 (UCAYALI):
UC03) Av 9 de Diciembre 646, Pucallpa – **UC04)** Jr Coronel Portillo 448-A, Pucallpa ☎61 573876 **W:** radiousa.com **E:** radiosuper103.3@gmail.com - **FM :** 103.3MHz – **UC05)** Zona San Fernando, Callería – **UC06)** Ca Padre Francisco Alvares s/n, Sephua - **FM:** 100.5MHz – **UC07)** Ca Iquitos 499, Villa Atalaya, Distrito de Raymondi, Prov de Atalaya ☎64 461240 **E:** rasat@terra.com.pe - **FM:** 95.5MHz – **UC09)** Carretera Federico Basadre Km 37, Los Pinos, Campoverde – **UC10)** Av Tupac Amaru 957, Calleria **W:** radiocielo.pe

FM in Lima (MHz): 88.3 R.Magica,San Isidro – **LM17)** 88.9 R.Felicidad – 89.7 Emisoras Peruánnos (RPP), San Isidro – 90.1 Cieneguilla – 90.1 R:Bethel, Ate-Amauta – 90.1 R.Silde, Lurigancho – 90.5 R.La Zona, Lurigancho – 91.1 R.San Borja – 91.5 R.Planicie – 91.5 R.del Sur,

Lurin — 91.5 R.Chalaca, Cieneguilla — 91.5 R.Andina, Ate-Huayacan - 91.9 Okey Radio, San Isidro — 92.5 R.Studio 92, San Isidro — 93.1 R.Ritmo Romantico, Chorrillos — **LM07)** 93.7 La Inolvidable — 94.3 R.Bravaza, San Isidro — 94.9 R.La Karibeña, Chorillos — 94.9 R.A, Corillos — 95.5 R.La Exitosa, Chorillos — 96.1 Z Rock & Pop, Chorillos — **LM45)** 96.7 R.Capital — 97.3 R.Moda, Chorillos — 97.7 R.Kandela, Ate — 97.7 R.Canto Grande, San Juan de Lurigancho — LM03) 97.7 R.Maria — 97.7 R.Sencación, Chaclayo — 97.7 R.Vitarte, Cieneguilla — **LM56)** 98.1 R.1160 — 98.7 R.Magica, Punta Hermosa — 98.7 R.Karibeña, San Luis — 99.1 R.Doble Nueve, Jesus Maria — 99.5 Ate-Huaycan — 99.5 Comas — 99.5 Cieneguilla — 99.5 Chaclacayo — 99.5 **LM43)** R.Imperial 2 — **LM22)** 100.1 R.Exito — 100.1 R.Oasis, San Isidro — 100.5 R.Enmanuel, Ate — 100.7 R.Satelite, Ventanilla — 100.7 R.La Familia, Carabayllo — **LM19)**101.1 R.Panamericana — **LM54)** 101.7 R.Cielo — **LM33)** 101.7 R.Comas — **LM54)** 101.7 R.Cielo — 101.7 R.Stereo Villa, Villa El Salvador — 101.7 Chaclavayo — 101.7 San Juan — **LM33)** 102.1 R.Oxigeno, San Isidro **LM51)** R.Nacional, Barranco — 103.3 R.Unión, Miraflores — **LM15)**103.9 R.Nacional, Lima —104.7 Viva FM, San isidro — **LM47)**105.1 R.Santa Rosa, Carabayllo — 105.5 R.Fiesta, Lince — **LM11)**106.3 R. Mar Plus, Chorillos — **LM58)** 107.1 R.Nueva Q, Chorillos — 107.7 R. Planeta, Chorillos

PHILIPPINES

L.T: UTC +8h — **Pop:** 101.8 million — **Pr.L:** Pilipino (Tagalog), English, Cebuano, Ilocano, Hiligaynon, Bicol — **E.C:** 60Hz, 220V — **ITU:** PHL

NATIONAL TELECOMMUNICATIONS COMMISSION (NTC) (Dept. of Transportation and Communications)
NTC Bldg., BIR Road, East Triangle, Diliman, Quezon City 1104 ☎ +63 2 9254651 or 9267722 **W:** ntc.gov.ph
L.P: Commissioner: Gamaliel A. Cordoba. Dep. Commissioners: Delilah F. Deles, Carlo Jose A. Martinez. Chief Broadcast Sces Div: Alvin Bernard N. Blanco

KAPISANAN NG MGA BRODKASTER NG PILIPINAS (KBP) (Assoc. of Broadcasters of the Philippines)
6th Flr, LTA Bldg, 118 Perea Str, Legaspi Village, Makati C, 1226 NCR ☎ +63 2 8151990/1/2 ≣ +63 2 8151993 **W:** kbp.org.ph
L.P: Chmn: Herman Z. Basbaño. Pres: Ruperto S. Nicdao, Jr. Most stns are KBP members

CATHOLIC MEDIA NETWORK (CMN)
Unit 201 Sunrise Condominium, 226 Ortigas Ave, North Greenhills, San Juan, Manila 1503 NCR ☎ +63 2 7249850 ≣ +63 2 7249962 **W:** catholicmedianetwork.org **L.P:** Pres: Fr. Francis B. Lucas. Chmn: Bishop Bernardino Cortez. (28 owned and affiliated stns on MW, 20 on FM)

PHILIPPINE BROADCASTING SERVICE (PBS, "Radyo ng Bayan") (Gov.)
4/F Media Center Bldg., Visayas Ave., Del Monte, Quezon C, 1105 NCR ☎ +63 2 9203968 **W:** pbs.gov.ph **L.P:** Dir. Gen: John S. Manalili. Dep. Dir. Gen: Monina S. Cespedes
Manila stns: DZRB Radyo Balita (news sce) 738 kHz, DZSR Sports Radio 918 kHz, DZRM Radyo Magasin 1278 kHz, DWBR-FM Business Radio 104.3MHz
Regional MW stns: DWBT, San Antonio, Basco, 3900 Batanes. **DWFB**, Mariano Marcos State University Campus, Laoag C, 2900 Ilocos Norte. **DWFR**, Multipurpose Bldg, Provincial Capitol Compound, Bontoc, 2616 Mountain Province. **DWLC**, Perez Park, Lucena C, 4301 Quezon Province. **DWPE**, CSU Campus, Caritan Highway, Tuguegarao, 3500 Cagayan. **DWRB**, City Civic Center, Taal Ave, Naga C, 4400 Camarines Sur. **DWRM**, City Hall Compound, Puerto Princesa C, 5300 Palawan. **DWRS**, Poblacion, Tayug, 2445 Pangasinan. **DXBN**, City Hall Compound, Brgy. Doongan, Butuan C, 8600 Agusan del Norte. **DXIM**, A. Velez Str, Cagayan de Oro C, 9000 Misamis Oriental. DXJS, Capitol Hills, Tandag, 8300 Surigao del Sur. DXJT, Brgy Maloro,Tangub C, 7214 Misamis Occidental. **DXMR**, Baliwasan Chico, Zamboanga C, 7000 Zamboanga del Sur. **DXPT**, Tubig Boh, Bongao, 7500 Tawi-Tawi. **DXRG**, Dugenio Str, Gingoog C, 9014 Misamis Oriental. **DXRP**, Door 5, PTA Complex, Magsaysay Park, 2nd District, Agdao, 8000 Davao C. **DXSM**, Camp Asturias, Jolo, 7400 Sulu. **DXSO**, Satellite Office, MSU Campus, Marawi C, 9700 Lanao del Sur. **DYES**, Capitol Compd, Borongan, 6800 Eastern Samar. **DYLL**, PNRC Youth Center Bldg, Bonifacio Drive, Iloilo C, 5000 Iloilo. **DYMP**, Govt Center, Candahug, Palo, Leyte. **DYMR**, CSCST Compound, Vicente Sotto, 6000 Cebu C. **DYOG**, Butel Building, Calbayog C, 6710 W. Samar. **DYSL**, Southern Leyte State University Compound, Sogod, 6606 Southern Leyte. **DZAG**, Don Mariano Marcos Memorial State University, Agoo, 2504 La Union. **DZEQ**, Polo Field, Pacdal Circle, Baguio C, 2600 Benguet. **DZER**, Boac, 4900 Marinduque. **DZMQ**, Tondaligan Beach, Dagupan

C, 2400 Pangasinan. **DZRK**, Capitol Compound, Tabuk, 3800 Kalinga. **DZVC** Virac, State College Campus, 4800 Catanduanes
See **PB)** entries in the MW frequency list below for frequencies and powers. Regional stns usually relay news from Manila on the h., and also carry networked prgrs at times.
NB: A number of stns are operating irr or are inactive.
Callsigns: _____-AM

MW	Call	kHz	kW	Net		MW	Call	kHz	kW	Net
67)	DXGH	531	5	dz		41)	DWWW	774	25	
118)	DYDW	‡531	10	cm		PB)	DXSM	774	10	
47)	DZBR	531	5			PB)	DXSO	774	10	
83)	DYRB	540	1			84)	DYRI	774	10	ag
54)	DZWT	540	10	cm		94)	DXRA	783	10	
PB)	DWRB	549	10			51)	DYME	783	5	
16)	DXHM	549	5	cm		75)	DZNL	783	5	ak
84)	DZXL	558	40			95)	DWES	792	5	
67)	DXCH	567	5	dz		38)	DWGV	792	5	
73)	DXMF	576	10	bo		PB)	DXBN	792	10	
PB)	DYMR	576	10			73)	DXPD	792	5	bo
PB)	DZMQ	576	5			66)	DYRR	792	5	
17)	DZHR	576	5	dz		58)	DXBL	801	1	ss
16)	DXCP	585	5	cm		22)	DXES	801	5	bo
PB)	DYLL	585	1	su		16)	DYKA	801	5	cm
16)	DXDB	594	5	cm		35)	DYWC	801	5	cm
60)	DYWR	‡594	10	bo		60)	DZNC	801	10	bo
36)	DZBB	594	20	su		PB)	DXRG	810	1	
10)	DZLL	603	10			90)	DZRJ	810	10	
84)	DXPR	603	5			58)	DWAR	819	5	ss
22)	DZVV	603	5	bo		114)	DWMG	819	1	
75)	DWSP	612	5	dz		101)	DXSC	‡819	1	
84)	DYHP	612	10			53)	DXUM	819	10	
84)	DXDC	621	10			50)	DYVL	819	10	ak
PB)	DZVC	621	1			39)	DWZR	828	5	
85)	DZTG	621	5			84)	DXCC	828	10	ag
2)	DZMM	630	35			135)	DZTC	828	1	
22)	DYWB	630	10/5	bo		PB)	DXJS	837	10	
84)	DXKR	639	5			58)	DXRE	837	5	ss
85)	DZRL	639	1			22)	DYFM	837	10	bo
67)	DWRH	648	10	dz		30)	DZXE	‡837	5	
PB)	DWRM	648	10			87)	DZRV	846	50	cm
84)	DXMB	648	3			67)	DXGO	855	5	ak
50)	DYRC	648	5	ak		42)	DXWG	‡855	1	
77)	DWRN	657	5			17)	DXZH	855	5	dz
130)	DXDD	657	5	cm		33)	DZGE	855	10	
PB)	DYES	657	1			58)	DWSI	864	5	ss
84)	DYVR	657	5			97)	DYHH	864	10	
98)	DZLU	657	1			140)	DZIP	864	10	
PB)	DXRP	666	10			58)	DZSP	864	5	ss
50)	DZRH	666	35			134)	DZMM	864	5	cm
103)	DXGD	675	1	cm		58)	DXRB	873	5	ss
85)	DYKC	675	5			58)	DXRT	‡873	5	
43)	DWJJ	684	5			127)	DYUP	873	5	
50)	DYEZ	684	10	ak		1)	DZPA	873	5	cm
33)	DZCV	684	5			33)	DZRC	873	5	
84)	DXBC	693	10	ag		3)	DWIZ	882	50	
85)	DXDX	693	1			62)	DXMS	882	10	cm
50)	DYKX	693	1	dz		PB)	DYOG	882	10	
50)	DYPH	693	10	dz		73)	DZGR	891	5	
106)	DZTP	693	10/5			63)	DWNE	900	5	
31)	DZAS	702	50			84)	DXRZ	900	5	ag
84)	DXIC	711	5	ag		22)	DYOW	900	5	bo
58)	DXRD	711	5	ss		115)	DYLA	909	5	
29)	DYBR	‡711	5			91)	DYSP	909	5	su
60)	DZVR	711	5	bo		16)	DZEA	909	5	cm
58)	DZYI	711	5			84)	DXRS	918	5	ag
50)	DYOK	720	1	ak		PB)	DZSR	918	50	
7)	DZJO	720	5			122)	DWRS	927	5	
60)	DZSO	720	5	bo		64)	DXDA	927	5	
PB)	DWPE	729	10			84)	DXMD	927	5	ag
60)	DXIF	729	10	bo		103)	DXMM	927	5	cm
84)	DXMY	729	5			73)	DZLG	927	5	bo
70)	DXOR	729	5			40)	DWIM	936	5	
72)	DZGB	729	5			111)	DXDN	936	5	uk
PB)	DZRB	738	60			PB)	DXIM	936	10	
62)	DXND	747	5	cm		84)	DYCC	936	1	
84)	DYHB	747	5			85)	DYKW	936	1	
50)	DZJC	747	10	ak		82)	DZXT	936	1	
PB)	DWRS	756	10			116)	DXDV	945	10	
9)	DWHL	756	1			58)	DXRO	945	5	
121)	DXBZ	756	10			4)	DWRO	‡945	5	
82)	DXJM	756	2			PB)	DWFB	954	10	
83)	DXGS	765	5			PB)	DXJT	954	1	
68)	DYAP	765	10			110)	DYMM	‡954	5	
58)	DYAR	765	5	ss		20)	DZEM	954	40	
58)	DZYT	765	5	ss		58)	DXYZ	963	5	ss

MW Call	kHz	kW	Net
73) DYMF	963	10	bo
136) DZNS	963	5	cm
PB) DWFR	972	5	
45) DWTI	972	5	
17) DXKH	972	5	dz
17) DYSM	972	1	ak
75) DWMT	981	5	dz
22) DXBR	981	10	bo
84) DXOR	981	5	ag
88) DXOW	981	10	
42) DYBQ	981	10	
58) DZRD	981	5	ss
107) DZIQ	990	10	
91) DXBM	990	5	su
67) DYTH	990	5	dz
67) DXMT	990	5	dz
45) DWMI	999	5	
84) DXHP	999	1	
PB) DXPT	999	1	
91) DYSS	999	5	su
PB) DZEQ	999	5	
16) DWBS	1008	5	cm
102) DWGO	1008	5	
85) DXXX	±1008	10	
42) DWDC	1017	5	
PB) DWLC	1017	5	
44) DXRR	1017	10	
138) DXSN	1017	5	cm
73) DXMC	1026	5	bo
58) DZAR	1026	10	ss
139) DXUZ	1035	5/1	
88) DYRL	1035	10	
22) DZWX	1035	5	bo
88) DXCO	1044	5	
81) DXLL	1044	5	uk
17) DYMS	±1044	5	ak
60) DZNG	±1044	10	bo
85) DXKD	1053	5	
112) DYSA	1053	10	cm
31) DXKI	1062	5	
46) DYEC	1062	10/5	
28) DZEC	1062	40	
85) DXKT	1071	5	
110) DYXT	1071	1	
123) DZSL	1071	1	
28) DWIN	1080	5	
83) DWRL	1080	5	
85) DXKS	1080	1	
67) DYBH	1080	5	dz
111) DXCM	1089	10	uk
39) DYHR	‡1089	1	
23) DWAD	1098	10	
58) DXCL	1098	5	ss
61) DWDY	1107	10	
141) DXBB	1107	5	
129) DYIN	1107	5	bo
8) DZOM	1107	1	
13) DYAG	1116	5	
31) DXAS	1116	5	
104) DYTR	1116	10	
113) DZLB	1116	5	
69) DXGL	1125	10	
91) DXGM	1125	5	su
22) DZWN	1125	10	bo
26) DWOM	1134	5	
95) DWJS	1134	5	
111) DXWN	1134	5	uk
79) DXOS	1134	10	
77) DYRM	±1134	1	
PB) DWBT	1134	1	
137) DYAF	1143	10	cm
31) DZOM	1143	10	
51) DYCM	1152	10	
75) DWCM	1161	10	
111) DXDS	1161	1	uk
84) DYKR	1161	5	ag
11) DYRD	1161	5	cm
72) DZMD	1161	5	
PB) DXMR	1170	10	
PB) DYSL	1170	10	
65) DZCA	±1170	10	
142) DWET	1179	10	
91) DXYK	1179	5	su
60) DYCX	1179	5	
36) DYSB	1179	5	su

MW Call	kHz	kW	Net
86) DZRS	1179	1	
22) DXLX	1188	5	bo
2) DYRV	‡1188	1	
82) DZLT	1188	5	
114) DXZO	1188	5	
98) DWBA	1197	5	
31) DXFE	1197	5	
4) DYRH	‡1197	5	
6) DWAN	‡1206	10	
118) DYRF	1215	10	cm
50) DWSR	1224	5	dz
28) DXED	1224	10	
PB) DZAG	1224	5	
87) DWRV	1233	5	cm
31) DYVS	1233	5	
32) DWBL	1242	20	
105) DXSY	1242	5	
27) DXZB	1242	5	
42) DYRG	1251	1	
72) DZMS	1251	2.5	
49) DWMC	1260	5	
97) DXRF	1260	5	dz
97) DYDD	1260	10	
28) DZEL	1260	5	
91) DWRC	1269	10	
PB) DZRM	1278	10	
50) DZZH	1287	5	dz
133) DWPR	1296	10	
2) DXAB	1296	10	
42) DYJJ	1296	5	
25) DWXI	1314	10	
57)DXAD	±1322	5	
19)DXHR	±1323	1	
36) DYSI	1323	10	su
52) DZRK	1323	10	
58) DWAY	1332	5	ss
85) DZKI	1332	1	
91) DXRL	‡1341	5	su
48) DWUN	1350	10	
PB) DZER	1350	5	
129) DYSJ	1359	1	
77) DZYR	1359	5	
58) DWTT	‡1368	5	
85) DXKO	1368	10	
85) DZBS	1368	2.5	
15) DZRA	1368	1	
85) DXKP	1377	10	
55) DXCR	1386	5	
85) DYVW	1386	5	cm
17) DYCH	1395	10	dz
132) DZVT	1395	5	cm
85) DXAQ	1404	-	ss
85) DYKB	1404	5	
91) DWRA	1413	5	su
33) DYXW	1413	5	
18) DXMU	1422	5	
11) DYZD	‡1422	5	
89) DYRS	‡1431	5	
50) DWDH	1440	10	dz
100) DXSI	1440	0.01	
52) DXSA	1449	5	
97) DYZZ	1458	10	
120) DZJV	1458	10	
87) DWVR	1467	1	cm
131) DXVP	1467	5	cm
92) DWRB	1476	1	
90) DXRJ	1476	10	
88) DZYA	1476	1	
67) DYDH	1485	5	dz
108) DWSS	1494	10	
83) DXOC	1494	5	
2) DYAB	1512	10	
125) DZAT	1512	10	
14) DZME	1530	25	
77) DZYM	1539	5	
36) DZSD	1548	10	su
16) DYDM	1548	5	cm
32) DXID	1566	10	
PB) DYMP	‡1566	7.8	
24) DWBR	1584	1	
124) DXSK	1593	10	
113) DZUP	1602	10	
37) DWGI	1638	0.6	
56) DZBF	1674	1	

‡ = r. inactive, ± = variable

SW Call	Location	kHz	kW	H of tr
PB)		6170±		2300-1300†
PB) DUR2	Marulas, Valenzuela	9580±	0.25	†

Alt. freq for 9580: 9620kHz (r. on 9619±). Operated by PBS, Philippine Broadc. Sce, these freqs. relay various PBS AM and FM sces. 6170kHz generally relays DZRM 1278kHz

GENERAL NOTES:

Station identifications: Generally, stn IDs are given on the h and half h The English alphabet is used for the call letters, while the freq. is usually expressed in Spanish- or English-language numerals. Extensive stn details are included in sign on and sign off Anns

Callsign assignments: DU = Shortwave only; DW = Luzon; DX = Mindanao and Sulu; DY = Visayas and Palawan; DZ = Luzon

Administrative divisions: Level 1: regions, 2: provinces, cities (C.), 3: municipalities, 4: barangays (brgy.). The National Capital Region (NCR) is also known as Metropolitan Manila or Metro-Manila.

NB: Cities may be referred to with or without "City", e.g. Baguio City or Baguio. Quezon City is always referred to by its full name.

Prgr. networks: ag=R. Agong, ak=Aksyon R. bo=Bombo R., cm=Catholic Media Network (CMN, see above and entry 16) below), dz=Radyo Ukay (key: 666kHz), ss=Sonshine R. (key: 1026kHz), su=Super R., uk=Radyo Ukay

Web addresses for broadcast networks: FEBC. **W:** febc.org – Bombo R. **W:** bomboradyo.com – R. Mindanao Netw **W:** rmn.ph – Manila Broadc. Co **W:** manilabroadcasting.com – Sonshine R. **W:** sonshineradio.com – DZRH: dzrh.com.ph

FM: A large number of FM stns are operating throughout the country. **Callsigns:** _____-FM

Manila FM(MHz): – 88.3 DWCT-FM "Jam 88.3" (Raven Broadc. Corp.) – 89.1 DWAV "Wave 89.1" (Blockbuster Broadc. System) – 89.9 DWTM "Magic 89.9" (Quest Broadc. Inc.) – 50) 90.7 DZMB "Love R." – 91.5 DWKY "Big R." (Mabuhay Broadc. System Inc.) – 92.3 DWFM "Radyo5 92.3 News FM" (Nation Broadc. Corp.) – 93.1 DWRX "Monster R." (Audiovisual Communicators Inc.) – 84) 93.9 DWKC "iFM" – 32) 94.7 DWLL "Mellow 947" – 28) 95.5 DWDM "Pinas FM" – 17) 96.3 DWRK "Easy Rock" – 36) 97.1 DWLS "Barangay LS" – 3) 97.9 DWQZ "97dot9 Home R." – 31) 98.7 DZFE "The Master's Touch" – 99.5 DWRT "Play FM" (Real R. Network Inc.) – 90) 100.3 DZRJ "RJ 100" – 67) 101.1 DWYS "Yes! FM" – 2) 101.9 DWRR "MOR 101.9 For Life!" – 73) 102.7 DWSM "Star FM" – 103.5 DWKX "K-Lite" (Advanced Media Broadc. Syst.) – PB) 104.3 DWBR "Business R." – 105.1 DWBM "Crossover" (Mareco Broadc. Network) – 105.9 DWLA "R. High 105.9" (All Youth Channels) – 106.7 DWET "Energy FM" (Ultrasonic Broadc. Syst. Inc.) – 141) 107.5 DWNU "Win R."

Cebu City FM (MHz): – 88.3 DWCT-FM "Mom's R." (Southern Broadc. Network) –16) 89.1 DYDW "Power 89" – 89.9 DYKI "Smooth FM" (Primaxx Broadc. Network) – 90.7 DYAC "Crossover" (Mareco Broadc. Network) – 91.5 DYHR "Yes! FM" – 92.3 DYBN "Magic 92.3" (Quest Broadc., Inc.) – 115) 93.1 DYWF "Brigada News FM"– 84) 93.9 DYXL "iFM"– 94.7 DYLL "Energy FM" (Ultrasonic Broadc. System) – 22) 95.5 DYMX "Star FM" – 96.3 DYRK "W- Rock" (Exodus Broadc. Co.) – 2) 97.1 DYLS "MOR" – 50) 97.9 DYBU "Love R." – 31) 98.7 DYFR "FR FM" – 91) 99.5 DYRT "Barangay RT" – 90) 100.3 DYRJ "RJ 100" – 101.1 DYIO "Y 101" (GVM Radio/TV Corp.) – 101.9 DYNC "Radyo5 News FM" (Nation Broadc. Corp.) – 17) 102.7 DYTC "Easy Rock" – 103.5 DYCD "Wild FM" (Ditan Communications/Univ. of Mindanao Broadc. Network) – 105.1 DYUR "UR FM" (Ultimate Entertainment) – 105.9 DYBT "Monster R." (Capricorn Production & Management Corp.) – 3) 106.7 DYQC "Home R." – 107.5 DYNU "Win R." (Progressive Broadc. Corp.)

Davao City FM (MHz): – 88.3 DXDR "Energy FM" (Ultrasonic Broadc. System) – 89.1 DXBE "Magic 89.1" (Quest Broadc. Inc) – 16) 89.9 DXGN – 50) 90.7 DXBM "Love R." – 82) 91.5 DXKX "Real FM" – 111) 92.3 DXWT "Wild 92.3" – 93.1 DXAC "Crossover" (Mareco Broadc. Network) – 84) 93.9 DXXL "Mellow" – 32) 94.7 DXLL "Mellow 94.7" – 107) 95.5 DXKR "Hit R." – 22) 96.3 DXFX "Star FM" – 97.1 DXUR "Mango R. UR 97.1" (Ultimate Entertainment Inc.) – 97.9 DXSS "Mom's R."(Southern Broadc. Network) – 3) 98.7 DXQM "Home R." – 99.5 DXBT "Monster R." (Ausiovisual Communicators Inc. – 90) 100.3 DXDJ "RJ 100" – 2) 101.1 DXRR "MOR" – 101.9 DXFM "Radyo5 News FM" (Nation Broadc. Corp.) – 102.7 DXDM (Multipoint Broadc. Network) – 91) 103.5 DXRV"Barangay 103.5" – 104.3 DXMA "The Edge" (United Christian Broadcasters) – 17) 105.1 DXYS "Easy Rock" – 105.9 DXMX "Mix FM" (Omarco Broadc. Corp.) – 106.7 DXET "Dream FM"(ABC Development Corp.) – 107.5 DXNU "Win R." (Progressive Broadc. Corp.)

Addresses
For each entry the organisation or company name is followed by the

call letters (in alphabetical order) and addresses of the stns licensed to the organisation. When contacting a stn, use Radio Station + the call letters as stn name. In some cases the stn may be operated by a different organisation than the licensee mentioned below.

PB) See separate listing for Philippine Broadc. Sce. Above. – **1)** Abra Community Btcg. Corp. DZPA R. Totoo, Blessed Arnold Janssen Communication Center, Zamora Str corner Rizal Str, Bangued, 2800 Abra – **2)** ABS-CBN Broadc. Corp (R. Patrol). DXAB, KM-4, Shrine Hills, Matina, 8000 Davao C. DYAB, ABS-CBN Broadc. Center, Jagobiao, Mandaue C, 6014 Cebu. DYRV, Catbalogan, 6700 Samar. DZMM, 15/F, Philcomcen Bldg, Ortigas Ave, Pasig C, NCR – **3)** Aliw Broadc. Corp. DWIZ, 5th Floor, Dominga Bldg, 2113 Pasong Tamo, Makati C, 1231 NCR – **4)** Allied Broadc. Center, Inc. DYRH, JTL Bldg, North Drive, Bacolod C, 6100 Negros Occidental. DYRO. Roxas C., Capiz – **5)** Association of Islamic Dev't. Cooperative. DXID, Banale Dist, Pagadian C, 7016 Zamboanga del Sur – **6)** Metropolitan Manila Development Authority (MMDA). DWAN MMDA Traffic Radio 1206, MMDA Communications and Command Center, EDSA corner Orense Str, Guadalupe Nuevo, Makati C, NCR – **7)** Bayanihan Broadc. Corp. DZJO, Infanta, 4336 Quezon Province – **8)** Ben Viduya (OMARCO). DZOM, Calapan C, 5200 Mindoro Oriental – **9)** Beta Broadc. Syst. DWHL R. Apo, 8 Kessing Str, Olongapo C, 2200 Zambales – **10)** Bicol Broadc. Syst. DZLL, BBS Bldg, Balagtas Road, Magsaysay Ave, Naga C, 4400 Camarines Sur – **11)** Bohol Chronicle Radio Corp. DYRD, Dejaresco Bldg, 56 Bernardino Inting Str, Tagbilaran C, 6300 Bohol. DYZD, Brgy Tapon, Ubay, 6315 Bohol – **13)** Cadiz Radio & TV Netw. DYAG, Cadiz C, 6121 Negros Occidental – **14)** Capitol Broadc. Center. DZME R. Uno, 5th Floor Victory Central Mall, Victory Liner Compound, 717 Rizal Avenue Extension, Monumento, Caloocan C, NCR – **15)** Catanduanes State College. DZRA, Virac, 4800 Catanduanes – **16)** Catholic Media Network (CMN). Most MW sts ID as R. Totoo. DWBS Radio Veritas, 2/F Landco Business Park, Legaspi C, 4500 Albay. DXCP, Lagao, Gen. Santos C, 9500 South Cotabato. DXDB Radyo Bandilyo, Communications Media Center, San Isidro Cathedral Compound, Malaybalay C, 8700 Bukidnon. DXHM, Clergy House Compound, Madang, Mati C., Davao Oriental. DYDM, SJC Extension Campus, Mambajao, Maasin C, 6600 Southern Leyte. DYKA, St Joseph Bldg, San Jose de Buenavista, 5700 Antique. DYYW, Clergy House, Baybay Blvd, Borongan, 6800 Eastern Samar. DZEA, Brgy. Nalbo, Laoag C, 2900 Ilocos Norte– **17)** Cebu Broadc. Co. DXKH, Cagayan de Oro C, 9000 Misamis Oriental. DXZH, Zamboanga C, 7000 Zamboanga del Sur. DYCH, Tanke, Talisay C, 6045 Cebu. DYMS, San Bartolome Str, Catbalogan, 6700 Samar. DYSM, Brgy. Cawayan, Catarman, 6400 Northern Samar. DZHR, Tuguegarao, 3500 Cagayan. – **18)** Central Mindanao University. DXMU, Musuan, 8710 Bukidnon – **19)** Gateway UHF Broadcasting (Seventh Day Adventist). DXHR Hope R., km 43 Baan Hwy, Butuan C., 8600 Agusan del Norte – **20)** Christian Era Broadc. Sce. DZEM, Maligaya Bldg 2, 887 EDSA, Quezon C – **22)** Consolidated Broadc. Syst, Inc. DXBR, Bombo R. Broadc. Center, Arujville Subd, Brgy. Libertad, Butuan C, 8600 Agusan del Norte. DXES Bombo R. Broadc. Center, Amao Rd, Brgy. Bula, Gen. Santos C, 9500 South Cotabato. DXLX, Tambo, Brgy. Hinaplon, Iligan C, 9200 Lanao del Norte. DYFM, Sky City Tower, Mapa Str, Jaro, Iloilo C, 5000 Iloilo. DYOW, Bombo R. Broadc. Center, Arnaldo Blvd, Roxas C, 5800 Capiz. DYWB, Bombo R. Broadcast Center, Lacson Str, Mandalagan, Bacolod C, 6100 Negros Occidental. DZVV, Bombo R. Broadc. Center, Brgy. Tamag, Vigan, 2700 Ilocos Sur. DZWN, Bombo R. Broadc. Center, Maramba Bankers' Village, Bonuan Catacdang, 2400 Dagupan C, Pangasinan. DZWX, Bombo R. Broadc. Center, 87 Lourdes Subdivision Rd, Baguio C, 2600 Benguet – **23)** Crusaders Broadc. Syst, R. Ngayon. DWAD, 209 E. de la Paz Str, Mandaluyong C, 1550 NCR – **24)** Dawnbreaker's Foundation. DWBR R. Baha'i, Bulac, Talavera, 3114 Nueva Ecija or P. O.Box 27, San José City 3121 – **25)** Delta Broadc. Syst. DWXI, Mathr Str, Multinational Village, Parañaque C, 1708 NCR – **26)** Dept. of National Defense, Armed Forces R.. DWDD, Camp Aguinaldo, EDSA, Quezon C, 1110 NCR – **27)** DXZB/TV13 Cooperative, Inc. DXZB, Zamboanga C, 7000 Zamboanga del Sur – **28)** Eagle Broadc. Corp. DWIN, Bo. Lucao, Dagupan C, 2400 Pangasinan. DXED, Cabiguio Ave, Agdao, 8000 Davao C. DZEC, R Aguila, Maligaya Bldg II, 887 EDSA, Quezon C. DZEL, Bo. Mayao, Lucena C, 4301 Quezon Province – **29)** East Visayan Broadc. DYBP, Sagcahan Rd, P.O. Box 80, Tacloban C, 6500 Leyte – **30)** Fairwaves Broadc. Netw. DZXE R. Tirador, Mira Hills, Vigan, 2700 Ilocos Sur – **31)** Far East Broadc. Co. . DXAS, P.O. Box 349, Tugbungan, Zamboanga C, 7000 Zamboanga del Sur. DXFE, Circumferential Rd, Dona Vicente Village, 8000 Davao C. DXKI, P.O. Box 8004, Brgy Morales, Koronadal C, 9506 South Cotabato. DYVS, P.O. Box 393, Km. 7, Pahanocoy, Bacolod C, 6100 Negros Occidental. DZAS, 62 Karuhatan Rd, Karuhatan, Valenzuela C, 1441 NCR. DZMR Missions Radio, Maharlika Highway, Sefton Village, Santiago City, 3311 Isabela – **32)** FBS Radio Netw. DWBL, Unit 908, Paragon Plaza, EDSA corner Reliance Str, Mandaluyong C, NCR – **33)** Filipinas Broadc. Netw. DYXW, Baruyan, San Jose, Tacloban C, 6500 Leyte. DZCV, Ugac Norte,

Tuguegarao, 3500 Cagayan. DZGE R. Numero Uno, Nordia Resort, Baras, Canaman, Naga C, 4400 Camarines Sur. DZRC R. Champion, Capt. Aquendes Drive, Legaspi C, 4500 Albay – **35)** Franciscan Broadc. Corp. DYWC R. Bandilyo, Parish Compound, St Anthony of Padua Parish, Sibulan, Dumaguete C, 6201 Negros Oriental – **36)** GMA Netw, Inc. DZSD, Arellano St., Dagupan C, 2400 Pangasinan. DYSB, Bacolod C, 6100 Negros Occidental. DYSI, GMA Compound, MacArthur Drive, Jaro, Iloilo C, 5000 Iloilo. DZBB, GMA Netw. Center, EDSA corner Timog Ave, Diliman, 1103 Quezon C – **37)** Guzman Institute of Tech. DWGI, 509 Z.P. de Guzman, Quiapo, Manila, NCR – **38)** GV Broadc. Syst. DWGV R. Centro, Rizal Extension, Cut-Cut, Angeles C, 2009 Pampanga – **39)** Hypersonic Broadc. Center. DWZR Zoom Radio, Penaranda Str, Legaspi C, 4500 Albay. DYHR, Calbayog C, 6710 W. Samar – **40)** Insular Broadc. Syst. DWIM R. Mindoro, Brgy. Bayanihan, Calapan, 5200 Mindoro Oriental – **41)** Interactive Broadcast Media, Inc. DWWW, 23 E. Rodriguez Sr. Blvd, Quezon C – **42)** Intercontinental Broadc. Corp, R. Budyong. DWDC, A.B. Fernandez Ave, Dagupan C, 2400 Pangasinan. DXWG, Iligan C, 9200 Lanao del Norte. DYBQ, Datu Puti Subdivision, ,Cubay, Jaro, Iloilo C, 5000 Iloilo. DYJJ, Roxas Ave, Roxas C, 5800 Capiz. DYRG, Roxas Ave Extension, Andagao, Kalibo, 5600 Aklan – **43)** Kaissar Broadc. Netw. DWJJ R.bisyon (Double J Ad Ventures), Celcor Compound, Bitas, Cabanatuan C, 3100 Nueva Ecija – **44)** Kalayaan Broadc. Syst. DXRR R. Rapido, Bug-ac, Matina, 8000 Davao C – **45)** Katigbak Enterprises (ConAmor Broadcasting Systems). DWMI, Calapan, 5200 Mindoro Oriental. DWTI, Broadcast Village, Ibabang Dupay, Lucena C, 4301 Quezon Province – **46)** Puerto Princesa Broadc. Co. DYEC Environment Radio, Puerto Princesa C, 5300 Palawan – **47)** Kumintang Broadc. Syst. DZBR R. Balisong, KBS Bldg, Capitol Hills, Batangas C, 4200 Batangas – **48)** Progressive Broadcasting Corporation. DWUN UNTV Radio La Verdad, UNTV Bldg, 907 EDSA, Brgy Philam, Quezon C – **49)** Magiliw Community Broadc. Co. DWMC, Tomana, Rosales, 2441 Pangasinan – **50)** Manila Broadc. Co. DWDH, Lucao District, Dagupan C, 2400 Pangasinan. DWSR, Lucena C, 4301 Quezon Province. DXRF, Matina, 8000 Davao C. DYEZ, Wilrose Building, Burgos Str, Bacolod C, 6100 Negros Occidental. DYKX, Kalibo, 5600 Aklan. DYOK, Suite 301Carlos Uy Bldg, Diversion Rd, Manurriao, Iloilo C, 5000 Iloilo. DYPH, Puerto Princesa C, 5300 Palawan. DYVL, J. Romualdez corner Real Streets, Tacloban C, 6500 Leyte. DYRC Radyo Cebu, 3rd Floor, Cinco Centrum Building, Fuente Osmeña Blvd, 6000 Cebu C. DZJC, Brgy. 29, Rizal Street, St. Joseph District, Laoag C, 2900 Ilocos Norte. DZRH, MBC Bldg, Vicente Sotto Str, CCP Complex, Pasay C, 1300 NCR. DZZH, Cabit-an, Sorsogon C, 4700 Sorsogon – **51)** Masbate Community Broadc. Co. DYCM, Bogo Amusement Complex, Taytayan, Bogo, 6010 Cebu. DYME, Tugbo Str, Masbate C, 5400 Masbate – **52)** Mindanao Broadc. Co, Inc. DXSA, Marawi C, 9700 Lanao del Sur – **53)** Univ. of Mindanao Broadcasting Netwk. DXUM R. Ukay, UMBN Broadcast Center, Multi-test Bldg, Ponciano Reyes St, 8000 Davao C – **54)** Mt. Province Broadc. Corp. DZWT, P.O. Box 156, Mount Beckel, La Trinidad, Baguio C, 2600 Benguet – **55)** Mt. View College. DXCR Hope R., MVC, Valencia, 8709 Bukidnon – **56)** Municipality of Marikina. DZBF, R. Marikina, Second Floor, City Hall, Shoe Avenue, Marikina C, NCR – **57)** Mindanao Dev. Multi-Purpose Coop. DXAD Radio Ranao, Marcos Blvd, Saduc, Marawi C, 9700 Lanao del Sur – **58)** Swara Sug Media Corporation. DWAR, Laoag C, 2900 Ilocos Norte. DWAY, Cabanatuan C, 3100 Nueva Ecija. DWSI, North Eastern Foundation College, Santiago, 3311 Isabela. DWTT, Tarlac C, 2300 Tarlac. DXBL, Mangagoy, Bislig C, 8311 Surigao del Sur. DXAQ, Philippine-Japan Friendship Hwy, Catitipan, Davao C. DXCL, Cagayan de Oro C, 9000 Misamis Oriental. DXRB, Brgy Libertad, Butuan C, 8600 Agusan del Norte. DXRD, J.P Laurel Ave, Bajada, 8000 Davao C. DXRE, Lagao, Gen. Santos C, 9500 South Cotabato. DXRO, Don Roman Vilo Str, Cotabato C, 9600 Maguindanao. DXRT, Jolo, 7400 Sulu. DXYZ, San Jose Rd, Baliwasan, 7000 Zamboanga C. DYAR, 3ʳᵈ Fl. Astron Gestus Bldg, Gorordo Ave, 6000 Cebu C. DZAR, Suite 3004, 30/F Jollibee Plaza Building, F Ortigas Jr Road, Ortigas Center, Pasig City, 1600 NCR. DZRD, Banuan Guesset, Dagupan C, 2400 Pangasinan. DZSP, San Pablo C, 4000 Laguna. DZYI, Calamagui 2nd, Ilagan, 3300 Isabela. DZYT, Cagayan Teachers College, Tuguegarao, 3500 Cagayan – **60)** Newsounds Broadc. Netw. DXIF, Bombo R. Broadc. Center, Corrales Ave, Cagayan de Oro C, 9000 Misamis Oriental. DYCX, San Jose de Buenavista, Antique. DYWR, Bombo R. Broadc. Center, Sto. Nino cor. Imelda Ave, Tacloban C, 6500 Leyte. DZNC, Bombo R. Broadc. Center, Barrio Menante II, Cauayan, 3305 Isabela. DZNG, Bombo R. Broadc. Center, Diversion Road, Brgy. Tabuko, Naga C, 4400 Camarines Sur. DZSO, Bombo R. Broadcast Center, Pennsylvania Ave, Parian, San Fernando C, 2500 La Union. DZVR, Bombo R. Broadcast Center, 48 A, Cabungaan Airport Ave, Laoag C, 2900 Ilocos Norte – **61)** Northeastern Broadc. Sce. DWDY, Ground Floor, Isabela Hotel, Mirante Uno, Cauayan, 3305 Isabela – **62)** Notre Dame Broadc. Corp. DXMS, Sinsuat Ave cor. Rizal Ave, Cotabato C, 9600 Maguindanao. DXND, Daang Maharlika, Kidapawan C, 9400 North Cotabato – **63)** Nueva Ecija

Provincial Gov. DWNE, Brgy Singalat, Palayan C, 3132 Nueva Ecija – **64)** Office of the Governor, Prov. of Agusan del Sur. DXDA R. Agusan, Patin-ay, Prosperidad, 8500 Agusan del Sur – **65)** Office of the Civil Defense. DZCA, Agham Rd. Science Garden, Pag-asa Planetarium, NCR – **66)** Ormoc Broadc. Co. DYRR, Bantigue, Ormoc C, 6541 Leyte – **67)** Pacific Broadc. Syst (subsidiary of Manila Broadc. Co.). DWRH, Santiago C, 3311 Isabela.. DXCH, Cotabato C, 9600 Maguindanao. DXGH, Purok Malakas, Lagao, Gen. Santos C, 9500 South Cotabato. DXGO, MBC Compound, Brgy. Duterte, R. Castillo Str, Agdao, 8000 Davao C. DYBH, Bacolod C, 6100 Negros Occidental. DYDH, Iloilo C, 5000 Iloilo. DYTH, Real Str, Tacloban C, 6500 Leyte. DZMT, Laoag C, 2900 Ilocos Norte – **68)** Palawan Broadc. Corp. DYAP, Rey Olivar Bldg., 61 Mabini St. Puerto Princesa C, 5300 Palawan. – **69)** PEC Broadc. Corp. DXGL, Butuan C, 8600 Agusan del Norte – **70)** Pedro N. Roa Broadc. DXOR, Don A. Velez Str, Cagayan de Oro C, 9000 Misamis Oriental – **72)** People's Broadc. Netw. DZGB, Mayona Building, Imperial Court Subdivision, Legaspi C, 4500 Albay. DZMD, Vinzons Ave, Daet, 4600 Camarines Norte. DZMS, Balobo Str, Sorsogon C, 4700 Sorsogon – **73)** People's Broadc. Sce. DXMC, Bombo R. Broadc. Center, Km 4 General Santos Drive, Koronadal C, 9506 South Cotabato. DXMF, Bombo R. Broadc. Center, San Pedro Str, 8000 Davao C. DXPD, Bombo R. Broadc. Center, North Diversion Road, Brgy. Banale, Pagadian C, 7016 Zamboanga del Sur. DYMF, 87-A. Borromeo Str, 6000 Cebu C. DZGR, Bombo R. Broadc. Center, Taft Str Extension, Brgy 5, Tuguegarao, 3500 Cagayan. DZLG, Bombo R. Broadc. Center, Tahao Road, Legaspi C, 4500 Albay. – **75)** Philippine Broadc. Corp. DWCM, Caranglaan District, Dagupan C, 2400 Pangasinan. DWMT, Naga C, 4400 Camarines Sur. DWSP, Tuding, Itogon, nr Baguio City, Benguet. DZNL, Brgy. Pagdalagan, San Fernando C, 2500 La Union. – **77)** Philippine Radio Corp. DWRN R. Asenso, Manipit Rd, Queborac Bagumbayan, Naga C, 4400 Camarines Sur. DYRM, Bo. Calindangan, Dumaguete C, 6200 Negros Oriental. DZYM R. Asenso, Puerto Gallenero, Pag-asa, San Jose, 5100 Mindoro Occidental. DZYR, Catbangen, San Fernando C, 2500 La Union – **79)** Public Affairs Sce, Armed Forces of the Philippines. DXOS, Basilan Island, Basilan – **81)** R.T. Broadc. Specialistns Philippines. DXLL, Campaner Str, Zamboanga C, 7000 Zamboanga del Sur – **82)** Radio Corp. of the Philippines. DXJM, J & M Bldg, Villakananga, Butuan C, 8600 Agusan del Norte. DZLT, Bo. Ibabang Dupay, Lucena C, 4301 Quezon Province. DZXT, MacArthur H-way, Tarlac C, 2300 Tarlac – **83)** DWRL Radio, Inc (subsidary of 82 above). DWRL, Purok 5, Rawis, Legaspi C, 4500 Albay. DXGS R. Asenso, NLSA Rd, Lagao, Gen. Santos C, 9500 South Cotabato. DXOC R. Asenso, Manabay, Catadman, Ozamis C, 7200 Misamis Occidental. DYRB, C. Padilla St., 6000 Cebu C – **84)** Radio Mindanao Netw. DXBC, Montilla Blvd, Butuan C, 8600 Agusan del Norte. DXCC, Canoy Bldg., Don Apolinar Velez Str, Cagayan de Oro C, 9000 Misamis Oriental. DXDC, San Vincente Bldg, cor. Anda & Bonifacio Stns, 8000 Davao C. DXDR, Bo. Mario Turno, Dipolog C, 7100 Zamboanga del Norte. DXHP, Flomencia Bldg. P. Castillo Mangagoy, Bislig C, 8311 Surigao del Sur. DXIC, Pafs Mejia Bldg, Roxas Str. cor Aguinaldo Str, Iligan C, 9200 Lanao del Norte. DXKR, Gen. Santos Drive, Koronadal C, 9506 South Cotabato. DXMB, Fortich Str, Malaybalay C, 8700 Bukidnon. DXMD, Bo. Obrero National Highway, Gen. Santos C, 9500 South Cotabato. DXMY, Esteros, RH 10, Cotabato C, 9600 Maguindanao. DXPR, Mercedes Str, San Jose Dist, Pagadian C, 7016 Zamboanga del Sur. DXRS, Km. 1 Rizal Str, Surigao C, 8400 Surigao del Norte. DXRZ, Zamaveco Bldg, Pilar Str, Zamboanga C, 7000 Zamboanga del Sur. DYCC, Brgy. Obrero, Calbayog C, 6710 W. Samar. DYHB, 4th Flt, SSS Bldg. Lacson Str, Bacolod C, 6100 Negros Occidental. DYHP. 2nd Flr, Gold Palace Bldg, 168 Osmeña Blvd, 6000 Cebu C. DYKR, C. Laserna Str, Kalibo, 5600 Aklan. DYRI, St Anne Bldg, Luna Str, La Paz, Iloilo C, 5000 Iloilo. DYVR, Punta, Tabuc, Roxas C, 5800 Capiz. DZXL, 4/F, Guadelupe Commerical Complex, Guadelupe Nuevo, Makati C, 1200 NCR – **85)** Radio Philippines Netw. DXDX R. Ronda, Acharon Blvd, Gen. Santos C, 9500 South Cotabato. DXKD, Gonzales corner Lopez Jaena Str, Biasong, Dipolog C, 7100 Zamboanga del Norte. DXKO R. Ronda, Gusa, National Hwy, Cagayan de Oro C, 9000 Misamis Oriental. DXKP R. Ronda, Araulio Str, Brgy Datoc, Pagadian C, 7016 Zamboanga del Sur. DXKS, Capitol Rd, Surigao C, 8400 Surigao del Norte. DXKT R. Ronda, Marfori Heights, 8000 Davao C. DXXX R. Ronda, Brgy Tugbungan, 7000 Zamboanga C. DYKB R. Ronda, Bo. Sumag, Bacolod C, 6100 Negros Occidental. DYKC, Maguikay, Mandaue C, 6014 Cebu. DYKW R. Ronda, Cagamayan, Binalbagan, 6107 Negros Occidental. DZBS R. Ronda, Agrix Supermarket cor Magsaysay Ave. & Bakawkan, Baguio C, 2600 Benguet. DZKI R. Ronda, San Agustin, Iriga C, 4431 Camarines Sur. DZRL R. Ronda, Bo. Kawayan, Batac, 2906 Ilocos Norte. DZTG, 46 Rizal Str, Tuguegarao, 3500 Cagayan – **86)** Radio Sorsogon Netw, Inc. DZRS, Don Luis Lee Bldg, Plaza Bonifacio, Sorsogon C, 4700 Sorsogon – **87)** Radio Veritas Global Broadc. Syst. DWRV, Maharlika Highway, Bayombong, 3700 Nueva Vizcaya. DWVR, San Jose C, 3121 Nueva Ecija. DZRV, R. Veritas, 20/F The Centerpoint Bldg 1, 162 West Ave

corner EDSA, Ortigas Center, Pasig C, 1600 NCR – **88)** R. Pilipino Corp (R. Asenso). DXCO, Atco Bldg, Capistrano & Gomez Str, Cagayan de Oro C, 9000 Misamis Oriental. DXOW, Mapa, 8000 Davao C. DYRL, Camaroli Av, Lupit Subd, Bacolod C, 6100 Negros Occidental. DZYA 2/F Tanglao Bldg, Balibago, Angeles C, 2009 Pampanga. – **89)** Ragde, Vicente & Sons. DYRS, Ragde Comp, Corner M. Endrinda Str and Broce Str, San Carlos C, 6127 Negros Occidental – **90)** Rajah Broadc. Netw (R. Bandido). DXRJ, RJ Clubhouse, Sta. Filomena, Iligan C, 9200 Lanao del Norte. DZRJ (The Voice of the Philippines), Ventures Bldg 1, Gen. Luna Str, Makati C, NCR – **91)** Republic Broadc. Syst. (owned by GMA Network Inc.) DWRA, Baguio C, 2600 Benguet. DWRC, San Nicolas, 2901 Ilocos Norte. DXBM, Cotabato C, 9600 Maguindanao. DXGM, Shrine Hills, Matina, 8000 Davao C. DXRL, 3/F Carisma Bldg., General Santos Drive, Koronadal C, 9506 South Cotabato. DXYK, Butuan C, 8600 Agusan del Norte. DYSP, Solid Rd, Brgy San Manuel, Puerto Princesa C, 5300 Palawan. DYSS, GMA Network Center, Nivel Hills, Apas, 6000 Cebu C – **92)** Ribbon Broadc. Netw. DWRB, 5/F, LCC Bldg, Lipa C, 4217 Batangas – **94)** RMC Broadc. Co, Inc (Rizal Memorial Colleges). DXRA R. Arangkada, A. Pichon St., 8000 Davao C – **95)** Rolin Broadc. Enterprises (sts relay RMN DWAR-FM 103.9MHz, Puerto Princesa). DWES, Narra, 5303 Palawan. DWJS, Roxas, 5308 Palawan – **97)** Sarraga Integration and Management Corp. (SIAM), El Nuevo Bantay R. DYHH Bantay R.DYDD, Lapu-Lapu C, 6015 Cebu. DYZZ, Bogo, 6010 Cebu. DYZZ, Guihulngan, 6214 Negros Oriental – **98)** Satellite Broadc. Corp. DWBA, Bangued, 2800 Abra. DZLU, National College of Technology Campus, Barangay 1, San Fernando C, 2500 La Union –**100)** Southern Institute of Tech. DXSI, Cagayan de Oro C, 9000 Misamis Oriental – **101)** Southern Philippines Mass Comm. DXSC, Camp Navarro, Calarian, 7000 Zamboanga C – **102)** Subic Broadc. Corp. DWGO Gabay ng Olangapo, 1 Kasarinlan Rd, Olongapo, 2200 Zambales – **103)** Sulu Tawi-Tawi Broadc. Foundation. DXGD Radio for Peace, Bongao, 7500 Tawi-Tawi. DXMM R. Totoo, Gandasuli Str, Jolo, 7400 Sulu – **104)** Tagbilaran Broadc. Corp. DYTR, CAP Bldg, CPG Ave crnr Borja Str, Dampas, Tagbilaran C, 6300 Bohol – **105)** Times Broadc. Corp. DXSY, Mariano Marcos, Ozamis C, 7200 Misamis Occidental – **106)** Tirad Pass R/TV Broadc. Netw. DZTP R. Tirad Pass, San Nicolas, Candon, 2710 Ilocos Sur – **107)** Trans-Radio Broadc. Corp. (operated by Philippine Daily Inquirer). DZIQ R. Inquirer, 2/F Media Resources Plaza, Pasong Tirad cor. Mola Str, Brgy La Paz, Makati C, NCR – **108)** Supreme Broadc. Systems. DWSS, Paragon Plaza, EDSA, Mandaluyong C, NCR – **110)** Universal Broadc. Syst (owned by Radio Mindanao Network). DYMM, Sunshine Village, Esperos Str, Tacloban C, 6500 Leyte. DYXT, Luna Str, Tagbilaran C, 6300 Bohol – **111)** University of Mindanao Broadc. Netwk (UMBN). DXCM, UM School Compound, Cotabato C, 9600 Maguindanao. DXDN, UM Tagum School Compound, Tagum C, 8100 Davao del Norte. DXDS, Digos C, 8002 Davao del Sur. DXMV, Mt. Kitangcad Cor. Kanlaon Street, Valencia, 8709 Bukidnon. – **112)** University of San Agustin. DYSA R. San Agustin, 2/F Univ. of S. Agustin, Gen. Luna Str, Iloilo C, 5901 Iloilo – **113)** University of the Philippines. DZLB, UP Los Banos College, 4031 Laguna. DZUP, Media Center, College of Mass Comunications, UP Campus Diliman, R, Magasay Ave corner Apacible Str, Quezon C, 1104 NCR – **114)** Vanguard Radio Netw (Radio Vanguard). DWMG, Solano, 3709 Nueva Vizcaya. DZXO, Ground Floor Diego Building, Maharlika Highway, Cabanatuan C, 3100 Nueva Ecija – **115)** Visayas Mindanao Confederation of Trade Unions. DYLA, Alu-Vimcontu Welfare Center, Pier Area, 6000 Cebu C – **116)** Vismin Radio & TV Broadc. Net. DXDV, Baan, Butuan C, 8600 Agusan del Norte – **118)** Word Broadc. Corp. DYDW Radio Diwa, Burayan, San José, Tacloban C, 6500 Leyte. DYRF R. Fuerza, Univ. of San Carlos, Pelaez Str, 6000 Cebu C – **120)** ZOE Broadc. Netw. DZJV, 140 Brgy Parian, Calamba, 4027 Laguna – **121)** Baganian Broadc. Corp. DXBZ R. Bagting, Bana Str, Sta Maria District, Pagadian C., 7015 Zamboanga del Sur – **122)** Solidnorth Broadcasting System. DWRS Commando Radio, Tamag, Vigan, 2700 Ilocos Sur – **123)** S.O.L. Telebroadcasting Station. DZSL, Purok 2, Talisay, Camarines Norte – **124)** Ranao Radio & TV Broadcast System Corp. DXSK R. Ranaw, Pangarungan Village, Marawi C, 9700 Lanao del Sur – **125)** End Time Mission (Pentecostal Missionary Church of Christ 4th Watch). DZAT, Purok Rosal, Bo. Silangan Mayao, Lucena C., 4301 Quezon Province – **127)** University of the Philippines in the Visayas. DYUP UPV Radio, Miagao, Iloilo – **129)** Inter-Island Broadc. Corp. (IBC), owned by 73) above. DYIN, Bombo R. Broadcast Center, Oyo Torong Str, cor. J. Magno. Str, Kalibo, 5600 Aklan. DYSJ, San Jose de Buenavista, Antique – **130)** Dan-ag sa Dakbayan Broadc. Corp. DXDD R. Kampana, New DXDD Bldg, Rizal. Str, Ozamis C, 7200 Misamis Occidental – **131)** Roman Catholic Archdiocese of Zamboanga Broadc. Network (RCA-ZBN). DXVP R. Verdadero, Sacred Heart Center, R.T. Lim Bvd, Zamboanga C, 7000 Zamboanga del Sur – **132)** Apostolic Vicariate of San Jose de Mindoro. DZVT R. Totoo, Labangan Poblacion, San Jose, 5100 Mindoro Occidental – **133)** Multipoint Broadc. Netwk. DWPR Power Radio, A.B. Fernandez Ave, Bolosan District, Dagupan C, 2400

Pangasinan – **134)** Alaminos City Broadc. Corporation. DZWM R. Totoo, St Joseph Cathedral Compound, Alaminos, 2404 Pangasinan – **135)** Government of Tarlac Province. DZTC, MacArthur Hwy, Tarlac C, 2300 Tarlac – **136)** Archdiocese of Nueva Segovia. DZNS R. Totoo, Brgy Pantay Fatima, Vigan, 2700 Ilocos Sur – **137)** Diocese of Bacolod. DYAF R. Veritas Bacolod, Rizal Str corner San Juan Str, Brgy. 11, Bacolod C, 6100 Negros Occidental – **138)** Silangan Broadcasting Corporation. DXSN R. Magbalantay or R. Totoo, 55 Jules Chevalier Str, Surigao C, 8400 Surigao del Norte – **139)**Universitad de Zamboanga. DXUZ R. Lipay, Ipil, 7001 Zamboanga Sibugay – **140)** Itransmission, Inc. DZIP R. Palaweño, Dimalanta Bldg, Rizal Ave, Puerto Princesa, Palawan – **141)** Sarangani Broadcasting Netwk. DXBB R. Alerto, Yumang Str, Brgy San Isidro, Gen. Santos C, 9500 South Cotabato – **142)** End-Time Mission Broadcasting Service. DWET Life R, Batal, Santiago C, 3311 Isabela

EXTERNAL SERVICES: R. Pilipinas, Radio Veritas Asia, FEBC International Service, VOA/IBB
see International Broadcasting section

PITCAIRN ISLANDS (UK)

L.T: UTC -8h — **Pop:** 67 — **Pr.L:** Pitcairn English — **E.C:** 50Hz, 240V — **ITU:** PTC

PITCAIRN ISLAND RADIO
✉ Adamstown, Pitcairn Island. **L.P:** Paul Warren. **FM:** 87.5MHz 0.0025kW. **Prgr:** local community radio
NB: Reported inactive

POLAND

L.T: UTC +1h (27 Mar-30 Oct: +2h) — **Pop:** 38.5 million — **Pr.L:** Polish — **E.C:** 50Hz, 230V — **ITU:** POL

KRAJOWA RADA RADIOFONII I TELEWIZJI (KRRiT) (National Broadcasting Council)
✉ Skwer kard. S.Wyszynskiego 9, 01-015 Warszawa ☎ +48 225973000 🖷 +48 225973180 **E:** krrit@krrit.gov.pl **W:** krrit.gov.pl **L.P:** Pres: Jan Dworak
NB. KRRiT is the regulatory authority for broadcasting.

POLSKIE RADIO S.A. (PR) (Pub)
✉ al. Niepodleglosci 77/85, 00-977 Warszawa ☎ +48 226459212 🖷 +48 226453993 **E:** public.relations@polskieradio.pl **W:** polskieradio.pl
L.P: Chmn: Andrzej Siezieniewski

LW	kHz	kW	Prgr		
Solec Kujawski	225	1200*	1	*) 1000kW at night	

FM (MHz)	1	2	3	4	kW
Bialogard (Slawoborze)	106.0	98.2	101.5	-	10/2x15
Bialystok (Cieszynska)	-	106.4	-	91.1	1/0.1
Bialystok (Krynice)	92.3	-	96.0	-	30
Bogatynia (G.Wysoka)	92.8	-	-	-	1
Bydgoszcz (Foton)	-	-	-	96.2	1
Bydgoszcz (Trzeciewiec)	106.6	97.6	102.1	-	60/2x120d
Czestochowa (Bleszno)	-	-	-	98.9	2
Czestochowa (Wreczyca)	87.5	90.6	91.7	-	10/2x60
Dzierzoniów	-	103.5	-	-	1
Elblag (Jagodnik)	-	102.3	-	101.2	5/0.25
Gdansk (Chwaszczyno)	95.7	-	99.9	-	120
Gdansk	-	89.5	-	93.4	1/0.1
Gdynia (Oksywie)	-	97.2	-	-	2
Gizycko (Milki)	97.1	92.6	94.4	-	6/2x10
Gorlice (Maslana Góra)	105.4	-	-	-	10
Gorzów Wlkp. (Janice)	94.9	-	-	105.4	0.1/1
Ilawa (Kisielice)	94.8	102.7	-	104.8	2x10/5
Jelenia Góra (Sniezne Kotly)	92.5	-	94.0	-	10
Kalisz (Mikstat)	100.0	95.6	102.5	94.2	10
Katowice (Kosztowy)	97.9	105.6	99.7	-	60
Kielce (Swiety Krzyz)	92.3	-	96.2	-	60
Kielce	-	102.7	-	87.6	1/0.1
Klodzko (Czarna Góra)	97.6	-	89.2	-	10
Klodzko	-	92.4	-	-	2
Konin (Zólwieniec)	87.7	-	103.3	-	30
Konin	-	95.0	-	-	1
Koszalin (Gologóra)	107.9	93.8	97.4	-	60
Kraków (Choragwica)	89.4	-	99.4	-	60
Kraków (Krzemionki)	-	102.0	-	97.2	1/0.4
Krosno (Sucha Góra)	88.0	-	92.0	-	120
Krynica (G.Jaworzyna)	106.4	89.6	-	98.4	1/0.1/1
Kutno	-	96.9	-	-	1

FM (MHz)	1	2	3	4	kW
Lebork (Skórowo Nowe)	100.5	88.2	106.3	107.5	2x10/5/10
Legnica	-	105.3	-	103.3	2/0.3
Lezajsk (Giedlarowa)	96.8	-	98.9	-	10
Lobez (Toporzyk)	-	-	-	100.6	3
Lódz	107.8	91.4	103.8	107.3	30/2x10/1.5
Lowicz	101.6	-	-	-	10
Lubaczów (Boble)	100.0	88.4	96.0	-	10
Luban (Nowa Karczma)	99.0	-	91.5	-	10/60
Lublin (Piaski)	90.8	-	104.2	-	30/90
Nowy Tomysl (Bolewice)	-	107.7	-	-	10
Olsztyn (Pieczewo)	93.0	93.7	99.1	97.9	30/2/120/0.1
Opole (Chrzelice)	88.3	94.5	90.3	-	60/10/60
Ostroleka (Lawy)	106.7	96.3	98.5	93.4	10/5/10/0.2
Pila (Staszyce)	-	102.5	-	-	10
Plock (Rachocin)	92.2	98.1	96.1	-	60/2.5/60
Poznan (Srem)	92.3	-	96.4	-	120
Przasnysz	105.9	107.1	-	-	10
Przemysl (Tatarska Góra)	87.8	94.1	99.6	91.0	5/1/5/1
Przysucha (Kozlowiec)	92.0	104.8	-	-	10
Rabka (G.Lubon Wielki)	93.4	90.4	-	-	5
Radom (Wacyn)	-	100.3	-	97.5	1/0.1
Radom	-	-	-	104.6	1
Ryki	105.1	88.7	-	-	10
Rzeszów (Baranówka)	-	105.8	-	91.5	1
Siedlce (Losice)	88.3	-	90.5	-	30
Slupsk	104.3	-	-	106.8	2.8/5
Solina (G.Jawor)	90.7	-	96.3	-	30
Stargard Szczeszinski	-	107.6	-	-	1
Suwalki (G.Krzemianucha)	105.5	92.0	96.6	-	20/2x30
Swieradów-Zdrój	-	93.2	-	90.5	10/1
Swinoujscie (Chrobrego)	107.7	-	-	-	10
Szczawnica (G.Prehyba)	88.0	-	94.7	-	10/5
Szczecin (Kolowo)	100.3	-	102.3	-	60
Szczecin (Warszewo)	-	96.3	-	88.4	1
Tarnów (G.Sw. Marcina)	-	-	-	99.9	2.5
Tarnów (Lichwin)	91.1	88.6	-	-	10
Wagrowiec (Golancz)	101.3	-	-	-	1
Walbrzych (G.Chelmiec)	-	87.9	99.8	94.3	2x5/0.5
Walcz (Rusinowo)	101.9	-	90.9	-	30
Warszawa (PKiN)	92.4	104.9	99.1	92.0	0.3/2.5/0.1/0.2
Warszawa (Raszyn)	102.4	-	98.8	-	120
Wisla (G.Skrzyczne)	91.5	-	100.8	-	10
Wloclawek (Szpetal Górny)	-	93.9	-	-	1
Wlodawa (Zolnierzy)	-	102.5	-	-	10
Wloszczowa (Dobromierz)	88.9	-	-	-	3.2
Wroclaw (G.Sleza)	98.8	-	100.2	-	120
Wroclaw (Zórawina)	-	87.7	-	107.5	10/5
Zagan (Wichów)	91.2	104.7	87.8	-	30
Zakopane (G.Gubalówka)	92.8	90.9	98.2	-	10/0.3/10
Zamosc (Feliksówka)	105.7	-	-	95.3	10/1
Zamosc (Tarnawatka)	-	87.6	91.3	-	30
Zielona Góra (Jemiolów)	105.0	89.9	94.1	-	60
Zielona Góra (Wilkanowo)	-	-	104.0	2	

NB: Sites with only txs below 1kW not listed.
D.Prgr: Prgr 1 (Jedynka): 24h. – **Prgr 2 (Dwójka):** 24h – **Prgr 3 (Trójka):** 24h. – **Prgr 4 (Czwórka):** 24h. – **PR24:** 24h. – **PR Rytm:** 24h.
External Service: see Int. Radio section.

PR Regional Stations
D.Prgr: All stations broadcast 24h. **PR R.Bialystok:** ul. Swierkowa 1, 15-328 Bialystok **E:** radiobia@radio.bialystok.pl. On (MHz) 87.9 (Lomza 0.2kW), 89.4 (Bialowieza 0.1kW), 96.8 (G.Krzemianucha 30kW), 99.4 (Krynice 30kW), 104.1 (Makarki 10kW), 176.640 (DAB+ 5B Krynice 2kW). – **PR R.Dla Ciebe (RDC):** ul. Mysliwiecka 3/5/7, 00-977 Warszawa **E:** radio@rdc.pl. On (MHz) 87.6 (Ostrów Mazowiecka 1kW), 89.1 (Wacyn 5kW), 100.8 (Ostroleka 0.25kW), 101.0 (Warszawa PKiN 13kW), 101.9 (Rachocin 60kW), 103.4 (Losice 120kW), 183.650 (DAB+ 6B Warszawa PKiN 6kW). – **PR R.Gdansk:** ul. Grunwaldzka 18, 80-006 Gdansk **E:** poczta@radio.gdansk.pl. On (MHz) 91.1 (Skórowo Nowe 10kW), 102.0 (Slupsk 1kW), 103.7 (Chwaszczyno 120kW), 106.0 (Kwidzyn 1kW), 107.0 (Bytów 10kW), 215.072 (DAB+ 10D Chwaszczyno 10kW). – **PR R.Katowice:** ul. Ligonia 29, 40-953 Katowice **E:** sekretariat@radio.katowice.pl. On (MHz) 89.3 (Zabrze 0.5kW), 97.0 (Raciborz 1kW), 98.4 (Wreczyca 60kW), 101.2 (Bytków 10kW), 102.2 (Kosztowy 60kW), 103.0 (G.Skrzyczne 10kW), 209.936 (DAB+ 10A Kosztowy 10kW). – **PR R.Kielce:** ul. Radiowa 4, 25-317 Kielce. **E:** radio@radio.kielce.com.pl. On (MHz) 90.4 (Kielce 0.25kW), 100.0 (Wloszczowa 1kW), 101.4 (Swiety Krzyz 120kW), 180.064 (DAB+ 10A SFN). – **PR R.Koszalin:** ul. Pilsudskiego 43-49, 75-502 Koszalin. **E:** radio@radio.koszalin.pl. On (MHz) 88.1 (Rusinowo 3kW), 91.0 (Kolobrzeg 0.1kW),

92.5 (Slawoborze 15kW), 95.3 (Slupsk 2kW)*, 97.8 (G.Chelmska 0.1kW), 103.1 (Gologóra 60kW), 229.072 (DAB+ 10D SFN). *) incl. prgrs from Slupsk studio. – **PR R.Kraków:** al. Slowackiego 22, 30-007 Kraków. **E:** radio@radio-krakow.pl. On (MHz) 87.6 (G. Lubon Wielki 5kW), 90.0 (G.Prehyba 10kW), 97.4 (Gorlice 2kW), 98.8 (Andrychów 1kW), 100.0 (G.Gubalówka 10kW), 101.0 (G. Sw. Marcina 10kW), 101.6 (Choragwica 60kW), 102.1 (G.Jaworzyna 1kW), 229.072 (DAB+ 12D Choragwica 10kW). – **PR R.Lódz:** ul. Narutowicza 130, 90-146 Lódz. **E:** studio@radiolodz.pl. On (MHz) 96.7 (Sieradz 0.5kW), 99.2 (Lódz 30kW), 104.0 (Wieruszów 1kW), 178.352 (DAB+ 5C Lodz 10kW). – **PR R.Lublin:** ul. Obronców Pokoju 2, 20-030 Lublin. **E:** poczta@radio.lublin.pl. On (MHz) 93.1 (Biala Podlaska 5kW), 102.2 (Piaski 90kW), 103.1 (Ryki 10kW), 103.2 (Feliksówka 30kW), 211.648 (DAB+ 10B SFN). Substation: **PR R.Freee: E:** redakcja@radiofreee.pl. On 89.9MHz (Lublin 1kW) + DAB. – **PR R.Merkury:** ul. Berwinskiego 5, 60-765 Poznan. **E:** office@radio-merkury.pl. On (MHz) 91.1 (Mikstat 10kW), 91.9 (Zólwieniec 30kW), 100.9 (Srem 120kW), 102.4 (Bolewice 3kW), 103.6 (Rusinowo 60kW), 220.352 (DAB+ 11C SFN). Local substation: **PR MC Radio: E:** redakcja@mcradio.pl. On 102.7MHz (Piatkowo 2kW) + DAB. – **PR R.Olsztyn:** ul. Radiowa 24, 10-206 Olsztyn. **E:** radio@ro.com.pl. On (MHz) 99.6 (Milki 10kW), 103.2 (Pieczewo 120kW), 103.4 (Jagodnik 0.5kW), 213.360 (DAB+ 10C Pieczewo 5.5kW). – **PR R.Opole** ul. Strzelców Bytomskich 8, 45-084 Opole. **E:** pro_fm@radio.opole. pl. On (MHz) 88.0 (Brzeg 1kW), 89.1 (Olesno 1kW), 92.6 (Paczków 1kW), 94.8 (Glubczyce 1kW), 96.3 (Kluczbork 30kW), 101.2 (Opole 1kW), 103.2 (Chrzelice 60kW), 105.1 (Strzelce Opolskie 1kW), 107.7 (Namyslów 1kW), 220.352 (DAB+ 11C SFN). – **PR R.PiK:** ul. Gdanska 48-50, 85-006 Bydgoszcz. **E:** radio@radiopik.pl. On (MHz) 100.1 (Trzeciewiec 120kW), 100.3 (Wloclawek 1kW), 106.9 (Brodnica 10kW), 220.352 (DAB+ 11C SFN). – **PR R.Rzeszów:** ul. Zamkowa 3, 35-032 Rzeszów. **E:** radiorz@radio.rzeszow.pl. On (MHz) 90.3 (Machów 1kW), 90.5 (Sucha Góra 120kW), 96.4 (Mielec 1kW), 99.2 (G.Jawor 5kW), 102.0 (Tatarska Góra 10kW), 102.9 (Giedlarowa 30kW), 103.7 (Boble 10kW), 106.7 (Magdalenka 2kW), 216.928 (DAB+ 11A SFN). – **PR R.Szczecin:** al. Wojska Polskiego 73, 70-481 Szczecin. **E:** sekretariat@radio.szczecin. pl. On (MHz) 92.0 (Kolowo 60kW), 98.7 (Slawoborze 10kW), 106.3 (Chrobrego 30kW), 216.928 (DAB+ 11A SFN). Substation: **PR R.94i4 FM: E:** sekretariat@szczecin.fm. On 94.4MHz (Warszewo 0.5kW) + DAB. – **PR R.Wroclaw:** ul. Karkonoska 8-10, 53-015 Wroclaw. **E:** sekretariatzarzadu@prw.pl. On (MHz) 89.0 (G.Wysoka 1kW), 95.5 (G.Chelmiec 5kW), 96.0 (Czarna Góra 10kW), 96.7 (Sniezne Kotly 10kW), 98.0 (G.Parkowa 0.1kW), 102.3 (G.Sleza 120kW), 103.6 (Nowa Karczma 60kW), 225.648 (DAB+ 12B Zórawina 10kW). Local substation: **PR R.RAM: E:** ram@prw.pl. On 89.8MHz (Zórawina 6kW) + DAB. – **PR R.Zachód:** ul. Kukulcza 1, 65-472 Zielona Góra. **E:** radio@zachod. pl. On (MHz) 103.0 (Jemiolów 120kW), 106.0 (Wichów 30kW), 223.936 (DAB+ 12C SFN). Local substations of R.Zachód: **PR R.Zielona Góra: E:** rzg@rzg.pl. On 97.1MHz (Zielona Góra 1kW) + DAB.

OTHER STATIONS

MW	kHz	kW	Location	Station
68A)	531	0.8	Wlodawa	R. AM Wlodawa
68B)	963	0.1	Lipsko	R. AM Lipsko
68C)	1062	0.8	Cmolas	R. AM Cmolas
68D)	1062	0.5	Jaroslaw	R. AM Jaroslaw
68E)	1062	0.8	Pulawy	R. AM Pulawy
68F)	1584	0.8	Andrychów	R. AM Andrychów
68G)	1584	0.1	Slupsk	R. AM Slupsk
68)	1602	0.8	Kraków	R. AM Kraków

FM	MHz	kW	Location	Station
27)	87.7	2	Bialystok	R. Akadera
3)	87.7	3	Miedzyzdroje	R. Maryja
1B)	87.8	1	Kraków	R. RMF Classic
3)	87.8	1	Biala Podlaska	R. Maryja
17)	87.9	25	Lublin	R. eR
3)	87.9	10	Lódz	R. Maryja
2A)	88.0	2	Wagrowiec	R. ZET
36)	88.1	1	Wielun	R. Fiat
1A)	88.2	120	Kielce	R. RMF FM
1A)	88.2	1	Polkowice	R. RMF FM
3)	88.2	1	Ostrów Wlkp.	R. Maryja
6A)	88.2	1	Torun	R. TOK FM
2A)	88.3	60	Zielona Góra	R. ZET
3)	88.3	1	Kutno	R. Maryja
3)	88.4	10	Bielsko-Biala	R. Maryja
6B)	88.4	5	Poznan	R. Zlote Przeboje
3)	88.5	10	Slupsk	R. Maryja
61)	88.6	1	Skierniewice	R. RSC
2A)	88.7	1	Koszalin	R. ZET
3)	88.7	1	Wagrowiec	R. Maryja
5A)	88.8	1	Lomza	R. Eska
3)	88.9	1	Gdansk	R. Maryja
3)	88.9	120	Wroclaw	R. Maryja

FM	MHz	kW	Location	Station
4)	88.9	15	Szczecin	R. Plus
3)	89.0	1	Warszawa	R. Maryja
39)	89.2	5	Bialystok	R. Jard
6A)	89.2	1	Elblag	R. TOK FM
1A)	89.3	60	Koszalin	R. RMF FM
1A)	89.3	30	Lublin	R. RMF FM
2A)	89.4	60	Luban	R. ZET
3)	89.4	2	Stargard Szczec.	R. Maryja
4)	89.5	10	Gniezno	R. Plus
5A)	89.5	1	Sanok	R. Eska
2D)	89.6	1	Lodz	Antyradio
33)	89.6	1	Opole	R. DOXA
3)	89.8	1	Mielec	R. Maryja
30)	89.8	1	Poznan	R. Emaus
6B)	89.8	1	Szczecin	R. Zlote Przeboje
19)	90.0	2	Rybnik	R. 90
6B)	90.0	4	Legnica	R. Zlote Przeboje
13)	90.1	10	Zamosc	Katolickie R. Zamosc
5A)	90.1	2	Lodz	R. Eska
9)	90.1	1	Koscierzyna	R. Kaszëbë
3)	90.2	10	Kamiensk	R. Maryja
43)	90.2	1	Kolobrzeg	R. Kolobrzeg
63)	90.2	1	Bielsko-Biala	R. Aniol Beskidów
3)	90.3	1	Zielona Góra	R. Maryja
6B)	90.4	1	Wroclaw	R. Zlote Przeboje
3)	90.6	5	Kraków	R. Maryja
32)	90.6	1	Slupsk	R. FAMA
4)	90.7	2	Gryfice	R. Plus
4)	90.7	5	Radom	R. Plus
5A)	90.7	2	Gdynia	R. Eska
16)	90.8	1	Mlawa	R. 7
1C)	90.8	1	Inowroclaw	R. RMF MAXXX
14)	90.9	1	Jelenia Góra	Muzyczne R.
14)	90.9	5	Walbrzych	Muzyczne R.
1A)	91.0	120	Warszawa	R. RMF FM
6B)	91.2	2	Katowice	R. Zlote Przeboje
1A)	91.3	10	Lobez	R. RMF FM
38)	91.4	1	Pelplin	R. Glos
1A)	91.5	15	Ostroleka	R. RMF FM
2A)	91.6	10	Ryki	R. ZET
4)	91.7	1	Zielona Góra	R. Plus
2A)	91.8	10	Swinoujscie	R. ZET
3)	91.8	1	Ciechanów	R. Maryja
1A)	91.9	30	Siedlce	R. RMF FM
2B)	92.0	1	Gdansk	R. ZET Chilli
59)	92.0	2.5	Wroclaw	R. Rodzina
2A)	92.1	1	Wlodawa	R. ZET
6B)	92.1	1	Bydgoszcz	R. Zlote Przeboje
2A)	92.2	10	Opole	R. ZET
55)	92.3	1	Laziska Gorna	R. Express FM
9)	92.3	2	Gdansk	R. Kaszëbë
6B)	92.5	1	Kraków	R. Zlote Przeboje
2A)	92.6	120	Lodz	R. ZET
42)	92.6	1	Sepólno Kraj.	R. Weekend
7)	92.6	1	Krosno	R. WAWA
3)	92.7	10	Lebork	R. Maryja
2C)	92.8	1	Torun	R. ZET Gold
6B)	92.8	1	Opole	R. Zlote Przeboje
1A)	92.9	10	Wroclaw	R. RMF FM
2A)	92.9	10	Gryfice	R. ZET
32)	92.9	1	Tomaszów Maz.	R. FAMA
1A)	93.0	60	Katowice	R. RMF FM
5A)	93.0	10	Poznan	R. Eska
3)	93.1	1	Krynica	R. Maryja
6B)	93.2	5	Jedrzejów	R. Zlote Przeboje
7)	93.2	2	Szczecin	R. WAWA
1A)	93.3	120	Bydgoszcz	R. RMF FM
5A)	93.3	1	Warszawa	R. Eska
25)	93.4	2	Gliwice	R. CCM
1A)	93.5	10	Lódz	R. RMF FM
2A)	93.6	120	Wroclaw	R. ZET
2B)	93.7	1	Kraków	R. ZET Chilli
1A)	93.8	60	Luban	R. RMF FM
52)	93.8	1	Kutno	R. Victoria
5A)	93.8	10	Gorzów Wlkp.	R. Eska
65)	93.8	1	Czestochowa	R. Jura
54)	93.9	1	Kedzierzyn-Kozle	R. Park FM
2C)	94.0	1	Warszawa	R. ZET Gold
4)	94.0	1	Konskie	R. Plus
12)	94.1	1	Jaslo	VIA – Kat. R. Rzeszów
5A)	94.1	1	Elblag	R. Eska
38)	94.2	1	Kartuzy	R. Glos
1A)	94.3	60	Plock	R. RMF FM
3)	94.3	1	Racibórz	R. Maryja
3)	94.4	1	Tarnobrzeg	R. Maryja
5A)	94.4	5	Bydgoszcz	R. Eska

FM	MHz	kW	Location	Station	FM	MHz	kW	Location	Station
6B)	94.4	1	Zary	R. Zlote Przeboje	5A)	99.0	1	Szczecinek	R. Eska
23)	94.5	1	Grodzisk Maz.	R. Bogoria	22)	99.2	5	Biala Podlaska	R. Racja
3)	94.5	1	Ustrzyki Dolne	R. Maryja	2A)	99.3	1	Rybnik	R. ZET
1A)	94.6	120	Poznan	R. RMF FM	42)	99.3	2	Chojnice	R. Weekend
5A)	94.6	1	Gdansk	R. Eska	2C)	99.4	2.5	Poznan	R. ZET Gold
36)	94.7	10	Czestochowa	R. Fiat	1A)	99.5	1	Kluczbork	R. RMF FM
52)	94.7	1	Rawa Maz.	R. Victoria	3)	99.5	1	Lipiany	R. Maryja
1A)	94.8	30	Zagan	R. RMF FM	4)	99.5	1	Slupsk	R. Plus
59)	94.8	2	Strzelin	R. Rodzina	6B)	99.5	1	Zmudz	R. Zlote Przeboje
31)	94.9	1	Sochaczew	R. Sochaczew	2C)	99.6	1	Konin	R. ZET Gold
4)	94.9	1	Jelenia Góra	R. Plus	1C)	99.7	1	Koszalin	R. RMF MAXXX
6A)	94.9	1	Kielce	R. TOK FM	3)	100.0	5	Zielona Góra	R. Maryja
2A)	95.0	20	Lezajsk	R. ZET	1A)	100.1	120	Krosno	R. RMF FM
3)	95.0	3	Szczecinek	R. Maryja	6B)	100.1	4	Warszawa	R. Zlote Przeboje
1A)	95.1	1.6	Suwalki	R. RMF FM	1A)	100.2	120	Bialystok	R. RMF FM
2C)	95.1	1	Zabrze	R. ZET Gold	3)	100.2	1	Gizycko	R. Maryja
2A)	95.2	60	Szczecin	R. ZET	64)	100.2	5	Zabrze	R. Fest
3)	95.2	1	Swieradów-Zdrój	R. Maryja	3)	100.3	1	Bogatynia	R. Maryja
3)	95.2	1	Sieradz	R. Maryja	48)	100.3	1	Racibórz	R. Vanessa
56)	95.2	1	Kraków	R. Bajka	3)	100.4	1	Jelenia Góra	R. Maryja
6A)	95.2	1	Gdynia	R. TOK FM	3)	100.4	10	Ostróda	R. Maryja
1A)	95.3	60	Olsztyn	R. RMF FM	3)	100.4	10	Ostrów Maz.	R. Maryja
1A)	95.3	60	Opole	R. RMF FM	3)	100.4	1	Nysa	R. Maryja
1A)	95.4	10	Tarnów	R. RMF FM	4)	100.4	5	Lódz	R. Plus
3)	95.4	5	Skierniewice	R. Maryja	3)	100.6	10	Torun	R. Maryja
3)	95.4	1	Gniezno	R. Maryja	3)	100.6	10	Krosno	R. Maryja
5B)	95.5	1	Katowice	R. Eska	3)	100.6	10	Glogów	R. Maryja
2A)	95.6	120	Bydgoszcz	R. ZET	3)	100.6	5	Parczew	R. Maryja
6B)	95.6	1	Lublin	R. Zlote Przeboje	40)	100.6	60	Czestochowa	R. Jasna Góra
2A)	95.7	10	Wisla	R. ZET	2A)	100.7	2	Zamosc	R. ZET
5B)	95.7	1	Szczecin	R. VOX FM	3)	100.7	5	Rabka	R. Maryja
6B)	95.7	1	Rzeszów	R. Zlote Przeboje	4)	100.7	10	Gorzów Wlkp.	R. Plus
1C)	95.8	1	Warszawa	R. RMF MAXXX	1A)	100.8	10	Jelenia Góra	R. RMF FM
1C)	95.8	2	Konin	R. RMF MAXXX	32)	100.8	5	Kielce	R. FAMA
3)	95.8	1	Hrubieszów	R. Maryja	1A)	100.9	10	Slupsk	R. RMF FM
48)	95.8	1	Krapkowice	R. Vanessa	3)	100.9	1	Wloclawek	R. Maryja
57)	95.9	1	Olsztyn	R. UWM FM	2D)	101.0	1	Kraków	Antyradio
5A)	95.9	1	Koszalin	R. Eska	1A)	101.1	30	Solina	R. RMF FM
1A)	96.0	60	Kraków	R. RMF FM	1C)	101.1	5	Walbrzych	R. RMF MAXXX
1C)	96.0	1	Olesnica	R. RMF MAXXX	3)	101.1	10	Zlotów	R. Maryja
53)	96.0	6	Lódz	R. Parada	5A)	101.1	2	Kalisz	R. Eska
1A)	96.1	1	Gorzów Wlkp.	R. RMF FM	1A)	101.2	10	Swinoujscie	R. RMF FM
1A)	96.1	1	Legnica	R. RMF FM	1C)	101.2	1	Bytów	R. RMF MAXXX
66)	96.2	2	Zabrze	R. Silesia	3)	101.2	10	Zagan	R. Maryja
1A)	96.4	15	Bialogard	R. RMF FM	58)	101.2	2.5	Nowy Sacz	R. RDN
1C)	96.4	1	Gdansk	R. RMF MAXXX	6A)	101.2	1	Plock	R. TOK FM
3)	96.5	10	Zamosc	R. Maryja	2C)	101.3	1	Kraków	R. ZET Gold
4)	96.5	10	Warszawa	R. Plus	3)	101.3	1	Lomza	R. Maryja
1A)	96.6	30	Walcz	R. RMF FM	6B)	101.3	10	Pabianice	R. Zlote Przeboje
2A)	96.6	10	Lebork	R. ZET	2A)	101.4	30	Suwalki	R. ZET
6B)	96.6	1	Zabrze	R. Zlote Przeboje	3)	101.4	10	Czersk	R. Maryja
1C)	96.7	2	Kraków	R. RMF MAXXX	5B)	101.5	1	Wroclaw	R. VOX FM
52)	96.7	1	Skierniewice	R. Victoria	1A)	101.6	10	Klodzko	R. RMF FM
7)	96.7	3	Torun	R. WAWA	2D)	101.6	1	Poznan	Antyradio
3)	96.9	7.5	Ilawa	R. Maryja	3)	101.6	10	Pisz	R. Maryja
5A)	96.9	1	Szczecin	R. Eska	3)	101.6	1	Szczecin	R. Maryja
2A)	97.0	30	Poznan	R. ZET	4)	101.7	120	Gdansk	R. Plus
3)	97.0	1	Lublin	R. Maryja	46)	101.7	120	Siedlce	Katolickie R. Podlasie
3)	97.0	2	Ciechanowiec	R. Maryja	62)	101.7	1	Kepno	R. Sud
1A)	97.1	12	Wloszczowa	R. RMF FM	1A)	101.8	60	Lezajsk	R. RMF FM
54)	97.1	1	Brzeg	R. Park FM	1A)	101.8	10	Zakopane	R. RMF FM
2A)	97.2	1	Walbrzych	R. ZET	28)	101.8	1	Jarocin	R. Elka
24)	97.2	1	Pulawy	R. Pulawy 24	10)	101.9	1	Jaslo	Trendy R.
2A)	97.3	60	Plock	R. ZET	1A)	102.0	10	Gizycko	R. RMF FM
5A)	97.3	1	Zamosc	R. Eska	3)	102.0	10	Bielsk Podl.	R. Maryja
6A)	97.4	1	Katowice	R. TOK FM	5A)	102.0	1	Leszno	R. Eska
1C)	97.5	1	Lomza	R. RMF MAXXX	3)	102.3	10	Lubaczów	R. Maryja
2A)	97.5	30	Zagan	R. ZET	4)	102.4	1	Kartuzy	R. Maryja
5A)	97.7	1	Kraków	R. Eska	6D)	102.4	1	Kraków	R. Pogoda
2A)	97.8	2.5	Szczawnica	R. ZET	8)	102.4	1	Mielec	R. Leliwa
2A)	97.9	60	Walcz	R. ZET	18)	102.6	1	Elk	R. 5 Elk
1A)	98.0	10	Kalisz	R. RMF FM	1C)	102.6	1	Czestochowa	R. RMF MAXXX
22)	98.1	60	Bialystok	R. Racja	3)	102.6	10	Tarnów	R. Maryja
52)	98.1	1	Mszczonów	R. Victoria	4)	102.6	1	Bydgoszcz	R. Plus
5A)	98.1	2	Tarnów	R. Eska	4)	102.6	1	Koszalin	R. Plus
34)	98.2	1	Przemysl	R. Fara	4)	102.6	20	Polkowice	R. Plus
28)	98.3	1	Polkowice	R. Elka	37)	102.7	1	Bialystok	R. Ortodoxia
1A)	98.4	120	Gdansk	R. RMF FM	4)	102.7	5	Rabka	R. Plus
28)	98.5	1	Leszno	R. Elka	51)	102.7	1	Skierniewice	R. Niepokalanów
2A)	98.6	1	Nysa	R. ZET	2A)	102.8	10	Ostroleka	R. ZET
51)	98.6	2	Lodz	R. Niepokalanów	2A)	102.8	5	Katowice	R. ZET
2A)	98.7	10	Ilawa	R. ZET	3)	102.8	1	Chelm	R. Maryja
3)	98.8	10	Gorzów Wlkp.	R. Maryja	3)	102.8	1	Kluczbork	R. Maryja
1A)	98.9	30	Konin	R. RMF FM	4)	102.8	1	Swieradów-Zdrój	R. Plus
9)	98.9	2	Reda	R. Kaszëbë	1A)	102.9	8	Walbrzych	R. RMF FM
1B)	99.0	1	Kielce	R. RMF Classic	1C)	102.9	1	Lebork	R. RMF MaXXX

FM	MHz	kW	Location	Station
2A)	102.9	12	Przysucha	R. ZET
2C)	102.9	1	Slupca	R. ZET Gold
3)	102.9	10	Gryfice	R. Maryja
6A)	102.9	1	Kraków	R. TOK FM
44)	103.0	3	Warszawa	R. Kolor 103 FM
6B)	103.0	2	Gdansk	R. Zlote Przeboje
2A)	103.1	30	Solina	R. ZET
60)	103.1	1	Kalisz	R. Rodzina Kalisz
1A)	103.2	10	Szczawnica	R. RMF FM
41)	103.3	1	Bialystok	R. i
5A)	103.3	1	Kielce	R. Eska
1A)	103.4	5	Lebork	R. RMF FM
1A)	103.4	1	Przemysl	R. RMF FM
2A)	103.4	60	Czestochowa	R. ZET
3)	103.5	3	Trzcinsko-Zdrój	R. Maryja
52)	103.5	5	Lowicz	R. Victoria
6C)	103.5	1	Bydgoszcz	Rock R.
21)	103.6	2	Nysa	R. Nysa FM
50)	103.6	10	Lomza	R. Nadzieja
58)	103.6	30	Tarnów	R. RDN
3)	103.7	3	Katowice	R. Maryja
67)	103.7	1	Wroclaw	R. MUZO.FM
12)	103.8	10	Rzeszów	VIA - Kat. R. Rzeszów
2A)	103.8	10	Klodzko	R. ZET
6C)	103.8	1	Kraków	Rock R.
39)	103.9	2	Bialystok	R. Jard 2
45)	103.9	1.5	Ciechanów	Kat. R. Diecezji Plockiej
2A)	104.0	10	Gizycko	R. ZET
3)	104.0	10	Swiecie	R. Maryja
1C)	104.1	5	Pila	R. RMF MaXXX
2A)	104.1	60	Kraków	R. ZET
32)	104.1	1	Zyrardów	R. FAMA
2A)	104.2	10	Bialogard	R. ZET
2A)	104.2	10	Jelenia Góra	R. ZET
3)	104.2	10	Elblag	R. Maryja
4)	104.3	1	Lipiany	R. Plus
45)	104.3	1	Plock	Kat. R. Diecezji Plockiej
2A)	104.4	10	Kalisz	R. ZET
3)	104.4	1	Stalowa Wola	R. Maryja
5B)	104.4	1	Gdansk	R. VOX FM
2C)	104.5	1	Lodz	R. ZET Gold
3)	104.5	10	Wlodawa	R. Maryja
3)	104.5	5	Wielen	R. Maryja
34)	104.5	1	Krosno	R. Fara
3)	104.6	2	Opole	R. Maryja
5A)	104.6	1	Torun	R. Eska
15)	104.7	2	Sieradz	Nasze R.
1A)	104.7	3	Rabka	R. RMF FM
3)	104.7	120	Bialystok	R. Maryja
3)	104.7	10	Lobez	R. Maryja
11)	104.9	1	Chelm	Bon Ton R.
1A)	104.9	1	Koszalin	R. RMF FM
2C)	104.9	1.5	Mragowo	R. ZET Gold
5A)	104.9	10	Krosno	R. Eska
5A)	104.9	60	Wroclaw	R. Eska
67)	104.9	1	Kraków	R. MUZO.FM
2A)	105.0	120	Gdansk	R. ZET
2D)	105.0	1	Bielsko-Biala	Antyradio
3)	105.1	1	Przemysl	R. Maryja
3)	105.1	30	Konin	R. Maryja
3)	105.1	10	Elk	R. Maryja
20)	105.2	1	Zakopane	R. Alex
3)	105.2	5	Wielun	R. Maryja
2A)	105.3	60	Kielce	R. ZET
2A)	105.3	30	Koszalin	R. ZET
3)	105.3	1	Plonsk	R. Maryja
2A)	105.4	30	Siedlce	R. ZET
6C)	105.4	1	Poznan	Rock R.
7)	105.5	1	Wroclaw	R. WAWA
3)	105.6	1	Kalisz	R. Maryja
5A)	105.6	1	Pila	R. Eska
5A)	105.6	3.2	Warszawa	R. Eska
5B)	105.6	1	Gdynia	R. VOX FM
6B)	105.6	1	Miedzyzdroje	R. Zlote Przeboje
2A)	105.7	20	Olsztyn	R. ZET
7)	105.7	1	Opole	R. WAWA
14)	105.8	10	Jelenia Góra	Muzyczne R.
1A)	105.9	60	Czestochowa	R. RMF FM
46)	106.0	1	Garwolin	Katolickie R. Podlasie
1C)	106.1	5	Bydgoszcz	R. RMF MaXXX
4)	106.1	10	Kraków	R. Plus
5B)	106.1	1	Lublin	R. VOX FM
6C)	106.1	10	Wroclaw	Rock R.
2C)	106.2	1	Opole	R. ZET Gold
3)	106.2	10	Lidzbark Warm.	R. Maryja
30)	106.2	1.5	Poznan	R. Emaus
35)	106.2	1	Warszawa	R. Warszawa
6B)	106.2	1	Jelenia Góra	R. Zlote Przeboje
2A)	106.3	10	Zakopane	R. ZET
3)	106.3	60	Plock	R. Maryja
3)	106.3	10	Klodzko	R. Maryja
3)	106.3	20	Lezajsk	R. Maryja
1A)	106.4	60	Zielona Góra	R. RMF FM
26)	106.4	10	Kalisz	R. Centrum Kalisz
2D)	106.4	1	Zabrze	Antyradio
1A)	106.5	10	Elk	R. RMF FM
1C)	106.5	20	Kielce	R. RMF MAXXX
5A)	106.5	1	Lobez	R. Eska
6C)	106.6	4	Opole	Rock R.
14)	106.7	5	Swieradów-Zd.	Muzyczne R.
1A)	106.7	60	Szczecin	R. RMF FM
1C)	106.7	3	Gdynia	R. RMF MaXXX
47)	106.7	1	Bielsko-Biala	R. Bielsko
3)	106.8	120	Poznan	R. Maryja
5A)	106.8	1	Bochnia	R. Eska
5A)	106.9	10	Radom	R. Eska
2A)	107.0	40	Lublin	R. ZET
2C)	107.0	1	Gizycko	R. ZET Gold
3)	107.0	5	Czestochowa	R. Maryja
5B)	107.1	1.6	Kraków	R. VOX FM
1B)	107.1	1	Gdynia	R. RMF Classic
2A)	107.1	30	Konin	R. ZET
3)	107.2	120	Kielce	R. Maryja
59)	107.2	2	Bystrzyca Klodzka	R. Rodzina
2A)	107.3	120	Bialystok	R. ZET
1A)	107.4	10	Ilawa	R. RMF FM
2A)	107.4	30	Krosno	R. ZET
3)	107.4	2.5	Walbrzych	R. Maryja
3)	107.4	1	Koszalin	R. Maryja
5B)	107.4	1	Poznan	R. VOX FM
2A)	107.5	30	Warszawa	R. ZET
49)	107.5	1	Naklo	R. Naklo
29)	107.6	60	Katowice	R. eM
1A)	107.7	15	Zamosc	R. RMF FM
3)	107.7	10	Siedlce	R. Maryja
3)	107.7	10	Olsztyn	R. Maryja
3)	107.8	10	Tarnów	R. ZET
29)	107.9	1	Kielce	R. eM
2A)	107.9	20	Przemysl	R. ZET
3)	107.9	20	Suwalki	R. Maryja
3)	107.9	10	Ryki	R. Maryja
33)	107.9	10	Opole	R. DOXA

NB: Txs below 1kW not listed.

Addresses & other information:

1A-C) al. Waszyngtona 1, 30-204 Kraków – **2A-D)** ul. Zurawia 8, 00-503 Warszawa – **3)** ul. Zwirki i Wigury 80, 87-100 Torun – **4)** ul. Zarawia 8, 00-503 Warszawa – **5A-C)** ul. Senatorska 13/15, 00-075 Warszawa – **6A-D)** ul. Czerska 14, 00-732 Warszawa – **7)** ul. Senatorska 12, 00-082 Warszawa – **8)** ul. Wyspianskiego 5 39-400 Tarnobrzeg – **9)** ul. Dabrowskiego 14D, 84-230 Rumia – **10)** Rynek 25, 38-400 Krosno – **11)** ul. Wojslawicka 7, 22-100 Chelm – **12)** ul. Zamkowa 4, 35-032 Rzeszów – **13)** ul. Hetmana J. Zamoyskiego 1, 22-400 Zamosc – **14)** pl. Ks. K. Wyszynskiego 45, 58-500 Jelenia Góra – **15)** ul. Rynek 14, 98-200 Sieradz – **16)** pl. Pilsudskiego 27, 09-300 Zuromin – **17)** ul. Jana Pawla II 11, 20-535 Lublin – **18)** ul. Bulwarowa 5, 16-400 Suwalki – **19)** Os. Dabrówki 1b, 44-286 Wodzislaw Sl. – **20)** ul. Smrekowa 26A, 34-500 Zakopane – **21)** ul. Podolska 22, 48-300 Nysa – **22)** ul. Ciepla 1/7, 15-472 Bialystok – **23)** ul. Kilinskiego 14, 05-825 Grodzisk Mazowiecki – **24)** Generala Stefana Grota-Roweckiego 4, 24-100 Pulawy – **25)** ul. Jana Pawla II 2, 44-100 Gliwice – **26)** ul. Lazienna 6, 62-800 Kalisz – **27)** ul. Zwierzyniecka 4, 15-333 Bialystok – **28)** ul. Spóldzielcza 6, 64-100 Leszno – **29)** ul. Jordana 39, 40-953 Katowice – **30)** ul. Zielona 2, 61-851 Poznan – **31)** ul. Narutowicza 1/1, 96-500 Sochaczew – **32)** ul. Piotrkowska 12/522, 25-510 Kielce – **33)** ul. Koraszewskiego 7-9, 45-011 Opole – **34)** pl. Katedralny 4, 37-700 Przemysl – **35)** ul. Florianska 3, 03-707 Warszawa – **36)** al. Najswietszej Marii Panny 54, 42-200 Czestochowa – **37)** ul. Antoniuk Fabryczny 13, 15-762 Bialystok – **38)** ul. Biskupa Dominika 11, 83-130 Pelplin – **39)** ul. Rzemieslnicza 4A, 15-703 Bialystok – **40)** ul. O. Augustyna Kordeckiego 2, 42-225 Czestochowa – **41)** ul. Ks. A.Abramowicza 1a, 15-872 Bialystok – **42)** ul. Jana Pawla II 1B, 89-804 Chojnice – **43)** ul. Janusza Korczaka 2, 78-100 Kolobrzeg – **44)** ul. Narbutta 41/43, 02-536 Warszawa – **45)** ul. Ks.Piotra Sciegiennego 18, 06-400 Ciechanów – **46)** ul. Pilsudskiego 62, 08-110 Siedlce – **47)** ul. Olszówka 62, 43-309 Bielsko-Biala – **48)** ul. Batorego 5, 47-400 Raciborz – **49)** ul. Mickiewicza 3, 89-100 Naklo nad Notecia – **50)** ul. Sadowa 3, 18-400 Lomza – **51)** ul. Zakroczymska 1, 00-225 Warszawa – **52)** ul. Seminaryjna 6A, 99-400 Lowicz – **53)** ul. Pilsudskiego 141, 92-318 Lódz – **54)** ul. Piastowska 1, 47-200 Kedzierzyn-Kozle – **55)** ul. Pilsudskiego 12, 43-100 Tychy – **56)** ul.

Bokserska 1, 02-682 Warszawa – **57)** ul. Kanafojskiego 1/14, 10-724 Olsztyn – **58)** ul. Bema 14, 33-100 Tarnów – **59)** ul. Katedralna 13, 50-328 Wroclaw – **60)** ul. Zlota 144, 62-810 Kalisz – **61)** ul. Wita Stwosza 2/4, 96-100 Skierniewice – **62)** ul. Jankowy 55, 63-600 Kepno – **63)** ul. Sw. Jana Chrzciciela 14, 43-346 Bielsko-Biala – **64)** ul. Jana Pawla II 2, 44-100 Gliwice – **65)** ul.Wilsona 6, 42-200 Czestochowa – **66)** Park Hutniczy 3-5, 41-800 Zabrze – **67)** ul. Ostrobramska 77, 04-175 Warszawa – **68)** ul. Fatimska 13a, 31-831 Kraków. Some stns may have own prgrs at times: **68A)** al. Pilsudskiego 10, 22-200 Wlodawa **E:** tr_wlodawa@wp.pl **68B)** ul. Ilzecka 6a, 27-300 Lipsko **E:** radio@lipsko.eu **68C)** ul. Cmolas 212a, 36-105 Cmolas **E:** radiocmolas@o2.pl **68D)** ul. Czarnieckiego 16, 37-500 Jaroslaw **68E)** ul. Mickiewicza 2a, 24-100 Pulawy **E:** radiopulawy@wp.pl **68F)** ul. Krakowska 74, 34-120 Andrychów **E:** radio@andrychow.eu **68G)** 76-200 Slupsk.

DAB Transmitters (DAB+)
Tx Operator: EmiTel **M:** PR1-4, PR24, PR Rytm, PR R. Poland, PR R. Chopin, PR R. Dzieciom, PR Regional stns

Block	MHz	kW	Location
5B	176.640	2	Bialystok (Krynice)
5C	178.352	10	Lódz
6B	183.650	6	Warszawa (PKiN)
10A	209.936	-	SFN (Katowice, Kielce)
10B	211.648	-	SFN (Lublin)
10C	213.360	5.5	Olsztyn (Pieczewo)
10D	215.072	10	Gdansk (Chwaszczyno)
11A	216.928	-	SFN (Krosno, Rzeszów)
11A	216.928	20	Szczecin (Kolowo)
11C	220.352	-	SFN (Bydgoszcz, Torun)
11C	220.352	-	SFN (Opole)
12A	223.936	-	SFN (Poznan)
12B	225.648	10	Wroclaw (Zórawina)
12C	223.936	-	SFN (Zielona Góra)
12D	229.072	-	SFN (Kolobrzeg, Koszalin)
12D	229.072	10	Kraków (Choragwica)

PORTUGAL

L.T: UTC (27 Mar-30 Oct: +1h) — **Pop:** 10.5 million — **Pr.L:** Portuguese — **E.C:** 50Hz, 220V — **ITU:** POR

ANACOM – Autoridade Nacional de Comunicações.
HQ: Avenida José Malhoa, 12, 1099-017 Lisboa ☎+351 21 721 10 00 +351 21 721 10 01 **W:** anacom.pt **E:** info@anacom.pt
Gov. body responsible for licensing & monitoring radio & TV txs

APR – Associação Portuguesa de Radiodifusão (Assoc. of Portuguese Broadcasters)
Avenida Defensores de Chaves, n.º 65 - 3º 1000-113 Lisboa ☎+351 213 015 453/+351 213 015 459/ +351 213 016 999 +351 21 301 65 36 **W:** apradiodifusao.pt **E:** apr@apradiofusao.pt

RTP-Rádio e Televisão de Portugal, SGPS (Pub)
Av. Marechal Gomes da Costa, 37, 1849-030 Lisboa ☎ +351 21 382 00 00 +351 21 382 00 98 **W:** rtp.pt **E:** info@rtp.pt **LP:** Chmn: Gonçalo Reis

Antena 1/Antena 2/Antena 3/RDP Africa/RDP Açores/RDP Madeira/RDP Internacional: ☎ +351 21 382 00 00. Antena 1 +351-21-382 00 70 +351-21-382 00 05, Antena 2 ☎+351-21-382 02 82 +351-21-382 01 99, Antena 3 +351-21-382 02 02 ☎ +351-21-382 00 17, RDP África ☎ +351-21-382 02 12 +351 21 382 00 81.
News Dept: ☎ +351 21 382 00 02 +351-21 382 01 83
LP: Chmn. bd of Dirs: Alberto da Ponte, Dir. of Antena 1/2/3:Rui Fernandes Pêgo, Dir. of RDP África: Jorge Oliveira Gonçalves, Reg. Dir (RDP Norte, Porto): José Alberto Lemos, Reg. Dir (RDP Centro, Coimbra): José Manuel Portugal, Reg. Dir (RDP Sul, Faro): Feliciano Estêvão, Reg. Dir. Açores & Madeira: see respective country entries, Dir. RDPi: Jorge Oliveira Gonçalves. Technical info. & support may be obtained from **E:** gabinete.tecnologias@rtp.pt
Ann: "Antena 1, a rádio que liga Portugal", "Antena 2, a rádio clássica", "Antena 3, a primeira vez é sempre na Três"

MW Antena 1	kHz	kW	MW Antena 1	kHz	kW
Miranda do Douro	630	2	Elvas	720	10
Montemor-o Velho	630	10	Faro	720	10
Bragança	666	2	Guarda	720	10
Castanheira do Ribatejo*	666	10	Miramar (Porto) ‡	720	10
Covilhã	666	10	Castelo Branco	720	10
Valença	666	10	Mirandela	720	10
Vila Real	666	10	Lamego	756	2
Viseu	666	10	Portalegre	1287	2

*) north of Lisbon; also known as "CEN" (Centro Emissor Nacional)

FM (MHz)	Ant. 1	Ant. 2	Ant. 3	kW
Alcoutim	88.9	91.5	101.9	0.2
Arestal (Aveiro)	106.7	95.2		0.5
Bornes (Bragança)	92.8	91.1	102.1	10
Braga (Sameiro)	91.3	88.0	103.0	10/2/10
Bragança	96.4	98.2	104.2	9
Castelo Branco	89.9	94.9	104.3	0.5
Coimbra C (a)	94.9			4
Elvas (Vª Boim)	103.8	93.2	101.6	5.4
Faro (S.Miguel) (b)	97.6	93.4	100.7	10
Gardunha	96.4	93.9	101.3	10
Grândola	99.2	90.6	103.6	10
Gravia (S. Pº do Sul)	104.5	106.8	107.9	0.1
Guarda	94.7	88.4	100.6	6.4
Janas (Sintra)	96.9	96.0	103.8	0.2
Leiria	98.7	104.2	106.4	1
Lisboa (Banática)	99.4	88.9	100.0	1/0.3/0.3
Lisboa (Monsanto)	95.7	94.4	100.3	36/36/32
Lousã	87.9	89.3	102.2	34/34/39
Manteigas	104.8	91.6	100.3	0.5
Marão (Vila Real)	95.2	99.8	101.5	9
Marofa §	97.2	93.4	104.6	20/20/10
Mendro	87.7	91.1	102.4	20/20/44
Mértola	90.9	92.2	100.1	0.4
Minhéu (V. P. Aguiar)*	94.9	88.0	104.7	10
Miranda do Douro	90.3	95.7	98.9	0.05
Moledo	102.9	88.0	92.3	0.5
Monchique (Fóia)	88.9	91.5	101.9	25
Montargil	93.6	99.6	105.0	3
Montejunto	98.3	88.7	105.2	10
Muro	88.3	94.6	102.0	10
Paredes de Coura	102.9		92.3	0.1
Pte. de Lima (Rendufe)	89.2	92.2	104.9	0.3
Portalegre	97.9	92.9	102.8	10
Porto (Mte. da Virgem)	96.7	92.5	100.4	44/44/50
Santarém	98.8			0.4
S. Domingos	87.9	89.3	103.7	0.2
Serra de Ossa	88.4	95.0	102.1	2/0.5/0.5
Tróia (Setúbal)	106.7	99.7	107.9	0.07
Valença	98.2	89.6	104.0	10
Viseu	88.2	97.5	101.8	0.5/0.5/0.7

* District of Vila Real; § District of Guarda

RDP África: a) 103.4MHz 1kW, **b)** 99.1MHz 1kW, **c)** 101.5MHz 4kW
D.Prgrs: 24h **Ant. 1**=Antena 1 (general pt rgrs, sport), **Ant. 2**=Antena 2 (serious music, culture), **Ant. 3**=Antena 3 (pop/rock music), **RDP Africa** (general prgrs aimed at the Portuguese-speaking African community
RDP Reg. Centres: N=RDP Norte: Rua Cândido dos Reis, 74, 4050-151 Porto ☎+351 22 339 99 00 +351 22 339 99 02. Dir. José Alberto Lemos. **C**=RDP Centro: Rua Dr. José Alberto Reis, 74, 3000-232 Coimbra ☎+351 23 979 89 00 +351 239 72 42 53 Dir. José Manuel Portugal **E:** rdpcentro@rdp.pt **S**=RDP Sul: Campo Senhora da Saúde, 8001-904 Faro +351 289 89 68 69 +351 289 80 21 92 **E:** rdpsul@rdp.pt Dir. Feliciano Estêvão
RDP abroad: txs in Cape Verde, Guinea-Bissau, São Tomé & Príncipe, Mozambique, all relaying RDP África, in Timor, relaying RDPi and airing a local prgr, and in Bosnia for the Portuguese peace-keeping force: this tx operated by the military (see respective country entries).
RDP África: Av. Marechal Gomes da Costa, 37, 1849-030 Lisboa ☎ +351 21 382 00 00 +351 21 382 00 81 **LP:** Dir: Jorge Oliveira Gonçalves **E:** rdpafrica@rtp.pt

Web Radio: Audio feeds at **W:** rtp.pt Antenas 1, 2 & 3 and RDP-África, RDP-Madeira and RDP-Açores. RTP web-only radios: 16 stns selectable at **W:** rtp.pt/play
SATELLITE: Europe, N. Africa & Mid. East: Hot Bird 13B (13° E), Transponder 111 (10.723GHz), Ku Band, H. Pol., FEC: ¾, SyR: 29.9 Ms/s, RDPi: PID 1230 (stereo), SID 4630. RDP Ant. 1: PID 1235, SID 4635, 24h. **Africa:** Intelsat 907 (27.5° W), Transponder 22/22, C Band, Right Circ. Pol., Symbol Rate 7.234 kSps. Freq. 3838 MHz; prgrs: RDP África: audio PID d 412, RDPi: audio PID d 413, Ant. 1: audio PID d 411. **Asia & Oceania:** Asiasat 5 (digital) (100.5°E), "European Bouquet", Transponder 10H (4GHz), C Band, Horiz. Pol. on 28.125 Ms/s, FEC ¾. RDP Int. stereo on the audio ch. 267, RDP Ant. 1 aired on the audio ch. 705. **N.America & Hawaii:** Galaxy 19 (digital) (97° W), Transponder 20, Frequency 12059.5 MHz, Ku Band, H. Pol., SyR 22.000 Ms/s, FEC ¾. RDP Int. audio PID: 4001 (stereo). **The Americas:** Intelsat 805 (55.5° W), DVB-S2 standard, Transponder 16 (4100.6 MHz), C Band, V. Pol., SyR 2.3196 Ms/s, FEC 8/9. RDP Int.: PID 413. **S.America:** Telstar 14 / Estrela do Sul 2 (63°W), transponder 13, 11710MHz, ku Band, Vert. Pol., Sy.Rate 3200, FEC 2/3. RDP Int.: PID 268.

DAB: RDP halted T-DAB broadcasts in June 2011. The network may be restored but there are no current plans to reactivate this service.

RÁDIO COMERCIAL, S.A. (Priv., comm.)
Owned by Media Capital Rádio – Radiofonia e Publicidade, S.A. **W:** http://mcr.clix.pt/index.asp
⌨ Rua Sampaio e Pina, 24-26, 1099-044 Lisboa ☎ +351 21 382 15 00 🖷 +351 21 382 15 89 **E:** info@radiocomercial.clix.pt, Northern office: Rua Tenente Valadim, 181, 4100 Porto ☎ +351 22 605 75 00 **W:** radiocomercial.clix.pt **LP:** Dir. Gen. MCR Rádios: Jordi Jordà

MW	kHz	kW	MW	kHz	kW
Avanca	#783	100	Cª. das Lezírias (Benavente)‡1035		*10

#) currently inactive but possibly to be reactivated. ‡) inactive *)
Nominal power **D.Prgr**: 24h

FM	MHz	kW	FM	MHz	kW
Fóia (Monchique)	88.1	10	Grândola	96.8	10
Lamego	88.7	10	Monsanto (Lisboa)	97.4	44
Minhéu (Vila Real)	88.9	10	Monte da Virgem (Porto)	97.7	44
Esposende	89.3	0.4	Gardunha	98.2	10
Lousã	90.8	44	Sintra	98.5	0.3
Bornes	91.9	10	Portalegre	98.9	10
Mendro	92.0	50	Valença	99.0	10
Bragança	93.9	10	Braga	99.2	10
Viseu	94.3	0.5	Montejunto	99.8	10
Mértola	95.8	0.4	Pico da Pena (Vouzela)	103.1	0.2
Guarda	96.1	10	Vila Boim (Elvas)	105.9	1
São Miguel (Faro)	96.1	10			

D.Prgr: 24h **Ann on FM:** Rádio Comercial. **Format:** music stn
Local FM stns in the same group:
M80: (see Southern network) – **Cidade (W:** cidadefm.clix.pt): txs in Lisboa 91.6MHz 5kW, Vila Nova de Gaia (Monte da Virgem, near Porto) 107.2MHz 0.5kW, Redondo (Alentejo province) 97.2MHz 0.5kW, Alcanena (Santarém) 99.3MHz 2kW, Penacova (Coimbra) & Loulé (Algarve province), 99.7MHz 1 / 2kW, Vale de Cambra (near Aveiro) 101.0 MHz 0.5kW, Viseu 102.8 MHz 2kW, Amares (Braga) 104.4MHz 1 kW, Montijo (Lisboa region) 106.2MHz 1kW – **Smooth FM (W:** smoothfm.clix.pt): txs in Lisboa 96.6 MHz 5kW, Barreiro (Lisboa region) 103.0MHz 2kW, Matosinhos (near Porto) 89.5MHz 1.5kW, Figueiró dos Vinhos (near Coimbra) 92.8MHz 1kW & Santarém 97.7MHz 2kW, – **Vodafone FM (W:** vodafone.fm): txs in Amadora (Lisboa reg.) 107.2MHz 1.5kW, Moita (near Lisboa) 101.1MHz 1.5kW, Maia (near Porto) 94.3MHz 1.5kW & Cantanhede (near Coimbra) 103.0MHz 2 kW – **MFM:** tx in Barreiro (Lisboa reg.) 96.2MHz 2kW

RÁDIO RENASCENÇA – Emissora Católica Portuguesa (Rlg/ Comm)
⌨ Rua Ivens, 14, 1249-108 Lisboa ☎ +351 21 323 92 00 🖷 +351 21 323 92 20 **E:** mail@rr.pt **PR**: **E:** rp@rr.pt **W:** rr.pt and rfm.pt and radiosim.pt
L.P: News Dir.: Drª Graça Franco, PD (R. Renascença): Dr Nelson Ribeiro, PD (RFM): Dr. António Mendes, PD (Rádio Sim): Dina Isabel

MW: Rádio Sim	kHz	kW	MW: Rádio Sim	kHz	kW
Braga ‡	576	10	Coimbra#	981	3
Muge §‡	594	1	Guarda‡	981	1
Vilamoura#	891	2.5	Chaves	1251	1
Évora ‡	927	1	Valongo ‡	1251	10
Seixal*	963	1	Castelo Branco	1251	1
Bragança‡	981	1	Viseu ‡	1251	10
Vila Real‡	981	1			

§ main tx: 100kW nominal (usually 60-80kW); 2x10kW stand by units
* 1x10 kW main tx; 1x1kW standby unit. R. Sim has been broadcasting the latter (spare tx). ‡ inactive *10 kW nominal

FM (MHz)	RR	RFM	R. Sim	kW
Aveiro	102.5	97.4		0.2
Arrábida	105.8	89.9		10/12
Bornes	89.6	101.1		10
Braga		89.7	101.1	1/10
Bragança	105.7	99.5		10
Elvas			102.3	0.1
Elvas/V.ª Boim		107.1	99.8	1
Fóia (Monchique)	98.6	104.9		12
Gardunha	103.4	99.5		10
Guarda	90.2	104.0		10
Lamego	98.6	106.2		12
Leiria		107.7	95.1	3/2
Lisboa	103.4	93.2		50
Lousã	106.0	91.7		50/56
Marofa	94.2	103.0		16/10
Mendro	96.5	100.9		50
Minhéu	89.8	102.6		10
Monte da Virgem	93.7	104.1		10
Montejunto	90.2	106.8		10
Muro	103.4	90.4		10/20

FM (MHz)	RR	RFM	R. Sim	kW
Pena (Vouzela)	93.8	95.0		0.4
Penafiel	90.2	102.5		1
S. Mamede	95.3	101.1		10
São Miguel	103.8	89.6		10
Serra de Ossa	98.5	89.7		2
Sintra	105.0	106.6		0.3
Valença	100.0	95.4		10
Valongo	104.5	106.2		0.4/1
Viseu	103.6	99.4		1

D.Prgr.: 24h. **Ann:** "Renascença - música e informação dia-a-dia.", "RFM - só grandes músicas"
Some prgs are simulcast on RR Canal 1 & R. Sim
Local FM stns of the R. Renascença group: Mega Hits (W: mega. fm): txs in Lisboa 92.4MHz 5kW, Sintra (west of Lisboa) 88.0MHz 1 kW, Coimbra 90.0MHz 5kW, Aveiro 96.5 MHz 2kW, Gondomar (Porto region) 90.6MHz 2kW and Braga 92.9 MHz 2kW
Local FM stns relaying Rádio Sim: R. Sim Pal - Palmela (near Lisboa): 102.2 MHz 2kW; **R. Sim Porto**- Maia (near Porto): tx in Valongo 100.8MHz 1.5kW; **R. Sim Rio Maior** - Rio Maior (near Santarém): 92.6MHz 1kW, 99.5MHz 0.050kW; **R.Sim NoAr** - Viseu: 106.4 MHz 2kW; **R. Sim Alentejo** – Portel (near Évora): 97.5 MHz 0.5kW

Regional FM networks:
Northern network
RÁDIO NOTÍCIAS, PRODUÇÕES E PUBLICIDADE, S.A.
⌨ Edifício "Alteio", Rua 3 da Matinha. 3º piso, sala 301, 1900-823 Lisboa ☎ +351 21 861 25 00 🖷 +351 21 861 25 07/8 **LP:** Chmn.: Joaquim Oliveira, TD: Jaime Silva, Dir tx network: José de Sousa TSF Northern office & Radiopress HQ: ⌨ Rua Gonçalo Cristóvão, 195, 4017-001 Porto ☎ +351 22 206 28 00 🖷 +351 22 206 28 03
E: tsf@tsf.pt **W:** tsf.pt
Station: TSF (priv., comm.)

FM	MHz	kW	FM	MHz	kW
Pena (Vouzela)	102.5	0.1	Guarda	106.6	10
Bornes	103.2	10	Minhéu	106.7	10
Gardunha	105.1	10	Braga	106.9	10
Valongo (Porto)	105.3	50	Bragança	107.0	10
Marofa	105.4	10	Lousã	107.4	50
Valença	105.7	10	Marão	107.6	10
Muro	106.5	10			

NB: the whole netw. relays key stn TSF 89.5MHz 5kW Lisboa . TSF broadcasts 24 hours/ day via **R. Jovem** 105.4MHz 2kW Évora , **R. Santa Maria** 101.6MHz 2kW Faro (Algarve) and **R. Caldas** 103.1 MHz 1kW Caldas da Rainha; in the Açores via **R. Comercial dos Açores-TSF** 99.4MHz 3kW Ponta Delgada (São Miguel isl.) and in Madeira via **R. Notícias-TSF** 100.0MHz 2kW Funchal.
Format: mainly news. **D.Prgr.:** 24h

Southern network
LICENSEE: RÁDIO REGIONAL DE LISBOA, S.A.
(Owned by Média Capital Rádio) ⌨ see R.Comercial **W:** m80.clix.pt
Station: M80 Rádio (priv., comm.)

FM	MHz	kW	FM	MHz	kW
Bragança# (Nogueira)	89.2	1	Coimbra #	98.4	5
Bragança#	90.0	0.05	Fafe #	103.8	1
Porto #	90.0	5	Monsanto (Lisboa)	104.3	50
Leiria#	93.0	2	Manteigas#	104.4	0.5
Mogadouro#	93.1	1	Valongo#	105.8	1.5
Aveiro#	94.4	2	São Miguel (Faro)	106.1	10
Penalva do Castelo#	95.6	0.5	Mendro	106.4	50
Montejunto	96.4	10	Portalegre	106.7	10
Sabugal#	96.8	0.5	Fóia (Monchique)	107.1	10
Vila Real #	97.4	1	Grândola	107.5	10

) txs of associated local stns. **Format:** music oldies from 1970s-90s.
N: every h on the h. **D.Prgr:** 24h **Ann:** "M80 Rádio"

Other networks:

Rádio 5FM (Priv., comm.)
⌨ Avenida Visconde de Barreiros, 89, 5º, 4470-151 Maia ☎+351 229 439 380 **E:** geral@radio5.pt **W:** radio5.pt
FM: txs in Póvoa de Varzim 89.0 MHz 2kW & Monte da Virgem (V. N. Gaia) 88.4 MHz 1kW **D.Prgr:** 24h
Associated local VHF-FM stns relaying Rádio 5:
R. Voz de Santo Tirso (Santo Tirso): 88.6 MHz 0.4kW Santo Tirso & **R. No Ar (Trofa)**: 107.8 MHz 1kW. All txs are located near Porto

Rádio Meo Music (Priv., comm.)
⌨ Rua Viriato nº25, 4º/6º-1050-234 Lisboa ☎+351 210 105 765 🖷+351 210 105 769 **W:** radiomeomusic.meo.pt **E:** geral@radiomeomusic.pt

FM: Almada (near Lisboa) 100.8 MHz 2kW & Monte da Virgem (Porto) 102.7 MHz 2kW **D.Prgr:** 24h **Format:** pop/dance music stn

Rádio Nostalgia (Priv., comm.)
✆ Rua Viriato nº 25 , 4º Dtº- 1050-234 Lisboa ☎+351 210 105 765 **W:** nostalgia.pt
FM: Lisboa 90.4 MHz 5kW & Porto 91.0 MHz 1.5kW **D.Prgr:** 24h **Format:** music oldies (1960s-1980s)

Rádio Amália (Priv., comm.)
✆ Rua Viriato nº 25 , 3º Esqº- 1050-234 Lisboa ☎+351 210 105 740 🖷+351 210 105 769 **W:** amalia.fm **E:** geral@amalia.fm
FM: Loures (near Lisboa) 92.0 MHz 2kW & Setúbal 100.6 MHz 2 kW **D.Prgr:** 24h **Format:** Portuguese music (Fado)

Rádio Nova Era (Priv., comm.)
✆ Rua das Camélias, 134 B, 4430-038 Vila Nova de Gaia ☎+351 223 770 180🖷+351 223 759 675 **W:** radionovaera.pt **E:** geral@radionovaera.pt
FM: Monte da Virgem (V. N. Gaia) 101.3 MHz 2kW & Paredes 100.1 MHz 2 kW (both near Porto) **D.Prgr:** 24h **Format:** dance music

Rádio Dom Bosco (Priv., comm.)
✆ Vilarinho da Tanha, 5000-011 Abaças - Vila Real ☎+351 254 905 108/+351 967 453 017
☎+351 223 770 180🖷+351 223 759 675 **W:** radiodombosco.pt **E:** radiodombosco@sapo.pt
FM: Lamego 94.1MHz 2kW & Trancoso 92.1 MHz 1 kW (near Guarda) **D.Prgr:** 24h **Format:** generalist station

Rádio NFM (Priv., comm.)
✆ NFM Global, Lda., Rua do Salgueirô, 69, 4585-208 Gandra PRD ☎+351 224 155 350 🖷+351 224 155 359 **E:** geral@nfm.pt **W:** radio.nfm.pt **FM:** 89.2 MHz 2 kW Amarante (near Porto), Bombarral 94.8 MHz 1kW & Ponte de Sor (near Portalegre) 96.0 MHz 2kW + 105.6 MHz 0.050kW. All frequencies carry also local prgs. **D.Prgr:** 24h

Local Stations (all priv. & comm.)
Radio Altitude
✆ Rua Batalha Reis, 6300-668 Guarda +351 271 22 19 95 🖷 +351 271 22 14 92 **E:** altitude@altitude.fm **W:** altitude.fm **LP:** Dir: Rui Isidro
MW: ‡1584kHz 1kW 24h (inactive, but planned to be reactivated)
FM: 90.9MHz 2kW 24h **Ann:** "Altitude FM"

Rádio Elvas
✆ Rua dos Chilões, n.º 1 R/C 7350-078 Elvas ☎+351 268 62 20 44 🖷 +351 268 62 20 46 **E:** radioelvas@radioelvas.com **W:** radioelvas.com
FM: 91.5 MHz 0.5kW Vila Boim (Elvas), 103.0 MHz 0.05kW São Vicente (Elvas), 104.3 MHz 0.05kW Elvas **D.Prgr:** 24h
Associated local VHF-FM stns relaying Rádio Elvas: R. Nova Antena (Montemor-o-Novo): 101.3 MHz 2kW (**W:** radionovaantena.com); **Rádio Campo Maior**: 95.9 MHz 0.5kW Campo Maior (near Elvas; **W:** radiocampomaior.com)

Other FM stations:

FM	MHz	kW	Station, location
50)	88.2	2	Ultra FM, Vila Franca de Xira
38)	88.6	2	R. Jornal de Setúbal, Setúbal: (effective 0.05kW)
51)	89.1	2	R. Lezíria, Vila Franca de Xira
1)	89.7	2	R. Antena Livre, Abrantes
46)	90.5	2	R. Cidade de Tomar, Tomar
47)	90.8	2	R. Geice, Viana do Castelo
9)	91.4	2	R. Iris FM, Benavente
39)	91.8	2	Algarve FM, Silves
30)	91.8	2	R. Clube de Penafiel, Penafiel
6)	91.9	2	R. Local de Barcelos, Barcelos
12)	92.0	2	R. Beira Interior, Castelo Branco
19)	92.1	2	R. Maiorca, Figueira da Foz
5)	92.7	2	ERA FM-Emissora Reg. de Amarante, Amarante
28)	92.8	2	Horizonte Tejo, Bobadela
3)	93.9	2	R. Mirasado, Alcácer do Sal (frequently inactive)
53)	94.0	2	R. Cidade Hoje, Vila Nova de Famalicão
25)	94.0	2	R. 94 FM, Leiria
16)	94.1	2	Diana FM, Évora
15)	94.5	2	R. Despertar, Estremoz
14)	94.7	2	Voz do Sorraia, Coruche
32)	94.8	5	R. Festival, Porto
44)	94.8	2	R. Gilão, Tavira
54)	95.5	2	R. Placard, Vila Nova de Gaia
21)	95.8	2	R. Fundação, Guimarães
34)	96.1	2	R. Onda Viva, Póvoa de Varzim
43)	96.9	2	R. Horizonte-Algarve, Tavira

FM	MHz	kW	Station, location
23)	97.0	2	R. Clube de Lamego, Lamego
4)	97.8	2	Radar, Almada
22)	98.0	2	R. Santiago, Guimarães
45)	98.0	2	R. Hertz, Tomar
11)	98.1	3	R. Marginal, Cascais
48)	98.4	2	R. XL FM, Vila do Conde
33)	98.9	5	R. Nova, Porto
37)	98.9	2	R. Azul, Setúbal: (effective power 0.25kW)
18)	99.1	2	R. Foz do Mondego, Figueira da Foz
2)	99.3	2	R. Soberania, Águeda
31)	100.5	2	R. Portalegre, Portalegre
24)	101.3	2	R. Liz, Leiria
7)	101.4	2	R. Pax, Beja
35)	101.7	2	R. Pernes, Santarém
27)	101.9	2	Estação Orbital, Loures (Sacavém)
36)	102.7	2	Antena Miróbriga, Santiago do Cacém
26)	103.1	2	Total FM, Loulé
17)	103.2	2	R. Telefonia do Alentejo, Évora
29)	103.7	2	R. Canção Nova, Ourém
8)	104.5	2	R. Voz da Planície, Beja
49)	104.6	2	R. Linear, Vila do Conde
52)	105.0	2	Digital FM, Vila Nova de Famalicão
55)	105.5	2	RCI-R. Clube do Interior, Viseu
20)	105.8	2	R. "F", Guarda
10)	106.0	2	R. Antena Minho, Braga
13)	107.9	2	R. Universidade de Coimbra, Coimbra

Some stns use 0.05kW repeaters + over 200 stns of less than 2kW

Addresses and other information:
Many stns have websites and may also have webcasting; most, if not all, have an email address. Add country code to tel. & fax nos
1) Rua General Humberto Delgado, Edifício Mira Rio cv, 2200-125 Abrantes ☎ 241 360170/1 🖷 241 360179 **E:** geral@antenalivre.pt **W:** antenalivre.pt – **2)** Rua José Sucena, 120-3º, 3750-157 Águeda ☎ 234 602133 🖷 241-624334 **W:** soberaniafm.com – **3)** Rua da Fábrica, Convento dos Frades, 7580-122 Alcácer do Sal ☎ 265 622981 🖷 265 622479 – **4)** Rua Viriato, 25-6.º D, S.Sebastião da Pedreira, 1050-234 Lisboa ☎ 21 0105790 / 21 0105769 **E:** geral@radarlisboa.fm **W:** radarlisboa.fm – **5)** Edifício de Sta. Luzia, Apartado 64, 4600-035 São Gonçalo, Amarante, ☎ 255 420480/9 🖷 255 425 405 **W:** erafm927.com **E:** geral@erafm927.com, info@erafm927.com – **6)** Centro Comercial Bolívar, lojas 45-49 / Apartado 129, 4750-180 Barcelos ☎ 253 823530 /1 🖷 253 181265 **E:** geral@radiobarcelos.com **W:** radiobarcelos.com.pt – **7)** Rua de Angola, Torre C-1º, 7800-468 Beja ☎ 284 325 011 🖷 284 326312 **E:** radio@radiopax.com, antonio-lucio@radiopax.com **W:** radiopax.com – **8)** Rua da Misericórdia, 4 / Apartado 368, 7800-285 Beja ☎ 284 311 330 🖷 284 321446 **E:** radio@vozdaplanicie.pt **W:** vozdaplanicie.pt – **9)** Rua dos Operários Agrícolas, 5B, 2135-322 Samora Correia, ☎ 263 650 730 🖷 263 650 739 **E:** director@irisfm.pt, informacao@irisfm.pt **W:** irisfm.pt – **10)** Praceta Escola do Magistério, 36, 4700-222 Braga ☎ 253 309560 🖷 253 309569 **E:** armindo.veloso@antena-minho.pt, antena-minho.pt **W:** antena-minho.pt – **11)** Rua Viriato nº 25 4ºE -105-234 Lisboa ☎21 0105742/63 🖷21 0105769 **E:** geral@marginal.fm **W:** marginal.fm – **12)** Avº 1º de Maio, 39, 3º Dtº / Apartado 178, 6000-909 Castelo Branco ☎ 272 321 050 🖷 272 320 488 **E:** radio.interior@netvisao.pt **W:** radiobeirainterior.radios.pt – **13)** Apartado 1178, 3001-501 Coimbra ☎ 239 851 058 🖷239 835 446 **E:** geral@ruc.pt, tecnica@ruc.pt **W:** ruc.pt – **14)** Rua do Couço, 29-r/c frt, 2100-169 Coruche ☎ 243 617436 & 243 617 100 🖷 243 617100 **E:** radiovozsorraia@sapo.pt,rvsinformacao@gmail.com **W:** radiovozsorraia.blogspot.com – **15)** Rua Bento de Jesus Caraça, Bloco C 1º Andar - Apartado 76 , 7100-104 Estremoz ☎ 268 339454 🖷 268 339456 **E:** radiodespertar.net **W:** radiodespertar.net – **16)** MARÉ, EE08, 7000-500 Évora ☎ 266 700333 🖷 266 700555 **E:** geral@dianafm.com **W:** dianafm.com – **17)** Estrada de Arraiolos - Edifício Diário do Sul, 7000 Évora ☎ 266 730415 🖷 266 730411 **E:** administracao@diariodosul.com.pt, telefonia@diariodosul.com **W:** imprensaregional.com.pt/diariodosul – **18)** Rua Detrás da Alfândega n.º 1-A ☎ 233 040620 🖷 233 428134 **E:** fozdomondego.secretariado@gmail.com **W:** rcfm.web.pt – **19)** Rua Poeta João de Lemos, 6, 3080-476 Maiorca ☎233930500 🖷233 930 499 ☎ 233 930 500 🖷 233 930499– **20)** Rua Soeiro Viegas, 2-B, 6300-758 Guarda ☎ 271 221468 🖷 271 221482 **E:** radiof@radiof.com **W:** radiof.com – **21)** Rua Arqueólogo Mário Cardozo, Ed. Guimarães Palace 411, Apartado 358, 4800-116 Guimarães ☎ 253 420520/2/5/6 🖷 253 420509 **E:** geral@radiofundacao.net **W:** radiofundacao.net – **22)** Edifício Santiago, Rua Dr. José Sampaio, 264, Apartado 485, 4810-275 Guimarães ☎ 253 421700 🖷 253 421709 **E:** santiago@guimaraesdigital.com, info@guimaraes-digital.com **W:** santiago.fm – **23)** Urbanização da Urtigosa, Bloco 6 - R/C, 5100-183 Lamego ☎ 254 609300/1 🖷 254 609309 **E:** geral@rclamego.pt **W:** rclamego.pt – **24)** Urbanização Quinta do Amparo, lote

4, R/C – Esq. /Quinta da Matinha / Apartado 525, 2415-583 Leiria ☎ 244 817 707 🖷 244 813951 E: radio@lizfm.pt W: lizfm.pt – 25) Av. dos Combatentes da Grande Guerra, Edifício Liz – 10º / Apartado 1113, 2400-122 Leiria ☎ 244 860090/4 🖷 244 860098 E: geral@radio94fm. pt W: radio94fm.pt – 26) Sítio do Troto, 8135-030 Almancil ☎ 289 396 065🖷 289 397110 E: 103.1@totalfm.pt W: totalfm.pt – 27) Travessa do Olival, 6, 2685-086 Sacavém ☎ 21 9401019 & 21 9427750 🖷 21 9427757 E: orbital@orbital.pt W: orbital.pt – 28) Rua da Boa Vista, N.º 2-B, 2685-027 Bobadela Loures ☎ 21 9559215 & 21 9553113 /219 🖷 21 9558465 W: horizontefm.pt – 29) Estrada da Batalha, 68, Edifício Canção Nova/ Apartado 199, 2495-405 Fátima ☎249 530600/3 🖷249 530609 E: direcaoradio@cancaonova.pt W: radio.cancaonova.pt – 30) Rua Alfredo Pereira, 14-2º / Apartado 14, 4564-909 Penafiel ☎ 255 710040 🖷 255 710049 E: info.mail@radioclube-penafiel.net W: radioclu-be-penafiel.pt – 31) Av. de Santo António, 22 , Edifício Régio 1, Atelier "A" e "B" /Apartado 154, 7300-074 Portalegre ☎ 245 300550 🖷 245 331630 E: geral@radioportalegre.pt W: radioportalegre.pt – 32) Rua da Alegria, 582 - 9 esqº, 4000-037 Porto ☎22 5370177 & 22 5101008 E: geral@radiofestival.pt W: radiofestival.pt – 33) Praça Coronel Pacheco, 2, 4050 - 453 Porto ☎ 226 151 000🖷 22 6151001 E: nova@radionova. fm W: radionova.fm – 34) Praça dos Combatentes, 15, 4990-439 Póvoa de Varzim ☎ 252 613686/888/878 & 252 299 570 🖷252 613898 E: radioondaviva@sapo.pt and geral@radioondaviva.pt W: radioondaviva. pt – 35) Rua Rádio Pernes, 1 / Apartado 22, 2001-701 Pernes & Rua Pedro de Santarém, 10 – 3º Dto., Apartado 511, 2001-906 Santarém☎ 243 332922 & 243 332004 🖷 243 332 998 E: pernesradio@gmail.com –36) Rua Condes de Avillez, 19-21, Apartado 45, 7540-909 Santiago do Cacém ☎ 269 829920/8 E: direcao.radio24@gmail.com W: ante-namirobriga.pt – 37) & 38) Rua Dr. António Rodrigues Manito, 58 - r/c "B", 2900-061 Setúbal ☎ 265 112023 🖷 265 089053 & 265 573639 E: radioazul98.9@gmail.com, radiojornal@sapo.pt – 39) Rua do Pacífico, lote 25/26/27, Cerro de Alagoa, 8200-166 Albufeira, ☎214 406 390/2 E: geral@algarvefm.pt, administracao@recordfm.com W: algarvefm.pt – 43) Quinta de S. Pedro, E. N. 125, 8800-903 Tavira ☎ 281 380 240 🖷 281 380 259 E: horizontesecretaria@gmail.com W: radiohorizonte. com – 44) Largo de Santana, 1, 8800-701 Tavira ☎ 281 320240 🖷281 325523 E: radiogilao@net.vodafone.pt, radiogilao@gmail.com W: radiogilao.com – 45) Rua Centro Republicano, 135, Apartado 133, 2300-909 Tomar ☎ 249 323100/20 🖷 249 316995 E: radiohertz@ radiohertz.pt W: radiohertz.pt – 46) Travessa da Cascalheira, n.º 27, 2300 Tomar ☎ 249 310010 🖷 249 310016 E: radio@cidadetomar.pt W: radio.cidadetomar.pt – 47) Rua José Espregueira Nº23 R/C, 4900-459 Viana do Castelo ☎ 258 800400 🖷 258 800409 E: geral@radiogeice. com W: radiogeice.com – 48) Av. Visconde Barreiros, 89 - 5º - 4470-151 Maia ☎ 229 439 393/5 🖷 229 439 394 W: radioxlfm.pt – 49) Rua das Donas, 3, 4480-910 Vila do Conde ☎ 252 642426/7/8/9 🖷 252 642303 E: radiolinear@gmail.com W: radiolinear.pt – R. Dr. Sousa Martins, Lote 2, 2725-461 Algueirão-Mem Martins☎ 218 008 247 E: geral@ ultrafm.pt W: ultrafm.pt – 52) Praça Marquês de Pombal, 2-7º,2600-222 Vila França de Xira ☎ 263 3286000 / 263 272 089 🖷 263 3286007 E: radioleziria@gmail.com – 52) Rua 8 de Dezembro, 214, Antas S. Tiago, Apartado 410, 4760-016 Vila Nova de Famalicão ☎ 252 308143/5/7 🖷 252 308144/9 E: comercial@opiniaopublica.pt, jfernandes@opiniao-publica.pt W: digitalfm.pt – 53) R. 5 de Outubro, Edifício Vilarminda, loja 204 / Apartado 89, 4764-976 Vila Nova de Famalicão ☎ 252 301 783 🖷 252 301789 E: radio@cidadehoje.pt W: cidadehoje.pt – 54) Rua Raimundo de Carvalho, 242 - Sala 1, 4430-185 Vila Nova de Gaia ☎ 22 3770840/3 🖷 22 3770849 E: geral@radioplacard.pt W: radioplacard. pt – 55) Rua do Comércio 58, 3º Andar, sala 6, 3500-110 Viseu ☎ 232 431 249 🖷 213 519 134 E: info@rci.pt W: rci.pt

Military Stations:
CINCSOUTHLANT-Commander-in-Chief South Atlantic Area/ **CINCIBERLANT**-Commander-in-Chief Iberian Atlantic Area / ☎2780 OEIRAS ☎. PR: +351 214 404106 - **FM** 88.4MHz 0.1kW (inactive) **D. Prgr:** AFN in English

PUERTO RICO (USA Commonwealth)

L.T: UTC -4h — **Pop**: 4 million — **Pr.L:** Spanish, English — **E.C:** 60Hz, 120V — **ITU:** PTR

FEDERAL COMMUNICATIONS COMMISSION (FCC)
see USA for details

ASOCIACIÓN DE RADIODIFUSORES DE PUERTO RICO
✉ P.O. Box 11208,The Atrium Business Center, Ave. Constitución 530, San Juan 00922 ☎+1 787 783 8810 **W:** radiodifusorespr.com **E:** radiodifu-sorespro@gmail.com

Most stns broadcast in Sp. only °= E or mainly E. d=directional antenna ‡ = inactive. Hrs of tr 24h except where indicated.

	MW Call	kHz	kW	Station, location, h. of tr.
1)	WPAB	550	5	WPAB 550, Ponce
2)	WKAQ	580	10/5	R. KAQ, San Juan
3)	WYEL	600	5	Mayagüez (r. WKAQ 580)
4)	WEXS	610	1/0.25	X-AM, Patillas
5)	WUNO	630	5	NotiUno, San Juan
6)	WAPA	680	10	Cadena WAPA R. "La Poderosa", San Juan: 0800-0300
6)	WA2XPA	680	0.4	Arecibo (synchr. WAPA)
7)	WKJB	710	10/0.75	KJB "Radio Isla", Mayagüez: 0915-0400
8)	WIAC	740	10	740 La Original, San Juan
8)	WIAC	740	0.5/0.1	740 La Original, Ponce (synchr)
9)	WORA	760	5	NotiUno, Mayagüez
10)	WKVM	810	50	R. Paz 810 AM, San Juan: 0900-0500
11)	WXEW	840	5/1	R. Victoria, Yabucoa: 0830-0300
12)	WABA	850	5/1	Waba "La Grande", Aguadilla
13)	WQBS	870	5	Vintage 870, San Juan: 0900-0400
14)	WYKO	880	1/0.5	La Poderosa 880, Sabana Grande
15)	WFAB	890	0.25	La Nave 890, Ceiba
16)	WPRP	910	4.4	NotiUno, Ponce
17)	WYAC	930	2.5	740 La Original, Cabo Rojo
18)	WIPR	940	10	Máxima 940 AM, San Juan
19)	WDNO	960	1/1.7	La Radio Que Te Bendice, Quebradillas
20)	WPRA	990	0.91	La Primera, Mayagüez: 0900-0400
21)	WOQI	1020	1/0.28	R. Coquí/La Señal de la Montaña, Adjuntas: 1000-0200
23)	WZNA	1040	9/0.25	Zona 1040, Moca
24)	WCGB	1060	5/0.5	Rock R. Netw., Juana Díaz (r. 1190) (°)
25)	WMIA	1070	0.5/2.5	R. Arecibo del Norte, Arecibo: 0925-0400 (Sun-0200)
26)	WLEY	1080	0.25	R. Isla 1080, Cayey
27)	WSOL	1090	0.25/0.07	La Nueva Sol 1090, San Germán: 0930(Sun 1000-) -0400
28)	WVJP	1110	2.5/0.5	R. Caguas, Caguas
29)	WMSW	1120	2.6/5	R. Once, Hatillo: 1000-0200
30)	WOIZ	1130	0.2/0.7	R. Antillas, Guayanilla: 0900-0200
31)	WQII	1140	10	Once Q Cadena Nacional, San Juan:1000-0400
32)	WBQN	1160	5/2.5	Super Borinquén, Barceloneta-Manatí: 1100-0200
33)	WLEO	1170	0.2	R. Leo, Ponce
34)	WBMJ	1190	10/5	Rock R. Netw. "La Roca", San Juan: (°)
35)	WGDL	1200	0.25/1	La mejor AM, Lares
36)	WHOY	1210	5	La Señal Activa de PR, Salinas: 0900-0330
37)	WNIK	1230	1	Única R., Arecibo
38)	WALO	1240	1/5	R. Oriental/Cad. R. Puerto Rico, Humacao
39)	WJIT	1250	0.25/1	R. Hit, Sabana
6)	WISO	1260	2.5/2	Cadena WAPA R, Ponce: 1000-0300
6)	WI3XSO	1260	2.5/0.9	Cadena WAPA R, Aguadilla (synchr)
6)	WI2XSO	1260	5/1.8	Cadena WAPA R, Mayagüez (synchr)
41)	WCMN	1280	5/1	NotiUno, Arecibo
42)	WTIL	1300	1	R. Util "La Voz Romántica", Mayagüez
43)	WSKN	1320	5/2.3	R. Isla 1320, San Juan
44)	WENA	1330	2/1.4	La Buena del Sur, Yauco
45)	WWNA	1340	0.95	R. Una 1340, Aguadilla: 0900-0300
46)	WEGA	1350	2.5	Faro de Santidad, Vega Baja
48)	WIVV	1370	5/1	Rock Radio Netw.,Vieques Isl.: (r. 1190): (°)
49)	WOLA	1380	1	Prócer, Voz de la Montaña, Barranquitas: 0900-0200
50)	WISA	1390	1	740 La Original, Isabela
51)	WIDA	1400	1	R. Vida AM, Carolina.
52)	WRSS	1410	1	R. Progreso, San Sebastián
2)	WUKQ	1420	1	Ponce (r. WKAQ 580)
53)	WNEL	1430	5	R.Tiempo/NotiUno, Caguas
55)	WCPR	1450	1	R. Coamo, Coamo
56)	WRRE	1460	0.5/0.3	Sonido Santidad, Juncos
57)	WLRP	1460	0.5	R. Raíces, San Sebastián: 0900-0400
58)	WKCK	1470	2/4	R. Cumbre, Orocovis: 0900-0200
59)	WMDD	1480	5	El 14-80 AM, Fajardo
60)	WDEP	1490	5/1	R. Isla, Ponce
61)	WMNT	1500	1/0.25	R. Atenas, Manatí: 1030-0200
62)	WBSG	‡1510	1	R. Voz, Lajas
63)	WVOZ	1520	25	Salud 1520 AM, San Juan
64)	WUPR	1530	1/0.25	Exitos 15-30, Utuado: 1000-0400
65)	WIBS	1540	1d	R. Voz/R. Caribe, Guayama
66)	WKFE	1550	0.25	La Isla/R. Café Dinámica Yauco
67)	WRSJ	1560	5/0.75	La Bachatera del Norte, Bayamón
68)	WPPC	1570	1/0.1	R. Felicidad, Peñuelas: 1300-2300
69)	WEKO	1580	5/2.5	R. Eko, Morovis
70)	WGYA	‡1590	1	Guayama (CP)

MW Call	kHz	kW	Station, location, h. of tr.
71) WCMA	1600	5	Cima 103.7, Bayamón: 1100-0500
46) WGIT	1660	10/1	Faro de Santidad, Canóvanas

Addresses and other information:
1) Box 7243, Ponce 00732-7243 **W:** wpabradio.com/index.html **E:** joselias@wpabradio.com - **FM:** WOQI 93.3MHz, WIOC 105 1MHz, WOYE 94 1MHz, Mayagüez – **2)** Box 364668, San Juan 00936-4668 **W:** wkaq580.univision.com - **FM:** KQ-105 La Primera 104.7MHz – **3)** Box 1370, Mayagüez 00681-1370 - **FM:** WAEL-FM 96.1MHz, Maricao – **4)** Box 640, Patillas 00723-0640 – **5)** Box 363222, San Juan 00936-3222 **W:** notiuno.com - **FM:** WFID 97.7MHz, Río Piedras – **6)** Urb Baldrich, 134 Domenech Ave, Hato Rey 00918-3502 **W:** waparadiopr.com – **7)** Box 1293, Mayagüez 00709-1293 **W:** radioisla1320.com - **FM:** WKJB-FM 99.1MHz – **8)** Box 9023916, San Juan 00902-3916 **W:** twitter.com/WIAC740 - **FM:** 102.5MHz – **9)** Box 43, Mayagüez 00681-0043 (or P.O.Box 363222, San Juan, PR 00936) **W:** notiuno.com – **10)** Urb. Roosevelt, 415 Calle Carbonell, Hato Rey 00918-2866 - **FM:** WORO 92.5MHz, Corozal – **11)** Box 100, Yabucoa 00767 **W:** victoria840.com – **12)** 6 Calle Munoz Rivera St., Aguadilla 00603-5154 (or P.O.Box 188, Aguadilla, PR 00605) **W:** waba.850.com – **13)** Calle Bori 1508, Urb Autonsanti, San Juan 00927 **W:** playtvpr.com/wqbs – **14)** Calle Dr. Felix Tio 34, Sabana Grande, PR 00637 – **15)** P.O.Box 318, Río Blanco, PR 00744. **W:** radiounidadcristiana.com – **16)** Box 7771, Ponce 00732-7771 – **17)** Box 681, Cabo Rojo 00623-0681 - **FM:** WMIO 102.3MHz – **18)** Box 190909, Hato Rey 00918-0909 **W:** prnet.pr/maxima/index.htm - **FM:** Allegro 91.3MHz – **19)** P.O.Box 846, Aguada, PR 00602. **W:** zona1040am.com – **20)** Box 1293, Mayagüez 00681-1293 **W:** wpra990.com – **21)** Box 704, Adjuntas 00601-0704 – **23)** Box 846, Aguada, PR 00602-0846 **W:** zona1040.com – **24)** Box 1414, Juana Díaz 00795-1414 (or P.O.Box 367000, San Juan, PR 00936) – Mon-Fri 1300-1700 local programming in Spanish – **W:** therockradio.org – **25)** Box 1055, Arecibo 00613-1055 – **26)** Box 1186, Cayey 00737-1186 (or 100 Gran Bulevar Paseo #403A, San Juan, PR 00926) **W:** radioisla1320.com – **27)** Box 5000, Suite 442, San Germán 00683-0442 **W:** radiosol.com – **28)** Box 207, Caguas 00726-0207 - **FM:** 103.3MHz, Criolla – **29)** 550 Calle Truncado, Hatillo 00659-2712 (or P.O.Box 140961, Arecibo, PR 00614) **W:** radioonce.com – **30)** Box 561130, Guayanilla 00656-1130 **W:** radioantillas.4t.com – **31)** Cobian's Plaza, Santurce 00909-1820 (or Box 193779, San Juan, PR 00919) – **32)** Box 1625 (or Calle 16 H-6 Urb. Flamboyan), Manatí 00674-1625 – **33)** Box 7213, Ponce 00732-7213 - **FM:** WZAR 101.9MHz – **34)** Box 367000, San Juan 00936-7000 (or Av Ponce de León N° 1409, P4, Santurce 00907) (// 48)) – Mon-Fri 2300-0540 Spanish, 0540-2300 English, Sun English 24h **W:** rockradionetwork.org **E:** radio@therockradio.org – **35)** Box 872, Lares, PR 00669 – **W:** wgdl1200am.com – **36)** Box 1148, Salinas 00751-1148 **E:** whoyam@coqui.net – **37)** Box 141526, Arecibo 00614 **W:** unicaradio1230.com - **FM:** 106.5MHz – **38)** Box 1240 (or P.O.Box 9230), Humacao 00792 **W:** waloradio.com – **39)** Box 316, Coamo 00769-0316 (or P.O.Box 878, Vega Alta, PR 00692) – **41)** Box 436, Arecibo 00613-0436 - **FM:** 107.3MHz, – **42)** Box 1360, Mayagüez 00681-1360. F.P.I: move to 960kHz. **W:** radioutil.net – **43)** Box 363222, San Juan 00936-3222 **W:** radioisla1320.com – **44)** Box 1330, Yauco 00698-1330 **W:** labuena1330.com – **45)** Box 7, Moca 00676-0007 **W:** radiouna1340.com – **46)** BHC 03 Box 12110, Carolina, P.R. 00987 **W:** farodesantidad.org – **48)** HC02 Box 13903, Vieques Island, PR 00765 – Sat 1000-1300 local programming in English **W:** and **E:** as 34) – **49)** Box 669-A, Barranquitas, PR 00794 – **50)** Box 750, Salinas 00662-0750 **W:** wisa1390.com **E:** wisa@prtc.net - **FM:** WKSA 101.5MHz – **51)** Box 188, Carolina 00986-0188 **W:** cadenaradiovida.com - **FM:** 90.5MHz – **52)** Box 1410, San Sebastián 00685-1410 – **54)** Box 487, Caguas 00726-0487 **W:** radiotiempo.net - **FM:** WPRM 98.5MHz, San Juan – **55)** Box 1863, Coamo 00769-1863 **W:** coamomall.com/coamomallradio – **56)** Box 1460, Las Piedras, PR 00771-1460 **W:** sonidosantidad.com – **57)** Box 1670, San Sebastián 00685-1670 – **58)** 10 Calle Pedro Arroyo, Orocovis 00720-2202 (or P.O.Box 1210, Orocovis, PR 00720) **W:** cumbre1470.com – **59)** Box 948, Fajardo 00738-0948. **W:** el1480am.net - **FM:** WDOY 96.5MHz – **60)** Box 7213, Ponce 00732-7213 **W:** radioisla1320.com – **61)** Box 6, Manatí 00674-0006 **W:** radioatenas.com – **62)** Box 593, Lajas 00667-0593 (has requested permission to move to San Germán) – **63)** Calle Bori 1554, San Juan, PR 00927. **W:** salud1520am.com - **FM:** 107.7MHz Carolina – **64)** Box 868, Utuado 00641-0868 **W:** wupr.com – **65)** Box 1540, Guayama 00785-1540 – **66)** Box 324, Yauco 00698-0324 (or 100 Gran Bulevar Paseo #403A, San Juan, PR 00926) **W:** radioisla1320.com – **67)** Box 4036, Carolina 00984-4036 (or Calle Bori 1554, San Juan, PR 00927) – **68)** Box 9064, Ponce 00732-9064 **W:** wppc1570am.org **E:** wpppcam@prtc.net – **69)** Calle Bori 1554, San Juan, PR 00927 – **70)** Calle Bori 1554, San Juan, PR 00927 – **71)** Box 9394, Santurce 00908-9394. **FM:** 103.7MHz
FM in San Juan (MHz): 89.7 WRTU University of San Juan – 91.3 WIPR-FM – 93.7 WZNT – 98.5 WPRM-FM – 99.1 WPRM-FM – 99.9

WIOA – 102.5 WIAC-FM – 104.7 WKAQ-FM – 105.7 WCAD

QATAR

L.T: UTC +3h — **Pop:** 850,000 — **Pr.L:** Arabic — **E.C:** 50Hz, 240V — **ITU:** QAT

SUPREME COUNCIL OF INFORMATION & COMMUNICATION TECHNOLOGY
P.O. Box 23264, Al Nassr Tower, Post Office Roundabout, Al Corniche St., Doha ☎+974 44 995333 🖷 +974 44 935913 **W:** ictqatar.qa **E:** info@ict.gov.qa

QATAR MEDIA CORPORATION (QMC, Gov.)
🖃 P.O. Box 1414, Doha ☎+974 44 894444 🖷 +974 44 882888 **W:** qatarbroadcast.qa **E:** contact@qna.org.qa **L.P:** Exec. Chmn: Sheikh Jabor Bin Yusuf Bin Jasim Al Thani. Dir. of Broadc: Mubarak Jaham Al-Kawari.

MW	kHz	kW	Prgr.	H. of tr.
Al Arish	675	600	A	24h

Main Arabic Prgr. (A): 24h. On **FM:** Al-Jumailiya 90.8MHz 40kW, Umm Said 93.4MHz, Al Kohr 97.6MHz 10kW, Al-Khaisah 102.6/103.4MHz, Al Ruwais 104.0MHz.
English prgr: Doha 97.5MHz 10kW.
Quran prgr: 103.4MHz
Oryx FM, Doha, 94.0MHz (joint QMC and RFI project in French.)
Sowt al-Khaleej(Vo the Gulf): Doha 88.0/99.0/100.8MHz. **W:** skr.fm
Sawt Al-Rayyan: Markhiyah 102.0MHz 10kW.
Al-Jazeera English TV audio: Doha 101.7MHz.
Al-Rayan TV audio: Doha 97.0MHz 20kW.
Ann: Main Arabic prgr: "Idha'at Qatar min al-Doha".

Other stations:
Emarat FM, Doha: 104.0MHz. See UAE – **Middle East BC,** Markhiya 92.0MHz – **QF R.,** Doha: 91.7MHz English, 93.7MHz Arabic. **W:** qfradio.org.qa – **AFN,** Al Udeid Airbase: 98.9/101.3MHz – **BBC World Sce,** Doha: 107.4MHz 8kW – **Monte Carlo Doualiya,** Doha: 99.6MHz 1kW – **R. Sawa,** Al-Jumailiya: 92.6MHz 20kW

RÉUNION (France)

L.T: UTC +4h — **Pop:** 800,000 — **Pr.L:** French — **E.C:** 50Hz, 220V — **ITU:** REU

RÉUNION LA PREMIÈRE
🖃 1 rue Jean-Chatel, FR-97716 St. Denis Messag Cédex 9 ☎+262 262406767 🖷 +262 262216484 **W:** reunion.la1ere.fr/radio **L.P:** Directrice Regional: Dominique Richard.
MW: St. Pierre 666kHz 20kW, St. André 1215kHz 5kW.

FM	MHz	kW	FM	MHz	kW
Petite-Ile	87.8	2	Saint-Paul	90.7	1
Saint-Denis	89.2	2	Saint-Leu	90.9	1
Le Tampon	89.6	3	Le Port	91.0	2
Plaine des Cafres	90.7	2	Saint-Benoît	106.7	2
+6 trs sub	1kW				

D.Prgr: 24h. During nighttime 2000-0100 relay of RFI.
Ann: "Réunion Première". **IS:** "Séga & Maloya" (Réunion Folklore).

Other Stations:

FM (MHz)	1	2	3	4	5	6	7	8	kW
Cilaos	103.5	98.8	107.6	-	-	-	88.5	100.7	0.2
Etang-Salé		89.3	-	-	-	-	-	94.7	1
La Possession		93.4	-	-	-	-	103.0	-	1
Le Port	91.6	93.4	94.2	105.2	93.8		103.3	-	1-2
Le Tampon	99.2	97.4	-	98.6	104.0	105.7	-	-	1-3
Petite-Ile	91.1	-	105.5	-	-	-	-	-	1-2
Plaine-des-Chafres	91.3	-	-	105.1	96.5	93.0	-	-	1-2
Plaine-des-Palm.	99.2	88.2	100.1	-	-	-	93.6	-	1-3
Saint-André		-	94.2	-	-	-	-	-	1
Saint-Benoit	97.5	101.3	-	-	88.5	-	105.2	0.2-1	
Saint-Denis	98.8	97.8	101.5	95.1	107.7	103.4	95.5	91.3	0.2-2
Sainte-Rose	99.8	-	87.6	107.5	89.0	93.6	102.1	-	0.1-2
Sainte-Suzanne	99.6	106.2	-	-	101.1	-	95.7	-	0.1-1
Saint-Joseph	107.8	-	98.8	98.0	107.0	90.5	103.5	88.3	0.1-1
Saint-Leu	91.5	95.0	-	105.3	96.7	92.8	103.1	106.8	1
Saint-Paul	-	107.1	103.7	105.7	96.6	89.6	90.0	87.6	1-2
Saint-Philippe	101.1	91.6	-	-	-	-	102.6	96.3	0.2-1
Salazie	93.2	101.7	89.0	104.4	-	103.2	-	105.7	0.2
Saline-les-Hauts		95.2	-	105.5	106.6	89.4	103.3	-	1
Trois Bassins	91.3	-	107.9	-	-	-	-	95.6	1
Vincendo		-	-	101.6	105.8	-	-	-	1

1) France Inter W: franceinter.fr – **2) R. Freedom W:** freedom.fr – **3) Kréol FM W:** radiokreol.com – **4) RER** (Radio ést Réunion) **W:** rer.re – **5) R. Festival W:** radiofestival.com – **6) Antenne Réunion Radio W:** antennereunion.fr – **7) Fun R. W:** funradio.re – **8) R. Arc en Ciel W:** 7afm.com

ROMANIA

L.T: UTC +2h (27 Mar-30 Oct: +3h) — **Pop:** 20.1 million — **Pr.L:** Romanian, Hungarian, German — **E.C:** 50Hz, 230V — **ITU:** ROU

CONSILIUL NATIONAL AL AUDIOVIZUALULUI (CNA)
✉ Bd. Libertatii nr. 14, sector 5, 050706 Bucuresti ☎ +40 21 3055350 📠 +40 21 3055354 **E:** cna@cna.ro **W:** cna.ro
L.P: Pres: Laura Corina Georgescu
NB. CNA is the regulatory authority for broadcasting.

SOCIETATEA ROMÂNA DE RADIODIFUZIUNE (SRR) (Pub)
✉ Str. Berthelot nr. 60-64, sector 1, 010171 Bucuresti ☎ +40 21 3031777 📠 +40 21 3031726 **E:** relatii.public@radioromania.ro **W:** radioromania.ro **L.P:** DG: Ovidiu Miculescu

LW/MW	kHz	kW	Prgr	MW	kHz	kW	Prgr
Brasov (Bod)	153	200	AS	Miercurea Ciuc	945	15	1
Petrosani	531	15	1	Iasi (Uricani)	1053	400	R
Urziceni	531	15	AS	Cluj (Jucu)	1152	400	1
Târgu Jiu	558	400	1	Bacau (Galbeni)	1179	400	1
Brasov (Bod)	567	50	1	Resita (Vascau)	1179	10	1
Satu Mare	567	50	1	Brasov (Bod)	1197	15	R+M
Botosani	603	50	1	Constanta (d)	1314	50	AS
Bucuresti (a)	603	30	AS+M	Craiova	1314	15	R
Oradea	603	50	1	Timisoara	1314	25	AS+M
Drobeta-T. Severin	603	15	R	Târgu Mures	1323	15	R+M
Timisoara (b)	630	400	R	Galati	1332	50	1
Voinesti	630	50	AS	Sighetul M.	1404	50	R/L+M
Sighetul M.	711	50	1	Sibiu	1404	15	1
Baia Mare	720	10	1	Olanesti	1422	10	1
Nufarul	720	15	1	Constanta (d)	1458	100	1
Sinaia	720	15	1	Nufarul	1530	15	R
Lugoj (Boldur)	756	400	1	Radauti	1530	15	1
Bucuresti (c)	855	400	1	Miercurea Ciuc	1593	15	R+M
Cluj (Jucu)	909	200	R+M	Ioan Corvin	1593	15	1
Timisoara	909	50	1	Oradea	1593	15	R+M
Constanta (d)	909	25	R	Sibiu	1593	10	R+M

(a) Herastrau (b) Ortisoara (c) Tâncâbesti (d) Valul lui Traian
R=Regional prgrs, L=Local prgr (substudio), M=Ethnic Minority Service in Hungarian/German

FM (MHz)	1	2	4	kW
Alexandria	91.8	89.7	-	10
Arad (Siria)	103.8	106.8	-	60
Bacau (Turn)	98.8	101.8	-	10
Baia Mare (Mogosa)	102.5	100.1	-	60
Baneasa (Dobrogea Sud)	106.6	89.1	-	30
Bârlad (Popeni)	103.9	102.8	-	10
Bihor (Curcubata Mare)	91.0	105.8	-	60
Bistrita (Heniu)	103.9	101.3	-	40
Botosani (Saveni)	100.8	106.0	-	10
Bucuresti (Herastrau)	105.3	101.3	104.8	2x100/2
Buzau (Dealul Istrita)	107.0	103.7	-	14
Calafat (Plenita)	90.2	101.1	-	10
Câmpulung M. (Rarau)	96.0	98.7	-	30
Cluj-Napoca (Feleac)	88.8	101.0	-	30
Comanesti (Laposi)	104.7	101.4	-	30
Constanta (Techirghiol)	105.5	-	-	60
Craiova	88.7	-	-	30
Deva (Magura Boiu)	103.4	105.0	-	30
Drobeta - T. Severin (Balota)	91.4	105.8	-	30
Faget	89.8	-	-	5
Focsani (Magura Odobesti)	102.5	101.0	-	60
Galati (Vacareni)	106.4	101.6	-	60
Gheorgheni (Harghita-Bai)	103.4	106.8	-	60
Iasi (Pietrarie)	101.1	103.1	-	100
Mahmudia	100.5	102.0	-	10
Novaci (Cerbu)	92.9	89.5	-	100
Oradea	104.1	96.1	-	10/60
Petrosani (Parâng)	88.1	90.6	-	10
Piatra Neamt (Pietricica)	103.6	100.3	-	30/10
Ploesti (Costila)	102.2	104.1	97.6	100
Ramnicu Vâlcea (Cozia)	103.4	102.5	-	30
Resita (Semenic)	102.5	-	-	100
Sibiu (Paltinis)	101.8	103.7	-	60
Suceava (Mihoveni)	99.6	101.6	-	30
Târgu Mures	93.6	104.9	-	10
Timisoara (Urseni)	106.4	100.7	-	15

FM (MHz)	1	2	4	kW
Tulcea	99.4	105.4	-	10
Tulcea (Topolog)	105.0	103.0	-	30
Turnu Magurele	105.1	-	-	30
Varatec	91.2	100.8	-	10
Zalau (Meses)	88.1	105.0	-	30

NB: Sites with only txs below 5kW not listed.
D.Prgr: Prgr 1 (R. România Actualitati): 24h. – **Prgr 2 (R. România Cultural):** 24h. – **Prgr 3 (R. România 3Net):** 24h via webcasting. – **Prgr 4 (R. România Muzical):** 24h. – **Antena Satelor (AS):** 24h. – **Service for Hungarian & German ethnic minorities (Bukaresti Rádió/R. Bukarest):** W 1200-1300 German & 1300-1400 Hungarian; Sun 0800-0820 Hungarian & 0820-0830 German.
International Service (R. Romania Int.): see Int. Radio section.

R. România Regional Services
✉ **R. România Regional,** Str. Berthelot nr. 60-64, sector 1, 010171 Bucuresti ☎ +40 21 3031469 📠 +40 21 3031860 **E:** radio.regional@radioromania.ro **W:** romaniaregional.ro
NB: All reg. stns relay news from national networks at times.
Bucuresti FM: Str. Berthelot nr. 60-64, 010171 Bucuresti. **E:** radiobucuresti@srr.ro. On 98.3MHz (Bucuresti 100kW): 24h. – **R. Cluj:** Str. Donath nr. 160, 400293 Cluj-Napoca. **E:** office@radiocluj.ro. On (MHz) 87.6 (Satu Mare 2kW), 93.3 (Negresti-Oas 2kW), 95.4 (Paltinis 0.1kW)*, 95.6 (Feleac 20kW), 101.7 (Sighetul 2kW): 24h; on (kHz) 909 (Cluj), 1404 (Sighetul M.)*, 1593 (Oradea & °Sibiu): 0400-2000 (*= except for prgrs from local substudios; °= W until 1900). For ethnic minorities: Hungarian ("Kolozsvári Rádió"): 0000-0200 (MF), 0600-0800 (W), 1300 (Sun 1200)-1600. Local substudios with own prgrs (otherwise rel. R. Cluj): **"Antena Sibiului"** Str. Brutarilor nr. 3, 550251 Sibiu. **E:** antena.sibiului@gmail.com. On 95.4MHz (Paltinis): 0900-1600 (MF); **"R. Sighet"** Str. Plevnei nr. 8, 435500 Sighetul Marmatiei. **E:** radiosighet@yahoo.com. On 1404kHz: 0400-0600 (MF), 0800 (Sun 0830)-1200, 1600-1900; for ethnic minorities: Hungarian ("Máramarosszigeti Rádió"): 0440-0450 (Mon), 0520-0525 (W), 1620-1630 (Tue), 1730-1755 (Thu); Ukrainian 1700-1755 (Fri). – **R. Constanta:** Vila nr. 1, 900001 Mamaia. **E:** secretariat@radioconstanta.ro. Prgr 1 ("Constanta FM") on (MHz) 90.8 (Techirghiol 30kW), Oct-May also on 106.2 (Sulina 2kW): 24h. Prgr 2 ("Constanta AM") on (kHz) 909 (Valul lui Traian), 1530 (Mahmudia): 0400-2200. Incl. prgrs in Armenian, Greek, Russian (for the Russo-Lipovanian ethnic minority), Tatar, Turkish: 1505-1800 (MF). Aromanian: 1610-1700 (Sun). Prgr 3 **"R. Vacanta"** (June-Sep for holidaymakers at the Black Sea coast; **E:** secretariat@radiovacanta.ro) on (MHz) 100.1 (Constanta 5kW, Mangalia 5kW), 106.2 (Sulina 2kW): 24h. N. (produced by SRR's "R.Romania International" service) in English, French, German, Italian, Russian: 1000 & 1700 (1 Jul - 31 Aug). – **R. Iasi:** Str. Lascar Catargi nr. 44, 700107 Iasi. **E:** secretariat@radioiasi.ro. Prgr 1 on (MHz) 90.8 (Rarau 30kW), 96.3MHz (Pietrarie 100kW) 24h; Prgr 2 on 1053kHz 0400-2000. For ethnic minorities (on MW/FM): Mon-Thu 1830-1900 Romany (Mon), Yiddish (Tue), Russian (for the Russo-Lipovanian ethnic minority) (Wed), Ukrainian (Thu). – **R. Oltenia Craiova:** Str. Stirbei Voda nr. 3, 200352 Craiova. **E:** office@radiocraiova.ro. On (kHz) 603 (Drobeta-Turnu Severin), 1314 (Craiova) + (MHz) 102.9 (Craiova 10kW), 105.0 (Cerbu 100kW): 0400-2200. – **R. Resita:** Str. Petru Maior nr. 71, 320111 Resita. **E:** contact@radioresita.ro. On 105.6MHz (Semenic 100kW): 24h. For ethnic minorities: 1710-1740 Ukrainian (Mon), Serbian (Tue), Hungarian (Wed), German (Thu), Croatian (Fri), Slovak (Sat), Czech (Sun). – **R. Târgu Mures:** Bd. 1 Decembrie 1918 nr. 109, 540445 Târgu Mures. **E:** office@radiomures.ro. On (MHz) 98.9 (Harghita-Bai 60kW), 102.9 (Târgu Mures 10kW): 0400-2000; on (kHz) 1197 (Brasov) 1323 (Târgu Mures), 1593 (Miercurea Ciuc) + 106.8MHz (Harghita 60kW): 0400-2200. For ethnic minorities: Hungarian ("Marosvásárhelyi Rádió"): MF 0400-1900, Sat 0500-1900, Sun 0500-2000; German ("R. Neumarkt"): W 1900-2000 (also via Sibiu 1593kHz). – **R. Timisoara:** Str. Pestalozzi nr. 14A, 300115 Timisoara. **E:** secretariat@radiotimisoara.ro. Prgr 1 ("Timisoara FM") on (MHz) 102.9 (Arad 2kW)*, 103.8 (Faget 5kW)*, 105.9 (Urseni 0.3kW): 24h (*= exc. for prgrs from substudio Arad); Prgr 2 ("Timisoara AM") on 630kHz: 24h. For ethnic minorities: German ("R. Temeswar"): 1100-1200 on MW & 1700-1800* on 105.9MHz (*= Italian on 1st Mon); Hungarian ("Temesvári Rádió"): 1200-1300 on MW & 1800-1900 on 105.9MHz; Serbian: 1300-1400 on MW & 1900-2000 on 105.9MHz; Sun, only on MW: 1430-1500 Czech, 1500-1600 Slovak, 1600-1700 Ukrainian, 1700-1800 Bulgarian, 1800-1900 Romany. Local substudio with own prgr **"Arad FM"** (otherwise rel. R.Timisoara): B-dul Revolutiei nr. 77, 310130 Arad. On (MHz) 102.9 (Arad 2kW), 103.8 (Faget 5kW): MF 1630-2000.

OTHER STATIONS

MW	kHz	kW	Location	Station
3)	1485	1	Botosani	R. Vocea Sperantei
3)	1485	1	Medias	R. Vocea Sperantei
3)	1485	1	Oradea	R. Vocea Sperantei
3)	1584	1	Iasi	R. Vocea Sperantei
3)	1584	1	Sighetul M.	R. Vocea Sperantei

MW	kHz	kW	Location	Station
3)	1584	1	Tecuci	R. Vocea Sperantei
3)	1584	1	Vatra Dornei	R. Vocea Sperantei
3)	1602	1	Piatra Neamt	R. Vocea Sperantei

FM	MHz	kW	Location	Station
4)	88.0	30	Bârlad	Kiss FM
1)	88.2	5	Botosani	Europa FM
43)	88.2	1	Oltenita	Stil FM
6)	88.3	3	Topolog	Itsy Bitsy
2A)	88.4	10	Varatec	Pro FM
2A)	88.5	100	Semenic	Pro FM
4)	88.5	2	Vaslui	Kiss FM
7A)	88.5	1	Constanta	R. 21
22)	88.6	1	Campina	Best FM
6)	88.7	2	Satu Mare	Itsy Bitsy
5)	88.9	2	Mahmudia	R. ZU
5)	89.0	3	Bucuresti	R. ZU
2A)	89.1	10	Târgu Mures	Pro FM
1)	89.2	2	Brasov	Europa FM
9)	89.2	1	Sulina	R. Trinitas
1)	89.3	4.5	Siria	Europa FM
41)	89.3	2	Sighetul M.	Sighet FM
5)	89.3	1	Pietricica	R. ZU
1)	89.4	2	Giurgiu	Europa FM
2C)	89.5	6	Bucuresti	Dance FM
6)	89.5	5	Tulcea	Itsy Bitsy
14)	89.7	22	Harghita-Bai	Mária Rádió Erdély
16)	89.8	2	Slobozia	Magic FM
2A)	89.9	1	Brasov	Pro FM
2A)	89.9	2	Medgidia	Pro FM
1)	90.0	4.5	Bistrita	Europa FM
2A)	90.0	60	Magura Odobesti	Pro FM
38)	90.1	2	Zimnicea	R. Z
9)	90.1	2	Toplita	R. Trinitas
5)	90.3	30	Laposi	R. ZU
1)	90.4	2	Râmnicu Vâlcea	Europa FM
1)	90.5	4.5	Baia Mare	Europa FM
7B)	90.6	1	Bacau	Vibe FM
5)	90.6	5	Topolog	R. ZU
1)	90.7	4	Târgu Mures	Europa FM
13)	90.7	30	Turnu Magurele	National FM
16)	90.8	2	Bucuresti	Magic FM
1)	90.9	2	Satu Mare	Europa FM
13)	90.9	5	Mahmudia	National FM
5)	90.9	2	Slobozia	R. ZU
4)	91.1	1	Constanta	Kiss FM
42)	91.1	1	Saveni	Sport Total FM
2A)	91.3	10	Urseni	Pro FM
4)	91.3	30	Dealul Istrita	Kiss FM
2A)	91.4	60	Harghita-Bai	Pro FM
7A)	91.5	5	Cozia	R. 21
13)	91.7	1	Bucuresti	National FM
A)	91.7	30	Feleac	RFI relay
2A)	91.8	10	Turn	Pro FM
2A)	92.0	60	Vacareni	Pro FM
4)	92.0	10	Heniu	Kiss FM
1)	92.1	4.5	Petrosani	Europa FM
7B)	92.1	2	Bucuresti	Vibe FM
1)	92.4	60	Paltinis	Europa FM
10)	92.5	10	Meses	R. Maria
5)	92.5	30	Dealul Istrita	R. ZU
9)	92.6	2	Zimnicea	R. Trinitas
9)	92.7	1	Iasi	R. Trinitas
23)	92.9	2	Constanta	C FM
44)	92.9	2	Slobozia	WYL FM
9)	93.0	60	Harghita-Bai	R. Trinitas
1)	93.2	4.5	Oradea	Europa FM
35)	93.2	2	Negresti	Smile FM
4)	93.3	1	Slobozia	Kiss FM
9)	93.3	3	Ceahlau	R. Trinitas
9)	93.4	2	Alexandria	Europa FM
13)	93.4	30	Heniu	National FM
3)	93.6	1	Tulcea	R. Vocea Sperantei
9)	93.6	30	Cozia	R. Trinitas
26)	93.8	2	Sighetul M.	R. eMaramures
4)	93.8	1	Draganesti-Olt	Kiss FM
2A)	93.9	30	Dobrogea Sud	Pro FM
13)	94.0	2	Zimnicea	National FM
13)	94.2	2	Constanta	National FM
37)	94.2	1	Bucuresti	R. Vocea Evangheliei
2A)	94.3	30	Cozia	Pro FM
9)	94.3	1	Mogosa	R. Trinitas
29)	94.5	2	Husi	Plus FM
12)	94.6	10	Meses	R. Transilvania
11)	94.7	10	Pietricica	Impact FM
16)	94.9	2	Satu Mare	Magic FM
2A)	94.9	60	Paltinis	Pro FM

FM	MHz	kW	Location	Station
6)	95.0	10	Saveni	Itsy Bitsy
5)	95.1	2	Medgidia	R. ZU
9)	95.3	100	Costila	R. Trinitas
8)	95.5	1	Calafat	R. Galaxy
8)	95.5	1	Craiova	R. Galaxy
1)	95.6	1	Darabani	R. Trinitas
2A)	95.7	10	Bârlad	Pro FM
31)	95.8	1	Tulcea	R. Delta
2A)	95.9	30	Magura Boiu	Pro FM
7A)	96.0	2	Negresti-Oas	R. 21
13)	96.1	2	Timisoara	National FM
4)	96.1	5	Bucuresti	Kiss FM
7B)	96.1	2	Zimnicea	Vibe FM
2A)	96.2	60	Techirghiol	Pro FM
8)	96.4	5	Cozia	R. Galaxy
9)	96.4	1	Nucet	R. Trinitas
2A)	96.5	2	Satu Mare	Pro FM
9)	96.5	60	Vacareni	R. Trinitas
9)	96.6	60	Paltinis	R. ZU
2A)	96.7	10	Saveni	Pro FM
27)	96.8	2	Dabuleni	Favorit FM
4)	96.8	2	Mahmudia	Kiss FM
28)	96.9	3.5	Bucuresti	Gold FM
33)	96.9	60	Mogosa	R. Impact
15)	97.0	10	Magura Odobesti	R. Focus FM
7A)	97.1	30	Mihoveni	R. 21
5)	97.2	2	Brasov	R. ZU
5)	97.3	30	Bârlad	R. ZU
32)	97.4	2	Sighetul M.	R. Galaxia
7A)	97.7	10	Meses	R. 21
2A)	97.9	3	Bucuresti	Pro FM
42)	97.9	3	Balota	Sport Total FM
25)	98.0	1	Bacau	Dream FM
3)	98.0	2	Negresti-Oas	R. Vocea Sperantei
13)	98.1	10	Varatec	National FM
9)	98.1	1	Hârsova	R. Trinitas
9)	98.2	1	Bailesti	R. Trinitas
2A)	98.5	30	Laposi	Pro FM
2A)	98.5	10	Parâng	Pro FM
4)	98.5	30	Canlia	Kiss FM
5)	98.5	60	Mogosa	R. ZU
9)	98.5	10	Balota	R. Trinitas
7A)	98.7	6	Dealul Istrita	R. 21
1)	98.8	1	Slatina	Europa FM
39)	98.9	2	Techirghiol	Realitatea FM
2A)	99.2	100	Pietrarie	Pro FM
4)	99.2	30	Cozia	Kiss FM
16)	99.3	30	Heniu	Magic FM
6)	99.3	2.5	Bucuresti	Itsy Bitsy
1)	99.5	5	Calarasi	Europa FM
2A)	99.6	30	Costila	Pro FM
1)	100.0	5	Bârlad	Europa FM
1)	100.0	2	Balota	Europa FM
1)	100.2	5	Harghita-Bai	Europa FM
7A)	100.2	25	Bucuresti	R. 21
1)	100.3	2	Buzau	Europa FM
1)	100.3	1	Vaslui	Europa FM
13)	100.6	2	Târgu Mures	National FM
17)	#100.6	6	Bucuresti	Rock FM
18)	100.6	30	Turnu Magurele	R. Sud
2A)	100.7	2	Brasov	Pro FM
2A)	100.7	100	Cerbu	Pro FM
1)	100.9	2	Slobozia	Europa FM
13)	100.9	5	Faget	National FM
19)	101.5	10	Parâng	R. Mondo FM
2A)	101.5	10	Meses	Pro FM
34)	101.7	2	Ploiesti	R. S.O.S.
40)	101.9	3	Bucuresti	Romantic FM
1)	102.0	2.5	Nucet	Europa FM
2A)	102.3	2	Toplita	Pro FM
1)	102.7	1.5	Câmpulung M.	Europa FM
1)	102.7	5	Meses	Europa FM
2A)	102.8	5	Bucuresti	Pro FM
22)	103.1	2	Dabuleni	R. Trinitas
1)	103.4	10	Galati	Europa FM
2A)	103.4	10	Mihoveni	Pro FM
3)	103.5	2	Cobadin	R. Vocea Sperantei
2B)	103.8	5	Bucuresti	Music FM
2A)	104.0	5	Satu Mare	Pro FM
4)	104.1	10	Parâng	Kiss FM
7A)	104.1	1	Mangalia	R. 21
1)	104.2	4	Turn	Europa FM
2A)	104.2	2	Voineasa	Pro FM
36)	104.3	5	Toplita	R. Son
1)	104.4	5	Timisoara	Europa FM
1)	104.5	2	Craiova	Europa FM

FM	MHz	kW	Location	Station
2A)	104.5	30	Feleac	Pro FM
3)	104.5	1	Zimnicea	R. Vocea Sperantei
1)	104.8	2	Negresti-Oas	Europa FM
2A)	104.8	30	Rarau	Pro FM
1)	105.1	4.5	Pietricica	Europa FM
7A)	105.2	30	Dobrogea Sud	R. 21
2A)	105.3	60	Siria	Pro FM
2A)	105.3	60	Mogosa	Pro FM
5)	105.3	2	Hârlau	R. ZU
1)	105.5	5	Mihoveni	Europa FM
2A)	105.5	30	Craiova	Pro FM
5)	105.5	2	Negresti	R. ZU
1)	105.8	7.5	Odobesti	Europa FM
13)	105.9	10	Parâng	National FM
1)	106.1	5	Constanta	Europa FM
1)	106.2	6	Paltinis	Europa FM
1)	106.3	5	Comanesti	Europa FM
24)	106.4	2	Satu Mare	City R.
1)	106.5	5	Iasi	Europa FM
1)	106.6	12	Feleac	Europa FM
21)	106.6	2	Moldova Noua	9FM
7A)	106.6	2	Draganesti-Olt	R. 21
1)	106.7	40	Bucuresti	Europa FM
1)	107.1	10	Cerbu	Europa FM
1)	107.1	2.5	Varatec	Europa FM
2A)	107.1	2	Mangalia	Pro FM
11)	107.2	10	Rarau	Impact FM
20)	107.3	5	Bucuresti	Smart FM
7A)	107.3	2	Zimnicea	R. 21
1)	107.4	5	Tulcea	Europa FM
2A)	107.4	2	Negresti-Oas	Pro FM
1)	107.5	100	Costila	Europa FM
1)	107.5	5	Resita	Europa FM
2A)	107.6	60	Oradea	Pro FM
9)	107.6	2	Voineasa	R. Trinitas
1)	107.7	5	Magura Boiu	Europa FM
2A)	107.8	10	Turn	Pro FM
2A)	107.8	30	Heniu	Pro FM
2A)	107.9	60	Curcubata Mare	Pro FM
2A)	107.9	30	Balota	Pro FM
30)	107.9	2	Moldova Noua	Popular FM
4)	107.9	2	Satu Mare	Kiss FM
7A)	107.9	1	Tulcea	R. 21

NB: Txs below 1kW not listed. #) HD Radio trial (Kiss FM, Magic FM, One FM, Rock FM)

Addresses & other information:
1) Str. Horia Macelariu nr. 36-28, sector 1, 013932 Bucuresti – **2A-C)** Bd. Pache Protopopescu nr. 109, 021409 Bucuresti – **3)** Str. Erou Iancu Nicolae nr. 38-38A, 077190 Voluntari. **E:** rvs@rvs.ro – **4)** Splaiul Independentei nr. 202A, sector 6, 060022 Bucuresti – **5)** Str. Maior Gheorghe Sontu nr. 8, sector 1, 011448 Bucuresti – **6)** Str. Leonida nr. 19, sector 2, 20556 Bucuresti – **7A,B)** Str. Horia Macelariu nr. 36-28, sector 1, 013932 Bucuresti – **8)** Bd. Carol nr. 43, 318688 Drobeta-Turnu Severin – **9)** Aleea Dealul Mitropoliei nr. 25, sector 4, 040163 Bucuresti – **10)** Str. Spartacus nr 33, 410466 Oradea – **11)** Str. Petru Rares nr. 19, 720011 Suceava – **12)** Bd. Dacia nr. 103, 410457 Oradea – **13)** Str. Fabricii nr. 46B, sector 6, 060823 Bucuresti – **14)** Str. Bârsei nr. 28, 410423 Oradea. In Hungarian – **15)** Bd. Nicolae Balcescu nr. 48, 120260 Buzau – **16)** Bd. Libertatii nr. 14, sector 5, 050706 Bucuresti – **17)** Splaiul Independentei nr. 319, sector 6, 060044 Bucuresti – **18)** Str. Campia Islaz nr. 97A, 200420 Craiova – **19)** Str. Institutului nr. 20A, 332006 Hunedoara – **20)** Str. Horia Macelariu 36-38, sector 1, 013937 Bucuresti – **21)** Str. Negru Voda, 115100 Campulung – **22)** Str. Teilor nr. 11, 105600 Campina – **23)** Bd. Alexandru Lapusneanu nr. 104, 900648 Constanta – **24)** Str. I.C. Bratianu nr. 1, 440010 Satu Mare. In Hungarian – **25)** Str. Drumul Muntele Gaina nr. 107-109, sector 1, 013913 Bucuresti – **26)** Bd. Bucuresti nr. 3, 430013 Baia Mare – **27)** Str. Ianus Pannonius nr. 25A, 410150 Oradea – **28)** Bd. Iuliu Maniu nr. 51, sector 6, 061077 Bucuresti – **29)** Str. Cpt. Ianculescu nr. 13C, 735100 Husi – **30)** Str. Grisellini nr. 43, 325550 Moldova Noua – **31)** Str. Podgoriilor nr. 32, 820185 Tulcea – **32)** Bd. Independentei nr. 4, 430123 Baia Mare – **33)** Str. DN1 Ploiesti-Campina km 5C, 107070 Blejoi – **35)** Str. Spiru Haret nr. 5, 730148 Vaslui – **36)** Str. Baratilor nr. 18, 545400 Sighisoara – **37)** Str. Orzari nr. 84, sector 2, 021554 Bucuresti – **38)** Bd. Mihai Viteazu nr. 17B, 145400 Zimnicea – **39)** Sos. Bucuresti-Ploiesti nr. 172-176B, sector 1, 013686 Bucuresti – **40)** Bd. Ficusului nr. 44A, sector 1, 013975 Bucuresti – **41)** Str. Xenopol nr. 46C, 435500 Sighetul M. – **42)** Str. Torentului nr. 2, sector 2, 012320 Bucuresti – **43)** Str. Bucuresti nr.149-151, 910011 Calarasi – **44)** Str. Torcatori nr. 2B, 100275 Ploiesti – **A)** Rel. RFI (France).

DAB Transmitter (Trial)
Tx Operator: Radiocom **M:** R. România Actualitati, România Cultural,

România Muzical, R. 3Net, Bucuresti FM **Tx:** Block 12A (223.936MHz) Bucuresti (Herastrau) 0.25kW

L.T: KA: UTC +2h; AD, AR, AS, BE, BR, CC, CV, DA, IN, IV, KB, KC, KD, KL, KO, KS, KT, KU, KV, KX, LI, MD, ME, MO, MU, NE, NN, NO, OL, PS, PZ, RO, RY, SA, SM, SO, SP, SR, ST, TA, TL, TS, TV, UD, UL, VG, VL, VN, VO, YA: +3h; BA, KO, OB, PR: +4h; CB, KG, KY, OM, SV, TY, YN: +5h; AK, KE, NS, RA, TO: +6h; KN, RK, RT: +7h; BU, IR, RS (Western), ZB: +8h; AM, KH, PM, RS (Central), YV: +9h; RS (Eastern), SL: +10h; CK, KM, MA: +11h. Crimea & Sevastopol: +3h. — **Pop:** 143.5 million — **Pr.L:** Russian; additional official languages in the republics: Abaza, Adyghe, Altay, Avar, Azeri, Bashkir, Buryat, Chechen, Chuvash, Erzya, Ingush, Kabardian, Kalmyk, Karachay-Balkar, Khakas, Komi-Zyrian, Lezgi, Mansi, Mari, Moksha, Nogai, Ossetic, Tatar, Tuvan, Udmurt, Yakut. Crimea & Sevastopol: Ukrainian, Crimean Tatar. — **E.C:** 50Hz, 220V — **ITU:** RUS

FEDERALNAYA SLUZHBA PO NADZORU V SFERE SVYAZI, INFORMATSIONNYKH TEKHNOLOGIY I MASSOVYKH KOMMUNIKATSII (ROSKOMNADZOR)
✉ 109074 Moskva, Kitaygorodskiy proyezd 7 ☎ +7 495 9876800 🖷 +7 495 9876801 **E:** rsoc_in@rsoc.ru **W:** rkn.gov.ru
L.P: Head: Aleksandr A.Zharov
NB: Licensing body for broadcasting.

VSEROSSIYSKAYA GOSUDARSTVENNAYA TELEVIZIONNAYA I RADIOVESHCHATELNAYA KOMPANIYA (VGTRK) (Gov)
✉ 125040 Moskva, Yamskogo polya 5-ya ul. 19/21 ☎ +7 495 2514050🖷 +7 495 2142347 **E:** vgtrk@vgtrk.com **W:** vgtrk.com
L.P: GD: Oleg B.Dobrodeyev
Abbreviations: RR = R. Rossii (D1 to D4 refer to the timeshifted editions Dubl 1 - 4, cf. D.Prgr); RM = Mayak; Reg = Regional prgrs (see "VGTRK Regional Services" chapter); VFM = Vesti FM; Rg = Region (decoding table see "VGTRK Regional Services" chapter); Geographical location: E = European part of Russia, S = Siberia, FE = Far Eastern part of Russia.

MW

Rg	Location	kHz	kW	Hrs of tr	Prgr
DA	Makhachkala, E	918	50	0300-2200	RM, Reg
OB	Matveyevka, E	936	5	0000-2000	RR-D4, Reg
KH	Nikolayevsk-na-A., FE	1224	5	2200-1400	RR-D2, Reg
BU	Bagdarin, S**	1278	5	2200-1800	RR-D3, Reg
RA	Ulagan, S*	1350	5	2200-1800	RR-D3, Reg
RA	Ust-Kan, S*	1350	5	2200-1800	RR-D3, Reg
OB	Buguruslan, E	1395	1	0000-2000	RR-D4, Reg
RA	Turochak, S*	1440	5	2200-1800	RR-D3, Reg
RA	Ust-Koksa, S*	1440	5	2200-1800	RR-D3, Reg
BU	Taksimo, S**	1584	1	2200-1800	RR-D3, Reg
BU	Novo-Ilinsk, S**	1602	1	2200-1800	RR-D3, Reg
BU	Ust-Barguzin, S**	1602	1	2200-1800	RR-D3, Reg

NB: Txs will be closed: *) by end of 2015 **) in 1st quarter of 2016 *) txs will be closed by end of 2015

FM (MHz)

Rg	Location	RM*	RM*	VFM*	kW
AD	Maykop	104.0	°66.32	-	4
AK	Barnaul	101.0	-	101.5	2/1
AM	Blagoveshchensk	72.86	-	-	4
AR	Arkhangelsk	106.0	-	-	1
AS	Astrakhan	101.2	-	-	1
BA	Steplitamak	106.7	-	-	2
BA	Ufa	101.2	-	102.1	0.5/1
BE	Belgorod	71.87	-	p89.6	4/1
BR	Bryansk	p90.6	°68.78	-	1/4
BU	Ulan-Ude	91.2	-	101.3	1/0.03
CB	Chelyabinsk	102.0	°69.65	107.8	1/4/1
CB	Kartaly	104.0	-	-	1
CC	Goragorskiy	104.1	-	103.3	1
CC	Groznyy	90.1	-	-	1
CC	Gudermes	104.9	-	-	1
CV	Cheboksary	72.89	-	-	1
DA	Makhachkala	98.6	-	100.3	1
IR	Bratsk	p99.9	-	p105.8	1/0.5
IR	Cheremkhovo	66.32	-	-	4
IR	Irkutsk	102.6	-	101.7	1/2
KA	Kaliningrad	102.5	-	95.1	4
KB	Nalchik	101.1	°72.23	p107.4	1/4/1
KC	Cherkessk	72.11	-	-	4
KD	Krasnodar	69.74	-	100.6	1
KD	Sochi	70.07	-	-	2

Rg	Location	RM*	RM*	VFM*	kW
KE	Kemerovo	102.3	-	90.6	1/0.5
KE	Novokuznetsk	103.0	-	-	1
KG	Kurgan	102.0	-	-	1
KH	Khabarovsk	106.8	°72.02	104.8	2/4/1
KL	Kaluga	68.60	-	-	4
KM	Petropavlovsk-Kam.	103.5	-	107.0	1
KN	Krasnoyarsk	106.6	-	94.0	1
KO	Syktyvkar	68.48	-	-	2
KT	Petrozavodsk	107.9	-	p106.3	0.5/1
KU	Kursk	102.0	-	-	1
KX	Elista	102.2	°69.14	-	1/4
KY	Khanty-Mansiysk	68.60	-	-	2
KY	Surgut	107.9	-	100.7	2/0.5
LI	Lipetsk	98.9	-	-	1
MA	Magadan	105.0	-	-	1
MD	Saransk	102.6	-	p90.6	1/-
ME	Yoshkar-Ola	102.7	°71.96	-	1/2
MO	Moskva	103.4	°67.22	97.6	5/10/5
MU	Murmansk	103.5	-	107.8	1
NN	N.Novgorod	71.45	-	98.6	4/1
NO	Pestovo	103.2	-	-	1
NO	V.Novgorod	101.2	-	-	5
NS	Novosibirsk	100.0	°69.26	104.6	1/4/2
OB	Buguruslan	102.8	-	-	1
OB	Orenburg	106.3	-	-	1
OB	Orsk	101.1	-	-	1
OM	Omsk	107.3	°66.86	88.6	1
OR	Oryol	p99.2	°72.05	p102.3	-/4/-
PE	Penza	72.23	-	p105.9	4/1
PM	Nakhodka	106.0	-	-	1
PM	Vladivostok	88.8	°69.68	89.8	2x5/1
PR	Perm	96.2	-	88.5	1
PS	Pskov	104.1	-	-	1
RA	Gorno-Altaysk	104.2	-	-	1
RK	Abakan	68.63	-	-	4
RO	Rostov-na-Donu	107.5	°71.39	-	1/4
RS	Yakutsk	72.08	-	-	2
RT	Kyzyl	103.4	-	-	1
RY	Mosolovo	107.5	-	-	1
RY	Ryazan	104.5	°71.39	-	1
SA	Zhigulyovsk	106.4	-	87.5	0.5/1
SL	Yuzhno-Sakhalinsk	103.5	-	102.7	5/-
SM	Roslavl	102.5	-	-	1
SM	Smogiri	67.13	-	-	4
SM	Vyazma	104.6	-	-	1
SO	Vladikavkaz	p89.6	°72.80	106.3	1/4/1
SP	St.Peterburg	107.0	-	89.3	5
SR	Saratov	90.2	°72.65	-	1/4
ST	Stavropol	104.3	°71.63	-	1/4
TA	Tambov	71.78	-	-	4
TL	Tula	103.9	°70.07	100.9	0.5/4/1
TO	Tomsk	106.6	°68.78	91.1	1/2/1
TS	Kazan	101.3	-	93.1	1
TS	Nab.Chelny	106.9	-	90.2	1/0.5
TY	Tyumen	100.0	°69.56	103.6	1/4/1
UD	Izhevsk	100.9	°69.62	p95.0	1/4/1
UL	Ulyanovsk	p100.6	°72.56	102.5	1/4/1
VG	Volgograd	p95.3	°72.11	106.8	1/4/1
VL	Vladimir	71.54	-	-	1
VN	Rossosh	106.5	-	-	1
VN	Voronezh	105.7	°69.38	-	1/4
VO	Vologda	102.4	°72.20	-	1 /2
YA	Yaroslavl	70.34	-	p99.9	4/1
YV	Birobidzhan	103.4	°66.32	-	0.5/4
ZB	Chita	67.88	-	101.5	1/1

NB: Sites with only txs below 1kW not listed. *) Txs may carry local/regional opt-outs °) Duplicated freqs in the OIRT FM band, to be closed P) Planned

R. Rossii: FM frqs see VGTRK Regional Services chapter; **R. Kultura:** Moskva 91.6MHz 5kW.

D.Prgr: R. Rossii: 24h. 0200-2200 via txs in European Russia, and in four time-shifted editions in other parts of the country: "Dubl 4" (RR-D4) via txs in the region between the Volga river and the Urals: 0000-2000, "Dubl 3" (RR-D3) for We.Siberia: 2200-1800, "Dubl 2" (RR-D2) for Ea.Siberia: 2000-1600, "Dubl 1" (RR-D1) for the Russian Far East: 1800-1400. NB: These editions are not announced on-air, and some prgrs may be carried simultaneously in several editions. — **Mayak, R. Kultura, Vesti FM:** 24h via webcasting; limited schedules may apply to FM/MW. – **YuFM:** 24h via webcasting. – **MW relay of Vesti FM for listeners in Ukraine:** see International Radio section.

VGTRK Regional Services

D.Prgr: Reg. prgrs produced by the regional VGTRK branches are generally broadcast at local prime time hours (morning/noon/early evening) on freqs shared with R. Rossii - on FM/MW (txs see below) & via the national DVB-T2 multiplex 1 (txs see National TV section). Some branches also have separate local or reg. outputs on exclusive freqs (txs see below). In addition, some branches broadcast short news bulletins and/or local advertsing via the freqs of Mayak or Vesti FM. (NB: GTRK=gosudarstvennaya teleradiokompaniya, state broadcasting company)

Ann: Typical identifications are: the name of the prgr as listed below; alternatively "Radio Rossii - (*)", "Govorit (*)" or "Vesti - (*)" (*= name of regional capital or region)", or similar.

AD) Respublika Adygeya: GTRK "Adygeya", 385000 Maykop, ul. Zhukovskogo 24. **E:** trkra@radnet.ru **Reg:** On (MHz) Guzeripl 68.00, Maykop 69.08, Krasnogvardeyskoye 69.38, Khamyshki 70.70, Koshekhabl 71.93, Takhtamukay 73.76, Sevastopolskaya 100.2, Ust-Sakhrayskiy 100.3, Dakhovskaya 100.8, Kamennomostskiy 101.1, Novoprokhladnoye & Novosvobodnaya 103.9 in Russian, Adyghe. Also via Krasnodar (KD) 67.58MHz. **SW prgr for the Circassian ethnic minority in the Near East:** see International Radio section.

AK) Altayskiy kray: GTRK "Altay", 656045 Barnaul, Zmeinogorskiy trakt 27a. **E:** altai@gtrk.ttb.ru **Reg:** On (MHz) Pavlovsk 66.53, Gornyak & Slavgorod & Mikhaylovka 66.59, Tselinnoye 66.74, Blagoveshchenka 66.95, Mamontovo 67.16, Rodino 67.43, Ust-Kalmanka 67.85, Zmeinogorsk 68.15, Togul 67.24, Ust-Kalmanka 67.85, Bystryy Istok 68.27, Pankrushikha & Pospelikha 68.36, Tyumentsevo 68.45, Barnaul 68.60/103.4, Galbshtadt 69.17, Zarinsk 69.53, Rubtsovsk 69.68, Novichikha 69.92, Kamen-na-Obi 70.31, Shipunovo 70.25, Shipunovo 70.35, Biysk 70.40, Volchikha 73.34, Biysk 104.7. Local channel "Heart FM" on Barnaul 69.80/105.9MHz.

AM) Amurskaya oblast: GTRK "Amur", 675000 Blagoveshchensk, per. Svyatitelya Innokentiya 15. **E:** info@gtrkamur.ru **Reg:** On (MHz) Skovorodino 67.22, Belogorsk 67.82, Zeya 68.24, Progress 68.36, Shimanovsk 68.72, Svobodnyy 69.92, Tynda 70.64, Blagoveshchensk 72.86.

AR) Arkhangelskaya oblast: GTRK "Pomorye", 163061 Arkhangelsk, ul. Popova 2. **E:** agtrk@pomorie.ru **Reg:** "R. Pomorye" on (MHz) Urdoma 66.38, Nizhneye Ustye 66.98, Kozmogorodskoye 67.10, Nyandoma 67.31, Karpogory 67.76, Konosha 67.91, Rogachevo 68.00, Pinega 68.30, Glubokiy 68.45, Mezen 68.48, Verkhneozersk 69.11, Plesetsk 69.23, Lekushonskoye 69.50, Vazhskiy 69.56, Sorga 69.71, Kizema 69.80, Pogost 69.92, Svetlyy 70.04, Pogor 70.19, Alferovskaya 70.34, Okulovskaya 70.55, Malozhma 70.64, Siya 70.73, Pervomayskiy 72.14, Stroyevskoye 72.38, Vershinino 72.50, Skarlakhta 73.10, Shangaly 73.19, Samkovo 73.37, Morshchikhinskaya 73.52, Arkhangelsk 102.0 (also relayed via txs in region NE).

AS) Astrakhanskaya oblast: GTRK "Lotos", 414000 Astrakhan, ul. Molodoy Gvardii 17. **E:** tvlotos@astranet.ru **Reg:** "R. Lotos" on (MHz) Astrakhan 66.02/104.5, Chernyy Yar 69.98, Tambovka 70.16.

BA) Respublika Bashkortostan: GTRK "Bashkortostan", 450076 Ufa, ul. Gafuri 9/1. **E:** vesti_rb@mail.ru **Reg:** "R. Bashkortostana" on (MHz) Tolbazy 65.96, Neftekamsk 66.47, Mesyagutovo & Dyurtyuli 66.86, Salavat 67.04, Baymak 67.16, Verkhneyarkeyevo & Verkhniy Avzyan 68.00, Ufa 68.24, Karaidel & Rayevka 68.42, Isyangulovo 68.66, Sharan 68.78, Uchaly 69.53, Inzer 70.01, Oktyabrskiy 70.28, Idelbakovo 70.58, Belebey 70.61, Birsk 70.76, Abzanovo 70.82, Bizhbulak 71.21, Starosubkhangulovo 71.36, Kugarchi 71.63, Burayevo 71.90, Beloretsk 72.05, Komsomolskiy 72.35, Krasnousolskiy 72.74, Tuymazy 73.37, Bakaly 103.7 in Bashkir, Russian.

BE) Belgorodskaya oblast: GTRK "Belgorod", 308009 Belgorod, pr. Slavy 60. **E:** trcblg@gtrktv.ru **Reg:** On (MHz) Stroitel 66.17, Selivanovo 66.80, Grayvoron 66.92, Rakitnoye 68.39, Biryuch 69.29, Belgorod 70.16, Volokonovka 70.49, Ivnya 70.64, Prokhorovka 70.76, Borisovka 71.03, Staryy Oskol 71.09, Borisovka 71.30, Alexeyevka 71.78, Chernyanka 72.02, Valuyki 73.64, Krasnoye 73.67.

BR) Bryanskaya oblast: GTRK "Bryansk", 241033 Bryansk, ul. Stanke Dimitrova 77. **E:** radio@br-tvr.ru **Reg:** On (MHz) Navlya 67.37, Bryansk 67.58, Shvedchiki 70.04, Unecha 70.55, Pocheb 71.54, Belaya Beryozka 71.73, Trubchevsk 73.94, Novozybkov 89.5.

BU) Respublika Buryatiya: GTRK "Buryatiya", 670000 Ulan-Ude, ul. Yerbanova 7. **E:** bgtrk@bgtrk.ru **Reg:** On (kHz) Bagdarin 1278, Taksimo 1584, Novoilinsk & Ust-Barguzin 1602 + (MHz) Kurumkan 66.08, Severobaykalsk 66.29, Zakamensk 66.68, Kyren 66.86, Gusinoozersk 67.16, Petropavlovka 67.46, Sulkhara 68.00, Babushkin 68.60, Sosnovo-Ozerskoye 69.56, Ulan-Ude 69.74, Kyakhta 70.16, Balakta 71.12, Bagdarin 71.66, B.Rechka + 7 sites 101.0, Barykino 101.5, Baykalo-Kudara & Podlopatki 102.0, Ust-Muya 102.2, Mukhorshibir & Posolskoye 102.5, Bichura 103.0, Kabansk 104.0, Turuntayevo 104.1, Kika & Tarbagatay 104.5, Tashir 105.0, Barguzin 105.5, Yelan 106.0, Gremyachinsk & Khorinsk & Sagan-Nur 106.5, Novoilinsk 107.0, Bayangol Barg + 7 sites

107.5 in Russian, Buryat. (* until 1st quarter of 2016)
CB) Chelyabinskaya oblast: GTRK "Yuzhnyy Ural", 454000 Chelyabinsk, ul. Ordzhonikidze 54b. **E:** radio@cheltv.ru **Reg:** "R. Yuzhnyy Ural" on (MHz) Kartaly 66.65, Kyshtym 67.13, Yuryuzan 67.25, Stepnoye 68.36, Mezhozernyy 68.68, Novoburino 70.82, Oktyabrskoye 70.91, Chelyabinsk 71.18, Zlatoust 71.69, Magnitogorsk 71.81. Local channel "Studiya 1" on Chelyabinsk 106.8MHz.
CC) Chechenskaya respublika: GTRK "Vaynakh", 364000 Grozny, ul. B. Khmelnitskogo 147. **E:** gtrkvainah@mail.ru **Reg:** "R. Vaynakh" on (MHz) Gvardeyskoye 68.84, Goragorskiy 72.44, Gukhoy 88.1, Tevzana 90.4, Guni 98.7, Ulus-Kert & Zony 100.0, Dyshne-Vedeno 100.2, Naurskaya 101.2, Zandak 101.6, Znamenskoye 101.7, Oyskhara 102.2, Tazbichi 102.5, Shelkovskaya & Tsa-Vedeno 103.1, Assinovskaya 103.2, Grozny 103.6, Khal-Kiloy & Nozhoay-Yurt 104.3, Kharachoy 105.0, Borzoy & Sayasan 105.1, Kargalinskaya 106.0, Terskoye 106.4, Gilyany 106.6, Dabrankhi 106.8, Benoy 106.9, Gudermes 107.3 in Russian, Chechen.
CK) Chukotskiy avtonomnyy okrug: GTRK "Chukotka", 686710 Anadyr, ul. Lenina 18. **E:** gtrk@anadyr.ru **Reg:** On (MHz) 100.5 (several txs), 101.6 (several txs), 102.8 (several txs), 104.7 (Anadyr & several other txs) in Russian, Chukchi.
CV) Chuvashskaya respublika - Chuvashiya: GTRK "Chuvashiya", 428003 Cheboksary, ul. Nikolayeva 4. **E:** chradio@tvr.chtts.ru **Reg:** "R. Chuvashii" on (MHz) Tsivilsk 67.04, Ibresi 70.85, Yadrin 71.12, Krasnyye Chetai 106.7 in Russian, Chuvash.
DA) Respublika Dagestan: GTRK "Dagestan", 367032 Makhachkala, ul. M.Gadzhiyeva 182. **E:** gtrk_dagestan@mail.ru **Reg:** On (MHz) Kochubey 67.04, Makhachkala 68.87, Gergebil 69.95 in Russian, Avar, Chechen, Kumyk, Lak, Nogai, Rutul, Tsakhur. On Makhachkala 918kHz in Russian, Aghul, Azeri, Dargwa, Lezgi, Tabassaran, Tat.
IN) Respublika Ingushetiya: GTRK "Ingushetiya", 386100 Nazran, per. Naberezhnyy 8. **E:** pressari@mail.ru **Reg:** On Nazran 104.0MHz in Russian, Ingush.
IR) Irkutskaya oblast: GTRK "Irkutsk", 664025 Irkutsk, ul. Gorkogo 15. **E:** news@vesti.irk.ru **Reg:** On (MHz) Zhmurovo 66.32, Ulkan 66.62, Yerbogachen 66.68, Tulun 66.74, Bodaybo & Slyudyanka 66.98, Chuna 67.10, Novaya Igirma 67.76, Cheremkhovo 67.88, Zheleznogorsk 68.12, Zhigalovo 68.24, Ust-Ilimsk 68.48, Mama 69.29, Tayshet 69.80, Baykalsk 69.86, Bayanday & Ust-Kut 70.64, Bokhan & Nizhneudinsk 70.82, Kachug 71.15, Bratsk 72.02, Zima 72.14, Yelantsy 72.26, Magistralnyy 101.0, Kirensk 101.9, Ilir 103.6, Irkutsk 105.0, Pokosnoye 106.5.
IV) Ivanovskaya oblast: GTRK "Ivteleradio", 153000 Ivanovo, ul. Teatralnaya 31. **E:** admin@ivtele.ru **Reg:** On (MHz) Rodniki 70.13, Ivanovo 71.21, Furmanov 73.64.
KA) Kaliningradskaya oblast: GTRK "Kaliningrad", 236016 Kaliningrad, ul. Klinicheskaya 19. **E:** tv-rv@baltnet.ru **Reg:** On (MHz) Veselovka 65.90, Kaliningrad 66.02, Bolshakovo 70.19.
KB) Kabardino-Balkarskaya respublika: GTRK "Kabardino-Balkariya", 360030 Nalchik, pr. Lenina 3. **E:** vestikbr@mail.ru **Reg:** On (MHz) Samarkovo 66.2, Nalchik 70.52, Zayukovo 73.49, Bulundu 73.70 in Russian, Kabardian, Karachay-Balkar.
KC) Karachayevo-Cherkesskaya respublika: GTRK "Karachayevo-Cherkesiya", 369000 Cherkessk, ul. Krasnoarmeyskaya 51. **E:** gtrk_kchr@rambler.ru **Reg:** On (MHz) Krasnogorskaya 66.98, Karachayevsk 67.34, Kavkazkiy 68.21, Adyge-Khabl 68.66, Zelenchuskaya 68.81, Pregradnaya 69.80, Ispravnaya 69.83, Ust-Dzheguta 69.98, Teberda 69.98, Arkhyz 70.07, Dombay 70.25, Cherkessk 70.31, V.Mara 71.06, Storozhevaya 71.72, Kurdzhinovo 71.81, Khabez 71.84, Urup 72.44 in Russian, Abaza, Karachay-Balkar, Nogai.
KD) Krasnodarskiy kray: GTRK "Kuban", 350038 Krasnodar, ul. Radio 5. **E:** owl@kubantv.ru **Reg:** "Radiostantsiya Kuban" on (MHz) Tbilisskaya 66.20, Goryachiy Klyuch 66.41, Abrau-Dyurso 66.62, Novorossiysk & Khadyzhensk 67.97, Gelendzhik 68.30, Kanevskaya 68.36, Armavir 68.57, Vyshestebliyevskaya 68.72, Primorsko-Ahktarsk 69.08, Kropotkin & Timashevsk 69.23, Pavlovskaya 69.59, Temryuk 70.22, Krasnyy Kut & Psebay 70.43, Tuapse 70.46, Adler 70.58, Yeysk 71.15, Gubskaya 71.21, Lazarevskoye 71.54, Krasnodar 71.81, Arkhipo-Osipovka 71.93, Sochi 71.93*, Apsheronsk 72.20, Imretinskaya 72.72, Otradnaya 72.98, Belaya Glina 102.0, Kushchevskaya 103.5. NB: *) Tx also carries prgrs by reg. substudio (Territorialnoye otdeleniye GTRK "Kuban"): 354000 Sochi, ul. Teatralnaya 11a. **E:** tv@sochi.com.
KE) Kemerovskaya oblast: GTRK "Kuzbass", 650000 Kemerovo, ul. Krasnoarmeyskaya 137a. **E:** director@gtrk.kuzbass.net **Reg:** "R. Kuzbassa" on (MHz) Yurga 66.11, Novokuznetsk 66.20, Kemerovo 66.56, Klyuchevaya 67.04, Leninsk-Kuznetskiy 69.71, Tashtagol 69.80, Anzhevo-Sudzhensk 70.40, Mezhdurechensk 70.64. Reg. channel "Kuzbass FM" on (MHz) Kemerovo 91.0, Klyuchevaya 101.2, Leninsk-Kuznetskiy 101.3, Anzhero-Sudzhensk 101.6, Mezhdurechensk 101.8, Novokuznetsk 102.0, Guryevsk 102.5, Yurga 103.6, Belovo 104.5, Sheregesh 105.7, Prokopyevsk 107.4.
KG) Kurganskaya oblast: GTRK "Kurgan", 640018 Kurgan, ul. Sovetskaya 105. **E:** report@gtrk-kurgan.ru **Reg:** On (MHz) Shumikha

66.89, Makushino 68.48, Shadrinsk 69.23, Shatrovo 71.18, Kurgan 71.87.
KH) Khabarovskiy kray: GTRK "Dalnevostochnaya", 680632 Khabarovsk, ul. Lenina 4. **E:** tv@dvtrk.com **Reg:** On Nikolayevsk-na-Amure 1224kHz + (MHz) Tyrma 66.32, Sovetskaya Gavan & Tsimmemanovka 66.74, Sukpay 67.31, Bogorodskoye 67.52, Troitskoye 67.73, Ayan & Nelkan 68.00, Chumikan 68.12, Duki 68.30, Komsomolsk-na-Amure 68.72*, Arka 69.20, Okhotsk 69.32, Glebovo 69.47, Vyazemskiy 69.83, Bikin 69.92, Chegdomyn & Nikolayevsk-na-Amure 70.16, im. P.Osipenko 70.64, Novaya Inya 71.42, De-Kastri 72.71, Khabarovsk 72.80 (also via txs in region YV). Local channel "R. 101.8" on Khabarovsk 101.8MHz. NB: *) Tx also carries reg. prgrs by reg. substudio (Territorialnoye otdeleniye GTRK "Dalnevostochnaya"): 681000 Komsomolsk-na-Amure, ul. Molodogvardeyskaya 7.
KL) Kaluzhskaya oblast: GTRK "Kaluga", 248021 Kaluga, Pole Svobody 40a. **E:** gtrk@kaluga.ru **Reg:** On (MHz) Kaluga 66.23, Lyudinovo 67.91, Medyn 68.03, Baryatino 70.79, Mosalsk 71.39, Spassk-Demensk 72.05, Zhizdra 72.92, Khvastovichi 73.07, Obninsk 73.13, Sukhinichi 101.3, Yukhnov 104.9.
KM) Kamchatskiy kray: GTRK "Kamchatka", 683000 Petropavlovsk-Kamchatskiy, ul. Sovetskaya 62. **Reg:** On (MHz) Ust-Bolsheretsk 69.56, Petropavlovsk-Kamchatskiy & Palana + 7 sites 69.68, Ust-Kamchatsk 71.12, Klyuchi 71.90, Milkovo 71.96, Sobolevo 72.86, Petropavlovsk-Kamchatskiy 102.0. Incl. prgrs in Koryak, Itelmen, Evenki produced by substudio (Territorialnoye otdeleniye GTRK "Kamchatka"): 684620 Palana, ul. Obukhova 4.
KN) Krasnoyarskiy kray: GTRK "Krasnoyarsk", 660028 Krasnoyarsk, ul. Mechnikova 44a. **E:** referent@kgtrk.ru **Reg:** On (MHz) Balakhta 66.32, Motygino 66.44, Karatuzskoye 67.37, Zelenogorsk 68.21, Solyanka 68.84, Uzhur 69.56, Pirovskoye 70.76 Tyukhtet 71.42, Krasnoturansk 71.48, Kodinsk 71.66, Igarka 72.00, Yeniseysk 72.74, Krasnoyarsk 94.5, Kansk 100.9, Norilsk 101.4*, Baykit & Tura 101.5**, Borodino 101.8, Anash 102.7, Lesosibirsk 102.8, Dudinka*** 103.7, Achinsk 104.0, Nazarovo 104.8, Sukhobuzimskoye 104.9, Kozulka 106.3, Divnogorsk & Minusinsk 107.9. NB: *) Tx also carries reg. prgrs by GTRK "Norilsk", 663300 Norilsk, nab. Urvantseva 10. **E:** secr@norilsk-tv.ru; **) Tx also carries prgrs by reg. substudio (Territorialnoye otdeleniye GTRK "Krasnoyarsk") in Russian, Evenki: 663370 Tura, ul. 50 let Oktyabrya 28. **E:** heglen@tura.evenkya.ru; ***) Tx also carries prgrs by reg. substudio (Territorialnoye otdeleniye GTRK "Norilsk") in Russian, Nenets: 647000 Dudinka, ul. Sovetskaya 15. **E:** gtrk@mail.smnet.ru.
KO) Respublika Komi: GTRK "Komi Gor", 167005 Syktyvkar, Oktyabrskiy pr. 164. **E:** komigor@komi.rfn.ru **Reg:** On (MHz) Yarashyu 65.90, Storozhevsk 66.2, Pechora 66.35, Ukhta 66.44, Vorkuta 66.60, Syktyvkar 66.80/91.6, Pechora 66.92, Ust-Tsilma 67.10, Sludka 67.16, Pomozdino 67.85, Kadzherom 68.30, N.Odes & Yaksha 68.36, Troitsko-Pechorsk 68.60, Shoshka 68.72, Aykino 68.78, Kartayol & Novyy Bor & Shchelyabozh 68.93, Meshchura 69.02, Mordino 69.05, Inta 69.08, Krasnobor 69.11, Okunevo 69.20, Usogorsk 69.56, Kosgorodok 69.74, Myyeldino & Kemdin 69.83, Ust-Kulom 70.16, Petrun 70.28, Vetyu 70.40, Voyvozh 70.64, Spasporub 70.73, Vuktyl 71.06, Kuratovo 71.09, B.Pyssa 71.15, Chukhlom 73.19, Usinsk & Vekshor 73.31 in Russian, Komi-Zyrian.
KS) Kostromskaya oblast: GTRK "Kostroma", 156961 Kostroma, pl. Konstitutsii 1. **E:** mail@kostroma.rfn.ru **Reg:** On (MHz) Bogovarovo 66.20, Vokhma 66.68, Kostroma 66.74, Sharya 67.10, Kologriv 68.66, Soligalich 69.02, Kostroma 69.86, Parfenyevo 70.01, Makaryev 71.60, Ostrovskoye 72.26, Pavino 73.10, Chukhloma 73.64, Pyshchug 73.88.
KT) Respublika Kareliya: GTRK "Kareliya", 185002 Petrozavodsk, ul. Pirogova 2. **E:** gtrk@petrozavodsk.rfn.ru **Reg:** "R. Karelii" on (MHz) Nadvoitsy 66.29, Sortavala 67.13, Naystenyarvi 69.80, Loukhi 70.07, Kostomuksha 70.28, Muyezerskiy 72.17, Medvezhyegorsk 72.47, Petrozavodsk 102.2 in Russian, Finnish, Karelian, Vepsian.
.KU) Kurskaya oblast: GTRK "Kursk", 305010 Kursk, ul. Sovetskaya 32. **E:** gtrk@kursk.rfn.ru **Reg:** On (MHz) Lgov 66.83, Kursk 69.71, Kshenskiy 72.41.
KV) Kirovskaya oblast: GTRK "Vyatka", 610000 Kirov, ul. Uritskogo 34. **E:** tv@gtrk-vyatka.ru **Reg:** On (MHz) Vyatskiye Polyarny 66.35, Kirov 66.92, Kirs 66.86, Sovetsk 67.07, Kyuchi 67.91, Falyonki 68.33, Pinyug & Nyr 70.55, Shmelevo 70.73, Urzhum 71.06, Omutninsk 71.33, Sanchursk 73.28.
KX) Respublika Kalmykiya: GTRK "Kalmykiya", 358000 Elista, ul. M.Gorkogo 34. **E:** kalmykiagtrk@mail.ru **Reg:** On (MHz) Sadovoye 66.95, Elista 67.28, Utta 68.24, Ulan-Kholl 69.59 in Russian, Kalmyk.
KY) Khanty-Mansiyskiy avtonomnyy okrug - Yugra: GTRK "Yugoriya", 628012 Khanty-Mansiysk, ul. Gagarina 4. **E:** gtrk@yugoria.tv **Reg:** "R. Yugry" on (MHz) Agirish 65.96, Khanty-Mansiysk 66.08, Kondinskoye 66.20, Kommunisticheskiy 66.32, Beloyarskiy 66.44, Oktyabrskoye 66.68, Bobrovskaya 66.77, Uray 67.22, Langepas 67.28, Kuminskiy 67.52, Igrim & Urmannyy 68.33, Surgut 68.84, Batovo 69.47, Mezhdurechenskiy 70.28, Vakhovsk 70.67, Nyagan 70.82,

Gornopravdinsk 71.00, Kogalym 71.30, Beryozovo 71.42, Yugorsk 71.78, Raduzhnyy 72.08, Nizhnevartovsk 72.56, Pyt-Yakh 72.86 in Russian, Khanti, Mansi. Txs also relay reg. prgrs by GTRK "Region-Tyumen", TY. (NB: KY is subordinated to region TY)

LI) Lipetskaya oblast: GTRK "Lipetsk", 398050 Lipetsk, pl. Plekhanova 1. **E:** teleradio@lipetsk.rfn.ru **Reg:** On (MHz) Lipetsk 66.53, Chernava 69.26, Izmalkovo 73.79, Yelets 101.7, Terbuny 101.9, Dankov 102.4, Ploty 102.6, Dobrinka 102.7, Dolgorukovo 102.9, Chaplygin 103.3, Lev Tolstoy 103.8, Usman 104.0, Volovo 104.4.

MA) Magadanskaya oblast: GTRK "Magadan", 685024 Magadan, ul. Kommuny 8/12. **E:** center@magtrk.ru **Reg:** On (MHz) Susuman 70.16, Evensk 100.5, Myandzha & Palatka & Seymchan & Sinegorye 101.0, Ola 101.3, Omchak & Omsukchan & Ust-Omchug & Yagodnoye 102.5, Stekolnyy 102.9, Magadan 103.5.

MD) Respublika Mordoviya: GTRK "Mordoviya", 430030 Saransk, ul. Dokuchayeva 29. **E:** radiomordovii@mail.ru **Reg:** On (MHz) Tengushevo 66.35, Saransk 66.68, Vechkusy 66.95, Dubenki 67.28, Krasnoslobodsk 67.31, B.Ignatovo 67.34, Ruzayevka 67.46, Yavas 67.67, Umet 68.33, B.Berezniki 68.42, Atyashevo 68.51, Torbeyevo 68.69, Chamzinka 68.75, Yelniki 68.78, Lyambir 68.96, Temnikov 68.99, Kovylkino 69.14, Kadoshkino 69.41, Ardatov 69.53, St.Shaygovo 69.65, Insar 71.03, Romodanovo 71.12, Atyuryevo 71.33 in Russian, Erzya, Moksha.

ME) Respublika Mariy El: GTRK "Mariy-El", 424031 Yoshkar-Ola, ul. Mashinostroiteley 7a. **E:** tv@tv.mari.ru **Reg:** On (MHz) Volzhsk 69.29, Yoshkar-Ola 70.34/106.0, Sovetskiy 71.21, Kozmodemyansk 72.20, Zvenigovo 73.16 in Russian, Mari.

MO) Moskva (Federal City) & Moskovskaya oblast: no regional branch of VGTRK.

MU) Murmanskaya oblast: GTRK "Murman", 183032 Murmansk, per. Rusanova 7. **E:** radio@tvmurman.com **Reg:** On (MHz) Murmansk 67.22/107.4, Kandalaksha 67.70, Revda 67.94, Alakurtti 69.50, Teriberka & Umba & Zapolyarnyy 69.74, Kaneva & Sosnovka 70.01, Tumannyy 70.19, Kirovsk & Prirechnyy 70.34, Lovozero 70.73, Krasnoshchelye 72.38, Ostrovnoy 106.1.

NE) Nenetskiy avtonomnyy okrug: Territorialnoye otdeleniye GTRK "Pomorye", 164700 Naryan-Mar, ul. Smidovicha 19. **E:** zapolyarie@mail.ru **Reg:** On (MHz) Naryan-Mar 66.20, Krasnyy 101.2, 102.0 (several txs), Velikovisochnyy 102.1, Nelmin Nos 102.2, Oksino & Khongurey 104.7 in Russian, Nenets. Txs also relay reg. prgrs by GTRK "Pomorye", Arkhangelsk, AR. (NB: NE is subordinated to region AR)

NN) Nizhegorodskaya oblast: GTRK "Nizhniy Novgorod", 603950 Nizhniy Novgorod, ul. Belinskogo 9a. **E:** radio@nnov.rfn.ru **Reg:** On (MHz) Vacha 66.65, Sokolskoye 66.92, Sergach 67.16, Semyonov 67.43, Pavlovo 67.85, N.Novgorod 67.94, Uren 68.84, Kovernino 69.53, Shakhunya 69.59, Arzamas 69.95, Lyskovo 70.43, Lukoyanov 70.52, Krasnyye Baki 70.64, Vyksa 71.09, Kstovo 73.97.

NO) Novgorodskaya oblast: GTRK "Slaviya", 173620 Velikiy Novgorod, ul. B.Moskovskaya 106. **E:** slavia-vn@yandex.ru **Reg:** "R. Slaviya" on (MHz) Borovichi 69.02, Proletariy 71.39, Zaluchye 71.93, Pestovo 100.0, Novgorod 102.2.

NS) Novosibirskaya oblast: GTRK "Novosibirsk", 630048 Novosibirsk, ul. Rimskogo-Korsakova 9. **E:** rrkc5@nsktv.ru **Reg:** On (MHz) B.Izyrak & Kundran 66.26, Novotroitsk 66.32, Vengerovo & Yegoryevskoye & Kiik & Chulym 66.35, Balman 66.44, Severnoye & Vorobyevo 66.50, Ust-Tarka 66.62, Suzun 66.68, Ordynskoye 66.74, Vdovino 66.89, Kargat 66.89, Maray 66.92, Kyshtovka 66.98, Novopreobrazhenka 67.01, Verkh-Iki 67.04, Chistoozernoye & Mezhovka 67.04, Kurilovo & Orlovskoye 67.13, B.Chernaya & Menshikovo 67.25, Dovolnoye 67.28, Kreshchenskoye 67.37, B.Kuliki 67.40, Biaza 67.43, Ichkala 67.49, Proletarskiy 67.52, Novoabyshevo 67.67, Novosibirsk 67.88/97.8, Gruzdeyevka 68.00, Bobrovka 68.18, Kordon 68.21, Aleksandro-Nevskoye 68.24, Vinograd 68.27, Boltovo 68.30, Bagan 68.36, Nikolayevka 68.54, Ogneva Zaimka 68.57, Ubinskoye 68.63, Korolevka 68.81, Ozero Karachi 68.84, Barabo-Yudino 68.90, Karasuk & Osinovskiy 68.93, Zdvinsk 68.96, Varvarovka & Yezhula & Zubkovo 68.99, Maslyanino 69.05, Vladimirovka 69.08, Vassino 69.11, Novosilish 69.32, Alekseyevka 69.44, Kuybyshev 69.68, Bitki 69.74, Mikhaylovka 69.77, Bolshenikolskoye & Kayly 69.83, Aksenikha 69.86, Zavyalovo 69.89, Kochki & Krasnozerskoye 69.95, Bazovo 69.96, Listvyanka 69.98, Novo-Baganenok 70.01, Cherepanovo 70.10, Moshkovo 70.22, Yermolayevka 70.40, Novokrasnoye 70.46, Musy 70.58, Kargan 70.61, Verkh-Miltyushi 70.67, Kruglikovo 70.70, Bergul 70.76, Minino & Orlovka (Kyshtovskiy rayon) 71.00, Krivoyazh 71.03, Krasnyy Yar & Novopokrovka 71.06, Lebedevo 71.48, Tatarsk 71.60, Bolotnoye 71.66, N.Matrenka 71.78, Novodubrovskoye 71.84, Bobrovichinsk 71.91, Beloye 72.08, Bortsovo 72.17, Zyryanka 72.23, Orlovka (Chistoozernyy rayon) 72.26, Raduga 72.29, Krugloozernoye 72.32, Verkh-Krasnoyarka 72.41, Zonovo 72.62, Novobibeyevo 72.71, Kourak 72.95.

OB) Orenburgskaya oblast: GTRK "Orenburg", 460024 Orenburg, per. Televizionnyy 3. **E:** gtrc@orenburg.rfn.ru **Reg:** On (kHz) Matveyevka 936, Buguruslan 1395 + (MHz) Orenburg 66.02, Buzuluk 66.62, Orsk

66.92, Yasnyy 69.71, Kuvandyk 70.04, Uralskoye 101.9, Sorochinsk 102.0, Bikkulovo 102.1, Tashla & Zhdanovka 102.6, Svetlyy 102.9, Pervomayskiy 103.0, Kvarkeno & Saraktash 103.1, Saraktash 103.3, Donetskoye 103.4, Izobilnoye 103.5, Ilek 103.6, Novosergiyevka 103.9, Sol-Iletsk 104.6, Abdulino 105.1, Pleshanovo 105.2, Akbulak 105.5, Sharlyk 106.4, Alekseyevo 106.5, Tyulgan 106.6, Ponomarevka 106.9, Severnoye 107.0, Orsk 107.5, Aleksandrovka 107.8 in Russian, Chuvash, Tatar.

OL) Orlovskaya oblast: GTRK "Oryol", 302028 Oryol, ul. 7 Noyabrya 43. **E:** post@ogtrk.oryol.ru **Reg:** On (MHz) Livny 67.19, Oryol 70.31.

OM) Omskaya oblast: GTRK "Irtysh", 644050 Omsk, pr. Mira 2. **E:** reklama@omsk.rfn.ru **Reg:** On (MHz) Isilkul 66.50, Ust-Ishim 67.04, Nazyvayevsk 67.28, Tara 68.39, Omsk 69.74/87.7, Khutora 70.43, Cherlak 71.06.

PM) Primorskiy kray: GTRK "Vladivostok", 690091 Vladivostok, ul. Uborevicha 20a. **E:** ptr@ptr-vlad.ru **Reg:** On (MHz) Nakhodka 66.74, Olga 67.58, Permskoye 67.79, Arsenyev 68.60, Kraskino 68.84, Kavalerovo 69.20, Dalnerechensk 69.32, Dalnegorsk 70.04, Novozhatkovo 70.64, Plastun & Terney 71.00, Vladivostok 71.84/102.1, Chkalovka 72.08, Nakhodka 101.4, Kamenka + 4 sites 101.5, Rudnyy 101.9, Moryak-Rybolov & Veselyy Yar & Zerkalnoye 102.0, Peretychikha & Ust-Sobolevka 102.1, Agzu & 5 sites 103.5, Ussuriysk 106.0.

PR) Permskiy kray: GTRK "Perm", 614090 Perm, ul. Tekhnicheskaya 7. **E:** main@t7.ru **Reg:** "R. Permskogo kraya" on (MHz) Kungur 66.65, Barda 67.10, Kudymkar 67.19*, Gayny 67.34*, Kizel 67.67, Keros 67.88*, Chastye 68.63, Oktyabrskiy 68.72, Vaya 68.78, Ust-Chernoye 68.84*, Ilyinskiy 68.93, Serebryanka 69.14, Uinskoye 69.38, Karagay 69.53, Osa 70.55, Chusovoy 70.67, Chernushka 70.70, Siva 70.73, Kochevo 70.82*, Krasnovishersk 71.33, Chaykovskiy 71.42, Berezniki 71.87, Ochyor 72.02, Kosa 73.10*, Yelovo & Nyrob 73.58, Perm 90.2. NB: *) Txs also carry prgrs by reg. substudio (Territorialnoye otdeleniye GTRK "Perm") in Russian, Komi-Permyak 617240 Kudymkar, ul. Volodarskogo 18. **E:** kudtv@mail.ru.

PS) Pskovskaya oblast: GTRK "Pskov", 180000 Pskov, ul. Nekrasova 50. **E:** tv@pvi.ru **Reg:** On (MHz) Pskov 66.05, V.Luki 67.25, Trutnevo 67.34, Novosokolniki 67.94, Sebezh 68.12, Dedovichi 69.86, Glubokoye 70.01.

PZ) Penzenskaya oblast: GTRK "Penza", ul. Lermontova 39, 440602 Penza. **E:** gtrk@penza-trv.ru **Reg:** On (MHz) Pachelma 66.80, Sosnovoborsk 68.51, Meshcherskoye 68.84, Blagodatka 69.08, Lopatino 70.22, Penza 70.67, Narovchat 70.88, Belinskiy 71.21, Issa 100.2, Gorodishche 100.4, Lunino 101.0, Neverkino 101.1, Issa 102.2, Nikolsk 106.1, Malaya Serdoba 106.4.

RA) Respublika Altay: GTRK "Gornyy Altay", 659000 Gorno-Altaysk, pr. Kommunisticheskiy 37. **E:** info@elaltay.ru **Reg:** On (kHz) Ulagan & Ust-Kan 1350*, Ust-Koksa & Turochak 1440* + (MHz) Turochak 66.02, Aktash & Tashanta & Shebalino 67.10, Gorno-Altaysk 67.22, Onguday & V.Tiyakhty 71.66 in Russian, Altai. (* until end of 2015)

RK) Respublika Khakasiya: GTRK "Khakasiya", 655017 Abakan, ul. Vyatkina 12. **E:** vgtrk2003@mail.ru **Reg:** "R. Khakasiya" on (MHz) Abakan 66.89/91.0, Kopyevo 68.00, Priiskovyy 68.51, Chernogorsk 69.50, Shira 70.16, Tashtyp & Vershina Tyoi 71.00, Bogdan 72.50, Askiz 72.59, Cheremushki 73.01, Sorsk 73.19, Sonskiy 73.52, Beya & Saragash 73.61, Kommunar 73.85, Sayanogorsk 102.7, Abaza 103.3 in Russian, Khakas.

RO) Rostovskaya oblast: GTRK "Don-TR", 344101 Rostov-na-Donu, ul. 1-ya Barrikadnaya 18. **E:** dontr2@dontr.ru **Reg:** On (MHz) Salsk 66.86, Morozovsk 67.07, Volgodonsk 70.13/99.0, Kamensk 70.28, Veshenskaya 72.23, Rostov-na-Donu 72.95/89.0.

RS) Respublika Sakha (Yakutiya): GTRK "Sakha", 677892 Yakutsk, ul. Ordzhonikidze 48. **E:** sakha@yandex.ru **Reg:** "R. Yakutii" on (MHz) Neryungri 66.68, Aldan 69.38, Lensk 70.28, Yakutsk 70.40/91.3, Olyokminsk 101.4, Pokrovsk 101.7, Belaya Gora & Ytyk-Kyuel 102.0 in Russian, Yakut.

RT) Respublika Tyva: GTRK "Tyva", 667003 Kyzyl, ul. Gornaya 31. **Reg:** On (MHz) Shagonar 70.64, Kyzyl 105.5 in Russian, Tuvinian.

RY) Ryazanskaya oblast: GTRK "Oka", 390006 Ryazan, ul. Skomoroshinskaya 20. **E:** zavtv@ryazan.rfn.ru **Reg:** "R. Ryazani" on (MHz) Kadom 68.03, Ryazan 69.32, Yermish 69.35, Lesnoye-Konobeyevo 72.35, Miloslavskoye 101.8, Mosolovo 103.5, Ryazhk 105.2, Skopin 106.9.

SA) Samarskaya oblast: GTRK "Samara", 443011 Samara, ul. Sovetskoy Armii 205. **E:** info@tvsamara.ru **Reg:** On (MHz) Sergeyevsk 66.71, Khvorostyanka 66.98, Zhigulyovsk 67.31, Chelno-Vershiny 67.43, Isakly 67.85, Neftegorsk 68.90, Chapayevsk 68.99, Pokhvistnevo 69.05, Kamyshla 69.47, Samara 70.31/95.3, Yelkhovka 70.76, B. Glushitsa 71.15, Shentala 71.33, Borskoye 73.04, Syzran 73.10, Klyavlino 73.70, Tavolzhanka 100.0, Oktyabrsk 100.4, Chetyrla 101.2, Kamyshla 102.6, Mordovo-Adelyakovo 103.0, Chelno-Vershiny 103.5, Androsovka 103.9, Alekseyevka & Shentala 104.0, Pokhvistnevo 104.1, Yelkhovka 104.2, Klyavlino & Maryevka 104.4, Koshki 105.1, Neftegorsk 105.2, Isakly

105.3, Novokurovka 105.5, Krasnoarmeyskoye 105.8, Sergiyevsk 105.9, Khvorostyanka 107.1, Kinel-Cherkassy 107.7.

SL) Sakhalinskaya oblast: GTRK "Sakhalin", ul. Komsomolskaya 209, 693000 Yuzhno-Sakhalinsk. **E:** gtrksakhalin@gmail.com **Reg:** On (MHz) Tymovskoye 66.08, 66.80 Khoe, Golovino 68.00, Malokurilskoye 68.24, Pyatirechye 68.39, Smirnykh 68.69, Okha 69.20, Aleksandrovsk-Sakhalinskiy 69.44, Gornozavodsk 69.50, Nogliki 69.56, Okhotskoye 69.65, Poronaysk 69.92, Tomari 70.16, Uglegorsk 70.40, Yuzhno-Kurilsk 70.94, Novikovo 71.12, Shebunino 71.63, Nevelsk 101.7, Dolinsk 102.0, Chekhov 104.0, Kholmsk 104.8, Yuzhno-Sakhalinsk 106.0, Korsakov 107.6. Incl. prgr in Korean.

SM) Smolenskaya oblast: GTRK "Smolensk", 214025 Smolensk, ul. Nakhimova 1. **E:** rukovodstvo@smolgtrk.rfn.ru **Reg:** On (MHz) Smolensk 68.54, Smogiri 68.96, Vyazma 69.20, Roslavl 70.91.

SO) Respublika Severnaya Osetiya - Alaniya: GTRK "Alaniya", 362007 Vladikavkaz, Osetinskaya gorka 2. **E:** mail@alaniatv.ru **Reg:** On (MHz) Verkhniy Fiagdon 69.47, Mozdok 71.78, Vladikavkaz 72.20 in Russian, Ossetic. Local channel "Alaniya FM" on Vladikavkaz 104.5MHz.

SP) Sankt Peterburg (Federal City) & Leningradskaya oblast: GTRK "Sankt-Peterburg", 197022 St.Peterburg, nab. reki Karpovki 43. **E:** info@rtr.spb.ru **Reg:** On (MHz) Tikhvin 66.14, St.Peterburg 66.30, Kingisepp 67.67, Podporozhye 69.95, Luga 70.88, Yefimovskiy 72.05.

SR) Saratovskaya oblast: GTRK "Saratov", 410004 Saratov, 2-ya Sadovaya ul. 7. **E:** top@gtrk.renet.ru **Reg:** On (MHz) Perelyub 66.44, Yershov & Yekaterinovka 68.48, Aleksandrov Gay 69.68, Balashov 70.16, Balakovo 70.52, Saratov 71.09, Lysyye Gory 101.8, Khvalynsk 102.8.

ST) Stavropolskiy kray: GTRK "Stavropolye", 355000 Stavropol, ul. Artema 35a. **E:** referent@stavropolye.tv **Reg:** On (MHz) Ipatovo 66.77, Pyatigorsk 68.96, Stavropol 69.53, Neftekumsk 70.01.

SV) Sverdlovskaya oblast: GTRK "Ural", 620026 Yekaterinburg, ul. Lunacharskogo 212. **E:** radio@sgtrk.ru **Reg:** "R. Urala" on (MHz) Talitsa 65.93, Novaya Lyalya 66.08, Petrokamenskoye 66.32, Alapayevsk 66.50, Talitsa 66.71, Zaykovo 66.83, Nevyansk 66.92, Nizhniye Sergi 67.01, Ivdel 67.76, Sankino 68.66, Basyanovskiy 68.69, Propokyevskaya Salda 68.72, Sredniy Bugalysh 68.93, Rezh & Shalya & Verkhoturye 69.17, Bisert 69.20, Baranchinskiy 69.29, Serov 69.65, Klevakinskoye 69.74, Useninovo 69.80, Andronovo 70.16, Andryushino 70.34, Afanasyevskoye & Azanka 70.43, Pelym 70.58, Arti 70.73, Yekaterinburg 71.06/95.5, Pyshma 71.24, Kamyshlov 72.53, Severouralsk 73.25, Turinsk 73.85, Krasnoufimsk 101.7.

TA) Tambovskaya oblast: GTRK "Tambov", 392000 Tambov, ul. Michurinskaya 8a. **E:** gtrk-tambov@bk.ru **Reg:** On (MHz) Tambov 71.00, Tokaryovka 103.3, Staroyuryevo 103.6.

TL) Tulskaya oblast: GTRK "Tula", 300600 Tula, Staronikitskaya ul. 1. **E:** info@tula.rfn.ru **Reg:** On (MHz) Efremov 66.92, Tula 71.15/91.3, Novomoskovsk 72.35, Suvorov 102.4.

TO) Tomskaya oblast: GTRK "Tomsk", 634050 Tomsk, ul. Pushkina 19. **E:** adm@tvtomsk.ru **Reg:** "R. Tomsk" on (MHz) Aleksandrovskoye 66.02, Pudino 66.74, Nadym 66.80, Kozhevnikovo 67.01, Krivosheino 67.31, Beregayevo & Lukashkin Yar & Novaya Burka 67.40, Staraya Yuvala & Ust-Bakchar 68.15, Voznesenka & Sredniy Vasyugan 68.33, Malinovka 68.39, Parabel 68.45, Kolpashevo 68.87, Klyukvinka 68.33, Strezhevoy 68.51, Vysokiy Yar 68.54, Teguldet 68.60, Yagodnyy 68.66, Koplashevo 68.87, Ulu-Yul 69.08, Podgornoye 69.20, Kyonga 69.29, Baturino 69.50, Belyy Yar 69.56, Parbig 69.80, Bakchar & Zyryanskoye 70.01, Malinovka 70.55, Novaya Tyuvinka 70.70, Komsomolsk 70.82, Novyy Vasyugan 70.94, Novonikolskoye 71.21, Oktyabrskiy & Sayga 71.33, Kargasok 71.42, Asino 71.57, Molchanovo 71.84, Krasnyy Yar 72.17, Chilino 72.20, Podgornoye 72.44, Zyryanskoye 73.01, Plotinkovo 73.22, Volodino 73.40, Novyy Tevriz & Filimonovka 102.0, Tomsk 102.9, Turuntayevo 106.3.

TS) Respublika Tatarstan (Tatarstan): GTRK "Tatarstan", 420015 Kazan, ul. M. Gorkogo 15. **E:** secret@trttv.ru **Reg:** "R.Tatarstana"/ "Tatarstan radiosi" on (MHz) Naberezhnyye Chelny 67.01, Sovkhoz im. Kirova 67.28, Baly 68.45, Kazan 68.48/99.4, Leninogorsk 68.63, Tetyushi 69.95, Bilyarsk 70.13, Aktanysh 70.22, Nurlat 70.46, Buinsk 70.61, Cheremshan 72.14, Nizhnekamensk & A.Saplyk 72.29, Abdakhmanovo 72.59, Almetyevsk 103.9, Bazarnyye Matabi 107.8 in Russian, Tatar.

TV) Tverskaya oblast: GTRK "Tver", 170000 Tver, ul. Vagzhanova 9. **E:** gtrktver@tvcom.ru **Reg:** On (MHz) Bologoye 66.39, Toropets 66.89, Kashin 66.95, Pogoreloye 67.55, Sharkovskiy 67.61, Beliy 68.06, Zapadnaya Dvina 69.35, Selizharovo 69.68, Rzhev 69.98, Maksatikha & Nelidovo 71.24, Kimry 71.48, Tver 72.32/93.5, Vesyegonsk 72.65.

TY) Tyumenskaya oblast: GTRK "Region-Tyumen", 625013 Tyumen, ul. Permyakova 6. **E:** gtrk@region-tyumen.ru **Reg:** On (MHz) Berdyuzhye 66.41, Aromashevo 66.68, Gagarino 66.89, Yarkovo 66.95, Sladkovo 68.33, Vagay 68.60, Armizonskoye 68.84, Masali 68.96, Yurginskoye 69.11, Demyanskoye 69.32, B.Sorokino 69.95, Nizhnyaya Tavda 70.34, Shabanovo 70.55, Uvat 71.42, Tyumen 71.66/90.8, Tobolsk 71.90, Uporovo 73.19, Zavodoukovsk 104.1, Baykalovo 105.5 (also relayed

via txs in region KY).

UD) Udmurtskaya respublika: GTRK "Udmurtiya", 426004 Izhevsk, ul. Komunarov 216. **E:** adm@udmtv.ru **Reg:** On (MHz) Izhevsk 68.06, Balezino 70.94, Kizner 71.81, Yar 72.11, Alashi 98.3, Karakulino 98.4, Debyesy 101.0, Vavozh 102.7, Kambarka & Yukamenskoye 103.6, Mozhga 104.0, Krasnogorodskoye 104.7, Valamaz 105.0, Syumsi 107.2 in Russian, Udmurt, Tatar, Mari.

UL) Ulyanovskaya oblast: GTRK "Volga", 432030 Ulyanovsk, ul. Simbirskaya 5. **E:** volgarek@mail.ru **Reg:** On (MHz) Novospasskoye 67.07, Dimitrovgrad 67.19, Kuzuvatovo 67.85, Pavlovka 69.47, Radishchevo 69.59, Staraya Kulatka 70.04, Veshkayma 70.40, Ulyanovsk 71.00/89.6, Inza 73.43, Gladchikha 73.49, Surskoye 73.58.

VG) Volgogradskaya oblast: GTRK "Volgograd-TRV", 400066 Volgograd, ul. Mira 9. **E:** radioinfo@volgograd-trv.ru **Reg:** (MHz) Mikhaylovka 66.83, Elton 66.95, Uryupinsk 67.17, Kamyshin 69.14, Chilekovo 69.44, Loboykovo & Uspenka 70.40, Volgograd 70.43/98.3, Yelan 70.49, Kletskiy 70.94, Surovikino 71.00, Zhirnovsk 71.51.

VL) Vladimirskaya oblast: GTRK "Vladimir", 600000 Vladimir, ul. Bol. Moskovskaya 62. **E:** adm@vladtv.ru **Reg:** On (MHz) Murom 66.32, Petushki 66.71, Aleksandrov 67.67, Suzdal 68.72, Gorokhovets 69.08, Sudogda 69.47, Melenki 70.25, Vyazniki 70.28, Sobinka 70.61, Kovrov 70.67, Kirzhach 71.03, Kolchugino 73.55, Gus-Khrustalnyy 103.1.

VN) Voronezhskaya oblast: GTRK "Voronezh", 394625 Voronezh, ul. Karl Marksa 114. **E:** tv@vgtv.vrn.ru **Reg:** On (MHz) Bobrov 67.04, Kalach 67.37, Rossosh 70.37, Borisoglebsk 70.82, Boguchar 71.90, Voronezh 72.11, Ertil 101.5.

VO) Vologodskaya oblast: GTRK "Vologda", 160000 Vologda, ul. Predtechenskaya 32. **E:** gtrk_vologda@pochta.ru **Reg:** On (MHz) Cherepovets 66.38/103.4, Sludno 66.77, Vitegra & Yakutino & Ozerki 66.86, Syamzha 67.88, Nyuksenitsa 68.03, Vologda 69.05, Verkhovazhye 69.08, Lipin Bor 69.65, Totma 69.71, Kurilovo 70.07, Andomskiy Pogost 100.8, Tarnogorskiy Gorodok 101.5, Kharovsk 102.2, Vozhega 102.5, Novaya Derevnya & Oshta 102.7, Shuyskouye 102.9.

YA) Yaroslavskaya oblast: GTRK "Yaroslaviya", 150014 Yaroslavl, ul. Bogdanovicha 20. **E:** gtrk@nordnet.ru **Reg:** On (MHz) Dubki 68.66, Volga 70.88, Yaroslavl 99.1, Lyubim 103.6, Danilov 104.3.

YN) Yamalo-Nenetskiy avtonomnyy okrug - Yugra: GTRK "Yamal", 626600 Salekhard, ul. Lambinykh 3. **E:** gtrk-yamal.ru **Reg:** On (MHz) Gubkinskiy 66.75, Muzhi 68.90, Yar-Sale 69.32, Kharp 70.76, Noyabrsk 70.46, Nadym 71.78, Salekhard 71.99/100.6. Txs also relay reg. prgrs by GTRK "Region-Tyumen", Tyumen, TY. (NB: YN is subordinated to region TY)

YV) Yevreyskaya avtonomnaya oblast: GTRK "Bira", 679016 Birobidzhan, ul. Oktyabrskaya 15. **E:** gtrkbira@biratv.rfn.ru **Reg:** On (MHz) Nikolayevka 66.02, Obluchye 66.32, Smidovich 66.80, Birobidzhan 67.88, Khingansk 68.33, Birakan 68.60, Pashkovo 69.89, Bidzhan & Teploozersk 70.07, Leninskoye 73.22, Kuldur 73.64.

ZB) Zabaykalskiy kray: GTRK "Chita", 672090 Chita, ul. Kostyushko-Grigorovicha 27. **E:** chrtv@chita.rfn.ru **Reg:** On (MHz) Kokuy & Petrovsk-Zabaykalskiy 66.14, Chita 66.32/91.6, Nerchinskiy Zavod 66.44, Krasnyy Chikoy 66.53, Kyra 68.00, Khilok 68.09, Karymskoye 68.81, Novopavlovka 69.05, Baley 69.17, Ulety 69.41, Khada-Bulak 69.56, Kholbon 69.80, Verkh-Usugli 69.98, Orlovskiy 70.07*, Krasnokamensk 70.67, Priargunsk 73.85, Narasun 101.9, Kurulga & Olinsk 102.4, Aleksandrovskiy Zavod + 6 sites 102.5, Kokuy 102.6, Tokhtor 102.8, Chara 103.0, Gazimurskiy Zavod & Drovyanaya & Shelopugino 103.6, Maleta & Zakharovo 103.7, Darasun & Mogoytuy 104.1, Batakan + 6 sites 104.2, Novokurgatay & Vershino-Shakhtaminskiy 104.4 in Russian, Buryat. NB: *) Tx also carries prgrs by reg. substudio (Territorialnoye otdeleniye GTRK "Chita"): ul. Bazara Rinchino 7, 687000 Aginskoye. **E:** abgtrk@aginsk.chita.ru.

RADIO ORFEY (Gov)

⌂ 115326 Moskva, ul. Pyatnitskaya 25 ☎ +7 495 9514340 🖷 +7 495 9594067 **E:** rgmc@muzcentrum.ru **W:** muzcentrum.ru
L.P: GD: Irina Gerasimova

Rg	Location	MHz	kW	Rg	Location	MHz	kW
PR	Perm	66.80	4	TL	Tula	71.93	4
SV	Yekaterinburg	69.92	1	MO	Moskva	99.2	5
LI	Lipetsk	70.07	4	SM	Smolensk	104.3	0.5
VG	Volgograd	71.33	2	KG	Kurgan	106.0	1
SP	St.Peterburg	71.66	5				

D.Prgr: 24h.

RUSSKAYA MEDIAGRUPPA (Semi-Gov)

⌂ 123298 Moskva, 3-ya Khoroshevskaya ul. 12 ☎ +7 499 5797709 🖷 +7 495 7480808 **E:** rusradio@rr.ru **W:** rmg.rusradio.ru
L.P: DG (acting): Roman Sarkisov
NB: In 2015, the state enterprise "Roskonsert" started the process to acquire the majority of shares in the media holding "Russkaya Mediagruppa". This includes the radio networks DFM, Hit FM, R.

Monte-Karlo, R. Maksimum, Russkoye R. (freqs see under "Other Stations").

OTHER STATIONS (¦=time-shared)

MW	kHz	kW	Rg	Location	Station
1)	531	5	SL	Yu-Sakhalinsk, FE	Avtoradio
86)	¦612	20	MO	Kurkino, E	Narodnoye R.
172)	¦612	20	MO	Kurkino, E	R. Radonezh
172)	684	10	SP	St.Peterburg, E	R. Radonezh
A)	738	5	MO	Kurkino, E	WRN relay
172)	738	50	PM	Tavrichanka, FE	R. Radonezh
117)	765	20	KH	Khabarovsk, FE	R. Vostok Rossii
117)	765	20	KH	Komsomolsk-na-A., FE	R. Vostok Rossii
117)	765	5	KH	Bikin, FE	R. Vostok Rossii
117)	765	5	KH	Bogorodskoye, FE	R. Vostok Rossii
117)	765	5	KH	Chegdomyn, FE	R. Vostok Rossii
117)	765	5	KH	De-Kastri, FE	R. Vostok Rossii
117)	765	5	KH	Nikolayevsk-na-A., FE	R. Vostok Rossii
117)	765	5	KH	Pereyaslavka, FE	R. Vostok Rossii
117)	765	5	KH	Sovetskaya Gavan, FE	R. Vostok Rossii
117)	765	5	KH	Troitskoye, FE	R. Vostok Rossii
117)	765	5	KH	Tsimmermanskoye, FE	R. Vostok Rossii
117)	765	5	KH	Vyazemskiy, FE	R. Vostok Rossii
117)	765	5	KH	Vysokogornyy, FE	R. Vostok Rossii
117)	765	5	KH	Yekaterinoslavka, FE	R. Vostok Rossii
117)	765	5	KH	Yagodnyy, FE	R. Vostok Rossii
117)	765	1	KH	Ayan, FE	R. Vostok Rossii
121)	¦828	10	SP	St.Peterburg, E	Radiogazeta Slovo
123)	¦828	10	SP	St.Peterburg, E	Pravoslavnoye R.
128)	1053	10	SP	Olgino, E	R. Mariya
132)	1089	50	SP	Krasnyy Bor, E	R. Teos
132)	1134	20	MO	Kurkino, E	R. Teos

FM	MHz	kW	Rg	Location	Station
14)	66.08	1	AK	Barnaul	R. Shanson
119)	66.23	1	TS	Nab. Chelny	Brezhnyev FM
19)	66.29	1	RO	Dyogtevo	Dorozhnoye R.
124C)	66.68	4	BA	Ufa	R. Ashkadar
16)	67.04	1	TY	Tyumen	Retro FM
187)	67.52	2	NS	Bagan	R. Slovo
223)	67.70	1	UL	Ulyanovsk	Tatarskoye R.
4)	67.70	1	CB	Magnitogorsk	Europa Plus
148)	67.79	1	TS	Nab. Chelny	R. Kunel
165)	67.79	4	SP	Vyborg	R. Peterburg
1)	68.00	1	MO	Moskva	Avtoradio
103B)	68.03	2	ME	Yoshkar-Ola	R. 3-y Kanal
4)	68.09	1	PZ	Penza	Europa Plus
5)	68.39	1	KG	Kurgan	Hit FM
60)	68.51	4	SV	Irbit	Kanal Voskreseniye
161)	68.57	1	NN	N.Novgorod	R. Obraz
168)	68.84	10	MO	Moskva	R. Nashe Podmoskovye
60)	68.87	4	SV	Nizhniye Sergi	Kanal Voskreseniye
95)	68.90	1	CV	Cheboksary	Otkrytoye R.
165)	68.93	4	SP	Kingisepp	R. Peterburg
3)	69.11	1	AK	Barnaul	Ekho Moskvy
4)	69.44	1	RO	Rostov-na-Donu	Ekho Moskvy
165)	69.47	5	SP	Sankt-Peterburg	R. Peterburg
218)	69.62	1	PE	Kungur	Soyuz FM
108)	69.68	1	BA	Ufa	R. 1-y Kanal
7)	69.74	1	UL	Ulyanovsk	Militseyskaya volna
6)	69.80	1	TY	Tomsk	Love R.
214)	69.86	4	CB	Magnitogorsk	Seven Skies
125)	70.64	1	SA	Tolyatti	R. Avgust
15)	70.70	1	CB	Chelyabinsk	DFM
86)	70.73	1	LI	Lipetsk	Narodnoye R.
16)	70.85	1	KV	Kirov	Retro FM
1)	70.94	1	NS	Kuybyshev	Avtoradio
3)	71.06	1	RK	Abakan	Ekho Moskvy
60)	71.21	4	SV	Nizhniy Tagil	Kanal Voskreseniye
88A)	71.24	15	SP	Sankt-Peterburg	R. Baltika
2)	71.30	2.5	MO	Moskva	Russkoye R.
216)	71.30	1	RS	Yakutsk	R. Viktoriya
27)	71.30	1	BA	Ufa	R. Dacha
4)	71.51	1	OB	Orsk	Europa Plus
4)	71.57	1	AK	Barnaul	Retro FM
60)	71.69	4	SV	Serov	Kanal Voskreseniye
14)	71.72	2	KL	Kaluga	R. Shanson
1)	71.84	1	KV	Kirov	Avtoradio
3)	71.93	1	KY	Surgut	Ekho Moskvy
14)	72.11	1	KA	Kaliningrad	R. Shanson
4)	72.11	4	SV	Afanasyevskoye	Kanal Voskreseniye
60)	72.11	4	SV	Tavda	Kanal Voskreseniye
99)	72.29	1	ZB	Chita	Populyarnoye R.
187)	72.38	2	NS	Tatarsk	R. Slovo

FM	MHz	kW	Rg	Location	Station
87)	72.41	4	CV	Ibresi	Natsionaln. R. Chuvashii
14)	72.44	1	KV	Kirov	R. Shanson
2)	72.83	1.5	SA	Samara	Russkoye R.
60)	72.83	4	SV	Yekaterinburg	Kanal Voskreseniye
86)	72.83	1	OR	Oryol	Narodnoye R.
172)	72.92	5	MO	Moskva	R. Radonezh
56)	73.10	15	SP	Sankt-Peterburg	Grad Petrov
172)	73.13	1	RO	Ryazan	R. Radonezh
2)	73.22	1	IR	Bratsk	Russkoye R.
16)	73.25	1	KL	Kaluga	Retro FM
86)	73.25	1	KD	Krasnodar	Narodnoye R.
14)	73.28	1	AK	Biysk	R. Shanson
69)	73.43	1	NN	Bor	Levyy Bereg
130B)	73.55	1	VN	Voronezh	R. Blagovestiye
55)	73.58	1	NS	Novosibirsk	Gorodskaya volna
18)	73.64	1	ST	Stavropol	Yumor FM
2)	73.76	1	IR	Irkutsk	Russkoye R.
10)	73.79	1	AK	Biysk	R. 7
16)	73.88	1	BE	St. Oskol	Retro FM
4)	73.88	1	MD	Saransk	Europa Plus
1)	73.91	1	VL	Vladimir	Avtoradio
3)	73.94	1	YA	Yaroslavl	Ekho Moskvy
3)	73.97	1	CB	Chelyabinsk	Ekho Moskvy
75)	73.97	1	KV	Kirov	Mariya FM
11)	87.5	1	SR	Saratov	R. Maksimum
19)	87.5	5	SP	Sankt-Peterburg	Dorozhnoye R.
19)	87.5	1	RO	Salsk	Dorozhnoye R.
223)	87.5	1	TS	Nab. Chelny	Tatarskoye R.
28)	87.5	5	MO	Moskva	Biznes FM
12)	87.6	1	BE	Belgorod	Sport FM
19)	87.6	1	IV	Kineshma	Dorozhnoye R.
21)	87.6	1	SV	Yekaterinburg	R. Zvezda
23)	87.6	1	PR	Perm	Detskoye R.
25)	87.6	1	KE	Kemerovo	R. Mir
1)	87.7	1	AM	Blagoveshchensk	Avtoradio
12)	87.7	1	SM	Smolensk	Sport FM
12)	87.8	1	PM	Vladivostok	Sport FM
12)	87.8	1	BA	Ufa	Sport FM
183)	87.8	1		Nizhnevartovsk	R. Sibir
12)	87.9	1	TY	Tyumen	Sport FM
16)	87.9	1	KH	Khabarovsk	Retro FM
24)	87.9	1	SR	Saratov	NRJ
31)	87.9	5	MO	Moskva	Like FM
45)	87.9	1	BR	Bryansk	Bryanskaya guberniya
14)	88.0	1	MA	Magadan	R. Shanson
16)	88.0	1	SP	Sankt-Peterburg	Retro FM
2)	88.0	1	SA	Tolyatti	Russkoye R.
21)	88.0	1	MU	Murmansk	R. Zvezda
231)	88.0	1	IN	Nazran	R. Ingushetiya
4)	88.0	1	KE	Kemerovo	Europa Plus
43)	88.0	1	PR	Perm	Bolid FM
19)	88.1	1	OM	Omsk	Dorozhnoye R.
19)	88.1	1	SM	Velizh	Dorozhnoye R.
151)	88.2	1	KE	Leninsk-Kuznetskiy	R. Leninsk
23)	88.2	1	RO	Rostov-na-Donu	Detskoye R.
24)	88.2	1	BA	Ufa	NRJ
5)	88.2	1	KY	Surgut	Hit FM
1)	88.3	2	PM	Vladivostok	Avtoradio
16)	88.3	5	MO	Moskva	Retro FM
16)	88.3	1	SL	Yuzhno-Sakhalinsk	Retro FM
17)	88.3	1	TS	Kazan	Serebryanyy dozhd
18)	88.3	1	TY	Tyumen	Yumor FM
19)	88.3	1	AK	Barnaul	Dorozhnoye R.
22)	88.3	1	KH	Khabarovsk	R. KP
23)	88.3	1	SR	Saratov	Detskoye R.
27)	88.3	1	AS	Astrakhan	R. Dacha
5)	88.3	1	YE	Yekaterinburg	Hit FM
5)	88.3	1	KD	Krasnodar	Militseyskaya volna
93)	88.3	1	NN	Sokolskoye	NN-R.
23)	88.4	1	SA	Tolyatti	Detskoye R.
36)	88.4	5	SP	Sankt-Peterburg	Avtoradio St-Peterburg
1)	88.5	1	KH	Komsomolsk-na-A.	Avtoradio
1)	88.5	1	MO	Yegoryevsk	Avtoradio
20)	88.5	1	YE	Severouralsk	R. Romantika
5)	88.6	1	UL	Dimitrovgrad	Hit FM
1)	88.7	2	KH	Khabarovsk	Avtoradio
12)	88.7	1	MU	Murmansk	Sport FM
134A)	88.7	1	SM	Safonovo	R. Vanya
14)	88.7	1	AM	Blagoveshchensk	R. Shanson
18)	88.7	5	MO	Moskva	Yumor FM
23)	88.7	1	KD	Krasnodar	Detskoye R.
26)	88.7	1	SR	Saratov	R. Rekord

FM	MHz	kW	Rg	Location	Station		FM	MHz	kW	Rg	Location	Station
7)	88.7	1	AK	Barnaul	Militseyskaya volna		14)	91.3	1	KE	Belovo	R. Shanson
12)	88.8	1	UL	Ulyanovsk	Sport FM		19)	91.3	1	VL	Murom	Dorozhnoye R.
167)	88.8	1	TY	Tyumen	R. Pobedy		4)	91.3	1	SA	Tolyatti	Europa Plus
17)	88.8	1	YE	Yekaterinburg	Serebryanyy dozhd		1)	91.4	1	MO	Shatura	Avtoradio
18)	88.9	5	PR	Perm	Yumor FM		12)	91.4	1	AS	Astrakhan	Sport FM
18)	88.9	5	SP	Sankt-Peterburg	Yumor FM		23)	91.4	1	UD	Izhevsk	Detskoye R.
26)	88.9	1	SL	Yuzhno-Sakhalinsk	R. Rekord		23)	91.4	1	OM	Omsk	Detskoye R.
14)	89.0	1	UL	Dimitrovgrad	R. Shanson		24)	91.4	1	UL	Ulyanovsk	NRJ
134A)	89.1	1	MU	Murmansk	R. Vanya		26)	91.4	1	BE	Belgorod	R. Rekord
139)	89.1	1	MO	Moskva	R. Jazz		3)	91.4	1	YE	Yekaterinburg	Ekho Moskvy
27)	89.1	1	AM	Blagoveshchensk	R. Dacha		4)	91.4	1	TS	Almetyevsk	Europa Plus
23)	89.2	1	YE	Yekaterinburg	Detskoye R.		131)	91.5	1	TS	Kazan	R. Bolgar
27)	89.2	1	KE	Kemerovo	R. Dacha		15)	91.5	1	BA	Ufa	DFM
27)	89.2	1	UL	Ulyanovsk	R. Dacha		17)	91.5	1	KE	Kemerovo	Serebryanyy dozhd
23)	89.3	1	TS	Kazan	Detskoye R.		180)	91.5	1	SA	Samara	Tok FM
25)	89.3	1	IR	Irkutsk	R. Mir		25)	91.5	1	TO	Tomsk	R. Mir
19)	89.4	1	PM	Vladivostok	Dorozhnoye R.		3)	91.5	5	SP	Sankt-Peterburg	Ekho Moskvy
27)	89.4	1	RK	Abakan	R. Dacha		25)	91.6	1	TS	Nab. Chelny	R. Mir
4)	89.4	1	PR	Perm	Europa Plus		25)	91.6	1	SO	Vladikavkaz	R. Mir
25)	89.5	1	MU	Murmansk	R. Mir		97)	91.8	1	PR	Perm	Pioner FM
76)	89.5	1	MO	Moskva	Megapolis FM		12)	91.9	1	TS	Kazan	Sport FM
2)	89.6	1	KH	Khabarovsk	Russkoye R.		159)	91.9	1	YE	Yekaterinburg	R. Norodnaya volna
24)	89.6	1	YE	Yekaterinburg	NRJ		25)	92.0	1	UD	Izhevsk	R. Mir
27)	89.6	1	TY	Tyumen	R. Dacha		80A)	92.0	5	MO	Moskva	Moskva FM
202)	89.7	4	SP	Sankt-Peterburg	R. Zenit		22)	92.3	1	YE	Yekaterinburg	R. KP
222)	89.7	1	TS	Kazan	Taksi FM		24)	92.3	2	TS	Kazan	NRJ
18)	89.8	1	RK	Abakan	Yumor FM		27)	92.4	5	MO	Moskva	R. Dacha
20)	89.8	1	PR	Perm	R. Romantika		236)	92.5	1	SA	Samara	Samarskoye Gub. R.
2)	89.9	1	SL	Yuzhno-Sakhalinsk	Russkoye R.		1)	92.6	1	MO	Orekhovo-Zuyevo	Avtoradio
98A)	89.9	1	SP	Vyborg	Piter FM		1)	92.6	1	MO	Taldom	Avtoradio
9A)	89.9	5	MO	Moskva	Slavyanskoye R.		12)	92.7	1	YE	Yekaterinburg	Sport FM
23)	90.0	1	UL	Ulyanovsk	Detskoye R.		20)	92.7	1	KN	Krasnoyarsk	R. Romantika
136)	90.1	5	SP	Sankt-Peterburg	R. Ermitazh		12)	92.8	3	NS	Novosibirsk	Sport FM
12)	90.2	1	KE	Kemerovo	Sport FM		141)	92.8	1	MO	Moskva	R. Karneval
134A)	90.2	1	TA	Tambov	R. Vanya		22)	92.8	1	NN	Nizhniy Novgorod	R. KP
185)	90.2	1	YE	Yekaterinburg	R. SK		13)	92.9	2	SP	Sankt-Peterburg	R. RSN
20)	90.2	1	SA	Saratov	R. Romantika		12)	93.2	5	MO	Moskva	Sport FM
27)	90.2	1	TS	Kazan	R. Dacha		12)	93.2	1	KE	Novokuznetsk	Sport FM
1)	90.3	5	MO	Moskva	Avtoradio		12)	93.5	1	KY	Krasnoyarsk	Sport FM
19)	90.3	2	KY	Surgut	Dorozhnoye R.		228)	93.5	1	TS	Kazan	Tartib FM
16)	90.4	1	SA	Tolyatti	Retro FM		10)	93.6	1	KA	Kaliningrad	R. 7
19)	90.4	1	KE	Leninsk-Kuznetskiy	Dorozhnoye R.		64)	93.6	5	MO	Moskva	Kommersant FM
49)	90.4	1	TY	Tyumen	Dobryye pesni		145)	94.0	5	MO	Moskva	Vostok FM
35)	90.5	1	OB	Omsk	R. Vera		18)	94.0	1	KA	Kaliningrad	Yumor FM
22)	90.6	1	SR	Saratov	R. KP		7)	94.2	1	NS	Novosibirsk	Militseyskaya volna
23)	90.6	1	BA	Ufa	Detskoye R.		81)	94.4	5	MO	Moskva	Vesna FM
24)	90.6	1	KD	Krasnodar	NRJ		212)	94.8	5	MO	Moskva	Govorit Moskva
28)	90.6	1	SA	Samara	Biznes FM		8)	94.8	1	YE	Yekaterinburg	Nashe R.
98B)	90.6	5	SP	Sankt-Peterburg	R. dlya dvoikh		24)	95.0	4	SP	Sankt-Peterburg	NRJ
1)	90.7	1	PR	Perm	Avtoradio		208)	95.2	5	MO	Moskva	Rock FM
19)	90.7	1	TL	Tula	Dorozhnoye R.		22)	95.3	1	CB	Chelyabinsk	R. KP
2)	90.7	1	TS	Kazan	Russkoye R.		19)	95.4	1	SP	Svetogorsk	Dorozhnoye R.
70)	90.7	1	LI	Lipetsk	Lipetsk FM		12)	95.5	1	SA	Tolyatti	Sport FM
8)	90.7	1	KY	Surgut	Nashe R.		16)	95.5	1	KA	Kaliningrad	Retro FM
11)	90.8	1	YE	Yekaterinburg	R. Maksimum		21)	95.6	10	MO	Moskva	R. Zvezda
207)	90.8	5	MO	Moskva	Relaks FM		23)	95.6	1	KE	Novokuznetsk	Detskoye R.
35)	90.8	1	KV	Kirov	R. Vera		64)	95.6	1	NN	N.Novgorod	Kommersant FM
61)	90.8	1	SO	Vladikavkaz	Kavkaz R.		171)	95.7	1	BE	Rakitnoye	R. Radio
25)	90.9	1	OM	Omsk	R. Mir		18)	95.7	1	SA	Samara	Yumor FM
6)	90.9	1	RS	Yakutsk	Love R.		20)	95.7	1	SP	Lyuban	R. Romantika
1)	91.0	1	MO	Volokalamsk	Avtoradio		21)	95.7	1	RY	Ryazan	R. Zvezda
10)	91.0	1	SA	Samara	R. 7		23)	95.7	1	VG	Volgograd	Detskoye R.
131)	91.0	1	TS	Alyoshkin Saplyk	R. Bolgar		12)	95.8	2	PR	Perm	Sport FM
134A)	91.0	1	KS	Kostroma	R. Vanya		158)	95.8	1	KA	Gusev	R. na Vostoke
18)	91.0	1	KH	Khabarovsk	Yumor FM		23)	95.8	1	NS	Novosibirsk	Detskoye R.
21)	91.0	1	KG	Kurgan	R. Zvezda		20)	95.9	1	YE	Yekaterinburg	R. Romantika
22)	91.0	1	KD	Krasnodar	R. KP		88B)	95.9	4	SP	Sankt-Peterburg	Neva FM
27)	91.0	1	SR	Saratov	R. Dacha		1)	96.0	1	SA	Tolyatti	Avtoradio
12)	91.1	1	AK	Barnaul	Sport FM		19)	96.0	5	MO	Moskva	Dorozhnoye R.
18)	91.1	1	TS	Kazan	Yumor FM		24)	96.0	1	CB	Chelyabinsk	NRJ
18)	91.1	1	KY	Surgut	Yumor FM		25)	96.0	1	KE	Novokuznetsk	R. Mir
19)	91.1	1	IR	Irkutsk	Dorozhnoye R.		47)	96.0	1	NN	N.Novgorod	Dinamit N.Novgorod
27)	91.1	1	LI	Lipetsk	R. Dacha		23)	96.1	1	RY	Ryazan	Detskoye R.
3)	91.1	1	BA	Ufa	Ekho Moskvy		5)	96.1	1	TV	Tver	Hit FM
8)	91.1	1	KY	Norilsk	Nashe R.		6)	96.1	1	VG	Volgograd	Love R.
9B)	91.1	10	SP	Sankt-Peterburg	Keks FM		18)	96.2	1	SP	Lyuban	Yumor FM
17)	91.2	1	TY	Tyumen	Serebryanyy dozhd		193)	96.2	1	KN	Krasnoyarsk	Krasnoyarsk FM
21)	91.2	1	RO	Rostov-na-Donu	Yumor FM		2)	96.2	2	NS	Novosibirsk	Russkoye R.
18)	91.2	1	ZB	Chita	Yumor FM		24)	96.2	1	UD	Izhevsk	NRJ
19)	91.2	1	SO	Vladikavkaz	Dorozhnoye R.		2)	96.3	1	KA	Kaliningrad	Russkoye R.
3)	91.2	5	MO	Moskva	Ekho Moskvy		20)	96.3	1	KE	Belovo	R. Romantika
3)	91.2	1	PR	Perm	Ekho Moskvy		65)	96.3	1	SA	Samara	Kot FM

FM	MHz	kW	Rg	Location	Station
14)	96.4	1	PZ	Penza	R. Shanson
16)	96.4	1	CB	Chelyabinsk	Retro FM
222)	96.4	5	MO	Moskva	Taksi FM
12)	96.5	1	TV	Tver	Sport FM
22)	96.5	1	VG	Volgograd	R. KP
27)	96.5	1	RY	Ryazan	R. Dacha
21)	96.6	1	KN	Krasnoyarsk	R. Zvezda
22)	96.6	1	PR	Perm	R. KP
38)	96.6	1	PR	Berezniki	Beloye R.
134A)	96.7	1	SP	Lyuban	R. Vanya
190)	96.7	1	DA	Makhachkala	R. Strana gor
27)	96.7	1	KE	Belovo	R. Dacha
23)	96.8	1	CB	Chelyabinsk	Detskoye R.
23)	96.8	5	MO	Moskva	Detskoye R.
24)	96.8	1	NN	N.Novgorod	NRJ
35)	96.8	1	SA	Samara	R. Vera
209)	96.9	1	RY	Ryazan	R. Den
16)	97.0	2	NS	Novosibirsk	Retro FM
23)	97.0	1	KY	Krasnoyarsk	Detskoye R.
27)	97.0	4	SP	Sankt-Peterburg	R. Dacha
22)	97.2	5	MO	Moskva	R. KP
235)	97.2	1	KA	Sovetsk	Russkiy kray
20)	97.4	2	NS	Novosibirsk	R. Romantika
25)	97.4	1	KN	Krasnoyarsk	R. Mir
8)	97.5	1	TV	Tver	Nashe R.
17)	97.6	1	KE	Belovo	Serebryanyy dozhd
24)	97.6	1	PR	Perm	NRJ
17)	97.7	1	KA	Kaliningrad	Serebryanyy dozhd
13)	97.8	1	UD	Izhevsk	R. RSN
67B)	97.8	1	VG	Leninsk	Belyy lebed
4)	97.9	1	SA	Syzran	Europa Plus
161)	98.0	1	NN	Nizhniy Novgorod	R. Obraz
181)	98.0	5	MO	Moskva	R. Shokolad
22)	98.3	1	NS	Novosibirsk	R. KP
26)	98.4	5	MO	Moskva	R. Rekord
12)	98.5	1	OL	Oryol	Sport FM
21)	98.5	1	TV	Tver	R. Zvezda
6)	98.5	1	SV	Yekaterinburg	Love R.
79)	98.5	1	BE	Borisovka	Mir Belogorya
1)	98.6	1	MO	Zaraysk	Avtoradio
16)	98.6	1	SA	Samara	Retro FM
219)	98.6	5	SP	Sankt-Peterburg	Nostalgia FM
1)	98.7	2	NS	Novosibirsk	Avtoradio
16)	98.7	1	KY	Krasnoyarsk	Retro FM
183)	98.7	1	KE	Novokuznetsk	R. Sibir
25)	98.7	1	ST	Stavropol	R. Mir
27)	98.7	1	CB	Chelyabinsk	R. Dacha
97)	98.7	1	PR	Berezniki	Pioner FM
20)	98.8	10	MO	Moskva	R. Romantika
24)	98.8	1	SP	Lyuban	NRJ
24)	98.8	1	VG	Volgograd	NRJ
8)	98.8	1	VO	Vologda	Nashe R.
17)	98.9	1	PR	Perm	Serebryanyy dozhd
19)	98.9	1	YE	Yekaterinburg	Dorozhnoye R.
25)	98.9	1	SA	Tolyatti	R. Mir
26)	98.9	1	KE	Leninsk-Kuznetskiy	R. Rekord
4)	98.9	1	PM	Arsenyev	Europa Plus
116B)	99.0	1	BA	Kumertau	R. Kabriolet
18)	99.0	1	MO	Taldom	Yumor FM
25)	99.0	1	KB	Nalchik	R. Mir
4)	99.0	1	TS	Chistopol	Europa Plus
1)	99.1	2	CB	Chelyabinsk	Avtoradio
113)	99.1	2	KY	Krasnoyarsk	R. 99.1 FM
18)	99.1	1	VN	Voronezh	Yumor FM
23)	99.1	1	NN	N.Novgorod	Detskoye R.
8)	99.1	1	TY	Tobolsk	Nashe R.
24)	99.1	2	NS	Novosibirsk	NRJ
3)	99.1	1	SA	Samara	Ekho Moskvy
11)	99.2	1	VG	Volgograd	R. Maksimum
19)	99.2	1	SR	Balakovo	Dorozhnoye R.
19)	99.2	1	SR	Balakovo	Dorozhnoye R.
22)	99.2	1	VO	Vologda	R. KP
6)	99.2	1	TS	Almetyevsk	Love R.
22)	99.3	1	TV	Tver	R. KP
4)	99.3	1	SP	Kingisepp	Europa Plus
5)	99.3	1	KE	Leninsk-Kuznetskiy	Hit FM
112)	99.4	1	TY	Golyshmanovo	R. 7 Tyumen
16)	99.4	5	PR	Perm	Retro FM
18)	99.4	1	LI	Lipetsk	Yumor FM
19)	99.4	1	SA	Tolyatti	Dorozhnoye R.
28)	99.4	2	YE	Yekaterinburg	Biznes FM
4)	99.4	1	MO	Kolomna	Europa Plus
40)	99.4	1	TS	Chistopol	BIM-R.
140)	99.5	2	KB	Nalchik	R. Kabardino-Balkariya
16)	99.5	1	TY	Tobolsk	Retro FM
18)	99.5	1	NS	Novosibirsk	Yumor FM
203)	99.5	1	RS	Aldan	Radiogora
23)	99.5	1	VN	Voronezh	Detskoye R.
3)	99.5	1	CB	Chelyabinsk	Ekho Moskvy
4)	99.5	1	KE	Novokuznetsk	Europa Plus
93)	99.5	1	NN	N.Novgorod	NN-R.
115)	99.6	1	TS	Almetyevsk	R. Aksu
16)	99.6	1	VO	Vologda	Retro FM
19)	99.6	1	SP	Lyuban	Dorozhnoye R.
19)	99.6	1	OL	Oryol	Dorozhnoye R.
22)	99.6	1	TY	Tyumen	R. KP
53)	99.6	10	MO	Moskva	Stolitsa FM
14)	99.8	1	KE	Mezhdurechensk	R. Shanson
230)	99.8	1	TV	Tver	R. Galaktika
27)	99.8	1	CB	Asha	R. Dacha
6)	99.8	1	SP	Vyborg	Love R.
102)	99.9	5	MO	Avsyunino	Prosto R.
25)	99.9	1	VN	Voronezh	R. Mir
4)	99.9	1	SA	Samara	Europa Plus
10)	100.0	1	NN	N.Novgorod	R. 7
104)	100.0	1	CB	Chelyabinsk	R. 100
16)	100.0	1	YE	Yekaterinburg	Retro FM
16)	100.0	1	SR	Balakovo	Retro FM
19)	100.0	2	RY	Mosolovo	Dorozhnoye R.
19)	100.0	1	AR	Plesetsk	Dorozhnoye R.
2)	100.0	1	OL	Oryol	Russkoye R.
217)	100.0	1	KA	Sovetsk	Mediakit FM
67A)	100.0	1	VG	Volgograd	R. Vedo
7)	100.0	1	OB	Akbulak	Militseyskaya volna
8)	100.0	1	PR	Perm	Nashe R.
1)	100.1	1	PR	Berezniki	Avtoradio
1)	100.1	1	KA	Kaliningrad	Avtoradio
17)	100.1	5	MO	Moskva	Serebryanyy dozhd
18)	100.1	1	CB	Magnitogorsk	Yumor FM
5)	100.1	1	RO	Rostov-na-Donu	Hit FM
6)	100.1	1	SA	Tolyatti	Love R.
7)	100.1	1	VL	Vladimir	Militseyskaya volna
83)	100.1	1	UD	Izhevsk	Moya Udmurtiya
116A)	100.2	1	BA	Kumertau	R. Aktan
18)	100.2	1	TS	Almetyevsk	Yumor FM
2)	100.2	1	SM	Vyazma	Russkoye R.
24)	100.2	1	LI	Khlebnoye	NRJ
4)	100.2	1	VO	Vologda	Europa Plus
4)	100.2	1	KU	Zheleznogorsk	Europa Plus
101)	100.3	1	KE	Mariinsk	Pravilnoye R.
18)	100.3	1	KN	Krasnoyarsk	Yumor FM
2)	100.3	2	SA	Samara	Russkoye R.
25)	100.3	1	IR	Irkutsk	R. Mir
36)	100.3	1	SP	Kingisepp	Avtoradio St-Peterburg
4)	100.3	1	BR	Bryansk	Europa Plus
4)	100.3	1	KS	Kostroma	Europa Plus
4)	100.3	1	KO	Syktyvkar	Europa Plus
4)	100.3	1	VN	Voronezh	Europa Plus
7)	100.3	1	OB	Sol-Iletsk	Militseyskaya volna
146)	100.4	4	CB	Chelyabinsk	R. Kontinental
166)	100.4	5	YE	Yekaterinburg	R. Pilot
17)	100.4	1	NN	N.Novgorod	Serebryanyy dozhd
2)	100.4	1	UL	Dimitrovgrad	Russkoye R.
27)	100.4	1	SM	Gagarin	R. Dacha
37)	100.4	1	KA	Sovetsk	Baltik plyus
4)	100.4	1	KT	Petrozavodsk	Europa Plus
51)	100.4	1	OL	Oryol	Ekspress R.
1)	100.5	1	TY	Tobolsk	Avtoradio
16)	100.5	1	TL	Tula	Retro FM
177)	100.5	1	RS	Aldan	R. Sakha
182)	100.5	1	YE	Nizhniy Tagil	R. Si
19)	100.5	1	VN	Bobrov	Dorozhnoye R.
2)	100.5	1	KS	Buy	Russkoye R.
2)	100.5	1	UD	Izhevsk	Russkoye R.
215)	100.5	1	PR	Solikamsk	SK FM
223)	100.5	1	TS	Kazan	Tatarskoye R.
34)	100.5	1	KE	Novokuznetsk	Apeks-Radio
39)	100.5	5	MO	Moskva	Best FM
4)	100.5	10	SP	Sankt-Peterburg	Europa Plus
7)	100.5	1	VL	Kovrov	Militseyskaya volna
101)	100.6	1	KE	Kemerovo	Pravilnoye R.
16)	100.6	1	VL	Murom	Retro FM
18)	100.6	1	SR	Saratov	Yumor FM
184)	100.6	1	TY	Tyumen	R. Siti

FM	MHz	kW	Rg	Location	Station		FM	MHz	kW	Rg	Location	Station
2)	100.6	1	BA	Kumertau	Russkoye R.		15)	101.2	10	MO	Moskva	DFM
2)	100.6	1	TV	Tver	Russkoye R.		16)	101.2	1	KD	Krasnodar	Retro FM
23)	100.6	1	AK	Barnaul	Detskoye R.		16)	101.2	1	RO	Rostov-na-Donu	Retro FM
232)	100.6	1	RA	Gorno-Altaysk	R. Iskatel		18)	101.2	1	CB	Chelyabinsk	Yumor FM
4)	100.6	1	MD	Saransk	Europa Plus		19)	101.2	1	MU	Monchegorsk	Dorozhnoye R.
4)	100.6	1	VG	Volgograd	Europa Plus		2)	101.2	1	KU	Kursk	Russkoye R.
6)	100.6	1	KL	Kaluga	Love R.		27)	101.2	1	AR	Arkhangelsk	R. Dacha
10)	100.7	1	ST	Stavropol	R. 7		4)	101.2	5	YE	Yekaterinburg	Europa Plus
124B)	100.7	1	BA	Davlekanovo	Sputnik FM		5)	101.2	1	KO	Pechora	Hit FM
137)	100.7	1	VN	Voronezh	R. Guberniya		16)	101.3	1	BA	Tuymazy	Retro FM
170)	100.7	1	DA	Makhachkala	R. Priboy		16)	101.3	1	VL	Vladimir	Retro FM
18)	100.7	1	KB	Nalchik	Yumor FM		18)	101.3	1	UD	Izhevsk	Yumor FM
18)	100.7	1	RY	Ryazan	Yumor FM		19)	101.3	1	RK	Abakan	Dorozhnoye R.
19)	100.7	1	MU	Apatity	Dorozhnoye R.		19)	101.3	1	TO	Tomsk	Dorozhnoye R.
19)	100.7	1	ZB	Chita	Dorozhnoye R.		2)	101.3	1	AK	Biysk	Russkoye R.
19)	100.7	1	KT	Peldozha	Dorozhnoye R.		2)	101.3	1	MD	Saransk	Russkoye R.
200)	100.7	3	NS	Novosibirsk	R. Yuniton		25)	101.3	1	AK	Rubtsovsk	R. Mir
229)	100.7	1	SA	Otradnyy	R. Ekstrim		3)	101.3	1	OB	Orenburg	Ekho Moskvy
234)	100.7	1	OB	Orsk	R. Tochka Ru		4)	101.3	1	LI	Lipetsk	Europa Plus
26)	100.7	1	RO	Rostov-na-Donu	R. Rekord		6)	101.3	2	KY	Krasnoyarsk	Love R.
27)	100.7	1	KU	Kursk	R. Dacha		6)	101.3	1	ST	Pyatigorsk	Love R.
4)	100.7	1	BR	Unecha	Europa Plus		8)	101.3	1	KA	Kaliningrad	Nashe R.
4)	100.7	1	PM	Ussuriysk	Europa Plus		1)	101.4	1	VN	Rossosh	Avtoradio
5)	100.7	5	PR	Perm	Hit FM		1)	101.4	1	BA	Steplitamak	Avtoradio
124A)	100.8	1	BA	Burayevo	R. Yuldash		1)	101.4	1	TV	Tver	Avtoradio
16)	100.8	1	BR	Bryansk	Retro FM		11)	101.4	1	PR	Berezniki	R. Maksimum
18)	100.8	1	VL	Vladimir	Yumor FM		116B)	101.4	1	KO	Ukhta	R. Kabriolet
19)	100.8	1	KY	Krasnoyarsk	Dorozhnoye R.		131)	101.4	2	TS	Bilyarsk	R. Bolgar
2)	100.8	4	KD	Tbilisskaya	Russkoye R.		14)	101.4	1	KH	Khabarovsk	R. Shanson
25)	100.8	2	KE	Leninsk-Kuznetskiy	R. Mir		16)	101.4	1	KS	Kostroma	Retro FM
26)	100.8	1	OB	Orenburg	R. Rekord		17)	101.4	1	PZ	Penza	Serebryanyy dozhd
28)	100.8	1	CB	Chelyabinsk	Biznes FM		19)	101.4	1	TY	Omutinskiy	Dorozhnoye R.
51)	100.8	1	OL	Livny	Ekspress R.		19)	101.4	1	ST	Stavropol	Dorozhnoye R.
6)	100.8	1	KM	Petropavlovsk-K.	Love R.		24)	101.4	1	TL	Tula	NRJ
1)	100.9	1	KD	Kushchevskaya	Avtoradio		5)	101.4	5	IR	Irkutsk	Hit FM
10)	100.9	1	IR	Irkutsk	R. 7		5)	101.4	1	NN	N.Novgorod	Hit FM
130B)	100.9	3	MO	Moskva	R. Vera		52)	101.4	10	SP	Sankt-Peterburg	Eldoradio
157)	100.9	1	KA	Kaliningrad	R. Monte-Karlo		55)	101.4	2	NS	Novosibirsk	Gorodskaya volna
16)	100.9	1	KD	Novorossiysk	Retro FM		7)	101.4	1	OL	Oryol	Militseyskaya volna
183)	100.9	1	ZB	Aginskoye	R. Sibir		1)	101.5	1	BR	Bryansk	Avtoradio
19)	100.9	1	LI	Lipetsk	Dorozhnoye R.		1)	101.5	1	CV	Cheboksary	Avtoradio
20)	100.9	1	RK	Abakan	R. Romantika		1)	101.5	1	TS	Nab. Chelny	Avtoradio
22)	100.9	1		Biysk	R. KP		1)	101.5	1	KY	Nyagan	Avtoradio
25)	100.9	1	TS	Kazan	R. Mir		110B)	101.5	3	VG	Volgograd	Volgograd FM
26)	100.9	5	NN	N.Novgorod	R. Rekord		14)	101.5	1	SR	Saratov	R. Shanson
4)	100.9	1	OL	Oryol	Europa Plus		18)	101.5	1	OM	Omsk	Yumor FM
4)	100.9	1	BA	Steplitamak	Europa Plus		18)	101.5	1	IR	Tayshet	Yumor FM
79)	100.9	1	BE	Belgorod	Mir Belogorya		19)	101.5	1	RY	Ryazan	Dorozhnoye R.
94)	100.9	1	PR	Kudymkar	Okrug FM		2)	101.5	1	KE	Yurga	Russkoye R.
98A)	100.9	10	SP	Sankt-Peterburg	Piter FM		2)	101.5	1	KD	Kanevskaya	Russkoye R.
126)	101.0	1	PM	Artyom	R. AVN		20)	101.5	1	MO	Shatura	R. Romantika
134A)	101.0	1	KO	Ukhta	R. Vanya		233)	101.5	1	PR	Perm	R. Nostagie
134B)	101.0	5	SP	Vyborg	Populyarnaya klassika		24)	101.5	1	KE	Novokuznetsk	NRJ
14)	101.0	1	TY	Ishim	R. Shanson		26)	101.5	2	SA	Samara	R. Rekord
14)	101.0	1	YE	Nizhniy Tagil	R. Shanson		27)	101.5	1	DA	Makhachkala	R. Dacha
14)	101.0	1	SA	Samara	R. Shanson		3)	101.5	1	AM	Blagoveshchensk	Ekho Moskvy
14)	101.0	1	TY	Tyumen	R. Shanson		4)	101.5	1	YE	Nizhniy Tagil	Europa Plus
19)	101.0	1	VO	Vologda	Dorozhnoye R.		62)	101.5	2	AD	Maykop	Kazak FM
19)	101.0	1	VO	Belozersk	Dorozhnoye R.		85)	101.5	1	NO	Malaya Vishera	MV Diapazon
19)	101.0	1	CB	Magnitogorsk	Dorozhnoye R.		1)	101.6	1	AR	Arkhangelsk	Avtoradio
2)	101.0	2	TS	Bugulma	Russkoye R.		10)	101.6	2	VN	Voronezh	R. 7
21)	101.0	1	PR	Berezniki	R. Zvezda		108)	101.6	1	BA	Ufa	R. 1-y Kanal
27)	101.0	1	OM	Omsk	R. Dacha		14)	101.6	1	YE	Krasnoturyinsk	R. Shanson
29)	101.0	1	KD	Otradnaya	Pervoye R.		14)	101.6	1	VG	Mikhaylovka	R. Shanson
3)	101.0	1	KV	Kirov	Ekho Moskvy		176)	101.6	1	RO	Rostov-na-Donu	R. Rostova
34)	101.0	2	KE	Kemerovo	Apeks-Radio		19)	101.6	1	PZ	Kuznetsk	Dorozhnoye R.
35)	101.0	5	RY	Mosolovo	R. Vera		2)	101.6	1	MU	Apatity	Russkoye R.
4)	101.0	1	MU	Murmansk	Europa Plus		2)	101.6	1	KS	Sharya	Russkoye R.
1)	101.1	1	KD	Sochi	Avtoradio		4)	101.6	1	CB	Chelyabinsk	Europa Plus
1)	101.1	1	RS	Yakutsk	Avtoradio		4)	101.6	1	UL	Dimitrovgrad	Europa Plus
10)	101.1	1	PR	Perm	R. 7		7)	101.6	1	OB	Pleshanovo	Militseyskaya volna
124A)	101.1	1	BA	Neftekamsk	R. Yuldash		7)	101.6	1	OB	Sarakbash	Militseyskaya volna
16)	101.1	1	ZB	Chita	Retro FM		1)	101.7	1	AS	Astrakhan	Avtoradio
171)	101.1	1	AK	Kamen-na-Obi	R. Radio		1)	101.7	1	VN	Borisoglebsk	Avtoradio
187)	101.1	1	NS	Kuybyshev	R. Slovo		10)	101.7	1	ST	Budyonnovsk	R. 7
19)	101.1	1	ME	Yoshkar-Ola	Dorozhnoye R.		10)	101.7	1	YA	Yaroslavl	R. 7
20)	101.1	1	DA	Makhachkala	R. Romantika		131)	101.7	1	TS	Bugulma	R. Bolgar
217)	101.1	1	KA	Chernyakhovsk	Mediakit FM		14)	101.7	1	KY	Krasnoyarsk	R. Shanson
24)	101.1	1	VN	Voronezh	NRJ		14)	101.7	1	SL	Yuzhno-Sakhalinsk	R. Shanson
3)	101.1	1	VG	Volgograd	Ekho Moskvy		15)	101.7	1	RK	Abakan	DFM
7)	101.1	1	KE	Novokuznetsk	Militseyskaya volna		15)	101.7	1	BA	Neftekamsk	DFM
14)	101.2	1	SA	Tolyatti	R. Shanson		19)	101.7	1	VO	Babayevo	Dorozhnoye R.

FM	MHz	kW	Rg	Location	Station
195)	101.7	5	PM	Vladivostok	R. VBC
2)	101.7	1	YV	Birobidzhan	Russkoye R.
27)	101.7	1	IR	Bratsk	R. Dacha
36)	101.7	1	SP	Lyuban	Avtoradio St-Peterburg
4)	101.7	1	UL	Ulyanovsk	Europa Plus
7)	101.7	1	AK	Kamen-na-Obi	Militseyskaya volna
8)	101.7	10	MO	Moskva	Nashe R.
9C)	101.7	1	BE	Belgorod	R. dlya druzey
1)	101.8	1	VN	Bobrov	Avtoradio
1)	101.8	1	PR	Chusovoy	Avtoradio
1)	101.8	1	KO	Syktyvkar	Avtoradio
10)	101.8	1	OL	Oryol	R. 7
105)	101.8	1	PZ	Penza	R. 101.8
12)	101.8	1	KV	Kirov	Sport FM
14)	101.8	1	TS	Chistopol	R. Shanson
15)	101.8	1	KE	Kemerovo	DFM
16)	101.8	1	UD	Izhevsk	Retro FM
16)	101.8	1	OB	Orenburg	Retro FM
16)	101.8	4	NO	V.Novgorod	Retro FM
19)	101.8	4	VL	Vladimir	Dorozhnoye R.
2)	101.8	1	KD	Krasnodar	Russkoye R.
2)	101.8	1	ST	Stavropol	Russkoye R.
25)	101.8	1	SA	Syzran	R. Mir
28)	101.8	1	KA	Kaliningrad	Biznes FM
4)	101.8	1	TV	Tver	Europa Plus
4)	101.8	1	KD	Tuapse	Europa Plus
4)	101.8	1	TY	Tyumen	Europa Plus
7)	101.8	1	OB	Buzuluk	Militseyskaya volna
1)	101.9	1	AK	Biysk	Avtoradio
1)	101.9	4	NN	N.Novgorod	Avtoradio
10)	101.9	5	KY	Surgut	R. 7
124B)	101.9	2	BA	Steplitamak	Sputnik FM
14)	101.9	1	AK	Barnaul	R. Shanson
19)	101.9	1	KO	Ukhta	Dorozhnoye R.
2)	101.9	1	DA	Makhachkala	Russkoye R.
23)	101.9	1	VO	Vologda	Detskoye R.
23)	101.9	1	BU	Ulan-Ude	Detskoye R.
26)	101.9	1	TS	Kazan	R. Rekord
4)	101.9	1	TS	Nab. Chelny	Europa Plus
4)	101.9	1	KD	Novorossiysk	Europa Plus
4)	101.9	1	OM	Omsk	Europa Plus
5)	101.9	1	IR	Tulun	Hit FM
8)	101.9	5	TL	Tula	Nashe R.
1)	102.0	1	VN	Boguchar	Avtoradio
1)	102.0	1	SR	Pugachyov	Avtoradio
1)	102.0	1	RY	Ryazan	Avtoradio
1)	102.0	1	TV	Zapadnaya Dvina	Avtoradio
10)	102.0	1	ST	Ipatovo	R. 7
112)	102.0	1	TY	Sladkovo	R. 7 Tyumen
17)	102.0	1	MU	Kirovsk	Serebryanyy dozhd
174)	102.0	10	SP	Sankt-Peterburg	R. Roks
18)	102.0	1	YE	Yekaterinburg	Yumor FM
183)	102.0	1	ZB	Kholbon	R. Sibir
183)	102.0	1	ZB	Krasnokamensk	R. Sibir
19)	102.0	1	BR	Bryansk	Dorozhnoye R.
19)	102.0	1	NS	Novosibirsk	Dorozhnoye R.
19)	102.0	5	PR	Perm	Dorozhnoye R.
19)	102.0	1	AR	Velsk	Dorozhnoye R.
26)	102.0	1	MU	Murmansk	R. Rekord
4)	102.0	1	ZB	Chita	Europa Plus
4)	102.0	1	SM	Smolensk	Europa Plus
4)	102.0	1	SO	Vladikavkaz	Europa Plus
5)	102.0	1	MD	Saransk	Hit FM
77)	102.0	1	CV	Cheboksary	MFM
92)	102.0	2	VG	Volgograd	Novaya volna
1)	102.1	1	LI	Lipetsk	Avtoradio
1)	102.1	1	SR	Saratov	Avtoradio
10)	102.1	1	KU	Kursk	R. 7
112)	102.1	1	TY	Yarkovo	R. 7 Tyumen
131)	102.1	2	TS	Leninogorsk	R. Bolgar
134A)	102.1	1	KE	Belovo	R. Vanya
134A)	102.1	1	KE	Mariinsk	R. Vanya
14)	102.1	1	IR	Bratsk	R. Shanson
14)	102.1	2	KY	Nizhnevartovsk	R. Shanson
154)	102.1	1	IR	Irkutsk	R. MCM
157)	102.1	5	MO	Moskva	R. Monte-Karlo
27)	102.1	1	SA	Samara	R. Dacha
33)	102.1	1	UL	Ulyanovsk	2x2 R.
4)	102.1	1	PS	Pskov	Europa Plus
1)	102.2	1	MO	Serebryanyye Prudy	Avtoradio
1)	102.2	1	SM	Vyazma	Avtoradio
112)	102.2	1	TY	Aromashevo	R. 7 Tyumen
16)	102.2	1	TV	Tver	Retro FM
16)	102.2	1	YA	Yaroslavl	Retro FM
17)	102.2	3	KY	Krasnoyarsk	Serebryanyy dozhd
171)	102.2	1	AK	Blagoveshchenka	R. Radio
182)	102.2	1	YE	Kamensk-Uralskiy	R. Si
19)	102.2	1	RY	Sasovo	Dorozhnoye R.
19)	102.2	1	NO	Valday	Dorozhnoye R.
19)	102.2	1	AR	Vazhskiy	Dorozhnoye R.
19)	102.2	1	SP	Volkhov	Dorozhnoye R.
2)	102.2	1	RK	Abakan	Russkoye R.
2)	102.2	1	BE	Belgorod	Russkoye R.
4)	102.2	1	KD	Krasnodar	Europa Plus
4)	102.2	1	KB	Nalchik	Europa Plus
4)	102.2	1	VO	Babayevo	Europa Plus
4)	102.2	1	KV	Kirov	Europa Plus
6)	102.2	2	AS	Astrakhan	Love R.
1)	102.3	1	KD	Armavir	Avtoradio
1)	102.3	1	AM	Belogorsk	Avtoradio
1)	102.3	2	OB	Orenburg	Avtoradio
1)	102.3	1	PZ	Penza	Avtoradio
112)	102.3	1	TY	Armizonskoye	R. 7 Tyumen
112)	102.3	1	TY	Uvat	R. 7 Tyumen
125)	102.3	1	SA	Tolyatti	R. Avgust
129)	102.3	1	MO	Kolomna	R. Blago
131)	102.3	2	TS	Shemordan	R. Bolgar
134A)	102.3	1	TL	Bogoroditsk	R. Vanya
19)	102.3	1	VN	Voronezh	Dorozhnoye R.
2)	102.3	1	BA	Neftekamsk	Russkoye R.
25)	102.3	1	KH	Khabarovsk	R. Mir
27)	102.3	1	IR	Usolye-Sibirskoye	R. Dacha
4)	102.3	1	BU	Ulan-Ude	Europa Plus
6)	102.3	1	KO	Syktyvkar	Love R.
1)	102.4	2	BA	Belebey	Avtoradio
1)	102.4	1	PM	Dalnegorsk	Avtoradio
112)	102.4	1	TY	Vikulovo	R. 7 Tyumen
12)	102.4	1	CB	Chelyabinsk	Sport FM
120)	102.4	1	VG	Mikhaylovka	R. Aprel
15)	102.4	1	AK	Barnaul	DFM
15)	102.4	1	TS	Nurlat	DFM
15)	102.4	1	VL	Vladimir	DFM
152)	102.4	5	IN	Nazran	ITT-veshchaniye
16)	102.4	1	TS	Kazan	Retro FM
19)	102.4	1	KS	Galich	Dorozhnoye R.
19)	102.4	1	NN	N.Novgorod	Dorozhnoye R.
19)	102.4	1	PS	Sebezh	Dorozhnoye R.
2)	102.4	1	KO	Ukhta	Russkoye R.
225)	102.4	1	PM	Luchegorsk	Vladivostok FM
27)	102.4	1	UD	Izhevsk	R. Dacha
29)	102.4	1	KD	Yeysk	Pervoye R.
30)	102.4	10	SP	Sankt-Peterburg	R. Metro
4)	102.4	1	DA	Makhachkala	Europa Plus
4)	102.4	1	PM	Nakhodka	Europa Plus
6)	102.4	1	TA	Tambov	Love R.
62)	102.4	1	KD	Novorossiysk	Kazak FM
1)	102.5	1	MU	Murmansk	Avtoradio
1)	102.5	4	IV	Rodniki	Avtoradio
122)	102.5	1	BA	Kumertau	R. Aris
14)	102.5	1	KD	Sochi	R. Shanson
14)	102.5	1	BA	Ufa	R. Shanson
146)	102.5	1	CB	Magnitogorsk	R. Kontinental
16)	102.5	1	YE	Serov	Retro FM
16)	102.5	5	KY	Surgut	Retro FM
16)	102.5	1	TO	Tomsk	Retro FM
18)	102.5	1	VN	Boguchar	Yumor FM
19)	102.5	1	PS	Dedovichi	Dorozhnoye R.
19)	102.5	1	KT	Kotkozero	Dorozhnoye R.
19)	102.5	1	SM	Safonovo	Dorozhnoye R.
199)	102.5	1	KY	Yugorsk	R. Yugra
2)	102.5	1	OM	Omsk	Russkoye R.
2)	102.5	1	TY	Tyumen	Russkoye R.
24)	102.5	5	SA	Samara	NRJ
27)	102.5	1	KM	Petropavlovsk-K.	R. Dacha
35)	102.5	1	RY	Ryazan	R. Vera
4)	102.5	1	AK	Biysk	Europa Plus
4)	102.5	1	CV	Cheboksary	Europa Plus
4)	102.5	1	RS	Yakutsk	Europa Plus
4)	102.5	1	SL	Yuzhno-Sakhalinsk	Europa Plus
46)	102.5	5	MO	Moskva	Comedy Radio
50)	102.5	5	YE	Yekaterinburg	Dzhem FM
62)	102.5	1	KD	Psebay	Kazak FM
1)	102.6	1	IR	Sayansk	Avtoradio
10)	102.6	1	SR	Saratov	R. 7

FM	MHz	kW	Rg	Location	Station
131)	102.6	2	TS	Nizhnekamsk	R. Bolgar
18)	102.6	1	VN	Ostrogozhsk	Yumor FM
183)	102.6	1	ZB	Chita	R. Sibir
19)	102.6	1	KT	Leppyasilta	Dorozhnoye R.
19)	102.6	1	KS	Makaryev	Dorozhnoye R.
19)	102.6	4	SP	Tikhvin	Dorozhnoye R.
2)	102.6	1	BR	Bryansk	Russkoye R.
2)	102.6	1	TY	Omutinskiy	Russkoye R.
2)	102.6	1	YA	Yaroslavl	Russkoye R.
26)	102.6	1	NS	Novosibirsk	R. Rekord
27)	102.6	1	KE	Novokuznetsk	R. Dacha
3)	102.6	1	PS	Pskov	Ekho Moskvy
4)	102.6	1	KL	Kaluga	Europa Plus
72)	102.6	1	PS	V. Luki	Luki FM
98B)	102.6	1	VG	Volgograd	R. dlya dvoikh
9C)	102.6	5	ST	Stavropol	R. dlya druzey
1)	102.7	1	AM	Progress	Avtoradio
1)	102.7	1	KU	Zheleznogorsk	Avtoradio
111)	102.7	1	NO	V.Novgorod	R. 53
124A)	102.7	1	BA	Baymak	R. Yuldash
124A)	102.7	1	BA	Narysh Tau	R. Yuldash
134A)	102.7	2	SA	Tolyatti	R. Vanya
14)	102.7	1	MU	Kandalaksha	R. Shanson
14)	102.7	1	VO	Vologda	R. Shanson
15)	102.7	5	PR	Perm	DFM
150)	102.7	5	PM	Vladivostok	R. Lemma
171)	102.7	1	AK	Zaraysk	R. Radio
196)	102.7	1	KH	Khabarovsk	Mix FM
227)	102.7	1	IR	Nizhneudinsk	Udachnoye R.
29)	102.7	5	KD	Krasnodar	Pervoye R.
4)	102.7	1	AS	Astrakhan	Europa Plus
5)	102.7	1	KO	Syktyvkar	Hit FM
96)	102.7	1	TV	Tver	Pilot R.
1)	102.8	1	PM	Arsenyev	Avtoradio
1)	102.8	1	RA	Gorno-Altaysk	Avtoradio
11)	102.8	10	SP	Sankt-Peterburg	R. Maksimum
124B)	102.8	1	BA	Uchaly	Sputnik FM
134A)	102.8	1	KE	Kemerovo	R. Vanya
14)	102.8	1	IR	Cheremkhovo	R. Shanson
14)	102.8	1	VN	Voronezh	R. Shanson
19)	102.8	1	KS	Ostrovskoye	Dorozhnoye R.
2)	102.8	1	AM	Belogorsk	Russkoye R.
21)	102.8	1	SO	Vladikavkaz	R. Zvezda
3)	102.8	1	BU	Ulan-Ude	Ekho Moskvy
4)	102.8	1	PR	Berezniki	Europa Plus
4)	102.8	1	NS	Kuybyshev	Europa Plus
4)	102.8	1	OB	Orsk	Europa Plus
4)	102.8	1	OM	Takmyk	Europa Plus
40)	102.8	1	TS	Kazan	BIM-R.
63)	102.8	1	KN	Krasnoyarsk	Avtoritetnoye R.
79)	102.8	1	BE	Valuyki	Mir Belogorya
82)	102.8	1	PZ	Penza	Most R.
1)	102.9	1	IR	Bratsk	Avtoradio
1)	102.9	1	PM	Nakhodka	Avtoradio
1)	102.9	1	RS	Neryungri	Avtoradio
1)	102.9	1	TA	Tambov	Avtoradio
134A)	102.9	1	NO	Borovichi	R. Vanya
15)	102.9	1	SA	Samara	DFM
18)	102.9	1	AK	Barnaul	Yumor FM
18)	102.9	1	SL	Yuzhno-Sakhalinsk	Yumor FM
19)	102.9	1	SP	Podporozhye	Dorozhnoye R.
2)	102.9	5	NN	N.Novgorod	Russkoye R.
224)	102.9	1	BU	Arshan	TD FM
224)	102.9	5	IR	Bayanday	TD FM
4)	102.9	1	VG	Mikhaylovka	Europa Plus
4)	102.9	1	VL	Vladimir	Europa Plus
58)	102.9	1	CB	Chelyabinsk	Intervolna
6)	102.9	1	KA	Kaliningrad	Love R.
62)	102.9	4	KD	Armavir	Kazak FM
75)	102.9	1	KV	Kirov	Mariya FM
1)	103.0	1	MA	Magadan	Avtoradio
112)	103.0	1	TY	Vagay	R. 7 Tyumen
124A)	103.0	1		Belyanka	R. Yuldash
14)	103.0	1	TS	Bugulma	R. Shanson
14)	103.0	10	MO	Moskva	R. Shanson
15)	103.0	1	CB	Magnitogorsk	DFM
160)	103.0	1	YN	Norilsk	R. Noyabrsk
175)	103.0	1	BA	Ufa	R. Roksana
179)	103.0	1	TV	Ostashkov	R. Seliger
19)	103.0	1	VN	Borisoglebsk	Dorozhnoye R.
19)	103.0	1	IV	Ivanovo	Dorozhnoye R.
19)	103.0	1	SP	Kirishi	Dorozhnoye R.

FM	MHz	kW	Rg	Location	Station
2)	103.0	1	UL	Ulyanovsk	Russkoye R.
204)	103.0	1	SR	Saratov	Radiola
21)	103.0	1	KH	Komsomolsk-na-A.	R. Zvezda
23)	103.0	1	CV	Cheboksary	Detskoye R.
4)	103.0	1	UD	Izhevsk	Europa Plus
5)	103.0	2	OB	Orenburg	Hit FM
8)	103.0	1	MU	Murmansk	Nashe R.
8)	103.0	1	PS	Pskov	Nashe R.
8)	103.0	1	EV	Birobidzhan	Nashe R.
8)	103.0	1	KM	Petropavlovsk-K.	Nashe R.
1)	103.1	1	CB	Ozyorsk	Avtoradio
1)	103.1	1	KT	Petrozavodsk	Avtoradio
1)	103.1	3	PM	Spass-Dalniy	Avtoradio
1)	103.1	1	VG	Volgograd	Avtoradio
112)	103.1	1	TY	Tyumen	R. 7 Tyumen
16)	103.1	1	YE	Krasnoturyinsk	Retro FM
16)	103.1	1	ST	Stavropol	Retro FM
164)	103.1	1	PZ	Kuznetsk	Svoye R.
18)	103.1	1	AK	Biysk	Yumor FM
18)	103.1	3	IR	Irkutsk	Yumor FM
197)	103.1	1	RS	Yakutsk	R. Viktoriya
2)	103.1	1	KD	Sochi	Russkoye R.
227)	103.1	2	KH	Khabarovsk	Udachnoye R.
4)	103.1	1	BE	St.Oskol	Europa Plus
6)	103.1	1	KS	Kostroma	Love R.
62)	103.1	1	KD	Primorsko-Akhtarsk	Kazak FM
7)	103.1	1	OB	Abdulino	Militseyskaya volna
7)	103.1	1	MU	Apatity	Militseyskaya volna
7)	103.1	1	OB	Kuvandyk	Militseyskaya volna
89)	103.1	1	KL	Kaluga	Nika FM
1)	103.2	1	KD	Krasnodar	Avtoradio
1)	103.2	1	NO	V.Novgorod	Avtoradio
11)	103.2	5	PR	Perm	R. Maksimum
112)	103.2	1	TY	Bolshoye Sorokino	R. 7 Tyumen
124A)	103.2	1	BA	Davlekanovo	R. Yuldash
14)	103.2	1	IR	Tayshet	R. Shanson
14)	103.2	4	PM	Vladivostok	R. Shanson
14)	103.2	1	YE	Yekaterinburg	R. Shanson
15)	103.2	1	SA	Tolyatti	DFM
18)	103.2	1	TS	Nab. Chelny	Yumor FM
18)	103.2	1	VN	Pavlovsk	Yumor FM
19)	103.2	1	MD	Saransk	Dorozhnoye R.
19)	103.2	1	SM	Vyazma	Dorozhnoye R.
2)	103.2	1	AS	Astrakhan	Russkoye R.
2)	103.2	1	ST	Pyatigorsk	Russkoye R.
21)	103.2	1	AR	Plesetsk	R. Zvezda
4)	103.2	1	VL	Kovrov	Europa Plus
4)	103.2	3	NS	Novosibirsk	Europa Plus
4)	103.2	1	RY	Ryazan	Europa Plus
5)	103.2	1	KG	Kurgan	Hit FM
1)	103.3	2	TS	Kazan	Avtoradio
1)	103.3	2	KY	Surgut	Avtoradio
124A)	103.3	1	BA	Bakaly	R. Yuldash
14)	103.3	1	KE	Kemerovo	R. Shanson
15)	103.3	1	PR	Berezniki	DFM
15)	103.3	1	VL	Murom	DFM
195)	103.3	1	PM	Nakhodka	R. VBC
2)	103.3	1	MU	Kandalaksha	Russkoye R.
2)	103.3	1	IR	Sayansk	Russkoye R.
225)	103.3	1	PM	Dalnerechensk	Vladivostok FM
24)	103.3	1	OB	Buzuluk	NRJ
24)	103.3	2	KY	Krasnoyarsk	NRJ
27)	103.3	1	SR	Balakovo	R. Dacha
27)	103.3	1	RO	Rostov-na-Donu	R. Dacha
27)	103.3	1	YA	Yaroslavl	R. Dacha
27)	103.3	1	OB	Orsk	R. Dacha
29)	103.3	4	KD	Tbilisskaya	Pervoye R.
37)	103.3	1	KA	Dobrovolsk	Baltik plyus
7)	103.3	1	TL	Tula	Militseyskaya volna
73)	103.3	1	BA	Salavat	M R.
8)	103.3	1	UD	Balezino	Nashe R.
99)	103.3	1	ZB	Chita	Populyarnoye R.
1)	103.4	1	KV	Kirov	Avtoradio
1)	103.4	1	MU	Kovdor	Avtoradio
1)	103.4	1	KL	Obinsk	Avtoradio
1)	103.4	1	NO	Valday	Avtoradio
1)	103.4	1	VN	Voronezh	Avtoradio
1)	103.4	1	KV	Vyatskiye Polyarny	Avtoradio
15)	103.4	5	SP	Sankt-Peterburg	DFM
173)	103.4	1	NN	N.Novgorod	R. Randevu
19)	103.4	1	AR	Arkhangelsk	Dorozhnoye R.
19)	103.4	1	RA	Gorno-Altaysk	Dorozhnoye R.

FM	MHz	kW	Rg	Location	Station
2)	103.4	1	VL	Vladimir	Russkoye R.
4)	103.4	1	TO	Tomsk	Europa Plus
1)	103.5	1	KA	Chernyakhovsk	Avtoradio
1)	103.5	1	KD	Labinsk	Avtoradio
1)	103.5	1	MO	Shakhovskaya	Avtoradio
1)	103.5	1	SO	Vladikavkaz	Avtoradio
109)	103.5	5	OM	Omsk	R. 3
134A)	103.5	1	OL	Oryol	R. Vanya
16)	103.5	1	CV	Cheboksary	Retro FM
16)	103.5	1	MU	Kirovsk	Retro FM
16)	103.5	1	KT	Petrozavodsk	Retro FM
19)	103.5	1	UL	Ulyanovsk	Dorozhnoye R.
2)	103.5	1	SM	Smolensk	Russkoye R.
206)	103.5	1	AR	Velsk	Region 29
207)	103.5	1	BA	Ufa	Relaks FM
221)	103.5	1	RS	Aldan	STV-Radio
225)	103.5	1	PM	Dalnegorsk	Vladivostok FM
225)	103.5	5	PM	Novozhatkovo	Vladivostok FM
4)	103.5	1	VO	Belozersk	Europa Plus
4)	103.5	1	SR	Saratov	Europa Plus
4)	103.5	1	KO	Ukhta	Europa Plus
41)	103.5	1	BR	Bryansk	BIT R.
7)	103.5	1	OB	Tyulgan	Militseyskaya volna
76)	103.5	1	KY	Norilsk	Megapolis FM
8)	103.5	1	CB	Chelyabinsk	Nashe R.
154)	103.6	1	IR	Cheremkhovo	R. MCM
155)	103.6	1	SA	Samara	R. Megapolis .
164)	103.6	1	PZ	Pachelma	Svoye R.
18)	103.6	1	RS	Yakutsk	Yumor FM
19)	103.6	1	VG	Volgograd	Dorozhnoye R.
19)	103.6	1	TV	Vyshniy Volochyok	Dorozhnoye R.
2)	103.6	1	TS	Nab. Chelny	Russkoye R.
27)	103.6	1	VL	Kolchugino	R. Dacha
4)	103.6	1	BE	Belgorod	Europa Plus
4)	103.6	1	VL	Gus-Khustalnyy	Europa Plus
4)	103.6	1	ST	Stavropol	Europa Plus
5)	103.6	1	CB	Magnitogorsk	Hit FM
8)	103.6	2	PR	Perm	Nashi pesni
1)	103.7	1	MD	Saransk	Avtoradio
10)	103.7	1	KD	Krasnodar	R. 7
11)	103.7	10	MO	Moskva	R. Maksimum
117)	103.7	2	KH	Khabarovsk	Vostok Rossii
12)	103.7	1	VO	Vologda	Sport FM
14)	103.7	1	AS	Astrakhan	R. Shanson
143)	103.7	1	OB	Orsk	R. Khit
149)	103.7	1	KU	Kursk	R. Kurs
157)	103.7	1	RO	Rostov-na-Donu	R. Monte-Karlo
16)	103.7	1	AK	Biysk	Retro FM
16)	103.7	1	AM	Shimanovsk	Retro FM
16)	103.7	1	PM	Vladivostok	Retro FM
18)	103.7	1	SR	Balakovo	Yumor FM
182)	103.7	5	YE	Yekaterinburg	R. Si
183)	103.7	1	RK	Abakan	R. Sibir
19)	103.7	1	KG	Kurgan	Dorozhnoye R.
19)	103.7	1	BU	Ulan-Ude	Dorozhnoye R.
19)	103.7	1	NN	Vorotynets	Dorozhnoye R.
2)	103.7	1	KE	Mezhdurechensk	Russkoye R.
2)	103.7	1	PM	Arsenyev	Russkoye R.
23)	103.7	1	SP	Sankt-Peterburg	Detskoye R.
236)	103.7	1	SA	Isakly	Samarskoye Gub. R.
27)	103.7	1	KD	Sochi	R. Dacha
4)	103.7	1	OB	Orenburg	Europa Plus
4)	103.7	1	NO	V.Novgorod	Europa Plus
1)	103.8	1	SA	Syzran	Avtoradio
103A)	103.8	1	ME	Yoshkar-Ola	Puls R.
124A)	103.8	1	BA	Steplitamak	R. Yuldash
14)	103.8	1	PR	Berezniki	R. Shanson
15)	103.8	1	TO	Tomsk	DFM
16)	103.8	1	KO	Syktyvkar	Retro FM
17)	103.8	1	KN	Yeniseysk	Serebryanyy dozhd
17)	103.8	1	TV	Tver	Serebryanyy dozhd
177)	103.8	1	RS	Neryungri	R. Sakha
19)	103.8	1	NO	Borovichi	Dorozhnoye R.
19)	103.8	1	YA	Yaroslavl	Dorozhnoye R.
2)	103.8	4	AR	Arkhangelsk	Russkoye R.
2)	103.8	1	RT	Kyzyl	Russkoye R.
4)	103.8	1	IR	Irkutsk	Europa Plus
4)	103.8	2	KY	Krasnoyarsk	Europa Plus
4)	103.8	1	PZ	Penza	Europa Plus
4)	103.8	1	ST	Pyatigorsk	Europa Plus
6)	103.8	1	VN	Voronezh	Love R.
8)	103.8	1	UD	Izhevsk	Nashe R.
89)	103.8	1	KL	Sukhinichi	Nika FM
1)	103.9	1	AK	Barnaul	Avtoradio
1)	103.9	1	PM	Dalnerechensk	Avtoradio
112)	103.9	1	TY	Isetskoye	R. 7 Tyumen
12)	103.9	1	SR	Saratov	Sport FM
12)	103.9	1	TA	Tambov	Sport FM
15)	103.9	1	MO	Lukhovitsy	DFM
15)	103.9	1	PR	Chusovoy	DFM
15)	103.9	2	NS	Novosibirsk	DFM
16)	103.9	1	VG	Mikhaylovka	Retro FM
18)	103.9	1	OL	Oryol	Yumor FM
183)	103.9	1	OM	Omsk	R. Sibir
2)	103.9	1	KV	Kirov	Russkoye R.
2)	103.9	1	KM	Petropavlovsk-K.	Russkoye R.
2)	103.9	1	PM	Dalnegorsk	Russkoye R.
4)	103.9	5	NN	N.Novgorod	Europa Plus
6)	103.9	1	PM	Partizansk	Love R.
7)	103.9	5	UL	Veshkayma	Militseyskaya volna
1)	104.0	1	YE	Kamensk-Uralskiy	Avtoradio
112)	104.0	1	TY	Ishim	R. 7 Tyumen
124B)	104.0	1	BA	Kugarchi	Sputnik FM
134A)	104.0	1	PZ	Pachelma	R. Vanya
14)	104.0	1	TS	Kazan	R. Shanson
14)	104.0	1	KE	Novokuznetsk	R. Shanson
16)	104.0	1	MU	Murmansk	Retro FM
16)	104.0	1	BA	Ufa	Retro FM
16)	104.0	1	VG	Volgograd	Retro FM
19)	104.0	1	TV	Rzhev	Dorozhnoye R.
19)	104.0	1	RS	Yakutsk	Dorozhnoye R.
26)	104.0	1	SA	Tolyatti	R. Rekord
27)	104.0	1	ST	Svetlograd	R. Dacha
4)	104.0	1	KY	Nizhnevartovsk	Europa Plus
8)	104.0	10	SP	Sankt-Peterburg	Nashe R.
91)	104.0	1	KD	Novorossiysk	Novaya Rossiya
1)	104.1	1	AR	Plesetsk	Avtoradio
1)	104.1	1	RO	Rostov-na-Donu	Avtoradio
118)	104.1	5	PR	Perm	R. Alfa
14)	104.1	1	VN	Borisoglebsk	R. Shanson
15)	104.1	1	TS	Chistopol	DFM
15)	104.1	1	OB	Orsk	DFM
15)	104.1	1	CB	Tryokhgornyy	DFM
188)	104.1	1	AS	Astrakhan	Yuzhnaya volna
2)	104.1	1	IR	Bratsk	Russkoye R.
2)	104.1	1	CB	Chelyabinsk	Russkoye R.
24)	104.1	1	RY	Ryazan	NRJ
27)	104.1	1	YE	Yekaterinburg	R. Dacha
4)	104.1	2	KY	Khanty-Mansiysk	Europa Plus
6)	104.1	1	YE	Krasnoturyinsk	Love R.
10)	104.2	1	UL	Ulyanovsk	R. 7
14)	104.2	1	KY	Surgut	R. Shanson
14)	104.2	1	CB	Zlatoust	R. Shanson
161)	104.2	4	NN	Arzamas	R. Obraz
167)	104.2	1	TY	Tobolsk	R. Pobedy
18)	104.2	2	TO	Tomsk	Yumor FM
18)	104.2	1	SM	Vyazma	Yumor FM
19)	104.2	1	SP	Kingisepp	Dorozhnoye R.
192)	104.2	1	VO	Babayevo	R. Transmit
192)	104.2	1	VO	Totma	R. Transmit
2)	104.2	1	CB	Magnitogorsk	Russkoye R.
24)	104.2	1	BE	Belgorod	NRJ
24)	104.2	10	MO	Moskva	NRJ
28)	104.2	1	KY	Krasnoyarsk	Biznes FM
4)	104.2	1	RK	Abakan	Europa Plus
4)	104.2	1	MU	Apatity	Europa Plus
4)	104.2	5	PM	Vladivostok	Europa Plus
5)	104.2	1	KD	Krasnodar	Hit FM
6)	104.2	1	CV	Cheboksary	Love R.
7)	104.2	1	OB	Tashla	Militseyskaya volna
1)	104.3	1	OL	Oryol	Avtoradio
11)	104.3	1	KT	Petrozavodsk	R. Maksimum
134A)	104.3	1	KV	Kirov	R. Vanya
15)	104.3	2	OB	Orenburg	DFM
15)	104.3	1	VN	Voronezh	DFM
16)	104.3	1	SR	Saratov	Retro FM
19)	104.3	1	KH	Khabarovsk	Dorozhnoye R.
19)	104.3	1	KE	Kemerovo	Dorozhnoye R.
19)	104.3	1	PZ	Penza	Dorozhnoye R.
2)	104.3	1	BA	Steplitamak	Russkoye R.
2)	104.3	1	KD	Tikhoretsk	Russkoye R.
213)	104.3	2	SA	Samara	Samara-Maksimum
22)	104.3	1	VL	Vladimir	R. KP
75)	104.3	1	NN	Krasnyye Baki	Mariya FM

FM	MHz	kW	Rg	Location	Station
1)	104.4	5	TL	Tula	Avtoradio
10)	104.4	1	BE	Ivnya	R. 7
101)	104.4	1	KE	Yurga	Pravilnoye R.
134A)	104.4	1	KE	Novokuznetsk	R. Vanya
14)	104.4	5	SP	Sankt-Peterburg	R. Shanson
146)	104.4	1	CB	Ozyorsk	R. Kontinental
16)	104.4	1	AK	Barnaul	Retro FM
16)	104.4	1	TA	Tambov	Retro FM
19)	104.4	1	NO	Khvoynaya	Dorozhnoye R.
19)	104.4	1	PS	Pushkinskiye gory	Dorozhnoye R.
19)	104.4	1	AM	Blagoveshchensk	Dorozhnoye R.
192)	104.4	1	VO	Nikolsk	R. Transmit
192)	104.4	2	VO	Vologda	R. Transmit
2)	104.4	1	PR	Chusovoy	Russkoye R.
26)	104.4	1	OM	Omsk	R. Rekord
4)	104.4	1	YN	Norilsk	Europa Plus
4)	104.4	5	KD	Sochi	Europa Plus
5)	104.4	1	BA	Tuymazy	Hit FM
6)	104.4	1	KA	Sovetsk	Love R.
6)	104.4	1	SL	Yuzhno-Sakhalinsk	Love R.
7)	104.4	1	VL	Murom	Militseyskaya volna
75)	104.4	2	TS	Shemordan	Mariya FM
1)	104.5	1	KM	Petropavlovsk-K.	Avtoradio
1)	104.5	1	BE	St.Oskol	Avtoradio
1)	104.5	1	YA	Yaroslavl	Avtoradio
100)	104.5	1	MU	Murmansk	Power Hit R.
114)	104.5	1	UD	Izhevsk	R. Adam
16)	104.5	1	MU	Kandalaksha	Retro FM
163)	104.5	1	CB	Chelyabinsk	R. Olimp
170)	104.5	1	DA	Kyzlyurt	R. Priboy
18)	104.5	1	VG	Volgograd	Yumor FM
19)	104.5	1	KT	Lakhdenpokhya	Dorozhnoye R.
191)	104.5	1	PM	Nakhodka	R. Svobodn. Nakhodka
199)	104.5	1	KY	Nyagan	R. Yugra
2)	104.5	1	BA	Ufa	Russkoye R.
210)	104.5	2	YE	Yekaterinburg	Rok-Arsenal
216)	104.5	1	RS	Yakutsk	R. Viktoriya
220)	104.5	1	MD	Saransk	Start FM
25)	104.5	1	NO	V.Novgorod	R. Mir
27)	104.5	2	NN	N.Novgorod	R. Dacha
29)	104.5	5	KD	Kanevskaya	Pervoye R.
33)	104.5	1	UL	Dimitrovgrad	2x2 R.
4)	104.5	1	KA	Kaliningrad	Europa Plus
4)	104.5	1	ME	Yoshkar-Ola	Europa Plus
5)	104.5	1	KO	Ukhta	Hit FM
7)	104.5	1	OB	Sharlyk	Militseyskaya volna
1)	104.6	1	KD	Tuapse	Avtoradio
1)	104.6	1	KV	Kilmez	Avtoradio
124A)	104.6	1	BA	Akyar	R. Yuldash
15)	104.6	1	RO	Rostov-na-Donu	DFM
16)	104.6	5	IR	Irkutsk	Retro FM
183)	104.6	1	IR	Bratsk	R. Sibir
183)	104.6	1	TO	Tomsk	R. Sibir
192)	104.6	1	VO	Cherepovets	R. Transmit
225)	104.6	1	PM	Arsenyev	Vladivostok FM
24)	104.6	1	KU	Kursk	NRJ
24)	104.6	1	SA	Syzran	NRJ
27)	104.6	1	KY	Krasnoyarsk	R. Dacha
40)	104.6	1	TS	Almetyevsk	BIM-R.
6)	104.6	1	PR	Berezniki	Love R.
6)	104.6	1	LI	Lipetsk	Love R.
66)	104.6	1	TY	Tyumen	Krasnaya Armiya
7)	104.6	1	RA	Zarinsk	Militseyskaya volna
98A)	104.6	1	SP	Volkhov	Piter FM
1)	104.7	1	RK	Abakan	Avtoradio
1)	104.7	1	CB	Magnitogorsk	Avtoradio
1)	104.7	1	KY	Nizhnevartovsk	Avtoradio
10)	104.7	5	MO	Moskva	R. 7
124A)	104.7	1	BA	Belebey	R. Yuldash
124B)	104.7	1	BA	Neftekamsk	Sputnik FM
131)	104.7	1	TS	Nurlat	R. Bolgar
15)	104.7	1	TS	Kazan	DFM
16)	104.7	1	KH	Komsomolsk-na-A.	Retro FM
18)	104.7	1	BE	Belgorod	Yumor FM
2)	104.7	1	KT	Petrozavodsk	Russkoye R.
26)	104.7	1	PR	Perm	R. Rekord
27)	104.7	5	PM	Vladivostok	R. Dacha
4)	104.7	1	KE	Mezhdurechensk	Europa Plus
8)	104.7	1	AR	Arkhangelsk	Nashe R.
8)	104.7	1	KD	Krasnodar	Nashe R.
97)	104.7	1	KS	Sharya	Pioner FM
98A)	104.7	1	SP	Luga	Piter FM
1)	104.8	1	SA	Samara	Avtoradio
1)	104.8	1	VL	Vladimir	Avtoradio
14)	104.8	1	TV	Tver	R. Shanson
16)	104.8	1	SM	Smolensk	Retro FM
16)	104.8	1	BA	Steplitamak	Retro FM
17)	104.8	1	SR	Saratov	Serebryanyy dozhd
172)	104.8	1	KD	Kushchevskaya	R. Radonezh
18)	104.8	1	MO	Kolomna	Yumor FM
19)	104.8	1	KB	Nalchik	Dorozhnoye R.
19)	104.8	1	OB	Orenburg	Dorozhnoye R.
19)	104.8	1	KO	Syktyvkar	Dorozhnoye R.
194)	104.8	1	DA	Makhachkala	R. Assa
2)	104.8	1	KE	Kemerovo	Russkoye R.
2)	104.8	1	KS	Kostroma	Russkoye R.
2)	104.8	1	PZ	Penza	Russkoye R.
2)	104.8	2	VN	Voronezh	Russkoye R.
24)	104.8	1	TS	Nab. Chelny	NRJ
5)	104.8	1	OL	Oryol	Hit FM
6)	104.8	1	MU	Monchegorsk	Love R.
7)	104.8	1	UL	Sengiley	Militseyskaya volna
88A)	104.8	5	SP	Sankt-Peterburg	R. Baltika
1)	104.9	1	YN	Norilsk	Avtoradio
124A)	104.9	1	BA	Beloretsk	R. Yuldash
131)	104.9	1	TS	Kutlu-Bukash	R. Bolgar
153)	104.9	1	SO	Vladikavkaz	R. MCC
16)	104.9	1	KV	Kirov	Retro FM
2)	104.9	1	VO	Vologda	Russkoye R.
23)	104.9	1	TA	Tambov	Detskoye R.
29)	104.9	5	KD	Novorossiysk	Pervoye R.
4)	104.9	1	TL	Tula	Europa Plus
6)	104.9	1	NN	N.Novgorod	Love R.
6)	104.9	1	TS	Bavly	Love R.
62)	104.9	1	KD	Yeysk	Kazak FM
7)	104.9	2	UL	Novoskapskoye	Militseyskaya volna
71)	104.9	1	CB	Chelyabinsk	L-Radio
1)	105.0	1	KE	Novokuznetsk	Avtoradio
1)	105.0	2	YE	Yekaterinburg	Avtoradio
10)	105.0	1	RY	Ryazan	R. 7
131)	105.0	1	PE	Barda	R. Bolgar
16)	105.0	1	PM	Nakhodka	Retro FM
16)	105.0	1	BU	Ulan-Ude	Retro FM
18)	105.0	1	VN	Arkhangelskoye	Yumor FM
18)	105.0	1	AS	Astrakhan	Yumor FM
198)	105.0	1	RS	Neryungri	R. Voyazh
199)	105.0	5	KY	Surgut	R. Yugra
221)	105.0	1	RS	Mirnyy	STV-Radio
24)	105.0	1	KD	Tuapse	NRJ
26)	105.0	1	KO	Ukhta	R. Rekord
27)	105.0	1	BA	Ufa	R. Dacha
29)	105.0	1	KD	Belaya Glina	Pervoye R.
29)	105.0	1	KD	Psebay	Pervoye R.
3)	105.0	1	TO	Tomsk	Ekho Moskvy
4)	105.0	1	PM	Artyom	Europa Plus
6)	105.0	1	OM	Omsk	Love R.
87)	105.0	2	CV	Tsivilsk	Natsionaln. R. Chuvashii
1)	105.1	1	ST	Stavropol	Avtoradio
110A)	105.1	1	VG	Volgograd	R. Sputnik
12)	105.1	1	LI	Lipetsk	Sport FM
124A)	105.1	1	BA	Kumertau	R. Yuldash
134A)	105.1	1	TV	Vyshniy Volochyok	R. Vanya
14)	105.1	1	PR	Perm	R. Shanson
14)	105.1	1	RO	Rostov-na-Donu	R. Shanson
16)	105.1	1	TY	Tyumen	Retro FM
16)	105.1	1	IR	Ust-Ilimsk	Retro FM
168)	105.1	1	MO	Shatura	R. Nashe Podmoskovye
2)	105.1	1	PR	Berezniki	Russkoye R.
4)	105.1	1	YA	Yaroslavl	Europa Plus
7)	105.1	1	KE	Leninsk-Kuznetskiy	Militseyskaya volna
1)	105.2	1	ZB	Chita	Avtoradio
2)	105.2	2	KY	Krasnoyarsk	Avtoradio
135)	105.2	1	PZ	Penza	R. Ekspress
149)	105.2	1	KU	Zheleznogorsk	R. Kurs
18)	105.2	1	KY	Megion	Yumor FM
2)	105.2	1	KO	Syktyvkar	Russkoye R.
27)	105.2	1	SA	Tolyatti	R. Dacha
27)	105.2	1	OB	Yasnyy	R. Dacha
37)	105.2	1	KA	Kaliningrad	Baltik plyus
5)	105.2	2	NS	Novosibirsk	Hit FM
6)	105.2	1	CB	Magnitogorsk	Love R.
62)	105.2	5	KD	Krasnodar	Kazak FM
8)	105.2	1	KD	Sochi	Nashe R.
80B)	105.2	5	MO	Moskva	Moscow FM

FM	MHz	kW	Rg	Location	Station	FM	MHz	kW	Rg	Location	Station
93)	105.2	1	NN	Koverino	NN-R.	28)	105.7	2	NS	Novosibirsk	Biznes FM
93)	105.2	1	NN	Sergach	NN-R.	29)	105.7	1	KD	Sochi	Pervoye R.
1)	105.3	1	KE	Kemerovo	Avtoradio	4)	105.7	1	RO	Rostov-na-Donu	Europa Plus
131)	105.3	1	TS	Absalmyanovo	R. Bolgar	5)	105.7	5	PM	Vladivostok	Hit FM
138)	105.3	1	SO	Vladikavkaz	R. Ir	10)	105.8	1	VL	Vladimir	R. 7
15)	105.3	5	PM	Vladivostok	DFM	11)	105.8	1	ST	Pyatigorsk	R. Maksimum
16)	105.3	1	VN	Voronezh	Retro FM	124A)	105.8	1	BA	Mesyagutovo	R. Yuldash
17)	105.3	1	NO	V.Novgorod	Serebryanyy dozhd	14)	105.8	1	BA	Neftekamsk	R. Shanson
171)	105.3	1	IR	Usolye-Sibirskoye	R. Radio	19)	105.8	1	SM	Roslavl	Dorozhnoye R.
18)	105.3	1	VN	Rossosh	Yumor FM	2)	105.8	1	KY	Krasnoyarsk	Russkoye R.
19)	105.3	1	UD	Izhevsk	Dorozhnoye R.	201)	105.8	1	KG	Shardinsk	R. Za oblakami
2)	105.3	1	SR	Saratov	Russkoye R.	205)	105.8	1	KS	Kostroma	RDV-FM
2)	105.3	1	TL	Tula	Russkoye R.	27)	105.8	1	KO	Ukhta	R. Dacha
27)	105.3	1	KS	Kostroma	R. Dacha	3)	105.8	1	TS	Kazan	Ekho Moskvy
27)	105.3	1	OB	Orenburg	R. Dacha	5)	105.8	1	OB	Orsk	Hit FM
6)	105.3	5	SP	Sankt-Peterburg	Love R.	59)	105.8	1	VN	Borisoglebsk	Kanal Melodiya (Vor.)
8)	105.3	1	RS	Yakutsk	Nashe R.	6)	105.8	4	TL	Tula	Love R.
1)	105.4	1	TO	Tomsk	Avtoradio	62)	105.8	1	KD	Tbilisskaya	Kazak FM
10)	105.4	1	CB	Chelyabinsk	R. 7	7)	105.8	1	OB	Buguruslan	Militseyskaya volna
12)	105.4	1	NN	N.Novgorod	Sport FM	7)	105.8	1	OB	Orenburg	Militseyskaya volna
124A)	105.4	1	BA	Uchaly	R. Yuldash	8)	105.8	1	IR	Usolye-Sibirskoye	Nashe R.
124A)	105.4	1	BA	Fyodorovka	R. Yuldash	1)	105.9	1	TS	Bugulma	Avtoradio
16)	105.4	1	AR	Arkhangelsk	Retro FM	14)	105.9	1	CB	Chelyabinsk	R. Shanson
16)	105.4	1	RY	Ryazan	Retro FM	14)	105.9	1	RY	Ryazan	R. Shanson
177)	105.4	1	RS	Mirnyy	R. Sakha	142)	105.9	1	KC	Karachayevsk	R. Kavkaz Khit
18)	105.4	1	VN	Kalach	Yumor FM	157)	105.9	5	SP	Sankt-Peterburg	R. Monte-Karlo
19)	105.4	1	KG	Shardinsk	Dorozhnoye R.	16)	105.9	1	SO	Vladikavkaz	Retro FM
2)	105.4	1	AK	Barnaul	Russkoye R.	18)	105.9	1	SA	Syzran	Yumor FM
20)	105.4	1	SA	Samara	R. Romantika	18)	105.9	1	TV	Tver	Yumor FM
29)	105.4	4	KD	Armavir	Pervoye R.	19)	105.9	1	VN	Kalach	Dorozhnoye R.
4)	105.4	1	NO	Borovichi	Europa Plus	19)	105.9	1	KA	Kaliningrad	Dorozhnoye R.
57)	105.4	1	CC	Groznyy	R. Groznyy	199)	105.9	1	KY	Nizhnevartovsk	R. Yugra
7)	105.4	1	OB	Pervomayskiy	Militseyskaya volna	2)	105.9	1	TA	Tambov	Russkoye R.
1)	105.5	1	YA	Rybinsk	Avtoradio	4)	105.9	1	KY	Surgut	Europa Plus
1)	105.5	1	MO	Uvarovka	Avtoradio	62)	105.9	1	KD	Tuapse	Kazak FM
106)	105.5	1	SL	Yuzhno-Sakhalinsk	R. ASTV	7)	105.9	1	NN	N.Novgorod	Militseyskaya volna
124A)	105.5	1	BA	Ufa	R. Yuldash	79)	105.9	1	BE	Svistovka	Mir Belogorya
131)	105.5	2	TS	Nab. Chelny	R. Bolgar	1)	106.0	1	MO	Kolomna	Avtoradio
144)	105.5	1	SP	Kirishi	R. Kirishi	12)	106.0	1	VG	Volgograd	Sport FM
15)	105.5	1	OL	Oryol	DFM	15)	106.0	1	KD	Krasnodar	DFM
16)	105.5	1	UL	Ulyanovsk	Retro FM	16)	106.0	1	YE	Nizhniy Tagil	Retro FM
171)	105.5	1	SV	Nizhniy Tagil	R. Radio	171)	106.0	1	IR	Nizhneudinsk	R. Radio
171)	105.5	1	AK	Rubtsovsk	R. Radio	18)	106.0	1	MA	Magadan	Yumor FM
183)	105.5	1	RA	Gorno-Altaysk	R. Sibir	18)	106.0	1	IR	Irkutsk	Yumor FM
19)	105.5	1	MA	Magadan	Dorozhnoye R.	19)	106.0	1	AS	Astrakhan	Dorozhnoye R.
192)	105.5	4	VO	Belozersk	R. Transmit	19)	106.0	1	MU	Murmansk	Dorozhnoye R.
2)	105.5	1	MU	Murmansk	Russkoye R.	2)	106.0	1	SR	Balakovo	Russkoye R.
2)	105.5	1	KB	Nalchik	Russkoye R.	4)	106.0	1	CB	Magnitogorsk	Europa Plus
2)	105.5	1	KE	Novokuznetsk	Russkoye R.	4)	106.0	1	KM	Petropavlovsk-K.	Europa Plus
2)	105.5	1	BE	St.Oskol	Russkoye R.	4)	106.0	1	BA	Ufa	Europa Plus
211)	105.5	1	IR	Ust-Kut	Lena FM	4)	106.0	1	SP	Vyborg	Europa Plus
221)	105.5	1	RS	Neryumgri	STV-Radio	5)	106.0	1	TS	Nab. Chelny	Hit FM
25)	105.5	1	BU	Ulan-Ude	R. Mir	1)	106.1	1	UD	Izhevsk	Avtoradio
42)	105.5	1	ME	Yoshkar-Ola	Blits FM	1)	106.1	1	TY	Tyumen	Avtoradio
6)	105.5	1	KD	Tuapse	Love R.	1)	106.1	1	VO	Vologda	Avtoradio
6)	105.5	1	TV	Tver	Love R.	101)	106.1	1	KE	Belovo	Pravilnoye R.
7)	105.5	1	OB	Kvarkeno	Militseyskaya volna	124A)	106.1	1	BA	Bikkulovo	R. Yuldash
88A)	105.5	1	SP	Vyborg	R. Baltika	124A)	106.1	1	BA	Kugarchi	R. Yuldash
1)	105.6	1	VN	Kantemirovka	Avtoradio	17)	106.1	1	KL	Kaluga	Serebryanyy dozhd
14)	105.6	5	IR	Irkutsk	R. Shanson	19)	106.1	2	SA	Samara	Dorozhnoye R.
2)	105.6	2	VG	Volgograd	Russkoye R.	2)	106.1	1	RS	Yakutsk	Russkoye R.
236)	105.6	1	SA	Kinel-Cherkassy	Samarskoye Gub. R.	24)	106.1	1	KD	Sochi	NRJ
25)	105.6	1	KO	Syktyvkar	R. Mir	25)	106.1	1	ZB	Chita	R. Mir
26)	105.6	1	TS	Almetyevsk	R. Rekord	26)	106.1	1	SP	Podporozhye	R. Rekord
29)	105.6	1	KD	Primorsko-Akhtarsk	Pervoye R.	7)	106.1	1	TO	Tomsk	Militseyskaya volna
3)	105.6	1	LI	Lipetsk	Ekho Moskvy	10)	106.2	1	LI	Lipetsk	R. 7
4)	105.6	5	KH	Khabarovsk	Europa Plus	112)	106.2	1	TY	Tobolsk	R. 7 Tyumen
48)	105.6	1	TY	Tyumen	Dipol FM	14)	106.2	1	OM	Omsk	R. Shanson
7)	105.6	1	OB	Novosergiyevka	Militseyskaya volna	16)	106.2	1	OB	Orsk	Retro FM
7)	105.6	1	MD	Saransk	Militseyskaya volna	16)	106.2	1	ST	Pyatigorsk	Retro FM
1)	105.7	1	MU	Apatity	Avtoradio	18)	106.2	1	KG	Shardinsk	Yumor FM
1)	105.7	1	BR	Unecha	Avtoradio	187)	106.2	2	NS	Novosibirsk	R. Slovo
124B)	105.7	1	BA	Oktyabrskiy	Sputnik FM	19)	106.2	1	KS	Kostroma	Dorozhnoye R.
14)	105.7	1	RK	Abakan	R. Shanson	19)	106.2	1	KU	Kursk	Dorozhnoye R.
147)	105.7	1	UD	Izhevsk	Gorod FM	19)	106.2	1	PZ	Pachelma	Dorozhnoye R.
18)	105.7	1	SA	Tolyatti	Yumor FM	19)	106.2	1	RA	Biysk	Dorozhnoye R.
19)	105.7	1	PR	Berezniki	Dorozhnoye R.	19)	106.2	1	KE	Novokuznetsk	Dorozhnoye R.
19)	105.7	1	NO	V.Novgorod	Dorozhnoye R.	2)	106.2	5	PR	Perm	Russkoye R.
2)	105.7	10	MO	Moskva	Russkoye R.	204)	106.2	5	YE	Yekaterinburg	Radiola
2)	105.7	1	YE	Yekaterinburg	Russkoye R.	21)	106.2	1	RK	Abakan	R. Zvezda
22)	105.7	1	ST	Stavropol	R. KP	222)	106.2	1	RK	Abakan	Taksi FM
221)	105.7	1	RS	Yakutsk	STV-Radio	225)	106.2	5	PM	Spass-Dalniy	Vladivostok FM

FM	MHz	kW	Rg	Location	Station
29)	106.2	1	KD	Pavlovskaya	Pervoye R.
4)	106.2	10	MO	Moskva	Europa Plus
6)	106.2	1	VL	Murom	Love R.
6)	106.2	1	UL	Ulyanovsk	Love R.
98A)	106.2	1	SP	Kingisepp	Piter FM
10)	106.3	1	TV	Tver	R. 7
124B)	106.3	1	BA	Baymak	Sputnik FM
15)	106.3	1	KY	Nizhnevartovsk	DFM
15)	106.3	1	MD	Saransk	DFM
16)	106.3	1	BE	Belgorod	Retro FM
17)	106.3	1	IV	Rodniki	Serebryanyy dozhd
178)	106.3	1	DA	Khasavyut	Khas FM
19)	106.3	1	IR	Bratsk	Dorozhnoye R.
19)	106.3	1	SR	Saratov	Dorozhnoye R.
19)	106.3	1	RO	Taganrog	Dorozhnoye R.
19)	106.3	1	CB	Chelyabinsk	Dorozhnoye R.
2)	106.3	1	SM	Roslavl	Russkoye R.
2)	106.3	1	KD	Goryachiy Klyuch	Russkoye R.
236)	106.3	1	SA	Khvorostyanka	Samarskoye Gub. R.
26)	106.3	5	SP	Sankt-Peterburg	R. Rekord
93)	106.3	1	NN	Shakhunya	NN-R.
1)	106.4	1	EV	Birobidzhan	Avtoradio
11)	106.4	1	AS	Astrakhan	R. Maksimum
11)	106.4	1	KA	Kaliningrad	R. Maksimum
11)	106.4	1	TL	Tula	R. Maksimum
12)	106.4	1	TS	Nab.Chelny	Sport FM
127)	106.4	10	IR	Irkutsk	R. Fresh (xAvtos)
134A)	106.4	1	KE	Mezhdurechensk	R. Vanya
134A)	106.4	1	PZ	Kuznetsk	R. Vanya
134A)	106.4	1	SV	Nizhniy Tagil	R. Vanya
16)	106.4	1	NN	N.Novgorod	Retro FM
17)	106.4	1	AK	Barnaul	Serebryanyy dozhd
19)	106.4	1	TA	Tambov	Dorozhnoye R.
225)	106.4	5	PM	Vladivostok	Vladivostok FM
4)	106.4	1	RA	Gorno-Altaysk	Europa Plus
59)	106.4	1	VN	Bobrov	Kanal Melodiya (Vor.)
98A)	106.4	1	SP	Tikhvin	Piter FM
1)	106.5	1	BA	Ufa	Avtoradio
15)	106.5	1	SR	Balakovo	DFM
16)	106.5	1	TS	Chistopol	Retro FM
16)	106.5	2	AD	Maykop	Retro FM
16)	106.5	1	KM	Petropavlovsk-K.	Retro FM
16)	106.5	1	ME	Yoshkar-Ola	Retro FM
168)	106.5	1	MO	Zaraysk	R. Nashe Podmoskovye
171)	106.5	1	KY	Achinsk	R. Radio
171)	106.5	5	IR	Zima	R. Radio
18)	106.5	1	BR	Bryansk	Yumor FM
19)	106.5	1	SP	Luga	Dorozhnoye R.
19)	106.5	1	KD	Tuapse	Dorozhnoye R.
19)	106.5	1	SL	Yuzhno-Sakhalinsk	Dorozhnoye R.
23)	106.5	1	SM	Smolensk	Detskoye R.
27)	106.5	1	OB	Kuvandyk	R. Dacha
3)	106.5	1	YA	Yaroslavl	Ekho Moskvy
4)	106.5	1	BA	Neftekamsk	Europa Plus
6)	106.5	1	TY	Tyumen	Love R.
68)	106.5	1	RS	Yakutsk	Lena R.
8)	106.5	1	MA	Magadan	Nashe R.
9C)	106.5	1	MU	Murmansk	R. dlya druzey
15)	106.6	1	KE	Leninsk-Kuznetskiy	DFM
19)	106.6	1	KS	Sharya	Dorozhnoye R.
199)	106.6	2	KY	Khanty-Mansiysk	R. Yugra
2)	106.6	1	ZB	Chita	Russkoye R.
25)	106.6	1	UL	Ulyanovsk	R. Mir
27)	106.6	1	PR	Berezniki	R. Dacha
28)	106.6	1	RO	Rostov-na-Donu	Biznes FM
4)	106.6	1	SP	Kirishi	Europa Plus
6)	106.6	10	MO	Moskva	Love R.
6)	106.6	3	SA	Samara	Love R.
1)	106.7	1	KD	Kropotkin	Avtoradio
1)	106.7	1	KU	Kursk	Avtoradio
1)	106.7	1	KD	Yeysk	Avtoradio
154)	106.7	1	IR	Listyanka	R. MCM
157)	106.7	1	PM	Nakhodka	R. Monte-Karlo
16)	106.7	1	RK	Abakan	Retro FM
18)	106.7	2	PZ	Penza	Yumor FM
19)	106.7	1	KV	Kirov	Dorozhnoye R.
19)	106.7	1	TV	Tver	Dorozhnoye R.
19)	106.7	1	SP	Vyborg	Dorozhnoye R.
26)	106.7	1	MU	Apatity	R. Rekord
26)	106.7	1	PM	Ussuriysk	R. Rekord
27)	106.7	1	NS	Novosibirsk	R. Dacha
29)	106.7	1	KD	Temryuk	Pervoye R.
4)	106.7	1	KV	Vyatskiye Polyarny	Europa Plus
6)	106.7	1	KO	Ukhta	Love R.
7)	106.7	1	TS	Bugulma	Militseyskaya volna
98B)	106.7	1	PS	Pskov	R. dlya dvoikh
9C)	106.7	1	RY	Ryazan	R. dlya druzey
1)	106.8	1	ZB	Krasnokamensk	Avtoradio
1)	106.8	1	YE	Nizhniy Tagil	Avtoradio
1)	106.8	1	OM	Omsk	Avtoradio
124B)	106.8	1	BA	Bakaly	Sputnik FM
14)	106.8	1	KD	Krasnodar	R. Shanson
168)	106.8	1	MO	Taldom	R. Nashe Podmoskovye
168)	106.8	1	MO	Volokalamsk	R. Nashe Podmoskovye
19)	106.8	5	BE	Belgorod	Dorozhnoye R.
19)	106.8	1	VN	Voronezh	Dorozhnoye R.
2)	106.8	1	YE	Serov	Russkoye R.
22)	106.8	1	AK	Barnaul	R. KP
25)	106.8	1	MD	Saransk	R. Mir
4)	106.8	2	TS	Kazan	Europa Plus
4)	106.8	1	VL	Murom	Europa Plus
59)	106.8	1	VN	Boguchar	Kanal Melodiya (Vor.)
6)	106.8	1	SR	Saratov	Love R.
8)	106.8	1	KE	Novokuznetsk	Nashe R.
90)	106.8	1	KY	Yugorsk	Nord FM
98B)	106.8	1	PS	V.Luki	R. dlya dvoikh
12)	106.9	1	VL	Vladimir	Sport FM
134A)	106.9	1	KE	Yurga	R. Vanya
14)	106.9	1	NN	N.Novgorod	R. Shanson
169)	106.9	1	VO	Vologda	R. Premyer
19)	106.9	1	KD	Sochi	Dorozhnoye R.
2)	106.9	1	SP	Tikhvin	Russkoye R.
3)	106.9	1	TL	Tula	Ekho Moskvy
32)	106.9	1	SA	Tolyatti	106.9 FM
44)	106.9	1	MU	Murmansk	Bolshoye R.
1)	107.0	1	KE	Belovo	Avtoradio
124B)	107.0	1	BA	Ufa	Sputnik FM
124B)	107.0	2	SV	Yekaterinburg	Sputnik FM
13)	107.0	5	MO	Moskva	R. RSN
131)	107.0	1	TS	Novosheshminsk	R. Bolgar
134A)	107.0	1	BR	Bryansk	R. Vanya
14)	107.0	1	SR	Balakovo	R. Shanson
15)	107.0	1	UD	Izhevsk	DFM
164)	107.0	1	PZ	Serdobsk	Svoye R.
19)	107.0	1	TY	Tyumen	Dorozhnoye R.
2)	107.0	1	CV	Cheboksary	Russkoye R.
2)	107.0	5	PM	Vladivostok	Russkoye R.
23)	107.0	1	YA	Yaroslavl	Detskoye R.
25)	107.0	1	PR	Berezniki	R. Mir
62)	107.0	5	KD	Kanevskaya	Kazak FM
92)	107.0	1	VG	Mikhaylovka	Novaya volna
1)	107.1	1	IR	Irkutsk	Avtoradio
124B)	107.1	1	BA	Kumertau	Sputnik FM
131)	107.1	1	TS	Abznakayevo	R. Bolgar
131)	107.1	2	TS	Bazarnyye Mataki	R. Bolgar
177)	107.1	2	RS	Yakutsk	R. Sakha
18)	107.1	1	VN	Borisoglebsk	Yumor FM
189)	107.1	1	DA	Makhachkala	R. Stolitsa
22)	107.1	1	KY	Krasnoyarsk	R. KP
27)	107.1	4	IV	Rodniki	R. Dacha
27)	107.1	4	TO	Tomsk	R. Dacha
7)	107.1	1	AK	Rubtsovsk	Militseyskaya volna
124B)	107.2	1	BA	Belebey	Sputnik FM
124B)	107.2	1	BA	Beloretsk	Sputnik FM
130A)	107.2	1	VN	Voronezh	R. Borneo
16)	107.2	1	KO	Ukhta	Retro FM
162)	107.2	1	RY	Ryazan	R. OK
19)	107.2	1	KT	Petrozavodsk	Dorozhnoye R.
19)	107.2	1	SM	Smolensk	Dorozhnoye R.
2)	107.2	1	OB	Orenburg	Russkoye R.
23)	107.2	1	SA	Samara	Detskoye R.
35)	107.2	1	IR	Bratsk	R. Vera
8)	107.2	1	CB	Snezhinsk	Nashe R.
84)	107.2	1	MD	Saransk	MS R.
1)	107.3	1	PM	Luchegorsk	Avtoradio
131)	107.3	1	TS	Manzelinsk	R. Bolgar
15)	107.3	1	CB	Chelyabinsk	DFM
156)	107.3	1	TS	Kazan	R. Millenium
19)	107.3	1	PS	Novosokolniki	Dorozhnoye R.
2)	107.3	1	VL	Murom	Russkoye R.
236)	107.3	1	SA	Sergiyevsk	Samarskoye Gub. R.
26)	107.3	1	SP	Luga	R. Rekord
5)	107.3	1	KE	Kemerovo	Hit FM
1)	107.4	1	KS	Kostroma	Avtoradio

FM	MHz	kW	Rg	Location	Station
171)	107.4	1	IR	Ust-Ilimsk	R. Radio
199)	107.4	1	TY	Tyumen	R. Yugra
2)	107.4	1	VN	Rossosh	Russkoye R.
206)	107.4	1	AR	Arkhangelsk	Region 29
21)	107.4	1	ZB	Chita	R. Zvezda
25)	107.4	1	YA	Rybinsk	R. Mir
28)	107.4	10	SP	Sankt-Peterburg	Biznes FM
5)	107.4	3	MO	Moskva	Hit FM
5)	107.4	3	KN	Achinsk	Hit FM
54)	107.4	2	TA	Tambov	Global FM
7)	107.4	1	OB	Ilek	Militseyskaya volna
74)	107.4	1	KD	Sochi	Maks FM
78)	107.4	1	VG	Mikhaylovka	Mikhaylovka FM
79)	107.4	1	BE	St.Oskol	Mir Belogorya
98B)	107.4	1	SR	Balakovo	R. dlya dvoikh
9C)	107.4	1	SA	Tolyatti	R. dlya druzey
1)	107.5	1	SM	Roslavl	Avtoradio
10)	107.5	1	RK	Abakan	R. 7
12)	107.5	1	KC	Karachayevsk	Sport FM
12)	107.5	1	KH	Khabarovsk	Sport FM
131)	107.5	1	TS	Bavly	R. Bolgar
14)	107.5	1	TL	Tula	R. Shanson
15)	107.5	1	TS	Nizhnekamsk	DFM
186)	107.5	1	YE	Irbit	R. Skit
19)	107.5	1	VO	Gryazovets	Dorozhnoye R.
2)	107.5	1	VL	Kovrov	Russkoye R.
2)	107.5	1	BU	Ulan-Ude	Russkoye R.
27)	107.5	1	IR	Irkutsk	R. Dacha
28)	107.5	1	BA	Ufa	Biznes FM
3)	107.5	1	PZ	Penza	Ekho Moskvy
5)	107.5	1	AK	Rubtsovsk	Hit FM
8)	107.5	1	KG	Kurgan	Nashe R.
1)	107.6	1	NN	Arzamas	Avtoradio
1)	107.6	1	KD	Kanevskaya	Avtoradio
12)	107.6	1	TO	Tomsk	Sport FM
133)	107.6	1	BR	Bryansk	R. Chistyye klyuchi
16)	107.6	1	RS	Yakutsk	Retro FM
19)	107.6	1	SP	Priozersk	Dorozhnoye R.
2)	107.6	1	KE	Leninsk-Kuznetskiy	Russkoye R.
22)	107.6	1	UD	Izhevsk	R. KP
226)	107.6	1	YE	Yekaterinburg	Gorod FM
24)	107.6	1	BA	Baymak	NRJ
1)	107.7	1	BE	Belgorod	Avtoradio
1)	107.7	1	KE	Mezhdurechensk	Avtoradio
107)	107.7	1	KD	Krasnodar	R. 107
12)	107.7	1	OB	Orenburg	Sport FM
124B)	107.7	1	BA	Burayevo	Sputnik FM
124B)	107.7	1	BA	Mesyagutovo	Sputnik FM
14)	107.7	2	NS	Novosibirsk	R. Shanson
16)	107.7	1	KD	Armavir	Retro FM
18)	107.7	1	SM	Smolensk	Yumor FM
26)	107.7	1	VL	Murom	R. Rekord
7)	107.7	1	OB	Yasnyy	Militseyskaya volna
8)	107.7	1	KO	Ukhta	Nashe R.
10)	107.8	1	KD	Novorossiysk	R. 7
16)	107.8	1	PR	Berezniki	Retro FM
16)	107.8	1	KY	Norilsk	Retro FM
19)	107.8	1	TY	Ishim	Dorozhnoye R.
19)	107.8	1	VN	Rossosh	Dorozhnoye R.
2)	107.8	10	SP	Sankt-Peterburg	Russkoye R.
28)	107.8	1	NN	N.Novgorod	Biznes FM
29)	107.8	1	KD	Kushchovskaya	Pervoye R.
4)	107.8	1	SR	Volsk	Europa Plus
6)	107.8	1	TS	Kazan	Love F.
7)	107.8	5	MO	Moskva	Militseyskaya volna
8)	107.8	1	SV	Krasnoturinsk	Nashe R.
1)	107.9	1	MU	Monchegorsk	Avtoradio
1)	107.9	5	PM	Novozhatkovo	Avtoradio
10)	107.9	1	BE	St.Oskol	R. 7
16)	107.9	1	KE	Kemerovo	Retro FM
16)	107.9	1	KD	Sochi	Retro FM
19)	107.9	1	TY	Tobolsk	Dorozhnoye R.
19)	107.9	1	BA	Ufa	Dorozhnoye R.
19)	107.9	1	NN	Sarov	Dorozhnoye R.
2)	107.9	1	RY	Ryazan	Russkoye R.
2)	107.9	1	SO	Vladikavkaz	Russkoye R.
27)	107.9	1	VL	Vladimir	R. Dacha
3)	107.9	1	SA	Tolyatti	Ekho Moskvy
36)	107.9	1	SP	Vyborg	Avtoradio St-Peterburg
7)	107.9	1	KD	Tikhoretsk	Militseyskaya volna

NB: Txs below 1kW not listed. +) Tests with DRM+ (Mayak)

Addresses and other information:

1) 127083 Moskva, ul. 8-go Marta 8 – **2)** 123298 Moskva, 3-ya Khoroshevskaya ul. 12 – **3)** 119992 Moskva, ul. Novyy Arbat 11 – **4)** 109004 Moskva, ul. Stanislavskogo 21 – **5)** 123298 Moskva, 3-ya Khoroshevskaya ul. 12 – **6)** 127299 Moskva, ul. Bolshaya Akademicheskaya 5a – **7)** 109180 Moskva, 3-y Golutinskiy per. 8/10 – **8)** 123060 Moskva, ul. Narodnogo Opolcheniya 39 – **9A-C)** 109004 Moskva, ul.Stanislavskogo 21 – **10)** 109004 Moskva, ul. Stanislavskogo 21 – **11)** 123298 Moskva, 3-ya Khoroshevskaya ul. 12 – **12)** 119435 Moskva, Savvinskaya nab. 23 – **13)** 127015 Moskva, Bumazhnyy proyezd 14 – **14)** 119049 Moskva, ul. Shabolovka 10 – **15)** 123298 Moskva, 3-ya Khoroshevskaya ul. 12 – **16)** 109004 Moskva, ul. Stanislavskogo 21 – **17)** 109004 Moskva, ul. Stanislavskogo 21 – **18)** 127083 Moskva, ul. 8-go Marta 8 – **19)** 199406 St.Peterburg, ul. Shevchenko 28 – **20)** 127083 Moskva, ul. 8-go Marta 8 – **21)** 129164 Moskva, pr. Mira 126 – **22)** 127993 Moskva, Staryy Petrovsko-Razumovskiy proyezd 1/23 – **23)** 129226 Moskva, ul. Vilgelma Pika 3 – **24)** 127083 Moskva, ul. 8-go Marta 8 – **25)** 107076 Moskva, ul. Krasnobogatyrskaya 44 – **26)** 198303 St.Peterburg, pr. Stachek 105 – **27)** 127299 Moskva, ul. B. Akademicheskaya 5a – **28)** 127287 Moskva, 2-ya Khutorskaya ul. 38a – **29)** 350038 Krasnodar, ul. Korolenko 2/1 – **30A,B)** 192007 St.Peterburg, Ligovskiy pr. 174 – **31)** 129226 Moskva, ul. Vilgelma Pika 3 – **32)** 445051 Tolyatti, Primorskiy bul. 2b – **33)** 432030 Ulyanovsk, ul. Narimanova 75 – **34)** 650007 Novokuznetsk, ul. Ordzhonikidze 35 – **35)** 107553 Moskva, B.Cherkizovskaya ul. 17 – **36)** 197376 St.Peterburg, ul. Ak.Pavlova 5 – **37)** 236000 Kaliningrad, ul. Narvskaya 58 – **38)** 618400 Berezniki, Klyuchevaya ul. 17 – **39)** 123060 Moskva, ul. Narodnogo Opolcheniya 39 – **40)** 420021 Kazan, ul. Gabdully Tukaya 91 – **41)** 241019 Bryansk, pr. Stanke Dimitrova 79 – **42)** 424038 Yoshkar-Ola, ul. Voinov-Internatsionalistov 37 – **43)** 614007 Perm, ul. Kuybysheva 37 – **44)** 183038 Murmansk, ul. Lenina 68 – **45)** 241007 Bryansk, ul. Duki 80 – **46)** 129272 Moskva, ul. Trifonovskaya 57 – **47)** 603022 N.Novgorod, Okskiy syezd 8 – **48)** 625000 Tyumen, ul. Geologorazvedchikov 28 – **49)** 625051 Tyumen, ul. Olimpiyskaya 9 – **50)** 620075 Yekaterinburg, pr. Lenina 41 – **51)** 302028 Oryol, ul. 7-ye Noyabrya 43 – **52)** 197376 St.Peterburg, ul. Prof.Popova 47 – **53)** 129164 Moskva, Zubarev per. 15 – **54)** 392020 Tambov, ul. Olega Koshevogo 14 – **55)** 630087 Novosibirsk, ul. Nemirovicha-Danchenko 122 – **56)** 199034 St.Peterburg, nab. L. Shmidta 39.– **57)** 364014 Groznyy, ul. Mayakovskogo 92 – **58)** 454091 Chelyabinsk, ul. Ordzhonikidze 81 – **59)** 394000 Voronezh, ul. Lenina 73 – **60)** 620086 Yekaterinburg, ul. Repina 6a – **61)** 362047 Vladikavkaz, ul. Vesennaya 5 – **62)** 350038 Krasnodar, ul. Korolenko 2/1 – **63)** 660075 Krasnoyarsk, ul. Severo-Yeniseyskaya 33 – **64)** 150008 Yaroslavl, ul. Vrubelya 4 – **65)** 443011 Samara, ul. Sovetskoy Armii 245e – **66)** 625019 Tyumen, ul. Respubliki 211a – **67A,B)** 400081 Volgograd, ul. Angarskaya 71 – **68)** 677000 Yakutsk, ul. Bestuzheva-Marlinskogo 9/3 – **69)** 660043 Krasnoyarsk, ul. Lunacharskogo 106 – **70)** 398050 Lipetsk, ul. Plekhanova 1 – **71)** 454091 Chelyabinsk, ul. Ordzhonikidze 41 – **72)** 182106 Velikiye Luki, pl. Chapayeva 5 – **73)** 453124 Steplitamak, ul. Khudaybердina 17 – **74)** 354000 Sochi, ul. Severnaya 12 – **75)** 610000 Kirov, Oktyabrskiy pr. 120 – **76)** 127015 Moskva, Bolshaya Novodmitrovskaya ul. 36 – **77)** 428022 Cheboksary, ul. Gagarina 36 – **78)** 403342 Mikhaylovka, ul. Belorusskaya 2a – **79)** 308000 Belgorod, pr. Slavy 60 – **80A,B)** 127137 Moskva, ul. Pravdy 24/2. 80B) in English – **81)** 129164 Moskva, per. Zubarev 15 – **82)** 440026 Penza, ul. Lermontova 39 – **83)** 426069 Izhevsk, ul. Pesochnaya 9 – **84)** 430011 Saransk, ul. Vasenko 32 – **85)** 174260 Malaya Vishera, ul. Moskovskaya 21 – **86)** 125009 Moskva, ul. Tverskaya 7. **E:** narodnoe-radio@mail.ru – **87)** 428003 Cheboksary, ul. Lenina 15 – **88A,B)** 197022 St.Peterburg, Kamenoostrovskiy pr. 67 – **89)** 248021 Kaluga, ul. Moskovskaya 189 – **90)** 628260 Yugorsk, ul. Lenina 18 – **91)** 353915 Novorossiysk, ul. Revolutsii 1905 goda 19 – **92)** 400131 Volgograd, ul. Komsomolskaya 8 – **93)** 603155 N.Novgorod, ul. B.Pecherskaya 33-1 – **94)** 619001 Kudymkar, ul. Polevaya 3 – **95)** 428022 Cheboksary, ul. Gagarina 36 – **96)** 170000 Tver, ul. Mednikovskaya 55/25 – **97)** 115035 Moskva, Sofiyskaya nab. 30 – **98A.B)** 199155 St.Peterburg, pr. KIMa 5/34 – **99)** 672010 Chita, ul. Amurskaya 36 – **100)** 183038 Murmansk, ul. Yegorova 14 – **101)** 650000 Kemerovo, pr. Kuznetskiy 33g – **102)** 142672 Likino-Dulevo, ul. Oktyabrskaya 42 – **103)** 424038 Yoshkar-Ola, ul. Voinov-Internatsionalistov 37 – **104)** 454084 Chelyabinsk, ul. Kalinina 21 – **105)** 440046 Penza, ul. Mira 1a – **106)** 693023 Yuzhno-Sakhalinsk, ul. Komsomolskaya 213a – **107)** 350000 Krasnodar, ul. Gimnazicheskaya 51 – **108)** 450075 Ufa, ul. Blyukhera 15 – **109)** 644010 Omsk, ul. Dekabristov 130 – **110A,B)** 400131 Volgograd, ul. Krasnoznamenskaya 25 – **111)** 173020 V.Novgorod, B.Moskovskaya ul. 106 – **112)** 625013 Tyumen, ul. Tekstilnaya 1 – **113)** 620151 Krasnoyarsk, ul. Baumana 22 – **114)** 426035 Izhevsk, ul. Avangardnaya 4b – **115)** 423400 Almetyevsk, ul. Radishcheva 12a – **116A,B)** 453300 Kumertau, PKiO im. Gagarina – **117)** 680000 Khabarovsk, ul. Lenina 4 – **118)** 514017 Perm, ul. Turgeneva 33a – **119)** 423810 Nab. Chelny, ul. 54-y kompleks 8 – **120)** 403348 Mikhaylovka, ul. Mira 81 – **121)** 197022 St.Peterburg, P.O.Box 122. **E:**

radioslovo@mail.ru – **122)** 453300 Kumertau, PKiO im. Gagarina – **123)** 196084 St.Peterburg, ul. Tsvetochnaya 16b **E:** radio_rusk@mail.ru – **124A-C)** 450076 Ufa, ul. Gafuri 9 124A,B) in Bashkir. – **125)** 445010 Tolyatti, ul. Sovetskaya 74a – **126)** 692760 Artyom, ul. Kirova 68 – **127)** 665831 Angarsk ul. Vesennyaya 2 – **128)** 190068 St.Peterburg, P.O.Box 732. **E:** pr@radiomaria.ru – **129)** 140400 Kolomna, ul. Shilova 9 – **130A,B)** 394071 Voronezh, ul. 20-letnaya Oktyabrya 66 – **131)** 420015 Kazan, ul. Gorkogo 15 – **132)** 190000 St.Peterburg, P.O.Box 110. **E:** spb@ radioteos.ru – **133)** 241037 Bryansk, ul. Dimitrova 70/1 – **134A,B)** 199406 St.Peterburg, ul. Shevchenko 28 – **135)** 440434 Penza, ul. Markina 1 – **136)** 194044 St.Peterburg, Krapivnyy per. 5 – **137)** 394036 Voronezh, ul. K.Marksa 67b – **138)** 362007 Vladikavkaz, ul. Osetinskaya gorka 2a – **139)** 125190 Moskva, Leningradskiy pr. 80 – **140)** 360000 Nalchik, pr. Lenina 5 – **141)** 115054 Moskva, ul. Valovaya 32/75 – **142)** 369200 Karachayevsk – **143)** 462411 Orsk, ul. Leninskogo Komsomola 4b – **144)** 187110 Kirishi, ul. Sovetskaya 20 – **145)** 129164 Moskva, Zubarev per. 15 – **146)** 454080 Chelyabinsk, ul. Ordzhonikidze 58a – **147)** 426011 Izhevsk, ul. Kholmogorova 11b – **148)** 423827 Nab.Chelny, bul. Yunykh Lenintsev 9 – **149)** 305004 Kursk, ul. Dimitrova 76 – **150)** 690091 Vladivostok, ul. Pologaya 53 – **151)** 652515 Leninsk-Kuznetskiy, ul. Pushkina 4 – **152)** 386102 Nazran, ul. Moskovskaya 29a – **153)** 362000 Vladikavkaz – **154)** 664012 Irkutsk, ul. Baykalskaya 106a – **155)** 443070 Samara, ul. Partizanskaya 19 – **156)** 420032 Kazan, ul. Tabeykina 19a – **157)** 123298 Moskva, 3-ya Khoroshevskaya ul. 12 – **158)** 238050 Gusev, ul. Shkolnaya 11 – **159)** 420053 Yekaterinburg, ul. Volgogradskaya 193 – **160)** 629807 Noyabrsk, ul. Lenina 47 – **161)** 603068 N.Novgorod, Yarmarochnyy proyezd 10 – **162)** 390023 Ryazan, ul. Tsiolkovskogo 20 – **163)** 454090 Chelyabinsk, ul. Tsvillinga 46a – **164)** 440034 Penza, ul. Markina 1.– **165)** 197375 St.Peterburg, ul. Chapygina 6 – **166)** 620075 Yekaterinburg, ul. Lenina 41 – **167)** 625013 Tyumen, ul. Permyakova 3a – **168)** 123007 Moskva, 5-ya Magistralnaya ul. 6 – **169)** 160035 Vologda, ul. Kozlenskaya 35 – **170)** 368120 Kyzylyurt, pr. Imama Shamilya 43/13 – **171)** 123001 Moskva, ul. Spolnyy per. 18 – **172)** 113326 Moskva, ul. Pyatnitskaya 25. **E:** radonezh@radonezh.ru – **173)** 603006 N.Novgorod, ul. Semashko 37 – **174)** 191123 St.Peterburg, ul. Kirochnaya 38 – **175)** 450075 Ufa, ul. Blyukhera 15.– **176)** 344002 Rostov-na-Donu, ul. Pushkinskaya 63 – **177)** 677027 Yakutsk, ul. Ordzhonikidze 48. **E:** sakharadio@mail.ru – **178)** 368006 Khasvyurt, ul. Energeticheskaya 1 – **179)** 172730 Ostashkov, ul. Konstantina Zaslonova 32a – **180)** 443093 Samara, ul. Myagi 10a – **181)** 127287 Moskva, 2-ya Khutorskaya ul. 38a – **182)** 620014 Yekaterinburg, ul. Lenina 41 – **183)** 634003 Tomsk, per. Mariniskiy 8 – **184)** 625013 Tyumen, ul. Permyakova 7 – **185)** 620109 Yekaterinburg, ul. Repina 15 – **186)** 623850 Irbit, ul. Zhukova 6a – **187)** 630011 Novosibirsk, ul. Kirova 3 – **188)** 414000 Astrakhan, ul. Nab. 1-ya Maya 75 – **189)** 367000 Makhachkala, ul. Gamidova 18 – **190)** 367032 Makhachkala, ul. M.Gadzhiyeva 188 – **191)** 692916 Nakhotka, ul. Koltsevaya 59 – **192)** 162610 Cherepovets, ul. Lenina 151 – **193)** 660028 Krasnoyarsk, ul. Baumana 22 – **194)** 367020 Makhachkala, ul. Nuradilova 2 – **195)** 690091 Vladivostok, ul. Uborevicha 20a – **196)** 680000 Krasnoyarsk, ul. Frunze 58 – **197)** 677027 Yakutsk, ul. Oktyabrskaya 16/2 – **198)** 678960 Neryungri, teletsentr – **199)** 628011 Khanty-Mansiysk, ul. Gagarina 4 – **200)** 630087 Novosibirsk, ul. Nemirovicha-Danchenko 122 – **201)** 640021 Kurgan, ul. Tobolnaya 54 – **202)** 197101 St.Peterburg, ul. Kronverskaya 23 – **203)** 678901 Aldan, Sportivnyy per. 2 – **204)** 620144 Yekaterinburg, ul. Khokhryakova 104 – **205)** 156005 Kostroma, ul. Lagernaya 15 – **206)** 163002 Arkhangelsk, Novgorodskiy pr. 32 – **207)** 129226 Moskva, ul. Vilgelma Pika 3 – **208)** 123060 Moskva, ul. Narodnogo Opolcheniya 39 – **209)** 390023 Ryazan, ul. Tsiolkovskogo 20 – **210)** 620075 Yekaterinburg, ul. Lenina 41 – **211)** 666784 Ust-Kut, ul. Kirova 88 – **212)** 123298 Moskva, 3-ya Khoroshevskaya ul. 12 – **213)** 443110 Samara, ul. Novo-Sadovaya 44 – **214)** 455040 Magnitogorsk, pr. K.Marksa 133 – **215)** 618551 Solikamsk, ul. Vseobucha 80 – **216)** 677000 Yakutsk, ul. Lenina 14 – **217)** 236010 Kaliningrad, pr. Mira 136 – **218)** 617470 Kungur, ul. Krasnaya 15 – **219)** 194044 Sankt-Peterburg, pr. Malyy Samsoniyevskiy 3a – **220)** 430000 Saransk, ul. Kommunisticheskaya 89 – **221)** 677007 Yakutsk, ul. Kirova 17/3 – **222)** 127299 Moskva, ul. Akademicheskaya 5a – **223)** 420094 Kazan, ul. Golubyatnikova 20a – **224)** 664007 Irkutsk, ul. K.Libknekhta 107d – **225)** 690091 Vladivostok, ul. Pologaya 60 – **226)** 620014 Yekaterinburg, pr. Lenina 24a – **227)** 680000 Khabarovsk, ul. Frunze 58 – **228)** 420034 Kazan, ul. Lenskaya 10 – **229)** 446300 Otradnyy, ul. Pervomayska 38a – **230)** 170100 Tver, ul. Medinkovskaya 55/25 – **231)** 386245 Stanitsa Troitskaya, ul. Krestyanskaya 4 – **232)** 649002 Gorno-Altaysk, pr. Kommunisticheskiy 1 – **233)** 614990 Perm, ul. Lenina 50-141 – **234)** 462431 Orsk, ul. Kutuzova 58-12 – **235)** 236040 Kaliningrad, Leninskiy pr. 10 – **236)** 443068 Samara, ul. Novo-Sadovaya 106 – **A)** Rel. WRN (UK). Full schedule see **W:** wrn.ru.

NON-PROFESSIONAL RADIO STATIONS
Upon application, the regulator Rozkomnadzor issues temporary, short-term licenses to non-professional radio stations ("Individualnoye

(Lyubitelskoye) veshchaniye"). These stns may operate with low power on specifically assigned MW frqs, usually 1584, 1593 or 1602kHz. Also the temporary use of SW freqs with low power has been granted in the past. Primarily technical universities have been organizing this type of transmitting activity, providing studio facilities and technical logistics. The prgrs are usually produced by students of these educational institutions.

DAB Transmitter (DAB+) (Trial)
Tx Operator: RTRS **M:** Mayak **Tx:** Block 11C (220.352MHz) Moskva; also other blocks may be tested.

Radio via DTT: see National TV section.

NB: The station listing for **Crimea** can be found at the end of the "Ukraine" chapter

RWANDA

LT: UTC +2h — **Pop:** 11 million — **Pr.L:** Kinyarwanda, Swahili, French, English — **E.C:** 50Hz, 230V — **ITU:** RRW

RWANDA UTILITIES REGULATORY AGENCY (RURA)
✉ B.P. 6929, Kigali ☎+250 252584562 🖷 +250 252584563 **W:** rura. gov.rw **E:** info@rura.gov.rw

RWANDA BROADCASTING AGENCY (RBA) (Gov)
✉ B.P. 83, Kigali ☎+250 252572276 **W:** rba.co.rw **E:** radiorwanda@ yahoo.com **L.P:** Dir. Broadc: Mweusi Karake. Dir. Prgrs: Paul Ndamage. Ag. Ch.Editor: Willy Rukundo. Tech. Dir: Charles Nahayo.
FM: Channel I (MHz): 89.8 Kinanira 0.5kW, 93.5 Nyarufubire 0.5kW, 95.1 Mugogo/Rushaki 0.5kW, 97.6 Karongi 1kW, 100.7 Mt. Jali 5kW, 103.2 Byumba 0.5kW, 103.9 Butare 0.5kW + 8 trs under 0.5kW.
Channel II (Magic FM): Kigali 90.7MHz 5kW.
D.Prgr in Kinyarwanda/Swahili/French/English: 24h. N. in English: 0515, 1830. **Ann:** F: "Vous écoutez Radio Rwanda émettant de Kigali".
R. Communautaires: Rubavu, 94.6, Nyagatare 95.5, Musanze 98.4, Huye 100.4, Rusizi 103.2MHz.

Other stations FM (MHz)
City R, Kigali: 88.3 1kW – **Contact FM:** Kigali 89.7 0.5kW – **Flash FM,** Kigali: 89.2 0.5kW – **KFM,** Kigali: 98.7 **W:** kfm.nationmedia.com (Cf. Kenya) – **KT R,** Kigali: 96.7 **W:** ktradio.rw – **R. Izuba,** Kibungo: 100.0 0.5kW –**R. Isango Star,** Kigali: 91.5 **W:** isangostar.rw – **R. Maria Rwanda:** Gitarama 88.6 1kW, Kigali 97.3 2kW, Karongi 99.8 **E:** radiomariar@yahoo.fr – **R. 10 FM:** Kigali (Mont Jari) 87.6 0.5kW **W:** danslevent.com/rwanda **E:** contact@danslevent.com – **R. Salus** (University R.), Butare: 97.0 1kW, Kigali 101.9 1kW. **W:** salus.nur.ac.rw – **R. Sana uRwanda** (Rlg.): Kigali 98.0 – **R. Umucyo,** Kigali: 102.8 0.1kW.
AWR: 106.4 0.3kW – **BBC African Sce:** Karongi 93.3, Kigali (Mont Jari) 93.9 3kW, Butare 106.1 3kW – **RFI Afrique:** Kigali 91.9 in French/Swahili – **Voice of America:** Kigali 104.3 2kW – **Deutsche Welle:** Kigali 96.0MHz 2kW

SABA (Netherlands)

LT: UTC -4h — **Pop:** 1,800 — **Pr.L:** Dutch (official), English — **E.C:** 60Hz, 110V — **ITU:** BES

Q93.9, The Voice of Saba
✉ PO Box 1,The Bottom, Saba ☎ +599 4 16 3213 🖷 +599 416 3308 **FM:** PJF1 93.9MHz 1kW **W:** q939fm.com

SAMOA

LT: UTC +13h (27 Sep 15-3 Apr 16, 25 Sep 16-2 Apr 17: +14h) — **Pop:** 193,000 —**Pr.L:** Samoan, English — **E.C:** 50Hz, 230/410V — **ITU:** SMO

OFFICE OF THE REGULATOR [Gov]
✉ Private Bag, Apia, Samoa. First Flr, G.Meredith Bldg, Tamaligi, Apia ☎ +685 30282 🖷 +685 30281 **W:** regulator.gov.ws **E:** admin@ regulator.gov.ws **L.P:** Regulator: Donnie de Freitas. Mgr Spectrum & Tech. Scs: Untoa Auelua Fonoti

MW	kHz	kW	MW	kHz	kW
1) 2AP Apia	540	5	1) 2AP Apia	747	5
FM	**MHz**	**kW**	**FM**	**MHz**	**kW**
2) Showers of Blessings FM	88.1	-	4) Mai FM	89.1	1
3) Talofa FM	88.5	0.25	2) Showers of Blessings FM	89.9	-

FM	MHz	kW	FM	MHz	kW
5) Aiga Fesilafa'i	90.5	1	3) Talofa FM	99.9	0.25
6) EFKS FM*	90.9	-	3) K-Lite FM	101.1	0.25
3) Talofa FM*	91.5	0.25	10) China R. Int.	100.4	-
7) Samoa FM	93.7	-	11) R. Australia	102.0	-
8) Laufou o le Talaleilei	95.1	-	8) Laufou o le Talaleilei	103.1	-
3) Star FM	96.1	0.25	7) Samoa FM*	104.1	-
3) Power FM	96.9	-	12) NUS Campus R.	105.0	-
2) Showers of Blessings FM	97.5	0.5	9) Power FM	106.7	-
3) Magik FM	98.1	0.3	6) EFKS FM	106.9	-
6) EFKS FM	98.9	-			

NB: Location Apia & Upoulu except *) Savai'i

Addresses and other information:
1) **NATIONAL RADIO 2AP (Gov)** ⌨ Ministry of Communications and Information Technology, Government of Samoa, Level 1, CA & CT Plaza, Savalolo, Apia, Samoa ☎ +685 26177 🖷 +685 24671 **W:** mcit.gov.ws **E:** mcit@mcit.gov.ws ⌨ 2AP Studio, Mulinu'u, Apia: +685 21422 **E:** a.ahsam@mcit.gov.ws **LP:** CEO: Tua'imalo Asamu Ah Sam, Senior Programmer: Vaasiliega Lupati Lagaia Samoan/English: 1700 (Sun 2200)-1000 on 540kHz Edu: brdcsts on some weekdays for Samoa and Tokelau 1930-2030 on 747kHz World N: 1800W, 1900W, 1930W. Local N: 1630W, 1730W, 1830W, 0730W Ann: "National Radio 2AP" or "Voice of the Nation" – 2) Samoa Worship Centre Church, PO Box 3026, Apia. ☎ +685 21447/23887/29153 🖷 +685 20657 **W:** samoa.worshipcentre-worldwide.org & facebook.com/uagaofaamanuiago/info incl live streaming audio. Prgr: Samoan/English religious – 3) R. Polynesia Ltd, P.O.Box 762, Svalalo, Apia ☎+685 25148/49/50 🖷 +685 25147 Brands: Magik FM - "Samoa's #1 Hit Music Station" (English) ☎ Studio +685 33981, Talofa FM "100% Local" (Samoan) Studio ☎+685 33999, K-Lite FM "Memories are Good" (English) ☎+685 33101 **N:** RNZI throughout the day, Star FM "Absolute Music Variety" (English) ☎ +685 33961 **W:** fmradio.ws **E:** corey@fmradio.ws **LP:** CEO Corey Keil D.Prgr: 24h – 4) Samoa Quality Broadcasters, Mulinu'u, Apia ☎+685 24790/91, 21735 🖷 +685 24789 CEO: Galuemalemana Ms Faresea Matafeo **E:** ceo@sbcl.ws **D.Prgr:** 24h (Samoan/English) Other: technical services for R. Australia 102.0FM – 5) Catholic Archdiocese of Samoa, PO Box 532, Muli'vai, Apia. ☎ +685 21156/21051/7521051 **E:** daman-auisavelio@yahoo.com Prgr: Samoan religious – 6) Ekalesia Faapotopototoga Kerisiano Samoa [EFKS] - Congregational Christian Church in Samoa, 5th Floor, John Williams Building, Tamalagi, Apia. ☎+685 24414 🖷: +685 20429 **W:** cccs.org.ws Prgr: Samoan religious Other: EFKS-TV – 7) Talamua Media & Publications Ltd, Level 2, Nia Mall, Fugalei, Apia. PO Box 1321, Apia. ☎ +685 7777937, 7513937 **W:** talamua.com **E:** samoafm93.7@gmail.com **LP:** MD: Angela Kronfeld-Polu. **ID:** "The People's Station" D.Prgr: 24h in Samoan/English – 8) Youth for Christ Samoa, PO Box 3706, Apia. ☎ +685 22663 **W:** yfcsamoa.org **LP:** Manasa Aloalii Prgr: Samoan religious – 9) Silver & Gold Radio Imaging Ltd, Vaea Street, Apia. ☎ 685 28894 **W:** facebook.com/power-969-1067-fm-samoa **ID:** "The Station that Rocks the Nation" Prgr: Samoan/English – 10) 24/7 English language via satellite from Beijing – 11) 24/7 Pacific English stream via satellite from Melbourne – 12) Faculty of Arts, Media & Journalism program, National University of Samoa, Le Papaigalagala Campus, To'omatgi ☎+685 20072 🖷 +685 25489 **E:** info@nus.edu.ws **W:** nus.edu.ws **LP:** Nora Tumua **E:** n.tumua@nus.edu.ws Vicky Lepou **E:** v.lepou@nus.edu.ws Prgr: student campus radio in Samoan/English

SAMOA (AMERICAN) (USA)

L.T: UTC -11h — **Pop:** 67,242 — **Pr.L:** Samoan, English — **E.C:** 60Hz, 120V — **ITU:** SMA

FEDERAL COMMUNICATIONS COMMISSION (FCC)
see USA for details

FM	MHz	Call	kW	FM	MHz	Call	kW
6)Tafuna	88.1	KGIF	1.5	10) Tafuna	94.5	KKAS-LP	0.1
7)PagoPago	88.9	KBTB	0.3	4) Ili'Ili	95.1	KULA-LP	0.1
8)Nu'uuli	89.7	KMOA	1.5	4) W. District	97.1	KULA-LP	0.011
9)Mapusaga	90.5	KPPO	0.75	4) C. District	99.1	KULA-LP	0.011
6)Utulei	91.3	KIOE	1.5	4) E. District	102.5	KULA-LP	0.023
3)Pago Pago	92.1	KSBS-FM	15.5	2) Fagaitua	103.1	WVUV-FM	1.3
2)Pago Pago	93.1	KKHJ-FM	1.1	5) Pago Pago	104.1	KNWJ	0.01*
2)Pavaiai	93.7	KKHJ-FM	0.01	5) Leone	104.7	KNWJ	0.28

* reported silent

Addresses and other information:
2) South Seas Broadcasting Inc, PO Box 6758, Pago Pago, American Samoa 96799. **LP:** Joey Cummings, GM ☎+1 684 633 4493 **W:** KKHJ-FM: khjradio.com **ID:** '93KHJ' **W:** WVUV-FM: wvuv.com **ID:** "WVUV-FM is V103 The People's Station" in Samoan/English, D.Prgr: both 24h **Other Media:** KKHJ-TV Island TV Cable 10 – 3) Samoa

Technologies Inc, PO Box 793, Pago Pago, American Samoa 96799-0793 ☎+1 684 633 7000 🖷+1 684 633 5727 **W:** ksbsfm92.com **E:** info@ksbsfm92.com **LP:** Esther Prescott, GM **ID:** 'Island 92 - The Station That Belongs to You' **News:** hourly bulletins from RNZI, R. Australia, BBC, NPR, VOA. D.Prgr: 24h – 4) Pacific Islands Bible School, PO Box 1268, Pago Pago, American Samoa 96799 – 5) Showers of Blessings R., PO Box 997777, Pago Pago, American Samoa 96799 ☎+1 684 699 8123. 🖷+1 684 699 8126 **W:** fm104.org **E:** info@fm104.org – 6) Leone Church of Christ, PO Box 5093, Pago Pago, American Samoa 96799 –7) Rev Shannon Cummings dba Pure Truth Ministries, PO Box 6008, Pago Pago, American Samoa 96799 – 8)Teen Challenge American Samoa P.O.Box 277, Pago Pago, American Samoa 96789. **LP:** Otto and Vickie Haleck ☎ +1 684 699 2635 **W:** globaltc.org – 9) Second Samoan Congregational Church of Long Beach, 655 Cedar Ave, Long Beach CA 90802-1222 – 10) Life Inc Ministry, PO Box 1744, Pago Pago, American Samoa 96799

SAN MARINO

L.T. UTC +1h (27 Mar-30 Oct: +2h) — **Pop.** 32,500 — **Pr.L:** Italian — **ITU:** SMR

SAN MARINO RTV (Gov)
⌨ Viale J.F.Kennedy 13, 47890 Repubblica di San Marino ☎ +378 0549 882000 🖷 +378 0549 882840 **E:** radio@sanmarinortv.sm **W:** smtvsanmarino.sm/radio **LP:** Dir. Carlo Romeo, Prgr.Dir.: Giuseppe Cesetti, T.Dir.: Fabio Pelliccioni
FM: 102.7MHz 30kW **D.Prgr:** 24h
San Marino Classic, **E:** classic@sanmarinortv.sm **FM:** 103.2MHz 30kW **D.Prgr:** 24h Also carries govt meetings, live service. Prgr. Dir. Stefano Coveri
F.PI. no plans to start on MW assigned freq. 711kHz
V: by QSL-card. Rpts to **E:** ufficiotecnico@sanmarinortv.sm

RADIO INTERNATIONAL SAN MARINO (Comm)
⌨ Europa Radiodiffusione S.r.l. Strada Rovereta 42 RSM-47891 Falciano ☎ +378 0549 909905 🖷 +378 0549 941580 **E:** info@radiointernational.sm **W:** radiointernational.sm
FM: 94.25MHz 1kW **D.Prgr:** 24h

SÃO TOMÉ E PRÍNCIPE

L.T: UTC — **Pop:** 210,000 — **Pr.L:** Portuguese, Crioulo — **E.C:** 50Hz, 220V — **ITU:** STP

RÁDIO NACIONAL DE SÃO TOMÉ E PRÍNCIPE (RNSTP, Gov)
⌨ Avenida Marginal 12 de Julho, C.P. 44, São Tomé ☎/🖷 +239 222 13 42 **W:** rnstp.st **E:** atendimento@rnstp.st
LP: Dir: Artur Meneses de Pinho. CE: Felisberto Garcia.
MW: Pinheira: 945kHz 20kW **FM:** 89.7/95.4/99.3MHz.
D.Prgr: 24h in Portuguese. **N:** 0700, 1300, 1630, 1930.
IS: one note gong, guitar.

RDP África: São Tomé 92.8MHz 3kW, Príncipe 101.9MHz 70W.
RFI Afrique: 102.8MHz in French/Portuguese.
VOA: São José 105.5MHz 0.2kW in English/Portuguese.
VOA relay station: MW 1530kHz 600kW 0300-0630, 1600-2200 & SW. For further details see International Radio section under USA

SAUDI ARABIA

L.T: UTC +3h — **Pop:** 29 million — **Pr.L:** Arabic — **E.C:** 60Hz, 127/220V — **ITU:** ARS

MINISTRY OF CULTURE & INFORMATION (MOCI)
⌨ Nasseriya Str, Riyadh 11161 ☎+966 1 4014440 🖷 +966 1 402 3570. **W:** moci.gov.sa **LP:** Dep. Min. of Eng. Affairs: Dr. Riyadh Najm.

SAUDI BROADCASTING CORPORATION (SBC, Gov.)
⌨ P.O. Box 61718, Riyadh 11575 or P.O. Box 8525, Riyadh 11492 ☎+966 1 4425170 🖷 +966 1 4041692 **W:** sr.sa **E:** saudi-radio@moci.gov.sa

MW	kHz	kW	H of tr & Prgr.
Bisha	531	10	24h (Q)
Ar-Rass	549	10	0300-2300 (R)
Gizan	549	1	0300-2300 (R)
Qurayyat	549	20	24h (R)
Rafha	549	20	24h (R)

MW	kHz	kW	H of tr & Prgr.
Abha	558	5	24h (Q)
Jeddah (Bahrah)	567	200	24h (Q)
Afif	567	15	24h (Q)
Gizan (Ahawagerh)	576	20	24h (Q)
Riyadh	585	1200	24h (R)
Al-Hufuf	594	10	0300-2300 (R)
Duba	594	2000	0300-1500 (R)
Makkah	594	50	24h (G/P)
Al-Aflaj	612	15	24h (Q)
Hail	612	5	24h (Q)
Gizan	630	20	0300-2200 (J)
Najran	630	10	24h (Q)
Jeddah (Khumra)	648	*2000	0300-2300 (R)
Rafha	657	20	24h (Q)
Abha	675	5	0300-2300 (R)
Afif	675	20	0300-2300 (R)
Jeddah (Bahrah)	684	200	24h (J)
Riyadh	684	10	24h (J)
Bisha	702	10	24h (J)
Duba	702	40	24h (J)
Najran	747	10	0300-2300 (R)
Buraidah	747	10	0300-2300 (J)
Al-Aflaj	765	20	24h (Q)
Al-Hufuf	765	10	24h (Q)
Qurayyat	765	20	24h (Q)
Ras al-Khair	783	100	24h (I)
Jeddah (An Nuziah)	792	50	24h (Q)
Abha	810	20	24h (J)
Ras al-Khair	855	100	24h (Q)
Ar-Rass	873	10	24h (Q)
Dammam	882	100	24h (Q)
Qurayyat II	900	1000	1200-0300 (I)
Al-Hufuf	927	20	24h (J)
Makkah	936	50	24h (Q)
Riyadh	936	50	24h (Q)
Hail	945	5	0300-2300 (R)
Madinah	981	20	24h (Q)
Duba	999	20	24h (Q)
Madinah	1017	20	24h (P)
Yanbu al-Bahr	1035	20	24h (J)
Bisha	1071	50	24h (R)
Najran	1080	10	0300-2200 (J)
Qurayyat	1089	20	24h (J)
Dammam	1098	100	24h (J)
Madinah	1116	20	24h (J)
Madinah	1215	20	24h (J)
Dammam	1260	500	24h (R)
Makkah	1287	5	24h (Q)
Riyadh	1422	20	24h (I)
Ras al-Khair	1440	1600	24h (R)
Jeddah (Bahrah)	1449	200	24h (R)
Hafar Al-Batin	1467	50	24h (R)
Jeddah (Khumra)	1512	1000	1500-0300 (Q)
Duba	1521	2000	1500-0300 (R)

*running on low power.

FM(MHz)	R	J	Q	I/M/E
Aflaj	93.3	96.5	99.8	
Al-Baha	98.0	88.4	91.5	
Ar-Rass	96.1	102.9	99.4	
Arafat	92.2	94.0	90.8	92.2
Arar	94.1	97.4	88.4	
Buraydah	89.3	95.6	93.2	99.0
Dammam	92.8/93.8	94.7	90.0	103.6
Duba	89.5	95.8	92.6	
Jeddah	92.0/99.5	93.0	89.9	96.2
Jizan	95.1	88.8	91.9	
Jubail	107.7	105.6	95.3	
Kharj	93.0	96.0	90.0	95.2
Mecca	94.7	98.0	91.5	
Medina	90.5	93.6	96.8	
Riyadh	91.2	94.4	100.0	97.7
Taif	96.5	93.3	99.8	106.9
Yanbu	97.4	93.6	90.9	

+ numerous low power stations under 10kW for local coverage.

R=R. Riyadh in Arabic: 24h. – **J=R. Jeddah in Arabic:** 24h, on most MW fqs 0300-2200. – **Q=Quran prgr:** 24h incl. Call of Islam 0100-0300 – **I=Call of Islam prgr:** 24h – **E=English prgr** (from either Riyadh or Jeddah studios): 0600-2100. – **M=Music prgr:** 24h. – **P=Pilgrimage Enlightment Radio:** 24h during two months of the "Haj" season in Arabic/E/F/Persian/Turkish/Hausa/Indonesian/Urdu

on MW and **FM:** 94.2/101.0MHz in Mina/Arafat/Muzdalifah.
Ann: R. Riyadh: "Idha'at ar-Riyadh", "Idha'atu'l-mamlakah al-arabiyah t'il-saudiayh min al-Riyadh". R. Jeddah: "Idha'at al-Jiddah", "Idha'atu'l-mamlakah al-arabiyah t'il-saudiayh min Jiddah". 'Quran prgr: "Idha-atu'l-Koran al-Kareem min al-mamlakah al-arabiyah t'il-saydiah". Call of Islam: "Idha'at Nidaa Al-Islam min Makka al-Mukaram". E: "This is Radio Riyadh/Jeddah".
IS: 'Ud' (oriental lute). Opens and closes with National Anthem.
F.PI: separate FM network for Call of Islam prgr.

EXTERNAL SERVICE: Saudi Radio: see International Radio section.

SAUDI ARAMCO RADIO (Serving the staff of Saudi Aramco Co.)
✉ P.O.Box 5000, Dhahran 31311 **W:** saudiaramco.com **E:** webmaster@aramco.com.sa
Studio 1 (pop, rock and country music): Udhailiyah 88.8MHz, Dhahran 91.4MHz, Safaniya/Tanajib/Haradh 103.8MHz – **Studio 2** (easy listening, jazz and classical music): Udhailiyah 91.9MHz, Dhahran 101.4MHz, Safaniya/Tanajib/Haradh 107.9MHz. **D.Prgr:** 24h in English.

Other stations (FM MHz):
Alif Alif FM: Riyadh 94.0, Jeddah 101.0, Dammam 107.5. **W:** alifaliffm.com – **MBC FM:** Dammam 101.9, Riyadh 102.0, Jeddah/Medina 103.0. **W:** mbc.net/mbcfm – **Mix FM:** Tabuk 93.0MHz, Riyadh & 5 sites 98.0, Jubayl 98.4, Nazran 101.0, Taif 101.4, Kharj/Skaka 103.0, Breida/Jeddah 105.5, Makkah & 3 sites 106.0, Majmaa 106.2, Baha/Rabegh 106.4. **W:** mixfm-sa.com – **Panorama FM:** Dammam 91.9, Riyadh 96, Tabuk 101.7, Jeddah 102, Madinah 102.3, Buraidah (Al Qassim) 103.3, Abha/Taif 104. See main entry under UAE – **R. Rotana:** Jeddah/Riyadh 88.0, Dammam 100.0. **W:** rotanafm.com – **uFM R.:** Riyadh 90.0, Madina 91.0, Al-Kharj/Ara'ar/Al-Dawadimi 91.5. **W:** ufmradio.com. **American Forces Network:** 93.7/100.7/103.9/107.8, Dammam 95.5, Makkah 95.8, Jeddah 97.0. New FM licenses granted to: Ghayat Al-Ibdah, Rotana, Electronic Resources and Shams R.

SENEGAL

LT: UTC — **Pop:** 14 million — **Pr.L:** French, Wolof, Mandinga, Soninké, Pular, others — **E.C:** 50Hz, 230V — **ITU:** SEN

CONSEIL NATIONAL DE REGULATION DE L'AUDIOVISUEL (CNRA)
✉ 15ème étage, Immeuble Fahd, Blvd Djily Mbaye, B.P. 50059, Dakar RP ☎ +221 33 8499120 📠 +221 33 8234785 **W:** cnra.sn
L.P: Chairperson: Nancy Ngom Ndiaye.

RADIODIFFUSION TÉLÉVISION SÉNÉGALAISE (Gov.)
✉ Triangle Sud x Avenue El-Hadj Malick SY, B.P. 1765, Dakar ☎ +221 33 8491212 📠 +221 33 8223490 **W:** rts.sn **E:** rts@rts.sn
L.P: DG: Babacar Diagne. Dir. Radio: Oumar Seck. Dir. New Tech. & Development: Papa Abdou Diallo.

FM	N	I	R	M	kW
Bakel	95.9	107.3			5
Dakar	95.7	92.5	94.5	95.2	10
Diourbel	97.6	96.6	101.1		2
Fatick	95.7		92.8		0.5/2
Goudiry	106.0		91.1		0.5
Kaolack	103.0	107.0	97.9		5
Kédougou	94.6	97.7	100.0		2
Kolda	100.0	102.2	92.2		2
Koungheul	89.7		107.0		1
Linguère	92.1	89.0			5
Louga	95.0	101.8	88.7		5/2
Matam	95.6	89.1	100.6		2
Ndioum		98.4	92.7		5
Ourossogui	96.5	89.1	105.3		5/2
Podor			100.6		0.25
Richard Toll			89.6		0.1
Saint-Louis	91.9	90.1	96.3		10/5
Tambacounda	102.0	88.1	92.0		5
Thiès	96.9	94.9	100.6		5
Touba			99.2		0.25
Vélingara	99.0	89.1	92.2		2
Ziguinchor	95.2	100.2	98.9		5

N=Chaîne Nationale: 24h in French, Wolof and other national languages – **I=R. Sénégal Internationale:** 24h in French, Arabic, Portuguese and other languages – **M=RTS Mag FM:** 24h in French – **R=Chaîne Régionale:** 0600-2400, regional programming for 9 to 18 hours a day depending on station.
Ann: N: "Radiodiffusion Télévision Sénégalaise émettant de Dakar". Int: "Radio Sénégal Internationale". **IS:** Melody on "Cora" (local harp).

Other stations (main networks):

FM	1)	2)	3)	4)	5)	6)	7)
Bakel			93.7	100.8			
Banlieue	91.7						
Bignona		91.4		88.3			
Dagana				91.7			
Dakar	98.5	94.0	88.9	101.0	103.9	98.7	97.8
Diourbel	91.1	92.4	90.9			106.0	105.5
Fatick		99.3	102.5		99.3		102.8
Joal			92.4				
Kaffrine		95.0	102.4				
Kaolack	94.6	93.9	105.0	92.7	99.7	93.1	91.9
Kébémer			91.5	101.3			
Kédogou		99.7	98.6	106.4			
Kidira			105.0				
Kolda	95.4	93.2	98.7	91.9	102.2	99.7	88.1
Linguere			102.8				
Louga		88.3	91.8		98.3	107.0	103.4
Matam	98.4	95.0		89.3	96.9	91.8	88.7
Mboro			98.6				
Mbour	106.9	95.8	102.8		104.1		
Ndioum	93.9						
Nioro		98.4					
Ourossogui			99.5				
Podor		100.0	98.7		95.4		
Richard Toll		99.0	106.0				
Saint-Louis	93.2	99.3	106.3	88.3	94.6	88.9	88.1
Sédhiou	88.0		95.3				
Tambacounda	98.5	93.2	91.0	94.0	105.6	100.5	90.3
Thiès	102.2	102.5	93.7	106.9	92.3	107.1	105.1
Toubambacké	92.8	92.4		89.1	106.2		
Velingara		96.4	102.4				
Ziguinchor	95.6	92.0	92.4			106.0	103.4

Addresses: 1) Sud FM Sen R, Immeuble Fahd, Bld. Djily Mbaye x rue Macodou Ndiaye (5ème étage), Dakar ☎+221 33 8650888 🖷 +221 33 8220250 **W:** sudfm.net – **2) Futurs Medias (RFM),** Rue 15x Corniche, Immeuble Elimane Ndour , B.P. 17795, Dakar ☎+221 33 8491640 **W:** futursmedias.net – **3) R. Dunyaa:** HLM 1, Rue 14 prolongée, Dakar ☎+221 33 8242424 **E:** dunyaa@sentoo.sn – **4) Express An-Nour FM – 5) Convergence FM,** Immeuble Lambert, Avenue Bourguiba, Dakar ☎+221 33 8253989 **W:** convergencefm.wordpress. com – **6) Océan FM – 7) Sénégal Info**
Community radio FM (MHz):
Afia FM, Dakar 107.0 – Biyen FM, Thiès 89.5 2kW – Ferlo FM, Dahra: 94.0 2kW – Gaynaako FM, Podor 99.4 0.5kW. **W:** gaynaakofm. org – Jéeri FM, Keur Momar Sarr 97.0 0.3kW – Manoore FM, Dakar: 89.4 5kW – R. Penc Mi, Fissel: 90.6 1kW. **E:** pencmi_fm@yahoo.fr – R. Tim-Timol, Matam: 91.8 1kW.

Other Stations (MHz):
BBC African Sce: Dakar 105.6 10kW. In French.
RFI Afrique: Ziguinchor 87.6 5kW, Tambacounda 88.9 2kW, Kaolack 91.5 5kW, Dakar 92.0 10kW, St-Louis 99.7 5kW, Thiès 100.2 5kW

SERBIA

L.T: UTC +1h (27 Mar-30 Oct: +2h) — **Pop:** 7.1 million — **Pr.L:** Serbian — **E.C:** 50Hz, 220V — **ITU:** SRB

UDRUZENJE RADIOTELEVIZIJE SRBIJE d.O.O.
🖃 Beogradska 70, 11000 Beograd ☎ +381 11 433718, 434688 🖷 +381 11 434023, 437280 **E:** yrtcoord@eunet.rs
LP: MD: Vjera Nikolic
Udruzenje Radiotelevizije Srbije comprises Radio-televizija Srbije and Voice of Serbia

JP. EMISIONA TEHNIKA I VEZE/ETV (PUBLIC ENTERPRISE BROADCASTING AND COMMUNICATION)
🖃 Kneza Viseslava 88, 11030 Belgrade ☎ +381 11 3693251 🖷 +381 11 3693260, Tech.: ☎ +381 11 3211610 **W:** etv.rs **E:** office@etv.rs, tehnika@etv.rs, etv@etv.rs **LP:** Dejan Smigic

RADIO-TELEVIZIJA SRBIJE
🖃 Takovska 10, 11000 Beograd ☎ +381 11 3212000 **E:** kontaktcentar@rts.rs **W:** rts.rs **LP:** DG: Dragan Bujosevic
R. Beograd: Hilendarska 2, 11000 Beograd ☎ +381 11 3248888 **LP:** Dir: Dusan Radulovic **W:** radiobeograd.co.rs

MW	kHz	kW	P	MW	kHz	kW	P
Bosilegrad	675	0.6	d	Negotin	693	0.5	d
Aleksinac	684	10	d	Nis	711	0.5	d

MW	kHz	kW	P	MW	kHz	kW	P
Medvedja	765	0.7	d	Tutin	1485	0.5	a
Beograd 2/3	1008	0.5		Beograd 202	1503	10	
Vranje	1296	7	d	Sjenica	1602	0.5	d
Crna Trava	1485	0.5	d				

P: a) Beograd1+ reg. prgr d) rel. Beograd 1

FM (MHz)	I	II/III	202	kW
Avala	95.3	97.6	104.0	75/75/130
Bajina Basta	91.9	93.0	94.0	2
Beograd	88.3			2
Besna Kobila	91.7	95.3	100.1	25/25/40
Bitovik	91.7	92.9	104.3	25
Crni Vrh	89.7	99.3	101.0	25
Crveni Cot	94.5	96.5	101.8	75/75.130
Deli Jovan	87.7	94.9	98.9	25/25/40
Jastrebac	96.9	89.3	103.5	100
Kopaonik	90.9	93.7	102.1	50/50/100
Ljubovija	104.0	94.0	105.6	25
Maljen	104.5	107.9	93.4	25
Nis	99.5			3.5
Ovcar	88.1	90.1	101.6	25
Pirot	98.5	102.5	101.0	15
Subotica	88.9	101.1	98.5	50/50/0.3
Tornik	90.6	97.5	100.2	15
Trgoviste	90.1	92.3	96.9	15
Tupiznica	92.5	96.1	100.4	25
Vrsac	95.7	98.1	104.0	30

Additional low power local stns not mentioned.

R. Beograd 1: 24h **N:** W 0303, 0330, 0400, 0430, 0500, 0540, 0700, 0800, 0900, 1000, 1100, 1200, 1300, 1400, 1600, 1700, 1830, 2100, 2200, 2300; Sun 0430, 0500, 0530, 0600, 0700, 0800, 0900, 1000, 1100, 1200, 1400, 1600, 1830, 2000, 2200, 2300 – **R. Beograd 2:** W 0400-1900 (Sun 0600-1900). **N:** W 1130, 1230, 1330, 1500, 1600, 1850. Sun 0630, 0730, 0930, 1055, 1130, 1330, 1730, 1850 – **R. Beograd 3:** 1900-2300 (Serious prgr.) – **R. Beograd 202:** 24h on 1503kHz, 104.0MHz + FM 202 – **Stereorama:** 0700-1900SS on FM 202. Other times rel. Beograd 202

Local stations:

FM	MHz	FM	MHz	FM	MHz
Arandjelovac	98.9	Leskovac	99.0	Smed. Palanka	88.3
Bor	91.7	Loznica	107.4	Smederevo	96.1
Cacak	92.8	Majdanpek	96.7	Soko Banja	90.5
Jagodina	97.3	Mladenovac	97.0	Uzice	92.0
Kladovo	89.0	Novi Pazar	90.0	Valjevo	88.6
Kragujevac	88.9	Pirot	95.8	Vranje	96.5
Kraljevo	87.6	Pozarevac	90.1	Vrnjacka Banja	96.5
Krusevac	92.2	Priboj	88.7	Zajecar	98.1
Lazarevac	89.3	Prijepolje	98.9		

E: R. Bella Amie: belami.rs **R. Vranje:** rtv-vranje.rs **R. Leskovac:** radioleskovac.rs **R. Kragujevac:** rtk.co.rs **R.Valjevo:** patak.co.rs

FM stations with national coverage:

FM	MHz	FM	MHz
Index	88.9	Play	92.5
Hit Music	98.5	R. S	94.9

All stns have relays
E: Index: indexradio.rs **Play:** b92.net **R.S:** radios.rs **Hit Music:** hitmusicfm.rs

Local FM stations in Beograd:

FM	MHz	FM	MHz	FM	MHz
Index	88.9	Radio S	94.9	Gradski	102.2
Bum Bum	89.4	TRI	95.8	Novosti	104.7
R. JAT	90.2	Prvi	96.2	Nostalgie	105.2
Pingvin	90.9	Naxi	96.9	Karolina	106.3
Pink	91.3	Hit FM	98.9	Top FM	106.8
TDI	91.8	Studio B	99.1	S.Ljube	107.3
Play	92.5	Sport FM	100.4	Antena	107.9
Laguna	93.7				

There are numerous local FM stns.

VOJVODINA (Autonomous Province)

RADIO TELEVIZIJA NOVI SAD
🖃 Ignjata Pavlasa 3, 21000 Novi Sad ☎ +381 21 210-1646 🖷 +381 21 423348 **E:** veroslava.pop@rtv.rs **W:** rtv.rs

MW	kHz	kW	Notes
Orlovat	1107	0.6	r. Beograd 1

MW	kHz	kW	Notes
Srbobran	1269	5	in Serbian
Novi Sad	1485	0.5	in Serbian

FM (MHz)	I	II	III	kW
Novi Sad	87.7	90.5	100.0	50
Subotica	99.3	92.5		50
Vrsac	99.6	91.7	107.1	30

I) in Serbian, II) in Hungarian, III) prgrs for national minorities
R. Novi Sad 1: 24h in Serbian **R. Novi Sad 2:** 0400-2305 in Hungarian

Local stations

FM	MHz	FM	MHz	FM	MHz
Apatin	98.7	Kovin	89.5	St. Pazova	91.5
B. Palanka	95.1	Odzaci	89.7	Subotica	91.5
B. Topola	97.8	Pancevo	92.1	Temerin	93.5
B. Petrovac	91.4	Ruma	102.7	Vrbas	95.5
Beocin	97.8	Sid	89.1	Vrsac	94.0
Indjija	96.0	Sombor	97.5	Zrenjanin	103.6
Kovacica	93.2	Srbobran	102.6		

There are numerous low-power local FM stns
E: R. Pancevo: rtvpancevo.rs **R. Panon:** pannonrtv.com **R. Zrenjanin:** radiozrenjanin.rs

SEYCHELLES

L.T: UTC +4h — **Pop:** 90,000 — **Pr.L:** Creole, English, French — **E.C:** 50Hz, 240V — **ITU:** SEY

MINISTRY OF INFORMATION TECHNOLOGY & COMMUNICATION (MITC)
✉ Telecom Division, P. O. Box 1389, Oceangate House, Room 16, Victoria, Mahé ☎+248 4382039 ▤ +248 4225325 **E:** telecom@sey-chelles.sc **L.P:** Dir: Dr. George Ah-Thew

SEYCHELLES BROADCASTING CORPORATION (SBC, Pub.)
✉ P.O. Box 321, Hermitage, Mahé ☎+248 4289600 ▤ +248 4225641
W: sbc.sc **E:** sbcradtv@seychelles.sc
L.P: MD: Mr. Ibrahim Afif. Prgr. Mgr.(Radio): Ms. Thelma Pool. CE: Mr. Joyvani Chetty. Marketing & PR Mgr: Mrs. Jacqueline Moustache.
MW: Victoria 1368kHz 10kW.
FM: Anse Soleil 93.6MHz 0.25kW, Fairyland 93MHz 0.25kW, St.Louis 93.6MHz 1kW, Praslin 100.8MHz 0.03kW.
D.Prgr: MW (spoken word): MF 0200-0930 & 1200-1800, SS 0200-1800. **N: English:** 0300, 0600, 0900, 1500. **French:** 0330, 0700, 1300, 1700. **Creole:** 0230, 0500, 0800, 1600.
FM: Paradise FM (musical prgr.): 24h.
Ann: E: "This is SBC Radio". F: "Ici la Radio SBC". C: "Isi Radyo SBC"
IS: Instrumental music.

RFI Afrique: St.Louis 103.8MHz 1kW, Anse Soleil 102.8MHz 0.25kW.
BBC African Sce: St.Louis 106.2MHz 0.5kW.
BBC Indian Ocean relay station: see International Radio section

SIERRA LEONE

L.T: UTC — **Pop:** 6.5 million — **Pr.L:** English, Krio, Limba, Mende, Temne, others — **E.C:** 50Hz, 230V — **ITU:** SRL

INDEPENDENT MEDIA COMMISSION (IMC)
✉ Kissy House, 54 Siaka Stevens Street, Freetown ☎+232 22 221835 **W:** imc-sl.org **E:** info@imc-sl.org
L.P: Commissioner: Augustine Garmoh.

SIERRA LEONE BROADCASTING CORPORATION (SLBC, Pub.)
✉ New England, Freetown ☎+232 22 241919 ▤ +232 22 240922
W: slbc.sl
L.P: DG: Elvis Gbanabom Hallowell. Dir. Eng.: K. Koroma.
FM: Freetown 100.0MHz 4kW. Regional stations (mostly own pro-gramming): Bo 96.5MHz 2kW, Kenema 93.5MHz 2kW, Kono 90.2MHz 1kW, Makeni 88.0MHz 1kW. In addition 4 trs under 1kW.
D.Prgr "Power FM": 0600-2400.

Other Stations FM (MHz):
Believers Broadcasting Network (BBN) (Rlg.), Freetown: 93.0 2kW. **W:** bbn-sl.org – **Capital R:** Freetown 104.9 4kW, Bo 102.3 50W. **W:** capitalradio.sl – **Eastern R:** Kenema 101.9, Kono 96.5 – **Kiss FM,** Bo: 104.0 (Also rel. VOA). – **R. Bintumani,** Kabala: 93.7 – **R. Bontico,** Bonthe: 96.9 – **R. Democracy,** Freetown: 98.1 – **R. Galaxy,** Mahera: 106.1 – **R. Gbafth,** Mile 91: 91.0 – **R. Kolenten,** Kambia: 92.4 – **R. Mankneh,** Makeni: 95.1 – **R. Moa,** Kailahun: 105.5 – **R. Modcar,** Moyamba: 94.8 – **R. Maria,** Makeni 101.1 0.5kW – **R. Mount Aureol,** Fourah Bay College, Freetown: 107.3MHz – **Njala University R,** Njala 92.5 – **R. Numbura,** Bumbuna: 102.5 – **R. One,** Freetown: 103.7 – **R. Wanjei,** Pujehun: 101.1 – **R. Viascity,** Waterloo: 100.6 – **Star R,** Freetown 103.5 – **Skyy R,** Freetown: 106.6 – **Unity R,** Freetown: 98.4 – **Voice of Islam,** Freetown: 102.0 – **VO the Handicapped,** Freetown: 96.2 (mostly rel. BBC) – **VO the Peninsula,** Tombo: 96.0 – **VO Women,** Mattru Jong: 88.5.
BBC African Sce: Freetown 94.3 8kW, Makeni 91.7 60W, Bo 94.5 120W, Kenema 95.3 60W – **RFI Afrique,** Freetown: 89.9 in French/English – **VOA,** Freetown: 102.4

SINGAPORE

L.T: UTC +8h — **Pop:** 5.7 million — **Pr.L:** English, Chinese, Malay, Tamil — **E.C:** 50Hz, 230V — **ITU:** SNG

MEDIA DEVELOPMENT AUTHORITY OF SINGAPORE (Government statutory board)
✉ 3 Fusionopolis Way, #16-22 Symbiosis, Singapore 138633 ☎ +65 6377 1700 ▤ +65 6577 3888 **W:** mda.gov.sg
L.P: Chmn: Mr Niam Chaing Meng, CEO: Ms Koh Lin-Net

MEDIACORP RADIO SINGAPORE PTE LTD (Comm.)
✉ Caldecott Broadcast Centre, Andrew Road, Singapore 299939 ☎ +65 6333 3888 ▤ +65 6359 7500 **W:** mediacorpradio.sg
L.P: Chmn: Mr Teo Ming Kian. CEO: Mr Shaun Seow. MD, MediaCorp R.: Ms Florence Lian
Stations: FM tx centre at Bukit Batok

	FM MHz	kW	Network	Format	Lang.
1)	89.7	6	Ria 89.7FM	CHR	Malay
2)	90.5	6	Gold 90FM	Gold	English
3)	92.4	10	Symphony 92FM	Classical	English
4)	93.3	6	Y.E.S. 93.3FM	AC	Chinese
5)	93.8	6	938LIVE	N./Info	English
6)	94.2	10	Warna 94.2FM	N./Info	Malay
7)	95.0	6	Class 95FM	AC	English
8)	95.8	10	Capital 95.8FM *	N./Info	Chinese
9)	96.3	6	Expat R. XFM	Int'l	A
10)	96.8	10	Oli 96.8FM	Full sce	Tamil
11)	97.2	6	Love 97.2FM **	Easy	Chinese
12)	98.7	6	987FM	CHR	English
13)	99.5	6	Lush 99.5FM	Urban	English

*) in Chinese: "Chengshi Pindao" **) in Chinese: "Zui'ai Pindao"
D.Prgr: all networks 24h Tr. powers shown are TRP
A = Mon-Fri 2300-0100 "Smile Wave" in Japanese. Mon-Fri 0100-0300 rel. R. France Int. in French. Daily 0900-1200 "Masti 96.3" in Hindi and 1200-1400 "Amar FM" in Bengali. Mon-Fri 1400-1600 rel. Deutsche Welle in German. At other times carries World Music.
Ownership: MediaCorp is wholly owned by Temasek Holdings, an investment company of the Government of Singapore.

SAFRA RADIO (Comm.)
Operated by the Singapore Armed Forces Reservists' Ass.
✉ Tower B #12-04, Defence Technology Towers, 5 Depot Rd, Singapore 109681 or Bukit Merah Central PO Box 1315, Singapore 911599 ☎ +65 6373 1920 ▤ +65 6278 3039 **W:** safraradio.com.sg
883JiaFM: 88.3MHz 5kW, 24h in Chinese
Power98FM: 98.0MHz 12kW, 24h in English

SPH UNIONWORKS PTE LTD (Comm.)
Joint venture of NTUC Media Co-operative (National Trade Unions Congress) & SPH MediaWorks (Singapore Press Holdings)
✉ 1000 Toa Payoh North, News Centre Podium Block Level 3, Singapore 318994 ☎ +65 6319 1900 ▤ +65 6319 1099 **W:** onefm.sg or kiss92.sg or ufm1003.sg **L.P:** Dir: Mr Patrick Daniel. Dep. Gen. Mgr: Mr Sim Hong Huat. Prgr Dir R. 91.3 & 92: Jamie R. Meldrum. Prgr Dir 100.3: Carine Ang CH
One FM: 24h in English on 91.3MHz **Kiss92 FM:** 24h in English on 92.0MHz **UFM 1003:** 24h in Chinese on 100.3MHz

BBC SINGAPORE 88.9 FM
24h rel. of BBCWS in English. The 5kW FM tx at Bukit Batok is oper-ated by MediaCorp.

FAR EASTERN RELAY STATION (Babcock Communications Ltd)
✉ 51 Turut Track, Singapore 718930 ☎ +65 6793 7511
See International Broadcasting section

SLOVAKIA

L.T: UTC +1h (27 Mar - 30 Oct: +2h) — **Pop:** 5.5 million — **Pr.L:** Slovak — **E.C:** 50Hz, 230V — **ITU:** SVK

ROZHLAS A TELEVÍZIA SLOVENSKA (Radio and Television of Slovakia) - RTVS
SLOVENSKY ROZHLAS (SLOVAK RADIO)
✉ Mytna 1 (P.O.Box 55), 817 55 Bratislava 15 ☎ + 421 2 57273111 🖷 + 421 2 57273559 **W:** rozhlas.sk **E:** info@rozhlas.sk **Radio FM: W:** radiofm.sk **E:** info@radiofm.sk **L.P:** DG: Václav Mika. PD: Vincent Štofaník. TD: Andrej Dolezal

MW	kHz	kW	Prgr
Kosice	702	5	S5 (daytime) + S3 (nighttime)
Nitra (Jarok)	1098	10	S5 (daytime) + S3 (nighttime)

FM (MHz)	S1	S2	S3	S4	kW
Banská Bystrica	90.1	101.5	102.0	105.4	100/100/0.1/2
Banská Stiavnica	99.0		102.6	20/20	
Bardejov	93.5	89.3	88.8	101.7	10/1/10/10
Borsky Mikulás			95.6	102.8	1
Bratislava	96.6	99.3	104.4	89.3	100/10/10/10
Cadca				91.8	0.5
Dolny Kubin				91.7	1
Dubnica n.V.	92.2				0.5
Kosice	96.6	100.3			100/35
Kosice (city)			96.2	101.2	0.5/1
Lucenec	103.6	88.2		98.0	10/2/10
Martin				91.8	0.5
Modry Kamen	90.9	88.5	103.1	98.3	10
Námestovo	102.4	100.4	88.7		10
Nitra	91.2	102.2			10/10
N. Mesto n.V.	103.2	100.7	90.8		10
Nové Zámky			94.6	102.8	1
Poprad	92.2	96.9	94.2	104.3	30
Presov			106.7	101.5	0.5
Rim. Sobota		95.0			1
Roznava	97.3	88.6	90.0	105.9	1/1/1/1
Ruzomberok	103.8	100.6	104.6	102.1	5
Snina	91.2		102.2	107.6	10
Stará Lubovna	89.1	102.3	96.1		10
Sturovo	96.3	91.7	106.2	103.7	10
Trebisov		89.2	106.7	101.3	10
Trencín		95.9	97.8	101.2	10
Trnava (F.P.I.)	90.8				10
Trstená				91.9	10
Zilina	103.5	100.1	97.2	91.9	20/20/30/1
Zvolen			99.8	89.0	0.5/1

Addresses and other information:
S1 = Radio Slovensko: 24h (national prgr news) **S2** = Radio Regina: 24h (regional prgrs + prgrs for national minorities in Hungarian, Ukrainian, Ruthenian, German, Czech, Polish and Gypsy/Roma + relays of Radio Slovensko – S1) **S2 BA** = Radio Regina Bratislava, ✉ Mytna 1, 817 55 Bratislava 15 **S2 BB** = Radio Regina Banská Bystrica ✉ L. Sáru 1, 975 68 Banská Bystrica **S2 KE** = Radio Regina Kosice ✉ Masarykova 7, 041 61 Kosice **S3** = Radio Devín: 24h (cultural prgr) on FM and 1700-0500 on 702 and 1098kHz **S4** = Radio FM: 24h (rock, pop and alternative music). N: on the h **S5** = Radio Patria – production of prgrs for national minorities in Hungarian, Ukrainian, Ruthenian, German, Czech, Polish, Gypsy/Roma relayed on S2 and S5 txs ✉ Slovensky Rozhlas, HRNEV, Moyzesova 7, 040 01 Kosice **E:** nev@slovakradio.sk Prgrs for minorities (S5): Hungarian 0500-1700 on 702 and 1098kHz. Prgrs for national minorities (S5) on Radio Regina (S2): Mon+Wed+Fri+Sat+Sun 1700-1800, Tue+Thu 1700-1800, 1900-2000

EXTERNAL SERVICE: Radio Slovakia International
See International Broadcasting section

MAJOR PRIVATE STATIONS/NETWORKS:
ASOCIÁCIA NEZÁVISLYCH ROZHLASOVYCH A TELEVÍZNYCH STANÍC
(Association of Independent Radio Stations)
✉ Gröslingova 63, 811 09 Bratislava ☎ +421 2 5296 2370 **W:** anrts. sk **E:** anrts@anrts.sk

FUN RADIO (Comm.) ✉ Leskova 5, 815 25 Bratislava ☎ +421 2 52494601 🖷 +421 2 52495535 **W:** funradio.sk – **RADIO JEMNÉ (Comm.)** ✉ Dr. Vladimíra Clementisa 10, 815 25 Bratislava ☎ +421 2 48484811 🖷 +421 2 52492701 **W:** jemne.sk **FM:** see list below **D.Prgr:** 24h – **RADIO EXPRES (Comm.)** ✉ Lamacská cesta 1, 841 04 Bratislava ☎ +421 2 59308900 🖷 +421 2 59308991 **W:** expres.sk **FM:** see list below **D.Prgr:** 24h – **EUROPA 2 (Comm.)** ✉ Seberíniho

1, 821 03 Bratislava ☎ +421 2 48224201 **W:** europa2.sk **FM:** see list below **D.Prgr:** 24h – **RADIO LUMEN (Relig.)** ✉ Kapitulská 2, 974 01 Banská Bystrica ☎ +421 48 4710800 🖷 +421 48 4710840 **W:** lumen.sk **FM:** see list below **D.Prgr:** 24h – **RADIO ANTÉNA ROCK (Comm.)** ✉ Dr. Vladimira Clementisa 10, 821 02 Bratislava ☎ +421 2 48484811 **W:** antenarock.sk **FM:** see list below **D.Prgr:** 24h – **RADIO VLNA (Comm.)** ✉ Siberiniho 1, 821 02 Bratislava ☎ +421 2 48484855 **W:** radiovlna.sk **FM:** see list below **D.Prgr:** 24h

Private Commercial FM Stations:

FM	MHz	kW	Station
Kosice	87.7	80	Fun R.
Banská Bystrica	87.7	10	R. Jemné
Nové Mesto n.V.	88.0	8.5	R. Jemné
Hlohovec	88.4	2	R. Expres
Ruzomberok	88.4	1	R. Expres
Snina	88.5	10	R. Vlna
Banská Bystrica	88.6	1	Rocková Republika
Nitra	88.8	10	R. Anténa Rock
Trencín	89.1	10	Fun R.
Rimavská Sobota	89.3	1	R. Expres
Ruzomberok	89.7	1	R. Lumen
Nitra	89.7	1	R. Expres
Banská Bystrica	90.5	2	R. One BB
Prievidza	90.5	1	R. WOW
Presov	90.8	2	R. Kosice
Zilina	90.8	1	R. One Rock
Moldava nad Bodvou	91.0	1	R. Expres
Ruzomberok	91.1	1	R. Vlna
Lucenec	91.6	10	Fun R.
Stropkov	92.4	1	R. Vlna
Zvolen	92.6	1	R. Expres
Zámky	92.7	1	R. Expres
Zilina	92.7	1	R. Vlna
Ruzomberok	92.8	1	R. Vlna
Trencín	93.3	10	R. Lumen
Banská Stiavnica	93.3	2	R. Lumen
Bratislava	93.8	6	R. Lumen
Košice	93.8	2	R. Best FM
Lehota p.Vtác.	93.9	1	R. Beta
Bratislava	94.3	100	Fun R.
Banská Bystrica	94.7	1	R. One Retro
Košice	94.8	1	R. Anténa Rock
Liptovsky Mikuláš	95.0	1	Fun R.
Nitra	95.2	10	Europa 2
Kosice	95.2	2	R. Expres
Levoca	95.3	1	R. Expres
Bardejov	95.6	1	R. Vlna
Roznava	95.7	1	R. Expres
Snina	95.9	10	R. Kiss
Lucenec	96.0	5	R. Vlna
Cadca	96.1	1	R. Frontinus
Martin	96.2	1	R. Frontinus
Partizánske	96.4	1	R. One Rock
Trstená	96.5	2	R. Expres
Zilina	96.5	1	R. Expres
Strázske	97.0	5	R. Kosice
Banská Bystrica	97.6	100	R. Anténa Rock
Stropkov	97.8	1	R. Kiss
Handlová	98.1	1	R. Lumen
Bardejov	98.2	1	R. Expres
Nové Mesto n.V.	98.5	8.8	Europa 2
Kosice	98.6	50	R. Jemné
Nové Zámky	98.7	1	R. Max
Ruzomberok	98.8	5	R. Anténa Rock
Michalovce	99.0	2	R. Vlna
Bardejov	99.1	1	R. Lumen
Zilina	99.2	20	Fun R.
Sturovo	99.4	10	R. Expres
Vychodna	99.5	1	R. Expres
Cadca	99.6	1	R. Vlna
Bratislava	100.3	1	R. Anténa Rock
Poprad	100.9	30	Europa 2
Lucenec	101.1	5	R. Expres
Roznava	101.4	1	R. Vlna
Bratislava	101.8	100	R. Vlna
Trencín	102.5	1	R. Expres
Poprad	102.5	1	Fun R.
Roznava	102.8	1	Fun R.
Strbské Pleso	102.9	2	R. Lumen
Kosice	102.9	1	Fun R.
Michalovce	103.3	2	R. Lumen
Presov	103.7	8	Europa 2
Banská Bystrica	104.0	100	Fun R.
Presov	104.1	1	R. Kiss

FM	MHz	kW	Station
Prievidza	104.5	1	R. One Rock
Zilina	104.6	1	R. Frontinus
Bratislava	104.8	50	Europa 2
Poprad	104.8	1	R. Vlna
Martin	104.9	1	R. Vlna
Banská Stiavnica	105.1	20	R. Vlna
Povazská Bystrica	105.2	1	R. Expres
Presov	105.2	1	R. Anténa Rock
Trencín	105.5	10	R. Expres
Stará Lubovna	105.7	10	R. Expres
Námestovo	105.8	10	R. Lumen
Presov	105.8	2	R. Vlna
Banská Bystrica	106.0	50	Europa 2
Kosice	106.2	20	R. Expres
Lucenec	106.3	3	R. Lumen
Roznava	106.3	1	R. Lumen
Modry Kamen	106.5	1	R. Expres
Bratislava	106.6	10	R.Jemné
Banská Bystrica	106.6	1	R. Vlna
Partizánske	106.7	1	R. WOW
Zilina	106.9	3	R.Jemné
Dobsiná	107.0	1	R. Vlna
Bardejov	107.1	10	Europa 2
Levice	107.1	4	Fun R.
Poprad	107.3	2	R. Anténa Rock
Prievidza	107.5	1	R. Expres
Bratislava	107.6	10	R. Expres
Stará Lubovna	107.7	1	R. Jemné

+ more than 60 relays of less than 1kW

SLOVENIA

L.T: UTC +1h (27 Mar – 30 Oct: +2h) — **Pop:** 2 million — **Pr.L:** Slovenian — **E.C:** 50Hz, 220V — **ITU:** SVN

AGENCIJA ZA KOMUNIKACIJSKA OMREZJA IN STORITVE (AKOS)

✉ Stegne 7, 1000 Ljubljana ☎+386 1 5836300 🖷+386 1 5111101 **W:** srdf.si akos-rs.si **E:** info.box@akos-rs.si

RADIOTELEVIZIJA SLOVENIJA (Pub.)

✉ Kolodvorska ulica 2, SI-1550 Ljubljana ☎+386 1 4752151 🖷 +386 1 4752150 **W:** rtvslo.si **E:** pr@rtvslo.si
L.P: DG: Marko Filli.

MW	kHz	kW	Prgr.	MW	kHz	kW	Prgr.
Beli Kriz	549	15	1/K	Domzale	918	300	1
Nemcavci	558	15	1/MMR	B. Kriz	1170	15	C

C=R. Capodistria in Italian, **K**=R. Koper in Slovenian, **MMR**=Muravideki Magyar R. in Hungarian.

FM (MHz)	Slo 1	Slo 2	Slo 3	Reg.	kW
Beli Kriz	92.0	94.1	96.1	104.3k/97.7c	5
	-	-	-	102.0si	1
Blejska Dobrava	-	-	-	100.4si	1
Boc	-	-	-	90.4m	2
Golnik	-	-	-	89.0si	1
Koper	92.2	-	-	104.1k	1
Krim	88.0	93.5	96.5	-	5
Krvavec	91.8	98.9	102.0	-	100
Kuk	90.8	87.8	96.4	100.6k	5
Kum	94.1	99.9	103.9	-	30
Ljubljana-Šance	-	-	-	100.8si	1
Nanos	92.9	95.3	105.7	88.6k	50/50/50/25
	-	-	-	103.1c	100
Pec	100.1	104.0	106.0	-	5
Pecarovci	-	-	-	87.6h	5
Plešivec	90.0	92.4	101.4	-	10
Pohorje	88.5	96.9	105.3	93.1m/102.8si	5/3/2/3/8
Skalnica	-	-	-	100.3k	2
Tinjan	89.3	98.9	98.1	107.6k/103.6c	6/6/6/6/5
	-	-	-	94.6si	0.2
Trdinov Vrh	90.9	97.6	100.6	-	7.5/10/11
Trstelj	92.6	94.3	102.2	96.7si	5

Reg. stns: c=R. Capodistria in Italian, h=MMR in Hungarian, k=R. Koper, m=R. Maribor, si=R. Slovenija Int.
R. Slovenija 1 "Prvi program": 24h. **N. in E & German:** 2130 – **R. Slovenija 2 "Val 202":** 0500 -2300. Other times relay R. Slovenija Int.. Pop + entertainment – **R. Slovenija 3 "Program ARS":** 24h. Serious music, educational – **R. SI, R. Slovenija International**, Ilichova ulica 33, SI-2000 Maribor. **W:** radiosi.eu . Music and entertainment channel 24h on **FM** ("si").

RADIO KOPER – CAPODISTRIA (Pub.)

✉ PO Box 117, SI-6000 Koper-Capodistria ☎+386 (5) 6685050 🖷 +386 (5) 6684500 (Slovenian Dept.) ☎+386 (5)6685440 (Italian Dept.) **W:** rtvslo.si/radio **E:** radio.koper@rtvslo.si radio.capodistria@rtvslo.si **R. Koper in Slovenian:** 0500-2300 on 549kHz + FM ("k"). Other times rel. Slovenija 1 – **R. Capodistria in Italian:** 24h on 1170kHz + FM ("c").

RADIO MARIBOR (Pub.)

✉ Ilichova ulica 33, SI-2000 Maribor ☎+386 2 4201555 **W:** rtvslo.si/radiomaribor **E:** radio.maribor@rtvslo.si **FM:** ("m"). **D.Prgr:** Mon-Sat 0440-2100, Sun 0600-2100. At other times rel. Slovenija 1.

MURAVIDEKI MAGYAR RADIO (Pub.)

✉ Kranjceva ulica 10, SI-9220 Lendava ☎+386 2 4299700 🖷+386 2 4299712 **W:** rtvslo.si/mmr **E:** mmr@rtvslo.si
MW 558kHz + **FM:** ("h"). **D.Prgr:** 0445-2300. At other times rel. Slovenia 1 on MW and R. SI on FM.

OTHER STATIONS:

MW	kHz	kW	Station	Location
A)	648	10	R. Murski Val	Nemcavci

A) Ul. Arhitekta Novaka 13, SI-9000 Murska Sobota **W:** radiomurskival.si **D.Prgr:** 24h. A joint night prgr. of Koroski R., Murski val, R. Celje, R. Kranj, R. Ptuj, R. Slovenske Gorice, R. Sora, R. Triglav, R. Univox and R. Velenje is broadcast.

FM	MHz	kW	Station	Location
1)	87.6	1	R. Europa 05	Ljubljana-Šance
2)	87.8	1	R. Salomon	Blejska Dobrava
3)	88.3	1	R. 1 Portoroz	Malija
3)	88.4	2	R. 1 Krvavec	Krvavec
5)	89.3	1	R. Študent	Ljubljana-Šance
18)	89.8	1	R. Ptuj	Majšperg
6)	90.0	5	R. Maxi	Ljutomer
3)	90.1	1	R. 1 Primorska	Nova Gorica
3)	90.2	1	R. Hit	Vrhnika
3)	90.6	1	R. 1 Orion	Krim
8)	91.7	1	R. Capris	Markovec
9)	92.6	1	R. S	Ljubljana-Šance
25)	93.1	1	R. Zeleni Val	Polzevo
10)	93.7	2	Štajerski Val	Boc
26)	93.8	1	R. Center	Markovec
40)	94.6	5	Murski Val	Pecarovci
43)	94.6	1	R. Sraka	Trdinov Vrh
11)	94.9	1	R. Veseljak	Ljubljana-Šance
41)	95.1	2	R. Celje	Boc
7)	95.6	3	R. Hit	Dobeno
6)	95.7	1	R. Maxi	Pecarovci
12)	95.9	1	R. MARŠ	Maribor
13)	96.0	1	R. Triglav	Ravni Valvazor
14)	97.2	1	Koroški R.	Plešivec
3)	97.3	1	R. 1 Primorska	Hrvatini
15)	97.3	1	R. Kranj	Smarjetna Gora
3)	97.4	1	R. 1 Štajerska	Ljubicna
21)	98.1	1	R. Aktual Kum	Kum
17)	98.2	1	R. 94	Postojna
18)	98.2	1	R. Ptuj	Ptuj
3)	99.1	5	R. 1 Primorska	Trstelj
20)	99.5	1	R. Robin	Nova Gorica
21)	99.5	1	R. City	Ljubljana-Šance
3)	99.6	5	R. 1 Primorska	Koper
20)	100.0	1	R. Robin	Trstelj
21)	100.2	5	R. Aktual	Krim
22)	100.2	1	Net FM	Maribor
23)	100.6	1	R. City	Maribor
23)	100.8	1	R. City	Topolšica
21)	101.2	1	R. Aktual	Ljubljana-Šance
19)	101.3	1	R. Pohorje	Maribor
2)	101.6	1	R. Salomon	Ljubljana-Šance
24)	101.8	1	R. Rogla	Konjiška Gora
3)	102.1	4	R. 1	M.Sobota/Bogojina
26)	102.4	1	R. Center	Ljubljana-Šance
21)	102.4	5	R. Aktual Obala	Hrvatini
21)	102.8	1	R. Aktual Obala	Portoroz/Šentanje
21)	103.0	5	R. Aktual Studio D	Trdinov Vrh
26)	103.2	1	R. Center	Rahtelov Vrh
31)	103.3	1	Rock Radio	Šmarna Gora
26)	103.7	1	R. Center	Maribor
42)	103.7	1	Primorski Val/R. Odmev	Javornik
17)	104.2	1	R. 94	Ilirska Bistrica
30)	104.5	100	R. Ognjišce	Krvavec
7)	104.5	5	R. Hit	Trstelj

FM	MHz	kW	Station	Location
21)	104.8	2	R. Aktual	Boc
26)	104.9	1	R. Center	Nova Gorica
3)	105.0	1	R. 1 Dolenjska	Krško
8)	105.1	5	R. Capris	Slavnik
32)	105.1	1	Primorski Val/Alpski Val	Kobariški Stol
33)	105.2	1	R. Laser	Rahtelov Vrh
34)	105.2	1	R. Antena	Ljubljana-Šance
40)	105.7	2	Murski Val	Zlatolicje
30)	105.9	5	R. Ognjišče	Kum
26)	106.4	6	R. Center	Tinjan
35)	106.4	4	R. Ekspres	Krim
36)	106.6	15	R. Krka	Trdinov Vrh
27)	106.8	1	R. Top	Maribor
37)	107.0	1	Moj R.	Topolšica
7)	107.0	1	R. Hit	Markovec
38)	107.1	1	R. 94 / R. NTR	Rovte
30)	107.3	2	R. Ognjišče	Boc
30)	107.5	2	R. Ognjišče	Skalnica
8)	107.9	1	R. Capris	Portoroz
3)	107.9	1	R. 1 Stajerska	Maribor
3)	107.9	1	R. 1 107.9	Ljubljana-Šance

NB: Txs below 1kW not mentioned.

Addresses: 1) Parmova ul. 53, 1000 Ljubljana **W:** radioeuropa05.si – **2)** Papirniški trg 17, 1260 Ljubljana-Polje. **W:** radiosalomon.si – **3)** Stegne 11B, 1000 Ljubljana **W:** radio1.si Loc.Prgr. 0100-0400 – **5)** Cesta 27. aprila 31, 1000 Ljubljana. **W:** radiostudent.si – **6)** Prešernova ul. 3, 9240 Ljutomer. **W:** radiomaxi.si – **7)** Ljubljanska Cesta 36, 1230 Domzale. **W:** radiohit.si – **8)** ul. 15.maja 10B, 6000 Koper. **W:** radiocapris.si – **9)** Stegne 11b, 1000 Ljubljana. **W:** radios.si – **10)** Drofenikova 1, 3230 Šentjur. **W:** stajerskival.si – **11)** Papirniški trg 17, 1260 Ljubljana-Polje. **W:** radioveseljak.si – **12)** Tkalski prehod 4, 2000 Maribor. **W:** radiomars.si – **13)** Trg Toneta Cufarja 4, 4270 Jesenice. **W:** radiotriglav.si – **14)** Meškova 21, 2380 Slovenj Gradec. **W:** koroski-radio.si – **15)** Stritarjeva 6, 4000 Kranj. **W:** radio-kranj.si – **17)** Kazarje 10, 6230 Postojna. **W:** radio94.si – **18)** Osojnikova cesta 3, 2250 Ptuj. **W:** radio-ptuj.si – **19)** Partizanska cesta 24, 2000 Maribor. **W:** radiopohorje.si – **20)** Kromberk, Industrijska cesta 5, 5000 Nova Gorica. **W:** robin.si – **21)** Papirniški trg 17, 1260 Ljubljana-Polje. **W:** radioaktual.si – **22)** Loška ul. 13, 2000 Maribor. **W:** radionet.si – **23)** Slovenska ul. 35, 2000 Maribor. **W:** radiocity.si – **24)** Škalska 7, 3210 Slovenske Konjice. **W:** radiorogla.si – **25)** Taborska cesta 38d, 1290 Grosuplje. **W:** zelenival.com – **26)** Zelezna cesta 14, 1000 Ljubljana. **W:** radiocenter.si – **27)** Partizanska cesta 24, 2000 Maribor. **W:** radiotop.fm – **30)** Trg Brolo Št 11, 6000 Koper. **W:** radio.ognjisce.si – **31)** Zelezna cesta 14, 1000 Ljubljana. **W:** rockradio.si – **32)** Poljubinj 89F, p.p.46, 5220 Tolmin **W:** primorskival.si D.Prgr: 1500-1900 Alpski Val. 1900-1500 Primorski Val (a joint programme of Alpski Val and R. Odmev) – **33)** Legen 101A, 2380 Slovenj Gradec. **W:** laserr.si – **34)** Cesta na Brdo 27, 1000 Ljubljana. **W:** radioantena.si – **35)** Stegne 21C, 1000 Ljubljana. **W:** radioekspres.si – **36)** Ljubljanska Cesta 26, 8000 Novo Mesto. **W:** radiokrka.com – **37)** Kidriceva 2B, 3320 Velenje **W:** mojradio.com – **38)** Tržaška 148, 1370 Logatec. D.Prgr: 2300-0500, other times r. R. 94 – **40)** **W:** primorskival.si D.Prgr: 1500-1900 R. Odmev & 1900-1500 Primorski Val (a joint programme of Alpski Val and R. Odmev) – **41)** Prešernova 19, 3000 Celje. **W:** radiocelje.com – **42)** see A) – **43)** Valanticevo 17, 8000 Novo Mesto. **W:** radiosraka.com

SOLOMON ISLANDS

L.T: UTC +11h — **Pop:** 571,890 — **Pr.L:** Pidgin, English — **E.C:** 50Hz, 240V — **ITU:** SLM

TELECOMMUNICATIONS COMMISSION OF THE SOLOMON ISLANDS (TCSI)
Suite 303, Level 3, Hyundai Mall, Honiara. ☎+677 23850 **W:** tcsi.org.sb **E:** ictpolicy@tcsi.org.sb
Regulator of broadcasting in the Solomon Islands

MW	kHz	kW	Station
1) Honiara, Guadalcanal	1035	6	R.Happy Isles

SW	kHz	kW	Station
1) Honiara, Guadalcanal	5020	10	R.Happy Isles
1) Honiara, Guadalcanal	9545	10	R.Happy Isles

FM	MHz	kW	Station
2) Gold Ridge, Guadalcanal	88.0	-	Gold Ridge FM
3) Honiara, Guadalcanal	88.1	-	Hope FM
4) Honiara, Guadalcanal	88.3	-	Gud Nius FM
5) Kia, Isabel	89.5	0.1	R.Kia
5) Tutuba, Isabel	89.5	0.1	R.Tutuba
6) Tetere, Guadalcanal	89.9	0.06	R.Bosco
5) Buala, Isabel	91.1	0.1	R.Buala

FM	MHz	kW	Station
5) Susubona, Isabel	91.1	0.1	R.Susubona
5) Kolotubi, Isabel	92.5	0.1	R.Kolotubi
5) Sigana, Isabel	92.5	0.1	R.Sigana
5) Lelegia, Isabel	94.3	0.1	R.Lelegia
5) Samasodu, Isabel	94.3	0.1	R.Samasodu
1) Gizo, Ghizo Isl	96.3	*1	R.Happy Lagoon
1) Honiara, Guadalcanal	96.3	-	R.Wantok
1) Kirakira, Makiri Isl	96.3	*0.5	
1) Lata, Nendo Isl	96.3	*0.5	R.Temotu
7) Honiara, Guadalcanal	97.7	-	Paoa FM
8) Honiara, Guadalcanal	100.0	-	ZFM
7) Honiara, Guadalcanal	101.7	-	Paoa FM
9) Honiara, Guadalcanal	105.6	-	BBC
10) Honiara, Guadalcanal	107.0	-	R.Australia

NB: * F.pl power increase or establishment late 2015.
Addresses and other information
1) SOLOMON ISLANDS BROADCASTING CORP. (Statutory Authority, Comm.) ◻ **Honiara:** P.O. Box 654, Honiara ☎ +677 20051 ▤ +677 23159. **Wantok FM** ☎ +677 29600 ▤ +677 29600 **Gizo:** P. O. Box 78, Gizo, Western Province ☎ +677 60160 **Lata:** P. O. Box 46, Lata, Santa Cruz ☎ +677 53047 **LP:** GM: Cornelius Rathamana **W:** sibconline.com.sb **E:** sibcnews@solomon.com.sb **MW:** R. Happy Isles (Voice of the Nation), Honiara 1035kHz **SW:** 5020kHz & 9545kHz (heard irr.) relay R.Happy Isles. **SW Schedule:** 5020kHz 0500-1200, 1900-2200, 9545kHz 2200-0500. **NB:** MW/SW gradually being phased out for primary coverage, but likely kept in some form for cyclone/tsunami/earthquake emergency coverage **FM:** Wantok FM, Honiara, R. Happy Lagoon, Gizo, R.Temotu, Lata, Kirakira, Makiri Isl. [planned] [+ other provincial FM stns planned for 2016]. Common urban breakout 0600 for Wantok FM network otherwise relay R.Happy Isles 1035 AM//5020 SW. **D.Prgr:** local 1900-0000, BBC 1300-1900 **N. in English:** 2000, 2200 (R. Australia), 0130W, 0200 (R. Australia), 0500, 0600 (BBC), 0730, 1000 (R. Australia), 1100 **Ann:** "This is the SIBC, Radio Happy Isles". **IS:** Drum and Bamboo Pipes **V.** by QSL-card – **2)** community radio funded through Gold Ridge Mining Ltd **Prgr:** 1900-1100 – **3)** Kukum SDA church, Honiara. Solomon Islands Mission Office, PO Box R145, Honiara ☎ +677 2281 [direct], 39267/39269/39281 **F:** +677 38862 **W:** facebook.com/hopefm88.1 **E:** hopefm88.1@sim.adventist.org.sb – **4)** UCB Pacific Partners, P.O. Box 1415, Honiara **W:** pacificpartners.org/christianradiointhesolomonislands **E:** solomons@pacificpartners.org **LP:** Tina Lemozi SM **F.PI:** FM relay at Gizo and Malaita – **5)** Isabel Province Community FM Network, c/o Office of the Premier, PO Box 4, Buala. **Prgr:** 0600-1100 daily **N:** SIBC R.Happy Isles 0730. Each stn operates independently otherwise apart from some shared prgrs – **6)** Don Bosco Rural Training Centre, Tetere, Guadalcanal **W:** radio@donbosco.org.sb **LP:** Father Ambrose Pereira – **7)** PO Box R331, Panatina Plaza, Prince Philip Hwy, Honiara ☎+677 38984 ▤+677 38980 **W:** solomonstarnews.com & facebook.com/paoafm **E:** paoafm@solomon.com.sb or paoafm.news@gmail.com **LP:** GM Joel Lamani, News Editor: Uriel Matangani **Other:** Pacific Star newspaper – **8)** P.O. Box 100, Honiara ☎+677 21100 ▤ +677 21100 **LP:** Sammy 'Sharzy' Saeni **E:** zfm@solomon.com.sb. – **9)** 24/7 Pacific stream via satellite from London – **10)** 24/7 Pacific stream via satellite from Melbourne

SOMALIA

L.T: UTC +3h — **Pop:** 10 million — **Pr.L:** Somali, Rahanwein (Maay), Arabic, English — **E.C:** 50Hz, 220V — **ITU:** SOM

BAR-KULAN RADIO (a joint project by Albany Associates, African Union Mission and United Nations) **W:** bar-kulan.com **E:** contactE@bar-kulan.com **L.P:** Dir: Abdirahman Omar Osman. Senior Editor: Salah Diriye.
FM: Bosaaso 89.5MHz, Galkayo 89.5MHz, Mogadishu 92.0MHz 3.5kW, Baidoa 92.0MHz.

Andalus R: Mogadishu 88.8MHz. **W:** radioandalus24.com
Dalsan R: Mogadishu 91.5MHz. **W:** dalsanradio.com
Goal R, Mogadishu: 99.0MHz.
Mogadishu City R, Mogadishu: 102.8MHz.
Mustaqbal R: Mogadishu 97.7MHz. **W:** mustaqbalradio.com
R. Al Furqaan: Mogadishu 106.5MHz. **W:** radioalfurqaan.com
R. Banadir: Mogadishu 103.5MHz. **W:** radiobanadir.com
R. Danan: Mogadishu 94.0MHz. **W:** radiodanan.net
R. Dhusamareb: Dhusamareb 88.5MHz.
R. Jubba: Mogadishu 99.5MHz. **W:** jubaradio.net
R. Kulmiye: Mogadishu 88.0MHz. **W:** kulmiyenews.com
R. Manta: Mogadishu 95.5MHz.
RADIO MOGADISHU ("Voice of the Republic of Somalia", controlled by the Transitional Federal Government). Mogadishu 90.0/99.9MHz. **W:** radiomuqdisho.net

R. Risaala: Mogadishu 102.2MHz. Also rel. BBC. **W:** risaala.net
R. Simba: Mogadishu 95.0MHz 1kW. **W:** simbanews.com **STAR FM,** Mogadishu: 97.0MHz. See main entry under Kenya.
STN R, Mogadishu: 98.5MHz.
Vo Democracy (R. Xamar): Mogadishu: 93.5MHz **W:** xamarradio.com
Xurmo R: Mogadishu 96.0MHz. **W:** xurmo.net

SOMALILAND
(self-declared autonomous state in northwest Somalia)

RADIO HARGEISA
✉ Nala soo xidhiidh, Head Quarter, Near SLNTV, Hargeisa. **E:** radio-hargeisa@yahoo.com **L.P:** Dir: Said Adam Ege.
Hargeisa: **MW:** 693kHz. **SW:** 7120kHz 100kW (irr.) **FM:** 89.0MHz.
D.Prgr in Somali: 0330-2100, SW 0330-0500, 0900-1400, 1500-1900. **N.** in **E:** 1300, 1930.
Ann: "Halkani wa Radio Hargeysa, codka jamhuriyada Somaliland".

BBC Somali Sce: Hargeisa 89.7MHz.
Voice of America: Hargeisa 88.0MHz.

PUNTLAND
(self-declared autonomous state in northeast Somalia)

PUNTLAND RADIO
✉ Garowe. **W:** puntlandradiotv.com **E:** puntlandradio1@gmail.com & **L.P:** CE: Ahmed Aden. **SW:** 6160kHz 0300-0600, 1500-1800 & 13800kHz 0600-1800. 10kW AM/U (irregular).

Al-Xikma R: Bacadweyn/Burtinle/Gaalkacyo/Garowe/Qardho 90.0MHz, Bosaso 92.0MHz. **W:** alxigma.piczo.com
Horseed R: Bosaso 89.2MHz 1kW. **W:** horseedmedia.net
One Nation R: Garowe 88.8MHz, Bosaso 89.5MHz.**W:** 1nationradio.com
R. Daljir: Burtinle/Garowe 88.0MHz, Bosaso/Buuhoodle/Cabudwaq/ Qardho 88.8MHz, Galkacyo 89.1MHz **W:** radiodaljir.com
R. Gaalkacyo: Gaalkacyo 88.2MHz, Garowe 89.0MHz.**W:** radiogaalkacyo.net
R. Garowe: Eyl 88.8MHz, Garowe 89.5MHz. **W:** garoweonline.com
R. Hobyo: Gaalkacyo 87.5MHz. **W:** hobyoradio.com
R. Midnimo: Bosaso 97.5MHz.
R. SBC: Garowe 88.5, Qardho 88.7, Bosaso 89.9MHz. **W:** allsbc.com
R. Voice of Mudug: Gaalkacyo 89.5MHz **W:** codkamudug.com
R. Voice of Peace: Gaalkacyo 88.8MHz, Bosaso 89.5MHz
Somali Public R: Dhahar, fq. not known. **W:** spr.fm

SOUTH AFRICA

L.T: UTC +2h — **Pop**: 54 million — **Pr.L:** English, Afrikaans, isiNdebele, isiXhosa, isiZulu, Sepedi, Sesotho, Setswana, siSwati, Tshivenda, xiTsonga — **E.C:** 50Hz, 230V — **ITU:** AFS

SOUTH AFRICAN BROADCASTING CORPORATION (SABC) (Pub)
✉ Private Bag X1, Auckland Park 2006 ☎ +27 11 714 9111 🖷 +27 11 714 9744 **W:** sabc.co.za **Regional offices:** PO Box 2551, Cape Town 8000 – PO Box 1588, Durban 4000 – PO Box 563, Bloemfontein 9300 – PO Box 1040, Port Elizabeth 6000 – PO Box 395, Polokwane 0700 – Private Bag X11301, Nelspruit 1200 – PO Box 1008, Kimberley 8300 – Private Bag X2158, Mafikeng 2735 – PO Box 1198, Hatfield (Pretoria) 0001. **LP:** Chmn: Prof. Mbulaheni Obert Maguvhe, Group CEO: Frans Matlala, COO: Hlaudi Motsoeneng
NB: All txs belong to SENTECH (the common carrier for broadcasting in South Africa), ✉ Private Bag X06, Honeydew 2040

MW HOME SERVICES (Comm.)

Location	Station	kHz	kW
Komga	Umhlobo Wenene FM	846	50

COUNTRYWIDE FM (Comm.)

Limpopo FM (MHz)	R. Sonder Grense	SAfm	R. 2000	5 FM	R. Metro
Blouberg	102.3	105.9	-	-	-
Hoedspruit	102.0	105.6	98.5	-	-
Louis Trichardt	100.7	104.3	97.2	-	-
Modimolle	102.9	106.5	-	-	-
Mokopane	101.4	105.0	97.9	91.4	106.7
Thabazimbi	101.9	105.5	98.4	-	-
Tzaneen	102.6	106.2	107.7	-	-

NW Province FM (MHz)	R. Sonder Grense	SAfm	R. 2000	5 FM	R. Metro
Christiana	103.6	107.2	-	-	-
Groot Marico	102.3	105.9	-	-	-
Klerksdorp	101.2	104.8	97.7	-	-
Piet Plessis	102.8	106.4	-	-	-
Pomfret	101.1	104.7	-	-	-
Rustenburg	100.7	104.3	97.2	-	-
Schweizer-Reneke	103.1	106.7	99.6	-	-
Zeerust	102.6	106.2	99.1	-	-

Gauteng FM (MHz)	R. Sonder Grense	SAfm	R. 2000	5 FM	R. Metro
Heidelberg	100.8	104.4	97.3	-	-
Helderkruin	-	-	-	104.0	-
Johannesburg	101.5	105.1	99.7	98.0	96.4
Menlo Park	102.1	105.7	98.6	-	-
Pretoria	101.0	104.6	97.5	89.9	92.4
Sunnyside	-	-	-	103.6	-
Welverdiend	102.0	105.6	104.1	107.3	-

Mpumalanga FM (MHz)	R. Sonder Grense	SAfm	R. 2000	5 FM	R. Metro
Carolina	103.0	106.6	-	-	-
Davel	103.5	107.1	100.0	90.4	-
Dullstroom	100.8	104.4	-	-	-
Lydenburg	102.8	106.4	-	-	-
eMalahleni	101.8	105.4	98.3	97.0	100.3
Nelspruit	102.5	106.1	99.0	91.1	-
Piet Retief	102.1	105.7	-	-	-
Sabie	104.2	107.9	-	-	-
Volksrust	102.6	106.2	-	-	-

Northern Cape FM (MHz)	R. Sonder Grense	SAfm	R. 2000	5 FM	R. Metro
Alexander Bay	102.2#	105.8#	98.7	92.2	-
Calvinia	101.5	105.1	-	-	-
Carnavon	102.5	106.1	-	-	-
Colesberg	103.8	107.5	-	-	-
De Aar	102.0	105.6	-	-	-
Douglas	102.9	106.5	-	-	-
Faans Grove	103.0	106.6	-	-	-
Garies	100.7#	104.3#	-	-	-
Kimberley	101.0	104.6	97.5	91.0	-
Kuruman Hills	102.4	106.0	-	-	-
Pofadder	102.8	106.4	-	-	-
Prieska	100.8	104.4	-	-	-
Sringbok	101.6	105.2	-	-	-
Upington	101.7	105.3	-	-	-
Victoria West	101.1	104.7	-	-	-
Williston	103.2	-	-	-	-

Free State FM (MHz)	R. Sonder Grense	SAfm	R. 2000	5 FM	R. Metro
Bethlehem	101.9	105.5	98.4	-	-
Bloemfontein	103.0	106.6	99.5	91.6	98.1
Boesmanskop	101.2	104.8	-	-	-
Ficksburg	103.7	107.3	-	-	-
Kroonstad	103.4	107.0	99.9	93.4	-
Ladybrand	102.1	105.7	-	-	-
Petrus Steyn	102.3	105.9	98.8	-	-
Senekal	101.1	104.7	97.6	-	-
Springfontein	102.6	106.2	99.1	-	-
Theunissen	102.5	106.1	99.0	92.5	-
Witsieshoek	101.3	104.9	-	-	-

Kwazulu Natal FM (MHz)	R. Sonder Grense	SAfm	R. 2000	5 FM	R. Metro
Donnybrook	102.7	106.3	99.2	-	-
Durban	100.8	104.4	97.3	89.9	93.0
Durban North	102.5	106.1	99.0	103.8	107.9
Eshowe	103.4	107.0	99.9	-	90.3
Glencoe	103.1	106.7	99.6	-	-
Greytown	101.7	105.3	98.2	-	-
Kokstad	101.0	104.6	-	-	-
Ladysmith	101.0	104.6	97.5	-	-
Matatiele	101.5	105.1	-	-	-
Mooi River	102.2	105.8	98.7	-	-
Nongoma	102.9	106.5	99.4	-	89.8
Pietermaritzburg	101.4	105.0	97.9	100.3	-
Port Shepstone	101.3	104.9	97.8	-	-
The Bluff	102.0	105.6	98.5	107.4	-
Ubombo	102.4	106.0	98.9	-	-
Vryheid	101.2	104.8	97.7	-	-

Western Cape FM (MHz)	R. Sonder Grense	SAfm	R. 2000	5 FM	R. Metro
Beaufort West	100.7@	104.3@	-	-	-
Constantiaberg	102.1	105.7	98.6	89.0	-
Ceres	103.7	107.3	-	-	-
Franschhoek	100.7	104.3	97.2	-	-
George	101.7	105.3	98.2	91.7	-

FM (MHz)	R. Sonder Grense	SAfm	R. 2000	5 FM	R. Metro
Grabouw	101.7	105.3	-	-	-
Hermanus	100.8	104.4	-	-	-
Hex River	102.0	105.6	-	-	-
Hout Bay	100.9	104.5	97.4	87.8	-
Kleinmond	104.2	107.9	-	-	-
Knysna	102.2	105.8	98.7	92.2	-
Ladysmith	101.4	105.0	-	-	-
Matjiesfontein	102.8	106.4	-	-	-
Montagu	104.2	107.9	-	-	-
Napier	102.4	106.0	-	-	-
Oudtshoorn	102.6	106.2	99.1	92.6	-
Paarl	101.6	105.2	98.1	88.5	-
Piketberg	101.1	104.7	97.6	-	-
Plettenberg	100.8	104.4	-	-	-
Riversdale	100.9	104.5	-	-	-
Sea Point	103.5	107.1	100.0	90.4	91.7
Simonstown	100.7	104.3	97.2	87.6	-
Stellenbosch	100.9	104.5	97.4	87.8	-
Table Mountain	102.6	106.2	99.1	89.9	88.6
Tygerberg	103.0	106.6	99.5	88.2	93.0
Uniondale	103.4	107.0	-	-	-
Vanrhynsdorp	103.4	107.0	-	-	-
Villiersdorp	100.9	104.5	99.8	-	-

Eastern Cape FM (MHz)	R. Sonder Grense	SAfm	R. 2000	5 FM	R. Metro
Aliwal North	101.7	105.3	-	-	-
Andrieskraal	103.2	106.8	-	-	-
Barkly East	100.9	104.5	-	-	-
Bedford	100.8	104.4	-	-	-
Burgersdorp	103.9	107.6	-	-	-
Butterworth	101.1	104.7	97.6	-	-
Cala	103.4	107.0	-	-	-
Cradock	102.7	106.3	-	-	-
East London	101.6	105.2	98.1	88.5	107.7
Elliot	101.4	105.0	-	-	-
Graaff-Reinet	103.3	106.9	-	-	-
Grahamstown	103.5	107.1	100.0	90.4	-
Hankey	101.0	104.6	-	-	-
Kareedouw	102.9	106.5	-	-	-
King Williams Tn	103.0	106.6	-	-	-
Mount Ayliff	103.2	106.8	99.7	-	-
Noupoort	101.4	105.0	-	-	-
Patensie	101.5	105.0	-	-	-
Parsons Hill (PE)	101.0	104.6	97.5	-	87.9
Paul Sauer Dam	103.6	107.2	-	-	-
Port Elizabeth	102.3	105.9	98.8	89.2	100.5
Port St.Johns	103.7	107.3	100.2	-	-
Queenstown	102.2	105.8	98.7	-	-
Suurberg	101.8	105.4	-	-	-
Ugie	102.6	106.2	-	-	-
Umtata	102.0	105.6	98.5	-	-
Willowmore	101.2	104.8	-	-	-

= mono – no RDS @ = mono RDS

NATIONAL SW SERVICES: Meyerton (G.C: 26S35 028E08): 4 x 100kW txs + 1 standby tx

kHz	Sce.	H of tr	kHz	Sce.	H of tr
3320	RSG	1700(1800*)-0500	9650	RSG	0800(0700*)-1700(1800*)
7285	RSG	0500-0800(0700*)			

* = from Oct.25, 2015 to Mar.27, 2016
RSG=R. Sonder Grense (tr for Northern Cape region) – details below.

SABC PUBLIC BROADCASTING SERVICES (PBS) (Comm.)
Ikwekwezi FM (isiNdebele): ✉ P.O.Box 11620, Hatfield 0028 **W:** ikwekwezifm.co.za ☎+27 12 431 5477 📠+27 12 431 5312 - **FM(MHz):** Middelburg 91.8/Pretoria 96.8/Dullstroom 107.7/Johannesburg 106.3/Davel 94.5 + 4 rel. — **Lesedi FM** (Sesotho): ✉ Private Bag X20707, Bloemfontein 9300 **W:** lesedifm.co.za ☎+27 51 503 3090 📠+27 51 503 3270 - **FM(MHz):** Bloemfontein 89.9/Durban 106.6/Johannesburg 88.4/Kroonstad 90.3MHz + 13 rel. — **Ligwalagwala FM** (siSwati): ✉ Private Bag X11301, Nelspruit 1200 **W:** ligwalagwalafm.co.za ☎+27 13 759 6600 📠+27 13 755 3865 - **FM(MHz):** Nelspruit 92.5/Pretoria 89.3MHz + 9 rel. — **Lotus FM** ✉ PO Box 1588, Durban 4000 **W:** lotusfm.co.za ☎+27 31 362 5202 📠+27 31 362 5202 - **FM(MHz):** Durban 87.7/Johannesburg 106.8/Pretoria 100.6 + 8 rel. — **Motsweding FM** (Setswana): ✉ Private Bag X2150, Mmabatho 2735 **W:** motswedingfm.co.za ☎+27 18 389 7111 📠+27 18 389 7326 - **FM(MHz):** Mmabatho 88.7/Johannesburg 89.6/Pretoria 91.0/Rustenburg 87.6MHz + 24 rel. — **Munghana**

Lonene FM (xiTsonga): ✉ PO Box 395, Polokwane 0700 **W:** munghanalonenefm.co.za ☎+27 15 290 0262 📠+27 15 290 0171 - **FM(MHz):** Johannesburg 103.2/Pretoria 95.6/Tzaneen 92.6/Nelspruit 89.4MHz + 4 rel. — **Phalaphala FM** (Tshivenda): ✉ PO Box 985, Polokwane 0700 **W:** phalaphalafm.co.za ☎+27 15 290 0260 📠+27 15 290 0170 - **FM(MHz):** Johannesburg 107.8/Tzaneen 99.1MHz + 4 rel. — **Radio Sonder Grense** (National service in Afrikaans): ✉ PO Box 91312, Auckland Park 2006 **W:** rsg.co.za ☎+27 11 714 2702 📠+27 11 714 3472 - on FM and SW as above — **Radio X-K FM** (in !Xun and Khwe languages for Khoi San communities in N.Cape): ✉ PO Box 1008, Kimberley 8300 ☎+27 53 831 8131 📠+27 53 831 8127 - **FM(MHz):** Schmidtsdrift 99.4/Kimberley 107.9 — **R.2000** ✉ Private Bag X1, Auckland Park 2006 **W:** radio2000.co.za ☎+27 11 714 4085 📠+27 11 714 2436 - **FM:** (as above) — **SAfm** (Nat. sce in English): ✉ PO Box 91162, Auckland Park 2006 **W:** safm.co.za ☎+27 11 714 4442 📠+27 11 714 5829 - **FM:** (as above) — **Thobela FM** (Sepedi): ✉ PO Box 395, Polokwane 0700 **W:** thobelafm.co.za ☎+27 15 297 0074 📠+27 15 290 0172 - **FM(MHz):** Johannesburg 90.1/Pretoria 87.9/Tzaneen 89.5MHz + 9 rel. — **TruFM** (isiXhosa & English): ✉ Private Bag X0037, Bhisho 5605 **W:** trufm.co.za ☎+27 40 609 1800 📠+27 40 636 4112 - **FM(MHz):** East London 104.1/Bhisho 100.0 + 2 rel. — **Ukhozi FM** (isiZulu): ✉ PO Box 1588, Durban 4000 **W:** ukhozifm.co.za ☎+27 31 362 5111 📠+27 31 362 5402 - **FM(MHz):** Durban 90.8, 92.0, 92.5/Johannesburg 91.5/Pretoria 102.4MHz + 21 rel. — **Umhlobo Wenene FM** (isiXhosa): ✉ PO Box 1040, Port Elizabeth 6000 **W:** umhlobowenene.co.za ☎+27 41 391 1911 📠 +27 41 374 3708 - **FM(MHz):** Port Elizabeth 92.3/King Williams Town 93.0/Durban 96.2/Johannesburg 93.2/Cape Town 92.1MHz + 47 FM rel. and on **MW** 846kHz (see above)

SABC COMMERCIAL BROADCASTING SERVICES (CBS) (Comm.)
Good Hope FM ✉ PO Box 2551, Cape Town 8000 ☎+27 21 430 8276 📠 +27 21 434 3392 **W:** goodhopefm.co.za – **FM:** Cape Town 95.3MHz + 7 rel — **R. Metro FM** ✉ PO Box 91136, Auckland Park 2006 **W:** metrofm.co.za ☎+27 89 110 3377 📠+27 11 714 4166 - **FM:** (as above) — **5 FM** ✉ PO Box 91555, Auckland Park 2006 ☎+27 11 714 2905 📠 +27 11 714 5714 **W:** 5fm.co.za - **FM:** (as above)

EXTERNAL SERVICE: Channel Africa: See Int. Broadc. Section

INDEPENDENT COMMUNICATIONS AUTHORITY OF SOUTH AFRICA (ICASA)
✉ Private Bag X10002, Sandton 2146 ☎ +27 11 566 3000 **E:** info@icasa.org.za **W:** icasa.org.za
The ICASA is the regulator of telecommunications and the broadcasting sectors. It issues licences for commercial and community stns.

PRIVATE STATIONS (Comm.)

MW	kHz	kW	Station	Location
20)	540	-	Sport 540 AM	Gauteng (F.Pl.)
1)	567	25	Cape Talk	Klipheuwel (Cape Town)
21)	702	-	LM R.	Welgedacht (F.Pl.)
22)	828	25	Magic 828 AM	Klipheuwel (Cape Town)

FM	MHz	kW	Station	Location
15)	88.1	-	Heart FM	Overberg
12)	88.6	-	Gagasi FM	Ladysmith
15)	88.8	-	Heart FM	Overstrand
2)	89.0	-	Rise FM	Piet Retief
12)	89.1	-	Gagasi FM	Mooi River
2)	89.7	-	Rise FM	Sabie
3)	89.8	-	North West FM	Rustenburg
4)	89.9	-	Capricorn FM	Thohoyandou
18)	90.4	-	Smile FM	Cape Town
7)	91.5	-	KFM	Camps Bay
4)	91.7	-	Capricorn FM	Polokwane
3)	91.8	-	North West FM	Mahikeng
3)	91.9	-	North West FM	Taung
5)	92.7	-	Talk R. 702	Johannesburg
3)	93.5	-	North West FM	Zeerust
6)	93.7	5	OFM	Sasolburg
7)	93.9	10	KFM	Beaufort West
7)	93.9	3	KFM	Garies
8)	93.9	6	R. Jacaranda	Rustenburg
8)	93.9	15	R. Jacaranda	Louis Trlchardt
9)	94.0	-	Algoa FM	Plettenberg Bay
4)	94.0	5	Algoa FM	Bedford
8)	94.0	10	R. Jacaranda	Dullstroom
9)	94.0	9	Algoa FM	Prieska
6)	94.0	-	OFM	Potchefstroom
10)	94.0	25	East Coast R.	Durban
11)	94.0	0.1	Highveld Stereo	Heidelberg
7)	94.0	0.1	KFM	Hermanus

FM	MHz	kW	Station	Location
7)	94.1	13	KFM	Riversdale
8)	94.2	33	R. Jacaranda	Pretoria
9)	94.2	0.1	Algoa FM	Hankey
10)	94.2	0.1	East Coast R.	Ladysmith
6)	94.2	-	OFM	Barkley West
6)	94.2	-	OFM	Boshof
6)	94.2	10	OFM	Kimberley
6)	94.3	-	OFM	Ventersburg
6)	94.3	12	OFM	Senekal
7)	94.3	10	KFM	Piketberg
2)	94.3	-	Rise FM	Nelspruit
9)	94.3	-	Algoa FM	Knysna
10)	94.4	10	East Coast R.	Vryheid
6)	94.4	10	OFM	Klerksdorp
10)	94.5	10	East Coast R.	Port Shepstone
7)	94.5	1.3	KFM	Tygerberg
7)	94.6	2.5	KFM	Ladismith
8)	94.6	10	R. Jacaranda	Mokopane
10)	94.6	0.3	East Coast R.	Pietermaritzburg
9)	94.6	-	Algoa FM	Steynsburg
9)	94.6	10	Algoa FM	Noupoort
9)	94.6	-	Algoa FM	Colesberg
9)	94.6	-	Algoa FM	Middelburg
12)	94.7	-	Gagasi FM	Ulundi
12)	94.7	-	Gagasi FM	Richards Bay
10)	94.7	12	East Coast R.	Matatiele
11)	94.7	38	Highveld Stereo	Johannesburg
7)	94.7	10	KFM	Calvinia
7)	94.8	17	KFM	Springbok
2)	94.8	-	Rise FM	Carolina
8)	94.8	0.3	R. Jacaranda	Enzelberg
9)	94.8	-	Algoa FM	Kei Mouth
9)	94.8	10	Algoa FM	East London
7)	94.9	-	KFM	Somerset West
7)	94.9	10	KFM	George
7)	94.9	-	KFM	Grabow
6)	94.9	8	OFM	Upington
10)	94.9	10	East Coast R.	Greytown
9)	94.9	10	Algoa FM	Aliwal North
9)	94.9	-	Algoa FM	Barkley East
9)	95.0	-	Algoa FM	Somerset East
9)	95.0	11	Algoa FM	Port Elizabeth
8)	95.0	11	R. Jacaranda	eMalahleni
8)	95.1	10	OFM	Bethlehem
8)	95.1	11	R. Jacaranda	Thabazimbi
8)	95.2	18	R. Jacaranda	Hoedspruit
7)	95.2	-	KFM	Hex River
11)	95.2	20	Highveld Stereo	Welverdiend
10)	95.2	0.1	East Coast R.	The Bluff
8)	95.3	-	R. Jacaranda	Pretoria East
8)	95.3	9	R. Jacaranda	Piet Retief
6)	95.3	10	OFM	Ladybrand
9)	95.4	12	Algoa FM	Queenstown
10)	95.4	10	East Coast R.	Mooi River
7)	95.4	-	KFM	Alexander Bay
7)	95.4	0.2	KFM	Knysna
8)	95.5	0.1	R. Jacaranda	Groot Marico
8)	95.5	0.2	R. Jacaranda	Blouberg
6)	95.5	11	OFM	Petrus Steyn
9)	95.5	-	Algoa FM	Cape St. Francis
9)	95.5	-	Algoa FM	Jeffreys Bay
9)	95.5	-	Algoa FM	Uitenhage
9)	95.5	16	Algoa FM	Port Elizabeth
10)	95.6	15	East Coast R.	Ubombo
6)	95.6	11	OFM	Kuruman Hills
7)	95.6	3	KFM	Napier
10)	95.7	6	East Coast R.	Durban North
8)	95.7	12	R. Jacaranda	Nelspruit
8)	95.7	10	OFM	Theunissen
6)	95.7	-	OFM	Welkom
7)	95.7	10	KFM	Carnavon
7)	95.8	9	KFM	Oudtshoorn
8)	95.8	10	R. Jacaranda	Volksrust
8)	95.8	11	R. Jacaranda	Zeerust
8)	95.8	12	R. Jacaranda	Tzaneen
6)	95.8	-	OFM	Colesberg
6)	95.8	-	OFM	Springfontein
10)	95.9	10	East Coast R.	Donnybrook
9)	95.9	12	Algoa FM	Cradock
13)	95.9	35	Kaya FM	Johannesburg
9)	96.0	-	R. Jacaranda	Lydenburg
9)	96.0	-	Algoa FM	Albertina
9)	96.0	-	Algoa FM	George
4)	96.0	-	Capricorn FM	Mokopane
7)	96.0	10	KFM	Matjiesfontein
7)	96.0	5	KFM	Pofadder
6)	96.1	9	OFM	Douglas
8)	96.1	0.2	R. Jacaranda	Modimole
10)	96.1	10	East Coast R.	Nongoma
9)	96.1	-	Algoa FM	Nature's Valley
9)	96.1	-	Algoa FM	Joubertina
9)	96.2	10	Algoa FM	King Williams Town
9)	96.2	-	Algoa FM	Bisho
6)	96.2	10	OFM	Bloemfontein
8)	96.2	9	R. Jacaranda	Carolina
10)	96.3	10	East Coast R.	Glencoe
6)	96.3	-	OFM	Warrenton
6)	96.3	-	OFM	Vryburg
6)	96.3	10	OFM	Schweitzer-Reineke
9)	96.5	-	Algoa FM	Aberdeen
9)	96.5	10	Algoa FM	Graaf-Reinet
7)	96.5	10	KFM	Villiersdorp
7)	96.6	17	KFM	Vanrhynsdorp
10)	96.6	10	East Coast R.	Eshowe
6)	96.6	10	OFM	Kroonstad
9)	96.7	-	Algoa FM	Port Elizabeth
9)	96.7	-	Algoa FM	Port Alfred
9)	96.7	10	Algoa FM	Grahamstown
8)	96.7	10	R. Jacaranda	Davel
6)	96.8	5,5	OFM	Christiana
10)	96.9	0.1	East Coast R.	Newcastle
7)	96.9	20	KFM	Ceres
6)	96.9	-	OFM	Ficksburg
3)	97.0	-	North West FM	Klerksdorp
8)	97.1	-	R. Jacaranda	Sabie
7)	97.1	-	KFM	Kleinmond
7)	97.1	-	KFM	Montagu
3)	97.3	-	North West FM	Vryburg
4)	97.6	-	Capricorn FM	Tzaneen
4)	98.0	-	Capricorn FM	Hoedspruit
12)	98.5	0.3	Gagasi FM	Pietermaritzburg
17)	98.7	11	Power FM	Johannesburg
14)	99.2	35	Y-FM	Johannesburg
3)	99.4	-	North West FM	Potchefstroom
12)	99.5	25	Gagasi FM	Durban
7)	100.1	-	KFM	Hout Bay
2)	101.6	-	Rise FM	Dullstroom
15)	102.7	0.1	Heart FM	Drakenstein
16)	102.7	35	Classic FM	Johannesburg
12)	103.5	-	Gagasi FM	Port Shepstone
19)	103.9	-	Vuma FM	Umhlanga
3)	103.9	-	North West FM	Pretoria
15)	104.9	1.3	Heart FM	Tygerberg
4)	105.4	-	Capricorn FM	Makhado
2)	105.8	-	Rise FM	Standerton
5)	106.0	-	Talk R. 702	Pretoria
15)	106.3	-	Heart FM	West Coast
2)	106.4	-	Rise FM	eMalahleni
7)	107.2	-	KFM	Stellenbosch
12)	107.9	-	Gagasi FM	Newcastle

Addresses and other information:
1) Private Bag X567, Vlaeberg 8018 ☎ +27 21 446 4700 🖷 +27 21 446 4800 **W**: capetalk.co.za **E**: feedback@capetalk.co.za – **2)** Shop 38, The Grove Shopping Centre, Cnr. R40 & George St., Riverside Park, Nelspruit, 1201 ☎ +27 13 757 0263 🖷 +27 13 757 0026 **LP**: Mark Schormann **W**: risefm.co.za **E**: info@risefm.co.za – **3)** 17 Kgwebo Ave., Unit 1 Delta Place, Mabe Business Park, Rustenburg 0300 ☎ +27 14 594 8960 🖷 +27 14 597 3345 **LP**: David Mobusela **W**: northwestfm. co.za **E**: admin@northwestfm.co.za – **4)** Postnet Suite 93, Private Bag X9676, Polokwane, 0700 ☎ +27 15 590 0900 **LP**: Simphiwe Mdlalose **W**: capricornfm.co.za **E**: info@capricornfm.co.za – **5)** PO Box 5572, Rivonia 2128. ☎ +27 11 506 3200 🖷 +27 (11) 506 3663 **W**: 702. co.za **E**: comment@702.co.za – **6)** PO Box 7117, Bloemfontein 9300 ☎ +27 51 505 0900 🖷 +27 51 505 0905 **LP**: Gary Stroebel **W**: ofm. co.za **E**: info@ofm.co.za – **7)** Private Bag X945, Cape Town, 8000 ☎ +27 21 446 4700 🖷 +27 21 446 4800 **W**: kfm.co.za **E**: kfm@kfm. co.za – **8)** PO Box 11961, Centurion 0046 ☎ +27 11 063 5700 **LP**: Alan Khan **W**: jacarandafm.com **E**: enquiries@jacarandafm.co.za – **9)** PO Box 5973, Walmer, 6065 ☎ +27 41 505 9497 🖷 +27 41 583 5555 **LP**: Dave Tiltmann **W**: algoafm.co.za **E**: dave.t@algoafm.co.za – **10)** P.O. Box 25095, Gateway, Umhlanga Rocks 4321 ☎ +27 31 570 9495 🖷 +27 86 679 4951. **LP**: Trish Taylor **W**: ecr.co.za **E**: auntyhazel@ecr. co.za – **11)** PO Box 3438, Rivonia 2128 ☎ +27 11 506 3947 🖷 +27 86

501 2014 **LP**: Tery Volkwyn **W**: 947.co.za **E**: webmaster947@947.co.za – **12)** 6 Zenith Drive, Solstice, Umhlanga New Town Centre 4319 ☎ +27 31 580 5300 🖹 +27 31 566 3403 **LP**: Pearl Sokhulu **W**: gagasifm. co.za **E**: management@gagasifm.co.za – **13)** PO Box 395, Parklands, 2112 **W**: kayafm.co.za ☎ +27 11 634 9500 🖹 +27 11 634 9574 **LP**: Charlene Deacon **E**: pr@kayafm.co.za – **14)** cor.Albury Rd. & Dunkeld Cresc., South West Blocks, Dunkeld West Ext.8, Sandton 2196 ☎ +27 11 772 0800 🖹 +27 11 280 0421 **LP**: Kanthan Pillay **W**: yworld.co.za **E**: kanthan@yfm.co.za – **15)** Second Floor, Media Centre, Greenpoint 8051 ☎ +27 21 406 8900 **LP**: Gavin Meiring **W**: 1049.fm **E**: info@1049.fm – **16)** PO Box 782, Auckland Park 2006 ☎ +27 11 403 1027 🖹 +27 11 408 5451 **LP**: Mike Ford **W**: classicfm.co.za **E**: info@classicfm.co.za – **17)** PO Box 3187, Houghton 2041 **W**: powerfm.co.za **E**: info@pow-erfm.co.za **LP**: Dawn Klatzko ☎ +27 11 014 9000 – **18)** PO Box 50194, Waterfront, 8002 ☎+27 21 818 8904 🖹+27 21 818 8810 **W**: smile904. fm **E**: studio@smile904.fm – **19)** 6th Floor, Centenary Building, Cnr. Equinox & Zenith Dr., Umhlanga New Town Centre, Unhlanga Rocks, 4319 ☎+27 31 833 3000 **W**: vumafm.co.za **E**: sales@vumafm.co.za – **20)** to be established **21)** Genesis House, 18 Wessel Road, Rivonia ☎+27 11 234 2691 **W**: lmradio.net **E**: sales@lmradio.net **22)**PO Box 119, Howard Place, 7450☎+27 87 828 0828 **W**: magic828.am **E**: tony. sanderson@magic828.am

COMMUNITY STATIONS
Numerous licences issued by ICASA with about 150 stns currently on the air, mainly on FM, most of them low power.

MW	kHz	kW	Station	Location
1)	576	50	R. Veritas	Meyerton
2)	657	50	R. Pulpit/R.Kansel	Meyerton
7)	729	25	Cape Pulpit	Cape Town
3)	1269	2	Arrowline Chinese R.	Edenvale
4)	1422	1	Hellenic R.	Bedfordview
2)	1440	10	R. Pulpit (DRM test)	Pretoria
5)	1485	1	R. Today	Honeydew
6)	1548	10	R. Islam	Lenasia
8	1584	0.25	R. 1584	Laudium (Pretoria)

Addresses and other information:
1) PO Box 4599, Edenvale 1610 **W**: radioveritas.co.za ☎ +27 11 663 4700 🖹 +27 11 452 7625 **LP**: Fr. Emil Blaser OP – **2)** 42 Jakobus Street, Kilner Park, 0186 **W**: radiokansel.co.za or radiopulpit.co.za **E**: gospel@radiopulpit.co.za ☎ +27 12 334 1200 🖹 +27 12 334 1400 Relig. prgrs in English, Afrikaans and other African languages, 24h – **3)** PO Box 2241, Edenvale 1610 **W**: arrowline.co.za **E**: info@arrowline.co.za ☎ +27 11 454 5808 🖹 +27 86 242 5838 prgrs in Chinese, 24h – **4)** PO Box 4077, Edenvale 1610 ☎ +27 11 453 3786 🖹 +27 11 453 3778 **W**: hellen-icradio.org.za **E**: info@hellenicradio.org.za **LP**: Tulla CritsotakisGeorge Zoulis, Prgrs in Greek and English 24h – **5)** PO Box 2820, Parklands 2121 **W**: 1485.org.za ☎ +27 11 880 0329 🖹 +27 86 601 2950 **E**: info@1485. org.za Prgrs in English for over 50s, rel. BBCWS 2300-0400, 24h – **6)** PO Box 2580, Lenasia, 1820 **W**: radioislam.org.za **E**: isv@radioislam. co.za ☎ +27 11 854 7022 🖹 +27 11 854 7024 Prgrs in English, 24h – **7)** Private Bag X18, Tyger Valley, 7536 ☎+27 21 917 7000 🖹+27 21 914 1351 **W**: capepulpit.co.za **E**: gospel@capepulpit.co.za, relig. prgrs in English, Afrikaans, Zulu and Xhoza, 24h – **8)** Carmine St., Laudium, 0037 ☎+27 12 374 1584 🖹+27 12 374 2488 **W**: radio1584.co.za **E**: islamic1584@gmail.com, prgrs of Institute for Islamic Services, 24h.

SOUTH SUDAN

LT: UTC +3h — **Pop**: 9 million — **Pr.L**: Dinka, Arabic — **E.C**: 50Hz, 240V — **ITU**: SSD

MINISTRY OF INFORMATION AND BROADCASTING
🖳 Juba ☎+211 922 260000 **W**: goss.org/index.php/ministries/infor-mation-broadcasting **L.P**: DG: Mr. Mustafa Biong Majak Koul.

SOUTH SUDAN NATIONAL RADIO (Gov.)
🖳 P.O. Box 126, Juba ☎+211 912 452275 **L.P**: DG: Mr. Arop Bagat. **MW**: Bentiu 558kHz‡, Juba 693kHz 40kW. **FM**: Bentiu 99.0MHz, Juba 105.0MHz, Kwajok 99.0MHz, Rumbek 98.0MHz. **D.Prgr**: 693kHz: 0330-1830.
Vo Eastern Equatoria State: Torit/Kapoeta 97.5MHz.
Yambio FM, Western Equatoria State: 90.0MHz 1kW.

RADIO MIRAYA (Joint project by UNMISS and Hirondelle Foundation)
🖳 c/o UNMISS, Tongping, Juba, Central Equatoria State ☎+211 912 062616 **W**: facebook.com/radiomiraya unmiss.unmissions.org/Default. aspx?tabid=3493&language=en-US **E**: mirayafm@un.org **L.P**: Chief of

Op: Quade Hermann. Head of Tech. Op: Sonam Tobgyal.
FM: Bor/Juba/Malakal/Rumbek/Wau 5kW, Aweil/Bentiu/Ezo/ Kapoeda/Maridi/Melut/Mundri/Naseer/Pibor/Torit/Yambio/Yei 1kW, all on 101.0MHz. 24h in Arabic and English.
Relays on shortwave: see Clandestines & Other Target Broadcasts section.

CATHOLIC RADIO NETWORK (Rlg.)
🖳 P.O. Box 258, Hai Jerusalem, Juba ☎ +211 924 217188 **W**: catholicradionetwork.org **E**: crn.director@gmail.com **L.P**: Dir: Enrica Valentini.
Stations: Bakhita R, Juba: 91.0 – **Easter R,** Yei: 94.0 1kW – **Good News R,** Rumbek: 89.0 2.5kW – **R. Anisa,** Yambio: 92.0 – **R. Don Bosco,** Tonj: 91.0 2kW – **R. Emmanuel,** Torit: 89.0 – **Vo Hope,** Wau: 88.6 – **Vo Love,** Malakal: 93.6 2kW – **Vo Peace,** Gidel: 107.9.

Internews stations: **R. Al-Mujtama,** Kurmuk 99.0 500W – **Mayardit FM,** Turalei 90.7 1kW – **Mingkaman 100 FM,** Mingkaman: 100.0 MHz – **Naath FM,** Leer/Nasir 88.0 1/2kW – **Nile FM,** Malakal: 98.0 600W – **Nhomlaau FM,** Malualkon 88.0 1kW – **VO Community,** Kauda: 88.0 300W. **W**: internews.org

Other Stations (FM MHz**):**
Capital FM, Juba: 89.0 **W**: capitalfmjuba.com – **City FM,** Juba: 88.4 **W**: cityfm.co – **Dream FM,** Juba: 90.6 **W**: facebook.com/pages/ Dream-FM-906-Juba/765092860188519 – **Eye R,** Juba: 98.6 2kW **W**: eyeradio.org **F.PI**: transmitters in Torit, Wau, Rumbek, Kwajok, Aweil, Bor and Yambio – **Liberty FM,** Juba/Yei: 90.0 – **Malakal FM,** Malakal: 105.0 – **Nehemiah Trumpet Call R,** Borongole: 97.3 **W**: operationsnehemiah.org/#!nehemiah-gospel-radio-973-fm/cis7 **F.PI**: shortwave operation – **R. Jonglei,** Bor: 95.9 **W**: facebook.com/ RadioJonglei959Fm – **R. Magwi,** Magwi: 92.5 – **Raja FM,** Raja: 95.0 – **Spirit FM,** Yei: 99.9 – **Wau FM,** Wau: 88.6
BBC World Sce: Juba 88.2 (English), Juba/Malakal/Wau 90.0 (Arabic).
R. France Int: Juba 91.4
Voice of America: Juba 93.5
F.PI: TWR relay station on mediumwave

SPAIN

LT: UTC +1h (27 Mar-30 Oct: +2h) — **Pop**: 40.5 million — **Pr.L**: Castilian, Catalan, Galician, Basque — **E.C**: 50Hz, 230V — **ITU**: E

MINISTERIO DE FOMENTO
Secretaría General de Comunicaciones
🖳 Paseo de la Castellana, 67, Palacio de Comunicaciones, 28071 Madrid **W**: www.fomento.gob.es **E**: fomento@fomento.es

RADIO NACIONAL DE ESPAÑA (RNE) (Pub)
🖳 Casa de la Radio, Avenida de la Radio y la Televisión, 4, Prado del Rey, 28223 Pozuelo de Alarcón
☎ +34 91 581 70 00 🖹 +34 91 346 1769 **W**: www.rne.es **E**: secretaria@rtve.es
RNE1 (R. Nacional) and **RNE5** (R. 5 Todo Noticias)

MW	kHz	kW	Net	Rg	Location
AS01)	531	20	RNE5	AS	Oviedo °
AN02)	531	10	RNE5	AN	Córdoba
GA02)	531	10	RNE5	GA	Pontevedra
NA01)	531	10	RNE5	NA	Pamplona °
VA01)	558	50	RNE5	VA	València °
GA01)	558	20	RNE5	GA	A Coruña °
EU02)	558	20	RNE5	EU	Donosti-San Sebastián
MU01)	567	50	RNE5	MU	Murcia °
CA01)	576	100	RNE5	CA	Barcelona °
MA01)	585	600	RNE1	MA	Madrid °
AN01)	603	50	RNE1	AN	Sevilla °
CL02)	603	10	RNE5	CL	Palencia
CA02)	612	10	RNE1	CA	Lleida (relay)
EU01)	612	10	RNE1	EU	Vitoria-Gasteiz °
AN04)	621	10	RNE1	AN	Jaén (relay)
BA01)	621	10	RNE1	BA	Palma de Mallorca °
CL03)	621	10	RNE1	CL	Avila (relay)
GA01)	639	300	RNE1	GA	A Coruña °
AR01)	639	50	RNE1	AR	Zaragoza °
EU03)	639	50	RNE1	EU	Bilbo-Bilbao (relay)
AN05)	639	20	RNE1	AN	Almería (relay)
CM03)	639	10	RNE1	CM	Albacete (relay)
EX02)	648	10	RNE1	EX	Badajoz (relay)
MA01)	657	50	RNE5	MA	Madrid °

MW	kHz	kW	Net	Rg	Location
AN01)	684	600	RNE1	AN	Sevilla °
AS01)	693	5	RNE1	AS	Boal (rel. of Oviedo)
CM01)	693	20	RNE1	CM	Toledo °
CA03)	693	10	RNE1	CA	Tortosa (rel.of Cataluña)
AS01)	729	100	RNE1	AS	Oviedo °
AN06)	729	20	RNE1	AN	Málaga
RI01)	729	20	RNE1	RI	Logroño °
CL01)	729	10	RNE1	CL	Valladolid °
CM04)	729	10	RNE1	CM	Cuenca
VA02)	729	10	RNE1	VA	Alacant-Alicante (relay)
CA01)	738	600	RNE1	CA	Barcelona °
AN07)	747	10	RNE5	AN	Cádiz
VA01)	774	100	RNE1	VA	València °
EX01)	774	60	RNE1	EX	Cáceres °
EU02)	774	50	RNE1	EU	Donosti-San Sebastián
GA03)	774	20	RNE1	GA	Ourense (relay)
AN08)	774	10	RNE1	AN	Granada (relay)
AN09)	774	10	RNE1	AN	La Línea (relay)
CL04)	774	10	RNE1	CL	León (relay)
CL05)	774	10	RNE1	CL	Soria (relay)
CM05)	801	25	RNE1	CM	Ciudad Real (relay)
GA04)	801	20	RNE1	GA	Lugo (relay)
CA04)	801	10	RNE1	CA	Girona (relay)
CL06)	801	10	RNE1	CL	Burgos
CL07)	801	10	RNE1	CL	Zamora
VA03)	801	10	RNE1	VA	Castelló (relay)
MU01)	855	300	RNE1	MU	Murcia °
CT01)	855	50	RNE1	CT	Santander °
CA03)	855	20	RNE1	CA	Tarragona (relay)
GA02)	855	20	RNE1	GA	Pontevedra (relay)
AN10)	855	10	RNE1	AN	Huelva (relay)
AR02)	855	10	RNE1	AR	Teruel (relay)
CL08)	855	10	RNE1	CL	Ponferrada (relay)
CL09)	855	10	RNE1	CL	Salamanca (relay)
NA01)	855	10	RNE1	NA	Pamplona-Iruñea °
AN03)	855	5	RNE1	AN	Marbella (relay)
CM02)	864	10	RNE1	CM	Socuellamos (rel.of Toledo)
BA01)	909	62	RNE5	BA	Palma de Mallorca °
AR01)	936	20	RNE5	AR	Zaragoza °
CL01)	936	20	RNE5	CL	Valladolid °
VA02)	936	10	RNE5	VA	Alacant-Alicante
AN11)	972	5	RNE1	AN	Cabra (rel.of Sevilla)
GA05)	972	2	RNE1	GA	Monforte de Lemos (relay)
AN08)	1017	10	RNE5	AN	Granada
CL06)	1017	10	RNE5	CL	Burgos°
AN05)	1098	25	RNE5	AN	Almería
GA04)	1098	20	RNE5	GA	Lugo
CL03)	1098	10	RNE5	CL	Avila
AN10)	1098	5	RNE5	AN	Huelva
RI01)	1107	25	RNE5	RI	Logroño °
CT01)	1107	20	RNE5	CT	Santander °
EX01)	1107	20	RNE5	EX	Cáceres °
AR02)	1107	10	RNE5	AR	Teruel (rel.of zaragoza)
CL08)	1107	10	RNE5	CL	Ponferrada (rel.of León)
CL05)	1125	10	RNE5	CL	Soria
CM01)	1125	10	RNE5	CM	Toledo °
EU01)	1125	10	RNE5	EU	Vitoria-Gasteiz °
VA03)	1125	10	RNE5	VA	Castelló
EX02)	1125	5	RNE5	EX	Badajoz °
AN06)	1152	20	RNE5	AN	Málaga
CA02)	1152	10	RNE5	CA	Lleida
CL07)	1152	10	RNE5	CL	Zamora
CM03)	1152	10	RNE5	CM	Albacete
MU02)	1152	10	RNE5	MU	Cartagena
GA03)	1305	25	RNE5	GA	Ourense
CM05)	1305	20	RNE5	CM	Ciudad Real
EU03)	1305	20	RNE5	EU	Bilbao-Bilbao
CL04)	1305	10	RNE5	CL	León
CM04)	1314	20	RNE5	CM	Cuenca
CA03)	1314	10	RNE5	CA	Tarragona
CL09)	1314	10	RNE5	CL	Salamanca
GA06)	1413	20	RNE5	GA	Vigo
AN04)	1413	10	RNE5	AN	Jaén
CA04)	1413	5	RNE5	CA	Girona
AN09)	1503	5	RNE5	AN	La Linea (rel.of Cádiz)
GA05)	1503	2	RNE5	GA	Monforte de Lemos (rel.of. Lugo)

°= regional key stn

FM	Location	RNE1	RNE2	RNE3	RNE4	RNE5	kW
Andalucía							
AN08)	Baza	92.6	97.3	-	-	-	5
AN02)	Cabra	95.1	89.5	103.8	-	88.0	1

FM	Location	RNE1	RNE2	RNE3	RNE4	RNE5	kW
AN02)	Córdoba	-	-	-	-	99.8	2
AN08)	Granada	104.2	96.4	94.4	-	98.5	1
AN01)	Guadalcanal	-	90.6	-	-	-	5
AN07)	Jerez	103.5	94.5	96.7	-	106.3	80
AN02)	Lagar de la Cruz	92.2	97.5	98.6	-	-	10
AN06)	Málaga	-	99.2	104.0	-	92.5	1
AN03)	Marbella	-	-	-	-	87.6	1
AN06)	Mijas	106.6	98.1	99.8	-	88.0	10
AN08)	Parapanda	103.0	91.1	93.9	-	-	5
AN05)	Pechina	100.9	92.4	94.9	-	106.7	70
AN10)	Punta Umbria	95.2	92.6	99.0	-	88.8	5
AN06)	Ronda	106.1	99.3	91.6	-	102.3	1
AN04)	Sierra Almadén	105.4	90.0	96.0	-	-	10
AN08)	Sierra Lújar	96.7	90.4	94.2	-	-	5
AN07)	Tajo	105.0	94.0	103.1	-	-	5
AN01)	Valencina	91.2	93.7	98.8	-	90.0	5
Aragon							
AR02)	Alcañiz	89.5	-	-	-	99.3	1
AR03)	Arguis	100.9	94.4	103.7	-	92.8	5
AR03)	Barbastro	89.6	97.4	105.1	-	100.2	1
AR01)	Caspe	90.2	99.0	-	-	103.7	1
AR03)	Ejea de los C.	94.8	98.9	106.4	-	91.2	
AR01)	Fraga	95.0	96.3	102.2	-	98.8	1
AR01)	Inogés	89.4	92.4	99.7	-	105.0	5
AR03)	Jaca	103.7	94.4	100.3	-	98.7	1
AR02)	Javalambre	-	90.0	93.9	-	-	1
AR01)	La Muela	94.5	90.9	96.3	-	103.6	10
AR02)	Montalban	90.5	92.7	96.4	-	105.1	
AR02)	Peracense	88.3	98.1	100.6	-	106.1	
AR02)	Teruel	104.7	89.2	94.5	-	95.6	1
Asturias							
AS01)	Avilés	100.0	87.9	95.6	-	102.9	1
AS01)	Boal	93.2	97.8	88.2	-	90.5	1
AS01)	Cangas Narcea	97.2	99.0	87.7	-	90.9	1
AS01)	Cangas Onis	88.8	92.5	104.0	-	100.3	1
AS02)	Gamoniteiro	102.5	92.2	94.4	-	104.4	10
AS02)	Gijón	99.2	98.5	102.0	-	89.9	5
AS01)	Ibias	95.8	98.7	102.9	-	105.1	1
AS01)	Llanes	106.1	-	-	-	97.3	1
AS01)	Los Oscos	89.7	104.0	105.7	-	96.1	1
AS01)	Luarca	96.8	93.8	100.3	-	-	1
AS01)	Mieres	-	-	-	-	101.8	1
AS01)	Oviedo	89.4	96.0	90.3	-	99.6	1
AS01)	Peñamelleras	93.9	96.4	100.7	-	104.6	
AS01)	San Martín	88.3	96.7	100.2	-	93.3	1
Baleares							
BA01)	Alfabia	90.1	87.9	92.3	-	104.5	10
BA01)	Ibiza	101.6	100.4	105.7	-	94.9	1
BA01)	Menorca	94.6	97.1	105.8	-	100.4	1
BA01)	Pollensa	93.2	95.4	97.4	-	99.7	1
Cantabria							
CT03)	Embalse Ebro	89.0	94.0	98.2	-	101.9	1
CT01)	Liérganes	96.9	93.0	102.9	-	105.0	10
CT02)	Torrelavega	99.5	97.9	103.4	-	89.4	1
Catalunya							
CA02)	Alpicat	94.6	89.2	97.8	87.9	-	10
CA02)	Baquéira	92.2	87.7	89.0	93.3	-	1
CA02)	Bossost	94.4	100.5	105.2	102.3	-	1
CA01)	Collserola	88.3	93.0	98.6	100.8	99.0	20
CA01)	Collsuspina	92.2	97.9	103.1	104.7	-	1
CA01)	Igualada	89.4	90.9	105.1	106.9	-	1
CA01)	Monte Caro	104.3	96.6	99.6	90.7	-	5
CA01)	Montserrat	94.3	99.0	-	103.8	98.8	2
CA03)	Musara	106.5	91.5	94.5	88.8	94.0	5
CA01)	Sant Pere Ribes	92.7	95.2	97.5	106.3	101.3	1
CA04)	Rocacorba	93.3	91.1	95.9	106.2	94.0	5
CA01)	Soriguera	99.9	103.6	106.4	90.6	97.2	1
CA03)	Ulldecona	95.0	-	-	-	-	1
CA02)	Viella	90.0	96.2	104.4	102.6	-	1
Castilla-León							
CL06)	Aranda Duero	90.0	92.7	101.6	-	106.2	1
CL03)	Arenas Pedro	102.4	90.3	-	-	-	1
CL09)	Béjar	87.6	92.0	97.8	-	102.4	1
CL07)	Benavente	87.8	91.3	97.9	-	100.2	1
CL05)	Burgo Osma	96.1	98.4	88.7	-	102.8	1
CL06)	Burgos	93.6	90.3	91.2	-	106.6	1
CL04)	Castropodame	103.3	93.0	99.9	-	105.9	5
CL02)	Cervera	88.6	94.8	97.3	-	100.4	1
CL09)	El Cabaco	102.9	92.4	95.4	-	-	5
CL02)	Guardo	89.8	105.6	-	-	104.0	1
CL04)	León	97.1	91.1	89.3	-	102.2	1

FM	Location	RNE1	RNE2	RNE3	RNE4	RNE5	kW
CL02)	Palencia	91.8	101.0	97.6	-	88.0	1
CL06)	Pancorbo	89.7	92.0	101.7	-	104.5	1
CL07)	Pbla Samabria	93.6	103.5	100.3	-	91.9	1
CL09)	Salamanca	94.5	88.1	91.4	-	102.2	1
CL10)	Segovia	97.0	-	-	-	91.5	1
CL05)	Soria	89.7	91.5	94.3	-	104.7	2
CL01)	Valladolid	97.3	93.1	92.2	-	95.1	5
CL04)	Villablino	98.1	89.0	91.4	-	99.4	1
CL06)	Villadiego	-	102.3	103.3	-	-	1
CL04)	Villafranca	90.9	89.7	97.5	-	104.1	1
CL07)	Zamora	101.8	96.7	98.5	-	88.8	5
Castilla La Mancha							
CM03)	Almansa	91.2	98.6	95.6	-	94.4	1
CM03)	Chincilla	91.8	93.6	99.0	-	106.3	5
CM05)	Ciudad Real	95.7	92.8	94.1	-	88.8	1
CM04)	Cuenca	105.6	93.0	92.0	-	96.1	1
CM06)	Guadalajara	103.7	93.5	96.9	-	102.1	1
CM05)	La Mancha	101.0	89.8	94.5	-	106.8	10
CM05)	Puertollano	93.1	99.1	91.8	-	101.8	5
CM05)	Socuéllamos	94.0	-	-	-	-	1
CM01)	Talavera	97.8	105.5	94.7	-	89.4	5
CM01)	Toledo	102.0	103.9	106.4	-	99.9	1
CM05)	Valdepeñas	92.6	95.5	97.3	-	102.1	1
Euskadi							
EU03)	Archanda	100.7	90.6	99.2	-	96.3	5
EU02)	Azcoitia	88.7	104.9	106.9	-	-	1
EU02)	Beasain	100.2	98.4	94.9	-	-	1
EU02)	Eibar	92.9	98.7	95.9	-	-	1
EU02)	Jaizquibel	104.7	90.0	92.1	-	-	10
EU02)	Monte Igueldo	87.6	99.5	98.9	-	93.3	1
EU03)	Oiz	106.4	105.3	102.1	-	-	5
EU01)	San León	-	-	-	-	93.3	1
EU03)	Sollube	105.9	93.9	95.4	-	-	5
EU02)	Tolosa	101.9	98.8	96.0	-	-	1
EU01)	Vitoria-Gasteiz	92.5	96.9	99.5	-	89.4	1
Extremadura							
EX02)	Badajoz	94.9	90.1	92.2	-	106.0	1
EX01)	Cáceres	95.1	101.7	93.7	-	88.2	1
EX02)	Mérida	-	-	-	-	101.3	1
EX01)	Montánchez	105.3	97.7	99.3	-	-	5
EX01)	Plasencia	88.6	-	99.3	-	104.4	1
Galicia							
GA03)	Barco	94.7	96.4	100.3	-	104.6	
GA02)	Domayo	90.1	92.1	97.4	-	-	5
GA04)	Monforte	-	-	-	-	88.8	1
GA03)	Monte Meda	102.8	91.2	94.3	-	106.8	5
GA01)	Monte Xalo	100.4	91.6	94.5	-	95.8	10
GA03)	Ourense	100.6	97.2	99.4	-	95.1	5
GA04)	Páramo	101.7	88.2	99.6	-	92.8	5
GA04)	Piedrafita	89.4	92.6	105.3	-	95.2	
GA02)	Pontevedra	-	88.3	-	-	-	1
GA07)	Santiago	103.1	98.1	99.0	-	93.7	5
GA03)	Verin	90.7	98.4	106.4	-	94.1	1
GA06)	Vigo	-	-	-	-	96.0	5
GA04)	Xistral	89.5	96.3	104.2	-	106.6	1
Madrid							
MA01)	Navacerrada	104.9	98.8	95.8	-	-	30
MA01)	Torrespaña	88.2	96.5	93.2	-	90.3	10
Murcia							
MU01)	Carrascoy	101.7	98.2	96.0	-	92.1	5
MU02)	Cartagena	102.9	94.5	97.5	-	103.5	1
MU01)	Jumilla	89.1	93.1	100.1	-	-	1
MU01)	Yecla	88.8	93.4	103.7	-	-	1
Navarra							
NA01)	Estella	89.0	101.2	100.5	-	90.9	1
NA01)	Gorramendi	88.3	99.0	100.6	-	95.3	1
NA01)	Ibañeta	89.6	93.8	103.4	-	101.9	1
NA01)	Isaba	90.3	95.1	103.0	-	91.8	1
NA01)	Leire	88.9	101.0	99.6	-	90.5	1
NA01)	Lesaka	90.6	94.8	97.0	-	102.2	1
NA01)	Monreal	106.1	97.5	93.0	-	95.7	5
NA01)	Pamplona	104.8	97.1	102.3	-	103.7	
NA01)	San Miguel	96.7	100.0	90.3	-	102.7	1
NA01)	Tudela	100.9	102.2	91.3	-	88.3	1
La Rioja							
RI01)	Logroño	95.4	88.1	89.9	-	97.2	1
RI01)	Moncalvillo	102.0	88.5	94.6	-	103.3	40
RI01)	Monte Yerga	87.6	106.8	96.5	-	105.4	1
Comunitat Valenciana							
VA02)	Aitana	104.8	88.6	99.7	-	-	10
VA02)	Alcoi	95.8	92.3	91.1	-	105.9	1
VA02)	Alicante	105.2	99.4	97.1	-	103.6	

FM	Location	RNE1	RNE2	RNE3	RNE4	RNE5	kW
VA03)	Benicasim	89.3	90.3	92.8	-	95.5	5
VA02)	Benidorm	87.6	97.8	102.1	-	-	
VA02)	Elda	93.9	88.1	97.6	-	-	1
VA01)	Monduber	97.4	99.3	100.1	-	-	5
VA01)	Monte Picayo	89.8	106.6	95.1	-	88.2	10
VA01)	Ontinyent	100.7	96.7	102.4	-	-	1
VA02)	Santa Pola	92.5	100.1	94.3	-	104.2	5
VA02)	Santa Pola	-	-	-	-	105.8	5
VA01)	Utiel	98.1	96.6	89.1	-	87.9	1
VA02)	Villena	90.7	97.1	101.1	-	-	1

RNE1 R. Nacional: (MW and FM): 24h. N: On the h. Regional prgrs from key stn of each region: Mon-Fri 0625-0630, 0650-0700 (//RNE5), 1210-1300, Sat & Sun 1230 –1300 (//RNE5),– RNE2 R.Clasica: (FM): Classical music & cultural prgrs: 24h. – RNE3: (FM): Young people's music prgr: 24h. – RNE4: (FM): Regional network in Catalunya: 24h. in Catalán. – RNE5: (MW and FM): Informacion -All news: : 24h. Regional: 0625-0630 (//RN), Regional: 0650-0700 (//RN), Local: 0745-0800, Regional: 0805-0810, Local 0830-0845, Regional: 1125-1130, Regional 1210-1200 (//RN), Regional 1830-1900. Sat & Sun 0805-0815, 1230-1300 (//RN).

Addresses for RNE regional key stns:
AN Andalucia: Edif.RTVE, Parque del Alamillo, Isla de la Cartuja,41092 Sevilla – **AR Aragón:** José Luís Albareda 1-3, 50004 Zaragoza – **AS Asturias:** Calle San Esteban de las Cruces 92, 33195 Oviedo – **BA Balears:** Aragó 26, 07006 Palma de Mallorca – **CA Catalunya:** C. Roc Boronat 127, 08018 Barcelona – **CL Castilla y León:** García Morato 27-29, 47007 Valladolid – **CM Castilla La Mancha:** Plaza de San Cristóbal s/n, 45002 Toledo – **CT Cantabria:** Polígono de Raos s/n, 39609 Camargo (Santander) – **EU Euskadi:** Plaza de Simón Bolívar 13, 01003 Vitoria-Gasteiz – **EX Extremadura:** Av. Ruta de la Plata 10, 10001 Cáceres – **GA Galicia:** Paseo Méndez Nuñez 12, 15006 A Coruña – **MA Madrid:** Casa de la Radio, Prado del Rey, 28223 Pozuelo de Alarcón – **MU Murcia:** La Olma 27-29, 30005 Murcia – **NA Navarra:** Calle Aoiz, 31004 Pamplona-Iruñea – **RI La Rioja:** Vara de Rey 42, 26002 Logroño – **VA Comunitat Valenciana:** Av.Colóm 13, 46004 València

OTHER STATIONS
Only stns with MW broadcasts and FM networks are listed. A number of other stns are heard irr. There are approx. 2,400 FM stns.

NATIONAL NETWORKS:
(COPE) CADENA DE ONDAS POPULARES ESPANOLAS (Comm)
✉ Alfonso XI N° 4, 28014 Madrid ☎ +34 91-3090000 ▤ +34 91-5317517 **W:** www.cope.es **E:** programas.madrid@cadenacope.net
Local and regional prgr on AM and FM stns: Mon-Fri 0555, 0624, 0650, 0724, 1809-1859, generally at xx27 and xx57 1700, 1930, 2030, 2130, 2230, 2255, 2357. Sat xx27 and xx57 0757-1400, 1557, 1657, 1810, 1840, 1910, 1940, 2040, 2257, 2330. Sun xx27 and xx57 0957-1300, xx10 and xx40 1510-1840, 2157, 2330 **(C100)Cadena 100** (music on FM only) **W:** www.cadena100.es **E:** jplane@cadena100.es **W sts list :** www.cadena100.es/emisoras.php **Gestiona Radio** (business prgr on FM only) **W:** www.gestionaradio.com **(MEGA) MegaStar FM** (music on FM only) **W:** http://megastar.fm (start in Sept.2013)
(D) CADENA DIAL (Comm) Part of Grupo Prisa
✉ Gran Vía 32, 28013 Madrid ☎ +34 91-3470880 ▤ +34 91-5211753 **W:** www.cadenadial.com **E:** ccampillo@cadenadial.com **W sts list:** www.cadenadial.com/nosotros/emisoras
(EFM) EUROPA FM (Comm) Part of Grupo Antena 3
✉ Fuerteventura 12, 28703 San Sebastian de los Reyes ☎+34 91-4366400 ▤+34 91-4366116 **W:** www.europafm.com **W stn list:** www.europafm.com/frecuencias
(ES) esRADIO (Comm)
✉ C/ Juan Esplandiú 13, 28007 Madrid **W:** www.esradio.fm ☎+34 91-4094766 ▤+34 91- 4094899 **W stn list:** www.esradio.fm/escuchenos.html
(LOCA) LOCA RADIO ESPAÑA (Comm) Part of RTL Group France
✉ C/ Enrique Larreta 12 bajo izq., 28036 Madrid **W:** www.locafm.com **E:** contacto@locaradio.es ☎+34 90-2302024
(HFM) Hit FM (Comm) Part of Grupo KISS Media
✉ José Isbert 6, Ciudad de la Imagen - 28223 Pozuelo de Alarcón **W:** www.hitfm.es
(IE) INTERECONOMÍA (Comm)
✉ Modesto Lafuente 42, 28003 Madrid. **W:** www.intereconomia.com **E:** redaccion@intereconomia.com ☎ +34 90-2996556 ▤+34 91- 5771314
(KFM) KISS FM (Comm)
✉ José Isbert 6, Ciudad de la Imagen - 28223 Pozuelo de Alarcón **W:** www.kissfm.es **E:** kissfm@kissfm.es **W st.list:** www.kissfm.es/contacta-kiss ☎+34 91-4440490 ▤+34 91-8379189

(L40) Los 40 Principales (Comm) Part of Grupo Prisa
Gran Vía 32, 7ª planta, 28013 Madrid **W:** www.los40.com **E:** los40@los40.com ☎ +34 91-3477700 ▤ +34 91-5228693
(MFM) MAXIMA FM (Comm) Part of Grupo Prisa
C/ Gran Vía 32, 7ª planta, 28013 Madrid **W:** www.maxima.fm **E:** ADSanchez@prisaradio.com ☎+34 91-3477624 ▤+34 91-5325808- Dir.: Toni Sánchez
(M80) M-80 RADIO (Comm) Part of Grupo Prisa
Gran Vía 32, 7ª planta, 28013 Madrid **W:** www.m80radio.com **E:** aalvarez@m80radio.com **W st list:** www.m80radio.com/emisoras/ciudad/ ☎ +34 91-3477700 ▤ +34 91-5228693 Dir.: Angel Alvarez
(OCR) ONDA CERO RADIO (Comm)
C/ Fuerteventura 12, 28703 San Sebastián de los Reyes, Madrid ☎ +34 91-4366400 ▤ +34 91-5386332 **W:** www.ondacero.es **E:** ondacero@ondacero.es **W st list:** www.ondacero.es/frecuencias **Prgrs:**. Onda Melodia. Local and regional programming on AM stations: Mon-Fri 0527, 0555, 0620, 0655, 0720, 0827, 0855, 0927, 0955, 1025, 1130, 1400, 1527, 1557, 1627, 1657, 1727, 1757, 1800, 2030, 2130, 2230, 2257, 2340, 0030. Sat-Sun 0527, 0727, 0757, 0827, 0857, 0927, 0957, 1027, 1227, 1457, 1850, 2255, 2320, 2340. Times vary.
(RA) RADIO TELEVISION AMISTAD (Rlg)
Apartado 269, 08211 Castellar del Vallés (Barcelona) ▤+34 93-7242380 **W:** www.rtvamistad.net **E:** info@rtvamistad.tv
(RKM) RKM RADIO (Rlg)
Carretera de Ajalvir a Daganzo km 1.7, Ajalvir, 28864 Madrid ☎ +34 91- 8844180 **W:** www.rkmradio.com **E:** madrid@rkmradio.com
(RM) RADIO MARIA (Rlg)
Paseo de Lanceros 2 (Centro Comercial), Planta 1ª, 28024 Madrid ☎+34 90-2500518 ▤ +34 91-7057727 **W:** www.radiomaria.es **E:** radiomaria@radiomaria.es
(RMA) RADIO MARCA (Comm)
AvenidadeSanLuís25,28033Madrid☎+3490- 2996111**W:** www. marca.com **E:** radiomarca@radiomarca.com Dir.: Francisco Garcia Caridad
(RO) Radiolé (Comm) Part of Grupo Prisa
Gran Vía 32, 7ª planta, 28013 Madrid ☎ +34 91-3477740 ▤ +34 91-5324769 **W:** www.radiole.com **W st list:** www.radiole.com/emisoras **E:** direccion@radiole.com Dir.: Miguel Ángel Corral Salas
(ROCK) ROCK FM (Comm) Part of Grupo COPE
Alfonso XI N° 4, 28014 Madrid ☎ +34 91-5951210 ▤ +34 91-3090721 **W:** www.rockfm.fm **W st list:** www.rockfm.fm/noticia.php5?id=641
(SER) SOCIEDAD ESPANOLA DE RADIODIFUSION (Comm) Part of Grupo Prisa
Gran Vía 32, 7ª planta, 28013 Madrid ☎ +34 91-3477700 ▤ +34 91-3470779 **W:** www.cadenaser.com **W st list:** www.cadenaser.com/emisoras **E:** redaccion@cadenaser.com **FM** stns Local and regional prgr AM stns: Mon-Fri 0550, 0620, 0650, 0720, 0827, 0855, 0930, 0957, 1003, 1030, 1057, 1120, 1410, 1530, 1630, 1720, 1810-1855, 1925, 2157, 2255, 2330, 0000, 0030, 0159, 0259. Sat-Sun 0750, 0855, 0955, 1055, 1105 and xx23 or xx53 in the evening. Times vary

REGIONAL NETWORKS:
(AR) ARAGÓN RADIO
María Zambrano 2, 50018 Zaragoza. ☎ +34 876-256500 ▤ +34 876-256519 **W:** www.aragonradio.es **E:** jmartinez@cartv.es Dir. Mktg : Javier Martinez López
(CR) CORPORACIO CATALANA DE MITJANS AUDIOVISUALS
Av. Diagonal 614-616, 08021 Barcelona ☎ +34 93-3069200 ▤ +34 93-3069201 **W:** www.catradio.cat **E:** catradio.com **Prgrs:** Catalunya Ràdio; Catalunya Informació; Catalunya Música
(CER) CANAL EXTREMADURA RADIO
Av. de las Américas 1, 1°, 06800 Mérida (Badajoz) ☎ +34 924-382000 **W:** http://radio.canalextremadura.es **E:** cexma@canalextremadura.es
(CLR) CASTILLA LEON RADIO
Calle Manuel Canesi Acevedo 1, ES-47016 Valladolid ☎ +34 98 3131313 ▤ +34 98 3131314 **W:** www.puntoradiocyl.com **E:** puntoradiocyl@edigrup.es
(CSR) CANAL SUR RADIO
Carretera Edificio Canal Sur. Avda. José Gálvez 1, 41092 Isla de la Cartuja, Sevilla ☎ +34 95-5054600 ▤ +34 95- 5054740 **W:** www.canalsur.es **E:** comunicacion@rtva.es Prgrs: Canal Fiesta: (Int. music and Spanish pop and rock music); Canal Sur Radio: (Andalucian and Spanish music, news and sports); Radio Andalucía Información.
(EI) EUSKA IRRATI TELEBISTA – RADIO TELEVISIÓN VASCA
EiTB Donostia: Paseo Miramon 122, 20014 Donostia-San Sebastián ☎ +34 94-30116 00 ▤ +34 94-301 1995 – EiTB Bilbao: Capuchinos de Basurto 2, 48013 Bilbo-Bilbao ☎ +34 94-6563000 ▤ +34 94-6563095 – EiTB Vitoria: Domingo Martinez de Aragón, 5-7 bajo, 01006 Vitoria-Gasteiz ☎ +34 94-5012500 ▤ +34 94-5012695

– EiTB Iruña: Calle Tomás Caballero 2, 31005 Pamplona-Iruña ☎ +34 94-8012200 ▤ +34 94-8153485.**Prgrs:** Euskadi Irratia (AM + FM), R. Euskadi (AM + FM), R. Vitoria (AM + FM), EiTB Músika (FM), Gaztea Irratia (FM) **W:** www.eitb.com **E :** info@eitb.com
(GR) GRUP FLAIX (Comm)
Passeig de Gràcia 55, novena planta, 08007 Barcelona ☎ +34 93-5055555 ▤ +34 93-4880776
Prgs: Flaix FM and Flaixbac **W:** www.flaixfm.cat and www.radioflaix-bac.com **E :** flaixfm@grupflaix.cat and flaixbac@grupflaix.cat
(IB3) IB3 RADIO C/ Manuel Azaña 7-A, 07006 Palma de Mallorca ☎ +34 971-139931 ▤ +34 971-139930 **W:** http://ib3tv.com/portada-radio **E :** info@eprtvib.com
(OC) ONA CATALANA (Comm) Part of Grupo Prisa
C/ Casp 6, 08010 Barcelona ☎ +34 93-3441400**W:** www.onafm.cat **E :** info@onafm.cat
(OM) ONDA MADRID
Paseo del Príncipe 3, 28223 Pozuelo de Alarcón (Madrid) ☎ +34 91-5128200 ▤ +34 91-5128300
W: www.ondamadrid.es **E :** ondamadrid@ondamadrid.es
(ORM) ONDA REGIONAL MURCIA
Avda. Libertad 6, 30009 Murcia ☎+34 968-200000 ▤+34 968-272665 **W:** www.orm.es **E :** info@orm.es
(RAC) RAC (Comm) Belong Grupo Godò
Av. Diagonal 477, Planta 15, 08036 Barcelona ☎+34 93-2704400 ▤+34 93-2704464 **Prgrs:** RAC1 and RAC 105 **W:** www.rac1.cat and www.rac105.cat **E :** rac1@rac1.net and rac105@rac105.net
(RCM) RADIO CASTILLA-LA MANCHA
Edificio RTVCM, C/ Río Alberche s/n, Polígono Santa María de Benquerencia, 45007 Toledo. ☎ +34 925-288600 ▤ +34 925-288607**W:** www.rtvsm.es **E:** comercial@rtvcm.es
(RCL) RADIO CASTILLA Y LEÓN
Edificio Promecal Burgos, Avenida Castilla y León 62-64, 09006 Burgos ☎ +34 947-266868 ▤ +34 947-202752 **W:** www.rtvcyl.es **E :** burgos@rtvcyl.es
(RE) RADIO ESTEL (Rlg)
Comtes de Bell-lloc 67-69, 08014 Barcelona ☎ +34 93-4092770 ▤ +34 93-4092775 **W:** www.radioestel.com **E :** estudis@radioestel.com Dir.: Jaume Aymar
(RG) RADIO GALEGA – COMPAÑÍA DE RADIO TELEVISION DE GALICIA
Casa da Radio, Edificio de Usos Múltiples San Marcos, 15820 Santiago de Compostela ☎ +34 981-540640 ▤ +34 981-540949 **W:** www.crtvg.es/rg **E :** info@crtvg.es
(RP) RADIO POPULAR - HERRI IRRATIA
Alameda Mazarredo 47, 48009 Bilbo-Bilbao ☎+34 94-4239200 ▤+34 94-4234703 **W:** www.radiopopular.com **E:** direccion@radio-popular.com
(RPA) RADIO DEL PRINCIPADO DE ASTURIAS
Camino de las Clarisas 263, 33203 Gijón ☎+34 985-185900 ▤ +34 985-185939 **W:** www.rtpa.es/radio **E :** comunicacion@rtpa.es
(RTT) RADIO TELE TAXI (Comm)
C/ Sant Carles 40, 08922 Sta Coloma de Gramenet (Barcelona) ☎+34 93-4665656 ▤ +34 93-4661534 **W:** www.radioteletaxi.com **E:** radioteletaxi@radioteletaxi.com
(RV) RADIO VOZ
Av. De la Prensa 84-85, Arteixo, 15142 A Coruña ☎ +34 981-180600 ▤ +34 981-180477 **W:** www.radiovoz.com **E:** director@radiovoz.com
(XAR) La XARXA (Comm)
Travessera de les Corts 131-159, 08028 Barcelona ☎ +34 93-5080600 **W:** www.xarxaradio.cat **E:** laxarxa@laxarxa.com

MW	kHzkW	Net	Rg	Station, location	FM (MHz)
CA07	540 50	OCR	CA	Onda Cero Catal., Barcelona	93.5
CA08	666 50	SER	CA	R. Barcelona, Barcelona	93.9
MU05	711 5	COPE	MU	COPE, Murcia	89.7
CA09	783 50	COPE	CA	COPE Catalunya i Andorra, Barcelona	
AN15	792 50	SER	AN	R. Sevilla, Sevilla	97.1
MA05	810 20	SER	MA	R. Madrid, Madrid	93.9
CA13	828 5	HFM	CA	HIT FM Catalunya, Terrassa	95.5
AN16	837 10	COPE	AN	COPE, Sevilla	99.6
CL15	837 10	COPE	CL	COPE, Burgos	95.5
GA09	837 5	COPE	GA	COPE, El Ferrol	88.7
AR05	873 25	SER	AR	R. Zaragoza, Zaragoza	95.3
GA10	873 10	SER	GA	R. Galicia, Stgo de Comp.	90
VA07	882 10	COPE	VA	COPE, Alacant-Alicante	95.6
AN17	882 5	COPE	AN	COPE, Málaga	89.4
AS05	882 5	COPE	AS	COPE, Gijón	103.6
CL16	882 5	COPE	CL	COPE, Valladolid	88.5
EU10	900 10	RP	EU	R. Popular, Bilbo-Bilbao	97.8

MW	kHz	kW	Net	Rg	Station, location	FM (MHz)
AN18)	900	5	COPE	AN	COPE, Granada	88.2
GA11)	900	5	COPE	GA	COPE, Vigo	87.8
MA06)	918	20	IE	MA	R. Inter, Madrid	95.1
MA13)	954	50	OCR	MA	Onda Cero R., Madrid	98.0
EU11)	990	10	SER	EU	R. Bilbao, Bilbo-Bilbao	89.5
AN19)	990	5	SER	AN	R. Cádiz, Cádiz	89.4
MA08)	999	50	COPE	MA	COPE, Madrid	99.5
CA11)	1008	10	SER	CA	R. Girona, Girona	98.5
EX06)	1008	5	SER	EX	R. Extremadura, Badajoz	96.9
VA08)	1008	5	SER	VA	R. Alacant, Alacant-Alicante	91.0
CA12)	1026	10	SER	CA	R. Reus, Reus	97.7
AS06)	1026	5	SER	AS	R. Asturias, Oviedo	97.5
GA12)	1026	5	SER	GA	R. Vigo, Vigo	99.4
AN20)	1026	5	SER	AN	R. Jaén, Jaén	96.9
AN21)	1026	5	SER	AN	R. Jerez, J. de la Frontera	97.8
CL17)	1026	5	SER	CL	R. Salamanca, Salamanca	96.9
EU12)	1044	10	SER	EU	R. San Sebastián, Donosti-S Se	97.2
CL18)	1044	5	SER	CL	R. Valladolid, Valladolid	90.9
AR06)	1053	25	COPE	AR	COPE, Zaragoza	88.5
VA09)	1053	5	COPE	VA	COPE, Vila-Real	91.7
AN22)	1080	10	SER	AN	R. Granada, Granada	95.4
AR07)	1080	10	SER	AR	R. Huesca, Huesca	96.9
BA06)	1080	5	SER	BA	R. Mallorca, P. de Mallorca	94.1
CM11)	1080	5	OCR	CM	Onda Cero R., Toledo	100.8
GA13)	1080	5	SER	GA	R. Coruña, A Coruña	91.0
CM12)	1116	5	SER	CM	R. Albacete, Albacete	89.6
GA14)	1116	5	SER	GA	R. Pontevedra, Pontevedra	89.1
CL19)	1134	10	COPE	CL	COPE, Salamanca	90.0
AN23)	1134	5	COPE	AN	COPE, Jerez de la Frontera	92.4
BA07)	1134	5	COPE	BA	COPE, Ciutadella	89.6
CL20)	1134	5	COPE	CL	COPE, Astorga	87.6
CM13)	1134	5	COPE	CM	COPE, Puertollano	97.5
NA05)	1134	5	COPE	NA	COPE, Pamplona-Iruñea	87.9
AN24)	1143	5	COPE	AN	COPE, Jaén	88.8
CA14)	1143	5	COPE	CA	COPE, Reus	89.7
GA15)	1143	5	COPE	GA	COPE, Ourense	92.4
VA10)	1179	50	SER	VA	R. Valéncia, València	94.2
RI05)	1179	2	SER	RI	R. Rioja, Logroño	91.7
AN25)	1215	5	COPE	AN	COPE, Córdoba	87.6
CL21)	1215	5	COPE	CL	COPE, León	97.7
CT05)	1215	5	COPE	CT	COPE Cantabria, Santander	88.4
MU06)	1215	5	COPE	MU	COPE, Lorca	89.2
AN26)	1224	5	COPE	AN	COPE, Huelva	91.9
AN27)	1224	5	COPE	AN	COPE, Almería	97.1
BA08)	1224	5	COPE	BA	COPE, Palma de Mallorca	97.6
CA15)	1224	5	COPE	CA	COPE, Lleida	97.4
CM14)	1224	5	COPE	CM	COPE, Albacete	95.4
AN28)	1260	5	SER	AN	R. Algeciras, Algeciras	95.7
MU07)	1260	5	SER	MU	R. Murcia, Murcia	91.3
CM15)	1269	10	COPE	CM	COPE, Ciudad Real	93.6
CL22)	1269	5	COPE	CL	COPE, Zamora	94.9
EX07)	1269	5	COPE	EX	COPE, Badajoz	89.1
CA17)	1287	10	SER	CA	R. Lleida, Lleida	93.4
CL23)	1287	5	SER	CL	R. Castilla, Burgos	89.1
GA17)	1287	5	SER	GA	R. Lugo, Lugo	91.8
VA11)	1296	50	COPE	VA	COPE, València	99.0
AN29)	1341	10	OCR	AN	Onda Cero R., Almería	93.8
CL24)	1341	5	SER	CL	R. León, León	88.2
CM16)	1341	5	OCR	CM	Onda Cero R., Ciudad Real	92.1
CL25)	1485	10	SER	CL	R. Zamora, Zamora	89.8
CT06)	1485	10	SER	CT	R. Santander, Santander	90.9
VA12)	1485	5	SER	VA	R. Alcoi, Alcoi	96.3
VA13)	1521	5	SER	VA	R. Castelló, Castelló	94.8
VA14)	1539	6	SER	VA	R. Elche - R. Elx, Elx	99.1
CA19)	1539	5	SER	CA	R. Manresa, Manresa	95.8
NA06)	1575	10	SER	NA	R. Pamplona, Pamplona	92.2
AN31)	1575	5	SER	AN	R. Córdoba, Córdoba	96.6
GA18)	1584	5	SER	GA	R. Ourense, Ourense	87.6
VA15)	1584	5	SER	VA	R. Gandia, Gandia	96.5
AN32)	1602	5	SER	AN	R. Linares, Linares	94.9
CL26)	1602	5	SER	CL	R. Segovia, Segovia	93.6
MU08)	1602	5	SER	MU	R. Cartagena, Cartagena	102.3
VA16)	1602	5	SER	VA	R. Ontinyent, Ontinyent	95.3

‡ = inactive

FM	MHz	kW	Net	Rg	Station, location
AN41)	87.6	5	CSR	AN	Canal Sur R., Santo Pitar,Málaga
AN35)	87.7	6	HIT	AN	HIT FM, Jerez de Frontera
CA34)	87.7	20	RAC	CA	RAC1, Barcelona Collserola
AN36)	87.9	5	SER	AN	R. Morón, Morón de la Frontera ,Sevilla
CA37)	88.0	25	CR	CA	Catalunya R., La Mussara, Tarragona

FM	MHz	kW	Net	Rg	Station, location
EU25)	88.0	5		EU	R. Nervión, Bilbao
AN37)	88.3	5	CSR	AN	Canal Fiesta R., Algeciras
CA25)	88.4	5	CR	CA	Catalunya R., Montcaro, Tortosa
CA25)	88.6	20	CR	CA	Catalunya Música, Soriguera, Lleida
CA35)	88.7	10		CA	R. RM, Barcelona Collserola
AN70)	88.8	40		AN	Stereo Vision, Sevilla
CA38)	88.9	25	CR	CA	Catalunya R., Rocacorba, Girona
EU07)	88.9	20	EI	EU	Euskadi Irratia, Bilbo-Bilbao
MU17)	88.9	5	RMA	MU	R,Marca, Murcia
MA05)	89.0	20	M80	MA	M80, Madrid
CA07)	89.1	8	RMA	CA	R,Marca,. Barcelona Collserola
EU10)	89.2	5	ROCK	VA	ROCKFM. Bilbo-Bilbao
EU26)	89.2	5		EU	Segura Irratia, Segura, Vitoria
GA29)	89.2	8	RMA	GA	R. Marca, A Coruña
VA21)	89.2	8	KFM	VA	Kiss FM, Alacant-Alicante
NA11)	89.3	6	KFM	NA	Kiss FM, Pamplona
GA28)	89.4	6	RA	GA	Ondas de Vida, R. Amistad, Vigo
MU14)	89.4	6	COPE	MU	COPE, Cartagena
AN42)	89.5	20	CSR	AN	Canal Fiesta R., Huelva
BA11)	89.5	8	KFM	BA	Kiss FM, Palma de Mallorca
EX11)	89.5	6	KFM	EX	Kiss FM, Cáceres
AR13)	89.7	40	ROCK	AR	ROCKFM.Zaragoza
AN43)	89.8	8	CSR	AN	RAI R.Andalucía Informacion, Granada
CA09)	89.8	10	ROCK	CA	ROCKFM., Barcelona Collserola
AS03)	89.8	8	RPA	AS	RPA, R.Principado Asturias, Gijón
CA36)	89.9	10	ROCK	CA	ROCKFM., Rocacorba, Girona
VA08)	90.0	8	MFM	VA	Maxima FM, Alicante
AN38)	90.1	8	KFM	AN	Kiss FM, Málaga
VA30)	90.1	5		VA	Peque V., Valencia
CA25)	90.2	10	CR	CA	Catalunya R., Sant Celoni, Barcelona
AN35)	90.3	6	OCR	AN	Onda Cero R., Jerez de la Frontera
EX12)	90.4	5	OCR	EX	Onda Cero Melodía, Mérida
AN57)	90.5	70	CSR	AN	RAI R.Andalucía Informacion, Almería
CA08)	90.5	8	M80	CA	M80, Barcelona Collserola
CL31)	90.5	5	SER	CL	SER R. Miranda, Miranda de Ebro Burgos
AN39)	90.8	5	SER	AN	SER R. Puerto, El Puerto de S.M., Cadiz
AN38)	90.8	10	OCR	AN	Onda Cero R., Málaga
AN59)	90.8	64	CSR	AN	RAI R.Andalucía Informacion, Sevilla
GA29)	90.8	5	RG	GA	R. Galega Música, Vigo
EU09)	90.9	20	EI	EU	R. Euskadi, Vitoria
MA11)	91.0	100	EFM	MA	Europa FM, Madrid
AS06)	91.1	6	D	AS	Cadena Dial Asturias, Oviedo
RI02)	91.1	6	COPE	RI	COPE Rioja, Logroño
EU07)	91.2	20	EI	EU	Euskadi Gaztea, Bilbo-Bilbao
CM08)	91.3	5	RCM	CM	R. Castilla-La Mancha, Guadalajara
AR04)	91.4	40	HIT	AR	HIT FM, Zaragoza
EX13)	91.4	10	SER	EX	Los 40, Plasencia
AN40)	91.4	8	EFM	AN	Europa FM, Córdoba
CL27)	91.5	8	KFM	CL	Kiss FM, Astorga
EU21)	91.5	8	KFM	EU	Kiss FM, Donosti-San Sebastián
EX05)	91.6	6	COPE	EX	COPE, Cáceres
VA17)	91.6	10	EFM	VA	Europa FM, La RIbera València
EU07)	91.7	20	EI	EU	R. Euskadi, Bilbo-Bilbao
MA05)	91.7	100	D	MA	Cadena Dial, Madrid
CL40)	91.7	5	KFM	CL	Kiss FM, Salamanca
VA08)	91.7	8	SER	VA	SER R. Alicante, Alicante
CA25)	91.9	15	CR	CA	Catalunya Música, Alpicat, Lleida
CA34)	91.9	10	RAC	CA	RAC105, Rocacorba, Girona
CM08)	91.9	5	RCM	CM	R. Castilla-La Mancha, Toledo
CT11)	91.9	10	OCR	CT	Onda Cero R., Santander
AR05)	92.0	40	MFM	AR	Máxima FM, Zaragoza
CA25)	92.0	100	CR	CA	Catalunya Informació, Barcelona Collserola
VA29)	92.0	10	MEGA	VA	MegaStar FM , València
EU10)	92.2	24	RP	EU	Popular Irratia Bilbo-Bilbao
MA05)	92.4	14	SER	MA	Radiolé, Madrid
CA25)	92.5	100	CR	CA	Catalunya R. Barcelona Collserola
EX08)	92.6	8	SER	EX	Los 40, Cáceres
GA21)	92.6	8	RV	GA	R. Voz, A Coruña
CM21)	92.8	8	KFM	CM	Kiss FM, Albacete
AN22)	92.8	8	D	AN	Cadena Dial, Granada
VA18)	92.8	8	EFM	VA	Europa FM, Elx-Elche
CL34)	92.9	6	CLR	CL	Castilla Leon R ., Burgos
AN43)	93.1	5	CSR	AN	Canal Fiesta R. Baza, Granada
AN72)	93.1	8	D	AN	Cadena Dial, Málaga
EU18)	93.1	8		EU	R.Gorbea, Vitoria-Gasteiz
GA22)	93.1	5	RV	GA	R. Voz,. Pontevedra
VA11)	93.1	5	ROCK	VA	ROCK FM, València
AN73)	93.2	5	ROCK	VA	ROCKFM , Sevilla
VA08)	93.2	8	D	VA	Cadena Dial, Alicante
CA25)	93.3	5	CR	BA	Catalunya R., Alfabia, Palma M.

FM	MHz	kW	Net	Rg	Station, location
GA13)	93.4	8	SER	GA	SER R. Coruña, A Coruña
CA30)	93.4	5	SER	CA	SER, R. LLeida
AR05)	93.5	8	SER	AR	R. Zaragoza 2, Zaragoza
CA25)	93.5	20	OCR	CA	Onda Cero R., Collserola Barcelona
AN47)	93.8	5	EFM	AN	Europa FM, Almería
AN72)	93.8	5	RO	AN	Radiolé, Málaga
MA05)	93.9	100	SER	MA	Los 40, Madrid
CA08)	93.9	8	SER	CA	Los 40, Collserola Barcelona
AN42)	94.0	10	CSR	AN	Canal Sur R., Huelva
GA23)	94.0	6	OCR	GA	Kiss FM, Vigo
GA07)	94.1	20	RG	GA	R. Galega, Santiago de Compostela
AN12)	94.2	5	ROCK	AN	ROCKFM ., Jaén
CT03)	94.2	6	RMA	CT	R. Marca, Santander
AN59)	94.3	20	CSR	AN	RAI R.Andalucía Informacion., Sevilla
AN55)	94.3	10	CSR	AN	Canal Sur R., Córdoba
CL23)	94.3	6	D	CL	Cadena Dial, Burgos
CA11)	94.4	10	MFM	CA	Maxima FM,. Girona, Rocacorba
CL39)	94.4	8	EFM	CL	Europa FM, Valladolid
EU08)	94.4	2	EI	EU	Euskadi Irratia,Donosti-S Sebastián
EX08)	94.4	4	SER	EX	SER, Cáceres
CA25)	94.5	5	CR	CA	Catalunya Informació, Collsuspina Barcelona
AN43)	94.6	5	CSR	AN	Canal Fiesta R., Loja,Granada
EU07)	94.7	20	EI	EU	Euskadi Gaztea, Bilbo-Bilbao
AN15)	94.8	40	M80	AN	M80, Sevilla
AN41)	94.9	60	CSR	AN	RAI R.Andalucía Informacion. Málaga
CA07)	94.9	20	EFM	CA	Europa FM, Collserola Barcelona
CM10)	95.0	6		CM	R. Surco, Albacete
EU09)	95.0	20	EI	EU	Euskadi Irratia, Vitoria-Gasteiz
AN43)	95.1	5	CSR	AN	Canal Sur R., Granada
CA11)	95.1	10	D	MA	Cadena Dial Girona, Rocacorba
MA17)	95.1	100	IE	MA	R. Inter, Madrid
AS08)	95.2	6	OCR	AS	Onda Cero R., Oviedo
AR05)	95.3	13	SER	AR	Los 40, Zaragoza
CA31)	95.3	5	OCR	CA	Onda Cero R., Tarragona
AS03)	95.4	10	RPA	AS	RPA,R.Principado Asturias, Boal
AN44)	95.4	8	KFM	AN	Kiss FM, Cádiz
AN52)	95.6	8	KFM	AN	Kiss FM, Córdoba
BA02)	95.8	5		BA	Insel R., Mallorca
CA28)	95.8	20	KFM	CA	Kiss FM, Barcelona
AN45)	95.9	40	OCR	AN	Onda Cero R., Sevilla
CA32)	95.9	5	RTT	VA	R. Tele Taxi, Benicassim, Valencia
CA08)	96.0	20	RO	CA	Radiolé, Collserola Barcelona
MA02)	96.0	20	FUN	MA	FUN RADIO Madrid
RI03)	96.0	6	KFM	RI	Kiss FM, Logroño
EU04)	96.1	20	EI	EU	Euskadi Gaztea, Zaldiaran
VA10)	96.1	10	M80	VA	M80, València
CL32)	96.2	6	OCR	CL	Europa FM, Salamanca
AN67)	96.2	6	D	AN	Cadena Dial Almería, Almería
AN33)	96.3	8	OCR	AN	Onda Melodía, Malaga
MU03)	96.3	5	AMC	MU	R. 5, Cartagena
CM12)	96.4	6	RO	CM	Radiolé, Albacete
EU08)	96.5	20	EI	EU	R. Euskadi, Donosti-San Sebastián
AS09)	96.5	8	SER	AS	R. Gijón, Gijón
VA22)	96.5	8	R9	VA	R. Nou, Alacant-Alicante
CL35)	96.5	5	KFM	CL	Kiss FM, León
AN43)	96.6	5	CSR	AN	Canal Sur R., Loja, Granada
GA08)	96.6	6	RG	GA	R. Galega Música, Friol
CA25)	96.7	25	CR	CA	Catalunya Música, Girona, Rocacorba
MU11)	96.7	6	KFM	MU	Kiss FM, Cartagena
AN22)	96.8	3	RO	AN	Radiolé, Madrid
VA25)	96.9	20	KFM	VA	Kiss FM, València
CA08)	96.9	8	SER	CA	R. Barcelona 2, Collserola Barcelona
MA16)	96.9	20	RM	MA	R. María España, Madrid
EX08)	97.0	6	D	EX	Cadena Dial, Cáceres
AN15)	97.1	40	SER	AN	Los 40, . Sevilla
AN43)	97.1	30	CSR	AN	Canal Fiesta R., Granada
AR05)	97.1	40	D	AR	CadenaDial Zaragoza, Zaragoza
CL23)	97.1	6	SER	CL	R. Castilla, Burgos
MU04)	97.1	5		MU	Onda Mediterranea R., Cartagena
MA07)	97.2	100		MA	Top Radio Latina , Madrid
CA25)	97.3	10	CR	CA	Catalunya R., Montserrat Barcelona
EU05)	97.3	8	C100	EU	Cadena 100, Vitoria-Gasteiz
EU06)	97.3	5		EU	Fórmula Hit, Portugalete, Gipuzcoa
VA 05)	97.3	8	OCR	VA	Onda Melodía, Altea.Alicante
CA11)	97.4	10	ONA	CA	FM, Figueres, Girona
AR06)	97.5	40	COPE	AR	COPE, Zaragoza
GA13)	97.6	8	M80	GA	M80, A Coruña
MA18)	97.6	4	OCR	MA	Onda Cero R., Alcalá de Henares, Madrid
CL32)	97.6	6	OCR	CL	Onda Cero R., Salamanca
CA32)	97.7	20	RTT	CA	R. Tele Taxi, Collserola Barcelona
VA27)	97.7	20	VA	LA	97 Punto 7, València
EU10)	92.2	24	RP	EU	Popular Irratia Bilbo-Bilbao
AN48)	97.9	30	CSR	AN	Canal Fiesta R., Jaén
AR06)	97.9	40	C100	AR	Cadena 100, Zaragoza
AN13)	98.0	30	COPE	AN	COPE, Alanis, Sevilla
EU13)	98.0	8	MEGA	EU	MegaStar FM, Donosti-San Sebastián
EU15)	98.0	8		EU	R. Álava,Onda Vasca, Vitoria-Gasteiz
MA13)	98.0	100	OCR	MA	Onda Cero R., Madrid
AN49)	98.1	5	SER	AN	R. Huelva, Huelva
CL18)	98.1	8	MFM	CL	Maxima FM, Valladolid
EX03)	98.1	5	CER	EX	Canal Extremadura R., Zafra, Badajoz
VA07)	98.1	10	ROCK	VA	ROCK FM, Alicante
RI04)	98.2	8	MEGA	RI	MegaStar FM, Logroño
CA25)	98.3	10	CR	CA	Catalunya Informació, Montserrat Barcelona
CM25)	98.3	5	KFM	CM	Kiss FM, Toledo
NA02)	98.3	6		NA	98.3 R., Pamplona
BA06)	98.4	5	MFM	BA	Maxima FM, Alfábia, Palma M.
VA10)	98.4	20	D	VA	Cadena Dial Mediterraneo, València
CA25)	98.5	5	CR	CA	Catalunya Informació, Montcaro, Tortosa
CA40)	98.5	10	SER	CA	SER, Girona
CT11)	98.5	5	KFM	CT	Kiss FM, Santander
CM22)	98.5	5	OCR	CM	Onda Cero R., Talavera de la Reina, Toledo
AR05)	98.6	40	M80	AR	M80, Zaragoza
CL36)	98.6	8		CL	R. Arlanzón, Burgos
CM08)	98.6	5	RCM	CM	R. Castilla-La Mancha, Valdepeñas, Ciudad Real
EU11)	98.8	5	M80	EU	M80, Bilbao
MU17)	98.8	6	RMA	MU	Solo R. R, Marca , Cartagena
BA16)	98.8	5	ROCK	BA	ROCK FM, Ultima Hora., Palma de Mallorca
CA22)	98.9	10	OCR	CA	Onda Cero R., Rocacorba Girona
VA26)	98.9	5	COPE	VA	COPE, R.Sirena, Benidorm
VA11)	99.0	40	C100	VA	Cadena 100, València
CL42)	99.1	5	KFM	CL	Kiss FM, Zamora
EU04)	99.1	5		EU	Euskadi Gaztea Vitoria-Gasteiz
MA03)	99.1	10	ES	MA	esRadio, Madrid
CL17)	99.3	6	D	CL	Cadena Dial, Salamanca
MU09)	99.3	8	KFM	MU	Kiss FM, Murcia
AN74)	99.4	30	CSR	AN	RAI R. Andalucía Informacion., Cádiz
AN55)	99.4	60	CSR	AN	RAI R. Andalucía Informacion., Córdoba
AR12)	99.4	40	OCR	AR	Onda Cero R., Zaragoza
CA08)	99.4	10	D	CA	Cadena Dial Barcelona, Barcelona
CL33)	99.4	8	KFM	CL	Kiss FM, Valladolid
AN51)	99.5	8	EFM	AN	Europa FM, Granada
MA08)	99.5	100	C100	MA	Cadena 100, Madrid
CA05)	99.6	10	GR	CA	Flaix FM, Girona, Rocacorba
CA25)	99.7	5	CR	CA	Catalunya R., Collsuspina, Barcelona
MA04)	99.8	10		MA	R. Sol XXI, Madrid
AN19)	99.8	8	D	AN	Cadena Dial Bahía, Cádiz
BA18)	99.9	8	RM	BA	R. Maria, Palma de Mallorca
AS03)	100.0	8	RPA	AS	R.Principado Asturias, Los Oscos
CA09)	100.0	20	C100	CA	Cadena 100, Collserola Barcelona
CA25)	100.1	10	CR	CA	Catalunya R., Girona, Rocacorba
EU07)	100.1	20	EI	EU	EITB IrratiaMusika, Bilbo-Bilbao
CA25)	100.2	35	CR	CA	Catalunya R., La Mussara,Tarragona
GA08)	100.2	5	RG	GA	R. Galega Música, Xistral
AN58)	100.3	40	KFM	AN	Kiss FM, Sevilla
CM12)	100.3	5	SER	CM	SER Albacete
AN72)	100.4	8	SER	AN	SER, Málaga
CL18)	100.4	8	D	CL	Cadena Dial, Valladolid
EU22)	100.4	5	SER	EU	Los 40, Vitoria-Gasteiz
MA09)	100.4	5		MA	R. Círculo, Madrid
VA10)	100.4	20	SER	VA	R. Valencia 2, Valencia
AR12)	100.5	10	EFM	AR	Europa FM, Zaragoza
AS03)	100.5	20	RPA	AS	R.Principado Asturias, Gijón
CA25)	100.5	5	CR	CA	Catalunya Música, Collsuspina, Barcelona
CM08)	100.5	5	RCM	CM	R. Castilla-La Mancha, Guadalajara
CM23)	100.5	5		CM	R. Santa María, Toledo
GA12)	100.6	8	SER	GA	SER. Vigo 2, Vigo
AN48)	100.6	30	CSR	AN	Canal Sur R., Jaén
BA16)	100.6	5	GR	BA	Flaix FM, Mallorca
GA08)	100.6	5	RG	GA	R. Galega Música, Monte Páramo
CA25)	100.7	80	CR	CA	Catalunya R., Alpicat, Lleida
CA05)	100.7	10	GR	CA	Flaixbac FM, Girona, Rocacorba
MA08)	100.7	20	MEGA	MA	MegaStar FM, Madrid
AN55)	100.8	5	CSR	AN	Canal Sur R., Córdoba
EX03)	100.8	5	CER	EX	Canal Extremadura R., Badajoz
VA19)	100.8	5	COPE	VA	COPE,Elche
GA24)	100.9	30	RG	GA	R. Galega, Xesteiras, Pontevedra
BA11)	101.0	5	OCR	BA	Onda Melodía Mallorca
CA34)	101.0	5	RAC	CA	Catalunya R., Mont Caro, Tortosa

FM	MHz	kW	Net	Rg	Station, location
EU05	101.0	8	COPE	EU	COPE, Vitoria
AN72	101.1	10	M80	AN	M80, Málaga
CT06	101.1	6	M80	CT	M80, Santander
VA23	101.2	20	OCR	VA	Onda Cero R., València
AN56	101.2	5	OCR	AN	Onda Cero R., Huelva
GA12	101.2	6	M80	GA	M80, Vigo
MA14	101.3	100		MA	Onda Madrid, Madrid
AN55	101.3	30	CSR	AN	Canal Fiesta R., Córdoba
AN43	101.3	5	CSR	AN	RAI R.Andalucía Informacion Loja, Granada
AS03	101.4	10	RPA	AS	R.Principado Asturias, Avilés
RI02	101.4	6	COPE	RI	Cadena 100, Logroño
AN15	101.5	40	SER	AN	Radiolé, Sevilla
CA25	101.5	8	CR	CA	Catalunya Música, Collserola Barcelona
EU07	101.5	24	OCR	EU	Onda Cero R., Bilbo-Bilbao
AN53	101.6	5	EFM	AN	Europa FM Costa del Sol, Mijas, Malaga
CM08	101.6	5	CLR	CM	Castilla Leon R, Cuenca
CA38	101.7	25	CR	CA	Catalunya Informació, Girona, Rocacorba
AN67	101.8	6	SER	AN	Los 40, Almería
CA06	101.8	5	GR	CA	Flaix FM, Tarragona
AN59	101.8	60	CSR	AN	Canal Fiesta R., Sevilla
EU04	101.9	8	EI	EU	Euskadi Irratia, Amurrio,Alava
GA30	101.9	6	RMA	GA	R. Marca, Vigo
AN14	102.0	8	COPE	AN	COPE, Cádiz
CA09	102.0	20	COPE	CA	COPE, Barcelona
CA25	102.2	25	CR	CA	Catalunya R, Girona, Rocacorba
AN42	102.2	30	CSR	AN	Canal Fiesta R., Huelva
BA06	102.3	4	M80	BA	M80 Mallorca, Palma de Mallorca
CA42	102.3	10	FUN	CA	FUN RADIO, Barcelona
GA25	102.3	40	RG	GA	R. Galega, Domaio
AN68	102.4	40	D	AN	Cadena Dial Sevilla, Sevilla
CA25	102.4	10	CR	CA	Catalunya Música, Montserrat, Barcelona
CT06	102.4	6	SER	CT	SER, Liérganes, Santander
EU28	102.4	6	OCR	EU	Onda Cero R., Vitoria
AN57	102.5	70	CSR	AN	Canal Fiesta R., Almería, Pechina
CA25	102.5	10	CR	CA	Catalunya Música, Mont Caro, Tortosa
CM08	102.5	12	RCM	CM	R. Castilla-La Mancha, Ciudad Real
EU29	102.5	8	OCR	EU	Onda Cero R., Donosti-San Sebastián
AN22	102.5	8	D	AN	Cadena Dial, Granada
EX03	102.6	60	CER	EX	Canal Extremadura R., Montánchez
EU23	102.6	15	COPE	EU	Bizkaia Irratia, Bilbo-Bilbao
MA13	102.7	100	KFM	MA	Kiss FM, Madrid
GA26	102.8	8	ES	GA	esRADIO,.A Coruña
AN72	102.8	8	SER	AN	Los 40,, Mijas, Málaga
CA25	102.8	100	CR	CA	Catalunya Música, Collserola Barcelona
CL43	102.8	8	CLR	CL	Castilla Leon R,, Valladolid
BA15	102.8	5	SER	BA	SER Ibiza, Ibiza
VA32	102.8	90	R9	VA	Sí R., Benicassim
AN71	103.1	5		AN	R. Pinomar, Málaga
AN15	103.2	28	SER	AN	SER Sevilla 2, Sevilla
EU07	103.2	20	EI	EU	R. Euskadi, Bilbo-Bilbao
MA22	103.2	5		MA	RTC - Radio TV Cristiana, Madrid
VA23	103.2	10	EFM	VA	Europa FM, València
AN22	103.3	8	MFM	AN	Maxima FM, Granada
CA29	103.4	10	RE	CA	R. Estel, Girona, Rocacorba
CL37	103.4	6	CLR	CL	Castilla Leon R, Salamanca
CM08	103.4	5	RCM	CM	R. Castilla-La Mancha, Puertollano, Ciudad Real
EU09	103.4	20	EI	EU	EITB Musika, Vitoria-Gasteiz
AN43	103.5	60	CSR	AN	Canal Sur R., Sierra de Lújar, Córdoba
CA08	103.5	20	SER	CA	Ona FM, ., Collserola Barcelona
EU08	103.5	20	EI	EU	Euskadi Gaztea,Donosti-S. Sebastián
AN55	103.6	30	CSR	AN	Canal Sur R., Córdoba
EU30	103.7	24	ROCK	EU	ROCK FM , Bilbo-Bilbao
GA08	103.7	70	RG	GA	R.Galega, Monte Páramo
GA30	103.8	6	RV	GA	R. Voz, Vigo
AN59	103.9	30	CSR	AN	Canal Fiesta R., Sevilla, Valencina
GA25	103.9	40	RG	GA	R. Galega, Monte Faro
MA05	103.9	30		MA	Ke Buena FM, Madrid
MU07	103.9	8	D	MU	Cadena Dial, Murcia, Murcia
CM08	104.0	10	RCM	CM	R. Castilla-La Mancha, Chinchilla, Albacete
EX03	104.0	5	CER	EX	Canal Extremadura R., Cáceres
AN24	104.1	5	ROCK	AN	ROCK FM, Córdoba
AN63	104.1	6	KFM	AN	Kiss FM, Almería
EU09	104.1	20	EI	EU	R. Vitoria/Gasteiz Irratia, Vitoria-Gasteiz
AN43	104.2	8	CSR	AN	Canal Sur R., Granada
AS11	104.2	5		AS	R. Amistad, Hevia-Siero, Gijón
CA08	104.2	37	SER	CA	Máxima FM, Collserola Barcelona
GA31	104.2	5	RG	GA	R. Galega Música, Santiago de Compostela
MA05	104.3	37	MFM	MA	Máxima FM, Madrid
AN42	104.4	30	CSR	AN	Canal Sur R., Huelva
EU07	104.4	20	EI	EU	Euskadi Irratia, Bilbo-Bilbao
CA25	104.5	2	CR	CA	Catalunya Informació, La Mussara, Tarragona
AN41	104.6	30	CSR	AN	Canal Sur R., Málaga
AN59	104.6	60	CSR	AN	RAI R.Andalucía Informacion, Sevilla
MU16	104.6	6	ORM	MU	Onda Regional Murcia, Cartagena
VA20	104.7	5	LOCA	VA	LOCA RADIO, Elx
GA12	104.7	6	MFM	GA	Máxima FM, Vigo
AN37	104.8	30	CSR	AN	Canal Sur R., Jerez de la Frontera
AN37	104.8	20	CSR	AN	Canal Sur R., Almería
AR14	104.8	10	RKM	AR	RKM, Zaragoza
EU31	104.8	5	RKM	EU	RKM, Vitoria-Gasteiz
GA25	104.8	40	RG	GA	R. Galega, Monte Meda
AN43	104.9	30	CSR	AN	Canal Sur R., Granada
EU23	104.9	8	EI	EU	Euskadi Gaztea, Amurrio
CA34	105.0	20	RAC	CA	RAC105, Collserola Barcelona
AN59	105.1	30	CSR	AN	Canal Sur R., Sevilla
CA32	105.1	10	RTT	CA	R. Tele Taxi, Girona, Rocacorba
MA10	105.1	5		MA	Super Q FM , Madrid
BA18	105.2	30	RM	BA	R. Maria, Alfabia, Palma M.
CL39	105.2	8	OCR	CL	Onda Cero R., Valladolid
MU16	105.3	60	ORM	MU	Onda Regional, Murcia
AS03	105.4	8	RPA	AS	R.Principado Asturias, Oviedo
CA25	105.4	20	CR	CA	Catalunya Música, La Mussara, Tarragona
MA05	105.4	100	SER	MA	SER Madrid 2, Madrid
AN55	105.5	6	CSR	AN	Canal Fiesta R. Cabra, Cordoba
CL38	105.5	6	KFM	CL	Kiss FM, Burgos
AN60	105.6	16	CSR	AN	Canal Sur R., Algeciras
EU32	105.6	8	C100	EU	Cadena 100,, Vitoria-Gasteiz
CA41	105.7	20	GR	CA	Flaix FM, Collserola Barcelona
AR12	105.8	40	KFM	AR	Kiss FM, Zaragoza
AN41	105.8	30	CSR	AN	Canal Fiesta R., Málaga
MA14	106.0	30		MA	Onda Madrid R., Madrid
AN55	106.1	6	CSR	AN	RAI R.Andalucía Información, Cabra, Cordoba
BA06	106.1	8	D	BA	Cadena Dial, Palma de Mallorca
CA41	106.1	20	GR	CA	Faixbac FM, Collserola Barcelona
GA27	106.1	6	RV	GA	R. Voz, Santiago de Compostela
EU33	106.2	8	C100	EU	CADENA100,, Donosti-San Sebastián
MA08	106.3	10	COPE	MA	COPE , Madrid
AS03	106.4	60	RPA	AS	R.Principado Asturias, Gamoniteiro
VA28	106.5	5	OCR	VA	Onda Cero Alicante, Alicante
AN76	106.9	20	RMA	AN	R. Marca, Sevilla
CA29	106.6	20	RE	CA	R. Estel, Collserola Barcelona
EU34	106.7	8	KFM	EU	Kiss FM, Vitoria-Gasteiz
BA09	106.8	100	IB3	BA	IB3, Alfábia, Palma M.
CA04	106.8	10	EFM	CA	Europa FM, Girona, Rocacorba
CA43	106.9	5		CA	RKB, R. Kanal Barcelona
MU18	106.9	8	ROCK	MU	ROCK FM , Murcia
MA27	107.0	2		MA	Libertad FM, Madrid
AN65	107.1	5		AN	R. Guadalate, Bornos, Jerez de la F.
MA20	107.2	15		MA	Fiesta FM, Madrid
CA20	107.9	15	RA	CA	R. Amistad,Barcelona.Turó d'en Fotjà

NB: stns less than 5kW omitted

Addresses and other information:
AN00) ANDALUCIA

AN01) Edif.RTVE, Parque del Alamillo, 41092 Sevilla. – **AN02)** Góngora 3, 14002 Córdoba. – **AN03)** Av.Ricardo Soriano 11, 29600 Marbella. – **AN04)** Av.de Granada 57, P1, 23001 Jaén. – **AN05)** Hermanos Machado 23, 04004 Almería. – **AN06)** Av.de la Aurora 40, 29006 Málaga. – **AN07)** Av.de Andalucía 67, 11007 Cádiz. – **AN08)** Plaza Carretas 5, 18009 Granada. – **AN09)** Plaza de Europa s/n, 11300 La Línea de la Concepción. – **AN10)** La Fuente 4, 21004 Huelva. – **AN11)** Cervantes 11, 14940 Cabra. – **AN12)** C/ Bartolomé 32 bajo, 23001 Jaén. – **AN13)** C/ Triana 8, 41380 Alanis. – **AN14)** C/ Algeciras 1, 2° módulo 8 "Edificio Fenicia", 11011 Cádiz. – **AN15)** Rafael González Abreu 6, 41001 Sevilla **E:** radiosevilla@cadenaser.com – **AN16)** Rioja 4, 41001 Sevilla. **E:** sevilla@cadenacope.net – **AN17)** Linaje 2, 29001 Málaga **E:** malaga@cadenacope.net – **AN18)** Gran Vía de Colón 28, 18001 Granada **E:** granada@cadenacope.net – **AN19)** Paseo Marítimo 1, Edif.Reina Victoria, 11010 Cádiz **E:** sercadiz@cadenaser.com – **AN20)** Obispo Aguilar 1, 23001 Jaén. **W:** www.radiojaen.com – **AN21)** Guadalete 12, 11403 Jerez de la Frontera. **W:** www.radiojerez.com – **AN22)** Santa Paula 2 (or: Ap.158), 18001 Granada **W:** www.radio-granada.es **E:** radiogranada@radiogranada.es – **AN23)** San Agustín 11 (or: Ap.364), 11403 Jerez de la Frontera **E:** jerez@cadenacope.net – **AN24)** Federico Mendizábal 10, 23001 Jaén **E:** jaen@cadenacope.net – **AN25)** Plaza Cardenal Toledo 4, 14001 Córdoba **E:** cordoba@cadenacope.net – **AN26)** José María Amoz 2, 21001 Huelva **E:** huelva@cadenacope.net – **AN27)** Padre Luque 11, 04001 Almería. **E:** almeria@cadenacope.net – **AN28)** General Castaños 2, 11201 Algeciras. **E:** radioalgeciras@unionradio.es – **AN29)** Av.Federico García Lorca 105, 04005 Almería. – **AN30)** San Agustín 4, 29200 Antequera. – **AN31)** García Lovera 3, 14002 Córdoba. **W:** www.radiocordoba.com –**AN32)**

Plaza Ramón y Cajal 8, 23700 Linares **E:** radiolinares@unionradio.es – **AN33)** C/ Peregrinos 3 "Edif. Galaxia 2º" Puerta 7, 29002 Málaga **AN35)** Gaitan 10, 11402 Jerez de la Frontera. – **AN36)** Pozo Nuevo 40 bajo, 41530 Morón de la Frontera. – **AN37)** C/ Carpinteros de Ribera 2, 11007-Cádiz. – **AN38)** C/ Peregrinos 3 "Edif. Galaxia 2º" Puerta 7, 29002 Málaga. – **AN39)** Misericordia 10, 11500 Puerto de Santa María. – **AN40)** C/ Doctor Manuel Ruiz Maya 8,5º, 14004 Córdoba – **AN41)** Avenida Velazquez 307, 29004 Malaga – **AN42)** Carretera Huelva-San Juan del Puerto, km. 6,36. 21007 Huelva. – **AN43)** Urb. Bola de Oro, C/ Laguna de Aguas Verdes 11, 18008 Granada. – **AN44)** C/ Dr. Manuel Ruíz Maya 8, 11004 Cádiz. – **AN45)** Pabellón Once, Isla de Cartuja, 41092 Sevilla. – **AN46)** Plaza de España 15, 11006 Cádiz. – **AN47)** Avenida Federico García Lorca 105, 04005 Almería. – **AN48)** Prolongación Av. De Granada s/n, Recinto Institución Ferial, 23009 Jaén. – **AN49)** Mendez Nuñez 15-5-6, 21001 Huelva. – **AN50)** Corredera 53, 11402 Jerez de la Frontera. – **AN51)** Recogidas 37, 18005 Granada. – **AN52)** Barroso 4-2, 14003 Córdoba. – **AN53)** C/ Ramón Gómez de la Serna 22 "Edificio King Edward II", 29600 Marbella. –**AN55)** Glorieta de Guadalhorce s/n, "Antigua Estación de RENFE", 14008 Córdoba. – **AN56)** Arquitecto Pérez Carasa 14-16, 21001 Huelva. – **AN57)** Centro Residencial Oliveros, C/ Maestro Serrano 9, 2º-B, 04004 Almería. — – **AN58)** Sevilla. – **AN59)** Edificio Canal Sur, Av. José Gálvez 1, 41092 Isla de la Cartuja (Sevilla). – **AN60)** C/ Patriaca Pérez Rodríguez 36, 11201 Algeciras. – **AN61)** Placentines 2, 41004 Sevilla. – **AN62)** Av.de la Borbolla 47, 41013 Sevilla. – **AN63)** Almería. – **AN65)** San Jerónimo 7, 11640 Bornos. –**AN67)** Av. Mediterráneo 159, 2º "Edificio Laura", 04007 Almería– **AN68)** Rafael Gonzáles Abreu 6, 41001 Sevilla. – **AN69)** C/ San Agustín 4, 29200 Antequera. –**AN70)** Pasaje Comercial, Gran Plaza Letra F, 41005 Sevilla **W:** www.ministeriosels-haddaisevilla.net – **AN71)** CL. Coín Parcela 1273, 29130 Alhaurín de la Torre (Málaga). – **AN72)** C/ Dr. Manuel Domínguez "Ed. Bulevar 2", 29001 Málaga. – **AN73)** Edificio de Oficinas del Estadio Olímpico, Isla de la Cartuja, 41092 Sevilla. – **AN74)** C/ Capinteros de Ribera 2, 11002 Cádiz. –**AN76)** Av. República Argentina 25-9º-B, 41011 Sevilla.

AR00) ARAGON
AR01) José Luís Albareda 1-3, 50004 Zaragoza. – **AR02)** Nueva 1, 44001 Teruel. – **AR03)** José Gil Caves 1, 22005 Huesca. **AR04)** Zaragoza. **W:** www.hitfm.es– **AR05)** Paseo de la Constitución 21, 50001 Zaragoza **E:** radiozaragoza@unionradio.es – **AR06)** Paseo de Sagasta 50 (or: Ap.42), 50006 Zaragoza. **E:** programas.zaragoza@ cadenacope.net – **AR07)** Calle Alcalde Carderera 1, 22080 Huesca. **W:** www.radiohuesca.com – **AR11)** Coso 46, 50004 Zaragoza. – **AR12)** Zaragoza. – **AR13)** Calle Bilbao, 2, 1ª planta, 50004 Zaragoza. – **AR14)** REMAR, Av. Cataluña 225, 50003 Zaragoza.

AS00) ASTURIAS
AS01) C/ San Esteban de las Cruces 92, 33195 Oviedo. – **AS02)** Plaza del Instituto 3, 33201 Gijón. – **AS03)** Camino de las Clarisas 263, 33203 Gijón. –**AS05)** Carr.de la Costa 87 (or: Ap.235), 33205 Gijón. – **AS06)** Asturias 19, Bajo, 33004 Oviedo. **W:** www. radioasturias. com – **AS07)** Prado Picón 16, 33008 Oviedo. **W:** www.copeasturias. com **E:** c-oviedo@arrakis.es **AS08)** C/ Cervantes 27, 5º,33003 Oviedo. – **AS09)** Jovellanos 1, 33202 Gijón. – **AS11)** C/ Lugar Orial 16, 33187 Hevia-Siero

BA00) BALEARES
BA01) Aragó 26, 07006 Palma de Mallorca. – **BA02)** Paseo Marítimo 26, 07014 Palma de Mallorca. – **BA03)** C/ Font i Monteros 21, 07003 Palma de Mallorca**. – BA05)** Felip II Nº 28, 07800 Eivissa **E:** ibiza@ cadenacope.net – **BA06)** Rector Bertomeu Martorell 35, Son Xigala, 07013 Palma de Mallorca **E:** informativos.mallorca@cadenaser.com – **BA07)** Av.Negrete 3, 07760 Ciutadela **W:** www.telyse.net/cope-menorca **E:** menorca@cadenacope.net – **BA08)** Av.Jaume III Nº 18, 07012 Palma de Mallorca **E:** mallorca@cadenacope.net **BA09)** C/ Manuel Azaña 7-A, 07006 Palma de Mallorca. – **BA11)** Forners 7, Edif.Once, 07002 Palma de Mallorca. – **BA13)** Menacor 171, 07007 Palma de Mallorca. **BA15)** Avenida Sant Jordi s/n, 07800 Figueretes (Ibiza). – **BA16)** C/ Gremi Selleters i Basters 14, "Polígon Son Castelló", 07009 Palma de Mallorca. – **BA18)** Mallorca.

CA00) CATALUNYA
CA01) C. Roc Boronat 127, 08018 Barcelona. – **CA02)** Carrer Lluis Companys 1, 25003 Lleida. – **CA03)** Rambla Nova 23, 43003 Tarragona. – **CA04)** Gran Vía Jaume I Nº 60, 17001 Girona. E-mail: emisora.girne@rtve.es – **CA05)** Av. Jaume I 76, 17002 Girona. – **CA06)** Plaça del Pati 2, entlo, 43800 Valls – **CA07)** Av. Diagonal 460, 3º, 08006-Barcelona **W:** www.radiomarcabarcelona.com **E:** info@radiomarcabarcelona.com – **CA08)** Casp 6, 08010 Barcelona. **E:** radiobarcelona@unionradio.es **W:** www.radiobarcelona.cat – **CA09)** Diputació 238, 08013 Barcelona **W:** www.fm/copebarcelona **E:** barcelona@cadenacope.net – **CA10)** Travessera de les Corts 131-159, Recinte Martenitat, Pavello Cambo, 08028 Barcelona **W:** www.comradio.com – **CA11)** Placa Josep Pla 2, 17001 Girona. **E:** radiogirona@ unionradio.es – **CA12)** Tomàs Bergadà 3, 43204 Reus **E:** radioreus@

unionradio.es – **CA13)** Carrer de Aragón 390-394, 2a planta, 08013 Barcelona – **CA14)** Llovera 54-56, 43204 Reus **E:** reus@cadenacope. net – **CA15)** Acadèmia 14, 25002 Lleida. **W:** www.copelleida.com **E:** lerida@cadenacope.net – **CA16)** Sèquia 3, 17001 Girona **E:** girona@ cadenacope.net – **CA17)** Vila Antònia 5, 25007 Lleida **E:** lleida@ cadenaser.com – **CA18)** Relay Onda Rambla Barcelona (Local adress: Rambla Nova 69, 43003 Tarragona) – **CA19)** Calle Nou 47, 08240 Manresa **E:** informatius@els40.com – **CA20)** Apartado 269, 08211 Castellar del Vallès – **CA21)** Avda. Diagonal 441, 1º, 08006-Barcelona – **CA22)**Avda. Jaume I, 37, 7é 2a, 17001 Girona – **CA25)** El Palau Nou, Ramblas 88-94, 4ª, 08002-Barcelona **CA25)** Av Diagonal 614-616, 08021 Barcelona. **E:** info@catradio.cat – **W:** www.catradio.cat – **CA27)** Bulidor s/n, Polígono Industrial 1, 08960 St Just D (Barcelona) – **CA28)** Aragó 390-394, P2, 08013 Barcelona. **E:** onamusica@onaca-taluna.com – **CA29)** C/ Comtes de Bell-lloc 67-69, 08014 Barcelona **E:** radioestel@radioesteI.com – **CA30)** Del Riu 6, 25007 Lleida. – **CA31)** Rambla Nova 38, 43004 Tarragona – **CA32)** C/ Sant Carles 40, 08922 Sta Coloma de Gramenet (Barcelona). – **CA34)** Av. Diagonal 477, 15ª, 08006 Barcelona. – **CA35)** Camí Real 551, 1º, 08302 Mataró. – **CA36)** Rambla de la Llibertat 6, 17004 Girona. – **CA37)** C/ Ramón y Cajal 36, 3º, 43001 Tarragona. – **CA38)** Carretera de Barcelona 33, 4º, 17001 Girona. – **CA39)** Rambla d'Arago 43, 1º, 25003 Lleida.– **CA40)** Gran via de Jaume I 29-2º, 17001 Girona. – **CA41)** Paseo de Gràcia 55-57, 9º, 08007 Barcelona. – **CA42)** Barcelona. **W:** www.facebook. com/Locafuncatalunya – **CA43)** Gran vía de les Corts Catalanes 645, 2º-1, 08007 Barcelona.

CL00) CASTILLA Y LEÓN
CL01) García Morato 27-29, 47007 Valladolid. – **CL02)** Becerro de Bengoa 9, 34002 Palencia. – **CL03)** Santa Clara 2, 05001 Avila. – **CL04)** Ordoño II Nº 28, 24001 León. – **CL05)** Campo 5, 42001 Soria. – **CL06)** Calle Barrio Gimeno 11, 09004 Burgos. – **CL07)** Av.de Requejo 21, 49012 Zamora. – **CL08)** Ave María 11, (or Apartado de Correos 105, 24480 Ponferrada) 24400 Ponferrada – **CL09)** Plaza de Colón 4, 37001 Salamanca. – **CL10)** Paseo Ezequiel Gonzales 24, 40002 Segovia. – **CL15)** Av.del Cid 8, 09005 Burgos **E:** informativos.burgos@cadenaser.net – **CL16)** Duque de la Victoria 23, 47001 Valladolid **E:** direccion.valladolid@cadenacope.net – **CL17)** C/ Veracruz 2 bajo, 37008 Salamanca **W:** www.radiosalamanca. com – **CL18)** C/ La Estación 3, 47004 Valladolid **E:** radiovalladolid@ cadenaser.com – **CL19)** Sol Oriente 11-15, 37002 Salamanca **E:** salamanca@cadenacope.net – **CL20)** Hermanos La Salle 2, 24700 Astorga **E:** astorga@cadenacope.net – **CL21)** Lope de Vega 1, 24002 León **W:** www.copeleon.net **E:** leon@cadenacope.net – **CL22)** Plaza Fernández Duró 3 (or: Ap.42), 49001 Zamora **E:** zamora@cadenacope. net – **CL23)** Plaza de España 3, 09005 Burgos **E:** radiocastilla.redaccion@unionradio.es – **CL24)** Villafranca 6, 24001 León **W:** www. radioleon.net **E:** radioleon@radioleon.com – **CL25)** Calle Santa Ana 6, 49006 Zamora **E:** radioz@teleline.es – **CL26)** Plaza Cirilo Rodríguez 2, 40001 Segovia **W:** www.radiosegovia.com – **CL27)** Astorga. – **CL31)** Vitoria 24, 09200 Miranda de Ebro. – **CL32)** Bermejeros 14, 37001 Salamanca. – **CL33)** Rastrojo 5, 47014 Valladolid. – **CL34)** Plaza de Aragón 5, 09001 Burgos. – **CL35)** Julio del Campo 4-6, 24002 León. – **CL36)** Plaza de los Vadillos 5, 09005 Burgos. **W:** www. radioarlanzon.com – **CL37)** Aliso 2 bajo, 37004 Salamanca. – **CL38)** Burgos. – **CL39)** Edif.Promecal, c/los Astros s/n, 47009 Valladolid. **CL40)** Salamanca. – **CL41)** Valladolid. – **CL42)** Zamora. – **CL43)** C/ Manuel Canesi Acevedo 1, 4706 Valladolid.

CM00) CASTILLA-LA MANCHA
CM01) Paseo de San Cristóbal s/n, 45002 Toledo. – **CM02)** Ramiro Ledesma 8, 13630 Socuéllamos. – **CM03)** Nuestra. Sra. De Araceli 1, Edif.Las Torres, 02002 Albacete. – **CM04)** Radio Nacional de España 2 (or: Ap.18), 16003 Cuenca. – **CM05)** Ronda del Carmen s/n (or: Ap.150), 13002 Ciudad Real **E:** emisora.cr.rne@rtve.es – **CM06)** Plaza de Consejo, Centro Civico, 19001 Guadalajara. – **CM07)** Ronda del Canillo 35, 45600 Talavera de la Reina. – **CM08)** Polígono Santa María de Benquerencia, C/ Río Alberche s/n, 45007 Toledo. – **CM10)** C/ Gaona 8 , 4º-B, 02001 Albacete. – **CM11)** www.radiosurco.es – **CM12)** Avenida de la Estación 5, 02001 Albacete. **E:** radioalbacete@ unionradio.es – **CM13)** Alejandro Prieto 2, 13500 Puertollano **E:** puertollano@cadenacope.net – **CM14)** Tesifonte Gallego 9, 02002 Albacete: albacete@cadenacope.net – **CM15)** Pasaje San Isidro 3, 13001 Ciudad Real **E:** ciudadreal@cadenacope.net – **CM21)** Av.de la Estación 5, 02001 Albacete. – **CM22)** C/ Joaquina Santander 13, 1º, 45600 Talavera de la Reina. – **CM23)** Calle Trinidad 12, 45002 Toledo. **W:** www.rtvd.org/radio.htm **E:** rtvdiocesana@planalfa.es – **CM24)** 02001 Albacete. – **CM25)** Toledo.

CT00) CANTABRIA
CT01) Polígono de Raos s/n, 39609 Camargo (Santander) – **CT02)** Av.del Besaya 1 (or: Ap.46), 39300 Torrelavega – **CT03)** C/ José María Pereda 23, 39100 Santa Cruz de Bezana. - **CT05)** Rualasal 5, 39001 Santander **E:** santander@cadenacope.net – **CT06)** Pasaje de la Peña

2, int 7, Edif.Simeon 39008 Santander **W**: www.radiosantander.com **E**: informativos@radiosantander.com – **CT11)** Fernandez de Isla 14,2°, 39008 Santander.
EU00) EUSKADI
EU01) Plaza de Simón Bolívar 13, 01003 Vitoria-Gasteiz – **EU02)** Paseo de los Fueros 2, 20006 Donosti-San Sebastián **E**: emisora.ss.rne@the.es – **EU03)** Licenciado Poza 55, 48013 Bilbo-Bilbao. – C/ Polorínviejo 4, 01003 Vitroria-Gasteiz. – **EU04)** C/ Domingo Martínez de Aragón 5-9, 01006 Vitoria-Gasteiz. **W**: www.eitb.com/eu/gaztea – **EU05)** C/ San Antonio 2 bajo, 01005 Vitoria-Gasteiz. – **EU06)** C/ Alonso Allende 21, Lonja izquierda, 48920 Portugalete. – **EU07)** Capuchinos de Basurto 2, Edificio Bami, 48013 Bilbo-Bilbao **E**: radio_euskadi@eitb.com – **EU08)** Miramón 172, 20004 Donostia-San Sebastián **W**: www eitb.com/euskara/ – **EU09)** C/ Domingo Martínez de Aragón 5-9, 01006 Vitoria-Gasteiz **W**: www.eitb.com/radiovitoria – **EU10)** Calle Alameda Mazarredo 47,7°, 48009 Bilbo-Bilbao **W**: www.radiopopular.com – **EU11)** C/ Epalza 8, 48007 Bilbo-Bilbao **E**: radiobilbao@unionradio.es – **EU12)** Paseo Portuetxe 51, Edificio ACB, 20018 Donostia-San Sebastián **E**: radiosansebastian@cadenaser.com – **EU13)** Miracruz 9, 20001 Donostia-San Sebastián –**EU15)** C/Portal de Gamarra, 23. Pabellón A, 01002 Vitoria-Gasteiz . **W**: www.ondavasca.com – **EU17)** Vitoria-Gasteiz. – **EU20)** Bulevar de Beurko 4, local 2, 48902-Barakaldo. **EU18)** C/ La Habana 1, 01012 Vitoria **W**: www.radiogorbea.com **EU21)** Av.de la Libertad 17, 20004 -Donosti-San Sebastián – **EU22)** General Alava 10-6 Depto 9, 01005 Vitoria-Gasteiz – **EU23)** Fontecha y Salazar 9-5, 48007 Bilbo-Bilbao – **EU24)** Eziago Poligonoa 10B, 20120 Hernani. – **EU25)** C. Hurtado de Amezaga 27,17piso, 48008 Bilbo-Bilbao. – **EU26)** C/ Esteban Zurbano 20, 20214 Segura (Guipúzcoa). – **EU27)** Gordóniz 44, 12°, 48002 Bilbao. – **EU28)** C/ San Prudencio 8-A,, 5°, 01005 Vitoria-Gasteiz. – **EU29)** Paseo Federico García Lorca 10, 4°, Puerta 1-2, 20014 Donosti-San Sebastián. – **EU30)** Ribera de Elorrieta 7, 48015 Bilbo-Bilbao. – **EU31)** C/ José Lejarreta 11, 01003 Vitoria-Gasteiz. – **EU32)** C/ Portal de Legutiano 6, 01002 Vitoria-Gasteiz . **EU33)** Parque Empresarial Zuazu, Ed. Ulía 8, 20018 Donosti-San Sebastián. – **EU34)** Vitoria-Gasteiz.
EX00) EXTREMADURA
EX01) Av.Ruta de la Plata 10, 10001 Cáceres – **EX02)** Plaza de España 5, 06002 Badajoz. – **EX03)** Avenida de las Américas 1, 1°, 06800 Mérida. – **EX05)** C/ Comandante Sánchez Herrero 2, 1°, 10004 Cáceres **E**: caceres@cadenacope.net – **EX06)** Ramón Albarrán 2, 06002 Badajoz **E**: radioextremadura@unionradio.es – **EX07)** Menacho 12, 06001 Badajoz **E**: badajoz@cadenacope.net – **EX08)** C/ Profesor Rodríguez Moñino 1, 8°-A, 10003 Cáceres. - **EX11)** Av.de España 9-6, 10004 Cáceres – **EX12)** Av.de Portugal s/n, Ctro Comercial El Foro, 06800 Mérida – **EX13)** Santa Isabel 4, 10600 Plasencia – **EX16)** Luis Alvarez Lancero 8, 10001 Cáceres.
GA00) GALICIA
GA01) Paseo Méndes Nuñez 12, (or: Ap.199), 15006 A Coruña – **GA02)** Lepanto 7, 36001 Pontevedra – **GA03)** Rua de Progreso 115 (or: Ap.268), 32003 Ourense – **GA04)** Ourense 59-63 (or: Ap.73), 27004 Lugo – **GA05)** Plaza de España 4, 27400 Monforte de Lemos – **GA06)** Av.García Barbón 36, 36201 Vigo – **GA07)** San Marcos s/n, Edif.TVE, 15780 Santiago de Compostela. – **GA08)** Rúa Pascual Veiga 12-14 baixo dereita, 27002 Lugo. – **GA09)** Plaza de España 5-6, 15403 El Ferrol **E**: ferrol@cadenacope.net – **GA10)** San Pedro de Mezonzo 3 (or: Ap 469), 15701 Santiago de Compostela **E**: radiogalicia@unionradio.es – **GA11)** Principe 57, 36202 Vigo **E**: vigo@cadenacope.net – **GA12)** Areal 6-8, 36201 Vigo **W**: www.radiovigo.es – **GA13)** Plaza de Ourense 3, 15004 A Coruña **W**: www.radiocoruna.com – **GA14)** Castelao 3 B, 36001 Pontevedra **E**: ser@radiopontevedra.net – **GA15)** Rua de Progreso 89, 32003 Ourense **E**: orense@cadenacope.net – **GA16)** Rua de Valiño s/n, 27002 Lugo **E**: lugo@cadenacope.net – **GA17)** Plaza de Santo Domingo 3, 27001 Lugo **W**: www.radiolugo.com – **GA18)** Rua do Paseo 30 (or: Ap.1017), 32003 Ourense **W**: www.radioourense.com **E**: cadenaser@radioourense.com – **GA21)** Ronda de Outeiro, N°1 y 3 Bajo, 15006 A Coruña– **GA22)** Salvador Moreno 30, 36001 Pontevedra – **GA23)** Av.García Barbón 104, 36201 Vigo – **GA24)** Rúa Benito Corbal 14, 2°, 36001 Pontevedra – **GA25)** Casa de la Radio, San Marcos, 15820 Santiago de Compostela – **GA26)** . **W**: www.esradio.fm – **GA27)** Salguiriños de Arriba 44, bajo, 15890 Santiago de Compostela. – **GA28)** Apartado de Correos 3114, 36208 Vigo. **W** : www.ondasdevida.org - **GA29)** C/ Torreiro 13-15, 3°-E, 15005 A Coruña. – **GA30)** Av. García Barbón 28, 36201 Vigo. – **GA31)** Rúa Costa Rica 6, 7°, 15005 A Coruña.
MA00) MADRID
MA01) Casa de la Radio, Prado del Rey, 28223 Pozuelo de Alarcón – **MA02)** C/ Enrique Larreta 12, 28036 Madrid. – **MA03)** C/ Juan Esplandiú 15, 2ª, 28007 Madrid. – **MA04)** C/ San Bernardo 20, 3°, Centro, 28015 Madrid – **MA05)** Gran Vía 32, 28013 Madrid **E**: redaccion@cadenaser.com – **MA06)** Modesto Lafuente 42, 28003 Madrid

W: www.radiointer.com **E**: radiointer@radiointer.com – **MA07)** C/ Juan Esplandiú 15, 2ª, 28007 Madrid – **MA08)** Alfonso XI N° 4, 28014 Madrid **W**: www.cope.es **E**: programas.madrid@cadenacope.net – **MA09)** Círculo de Bellas Artes, C/ Alcalá 42, 5 planta, 28014 Madrid.– **MA10) W**: www.superqfm.es – **MA11)** Bueso Pineda 7, 28043 Madrid – **MA13)** José Isbert 6, Ciudad de la Imagen - 28223 Pozuelo de Alarcón **W**: www.kissfm.es **E**: kissfm@kissfm.es – **MA14)** Pso del Principe 3, Cd.de la Imagem, 28223 Pozuelo de Alarcón **W**: www.telemadrid.com – **MA16)** Av.de los Arqueros s/n, 28024 Madrid **E**: radiomaria@arsenet.com – **MA17)** Paseo de la Castellana 36-38, 28046 Madrid **W**: www.intereconomia.com – **MA18)** Sta Clara 7, 28801 Alcalá de Henares –**MA20)** C/ Juan Español 47, local bajo, 28026 Madrid. **W**: www.fiestafm.net. – **MA21)** C. Francisco Silvela 122 bajo, 28002 Madrid. –**MA22)** Calle de Secoya 29, Planta 3 Puerta 1, 28054 Madrid – **MA24)** C/ Orense 18, piso 8, of. 9, 28020 Madrid. **W**: www.rtcespana.es – **MA26)** Juan Ignacio Luca de Tena 7, 28027 Madrid. –**MA27)** Paseo de la Castellana 129, 1°-C, 28046-Madrid **W**: http://radiolibertad.com .
MU00) MURCIA
MU01) La Olma 27-29, 30005 Murcia **E**: emisora.mu.rne@rtve.es – **MU02)** Paseo Alfonso XIII N° 51, 30203 Cartagena. – **MU03)** C/ Bucarest 29, 30391 Cartagena. **MU04)** C/ Carmen Conde 46, 1°, 30203 Cartagena. – **MU05)** Arco de Santo Domingo 2-3, Edif.Fontanar, 30001 Murcia **E**: murcia@cadenacope.net – **MU06)** Av.Juan Carlos I N° 63, 30800 Lorca **E**: lorca@cadenacope.net – **MU07)** Calle Radio Murcia 4, 30001 Murcia **E**: radiomurcia@unionradio.es – **MU08)** Real 70, 30201 Cartagena **E**: informativos.cartagena@cadenaser.com – **MU09)** Murcia – **MU11)** Edif.Mediterráneo, Puerta Murcia 11, 30201 Cartagena – **MU12)** C/ Carmen 51, 1° A, 30201 Cartagena – **MU13)** Madre de Dios 15, 30004 Murcia – **MU14)** Mayor 31, 30280 Cartagena – **MU16)** Av.Libertad 6, bajo, 30009 Murcia. – **MU17)** Pza de los Apóstoles 7, 30001 Murcia. – **MU18)** Ed.del Periódico La Verdad, Camino Viejo de Monteagudo s/n, 30160 Murcia.
NA00) NAVARRA
NA01) Emilio Arrieta 8, P8, 31002 Pamplona-Iruñea **NA02)** Aoiz 17, 31004 Pamplona-Iruñea – **NA03)** Ed. Ciencias Sociales, Universidad de Navarra, Campus Universitario s/n, 31080 Pamplona.-Iruñea **W**: www.unav.es/98.3 – **NA05)** Amaya 2-B, 31002 Pamplona-Iruñea **E**: pamplona@cadenacope.net – **NA06)** Polígono Plazaola, Manzana F, 2° A, 31195 Aizoain (or Apartado de Correos 71, 31080 Pamplona) **E**: informativosnavarra@cadenaser.com – **NA11)** Plaza del Castillo 43, 31001 Pamplona-Iruñea – **NA12)** Cortes de Navarra 1, 31002 Pamplona-Iruñea.
RI00) LA RIOJA
RI01) Vara de Rey 42, (or: Ap.247), 26002 Logroño – **RI02)** Residencia Universitaria Francisco Jordán, Av. Madre de Dios 17, 26001 Logroño - **RI03)** C/ Estambrera 36, 1°, 26006 Logroño. – **RI04)** C/ General Vara del Rey 74, 26002 Logroño. – **RI05)** Av.de Portugal 12 (or: Ap.149), 26001 Logroño **W**: www.radiorioja.com – **RI11)** Logroño – **RI12)** Miguel Villanueva 2, Ofc.5, 26001 Logroño
VA00) CUMUNITAT VALENCIANA
VA01) Av Colóm 13, 46004 València – **VA02)** Angel Lozano 18, 03001 Alacant-Alicante – **VA03)** Passeig de la Ribalta 5, 12001 Castelló – **VA04)** Juan Carlos I 37, 03202 Elx. - **VA05)** Plaça dels Sports 7-8, Ed. Sabater, 03590 Altea – **VA07)** Rambla de Méndez Nuñez 45, 03002 Alacant-Alicante **E**: alicante@cadenacope.net – **VA08)** Calderón de la Barca 26, 03004 Alacant-Alicante **E**: alicante@cadenaser.com – **VA09)** Av.Francisco Tàrrega 69, 12540 Vila-Real **E**: castellon@cadenacope.net – **VA10)** Don Juan de Austria 3, 46002 València **E**: valencia@cadenaser.com – **VA11)** Passatge Dr.Sierra 2, 46004 València **W**: www.cope.es/valencia – **VA12)** Doctor Sempere 16B y C, Bajos, 03803 Alcoi **E**: radioalcoy@radioalcoy.com – **VA13)** Moyano 5, 12002 Castelló **W**: www.radiocastellon.comdc – **VA14)** Dr.Caro 43, 03201 Elx **W**: www.radioelche.com – **VA15)** Calle Loreto 32, 46700 Gandia **E**: ser@radiogandia.net – **VA16)** Ereta 2A (or: Ap.84), 46870 Ontinyent **W**: www.radioontinyent.com – **VA 17)** C/ Hort dels Frares 12, 46600 Alzira. – **VA18)** C/ Doctor Caro 18 entresuelo derecha, 03201 Elx. – **VA19)** C/ La Fira 10, 03202 Elx. **VA20)** C/ Almorida 2, 4° derecha, 03201 Elx. – **VA21)** Alacant-Alicante. **E** : alicante@kissfm.es – **VA23)** C/ San Vicente 16, entreplanta 1°, 46001 València – **VA24)** Av.Blasco Ibañez 136, 46022 València – **VA25)** València – **VA26)** Vía Emilia Ortuño 5, 3°, 03500 Benidorm – **VA27)** Edificio Levante. Polígono Vara de Quart. Calle Traginers, 7 46014 València **W**: www.la977.com **VA28)** Paseo Explanada de España 26, 03001 Alicante – **VA29)** C/ Els Gremis 1, Polígono Vara de Quart, 46014 Valencia **W**: www.abc.es/radio – **VA30)** C.C. Alfafar, Pl. Alquería de la Culla 4, Planta14, of.01, 46910 Alfafar,Valencia. **W**: www.pequeradio.es – **VA32)** Av. Blasco Ibáñez 134, 46022 València. – **VA33)** Av. Aragón 30, 46031 València.
For more information see W: www.lalistadelafm.com

AMERICAN FORCES RADIO & TV SERVICE (Mil.)
ZFM 92.1MHz, Morón de la Frontera ✉ APO AE 09643 Moron de la Frontera (Sevilla). – **FM102 Navy** 102.5MHz, Rota. ✉ FPO AE 09645 – 0019 Base Naval, Rota (Cadiz) **D.Prgr:** All stns 24h

SRI LANKA

L.T: UTC +5½h — **Pop:** 19 million — **Pr.L:** Sinhala, Tamil, English — **E.C:** 50Hz, 230V — **ITU:** CLN

SRI LANKA BROADCASTING CORPORATION (Pub)
✉ P.O. Box 574, Independence Square, Colombo 7 ☎+94 11 2697491 📠 +94 11 2691568 **E:** ddge@slbc.lk **W:** slbc.lk
L.P: Chairman Nanda Muruttetuwegama, DG: Erananda Hettiarachchi, Dir (Eng.) H. M. Jackson, Dir. News: Indika Jayarathna, Sup. Eng. (VHF): M.G.W.Priyadarshana

FM (MHz)	A	B	C	D	E	F
Colombo	91.7	94.3	102.1	104.7	97.6	89.8
Deniyaya	91.9	94.5	102.3	104.9	97.4	89.6
Haputale	91.9	94.5	-	104.9	97.4	89.6
Hunasgiriya	91.7	94.3	102.1	104.7	97.4	89.6
Karaghatenna	91.7	94.3	102.3	104.9	97.4	89.6
Kovavil	-	-	102.1	-	97.6	89.6
Palali	-	-	104.9	-		
Radella	91.7	94.3	102.3	104.7	97.6	89.8
Yatiyantota	91.9	94.5	102.3	104.9	97.4	89.6

A = Sinhala National Sce 2300-1600., **B** = Sinhala Commercial Sce 24h, **C** = Tamil National Sce 2300-1715, **D** = Tamil Commercial Sce 2300-1700, **E** = English Sce 0000-1700 (includes rel. of BBC World Sce), **F** = City FM 24h.
Sports Sce: operates irregularly as required using freqs of Vidula Sce and also YAL FM.
Vidula (Children's channel): Colombo 107.3MHz,Yatiyantota 107.5MHz: 0000-1630 in Sinhala, Tamil and English.
Regional services:
MW: Iratperiyakulam (Wanni service in Sinhala and Tamil) 855kHz (currently inactive)
FM: Akkaraipattu: Haputale 102.1MHz (Thirayi Sevaya) – **Anuradhapura:** Karaghatenna 107.3MHz (Rajarata Sevaya) – **Batticaloa:** Karaghatenna 90.1MHz (Pirai FM in Tamil) – **Jaffna:** 90.1MHz (Palali Sevaya/YAL FM) – **Kandy:** Radella & Hunasgiriya 107.3MHz (Kandurata Sevaya) – **Kurunegala:** Karaghatenna 90.1MHz (Wayamba Handa) – **Matara:** Haputale 107.5MHz, Deniyaya 107.3MHz 5kW (Ruhunu Sevaya).
Regional Sce operates 2300-0230 & 1000-1530.
Community Stations: Badulla 107.3MHz, Girandurukotte 95.8MHz, Mawathura 97.6MHz 0.3kW- Kothmale FM
Ann: A: "Me Sri Lanka Guwan Viduli Sansthave Welanda Sevaya". **B:** "Me Sri Lanka Guwan Viduli Sansthava Swadeshiya Sevaya". **C:** "Illangar Oliparappu Kootuthapanam Tamil Sevai". **E:** "This is the Sri Lanka Broadcasting Corporation"

EXTERNAL SERVICE: SLBC see International Broadcasting section

MAJOR COMMERCIAL NETWORKS (All FM MHz):
ASSET RADIO BROADCASTING (Pvt) Ltd
✉ 09C Ocean Tower Building, Station Road, Bambalapitya, Colombo 4 ☎+94 11 2507080 📠 +94 11 5342434 **E:** eng@nethfm.com **W:** nethfm. com **Stn: Neth FM** in Sinhala: Gongala/Hunasgiriya/Laggala 94.8, Colombo/Nayabedda/Magalkanda 95.0.
COLOMBO COMMUNICATIONS (Pvt) Ltd
✉ 686 Galle Road, Colombo 3 ☎+94 11 5577777 📠 +94 11 2505796 **E:** info@efm.lk **W:** efm.lk **Stns: E! FM:** Colombo/Gongala/Hunasgiriya 88.3 – **RAN FM:** Nayabedda/Gongala/Gammaduwa/Ratnapura 88.1, Colombo 100.5 – **Shree FM:** Colombo/Magalkanda 100.0, Gongala/Hunasgiriya/Nayabedda/Ratnapura 100.2
HIRU MEDIA NETWORKS
✉ Asia Broadcasting Corporation Private Ltd, 35th Floor, East Tower, World Trade Center, Colombo 1 ☎+94 11 233 7555 📠+94 11 234 6870 **E:** md@abcradio.lk **W:** abcradio.lk **Stns: Gold FM:** Colombo/Gongala/Hunasgiriya 93.2, Gammaduwa/Nuwara Eliya 93.0 – **Hiru FM:** Hunasgiriya/Gammaduwa/Nuwara Eliya 96.1, Colombo/Gongala/Madolsima 96.3 – **Shaa FM:** Colombo/Nuwara Eliya 90.9, Hunasgiriya/Gammaduwa/Gongala 91.1 – **Sooriyan FM:** Colombo/Gongala/Madolsima 103.4, Jaffna/Gammaduwa/Hunasgiriya/Nuwara Eliya 103.6 – **Sun FM:** Nuwara Eliya/Magalkanda/Hunasgiriya 98.9, Colombo/Gammaduwa/Gongala 98.7
INDEPENDENT TELEVISION NETWORK
✉ Wickramasinghepura, Battaramulla 10120 ☎+94 11 2774424 📠+94 11 2774591 **E:** itn@slt.lk **W:** itn.lk **L.P:** Chmn.: Rosmand Senarathna, Gen Mgr: W Wijesinghe. **Stns: Lakhanda:** Karaghatenna/

Nayabedda/Yatiyantota 93.5, Colombo/Kovavil/Deniyaya/ Hunasgiriya 93.7 – **Vasantham:** Colombo/Jaffna/Karagahatenna 102.6, Kaluthara/Magalkanda/Kovavil 102.8
LAKVIEW BROADCASTING (Pvt) Ltd
✉ 965 Bulugaha Junction, Wedamulla, Kelaniya, Colombo ☎+94 11 7920930 📠+94 11 7920935. **Stn: Lak FM:** Colombo/Nayabedda/Karaghatenna/Magalkanda 106.0, Nuwara Eliya 106.2
MBC NETWORKS (Pvt) Ltd
✉ PO Box 25, 36 Araliya Uyana, Depanama, Pannipitiya ☎+94 11 2851371 📠+94 11 2851373. **Stns: Shakthi FM:** ✉ 7 Braybrooke Place, Colombo. Colombo/Gammaduwa/Gongala 103.9, Nayabedda/Hunasgiriya/Jaffna/Mt Oliphant/Nuwara Eliya 104.1 – **Sirasa FM:** ✉ PO Box 25, Araliya Uyana. Colombo/Gongala/Nayabedda 106.5 Pannipitiya. Nuwara Eliya/Gammaduwa/Hunasgiriya 106.7 – **Y FM:** ✉ 7 Braybrooke Place, Colombo. Colombo/Gammaduwa/Hantana/Nayabedda 93.7 – **Yes FM:** ✉ as MBC Networks. Colombo/Gongala/Hunasgiriya 100.8, Mt Oliphant/Nuwara Eliya 101.0
TNL RADIO NETWORK (Telshan Networks Ltd)
✉ 7B Tower Building, 25.Station Road, Colombo.4 ☎+94 11 2706128 **L.P:** Chmn. & MD: Shan Wickremesinghe, Comm. Dir: Ms. Ishini Wickremesionghe. **Stns: Rhythm FM:** Chilaw/Karagahatenna/Gongala 95.6, Colombo 95.8 – **Lite FM:** Colombo/Nuwara Eliya 87.6, Gongala/Hantana 87.8 – **TNL Rocks:** ✉ 52, 5th Lane, Colombo 3 ☎+94 11 7777555. Colombo/Hanthana 99.2, Gongala 101.8.

Other Stations:
SLBC transmitting station Puttalam 1125kHz 50kW Available for hire by international broadcasters
Trans World Radio India MW: Puttalam 882kHz 400kW Broadc. for Sri Lanka and southern India. See International section for details.
IBB RELAY STATION see International Broadcasting section

ST BARTHÉLEMY (France)

L.T: UTC -4h — **Pop:** 7,500 — **Pr. L:** French, Creole, English — **E.C:** 50Hz, 230V — **ITU:** BLM

GUADELOUPE PREMIÈRE (Pub)
✉ c/o Morne Bernard-Destrellan, B.P. 180, 97122 Baie-Mahault, Guadeloupe. ☎+590 590939696 📠 +590 590939682.
FM: 88.6MHz 0.3kW

RADIO SAINT-BARTH
✉ BP 1113, 97014 St Barthélemy. ☎+590 590 27 74 74 📠 +590 590 27 74 10. **L.P:** Président Clemenceau Magras
FM: 98.7MHz 0.3kW, 100.7MHz 0.3kW, 103.7MHz 0.3kW.

R. France Internationale: via R. St. Barth 100.7MHz

ST EUSTATIUS (Netherlands)

L.T: UTC -4h — **Pop:** 3,900 — **Pr.L:** Dutch (official), English — **E.C:** 60Hz, 110V — **ITU:** BES

PJB-50 RADIO STATIA,
Sint Eustatius Broadcasting Foundation
✉ Statia Mall, Chaple Piece ☎ +599 318 2722 📠 +599 318 2168 **L.P.:** Dir: Ivan Rivers; English prgrs **W:** radiostatia.com **E:** radio_statia@yahoo.com
FM: PJB50 92.3MHz, 0.5 kW, 24h

ST HELENA (UK)

L.T: UTC — **Pop:** 4,000 — **Pr. L:** English — **E.C:** 50Hz, 240V — **ITU:** SHN

SOUTH ATLANTIC MEDIA SERVICES LIMITED (SAMS)
✉ The Media Centre, Castle Gardens, Jamestown, St Helena STHL 1ZZ ☎+290 22727 **L.P:** CEO: Richard Wallis, SM: vacant
E: news@sams.sh **W:** sams.sh (live audio stream)
FM(MHz): **SAMS Radio 1:** High Knoll Fort 90.5, Jamestown 102.7, Levelwood 105.1, Blue Hill 105.3 **SAMS Radio 2** (rel. BBC World Service): High Knoll Fort 88.1, Jamestown 100.7

Saint FM Community Radio
✉ Association Hall, Main St, Jamestown, St Helena STHL 1ZZ. ☎+290 22667 **E:** admin.fm@helanta.co.sh **W:** saint.fm (live audio stream) **L.P:** Chair: Julie Thomas, SM: Donna Crowie
FM(MHz): Half Tree Hollow 93.1 0.25kW, Deadwood Plain 95.1 0.05kW, Jamestown 106.7 0.05kW.
F.PI: Sandy Plain or Blue Hill 91.1MHz 0.05kW.

ST KITTS & NEVIS

L.T: UTC -4h — **Pop:** 56,000 — **Pr.L:** English — **E.C:** 60Hz, 220V — **ITU:** SCN

NATIONAL BROADCASTING CORPORATION OF ST.KITTS & NEVIS (Gov. Comm.)
✉ PO Box 331, Springfield, Basseterre, St. Kitts ☎ +1 869 465 2621 🖷 +1 869 466 2159 **L.P.:** GM: Clement O'Garro **E:** info@zizonline.com **W:** zizonline.com
FM: Radio ZIZ 95.9/96.1/96.9MHz – **Big Wave 96.7 FM** 96.7MHz

RADIO PARADISE (Rlg.)
✉ Flowing Streams Church, PO Box 690069, Vero Beach FL 32969-0069, USA ☎ +1 772 569 8880 **E:** info@trunews.com **W:** trunews.com **L.P.:** Don Burkhart
MW: Conaree, St. Kitts 820kHz 50kW. Inactive

VOICE OF NEVIS (Comm.)
✉ Bath Plains, PO Box 195, Charlestown, Nevis ☎ +1 869 469 1616/1700 🖷 +1 869 469 5329 **W:** vonradio.com
L.P: GM: Evered Herbert
MW: 860kHz 10kW **D.Prgr:** 24h **Ann:** "This is Von Radio on 860 AM"

Other stations:
Choice FM, Ram's, Stoney Grove, PO Box 923, Charlestown, Nevis 00109 ☎ +1 869 469 1049 🖷 +1 869 469 0662 **E:** choicefm1053@gmail.com **W:** sknclt.com FM: 105.3/105.5MHz – **CSS Caribbean Superstation, W:** yourcss.net FM: 93.1MHz (Relay Trinidad) – **Dominion Radio,** PO Box 513, Basseterre ☎ +1 869 465 1597 **W:** dominionradioskn.com FM: 91.5MHz. Format: Rlg. – **Freedom FM,** The Cable Bldg., Suite 2, Cayon St., Basseterre. **W:** freedomskn.com **L.P.:** CEO Clement Juni Liburd. FM: 106.5MHz – **Goodwill Radio,** P.O. Box 98, Lodge Village, St. Kitts ☎ +1 869 465 7795 🖷 +1 869 465 9556 FM: 103.3MHz (Nevis) & 104.5MHz (St. Kitts). Format: Rlg. – **Kyss FM - The Love FM,** 51A Stadium View, Sandy Point ☎ +1 869 466 5978 **E:** info@kyssonline.com **W:** kyssonline.com FM: 102.3/102.5MHz – **Praise FM,** Hamilton Estate, 00265 Charlestown, Nevis ☎ +1 869 667 0351 **W:** praisefmnevis.org **L.P.:** Steve Huggins. FM: 99.3MHz. Format: Gospel – **Radio One,** St. Kitts & Nevis Broadcasting Corp., Bakers Corner, Basseterre ☎ +1 869 466 0941 FM: 94.1MHz – **Radio St. Kitts Nevis,** Victoria Rd, Basseterre and Reef Broadcasting, #79 Castle Coakley, Christiansted, VI 99820, USA ☎ +1 869 465 528 **W:** reefradiostkittsnevis.com FM: 90.7MHz (relays WAXJ 103.5, US Virgin Isl.) – **Sugar City 90.3,** 8 Green Land's Park, Basseterre ☎ +1 869 466 1113 **W:** sugarcityfm.com FM: 90.3MHz – **Winn FM,** Unit C24, Newtown Bay Rd, Basseterre, St. Kitts ☎ +1 869 466 9586 **E:** info@winnfm.com **W:** winnfm.com FM: 98.9MHz

ST LUCIA

L.T: UTC -4h — **Pop:** 185,000 — **Pr.L:** English, Creole — **E.C:** 50Hz, 220V — **ITU:** LCA

RADIO ST. LUCIA COMPANY LTD. (Gov. Comm.)
✉ Morne Fortune, PO Box 660, Castries ☎ +1 758 452 2337 🖷 +1 758 453 1568 **E:** info@rslonline.com **W:** rslonline.com
L.P: MD: Claude Emmanuel. CEN: Othneil Robinson. PM: Garfield Alexander
FM: 97.3MHz 2kW (North), 97.7MHz 0.3kW (South). **D.Prgr:** 24h **N:** 1030, 1600 & 2200

Other stations:
CATHOLIC TV BROADCASTING SERVICE, Micoud Str, Castries ☎ +1 758 452 7050 FM: 87.75MHz (TV sound of EWTN, USA) – **HOT FM/KISS FM,** Old Victoria Rd, Morne Fortune, PO Box MF 7096, Castries ☎ +1 758 452 6040 🖷 +1 758 458 1462 **W:** caribbeanhotfm.com & caribbeankissfm.com CEO: Patrick Smith. Mgr.: Sandra Recai. Stns: **Hot FM:** 96.1(South)/105.3(North)MHz, **Kiss FM:** 105.5(South)/105.9(North)MHz – **IBAS RADIO,** Darling Rd, Castries ☎ +1 758 4599 0645 **W:** ibasradio.com FM: 104.5/106.7MHz. Format: C&W – **JOY FM,** PO Box MF 7149, Castries ☎ +1 758 453 6962 FM: 90.1 (North)/96.9 (South) MHz. Format: Rlg – **KAIRI FM,** Morne Du Don, PO Box 1730 Castries ☎ +1 758 451 1079 **W:** kairifm758.com FM: 107.1/107.9MHz – **LOVE-FM,** Beanefield, PO Box 520, Vieux-Fort ☎ +1 758 454 5683 **W:** lovefmstlucia.com FM: 103.9MHz(South)/ 94.9MHz (North)/91.9MHz(West) – **PRAYZ FM RADIO,** Sir John Compton Highway, Sans Soucis, PO Box CP6141, Castries ☎ +1 758 452 1022 **W:** prayzfm.org FM: 92.5/98.5MHz Format: Rlg., Adventist – **RADIO CARIBBEAN INTERNATIONAL,**

11 Mongiraud St., PO Box 121, Castries ☎ +1 758 452 2636 🖷 +1 758 452 2637 **W:** rcistlucia.com LP: GM: Mr. Antonius Secra Gibson. SM: Peter Ephraim. FM: 99.1(South)/101.1(North) MHz – **RADIO 100 HELEN FM,** Morne Fortune, PO Box 621, Castries ☎ +1 758 452 4982 🖷 +1 758 453 1737 **W:** htsstlucia.org **L.P.:** PD: Valerie Albert-Fevrier. FM: 100.1(Castries)/100.3(North)/103.5(South)MHz – **REAL 91.3 FM,** PO Box CP 6279, Castries ☎ +1 758 453 7458 **W:** realfm913fm.com L.P.: Almus McDowall. FM: 91.3/91.5MHz – **RADIO FREE IYANOLA (RFI),** 22 Delieu St, Soufriere ☎ +1 758 489 1021 **W:** rfi1021slu.com FM: 102.1MHz. Format: Reggae – **RHYTHM FM/BLAZIN FM INC.,** Julian Charles Rd., PO Box 584, Castries ☎ +1 758 450 9494 🖷 +1 758 451 6217 **W:** rhythmfm.net & blazinfm.com L.P.: MD Dwayne Mendes. PD: Irvin 'Ace' Loctar. Stns: **Rhythm FM:** 95.5/99.5MHz, **Blazin FM:** 99.3MHz – **RIZZEN 102FM,** McVane Drive, Sans Soucis, Castries ☎ +1 758 451 3057 🖷 +1 758 451 3011 **W:** rizzen102.com FM: 99.7/102.5/102.9MHz. Format: Rlg. – **SOUFRIERE FM,** Sulphur Springs Park, PO Box 272, Soufriere ☎ +1 758 459 7885 🖷 +1 758 457 1071 **W:** 885soufrierefm.com FM: 88.5MHz (local community stn) – **THE WAVE,** Karlione Court, Rodney Bay. PO Box CP5631, Castries ☎+1 758 451 6400 🖷+1 758 452 2633 **W:** thewavestlucia.com L.P.: GM: Sue Monplaisir. PD: Michael Rogers. FM: 93.7 (South) /94.5 (North) MHz – **WVENT,** Karlione Court, Rodney Bay ☎ +1 758 451 6400 **W:** wventradio.com FM: 93.5(North)/94.7(South)MHz – **YES FM,** Sunny Acres, PO Box 1817, Castries ☎ +1 758 451 3736. FM: 101.5(South)/101.7(North)MHz. Format: Rlg.

ST MAARTEN (Netherlands)

L.T: UTC -4h — **Pop:** 37,500 — **Pr.L:** Dutch (official), English — **E.C:** 60Hz, 120V — **ITU:** SXM

BUREAU TELECOMMUNICATIONS AND POST
✉ Cannegieter Street 15 – Unit 5.1, Philipsburg, St. Maarten ☎ +1 721 542 4699 🖷 +1 721 542 4817 **W:** sxmregulator.sx **E:** info@sxmregulator.sx

MW Call	kHz	kW	Station, location
1) PJD-2	1300	1	The Voice of St. Maarten, Philipsburg

FM	MHz	kW	Station, location
4)	91.9		Island 92, Simpson Bay
6)	94.7	3	Mix 94.7, Philipsburg
6)	96.3	3	Oasis 96.3, Philipsburg
8)	98.1		Pearl FM, Philipsburg
3)	99.9		Soualiga Broadcasting,Choice FM, Philipsburg
6)	101.1	3	Laser 101 FM
1)	102.7	3.5	PJD3, The V of St. Maarten/Power 102.7, Philipsburg
7)	104.3		PJM1, X 104.3, Philipsburg
5)	105.5	3	Tropixx 105.5, Philipsburg
5)	106.3		Inspire 106.3 FM, Philipsburg
2)	107.9	1	Gov. R., Philipsburg

Addresses and other information
1) Back Street 187, P.O. Box 366, Philipsburg ☎ +1 721 542 2580, +1 721 542 2764, +1 721 542 2141 +721 542 2356 **W:** pdj2radio.com – **2)** PO Box 943, Clem Lebaga Square, Philipsburg ☎+1 721 542 2233 – **3)** Backstreet 29, Philipsburg ☎ +1 721 542 2049 🖷 +1 721 542 5791 **W:** sxmradio.com/choicefm.html – **4)** 2nd Floor, Express Building, Simpson Bay ☎ +1 721 544 3377 **E:** info@island92.com **W:** island92.com – **5) W:** radio-inspire.fm – **6)** A.Th. Illidge Road 106 Philipsburg ☎+ +1 721 543 2200 ☎ +1 721 543 2229; Oasis, Laser and Mix: 24h in English; Tropixx: 24h in English, Papiamentu and Spanish; Laser,Tropixx and Mix: Dir: Gary Euton; Oasis: Dir: Phyllis Meit **E:** marketing@philbroad.com **W:** oasis963. **W:** laser101.fm **W:** tropixx.fm – **7)** Media One Corporation, 9, Walter Nisbeth Road, Suite B, Philipsburg ☎+1 721 543 8104 24h in English, Dir. Mr E. Brown, **W:** x1043.com **E:** info@mediaoneco.com – **8)** Fort Belair Road 3, Philipsburg ☎+1 721 5430 462 🖷 +1 721 5430 462 **W:** pearlfmradio.sx

ST MARTIN (France)

L.T: UTC -4h — **Pop:** 36,000 — **Pr. L:** French, Creole, English, Dutch — **E.C:** 50Hz, 230V — **ITU:** MAF

GUADELOUPE 1ÈRE
✉ Quartier Bellevue-Marigot, 97100 Saint Martin ☎+590 590291716 **FM:** St. Martin 88.9MHz 0.3kW

RADIO SAINT MARTIN (Comm.)
✉ Port de Marigot, 97150 Saint Martin **L.P.:** Mgr: H. Cocks.
FM: 101.5MHz 0.3kW **D.Prgr:** 1000-0500(Sun -0400) in French & English exc. Spanish: 2000-2100W.
RADIO CALYPSO
✉ 10, rue du Général de Gaule, 97150 Saint Martin

☎+590 590 522222 🖷 +590 590 52 22 23 **W:** radiocalypso.net **E:** calypsopub@powerantilles.com **FM:** 102.1MHz 1kW

Other Stations:
R. Laser Îles du Nord 89.9MHz 1kW – **Youth R.** 92.5MHz 1kW – **R.** 94.3MHz 1kW – **R. Music FM** 95.1MHz 1kW – **R. SOS** 95.9MHz 1kW – **R. Maranatha** 100.3MHz 1kW – **R. Tropik FM** 104.7MHz 1kW – **Sun FM Music** 107.1MHz 1kW

ST PIERRE ET MIQUELON (France)

L.T: UTC -3h (13 Mar-6 Nov: -2h) — **Pop:** 7,000 — **Pr.L:** French — **E.C:** 50Hz, 220V — **ITU:** SPM

RADIO ST PIERRE ET MIQUELON PREMIÈRE
🖃 B.P. 4227-97500 St. Pierre et Miquelon. ☎+508 508413824.
L.P: Dir: Joseph Edern. Dir. Tec: Daniel Beugin. Head of N: Jacques Barret. **FM:** St. Pierre 97.9MHz 10W, 99.9MHz 0.5kW, Miquelon 98.9MHz 50W.
D.Prgr: 0930-0230. **Rel. France-Inter:** 0230-0930. **N (local):** 1000, 1530, 2200, **(Rel. France-Inter:)** 1100, 1200, 1300, 1400, 1800, 1900 **Ann:** "Ici Radio Saint-Pierre et Miquelon Première"
IS: La Marseillaise **V.** by QSL-card. Rec. acc.

R. Atlantique 🖃 B.P. 1282-97500 ☎+508 508412493 **W:** cheznoo. net/radioatlantique **FM:** 102.1MHz (also rel. R. France Int.)

ST VINCENT & THE GRENADINES

L.T: UTC -4h — **Pop:** 110,000 — **Pr.L:** English — **E.C:** 50Hz, 230V — **ITU:** VCT

NATIONAL BROADCASTING CORPORATION RADIO ST. VINCENT AND THE GRENADINES – NBCSVG (Gov. Comm.)
🖃 Richmond Hill, PO. Box 705, Kingstown ☎ +1 784 457 1111 🖷 +1 784 456 2749 **W:** nbcsvg.com **E:** nbcsvgadmin@vincysurf.com
L.P: Chmn: Elson Crick. GM: Corletha Ollivierre. Dep. GM: Raphael King. Ag. PM: Colvin Harry. Tech Dir: Lynford Byron. N Ed: Lesley De Bique
FM: 90.7MHz 1kW, 107.5MHz 1kW
D.Prgr: 24h. Relays BBC 0400-0930. **N:** 1130, 1630, 2230 – Su 1230 only. **Ann:** "NBC Radio"

Other Stations (FM MHz):
ADORATION FM, North Union, Charlotte. E: adoration88@gmail. com. W: adoration88.com. FM: 88.9MHz. Format: Rlg – **BEQUIA COMMUNITY HIGH SCHOOL**, PO Box 75BQ, Bequia. FM: 89.3 – **CROSS COUNTRY RADIO,** 50 Vigie Highway, PO Box 1000, Kingstown ☎ +1 784 456 4413 🖷 +1 784 456 4117 **W:** ccrradiosvg. com FM: 88.5/104.3 Format: Rlg – **E-ZEE RADIO,** Dorsetshire Hill, PO Box 617, Kingstown ☎ +1 784 456 1078 **W:** ezeeradiosvg.com. FM: 91.1/100.5/102.7 Format: Easy listening – **HITZ-FM,** St Vincent Broadcasting Corp., Dorsetshire Hill, P.O. Box 617, Kingstown ☎ +1 784 456 1078 🖷 +1 784 456 1015 **W:** hitz1037.com FM: 91.5/103.7. Format: Urban Caribbean – **ISLAND VIBZ,** Green Hill, PO Box 473, Kingstown ☎ +1 784 455 1723 **W:** islandvibz953.com FM: 95.3 – **HOT 97FM,** 1 Melville Street, PO Box 1716, Kingstown ☎ +1 784 452 9797 🖷 +1 784 456 2462 **W:** hot97svg.com FM: 93.1/97.1. Format: Urban Caribbean – **JEM RADIO,** Hopewell Rd, PO Box 1419, Kingstown ☎ +1 784 451 3827 **W:** jemradio.com FM: 89.1. Format: Rlg. – **NICE RADIO,** BDS Company Ltd., Dorsetshire Hill, PO Box 324, Kingstown ☎ +1 784 458 1013 🖷 +1 784 456 5556 **W:** niceradio.info L.P: Mgr: Douglas Defreitas. FM: 90.3/96.7/101.3 – **PRAISE FM,** Sion Hill, P.O.Box 443, Kingstown ☎ +1 784 456 1057 🖷 +1 784 456 1696 **W:** praisefmsvg.com L.P.: PD Donny Daniel. FM: 95.7/105.7 Format: Rlg – **STAR FM,** Murray's Rd, McKies Hill, PO Box 1651, Kingstown ☎ +1 784 453 7827 🖷 +1 784 485 7827 **W:** star983fm.com FM: 98.3/104.7 – **TOTAL FM,** 6 Mckies Hill, PO Box 360, Kingstown ☎ +1 784 457 1234. FM: 100.5 – **WEFM,** Windy Point, Lower Questelles, PO Box 1346, Kingstown ☎ +1 784 457 9994 🖷 +1 784 457 7123 **E:** wefm@vincysurf.com **W:** 999wefm.com FM: 99.9

SUDAN

L.T: UTC +3h — **Pop:** 34 million — **Pr.L:** Arabic, Nubian, Bedawi — **E.C:** 50Hz, 240V — **ITU:** SDN

MINISTRY OF INFORMATION & COMMUNICATION
L.P: Minister: Al-Zahawi Ibrahim Malek

SUDAN RADIO & TV CORPORATION - SUDAN RADIO (Gov.)
🖃 P.O. Box 1094, Mulazmin, Omdurman ☎+249 1 87572956 🖷 +249 1 87556006. **W:** sudanradio.info **E:** info@sudanradio.info
L.P: Dep. Dir: Mr. Abdul Azim Awad. DG Eng. & Tech. Sces: Abbas Sidig.

MW	kHz	kW	Prgr.	MW	kHz	kW	Prgr.
Nyala	540	50	R	Wadi Halfa	873	5	R
Al-Ubayyid	639	10	R	Singa	891	5	R
Kassala	666	10	R	Al-Foula	945	5	R
Khartoum	747	10	R	Khartoum	963	100	S/G/Q
Port Sudan	747	5	R	Al-Damazin	1026	5	R
Omdurman	765	50	G	Reiba (Sennar)	1296	600	G
Atbara	783	5	R	Al Qadarif	1485	12	R
Al-Fashir	801	5	R	Kosti	1584	5	R
Dongola	819	10	R	Kadugli	1602	5	R
Wad Madani	873	10	R				

SW: Khartoum (Al-Aitahab) 100kW (irr.) General prgr: 7205kHz 0230-0400, 1500-1630, 1930-2100. 9505kHz: 0900-1500.
FM: Khartoum: 88.6MHz (W), 90.0MHz (S/Q), 93.0MHz (Y), 95.0MHz (G), 98.0MHz (E/U), 100.0MHz (N), 105.0MHz (Q), 107.0MHz (local). Prgr. S: Khartoum 90.0MHz & Darfur: Al-Fashir/Al-Junayna 95.0MHz, Nyala 98.0MHz.
Regional stations: Al-Gadarif/Dongola/El Obeid/Kassala/Nyala/Sinja 98.0MHz, Port Sudan 105.0MHz.
F.PI: 4 FM stations in Darfur.
Prgrs: G=General Prgr (incl. **National Unity R.** 1000-1200) in Arabic: 24h. 963kHz 0200-2100. **H=Quran R:** 0200-1000. **K=Khartoum State R:** 0300-0700, 1300-1900. **N="Sudan Home Radio":** 24h. **S=R. As-Salam** (Peace): 0530-0830, 1300-2100 on 90.0MHz, 963 & 7205kHz. **U="Nation's Memory Radio":** 1100-1500, 1900-2300. **E=European prgr.** in English/French: 1500-1900. **W: Wadi al-Nil** (Nile Valley R.). **Y=Youth & Sports R.**
R=Regional stations.D.Prgr: mostly 0300-2100. Also relay **G** prgr.
VO the Armed Forces, Khartoum: 97.0MHz. **W:** mod.gov.sd
VO the Police, Khartoum: 99.6MHz. **W:** moi.gov.sd
Ann: "Huna Omdurman, Idha'atu-l-Gumhuriya as-Sudan"
IS: Sudanese music.**F.PI:**
External sce: see International radio section.

Other Stations (FM MHz):
Al-Basirah R, Khartoum 96.3, Al-Jazirah 96.6 **W:** elbasiera.net – **Al-Furqan R** (rlg.), Khartoum 99.0 **W:** furqan.org – **Al-Kawthar R.**(rlg.), Khartoum 92.0 **W:** kawther.sd – **Al-Rabiyah FM,** Khartoum 94.0. Owned by Channel 4, UAE. **W:** alrabaafm.com – **Al-Tibbiyah FM,** Khartoum 99.3. **W:** altbia.fm – **BNFM** (tv audio), Khartoum: 91.0 **W:** bnile.tv – **Bokra FM,** Khartoum: 104.6. **W:** facebook. com/BokraFm1046 – **Capital R,** Khartoum: 91.6 **W:** capitalfmsudan. com – **Hala FM,** Khartoum: 96.0 **W:** hala96.fm – **Hawa al-Sudan,** Khartoum: 88.3MHz – **Khartoum FM,** Khartoum: 89.0. **W:** kfm89.net – **Life and Health R,** Khartoum: 106.0 – **Mango FM,** Khartoum/Port Sudan/Wad Madani: 96.0. **W:** mango96.com Also rel. BBC – **OUS R,** Khartoum: 89.5. **W:** ousmedia.net – **R. Darfur:** 90.3 **W:** darfurfm. net – **R. Darfur:** 90.3 **W:** darfurfm.net – **R. Tonight,** Khartoum: 101.0 – **Sports FM,** Khartoum: 104.0. **W:** sporttsfm104.net – **Tayba FM** (rlg.), Khartoum: 103.0. **W:** tayba.fm – **Vision FM,** Khartoum 101.3. **W:** facebook.com/vision1013FM
R. Sawa, Khartoum: 97.5MHz.
UNAMID R, Darfur. **W:** unamid.unmissions.org . Relayed twice daily via R. As-Salam and Darfur stations

SURINAME

L.T: UTC -3h — **Pop:** 540,000 — **Pr.L:** Dutch, English, Sranang Tongo, Sarnami Hindi, Javanese — **E.C:** 60Hz, 110/115/127/220V — **ITU:** SUR – **Int. dialling code:** 597

TELECOMMUNICATE BEDRIJF SURINAME (TELESUR) (Gov)
🖃 P.O. Box 1839, Paramaribo ☎ 474242/473944 🖷 404800 **W:** telesur.sr **E:** telesur@sr.net

STICHTING RADIO-OMROEP SURINAME (SRS)
🖃 P.O. Box 271, Paramaribo ☎ 498115 🖷 498116 **W:** radiosrs.com **E:** adm@radiosrs.com
FM: Paramaribo 96.3MHz 1kW, Coronie, Nickerie, Moengo, Brokopondo 94.7MHz 0.1kW, Wageningen 95.6 MHz, Albina 105.7MHz 0.1kW **D.Prgr:** 0900-0700

PRIVATE COMMERCIAL STATIONS:
SW: 8) R. Apintie, Paramaribo 4990kHz 1kW (irregular)

FM: 1) R. 10 88.1, 88.7 & 103.7MHz – **2) Radika** 98.3MHz – **3) R. Garuda** 97.5, 103.4 & 105.7MHz – **4) Sky R.** 94.1 & 102.7MHz – **5) R. Katoilica** 93.1MHz – **6) R. Trishul** 90.5MHz – **7) R. Zon** 107.5 MHz – **8) R. Apintie** 97.1MHz – **9) R. Ishara** 100.7MHz – **10) R. Noer** 92.1MHz – **11) R. Paramaribo Rapar "The Hot-One"** 89.7MHz – **12) RP Acme** 91.3MHz – **13) RTV Mustika** 106.5MHz – **14) Sangeetmala R.** 99.3 & 100.1MHz – **15) R. Shalom** 94.5MHz – **16) R. Pertjajah** 95.3MHz – **17) R. Koyeba** 104.9MHz – **18) Rasonic R.** 102.3 & 105.3MHz – **19) Kara´s Broadcasting Corp.** 101.1 & 103.1 MHz – **20) R. ABC** 101.7MHz

Addresses:
1) Stadionlaan 3 (P.O.Box 110), Paramaribo ☎ 410881 🖷 422294 **W:** radio10.sr **E:** info@radio10.sr – **2)** Indira Gandhiweg 165, Paramaribo ☎ 482800 – **3)** Goudstraat 20 Maretrait 4, Paramaribo 454 926 **W:** rtvgaruda.com **E:** info@rtv-garuda.com – **4)** Ormosiastraat 2 (P.O.Box 1597), Paramaribo ☎ 530015 **W:** skyradioasuriname.com **E:** info@skyradio.sr – **5)** Paramaribo – **6)** Flocislaan 4, Boyen ☎ 439500 **W:** trishul.sr **E:**info@trishul.sr – **7)** Burenstraat No 60, Paramaribo ☎475261 🖷 420233 **W:** radiozon.com **E:**admin@radiozon.com – **8)** verl. Gemenelandsweg 37, Paramaribo ☎ 400455 🖷 400684 **W:** apintie.sr **E:** apintie@sr.net – **9)** 109 Fredericiweg, Nickerie ☎231244 **W:** isharafm.com **E:** info@isharafm.com – **10)** Zwartenhovenbrugstraat 154, Paramaribo **W:** dbsuriname.com/radionoer.php **E:** radionoer@gmail.com – **11) 18)** Coppenamstraat 34 (P.O. Box 975), Paramaribo ☎ 497774 Paramaribo **W:** dbsuriname.com/radiorpthehotone.php **E:** rpthehot1@gmail.com – **12)** Zwartenhovenbrugstraat 154, Paramaribo **W:** dbsuriname.com/radiorpthehotone.php – **13)** Paramaribo **W:** rtv-mustika.net **E:** rtvmustikacontact@gmail.com – **14)** Indira Gandhiweg No 40, Wanicxa ☎ 482392 **W:** sgmsuriname.com **E:** info@sgm-suriname.com – **15)** Malebatrumstraat 10-12 BV, Paramaribo ☎ 422630 🖷 422737 **W:** shalomsuriname.com **E:** shalom@sr.net – **16)** Gemenlandsweg/Daneil Coutinhostraat 31, Paramaribo **W:**http://twitter.com/#!/PertjajahLuhur – **17)** van`t Hogerhuystraat 88 ☎ 403115 **W:**radiokoyebasuriname.com **E:** odjahh@yahoo.com – **18)** Bataviastraat 25, NW. Nickerie ☎ 231447 **W:** rasonictv.com – **19)** Verlengde Gemenelandsweg 177, Paramaribo ☎ 4300666 – **20)** Maystraat 57, Paramaribo ☎ 465092 **W:** abcsuriname.com **E:** info@abcsuriname.com

SWAZILAND

LT: UTC +2h — **Pop:** 1.1 million — **Pr.L:** English, Siswati — **E.C:** 50Hz, 230V — **ITU:** SWZ

SWAZILAND POSTS & TELECOMMUNICATIONS CORPORATION (SPTC)
🖃 Phutfumani Bldg, Warner St, P.O Box 125, Mbabane ☎+268 2405 2000 🖷 +268 24052020 **W:** sptc.co.sz **E:** info@sptc.co.sz **L.P:** MD: Nathi Dlamini.

SWAZILAND BROADCASTING AND INFORMATION SERVICES (Gov)
🖃 P.O. Box 338, Corner Gwamile & Dzeliwe Streets, Mbabane H100 ☎+268 24042761 🖷 +268 24042774 **W:** gov.sz/index. php?option=com_content&id=388&Itemid=402 **E:** sbisnews@afric-aonline.co.sz
L.P: Dir: Percy Simelane. Asst. Principal prgrs Officer: Phesheya Dube. A/Prgr. Coordinator: Austin Dlamini. A/Tr. Engineer: Christopher Motsa.
FM: 88.5/91.6/93.6/105.2MHz 10kW + 4 low power relays.
English Sce: 0255-1800 on FM 91.6/93.6MHz. **N:** 0400, 0500, 1600.
Siswati Sce: 0255-2100 on FM 88.5/105.2MHz.
Ann: E: "This is the English sce. of Radio Swaziland." Siswati: "Lona ngu Mawakato waka Ngwane".
IS: at s/on, Cilongo (Swazi instrument). English Sce: cock crow, fanfare, spoken ID, instrumental theme.

TRANS WORLD RADIO - VOICE OF THE CHURCH
🖃 P.O. Box 4544, Corner Martin & Tenbergen St,Manzini **W:** vocfm. org **W:** info@voc.org.sz ☎+268 25054845 🖷 +268 25054809 **L.P:** Nat. Dir: Nelson Vilakati, Adm: Tryphinah Dlamini, PM: Abel Vilakati.
FM: 95.0/96.0/97.0/101.0MHz.
MW: TWR Africa, Mpangela Ranch 1170kHz 50kW 1800-2155 & SW. For further details see International Radio section

SWEDEN

LT: UTC +1h (27 Mar-30 Oct: +2h) — **Pop:** 9.8 million — **Pr.L:** Swedish — **E.C:** 50Hz, 230V — **ITU:** S

TERACOM AB
Responsible for distribution of prgrs produced by Sveriges Radio (Swedish Broadcasting Corporation) and by most of the commercial radio stns and community radio associations.
HQ: 🖃 Box 30150, SE-10425 Stockholm ☎ +46 8 55542000 🖷 +46 8 55542001 **W:** teracom.se **E:** kundtjanst@teracom.se
L.P: MD Johnny Svedberg

PTS
PTS (Post-och telestyrelsen) is the authority that supervises activities in radio, telecom and datacom.
🖃 Box 5398, SE-10249 Stockholm ☎ +46 8 6785500 **W:** pts.se **E:** pts@pts.se **L.P:** Dir. Gen. Göran Marby

SVERIGES RADIO AB
(Swedish Broadcasting Corporation) (Pub)
🖃 Radiohuset, Oxenstiernsgatan 20, Stockholm (🖃SE-10510 Stockholm) ☎ + 46 8 7845000 🖷 + 46 8 7841500 **W:** sr.se **E:** lyssnarservice@sverigesradio.se **L.P:** MD: Cilla Benkö

FM (MHz)		1	2	3	4	kW
24)	Arvidsjaur	89.4	94.2	97.1	100.6	60
20)	Bollnäs	88.4	91.7	96.0	103.8	60
19)	Borlänge	89.4	93.0	97.7	101.3	60
25)	Borås	88.5	94.6	97.9	102.9	10
14)	Bäckefors	92.7	96.8	99.1	102.2	60
6)	Emmaboda	93.0	96.7	99.7	101.8	60
7)	Emmaboda				95.6	60
5)	Finnveden	90.1	94.2	99.9	103.4	30
24)	Gällivare	88.3	94.9	98.5	100.9	60
20)	Gävle	88.1	97.4	99.8	102.0	60
13)	Göteborg	89.3	96.3	99.4	101.9	60
12)	Halmstad	87.7	91.2	95.4	97.3	60
10)	Halmstad				102.6	3
11)	Helsingborg	89.8	95.7	98.4	103.2	6
20)	Hudiksvall	87.6	90.2	93.8	100.7	60
11)	Hörby	88.8	92.4	97.0	101.4	60
11)	Hörby				89.5	5
5)	Jönköping	91.6	93.7	97.1	100.8	3
24)	Kalix	91.3	93.6	97.9	102.2	60
9)	Karlshamn	90.3	93.4	98.3	100.4	15
9)	Karlskrona	89.1	95.0	97.7	100.7	10
17)	Karlstad	90.5	94.2	96.5	103.5	15
24)	Kiruna	89.1	92.7	96.4	102.7	60
4)	Kisa	90.5	92.5	96.9	103.6	30
23)	Lycksele	92.9	95.4	98.7	103.3	60
11)	Malmö	87.9	93.3	98.0	102.0	6
11)	Malmö*				100.6	6
19)	Mora	92.2	96.7	99.0	101.0	60
4)	Motala	91.1	94.0	98.2	101.2	20
3)	Norrköping	90.0	93.5	98.7	102.3	60
3)	Norrköping				94.8	60
5)	Nässjö	89.6	92.1	99.0	102.1	60
24)	Pajala	90.8	93.0	95.9	100.2	60
23)	Skellefteå	93.8	96.3	100.0	103.9	60
16)	Skövde	88.9	95.1	97.5	100.3	60
21)	Sollefteå	89.3	93.5	98.1	101.2	60
1)	Stockholm	92.4	96.2	99.3	103.3	60
1)	Stockholm**		89.6			0.9
1)	Stockholm***				93.8	0.9
23)	Storuman	87.6	91.2	99.0	102.5	60
21)	Sundsvall	92.7	96.9	99.2	102.8	60
16)	Sunne	90.9	94.5	98.5	101.8	60
22)	Sveg	90.6	94.9	97.9	102.2	60
22)	Tåsjö	89.9	94.7	97.5	100.8	60
23)	Tåsjö				88.2	60
14)	Uddevalla	89.9	98.1	97.2	103.2	8
2)	Uppsala	90.3	93.3	96.6	102.5	20
12)	Varberg	90.4	93.6	98.8	103.8	10
8)	Visby	87.6	94.1	97.2	102.4	60
6)	Vislanda	88.0	90.6	94.7	101.0	20
23)	Vännäs	88.5	92.1	95.8	103.6	60
14)	Västervik	88.3	91.8	96.0	102.7	60
15)	Västerås	90.7	95.8	98.0	100.5	60
21)	Ånge	93.2	95.6	99.6	103.1	60
22)	Ånge				94.5	60
24)	Älvsbyn	90.6	94.5	99.4	102.9	60
17)	Örebro	87.9	91.5	99.6	102.8	60
21)	Örnsköldsvik	90.8	94.4	97.8	100.1	60
24)	Östersund	87.9	91.5	94.0	100.4	60
2)	Östhammar	89.1	92.8	95.5	101.6	60
24)	Överkalix	88.9	91.7	99.0	103.2	15

+ 360 low power txs. A comprehensive list of all stns is available on **W:** teracom.se
*) Broadc. "Din Gata", a local P3-prgr for the Malmö-area. **) P6

Stockholm International. Prgr for immigrant and minority langs, mix of music and rel. of foreign broadc., BBC, Deutsche Welle, CBC etc. 24h. 2200-0200 and 0300-0600 rel. BBC WS. ***) SR Metropol. Music for young people, 24h (add. frqs in greater Stockholm area: 97.6, 102.9 MHz)

First Prgr. W: sr.se/p1 (news & spoken word): MF 0429-0045,SS0455-0030. News:MF 0430, 0500, 0530, 0600, 0630, 0700, 0800, 0900, 1000, 1130, 1300, 1400, 1445, 1545, 1645, 1800, 1900, 2000, 2100, 2200, 2300,2400. **Wrp** (incl. forecast for Swedish waters): 0455, 0555, 0655, -1200 (SS 1150), 1455, 2050 – **Second Prgr. W:** sr.se/p2 24h: Classical music and jazz prgrs, Sami, Finnish and prgrs for immigrants – **Third Prgr. W:** sr.se/p3: light music, entertainment, current affairs, news for listeners under 40: 24h – **Fourth Prgr. W:** sr.se/p4 24h: Regional network 0459 - 1700. 1700-0459 relay of P4 network from Stockholm (frqs as above, addresses given below) – **P4 Radio Stockholm. W:** sr.se/stockholm 103.3 MHz Local prgrs for Stockholm area. 0503-2303. 2303-0503 Relay of main P4 prgr
Ann: Nat. Prgr. "Sveriges Radio" and the sce e.g. "Sveriges Radio P1"

Digital Radio (DAB): Channels are used: 12B, 12C, 13C & 13F.

Location	Ch	kW	Location	Ch	kW	Location	Ch	kW
Älvsbyn	12B	4	Malmö	12B	4	Stockholm	12C	10
Enköping	12B	4	Sigtuna	12B	0.2	Uppsala	12B	2
Gävle	13F	20	Södertälje	12B	2	Uppsala	13C	20
Göteborg	12B	2	Stockholm	12B	4			

Progr: 12B: SR Klassiskt, SR Knattekanalen, SRP1, SRP3 Star, SRP4, SRP7 Sisuradio & SR Världen. 12C 13C & 13F: Bandit, Lugna Favoriter, Mix Megapol, NRJ, RixFM, Rockklassisker, Skärgårdsradion, SRP2, SRP3, SRP4 Stockholm & Vinyl.

Addresses of Regional Centres
1) SR Stockholm, Pipersgatan 45, 107 80 Stockholm – **2)** SR Uppland, Box 1552, 751 45 Uppsala – **3)** SR Sörmland, Box 641, 631 08 Eskilstuna – **4)** SR Östergötland, Box 500, 601 07 Norrköping – **5)** SR Jönköping, 551 92 Jönköping – **6)** SR Kronoberg, Box 62, 351 03 Växjö – **7)** SR Kalmar, 391 83 Kalmar – **8)** SR Gotland, Box 1324, 621 24 Visby – **9)** SR Blekinge, Box 305, 371 25 Karlskrona – **10)** SR Kristianstad, Box 505, 291 25 Kristianstad – **11)** SR Malmöhus, 211 01 Malmö – **12)** SR Halland, Box 133, 301 04 Halmstad – **13)** SR Göteborg, Pumpvägen 2, 405 13 Göteborg – **14)** SR Väst, Box 654, 451 24 Uddevalla – **15)** SR Västmanland, Box 850, 721 22 Västerås – **16)** SR Skaraborg, 541 24 Skövde – **17)** SR Värmland, Box 98, 651 03 Karlstad – **18)** SR Örebro, Västra Bangatan 15, 701 80 Örebro – **19)** SR Dalarna, Box 123, 791 23 Falun – **20)** SR Gävleborg, Box 6702, 801 74 Gävle – **21)** SR Västernorrland, 851 79 Sundsvall – **22)** SR Jämtland, Lingonvägen 7 B, 831 62 Östersund – **23)** SR Västerbotten, Mariehemsvägen 4, 906 15 Umeå – **24)** SR Norrbotten, Nygatan 3, 971 71 Luleå – **25)** SR Sjuhärad, Box 27, 503 05 Borås

Sami **R.**, Österleden 21, SE-98131 Kiruna. MD: Ole-isak Mienna **W:** sverigesradio.se/sameradion **E:** sameradion@sverigesradio.se
Sisuradio, Oxenstiernsgatan 20 RH-4A, SE 10510 Stockholm. Regional prgrs in Finnish 1710-1800 via P4 transmitters, **E:** sisuradio@sr.se
SR Metropol, Pipersgatan 45, SE-107 80 Stockholm **E:** metropol@sr.se
Further information about main addresses, tel numbers and prgrs can be found at **W:** sr.se & onair.nu

SVERIGES UTBILDNINGSRADIO AB (Pub)
(Swedish Educational Broadcasting Company)
✉ UR, Tulegatan 7, SE-113 95 Stockholm ☎ + 46 8 7840000
W: ur.se **E:** kundtjanst@ur.se **LP:** MD:Erik Fichtelius **FM:** See Swedish Radio **UR** produces educational prgrs for radio & television

Local Commercial Radio:

Location	MHz	kW	Net	Location	MHz	kW	Net
Skellefteå	92.4	1	C	Gällivare	105.2	8	A
Södertälje	100.8	3	A	Malmö	105.2	5	B
Linköping	101.7	3	C	Uppsala	105.3	5	A
Borlänge	102.6	1	B	Stockholm	105.5	1	C
Södertälje	103.9	4	C	Luleå	105.6	5	C
Halmstad	104.2	1	A	Avesta	105.8	1	B
Kalix	104.3	8	A	Göteborg	105.9	3	C
Växjö	104.3	5	C	Kristianstad	105.9	1	B
Karlstad	104.4	10	C	Jönköping	106.0	5	C
Eskilstuna	104.5	10	C	Luleå	106.3	5	A
Östersund	104.5	1	A	Karlshamn	106.4	5	B
Mora	104.5	5	B	Norrköping	106.5	3	C
Örnsköldsvik	104.8	10	A	Uppsala	106.5	5	C
Trollhättan	105.0	3	C	Malmö	106.7	1	C

Location	MHz	kW	Net	Location	MHz	kW	Net
Skellefteå	106.7	4	B	Halmstad	107.2	1	B
Finnveden	106.8	3	B	Östersund	107.2	3	C
Trollhättan	106.9	1	A	Kristianstad	107.3	1	C
Hudiksvall	107.0	10	B	Helsingborg	107.6	1	C
Borås	107.1	3	C	Skövde	107.6	5	B
Örnsköldsvik	107.1	5	B	Nyköping	107.7	10	C

+ 30 stns below 1kW. **NB:** These stns belong to networks. There are a number of commercial local stns on FM. A comprehensive list can be found on **W:** teracom.se & onair.nu

Addresses and other information:
A) MIX MEGAPOL, 115 78 Stockholm **W:** mixmegapol.se **E:** info@mixmegapol.se – **B) NRJ,** P.O. Box17115, SE-10462 Stockholm ☎ +46 856272000 **W:** nrj.se **E:** info@nrj.se – **C) RIX FM,** Box 17820, 118 94 Stockholm ☎ +46 8 56272000 📠+46 8 56272080 **W:** rixfm.com **E:** rix@rixfm.com

MTG Modern Times Group
✉ Box 17115, 10462 Stockholm **W:** bandit.se
Bandit Rock Stockholm: 106.3MHz 1kW – **Bandit Rock Uppsala** 106.5MHz 4kW - **Bandit Rock Skåne:** 95.9 & 105.9MHz 1kW – **Bandit Rock Västra Götaland:** 90.8, 104.8, 106.8 & 106.9MHz. 0.04-1kW – **Bandit Rock Norrbotten:** 95.3, 103.6 & 106.3MHz. 0.25-5kW

Private stations in the Stockholm area
FM(MHz): 88.0 City 1, 96.3 City 2, 97.3 Solna-Sundbyberg, 101.1 R. Sydost, 101.9 Star FM, 104.3 Mix Megapol, 104.7 Lugna Favoriter, 105.1 Energy, 105.5 Rix FM, 105.9 The Voice, 106.3 Bandit, 106.7 Rockklassiker, 107.1 Vinyl, 107.5 Studio

COMMUNITY STATIONS
Närradio is open for any non-commercial organization, whose main activity is other than broadcasting. The organization may obtain a permit for community radio broadcasting by PTS. The txs are made available at a nominal fee and built and operated by Teracom AB. The txs have powers of 10-400W and the target is the local community. There are more than 200 txs in operation. Frequency range: 88-108MHz. A few Närradio stns also broadcast commercial prgrs. A comprehensive list of Närradio-stns is at **W:** teracom.se
Närradio in greater Stockholm area:
FM(MHz):, 88.2 R. Sigtuna, 88.9 Sydväst, 90.5 MRS, 91.4 Tyresö, 91.6 BMU, 94.2 Järfälla, 94.5 Hit FM, 94.6 Sollentuna, 95.3 City 2, 97.3 Solna/Sbg, 97.8 Lidingö, 98.3 R. Nord, 08.5 Haninge, 99.9 Nacka, 101.4 R. Viking, 103.7 R. Österåker and 107.8 R. Roslagen

SWITZERLAND

L.T: UTC +1h (27 Mar-30 Oct: +2h) — **Pop:** 8 million — **Pr.L:** Swiss (Alemannic) German, German, French, Italian, Rumantsch — **E.C:** 50Hz, 230V — **ITU:** SUI

BUNDESAMT FÜR KOMMUNIKATION (BAKOM)
✉ Zukunftstrasse 44, 2501 Biel ☎+41 32 3275511 📠+41 32 3275555
E: info@bakom.admin.ch **W:** bakom.admin.ch
LP: Dir: Philipp Metzger
NB: BAKOM is the regulatory authority for broadcasting

SRG SSR (Pub)
✉ Giacomettistrasse 1, 3000 Bern 31 ☎+41 31 3509111 📠+41 31 3509256 **E:** info@srgssr.ch **W:** srgssr.ch
LP: Pres: Viktor Baumeler (interim); DG: Roger de Weck
NB: SRG SSR is the administrative holding for the regional branches Schweizer Radio und Fernsehen (SRF), Radiotelevisiun Svizra Rumantscha (RTR), Radio Télévision Suisse (RTS) and Radiotelevisione svizzera (RSI).

Schweizer Radio und Fernsehen (SRF)
✉ Fernsehstrasse 1-4, 8052 Zürich ☎+41 44 3056611 📠 +41 44 3055635 **E:** srf@srf.ch **W:** srf.ch **LP:** Dir: Rudolf Matter
✉ Radio studios: Brunnenhofstrasse 22, 8057 Zürich (exc. R. SRF 2 Kultur, R. SRF 4 News); Novarastrasse 2, 4002 Basel (R. SRF 2 Kultur), Schwarztorstrasse 21, 3007 Bern (R. SRF 4 News), subreg. studios.

FM (MHz)	1	2	3	kW
Arth (Rigi-Kulm)	90.9	96.6	103.8	20
Beatenberg (Niederhorn)	93.6	97.2	105.8	4
Bettingen (St. Chrischona)	90.6	99.0	103.6	32
Bolligen (Bantiger)	88.2	93.2	99.3	5
Bregenz (Pfänder)**	96.3	97.7	107.5	2
Carona (Monte San Salvatore)	96.3			20

FM (MHz)	1	2	3	kW
Castel San Pietro (Caviano)	93.0	-	-	10
Celerina (Laret)	91.9	100.3	106.3	2
Evilard (Hohmatt)	96.0	99.7	91.7	0.1/1/0.1
Feschel (Wilerzälg)	88.2	90.3	101.5	1.6
Gerra (Lutri)	95.4	-	-	1.3
Haute-Nendaz (La Crête)	92.0	-	-	2
Ins (Schaltenrain)	90.7	-	-	1
Lostorf (Froburg)	96.0	98.7	91.3	1.3
Martigny (Ravoire)	107.7	-	-	2
Mt. Salève*	87.8	-	-	2
Nods (Chasseral)	103.0	-	105.3	20
Oberdorf (Nesselboden)	89.7	-	-	1.6
Pianezzo (Monti di Paudo)	96.9	-	-	2.5
Port Valais (Chalavornaire)	93.6	-	-	1
Schattenhalb (Geissholzli)	95.4	98.4	105.6	2
Tarasp (Sparsels)	101.3	103.9	95.1	1.3
Thollon (Leucel)*	88.1	-	-	6.3
Valzeina (Mittagplatte)	93.8	102.5	104.3	1.6
Visperterminen (Gebidem)	89.4	93.9	103.9	2.5
Widen (Gugelholz)	98.3	-	-	1
Wildhaus (Säntis)	101.5	95.4	105.6	63
Zürich (Uetliberg)	94.6	106.4	105.8	2/0.6/2

NB: Sites with only txs below 1kW not listed. *) Located in France **) Located in Austria
D.Prgr (in Swiss German, exc. news/traffic info and *= in German): **Prgr 1 (R. SRF 1):** 24h. **Subregional prgrs:** 0632-0637 (MF), 0732-0737 (MF), 1103-1110 (MF), 1630-1700 (Sun-Fri), 1630-1640 (Sat), 1655-1700 (Sat; Graubünden only) – **Prgr 2 (R. SRF 2 Kultur)*:** 24h – **Prgr 3 (R. SRF 3):** 24h – **Prgr 4 (R. SRF 4 News)*:** 24h – **Prgr 5 (R. SRF Musikwelle):** 24h – **Prgr 6 (R. SRF Virus):** 24h.

Radiotelevisiun Svizra Rumantscha (RTR)
📧 Via da Masans 2, 7002 Cuira ☎+41 81 2557575 📠 +41 81 2557500
E: esther.bigliel@rtr.ch **W:** rtr.ch **L.P:** Dir: Ladina Heimgartner

FM	MHz	kW	FM	MHz	kW
Celerina (Laret)	89.1	2	Tarasp (Sparsels)	98.7	1.3
Valzeina (Mittagplatte)	90.3	1.6	**NB:** Txs below 1kW not listed.		

D.Prgr (in Rumantsch): **R. Rumantsch:** 24h. Incl. relay of selected R.SRF prgrs in Swiss German/German.

Radio Télévision Suisse (RTS)
📧 Administration/studios: Quai Ernest-Ansermet 20, 1211 Genève 8 ☎+41 58 2367444 📠 +41 58 2367454 **E:** manon.romerio@rts.ch **W:** rts.ch **L.P:** Dir: Gilles Marchand
📧 Radio studios: Avenue du Temple 40, 1010 Lausanne.

FM (MHz)	1	2	3	4	-	kW
Abbaye (Pont-Agouillons)	99.5	87.6	101.4	-	-	1
Bolligen (Bantiger)	95.1	-	-	-	-	5
Bourrignon (Ordons)	94.2	99.6	104.8	-	-	10
Carona (Monte San Salvatore)	104.0	-	-	-	-	20
Castel San Pietro (Caviano)	87.8	-	-	-	-	10
Chardonne (Mt. Pèlerin)	91.6	101.5	90.6	-	-	1.6
Chaux-de-Fonds (Cornu)	92.3	96.3	103.4	-	-	1.3
Cudrefin (Tremblex)	91.3	92.0	89.1	-	-	4
Feschel (Wilerzälg)	91.4	96.1	107.4	-	-	1.6
Gerra (Lutri)	93.2	-	-	-	-	1.6
Gingins (Barillette)	91.2	100.1	105.6	-	-	20
Haute-Nendaz (La Crête)	94.4	96.5	106.0	-	-	2
Ins (Schaltenrain)	96.9	-	-	-	-	1
Martigny (Ravoire)	93.2	106.9	100.5	-	-	2
Mt. Salève*	94.9	100.7	104.4	90.8	-	1
Nods (Chasseral)	102.3	100.3	104.2	-	-	20
Ollon (Chamossaire)	98.1	95.0	88.6	-	-	1
Ollon (Chamossaire)	105.1	-	-	-	-	0.3
Pianezzo (Monti di Paudo)	105.3	-	-	-	-	2.5
Premier (Buclards)	94.7	100.8	104.7	-	-	10
Saint-Sulpice (Haut de la Vy)	102.0	95.3	104.5	-	-	1
Sorens (Gibloux)	91.0	92.5	88.6	-	-	4
Thollon (Leucel)*	102.6	96.2	98.5	-	-	6.3
Visperterminen (Gebidem)	90.8	-	-	-	-	2.5
Wildhaus (Säntis)	99.9	-	-	-	-	63

NB: Sites with only txs below 1kW not listed. *) Located in France
D.Prgr (in French): **Prgr 1 (La 1ère):** 24h – **Prgr 2 (Espace 2):** 24h **Prgr 3 (Couleur 3):** 24h – **Prgr 4 (Option Musique):** 24h.

Radiotelevisione svizzera (RSI)
📧 Via Canevascini 5, 6900 Lugano ☎+41 91 8035111 📠 +41 91 8035355 **E:** info@rsi.ch **W:** rsi.ch **L.P:** Dir: Maurizio Canetta

FM (MHz)	1	2	3	kW
Arth (Rigi-Kulm)	106.2	-	-	20
Carona (Monte San Salvatore)	88.1	91.5	106.0	20

FM (MHz)	1	2	3	kW
Castel San Pietro (Caviano)	88.8	98.8	104.5	10
Celerina (Laret)	104.3	-	-	2
Gerra (Lutri)	92.5	94.1	99.2	1.3
Mt. Salève*	97.1	-	-	2
Nods (Chasseral)	107.3	-	-	20
Pianezzo (Monti di Paudo)	89.4	93.5	107.4	2.5
Thollon (Leucel)*	97.8	-	-	6.3
Valzeina (Mittagplatte)	95.8	-	-	1.6
Visperterminen (Gebidem)	96.7	-	-	2.5
Wildhaus (Säntis)	107.8	-	-	63

NB: Sites with only txs below 1kW not listed *) Located in France
D.Prgr (in Italian): **Prgr 1 (Rete Uno):** 24h – **Prgr 2 (Rete Due):** 24h **Prgr 3 (Rete Tre):** 24h.

OTHER STATIONS

	FM	MHz	kW	Location	Station
16B)		87.6	2	Stockeren	RadioFR.
24)		88.0	2.5	Michelskreuz	R. Sunshine
7)		88.4	2	Petite Gorge*	LFM
24)		88.8	1	Schüppenloch	R. Sunshine
24)		88.8	2	Gugelholz	R. Sunshine
3)		88.9	4	Dornegg	R. 32
10)		89.2	1	Utzenstorf	R. Bern1
15)		89.3	1	Rorschacherberg	R. FM1
16A)		89.4	1.6	Gibloux	RadioFR.
19)		89.8	1	Lenzerheide	R. Südostschweiz
25)		90.0	1	St. Gallen	R. Top
14)		90.6	1	Monti di Paudo	R. Fiume Ticino
8)		91.6	2	Gugelholz	R. Argovia
18)		91.8	2	Mt. Salève*	Yes FM
2)		92.1	1	Honegg	R. 24
13)		92.2	1	Mt. Salève*	R. Cité Genève
18)		92.3	4	Champs Maître	Yes FM
12)		92.6	1	Giettes	R. Chablais
27A)		92.8	1	Elemoos	Canal 3
14)		93.0	1	Monte Laura	R. Fiume Ticino
27B)		93.9	1	Elemoos	Canal 3
18)		94.0	1	Champs Lequet	Yes FM
28)		94.5	1	St. Chrischona	R. X
18)		95.6	6	Leucel*	Yes FM
4)		96.5	4	Alpe Tiglio	R. 3i
1)		97.0	1	Champs Lequet	One FM
12)		97.1	1	Chamossaire	R. Chablais
7)		97.4	4	Champs Maître	LFM
20)		97.6	2	Petite Gorge*	Rouge FM
10)		97.7	1.6	Bantiger	R. Bern1
11)		99.2	1.6	Michelskreuz	R. Central
1)		99.3	2	Grand Devin	One FM
24)		100.0	6.3	Monte San Salvatore	R. Sunshine
11)		100.1	1	Sonnenberg	R. Central
17)		100.6	1	Loge	RFJ
6)		100.6	1	Schaltenrain	GRRIF
17)		100.6	6.3	Ordons	RFJ
5B)		101.0	1	Utzenstorf	Energy Bern
23)		101.7	1	Loge	R. RTN
5A)		101.7	4	St.Chrischona	Energy Basel
5B)		101.7	1.6	Bantiger	Energy Bern
28)		101.9	4	Tresillet	Rouge FM
21)		102.1	1.6	Michelskreuz	R. Pilatus
22)		102.2	1.6	Gebidem	R. Rottu Oberwallis
11)		102.6	2	Urmiberg	R. Central
11)		103.0	1.6	Alpnach	R. Central
7)		103.3	6.3	Leucel*	LFM
21)		104.9	1	Sonnenberg	R. Pilatus
20)		106.5	6.3	Leucel*	Rouge FM
4)		106.5	10	Caviano	R. 3i
26)		106.7	1	Uetliberg	R. Zürisee
4)		106.8	2.5	Monte San Salvatore	R. 3i
1)		107.0	2	Petite Gorge*	One FM
19)		107.0	3.2	Mittagplatte	R. Südostschweiz
14)		107.1	4	Lutri	R. Fiume Ticino
1)		107.2	3.2	Publier*	One FM
23)		107.6	1	Montela	R. RTN
9)		107.6	4	St.Chrischona	R. Basilisk
1)		107.9	4	Champs Maître	One FM

NB: Txs below 1kW not listed. *) Located in France
Addresses & other information:
NB. Stns broadcast in Swiss German/German exc. where indicated otherwise. **1)** Rue des Bains 33, 1205 Genève. In French. – **2)** Limmatstrasse 264, 8005 Zürich – **3)** Zuchwilerstrasse 21, 4501 Solothurn – **4)** Via Carona 15, 6815 Melide. In Italian. – **5A)**

Münchensteinerstrasse 43, 4052 Basel, **5B)** Optingenstrasse 56, 3001 Bern – **6)** Rue du Marché 3, 2800 Delémont. In French. – **7)** Chemin de Mornex 1 Bis, 1003 Lausanne. In French. – **8)** Bahnhofstrasse 41, 5001 Aarau – **9)** Marktgasse 8, 4001 Basel – **10)** Dammweg 9, 3001 Bern – **11)** Postfach 464, 6440 Brunnen – **12)** Rue des Fours 11A, 1870 Monthey 1. In French. – **13)** Rue du Pré-de-la-Fontaine 2, 1217 Meyrin 2. In French. – **14)** Via Varenna 18, 6600 Locarno. In Italian. – **15)** Bionstrasse 4, 9001 St.Gallen – **16A,B)** Rue de Romont 35, 1701 Fribourg. 16A) in French. – **17)** Rue du 23-Juin 20, 2800 Delémont. In French. – **18)** Route des Jeunes 12, 1227 Carouge. In French. – **19)** Sommeraustrasse 32, 7007 Chur – **20)** En Budron A6, 1052 Le-Mont-sur-Lausanne. In French. – **21)** Zürichstr. 5, 6004 Luzern – **22)** Treichweg 1, 3930 Visp – **23)** Champs-Montants 16a, 2074 Marin. In French. – **24)** Erlenstrasse 2, 6343 Rotkreuz – **25)** Bürglistrasse 31a, 8401 Winterthur – **26)** Bahnhofplatz 1, 8640 Rapperswil – **27A,B)** Robert-Walser-Platz 7, 2501 Biel. 27B) in French. – **28)** Oslostrasse 10, 4142 Münchenstein.

DAB Transmitters (DAB+ exc.*= dual DAB/DAB+)
Licensee: SRG SSR **M1:** R. SRF 1*, R. SRF 2 Kultur, R. SRF 3, R. SRF 4 News, R. SRF Musikwelle*, R. SRF Virus, Swiss Pop, Swiss Classic, Swiss Jazz, RTS La 1ère, RSI Rete Uno, RTR R. Rumantsch **M2:** RTS La 1ère*, RTS Espace 2, RTS Couleur 3, RTS Option Musique*, Swiss Pop, Swiss Classic, Swiss Jazz, R. SRF 1, R. SRF Musikwelle, RSI Rete Uno, RTR R. Rumantsch, WRS **M3:** RSI Rete Uno*, RSI Rete Due*, RSI Rete Tre*, Swiss Pop, Swiss Classic, Swiss Jazz, R. SRF 1, R. SRF Musikwelle, RTS La 1ère, RTS Option Musique, RTR R. Rumantsch **M4:** R. SRF 1*, R. SRF 2 Kultur, R. SRF 3, R. SRF 4 News, R. SRF Musikwelle*, R. SRF Virus, Swiss Pop, Swiss Classic, Swiss Jazz, RTS La 1ère, RSI Rete Uno, RTR R. Rumantsch* – **Licensee:** SwissMediaCast AG **M5:** Lifechannel, R. Inside, Energy Zürich, Energy Basel, Eviva, Top Two, R. Top, R. 24, R. FM1, ERF Plus, R. Maria, R. Central, R. Argovia, R. Pilatus, Landliebe R., RTS Espace 2, RTS Option Musique, RSI Rete Tre **M6a-c:** **Regional muxes** (all on muxes: SRG R. SRF 1 (subregional editions), R. Zürisee) **M6a:** R. Sunshine, Basilisk **M6b:** Energy Bern, R. Bern1, R. FR. Freiburg, R. 32 **M6c:** R. L (Liechtenstein), R. Melody – **Licensee:** Romandie Médias SA **M7:** RSI Rete Tre, SRG R. SRF 4 News, Rhone FM, R. Chablais, LFM+, One FM, Rouge FM, Yes FM, Vertical, RadioFR., RadioFR. Music, BNJ-RJB, BNJ-RTN, BNJ-RFJ, GRIFF – **Licensee:** Digris AG **M:** Local muxes in key agglomerations. New muxes planned for Bern and Aarau. **M-GE (Genève):** Backstage R., Fréquence Banane, LaFabrik, 7radio, Magic R., Spoon R., R. 74, Global FM, IP Music, Maxxima, Open Broadcast, Traxx FM, R. Vostok, Plein Air, WRS **M-LA (Lausanne):** Open Broadcast, Global FM, IP Music, Maxxima, 7radio **M-OW (Oberwallis):** RRO, Global FM, Vibration 108, lischers R., Open Broadcast **M-ZH (Zürich):** Backstage R., R. 4TNG, Kanal K, Lora, Open Broadcast, Planet 105, R. 74, R. Industrie, rundfunk.fm, R. X, Spoon R., R. Stadtfilter, Txoxic FM, Traxx FM.

Block	MHz	kW	Location	Mux
7A	188.928	-	SFN (Nordschweiz)	6a
7D	194.064	-	SFN (Deutschschweiz)	5
8B	197.648	-	SFN (Mittelland)	6b
8C	199.360	10	Reyvroz (Mont. des Sœurs)**	Digris LA
9A	202.928	1	Felsenegg (Stigberg)	Digris ZH
9D	208.064	-	SFN (Ostschweiz)	6c
9D	208.064	-	SFN (Oberwallis)	Digris OW
10B	211.648	-	SFN (Romandie)	7
10D	215.072	0.6	Crozet (Fierney)**	Digris GE
12A	225.648	-	SFN (Romandie)	2
12A	225.648	-	SFN (Ticino)	3
12C	227.360	-	SFN (Deutschschweiz¹)	1
12D	229.072	-	SFN (Graubünden)	4

**) Located in France ¹) exc. Graubünden

SYRIA

L.T: UTC +2h (25 Mar-28 Oct: +3h; subject to confirmation) — **Pop:** 20 million — **Pr.L:** Arabic — **E.C:** 50Hz, 220V — **ITU:** SYR

MINISTRY OF INFORMATION
✉ Mezzeh Autostrad, Dar al Ba'th Building, Damascus ☎+963 11 6664681 🖷 +963 11 6664681 **W:** moi.gov.sy **E:** info@moi.gov.sy **L.P:** Talib Qadi Amin, Asst. Minister.

SYRIAN RADIO AND TV (Gov.)
✉ Radio & TV Directorate, Ommayad Square, Damascus ☎+963 11 2720700 🖷 +963 11 2234930 **W:** rtv.gov.sy **L.P:** DG: Fayez Al Sayegh. Dir. Eng: Adnan Salhah. Dir. Radio: Mahmoud Al Joma'at.

MW	kHz	kW	Prgr	MW	kHz	kW	Prgr
Adra	567	300	1	Tartus	783	300	1/E
Sabboura	666	50	2	Deir ez-Zor	828	200	1

MW	kHz	kW	Prgr	MW	kHz	kW	Prgr
Tartus	1071	100	*	Aleppo	1314	50	1

*relays R. Al-Nour, LBN

FM	1	2/M	Y	kW
Abu Kamal	-	-	92.6	
Afrin	93.0	90.3	96.6	
Al-Hassake	89.9	93.0	99.5	
Aleppo	96.1	99.4	89.9	10
Ayn al-Arab	89.4	-	105.1	
Bloudan	93.5	-	96.7	
Damascus	95.5	98.3	88.7	
Deir ez-Zor	90.0	94.1	87.8	150/1
Homs	-	-	99.3	
Maliqiyah	89.4	92.1	99.0	
Nabi Saleh	89.0	93.0	98.8	
Raqqah	103.7	96.9	93.7	
Slenfe	94.9	91.7	88.6	150
Suwayda	92.6	87.8	100.9	150
Tartus	-	-	95.5	
Yabrud	-	-	93.0	

General Prgr (1): 24h. Incl. **VO Armed Forces:** 1630-1700 and **R. Palestine** prgr: 1700-1730.
Voice of the People (2): 24h. **Voice of Youth (Y)** 0400-2400. **Aleppo local prgr (A):** 1300-1600. **E:** External Service. 666 and 783kHz heard also relaying TV audio.
Ann: 1: "Idha'at Dimashq". 2: "Huna Idha'at Sowt as-Sha'ab min Dimashq". Y: "Huna Sowt as-Shabab". R. Palestine: "Idha'at Falasteen min Dimashq". Aleppo: "Idha'at al-Halab".

EXTERNAL SERVICE: R. Damascus: see International Radio section.

Other stations:
Al Madina FM: Slenfe 100.5MHz, Aleppo/Damascus 101.5MHz. **W:** almadinafm.com – **Arabesque FM:** Aleppo/Damascus 102.3MHz, Slenfe 106.9MHz. **W:** arabesque.fm – **Fann FM:** Aleppo/Damascus 89.0MHz, Slenfe 106.1MHz. **W:** fann-fm.com – **Farah FM:** Aleppo/Damascus 97.3MHz. **W:** farah.fm – **R. Gecko (UN)**, Camp Faouar, Golan: 103.8MHz. **W:** radio-gecko.com – **Melody FM:** Aleppo/Damascus 97.9MHz. **W:** melodysyria.com – **Mix FM:** Damascus: 105.7MHz. **W:** mixfmsyria.com – **Ninar FM:** Aleppo 88.3MHz, Slenfe 89.6MHz, Damascus 93.8MHz. **W:** ninarweb.com – **Rotana Style FM:** Slenfe 103.3MHz, Aleppo/Damascus 105.0MHz. **W:** rotanastyle.com – **Sawt el-Ghad,** Damascus: 99.9MHz. **W:** sawtelghad.com – **Shahba FM,** Aleppo 94.0MHz. **W:** shahbafm.com – **Sham FM:** Damascus 92.3MHz, Aleppo 95.3MHz, Slenfe 101.8MHz. **W:** shamfm. fm – **Syria Al-Ghad:** Damascus 104.2MHz, Aleppo 104.4MHz, Slenfe 107.4MHz. **W:** syriaalghad.com
– **Version FM:** Damascus 94.4MHz. **W:** versionfm.com
NB: many stns and transmitters reported off the air or operating irregularly. An increasing number of of unlicensed stations are in operation.
Nasaem FM: Aleppo 98.5MHz. Tx believed to be in Turkey. **W:** nasaem-syria.com **E:** info@nasaem-syria.com
Watan FM reported in Damascus, operated by the opposition.
W: facebook.com/fm.watan **E:** watan.sy.info@gmail.com
Rozana R. W: rozana.fm **F.PI:** relays via FM stations in Syria and shortwave transmissions

TAIWAN (Rep. of China)

L.T: UTC +8h — **Pop:** 23.3 million — **Pr.L:** Mandarin (Chinese), Taiwanese (Amoy), Hakka — **E.C:** 60Hz, 110V — **ITU:** CHN (**WRTH:** TWN)

NATIONAL COMMUNICATIONS COMMISSION (NCC)
RenAi Rd. Office: ✉ No. 50, Sec. 1, RenAi Rd., Taipei 10052 ☎ + 886 800 177177 🖷 + 886 2 2343 3994 **W:** ncc.gov.tw **E:** po2@ncc.gov.tw
L.P: Chairperson: Howard S. H. Shyr

CHUNGKUO KUANGPO KUNGSSU (Broadcasting Corporation of China - BCC) (Priv. Comm.)
✉ 375 Sungchiang Rd, Chungshan Ward, Taipei 104 ☎ + 886 2 2501 9688 🖷 + 886 2 2501 8834 **W:** bcc.com.tw **E:** pr@bcc.com.tw
L.P: Chairman: Chao Shao Kang
Call: BE followed by the callsign below

	MW	Call	Location	kHz	kW	Netw.
1)		D57	Taipei (Tucheng)	531	10	L
10)		D65	Ilan	630	10	N
10)		D34	Taipei (Tucheng)	648	20	N
6)		D92	Tainan	711	10	C
4)		D58	Taichung	720	10	N

MW	Call	Location	kHz	kW	Netw.
8)	D28	Taitung	819	10	N
9)	D27	Hualien	855	10	N
7)	D25	Kaohsiung	864	10	N
2)	G77	Hsinchu	882	10	N
6)	D24	Tainan	891	10	L
4)	D43	Taichung	927	10	C
1)	D55	Taipei (Tucheng)	963	20	C
8)	D88	Taitung	1008	10	C
2)	D53	Hsinchu	1017	10	C
5)	D26	Chia-i	1035	10	C
4)	D23	Taichung	1062	10	L
11)	D72	Yuli*	1116	3.5	C
12)	D68	Puli*	1152	1	C
10)	D86	Ilan	1161	10	C
3)	D89	Miaoli	1161	10	C
9)	D32	Hualien	1188	10	C
7)	D52	Kaohsiung	1224	10	C
6)	D47	Tainan	1296	10	N
5)	D63	Chia-i	1350	10	N
11)	D74	Yuli*	1386	3.5	N
3)	D54	Miaoli	1413	10	N
12)	D67	Puli*	1413	1	N

N=News Netw, C=Country Netw, , L=local

FM	Location	P	F	M	kW
1)	Taipei	103.3	105.9	96.3	35/10/35
3)	Huoyenshan	102.9	101.5	96.1	10/10/10
4)	Taichung	102.1	106.9	96.3	35/10/35
5)	Chentoushan	103.1	104.3	96.1	10/10/5
7)	Kaohsiung	103.3	105.9	96.3	35/10/35
8)	Taitung	102.1	106.9	96.3	5/2.5/2.5
9)	Hualien	102.1	106.9	96.3	5/2.5/5
10)	Ilan	102.1	102.9	96.1	2.5/2.5/2.5
11)	Yuli*	103.3	105.7		1/2.5
12)	Puli*	107.3			1
13)	Kinmen*	96.3			10

P=Pop Netw, F=Formosa Netw, M=Music Netw. *) relay stn

D.Prgr: News Network: 24h in Mandarin – **Country Network:** 24h in Amoy – **Taipei Local R. (i go 531):** 24h mainly in Mandarin/Hakka – **Pop Network(i like radio):** 24h in Mandarin – **Formosa Network:** 24h in Amoy – **Music Network (i radio):** 24h in Mandarin
Addresses of local stations:
2) 125-1, Chingpu Rd, Chiingpu, Hsinfeng Village, Hsinchu 304 – **3)** 78, Lane 1008, Chungshan Rd, Kaomiao Li, Miaoli 360 – **4)** 35th Flr, 758 Chungming So. Rd, Taichung 402 – **5)** 121 Wufeng So. Rd, Chia-i 600 – **6)** 5, 19th Flr, 248, Sec. 2, Yunghua Rd, Anping, Tainan 708 – **7)** 1, 24th Flr, 91 Chungshan 2nd Rd, Chienchen, Kaohsiung 806 – **8)** 23, Lane 52, Kuilin No. Rd, Taitung 950 – **9)** 25 Shuiyuan Str, Hualien 970 – **10)** 8 Kuchie Rd, Chuangwei Village, Ilan 263 – **11)** Yuli (relay st.) – **12)** Puli (relay st.) – **13)** Kinmen (relay st.), relays also News Netw at certain times
Ann: Mandarin: "Chungkuo Kuangpo Kungssu" or "Chungkuo Kuangpo Kungssu, (location) Kuangpo Tientai", Amoy: "Tiyon Gok Kon Po Kon Sih, (location) Kon Po Den Tai"

EXTERNAL SERVICES: Radio Taiwan International
see International Broadcasting section

HAN SHENG KUANGPO TIENTAI (Voice of Han Broadcasting Networking) (Gov)
(operated by General Political Warfare Bureau, Ministry of National Defense)
✉ B, 5th Flr, 3, Sec. 1, Hsin-i Rd, Chungcheng Ward, Taipei 10048 ☎ + 886 2 2321 5191 📠 + 886 2 2396 2657 **W:** voh.com.tw

MW	Call	Location	kHz	kW
1)	C22	Taipei	684	10
1b)	C25	Taoyuan	693	10
2b)	C32	Tainan	693	8
4)	C33	Hualien	792	10
2c)	C38	Penghu	846	10
1b)		Taoyuan	936	5
3b)	C31	Yunlin	1089	10
1)	C22	Taipei	1116	10
4b)	C30	Ilan	1116	10
2)		Kaohsiung	1251	10
2c)	C44	Penghu	1269	10
3)	C27	Taichung	1287	10
2)	C36	Kaohsiung	1332	10
4)	C40	Hualien	1359	5

FM	Call	Location	MHz	kW
2b)	C28	Tainan(Chentoushan)	101.3	35
1)	C26	Miaoli (Huoyenshan)	104.5	35

FM	Call	Location	MHz	kW
4)	C35	Hualien	104.5	3
4c)	C39	Taitung	105.3	3
1)	C24	Taipei	106.5	35
4b)		Ilan*	106.5	
2)	C34	Kaohsiung	107.3	35
4)	C37	Hualien	107.3	3
1c)		Kinmen*	107.3	0.1

*) relay stn
D.Prgr: MW: 2100-1600, FM 24h. Rel. RTI "Voice of Taiwan" domestic foreign language sce: **D:** Mon-Fri 0500-0600&1500-1600, Fri&Sat 2200-0000 on FM – **1b)** Taoyuan **1c)** Kinmen (relay Taipei) – **2)** 40 Mingte New Village, Tsoying, Kaohsiung 813 – **2b)** Tainan 2c) 1 Makong, Penghu (relay Kaohsiung) – **3)** 78 Chenhsing Rd, Taichung 401 – 4) 643 Chungcheng Rd, Hualien 970 – 4b) Ilan 4c)Taitng (relay Hiualien)

BROADCASTS TO MAINLAND:
KUANGHUA CHIH SHENG (Voice of Kuanghua)
✉ P.O.Box 1700, Taipei ☎ + 886 2 2603 0429 📠 + 886 2 2603 0433
W: khmusic.com.tw

MW Location	kHz	kW	Location	kHz	kW
Hsinfeng	711	250	Kuanyin	846	250
Kuanyin	801	250	Hsinfeng	981	250

D.Prgr. 24h

SW Location	kHz	kW
Kuanyin	‡9745	250

D.Prgr. 0755-0005 **Ann:** "Kuanghua chih Sheng"

FU HSING KUANGPO TIENTAI (Fu Hsing Broadcasting Station) (Gov)
(operated by Ministry of National Defense)
✉ 5, Lane 280, Sec. 5, Chungshan No. Rd, Shihlin Ward, Taipei 111
☎ + 886 2 2882 3450 📠 + 886 2 2881 8218 **W:** fhbs.com.tw

MW	Call	Location	kHz	kW
1)	H7	Taipei 1	558	1
2)	H2	Taipei 2	594	10
3)	H38	Taichung 2	594	5
3)	H44	Kaohsiung 1	594	10
3)	H56	Kaohsiung 2	846	10
1)	H3	Taipei 1	909	10
1)	H5	Taipei2	1089	5
2)	H34	Taichung 2	1089	10

SW	Call	Location	kHz	kW
1)		Kuanyin	9410	10
1)		Kuanyin	9774	10
1)		Kuanyin	15375	10

FM	Call	Location	MHz	kW
1)	I44	Taichung 1	107.8	10

D.Prgr: 1st Netw on 558/909kHz, **2nd Netw.** on 594/1089kHz, both 24h **Shortwave Netw.** on 9410/9774/15375kHz 2300-0100, 0400-0600, 0800-1000, 1100-1300 for China Mainland. At present time only 9410kHz audible occasionally.
Local Stations: 2) 81 Chungtai Rd, Chunshe Li, Nantun, Taichung 408. **1st Netw.** on 107.8MHz **2nd Netw.** on 594/1089kHz – **3)** 819 Chengching Rd, Niaosung Village, Kaohsiung 833. **1st Netw.** on 594kHz **2nd Netw.** on 846kHz **Ann:** "Fu Hsing Kuangpo Tientai, (location) Tai"

OTHER PUBLIC & COMMERCIAL STATIONS (Call: BE.)

MW	Call	Station	Location	kHz	kW
6a)		Taiwan	Tahsi	621	1
6c)		Taiwan	Sungling	630	10
7b)	V59	Cheng Sheng	Taichung 2	657	20
7c)		Cheng Sheng	Peikang	675	5
8)	E43	Shih Hsin	Taipei	729	0.5
2)	L2	Yuyeh	Penghu	738	100
9)		Sheng Li	Makung	756	1
6b)	V94	Taiwan	Taichung	774	20
10)	V88	Hsien Sheng	Taoyuan	774	20
9)	V56	Sheng Li	Tainan 1	774	1
11)	V79	Keelung	Keelung	792	1
12)		Chien kuo	Hsinhua	801	1
13)	V54	Kuo Sheng	Changhua	810	10
7)	V35	Cheng Sheng	Taipei	819	5
7a)	V72	Cheng Sheng	Chia-i	855	1
14)	V24	Min Pen	Taipei 2	855	1
15)		Feng Ming	Penghu	882	1
16)	V98	Cheng Kung	Kaohsiung	936	1
12)	V85	Chien Kuo	Hsinying	954	10
6c)	V84	Taiwan	Chunghsing	963	10
15)	V68	Feng Ming	Kaohsiung 2	981	3
7b)	V58	Cheng Sheng	Taichung 1	990	20
17)	V92	Tien Nan	Taipei	999	1

MW	Call	Station	Location	kHz	kW
7f)	V60	Cheng Sheng	Kaohsiung	1008	1
18)		Tien Sheng	Yuanli	1026	1
19)	V51	Chung Hua	Sanchung 2	1026	1
20)	V64	Yen Sheng	Hualien 1	1044	5
7d)	V82	Cheng Sheng	Ilan	1062	1
21)	V74	Min Li	Pingtung	1062	5
6a)		Taiwan	Kuanhsi	1062	1
22)	V96	Tien Sheng	Tainan	1071	1
5)	G28	Kaohsiung	Kaohsiung	1089	10
7c)	V36	Cheng Sheng	Yunlin	1125	5
4)	G26	Taipei	Taipei	1134	10
3)	L3	Yuyeh	Penghu	1143	100
23)	V70	Hua Sheng	Taipei 1	1152	5
15)	V67	Feng Ming	Kaohsiung 1	1161	1.2
13)		Kuo Sheng	Erhlin	1179	2.5
6)	V46	Taiwan	Taipei 2	1188	1
9)	V57	Sheng Li	Tainan 2	1188	1
6a)	V62	Taiwan	Hsinchu	1206	10
18)		Tien Sheng	Pengshan	1215	1
23)	V71	Hua Sheng	Taipei 2	1224	1
19)		Chung Hua	Juifang	1233	1
20)		Yen Sheng	Hualien 2	1242	1
7a)		Cheng Sheng	Taipao	1260	1
7e)	V37	Cheng Sheng	Taitung	1269	1
24)		Fuhsingkang	Peitou	1278	1
21)		Min Li	Fangliao	1287	1
14)	V23	Min Pen	Taipei 1	1296	1
1c)	P33	Ching Cha	Tainan	1314	1
18)	V76	Tien Sheng	Chunan	1314	10
6)	V45	Taiwan	Taipei 1	1323	1
6c)		Taiwan	Puli	1332	1
19)	V50	Chung Hua	Sanchung 1	1350	2.5
25)		Chin Hsi	Kaohsiung	1368	1
7f)		Cheng Sheng	Tafa	1395	1
26)	V78	Yi Shih	Keelung	1404	10
12)		Chien Kuo	Kuanyin	1422	1
2)	E32	Chiao Yu	Taipei	1494	10
2a)	E34	Chiao Yu	Changhua	1494	5
1a)		Ching Cha	Hsinchu	1512	1
3a)		Yuyeh	Ilan	1593	1

FM	Call	MHz	kW	FM	Call	MHz	kW	FM	Call	MHz	kW
8)		88.1		56)		97.7	3	31c)		100.8	
2f)		88.9	1	57)		97.7	3	82)		101.1	3
2l)		88.9	1	58)		97.9	3	1f)	P35	101.3	1.5
2n)		91.5		59)		97.9	3	1e)	P39	101.3	1
32)		92.1	3	2i)		98.1	3	1g)	P37	101.3	1.5
33)		92.1	3	60)	M23	98.1	3	2)	E33	101.7	30
34)		92.3	3	61)		98.3	3	2b)	E36	101.7	30
35)		92.7	3	62)		98.3	3	83)		102.3	3
36)		92.9	3	63)		98.3	3	84)	M27	102.5	3
37)		92.9	3	64)		98.5	3	2d)	E38	102.9	5
1d)	P42	93.1	25	65)		98.5	3	2a)	E35	103.5	30
4)	G25	93.1	10	66)		98.7	3	2g)	E40	103.5	10
38)		93.3	3	67)		98.7	3	2c)	E37	103.7	5
39)		93.5	3	68)		98.7	3	2h)	E41	103.9	3
40)		93.5	3	69)	M31	98.9	3	85)		103.9	3
41)		93.7	3	70)		98.9	3	87)	M22	104.1	3
42)		93.7	3	2k)		99.1	4	1)	P29	104.9	35
43)		93.7	3	71)		99.1	3	1c)	P31	104.9	
44)		93.9	3	72)		99.1	3	1d)	P32	104.9	12
1)	P41	94.3	10	2m)		99.3	3	1c)		104.9	8
1f)	P44	94.3	5	73)		99.3	3	1b)	P30	105.1	35
1g)	P45	94.3	5	74)	M24	99.5	3	2k)		105.3	3
5)	G29	94.3	16	75)	N77	99.5	3	86)		105.5	3
1b)	P43	94.5	30	76)		99.5	3	87)		105.5	3
45)		96.7	3	77)		99.7	3	88)		105.7	3
46)		96.7	3	78)		99.7	3	89)	M29	106.1	3
47)		96.9	3	79)	M30	99.9	3	1f)	P36	106.5	1.5
48)		96.9	3	2e)		100.1		90)		106.5	3
49)	N61	97.1	3	31b)		100.1	13	91)		106.7	3
50)		97.1	3	2f)	E39	100.3	1	92)	M28	106.9	3
51)		97.1	3	80)		100.3	3	93)		107.1	3
53)		97.3	3	2d)		100.5	3	94)		107.3	3
2c)		97.3	3	81)	M26	100.7	3	95)		107.7	3
52)		97.3	3	31)	M3	100.7	30	2j)		107.7	3
54)	N74	97.5	1	31a)		100.7	27	96)	M25	107.7	3
55)		97.5	3								

NB: + more than 80 low-powered community FM stns

Addresses and other information: under **30)** AM or AM/FM stn(s), above **30)** only FM stn(s)

1) Chingcha Kuangpo Tientai (Police Broadcasting Service), 17 Kuangchou Str, Chungcheng, Taipei 10066. Three networks in 24h: AM Reg. Public Security Traffic Netw. (ARS), FM Nat. Public Security Traffic Netw. (FNS) and FM Reg. Public Security Traffic Netw. (FRS). FNS on 104.9MHz,FRS on 94.3MHz – **1a)** 389 Sec.2, Hsinglung Rd, Chupei City, Hsinchu 302. ARS on 1512kHz – **1b)** 99 Po-ai Str, Nantun, Taichung 408. FNS on 105.1MHz, FRS on 94.5MHz – **1c)** 85-21, Nanshih, Nanshih Li, Matou, Tainan 721. ARS on 1314kHz, FNS on 104.9MHz – **1d)** 455 Po-ai 4th Rd, Tsoying Ward, Kaohsiung 813. FNS on 104.9MHz, FRS on 93.1MHz – **1e)** 89 Sec. 2, Minchuan Rd. Ilan 26049. FRS on 101.3MHz – **1f)** 21-2 Fuchien Rd, Hualien 970. , FNS on 101.3, 106.5MHz, FRS on 94.3MHz – **1g)** 289, Chungshan Rd. Taitung 950. FNS on 101.3MHz, FRS on 94.3MHz **W:** pbs.gov.tw – **2)** Chiao Yu Broadc. System – National Education R., 41 Nanhai Rd, Taipei 10066. On MW, FM both 24h **Ann:** "Chiao Yu chih Sheng, Chiao Yu Kuangpo Tientai" – **2a)** 5-1 Hukang Rd, Changhua 50080 – **2b)** 380 Kuangtung 3rd Rd, Kaohsiung 80656 – **2c)** 457 Tunghsing Rd, Hualien 97063. 1st prgr on 103.7MHz, 2nd prgr on 97.3MHz – **2d)** 135, Ma Hengheng Rd, Taitung 95047. 1st prgr on 102.9MHz, 2nd prgr on 100.5MHz – **W:** ner.gov.tw – **2e)** Keelung – **2f)** Yuli (1st prgr on 100.3MHz, 2nd prgr on 88.9MHz) relay Hualien – **2g)** Ilan – **2h)** Miaoli – **2i)** Nantou relay Changhua – **2j)** Chia-I relay Kaohsiung – **2k)** Penghu (1st prgr on 99.1MHz, 2nd prgr on 105.3MHz) – **2l)** Kinmen relay Taipei – **2m)** Hengchun relay Kaohsiung – **2n)** Matzu relay Taipei – **3)** Yuyeh Broadc. St (Fishery R. Station), 5 Yukang No. 1 Rd, Chienchen Ward, Kaohsiung 806. 24h Weather rpt. at every h External service: see Internationl Broadcasting section. **Ann:** "Hi-giap Kong-po'-tian-tai" **W:** frs.gov.tw – **3a)** Ilan (relay stn) – **4)** Taipei Broadc. St, 4th Flr, 62-2, Sec. 3, Chungshan No. Rd, Taipei 10452 (operated by Taipei City Council). AM "Ho Hi Yan" Ch. on 1134kHz, 2300-1600. FM "City Info" Ch. on 93.1MHz, 24h. **Rel:** BBC-WS: MF1400-1500, Sun-Thu2200-2300. **W:** radio.taipei.gov.tw – **5)** Kaohsiung Broadc. St, 90 Hsinchiang Rd, Kushan, Kaohsiung 80472 (operated by Kaohsiung City Council). Two prgr on 1089kHz, 94.3MHz, both 2200-1800 **W:** kbs.gov. tw – **6)** Taiwan Broadc. Co, 9th Flr, 2, Sec 2, Jen-ai Rd, Chungcheng, Taipei 100. 1st prgr on 1323kHz, 24h 2nd prgr on 1188kHz, 24h **W:** taiwanradio.com.tw – **6a)** 2, Lane 506, Kaofeng Rd, Hsinchu 300. 24h – **6b)** 25th Flr, 787, Chungming So. Rd, Taichung. 24h – **6c)** 258-1 Fentsao Rd, Tsaotun Town, Nantou 542. 24h – **7)** Cheng Sheng Broadc. Corp., 7th Flr, 1, Lane 66, Sec. 1, Chungching So. Rd, Taipei 10045. 819kHz, 104.1MHz both 24h – **7a)** 17,Chuiyang Rd. Chia-i 60043. 24h – **7b)** 760, Sec. 2, Chunghsing Rd, Tali Ward, Taichung 41244. 1st prgr on 990kHz, 2nd prgr on 657kHz, both 24h. – **7c)** 3rd Flr 32, Lane 416, 1 Sec. Linsen Rd, Huwei Town, Yunlin 63243 – **7d)** 45 Chienchun Rd, Ilan 26051. 24h – **7e)** 21, Lane 380, Hsinsheng Rd, Taitung 95052. 24h – **7f)** 838 Chengching Rd, Niaosung , Kaohsiung 83347. Kaohsiung St. on 1008kHz, Tafa St. on 1395kHz, both 24h **W:** csbc.com.tw – **8)** Shih Hsin Radio St, 1, Lane 17, Sec. 1, Mushan Rd, Wenshan Ward, Taipei 11604. AM: and FM both 2255-1605(Sun 1305) **W:** shrs.shu.edu.tw – **9)** Shengli chih Sheng (Voice of Victory) Broadc. Co, 22, Sec. 1, Chienkang Rd, Chunghsi Ward, Tainan 700. 1st Prgr. on 774kHz, 24h 2nd Prgr. on 1188kHz, 24h Makung St. on 756kHz, 24h **Ann:** "Tainan Sheng Li chih Sheng Kuangpo Tientai" **W:** e-go.org.tw/victor/ – **10)** Hsien Sheng Broadc. Co, 1, 16th Flr, Lane 505, Chungshan Rd, Taoyuan Ward, Taoyuan 330. 24h **W:** am774.myweb.hinet.net – **11)** Keelung Broadc. St, 12th Flr, 13 Chungsu Rd, Keelung 200. 24h – **12)** Chien Kuo Broadc. St, 78 Chienkuo Rd, Hsinying , Tainan 730. 24h– **13)** Kuo Sheng Broadc. Co, 35 Wenchuan Rd, Pakuashan, Changhua 500. 24h – **13a)** 2 Taiping Rd, Erhlin Town, Changhua 526 – **14)** Min Pen Broadc. Co, 6th Flr, 325, Sec. 3, Huanho So. Rd, Wanhua Ward, Taipei 108. 1st Prgr on 1296kHz, 2nd Prgr on 855kHz, both 24h **W:** mingpen.com.tw – **15)** Feng Ming Broadc. Co, 492 Chiuju 2nd Rd, Sanmin Ward, Kaohsiung 807. 1st Prgr on 1161kHz, 2nd Prgr on 981kHz, both 24h **W:** fengmin.com.tw – **15a)** Chentieh Hsien, Li 38, Makung, Penghu – **16)** Chengkung Broadc. St, 63 Chunghua 3rd Rd, Kaohsiung 801. 24h (exc. Sun 1600-2100). – **17)** Tien Nan Broadc. St, 7th Flr. 235, Sec. 4, Chengte Rd, Shihlin Ward, Taipei 111. 24h **W:** tnbcam999. myweb.hinet.net– **18)** T'ien Sheng Broadc. St, 285 Kungyi Rd, Chunan Town, Miaoli 350. 24h – **18a)** 8, Kozhuang, Chungshue Rd, Yuanli Town, Miaoli 358. Yuanli St. on 1026kHz, Pengshan St. on 1215kHz, both 24h – **19)** Chung Hwa (China) Broadc. Co, 6th Flr, 238 Hopien No. Str, Sanchung, New Taipei 241. 1st Prgr on 1350kHz, 2nd prgr on 1026kHz, both 24h **Ann:** "Chung Hua Kuangpo Tientai Ti I/Erh Tai". Juifang St,. relays 2nd prgr on 1233kHz, 24h **W:** chbc. wunme.com – **20)** Yen Sheng Broadc. St, 31, Sec. 1, Nanpin Rd, Tungchang, Chi-an Village, Hualien 973. On 1044, 1242kHz, both 24h **W:** ysbc.myweb. hinet. net – **21)** Min Li Broadc. St, 57-20 Minsheng Rd, Pingtung 900. 24h – **22)** Tien Sheng Broadc. St, 11th Flr, 149, Sec. 1, Linsen Rd, Ea. Ward Tainan 701. 24h (exc. Sun 1600-2155) **W:** am1071. com.tw – **23)** Hua Sheng Broadc. Co, 18 Huasheng Str, Shihlin Ward, Taipei 111. 1st Prgr on 1152kHz, 2nd Prgr on 1224kHz, both 24h **W:** hsradio.com.tw – **24)** Fuhsingkang Broadac. Stn. 70, Sec .2, Chungyang Rd, Peitou, Taipei 112 – **25)** Chin Hsi Broadc. Co, 2nd Flr, 461 Wenfu Rd,

Tsoying, Kaohsiung 804. 24h **W:** am1368 com.tw – **26)** Yi Shih Broadc. St, 75 Paisan Str, Chitu Ward, Keelung 206. 24h **Ann:** "Keelung Yi Shih Kuangpo Tientai" **W:** yishih.ehosting.com.tw **31)** International Community R. Taipei (ICRT), 19-5F, No.5 Sec 3, New Taipei Rd, Hsinchuang Ward, New Taipei 24250. 24h in English Rel. BBC News Sun-Thu 2200-2230 – **31a)** Kaohsiung – **31b)** Taichung – **31c)** Chia-i **W:** icrt.com.tw – **32)** Fei Tieh (UFO) Broadc. Co (UFO Netw), 25th Flr, 102, Sec. 2, Lossufou Rd, Chungcheng Ward, Taipei 100. 24h **W:** uforadio. com.tw UFO Netw: Miaoli 91.3MHz, Taichung 89.9MHz, Yunlin & Chia-i district 90.5MHz, Kaohusing 103.9MHz, Ilan 89.9MHz, Hualien 91.3MHz, Taitung 91.3MHz, Penghu 89.7MHz – **33)** Chin Sheng Broadc. St, 25th Flr, 206 Kuanghua 1st Rd, Lingya, Kaohsiung 802. 24h – **34)** Chia-i (Chia Le Broadc St), 1, 16th Flr, 193, Hsiaoya Rd, Chia-i 600. – **35)** Yachou (Asia) Broadc. St (Asia FM Netw), 2, 22nd Flr, 102 Chungping Rd, Taoyuan Ward, Taoyuan 330. 24h **W:** asiafm.com.tw – **36)** Cheng Shih Broadc. St, 28th Flr, 758 Chungming So. Rd, So. Ward, Taichung 402 **W:** goldfm.com.tw – Other Gold FM Netw st: Taipei 90.1MHz, Miaoli 98.3MHz, Tainan 97.1MHz – **37)** Taiwu chih Chun Broadc.(Yes R.) St. 9, Lane 240, Sec. 1, Poyu Rd. Panglin, Chinning, Kinmen 893 – **38)** Yun Chia Broadc. St, 9th Flr, 617 Chungshan Rd, Chia-i 600. 24h **W:** fm933.com. tw – **39)** Hsin Kechia Broadc. St, 1, 16th Flr, 411 Huannan Rd, Pingchen Ward, Taoyuan 324. 24h – **40)** Lien Hua Broadc. St. (Best 935) 3, 8th Flr. 65, Kuolienssu Rd. Hualien 970 – **41)** Pao Tao Kechia Broadc. St, (Formosa Hakka R. Stn.) 2, 17th Flr, 91, Sec. 2, Lossufu Rd, Ta'an Ward, Taipei 10646. 24h **W:** formosahakka.org.tw – **42)** Sheng Tu Broadc. Co, 233 Fentsao Rd, Tsaotun Town, Nantou 542. 24h **W:** fm937.com.tw – **43)** Ling Hsiu Broadc. St, – 10, 20th Flr. 149, Sec. 1, Linsen Rd. Tainan 701 – **44)** Ta Ti chih Sheng Broadc. St. 10, Chengpei Village, Huhsi, Makung, Penghu 880 – **45)** Huan Yu Broadc. Co (Uni R.), 3, 6th Flr, 675, Sec. 1, Chingkuo Rd, Hsinchu 300. 24h **W:** turc967.com.tw – **46)** Penghu Broadc. St. 2nd Flr. 1-204, I-lin Shihchuan-li, Makung, Penghu 880 – **47)** Tien Tien (Sky) Broadc. St, 42nd Flr, 760 Chungming So. Rd, So. Ward, Taichung 402. 24h **W:** tw.myblog.yahoo.com/sky9692004 – **48)** Chu Jen (Boss) Broadc. St, 17th Flr, 155, Fujen Rd, Lingya, Kaohsiung 802. 24h – **49)** Ta Han chih Yin (Voice of Hakka) Broadc. St, 1-1 Hsintung Rd, Toufen Town, Miaoli 351. 24h **W:** fm971.com.tw – **50)** Tainan chih Yin Broadc. St, 1-134 Chunghua Rd, Yongkang, Tainan 710 – **51)** Ilan chih Sheng (Voice of Ilan) Chung Shan Broadc. Co, 2nd Flr, 289-2 Kungcheng Rd, Lotung Town, Ilan 265. 24h **W:** super971.com.tw – **52)** Green Peace Broadc. St, 1, 14th Flr, 97, Sec. 4, Chunghsing Rd, Sanchung New Taipei 241. 24h **W:** greenpeace.com.tw – **53)** Ai Yu chih Sheng Broadc. St, 7, Lane 828, Sec. 3, Chinma Rd, Changhua 500. 24h **W:** tw.myblog.yahoo. com/fm973-fm973 – **54)** IC chih Yin, IC Broadc. Co. Ltd., 2, 11th Flr, 287, Sec. 2, Kuangfu Rd, Hsinchu 30071. 24h **W:** ic975.com – **55)** Kuai Le (Happy) Broadc. St, 1st Flr, 70, Ling-an Rd, Lingya, Kaohsiung 802. 24h. Happy R. Netw: Taipei 89.3MHz, Taichung 89.5MHz, Chia-I 92.3MHz, Hualien 98.3MHz, Penghu 91.3MHz & 96.7MHz – **56)** Taiwan Sheng Yin Broadc. St. 9th Flr. 76, Sec. 1, Minchuan Rd. Chungshan Ward, Taipei, 104. 24h – **57)** Hao Chia Ting Broadc. Co (Family 977 Broadc. Network), 37th Flr, 789 Chungming So. Rd. So. Ward, Taichung 402. 24h **W:** family977.com.tw – **58)** Tainan Kaihsuan Broadc. St, 2, 21th Flr, 425 Chunghua Rd, Yungkang, Tainan 710 – **59)** Ka Ma Lan Broadc. St, 46, Lane 455, Kangnuan Rd, Ilan 260 – **60)** Taiwan Chuan Min Broadc. St (News 98), 1, 25th Flr, 100, Sec. 2, Lossufu Rd, Chungcheng Ward, Taipei 100. 24h – **61)** Ta Miaoli FM Broadc. St, 3, 16th Flr, 1 Chanchien, Shangmiao Li, Miaoli 360. – **62)** Kang Tu Broadc. St (Best R.), 1, 34th Flr, 80 Mintsu 1st Rd, Sanmin Ward, Kaohsiung 807. 24h **W:** bestradio.com. tw Haoshih (Best) Netw: Taipei 98.9MHz, Taichung 90.3MHz, Hualien 93.5MHz – **63)** Hualien (Huan Le Broadc St), 3rd Flr, 196, Linsen Rd, Hualien 970 – **64)** Pao Tao Hsin Sheng (Super FM 98.5) Broadc. St, 1, 2nd Flr, 3, Sec. 1, Tunhua So. Rd, Sungshan Ward, Taipei 105. 24h **W:** superfm98-5.com.tw – **65)** Feifanyin Broadc. St (Libra R.), 40, Lane 40, Sec. 2, Shuangshih Rd. No. Ward, Taichung 40455. 24h **W:** libraradio. com.tw – **66)** Mei Jih Broadc. Co (Sakura R.), 1, 7th Flr, 1-67 Wuchuan Rd, We. Ward, Taichung 403. 24h **W:** fm987.com.tw – **67)** Ching Chun Broadc. St, 15-2, 53, Sec. 2, Lin'an Rd, No. Ward, Tainan 704. – **68)** Tung Min Broadc. St. 156, Fuyu Rd. Chihpen, Taitung 950. – **69)** Chin Yue Broadc. St (Best 989), 6th Flr, 88, Sec. 2, Chunghsiao East Rd, Chungcheng, Taipei 100. 24h – **70)** Cheng Kang Broadc. St. 2, 4th Flr. 73, Teming Rd. Chia-i, 600 – **71)** Ta Chien Broadc. St (Super 99.1), 2,22nd Flr. 309 Sec. 2, Taiwan Tatao, We. Ward, Taichung 403 **W:** superfm99-1. com.tw – **72)** Yang Kuang Broadc. St, 6, 21st Flr, 3, Tzuchiang 3rd Rd, Lingya, Kaohsiung 802. – **73)** Hsin Sheng FM Broadc. St, 1, 19th Flr, 37 Chianchung 1st Rd, Hsinchu 300 **W:** ss-radio.com.tw – **74)** Shen Nong (Farmer R.) Broadc. Co, 10th Flr, 234 Peiping Rd, Huwei Town, Yunlin 632.24h **W:** fm995.com.tw – **75)** Tong Fang Broadc. St, 13rd Flr, 168, Sec. 3, Chunching Rd, Lotung Town, Ilan 265. 24h – **76)** Lan Yu Broadc. St, 147, Yujen, Hongtou, Lanyu Village, Taitung 95241.24h **W:** lanan.org. tw/radeo.htm – **77)** Taipei Ai Yue Broadc. Co, 17th Flr, 47 Tunghsing Rd, Hsin-i, Taipei 110. 24h **W:** prtmusic.com.tw – **78)** Nantou Broadc. St, 1A, 37th Flr, 760 Chungming So. Rd, So. Ward, Taichung 402 – **79)** Ta

Chung Broadc. Co (Kiss R.), 2, 34th Flr, 6 Minchuan 2nd Rd, Chienchen Ward, Kaohsiung 806. 24h **W:** kiss.com.tw – Kiss R. Netw: Nantou 99.7MHz. – **80)** Pao Tao Broadc. St. 1, 12th Flr. 287, Wenya St. Chia-i 600. – **81)** Taichung Broadc.Co, 21st Flr, 489, Sec. 2, Taiwan Tatao, We. Ward, Taichung 403. 24h **W:** lucky7.com.tw – **82)** Ching Shan Broadc. St. A-12-7, 20, Talung Rd. We. Ward, Taichung 403 – **83)** Ai Miao Broadc. St, 78, Huatung Str, Chunan Town, Miaoli 350. 24h – **84)** Ku Tu Broadc. Co, 1, 15th Flr, 77, Sec. 2, Chunghua East Rd, Tainan 701. 24h **W:** fm1025.com.tw – **85)** Nan Taiwan chih Sheng (Voice of South Taiwan), 38th Flr, 38, Hsinkuang Rd, Lingya, Kaohsiung 802. – **86)** Huanhsi chih Sheng (Happy R.) Broadc. St, 37th Flr, 760 Chungming So. Rd, So. Ward, Taichung. 24h **W:** happy1055.com.tw – **87)** Tung Shan He FM Broadc. St, 13th Flr, 162-5, Sec. 3, Chunching Rd, Lotung Town, Ilan 265 – **88)** Tzumei (Sister R.) Broadc. St, 4th Flr, 32, Lane 416, Sec. 1, Linsen Rd, Huwei Town, Yunlin 632. 24h **W:** sister-radio.com.tw – **89)** Chuan Kuo Broadc. Co, 1, 8th Flr, 659, Sec.2, Taiwan Tatao, We. Ward, Taichung 403. 24h **W:** taichungnet.com.tw – **90)** Chih Nan Broadc. St,15th Flr, 53, Sec.2, Lin-an Rd, No. Ward, Tainan 704 – **91)** Kao Ping Hsi Broadc. St, 17th Flr, 161-53 Chiuta Rd, Chiuchu, TashuWard, Kaohsiung 842 – **92)** Taoyuan Broadc. St (TBC R.), 9th Flr, 859, Sec. 1, Chunghua Rd, Chungli, Taoyuan 320. 24h **W:** tbcradio.com.tw – **93)** Chia-i Huanchiu Broadc. St, 1, 19th Flr, 25 Pingtien, Chianghsi Village, Fanlu, Chia-i 600 – Other Smile Netw sts: Hsinchu on 90.3, Nantou on105.5, Tainan on 97.9, Kaohsiung on 90.5, Pingtung on 90.9/91.3/92.5MHz – **94)** Lan Yang FM Broadc. St, 12th Flr, 186, Sec. 3, Chungcheng Rd, Wuchie Village, Ilan 268. 24h – **95)** Taipei chih Yin Broadc. Co, (Hito R.) 15-1, Sec. 1, Hanchou So. Rd, Chungcheng Ward, Taipei 10050. 24h Hit FM Netw: Taichung 91.5MHz Kaohsiung 90.1MHz **W:** hitfm.com.tw – **96)** Tung Taiwan Broadc. St, 31, Sec. 1, Nanpin Rd, Tungchang, Chi-an Village, Hualien 973.

TAJIKISTAN

L.T: UTC +5h — **Pop:** 8 million — **Pr.L:** Tajik, Uzbek — **E.C:** 50Hz, 220V — **ITU:** TJK

KUMITAI TELEVIZION VA RADIOI
(State Committee for Radio & TV)
✉ k. Chapaev 31, 734025 Dushanbe ☎ +992 37 2277497
E: radiotoj@mail.ru; info@ktr.tj **W:** ktr.tj
LP: Chmn: Asadulloi Rahmon
NB: In addition to being a state broadcaster, the committee is also responsible for issuing licenses to private radio stations in Tajikistan.

MW	kHz	kW	Prgr	MW	kHz	kW	Prgr
Dushanbe	549	40	2	Dushanbe (a)	1143	150	F
Orzu	702	150	1	Orzu	1161	40	2
Khujand	819	15	1	Dushanbe	1323	7	1

(a) Yangiyul F=International Service

SW	kHz	kW	Prgr
Dushanbe (Yangiyul)	4765	50	1 (2300-2000)

FM (MHz)	1	2	3	kW
Ayvanj	-	107.8	-	-
Dushanbe	104.7	102.2	106.5	2x4/-
Khorugh*	104.5	104.0	103.0	
Khujand	102.7	-	106.1	4
Panj	-	100.3	-	-
Qurghonteppa	67.88	66.32	-	4

+ low power txs. *) Located in Kuhistan-Badakhshan (autonomous province)

D.Prgr: Prgr 1 (Radioi Tojikiston): 24h. – **Prgr 2 (Sadoi Dushanbe):** 24h. For ethnic minorities: 0600-0900 (Russian). – **Prgr 3 (Radioi Farhang):** 24h. – **Regional Stations: R. Badakhshon (Khorugh) + R. Khatlon (Qurghonteppa):** FM planned. **R. Sughd (Khujand)** on Khujand 101.1MHz.
International Service (Ovozi Tojik): see International Radio section. On FM: Dushanbe 105.5MHz.

OTHER STATIONS

MW	kHz	kW	Location	Station
A)	1296	300	Orzu	R.Rossii relay

FM	MHz	kW	Location	Station
16)	88.8	-	Khujand	Love R.
18)	92.2	-	Istaravshan	Dunyo FM
15)	93.3	-	Chkalov	R. Salom
12)	95.5	-	Isfara	R. Diyor
17)	97.7	-	Khujand	R. Shahri Man
B)	100.3	-	Dushanbe	R. Sputnik relay
14)	100.6	-	Khujand	R. Payvand
4)	101.5	0.2	Kulob	R. Mavji ozod
9)	101.5	-	Dushanbe	FM Khovar
10)	101.5	-	Panjakent	Sadoi Panjakent

FM	MHz	kW	Location	Station
2)	102.4	-	Qurghonteppa	R. Vatan
7A)	103.0	-	Dushanbe	R. Rusii Oriyono
7B)	103.0	-	Khujand	R. Imruz
2)	103.3	-	Khujand	R. Vatan
1A)	103.7	0.3	Khujand	R. Tiroz
5)	104.0	-	Dushanbe	AFM
3B)	104.4	-	Khujand	R. Aziya Plus
3A)	104.5	0.3	Dushanbe	R. Aziya FM
2)	105.0	-	Khorugh*	R. Vatan
11)	105.2	-	Isfara	R. Isfara
12)	105.5	-	Asht	R. Diyor
13)	105.7	-	Khujand	Sadoi Khujand
4)	105.9	-	Isfara	R. Mavji ozod
2)	106.0	0.1	Dushanbe	R. Vatan
6)	106.1	-	Istaravshan	R. AVIS-Plus
1B)	106.7	-	Khujand	Tirozi Javoni
18)	106.8	1	Tursunzade	Sadoi Osiyo
3B)	107.0	0.1	Dushanbe	R. Aziya Plus
3B)	107.0	-	Qurghonteppa	R. Aziya Plus
B)	107.1	-	Khujand	R. Sputnik relay
7B)	107.4	-	Dushanbe	R. Imruz
7B)	107.4	-	Kulob	R. Imruz
7B)	107.4	-	Qurghonteppa	R. Imruz
8)	107.5	1	Ghafurov	R. Jahonori

*) Located in Kuhistan-Badakhshan (autonomous province)

Addresses & other information:
1A,B) k. Tiroz 9, 735700 Khujand **E:** radio@tiroz.org – **2)** pr. S.Sherozi 16, 734018 Dushanbe **E:** info@vatan.tj – **3A,B)** pr. S.Sherozi 16, 734018 Dushanbe **E:** radio@asiaplus.tj – **4)** k. Umari Hazom 18, 735330 Vose – **5)** pr. S.Ayni 27/17, 734000 Dushanbe **E:** info@afm.tj – **6)** k. A.Mirrajabov 10, 735610 Istaravshan **E:** avis@avis.tj – **7A,B)** pr. Rudaki 100, 734001 Dushanbe **E:** info@orionomedia.tj. 7A) rel. Russkoye R. (Russia) – **8)** k. Lenin 22, 735690 Ghafurov – **9)** Dushanbe. **E:** sadrshamsi67@mail.ru – **10)** k. Bobodajarov 7a, 735500 Panjakent **E:** simo-tv@mail.ru – **11)** k. Markazi 40, 735920 Isfara **E:** sahbon@mail. ru – **12)** k. I.Somoni 91a, Shaydon **E:** radio@diyorfm.com – **13)** 735700 Khujand – **14)** k. Lenin 303a, 735700 Khujand **E:** akram_urunov@mail. ru – **15)** 735730 Chkalov **E:** radiosalom@mail.ru – **16)** 735700 Khujand – **17)** k. Tanburi 19, 735700 Khujand **E:** shahriman.97.70@gmail.com – **17)** k. Lenin 134, 735000 Tursunzade– **18)** 1. Mikrorayon 6-65, 735000 Tursunzade – **A)** Rel. R. Rossii (Russia). – **B)** Rel. R. Sputnik (Russia).

Int. relays on MW: (txs operated by Teleradiokom) Dushanbe (Yangiyul) 1251kHz 100kW; Orzu 927kHz 300kW & operated on behalf of IBB (USA): 972kHz 800kW. See Int. Radio section.

TANZANIA

L.T: UTC +3h — **Pop:** 41 million — **Pr.L:** Swahili, English — **E.C:** 50Hz, 230V — **ITU:** TZA

TANZANIA COMMUNICATIONS REGULATORY AUTHORITY (TCRA)
Mawasiliano House, Plot 304, Ali Hassan Mwinyi/Nkomo Rd, P.O Box 474, Dar es Salaam ☎+255 22 2118947 ▤ +255 22 2116664 **W:** tcra.go.tz **E:** dg@tcra.go.tz
L.P: DG: John Nkoma. Dir. Broadc. Affairs: Habbi Gunze.

TANZANIA BROADCASTING CORPORATION (TBC, Gov)
P. O. Box 9191, Nyerere Rd, Dar es Salaam ☎+255 22 2860760 ▤ +255 22 2866383 **W:** tbc.go.tz **E:** info@tbc.go.tz
L.P: DG: Dunstan Tido Mhando. Dir. Radio: Ms. Edah Sanga. TD: Harold Limo. Dir. News: Ms. Susan Mungi. Dir. PR: Ngalimecha Ngayoma.

MW	kHz	kW	MW	kHz	kW
Dodoma	603	100/10	Mwanza	720	50/10
Mbeya	621	50/10	Kunduchi	837	1
Nachingwea	‡648	100/10	Songea	‡990	100/10
Kunduchi	‡657	100	Arusha	1215	50/10
Kigoma	711	100/10			

‡) inactive
FM (MHz): Arusha 91.6, Dar es Salaam 89.9/92.35, Dodoma 87.7, Kigoma 88.4, Lindi 93.5, Mbeya/Masasi/Nachingwea 92.3, Mwanza 89.2, Songea 98.7, Dar es Salaam 94.6/95.3MHz.
TBC Taifa in Swahili on MW: 0200-2100 on 675/711/837kHz, others 24h. N. on the hour. Relayed also from Zanzibar at 1600. **TBC FM in Swahili:** 24h. MW & FM channels may opt out at times to carry regional prgrs. **TBC International in English:** Dar es-Salaam 95.3MHz.

PRIVATE STATIONS
RADIO ONE, P.O. Box 4374, Dar es Salaam. **W:** radio1.co.tz **MW:** Moshi 1323kHz 10kW (Swahili 24h), Dar es Salaam 1440kHz 10kW (English, but rep. inactive). **FM** (all 5kW): Dar es Salaam 89.7MHz, Mwanza 102.5MHz, Dodoma 100.8MHz, Arusha 95.3MHz.
RADIO FREE AFRICA, P.O. Box 1732, Post Road, Mwanza. **W:** radiofreeafricatz.com **E:** info@radiofreeafricatz.com Swahili Sce: **MW:** Mwanza 1377kHz 50kW (irr.). **FM:** Katavi 87.9, Himo/Msinga 88.2MHz, Singida 88.3, Geita 88.4, Mbeya 88.8, Iringa/Simiu 88.9, Arusha/Bukoba/Dodoma/Kigoma/Mtwara 89.0, Sumbawanga 89.1, Manyara/Songea 89.6, Mwanza 89.8, Njoluma 89.9, Kagera/Tabora 90.0, Musoma 93.5, Morogoro 93.8, Lindi 96.7, Dar es-Salaam/Pwanii/ Zanzibar 98.6, Pemba/Tanga 99.3.
English sce: **Kiss FM:** Mbeya 88.2MHz, Mwanza 88.7MHz, Arusha 89.9MHz, Dar es Salaam 89MHz, Shinyanga 96.4MHz.

Other Stations:
Capital R, Plot No.130, Mikocheni, Light Industrial Area, P.O. Box 4374 Dar Es Salaam. **W:** capitalradio.co.tz - Morogoro 88.9, Bukoba 95.3, Mbeya 96.4, Dodoma 97.3, Dar es Salaam 101.3, Mwanza 101.2, Arusha 102.1, Moshi 103.3 – **Clouds FM**, P.O. Box 31513, Dar es Salaam - Dar es Salaam 88.4MHz, Arusha 98.6MHz, Mwanza 99.4MHz – **East Africa R**, P.O.Box 4374, Dar es Salaam - Dar es Salaam 87.8, Bukoba 89.8, Moshi 93.4, Arusha 93.6, Tanga 97.8, Dodoma 99.6, Mbeya 100.0, Morogoro 102.8, Tabora 105.2. (also relayed on FM in Kampala, Uganda, & Nairobi, Kenya) **W:** eastafricaradio.com – **Moshi FM**, P.O. Box 933, Moshi: 90.2MHz. **W:** facebook.com/90.2mhz – **R. Five**, P.O. Box 11843, Arusha: 105.7MHz. **E:** impala@cybernet.co.tz – **R. Imaan** (Rlg.): Morogoro 96.0MHz – **R. Kheri** (Rlg.) Dar es Salaam 104.1MHz – **R. Kwizera**, P.O. Box 154, Ngara Field Office, Ngara. **W:** jrs.net/countries/eaf.php?lang=en - 97.9MHz (in Swahili, also rel. RFI Afrique in English) – **R. Kili FM**, Soweto, Moshi, Kilimanjaro 0000 - Moshi 87.5MHz. **W:** radiokilifm.com – **R. Maria Tanzania**, P.O. Box 34573, Dar es Salaam - Songea 89.1MHz, Iringa 90.4MHz, Mbeya 91.9MHz, Morogoro 102.0MHz, Unguja/Pemba 103.5MHz, Mwanza 106.0MHz, Arusha 106,7MHz. Arusha 2kW, Pemba 0.5kW, others 1kW. **W:** radiomariatanzania.co.tz – **R. Sauti ya Injili** (Rlg.): Lutheran R. Centre, P.O. Box 777, Moshi **W:** sautiyainjili.org - Moshi 92.2, Tanga 96.0, Arusha 96.2, Rombo 96.4, Tanga 96.5, Morogoro 99.9, Same 100.4, Usambara 102.6, Kibaya 102.9MHz – **R. Sauti ya Quran** (Rlg.) Dar es Salaam: 102.0MHz – **R. Tumaini Int**: P.O. Box 9916, Dar es Salaam - Dar es Salaam 96.3/105.9MHz, Kibahe 91.4MHz.

ZANZIBAR
(semi-autonomous archipelago)

ZANZIBAR BROADCASTING CORPORATION (Pub.)
P.O. Box 314, Zanzibar, Tanzania ☎+255 24 2330000 **W:** zbc.co.tz
L.P: DG: Hassan Abdallah Massawi; Dir (Radio): Rafi Haji Makame.
MW: Chumbuni 585kHz 50kW.
SW: Dole: 6015 & 11735kHz 50kW.
FM: Unguja 97.4MHz, Pemba 90.5MHz.
D.Prgr in Swahili: 0900-2100 on 585kHz. FM ("Spice FM"): 0300-2100. **N:** Local bulletins at 0400, 1200, 1600, 1800, 1900. Rel. R.Tanzania from Dar es Salaam at 1700, 1900. **In English:** irr. 1800. **Relays on shortwave:** see International Radio section.

Other stations:
Al-Noor FM (Rlg.), Zanzibar: 92.6MHz 2kW. **W:** alnoorcharity.org
Chuchu FM, Zanzibar: 90.9MHz. **W:** chuchufm.com
R. Adhana (Rlg.). Zanzibar: 104.9MHz. **W:** facebook.com/Adhana-fm-1487495931462046
R. Maria Tanzania (Rlg.) Pemba: 103.5MHz.
R. Tumaini 2, Zanzibar: 105.9MHz.
BBC African Sce: Zanzibar 94.1MHz, Pemba 93.5MHz.
China R. Int: Zanzibar 99.7MHz.
RFI Afrique: Dar es Salaam 94.6MHz in F/E/Swahili

THAILAND

L.T: UTC +7h — **Pop:** 67.8 million — **Pr.L:** Thai — **E.C:** 50Hz, 220V — **ITU:** THA

NATIONAL BROADCASTING AND TELE-COMMUNICATIONS COMMISSION (NBTC)
87 Phahonyotin Rd. Soi 8, Samsen Nai,Phayatai Bangkok 10400 ☎ +66 2271-0151 ▤ +66 2290-5240 **W:** nbtc.go.th
L.P: Chmn: Col. Natee Sukonrat
The NBTC controls administrative, legal, technical and programming aspects of broadcasting in Thailand.

GOVERNMENT PUBLIC RELATIONS DEPT. (Gov.)

✉ Soi Aree Samphan, Rama VI Road, Bangkok 10400
☎ +66 2618-2323 🖷 +66 2618-2364/2399 **W:** thailand.prd.go.th (general info in English). This body operates the NBT radio & TV services (R.Thailand & Television Thailand).
L.P: DG: Mr Apinan Juntarungsri

THE NATIONAL BROADCASTING SERVICES OF THAILAND (NBT) – RADIO THAILAND (Sathaanii Witthayu Krachaisiang Haeng Pratheet Thai, Sor. Wor. Thor.) (Gov.)

✉ 236 Vibhavadi Rangsit Superhighway, Din Daeng, Huay Khwang, Bangkok 10320 ☎ +66 2277-4020 🖷 +66 2277-2809
W: nbt.prd.go.th
L.P: Exec. Dir. R. Thailand: Ms Pitchaya Muangnow

MW STATIONS:

kHz	kW	Location +)	kHz	kW	Location +)
531	25	Maha Sarakham	981	25	Yala
549	10	Mukdahan	1026	25	Phitsanulok
558	10	Kanchanaburi	1026	10	Betong (Yala)
639	10	Chiang Mai $	1062	10	Phuket
639	20	N. Si Thammarat	1098	10	Mae Sot
648	25	Khon Kaen	1116	10	Takua Pa (Phang Nga)
720	5/10	‡Krabi	1125	25	Chanthaburi
729	25	N. Ratchasima	1134	10	Lampang
783	10	Ranong	1215	25	Surat Thani
810	10	Nong Khai	1260	25	Chiang Rai
810	10	Sangkhlaburi%	1296	10	‡Pattani
819	10	Pathum Thani#	1341	20	Loei
837	10	Pathum Thani#	1341	25	U. Ratchathani
846	10	Phetchabun	1341	10	Phangnga
864	10	Tak	1368	25	Nan
864	10	Si Sa Ket	1368	10	Buri Ram
891	1000	Sara Buri#	1377	10	Chumphon
909	10	Dansai (Loei)	1404	25	Songkhla
909	25	Surin	1422	10	Amnat Charoen
918	100	Bangkok	1476	50	Chiang Mai $
981	25	Mae Hong Son	1557	10	Trat
981	20	N. Phanom	1593	10	Ratchaburi

‡) r. inactive at editorial deadline +) N.=Nakhon, U.=Ubon. %) Kanchanaburi Province. #) Bangkok area. $) tr. located in Lamphun Province

D.Prgr:

AM 891: 2200-1700 on 891kHz (tx site: Nong Khae, Sara Buri) and in full or in part on many RT regional AM stns. N: On the h –AM 819: 2200-1700 on 819kHz (tx site: Rangsit, Pathum Thani), also in part on many RT regional MW stns – AM 837: 2300-1700 on 837kHz (tx site: Bang Phun, Pathum Thani).– AM 918 (tx site: Rangsit, Pathum Thani): 2200-1700 ASEAN languages sce. in English & Thai exc. Malay: 0600-0730, Chinese: 0730-0900, Lao: 0910-1000, Burmese: 1010-1100, Khmer: 1110-1200, on 918kHz, also in part on some RT regional FM stns inc. Chiang Mai 98MHz, Phuket 90.5MHz, Samui 96.75MHz, Songkhla 102.25MHz – Bangkok FM prgrs: 88.0MHz Foreign Lang Prgr in English (10kW), 92.5MHz (10kW), 93.5MHz "Digital R. HD One" (10kW), 95.5MHz "Virgin Hitz"in English (10 kW), 97.0MHz (10kW) "Quality News Station.", 105.0MHz (10kW) prgr for young people and families.

Selected Reg. Stations: ✉ 49 Prachasamphan Rd., Tambon Chang Khlan, Muang Dist., Chiang Mai 50100 **FM:** 93.25 & 98.0MHz; 1476 kHz: Prgr in Thai and minority langs for hill tribes 2200-1600 ✉ Kasikon Thungsang Rd, Muang Dist., Khon Kaen 40000 **FM:** 98.5 & 99.5MHz. ✉ Soi Sathaban Ratchaphat Phuket, Thepkasatri Rd, Tambon Ratsada, Muang Dist., Phuket 83000 **FM:** 90.5 "Blue Wave" & 96.75MHz "Sunshine R.". ✉ 439 Mu 2, Songkhla - Ko Yo Road, Tambon Phawong, Muang Dist., Songkhla 90100 **FM:** 89.5, 90.5 & 102.25MHz

Addresses of other regional stations: Most stns can be reached by quoting "Sathaanii Witthayu Sor. Wor. Thor." or "Radio Thailand" and the location given in the freq. list. **D.Prgr** of reg. sts: generally 2200-1700

EXTERNAL SERVICE: Radio Thailand
see International Broadcasting section

NATIONAL EDUCATION RADIO (Sathaanii Witthayu Krachaisiang Haeng Pratheet Thai Pheua Kaan Seuksaa, Sor. Wor. Sor.)

✉ Soi Aree Samphan, Rama VI Rd, Samsen, Phaya Thai, Bangkok 10400
☎ +66 2271-3448 🖷 +66 2245-7083 **W:** edu.prd.go.th

D.Prgr: 2200-1700 on 1467kHz in the Bangkok area. Regional stns carry own prgrs and relay Bangkok.

MW:

kHz	kW	Location	kHz	kW	Location
549	100	Lampang	936	50	Nakhon Sawan
558	50	‡Songkhla	963	25	Krabi
621	100	Khon Kaen	1242	50	Surat Thani
711	20	Ubon Ratchathani	1467	100	Pathum Thani
927	20	Chanthaburi			

‡) inactive at editorial deadline

OTHER STATIONS:

	MWkHz	kW	Province +)		MWkHz	kW	Province +)
39)	540	5	Bangkok	6)	1107	10	Khon Kaen
24)	567	5	Chaiyaphum	7)	1116	10	Phitsanulok
17)	576	5	Bangkok	6)	1134	10	N. Ratchasima
7)	585	5	Phrae	27)	1143	10	Bangkok
32)	585	5	Chumphon	37)	1152	10	Chiang Mai
9)	594	5	Bangkok	37)	1152	10	Khon Kaen
32)	603	5	Khon Kaen	20)	1161	20	Bangkok
10)	612	5	Lop Buri	29)	1161	10	U. Ratchathani
25)	612	5	Chiang Mai	29)	1170	10	Chanthaburi
1)	630	5	Bangkok	29)	1170	10	Phitsanulok
24)	657	5	Bangkok	36)	1179	10	Bangkok
7)	666	5	Tak	34)	1179	10	Chiang Rai
6)	666	5	Surin	35)	1188	10	Sakon Nakhon
29)	675	5	Bangkok	7)	1188	10	Phitsanulok
8)	684	5	N. Si Thammarat	5)	1188	10	Sa Kaeo
39)	684	5	Udon Thani	26)	1197	10	Lop Buri
11)	693	5	Saraburi	5)	1206	10	Prachuap KK
19)	711	5	Chiang Mai	35)	1215	10	Phrae
10)	711	5	Lop Buri	6)	1215	10	U. Ratchathani
29)	720	5	Chon Buri	12)	1224	10	Chiang Rai
32)	738	5	Chiang Mai	12)	1224	10	N. Sawan
32)	738	5	Songkhla	12)	1233	10	Bangkok
37)	747	5	Bangkok	32)	1233	10	Udon Thani
6)	747	5	Udon Thani	7)	1242	10	Phetchabun
34)	756	5	Narathiwat	12)	1251	10	Roi Et
35)	756	5	Surin	12)	1251	5	Bangkok
31)	765	5	Lampang	25)	1269	10	Songkhla
12)	765	5	Lop Buri	15)	1269	10	Bangkok
18)	774	5	Rayong	28)	1287	10	Samut Prakan#
36)	774	5	Udon Thani	32)	1287	10	U. Ratchathani
7)	783	5	Kamphaeng Phet	39)	1305	10	Sara Buri
19)	792	5	Bangkok	25)	1314	10	Khon Kaen
3)	801	5	N. Sawan	12)	1323	10	Chiang Mai
12)	801	5	Chiang Rai	12)	1323	10	Surat Thani
12)	801	5	U. Ratchathani	14)	1332	10	Bangkok
32)	828	5	N. Si Thammarat	12)	1332	10	Maha Sarakham
7)	828	5	Sukhothai	7)	1350	10	Trang
34)	837	5	Sakon Nakhon	33)	1350	10	Bangkok
2)	855	5	Prachin Buri	6)	1359	10	Sakhon Nakhon
16)	873	5	Bangkok	12)	1368	10	N. Pathom
30)	918	10	Chiang Mai	22)	1377	10	Phitsanulok
8)	936	10	Pattani	13)	1386	10	Pathum Thani#
12)	945	10	Bangkok	34)	1395	10	Chiang Rai
6)	945	10	Kalasin	24)	1404	10	Yasothon
12)	954	10	Phitsanulok	5)	1404	10	Suphan Buri
12)	954	10	Chanthaburi	33)	1422	10	Bangkok
18)	963	10	Bangkok	30)	‡1422	10	Phitsanulok
34)	972	10	Phetchabun	12)	1431	10	N. Ratchasima
38)	981	10	Pathum Thani#	29)	1431	5	Songkhla
30)	990	10	N. Ratchasima	6)	1440	10	N. Phanom
7)	999	10	Chiang Rai	32)	1440	10	Samut Sakhon
33)	999	10	Bangkok	7)	1449	10	Phichit
32)	1008	10	N. Ratchasima	10)	1449	10	Chumphon
12)	1017	10	Prachuap KK	24)	1458	10	Si Sa Ket
31)	1035	10	Bangkok	29)	1458	10	Phuket
35)	1044	10	Khon Kaen	27)	1494	10	Bangkok
8)	1044	10	N. Si Thammarat	24)	1503	10	Surat Thani
1)	1053	10	Bangkok	35)	1512	10	Phayao
12)	1062	10	Udon Thani	12)	1512	10	Songkhla
4)	1071	10	Bangkok	34)	1521	10	Bangkok
32)	1080	10	Chiang Rai	32)	1530	10	Uttaradit
32)	1080	10	N. Sawan	5)	1530	10	Chanthaburi
32)	1080	10	Yala	23)	1539	10	Kanchanaburi
31)	1089	10	Udon Thani	11)	1557	10	Phetchabun
30)	1098	10	Songkhla	–)	15751000		Ayutthaya
25)	1107	10	Samut Sakhon#				

‡) r. inactive. +) N.=Nakhon, U.=Ubon, KK=Khiri Khan. #) Bangkok area

GENERAL NOTES: News: Stns are generally required to relay N. from R. Thailand at 0000 & 1200 daily, each 30 mins, and to relay time signal and national anthem at 0000 and 1100. **Station IDs:** Both short names, e.g. Wor. Por. Tho, and long names may serve as stn identifications, usually preceded by "Thiinii" ("This is"), "Thiinii Sathaanii Witthayu (Krachaisiang)" ("This is R. St.") or "Khun kamlang rap fang" ("You are listening to"). Changwat=province. Amphoe=district (dt.). Prgrs are often supplied by separate production companies. The Thai name for Bangkok is 'Krung Thep' or 'Krung Thep Mahanakhon'. **Thai numerals:** 0 = suun, 1 = neung (et), 2 = song, 3 = saam, 4 = sii, 5 = haa, 6 = hok, 7 = jet, 8 = paet, 9 = kao, 10 = sip, 20 = yi sip, 100 = roi, 1000 = phan; thii = number, jut = decimal point

1) Mor. Thor. Bor. Sip Et (Monthon Thahaan Bok Thii Sip Et, 11th Military Circle) 145 Rama V Rd, Dusit Region, Bangkok 10300 Ann: "Suan Mitsakawan" – **2) Mor. Thor. Bor. Sip Song** (Monthon Thahaan Bok Thii Sip Song, "Siang Khai Chakkrapong", 12th Military Circle, "Voice of Chakkrapong Camp") Chakkrapong Camp, Dong Phra Ram, Prachin Buri 25000 – **3) Mor. Thor. Bor. Thii Saam Sip Et** (Monthon Thahaan Bok Thii Saam Sip Et, 31st Military Circle). Jiraprawat Camp, Nakhon Sawan 60000 – **4) Sathaanii Witthayu Rattasapha** (Parliament R. Station). ☞ Parliament House, Uthong Nai Rd, Dusit Region, Bangkok 10300 – **5) Thor. Phor. Neung** (Kongthap Phaak Thii Neung, 1st Army Area). HQ: ☞ Headquarters of the 1st Army Area, Suan Mitsakawan, Rajchadamnern Nok Ave, Dusit Region, Bangkok 10300. **Regional stns:** 9 Mu 4, Bang Kacha, Chanthaburi 22000 – Phairirayodet Camp, Suwansri Rd, Tha Kasem, Sa Kaeo 27000 – Kao Kuat, Kraw Plub Pla, Ratchaburi 70000 – Ban Sam Liam, Mu 4, Don Pho Thong, Suphan Buri 72000 – **6) Thor. Phor. Song** (Kongthap Phaak Thii Song, 2nd Army Area). HQ: ☞ Suranari Camp, Ratchadamnoen Rd, Nong Phailom, Nakhon Ratchasima 30000. **Regional stns:** Aphai Rd, Nai Muang, Kalasin 46000 – Si Phatcharin Camp, Sila, Khon Kaen 40000 – Phra Yot Muang Khwang Camp, Nakhon Phanom-Sakon Nakhon Rd, Khurukhu, Nakhon Phanom 48000 – Krit Siwara Camp, That Naveng, Sakon Nakhon 47000 – Wirawatyothin Camp, Phakdichumphon Rd, Nok Muang, Surin 32000 – Sapphasiti Prasong Camp, Warin Chamrap District, Ubon Ratchathani 34190 – Yutthasin Prasit Camp, Non Sung Rd, Udon Thani 41330 – **7) Thor. Phor. Saam** (Kongthap Phaak Thii Saam, 3rd Army Area). ☞ Headquarters of the 3rd Army Area, Somdet Phra Ekathosarot Camp, Aranyik, Phitsanulok 65000. **Regional stns:** Mengrai Maharat Camp, Chiang Rai 57000 – 236/5 Mu 3, Nakhon Sawan - Kamphaeng Phet Rd, Nakhon Chum, Kamphaeng Phet 62000 – Khalang Nakhon Camp, Nong Krating, Lampang 52000 – Phokun Pha Muang Camp, 166/1 Mu 1, Wat Pa, Lom Sak District, Phetchabun 67110 – 104/1 Mu 5, Ban Krot Ngam, Ban Na, Wachirabarami District, Phichit 66140 – Ban Mai, Ratsadon Uthit Rd, Nai Wiang, Phrae 54000 – Bypass Road, Pak Khwae, Sukhothai 64000 – Charot Withithong Rd, Nam Ruem, Tak 63000 – **8) Thor. Phor. Sii** (Kongthap Phaak Thii Sii, 4th Army Area). HQ: ☞ Wachirahwud Camp, Ratchadamnoen-Pak Nun Rd, Nakhon Si Thammarat 80000. **Regional stns:** Senanarong Camp, Kho Hong, Hat Yai District, Songkhla 90110 – Ban Na San District, Surat Thani 84120 – Charoen Pradit Rd, Rusamilae, Pattani 94000 – **9) Phon Por. Thor. Or.** (Kong Phon Thahaan Peun Yai Tosue Akart Yaan, Anti-Aircraft Artillery Division), ☞ Kiak Kay Junction, Thahaan Road, Bangsue, Dusit Region, Bangkok 10300 – **10) Wor. Sor. Por.** (Witthayu Suun Karn Thahaan Peun Yai, Artillery Centre R. St.). ☞ 301 Phahonyothin Camp, Artillery Centre, Khao Phra Ngam, Lop Buri 15160. Regional st: Khet Udomsak Camp, Wang Mai, Chumphon 86000 – **11) Siang Adison** (Suun Kaan Thahaan Maa, Cavalry Centre, "Voice of Adison"). ☞ Saraburi Cavalry Centre, Adison Camp, Mitraphap Rd, Pak Phrieo, Saraburi 18000. Regional st: Saraburi-Lom Sak Rd, Nong Khwai, Lom Sak District, Phetchabun 67110 – **12) Thor. Or.** (Thahaan Akart, Royal Thai Airforce). ☞ Tor. Or. 01, 1233kHz, Don Muang: 171 Mu 2, Phahonyothin Rd, Khlong Thanon, Sai Mai, Bangkok 10220. Tor. Or. 01, 945kHz, Min Buri: 74 Mu 2, Nimit Mai, Sai Kong Tin, Min Buri, Bangkok 10510. Tor. Or. 06, 1251kHz: The Empress Hotel, 1091/343 Phetchaburi Tat Mai Road, Charurat, Makassan, Ratcha Thewi, Bangkok 10400. **Regional stns:** Thor. Or. 02: 301 Wing 2, 1st Air Division, Khao Phra Ngam Rd, Lop Buri 15160 – Thor. Or. 03: Wing 1, Mu 3, Nong Phai Lom, Nakhon Ratchasima 30000 – Thor. Or. 04: 305 Mu 4, Wing 4, 3rd Air Division, Takhli District, Nakhon Sawan 60140 – Thor. Or. 05: Wing 53, 4th Air Division, Ko Lak, Prachuap Khiri Khan 77000 – Thor. Or. 7: Surat Thani Airport Entrance, Huatoey, Phunphin District, Surat Thani 84130 – Thor. Or. 08: 38 Mu 14, Ban Nongphai, Chayangkun Rd, Khamyai, Ubon Ratchathani 34000 – Thor. Or. 09: 549 Mu 9, Wing 23, Thahaan Rd, Makkhaeng, Udon Thani 41000 – Thor. Or. 10: Wing 46, 3rd Air Division, Yaek Khok Matum, Phitsanulok - Wangthong Rd, Na – **13) Sathaanii Witthayu Pheua Kaan Kaset** (Agricultural R. St.). ☞ Agricultural Radio Section, 2143/1 Phahonyothin Road, Lat Yao, Bang Khen Region, Bangkok 10900 – **14) Or. Sor.** (Sathaanii Witthayu Amphon Sathaan, Phraratchawang Dusit, Amphon Sathan Throne Radio Station). ☞ Dusit Palace, Ratchawithi Rd, Chitralada, Dusit

Region, Bangkok 10303 D.Prgr: Tu-Sa 0330-0500, 0900-1200, Su 0230-0500, M silent – **15) Kho. Sor. Thor. Bor.** (Kromkarn Khon Song Thahaan Bok, Army Transportation Dept.). ☞ Army Transportation Broadcasting Station, Transport School Compound, Thahaan Road, Dusit Region, Bangkok 10300 – **16) Wor. Kor. Thor. Mor.** (Sathaanii Witthayu Krung Theep Mahaanakhon, Bangkok Radio Station), ☞ 192 Sarasin Rd, Lumphini Park, Pathum Wan Region, Bangkok 10330 – **17) Tor. Chor. Dor.** (Tamruat Trawen Chaidaen, Border Patrol Police). ☞ Bang Khen Police Dept. Club, Vibhavadi-Rangsit Rd, Bang Khen Bangkok 10210 – **18) Phon Mor. Song** (Sathaanii Witthayu Kong Phan Thahaan Maa Thii Song, 2nd Cavalry Division), ☞ Samsen Rd, Bang Krabeu, Dusit Region, Bangkok 10300 Bangkok. Regional st: Rayong-Ban Khai Rd, Nam Khok, Rayong 21000 – **19) Wor. Phor. Thor.** (Witthayu Kromkarn Phalang Ngan Thahaan, Defence Energy Dept. R. St.). ☞ New Building, Sukhumvit 24, Phra Khanong, Bangkok 10250. Regional st: 141/3 Mu 4, Don Kaeo Rd, Chotana, Mae Rim District, Chiang Mai 50180 – **20) Wor. Sor. Sor.** (Witthayu Seuksa, Educational Radio). ☞ Educational Technology Centre, Si Ayutthaya Rd, Ratcha Thewi, Bangkok 10400 – **22) Wor. Phon Sii** (Witthayu Kong Phon Thii Sii, 4th Infantry Division). ☞ Headquarters of the 4th Infantry Division, Somdet Phra Naresuan Maharat Camp, Phitsanulok 65000 – **23) Phon Ror. Kao** (Kong Phon Thahaan Raap Thii Kao, 9th Infantry Division), ☞ Surasi Camp, Kanchanaburi 71190 – **24) Jor. Sor.** (Krom Jaye Thahaan Suesarn, Army Signals Department). ☞ Jor. Sor. 1, Rama V Rd, Saphan Daeng, Bangsue, Dusit Region, Bangkok 10300. **Regional stns:** Jor. Sor. 2, Tharathibodi Rd, Thakham, Phunphin District, Surat Thani 84130 – Jor. Sor. 3, Prasert Songkhram Camp, Kongphon Si Rd, Nua Muang, Roi Et 45000 – Jor. Sor. 4, 104 Thetsaban 1 Rd, Nai Muang, Yasothon 35000 – Jor. Sor. 5, 5 Mu 2 Ban Lao, Ban Lao, Chaiyaphum 36000 – Jor. Sor. 6, 1543/23 Srisumang Rd, Muang Tai, Si Sa Ket 33000 – **25) Mor. Kor.** (Mahaawitthayalai Kasetsart, Kasetsart University). HQ: ☞ 50 Phahonyothin Rd, Bang Khen, Chatuchak, Bangkok 10900. Bangkok. Tr. located at Nongkhaem in Samut Sakhon province. **Regional stns:** 301/1 Mu 5, Paphai, Sansai District, Chiang Mai 50210 – 86/8 Maliwan Rd, Muang Kao, Sitan, Khon Kaen 40000 – 424 Mu 3, Kanchanawanit Rd, Phawong, Songkhla 90100 – **26) Jor. Tor. Lor.** (Jangwat Thahaan Bok Lop Buri, Lop Buri Army Province). ☞ 13th Military Circle, Narai Maharat Rd, Lop Buri 15000 – **27) Or. Sor. Mor. Thor.** (Ongkarn Suesarn Muanchon Haeng Pratheet Thai, Mass Communications Org. of Thailand, MCOT "Modern Radio"). ☞ 63/1 Rama IX Rd, Huay Khwang, Bangkok 10320 – **28) Sor. Or. Thor.** (Sathaanii Witthayu Krom Utiniyom Witthayaa, Meteorological Department R. St.), ☞ 4353 Sukhumvit Rd, Bangna, Bangkok 10260 – **29) Sor. Thor. Ror.** (Siang Chaak Thahaan Reua, Voice of the Navy). ☞ Sor. Thor. Ror. 2: Phutianan Stadium, Phra Khanong, Bangna District, Bangkok 10260. **Regional stns:** Sor. Thor. 3: 99/1 Mu 1, Phuket 83000 – Sor. Thor. Ror. 4: 9/9 Thetsaban-Phatthana Rd, Wat Mai, Chanthaburi 22000 – Sor. Thor. Ror. 5: 652 Mu 2, Sattahip District, Chon Buri 20180 – Sor. Thor. Ror. 6: Songkhla Naval Station, Thale Luang Rd, Bo Yang, Songkhla 90000 – Sor. Thor. Ror. 7: Mae Klang River Operation Unit, Nakhon Phanom 48000 – Sor. Thor. Ror. 8: Ban Khlong Mek, Tha Chang, Phrom Phiram District, Phitsanulok 65150 – Sor. Thor. Ror. 9: Ban Thung Sawang, Ubon-Takan Rd, Rai Noi, Ubon Ratchathani 34000 – **30) Sor. Wor. Phor.** (Sathaanii Witthayu Phitaksantirat, Police R. St.). ☞ Radio Broadcasting Section, 2nd Communication Division, Directorate of Police Communications, Police Department, Bang Khen Region, Bangkok 10900. **Regional stns:** 40 Mu 1, Chotana Rd, Maesa, Mae Rim District, Chiang Mai 50180 – Sor. Wor. Phor. 2, Suranarai Rd, Cho Ho, Nakhon Ratchasima 30310 – Sor. Wor. Phor. 3, Banphru, Hat Yai District, Songkhla 90250 – Sor. Wor. Phor. 4, Pracha Uthit Rd, Nai Muang, Phitsanulok – **31) Neung. Por. Nor.** (Krom Praisanii Thoralek, Post & Telegraph Dept.). ☞ Chaengwattana-Thungsonghong Rd, Don Muang, Bangkok 10210. 1035kHz=Phaak Phiset, 1089kHz=Mor. Sor. Thor. **Regional stns:** 219 Mu 4, Lampang-Hang Chat Rd, Pong Yang Khok, Hang Chat District, Lampang 52190 – Ban Nong Bu, Rop Muang Rd, Samphrao, Udon Thani 41000 – **32) Wor. Por. Tho.** (Witthayu Prachaam Thin, Local R, Communications Division, Signals Dept, Royal Thai Army) – Wor. Por. Tho. 8: Kamphaeng Phet Akkharayothin Camp, Suan Luang, Krathum Baen District, Samut Sakhon 74110. **Regional stns:** Wor. Por. Tho. 2: Kawila Camp, Kongsai, Wat Ket, Chiang Mai 50000 – Wor. Por. Tho. 3: 001 Na Khai Suranari, Phanibut Rd, Pho Klang, Nakhon Ratchasima 30000 – Wor. Por. Tho. 4: Thep Sattri Si Sunthon Camp, Kabang, Thung Song District, Nakhon Si Thammarat 80310 – Wor. Por. Tho. 5: 5 Kanchanawanit Rd, Hat Yai District, Songkhla 90110 – Wor. Por. Tho. 6: Sapphasiti Prasong Camp, Warin Chamrap District, Ubon Ratchathani 34190 – Wor. Por. Tho. 7: Khai Prachak Sinlaprakhom, Thahaan Rd, Mak Khaeng, Udon Thani 41000 – Wor. Por. Tho. 9: Chiraprawat Camp, Na Khai Chiraprawat Rd, Nakhon Sawan 60000 – Wor. Por. Tho. 10: Mengrai Maharat Barracks, Chiang Rai 57000 – Wor. Por. Tho. 12: 140 Kasikonthungsang Rd, Sila, Khon Kaen 40000 – Wor. Por. Tho. 14: Phichai Dap Hak Camp, 13/7

Prachanimit Rd, Tha It, Uttaradit 5 – **33) Phon Neung Ror. Or.** (Kong Phon Thii Neung Raksaa Phra Ong, 1st Infantry Division, Royal Guard). ☒ Phitsanulok Rd, Dusit Region, Bangkok 10300. 999kHz=Phaak Phiset, 1350kHz=Phaak Pokkati (tr. on 1350kHz r. relocated to Saraburi Prov.) – **34) Nor. Thor. Phor.** (Nuai Bannachakaan Thahaan Phatthanaa, Armed Forces Development Command AFDC, Royal Thai Armed Forces HQ). ☒ Sathaanii Witthayu 919, Phitsanulok Rd, Dusit Region, Bangkok 10300. **Regional Stns:** Sathaanii Witthayu 914, Suan Sak Kieo Tap Yong, Ban Pong 00, Mae Chan, Mae Chan District, Chiang Rai 57110. 1395kHz in Thai, 1179kHz prgr in Thai and minority langs for hilltribes – Sathaanii Witthayu 912, 13 Chan Uthit Rd, Bang Nak, Narathiwat 96000 in Thai and Malay – Sathaanii Witthayu 921, 114 Mu 1, Na Saeng, Lom Kao District, Phetchabun 67120 – Sathaanii Witthayu 909, Ban Rung Phatthana, Sakon Nakhon-Nakhon Phanom Rd, That Naweng, Sakon Nakhon 47000 – **35) Kor. Wor. Sor.** (Kitkarn Witthayu Krachaisiang, Radio & TV Division, Army Signals Dept). HQ: ☒ Radio Broadcasting & Television Division, Signals Department, Royal Thai Army, Rama V Rd, Saphan Daeng, Bangsue, Dusit Region, Bangkok 10300. **Regional stns:** Kor. Wor. Sor. 1, Surin-Prasat Rd, Nok Muang, Surin 32000 – Kor. Wor. Sor. 2, Yantarakit Sokon Rd, Sung Men District, Phrae 54130 – Kor. Wor. Sor. 3, 1879 Mu 14, That Choeng Chum, Sakon Nakhon 47000 – Kor. Wor. Sor. 4, 383 Super Highway, Ban Dom, Phayao 56000 – Kor. Wor. Sor. 5, 252 Mitraphap Rd, Ban Phai District, Khon Kaen 40110 – **36) Sor. Sor. Sor.** (Siang Sam Yot, Crime Suppression Division, Royal Thai Police). ☒ Section 1, Superintendency 2, Command Division, Crime Suppression Division, Phahonyothin Rd, Bangkok 10900. Regional st: 195 Mu 8, Udon-Nong Samrong Rd, Mumon, Udon Thani 41000 – **37) Ror. Dor.** (Kromkarn Raksaa Dindaen, Territorial Defence Dept.). HQ: ☒ 2 Charoen Krung Rd, Suan Chaochet, Phra Nakhon Region, Bangkok 10200. **Regional stns:** Nong Ho, Chotana Rd, Chang Peuak, Chiang Mai 50000 – Sri Phatcharin Camp, Raat Khaneung Rd, Nai Muang, Khon Kaen 40000 – **38) Mahaawitthayalai Thammasat** (Thammasat University), ☒ Faculty of Journalism and Mass Communications, Thammasat University, Prachan Rd, Phra Nakhon Region, Bangkok 10200 – **39) Yaan Kraw** (4th Cavalry Battalion, Armoured Unit, Royal Guard). HQ: ☒ Military Armoured Car School, 1156 Samsen Road, Bangkabrue, Dusit Region, Bangkok 10300. **Regional stns:** Saraburi Cavalry Centre, Adison Camp, Mitraphap Rd, Pak Phrieo, Saraburi 18000 – Mitraphap Rd, Nong Bua Udon Thani 41000

FM STATIONS IN SELECTED CITIES (MHz) (exc. R. Thailand and community radio stns):
Bangkok: 87.5 Sathaanii Witthayu Ratthasapha (Parliament R. St.) – 88.5 Sor. Thor. Ror. 1, "Sabaidee R." – 89.0 Yaan Kraw "Chill FM" – 89.5 Rajamangala University of Technology "Sweet FM" – 90.0 Phon Neung Ror. Or. "Luukthung Rak Thai" – 90.5 Wor. Phor. Thor. – 91.0 Sor. Wor. Phor. – 91.5 Yaan Kraw, "Fresh 91.5" – 92.0 Wor. Sor. Sor. – 93.0 Sor. Thor. Ror. 1, "Cool 93 Fahrenheit" – 94.0 Thor. Thor. Bor. (Sathaanii Witthayu Thorathat Kongthap Bok, Army TV Station), "EFM" – 94.5 Jor. Sor. "Luukthung Easy" – 95.0 Or. Sor. Mor. Thor "Luukthung Mahaanakhon" – 96.0 Ror. Dor. "Sport R." – 96.5 Or. Sor. Mor. Thor, "Khleun Khwaam Khit" – 97.5 Or. Sor. Mor. Thor, "Modern Radio Seed 97.5 FM" – 98.0 Phon Neung Ror. Or. "Virgin Star" – 98.5 Neung Por. Nor, "Click FM" – 99.0 Or. Sor. Mor. Thor, "Active R." – 99.5 Sathaanii Witthayu 9-1-9, "Traffic Radio Society (TRS)" – 100.0 Jor. Sor. Roi – 100.5 Or. Sor. Mor. Thor. "Modern R. News Network" – 101.0 Sathaanii Witthayu Kong Banchakaan Thahaan Suungsut (Royal Thai Armed Forces Command HQ), "101 Radio Report One" – 101.5 Sathaanii Witthayu Chulaa or "Witthayu Chulaa" or "CU FM" (Chulalongkorn Univ.) – 102.0 Khor. Sor. Thor. Bor. "Working Station" – 102.5 Thor. Or, "Get 102.5" – 103.0 Jor. Sor "Like FM" – 103.5 Thor. Thor. Bor, "FM One" – 104.0 Or. Sor. – 104.5 Phon Por. Thor. Or. (Kong Phon Thahaan Peun Yai Tosue Akart Yaan, Anti-Aircraft Artillery Division), "Love Radio" – 105.5 Or. Sor. Mor. Thor "Eazy FM" – 106.0 Sor. Thor. Ror. 1 – 106.5 Neung Por. Nor, "Green Wave" – 107.0 Or. Sor. Mor. Thor, "Met 107".
Chiang Mai: 88.0 Sor. Thor. Ror. – 100.0 Mor. Chor. (Chiang Mai Univ.) – 100.75 Or. Sor. Mor. Thor. – 101.5 Thor.Phor. Saam – 102.5 Thor. Or 013 "Get 102.5" – 105.75 Sor. Sor. Sor. – 106.75 Sathaanii Witthayu Ratthasapha (Parliament R. St.)
Khon Kaen: 88.25 Thor. Phor. Song "KCS Radio" – 90.75 Or. Sor. Mor. Thor. – 103.0 Mor. Khor. (Khon Kaen Univ.) – 104.5 Wor. Phor. – 107.0 Thor Or. 020
Phuket: 88.0 Sor. Thor. Ror. "Nice Peak FM" – 89.0 Neung Por. Nor "Power Zone FM"– 95.0 Sor. Sor. Sor, "Kiss FM" – 99.25 Sathaanii Witthayu Ratthasapha (Parliament R. St.) – 101.5 Or. Sor. Mor. Thor. – 102.5 Ror. Dor. – 107.25 Sor. Or. Thor. "Smart R."
Songkhla/Hat Yai: 88.0 Mor. Or. (Prince of Songkhla Univ.), Hat Yai – 94.5 Sor. Thor. Ror. 6 – 96.5 Or. Sor. Mor. Thor., Hat Yai – 103.25 Sathaanii Witthayu Ratthasapha (Parliament R. Stn) – 104.0 Tor. Chor.

Dor., Hat Yai – 107.0 Thor. Or. 011, Khlong Hoi Khong – 107.75 Thor. Phor. Sii, Hat Yai "Smart R."

OTHER FM STATIONS: A large number of FM stns belonging to R. Thailand and other operators are on air throughout Thailand. Approx. 6000 community radio stns with max. permitted tx power 30W were operating in early 2014, but at editorial deadline many community stns were off air following the military coup of May 2014.

International Relays: See International radio section

LT: UTC +9h — **Pop:** 1.2 million — **Pr.L:** Tetun, Portuguese, Indonesian — **E.C:** 50 Hz, 220V — **ITU:** TLS

AUTORIDADE NACIONAL DE COMUNICAÇÕES (ANC)
☒ Ground Floor, Telecom Building, Av. Bispo de Medeiros 8, Caicoli, Díli ☎ +670 3339330 **W:** anc.tl **L.P:** Exec. Pres: António Brígido Correia

RÁDIO E TELEVISÃO DE TIMOR-LESTE (RTTL) (Pub.)
☒ Edifício da Rádio e Televisão, Rua Mercado Municipal, Caixa Postal 114, Díli ☎ +670 3321827 **W:** rttlep.tl **E:** info@rttlep.tl **L.P:** Dir: Milena Soares Abrantes. RTTL administers R. Timor-Leste (RTL) and TV Timor-Leste (TVTL)

RÁDIO TIMOR-LESTE (RTL) (Pub.)
☒ Rua Mercado Municipal, Caixa Postal 114, Díli ☎ +670 3321826 or +670 3321827 **W:** rttlep.tl **E:** radiotimorleste@gmail.com **L.P:** Dir: Rosário Maia Martins. PD: Martinho Tavares

FM (MHz)	kW	Location	FM (MHz)	kW	Location
88.9	0.5	Maliana	95.0	0.3	Manatuto
90.3	0.3	Aileu	96.8	0.5	Lospalos
90.6		Ermera	97.0	1	Same
90.9		Ainaro	97.6		Díli (Generation FM)
91.7	4	Díli	98.9	0.3	Viqueque
92.1	0.3	Oecussi	99.1		Liquisa
92.6		Kutulau	105.4	1	Baucau
93.3	0.3	Suai			

D.Prgr in Tetun, Portuguese and Indonesian: 2100-1500.
N. in **Tetun/Portuguese/Indonesian:** 2200-2300, 0330-0430, 1100-1200

RÁDIO MAUBERE (Operated by Fretilin Party)
☒ Avenida dos Mártires da Pátria, Lurumata, Díli ☎ +670 3322599 **W:** https://facebook.com/radiomaubere **E:** radio-maubere@live.com **FM (MHz):** Manatuto 93.8, Viqueque 94.8. Baucau 96.0, Oecusse 96.2, Ermera 96.4, Suai 96.5, Aileu & Ainaro 97.9, Liquisa 97.9, Lospalos 98.0, Same 98.2, Maliana 99.5, Díli 99.9

TIMOR-LESTE ASSOCIATION OF COMMUNITY RADIO STATIONS (Asosiasaun Radio Komunidade Timor-Leste)(ARKTL)
☒ National Press Centre, Rua Martires da Patria, Fatuhada, Dili ☎ +670 77239945 **W:** arktl.org **E:** arktl.info@gmail.com **L.P:** Pres: Prezado Ximenes. ARKTL's main role is as advocate for all community and independent stns. Member stns: 4, 8, 10, 11, 12, 15, 17, 19, 21, 22, 23, 25, 26, 27, 28 and 30.

COMMUNITY RADIO CENTRE (Centru Radio Comunidade) (CRC)
☒ CNE Building, Rua Bispo de Medeiros, Kintal Ki'ik, PO Box 160, Santa Cruz, Díli ☎ +670 3310127 or +670 77237890 **W:** crc-tl.org **E:** info@crc-tl.org **L.P:** Mgr: Luis Evaristo dos Santos. CRC supports stns 4, 8, 10, 11, 12, 15, 16, 17, 19, 21, 22, 23, 26, 27 and 30.

COMMUNITY AND INDEPENDENT STATIONS

MW	kHz	kW	Station
1)	*1404	2.5/5	R. Timor Kmanek, Díli
FM	**MHz**	**kW**	**Station**
2)	88.8	0.15	M3 R., Díli
3)	89.5	0.5	Voz FM, Díli
4)	89.7		R. Comunidade Maubisse Mau-Loko, Maubisse
5)	90.0		R. Akademika, Universidade Nal de Timor-Leste, Díli
6)	90.6		R. Lian Dame, Universidade da Paz, Díli
7)	91.2		R. Lalenok Ba Ema Hotu (Labeh), Díli
8)	91.7	0.2	R. Comunidade Maliana, Maliana
9)	92.3		R. Advent Suara Pengharapan, Díli
10)	92.3	0.1	R. Comunidade Café Ermera, Gleno
11)	92.3	0.1	R. Comunidade Tokodede, Liquisa
12)	93.3	0.1	R. Comunidade Atoni Lifau, Oecussi
13)	93.5		Jojo R., Díli

FM	MHz	kW	Station
14)	94.1		R. Comunidade Comoro, Díli
15)	94.1	0.1	R. Comunidade Cova Taroman, Suai
16)	94.7	0.3	R. Metro, Díli
17)	95.1	0.1	R. Comunidade 1912 Dom Boaventura, Same
18)	95.8		Liberdade FM, Díli
19)	96.1	0.1	R. Comunidade Ili Uai, Manatuto
20)	97.0		R. Suara Timor Lorosae, Díli
21)	97.1	0.1	R. Comunidade Rai Husar, Aileu
22)	97.9	0.8	R. Povo Viqueque, Viqueque
23)	98.1	0.1	R. Comunidade Lian Tatamailau, Ainaro
1)	98.5	0.1	R. Timor Kmanek, Díli
24)	98.9		R. Kolejiu Fatumaka, Fatumaka
25)	99.5	0.16	R. Rakambia, Díli
26)	99.9	0.1	R. Comunidade Lian Matebian, Baucau
27)	100.1	0.3	R. Comunidade Lospalos (Vox Populi), Lospalos
28)	100.5	0.1	R. Lorico Lian, Díli
29)	102.0		R. Klibur, Díli
30)	102.5	0.15	R. Popular Kolele Mai, Bukoli
31)	107.9		R. Fini Lorosae, Baucau
32)	--		R. Nain Feto, Laleia

RELAYS OF INTERNATIONAL STATIONS:
RDP Internacional, Díli 105.3MHz 1 KW irr. –**BBC World Service**, Díli 95.3MHz – **R. Australia**, Díli 106.4MHz

TOGO

L.T: UTC — **Pop:** 6 million — **Pr.L:** French, Ewé, Kabyè, Kotokoli, Mina — **E.C:** 50Hz, 127(Lomé)/220V — **ITU:** TGO

HAUTE AUTORITÉ DE L'AUDIOVISUEL ET DE LA COMMUNICATION (HAAC)
Lomé. **L.P:** Pres: Philippe Evegno, Vice Pres: Wiyao Dadja Pouwi

RADIODIFFUSION-TÉLÉVISION TOGOLAISE (Gov.)
RADIO LOMÉ B.P. 434, Lomé +228 2221 2493 +228 2221 3673 **W:** radiolome.tg **E:** radiolome@radiolome.tg
L.P: Dir: Bawa Semedo. CE: Dodzi Soares.
FM: Agou 88.3MHz, Alédjo 92.7MHz, Dapaong 88.3MHz, Badou 99.3MHz, Lomé 99.5MHz.
D.Prgr: French/Ethnic: 24h. **English:** 1940. **Ann:** "Radio Lomé". **IS:** Soft tempo chime.

RADIO KARA (Regional station)
B.P. 21, Kara. **L.P:** Dir: Kao Pérézi. CE: Tete Anani
FM: Kara 91.5MHz, Dapaong 91.9MHz, Agou 94.5MHz, Alédjo 99.3MHz, Lomé 101.5MHz.
D.Prgr: 0525-0905, 1200-1435, 1625-2105. **Ann:** "Radiodiffusion Kara".

Other Stations (FM MHz):
R. Avenir, 76 Blvd. de la Kara, Quartier Doumassessé, B.P. 20183, Lomé: 104.3 – **R. de L'Evangile**, Lomé: 100.3. – **R. Delta Santé**, Aneho: 106.1. (Also rel. RFI) – **R. Evangile Jésus Vous Aime**, Bretelle de Kilmamé, B.P. 2313, Lomé. **FM:** Lomé 100.2, Agou 104.1 – **R. Maria Togo**, n°155 de la rue 158, Hédzranawoé, B.P. 30162, Lomé **W:** radiomaria.org **E:** rmariatg@ids.tg **FM:** Dapaong 88.5 0.25kW, Lomé 98.8, Kara 101.5, Kpalimé/Sokodé 104.5 – **R. Missionnaire**, Quartier Tomdé Kara, B.P. 170, Kara: 106.3. **E:** emc_kara@yahoo.com – **R. Nana FM**, Angle Rues Tanou et Djossi, B.P. 6035, Lomé: 95.5. **E:** petdog2@yahoo.fr – **Océan FM**, Aneho: 93.1 – **R. Rurale:** Pagouda 88.9, Notsè 100.1, Dapaong 102.5 – **Sport FM**, Tokoin Habitat, B.P. 8675, Lomé: 91.9 **W:** radiosportfm.com – **R. Tropik FM**, Quartier Wuiti, B.P. 2276, Lomé: 93.1. **E:** tropikfm@nomade.fr – **Zephyr FM**, B.P. 20017, Lomé. **W:** zephyr.tg **E:** zephyr@zephyr.tg **FM:** Lomé 92.3, Kara 95.5, Atakpamé 102.9 – **R. Zion**, Adidogomé, B.P. 13853, Lomé. **FM:** Lomé 94.3, Kpalimé 102.5.
BBC African Sce in English/French: Lomé 97.5
RFI Afrique: Lomé 91.5, Aledjo 95.9, Agou 98.3

TOKELAU (New Zealand)

L.T: UTC +11h — **Pop:** 1,411 — **Pr.L:** Tokelauan, English — **E.C:** 50Hz, 240V — **ITU:** TOK

TOKELAU COMMUNITY RADIO
Office of the Council for the Ongoing Government, Tokelau Office, PO Box 3298 Apia, Samoa **LP:** GM: Jovilisi Suveinakama +685 20822 **W:** tokelau.org.nz
Prgr: local community news and information, educational talks, weather reports and music. Each stn operates independently, with studios on each atoll.

FM	MHz	kW	Station
Atafu Atoll	107.5	0.005	R. Atafu FM
Fakaofo Atoll	107.5	0.005	R. Fakaofo FM
Nukunonu Atoll	107.5	0.005	R. Nukunonu FM

NB: R. Atafu rep. silent (2015) and studio facilities no longer existing. A late 2014 review recommended reintroduction of FM services to each atoll in association with a local 3G mobile telephone service. AM services discounted because of limited power supply to provide 5-10kW service and technical issues with the necessary height of tower.

TONGA

L.T: UTC +13h — **Pop:** 105,916 — **Pr.L:** Tongan, English — **E.C:** 50Hz, 240V — **ITU:** TON

MINISTRY OF INFORMATION & COMMUNICATIONS
P.O. Box 1380, Nuku'alofa +676 28170 +676 24861 **W:** mic.gov.to **E:** enquiries@mic.gov.to **CEO:** Paula Ma'u
MIC is the government ministry responsible for broadcasting policy and radio spectrum administration.

MW	Location	KHz	kW	Station
1)	Nuku'alofa*	1017	10	A3Z
FM	**Location**	**MHz**	**kW**	**Station**
2)	Vaipoa**	88.0	-	A3NTT R. Niuatoputapu
3)	Nuku'alofa*	88.1	-	FM88
4)	Nuku'alofa*	88.6	-	R. Nuku'alofa
5)	Neiafu, Vava'u	88.6	-	R. Waves of Vava'u
6)	Nuku'alofa*	87.5	-	(F.P.I.)
7)	Neiafu, Vava'u	87.9	-	89.5FM
8)	Neiafu. Vava'u	89.0	-	Letio Faka-Kalistiane 89FM
9)	Nuku'alofa*	89.1	-	A3V Tonga R. Magic 89.1
10)	Neiafu, Vava'u	89.3	-	PIG FM
7)	Nuku'alofa*	89.5	-	89.5 FM
1)	Neiafu, Vava'u	90.0	-	Vava'u Kool FM
1)	Nuku'alofa*	90.0	0.1	Kool FM
11)	Nuku'alofa*	93.1	0.2	A3R Letio Faka-Kalistiane 93FM
12)	Nuku'alofa*	98.0	0.1	Le'o 'o e Kakai
9)	Neifu, Vava'u	101.1	-	A3V Vava'u R.
13)	Nuku'alofa*	103.0	-	R. Australia

*) Nuku'alofa,Tongatapu **) Vaipoa, Niuatoputapu

Addresses and other information
1) TONGA BROADCASTING COMMISSION (Independent Statutory Board, part-comm.) P.O. Box 36, Nuku'alofa +676 23295, 23555, 23556 +676 24417 Fangatongo, Neiafu, Vava'u +676 70827, 70843 **W:** tonga-broadcasting.net **E:** tbc_news@tonga-broadcasting.net **L.P:** GM: 'Elenoa 'Amanaki DepGM: Nanise Fifita Chief Prgr Officer: Viola Ulakai C.E: Salomone Finau **Tongatapu:** **MW:** A3Z 1017kHz 10kW **FM:** 90.0MHz 0.1kW (Kool FM) **Vava'u:** 90.0MHz Vava'u Kool FM **R. Tonga** "The Call of the Friendly Isles" on 1017kHz: **D.Prgr:** 1900-1100. **N. in English:** 1800 (BBC), 1900 (ABC), 0000 (ABC or RNZI), 0700 (local), 0715 (ABC) **Kool FM** "Kool 90FM" & "Vava'u Kool 90FM" **N:** local and RNZI **D.Prgr:** 24h – **2)** Old Catholic Priests residence, Vaipoa, Niuatoputapu, Northern Tonga. Community radio post-earthquake funded by South Pacific Commission – **3)** Taimi Media Network, Vaiola Motu'a, Nuku'alofa +676 25133/27477 **W:** taimi-online.com **E:** kalafim@yahoo.com.au **LP:** CEO Kalafi Moala **Prgr:** news/talk/talkback – **4)** Teufaiva, Nuku'alofa +676 26262 **W:** facebook.com/radio-nukualofa-886fm **Prgr:** 24/7 – **5)** +676 71128 – **6)** Sovereign Distributors Ltd, PO Box 86, Nuku'alofa +676 23283 **F:** +676 22915 **LP:** MD Lupe 'Ilaiu (licence issued – **7)** Broadcom Ltd, Ngeieia, Nuku'alofa. Vava'u studio: +676 22296 **W:** facebook.com/895fm **LP:** MD Katalina Tohi, C.Ops Mgr Siaosi Lavaka **Prgr:** 24/7 in Tongan/English **Other:** affiliated and shares Tongan language religious programs with R.Tama Ohi network in NZ **W:** tamaohi.org and Radio Tonga Vake-Tali-Folau in San Francisco **W:** radiotongavt-fusa.com with internet audio also targeted at Australia and Europe – **8)** UCB Pacific Partners, PO Box 95, Neiafu **W:** pacificpartners.org **Prgr:** 24/7 Tongan religious – **9)** 13 Vaha'akolo Road, Kaipongipongi, Nuku'alofa +676 25891 +676 25600 **W:** tongaradio.com **E:** a3v@tongaradio.com or magic@tongaradio.com **LP:** Mgr Phillip Vea – **10) T:** +676 71479 **W:** facebook.com/pigfm-893 **LP:** Greg Carlson **Prgr:** eclectic 'Radio that Rocks the South Pacific' – **11)** UCB Pacific Partners, PO Box 478, Nuku'alofa **W:** pacificpartners.org **E:** tonga@pacificpartners.org **Prgr:** 24/7 Tongan religious – **12)** Voice of the People, Ma'a Fafine moe Famili Inc, Community Media Centre, Fasi, Nuku'alofa. **LP:** Bale Huni **Prgr:** community radio – **13)** 24/7 Pacific stream in English via satellite from Melbourne.

TRINIDAD & TOBAGO

L.T: UTC -4h — **Pop:** 1.3 million — **Pr.L:** English — **E.C:** 60Hz, 115V — **ITU:** TRD

CARIBBEAN NEW MEDIA GROUP LTD. (Gov. Comm.)
⌨ 11a Maraval Rd, Port of Spain ☎ +1 868 622 4141 **W:** talkcity91fm.com & next99fm.com & sweet100fm.com
FM: Talk City 91.1MHz – **Next** 99.1MHz – **Sweet** 100.1MHz

TRINIDAD BROADCASTING COMPANY (Comm.)
⌨ Second Floor, Guardian Building, 22-24 St. Vincent St, P.O. Box 716, Port of Spain ☎ +1 868 623 3802-5 ▤ +1 868 625 1782 **W:** 951thebestmix.co.tt & vibect105.co.tt & inspirationalradio730.co.tt
L.P: GM: Steve Dipnarine
MW: Inspirational 7-30 AM: 730kHz 20kW, 24h (Gospel). **N:** On the h 0600-1900
FM: The Best Mix: 95.1MHz 100kW (A/C) – **The Vibe CT 105:** 105.1MHz (Local music + sport) – **Sangeet:** 106.1MHz (Chutney + Current Affairs) – **Aakash Vani:** 106.5MHz (Easy Listening) – **SLAM:** 100.5MHz (Progressive Urban) – **SKY:** 99.5MHz (Rlg.)

ONE CARIBBEAN MEDIA (Comm.)
⌨ 5 Rosalina St, Woodbrook,, Port of Spain ☎ +1 868 625 8426 ▤ +1 868 624 3234 **L.P:** CEO: Vic Fernandes. GM: Richard Purcell. PD: Wayne LeBlanc **W:** onecaribbeanmedia.net
FM: Hott 93: 93.1MHz (Tobago), 93.5MHz (Port of Spain) – **Caribbean SuperStation (CSS)** Txs in Montserrat (also serving Antigua), Virgin Islands (British), and St. Kitts. F.pl: Tx in Antigua – **i95.5 FM:** 95.5MHz (News, talk, current affairs) – **Red 96.7:** 96.7MHz (Urban) – **W107.1 The Word:** 107.1MHz (Gospel) – **The Wave:** Tx in St.Lucia – **Taj92.3 FM:** 92.3MHz (East Indian)

HCU COMMUNICATIONS GROUP (Comm.)
⌨ 112 Montrose Main Rd, 3rd Floor, Chaguanas ☎ +1 868 665 3630 ▤ +1 868 672 1059 **W:** hotlikepepperradio.com & masala101.com **L.P:** Chmn: Mohan Jaikaran. CEO: Marcel Mahabir. SM: Joy Mahabir
FM: U97.5 Hot Like Pepper: 97.5MHz – **Win Radio 101 Trinidad:** 101.1MHz 25kW. Format: East Indian

C.L. COMMUNICATIONS GROUP (Comm.)
⌨ #4 Herbert St, St. Clair, Port of Spain ☎ +1 868 622 4124 Radio 90.5: 622 0451, Music Radio 9-7: 622 9797, Heartbeat: 622 1035 & Ebony: 622 3104 ▤ +1 868 622 6693 **E:** radio90fm@homeviewtnt.com andradio97@wow.net, radio104@tstt.net.tt **W:** clcommunications.com
FM: Radio 90.5: 90.5MHz (East Indian Stn) – **Music Radio 9-7:** 97.1/97.9MHz – **Heartbeat 103.5:** 103.5MHz (For women) – **Ebony 104:** 104.1MHz

TRINIDAD & TOBAGO RADIO NETWORK (Comm.)
⌨ 153 Tragarete Rd, Newtown, Port of Spain ☎ +1 868 628 6937/6044 **W:** star947tt.com and 96wefm.com and 1077musicforlife.com **L.P:** MD: Tony Chow Lin On. SM: Robert Dash. PD: Paul Richards
FM: Star 94.7 HD: 94.7MHz (Rock) – **W.E.F.M:** 96.1MHz (Urban Caribbean) – **Music for Life:** 107.7 (Soul)

RADIO VISION LIMITED (Comm.)
⌨ 88-90 Abercromby St., Port of Spain ☎ +1 868 627 6937 **W:** city94fm.com & power102fm.com **L.P:** CEP: O'Brian Haynes. MD Brian Knight
FM: Boom Champions 94.1MHz – **POWER 102:** 102.1/102.5

Other stations:
BBC FM: 98.7MHz – **HERITAGE RADIO,** 104 Woodford St, New Town, Port of Spain ☎ +1 868 622 3312 ▤ +1 868 657 9248 **W:** heritageradiott.com. FM: 101.7MHz (Multicultural/rlg.) – **ISAAC 98.1,** 105a Woodford Street, Newtown, Port of Spain ☎ +1 868 628 0904 **W:** isaac981.com **L.P:** CEO Margaret Elcock. FM: 98.1MHz (Rlg) – **LIFE RADIO,** 6A Naparima Mayaro Rd, Cocoyea Village, San Fernando ☎ +1 868 653 0237. FM: 99.5MHz (Rlg) – **MAD 91.5 FM,** Bolan Amar Building, Pole Carew Street, Woodbrook ☎ +1 868 628 0827. FM: 91.5MHz (Urban) – **MORE FM,** 177 Tragarete Rd., Woodbrook ☎ +1 868 628 9595 **W:** morefmtrinidad.com FM: 104.7/107.5MHz (Top 40) – **103FM,** Level 4, Long Circular Mall, Long Circular Road, St. James ☎ +1 868 628 9222/23/24 **W:** 103fm.net FM: 103.1 (East Indian) – **PARLIAMENT OF THE REPUBLIC OF TRINIDAD & TOBAGO,** Abercromby St, Port of Spain: FM: 105.5MHz – **RADIO JAAGRITI,** Corner Pasea Main Road Ext and Churchill Roosevelt Highway,

Tunapuna ☎ +1 868 663 8743 ▤ +1 868 645 0613 **W:** jaagriti.com **L.P:** MD: Sat Maharaj. FM: 102.7MHz. (Rlg. hindu) – **RADIO TAMBRIN,** 3 Picton Street, Scarborough, Tobago ☎ +1 868 639 3437 ▤ +1 868 660 7351 **E:** tambrin@tstt.net.tt **W:** tambrintobago.com **L.P:** GM: George Leacock. FM: 92.7MHz – **RADIO TOCO,** Galera Road, Toco ☎ +1 868 670 0068 **L.P:** CEO: Michael Als. FM: 106.7MHz 1.2kW. Community Radio for NE Trinidad – **THE STREET,** 56 Maraval Road, Port of Spain ☎ +1 868 628 3460 **W:** thestreet919fm.com FM: 91.9MHz – **WACK FM,** 129c Coffee Street, San Fernando ☎ +1 868 652 9774 **W:** wackradio901fm.com **L.P:** CEO: Kenny Phillips. FM: 90.1MHz

TRISTAN DA CUNHA (UK)

L.T: UTC — **Pop:** 275 — **Pr.L:** English — **E.C:** 50Hz, 220V — **ITU:** TRC

TRISTAN BROADCASTING SERVICE (Gov.)
⌨ The Administrator, Tristan da Cunha, So. Atlantic via Cape Town, South Africa. **E:** tristan.radio@yahoo.co.uk **L.P:** Head of Telecommunications: Andy Repetto.
FM: Atlantic FM, 93.5MHz 25W **D.Prgr:** Sun 1000-1200

Other stations:
Satellite relay of **BFBS 1** probably rebroadcast on 93.5MHz

TUNISIA

L.T: UTC +1h — **Pop:** 10.5 million — **Pr.L:** Arabic — **E.C:** 50Hz, 115/220V — **ITU:** TUN

HAUTE AUTORITÉ INDÉPENDANTE DE LA COMMUNICATION AUDIOVISUELLE (HAICA)
⌨ 50 Ave de l'Indépendance, Le Bardo 2000 ☎+216 7166 0177 **W:** haica.tn **E:** contact@haica.tn

RADIO TUNISIENNE (Gov.)
⌨ 71 Ave. de la Liberté, TN-1002 Tunis ☎+216 71847300 ▤+216 71785146 **W:** rtci.tn **E:** ittisal@ertt.nat.tn
L.P: DG Radio: Chaouki Aloui. Dir. Tech. Radio: Moncef Fathallah.

MW	kHz	kW		Prgr.	Times
Gafsa	585	350		N	0400-2400
Tunis	630	300		N	24h
Medenine	684	10		N	0400-2400
Tunis	963	100		I	24h

FM (MHz)	N	C	I	Y	kW
Ain Draham	90.3		93.4	96.6	6
Biadha		105.4	101.8	95.0	50
Gabes		93.3			1
Ghraba (Sfax)	93.0	103.0	99.5	93.0	60
Gorrâa	89.1		95.4	89.1	4
Harkoussia				92.5	
Kasserine			99.2	89.6	49
Kchabta	102.6		93.8	97.0	
Kef Errand	89.8			99.4	
Remada	103.4	99.9	94.3	90.3	80
Souk Jomaa				91.3	
Trozza		87.7		90.8	
Tunis	105.3		98.2	88.6	1
Zaghouan	94.3	101.1	94.3	96.5	20
Zarzis		90.7	97.2	93.9	72

National Channel (N) in Arabic: 24h. **N.** on the h. – **Cultural channel (C)** in Arabic: 1100-2400 on 963kHz & FM. – **R. Tunis Chaîne Internationale (RTCI) (I):** French 0500-0100 except English 1403-1430, German 1430-1500, Italian 1900-1930, Spanish 1930-2000. – **R. Jeunes** (Youth R.) **(Y):** 24h.
Regional stations (FM MHz): R. Gafsa, Avenue Habib Bourguiba, 2100 **FM:** Gafsa: 88.3, 89.0 40kW, Biadha 91.8, Chambi 92.7 50kW, 93.5 – **R. Le Kef,** Rue Mongi Slim, 7100 Le Kef. **FM:** Souk-Jomaa 90.0, 92.2 50kW, Ain Draham 90.3, Ghardimaou 94.1, Sidi Youssef 95.8, Sidi Salem 96.2, Le Kef 96.8, Nefta 99.6, Nebeur 100.1, Goraa 102.2, 103.1, 106.7 – **R. Monastir,** Rue Farhat Hached, 5019 Monastir. **FM:** Harkoussia 95.7, Trozza 97.3 5kW, Sousse 99.0, Zaghouan 104.7, Monastir 106.1 – **R. Sfax,** Route de Menzel Chaker Road, 3058 Sfax. **FM:** Djerba 89.0, Ksour-Essaf 100.0, Trozza 100.8, Sfax 105.2 – **R. Tataouine,** Cité 7 Novembre, 3263 **FM:** Tataouine: 87.6 70kW, Techout 89.5, 92.2, 94.3 80kW, 96.6 80kW, 102.6.
Ann: National Channel: "Huna Tunis, Idha'atu-l-Wataniya at-Tunisiya". Cultural Channel: "Huna idha'at-Tunis at-thakafiya". F: "Ici Radio Tunisie Internationale".

Other Stations (FM MHz):
Cap FM: Kef-Errand 91.5, Hammamet 95.2/105.6. **W:** capradio.tn

– Chambi FM: Kasserine 95.9. **W:** chambi-fm.net – **R. Express FM,** Tunis: 103.6. **W:** radioexpressfm.com – **R. Med,** Nabeul: 100.0, Cap Bon 104.1. **W:** radiomed.tn – **R. Mosaïque FM,** Immeuble Montplaisir, Tunis. Hammamet 88.9, Sidi Bou Said 90.3 0.1kW, Nabul 92.9, Tunis 94.9 5kW. D.Prgr: 24h in French and English. **W:** mosaiq-uefm.net – **R. Jawhara FM,** Kairouan 89.4, Sousse 102.5/107.3 1kW. 0500-2400. **W:** jawharafm.net – **Shems FM:** Gafsa 88.7, Monastir 90.6, Sousse 93.7, Bizerta 95.7, Sfax 96.2, Tunis 101.7, Cap Bon 106.5, Kairouan 107.0. **W:** shemsfm.net – **Zitouna FM**: El Ghraba 89.9 60kW, Nefta 91.4 1kW, Gorraa 92.2 3kW, Trozza 94.0 5kW, Tataouine 94.4 1kW, Ksour-Essaf 96.9, Zaghouan 97.6 80kW, Souk-Jomaa 97.8, Biadha 98.3 35 kW, Bizerte 99.1 5kW, Gabes 99.8 1kW, Ain Draham 100.4 5kW, Zarziz 100.7 63kW, Tozeur 102.3 1kW, Nabeul 102.9 7kW, Remada 103.4 80kW, Sidi Bou Said 106.9. **W:** zitounafm.net

TURKEY

L.T: UTC +2h (27 Mar-30 Oct: +3h) — **Pop:** 73 million — **Pr.L:** Turkish — **E.C:** 50Hz, 230V — **ITU:** TUR

SUPREME BOARD OF RADIO AND TELEVISION(RTÜK)
Bilkent Plaza B2 Blok, 06530 Bilkent/Ankara ☎+90 312 2975000
W: rtuk.gov.tr **E:** rtuk@rtuk.gov.tr **LP:** Pres: Davut Dursun

TÜRKIYE RADYO-TELEVIZYON KURUMU (TRT)
(Turkish Radio-Television Corporation)
TRT Genel Mudurlugu, Turan Günes Bulvarı, 06109 OR-AN, Ankara
☎+90 312 4634343 +90 312 4632335
W: radyo.trt.net.tr **E:** rdb@trt.net.tr
LP: DG: Senol Göka. Dep. DG (Eng.): Zeki Ciftci. Dep. DG (Radio): Erkan Durdu. Dir. Radio Dept: Amber Turkmen. Dir. Transmitters Dept: Recep Yurduseven.

MW	kHz	kW	N	MW	kHz	kW	N
Mersin	630	300	1/A	Izmir	927	200	1
Çatalca*	702	600	T	Trabzon	954	300	1
Antalya	891	300	1	Diyarbakir	1062	300	K

*) Istanbul. 1=TRT1, K=Kurdish, A=Arabic (Vo Turkey) for Syria 1800-2000, T=Türkü; 702kHz inactive, but expected to return late 2015.

FM	TRT1	TRT2	TRT3	TRT4	Türkü	Haber	Nagme	kW
Adana (c)	105.1	92.5	89.2	96.7		100.0		30
Adiyaman (d)	88.8	94.4		93.3	90.8		103.3	30
Afyon	97.0	93.0		94.0	92.0	96.2	94.0	5/30
Agri (e)	88.2	92.2			95.2		101.8	30
Amasya	94.7	93.9		107.3	101.9	99.6	98.9	30
Ankara-Cankaya	93.3	88.0		91.2	103.7	98.6 105.6	102.8	30
Ankara-Yenimehalle		100.3			107.8			30
Antalya (a)	100.6	95.6	91.6		88.4		92.1	30/1
Antalya-Alanya (a)	90.3	92.7		94.4				5
Antalya-Kas (a)	88.1	90.5	97.0	97.1				1/5
Aydin	98.5	91.7	97.6	101.5	95.0		106.3	30/5
Aydin-Dilek YA	98.7	90.2	93.5	103.8				30
Balikesir	92.6	98.4		99.3				30
Balikesir-Ayvalik	88.4	90.4		103.5	99.1	95.4	101.1	5
Bilecik	97.1	99.1		101.1				5
Bingöl (d)	99.2	97.2		105.0	99.6		97.6	30
Bitlis (d)	98.0	94.2		100.0	94.3	96.3		5
Bolu	89.6	92.6		98.9		94.8		30/5
Burdur (a)	94.0	89.6			102.4		99.2	5
Bursa	87.9	98.9	91.1	95.2		96.7		30/5
Çanakkale	93.0	89.5		97.0	100.3	106.3		30
Çankiri	88.4	91.6			98.8		100.8	30
Çorum	105.7	103.7			98.2		101.2	5
Denizli	95.2	93.2	90.0	101.5				30/5
Diyarbakir (d)	98.4	95.5		107.3				30
Edirne	97.9	89.0		103.7	91.0		100.9	1/30
Elazig (d)	94.8	92.8		102.2	107.5	89.6	102.7	30
Erzincan (e)	88.0	93.2		91.2	96.7			30
Erzurum (e)	90.8	98.8		102.6	96.8	92.7		30/5
Erzurum-Oltu (e)	95.6	93.6		89.1			98.1	5
Eskisehir	89.0	96.8	94.4	101.3				30
Eskisehir-Sivrihisar	90.2	98.4		104.4		96.2		30
Gaziantep (d)	92.0	97.6		101.9		95.2		30
Hatay (c)	93.6	91.2		88.0	100.0			30/5
Isparta (a)	94.0	89.6		105.5	102.4		99.2	30
Istanbul	95.6	91.4	88.2	103.4		101.6	100	100/5
Izmir	94.7	91.2	88.0		100.5		89.8	100/5
Izmir-Ödemis	92.9	97.9		87.8		95.8		5
Izmir-Karaburun	90.8	93.8	99.1	101.6	99.1	88.7	421.54	5
K.Maras (c)	99.8	105.8		87.8		107.9		5
K.Maras-Elbistan (c)	91.4	96.4		94.0				30
Karaman (c)	96.4	98.6		90.8		106.5		30
Kars (e)	100.8	89.5		103.3		91.3		30

FM	TRT1	TRT2	TRT3	TRT4	Türkü	Haber	Nagme	kW
Kastamonu	93.2	91.5		90.0			101.9	30/5
Kastamonu-Bozkurt	101.5	97.5		103.5				30
Kayseri	89.4	97.2		93.3		99.2		30
Kilis (d)	94.4	90.8		98.3			88.8	5
Kirklareli	94.5	90.0		92.0		103.6		110/30
Kirklareli-Demirköy	94.5	90.0		92.0		103.6		30
Kirsehir	97.6	92.0		88.8			102.5	30
Kocaeli-Gebze	105.5	100.9						30
Kocaeli-Izmit	90.5	96.0		100.5		103.6		30/100
Konya (c)	103.2	90.5		107.4			92.9	30/5
Konya-Aksehir	89.2	95.8		92.4			101.0	30
Kütahya	90.2	95.4		88.1		92.1		30
Mardin (d)	92.8	104.5		107.0				5
Mardin-Nusaybin(d)	96.8	93.4		91.0				30
Mersin-Icel (c)	93.1	90.0	95.8		92.0 104.3	102.1		5
Mersin-Silifke (c)	98.3	95.1		102.2			103.2	30/5
Mugla-Bodrum (a)	94.6	99.3	89.4		100.3		97.4	5
Mugla-Datça (a)	95.8	107.1	102.9	92.6	102.2		96.6	30
Mugla-Datça (c)	88.8							30
Mugla-Fethiye (a)	97.7	94.5	89.3	93.7	103.1		93.7	5
Mugla-Köycegiz (a)	105.1	99.8	95.4	92.8				30
Mugla-Marmaris (a)	98.2	90.9	95.0	101.0				5
Mugla-Yatagan (a)	88.8	92.0		102.2			96.6	30
Mus (d)	99.2	97.2		105.0	102.7			30
Nevsehir-Avanos	99.6	95.0	93.7	103.0	88.8		102.5	5
Nigde (c)	90.0	95.6		93.2			105.7	30
Ordu-Persembe (t)	99.9	95.6		97.6				30
Samsun (t)	95.2	92.8	93.2	96.8	91.3	90.8	97.5	30
Sanliurfa (d)	98.1	102.5						5/30
Sanliurfa-Suruc (d)	90.4	100.3		105.5				30
Siirt-Kurtalan (d)	99.6	105.6		101.6				30
Sirnak (d)	101.6							30
Sirnak-Cizre (d)	101.9	97.7		103.8				30
Sivas	93.6	98.3	100.9		90.4			30
Trabzon (t)	88.8	95.0		97.0	103.7	92.0	105.7	30
Tunceli (d)	89.2	92.4		106.9			101.1	30
Usak	105.5	101.9		98.4			95.7	30
Van (d)	94.8	89.3	100.3		92.8			30/5
Van-Özalp (d)	91.2	97.6		101.2			93.2	5
Yozgat	98.0	96.0		89.8	104.0			5
Zonguldak	88.8	97.2		93.4		99.2		5/30

+about 400 transmitters 1kW or less.

1 = Radyo Bir (spoken word): 24h on FM. **MW:** 0400-1115 on 630/891/927/954kHz. In Turkish. – **2 = (TRT-FM)** (popular music): 24h in Turkish – **3 = Radyo Üc** (classical music): 24h in Turkish exc. N. in English/French/German (3 min's each): 0503, 0803, 1003, 1303, 1503, 1803. Tourist Prgrs (3 min's each on Saturdays): English: 1715, French: 1515, German: 2015 – **4= Radyo Dört** (art & folk music): 24h on FM, 1100 (927kHz from 0800)-1600 on 630/927/954kHz – **TRT Türkü** (Turkish folk music channel): 24h on FM & 0400-2300 on 702 kHz) – **TRT Kurdî in Kurdish:** 0400-1600 on 1062kHz & 24h on **FM:** Adiyaman 88.4, Bingöl 90.2, Bitlis 90.6, Diyarbakir 88.4, Mardin 102.1, Mus 90.2, Siirt 103.6, Sirnak 94.5 & Van 102.3MHz – **TRT Radyo Haber:** news network; 24h on FM – **TRT Nagme** (Turkish Art Music Channel): 24h – **Regional prgrs** (Bölgesel R): via FM1 on txs near Antalya (a), Çukurova (c), Diyarbakir (d), Erzurum (e) and Trabzon (t) – **TRT Kent Radyo** (City R.): Izmir 99.1MHz, Ankara 105.6MHz & Istanbul 106.6MHz. 24h, r. TRT FM 2300-0500 – **Armenian Sce.** on 106.3MHz: 0530-0600 & 1600-1630 – MW txs may carry additional special prgr. during Ramazan month.
Ann: TRT-1: "Burasi TRT Radyo Bir", TRT-4: "Burasi TRT Radyo Dört". Reg.: e.g. Antalya: "Burasi TRT Antalya Radyosu."

EXTERNAL SERVICE: Voice of Turkey
See International Radio section.

Other stations; main networks:

FM (MHz)	1)	2)	3)	4)	5)	6)	7)	8)	9)	10)
Abant		104.5								
Adana	105.4	89.6	102.9	103.8	96.0		97.2	101.9	92.0	98.7
Adiyaman				92.0			100.5			91.2
Afyon		101.2	100,6	90.4		95.2		96.2		102.4
Agri					100.4			96.2		104.7
Akhisar			93.0				105.2			
Aksaray		100.0				95.7	97.2	105.0		107.3
Aksehir							105.0			
Alanya			100.0	89.3	98.0		89.9	93.5		
Amasya	92.8							101.6		89.1
Ankara	102.4	88.8	100.0	105.3	97.2	94.4	89.8	107.4	90.8	94.6

FM (MHz)	1)	2)	3)	4)	5)	6)	7)	8)	9)	10)
Antalya	90.2	89.7	100.0	89.3	102.6	90.9	101.2	95.3	94.2	95.8
Ardahan						95.5	98.0	99.0		103.7
Artvin								100.4		106.8
Aydin			100.0	92.3		95.8		91.1		93.2
Ayvalik				98.3		93.6			105.2	
Bafra								96.0	100.8	
Balikesir	98.7	88.8	100.0	90.7	93.5	94.3	97.2	88.5		99.6
Bandirma				89.3		107.7	106.2	107.0		87.8
Bartin						95.5	98.4	100.0		105.7
Batman								95.0		102.8
Bayburt						91.5		95.0		107.0
Bilecik								102.5		96.0
Bingöl								103.3		102.5
Bitlis								101.0		106.3
Bodrum	104.8	103.5	100.0	89.2	92.4					
Bolu		88.9	100.0	94.3		97.2	89.2	107.6	89.0	93.4
Boyabat								100.0		106.8
Boyabat								100.0		90.5
Bucak								100.0		
Burdur		93.5		92.0			88.0	104.5		93.8
Bursa	92.0	89.8	100.0	89.2	97.2	106.6	104.6	107.6	90.8	97.9
Ceyhan							107.7	88.9		93.6
Cizre							88.1			
Çanakkale		88.0		89.3		99.5	105.3	101.0		106.7
Çankiri						90.1		92.8		97.0
Çeşme		89.6	95.0	89.3	97.2					
Çorlu			100.0					91.3	93.3	
Çorum							91.3	89.5		90.7
Demirci							104.6			
Denizli		88.0	100.0	89.3	96.0	92.9	107.7	96.8		90.5
Develi							102.0	99.0	90.8	
Didim										
Dinar							94.9			
Diyarbakir	92.0	89.8	100.3	92.3		90.4	98.0	101.0		88.0
Dogubeyazit						100.5			97.5	
Düzce	92.0			97.4				107.6		93.4
Edirne				101.3	102.6	90.5	103.0	91.3	96.3	93.4
Edremit						90.7		96.0	98.4	
Elazig		89.9				104.4	92.4	94.1		101.2
Erzincan						89.5		93.8		107.2
Erzurum	91.8	90.4	100.7	89.3		94.6	91.5	94.0		89.6
Eskisehir	88.6	100.0	100.5	89.3	97.2	92.6	106.3	106.6		89.6
Fethiye	102.0	88.2	100.3	96.7	96.4		99.0	98.5		
Gaziantep	107.5	92.4	104.6	102.5	103.7	96.6	107.0	103.0	93.2	88.0
Gazipasa							97.5		99.3	104.8
Gebze	92.0							107.6		
Gerede		89.1				94.5	102.7	107.4	104.8	
Giresun						91.1		93.0		106.2
Gümüshane						92.0		102.5	90.8	101.8
Hakkari						98.0		90.0		91.8
Hatay		105.5				88.5	106.7	101.0		99.5
Igdir						95.5		99.5		89.8
Iskenderun			101.0				94.6	95.6		107.6
Isparta		92.5		91.8		96.0		100.0		87.7
Istanbul	92.0	89.8	100.0	89.2	97.2	94.1	104.6	107.6		102.6
Izmir	92.0	89.8	100.0	89.3	97.2	96.7	101.3	96.9	90.8	98.7
K.Maras		89.8		89.0			98.2	94.0	90.8	102.3
Karaman								103.9		96.1
Kars		102.0				90.6	104.6	102.7		100.4
Kastamonu			100.5				104.6	101.0		
Kayseri	93.9	105.0	100.0	88.7	98.9	104.7	100.2	88.5	96.2	106.7
Kirikkale						105.5		105.0		94.0
Kirklareli						89.8	107.6			100.3
Kirsehir								94.4		91.3
Kocaeli	92.0	89.8	100.0	89.2		94.2	104.6	107.6		99.5
Konya	95.1	89.9	95.7	89.3	101.7	98.0	92.1	102.0	93.4	96.1
Kusadasi	104.5		100.0	89.3	92.7					89.8
Kütahya		92.8	102.9	91.3		92.6	107.0	93.8	90.8	100.8
Ladik	92.0									
Malatya		89.9	103.3	97.8		91.7	104.6	105.5	94.5	91.3
Manisa		104.1	100.3	89.1		101.3	103.3	105.4	94.3	
Mardin		89.0				102.5	104.0	95.0		87.7
Marmaris	103.6	105.5	100.0	89.3	96.1					
Mersin		93.5	105.0	90.3		93.7		105.3		103.5
Milas							96.9			
Mugla			100.3	89.3			104.6	102.6	90.1	106.8
Mus						93.3		102.0		104.2
Nevsehir								101.8		91.3
Nigde	91.8					97.0		103.0		97.3
Ordu								92.5		96.5
Osmaniye		89.6				98.4	99.9	101.7		89.4
Rize				94.6				102.5		105.3

FM (MHz)	1)	2)	3)	4)	5)	6)	7)	8)	9)	10)
Sakarya	101.3	88.0	100.7	101.8	91.2		104.6	107.8	97.8	91.5
Samsun	99.7	106.2	100.0	88.0		89.1	94.1	103.0	96.3	105.8
Sanliurfa		104.4					92.0	93.5		103.6
Saraykoy							107.4			
Siirt								91.0		102.8
Sinop							94.2	99.0		107.4
Sivas	96.2			102.2			91.0	100.1		92.3
Sivrihisar							97.5	94.9		106.5
Soke								96.9	105.4	
Tekirdag	96.2		100.0	90.3	96.0		104.6	105.4	91.8	91.8
Tokat								96.0		
Trabzon		100.4	104.6	89.3		94.6	93.0	102.8	90.3	92.5
Tunceli							94.5	94.0		106.2
Usak							106.0	99.0		107.5
Van							104.6	96.0		103.3
Yalova			100.0				94.5			
Yozgat							102.0	100.4		106.6
Zile							98.0	96.4		
Zonguldak	96.0		101.5	90.0			104.6	107.0	91.0	94.1

Addresses and other information:
1) Kral FM ◫ Ahi Evran Cad. No 3, 34398 Maslak-Sisli-Istanbul ☎+90 212 3350000 **W:** kralfm.com.tr – **2) Show R.** ◫ Ust Zeren Sokak No 40, Levent-Besiktas-Istanbul ☎+90 212 3850000 **W:** showradyo.com.tr – **3) Power FM** ◫ Gumusyolu Cad. Kusbakisi Sk. No 43, Altunizade-Uskudar-Istanbul ☎+90 216 5540400 **W:** powerfm.com.tr – **4) Alem FM** ◫ Ayazaga Mah. Kemerburgaz Yolu Cendere Mevkii No 29, Sisli-Istanbul ☎+90 212 3318888 **W:** alemfm.com – **5) Metro FM** ◫ Büyükdere Cad. No 23, CEM Is Merkezi Kat. 4, Istanbul ☎+90 212 3686200 **W:** metrofm.com.tr – **6) Polis Radyosu** ◫ Necatibey Caddesi No 108, Anittepe-Ankara ☎+90 312 2306181 **W:** polisradyosu.net – **7) Radyo 7** ◫ Defterdar Mah. Otakcilar Cad. No 78, Eyup-Istanbul ☎+90 212 4378585 **W:** radyo7.com – **8) Akra FM** ◫ Barbaros Mah. Mutevelli Cesme Cad. No 21, Uskudar-Istanbul ☎+90 216 3252265 **W:** akradyo.net – **9) Akra FM** ◫ Barbaros Mah. Mutevelli Cesme Cad. No 21, Uskudar-Istanbul ☎+90 216 3252265 **W:** akradyo.net – **10) Diyanet Radyo** (Gov.) ◫ Üniversiteler Mah. Dumlupınar Bulv. No : 147/A 06800 Çankaya/Ankaral ☎+90 2957443 **W:** diyanetradyo.com Kuran R: Ankara 88.2, Istanbul 97.4, Izmir 90.3 & Konya 88.2
In addition there are about 30 national, 100 regional and 1000 local stations in operation on FM.

AFN INCIRLIK AIR BASE BROADCASTING STN (Mil.)
☎+90 322 3166421 **W:** incirlik.afneurope.net **E:** 39abw.pa@incirlik.af.mil **MW:** 1593kHz 5W. **FM:** 107.1MHz on cable

TURKMENISTAN

L.T: UTC +5h — **Pop:** 5.1 million — **Pr.L:** Turkmen — **E.C:** 50Hz, 220V — **ITU:** TKM

TELEWIDENIÝE, RADIOGEPLESIKLER WE KINEMATOGRAFIÝA BARAKDY DÖWLET KOMITET
(State Committee for TV, Radio and Cinematography)
◫ Magtymguly köçesi 89, 744000 Asgabat ☎ +993 12 351515 🖷 +993 12 394470 **L.P:** Chmn: A. Kakaýewi

LW/MW	kHz	kW	Prgr	MW	kHz	kW	Prgr
Asgabat	279	150	1	Serhetabat	1080	5	1
Asgabat	576	150	2/3	Asgabat	1125	20	1
Türkmenbasy	675	10	2/3	Syrttagta	1233	40	1
Ýekarça	720	1	1	Dasoguz	1233	5	1
Etrek	720	1	1	Türkmenbasy	1476	10	1
Türkmenabat	927	50	1				

FM (MHz)	1	2/3	1	2/3	4	kW
Arçabyl	-	-	102.3	-	100.3	4
Asgabat	71.12	69.68	103.2	104.4	101.3	2x4/3x10
Atamyrat	-	-	102.8	-	100.3	4
Baharly	-	70.64	101.6	104.1	-	4
Balkanabat	70.28	72.02	100.4	101.9	103.9	2x4/3x1
Baýramaly	-	70.27	-	-	-	4
Boldumsaz	-	-	105.6	106.9	104.0	4
Dasoguz	69.32	67.22	100.7	103.0	100.1	2x4/3x1
Magdanly	-	-	104.2	106.7	102.2	4
Mary	-	-	103.2	104.4	102.3	4
Tejen	70.52	72.14	-	-	-	4
Türkmenabat	66.95	68.77	104.4	106.0	100.8	4
Türkmenbasy	69.23	67.19	100.2	101.7	100.7	2x4/3x10
Uly Balkan Gersi	72.20	70.61	-	-	103.0	4

D.Prgr: Prgr 1 (Watan): 24h. – **Prgr 2 (Çar tarapdan):** 0200-0400,

0700-0900, 1400-1700. – **Prgr 3 (Miras):** 0400-0700, 0900-1400, 1700-2300. – **Prgr 4 (Owaz):** 24h. N. in English 0000, Turkmen 0100, Russian 0200; continued in 3h cycles.

DAB Transmitters (DAB+)
Tx Operator: Ministry of Communications **M:** Watan, Çar tarapdan, Miras, Owaz **Txs:** Block 7B (190.640MHz) & 13B (232.496MHz) Asgabat 3.1kW

TURKS & CAICOS ISLANDS (UK)

L.T: UTC -5h (13 Mar-6 Nov: -4h) — **Pop:** 31,500 — **Pr.L:** English — **E.C:** 60Hz, 110/220/440V — **ITU:** TCA

RADIO TURKS & CAICOS (Gov. Comm.)
✉ P.O. Box 69, Grand Turk ☎ +1 649 946 2010 🖷 +1 649 946 1600 **E:** teamrtc@rtc107fm.com **W:** rtc107fm.com
FM: 101.9MHz (Grand Turk/Salt Cay & South Caicos), 103.9MHz (North & Middle Caicos), 105.9MHz & 107.7MHz (Providenciales)
D.Prgr: 24h Local prgr: 1100-0300; at other times relays country satel-lite stn. On 105.9: "RTC" (Official Government News Radio)
Ann: "This is Radio Turks & Caicos on Grand Turk, Turks & Caicos Islands"

RADIO VISIÓN CRISTIANA (Rlg.)
✉ North End, So. Caicos **W:** radiovision.net
MW: So. Caicos 530kHz (Lp)(Unconfirmed)
D.Prgr. in Spanish: rel. WWRV 1330, NY, USA

WIV FM RADIO LTD (Comm.)
✉ WIV Building, Leeward Highway, Box 324, Providenciales ☎ +1 888 628 9391 **W:** praisehimfm.com & 939islandfm.com & power925fm.com **L.P.:** Kenny Caughlin
FM: PraiseHim FM: 90.5MHz (Gospel) – **Island FM:** 93.9MHz (Island music) – **KISS FM:** 102.5MHz (Light rock) – **Power 92.5 FM:** 92.5MHz (Hit music)

Other stations:
FAITH FM – ROCK OF JESUS NETWORK, Blue Hills Settlements, Five Cays, Providenciales ☎ +1 649 941 5451 **W:** rojnetwork.com FM: 98.9MHz – **JAMZ RADIO**, Connolly Production, PO Box 63, Tropicana Plaza, Providenciales. FM: 88.5MHz – **KIST**, Providenciales: 106.3MHz. Grand Turk: 94.9MHz 2kW. Format: Gospel – **LIFE RADIO - ZIBF**, Communication Network, Camron and Patrick St, So. Caicos. FM: Life R. 1:105.5MHz 0.6kW, Life R. 2: 107.1MHz (reported: 103.5MHz) – **RADIO EXAMPLE OF CHRIST**, PO Box 1095, Five Cays, Providenciales ☎ +1 649 941 7532 FM: 95.1MHz – **SIRIUS XM CLASSIC ROCK**. FM: 99.9MHz – **SMOOTH FM** smoothfm.tc FM: 88.1MHz – **TROPICAL VIBES**, The Bight, Stubbs Rd, Providenciales ☎ +1 649 941 8550 **W:** tropicalvibes.tci.com FM: 103.5/105.5MHz 0.5kW – **WDDR RADIO**, Box 262, Providenciales: 88.7MHz (0.25kW) – **ZVIC (Victory In Christ)**, PO Box 32, Providenciales. FM 96.7MHz

TUVALU

L.T: UTC +12h — **Pop:** 10,544 — **Pr.L:** Tuvaluan, English — **E.C:** 50Hz, 240V (Funafuti only) — **ITU:** TUV

TUVALU MEDIA CORPORATION (Gov.)
✉ Private Mail Bag, Vaiaku, Funafuti ☎ +688 20139 🖷 + 688 20732 **L.P:** GM Melali Taape **Prgr Prod:** Ms Afasene Pese, Head of Tech. **Sces:** John Sammons
W: tuvalu-news.tv **E:** meltaape@govt.tv, apese@govt.tv
Radio Tuvalu AM: MW: 621kHz 5kW Funafuti (nationwide coverage)
FM: Funafuti (local coverage) 100.1MHz 0.02kW
D.Prgr: 1830-2000, 2325-0100, 0625-10000 daily. **N. in English:** 1910, 0710 **Ann:** E: "This is Radio Tuvalu" **V:** by letter
BBC Pacific stream via satellite from London at other times: 2000-2325, 0100-0625, 1000-1830

UGANDA

L.T: UTC +3h — **Pop:** 33 million — **Pr.L:** Luganda, Swahili, English — **E.C:** 50Hz, 240V — **ITU:** UGA

UGANDA COMMUNICATIONS COMMISSION (UCC)
✉ 12th Floor, Communications House, Plot 1, Colville Street, P. O. Box 7376, Kampala ☎+256 41 4339000 🖷 +256 41 4348832
W: ucc.co.ug **E:** ucc@ucc.co.ug

UGANDA BROADCASTING CORPORATION(UBC, Pub.)
✉ P.O. Box 2038, Plot 17-19, Nile Ave, Kampala ☎+256 41 4257034 🖷 + 256 41 4257252 **W:** ubc.ug **E:** customerservice@ubc.ug **L.P:** Chmn: Chris B. Katuramu. Man. Dir: Musinguzi Mugasa. Commissioners: Radio Broadc: Jack Turyamwijuka. Ag. Contr. of Prgrs (Radio): Charles Byekwaso. Ag. Principal Eng. (Radio): Yona Hamala.

MW	kHz	kW	Ch.
Mityana	576	100	UBC West/Star FM
Kampala	909	20	West Nile FM
Kabale	999	100	UBC R. (irr.)

SW	kHz	kW	Ch.	Times
Kampala	4976	10	Red	0200-0500,1200-2105(occ. overnight)
Kampala	7195	10	Red	0500-1200

FM (MHz)	UBC R.	West	Butebo	Star FM	Magic
Fort Portal	-	98.8	-	-	-
Hoima	-	99.1	-	-	-
Jinja	-	-	-	95.7	-
Kabale	-	93.7	-	-	-
Kampala	98.0	107.5	107.3	87.5	100.0
Kisoro	-	97.7	-	-	-
Lira	100.0	-	-	-	-
Masaka	-	99.5	-	96.9	-
Mbale	-	-	96.9	-	-
Mbarara	-	97.4	-	-	-
Masindi	-	105.0	-	-	-
Soroti	-	-	96.7	-	-

UBC R. in English, Swahili, Luo and Nubian: 24h – **UBC West** in 5 ethnic languages: 0300-2105 – **Butebo Channel** in 11 ethnic lan-guages – **Star FM** in Luganda. **Magic FM** in English.
Buruli FM in 5 ethnic languages: Nakasongola 107.0MHz.
Mega FM in Luo/others: Gulu 102.1, Moro 103.1MHz 2kW.
Ngeya FM in 5 languages: Kasese 101.5MHz.
Vo Bundibugyo: Bundibugyo 93.3MHz.
West Nile FM: Arua 94.1MHz.

DUNAMIS SHORTWAVE (Rlg.)
(a joint project by High Adventure Canada and Dunamis FM).
✉ P.O. Box 4260, Kampala. **W:** biblevoice.org **E:** dunashortwave@outlook.com **L.P:** CE: David Firth.
SW: Mukono 4750kHz 1kW. **D.Prgr:** in English/Ethnic 1500-1900v.
Other stations (FM MHz):
African R, Kampala: 104.5 – **All Karamoja FM,** Moroto: 94.7 – **Arua One FM,** Arua: 88.7 2kW – **Bamboo FM,** Jinja: 107.6 – **Basoga Bainho,** Jinja: 87.7 – **Beat FM,** Kampala: 96.3 – **Bob FM,** Kampala: 92.7 **W:** facebook.com/927BobFM – **Buddu BS,** Masaka: 98.8 – **Bukedde FM:** Kampala 100.5, Masaka 106.8 **W:** bukedde.co.ug – **Bunuyoro BS,** Masindi: 98.2 – **Busiro FM,** Kakiri: 107.5 – **Busoga FM,** Jinja: 96.0 – **Campus FM,** Kampala: 106.6 – **Capital FM:** Kampala 91.3, Mbale 90.9, Mbarara 88.7 – **City FM,** Kampala: 98.1 – **Continental FM,** Kumi: 94.7 – **Dembe FM,** Kampala: 90.4 – **Dunamis FM,** Kampala: 103.0 – **East Africa R,** Kampala: 99 (cf. Tanzania) – **Eastern Voice,** Bugiri: 102.3 – **Elgon FM,** Kapchorwa 89.2 – **Etop R,** Soroti: 99.4 – **Eye FM,** Iganga: 98.8 – **Impact & Alpha FM,** Mbale 98.5, Masaka 101.5 1kW, Kampala 102.1 4kW. **W:** victoryuganda.org – **Juice FM,** Kampala: 103.4 **W:** facebook.com/1034-JUICE-FM-Sports-542359682519594 – **Kibaale Community R:** 91.7 – **Kiira FM,** Jinja: 88.6 – **Kings R,** Masindi 88.2 – **Liberty FM,** Hoima 89.0 – **Maranatha FM,** Jinja: 104.7 – **Mbale FM:** 90.1 – **Nehemiah Trumpet Call,** Nimule: 97.3MHz 350W – **Nile BS,** Jinja: 89.4 – **Open Gate FM,** Mbale: 103.2 – **Power FM,** Kampala: 104.1 – **Prime R,** Kampala: 91.9 – **R FM,** Iganga: 91.1 **W:** rfm.co.ug – **R. Apac,** Apac 92.9 0.4kW, Odokomit 106.5 0.1kW **W:** radioapac.tripod.com – **R. Kigezi,** Kabale 93.3 **W:** kfm.co.ug – **R. Kitara,** Masindi: 101.8 – **Kyoga Veritas R,** Soroti: 91.5 1kW. **W:** facebook.com – **R. Lira,** Lira: 95.3 – **R. Mama,** Kampala: 101.7. **W:** interconnection.org/umwa/community_radio.html – **R. Maria Uganda,** Masaka 94 40W, Mbale 101.8, Kampala 103.7 40W, Fort Portal 104.6, Mbarara 105.4. **W:** radiomaria.org – **R. One,** Kampala: 90.0 – **R. Pacis,** Arua: 90.9/94.5 1kW. **W:** radiopacis.org – **R. Paidha,** Nebbi: 87.8 – **R. Rukungiri:** 96.9 – **R. Rupiny:** Kampala 95.7, Lira 98.1 **W:** visiongroup.co.ug – **R. Sapientia,** Kampala 94.4 5kW. **W:** radiosapientia.com – **R. Simba,** Kampala: 97.3 **W:** simba.fm – **R. Skynet,** Mityana: 96.9 – **R. Two,** Kampala: 87.9 – **R. Unity,** Lira: 97.7 – **R. Wa,** Lira: 89.8 – **R. West FM:** Mbarara 102.2, Tooro 91.0, Kabale & Masak – **Rhino FM,** Lira: 96.1 – **Rock Mamba FM,** Tororo 106,8 – **Safari FM,** Mayuge 103.9 – **Sanyu FM,** Kampala 88.2 – **Speak FM,** Gulu 89.5 **W:** fowode.org – **Spirit FM,** Mukono: 96.6 – **Ssuubi FM,** Kampala 104.9, Masaka 88.1. **W:** ssuubifmradio.com – **Star FM,** Kampala: 100.0 – **Step FM,** Mbale: 99.8 – **Super FM,** Kampala: 88.5 – **Truth FM,** Mbale: 105.3 – **VO Africa:** Kampala 92.3 – **VO Kigezi,** Kabale 89.5 – **VO Life,** Arua: 100.9 **W:** vol-radio.net – **VO Teso,** Soroti: 88.4 – **Top R,** Kampala: 89.6 – **VO Toro,** Kampala 100.5, Fort Portal 101.0, Mbarara 95.0, Mubende 97.5 – **Touch FM,** Kampala: 95.9 1kW. **W:** touch.fm – **X FM:** Kampala: 94.8, Mbarara 96.6 **W:** xfm.co.ug

BBC African Sce: Kampala 101.3MHz, Mbale/Mbarara 107.3MHz in English/Swahili/Kinyarwanda.
China R. Int: Jinja 107.1, Kampala 107.3MHz.
RFI Afrique: Kampala 93.7MHz in F/E/Swahili

UKRAINE

L.T: UTC +2h (27 Mar-30 Oct: +3h); Crimea and Donets Basin (de facto): UTC +3h — **Pop:** 45.9 million — **Pr.L:** Ukrainian, Russian — **E.C:** 50Hz, 220V — **ITU:** UKR

NATSIONALNA RADA UKRAINY Z PYTAN TELEBACHENNIA I RADIOMOVLENNIA
(National Television and Radio Broadcasting Council)
✆ vul. Prorizna 2, 01001 Kyiv ☎ +380 44 2787575 ▤ +380 44 2787575 **E:** presa@nrada.gov.ua **W:** nrada.gov.ua
L.P: Chmn: Yurii Artemenko
NB: The council is the regulatory authority for broadcasting.

DERZHAVNYI KOMITET TELEBACHENNIA I RADIOMOVLENNIA UKRAINY (DERZHTELERADIO)
(State Committee for Television and Radio Broadcasting)
✆ vul. Prorizna 2, 01001 Kyiv ☎ +380 44 2785349 ▤ +380 44 2791170 **E:** pr@comin.gov.ua **W:** comin.kmu.gov.ua
L.P: Chmn: Oleh Nalyvaiko

NATSIONALNA SUSILNA TELERADIOKOMPANIIA UKRAINY (NSTU) (Pub)
✆ vul. Khreshchatyk 26, 01001 Kyiv ☎ +380 44 2396224 ▤ +380 44 2793477 **W:** nrcu.gov.ua
L.P: DG (acting): Anatolii Tabachenko
NB: The merger of the former state broadcasting company Natsionalna Radiokompaniia Ukrainy (NRKU) and the regional state broadcasting companies with the new public service broadcaster NSTU is still in progress.

MW	kHz	kW	Prgr*	MW	kHz	kW	Prgr*
Mykolaiv (a)	549	720	1	Mykolaiv	1377	3.5	MY
Kharkiv (b)	837	150	1,F	Vinnytsia	1377	7	VI
Chernivtsi	837	25	CV	Verkhovyna	1044	1	1,IF
Dnipropetrovsk	990	2.5	DN	Izmail	1404	10	1
Petrivka	1278	100	1,F	Mykolaiv (a)	1431	800	F

a) Luch (b) Taranivka *) Reg. services CV, DN, IF, MY, VI see below
F=International Service

FM (MHz) (Situation as of October 2015)

Rg	Location	1a**	1b**#	2	3	kW
ZH	Andriivka	103.4	-	71.90	72.68p	5/2x1
RI	Antopil	87.8	-	67.46	66.53p	0.5/2x1
CH	Bakhmach	-	66.38	-	-	2
VI	Bershad	105.1	-	-	71.93	1
CK	Buky	106.9	-	-	67.88p	0.5/1
CK	Cherkasy	91.4	-	70.64	72.20p	0.25/2x1
CH	Chernihiv	98.2	69.47	-	-	0.25/1
CV	Chernivtsi	91.8	69.26	67.19	-	0.25/2x1
DN	Dnipropetrovsk	-	68.36	-	66.74	3/1
VO	Horokhiv	106.5	-	-	-	1
IF	Ivano-Frankivsk	-	71.24	-	-	1
KA	Izium	102.5	-	-	70.46	0.25/2x1
OD	Kamianske	103.3	-	-	66.59p	0.1/1
KA	Kharkiv	-	67.13	67.91	-	1
KE	Kherson	100.6	-	-	71.90p	5/1
KM	Khmelnytskyi	104.6	-	70.46	67.70p	1
CH	Kholmy	106.1	-	68.27	-	0.5/1
ZK	Khust	101.2	-	71.90	-	0.1/1
KH	Kirovohrad	91.2	66.98	68.84	-	0.25/2x1
OD	Kotovsk	103.6	-	-	69.35	0.5/1
DO	Kramatorsk	-	69.41	-	-	1
PO	Krasnohorivka	106.3	-	68.60	66.08p	3/2x4
DN	Kryvyi Rih	-	71.63	-	69.56	1
KM	Kulchiivtsi	-	70.76	72.89	-	1
KY	Kyiv	105.0	68.51	71.30	72.98	5/15/5/4
TE	Lozova	87.7	69.83	71.75	-	0.25/2x1
LV	Lviv	103.3	-	68.99	67.04	0.5/2x1
VO	Liubeshiv	107.8	-	105.2	-	0.1/1
DO	Mariupol	-	67.34	-	69.44	1
ZP	Melitopol	-	68.72	-	-	1
MY	Mykolaiv	92.0	69.80	-	71.78	0.5/4/1
DN	Nikopol	-	69.38	-	-	1
CV	Novodnistrovsk	106.6	69.59	-	-	0.1/1
OD	Odesa	-	70.52	72.14	-	2/1
ZH	Olevsk	100.2	-	69.80	-	1
ZH	Ovruch	104.2	-	-	-	2
LU	Pidhorivka	-	69.65	-	71.66	1
MY	Pervomaisk	-	69.92	-	68.03	2/4
PO	Poltava	101.8	-	-	-	1

Rg	Location	1a**	1b**#	2	3	kW
CH	Pryluky	-	71.00	72.56	-	1
ZK	Rakhiv	102.2	-	72.71	70.19p	0.1/1/2
LU	Rovenky+	-	69.08	-	-	1
VO	Shatsk	101.5	-	-	-	1
SU	Shostka	107.8	-	67.49	65.93p	0.25/1/4
SU	Trostianets	104.1	-	69.92	68.75p	0.5/2x1
ZK	Uzhhorod	103.0	-	71.54	69.53p	0.5/2x1
KE	Vasylivka	105.8	-	-	69.23p	5/1
VI	Vinnytsia	88.6	71.69	68.57	-	0.5/2x1
KM	Volochysk	-	68.72	-	-	4
ZP	Zaporizhzhia	103.7	-	72.29	70.73p	1
VO	Zarichne	103.8	-	-	-	1
OD	Zhovten	-	68.99	-	-	1

NB: Sites with only txs below 1kW not listed. P=planned. **) Networks 1a/1b simulcast Prgr 1, but partly carry different regional outputs (see below) #) Most freqs to be re-assigned to Prgr 3 (R. Kultura) +) Tx is located in part of the Donets Basin controlled by "Luhansk People's Republic" (LPR)
D.Prgr: Prgr 1 (Ukrainske R.): 24h. – **Prgr 2 (R. Promin):** 24h. – **Prgr 3 (R. Kultura):** 24h.
International Service (R. Ukraine Int.): see Intern. Radio section.

NSTU REGIONAL SERVICES
D.Prgr: all branches broadcast via txs shared with Prgr 1 of NSTU; some branches produce additional output carried on exclusive freqs. Schedules may vary from branch to branch. "Reg 1" on network 1b (partly also via 1a) is generally broadcast: 0410-0430 (SS), 0445-0455 (MF), 0610-0630, 1340-1400 (MF), 1345-1400 (Sat), 1545-1600 (Sat), 1610-1700, 1800-1830. "Reg 2" is broadcast at various times on network 1a and/or exclusive freqs (see below). "Reg 1" services on network 1b are due to cease, as the freqs are being re-assigned to Prgr 3, or are to be taken off the air. (ODTRK=Oblasna derzhavna teleradiokompaniia)
CH) Chernihivska ODTRK: pr. Peremohy 62, 14000 Chernihiv **E:** tvodtrk@ukr.net. Reg 1: "R. Siver-Tsentr"/"Chernihivska khvylia" on 1a+1b. – **CK) Cherkaska ODTRK:** vul. B.Vishnevetskoho 35/1, 18002 Cherkasy **E:** rosradio@ua.fm. Reg 1: "R. Ros" on 1a+1b. – **CV) Chernivetska ODTR:** vul. Holovna 91, 58001 Chernivtsi **E:** bukdtrk-net@ukr.net. Reg 1: "R. Bukovyna" on 1a+1b; Reg 2: "R. Bukovyna" on 837kHz (Chernivtsi): 0600-1100 + 67.97MHz (Chernivtsi 1kW): 0600-2000. – **DN) Dnipropetrovska ODTRK:** vul. Televiziina 3, 49010 Dnipropetrovsk **E:** dodtrk@email.ua. Reg 1: "Dnipropetrovske oblasne R." on 1b; Reg 2: "R. Mryia" on 990kHz (Dnipropetrovsk): 1000-1200. – **DO) Donetska OTDRK:** pl. Lenina 2, 84313 Kramatorsk. **E:** dogtrk3@gmail.com Reg 1: "R. Donechchyna" on 1b (not on air). Substudio: Primorskyi park, 87525 Mariupol. **E:** R. Priazovia" on Mariupol 67.38MHz: Mon/Wed/Fri 1340-1400 (repeat 1610-1630). – **IF) Ivano-Frankivska ODTRK "Karpaty":** vul. Sichovykh striltsiv 30a, 76000 Ivano-Frankivsk **E:** radio@il.if.ua. Reg 1: "Ivano-Frankivske oblase R."/"R. Karpaty" on 1a+1b. Reg 2: "R. Karpaty" on 72.02MHz (Ivano-Frankivsk 1kW). – **KA) Kharkivska ODTRK:** maidan Svobody 5, 61506 Kharkiv. **E:** info@otb.com.ua. Reg 1: "Hovoryt Kharkiv" on 1b. – **KE) Khersonska ODTRK "Skifiia":** vul. Perekopska 10, 73000 Kherson **E:** khersonodtrk@skifiya.ks.ua. Reg 1: "R. Dnipro" on 1b; Reg 2: "R. Tavria" on 1a. – **KH) Kirovohradska ODTRK:** pl. Heroiv Maidanu 1, 25022 Kirovohrad **E:** kodtrk@rambler.ru. Reg 1: "R. Skifiia-Tsentr" on 1b. – **KM) Khmelnytska ODTRK "Podillia-Tsentr":** vul. Volodymyrska 92, 29000 Khmelnytskyi **E:** office@odtrk.km.ua. Reg 1: "Hovoryt Khmelnytskyi" on 1b; Reg 2: "R. Podillia-Tsentr" on 1a. – **KY) Kyivska ODTRK:** vul. Khreshchatyk 5v, 01001 Kyiv **E:** 1kdrtrk@list.ru. Reg 1: "Holos Kyieva" on 1b. Reg 2 (local prgr for Kyiv): "Maidan" on 72.08MHz (Kyiv 4kW): 0400 (SS 0600)-1800. – **LU) Luhanska ODTRK:** vul. Vilesova 1v, 93400 Severodonetsk. **E:** lgtrk@ukrpost.ua. Reg 1: "Luhanske Oblasne R." on 1b (not via Rovenky); Reg 2: "R. Puls" on (MHz) 99.5 (Shyrokyi 0.1kW), 100.6 (Pidhorivka 1kW): 0400-2000. – **LV) Lvivska ODTRK:** vul. Vysokyi Zamok 4, 79008 Lviv **E:** lodtrk12@gmail. com. Reg 1: "Lvivske R." on 1a+1b. – **MY) Mykolaivska ODTRK:** pr. Lenina 24-b, 54029 Mykolaiv **E:** nogtrk@gmail.com. Reg 1: "R. Buzka khvylia" on 1b; Reg 2: "R. Mykolaiv" on 1377kHz (Mykolaiv): 0800-0900. – **OD) Odeska ODTRK:** Fontanska doroha 3, 65963 Odesa **E:** odt@ukr.net. Reg 1:"Chornomorskyi maiak" on 1b; Reg 2: "Chornomorskyi maiak" on 72.02 (Odesa 0.1kW): 0700-1900. – **PO) Poltavska ODTRK "Ltava":** vul. R.Kyrychenko 1, 36000 Poltava **E:** info@ltava.poltava.ua. Reg 1: "R. Ltava" on 1b; Reg 2: "Vasha khvylia" on 1a. – **RI) Rivnenska ODTRK:** vul. Kotliarevskoho 20-a, 33028 Rivne **E:** radiokraj@mail. ru. Reg 1: "R. Krai" on 1b; Reg 2: "Rivne FM" on 1a. – **SU) Sumska ODTRK:** vul. Petropavlivska 125, 40030 Sumy **E:** trksumy@ukr.net. Reg 1: not on air; Reg 2: "Sloboda-FM"/"Hovoriat Sumy" on 1a+1b. – **TE) Ternopilska ODTRK:** bul. T.Shevchenka 17, 46021 Ternopil **E:** todtrk@poshta.te.ua. Reg 1: "Ternopilske oblasne R." on 1a+1b; Reg 2: "R. Lad" on 71.03MHz (Lozova 1kW): 1400-1900. – **VI) Vinnytska ODTRK "Vintera":** vul. Teatralna 15, 21100 Vinnytsia **E:** mail@vodtrk. com.ua. Reg 1: "Hovoryt Vinnytsia"/"R. Khylia" on 1a+1b. Reg 2: "R.

Khvylia" on 1377 (Vinnytsia): 0700-1515. – **VO) Volynska ODTRK:** vul. Slovatskoho 9, 43025 Lutsk **E:** admin@voltv.lutsk.ua. Reg 1: "Volynske R." on 1b; Reg 2: "R. Lutsk" on 1a. – **ZH) Zhytomyrska ODTRK:** vul. Teatralna 7, 10014 Zhytomyr **E:** tvradiozt@ukr.net. Reg 1: "Zhytomyrske oblasne R." on 1b; Reg 2: "Zhytomyrska khvylia" on 1a (Olevsk 101.9 & Andriivka 103.4MHz). – **ZK) Zakarpatska ODTRK:** Kyivska nab. 18, 88018 Uzhhorod **E:** tisafm@gmail.com. Reg 1: "R. Tysa" on 1a+1b. – **ZP) Zaporizka ODTRK:** vul. Matrosova 24, 69057 Zaporizhzhia **E:** zdtrk@zp.ukrtel.net. Reg 1: not on air; Reg 2:"Zaporizhzhia FM" on 1b.

OTHER STATIONS

MW	kHz	kW	Location	Station
60)	765	40	Petrivka	R. Mayak - Odessa

FM	MHz	kW	Location	Station
30)	67.82	1	Lviv	R. Emmanuil
55)	69.68	1	Kyiv	R. Maria
61)	71.40	4	Kyiv	Hromadske R.
41)	87.5	1	Odesa	Pervoye R. FM1
3)	87.9	1	Odesa	Era FM
19)	88.0	1	Kharkiv	Russkoye R. Ukraina
4)	88.1	1	Dnipopetrovsk	Europa Plus
17)	88.5	1	Dnipopetrovsk	Relax FM
18)	88.5	1	Odesa	Retro FM
7)	89.0	1	Ternopil	Kiss FM
11B)	89.7	1	Odesa	Prosto Rock
14)	90.2	1	Odesa	R. Roks Ukraina
10)	90.3	1	Sumy	Nashe R.
20)	90.9	1	Dnipopetrovsk	Stilnoye R. "Perets FM"
3)	90.9	1	Sumy	Era FM
20)	91.0	1	Cherkasy	Stilnoye R. "Perets FM"
5)	91.0	1	Odesa	Evropeiska stantsiia
1)	91.1	1	Kryvyi Rih	Avtoradio-Ukraina
19)	91.1	1	Lviv	Russkoye R. Ukraina
34)	91.2	2	Kharkiv	M-FM
18)	91.3	1	Sumy	Retro FM
9)	91.3	1	Vinnytsia	Lyubimoye R.
4)	91.4	2	Odesa	Europa Plus
18)	91.5	1	Berdiansk	Retro FM
8)	91.6	1	Kryvyi Rih	Lux FM
18)	92.4	1	Kyiv	Retro FM
4)	92.8	2	Kyiv	Europa Plus
24)	93.8	1	Kyiv	Biznes-R.
12)	94.2	1	Kyiv	R. 24
13)	95.2	1.5	Kyiv	R. Melodiya
27)	95.6	2	Kyiv	Dzhem FM
3)	96.0	2	Kyiv	Era FM
6)	96.4	2	Kyiv	Hit FM Ukraina
12)	96.5	1	Volnovakha	R. 24
2)	96.8	2	Kyiv	DJ FM
19)	97.0	2	Volnovakha	Russkoye R. Ukraina
45)	98.0	1	Kyiv	R. Kyiv
19)	98.5	2	Kyiv	Russkoye R. Ukraina
3)	98.9	1	Nikopol	Era FM
38)	99.0	2	Kyiv	Nostalgie
18)	99.1	1	Melitopol	Retro FM
18)	99.1	1	Poltava	Retro FM
4)	99.3	1	Vinnytsia	Europa Plus
31)	99.4	1.5	Kyiv	Lounge FM
8)	99.4	1	Kherson	Lux FM
1)	100.0	1	Poltava	Avtoradio-Ukraina
5)	100.0	4	Kyiv	Evropeiska stantsiia
41)	100.2	2	Kamianske	Pervoye R. FM1
5)	100.2	1	Kryvyi Rih	Evropeiska stantsiia
1)	100.3	1	Vinnytsia	Avtoradio-Ukraina
5)	100.3	1	Zaporizhzhia	Evropeiska stantsiia
18)	100.4	1	Ivano-Frankivsk	Retro FM
59)	100.4	1	Odesa	Avtoradio-Odesa
16)	100.5	1	Kharkiv	R. Vesti
37)	100.5	2	Kyiv	Narodnoye R.
8)	100.5	1	Dnipopetrovsk	Lux FM
56)	100.6	1	Pidhorivka	R. Puls
1)	100.6	1	Chernihiv	Avtoradio-Ukraina
57)	100.6	2	Korosten	Rekord FM
7)	100.6	1	Poltava	Kiss FM
10)	100.7	1	Antopil	Nashe R.
14)	100.8	1	Mykolaiv	R. Roks Ukraina
14)	100.8	1	Zaporizhzhia	R. Roks Ukraina
32)	100.8	1	Lviv	Lvivska khvylia
6)	100.8	1	Mariupol	Hit FM Ukraina
18)	100.9	1	Kremenchuk	Retro FM
18)	100.9	1	Lutsk	Retro FM
18)	100.9	1	Vinnytsia	Retro FM
15)	101.0	1	Kryvyi Rih	R. Shanson
3)	101.0	1	Kramatorsk	Era FM
51)	101.0	1	Sokal	R. Sokal

FM	MHz	kW	Location	Station
6)	101.0	1	Odesa	Hit FM Ukraina
12)	101.0	1	Cherkasy	R. 24
19)	101.1	1	Dnipopetrovsk	Russkoye R. Ukraina
21)	101.1	3	Kyiv	Piatnytsia
4)	101.1	1	Kharkiv	Europa Plus
3)	101.2	1	Melitopol	Era FM
7)	101.2	1	Kherson	Kiss FM
8)	101.2	1	Khmelnytskyi	Lux FM
20)	101.3	1	Poltava	Stilnoye R. "Perets FM"
20)	101.3	1	Zhytomyr	Stilnoye R. "Perets FM"
13)	101.4	1	Sumy	R. Melodiya
20)	101.4	1	Antopil	Stilnoye R. "Perets FM"
20)	101.4	1	Kryvyi Rih	Stilnoye R. "Perets FM"
21)	101.4	1	Odesa	Piatnytsia
17)	101.5	4	Kyiv	Relax FM
18)	101.5	1	Kirovohrad	Retro FM
19)	101.5	1	Krasnohorivka	Russkoye R. Ukraina
20)	101.5	1	Kharkiv	Stilnoye R. "Perets FM"
21)	101.5	1	Dnipopetrovsk	Piatnytsa
4)	101.6	1	Cherkasy	Europa Plus
54)	101.6	1	Kholmtsi	R. Versia
14)	101.7	1	Kramatorsk	R. Roks Ukraina
19)	101.7	1	Khmelnytskyi	Russkoye R. Ukraina
19)	101.7	1	Zhytomyr	Russkoye R. Ukraina
7)	101.7	1	Mariupol	Kiss FM
7)	101.8	1	Odesa	Kiss FM
15)	101.9	4	Kyiv	R. Shanson
20)	101.9	1	Kherson	Stilnoye R. "Perets FM"
28)	102.0	1	Pryluky	Halaktyka plius
6)	102.0	2	Dnipopetrovsk	Hit FM Ukraina
12)	102.1	1	Lviv	R. 24
18)	102.1	1	Khmelnytskyi	Retro FM
7)	102.1	1	Mykolaiv	Kiss FM
43)	102.2	1	Odesa	R. Fil
6)	102.3	1	Poltava	Hit FM Ukraina
14)	102.4	1	Cherkasy	R. Roks Ukraina
5)	102.4	1	Kholmtsi	Evropeiska stantsiia
7)	102.4	1	Kharkiv	Kiss FM
8)	102.4	1	Chernivtsi	Lux FM
11A)	102.5	2	Kyiv	Prosto R.
13)	102.5	1	Tokmak	R. Melodiya
20)	102.5	1	Khmelnytskyi	Stilnoye R. "Perets FM"
6)	102.5	1	Kherson	Hit FM Ukraina
18)	102.6	1	Lubny	Retro FM
6)	102.6	1	Vinnytsia	Hit FM Ukraina
10)	102.7	4	Kryvyi Rih	Nashe R.
10)	102.7	1	Zhytomyr	Nashe R.
20)	102.7	1	Kovel	Stilnoye R. "Perets FM"
9)	102.7	1	Poltava	Lyubimoye R.
10)	102.8	1	Mykolaiv	Nashe R.
20)	102.8	1	Kamianets-Podilskyi	Stilnoye R. "Perets FM"
23)	102.8	1	Mariupol	Best FM
48)	102.8	1	Pryluky	R. Planeta
10)	102.9	3	Dnipopetrovsk	Nashe R.
18)	103.0	1	Antopil	Retro FM
21)	103.0	1	Kharkiv	Piatnytsia
9)	103.0	1	Ivano-Frankivsk	Lyubimoye R.
10)	103.1	1	Khmelnytskyi	Nashe R.
12)	103.1	5	Kostiantynivka	R. 24
7)	103.1	1	Zaporizhzhia	Kiss FM
8)	103.1	5	Kyiv	Lux FM
9)	103.1	1	Kherson	Lyubimoye R.
21)	103.2	1	Melitopol	Piatnytsia
37)	103.2	2	Odesa	Narodnoye R.
4)	103.2	1	Kryvyi Rih	Europa Plus
2)	103.3	1.2	Dnipopetrovsk	DJ FM
3)	103.3	1	Cherkasy	Era FM
36)	103.4	2	Zhovten	Hrad FM
6)	103.4	1	Sumy	Hit FM Ukraina
13)	103.5	1	Kremenchuk	R. Melodiya
14)	103.5	1	Ternopil	R. Roks Ukraina
14)	103.6	1	Kyiv	R. Roks Ukraina
7)	103.6	1	Khmelnytskyi	Kiss FM
9)	103.6	2	Kryvyi Rih	Lyubimoye R.
19)	103.7	1	Cherkasy	Russkoye R. Ukraina
3)	103.7	1	Kherson	Era FM
52)	103.7	1	Vinnytsia	R. TAKT
6)	103.7	1	Antopil	Hit FM Ukraina
10)	103.8	1	Poltava	Nashe R.
19)	103.8	1	Kirovohrad	Russkoye R. Ukraina
20)	103.8	1	Bila Tserkva	Stilnoye R. "Perets FM"
36)	103.8	3	Odesa	Hrad FM
8)	103.8	1	Ivano-Frankivsk	Lux FM
18)	103.9	1	Kovel	Retro FM
19)	103.9	1	Kremenchuk	Russkoye R. Ukraina

FM	MHz	kW	Location	Station
3)	103.9	1	Zhytomyr	Era FM
4)	103.9	1	Lviv	Europa Plus
1)	104.0	1	Mariupol	Avtoradio-Ukraina
9)	104.0	1	Dnipopetrovsk	Lyubimoye R.
9)	104.0	4	Kyiv	Lyubimoye R.
12)	104.0	2	Kharkiv	R. 24
19)	104.1	1	Vinnytsia	Russkoye R. Ukraina
20)	104.1	1	Mykolaiv	Stilnoye R. "Perets FM"
10)	104.3	1	Chernihiv	Nashe R.
13)	104.3	1	Polohy	R. Melodiya
7)	104.3	1	Lviv	Kiss FM
8)	104.3	2	Odesa	Lux FM
21)	104.4	1	Kherson	Piatnytsia
35)	104.4	1	Dniprodzerzhynsk	Micomp R.
47)	104.4	1	Novovolynsk	R. Nova
10)	104.5	1	Kharkiv	Nashe R.
13)	104.5	1	Cherkasy	R. Melodiya
15)	104.5	1	Zaporizhzhia	R. Shanson
19)	104.5	1	Poltava	Russkoye R. Ukraina
8)	104.5	1	Ternopil	Lux FM
16)	104.6	2	Kyiv	R. Vesti
3)	104.6	1	Kirovohrad	Era FM
15)	104.7	1	Melitopol	R. Shanson
2)	104.7	1	Kryvyi Rih	DJ FM
6)	104.7	1	Chernihiv	Hit FM Ukraina
8)	104.7	1	Lviv	Lux FM
1)	104.8	1	Dnipopetrovsk	Avtoradio-Ukraina
10)	104.8	1	Lutsk	Nashe R.
19)	104.8	1	Kherson	Russkoye R. Ukraina
11A)	104.9	1	Zhytomyr	Prosto R.
19)	104.9	1	Odesa	Russkoye R. Ukraina
20)	104.9	1	Zarichne	Stilnoye R. "Perets FM"
15)	105.0	1	Poltava	R. Shanson
2)	105.1	1	Sumy	DJ FM
21)	105.1	1	Mykolaiv	Piatnytsia
9)	105.1	1	Zaporizhzhia	Lyubimoye R.
18)	105.2	1	Krasnohorivka	Retro FM
8)	105.2	1	Kharkiv	Lux FM
8)	105.2	1	Kholmtsi	Lux FM
11B)	105.3	4	Odesa	Prosto R. Odesa
15)	105.3	2	Dnipopetrovsk	R. Shanson
18)	105.3	1	Shostka	Retro FM
19)	105.3	1	Mariupol	Russkoye R. Ukraina
2)	105.3	1	Dubrovytsia	DJ FM / Euroradio
58)	105.3	1	Severodonetsk	STV
6)	105.3	1	Kirovohrad	Hit FM Ukraina
1)	105.4	1	Lviv	Avtoradio-Ukraina
40)	105.4	1	Khmelnytskyi	OK FM
8)	105.4	1	Chernihiv	Lux FM
20)	105.5	2	Kyiv	Stilnoye R. "Perets FM"
20)	105.5	1	Lutsk	Stilnoye R. "Perets FM"
10)	105.6	1	Zaporizhzhia	Nashe R.
18)	105.6	1	Zhytomyr	Retro FM
19)	105.6	1	Sumy	Russkoye R. Ukraina
6)	105.6	1	Ternopil	Hit FM Ukraina
18)	105.7	1	Kamianets-Podilskyi	Retro FM
9)	105.7	1	Kharkiv	Lyubimoye R.
11A)	105.8	1	Dnipopetrovsk	Prosto R.
13)	105.8	1	Poltava	R. Melodiya
2)	105.8	1	Kirovohrad	DJ FM
20)	105.8	1	Mariupol	Stilnoye R. "Perets FM"
19)	105.9	1	Kryvyi Rih	Russkoye R. Ukraina
10)	106.0	1	Lviv	Nashe R.
22)	106.0	1	Berdiansk	Azovskaya volna
29)	106.0	1	Kyiv	Holos Stolitsi
39)	106.0	1	Odesa	Odessa-Mama
1)	106.1	1	Kharkiv	Avtoradio-Ukraina
13)	106.1	1	Ternopil	R. Melodiya
8)	106.1	1	Cherkasy	Lux FM
10)	106.2	1	Kherson	Nashe R.
18)	106.2	1	Bila Tserkva	Retro FM
20)	106.2	1	Kirovohrad	Stilnoye R. "Perets FM"
4)	106.2	1	Zaporizhzhia	Europa Plus
13)	106.3	1	Melitopol	R. Melodiya
1)	106.4	1	Ivano-Frankivsk	Avtoradio-Ukraina
10)	106.4	1	Vinnytsia	Nashe R.
53)	106.4	2	Antopil	R. Trek
10)	106.5	1	Mariupol	Nashe R.
7)	106.5	2	Kyiv	Kiss FM
25)	106.6	1	Chernivtsi	Blysk FM
44)	106.6	2	Odesa	R. Glas
6)	106.6	1	Zaporizhzhia	Hit FM Ukraina
15)	106.7	1	Kirovohrad	R. Shanson
18)	106.7	1	Kherson	Retro FM
15)	106.8	1	Chernihiv	R. Shanson

FM	MHz	kW	Location	Station
50)	106.8	2	Debeslavtsi	R. Siaivo
7)	106.8	3	Dnipopetrovsk	Kiss FM
6)	106.9	1	Kryvyi Rih	Hit FM Ukraina
8)	106.9	1	Lutsk	Lux FM
18)	107.0	1	Zaporizhzhia	Retro FM
26)	107.0	1	Sumy	Diva-R.
3)	107.0	1	Kharkiv	Era FM
4)	107.0	1	Kyiv	Europa Plus
49)	107.0	1	Odesa	R. Shlyager
7)	107.0	1	Kramatorsk	Kiss FM
2)	107.1	1	Zarichne	DJ FM / Euroradio
8)	107.1	1	Mykolaiv	Lux FM
9)	107.1	1	Cherkasy	Lyubimoye R.
42)	107.2	1	Lviv	R. Brolos
18)	107.2	1	Kholmtsi	Retro FM
19)	107.2	1	Chernihiv	Russkoye R. Ukraina
46)	107.3	1	Dnipopetrovsk	R. Mix
1)	107.4	2.5	Kyiv	Avtoradio-Ukraina
12)	107.4	1	Odesa	R. 24
3)	107.4	1	Kryvyi Rih	Era FM
5)	107.4	1	Kharkiv	Evropeiska stantsiia
13)	107.5	1	Zaporizhzhia	R. Melodiya
20)	107.5	1	Dubrovytsia	Stilnoye R. "Perets FM"
14)	107.6	2	Kherson	R. Roks Ukraina
14)	107.7	1	Chernihiv	R. Roks Ukraina
16)	107.7	1	Dnipopetrovsk	R. Vesti
8)	107.7	1	Zhytomyr	Lux FM
3)	107.8	1	Mykolaiv	Era FM
1)	107.9	1	Sumy	Avtoradio-Ukraina
10)	107.9	1	Kirovohrad	Nashe R.
10)	107.9	5	Kyiv	Nashe R.
10)	107.9	1	Odesa	Nashe R.
12)	107.9	1	Novoaidar	R. 24
2)	107.9	1	Zaporizhzhia	DJ FM

NB: Txs less than 1kW not listed.

Addresses & other information:
1) vul. Bastionna 15, 01014 Kyiv – **2)** b-r T.Shevchenka 54/1, 01032 Kyiv – **3)** pr-t Povitrianoflotskyi 54, 03151 Kyiv – **4)** vul. Ivana Kudri 26, 01042 Kyiv – **5)** vul. Saksahanskoho 91, 01032 Kyiv – **6)** vul. V.Khvoiky 15/15, 04655 Kyiv – **7)** vul. V.Khvoiky 15/15, 04655 Kyiv – **8)** vul. Volodymyrska 61/11, 01033 Kyiv – **9)** b-r T.Shevchenka 54/1, 01032 Kyiv – **10)** vul. O.Shmidta 6, 04107 Kyiv – **11A,B)** 11A) vul. O.Shmidta 6, 04107 Kyiv, 11B) vul. Fontanska doroha 3, 65063 Odesa – **12)** pl. Halytska 15, 79008 Lviv – **13)** vul. V.Khvoiky 15/15, 04655 Kyiv – **14)** vul. V.Khvoiky 15/15, 04655 Kyiv – **15)** b-r T.Shevchenka 54/1, 01032 Kyiv – **16)** vul. O.Shmidta 6, 04107 Kyiv – **17)** vul. V.Khvoiky 15/15, 04655 Kyiv – **18)** vul. Elektrykiv 26, 04176 Kyiv – **19)** vul. V.Khvoiky 15/15, 04655 Kyiv – **20)** vul. Dovzhenka 14, 03057 Kyiv – **21)** vul. V.Khvoiky 15/15, 04655 Kyiv – **22)** Melitopolske shose 20, 77108 Berdiansk – **23)** vul. Chernyshevskoho 15, 61007 Kharkiv – **24)** b-r T.Shevchenka 54/1, 01032 Kyiv – **25)** vul. Eminesku 2, 58000 Chernivtsi – **26)** vul. Kharkivska 5, 40024 Sumy – **27)** vul. Kyrylivska 104a, 04080 Kyiv – **28)** vul. Piriatynska 129, 17500 Pryluky – **29)** vul. Kyrylivska 104a, 04080 Kyiv – **30)** vul. Velyka Vasylivska 131a, 03150 Kyiv – **31)** vul. Kyrylivska 104a, 04080 Kyiv – **32)** vul. Hutsulska 9a, 79008 Lviv – **33)** pr-t Illicha 100, 83052 Donetsk – **34)** vul. Petrovskoho 3, 61002 Kharkiv – **35)** vul. Komsomolskyi 15b, 51900 Dniprodzerzhynsk – **36)** vul. Balkivska 120/1, 65005 Odesa – **37)** vul. O.Shmidta 6, 04107 Kyiv – **38)** Y.Konovaltsiia 32a, 01133 Kyiv – **39)** vul. Zaslavskoho 10/12, 65004 Odesa – **40)** pr-t Miru 69, 29000 Khmelnytskyi – **41)** vul. Balkivska 120/1, 65005 Odesa – **42)** Pidvalna 3, 79008 Lviv – **43)** vul. Troitska 50, 65045 Odesa – **44)** vul. Kanatna 83, 65107 Odesa – **45)** vul. Khreshchatyk 44, 01044 Kyiv – **46)** vul. Suchkova 2a, 51200 Novomoskovsk – **47)** pr-t Druzhby 27, 45400 Novovolynsk – **48)** vul. Piriatynska 129, 17500 Pryluky – **49)** vul. Tereshkovoi 15, 65078 Odesa – **50)** vul. Sichovykh striltsiv 23, 78200 Kolomyia – **51)** Sichovykh striltsiv 18, 80000 Sokal – **52)** vul. Soborna 59, 21050 Vinnytsia – **53)** vul. Kavkazka 2, 33013 Rivne – **54)** vul. Erdeli 1, 88018 Uzhhorod – **55)** vul. Sribnokilska 8, 02095 Kyiv – **56)** vul. Vilnesova 1v, 93400 Severodonetsk – **57)** vul. Rylskoho 9, 10014 Zhytomyr – **58)** vul. Haharina 93, 93400 Severodonetsk – **59)** vul. Kanatna 83, 65107 Odesa – **60)** vul. Fontanska doroha 33, 65009 Odesa. **E:** mayak36@ukr.net – **61)** vul. Holosiivska 7, 03039 Kyiv.

NON-PROFESSIONAL RADIO STATION

SW	kHz	kW	Location	Station
1)	†11980*	0.25	Zaporizhzhia	Dniprovska khvylia

Address & other information: †=irreg. *=AM/USB
1) TRK "Aleks TV", pr-t. Motorobudivnykiv 48, 69068 Zaporizhzha. **E:** radiodh@rambler.ua. SS 0500-0800 (tr times are variable). No own prgrs: trs consist of rel. Ukrainian Public Radio (Prgr 1) and occ. own IDs.
NB: Not licensed as broadcasting station (mass medium); trs are made with amateur radio equipment on the basis of an exceptional technical permission.

DONETS BASIN

Part of Donetsk oblast controlled by "DPR":

R. Respublika (¹): vul. Kuibysheva 61, 83016 Donetsk (mail: via Russia). On Donetsk 99.0MHz (0.5kW), incl. rel. Vesti FM (Russia). Run by the "DPR" administration.

OTHER STATIONS

FM MHz	kW	Location	Station
99.4	1	Donetsk	Relax FM*
100.5	1	Donetsk	R. Sputnik relay*
101.2	1	Donetsk	R. Donbass FM
103.5	1	Donetsk	R. Melodiya*
104.7	1	Donetsk	R. Vanya*
105.1	2	Donetsk	Hit FM*
106.8	3	Donetsk	R. Novorossiya - Roks

NB: Txs below 1kW not listed. *) Relays from Russia

Part of Luhansk oblast controlled by "LPR":

GTRK LNR (²): vul. Demokhina 25, 91000 Luhansk (mail: via Russia). **W:** radio.lnr.tv. **D.Prgr:** "Svoye R." on 103.6MHz (Luhansk 1kW). Run by the "LPR" administration.

OTHER STATIONS

FM MHz	kW	Location	Station
100.4	1	Luhansk	Vesti FM relay*
102.3	1	Luhansk	R. Sputnik relay*
106.5	1	Luhansk	R. Respublika relay**

NB: Txs below 1kW not listed. **) Relays from Russia **) Rel. R. Respublika.

(¹) (²) The studios are located in the premises of the former regional state broadcasting companies "Donetska ODTRK" (now relocated to Kramatorsk) and "Luhanska ODTRK" (now relocated to Severodonetsk). – The (re)transmission of radio stns on the territories of the Donets Basin controlled by the administrations of the soi-disant "Donetsk People's Republic" (DPR) and "Luhansk People's Republic" (LPR) is de facto subject to authorisation by these administrations.

CRIMEA
(under Russian administration)

L.T: UTC +3h — **Pop:** 2.4 million — **Pr.L:** Russian, Ukrainian, Crimean Tatar

VSEROSSIYSKAYA GOSUDARSTVENNAYA TELEVIZIONNAYA I RADIOVESHCHATELNAYA KOMPANIYA (VGTRK) (Gov)

Contact details see under "Russia"

FM (VFM)	MHz	kW	FM (VFM)	MHz	kW
Krasnoperekopsk	°68.48	4	Sevastopol	102.0	1
Simferopol	p87.5	1	Krasnoperekopsk	102.6	1
Kerch	p91.6	1			

NB: Txs below 1kW not listed. P=Planned °) To be closed
D.Prgr: Vesti FM (VFM): see under "Russia".

TELERADIOKOMPANIYA "KRYM" (Gov)

295001 Simferopol, ul. Studencheskaya 14 ☎ +7 652 546406 **E:** tv@tv.crimea.ru **W:** 1tvcrimea.ru **L.P:** DG: Yekaterina Kozyr

FM (MHz)	1	2	kW	FM	1	2	kW
Sevastopol	91.3	90.4	1/0.5	Simferopol	100.1	100.6	1

NB: Txs below 1kW not listed.
D.Prgr: Prgr 1 ("R. Krym") 24h, Prgr 2 ("R. Morye") 24h.

OBSHCHESTVENNAYA KRYMSKO-TATARSKAYA TELERADIOKOMPANIYA (OKTT) (Pub)

295011 Simferopol, ul. Kozlova 45a **L.P:** DG: Seyran Mambetov

FM	MHz	kW
Simferopol	106.6	1

NB: Txs below 1kW not listed.
D.Prgr: "Vatan Sedasi" 24h in Crimean Tatar, Russian.

OTHER STATIONS

FM MHz	kW	Location	Station
27) 88.0	1	Simferopol	R. Dacha
21) 88.3	1	Sevastopol	R. Zvezda
16) 90.1	1	Simferopol	Retro FM
8) 91.1	1	Simferopol	Nashe R.
21) 98.3	1	Simferopol	R. Zvezda
10) 101.2	1	Simferopol	R. 7
4) 101.4	1	Kerch	Europa Plus
18) 101.7	1	Simferopol	Yumor FM
102.3	1	Simferopol	R. Sputnik
62) 104.3	1	Simferopol	Kazak FM
105.1	1	Krasnoperekopsk	R. Sputnik
14) 105.4	1	Simferopol	R. Shanson
2) 106.1	1	Simferopol	Russkoye R.
10) 107.0	1	Sevastopol	R. 7

NB: Txs below 1kW not listed.
Addresses & other information:
Contact details see "Other Stations" chart under "Russia" (stn numbers refer to that chart)

Radio via DTT: see National TV section.

NB: Radio stations in Crimea are currently regulated by mass media & telecommunication laws of the Russian Federation. See under "Russia" for information on regulatory authorities.

UNITED ARAB EMIRATES

L.T: UTC +4h — **Pop:** 5 million — **Pr.L:** Arabic — **E.C:** 50Hz, 220V — **ITU:** UAE

NATIONAL MEDIA COUNCIL

P.O. Box 17, Abu Dhabi ☎ +971 2 4453000 🖷 +971 2 4452504 **W:** uaeinteract.com **L.P:** Chmn: Saqr Ghubash Saeed Ghubash.

ABU DHABI MEDIA COMPANY (Pub.)

4th St, Sector 18, Zone 1, Abu Dhabi ☎ +971 2 4144000 🖷 +971 2 4144001 **W:** admedia.ae **L.P:** CEO: Ahmed Ali Mohamed Al Bloushi. Dir. Radio: Jaber Obaid. Head R&TV Eng: Mahmood Al-Redha.

MW	kHz	kW	Prgr	Times
Maqtaa	810	50	A	24h
Al-Ain	828	1	A	24h

Irregular tests on 1170 and 1539 kHz.
A=Abu Dhabi R. in Arabic: On MW & FM(MHz): Ras al-Khaimah 89.7, Abu Dhabi 90.0, Jabal Al-Dhanna 97.3, Dubai 98.4, Habshan 100.1, Liwa 103.7, Fujairah 106.0.
FM (MHz): Capital FM: Dubai 88.8MHz, Abu Dhabi 97.3MHz – **Classic FM** (in english): Dubai 87.9. Abu Dhabi 91.6, Al Ain 105.2 – **Emarat FM:** 24h on FM (MHz): Ras al-Khaimah 88.5, Jabal al-Dhanna 92.4, Al-Ain 94.9, Abu Dhabi 95.8, Liwa 95.6, Dubai 97.1, Habshan 98.4, Fujairah 103.9 – **Holy Quran R:** 24h on FM (MHz): Jabel Dhana 87.7, Dubai 88.2, Al-Ain 88.6, Habshan 88.8, Liwa 89.3, Fujairah 97.6, Abu Dhabi 98.1MHz, Ras al-Khaimah 105.2 – **R. Mirchi:** Dubai/Sharjah 88.8MHz, Al-Ain 95.6MHz, Abu Dhabi 97.3MHz. **W:** radiomirchi.com – **Star FM:** Abu Dhabi 92.4MHz, Dubai 99.9MHz. Al-Ain 100.1MHz.

GULF NEWS BROADCASTING

P.O. Box 6519, Dubai ☎ +971 4 3446366 🖷 +971 4 3448185 **W:** gnbroadcasting.com
FM: R. 1 (Arabic): Abu Dhabi 100.5MHz 1kW, Dubai 104.1MHz 10kW – **R. 2** (Arabic): Dubai 99.3MHz 10kW, Abu Dhabi 106.0MHz 1kW – **Hayat FM** (Arabic): Umm al-Quwain 95.6MHz – **Josh FM** (English): Umm al-Quwain 95.6MHz

RAS AL-KHAIMAH BROADCASTING STATION

RAK Media, P.O. Box 141, Ras al Khaimah ☎ +971 7 851151 🖷 +971 7 353441
MW: 1152kHz 200kW. **FM:** 95.3MHz (Arabic).
MW: r. VO Kerala (**W:** radiovok.com) 0130v-2100v in Malayalm (Also r. 1800-1900 Radio SIP in Indonesian: **W:** sipradioindonesia.com).

SHARJAH MEDIA CORPORATION

P.O. Box 111, Sharjah ☎ +971 6 566 1111 🖷 +971 6 566 9999 **W:** smc.ae **E:** info@smc.ae
R. Sharjah in Arabic: Sharjah 94.4MHz, unk. loc 95.0MHz, Abu Dhabi 96.3, Khor Fakkan 107.6MHz, Kalba 107.7MHz.

UMM AL QUWAIN BROADCASTING STATION

Shamal Media Services, P.O. Box 1106, Umm al Quwain ☎ +971 6 5657106 🖷 +971 6 5651806
MW: Holy Quran R: 846kHz 20kW 24h.
FM: UAQ FM: 97.8MHz in Arabic. **W:** uaqfm.com – **Hum FM:** 106.2MHz in Hindi/Urdu. **W:** humfm.com

ASIANET RADIO

Asianet Global FZ LLC, P.O. Box 62787, Boutique No. 10, Dubai Media City ☎ +971 4 3914150 🖷 +971 4 3918045 **W:** asianetradio. me **E:** radio657@asianetworld.tv

MW: Al-Dhabbiya 657kHz 100kW. **D.Prgr:** 24h in Malayalam.

RADIO ASIA NETWORK
✉ Dolphin Recording Studio, P.O. Box 4300, Dubai ☎+971 4 4534950 🖷 +971 4 3421387 **L.P:** GM: Brij Bhalla. PD: Vettoor G. Sreedharan. **W:** radioasiauae.com **E:** am@radioasia.ae
MW: Radioasia: Ras al Khaimah 1269kHz 200kW. **D.Prgr:** 24h in Malayalam.
FM: Super FM: Ras al-Khaimah 94.7MHz 20kW in Malayalam/Tamil. **W:** super947.fm — **Suno FM:** 102.4MHz in Hindi/Urdu. **W:** suno1024. com **Ann:** "Radio Asia 1269 AM".

ARABIAN RADIO NETWORK (ARN)
✉ P.O. Box 502255, CNN Bldg, Media City 103, Dubai ☎+971 4 3912000 🖷 +971 4 3912007 **W:** arn.ae **E:** amghrteam@arabmedia-group.ae **L.P:** GM: Mahmoud Al-Rasheed. COO: Steve Smith.
FM: Tag 91.1: 91.1MHz in Filipino – **Dubai 92:** 92.0MHz 5kW in English – **R. Shoma:** 93.4MHz in Farsi – **Hit FM:** 96.7MHz 5kW in Malayalam – **Al-Arabiya:** 99.0MHz 10kW in Arabic – **Al-Khaleejiya:** 100.9MHz 5kW in Arabic – **City FM:** 101.6MHz 5kW in Hindi – **Dubai Eye:** 103.8MHz 5kW in English – **Virgin R:** Dubai 104.4MHz 30kW.

DUBAI MEDIA INCORPORATED (DMI)
W: dmi.ae **Dubai FM:** 93.0MHz. **Noor Dubai:** 93.9MHz 5kW.

CHANNEL 4 RADIO NETWORK
✉ P.O Box 442, Ajman ☎+971 6 746 1444 **L.P:** MD: Mohammad Murad. Prgr. Controller: Peter Gowers. **W:** ch4network.com
FM: all in Ajman. **R. 4 FM:** 89.1MHz in English/Hindi – **Channel 4 FM:** 104.8 & 106.5MHz 1kW in English – **Gold FM:** 101.3MHz in Hindi – **Al Rabia FM:** 107.8MHz 1kW in Arabic.

FUJAIRAH MEDIA GROUP
✉ Fujairah ☎971 9 2244100 🖷 +971 9 2244101 **W:** fmg.ae
FM: Coast FM: Ajman 103.2MHz (English) – **Fujairah FM:** 92.6MHz (Arabic) – **Jazz R.** 106.8MHz (German) – **R. Spice FM:** 105.4MHz (English/Hindi/Tamil) – **Rock R:** 90.9MHz – **Russkoye R:** 96.3MHz (Russian)

MALAR GLOBAL MEDIA
R. Hello: 89.5MHz in Telugu. **W:** radio895.com – **R. Me:** Dubai 100.3MHz in Malayalam. **W:** radiomeonline.com – **R. Salaam,** 106.5MHz in Tamil. **W:** salaam.fm – **Wow FM,** 107.0MHz in Flipino. **W:** wowfm.ae

MBC FM & PANORAMA FM
✉ P.O. Box 75335, MBC Building, Media City, Dubai ☎+971 4 3919713 🖷 +971 4 3916683 **W:** mbc.net **E:** contactus@mbc.ae
L.P: Dir: Hassan Muawad. **FM:** Txs in Bahrain, Iraq, Jordan, Kuwait, Qatar, Saudi Arabia, Sudan and Palestine West Bank.

Sky News Arabia, Abu Dhabi: 90.3MHz. **W:** skynewsarabia.com
Sowt al-Khaleej, Abu Dhabi: 105.2MHz. See Qatar for main entry.
Zayed R. for Quran: Fujairah 97.4 & 97.6MHz. **W:** zayedquran.gov.ae
BBG - R. Sawa: Dubai 90.5MHz 5kW, Abu Dhabi 98.7MHz 10kW.
BBG - R. Farda: Al-Dhabbiya 1575kHz 800kW 24h. For further details see Int. radio section under USA.
Monte Carlo Doualiya: Dubai 95.3MHz
F.PI: Pravasi Bharathi in Malayalam: 810kHz 200kW DRM. **W:** pravasibharathi.com

UNITED KINGDOM

L.T: UTC (27 Mar-30 Oct: +1h) — **Pop:** 65 million — **Pr.L:** English Welsh — **E.C:** 50Hz, 230V — **ITU:** G — **Int.Dialling Code:** +44

CROWN DEPENDENCIES
NB: The Channel Islands and the Isle of Man are dependencies of the British Crown and are not part of the United Kingdom. They are included here for editorial convenience.

BRITISH BROADCASTING CORPORATION (Pub)
The BBC is an independent body created by Royal Charter and operates under licence.
✉ Broadcasting House, Portland Place, London W1A 1AA. ☎ 20 7580 4468 **W:** bbc.co.uk **L.P:** DG: Tony Hall; Dir Radio: Helen Boaden; Dir TV: Danny Cohen; Dir News: James Harding; Dir Strategy & Digital: James Purnell; CEO BBC Worldwide: Tim Davie

LW/MW:

Radio 4	kHz	kW	Radio 4	kHz	kW
Burghead	198	50	Droitwich	198	500

Radio 4	kHz	kW	Radio 4	kHz	kW
Westerglen	198	50	Redruth	756	2
Newcastle	603	2	Enniskillen	774	1
Londonderry	720	0.25	Plymouth	774	1
Lisnagarvey	720	10	Redmoss	1449	2
Crystal Palace	720	0.8	Carlisle	1485	1

Radio 5 Live	kHz	kW	Radio 5 Live	kHz	kW
Barrow	693	1	Clevedon	909	50
Bexhill	693	1	Exeter	909	1
Brighton	693	1	Fareham	909	1
Burghead	693	25	Lisnagarvey	909	10
Droitwich	693	150	Londonderry	909	1
Enniskillen	693	1	Bournemouth	909	0.25
Folkestone	693	1	Moorside Edge	909	200
Postwick	693	10	Redruth	909	2
Redmoss	693	1	Westerglen	909	50
Stagshaw	693	50	Whitehaven	909	1
Start Point	693	50	Tywyn	990	1
Brookmans Park	909	150			

England, Isle of Man, Channel Is FM (all stereo)

FM	R1	R2	R3	R4	kW
Barnstaple	98.1	88.5	90.7	92.9	1
Beacon Hill	98.4	88.7	90.9	93.1	1
Belmont	98.3	88.8	90.9	93.1	16
Bilsdale	98.6	89.0	91.2	93.4	5
Bow Brickhill	98.2	88.6	90.8	93.0	10
Bristol	98.9	89.3	91.5	93.7	1.3
Chatton	99.7	90.1	92.3	94.5	5.6
Crystal Palace	98.8	88.8	91.0	93.2	4
Douglas (I.O.M.)	98.0	88.4	90.6	92.8	11
Guildford	97.7	88.1	90.3	92.5	3
Caversham	99.4	89.8	92.0	94.2	1
Holme Moss	98.9	89.3	91.5	93.7	250
Keighley	98.5	88.9	91.1	93.3	1
Les Platons (C.I.)	97.1	89.6	91.1	94.8	16
Manningtree	97.7	88.1	90.3	92.5	5
Morecambe Bay	99.6	90.0	92.2	94.4	10
North Hessary Tor	97.7	88.1	90.3	92.5	160
Oxford	99.1	89.5	91.7	93.9	46
Pendle Forest	97.8	90.2	92.6	94.6	1
Peterborough	99.7	90.1	92.3	94.5	40
Pontop Pike	98.1	88.5	90.7	92.9	134
Redruth	99.3	89.7	91.9	94.1	25
Ridge Hill	98.2	88.6	90.8	93.0	10
Rowridge	98.2	88.5	90.7	92.9	250
Sandale	97.7	88.1	90.3	92.5	250
Stanton Moor	99.4	89.8	92.0	94.2	1.2
Sutton Coldfield	97.9	88.3	90.5	92.7	250
Swingate (Dover)	99.5	90.0	92.4	94.4	11
Tacolneston	99.3	89.7	91.9	94.1	250
Winter Hill	98.2	88.6	90.8	93.0	4
Woolmoor	99.6	90.2	92.2	94.4	1
Wrotham	*98.8	89.1	91.3	93.5	125*/250

+ 74 low power txs less than 1kW

STATIONS: Radio 1: New music for youth audience 24h **N:** Newsbeat M-F 1245, 1745 – **Radio 1Xtra** (digital only) – **Radio 2:** Adult contemporary and specialist music: 24h **N:** on the h – **Radio 3:** Classical music, jazz, world music, arts: 24h **N:** 0700, 0800, 0900(SS), 1300, 1700(MF), 1800(MF) – **Radio 4:** News, documentaries, drama, entertainment, and cricket on LW/MW in season: 0520-0100; relays BBCWS 0100-0520 **N:** 0530, then on the h (not 1000 Sun, 1100 Sun, 1500 Sat) – **Radio 4Extra** (digital only) – **Radio 5 Live:** News & sport: 24h **N:** on the h and half h – **Radio 6 Music:** New and archive music: 24h (digital only)

BBC LOCAL RADIO

MW	Station	Location	kHz	kW
1)	Three Counties R.	Luton	630	0.2
6)	R. Cornwall	Redruth	630	2
6)	R. Cornwall	Bodmin	657	0.5
37)	R. York	Fulford	666	0.5
11)	Essex	Manningtree	729	0.2
15)	Hereford & Worcs	Worcester	738	0.037
8)	R. Cumbria	Carlisle	756	1
11)	Essex	Chelmsford	765	0.5
18)	R. Kent	Littlebourne	774	0.7
20)	R. Leeds	Farnley	774	0.5
10)	R. Devon	Barnstaple	801	2
8)	R. Cumbria	Barrow	837	1
19)	R. Lancashire	Preston	855	1
26)	R. Norfolk	Postwick	855	1.5
26)	R. Norfolk	West Lynn	873	0.3

MW	Station	Location	kHz	kW
10)	R. Devon	Exeter	990	1
33)	R. Solent	Fareham	999	1
4)	R. Cambridgeshire	Chesterton Fen	1026	0.5
17)	R. Jersey	Trinity	1026	1
31)	R. Sheffield	Sheffield	1035	1
9)	R. Derby	Burnaston Lane	1116	1
14)	R. Guernsey	Rohais	1116	0.5
30)	Sussex	Bexhill	1161	1
1)	Three Counties R.	Bedford	1161	0.1
37)	R. York	Scarborough	1260	0.5
36)	Wiltshire	Lacock	1332	0.4
33)	R. Solent for Dorset	Bournemouth	1359	0.85
30a)	Surrey	Duxhurst	1368	0.5
36)	Wiltshire	Swindon	1368	0.1
22)	R. Lincolnshire	Lincoln	1368	2
12)	R. Gloucestershire	Berkeley Heath	1413	0.5
12)	R. Gloucestershire	Bourton-on-the-Water	1413	0.5
8)	R. Cumbria	Whitehaven	1458	0.5
10)	R. Devon	Torquay	1458	2
25)	Newcastle	Wrekenton	1458	2
16)	R. Humberside	Hull	1485	2
30)	Sussex	Brighton	1485	1
23)	R. Merseyside	Wallasey	1485	2
34)	R. Stoke	Sideway	1503	1
11)	Essex	Southend-on-Sea	1530	0.15
3)	R. Bristol	Mangotsfield	1548	5
19)	R. Lancashire	Oxcliffe	1557	0.25
3)	Somerset & R. Bristol	Taunton	1566	1
28)	R. Nottingham	Clipstone	1584	2
15)	Hereford & Worcester	Woofferton	1584	0.3
18)	R. Kent	Rusthall	1602	0.25

Note: some BBC MW local radio trs. may close

FM	Station	Location	MHz	kW
31)	R. Sheffield	Sheffield	88.6	0.3
17)	R. Jersey	Les Platons	88.8	3.8
1)	Three Counties R.	Epping Green	90.4	0.1
20)	R. Leeds	Holme Moss	92.4	5.6
14)	R. Guernsey	Les Touillets	93.2	1
34)	R. Stoke	Alsagers Bank	94.6	6.1
2)	R. Berkshire	Henley	94.6	0.25
15)	Hereford & Worcester	Ridge Hill	94.7	2
1)	Three Counties R.	Aylesbury	94.7	0.2
31)	R. Sheffield	Chesterfield	94.7	0.4
7)	Coventry & Warwicks.	Meriden	94.8	2.2
10)	R. Devon	Huntshaw Cross	94.8	0.675
24)	R. London	Crystal Palace	94.9	4
3)	R. Bristol	Dundry Lane	94.9	0.5
22)	R. Lincolnshire	Belmont	94.9	6
30)	Sussex	Newhaven	95.0	0.1
5)	Tees	Bilsdale	95.0	10
12)	R. Gloucestershire	Stroud	95.0	0.1
13)	R. Manchester	Holme Moss	95.1	5.6
28)	R. Nottingham	Newark	95.1	0.2
26)	R. Norfolk	Stoke Holy Cross	95.1	4
6)	R. Cornwall	Caradon Hill	95.2	4.3
8)	R. Cumbria	Kendal	95.2	0.1
29)	R. Oxford	Beckley	95.2	5.8
11)	Essex	South Benfleet	95.3	1.2
30)	Sussex	Brighton	95.3	1.2
9)	R. Derby	Stanton Moor	95.3	1.2
20)	R. Leeds	Luddenden	95.3	0.083
2)	R. Berkshire	Windsor	95.4	0.5
25)	Newcastle	Pontop Pike	95.4	10
1)	Three Counties R.	Sandy Heath	95.5	1
3)	Somerset & R. Bristol	Mendip	95.5	9
19)	R. Lancashire	Hameldon Hill	95.5	1.6
28)	R. Nottingham	Mansfield	95.5	2
35)	R. Suffolk	Lowestoft	95.5	2
37)	R. York	Olivers Mount	95.5	0.25
26)	R. Norfolk	West Runton	95.6	2
8)	R. Cumbria	Sandale	95.6	15
38)	WM (West Midlands)	Sutton Coldfield	95.6	11
4)	R. Cambridgeshire	Peterborough	95.7	5.1
10)	R. Devon	Plymouth	95.7	1
23)	R. Merseyside	Allerton Park	95.8	8
5)	Tees	Whitby	95.8	0.1
10)	R. Devon	Exeter	95.8	0.4
35)	R. Suffolk	Aldeburgh	95.9	2
16)	R. Humberside	High Hunsley	95.9	9.6
4)	R. Cambridgeshire	Cambridge	96.0	1
9)	R. Derby	Buxton	96.0	1.5

FM	Station	Location	MHz	kW
32)	R. Shropshire	The Wrekin	96.0	4.8
25)	Newcastle	Chatton	96.0	5.6
8)	R. Cumbria	Morecambe Bay	96.1	3.2
33)	R. Solent	Rowridge	96.1	10
18)	R. Kent	Wrotham	96.7	8.7
18)	R. Kent	Folkestone	97.6	0.1
1)	Three Counties R.	High Wycombe	98.0	0.2
20)	R. Leeds	Keighley	102.7	0.5
10)	R. Devon	North Hessary Tor	103.4	15
11)	Essex	Great Braxted	103.5	12
36)	Wiltshire	Salisbury	103.5	1
3)	R. Bristol	Weston-S-Mare	103.6	0.1
36)	Wiltshire	Swindon	103.6	0.5
27)	R. Northampton	Geddington	103.6	0.8
7)	Coventry & Warwicks.	Lark Stoke	103.7	1.4
37)	R. York	Acklam Wold	103.7	2
25)	Newcastle	Hexham	103.7	0.1
1)	Three Counties R.	Zouches Farm	103.8	0.5
28)	R. Nottingham	Mapperley Ridge	103.8	1
33)	R. Solent (Dorset)	Bincombe Hill	103.8	0.5
6)	R. Cornwall	Redruth	103.9	18
19)	R. Lancashire	Winter Hill	103.9	2
20)	R. Leeds	Beecroft Hill	103.9	0.1
35)	R. Suffolk	Manningtree	103.9	5
15)	Hereford & Worcester	Great Malvern	104.0	2
30a)	Surrey	Reigate	104.0	3.8
8)	R. Cumbria	Whitehaven	104.1	1
31)	R. Sheffield	Holme Moss	104.1	4.4
34)	R. Stoke	Stafford	104.1	0.075
2)	R. Berkshire	Hannington	104.1	3
18)	R. Kent	Swingate	104.2	10
27)	R. Northampton	Northampton	104.2	4
36)	Wiltshire	Naish Hill	104.3	0.6
10)	R. Devon	Beacon Hill	104.3	1
37)	R. York	Woolmoor	104.3	0.5
2)	R. Berkshire	Reading	104.4	1
26)	R. Norfolk	Great Massingham	104.4	4.2
15)	Hereford & Worcester	Redditch	104.4	0.1
30)	Sussex	Heathfield	104.5	10
1)	Three Counties R.	Bow Brickhill	104.5	2.2
9)	R. Derby	Drum Hill	104.5	5.4
19)	R. Lancashire	Lancaster	104.5	2
13)	R. Manchester	Saddleworth	104.6	0.1
15)	Hereford & Worcester	Kidderminster	104.6	0.5
30a)	Surrey	Guildford	104.6	3
3)	R. Bristol	Bath	104.6	0.082
35)	R. Suffolk	Great Barton	104.6	2
12)	R. Gloucestershire	Churchdown Hill	104.7	2
30)	Sussex	Burton Down	104.8	2
21)	R. Leicester	Copt Oak	104.9	8
36)	Wiltshire	Marlborough	104.9	0.1

+ 15 low power txs less than 0.1kW

Addresses

1) Unit 4 Grove Park, Court Drive, Dunstable LU5 4GP ☎1582 636900 **E:** threecounties@bbc.co.uk – **2)** Caversham Park, Peppard Rd, Reading RG4 8TZ ☎118 9464200 **E:** radio.berkshire.news@bbc.co.uk – **3)** Whiteladies Rd, Bristol BS8 2LR ☎117 9741111 **E:** radio.bristol@bbc. co.uk; BBC Somerset, Broadcasting House, Park Street, Taunton TA1 4DA ☎1823 323956 **E:** somerset@bbc.co.uk – **4)** Cambridge Business Park, Cowley Rd, Cambridge CB4 0WZ ☎1223 259696 **E:** cambs@ bbc.co.uk– **5)** Broadcasting House, Newport Rd, Middlesbrough TS1 5JA ☎1642 225211 **E:** tees@bbc.co.uk– **6)** Phoenix Wharf, Truro TR1 1UA ☎1872 275421 **E:** radio.cornwall@bbc.co.uk – **7)** Priory Place, Coventry CV1 5SQ ☎24 76551000 **E:** coventry.warwickshire@bbc. co.uk– **8)** Annetwell Street, Carlisle CA3 8BB ☎1228 592444 **E:** radio. cumbria@bbc.co.uk – **9)** 56 St Helen's Str, Derby DE1 3HY ☎1332 361111 **E:** radio.derby@bbc.co.uk – **10)** PO Box 1034, Plymouth PL3 5YQ ☎1752 260323 **E:** radio.devon@bbc.co.uk – **11)** PO Box 765, Chelmsford CM2 9XB ☎1245 616000 **E:** essex@bbc.co.uk– **12)** London Rd, Gloucester GL1 1SW ☎1452 308585 **E:** radio.gloucestershire@ bbc.co.uk – **13)** Quay House, BBC Media City UK, Salford M50 2QH ☎161 335 6000 **E:** radio.manchester@bbc.co.uk – **14)** Bulwer Ave, St Sampson, Guernsey GY2 4LA ☎ 1481 200600 **E:** bbcguernsey@ bbc.co.uk – **15)** Hylton Rd, Worcester WR2 5WW ☎1905 748485 **E:** bbchw@bbc.co.uk and 43 Broad Street, Hereford HR4 9HH ☎1432 355255 – **16)** Queens Court, Queens Gardens, Hull HU1 3RH ☎1482 323232 **E:** radio.humberside@bbc.co.uk – **17)** 18-21 Parade Rd, St. Helier, Jersey JE2 3PL ☎1534 870000 **E:** radiojersey@bbc.co.uk – **18)** The Great Hall, Mount Pleasant Rd, Tunbridge Wells TN1 1QQ ☎1892 670000 **E:** radio.kent@bbc.co.uk – **19)** 20-26 Darwen Street, Blackburn

BB2 2EA ☎1254 262411 **E**: radio.lancashire@bbc.co.uk – **20)** 2 St Peters Square, Leeds LS9 8AH ☎113 244 2131 **E**: radioleeds@bbc.co.uk – **21)** 9 St Nicholas Place, Leicester LE1 5LB ☎116 251 6688 **E**: radioleicester@bbc.co.uk – **22)** Radion Buildings, Newport, Lincoln LN1 3XY ☎1522 511411 **E**: radio.lincolnshire@bbc.co.uk – **23)** 31 College Lane, Liverpool L1 3DS ☎151 708 6161 **E**: radio.merseyside@bbc.co.uk – **24)** Egton Wing, Broadcasting House, Portland Place, London W1A 1AA ☎20 8743 8000 **E**: yourlondon@bbc.co.uk – **25)** Broadcasting Centre, Barrack Rd, Newcastle-Upon-Tyne NE99 1RN ☎191 222 4141 **E**: bbcnewcastle@bbc.co.uk – **26)** The Forum, Millennium Plain, Norwich NR2 1BH ☎1603 619331 **E**: norfolk@bbc.co.uk – **27)** Broadcasting House, Abington Street, Northampton NN1 2BH ☎1604 239100 **E**: northampton@bbc.co.uk – **28)** London Rd, Nottingham NG2 4UU ☎115 955 0500 **E**: radio.nottingham@bbc.co.uk – **29)** 269 Banbury Rd, Oxford OX2 7DW ☎8459 311444 **E**: oxford@bbc.co.uk – **30)** Broadcasting House, 40-42 Queen's Rd, Brighton BN1 3XB **E**: sussex@bbc.co.uk – **30a)** Broadcasting Centre, Guildford GU2 7AP ☎1483 306306 **E**: surrey@bbc.co.uk – **31)** 54 Shoreham Street, Sheffield S1 4RS ☎114 2731177 **E**: radio.sheffield@bbc.co.uk – **32)** 2-4 Boscobel Drive, Shrewsbury SY1 3TT ☎1743 248484 **E**: shropshire@bbc.co.uk – **33)** Broadcasting House, 10 Havelock Rd, Southampton SO14 7PW ☎23 8063 1311 **E**: radio.solent@bbc.co.uk – **34)** Cheapside, Hanley, Stoke-on-Trent ST1 1JJ ☎01782 08080 **E**: radio.stoke@bbc.co.uk– **35)** Broadcasting House, St. Matthew's Street, Ipswich IP1 3EP ☎1473 250000 **E: radio**suffolk@bbc.co.uk– **36)** 56-58 Prospect Place, Swindon SN1 3RW ☎ 1793 513626 **E**: wiltshire@bbc.co.uk – **37)** 20 Bootham Row, York Y030 7BR ☎1904 641 351 **E**: northyorkshire.news@bbc.co.uk – **38)** The Mailbox, Wharfside Street, Birmingham B1 1AY ☎121 567 6767 **E**: radio.wm@bbc.co.uk
D.Prgr: Stns generally carry local or regional prgrs from 0600-0100, then BBC Radio 5 Live overnight

BBC SCOTLAND

🖵40 Pacific Quay, Glasgow G51 1DA ☎ 141 422 6000
W: bbc.co.uk/radioscotland
MW: R. Scotland: Burghead 810kHz 100kW, Westerglen 810kHz 100kW, Redmoss 810kHz 5kW, Dumfries 585kHz 2kW

FM stereo	R1	R2	R3	R4	RS/L	kW
Ashkirk	98.7	89.1	91.3	103.9	93.5f	50
Ben Gullipen	98.3	88.7	90.9	104.9	93.1	1
Black Hill	99.5	89.9	92.1	*95.8	94.3	250/*200
Bressay	97.9	88.3	90.5	94.9	92.7ac	43
Clettraval	97.7	88.1	90.3	95.1	92.5d	2
Daliburgh	98.9	89.3	91.5	95.9	93.7d	1
Darvel	99.1	89.5	91.7	104.3	93.9	10
Durris	99.0	89.4	91.6	95.9	93.8a	2.1
Eitshal	99.4	89.8	92.0	95.1	94.2d	2
Forfar	97.9	88.3	90.5	94.9	92.7	17
Fort William	98.9	89.3	91.5	95.9	93.7d	3
Glengorm	99.1	89.5	91.7	96.1	93.9d	5
Keelylang Hill	98.9	89.3	91.5	96.0	93.7ab	41
Kirkton Mailer	98.6	89.0	91.2	94.6	93.4	1
Meldrum	98.3	88.7	90.9	95.3	93.1a	150
Melvaig	98.7	89.1	91.3	95.7	93.5d	50
Oban	98.5	88.9	91.1	95.3	93.3d	3.6
Rosemarkie	99.2	89.6	91.8	103.6	94.0d	20
Rumster Forest	99.7	90.1	92.3	95.6	94.5d	10
Sandale	97.7	88.1	90.3	92.5	94.7e	250
Skriaig	98.1	88.5	90.7	94.8	92.9d	30
So. Knapdale	98.9	89.3	91.5	95.6	93.7	2.2

+ 32 low power txs less than 1kW
RS/L=R. Scotland + local news – a) RS: Aberdeen – b) RS: Orkney – c) RS: Shetland – d) RS: Inverness – e) RS: Dumfries – f) RS: Selkirk.
D.Prgr: R.Scotland 0530(SaSu0600)-0100. Rel. BBC Radio 5 overnight

Local Services (FM only). Freqs as above.
a) Beechgrove Terrace, Aberdeen AB15 5ZT. M-F: 0630, 0730, 0830, 1230, 1630, 1730. **W:** bbc.co.uk/northeastscotland – b) Castle Str, Kirkwall, Orkney KW15 1DF: M-F 0730-0800, Fri 1810-1900 – c) Pitt Lane, Lerwick, Shetland ZE1 0DW: M-F 1730-1800, Fri 1810-1900 – d) 7 Culduthel Rd, Inverness IV2 4AD M-F: 0630, 0730, 0830, 1230, 1630, 1730 – e) Elmbank, Lovers Walk, Dumfries DG1 1NZ: M-F: 0630, 0730, 0830, 1230, 1630, 1730. **W:** bbc.co.uk/southscotland – f) Ettrick Riverside, Dunsdale Rd, Selkirk TD7 5EB M-F 0630, 0730, 0830, 1230, 1630, 1730

BBC RADIO NAN GAIDHEAL

🖵 54 Seaforth Rd., Stornoway HS1 2SD ☎ 1851 705000 🖷 1851 704633 **W:** bbc.co.uk/radionangaidheal
MW: Redmoss 990kHz 1kW

FM	MHz	kW	FM	MHz	kW
Glengorm	103.5	5	Meldrum	104.2	150
Clettraval	103.7	2	Eitshal	104.3	2
So. Knapdale	103.7	2.2	Kirkton Mailer	104.5	1
Forfar	103.7	17	Rumster Forest	104.5	10
Melvaig	103.9	50	Oban	104.6	3.6
Craigkelly	104.1	5	Black Hill	104.7	10
Daliburgh	104.2	1	Skriaig	104.7	30
Fort William	104.2	3	Rosemarkie	104.9	20

+ 16 low power txs less than 1kW
D.Prgr: Own prgrs in Gaelic and relays of BBC R. Scotland

BBC CYMRU WALES

🖵 Broadcasting House, Llantrisant Rd, Llandaff, Cardiff CF5 2YQ
☎ 29 2032 2000 🖷 29 2055 5960
E: radiowales@bbc.co.uk **W:** bbc.co.uk/radiowales

FM stereo	R1	R2	R3	R4	kW
Blaenplwyf	98.3	88.7	90.9	104.0	250
Carmel	98.0	88.4	90.6	92.8	2.5
Haverfordwest	98.9	89.3	91.5	104.9	20
Kilvey Hill	99.1	89.5	91.7	94.6	1
Llanddona	99.4	89.8	92.0	103.6	21
Llandrindod Wells	98.7	89.1	91.3	103.8	2.8
Llangollen	98.5	88.9	91.1	93.3	15.6
Wenvoe	99.5	89.9	92.1	94.3	250

FM stereo	R. Wales	R.Cymru	kW
Blaenplwyf	95.3	93.1	250/120
Carmel	95.1	104.6	3/3.2
Haverfordwest	95.9	93.7	20
Kilvey Hill	93.9	104.2	1
Llanddona	94.8	94.2	21/10
Llandrindod Wells	-	93.5	2.8
Llangollen	-	104.3	15.6
Wenvoe	103.9	-	40
Wenvoe	-	96.8	250

+ 42 low power txs less than 1kW
MW R. Wales: Forden 882kHz 1kW, Llandrindod Wells 1125kHz 1kW, Penmon 882kHz 10kW, Tywyn 882kHz 5kW, Washford 882kHz 100kW, Wrexham 657kHz 2kW
D.Prgr: R Wales: 0530(SaSu0500)-0100. Rel. BBC WS overnight. **R Cymru:** 0530-0000. Rel. BBC Radio 5 overnight

BBC NORTHERN IRELAND

🖵 Broadcasting House, 25-27 Ormeau Avenue, Belfast BT2 8HQ ☎ 28 9033 8000 🖷 28 9032 6453 **W:** bbc.co.uk/radioulster
MW: Enniskillen 873kHz 1kW, Lisnagarvey 1341kHz 100kW

FM stereo	R1	R2	R3	R4	R.Ulster	kW
Brougher Mountain	99.0	89.4	91.6	95.6	93.8	9.8
Camlough	98.3	88.7	90.9	104.6	93.1	4
Divis	99.7	90.1	92.3	96.0	94.5	250/125
Limavady	99.2	89.6	91.8	94.0	95.4	3.4
Londonderry	98.3	88.7	90.9	94.9	93.1h	31/10

+ 5 low power txs of less than 1kW – h) **R. Foyle** (see below)
R. Ulster: Enniskillen 873kHz 1kW, Lisnagarvey 1341kHz 100kW.
D.Prgr: MF 0630(SaSu0700)-0000. Other times rel. BBC R5

BBC RADIO FOYLE

🖵 8 Northland Rd, Londonderry BT48 7GD ☎ 28 7137 8600 **W:** bbc.co.uk/radiofoyle
E: radio.foyle@bbc.co.uk
MW: Londonderry 792kHz 1kW **FM:** 93.1MHz 31kW
D.Prgr: 24h. Own prgs. and relay BBC R. Ulster. Local N. M-F hourly 0700-1700

BBC ASIAN NETWORK

🖵 New Broadcasting House, London W1A 1AA ☎ **E:** asiannetwork-news@bbc.co.uk **W:** bbc.co.uk/asiannetwork

MW	kHz	kW	MW	kHz	kW
Sedgley	828	0.2	Gunthorpe	1449	0.15
Freemen's Common	837	0.5	Langley Mill	1458	5

D.Prgr: 0600-2400, mainly in English. Relays BBC Radio 5 Live overnight.

BBC Asian Network relays

MW	kHz	kW	MW	kHz	kW
R. Leeds	774a	0.7	R. Derby	1116c	1
R. Sheffield	1035b				

Key: a) Mon-Fri 1900-0100, b) Mon-Fri 1600-0100, c) Mon-Fri 1900-0100, SS 1800-0030. Local Asian programming is also carried on some BBC local radio stns at various times.

ARQIVA
✉ Crawley Court, Winchester SO21 2QA ☎1962 823434
W: arqiva.com Operates most BBC domestic and many commercial radio tx sites. Formerly National Grid Wireless.

EXTERNAL SERVICE: BBC World Service
See International Broadcasting section

OFFICE OF COMMUNICATIONS (Ofcom) (Regulatory Authority)
✉ Riverside House, 2A Southwark Bridge Rd, London SE1 9HA
☎20 7981 3040 ▤20 7981 3333 **W:** ofcom.org.uk **L.P:** CEO: Sharon White

RADIO CENTRE
✉ 6th Floor, 55 New Oxford Str., London W1A 1BS ☎20 7010 0600
▤20 7306 7801 **W:** radiocentre.org - Radio Centre represents commercial radio to Government, Ofcom, Copyright Societies and other organizations concerned with radio.

DIGITAL RADIO (DAB): DAB trs are on Band 3. **BBC Digital Radio:** BBC Radios 1, 1Xtra, 2, 3, 4, 4 Extra, 5 Live, 5 Live Sports Extra, 6 Music, Asian Network and World Service are on a single frequency network on 225.648MHz. **Digital One:** ✉ UK House, 4th Floor, 2-5 Gt Titchfield Str, London W1W 8BB **W:** ukdigitalradio.com Progr includes: Absolute, Absolute 80s, BFBS, Capital Xtra, Classic FM, Kiss, LBC, Planet Rock, Premier Christian Radio, Smooth Extra, talkSPORT, UCB UK. **All prgrs** are in a single frequency network for England, Wales & Northern Ireland on 222.064MHz, block 11D, and for Scotland on 223.936MHz, Block 12A. **Local multiplexes: Bauer:** Central Lancashire, Humberside, Leeds, Liverpool, South Yorkshire, Teesside, Tyne & Wear. **CE Digital:** Greater London, Birmingham, Manchester. **Digital Radio Group:** Greater London. **MuxCo:** Chester, Wrexham & Liverpool, Gloucestershire, Lincolnshire, Hereford & Worcester, Mid & W Wales, NE Wales & W Cheshire, Surrey, Somerset, N Yorkshire*, Oxford. **Now Digital:** Ayr, Bournemouth, Bristol & Bath, Cambridge, Cardiff & Newport, Coventry, Derbyshire, Exeter & Torbay, Herts, Beds, Bucks & Northants, Kent, Leicester, Norwich, Nottingham, Peterborough, Reading & Basingstoke, So. Hampshire, Southend & Chelmsford, Sussex Coast, Swindon & West Wiltshire, Wolverhampton/Shrewsbury & Telford. **Score Digital:** Dundee & Perth, Edinburgh, Glasgow, Inverness, Northern Ireland. **South West Digital Radio:** Plymouth & Cornwall. **Switchdigital:** Aberdeen, Central Scotland, Greater London. **UTV-Bauer:** Bradford & Huddersfield, Stoke-on-Trent, Swansea. **3G:** Isle of Man. (*planned)

NATIONAL COMMERCIAL STATIONS:

ABSOLUTE RADIO
✉ 1 Golden Square, London W1F 9DJ ☎20 7434 1215 ▤20 7434 1197 **W:** absoluteradio.co.uk

MW	kHz	kW	MW	kHz	kW
Bournemouth	1197	0.3	Plymouth	1215	1
Brighton	1197	1	Redmoss	1215	2.3
Cambridge	1197	0.2	Redruth	1215	2
Torbay	1197	1	Washford	1215	100
Trowell	1197	1	Westerglen	1215	100
Wallasey	1197	0.4	Wrekenton	1215	2
Gloucester	1197	0.3	Kings Heath	1233	1
Hoo (Kent)	1197	2	Manningtree	1233	1
Oxford	1197	0.3	Sheffield	1233	0.3
Brookmans Park	1215	125	Swindon	1233	0.1
Dartford Tunnel	1215	0.004	Boston	1242	2
Droitwich	1215	105	Dundee	1242	1
Fareham	1215	1	Sideway	1242	1
Hull	1215	0.3	Stockton	1242	1
Lisnagarvey	1215	16	Guildford	1260	1
Moorside Edge	1215	200	Lydd	1260	1
Norwich	1215	1			

D.Prgr: 24h (rock & contemporary music). **N:** on the h
FM: West Midlands (Sutton Coldfield) 105.2 MHz, 11kW; London (Crystal Palace) 105.8MHz 4kW

CLASSIC FM
✉30 Leicester Square, London WC2H 7LA ☎ 20 7343 9000 **W:** classicfm.com

FM	MHz	kW	FM	MHz	kW
Cumbria	99.9	250	Bath	100.2	0.2
No.Hessary Tor	100.0	160	Douglas I.O.M.	100.2	1
Angus	100.1	10.3	Bradford	100.3	0.5
Sutton Coldfield	100.1	250	Pontop Pike	100.3	130

FM	MHz	kW	FM	MHz	kW
Rowridge	100.3	250	Swansea	101.3	1
Milton Keynes	100.4	10	Bristol	101.4	0.2
Ridge Hill	100.4	5	Inverness	101.4	11
Belmont	100.5	6.2	Tacolneston	101.5	250
Londonderry	100.5	31	Redruth	101.5	10
Meldrum	100.5	150	Gt. Ormes Head	101.6	2.5
Presely	100.5	7.13	Bilsdale	101.6	2
Crystal Palace	100.6	2	Leeds	101.6	0.5
Arfon	100.7	18.75	Black Hill	101.7	250
Swindon	100.8	0.72	Sheffield	101.7	0.5
Selkirk	100.9	10	Wenvoe	101.7	250
Wrotham	100.9	250	Dover	101.8	5.2
Fenham	101.0	0.05	Morecambe Bay	101.8	6.4
Blaen Plwyf	101.1	10	Reading	101.8	0.5
Holme Moss	101.1	250	Brighton	101.8	0.4
Darvel	101.3	8	Divis	101.9	250
Oxford	101.3	46	Peterborough	101.9	35

D.Prgr: 24h **N:** on the h

HEART
✉ 30 Leicester Square, London WC2H 7LA ☎20 7766 6000 **W:** heart.co.uk

FM	MHz	kW	Location	FM	MHz	kW	Location
100)	88.0	1.4	Wrexham	43)	102.3	2	Bournemouth
40)	95.9	0.27	Thanet	41)	102.4	8.2	Eastbourne
40)	96.1	0.2	Ashford	76)	102.4	2	Gloucester
92)	96.1	0.5	Colchester	104)	102.4	3.3	Norwich
82)	96.2	2.5	N Devon	92)	102.6	2	Chelmsford
86)	96.3	2	Bristol	89)	102.6	9	Oxford
92)	96.3	1	Southend	86)	102.6	4	Mendip
82)	96.4	1.6	Torbay	41)	102.7	3.6	Reigate
104)	96.4	2	Bury St.Eds	88)	102.7	4	Peterborough
86)	96.5	0.1	Taunton	40)	102.8	1	Dunkirk
72)	96.6	4	Northampton	100)	102.8	0.2	Long Mountain
16)	96.6	0.5	Watford	89)	102.9	3.4	Hannington
43)	96.7	0.5	Winchester	88)	103.0	1	Cambridge
72)	96.9	0.9	Bedford	82)	103.0	1	Stockland Hl
41)	96.9	0.1	Newhaven	76)	103.0	0.1	Stroud
40)	97.0	0.5	Dover	86)	103.0	1	Weston-S-Mare
82)	97.0	1	Exeter	40)	103.1	4	Maidstone
89)	97.0	1	Reading	122)	103.3	0.5	Penicuik
82)	97.0	2	Plymouth	72)	103.3	2	Milton Keynes
86)	97.1	0.2	W.Somerset	89)	103.4	0.1	Henley-on-Th
104)	97.1	3.4	Ipswich	41)	103.5	1	Brighton
87)	97.2	0.7	Swindon	85)	105.1	2.5	E.Cornwall
82)	97.3	0.1	Ilfracombe	42)	105.2	3	Carmel
89)	97.4	0.3	Banbury	45)	105.4	5	Winter Hill
43)	97.5	0.85	Portsmouth	42)	105.4	5	Cardiff
72)	97.6	1	Luton	42)	105.7	9.4	Preseley
122)	100.3	20	Black Hill	100)	105.7	1.25	Llandudno
82)	100.5	0.3	Totnes	42)	105.9	1	Newport
34)	100.7	11	Birmingham	42)	106.0	1	Swansea
36)	100.7	10	Bilsdale	49)	106.2	3.1	Emley Moor
82)	100.8	0.1	Dartmouth	42)	106.2	0.5	Fishguard
122)	101.1	10	Edinburgh	33)	106.2	4	London
36)	101.2	0.2	Hexham	100)	106.9	0.44	Meol-y-Parc
82)	101.2	1.15	Salcombe	85)	107.0	11	W.Cornwall
92)	101.7	0.1	Harlow	100)	107.2	3.1	Arfon
36)	101.8	8.5	Burnhope	100)	107.3	0.15	Bargoed
82)	101.9	0.5	Ivybridge	49)	107.6	2	Bradford
41)	102.0	0.2	Hastings	100)	107.7	10.25	Blaenplwyf
87)	102.2	0.5	W Wiltshire	49)	107.7	0.2	Sheffield
42)	102.3	5	Pontypridd				

D.Prgr: 24h **N:** on the h (No. refer to local studio address - see list)

SMOOTH RADIO
✉ 30 Leicester Square, London WC2H 7LA ☎20 7766 6000 **W:** smoothradio.com

MW	kHz	kW	Location	MW	kHz	kW	Location
40)	603	0.4	Littlebourne	40)	1242	0.32	Maidstone
76)	774	0.14	Gloucester	104)	1251	0.76	Bury St.Eds.
72)	792	0.28	Bedford	86)	1260	1.6	Bristol
43)	828	0.27	Bournemouth	100)	1260	0.64	Wrexham
72)	828	0.2	Luton	42)	1305	0.2	Newport
87)	936	0.18	Naish Hill	41)	1323	0.5	Brighton
41)	945	0.7	Bexhill	88)	1332	0.6	Peterborough
104)	1152	0.83	Norwich	42)	1359	0.2	Cardiff
82)	1152	0.32	Plymouth	92)	1359	0.28	Chelmsford
87)	1161	0.16	Swindon	92)	1431	0.35	S'thend-on-Sea
104)	1170	0.28	Ipswich	72)	1557	0.76	Northampton
43)	1170	0.12	Portsmouth	92)	1557	0.5	Southampton

FM

FM		MHz	kW	FM		MHz	kW
36)	Newton	96.4	0.2	122)	Glasgow	105.2	30
36)	Burnhope	97.5	9	9)	Sutton Coldfield	105.7	11
37)	Winter Hill	100.4	5	69)	Waltham	106.6	10.8
69)	Derby	101.4	0.2	36)	Eston Nab	107.7	5
33)	Croydon	102.2	4				

D.Prgr: 24h (Numbers refer to local studio address - see list below)

TALKSPORT

📠 18 Hatfields, London SE1 8DJ ☎20 7959 7800 📠20 7959 7808
W: talksport.com

MW	kHz	kW	MW	kHz	kW
Bournemouth	1053	1	Brookmans Park	1089	400
Brighton	1053	2	Dartford Tunnel	1089	0
Droitwich	1053	500	Lisnagarvey	1089	13
Dumfries	1053	10	Moorside Edge	1089	400
Londonderry	1053	1	Redmoss	1089	2
Plymouth	1053	1	Redruth	1089	2
Postwick	1053	18	Washford	1089	80
Stockton	1053	1	Westerglen	1089	125
Tonbridge	1053	4	Boston	1107	1
Dundee	1053	1	Fareham	1107	1
Exeter	1053	1	Lydd	1107	2
Hull	1053	1	Reigate/Crawley	1107	1
Inverness	1053	1	Torbay	1107	1
Clipstone	1071	1	Wallasey	1107	1
Newcastle	1071	1			

D.Prgr: 24h

LOCAL RADIO STATIONS:

MW	kHz	kW	Station or Slogan	Location
-)	531	0.001	occasional RSLs	
120)	558	1	Spectrum R.	London
56)	828	0.12	R. Aire 2	Leeds
128)	855	0.15	Sunshine R.	Ludlow
-)	936	0.1	Dales R*	Hawes
69)	945	0.2	Gold	Derby
1)	963	0.95	Sunrise R	E. London
93)	963	0.2	Asian Sound R.	Haslingden
1)	972	1	Sunrise R.	W. London
34)	990	0.09	Free R. 80s	Wolverhampton
53)	990	0.25	Hallam 2	Doncaster
60)	999	0.8	Rock 2	Preston
69)	999	0.25	Nottingham	Gold
34)	1017	0.63	Free R. 80s	Shrewsbury
153)	1026	1.7	Downtown R.	Belfast
155)	1035	0.78	Northsound 2	Aberdeen
160)	1035	0.32	West Sound AM	Ayr
167)	1035	2.5	Lyca Dilse	London
161)	1107	1.5	MFR 2	Inverness
-)	1134	0.001	LPAMs	
33)	1152	23.5	LBC	London
158)	1152	3.6	Clyde 2	Glasgow
34)	1152	3	Free R. 80s	Birmingham
51)	1152	1.5	Key 2	Manchester
61)	1152	1.8	Metro 2	Newcastle
54)	1161	0.35	Viking 2	Hull
156)	1161	1.4	Tay 2	Dundee
127)	1170	0.58	Swansea Sound	Swansea
59)	1170	0.32	TFM 2	Stockton
35)	1170	0.2	Signal 2	Stoke-on-Trent
-)	1251	0.001	LPAMs	
151)	1260	0.29	Sabras R.	Leicester
106)	1278	0.43	Pulse 2	Bradford
-)	1278	0.001	LPAMs/RSLs	
-)	1287	0.001	LPAMs	
131)	1287	0.004	R Glan Clwyd*	Bodelwyddan
148)	1296	10	R. XL	Birmingham
53)	1305	0.15	Hallam 2	Barnsley
98)	1305	0.5	Premier Christian R.	Epsom
98)	1305	0.5	Premier Christian R.	Chingford
180)	1323	0.002	Akash R*	Leeds
98)	1332	1	Premier Christian R.	London
-)	1350	0.001	LPAMs	
34)	1359	0.27	Free R. 80s	Coventry
93)	1377	0.08	Asian Sound R.	Ashton Moss
24)	1386	0.1	R. JCom*	Leeds
-)	1386	0.001	LPAMs	
-)	1404	0.001	LPAMs	
98)	1413	0.5	Premier Christian R.	Heathrow
98)	1413	0.5	Premier Christian R.	Dartford Marshes
-)	1431	0.001	LPAMs	
-)	1449	0.001	LPAMs	

MW	kHz	kW	Station or Slogan	Location
167)	1458	125	Lyca R.	W.London
45)	1458	5	Gold	Manchester
81)	1503	0.1	Betar Bangla*	E.London
234)	1521	0.07	Flame CCR*	Wirral
106)	1530	0.74	Pulse 2	Huddersfield
33)	1548	97.5	Gold	London
53)	1548	0.74	Hallam 2	Sheffield
52)	1548	1	R. City 2	Liverpool
159)	1548	2.2	Forth 2	Edinburgh
98)	1566	0.8	Premier Christian R	Guildford
-)	1575	0.001	LPAMs/RSLs	
156)	1584	0.21	Tay 2	Perth
11)	1584	0.2	Panjab R.	N.London
83)	1602	0.07	Desi R.*	Southall
-)	1602	0.001	occasional RSLs	

*community radio stns

FM	MHz	kW	Name or Slogan	Location
-)	87.7	-	RSLs/LPFMs	
-)	87.9	-	RSLs	
100)	88.0	1.4	Heart - N Wales	Wrexham
172)	94.0	0.125	Voice of Africa R.*	E. London
91)	95.2	0.2	Kingdom FM	Dunfermline
33)	95.8	4	Capital FM	London
91)	96.1	0.5	Kingdom FM	Glenrothes
108)	96.1	0.2	Rother FM	Rotherham
124)	96.2	4	SIBC	Shetland
63)	96.2	0.2	KMFM	Tonbridge
99)	96.2	1	Mix 96	Aylesbury
77)	96.2	2.6	North Norfolk R.	Stody
138)	96.2	0.1	The Revolution	Oldham
145)	96.2	0.625	Yorkshire Coast R.	Scarborough
116)	96.2	0.1	Touch FM	Coventry
69)	96.2	1	Capital FM	Nottingham
56)	96.3	2.5	R. Aire	Leeds
100)	96.3	1.25	Capital FM	Llandudno
184)	96.3	0.1	The Bee	Chorley
153)	96.4	2	Downtown R.	Limavady
34)	96.4	10	Free R,	Birmingham
127)	96.4	1.5	The Wave	Swansea
154)	96.4	3	The Eagle	Guildford
156)	96.4	0.8	Tay FM	Perth
35)	96.4	0.25	Signal 1	Congleton
163)	96.4	3	CFM	Carlisle
63)	96.4	0.2	KMFM	Folkestone
112)	96.4	0.1	Compass FM	Grimsby
47)	96.5	0.4	R. Wave	Blackpool
157)	96.5	0.12	West Sound	Stranraer
153)	96.6	8.2	Downtown R.	Brougher Mountain
84)	96.6	0.1	The Breeze	Blandford
26)	96.6	0.2	RNA FM	Arbroath
59)	96.6	10	TFM R.	Bilsdale
31)	96.6	0.4	R. Ceredigion	Lampeter
142)	96.6	0.45	Nevis R.*	Fort William
161)	96.6	0.45	MFR	Cairngorm
25)	96.6	0.4	Spirit FM	Chichester
160)	96.7	2.2	West FM	Ayr
52)	96.7	8	R. City	Liverpool
144)	96.7	0.55	Q Radio	Belfast
115)	96.7	3	KL.FM	King's Lynn
96)	96.7	0.2	Ashbourne R.	Ashbourne
70)	96.7	0.1	Free R.	Kidderminster
161c)	96.7	0.1	MFR / Kinnaird*	Fraserburgh
162)	96.8	5	R. Borders	Selkirk
125)	96.8	0.5	Lochbroom FM	Polbain
54)	96.9	9.4	Viking FM	Hull
155)	96.9	11	Northsound 1	Aberdeen
35)	96.9	0.2	Signal 1	Stafford
109)	96.9	3.2	The Bay	Morecambe Bay
142)	97.0	0.25	Nevis R.*	Glencoe
157)	97.0	1	West Sound	Dumfries
34)	97.0	1.8	Free R.	Coventry
61)	97.1	10	Metro R.	Newcastle
100)	97.1	1	Capital FM	Wirral
121)	97.1	0.3	NECR	Braemar
121)	97.1	0.1	NECR	Turriff
133)	97.1	0.275	The Breeze	Haslemere
153)	97.1	0.08	Downtown R.	Larne
66)	97.1	3	R. Carmarthenshire	Carmel
136)	97.2	0.14	Connect FM	Wellingborough
34)	97.2	0.2	Free R.	Wolverhampton
58)	97.2	0.2	Kiss	Bristol
135)	97.2	0.31	Q Radio	Coleraine

FM	MHz	kW	Name or Slogan	Location	FM	MHz	kW	Name or Slogan	Location
118)	97.2	0.7	Wessex FM	Dorchester/Weymouth	53)	102.9	0.45	Hallam FM	Barnsley
147)	97.2	1	Stray FM	Harrogate	135)	102.9	3.14	Q102.9	Londonderry
33)	97.3	4	LBC	London	100)	103.0	5	Capital FM	Caernarfon
159)	97.3	9.8	Forth 1	Edinburgh	51)	103.0	4	Key 103	Manchester
161)	97.4	6.25	MFR	Inverness	143)	103.0	4	Isles FM	Stornoway
60)	97.4	2	Rock FM	Preston/Blackpool	155)	103.0	0.174	Northsound 1	Peterhead
153)	97.4	3.2	Cool FM	Belfast	166)	103.0	0.1	Your R.	Dumbarton
42)	97.4	0.5	Capital FM	Newport	157)	103.0	0.7	West Sound	Kirkcudbright
53)	97.4	0.4	Hallam FM	Sheffield	34)	103.1	2.7	Free R.	Shrewsbury
31)	97.4	0.4	R. Ceredigion	Penwaun	14)	103.1	0.5	Central FM	Stirling
84)	97.4	0.125	The Breeze	Shaftesbury	153)	103.1	1.8	Downtown R.	Newry
134)	97.4	0.24	The Beach	Southwold	77)	103.2	0.25	North Norfolk R. (2 txs)	N. Norfolk
106)	97.5	0.5	Pulse 1	Bradford	42)	103.2	2	Capital FM	Cardiff
28)	97.5	0.4	Heartland FM	Pitlochry	43)	103.2	2	Capital FM	Southampton
160)	97.5	0.15	West FM	Girvan	32)	103.2	0.1	Mansfield 103.2	Mansfield
66)	97.5	0.2	Scarlet FM	Llanelli	109)	103.2	0.1	The Bay	Kendal
70)	97.6	0.8	Free R.	Hereford	123)	103.2	0.4	Sunrise FM	Bradford
159)	97.6	0.1	Forth 1	Edinburgh	150)	103.2	0.4	Star R - NE	Darlington
33)	97.7	1	Radio X	Manchester	61)	103.2	0.12	Metro R.	Hexham
15)	99.8	0.75	2BR	Burnley	121)	103.2	0.3	NECR	Colpy
68)	99.8	0.75	KCFM	Hull	74)	103.3	0.17	High Peak R.	Buxworth
50)	99.9	0.5	R. Norwich	Stoke Holy Cross	74)	103.3	0.1	High Peak R.	Hope Valley
58)	100.0	4	Kiss	London	114)	103.3	0.1	London Greek R.	London
101)	100.1	0.2	Lakeland R.	Kendal	31)	103.3	5.8	R. Ceredigion	Blaenplwyf
12)	100.2	2	Dream 100	Clacton-on-Sea	158)	103.3	0.1	Clyde 1	Rosneath
135)	100.5	1	Q Radio	Newry	6)	103.3	0.4	Oban FM	Oban
101)	100.8	0.12	Lakeland R.	Windermere	100)	103.4	1.4	Capital FM	Wrexham
84)	100.8	0.13	The Breeze	Porlock	53)	103.4	1.6	Hallam FM	Doncaster
58)	101.0	40	Kiss	Mendip	153)	103.4	0.2	Downtown R.	Newcastle
135)	101.1	0.4	Q Radio	Newry	162)	103.4	0.5	R. Borders	Eyemouth
64)	101.2	1.65	Waves R.	Peterhead	39)	103.4	0.16	Sun FM	Sunderland
135)	101.2	6.26	Q Radio	Brougher Mountain	163)	103.4	0.4	CFM	Whitehaven
101)	101.4	0.1	Lakeland R	Keswick	134)	103.4	2	The Beach	Lowestoft
133)	101.6	0.1	The Breeze	Alton	150)	103.5	0.2	Star R - NE	Northallerton
63)	101.6	0.4	KMFM	Wrotham	21)	103.7	4	Channel 103 FM	Jersey
133)	101.8	0.11	The Breeze	Petersfield	141)	104.7	2.5	Minster FM	York
121)	101.9	0.22	NECR	Tullich	5)	104.7	1.25	Island FM	Guernsey
105)	102.0	1	Town FM	Ipswich	140)	104.9	0.64	Imagine FM	Stockport
108)	102.0	0.45	Dearne FM	Barnsley	33)	104.9	2.9	Radio X	London
130)	102.0	0.1	Peak FM	Matlock	49)	105.1	3.1	Capital FM	Emley Moor
45)	102.0	0.5	Capital FM	Manchester	95)	105.1		Southend R.	Southend-on-Sea
146)	102.0	1.25	Spire FM	Salisbury	58)	105.2	11	Absolute R	Sutton Coldfield
133)	102.0	0.1	The Breeze	Alton	164)	105.2	10	Wave 105	Solent
116)	102.0	2.6	Touch FM	Stratford upon Avon	181)	105.2	0.8	An R*	Benbecula
73)	102.0	0.2	Wave 102	Dundee	36)	105.3	8.4	Capital FM	Burnhope
121)	102.1	1.25	NECR	Inverurie	69)	105.4	5	Capital FM	Leicester
78)	102.1	1.2	Nation Hits	Swansea	91)	105.4	0.1	Kingdom FM	Fife
159)	102.2	1	Forth 1	Penicuik	58)	105.4	4	Magic 105.4	Croydon
112)	102.2	6.4	Lincs FM	Belmont	111)	105.5	1.6	The Breeze	Torbay
165)	102.2	2.5	Pirate FM	Caradon Hill	58)	105.6	1	Kiss	Cambridge
9)	102.2	1	Capital FM	Birmingham	49)	105.6	0.5	Capital FM	Bradford
163)	102.2	0.815	CFM	Workington	49)	105.6	0.25	Capital FM	Sheffield
125)	102.2	0.7	Lochbroom FM	Ullapool	79)	105.6	0.4	The Breeze	Yeovil
158)	102.3	0.6	Clyde 1	Rothesay	63)	105.6	0.5	KMFM	Maidstone
25)	102.3	0.5	Spirit FM	Littlehampton	29)	105.6	0.1	The Breeze	Newbury
153)	102.3	0.5	Downtown R.	Ballymena	44)	105.7	10	Capital FM	Edinburgh
142)	102.3	0.8	Nevis R.*	Fort William	10)	105.8	1.9	U105	Belfast
4)	102.4	0.1	Touch FM	Burton	36)	105.8	0.2	Capital FM	Hexham
84)	102.4	2	The Breeze	Minehead	164)	105.8	0.625	Wave 105	Poole
153)	102.4	10	Downtown R.	Londonderry	49)	105.8	9.6	Capital FM	Hull
158)	102.4	0.6	Clyde 1	Rosneath	52)	105.9	7.5	City Talk	Liverpool
145)	102.4	0.1	Yorkshire Coast R.	Bridlington	128)	105.9	1	Sunshine R.	Woofferton
22)	102.4	0.1	Wish FM	Wigan	107)	106.0	4	Sam FM	Solent
142)	102.4	0.8	Nevis R.*	Glenachulish	38)	106.0	8	Gem 106	Copt Oak
158)	102.5	24.5	Clyde 1	Glasgow	135)	106.0	0.6	Q. R.	Cookstown
106)	102.5	2	Pulse 1	Halifax	63)	106.0	0.1	KMFM	Canterbury
161a)	102.5	1.2	MFR / Caithness*	Thurso	75)	106.0	0.6	Two Lochs R.	Gairloch
102)	102.5	20	R. Pembrokeshire	Haverfordwest	58)	106.1	4	Kiss	Stoke Holy Cross
163)	102.5	0.1	CFM	Penrith	44)	106.1	20	Capital FM	Glasgow
176)	102.5	0.2	Mon FM*	Anglesey	37)	106.1	1	Real R. XS	Manchester
35)	102.6	4	Signal 1	Stoke-on-Trent	177)	106.1	0.17	The Hub*	Tregony
61)	102.6	0.125	Metro R.	Alnwick	103)	106.2	1.5	Sunshine R.	Hereford
121)	102.6	0.3	NECR	Kildrummy	91)	106.3	0.15	Kingdom FM	Fife
150)	102.6	0.1	Star R. NE	Richmond	30)	106.3	0.9	Bridge FM	Bridgend
62)	102.7	9	Cuillin FM	Isle of Skye	19)	106.3	0.175	Original 106	Peterhead
150)	102.8	0.5	Star R. NE	Burnhope	27)	106.3	0.2	Dee	Chester
69)	102.8	0.9	Capital FM	Derby	58)	106.4	20	Kiss	Mendelsham
70)	102.8	1	Free R.	Worcester	36)	106.4	10	Capital FM	Bilsdale
156)	102.8	5	Tay FM	Dundee	121)	106.4	0.3	NECR	Cock Bridge
165)	102.8	10	Pirate FM	Redruth	94)	106.4	0.4	Bright FM	Haywards Heath
147)	102.8	1	Stray FM	Skipton	74)	106.4	0.25	High Peak R.(2 txs)	Buxton/Glossop
161)	102.8	1	MFR	Keith	117)	106.4	0.1	The Breeze	Andover

FM	MHz	kW	Name or Slogan	Location
177)	106.4	0.2	The Hub*	St Mawes
13)	106.5	0.5	Argyll FM	Campbeltown
3)	106.5	0.5	Signal 107	Shrewsbury
84)	106.5	1	Sam FM	Bristol
15)	106.5	0.1	The Bee	Preston
107)	106.6	0.3	Sam FM	Poole
79)	106.6	0.25	The Breeze	Chard
75)	106.6	2	Two Lochs R.	Loch Ewe
25)	106.6	0.4	Spirit FM	Midhurst
28)	106.6	0.25	Heartland FM	Perth
168)	106.6	0.2	BCB*	Bradford
23)	106.7	0.1	Bob FM	Stevenage
160)	106.7	0.6	West FM	Rothesay
18)	106.7	0.62	R Plymouth	Ft Staddon
8)	106.8	4	Nation R.	Cardiff
94)	106.8	0.1	Bright FM	Lewes
150)	106.8	0.1	Star R. - NE	Durham
63)	106.8	0.4	KMFM	Dover
136)	106.8	0.2	Connect FM	Peterborough
108)	106.8	0.5	Ridings FM	Wakefield
65)	106.8	0.3	Jack FM	Oxford
19)	106.8	19	Original FM	Aberdeen
175)	106.8	0.15	Rinse FM*	SE London
23)	106.9	0.28	Bob FM	Hertford
152)	106.9	0.3	Silk FM	Macclesfield
166)	106.9	0.1	Your R.	Helensburgh
15)	107.0	0.5	The Bee	Blackburn
113)	107.0	0.1	Isle of Wight R.	Chillerton Down
4)	107.0	0.1	Oak FM	Loughborough
90)	107.0	0.2	Jack FM Berks	Reading
135)	107.0	0.62	Q Radio	Ballymena
103)	107.0	1	Sunshine R.	Monmouth
33)	107.1	0.16	Capital Xtra	N. London
108)	107.1	0.5	Trax FM	Doncaster
48)	107.1	0.14	Speysound R*	Aviemore
46)	107.1	0.12	Star R.	Ely
147)	107.1	0.1	Stray FM	Ilkley & Pateley Br.
13)	107.1	0.625	Argyll FM	Ballygroggan
116)	107.1	0.1	Rugby FM	Rugby
3)	107.1	0.1	Signal 107	Oswestry
181)	107.2	0.6	An R*	Daliburgh
135)	107.2	0.25	Q Radio	Dungannon
107)	107.2	0.2	The Breeze	Winchester
22)	107.2	0.18	Wire FM	Warrington
110)	107.2	0.2	Rutland R.	Oakham
137)	107.2	0.2	Juice	Brighton
63)	107.2	0.1	KMFM	Thanet
84)	107.2	0.66	The Breeze	Bristol
3)	107.2	0.2	Signal 107	Kidderminster
119)	107.3	1	R. Exe	Exeter
116)	107.3	0.2	Touch FM	Warwick
8)	107.3	1.25	Nation R.	Swansea
174)	107.3	0.18	Reprezent*	S. London
136)	107.4	0.2	Connect FM	Kettering
84)	107.4	0.1	The Breeze	Bridgwater
130)	107.4	0.2	Peak FM	Chesterfield
3)	107.4	0.1	Signal 107	Telford
22)	107.4	0.18	Tower FM	Bolton
107)	107.4	0.2	The Breeze	Portsmouth
102)	107.5	0.1	R. Pembrokeshire	Fishguard
80)	107.5	0.1	The Breeze	Cheltenham
126)	107.5	0.6	Time	Romford
7)	107.5	0.15	Sovereign FM	Eastbourne
84)	107.5	0.1	The Breeze	Warminster
17)	107.6	0.4	Juice FM	Liverpool
133)	107.6	0.1	The Breeze	Basingstoke
173)	107.6	0.2	Vibe*	Watford
107)	107.6	1	Fire R.	Bournemouth
67)	107.6	0.2	Banbury Sound	Banbury
63)	107.6	0.5	KMFM	Ashford, Kent
129)	107.7	0.85	KCR*	Keith
2)	107.7	0.2	Sam FM	Swindon
84)	107.7	0.1	The Breeze	Weston Super Mare
95)	107.7	0.1	Chelmsford R.	Chelmsford
58)	107.7	0.2	Kiss	Peterborough
55)	107.7	0.1	Splash FM	Worthing
3)	107.7	0.17	Signal 107	Wolverhampton
13)	107.7	0.5	Argyll FM	South Knapdale
179)	107.7	1	KCR*	Keith
149)	107.8	0.1	Arrow FM	Hastings
139)	107.8	0.8	R. Jackie	SW London
107)	107.8	0.9	The Breeze	Southampton

FM	MHz	kW	Name or Slogan	Location
147)	107.8	1	Stray FM	Skipton
4)	107.9	0.2	Oak FM	Hinckley
108)	107.9	0.1	Trax FM	Worksop
198)	107.9	0.1	Star R.	Cambridge
57)	107.9	0.2	The Breeze	Bath
65)	107.9	0.2	Jack 2	Oxford
63)	107.9	0.2	KMFM	Medway
170)	107.9	0.1	R Scilly*	St Mary's
178)	107.9	0.1	GTFM*	Pontypridd
169)	107.9	0.1*	The Cat	Crewe

+approx 250 stns of less than 0.1kW *community radio stns
H. of tr: Most stns operate 24h Some stns carry automated prgrs outside peak hours

MAJOR COMMERCIAL RADIO GROUPS:

CELADOR RADIO ✉ 39 Long Acre, London WC2E 9LG ☎ 20 7845 6800 **W:** celador.co.uk
BAUER MEDIA RADIO ✉ 1 Golden Square, London W1W 9DJ ☎ 20 7434 1215 **W:** bauermedia.co.uk
GLOBAL RADIO ✉ 30 Leicester Square, London WC2H 7LA ☎ 20 7766 6000 🖷 20 7766 6111 **W:** thisisglobal.com/radio
UKRD GROUP Ltd ✉ Unit 10, Barncoose Ind. Est, Redruth TR15 3RQ ☎ 1209 310435 🖷 1209 310406 **W:** ukrd.com
UTV MEDIA plc ✉ Ormeau Rd., Belfast BT7 1EB ☎ 28 9032 8122 🖷 9024 6695 **W:** utvmedia.com

Addresses & other information

1) Radio House, Bridge Rd, Southall UB2 4AT ☎ 20 8574 6666 **W:** sunriseradio.com – **2)** Lime Kiln, Royal Wootton Bassett, Swindon SN4 7HF ☎ 1793 858222 **W:** samfm.co.uk/swindon/ – **3)** 2nd Floor, Mander House, Wolverhampton WV1 3NB ☎ 1902 571070 **W:** signal107.co.uk – **4)** 3 Martins Court, Telford Way, Coalville LE67 3HD ☎ 1530 278200 **W:** oakfm.co.uk touchfm.co.uk – **5)** 12 Westerbrook, St Sampsons, Guernsey GY2 4QQ ☎ 1481 242000 **W:** islandfm.com – **6)** 132 George Street, Oban PA34 5NT ☎ 1631 570057 **W:** obanfm.com – **7)** 14 St Mary's Walk, Hailsham BN27 1AF ☎ 1323 442700 **W:** sovereignfm.com – **8)** St Hilary Transmitter, St Hilary, Cowbridge, CF71 1DP ☎ 29 21414100 **W:** nationradio.com – **9)** Eleven Brindley Place, 2 Brunswick Square, Birmingham B1 2LP ☎ 121 695 0000 **W:** capitalfm.co.uk heart.co.uk smoothradio.com – **10)** UTV, Ormeau Rd, Belfast BT7 1EB ☎ 28 9033 2105 **W:** u105.com – **11)** Springfield Rd, Hayes UB4 0TH ☎ 20 8848 8877 **W:** panjabradio.co.uk – **12)** Northgate House, St Peters Street, Colchester CO1 1HT ☎ 1206 764466 **W:** dream100.com – **13)** 27-29 Longrow, Campbeltown PA28 6ER ☎ 1586 551800 **W:** argyllfm.com – **14)** 9 Munroe Rd., Stirling FK7 7UU ☎ 1324 611164 **W:** centralfm.co.uk – **15)** 2A Petre Court, Petre Rd, Clayton-le-Moors, Accrington BB5 5HH ☎ 1282 690000 **W:** 2br.co.uk thebee.co.uk – **16)** Unit 5 Metro Centre, Dwight Rd, Watford WD18 9UD ☎ 1923 205480 **W:** heart.co.uk/watfordhemel – **17)** 33-39 Strand Str., Liverpool L1 8LT ☎ 151 242 0600 **W:** juicefm.com – **18)** 3 Crescent Ave. Mews, Plymouth PL1 3AP ☎ 1752 389532 **W:** radioplymouth.com – **19)** Craigshaw Rd, Aberdeen AB12 3AR ☎ 1224 294860 **W:** originalfm.com – **20)** 5-6 Aldergate, Tamworth, B79 7DJ ☎ 1827 318000 **W:** touchfm.co.uk – **21)** 6 Tunnell Street, St Helier, Jersey JE2 4LU ☎ 1534 888103 **W:** channel103.com – **22)** Orrell Lodge, Orrell Rd, Wigan WN5 8HJ ☎ 1942 761024 **W:** wishfm.net towerfm.co.uk wirefm.co.uk – **23)** The Pumphouse, Knebworth Park SG3 6HQ ☎ 1438 810900 **W:** bobfm.co.uk – **24)** MAZCC, 311 Stonegate Rd, Leeds LS17 6AZ ☎ 113 218 5836 **W:** radiojcom.com – **25)** 9/10 Dukes Court, Bognor Rd, Chichester PO19 8FX ☎ 1243 773600 **W:** spiritfm.net – **26)** Arbroath Infirmary, Rosemount Rd, Arbroath DD11 2AT ☎ 1241 879660 **W:** radionorthangus.co.uk – **27)** 2 Chantry Court, Chester CH1 4QN ☎ 1244 391000 **W:** dee1063.com – **28)** 9 Alba Place, Pitlochry PH16 5BH ☎ 1796 474040 **W:** heartlandfm.co.uk – **29)** Portway, Newbury RG14 1AY ☎ 1635 841600 **W:** thebreeze.com – **30)** PO Box 1063, Bridgend CF35 6WY ☎ 1656 838620 **W:** bridge.fm – **31)** Merlin House, Parc Merlin, Glan Yr Afon Ind. Est., Aberystwyth SY23 3FF ☎ 1970 229110 **W:** ceredigionradio.co.uk – **32)** Unit 4, Brunts Business Centre, Samuel Brunts Way, Mansfield NG18 2AH ☎ 1623 646666 **W:** mansfield103.co.uk – **33)** 30 Leicester Square, London WC2H 7LA ☎ 20 7766 6000 **W:** capitalfm.com Capital Xtra: capitalxtra.com Gold: mygoldmusic.co.uk LBC: lbc.co.uk XFM: radiox.co.uk – **34)** 9 Brindleyplace, 4 Oozells Square, Birmingham B1 2DJ ☎ 121 566 5200 **W:** freeradio.co.uk freeradio80s.co.uk – **35)** 67-73 Stoke Rd, Stoke-on-Trent ST4 2SR ☎ 1782 441 300 **W:** signal1.co.uk – **36)** Wellbar Central, 36 Gallowsgate, Newcastle NE1 4TD ☎ 191 440 7500 **W:** realradionorth heart.co.uk – **37)** Laser House, Waterfront Quay, Salford M50 3XW ☎ 161 662 4602 **W:** smoothradio; and realradioxs.co.uk – **38)** City Link, Nottingham NG2 4NG ☎ 115 910 6100 **W:** gem106.co.uk – **39)** Business & Innovation Centre, Sunderland Enterprise Park, Sunderland SR5 2TA ☎

191 548 1034 **W:** sun-fm.com – **40)** Radio House, John Wilson Business Park, Whitstable CT5 3QX ☎ 1227 772004 – **41)** Radio House, Franklin Rd., Brighton BN41 1AF ☎ 1273 316900 – **42)** Radio House, Atlantic Wharf, Cardiff CF10 4DJ ☎ 29 2094 2900 **W:** capitalfm.co.uk heart.co.uk – **43)** Apple Ind. Estate, Whittle Ave, Fareham PO15 5SX ☎ 1489 587600 **W:** capitalfm.co.uk – **44)** Four Winds Pavilion, 1 Pacific Quay, Glasgow G51 1EB ☎ 141 566 6106 **W:** capitalfm.co.uk – **45)** Suite 1.1, 4 Exchange Quay, Salford M5 3EE ☎ 161 662 4700 **W:** capitalfm.co.uk; mygoldmusic.co.uk – **46)** 20 Mercers Row, Cambridge CB5 8HY ☎ 1223 305107 **W:** star107.co.uk – **47)** Mowbray Drive, Blackpool FY3 7JR ☎ 1253 650300 **W:** wave965.com – **48)** Plot 4A, Dalfaber Industrial Estate, Aviemore PH22 1ST ☎ 1479 811888 **W:** speysound-radio.com – **49)** 2a Joseph's Well, Hanover Walk, Leeds LS3 1AB ☎ 113 308 5100 **W:** capitalfm.co.uk – **50)** 29 Yarmouth Rd, Norwich NR7 0EE ☎ 1603 703300 **W:** norwich999.com – **51)** Castle Quay, Castlefield, Manchester M15 4PR ☎ 161 288 5000 **W:** key103.co.uk key2radio.co.uk – **52)** St Johns Beacon, 1 Houghton Street, Liverpool L1 1RL ☎ 151 472 6800 **W:** radiocity.co.uk radiocity2.co.uk – **53)** 900 Herries Rd, Sheffield S6 1RH ☎ 114 2091000 **W:** hallamfm.co.uk hallam2.co.uk – **54)** The Boathouse, Commercial Rd, Hull HU1 2SG ☎ 1482 325141 **W:** vikingfm.co.uk viking2.co.uk – **55)** Guildbourne Centre, Worthing BN11 1LZ ☎ 1903 210772 **W:** splashfm.com – **56)** PO Box 2000, 51 Burley Rd, Leeds LS3 1LR ☎ 113 283 5500 **W:** radioaire.co.uk – **57)** The Tramshed, Beehive Yard, Walcot St, Bath BA1 5BB ☎ 1225 731318 **W:** thebreeze.com – **58)** 1 Golden Square, London W1F 9DJ ☎ 20 7434 1215 **W:** Magic: magic.co.uk Kiss: kissfmuk.com Absolute: absoluteradio.co.uk – **59)** Addr as 61 **W:** tfmradio.co.uk tfm2.co.uk – **60)** St Paul's Square, Preston PR1 1XA ☎ 1772 477700 **W:** Rock FM: rockfm.co.uk rockfm2.co.uk – **61)** 55 Degrees North, Pilgrim St., Newcastle upon Tyne NE1 6BF ☎ 191 230 6100 **W:** metroradio.co.uk metroradio2.co.uk – **62)** Stormyhill Rd, Portree IV51 9DT ☎ 1478 611796– **W:** cuillinfm.co.uk – **63)** Medway House, Sir Thomas Longley Rd, , Medway City Estate, Rochester ME2 4DU ☎ 1634 711079 **W:** kmfm.co.uk – **64)** 7 Blackhouse Circle, Blackhouse Industrial Estate, Peterhead AB42 1BN ☎ 1779 491012 **W:** wavesfm.com – **65)** 270 Woodstock Rd, Oxford OX2 7NW ☎ 1865 315980 **W:** jackfmoxfordshire.co.uk – **66)** PO Box 971, Llanelli SA15 1YH ☎ 1267 679250 **W:** radiocarmarthenshire.co.uk scarletfm.com – **67)** Colin Saunders Innovation Centre, Mewburn Rd., Banbury OX16 9PA ☎ 1295 661070 **W:** banburysound.co.uk – **68)** Planet House, 2 Woodhouse St. Hull HU9 1RJ ☎ 1482 333999 **W:** kcfm.co.uk – **69)** Chapel Quarter, Maid Marian Way, Nottingham NG1 6HQ ☎ 115 986 1066 **W:** capitalfm.co.uk; mygoldmusic.co.uk – **70)** Kirkham House, John Comyn Drive, Worcester WR3 7NS ☎ 1905 545510 **W:** freeradio.co.uk – **71)** 5 Abbey Court, Fraser Rd, Bedford, MK44 3WH ☎ 1234 235010 – **72)** 4ᵗʰ Floor CBX 2 East, Midsummer Blvd, Milton Keynes MK9 2EA ☎ 1908 591600 – **73)** 11 Buchanan Str., Dundee, DD4 6SD ☎ 1382 901000 **W:** wave102.co.uk – **74)** PO Box 106, High Peak SK23 0DJ ☎ 1298 813144 **W:** highpeakradio.co.uk – **75)** Mansegate, Gairloch IV21 2LR ☎ 870 712106 **W:** 2lr.co.uk – **76)** Bridge Studios, Eastgate Centre, Gloucester GL1 1SS ☎ 1452 572400 – **77)** Breck Farm, Stody, Norfolk NR24 2ER ☎ 1263 860808 **W:** northnorfolkradio.com – **78)** PO Box 1021, Neath SA11 9BF **W:** nationhits.com – **79)** 72 Middle Street, Yeovil BA20 1DJ ☎ 1935 848488 **W:** thebreeze.com – **80)** 309 High Str. , Cheltenham GL50 3HW ☎ 1242 227559 **W:** thebreeze.com – **81)** Unit 6, 10-14 Hollybush Gdns., London E2 9QP ☎ 20 7729 4333 **W:** betarbangla.org.uk – **82)** Hawthorn Hse., Exeter Business Park, Exeter EX1 3QS ☎ 1392 444444 – **83)** Panjabi Centre, 30 Sussex Rd, Southall UB2 5EG ☎ 20 8564 9591 **W:** desiradio.org.uk – **84)** County Gates, Ashton Rd, Bristol BS3 2JH ☎ 117 966 6107 **W:** thebreeze.com – **85)** 10 Wheal Kitty Workshops, St Agnes TR5 0RD ☎ 1872 554400 – **86)** 1 Passage Str., Bristol BS2 0JF ☎ 117 984 3200 – **87)** Chiseldon House, Stonehill Green, Westlea, Swindon SN5 7HB ☎ 1793 663000 – **88)** 2 Enterprise House, Chivers Way, Histon, Cambridge CB24 9ZR ☎ 1233 623800 – **89)** The Chase, Calcot, Reading RG31 7RB ☎ 118 9454400 – **90)** Radio House, Madejski Stadium, Reading RG2 0FN ☎ 118 986 2555 **W:** jackfmberkshire.com – **91)** Haig House, Haig Business Park, Markinch, Fife KY7 6AQ ☎ 1592 753753 **W:** kingdomfm.co.uk – **92)** 31 Glebe Rd, Chelmsford CM1 1QG ☎ 1254 524500 – **93)** 42 Southall Str, Manchester M3 1LQ ☎ 161 288 1000 **W:** asiansoundradio.co.uk – **94)** 10 Station Rd., Burgess Hill RH15 9DQ ☎ 1444 301064 **W:** brightfm.net – **95)** Icon Bldg., Western Esplanade, Southend-on-Sea SS1 1EE ☎ 1702 455070 **W:** southendradio.com chelmsfordradio.co.uk – **96)** St Monicas House, Windmill Lane, Ashbourne DE6 1EY ☎ 1335 346967 **W:** ashbourneradio.co.uk – **97)** The Stanley Centre, Kelvin Way, Crawley RH10 9SE ☎ 1293 636000 **W:** mercuryfm.co.uk – **98)** 22 Chapter Street, London SW1P 4NP ☎ 20 7316 1300 **W:** premier.org.uk – **99)** Friars Square Studios, 11 Bourbon Street, Aylesbury HP20 2PZ ☎ 1296 399396 **W:** mix96.co.uk – **100)** The Studios, Mold Rd, Wrexham LL11 4AF ☎ 1978 752200 **W:** capitalfm.com – **101)** Lakeland Food Park, Crook Rd, Kendal LA8 0QJ ☎ 1539 737 380 **W:** lakelandradio.

co.uk – **102)** Unit 14, Old School Estate, Station Rd, Narberth SA67 7DU ☎ 1834 887160 **W:** radiopembrokeshire.com – **103)** Suite 5, Penn House, Broad Str. Hereford HR4 9AP ☎ 1432 360246 **W:** sunshineradio.co.uk – **104)** St George's Plain, 47-49 Colegate, Norwich NR3 1DB ☎ 1603 671100 – **105)** Radio House, Orion Court, Gt Blakenham, Ipswich IP6 0LW ☎ 473 836102 **W:** town102.com – **106)** New Augustus Str., Bradford BD1 5LL ☎ 1274 203040 **W:** pulse.co.uk, pulse2.net – **107)** Roman Landing, Kingsway, Southampton SO14 1BN ☎ 845 466 1107 **W:** samfm.co.uk/southcoast/ jackradio.com fireradio.co.uk – **108)** 5 Sidings Court, Doncaster DN4 5NU ☎ 1302 341166 **W:** dearnefm.co.uk ridingsfm.co.uk rotherfm.co.uk traxfm.co.uk – **109)** PO Box 969, 24 St George's Quay, Lancaster LA1 3LD ☎ 1524 848747 **W:** thebay.co.uk – **110)** 40 Melton Rd, Oakham LE15 6AY ☎ 1572 757868 **W:** rutlandradio.co.uk – **111)** Marble Court, Lymington Rd, Torquay TQ1 4FB ☎ 1803 321055 – **112)** Witham Park, Waterside South, Lincoln LN5 7JN ☎ 1522 549900 **W:** lincsfm.co.uk compassfm.co.uk – **113)** Dodnor Park, Newport, Isle of Wight PO30 5XE ☎ 1983 822557 **W:** iwradio.co.uk – **114)** LGR house, 437 High Rd, London N12 0AP ☎ 20 8349 6950 **W:** lgr.co.uk – **115)** 18 Blackfriars Street, Kings Lynn PE30 1NN ☎ 1553 772777 **W:** klfmradio.co.uk – **116)** Holly Farm Business Park, Honily, Kenilworth CV8 1NP ☎ 1926 485600 **W:** touchfm.co.uk rugbyfm.co.uk **117)** 3 Eastgate House, Andover SP10 1EP ☎ 11264 336000 **W:** thebreeze.com – **118)** 18 Trinity Street, Dorchester DT1 1DJ ☎ 1305 250333 **W:** wessexfm.co.uk – **119)** 6a Cranmere Court, Lustleigh Close, Exeter EX2 8PW ☎ 1392 823557 **W:** radioexe.co.uk – **120)** 4 Ingate Place, London SW8 3NS ☎ 20 7627 4433 **W:** spectrumradio.net – **121)** The Shed, School Rd, Kintore, Inverurie AB51 0UX ☎ 1467 632909 **W:** necrfm.co.uk – **122)** Unit 1130, Parkway Court, Glasgow Business Park, Glasgow G69 6GA ☎ 141 781 1011 **W:** heart.co.uk smoothradio.com – **123)** 55 Leeds Rd, Bradford BD1 5AF ☎ 1274 735043 **W:** sunriseradio.fm – **124)** Market Street, Lerwick, Shetland ZE1 0JN ☎ 1595 695299 **W:** sibc.co.uk – **125)** Mill Street Industrial Estate, Ullapool IV26 2UN ☎ 1854 613131 **W:** lochbroomfm.com – **126)** Lambourne House, 7 Western Rd, Romford RM1 3LD ☎ 1708 731643 **W:** time1075.net – **127)** Victoria Rd, Gowerton, Swansea SA4 3AB ☎ 1792 511964 **W:** swanseasound.co.uk thewave.co.uk – **128)** Unit 11, Burway Trading Estate, Ludlow SY8 1EN ☎ 1584 873795 **W:** sunshineradio.co.uk – **129)** 59a Land Street, Keith AB55 5AN ☎ 1542 866080 **W:** kcr.fm – **130)** Radio House, Foxwood Rd, Chesterfield S41 9RF ☎ 1246 269107 **W:** peakfm.co.uk – **131)** Glan Clwyd Hospital, Bodelwyddan, Rhyl LL18 5UJ ☎ 1745 584229 **W:** rygc.co.uk – **133)** Paddington House, Festival Place, Basingstoke RG21 7LJ ☎ 1256 694000 **W:** thebreeze.com – **134)** PO Box 103.4, Lowestoft NR32 2TL ☎ 845 3451035 **W:** thebeach.co.uk – **135)** Woodside Rd Industrial Estate, Ballymena BT42 4QJ ☎ 28 2564 8777 **W:** qonair.com – **136)** 55 Headlands, Kettering NN15 7EY ☎ 1536 513664 **W:** connectfm.com – **137)** 170 North Street, Brighton BN1 1EA ☎ 1273 387107 **W:** juice-brighton.com – **138)** Sarah Moor Studios, Henshaw Str, Oldham OL1 3EN ☎ 161 621 6500 **W:** revolutiononline.co.uk – **139)** 110 Tolworth Broadway, Surbiton KT6 7JD ☎ 20 8288 1300 **W:** radiojackie.com – **140)** 1 Waterloo Place, Watson Square, Stockport SK1 3AZ ☎ 161 476 7340 **W:** imaginefm.net – **141)** PO Box 123, Dunnington, York YO19 5ZX ☎ 1904 488888 **W:** minsterfm.co.uk – **142)** Ben Nevis Estate, Claggan, Fort William PH33 6PR ☎ 1397 700007 **W:** nevisradio.co.uk – **143)** 50 Seaforth Rd, Stornoway, Isle of Lewis HS1 2SH ☎ 1851 703333 **W:** isles.fm – **144)** Arena Bldg., 85 Ormeau Rd, Belfast BT7 1SH ☎ 28 9023 4967 **W:** qonair.com – **145)** PO Box 962, Scarborough YO11 3ZP ☎ 1723 581700 **W:** yorkshirecoastradio.com – **146)** City Hall Studios, Malthouse Lane, Salisbury SP2 7QQ ☎ 1722 416644 **W:** spirefm.co.uk – **147)** The Hamlet, Hornbeam Park Avenue, Harrogate HG2 8RE ☎ 1423 522972 **W:** strayfm.com – **148)** KMS House, Bradford Street, Birmingham B12 0JD ☎ 121 753 5353 **W:** radioxl.net – **149)** Century House, 100 Menzies Rd, St Leonards-on-Sea, TN38 9BB ☎ 1424 410078 **W:** arrowfm.co.uk – **150)** Radio House, 11 Woodland Rd, Darlington DL3 7BJ ☎ 1325 341801 **W:** starradionortheast.co.uk – **151)** Radio House, 63 Melton Rd, Leicester LE4 6PN ☎ 116 261 0666 **W:** sabrasradio.com – **152)** 140 Moss Lane, Macclesfield SK11 7XE ☎ 1625 268000 **W:** silk1069.com – **153)** Kiltonga Ind. Estate, Newtownards, Co Down BT23 4ES ☎ 28 9181 5555 **W:** downtown.co.uk, coolfm.co.uk – **154)** Dolphin House, North Street, Guildford GU1 4AA ☎ 1483 300964 **W:** 964eagle.co.uk – **155)** Abbottswell Rd, West Tullos, Aberdeen AB12 3AJ ☎ 1224 337000 **W:** northsound1.co.uk – **156)** 6 North Isla Street, Dundee DD3 7JQ ☎ 1382 200800 **W:** tayfm.co.uk tay2.co.uk – **157)** Unit 40, Loreburn Centre, High Street, Dumfries DG1 2BD ☎ 1387 250999 **W:** westsoundradio.com – **158)** Clydebank Business Park, Clydebank, Glasgow G81 2RX ☎ 141 565 2200 **W:** clyde1.com – **159)** Forth House, Forth Street, Edinburgh EH1 3LE ☎ 131 556 9255 **W:** forthone.com – **160)** Radio House, 54a Holmston Rd, Ayr KA7 3BE ☎ 1292 283662 **W:** westsound.co.uk, westfm.co.uk – **161)** Scorguie Place, Inverness IV3 8UJ ☎ 1463 224433 **W:** mfr.co.uk – **161a)** Neil Gunn Drive, Thurso KW14 7QU ☎ 01847 890000 **W:** caithnessfm.co.uk –**161c)** Old Thomas Walker Hospital, Charlotte Street, Fraserburgh AB43 9LS ☎ 1346 512010 – **162)** Tweedside Park, Galashiels TD1 3TD ☎ 1896 759444 **W:** radioborders.com – **163)** PO Box 964, Carlisle CA1 3NG ☎ 1228 818964 **W:** cfmradio.com – **164)** 5 Manor Court, Barnes Wallis Rd, Segensworth East, Fareham PO15 5TH ☎ 1489 481050 **W:** wave105.com – **165)** Barncoose Ind. Estate, Wilson Way, Redruth TR15 3XX ☎ 1209 314400 **W:** piratefm.co.uk – **166)** Carus House, 201 Dumbarton Rd, Clydebank G81 4XJ ☎ 1389 744435 **W:** yourradiofm.com – **167)** 4 Ingate Place, London SW8 3NS ☎ 20 7627 4433 **W:** lycadilse.com, radio1458.com – **168)** 11 Rawson Rd, Bradford BD1 3SH ☎ 1274 771677 **W:** bcbradio.co.uk – **169)** C206 South Cheshire College, Danebank Ave., Crewe CW2 8AB ☎ 1270 654686 **W:** thisisthecat.com – **170)** Porthmellon, St Mary's, Isles of Scilly TR21 0JY ☎1720 423417 **W:** scillytoday.com – **171)**–**172)** 24 Swete Str., London E13 0BS ☎ 20 8471 9111 **W:** voiceofafricaradio.com – **173)** 59 Clarendon Rd, Watford WD17 1LA ☎1923 888650 **W:** vibe1076.co.uk – **174)** 91-93 Queens Rd, London SE15 2EZ ☎20 7639 8512 **W:** reprezent.org.uk – **175)** Old Truman Brewery, 91 Brick Lane, London E1 6QL ☎ 20 7247 7252 **W:** rinse.fm – **176)** 12 Ffordd yr Efail, Llangefni LL77 7ER ☎ 1248 722224 **W:** monfm.net – **177)** Unit A, Tregony Industrial Estate, Truro TR2 5TL ☎1872 248494 **W:** thehubradio.co.uk – **178)** Pinewood Studios, Pinewood Ave, Rhydyfelin, Pontypridd CF37 5EA ☎1443 406111 **W:** gtfm.co.uk – **179)** 59a Land Street, Keith AB55 5AN ☎ 1542 886080 **W:** kcr.fm **180)** 122 Potternewton Lane, Leeds, LS7 2EG ☎113 217 4906 **W:** akashradioleeds.co.uk – **181)** The Bunker, East Camp, Balivanich, Isle of Benbecula HS7 5LA **W:** anradio.info

MANX RADIO (Comm.)
✉ Broadcasting House, Douglas Head, Douglas, Isle of Man IM1 5BW ☎ 1624 682600 🖶 1624 682604 **W:** manxradio.com **E:** reception@manxradio.com **L.P:** MD: Anthony Pugh
MW: 1368kHz Foxdale 20kW **FM:** 89.0MHz Snaefell 4kW / 97.2MHz Carnane 11kW / 103.7MHz Jurby 4kW
D.Prgr: 24h Separate prgrs on MW at various times & during Manx TT motorcycle events

ENERGY FM (Comm.)
✉ PO Box 986, Douglas, Isle of Man IM99 2TB ☎ 1624 611936 **W:** energyfm.net **FM:** 91.2MHz Snaefell 1.2kW, 93.4MHz Jurby 1.2kW, 98.6MHz Carnane 2kW (+ relays on 98.4/102.4/105.2) **D.Prgr:** 24h
3FM (Comm.)
✉ 45 Victoria Street, Douglas, Isle of Man IM1 3RS ☎ 1624 616333 🖶 1624 614333 **W:** three.fm
FM: 104.2MHz (Ramsey & Mull Hill), 105MHz (Carnane 2kW), 106.6MHz (Snaefell), 106.2MHz (Peel) **D.Prgr:** 24h

BRITISH FORCES BROADCASTING SERVICE
(a division of Services Sound & Vision Corp.)
✉ SSVC, Narcot Lane, Gerrards Cross SL9 8TN ☎ 1494 878354 🖶 1494 878552 **E:** adminofficer@bfbs.com **W:** bfbs.com/radio/
L.P: Contr BFBS Radio: Nicky Ness
BFBS UK in English **FM:** 89.3MHz (Blandford), 98.5MHz (Edinburgh), 100.6MHz (Lisburn), 101MHz (Belfast), 102.5MHz (Aldershot), 106.5MHz (Antrim), 106.8MHz (Salisbury), 106.9MHz (Catterick), 107MHz (Colchester). **MW:** Low power relays on 1287kHz (BovingtonGlencourse). **DAB:** Digital One (national); Brize Norton (Oxon)
BFBS Gurkha Radio in Nepali, news hourly in English. **MW:** Low power sce on 1134kHz (Bramcote, Catterick, Sandhurst), 1251kHz (York), 1278kHz (Folkestone-main studio & Stafford), 1287kHz (Blandford, Brecon, Maidstone)
See Ascension Island, Belgium, Bosnia, British Indian Ocean Territory, Brunei, Canada, Cyprus, Falkland Islands, Germany, Gibraltar, Nepal, Netherlands for other BFBS sces.

Restricted Service Licences (RSL) Licences are granted for low power special event stns operating for up to 28 days (occ. longer) usually on FM (occ. on MW)
LPAM (Low Power AM stations) There are currently about 45 stns on the air (including BFBS relays - see above) with txs of 0.001kW e.r.p. Freqs used: 1134, 1251, 1278, 1287, 1350, 1386, 1404, 1431, 1449, 1575kHz
LPFM (Low Power VHF/FM stations) There are currently about 20 stns on the air, most on 87.7MHz, with txs of typically 50mW

COMMUNITY RADIO Small-scale, low-power, non-profit community radio sces to serve a particular neighbourhood. Most on FM with 25W. approx 235 stns on air as of October 2015. MW community radio sces and FM sces above 100W are included in the main frequency lists above. For updated listing of short-term RSLs, long-term

RSLs (LPAMs) and Community Radio see Radio Broadcast Licensing at **W:** licensing.ofcom.org.uk

Community Audio Distribution Systems (CADS) licence-exempt service for religious and community events using 27MHz Citizens Band

UNITED STATES OF AMERICA

L.T: See World Time Table (DST where applicable: 13 Mar - 6 Nov) — **Pop:** 319 million — **Pr.L:** English — **E.C:** 60Hz, 110V — **ITU:** USA

FEDERAL COMMUNICATIONS COMMISSION (FCC)
(Independent U.S. Govt. agency)
✉ 455 12th St SW, Washington, D.C 20554 ☎ +1 888 2255322 🖶 +1 866 4180232 **E:** fccinfo@fcc.gov **W:** fcc.gov
L.P: Chmn: Tom Wheeler; Commissioners: Mignon Clyburn, Ajit Pay, Michael O'Rielly, Jessica Rosenworcel
The FCC regulates communications by radio, television, wire, satellite, and cable in all 50 U.S. states, the District of Columbia and U.S. territories.

NATIONAL ASSOCIATION OF BROADCASTERS (NAB)
✉ 1771 N St NW, Washington DC 20036 ☎ +1 202 4295300 **E:** nab@nab.org **W:** nab.org **L.P:** Pres/CEO: Gordon H. Smith
The NAB is a trade association for broadcasters that advances the interests of its members (more than 8,300 local radio & TV stns, as well as networks) in federal government, industry and public affairs.

NATIONAL ASSOCIATION OF SHORTWAVE BROADCASTERS, Inc (NSAB)
✉ 175 Fontainebleau Blvd., Suite 1N4, Miami, FL 33172 ☎ +1 863 7630281 🖶 +1 863 7631034 **E:** nasbshortwave@gmail.com **W:** shortwave.org **L.P:** Pres: Glenn W. Tapley, Vice Pres: Brady Murrey
The NASB represents the privately-owned shortwave radio stations in the United States and promotes shortwave broadcasting in the U.S. and around the world.

NATIONAL FEDERATION OF COMMUNITY BROADCASTERS (NFCB)
✉ 1308 Clear Fork Rd, Crawford, CO 81415 ☎ +1 970 2793411 **W:** nfcb.org **L.P:** Pres: Beverly Hacker

NATIONAL RELIGIOUS BROADCASTERS (NRB)
✉ 9510 Technology Drive, Manassas, VA 20110 ☎🖶 +1 703 3307000 **E:** info@nrb.org **W:** nrb.org **L.P:** Pres/CEO: Jerry A. Johnson

MAJOR PRODUCERS/DISTRIBUTORS OF NETWORK PROGRAMMING FOR LOCAL STATIONS

ABC RADIO (ABC, Inc - a division of The Walt Disney Co)
✉ 125 West End Avenue, New York, NY 10023 ☎ +1 212 4565101 **W:** abcradio.com **L.P:** Vice Pres/GM: Steve Jones

AMERICAN PUBLIC MEDIA GROUP (Non-Comm)
✉ 480 Cedar St, St. Paul, MN 55101 ☎ +1 651 2901373 🖶 +1 651 2901415 **W:** americanpublicmedia.org
L.P: Pres/CEO: Jon McTaggart

AMERICAN URBAN RADIO NETWORKS (SHERIDIAN BROADCASTING CORP)
✉ 960 Penn Avenue, Suite 200, Pittsburgh, PA 15222 ☎ +1 412 4564018 🖶 +1 412 4564022 **W:** aurn.com
L.P: Chmn/GM (Sheridian Broadcasting Corp): Ronald R. Davenport

BIBLE BROADCASTING NETWORK, Inc (Rlg)
✉ 7315 Pineville Matthews Rd, Charlotte, NC 28226 ☎ +1 704 5416446 **W:** bbnradio.org **L.P:** Pres: Lowell Davey

BOTT RADIO NETWORK (BOTT COMMUNICATIONS, Inc) (Rlg)
✉ 10550 Barkley St, Suite 100, Overland Park, KS 66212 ☎ +1 913 6427770 🖶 +1 913 6421319 **E:** comments@bottradionetwork.com **W:** bottradionetwork.com **L.P:** Pres/CEO (Bott Comm.): Rich Bott

CBS RADIO, Inc (Division of CBS Corporation)
✉ 1271 Avenue of the Americas, 44th floor, New York, NY 10020 ☎ +1 212 6499600 **W:** cbsradio.com **L.P:** CEO: Andre J. Fernandez

COMPASS MEDIA NETWORKS, LLC
✉ 32 Elm Place, Rye, NY 10580 ☎ +1 914 6005099 🖶 +1 914 8404137 **W:** compassmedianetworks.com **L.P:** CEO: Peter Kosann

CUMULUS MEDIA, Inc
3280 Peachtree Rd NW, Suite 2300, Atlanta, GA 30305 ☎ +1 404 9490700 📠 +1 404 9490740 **W:** cumulus.com
L.P: Pres/CEO: Mary G.Berner

DISNEY AND ESPN MEDIA NETWORKS, Inc
(Division of The Walt Disney Company)
3800 W Alameda Ave, Ste B, Burbank, CA 91505 ☎ +1 818 5697500 **W:** espnradioaffiliatezone.com
L.P: Affiliate Sales & Marketing: Justin Connolly

FAMILY LIFE NETWORK (FAMILY LIFE MINISTRIES, Inc) (Rlg)
7634 Campbell Creek Rd, Bath, NY 14810 ☎ +1 607 7764151 📠 +1 607 7766929 **W:** fln.org
L.P: Pres (Family Life Ministries): Rick Snavely

FAMILY LIFE RADIO (FAMILY LIFE COMMUNICA-TIONS, Inc) (Rlg)
7355 N. Oracle Rd, Tucson, AZ 85704 ☎ +1 520 7426976 📠 +1 520 7426979 **E:** correspondence@flc.org **W:** myflr.org; flc.org **L.P:** Pres (Family Life Communications): Randy Carlson

FOX NEWS RADIO (Fox Entertainment Group, Inc - a subsidiary of 21st Century Fox, Inc)
1211 Avenue of the Americas, 18th floor, New York, NY 10036 ☎ +1 212 3015439 **E:** foxnewsradio@foxnews.com **W:** radio.foxnews.com **L.P:** Chmn/CEO (Fox News Channel): Roger Ailes

GENESIS COMMUNICATIONS NETWORK (GENESIS COMMUNICATIONS, Inc)
4300 West Cypress St, Suite 1040, Tampa, FL 33607 ☎ +1 813 2811040 📠 +1 813 2811948 **W:** gcnlive.com; radiogenesis.com **L.P:** CEO (Genesis Communications): Bruce Maduri

IHEARTMEDIA, Inc
200 E. Basse Rd, San Antonio, TX 78209 ☎ +1 210 8222828 📠 +1 210 8222299 **W:** iheartmedia.com **L.P:** Pres: John E. Hogan

NATIONAL PUBLIC RADIO, Inc (Non-Comm)
635 Massachusetts Avenue NW, Washington, DC 20001 ☎ +1 202 5133232 📠 +1 202 5133329 **W:** npr.org **L.P:** CEO: Jarl Mohn

PREMIERE RADIO NETWORKS, Inc (Subsidiary of iHeartMedia, Inc)
15260 Ventura Boulevard, Suite 400, Sherman Oaks, CA 91403 ☎ +1 818 3775300 📠 +1 818 4615490 **E:** sales@premiereradio.com **W:** premiereradio.com **L.P:** Chmn/CEO: Steve C. Lehman

RADIO 74 (RADIO 74 INTERNATIONALE) (Rlg)
1209 West Robert Avenue, Ridgecrest, CA 93556-0716 ☎ +1 760 3752355 **E:** contact@radio74.org **W:** radio74.net
L.P: Pres: Everet W. Witzel

RELEVANT RADIO (STARBOARD MEDIA FOUNDA-TION, Inc) (Rlg)
1496 Bellevue St, Suite 202, Green Bay, WI 54311 ☎ +1 920 8841460 📠 +1 920 4659986 **E:** info@relevantradio.com **W:** relevantradio.com
L.P: Chmn/CEO (Starboard Media Found.): Thomas Vorpahl

SALEM RADIO NETWORK (SALEM MEDIA GROUP, Inc)
4880 Santa Rosa Rd, Camarillo, CA 93012 ☎ +1 805 9870400 **W:** salemmedia.com **L.P:** CEO (Salem Media Group): Edward G. Atsinger

UNIVISION RADIO (UNIVISION COMMUNICATIONS, Inc)
605 Third Avenue, 33rd Floor, New York, NY 10158 ☎ +1 212 4555200 **W:** univision.com
L.P: CEO/Pres/Dir (Univision Communications): Randy Falco
Univision Radio is a Spanish language network.

USA RADIO NETWORKS (CROSS PLATFORM MEDIA, LLC)
819 W. Hargett St, Raleigh, NC 27603 ☎ +1 844 5000812 **E:** info@usaradionetworks.com **W:** usaradionetworks.com
L.P: CEO (Cross Platform Media): Sam Hassell

WESTWOOD ONE, Inc (Subsidiary of Cumulus Media, Inc)
220 West 42nd St, Candler Tower, New York, NY 10036 ☎ +1 212 9672888 **W:** westwoodone.com **L.P:** CEO/Dir: Paul Caine

LOCAL STATIONS
There are more than 16,600 local stns operating on AM and FM. As of June 30, 2015: 4,698 AM stns; 6,666 FM (Full Power) Commercial stns; 4,091 FM (Full power) Educational stns; 1,149 FM Low power stns (LPFM). In addition, there are 6,366 FM translators and boosters.

Call Letter Assigments: For broadcasting stns in the U.S., callsigns consist of four letters, beginning with K or W, to which "-FM" or "-LP" may be added for FM stns. Calls with leading K are assigned to stns west of the Mississippi River (incl. Guam and No. Mariana Is), while a leading W is assigned to broadcast stns east of the Mississippi (incl. Puerto Rico). Exceptions: a few stns east of the Mississippi using a "K" callsign and stns west of the Mississippi using a "W" callsign will be noted. These are old callsigns that were assigned for various reasons (e.g. reflecting the initial geographic division in the early days of U.S. radio, or were requested by the stn owner) and are retained by special permission. Similarly some very old callsigns using only three letters may be retained by the stns that were once assigned these callsigns.
Program Formats: Especially in multi-station markets, **commercial radio stns** concentrate their prgrs to appeal to a given segment of the population or a given listening taste. Many stns devote their entire broadcast day to news and/or talk prgrs, or sports coverage. Others specialize in various types of music: Hit music (e.g. Contemporary Hit Radio), Country music, Classic Hits or Oldies, African American music (e.g. Urban Contemporary), Latin music (e.g. Mexican Regional), Classical music, etc. The number of Spanish language stns targeting the Hispanic audience has increased considerably in recent years. Some stns address other ethnic communities (e.g. African, Asian, European), incl. relays of foreign radio prgrs. Many stns change to a new format from time to time. **Non-commercial Educational radio stns** include public radio, religious radio, community radio, college radio, high school radio, etc.
Local radio stns make extensive use of programming produced and/or distributed by network providers (typically fed by satellite), and many may have only one local identification per hour, usually on top of the hour.
AM Stations: In the U.S. the AM band 540-1600kHz & expanded band 1610-1700kHz is divided into "clear", "regional" and "local" channels, and the AM stns into domestic classes A, B, C, D. "Clear channel" stns in the highest class A today have a protected area extending to 750 miles (ca 1200 km). Outside this area, the frequencies are also used by other stns. In order to combat interference from neighbouring countries, a few stns have been granted temporary licenses for increased powers, and many daytime stns may now operate after local sunset, using low or very low powers. 530kHz is reserved for very low power Travelers' Information Stations (TIS).
Developments: With the large decrease in AM listening in favour of FM, an increasing number of AM stns go off the air for a longer or shorter period due to economic difficulties. After a silence period of 12 consecutive months, the license expires. Stns on the so-called "regional channels", previously limited to 5kW power, may now apply for up to 50kW (1610-1700kHz: up to 10kW), limited only by the required protection of other stns. Relaxed ownership rules have allowed groups of co-owned stns to form in larger markets with the group stns often broadcasting from a common studio address.
Travelers' Information Stations (TIS): State and local governments may create state-wide networks to provide non-commercial public safety information via radio using LPFM stations or AM stns (530-1700kHz) of up to 10 Watts.
Low Power FM Stations (LPFM): This type of FM license is open to non-commercial educational entities and public safety/travelers' information entities, but not individuals or commercial operations.
Digital Broadcasting: A number of stns are transmitting digital audio in the FM or AM band (as regular service or test), using the IBOC system. With this hybrid system digital signals are emitted on both sides of a transmitter's analogue signal, so that both analogue and digital receivers can recover the audio. Analogue listeners may experience the IBOC signal as an increased noise level on freqs adjacent to the nominal channel of the emitting transmitter. While in the AM band the IBOC signal is limited to one digital audio channel, IBOC in the FM band offers the option for multicasting on several digital subchannels. Most stns are using this possibility to transmit various additional programme feeds. As of 31 August, 2015 there were 240 AM and 1835 FM stns licensed to air digital signals. A directory of stns carrying IBOC transmissions and the content of their subchannels can be found on **W:** hdradio.com/stations, a list of AM stns with IBOC trs: **W:** topazdesigns.com/iboc/station-list.html.

MEDIUMWAVE
Call: Station call letters. All stns are required to announce their actual call letters and city of licence once per hour as close as possible to the top of the hour.
Ant: Type of licence and use of directional antenna. The symbols mean as follows: **U** means Unlimited Time operation, i.e. up to 24 hours a day. **U1** without directional antenna, **U2** with directional antenna at night, **U3** with directional antenna at all hours, same pattern, day and night, **U4** with directional antenna at all hours, different patterns day

and night, **U5** with directional antenna daytime, non-directional at night, **U6** with directional antenna at night and during critical hours, **U7** with different directional patterns for day, critical hours and night, **U8** as U7 but non-directional day, **U9** means directional day and night (different patterns), but non-directional during critical hours (usually on reduced power), **U10** means directional during critical hours only, **U11** means separate patterns for daytime and critical hours, nondirectional nights. **D** is daytime operation (between local sunrise and local sunset. The symbols mean as follows: **D1** without directional antenna, **D2** with directional antenna during critical hours only, **D3** with directional antenna, **D4** with directional antenna, differenct patterns during critical and non-critical hours, **D5** with directional antenna except during critical hours. **L** is limited time, and means a stn West of the dominant stn can operate from as early as sunrise at the dominant stns location; A stn East of the dominant stn can operate as late as the dominant stns sunset. Number indicates directional pattern as under "U" above.

D: Daytime power in kW. **N:** Nighttime power in kW.

City of License and Sta: City and State that the license has been issued to. **NB:** Hawaii and Alaska are listed under separate country headings.

Scope: Due to the large number of stns in operation, the listing has been limited to stns operating at 2.5kW or more during daytime. Stations on 530 (TIS) and on the "local channels" 1230, 1240, 1340, 1400, 1450, 1490 kHz have been omitted due to their low power.

STATES: AL Alabama, AR Arkansas, AZ Arizona, CA California, CO Colorado, CT Connecticut, DE Delaware, FL Florida, GA Georgia, IA Iowa, ID Idaho, IL Illinois, IN Indiana, KS Kansas, KY Kentucky, LA Louisiana, MA Massachusetts, ME Maine, MI Michigan, MN Minnesota, MO Missouri, MS Mississippi, MT Montana, NC North Carolina, ND North Dakota, NE Nebraska, NH New Hampshire, NJ New Jersey, NM New Mexico, NV Nevada, NY New York, OH Ohio, OK Oklahoma, OR Oregon, PA Pennsylvania, RI Rhode Island, SC South Carolina, SD South Dakota, TN Tennessee, TX Texas, UT Utah, VA Virginia, VT Vermont, WA Washington, WI Wisconsin, WV West Virginia, WY Wyoming.

Digital Broadcasting: # Stns reported transmitting IBOC signals (regularly or intermittently) at day- and/or nighttime

MW	Call	kHz	Ant.	D	N	Sta	City of License
		530	Various stns of 0.01kW or less (TIS)				
1	KMLB	540	U1	4	0.02	LA	Monroe
2	KNMX	540	U3	5	0.02	NM	Las Vegas
3	KRXA	540	U4	10	0.5	CA	Carmel Valley
4	KVIP	540	U1	2.5	0.01	CA	Redding
5	KWMT	540	U3	5	0.17	IA	Fort Dodge
6	WASG	540	U1	2.5	0.01	AL	Daphne
7	WDAK	540	U1	4	0.03	GA	Columbus
8	WETC	540	U4	4	0.5	NC	Wendell-Zebulon
9	WFLF	540	U4	50	46	FL	Pine Hills
10	WKFN	540	U1	4	0.05	TN	Clarksville
11	WLIE	540	U4	10	0.22	NY	Islip
12	WRGC	540	U1	5	0.14	NC	Sylva
13	WWCS	540	U4	5	0.5	PA	Canonsburg
14	KARI	550	U4	5	2.5	WA	Blaine
15	KBOW	550	U2	5	1	MT	Butte
16	KCRS	550	U4	5	1	TX	Midland
17	KFRM	550	U3	5	0.11	KS	Salina
18	KFYI	#550	U1	5	1	AZ	Phoenix
19	KFYR	550	U2	5	5	ND	Bismarck
20	KOAC	550	U4	5	5	OR	Corvallis
21	KRAI	550	U2	5	0.5	CO	Craig
22	KTRS	550	U2	5	5	MO	Saint Louis
23	KTSA	550	U2	5	5	TX	San Antonio
24	KUZZ	550	U4	5	5	CA	Bakersfield
25	WAYR	550	U4	5	0.5	FL	Fleming Island
26	WDEV	550	U4	5	1	VT	Waterbury
27	WDUN	550	U4	10	2.5	GA	Gainesville
28	WGR	550	U2	5	5	NY	Buffalo
29	WKRC	550	U4	5	1	OH	Cincinnati
30	WSAU	550	U4	15	20	WI	Wausau
31	WSVA	550	U2	5	1	VA	Harrisonburg
32	KLVI	560	U2	5	5	TX	Beaumont
33	KLZ	#560	U3	5	5	CO	Denver
34	KMON	560	U4	5	5	MT	Great Falls
35	KPQ	560	U4	5	5	WA	Wenatchee
36	KSFO	560	U2	5	5	CA	San Francisco
37	KWTO	560	U4	5	4	MO	Springfield
38	WEBC	560	U4	5	5	MN	Duluth
39	WFIL	560	U4	5	5	PA	Philadelphia
40	WFRB	560	U1	5	0.05	MD	Frostburg
41	WGAN	560	U4	5	5	ME	Portland
42	WHBQ	560	U4	5	1	TN	Memphis
43	WHYN	560	U3	5	1	MA	Springfield
44	WIND	560	U4	5	5	IL	Chicago
45	WJLS	560	U2	4.5	0.47	WV	Beckley
46	WMIK	560	U1	2.5	0.08	KY	Middlesboro
47	WNSR	560	U4	4.5	0.07	TN	Brentwood
48	WOOF	560	U1	5	0.11	AL	Dothan
49	WQAM	560	U1	5	1	FL	Miami
50	WVOC	560	U2	5	5	SC	Columbia
51	KCFJ	570	U1	5	0.04	CA	Alturas
52	KLAC	570	U2	5	5	CA	Los Angeles
53	KLIF	570	U2	5	5	TX	Dallas
54	KNRS	570	U3	5	5	UT	Salt Lake City
55	KVI	570	U1	5	5	WA	Seattle
56	KWML	570	U2	5	0.15	NM	Las Cruces
57	WAAX	570	U2	5	0.5	AL	Gadsden
58	WKBN	570	U2	5	5	OH	Youngstown
59	WMCA	570	U3	5	5	NY	New York
60	WNAX	570	U2	5	5	SD	Yankton
61	WSPZ	570	U4	5	1	MD	Bethesda
62	WSYR	570	U2	5	5	NY	Syracuse
63	WTBN	570	U4	5	5	FL	Pinellas Park
64	WWNC	570	U1	5	5	NC	Asheville
65	KIDO	580	U2	5	5	ID	Nampa
66	KJMJ	580	U2	5	1	LA	Alexandria
67	KMJ	580	U3	50	50	CA	Fresno
68	KSAZ	580	U2	5	0.39	AZ	Marana
69	KUBC	580	U2	5	1	CO	Montrose
70	WCHS	580	U2	5	5	WV	Charleston
71	WDBO	580	U2	5	5	FL	Orlando
72	WGAC	#580	U2	5	0.84	GA	Augusta
73	WHP	#580	U2	5	5	PA	Harrisburg
74	WIBW	580	U2	5	5	KS	Topeka
75	WILL	580	U3	5	0.1	IL	Urbana
76	WKSK	580	U1	5	0.03	NC	West Jefferson
77	WKTY	580	U4	5	0.74	WI	La Crosse
78	WTAG	#580	U4	5	5	MA	Worcester
79	WTCM	580	U4	50	1.1	MI	Traverse City
80	WYHM	580	U1	5	0.04	TN	Rockwood
81	KID	590	U2	5	1	ID	Idaho Falls
82	KLBJ	590	U2	5	1	TX	Austin
83	KQNT	#590	U1	5	5	WA	Spokane
84	KSUB	590	U2	5	1	UT	Cedar City
85	KTHO	590	U2	2.5	0.5	CA	South Lake Tahoe
86	KTIE	590	U4	2.5	0.96	CA	San Bernardino
87	KUGN	590	U2	5	5	OR	Eugene
88	KXSP	590	U1	5	5	NE	Omaha
89	KZHS	590	U1	5	0.06	AR	Hot Springs
90	WARM	590	U3	5	5	PA	Scranton
91	WDIZ	590	U2	1.7	2.5	FL	Panama City
92	WDWD	590	U4	12	4.5	GA	Atlanta
93	WEZE	590	U3	5	5	MA	Boston
94	WJMS	590	U2	5	1	MI	Ironwood
95	WKZO	590	U4	5	5	MI	Kalamazoo
96	WROW	590	U4	5	1	NY	Albany
97	WVLK	590	U2	5	1	KY	Lexington
98	WCOL	600	U2	5	0.5	CO	Wellington
99	KGEZ	600	U4	5	1	MT	Kalispell
100	KOGO	#600	U4	5	5	CA	San Diego
101	KROD	600	U2	5	5	TX	El Paso
102	KSJB	600	U3	5	5	ND	Jamestown
103	KTBB	600	U2	5	2.5	TX	Tyler
104	WBOB	600	U2	5	1.8	FL	Jacksonville
105	WCAO	#600	U3	5	5	MD	Baltimore
106	WFST	600	U1	5	0.12	ME	Caribou
107	WKYH	600	U1	5	0.04	KY	Paintsville
108	WMT	600	U2	5	5	IA	Cedar Rapids
109	WREC	600	U2	5	5	TN	Memphis
110	WSJS	600	U4	5	5	NC	Winston-Salem
111	KAVL	610	U4	4.9	4	CA	Lancaster
112	KCSP	610	U2	5	5	MO	Kansas City
113	KDAL	610	U2	5	5	MN	Duluth
114	KEAR	610	U1	5	5	CA	San Francisco
115	KILT	610	U2	5	5	TX	Houston
116	KNML	610	U2	5	5	NM	Albuquerque
117	KONA	610	U4	5	5	WA	Kennewick-Richland-Pasco
118	KRTA	610	U2	2.5	5	OR	Medford
119	KVLE	610	U1	5	0.21	CO	Vail
120	KVNU	610	U2	10	1	UT	Logan
121	WAGG	610	U2	5	0.61	AL	Birmingham

MW	Call	kHz	Ant.	D	N	Sta	City of License
122	WFNZ	#610	U4	5	1	NC	Charlotte
123	WGIR	610	U4	5	1	NH	Manchester
124	WIOD	610	U4	5	5	FL	Miami
125	WTEL	610	U3	5	5	PA	Philadelphia
126	WTVN	610	U2	5	5	OH	Columbus
127	WVBE	610	U4	5	1	VA	Roanoke
128	KJOL	620	U1	5	0.07	CO	Grand Junction
129	KMKI	620	U2	5	4.5	TX	Plano
130	KPOJ	620	U2	25	10	OR	Portland
131	KTAR	#620	U2	5	5	AZ	Phoenix
132	WDAE	620	U2	5.6	5.5	FL	Saint Petersburg
133	WDNC	620	U4	5	1	NC	Durham
134	WGCV	620	U1	2.5	0.12	SC	Cayce
135	WHEN	620	U2	5	1	NY	Syracuse
136	WJDX	620	U2	5	1	MS	Jackson
137	WKHB	620	U1	5.5	0.05	PA	Irwin
138	WRJZ	620	U2	5	5	TN	Knoxville
139	WSNR	620	U4	3	7.6	NJ	Jersey City
140	WTMJ	#620	U4	50	10	WI	Milwaukee
141	WTRP	620	U1	2.5	0.12	GA	La Grange
142	WVMT	620	U4	5	5	VT	Burlington
143	WWNR	620	U1	5	0.02	WV	Beckley
144	WZON	620	U2	5	5	ME	Bangor
145	KCIS	630	U2	5	2.5	WA	Edmonds
146	KFXD	630	U4	5	5	ID	Boise
147	KHOW	630	U4	5	5	CO	Denver
148	KPLY	630	U2	5	1	NV	Reno
149	KSLR	630	U4	5	4.3	TX	San Antonio
150	KYFI	630	U4	5	5	MO	Saint Louis
151	WBMQ	630	U1	4.8	0.04	GA	Savannah
152	WLAP	630	U4	5	1	KY	Lexington
153	WMAL	630	U4	10	5	DC	Washington
154	WNEG	630	U1	5	0.04	GA	Toccoa
155	WPRO	630	U2	5	5	RI	Providence
156	KFI	640	U1	50	50	CA	Los Angeles
157	KTIB	640	U4	5	1	LA	Thibodaux
158	KWPN	#640	U4	5	1	OK	Moore
159	WCRV	640	U2	50	0.48	TN	Collierville
160	WFNC	640	U1	10	1	NC	Fayetteville
161	WGST	640	U4	50	1	GA	Atlanta
162	WHLO	640	U4	5	0.5	OH	Akron
163	WMEN	640	U4	7.5	0.46	FL	Royal Palm Beach
164	WNNZ	640	U4	50	1	MA	Westfield
165	WOI	640	U2	5	1	IA	Ames
166	WWJZ	640	U4	50	0.95	NJ	Mount Holly
167	WXSM	640	U2	10	0.81	TN	Blountville
168	KGAB	650	U2	8.5	0.5	WY	Orchard Valley
169	KMTI	650	U1	0.9	0.9	UT	Manti
170	KSTE	650	U4	21.4	0.92	CA	Rancho Cordova
171	WNMT	650	U2	10	1	MN	Nashwauk
172	WSM	650	U1	50	50	TN	Nashville
173	KAPS	660	U4	10	1	WA	Mount Vernon
174	KEYZ	660	U4	5	5	ND	Williston
175	KSKY	660	U4	20	0.7	TX	Balch Springs
176	KTNN	660	U2	50	50	AZ	Window Rock
177	KWVE	660	U4	8	6	CA	Oildale
178	KXOR	660	U1	10	0.07	OR	Junction City
179	WBHR	660	U4	10	0.5	MN	Sauk Rapids
180	WFAN	660	U1	50	50	NY	New York
181	WLFJ	660	D1	50		SC	Greenville
182	WORL	660	U4	3.5	1	FL	Altamonte Springs
183	WXQW	660	U2	10	0.85	AL	Fairhope
184	KBOI	670	U2	50	50	ID	Boise
185	KHGZ	670	D1	5		AR	Glenwood
186	KIRN	670	U3	5	3	CA	Simi Valley
187	KLTT	#670	U4	50	1.4	CO	Commerce City
188	KMZQ	670	U4	30	0.6	NV	Las Vegas
189	WIEZ	670	D1	5.4		PA	Lewistown
190	WMTY	670	D1	2.5		TN	Farragut
191	WRJR	670	U5	20	0.003	VA	Claremont
192	WSCR	#670	U1	50	50	IL	Chicago
193	WWFE	670	U4	50	1	FL	Miami
194	WYLS	670	D1	4.8		AL	York
195	KFEQ	680	U4	5	5	MO	Saint Joseph
196	KKGR	680	D1	5		MT	East Helena
197	KKYX	680	U2	50	10	TX	San Antonio
198	KNBR	680	U1	50	50	CA	San Francisco
199	KOMW	680	D1	5		WA	Omak
200	WCBM	680	U4	50	20	MD	Baltimore
201	WCNN	680	U4	50	10	GA	North Atlanta
202	WDBC	680	U4	10	1	MI	Escanaba
203	WINR	680	U4	5	0.5	NY	Binghamton

MW	Call	kHz	Ant.	D	N	Sta	City of License
204	WKAZ	680	U4	10	0.22	WV	Charleston
205	WMFS	680	U2	8	5	TN	Memphis
206	WNZKn	680	N2	0	2.5	MI	Dearborn Heights
207	WOGO	680	U4	2.5	0.5	WI	Hallie
208	WPTF	680	U2	50	50	NC	Raleigh
209	WRKO	680	U4	50	50	MA	Boston
210	KGGF	690	U4	10	5	KS	Coffeyville
211	KTSM	690	U4	10	10	TX	El Paso
212	WADS	690	D3	3.2		CT	Ansonia
213	WELD	690	U1	3	0.01	WV	Fisher
214	WJOX	690	U2	50	0.5	AL	Birmingham
215	WNZK	690	D3	2.5		MI	Dearborn Heights
216	WOKV	690	U2	50	25	FL	Jacksonville
217	WQNO	690	U4	10	5	LA	New Orleans
218	WZAP	690	U1	10	0.01	VA	Bristol
219	KALL	700	U4	50	10	UT	North Salt Lake City
220	KGRV	700	U1	23	0.47	OR	Winston
221	KMBX	700	U1	2.5	0.7	CA	Soledad
222	KSEV	700	U4	15	1	TX	Tomball
223	KXLX	700	U2	10	0.6	WA	Airway Heights
224	WDMV	700	D3	5		MD	Walkersville
225	WFAT	700	D1	2.5		MA	Orange-Athol
226	WLW	700	U1	50	50	OH	Cincinnati
227	KBMB	710	U4	22	3.9	AZ	Black Canyon City
228	KCMO	710	U4	10	5	MO	Kansas City
229	KEEL	710	U4	50	5	LA	Shreveport
230	KFIA	710	U4	25	1	CA	Carmichael
231	KGNC	710	U4	10	10	TX	Amarillo
232	KIRO	710	U2	50	50	WA	Seattle
233	KNUS	710	U3	5	5	CO	Denver
234	KSPN	710	U4	50	10	CA	Los Angeles
235	KXMR	710	U7	50	4	ND	Bismarck
236	WAQI	710	U4	50	50	FL	Miami
237	WDSM	710	U2	10	5	WI	Superior
238	WEGG	710	D1	2.5		NC	Rose Hill
239	WEKC	710	D1	4.2		KY	Williamsburg
240	WFNR	710	D3	10		VA	Blacksburg
241	WOR	#710	U4	50	50	NY	New York
242	WUFF	710	D1	2.5		GA	Eastman
243	KDWN	#720	U2	50	50	NV	Las Vegas
244	KFIR	720	U1	10	0.18	OR	Sweet Home
245	KSAH	720	U4	10	0.89	TX	Universal City

MW	Call	kHz	Ant.	D	N	Sta	City of License
246	WGCR	720	D1	50		NC	Pisgah Forest
247	WGN	720	U1	50	50	IL	Chicago
248	WRZN	720	U2	10	0.25	FL	Hernando
249	WVCC	720	D1	7.97		GA	Hogansville
250	KNFL	**730**	U4	15	0.5	ID	Boise
251	KYYA	730	U1	5	0.23	MT	Billings
252	WACE	730	U1	5	0.008	MA	Chicopee
253	WLTQ	730	U1	5	0.1	SC	Charleston
254	WPIT	730	U1	5	0.02	PA	Pittsburgh
255	WSTT	730	U1	5	0.02	GA	Thomasville
256	WTNT	730	U1	8	0.02	VA	Alexandria
257	WZGV	730	U1	10	0.19	NC	Cramerton
258	KBRT	**#740**	U4	50	0.19	CA	Costa Mesa
259	KCBS	#740	U4	50	50	CA	San Francisco
260	KRMG	740	U4	50	25	OK	Tulsa
261	KTRH	740	U4	50	50	TX	Houston
262	KVOR	#740	U4	3.3	1.5	CO	Colorado Springs
263	KVOX	740	U7	50	0.94	ND	Fargo
264	WDGY	#740	D3	5		WI	Hudson
265	WMSP	740	U4	10	0.23	AL	Montgomery
266	WNOP	740	U4	2.5	0.03	KY	Newport
267	WNYH	740	U4	25	0.04	NY	Huntington
268	WPAQ	740	U1	10	0.007	NC	Mount Airy
269	WSBR	740	U3	2.5	0.94	FL	Boca Raton
270	WYGM	740	U4	50	50	FL	Orlando
271	KAMA	**750**	U4	10	1	TX	El Paso
272	KBNN	750	D1	5		MO	Lebanon
273	KERR	750	U2	50	1	MT	Polson
274	KHWG	750	U1	10	0.25	NV	Fallon
275	KMMJ	750	L3	10.5		NE	Grand Island
276	KOAL	#750	U2	10	6.8	UT	Price
277	KXTG	750	U4	50	20	OR	Portland
278	WNDZ	750	D3	15		IN	Portage
279	WSB	750	U1	50	50	GA	Atlanta
280	KCCV	**760**	U4	6	0.2	KS	Overland Park
281	KFMB	760	U2	5	50	CA	San Diego
282	KKZN	760	U4	50	1	CO	Thornton
283	KMTL	760	D1	10		AR	Sherwood
284	KTKR	760	U4	50	1	TX	San Antonio
285	WCHP	760	U4	35	0.01	NY	Champlain
286	WCIS	760	D1	3.5		NC	Morganton
287	WEFL	760	U4	3	1.5	FL	Tequesta
288	WJR	760	U1	50	50	MI	Detroit
289	WLCC	760	U4	10	1	FL	Brandon
290	WVNE	760	D1	25		MA	Leicester
291	KAAM	**770**	U4	10	1	TX	Garland
292	KATL	770	U2	10	1	MT	Miles City
293	KCBC	#770	U4	50	4.1	CA	Manteca
294	KKOB	770	U4	50	50	NM	Albuquerque
295	KTTH	770	U4	50	5	WA	Seattle
296	KUOM	770	D1	5		MN	Minneapolis
297	WABC	770	U1	50	50	NY	New York
298	WJBX	770	U4	10	0.63	FL	North Fort Myers
299	WLWL	770	D1	5		NC	Rockingham
300	WTOR	770	D3	13		NY	Youngstown
301	WVNN	770	U2	7	0.25	AL	Athens
302	WYRV	770	D1	5		VA	Cedar Bluff
303	KAZM	**780**	U2	5	0.25	AZ	Sedona
304	KKOH	780	U2	50	50	NV	Reno
305	WAVA	780	D1	12		VA	Arlington
306	WBBM	#780	U1	50	50	IL	Chicago
307	WCKB	780	U1	7	0.001	NC	Dunn
308	WIIN	780	D1	5		MS	Ridgeland
309	WWOL	780	D1	10		NC	Forest City
310	WXME	780	U1	5	0.06	ME	Monticello
311	WZZX	780	D1	5		AL	Lineville
312	KABC	**#790**	U2	5	5	CA	Los Angeles
313	KBME	790	U4	5	5	TX	Houston
314	KFGO	790	U2	5	5	ND	Fargo
315	KFPT	790	U4	5	2.5	CA	Clovis
316	KFYO	790	U4	5	1	TX	Lubbock
317	KGHL	790	U1	5	1.8	MT	Billings
318	KGMI	790	U2	5	1	WA	Bellingham
319	KJRB	790	U4	5	3.8	WA	Spokane
320	KNST	790	U4	5	0.5	AZ	Tucson
321	KURM	790	U2	5	0.5	AR	Rogers
322	KWSW	790	U1	5	0.11	CA	Eureka
323	KXXX	790	U1	5	0.02	KS	Colby
324	WAEB	790	U4	3.6	1.5	PA	Allentown
325	WAXY	790	U4	5	5	FL	South Miami
326	WAYY	790	U2	5	5	WI	Eau Claire
327	WBLO	790	U1	10	0.02	NC	Thomasville
328	WETB	790	U1	5	0.07	TN	Johnson City
329	WKRD	790	U4	5	1	KY	Louisville
330	WLBE	790	U2	5	1	FL	Leesburg-Eustis
331	WMC	790	U2	5	5	TN	Memphis
332	WNIS	790	U3	5	5	VA	Norfolk
333	WPRV	790	U2	5	5	RI	Providence
334	WQXI	790	U2	28	1	GA	Atlanta
335	WSGW	790	U4	5	1	MI	Saginaw
336	WTSK	790	U1	5	0.03	AL	Tuscaloosa
337	KBRV	**800**	U1	10	0.15	ID	Soda Springs
338	KQCV	800	U4	2.5	1	OK	Oklahoma City
339	WDUX	800	U3	5	0.5	WI	Waupaca
340	WNNW	800	U1	3	0.24	MA	Lawrence
341	WSVS	800	U1	10	0.27	VA	Crewe
342	WTMR	800	U1	5	0.5	NJ	Camden
343	WVAL	800	U4	2.6	0.85	MN	Sauk Rapids
344	WVHU	800	U1	5	0.18	WV	Huntington
345	KBHB	**810**	U1	25	0.06	SD	Sturgis
346	KGO	810	U3	50	50	CA	San Francisco
347	KSWV	810	U1	5	0.01	NM	Santa Fe
348	KTBI	810	D1	50		WA	Ephrata
349	WCKA	810	U4	50	0.5	AL	Jacksonville
350	WEKG	810	D1	5		KY	Jackson
351	WGY	#810	U1	50	50	NY	Schenectady
352	WHB	810	U2	50	5	MO	Kansas City
353	WMGC	810	U1	5	0.006	TN	Murfreesboro
354	WMJH	810	D1	3.6		MI	Rockford
355	WPIN	810	D1	4.2		VA	Dublin
356	WQIZ	810	D1	5		SC	Saint George
357	WRSO	810	U4	20	0.4	FL	Orlovista
358	WSJC	810	U2	50	0.5	MS	Magee
359	WZYN	810	D1	2.5		GA	Hahira
360	KGNW	**820**	U4	50	5	WA	Burien-Seattle
361	KUTR	820	U8	50	2.5	UT	Taylorsville
362	WBAP	820	U1	50	50	TX	Fort Worth
363	WBKK	820	U4	10	0.75	MN	Wilton
364	WCPT	820	U2	5	1.5	IL	Willow Springs
365	WNTW	820	U4	10	1	VA	Chester
366	WNYC	820	U4	10	0.93	NY	New York
367	WVSG	#820	U2	6.5	0.79	OH	Columbus
368	WWBA	820	U4	50	1	FL	Largo
369	WWFD	820	U4	4.3	0.43	MD	Frederick
370	WWLZ	820	U2	4.1	0.85	NY	Horseheads
371	KFLT	**830**	U2	50	1	AZ	Tucson
372	KLAA	830	U2	50	20	CA	Orange
373	KNCO	830	U2	5	5	CA	Grass Valley
374	KUYO	830	D1	25		WY	Evansville
375	WCCO	#830	U1	50	50	MN	Minneapolis
376	WCRN	830	U4	50	50	MA	Worcester
377	WEEU	830	U4	20	6	PA	Reading
378	WFNO	830	U4	5	0.75	LA	Norco
379	WGUE	830	D1	3		TN	Memphis
380	WTRU	830	U4	10	10	NC	Kernersville
381	KMAX	**840**	U4	10	0.28	WA	Colfax
382	KMPH	840	U4	5	5	CA	Modesto
383	KTIC	840	D1	5		NE	West Point
384	KVJY	840	U4	5	1	TX	Pharr
385	KWDF	840	D1	8		LA	Ball
386	KXNT	#840	U4	50	25	NV	North Las Vegas
387	WBHY	840	D1	10		AL	Mobile
388	WCEO	840	D3	50		SC	Columbia
389	WHAS	840	U1	50	50	KY	Louisville
390	WHGH	840	D1	10		GA	Thomasville
391	WKTR	840	D3	8.2		VA	Earlysville
392	KEYH	**850**	U4	10	0.18	TX	Houston
393	KFUO	#850	D1	5		MO	Clayton
394	KHHO	850	U4	10	1	WA	Tacoma
395	KJON	850	D3	5		TX	Carrollton
396	KOA	850	U1	50	50	CO	Denver
397	WAIT	850	D3	2.5		IL	Crystal Lake
398	WAXB	850	D1	2.5		CT	Ridgefield
399	WEEI	850	U4	50	50	MA	Boston
400	WFTL	850	U4	5	1	FL	West Palm Beach
401	WKGE	850	U3	10	10	PA	Johnstown
402	WKNR	850	U4	50	4.7	OH	Cleveland
403	WKVL	850	D3	50		TN	Knoxville
404	WPTK	850	U2	10	5	NC	Raleigh
405	WQRM	850	D1	10		MN	Duluth
406	WRUF	850	U2	5	5	FL	Gainesville
407	WTAR	850	U4	50	25	VA	Norfolk
408	WXJC	#850	U4	50	1	AL	Birmingham
409	KKAT	**860**	U1	10	0.19	UT	Salt Lake City

MW	Call	kHz	Ant.	D	N	Sta	City of License
410	KKOW	860	U2	10	5	KS	Pittsburg
411	KONO	860	U2	5	0.9	TX	San Antonio
412	KPAM	860	U2	50	15	OR	Troutdale
413	KTRB	860	U2	50	50	CA	San Francisco
414	WAEC	860	U12	5	0.5	GA	Atlanta
415	WDMG	860	U2	5	5	GA	Douglas
416	WFSI	860	U4	2.5	0.06	MD	Baltimore
417	WGUL	860	U4	5	1.5	FL	Dunedin
418	WOAY	860	U1	10	0.01	WV	Oak Hill
419	WSBS	860	U1	2.7	0.004	MA	Great Barrington
420	WWDB	860	D3	10		PA	Philadelphia
421	KFLD	870	U1	10	0.25	WA	Pasco
422	KLSQ	870	U2	5	0.43	NV	Whitney
423	KPRM	870	U2	50	1	MN	Park Rapids
424	KRLA	870	U4	50	3	CA	Glendale
425	WHCU	870	U2	5	1	NY	Ithaca
426	WKAR	870	D3	10		MI	East Lansing
427	WLVP	870	U4	10	1	ME	Gorham
428	WPWT	870	D1	10		TN	Colonial Heights
429	WQRX	870	D1	10		AL	Valley Head
430	WTCG	870	D1	5		NC	Mount Holly
431	WWL	870	U3	50	50	LA	New Orleans
432	KHAC	880	U1	10	0.43	NM	Tse Bonito
433	KIXI	880	U4	50	10	WA	Mercer Island-Seattle
434	KJJR	880	U1	10	0.5	MT	Whitefish
435	KJOZ	880	U4	10	1	TX	Conroe
436	KKMC	880	U4	10	10	CA	Gonzales
437	KLRG	880	U2	50	0.22	AR	Sheridan
438	KRVN	880	U2	50	50	NE	Lexington
439	KWIP	880	U1	5	1	OR	Dallas
440	WBKZ	880	D1	5		GA	Jefferson
441	WCBS	#880	U1	50	50	NY	New York
442	WMDB	880	U1	2.5	0.002	TN	Nashville
443	WMEQ	880	U2	10	0.21	WI	Menomonie
444	WPEK	880	D1	5		NC	Fairview
445	WRFD	880	D1	23		OH	Columbus-Worthington
446	WZAB	880	U4	4	5	FL	Sweetwater
447	KDXU	890	U2	10	10	UT	Saint George
448	KIHC	890	U4	5	5	CA	Arroyo Grande
449	KJME	890	U4	5	0.58	CO	Fountain
450	KMJE	890	U4	10	0.48	CA	Olivehurst
451	KTXV	890	U4	20	0.25	TX	Mabank
452	KVOZ	890	U2	10	1	TX	Del Mar Hills
453	KYWN	890	U2	50	0.25	ID	Meridian
454	WAMG	890	U4	25	6	MA	Dedham
455	WBAJ	890	D1	50		SC	Blythewood
456	WHJA	890	D1	10		MS	Laurel
457	WJTP	890	D1	5		GA	Lithia Springs
458	WKNV	890	D3	10		VA	Fairlawn
459	WLS	890	U1	50	50	IL	Chicago
460	WYAM	890	D1	2.5		AL	Hartselle
461	KALI	900	U4	5	0.15	CA	West Covina
462	KREH	900	U4	5	0.01	TX	Pecan Grove
463	KTIS	900	U4	50	0.5	MN	Minneapolis
464	WCPA	900	U4	2.5	0.5	PA	Clearfield
465	WJLG	900	U1	4.35	0.15	GA	Savannah
466	WJWL	900	U4	10.5	1.08	DE	Georgetown
467	WKDA	900	U1	5	0.13	TN	Lebanon
468	WKDW	900	U1	2.5	0.12	VA	Staunton
469	WLSI	900	U1	3.5	0.12	KY	Pikeville
470	WMOP	900	U1	2.7	0.02	FL	Ocala
471	WYCV	900	U1	2.5	0.25	NC	Granite Falls
472	KCJB	910	U4	5	5	ND	Minot
473	KECR	910	U4	5	5	CA	El Cajon
474	KGME	#910	U2	5	5	AZ	Phoenix
475	KKBE	910	U2	5	0.5	NM	Roswell
476	KKSF	910	U2	20	5	CA	Oakland
477	KLCN	910	U1	5	0.08	AR	Blytheville
478	KMTT	910	U4	3.3	4.3	WA	Vancouver
479	KOXR	910	U3	5	1	CA	Oxnard
480	KPOF	#910	U1	5	1	CO	Denver
481	KRIO	910	U4	5	5	TX	McAllen
482	KWDZ	910	U4	5	1	UT	Salt Lake City
483	WAEI	910	U2	5	5	ME	Bangor
484	WALT	910	U1	5	1	MS	Meridian
485	WAVL	910	U4	5	0.06	PA	Apollo
486	WEPG	910	U1	5	0.09	TN	South Pittsburg
487	WFDF	#910	U4	50	25	MI	Farmington Hills
488	WHSM	910	U1	5	0.07	WI	Hayward
489	WJCW	910	U2	5	1	TN	Johnson City
490	WLAT	910	U2	5	5	CT	New Britain
491	WLTP	910	U5	5	0.04	OH	Marietta

MW	Call	kHz	Ant.	D	N	Sta	City of License
492	WOLI	910	U4	3.6	0.89	SC	Spartanburg
493	WRFV	910	U2	5	5	GA	Valdosta
494	WRNL	910	U2	5	1.5	VA	Richmond
495	WSBA	910	U4	5	1	PA	York
496	WSRP	910	U2	5	5	NC	Jacksonville
497	WSUI	910	U2	5	4	IA	Iowa City
498	WTWD	910	U3	5	5	FL	Plant City
499	KARN	#920	U2	5	5	AR	Little Rock
500	KBAD	920	U2	5	0.5	NV	Las Vegas
501	KDHL	920	U4	5	5	MN	Faribault
502	KGTK	920	U2	3	0.007	WA	Olympia
503	KIHM	920	U2	4.8	0.85	NV	Reno
504	KKLS	920	U3	5	0.11	SD	Rapid City
505	KLMR	920	U2	5	0.5	CO	Lamar
506	KPSI	920	U4	5	1	CA	Palm Springs
507	KVEL	920	U2	5	1	UT	Vernal
508	KVIN	920	U4	0.5	2.5	CA	Ceres
509	KXLY	920	U1	20	5	WA	Spokane
510	KYFR	920	U4	5	2.5	IA	Shenandoah
511	KYST	920	U4	5	1	TX	Texas City
512	WBAA	#920	U2	5	1	IN	West Lafayette
513	WDMC	920	U2	5	1	FL	Melbourne
514	WGHQ	920	U4	5	0.07	NY	Kingston
515	WGKA	920	U1	14	0.49	GA	Atlanta
516	WHJJ	920	U2	5	5	RI	Providence
517	WIRD	920	U1	5	0.08	NY	Lake Placid
518	WMMN	920	U1	5	0.2	WV	Fairmont
519	WOKY	920	U4	5	1	WI	Milwaukee
520	WPCM	920	U1	5	0.05	NC	Burlington - Graham
521	WTCW	920	U1	4.2	0.04	KY	Whitesburg
522	WURA	920	U4	7	0.97	VA	Quantico
523	KAFF	930	U1	5	0.03	AZ	Flagstaff
524	KAGI	930	U1	5	0.12	OR	Grants Pass
525	KAPR	930	U1	2.5	0.07	AZ	Douglas
526	KHJ	930	U2	5	5	CA	Los Angeles
527	KIUP	930	U1	5	0.1	CO	Durango
528	KKIN	930	U1	2.5	0.36	MN	Aitkin
529	KLUP	930	U2	5	1	TX	Terrell Hills
530	KMPT	930	U2	5	1	MT	East Missoula
531	KRKY	930	U1	4.5	0.12	CO	Granby
532	KROE	930	U1	5	0.11	WY	Sheridan
533	KSDN	930	U4	5	1	SD	Aberdeen
534	KSEI	930	U2	5	5	ID	Pocatello
535	KWOC	930	U2	5	0.5	MO	Poplar Bluff
536	KYAK	930	U1	10	0.12	WA	Yakima
537	WBEN	930	U2	5	5	NY	Buffalo
538	WDLX	930	U2	5	1	NC	Washington
539	WEZZ	930	U1	5	0.04	AL	Monroeville
540	WFMD	930	U4	5	2.5	MD	Frederick
541	WFXJ	#930	U2	5	5	FL	Jacksonville
542	WGAD	930	U2	5	0.5	AL	Rainbow City
543	WKBM	930	U4	2.5	4.2	IL	Sandwich
544	WKCT	930	U2	5	0.5	KY	Bowling Green
545	WKY	930	U2	5	5	OK	Oklahoma City
546	WLBL	#930	U1	5	0.07	WI	Auburndale
547	WLLL	930	U1	9	0.04	VA	Lynchburg
548	WLSS	930	U4	5	3	FL	Sarasota
549	WMGR	930	U2	5	0.5	GA	Bainbridge
550	WPAT	930	U2	5	5	NJ	Paterson
551	WPKX	930	U2	5	5	NH	Rochester
552	WRVC	930	U2	5	1	WV	Huntington
553	WSEV	930	U1	5	0.14	TN	Sevierville
554	WSFZ	930	U2	3.8	3.1	MS	Jackson
555	WTAD	930	U2	5	1	IL	Quincy
556	WTOU	930	U4	5	1	MI	Battle Creek
557	WYFQ	930	U2	5	1	NC	Charlotte
558	KCMC	940	U1	2.5	0.01	TX	Texarkana
559	KFIG	940	U4	50	50	CA	Fresno
560	KICE	940	U4	10	0.06	OR	Bend
561	KIXZ	940	U4	5	1	TX	Amarillo
562	KOBY	940	U1	10	0.03	UT	Cedar City
563	KPSZ	940	U4	10	5	IA	Des Moines
564	KVSH	940	U1	5	0.01	NE	Valentine
565	WCPC	940	U4	31	0.007	MS	Houston
566	WECO	940	U1	5	0.01	TN	Wartburg
567	WIDG	940	U1	5	0.004	MI	Saint Ignace
568	WINZ	940	U2	50	10	FL	Miami
569	WKGM	940	U2	10	3.1	VA	Smithfield
570	WKYK	940	U2	4.6	0.25	NC	Burnsville
571	WMAC	940	U2	50	10	GA	Macon
572	WMIX	940	U4	5	1.5	IL	Mount Vernon
573	WNRG	940	U1	5	0.01	VA	Grundy

MW	Call	kHz	Ant.	D	N	Sta	City of License
574	WYLD	940	U4	10	0.5	LA	New Orleans
575	KAHI	950	U4	5	5	CA	Auburn
576	KCAP	950	U2	5	5	MT	Helena
577	KDCE	950	U1	4.2	0.08	NM	Española
578	KJR	950	U4	50	50	WA	Seattle
579	KJTV	950	U4	5	0.5	TX	Lubbock
580	KMHR	950	U1	3.5	0.03	ID	Boise
581	KNFT	950	U1	5	0.22	NM	Bayard
582	KOEL	950	U4	5	0.5	IA	Oelwein
583	KOZE	950	U4	5	1	ID	Lewiston
584	KPRC	950	U2	5	5	TX	Houston
585	KRWZ	#950	U3	5	5	CO	Parker
586	KTBR	950	U1	3.4	0.02	OR	Roseburg
587	KWOS	950	U2	5	0.5	MO	Jefferson City
588	KXJK	950	U1	5	0.08	AR	Forrest City
589	WAKM	950	U4	5	0.08	TN	Franklin
590	WBES	950	U2	5	1	WV	Charleston
591	WCTN	950	U3	2.5	0.35	MD	Potomac - Cabin John
592	WGTA	950	U1	5	0.11	GA	Summerville
593	WGUN	950	U1	3.5	0.06	GA	Valdosta
594	WHSY	950	U1	5	0.06	MS	Hattiesburg
595	WIBX	950	U3	5	5	NY	Utica
596	WJKB	950	U4	10	6	SC	Moncks Corner
597	WKDN	950	U4	43	21	PA	Philadelphia
598	WNTD	950	U2	1	5	IL	Chicago
599	WORD	950	U2	5	5	SC	Spartanburg
600	WROL	950	U1	5	0.09	MA	Boston
601	WTLN	950	U2	12	5	FL	Orlando
602	WWJ	#950	U4	50	50	MI	Detroit
603	WXGI	950	U1	3.9	0.04	VA	Richmond
604	WXLW	950	U4	5	0.03	IN	Indianapolis
605	KALE	960	U2	5	1	WA	Richland
606	KCGS	960	U1	5	0.04	AR	Marshall
607	KFLN	960	U1	5	0.09	MT	Baker
608	KGKL	960	U2	5	1	TX	San Angelo
609	KIXW	960	U1	5	0.02	CA	Apple Valley
610	KKNT	960	U2	5	5	AZ	Phoenix
611	KLAD	960	U2	5	5	OR	Klamath Falls
612	KLTF	960	U1	5	0.03	MN	Little Falls
613	KMA	960	U2	5	5	IA	Shenandoah
614	KNDN	960	U1	5	0.16	NM	Farmington
615	KNEB	960	U4	5	0.35	NE	Scottsbluff
616	KNEW	#960	U3	5	5	CA	Oakland
617	KOVO	960	U2	5	1	UT	Provo
618	KZIM	960	U2	5	0.5	MO	Cape Girardeau
619	WATS	960	U1	5	0.05	PA	Sayre
620	WCRU	960	U4	10	5	NC	Dallas
621	WEAV	960	U4	5	5	NY	Plattsburgh
622	WELI	#960	U2	5	5	CT	New Haven
623	WERC	960	U2	5	5	AL	Birmingham
624	WFGL	960	U4	2.5	1	MA	Fitchburg
625	WFIR	960	U2	5	5	VA	Roanoke
626	WHAK	960	U1	5	0.13	MI	Rogers City
627	WHYL	960	U4	5	0.02	PA	Carlisle
628	WJYZ	960	U4	5	0.39	GA	Albany
629	WLPR	960	U1	6	0.03	AL	Prichard
630	WPRT	960	U1	3.8	0.01	KY	Prestonsburg
631	WRFC	960	U2	5	2.5	GA	Athens
632	WRNS	960	U2	5	1	NC	Kinston
633	WSBT	960	U4	5	5	IN	South Bend
634	WTGM	960	U4	5	5	MD	Salisbury
635	KBUL	970	U2	5	5	MT	Billings
636	KCFO	970	U4	2.5	1	OK	Tulsa
637	KFEL	970	U1	3.2	0.18	CO	Pueblo
638	KHTY	970	U4	1	5	CA	Bakersfield
639	KJLT	970	U1	5	0.05	NE	North Platte
640	KNIH	970	U4	5	0.5	NV	Paradise
641	KNWZ	970	U4	5	1	CA	Coachella
642	KQAQ	970	U3	5	5	MN	Austin
643	KTTO	970	U2	5	1	WA	Spokane
644	KUFO	970	U2	5	5	OR	Portland
645	KVWM	970	U1	5	0.19	AZ	Show Low
646	KXTA	970	U2	5	0.9	ID	Rupert
647	WBGG	970	U4	5	5	PA	Pittsburgh
648	WDAY	970	U4	10	10	ND	Fargo
649	WDCZ	970	U3	5	5	NY	Buffalo
650	WERH	970	D1	5		AL	Hamilton
651	WFLA	#970	U4	25	11	FL	Tampa
652	WFSR	970	U1	5	0.02	KY	Harlan
653	WFUN	970	U4	5	1	OH	Ashtabula
654	WGTK	970	U4	5	5	KY	Louisville
655	WHA	#970	U1	5	0.05	WI	Madison
656	WKCI	970	U4	5	1	VA	Waynesboro
657	WNIV	970	U1	5	0.03	GA	Atlanta
658	WNYM	970	U4	50	5	NJ	Hackensack
659	WTBF	970	U1	5	0.04	AL	Troy
660	WVOP	970	U1	4	0.06	GA	Vidalia
661	WWRK	970	U1	10	0.03	SC	Florence
662	WYSE	970	U1	5	0.03	NC	Canton
663	WZAM	970	U1	5	0.06	MI	Ishpeming
664	WZAN	970	U2	5	5	ME	Portland
665	KCAB	980	U1	5	0.03	AR	Dardanelle
666	KDBV	980	U4	10	10	CA	Salinas
667	KDSJ	980	U2	5	1	SD	Deadwood
668	KEJY	980	U2	5	0.5	CA	Eureka
669	KFWB	#980	U1	5	5	CA	Los Angeles
670	KKMS	980	U3	5	5	MN	Richfield
671	KMBZ	980	U2	5	5	MO	Kansas City
672	KMIN	980	U1	5	0.23	NM	Grants
673	KOKA	980	U1	5	0.07	LA	Shreveport
674	KQUE	980	U4	5	4	TX	Rosenberg-Richmond
675	KSPZ	980	U4	5	1	ID	Ammon
676	KSVC	980	U2	10	1	UT	Richfield
677	KTCR	980	U4	5	0.5	WA	Selah
678	KVLV	980	D1	5		NV	Fallon
679	WAAV	980	U2	5	5	NC	Leland
680	WAKK	980	U1	5	0.15	MS	McComb
681	WCAP	980	U4	5	5	MA	Lowell
682	WCUB	980	U4	5	5	WI	Two Rivers
683	WDVH	980	U1	5	0.16	FL	Gainesville
684	WFHG	980	U2	5	1	VA	Bristol
685	WHAW	980	U1	25	0.04	WV	Lost Creek
686	WHSR	980	U4	5	2.2	FL	Pompano Beach
687	WILK	980	U2	5	1	PA	Wilkes-Barre
688	WOFX	#980	U2	5	5	NY	Troy
689	WONE	#980	U2	5	5	OH	Dayton
690	WPGA	980	U1	2.6	0.08	GA	Perry
691	WRNE	980	U2	4	1	FL	Gulf Breeze
692	WTEM	980	U4	50	5	DC	Washington
693	WULR	980	U3	3	0.16	SC	York
694	WYFN	980	U2	5	5	TN	Nashville
695	KATD	#990	U4	10	5	CA	Pittsburg
696	KFCD	990	U4	7	0.92	TX	Farmersville
697	KRKS	990	U2	6.5	0.39	CO	Denver
698	KRMO	990	U4	2.5	0.04	MO	Cassville
699	KTKT	990	U4	10	0.49	AZ	Tucson
700	KTMS	990	U4	5	0.5	CA	Santa Barbara
701	KWAM	990	U4	10	0.45	TN	Memphis
702	WALE	990	U4	50	5	RI	Greenville
703	WDCX	#990	U4	5	2.5	NY	Rochester
704	WDEO	990	U4	9.2	0.25	MI	Ypsilanti
705	WDYZ	990	U4	5	14	FL	Orlando
706	WEEB	990	U1	10	0.02	NC	Southern Pines
707	WLLI	990	U3	10	0.1	PA	Somerset
708	WMYM	990	U4	5	5	FL	Miami
709	WNML	990	U2	10	10	TN	Knoxville
710	WNRV	990	U1	5	0.01	VA	Narrows-Pearisburg
711	WNTP	990	U4	50	10	PA	Philadelphia
712	WXCT	990	U4	2.5	0.08	CT	Southington
713	KCEO	1000	U5	10	0.9	CA	Vista
714	KKIM	1000	U1	10	0.03	NM	Albuquerque
715	KOMO	1000	U2	50	50	WA	Seattle
716	KTOK	1000	U4	5.8	5.8	OK	Oklahoma City
717	KXRB	1000	U4	10	0.1	SD	Sioux Falls
718	WLNL	1000	D1	5		NY	Horseheads
719	WMVP	1000	U4	50	50	IL	Chicago
720	WRQR	1000	D4	5		TN	Paris
721	WXTN	1000	D1	5		MS	Benton
722	WYBT	1000	D1	5		FL	Blountstown
723	KBBW	1010	U4	10	2.5	TX	Waco
724	KCHJ	1010	U4	5	1	CA	Delano
725	KIHU	1010	U13	50	0.19	UT	Tooele
726	KIQI	1010	U3	10	0.5	CA	San Francisco
727	KLAT	1010	U4	5	3.6	TX	Houston
728	KOOR	1010	D1	4.5		OR	Milwaukie
729	KSIR	1010	U3	25	0.28	CO	Brush
730	KTNZ	1010	U4	5	0.5	TX	Amarillo
731	KXEN	1010	U4	50	0.5	MO	Saint Louis
732	KXPS	1010	U4	3.6	0.4	CA	Thousand Palms
733	KXXT	1010	U5	15	0.25	AZ	Tolleson
734	WCNL	1010	U1	10	0.03	NH	Newport
735	WHFS	1010	U4	50	5	FL	Seffner
736	WHIN	1010	U1	5	0.04	TN	Gallatin
737	WINS	#1010	U3	50	50	NY	New York

MW	Call	kHz	Ant.	D	N	Sta	City of License	MW	Call	kHz	Ant.	D	N	Sta	City of License
738	WJXL	1010	U4	50	30	FL	Jacksonville Beach	820	WXNC	1060	D1	4		NC	Monroe
739	WKJW	1010	U10	47	0.09	NC	Black Mountain	821	KATQ	1070	U1	5	0.05	MT	Plentywood
740	WMOX	1010	U4	10	1	MS	Meridian	822	KFTI	1070	U2	10	1	KS	Wichita
741	WPMH	1010	U3	5	0.44	VA	Portsmouth	823	KHMO	1070	U4	5	1	MO	Hannibal
742	WTZA	1010	U1	50	0.07	GA	Atlanta	824	KNTH	1070	U4	10	5	TX	Houston
743	KCKN	1020	U4	50	50	NM	Roswell	825	KNX	#1070	U1	50	50	CA	Los Angeles
744	KDKA	1020	U1	50	50	PA	Pittsburgh	826	KSKK	1070	U2	10	5	MN	Verndale
745	KDYK	1020	U5	4	0.4	WA	Union Gap	827	KWEL	1070	D1	2.5		TX	Midland
746	KMMQ	1020	U4	50	1.4	NE	Plattsmouth	828	WAPI	1070	U2	50	5	AL	Birmingham
747	KTNQ	1020	U4	50	50	CA	Los Angeles	829	WBKW	1070	D1	10		WV	Beckley
748	WHDD	1020	D1	2.5		CT	Sharon	830	WCSZ	1070	U4	50	1.5	SC	Sans Souci
749	WRIX	1020	D1	10		SC	Homeland Park	831	WDIA	1070	U4	50	5	TN	Memphis
750	WURN	1020	U4	8.9	0.98	FL	Kendall	832	WFLI	1070	U4	50	2.5	TN	Lookout Mountain
751	KBUF	1030	U2	2.5	1.2	KS	Holcomb	833	WFNI	#1070	U4	50	10	IN	Indianapolis
752	KCTA	1030	D1	50		TX	Corpus Christi	834	WFRF	1070	D1	10		FL	Tallahassee
753	KCWJ	1030	U4	5	0.5	MO	Blue Springs	835	WINA	1070	U2	5		VA	Charlottesville
754	KDUN	1030	U1	50	0.63	OR	Reedsport	836	WKOK	1070	U2	10	1	PA	Sunbury
755	KFAY	1030	U4	6	1	AR	Farmington	837	WNCT	#1070	U4	50	10	NC	Greenville
756	KJDJ	1030	U1	2.5	0.7	CA	San Luis Obispo	838	WNVY	1070	U1	15	0.02	FL	Cantonment
757	KMAS	1030	U1	10	1	WA	Shelton	839	WSCP	1070	D1	2.5		NY	Sandy Creek-Pulaski
758	KTWO	1030	U2	50	50	WY	Casper	840	WTSO	1070	U4	10	5	WI	Madison
759	KVOI	1030	U4	10	1	AZ	Cortaro	841	WTWK	1070	D1	5		NY	Plattsburgh
760	WBGS	1030	D5	10		WV	Point Pleasant	842	KFXX	1080	U4	50	9	OR	Portland
761	WBZ	#1030	U3	50	50	MA	Boston	843	KRLD	1080	U2	50	50	TX	Dallas
762	WCTS	1030	U4	50	1	MN	Maplewood	844	KSCO	1080	U2	10	5	CA	Santa Cruz
763	WDRU	1030	D3	50		NC	Creedmoor	845	KSLL	1080	D1	10		UT	Price
764	WEBS	1030	U1	5	0.003	GA	Calhoun	846	KVNI	1080	U2	10	1	ID	Coeur d'Alene
765	WGSF	1030	U12	50	1	TN	Memphis	847	WALD	1080	D1	9		SC	Johnsonville
766	WNOW	1030	D3	9.4		NC	Mint Hill	848	WFTD	1080	D4	50		GA	Marietta
767	WNVR	1030	U7	10	0.12	IL	Vernon Hills	849	WHIM	1080	U4	50	10	FL	Coral Gables
768	WONQ	1030	U2	45	1.7	FL	Oviedo	850	WHOO	1080	U7	19	0.19	FL	Kissimmee
769	WUFL	1030	D3	5		MI	Sterling Heights	851	WKAC	1080	D1	5		AL	Athens
770	WWGB	1030	D3	50		MD	Indian Head	852	WKGX	1080	D1	5		NC	Lenoir
771	KCBR	#1040	D1	15		CO	Monument	853	WKJK	1080	U4	10	1	KY	Louisville
772	KGGR	1040	D1	3.3		TX	Dallas	854	WNWI	1080	U2	3	2.6	IL	Oak Lawn
773	WCHR	1040	U7	15	1.5	NJ	Flemington	855	WTIC	#1080	U2	50	50	CT	Hartford
774	WHBO	1040	U2	3.6	0.42	FL	Pinellas Park	856	WWNL	1080	D4	50		PA	Pittsburgh
775	WHO	1040	U1	50	50	IA	Des Moines	857	KAAY	1090	U2	50	50	AR	Little Rock
776	WJBE	1040	D1	10		TN	Powell	858	KBOZ	1090	U2	5	5	MT	Bozeman
777	WJTB	1040	D1	5		OH	North Ridgeville	859	KEXS	1090	D4	8		MO	Excelsior Springs
778	WLVJ	1040	U4	25	1.1	FL	Boynton Beach	860	KFNQ	1090	U4	50	50	WA	Seattle
779	WPBS	1040	D1	50		GA	Conyers	861	KLWJ	1090	D1	2.5		OR	Umatilla
780	WSGH	1040	U4	9.1	0.18	NC	Lewisville	862	KMXA	#1090	U4	50	0.5	CO	Aurora
781	WYSL	1040	U7	20	0.5	NY	Avon	863	KNCR	1090	D1	10		CA	Fortuna
782	WZSK	1040	D1	10		PA	Everett	864	KVOP	1090	U4	5	0.5	TX	Plainview
783	KBLE	1050	U1	5	0.44	WA	Seattle	865	WAQE	1090	D1	5		WI	Rice Lake
784	KEYF	1050	U1	5	0.26	WA	Dishman	866	WBAL	1090	U2	50	50	MD	Baltimore
785	KJPG	1050	U5	10	0.007	CA	Frazier Park	867	WCZZ	1090	D1	5		SC	Greenwood
786	KLOH	1050	U4	9.38	0.43	MN	Pipestone	868	WFCV	1090	D4	2.5		IN	Fort Wayne
787	KMTA	1050	U1	10	0.13	MT	Miles City	869	WHGG	1090	D1	10		TN	Kingsport
788	KORE	1050	U1	5	0.14	OR	Springfield-Eugene	870	WILD	1090	D1	4.8		MA	Boston
789	KTCT	#1050	U4	50	10	CA	San Mateo	871	WTSB	1090	D1	9		NC	Selma
790	WADC	1050	U1	5	0.14	WV	Parkersburg	872	KAFY	1100	U2	4.2	0.8	CA	Bakersfield
791	WBQH	1050	U1	10	0.04	MD	Silver Spring	873	KDRY	1100	U2	11	1	TX	Alamo Heights
792	WBRG	1050	U1	3.8	0.09	VA	Lynchburg	874	KFAX	1100	U3	50	50	CA	San Francisco
793	WEPN	1050	U4	50	50	NY	New York	875	KFNX	1100	U4	50	1	AZ	Cave Creek
794	WFAM	1050	U1	5	0.08	GA	Augusta	876	KKLL	1100	D1	5		MO	Webb City
795	WFSC	1050	U1	5	0.15	NC	Franklin	877	KNZZ	1100	U12	50	10	CO	Grand Junction
796	WHSC	1050	U3	5	0.47	SC	Conway	878	KWWN	1100	U4	22	2	NV	Las Vegas
797	WJSB	1050	D1	3.1		FL	Crestview	879	WCGA	1100	D1	10		GA	Woodbine
798	WROS	1050	U4	5	0.01	FL	Jacksonville	880	WHLI	1100	D3	10		NY	Hempstead
799	WSEN	1050	U3	2.5	0.01	NY	Baldwinsville	881	WISS	1100	D1	2.5		WI	Berlin
800	WTKA	1050	U3	10	0.5	MI	Ann Arbor	882	WTAM	1100	U1	50	50	OH	Cleveland
801	WVXX	1050	U3	5	0.35	VA	Norfolk	883	WTWN	1100	D1	5		VT	Wells River
802	KBGN	1060	D1	10		ID	Caldwell	884	WWWE	1100	D1	5		GA	Hapeville
803	KDUS	1060	U2	5	0.5	AZ	Tempe	885	WZFG	1100	U2	50	0.44	MN	Dilworth
804	KDYL	1060	U1	10	0.14	UT	South Salt Lake	886	KBND	1110	U12	10	5	OR	Bend
805	KFOY	1060	U2	10	0.25	NV	Sparks	887	KDIS	1110	U4	50	20	CA	Pasadena
806	KGFX	1060	U4	10	1	SD	Pierre	888	KEJL	1110	D1	5		NM	Humble City
807	KIJN	1060	D3	10		TX	Farwell	889	KFAB	1110	U2	50	50	NE	Omaha
808	KKVV	1060	U1	5	0.04	NV	Las Vegas	890	KGFL	1110	D1	5		AR	Clinton
809	KRCN	1060	U1	50	0.11	CO	Longmont	891	KLIB	1110	U4	5	0.5	CA	Roseville
810	KTNS	1060	U1	5	0.02	CA	Oakhurst	892	KTEK	1110	D3	2.5		TX	Alvin
811	KXPL	1060	D1	10		TX	El Paso	893	KVTT	1110	D4	50		TX	Mineral Wells
812	KYW	#1060	U3	50	50	PA	Philadelphia	894	WBT	1110	U2	50	50	NC	Charlotte
813	WHFB	1060	U1	5	0.001	MI	Benton Harbor-St Joseph	895	WCCM	1110	D3	5		NH	Salem
814	WILB	1060	D4	15		OH	Canton	896	WGNZ	1110	U7	5	0.002	OH	Fairborn
815	WIXC	1060	U7	50	5	FL	Titusville	897	WJML	1110	U3	10	0.01	MI	Petoskey
816	WKNG	1060	D1	50		GA	Tallapoosa	898	WKQA	1110	D3	50		VA	Norfolk
817	WLNO	1060	U4	50	5	LA	New Orleans	899	WMBI	1110	D1	4.2		IL	Chicago
818	WMCL	1060	U3	2.5	0.002	IL	McLeansboro	900	WNAP	1110	D5	4.8		PA	Norristown
819	WQOM	1060	U4	50	2.5	MA	Natick	901	WPMZ	1110	D3	5		RI	East Providence

MW	Call	kHz	Ant.	D	N	Sta	City of License
902	WSLV	1110	D1	2.5		TN	Ardmore
903	WTIS	1110	D3	10		FL	Tampa
904	WTOF	1110	D1	10		AL	Bay Minette
905	WUPE	1110	D3	5		MA	Pittsfield
906	KANN	**1120**	U4	10	1.1	UT	Roy
907	KETU	1120	D4	10		OK	Catoosa
908	KMOX	#1120	U1	50	50	MO	Saint Louis
909	KPNW	1120	U3	50	50	OR	Eugene
910	KTXW	1120	U4	5.6	0.15	TX	Manor
911	KZSJ	1120	U1	5	0.15	CA	San Martin
912	WBNW	1120	U4	5	1	MA	Concord
913	WKAJ	1120	U4	10	0.4	NY	Saint Johnsville
914	WSME	1120	D1	6		NC	Camp Lejeune
915	WTWZ	1120	D1	10		MS	Clinton
916	WUST	1120	D1	20		DC	Washington
917	KBMR	**1130**	U1	10	0.02	ND	Bismarck
918	KRDU	1130	U4	5	6.2	CA	Dinuba
919	KSDO	1130	U4	10	10	CA	San Diego
920	KTLK	1130	U4	50	25	MN	Minneapolis
921	KTMR	1130	D3	25		TX	Converse
922	KWKH	1130	U2	50	50	LA	Shreveport
923	KXET	1130	U4	25	0.49	OR	Mount Angel
924	WALQ	1130	D1	25		AL	Carrville
925	WBBR	1130	U2	50	50	NY	New York
926	WDFN	1130	U4	50	10	MI	Detroit
927	WEAF	1130	U1	5	0.007	SC	Camden
928	WISN	#1130	U4	50	10	WI	Milwaukee
929	WLBA	1130	D1	10		GA	Gainesville
930	WPYB	1130	D1	6.5		NC	Benson
931	WWBF	1130	U2	2.5	0.5	FL	Bartow
932	KCXL	**1140**	U1	4	0.006	MO	Liberty
933	KGEM	1140	U2	10	10	ID	Boise
934	KHFX	1140	U4	5	0.71	TX	Cleburne
935	KHTK	#1140	U4	50	50	CA	Sacramento
936	KLTK	1140	D1	5		AR	Centerton
937	KNWQ	1140	U4	10	2.5	CA	Palm Springs
938	KSOO	1140	U2	10	5	SD	Sioux Falls
939	KXST	1140	U2	10	2.5	NV	North Las Vegas
940	KYOK	1140	D3	5		TX	Conroe
941	KZMQ	1140	D1	10		WY	Greybull
942	WBXR	1140	D4	15		AL	Hazel Green
943	WCJW	1140	D4	8		NY	Warsaw
944	WNWF	1140	U1	3	0.01	FL	Destin
945	WQBA	1140	U4	50	10	FL	Miami
946	WRMQ	1140	U2	5	0.008	FL	Orlando
947	WRVA	1140	U3	50	50	VA	Richmond
948	WSAO	1140	D1	5		MS	Senatobia
949	WVEL	#1140	D1	5		IL	Pekin
950	WVHF	1140	D3	5		MI	Kentwood
951	WXLZ	1140	D1	2.5		VA	Saint Paul
952	KAGO	**1150**	U2	5	1	OR	Klamath Falls
953	KCKY	1150	U4	5	1	AZ	Coolidge
954	KDEF	1150	U2	5	0.5	NM	Albuquerque
955	KEIB	1150	U4	50	44	CA	Los Angeles
956	KGDD	1150	U1	5	0.01	OR	Portland
957	KHRO	1150	U1	5	0.38	TX	El Paso
958	KIMM	1150	U2	5	0.5	SD	Rapid City
959	KKNW	1150	U2	10	6	WA	Seattle
960	KNRV	1150	U4	10	1	CO	Englewood
961	KQQQ	1150	U1	11	0.02	WA	Pullman
962	KSAL	1150	U2	5	5	KS	Salina
963	KSEN	1150	U4	10	5	MT	Shelby
964	KWKY	1150	U4	2.5	1	IA	Des Moines
965	WAVO	1150	U1	5	0.05	SC	Rock Hill
966	WCRK	1150	U2	5	0.5	TN	Morristown
967	WCUE	1150	U3	5	5	OH	Cuyahoga Falls
968	WDEL	1150	U4	5	5	DE	Wilmington
969	WEAQ	1150	U1	5	0.04	WI	Chippewa Falls
970	WELC	1150	D1	5		WV	Welch
971	WGBR	1150	U4	5	0.8	NC	Goldsboro
972	WGGH	1150	U4	5	0.04	IL	Marion
973	WGOW	1150	U2	5	1	TN	Chattanooga
974	WHBY	1150	U4	20	25	WI	Kimberly
975	WHUN	1150	U1	5	0.03	PA	Huntingdon
976	WJBO	1150	U4	15	5	LA	Baton Rouge
977	WJEM	1150	U3	5	0.1	GA	Valdosta
978	WJRD	1150	U2	20	1	AL	Tuscaloosa
979	WMRD	1150	U1	2.5	0.04	CT	Middletown
980	WMST	1150	U1	2.5	0.03	KY	Mount Sterling
981	WNLR	1150	U1	2.5	0.03	VA	Churchville
982	WSNW	1150	U1	5	0.05	SC	Walhalla
983	WTMP	1150	U4	10	0.5	FL	Egypt Lake
984	WWDJ	1150	U4	5	5	MA	Boston
985	KCTO	**1160**	U4	5	0.23	MO	Cleveland
986	KRDY	1160	U4	10	1	TX	San Antonio
987	KSL	#1160	U1	50	50	UT	Salt Lake City
988	KVCE	1160	U4	35	1	TX	Highland Park
989	WAIX	1160	U1	5	0.57	NY	Mechanicville
990	WBYN	1160	U4	4	1	PA	Lehighton
991	WCCS	1160	U4	10	1	PA	Homer City
992	WCFO	1160	U4	50	0.16	GA	East Point
993	WCRT	1160	U2	50	1	TN	Donelson
994	WCVX	1160	U4	5	0.99	KY	Florence
995	WEWC	1160	U5	5	0.25	FL	Callahan
996	WIWA	1160	U4	2.5	0.5	FL	Saint Cloud
997	WKCM	1160	U2	2.5	1	KY	Hawesville
998	WMET	1160	U4	50	1.5	MD	Gaithersburg
999	WOBM	1160	U4	5	8.9	NJ	Lakewood Township
1000	WODY	1160	U2	5	0.25	VA	Fieldale
1001	WPIE	1160	U4	5	0.31	NY	Trumansburg
1002	WSKW	1160	U1	10	0.73	ME	Skowhegan
1003	WVNJ	1160	U4	20	2.5	NJ	Oakland
1004	WWQT	1160	U2	25	0.5	NC	Tryon
1005	WYDU	1160	U1	5	0.25	NC	Red Springs
1006	WYLL	1160	U4	50	50	IL	Chicago
1007	KCBQ	**1170**	U4	50	2.9	CA	San Diego
1008	KFAQ	#1170	U4	50	50	OK	Tulsa
1009	KLOK	1170	U4	50	5	CA	San Jose
1010	KOWZ	1170	U1	2.5	0.005	MN	Waseca
1011	KPUG	1170	U2	10	5	WA	Bellingham
1012	KYET	1170	U1	6	0.001	AZ	Golden Valley
1013	WAVS	1170	U2	5	0.25	FL	Davie
1014	WCLN	1170	D1	5		NC	Clinton
1015	WCXN	1170	D1	7.7		NC	Claremont
1016	WDEK	1170	D1	10		SC	Lexington
1017	WGMP	1170	U4	10	0.004	AL	Montgomery
1018	WLBH	1170	D3	5		IL	Mattoon
1019	WWVA	1170	U2	50	50	WV	Wheeling
1020	KCKQ	**1180**	U2	4	0.19	NV	Sparks
1021	KERN	1180	U4	50	10	CA	Wasco - Greenacres
1022	KGOL	1180	U4	50	3	TX	Humble
1023	KLAY	1180	U2	5	1	WA	Lakewood
1024	KOFI	1180	U2	50	10	MT	Kalispell
1025	KYES	1180	U7	50	5	MN	Rockville
1026	KZOT	1180	U4	25	1	NE	Bellevue
1027	VOA	1180	U3	100	100	FL	Marathon
1028	WFGN	1180	D1	2.5		SC	Gaffney
1029	WHAM	#1180	U1	50	50	NY	Rochester
1030	WJNT	1180	U12	50	0.5	MS	Pearl
1031	WLTT	1180	D3	10		NC	Carolina Beach
1032	WUMY	1180	U7	5	0.02	AR	Turrell
1033	WVLZ	1180	D1	10		TN	Knoxville
1034	WXLA	1180	D4	10		MI	Dimondale
1035	WZQZ	1180	D1	5		GA	Trion
1036	KDMR	**1190**	U2	5	0.5	MO	Kansas City
1037	KDYA	1190	D3	3		CA	Vallejo
1038	KEX	#1190	U2	50	50	OR	Portland
1039	KFXR	1190	U4	50	5	TX	Dallas
1040	KGBN	1190	U4	20	1.3	CA	Anaheim
1041	KJJI	1190	U2	25	0.35	AR	White Hall
1042	KKOJ	1190	D3	5		MN	Jackson
1043	KNUV	1190	U4	5	0.25	AZ	Tolleson
1044	KQQZ	1190	U4	10	0.02	MO	De Soto
1045	KREB	1190	D1	5		AR	Bentonville-Bella Vista
1046	KVCU	1190	U1	6.8	0.11	CO	Boulder
1047	KXKS	1190	U1	10	0.02	NM	Albuquerque
1048	WAFS	1190	D1	25		GA	Atlanta
1049	WAMT	1190	U2	4.7	0.23	FL	Pine Castle - Sky Lake
1050	WCRW	1190	D3	50		VA	Leesburg
1051	WEUV	1190	D1	2.5		AL	Moulton
1052	WIXE	1190	U1	5	0.07	NC	Monroe
1053	WLIB	1190	U4	10	30	NY	New York
1054	WMEJ	1190	D1	5		MS	Bay Saint Louis
1055	WNWC	1190	U4	4.8	0.02	WI	Sun Prairie
1056	WOWO	#1190	U2	50	9.8	IN	Fort Wayne
1057	WSDQ	1190	D1	5		TN	Dunlap
1058	WVUS	1190	U1	4.5	0.02	WV	Grafton
1059	KFNW	**1200**	U4	50	13	ND	West Fargo
1060	KPSF	1200	U4	5	1.3	CA	Cathedral City
1061	KYAA	1200	U2	25	10	CA	Soquel
1062	WAMB	1200	D1	50		TN	Nashville
1063	WCHB	1200	U4	50	15	MI	Taylor
1064	WJUA	1200	U4	50	1	FL	Pine Island Center
1065	WKST	1200	U2	5	1	PA	New Castle

MW	Call	kHz	Ant.	D	N	Sta	City of License
1066	WMIR	1200	U1	6.5	0.01	SC	Atlantic Beach
1067	WOAI	#1200	U1	50	50	TX	San Antonio
1068	WRKK	1200	U4	10	0.25	PA	Hughesville
1069	WRTO	1200	U4	20	4.5	IL	Chicago
1070	WSML	1200	U2	10	1	NC	Graham
1071	WXIT	1200	D1	10		NC	Blowing Rock
1072	WXKS	1200	U4	50	50	MA	Newton
1073	WZPS	1200	U1	22	0.009	WV	Huntington
1074	KEBR	1210	U5	5	0.5	CA	Rocklin
1075	KEVT	1210	U2	10	1	AZ	Sahuarita
1076	KGYN	1210	U2	10	10	OK	Guymon
1077	KHAT	1210	U2	10	1	WY	Laramie
1078	KHKR	1210	U1	10	0.25	UT	Washington
1079	KMIA	1210	U4	27.5	10	WA	Auburn-Federal Way
1080	KOKK	1210	U4	5	0.87	SD	Huron
1081	KPRZ	1210	U4	20	10	CA	San Marcos
1082	KQEQ	1210	U5	5	0.37	CA	Fowler
1083	KRSV	1210	U1	5	0.25	WY	Afton
1084	KUBR	1210	U4	10	5	TX	San Juan
1085	WANB	1210	D1	5		PA	Waynesburg
1086	WDGR	1210	D1	10		GA	Dahlonega
1087	WILY	1210	U11	10	0.003	IL	Centralia
1088	WJNL	1210	D1	50		MI	Kingsley
1089	WLRO	1210	U2	10	1	LA	Denham Springs
1090	WMPS	1210	U4	10	0.25	TN	Bartlett
1091	WNMA	1210	U4	47	2.5	FL	Miami Springs
1092	WPHT	1210	U1	50	50	PA	Philadelphia
1093	WSBI	1210	D1	10		TN	Static
1094	WTXK	1210	U1	10	0.003	AL	Pike Road
1095	KDOW	1220	U1	5	0.14	CA	Palo Alto
1096	KLBB	1220	U1	5	0.25	MN	Stillwater
1097	WDYT	1220	U5	25	0.1	NC	Kings Mountain
1098	WENC	1220	U1	5	0.15	NC	Whiteville
1099	WFAX	1220	U1	5	0.04	VA	Falls Church
1100	WGNY	1220	U4	10	0.18	NY	Newburgh
1101	WHKW	1220	U3	50	50	OH	Cleveland
1102	WSLM	1220	U3	5	0.08	IN	Salem
		1230					Various stns of 1kW or less
		1240					Various stns of 1kW or less
1103	KBRF	1250	U2	5	2.2	MN	Fergus Falls
1104	KDEI	1250	U2	5	1	TX	Port Arthur
1105	KHIL	1250	U1	5	0.19	AZ	Willcox
1106	KIKC	1250	U1	5	0.13	MT	Forsyth
1107	KKDZ	#1250	U2	5	5	WA	Seattle
1108	KLLK	1250	U4	5	2.5	CA	Willits
1109	KNEU	1250	U1	5	0.12	UT	Roosevelt
1110	KWSU	#1250	U1	5	5	WA	Pullman
1111	KYYS	1250	U4	25	3.7	KS	Kansas City
1112	KZDC	1250	U4	25	0.92	TX	San Antonio
1113	KZER	1250	U4	2.5	1	CA	Santa Barbara
1114	WARE	1250	U4	5	2.5	MA	Ware
1115	WBRM	1250	U1	5	0.05	NC	Marion
1116	WDVA	1250	U2	5	5	VA	Danville
1117	WGAM	1250	U4	5	5	NH	Manchester
1118	WGHB	1250	U4	5	2.5	NC	Farmville
1119	WHHQ	1250	U4	5	1.1	MI	Bridgeport
1120	WHNZ	#1250	U4	25	5.9	FL	Tampa
1121	WLEM	1250	U1	2.5	0.03	PA	Emporium
1122	WMTR	1250	U4	5	7	NJ	Morristown
1123	WPGP	1250	U2	5	5	PA	Pittsburgh
1124	WRBZ	1250	U1	5	0.08	AL	Wetumpka
1125	WRCW	1250	U3	3	0.12	VA	Warrenton
1126	WSSP	1250	U4	5	5	WI	Milwaukee
1127	WTMA	1250	U2	5	1	SC	Charleston
1128	WYKM	1250	D1	5		WV	Rupert
1129	WZOB	1250	U1	5	0.12	AL	Fort Payne
1130	KBRH	1260	U1	5	0.12	LA	Baton Rouge
1131	KBSZ	1260	U1	4.5	0.05	AZ	Apache Junction
1132	KDLF	1260	U3	5	0.03	IA	Boone
1133	KEIR	1260	U1	5	0.06	ID	Idaho Falls
1134	KMZT	1260	U4	20	7.5	CA	Beverly Hills
1135	KPOW	1260	U2	5	1	WY	Powell
1136	KSFB	1260	U1	5	1	CA	San Francisco
1137	KSGF	1260	U2	5	5	MO	Springfield
1138	KSML	1260	U1	4.5	0.07	TX	Diboll
1139	KTRC	1260	U1	1	1	NM	Santa Fe
1140	KWEI	1260	U1	8.4	0.03	ID	Weiser
1141	KWYR	1260	U1	5	0.14	SD	Winner
1142	WCCR	1260	U4	10	5	OH	Cleveland
1143	WCHV	1260	U4	5	2.5	VA	Charlottesville
1144	WDKN	1260	U1	5	0.01	TN	Dickson
1145	WFJS	1260	U4	5	2.5	NJ	Trenton
1146	WFTW	1260	U1	2.5	0.13	FL	Fort Walton Beach
1147	WHYM	1260	U1	5	0.05	SC	Lake City
1148	WKXR	1260	U4	5	0.5	NC	Asheboro
1149	WMKI	1260	U2	5	5	MA	Boston
1150	WNDE	1260	U2	5	5	IN	Indianapolis
1151	WNOO	1260	U1	5	0.02	TN	Chattanooga
1152	WNXT	1260	U4	5	1	OH	Portsmouth
1153	WPHB	1260	U1	5	0.03	PA	Philipsburg
1154	WPJF	1260	U1	5	0.01	SC	Greenville
1155	WPNW	1260	U4	10	1	MI	Zeeland
1156	WRIE	1260	U4	5	5	PA	Erie
1157	WSDZ	#1260	U4	20	5	IL	Belleville
1158	WSKO	1260	U2	5	5	NY	Syracuse
1159	WSUA	1260	U4	50	20	FL	Miami
1160	WUFE	1260	D1	5		GA	Baxley
1161	WWRC	1260	U4	35	5	DC	Washington
1162	WWVT	#1260	U1	5	0.02	VA	Christiansburg
1163	WXCE	1260	U4	5	5	WI	Amery
1164	WYDE	1260	U1	5	0.04	AL	Birmingham
1165	KAJO	1270	U1	10	0.04	OR	Grants Pass
1166	KBAM	1270	U1	5	0.08	WA	Longview
1167	KBZZ	1270	U2	13	5	NV	Sparks
1168	KDJI	1270	U1	5	0.13	AZ	Holbrook
1169	KFAN	1270	U4	5	1	MN	Rochester
1170	KFLC	#1270	U4	50	5	TX	Benbrook
1171	KFSQ	1270	U4	5	0.75	CA	Thousand Palms
1172	KIML	1270	U2	5	1	WY	Gillette
1173	KJUG	1270	U2	5	1	CA	Tulare
1174	KNWC	1270	U4	5	2.3	SD	Sioux Falls
1175	KSCB	1270	U1	5	0.02	KS	Liberal
1176	KTFI	1270	U1	5	1	ID	Twin Falls
1177	KTUZ	1270	U4	5	1	OK	Claremore
1178	WBOJ	1270	U1	5	0.18	GA	Columbus
1179	WCBC	1270	U4	5	1	MD	Cumberland
1180	WCGC	#1270	U4	10	0.5	NC	Belmont
1181	WCMR	1270	U4	5	1	IN	Elkhart
1182	WDLA	1270	U1	5	0.08	NY	Walton
1183	WHEO	1270	D1	5		VA	Stuart
1184	WHGS	1270	U1	10	0.21	SC	Hampton
1185	WHLD	1270	U3	5	1	NY	Niagara Falls
1186	WIJD	1270	U1	5	0.1	AL	Prichard
1187	WJJC	1270	U1	5	0.17	GA	Commerce
1188	WKBF	1270	U2	5	5	IL	Rock Island
1189	WLBR	1270	U4	5	1	PA	Lebanon
1190	WLIK	1270	U2	5	0.5	TN	Newport
1191	WMKT	1270	U2	27	5	MI	Charlevoix
1192	WMPM	1270	U1	5	0.14	NC	Smithfield
1193	WNLS	1270	U1	5	0.11	FL	Tallahassee
1194	WNOG	1270	U4	5	5	FL	Naples
1195	WRLZ	1270	U4	25	5	FL	Eatonville
1196	WSPR	1270	U4	5	1	MA	Springfield
1197	WTSN	1270	U4	5	5	NH	Dover
1198	WWWI	1270	U2	5	5	MN	Baxter
1199	WXYT	#1270	U4	50	50	MI	Detroit
1200	KBNO	1280	U4	5	5	CO	Denver
1201	KIT	1280	U1	5	1	WA	Yakima
1202	KQLL	1280	U1	5	0.02	NV	Henderson
1203	KRVM	1280	U4	5	1.5	OR	Eugene
1204	KRZE	1280	U1	5	0.1	NM	Farmington
1205	KVXR	1280	U4	5	1	MN	Moorhead
1206	KXEG	1280	U1	2.5	0.04	AZ	Phoenix
1207	KXTK	1280	U4	10	2.5	CA	Arroyo Grande
1208	KZFS	1280	U4	5	0.12	WA	Spokane
1209	KZNS	1280	U4	50	0.67	UT	Salt Lake City
1210	WADO	1280	U4	50	7.2	NY	New York
1211	WANS	1280	U2	5	1	SC	Anderson
1212	WDSP	1280	U1	5	0.04	FL	De Funiak Springs
1213	WGBF	1280	U2	5	1	IN	Evansville
1214	WHTK	1280	U2	5	5	NY	Rochester
1215	WHVR	1280	U4	5	0.5	PA	Hanover
1216	WIHB	1280	U1	5	0.09	GA	Macon
1217	WJAY	1280	U1	4.2	0.27	SC	Mullins
1218	WJST	1280	U2	4.9	1	PA	New Castle
1219	WJYE	1280	U2	5	5	ME	Gardiner
1220	WMCP	1280	U1	5	0.5	TN	Columbia
1221	WMXB	1280	U2	5	0.5	AL	Tuscaloosa
1222	WNAM	1280	U4	5	5	WI	Neenah-Menasha
1223	WODT	1280	U3	5	5	LA	New Orleans
1224	WPKZ	1280	U4	5	1	MA	Fitchburg
1225	WWTC	1280	U2	5	5	MN	Minneapolis
1226	WYAL	1280	D1	5		NC	Scotland Neck
1227	WYVE	1280	U1	2.5	0.16	VA	Wytheville

MW	Call	kHz	Ant.	D	N	Sta	City of License
1228	KAZA	1290	U4	5	0.08	CA	Gilroy
1229	KDMS	1290	U1	2.5	0.1	AR	El Dorado
1230	KGVO	1290	U2	5	5	MT	Missoula
1231	KIVY	1290	U1	2.5	0.17	TX	Crockett
1232	KKDD	1290	U4	5	5	CA	San Bernardino
1233	KMMM	1290	U4	5	0.5	KS	Pratt
1234	KOIL	1290	U2	5	5	NE	Omaha
1235	KOUU	1290	U5	50	0.02	ID	Pocatello
1236	KOWB	1290	U4	5	1	WY	Laramie
1237	KPAY	1290	U2	5	5	CA	Chico
1238	KRGE	1290	U2	5	5	TX	Weslaco
1239	KUMA	1290	U2	5	5	OR	Pendleton
1240	KUOA	1290	U1	5	0.03	AR	Siloam Springs
1241	KWFS	1290	U1	5	0.07	TX	Wichita Falls
1242	WCBL	1290	U1	5	0.05	KY	Benton
1243	WCHK	1290	U2	10	0.5	GA	Canton
1244	WDZY	1290	U1	25	0.04	VA	Colonial Heights
1245	WFBG	1290	U2	5	1	PA	Altoona
1246	WHIO	1290	U2	5	5	OH	Dayton
1247	WHKY	1290	U4	50	1	NC	Hickory
1248	WIRL	1290	U4	5	5	IL	Peoria
1249	WJCV	1290	U1	5	0.04	NC	Jacksonville
1250	WJNO	1290	U4	10	4.9	FL	West Palm Beach
1251	WKBK	1290	U3	5	5	NH	Keene
1252	WKLB	1290	U1	5	0.03	KY	Manchester
1253	WKLJ	1290	U1	5	0.05	WI	Sparta
1254	WNBF	1290	U2	9.3	5	NY	Binghamton
1255	WNBN	1290	U1	2.5	0.09	MS	Meridian
1256	WOPP	1290	U4	2.5	0.5	AL	Opp
1257	WRNI	1290	U4	10	10	RI	Providence
1258	WTKS	1290	U2	5	5	GA	Savannah
1259	WVOW	1290	U2	5	1	WV	Logan
1260	WWTX	#1290	U1	2.5	0.03	DE	Wilmington
1261	WZTI	1290	U4	5	5	WI	Greenfield
1262	KAKC	1300	U4	5	1	OK	Tulsa
1263	KAPL	1300	U2	20	5	OR	Phoenix
1264	KAZN	1300	U4	23	4.2	CA	Pasadena
1265	KBRL	1300	U3	5	0.13	NE	McCook
1266	KCMY	1300	U2	5	5	NV	Carson City
1267	KCSF	#1300	U1	5	1	CO	Colorado Springs
1268	KGLO	1300	U4	5	5	IA	Mason City
1269	KKOL	1300	U4	50	47	WA	Seattle
1270	KLER	1300	U2	5	1	ID	Orofino
1271	KOLY	1300	U1	5	0.11	SD	Mobridge
1272	KPMI	1300	U2	2.5	0.6	MN	Bemidji
1273	KPMO	#1300	U1	5	0.07	CA	Mendocino
1274	KSMD	1300	D1	5		AR	Searcy
1275	KSYB	1300	U1	5	0.03	LA	Shreveport
1276	KVET	1300	U4	5	1	TX	Austin
1277	KWRU	1300	U2	5	1	CA	Fresno
1278	WCLG	1300	U1	2.5	0.04	WV	Morgantown
1279	WFFG	1300	U2	2.5	2.5	FL	Marathon
1280	WGDJ	1300	U4	10	8	NY	Rensselaer
1281	WIBR	1300	U4	5	1	LA	Baton Rouge
1282	WIMG	1300	U4	3.2	1.3	NJ	Ewing
1283	WJMO	1300	U3	5	5	OH	Cleveland
1284	WJZ	1300	U4	5	5	MD	Baltimore
1285	WKCY	1300	U1	6.4	0.005	VA	Harrisonburg
1286	WKZN	1300	U4	5	0.5	PA	West Hazleton
1287	WLXG	1300	U2	2.5	1	KY	Lexington
1288	WMEL	1300	U4	5	1	FL	Cocoa Beach
1289	WMTM	1300	U1	5	0.06	GA	Moultrie
1290	WMTN	1300	U1	5	0.09	TN	Morristown
1291	WNQM	1300	U2	50	5	TN	Nashville
1292	WOAD	1300	U1	5	1	MS	Jackson
1293	WOOD	1300	U3	20	20	MI	Grand Rapids
1294	WPNH	1300	U1	5	0.08	NH	Plymouth
1295	WQBN	1300	U5	5	0.16	FL	Temple Terrace
1296	WRDZ	1300	U4	4.5	4	IL	La Grange
1297	WSYD	1300	U2	5	1	NC	Mount Airy
1298	WXRL	1300	U4	5	2.5	NY	Lancaster
1299	KAHL	1310	U3	5	0.28	TX	San Antonio
1300	KEIN	1310	U1	5	1	MT	Great Falls
1301	KFKA	1310	U2	5	1	CO	Greeley
1302	KGLB	1310	U4	2.5	0.27	MN	Glencoe
1303	KIHP	1310	U2	5	0.5	AZ	Mesa
1304	KIQQ	1310	U3	5	0.11	CA	Barstow
1305	KKNS	1310	U2	5	0.5	NM	Corrales
1306	KLIX	1310	U2	5	2.5	ID	Twin Falls
1307	KMBS	1310	U1	5	0.04	LA	West Monroe
1308	KMKY	#1310	U3	5	5	CA	Oakland
1309	KNOX	1310	U2	5	5	ND	Grand Forks
1310	KNPT	1310	U2	5	1	OR	Newport
1311	KTCK	1310	U4	25	5	TX	Dallas
1312	KZRG	1310	U4	5	1	MO	Joplin
1313	KZXR	1310	U1	5	0.06	WA	Prosser
1314	WADB	1310	U4	2.5	1	NJ	Asbury Park
1315	WAUC	1310	U3	5	0.5	FL	Wauchula
1316	WBFD	1310	U1	2.5	0.08	PA	Bedford
1317	WCCW	1310	U4	15	7.5	MI	Traverse City
1318	WDCT	1310	U4	5	0.5	VA	Fairfax
1319	WDKD	1310	U1	5	0.06	SC	Kingstree
1320	WDOC	1310	U1	5	0.02	KY	Prestonsburg
1321	WDTW	1310	U4	5	5	MI	Dearborn
1322	WDXI	1310	U2	5	1	TN	Jackson
1323	WGH	1310	U4	20	5	VA	Newport News
1324	WGSP	1310	U2	5	0.24	NC	Charlotte
1325	WHEP	1310	U1	2.5	0.04	AL	Foley
1326	WIBA	1310	U4	5	5	WI	Madison
1327	WICH	1310	U4	5	5	CT	Norwich
1328	WISE	1310	U2	5	1	NC	Asheville
1329	WJUS	1310	U1	5	0.03	AL	Marion
1330	WLOB	1310	U4	5	5	ME	Portland
1331	WNAE	1310	U1	5	0.09	PA	Warren
1332	WOKA	1310	U1	3.9	0.03	GA	Douglas
1333	WORC	1310	U4	5	1	MA	Worcester
1334	WPBC	1310	U1	2.5	0.03	GA	Decatur
1335	WRVP	1310	U3	5	0.03	NY	Mount Kisco
1336	WSLW	1310	D1	5		WV	White Sulphur Springs
1337	WTIK	1310	U4	5	1	NC	Durham
1338	WTLB	1310	U4	5	0.5	NY	Utica
1339	WTLC	#1310	U2	5	1	IN	Indianapolis
1340	WYND	1310	U1	10.4	0.11	FL	DeLand
1341	KCTC	1320	U4	5	5	CA	West Sacramento
1342	KELO	1320	U2	5	5	SD	Sioux Falls
1343	KFNZ	1320	U3	5	5	UT	Salt Lake City
1344	KHRT	1320	U1	2.5	0.31	ND	Minot
1345	KNCB	1320	U1	5	0.05	LA	Vivian
1346	KOLT	1320	U2	5	1	NE	Scottsbluff
1347	KOZY	1320	U2	5	5	MN	Grand Rapids
1348	KSIV	1320	U2	4.6	0.27	MO	Clayton
1349	KWHN	1320	U2	5	5	AR	Fort Smith
1350	KXRO	1320	U2	5	1	WA	Aberdeen
1351	KXYZ	1320	U4	10	5	TX	Houston
1352	WARA	1320	U4	5	5	MA	Attleboro
1353	WATR	1320	U4	5	1	CT	Waterbury
1354	WCOG	1320	U4	5	5	NC	Greensboro
1355	WDDV	1320	U4	5	1	FL	Venice
1356	WDER	1320	U4	10	1	NH	Derry
1357	WDMJ	1320	U1	5	0.13	MI	Marquette
1358	WENN	1320	U1	5	0.11	AL	Birmingham
1359	WFHR	1320	U2	5	0.5	WI	Wisconsin Rapids
1360	WGOC	1320	U2	5	0.5	TN	Kingsport
1361	WHIE	1320	U1	5	0.08	GA	Griffin
1362	WILS	1320	U4	25	1.9	MI	Lansing
1363	WISW	1320	U2	5	2.5	SC	Columbia
1364	WJAS	1320	U4	7	3.3	PA	Pittsburgh
1365	WJNJ	1320	U2	50	5	FL	Jacksonville
1366	WKRK	1320	U1	5	0.06	NC	Murphy
1367	WLQY	1320	U4	5	5	FL	Hollywood
1368	WMSR	1320	U1	5	0.07	TN	Manchester
1369	WRJW	1320	U1	5	0.07	MS	Picayune
1370	WVNZ	1320	U4	5	0.008	VA	Richmond
1371	KCKM	1330	U2	12	1	TX	Monahans
1372	KGAK	1330	U2	5	1	NM	Gallup
1373	KKPZ	#1330	U3	5	5	OR	Portland
1374	KLBS	1330	U2	0.42	5	CA	Los Banos
1375	KMBI	1330	D1	5		WA	Spokane
1376	KNSS	1330	U2	5	5	KS	Wichita
1377	KOVE	1330	U1	5	0.25	WY	Lander
1378	KPTY	1330	U4	5	5	IA	Waterloo
1379	KVOL	1330	U2	5	1	LA	Lafayette
1380	KWFM	1330	U2	2	5	AZ	South Tucson
1381	KWKW	1330	U2	5	5	CA	Los Angeles
1382	WBTM	1330	U2	5	1	VA	Danville
1383	WCVC	1330	D1	5		FL	Tallahassee
1384	WEBO	1330	U1	5	0.03	NY	Owego
1385	WEBY	1330	U5	25	0.07	FL	Milton
1386	WESR	1330	U1	5	0.05	VA	Onley-Onancock
1387	WFNN	1330	U4	5	5	PA	Erie
1388	WHBL	1330	U4	5	1	WI	Sheboygan
1389	WHGM	1330	U2	5	0.5	MD	Havre de Grace
1390	WITM	1330	U1	5	0.03	VA	Marion
1391	WJNX	1330	U4	5	1	FL	Fort Pierce

MW	Call	kHz	Ant.	D	N	Sta	City of License	MW	Call	kHz	Ant.	D	N	Sta	City of License
1392	WKDP	1330	U4	5	0.01	KY	Corbin	1473	WGIV	1370	U1	16	0.04	NC	Pineville
1393	WKTA	1330	U4	5	0.11	IL	Evanston	1474	WGOH	1370	U1	5	0.02	KY	Grayson
1394	WLOL	1330	U4	9.7	5.1	MN	Minneapolis	1475	WHEE	1370	D1	5		VA	Martinsville
1395	WPJS	1330	U1	3.2	0.02	SC	Conway	1476	WJIP	1370	D1	5		NY	Ellenville
1396	WRCA	1330	U4	25	17	MA	Watertown	1477	WKMC	1370	U3	5	0.03	PA	Roaring Spring
1397	WTRX	1330	U4	5	1	MI	Flint	1478	WLJW	1370	U4	5	1	MI	Cadillac
1398	WVHI	1330	U2	5	1	IN	Evansville	1479	WLLN	1370	U3	5	0.04	NC	Lillington
1399	WWRV	1330	U4	10	5	NY	New York	1480	WLOP	1370	U1	5	0.03	GA	Jesup
1400	WYRD	1330	U2	5	5	SC	Greenville	1481	WOCA	1370	U1	5	0.03	FL	Ocala
1401	WZCT	1330	U1	5	0.03	AL	Scottsboro	1482	WQLL	1370	U4	50	24	MD	Pikesville
		1340	Various stns of 1kW or less					1483	WSHV	1370	U1	4.2	0.41	VA	South Hill
1402	KABQ	**1350**	U5	5	0.5	NM	Albuquerque	1484	WSPD	1370	U2	5	5	OH	Toledo
1403	KCOR	1350	U2	5	5	TX	San Antonio	1485	WTAB	1370	U1	5	0.1	NC	Tabor City
1404	KCOX	1350	U1	5	0.03	TX	Jasper	1486	WVLY	1370	U1	5	0.02	WV	Moundsville
1405	KRLC	1350	U1	5	1	ID	Lewiston	1487	WVMR	1370	D1	5		WV	Frost
1406	KRNT	1350	U2	5	5	IA	Des Moines	1488	WXXI	1370	U1	5	5	NY	Rochester
1407	KSRO	1350	U2	5	5	CA	Santa Rosa	1489	KCNW	**1380**	U1	2.5	0.02	KS	Fairway
1408	KTDD	1350	U4	5	0.6	CA	San Bernardino	1490	KDXE	1380	U4	5	2.5	AR	North Little Rock
1409	KTIK	1350	U4	5	0.6	ID	Nampa	1491	KHEY	1380	U1	5	0.5	TX	El Paso
1410	KZTD	1350	U1	2.5	0.07	AR	Cabot	1492	KLIZ	1380	U2	5	5	MN	Brainerd
1411	WARF	#1350	U3	5	5	OH	Akron	1493	KLPZ	1380	U1	2.5	0.05	AZ	Parker
1412	WBLT	1350	U1	5	0.04	VA	Bedford	1494	KMUS	1380	U4	7	0.25	OK	Sperry
1413	WEZS	1350	U1	5	0.11	NH	Laconia	1495	KOTA	1380	U2	5	5	SD	Rapid City
1414	WFNS	1350	U1	2.5	0.11	GA	Blackshear	1496	KRCM	1380	U1	2.8	0.06	TX	Shenandoah
1415	WGPL	1350	U4	5	5	VA	Portsmouth	1497	KRKO	#1380	U2	50	50	WA	Everett
1416	WHWH	1350	U4	5	5	NJ	Princeton	1498	KSRV	1380	U2	5	1	OR	Ontario
1417	WINY	1350	U1	5	0.07	CT	Putnam	1499	KTKZ	1380	U4	5	5	CA	Sacramento
1418	WIOU	1350	U4	5	1	IN	Kokomo	1500	KWMF	1380	U5	4	0.16	TX	Pleasanton
1419	WNVA	1350	U1	5	0.03	VA	Norton	1501	KXFN	1380	U4	5	1	MO	Saint Louis
1420	WOYK	1350	U2	5	5	PA	York	1502	WABH	1380	U4	10	0.45	NY	Bath
1421	WTDR	1350	U2	5	1	AL	Gadsden	1503	WAOK	1380	U2	25	4.2	GA	Atlanta
1422	WWWL	1350	U2	5	5	LA	New Orleans	1504	WBEL	1380	U2	5	5	IL	South Beloit
1423	WYPZ	1350	U2	15	0.05	GA	Warner Robins	1505	WBTK	1380	U4	5	5	VA	Richmond
1424	WZGM	1350	U1	10	0.05	NC	Black Mountain	1506	WELE	1380	U4	5	2.5	FL	Ormond Beach
1425	KBUY	**1360**	U1	5	0.2	NM	Ruidoso	1507	WFNW	1380	U4	3.5	0.35	CT	Naugatuck
1426	KDJW	1360	U4	6	0.32	TX	Amarillo	1508	WHEW	1380	D1	2.8		TN	Franklin
1427	KFIV	1360	U4	4	0.95	CA	Modesto	1509	WKDM	1380	U3	5	5	NY	New York
1428	KHNC	1360	U4	10	1	CO	Johnstown	1510	WKJG	1380	U4	5	5	IN	Fort Wayne
1429	KKBJ	1360	U2	5	2.5	MN	Bemidji	1511	WKJV	1380	U2	25	1	NC	Asheville
1430	KKMO	1360	U1	5	5	WA	Tacoma	1512	WLRM	1380	U4	2.5	1	TN	Millington
1431	KLSD	1360	U1	5	1	CA	San Diego	1513	WMJR	1380	U1	5	0.03	KY	Nicholasville
1432	KMNY	1360	U4	50	0.89	TX	Hurst	1514	WNRI	1380	U1	2.5	0.01	RI	Woonsocket
1433	KOHU	1360	U2	4.3	0.5	OR	Hermiston	1515	WNRR	1380	U1	4	0.07	SC	North Augusta
1434	KPXQ	1360	U2	50	1	AZ	Glendale	1516	WOTE	1380	U3	3.9	1.8	WI	Clintonville
1435	KRKK	1360	U2	5	1	WY	Rock Springs	1517	WPHM	1380	U4	5	5	MI	Port Huron
1436	KSCJ	1360	U2	5	5	IA	Sioux City	1518	WPYR	1380	U4	5	0.06	LA	Baton Rouge
1437	KUIK	1360	U2	5	5	OR	Hillsboro	1519	WSYB	1380	U2	5	1	VT	Rutland
1438	KWWJ	1360	U4	5	1	TX	Baytown	1520	WTOB	1380	U4	5	2.5	NC	Winston-Salem
1439	WCGL	1360	U1	5	0.08	FL	Jacksonville	1521	WVSA	1380	U1	5	0.03	AL	Vernon
1440	WCHL	1360	U2	5	1	NC	Chapel Hill	1522	WWMI	1380	U2	9.8	6.5	FL	Saint Petersburg
1441	WDRC	1360	U2	5	5	CT	Hartford	1523	KBBO	**1390**	U4	5	0.39	WA	Yakima
1442	WELP	1360	U1	5	0.03	SC	Easley	1524	KENN	1390	U2	5	1.3	NM	Farmington
1443	WGBN	1360	U2	5	1	PA	McKeesport	1525	KFFK	1390	U1	5	0.03	AR	Rogers
1444	WHBG	1360	U1	5	0.009	VA	Harrisonburg	1526	KGNU	#1390	U1	5	0.13	CO	Denver
1445	WHNR	1360	U4	5	2.5	FL	Cypress Gardens	1527	KHOB	1390	U2	5	0.5	NM	Hobbs
1446	WIXI	1360	U1	12	0.04	AL	Jasper	1528	KJPW	1390	U1	5	0.11	MO	Waynesville
1447	WKAT	1360	U1	5	1	FL	North Miami	1529	KLGN	1390	U2	5	0.5	UT	Logan
1448	WKMI	1360	U2	5	1	MI	Kalamazoo	1530	KLOC	1390	U4	5	5	CA	Turlock
1449	WMOB	1360	U4	9	0.2	AL	Mobile	1531	KLTX	1390	U4	5	3.6	CA	Long Beach
1450	WMOV	1360	D1	5		WV	Ravenswood	1532	KRRZ	1390	U1	5	1	ND	Minot
1451	WNJC	1360	U4	5	0.8	NJ	Washington Twnshp	1533	KXSS	1390	U4	2.5	1	MN	Waite Park
1452	WPPA	1360	U4	5	0.5	PA	Pottsville	1534	KZZD	1390	U1	5	0.69	OR	Salem
1453	WSAI	1360	U2	5	5	OH	Cincinnati	1535	WAJD	1390	U1	5	0.05	FL	Gainesville
1454	WTAQ	1360	U4	10	5	WI	Green Bay	1536	WCAT	1390	U2	5	5	VT	Burlington
1455	WWOW	1360	U1	5	0.03	OH	Conneaut	1537	WEED	1390	U1	5	0.03	NC	Rocky Mount
1456	WWWJ	1360	U1	5	0.03	VA	Galax	1538	WEGP	1390	U4	25	10	ME	Presque Isle
1457	WYOS	1360	U1	5	0.5	NY	Binghamton	1539	WEOK	1390	U3	5	0.1	NY	Poughkeepsie
1458	KDTH	**1370**	U2	5	5	IA	Dubuque	1540	WFBL	1390	U4	5	5	NY	Syracuse
1459	KGNO	1370	U1	5	0.23	KS	Dodge City	1541	WGRB	1390	U4	5	5	IL	Chicago
1460	KJCE	1370	U4	5	0.5	TX	Rollingwood	1542	WHMA	1390	U2	5	1	AL	Anniston
1461	KRAC	1370	U4	4	0.2	CA	Red Bluff	1543	WKPA	1390	U1	4.7	0.03	VA	Lynchburg
1462	KSOP	1370	U2	5	0.5	UT	South Salt Lake	1544	WLCM	1390	U4	5	4.5	MI	Holt
1463	KWRM	1370	U4	5	2.5	CA	Corona	1545	WMER	1390	U4	5	0.1	MS	Meridian
1464	KWTL	1370	U1	12	0.27	ND	Grand Forks	1546	WMPO	1390	U1	5	0.12	OH	Middleport-Pomeroy
1465	KXTL	1370	U1	5	5	MT	Butte	1547	WNIO	#1390	U2	9.5	4.8	OH	Youngstown
1466	KZSF	1370	U3	5	5	CA	San Jose	1548	WPLM	1390	U4	5	5	MA	Plymouth
1467	WCCN	1370	U1	5	0.04	WI	Neillsville	1549	WRIG	1390	U4	10	7.2	WI	Schofield
1468	WCOA	1370	U2	5	5	FL	Pensacola	1550	WROA	1390	U4	5	5	MS	Gulfport
1469	WDEA	1370	U4	5	5	ME	Ellsworth	1551	WSPO	1390	U2	5	5	SC	Charleston
1470	WDEF	1370	U4	5	5	TN	Chattanooga	1552	WTJS	1390	U2	5	1	TN	Jackson
1471	WFEA	1370	U4	5	5	NH	Manchester	1553	WYXI	1390	U1	2.5	0.06	TN	Athens
1472	WGCL	1370	U4	5	0.5	IN	Bloomington	1554	WZHF	1390	U4	5	5	VA	Arlington

MW	Call	kHz	Ant.	D	N	Sta	City of License
1555	WZQQ	1390	D1	5		KY	Hazard
		1400	Various stns of 1kW or less				
1556	KBNP	**1410**	U1	5	0.009	OR	Portland
1557	KCAL	1410	U2	5	4	CA	Redlands
1558	KGSO	1410	U4	5	1	KS	Wichita
1559	KKLO	1410	U4	5	0.5	KS	Leavenworth
1560	KMYC	1410	U4	5	1	CA	Marysville
1561	KOOQ	1410	U2	5	0.5	NE	North Platte
1562	KQV	1410	U4	5	5	PA	Pittsburgh
1563	KWYO	1410	U1	5	0.35	WY	Sheridan
1564	WDOV	1410	U4	5	5	DE	Dover
1565	WELM	1410	U2	5	1	NY	Elmira
1566	WHBT	1410	U1	5	0.01	FL	Tallahassee
1567	WHLN	1410	U1	5	0.04	KY	Harlan
1568	WING	1410	U2	5	5	OH	Dayton
1569	WIQR	1410	U4	5	1	AL	Prattville
1570	WIZM	1410	U2	5	5	WI	La Crosse
1571	WKKP	1410	U1	2.5	0.05	GA	McDonough
1572	WLSH	1410	D3	5		PA	Lansford
1573	WMYR	1410	U2	5	5	FL	Fort Myers
1574	WNER	1410	U1	3.5	0.05	NY	Watertown
1575	WNGL	1410	U2	5	4.6	AL	Mobile
1576	WPOP	1410	U4	5	5	CT	Hartford
1577	WQBQ	1410	U1	5	0.09	FL	Leesburg
1578	WRJD	1410	U4	5	0.29	NC	Durham
1579	WRTZ	1410	U1	5	0.07	VA	Roanoke
1580	WSCW	1410	D1	5		WV	South Charleston
1581	KBHS	**1420**	U1	5	0.08	AR	Hot Springs
1582	KIGO	1420	U1	32	0.01	ID	Saint Anthony
1583	KITI	1420	U4	5	5	WA	Centralia - Chehalis
1584	KMOG	1420	U2	2.5	0.5	AZ	Payson
1585	KSTN	1420	U4	5	1	CA	Stockton
1586	KTOE	1420	U2	5	5	MN	Mankato
1587	KUJ	1420	U1	5	0.9	WA	Walla Walla
1588	WACK	1420	U4	5	0.5	NY	Newark
1589	WACT	1420	U1	5	0.1	AL	Tuscaloosa
1590	WASR	1420	U1	5	0.13	NH	Wolfeboro
1591	WBRD	1420	U4	2.5	1	FL	Palmetto
1592	WBSM	1420	U3	5	1	MA	New Bedford
1593	WCED	1420	U1	4.2	0.005	PA	Du Bois
1594	WCOJ	1420	U2	5	5	PA	Coatesville
1595	WDJA	1420	U4	5	0.5	FL	Delray Beach
1596	WEMB	1420	U1	5	0.02	TN	Erwin
1597	WHK	1420	U2	5	5	OH	Cleveland
1598	WIGG	1420	U1	5	0.07	MS	Wiggins
1599	WIMS	1420	U4	5	5	IN	Michigan City
1600	WKCW	1420	U4	22	0.06	VA	Warrenton
1601	WKWN	1420	U1	2.5	0.11	GA	Trenton
1602	WLIS	1420	U2	5	0.5	CT	Old Saybrook
1603	WLNA	1420	U4	5	1	NY	Peekskill
1604	WOC	1420	U4	5	5	IA	Davenport
1605	WRCG	1420	U1	5	0.07	GA	Columbus
1606	WTCR	1420	U2	5	0.5	WV	Kenova
1607	KBRC	**1430**	U2	5	1	WA	Mount Vernon
1608	KCKL	1430	U4	5	1	WA	Asotin
1609	KCRX	1430	U2	5	1	NM	Roswell
1610	KEES	1430	U2	5	1	TX	Gladewater
1611	KEZW	1430	U2	10	5	CO	Aurora
1612	KLO	1430	U4	25	5	UT	Ogden
1613	KMRB	1430	U4	50	9.8	CA	San Gabriel
1614	KRGI	1430	U2	5	1	NE	Grand Island
1615	KSHJ	1430	U4	5	1	TX	Houston
1616	KTBZ	1430	U4	25	5	OK	Tulsa
1617	KVVN	1430	U4	1	2.5	CA	Santa Clara
1618	KYKN	1430	U2	5	5	OR	Keizer
1619	KYNO	1430	U3	5	5	CA	Fresno
1620	KZQZ	1430	U4	50	5	MO	Saint Louis
1621	WBLR	1430	U1	5	0.16	SC	Batesburg
1622	WCWC	1430	U1	4.6	0.03	KY	Williamsburg
1623	WDAL	1430	U1	2.5	0.07	GA	Dalton
1624	WDEX	1430	U4	2.5	0.5	NC	Monroe
1625	WDIC	1430	U1	5	0.05	VA	Clinchco
1626	WDJS	1430	U4	10	5	NC	Mount Olive
1627	WENE	1430	U2	5	5	NY	Endicott
1628	WFHK	1430	D1	5		AL	Pell City
1629	WGFS	1430	U1	3.9	0.21	GA	Covington
1630	WION	1430	U2	4.7	0.33	MI	Ionia
1631	WKOX	1430	U2	5	1	MA	Everett
1632	WLKF	1430	U1	5	1	FL	Lakeland
1633	WLTG	1430	U4	5	5	FL	Panama City
1634	WMNC	1430	U1	2.7	0.04	NC	Morganton
1635	WNAV	1430	U2	5	1	MD	Annapolis
1636	WNSW	1430	U4	10	7	NJ	Newark
1637	WOIR	1430	U2	5	0.5	FL	Homestead
1638	WOWW	1430	U2	2.5	2.5	TN	Germantown
1639	WPLN	1430	U2	15	1	TN	Madison
1640	WPNI	1430	U4	5	0.01	MA	Amherst
1641	WTMN	1430	U1	10	0.04	FL	Gainesville
1642	WVAM	1430	U2	5	1	PA	Altoona
1643	WXNT	1430	U2	5	5	IN	Indianapolis
1644	KAZG	**1440**	U1	5	0.05	AZ	Scottsdale
1645	KDIZ	#1440	U2	5	0.5	MN	Golden Valley
1646	KETX	1440	U1	5	0.09	TX	Livingston
1647	KMAJ	1440	U3	5	1	KS	Topeka
1648	KMED	1440	U1	5	1	OR	Medford
1649	KODL	1440	U2	5	1	OR	The Dalles
1650	KPTO	1440	U4	2.5	0.35	ID	Pocatello
1651	KPUR	1440	U2	5	1	TX	Amarillo
1652	KRDZ	1440	U1	5	0.21	CO	Wray
1653	KTNO	1440	U4	50	0.35	TX	University Park
1654	KTUV	1440	U2	5	0.24	AR	Little Rock
1655	KUHL	1440	U2	5	1	CA	Santa Maria
1656	KVON	1440	U4	5	1	CA	Napa
1657	WAJR	1440	U4	5	0.5	WV	Morgantown
1658	WBLA	1440	U1	5	0.19	NC	Elizabethtown
1659	WCDL	1440	U1	5	0.03	PA	Carbondale
1660	WFNY	1440	U2	5	0.5	NY	Gloversville
1661	WGEM	1440	U4	5	1	IL	Quincy
1662	WGIG	1440	U2	5	1	GA	Brunswick
1663	WGMI	1440	U1	2.5	0.06	GA	Bremen
1664	WGVL	1440	U2	5	5	SC	Greenville
1665	WHIS	1440	U1	5	0.5	WV	Bluefield
1666	WHKZ	1440	U4	5	5	OH	Warren
1667	WKLV	1440	U1	5	0.07	VA	Blackstone
1668	WKPR	1440	U1	2.7	0.02	MI	Kalamazoo
1669	WLWI	1440	U2	5	1	AL	Montgomery
1670	WLXN	1440	U2	5	1	NC	Lexington
1671	WMAX	1440	U4	5	2.5	MI	Bay City
1672	WNFL	1440	U4	5	0.5	WI	Green Bay
1673	WNPV	1440	U4	2.5	0.5	PA	Lansdale
1674	WPRD	1440	U2	5	1	FL	Winter Park
1675	WRED	1440	U2	5	5	ME	Westbrook
1676	WROK	1440	U5	5	0.27	IL	Rockford
1677	WVEI	1440	U2	5	5	MA	Worcester
1678	WVGG	1440	D1	5		MS	Lucedale
1679	WWCL	1440	U4	5	1	FL	Lehigh Acres
1680	WZYX	1440	U1	5	0.06	TN	Cowan
		1450	Various stns of 1kW or less				
1681	KARR	**1460**	U4	5	2.5	WA	Kirkland
1682	KBRZ	1460	U1	5	0.12	TX	Missouri City
1683	KCLE	1460	U4	11	0.7	TX	Burleson
1684	KENO	1460	U4	10	0.62	NV	Las Vegas
1685	KHOJ	1460	U4	12	0.21	MO	Saint Charles
1686	KION	1460	U3	10	10	CA	Salinas
1687	KKAQ	1460	U1	2.5	0.15	MN	Thief River Falls
1688	KLTC	1460	U2	5	5	ND	Dickinson
1689	KTYM	1460	U4	5	0.5	CA	Inglewood
1690	KUTI	1460	U2	5	3.7	WA	Yakima
1691	KXNO	#1460	U2	5	5	IA	Des Moines
1692	KXPN	1460	U1	5	0.05	NE	Kearney
1693	KZNT	1460	U2	5	0.54	CO	Colorado Springs
1694	WBNS	1460	U2	5	1	OH	Columbus
1695	WBRN	1460	U2	5	2.5	MI	Big Rapids
1696	WBUC	1460	U1	5.5	0.02	WV	Buckhannon
1697	WEKB	1460	U1	5	0.11	KY	Elkhorn City
1698	WEWO	1460	U4	5	5	NC	Laurinburg
1699	WGMF	1460	U4	5	1	PA	Tunkhannock
1700	WHAL	1460	U1	4	0.14	AL	Phenix City
1701	WHBK	1460	U1	5	0.13	NC	Marshall
1702	WHIC	1460	U2	3.7	5	NY	Rochester
1703	WIFI	1460	U3	5	0.5	NJ	Florence
1704	WKAM	1460	U2	2.5	0.5	IN	Goshen
1705	WKDV	1460	U4	5	5	VA	Manassas
1706	WMCJ	1460	U2	5	0.5	AL	Cullman
1707	WNPL	1460	U4	7	2	FL	Golden Gate
1708	WOPG	1460	U2	5	5	NY	Albany
1709	WQOP	1460	U2	15	5	FL	Jacksonville
1710	WQXM	1460	U5	10	0.15	FL	Bartow
1711	WRAD	1460	U1	5	0.03	VA	Radford
1712	WTKT	1460	U4	5	4.2	PA	Harrisburg
1713	WXBR	1460	U2	5	1	MA	Brockton
1714	WXEM	1460	U1	5	0.19	GA	Buford
1715	WXOK	1460	U1	4.7	0.29	LA	Port Allen
1716	WZEP	1460	U1	10	0.18	FL	Defuniak Springs

MW	Call	kHz	Ant.	D	N	Sta	City of License
1717	KBSN	**1470**	U4	5	1	WA	Moses Lake
1718	KELA	1470	U1	5	1	WA	Centralia-Chehalis
1719	KIID	1470	U4	5	1	CA	Sacramento
1720	KLCL	1470	U1	5	0.5	LA	Lake Charles
1721	KMNQ	1470	U4	5	5	MN	Brooklyn Park
1722	KNXN	1470	U1	2.5	0.03	AZ	Sierra Vista
1723	KUTY	1470	U1	5	5	CA	Palmdale
1724	KVSL	1470	U1	5	0.08	AZ	Show Low
1725	KWRD	1470	D1	5		TX	Henderson
1726	KWSL	1470	U4	5	5	IA	Sioux City
1727	KYYW	1470	U2	5	1	TX	Abilene
1728	WAZN	1470	U4	1.4	3.4	MA	Watertown
1729	WBFC	1470	U1	2.5	0.02	KY	Stanton
1730	WBKV	1470	U4	2.5	2.5	WI	West Bend
1731	WBTX	1470	U4	5	0.03	VA	Broadway-Timberville
1732	WFNT	1470	U4	5	1	MI	Flint
1733	WJDY	1470	U3	5	0.04	MD	Salisbury
1734	WLAM	1470	U3	5	5	ME	Lewiston
1735	WMBD	1470	U4	5	5	IL	Peoria
1736	WMGG	1470	U1	5	0.5	FL	Dunedin
1737	WMMW	1470	U4	2.5	2.5	CT	Meriden
1738	WNAU	1470	U2	2.5	0.5	MS	New Albany
1739	WNYY	1470	U2	5	1	NY	Ithaca
1740	WQXL	1470	U1	11	0.1	SC	Columbia
1741	WRGA	1470	U2	5	5	GA	Rome
1742	WSAN #	1470	U2	5	5	PA	Allentown
1743	WTOE	1470	U1	5	0.1	NC	Spruce Pine
1744	WTZE	1470	D1	5		VA	Tazewell
1745	WVOL	1470	U4	5	1	TN	Berry Hill
1746	WWBG	1470	U4	10	5	NC	Greensboro
1747	WWNN	1470	U4	50	2.5	FL	Pompano Beach
1748	KBMS	**1480**	U2	1	2.5	WA	Vancouver
1749	KBXD	1480	U4	5	1.9	TX	Dallas
1750	KCHL	1480	U3	2.5	0.09	TX	San Antonio
1751	KGOE	1480	U1	5	1	CA	Eureka
1752	KKCQ	1480	U1	5	0.09	MN	Fosston
1753	KLVL	1480	U4	5	0.5	TX	Pasadena
1754	KPHX	1480	U2	5	0.5	AZ	Phoenix
1755	KQAM	1480	U4	5	1	KS	Wichita
1756	KRXR	1480	U1	5	0.09	ID	Gooding
1757	KTHS	1480	U1	5	0.06	AR	Green Forest
1758	KVNR	1480	U4	5	5	CA	Santa Ana
1759	KYOS	1480	U2	5	5	CA	Merced
1760	WBBP	1480	U1	5	0.04	TN	Memphis
1761	WCFR	1480	U1	5	0.02	VT	Springfield
1762	WDAS	1480	U4	5	5	PA	Philadelphia
1763	WDJO	1480	U4	4.5	0.3	OH	Cincinnati
1764	WERM	1480	U2	5	4.4	AL	Mobile
1765	WGFY #	1480	U4	4.4	5	NC	Charlotte
1766	WGVU #	1480	U2	2	5	MI	Kentwood
1767	WHBC	1480	U4	15	5	OH	Canton
1768	WKGC	1480	U1	5	0.03	FL	Southport
1769	WLEA	1480	U1	2.5	0.01	NY	Hornell
1770	WLMV	1480	U4	5	5	WI	Madison
1771	WPFJ	1480	U1	5	0.01	NC	Franklin
1772	WPFR	1480	U4	5	1	IN	Terre Haute
1773	WPWC	1480	U4	5	0.5	VA	Dumfries-Triangle
1774	WQOH	1480	U1	5	5	AL	Irondale
1775	WQTM	1480	U1	10	0.04	NC	Fair Bluff
1776	WRCK	1480	D1	5		NY	Remsen
1777	WSAR	1480	U3	5	5	MA	Fall River
1778	WSDS	1480	U4	0.75	3.8	MI	Salem Township
1779	WTOX	1480	U4	6.3	1.5	VA	Glen Allen
1780	WTOY	1480	U1	5	0.02	VA	Salem
1781	WUKB	1480	D1	5		KY	Neon
1782	WYZE	1480	U1	10	0.04	GA	Atlanta
1783	WZRC	1480	U4	5	5	NY	New York
		1490	Various stns of 1kW or less				
1784	KSJX	**1500**	U4	10	5	CA	San Jose
1785	KSTP	1500	U2	50	50	MN	Saint Paul
1786	WBRI	1500	D3	5		IN	Indianapolis
1787	WDPC	1500	D4	5		GA	Dallas
1788	WFED	1500	U4	50	50	DC	Washington
1789	WFIF	1500	D3	5		CT	Milford
1790	WLQV	1500	U4	50	10	MI	Detroit
1791	KBED	**1510**	D3	5		TX	Nederland
1792	KCKK	1510	U4	10	25	CO	Littleton
1793	KCTE	1510	D3	10		MO	Independence
1794	KFNN	1510	U3	22	0.1	AZ	Mesa
1795	KGA	1510	U4	50	15	WA	Spokane
1796	KIRV	1510	D3	10		CA	Fresno
1797	KLLB	1510	D1	10		UT	West Jordan
1798	KMRF	1510	D4	5		MO	Marshfield
1799	KMSD	1510	U1	5	0.01	SD	Milbank
1800	KOAZ	1510	U1	5	0.02	NM	Isleta
1801	KSFN	1510	U4	8	2.4	CA	Piedmont
1802	KSPA	1510	U4	10	1	CA	Ontario
1803	WFAI	1510	D3	2.5		NJ	Salem
1804	WLAC	1510	U2	50	50	TN	Nashville
1805	WMEX	1510	U7	50	50	MA	Boston
1806	WPGR	1510	U4	5	0.001	PA	Monroeville
1807	WRRD	1510	D4	23		WI	Waukesha
1808	WWBC	1510	D4	50		FL	Cocoa
1809	WWSM	1510	D3	5		PA	Annville-Cleona
1810	KFXZ	**1520**	U6	10	0.5	LA	Lafayette
1811	KKXA #	1520	U2	50	50	WA	Snohomish
1812	KKZZ	1520	U4	10	1	CA	Port Hueneme
1813	KMPG	1520	D4	5		CA	Hollister
1814	KOKC	1520	U2	50	50	OK	Oklahoma City
1815	KOLM	1520	U8	10	0.8	MN	Rochester
1816	KQQB	1520	D3	2.5		TX	Stockdale
1817	KQRR	1520	U3	50	15	OR	Oregon City
1818	KRHW	1520	U7	5	1.6	MO	Sikeston
1819	KYND	1520	D4	25		TX	Cypress
1820	WARR	1520	D1	5		NC	Warrenton
1821	WBZW	1520	U4	5	0.35	FL	Apopka
1822	WDCY	1520	D1	2.5		GA	Douglasville
1823	WDSL	1520	D1	5		NC	Mocksville
1824	WEXY	1520	U2	5	0.8	FL	Wilton Manors
1825	WHOW	1520	D1	5		IL	Clinton
1826	WIZZ	1520	D3	10		MA	Greenfield
1827	WLGC	1520	D1	5		KY	Greenup
1828	WTRI	1520	D3	17		MD	Brunswick
1829	WWKB	1520	U3	50	50	NY	Buffalo
1830	KFBK #	**1530**	U4	50	50	CA	Sacramento
1831	KGBT	1530	U8	50	10	TX	Harlingen
1832	KKHI	1530	U1	15	0.01	CO	Colorado Springs
1833	KLBW	1530	D1	2.5		TX	New Boston
1834	KQSP	1530	U3	8.6	0.01	MN	Shakopee
1835	KVDW	1530	D1	2.5		AR	England
1836	KXTD	1530	D3	5		OK	Wagoner
1837	KZNX	1530	U7	10	0.22	TX	Creedmoor
1838	WCKY #	1530	U2	50	50	OH	Cincinnati
1839	WDJZ	1530	D3	5		CT	Bridgeport
1840	WLCO	1530	D3	5		MI	Lapeer
1841	WLLQ	1530	D3	10		NC	Chapel Hill
1842	WTTI	1530	D4	10		GA	Dalton
1843	WVBF	1530	U14	5	0.004	MA	Middleborough Center
1844	WYMM	1530	D3	50		FL	Jacksonville
1845	KASA	**1540**	U3	10	0.01	AZ	Phoenix
1846	KEDA	1540	U4	5	1	TX	San Antonio
1847	KGBC	1540	U4	2.5	0.25	TX	Galveston
1848	KMPC	1540	U4	50	37	CA	Los Angeles
1849	KXEL	1540	U2	50	50	IA	Waterloo
1850	KXPA	1540	U2	5	5	WA	Bellevue
1851	KZMP	1540	U4	32	0.75	TX	University Park
1852	WACA	1540	D1	5		MD	Wheaton
1853	WDCD	1540	U3	50	50	NY	Albany
1854	WECZ	1540	D1	5		PA	Punxsutawney
1855	WKVQ	1540	D1	10		GA	Eatonton
1856	WNWR	1540	D3	50		PA	Philadelphia
1857	WREJ	1540	U4	10	0.007	VA	Richmond
1858	WTBI	1540	D1	5		SC	Pickens
1859	WXEX	1540	U1	5	0.003	NH	Exeter
1860	WYNC	1540	D1	2.5		NC	Yanceyville
1861	KAPE	**1550**	U3	5	0.04	MO	Cape Girardeau
1862	KESJ	1550	U2	2.5	0.5	MO	Saint Joseph
1863	KKOV	1550	U2	50	12	WA	Vancouver
1864	KLFJ	1550	U1	5	0.02	MO	Springfield
1865	KMRI	1550	U1	10	0.34	UT	West Valley City
1866	KRKE	1550	U1	10	0.02	NM	Albuquerque
1867	KRPI	1550	U4	50	10	WA	Ferndale
1868	KUAZ	1550	D1	50		AZ	Tucson
1869	KWRN	1550	U2	5	0.5	CA	Apple Valley
1870	KXEX	1550	U4	5	2.5	CA	Fresno
1871	KXTO	1550	U1	2.5	0.09	NV	Reno
1872	KYAL	1550	U3	2.5	0.04	OK	Sapulpa
1873	KZDG	1550	U4	10	10	CA	San Francisco
1874	WAMA	1550	U1	10	0.13	FL	Tampa
1875	WAZX	1550	U4	50	0.01	GA	Smyrna
1876	WHIT	1550	D3	5		WI	Madison
1877	WIGN	1550	U1	35	0.006	TN	Bristol
1878	WITK	1550	U4	10	0.5	PA	Pittston
1879	WKBA	1550	D3	10		VA	Vinton

MW	Call	kHz	Ant.	D	N	Sta	City of License
1880	WKTF	1550	U1	10	0.02	GA	Vienna
1881	WLOR	1550	U4	50	0.04	AL	Huntsville
1882	WMRE	1550	U1	5	0.006	WV	Charles Town
1883	WNTN	1550	U1	10	0.003	MA	Newton
1884	WNZF	1550	U2	11	0.25	FL	Bunnell
1885	WPFC	1550	U1	5	0.04	LA	Baton Rouge
1886	WRHC	1550	U4	10	0.5	FL	Coral Gables
1887	WSDK	1550	U4	5	2.4	CT	Bloomfield
1888	WTHB	1550	U1	5	0.01	GA	Augusta
1889	WVAB	1550	U1	5	0.009	VA	Virginia Beach
1890	KGOW	**1560**	U4	46	15	TX	Bellaire
1891	KKAA	1560	U4	10	10	SD	Aberdeen
1892	KLNG	1560	D1	10		IA	Council Bluffs
1893	KNZR	1560	U2	25	10	CA	Bakersfield
1894	KTXZ	1560	U4	2.5	2.5	WA	West Lake Hills
1895	KVAN	1560	U4	10	0.7	WA	Burbank
1896	KZIZ	1560	U2	5	0.9	WA	Pacific
1897	WCNW	1560	D3	5		OH	Fairfield
1898	WFME	1560	U4	50	50	NY	New York
1899	WLZR	1560	D1	5		FL	Melbourne
1900	WNWN	1560	D3	4.1		MI	Portage
1901	WPAD	1560	U7	10	5	KY	Paducah
1902	WSBV	1560	D1	2.5		VA	South Boston
1903	WYZD	1560	D1	4.2		NC	Dobson
1904	KAKK	**1570**	U1	9.5	0.25	MN	Walker
1905	KBCV	1570	U4	5	3	MO	Hollister
1906	KCVR	#1570	U4	5	0.5	CA	Lodi
1907	KKCL	1570	U1	7	0.01	CO	Loveland
1908	KPRO	1570	U3	5	0.19	CA	Riverside
1909	KTGE	1570	U4	5	0.5	CA	Salinas
1910	KYCR	1570	U1	3.8	0.23	MN	Golden Valley
1911	WCLE	1570	U1	5	0.08	TN	Cleveland
1912	WCRL	1570	U1	2.5	0.06	AL	Oneonta
1913	WECU	1570	U1	8	0.2	NC	Winterville
1914	WFLR	1570	U1	5	0.44	NY	Dundee
1915	WFRL	1570	U3	5	0.5	IL	Freeport
1916	WIGO	1570	U1	5	0.05	GA	Morrow
1917	WISP	1570	U1	5	0.9	PA	Doylestown
1918	WIZK	1570	D1	3.2		MS	Bay Springs
1919	WLKD	1570	U1	5	0.5	WI	Minocqua
1920	WMVX	1570	U1	30	0.08	MA	Beverly
1921	WNCA	1570	U1	5	0.28	NC	Siler City
1922	WNST	1570	U1	5	0.23	MD	Towson
1923	WPGM	1570	U1	2.5	0.22	PA	Danville
1924	WTWB	1570	U1	5	0.01	FL	Auburndale
1925	WVOJ	1570	U1	10	0.03	FL	Fernandina Beach
1926	WYTI	1570	U1	2.5	0.22	VA	Rocky Mount
1927	KBLA	**1580**	U4	50	50	CA	Santa Monica
1928	KFCS	1580	U1	10	0.04	CO	Colorado Springs
1929	KGAL	1580	U2	5	1	OR	Lebanon
1930	KMIK	1580	U2	50	50	AZ	Tempe
1931	WDAB	1580	U1	5	0.01	SC	Travelers Rest
1932	WJFK	1580	U4	50	0.27	MD	Morningside
1933	WLIJ	1580	U1	5	0.01	TN	Shelbyville
1934	WLIM	1580	U2	10	0.5	NY	Patchogue
1935	WNPZ	1580	D1	5		TN	Knoxville
1936	WNTF	1580	D3	10		FL	Bithlo
1937	WPMO	1580	U4	5	0.05	MS	Pascagoula-Moss Point
1938	WSRF	1580	U4	10	1.5	FL	Fort Lauderdale
1939	WTCL	1580	D1	10		FL	Chattahoochee
1940	WTTN	1580	U5	5	0.004	WI	Columbus
1941	WVKO	1580	U4	3.2	0.29	OH	Columbus
1942	WVOK	1580	U1	2.5	0.02	AL	Oxford
1943	WWTF	1580	U3	10	0.04	KY	Georgetown
1944	KBJT	**1590**	U1	4.7	0.03	AR	Fordyce
1945	KCTY	1590	U3	2.5	0.04	NE	Wayne
1946	KELP	1590	U4	5	0.8	TX	El Paso
1947	KGAS	1590	U1	2.5	0.12	TX	Carthage
1948	KGFK	1590	U4	5	1	MN	East Grand Forks
1949	KLFE	1590	U2	5	5	WA	Seattle
1950	KLIV	1590	U2	5	5	CA	San Jose
1951	KLRK	1590	U4	2.5	0.06	TX	Mexia
1952	KMIC	1590	U2	5	5	TX	Houston
1953	KTIL	1590	U2	5	1	OR	Netarts
1954	KVGB	1590	U2	5	5	KS	Great Bend
1955	KVTA	1590	U4	5	5	CA	Ventura
1956	KYNG	1590	U1	2.5	0.05	AR	Springdale
1957	WAIK	1590	U4	5	0.05	IL	Galesburg
1958	WAKR	1590	U2	5	5	OH	Akron
1959	WALG	1590	U4	5	1	GA	Albany
1960	WARV	1590	U4	8	5	RI	Warwick
1961	WCGO	1590	U2	10	2.5	IL	Evanston
1962	WCSL	1590	U1	10	0.03	NC	Cherryville
1963	WFTH	1590	U1	5	0.01	VA	Richmond
1964	WGBW	1590	U4	10	0.5	WI	Denmark
1965	WGGO	1590	U1	5	0.01	NY	Salamanca
1966	WHGT	1590	U4	15	0.05	MD	Maugansville
1967	WHPY	1590	U3	5	0.02	NC	Clayton
1968	WIXK	1590	U1	5	0.09	WI	New Richmond
1969	WKTP	1590	U3	5	5	TN	Jonesborough
1970	WNTS	1590	U4	5	0.5	IN	Beech Grove
1971	WPSL	1590	U1	5	0.06	FL	Port Saint Lucie
1972	WPSN	1590	U1	2.5	0.01	PA	Honesdale
1973	WPWA	1590	U2	2.5	1	PA	Chester
1974	WQCH	1590	D1	5		GA	Lafayette
1975	WRXB	1590	U4	5	1	FL	Saint Pete Beach
1976	WSMN	1590	U3	5	5	NH	Nashua
1977	WTVB	1590	U2	5	1	MI	Coldwater
1978	WVNA	1590	U2	5	1	AL	Tuscumbia
1979	WXRS	1590	U1	2.5	0.02	GA	Swainsboro
1980	KAHZ	**1600**	U2	5	5	CA	Pomona
1981	KATZ	1600	U2	6	3.5	MO	Saint Louis
1982	KEPN	#1600	U2	5	5	CO	Lakewood
1983	KGST	1600	U2	5	5	CA	Fresno
1984	KGYM	1600	U2	5	5	IA	Cedar Rapids
1985	KIVA	1600	U1	10	0.17	NM	Albuquerque
1986	KLEB	1600	U4	5	0.25	LA	Golden Meadow
1987	KOKE	1600	U4	5	0.7	TX	Pflugerville
1988	KOPB	1600	U2	5	1	OR	Eugene
1989	KPNP	1600	U3	5	5	MN	Watertown
1990	KRVA	1600	U4	25	0.93	TX	Cockrell Hill
1991	KTUB	1600	U2	5	1	UT	Centerville
1992	KUBA	1600	U2	5	2.5	CA	Yuba City
1993	KVRI	1600	U4	50	10	WA	Blaine
1994	WAAM	1600	U4	5	5	MI	Ann Arbor
1995	WAOS	1600	U1	20	0.06	GA	Austell
1996	WATX	1600	U1	2.5	0.02	TN	Algood
1997	WAYC	1600	U1	2.7	0.01	PA	Bedford
1998	WCPK	1600	U1	4.2	0.02	VA	Chesapeake
1999	WEHH	1600	U4	5	0.17	NY	Elmira Heights-Horseheads
2000	WHIY	1600	U2	5	0.5	AL	Huntsville
2001	WHNP	1600	D1	2.5		MA	East Longmeadow
2002	WHTY	1600	U4	5	4.7	FL	Riviera Beach
2003	WIDU	1600	U4	5	0.14	NC	Fayetteville
2004	WKKX	1600	U1	5	0.03	WV	Wheeling
2005	WKZK	1600	U1	4	0.02	SC	North Augusta
2006	WMQM	1600	U1	50	0.03	TN	Lakeland
2007	WRJE	1600	U4	5	1	DE	Dover
2008	WRPN	1600	U4	5	5	WI	Ripon
2009	WTZQ	1600	U1	5	0.03	NC	Hendersonville
2010	WUNR	1600	U3	20	20	MA	Brookline
2011	WWRL	1600	U4	25	5	NY	New York
2012	WXMY	1600	D1	5		VA	Saltville
2013	WXVI	1600	U4	5	1	AL	Montgomery
2014	WZNZ	1600	U1	5	0.08	FL	Atlantic Beach
2015	WZZW	1600	U1	5	0.02	WV	Milton
2016	KOZN	**1620**	U1	10	1	NE	Bellevue
2017	KSMH	1620	U1	10	1	CA	West Sacramento
2018	KYIZ	1620	U1	10	1	WA	Renton
2019	WDND	1620	U1	10	1	IN	South Bend
2020	WNRP	1620	U1	10	1	FL	Gulf Breeze
2021	WTAW	1620	U1	10	1	TX	College Station
2022	KCJJ	**1630**	U1	10	1	IA	Iowa City
2023	KKGM	1630	U1	10	1	TX	Fort Worth
2024	KRND	1630	U1	10	1	WY	Fox Farm
2025	WRDW	1630	U1	10	1	GA	Augusta
2026	KBJA	**1640**	U1	10	1	UT	Sandy
2027	KDIA	1640	U2	10	10	CA	Vallejo
2028	KDZR	1640	U1	10	1	OR	Lake Oswego
2029	KZLS	1640	U4	10	1	OK	Enid
2030	WSJP	1640	U1	10	1	WI	Sussex
2031	WTNI	1640	U1	10	1	MS	Biloxi
2032	KBJD	**1650**	U1	10	1	CO	Denver
2033	KCNZ	1650	U1	10	1	IA	Cedar Falls
2034	KFOX	1650	U1	10	0.49	CA	Torrance
2035	KSVE	1650	U1	8.5	0.85	TX	El Paso
2036	KYHN	1650	U1	10	1	AR	Fort Smith
2037	WHKT	1650	U1	10	1	VA	Portsmouth
2038	KQWB	**1660**	U1	10	1	ND	West Fargo
2039	KRZI	1660	U1	10	1	TX	Waco
2040	KTIQ	1660	U1	10	1	CA	Merced
2041	KWOD	1660	U1	10	1	KS	Kansas City
2042	KXOL	1660	U1	10	1	UT	Brigham City
2043	WBCN	1660	U1	10	1	NC	Charlotte

MW	Call	kHz	Ant.	D	N	Sta	City of License
2044	WCNZ	1660	U1	10		1	FL	Marco Island
2045	WQLR	1660	U1	10		1	MI	Kalamazoo
2046	WWRU	1660	U4	10		10	NJ	Jersey City
2047	KHPY	**1670**	U4	10		9	CA	Moreno Valley
2048	KNRO	1670	U1	10		1	CA	Redding
2049	WPLA	1670	U1	10		1	GA	Dry Branch
2050	WUSW	1670	U1	10		1	WI	Madison
2051	KGED	**1680**	U1	10		1	CA	Fresno
2052	KNTS	1680	U1	10		1	WA	Seattle
2053	KRJO	1680	U1	10		1	LA	Monroe
2054	WOKB	1680	U1	10		1	FL	Winter Garden
2055	WPRR	1680	U1	10	0.68	1	MI	Ada
2056	WTTM	1680	U1	10		1	NJ	Lindenwold
2057	KDDZ	**#1690**	U1	10		1	CO	Arvada
2058	KFSG	1690	U1	10		1	CA	Roseville
2059	WMLB	1690	U1	10		1	GA	Avondale Estates
2060	WPTX	1690	U1	10		1	MD	Lexington Park
2061	WVON	#1690	U1	10		1	IL	Berwyn
2062	KBGG	**1700**	U1	10		1	IA	Des Moines
2063	KKLF	1700	U1	10		1	TX	Richardson
2064	KVNS	1700	U1	8.8	0.88	1	TX	Brownsville
2065	WEUP	1700	U1	10		1	AL	Huntsville
2066	WJCC	1700	U1	10		1	FL	Miami Springs
2067	WRCR	1700	U1	10		1	NY	Ramapo

Addresses:
– 1) 1109 Hudson Lane, Monroe, LA 71201-6003 – 2) 304 S Grand Ave, Las Vegas, NM 87701-3873 – 3) 20720 Marilla St, Chatsworth, CA 91311-4407 – 4) 1139 Hartnell Ave, Redding, CA 96002-2113 – 5) 200 N 10th St, Fort Dodge, IA 50501-3925 – 6) 273 Azalea Rd, Mobile, AL 36609-1970 – 7) 1501 13th Ave, Columbus, GA 31901-1908 – 8) 164 Southeast Blvd, Clinton, NC 28328-4758 – 9) 2500 Maitland Center Pkwy #401, Maitland, FL 32751-4122 – 10) 1640 Old Russellville Pike, Clarksville, TN 37043-1709 – 11) 2395 Ocean Ave #3, Ronkonkoma, NY 11779-5670 – 12) 1846 Skyland Dr, Sylva, NC 28779-8008 – 13) 32500 Parklane St, Garden City, MI 48135-1572 – 14) 4840 Lincoln Rd, Blaine, WA 98230-9602 or PO Box 75150 RPO White Rock, White Rock, BC V4B 5L3 – 15) 660 Dewey Blvd, Butte, MT 59701-2318 – 16) 1330 E 8th St #207, Odessa, TX 79761-4731 – 17) 1815 Meadowlark Rd, Clay Center, KS 67432-8201 – 18) 4686 E Van Buren St #300, Phoenix, AZ 85008-6967 – 19) 3500 E Rosser Ave, Bismarck, ND 58501-3398 – 20) 7140 SW Macadam Ave, Portland, OR 97219-3013 – 21) 1111 W Victory Way, Craig, CO 81625-2950 – 22) 638 West Port Plaza, Saint Louis, MO 63146-3106 – 23) 4050 Eisenhauer Rd, San Antonio, TX 78218-3409 – 24) 3223 Sillect Ave, Bakersfield, CA 93308-6329 – 25) 2500 Russell Rd, Green Cove Springs, FL 32043-9492 – 26) 9 Stowe St, Waterbury, VT 05670-1820 – 27) 1102 Thompson Bridge Rd, Gainesville, GA 30501-1706 – 28) 500 Corporate Parkway #200, Buffalo, NY 14226-1263 – 29) 8044 Montgomery Rd #650, Cincinnati, OH 45236-2959 – 30) 557 Scott St, Wausau, WI 54403-4829 – 31) 1820 Heritage Center Way, Harrisonburg, VA 22801-8451 – 32) 2885 Interstate 10 E, Beaumont, TX 77702-1001 – 33) 2821 S Parker Rd #1205, Aurora, CO 80014-2708 – 34) 20 3rd St N #231, Great Falls, MT 59401-3188 – 35) 231 N Wenatchee Ave, Wenatchee, WA 98801-2009 – 36) 55 Hawthorne St #1000, San Francisco, CA 94105-3966 – 37) 3000 Chestnut Expressway, Springfield, MO 65802-2528 – 38) 14 E Central Entrance, Duluth, MN 55811-5508 – 39) 117 Ridge Pike, Lafayette Hill, PA 19444-1900 – 40) 242 Finzel Rd, Frostburg, MD 21532-4009 – 41) 420 Western Ave, South Portland, ME 04106-1704 – 42) 6080 Mount Moriah Rd Ext, Memphis, TN 38115-2698 – 43) 1331 Main St, Springfield, MA 01103-1669 – 44) 25 NW Point Blvd #400, Elk Grove, IL 60007-1030 – 45) 102 N Kanawha St, Beckley, WV 25801-4715 – 46) PO Box 608, Middlesboro, KY 40965-0608 – 47) 1815 Division St #110, Nashville, TN 37203-2753 – 48) 2518 Columbia Hwy, Dothan, AL 36303-5402 – 49) 194 NW 187th St, Miami, FL 33169-4050 – 50) 316 Greystone Blvd, Columbia, SC 29210-8007 – 51) PO Box 580, Alturas, CA 96101-0580 – 52) 3090 Olive Ave #550, Burbank, CA 91505-5544 – 53) 3090 Olive St #400, Dallas, TX 75219-7640 – 54) 2801 Decker Lake Dr, West Valley City, UT 84119-2330 – 55) 140 4th Ave N #340, Seattle, WA 98109-4932 – 56) 1355 California Ave, Las Cruces, NM 88001-4130 – 57) 6510 Whorton Bend Rd, Gadsden, AL 35903-8873 – 58) 7461 South Ave, Youngstown, OH 44512-5789 – 59) 111 Broadway, New York, NY 10006-1901 – 60) WNAX Bldg - 1609 E Hwy 50, Yankton, SD 57078-6406 – 61) 1801 Rockville Pike #405, Rockville, MD 20852-5604 – 62) 500 Plum St #100, Syracuse, NY 13204-1427 – 63) 5211 W Laurel St #101, Tampa, FL 33607-1725 – 64) 13 Summerlin Rd, Asheville, NC 28806-2800 – 65) 2414 Park Blvd #1001, Boise, ID 83712-7781 – 66) 601 Washington St, Alexandria, LA 71301-8028 – 67) 1077 W Shaw St, Fresno, CA 93771-3702 – 68) 1110 S Park Ave, Tucson, AZ 85719-6745 – 69) 106 Rose Lane, Montrose, CO 81401-3823 – 70) 1111

Virginia St E, Charleston, WV 25301-2406 – 71) 4192 N John Young Pkwy, Orlando, FL 32804-2696 – 72) 4051 Jimmie Dyess Pkwy, Augusta, GA 30909-9469 – 73) 600 Corporate Cir #100, Harrisburg, PA 17110-9787 – 74) 1200 SW Executive Dr, Topeka, KS 66615-3850 – 75) Campbell Hall - 300 N Goodwin Ave, Urbana, IL 61801-2316 – 76) 240 Radio Road, West Jefferson, NC 28694-ND – 77) 201 State St, La Crosse, WI 54601-3246 – 78) 96 Stereo Lane, Paxton, MA 01612-1376 – 79) 314 E Front St, Traverse City, MI 49684-2528 – 80) 319 W Rockwood St, Rockwood, TN 37854-2245 – 81) 1406 Commerce Way, Idaho Falls, ID 83401-1233 – 82) 8309 N Interstate 35, Austin, TX 78753-5771 – 83) 808 E Sprague Ave, Spokane, WA 99202-2126 – 84) 750 Ridgeview Dr #204, St. George, UT 84770-2697 – 85) 1001 Heavenly Village Way #36A, South Lake Tahoe, CA 96150-6985 – 86) 701 N Brand Blvd #550, Glendale, CA 91203-1235 – 87) 1200 Executive Pkwy #440, Eugene, OR 97401-2169 – 88) 10714 Mockingbird Dr, Omaha, NE 68127-1942 – 89) 2800 Buena Vista Rd, Hot Springs, AR 71913-8208 – 90) 600 Baltimore Dr, Wilkes-Barre, PA 18702-7901 – 91) 1834 Lisenby Ave, Panama City, FL 32405-3713 – 92) 900 Circle 75 Pkwy SE #1320, Atlanta, GA 30339-3095 – 93) 500 Victory Rd #2, Quincy, MA 02171-3132 – 94) 222 S Lawrence St, Ironwood, MI 49938-2524 – 95) 4200 W Main St, Kalamazoo, MI 49006-2766 – 96) 6 Johnson Rd, Latham, NY 12110-5638 – 97) 300 W Vine St 3rd Flr, Lexington, KY 40507-1807 – 98) 4270 Byrd Dr, Loveland, CO 80538-7074 – 99) 2995 US Highway 93 S, Kalispell, MT 59901-8640 – 100) 9660 Granite Ridge Dr, San Diego, CA 92123-2657 – 101) 4180 N Mesa St, El Paso, TX 79902-1420 – 102) 2400 8th Ave SW #D1, Jamestown, ND 58401-6623 – 103) 1001 E Southeast Loop 323 #455, Tyler, TX 75701-9600 – 104) 4190 Belfort Rd #450, Jacksonville, FL 32216-1405 – 105) 711 W 40th St #350, Baltimore, MD 21211-2190 – 106) 670 Sweden St, Caribou, ME 04736-3419 – 107) 330 2nd Ave, Paintsville, KY 41240-1034 – 108) 600 Old Marion Rd NE, Cedar Rapids, IA 52402-2152 – 109) 2650 Thousand Oaks Blvd #4100, Memphis, TN 38118-2451 – 110) 875 W 5th St, Winston-Salem, NC 27101-2505 – 111) 352 "E" Ave #K4, Lancaster, CA 93535-4505 – 112) 7000 Squibb Rd, Mission, KS 66202-3233 – 113) 11 E Superior St #380, Duluth, MN 55802-3016 – 114) 260 Hegenberger Rd, Oakland, CA 94621-1491 – 115) 24 E Greenway Plaza #1900, Houston, TX 77046-2428 – 116) 500 4th St NW, Albuquerque, NM 87102-5324 – 117) 2823 W Lewis St, Pasco, WA 99301-6700 – 118) 511 Rossanley Dr, Medford, OR 97501-1771 – 119) 614 Kimbark St, Longmont, CO 80501-4911 – 120) 810 W 200 N, Logan, UT 84321-3726 – 121) 2700 Corporate Dr #115, Birmingham, AL 35242-2735 – 122) 1520 South Blvd #300, Charlotte, NC 28203-3701 – 123) 195 McGregor St #810, Manchester, NH 03102-3755 – 124) 7601 Riviera Blvd, Miramar, FL 33023-6574 – 125) 555 E City Ave #330, Bala Cynwyd, PA 19004-1137 – 126) 2323 W 5th Ave #200, Columbus, OH 43204-4988 – 127) 3934 Electric Rd, Roanoke, VA 24018-4513 – 128) 1354 E Sherwood Dr, Grand Junction, CO 81501-7546 – 129) 13725 Montfort Dr, Dallas, TX 75240-4455 – 130) 13333 SW 68th Pkwy, Tigard, OR 97223-8304 – 131) 7740 N 16th St #200, Phoenix, AZ 85020-4482 – 132) 4002 W Gandy Blvd, Tampa, FL 33611-3410 – 133) 3100 Highwoods Blvd #140, Raleigh, NC 27604-1065 – 134) 2440 Millwood Ave, Columbia, SC 29205-1128 – 135) 500 Plum St #100, Syracuse, NY 13204-1427 – 136) 1375 Beasley Rd, Jackson, MS 39206-2018 – 137) 1918 Lincoln Hwy, North Versailles, PA 15137-2706 or PO Box 990, Greensburg, PA 15601-0990 – 138) 1621 E Magnolia Ave, Knoxville, TN 37917-7825 – 139) 2508 Coney Island Ave 2nd Flr, Brooklyn, NY 11223-5026 – 140) 720 E Capitol Dr, Milwaukee, WI 53212-1308 – 141) 806 New Franklin Rd, La Grange, GA 30240-1859 – 142) 118 Malletts Bay Ave, Colchester, VT 05446-2009 – 143) 306 S Kanawha St, Beckley, WV 25801-5619 – 144) 861 Broadway, Bangor, ME 04401-2916 – 145) 19319 Fremont Ave N, Shoreline, WA 98133-3800 – 146) 827 Park Blvd #100, Boise, ID 83712-7782 – 147) 4695 S Monaco St, Denver, CO 80237-3403 – 148) 2900 Sutro St, Reno, NV 89512-1616 – 149) 9601 McAllister Freeway #1200, San Antonio, TX 78216-4686 – 150) 10845 Olive Blvd #160, Saint Louis, MO 63141-7792 or PO Box 7300, Charlotte, NC 28241-7300 – 151) 214 Television Circle, Savannah, GA 31406-4519 – 152) 2601 Nicholasville Rd, Lexington, KY 40503-3307 – 153) 4400 Jenifer St NW #400, Washington, DC 20015-2183 – 154) 145 N Alexander St, Toccoa, GA 30577-2371 – 155) 1502 Wampanoag Trail, Riverside, RI 02915-1075 – 156) 3400 Olive Ave #550, Burbank, CA 91505-5544 – 157) 108 Green St, Thibodaux, LA 70301-3144 – 158) 4045 NW 64th St #600, Oklahoma City, OK 73116-2615 – 159) 6401 Poplar Ave #640, Memphis, TN 38119-4800 – 160) 1009 Drayton Rd, Fayetteville, NC 28303-3887 – 161) 1819 Peachtree Rd NE #700, Atlanta, GA 30309-1849 – 162) 7755 Freedom Ave NW, North Canton, OH 44720-6905 – 163) 2100 Park Central Blvd #100, Pompano Beach, FL 33064-2219 – 164) 131 County Circle, Amherst, MA 01003-9257 – 165) 204 Communications Bldg - Iowa State Univ, Ames, IA 50011-0001 – 166) 501 Office Center Dr #190, Fort Washington, PA 19034-3268 – 167)

162 Free Hill Rd, Gray, TN 37615-3144 – **168)** 1912 Capitol Ave #300, Cheyenne, WY 82001-3659 – **169)** 1600 W 500 N, Manti, UT 84642-5503 – **170)** 1545 River Park Dr #500, Sacramento, CA 95815-4693 – **171)** 807 W 37th St, Hibbing, MN 55746-2856 – **172)** 2644 McGavock Pike, Nashville, TN 37214-1202 – **173)** 2029 Freeway Dr, Mount Vernon, WA 98273-5470 – **174)** 410 E 6th St, Williston, ND 58801-5552 – **175)** 6400 N Belt Line Rd #110, Irving, TX 75063-6065 – **176)** PO Box 2569, Window Rock, AZ 86515-2569 – **177)** 3000 W MacArthur Blvd #500, Santa Ana, CA 92704-7947 – **178)** 2911 Tennyson Ave, #400, Eugene, OR 7408-4811 or PO Box 40231, Downey, CA 90239-1231 – **179)** 1010 2nd St N, Sauk Rapids, MN 56379-2527 – **180)** 345 Hudson St Fl10, New York, NY 10014-4502 – **181)** 2420 Wade Hampton Blvd, Greenville, SC 29615-1107 – **182)** 1188 Lake View Dr, Altamonte Springs, FL 32714-2713 – **183)** 2800 Dauphin St #104, Mobile, AL 36606-2400 – **184)** 1419 W Bannock St, Boise, ID 83702-5234 – **185)** 108 Highway 70 E #11, Glenwood, AR 71943-8800 – **186)** 3301 Barham Blvd #300, Los Angeles, CA 90068-1477 – **187)** 2821 S Parker Rd #1205, Aurora, CO 80014-2708 – **188)** 3999 Las Vegas Blvd S #K, Las Vegas, NV 89119-1097 – **189)** 12½ E Market St, Lewistown, PA 17044-2123 – **190)** 517 Watt Rd, Knoxville, TN 37922-1110 – **191)** 6223 Old Mendenhall Rd, High Point, NC 27263-3940 – **192)** 180 N Stetson St #1250, Chicago, IL 60601-6732 – **193)** 330 SW 27th Ave #207, Miami, FL 33135-2957 – **194)** 11474 US Hwy 11, York, AL 36925-9764 – **195)** 4104 Country Lane, Saint Joseph, MO 64506-4921 – **196)** 1400 11th Ave #3, Helena, MT 59601-7996 – **197)** 8122 Datapoint Dr #600, San Antonio, TX 78229-3446 – **198)** 55 Hawthorne St #1100, San Francisco, CA 94105-3932 – **199)** 320 Emery Dr, Omak, WA 98841-9237 – **200)** 1726 Reisterstown Rd #117, Pikesville, MD 21208-2986 – **201)** 780 Johnson Ferry Rd NE #500, Atlanta, GA 30342-1436 – **202)** 604 Ludington St, Escanaba, MI 49829-3830 – **203)** 320 N Jensen Rd, Vestal, NY 13850-2111 – **204)** 1111 Virginia St E, Charleston, WV 25301-2406 – **205)** 1835 Moriah Woods Blvd, Memphis, TN 38117-7122 – **206)** Tower 14-21700 Northwestern Hwy #1190, Southfield, MI 48075-4923 – **207)** 2396 Hallie Rd, Chippewa Falls, WI 54729-7519 – **208)** 3012 Highwoods Blvd #201, Raleigh, NC 27604-1031 – **209)** 20 Guest St 3rd Flr, Brighton, MA 02135-2040 – **210)** 306 W 8th St, Coffeyville, KS 67337-5829 – **211)** 4045 N Mesa St, El Paso, TX 79902-1526 – **212)** 261 Portsea St, New Haven, CT 06519-2104 – **213)** 126 Kessel Rd, Fisher, WV 26818-4012 – **214)** 244 Goodwin Crest Dr #300, Birmingham, AL 35209-3700 – **215)** Tower 14-21700 Northwestern Hwy #1190, Southfield, MI 48075-4923 – **216)** 8000 Belfort Parkway #100, Jacksonville, FL 32256-6971 – **217)** 8230 Summa Ave, Baton Rouge, LA 70809-3421 – **218)** 11373 Wallace Pike, Bristol, VA 24202-2743 – **219)** 50 W Broadway #200, Salt Lake City, UT 84101-2024 – **220)** 196 Main St, Winston, OR 97496-ND – **221)** 67 Garden Court, Monterey, CA 93940-5302 – **222)** 11451 Katy Freeway #125, Houston, TX 77079-2004 – **223)** 500 W Boone Ave, Spokane, WA 99201-2404 – **224)** 702 Russell Ave #306, Gaithersburg, MD 20877-2606 or PO Box 2195, Manassas, VA 20108-2195 – **225)** 30 How St, Haverhill, MA 01830-6131 – **226)** 8044 Montgomery Rd #600, Cincinnati, OH 45236-2959 – **227)** 501 N 44th St #425, Phoenix, AZ 85008-6587 – **228)** 5800 Foxridge Dr #600, Mission, KS 66202-2347 – **229)** 6341 W Port Ave, Shreveport, LA 71129-2415 – **230)** 1425 River Park Dr #520, Sacramento, CA 95815-4524 – **231)** 3505 Olsen Blvd #117, Amarillo, TX 79109-3096 – **232)** 1820 Eastlake Ave S, Seattle, WA 98102-3711 – **233)** 3131 S Vaughn Way #601, Aurora, CO 80014-3516 – **234)** 800 W Olympic Blvd #A-200, Los Angeles, CA 90015-1360 – **235)** 3500 E Rosser Ave, Bismarck, ND 58501-3398 – **236)** 800 S Douglas Rd #111, Coral Gables, FL 33134-3187 – **237)** 11 E Superior St #380, Duluth, MN 55802-3016 – **238)** 3228 S US Hwy 117, Rose Hill, NC 28458-8498 – **239)** 402 Main St, Williamsburg, KY 40769-1126 – **240)** 7080 Lee Highway, Fairlawn, VA 24141-8416 – **241)** 32 Ave of the Americas 3 Floor, New York, NY 10013-2473 – **242)** 855 College St, Eastman, GA 31023-6771 – **243)** 2920 S Durango Dr, Las Vegas, NV 89117-4412 – **244)** 28041 Pleasant Valley Rd, Sweet Home, OR 97386-9599 – **245)** 4050 Eisenhauer Rd, San Antonio, TX 78218-3409 – **246)** 3232 Hendersonville Hwy, Pisgah Forest, NC 28768-7806 – **247)** 435 N Michigan Ave, Chicago, IL 60611-4076 – **248)** 100 NW 76th Dr #2, Gainesville, FL 32607-6659 – **249)** 154 Boone Dr, Newman, GA 30263-2801 – **250)** 5660 E Franklin Rd # 200, Nampa, ID 83687-5133 – **251)** 2075 Central Ave, Billings, MT 59102-4956 – **252)** 326 Chicopee St, Chicopee, MA 01013-1797 or PO Box 1, Springfield, MA 01101-0001 – **253)** 2 Beeco Rd, Greer, SC 29650-1004 – **254)** 7 Parkway Center #625, Pittsburgh, PA 15220-3707 – **255)** 2194 US Hwy 319 S, Thomasville, GA 31792-1417 – **256)** 11240 Waples Mill Rd #405, Fairfax, VA 22030-6078 – **257)** 1366 Startown Rd, Lincolntown, NC 28152-5033 – **258)** 3183 Airway Ave #D, Costa Mesa, CA 92626-4611 – **259)** 865 Battery St, San Francisco, CA 94111-1503 – **260)** 7136 S Yale Ave #500, Tulsa, OK 74136-6325 – **261)** 2000 West Loop S #300, Houston, TX 77027-3510 – **262)** 6805 Corporate Dr #130, Colorado Springs, CO 80919-5903 – **263)** 1020 S 25th St, Fargo, ND 58103-2312 – **264)** 300 St Croix Trail S, Lakeland, MN 55043-ND or PO Box 25130, Saint Paul, MN 55125-0130 – **265)** 1 Commerce St #300, Montgomery, AL 36104-3542 – **266)** 5440 Moeller Ave, Cincinnati, OH 45212-1211 – **267)** PO Box 2000012, Brooklyn, NY 11220-0012 – **268)** 2147 Springs Rd, Mount Airy, NC 27030-2447 – **269)** 1650 S Dixie Hwy, Boca Raton, FL 33432-7462 – **270)** 2500 Maitland Center Pkwy #401, Maitland, FL 32751-4179 – **271)** 2211 E Missiouri Ave # S-300, El Paso, TX 79903-3831 – **272)** 18553 Gentry Rd, Lebanon, MO 65536-5748 – **273)** 36581 N Reservoir Rd, Polson, MT 59860-8677 – **274)** 1050 W Williams Ave, Fallon, NV 89406-2634 – **275)** 128 S 4th St, O'Neill, NE 68763-1814 or PO Box 8, Aurora, NE 68818-0008 – **276)** 1899 Carbonville Rd, Helper, UT 84526-ND or PO Box 875, Price, UT 84501-0875 – **277)** 1211 SW 5th Ave 6 Flr, Portland, OR 97204-3735 – **278)** 5625 N Milwaukee Ave, Chicago, IL 60646-6221 – **279)** 1601 W Peachtree St NE, Atlanta, GA 30309-2663 – **280)** 10550 Barkley St, Overland Park, KS 66212-1824 – **281)** 7677 Engineer Rd, San Diego, CA 92111-1582 – **282)** 4695 S Monaco St, Denver, CO 80237-3408 – **283)** 301 Brookswood Rd #208, Sherwood, AR 72120-4200 – **284)** 6222 West Interstate 10, San Antonio, TX 78201-2097 – **285)** 137 Rapids Rd, Champlain, NY 12919-4945 – **286)** 2828 NC 126, Morganton, NC 28655-8264 – **287)** 2090 Palm Beach Lake Blvd #801, West Palm Beach, FL 33409-6508 – **288)** 3011 W Grand Blvd #800, Detroit, MI 48202-3086 – **289)** 5211 W Laurel St #101, Tampa, FL 33607-1725 – **290)** 70 James St #201, Worcester, MA 01603-1045 – **291)** 3201 Royalty Row, Irving, TX 75062-4961 – **292)** 818 Main St, Miles City, MT 59301-3221 – **293)** 10948 Cleveland Ave, Oakdale, CA 95361-9709 – **294)** 500 4th St NW, Albuquerque, NM 87102-2102 – **295)** 1820 Eastlake Ave E, Seattle, WA 98102-3711 – **296)** 330 21st Ave S #610, Minneapolis, MN 55455-4550 – **297)** 2 Penn Plaza #1700, New York, NY 10121-0085 – **298)** 20125 S Tamiami Trail, Estero, FL 33928-2117 – **299)** 275 River Rd, Rockingham, NC 28380-1536 – **300)** 904 Center St, Lewiston, NY 14092-1737 or 600 The East Mall #400, Toronto, ON M9B 4B1 – **301)** 1717 US Hwy 72 E, Athens, AL 35611-4413 – **302)** 504 Middle Creek Rd, Cedar Bluff, VA 24609-ND – **303)** 3400 W Highway 89a, Sedona, AZ 86336-4914 – **304)** 595 E Plumb Lane, Reno, NV 89502-3503 – **305)** 1901 N Moore St #200, Arlington, VA 22209-1746 – **306)** 180 N Stetson St #1100, Chicago, IL 60601-6723 – **307)** 17336 US Highway 421 S, Dunn, NC 28334-5580 – **308)** 265 Highpoint Dr, Ridgeland, MS 39157-6018 – **309)** 1381 W Main St, Forest City, NC 28043-2525 – **310)** 274 Britton Rd, Monticello, ME 04760-3110 – **311)** 801 Noble St #30, Anniston, AL 36201-5698 – **312)** 3321 S La Cienega Blvd, Los Angeles, CA 90016-3114 – **313)** 2000 West Loop S #300, Houston, TX 77027-3510 – **314)** 1020 S 25th St, Fargo, ND 58103-3212 – **315)** 1415 Fulton St, Fresno, CA 93721-1609 – **316)** 4413 82nd St #300, Lubbock, TX 79424-3395 – **317)** 600 First Ave N, Billings, MT 59101-2654 or PO Box 1742, Billings, MT 59103-1742 – **318)** 2219 Yew St Rd, Bellingham, WA 98229-8898 – **319)** 1601 E 57th Ave, Spokane, WA 99223-6623 – **320)** 3202 N Oracle Rd, Tucson, AZ 85705-3820 – **321)** 113 E New Hope Rd, Rogers, AR 72758-6058 – **322)** 1101 Marsh Rd, Eureka, CA 95501-1574 – **323)** 1065 S Range Ave, Colby, KS 67701-3505 – **324)** 1541 Alta Dr #400, Whitehall, PA 18052-5632 – **325)** 20450 NW 2nd Ave, Miami, FL 33169-2505 – **326)** 944 Harlem St, Altoona, WI 54720-1127 – **327)** 4801 E Independence Blvd #815, Charlotte, NC 28212-5490 – **328)** 231 Brandonwood Dr, Johnson City, TN 37604-2156 – **329)** 4000 Radio Drive #1, Louisville, KY 40218-4568 – **330)** 32900 Radio Road, Leesburg, FL 34788-3903 – **331)** 1835 Moriah Woods Blvd, Memphis, TN 38117-7122 – **332)** 500 Dominion Tower - 999 Waterside Dr, Norfolk, VA 23510-3300 – **333)** 1502 Wampanoag Trail, Riverside, RI 02915-1075 – **334)** 210 Interstate North Cir SE #100, Atlanta, GA 30339-2206 – **335)** 1795 Tittabawassee Rd, Saginaw, MI 48604-9431 – **336)** 142 Skyland Blvd E, Tuscaloosa, AL 35405-4096 – **337)** 213 E 2nd St, Soda Springs, ID 83276-1411 – **338)** 1919 N Broadway Ave, Oklahoma City, OK 73103-4499 – **339)** 200 Tower Rd, Waupaca, WI 54981-1699 – **340)** 462 Merrimack St, Methuen, MA 01844-5804 – **341)** 1032 Melody Lane, Crewe, VA 23930-ND – **342)** 2775 Mt Ephraim Ave, Camden, NJ 08104-3295 – **343)** 1010 2nd St N, Sauk Rapids, MN 56379-2527 – **344)** 134 4th Ave, Huntington, WV 25701-1253 – **345)** 1612 Junction Ave #1, Sturgis, SD 57785-2166 – **346)** 55 Hawthorne St #1000, San Francisco, CA 94105-3966 – **347)** 102 Taos St, Santa Fe, NM 87505-3832 – **348)** 55 Alder St NW #3, Ephrata, WA 98823-1663 – **349)** 188 John Turner Broadcast Blvd, Jacksonville, AL 36265-6659 or PO Box 8, Anniston, AL 36202-0008 – **350)** 1501 Hargis Lane, Jackson, KY 41339-1102 – **351)** 1203 Troy-Schenectady Rd #201, Latham, NY 12110-1046 – **352)** 6721 W 121st St, Overland Park, KS 66209-2003 – **353)** 2514 Eugenia Ave, Nashville, TN 37211-2117 – **354)** 2422 Burton St SE, Grand Rapids, MI 49546-4806 – **355)** 145 Jackson St NE, Blacksburg, VA 24060-3931 – **356)** 2 Beeco Rd, Greer, SC 29650-1004 – **357)** 999 Douglas Ave #3318, Altamonte Springs, FL 32714-5213 – **358)** 130 Radio Station Drive, Magee, MS 39111-4399

– 359) 4198 Rebecca Circle, Valdosta, GA 31606-2201 **– 360)** 2201 6th Ave #1500, Seattle, WA 98121-1840 **– 361)** 3701 Harrison Rd, Ogden, UT 84403-2059 **– 362)** 3090 Olive St #400, Dallas, TX 75219-7640 **– 363)** 17487 Driftwood Ln, Park Rapids, MN 56470-2739 **– 364)** 5475 N Milwaukee Ave, Chicago, IL 60630-1249 **– 365)** 4301 W Hundred Rd, Chester, VA 23831-1737 **– 366)** 160 Varick St, New York, NY 10013-1220 **– 367)** 4673 Winterset Dr, Columbus, OH 43220-8113 **– 368)** 800 8th Ave SE, Largo, FL 33771-2162 **– 369)** 3400 Idaho Ave NW #200, Washington, DC 20016-3000 **– 370)** 2205 College Ave #3, Elmira, NY 14903-1223 **– 371)** 7355 N Orcale Rd #102, Tucson, AZ 85704-6353 **– 372)** 2000 E Gene Autry Way, Anaheim, CA 92806-6143 **– 373)** 1255 E Main St #A, Grass Valley, CA 95945-5711 **– 374)** 1423 S Beverly St, Casper, WY 82609-4131 **– 375)** 625 2nd Ave S #200, Minneapolis, MN 55402-1961 **– 376)** 82 Franklin St, Worcester, MA 01608-1917 **– 377)** 34 N 4th St, Reading, PA 19601-3996 **– 378)** 3500 N Causeway Blvd #830, Metairie, LA 70002-3561 **– 379)** 230-2 Goodman Rd E #202, Southaven, MS 38671-5151 **– 380)** 4405 Providence Lane #D, Winston-Salem, NC 27106-3226 **– 381)** 1114 N Almon St, Moscow, ID 83843-8507 **– 382)** 3256 Penryn Rd #100, Loomis, CA 95650-8052 **– 383)** 1011 N Lincoln St, West Point, NE 68788-1003 **– 384)** 1201 N Jackson Ave #900, McAllen, TX 78501-5764 **– 385)** 3735 Rigolette Rd, Pineville, LA 71360-7365 **– 386)** 7255 S Tenaya Way #100, Las Vegas, NV 89113-1900 **– 387)** 6530 Spanish Fort Blvd #B, Spanish Fort, AL 36527-5014 or PO Box 1328, Mobile, AL 36633-1328 **– 388)** 4801 E Independence Blvd #815, Charlotte, NC 28212-5490 **– 389)** 4000 Radio Drive #1, Louisville, KY 40218-4568 **– 390)** 221 Pall Bearer Rd, Thomasville, GA 31792-1101 **– 391)** PO Box 7111, Charlottesville, VA 22906-7111 **– 392)** 3000 Bering Dr, Houston, TX 77057-5708 **– 393)** 1333 S Kirkwood Rd St, Saint Louis, MO 63122-7266 **– 394)** 645 Elliott Ave W #400, Seattle, WA 98119-3911 **– 395)** 8828 N Stemmons Fwy #106, Dallas, TX 75247-3720 **– 396)** 4695 S Monaco St, Denver, CO 80237-3403 **– 397)** 5625 N Milwaukee Ave, Chicago, IL 60646-6221 **– 398)** 98 Mill Plain Rd, Danbury, CT 06811-6101 **– 399)** 20 Guest St 3rd Flr, Brighton, MA 02135-2040 **– 400)** 2100 Park Central Blvd #100, Pompano Beach, FL 33064-2219 **– 401)** 104 S Center St #400, Ebensburg, PA 15931-1656 **– 402)** 1301 E 9th St #252, Cleveland, OH 44114-1800 **– 403)** 261 Hannum St, Alcoa, TN 37701-2451 **– 404)** 3012 Highwoods Blvd #201, Raleigh, NC 27604-1031 **– 405)** 3434 W Kilbourn Ave, Milwaukee, MN 53208-3313 **– 406)** 1200 Weimer Hall, Gainesville, FL 32611 **– 407)** 500 Dominion Tower - 999 Waterside Dr, Norfolk, VA 23510-3300 **– 408)** 120 Summit Pkwy #200, Birmingham, AL 35209-4741 **– 409)** 434 Bearcat Dr, Salt Lake City, UT 84115-2520 **– 410)** 1162 E Hwy 126, Pittsburg, KS 66762-8712 **– 411)** 8122 Datapoint Dr #600, San Antonio, TX 78229-3446 **– 412)** 6605 SE Lake Rd, Portland, OR 97222-2161 **– 413)** 300 Broadway #8, San Francisco, CA 94133-4545 **– 414)** 1465 Northside Dr NW #218, Atlanta, GA 30318-4239 **– 415)** 601 W Roanoke Dr, Fitzgerald, GA 31750-3633 **– 416)** 305 Washington Ave 4th Flr, Towson, MD 21204-4748 **– 417)** 5211 W Laurel St #101, Tampa, FL 33607-1725 **– 418)** 240 Central Ave, Oak Hill, WV 25901-3006 **– 419)** 425 Stockbridge Rd, Great Barrington, MA 01230-1233 **– 420)** 555 E City Ave #330, Bala Cynwyd, PA 19004-1137 **– 421)** 2621 West A St, Pasco, WA 99301-4702 **– 422)** 6767 W Tropicana Ave #102, Las Vegas, NV 89103-4755 **– 423)** PO Box 49, Park Rapids, MN 56470-0049 **– 424)** 701 N Brand Blvd #550, Glendale, CA 91203-1235 **– 425)** 1751 Hanshaw Rd, Ithaca, NY 14850-9105 **– 426)** 283 Comm Arts Bldg - MSU, East Lansing, MI 48824-1212 **– 427)** 477 Congress St #900, Portland, ME 04101-3432 **– 428)** 340 Martin Luther King Blvd, Bristol, TN 37620-3996 **– 429)** 2278 Wortham Lane, Grovetown, GA 30813-5103 **– 430)** 1115 Honeysuckle Dr, Keene, TX 76059-2101 **– 431)** 400 Poydras St #800, New Orleans, LA 70130-3245 **– 432)** PO Box 9090, Window Rock, AZ 86515-9090 **– 433)** 3650 131st SE #550, Bellevue, WA 98006-1334 **– 434)** 2432 US Hwy 2 E, Kalispell, MT 59901-2310 **– 435)** 1600 Pasadena Blvd, Pasadena, TX 77502-2402 **– 436)** 30 E San Joaquin St #105, Salinas, CA 93901-2946 **– 437)** 10000 Warden Rd, North Little Rock, AR 72120-3656 **– 438)** 1007 Plum Creek Parkway , Lexington, NE 68850-2621 **– 439)** 1405 E Ellendale Ave, Dallas, OR 97338-1709 **– 440)** 1186 W Broad St, Athens, GA 30606-3050 **– 441)** 345 Hudson St Flr 11, New York, NY 10014-4502 **– 442)** 3715 N Natchez Ct, Nashville, TN 37211-3421 **– 443)** 619 Cameron St, Eau Claire, WI 54703-4700 **– 444)** 13 Summerlin Rd, Asheville, NC 28806-2800 **– 445)** 8101 N High St #360, Columbus, OH 43235-1442 **– 446)** 2828 W Flagler St, Miami, FL 33135-1337 **– 447)** 750 Ridgeview Dr #204, Saint George, UT 84770-2665 **– 448)** 560 Higuera St #G, San Luis Obispo, CA 93401-3850 **– 449)** 965 S Irving St, Denver, CO 80219-3422 **– 450)** 1442 Ethan Way #101, Sacramento, CA 95825-2232 **– 451)** 10613 Bellaire Blvd #900, Houston, TX 77072-5221 **– 452)** 4501 N McColl Rd, McAllen, TX 78504-2431 **– 453)** PO Box 490, Cauldwell, ID 83606-0490 **– 454)** 122 Green St #2L, Worcester, MA 01604-4138 **– 455)** 243 Riverchase Way #A, Lexington, SC 29072-9470 **– 456)** 37 Ellisville Blvd, Laurel, MS 39440-4523 **– 457)** 2800 Shallowford Rd NE, Atlanta, GA 30341-5217 **– 458)** 145

Jackson St NE, Blacksburg, VA 24060-3931 **– 459)** 190 N State St, Chicago, IL 60601-3398 **– 460)** 1301 Central Pkwy SW, Decatur, AL 35601-4817 **– 461)** 747 E Green St #400, Pasadena, CA 91101-2148 **– 462)** 10613 Bellaire Blvd #900, Houston, TX 77072-5221 **– 463)** 3003 Snelling Ave N, Saint Paul, MN 55113-1599 **– 464)** 801 E DuBois Ave, DuBois, PA 15801-3643 **– 465)** 214 Television Circle, Savannah, GA 31406-4519 **– 466)** 233 NE Front St, Milford, DE 19963-1431 **– 467)** 2514 Eugenia Ave, Nashville, TN 37211-2117 **– 468)** 207 University Blvd #200, Harrisonburg, VA 22801-3752 **– 469)** 1240 Radio Drive, Pikeville, KY 41501-4779 **– 470)** 2320 NE 2nd St #5, Ocala, FL 34470-6992 **– 471)** 398 S Main St, Granite Falls, NC 28630-8535 **– 472)** 1000 20th Ave SW, Minot, ND 58701-6447 **– 473)** 11865 Moreno Ave, Lakeside, CA 92040-1110 **– 474)** 4686 E Van Buren St #300, Phoenix, AZ 85008-6967 **– 475)** 1301 N Main St, Roswell, NM 88201-5013 **– 476)** 340 Townsend St #4, San Francisco, CA 94107-1698 **– 477)** 125 S 2nd St, Blytheville, AR 72315-3413 **– 478)** 0700 SW Bancroft St, Portland, OR 97239-4226 **– 479)** 200 S A St #400, Oxnard, CA 93030-5717 **– 480)** 3455 W 83rd Ave, Westminster, CO 80030-4005 **– 481)** 4300 S US Highway 281, Edinburg, TX 78539-9650 **– 482)** 2801 Decker Lake Dr #100, West Valley City, UT 84119-2330 **– 483)** 184 Target Industrial Circle #207, Bangor, ME 04401-5718 **– 484)** 4307 Highway 39 N, Meridian, MS 39301-1007 **– 485)** 114 S Jefferson St, Kittanning, PA 16201-2408 **– 486)** 105 N Ash Ave, South Pittsburg, TN 37380-1565 **– 487)** 20733 W 10 Mile Rd, Southfield, MI 48075-1086 **– 488)** 16880 W US Highway 63, Hayward, WI 54843-7186 **– 489)** 162 Freehill Rd, Gray, TN 37615-3144 **– 490)** 135 Burnside Ave, East Hartford, CT 06108-3466 **– 491)** 6006 Grand Central Ave, Parkersburg, WV 26105-9125 or PO Box 5559, Vienna, WV 26105-5559 **– 492)** 225 S Pleasantburg Dr #3B, Greenville, SC 29607-2533 **– 493)** 3765 N John Young Parkway, Orlando, FL 32804-3213 **– 494)** 3245 Basie Rd, Richmond, VA 23228-3404 **– 495)** 5989 Susquehanna Plaza Dr, Hellam, PA 17406-8910 **– 496)** 1223 W New Bern Rd, Kinston, NC 28504-4713 **– 497)** 710 S Clinton St, Iowa City, IA 52242-4214 **– 498)** 5211 W Laurel St, Tampa, FL 33607-1736 **– 499)** 700 Wellington Hills Rd, Little Rock, AR 72211-2026 **– 500)** 8755 W Flamingo Rd, Las Vegas, NV 89147-8667 **– 501)** 601 Central Ave N, Faribault, MN 55021-1307 **– 502)** 1700 SE Mile Hill Dr #243, Port Orchard, WA 98366-3507 **– 503)** 3256 Penryn Rd #100, Loomis, CA 95650-8052 **– 504)** 660 Flormann St #100, Rapid City, SD 57701-4679 **– 505)** 7350 US Hwy 50, Lamar, CO 81052-9563 **– 506)** 2100 E Tahquitz Canyon Way, Palm Springs, CA 92262-7046 **– 507)** 2495 N Vernal Ave, Vernal, UT 84078-ND **– 508)** 961 N Emerald Ave #A, Modesto, CA 95351-1556 **– 509)** 500 W Boone Ave, Spokane, WA 99201-2497 **– 510)** 290 Hegenberger Rd, Oakland, CA 94621-1436 **– 511)** 7322 Southwest Frwy #500, Houston, TX 77074-2084 **– 512)** 712 3rd St, West Lafayette, IN 47907-2005 **– 513)** 1800 Turtle Mound Rd, Melbourne, FL 32934-8105 **– 514)** 67 Main St, Sharon, CT 06069-2018 **– 515)** 2970 Peachtree Rd NW #700, Atlanta, GA 30305-4919 **– 516)** 75 Oxford St, Providence, RI 02905-4722 **– 517)** 159 Santanoni Ave, Saranac Lake, NY 12983-2478 **– 518)** 450 Leonard Ave Extension, Fairmont, WV 26554-3878 **– 519)** 12100 W Howard Ave, Greenfield, WI 53228-1851 **– 520)** 1109 Tower Dr, Burlington, NC 27215-4425 **– 521)** PO Box 228, Mayking, KY 41837-0228 **– 522)** 1770 Van Buren Dr, Dumfries, VA 22025-2036 **– 523)** 1117 W Route 66, Flagstaff, AZ 86001-6213 **– 524)** 1250 Siskiyou Blvd, Ashland, OR 97520-5010 **– 525)** PO Box 1179, Douglas, AZ 85608-1179 **– 526)** 1845 W Empire Ave, Burbank, CA 91504-3402 **– 527)** 190 Turner Dr #G, Durango, CO 81303-8231 **– 528)** 37208 US Hwy 169, Aitkin, MN 56431-4195 **– 529)** 9601 McAllister Freeway #1200, San Antonio, TX 78216-4686 **– 530)** 3250 S Reserve St #200, Missoula, MT 59801-8236 **– 531)** PO Box 7069, Breckenridge, CO 80424-7069 **– 532)** 1716 KROE Lane, Sheridan, WY 82801-9681 **– 533)** 3304 S Highway 281, Aberdeen, SD 57401-8792 **– 534)** 544 N Arthur Ave, Pocatello, ID 83204-3002 **– 535)** 1015 W Pine St, Poplar Bluff, MO 63901-4839 **– 536)** PO Box 31000, Spokane, WA 99223-3016 **– 537)** 500 Corporate Parkway #200, Buffalo, NY 14226-1263 **– 538)** 525 Evans St, Greenville, NC 27858-2311 **– 539)** 2711 Pelham Pkwy, Pelham, AL 35124-1704 **– 540)** 5966 Grove Hill Rd, Frederick, MD 21703-6012 **– 541)** 11700 Central Pkwy, Jacksonville, FL 32224-2600 **– 542)** 1913 Barry St, Oxford, AL 36203-2319 **– 543)** 1496 Bellevue St #202, Green Bay, WI 54311-4205 **– 544)** 804 College St, Bowling Green, KY 42101-2133 **– 545)** 4045 NW 64th St #600, Oklahoma City, OK 73116-2615 **– 546)** 821 University Ave, Madison, WI 53706-1412 **– 547)** 105 Whitehall Rd, Lynchburg, VA 24501-6706 **– 548)** 5211 W Laurel St, Tampa, FL 33607-1736 **– 549)** 521 S Scott St, Bainbridge, GA 39819-4101 **– 550)** 27 William St 11th Flr, New York, NY 10005-2718 **– 551)** 815 Lafayette Rd, Portsmouth, NH 03801-5406 **– 552)** 401 11th St #200, Huntington, WV 25701-2235 **– 553)** 430 State Highway 165 #C, Branson, MO 65616-3541 **– 554)** 4908 Ridgewood Rd, Jackson, MS 39211-5422 **– 555)** 329 Maine St, Quincy, IL 62301-3928 **– 556)** 390 Golden Ave, Battle Creek, MI 49015-4598 **– 557)** 11530 Carmel Commons Blvd, Charlotte, NC 28226-3976

– **558)** 615 Olive St, Texarkana, TX 75501-5512 – **559)** 1415 Fulton St, Fresno, CA 93721-1609 – **560)** 345 SW Cyber Dr #100, Bend, OR 97702-1045 – **561)** 6214 W 34th Ave, Amarillo, TX 79109-4006 – **562)** 1105 N Iron Springs Rd, Cedar City, UT 84720-6526 – **563)** 1416 Locust St, Des Moines, IA 50309-3014 – **564)** 126 W 3rd St, Valentine, NE 69201-1826 – **565)** 1189 N Jackson St, Houston, MS 38851-8273 – **566)** 305 N Church St, Wartburg, TN 37887-3164 – **567)** 7119 W M-68, Indian River, MI 49749-9472 – **568)** 7601 Riviera Blvd, Miramar, FL 33023-6574 – **569)** 13379 Great Springs Rd, Smithfield, VA 23430-6930 – **570)** 401 Saw Mill Hollow Rd, Burnsville, NC 28714-9789 – **571)** 544 Mulberry St #500, Macon, GA 31201-8258 – **572)** 3501 Broadway St, Mount Vernon, IL 62864-2202 – **573)** 1011 Radio Drive, Grundy, VA 24614-6157 – **574)** 929 Howard Ave, New Orleans, LA 70113-1148 – **575)** 985 Lincoln Way #103, Auburn, CA 95603-5255 – **576)** 100 W Lyndale Ave #B, Helena, MT 59601-2999 – **577)** 403 W Pueblo Dr, Española, NM 87532-2530 – **578)** 351 Elliott Ave W #400, Seattle, WA 98119-3911 – **579)** 9800 University Ave, Lubbock, TX 79423-5302 – **580)** 624 3rd St S, Nampa, ID 83651-3840 – **581)** 1560 N Corbin St, Silver City, NM 88061-6526 – **582)** 2502 S Frederick Ave, Oelwein, IA 50662-3116 – **583)** 2560 Snake River Ave, Lewiston, ID 83501-9685 – **584)** 2000 West Loop S #300, Houston, TX 77027-3510 – **585)** 7800 E Orchard Rd #400, Greenwood Village, CO 80111-2599 – **586)** 1250 Siskiyou Blvd, Ashland, OR 97520-5010 – **587)** 3109 S 10 Mile Dr, Jefferson City, MO 65109-1012 – **588)** 501 E Broadway St, Forrest City, AR 72335-3801 – **589)** 222 Mallory Station Rd, Franklin, TN 37067-0201 – **590)** 817 Suncrest Place, Charleston, WV 25303-2302 – **591)** 7825 Tuckerman Ln #217, Potomac, MD 20854-3241 – **592)** 6320 Sunbriar Dr, Cumming, GA 30040-7078 – **593)** 2973 US Hwy 84 W, Valdosta, GA 31601 – **594)** 63 Braswell Rd, Hattiesburg, MS 39401-9730 – **595)** 9418 River Rd, Marcy, NY 13403-2071 – **596)** 60 Markfield Dr #4, Charleston, SC 29407-7907 – **597)** 1 Bala Plaza #424, Bala Cynwyd, PA 19004-1403 – **598)** 1496 Bellevue St #202, Green Bay, WI 54311-4205 – **599)** 25 Garlington Rd, Greenville, SC 29615-4613 – **600)** 500 Victory Rd #2, Quincy, MA 02171-3132 – **601)** 1188 Lake View Dr, Altamonte Springs, FL 32714-2713 – **602)** 26495 American Dr, Southfield, MI 48034-6114 – **603)** 701 German School Rd, Richmond, VA 23225-5357 – **604)** 645 Industrial Dr, Franklin, IN 46131-9617 – **605)** 4304 W 24th Ave Suite 200, Kennewick, WA 99338 – **606)** 260 Battle St, Marshall, AR 72650-9440 – **607)** 3600 Highway 7 N, Baker, MT 59313-ND – **608)** 1301 S Abe St, San Angelo, TX 76903-7245 – **609)** 12730 Hesperia Rd #16, Victorville, CA 92392-5808 – **610)** 2425 E Camelback Rd #570, Phoenix, AZ 85016-4250 – **611)** 404 Main St #4, Klamath Falls, OR 97601-6021 – **612)** 16405 Haven Rd, Little Falls, MN 56345-6400 – **613)** 209 N Elm St, Shenandoah, IA 51601-1139 – **614)** 1515 W Main St, Farmington, NM 87401-3896 – **615)** 1928 E Portal Place, Scottsbluff, NE 69361-2727 – **616)** 340 Townsend St #4, San Francisco, CA 94107-1698 – **617)** 50 W Broadway #200, Salt Lake City, UT 84101-2024 – **618)** 324 Broadway St, Cape Girardeau, MO 63701-7331 – **619)** 193 S Keystone Ave, Sayre, PA 18840-1330 – **620)** 4405 Providence Lane #D, Winston-Salem, NC 27106-3226 – **621)** 265 Hegeman Ave, Colchester, VT 05446-3174 – **622)** 495 Benham St, Hamden, CT 06514-2009 – **623)** 600 Beacon Parkway W #400, Birmingham, AL 35209-3118 – **624)** 356 Broad St, Fitchburg, MA 01420-3030 – **625)** 3934 Electric Rd, Roanoke, VA 24018-4513 – **626)** 1491 M-32 West, Alpena, MI 49707-8194 – **627)** 1703 Walnut Bottom Rd, Carlisle, PA 17015-9151 – **628)** 809 S Westover Blvd, Albany, GA 31707-4953 – **629)** 6530 Spanish Fort Blvd #B, Spanish Fort, AL 36527-5014 or PO Box 1328, Mobile, AL 36633-1328 – **630)** 1240 Radio Drive, Pikeville, KY 41501-4779 – **631)** 1010 Tower Place, Bogart, GA 30622-3052 – **632)** 1361 Colony Dr, New Bern, NC 28562-4129 – **633)** 1301 E Douglas Rd, Mishawaka, IN 46545-1732 – **634)** 351 Tilghman Rd, Salisbury, MD 21804-1920 – **635)** 27 N 27th St, Billings, MT 59101-2357 – **636)** 5800 E Skelly Dr #150, Tulsa, OK 74135-6416 – **637)** 200 N Industrial Park Rd, Excelsior Springs, MO 64024-1736 – **638)** 1100 Mohawk St #280, Bakersfield, CA 93309-7417 – **639)** 201 S Bailey Ave, North Platte, NE 69101-5406 – **640)** 1455 E Tropicana Ave #550, Las Vegas, NV 89119-6592 – **641)** 1321 N Gene Autry Trail, Palm Springs, CA 92262-5473 – **642)** 109 E Clark St, Albert Lea, MN 56007-2420 – **643)** PO Box 2482, Kirkland, WA 98083-2482 – **644)** 1211 SW 5th Ave 6th Fl, Portland, OR 97204-3735 – **645)** 1838 Commerce Dr #A, Lakeside, AZ 85929-7007 – **646)** 3219 Laurelwood Dr, Twin Falls, ID 83301-8106 – **647)** 200 Fleet St 4th Flr, Pittsburgh, PA 15220-2910 – **648)** 301 8th St S, Fargo, ND 58103-1826 – **649)** 625 Delaware Ave #308, Buffalo, NY 14202-1007 – **650)** 1597 Military St S, Hamilton, AL 35570-5026 – **651)** 4002 W Gandy Blvd #A, Tampa, FL 33611-3410 – **652)** 125 S Main St, Harlan, KY 40831-2109 – **653)** 3226 Jefferson Rd, Ashtabula, OH 44004-9112 – **654)** 9960 Corporate Campus Dr #3600, Louisville, KY 40223-4070 – **655)** 821 University Ave, Madison, WI 53706-1412 – **656)** 207 University Blvd #200, Harrisonburg, VA 22801-3752 – **657)** 2970 Peachtree Rd NW #700, Atlanta, GA 30305-4919 – **658)** 111

Broadway, New York, NJ 10006-1901 – **659)** 67 W Court Square, Troy, AL 36081-2611 – **660)** 1501 Mount Vernon Rd, Vidalia, GA 30474-3031 – **661)** 181 E Evans St #311, Florence, SC 29506-2512 – **662)** 1190 Patton Ave, Asheville, NC 28806-2706 – **663)** 121 N Front St, Marquette, MI 49855-4300 – **664)** 420 Western Ave, South Portland, ME 04106-1704 – **665)** 2705 E Parkway Dr, Russellville, AR 72802-2006 – **666)** 229 Pajaro St #205, Salinas, CA 93901-3499 – **667)** 745 Main St, Deadwood, SD 57732-1015 – **668)** 1101 Marsh Rd, Eureka, CA 95501-1574 – **669)** 5670 Wilshire Blvd #200, Los Angeles, CA 90036-5611 – **670)** 2110 Cliff Rd, St Paul, MN 55122-3522 – **671)** 7000 Squibb Rd, Mission, KS 66202-3233 – **672)** 733 E Roosevelt Ave, Grants, NM 87020-2113 – **673)** 208 N Thomas Dr, Shreveport, LA 71107-6520 – **674)** 1600 Pasadena Blvd, Pasadena, TX 77502-2404 – **675)** 854 Lindsay Blvd, Idaho Falls, ID 83402-1820 – **676)** 390 E Annabella Rd, Richfield, UT 84701-2692 – **677)** 1200 Chesterly Dr #160, Yakima, WA 98902-7345 – **678)** 1155 Gummow Dr, Fallon, NV 89406-9453 – **679)** 3233 Burnt Mill Dr #4, Wilmington, NC 28403-2676 – **680)** 206 N Front St, McComb, MS 39648-3916 – **681)** 243 Central St, Lowell, MA 01852-2214 – **682)** 1915 Mirro Dr, Manitowoc, WI 54220-6715 – **683)** 100 NW 76th Dr #2, Gainesville, FL 32607-6659 – **684)** 901 E Valley Dr, Bristol, VA 24201-4903 – **685)** 300 Harrison Ave, Weston, WV 26452-2100 – **686)** 1650 S Dixie Hwy, Boca Raton, FL 33432-7462 – **687)** 305 Hwy 315, Pittston, PA 18640-3987 – **688)** 1203 Troy-Schenectady Rd #201, Latham, NY 12110-1046 – **689)** 101 Pine St, Dayton, OH 45402-2925 – **690)** 1691 Forsyth St, Macon, GA 31201-1407 – **691)** 312 E Nine Mile Rd #29D, Pensacola, FL 32514-1475 – **692)** 1801 Rockville Pike #405, Rockville, MD 20852-5604 – **693)** 6223 Old Mendenhall Rd, High Point, NC 27263-3940 – **694)** 11530 Carmel Commons Blvd, Charlotte, NC 28226-3976 – **695)** 44 Gough St #301, San Francisco, CA 94103-5424 – **696)** 12900 Preston Rd #200, Dallas, TX 75230-1380 – **697)** 3131 S Vaughn Way #601, Aurora, CO 80014-3516 – **698)** 1569 N Central Ave, Monett, MO 65708-1104 – **699)** 3871 N Commerce Dr, Tucson, AZ 85705-2983 – **700)** 414 E Cota St, Santa Barbara, CA 93101-1624 – **701)** 5495 Murray Rd, Memphis, TN 38119-3703 – **702)** 1185 N Main St, Providence, RI 02904-1824 – **703)** 625 Delaware Ave #308, Buffalo, NY 14202-1007 – **704)** 24 Frank Lloyd Wright Dr, Ann Arbor, MI 48105-9755 – **705)** 610 Sycamore St #220, Celebration, FL 34747-4996 – **706)** 1650 Midland Rd, Southern Pines, NC 28387-2111 – **707)** 109 Plaza Dr #2, Johnstown, PA 15905-1212 – **708)** 2150 W 68th St #202, Hialeah, FL 33016-1802 – **709)** 4711 Old Kingston Pike, Knoxville, TN 37919-5207 – **710)** 1535 Narrows Rd, Narrows, VA 24124-ND – **711)** 117 Ridge Pike, Lafayette Hill, PA 19444-1900 – **712)** 34 Sylvan St, West Springfield, MA 01089-3444 – **713)** 3256 Penryn Rd #100, Loomis, CA 95650-8052 – **714)** 4125 Carlisle Blvd NE, Albuquerque, NM 87107-4848 – **715)** 140 4th Ave N #340, Seattle, WA 98109-4932 – **716)** 1900 NW Expressway St #1000, Oklahoma City, OK 73118-1854 – **717)** 5100 S Tennis Lane, Sioux Falls, SD 57108-2212 – **718)** 3134 Lake Rd, Horseheads, NY 14845-3103 – **719)** 190 N State St, Chicago, IL 60601-3302 – **720)** 110 India Rd, Paris, TN 38242-7565 – **721)** PO Box 1336, Yazoo, MS 39194-1336 – **722)** 20872 NE Kelley Ave, Blountstown, FL 32424-1115 – **723)** 1019 Washington Ave, Waco, TX 76701-1256 – **724)** 5100 Commerce Dr, Bakersfield, CA 93309-0684 – **725)** 3256 Penryn Rd #100, Loomis, CA 95650-8052 – **726)** 44 Gough St #301, San Francisco, CA 94103-5424 – **727)** 5100 Southwest Freeway, Houston, TX 77056-7308 – **728)** 5110 SE Stark St, Portland, OR 97215-1751 – **729)** 220 State St #106, Fort Morgan, CO 80701-2116 – **730)** 3639 Wolfin Ave, Amarillo, TX 79102-2119 – **731)** 5615 Pershing Ave #12, Saint Louis, MO 63112-1757 – **732)** 75153 Merle Dr #D, Palm Desert, CA 92211-5197 – **733)** 2800 N 44th St #100, Phoenix, AZ 85008-1560 – **734)** 103 Hanover St, Newport, NH 03766-1098 or PO Box 2295, New London, NH 03257-2295 – **735)** 9721 Executive Center Dr N #200, St Petersburg, FL 33702-2439 – **736)** 1625 Hwy 109 N, Gallatin, TN 37066-8135 – **737)** 345 Hudson St Fl 11, New York, NY 10014-4502 – **738)** 9090 Hogan Rd, Jacksonville, FL 32216-4648 – **739)** 70 Adams Hill Rd, Asheville, NC 28806-3841 or PO Box 159, Black Mountain, NC 28711-0159 – **740)** 451 Highway 11 & 80, Meridian, MS 39301-2779 – **741)** 2202 Jolliff Rd, Chesapeake, VA 23321-1416 – **742)** 1570 Northside Dr NW Bldg 200, Atlanta, GA 30318-4204 – **743)** 1700 La Luz Rd, Roswell, NM 88201-ND – **744)** Foster Plaza 5, 651 Holiday Dr, Pittsburgh, PA 15220-2740 – **745)** 706 Butterfield Rd, Yakima, WA 98901-2021 – **746)** 5011 Capitol Ave, Omaha, NE 68132-2921 – **747)** 5999 Center Dr, Los Angeles, CA 90045-8901 – **748)** 67 Main St, Sharon, CT 06069-2018 – **749)** 100 W Shockley Ferry Rd, Anderson, SC 29624-3746 – **750)** 2555 Ponce De Leon Blvd #225, Coarl Gables, FL 33134-6033 – **751)** 1402 E Kansas Ave, Garden City, KS 67846-5806 – **752)** 1602 S Brownlee Blvd, Corpus Christi, TX 78404-3134 – **753)** 18920 E Valley View Pkwy #C, Independence, MO 64055-7020 – **754)** 136 N 7th St, Reedsport, OR 97467-1503 – **755)** 4209 N Frontage Rd, Fayetteville, AR 72703-5002 – **756)** 121 W Alvin Ave, Santa Maria, CA 93458-3002 – **757)** 210 W Cota St, Shelton, WA

98584-2264 – **758)** 150 Nichols Ave, Casper, WY 82601-1816 – **759)** 3222 S Richey Ave, Tucson, AZ 85704-7738 – **760)** 303 8th St, Point Pleasant, WV 25550-1209 – **761)** 1170 Soldiers Field Rd, Allston, MA 02134-1092 – **762)** 900 Forestview Lane N, Plymouth, MN 55441-5934 – **763)** 4405 Providence Lane #D, Winston-Salem, NC 27106-3226 – **764)** 427 S Wall Sreet, Calhoun, GA 30701-2431 – **765)** 3654 Park Ave, Memphis, TN 38111-5626 – **766)** 4321 Stuart Andrew Blvd #E, Charlotte, NC 28217-1588 – **767)** 3656 W Belmont Ave, Chicago, IL 60618-5328 – **768)** 1355 E Altamonte Dr, Altamonte Springs, FL 32701-5011 – **769)** 42669 Garfield Rd #328, Clinton Township, MI 48038-5024 or PO Box 1030, Sterling Heights, MI 48311-1030 – **770)** 6710 Oxon Hill Rd #100, Oxon Hill, MD 20745-1158 – **771)** 5050 Edison Ave #218, Colorado Springs, CO 80915-3450 – **772)** 5787 S Hampton Rd #285, Dallas, TX 75232-2290 – **773)** 619 Alexander Rd Fl 3, Princeton, NJ 08540-6000 – **774)** 800 8th Ave SE, Largo, FL 33771-2162 – **775)** 2141 Grand Ave, Des Moines, IA 50312-5303 – **776)** 2340 Martin Luther King Jr Ave, Knoxville, TN 37915-1625 – **777)** 105 Lake Ave, Elyria, OH 44035-5013 – **778)** 2555 Ponce De Leon Blvd #225, Coral Gables, FL 33134-6033 – **779)** 3230 Steve Reynolds Blvd #219, Duluth, GA 30096-8833 – **780)** 4321 Stuart Andrew Blvd #E, Charlotte, NC 28217-1588 – **781)** 5620 S Lima Rd, Avon, NY 14414-9791 – **782)** 151 E 1st Ave, Everett, PA 15537-1351 – **783)** PO Box 2482, Kirkland, WA 98083-2482 – **784)** 1601 E 57th Ave, Spokane, WA 99223-6623 – **785)** 3256 Penryn Rd #100, Loomis, CA 95650-8052 – **786)** 608 State Highway 30, Pipestone, MN 56164-1458 – **787)** 508 Main St, Miles City, MT 59301-3047 – **788)** 2080 Laura St, Springfield, OR 97477-2197 – **789)** 55 Hawthorne St #1100, San Francisco, CA 94105-3914 – **790)** 5 Rosemar Circle, Parkersburg, WV 26104-1203 – **791)** 3400 Idaho Ave NW #200, Washington, DC 20016-3000 – **792)** 539 Ragland Rd, Madison Heights, VA 24572-ND or PO Box 1079, Lynchburg, VA 24505-1079 – **793)** 125 West End Ave 6th Flr, New York, NY 10023-6387 – **794)** 552 Laney-Walker Extension, Augusta, GA 30901-3014 – **795)** 180 Radio Hill Road, Franklin, NC 28734-6927 – **796)** 11640 Highway 17 Bypass, Murrells Inlet, SC 29576-9332 – **797)** 506 W 1st Ave, Crestview, FL 32536-2420 – **798)** 5590 Rio Grande Ave, Jacksonville, FL 32254-1354 – **799)** 8456 Smokey Hollow Rd, Baldwinsville, NY 13027-8222 – **800)** 1100 Victors Way #100, Ann Arbor, MI 48108-5220 – **801)** 700 Monticello Ave #301, Norfolk, VA 23510-2538 – **802)** 3303 E Chicago St, Caldwell, ID 83605-6904 – **803)** 1900 W Carmen St, Guadalupe, AZ 85283-2559 – **804)** 3606 S 500 W, Salt Lake City, UT 84115-4208 – **805)** 2900 Sutro St, Reno, NV 89512-1616 – **806)** 214 W Pleasant Dr, Pierre, SD 57501-2472 – **807)** 205 9th St, Farwell, TX 79325-ND – **808)** 3185 S Highland Dr #13, Las Vegas, NV 89109-1029 – **809)** 614 Kimbark St, Longmont, CO 80501-4911 – **810)** 40356 Oak Park Way, Oakhurst, CA 93612-8872 – **811)** 2211 E Missiouri Ave #N-300, El Paso, TX 79903-3807 – **812)** 1555 Hamilton St Fl 6, Philadelphia, PA 19130-4085 – **813)** 2100 Fairplain Ave, Benton Harbor, MI 49022-6828 – **814)** 4365 Fulton Dr NW, Canton, OH 44718-2823 – **815)** 800 8th Ave SE, Largo, FL 33771-2162 – **816)** 102 Parkwood Circle, Carrollton, GA 30117-8353 – **817)** 401 Whitney Ave #160, Gretna, LA 70056-2573 – **818)** PO Box 818, Benton, IL 62812-0818 – **819)** 350 Mass Ave #145, Arlington, MA 02474-6713 – **820)** 4801 E Independence Blvd #815, Charlotte, NC 28212-5490 – **821)** 112 E 3rd Ave, Plentywood, MT 59254-2223 – **822)** 4200 N Old Lawrence Rd, Wichita, KS 67219-3211 – **823)** 119 N 3rd St, Hannibal, MO 63401-0711 – **824)** 6161 Savoy Dr #1200, Houston, TX 77036-3363 – **825)** 5670 Wilshire Blvd #200, Los Angeles, CA 90036-5611 – **826)** 11 Bryant Ave SE, Wadena, MN 56482-1543 – **827)** 310 W Wall St #104, Midland, TX 79701-5123 – **828)** 244 Goodwin Crest Dr #300, Birmingham, AL 35209-3700 – **829)** 306 S Kanawha St, Beckley, WV 25801-5619 – **830)** 6304 White Horse Rd #B-5, Greenville, SC 29611-3203 – **831)** 2650 Thousand Oaks Blvd #4100, Memphis, TN 38118-2451 – **832)** 621 O'Grady Dr, Chattanooga, TN 37419-1305 – **833)** 40 Monument Circle #600, Indianapolis, IN 46204-3011 – **834)** 4015 N Monroe St, Tallahassee, FL 32303-2139 – **835)** 1140 Rose Hill Dr, Charlottesville, VA 22903-5128 – **836)** 1227 County Line Rd, Selinsgrove, PA 17870-8188 or PO Box 1070, Sunbury, PA 17801-0870 – **837)** 2929 Radio Station Road, Greenville, NC 27834-0864 – **838)** 2070 N Palafox St, Pensacola, FL 32501-2145 – **839)** 235 Walton St, Syracuse, NY 13202-1533 – **840)** 2651 S Fish Hatchery Rd, Fitchburg, WI 53711-5410 – **841)** 372 S Dorset St, South Burlington, VT 05403-6363 – **842)** 0700 SW Bancroft St, Portland, OR 97239-4226 – **843)** 4131 N Central Expressway #1000, Dallas, TX 75204-2121 – **844)** 2300 Portola Dr, Santa Cruz, CA 95062-4203 – **845)** 6 E Main St, Price, UT 84501-3032 – **846)** 500 W Boone Ave, Spokane, WA 99201-2404 – **847)** PO Box 2355, West Columbia, SC 29171-2355 – **848)** 3490 Shallowford Rd NE #302, Atlanta, GA 30341-2934 – **849)** 2828 W Flagler St, Miami, FL 33135-1337 – **850)** 1160 S Semoran Blvd #A, Orlando, FL 32807-1461 – **851)** 19245 Hwy 127, Athens, AL 35614-6805 – **852)** 827 Fairview Dr SW, Lenoir, NC 28645-6023 – **853)** 4000 Radio Drive #1, Louisville, KY 40218-1568 – **854)** 934 W 138th St,

Riverdale, IL 60827-1673 – **855)** 10 Executive Dr, Farmington, CT 06032-2841 – **856)** 2652 Library Rd #3, Pittsburgh, PA 15234-3127 – **857)** 700 Wellington Hills Rd, Little Rock, AR 72211-2026 – **858)** 5445 Johnson Rd, Bozeman, MT 59718-8333 – **859)** 201 Industrial Park Rd, Excelsior Springs, MO 64024-1736 – **860)** 1000 Dexter Ave N #100, Seattle, WA 98109-3582 – **861)** 80898 Powerline Rd, Umatilla, OR 97882-9309 – **862)** 1907 Mile High Stadium West Cir, Denver, CO 80204-1908 – **863)** 2200 Smith Lane, Fortuna, CA 95540-2771 or PO Box 109, Eureka, CA 95502-0109 – **864)** 3218 Quincy St, Plainview, TX 79072-1906 – **865)** 1859 21st Ave, Rice Lake, WI 54868-9502 – **866)** 3800 Hooper Ave, Baltimore, MD 21211-1313 – **867)** 210 Montague Ave, Greenwood, SC 29649-1935 – **868)** 3737 Lake Ave, Fort Wayne, IN 46805-5554 – **869)** 340 Martin Luther King Blvd, Bristol, TN 37620-2313 – **870)** 500 Victory Rd, Quincy, MA 02171-3139 – **871)** PO Box 90, Smithfield, NC 27577-0090 – **872)** 4043 Geer Rd, Hughson, CA 95326-9715 – **873)** 16414 San Pedro Ave #575, San Antonio, TX 78232-2277 – **874)** 39138 Fremont Blvd 3rd Flr, Fremont, CA 94538-1305 – **875)** 2001 N 3rd St #102, Phoenix, AZ 85004-1439 – **876)** 1411 Locust St, Saint Louis, MO 63103-2332 – **877)** 1360 E Sherwood Dr, Grand Junction, CO 81501-7546 – **878)** 8755 W Flamingo Rd, Las Vegas, NV 89147-8667 – **879)** 714 Narrow Way, Saint Simons Island, GA 31522-9712 – **880)** 234 Airport Plaza Blvd #5, Farmingdale, NY 11735-3938 – **881)** 112 N Pearl St, Berlin, WI 54923-1570 – **882)** 6200 Oak Tree Blvd 4th Flr, Independence, OH 44131-2510 – **883)** 1047 Route 302, Wells River, VT 05081-9742 – **884)** 1465 Northside Dr NW #218, Atlanta, GA 30318-4220 – **885)** 3301 University Dr S, Fargo, ND 58104-6289 – **886)** 63088 NE 18th St #200, Bend, OR 97701-7102 – **887)** 3800 W Alameda Ave, Burbank, CA 91505-4300 – **888)** 1423 W Bender Blvd, Hobbs, NM 88240-9252 – **889)** 5010 Underwood Ave, Omaha, NE 68132-2297 – **890)** 360 Main St, Clinton, AR 72031-6622 – **891)** 3463 Ramona Ave #15, Sacramento, CA 95826-3827 – **892)** 6161 Savoy Dr #1200, Houston, TX 77036-3363 – **893)** 6545 Crown Forest Dr, Plano, TX 75024-7489 or PO Box 1629, Cleburne, TX 76033-1629 – **894)** 1 Julian Price Place, Charlotte, NC 28208-5211 – **895)** 462 Merrimack St, Methune, MA 01844-5804 – **896)** 8010 N Main St, Dayton, OH 45405-2249 – **897)** 2175 Click Rd, Petoskey, MI 49770-8818 – **898)** 700 Monticello Ave #311, Norfolk, VA 23510-2523 – **899)** 820 N LaSalle St, Chicago, IL 60610-3214 – **900)** 2311 Old Arch Rd, Norristown, PA 19401-2013 – **901)** 1270 Mineral Spring Ave, North Providence, RI 02904-4637 – **902)** 26321 Stateline Rd W, Ardmore, TN 38449-3083 – **903)** 311 112th Ave NE, St Petersburg, FL 33716-3394 – **904)** 2500 Battleship Pkwy, Mobile, AL 36602-8003 – **905)** 211 Jason St, Pittsfield, MA 01201-5998 – **906)** 2201 S 6th St, Las Vegas, NV 89104-2999 – **907)** 7700 S Lewis Ave, Tulsa, TX 74136-7701 – **908)** 1220 Olive St, 3rd Floor, Saint Louis, MO 63103-2324 – **909)** 1500 Valley River Dr #350, Eugene, OR 97401-2163 – **910)** 314 E Highland Mall Blvd #250, Austin, TX 78752-3725 – **911)** 1630 Oakland Rd #A109, San Jose, CA 95131-2450 – **912)** 144 Gould St #155, Needham Heights, MA 02494-2338 – **913)** 1250 Riverfront Center, Saint Johnsville, NY 12010-4602 – **914)** 410 New Bridge St #3B, Jacksonville, NC 28540-4759 – **915)** 4611 Terry Rd #C, Jackson, MS 39212-5646 – **916)** 2131 Crimmins Lane, Falls Church, VA 22043-1962 – **917)** 3500 E Rosser Ave, Bismarck, ND 58501-3398 – **918)** 83 E Shaw Ave #150, Fresno, CA 93710-7622 – **919)** 136 S Oak Knoll Ave #300, Pasadena, CA 91101-2624 – **920)** 1600 Utica Ave S #400, Minneapolis, MN 55416-1480 – **921)** 1302 N Shepherd Dr, Houston, TX 77008-3752 – **922)** 6341 W Port Ave, Shreveport, LA 71129-2415 – **923)** 5110 SE Stark St, Portland, OR 97215-1751 – **924)** 320 Barnett Blvd, Tallassee, AL 36078-1506 – **925)** 731 Lexington Ave, New York, NY 10022-1331 – **926)** 27675 Halsted Rd, Farmington Hills, MI 48331-3511 – **927)** 2440 Millwood Ave, Columbia, SC 29205-1128 – **928)** 12100 W Howard Ave, Milwaukee, WI 53228-1851 – **929)** 5815 Westside Rd, Austell, GA 30106-3179 – **930)** 2234 Hodges Chapel Rd, Benson, NC 27504 – **931)** 1130 Radio Road, Bartow, FL 33830-7600 – **932)** 310 S La Frenz Rd, Liberty, MO 64068-7944 – **933)** 5601 Cassia St, Boise, ID 83705-1836 – **934)** 1302 N Shepherd Dr, Houston, TX 77008-3752 – **935)** 5244 Madison Ave, Sacramento, CA 95841-3004 – **936)** 305 N 2nd St, Rogers, AR 72756 – **937)** 1321 N Gene Autry Trail, Palm Springs, CA 92262-5473 – **938)** 5100 S Tennis Lane, Sioux Falls, SD 57108-2212 – **939)** 7255 S Tenaya Way #100, Las Vegas, NV 89113-1900 – **940)** 4638 Decker Dr, Baytown, TX 77520-1418 – **941)** 1949 Mountain View Dr, Cody, WY 82414-4932 – **942)** 2926 Huntsville Hwy #D, Fayetteville, TN 37334-6687 – **943)** 3258 Merchant Rd, Warsaw, NY 14569-9320 – **944)** 641 Bayou Blvd, Pensacola, FL 32503-6329 – **945)** 800 S Douglas Rd #111, Coral Gables, FL 33134-3187 – **946)** 1355 E Altamonte Dr, Altamonte Springs, FL 32701-5011 – **947)** 3245 Basie Rd, Richmond, VA 23228-3404 – **948)** 15963 Highway 4 E, Senatobia, MS 38668-5786 – **949)** 120 Eaton St, Peoria, IL 61603-4217 – **950)** 2504 Ardmore St SE, Grand Rapids, MI 49506-4901 – **951)** PO Box 1299, Lebanon, VA 24266-1299 – **952)** 404 Main St, Klamath Falls, OR 97601-6021 – **953)** 1445 W Baseline Rd, Phoenix, AZ 85041-

7010 – **954)** 10424 Edith Blvd NE, Albuquerque, NM 87113-2408 – **955)** 3400 Olive Ave #550, Burbank, CA 91505-5544 – **956)** 5110 SE Stark St, Portland, OR 97215-1751 – **957)** 5426 N Mesa St, El Paso, TX 79912-5421 – **958)** 11 Main St, Rapid City, SD 57701-2831 – **959)** 3650 131st Ave #550, Bellevue, WA 98006-1334 – **960)** 1582 S Parker Rd #204, Denver, CO 80231-2716 – **961)** 801 Old Wawawai Rd, Pullman, WA 99163-9002 – **962)** 131 N Santa Fe Ave, Salina, KS 67401-2615 – **963)** 830 Oilfield Ave, Shelby, MT 59474-1641 – **964)** 6626 Dubuque Trail, Norwalk, IA 50211-9645 or PO Box 838, Des Moines, IA 50304-0838 – **965)** 5732 N Tryon St, Charlotte, NC 28213-6802 – **966)** 510 W Economy Rd, Morristown, TN 37814-3223 – **967)** 290 Hegenberger Rd, Oakland, CA 94621-1436 – **968)** 2727 Shipley Rd, Wilmington, DE 19810-3299 – **969)** 944 Harlem St, Altoona, WI 54720-1127 – **970)** 494 Blue Prince Rd, Bluefield, WV 24701-9577 – **971)** 2581 US Hwy 70 W, Goldsboro, NC 27530-9553 – **972)** 1801 E Main St, Marion, IL 62959-5115 – **973)** 821 Pineville Rd, Chattanooga, TN 37405-2633 – **974)** 2800 E College Ave, Appleton, WI 54915-3255 – **975)** 1 Forever Dr, Holidaysburg, PA 16648-3029 – **976)** 5555 Hilton Ave #500, Baton Rouge, LA 70808-2564 – **977)** 118 N Patterson St, Valdosta, GA 31601-5570 – **978)** 5455 Jug Factory Rd, Tuscaloosa, AL 35405-4213 – **979)** 777 River Rd, Middletown, CT 06457-3922 – **980)** 22 W Main St, Mount Sterling, KY 40353-1314 – **981)** 35 Eagle Rock Lane, Churchville, VA 24421 – **982)** 103 Ram Cat Alley, Seneca, SC 29678-3243 – **983)** 407 N Howard Ave #200, Tampa, FL 33606-1575 – **984)** 500 Victory Rd #2, Quincy, MA 02171-3132 – **985)** 310 S La Frenz Rd, Liberty, MO 66105-2003 – **986)** 9601 McAllister Fwy #1200, San Antonio, TX 78216-4695 – **987)** 55 N 300 W, Salt Lake City, UT 84180-1109 – **988)** 6400 N Belt Line Rd #110, Irving, TX 75063-6065 – **989)** 100 Saratoga Village Blvd #21, Malta, NY 12020-3703 – **990)** 619 Alexander Rd, Princeton, NJ 08540-6000 – **991)** 840 Philadelphia St #100, Indiana, PA 15701-3922 – **992)** 1100 Spring St #610, Atlanta, GA 30309-2828 – **993)** 15 Century Blvd #101, Nashville, TN 37214-3692 – **994)** 635 W 7th St #400, Cincinnati, OH 45203-1549 – **995)** 9831 Beach Blvd #7, Jacksonville, FL 32207-7229 – **996)** PO Box 593642, Orlando, FL 32859-3642 – **997)** 1115 Tamarack Rd #500, Owensboro, KY 42301-6988 – **998)** 8121 Georgia Ave #806, Silver Spring, MD 20910-4945 – **999)** 8 Robbins St #201, Toms River, NJ 08753-7668 – **1000)** 1675 Grandview Rd, Martinsville, VA 24112-2319 – **1001)** 3100 N Triphammer Rd #100, Lansing, NY 14882-8906 – **1002)** 208 Middle Rd, Skowhegan, ME 04976-5023 – **1003)** 1086 Teaneck Rd #4F, Teaneck, NJ 07666-4858 – **1004)** PO Box 52, Greenville, SC 29602-0052 or , Tryon, NC – **1005)** PO Box 711, Red Springs, NC 28377-0711 – **1006)** 25 NW Point Blvd #400, Elk Grove Village, IL 60007-1030 – **1007)** 9255 Towne Centre Dr #535, San Diego, CA 92121-3038 – **1008)** 4590 E 29th St, Tulsa, OK 74114-6208 – **1009)** 2905 King St, San Jose, CA 95122-1518 – **1010)** 255 Cedardale Dr SE, Owatonna, MN 55060-4425 – **1011)** 2219 Yew St Rd, Bellingham, WA 98229-8855 – **1012)** 812 E Beale St, Kingman, AZ 86401-5925 – **1013)** 6360 SW 41st Place, Davie, FL 33314-3412 – **1014)** 118 E Main St, Clinton, NC 28328-4029 – **1015)** 4321 Stuart Andrew Blvd #E, Charlotte, NC 28217-1588 – **1016)** 109 Old Chapin Rd #Q, Lexington, SC 29072-2065 – **1017)** 4101 Wall St #A, Montgomery, AL 36106-3656 – **1018)** PO Box 322, Mattoon, IL 61938-0322 – **1019)** 1015 Main St, Wheeling, WV 26003-2782 – **1020)** 2900 Sutro St, Reno, NV 89512-1616 – **1021)** 1400 Eon Dr #144B, Bakersfield, CA 93309-9404 – **1022)** 5353 W Alabama St #450, Houston, TX 77056-5922 – **1023)** 10025 Lakewood Dr SW #B, Tacoma, WA 98499-3897 – **1024)** 317 First Ave E, Kalispell, MT 59901-9601 – **1025)** 1310 2nd St NW #A, Sauk Rapids, MN 56379-2532 – **1026)** 5011 Capitol Ave, Omaha, NE 68132-2921 – **1027)** VOA - 330 Independence Ave SW, Washington, DC 20547-0003 – **1028)** 470 Leadmine Rd, Gaffney, SC 29340-4037 – **1029)** 100 Chestnut St #1700, Rochester, NY 14604-2418 – **1030)** 731 S Pear Orchard Rd #27, Ridgeland, MS 39157-4839 – **1031)** 122 Cinema Dr, Wilmington, NC 28403-1490 – **1032)** 230 Goodman Rd E #202, Southaven, TN 38671-5151 – **1033)** 9040 Executive Dr #303, Knoxville, TN – **1034)** 600 W Cavanaugh Rd, Lansing, MI 48910-5254 – **1035)** 10143 Commerce St, Summerville, GA 30747-1356 – **1036)** 201 Industrial Park Rd, Kansas City, MO 64024-1736 – **1037)** 3260 Blume Dr #520 Plaza II, Richmond, CA 94806-5715 – **1038)** 13333 SW 68th Pkwy, Tigard, OR 97223-8304 – **1039)** 14001 Dallas Pkwy #300, Dallas, TX 75240-7369 – **1040)** 621 S Virgil Ave #400, Los Angeles, CA 90005-4043 – **1041)** 5183 N 35th St, Milwaukee, WI 53209-5399 – **1042)** 71991 US Hwy 71 S, Jackson, MN 56143-ND – **1043)** 1601 N 7th St #310, Phoenix, AZ 85006-2481 – **1044)** 6500 W Main St #315, Belleville, IL 62223-3700 – **1045)** 1780 W Holly St, Fayetteville, AR 72703-1307 – **1046)** UMC Campus Box 207, Boulder, CO 80309-1001 – **1047)** 2000 Randolph Rd SE #103, Albuquerque, NM 87106-2146 – **1048)** 2970 Peachtree Rd NW #700, Atlanta, GA 30305-4919 – **1049)** 1160 S Semoran Blvd, Orlando, FL 32807-1461 – **1050)** 2131 Crimmins Lane, Falls Church, VA 22043-1962 – **1051)** 2609 Jordan Lane NW, Huntsville, AL 35816-1030 – **1052)** 1700 Buena Vista Dr, Monroe, NC

28112-6306 – **1053)** 395 Hudson St Fl 7, New York, NY 10014-7452 – **1054)** 1190 Hollywood Blvd, Bay Saint Louis, MS 39520-1662 – **1055)** 5606 Medical Circle, Madison, WI 53719-1232 – **1056)** 2915 Maples Rd, Fort Wayne, IN 46816-3199 – **1057)** 105 Ash Ave, South Pittsburg, TN 37380-1513 – **1058)** 132 Carubia Dr, Core, WV 26541-7137 – **1059)** 5702 52nd Ave S, Fargo, ND 58104-5605 – **1060)** 75-153 Merle Dr #D, Palm Desert, CA 92211-5197 – **1061)** 2336 Penryn Rd #100, Loomis, CA 95650-8052 – **1062)** 2514 Eugenia Ave, Nashville, TN 37211-2117 – **1063)** 3250 Franklin St, Detroit, MI 48207-4219 – **1064)** 2824 Palm Beach Blvd, Fort Myers, FL 33916-1503 – **1065)** 219 Savannah-Gardner Rd, New Castle, PA 16101-5546 – **1066)** 4337 Big Barn Dr, Little River, SC 29566-6802 – **1067)** 6222 West Interstate 10, San Antonio, TX 78201-2097 – **1068)** 1559 W 4th St, Williamsport, PA 17701-5650 – **1069)** 625 N Michigan Ave #300, Chicago, IL 60611-3163 – **1070)** 875 W 5th St, Winston-Salem, NC 27101-2505 – **1071)** 738 Blowing Rock Rd, Boone, NC 28607-4840 – **1072)** 10 Cabot Rd #302, Medford, MA 02155-5173 – **1073)** 703 3rd Ave, Huntington, WV 25701-1421 – **1074)** 4135 Northgate Blvd, Sacramento, CA 95834-1226 – **1075)** 2919 E Broadway Blvd #235, Tucson, AZ 85716-5301 – **1076)** 2300 N Lelia St, Guymon, OK 73942-2840 – **1077)** 302 S 2nd St #204, Laramie, WY 82070-3650 – **1078)** 750 Ridgeview Dr #204, Saint George, UT 84770-2665 – **1079)** 1400 W Main St, Auburn, WA 98001-5230 – **1080)** 1726 Dakota Ave S, Huron, SD 57350-4024 – **1081)** 9255 Towne Centre Dr #535, San Diego, CA 92121-3038 – **1082)** 139 W Olive Ave, Fresno, CA 93728-3035 – **1083)** 10399 State Hwy 238, Afton, WY 83110-ND – **1084)** 4501 N McColl Rd, McAllen, TX 78504-2431 – **1085)** 369 Tower Rd, Waynesburg, PA 15370-3663 or PO Box 990, Greensburg, PA 15601-0990 – **1086)** PO Box 2964, Duluth, GA 30096-2964 – **1087)** 302 S Poplar St, Centralia, IL 62801-3900 – **1088)** 2175 Click Rd, Petoskey, MI 49770-8818 – **1089)** 5555 Hilton Ave #500, Baton Rouge, LA 70808-2564 – **1090)** 6080 Mt Moriah Rd Ext, Memphis, TN 38115-2645 – **1091)** 350 NW 71st St, Miami, FL 33138-5530 – **1092)** 400 Market St Fl 10, Philadelphia, PA 19106-2530 – **1093)** 1079 E Trinity Lane, Nashville, TN 37216-3043 – **1094)** 1359 Carmichael Way, Montgomery, AL 36106-3629 – **1095)** 39138 Fremont Blvd 3rd Flr, Fremont, CA 94538-1305 – **1096)** 104 Main St N, Stillwater, MN 55082-5076 – **1097)** 6223 Old Mendenhall Rd, High Point, NC 27263-3940 – **1098)** 108 Radio Station Rd, Whiteville, NC 28472-4906 – **1099)** 161 Hillwood Ave #B, Falls Church, VA 22046-2983 – **1100)** 661 Little Britain Rd, Newburgh, NY 12553-6150 – **1101)** 4 Summit Park Dr #150, Independence, OH 44131-6921 – **1102)** 1308 E Hwy 56, Salem, IN 47167-9690 – **1103)** 728 Western Ave, Fergus Falls, MN 56537-1095 – **1104)** 601 Washington St, Alexandria, LA 71301-8028 – **1105)** 900 Patte Rd, Willcox, AZ 85643-3408 – **1106)** 210 W Front St, Forsyth, MT 59327-ND – **1107)** 200 1st Ave W #104, Seattle, WA 98119-4291 – **1108)** 140 N Main, Lakeport, CA 95453-4815 – **1109)** 2242 E 1000 S, Roosevelt, UT 84066-4554 – **1110)** Murrow Comm Cntr - WSU, Pullman, WA 99163-ND – **1111)** 1701 S 55th St, Kansas City, KS 66106-2241 – **1112)** 4050 Eisenhauer Rd, San Antonio, TX 78218-3409 – **1113)** 200 South "A" St #400, Oxnard, CA 93030-5717 – **1114)** 3 Converse St #101, Palmer, MA 01069-1538 – **1115)** 147 N Garden St, Marion, NC 28752-3709 – **1116)** 1 Radio Lane, Danville, VA 24541-5235 – **1117)** 149 Main St #210, Nashua, NH 03060-2725 – **1118)** 525 Evans St, Greenville, NC 27858-2311 – **1119)** PO Box 504, Ann Arbor, MI 48106-0504 – **1120)** 4002 W Gandy Blvd, Tampa, FL 33611-3410 – **1121)** 241 W 4th St, Emporium, PA 15834-1047 – **1122)** 55 Horsehill Rd, Cedar Knolls, NJ 07927-2003 – **1123)** 7 Parkway Center #625, Pittsburgh, PA 15221-3019 – **1124)** 2821 US Highway 231, Wetumpka, AL 36093-1222 – **1125)** 1901 N Moore St #200, Arlngton, VA 22209-1746 – **1126)** 11800 W Grange Ave, Hales Corners, WI 53130-1099 – **1127)** 4230 Faber Place Dr #100, North Charleston, SC 29405-8512 – **1128)** 714 Nicholas St, Rupert, WV 25984 – **1129)** PO Box 680748, Fort Payne, AL 35968-1608 – **1130)** 2825 Government St, Baton Rouge, LA 70806-5412 – **1131)** 4501 Broadway, Miami, AZ 85539-3800 – **1132)** 1541 E Grand Ave, Des Moines, IA 50316-3542 – **1133)** 400 W Sunnyside Rd, Idaho Falls, ID 83402-4613 – **1134)** 1500 Cotner Ave, Los Angeles, CA 90025-3303 – **1135)** 912 Lane 11½, Powell, WY 82435-9222 – **1136)** 3256 Penryn Rd #100, Loomis, CA 95650-8052 – **1137)** 2330 W Grand St, Springfield, MO 65802-4900 – **1138)** 121 S Cotton Square, Lufkin, TX 75904-2933 – **1139)** 2502 Camino Entrada #C, Santa Fe, NM 87507-4911 – **1140)** 1156 N Orchard St, Boise, ID 83706-2234 – **1141)** 346 S Main St, Winner, SD 57580-1832 – **1142)** 175 Ken Mar Industrial Pkwy, Broadview Heights, OH 44147-2950 – **1143)** 1150 Pepsi Place #300, Charlottesville, VA 22901-2865 – **1144)** 108 W College St, Dickson, TN 37055-1936 – **1145)** PO Box 7509, Trenton, NJ 08628-0509 – **1146)** 225 Hollywood Blvd NW, Fort Walton Beach, FL 32548-4725 – **1147)** 51 Commerce St, Sumter, SC 29150-5014 or PO Box 6344, Florence, SC 29501-6344 – **1148)** 1119 Eastview Dr, Asheboro, NC 27203-4576 – **1149)** 309 Waverly Oaks Rd #103, Waltham, MA 02452-8403 – **1150)** 6161 Fall Creek Rd, Indianapolis, IN 46220-5032

– **1151)** 1108 Hendricks St, Chattanooga, TN 37406-3159 – **1152)** 604 Chillicothe St #405, Portsmouth, OH 45662-4024 – **1153)** 315 S Atherton St, State College, PA 16801-4045 – **1154)** 6223 Old Mendenhall Rd, High Point, NC 27263-3940 – **1155)** 425 Centerstone Ct #1, Zeeland, MI 49464-2249 – **1156)** 471 Robison Rd W, Erie, PA 16509-5425 – **1157)** 1978 Interbelt Business Center Dr, Saint Louis, MO 63114-5760 – **1158)** 1064 James St, Syracuse, NY 13203-2704 – **1159)** 2100 Coral Way #200, Coral Gables, FL 33145-2639 – **1160)** 4005 Golden Isle W, Baxley, GA 31513-7972 – **1161)** 1901 N Moore St #200, Arlington, VA 22209-1706 – **1162)** 3520 Kingsbury Cir, Roanoke, VA 24014-1356 – **1163)** 328 100th St, Amery, WI 54001-4024 – **1164)** 120 Summit Pkwy #200, Birmingham, AL 35209-4719 – **1165)** 888 Rogue River Highway, Grants Pass, OR 97527-5209 – **1166)** 1130 14th Ave, Longview, WA 98632-3017 – **1167)** 961 Matley Lane #120, Reno, NV 89502-2119 – **1168)** 1838 Commerce Dr #A, Lakeside, AZ 85929-7007 – **1169)** 1530 Greenview Dr SW #200, Rochester, MN 55902-1080 – **1170)** 7700 Carpenter Freeway Fl2, Dallas, TX 75247-4829 – **1171)** 1321 N Gene Autry Trail, Palm Springs, CA 92262-5473 – **1172)** 2810 Southern Dr, Gillette, WY 82718-9369 – **1173)** 1401 W Caldwell Ave, Visalia, CA 93277-7725 – **1174)** 6300 S Tallgrass Ave, Sioux Falls, SD 57108-8184 – **1175)** 1410 N Western Ave, Liberal, KS 67901-2212 – **1176)** 630 Falls Ave, Twin Falls, ID 83301-3300 – **1177)** 5101 S Shields Blvd, Oklahoma City, OK 73129-3217 – **1178)** 1501 13th Ave, Columbus, GA 31901-1908 – **1179)** 35 Baltimore St, Cumberland, MD 21502-3024 – **1180)** 5732 N Tryon St, Charlotte, NC 28607-4835 – **1181)** 25802 County Road 26, Elkhart, IN 46517-9132 – **1182)** 34 Chestnut St, Oneonta, NY 13820-2466 – **1183)** 3824 Wayside Rd, Stuart, VA 24171-2506 – **1184)** 1816 Savannah Hwy, Hampton, SC 29924-6545 – **1185)** 50 James E Casey Dr, Buffalo, NY 14206-2367 – **1186)** 273 Azalea Rd #403, Mobile, AL 36609-1970 – **1187)** 1801 N Elm St, Commerce, GA 30529-2347 – **1188)** 1035 Lincoln Rd #205, Bettendorf, IA 52722-4149 – **1189)** 440 Rebecca Lane, Lebanon, PA 17046-1734 – **1190)** 640 W Hwy 25/70, Newport, TN 37821-8068 – **1191)** 2095 S US Highway 131, Petoskey, MI 49770-9216 – **1192)** PO Box 57, Smithfield, NC 27577-0057 – **1193)** 325 John Knox Rd #G, Tallahassee, FL 32303-4161 – **1194)** 2824 Palm Beach Blvd, Ft Myers, FL 33916-1503 – **1195)** 6106 Hoffner Ave, Orlando, FL 32822-4906 – **1196)** 34 Sylvan St, West Springfield, MA 01089-3444 – **1197)** 101 Back Rd, Dover, NH 03820-5012 – **1198)** 305 W Washington St, Brainerd, MN 56401-2923 – **1199)** 26455 American Dr, Southfield, MI 48034-6114 – **1200)** 600 Grant St #600, Denver, CO 80203-3540 – **1201)** 4010 Summitview Ave, Yakima, WA 98908-2966 – **1202)** 150 Spectrum Blvd, Las Vegas, NV 89101-4860 – **1203)** 1574 Coburg Rd PMB 237, Eugene, OR 97401-4802 – **1204)** 204 E Broadway, Farmington, NM 87401-6418 – **1205)** 216 Belmont Rd, Grand Forks, ND 58201-4620 – **1206)** 2800 N 44th St #100, Phoenix, AZ 85008-1559 – **1207)** 880 Via Esteban #C, San Luis Obispo, CA 93420-2462 – **1208)** 808 E Sprague Ave, Spokane, WA 99202-2126 – **1209)** 301 W South Temple, Salt Lake City, UT 84101-1216 – **1210)** 485 Madison Ave, New York, NY 10022-5803 – **1211)** 106 E Shockley Ferry Rd, Anderson, SC 29624-3746 – **1212)** 500 Grand Ave #210, Destin, FL 32541-1410 – **1213)** 117 SE 5th St, Evansville, IN 47708-1639 – **1214)** 100 Chestnut St#1700, Rochester, NY 14604-2418 – **1215)** 275 Radio Road, Hanover, PA 17331-1140 – **1216)** 7080 Industrial Way, Macon, GA 31206-7538 – **1217)** 3004 E Highway 76, Mullins, SC 29574-7396 or PO Box 1020, Marion, SC 29571-1020 – **1218)** 219 Savannah-Gardner Rd, New Castle, PA 16101-5546 – **1219)** PO Box 308, Bath, ME 04530-0308 – **1220)** 886 Mt Olivet Rd, Columbia, TN 38401-8031 – **1221)** 601 Greensboro Ave #507, Tuscaloosa, AL 35401-1795 – **1222)** 491 S Washburn St #400, Oshkosh, WI 54904-6733 – **1223)** 929 Howard Ave, New Orleans, LA 70113-1148 – **1224)** 762 Water St, Fitchburg, MA 01420-6481 – **1225)** 2110 Cliff Rd, Saint Paul, MN 55122-2347 – **1226)** 25539 NC Hwy 125, Scotland Neck, NC 27874-ND – **1227)** 110 W Spiller Ave, Wytheville, VA 24382-1953 – **1228)** 1982 Senter Rd, San Jose, CA 95112-2603 – **1229)** 1904 W Hillsboro St, El Dorado, AR 71730-6806 – **1230)** 3250 S Reserve St #200, Missoula, MT 59801-8236 – **1231)** 102 S 5th St, Crockett, TX 75835-2037 – **1232)** 2030 Iowa Ave #A, Riverside, CA 92507-7412 – **1233)** 30129 E US Hwy 54, Pratt, KS 67124-8304 – **1234)** 5011 Capitol Ave, Omaha, NE 68132-2921 – **1235)** 436 N Main St, Pocatello, ID 83204-3018 – **1236)** 3525 Soldier Springs Rd, Laramie, WY 82070-8903 – **1237)** 2654 Cramer Lane, Chico, CA 95928-8838 – **1238)** 2720 Highway 83, Weslaco, TX 78596-1225 – **1239)** 2003 NW 56th St, Pendleton, OR 97801-4593 – **1240)** 2250 W Sunset Ave #3, Springdale, AR 72762-5187 – **1241)** 2525 Kell Blvd #200, Wichita Falls, TX 76308-1008 – **1242)** 1039 Eggners Ferry Rd, Benton, KY 42025-8070 – **1243)** 1176 Satellite Blvd NW #200, Suwanee, GA 30024-2868 – **1244)** 2602 Whitehouse Rd #E, South Chesterfield, VA 23834-5398 – **1245)** 1 Forever Dr, Holidaysburg, PA 16648-3029 – **1246)** 1611 S Main St, Dayton, OH 45409-2547 – **1247)** 526 Main Ave SE, Hickory, NC 28602-1103 – **1248)** 331 Fulton St #1200, Peoria, IL 61602-1475 – **1249)** 907 Lejeune Blvd, Jacksonville, NC 28540-5916 – **1250)** 3071 Continental Dr, West Palm Beach, FL 33407-3274 – **1251)** 69 Stanhope Ave, Keene, NH 03431-1577 – **1252)** 219 Main St, Manchester, KY 40962-1259 – **1253)** 113 W Oak St, Sparta, WI 54656-1712 – **1254)** 59 Court St #100, Binghamton, NY 13901-3293 – **1255)** 266 23rd St, Meridian, MS 39301-1728 – **1256)** 1101 Cameron Rd, Opp, AL 36467-2407 – **1257)** 1246 Cranston St, Cranston, RI 02920-7318 – **1258)** 245 Alfred St, Savannah, GA 31408-3205 – **1259)** 204 Main St #201, Logan, WV 25601-3943 – **1260)** 920 W Basin Rd #400, New Castle, DE 19720-1013 – **1261)** N72 W12922 Good Hope Rd, Menomonee Falls, WI 53051-4441 – **1262)** 2625 S Memorial Dr #A, Tulsa, OK 74129-2623 – **1263)** 7590 Highway 238, Jacksonville, OR 97530-9728 – **1264)** 747 E Green St #400, Pasadena, CA 91101-2148 – **1265)** 1811 W O St, McCook, NE 69001-4264 – **1266)** 1960 Idaho St, Carson City, NV 89701-5324 – **1267)** 6805 Corporate Dr #130, Colorado Springs, CO 80919-1977 – **1268)** 341 S Yorktown Pike, Mason City, IA 50401-4533 – **1269)** 2201 6th Ave #1500, Seattle, WA 98121-1840 – **1270)** 3110 Upper Fords Creek Rd, Orofino, ID 83544-9629 – **1271)** 118 E 3rd St E, Mobridge, SD 57601-2511 – **1272)** 2115 Washington Ave S, Bemidji, MN 56601-8918 – **1273)** 1250 Siskiyou Blvd, Ashland, OR 97520-5010 – **1274)** 111 N Spring St, Searcy, AR 72143-7712 – **1275)** 1526 Corporate Dr, Shreveport, LA 71107-6338 – **1276)** 3601 S Congress Ave #F, Austin, TX 78704-7280 – **1277)** 44 Gough St #301, San Francisco, CA 94103-5424 – **1278)** 343 High St, Morgantown, WV 26505-5515 – **1279)** 1 Boot Key, Marathon, FL 33050 – **1280)** 51 S Pearl St, Albany, NY 12207-1500 – **1281)** 631 Main St, Baton Rouge, LA 70801-1911 – **1282)** 1842 S Broad St, Trenton, NJ 08610-6002 – **1283)** 6555 Carnegie Ave #100, Cleveland, OH 44103-4619 – **1284)** 1423 Clarkview Rd, Baltimore, MD 21209-2134 – **1285)** 207 University Blvd #200 , Harrisonburg, VA 22801-3752 – **1286)** 305 Hwy 315, Pittston, PA 18460-3987 – **1287)** 401 W Main St #301, Lexington, KY 40507-1646 – **1288)** 2355 Pluckebaum Rd, Cocoa, FL 32926-5179 – **1289)** 100 WMTM Road, Moultrie, GA 31788-4104 – **1290)** 510 W Economy Rd, Morristown, TN 37814-3223 – **1291)** 1300 WWCR Ave, Nashville, TN 37218-3800 – **1292)** 731 S Pear Orchard Rd #27, Ridgeland, MS 39157-4839 – **1293)** 77 Monroe Center NW #1000, Grand Rapids, MI 49503-2912 – **1294)** 110 Babbitt Rd, Franklin, NH 03235-2105 – **1295)** PO Box 151300, Tampa, FL 33684-1300 – **1296)** 401 N Michigan Ave #2010, Chicago, IL 60611-4206 – **1297)** 2147 Springs Rd, Mount Airy, NC 27030-ND – **1298)** 5426 William St, Lancaster, NY 14086-9320 – **1299)** 8023 Vantage Dr #840, San Antonio, TX 78230-4771 – **1300)** 3313 15th St #F, Great Falls, MT 59405-ND – **1301)** 820 11th Ave, Greeley, CO 80631-3246 – **1302)** 20132 Highway 15, Glencoe, MN 55350-5643 – **1303)** 3256 Penryn Rd #100, Loomis, CA 95650-8052 – **1304)** 650 S E St #H, San Bernadino, CA 92408-1946 – **1305)** 1606 Central Ave SE #104, Albuquerque, NM 87106-4478 – **1306)** 415 Park Ave, Twin Falls, ID 83301-7752 – **1307)** 613 N 5th St, West Monroe, LA 71291-1726 – **1308)** 900 Front St, San Francisco, CA 94111-1427 – **1309)** 1185 9th St NE, Thompson, ND 58278-9343 – **1310)** 906 SW Alder St, Newport, OR 97365-4712 – **1311)** 3090 Olive St #400, Dallas, TX 75219-7640 – **1312)** 2702 E 32nd St, Joplin, MO 64804-4307 – **1313)** 152101 W County Road 12, Prosser, WA 99350-7265 – **1314)** 8 Robbins St #201, Toms River, NJ 08753-7668 – **1315)** 1310 S Florida Ave, Wauchula, FL 33873-9479 – **1316)** 134 E Pitt St, Bedford, PA 15522-1311 – **1317)** 300 E Front St #450, Traverse City, MI 49684-5720 – **1318)** 3231 Old Lee Highway #506, Fairfax, VA 22030-1504 – **1319)** 51 Commerce St, Florence, SC 29501-6344 or PO Box 6344, Sumter, SC 29151-1269 – **1320)** 95 Jackson St, Prestonsburg, KY 41653-1010 – **1321)** 23300 Goddard Rd, Taylor, MI 48180 – **1322)** 1 WDXI Drive, Jackson, TN 38305-4124 – **1323)** 5589 Greenwich Rd #200, Virginia Beach, VA 23462-6565 – **1324)** 4801 E Independence Blvd #815, Charlotte, NC 28212-5497 – **1325)** PO Box 1747, Foley, AL 36536-1747 – **1326)** 2651 S Fish Hatchery Rd, Madison, WI 53711-5400 – **1327)** 40 Cuprak Rd, Norwich, CT 06360-2008 – **1328)** 1190 Patton Ave, Asheville, NC 28806-2706 – **1329)** 16 Martin Luther King St, Selma, AL 36703-3109 – **1330)** 779 Warren Ave, Portland, ME 04103-1176 – **1331)** 310 2nd Ave, Warren, PA 16365-2407 – **1332)** 1310 Walker St W, Douglas, GA 31533-7952 – **1333)** 122 Green St #2L, Worcester, MA 01604-4138 – **1334)** 2215 Perimeter Park Dr, Atlanta, GA 30341-1307 – **1335)** 419 Broadway, Paterson, NJ 07501-2104 – **1336)** 276 Seneca Trail, Ronceverte, WV 24970-1043 – **1337)** 707 Leon St, Durham, NC 27704-4125 – **1338)** 39 Kellogg Rd, New Hartford, NY 13413-2849 – **1339)** 21 E St Joseph St, Indianapolis, IN 46204-1025 – **1340)** 316 E Taylor Rd, DeLand, FL 32724-7817 – **1341)** 5345 Madison Ave, Sacramento, CA 95841-3141 – **1342)** 500 S Phillips Ave, Sioux Falls, SD 57104-6825 – **1343)** 434 Bearcat Dr, Salt Lake City, UT 84115-2520 – **1344)** 3600 County Road 19 S, Minot, ND 58701-ND – **1345)** 17525 Highway 1, Vivian, LA 71082-9526 – **1346)** 2002 Char Ave, Scottsbluff, NE 69361-2255 – **1347)** 507 SE 11th St, Grand Rapids, MN 55744-3950 – **1348)** 1750 S Brentwood Blvd #811, Saint Louis, MO 63144-1344 –

1349) 311 Lexington Ave, Fort Smith, AR 72901-3842 – **1350)** 1308 Coolidge Rd, Aberdeen, WA 98520-6317 – **1351)** 1782 W Sam Houston Pkwy N, Houston, TX 77043-2723 – **1352)** 127 Dorrance St Fl 5, Providence, RI 02903-2828 – **1353)** 79 Baldwin Ave, Waterbury, CT 06706-1854 – **1354)** 875 W 5th St, Winston Salem, NC 27101-2505 – **1355)** 1779 Independence Blvd, Sarasota, FL 34234-2106 – **1356)** 8 Lawrence Rd , Derry, NH 03038-4191 – **1357)** 1009 W Ridge St #A, Marquette, MI 49855-3963 – **1358)** 2700 Corporate Dr #115, Birmingham, AL 35242-2735 – **1359)** 645 25th Ave N, Wisconsin Rapids, WI 54495-3294 – **1360)** 162 Free Hill Rd, Gray, TN 37615-3144 – **1361)** 1000 Memorial Dr, Griffin, GA 30223-4446 – **1362)** 600 W Cavanaugh Rd, Lansing, MI 48910-5254 – **1363)** 1801 Charleston Hwy #J, Cayce, SC 29033-2019 or PO Box 5106, Columbia, SC 29250-0626 – **1364)** 900 Parish St 3rd FLR, Pittsburgh, PA 15220-3407 – **1365)** 2360 St Johns Bluff Rd S #2, Jacksonville, FL 32246-2310 – **1366)** 427 Hill St, Murphy, NC 28906-3509 – **1367)** 1055 NE 125th St, North Miami, FL 33161-5804 – **1368)** 1030 Oakdale St, Manchester, TN 37355-5618 – **1369)** 2438 Highway 43 S, Picayune, MS 39466-7486 – **1370)** 306 W Broad St, Richmond, VA 23220-4219 – **1371)** 1200 S Stockton Ave, Monahans, TX 79756-4060 – **1372)** 401 E Coal Ave, Gallup, NM 87301-6099 – **1373)** 9700 SE Eastview Dr, Happy Valley, OR 97086-6975 – **1374)** 401 Pacheco Blvd, Los Banos, CA 93635-4227 – **1375)** 5408 S Freya St, Spokane, WA 99223-7114 – **1376)** 2120 N Woodlawn St #352, Wichita, KS 67208-1881 – **1377)** 1530 Main St, Lander, WY 82520-2658 – **1378)** 514 Jefferson St, Waterloo, IA 50701-5422 – **1379)** PO Box 159, Carencro, LA 70520-0159 – **1380)** 4433 E Broadway Blvd #210, Tucson, AZ 85711-3536 – **1381)** 3301 Barham Blvd #201, Los Angeles, CA 90068-1477 – **1382)** 710 Grove St, Danville, VA 24541-1704 – **1383)** PO Box 866, Pensacola, FL 32591-0866 – **1384)** 60 North Ave, Owego, NY 13827-1325 – **1385)** 7179 Printers Alley, Milton, TN 32583-5347 – **1386)** 22479 Front St, Accomac, VA 23301-1641 or PO Box 460, Onley, VA 23418-0460 – **1387)** 1 Boston Store Place, Erie, PA 16501-2312 – **1388)** 2100 Washington Ave, Sheboygan, WI 53081-7042 – **1389)** 13321 New Hampshire Ave #207, Silver Spring, MD 20904-3450 – **1390)** 2340 Martin Luther King Jr Ave, Knoxville, TN 37915-1625 – **1391)** 4100 Metzger Rd, Fort Pierce, FL 34947-1712 – **1392)** 821 Adams Rd, Corbin, KY 40701-4708 – **1393)** 4320 Dundee Rd, Northbrook, IL 60062-1703 – **1394)** 1496 Bellevue St #202, Green Bay, WI 54311-4205 – **1395)** 1516 4th Ave #B, Conway, SC 29526-5032 – **1396)** 552 Massachusetts Ave #201, Cambridge, MA 02139-4088 – **1397)** 6317 Taylor Dr, Flint, MI 48507-4683 – **1398)** 2207 E Morgan Ave #J, Evansville, IN 47711-4355 – **1399)** 419 Broadway, Paterson, NJ 07501-2104 – **1400)** 25 Garlington Rd, Greenville, SC 29615-4613 – **1401)** 1111 E Willow St, Scottsboro, AL 35768-2210 – **1402)** 5411 Jefferson St NE #100, Albuquerque, NM 87109-3485 – **1403)** 12451 Network Blvd #140, San Antonio, TX 78249-3445 – **1404)** 1408 E Gibson St, Jasper, TX 75951-6123 – **1405)** 805 Stewart Ave, Lewiston, ID 83501-4709 – **1406)** 1416 Locust St, Des Moines, IA 50309-3014 – **1407)** 1410 Neotomas Ave #200, Santa Rosa, CA 95405-7533 – **1408)** 2030 Iowa Ave #A, Riverside, CA 92507-7412 – **1409)** 1419 W Bannock St, Boise, ID 83702-5234 – **1410)** 2222 Main St, North Little Rock, AR 72114-2302 – **1411)** 7755 Freedom Ave NW, North Canton, OH 44720-6905 – **1412)** 1035 Avalon Dr, Forest, VA 24551-2970 – **1413)** 277 Union Ave #205, Laconia, NH 03246-3114 – **1414)** 436 Mall Blvd, Brunswick, GA 31525-1819 – **1415)** 645 Church St #400, Norfolk, VA 23510-1712 – **1416)** 27 Wiliam St 11th Flr, New York, NY 10005-2718 – **1417)** 45 Pomfret St, Putnam, CT 06260-1827 – **1418)** 671 E County Road 400 S, Kokomo, IN 46902-8101 – **1419)** 214 Walnut Dr SE, Wise, VA 24293-ND – **1420)** 5 Brooks Robinson Way, York, PA 17401-2401 – **1421)** 1913 Barry St, Oxford, AL 36203-2319 or PO Box 1350, Gadsden, AL 35902-1350 – **1422)** 400 Poydras St #800, New Orleans, LA 70130-3245 – **1423)** 6174 GA Hwy 57, Macon, GA 31217-3405 or PO Box 2127, Warner Robins, GA 31099-2127 – **1424)** 46 Haywood St #352, Asheville, NC 28801-2749 – **1425)** 1096 Mechem Dr #G3, Ruidoso, NM 88345-7057 – **1426)** 701 S Pierce St #101, Amarillo, TX 79101-2428 – **1427)** 2121 Lancey Dr, Modesto, CA 95355-3000 – **1428)** 2 S Parish Ave, Johnstown, CO 80534-7800 – **1429)** 2115 Washington Ave S, Bemidji, MN 56601-8918 – **1430)** 1040 S Henderson St, Seattle, WA 98108-4720 – **1431)** 9660 Granite Ridge Dr, San Diego, CA 92123-2657 – **1432)** 5801 Marvin D Love Freeway #409, Dallas, TX 75237-2319 – **1433)** 80404 Cooney Lane, Hermiston, OR 97838-6613 – **1434)** 2425 E Camelback Rd #570, Phoenix, AZ 85016-4250 – **1435)** 2717 Yellowstone Rd, Rock Springs, WY 82901-2813 – **1436)** 2000 Indian Hills Dr, Sioux City, IA 51104-1602 – **1437)** 3355 NE Cornell Rd, Hillsboro, OR 97124-5018 – **1438)** 4638 Decker Dr, Baytown, TX 77520-1418 – **1439)** 3890 Dunn Ave #804, Jacksonville, FL 32218-6429 – **1440)** 88 Vilcom Center Dr #130, Chapel Hill, NC 27514-1660 – **1441)** 869 Blue Hills Ave, Bloomfield, CT 06002-3710 – **1442)** 100 Cross Hill Way, Easley, SC 29640-8854 – **1443)** 560 7th St, New Kensington, PA 15068-6527 – **1444)** 1820 Heritage Center Way, Harrisonburg, VA 22801-8451 – **1445)** 1505 Dundee Rd, Winter Haven, FL 33884-1013 – **1446)** PO Box 19123, Birmingham, AL 35219-9123 or PO Box 622, Jasper, AL 35502-0622 – **1447)** 2828 W Flagler St, Miami, FL 33135-1337 – **1448)** 4154 Jennings Dr, Kalamazoo, MI 49048-1087 – **1449)** 2500 Battleship Pkwy, Mobile, AL 36602-8003 – **1450)** 527 Gibbs St, Ravenswood, WV 26164-1011 – **1451)** 123 Egg Harbor Rd #302, Sewell, NJ 08080-9406 – **1452)** 212 S Centre St, Pottsville, PA 17901-3532 – **1453)** 8044 Montgomery Rd #650, Cincinnati, OH 45236-2959 – **1454)** 1420 Bellevue St, Green Bay, WI 54311-5649 – **1455)** 229 Broad St, Conneaut, OH 44030-2616 – **1456)** 325 Poplar Knob Rd, Galax, VA 24333-4106 – **1457)** 59 Court St #100, Binghamton, NY 13901-3293 – **1458)** 346 W 8th St, Dubuque, IA 52001-4649 – **1459)** 2601 Central Ave #C, Dodge City, KS 67801-6212 – **1460)** 4301 Westbank Dr #301, Austin, TX 78746-4400 – **1461)** PO Box 669, Marysville, CA 95901-0018 – **1462)** 1285 W 2320 S, Salt Lake City, UT 84119-1448 – **1463)** 210 Radio Road, Corona, CA 92879-1722 – **1464)** 216 Belmont Rd, Grand Forks, ND 58201-4620 – **1465)** 750 Dewey Blvd #1, Butte, MT 59701-3200 – **1466)** 2347 Bering Dr, San Jose, CA 95131-1125 – **1467)** 1201 E Division St, Neillsville, WI 54456-2123 – **1468)** 6565 North W St #270, Pensacola, FL 32505-1797 – **1469)** 49 Acme Rd, Brewer, ME 04412-1545 – **1470)** 2615 Broad St, Chattanooga, TN 37408-3100 – **1471)** 500 N Commercial St, Manchester, NH 03101-1151 – **1472)** 120 W 7th St #400, Bloomington, IN 47404-3869 – **1473)** 9349 China Grove Church Rd, Pineville, NC 28134-8531 – **1474)** PO Box 487, Grayson, KY 41143-0487 – **1475)** 1129 Chatham Heights, Martinsville, VA 24112-2149 – **1476)** 20 Tucker Dr, Poughkeepsie, NY 12603-1644 – **1477)** 2513 6th Ave, Altoona, PA 16602-2129 – **1478)** 1101 S Cass St, Traverse City, MI 49684-3235 – **1479)** 910 E McNeill St, Lillington, NC 27546-7483 – **1480)** 2420 Waycross Highway, Jesup, GA 31545-2332 – **1481)** 1515 E Silver Springs Blvd #134, Ocala, FL 34470-6830 – **1482)** 1726 Reisterstown Rd #117, Pikesville, MD 21208-2986 – **1483)** 26256 Highway 47, South Hill, VA 23970-ND – **1484)** 125 S Superior St, Toledo, OH 43602-1790 – **1485)** PO Box 127, Tabor City, NC 28463-0127 – **1486)** 1201 Main St, Moundsville, WV 26003-2844 – **1487)** RR1 Box 139, Dunmore, WV 24934-9712 – **1488)** 280 State St, Rochester, NY 14614-1033 – **1489)** 4535 Metropolitan Ave, Kansas City, KS 66106-2599 – **1490)** PO Box 55450, North Little Rock, AR 72215-5450 – **1491)** 4045 N Mesa St, El Paso, TX 79902-1526 – **1492)** 13225 Dogwood Dr, Baxter, MN 56425-8669 – **1493)** 816 W 6th St, Parker, AZ 85344-4599 – **1494)** 1232 E 2nd St, Tulsa, OK 74120-2010 – **1495)** 518 St Joseph St, Rapid City, SD 57701-2717 – **1496)** 1600 Pasadena Blvd, Pasadena, TX 77502-2404 – **1497)** 2707 Colby Ave #1380, Everett, WA 98201-3568 – **1498)** 1725 N Oregon St, Ontario, OR 97914-1541 – **1499)** 1425 River Park Dr #520, Sacramento, CA 95815-4524 – **1500)** 3308 Broadway St #401, San Antonio, TX 78209-6550 – **1501)** 1300 Hampton Ave #100, Saint Louis, MO 63139-3163 – **1502)** 7035 E Washington St Ext, Bath, NY 14810-ND – **1503)** 400 Colony Sq NE #800, Atlanta, GA 30361-6318 – **1504)** 1 Parker Place #485, Janesville, WI 53545-4078 – **1505)** 2809 Emerywood Pkwy #540, Henrico, VA 23294-3745 – **1506)** 432 S Nova Rd, Ormond Beach, FL 32174-6121 – **1507)** 175 Church St, Naugatuck, CT 06770-4180 – **1508)** 1811 Carters Creek Pike, Franklin, TN 37064-6823 – **1509)** 27 Wiliam St 11th Flr, New York, NY 10005-2718 – **1510)** 2915 Maples Rd, Fort Wayne, IN 46816-3199 – **1511)** 70 Adams Hill Rd, Asheville, NC 28806-3841 – **1512)** 3704 Whittier Rd, Millington, TN 38108-2649 – **1513)** 110 Dennis Dr, Lexington, KY 40503-2917 – **1514)** 786 Diamond Hill Rd, Woonsocket, RI 02895-1499 – **1515)** 445 Carolina Springs Rd, North Augusta, SC 29841-8801 – **1516)** 1456 E Green Bay St, Shawano, WI 54166-2258 – **1517)** 808 Huron Ave, Port Huron, MI 48060-3705 – **1518)** 8230 Summa Ave, Baton Rouge, LA 70809-3421 – **1519)** 67 Merchants Row, Rutland, VT 05701-5910 – **1520)** 3720 Reynolda Rd, Winston-Salem, NC 27106-2232 – **1521)** PO Box 630, Vernon, AL 35592-0630 – **1522)** 11300 4th St N #143, Saint Petersburg, FL 33716-2939 – **1523)** 1200 Chesterly Dr #160, Yakima, WA 98902-7345 – **1524)** 212 W Apache St, Farmington, NM 87401-6235 – **1525)** 1780 W Holly St, Fayetteville, AR 72703-1307 – **1526)** 4700 Walnut St, Boulder, CO 80301-2548 – **1527)** 1304 W Broadway Pl, Hobbs, NM 88240-5508 – **1528)** 313 Old Route 66, Saint Robert, MO 65584-ND or PO Box D, Waynesville, MO 65583-0480 – **1529)** 810 W 200 N, Logan, UT 84321-3726 – **1530)** 4043 Geer Rd, Hughson, CA 95326-9715 – **1531)** 136 S Oak Knoll Ave #300, Pasadena, CA 91101-2624 – **1532)** 1000 20th Ave SW, Minot, ND 58701-6447 – **1533)** 640 Lincoln Ave SE, Saint Cloud, MN 56304-1024 – **1534)** 285 Liberty St NE #365, Salem, OR 97301-0034 – **1535)** 7120 SW 24th Ave, Gainesville, FL 32607-3705 – **1536)** 372 Dorset St, South Burlington, VT 05403-6212 – **1537)** 115 N Church St, Rocky Mount, NC 27804-5402 – **1538)** 28 Houlton Rd, Presque Isle, ME 04769-5206 – **1539)** 2 Pendell Rd, Poughkeepsie, NY 12601-1500 – **1540)** 8456 Smokey Hollow Rd, Baldwinsville, NY 13027-8222 – **1541)** 233 N Michigan Ave #2800, Chicago, IL 60601-5519 – **1542)** 801 Noble St #30,

Anniston, AL 36201-5698 – **1543)** 2043 10th St NE, Roanoke, VA 24012-5309 – **1544)** 1613 Lawrence Hwy , Charlotte, MI 48813-8844 – **1545)** 315 A Street, Meridian, MS 39301-4512 – **1546)** 39540 Bradbury Rd, Middleport, OH 45760-9703 – **1547)** 7461 South Ave, Youngstown, OH 44512-5789 – **1548)** 17 Columbus Rd, Plymouth, MA 02360-4810 – **1549)** 557 Scott St, Wausau, WI 54403-4829 – **1550)** 10250 Lorraine Rd, Gulfport, MS 39503-6005 – **1551)** 2294 Clements Ferry Rd, Charleston, SC 29492-7729 – **1552)** 122 Radio Road, Jackson, TN 38301-3465 – **1553)** 104 Cherry St, Athens, TN 37303-ND – **1554)** 1325 G Street #750, Washington, DC 20005-3104 – **1555)** 516 Main St, Hazard, KY 41701-1775 – **1556)** 278 SW Arthur St, Portland, OR 97201-4745 – **1557)** 1950 S Sunwest Lane #302, San Bernadino, CA 92408-3227 – **1558)** 1632 S Maize Rd, Wichita, KS 67209-3912 – **1559)** 1411 Locust St, Saint Louis, MO 63103-2332 – **1560)** 1605 Simpson Lane, Marysville, CA 95901-9747 – **1561)** 1301 E 4th St, North Platte, NE 69101-4302 – **1562)** Centre City Towers - 650 Smithfield St #620, Pittsburgh, PA 15222-3913 – **1563)** 1716 KROE Lane, Sheridan, WY 82801-9681 – **1564)** 1575 McKee Rd #206, Dover, DE 19904-1382 – **1565)** 1705 Lake St, Elmira, NY 14901-1299 – **1566)** 3411 W Tharpe St, Tallahassee, FL 32303-1139 – **1567)** 100 Eversole St #1 , Harlan, KY 40831-2346 – **1568)** 717 E David Rd, Dayton, OH 45429-5218 – **1569)** 800 County Road 4 E, Prattville, AL 36067-6610 – **1570)** 201 State St, La Crosse, WI 54601-3246 – **1571)** 940 Brownlee Rd, Jackson, GA 30233-2418 – **1572)** 2147 Market St, Nesquehoning, PA 18240-1422 or PO Box D, Lansford, PA 18232-0801 – **1573)** 1061 Collier Center Way #9, Naples, FL 34110-8403 – **1574)** 134 Mullin St, Watertown, NY 13601-3616 – **1575)** 366 S Section St, Fairhope, AL 36532-ND – **1576)** 10 Columbus Blvd #24, Hartford, CT 06106-1973 – **1577)** 3765 N John Young Pkwy, Orlando, FL 32804-3213 – **1578)** 707 Leon St, Durham, NC 27704-4125 – **1579)** 219 Luckett St NW, Roanoke, VA 24017-6812 – **1580)** 100 Kanawha Terrace, Saint Albans, WV 25177-2771 – **1581)** 208 Buena Vista Rd, Hot Springs, AR 71913-8208 – **1582)** PO Box 84, Jerome, ID 83338-0084 – **1583)** 1133 Kresky Ave, Centralia, WA 98531-3789 – **1584)** 500 E Tyler Pkwy, Payson, AZ 85541-3276 – **1585)** 2171 Ralph Ave, Stockton, CA 95206-3699 – **1586)** 59346 Madison Ave, Mankato, MN 56001-8518 – **1587)** 45 Campbell Rd, Walla Walla, WA 99362-9597 – **1588)** 187 Vienna Rd, Newark, NY 14513-9124 – **1589)** 3900 11th Ave, Tuscaloosa, AL 35401-7056 – **1590)** 73 Varney Rd #A, Wolfeboro, NH 03894-ND – **1591)** 1800 Northgate Blvd #A10, Sarasota, FL 34234-2157 – **1592)** 22 Sconticut Neck Rd, Fairhaven, MA 02719-1930 – **1593)** 12 W Long Ave, Du Bois, PA 15801-2100 – **1594)** 40 Rickert Rd, Doylestown, PA 18901-2326 – **1595)** 2710 W Atlantic Ave, Delray Beach, FL 33445-4431 – **1596)** 101 Riverview Rd, Erwin, TN 37650-8722 – **1597)** 4 Summit Park Dr #150, Independence, OH 44131-6921 – **1598)** 959 Magnolia Dr N, Wiggins, MS 39577-3630 – **1599)** 685 E 1675 N, Michigan City, IN 46360-9503 – **1600)** 7351 Hunton St, Warrenton, VA 20187-2222 – **1601)** 12544 N Main St, Trenton, GA 30752-2227 – **1602)** 777 River Rd, Middletown, CT 06457-3922 – **1603)** 715 Route 52, Beacon, NY 12508-1047 – **1604)** 3535 E Kimberly Rd, Davenport, IA 52807-2583 – **1605)** 1820 Wynnton Rd, Columbus, GA 31906-2930 – **1606)** 134 4th Ave, Huntington, WV 25701-1220 or , Kenova, WV – **1607)** 2029 Freeway Dr, Mount Vernon, WA 98273-5470 – **1608)** 403 Capital St, Lewiston, ID 83501-1815 – **1609)** 200 W 1st St, Roswell, NM 88203-4668 – **1610)** 4638 Decker Dr, Baytown, TX 77520-1418 – **1611)** 4700 S Syracuse St #1050, Denver, CO 80237-2713 – **1612)** 257 E 200 S #400, Salt Lake City, UT 84111-2073 – **1613)** 747 E Green St #400, Pasadena, CA 91101-2148 – **1614)** 3205 W North Front St, Grand Island, NE 68803-4024 – **1615)** 3308 Broadway St #401, San Antonio, TX 78209-6550 – **1616)** 2625 S Memorial Dr, Tulsa, OK 74129-2600 – **1617)** 342 Day St, San Francisco, CA 94131-2313 – **1618)** 4205 Cherry Ave NE, Keizer, OR 97303-4856 or PO Box 1430, Salem, OR 97308-1430 – **1619)** 1415 Fulton St, Fresno, CA 93721-1609 – **1620)** 6500 W Main St #315, Belleville, IL 62223-3700 – **1621)** 2278 Wortham Lane, Grovetown, GA 30813-5103 or PO Box 510, Appling, GA 30802-0510 – **1622)** 116 N 4th St, Williamsburg, KY 40769-1115 – **1623)** 613 Silver Circle, Dalton, GA 30721-4551 – **1624)** 3901 Weddington Rd, Monroe, NC 28110-9513 – **1625)** 2298 Rose Ridge, Clintwood, VA 24228-7738 – **1626)** 990 N Center St Extension, Mount Olive, NC 28365-2704 – **1627)** 320 N Jensen Rd, Vestel, NY 13850-2111 – **1628)** 22 Cogswell Ave, Pell City, AL 35125-2438 – **1629)** PO Box 2419, Covington, GA 30015-7419 – **1630)** 1150 Haynor Rd, Ionia, MI 48846-8532 – **1631)** 10 Cabot Rd #302, Medford, MA 02155-5173 – **1632)** 404 W Lime St, Lakeland, FL 33815-4651 – **1633)** 3100 E 15th St, Panama City, FL 32405-7421 – **1634)** 1103 N Green St, Morganton, NC 28655-9003 – **1635)** 236 Admiral Dr, Annapolis, MD 21401-3123 – **1636)** 1496 Bellevue St #202, Green Bay, WI 54311-4205 – **1637)** 13085 SW 133rd Ct, Miami, FL 33186-5850 – **1638)** 230 Goodman Rd E #202, Southaven, MS 38671-5151 – **1639)** 630 Mainstream Dr, Nashville, TN 37228-1204 – **1640)** 100 William T Morrissey Blvd, Dorchester, MA 02125-3300 – **1641)** 100 NW 76th Dr

#2, Gainesville, FL 32607-6659 – **1642)** 1 Forever Dr, Holidaysburg, PA 16648-3029 – **1643)** 9245 N Meridian St #300, Indianapolis, IN 46260-1832 – **1644)** 4343 E Camelback Rd #300, Phoenix, AZ 85018-8306 – **1645)** 1300 Godward St NE #1440, Minneapolis, MN 55413-3089 – **1646)** 115 Radio Road, Livingston, TX 77351-7702 – **1647)** 825 S Kansas Ave #100, Topeka, KS 66612-1233 – **1648)** 3624 Avion Dr, Medford, OR 97504-4011 – **1649)** 404 E 2nd St, The Dalles, OR 97058-2412 – **1650)** 1192 E Draper Pkwy #462, Draper, UT 84020-9356 – **1651)** 301 S Polk St #100, Amarillo, TX 79101-1404 – **1652)** 32992 US Highway 34, Wray, CO 80758-9161 – **1653)** 6400 N Belt Line Rd #110, Irving, TX 75063-6065 or QSL's to CE Mortenson Broadcasting Co 3270 Blazer Pkwy #101, Lexington, KY 40509-1847 – **1654)** 8211 Geyer Springs Rd #P6, Little Rock, AR 72209-4909 – **1655)** 1101 S Broadway #C, Santa Maria, CA 93454-6660 – **1656)** 1124 Foster Rd, Napa, CA 94558-6520 – **1657)** 1251 Earl L Core Rd, Morgantown, WV 26505-5881 – **1658)** 512 Peanut Rd, Elizabethtown, NC 28337-8811 – **1659)** 1049 N Sekol Ave, Scranton, PA 18504-1098 – **1660)** 101 S Main St, Gloversville, NY 12078-3820 – **1661)** 513 Hampshire St, Quincy, IL 62301-2928 – **1662)** 3833 US Highway 82, Brunswick, GA 31523-7735 – **1663)** 613 Tallapoosa St W, Bremen, GA 30110-1838 – **1664)** 101 N. Main St #1000, Greenville, SC 29601-4852 – **1665)** 900 Bluefield Ave, Bluefield, WV 24701-2760 – **1666)** 4 Summit Park Dr #150, Independence, OH 44131-6921 – **1667)** 950 Kenbridge Rd, Blackstone, VA 23824-3105 – **1668)** 2244 Ravine Rd, Kalamazoo, MI 49004-3506 – **1669)** 1 Commerce St #300, Montgomery, AL 36104-3549 – **1670)** 200 Radio Drive, Lexington, NC 27292-8010 – **1671)** 24 Frank Lloyd Wright Dr, Ann Arbor, MI 48105-9755 – **1672)** 1420 Bellevue St, Green Bay, WI 54311-5649 – **1673)** 1210 Snyder Rd, Lansdale, PA 19446-4614 – **1674)** 222 Hazard St, Orlando, FL 32804-3030 – **1675)** 779 Warren Ave, Portland, ME 04103-1007 – **1676)** 3901 Brendenwood Rd, Rockford, IL 61107-2200 – **1677)** 1350 Main St #1206, Springfield, MA 01103-1667 – **1678)** PO Box 1369, Pascagoula, MS 39568-1369 – **1679)** 419 Broadway, Paterson, NJ 07501-2104 – **1680)** 540 Cumberland St W, Cowan, TN 37318-3115 – **1681)** 290 Hegenberger Rd, Oakland, CA 94621-1436 – **1682)** 10614 Rockley Rd, Houston, TX 77099-3514 – **1683)** 919 N Main St, Cleburne, TX 76033-3853 – **1684)** 8755 W Flamingo Rd, Las Vegas, NV 89147-8667 – **1685)** 4424 Hampton Ave, Saint Louis, MO 63109-2232 – **1686)** 903 N Main St, Salinas, CA 93906-3912 – **1687)** 1433 Main Ave N, Thief River Falls, MN 56701-1141 – **1688)** 11291 39th St SW, Dickinson, ND 58601-9206 – **1689)** 6803 West Blvd, Inglewood, CA 90302-1895 – **1690)** 4010 Summitview Ave, Yakima, WA 98908-2966 – **1691)** 2141 Grand Ave, Des Moines, IA 50312-5303 – **1692)** 403 E 25th St, Kearney, NE 68847-5515 – **1693)** 7150 Campus Dr #150, Colorado Springs, CO 80920-3157 – **1694)** 605 S Front St #300, Columbus, OH 43215-5626 – **1695)** 18720 16 Mile Road, Big Rapids, MI 49307-9303 – **1696)** 1065 Radio Park Dr, Mt. Clare, WV 26408-9516 – **1697)** 1240 Radio Drive, Pikeville, KY 41501-4779 – **1698)** 1338 Bragg Blvd, Fayetteville, NC 28301-4202 – **1699)** PO Box 701, Tunkhannock, PA 18657-0701 – **1700)** 1501 13th Ave, Columbus, GA 31901-1908 – **1701)** 1055 Skyway Dr, Marshall, NC 28753-3809 – **1702)** 6325 Sheridan Dr, Williamsville, NY 14221-4801 – **1703)** 123 Egg Harbor Rd #302, Sewell, NJ 08080-9406 – **1704)** 930 E Lincoln Ave, Goshen, IN 46528-3504 – **1705)** 11240 Waples Mill Rd #405, Fairfax, VA 22030-6078 – **1706)** 1707 Warnke Rd NW, Cullman, AL 35055-2231 – **1707)** 2824 Palm Beach Blvd, Fort Myers, FL 33916-1503 – **1708)** 105 Kenwood Ave, Bethlehem, NY 12148-ND or PO Box 89, Rexford, NY 12148-0089 – **1709)** 1611 Atlantic Blvd, Atlantic Beach, FL 32233-2516 or PO Box 51585, Jacksonville Beach, FL 32240-1585 – **1710)** 1355 N Maple Ave, Bartow, FL 33830-3024 or PO Box 452905, Miami, FL 33245-2905 – **1711)** 7080 Lee Highway , Fairlawn, VA 24141-8416 – **1712)** 600 Corporate Cir #100, Harrisburg, PA 17110-9787 – **1713)** 250 Belmont St, Brockton, MA 02301-5178 – **1714)** 5815 Westside Rd, Austell, GA 30106-3179 – **1715)** 501 Main St, Baton Rouge, LA 70801-1911 – **1716)** 449 N 12th St, Defuniak Springs, FL 32433-0411 – **1717)** 2241 W Main St, Moses Lake, WA 98837-2826 – **1718)** 1635 S Gold St, Centralia, WA 98531-8997 – **1719)** 8265 Sierra College Blvd #312, Roseville, CA 95661-9403 – **1720)** 900 N Lake Shore Dr, Lake Charles, LA 70601-2120 – **1721)** 3003 27th Ave S #400, Minneapolis, MN 55406-1914 – **1722)** 3222 S Richey Ave, Tucson, AZ 85713-5453 – **1723)** 570 E Avenue Q9, Palmdale, CA 93550-2354 – **1724)** 1838 Commerce Dr #A, Lakeside, AZ 85929-7007 – **1725)** 1101 Kilgore Dr, Henderson, TX 75652-5129 – **1726)** 1113 Nebraska St, Sioux City, IA 51105-1438 – **1727)** 3911 S 1st St, Abilene, TX 79605-1639 – **1728)** 500 W Cummings Park #2600, Woburn, MA 01801-6503 – **1729)** 2401 Paint Creek Rd, Stanton, KY 40380-9272 – **1730)** 2410 S Main St #A, West Bend, WI 53095-5270 – **1731)** 166 N Main St, Broadway, VA 22815-9702 – **1732)** 3338 E Bristol Rd, Burton, MI 48529-1408 – **1733)** 351 Tilghman Rd, Salisbury, MD 21804-1920 – **1734)** 447 Congress St #3B, Portland, ME 04101-3505 – **1735)** 331 Fulton St #1200, Peoria, IL 61602-1475 – **1736)** 800 8th Ave SE, Largo, FL 33771-2162 – **1737)**

869 Blue Hills Ave, Bloomfield, CT 06002-3789 – **1738)** 240 Moss Hill Dr, New Albany, MS 38652-3400 – **1739)** 1751 Hanshaw Rd, Ithaca, NY 14850-9105 – **1740)** 2440 Millwood Ave, Columbia, SC 29205-1128 – **1741)** 20 John Davenport Dr NW, Rome, GA 30165-2536 – **1742)** 1541 Alta Dr #400, Whitehall, PA 18052-5622 – **1743)** 401 Saw Mill Hollow Rd, Burnsville, NC 28714-9789 – **1744)** 900 Bluefield Ave, Bluefield, WV 24701-2760 – **1745)** 1320 Brick Church Pike, Nashville, TN 37207-5038 – **1746)** 4321 Stuart Andrew Blvd #E, Charlotte, NC 28217-1588 – **1747)** 1650 S Dixie Hwy, Boca Raton, FL 33432-7462 – **1748)** 601 Main St #400, Vancouver, WA 98660-3404 – **1749)** 8035 E R L Thornton Fwy #607, Dallas, TX 75217-5129 – **1750)** 1211 W Hein Rd, San Antonio, TX 78220-3301 – **1751)** 5640 S Broadway St, Eureka, CA 95503-6997 – **1752)** 35006 US Highway 2 E, Fosston, MN 56542-9268 – **1753)** 6161 Savoy Dr #1140, Houston, TX 77036-3323 – **1754)** 824 E Washington St, Phoenix, AZ 85034-1088 – **1755)** 1632 S Maize Rd, Wichita, KS 67209-3912 – **1756)** PO Box 786, Jerome, ID 83338-5483 – **1757)** 1 Radio Drive, Berryville, AR 72616-ND – **1758)** 13749 Beach Blvd, Westminster, CA 92683-3204 – **1759)** 1020 W Main St, Merced, CA 95340-4521 – **1760)** 369 E GE Patterson Ave, Memphis, TN 38126-3301 – **1761)** 10 Clinton St #10, Springfield, VT 05156-3310 – **1762)** 111 Presidential Blvd #100, Bala Cynwyd, PA 19004-1009 – **1763)** 635 W 7th St #201A, Cincinnati, OH 45203-1513 – **1764)** 1551 Springhill Ave #A, Mobile, AL 36604-3283 – **1765)** 1100 S Tryon St #210, Charlotte, NC 28203-4297 – **1766)** 301 Fulton St W, Grand Rapids, MI 49404-6492 – **1767)** 550 Market Ave S, Canton, OH 44702-2103 – **1768)** 5230 W Highway 98, Panama City, FL 32401-1058 – **1769)** 5942 County Route 64, Hornell, NY 14843-9730 – **1770)** 730 Ray O Vac Lane, Madison, WI 53711-2472 – **1771)** 292 Old Clarkesville Rd, Toccoa Falls, NC 30577-ND – **1772)** 3775 W Dugger Ave W, Terre Haute, IN 47885-9794 – **1773)** 4415 39th Place, Brentwood, MD 20772-1106 – **1774)** 40 Park Rd #B, Pleasant Grove, AL 35127-1910 – **1775)** 804 Perryman St, Fair Bluff, NC 36401-1902 – **1776)** 185 Genesee St #1501, Utica, NY 13501-2109 – **1777)** 1 Home St, Somerset, MA 02720-5229 – **1778)** 28084 Van Born Rd, Westland, MI 48186-5159 – **1779)** 306 W Broad St, Richmond, VA 23220-4219 – **1780)** 504 23rd St NW, Roanoke, VA 24017-5414 – **1781)** 486 Lakeside Dr, Jenkins, KY 41537-8917 – **1782)** 1111 Boulevard SE, Atlanta, GA 30312-3895 – **1783)** 27 Wiliam St 11th Flr, New York, NY 10005-2718 – **1784)** 44 Gough St #301, San Francisco, CA 94103-5424 – **1785)** 3415 University Ave SE, Minneapolis, MN 55114-3327 – **1786)** 4802 E 62nd St, Indianapolis, IN 46220-5296 – **1787)** 8451 S Cherokee Blvd #B, Douglasville, GA 30134-8520 – **1788)** 3400 Idaho Ave NW #200, Washington, DC 20016-3000 – **1789)** 90 Kay Ave, Milford, CT 06460-5495 – **1790)** 2 Radio Plaza St, Ferndale, MI 48220-2129 – **1791)** 755 S 11th St #102, Beaumont, TX 77701-3723 – **1792)** 1032 S Union Blvd #100, Lakewood, CO 80228-3374 – **1793)** 6721 W 121st St, Overland Park, KS 66209-2003 – **1794)** 8145 E Evans Rd #8, Scottsdale, AZ 85260-3645 – **1795)** 1601 E 57th Ave, Spokane, WA 99223-6623 – **1796)** PO Box 6326, Santa Maria, CA 93456-6326 – **1797)** 1510 S Richards St, Salt Lake City, UT 84107-7650 – **1798)** 1411 Locust St, Saint Louis, MO 63103-2332 – **1799)** 15096 South Dakota Highway 15 , Milbank, SD 57252-5954 – **1800)** 1213 San Pedro Dr NE, Albuquerque, NM 87110-6725 – **1801)** 2600 El Camino Real #224, Palo Alto, CA 94306-1721 – **1802)** 8729 9th St #110, Rancho Cucamonga, CA 91730-4312 – **1803)** 704 N King St #604, Wilmington, DE 19801-3535 – **1804)** 55 Music Square W, Nashville, TN 37203-3207 – **1805)** 308 Victory Rd, Quincy, MA 02171-3129 – **1806)** 3660 Route 30 #D, Latrobe, PA 15650-4309 – **1807)** 310 W Wisconsin Ave #100, Milwaukee, WI 53203-2224 – **1808)** 1150 W King St, Cocoa, FL 32922-8618 – **1809)** 277 Gravel Hill Rd, Palmyra, PA 17078-8535 – **1810)** PO Box 159, Carencro, LA 70520-0159 – **1811)** 2707 Colby Ave #1380, Snohomish, WA 98201-3568 – **1812)** 2284 S Victoria Ave #2-G, Ventura, CA 93003-6626 – **1813)** PO Box 2245, Watsonville, CA 95077-2245 – **1814)** 400 E Britton Rd, Oklahoma City, OK 73114-7507 – **1815)** 122 4th Ave SW, Rochester, MN 55902-3339 – **1816)** 111 N Main St, Hallettsville, TX 77964-2796 – **1817)** 5110 SE Stark St, Portland, OR 97215-1751 – **1818)** 125 S Kingshighway St, Sikeston, MO 63801-2943 – **1819)** 3 Hickory Ridge Dr, Houston, TX 77024-6229 – **1820)** 824 US Hwy 158 W Bypass, Warrenton, NC 27589-9796 – **1821)** 1188 Lake View Dr, Altamonte Springs, FL 32714-2713 – **1822)** 8451 S Cherokee Blvd #B, Douglasville, GA 30134-8520 – **1823)** 431 Eaton Rd, Mocksville, NC 27028-8653 – **1824)** 412 W Oakland Park Blvd, Wilton Manors, FL 33311-1712 – **1825)** 2980 US Highway 51, Clinton, IL 61727-9479 – **1826)** 369 Shelburne Rd, Greenfield, MA 01301-9653 – **1827)** 1524 Winchester Ave, Ashland, KY 41101-7637 – **1828)** 10 Radio Lane, Brunswick, MD 21788-1645 – **1829)** 500 Corporate Parkway #200, Buffalo, NY 14226-1265 – **1830)** 1545 River Park Dr #500, Sacramento, CA 95815-4693 – **1831)** 200 S 10th #600, McAllen, TX 78501-4869 – **1832)** 5050 Edison Ave #218, Colorado Springs, CO 80915-3540 – **1833)** 1190 Daniels Chapel Rd, New Boston, TX 75570-ND – **1834)** 919 Lilac Dr N, Golden Valley, MN 55422-4615 – **1835)**

4317 E Broadway St, North Little Rock, AR 72117-4124 – **1836)** 5807 S Garnett St #K, Tulsa, OK 74146-6847 – **1837)** 9570 Pan American Dr, El Paso, TX 79927-2001 – **1838)** 8044 Montgomery Rd #650, Cincinnati, OH 45236-2959 – **1839)** 211 State St Fl 3, Bridgeport, CT 06604-4808 – **1840)** 3338 E Bristol Rd, Burton, MI 48529-1408 – **1841)** 3025 Waughtown St #G, Winston-Salem, NC 27107-1634 – **1842)** PO Box 216, Dalton, GA 30722-0216 – **1843)** 123 Broadway, Taunton, MA 02780-2507 or PO Box 329, Middleborough Center, MA 02346-2329 – **1844)** 5900 Pickettville Rd, Jacksonville, FL 32254-1172 – **1845)** 1445 W Baseline Rd, Phoenix, AZ 85041-7010 – **1846)** 1246 W Laurel #200, San Antonio, TX 78201-6431 – **1847)** 3 Hickory Ridge Dr, Houston, TX 77024-6229 – **1848)** 3700 Wilshire Blvd #600, Los Angeles, CA 90010-3013 – **1849)** 514 Jefferson St, Waterloo, IA 50701-5422 – **1850)** 114 Lakeside Ave, Seattle, WA 98122-6542 – **1851)** 400 Las Colinas Blvd E #1033, Irving, TX 75039-5599 – **1852)** 2730 University Blvd W #200, Wheaton, MD 20902-4658 – **1853)** 4243 Albany St, Albany, NY 12205-4609 – **1854)** 904 N Main St, Punxsutawney, PA 15767-2641 – **1855)** 869 Church St, Eatonton, GA 31024-6452 – **1856)** 200 Monument Rd #6, Bala Cynwyd, PA 19004-1726 – **1857)** 306 W Broad St, Richmond, VA 23220-4219 – **1858)** 3931 Whitehorse Rd, Greenville, SC 29611-5599 – **1859)** PO Box 1540, Exeter, NH 03833-1540 – **1860)** 545 Fire Tower Rd, Yanceyville, NC 27379-ND – **1861)** 901 S Kingshighway, Cape Girardeau, MO 63703-8003 – **1862)** 4104 Country Lane, Saint Joseph, MO 64506-4921 – **1863)** 6605 SE Lake Rd, Portland, OR 97222-2161 – **1864)** 430-C State Highway 165 S, Branson, MO 65616-3541 – **1865)** 314 S Redwood Rd, Salt Lake City, UT 84104-3536 – **1866)** 1213 San Pedro Dr NE, Albuquerque, NM 87110-6725 – **1867)** PO Box 3213, Ferndale, WA 98248-3213 – **1868)** Univ of Arizona, Tucson, AZ 85721-0067 – **1869)** 15165 7th St #D, Victorville, CA 92392-3816 – **1870)** 139 W Olive Ave, Fresno, CA 93728-3035 – **1871)** 5166 Meadowood Mall Circle, Reno, NV 89502-6502 – **1872)** 2448 E 81st St #5500, Tulsa, OK 74137-4201 – **1873)** 40931 Freemont Blvd, Freemont, CA 94538-4307 – **1874)** 4107 W Spruce St #250, Tampa, FL 33607-2327 – **1875)** 5495 Jimmy Carter Blvd #C2, Norcross, GA 30093-1519 – **1876)** 730 Ray O Vac Lane, Madison, WI 53711-2472 – **1877)** 101 Lee St, Bristol, VA 24201-4355 – **1878)** 944 Exeter Ave, Exeter, PA 18643-1215 – **1879)** 2043 10th St NE, Roanoke, VA 24012-5309 – **1880)** 7120 US Highway 41, Vienna, GA 31092-4605 – **1881)** 1550 The Boardwalk #1, Huntsville, AL 35816-ND – **1882)** 510 Pegasus Court, Winchester, VA 22602-4596 – **1883)** 143 Rumford Ave, Auburndale, MA 02466-1311 – **1884)** 2405 E Moody Blvd #402, Bunnell, FL 32110-5994 – **1885)** 6943 Titian Dr, Baton Rouge, TX 70806-2767 – **1886)** 330 SW 27th Ave #207, Miami, FL 33135-2957 – **1887)** 160 Chapel Rd #103, Manchester, CT 06042-8929 – **1888)** 411 Radio Station Road, North Augusta, SC 29841-9411 – **1889)** 2202 Jolliff Rd, Chesapeake, VA 23321-1416 – **1890)** 5353 W Alabama #415, Houston, TX 77056 – **1891)** 3980 S Dakota St, Aberdeen, SD 57401-8585 – **1892)** 120 S 35th St #2, Council Bluffs, IA 51501-3203 – **1893)** 3561 Pegasus Dr #107, Bakersfield, CA 93308-0658 – **1894)** 9434 Parkfield Dr, Austin, TX 78758-6227 – **1895)** 9834 17th Ave SW, Seattle, WA 98106-2713 – **1896)** 2600 S Jackson St, Seattle, WA 98144-2499 – **1897)** 8686 Michael Lane, Fairfield, OH 45014-3096 – **1898)** 290 Hegenberger Rd, Oakland, CA 94621-1436 – **1899)** 1800 W Hibiscus Blvd #138, Melbourne, FL 32901-2624 – **1900)** 4200 W Main St, Kalamazoo, MI 49006-2766 – **1901)** 6000 Bristol Dr, Paducah, KY 42003-9213 – **1902)** PO Box 778, South Boston, VA 24592-0778 – **1903)** 121 W Atkins St, Dobson, NC 27017-8709 – **1904)** PO Box 49, Park Rapids, MN 56470-0049 – **1905)** 1111 S Glenstone Ave #3-102,, Springfield, MO 65804 – **1906)** 6820 Pacific Ave #3A, Stockton, CA 95207-2604 – **1907)** 201 N Industrial Park Rd, Excelsior Springs, MO 64024-1736 – **1908)** 7351 Lincoln Ave, Riverside, CA 92504-4618 – **1909)** 548 E Alisal St, Salinas, CA 93905-2760 – **1910)** 2110 Cliff Rd, Eagan, MN 55122-2347 – **1911)** 1860 Executive Park NW #E, Cleveland, TN 37312-2743 – **1912)** 215 3rd Street S, Oneonta, AL 35121-2184 – **1913)** 3105 Evans St #E, Greenville, NC 27834-6899 – **1914)** 3568 Lenox Rd, Geneva, NY 14456-2058 – **1915)** 834 N Tower Rd, Freeport, IL 61032-8650 – **1916)** 2424 Old Rex Morrow Rd, Ellenwood, GA 30294-3901 – **1917)** 40 Rickert Rd, Doylestown, PA 18901-2326 – **1918)** PO Box 1071, Bay Springs, MS 39422-1071 – **1919)** 3616 State Highway 47, Rhinelander, WI 54501-8819 – **1920)** 462 Merrimack St, Methuen, MA 01844-5804 – **1921)** 17890 US Hwy 64 W, Siler City, NC 27344-1631 – **1922)** 1550 Hart Rd, Towson, MD 21286-1697 – **1923)** 8 E Market St, Danville, PA 17821-2917 – **1924)** 127 Glenn Rd, Auburndale, FL 33823-2401 – **1925)** 9831 Beach Blvd #7, Jacksonville, FL 32246-4703 – **1926)** 275 Glenwood Dr, Rocky Mount, VA 24151-2136 – **1927)** 747 E Green St #400, Pasadena, CA 91101-2148 – **1928)** 5050 E Edison Ave #218, Colorado Springs, CO 80915-3540 – **1929)** 36991 KGAL Drive, Lebanon, OR 97355-9666 – **1930)** 4602 E University Dr #150, Phoenix, AZ 85034-7423 – **1931)** 830 Old Buncombe Rd, Travelers Rest, SC 29690-9467 – **1932)** 4200 Parliament Place #300, Lanham, MD 20706-

1881 – **1933)** 236 Woodland Dr, Shelbyville, TN 37160-6759 – **1934)** 41 Pennsylvania Ave, Medford, NY 11763-3717 – **1935)** 4284 Memorial Dr Ste B, Decatur, GA 30032-1220 – **1936)** 3765 N John Young Parkway, Orlando, FL 32804-3213 – **1937)** 5115 Telephone Rd, Pascagoula, MS 39567-1130 – **1938)** 1510 NE 162nd St, North Miami Beach, FL 33162-4716 – **1939)** PO Box 2312, Quincy, FL 32353-2312 – **1940)** 100 Stoddart St, Beaver Dam, WI 53916-1306 – **1941)** 3360 E Livingston Ave #2A, Columbus, OH 43227-1961 – **1942)** 1215 Church St, Oxford, AL 36203-1639 – **1943)** 2601 Nicholasville Rd, Lexington, KY 40503-3307 – **1944)** 303 N Spring St, Fordyce, AR 71742-3317 – **1945)** 85592 574th Ave, Wayne, NE 68787-7043 – **1946)** 6900 Commerce Ave, El Paso, TX 79915-1102 – **1947)** 215 S Market St, Carthage, TX 75633-2623 – **1948)** 1185 9th St NE, Thompson, ND 58278-9343 or PO Box 13638, Grand Forks, ND 58208-3638 – **1949)** 2201 6th Ave #1500, Seattle, WA 98121-1840 – **1950)** 750 Story Rd, San Jose, CA 95122-2604 – **1951)** 5501 Bagby Ave, Waco, TX 76711-2300 – **1952)** 3120 Southwest Freeway #610, Houston, TX 77098-4521 – **1953)** 170 3rd St, Netarts, OR 97141-9489 – **1954)** 1200 Baker Ave, Great Bend, KS 67530-4523 – **1955)** 2284 Victoria Ave #2-G, Ventura, CA 93003-6626 – **1956)** 4209 N Frontage Rd, Fayetteville, AR 72703-5002 – **1957)** 55 Public Square, Monmouth, IL 61462-1755 – **1958)** 1795 W Market St, Akron, OH 44313-7001 – **1959)** 1104 W Broad Ave, Albany, GA 31707-4340 – **1960)** 19 Luther Ave, Warwick, RI 02886-4615 – **1961)** 2100 Lee St, Evanston, IL 60202-1539 – **1962)** 1416 Shelby Highway, Cherryville, NC 28021-8356 – **1963)** 227 E Belt Blvd, Richmond, VA 23224-1205 – **1964)** 1414 16th St, Two Rivers, WI 54241-3031 or PO Box 100, Denmark, WI 54208-0100 – **1965)** 231 N Union St, Olean, NY 14760-2663 – **1966)** 16221 National Pike, Hagerstown, MD 21740-2150 – **1967)** 911 W Main St, Clayton, NC 27520-1620 – **1968)** 125 E 3rd St, New Richmond, WI 54017-1800 – **1969)** 222 Commerce St, Kingsport, TN 37660-4319 – **1970)** 1800 N Meridian St #603, Indianapolis, IN 46202-1433 – **1971)** 4100 Metzger Rd, Fort Pierce, FL 34947-1712 – **1972)** 575 Grove St, Honesdale, PA 18431-1041 – **1973)** 12 Kent Rd, Aston, PA 19014-1498 – **1974)** PO Box 746, Lafayette, GA 30728-0746 – **1975)** 3551 42nd Ave S #B106, Saint Petersburg, FL 33711-4369 – **1976)** 149 Main St #210, Nashua, NH 03060-2725 – **1977)** 182 N Angola Rd, Coldwater, MI 49036-9554 – **1978)** 509 N Main St, Tuscumbia, AL 35674-2048 – **1979)** 2 Radio Loop, Swainsboro, GA 30401-5673 – **1980)** 747 E Green St #400, Pasadena, CA 91101-2148 – **1981)** 1001 Highlands Plaza Dr W #100, Saint Louis, MO 63110-1339 – **1982)** 7800 E Orchard Rd #400, Greenwood Village, CO 80111-2599 – **1983)** 1110 E Olive Ave, Fresno, CA 93728-3535 – **1984)** 1110 26th Ave SW, Cedar Rapids, IA 52404-3430 – **1985)** 1213 San Pedro Dr NE, Albuquerque, NM 87110-6725 – **1986)** 11603 Highway 308, Larose, LA 70373 – **1987)** 9434 Parkfield Dr, Austin, TX 78758-6227 – **1988)** 7140 SW Macadam Ave, Portland, OR 97219-3013 – **1989)** 6500 Brooklyn Blvd, Brooklyn Center, MN 55429-1754 – **1990)** PO Box 300901, Arlington, TX 76007-0901 – **1991)** 2722 S Redwood Rd #1, Salt Lake City, UT 84119-8410 – **1992)** 1479 Sanborn Rd, Yuba City, CA 95993-6042 – **1993)** 4840 Lincoln Rd, Blaine, WA 98230-9602 or PO Box 75150 RPO White Rock, White Rock, BC V4B 5L3 – **1994)** 4230 Packard St, Ann Arbor, MI 48108-1597 – **1995)** 5815 Westside Rd SW , Austell, GA 30106-3179 – **1996)** 259 S Willow Ave #A, Cookeville, TN 38501-3140 – **1997)** 134 E Pitt St, Bedford, PA 15522-1311 – **1998)** 645 Church St #400, Norfolk, VA 23510-1712 – **1999)** 1705 Lake St, Elmira, NY 14901-1299 – **2000)** 2609 Jordan Lane NW, Huntsville, AL 35816-1030 – **2001)** 15 Hampton Ave, Northampton, MA 01060-3809 – **2002)** 2475 Mercer Ave #104, West Palm Beach, FL 33401-7447 – **2003)** 1338 Bragg Blvd, Fayetteville, NC 28301-4202 – **2004)** 1201 Main St, Wheeling, WV 26003-2844 – **2005)** 2 Milledge Rd, Augusta, GA 30904-3063 – **2006)** 3704 Whittier Rd, Memphis, TN 38108-2649 – **2007)** 1076 S Chapel St, Newark, DE 19702-1304 – **2008)** N7502 Radio Road, Ripon, WI 54971-9231 – **2009)** 418 Duncan Rd, Flat Rock, NC 28731-4712 or PO Box 462, Hendersonville, NC 28793-0462 – **2010)** 60 Temple Pl #200, Boston, MA 02111-1324 – **2011)** 333 7th Ave #1401, New York, NY 10001-5021 – **2012)** 188 Valley Rd, Saltville, VA 24370-ND or PO Box 5555, Chilhowie, VA 24319-6555 – **2013)** 912 S Perry St, Montgomery, AL 36104-5002 – **2014)** 4190 Belfort Rd #450, Jacksonville, FL 32233-2516 – **2015)** 134 4th Ave, Huntington, WV 25701-1253 – **2016)** 5011 Capitol Ave, Omaha, NE 68132-2921 – **2017)** 3256 Penryn Rd #100, Loomis, CA 95650-8052 – **2018)** 2600 S Jackson St, Seattle, WA 98144-2499 – **2019)** 3371 W Cleveland Rd Ext #300, South Bend, IN 46628-9780 – **2020)** 7251 Plantation Rd, Pensacola, FL 32504-6334 – **2021)** 2700 Earl Rudder Freeway S #5000, College Station, TX 77845-5011 or PO Box 3248, Bryan, TX 77805-3248 – **2022)** 4404 Napoleon Street SE, Iowa City, IA 52240-8143 – **2023)** 5787 S Hampton Rd #108, Dallas, TX 75232-6377 or QSL's to CE Mortenson Broadcasting Co 3270 Blazer Pkwy #101, Lexington, KY 40509-1847 – **2024)** PO Box 1531, Broomfield, CO 80038-1531 – **2025)** 4051 Jimmie Dyess Pkwy, Augusta, GA 30909-9469 – **2026)** 1762 S Main St, Salt Lake City, UT

84115-1912 – **2027)** 3260 Blume Dr #520 Plaza II, Richmond, CA 94806-5715 – **2028)** 3030 SW Moody Ave #210, Portland, OR 97201-4868 – **2029)** 4045 NW 64th St #306, Oklahoma City, OK 73116-2616 – **2030)** 1496 Bellevue St #202, Green Bay, WI 54311-4205 – **2031)** 1909 East Pass Rd #D11, Gulfport, MS 39507-3778 – **2032)** 3131 S Vaughn Way #601, Aurora, CO 80014-3516 – **2033)** 721 Shirley St, Cedar Falls, IA 50613-1513 – **2034)** 4525 Wilshire Blvd 3rd Flr, Los Angeles, CA 90010-3845 – **2035)** 5426 N Mesa St, El Paso, TX 79912-5442 – **2036)** 333 S Kerr Blvd, Sallisaw, OK 74955-7212 – **2037)** 2202 Mt Jolliff Rd, Chesapeake, VA 23321-1416 – **2038)** 2720 S 7th Ave SW, Fargo, ND 58103-8710 – **2039)** 5501 Bagby Ave, Waco, TX 76711-2300 – **2040)** 1020 W Main St, Merced, CA 95340-4521 – **2041)** 7000 Squibb Rd, Mission, KS 66202-3233 – **2042)** 515 S 700 E #1C, Salt Lake City, UT 84102-2802 – **2043)** 1520 South Blvd #300, Charlotte, NC 28203-3701 – **2044)** 1061 Collier Center Way #9, Naples, FL 34110-8403 – **2045)** 4200 W Main St, Kalamazoo, MI 49006-2749 – **2046)** 27 Wiliam St 11th Flr, New York, NY 10005-2718 – **2047)** 20720 Marilla St, Chatsworth, CA 91311-4407 – **2048)** 3360 Alta Mesa Dr, Redding, CA 96002-2831 – **2049)** 7080 Industrial Way, Macon, GA 31216-7538 – **2050)** 730 Ray O Vac Lane, Madison, WI 53711-2472 – **2051)** 139 W Olive Ave, Fresno, CA 93728-3035 – **2052)** 2201 6th Ave #1500, Seattle, WA 98121-1840 – **2053)** 1109 Hudson Lane, Monroe, LA 71201-6003 – **2054)** 3765 N John Young Parkway, Orlando, FL 32804-3213 – **2055)** 3777 44th St SE, Grand Rapids, MI 49512-3945 – **2056)** 27 William St Fl 11, New York, PA 19125-4347 – **2057)** 12136 Bayaud Ave #125, Lakewood, CO 80228-2115 – **2058)** 3463 Ramona Ave #15, Sacramento, CA 95826-3827 – **2059)** 1100 Spring St #610, Atlanta, GA 30309-2828 – **2060)** 28095 Three Notch Rd #2B, Mechanicsville, MD 20659-3373 – **2061)** 1000 E 87th St, Chicago, IL 60619-6397 – **2062)** 4143 109th St, Urbandale, IA 50322-7925 – **2063)** 11737 Nelon Dr, Corpus Christi, TX 78410-3028 – **2064)** 901 E Pike Blvd, Weslaco, TX 78596-4937 – **2065)** 2609 Jordan Lane NW, Huntsville, AL 35816-1030 – **2066)** 75 NW 167th St, North Miami Beach, FL 33169-6017 – **2067)** 5 Provident Bank Park Dr, Pomona, NY 10970-3540

FM STATIONS IN MAJOR METROPOLITAN AREAS:

FM Callsign	MHz	Location	kW
Atlanta Area			
WJSP	88.1	Jasper Springs	42
WRAS	88.5	Atlanta	100
WRFG	89.3	Atlanta	65
WYFW	89.5	Winder	6
W209CG	89.7	Tallapoosa	0.01
WWBM	89.7	Yates	1
WABE	90.1	Atlanta	96
W213BE	90.5	Snellville	0.01
WUWG	90.7	Carrollton	0.43
WMVV	90.7	Griffin	18
WREK	91.1	Atlanta	40
WWEV-FM	91.5	Cumming	8.9
WMVW	91.7	Peachtree City	13
WCLK	91.9	Atlanta	6
WBTR-FM	92.1	Carrollton	0.58
W221AZ	92.1	Lilburn	0.03
W222AF	92.3	Marietta	0.02
W233BP	92.5	Lithia Springs	0.12
W249CK	92.5	Duluth	0.25
WZGC	92.9	Atlanta	66
WVFJ	93.3	Manchester	270
W229AG	93.7	Atlanta	0.22
WSTR	94.1	Smyrna	100
W233BF	94.5	Atlanta	0.12
WUBL	94.9	Atlanta	100
WSBB-FM	95.5	Doraville	100
WWPW	96.1	Atlanta	100
W243CE	96.5	Winder	0.25
WRDG	96.7	Peachtree City	2.15
WSRV	97.1	Gainesville	100
WUMJ	97.5	Fayetteville	7.9
W250BC	97.9	Atlanta	0.25
WSB-FM	98.5	Atlanta	100
W255CJ	98.9	Atlanta	0.25
WRGU	99.1	Riverdale	0.1
WWWQ	99.7	Atlanta	100
W261BG	100.1	Morrow	0.01
WNNX	100.5	College Park	13.5
W265AV	100.9	Woodstock	0.25
WKHX-FM	101.5	Marietta	100
W270AS	101.9	Carrollton	0.01
WLKQ-FM	102.3	Buford	4.2

FM Callsign	MHz	Location	kW
WPZE	102.5	Mableton	3
W275BK	102.9	Decatur	0.16
WVEE	103.3	Atlanta	100
WALR-FM	104.1	Greenville	100
WFSH-FM	104.7	Athens	23.5
WBZY	105.3	Bowdon	70
WRDA	105.7	Canton	20
W290AG	105.9	Griffin	0.03
WNGC	106.1	Arcade	100
WYAY	106.7	Gainesville	77
WTSH	107.1	Aragon	100
W269BB	107.1	Jonesboro	0.25
WAMJ	107.5	Roswell	33
WPCG-LP	107.9	Canton	0.1
WHTA	107.9	Hampton	33

Baltimore Area

FM Callsign	MHz	Location	kW
WYPR	88.1	College Park	0.01
WAMU	88.5	Washington	50
WEAA	88.9	Baltimore	12.5
W205BL	88.9	Frederick	0.2
WPFW	89.3	Washington	50
WTMD	89.7	Towson	10
WCSP-FM	90.1	Washington	36
WKHS	90.5	Worton	17.5
WZXY	90.7	Spring Grove	0.2
W215BY	90.9	Church Hill	0.03
WETA	90.9	Washington	75
WHFC	91.1	Bel Air	1.1
WBJC	91.5	Baltimore	50
WGTS	91.9	Takoma Park	27
WERQ-FM	92.3	Baltimore	37
WWXT	92.7	Prince Frederick	2.85
WPOC	93.1	Baltimore	19.5
WTTZ-LP	93.5	Baltimore	0.04
WKYS	93.9	Washington	25
W231BG	94.1	Sunnyburn	0.03
WIAD	94.7	Bethesda	50
WRBS-FM	95.1	Baltimore	50
WPGC-FM	95.5	Morningside	50
WWIN-FM	95.9	Arbutus	6
WSOX	96.1	Red Lion	13.5
W241AO	96.1	Wye Mills	0.08
WHUR-FM	96.3	Washington	16.5
WCEI-FM	96.7	Easton	12.5
WLAN	96.9	Lancaster	50
WASH	97.1	Washington	17.5
W248AO	97.5	Baltimore	0.25
WIYY	97.9	Baltimore	13.5
W252BR	98.3	Edgemere	0.25
WYCR	98.5	York-Hanover	10.5
WMZQ-FM	98.7	Washington	50
WNEW	99.1	Bowie	45
WIHT	99.5	Washington	50
W260BV	99.9	Aberdeen	0.01
W260BM	99.9	Annapolis	0.01
W261CD	100.1	Baltimore	0
WBIG-FM	100.3	Washington	50
WZBA	100.7	Westminster	25
W265BG	100.9	North East	0.01
WWDC	101.1	Washington	25
W268BA	101.5	Church Hill	0.25
WLIF	101.9	Baltimore	13.5
WMMJ	102.3	Bethesda	2.9
W272BJ	102.3	Fairlee	0.25
WQSR	102.7	Baltimore	50
WRNR-FM	103.1	Grasonville	6
WTOP-FM	103.5	Washington	44
WXCY	103.7	Havre de Grace	37
WPRS-FM	104.1	Waldorf	0.45
WZFT	104.3	Baltimore	29
W284BE	104.7	Havre de Grace	0.01
W285EJ	104.9	White Marsh	0.25
WAVA-FM	105.1	Arlington	33
W288BS	105.5	Reston	0.1
WJZ-FM	105.7	Catonsville	50
WVRX	105.9	Woodbridge	40
W291BA	106.1	Baltimore	0.24
WWMX	106.5	Baltimore	16.5
WJFK-FM	106.7	Manassas	22.5
WMVK-LP	107.3	Perryville	0.01
WROX	107.3	Washington	21.5
WGTY	107.7	Gettysburg	16

FM Callsign	MHz	Location	kW
WLZL	107.9	Annapolis	50

NB: see also Washington list.

Boston Area

FM Callsign	MHz	Location	kW
WMBR	88.1	Cambridge	0.72
WBMT	88.3	Boxford	0.66
WIQH	88.3	Concord	0.1
WGAO	88.3	Franklin	0.18
WRPS	88.3	Rockland	0.11
WERS	88.9	Boston	4
WHAB	89.1	Acton	0.01
WGBH	89.7	Boston	100
WZBC	90.3	Newton	1
WBUR-FM	90.9	Boston	40
WSHL-FM	91.3	Easton	0.1
WDJM-FM	91.3	Framingham	0.1
WBIM-FM	91.5	Bridgewater	0.18
WUML	91.5	Lowell	1.4
WMFO	91.5	Medford	0.13
WMLN-FM	91.5	Milton	0.17
WZLY	91.5	Wellesley	0.01
WUMT	91.7	Marshfield	1.1
WAVM	91.7	Maynard	0.5
WMWM	91.7	Salem	0.13
WUMG	91.7	Stow	0.5
WUMB-FM	91.9	Boston	0.66
W275BH	92.1	Newton	0.06
WPRO	92.3	Providence	39
WXRV	92.5	Andover	25
WBOS	92.9	Brookline	18.5
WSNE	93.3	Taunton	31
WEEI-FM	93.7	Lawrence	42
WHJY	94.1	Providence	50
WJMN	94.5	Boston	9.2
WHRB	95.3	Cambridge	3
WATD-FM	95.9	Marshfield	1.6
W242AA	96.3	Beacon Hill	0.01
W243DC	96.5	Needham	0.01
WBQT	96.9	Boston	22.5
WJFD	97.3	New Bedford	50
WKAF	97.7	Brockton	2.7
WYAJ	97.7	Sudbury	0.004
WCTK	98.1	New Bedford	47
WBZ-FM	98.5	Boston	16
WPLM	99.1	Plymouth	50
WCRB	99.5	Lowell	37
WHHB	99.9	Holliston	0.02
WBRS	100.1	Waltham	0.03
WZLX	100.7	Boston	21.5
WWBB	101.5	Providence	13.5
WBWL	101.7	Lynn	1.7
WKLB-FM	102.5	Waltham	14
W275BH	102.9	Lawrence	0.25
WODS	103.3	Boston	15.5
W279BQ	103.7	Gloucester	0.08
WBMX	104.1	Boston	21
WXLO	104.5	Fitchburg	37
WRBB	104.9	Boston	0.02
WBOQ	104.9	Gloucester	3.2
WROR-FM	105.7	Framingham	23
WWKX	106.3	Woonsocket	1.15
WMJX	106.7	Boston	21.5
WAAF	107.3	Worcester	9.6
WXKS-FM	107.9	Medford	20.5

Charlotte Area

FM Callsign	MHz	Location	kW
WPIR	88.1	Hickory	26.5
W202BW	88.3	Harrisburg	0.01
WFDD	88.5	Winston-Salem	60
WNSC	88.9	Rock Hill	97.9
WDAV	89.9	Davidson	100
WRBK	90.3	Richburg	7.5
WFAE	90.7	Charlotte	100
W217AX	91.3	Harrisburg	0.01
WFBK	91.5	Fort Mill	0.14
WSGE	91.7	Dallas	7.5
W219CH	91.7	Lowrys	0.01
W220DL	91.9	Statesville	0.04
WRCM	91.9	Wingate	30
WKRR	92.3	Asheboro	100
WQNC	92.7	Harrisburg	6
W225BD	92.9	Statesville	0.25
WRHJ-LP	93.1	Rock Hill	0.04
WTPT	93.3	Forest City	93

FM Callsign	MHz	Location	kW
WYFQ-FM	93.5	Wadesboro	8.7
WWLV	94.1	Lexington	43
W232AX	94.3	Rock Hill	0.05
WNKS	95.1	Charlotte	100
WXRC	95.7	Hickory	100
WHQC	96.1	Shelby	100
W243BY	96.5	Charlotte	0.25
WKKT	96.9	Statesville	100
WKBC	97.3	N. Wilkesboro	100
WPEG	97.9	Concord	95
W252BU	98.3	Dallas	0.25
W254AZ	98.7	Belmont	0.09
W256BP	99.1	Charlotte	0.01
WBT-FM	99.3	Chester	7.7
WRFX	99.7	Kannapolis	84
W261AP	100.1	Kings Mountain	0.01
W262BM	100.3	Charlotte	0.01
WQNC	100.9	Indian Trail	6
WWGT-LP	100.9	Lincolnton	0.1
W267AG	101.3	Salisbury	0.04
WBAV-FM	101.9	Gastonia	100
WGSP-FM	102.3	Pageland	2.55
WLKO	102.9	Hickory	31
W277CB	103.3	Charlotte	0.25
WSOC-FM	103.7	Charlotte	100
W282BP	104.3	Charlotte	0.25
WKQC	104.7	Charlotte	100
WOSF	105.3	Gaffney	51
W289BO	105.7	Rock Hill	0.25
WOLS	106.1	Waxhaw	21
WEND	106.5	Salisbury	84
WRHM	107.1	Lancaster	2.4
WLNK	107.9	Charlotte	100
Chicago Area			
WWTG	88.1	Carpentersville	2
WSSD	88.1	Chicago	0.01
WCRX	88.1	Chicago	0.1
WBMF	88.1	Crete	0.09
WLTL	88.1	La Grange	0.18
WAES	88.1	Lincolnshire	0.15
WLRA	88.1	Lockport	0.14
WTZI	88.1	Rosemont	0.3
WETN	88.1	Wheaton	0.25
WNTH	88.1	Winnetka	0.1
WCLR	88.3	Arlington Hts.	1
WDSO	88.3	Chesterton	0.4
WZRD	88.3	Chicago	0.1
WXAV	88.3	Chicago	0.15
WDGC-FM	88.3	Downers Grove	0.25
WHCM	88.3	Palatine	0.1
WHPK-FM	88.5	Chicago	0.1
WHFH	88.5	Flossmoor	1.5
WGBK	88.5	Glenview	0.19
WHSD	88.5	Hinsdale	0.13
W203AJ	88.5	Michigan City	0.01
WSEH	88.5	South Elgin	0.67
WLUW	88.7	Chicago	0.1
WRSE	88.7	Elmhurst	0.32
WGVE-FM	88.7	Gary	2.1
WCSF	88.7	Joliet	0.1
WEGN	88.7	Kankakee	5
WSRI	88.7	Sugar Grove	0.6
WIIT	88.9	Chicago	0.01
WEPS	88.9	Elgin	0.74
WMXM	88.9	Lake Forest	0.35
WMXM	88.9	Lake Forest	0.29
WOTW	88.9	Monee	0.1
WRRG	88.9	River Grove	0.1
WARG	88.9	Summit	0.5
W206AI	89.1	Lake Villa	0.08
WLPR-FM	89.1	Lowell	2.4
W206BL	89.1	Mount Prospect	0.12
WONC	89.1	Naperville	1.5
WJLV	89.1	Round Lake Bch.	1.9
WKKC	89.3	Chicago	0.28
WNUR-FM	89.3	Evanston	7.2
W207BI	89.3	University Park	0.01
WBEW	89.5	Chesterton	4
WMBI-FM	90.1	Chicago	100
WRTE	90.5	Chicago	0.07
WRTW	90.5	Crown Point	3.1
WMTH	90.5	Park Ridge	0.01

FM Callsign	MHz	Location	kW
WDCB	90.9	Glen Ellyn	5
W216AC	91.1	Valparaiso	0.001
W217BM	91.3	Elgin	0.01
WBEZ	91.5	Chicago	7.5
W219CD	91.7	Elgin	0.01
WJCH	91.9	Joliet	50
W221BY	92.1	Elgin	0.02
WPWX	92.3	Hammond	50
WCPY	92.7	Arlington Hts.	1.8
WXRT	93.1	Chicago	14
WVIX	93.5	Lemont	6
WITW-LP	93.5	Valparaiso	0.05
WLIT-FM	93.9	Chicago	6
WJKL	94.3	Glendale Hts.	3.5
W232BL	94.3	Joliet	0.01
WLS-FM	94.7	Chicago	20.5
W236BD	95.1	Michigan City	0.01
WIIL	95.1	Union Grove	50
WVUR-FM	95.1	Valparaiso	0.03
WEBG	95.5	Chicago	8.3
WERV-FM	95.9	Aurora	3
W240BJ	95.9	Crown Point	0.01
WEFM	95.9	Michigan City	3
WBBM-FM	96.3	Chicago	19
WSSR	96.7	Joliet	3.1
WCOE	96.7	La Porte	3
W244BQ	96.7	Park Ridge	0.01
WWDV	96.9	Zion	50
WDRV	97.1	Chicago	8.3
W248AP	97.5	Chesterton	0.1
W248BB	97.5	Hillside	0.25
WLUP-FM	97.9	Chicago	6
WCCQ	98.3	Crest Hill	3
W252AW	98.3	Ridgefield	0.25
WRLR-LP	98.3	Round Lake Hts.	0.09
WVLP-LP	98.3	Valparaiso	0.1
WFMT	98.7	Chicago	6
WUSN	99.5	Chicago	24.2
WCPQ	99.9	Park Forest	50
W260BL	99.9	Waukegan	0.01
WSHE	100.3	Chicago	8.3
WRXQ	100.7	Coal City	2.45
W264BF	100.7	Englewood	0.002
WKQX	101.1	Chicago	8.3
WLGS-LP	101.5	Lake Villa	0.1
W268AY	101.5	Seward Township	0.02
WTMX	101.9	Skokie	4.2
WYCA	102.3	Crete	1.05
W272BZ	102.3	Portage	0.03
WXLC	102.3	Waukegan	3
WVAZ	102.7	Oak Park	35
WVIV-FM	103.1	Highland Park	6
W276BM	103.1	Park Forest	0.01
WKSC-FM	103.5	Chicago	17
WLMM-LP	103.9	Channahon	0.1
W280EM	103.9	Chicago	0.17
WXRD	103.9	Crown Point	3
WWYW	103.9	Dundee	2.55
WJMK	104.3	Chicago	24.2
WOJO	105.1	Evanston	8.4
WLJE	105.5	Valparaiso	1.25
WZSR	105.5	Woodstock	1.6
WCFS-FM	105.9	Elmwood Park	25.1
W292DJ	106.3	Lake Bluff	0.01
WSRB	106.3	Lansing	4.1
WPPN	106.7	Des Plaines	50
W294BA	106.7	Valparaiso	0.05
W295AF	106.9	La Porte	0.01
WZVN	107.1	Lowell	2.65
WGCI-FM	107.5	Chicago	6
WLEY-FM	107.9	Aurora	21
Dallas & Fort Worth Area			
KNTU	88.1	McKinney	100
KJRN	88.3	Keene	23
KEOM	88.5	Mesquite	61
KTCU-FM	88.7	Fort Worth	10
KNON	89.3	Dallas	55
KAWA	89.7	Sanger	14
KERA	90.1	Dallas	100
KTXG	90.5	Greenville	38
KCBI	90.9	Dallas	100
KDKR	91.3	Decatur	40

FM Callsign	MHz	Location	kW
K218EB	91.5	Greenville	0.25
KKXT	91.7	Dallas	100
KZPS	92.5	Dallas	100
KLIF-FM	93.3	Haltom City	50
KNOR	93.7	Krum	43
KLNO	94.1	Fort Worth	100
KSOC	94.5	Gainesville	9.8
KLTY	94.9	Arlington	100
KHYI	95.3	Howe	16.9
K240DS	95.9	Garland	0.12
KSCS	96.3	Fort Worth	100
KTCK	96.7	Flower Mound	90
KEGL	97.1	Fort Worth	100
K248BC	97.5	Dallas	0.05
KBFB	97.9	Dallas	100
KBOC	98.3	Bridgeport	93
KLUV	98.7	Dallas	100
KDXX	99.1	Denton	100
KPLX	99.5	Fort Worth	100
K260BP	99.9	Irving	0.25
KJKK	100.3	Dallas	100
KWRD	100.7	Highland	98
WRR	101.1	Dallas	100
W268CL	101.5	Garland	0.25
KYDA	101.7	Azle	92
KDGE	102.1	Fort Worth-Dallas	100
K273BJ	102.5	Dallas	0.25
KDMX	102.9	Dallas	100
KESN	103.3	Allen	98
KVIL	103.7	Highland Park-Dallas	100
KESC-LP	104.1	Dallas	0.1
KTDK	104.1	Sanger	6.2
KKDA-FM	104.5	Dallas	100
KRLD-FM	105.3	Dallas	100
KRNB	105.7	Decatur	4.3
KHKS	106.1	Denton	100
KZZA	106.7	Muenster	75
KESS	107.1	Benbrook	0.2
KMVK	107.5	Fort Worth	53
KFZO	107.9	Lewisville	5
Denver Area			
KVOD	88.1	Lakewood	1.2
KGNU-FM	88.5	Boulder	4
KDAB	88.9	Central City	0.01
KUVO	89.3	Denver	22.5
KXGR	89.7	Loveland	80
KCFR-FM	90.1	Denver	50
K213EG	90.5	Littleton	0.003
KGUD	90.7	Longmont	0.1
KLDV	91.1	Morrison	100
K219LF	91.7	Idaho Springs	0.03
K220IY	91.9	Lafayette	0.12
KJMN	92.1	Castle Rock	42
KWOF	92.5	Broomfield	57
KKPK	92.9	Colorado Springs	60
KTCL	93.3	Wheat Ridge	71
K229BS	93.7	Lakewood	0.1
K229AC	93.7	Ward	0.03
KILO	94.3	Colorado Springs	59.2
KRKS-FM	94.7	Lafayette	100
KATC	95.1	Colorado Springs	58
KPTT	95.7	Denver	100
KXPK-FM1	96.5	Boulder	0.5
KXPK	96.5	Evergreen	100
KCCY	96.9	Pueblo	58
KBCO	97.3	Boulder	100
KKFM	98.1	Colorado Springs	71
KYGO-FM1	98.5	Boulder	0.5
KYGO-FM	98.5	Denver	100
KQMT	99.5	Denver	100
KVUU	99.9	Pueblo	57
KIMN-FM1	100.3	Boulder	0.58
KGFT	100.7	Pueblo	77
KIMN	100.3	Denver	100
KOSI	101.1	Denver	100
KJHM	101.5	Strasburg	20
K269AE	101.7	Boulder	0.1
K269CL	101.7	Evergreen	0.04
KAMV-LP	101.9	Brighton	0.1
KXWA	101.9	Centennial	9.5
KRKY-FM	102.1	Estes Park	0.18
KDSP-FM2	102.3	Boulder	0.25

FM Callsign	MHz	Location	kW
KVOQ	102.3	Greenwood Village	1
K274BW	102.7	Berthoud	0.25
KBIQ	102.7	Manitou Springs	57
K276FK	103.1	Pinecliffe	0.25
KRFX	103.5	Denver	100
KKFN	104.3	Longmont	100
KXKL-FM1	105.1	Boulder	1.5
KXKL-FM	105.1	Denver	100
KJAC-FM1	105.5	Boulder	0.1
KALC	105.9	Denver	100
K292FM	106.3	Denver	0.1
KBPI	106.7	Denver	100
KFCO	107.1	Bennett	93
KQKS	107.5	Lakewood	100
K300CP	107.9	Denver	0.25
Detroit Area			
WBFH	88.1	Bloomfield Hills	0.36
WHPR-FM	88.1	Highland Park	0.01
WSMF	88.1	Monroe	1.2
WSDP	88.1	Plymouth	0.2
WCBN-FM	88.3	Ann Arbor	3
WXOU	88.3	Auburn Hills	0.11
WDTE	88.3	Grosse Pt. Shores	5.5
WSHJ	88.3	Southfield	0.11
WSHM	88.3	Wixom	0.1
WDTR	88.9	Imlay City	6
W206BI	89.1	Hamtramck	0.01
WPHS	89.1	Warren	0.1
WEMU	89.1	Ypsilanti	16
WHFR	89.3	Dearborn	0.27
WBLD	89.3	Orchard Lake	0.02
WAHS	89.5	Auburn Heights	0.1
WDTP	89.5	Huron Township	50
WOVI	89.5	Novi	0.1
W208BB	89.5	Royal Oak	0.05
WDTP	90.1	Huron Township	0.7
WRCJ-FM	90.9	Detroit	42
WVMV	91.5	China Township	1.05
WUOM	91.7	Ann Arbor	93
WMXD	92.3	Detroit	45
W244CC	92.7	Detroit	0.25
WDRQ	93.1	Detroit	26.5
W228CJ	93.5	Detroit	0.04
W284BQ	93.9	Detroit	0.25
W232CA	94.3	Detroit	0.1
W232BH	94.3	Holly	0.01
WCSX	94.7	Birmingham	14
WKQI	95.5	Detroit	100
WDVD	96.3	Detroit	21
WXYT-FM	97.1	Detroit	50
W248AQ	97.5	Harrison	0.001
WYDM	97.5	Monroe	41
WJLB	97.9	Detroit	50
W252BX	98.3	Detroit	0.17
WDZH	98.7	Detroit	50
W256AY	99.1	Detroit	0.04
WYCD	99.5	Detroit	17.5
W206CB	99.9	Hamtramck	0.25
WNIC	100.3	Dearborn	50
WRIF	101.1	Detroit	27
WDET-FM	101.9	Detroit	48
W272CA	102.3	Detroit	0.04
WPZR	102.7	Mount Clemens	50
WWWW-FM	102.9	Ann Arbor	15
WMUZ	103.5	Detroit	50
WOMC	104.3	Detroit	190
W284BQ	104.7	Detroit	0.25
WMGC-FM	105.1	Detroit	50
W288BK	105.5	Rochester Hills	0.04
WDMK	105.9	Detroit	20
W292DK	106.3	Westland	0.01
WDTW-FM	106.7	Detroit	61
WQKL	107.1	Ann Arbor	3
WGPR	107.5	Detroit	50
WCRZ	107.9	Flint	50
+16 Canadian stations within 65 kilometers (see Canada listing)			
Houston-Galveston Area			
K201FA	88.1	Freeport	0.05
201EU	88.1	Katy	0.25
KFTG	88.1	Pasadena	0.7
K201DZ	88.1	Port Bolivar	0.12
KAFR	88.3	Conroe	100

FM Callsign	MHz	Location	kW	FM Callsign	MHz	Location	kW
KUHF	88.7	Houston	100	K212FA	90.3	Temple City	0.01
KSBJ	89.3	Humble	100	KPFK	90.7	Los Angeles	110
KZBJ	89.5	Bay City	35	KPFK-FM1	90.7	Malibu	1.5
K208DG	89.5	Galveston	0.25	K216EM	91.1	Arcadia	0.01
KACC	89.7	Alvin	5.6	K216FA	91.1	Quartz Hill	0.01
K210DF	89.9	Lake Jackson	0.25	KDSC	91.1	Thousand Oaks	4.8
KPFT	90.1	Houston	100	K216FM	91.1	Van Nuys	0.01
KJIC	90.5	Santa Fe	36	KUSC	91.5	Los Angeles	39
KGBV	90.7	Hardin	0.45	KUSC-FM1	91.5	Santa Clarita	0.2
KTSU	90.9	Houston	18.5	K220FR	91.9	Simi Valley	0.01
KYBJ	91.1	Lake Jackson	17.5	K220HC	91.9	Sun Valley	0.01
K217GB	91.3	Houston	0.25	KRRL	92.3	Los Angeles	40
KPVU	91.3	Prairie View	31	KJLL-FM	92.7	Fountain Valley	0.69
K218EJ	91.5	Galveston	0.25	KHJL-FM1	92.7	Malibu Vista	0.04
K218DA	91.5	Houston	0.01	KYRA	92.7	Thousand Oaks	3.1
KUHA	91.7	Houston	50	KCBS-FM	93.1	Los Angeles	27.5
KROI	92.1	Seabrook	24	KXRN-LP	93.5	Laguna Niguel	0.05
KKBQ-FM	92.9	Pasadena	100	KDEY-FM	93.5	Ontario	5
K227BD	93.3	Freeport	0.2	KDAY	93.5	Redondo Beach	4.2
KQBU-FM	93.3	Port Arthur	100	KDAY	93.5	Redondo Beach	0.75
KQBT	93.7	Houston	100	KXOS	93.9	Los Angeles	35
K231CN	94.1	Richmond	0.25	KXOS-FM1	93.9	Santa Clarita	0.25
KTBZ-FM	94.5	Houston	100	KEBN	94.3	Garden Grove	6
K236AR	95.1	Angleton	0.04	KBUA	94.3	San Fernando	6
KKHH	95.7	Houston	100	KBUA-FM1	94.3	Valencia & Newhall	0.04
KHMX	96.5	Houston	100	KTWV	94.7	Los Angeles	58
KTHT	97.1	Cleveland	0.8	K236AW	95.1	Lancaster	0.01
KFNC	97.5	Beaumont	8	KFRG	95.1	San Bernardino	50
KBXX	97.9	Houston	100	KBBY-FM	95.1	Ventura	12.5
KTJM	98.5	Port Arthur	100	KLOS	95.5	Los Angeles	72
KODA	99.1	Houston	100	KFSH-FM	95.9	La Mirada	6
K258BZ	99.5	Sugar Land	0.1	K241AJ	96.1	Palmdale	0.01
KHGV-LP	99.7	Houston	0.1	KXOL-FM	96.3	Los Angeles	22
KVST	99.7	Willis	2.95	KWIZ	96.7	Santa Ana	6
KSHN	99.9	Liberty	26.5	KLJR-FM	96.7	Santa Paula	0.28
KILT-FM	100.3	Houston	100	KAMP-FM	97.1	Los Angeles	21
KKHT-FM	100.7	Winnie	100	KLYY	97.5	Riverside	72
KLOL	101.1	Houston	100	KLAX-FM	97.9	East Los Angeles	33
KSTB	101.5	Crystal Beach	6	KRCV-FM1	98.3	San Dimas	0.75
KMJQ	102.1	Houston	100	KRCV	98.3	West Covina	6
KLTN	102.9	Houston	100	KYSR	98.7	Los Angeles	75
KJOJ	103.3	Freeport	100	KKLA-FM	99.5	Los Angeles	10
KHJK	103.7	La Porte	100	KOLA	99.9	San Bernardino	29.5
KRBE	104.1	Houston	100	K261AB	100.1	Newhall, etc.	0.01
KAMA-FM	104.9	Deer Park	10.6	KSWD	100.3	Los Angeles	15
KORG-LP	105.3	Cleveland	0.07	K264AF	100.7	Guasti	0.01
KPTY	105.3	Crystal Beach	6	KHAY	100.7	Ventura	39
KTWL	105.3	Hempstead	92	KRTH	101.1	Los Angeles	54
KHCB-FM	105.7	Houston	100	KORM-LP	101.5	Corona	0.1
K291CE	106.1	Sugar Land	0.12	KWVS-LP	101.5	Malibu	0.1
KOVE-FM	106.5	Galveston	100	KOCI-LP	101.5	Newport Beach	0.04
K294BH	106.7	Simonton	0.25	KSCA	101.9	Glendale	11.5
KHPT	106.9	Conroe	100	KJLH	102.3	Compton	5.6
KGLK	107.5	Lake Jackson	100	K272DI	102.3	Fillmore	0.01
KQQK	107.9	Beaumont	100	KJLH-FM1	102.3	Hollywood	0.01
KBCP-LP	107.9	Brookshire	0.06	KIIS-FM	102.7	Los Angeles	8
Los Angeles Area				K276EF	103.1	Muscoy	0.01
KKJZ	88.1	Long Beach	41	KDLE	103.1	Newport Beach	0.3
KQRU	88.3	Acton	0.1	KDLD	103.1	Santa Monica	3.7
KCLU-FM	88.3	Thousand Oaks	3.2	KOST	103.5	Los Angeles	12.5
K203FC	88.5	North Edwards	0.25	KRCD	103.9	Inglewood	4.1
KCSN	88.5	Northridge	0.37	K280DT	103.9	Thousand Oaks	0.01
KCSN-FM1	88.5	West Los Angeles	1.28	KBIG-FM	104.3	Los Angeles	65
KISL	88.7	Avalon	0.2	KCAQ-FM1	104.7	Calabasas	0.09
KSPC	88.7	Claremont	3	KCAQ-FM2	104.7	Granada Hills	0.5
KUCI	88.9	Irvine	0.2	KXRN-LP	104.7	Laguna Niguel	0.04
K205EP	88.9	La Canada	0.01	KCAQ-FM5	104.7	Las Flores Canyon	0.5
KXLU	88.9	Los Angeles	2.9	KCAQ	104.7	Oxnard	4.5
K206AA	89.1	Laguna Beach	0.04	KKGO	105.1	Los Angeles	35
KCRU	89.1	Oxnard	0.92	KKGO-FM1	105.1	Santa Clarita	0.06
KPCC	89.3	Pasadena	0.6	KGIC-LP	105.5	Corona	0.06
KPCC-FM1	89.3	Santa Clarita	0.01	KBUE	105.5	Long Beach	3.9
K208AM	89.5	Newport Beach	0.08	KPWR	105.9	Los Angeles	25
KCRW	89.9	Santa Monica	6.9	KGMX	106.3	Lancaster	3
K210EO	89.9	Santa Paula	0.01	KALI-FM	106.3	Santa Ana	6
KBPK	90.1	Buena Park	0.02	K292CR	106.3	Simi Valley	0.004
K211EY	90.1	Palmdale	0.01	KROQ-FM	106.7	Pasadena	6.5
K211DK	90.1	Santa Ana	0.01	KSSE	107.1	Arcadia	6
KSAK	90.1	Walnut	0.004	KSSE-FM1	107.1	San Fernando	0.02
KMRO-FM1	90.3	Camarillo	2	KLVE	107.5	Los Angeles	32
KMRO-FM3	90.3	Camarillo	0.02	KWVE-FM	107.9	San Clemente	0.53
K205DZ	90.3	Devore	0.002	KWVE-FM4	107.9	San Clemente	0.02

FM Callsign	MHz	Location	kW
KNJR-LP	107.9	Thousand Oaks	0.1

Miami-Fort Lauderdale Area

FM Callsign	MHz	Location	kW
WRGP	88.1	Homestead	0.17
WGNK	88.3	Pennsuco	6
WMFL	88.5	Florida City	7.7
WKPX	88.5	Sunrise	25
WDNA	88.9	Miami	7.4
WRMB	89.3	Boynton Beach	100
WMLV	89.7	Miami	100
WYBP	90.3	Ft Lauderdale	3
WVUM	90.5	Coral Gables	5.9
WLFE	90.9	Cutler Bay	100
WLRN-FM	91.3	Miami	47
W220DU	91.7	W Deerfield Bch	0.25
WMKL	91.9	Hammocks	25
WCMQ-FM	92.3	Hialeah	31
WFEZ	93.1	Miami	100
W228BY	93.5	Allapattah	0.12
W228BV	93.5	Ft Lauderdale	0.17
W228AY	93.5	Key Largo	0.02
WMIA-FM	93.9	Miami Beach	100
W233AP	94.5	Oakland Park	0.09
WMGE	94.9	Miami Beach	100
WURN-FM	95.3	Key Largo	21
W237CP	95.3	Miami	0.07
W237BD	95.3	Pompano Beach	0.25
WRMA	95.7	N Miami Beach	40
W241AX	96.1	Boca Raton	0.25
WPOW	96.5	Miami	100
W245BC	96.9	Lauderdale Lks.	0.07
W245BF	96.9	North Miami	0.1
WFLC	97.3	Miami	100
WRMF	97.9	Palm Beach	100
WRTO-FM	98.3	Goulds	100
WEDR	99.1	Miami	100
WKIS	99.9	Boca Raton	100
WCTH	100.3	Plantation Key	100
WHYI-FM	100.7	Ft Lauderdale	100
WLYF	101.5	Miami	100
WKLG	102.1	Rock Harbor	100
WMXJ	102.7	Pompano Beach	100
WMIB	103.5	Ft Lauderdale	100
WORZ-LP	104.3	Key Largo	0.1
WSFS	104.3	West Palm Beach	100
WHQT	105.1	Coral Gables	100
WWWK	105.5	Islamorada	50
WBGG-FM	105.9	Ft Lauderdale	100
WRAZ-FM	106.3	Leisure City	50
WXDJ	106.7	Ft Lauderdale	100
WURN	107.1	Key Largo	6.1
WAMR-FM	107.5	Miami	95
WEAT	107.9	West Palm Beach	100

Minneapolis-St Paul Area

FM Callsign	MHz	Location	kW
WAJC	88.1	Newport	1.2
KRLX	88.1	Northfield	0.1
KJGT	88.3	Waconia	11
KBEM-FM	88.5	Minneapolis	2.9
WUSG-LP	88.7	Cambridge	0.1
WRFW	88.7	River Falls	3
KCMP	89.3	Northfield	100
KPCS	89.7	Princeton	40
KMOJ	89.9	Minneapolis	6.2
KFAI	90.3	Minneapolis	0.9
KMKL	90.3	North Branch	15
K214DF	90.7	Golden Valley	0.01
KNOW-FM	91.1	Minneapolis	100
K218DK	91.5	Bloomington	0.22
WMCN	91.7	St. Paul	0.01
K220JP	91.9	Minneapolis	0.01
W220DN	91.9	North Branch	0.04
K221ES	92.1	Albertville	0.25
W221BS	92.1	Waite	0.06
KQRS-FM	92.5	Golden Valley	100
W225AP	92.9	St. Paul	0.17
W227BF	93.3	Shoreview	0.01
KXXR	93.7	Minneapolis	100
KSTP-FM	94.5	St. Paul	100
KNOF	95.3	St. Paul	6
KRDS-FM	95.5	New Prague	6
WDMO	95.7	Baldwin	4
W239AM	95.7	Hudson	0.25
KQCL	95.9	Faribault	3

FM Callsign	MHz	Location	kW
WLKX-FM	95.9	Forest Lake	3
KTWN	96.3	Edina	19
W239AM	96.7	Hudson	0.17
KTCZ-FM	97.1	Minneapolis	100
K249ED	97.7	Albertville	0.17
KTIS-FM	98.5	Minneapolis	100
KSJN	99.5	Minneapolis	100
K260BA	99.9	Coon Rapids	0.25
KFXN-FM	100.3	Minneapolis	100
W264BR	100.7	Falcon Heights	0.09
KDWB-FM	101.3	Richfield	100
KALY-LP	101.7	Minneapolis	0.1
KEEY-FM	102.1	St. Paul	100
K273BH	102.5	Fridley	0.25
KMNB	102.9	Minneapolis	100
K277AS	103.3	Big Lake	0.01
K278BP	103.5	Cottage Grove	0.17
KZJK	104.1	St. Louis Park	100
K283BG	104.5	Minneapolis	0.1
WGVX	105.1	Lakeville	2.6
WGVY	105.3	Cambridge	25
WGVZ	105.7	Eden Prarie	3.8
KLCI	106.1	Elk River	9.1
WEVR-FM	106.3	River Falls	6
K293BA	106.5	Elko	0.2
KDXL	106.5	St. Louis Park	0.01
KUOM-FM	106.5	St. Louis Park	0.01
K294AM	106.7	West St. Paul	0.17
KTMY	107.1	Coon Rapids	22
KQQL	107.9	Anoka	100

New York Area

FM Callsign	MHz	Location	kW
WYGG	88.1	Asbury Park	0.92
WXBA	88.1	Brentwood	0.18
WCWP	88.1	Brookville	0.1
WDNJ	88.1	Hopatcong	0.5
WARY	88.1	Valhalla	0.04
WBGO	88.3	Newark	4.5
W202AR	88.3	Newburgh	0.01
WVOF	88.5	Fairfield	0.1
W203BB	88.5	Norwalk	0.01
WPOB	88.5	Plainview	0.12
WEDW-FM	88.5	Stamford	2
WNJP	88.5	Sussex	0.45
WKWZ	88.5	Syosset	0.12
WRHU	88.7	Hempstead	0.47
WRSU-FM	88.7	New Brunswick	1.35
WNYK	88.7	Nyack	0.01
WPSC-FM	88.7	Wayne	0.2
WMNJ	88.9	Madison	0.01
WWES	88.9	Mount Kisco	0.2
WFRS	88.9	Smithtown	1.5
WSIA	88.9	Staten Island	0.01
WMCX	88.9	W. Long Branch	1
WNYU-FM	89.1	New York	8.3
WNYU-FM1	89.1	New York	0.01
WFDU	89.1	Teaneck	0.55
WGSS	89.3	Copiague	0.03
WFJS-FM	89.3	Freehold	3.8
WDDM	89.3	Hazlet	0.01
WLJP	89.3	Monroe	1.58
WNJY	89.3	Netcong	0.52
W208AU	89.5	Massapequa	0.23
WSOU	89.5	South Orange	2.4
WRDR	89.7	Freehold Township	5
WOBH	89.7	Lindenhurst	1.8
W209CJ	89.7	Mount Kisco	0.03
WKCR-FM	89.9	New York	1.35
WJZZ	90.1	North Salem	0.1
W211AI	90.1	Stamford	0.25
WUSB	90.1	Stony Brook	3.6
WKRB	90.3	Brooklyn	0.01
WHPC	90.3	Garden City	0.5
WRPR	90.3	Mahwah	0.1
WHCR-FM	90.3	New York	0.01
W212CC	90.3	Newburgh	0.01
WDFH	90.3	Ossining	0.05
WVPH	90.3	Piscataway	0.1
WKNJ-FM	90.3	Union Township	0.01
WMSC	90.3	Upper Montclair	0.001
WWPT	90.3	Westport	0.33
WBJB-FM	90.5	Lincroft	0.9
WJSV	90.5	Morristown	0.12

FM Callsign	MHz	Location	kW
WFUV	90.7	New York	47
WFUV-FM3	90.7	New York	2.5
WFMU	91.1	East Orange	1.25
WFMU-FM1	91.1	New York	0.02
WOSS	91.1	Ossining	0.01
W217AF	91.3	Huntington Stn.	0.25
WNYE	91.5	New York	2
WXCI	91.7	Danbury	3
W219DQ	91.7	Dillyville	0.04
W220AC	91.9	Fairfield	0.01
WNTI	91.9	Hackettstown	5.6
WSHR	91.9	Lk. Ronkonkoma	6
WSLX	91.9	New Canaan	0.01
W219DQ	91.9	New City	0.01
W220AA	91.9	Parlin	0.01
WBMP	92.3	New York	18
WQBU-FM2	92.7	Brooklyn	1.2
WQBU-FM	92.7	Garden City	2
WQBU-FM1	92.7	New York	0.08
WPAT-FM	93.1	Paterson	22
WVIP	93.5	New Rochelle	1.75
W228CG	93.5	Warwick	0.25
W229BH	93.7	Newburgh	0.01
WNYC-FM	93.9	New York	11
W231BP	94.1	Chester	0.25
WJLK	94.3	Asbury Park	1.3
W232AL	94.3	Pomona	0.03
WWSK	94.3	Smithtown	3
W233BM	94.5	Beacon	0.01
WNSH	94.7	Newark	37.2
W235BB	94.9	Hauppauge	0.01
WRKI-FM2	95.1	Bridgeport	0.23
WRKI-FM1	95.1	Norwalk	0.6
WPLJ	95.5	New York	19
WFOX	95.9	Norwalk	3
WRAT	95.9	Point Pleasant	6
WXNY-FM	96.3	New York	26
W244AS	96.7	Oakhurst	0.01
WKLV-FM	96.7	Port Chester	3.1
W245BA	96.9	Manorville	0.01
WQHT	97.1	New York	29.5
WALK-FM	97.5	Patchogue	39
WSKQ-FM	97.9	New York	6
WDAQ	98.3	Danbury	1.3
WKJY	98.3	Hempstead	3
WMGQ	98.3	New Brunswick	1.2
WEPN	98.7	New York	6
WAWZ	99.1	Zarephath	28
WBAI	99.5	New York	4.3
WHTZ	100.3	Newark	13
W264BT	100.7	Edison	0.01
WHUD	100.7	Peekskill	50
WCBS-FM	101.1	New York	16.8
W268AN	101.5	Plainview	0.01
WFAN	101.9	New York	29.5
WUPC-LP	102.3	Arrowhead Vlg	0.1
WBAB	102.3	Babylon	6
WSUS	102.3	Franklin	0.6
WWFS	102.7	New York	50
WBZO	103.1	Bay Shore	3
W276AQ	103.1	Fort Lee	0.04
W276BV	103.1	Greenwich	0.002
WJGK	103.1	Newburgh	6
W276AV	103.1	Stamford	0.003
WKTU	103.5	Lake Success	17
WNNJ	103.7	Newton	0.5
W280DJ	103.9	Beacon	0.01
WNBM	103.9	Bronxville	1.3
WAXQ	104.3	New York	17
W283BA	104.5	Selden	0.01
W284BW	104.7	Franklin Township	0.01
W284AQ	104.7	Hackettstown	0.21
WSPK	104.7	Poughkeepsie	7.4
W285DE	104.9	Bridgeport	0.02
WWPR-FM	105.1	New York	17
W287AZ	105.3	Southport	0.05
WDHA-FM	105.5	Dover	1
W289AD	105.7	Selden	0.25
WQXR-FM	105.9	Newark	1.59
WBLI	106.1	Patchogue	49
WKMK	106.3	Eatontown	1.1
W292DV	106.3	New York	0.25

FM Callsign	MHz	Location	kW
WFME	106.3	Mount Kisco	0.98
W292DV	106.3	New York	0.09
W293AE	106.5	Newburgh	0.01
WLTW	106.7	New York	17
WXPK	107.1	Briarcliff Manor	1.9
WWZY	107.1	Long Branch	5
W296BD	107.1	Warwick	0.01
W297AN	107.3	Danbury	0.02
WBLS	107.5	New York	4.2
W299AG	107.7	Newburgh	0.01
WMDI-LP	107.9	Lakewood	0.1
WMNJ	107.9	Madison	0.01
WWPH	107.9	Princeton Jct.	0.02
WEBE	107.9	Westport	50
Philadelphia Area			
WNJS-FM	88.1	Berlin	0.08
WPEB	88.1	Philadelphia	0.001
WMHS	88.1	Pike Creek	0.09
WNJT-FM	88.1	Trenton	0.11
WXPN	88.5	Philadelphia	3.2
WBZC	88.9	Pemberton	10
WBYO	88.9	Sellersville	4.5
WXHL-FM	89.1	Christiana	1.2
WYBF	89.1	Radnor Township	0.7
WWFM	89.1	Trenton	1.15
WXVU	89.1	Villanova	0.1
WNJB-FM	89.3	Bridgeton	2.5
WRTJ	89.3	Coatesville	0.46
WRDV	89.3	Warminster	1.6
WYPA	89.5	Cherry Hill	2
WDNR	89.5	Chester	0.01
WGLS-FM	89.7	Glassboro	0.75
WRTI	90.1	Philadelphia	11
WVBV	90.5	Medford Lakes	21
WHYY-FM	90.9	Philadelphia	13.5
WVUD	91.3	Newark	6.8
WTSR	91.3	Trenton	1.5
WDBK	91.5	Blackwood	0.1
WSRN-FM	91.5	Swarthmore	0.11
WLBS	91.7	Bristol	0.1
WKDU	91.7	Philadelphia	0.8
WBMR	91.7	Telford	0.5
WCUR	91.7	West Chester	0.1
WMPH	91.7	Wilmington	0.1
W220AG	91.9	Lawrenceville	0.01
WVLT	92.1	Vineland	6
WXTU	92.5	Philadelphia	15
WMMR	93.3	Philadelphia	25
WSTW	93.7	Wilmington	47.1
WIP-FM	94.1	Philadelphia	15
WPST	94.5	Trenton	50
WRSD	94.9	Folsom	0.01
W235AP	94.9	Radnor	0.002
W236AF	95.1	Burlington	0.12
WBEN-FM	95.7	Philadelphia	11
WCTO	96.1	Easton	50
WZMP	96.5	Philadelphia	9.6
W245AG	96.9	Glenside	0.01
W246AR	97.1	Bensalem	0.07
W246AQ	97.1	Collingswood	0.01
WZZE	97.3	Glen Mills	0.02
WPEN-FM	97.5	Burlington	26
W249BY	97.7	Bridgeton	0.01
WOGL	98.1	Philadelphia	10
WZFI-LP	98.5	Bridgeton	0.08
WUSL	98.9	Philadelphia	32
WJBR-FM	99.5	Wilmington	50
W260BW	99.9	Egg Harbor	0.12
WHHS	99.9	Havertown	0.01
WRNB	100.3	Media	33
WLEV	100.7	Allentown	11
WBEB	101.1	Philadelphia	14
WKXW	101.5	Trenton	15.5
WJKS	101.7	Canton	4.1
W269BL	101.7	Coatesville	0.003
W269BT	101.7	Pottstown	0.02
WIOQ	102.1	Philadelphia	32
WRFY	102.5	Reading	10
WMGK	102.9	Philadelphia	43
W277BA	103.3	Millville	0.02
W277BL	103.3	New Castle	0.003
WPRB	103.3	Princeton	14

FM Callsign	MHz	Location	kW
W278AK	103.5	Village Green	0.08
WPPZ-FM	103.9	Jenkintown	0.37
W280CP	103.9	Wagontown	0.01
WRFF	104.5	Philadelphia	11
WSJO	104.9	Egg Harbor City	10
WDAS-FM	105.3	Philadelphia	42
W289AZ	105.7	Trenton	0.01
WISX	106.1	Philadelphia	22.5
WKVP	106.9	Camden	38
W297AD	107.3	Philadelphia	0.02
WBYN-FM	107.5	Boyertown	5.5
WRRC	107.7	Lawrenceville	0.02
W299BH	107.7	Marshallton	0.25
WPOV-LP	107.7	Vineland	0.04
W300AC	107.9	Chatsworth, etc.	0.04
WPHI-FM	107.9	Pennsauken	0.78

Phoenix Area

FM Callsign	MHz	Location	kW
KNAI	88.3	Phoenix	22.5
KPHF	88.3	Phoenix	22.5
KPNG	88.7	Chandler	15
K204DR	88.7	Laveen	0.01
K205CI	88.9	Phoenix	0.01
KLVK	89.1	Fountain Hills	30
KBAQ	89.5	Phoenix	30
K209DV	89.7	Scottsdale	0.01
K210DY	89.9	Black Canyon City	0.25
KZAI	89.9	Superior	45
KFLR-FM	90.3	Phoenix	100
KVIT	90.7	Apache Jct	2
K214DN	90.7	Surprise	0.01
K216FO	91.1	Guadalupe	0.01
KJZZ	91.5	Phoenix	100
K219DZ	91.7	Rio Verde	0.01
KTAR-FM	92.3	Glendale	100
K224CJ	92.7	Phoenix	0.01
KDKB	93.3	Mesa	100
KWSS-LP	93.9	Scottsdale	0.003
KOOL-FM	94.5	Phoenix	100
KVIB	95.1	Sun City West	41
KYOT-FM	95.5	Phoenix	100
K240DC	95.9	Buckeye	0.06
K241BQ	96.1	Ft Mcdowell	0.25
KSWG	96.3	Wickenburg	6.4
K243BN	96.5	Laveen	0.25
KMXP	96.9	Phoenix	100
K247BH	97.3	Goodyear	0.04
KMVA	97.5	Dewey	42
KUPD	97.9	Tempe	100
KKFR	98.3	Mayer	41
KMVP	98.7	Phoenix	100
K257CD	99.3	Phoenix	0.02
K258BY	99.5	Tortilla Flat	0.01
K258BY	99.5	Tortilla Flat	0.12
KRPH-FM1	99.5	Wittmann	0.45
KESZ	99.9	Phoenix	100
KCWG-LP	100.3	Crown King	0.001
KQMR	100.3	Globe	90
KSLX-FM	100.7	Scottsdale	100
KNRJ	101.1	Cordes Lakes	40
KZON	101.5	Phoenix	100
K270BA	101.9	Wickenburg	0.12
KAHM	102.1	Spring Valley	25.5
KNIX-FM	102.5	Phoenix	100
KLNZ	103.5	Glendale	62
KEXX	103.9	Gilbert	43
KAJM	104.3	Camp Verde	40
K282BC	104.3	Sunflower	0.01
KZZP	104.7	Mesa	100
K282BC	104.9	Sunflower	0.01
KHOV	105.1	Wickenburg	100
KLVA	105.5	Casa Grande	50
KHOT-FM	105.9	Paradise Valley	36
KQMR	106.3	Sun City	23
KKMR	106.5	Arizona City	8.6
KWSS-LP	106.7	Scottsdale	0.01
KDVA	106.9	Buckeye	6
KVVA-FM	107.1	Apache Jct	23.5
KMLE	107.9	Chandler	100

Portland Area

FM Callsign	MHz	Location	kW
KBVM	88.3	Portland	3.5
KMUZ	88.5	Turner	0.04
KTFH	88.7	Lees Camp	0.1

FM Callsign	MHz	Location	kW
KZRI	88.7	Sandy	3.7
KMHD	89.1	Gresham	7.9
KJVH	89.5	Longview	0.1
KPFR	89.5	Pine Grove	7
KQAC	89.9	Portland	5.9
KLWO	90.3	Longview	0.4
KSLC	90.3	Mcminnville	0.75
KWBX	90.3	Salem	0.14
KBOO	90.7	Portland	26.5
KOPB-FM	91.5	Portland	73
K220IN	91.9	Portland	0.01
KXRY	91.9	Portland	0.007
KGON	92.3	Portland	100
K224DD	92.7	Portland	0.02
K225BF	92.9	Turner	0.02
KRYP	93.1	Gladstone	1.6
KKJC-LP	93.5	Mcminnville	0.1
K228EU	93.5	Portland	0.1
KPDQ-FM	93.9	Portland	52
K231AM	94.1	Woodland	0.12
KZZR	94.3	Government Camp	3.4
KLYK	94.5	Kelso	3
KNRK	94.7	Camas	6.3
KISN-LP	95.1	Portland	0.0002
KBFF	95.5	Portland	100
K240DA	95.9	Stevenson	0.09
K240CZ	95.9	Tigard	0.02
KQRZ-LP	96.3	Hillsboro	0.1
KKJC-LP	96.3	Mcminnville	0.1
KQSO-LP	96.3	Newberg	0.001
K242AF	96.3	Portland	0.03
K242AB	96.3	Salem	0.25
KWLZ-FM	96.3	West Linn	4.1
KPVN-LP	96.3	Woodburn	0.03
KYCH-FM	97.1	Portland	100
K248BS	97.5	Newberg	0.003
KLVP	97.9	Aloha	10
K250AE	97.9	Longview	0.25
KLVC	97.9	Portland	0.01
KPPK	98.3	Rainier	1.6
KUPL	98.7	Portland	25
KPQR-LP	99.1	Portland	0.1
KSFL-LP	99.1	Portland	0.1
KWJJ-FM	99.5	Portland	52
KRKT	99.9	Albany	100
KKRZ	100.3	Portland	100
KXL-FM	101.1	Portland	100
K268BN	101.5	Eufaula/Longview	0.25
KINK	101.9	Portland	100
K272EL	102.3	Portland	0.1
K273AI	102.5	Ariel	0.01
K273AJ	102.5	Elwood	0.01
K274AR	102.9	Gresham	0.99
KKCW	103.3	Beaverton	100
K279BO	103.7	Portland	0.99
KFIS	104.1	Scappoose	7
K283BL	104.5	Portland	0.1
K284BM	104.7	Longview	0.04
KRSK	105.1	Molalla	22.5
KUKN	105.5	Longview	0.7
K288FT	105.5	Portland	0.05
KFBW	105.9	Vancouver	22.5
KLTH	106.7	Lake Oswego	100
KLVU-FM2	107.1	Family Camp	0.05
KRQT-FM1	107.1	Longview	2
K296FT	107.1	West Haven	0.03
KXJM	107.5	Banks	71
KHPE	107.9	Albany	100

San Diego Area

FM Callsign	MHz	Location	kW
KSDS	88.3	San Diego	22
KSBR	88.5	Mission Viejo	0.6
KSDW	88.9	Temecula	1.15
KNSJ	89.1	Descanso	0.33
K206AC	89.1	San Diego	0.04
KPBS-FM	89.5	San Diego	26
K210CL	89.9	Lemon Grove	0.001
KOPA	91.3	Pala	0.1
KSOQ-FM	92.1	Escondido	0.58
K225BA	92.9	Borrego Springs	0.05
KXFG	92.9	Sun City	6
KHTS-FM	93.3	El Cajon	50
K229BO	93.7	Rancho Bernardo	0.01

FM Callsign	MHz	Location	kW	FM Callsign	MHz	Location	kW
KMYI	94.1	San Diego	77	KISQ-FM2	98.1	Pleasanton	10
KMYT	94.5	Temecula	0.54	KISQ	98.1	San Francisco	75
KBZT	94.9	San Diego	26.5	KUFX-FM3	98.5	Pleasanton	0.15
KSSX	95.7	Carlsbad	28	KSOL-FM3	98.9	Pleasanton	0.18
KYDO	96.1	Campo	25	KSOL	98.9	San Francisco	6.1
KSIQ-FM1	96.1	Santee	5	KSOL-FM2	98.9	Sausalito	0.15
KYXY	96.5	San Diego	26.5	KVYN-FM1	99.3	Cordelia	0.01
K245AI	96.9	San Pasqual	0.01	K257BE	99.3	Los Gatos	0.01
KSON	97.3	San Diego	50	KMVQ-FM	99.7	San Francisco	45
KIFM	98.1	San Diego	26.5	KMVQ-FM3	99.7	Walnut Creek	0.18
K252BF	98.3	Temecula	0.003	KZST-FM1	100.1	Petaluma	0.04
K253AD	98.5	Oceanside	0.01	KBRG	100.3	San Jose	14.5
KLVJ	100.1	Julian	0.11	KSFH	100.7	Mountain View	0.01
KFMB-FM	100.7	San Diego	30	K264AQ	100.7	Mountain View	0.002
KGB-FM	101.5	San Diego	50	KVVZ	100.7	San Rafael	6
KPRI	102.1	Encinitas	30	K265CV	100.9	Fremont	0.01
KLQV	102.9	San Diego	30	K265DI	100.9	Sausalito	0.08
KTMQ	103.3	Temecula	1.25	KIOI	101.3	San Francisco	125
KEGY	103.7	San Diego	26.5	KIOI-FM1	101.3	Walnut Creek	0.15
KIOZ	105.3	San Diego	26	K269FB	101.7	Daly City	0.01
KLNV-FM1	106.5	Rancho Bernardo	0.004	KKIQ-FM1	101.7	Hayward	0.85
KLNV	106.5	San Diego	50	KHTH-FM1	101.7	Petaluma	0.04
KSSD	107.1	Fallbrook	3	KRBQ	102.1	San Francisco	33
KRLY-LP	107.9	Alpine	0.002	KRBQ	102.1	San Francisco	1
+16 Mexican stations serving this market				KBLX-FM	102.9	Berkeley	7
San Francisco Area				KBLX-FM2	102.9	Pleasanton	0.18
K201BV	88.1	Benicia-Martinez	0.004	K277CH	103.3	San Francisco	0.01
KECG	88.1	El Cerrito	0.02	KOSF-FM1	103.7	Pleasanton	0.18
K215FB	88.1	Napa	0.01	KOSF	103.7	San Francisco	10
KSRH	88.1	San Rafael	0.01	K281BB	104.1	Vacaville	0.01
KQED-FM	88.5	San Francisco	110	KFOG-FM3	104.5	Pleasanton	0.18
KQED-FM2	88.5	Walnut Creek	0.06	KFOG	104.5	San Francisco	13.5
K205BM	88.9	San Rafael	0.01	KMHX-FM2	104.9	Glen Ellen	0.95
KCEA	89.1	Atherton	0.1	KITS-FM4	105.3	Antioch	0.33
KPFB	89.3	Berkeley	0.46	KITS-FM2	105.3	Pleasanton	0.04
K207EP	89.3	Concord	0.01	KITS-FM3	105.3	San Francisco	0.03
KOHL	89.3	Fremont	0.15	KITS	105.3	San Francisco	16.5
KRSA	89.3	Moss Beach	0.04	KITS-FM1	105.3	Walnut Creek	0.61
KPDO	89.3	Pescadero	0.1	K289AS	105.7	Napa	0.25
KSMC	89.5	Moraga	0.8	KVVF	105.7	Santa Clara	50
KPOO	89.5	San Francisco	0.3	KMEL	106.1	San Francisco	69
KZCT	89.5	Vallejo	0.01	KMEL-FM2	106.1	Walnut Creek	6.5
KFJC	89.7	Los Altos	0.11	KEZR	106.5	San Jose	42
K210EH	89.9	Bolinas	0.01	KFRC-FM1	106.9	Pleasanton	4.8
KCRH	89.9	Hayward	0.02	KFRC-FM	106.9	San Francisco	80
KZSU	90.1	Stanford	0.5	KLVS	107.3	Livermore	8.1
K212BJ	90.3	Dublin	0.2	KSAN-FM1	107.7	Pleasanton	0.18
KOSC	90.3	San Francisco	2.85	KSAN	107.7	San Mateo	8.9
KVHS	90.5	Concord	0.41	**Seattle-Tacoma Area**			
KWMR-FM2	90.5	Inverness Pk.	0.004	K201EN	88.1	Everett	0.01
KWMR	90.5	Pt. Reyes Stn.	0.24	K201EX	88.1	Greenwater	0.01
KALX	90.7	Berkeley	0.5	KWAO	88.1	Ocean Park	76
K214CS	90.7	Sonoma	0.004	K201EM	88.1	Olympia	0.14
K215FB	90.9	Napa	0.01	K201AB	88.1	West Seattle	0.12
K216FV	91.1	Concord	0.01	KPLU-FM	88.5	Tacoma	68
KCSM	91.1	San Mateo	11	KMIH	88.9	Mercer Island	0.03
KDVZ	91.3	Point Reyes	0.1	K206DM	89.1	Bremerton	0.01
KSVY	91.3	Sonoma	2.5	K206DO	89.1	Cape George	0.002
KXCF	91.5	Marshall	0.1	K206DL	89.1	Granite Falls	0.01
KALW	91.7	San Francisco	1.9	K206CJ	89.1	Issaquah	0.003
K220JV	91.9	Byron	0.01	K207AZ	89.3	Gig Harbor	0.03
KKDV-FM3	92.1	Martinez	0.25	KAOS	89.3	Olympia	1.25
K221DQ	92.1	Petaluma	0.01	K207AP	89.3	Sumner & Lake Tapps	0.02
KKDV	92.1	Walnut Creek	3	KNHC	89.5	Seattle	15
KSJO	92.3	San Jose	32	KWFJ	89.7	Roy	1
KREV	92.7	Alameda	3.6	KGRG-FM	89.9	Auburn	0.25
KRZZ-FM1	93.3	Pleasanton	0.19	KASB	89.9	Bellevue	0.06
KRZZ	93.3	San Francisco	33	KXIR	89.9	Freeland	1.8
KPFA	94.1	Berkeley	59	KGHP	89.9	Gig Harbor	1.35
KPFA-FM3	94.1	Oakley	0.04	KPLI	90.1	Olympia	0.1
KBAY	94.5	Gilroy	44	K211FH	90.1	Shelton	0.05
KYLD-FM1	94.9	Pleasanton	0.18	KUPS	90.1	Tacoma	0.1
KYLD	94.9	San Francisco	30	KEXP-FM	90.3	Seattle	4.7
KUIC-FM2	95.3	Vallejo	0.17	KSER	90.7	Everett	5.8
KGMZ	95.7	San Francisco	6.9	KVTI	90.9	Tacoma	51
KGMZ-FM1	95.7	Walnut Creek	0.18	KROH	91.1	Port Townsend	1.15
KOIT-FM3	96.5	Martinez	3.3	KBCS	91.3	Bellevue	8
KOIT	96.5	San Francisco	24	KQXI	91.5	Granite Falls	1.6
KLLC-FM2	97.3	Pleasanton	4.8	KSQM	91.5	Sequim	2.4
KLLC	97.3	San Francisco	82	KYFQ	91.7	Tacoma	23
KFFG	97.7	Los Altos	3.3	K220HD	91.9	Fall City	0.004
K249DJ	97.7	San Pablo	0.01	K221FJ	92.1	Tacoma	0.15

FM Callsign	MHz	Location	kW
KQMV	92.5	Bellevue	60
KUBE	93.3	Seattle	100
KANY	93.7	Montesano	14
KLSY	93.7	Montesano	32
KMPS-FM	94.1	Seattle	73
K233BU	94.5	White Center	0.06
KUOW-FM	94.9	Seattle	100
KJR-FM	95.7	Seattle	100
KXXO	96.1	Olympia	37
KJAQ	96.5	Seattle	53
KWPA-LP	96.9	Coupeville	0.03
KGY-FM	96.9	Mccleary	11
KIRO-FM	97.3	Tacoma	55
KOMO-FM	97.7	Belfair	69
K249DX	97.7	Redmond	0.08
KING-FM	98.1	Seattle	68
KLCK-FM	98.9	Seattle	68
KDDS-FM	99.3	Elma	64
K258BJ	99.5	Everett	0.01
KISW	99.9	Seattle	68
KKWF	100.7	Seattle	68
KPLZ-FM	101.5	Seattle	100
K271AH	102.1	Camano	0.12
K272ER	102.3	Sequim	0.2
KZOK-FM	102.5	Seattle	73
KYNW	102.9	Centralia	70
K277AE	103.3	Seattle	0.25
KHTP	103.7	Tacoma	68
K281AD	104.1	Olympia	0.05
KLSW	104.5	Covington	7.1
KZFX-LP	104.5	Fall City	0.1
KKBW	104.9	Eatonville	17
KCMS	105.3	Edmonds	54
K289AK	105.7	Orting	0.01
KBKS-FM	106.1	Tacoma	73
K293AY	106.5	Enumclaw	0.01
KOWA-LP	106.5	Olympia	0.02
KRWM	106.9	Bremerton	49
K201EX	107.3	Greenwater	0.002
KNDD	107.7	Seattle	68

St Louis Area

FM Callsign	MHz	Location	kW
KDHX	88.1	St. Louis	42
WSIE	88.7	Edwardsville	50
W206AN	89.1	Carlinville	0.08
KCLC	89.1	St. Charles	50
KTBJ	89.3	Festus	25
KNLH	89.5	Cedar Hill	0.06
WARW	89.5	Dorsey	1.5
KCFV	89.5	Ferguson	0.1
WGRN	89.5	Greenville	0.3
KGNX	89.7	Ballwin	0.12
WCBW-FM	89.7	East St. Louis	0.25
KGNA-FM	89.9	Arnold	0.15
WLCA	89.9	Godfrey	1.5
KGNV	89.9	Washington	1
W211AD	90.1	Granite City	0.06
KRHS	90.1	Overland	0.01
KWUR	90.3	Clayton	0.01
KWMU	90.7	St. Louis	100
KSIV-FM	91.5	St. Louis	85
K220HT	91.9	St. Louis	0.09
WIL-FM	92.3	St. Louis	100
W224BJ	92.7	Carlyle	0.17
W226BC	93.1	Brighton	0.02
KBDZ	93.1	Perryville	50
KQQX	93.3	Hermann	50
KSD	93.7	St. Louis	74
KSHE	94.7	Crestwood	100
K236AZ	95.1	Gray Summit	0.02
WFUN-FM	95.5	Bethalto	24.5
WOLG	95.9	Carlinville	6
KNOU	96.3	St. Louis	100
WCXO	96.7	Carlyle	2.1
K241BS	96.7	St. Louis	0.1
KFTK	97.1	Florissant	100
WDLJ	97.5	Breese	2.5
KHZR	97.7	Potosi	26.5
KYKY	98.1	St. Louis	90
KLJY	99.1	Clayton	100
KTGP-LP	99.5	St. Louis	0.08
WZJM-LP	99.9	Freeburg	0.1
KFAV	99.9	Warrenton	10.5
KDJR	100.1	De Soto	2
KMJM	100.3	Bridgeton	17
KFNS-FM	100.7	Troy	6
WXOS	101.1	East St. Louis	100
K268BF	101.5	Bellefontaine	0.09
KXQX	101.7	Elsberry	3.1
WGEL	101.7	Greenville	6
KEZK-FM	102.5	St. Louis	100
KLOU	103.3	St. Louis	90
W279AQ	103.7	Mascoutah	0.01
W280DR	103.9	Greenville	0.25
WHHL	104.1	Hazelwood	50
KSLQ-FM	104.5	Washington	3
WNSV	104.7	Nashville	3.4
KBWX	104.9	Columbia	7.8
W286AJ	105.1	Jerseyville	0.12
K286BG	105.1	Washington	0.01
WAOX	105.3	Staunton	6
KPNT	105.7	St. Genevieve	100
WSMI-FM	106.1	Litchfield	39
WARH	106.5	Granite City	90
K297BI	107.3	St. Louis	0.25
KSLZ	107.7	St. Louis	100

Tampa-St Petersburg Area

FM Callsign	MHz	Location	kW
WJIS	88.1	Bradenton	100
W202CB	88.3	Bayonet Point	0.03
WMNF	88.5	Tampa	7
WMYZ	88.7	Clermont	1.2
WYFE	88.9	Tarpon Springs	60
WSMR	89.1	Sarasota	54
W207BU	89.3	Bayonet Point	0.25
WFLJ	89.3	Frostproof	10
WKFA	89.3	St. Catherine	3.9
WUSF	89.7	Tampa	100
WJUF	90.1	Inverness	21
WLVF-FM	90.3	Haines City	0.75
WBVM	90.5	Tampa	77
WKES	91.1	Lakeland	100
WCIE	91.5	New Port Richey	75
WHGN	91.9	Crystal River	41
WYFO	91.9	Lakeland	25
WLTQ-FM	92.1	Venice	11.5
WYUU	92.5	Safety Harbor	50
WFLZ-FM	93.3	Tampa	100
WSEU-LP	93.7	Lakeland	0.1
W229BM	93.7	Riverview	0.23
WLLD	94.1	Lakeland	100
W233AV	94.5	Gulfport	0.25
WWRM	94.9	Tampa	100
WXCV	95.3	Homosassa Spgs	6
W237CW	95.3	Pinellas Park	0.01
W237DI	95.3	West Tampa	0.12
WBTP	95.7	Clearwater	100
W254AI	95.9	Auburndale	0.25
WAPQ-LP	95.9	Avon Park	0.1
WLAS-LP	96.1	Bartow	0.1
WTMP-FM	96.1	Dade City	2.8
W242AK	96.3	Lakeland	0.25
WULB-LP	96.3	Longboat Key	0.1
WSCQ	96.3	Sun City Center	0.08
W243AK	96.5	Bradenton	0.08
WSLR-LP	96.5	Sarasota	0.02
WYXZ	96.5	Tampa	0.1
W244BE	96.7	Brandon	0.08
WEKJ-LP	96.7	Chassahowitzka	0.05
WZPH-LP	96.7	Dade City	0.1
W244BJ	96.7	Frostproof	0.02
WCFQ-LP	96.7	Inverness	0.08
W244BJ	96.9	Frostproof	0.25
W245AZ	96.9	Leesburg	0.27
WSUN-FM	97.1	Holiday	22
W247AF	97.3	Sarasota	0.08
WPCV	97.5	Winter Haven	100
WXTB	97.9	Clearwater	100
WWRZ	98.3	Fort Meade	27
W254AI	98.7	Auburndale	0.05
WBRN	98.7	Holmes Beach	50
WBCG	98.9	Murdock	5.5
W255CC	98.9	Sarasota	0.05
WWOJ	99.1	Avon Park	10
W202CB	99.1	Bayonet Point	0.25
WVVD-LP	99.1	East Tampa	0.1

FM Callsign	MHz	Location	kW
WVVD-LP	99.1	Seffner	0.06
WQYK-FM	99.5	St. Petersburg	100
W207BU	99.9	Bayonet Point	0.25
WXJB	99.9	Homosassa	9.5
W260CA	99.9	Sebring	0.05
WBPV-LP	100.1	Bradenton	0.1
WGGF-LP	100.1	Sun City Center	0.1
WVVF-LP	100.1	Town-N-Country	0.075
WMTX	100.7	Tampa	100
W265BJ	100.9	Crystal River	0.05
W266AI	101.1	Chassahowitzka	0.17
WUDN-LP	101.1	Sarasota	0.1
WPOI	101.5	St. Petersburg	100
WOPC-LP	102.1	Bradenton	0.1
WWFH-LP	102.1	Land O' Lakes	0.054
WPBW	102.1	St. Petersburg	0.015
WHPT	102.5	Sarasota	100
W274BB	102.7	Haines City	0.01
W275AX	102.9	Fort Meade	0.14
W221CE	102.9	Wesley Chapel	0.2
WHKQ	103.1	Windermere	22
WFUS	103.5	Gulfport	100
W280DK	103.9	Inverness	0.25
W280DW	103.9	Tampa	0.25
WZIG-LP	104.1	Palm Harbour	0.1
W283AM	104.3	Arcadia	0.03
WKZM	104.3	Sarasota	25
W283AM	104.5	Arcadia	0.02
WRBQ-FM	104.7	Tampa	100
WCFQ-LP	104.9	Inverness	0.08
WVDV-LP	104.9	Sebring	0.07
WZSP	105.3	Nocatee	4.1
WDUV	105.5	New Port Richey	47
WTZB	105.9	Englewood	25
W290BJ	105.9	West Tampa	0.25
W291AG	106.1	Highland City	0.17
WGHR	106.3	Spring Hill	25
W239CK	106.5	Clearwater	0.09
WCTQ	106.5	Sarasota	13
WXXL	106.7	Tavares	100
W295BH	106.9	Sarasota	0.05
WZZS	106.9	Zolfo Springs	5
WXGL	107.3	St. Petersburg	100
W298AV	107.5	Englewood	0.08
W299AU	107.7	Zolfo Springs	0.01
WWMA-LP	107.9	Avon Park	0.1
WEKJ-LP	107.9	Chassahowitzka	0.05
WSRZ-FM	107.9	Coral Cove	47
WPHC-LP	107.9	Spring Hill	0.1

Washington DC Area

FM Callsign	MHz	Location	kW
WYPR	88.1	Baltimore	15.5
WMUC-FM	88.1	College Park	0.01
WAMU	88.5	Washington	50
WPFW	89.3	Washington	50
W209BY	89.7	Woodbridge	0.01
WCSP-FM	90.1	Washington	36
WETA	90.9	Washington	75
WBJC	91.5	Baltimore	50
WGTS	91.9	Takoma Park	27
WERQ-FM	92.3	Baltimore	37
WWXT	92.7	Prince Frederick	2.8
WPOC	93.1	Baltimore	19.5
WD2XAB	93.5	Columbia	2
WKYS	93.9	Washington	25
WIAD	94.7	Bethesda	50
WRBS-FM	95.1	Baltimore	50
WPGC-FM	95.5	Morningside	50
WWIN-FM	95.9	Arbutus	6
W240BH	95.9	Gainesville	0.004
WHUR-FM	96.3	Washington	16.5
WASH	97.1	Washington	17.5
W248BN	97.5	Alexandria	0.25
W249BE	97.7	Alexandria	0.01
WIYY	97.9	Baltimore	13.5
W252BR	98.3	Edgemere	0.25
WSMD-FM	98.3	Mechanicsville	3
WMZQ-FM	98.7	Washington	50
WNEW	99.1	Bowie	45
WIHT	99.5	Washington	50
W260BM	99.9	Annapolis	0.01
WFRE	99.9	Frederick	7.6
W261CD	100.1	Baltimore	0.002

FM Callsign	MHz	Location	kW
WBIG-FM	100.3	Washington	50
WZBA	100.7	Westminster	25
WWDC	101.1	Washington	25
WDQB	101.5	Fredericksburg	50
WLIF	101.9	Baltimore	13.5
WMJS-LP	102.1	Prince Frederick	0.08
WMMJ	102.3	Bethesda	2.9
WQSR	102.7	Baltimore	50
W275B0	102.9	Chantilly	0.01
WTOP-FM	103.5	Washington	44
WPRS-FM	104.1	Waldorf	50
W282BA	104.3	Leesburg	0.1
W285FA	104.7	Washington	0.25
WAVA-FM	105.1	Arlington	33
W288BS	105.5	Reston	0.09
WJZ	105.7	Catonsville	50
WMAL	105.9	Woodbridge	40
W291BA	106.1	Baltimore	0.23
WJFK-FM	106.7	Manassas	40
WRQX	107.3	Washington	21.5
WWWT	107.7	Manassas	29
WLZL	107.9	College Park	50

NB: see also Baltimore list.

URUGUAY

L.T: UTC -3h — **Pop:** 3.3 million — **Pr.L:** Spanish — **E.C:** 50Hz, 220V — **ITU:** URG — **Int. dialling code:** +598

DIRECCION NACIONAL DE TELECOMUNICACIONES Y SERVICIOS DE COMUNICACIÓN AUDIOVISUAL
Ministerio de Industria, Energía y Minería
✉ Av. Uruguay 988 (Casilla de Correo 927), 11100 Montevideo Edificio Ciudadela Sarandí 690 D, 2º entrepiso ☎ 2915 0856 **E:** info@dinatel.miem.gub.uy **W:** dinatel.gub.uy

UNIDAD REGULADORA DE SERVICIOS DE COMUNICACIONES (URSEC)
✉ Av. Uruguay 988 (Casilla de Correo 927), 11100 Montevideo ☎ 2902 8082, 2900 5708 **E:** radiodifusion@ursec.gub.uy
W: ursec.gub.uy **L.P:** Ing. Gabriel Lombide

ASOCIACION NACIONAL DE BROADCASTERS URUGUAYOS (ANDEBU)
✉ Carlos Quijano 1264, 11100 Montevideo ☎ 2902 1525, 2908 0037 🖷 2902 1540 **E:** andebu@adinet.com.uy **W:** andebu.org

COOPERATIVA DE RADIO EMISORAS DEL INTERIOR (CORI)
✉ Av. 18 de Julio 948, Oficina 603, 11000 Montevideo 🖷 2902 9047 **W:** cori.com.uy **E:** coriamfm@adinet.com.uy

RADIOS AM DEL INTERIOR (RAMI)
✉ Nueva York 1618, 11800 Montevideo ☎ 29246722 / 9241310 🖷29247279 **E:** rami@adinet.com.uy **W:** rami.com.uy
W: ramiradiosdelinterior.com **E:** rami@adinet.com.uy

RED ORO
✉ Rio Negro 1337, Esc. 209, 11100 Montevideo ☎ 2903 1678 🖷 2 900 3916 **E:** redoro@adinet.com.uy

ASOCIACION MUNDIAL DE RADIOS COMUNITARIAS (AMARC URUGUAY)
✉ Germán Barbato 1480, 11000, Montevideo ☎ 29021236 **W:** sitio. amarcuruguay.org **E:** mesanacional@amarcuruguay.org

RADIODIFUSIÓN NACIONAL DEL URUGUAY (RNU) (Gov)
✉ Sarandí 450, 11000 Montevideo ☎ 2 1768 2 915 5378 **W:** rnu. com.uy **E:** organizacion@rnu.uy
L.P: Dir:. Pedro Ramela Tech. Dir: José Cuello **E:** departamentotecnico@rnu.uy

MW Call		kHz	kW	Station, location, h. of tr.
CO01)	CW1	550	25	R. Colonia, Colonia: 24h
MO01)	CX58	580	2	R. Clarín, Montevideo: 24h
MO02)	CX4	610	50	R. Rural, Montevideo: 0900-0400
MO03)	CX6	650	25	Radiodifusión Nacional del Uruguay "R. Clásica", Montevideo: 24h
RN01)	CW68	680	1	R. Young, Young: 0900-0300
MO04)	CX8	690	25	R. Sarandí, Montevideo: 24h

MW Call	kHz	kW	Station, location, h. of tr.
MO05) CX10	730	5/2.5	R. Continente, Montevideo: 24h
SA01) CW27	740	5	R. Tabaré, Salto: 0900-0300
MO06) CX12	770	100/25	R. Oriental, Montevideo: 24h
MO07) CX14	810	50/25	R. El Espectador, Montevideo: 0800-0500
SA02) CW23	‡820	1/0.5	R. Cultural, Salto
MO08) CX16	850	50	R. Carve, Montevideo: 0825-0300
MO09) CX18	890	50/10	R. Sport 890, Montevideo: 0900-0300 SS 24h
AR1) CW17	900	3	R. Frontera, Artigas
MO10) CX20	930	50	R. Monte Carlo, "la Super R.", Montevideo: 24h
DU01) CW96	960	2/1	R. Yi, Durazno: 1000-0200
MO11) CX22	970	20/3	R. Universal, Montevideo: 1030-0100
MO12) CX24	1010	25	R. 1010AM, Montevideo: 0900-0400
SA03) CW102	1020	0.1	R. Libertadores, Salto: 0700-0300
MO03) CX26	1050	25	Radiodifusión Nacional del Uruguay "R. Uruguay", Montevideo: 24h
MO14) CX28	1090	15	R. Imparcial, Montevideo: 24h
TA01) CX111	1110	3	R. Paso de los Toros, Paso de los Toros: 1100-0200
SA04) CW31	1120	10	R. Salto, Salto: 0900-0300
MO15) CX30	1130	20	R. Nacional, Montevideo: 24h
TT01) CW116	1160	2/1	R. Agraria del Uruguay, Cerro Chato: 0800-0100
MO16) CX32	1170	10	Radiomundo, Montevideo: 1100-0300
AR02) CX118	1180	10	LV de Artigas, Artigas: 0900-0300
FL01) CW33	1200	1	La Nueva R., Florida: 0900(SS 1000)-0300
SO02) CX121	1210	2/1	Difusora Soriano, Mercedes: 24h
MA01) CV121	1210	2/1	R. RBC, Piriápolis: 24h
TT02) CV121	1210	0.25	R. El Libertador, Villa Vergara
RI05) CX122	1220	1/0.5	R. Reconquista, Rivera: 1100-0400
PA01) CW35	1240	5/1	R. Paysandú, Paysandú: 0900-0400
MO17) CX36	1250	10	R. Centenario, Montevideo:24h
AR03) CW125	1250	5	R. Bella Unión, Bella Unión: 24h
RO01) CW37	1260	3	Dif. Rochense, Rocha: 0900-0300
AR04) CV127	1270	4/2	R. Cuareim, Artigas: 0900-0300
TA02) CX128	1280	3/1	R. Tacuarembó, Tacuarembó: 0845-0300
MO03) CX38	1290	10	Radiodifusión Nacional del Uruguay "Em. del Sur", Montevideo: 24h
PA02) CW39	1320	1/0.5	R. LV de Paysandú, Paysandú: 0900-0300
RO02) CW132	1320	1/0.5	R. Fortaleza, Rocha: 1000-0200
MO19) CX40	1330	5	R. Fénix, Montevideo: 1000-0600
CL01) CW53	1340	10/1	LV de Melo, Melo: 0800-0300
CL02) CW136	1360	1	R. Río Branco, Río Branco: 1055-0200
SJ01) CW41	1360	2.5	R. 41, San José: 24h
MO20) CX42	1370	5.3/2.5	Em. Ciudad de Montevideo: 1100-0300
RI01) CV137A	1370	0.5	R. Real, Minas de Corrales: 0930-0130
RN02) CW137	1370	1/0.5	Nueva R. San Javier, San Javier: 24h
TT03) CW45	±1390	5	Dif. Treinta y Tres, Treinta y Tres: 0800-0300
TA03) CX140	1400	25	R. Zorrilla de San Martín, Tacuarembó: 0900-0300
MO21) CX44	1410	10/5	AM Libre, Montevideo: 24h
SA05) CW141	1410	2/0.5	R. 1410, Salto: 0900-0300
LA01) CW43	1420	5	R. Lavalleja, Minas: 0900-0300
PA03) CX142	1420	1/0.5	R. Felicidad, Paysandú: 0830-0130
DU02) CW25	1430	20/5	R. Durazno, Durazno: 0830-0300
RI02) CX144	1440	3/0.5	R. Rivera, Rivera: 0830(Su: 1000)-0300
MO22) CX46	1450	10/5	R. América, Montevideo: (0930-0630)
SA06) CW145	1450	1/0.25	R. Arapey, Salto: 24h
CO02) CX146	1460	1	R. Carmelo, Carmelo: 0930-0030 (Su: 1000-0100)
LA02) CV146	1460	0.25	R. José Batlle y Ordóñez, José Batlle y Ordóñez
CA01) CX147	1470	2	R. Cristal del Uruguay,Las Piedras: 24h
CL03) CW147	1470	1	R. Maria, Melo: 24h
RO04) CW148	1480	3	R. Universo, Castillos: 0900-0300
RI03) CW43B	1480	3/0.5	R. Internacional, Rivera: 0800-0300
RN03) CX148	1480	1	Difusora Rio Negro, Young:0900-0300
AR05) CV149	1490	1/0.25	R. del Centro, Baltasar Brum: 0900-0100 (Su: 1000-0200)
CO03) CX149	1490	1	R. del Oeste, Nueva Helvecia: 0930-0300
RN04) CX151	1510	1/0.5	R. Rincón, Fray Bentos: 0915-0230
MA02) CW57	1510	2/0.5	R. San Carlos, San Carlos: 0800-0400
TA04) CW151	1510	0.5	R. Ibirapitá, San Gregorio de Polanco: 1000-0200
CL04) CX152	1520	2	R. Acuarela, Melo: 0900-0300
SO03) CV152	1520	1/0.5	R. Paz, "La Nueva R.", Guichón: 1000-0030
CO4) CW153	1530	0.25	Em. Cono Sur, Nueva Palmira: 0900-0300
PA04) CW154	1540	1	R. Charrúa, Paysandú: 1000-0300
TT04) CX154	1540	05/025	R. Patria, Treinta y Tres: 0800-0300
S001) CV154	1540	1	R. Centro, Cardona: 0900-0200
SO04) CW155	1550	0.25	R. Agraciada, Mercedes: 24h
DU03) CW155	1550	2/0.5	R. Sarandí del Yí, Sarandí del Yí: 1030-0130
MA03) CW51	1560	3/0.5	R. Maldonado, Maldonado: 24h
FO01) CX156	1560	2/0.5	Dif. Americana, Trinidad: 0930-0300

MW Call	kHz	kW	Station, location, h. of tr.
RI04) CV156	1560	1	R. Vichadero: 1000-0200
CA02) CX157	1570	2/0.5	R. Canelones: 0930-0230
AR06) CW157A	1570	1	Em. Celeste, Tomás Gomensoro: 0830-0100)
LA03) CW54	1580	2/0.5	Emisoras del Este, Minas: 0800-0200
SO05) CW158	1580	1/0.5	R. San Salvador, Dolores: 24h
RO05) CW159	1590	1/0.25	R. Nueva Radio Lascano, Lascano
CO06) CX159	1590	1	R. Real, Colonia: 0930-0300
CA03) CV160	1600	1	R. Continental, Pando: 0915-0300
RN05) CX160	1600	1	R. Litoral, Fray Bentos: 0900-0300

SW Call	kHz	kW	Station, location
MO04) CXA61	‡6045	0.3	R. Sport 890, Montevideo: (LSB)
RO04) CWA148	6055	0.3	R. Universo, Castillos
AR02) CXA3	6075	1	LV de Artigas, Artigas: irr.
MO03) CXA4	6125	0.3	Radiodifusión Nacional del Uruguay, "R. Uruguay", Montevideo: 24h

‡ = inactive, ± = varying freq,

Addresses and other information

AR00) ARTIGAS
AR01) Av Lecueder 803, 55000 Artigas ☎4772 1230 ▤4773 2164 **W:** radiofronterafm.blogspot.com - **FM:** 88.3MHz "Frontera FM" – **AR02)** Av Lecueder 483, 55000 Artigas ☎4772 2447 ▤4772 4744 **W:** radioartigas.com **E:** radioartigas118@gmail.com – **FM:** 90.7MHz "Amatista FM", 105.5MHz "Norte FM" – **AR03)**Enrique Ferreira 1550, 55100 Bella Unión ☎4779 2058 ▤4772 4744 **W:** radiobellaunion. com **E:** radiobellaunion@gmail.com or informativoradiobu@gmail. com - **FM:** 105.5MHz "Stereo Norte FM" – **AR04)** Av Lecueder 167, 55000 Artigas ☎4772 2867 **W:** radiocuareim.com **E:** racua@adinet. com.uy – **AR05)** Batlle y Ordóñez y 25 de Agosto, 55001 Baltasar Brum, Artigas ☎4776 2109 **W:** radiodelcentro.com **E:** radiodelcentro_95@hotmail.com – **AR06)** 18 de Julio y 19 de Abril, 55002 Tomás Gomensoro ☎4777 2157 ▤4777 3059 **W:** radioceleste1570.com **E:** radioceleste@hotmail.com

CA00) CANELONES
CA01) Av Artigas 781, 90200 Las Piedras, Canelones ☎4236 44775 ▤4236 44814 **W:** radiocristaldeluruguay.com.uy **E:** cx147cristal@ adinet.com.uy – **CA02)** Gral. Fructuoso Rivera 216, 90000 Canelones ☎4332 1570 **W:** radiocanelones.com.uy **E:** 1570amsrl@gmail.com – **CA03)** Av Artigas 977, 91000 Pando ☎4229 22512 ▤4229 24440 **W:** radiocontinental.com.uy **E:** administracion@radiocontinental.com. uy or programación@radiocontinental.com.uy

CL00) CERRO LARGO
CL01) Remigio Castellanos 721, 37000 Melo ☎4642 2397 ▤4642 3226 **W:** lavozdemelo.com **E:** director@lavozdemelo.com – **CL02)** Virrey Arredondo 986, 37100 Rio Branco ☎4675 2009 **E:** am1360@ adinet.com.uy **CL03)** Treinta y Tres 949, 37100 Melo ☎4642 2387 **W:** radiomaria.org.uy **E:** info.ury@radiomaria.org – **CL04)** José Pedro Varela 750, Melo ☎4642 2051 ▤4642 1264 **W:** radioacuarela.blogspot.com **E:** acuarelaradio@yahoo.com

CO00) COLONIA
CO01) Rivadavia 383, 70000 Colonia ☎4522 2006 ▤4522 2961 **W:** radiocolonia.com **E:** cw1@adinet.com.uy - **FM:** 93.5MHz "FM Mágica" – **CO02)**19 de Abril 444, 70100 Carmelo ☎4542 3558 ▤4542 2520 **W:** radiocarmelo.com **E:** radiocarmelo@adinet.com. uy – **CO03)** Calle Berna 1375, 70201 Nueva Helvecia **W:** ro.com. uy ☎4554 4217 ▤4554 4409 **E:**1490@ro.com.uy - **FM:** 90.7MHz "Reflejos" – **CO04)** Chile 1162 y Gral Artigas, 70101 Nueva Palmira, Depto de Colonia ☎4544 6053 **W:**emisoraconosur1530.com **E:** emisoraconosur@gmail.com / emisoraconosurventas@gmail.com – **CO06)** Av Gral Flores 472, 70000 Colonia ☎4522 2030

DU00) DURAZNO
DU01) Zorrilla de San Martín 875, 97000 Durazno ☎4362 2701 ▤4362 3297 **W:** am960.com.uy **E:** multimyi@adinet.com.uy – **DU02)** Br. Gral. Fructuoso Rivera 501, 97000 Durazno ☎4362 2015 ▤4362 2058 **W:** radiodurazno.com **E:** am1430@adinet.com.uy **W:**radiodurazno.com director@radiodurazno.com – **FM:** 95.1MHz "Radio City" – **DU03)** Calle Sarandí del Yí 428, 97100 Sarandí del Yí ☎▤4367 9155 **E:** norasan@adinet.com.uy - **FM:** 89.5MHz "Scala FM"

FL00) FLORIDA
FL01) Antonio Ma Fernández 800, 94000 Florida ☎4352 2026 **W:** cw33florida.com.uy **E:** cw33@adinet.com.uy - **FM:** 88.7MHz "Claridad"

FO00) FLORES
FO01) Herrera 435, 85000 Trinidad ☎4364 2229 ▤364 37550 **W:** agenda.org.uy/difusoraamericana **E:** am1560@hotmail.com

LA00) LAVALLEJA
LA01) José E Rodó 530, 30000 Minas ☎4442 2304 – **W:** radiolavalleja.jimdo.com **E:** cw43radiolavalleja@gmail.com – **LA02)** Camino Nacional s/n, 30200 José Batlle y Ordóñez ☎▤4469 2132 – **LA03)** Treinta y Tres 632, 30000 Minas **W:** federalfm.uy/cw54. php ☎4442 3092 ▤442 8714 **E:** federalfm@federalfm.uy - **FM:**

107.3MHz "Federal FM"
MA00) MALDONADO
MA01) Chacabuco y Moreno, 20200 Piriápolis ☎4432 2771 **W:** radiorbc.com **E:** radiorbc@adinet com.uy – **MA02)** Calle Sarandí 775, entre 18 de Julio y Treinta y Tres, 20400 San Carlos ☎426 6426 64050📠4426 69162 **E:** rscaudio@adinet.com.uy – **MA03)** Zelmar Michelini 819, 20000 Maldonado ☎4422 3872 📠4422 2555 **W:** radiomaldonado.com.uy **E:** am1560@hotmail.com or am1560@adinet. com.uy **N:** every ½h - **FM:** 103.5MHz "Aspen FM"
MO00) MONTEVIDEO
MO01) Av. 18 de Julio 1516, P.9, Esc 7, 11200 Montevideo ☎240 06877 📠240 15841 **W:** radioclarin.com **E:** clarinam580@adinet.com. uy – **MO02)** Joaquín Suarez 3409, 11700 Montevideo ☎233 60610 **W:** cx4radiorural.com **E:** rural@cx4radiorural.com – **MO03)** Sarandí 430, 11000 Montevideo **W:** rnu.com.uy **E:** organizacion@rnu.uy–☎2 1768 - CX6: - Clásica: - 24h - CX26: - Uruguay – 24h ~~0900-0300~~📠direccionradiouruguay@rnnu.uy – CX38 24h Uruguayan music **W:** emisoradelsur947@gmail.com Media Prgr: SS1400-1500, 0200-0300 "Radioactividades" on 1050kHz Rpt. to Cas, 7011, 11000 Montevideo. **E:** lmoreira@montevideo.com.uy **FM:** 103.9MHz Colonia. 100.1MHz, Bella Unión, 98.7MHz Artigas. 104.3MHz Salto, 103.5MHz . Paysandú, 92.1MHz. 94.7MHz Montevideo. 107.7MHz Rocha, 93.5MHz Chuy. 106.9MHz Melo. 93.9MHz Rivera. 97.1MHz Montevideo. 100.9MHz Maldonado 92.1MHz Mercedes. 102.9MHz Fray Bentos. 92.7MHz Treinta y Tres. 105.1MHz Durazno 103.7MHz Tacuarembó 106.1 Minas – **MO04)** Enriqueta Compte y Riquet 1250, 11800 Montevideo ☎220 82612 📠220 36906 **W:** sarandi.com.uy **E:** direccion@sarandi690.com. uy – **MO05)** Germán Barbato 1472, 11100 Montevideo ☎2902 4038 📠290 24038 **E:** cx10.730.continente@adinet.com.uy – **MO06)** Cerrito 475, 11000 Montevideo **W:** oriental.com.uy **E:** via oriental770.com/ contacto ☎291 61130 – **MO07)** Río Branco 1481, 11100 Montevideo ☎290 23531 📠290 83044 **W:** espectador.com **E:** am810@espectador. com.uy – **MO08)** Mercedes 973, 11100 Montevideo ☎2902 6162 📠290 20126 **W:** carve850.com.uy **E:** matiasreyesroque@gmail.com (Matías Reyes Roque, stn mgr) prensacarve@gmail.com – **MO09)** Enriqueta Compte y Riquet 1250, 11800 Montevideo ☎220 4163 📠220 3786 **W:** sport890.com.uy **E:** sport890@sport890.com.uy – Rpt. to: fgopar34@gmail.com – **MO10)** Av 18 de Julio 1224, 11100 Montevideo ☎290 14433 **W:** radiomontecarlo.com.uy **E:** cx20@ radiomontecarlo.com.uy – **MO11)** Av 18 de Julio, 1220, 3er piso, 11100 Montevideo ☎290 26022 📠290 26050 **W:** 970universal. com **E:** 970universal.com/contacto – **MO12)** Mercedes 973, 11100 Montevideo **W:** radio1010.com.uy ☎2902 6712 📠2902 9110 **E:** radio1010.uy/contacto or programacion@sadrep.com.uy – **MO14)** Av del Libertador Brig Gral. Lavalleja 1708, ap 101, Edificio Carioca, 11800 Montevideo ☎292 41514 📠292 42323 **W:** radioimparcial. com **E:** radioimparcial@adinet.com.uy – **MO15)** Plaza Independencia 846, EP, 11100 Montevideo ☎290 25640 📠290 83584 **W:** la30.com. uy **E:** prensa@radionacional.com.uy – **MO16)** Rambla Armenia 1647, Montevideo ☎262 89626 📠262 89627 – **MO17)** Av 18 de Julio 1357, Oficina 202, 11200 Montevideo ☎290 30302 📠290 30307 **E:** radio36@gmail.com – **MO19)** Canelones 1969, 11200 Montevideo ☎240 83292 **W:** cx40radiofenix **E:** radiofenix@adinet.com.uy – **MO20)** Arenal Grande 2093, 11800 Montevideo ☎292 40142 📠292 90094 **W:** emisoraciudaddemontevideo.com.uy **E:** CX42@emisoraciudaddemontevideo.com.uy – **MO21)** Garibaldi 2579, Montevideo **W:** 1410amlibre.com.uy **E:** via www.3.1410amlibre.com/ contacto.php ☎248 73565 – **MO22)** Emilio Frugoni 1312, Montevideo **W:** cx46.com ☎240 90094 📠240 89314 **E:** correo@cx46.com
PA00) PAYSANDÚ
PA01) Av España 1629, 60000 Paysandú **E:** am1240@adinet.com.uy / correo@radiocw39.com ☎4722 3617 📠4722 2954 **W:** radiocw39. com – **PA02)** 18 de Julio 614, 60000 Paysandú ☎4722 2267 📠4722 4970 **E:** correo@radiocw39.com – **PA03)** 33 Orientales 946,1° piso, 60000 Paysandú ☎4722 4020 📠4722 4020 **W:** paysandu.com/radiofelicidad **E:** radiofelicidad@radiofelicidad.com.uy – **PA04)** Tte. Cnel Francisco Bicudo y Ruta 3 Gral Artigas, 60000 Paysandú ☎ 📠4722 4856 **E:** cw154@adinet.com.uy
RI00) RIVERA
RI01) Dr Dávison s/n, 40002 Minas de Corrales ☎4658 2073 **W:** radioreal.com.uy **E:** eduardo.andina@gmail.com– **RI02)** Dr Gabriel Anolles 441, 40000 Rivera ☎4622 3230 - **E:** radiorivera@gmail. com – **RI03)** Av Sarandí 792, 40000 Rivera ☎4622 3259 📠4622 3422 **W:** internacionalamyfm.com **E:** internac@gmail.com - **FM:** 94.5MHz – **RI04)** Bulevar Artigas casi Rivera, 40003 Vichadero ☎4654 2018 **W:** radiovichadero.com **E:** radiosamfm@hotmail.com – **RI05)** Francisco Acuña de Figueroa 887, 40000 Rivera ☎4622 5893 **W:** multimediadelnorte.com/reconquista **E:** reconquista1220@hotmail. com – **FM:** 90.6MHz
RN00) RIO NEGRO
RN01) Rincón 1689, 65100 Young 📠4567 2071 **W:** radioyoung680.

listen2myradio.com/ (streaming audio) **E:** am680@adinet.com.uy – **RN02)** 27 de Julio casi Basilio Lubkov, San Javier ☎4569 2005 📠4569 2089 **W:** 1370am.com.uy/ **E:** radiosanjavier@hotmail.com – **RN03)** Rincón 1811, 65100 Young ☎4567 5143 **E:** imagenfm@ adinet.com.uy **W:** 89.1MHz "Imágen FM" – **RN04)** 25 de Mayo 3164 al 3168, 65000 Fray Bentos ☎4562 2022 📠4562 2653 **W:** agenda.org.uy/radiorincon **E:** rinconprensa@adinet.com or prensa. rincon@gmail.com – **RN05)** 18 de Julio y 25 de Agosto, 65000 Fray Bentos ☎4562 3100 & 4562 3100 📠4562 3528 **W:** radiolitoral.com. uy **E:** litoral@adinet.com.uy
RO00) ROCHA
RO01) Ramírez 127, 27000 Rocha ☎4472 2250 📠4472 2650 **W:** difusorarochense.com.uy **E:** difusorarochense@gmail.com – **FM:** 91.5MHz & 106.3MHz – **RO02)** Zorrilla de S Martin 200, 27000 Rocha ☎4472 1198 📠4472 3973 **W:** https://facebook.com – Radio Fortaleza **E:** fortaleza1320@gmail.com – **RO04)** 18 de Julio 1322, 27200 Castillos ☎4475 8054 📠4475 8755 **W:** universoam.com **E:** am1480@ adinet.com.uy (radio) grupouniverso@adinet.com.uy (dir.) – **RO05)** Nicolás Corbo 1152, 27300 Lascano **W:** nuevaradiolascano.com **E:** lanuevaradio@adinet.com.uy ☎4456 9280 & 4456 4380
SA00) SALTO
SA01) Uruguay 1416, 50000 Salto ☎4734 0298 📠4733 3222 **W:** radiotabare.com.uy **E:** info@radiotabare.com.uy or amtabare@adinet. com.uy – **SA02)** Lavalleja 48, 50000 Salto ☎📠4732 4330 - **FM:** 106.5MHz "Emisora del Éxodo" – **SA03)** Uruguay 1416, 50000 Salto ☎📠4733 3222 **W:** amlibertadores.com **E:** amlibertadores@adinet. com.uy – **SA04)** Brasil 715, 50000 Salto ☎4733 2615 📠4733 3414 **W:** agenda.org.uy/radiosalto **E:** cw31salt@adinet.com.uy & radiosalto@ adinet.com.uy – **FM:** 88.3MHz "Emisora del Lago" – **SA05)** Brasil 792, 50000 Salto ☎473 3752 7759 📠4732 6264 **W:** 10minutos. com.uy **E:** http://10minutos.com.uy/?page_id=2 – **SA06)** Artigas 101, 50000 Salto ☎4732 6264 **W:** 10minutos.com.uy **E:** amarapey@ adinet.com.uy
SJ00) SAN JOSÉ
SJ01) Evaristo Ciganda 511, 80000 San José ☎📠4342 6444 **W:** radio41.com.uy **E:** 1360am@radio41.com.uy
SO00) SORIANO
SO02) Calle Joaquín Suárez al final, 75.200 Cardona ☎📠4536 9315 **W:** radiocentrocardona.blogspot.com/ **E:** radiocentro@adinet.com. uy – **SO03)** Luis Alberto de Herrera 346, 60008 Guichón, Depto de Paysandú ☎4742 2053 📠4742 2297 **W:** pazlanuevaradio.net **E:** lanuevapaz@adinet.com.uy – **SO04)** Colón 319 Planta Alta, 75000 Mercedes ☎4532 8536 (Adm.), 4532 8538 (AM Studio) **W:** http:// enterarte.info/agraciadanueva/noticias.php **E:** radioagraciada1550@ hotmail.com - **FM:** 100.3MHz "Galicia" – **SO05)** Av Asencio 1695, 75100 Dolores, Depto de Soriano ☎4534 2110 📠4534 2691 **W:** radiosansalvador.com.uy **E:** administracion@radiosansalvador.com.uy - **FM:** 89.7MHz "Skorpio"
TA00) TACUAREMBÓ
TA01) 18 de Julio 743, 45100 Paso de los Toros ☎📠4664 5146 **W:** ampasodelostoros.com **E:** am1110@adinet.com.uy or radiopasodelostoros@pasodelostoros.com - **FM:** 91.9MHz "Toros FM" – **TA02)** 18 de Julio 112, 45000 Tacuarembó ☎4263 22898 📠4263 2495 **W:** radiotacuarembo.com **E:** radiotbclientes@hotmail.com– **FM:** 92.5MHz, 104.5MHz – **TA03)** 18 de Julio 302, 45000 Tacuarembó ☎4632 2605 📠4622 2779 – **W:** radiozorrilla.com **E:** zsm@adinet.com. uy - **FM:** 88.9MHz "Em de la Música" – **TA04)** Gral Artigas 193, 42500 San Gregorio de Polanco, Tacuarembó ☎4639 4547 📠4639 2495 **W:** radioibirapita1510am.blogspot.com **E:** radioibirapita1510am@yahoo. com
TT00) TREINTA Y TRES
TT01) Juan Muñoz s/n, 30204 Cerro Chato, Depto Treinta y Tres ☎4466 2200 📠4466 2225 **W:** radioagraria.com **E:** radioagraria@hotmail.com Rpts. to: cx2ua@hotmail.com – **TT02)** Marcelo Barreto s/n, Villa Vergara, 33000 Treinta y Tres ☎4458 2917 **W:** ellibertador.com. uy **E:** ellibertador@adinet.com.uy – **TT03)** Pablo Zufriátegui 1076, 33000 Treinta y Tres ☎4452 22476 📠4452 2340 **W:** difusoratreintaytres.com.uy **E:** cw45@adinet.com.uy – **TT04)** Atanasio Sierra 1092 casi Juan A.Lavalleja, 33000 Treinta y Tres ☎4452 3532 📠452 3533 **W:** radiopatria.com.uy **E:** radiopatria@gmail.com

FM in Montevideo (MHz): all stns 10-100kW
89.1 Uni-Radio (LP stn) – 90.3 FM Oldies – 91.1 R.Futura – 91.5 ZOE Gospel Music – 91.9 R.Disney – 92. MO7)93. Urbana FM – **MO7)** 92.5 El Espectador – 93.9 Océano – **MO03)** 94.7 Emisora del Sur (SODRE) – 95.5 Em. Del Plata – 96.3 Alfa FM – **MO03)** 97.1 Babel (SODRE) – 97.9 M24 – 98.7 Diamante FM – 99.5 Em. del Sol – 100.3 Aire FM – 101.3 Nuevo Tiempo – 101.9 Azul FM – 103.7 Latina FM – 104.3 Radiocero – 105.9 Galaxia FM – 106.7 La Ley FM.
NB: In the rest of the country there are 165 FM outlets. There are also 156 authorised Community LPFM stns in the country.

UZBEKISTAN

L.T: UTC +5h — **Pop:** 30.2 million — **Pr.L:** Uzbek — **E.C:** 50Hz, 220V — **ITU:** UZB

O'ZBEKISTON RESPUBLIKASI AXBOROT TEXNOLOGIYALARI VA KOMMUNIKATSIYALARINI RIVOJLANTIRISH VAZIRLIGI
(Ministry for Information Technology & Communications)
✉ Amir Temur sho ko'chasi 4, 100047 Toshkent ☎ +998 71 2384107 📠 +998 71 2398782 **E:** info@mitc.uz **W:** mitc.uz
L.P: Minister: Xurshid Mirzaxidov
NB: The ministry issues broadcasting licenses.

O'ZBEKISTON MILLY TELERADIOKOMPANIYASI (Gov)
✉ Navoiy ko'chasi 69, 100011 Toshkent ☎ +998 71 2141250 📠 +998 71 2441332.**E:** info@mtrk.uz **W:** mtrk.uz
✉ Radio studios: Xorazm ko'chasi 49, 100047 Toshkent
L.P: Pres: Alisher Xadjayev

FM	1*	2	3	kW
Andijon	-	105.2	-	1
Buxoro	102.0c	103.9	105.4	2
Namangan	-	105.2	-	2
Navoi	106.6g	104.0	105.8	2
Nukus**	103.1f	104.6	-	2
Qarshi	102.3e	103.1	105.6	1
Toshkent	103.1	104.0	107.8	4
Samarqand	105.2i	101.9	-	1
Urganch	103.5l	101.5	-	4

+ translators. *) incl. reg prgrs (see below) **) Located in Karakalpakstan (autonomous province)
D.Prgr: Prgr 1 (O'zbekiston): 24h. For ethnic minorities: 1300-1315 & Sat 1800-1830 Russian, 1830-1900 Karakalpak (Fri), Kazakh (Sat). – **Prgr 2 (Yoshlar):** 2300-2100. – **Prgr 3 (Mahalla):** 0000-2200. – **Local Station: "Toshkent"** on Toshkent 87.9 (4kW): 0000-2200 in Uzbek, Russian.

O'zbekiston MTRK Regional Services
D.Prgr: via Prgr 1 txs. Some branches also transmit on exclusive freqs, see below. **a) Andijon TRK:** Istiqlol ko'chasi 9, 170120 Andijon **E:** andijon@mtrk.uz – **b) Buxoro TRK:** Eshanov ko'chasi 20, 200120 Buxoro **E:** buxorotv@mtrk.uz – **c) Farg'ona TRK:** 150100 Farg'ona **E:** fargona@mtrk.uz – **d) Jizzax TRK:** Rashidov maydon, 130100 Jizzax **E:** jizzaxtvr@mtrk.uz. "R. Sanzar" on 105.4MHz: 24h. – **e) Qashqadaryo TRK:** 180100 Qarshi **E:** qashqadaryo_trk@mtrk.uz – **f) Qoraqalpog'iston TRK:** Dustnazarov ko'chasi 20, 230100 Nukus – **g) Navoi TRK:** Xalklar Do'stligi ko'chasi 32, 210100 Navoiy **E:** ntrk.nazorat@mtrk.uz – **h) Namangan TRK:** Holhanov ko'chasi 1, 160136 Namangan **E:** namangan@mtrk.uz – **i) Samarqand TRK:** 140100 Samarqand. "R. Jahon" on 105.2MHz: 24h. – **j) Sirdaryo TRK:** 120100 Guliston **E:** svtrk@mtrk.uz – **k) Surxondaryo TRK:** 190100 Termiz. – **l) Xorazm TRK:** 220100 Urganch. **E:** xorazmtvr@mtrk.uz.

OTHER STATIONS

FM	MHz	kW	Location	Station
8)	88.4	1	Toshkent	Navro'z FM
4C)	90.0	1	Toshkent	A'lo FM
11)	100.4	2	Nukus*	Nukus-FM
1B)	100.5	2	Toshkent	Oriat FM
10)	100.5	1	Farg'ona	Ruxsor FM
3)	101.0	1	Toshkent[1]	O'zbegim taronasi
2)	101.5	1	Toshkent	R. Grand
5)	102.0	2	Toshkent	R. Hamroh
6)	102.7	1	Toshkent[1]	Vodiy sadosi
9A)	103.5	1	Toshkent	R. Poytaxt
9A)	104.5	1	Samarqand	R. Poytaxt
4A)	105.0	4	Toshkent	R. Terra
4B)	105.8	1	Toshkent	Zamin FM
1A)	106.5	4	Toshkent	Oriat Dono
6)	106.9	1	Angren[1]	Vodiy sadosi
9B)	107.2	1	Toshkent	R. Poytaxt-Inform
7)	107.2	1	Samarqand	STV Radio
4B)	107.3	1	Andijon	Zamin FM
4B)	107.4	1	Buxoro	Zamin FM

NB: Txs below 1kW not listed. *) Located in Karakalpakstan (autonomous province) [1]) + txs in other towns on same freq. (synchr. network)
Addresses & other information:
1A,B) Istikbol ko'chasi 6, 100000 Toshkent. 1A) in Uzbek, **E:** radio@oriatdono.uz; 1B) in Russian, **E:** fm@oriat.uz – **2)** Bunyodkor ko'chasi 15, 100043 Toshkent **E:** radio@grand.uz – **3)** Shaxrisabz ko'chasi 16a, 100000 Toshkent **E:** ut101@mail.ru – **4A-C)** Xamid Olimjon maydon 13A, 10000 Toshkent –**5)** Shayxontohur ko'chasi 36, 100007 Toshkent **E:** hamroh@mail.ru – **6)** Mirobod ko'chasi 39/1A, 100000 Toshkent **E:**

mtrk@intal.uz – **7)** Firdavskiy ko'chasi 1, 140100 Samarqand **E:** info@stv.uz – **8)** Muqumiy ko'chasi 178, 100096 Toshkent **E:** info@navruzfm.uz – **9A,B)** Movaraunnahr ko'chasi 14, 100000 Toshkent **E:** radio1072@rambler.ru 9B) in Russian. – **10)** Marg'ilon ko'chasi 76, 150100 Farg'ona **E:** 100_5@inbox.ru – **11)** Nukus

VANUATU

L.T. UTC + 11h — **Pop:** 224,564 — **Pr.L:** Bislama, English, French — **E.C:** 50Hz, 230V — **ITU:** VUT

TELECOMMUNICATIONS AND RADIO COMMUNICATIONS REGULATOR
W: trr.vu [note: currently under operational review and website unavailable]

MW	kHz	kW	Station
1) Emten Lagoon, Efate	1125	2.5	R.Vanuatu
1) Luganville, Espiritu Santo	1179	10	R.Vanuatu*

SW	kHz	kW	Station
1) Emten Lagoon, Efate	3945	1.5-2	R.Vanuatu
1) Emten Lagoon, Efate	7260	1.5-2	R.Vanuatu

FM	MHz	kW	Station
2) Aniwa Isl.	89.0	0.1	CRST FM104
3) Siviri, Efate	89.0	-	Taleva 89FM
4) Port Vila, Efate	90.0	0.3	Laef 90FM
5) Port Vila, Efate	96.0	-	BUZZ FM
1) Luganville, Espiritu Santo	98.0	0.25	Halo FM
1) Port Vila, Efate	98.0	0.2	Paradise FM
6) Luganville, Espiritu Santo	99.0	0.25	BBC
6) Port Vila, Efate	99.0	0.25	BBC
7) Port Vila, Efate	100.0	0.2	France Inter
8) Luganville, Espiritu Santo	102.0	-	China R. Int.
8) Port Vila, Efate	102.0	-	China R. Int.
9) Port Vila, Efate	103.0	0.2	R.Australia
2) Isangel, Tanna	104.0	0.1	CRST FM104
8) Lakatoro, Malakula	106.0	-	China R. Int.
10) Port Vila, Efate	107.0	0.3	Capital FM107

* currently silent after cyclone damage
Addresses and other information
1) VANUATU BROADCASTING AND TELEVISION CORPORATION (VBTC) ✉PMB 9049, Port Vila ☎ +678 23615/22999 Ext 127/128 📠 +678 22026 **L.P:** AGM: Fred Vuroberavu, Mgr Radio: Samuel Seiragi, Mgr-Tech. Srvcs: Warren Robert **W:** facebook.com/radiovanuatu [note: VBTC website currently unavailable for technical reasons] **E:** technical@vbtc.com.vu National Radio Service: **Radio Vanuatu D.Prgr:** Mon-Sat 1815-0030, Sun 1815-1030 other times relay Paradise FM **Schedule:** 3945kHz [overnight] 0400-2200 7260 [daytime] 2200-0400 [note: SW schedule may vary depending on technical requirements and rebuilding services after cyclone damage] **MW:** 24/7 including relay Paradise FM **FM:** Halo FM Luganville **Paradise FM** Port Vila **Prgr:** commercial 24/7 [**Note:** VBTC operations are currently under review because of systemic failures in operations and management which came to a head after Cyclone Pam in mid-2015] – **2)** CRST [aka known as CREST], Community R.Society of Tanna, Isangel, Tanna ☎ +678 68054 **W:** facebook.com/tannaradio **E:** gudfella@vanuatu.com.vu local community radio **Network:** Aniwa Isl and r. 3 locations in Tafea Province – **3)** Siviri, North Efate, local community radio – **4)** Vanuatu Christian Broadc. Netw. [VCBN], PO Box 674, Port Vila ☎ +678 26408 **E:** nenes@vanuatu.com.vu **W:** vcbn.org **L.P:** CEO: Jenny Joy James **Other:** associated with UCB International [Auckland, NZ] – **5)** Port Vila ☎ +678 23224 **L.P:** Marc Neil-Jones **W:** facebook.com/buzz-96fm **E:** advertising@fm96.vu **ID:** Today's Best Music & News **Prgr:** 24/7 **Other:** associated with Vanuatu Daily Post – **6)** 24/7 Pacific stream via satellite from London – **7)** 24/7 French language stream via satellite from Paris – **8)** 24/7 English language stream via satellite from Beijing – **9)** 24/7 English and French languages stream via satellite from Melbourne – **10)** Top Flr, Laguna Bldg, Port Vila [PO Box 258, Port Vila] ☎ +678 23847 **E:** sales@fm107vanuatu.com **W:** fm107vanuatu.com includes live audio streaming 24/7 & facebook.com/fm107vanuatu **L.P:** GM Arthur Knight Dir. Sabie Natonga **ID:** "Capital FM107" **D.Prgr:** 24/7
NB: Several other LP FM stns in Port Vila region rep. including 24/7 rel. of RNZI which recently sustained major cyclone damage. Status of FM community stn for Saratamata, Penama province currently unknown.

VATICAN CITY STATE

L.T: UTC +1h (27 Mar-30 Oct: +2h) — **Pop:** 900 — **E.C:** 50Hz, 220V — **ITU:** CVA

RADIO VATICANA (Rlg.)
✉ Vatican Radio, 00120 Vatican City ☎ +39 06 6988 3551 Int. Rel:

☎ +39 06 6988 3551 ▤ +39 06 6988 4565 **W:** radiovaticana.org **E:** promo@vatiradio.va
L.P: DG: Rev. Federico Lombardi S.J.; TD: Sandro Piervenanzi; CE: Maurizio Venuti; Head of Int. Rel: Giacomo Ghisani; Vatican Radio Museum, guided visiting tour c/o Palazzo Pio XII, Piazza Pia 3 ☎ +39 06 6988 3995 **E:** museo_rv@vaticanradio.org **W:** radiovaticana. org/museo_tecnico/it/index.asp
MW: 585kHz 5kW, 1260kHz 5kW **FM:** 93.3 10kW/103.8 0.2kW/105.0MHz 10kW
Progr: Europa Programma 1 93.3MHz 24h 1260kHz (1000-2030) **W:** radiovaticana.org/it1/sched_eur1.asp **Italia Programma 2** 105.0MHz 24h (Multil.) 585kHz 24h **W:** radiovaticana.va/105/it_palinsesto.asp
DAB+: Channel 7B (Roma) Channel 13E (Milano)
Ann: Before all transmissions: Latin: "Laudetur Jesus Christus" (Praised be Jesus Christ), repeated in the language of the broadcast, then stn identification. **IS:** "Christus Vincit". **V.** by QSL-card

EXTERNAL SERVICE: Vatican Radio see International Radio section

VENEZUELA

L.T: UTC -4½h — **Pop:** 30 million — **Pr.L:** Spanish — **E.C:** 60Hz, 120V — **ITU:** VEN

COMISION NACIONAL DE TELECOMUNICACIONES (CONATEL)
▤ Avenida Veracruz con Calle Cali, Edificio CONATEL, Urb. Las Mercedes, Caracas 1060 ▤ 212 993 8801 **W:** conatel.gob.ve **E:** conatel@conatel.gob.ve

CAMARA VENEZOLANA DE LA INDUSTRIA DE RADIODIFUSION
▤ Ap. 3955, Caracas 1060 ☎ +58 212 2634855, 2634528 ▤ +58 212 2614783.

MW	Call	kHz	kW	Station, location, h. of tr.
AM01)		540	10	LV de Manapiare, San Juan de Manapiare
ZU01)	OY	540	50/25	R. Perijá, La Villa del Rosario: 0930-0430
DC01)	KE	550	50	R. Mundial, Caracas
DC02)	RH	560	50	RNV El Informativo, Pto.Ordaz: 1030-0430
AR09)	LX	570	100	R. La Villa, Villa de Cura
ZU02)	MJ	‡580	50/10	LV de la Fe, Maracaibo
DC02)		580		RNV El Informativo, Barinas
DC04)	KL	590	20	R. Continente, Caracas
BA01)	SW	600	15	R. Alto Llano, Sta Bárbara de Barinas
AN01)	XY	610	10	R. Centro, Cantaura
LA01)	SE	610	10	R. Cristal, Barquisimeto
AP01)	ZC	620	50/25	R. Fe y Alegría,Guasdualito 0930-0430
ZU03)	NO	620	10	R. Libertad, Cabimas: 0930-0430
DC02)	KA	630	50/25	RNV El Informativo, Caracas: 1030-0430
AN02)	QO	640	30	Deportes Unión R., Puerto La Cruz
LA02)	MU	640	10/5	R. Carora, Carora: 1030-0430
AN03)	QZ	660	10	R. Anaco, Anaco: 0930-0430
FA01)	NA	660	10	Ondas de los Medanos, Coro: 0930-0430
DC03)	LL	670	100	R. Rumbos, Caracas (also r. LV de la Lib.)
SU02)	QR	680	10	R. Continente, Cumaná: 1030-0530
LA03)	MR	690	50/20	R. Barquisimeto, Barquisimeto
BO01)	PQ	700	5/2	R. Sur, Puerto Ordaz
ZU04)	MH	700	10	R. Popular, Maracaibo: 1030-0430
DC05)	KY	710	50/20	R. Capital, Caracas: 1030-0630
AP02)	XE	720	10	R. Elorza, Elorza
NE01)	QE	720	50	R. Venezuela Oriente, Porlamar
LA04)	MT	730	10	R. Universo, Barquisimeto
BO02)	NQ	740	50	R. Caroni "Q-FM", Puerto Ordaz
ZU05)	NC	740	10	Unión R., Maracaibo: 0930-0430
DC06)	KS	750	100	RCR 750 Radio Caracas Radio, Caracas
TR01)	SO	760	10	R. Simpática 760, Trujillo
DC02)	KK	770	50/20	RNV El Informativo, Valencia (Campo Carabobo) 1030-0430
FA02)	MN	780	15	R. Coro, Coro
TA03)	OD	780	50/20	Ecos del Torbes, San Cristóbal: 0930-0430(SS -0630)
DC02)		790		RNV El Informativo, Cd. Bolívar: 1030-0430
DC07)	KC	790	10	R. Venezuela, Caracas
LA05)	XM	790	50	R. Minuto, Barquisimeto
BO03)	SH	820	50	R. Guayana, Guayana
DC08)	LT	830	25	R. Sensación, Caracas(also r.LV de la Lib.)
LA04)	MY	840	10	8-40 AM, Barquisimeto
MO01)	UZ	840	10/5	Guarapiche 8-40 "La Primera", Maturín
CA02)	RV	850	10	RV-850, Valencia
ZU06)	ZC	850	10	R. Fe y Alegría, Maracaibo: 0930-0530
GU01)	YE	860	20/10	Enlace 8-60, Valle de la Pascua

MW	Call	kHz	kW	Station, location, h. of tr.
TA05)	OL	860	10	R. Mundial, San Cristóbal: 0930-0530
LA11)	MP	870	10	Unión R. Noticias, Barquisimeto: 1030-0430
BA02)	ZD	‡880	20/10	R. Venezuela Barinas, Barinas
DC02)	KV	880	10	RNV Musical, Caracas: 1030-0430
FA04)		880	10	R. Paraguaná, Punto Fijo
CA03)	LW	890	25	Reloj R. América, Valencia: 0930-0430
ZU07)	MD	900	25	R. Venezuela Mara Ritmo, Maracaibo
DC10)	RQ	910	50/20	RQ 910 AM Center, Caracas
CO01)	QU	920	10/5	R. San Carlos, San Carlos
NE02)	QX	920	20	R. Nueva Esparta, Porlamar: 1030-0430
AR02)	LJ	930	10	R. Maracay, Maracay: 1030-0630
AN08)	LU	940	10	R. Fe y Alegría, El Tigre(Campo Mata): 0930-0330
FA05)	NN	940	10	R. Punto Fijo, Punto Fijo: 0930-0430
MO02)	RB	960	50/20	R. Monagas, Maturín
TA06)	SS	960	10	R. San Sebastián, San Cristóbal: 1030-0530
AR03)	LR	970	10	R. Continente 970, Maracay: 0930-0430
TR02)	SD	970	15	R. Turismo, Valera: 0930-0430
AN10)	QM	980	10	Unión R. Notícias, El Tigre: 1030-0430
DC12)	RT	990	20	R. Tropical, Caracas(r. LV de la Liberación)
CA04)	NM	1000	10	R. Caribeña Mil AM (Continente), Morón: 0930-0430
TA11)	OA	1000	10	Deportes Unión R, San Cristóbal:1030-0430
AR04)	PC	1010	10	R. Aragua, Cagua: 0930-0430
BO05)	QF	1010	10	R. Venezuela Bolívar, Cd. Bolívar
NE03)	RS	1020	10	R. Mundial Margarita, La Asunción: 1030-0530
YA01)	TW	1020	25	R. Alegría, Chivacoa
ZU08)	MX	1020	50/10	R. Calendario Zulia, Maracaibo
MI01)	TD	1030	25/10	R. Valles del Tuy, Ocumare del Tuy: 0930-0430
PO02)	QY	1030	20	R. Onda 1030, Guanare: 0930-0630
CA05)	LB	‡1040	20	LV de Carabobo, Valencia: 0930-0430
ME01)	ON	1040	20/10	R. Mundial Los Andes, Mérida
DC02)	RO	1050	20	RNV El Informativo, Cabudare: 1030-0430
GU02)	LN	1060	10	R. Guárico, San Juan de los Morros: 1030-0330
TA07)	OE	1060	10	Unión R. Noticias, San Cristóbal
AP03)		1070	10	Superior 1070 Biruaca, S. Fernando de Apure
PO03)		1070	25	Contacto 1070, Ospino: 1030-0430
ZU09)	MA	1070	10	R. Mundial Zulia, Maracaibo
AN11)	QJ	1080	10	R. Barcelona, Barcelona
AR05)	NR	1080	10	R. Venezuela, Maracay
DC13)	SZ	1090	20	Deportes Unión R., Caracas
YA02)	PB	1090	10	R. Yaracuy "Operadora 1090 AM", S. Felipe
BO06)	SV	1100	10	R. Angostura, Cd.Bolívar
CA06)	RX	1110	10	Deportes Unión R., Valencia
SU03)	QT	1110	10	R. Venezuela, Carúpano: 0930-0430
AN02)	SK	1120	20/10	R. Dif.del Sur, San Fernando de Apure
MO03)	XZ	1120	5	R. República "La Estación Feliz", Maturín
LA07)	KQ	1130	10	R. Popular, Barquisimeto: 0930-0430
DC16)	RL	1130	20/10	R. Ideal, Caracas
BO07)	QD	1150	10	Ecos del Orinoco, Cd.Bolívar
FA06)	MV	1150	10	R. Venezuela Caribe, Punto Fijo
ME03)	OK	1160	1	R. Universidad, Mérida
MI02)	RR	1160	20/10	R. Industrial, Guarenas
VA01)	KW	1170	10	R. Bolivariana "R. 1070", Maiquetía: 1030-0430
AR06)	LQ	1180	10	Super Suave 11-80, La Victoria
MO04)	OR	1180	10	R. Maturín, Maturín: 0930-0430
BO08)	PF	1190	20/10	Ondas de Libertad, San Felix: 0930-0330
TA09)	ZD	1190	10	La Cultural del Táchira, San Cristóbal
DC14)	OZ	1200	10	R. Tiempo, Caracas
MO05)	SF	1200	10	R. Dimensión, Caripito: 1030-0330
AP05)	RD	1220	10	LV de Apure, San Fernando de Apure
CA07)	VM	1220	10/5	Valencia 1220 - Circuito R. Venezuela, Valencia
ZU14)	ZO	1220	20/10	R. Aeropuerto 1220, Maracaibo
TR03)	OH	1230	10	R. Valera, Valera: 0930-0430
BO09)	PZ	1250	10	Latina 12-50, Pto Ordaz: 0930-0430
DC15)	RM	1260	10	BBN R, Caracas
ME04)	OU	1270	10	R. Ondas Panamericanas, El Vigía
GU03)	QS	1280	10	R. Zaraza, Zaraza: 1030-0330
TR04)	OF	1280	10	R. Trujillo, Trujillo
CA08)	LF	1290	10	R. Puerto Cabello, Puerto Cabello
DC10)	KH	1300	10/8	R. Recuerdos AM Center, Caracas
ZU16)	NS	1300	10	R. Reloj, Maracaibo: 1000-0500
DC02)	SM	1310	10	RNV El Informativo, Barcelona: 1030-0430
DC02)	SL	1310	1	RNV El Informativo, Guri: 1030-0430
DC02)		1310		RNV El Informativo, Sta. Elena: 1030-0430
TR05)	TS	1310	5	R. Andina "Sonido 13-10", Isnotú: 0930-0530
AR07)	WP	1320	10/5	R. Apolo, Turmero
LA08)	SG	1320	10	R. Colonial, El Tocuyo
DC02)		1330		RNV El Informativo, La Paragua: 1030-0430
GU04)	OY	1330	5	R. Los Llanos, Calabozo: 0930-0330
DC01)		‡1340		R Mundial, Barinas

MW	Call	kHz	kW	Station, location, h. of tr.
DC17)	NE	1340	10	R. Uno, Caracas
AN13)	ZZ	1350	5	R. Eclipse, El Tigrito
FA07)	TJ	1350	5	R. Falcón, Puerto Cumarebo
MI04)	TZ	±1360	5	R. Armonía, Charallave: 1030-0330
GU05)	OQ	1370	5	Unión R. Notícias, Valle de la Pascua: 1030-0430
ME05)	JI	1370	10	R. Continente Cumbre, Mérida: 1030-0430
PO05)	SV	1370	5	RNV Portuguesa, Acarigua: 1030-0430
BO10)	ME	1380	5	R. Revelación, Cd.Bolivar
CA09)	NG	1380	10	Ondas del Mar, Puerto Cabello: 0930-0430
DC18)	ZA	1390	20	R. Fe y Alegría, Caracas
ZU20)	ZO	1390	10	R. Lumen, Maracaibo: 1030-0530
GU06)	NF	1400	1	R. Sabana, El Sombrero: 1030-0230
PO06)	ST	1410	5	R. Turén, Turén: 0930-0430
TR01)	SP	1410	10	R. Simpatía, Valera
DC21)		1420	5	R. Sintonía, Caracas
LA10)	RW	1420	10/5	R. Cardenal, Carora: 1030-0430
AN14)	TP	1430	25	R. Bahía, Puerto La Cruz
BO11)	TM	1430	10/5	R. Caicara, Caicara del Orinoco
CA10)	NB	±1430	10	Llanerísima, Guacara
GU07)	RF	1440	10	R. Orituco, Altagracia del Orituco
PO07)	ZI	1440	10	R. Estelar 14-40, Guanare: 0930-0430
BO12)	XC	1450	10/5	R. Mega Visión, San Felix
VA02)	KJ	1450	10/8	R. María, Caracas
TR07)	RJ	1460	5	R. Jardín, Boconó
CA11)	JW	1470	10	Union R. Cultural, Valencia
SU04)	SY	1470	10	Union R. Vibración, Carúpano
FA08)		1480		R. Cumarebo, Cumarebo
DC19)	XD	1490	10	R. Dinámica, Caracas
ME06)	SQ	1490	1	R. Mérida 14-90, Mérida
SU05)	RZ	1500	10/5	R. 2000, Cumaná: 1030-0430
DC02)		1510		RNV El Informativo, Güigüe
YA04)	NP	1530	10	R. San Felipe el Fuerte, San Felipe
ZU24)	XO	1550	10/5	R. Impacto La Poderosa, Cd. Ojeda
DC02)	LZ	1560	10/5	RNV El Informativo, Mérida
GU08)	YV	1580	10/5	R. Venezolana, Calabozo: 1030-0230
DC20)	UD	1590	10	R. Deporte, Caracas

Hrs of tr: 24h unless shown. **Call:** YV—, ‡=inactive, (r)=repeater, ±=variable frequency. **NB:** Many trs operate irr. or on lower power.

Networks:
CNB - CIRCUITO NACIONAL BELFORT
🖃 Quinta CNB, Av.Los Naranjos, La Florida, Caracas **W:** cnb.com.ve
CIRCUITO AM CENTER
🖃 CentroComercialConcresa, Nivel 1, Circuito Center, Prados del Este, Caracas 1080, Edo.Miranda ☎ +58 212 976-2013 **E:** feloespinosa@cantv.et.
CIRCUITO RADIAL ALFA OMEGA
🖃 Calle 25, Con Calle 67, Sector El Paraíso, frente Al Colegio La Epifanía, Maracaibo, Edo.Zulia ☎ +58 261 783-2524
CIRCUITO POPULAR
🖃 Boulevard de Sabana Grande, Torre Provincial, P10, Sabana Grande, Caracas 1050 ☎ +58 212 762 5052
CIRCUITO RADIO CARACAS RADIO
🖃 Av.Páez, Quinta RCR, El Paraíso, Caracas 1021 ☎ +58 212 481-3590
CIRCUITO RADIAL CONTINENTE
🖃 Calle La Joya, Edif.Cosmos, PH, Chacao, Caracas 1060, Edo. Miranda ☎ +58 212 267-3132 🖷 +58 212 267-1223 **W:** radiocontinente.jimdo.com **E:** produccion@radiocontinente zzn.com
CIRCUITO RADIO VENEZUELA
🖃 Av.Rómulo Gallegos, Edif.KLM, P12, Ofcs CyD, Los Palos Grandes, Caracas 1062, Edo.Miranda ☎ +58 212 286-8492 **W:** radiovenezuela. com.ve **E:** radiovenezuela@hotmail.com
CIRCUITO SATELITAL RUMBOS
🖃 Av.Francisco de Miranda, Multicentro Empresarial del Este, Edif. Libertador, Núcleo A, P7, Chacao, Caracas 1060, Edo.Miranda ☎ +58 212 263-3236 🖷 212 263-2212 **E:** radiorumbos@ip-net.work.net
CIRCUITO UNION RADIO
🖃 Av.Mohedano, Entre Calle Los Granados y 1ª transversal, Edif. Splendor, La Castellana, Caracas 1060, Edo.Miranda ☎ +58 212 263-5133 **W:** unionradio.com
CORPORACIÓN REGIONAL BRADCASTING
🖃 Calle 74, Entre Avre. 3Dy3E, Edif.Televisa, Sector La Lago, Maracaibo 4002, Edo. Zulia ☎ +58 261 792-9217
GRUPO RADIAL DE ORIENTE
🖃 Urb.Tricentenaria, Centro ComercialTricentenaria, P2, Ofcs 03y09, Barcelona 6001, Edo.Anzoátegui ☎ +58 281 277-1743 🖷 281 277-1776 **E:** radioanzoategui@hotmail.com
SISTEMA RADIO MUNDIAL
🖃 Calle Nueva York, Edif.Manzanillo, P2, Las Mercedes, Caracas

1060, Edo.Miranda ☎ 212 993-9391 **W:** radiomundial.com.ve **E:** prensayvke@cantv.net

State abbreviations: AM = Amazonas, AN = Anzoátegui, AP = Apure, AR = Aragua, BA = Barinas, BO = Bolívar, CA = Carabobo, CO = Cojedes, DA = Delta Amacuro, DC = Distrito Capital, FA = Falcón, GU = Guárico, LA = Lara, ME = Mérida, MI = Miranda, MO = Monagas, NE = Nueva Esparta, PO = Portuguesa, SU = Sucre, TA = Táchira, TR = Trujillo, VA = Vargas, YA = Yaracuy, ZU = Zulia.
N.B: These abbreviations are not officially recognized by the Venezuelan Post Office. Letters should therefore carry the full name.

Addresses and other information:
AM00) AMAZONAS
AM01) San Juan de Manapiare.
AAN00) ANZOÁTEGUI
AN01) Av Hospital cruce con Calle Freites, Edif.Radio Centro, Cantura 6007 – **AN02)** Av 5 de Julio, Edif Los Angeles, Sotanos 1y2, Puerto La Cruz 6023. **W:** unionradio.net/deportes – **AN03)** Calle Cajigal cruce con Av.Nueva Esparta N° 39, Edif.Radio City, planta baja, Anaco 6003 – **AN08)** Av.Simon Rodríguez con 8va Calle Norte, Complejo Cultural Simón Rodríguez, El Tigre 6034 **W:** feyalegria.org – **AN10)** Av Francisco de Miranda N° 196, Al lado del Banco Provincial, El Tigre 6034 – **AN11)** Av Miranda cruce con Av.San Carlos, Edif.Radio Barcelona, P2, Barcelona 6001 – **AN13)** Av.Intercomunal El Tigre El Tigrito, Detrás de Elite Motors, Casa Amarilla, El Tigrito 6035 – **AN14)** Av Municipal, Torre Pelicano, P8, Apto 8-4, Puerto La Cruz 6023.
AP00) APURE
AP01) Carr Nacional, Vía Elorza La Arenosa, Edif. Fe y Alegría, Guasdualito 5063. **W:** feyalegria.org – **AP02)** Calle 9 con Cra 4, Municipio Rómulo Gallegos, Elorza 7007 – **AP03)** Av.Fuerzas Armadas, Edif.Superior, P1, San Fernando de Apure 7001 0930-0400 – **AP04)** Calle Carlos Rodríguez Rincones, Gobernación del Estado Apure, San Fernando de Apure 7001 – **AP05)** Av Miranda, Edif.Don António Cestari, San Fernando de Apure 7001.
AR00) ARAGUA
AR02) Calle Boyacá, Edif Centro, P9, Ofc 1, Maracay 2101 – **AR03)** Av Miranda Oeste N° 149, Entre Carabobo y Pinhincha, Edif.Canaobre, PH, Maracay 2101 **W:** radiocontinente.jimdo.com – **AR04)** Calle Sucre, Edificio Comercial y Profesional Sucre, Piso 2, Oficina #3, Cagua 2122 **W:** radioaragua.com – **AR05)** Urb.Calicanto, Calle Coromoto, Norte 6, Detrás de la Maestranza Cesar Girón, Maracay 2101 **W:** radiovenezuela.com.ve – **AR06)** Edif Veliz, Calle Aldao, frente a la Plaza Rivas, La Victoria 2126 – **AR07)** Av.Bermúdez, Torre Apolo, PB, entre Mariño y Bolívar, Turmero 2115 **W:** apolo1320am.venesur.com – **AR09)** Calle Páez, N° 138, Detrás del Teatro de la Opera, Maracay 2126
BA00) BARINAS
BA01) Cra 1 N° 7-39, entre Calles 7 y 8, Santa Bárbara de Barinas 5210 – **BA02)** Av. 23 de Enero, Centro Comercial Central Plaza, Local 27, Barinas 5201 **W:** radiovenezuela.com.ve
B000) BOLIVAR
BO01) Av.Guasipati, Edif Piarde, PH, Puerto Ordaz 8015 – **BO02)** Urb. Altavista Calle Caura, Edif Los Bancos, P4, Puerto Ordaz 8015 – **BO03)** Av.Raúl Leoni, Edif.Antonelli, PB, Upatá 8026 – **BO05)** Calle Dalla Costa, Alto N° 5, Cd Bolívar 8001 - 0900-0400 **W:** radiovenezuela.com. ve – **BO06)** Final Paseo Heres, Edif.Tovar, P2, Cd Bolívar 8001 – **BO07)** Paseo Meneses, Centro Comercial Meneses, PA, Locales 11 y 12, Cd Bolívar 8001 – **BO08)** Calle México, Parcela El Roble, Detrás de la Estación de Servicio Volfo, Sector La Antena, San Félix 8024 – **BO09)** Calle El Tocuyo, Centro Comercial Plaza, P2, Pto Ordaz 8015 – **BO10)** Av 19 de Abril, Edif La Disinca, P.B., Cd Bolívar 8001 – **BO11)** Calle Constitución N° 78, Caicara del Orinocco 7107 – **BO12)** Av.Della Costa, Edif.Flor Motors, PB, San Felix 8024.
CA00) CARABOBO
CA02) Av Bolívar Norte, Edif Felpo, P7, Ofc 3-3, Valencia 2001 – **CA03)** Calle Girardot, Entre Urdaneta y Boyacá N° 98-28, Valencia 2001 **W:** america890.net – **CA04)** Carr.Panamericana, Edif.Radio Mil, Morón – **CA05)** Av Rosarito, Torre Trebol, P1, Ofc 13, Calle Mones del Este, Valencia 2001 – **CA06)** Av.Bolívar Norte, Torre Banavén, P12, Ofc.12-9, Valencia 2001 **W:** deportesunionradio.net – **CA07)** Av.Rosario, Edif.El Parque, PB Local 2, Urb.Lomas del Este, Valencia 2001 **W:** radiovenezuela.com.ve – **CA08)** Av.Marina, Edif.Diproca, PB, Local 3, Puerto Cabello 2024. **W:** radiopuertocabello.com – **CA09)** Av Bolívar, Edif Sabatino, P1, Urb.Rancho Grande, Puerto Cabello 2024 – **CA10)** Final de La Calle Jacinto con Calles Ricaurte y Girardot, Edif.Radio Satélite, Guacara 2015 – **CA11)** Av.Montes de Oca, Edif.Don Pelayo, P12, Valencia 2001 **W:** unionradio.net/cultural - **FM:** 99.1MHz.
C000) COJEDES
C001) Av.Sucre, Edif.General Manuel Manrique, P3, Local 46, San Carlos 2201 - 0955-0400 **W:** unionradio.net
DC00) DISTRITO CAPITAL
DC01) Calle Nueva York Cruce con Av.Rio de Janeiro, Edif YVKE

Mundial, P1, Las Mercedes, Caracas 1060, Edo.Miranda **W:** radiomundial.com.ve – **DC02)** Final Calle Las Marías, Edif. Radio Nacional de Venezuela, entre Chapellín y Country Club, La Frorida, Caracas 1050, Edo. Miranda **W:** rnv.gov.ve **E:** infornv@gmail.com – **DC03)** Av.Francisco de Miranda, Multicentro Empresarial del Este, Edif. Libertador, P7, Núcleo A Chacao, Caracas 1060, Edo Miranda – **DC04)** Calle La Joya, Edif Cosmos PH, Chacao, Caracas 1060, Edo Miranda **W:** radiocontinente.jimdo.com – **DC05)** Av.Francisco de Miranda, Centro Comercial Los Ruices, P3, Los Ruices, Caracas 1071, Edo Miranda – **DC06)** Av José A Paez, Quinta RCR, El Paraiso, Caracas 1021, Distrito Capital – **DC07)** Av.Rómulo Gallegos, Edif.KLM, P12, Ofc CyD, Los Palos Grandes, Caracas 1062, Edo Miranda. **W:** radiovenezuela. com.ve – **DC08)** Av Santiago de Chile, Quinta Radio Sensación, Los Caobos, Caracas 1050 – **DC10)** Centro Comercial Concresa, Nivel 1, Circuito Center, Prados del Este, Caracas 1080, Edo.Miranda. **W:** fmcenter.com.ve/amcenter.aspx – **DC12)** Puente Nuevo a Puerto Escondido, Edif.Torre del Oeste, P1, El Silencio, Caracas 1010, Distrito Capital (or Ap.3674, Caracas 1010-A) **W:** ipdave.com.ve facebook. com/La-Voz-De-La-Liberacion-Venezuela-1513240865583338 – **DC13)** Av.Mohedano, Entre Calle Los Granados y 1ª transversal, Edif.Splendor, La Castellana, Caracas 1060, Edo.Miranda. **W:** unionradio.net/deportes – **DC14)** Av Los Mangos N° 49, Qta.Radio Tiempo, La Florida, Caracas 1050-A, Edo.Miranda **W:** radiotiempo.com.ve – **DC15)** Av Los Mangos con Av.Valencia Parpacén, Qta. Marisabel (BBN), La Florida, Caracas 1050, Edo.Miranda **W:** bbnradio.org/wcm4/spanish/Radio/Emisoras/tabid/646/StationID/236/Default.aspx – **DC16)** Centro Comercial Uslar, P15, Ofc 152, Montalbán, Caracas 1021, Distrito Capital **W:** radioideal.com.ve – **DC17)** Edif Mundial, Av Tamanaco, El Rosal, Caracas 1060. **W:** radiouno.com.ve – **DC18)** Calle 3B, Edif.C-207, P2, (detrás del McDonald's), La Castra, Caracas 1070, Edo.Miranda **W:** feyalegria.org comunicamundi.net/live/irfa.html – **DC19)** Av.Boulevard Brasil N° 74, de Santa Ana a Providencia La Pastora, Caracas 1010, Distrito Capital. **W:** radiodinamica.com – **DC20)** Av Circunvalación del Sol, Centro Profesional Sta Paula, Torre A, P5 Ofc 51, Caracas 1061, Edo.Miranda. **W:** radiodeporte.com – **DC21)** Calle La Joya, Torre Cosmos, P9, Ofc 9A, Chacao, Caracas 1060, Edo.Miranda (or Centro Comercial El Pichacho, P8, San António de los Altos 1204). **W:** radiosintonia1420.com.ve

FA00) FALCÓN
FA01) Calle Bolívar, Edif.Don Cosme, P2, Coro 4101 – **FA02)** Avenida Manaure esquina Maparari, Edificio Pepelupe, Coro 4101. **W:** radiocoro.com – **FA04)** Urb Los Caciques, Calle Falcón, Qta.Paraguaná, Punto Fijo 4102 – **FA05)** Calle Talavera, entre Calles Comercio y Arismendi, Edif.Radio Punto Fijo, Punto Fijo 4102 – **FA06)** Av.Ecuador, Entre Calles Comercio y Arismendi, Punto Fijo 4102 – **FA07)** Av.Bolívar, Edif.Colonial Planta Baja, Urb.Alta Vista, Puerto Cumarebo 4167 – **FA08)** Centro Ciudad Comercial Tamanaco (CCCT), Torre B, P7, Ofc 704, Chuao, Caracas 1060, Edo Miranda

GU00) GUÁRICO
GU01) Av RómuloGallegos, Edif.Flor de Pascua, Loc 2, Valle de la Pascua 2307. **W:** enlace860am.tk – **GU02)** Av Principal La Moreras, Edif.Ghersy N° 28, San Juan de los Morros 2301 – **GU03)** Calle Concordia, Qta Puerto Arturo N° 35, Zaraza 2332 – **GU04)** Cra 12, Altos del Teatro Paez, Frente a la Bomba, Calabozo 2312 – **GU05)** Av 5 de Julio N° 20, Valle de la Pascua 2307 **W:** unionradio.net – **GU06)** Calle Alegría, Qta.Galia, El Sombrero 2319 – **GU07)** Calle Andrés Eloy Blanco, Altagracia de Orituco 2320 – **GU08)** Cra 12, Entre Calles 3 y 4 N° 3-57, Calabozo 2312

LA00) LARA
LA01) Av Venezuela con Calles 13 y 14, Edif.Radio Cristal, Barquisimeto 3001 – **LA02)** Calle Sucre Entre Cras 7 y 8, La Casita, Carora 3040 - **FM:** 100.5MHz – **LA03)** Calle 4 con Cra 3, Qta.Técnica, Urb.del Este, Barquisimeto 3002 – **LA04)** Av Venezuela con Calles 32 y 33, Edif. Don Martín, P4, Apto 4-A, Barquisimeto 3001 – **LA05)** Av.Pedro León Torres, Centro Comercial Venrol, locales 29 y 30, Barquisimeto 3001. **W:** radiominuto.net – **LA07)** Calle 29, Entre Calles 18 y 19, Casa N° 18-74, Barquisimeto 3001 – **LA08)** Calle 10 cruce con Calle 9, Casa S/N, El Tocuyo 3018 – **LA10)** Av Bolívar, Edif Guillermo, Locales 2 y 3, Carora 3040 – **LA11)** Av Los Leones, Centro Empresarial Caracas, P5, Ofc 5-2, Barquisimeto 3002 **W:** unionradio.net

ME00) MÉRIDA
ME01) Calle 44 N° 3-57, Diagonal al Colegio de Médicos, Mérida 5101 **W:** radiomundial.com.ve – **ME03)** Av Gonzalo Pico, Bajando por La Facultad de Ingeniería, Qta.Radio Universidad, Mérida 5101 – **ME04)** Av Bolívar, Esquina Calle 11, N° 10-87, El Vigía 5145 – **ME05)** Av.Andrés Bello, Centro Comercial Las Tapias, P3, Ofc.40-41, Mérida 5101 **W:** radiocontinente.jimdo.ve – **ME06)** Av 3, Esquina con Calle 22, Mérida 5101

MI00) MIRANDA
MI01) Calle Urdaneta N° 29, Edif Radio Valles del Tuy, P1, Ocumare del Tuy 1209 – **MI02)** Edif. Electricidad De Caracas, Semi Sotano, Frente a

La Plaza Bolívar, Guarenas 1220 – **MI04)** Final Av.Tosta Gracía, Resd. Boal, Mezz.2, Charallave 1200.

MO00) MONAGAS
MO01) Cra 5 N° 33, Antigua Calle Boyacá, Maturín 6201 – **MO02)** Av Bolívar,Edif.Radio Monagas, P1, Maturín 6201 - **FM:** 93.5MHz – **MO03)** Calle Monagas, Edif Isnotú, PB, Maturín 6201 – **MO04)** Calle Sucre, Edif.Radio Maturín, PB, Maturín 6201 – **MO05)** Av Bolívar, Edif.Radio Dimensión, PB, Caripito 6211

NE00) NUEVA ESPARTA
NE01) Calle La Marina, Edif.Sta Rita, Nivel 3, Porlamar 6301 **W:** radiovenezuela.com.ve – **NE02)** Av Miranda, Edif.Best, P2, Porlamar 6301 – **NE03)** Calle Girardot, Urb.Cocheima, Edif Doña Teresa, P3, La Asunción 6311 **W:** radiomundial.com.ve

P000) PORTUGUESA
PO02) Cra 9, Esq Calle 15, Edif D'Zonno, P3, Apto 8, Guanare 3310 – **PO03)** Intercepción de la Autopista José António Páez con Carr. Nacional, Ospino 3319 – **PO05)** Av. 28 entre calles 26 y 27 del sector Campo Lindo del Municipio Páez, Acarigua – **PO06)** Av Peñalver con Calle 31, Edif.Los Andes, PB, Turén 3308 – **PO07)** Av Los Próceres, Urb. Francisco de Miranda, Edif.Radial, Guanare 3310

SU00) SUCRE
SU02) Av.Gran Mariscal Sucre N° 30, Cumaná 6101 **W:** circuito-radiocontinente.com – **SU03)** Calle Independencia con Calle Páez, Multinacional, P5, Radio Venezuela, Carúpano 6124 **W:** radiovenezuela. com.ve – **SU04)** Av Independencia 141, Edif Plaza, PB, Carúpano 6124 **W:** unionradio.net – **SU05)** Av Santa Rosa 18, Sector La Copita, frente a la Iglesia Santa Rosa de Lima, Cumaná 6101 **W:** radio2000.com.ve

TA00) TACHIRA
TA03) Calle 9 N° 8-16, San Cristóbal 5001 **W:** ecosdeltorbes.net – **TA05)** Av Las Lomas, Edif.Primo Centro, Locales 3-12 y 3-13, San Cristóbal 5001 – **TA06)** Av 19 de Abril, Qta.Circuito Lider, San Cristóbal 5001 – **TA07)** Pasaje Acueducto N° 24-60, Barrio Obrero, San Cristóbal 5001 **W:** unionradio.net – **TA09)** Av 19 de Abril con Av 8, La Concordia, San Cristóbal 5001 **W:** laculturalfm.com.ve – **TA11)** Cra 9 cruce con Calle 9, Edif.El Ciclón, P4, San Cristóbal 5001.

TR00) TRUJILLO
TR01) Av 11, entre Calles 12y13 N° 12-56, Valera 3101 – 1045-0400 **W:** radiosimpatia.com.ve – **TR02)** Av Bolívar con Calle 15, Edif.Grasso, P1, Valera 3101 – **TR03)** Av 10 entre Calles 9y10, Edif.Radio Valera, Local 9-31, Valera 3101 – **TR04)** Calle Independencia N° 10-11, Trujillo 3102 – **TR05)** Calle Iglesia, José Gregorio Hernández, Isnotu 3109 – **TR07)** CalleBolívar, Plaza la Alameda, Edif.Radio Jardín, Boconó 3103.

VA00) VARGAS
VA01) Av Soublette, Edif Las Américas B, P16, Maiquetía 1161 – **VA02)** 3era Norte Av Guaicaipuro, Quinta Mirna, Caracas **W:** radiomaria.org.ve

YA00) YARACUY
YA01) Av 10, Entre Calles 7y8, Edif.Alegría, Chivacoa 3202 – **YA02)** Prolongación 5ta Av.Urb.Andrés Eloy Blanco, Sector la Aduana, San Felipe 3201 – **YA04)** Av.Cartagena, entre Calles 19 y 20, Edif.Radio San Felipe, San Felipe 3201.

ZU00) ZULIA
ZU01) Calle Central, Edif.Radio Perijá, P2, La Villa del Rosario 4047 – **ZU02)** Calle 64 Esq.Av 3e, Edif.La Voz de la Fe, Sector Don Bosco, Maracaibo 4002 (or P.O.Box 459, Maracaibo 4002-A) – **ZU03)** Av El Muelle N° 1, Edif.Radio Libertad, frente a la Plaza Bolívar, Cabimas 4013 – **ZU04)** Av 11 N° 87-46, Edif 95.5, PB, Sector Veritas, Maracaibo 4002 – **ZU05)** Av 25 con Calle Paraíso N° 24-88, Maracaibo 4005 – **ZU06)** Av 3-E N° 63-50, Sector Don Bosco, Maracaibo 4002 **W:** feyalegria.org – **ZU07)** Calle 67 cruce con Av 27, detrás del Colegio La Epifanía, Sector Santa María, Maracaibo 4005 **W:** radiovenezuela.com. ve – **ZU08)** Av Edif.Radio Calendario, Sector Grano de Oro, frente al Stadium Alejandro Borges, Maracaibo 4005. **W:** radiocontinente.jimdo. ve – **ZU09)** Calle Radio Zulia, Av 23 con Calle 79 1 de Mayo,Maracaibo 4005 **W:** radiomundial.com.ve – **ZU14)** Av 3H, Edif.Plaza, Local 2, Sierra Maestra, Maracaibo 4008 – **ZU16)** Av 8 Esq Calle 73, N° 72-75, Edif Radiolandia, Sector Santa Rita, Maracaibo 4020 – **ZU20)** Iglesia de María en Pentecostés, Urb.San Jacinto, primera entrada, vía El Moján, Maracaibo 4005 – **ZU24)** Cra N Con Av.51, Zona Industrial, Cd.Ojeda 4019.

FM in Caracas (MHz): 88.1 Imagen – 88.9 Romántica – 89.7 X FM – 90.3 Unión Noti– 91.1 RNV Clásica – 91.9 Candela Pura Estrella – 92.9 Tu FM – 93.5 Melodía Stereo – 94.1 Hot 94 – 94.9 Clásicos FM – 95.5 Jazz – 96.3 Alba Ciudad – 96.9 X FM – 97.7 Em.Cultural – 98.5 La Radio del Sur– 99.1 La Nueva Mágica – 99.9 Éxitos – 100.7 Ateneo – 101.5 Kys – 101.9 Tiuna – 102.3 AN Radio, La Voz de la Asamblea Nacional – 102.7 Original – 103.3 Radiorama Stereo – 103.9 RNV Activa/Canal Juvenil – 104.5 Rumbera – 105.3 Planeta – 105.9 Sonera – 106.5 Fiesta 106 – 106.9 Playa 107 – 107.3 La Mega Estación107 – 107.9 Onda

VIETNAM

L.T: UTC +7h — **Pop:** 94.4 million — **Pr.L:** Vietnamese, ethnic — **E.C:** 50Hz, 220V — **ITU:** VTN

DÀI TIẾNG NÓI VIỆT NAM
(VOV, RADIO THE VOICE OF VIETNAM) (Gov.)
✉ 58 Quan Su Str, Hanoi ☎ +84 (4) 8255694 📠 +84 4 8265875
W: vov.vn **E:** qhqt.vov@hn.vnn.vn
L.P: DG: Nguyen Dang Tien. Dir Editorial Sce: Uong Ngoc Dau. Dir Tech Sce: Nguyen Xuan Huy

MW	kHz	Net	kW	Station, location, h of tr
1)	549	2	200	Hung Yen, (Site: My Hao): 2145-1700
1)	558	2	100	Ho Chi Minh C., Quan Tre: 2145-1700
1)	576	2,P	50	Khanh Hoa, Nha Trang: 2145-1700
1)	594	1	50	Danang, (Site: An Hai): 2145-1700
3)	610	H	20	Ho Chi Minh City, Tang Nhon Phu: 2100-1700
1)	630	1	200	Quang Binh, Dong Hoi: 2145-1700
1)	648	1	50	Binh Dinh, Quy Nhon, (Site: An Nhon): 2145-1700
1)	657	1	100	Ho Chi Minh C., Quan Tre: 2145-1700
1)	666	1	50	Khanh Hoa, Nha Trang: 2145-1700
1)	675	1	500	Hung Yen, (Site: My Hao): 2145-1700
4)	702	2,Q,D	50	Danang, (Site: An Hai): 2145-1700
1)	711	1	500	Can Tho, Thoi Long: 2145-1700
5)	±720	P	10	Dong Nai: 2200-1500 (Site: Quan Tre, Ho Chi Minh C)
1)	729	2	200	Quang Binh, Dong Hoi: 2145-1700
6)	740	2,P	50	Binh Dinh, Quy Nhon, (Site: An Nhon): 2145-1700
7)	756	P	10	Long An, Tan An: 2200-1100§
1)	783	2	500	Can Tho, Thoi Long: 2145-1700
1)	819	4	20	Dac Lac, Buon Ma Thuot: 2200-1600§
8)	828	P	10	Son La: 2200-1400§
9)	837	P	10	Can Tho: 2200-1200§
10)	846	P	10	Thanh Hoa: 0400-1030§
1)	873	1,3,4	500	Can Tho, Thoi Long: 2155-1700
11)	±900	P	10	Ha Tinh: 2200-1200§
12)	900	1,P	10	Kon Tum: 2200-1600§
5)	909	P	10	Dong Nai: 2200-1500
13)	972	1,P	10	Quang Ngai: 2155-1600§
14)	‡1035	P	10	Hoa Binh: 2215-1100§
15)	1089	P	10	Kien Giang, Rach Gia: 2200-1200§
16)	1089	P	10	Cao Bang
17)	1098	1,P	10	Binh Thuan (Phan Thiet): 2200-1100§
18)	1098	P	10	Thua Thien Hue, Hue: 2145-1145/1310§
19)	1125		5	Tay Ninh: 2200-1200§
20)	1170	P	10	An Giang, Long Xuyen: 2200-1330§
1)	1242	E	500	Can Tho, Thoi Long: 1300-1600

‡) r. inactive ±) variable fq. §) split schedule, see Regional stns below for details

SW	kHz	Net	kW	Location, h. of tr
1)	5925	2	50	Xuan Mai: 2145-1700
1)	5975	1	50	Hanoi: 2145-1700
1)	6020	4	20	Buon Ma Thuot: 2200-1600
1)	6165	1	50	Xuan Mai: 2200-2300, 2330-2400, 1130-1400
1)	7210	1	20	Buon Ma Thuot: 2145-1700
1)	9530	1	50	Xuan Mai: 2145-1700
1)	9635	1	100	Son Tay: 24h+
1)	9850	4	50	Xuan Mai: 0400-0600

+) transmission for Gulf of Tonkin area ‡) r. inactive at editorial deadline

SW Stations: Hanoi 50kW (Me Tri, G.C: 105.47E 21.01N). Xuan Mai (also known as CK2) 50kW (GC: 105.36E 20.53N). Buon Me Thuot 2x20kW (G.C: 108.03E 12.41N). Son Tay (see Int Radio section)
Netw.: 1/2/3: Voice of Vietnam 1st/2nd/3rd national prgr — **4:** Voice of Vietnam minorities network — **D:** Radio & TV Danang — **E:** Voice of Vietnam external sces — **H:** Voice of the People of Ho Chi Minh City — **P:** Provincial sce — **Q:** Radio & TV Quang Nam (Hoi An, Quang Nam Province).

FM: Most services are also carried by numerous FM stns. Details for Hanoi and Ho Chi Minh City are shown here, others in the address section where known. All FM powers shown are TRP.

FM(MHz)	Local	kW	VOV1	kW	VOV2	kW	VOV3	kW	VOV5	kW
Hanoi	90.0	10	100.0m	10	96.5t	10	102.7t	20	105.5m	5
Hanoi	96.0h	2								
HCMC	99.9	20	94.0d	10			104.5q	10	105.7q	10
HCMC	95.6	20								

Hanoi Radio & TV Station: ✉ 5 Huynh Thuc Khang, Dong Da District, Hanoi. d) Dong Hung Thuan, Hoc Mon. h) 2nd prgr, tx in Ha Dong. m) Me Tri. q) Quan Tre. t) Tam Dao in Vinh Phuc province
Prgrs. from Hanoi
VOV1, news & current affairs: 2145-1700. **FM:** Hanoi 100.0MHz,

Ho Chi Minh C. 94.0MHz, and also relayed in part by many regional sts. **N:** 2205, 2300, 0100, 0300, 0500, Mon-Sat 0630, 0700, Mon-Sat 0730, 0800, Mon-Sat 1000, 1100, 1230, MF 1330, 1430. SW freqs marked + relay VOV3 1700-2145
VOV2, economic, social, cultural & education prgrs: 2145-1700.
FM: Hanoi 96.5MHz 10kW, Son La (Deo Pha Din) 93.5MHz 20kW, Phu Yen 102.7MHz 5kW, Buon Ma Thuot 102.7MHz 5kW. **LL:** English 0600, French 0615, Chinese/Japanese/Vietnamese through English 0630 (repeated Mon-Sat 1600-1645)
VOV3, news & music prgrs: 24h on FM (freqs in MHz) Hanoi 102.7 20kW, Thanh Hoa 94.9, Quang Binh 96.1 MHz 5kW, Vinh 98.0 0.5kW, Hue 106.1MHz 10kW, Danang (Ba Na) 102.5MHz 10kW, Qui Nhon 103.1 10kW, Phu Yen (Tuy Hoa) 96.0 2.5kW, Dac Nong (Gia Nghia) 96.6 5kW, Dac Lac 102.7, Bing Thuan (Phan Thiet) 102.0MHz 5kW, Ho Chi Minh C. 104.5MHz 10kW, Tay Ninh 101.0MHz 20kW, An Giang (Nui Cam) 91.5MHz 20kW, Can Tho 90.0. Inc. **Hot Radio:** Mon-Sat 0200-0300, Sun 0300-0400; **Xone FM:** music prgrs for young people, 2300-0200, 0600-1600
VOV4, prgrs for ethnic minorities: Bana, Ede, Giarai, Hmong, K'Hor (Koho), Sedang, Thai, M'Nong: 2200-1600 on 819kHz, 6020kHz, Dac Lac (Buon Ma Thuot) 100.0MHz 5kW & Dac Nong (Gia Nghia) 101.5MHz 5kW for Central Highlands. **Dao, H'Mong (Ho Mong), Thai:** 2150-2300, 0000-0030, 1145-1400 on 6165kHz, 0400-0530 on 9850kHz for Northern Vietnam, also in whole or in part on Cao Bang (Phan Thanh) 97.0MHz 10kW, Dien Bien Phu 98.0MHz 2kW, Ha Giang (Quan Ba) 103.2MHz 10kW, Lai Chau (Muong Te) 101.5MHz 2kW, Lang Son (Mau Son) 101.0MHz 10kW, Son La (Deo Pha Din) 104.3MHz 10kW (FM freqs relay VOV1 or provincial stns at other times). **Co Tu:** 2330-2400, 0420-0450, 1230-1300 on Danang (Ba Na) 100.0MHz 10kW (freq. relays VOV1 at other times). **Cham, Khmer (Kho Me), Vietnamese:** 2155-1330 on 873kHz for the Mekong Delta (inc. relays of VOV1)
VOV5, prgrs for foreigners: Hanoi 105.5MHz, Ho Chi Minh City 105.7MHz. **Cambodian:** 0800-0830. **Chinese:** 0400-0430, 1100-1130. **English:** 0030-0130, 0500-0600, 0900-1030, 1200-1300, 1400-1500, 1600-1730. **French:** 0130-0230, 0600-0700, 1300-1330. **German:** 0000-0030 **Indonesian:** 0730-0800. **Japanese:** 0430-0500, 1330-1400. **Lao:** 0700-0730. **Russian:** 0230-0300, 0830-0900. **Spanish:** 1030-1100. **Thai:** 1130-1200. **Vietnamese:** 0300-0400, 1500-1600
VOV Traffic Channel (VOV Giao Thông): 2230-1800. **FM:** Hanoi (Me Tri) 91.0MHz 5kW, Ho Chi Minh C. (Quan Tre) 91.0MHz 5kW
VOV 24/7: 2300-1700 in English. **FM:** Hanoi/Ho Chi Minh C. 104.0MHz.
Ann: "Dây là Tiếng Nói Việt Nam, phát thanh tù Hà Nôi, thu dô nước Công Hòa Xã Hôi Chu Nghia Việt Nam"". Khmer: "Thini Vithayu Samlang Vietnam"

Regional stations

General remarks: Schedules shown are for provincial services on MW. Stns may also relay VOV1, especially at 2300-2330, 0500-0545/0600 and 1100-1130/1145 if they are on air at those times, but relays of VOV as a rule are not included in the schedules below. Several hundred FM stns are operated by local governments of county-level administrative divisions (*huyen* or counties, *thi xa* or county-level towns, and *quan* or urban districts). These generally transmit with powers in the 50-500W range and with limited hours, and in many cases relay the provincial stn or Hanoi at times.
Ann: Provincial sces usually identify as "Radio & TV (name of province)", in Vietnamese: "Dài Phát Thanh Truyên Hình (name)"

Addresses and other information:
1) National freqs. See above for details – **2)** 70 Tran Phu, Nha Trang. 2230-2200, 0430-0500, 1030-1100 - **FM:** 103.3MHz 0.1kW/106.5MHz 2kW + relays – **3)** 3 Nguyen Dinh Chieu, Dist. 1, Ho Chi Minh City. H: 2100-1700 in Vietnamese/Khmer - **FM:** 95.6/99.9MHz. Districts: Hoc Mon 93.0MHz, Nha Be 95.6MHz, Binh Chanh 103.4MHz, Can Gio 105.0MHz, Cu Chi 106.5MHz – **4)** Q: Tran Phu Road, Tan Thanh Ward, Tam Ky Town, Quang Nam: 2220-2245, 0400-0430, 1145-1215 - **FM:** 97.6MHz 2kW. D: 33 Le Loi, Hai Chau Ward, Da Nang. 2245-2300, 0430-0445, 1215-1315(SS 1400) - **FM:** 96.3MHz 5kW – **5)** Dong Khoi Road, Tam Hoa, Bien Hoa, Dong Nai - **FM:** 97.5MHz 10kW – **6)** 23 Mai Xuan Thuong, Quy Nhon City. 2230-2300, 0430-0500, 1145-1230 - **FM:** 97.0MHz 5kW, (Huai Nhon)99.9MHz 1kW – **7)** 125 National Road 1A, Ward 4, Tan An City. 2200-0030(Sat 0100, Sun 0315), 0430-0530, 1000-1110/1210 - **FM:** 96.9MHz 3kW – **8)** Group 12, Quyet Thang Ward, Son La Town. 2200-2400, 0400-0600, 1200-1400 in Vietnamese/Hmong - **FM:** 96.0MHz 2kW + relays – **9)** 213 30 Thang 4 St, Can Tho City. 2200-2400, 0400-0600, 0900-1100 - **FM:** 97.3MHz 5kW – **10)** 8 Hac Thanh St, Thanh Hoa City. 2200-2300, 0250-0600, 0930-1045 – **11)** 28 Phan Dinh Phung, Ha Tinh Town. 2200-2330, 0400-0600, 1000-1200 - **FM:** 93.6MHz 0.05kW – **12)** 258A Phan Dinh Phung St, Kon Tum. 2215-

2300, 2330-2400, 0345-0500, 1015-1100, 1145-1215 - **FM:** 95.1MHz 2kW – **13)** 165 Hung Vuong St, Quang Ngai City. 2230-2300, 0200-0300, 0400-0500, 0530-0545/0600, 0830-0900, 1000-1100 in Vietnamese/Kor - **FM:** 102.9MHz 5kW – **14)** 115 Tran Hung Dao St, Phuong Lam Ward, Hoa Binh City - **FM:** 97.5MHz 0.2kW – **15)** 39 Dong Da, Vinh Lac, Rach Gia Town. 2230-0030(Sun 0230), 0400-0600, 0900-1145/1200 in Vietnamese/Khmer - **FM:** 99.4MHz 5kW – **16)** 87 Be Van Dan Rd, Cao Bang Town. 2200-2300, 0300-0500, 1200-1400 - **FM:** 99.0MHz 5kW – **17)** 339-341 Thu Khoa Huan, Phan Thiet City, Binh Thuan Province. 2200-2300, 0400-0500, 1000-1100 - **FM:** 92.3MHz 5kW – **18)** 58 Huong Vong St, Hue. 2230-2300, 0400-0500, 0955-1100, occ. 1145-1310 - **FM:** 93.0MHz 2kW & 96.0MHz 0.02kW – **19)** 188 Ward 3, 30/4 Rd, Tay Ninh. 2200-2400(Sun 0230), 0400-0500, 1000-1200 - **FM:** 103.1MHz 5kW – **20)** 45/1 Tran Hung Dao, Long Xuyen City, An Giang Province. 2200-0015 (Sun 0145), 0330-0600, 0900-1330 in Vietnamese/Khmer. **FM:** 90.1MHz 0.1kW

Provincial sces operating on FM only (MHz):
Bac Giang 98.4 5kW; Bac Kan 99.3 2kW; Bac Lieu 93.8 2kW; Bac Ninh 92.1 2kW; Ba Ria Vung Tau (Nui Nho) 92.0 5kW; Ben Tre 97.9 2kW; Bing Duong (Thu Dau Mot) 92.5 10kW; Binh Phuoc (Dong Xoai) 89.4 2kW; Dac Lac (Buon Ma Thuot) 94.7 5kW; Ca Mau 94.6MHz 5kW; Dac Nong (Gia Nghia) 88.8 2kW, (Dak Mil) 95.5 2kW; Dien Bien (Dien Bien Phu) 96.3 1kW; Gia Lai (Pleiku) 93.7 2kW + relays; Ha Giang 92.0 2kW + relays; Hai Duong 104.5 5kW; Hai Phong 93.7 3kW; Ha Nam (Phu Ly) 93.3 2kW; Hau Giang 89.6 3kW; Hung Yen 92.7 2kW; Lam Dong (Da Lat) 97.0 2kW + relays; Lang Son 88.2MHz 1kW, (Mau Son) 101.0MHz 10kW; Lao Cai 91.0 5kW, 95.2 1kW & 97.0 10kW; Nam Dinh 95.1 2kW; Nghe An (Vinh) 99.6 10kW + relays; Ninh Binh 98.1 2kW; Ninh Thuan (Phan Rang Thap Cham) 95.0 5kW & 99.6 2kW; Phu Tho (Viet Tri) 106.0 5kW; Phu Yen 96.0 2.5kW; Quang Binh (Dong Hoi) 94.1 1kW; Quang Ninh (Ha Long) 97.8 10kW; Quang Tri (Dong Ha) 92.5 5kW;Soc Trang 100.4 2kW; Thai Binh 91.7 3.3kW; Tieng Giang (My Tho) 96.2 2kW; Thai Nguyen 106.5MHz 1kW; Tra Vinh 92.7 2kW; Tuyen Quang 95.6 2kW;Vinh Long 90.2 1kW; Vinh Phuc 102.7 2kW; Yen Bai 92.1 2kW + relays.

VIRGIN ISLANDS (AMERICAN) (USA)

L.T: UTC -4h — **Pop:** 106,000 — **Pr.L:** English, Spanish, Creole — **E.C:** 60Hz, 110V — **ITU:** VIR

FEDERAL COMMUNICATIONS COMMISSION (FCC)
see USA for details

MW	Call	kHz	kW	MW	Call	kHz	kW
1)	WSTX	970	5/1	5)	WSTA	1340	1
2)	WVWI	1000	5/1	4)	WDHP	1620	10/1
18)	WUVI	1090	0.25	3)	WIGT	1690	0.9
FM	**Call**	**MHz**	**kW**	**FM**	**Call**	**MHz**	**kW**
6)	WIVH	89.9	1.4	1)	WSTX	100.3	50
7)	WXZT	90.7	10	2)	WWKS	101.3	50
8)	WTJX	93.1	1.3	13)	WEVI	102.1	3.5
9)	WVSE	91.9	7.4	14)	WIUJ	102.9	1.5
10)	WVVI	93.5	9.6	4)	WAXJ	103.5	6
11)	WJKC	95.1	50	15)	WZIN	104.3	44
2)	WIVI	96.1	2.4	16)	WMNG	104.9	6
3)	WGOD	97.9	50	2)	WVJZ	105.3	30
12)	WMYP	98.3	1.9	17)	WVIE	107.3	1.7
11)	WVIQ	99.5	32	18)	WLDV	107.9	3.6

Addresses and other information
1) 2111 Company St, Suite 3, Christiansted, St. Croix 00820 ☎ +1 340 643-9789 **W:** wstxradio.com Stns: WSTX-AM on 970kHz: (news/sport/talk) & WSTX-FM on 100.3MHz (reggae) – **2)** Gark LLC, 13 Crown Bay Fill, PO Box 302179, Charlotte Amalie, St. Thomas 00803 ☎ +1 340 776 1000 **W:** amg.vi Stns: Pirate Radio on 96.1 (Top 40), KISS 101.3 FM (A/C), 105 JAMZ on 105.3 (CHR/rythmic) and Radio One on 1000kHz (News/talk/sport) – **3)** 22A Estate Dorothea, Box 305012, Charlotte Amalie, St. Thomas 00803 ☎ +1 340 774 4498 **W:** wgodvi.org Ann: WGOD–"The Word of God in The Caribbean – **4)** Reef Broadcasting Inc., 79A Castle Coakley, Christiansted, St. Croix 00820 ☎ +1 340 719 1620 📠 +1 340 778 1686 **W:** reefbroadcasting.com Stns: WAXJ 'The Reef' on 103.5MHz (News/talk) & WDHP on 1620kHz (Local Information/Music) – **5)** 121 Sub Base, St. Thomas 00802 ☎ +1 340 774 1340 **W:** lucky13wsta.com Ann: Lucky 13 – WSTA – **6)** Missionary Radio, 5007 Mt. Washington, Christiansted, St. Croix 00820 ☎ +1 340 718 2852 **W:** wivh.org Ann: "WIVH The Voice Of Hope" (Rlg.) – **7)** PO Box 8294, Christiansted 00823, St. Croix ☎ +1 340 277 7821. Ann: "Radio Latino 90.7" – **8)** PO Box7879, St. Thomas, VI 00801 & PO Box 808, St. Croix VI00821 ☎ +1 340 774 6255/718 3339 **W:** wtjx.org Ann: National Public Radio – **9)** Ste. 101 Barren Spot, Village Mall, Christiansted, St. Croix **W:** radiopapilove.com Ann: "Radio Papilove" (Spanish; Rlg)

– **10)** PO Box 25387, Christiansted, St. Croix 00824 ☎ +1 340 773 5935 Ann: "Caribbean Country" – **11)** JKC Communications/Radio 95, 5020 Anchors Way, PO Box 25680, Christiansted, St. Croix 00824 ☎ +1 340 773 0995 **W:** isle95.com Stns: Isle 95 on 95.1MHz (Urban/reggae) & Sunny 99.5 (A/C) – **12)** PO Box 25387, Christiansted, St. Croix 00824 ☎ +1 340 773 0995 Ann: Rumba 98.3 (Spanish/Tropical/Variety) – **13)** Lifeline, 15 Peter's Rest, Christiansted 00820 – ☎ +1 340 713 5433 Ann: Life Radio (Rlg.) – **14)** Virgin Isl. Youth Development Radio, PO Box 2477, Charlotte Amalie, St. Thomas 00803 ☎ +1 340 776 1029 **W:** wiuj.com (Pub./Educ.) – **15)** PO Box 306117, Charlotte Amalie, St. Thomas 00803 ☎ +1 340 776 1043 Ann: "The Buzz" (Active Rock) – **16)** Clara Communications Corp., PO Box 25680, Christiansted, St. Croix 00824 ☎ +1 340 713 9666 Ann: "Mongoose 104.9 FM" (Classic hits) – **17)** Virgin Islands Radio Entertainment Detroit, 160 Victor St, Highland Park, MI 48203-3130 ☎ +1 313 868 6612 **W:** wviefm1073.com – **18)** 1013 Western Suburbs, Christiansted, St. Croix ☎ +1 340 713 1079 **W:** dav-ybe.com Ann: "Da Vybe" – **19)** Penha House 3rd floor, 2 John Brewer's Bay, St. Thomas 00802 ☎ +1 340 643 1099 **E:** wuviradio@gmail.com **W:** wuvi.am Ann: "The Voice of the University" (College radio/rlg)

VIRGIN ISLANDS (BRITISH) (UK)

L.T: UTC -4h — **Pop:** 28,000 — **Pr.L:** English — **E.C:** 60Hz, 110V — **ITU:** VRG

VIRGIN ISLANDS BROADCASTING LTD. (Comm.)
✉ Baughers Bay, P.O. Box 78, Road Town, Tortola, BVI ☎ +1 284 494 2250/2430/6994 📠 +1 284 494 1139 **E:** zbvi@surfbvi.com **W:** zbviradio.com **LP:** MD: Meritt Herbert. GM: Harvey Herbert. Ops Mgr: Sandra Warrican. Production Mgr: Iris Jones
MW: ZBVI 780kHz 10kW **D.Prgr:** MF 0930-0130, SS 1100-0130.
Ann: "This is ZBVI Radio from Tortola"

Other Stations:
CSS - CARIBBEAN SUPER STATION: 90.9MHz 1kW (rel. Trinidad) – **ZCBN TRADEWINDS RADIO,** 2nd Floor Chevelle Center, Road Town, Tortola ☎ +1 284 340 3461 **W:** tradewinds923.com FM: 92.3MHz – **ZCCR,** Little Dix Hill Rd, East End, PO Box 41, Tortola ☎ +1 284 495 2861/2161/0461 📠 +1 284 495 1461 **W:** zccrfm.com FM: 94.1MHz 8.5kW. Ann: CCR Your Caribbean Christian Station. Format: Gospel – **ZJKC** FM: 90.9MHz (rel. Isle 95 WJKC, US Virgin Island) – **ZKING,** Christian Broadcasting Network, Horsepath, Road Town, Tortola ☎ +1 284 494 4600 📠 +1 284 494 8747. FM: 100.9MHz. Format: Rlg. – **ZROD,** 19 Flemming St.,P.O. Box 992, Road Town, Tortola ☎ +1 284 494 1037 📠 +1 284 494 4564. L.P: GM: Rodney Herbert. FM: 103.7MHz. Ann.: Z-Rod The Virgin Islands Best Music Mix – **Z.V.C.R.,** Main St., P.O.Box 43, Road Town, Tortola ☎ +1 284 494 6995/7305 **W:** zvcr1069fm.com FM: 106.9MHz

WAKE ISLAND (USA)

L.T: UTC +12h — **Pop:** 150 — **Pr.L:** English — **E.C:** 60Hz, 110V — **ITU:** WAK

THE QUAKE
✉ USAF Detachment 3, 13AF, PACAF/Chugach Federal Solutions Inc. PO Box 187, Wake Island 96898 ☎ +1 808 424 2101 **E:** baseops@ wakeisland.net **LP:** Comms Mgr: Colin Bradley **Prgr:** Local prgrs and automated music 24/7
FM: 104.5MHz
NB: Another 4 FM satellite radio prgr feeds are supplied from Armed Forces Radio

WALLIS & FUTUNA (France)

L.T: UTC +12h — **Pop:** 13,000 — **Pr.L:** French, Wallisian — **E.C:** 50Hz, 220V — **ITU:** WAL

WALLIS ET FUTUNA PREMIÈRE (Gov)
✉ B.P.102, Pointe Matala, 98600 Mata-Utu, Uvea, Iles de Wallis et Futuna (par Nouméa, Nouvelle-Calédonie) ☎ +681 681721300 📠 +681 681722346 **W:** wallisfutuna.la1ere.fr (live streaming) **D.Prgr:** 24h local and satellite relay from Paris

FM	MHz	FM	MHz
Sigave, Futuna	89.0	Hihifo, Uvea	101.0
Sigave, Futuna	90.0	Mua/Hahake, Uvea	103.0
Alo, Futuna	91.0		

RADIO Ô (Gov)
W: radioo.fr **D.Prgr:** 24h satellite relay from Paris
FM: Mua/Hahake, Uvea, 100.0MHz

YEMEN

L.T: UTC +3h — **Pop:** 24 million — **Pr.L:** Arabic — **E.C:** 50Hz, 220/230V — **ITU:** YEM

MINISTRY OF INFORMATION
P.O. Box 19560, Al-Zubairy St, San'a ☎+967 1 215116/7/8 +967 1 207716 **W:** yemeninfo.gov.ye **E:** yemen-info@y.net.ye
L.P: Nadia Al-Safaq, Minister of Information.

YEMEN GENERAL CORPORATION FOR RADIO & TV (YGCRT) (Gov.)
Tech. Dept, 26 September St, PO Box 2371, San'a ☎+967 1 282060 +967 1 282053 **W:** yemenrtv.net sanaaradio.net adenradio.net **E:** info@yemenradio.net, adenradio@yemen.net.ye
L.P: Mgr. Op. & Maintenance: Ali Al-Shiaani. Dir. Eng: Ali Al-Shyani. Head Tr. Station: Ismail Hussein Al-Nono.

MW	kHz	kW	Netw.	Times
Unknown location	602		G	-2300
San'a	711	200	G	1900-0300
Mukalla	756	50	G/L	1500-2300
Al-Hiswah	792	100	2	0300-0800,1100-2100
San'a	838	30	G	0300-1700v
Taiz	891		L	0300-2100
Hudaydah	909	750	G	1500-0300
San'a	1008	600	G	1400-2100
Taiz	1071	30	G	0300-0300
Hudaydah	1125	50	L	0300-2300
Al-Hiswah	1188	100	G	0300-2300

N.B: only 711 and 838 kHz have been reported active recently.
FM (MHz): Ad-Dali 96.7 5kW, Ad-Damigh 99.9 5kW, Aden 99.0 (G)/102.5 (2), Al-Ashmur 92.6 5kW, Al Hudah 88.6/98.0, Hudaydah 90.4 (L)/107.0 (G), Ibb 96.0 (G)/98.4 (L), Mukalla 91.5 (L)/98.5 (G), Riam 92.4 5kW, San'a 88.1 (G)/89.9 (L)/92.5 (2)/96.5 (Y), Sayun 89.5 (G)/95.4 (L), Taiz 88.1 (G)/89.0 (L), Shabwa 98.7MHz (L).
G=General prgr. from San'a: 0300-2215. **English:** 1800-1900.
2=Second prgr. from Aden: 0300-0800, 1100-2130 (Fri 0255-2130). **English:** 1600-1630. **French:** 1705-1725.
Y=Youth prgr. on 837kHz, 89.9/96.5MHz + 3 other trs.
L=Local prgr; times vary by station, between 0600-2100, also rel. General prgr. Mukalla R. frequencies are shared by Sayun R.
IS: Flute. **Ann:** "Idha'atu-I-Jumhuriyah al-Yamaniyah min San'a", Huna Adan, Idha'atu-I-Jumhuriyah al-Yamaniyah, il-barnamig at-thani". E: "This is Republic of Yemen Radio broadcasting from (town: San'a/Aden)"

ZAMBIA

L.T: UTC +2h — **Pop:** 12 million — **Pr.L:** English, Bemba, Lozi, Lunda, Nyanja, Tonga, Chichewa, others — **E.C:** 50Hz, 230V — **ITU:** ZMB

MINISTRY OF INFORMATION AND BROADCASTING SERVICES (MIBS)
P.O. Box 32020, Lusaka ☎/ +260 211 235410 **W:** mibs.gov.zm
L.P: Minister: Mike Mulongoti.

ZAMBIA NATIONAL BROADCASTING CORPORATION (ZNBC, Pub)
P.O. Box 50015, Mass Media Complex, Alick Nkhata Rd, Lusaka 10101 ☎+260 21 1251983 +260 21 1254920 **W:** znbc.co.zm (streaming: coppernet.zm) **L.P:** DG: Chibamba Kanyama. Actg. Dir. Tech. Sces: Mr. Malolela Lusambo. PD: Kenneth Maduma. PR Officer: Masuzyo Ndhlovu.

SW	kHz	kW	Sce.	Times
Lusaka	5915	100	R1	0245-2205
Lusaka	‡6165	100	R2	0245-2205

NB: 6165kHz expected to reactivate in the near future.

FM(MHz)	R1	R2	N	R4	kW
Chipata	93.3	96.5	94.9		1
Choma			105.7		
Kabwe				92.1	0.5
Kapiri Mposhi	97.5	94.3	91.1		1
Kasama	88.3	92.3	91.5		1
Kitwe	98.5	95.7	94.1	88.1	2
Livingstone	89.3	97.3	100.5	95.7	1/0.5
Lusaka	102.9	95.7	92.5	88.1	2
Mansa	88.3	92.3	91.5		1
Mongu	94.9	91.7	98.1		1
Solwezi	95.3	91.3	93.3		1

R. One in 7 Zambian languages: 0245-2205. – **R. Two in English:**

0245-2205. Relays VOA 2000-2100. – **N=National Assembly Channel – R. Four (music channel) in English:** 0240-2205. Also relays VOA.
Ann: E: "This is Radio Two of ZNBC broadcasting from Lusaka". Chichewa: "Kuno ndi ku Zambia National Broadcasting Corporation wa Lusaka." **IS:** "Call of the Fish Eagle".

Other stations (FM: MHz):
Breeze FM, Chipata: 99.6. **W:** breezefm.com – **Chikuni Community R**, Monze: 91.8 0.5kW. **W:** chikuniradio.org – **Choice FM**, Lusaka: 107.8. **E:** choice@microlink.zm – **Falls FM**, Livingstone: 90.1 – **Flava FM**, Kitwe: 96.4. **W:** flavafm.co.zm – **Horn FM**, Lusaka: 94.2 – **Pan African R**, Lusaka: 105.1. **W:** panafricanradio.org – **R. Christian Voice: FM:** Ndola 98.9, Kapiri 101.5, Kitwe 105.3, Lusaka 106.1. **W:** radiochristianvoicezambia.com – **R. Icengelo**, Kitwe: 89.1 – **R. Liambayi**, Mongu 101.9 – **R. Maria Zambia**, Chipata. **FM:** Kanjala 90 0.3kW. **E:** info.zam@radiomar.org F.PI: another tr in Lusaka – **R. Musi O Tunya**, Livingstone: 106 – **R. Phoenix**, 12th Floor, ZIMCO House, Cairo Rd, Private Bag E702, Lusaka. **W:** radiophoenix.co.zm **FM:** Lusaka 89.5, Kabwe 100, Kitwe 100.5, Chingola 104, Kapiri/Mposhi 104.5, Ndola/Luanshya 107.6 – **R. Q-FM**, 15th floor Indeco House, P.O. Box 30896, Lusaka **FM:** qfmradio.com **FM:** Lusaka 93.2, Kabwe 96.7, Choma 89.8, Kitwe 90.0, Mumbwa 89, Namwala 90.6 – **Sky FM**, P.O. Box 31165, Plot 55, Luwato Rd, Roma, Lusaka. **FM:** Choma 88.8, Zimba 93.8, Monze 95.1, Livingstone 102.4, Lusaka 104. **E:** skyfmbcast@zamtel.zm – **Yatsani R**, P.O. Box 320147, Bauleni, Lusaka: 99.1 2kW. **W:** yatsani.com
BBC African Sce: Kitwe/Lusaka 98.1 2kW.
RFI Afrique: Lusaka 100.5 2kW, Kitwe 92.5 1kW

ZIMBABWE

L.T: UTC +2h — **Pop:** 11 million — **Pr.L:** English, Shona, Ndebele, Chewa — **E.C:** 50Hz, 220V — **ITU:** ZWE

BROADCASTING AUTHORITY OF ZIMBABWE (BAZ)
1 Pennefather , Media Centre, Rainbow Towers Grounds, P.O. Box CY496, Causeway, Harare ☎+263 4 797382-5 +263 4 797375 **W:** baz.co.zw **E:** baz@comone.co.zw **L.P:** Chief Exec: Obert Muganyara.

ZIMBABWE BROADCASTING CORPORATION (ZBC, Gov)
P.O. Box HG 444, Broadcasting Centre, Pockets Hill, Highlands, Harare ☎+263 4 498610 **W:** zbc.co.zw **L.P:** DG: Henry Muradzikwa. CEO: Happison Muchechetere. Head Radio & TV: Abigail Mvududu.

FM (MHz)	R1	R2	R3	R4	kW
Beithbridge	-	98.1	-	105.2	
Bulawayo	90.0	96.3	99.6	103.1	10
Chiredzi	93.3	95.5	98.8	102.3	
Chivhu	93.3	96.5	103.3	106.8	
Gokwe	-	96.8	89.6	103.5	
Gwanda	105.8	95.4	98.7	102.2	
Gweru	90.7	93.9	97.2	100.7	5
Harare	92.8	96.0	99.3	102.8	10
Hwange	91.5	98.2	94.7	-	
Kadoma	88.5	94.8	98.1	101.6	10
Karoi	99.9	96.6	93.4	90.3	
Kenmur	90.4	93.5	96.7	-	
Lowveld	101.1	88.0	91.1	94.3	
Masvingo	106.5	92.9	99.4	102.9	
Mount Darwin	-	95.2	99.2	102.0	
Mutare	105.3	89.1	98.7	105.8	3
Mutorashanga	104.7	94.3	91.1	101.1	
Nyanga	105.5	91.7	94.9	101.7	
Sabi/Chipinge	94.5	97.8	101.3	-	
Victoria Falls	92.9	96.1	99.4	-	

F.PI: community radio stations: Sunshine R. in Harare and Skies R. in Bulawayo.
1) S-FM: mainly in English: 24h – **2) R. Zimbabwe:** in Shona/Ndebele/English: 24h – **3) Power FM:** youth programme in English: 24h. **N:** on the h. – **4) National FM:** in 14 minority languages: 24h. **Ann:** In addition to programme names: "ZBC".

Other stations:
Star FM: Harare 89.7MHz, Bulawayo 93.1MHz. **W:** starfm.co.zw
Zi FM: Mutare 95.4MHz, Masvingo 96.1MHz, Mutorashanga 97.6MHz, Nyanga 98.2MHz, Beitbridge 101.6MHz, Gweru 104.3MHz, Kadoma 1052.MHz, Harare 106.4MHz, Victoria Falls 106.5MHz, Bulawayo 106.7MHz. **W:** zifmstereo.co.zw
F.PI: **Breeze FM**, Victoria Falls. **Diamond FM**, Mutare. **Faya FM**, Gweru. **Gogogoi FM**, Masvingo. **KE 100.4 FM**, Harare. **Nyaminyami FM**, Kariba. **Skyz Metro FM**, Bulawayo. **Ya FM**, Zvishavane

INTERNATIONAL RADIO

Section Contents

Initial entries for each letter,
see Main Index for full details.

NB: The copy deadline for this section was 20 November 2015

Features & Reviews

National Radio

International Radio

Frequency Lists

National Television

Reference

Notes for the International Radio section

Country abbreviation codes are shown after the country name. The three-letter codes after each frequency are transmitter site codes. These, and the Area/Country codes in the Area column, can be decoded by referring to the tables in the Reference Section.

Where a frequency has an asterisk (*) etc. after it, see the '**KEY**' section at the end of the schedule entry.

The following symbols are used throughout this section:
† = Irregular transmissions/broadcasts;
‡ = Inactive at editorial deadline;
± = variable frequency;
+ = DRM (Digital Radio Mondiale) transmission.

Where transmitter details are given for a particular entity, the number of units shown represent the installed capability of the site, but do not reflect any details of txs being coupled/bridged (to increase overall power output), run at reduced power or remaining unused.
Should a site become decommissioned or dismantled, it is removed from the entry but if a site is merely dormant/inactive, it is then marked with the 'inactive' symbol, shown above.

If **Webcast:** is shown, the letter(s) after indicate the type of service(s) available: **D** = On Demand audio; **L** = Live audio; **P** = Podcast. For international services we have shown, where possible, languages available only via webcast. We do not include those broadcasters that have a foreign service available only via the internet, and are no longer broadcasting via MW/SW radio.

An alphabetical listing of **Religious Broadcasters**, cross-referenced by country, is given at the end of the section.

AFGHANISTAN (AFG)

RADIO TELEVISION AFGHANISTAN (Tx Operator)
⌨ See National Radio section.
E: radioafghanistan@yahoo.com **W:** www.rta.org.af
L.P: DG (R. Afghanistan): Abdul Ghaney Mudaqiq.
MW: [KAB] Kabul, Pol-e Charkhi: 1296kHz 400kW; [KHO] Khost, Tani: 621kHz 200kW (Both txs operated on behalf of IBB).
SW: [KAB] Kabul, Yakatut ‡: 1 x 100kW
Key: ‡ Inactive at time of publication.
Notes: RTA provides MW facilities for IBB (USA).

ALASKA (ALS)

KNLS INTERNATIONAL (Rlg)
⌨ P.O. Box 473, Anchor Point, AK 99556, USA. (Transmitting station)
☎ +1 907 2352326. 🖷 +1 907 2352326.
E: knls@aol.com **W:** www.knls.org (English); www.knls.net (Russian); www.smzg.org (Chinese)
Webcast: D
⌨ 605 Bradley Court, Franklin, TN 37067, USA. (World Christian Broadcasting HQ & studios)
☎ +1 615 3718707. 🖷 +1 615 3718791.
L.P: SM: Dave Dvorak; Chief Engineer: Kevin K. Chambers.
SW: [NLS] Anchor Point, AK: 2 x 100kW.
kHz: *6190, 7355, 9615, 9655, 9680*

Winter Schedule 2015/2016

Chinese	Days	Area	kHz
0800-1200	daily	EAs	7355nls
1300-1400	daily	EAs	9655nls, 9680nls
1400-1800	daily	EAs	9655nls
English	**Days**	**Area**	**kHz**
0800-0900	daily	EAs	9615nls
1000-1100	daily	EAs	9615nls
1200-1300	daily	EAs	7355nls, 9615nls
1400-1500	daily	EAs	9615nls
Russian	**Days**	**Area**	**kHz**
0900-1000	daily	EAs	9680nls
1100-1200	daily	EAs	9680nls
1500-1600	daily	EAs	9680nls
1600-1800	daily	EAs	6190nls

Ann: English: "This is Alaska calling. You are listening to station KNLS, Anchor Point, Alaska, United States of America."
V: QSL-card.

Notes: On air since 23 Jul 1983. KNLS is a SW transmitting station owned by World Christian Broadcasting, Inc. (WCB). See under USA for corporate details. FPI: 2nd transmitter to return on the air in spring 2015.

ALBANIA (ALB)

RADIO TIRANA (Pub)
⌨ Rruga Ismail Qemali 11, Tirana, Albania.
☎ +355 4 2223650. 🖷 +355 4 2223650.
E: radiotiranaenglish@live.com **W:** www.rtsh.al
Webcast: L
L.P: Dir: Alfons Zeneli; Technical Dir, RTSH: Agron Aranitasi; Head of RTV Monitoring: Mrs. Drita Çiço. (drita.cico@yahoo.com)
MW: [FLA] Fllaka: 1215/1395/1458kHz 500kW.
SW: [SHI] Shijak: 2 x 100kW.
kHz: *1395, 1458, 7390, 7465, 7470*

Winter Schedule 2015/2016

Albanian	Days	Area	kHz
0000-0100	daily	NAm	7465shi
0800-1000	daily	Eu	7390shi
0900-1000	daily	Eu	1395fla
1500-1630	daily	Eu	1458fla
English	**Days**	**Area**	**kHz**
0230-0300	.twtfss	NAm	7470shi
2100-2130	mtwtfs.	Eu	7465shi
French	**Days**	**Area**	**kHz**
1830-1900	mtwtfs.	Eu	7465shi
German	**Days**	**Area**	**kHz**
2030-2100	mtwtfs.	Eu	7465shi
Greek	**Days**	**Area**	**kHz**
1645-1700	mtwtfs.	Eu	1458fla
Italian	**Days**	**Area**	**kHz**
1900-1930	mtwtfs.	Eu	7465shi
Serbian	**Days**	**Area**	**kHz**
2115-2130	mtwtfs.	Eu	1458fla
Turkish	**Days**	**Area**	**kHz**
1930-2000	mtwtfs.	ME	1458fla

Ann: Albanian: "Radio Tirana per Bashkatdhetaret"; English: "This is Radio Tirana"; French: "Ici Tirana"; German: "Hier ist Radio Tirana"; Greek: "Sas milun ta Tirana"; Italian: "Parla Tirana"; Serbian: "Govori Tirana"; Turkish: "Burasi Tiran Radyosu".
V: QSL-card.

Notes: Radio Tirana (Radio Tirana 3) is the External Sce of the public broadcaster Albanian Radio & TV (Radiotelevizioni Shqiptar - RTSH)
CHINA RADIO INTERNATIONAL (CRI) RELAY
L.P: Mgr: Zhang Tianwei.
SW: [CER] Cërrik, Shtërmen: 6 x 150kW.
Notes: The Cërrik transmitting stn is owned by Radiotelevizioni Shqiptar (RTSH), and was leased to China Radio International for 15 years in 2003.

ALGERIA (ALG)

RADIO ALGÉRIENNE (Pub)
🖃 21 Boulevard des Martyrs, 16000 Algiers, Algeria.
☎ +213 21483790. 🖷 +213 21230823.
E: radionet@radioalgerie.dz **W:** www.radioalgerie.dz
Webcast: L
L.P: (ENRS) DG: Tewik Khelladi; Dir, Technical Services: Chibab Benchikh El Hocine.
SAT: Badr 6, Eutelsat 5WA/Hot Bird 13D, Galaxy 19, Nilesat 201.
kHz: *5865, 6145, 7295, 9380, 11775, 11985*

Winter Schedule 2015/2016

Arabic/French	Days	Area	kHz
0400-0700	daily	CAf,WAf	5865iss
0500-0600	daily	CAf,WAf	7295iss
1800-2000	daily	CAf,WAf	11985iss
1900-2100	daily	NAf,WAf	11775iss
2000-2200	daily	CAf,WAf	9380iss
2100-2300	daily	NAf,WAf	6145iss

Ann: Arabic: "Huna Al-Djazair".
V: QSL-card.
Notes: Relays of ENRS (Entreprise Nationale de Radiodiffusion Sonore) Home Sce 'Koran' prgr and Chaîne 1/3.

TÉLÉDIFFUSION D'ALGÉRIE (TDA) ‡ (Tx Operator)
🖃 BP 50, 16340 Alger, Algeria.
☎ +213 23181065. 🖷 +213 23181045.
E: contact@tda.dz **W:** www.tda.dz
L.P: DG: Abdelmalek Houyou.
SW: [BEC] Béchar: 1 x 250kW ‡; [ORG] Ouargla: 1 x 250kW ‡. F.pl: new SW tx centre at Sid Belabbes.
Key: ‡ Inactive at time of publication.
Notes: Télédiffusion d'Algérie is the national transmitter network operator. The tx centres at Béchar and Ouargla are under construction, completion not expected until c2016. A new External Service tx centre at Sid Belabbes is in the planning stage.

ANGOLA (AGL)

ANGOLAN NATIONAL RADIO (Pub)
🖃 C.P. 1329, Luanda, Angola.
☎ +244 222323172. 🖷 +244 222324647.
E: rna@rna.ao **W:** www.rna.ao
L.P: Chmn (RNA): Sebastiao Lino.
MW: [MUL] Luanda, Mulenvos: 945kHz 25kW.
SW: [MUL] Luanda, Mulenvos: 1 x 15kW.‡
kHz: *945*

Winter Schedule 2015/2016

English	Days	Area	kHz
2200-2300	daily	SAf	945mul
French	**Days**	**Area**	**kHz**
2100-2200	daily	SAf	945mul
Lingala	**Days**	**Area**	**kHz**
2000-2100	daily	SAf	945mul
Portuguese	**Days**	**Area**	**kHz**
2300-2400	daily	SAf	945mul

Key: ‡ Inactive at time of publication.
Ann: English: "International Service of Angolan National Radio".
V: QSL-card.

ANGUILLA (AIA)

CARIBBEAN BEACON (UNIVERSITY NETWORK RELAY)
🖃 P.O. Box 690, The Valley, Anguilla.
☎ +1 809 4974340. 🖷 +1 809 4974311.
E: beacon@anguillanet.com

L.P: SM/Chief Engineer: Eddie Sutton.
MW: [AIA] The Valley: 1610kHz 50kW.
SW: [AIA] The Valley: 1 x 100kW.
FM/DAB: FM: 100.1MHz (The Valley, 35kW), 0000-2400.
V: QSL-card.
Notes: Transmitting station owned by Melissa Scott (USA), carrying "University Network" programming (see main entry under "USA" for schedules).

ANTARCTICA (ATA)

RADIO NACIONAL ARCANGEL SAN GABRIEL (LRA36) (Gov)
🖃 Base Antártica Esperanza, CP 9411-Antártida Argentina, Argentina.
☎ +54 2974 445304.
E: lra36@hotmail.com
SW: [LRA] Base Antártica Esperanza: 1 x 10kW.
FM/DAB: FM: 97.6MHz (Base Antártica Esperanza, 24hrs)
kHz: *15476*

Winter Schedule 2015/2016

Spanish	Days	Area	kHz
1830-2130	mtwtf..	SAm	15476lra†

Key: † Irregular.
V: QSL-card/Letter. Rp. (1 IRC)
Notes: On air since 20 October 1979. Station is used as a way of keeping contact between servicemen/scientists stationed in the Antarctic, and their families in mainland Argentina and elsewhere.

ARGENTINA (ARG)

RADIODIFUSIÓN ARGENTINA AL EXTERIOR (RAE) (Pub)
🖃 Casilla de Correo 555, Correo Central, C1000WAF Buenos Aires, Argentina.
☎ +54 11 43256368. 🖷 +54 11 43259433.
E: rae@radionacional.gov.ar; argentinainternationalradio@gmail.com (English Sce) **W:** rae.com.ar
Webcast: L
L.P: Dir: Luis María Barassi.
SW: [BUE] Buenos Aires, General Pacheco: 2 x 50, 1 x 100kW.
kHz: *6060, 11710, 15345*

Winter Schedule 2015/2016

English	Days	Area	kHz
1800-1900	mtwtf..	Eu	15345bue
French	**Days**	**Area**	**kHz**
2000-2100	mtwtf..	Eu	15345bue
German	**Days**	**Area**	**kHz**
1700-1800	mtwtf..	Eu	15345bue
2100-2200	mtwtf..	Eu	15345bue
Italian	**Days**	**Area**	**kHz**
1900-2000	mtwtf..	Eu	15345bue
Spanish	**Days**	**Area**	**kHz**
1300-1530	mtwtf..	SAm	6060bue
1300-1530	mtwtf..	Eu	15345bue
1800-0000	.....ss	SAm	6060bue**
1800-0000	.....ss	Am	15345bue*
2200-2400	mtwtf..	SAm	6060bue
2200-2400	mtwtf..	Eu	15345bue
2200-2400	mtwtf..	Am	11710bue

Key: * Relay of RNA 870kHz, timing varies. ** Relay of R. Nacional Rock. Timings vary.
Ann: English: "This is RAE, the International Service of the Argentine Radio", "RAE, Buenos Aires". **V:** QSL-card.
Notes: RAE is the External Sce of the national public-service broadcaster Radio y Televisión Argentina (RTA S.E.).

ARMENIA (ARM)

PUBLIC RADIO OF ARMENIA (FOREIGN SERVICE) (Pub)
🖃 A. Manoogian Street 5, 0025 Yerevan, Armenia.
☎ +374 10 558010. 🖷 +374 10 551513.
E: ak@arradio.am **W:** armradio.info
Webcast: D
L.P: Dir, Foreign Service: Amasia Hovhannisyan.

MW/SW: Via Gavar transmitting station.
kHz: *1314, 4810*

Winter Schedule 2015/2016

Arabic	Days	Area	kHz
1900-1930	daily	ME	4810erv

Assyrian	Days	Area	kHz
1530-1545	daily	ME	4810erv

Azeri	Days	Area	kHz
1145-1200	daily	ME	1314erv, 4810erv
1200-1215	mtwtf..	ME	1314erv, 4810erv

Farsi	Days	Area	kHz
1430-1500	daily	ME	4810erv

Greek	Days	Area	kHz
1615-1630	daily	ME	4810erv

Kurdish	Days	Area	kHz
1230-1300	daily	ME	1314erv
1545-1615	daily	ME	4810erv

Turkish	Days	Area	kHz
1200-1215	.....ss	ME	1314erv, 4810erv
1215-1230	daily	ME	1314erv, 4810erv

Yezidi*	Days	Area	kHz
0600-0630	daily	ME	1314erv
1500-1530	daily	ME	4810erv

Key: * Kurmanji Kurdish (designated "Yezidi" in Armenia).
Ann: Arabic: "Huna Idha'at Jumhuriyat al-Yermaniyah min Yerevan".
V: QSL-card. Rp. (1 IRC)
Notes: Times may be changed or broadcasts may be cancelled without notice. In some languages the prgrs identify as "Voice of Armenia".

AR RADIO INTERCONTINENTAL (Tx Operator)
✉ A.Manoogian Street 5, 0025 Yerevan, Armenia.
☎ +374 10 551143. 🖷 +374 10 554600.
E: aa@arradio.am **W:** www.arradio.am
LP: DG: Armen Amiryan; CEO: Hrachya Kostanyan.
MW: [ERV] Gavar, Noratus: 864/1350/1377kHz 1000kW.

RADIO CJSC (Tx Operator)
✉ 3333 Noratus, Armenia.
☎ +374 99 706767.
E: info@radio-int.am **W:** www.radio-int.am
LP: Dir: Gagik Aloyan.
MW: [ERV] Gavar, Noratus: 1314kHz 1000kW ‡, 1395kHz 500kW.
SW: [ERV] Gavar, Noratus: 4 x 100, 3 x 1000kW
Notes: Radio CJSC is the operator of high power transmitting facilities in Armenia.

ASCENSION ISLAND (ASC)

BBC ATLANTIC RELAY STATION
✉ English Bay, Ascension Island, ASCN 1ZZ.
☎ +247 4458. 🖷 +247 6117.
SW: [ASC] English Bay: 6 x 250kW.
V: QSL-letter. (For direct report)
Notes: Owned by the BBC and operated by Babcock Media Services (see under United Kingdom).

AUSTRALIA (AUS)

ABC RADIO AUSTRALIA (Pub)
✉ G.P.O Box 9994, Melbourne, VIC 3001, Australia.
☎ +61 3 96261500. 🖷 +61 3 96261899.
E: Via website. **W:** www.radioaustralia.net.au
Webcast: D/L/P
LP: CEO (ABC International): Lynley Marshall; COO (ABC Int'l): Anne Milne; Head (Eng): Adrian Potter.
SW: Leased from Broadcast Australia.
SAT: Intelsat 18/20, SES 7.
kHz: *9580, 12065, 12085, 15240, 15415, 17840*

Winter Schedule 2015/2016

English	Days	Area	kHz
0630-0700	.....ss	Pac	15240shp, 15415shp, 17840shp
0700-0800	daily	Pac	15240shp, 15415shp, 17840shp

English	Days	Area	kHz
0800-0805	.....ss	Pac	15240shp, 15415shp, 17840shp
0805-0900	daily	Pac	15240shp, 15415shp, 17840shp
0900-0930	.....ss	Pac	9580shp, 12065shp, 12085shp
0930-2100	daily	Pac	9580shp, 12065shp, 12085shp
2100-0630	daily	Pac	15240shp, 15415shp, 17840shp

French	Days	Area	kHz
0800-0805	mtwtf..	Pac	15240shp, 15415shp, 17840shp

Tok Pisin	Days	Area	kHz
0630-0700	mtwtf..	Pac	15240shp, 15415shp, 17840shp
0900-0930	mtwtf..	Pac	9580shp, 12065shp, 12085shp

Ann: English: "This is Radio Australia broadcasting from studios in Melbourne, Victoria".
IS: "Waltzing Matilda" prior to opening, on all freqs. Foreign language broadcasts start with the laugh of the Kookaburra.
V: Does not verify reception reports, and no longer issues QSL cards.
Notes: Radio Australia is the External Sce of the public service Australian Broadcasting Corporation (ABC).

REACH BEYOND AUSTRALIA (Rlg)
✉ P.O. Box 291, Kilsyth, VIC 3137, Australia.
☎ +61 3 87208000. 🖷 +61 3 87208020.
E: radio@reachbeyond.org.au **W:** www.reachbeyond.org.au
Webcast: P
✉ Lot 579, Packsaddle Rd, Kununurra, WA 6743, Australia. (Transmitter Site)
☎ +61 8 91669000. 🖷 +61 8 91669001.
LP: CEO: Dale Stagg; Frequency Mgr: Ken Lingwood.
SW: [KNX] Kununurra: 4 x 100kW.
kHz: *9625, 9695, 9720, 15340, 15400, 15430, 15525, 15550, 17760*

Winter Schedule 2015/2016

Bengali	Days	Area	kHz
1315-1330	.....s.	As	15340knx
1400-1415	m......	As	15340knx
1415-1430	m......	As	9720knx

Bhojpuri	Days	Area	kHz
1315-1330	.t.....	As	15340knx

Burmese	Days	Area	kHz
1130-1145	.t.t...	As	15430knx

Cantonese	Days	Area	kHz
1145-1215	mtwtf..	As	15550knx
2300-2330	mtwt.s	As	15525knx

Chhattisgarhi	Days	Area	kHz
1400-1415	.....ss	As	9720knx

Chin (Falam)	Days	Area	kHz
1115-1145	..w..s.	As	15430knx

Chin (Haka)	Days	Area	kHz
1130-1145	m..f..	As	15430knx

Chinese	Days	Area	kHz
1145-1245	.....ss	As	15550knx
1215-1245	mtwtf..	As	15550knx
2230-2300	mtwt.s	As	15525knx
2300-2400	....fs.	As	15525knx

Dzongkha	Days	Area	kHz
1300-1315	...f..	As	15340knx

English	Days	Area	kHz
1115-1130	mt.tf.s	As	15430knx
1130-1145	......s	As	15430knx
1330-1345	....f..	As	9720knx, 15340knx
1445-1600	daily	As	15340knx

Gujarati	Days	Area	kHz
1400-1415	...f..	As	15340knx
1415-1430	...f..	As	9720knx

Hindi	Days	Area	kHz
1330-1345	mtwt.ss	As	9720knx
1330-1400	mtwt.ss	As	15340knx

Hindi	Days	Area	kHz
1345-1400	...f..	As	15340knx
1345-1400	daily	As	9720knx
1400-1415	..w..s	As	15340knx
1415-1430	..w....	As	9720knx

Indonesian	Days	Area	kHz
1215-1245	mtwtfs.	As	9695knx
1245-1300	daily	As	9695knx
2230-2245	daily	As	9625knx

Japanese	Days	Area	kHz
1100-1130	.....ss	As	15400knx
2230-2300	...fs.	As	17760knx

Kuruk	Days	Area	kHz
1315-1330	..w....	As	15340knx
1400-1415	..w....	As	9720knx

Malayalam	Days	Area	kHz
1400-1415	m......	As	9720knx
2200-2230	......s	As	9625knx

Malaysian	Days	Area	kHz
1215-1245	......s	As	9695knx

Marathi	Days	Area	kHz
1315-1330	....f..	As	15340knx
1400-1415	....f..	As	9720knx

Marwari	Days	Area	kHz
1400-1415	.t.....	As	15340knx
1415-1430	.t.....	As	9720knx

Nepali	Days	Area	kHz
1300-1315	.twt..s	As	15340knx
1300-1330	m......	As	15340knx

Oriya	Days	Area	kHz
1300-1315	.....s.	As	15340knx

Punjabi	Days	Area	kHz
1315-1330	.....s	As	15340knx

Rawang	Days	Area	kHz
1145-1215	daily	As	15430knx

Tamil	Days	Area	kHz
1415-1430	.....ss	As	9720knx
1430-1445	mtwtf.s	As	9720knx

Telugu	Days	Area	kHz
1400-1415	.t.t...	As	9720knx
1415-1430	...t...	As	9720knx

Tibetan	Days	Area	kHz
1100-1115	......s	As	15430knx
1315-1330	...t...	As	15340knx

Urdu	Days	Area	kHz
1400-1415	.....s.	As	15340knx
1400-1415	...t...	As	15340knx
1415-1445	daily	As	15340knx
1430-1445	.....s.	As	9720knx

Vietnamese	Days	Area	kHz
1100-1115	.t.f..	As	15340knx

Ann: English: "This is Reach Beyond Australia".
V: QSL-card.
Notes: Former name: HCJB Australia. Partner organisation of World Radio Missionary Fellowship, Inc (USA) and its media ministry Reach Beyond.

BROADCAST AUSTRALIA (Tx Operator)
✉ P.O. Box 1212, Crows Nest, NSW 1585, Australia.
☎ +61 2 8113 4666. 🖷 +61 2 8113 4646.
E: info@broadcastaustralia.com.au
W: www.broadcastaustralia.com.au
✉ Level 10, Tower A, 799 Pacific Highway, Chatswood, NSW 2067, Australia. (HQ)
L.P: Chmn: Gerry Moriarty; Group CEO: Jim Hassell.
SW: [BRN] Brandon: 3 x 10kW; [SHP] Shepparton: 7 x 100kW.
Notes: Broadcast Australia is the national transmitter network operator and is owned by Canada Pension Plan Investment Board (CPPIB). Has purchased 2 x100kW DRM-ready transmitters for use at Shepparton and Tenant Creek.

AUSTRIA (AUT)

RADIO Ö1 INTERNATIONAL (ORF) (Pub)
✉ Argentinierstrasse 30a, A-1040 Wien, Austria.
☎ +43 1 5010116060. 🖷 +43 1 5010116066.
E: roi.service@orf.at **W:** oe1.orf.at
Webcast: D/L/P
L.P: DG (ORF): Dr. Alexander Wrabetz.
SW: Uses txs provided by ORS.
SAT: Astra 1N.
kHz: 6155

Winter Schedule 2015/2016

German	Days	Area	kHz
0600-0715	daily	Eu,NAf,ME	6155mos

V: QSL-letter.
Notes: Relays of ORF's domestic service "Österreich 1" (Ö1).

TWR EUROPE (Rlg)
✉ Postfach 141, A-1235 Wien, Austria.
☎ +43 1 863120. 🖷 +43 1 8631220.
E: twre@twr.com **W:** www.twreurope.org
Webcast: D
✉ Other European branches: P.O. Box 176, 3780 BD Voorthuizen, The Netherlands; P.O. Box 12, 820 02 Bratislava 22, Slovakia.
L.P: Dir: Felix Widme.
SAT: Astra 2G (TWR UK)
kHz: 864, 999, 1035, 1233, 1287, 1350, 1377, 1395, 1467, 1548, 5910, 7215, 7300, 7320, 7375, 9470

Winter Schedule 2015/2016

Arabic	Days	Area	kHz
2000-2100	daily	ME	1377erv
2025-2155	daily	RUS	1233cgr
2230-2315	daily	NAf,ME	1467rou

Belarusian	Days	Area	kHz
1500-1530	m......	Eu	7375nau, 9470mos
2000-2100	m......	Eu	999kch

Bosnian	Days	Area	kHz
1945-2030	......s	Eu	1395fla

Bulgarian	Days	Area	kHz
1800-1830	daily	Eu	1548kch

Chechen	Days	Area	kHz
1740-1755	...t...	RUS	864erv

Croatian	Days	Area	kHz
1915-2030	.....s.	Eu	1395fla
1930-1945	.....s.	Eu	1395fla
1930-2000	mtwtf..	Eu	1395fla

English	Days	Area	kHz
1445-1500	daily	CAs	1287bis

Farsi	Days	Area	kHz
1815-1830	mtwt.ss	ME	1377erv
1830-2000	daily	ME	1377erv

Hebrew	Days	Area	kHz
1845-1915	mtwt.ss	ME	1350erv

Hungarian	Days	Area	kHz
0930-1000	daily	Eu	7215nau
1825-1900	daily	Eu	1395fla

Kabyle	Days	Area	kHz
2115-2145	mtw.fs.	NAf	1467rou
2115-2200	...t..s	NAf	1467rou

Karakalpak	Days	Area	kHz
1640-1655	.....ss	RUS	864erv
1655-1710	.....s.	RUS	864erv

Kazakh	Days	Area	kHz
1500-1530	daily	CAs	1287bis
1625-1640	daily	CAs	864erv

Kumyk	Days	Area	kHz
1740-1755	....f..	RUS	864erv

Kurdish (Kurmanji)	Days	Area	kHz
1800-1815	daily	ME	1350erv

Kurdish (Sorani)	Days	Area	kHz
1800-1815	daily	ME	1377erv

Lak	Days	Area	kHz
1740-1755	..w....	RUS	864erv

Lezgi	Days	Area	kHz
1740-1755	.t.....	RUS	864erv

Montenegrin	Days	Area	kHz
1945-2000	.....s.	Eu	1548kch

Polish	Days	Area	kHz
0645-0700	mtwtf..	Eu	5910mos

Polish	Days	Area	kHz
0800-0815	mtwtf..	Eu	7320mos
1900-1915	.....s.	Eu	1395fla
1900-1930	mtwtf.s	Eu	1395fla
Qashqai	**Days**	**Area**	**kHz**
1815-1830	....f..	ME	1377erv
Romani (Balkan)	**Days**	**Area**	**kHz**
1830-1845	daily	Eu	1548kch
Romani (Vlax)	**Days**	**Area**	**kHz**
1915-1945	mtwtf..	Eu	1548kch
Romanian	**Days**	**Area**	**kHz**
1845-1915	mtwtf..	Eu	1548kch
1845-1945	.....ss	Eu	1548kch
Russian	**Days**	**Area**	**kHz**
0200-0400	daily	RUS	1035ttu
1500-1530	.twtfss	RUS	7300nau, 9470mos
1600-1700	m.w.f.	RUS	1035ttu
1630-1700	daily	CAs	1287bis
1640-1710	mtwtf.	RUS	864erv
1715-1730	daily	CAs	1287bis
1800-2000	daily	RUS	1035ttu
1845-1915	....f..	RUS	1350erv
1930-2000	m......	RUS	999kch
1930-2030	.t....s	RUS	999kch
1945-2015	.....s.	RUS	999kch
2000-2030	..wtf..	RUS	999kch
Serbian	**Days**	**Area**	**kHz**
1945-2000	mtwtfs.	Eu	1548kch
2000-2030	mtwtf..	Eu	1395fla
Sous/Tachelhit	**Days**	**Area**	**kHz**
2145-2200	....f..	NAf	1467rou
Tabassaran	**Days**	**Area**	**kHz**
1740-1755	m......	RUS	864erv
Tachawit	**Days**	**Area**	**kHz**
2145-2200	.....s.	NAf	1467rou
Tajik	**Days**	**Area**	**kHz**
1700-1715	daily	CAs	1287bis
Tamazight	**Days**	**Area**	**kHz**
2145-2200	m.w....	NAf	1467rou
Tarifit	**Days**	**Area**	**kHz**
2145-2200	.t.....	NAf	1467rou
Tatar	**Days**	**Area**	**kHz**
1740-1755	.....s.	RUS	864erv
Turkish	**Days**	**Area**	**kHz**
1815-1845	daily	ME	1350erv
Turkmen	**Days**	**Area**	**kHz**
1610-1625	daily	CAs	864erv
Ukrainian	**Days**	**Area**	**kHz**
1900-1930	mt....s	Eu	999kch
1900-1945	.....s.	Eu	999kch
1900-2000	..wtf..	Eu	999kch
2015-2030	.....s.	Eu	999kch
Uyghur	**Days**	**Area**	**kHz**
1600-1630	daily	CAs	1287bis
Uzbek	**Days**	**Area**	**kHz**
1530-1600	daily	CAs	1287bis
1655-1740	.....s	CAs	864erv
1710-1740	mtwtfs.	CAs	864erv
1730-1745	daily	CAs	1287bis

Ann: English: "This is Trans World Radio. The following programme is in the ... language".
V: QSL-card.
Notes: TWR regional division, covering Europe, Russia, Central Asia, the Near & Middle East. For corporate details, see under TWR (USA).

ÖSTERREICHISCHE RUNDFUNKSENDER GMBH & CO KG (ORS) (Tx Operator)
✉ Würzburggasse 30, A-1136 Wien, Austria.
☎ +43 1 87012680. 🖷 +43 1 8704012773.
E: office@ors.at **W:** www.ors.at
LP: CEO: Michael Wagenhofer, MD: Norbert Grill.
SW: [MOS] Moosbrunn: 4 x 100, 2 x 500kW.
Notes: ORS is the national transmitter network operator.

AZERBAIJAN (AZE)

VOICE OF AZERBAIJAN (Gov)
✉ M. Hüseyn Street 1, AZ 1011 Baki, Azerbaijan.
☎ +994 12 4927851. 🖷 +994 12 4398505.
E: info@aztv.az **W:** www.aztv.az
LP: PD: Hafiz Nagioglu.
MW: Leased from Teleradio IB.
SAT: AzerSpace 1/Africasat 1A.
kHz: *1296*

Winter Schedule 2015/2016

Arabic	Days	Area	kHz
1700-1800	daily	Cau,WAs	1296hqb
Armenian	**Days**	**Area**	**kHz**
0900-1000	daily	Cau,WAs	1296hqb
Azeri	**Days**	**Area**	**kHz**
0500-0800	daily	Cau,WAs	1296hqb
1400-1700	daily	Cau,WAs	1296hqb
Azeri/Armenian	**Days**	**Area**	**kHz**
1300-1400	daily	Cau,WAs	1296hqb*
Farsi	**Days**	**Area**	**kHz**
1100-1200	daily	Cau,WAs	1296hqb
Russian	**Days**	**Area**	**kHz**
1800-1830	daily	Cau,WAs	1296hqb
Turkish	**Days**	**Area**	**kHz**
0800-0900	daily	Cau,WAs	1296hqb
1000-1100	daily	Cau,WAs	1296hqb
1200-1300	daily	Cau,WAs	1296hqb

Key: * Prgr "Vätan" (Homeland) for listeners in Mountainous Karabagh.
Notes: External Sce of the national, state-owned broadcasting company "Azerbaijan TV and Radio Broadcasting". During 1992-1998 the transmissions also identified as "R. Dada Gorgud". The schedule is based on monitoring sources and is not complete; not all details have been confirmed at editorial deadline (official schedule not received), some trs may not be daily. Additional languages (times yet to be established): Georgian (three times a week 15min), as well as broadcasts for ethnic minorities in Azerbaijan in Kurdish, Lezgian and Talysh (twice a week each for 15-20min).

TELERADIO IB (Tx Operator)
✉ A. Abbaszadä küç 2, AZ 1004 Baki, Azerbaijan.
☎ +994 12 4988066. 🖷 +994 12 4988397.
E: info@teleradio.az **W:** teleradio.az
LP: DG: Äflatun M. Särifov.
MW: [HQB] Haciqabul, Pirsaat: 1296kHz 125kW.
Notes: Teleradio IB, a subsidiary of the Azerbaijani Ministry of Communications and High Technologies, is the owner of the transmitter facilities in Azerbaijan.

BAHRAIN (BHR)

RADIO BAHRAIN (Gov)
✉ See National Radio section.
Webcast: L (www.bna.bh/portal/radio)
LP: CEO: Ahmed Najim; Dir, Broadcasting: Hamad Al-Manai; Dir, Technical: Abdulla Ahmed Al-Balooshi.
SW: [ABH] Abu Hayan: 2 x 60kW.
SAT: Badr 4.
kHz: *9745*

Winter Schedule 2015/2016

Arabic	Days	Area	kHz
0000-2400	daily	ME	9745abh*

Key: * H3E (AM/U) mode, relays Shabab FM.
Ann: Arabic: "Idhaat al-Bahrain".
IS: Local composition, played on guitar and violin.
V: QSL-letter.
Notes: Relays Home Sce prgrs.

BANGLADESH (BGD)

BANGLADESH BETAR (Pub)
✉ 121 Kazi Nazrul Islam Avenue, Shah Bagh, Dhaka-1000, Bangladesh.
☎ +880 2 8618119. (Ext. Sce) 🖷 +880 2 8612012.
E: ts-betar@bdonline.com; betar.external@yahoo.com (Dir, Ext Sce)

W: www.betar.gov.bd
Webcast: D/L
☎ +880 2 8651083. (DG) 🖷 +880 2 9662600. (DG)
L.P: DG: Kazi Akhtar Uddin Ahmed; Deputy DG (Prgr): A. S. M. S. Apel Mahmood; Dir, External Sce: Setab Uddin Ahmed.
SW: [DKA] Dhaka, Khabirpur: 2 x 250kW.
kHz: 7250, 9455, 13580, 15105, 15505

	Winter Schedule 2015/2016		
Arabic	**Days**	**Area**	**kHz**
1600-1630	daily	ME	7250dka
Bengali	**Days**	**Area**	**kHz**
1630-1730	daily	ME	7250dka
1915-2000	daily	Eu	13580dka
English	**Days**	**Area**	**kHz**
1230-1300	daily	SEA	15105dka
1745-1900	daily	Eu	13580dka
Hindi	**Days**	**Area**	**kHz**
1515-1545	daily	SAs	15505dka
Nepali	**Days**	**Area**	**kHz**
1315-1345	daily	SAs	9455dka
Urdu	**Days**	**Area**	**kHz**
1400-1430	daily	SAs	15505dka

Ann: English: "This is the External Service of Bangladesh Betar".
IS: Local composition, played on violin and tanpura.
V: QSL-card (Rpt to Senior Engineer, Research and Receiving Centre. Email rpt to: rrc@dhaka.net)
Notes: External service of the national public broadcaster Bangladesh Betar, which began broadcasting on 1 Jan 1972.

BELARUS (BLR)

BELARUSKAJE RADYJO (Gov)
🖃 See National Radio section.
Webcast: L
kHz: 1170, 6080, 7255

	Winter Schedule 2015/2016		
Belarusian	**Days**	**Area**	**kHz**
0400-0700	daily	RUS	1170sas, 7255mns
1500-1700	daily	RUS	7255mns
1500-2100	daily	UKR	6080mns

V: QSL-card.

RADIO BELARUS (Gov)
🖃 Cyrvonaja Street 4, 220807 Minsk, Belarus.
☎ +375 17 2395852. 🖷 +375 17 2848574.
E: radio_belarus@tvr.by **W:** www.radiobelarus.tvr.by
Webcast: D/L
L.P: Dir: Navum Halpiarovic; Head, Foreign Language Dept: Vjacaslaú Lakcjušyn.
MW/SW: Leased from Belaruski Radyjotelevizijny Peredajucy Centr.
FM/DAB: See National Radio section.
kHz: 1170, 3985, 6005, 11730, 11930

	Winter Schedule 2015/2016		
Belarusian	**Days**	**Area**	**kHz**
1100-1400	daily	Eu	11730mns
English	**Days**	**Area**	**kHz**
2000-2200	.tw.f..	Eu	11730mns, 11930mns
2020-2200	m..t.ss	Eu	11730mns, 11930mns
French	**Days**	**Area**	**kHz**
1940-2000	m..t.ss	Eu	11730mns, 11930mns
German	**Days**	**Area**	**kHz**
0700-0900	mtwtf..	Eu	6005kll*
0700-0900	daily	Eu	3985kll*
1800-1940	m..t.ss	Eu	11730mns, 11930mns
1800-2000	.tw.f..	Eu	11730mns, 11930mns
2100-2300	daily	Eu	3985kll*
Polish	**Days**	**Area**	**kHz**
1600-1800	daily	Eu	1170sas, 11730mns
1705-1800	daily	Eu	11930mns
Russian	**Days**	**Area**	**kHz**
1400-1600	daily	Eu	11730mns
2200-2300	daily	Eu	11730mns, 11930mns
Spanish	**Days**	**Area**	**kHz**
2000-2020	m..t.ss	Eu	11730mns, 11930mns

Key: * Additional relay, initiated by and courtesy of Funkhaus

Euskirchen e.V. in Germany (part of the Kall SW relay platform)
Ann: Belarusian: "Havoryc Radyjo Belarus"; English: "This is Radio Belarus", "You are listening to Radio Belarus"; German: "Hier ist Radio Belarus".
V: QSL-card.
Notes: Radio Belarus is the External Sce of the National State Radio-TV Company of Belarus.

BELARUSKI RADYJOTELEVIZIJNY PEREDAJUCY CENTR (Tx Operator)
🖃 vul. Engelsa 22, 220030 Minsk, Belarus.
☎ +375 17 2270845. 🖷 +375 17 2271084.
E: inbox@brtpc.by **W:** www.brtpc.by
L.P: DG: Ihar Biazruconak.
MW: [SAS] Sasnovy: 1170kHz 1000kW (run at 700kW).
SW: [MNS] Minsk, Kalodziščy: 1 x 75, 1 x 150, 1 x 250kW.
Notes: Belaruski Radyjotelevizijny Peredajucy Centr, a subsidiary of the Ministry of Telecommunications & Informatisation, is the national transmitter network operator.

BELGIUM (BEL)

RTBF INTERNATIONAL (Pub)
🖃 Local 3P09, 52 Bd Reyers, B-1044 Bruxelles, Belgium.
☎ +32 2 7374014. 🖷 +32 2 7373032.
E: rtbfi@rtbf.be **W:** www.rtbf.be/rtbfi
Webcast: L
L.P: Dir/GM (RTBF): Jean-Paul Philippot.
MW: [WAV] Wavre: 621kHz 300kW.
FM/DAB: FM: 99.2MHz (Kinshasa, Dem. Rep. of Congo).
SAT: Eutelsat 5WA.
kHz: 621

	Winter Schedule 2015/2016		
French	**Days**	**Area**	**kHz**
0400-2310	daily	WEu	621wav

V: QSL-card. (sent only by email)
Notes: Transmissions are relays of RTBF network programmes (including La Première and Vivacité, and others).

RADIO 700 (Comm)
🖃 Morsheck 3, B-4760 Büllingen, Belgium.
☎ +32 80 480105.
E: info@radio700.eu **W:** www.radio700.eu; www.radio700.de
Webcast: L
SW: Via Radio 700 Kurzwellendienst. (Germany)
FM/DAB: see National Radio section. (Belgium, Germany)
kHz: 3985, 6005, 7310

	Winter Schedule 2015/2016		
German	**Days**	**Area**	**kHz**
0900-1000	......s	Eu	7310kll
0900-1400	mtwtf..	Eu	6005kll
0900-1530	mtwtfs.	Eu	7310kll
0900-1730	daily	Eu	3985kll
1100-1400	......s	Eu	6005kll
1300-1400	.....s.	Eu	6005kll
1500-1530	......s	Eu	7310kll
1600-1800	.....ss	Eu	6005kll
1700-1800	mtwtf..	Eu	6005kll
1800-1900	.....ss	Eu	3985kll
2300-0700	daily	Eu	3985kll

V: QSL-card.
Notes: Radio 700 - "Schlager und Oldies" is licensed to VoG Privater Rundfunk in Ostbelgien (PRiO) and is primarily targeting German speaking listeners on both sides of the Belgian-German border. Radio 700 was founded 2002 as local radio project of Funkhaus Euskirchen e.V. in Euskirchen, Germany.

BROADCAST BELGIUM (Consultants) (Broker)
🖃 P.O. Box 1, B-2310 Rijkevorsel, Belgium.
☎ +32 33 147800.
E: info@broadcast.be **W:** www.broadcast.be
L.P: Managing Director: Ludo Maes.
V: QSL-card (For brokered transmissions). Rp.
Notes: Broadcast Belgium (formerly TDP) is an international radio consultancy that, in conjunction with their sister company (Alyx & Yeyi, see under USA) provides services and brokers airtime etc. for radio stations with political, religious, commercial and NGO backgrounds.

BENIN (BEN)

TWR RELAY STATION
✉ B.P. 1039, Parakou, Benin.
☎ +229 23102055.
E: 1566@twr.org **W:** www.twrbenin.com
L.P: SM: Garth Kennedy.
MW: [PAR] Parakou: 1566kHz 100kW.
SW: [PAR] Parakou: 1 x 100kW (Planned). ‡
Key: ‡ Inactive at time of publications.
Notes: Owned by TWR. For corporate details, see under TWR (USA). For schedule, see TWR Africa (South Africa). F.PI: SW tx to be installed at site (pending licensing/construction permits and funding).

BONAIRE (BES)

TWR BONAIRE (Rlg)
✉ P.O. Box 388, Kralendijk, Bonaire, Carribean Netherlands..
☎ +599 7178800. 🖶 +599 7178808.
E: 800am@twr.org **W:** www.twrbonaire.com
Webcast: D/L
L.P: Dir: Dick Veldman.
MW: [TWB] Bonaire, Belnem: 800kHz 100kW. F.pl: 450kW.
FM/DAB: FM: 89.5MHz (Bonaire).
kHz: 800

Winter Schedule 2015/2016

Baniua	Days	Area	kHz
0845-0900	.....s.	SAm	800twb
English	**Days**	**Area**	**kHz**
2300-0030	daily	SAm	800twb
Macuxi	**Days**	**Area**	**kHz**
0845-0900	......s	SAm	800twb
Portuguese	**Days**	**Area**	**kHz**
0700-0845	.....ss	SAm	800twb
0700-0900	mtwtf..	SAm	800twb
Spanish	**Days**	**Area**	**kHz**
0030-0700	daily	SAm	800twb
0900-1230	daily	SAm	800twb
2130-2300	daily	SAm	800twb

Ann: English: "This is the international sound of the Caribbean, Trans World Radio, Bonaire".
V: QSL-card.
Notes: Branch and transmitting station. Owned by TWR, for corporate details, see under USA.

BOTSWANA (BOT)

IBB RELAY STATION BOTSWANA
✉ IBB Transmitting Station, Private Bag 38, Selebi-Phikwe, Botswana.
☎ +267 2610932. 🖶 +267 2610185.
L.P: SM: George O. Miller.
MW: [BOT] Selebi-Phikwe, Moepeng Hill: 909kHz 600kW. Reserve: 50kW.
SW: [BOT] Selebi-Phikwe, Moepeng Hill: 4 x 100kW.
V: QSL-card (Email rpt to manager_botswana@bot.ibb.gov)

BULGARIA (BUL)

RADIO BULGARIA (Pub)
✉ bul. Dragan Tsankov 4, 1040 Sofia, Bulgaria.
☎ +359 29336633.
E: digitalbroadcasting@bnr.bg; german@bnr.bg (German section)
W: bnr.bg
Webcast: D/L
L.P: Dir (BNR Multimedia Programmes): Anton Mitov.
SW: via Radio 700 Kurzwellendienst (Germany).
kHz: 3985, 6005, 7310

Winter Schedule 2015/2016

German	Days	Area	kHz
0830-0900	daily	Eu	7310kll*
1530-1600	daily	Eu	6005kll*
1730-1800	daily	Eu	3985kll*

Key: * The relay is an initiative of Funkhaus Euskirchen e.V. in Germany (part of the Kall SW relay platform).

Notes: Radio Bulgaria is produced by the "Multimedia programmes" department of Bulgarian National Radio (BNR).

SPACELINE LTD (Broker)
✉ bul. James Bourchier 71, 6th Floor, 1407 Sofia, Bulgaria.
☎ +359 2 9625962.
E: info@spaceline.bg **W:** www.spaceline.bg
L.P: GM: Dimitar Todorov.
Notes: Spaceline Ltd brokers air time for SW facilities in Bulgaria and Armenia.

NURTS BULGARIA (Tx Operator)
✉ bul. Peyo K. Yavorov 2, 1164 Sofia, Bulgaria.
☎ +359 2 8069300. 🖶 +359 2 8069309.
E: office@nurts.bg **W:** www.nurts.bg
L.P: CEO's: Emil Atanasov, Svilen Popov.
SW: [SOF] Sofia, Kostinbrod: 5 x 50 (4 x 50 used in parallel as 2 x 100kW); DRM capable: 1 x 70kW.
Notes: NURTS, a subsidiary of Bulgarian Telecommunications Company EAD, is the Bulgarian national transmitter operator.

CAMEROON (CME)

SAWTU LINJIILA (VOICE OF THE GOSPEL) (Rlg)
✉ B.P. 02, Ngaoundéré, Cameroon.
E: sawtulinjiila@yahoo.fr
W: www.oseelc.org (EELC); nms.no (NMS); www.lutheranworld.org (LWF)
L.P: Dir: Rev Yaya Bournang.
FM/DAB: FM: txs in Cameroon, Chad and Central African Republic.
kHz: 9800

Winter Schedule 2015/2016

Fulfulde	Days	Area	kHz
1830-1900	daily	WAf	9800iss, 9800iss

Ann: Fulfulde: "Sawtu Linjiila".
V: QSL-email.
Notes: Multimedia ministry for Fulfulde (Fulani) speakers in West Africa. The project is funded by the Evangelical Lutheran Church of Cameroon (EELC), the Norwegian missionary organisation Det Norske Misjonsselskap (NMS) and the Lutheran World Federation (LWF). Launched on 6 November 1966, initially broadcast on shortwave via Trans World Radio.

CANADA (CAN)

BIBLE VOICE BROADCASTING (BVB) (Rlg)
✉ P.O. Box 95561, Newmarket, ON L3Y 8J8, Canada.
☎ +1 905 8982500.
E: mail@bvbroadcasting.org **W:** www.bvbroadcasting.org
Webcast: D/P
✉ 350 Davis Drive, Newmarket, ON L3Y 2N7, Canada. (HAGCM)
☎ +1 905 8985447. 🖶 +1 905 8982500.
W: www.hagcm.org
L.P: International Ministry Coordinator: Mrs. Marty McLaughlin.
kHz: 5940, 5950, 5980, 6030, 6260, 7220, 7325, 7365, 9440, 9450, 9470, 9515, 9715, 9925, 11700, 11790, 11875, 11915, 13630, 15335, 17510, 17540, 17820, 17860, 21480

Winter Schedule 2015/2016

Amharic	Days	Area	kHz
1630-1700	m.w.f..	EAf	15335nau
1630-1800	.t.....	EAf	15335nau
1630-1830	...t....	EAf	15335nau
1700-1730	.....s.	EAf	15335nau
1700-1800	......s	EAf	15335nau
1730-1800	..w....	EAf	15335nau
Arabic	**Days**	**Area**	**kHz**
0300-0315	daily	ME	7325nau
0430-0445	.....ss	ME	5980nau
0430-0450	mtwtf..	ME	5980nau
0500-0515	...f...	ME	9450nau
0600-0615	daily	NAf	9440nau
0830-0900	...f...	NAf	17540nau
0900-0915	.....s.	NAf	17540nau
1700-1715	...t.ss	ME	11700sof
1700-1715	...f...	ME	11915nau
1700-1745	.t.....	ME	11700sof
1700-1745	...s.	ME	11915nau

Arabic	Days	Area	kHz
1700-1800	m.w.f..	ME	11700sof
1830-1900	.....s	ME	9715nau
2000-2015	daily	ME	5940nau
2030-2045	daily	NAf	9515nau

Dinka	Days	Area	kHz
1700-1730	daily	SDN	11875nau

English	Days	Area	kHz
0200-0215	.t..f..	SAs	11790mdc
0200-0230	...t..s	SAs	11790mdc
0200-0300	.....s	SAs	11790mdc
0445-0515	.....s	ME	5980nau
0800-0830	.....ss	WEu	7220nau
0900-1000	....f..	NAf	17540nau
1115-1130	.....s	FE	21480mdc
1200-1215	.....s	SEA	17820tac**, 17860tac**
1200-1230	.....s	FE	21480mdc
1200-1300	.....s.	FE	21480mdc
1400-1430	...f..	SAs	6260tac
1400-1500	....s.	SAs	17510iss
1515-1545	....s.	SAs	13630nau
1800-1830	...t..s	ME	9715nau
1800-1845	....f..	ME	9715nau
1800-1900	m......	ME	9715mos
1800-2000	.....s.	ME	9715nau
1815-1830	.....s	IRN	7365nau
1830-2000	.....s	EEu,RUS	6030nau
1900-2000	.....s	ME	9715nau
1915-1945	.....s	ME	9470nau
1930-1945	.....s.	EEu,RUS	6030nau
1930-2015	.....s	ME	9925sof

Farsi	Days	Area	kHz
1730-1830	daily	IRN	11700sof*
1800-1830	....f..	IRN	7365nau
1800-1900	...t...	IRN	7365nau
1830-1900	.t...s	IRN	7365nau

Hadiyaa	Days	Area	kHz
1730-1800	.....s.	EAf	15335nau

Japanese	Days	Area	kHz
1130-1145	.....s	FE	21480mdc

Luri	Days	Area	kHz
0400-0430	m....ss	IRN	5950nau

Nuer	Days	Area	kHz
1630-1700	daily	SDN	11875nau

Oromo	Days	Area	kHz
1600-1630	mt....s	EAf	15335nau

Russian	Days	Area	kHz
1900-1915	...f..	EEu,RUS	6030nau
1900-1930	.t.....	EEu,RUS	6030nau

Somali	Days	Area	kHz
1630-1700	.....ss	EAf	15335nau

Tamil	Days	Area	kHz
1515-1530	...f..	SAs	13630nau

Tigrinya	Days	Area	kHz
1700-1730	m.w....	EAf	15335nau
1800-1830	.t.....	EAf	15335nau

Ukrainian	Days	Area	kHz
1900-1915	...t...	EEu,RUS	6030nau

Urdu	Days	Area	kHz
1530-1600	...f..	SAs	13630nau

Key: * Alt freq: 15570kHz; ** Unconfirmed at time of publication.
V: QSL-card.
Notes: BVB is operated by High Adventure Gospel Communication Ministries (Canada), in cooperation with Bible Voice (UK) and High Adventure Gospel Communication Ministries, Inc (USA). BVB's SW transmissions consist of religious paid programming, produced by small religious organisations, or individuals.

CHINA (CHN)

CHINA RADIO INTERNATIONAL (CRI) (Gov)
16a, Shijingshan Rd, Beijing 100040, P.R. China.
☎ +86 10 68891000, 68891001. 🖷 +86 10 68892738, 68891582.
E: aboutcri@cri.com.cn; crieng@cri.com.cn **W:** www.cri.com.cn, www.cri.cn

Webcast: D/L
L.P: GD: Wang Gengnian; CE: Wang Lian; Dir, English Sce: Yang Lei.
MW: See SARFT for tx information.
SW: See SARFT for tx information.
SAT: Apstar 6, Intelsat 14/19/20/21, Superbird C2, Telstar 11N, Yamal 202.
kHz: 603, 684, 900, 963, 1017, 1044, 1080, 1188, 1269, 1296, 1323, 1341, 1422, 1440, 1521, 5905, 5910, 5915, 5955, 5960, 5965, 5970, 5975, 5980, 5985, 5990, 6010, 6020, 6025, 6040, 6055, 6060, 6065, 6070, 6075, 6080, 6090, 6095, 6100, 6105, 6110, 6115, 6135, 6140, 6145, 6150, 6155, 6160, 6165, 6175, 6180, 6185, 7205, 7210, 7215, 7220, 7225, 7235, 7240, 7245, 7250, 7255, 7260, 7265, 7275, 7285, 7290, 7295, 7300, 7305, 7315, 7320, 7325, 7330, 7335, 7340, 7345, 7350, 7360, 7365, 7370, 7380, 7385, 7390, 7395, 7400, 7405, 7410, 7415, 7420, 7425, 7430, 7435, 7440, 7445, 9410, 9415, 9425, 9430, 9435, 9440, 9450, 9455, 9460, 9470, 9490, 9515, 9525, 9535, 9540, 9550, 9555, 9560, 9565, 9570, 9580, 9585, 9590, 9600, 9610, 9615, 9620, 9640, 9645, 9655, 9665, 9675, 9685, 9690, 9695, 9705, 9710, 9720, 9730, 9745, 9760, 9765, 9770, 9785, 9790, 9795, 9800, 9825, 9855, 9860, 9865, 9870, 9875, 9880, 11610, 11635, 11640, 11650, 11665, 11680, 11690, 11700, 11710, 11720, 11725, 11730, 11750, 11760, 11770, 11780, 11785, 11790, 11795, 11805, 11820, 11855, 11860, 11870, 11875, 11885, 11895, 11900, 11910, 11920, 11945, 11955, 11975, 11980, 11990, 12015, 12035, 12070, 13570, 13580, 13590, 13600, 13610, 13640, 13645, 13650, 13655, 13660, 13665, 13670, 13710, 13715, 13720, 13730, 13740, 13750, 13770, 13780, 13790, 13800, 13810, 13850, 13855, 15110, 15120, 15125, 15130, 15135, 15140, 15145, 15160, 15170, 15185, 15190, 15205, 15210, 15220, 15225, 15250, 15335, 15340, 15350, 15425, 15430, 15435, 15440, 15445, 15465, 15505, 15525, 15550, 15560, 15620, 15665, 15700, 17485, 17490, 17510, 17520, 17540, 17560, 17570, 17615, 17630, 17640, 17650, 17670, 17680, 17690, 17710, 17720, 17730, 17735, 17740, 17750, 17855*

Winter Schedule 2015/2016

Albanian	Days	Area	kHz
1900-2000	daily	Eu	6020szg, 7385kas

Amoy	Days	Area	kHz
0100-0200	daily	SAs	9610kun
0100-0200	daily	SEA	9460kun, 9550kun, 9860jin, 11945kun, 11980kun
0100-0300	daily	SEA	15425xia, 17490bei
1200-1300	daily	SEA	11910bei
1400-1500	daily	SEA	9655kun, 11650kun

Arabic	Days	Area	kHz
0500-0700	daily	ME	9590cer
0500-0700	daily	ME,NAf	17485kas
0500-0700	daily	NAf	5985cer, 7210cer
1600-1700	daily	NAf,WAf	15125bko
1600-1800	daily	ME,NAf	7300kas
1600-1800	daily	NAf	9555cer, 11725cer
1830-1930	daily	WAf	11640bko
2000-2200	daily	ME,NAf	6100xia, 6185cer, 7215cer

Bengali	Days	Area	kHz
0200-0300	daily	SAs	9655kun, 11640kun
1300-1400	daily	SAs	1188kun, 9600bji
1300-1500	daily	SAs	9490kun, 11610kun
1400-1500	daily	SAs	1269xuw
1500-1600	daily	SAs	9610kun, 9690kun

Bulgarian	Days	Area	kHz
1100-1200	daily	Eu	7220cer
1830-1900	daily	Eu	6020szg, 7265uru, 9695kun
2030-2100	daily	Eu	7320uru, 9720uru

Burmese	Days	Area	kHz
0200-0300	daily	BRM	900deh
0700-0800	daily	BRM	900deh
1100-1200	daily	SEA	1188kun, 9880kun
1300-1400	daily	SEA	9880kun
1300-1500	daily	SEA	7400kun
1400-1500	daily	BRM	900deh

Cantonese	Days	Area	kHz
0000-0100	daily	SEA	11820xia, 17490bei
0400-0500	daily	EAs	15160jin

Cantonese	Days	Area	kHz
0400-0500	daily	NAm	9790hab
0400-0600	daily	EAs	13655xia
0500-0600	daily	EAs	15170jin
0700-0800	daily	EAs	11640jin, 13610xia
1000-1100	daily	Pac	15440kun, 17670kun
1100-1200	daily	Pac	9540bei, 13580kun
1100-1200	daily	SEA	603dof, 7370nnn, 9590kun, 9645bei
1200-1300	daily	NAm	9570hab
1700-1800	daily	EAf	7220xia
1700-1800	daily	SAf	7325uru
1900-2000	daily	Eu	7215bei, 9770kas
2300-2400	daily	SEA	6140kun, 6180kun, 7325uru, 9425jin, 11945kun

Chaozhou	Days	Area	kHz
0700-0800	daily	SEA	15145xia, 17750xia
1100-1200	daily	SEA	9440kun, 11875kun
1800-1900	daily	Eu	6010uru, 7285xia

Chinese	Days	Area	kHz
0000-0100	daily	SEA	9435kun, 11975kun, 12035xia
0000-0100	daily	EAs	11780jin, 11900bei
0000-0200	daily	SEA	13580bei
0000-0400	daily	EAs	13655xia
0100-0200	daily	SAs	7250uru, 7300kas
0100-0200	daily	SEA	9655nnn, 11640xia, 11770nnn
0100-0400	daily	EAs	15160jin
0200-0300	daily	NAm	9580hab
0200-0300	daily	NAm,CAm	9690nob
0200-0300	daily	SAm	7330kas, 15140bei
0200-0300	daily	SAs	9825kas
0200-0400	daily	NAm	6020cer, 9570cer
0300-0400	daily	SAs	9450kas, 17540bei
0300-0600	daily	EAs	15130bei
0400-0500	daily	SAs	13640kas, 15170kas
0500-0600	daily	SAs	15110kas
0500-0700	daily	EAs	13570xia, 15120bei
0600-0700	daily	EAs	13655xia, 15170jin
0600-0800	daily	SEA	11710nnn, 13750kun, 17740xia
0600-0900	daily	Eu	7650kas
0700-0800	daily	SAs	17520kas
0700-0800	daily	SEA	11875nnn
0700-0900	daily	Eu	11855cer
0800-0900	daily	SAs	15550kas
0800-0900	daily	EAs	9880bei, 11640jin, 13610xia
0800-1000	daily	CAs,Cau	15560xia, 17560xia
0900-1000	daily	Pac	15440kun, 17670kun
0900-1000	daily	SEA	11895nnn
0900-1000	daily	EAs	7430jin, 9440xia
0900-1100	daily	EAs	5965bei
0900-1100	daily	SAs	13780kas, 15525uru
0900-1100	daily	SEA	9460nnn, 11980kun, 13850bei, 15250kun, 15340xia
1000-1100	daily	EAs	7255xia, 9880bei
1000-1300	daily	Eu	17650kas
1100-1200	daily	SAs	9515kas, 11980kas
1100-1200	daily	EAs	7435bei
1100-1200	daily	Pac	11750bei, 15440kun
1200-1300	daily	SAs	7205kas, 9655kas
1200-1300	daily	EAs	7390bei
1200-1300	daily	ME	15110uru
1200-1400	daily	ME,NAf	11790kas*, 13810kas*
1200-1400	daily	SAs	9540kun
1200-1400	daily	SEA	7440nnn, 9855bei
1300-1400	daily	EAs	7205bei
1300-1400	daily	Eu	13855kas
1300-1400	daily	ME	12015uru
1300-1400	daily	SEA	7215xia
1400-1500	daily	SEA	6040xia, 7410bei

Chinese	Days	Area	kHz
1400-1500	daily	SAs	9730kas
1400-1500	daily	EAs	7210bei
1400-1500	daily	Eu	9430kas, 11785kas
1400-1500	daily	ME	11610uru
1400-1600	daily	SAs	7235kas
1500-1600	daily	EAs	7255bei
1500-1600	daily	Eu	9590kas, 9705kas
1500-1600	daily	SAs	9560kas
1500-1600	daily	SEA	5910bei, 9455kun
1730-1830	daily	Eu	6150szg, 7445uru
1730-1830	daily	ME,NAf	7275uru, 7315kun, 9695kun
2000-2100	daily	ME,NAf	7245kas, 9865kun
2000-2100	daily	SAf	7405xia
2000-2100	daily	Eu	7335szg, 7440bei
2200-2300	daily	NAf,ME	7265kun, 7395uru
2200-2300	daily	SAf	5975bei, 7430jin
2200-2300	daily	SEA	6100kun, 6140kun, 6180kun, 7325kun
2200-2300	daily	EAs	7305bei
2230-2300	daily	CAf	15505bko
2300-2400	daily	EAs	9555bei
2300-2400	daily	Eu	7300uru

Croatian	Days	Area	kHz
1700-1800	daily	Eu	7335bei, 9435kas
2100-2200	daily	Eu	6135bei, 7225bei

Czech	Days	Area	kHz
1100-1200	daily	Eu	15225kas, 17570kas
1900-1930	daily	Eu	7325szg
1900-2000	daily	Eu	7415uru

English	Days	Area	kHz
0000-0100	daily	EAs	9425bei
0000-0100	daily	SAs	7425kas
0000-0200	daily	NAm	6020cer, 9570cer
0000-0200	daily	SAs	6075kas, 6180kas
0000-0200	daily	SEA	11885xia, 15125bei
0100-0200	daily	Eu	9675kas
0100-0200	daily	NAm	9580hab
0100-0200	daily	SAs	7370kas
0200-0300	daily	SAs	9610kas
0200-0400	daily	SAs	11770kas
0300-0400	daily	NAm	9790hab
0300-0400	daily	SAs	13800kas
0300-0500	daily	EAs	13570xia, 13590bei, 15120bei
0400-0600	daily	CAs	17855bei
0400-0600	daily	CAs,Eu	17730xia
0500-0700	daily	ME,NAf	17510kas
0500-0700	daily	SAs	15430kas
0500-0900	daily	SAs	11895kas, 15465kas
0500-1100	daily	SAs	15350kas
0600-0700	daily	ME	11870kas, 15145kas
0600-0700	daily	NAf	11750cer
0600-0700	daily	SEA	13645xia
0600-0800	daily	SEA	17710bei
0700-0800	daily	SEA	13660xia
0700-0900	daily	ME,NAf	17670kas
0700-0900	daily	Eu	11785cer
0700-1000	daily	SAs	15185kas
0700-1300	daily	Eu	17490kas
0800-1000	daily	EAs	9415xia
0900-1000	daily	Eu	17570uru, 17690jin
0900-1100	daily	Pac	15210kun, 17690jin
1000-1100	daily	EAs	5955xia, 7215xia, 11635bei
1000-1100	daily	SAs	15190kas
1000-1200	daily	SEA	13590xia, 13720xia
1100-1200	daily	SAs	11795kas
1100-1300	daily	Eu	13665cer
1100-1300	daily	SAs	7250kas, 11650uru, 12015kas
1100-1300	daily	SEA	1269xuw
1100-1600	daily	EAs	5955bei
1200-1300	daily	CAs	11690xia

English

English	Days	Area	kHz
1200-1300	daily	Pac	9760kun
1200-1300	daily	SAs	9460kas
1200-1300	daily	SEA	684dof, 1188kun, 9600kun, 9645bei, 9730kun
1200-1400	daily	Eu	13790uru
1200-1400	daily	Pac	11760kun
1200-1400	daily	SEA	1341hdu, 11980kun
1300-1400	daily	NAm	9570hab
1300-1400	daily	SEA	9730bei, 11910bei
1300-1400	daily	Eu	13670kas
1300-1400	daily	SAs	7300kas, 9655kas
1300-1400	daily	Pac	11900bei
1300-1500	daily	CAs,Eu	9765bji
1300-1600	daily	SEA	9870xia
1400-1500	daily	CAs,Eu	11665uru
1400-1500	daily	Eu	9795uru, 13710kas
1400-1500	daily	SAs	7300uru, 9460uru
1400-1600	daily	EAf,WAf	17630bko
1400-1600	daily	NAm	15700hab
1500-1600	daily	NAf,ME	6095kas, 9720uru
1500-1600	daily	SAs	1188kun, 7395uru, 9785jin
1500-1600	daily	Eu	9525kas
1500-1600	daily	SEA	7325bei
1500-1700	daily	Eu	9435kas
1500-1800	daily	SAs	1323uru
1500-1800	daily	SEA	9880nnn
1600-1700	daily	Eu	9875kas
1600-1700	daily	NAf,ME	7420uru
1600-1700	daily	SEA	6060kun
1600-1800	daily	Eu	7255kas
1600-1800	daily	SAf	7435jin, 9570bei
1600-1800	daily	SAs	7235kas
1600-1800	daily	SEA	1080xuw, 6175nnn
1700-1800	daily	SAs	6140kas, 7410kas
1700-1800	daily	SEA	6090kun, 7420kun
1700-1800	daily	ME	6165bei
1700-1900	daily	Eu	6100bei
1800-1900	daily	Eu	7405bei
1900-2100	daily	ME,NAf	7295kas, 9440kun
2000-2100	daily	SAf	5985bei
2000-2200	daily	Eu	5960cer, 7285cer, 7415kas, 9600kas
2100-2200	daily	SAf	7205xia, 7325bei
2200-2300	daily	EAs	5915bei
2300-0100	daily	SEA	11790xia
2300-0200	daily	Eu	7350kas
2300-2400	daily	EAs	6145bei
2300-2400	daily	SEA	9535kun
2300-2400	daily	NAm,CAm	5990hab
2300-2400	daily	SAs	5915kas, 7410kas

Esperanto

Esperanto	Days	Area	kHz
1100-1200	daily	EAs	7210uru, 9450uru
1300-1400	daily	SEA	9440nnn, 11650bei
1700-1800	daily	Eu	7205bei, 7245xia
1930-2030	daily	Eu	7265uru, 9745uru
2200-2300	daily	SAm	7315kas, 9860kas

Filipino

Filipino	Days	Area	kHz
1130-1200	daily	SEA	1341hdu, 5910bei, 7410jin, 12070xia
1130-1230	daily	SEA	11955kun
1200-1230	daily	SEA	9720xia
1430-1500	daily	SEA	1341hdu, 7325bei, 11640bei

French

French	Days	Area	kHz
0600-0800	daily	Eu	15220kas
1200-1400	daily	Eu	15205kas
1300-1400	daily	Eu	17650kas
1400-1500	daily	WAf	11920cer, 13670cer
1600-1800	daily	Eu	7350kas
1800-2000	daily	Eu	5970cer, 7360cer
1800-2000	daily	NAf,WAf	6055cer, 7385cer
1830-2030	daily	WAf	7350uru, 9645kun
2030-2230	daily	Eu	6115bei, 7350uru

German

German	Days	Area	kHz
0600-0800	daily	Eu	17615uru, 17720kas
0600-1100	daily	Eu	1440mrn**
1600-1800	daily	Eu	5970cer, 7380cer
1800-2000	daily	Eu	6160xia, 7395kas, 9615uru
1800-2300	daily	Eu	1440mrn**

Hakka

Hakka	Days	Area	kHz
0000-0100	daily	SEA	9460kun, 9550kun, 9610kun, 9860jin
0400-0500	daily	SAs	13740kas, 15350kas
0400-0500	daily	SEA	17510xia, 17710bei
1600-1700	daily	SAf	6090xia, 7325uru

Hausa

Hausa	Days	Area	kHz
0800-0900	daily	WAf	7295bko
1630-1730	daily	WAf	9620kas, 9665kun
1730-1830	daily	WAf	9450kas, 9685kun
1800-1830	daily	WAf	11640bko

Hindi

Hindi	Days	Area	kHz
0300-0400	daily	SAs	11640kas, 11700kas, 13720kas, 15350kas
1300-1400	daily	SAs	1269xuw, 1422kas, 7265uru, 9450kas
1500-1600	daily	SAs	7225uru, 7265kas
1600-1700	daily	SAs	1188kun, 1422kas, 5915kas, 7395kun
1600-1800	daily	SAs	1269xuw

Hungarian

Hungarian	Days	Area	kHz
1000-1100	daily	Eu	15220kas, 17570kas
1900-1930	daily	Eu	7435xia, 9560uru
2030-2100	daily	Eu	7390jin, 9585kas
2130-2200	daily	Eu	7445uru

Indonesian

Indonesian	Days	Area	kHz
0830-0930	daily	SEA	15135kun, 17735kun
1030-1130	daily	SEA	11700kun, 15135kun
1330-1430	daily	SEA	11805kun, 11955kun

Italian

Italian	Days	Area	kHz
0600-0700	daily	Eu	15620kas
1800-1900	daily	Eu	7340kas, 7435jin
2030-2130	daily	Eu	7265uru, 7345xia

Japanese

Japanese	Days	Area	kHz
1000-1100	daily	EAs	9440xia
1000-1300	daily	EAs	7325jin
1100-1300	daily	EAs	7260xia
1100-1600	daily	EAs	1044hnl
1300-1400	daily	EAs	7215jin, 7325xia
1400-1500	daily	EAs	7395xia, 7410jin
1500-1600	daily	EAs	5980xia, 7220jin
2200-2300	daily	EAs	5985xia, 7440jin
2300-2400	daily	EAs	9435xia, 9695jin

Khmer

Khmer	Days	Area	kHz
0000-0100	daily	SEA	11990nnn
1030-1130	daily	SEA	684dof, 15160nnn, 17680kun
1200-1300	daily	SEA	9440kun, 11680nnn
1400-1500	daily	SEA	6055nnn, 9880nnn
2300-0100	daily	SEA	9765nnn
2300-2400	daily	SEA	7395nnn

Korean

Korean	Days	Area	kHz
1100-1500	daily	EAs	1017cah, 1323hdn, 5965xia
2100-2300	daily	EAs	1017cah, 1323hdn, 7290xia

Lao

Lao	Days	Area	kHz
1230-1330	daily	SEA	7360kun, 9785kun
1430-1530	daily	SEA	1080xuw, 7360kun, 9675kun

Malay

Malay	Days	Area	kHz
0930-1030	daily	SEA	15135kun, 17680kun
1230-1330	daily	SEA	11700kun, 11955kun

Mongolian

Mongolian	Days	Area	kHz
0000-0100	daily	EAs	9470xia, 11875bei
1100-1200	daily	EAs	6100uru, 7390huh

Mongolian	Days	Area	kHz
1200-1300	daily	EAs	1323uru, 5915huh, 5990huh
1300-1400	daily	EAs	6100uru, 7285bei
1400-1500	daily	EAs	5915huh, 5990huh
2300-2400	daily	EAs	6185xia, 7205xia

Nepali	Days	Area	kHz
0130-0230	daily	SAs	11860kun
0130-0330	daily	SAs	13780kun
0230-0330	daily	SAs	11730kun
1400-1500	daily	SAs	1188uru, 7220xia, 7435kun
1500-1600	daily	SAs	1269xuw, 7215kun, 9535xia

Pashto	Days	Area	kHz
0200-0230	daily	WAs	6065kas, 7350kas, 15435xia
1500-1600	daily	WAs	7435kun, 9665kas
1530-1600	daily	WAs	6165uru

Persian	Days	Area	kHz
1500-1530	daily	ME	6165uru, 9600kas
1800-1900	daily	ME	7325bei, 7415xia

Polish	Days	Area	kHz
2000-2100	daily	Eu	6020szg, 7305uru

Portuguese	Days	Area	kHz
0000-0100	daily	SAm	9710kas
1900-2000	daily	Eu	7335jin, 9730kas
1900-2000	daily	SAf	5985bei, 7365bei, 7405xia, 9535bji
2200-2300	daily	Eu	6175cer, 7260uru
2200-2300	daily	SAm	9410kas, 9685kas
2300-0100	daily	SAm	6100bei
2300-2400	daily	SAm	13650hab

Romanian	Days	Area	kHz
0900-1000	daily	Eu	7285cer, 9460cer
1900-2000	daily	Eu	6090uru
1930-2000	daily	Eu	7435xia

Russian	Days	Area	kHz
0000-0200	daily	CAs	1521uru
0100-0200	daily	CAs	5905kas
0100-0200	daily	CAs,Eu	13600xia
0200-0300	daily	CAs	5915kas
0200-0500	daily	CAs,Eu	17640xia
0300-0400	daily	CAs	11710uru
0300-0400	daily	CAs,Eu	17710jin
0300-0500	daily	CAs	7325kas
0400-0600	daily	CAs,Eu	15445kas, 15665uru
0800-1000	daily	CAs,Eu	15335kas, 15665uru
1000-1100	daily	EAs	7390huh
1000-1200	daily	EAs	5915huh, 7290szg
1000-1600	daily	EAs	963hdn
1100-1200	daily	CAs	6080bei
1100-1200	daily	EAs	1323uru
1100-1600	daily	EAs	1323hei
1100-2000	daily	CAs	1521uru
1200-1300	daily	CAs,Eu	7215xia, 9590szg, 9685uru
1200-1300	daily	EAs	6100bei, 7410szg
1200-1700	daily	CAs	5905kas
1300-1400	daily	CAs,Eu	9665xia
1300-1400	daily	EAs	5915huh, 5990huh, 7255szg
1300-1500	daily	EAs	1323uru
1400-1500	daily	CAs,Eu	7330xia
1400-1500	daily	EAs	7435szg
1500-1600	daily	CAs,Eu	6025xia, 6105szg, 6180uru
1500-1600	daily	EAs	5915huh, 5965bei, 5990huh
1600-1700	daily	CAs,Eu	7215szg, 7265bei
1600-1700	daily	Eu	6070kas
1600-1800	daily	CAs,Eu	6040uru
1700-1800	daily	CAs,Eu	6070xia, 7265uru, 7410szg
1800-1900	daily	CAs,Eu	6070bei, 7210uru, 7255szg

Russian	Days	Area	kHz
1900-2000	daily	CAs,Eu	6100bei, 6110xia, 7245bji
2000-2100	daily	CAs,Eu	6155bei, 7255bji
2300-0100	daily	EAs	5990huh, 7405huh

Serbian	Days	Area	kHz
1200-1300	daily	Eu	7345cer
2000-2030	daily	Eu	7325uru, 7390xia, 9585kas
2100-2130	daily	Eu	7325xia, 7445kun

Sinhala	Days	Area	kHz
1400-1500	daily	SAs	7265kas, 9665jin
2330-0030	daily	SAs	6100kun, 7260kas

Spanish	Days	Area	kHz
0000-0100	daily	NAm,CAm	5990hab
0000-0100	daily	SAm	15120hab
0100-0300	daily	SAm	9710kas
0600-0800	daily	Eu	15135kas
2100-2300	daily	Eu	6020szg, 9640kas
2200-2300	daily	SAm	6100bei
2200-2400	daily	Eu	7210cer, 7250uru
2300-0100	daily	SAm	9800kas
2300-0300	daily	SAm	9590kas
2300-2400	daily	Eu	6175cer

Swahili	Days	Area	kHz
1600-1700	daily	EAf	7245xia
1600-1800	daily	EAf	5985bei
1700-1800	daily	CAf,EAf	15125bko
1700-1800	daily	EAf	7400xia

Tamil	Days	Area	kHz
0200-0300	daily	SAs	11870kas, 13715kas
0300-0400	daily	SAs	13600kun, 13730kas
1400-1500	daily	SAs	9570kas, 9610kas
1500-1600	daily	SAs	9490kas, 9730kas

Thai	Days	Area	kHz
1130-1230	daily	SEA	1080xuw, 7360kun, 9785kun
1330-1430	daily	SEA	1080xuw, 7360kun, 9785kun

Turkish	Days	Area	kHz
1500-1600	daily	ME	7345cer, 9565cer
1600-1700	daily	ME	6165uru, 7325kun
1900-2000	daily	ME	7255kun, 9655kun

Urdu	Days	Area	kHz
0100-0200	daily	SAs	7240kas
0100-0300	daily	SAs	6020kas
0200-0300	daily	SAs	7290kas
1400-1500	daily	SAs	7285kas
1400-1600	daily	SAs	1422kas, 6075kas
1500-1600	daily	SAs	7285kas

Vietnamese	Days	Area	kHz
0000-0100	daily	SEA	11770bei, 13770xia
0400-0600	daily	SEA	603dof, 11650kun, 17740xia
0500-0600	daily	SEA	11640kun
1100-1200	daily	SEA	11785bji, 11990xia
1100-1600	daily	SEA	9550bei
1100-1700	daily	SEA	1296kun
1200-1300	daily	SEA	11640xia, 11720bji
1300-1400	daily	SEA	9685xia
1300-1600	daily	SEA	603dof
1400-1500	daily	SEA	9685bji
1400-1600	daily	SEA	684dof
1600-1700	daily	SEA	6010bei, 7315kun
2300-2400	daily	SEA	603dof
2300-2400	daily	SEA	7220xia, 9415bei

Key: * Relay of CRI News Radio; ** expected to stop at end of 2015.
Ann: Arabic: "Idha'at as-Sin ad-Duwaliyah"; Chinese: "Zhongguo guoji guangbo diantai"; English: "This is China Radio International, broadcasting from Beijing"; German: "Hier ist Radio China International"; Indonesian: "Inilah Radio CRI, China Radio International"; Japanese: "Kochirawa Pekin Hoso, Chugoku Kokusai Hosokyoku desu"; Korean: "Jungguk gukje bangsonggugimnida"; Malay: "Inilah Radio Antarabangsa China, dalam bahasa Melayu"; Mongolian: "Hyatadyn Olon Ulsyn Radio"; Russian: "Govorit Meždunarodnoye Radio Kitaya".

Spanish: "Esta es Radio Internacional de China"; Swahili: "Hii ni Radio China kimataifa"; Vietnamese: "Day la dai phatthanh quoc te Trung quoc".
IS: First bars of the National Anthem.
V: QSL-card.
Notes: Founded on 3 Dec 1941. China Radio International is the External Sce produced under the roof of the State Administration of Radio, Film and Television of the P.R. of China (SARFT).

VOICE OF GUANGXI BEIBU WAN, BEIBU BAY RADIO (Gov)
✉ 75 Minzu Dadao, Nanning, Guangxi 530022, P.R.China.
☎ +86 771 5802999. 🖷 +86 771 5802555.
E: floatingsea@139.com **W:** www.bbrtv.com
Webcast: L
SW: See SARFT, for tx information.
kHz: 5050, 9820

Winter Schedule 2015/2016			
Cantonese	**Days**	**Area**	**kHz**
1100-1200	daily	SEA	5050nnn, 9820nnn
English/Thai/			
Khmer	**Days**	**Area**	**kHz**
2300-2400	daily	SEA	5050nnn, 9820nnn
Khmer	**Days**	**Area**	**kHz**
1500-1600	daily	SEA	5050nnn, 9820nnn
Thai	**Days**	**Area**	**kHz**
1300-1400	daily	SEA	5050nnn, 9820nnn
Vietnamese	**Days**	**Area**	**kHz**
1000-1100	daily	SEA	5050nnn, 9820nnn
1200-1300	daily	SEA	5050nnn, 9820nnn
1400-1500	daily	SEA	5050nnn, 9820nnn

Ann: Chinese: "Guangxi Bei-bu Wan zhi sheng"; English: "Learn about the world. Know China. This is Guangxi Beibu Bay Radio"; Vietnamese: "Tieng noi vinh bac phong guang tay".
V: QSL-letter.
Notes: Beibu Bay Radio is a joint External Service project of the provincial Guanxi People's Broadcasting Station and China Radio International.

VOICE OF THE SOUTH CHINA SEA ‡ (Gov)
✉ See China Radio International for contact details.
W: vscs.cri.cn
Webcast: L
FM/DAB: FM: 101.0MHz Sansha, 10kW; 102.0MHz Qionghai (24h)
Key: ‡ Inactive at time of publication.
Notes: Produced by China Radio International (CRI). Voice of the South China Sea, is a service aimed at countries around the South China Sea, will eventually broadcasts in 6 languages: Chinese, English, Filipino, Indonesian, Malaysian and Vietnamese. The inaugural broadcast was on April 9, 2013. Currently using 10kW FM transmitters. Expected to add MW transmissions, on 1008 kHz.

YUNNAN PEOPLE'S BROADCASTING STATION – THE VOICE OF SHANGRI–LA (Gov)
✉ Voice of Shangri-la, 182 Renmin Xi Lu, Kunming, Yunnan 650031, P.R.China.
☎ +86 871 5310211. 🖷 +86 871 5361744.
E: admin@ynradio.net **W:** www.ynradio.com
Webcast: D/L
SW: See SARFT for tx information.
kHz: 6035

Winter Schedule 2015/2016			
Chinese	**Days**	**Area**	**kHz**
1100-1200	daily	SEA	6035sha
1300-1400	daily	SEA	6035sha
Vietnamese	**Days**	**Area**	**kHz**
1000-1100	daily	SEA	6035sha
1200-1300	daily	SEA	6035sha
1400-1500	daily	SEA	6035sha

Ann: Chinese: "Xianggelila zhi sheng"; English: "Yunnan Radio and Television International, The Voice Shangri-la".
V: QSL-letter.
Notes: External Service of the provincial Yunnan People's Broadc.Stn.

STATE ADMINISTRATION OF RADIO, FILM AND TV (SARFT) (Tx Operator)
✉ 2 Fuxingmenwai Street, Xicheng District, Beijing 100866, P.R.China.

☎ +86 10 66093114. 🖷 +86 10 86092437.
E: sarft@chinasarft.gov.cn
W: www.sarft.gov.cn; www.chinasarft.gov.cn
LP: Minister: Cai Fuchao.
MW: [CAH] Changchun, Jilin prov.: 1017kHz 100kW; [DEH] Luxi, Dehong pref., Yunnan prov.: 900kHz 100kW; [DOF] Dongfang, Hainan prov.: 603/684kHz 600kW; [HDN] Huadian, Jilin prov.: 963/1323kHz 600kW; [HDU] Guangzhou, Liantang, Huadu district, Guangdong prov.: 1341kHz 300kW; [HEI] Shuangyashan, Heilongjiang prov.: 1323 kHz 200kW; [HNL] Changzhou, Henglin, Jiangsu prov.: 1044kHz 600kW; [KAS] Kashgar (Kashi), Sayibage, Xinjiang Uighur autonomous region: 1422kHz 600kW; [KUN] Kunming, Anning, Yunnan prov.: 1188/1296kHz 300kW; [URU] Ürümqi, Hutubi, Xinjiang Uighur autonomous region: 1323/1521kHz 500kW; [XUW] Xuanwei, Yunnan prov.: 1080/1269kHz 600kW.
SW: [BEI] Beijing, Doudian: 150/500kW; [BJI] Baoji, Qishan, Shaanxi prov.: 150kW; [HUH] Hohhot, Bikeqi, Nei Menggu autonomous region: 4 x 100kW; [JIN] Jinhua, Lanxi, Zhejiang prov.: 2 x 100, 3 x 500kW; [KAS] Kashgar (Kashi), Sayibage, Xinjiang Uighur autonomous region: 2 x 100, 8 x 500kW; [KUN] Kunming, Anning, Yunnan prov.: 4 x 150, 4 x 500kW; [NNN] Nanning, Guangxi Zhuang autonomous region: 2 x 15; 2 x 100kW; [SHA] Kunming, Shalang, Yunnan prov.: 1 x 50kW; [SZG] Shijiazhuang, Nanpozhuang, Hebei prov.: 2 x 500kW; [URU] Ürümqi, Hutubi, Xinjiang Uighur autonomous region: 9 x 100, 8 x 500kW; [XIA] Xi'an, Xianyang, Shaanxi prov.: 150/500kW; [XUW] Xuanwei, Yunnan prov.: 4 x 100kW.
Notes: SARFT in an executive branch under the State Council of the People's Republic of China.

CUBA (CUB)

RADIO HABANA CUBA (RHC) (Gov)
✉ Apartado 6240, La Habana 10600, Cuba.
☎ +53 7 877 5524. 🖷 +53 7 8776531.
E: inforhc@enet.cu **W:** www.radiohc.cu
Webcast: L
LP: DG: Lic. Isidro Fardales; Chief Eng: Ing. Luis Pruna Amer; Advisor Consultant to DG: Prof. Arnaldo Coro Antich.
SW: Uses txs operated by Radiocuba.
FM/DAB: FM: 102.5MHz (Havana).
SAT: Hispasat 1D.
kHz: 5040, 6000, 6060, 6075, 6100, 6165, 9535, 9550, 9640, 9710, 9820, 9850, 11670, 11760, 11840, 11880, 11950, 13740, 15230, 15370, 17580, 17730, 17750

Winter Schedule 2015/2016			
Arabic	**Days**	**Area**	**kHz**
1900-1930	daily	NAm	11670hab
2030-2100	daily	Eu	15370hab
Creole	**Days**	**Area**	**kHz**
0100-0130	daily	Car	5040hab
1930-2000	daily	NAm	11670hab
2300-2330	daily	SAm	17730hab
English	**Days**	**Area**	**kHz**
0000-0100	daily	CAm	5040hab
0100-0700	daily	NAm	6000hab, 6165hab
0500-0700	daily	NAm	6060hab, 6100hab
0600-0700	daily	CAm	5040hab
2000-2100	daily	NAm	11670hab
2200-2300	daily	Af	11880hab
Esperanto	**Days**	**Area**	**kHz**
0700-0730	......s	NAm	6100hab
1600-1630	......s	Am	11760hab
2230-2300	......s	SAm	17730hab
French	**Days**	**Area**	**kHz**
0130-0200	daily	Car	5040hab
1930-2000	daily	Eu	15370hab
2100-2130	daily	Af	11880hab
2100-2130	daily	NAm	11670hab
2230-2300	mtwtfs.	SAm	17730hab
Portuguese	**Days**	**Area**	**kHz**
2000-2030	daily	Eu	15370hab
2130-2200	daily	Af	11880hab
2300-2400	daily	SAm	15230hab
2330-2400	daily	SAm	17730hab
Quecha	**Days**	**Area**	**kHz**
0000-0030	daily	SAm	17730hab

Spanish	Days	Area	kHz
0000-0100	.twtfs.	NAm	6000hab*, 11950hab*
0000-0500	daily	NAm	6060hab
0000-0600	daily	SAm	11670hab
0000-0700	daily	SAm	15230hab
0200-0600	daily	CAm	5040hab
1200-1400	daily	Am	6000hab
1200-1400	daily	NAm	9850hab
1200-1500	daily	NAm	9710hab
1200-1500	daily	SAm	17580hab
1200-1600	daily	Car	9640hab
1200-1600	daily	SAm	17730hab, 17750hab
1200-1600	daily	CAm	9820hab
1200-1600	......s	Am	11760hab
1200-1900	mtwtfs.	Am	11760hab
1400-1500	daily	CAm	9550hab
1400-1600	daily	NAm	15370hab
1630-1900	......s	Am	11760hab
2200-0300	daily	Am	11760hab
2200-0500	daily	CAm	9535hab
2200-0500	daily	SAm	13740hab
2200-0600	daily	Car	6075hab
2200-0600	daily	SAm	11840hab
2200-2400	daily	Eu	15370hab
2200-2400	daily	CAm	5040hab

Key: * Mesa Redonda Prgr.
Ann: English: "This is Radio Havana Cuba".
V: QSL-card and letter. (Email to: radiohc@enet.cu)
Notes: Radio Habana Cuba is the External Sce of the state-owned Instituto Cubano de Radio y Television (ICRT). Frequencies and schedule are variable.

RADIOCUBA (Tx Operator)
✉ Habana No 406, e/ Obispo y Obrapía, Habana Vieja, Ciudad de La Habana, Cuba.
☎ +53 7 8607181. 📠 +53 7 8603107.
E: dirgeneral@radiocuba.cu
LP: DG: Justo Moreno García.
SW: [HAB] La Habana, two sites: Bauta, Corralillo (G.C. 22N57 082W33): 1 x 50, 6 x 100kW; Quivicán, San Felipe (G.C. 22N50 082W18): 5 x 250kW.
Notes: Radiocuba, a state operated company that forms part of the Ministry of Information and Communications, is the national transmitter network operator.

CYPRUS (CYP)

FG RADIO (EX EUROPEAN NEWS NETWORK) (Comm)
✉ Based in Nicosia, Cyprus.
☎ +357 22007961.
E: broadcast@cytanet.com.cy (radio production office); news@famagusta-gazette.com/FG.radio-158.htm
✉ P.O.Box 30582, 5344 Famagusta, Cyprus. (Famagusta Gazette)
LP: Chief editor (Famagusta Gazette): Paul Wood.
kHz: 5850, 7570, 9955, 11580, 15770

Winter Schedule 2015/2016			
English	Days	Area	kHz
0115-0130	......s	NAm	11580yfr
0215-0230	......s	NAm	11580yfr
0245-0300	..w....	LAm	9955yfr
0515-0530	..w.f..	LAm	9955yfr
1230-1245	......s	LAm	9955yfr
1400-1415	..w....	LAm	9955yfr
1445-1500	..t.....	LAm	9955yfr
2100-2115	..w....	NAm	7570yfr, 15770yfr
2145-2200	.....s.	NAm	15770yfr
2300-2315	..t.t...	NAm	5850yfr, 11580yfr

IS: Instrumental Waltz.
Notes: Weekly prgr with Europe related news, produced by the team of the online news portal "Famagusta Gazette".

BBC EAST MEDITERRANEAN RELAY STATION
✉ P.O. Box 54912, 3729 Limassol, Cyprus.
☎ +357 24332511. 📠 +357 24332595.
LP: SM: Andreas Themistocleous.

MW: [ZAK] Zakaki (located at Lady's Mile in the Akrotiri Sovereign Base Area): 639/720kHz 500kW.
V: QSL-card. (For direct report)
Notes: Owned by the BBC and operated by Babcock Media Services (see under United Kingdom). The Zygi site closed at the end of April 2015.

FMM RELAY STATION
✉ Cape Gkreko, Cyprus.
☎ +357 23831344. 📠 +357 23831344.
E: psardos@aol.com
LP: Technical Manager: Philippe Sardos.
MW: [CGR] Cape Gkreko: 990kHz 600kW (leased by IBB), 1233kHz 600kW.
V: QSL-letter. (for relayed prgrs)
Notes: Transmitting station owned by the French External Services holding company France Médias Monde (FMM), formerly Audiovisuel extérieur de la France (AEF).

CZECH REPUBLIC (CZE)

RADIO PRAGUE (Pub)
✉ Vinohradská 12, 120 99 Praha 2, Czech Republic.
☎ +420 2 21552933. 📠 +420 2 21552903.
E: cr@radio.cz **W:** www.radio.cz
Webcast: D/L/P. Web-only languages: Czech, French, German, Russian.
LP: Dir: Miroslav Krupicka; Editor-in-Chief: Gerald Schubert.
SW: Leases airtime on WRMI (See under USA).
SAT: Astra 3A (Also on WRN via Eurobird 1, Galaxy 25, Hot Bird 6).
kHz: 738, 9955

	Winter Schedule 2015/2016		
English	Days	Area	kHz
0130-0200	.twtfs.	LAm	9955yfr
0400-0430	m.....s	LAm	9955yfr
1300-1330	mtwtfs.	LAm	9955yfr
Russian	Days	Area	kHz
0030-0100	mtwtfs.	RUS	738msk
0200-0230	daily	RUS	738msk
0530-0600	daily	RUS	738msk
0830-0900	daily	RUS	738msk
1230-1300	daily	RUS	738msk
1800-1830	daily	RUS	738msk
Spanish	Days	Area	kHz
0300-0330	daily	LAm	9955yfr
1100-1130	mtwtf..	LAm	9955yfr

Ann: English: "Welcome to Radio Prague, the External Service of Czech Radio".
IS: Fanfare from Dvořák's 9th Symphony ("From the New World"), played on French horn.
V: QSL-card. Rec. acc. (Online form at: www.radio.cz/en/report)
Notes: Radio Prague (Ceský Rozhlas 7) is the External Sce of the public service Czech Radio (Ceský Rozhlas).

DJIBOUTI (DJI)

IBB RELAY STATION DJIBOUTI
✉ IBB Transmitting Station, Djibouti.
MW: [DJI] Djibouti, Dorale: 1431kHz 600kW.

ECUADOR (EQA)

VOZANDES MEDIA (Rlg)
✉ Casilla 17-17-691, Quito, Ecuador.
☎ +593 2 6101779.
E: hcjb@andenstimme.org **W:** andenstimme.org
✉ Jacinto de la Cuava Oe4-33, y Av. Brasil, Quito, Ecuador
SW: [QUI] Quito, Mount Pichincha: 1 x 10kW.
kHz: 6050

	Winter Schedule 2015/2016		
Chachi	Days	Area	kHz
2130-2200	mtwtf..	LAm	6050qui
Cofan	Days	Area	kHz
0000-0030	daily	LAm	6050qui
Quechua	Days	Area	kHz
0030-0100	mtwtf..	LAm	6050qui

Quechua	Days	Area	kHz
0100-0300	.....ss	LAm	6050qui
0825-1100	mtwtf..	LAm	6050qui
0825-1130	.....ss	LAm	6050qui

Shuar	Days	Area	kHz
2330-2400	mtwtf..	LAm	6050qui

Spanish	Days	Area	kHz
0130-0500	mtwtf..	LAm	6050qui
0300-0500	.....ss	LAm	6050qui
1100-1500	mtwtf..	LAm	6050qui
1130-1500	.....ss	LAm	6050qui
1900-2130	mtwtf..	LAm	6050qui
1900-2400	.....ss	LAm	6050qui
2200-2330	mtwtf..	LAm	6050qui

Waorani	Days	Area	kHz
0030-0100	.....ss	LAm	6050qui
0100-0130	mtwtf..	LAm	6050qui

V: QSL-card.
Notes: The Ecuador-registered Asociación Vozandes Media was founded in 2009 by the staff of former, the Quito-based HCJB German language service, and took over the operation of the SW transmitter in Quito. Vozandes Media produces prgrs in the German and Low German languages and in languages of the indigenous population in Ecuador. Vozandes Media is a partner organisation of World Radio Missionary Fellowship, Inc. (USA) and its media ministry Reach Beyond, Radio HCJB - La Voz des los Andes (Ecuador) and Radio HCJB Deutschland (Germany).

EGYPT (EGY)

RADIO CAIRO (Gov)
P.O. Box 1186, 11511 Cairo, Egypt.
+20 2 25789461. +20 2 25789461.
E: egyptianoverseas_english@hotmail.com; enginfo@ertu.org (ERTU Engineering) **W:** ertu.org
L.P: (ERTU) Pres/Chmn: Esam El Amir; Head of Overseas Broadcasting Service: Mrs. Sana Selim El Shafae.
MW: [ELA] El Arish: 1008kHz, 100kW
SW: [ABS] Abis: 8 x 250, 1 x 500kW; [ABZ] Abu Zaabal: 13 x 100, 1 x 250, 4 x 500kW.
kHz: *1008, 9435, 9570, 9745, 9860, 9885, 9900, 9965, 11665, 11750, 11790, 12070, 13580, 13670, 15285, 15290, 15300, 15345, 15450, 15535, 15610, 15710*

Winter Schedule 2015/2016

Afar	Days	Area	kHz
1600-1700	daily	EAf	15450abz

Albanian	Days	Area	kHz
1500-1600	daily	Eu	13580abs

Amharic	Days	Area	kHz
1730-1900	daily	EAf	15285abz

Arabic	Days	Area	kHz
0030-0430	daily	NAm	9965abs
0200-0700	daily	Eu,NAm	9745abs*
0600-1500	daily	ISR	1008ela
1300-1600	daily	WAf	15535abs
2330-0045	daily	CAm	12070abs

Dari	Days	Area	kHz
1300-1400	daily	WAs	11665abs

English	Days	Area	kHz
0200-0330	daily	NAm	9860abs
1600-1640	daily	ISR	1008ela
1600-1800	daily	CAf,SAf	15345abs
1900-2030	daily	WAf	15290abs
2115-2245	daily	Eu	9900abs
2300-0030	daily	NAm	9965abs

Farsi	Days	Area	kHz
1330-1530	daily	ME	15300abz

French	Days	Area	kHz
1640-1700	daily	ISR	1008ela
2000-2115	daily	Eu	9900abs
2100-2300	daily	WAf	13580abs

German	Days	Area	kHz
1900-2000	daily	Eu	9570abs

Hausa	Days	Area	kHz
1800-2100	daily	WAf	15710abs

Hebrew	Days	Area	kHz
1700-2200	daily	ISR	1008ela

Indonesian	Days	Area	kHz
1230-1400	daily	SEA	15710abs

Italian	Days	Area	kHz
1800-1900	daily	Eu	9435abs

Russian	Days	Area	kHz
1500-1600	daily	ISR	1008ela
1900-2000	daily	Eu	9885abs

Somali	Days	Area	kHz
1700-1730	daily	EAf	15285abz

Spanish	Days	Area	kHz
0045-0200	daily	LAm	11750abs, 12070abs
0045-0200	daily	NAm	9860abs

Swahili	Days	Area	kHz
0400-0600	daily	EAf,CAf	15610abz

Turkish	Days	Area	kHz
1700-1900	daily	ME	9745abs

Urdu	Days	Area	kHz
1600-1800	daily	SAs	13670abs

Uzbek	Days	Area	kHz
1500-1600	daily	CAs	11790abs

Key: * Relay of HS General prgr.
Ann: English: "You are tuned to Radio Cairo"; Arabic: "Sout al-Arab, min al Qahira", "Sowt-il Afrikiy min al-Qahira".
V: QSL-card. (Send to: P.O. Box 566, 11511 Cairo, Egypt). Email rpt to freqmeg@yahoo.com
Notes: Radio Cairo is the External Sce of the Egyptian Radio & TV Union (ERTU).

ESTONIA (EST)

TARTU PERERAADIO (Rlg)
See National Radio section.
Webcast: D/L (radioeli.ru)
MW: [TTU] Tartu, Kavastu: 1035kHz 200kW.
Notes: Tartu Pereraadio is an Estonian evangelical broadcaster. Its transmissions include TWR broadcasts, see TWR Europe schedule (under Austria).

ETHIOPIA (ETH)

ETHIOPIAN BROADCASTING CORPORATION (EBC) (RADIO ETHIOPIA) (Gov)
P.O. Box 654, Addis Ababa, Ethiopia.
+251 11 5524079. +251 11 5512686.
E: info@erta.gov.et **W:** www.ebc.et
L.P: Head, Foreign Languages Dept: Melesse Edea Beyi.
SW: [GJW] Geja: 3 x 100kW.
kHz: *7236*

Winter Schedule 2015/2016

Afar	Days	Area	kHz
1300-1400	daily	EAf,ME	7236gjw±,†

Arabic	Days	Area	kHz
1400-1500	daily	EAf,ME	7236gjw±,†

English	Days	Area	kHz
1600-1700	daily	EAf,ME	7236gjw±,†

French	Days	Area	kHz
1700-1800	daily	EAf,ME	7236gjw±,†

Somali	Days	Area	kHz
1200-1300	daily	EAf,ME	7236gjw±,†

Key: ± Variable Frequency; † Irregular.
Ann: English: "You are tuned to the External Service of Radio Ethiopia"; "Ethiopian Broadcasting Corporation"; "EBC".
V: QSL-card.
Notes: External Sce of the national state broadcaster Ethiopian Broadcasting Corporation (EBC).

FINLAND (FIN)

SCANDINAVIAN WEEKEND RADIO (SWR)
P.O. Box 99, FI-34801 Virrat, Finland.
+358 3 4755776. (studio, during broadcast only)
+358 3 4755776.
E: info@swradio.net **W:** www.swradio.net
Webcast: L (www.radioverkko.fi, 0800-1800 only)/P

L.P: Chief Editor: Esa Saunamäki; QSL Mgr: Tapani Häkkinen.
MW: [VIR] Virrat, Liedenpohja: 1602kHz 0.4kW.
SW: [VIR] Virrat, Liedenpohja: 2 x 0.1kW.
FM/DAB: FM: Virrat, Liedenpohja 94.9MHz
kHz: *1602, 5980, 6170, 11690, 11720*

Winter Schedule 2015/2016

English/Finnish	Days	Area	kHz
0600-0900	.....s.	Eu	5980vir
0800-1400	'....s.	Eu	11720vir
0900-1500	.....s.	Eu	6170vir
1400-1700	.....s.	Eu	11690vir
1500-1900	.....s.	Eu	5980vir
1700-1900	.....s.	Eu	11720vir
1900-2200	.....s.	Eu	6170vir, 11690vir
2200-0600	....fs.	Eu	6170vir
2200-2200	....fs.	Eu	1602vir
2200-2300	...f..	Eu	11720vir
2300-0800	...fs.	Eu	11690vir

Ann: English: "You are listening to Scandinavian Weekend Radio".
V: QSL-card (for written rpt; pdf/doc rpt form downloadable from website) Rp (2 IRCs/EUR/USD); QSL-email (for web report via website)
Notes: On air since 1 July 2000. Run by radio hobbyists of the radio amateur club Vaihtoehtoisen radiotoiminnan tukiyhdistys ry (OH6SWR). The stn is operated on the basis of a series of short-term temporary licences (24h/month, three months in a row), on the first Fri-Sat of the month. Transmissions have to pause for a month before the club is entitled to a new series of licences. There is also a special event broadcast on Midsummer Day in Finland.

FRANCE (F)

MONTE CARLO DOUALIYA (Pub)
✉ 80 rue Camille Desmoulins, F-92130, Issy les Moulineaux, France.
☎ +33 1 84228484.
E: darine.sahnoun@mc-doualiya.com (head of PR, FMM); Via website.
W: www.mc-doualiya.com
Webcast: D/L/P
L.P: Dir: Souad El Tayeb.
MW: via FMM transmitting station Cape Gkreco, Cyprus.
FM/DAB: FM: Txs in Bahrain, Djibouti, Iraq, Jordan, Kuwait, Lebanon, Mauritania, Palestinian Territories and Qatar. (See National Radio section)
SAT: Astra 1N, Badr 4/6, Eutelsat 5WA/7B/9A, Nilesat 201.
kHz: *1233*

Winter Schedule 2015/2016

Arabic	Days	Area	kHz
0330-2020	daily	NAf,ME	1233cgr

Ann: Arabic: "Monte Carlo Doualiya".
V: QSL-card.
Notes: Produced under the umbrella of the External Services holding France Médias Monde (FMM), formerly Audiovisuel extérieur de la France (AEF).

RADIO FRANCE INTERNATIONALE (RFI) (Pub)
✉ 80 rue Camille Desmoulins, F-92130, Issy les Moulineaux, France.
☎ +33 1 84228484.
E: english.service@rfi.fr **W:** www.rfi.fr
Webcast: L/P
✉ B.P. 9516, F-75016 Paris Cedex 16, France.
L.P: Pres/DG (FMM): Marie-Christine Saragosse; Managing Dir (RFI): Geneviève Goëtzinger.
MW/SW: Leased from TDF & foreign relays.
SAT: Anik F1R/F2/F3, Arabsat 5C, AsiaSat 7, Astra 1N, Badr 4/6, Eutelsat 5WA/9BA/16A/36B/Hot Bird 13B, Galaxy 3C&Intelsat 11, Hispasat 1E, Intelsat18/20/30/903, Nimiq 6, SES 5/6/7, Superbird C2.
kHz: *3965, 5925, 7205, 7295, 7390, 9540, 9665, 9675, 9790, 9805, 11580, 11700, 11995, 13685, 13695, 13740, 13750, 15300, 15315, 15360, 15455, 15770, 17615, 17620, 17660, 17685, 17850, 21580, 21620, 21690*

Winter Schedule 2015/2016

English	Days	Area	kHz
0100-0200	..w.fs.	NAm	11580yfr
0200-0300	..w.fs.	NAm	11580yfr
0600-0700	daily	WAf,CAf	9675iss, 13695iss
2100-2200	mt.....	NAm	15770yfr
2115-2200	...w....	NAm	15770yfr

English	Days	Area	kHz
2130-2200	...t...	NAm	15770yfr

French	Days	Area	kHz
0000-2400	daily	Eu	3965iss+
0400-0600	daily	CAf,EAf	7390iss, 9790iss
0500-0600	daily	CAf,EAf	11700iss
0600-0700	daily	WAf	9790iss**
0600-0700	daily	CAf,EAf	11700iss**
0600-0700	daily	NAf,WAf	5925iss*, 7390iss*
0600-0900	daily	Af	15300iss
0700-0800	daily	NAf,WAf	9790iss
0700-0800	daily	WAf,CAf	11700iss, 13695iss*
0700-0900	daily	CAf	17850iss
0800-0900	daily	CAf	21580iss
0800-0900	daily	NAf,WAf	13695iss
1200-1300	daily	WAf,CAf	17660iss
1200-1300	daily	CAf	21580iss, 21690mdc
1200-1300	daily	NAf,WAf	17620iss
1700-1800	daily	CAf	17850iss, 21580iss
1700-1800	daily	WAf,CAf	17620iss
1700-1900	daily	NAf,WAf	13740iss
1700-2000	daily	WAf,CAf	15300iss
1800-2100	daily	WAf,CAf	11995iss
1900-2000	daily	WAf,CAf	13695iss
1900-2200	daily	WAf,CAf	9790iss
2000-2200	daily	WAf,CAf	7205iss

Hausa	Days	Area	kHz
0600-0630	daily	WAf,CAf	7295iss*, 9805iss, 13750iss**
0700-0730	daily	WAf,CAf	13685iss, 15315iss
1600-1700	daily	WAf,CAf	17615iss
2000-2030	daily	WAf,CAf	9540iss

Mandinka	Days	Area	kHz
0800-0830	mtwtf..	WAf,CAf	15455iss
1200-1230	mtwtf..	WAf,CAf	21620iss

Portuguese	Days	Area	kHz
1700-1730	daily	CAf	17685iss
1900-1930	daily	CAf	15360iss

Swahili	Days	Area	kHz
0430-0500	daily	EAf,CAf	9665iss
1500-1600	daily	EAf,CAf	21690iss

Key: + DRM; * Nov-Feb; ** March.
Ann: French: "Ici Paris, Radio France Internationale".
V: QSL-card.
Notes: RFI is produced under the umbrella of the External Services holding France Médias Monde (FMM), formerly Audiovisuel extérieur de la France (AEF). For FMM programming in Arabic, see Monte Carlo Doualiya.

ECHO OF EUROPE ‡
✉ 9 rue de Sébastopol, BP 21531, F-31015 Toulouse Cedex 6, France.
E: contact@echoofeurope.eu **W:** echoofeurope.eu
Webcast: P
L.P: Editor-in-Chief: Simon Marty.
Key: ‡ Inactive at time of publication.
Ann: English: "Echo of Europe, your European news radio"; French: "Vous êtes à l'écoute du programme en Français de Echo of Europe".
Notes: Active since December 2012.

TÉLÉDIFFUSION DE FRANCE S.A.S. (TDF) (Tx Operator)
✉ 106 Avenue Marx Dormoy, 92541 Montrouge Cedex, France.
☎ +33 149651000.
W: www.tdf.fr; www.tdf-group.com
✉ 10 rue d'Oradour-sur-Glane, F-75732 Paris Cedex 15, France. (Radio Division)
☎ +33 155951000. 🖷 +33 155952233.
L.P: (TDF Group) Pres: Olivier Huart; DG: Benoit Mérel.
SW: [ISS] Issoudun: 17 x 500kW.
V: QSL-card. (For RFI and other broadcaster relays via ISS)
Notes: TDF S.A.S., part of the TDF group, is the national French transmitter network operator with shortwave transmitting facilities in Issoudun. The TDF tx centre at Montsinéry (French Guiana) has closed. For other members of the TDF group, see under Germany (Media Broadcast) and Monaco (Monte Carlo Radiodiffusion).

GERMANY (D)

DEUTSCHE WELLE (DW) (Pub)
✉ Kurt-Schumacher-Str. 3, D-53113 Bonn, Germany.
☎ +49 228 4290. 🖷 +49 228 4293000.
E: info@dw.de **W:** www.dw.com
Webcast: D/L/P. Web only languages (some of which may also be broadcast on local FM affiliate stns): Albanian, Arabic, Bosnian, Bulgarian, Croatian, Farsi, Greek,. Hindi, Macedonian, Polish, Portuguese, Romanian, Russian, Serbian, Spanish, Turkish & Ukrainian.
✉ Voltastr. 6, D-13355 Berlin.
☎ +49 30 46460.
L.P: DG: Peter Limbourg; PD: Gerda Meuer; MD, Distribution, Marketing and Technology: Guido Baumhauer; Dir, Int Relations: Klaus Bergmann.
SAT: Badr 4, Eutelsat 5WA/7B/Hot Bird 13B, Intelsat 20, Nilesat 201, SES 3/5.
kHz: *6125, 9800, 9830, 11810, 12005, 13610, 15215, 15275, 15430, 15520, 15530, 15560, 17710, 17800, 21780*

Winter Schedule 2015/2016

Amharic	Days	Area	kHz
1600-1700	daily	ETH	15275trm, 15560dha

Dari	Days	Area	kHz
1330-1400	daily	AFG	15215trm, 15430dha

English	Days	Area	kHz
0400-0500	daily	EAf	9800mey, 11810mdc
0500-0600	daily	SAf	9800mey, 15520mdc
0700-0800	daily	WAf	15530iss, 17800dha

French	Days	Area	kHz
1700-1800	daily	Af	15275iss, 15560iss, 17800asc

Hausa	Days	Area	kHz
0630-0700	daily	WAf	9800iss, 9830sao, 15275mey, 21780dha
1300-1400	daily	WAf	9830sao, 17800iss, 21780dha
1800-1900	daily	WAf	9830sao, 12005iss, 13610iss

Pashto	Days	Area	kHz
1400-1430	daily	AFG	15215trm, 15430dha

Swahili	Days	Area	kHz
0300-0400	daily	EAf	6125mey, 9800iss
1000-1100	daily	EAf	15275mdc, 17710mey
1500-1600	daily	EAf	15275trm, 17710dha

Ann: English: "DW - Deutsche Welle".
V: QSL-card. (Rpt to DW Customer Service)
Notes: Deutsche Welle is a public service External broadcaster.

EVANGELISCHE MISSIONS–GEMEINDEN (Rlg)
✉ Lauenburger Strasse 12, D-51709 Marienheide, Germany.
☎ +49 2264 3625.
E: info@missionsbote.de **W:** www.missionsbote.de
Webcast: D
L.P: Head of missionary society: Andreas Herzog.
kHz: *6055*

Winter Schedule 2015/2016

German	Days	Area	kHz
1130-1200	.....ss	Eu	6055nau

V: QSL-card.
Notes: Produced by Missionswerk Evangelische Missions-Gemeinden in Deutschland e.V.

LUTHERISCHE STUNDE (Rlg)
✉ Postfach 1162, D-27363 Sottrum, Germany.
☎ +49 4264 2436. 🖷 +49 4264 2437.
E: info@lutherischestunde.de **W:** www.lutherischestunde.de
Webcast: D
L.P: MD (Lutherische Stunde e.V.): Petra Schmid.
kHz: *1440, 3995, 7365*

Winter Schedule 2015/2016

German	Days	Area	kHz
0725-0730	daily	Eu	7365wnm
1825-1830	..w....	Eu	1440mrn*
1855-1900	daily	Eu	3995wnm

Key: * Until 31 Dec 2015.
V: QSL-card. (Email to: p.schmid@lutherischestunde.de)
Notes: Produced by Lutherische Stunde e.V.

MISSIONSWERK FRIEDENSSTIMME (Rlg)
✉ Gimborner Str. 20, D-51709 Marienheide, Germany.
☎ +49 2261 60170. 🖷 +49 2261 60173.
E: redaktion@mwfst.de; info@mwfst.de
kHz: *9465, 13710*

Winter Schedule 2015/2016

Russian	Days	Area	kHz
1200-1230	.....s.	RUS	13710nau
1600-1630	.....s.	RUS	9465nau

Notes: Produced by Missionswerk Friedensstimme der Vereinigung der Evangeliums-Christen-Baptisten e.V.

MISSIONSWERK HEUKELBACH (Rlg)
✉ Sülemickerstraße 15, D-51700 Bergneustadt, Germany.
☎ +49 2261 9450. 🖷 +49 2261 94537.
E: info@missionswerk-heukelbach.de
W: www.missionswerk-heukelbach.de
Webcast: D
L.P: Head of missionary organisation: Rudi Joas.
kHz: *3995, 7365*

Winter Schedule 2015/2016

German	Days	Area	kHz
0600-0630	daily	Eu	3995wnm, 7365wnm
1630-1700	daily	Eu	3995wnm, 7365wnm

V: QSL-card.
Notes: Produced by Missionswerk Werner Heukelbach e.V.

RADIO HCJB DEUTSCHLAND (Rlg)
✉ Arbeitsgemeinschaft Radio HCJB e.V., Postfach 8025, D-32736 Detmold, Germany.
☎ +49 5232 7980816. 🖷 +49 30 61090010376.
E: info@hcjb.de; hoffnungswelle@gmx.de **W:** www.hcjb.de
Webcast: L/P
✉ Casilla 17-17-691, Quito, Ecuador. (Vozandes Media)
☎ +593 2 2266808. 🖷 +593 2 2267263.
E: deutsch@andenstimme.org (Vozandes Media)
W: www.andenstimme.org (Vozandes Media)
L.P: Dir: Marco Schaa.
SW: [WNM] Weenermoor: 1 x 1, 1 x 1.5kW
SAT: Astra 1N
kHz: *3995, 7365*

Winter Schedule 2015/2016

English	Days	Area	kHz
0500-1700	daily	Eu	3995wnm
1730-2000	daily	Eu	3995wnm
2030-2300	daily	Eu	3995wnm

German	Days	Area	kHz
0500-1700	daily	Eu	7365wnm
1730-2000	daily	Eu	7365wnm
2030-0400	daily	Eu	7365wnm

German (Low)	Days	Area	kHz
1700-1730	daily	Eu	3995wnm, 7365wnm
2000-2030	daily	Eu	3995wnm, 7365wnm

Russian	Days	Area	kHz
0400-0500	daily	Eu	3995wnm, 7365wnm

Key: * Overnight relays Life FM (Cork, Ireland), in English.
V: QSL-card.
Notes: Arbeitsgemeinschaft Radio HCJB e.V. is a partner organisation of Vozandes Media (Ecuador) and World Radio Missionary Fellowship, Inc. (USA). The 24h programming is produced by various small (mainly religious) prgr producers.

CHANNEL 292
✉ Rudolf-Diesel-Str. 1, D-85296 Rohrbach, Germany.
☎ +49 8442 953901. 🖷 +49 8442 954893.
E: info@channel292.de **W:** www.channel292.de
L.P: CEO (Intermedicom GmbH): Rainer Ebeling (DB8QC).
SW: [ROB] Rohrbach, Waal: 1 x 0.01kW.
kHz: *6070*

Winter Schedule 2015/2016

German/English	Days	Area	kHz
0000-2400	daily	Eu	6070rob†*

Key: † Irregular; * Schedule shows available slots for airtime booking;

actual schedule of relayed third-party prgrs varies constantly, most current schedule on stn website.
V: QSL-email. Rpt to qsl@channel292.de
Notes: The operation of the station (initially launched as "R. 6150" in 2012) is licensed to the company Intermedicom GmbH; behind the station is a group of radio amateurs. The programming consists of relays of third-party prgrs/radio shows; vacant tr hours are sometimes filled with rebroadcasts of vintage radio shows related to offshore radio.

DEUTSCHER WETTERDIENST (DWD)
✉ Frankfurter Str. 135, D-63067 Offenbach, Germany.
☎ +49 69 80610. 🖷 +49 69 80624474.
E: info@dwd.de **W:** www.dwd.de
✉ Transmitter site: DWD Wetterfunkstelle, Haidkamp 10, D-25421 Pinneberg, Germany.
LP: Pres: Prof. Dr. Gerhard Adrian.
SW: [PIN] Pinneberg: 1 x 10kW.
kHz: 5905

	Winter Schedule 2015/2016		
German	**Days**	**Area**	**kHz**
0600-0630	daily	Eu	5905pin*
1200-1230	daily	Eu	5905pin*

Key: * AM/USB
V: QSL-card. Email rpt to seeschifffahrt@dwd.de

DPØ7 SEEFUNK ‡
✉ Estedeich 84, D-21129 Hamburg, Germany.
☎ +49 40 23855780. 🖷 +49 40 74134242.
E: info@dp07.com
W: www.dp07.com/unser-service/kurzwellen-funkbetrieb.html
LP: Company owner: Reiner Dietzel.
SW: Via Radio 700 Kurzwellendienst (airtime lease).
V: QSL-card.
Notes: Maritime weather forecasts for Baltic & North Sea, produced by the company Reiner Horst Dietzel - DP07 Seefunk-. On the air during the leisure time boating season. Seasonal trs ended on 18 October 2015, the relays are planned to resume on 25 March 2016.

EUROPA 24
✉ c/o Interessengemeinschaft Hochfrequenztechnik e.V., Johann-Strauß-Str. 22, D-45711 Datteln, Germany.
E: europa24onshortwave@yahoo.com
SW: [DAT] Datteln (unconfirmed low power).
kHz: 6150

	Winter Schedule 2015/2016		
German	**Days**	**Area**	**kHz**
0700-1800	daily	Eu	6150dat†

Key: † Irregular.
Ann: English: "This is Europe Twenty Four"; German: "Hier ist Europa vierundzwanzig".
V: QSL-card.

HAMBURGER LOKALRADIO
✉ Max-Eichholz-Ring 18, D-21031 Hamburg, Germany. (Editorial Office)
☎ +49 40 7382417. 🖷 +49 40 7382417.
E: redaktion@hamburger-lokalradio.de **W:** www.hhlr.de
✉ c/o Kulturzentrum Lola, Lohbrügger Landstrasse 8, D-21031 Hamburg, Germany. (Studio)
☎ +49 40 72692422. 🖷 +49 40 72692423.
LP: Editor-in-Chief: Michael Kittner.
SW: via tx of MV Baltic Radio. (airtime lease)
kHz: 6190, 7265, 9485

	Winter Schedule 2015/2016		
German/Various	**Days**	**Area**	**kHz**
0700-0900	.....s.	Eu	7265goh
0900-1200	.....s.	Eu	6190goh
1200-1600	.....s.	Eu	7265goh
1200-1600	......s	Eu	9485goh

V: QSL-card.
Notes: Community radio prgr, produced by Anbietergemeinschaft Hamburger Lokalradio e.V.

MV BALTIC RADIO
✉ Seestrasse 17, D-19089 Göhren, Germany.
☎ +49 3861 301380. 🖷 +49 3861 3029720.
E: info@mvbalticradio.de

LP: Mgr: Roland Rohde.
SW: [GOH] Göhren: 1 x 1kW.
kHz: 7265, 9485

	Winter Schedule 2015/2016		
German/Various	**Days**	**Area**	**kHz**
0800-0900	......s	Eu	7265goh*
0900-1000	......s	Eu	9485goh*

Key: * Not every Sun, alternates with other stations.
V: QSL-card.
Notes: Run by R&R Medienservice. Variable schedule. Sells its airtime to small prgr producers (see also under Hamburger Lokalradio).

RADIO 700 KURZWELLENDIENST
✉ Kuchenheimer Str. 155, D-53881 Euskirchen, Germany.
☎ +49 2251 921300. 🖷 +49 2251 921303.
E: info@funkhaus-euskirchen.de **W:** www.shortwaveservice.com; www.classicbroadcast.de; www.radio360.eu
Webcast: L/P (P: www.radio360.eu)
LP: Project coordinator: Christian Millig.
SW: [KLL] Kall, Krekel: 4 x 1, 1 x 20kW.
V: QSL-card. (for relayed prgrs)
Notes: Shortwave relay service and podcast Internet portal, provided by Funkhaus Euskirchen e.V. Frequently changing schedule, details at www.shortwaveservice.com.

RADIO DARC
✉ c/o Rainer Englert (DF2NU), Dorfstrasse 14, D- 85567 Bruck-Alxing, Germany.
☎ +49 8092 83246. 🖷 +49 8092 83247.
E: radio@darc.de **W:** www.darc.de
kHz: 6070

	Winter Schedule 2015/2016		
German	**Days**	**Area**	**kHz**
1000-1100	......s	Eu	6070rob
1600-1700	m......	Eu	6070rob
2000-2100	m......	Eu	6070rob

V: QSL-card.
Notes: Prgr produced by association of German radio amateurs, Deutscher Amateur-Radio-Club e.V. (DARC). On SW since 22 March 2015.

RADIO GLORIA INTERNATIONAL
✉ Postfach 540109, D-01311 Dresden, Germany.
E: radiogloria@aol.com
Webcast: L (www.shortwaveservice.com)
LP: Prgr Host: Armin Mothes.
kHz: 6005, 7265, 7310, 9485

	Winter Schedule 2015/2016		
English/German	**Days**	**Area**	**kHz**
0700-0800	......s	Eu	9485goh*
0800-0900	......s	Eu	7265goh*
0900-1000	......s	Eu	9485goh*
1100-1200	......s	Eu	7310kll*
1600-1700	......s	Eu	6005kll*

Key: * Every 4th Sun; B15 schedule: 26 Dec 2015, 24 Jan & 28 Feb 2016.
V: QSL-card (Rp. 2USD).
Notes: Monthly music show with DJ Armin Mothes.

RADIO JOYSTICK
✉ Postfach 2331, D-55512 Bad Kreuznach, Germany.
☎ +49 179 3615394. 🖷 +49 3212 1154964.
E: chapri@radiojoystick.de **W:** www.radiojoystick.de
Webcast: D/L (via www.play.fm)
LP: Presenter: Jens F. Hofstadt. (a.k.a "Charlie Prince")
kHz: 7330

	Winter Schedule 2015/2016		
German	**Days**	**Area**	**kHz**
1100-1200	......s	Eu	7330mos*

Key: * 1st Sunday of month.
Ann: English: "Radio Joystick, funky sounds for Central Europe".
V: QSL-card.
Notes: Monthly broadcast of the "Charlie-Prince-Show". R. Joystick was founded in 1985; the show has been relayed on SW via various rebroadcasters over the years.

RADIO ÖÖMRANG
Tanenwai 24, D-25946 Nebel-Westerheide, Germany.
☎ +49 4682 2688. 🖷 +49 4682 2262.
E: familie-koelzow@t-online.de
L.P: Producer: Gernot Schrader.
Ann: English: "This is Radio Öömrang, the free voice of the Frisian people".
V: Does not verify.
Notes: The prgr "Radio Öömrang" ("Radio Amrum") is broadcast each year on 21 February (a major North Frisian holiday). The prgr was founded by the radio amateur Arjan Kölzow on the island of Amrum in North Germany. The first SW broadcast was on 21 February 2006. The prgr is in the North Frisian language (Öömrang dialect) as well as Standard German, and is aimed at the descendants of North Frisian immigrants in North America.

IBB RELAY STATIONS GERMANY
IBB Transmitting Station Lampertheim, Postfach 1145, D- 68601 Lampertheim, Germany.
☎ +49 6206 1590
L.P: SM: Michael R. Hardegen.
SW: [BIB] Biblis: 11 x 100kW; [LAM] Lampertheim: 9 x 100kW.
V: QSL-card.

MEDIA BROADCAST GMBH (Tx Operator)
Erna-Scheffler-Str. 1, D-51103 Köln, Germany.
☎ +49 221 71015000.
E: info@media-broadcast.com **W:** www.media-broadcast.com
Joseph-Lammerting-Allee 8 - 10, 50933 Köln, Germany.
L.P: Chairman: Dr. Marcus Englert; CEO: Wolfgang Breuer; Head of SW Sales: Michael Pütz.
SW: [NAU] Nauen: 2 x 100, 4 x 500kW.
V: QSL-card. (For relayed stns. Email rpts: qsl-shortwave@media-broadcast.com).
Notes: Media Broadcast GmbH, part of the TDF Group (France), is a major transmitter network operator in Germany and owns the SW transmitting centre in Nauen.

GREECE (GRC)

ERT (I FONI TIS ELLADAS) (Pub)
Mesogeion Ave. 432, Office P 211, 15342 Agia Paraskevi, Greece.
☎ +30 2106066439.
E: thevoiceofgreece@ert.gr
W: www.ert.gr; www.ert.gr/i-foni-tis-elladas
Webcast: L (webradio.ert.gr/i-foni-tis-elladas)
L.P: Dir: Mrs Gianna Triantafilli.
SW: [AVL] Vathy (Avlida municipality), Kalochori-Pantichi: 2 x 100kW, 1 x 250kW.
kHz: 9420, 9935, 11645

Winter Schedule 2015/2016

Greek	Days	Area	kHz
0400-0800	daily	Eu,Af	11645avl‡
1800-0500	daily	Eu,Am	9935avl‡
1800-0800	daily	Eu,Am	9420avl‡

Key: ‡ Inactive at time of publication.
Ann: Greek: "I Foni tis Elladas".
Notes: SW transmission hours are highly variable and may include short news bulletins in multiple languages. ERT resumed official broadcasts in July 2015, after a hiatus of 2 years.

GUAM (GUM)

KSDA (AWR ASIA/PACIFIC RELAY STATION)
P.O. Box 8990, Agat, Guam 96928. (Transmitting station)
☎ +1 671 5652000. 🖷 +1 671 5652983.
E: guam@awr.org
EIS Building B, Unit 1101, 71/15 Soi Pridi Banomyong 37, Sukhumvit 71 Road, Klongton Nua, Vadhana District, Bangkok 10110, Thailand (AWR Asia/Pacific branch & studios)
☎ +66 223818869.
W: www.awr.org
L.P: SM: Victor Shepherd; Chief Engineer: Brook Powers.
SW: [SDA] Agat, Facpi Point: 5 x 100kW.
Ann: English: "From the beautiful island of Guam in the West Pacific, this is Adventist World Radio, the Voice of Hope".

V: QSL-card (Rpt to AWR Asia/Pacific Branch in Thailand).
Notes: Transmitting station owned by Adventist Broadcasting Service, Inc., see USA for corporate details. For schedules, see AWR Asia/Pacific (Indonesia).

KTWR (TWR RELAY STATION)
P.O.Box 6095, Merizo, Guam 96916-0395. (Transmitting station)
☎ +1 671 8288637. 🖷 +1 671 8288636.
E: ktwrfcd@twr.org **W:** www.ktwr.net
85 Playfair Road #04-01, Tong Yuan Industrial Building, Singapore 368000. (TWR Asia branch & studios)
☎ +65 65015150. 🖷 +65 64443053.
E: info@twr.asia **W:** www.twr.asia
L.P: Stn Dir: George Ross; Chief Engineer: Mike Sabin.
SW: [TWR] Merizo: 3 x 100, 2 x 250kW.
Ann: English: "This is your Station for Inspiration, KTWR, Agana".
IS: "We've a story to tell the Nations", played on an organ.
V: QSL-card. Rp. (3 IRCs)
Notes: Transmitting station owned by TWR, Inc. See USA for corporate details. For schedule, see TWR Asia (Singapore).

INDIA (IND)

ALL INDIA RADIO (AIR) (Pub)
External Services Division, P.O. Box 500, New Delhi-110001, India.
☎ +91 11 23421220. 🖷 +91 11 23421220.
E: esd.gos@air.org.in
W: www.allindiaradio.gov.in; airworldservice.org
New Broadcasting House, 27 Mahadev Road, New Delhi-110001, India. (Studio)
E: gosesdair@yahoo.co.in; adg.esd@air.org.in
W: www.newsonair.com (News)
L.P: Minister for Information & Broadcasting: Arun Jaitely; Minister of State for I&B: Col. Rajyavardhan Rathore; Chmn (Prasar Bharati Corp): Dr. A. Surya Prakash; CEO: Jawhar Sircar; Addl DG, AIR Ext Sces: Dr. Manoj Kr. Patairiya; Engineer-in-Chief: Animesh Chakrborty.
MW: [JAL] Jalandhar: 702kHz 300kW; [KKT] Chinsurah: 594/1134kHz 1000kW; [RAJ] Rajkot 1071kHz 1000kW; [TUT] Tuticorin: 1053kHz 200kW.
SW: [ALG] Aligarh: 4 x 250kW; [BGL] Bengaluru, Doddaballapur: 6 x 500kW (www.airbengaluru.com); [DEL] Delhi, two sites: Khampur (G.C. 28N49 077E07): 7 x 250kW (www.hptkhampur.wix.com/airkhampur); Kingsway (G.C. 28N43 077E12): 2 x 100kW; [MUM] Mumbai: 1 x 100kW; [PAN] Panaji: 2 x 250kW (www.airpanaji.gov.in).
kHz: 594, 702, 1053, 1071, 1134, 4870, 5990, 6145, 6165, 7250, 7270, 7340, 7350, 7370, 7505, 7520, 7550, 7555, 9445, 9575, 9595, 9620, 9635, 9690, 9705, 9800, 9810, 9820, 9835, 9910, 9940, 9950, 11560, 11620, 11645, 11670, 11710, 11715, 11740, 11775, 11840, 11845, 11850, 11935, 11985, 12025, 13605, 13640, 13645, 13695, 13710, 13795, 15030, 15040, 15050, 15120, 15140, 15175, 15185, 15210, 15410, 15770, 17510, 17670, 17705, 17715, 17875, 17895

Winter Schedule 2015/2016

Arabic	Days	Area	kHz
0430-0530	daily	ME	11670alg, 15210pan, 15770del
1730-1945	daily	ME	9620alg, 11710del, 13640bgl

Baluchi	Days	Area	kHz
1500-1600	daily	SAs	1071raj, 6165del, 7340mum, 9620alg

Burmese	Days	Area	kHz
1215-1315	daily	SAs	1134kkt
1215-1315	daily	SEA	9940bgl, 11710del

Chinese	Days	Area	kHz
1145-1315	daily	EAs	11845del**, 15040bgl+, 17705bgl**

Dari	Days	Area	kHz
0300-0345	daily	WAs	7350alg, 9910del, 11560pan
1315-1415	daily	WAs	11560pan

English	Days	Area	kHz
0230-0300	daily	SAs	7505del
1000-1100	daily	SAs	1053tut, 7270cni
1000-1100	daily	EAs	13605bgl, 15030alg, 15410bgl

English	Days	Area	kHz
1000-1100	daily	Pac	13695bgl, 17510del, 17895bgl+
1330-1500	daily	SEA	9690bgl, 11620del, 13710bgl
1530-1545	daily	EAf	7555del
1530-1600	daily	SAs	1053tut
1745-1945	daily	EAf	11935mum, 13695bgl, 17670del
1745-1945	daily	Eu	9950del+, 11670bgl
1745-1945	daily	NAf,WAf	9445del
2045-2230	daily	Eu	9445bgl, 9950del+, 11670bgl
2045-2230	daily	Pac	9910alg, 11620bgl, 11740pan
2245-0045	daily	EAs	9690del, 11645del+, 13605bgl+
2245-0045	daily	SEA	9705pan, 11710del

English/Hindi	Days	Area	kHz
0230-0300	daily	SAs	594kkt
1515-1600	daily	SAs	1134kkt

Farsi	Days	Area	kHz
0400-0430	daily	ME	11670bgl, 15210pan, 15770del
1615-1730	daily	ME	9620alg, 11710del, 13640bgl

French	Days	Area	kHz
1945-2030	daily	NAf,WAf	9620alg, 11710del, 13640bgl

French/Hindi	Days	Area	kHz
1945-2030	daily	Eu	7550bgl+*

Gujarati	Days	Area	kHz
0415-0430	daily	EAf	15120bgl, 15185pan, 17715del+
1515-1600	daily	EAf	11620bgl, 13640bgl, 15175pan

Hindi	Days	Area	kHz
0315-0415	daily	EAf	15120bgl+, 15185pan, 17715del+
0315-0415	daily	ME	11840del, 13695bgl, 15120pan
0430-0530	daily	EAf	15120bgl, 15185pan, 17715del+
1515-1530	daily	EAf	7555del
1615-1730	daily	EAf	7505pan, 9950bgl, 13605bgl, 17670del
1615-1730	daily	ME	9445del, 12025pan
1945-2045	daily	Eu	9950del+, 11670bgl
2300-2400	daily	SEA	9910alg, 11740pan, 13795bgl

Hindi/English	Days	Area	kHz
1745-1945	daily	Eu	7550bgl+*
2045-2230	daily	Eu	7550bgl+*

Indonesian	Days	Area	kHz
0845-0945	daily	SEA	15770pan, 17510del, 17875bgl

Kannada	Days	Area	kHz
0215-0300	daily	ME	13695bgl, 15120bgl

Malayalam	Days	Area	kHz
1730-1830	daily	ME	7505pan, 12025pan

Nepali	Days	Area	kHz
0130-0230	daily	SAs	594kkt, 7505del, 9800del, 11715del
0700-0800	daily	SAs	594kkt, 7520del, 9940del, 11850del
1330-1430	daily	SAs	1134kkt, 4870del, 7555del, 11775pan

Pashto	Days	Area	kHz
0215-0300	daily	WAs	7350alg, 9910del, 11560pan
1415-1530	daily	WAs	11560pan

Punjabi	Days	Area	kHz
0800-0830	daily	SAs	702jal
1130-1230	daily	SAs	702jal
1300-1430	daily	SAs	702jal

Russian	Days	Area	kHz
1615-1715	daily	Eu	9595bgl, 11620bgl+, 15140del

Saraiki	Days	Area	kHz
1230-1300	daily	SAs	702jal

Sindhi	Days	Area	kHz
0100-0200	daily	SAs	1071raj, 5990del, 7370del, 9635alg
1230-1500	daily	SAs	1071raj, 6165del, 7340mum, 9620alg

Sinhala	Days	Area	kHz
0045-0115	daily	SAs	1053tut, 7270cni, 11740pan, 11985del
1300-1500	daily	SAs	1053tut, 7270cni, 9820del, 15050del+

Swahili	Days	Area	kHz
1515-1615	daily	EAf	9950bgl, 13605bgl, 17670del

Tamil	Days	Area	kHz
0000-0045	daily	SAs	1053tut, 7270cni, 9835del, 11985del
0000-0045	daily	SEA	11740pan, 13795bgl
0115-0330	daily	SAs	1053tut
1100-1300	daily	SAs	1053tut
1115-1215	daily	SAs	1134kkt, 7270cni, 17510del
1115-1215	daily	SEA	9810pan, 13695bgl
1500-1530	daily	SAs	1053tut

Telugu	Days	Area	kHz
1215-1245	daily	SEA	9810pan, 13695bgl

Thai	Days	Area	kHz
1115-1200	daily	SEA	11670bgl, 13645alg, 15410pan

Tibetan	Days	Area	kHz
1215-1330	daily	SAs	7555del, 9575bgl, 11775pan, 15040bgl+

Urdu	Days	Area	kHz
0015-0100	daily	SAs	1071raj
0015-0430	daily	SAs	702jal, 6145alg, 7340mum, 7520del, 11620bgl
0200-1230	daily	SAs	1071raj
0800-1130	daily	SAs	7250del
0830-1130	daily	SAs	702jal, 7340mum, 9940del, 11620del
0830-1930	daily	SAs	7520del
1430-1930	daily	SAs	702jal
1600-1930	daily	SAs	1071raj

Key: + DRM; +* DRM Simulcast ** Jammed.

Ann: Dari: "Inja Delhi"; English: "This is the General Overseas Service of All India Radio"; Hindi: "Yeh Akashvani ki videsh prasaran sewa hai"; Nepali: "Yo All India Radio ho"; Sinhala: "Me All India Radio videshiya sevayai"; Tamil: "Idi Akashvani videsh sewai".

V: QSL-card. Rpt to Dpty. Director General (Spectrum Management & Synergy), All India Radio, Room No.204, Akashvani Bhavan, New Delhi-110001. Tel: 91-11-23421062, 23421145; E: spectrum-manager@air.org.in

Notes: External Sce of the national public broadcaster Prasar Bharati Corporation. Began broadcasting on 1 October 1939.

ATHMIK YATRA RADIO (Rlg)

✉ P.O. Box 12, Manjadi Junction P.O., Tiruvalla-5, Kerala 689 105, India.
☎ +91 469 2630654.
E: ayradio4567@gmail.com; atmikyatra@aynepal.com (Nepali)
W: www.ayradio.com; www.aynepal.com (Nepali)
Webcast: D
✉ P.O.Box 3342, Kathmandu, Nepal.
L.P: Pres: Dr K.P. Yohannan.
kHz: *1548, 7215, 9520, 15150, 15235, 15285*

	Winter Schedule 2015/2016		
Ao	**Days**	**Area**	**kHz**
1400-1415	.....s.	As	15235nau
Awadhi	**Days**	**Area**	**kHz**
1600-1615	mtw....	As	15150nau

	Days	Area	kHz
Bagheli	**Days**	**Area**	**kHz**
1545-1600	.wtf..	As	15150nau
Bagri	**Days**	**Area**	**kHz**
0030-0045	mt.....	As	7215nau
Banjara	**Days**	**Area**	**kHz**
0015-0030	m......	SAs	1548trm
1415-1430	.....ss	As	15285nau
Bantawa	**Days**	**Area**	**kHz**
2330-2345	.....s	As	9520nau
Bengali	**Days**	**Area**	**kHz**
0015-0030	.....ss	As	9520nau
1515-1530	....fss	As	15235nau
1515-1530	mtwtf..	SAs	1548trm
Bhili	**Days**	**Area**	**kHz**
0115-0130	m......	As	7215nau
1400-1415	...t...	As	15285nau
Bhojpuri	**Days**	**Area**	**kHz**
1415-1430	....fs.	SAs	1548trm
1445-1500	.....ss	As	15285nau
Bodo	**Days**	**Area**	**kHz**
0000-0015	mt.....	As	9520nau
Bondo	**Days**	**Area**	**kHz**
1400-1415	..w....	As	15285nau
Bundelkhandi	**Days**	**Area**	**kHz**
0030-0045	...f...	As	7215nau
1545-1600	mt.....	As	15150nau
Burmese	**Days**	**Area**	**kHz**
1330-1345	.....s	SAs	1548trm
2345-2400	.twt...	As	9520nau
Chakma	**Days**	**Area**	**kHz**
0015-0030	mt.....	As	9520nau
1415-1430	......s	SAs	1548trm
Chhattisgarhi	**Days**	**Area**	**kHz**
1345-1400	mt.....	SAs	1548trm
1530-1545	mt.....	As	15150nau
Chin	**Days**	**Area**	**kHz**
1345-1400	.....s	SAs	1548trm
2345-2400	m.....s	As	9520nau
Chowdhari	**Days**	**Area**	**kHz**
1330-1345	...t...	SAs	1548trm
Dari	**Days**	**Area**	**kHz**
1545-1615	.....s.	As	15150nau
Deori	**Days**	**Area**	**kHz**
1345-1400	...tf..	As	15235nau
Deshiya	**Days**	**Area**	**kHz**
1345-1400	..wt...	As	15285nau
Dogri	**Days**	**Area**	**kHz**
0045-0100	...tf..	As	7215nau
Dzongkha	**Days**	**Area**	**kHz**
1430-1445	mtw....	As	15235nau
Gamit	**Days**	**Area**	**kHz**
1400-1415	..t....	SAs	1548trm
1415-1430	..wt...	As	15285nau
Garhwali	**Days**	**Area**	**kHz**
0030-0045	.....ss	As	7215nau
Garo	**Days**	**Area**	**kHz**
1415-1430	.....ss	As	15235nau
Gojri	**Days**	**Area**	**kHz**
1230-1245	m......	As	15285nau
Gondi	**Days**	**Area**	**kHz**
1400-1415	...f...	As	15285nau
Gujarati	**Days**	**Area**	**kHz**
1245-1300	...tf..	As	15285nau
1345-1400	..wt...	SAs	1548trm
Gurung	**Days**	**Area**	**kHz**
2330-2345	.tw....	As	9520nau
Halam	**Days**	**Area**	**kHz**
1400-1415	mt.....	As	15235nau
1430-1445	......s	SAs	1548trm
Haryanvi	**Days**	**Area**	**kHz**
1430-1445	.....ss	As	15285nau
Hindi	**Days**	**Area**	**kHz**
1315-1330	.....ss	As	15285nau
Hindi	**Days**	**Area**	**kHz**
1445-1500	.....ss	SAs	1548trm
1445-1500	mtwtf..	As	15285nau
1500-1515	...fss	SAs	1548trm
1615-1630	daily	As	15150nau
Ho	**Days**	**Area**	**kHz**
0015-0030	...f...	As	9520nau
1445-1500	..w....	SAs	1548trm
Kangri	**Days**	**Area**	**kHz**
0045-0100	.....ss	As	7215nau
Kannada	**Days**	**Area**	**kHz**
0000-0015	..wtfss	SAs	1548trm
Karbi	**Days**	**Area**	**kHz**
1400-1415	...tf..	As	15235nau
2345-2400	....fs.	As	9520nau
Kashmiri	**Days**	**Area**	**kHz**
1230-1245	..wt...	As	15285nau
Kaubru	**Days**	**Area**	**kHz**
1345-1400	..w....	As	15235nau
Khandesi	**Days**	**Area**	**kHz**
1315-1330	..w....	As	15285nau
Khariya	**Days**	**Area**	**kHz**
0030-0045	..w....	As	7215nau
1415-1430	..w....	SAs	1548trm
Khasi	**Days**	**Area**	**kHz**
1430-1445	.....ss	As	15235nau
Khota	**Days**	**Area**	**kHz**
1415-1430	m......	SAs	1548trm
Khurukh	**Days**	**Area**	**kHz**
0000-0015	..wt...	As	9520nau
1430-1445	mt.....	SAs	1548trm
Kinnauri	**Days**	**Area**	**kHz**
0100-0115	.....ss	As	7215nau
Kokborok	**Days**	**Area**	**kHz**
1345-1400	mt.....	As	15235nau
1400-1415	.....ss	SAs	1548trm
Konkani	**Days**	**Area**	**kHz**
0000-0015	.t.....	SAs	1548trm
Konyak	**Days**	**Area**	**kHz**
1430-1445	...tf..	As	15235nau
Kotwalia	**Days**	**Area**	**kHz**
0115-0130	..w....	As	7215nau
1415-1430	...t...	SAs	1548trm
1430-1445	....f..	As	15285nau
Koya	**Days**	**Area**	**kHz**
0015-0030	.t.....	SAs	1548trm
1245-1300	.....ss	As	15285nau
Kui	**Days**	**Area**	**kHz**
1330-1345	....fs.	SAs	1548trm
1415-1430	mt.....	As	15285nau
Kuki (Thadou)	**Days**	**Area**	**kHz**
1345-1400	.....ss	As	15235nau
Kukna	**Days**	**Area**	**kHz**
0115-0130	.t.....	As	7215nau
1415-1430	...f...	As	15285nau
1430-1445	...t...	SAs	1548trm
Kupiya	**Days**	**Area**	**kHz**
1400-1415	......s	As	15285nau
Ladakhi	**Days**	**Area**	**kHz**
1230-1245	.t.....	As	15285nau
Lepcha	**Days**	**Area**	**kHz**
1500-1515	.tw....	As	15235nau
Limbu	**Days**	**Area**	**kHz**
2330-2345	....fs.	As	9520nau
Lungeli-Magar	**Days**	**Area**	**kHz**
2330-2345	m......	As	9520nau
Magahi	**Days**	**Area**	**kHz**
0045-0100	..w....	As	7215nau
1430-1445	....fs.	SAs	1548trm
1500-1515	...tf..	As	15235nau
Maithili	**Days**	**Area**	**kHz**
1530-1545	..wtf..	As	15150nau
Malayalam	**Days**	**Area**	**kHz**
0030-0045	daily	SAs	1548trm

Malto	Days	Area	kHz
1330-1345	...f..	As	15285nau
1330-1345	...t..	As	15285nau
1415-1430	.t.....	SAs	1548trm

Marathi	Days	Area	kHz
1315-1330	...tf..	As	15285nau
1330-1345	mtw....	SAs	1548trm

Marwari	Days	Area	kHz
0100-0115	mt.....	As	7215nau
1345-1400	mt.....	As	15285nau

Meitei	Days	Area	kHz
1330-1345	mtw....	As	15285nau
1500-1515	.....ss	As	15235nau

Mising	Days	Area	kHz
0000-0015	...fss	As	9520nau
1415-1430	..wtf..	As	15235nau

Mouchi	Days	Area	kHz
1430-1445	...t..	As	15285nau

Mundari	Days	Area	kHz
1430-1445	..w....	SAs	1548trm
1515-1530	..wt...	As	15235nau

Nepali	Days	Area	kHz
1300-1315	daily	As	15285nau

Netakani	Days	Area	kHz
1345-1400	.....s	As	15285nau

Newari	Days	Area	kHz
1445-1500	...tf..	As	15235nau

Nockte	Days	Area	kHz
1330-1345	mt.....	As	15235nau

Oriya	Days	Area	kHz
1230-1245	....fss	As	15285nau
1345-1400	....fs.	SAs	1548trm

Pashto	Days	Area	kHz
1545-1615	.....s	As	15150nau

Punjabi	Days	Area	kHz
0100-0115	...tf..	As	7215nau
1245-1300	mtw....	As	15285nau

Rajasthani	Days	Area	kHz
0045-0100	mt.....	As	7215nau

Rengma	Days	Area	kHz
1400-1415	..w....	As	15235nau

Rongmei	Days	Area	kHz
1330-1345	......s	As	15235nau

Sadri	Days	Area	kHz
1445-1500	mt.....	SAs	1548trm
1600-1615	...tf..	As	15150nau

Sambalpuri	Days	Area	kHz
1400-1415	....f..	SAs	1548trm
1430-1445	mt.....	As	15285nau

Santhali	Days	Area	kHz
0015-0030	..wt...	As	9520nau
1315-1330	m......	As	15285nau
1400-1415	mtw....	SAs	1548trm
1415-1430	mt.....	As	15235nau

Sarchopa	Days	Area	kHz
1445-1500	mtw....	As	15235nau

Sherpa	Days	Area	kHz
1500-1515	m......	As	15235nau
2330-2345	...t...	As	9520nau

Sindhi	Days	Area	kHz
0100-0115	..w....	As	7215nau
1530-1545	.....ss	As	15150nau

Sinhala	Days	Area	kHz
2345-2400	m....s	SAs	1548trm

Soura	Days	Area	kHz
1400-1415	mt.....	As	15285nau
1445-1500	....f..	SAs	1548trm

Sumi	Days	Area	kHz
1400-1415	......s	As	15235nau

Tamang	Days	Area	kHz
1515-1530	mt.....	As	15235nau

Tamil	Days	Area	kHz
2345-2400	.twtfs.	SAs	1548trm

Tangkhul	Days	Area	kHz
1330-1345	....fs.	As	15235nau

Telugu	Days	Area	kHz
0015-0030	..wtfss	SAs	1548trm

Tharu	Days	Area	kHz
1330-1345	..wt...	As	15235nau

Tibetan (Amdo)	Days	Area	kHz
1330-1345	.....s.	As	15285nau

Tibetan (Khams)	Days	Area	kHz
1445-1500	.....ss	As	15235nau

Tibetan (Lhasa)	Days	Area	kHz
1330-1345	......s	As	15285nau

Tulu	Days	Area	kHz
0000-0015	m......	SAs	1548trm

Urdu	Days	Area	kHz
1345-1400	....fs.	As	15285nau
1515-1530	.....ss	SAs	1548trm

Vadari	Days	Area	kHz
0115-0130	...t...	As	7215nau
1315-1330	.t.....	As	15285nau

Varli	Days	Area	kHz
0115-0130	....f..	As	7215nau

Varti	Days	Area	kHz
1430-1445	..w....	As	15285nau

Vasavi	Days	Area	kHz
0030-0045	...t...	As	7215nau
1445-1500	...t...	SAs	1548trm

Yerukala	Days	Area	kHz
1400-1415	.....s.	As	15285nau

Ann: Malayalam: "Athmeeya Yathra".
V: QSL-card.
Notes: Athmik Yatra Radio ("AY Radio") is the radio mission of the Believers Church (a network of Pentecostal Churches in India). Successor station to "Gospel For Asia" (GFA). The name of the service originates in the prgr "Athmik Yatra" ("Spiritual Journey"), hosted by K.P. Yohannan, and transmitted for Malalayam speakers in India via Trans World Radio since 1985.

FEBA INDIA (Rlg)

✉ 7 Commissariat Road, P.O Box: 25066, Bangalore 560 025, India. (Head Office & Studio)
☎ +91 80 25328191; +91 80 25559063. 🖷 +91 80 25585098.
E: febaindia@vsnl.com **W:** febaindia.org
Webcast: febaonline.org
✉ A-42-44, Manushree Building, Commercial Complex, Dr.Mukerjee Nagar, New Delhi 110 009, India.(Branch Office & Studio)
☎ +91 11 27652426; +91 11 27652084.
L.P: Dir: Christian Benjamin.
kHz: 873, 1125, 9540, 9775

Winter Schedule 2015/2016

English	Days	Area	kHz
1330-1345	m......	As	9775trm

Hindi	Days	Area	kHz
1330-1345	.....s.	As	9775trm
1430-1500	daily	As	9540tac

Kannada	Days	Area	kHz
1330-1400	....f..	As	9775trm

Kuvi	Days	Area	kHz
1345-1400	.t.....	As	9775trm

Malayalam	Days	Area	kHz
1330-1345	...t...	As	9775trm
1345-1400	..wtfs.	As	9775trm

Tamil	Days	Area	kHz
0030-0100	mt...s	As	1125put
0130-0215	......s	As	873put
1330-1400	......s	As	9775trm
1345-1400	m......	As	9775trm

Telugu	Days	Area	kHz
1330-1345	.tw....	As	9775trm

V: QSL-email. E-mail rpt to: kenneth@febaindia.org (Kenneth Edward)
Notes: Far East Broadcasting Associates of India (FEBA India) is regional partner of Far East Broadcasting Company, Inc (USA) (see USA for FEBC corporate details), targeting the Indian subcontinent.

TWR INDIA (Rlg)

✉ 1st Floor, 24/46, Aspiran Garden 1st St, Aspiran Garden Colony, Kilpauk, Chennai, Tamil Nadu 600010, India.
☎ +91 11 26515790. 📠 +91 11 6868049.
E: info@twr.in **W:** twr.in; radio882.com
Webcast: D/L
L.P: CEO: George Philip.
kHz: 882, 1467, 7280, 7505, 12025, 15225, 15240, 15280, 15360, 15755

Winter Schedule 2015/2016

Awadhi	Days	Area	kHz
1400-1415	.t.....	As	15755tac

Banjara	Days	Area	kHz
1215-1230	.t.....	SAs	882put

Bengali	Days	Area	kHz
0030-0045	mtwtf..	As	7280tac
1315-1330	.....s.	As	12025erv
2230-2300	daily	SAs	882put

Bhili	Days	Area	kHz
1500-1515	.tw....	As	12025erv

Bhojpuri	Days	Area	kHz
0045-0115	mtwtf..	As	7280tac

Bondo	Days	Area	kHz
1330-1345	.....s	As	12025erv

Braj Bhasha	Days	Area	kHz
1315-1330	....f..	As	12025erv

Bundeli	Days	Area	kHz
1345-1415	.....s.	As	12025erv

Chhattisgarhi	Days	Area	kHz
1230-1245	m......	SAs	882put
1245-1315	mtwtf..	SAs	882put
1300-1315	.....ss	SAs	882put

Chodri	Days	Area	kHz
1445-1500	.....ss	As	12025erv

Dari	Days	Area	kHz
1530-1600	daily	WAs	1467bis

Deccani	Days	Area	kHz
1215-1230	...f..	SAs	882put
1315-1345	mtwtf..	SAs	882put

Dhodiya	Days	Area	kHz
1515-1530	..wt...	As	12025erv

Dogri	Days	Area	kHz
1315-1330	mtwtf..	As	15755tac

Dzongkha	Days	Area	kHz
0115-0130	mtw...s	As	7280tac

English	Days	Area	kHz
0030-0045	m...fss	SAs	882put
0115-0130	..wt...	SAs	882put
1200-1215	daily	SAs	882put
1215-1230	.....s.	SAs	882put
1230-1245	.....s.	SAs	882put
1545-1615	.....ss	SAs	882put

Gamit	Days	Area	kHz
1500-1515	m......	As	12025erv
1500-1530	.....ss	As	12025erv

Garhwali	Days	Area	kHz
1330-1345	.....s.	As	12025erv
1415-1430	mtwtf..	As	15755tac

Gondi	Days	Area	kHz
1215-1230	.....s	SAs	882put
1545-1615	mtwtf..	SAs	882put

Gujarati	Days	Area	kHz
1230-1245	..wt...	SAs	882put
1315-1345	.....s.	SAs	882put
1345-1415	.....s	SAs	882put
1400-1415	.....s.	SAs	882put
1430-1445	.....s.	SAs	882put
2300-2330	..wtfss	SAs	882put

Haryanvi	Days	Area	kHz
1330-1345	....f..	As	12025erv

Hindi	Days	Area	kHz
0100-0115	.....s	As	7280tac
1315-1430	.....ss	As	15755tac
1330-1400	.....s	As	1467bis
1330-1400	mtwtf..	As	15755tac
1400-1415	m.wtf..	As	15755tac
1430-1445	daily	As	7505tac
1445-1515	mtwtfs.	As	7505tac

Ho	Days	Area	kHz
1300-1315	.....s.	As	12025erv

Kannada	Days	Area	kHz
0100-0115	...fs.	SAs	882put
0115-0130	.....s.	SAs	882put
1415-1445	mtwtf.s	SAs	882put

Kashmiri	Days	Area	kHz
1330-1345	.....s.	As	1467bis
1330-1345	..w....	As	12025erv

Kharia	Days	Area	kHz
1400-1415	.....s	As	12025erv

Kokborok	Days	Area	kHz
1230-1300	mtwtf..	As	15240twr
1245-1300	.....s	As	15240twr

Konkani	Days	Area	kHz
0045-0100	.....s.	SAs	882put
1215-1230	..w....	SAs	882put

Kotwalia	Days	Area	kHz
2315-2330	m......	SAs	882put

Koya	Days	Area	kHz
1215-1230	m......	SAs	882put

Kui	Days	Area	kHz
1245-1300	.....s.	As	12025erv

Kukna	Days	Area	kHz
2300-2315	mt.....	SAs	882put

Kumauni	Days	Area	kHz
1300-1315	.....s	As	12025erv
1345-1355	.....s.	As	1467bis

Kuruk	Days	Area	kHz
1345-1400	.....s	As	12025erv
1415-1430	..tfs.	As	12025erv

Kutchi	Days	Area	kHz
2315-2330	.t.....	SAs	882put

Magahi	Days	Area	kHz
1415-1430	m.....s	As	12025erv

Maithili	Days	Area	kHz
1330-1345	mt.....	As	12025erv
1345-1415	mtwtf..	As	12025erv

Malayalam	Days	Area	kHz
0100-0130	.....s	SAs	882put
1230-1245	.....s	SAs	882put
2330-2400	daily	SAs	882put

Malvi	Days	Area	kHz
0115-0130	...f..	SAs	882put

Manipuri	Days	Area	kHz
1330-1345	.....s	As	15225twr

Marathi	Days	Area	kHz
1430-1500	.....s.	SAs	882put
1445-1515	mtwtf..	SAs	882put

Marwari	Days	Area	kHz
1315-1330	mt...s	As	12025erv

Mawchi	Days	Area	kHz
1515-1530	mt.....	As	12025erv

Mewadi	Days	Area	kHz
1315-1330	..wt...	As	12025erv

Mundari	Days	Area	kHz
1415-1430	.tw....	As	12025erv

Nepali	Days	Area	kHz
0115-0130	...t...	As	7280tac
1400-1500	daily	As	15280twr

Oriya	Days	Area	kHz
0100-0115	..w....	SAs	882put
1415-1430	.....s.	SAs	882put
1500-1530	.....s.	SAs	882put
1500-1545	.....s	SAs	882put
1515-1545	mtwtf..	SAs	882put

Pashto	Days	Area	kHz
1500-1530	daily	WAs	1467bis
1600-1630	daily	WAs	1467bis

Punjabi	Days	Area	kHz
1330-1400	mtwtf..	As	1467bis
1355-1430	.....s.	As	1467bis
1400-1430	mtwtf.s	As	1467bis
1445-1515	.....s	As	7505tac
1500-1515	m...s.	As	1467bis
1500-1530	..t...	As	1467bis
1515-1545	daily	As	7505tac
1545-1615	mtwtf..	As	7505tac
Sadri	**Days**	**Area**	**kHz**
1430-1445	....ss	As	12025erv
Santhali	**Days**	**Area**	**kHz**
1245-1300	......s	As	12025erv
1300-1315	daily	As	15240twr
1315-1330	.....s	As	15225twr
Sindhi	**Days**	**Area**	**kHz**
1430-1500	mtwtf..	As	12025erv
Soura	**Days**	**Area**	**kHz**
1245-1300	....ss	SAs	882put
Tamil	**Days**	**Area**	**kHz**
0000-0030	daily	SAs	882put
0030-0045	.twt...	SAs	882put
0045-0100	mtwtf..	SAs	882put
0100-0130	mt.....	SAs	882put
Telugu	**Days**	**Area**	**kHz**
0100-0115	...t...	SAs	882put
1315-1345	......s	SAs	882put
1345-1400	....s.	SAs	882put
1345-1415	mtwtf..	SAs	882put
1530-1545	.....s.	SAs	882put
Tibetan	**Days**	**Area**	**kHz**
1330-1345	...t...	As	12025erv
Tulu	**Days**	**Area**	**kHz**
0045-0100	......s	SAs	882put
Urdu	**Days**	**Area**	**kHz**
1330-1400	.....s.	As	1467bis
1400-1415	daily	As	15360man
1430-1500	daily	As	1467bis
1500-1530	.tw....	As	1467bis
1515-1530	m......	As	1467bis
1530-1600	....ss	As	12025erv
Varli	**Days**	**Area**	**kHz**
1230-1245	.t.....	SAs	882put
Vasavi	**Days**	**Area**	**kHz**
1500-1515	...tf..	As	12025erv

V: QSL-card.
Notes: TWR regional division, covering the Indian subcontinent. For corporate details, see under TWR (USA).

INDONESIA (INS)

VOICE OF INDONESIA (VOI) (Pub)
✉ P.O. Box 1157, Jakarta 10110, Indonesia.
☎ +62 21 3456811. 🖷 +62 21 3500990.
E: english@voi.co.id **W:** www.voi.co.id
Webcast: D/L
✉ Physical address: 4-5 Jalan Medan Merdeka Barat, Jakarta 10110, Indonesia.
L.P: Dir, Broadcasting: Kabul Budiono.
SW: [JAK] Jakarta, Cimanggis: 2 x 50, 3 x 100, 9 x 250kW.
kHz: 9526

Winter Schedule 2015/2016

Arabic	Days	Area	kHz
1600-1700	daily	Eu,NAf,ME	9526jak†
Chinese	**Days**	**Area**	**kHz**
1100-1200	daily	As,Pac	9526jak†
1500-1600	daily	As,Pac	9526jak†
English	**Days**	**Area**	**kHz**
1000-1100	daily	As,Pac	9526jak†
1300-1400	daily	As,Pac	9526jak†
1900-2000	daily	Eu,NAf,ME	9526jak†
French	**Days**	**Area**	**kHz**
2000-2100	daily	Eu,NAf,ME	9526jak†
German	**Days**	**Area**	**kHz**
1800-1900	daily	Eu	9526jak†

Indonesian	Days	Area	kHz
1400-1500	daily	As,Pac	9526jak†
Japanese	**Days**	**Area**	**kHz**
1200-1300	daily	As,Pac	9526jak†
Spanish	**Days**	**Area**	**kHz**
1700-1800	daily	Eu	9526jak†

Key: † Irregular.
Ann: English: "This is the Voice of Indonesia, in Jakarta"; Spanish: "La Voz de Indonesia en Jakarta".
V: QSL-card. (Online rpt form available)
Notes: The Voice of Indonesia is the External Sce of the state broadcaster Radio Republik Indonesia.

IRAN (IRN)

VOICE OF THE ISLAMIC REPUBLIC OF IRAN (VOIRI) (Gov)
✉ P.O. Box 19395-6767, Tehran, Iran.
☎ +98 21 22013687; +98 21 22162731. 🖷 +98 21 22044287.
E: englishradio@irib.ir; bm@irib.ir; prworld@irib.ir
W: worldservice.irib.ir
Webcast: D/L
☎ +98 21 22013720.
L.P: IRIB) Pres: Mohammad Sarafraz; DG, Int. Affairs: Abbas Naseri Taheri.
MW: [AHW] Ahwaz, Bandar-e Mahshar: 576/1080kHz 750kW; 1530kHz 50kW; [BNB] Bonab: 639kHz 400kW; [BNT] Bandar-e Torkaman: 1449kHz 400kW; [CHB] Chabahar: 765kHz 1000kW; [JOL] Jolfa 1323kHz 50kW; [KER] Kerman: 1224kHz 600kW; [KIA] Bandar-e Kiashahr: 702kHz 500kW; [QSH] Qasr-e Shirin: 612/1161kHz 600kW; [TYB] Tayebad: 720kHz 400kW; [ZAB] Zabol: 1098kHz 200kW
SW: [AHW] Ahwaz, Bandar-e Mahshar: 2 x 250kW; [KAM] Tehran, Kamalabad: 10 x 100, 3 x 250, 1 x 350, 12 x 500kW; [SIR] Sirjan: 10 x 500kW; [ZAH] Zahedan: 2 x 500kW.
SAT: Eutelsat 3B, Eutelsat Hot Bird 13C, Galaxy 19, Intelsat 902.
kHz: 576, 612, 639, 702, 720, 765, 1080, 1098, 1161, 1224, 1323, 1395, 1449, 5900, 5920, 5925, 5930, 5935, 5940, 5945, 5950, 5965, 5995, 6005, 6040, 6055, 6060, 6075, 6085, 6090, 6100, 6110, 6120, 6135, 6140, 6145, 6175, 6195, 7220, 7225, 7270, 7280, 7285, 7290, 7300, 7305, 7315, 7320, 7325, 7330, 7345, 7350, 7360, 7370, 7375, 7380, 7390, 7400, 7425, 7445, 9445, 9480, 9490, 9500, 9510, 9515, 9545, 9550, 9580, 9585, 9590, 9630, 9710, 9740, 9755, 9800, 9850, 9875, 9895, 11675, 11720, 11730, 11760, 11780, 11810, 11825, 11830, 11880, 11925, 11940, 11955, 12040, 13570, 13680, 13730, 13735, 13740, 13750, 13780, 13785, 13790, 13820, 13830, 13865, 15085, 15140, 15170, 15175, 15220, 15240, 15300, 15330, 15360, 15400, 15450, 15460, 15490, 15525, 15530, 15615, 15750, 17560, 17640, 17660, 17670, 17685, 17690, 17710, 17715, 17820, 17865, 21510, 21520, 21600

Winter Schedule 2015/2016

Albanian	Days	Area	kHz
0620-0720	daily	Eu	13820kam, 15490sir
1820-1920	daily	Eu	5925sir, 9850kam
2020-2120	daily	Eu	5935sir, 9630kam
Arabic	**Days**	**Area**	**kHz**
0000-2400	daily	ME	1224kih
0130-0420	daily	ME	1161qsh
0220-1250	daily	ME	765chb
0230-0530	daily	ME	6055kam
0230-0530	daily	NAf,ME	7370kam, 9895zah
0320-0420	daily	ME	6175kam*, 7425sir*
0330-1630	daily	ME	576ahw
0520-1630	daily	ME	612qsh
0530-0830	daily	ME	13780kam
0530-1030	daily	NAf,ME	15360sir
0530-1420	daily	NAf,ME	15750zah
0830-1430	daily	ME	13750kam
1030-1130	daily	NAf,ME	11760sir, 13790kam
1030-1430	daily	NAf,ME	13570kam
1430-1700	daily	NAf,ME	6120kam
1430-1730	daily	ME	9515kam
1530-0330	daily	ME	1080ahw
1620-0120	daily	ME	765chb
1630-2030	daily	ME	1161qsh
1700-0230	daily	NAf,ME	6060zah
1730-2030	daily	ME	7285kam

Armenian	Days	Area	kHz
0250-0320	daily	Cau	6145sir, 7300sir
0920-0950	daily	Cau	11825sir, 15220sir
1620-1720	daily	Cau	5945sir, 7290sir

Azeri	Days	Area	kHz
0320-0520	daily	ME	1323jol, 7380sir
0320-0520	daily	Cau	702kia
1420-1650	daily	ME	702kia, 1323jol, 7360zah

Azeri (Aran)	Days	Area	kHz
0530-0930	daily	Cau	702kia

Bengali	Days	Area	kHz
1420-1520	daily	ME	7320sir
1420-1520	daily	SAs	9800sir, 11760kam
1620-1650	daily	SAs	7375kam, 9740kam

Bosnian	Days	Area	kHz
0520-0620	daily	Eu	13735kam, 15330sir
1720-1820	daily	Eu	6175sir, 9850kam
2120-2220	daily	Eu	5950sir, 9590kam

Chinese	Days	Area	kHz
1150-1250	daily	EAs	15140kam, 15525kam, 17560sir, 17670sir
2320-0020	daily	EAs	6090sir, 6110sir, 9490kam

Dari	Days	Area	kHz
0250-0620	daily	WAs	9480ahw, 11925sir
0300-0630	daily	ME	1098zab
0300-1500	daily	WAs	720tyb
0620-0820	daily	WAs	15400kam
0820-1150	daily	WAs	15300kam
0820-1420	daily	WAs	13830ahw
0820-1450	daily	WAs	1098zab
1150-1450	daily	WAs	11720kam

English	Days	Area	kHz
0320-0420	daily	NAm	7325kam**, 9710sir**
1020-1120	daily	ME	702kia
1020-1120	daily	SAs	17560kam, 21510kam
1520-1620	daily	SAs,SEA	11940kam, 13785sir
1920-2020	daily	Eu	6040sir, 7425kam
1920-2020	daily	SAf	13735kam, 15460sir

French	Days	Area	kHz
0620-0720	daily	Eu,NAf	15450kam, 17865kam
1820-1920	daily	Eu	5935sir, 6135kam
1820-1920	daily	WAf	11955sir

German	Days	Area	kHz
0720-0820	daily	Eu	15175kam, 17690sir
1720-1820	daily	Eu	5900kam, 7425sir

Hausa	Days	Area	kHz
0550-0650	daily	WAf	17560sir
1120-1150	daily	WAf	21520sir, 21600sir
1820-1920	daily	WAf	9545kam, 12040sir

Hebrew	Days	Area	kHz
0420-0450	daily	ME	9755sir, 11780sir
1150-1220	daily	ME	13740kam, 15240sir

Hindi	Days	Area	kHz
0150-0250	daily	SAs	6085sir, 7280sir
1420-1520	daily	SAs	11730kam, 13790sir

Indonesian	Days	Area	kHz
1220-1320	daily	SEA	15360kam, 17715sir
2220-2320	daily	SEA	9490kam, 11830sir

Italian	Days	Area	kHz
0620-0720	daily	Eu	15085kam, 17660sir
1920-1950	daily	Eu	6135kam, 7305sir

Japanese	Days	Area	kHz
1320-1420	daily	EAs	9585sir, 12040kam
2050-2150	daily	EAs	5965sir, 7425sir

Kazakh	Days	Area	kHz
0920-1020	daily	CAs	15615kam, 17660sir
1520-1620	daily	CAs	7380ahw, 9480sir

Kurdish	Days	Area	kHz
0420-0520	daily	ME	639bnb, 7350kam, 9875sir
0430-0520	daily	ME	612qsh

Kurdish	Days	Area	kHz
1320-1620	daily	ME	639bnb, 5920kam

Pashto	Days	Area	kHz
0220-0320	daily	WAs	6075sir, 7390kam
0720-0820	daily	WAs	1098zab, 11810sir, 13730sir
1220-1320	daily	WAs	7360sir, 9510kam
1250-1320	daily	WAs	765chb
1620-1720	daily	WAs	5935sir, 7345ahw

Russian	Days	Area	kHz
0820-0920	daily	Eu	17685kam
0820-0920	daily	Eu,CAs	15170sir, 17820sir
1420-1520	daily	Cau,CAs	1449bnt, 11880sir
1420-1520	daily	Eu,CAs	7350kam, 9580ahw
1650-1750	daily	Eu,Cau	6110ahw, 7375kam
1750-1850	daily	Eu,Cau	6110kam, 7220sir
1920-2020	daily	Eu,Cau	702kia, 6195kam, 7225sir

Spanish	Days	Area	kHz
0020-0220	daily	LAm	9445kam
0020-0320	daily	LAm,Eu	7225kam
0520-0620	daily	Eu	13865sir, 15530kam
2020-2120	daily	Eu	6195kam, 7400sir

Swahili	Days	Area	kHz
0350-0450	daily	CAf,EAf	11825sir, 13680sir
0820-0920	daily	CAf,EAf	17640kam, 17710sir
1720-1820	daily	CAf,EAf	13750sir
1720-1820	daily	EAf,ME	11830kam

Tajik	Days	Area	kHz
0050-0220	daily	CAs	720tyb, 5950sir, 7270kam
1550-1720	daily	CAs	720tyb, 6005sir, 7445kam
1550-1720	daily	WAs	1098zab

Talysh	Days	Area	kHz
1720-1820	daily	ME	702kia

Turkish	Days	Area	kHz
0420-0550	daily	ME	7330kam, 9550kam
1550-1720	daily	ME	5995kam, 7315kam
1820-1920	daily	ME	639bnb, 702kia

Turkmen	Days	Area	kHz
1250-1420	daily	CAs	1449bnt
1520-1920	daily	CAs	1395-***, 1449bnt

Urdu	Days	Area	kHz
0120-0220	daily	SAs	6100kam, 6140ahw, 7360kam
0130-0230	daily	ME	1098zab
0130-0230	daily	SAs	765chb
1250-1420	daily	ME	11675kam
1250-1420	daily	SAs	9500sir, 11730kam
1320-1420	daily	SAs	765chb
1520-1620	daily	SAs	5940sir
1520-1720	daily	SAs	765chb

Uzbek	Days	Area	kHz
0220-0250	daily	CAs	5950kam, 7300sir
1450-1550	daily	SAs	7445sir
1450-1550	daily	CAs,SAs	5930kam

Key: * "VO Palestine" prgr; ** "VO Justice" prgr. *** Tx site and power unknown, but thought to be in, or near, the Golestan district of Iran.

Ann: Arabic: "Huna Tahran - Sawt al Jumhuriya al Islamiya fi Iran"; English: "This is the Voice of the Islamic Republic of Iran", V.O.J. prgr: "This is the Voice of Justice"; French: "Ici Tehran, la Voix de la République Islamique de l'Iran"; Russian: "Govorit Tegeran, Golos Islamskoy Respubliki Iran".

IS: "Love's Rainfall", by Nasser Cheshmazar.

V: QSL-card.

Notes: The Voice of the Islamic Republic of Iran is the External Sce of the state broadcaster IRIB. The prgr "Voice of Justice" is aimed at listeners in the USA. The "Voice of the Palestinian Islamic Revolution" prgr targets listeners in the territories under Palestinian Authority. External Sce in Farsi/Persian is known as "Seda-ye Ashena" (www.sedayeashna.ir) and is not available via terrestrial broadcasting methods.

IRELAND (IRL)

RTÉ RADIO WORLDWIDE (Pub)
✉ RTÉ, Donnybrook, Dublin 4, Ireland.
☎ +353 1 208 3111. 🖷 +353 1 208 3080.
E: hearus@rte.ie
W: www.rte.ie/radio/page/138546-rte-radio-worldwide
Webcast: D/L/P
L.P: DG, RTÉ: Noel Curran; MD, Radio: Jim Jennings.
SAT: (via WRN English) Eutelsat 28A/36B/Hot Bird 13A, Intelsat 7/10, Galaxy 19, Sirius FM 5, Superbird C2, Telstar 18, XM3/4.
kHz: 5820

Winter Schedule 2015/2016

English/ Irish Gaelic	Days	Area	kHz
1930-2000	mtwtf..	Af	5820mdc

Ann: English: "RTÉ Ireland, a production of RTÉ Radio One".
V: QSL-card.
Notes: RTÉ is Ireland's national Public Service broadcaster.

ITALY (I)

IRRS–SHORTWAVE (NEXUS–IBA)
✉ P.O. Box 10980, I-20110 Milano, Italy.
☎ +39 02 2666971. 🖷 +39 02 70638151.
E: info@nexus.org **W:** www.nexus.org (General); www.egradio.org (Religious relays)
Webcast: L (mp3.nexus.org)
L.P: Pres: Alfredo E. Cotroneo.
SW: Via tx leased from Radiocom (Romania).
kHz: 7290, 9510, 15190, 15515

Winter Schedule 2015/2016

English	Days	Area	kHz
0900-1000	.....s.	Eu,ME,NAf	9510sof
1030-1300	.....s	Eu,ME,NAf	9510sof
1500-1600	.....s	ME,As,AUS	15190sof
1900-2000	....fss	Eu,ME,NAf	7290sof
Oromo	**Days**	**Area**	**kHz**
1500-1530	.....s.	EAf	15515sof

Ann: English: "This is IRRS shortwave in Milano - signing on".
IS: S/on: Triumphal Scene from Aida (Verdi); S/off: Prisoners' Chorus (Verdi).
V: QSL-card. Rp. (Rpt by email to: reports@nexus.org)
Notes: NEXUS-IBA is a provider of relay services for prgr producers and broadcasters, via Internet (24/7) and leased tx facilities in Bulgaria. Some prgs are relayed via Challenger Radio (Northern Italy) 1368kHz.

JAPAN (J)

RADIO JAPAN (NHK WORLD) (Pub)
✉ 2-1, Jinnan 2-chome, Shibuya-ku, Tokyo. 150-8001, Japan.
☎ +81 3 34651111. 🖷 +81 3 34811350.
E: nhkworld@nhk.jp **W:** www.nhk.or.jp/nhkworld
Webcast: D/L/P
L.P: DG (NHK International, Inc): Yoshinori Nemoto; Pres (NHK): Katsuto Momii; DG, Broadcasting (NHK): T.Sakamoto.
SW: Leased from KDDI & foreign relays.
SAT: Badr 5, Eutelsat Hot Bird 13D, Intelsat 19/20/21.
kHz: 738, 927, 1386, 5910, 5960, 5985, 6075, 6090, 6190, 6195, 7330, 7395, 9395, 9560, 9575, 9620, 9625, 9670, 9680, 9700, 9730, 9750, 9760, 9765, 9770, 9855, 11665, 11685, 11730, 11740, 11790, 11800, 11815, 11910, 11925, 11945, 11975, 12015, 13640, 13650, 13725, 13730, 13840, 13870, 15130, 15195, 15290, 15590, 15720, 17540, 17585, 17810

Winter Schedule 2015/2016

Arabic	Days	Area	kHz
0600-0630	daily	ME,NAf	11975iss
Bengali	**Days**	**Area**	**kHz**
1300-1345	daily	SAs	11685sng
Burmese	**Days**	**Area**	**kHz**
1030-1100	daily	SEA	11740sng
1430-1500	daily	SEA	11740sng
1445-1500	daily	SEA	5985yan*
2340-2400	daily	SEA	13650yam

Chinese	Days	Area	kHz
0900-0930	daily	As	6090yam
1200-1230	daily	As	6090yam
1300-1330	daily	As	6190yam
1400-1430	daily	As	6190yam
1530-1600	daily	As	9575yam
2230-2250	daily	As	9560yam
English	**Days**	**Area**	**kHz**
0500-0530	daily	Eu	13640dha
0500-0530	daily	SAf	9770iss
0710-0725	daily	SEA	9730yan*
1000-1030	daily	Pac	9625yam
1100-1130	....f..	Eu	9760wof+
1200-1230	daily	SEA	11740sng
1400-1430	daily	SEA	11925hbn
1400-1430	daily	SAs	11685tac
1540-1600	daily	SEA	5985yan*
1800-1830	m......	Am	9395yfr
1800-1830	daily	CAf	11800mey
French	**Days**	**Area**	**kHz**
0530-0600	daily	CAf,WAf	11730iss, 13840mdc
2030-2100	daily	WAf	9855mdc
Hindi	**Days**	**Area**	**kHz**
0100-0130	daily	SAs	7330tac
1430-1515	daily	SAs	15720mdc
Indonesian	**Days**	**Area**	**kHz**
1115-1200	daily	SEA	9625hbn
1315-1400	daily	SEA	11925hbn
2130-2200	daily	SEA	6075yam
Japanese	**Days**	**Area**	**kHz**
0200-0500	daily	SEA	17810yam
0200-0500	daily	As	15195yam
0200-0500	daily	SAs	15590yam
0300-0500	daily	CAm	5960iss
0300-0500	daily	ME,NAf	9620nau
0700-0800	daily	EAs	11790yam
0800-0900	daily	SEA	17585yam
0800-1000	daily	SAm	12015asc
0800-1000	daily	WAf	15290iss
0800-1700	daily	As	9750yam
0900-1500	daily	SEA	11815yam
1500-1700	daily	SAs	9680yam
1700-1900	daily	ME,NAf	9765nau
1700-1900	daily	SAf	11945iss
1900-2100	daily	CAf	15130iss
1900-2100	daily	ME,NAf	9670yam
2000-2100	daily	Pac	9625yam
2100-2300	daily	SEA	11665yam
2100-2400	daily	As	11910yam
Korean	**Days**	**Area**	**kHz**
0915-0945	daily	EAs	9700yam
1130-1200	daily	EAs	6090yam
1230-1300	daily	EAs	6190yam
1330-1400	daily	EAs	6190yam
1430-1500	daily	EAs	6190yam
2210-2230	daily	EAs	9560yam
Persian	**Days**	**Area**	**kHz**
0400-0430	daily	ME	11730tac
1430-1500	daily	ME	13725iss
1630-1700	daily	ME	927dsb
Portuguese	**Days**	**Area**	**kHz**
0900-0930	daily	SAm	6195hri
2130-2200	daily	SAm	17540hri
Russian	**Days**	**Area**	**kHz**
0330-0400	daily	RUS	738msk
0330-0400	daily	Eu	1386sit
0430-0500	daily	Eu	5910sit
0530-0600	daily	EAs	11790yam
1100-1130	daily	EAs	6090yam
1100-1130	daily	RUS	738msk
1130-1200	....f..	Eu	9760wof+
1600-1630	daily	CAs	927dsb
1600-1630	daily	RUS	738msk
1730-1800	daily	Eu	1386sit
2200-2230	daily	RUS	738msk

Spanish	Days	Area	kHz
0400-0430	daily	LAm	5985yfr, 6195hri
0930-1000	daily	SAm	6195hri

Swahili	Days	Area	kHz
0315-0400	daily	EAf	7395mdc
1730-1800	daily	EAf	13730mdc

Thai	Days	Area	kHz
1130-1200	daily	SEA	11740sng
1230-1300	daily	SEA	11740sng
2300-2320	daily	SEA	13650yam

Urdu	Days	Area	kHz
1515-1600	daily	SAs	13870dha
1700-1745	daily	SAs	927dsb

Vietnamese	Days	Area	kHz
1100-1130	daily	SEA	11740sng
1300-1330	daily	SEA	11740sng
2320-2340	daily	SEA	13650yam

Key: + DRM; * via MRTV Yangon.

Ann: Chinese: "Zheli shi riben guoji guangbo diantai, NHK huan-qiu guangbowang"; English: "This is NHK World, Radio Japan in Tokyo"; Indonesian: "Inilah Radio Jepang, NHK World, siaran bahasa Indonesia"; Japanese: "Kochirawa NHK Warudo, Rajio Nippon, NHK no kokusaihoso desu"; Korean: "Yeogineun NHK World, Radio Ilbonimnda".

IS: Melody "Kazoe Uta".

V: QSL-card.

Notes: Radio Japan is the External Sce of the public broadcaster NHK, produced by its subsidiary NHK International, Inc. The Japanese programmes include relays of NHK domestic Radio 1. Radio Japan is also broadcast on FM & AM (MW) in the following cities and countries: Arabic, to IRQ: 2000-2030 on 88.3MHz (Baghdad + 4 cities), to West Bank: 2100-2130 on 87.8MHz (Ramallah + 3 cities); Burmese, to BRM: 1445-1500 Mon-Wed (Thu & Fri-1505) on 576kHz (Yangon) and 594kHz (Naypyidaw); Bengali, to BGD: 1500-1545 on 104.0MHz (Dhaka + 6 cities); English, to BRM: 0710-0725 Sat & Sun, 1540-1600 Thu & Fri on 576kHz (Yangon) & 594kHz (Naypyidaw); French, to COD: 0530-0600 & 2030-2100 on 103.0MHz (Uvira), 0630-0700 & 2145-2215 on 89.5MHz (Beni); Indonesian, to INS: 1200-1215 on 90.0MHz (Jakarta + 7 cities), 1406-1451 on 92.5MHz (Muaro Jambi, 93.9MHz (Maros), 98.8MHz (Wonosobo), 105.5MHz (Bandung + 34 cities); Persian, to AFG: 1430-1500 on 88.0MHz (Kabul & Herat); Portuguese, to B: 2030-2100 on 1370kHz (Sao Paulo + 2 cities) & 96.5MHz (Campinas); Swahili, to TZA: 0315-0400 on 98.2MHz (TZA: Mwanza), 1730-1800 on 94.6MHz (Dar es Salaam + 22 cities), & to COD: 0530-0615 & 1900-1930 on 89.5MHz (Beni); Thai, to THA: 0100-0130 Mon-Fri on 107.25MHz (Phitsanulok), 1230-1300 Mon-Fri on 981kHz (Bangkok) & 102.25MHz (Mahasarakham); Vietnamese to VTN: 1300-1315 (Sun & Mon-1320) on 91.0MHz (Hanoi, Ho Chi Minh City, Can Tho and Quang Binh).

KDDI CORPORATION (Tx Operator)

✉ Garden Air Tower, 10-10, Iidabashi 3-chome, Chiyoda-ku, Tokyo 102-8460, Japan.

☎ +81 3 33470077. 🖨 +81 3 33475845.

W: www.kddi.com

L.P: Pres: Takashi Tanaka.

SW: [YAM] Koga, Yamata, Ibaraki prefecture: 4 x 100, 7 x 300kW.

Notes: KDDI Corporation is a major national telecommunications provider.

KOREA, (D.P.R.) (KRE)

VOICE OF KOREA (VOK) (Gov)

✉ Pyongyang, Democratic People's Republic of Korea.

☎ +850 2 3816035. 🖨 +850 2 3814416.

E: vok@star-co.net.kp **W:** www.vok.rep.kp

Webcast: D

MW/SW: Uses txs provided by the Ministry of Post & Telecommunications.

SAT: Thaicom 5.

kHz: 621, 3250, 6070, 6170, 6185, 7210, 7220, 7235, 7570, 7580, 9425, 9435, 9445, 9650, 9730, 9850, 9875, 9890, 11635, 11645, 11710, 11735, 11910, 12015, 13650, 13760, 15105, 15180, 15245

Winter Schedule 2015/2016

Arabic	Days	Area	kHz
1530-1630	daily	ME,NAf	9890kuj, 11645kuj
1730-1830	daily	ME,NAf	9890kuj, 11645kuj

Chinese	Days	Area	kHz
0330-0430	daily	SEA	13650kuj, 15105kuj
0530-0630	daily	EAs	7220kuj, 9445kuj, 9730kuj
0630-0730	daily	SEA	13650kuj, 15105kuj
0830-0930	daily	EAs	7220kuj, 9445kuj
1130-1230	daily	EAs	7220kuj, 9445kuj
1330-1430	daily	SEA	6185kuj, 9850kuj
2130-2330	daily	EAs	7235kuj, 9445kuj, 9875kuj, 11635kuj

English	Days	Area	kHz
0430-0530	daily	EAs	7220kuj, 9445kuj, 9730kuj
0430-0530	daily	LAm	11735kuj, 13760kuj, 15180kuj
0530-0630	daily	SEA	13650kuj, 15105kuj
0630-0730	daily	EAs	7220kuj, 9445kuj, 9730kuj
1030-1130	daily	LAm	6170kuj, 9435kuj
1030-1130	daily	SEA	6185kuj, 9850kuj
1330-1430	daily	NAm	9435kuj, 11710kuj
1330-1430	daily	Eu	7570kuj, 12015kuj
1530-1630	daily	Eu	7570kuj, 12015kuj
1530-1630	daily	NAm	9435kuj, 11710kuj
1630-1730	daily	ME,NAf	9890kuj, 11645kuj
1830-1930	daily	Eu	7570kuj, 12015kuj
1930-2030	daily	ME,NAf	9875kuj, 11635kuj
1930-2030	daily	SAf	7210kuj, 11910kuj
2130-2230	daily	Eu	7570kuj, 12015kuj

French	Days	Area	kHz
0430-0530	daily	SEA	13650kuj, 15105kuj
0630-0730	daily	LAm	11735kuj, 13760kuj, 15180kuj
1130-1230	daily	LAm	6170kuj, 9435kuj
1130-1230	daily	SEA	6185kuj, 9850kuj
1430-1530	daily	NAm	9435kuj, 11710kuj
1430-1530	daily	Eu	7570kuj, 12015kuj
1630-1730	daily	Eu	7570kuj, 12015kuj
1630-1730	daily	NAm	9435kuj, 11710kuj
1830-1930	daily	ME,NAf	9875kuj, 11635kuj
1830-1930	daily	SAf	7210kuj, 11910kuj
2030-2130	daily	Eu	7570kuj, 12015kuj

German	Days	Area	kHz
1630-1730	daily	Eu	6170kuj, 9425kuj
1830-2030	daily	Eu	6170kuj, 9425kuj

Japanese	Days	Area	kHz
0730-1320	daily	EAs	621chj, 3250pyo, 7580kuj, 9650kuj
0930-1320	daily	EAs	6070kng
2130-0020	daily	EAs	621chj, 3250pyo, 7580kuj, 9650kuj

Korean	Days	Area	kHz
0930-1020	daily	EAs	7220kuj, 9445kuj
1230-1320	daily	LAm	6170kuj, 9435kuj
1230-1320	daily	SEA	6185kuj, 9850kuj
1430-1520	daily	SEA	6185kuj, 9850kuj
1730-1820	daily	Eu	7570kuj, 12015kuj
1730-1820	daily	NAm	9435kuj, 11710kuj
2030-2120	daily	Eu	6170kuj, 9425kuj
2030-2120	daily	ME,NAf	9875kuj, 11635kuj
2030-2120	daily	SAf	7210kuj, 11910kuj
2330-0020	daily	EAs	7235kuj, 9445kuj, 9875kuj, 11635kuj
2330-0020	daily	Eu	7570kuj, 12015kuj

Russian	Days	Area	kHz
0730-0930	daily	EAs	9875kuj, 11735kuj
0730-0930	daily	Eu	13760kuj, 15245kuj
1430-1630	daily	Eu	6170kuj, 9425kuj
1730-1830	daily	Eu	6170kuj, 9425kuj

Spanish	Days	Area	kHz
0330-0430	daily	LAm	11735kuj, 13760kuj, 15180kuj
0530-0630	daily	LAm	11735kuj, 13760kuj, 15180kuj
1930-2030	daily	Eu	7570kuj, 12015kuj

Spanish	Days	Area	kHz
2230-2330	daily	Eu	7570kuj, 12015kuj

Ann: Arabic: "Huna Sowt al Koriya"; Chinese: "Chaoxian zhi sheng guangbo diantai"; English: "This is the Voice of Korea"; French: "La Voix de la Corée"; German: "Hier ist die Stimme Koreas"; Japanese: "Choson no koe hoso desu"; Korean: "Joson Jung-ang Pangsong-imnida", "Pyongyang Pangsong-imnida"; Russian: "Govorit Golos Korei"; Spanish: "Aqui la Voz de Corea".
IS: Song of General Kim Il Sung. Opening music: National Anthem.
V: QSL-card.
Notes: Voice of Korea is the External Sce of the Radio & TV Broadcasting Committee of the Democratic People's Republic of Korea.

PYONGYANG BROADCASTING STATION (PYONGYANG PANGSONG)

Pyongyang, Democratic People's Republic of Korea.
W: www.gnu.rep.kp
Webcast: D
MW/SW: Uses txs provided by the Ministry of Post & Telecommunications.
kHz: 621, 657, 801, 855, 1053, 3250, 3320, 6400

Winter Schedule 2015/2016

Korean	Days	Area	kHz
0330-0730	daily	EAs	621chj, 3250pyo
0830-1430	daily	EAs	1053hju
1330-2030	daily	EAs	621chj
1330-2100	daily	EAs	3250pyo
2130-1900	daily	EAs	3320pyo, 6400kng†
2130-2100	daily	EAs	657kan, 801hwd, 855swo
2230-1430	daily	EAs	1053hju

Key: † Irregular.
Ann: Korean: "Pyongyang Pangsong-imnida".
IS: Song of General Kim Il Sung. Opening & closing music: National Anthem.
Notes: Timings and frequency use variable.

MINISTRY OF POST & TELECOMMUNICATIONS (Tx Operator)

Oesong-dong, Central District, Pyongyang, Democratic People's Republic of Korea.
☎ +850 2 3813180. 🖷 +850 2 3814418.
E: mptird@star-co.net.kp
L.P: Minister: Kwang Chol Kim.
MW: [CHJ] Chongjin: 621kHz 500kW; [HJU] Haeju: 1053kHz 1000kW; [HWD] Kimchaek, Hwadae county: 801kHz 500kW; [KAN] Kangnam: 657kHz 1500kW; [SAG] Samgo: 684kHz 250kW; [SEP] Sepo: 729kHz 50kW; [SWO] Sangwon: 855kHz 500kW.
SW: [CHJ] Chongjin: 1 x 5kW; [KNG] Kanggye: 1 x 250kW; [KUJ] Kujang: 10 x 200kW; [PYO] Pyongyang: 1 x 100kW. New Chinese-made txs (20/50/100/150kW) are currently being installed.
Notes: The Ministry of Post and Telecommunications owns and operates the transmitter network in the Democratic People's Republic of Korea.

KOREA, Rep. of (KOR)

KBS WORLD RADIO (Pub)

13, Yeouigongwon-ro, Yeongdeungpo-gu, Seoul, 07235, Rep. of Korea.
☎ +82 2 7813885. (English) 🖷 +82 2 7813694.
E: rki@kbs.co.kr; english@kbs.co.kr **W:** world.kbs.co.kr
Webcast: D/L/P
L.P: Pres: Cho Dae-hyun; Exec. Producer, World Radio: Paek Seung Yeop.
MW: [DAN] Dangjin (HLCA): 972kHz 1500kW; [KIM] Gimje (HLSR): 1170kHz 500kW.
SW: [KIM] Gimje: 8 x 100, 3 x 250kW; [HWA] Hwaseong: 1 x 100kW.
kHz: 738, 1170, 3955, 5950, 6015, 6045, 6095, 6155, 7215, 7235, 7275, 9515, 9570, 9580, 9605, 9640, 9645, 9690, 9740, 9760, 9770, 9805, 9840, 11795, 11810, 15160, 15575

Winter Schedule 2015/2016

Arabic	Days	Area	kHz
2000-2100	daily	ME,Af	9840dha

Chinese	Days	Area	kHz
1130-1230	daily	EAs,SEA	6095kim, 9770kim
1300-1400	daily	EAs	1170kim, 7275kim
2300-2400	daily	EAs,SEA	7215kim, 9805kim

English	Days	Area	kHz
0200-0300	daily	SAm	9580kim
0200-0300	daily	SEA	9690kim
0800-0900	daily	SEA	9570kim
1100-1130	.....s.	Eu	9760wof+
1230-1330	daily	EAs	6095kim
1300-1400	daily	NAm	15575kim
1300-1400	daily	SEA	9570kim
1400-1500	daily	SEA	9640kim
1600-1700	daily	SEA	9640kim
1600-1700	daily	Eu	9515kim
1800-1900	daily	Eu	7275kim
2200-2300	daily	Eu	11810kim

French	Days	Area	kHz
2000-2100	daily	Af	5950iss
2100-2200	daily	Eu	3955wof

German	Days	Area	kHz
2000-2100	daily	Eu	3955wof

Indonesian	Days	Area	kHz
1200-1300	daily	SEA	9570kim
1400-1500	daily	SEA	9570kim
1600-1700	daily	SEA	9805kim
2200-2300	daily	SEA	9805kim

Japanese	Days	Area	kHz
0100-0200	daily	EAs	9580kim
0200-0300	daily	EAs	11810kim
0800-0900	daily	EAs	7275kim
0800-0900	daily	EAs	6155kim
0900-1100	daily	EAs	6095kim
1100-1300	daily	EAs	1170kim

Korean	Days	Area	kHz
0300-0400	daily	SAm	11810kim
0350-2400	daily	EAs	6015hwa*
0700-0800	daily	Eu	6045wof
0900-1000	daily	Eu,ME,Af	15160kim
0900-1100	daily	EAs,SEA	7275kim, 9570kim
1000-1100	daily	EAs	1170kim
1200-1300	daily	EAs	7275kim
1400-0400	daily	EAs	1170kim**
1400-1500	daily	NAm	15575kim
1600-1800	daily	Eu	7275kim
1600-1800	daily	ME,Af	9740kim
1700-1900	daily	Eu	9515kim

Russian	Days	Area	kHz
0230-0300	daily	RUS	738msk
0630-0700	daily	RUS	738msk
0800-0830	mtwtfs.	RUS	738msk
1030-1100	daily	RUS	738msk
1300-1400	daily	Eu,CAs	9645msk
1330-1400	daily	RUS	738msk
1730-1800	daily	RUS	738msk
1800-1900	daily	Eu	7235wof
2000-2030	daily	RUS	738msk
2230-2300	daily	RUS	738msk

Spanish	Days	Area	kHz
0100-0200	daily	SAm	9605hri, 11810kim
0200-0300	daily	NAm	15575kim
1100-1200	daily	SAm	11795kim
1800-1900	daily	Eu,Af	9740kim

Vietnamese	Days	Area	kHz
0100-0200	daily	SEA	9690kim
1030-1130	daily	SEA	9770kim
1500-1600	daily	SEA	9640kim

Key: + DRM; * 1st Global Korean Network; ** 2nd Global Korean Network.
Ann: Arabic: "Huna KBS World Radio min Si'ul"; Chinese: "Zheli shi Hanguo guoji guangbo diantai, zai Dahanminguo shoudu Shou'er wei nin boyin"; English: "This is KBS World Radio, the overseas service of the Korean Broadcasting System, coming to you from Seoul, the capital of the Republic of Korea"; German: "Hier ist KBS World Radio aus Seoul, der Auslandssender der Republik Korea"; Indonesian: "Inilah siaran bahasa Indonesia, KBS World Radio, yang dipancarkan langsung dari ibu kota Republik Korea, Seoul"; Japanese: "Kochirawa Kankoku Souru kara okurishiteimasu KBS no rajio kokusai hoso, KBS

warudo rajio desu"; Korean: "Yeogineun Daehan Minguk Seoul-eseo bonaedeurineun KBS World Radio urimal bangsong-imnida"; Spanish: "Esto es KBS World Radio, emitiendo desde Seúl, Republica de Corea."; Vietnamese: "Day la chuong trinh phat thanh tieng Viet cua dai KBS World Radio phat thanh tu Seoul Han quoc". Global Korean Network 1:"Jungpa Gubaek-chilsib-i(972)kHz, Hanminjok Neteuwokeu Chaeneol, KBS Hanminjok Je-il Bangsong-imnida"; Global Korean Network 2:"Jungpa Cheonbaek-chilsip(1170)kHz, Daehan Mingook Seoureseo Bonae Deurineun Hanminjok Neteuwokeu Chaeneol, KBS Hanminjok Je-I Bangsong-imnida".
IS: Korean children's song "Dar-a Dar-a Balgeun Dar-a (Oh, Bright Moon)", played on a glockenspiel. Original music "Dawn" composed by Kim Hee Jyo, with KBS symphony orchestra.
V: QSL-card. Online-form available on website.
Notes: KBS World Radio is the External Sce of the public broadcaster Korean Broadcasting System (KBS). KBS Global Korean Network Programmes are services for ethnic Koreans living outside of the Republic of Korea. Indonesian is broadcast daily from 1200-1300 on 102.6MHz in Jakarta (Indonesia) and Spanish is broadcast mon-fri from 0100-0155 on 94.7MHz in Buenos Aires (Argentina).

FEBC KOREA (Rlg)
✉ P.O. Box 88, Seoul 04067, Republic of Korea.
☎ +82 2 3200114. 🖷 +82 2 3200229.
E: febcadm@febc.net **W:** www.febc.or.kr; www.febc.net (Korean); english.febc.net (English)
Webcast: L
✉ Yeongdeungpo-dong 6-ga 8-1, Yeongdeungpo-gu, Seoul 150-036, Republic of Korea.
L.P: Pres: Dr Billy Kim.
MW: [JEJ] Jeju (HLAZ): 1566kHz 250kW; [SEO] Seoul, Incheon (HLKX): 1188kHz 100kW.
kHz: *1188, 1566*

Winter Schedule 2015/2016

Chinese	Days	Area	kHz
1100-1230	daily	EAs	1566jej
1345-1600	daily	EAs	1566jej
1830-1900	daily	EAs	1566jej
1900-2000	daily	As	1188seo
English	**Days**	**Area**	**kHz**
1000-1100	mtwtf..	As	1188seo
Japanese	**Days**	**Area**	**kHz**
1230-1345	daily	J	1566jej
Korean	**Days**	**Area**	**kHz**
1600-1830	daily	EAs	1566jej
1900-1100	daily	EAs	1566jej
2000-1000	daily	As	1188seo

Ann: Chinese: "HLKX. Zheli shi zhongpo 1188 (yao yao ba ba) qianhe, Yiyou Diantai di 2 (er) dai.", "HLAZ. Zheli shi zhongbo 1566 (yao wu liu liu) qianhe, Yiyou Diantai di 1 (yi) dai"; English: "It's 8 o'clock and time for daily English segment on HLKX 1188 on your am radio dial"; Japanese: "Kochirawa kirisutokyo hosokyoku FEBC desu"; Korean: "Jungpa Cheonbaek-palsip-pal (1188) kHz, Pyojun FM Paeng-nyuk-jeom-gu (106.9) MHz, Jungpa Cheon-o-baeng-nyuk-sim-nyuk (1566) kHz, Seogwipo FM Baeg-il-jeom-il (101.1) MHz, Tong-il-eul Wihae Gidohaneun Jeju Geukdong Bangsong-imnida. HLAZ".
V: QSL-card.
Notes: FEBC Korea is a regional division of Far East Broadcasting Company, Inc (FEBC) (USA), targeting Korea, China, Mongolia, and the Far Eastern parts of Russia. See USA for FEBC corporate details. The transmissions may include prgrs provided by small religious prgr producers and broadcast under own labels.

KUWAIT (KWT)

RADIO KUWAIT ‡ (Gov)
✉ See National Radio section.
SW: [KBD] Kuwait, Kabd: 5 x 500kW ‡
SAT: Arabsat 5C, AsiaSat 5, Badr 4, Eutelsat Hot Bird 13C, Galaxy 19, Hispasat 1E, Nilesat 201.
Key: ‡ Inactive at time of publication.
Ann: Arabic: "Huna al-Kuwait".
V: QSL-card.
Notes: Arabic prgrs are relays of Home Sce networks.

IBB KUWAIT "GEORGE A. MOORE JR" TRANSMITTING STATION
✉ IBB Transmitting Station, c/o US Embassy, P.O. Box 77, Safat 13001, Kuwait City, Kuwait.

L.P: SM: Gaines Johnson.
MW: [KWT] Kuwait, Umm Al-Rimam: 1548kHz 600kW; 1593kHz 150kW.
SW: [KWT] Kuwait, Umm Al-Rimam: 6 x 250kW.
V: QSL-card.

KYRGYZSTAN (KGZ)

SHORTWAVE RELAY SERVICE (Rlg)
✉ Bishkek, Kyrgyzstan.
SW: Leased from Kyrgyztelecom.
kHz: *5130*

Winter Schedule 2015/2016

Persian	Days	Area	kHz
1500-1800	daily	WAs	5130bis†

Key: † Irregular, schedule dependent on airtime bookings.
Notes: Rebroadcasts paid religious programming in Central Asian languages.

KYRGYZTELECOM (Tx Operator)
✉ Chui avenue 96, 720000 Bishkek, Kyrgyzstan.
☎ +996 312 681616. 🖷 +996 312 662424.
E: info@kt.kg **W:** www.kt.kg
L.P: DG: Salavat Iskakov.
MW: [BIS] Bishkek, Krasnaya Rechka: 1287kHz 150kW; operated on behalf of TWR: 1467kHz 500kW.
SW: [BIS] Bishkek, Krasnaya Rechka: 1 x 15kW. (Estimated power)
Notes: Kyrgyztelecom is the national tx operator.

LAOS (LAO)

LAO NATIONAL RADIO (Gov)
✉ See National Radio Section.
Webcast: D
MW: [VIE] Vientiane 567kHz 200kW.
SW: [VIE] Vientiane 1 x10kW.
FM/DAB: FM: 97.25MHz (Vientienne, 2kW)
kHz: *567, 6130*

Winter Schedule 2015/2016

English	Days	Area	kHz
1400-1430	daily	SEA	567vie, 6130vie
French	**Days**	**Area**	**kHz**
1430-1500	daily	SEA	567vie, 6130vie
Khmer	**Days**	**Area**	**kHz**
1530-1600	daily	SEA	567vie, 6130vie
Thai	**Days**	**Area**	**kHz**
1330-1400	daily	SEA	567vie, 6130vie
Vietnamese	**Days**	**Area**	**kHz**
1500-1530	daily	SEA	567vie, 6130vie

IS: National Anthem.
V: QSL-Card.
Notes: Times variable.

LITHUANIA (LTU)

RADIO BALTIC WAVES INTERNATIONAL (RBWI)
✉ Algirdo g. 13-9, LT-03219 Vilnius, Lithuania.
☎ +370 699 05074.
E: riplei@takas.lt
L.P: Dir: Rolandas Stirblys; Project Coordinator: Rimantas Pleikys.
MW: Leased from LRTC.
V: No longer issues QSL-cards.
Notes: RBWI markets air time on MW relay facilities in Lithuania for foreign broadcasters.

ZILIONIS RADIO TV CONSULTING (Broker)
✉ P.O. Box 3300, LT-02003 Vilnius 13, Lithuania.
☎ +370 685 76840. 🖷 +370 526 52532.
E: consult@zilionis.com **W:** www.zilionis.com/airtime
L.P: Dir: Sigitas Zilionis.

LIETUVOS RADIJO IR TELEVIZIJOS CENTRAS (LRTC) (Tx Operator)
✉ Sausio 13-osios g. 10, LT-04347 Vilnius, Lithuania.
☎ +370 5 2040300. 🖷 +370 5 2040325.

E: info@telecentras.lt **W:** www.telecentras.lt
L.P: GD: Remigijus Šeris.
MW: [SIT] Kaunas, Sitkunai: 1386kHz 75/150kW.
SW: [SIT] Kaunas, Sitkunai: 1 x 100kW.
Notes: LRTC is the national transmitter network operator.

LUXEMBOURG (LUX)

RTL RADIO (Comm)
✉ 45, boulevard Pierre Frieden, L-1543 Luxembourg.
☎ +352 421423500. 🖷 +352 421422738.
E: oliver.fahlbusch@rtlgroup.com **W:** www.rtlgroup.com
Webcast: L (rtl1440.com)
✉ Kurfürstendamm 207, D-10719 Berlin, Germany.
☎ +49 30 884840.
W: www.rtlradio.de
L.P: (RTL Group) CEOs: Guillaume de Posch, Anke Schäferkordt; Senior Vice Pres. Corporate Communications & Marketing: Oliver Fahlbusch.
MW/SW: Uses txs provided by Broadcasting Center Europe.
SAT: Astra 1M.
kHz: *1440*

German	Winter Schedule 2015/2016		
	Days	Area	kHz
0400-0600	......s	Eu	1440mrn*
0400-0700	mtwtfs.	Eu	1440mrn*
0630-0700	......s	Eu	1440mrn*
1200-1210	daily	Eu	1440mrn*
1655-1825	..w....	Eu	1440mrn*
1655-1830	mt.tfss	Eu	1440mrn*

Key: * Until 31 Dec 2015
Ann: German: "RTL - Deutschlands Hit-Radio".
Notes: RTL Radio is part of RTL Group, a multinational TV, radio and media production holding, majority-owned by Bertelsmann AG (Germany). In July 2015, the main studio of RTL Radio was moved from Luxembourg to Berlin, Germany.

BROADCASTING CENTER EUROPE (BCE) (Tx Operator)
✉ 45, boulevard Pierre Frieden, L-1543 Luxembourg.
☎ +352 24801. 🖷 +352 24806609.
E: contact@bce.lu **W:** www.bce.lu
L.P: CEO: Frédéric Lemaire.
LW: [BDW] Beidweiler: 234kHz 1500kW. Standby: 2x1000kW.‡
MW: [MRN] Marnach: 1440kHz 2x300kW. Standby: 2x600kW. (Site will be closed on 31 Dec 2015).
Key: ‡ Inactive at time of publication.
V: QSL-card.
Notes: BCE is part of RTL Group's Technical Division. It was founded in January 2000, as a result of the merger of various technical entities of the RTL Group.

MACEDONIA (MKD)

RADIO MAKEDONIJA (Pub)
✉ blvd. "Goce Delcev" bb, 1000 Skopje, Macedonia.
☎ +389 2 5119874.
E: radiomakedonija@mrt.com.mk **W:** mrt.com.mk
Webcast: L
L.P: Editor: Vangel Borozinovski.
MW: Leased from Makedonska Radiodifuzija.
kHz: *810*

Albanian	Winter Schedule 2015/2016		
	Days	Area	kHz
2000-2030	mtwtf..	Eu	810sko
Bulgarian	**Days**	**Area**	**kHz**
1900-1930	mtwtf..	Eu	810sko
French/			
Macedonian	**Days**	**Area**	**kHz**
1830-1900	mtwtf..	Eu	810sko
Greek	**Days**	**Area**	**kHz**
1930-2000	mtwtf..	Eu	810sko
Macedonian	**Days**	**Area**	**kHz**
1830-2100	.....s.	Eu	810sko
2100-0200	mtwtf..	Eu	810sko
Serbian	**Days**	**Area**	**kHz**
2030-2100	mtwtf..	Eu	810sko

Ann: Macedonian: "Radio Makedonija".

V: QSL-letter.
Notes: External Sce of the public service broadcaster Makedonska Radio Televizija (MRT).

MAKEDONSKA RADIODIFUZIJA (Tx Operator)
✉ blvd. "Goce Delcev" 18, 1000 Skopje, Macedonia.
☎ +389 2 3297100. 🖷 +389 2 3225520.
E: makedonska.radiodifuzija@jpmrd.gov.mk **W:** www.jpmrd.gov.mk
MW: [SKO] Skopje, Sveti Nikole: 810kHz 100kW.
V: QSL-letter.
Notes: Makedonska Radiodifuzija is the national transmitter network provider.

MADAGASCAR (MDG)

MADAGASCAR WORLD VOICE ‡ (Rlg)
✉ World Christian Broadcasting, Immeuble Assist, 7ème etage, 101 Antananarivo, Madagascar.
✉ 4344 Livingston Ave, Dallas, TX 75205-2608, USA.
E: info@worldchristian.org **W:** www.worldchristian.org
L.P: Pres/CEO: Earl Young; SM: Mahefa Rakotomamonjy; Engineer: Kevin Chambers.
SW: [MWV] Mahajanga: 2 x 100kW
Key: ‡ Inactive at time of publication.
Notes: Transmitting station owned World Christian Broadcasting, Inc (WCB). See USA for corporate details. Transmissions are due to start in late 2015 or early 2016.

MALAGASY GLOBAL BUSINESS S.A. (MGLOB) (Tx Operator)
✉ Lot Bonnet 88, Ivandry, 101 Antananarivo, Madagascar.
☎ +261 202242222. 🖷 +261 202243184.
L.P: Director: Ms Flore Ravelojaona (flore@mglob.mg); Technical Mgr: Tovonirina Razananaivo (tovo@mglob.mg); Sales & frequency mgr: Rocus de Joode (rocus@mglob.mg).
SW: [MDC] Talata Volonondry: 3 x 250kW.
V: QSL-card (for relayed prgrs). Email rpt to monitoring@mglob.mg
Notes: Malagasy Global Business S.A. (MGlob) was established in October 2012 by staff members of the former Radio Netherlands Worldwide Relay Station at Talata Volonondry, and is the new operator of the transmitting station.

MALI (MLI)

CHINA RADIO INTERNATIONAL (CRI) RELAY
SW: [BKO] Bamako, Kati: 2 x 100kW.
V: QSL-card. (Rpt to CRI, in China)
Notes: The shortwave facilities are leased to CRI by Radiodiffusion-Télevision du Mali.

MOLDOVA Transnistria (MDA)

PRIDNESTROVSKIY RADIOTELETSENTR (Tx Operator)
✉ MD-4006 Maiac, Pridnestrovian Moldavian Republic, Moldova.
☎ +373 210 66500.
E: prtc@idknet.com
L.P: DG: Vitaliy Kucherenko; Technical Dir: Sergey Omelchenko.
MW: [KCH] Grigoriopol, Maiac: 621kHz 150kW, 999/1413/1548kHz 1000kW.
SW: [KCH] Grigoriopol, Maiac: 5 x 1000kW.
V: QSL-email.
Notes: Pridnestrovskiy Radioteletsentr (owned by RTRN, Russia) provides high power MW & SW transmitting facilities.

MONACO (MCO)

RADIO MONACO (Comm)
✉ 7 rue du Gabian, Gildo Pastor Center, 98000 Monaco.
☎ +377 97985050. 🖷 +377 97985051.
E: info@radio-monaco.com **W:** radio-monaco.com
SW: Via Monaco Radio (NAYA) utility station.
kHz: *4363, 8728, 13146*

French	Winter Schedule 2015/2016		
	Days	Area	kHz
1200-1203	mtwtf..	Atl,Med	4363mcr*, 8728mcr*, 13146mcr*,‡

Key: * USB, ‡ Inactive at time of publication.

Ann: French: "Radio Monaco".
V: QSL-email.
Notes: Relay of newscasts, for ships, via Monaco Radio/Naya Radio utility station.

MONACO RADIO (NAYA) (Tx Operator)
⌨ 1, Chemin du Fort Antoine, 98000 Monte Carlo, Monaco.
☎ +377 97980000. 🖷 +377 93301300.
E: info@naya.mc **W:** www.naya.mc
SW: [MCO] Fontbonne, Mont Agel (France): 4 x 10kW.
Notes: Monaco Radio (call sign 3AC) is a costal radio utility station, operated by NAYA.

MONTE CARLO RADIODIFFUSION (MCR) (Tx Operator)
⌨ 10-12 quai Antoine 1er, MC-98000 Monte Carlo, Monaco.
☎ +377 97974700. 🖷 +377 97974707.
E: contact@mcr.mc **W:** www.mcr.mc
L.P: Chmn: Jean Pastorelli; Managing Dir: Pierre Medicin.
LW: [ROU] Roumoules (France): 216kHz 2000kW.
MW: [CDM] Col de la Madone (France): 702kHz 400kW (run at 200kW); [ROU] Roumoules (France): 1467kHz 1000kW.
Notes: MCR (a subsidiary of Télédiffusion de France) is the national transmitter network owner in Monaco and also maintains high power transmitting centres in France (at the France/Monaco border area).

MONGOLIA (MNG)

VOICE OF MONGOLIA (Pub)
⌨ P.O. Box 365, Ulaanbaatar 13, Mongolia.
☎ +976 11 327900. 🖷 +976 11 323096.
E: vom_english@yahoo.com **W:** www.vom.mn; www.mnb.mn
Webcast: D (vom.mn)/L (mnb.mn)
L.P: Dir, Foreign Sce: Mrs Narantuya B; Mail Editor: Bolorchimeg E.
MW/SW: Leased from MRTBN.
kHz: 3985, 6005, 7310, 12015, 12035

Chinese	Days	Area	kHz
	Winter Schedule 2015/2016		
1000-1030	daily	As	12035uba
1430-1500	daily	As	12015uba
English	**Days**	**Area**	**kHz**
0800-0830	daily	Eu	7310kll*
0900-0930	daily	As	12035uba
1500-1530	daily	Eu	6005kll*
1530-1600	daily	As	12015uba
2000-2030	mtwtf.s	Eu	3985kll*
Japanese	**Days**	**Area**	**kHz**
1030-1100	daily	As	12035uba
1500-1530	daily	As	12015uba
Mongolian	**Days**	**Area**	**kHz**
0930-1000	daily	As	12035uba
1400-1430	daily	As	12015uba

Key: * Additional relay, initiated by and courtesy of Funkhaus Euskirchen e.V. in Germany (part of the Kall SW relay platform)
Ann: English: "This is the Voice of Mongolia"; Mongolian: "Ulaanbaataraas yarij baina".
V: QSL-card. Rp (2 IRCs or 1 USD) appreciated.
Notes: The Voice of Mongolia is the External Sce of the Mongolian National Radio & TV.

RADIO AND TELEVISION BROADCASTING NETWORK (RTBN) (Tx Operator)
⌨ Bayangol district, 17th subdistrict, Amarsanaagiin St., Ulaanbaatar, Mongolia.
☎ +976 77 003111. 🖷 +976 77 003119.
E: info@rtbn.gov.mn **W:** rtbn.gov.mn
L.P: CEO: Ch. Oyuünbaatar.
SW: [UBA] Ulaanbaatar, Honhor: 1 x 250kW.
Notes: RTBN is the national transmitter operator in Mongolia.

MOROCCO (MRC)

RADIO MÉDITERRANÉE INTERNATIONALE (MEDI 1) (Comm)
⌨ 3/5 Rue M'Sallah, 90000 Tanger, Morocco.
☎ +212 539936363. 🖷 +212 539936363.
E: medi1@medi1.com **W:** www.medi1.com
Webcast: D/L/P
L.P: CEO: Hassan Khiyar.
LW: [NAD] Nador: 171kHz 1600kW.
SW: [NAD] Nador: 2 x 250kW.
FM/DAB: FM: Transmitters in Morocco, France and Belgium.
SAT: Arabsat 5A, Eutelsat 21B/Hot Bird 13D.
kHz: 171, 9575

Arabic/French	Days	Area	kHz
	Winter Schedule 2015/2016		
0000-2400	daily	NAf,ME,Eu	171nad, 9575nad

Ann: Arabic: "Mahataat Medi an"; French: "Ici Medi 1, Radio Méditerranée Internationale".
V: QSL-card.
Notes: Medi 1 Radio is produced by the Moroccan-French joint venture Société Radio Méditerranée Internationale.

NETHERLANDS (HOL)

TRANSPORT RADIO (Comm)
⌨ P.O. Box 1010, 8200 BA Lelystad, The Netherlands.
☎ +31 653 367364.
E: info@transportradio.nl **W:** www.transportradio.nl
Webcast: L/P
L.P: Producer: Eric van Willegen.
kHz: 6095

Dutch	Days	Area	kHz
	Winter Schedule 2015/2016		
0900-1100	m..tf..	Eu	6095nau

Ann: Dutch: "Transport Radio".
V: QSL-card.
Notes: Internet radio station aimed at Dutch hauliers, focussing on transport related news and information.

THE MIGHTY KBC
⌨ Argonstraat 6, NL-6718 WT Ede, Netherlands.
☎ +31 318 552491. 🖷 +31 318 437801.
E: themightykbc@gmail.com **W:** www.kbcradio.eu
Webcast: L
L.P: Producer: Eric van Willegen; Freq Mgr: Jan Oosterveen.
kHz: 6095, 7395

English	Days	Area	kHz
	Winter Schedule 2015/2016		
0900-1600	......s	Eu	6095nau
2300-0200	......s	NAm	7395nau

V: QSL-card. Rp. ($2 USD/2 IRCs)
Notes: Produced by KBC Import/Export.

NEW ZEALAND (NZL)

RADIO NEW ZEALAND INTERNATIONAL (RNZI) (Pub)
⌨ P.O. Box 123, Wellington, New Zealand.
☎ +64 4 4741437. 🖷 +64 4 4741433.
E: info@rnzi.com **W:** www.rnzi.com; www.radionz.co.nz/international
Webcast: D/L/P
L.P: Mgr: Linden Clark; Technical Mgr: Adrian Sainsbury; Transmission Engineer: Andy Anderson.
SW: [RAN] Rangitaiki: 2 x 100kW. F.pl: new 300kW tx (DRM-capable)
kHz: 7330, 9700, 9765, 9780, 11690, 11725, 13840, 15720, 17675

English	Days	Area	kHz
	Winter Schedule 2015/2016		
0250-0400	mtwtf..	Pac	17675ran+
0500-0800	daily	Pac	11725ran
0650-0800	mtwtf..	Pac	11690ran+
0800-1100	daily	Pac	9765ran
1100-1300	daily	Pac	13840ran
1300-1745	daily	Pac	9700ran
1550-1650	mtwtf..	Pac	7330ran+
1650-1745	mtwtf..	Pac	9780ran+
1745-1950	mtwtf..	Pac	11690ran+
1745-2150	daily	Pac	11725ran
1950-2150	mtwtf..	Pac	15720ran+
2150-0500	daily	Pac	15720ran
2255-0200	mtwtf..	Pac	17675ran+

Key: + DRM

Ann: English: "This is Radio New Zealand International, the Voice of the Pacific"; Maori: "Te reo irirangi o Aotearoa, o te Moana-nui-a-Kiwa".
V: QSL-card. Rp (2 IRC or 2 USD); QSL-email (via online form)
Notes: Schedule is variable. RNZI is the External Sce of the public broadcaster Radio New Zealand. The SW transmissions are in English, with news in various Pacific languages. Increased programming and languages, plus local FM relays in major Pacific urban centers are planned. 1st & 3rd Thursdays of each month are site maintenance days and transmissions may be reduced or there may be test transmissions during this period.

NIGERIA (NIG)

VOICE OF NIGERIA (VON) (Pub)
6th and 7th Floors, Radio House, Herbert Macaulay Way, Area 10, Garki, Abuja, Nigeria. (Headquarters)
☎ +234 9 2344016. 🖷 +234 9 2346970.
E: info@voiceofnigeria.org.ng **W:** www.voiceofnigeria.org.ng
Webcast: L/P
Broadcasting House, Ikoyi, P.M.B. 40003, Falomo, Lagos, Nigeria.
☎ +234 1 2693076. 🖷 +234 1 2691944.
L.P: DG: Sam O. Worlu; PD: Yusuf A. Yusuf.
SW: [AJA] Abuja, Lugbe: 3 x 250kW; [IKO] Ikorodu: 3 x 250kW.
kHz: 7255, 9690, 15120

Winter Schedule 2015/2016

English	Days	Area	kHz
0800-0900	daily	WAf	7255aja†,*
1800-1930	daily	WAf	7255aja†,*
1800-1930	daily	Eu	15120aja+,†
French	**Days**	**Area**	**kHz**
0700-0730	daily	WAf	7255aja†,*
Fulfulde	**Days**	**Area**	**kHz**
0730-0800	daily	WAf	7255aja†,*
1930-2000	daily	WAf	7255aja†,*
Hausa	**Days**	**Area**	**kHz**
0600-0700	daily	WAf	7255aja†,*, 9690aja†,*
2000-2100	daily	WAf	7255aja†,*

Key: * Alternative freq: 9690kHz; + DRM; † Irregular, with varying schedule.
Ann: English: "You're listening to the Voice of Nigeria, Lagos".
IS: As Home Sce. Also bells playing the first bars of the National Anthem, 15 minutes before the commencement of each transmission block.
V: QSL-card.
Notes: The Voice of Nigeria is the External Sce of the Federal Radio Corporation of Nigeria (FRCN).

NORTHERN MARIANA ISL. (MRA)

IBB "ROBERT E. KAMOSA" TRANSMITTING STATION
P.O. Box 504969, Saipan, MP 96950, USA.
☎ +1 670 2331624. 🖷 +1 670 2331614.
L.P: SM: David Strawman.
SW: [SAI] Saipan, Aginga Point: 3 x 100kW; [TIN] Tinian: 2 x 250, 6 x 500kW.
V: QSL-card.
Notes: IBB owned transmitting station. Maintained & operated by Rome Research Corporation (RRC).

NORWAY (NOR)

LKB LLE BERGEN KRINGKASTER (Comm)
PO Box 100, N5331 RONG, Norway.
☎ +47 56324985.
E: styret@bergenkringkaster.no **W:** www.bergenkringkaster.no
Grensedalen 59, N5306 Erdal, Norway. (Site and Studio)
L.P: Chmn: Per Dagfinn Green (LA1TNA); Chief Eng: Øystein Ask (LA7CFA); Chief Editor: Svenn Martinsen.
MW: [ERD] Bergen, Erdal: 1314kHz 0.18kW (FPI: 1611kHz 0.075kW)
SW: [ERD] Bergen, Erdal: 1 x 0.05kW
FM/DAB: FM: 103.8MHz Erdal, 0.1kW.
kHz: 1314, 5895

Winter Schedule 2015/2016

English	Days	Area	kHz
0600-0800	mtwtf..	Eu	1314erd*, 5895erd*
1300-1500	mtwtf..	Eu	1314erd*, 5895erd*
2200-0800	.....ss	Eu	1314erd*, 5895erd*

Key: * Ongoing test transmissions.
Ann: English: "You are listening to LKB LLE Bergen Broadcasting Station".
IS: "MacGyver in Space" by Øyvind Ask.
V: QSL-card, e-mail or letter. Rp. (E-mail reception reports to: report@bergenkringkaster.no)
Notes: Owned by Foreningen Bergen Kringkaster(Bergen Broadcasting Association). Leases facilities of the ex-NRK Broadcasting stations LKB LLE, at Frudalsmyrene in Askøy Municipality, Norway. Schedule subject to variation during test period.

RADIO NORTHERN STAR (Comm)
PO Box 100, N5331 RONG, Norway.
☎ +47 56324985.
E: 1000@northernstar.no **W:** www.northernstar.cc
Webcast: L
P7 Kristen Riksradio (Norwegian Christian Radio), Skjenet 2, N5353 Straume, Norway.(Studio)
L.P: MD: Svenn Martinsen.
MW: [ERD] Bergen, Erdal: 1314kHz 0.18kW. (FPI: 1611kHz 0.075kW)
SW: [ERD] Bergen, Erdal: 1 x 0.05kW
kHz: 1314, 5895

Winter Schedule 2015/2016

English/Norwegian	Days	Area	kHz
0100-0200	.t.....	Eu	1314erd*, 5895erd*
0800-0815	.....ss	Eu	1314erd*, 5895erd*
0900-0920	.....ss	Eu	1314erd*, 5895erd*
1000-1130	.....ss	Eu	1314erd*, 5895erd*
1800-1900	.....s.	Eu	1314erd*, 5895erd*
1900-1945	mtwtf..	Eu	1314erd*, 5895erd*
1900-1945	.....ss	Eu	1314erd*, 5895erd*
2000-2200	m..t...	Eu	1314erd*, 5895erd*

Key: * Ongoing test transmissions.
Ann: English: ""This is Radio Northern Star-Your Radio Heartland of Music"; "You're on Digital Radio for Europe and the World - The Northern Star".
IS: "Northern Star" by Ann Reed.
V: QSL-email or letter. Rp.
Notes: Owned and operated by Northern Star Media Services AS. Using facilities of former LKB/LLE Bergen Broadcasting stn. Sister Station of "LKB LLE Bergen Kringkaster". Schedule subject to variation during test period.

OMAN (OMA)

RADIO SULTANATE OF OMAN (Pub)
P.O. Box 397, 113 Muscat, Oman.
☎ +968 24603888. 🖷 +968 24604629.
E: Via website. **W:** part.gov.om
Webcast: L
English FM, P.O.Box 398, 113 Muscat, Oman. (English prgr)
L.P: Dir, Foreign Sce: Salim Mohammed Al-Ghammari; Dir, Engineering: Mohammed Salim Al-Marhouby; Frequency Mgr: Salim Al-Nomani.
SW: [SEB] Seeb ‡: 1 x 100kW planned; [THU] Thumrait: 1 x 100kW
SAT: Arabsat 5C, AsiaSat 5, Badr 6, Eutelsat 7WA/Hot Bird 13C, Galaxy 19, Hispasat 1C, Nilesat 201, Optus D2
kHz: 9540, 11650, 13600, 15140

Winter Schedule 2015/2016

Arabic	Days	Area	kHz
0200-0300	daily	EAf	9540thu
0400-1000	daily	EAf	13600thu
1500-2200	daily	Eu,ME	15140thu
2200-0200	daily	Eu,ME	11650thu
English	**Days**	**Area**	**kHz**
0300-0400	daily	EAf	9540thu
1400-1500	daily	Eu,ME	15140thu

Key: ‡ Inactive at time of publication.
Ann: Arabic: "Idha'atu Saltanat Oman min Muscat"; English: "Radio Sultanate of Oman".
V: QSL-folder.
Notes: On air since 30 July 1970. Relays of Home Sce programmes in Arabic and English.

BBC EASTERN RELAY STATION
P.O. Box 40, 422 Al Ashkarah, Oman.
E: opsaseela@yahoo.com; rebers@omantel.net.com
LP: Senior Transmitter Engineer: Khalid Nasser.
MW: [SLA] A'Seela: 702/1413kHz 800kW.
SW: [SLA] A'Seela: 3 x 250kW.
V: QSL-card. (For direct report)
Notes: Owned by the BBC and operated by Babcock Media Services (see under United Kingdom).

PAKISTAN (PAK)

RADIO PAKISTAN (Gov)
Broadcasting House, Constitution Avenue, Islamabad 44000, Pakistan.
☎ +92 51 9210689. (News Room) 🖷 +92 51 9222432.
E: info@radio.gov.pk **W:** www.radio.gov.pk
LP: DG (Pakistan Broadcasting Corp.): Syed Imran Gardezi.
SW: [ISL] Islamabad, Rawat: 5 x 100, 2 x 250kW; [KAC] Karachi, Landhi ‡: 2 x 100kW (under construction).
kHz: 5885, 6095, 7470, 9670, 9700, 9745, 9795, 11530, 11570, 11600, 11805, 11860, 11875, 11905, 15725, 15730, 17700

Winter Schedule 2015/2016

Balti	Days	Area	kHz
0045-0530	daily	SAs	7470isl‡
Bengali	**Days**	**Area**	**kHz**
0900-1000	daily	SAs	9745isl‡, 11875isl‡
Chinese	**Days**	**Area**	**kHz**
1200-1300	daily	EAs	9670isl†, 11905isl†
Dari	**Days**	**Area**	**kHz**
1445-1545	daily	WAs	5885isl‡
Farsi	**Days**	**Area**	**kHz**
1700-1800	daily	ME	6095isl‡, 7470isl‡
Gujarati	**Days**	**Area**	**kHz**
1145-1215	daily	SAs	9700isl‡, 11860isl‡
Hindi	**Days**	**Area**	**kHz**
1045-1145	daily	SAs	9700isl‡, 11860isl‡
Nepali	**Days**	**Area**	**kHz**
1000-1030	daily	SAs	9795isl‡, 11875isl‡
Pashto	**Days**	**Area**	**kHz**
1345-1445	daily	WAs	5885isl‡
Sheena	**Days**	**Area**	**kHz**
0530-0615	daily	SAs	7470isl‡
Sinhala	**Days**	**Area**	**kHz**
1230-1300	daily	SAs	9795isl‡, 11805isl‡
Tamil	**Days**	**Area**	**kHz**
1300-1330	daily	SAs	9795isl‡, 11805isl‡
Urdu	**Days**	**Area**	**kHz**
0045-0215	daily	SEA	11600isl†, 15730isl†
0500-0700	daily	ME	11570isl†, 15730isl†
0830-1105	daily	Eu	15730isl†,*, 17700isl‡,*
1330-1530	daily	ME	11530isl‡, 15725isl†
1700-1900	daily	Eu	11570isl†, 15725isl†

Key: ‡ Inactive at time of publication; † Irregular; * News in English 1100-1105v.
Ann: English: "This is Radio Pakistan"; Urdu: "Ye Radio Pakistan hai".
V: QSL-card. Email reports to: fmcell@radio.gov.pk
Notes: Some transmissions are irregular.

PALAU (PLW)

T8WH – WORLD HARVEST RADIO (WHR) (Rlg)
P.O. Box 66, Koror, PW 96940, Republic of Palau.
61300 S Ironwood Rd, South Bend, IN 46614, USA. (LeSEA Broadcasting Corp.)
E: whr@lesea.com **W:** lesea.com/whr
LP: Chief Engineer: Gary Shirk.
SW: [HBN] Medorm, Babeldaob Island: 4 x 100kW.
FM/DAB: KRST-FM 102.5MHz (Koror 0.75kW)
SAT: Apstar 7, Galaxy 16, Intelsat 19.
kHz: 9930, 15565, 17725

Winter Schedule 2015/2016

English	Days	Area	kHz
0100-0300	......s	SEA,CAf	17725hbn
0300-0400	mtwtf.s	SEA,CAf	17725hbn
0800-0815	mtwtf.s	As	9930hbn
0815-0830	......s	As	9930hbn
0830-0900	mtwtf.s	As	9930hbn
0900-1000	daily	As	9930hbn
1000-1400	daily	As	9930hbn
1430-1530	.....ss	SEA,CAf	15565hbn
1530-1600	.....s.	SEA,CAf	15565hbn
Japanese	**Days**	**Area**	**kHz**
0800-0900	.....s.	As	9930hbn

Ann: English: "This is T8WH, Palau. This is World Harvest Radio, the international voice of LeSEA Broadcasting".
V: QSL-card. (Rpts should be sent to LeSEA Broadcasting Corp. address in USA). Rp (IRC/USD) appreciated.
Notes: Transmitting station owned by LeSEA Broadcasting Corp. (USA). Historical callsigns (licensed to previous owners): T8BZ, KHBN. Actual schedule may vary during the course of the season, depending on airtime sales/tx lease. T8WH transmits prgrs of World Harvest Radio (see USA).

PHILIPPINES (PHL)

RADYO PILIPINAS OVERSEAS (DZRP) (Gov)
4th Floor, PIA Bldg, Visayas Ave, Quezon City, Metro Manila 1100, Philippines.
☎ +63 2 7727716.
E: dzrp_pbs@yahoo.com; radyo_pilipinas_overseas@yahoo.com
W: www.pbs.gov.ph
Webcast: L
LP: Acting SM: Remigio L. Sampang.
SW: Uses facilities provided by IBB.
kHz: 9925, 12120, 15190, 15640, 17700, 17820

Winter Schedule 2015/2016

English	Days	Area	kHz
0200-0330	daily	ME	15640pht, 17700pht, 17820pht
Filipino	**Days**	**Area**	**kHz**
1730-1930	daily	ME	9925pht, 12120pht, 15190pht

Ann: English: "This is Radyo Pilipinas, the Overseas Service of the Philippines Broadcasting Service, PBS. Radyo Pilipinas is reaching you from Manila, Philippines", "Radyo Pilipinas Overseas Service, The Voice of the Philippines".
V: QSL-card. Rp (2 IRCs). Rec. acc.
Notes: Radyo Pilipinas Overseas is the External Sce of the Philippine Broadcasting Service (PBS), organized under the Philippine government Bureau of Broadcast Services (BBS). Broadcasts include relays of PBS's domestic services Radyo ng Bayan and Radyo Magasin.

FEBC PHILIPPINES (Rlg)
P.O.Box 14205, Ortigas Center Post Office, Pasig City 1605, Philippines.
☎ +63 2 6543322. 🖷 +63 2 6540894.
E: info@febc.org.ph **W:** febc.ph
46/F One Corporate Centre, Dona Julia Vargas cor. Meralco Avenues, Ortigas Center, Pasig City 1605, Philippines.
LP: Pres: Dan Andrew S. Cura.
SW: [BOC] Bocaue, Bulacan prov: 4 x 100kW; [IBA] Iba, Zambales prov: 2 x 100kW.
kHz: 7410, 9345, 9400, 9405, 9430, 9465, 9795, 9920, 9940, 11650, 11750, 11825, 12055, 12070, 12095, 12120, 15330, 15435, 15450, 15560, 15580, 15620, 15640

Winter Schedule 2015/2016

Achang	Days	Area	kHz
1230-1245	daily	As	12095boc
Akha	**Days**	**Area**	**kHz**
1215-1230	daily	As	12120boc
Bahnar	**Days**	**Area**	**kHz**
1230-1300	m.w.f..	As	9920iba
Bai (Southern)	**Days**	**Area**	**kHz**
1000-1030	daily	As	15640boc
Buginese	**Days**	**Area**	**kHz**
0930-1000	daily	As	15580boc
Burmese	**Days**	**Area**	**kHz**
1330-1400	daily	As	12120boc

Burmese	Days	Area	kHz
2330-0030	daily	As	15640boc

Chin (Daai)	Days	Area	kHz
1245-1259	daily	As	12120boc

Chin (Mro)	Days	Area	kHz
0030-0045	daily	As	15640boc

Chinese	Days	Area	kHz
0900-1600	daily	As	9430boc
1000-1400	daily	As	9400iba
1400-1600	daily	As	9345iba
2230-0030	daily	As	9405boc
2300-0100	daily	As	12070iba

Hmong (Black)	Days	Area	kHz
1300-1330	daily	As	12095boc

Hmong (Blue/Njua)	Days	Area	kHz
1100-1130	.....ss	As	12095boc
2300-2330	.....ss	As	12095boc

Hmong (White/Daw)	Days	Area	kHz
1100-1130	mtwtf..	As	12095boc
2300-2330	mtwtf..	As	12095boc

Hre	Days	Area	kHz
1230-1300	.t.t.s.	As	9920iba

Hui zu	Days	Area	kHz
0900-0930	daily	As	9400iba

Iu Mien	Days	Area	kHz
1200-1230	daily	As	12095boc
2300-2330	daily	As	9430boc

Jarai	Days	Area	kHz
1200-1230	...tfs.	As	9920iba

Javanese	Days	Area	kHz
0100-0130	daily	As	15560boc
1400-1430	daily	As	15620boc

Jingpho	Days	Area	kHz
0045-0100	daily	As	15640boc

Karen (Pa'o)	Days	Area	kHz
1145-1200	daily	As	15330boc

Khmer	Days	Area	kHz
1200-1300	daily	As	7410boc

Khmu	Days	Area	kHz
0000-0015	daily	As	9795iba
1330-1400	daily	As	12095boc

Koho	Days	Area	kHz
1300-1330	daily	As	9920iba

Lahu	Days	Area	kHz
0015-0045	daily	As	12055boc
1400-1430	daily	As	11750boc

Lao	Days	Area	kHz
1130-1200	daily	As	12095boc
2330-2400	daily	As	9795iba

Lisu	Days	Area	kHz
1300-1330	daily	As	12120boc

Lu	Days	Area	kHz
1030-1100	daily	As	12095boc
2345-0015	daily	As	12055boc

Makassarese	Days	Area	kHz
0900-0930	daily	As	15580boc

Minangkabau	Days	Area	kHz
0930-1000	daily	As	15450boc

Mon	Days	Area	kHz
1115-1145	daily	As	15330boc
2300-2330	daily	As	9795iba

Mongolian	Days	Area	kHz
0830-0900	daily	As	15450iba

Naga	Days	Area	kHz
1230-1245	daily	As	12120boc

Palaung/Pale	Days	Area	kHz
2330-2345	daily	As	12055boc

Rade	Days	Area	kHz
1200-1230	mtw...s	As	9920iba

Rawang	Days	Area	kHz
1200-1215	daily	As	12120boc

Russian	Days	Area	kHz
1500-1600	mtwtfs.	RUS	11650boc

Sasak	Days	Area	kHz
1030-1100	daily	As	15580boc

Shan	Days	Area	kHz
0000-0045	daily	As	15435boc

Sundanese	Days	Area	kHz
1000-1030	daily	As	15580boc

Tai (Dam)	Days	Area	kHz
1245-1300	daily	As	12095boc

Tai (Nua)	Days	Area	kHz
0045-0100	daily	As	15435boc

Tibetan (Khams)	Days	Area	kHz
1300-1330	daily	As	11825boc

Uyghur	Days	Area	kHz
1430-1500	daily	As	9940boc

Vietnamese	Days	Area	kHz
1100-1200	daily	As	9795iba

Wa	Days	Area	kHz
0045-0100	daily	As	12055boc

Yunnan	Days	Area	kHz
1330-1400	daily	As	9465boc

Zhuang (Northern)	Days	Area	kHz
0930-1000	daily	As	9400iba

Ann: English: "This is FEBC Radio, broadcasting from Manila, Philippines".
V: QSL-card. Rp. preferred (3 IRCs)
Notes: Far East Broadcasting Company (Philippines), Inc is a regional division of Far East Broadcasting Company, Inc (FEBC) (USA), targeting Asia and Russia. See USA for FEBC corporate details. The transmissions may include prgrs provided by small religious prgr producers and broadcast under own labels.

RADIO VERITAS ASIA (Rlg)
🖃 Buick St., Fairview Park, Quezon City, Metro Manila 1106, Philippines.
☎ +63 2 9390011. 🖷 +63 2 9390011.
E: rvaprogram@rveritas-asia.org **W:** www.rveritas-asia.org
Webcast: D/L
LP: GM: Fr. Carlos S. Lariosa; PD: Rev. Msgr. Gabriel Htun Myint; Technical Dir: Engr. Alex M. Movilla.
SW: [PUG] Palauig: 1 x 50, 2 x 250kW.
kHz: 6115, 9520, 9645, 9670, 9720, 11640, 11750, 11850, 11855, 11870, 11935, 11945, 15225, 15255, 15265, 15280, 15330, 15355, 15450, 15530, 15620, 17860

Winter Schedule 2015/2016			
Bengali	Days	Area	kHz
0030-0100	daily	As	15265pug
1400-1430	daily	As	11870pug

Burmese	Days	Area	kHz
1130-1200	daily	As	15450pug
2330-2400	daily	As	9720pug

Chin	Days	Area	kHz
1330-1400	daily	As	9520pug

Chin (Teddi)	Days	Area	kHz
0130-0200	mtw....	As	15255pug

Chin (Zomi)	Days	Area	kHz
0130-0200	...tfss	As	15255pug

Chinese	Days	Area	kHz
1000-1130	daily	As	11945pug
2100-2230	daily	As	6115pug

Hindi	Days	Area	kHz
0030-0100	daily	As	15280pug
1330-1400	daily	As	11640pug

Hmong	Days	Area	kHz
1200-1230	daily	As	11935pug

Kachin	Days	Area	kHz
1230-1300	daily	As	15225pug
2330-2400	daily	As	9645pug

Karen	Days	Area	kHz
0000-0030	daily	As	11935pug
1200-1230	daily	As	15225pug

Khmer	Days	Area	kHz
1000-1030	daily	As	11850pug

Sinhala	Days	Area	kHz
0000-0030	daily	As	11855pug
Tagalog	**Days**	**Area**	**kHz**
1500-1555	daily	As	15620smg
2300-2330	daily	As	15355pug
Tamil	**Days**	**Area**	**kHz**
1400-1430	daily	As	9520pug
Telugu	**Days**	**Area**	**kHz**
0100-0130	daily	As	15530pug
1430-1500	daily	As	11750pug
Urdu	**Days**	**Area**	**kHz**
0100-0130	daily	As	15280pug, 17860pug
1430-1500	daily	As	15330smg
Vietnamese	**Days**	**Area**	**kHz**
0130-0230	daily	As	15530pug
1300-1400	daily	As	11850pug
2330-2400	daily	As	9670pug

V: QSL-card.
Notes: Catholic station, on air since 11 April 1969. Owned by the "Philippine Radio Educational and Information Center" (PREIC), composed of Filipino bishops and professionals.

IBB RELAY STATIONS PHILIPPINES
P.O.Box 151, CPO 1099, 1050 Manila, Philippines.
☎ +63 45 9820254. 🖷 +63 45 9821402.
L.P: SM: David Strawman.
SW: [PHT] Tinang: 3 x 50, 12 x 250kW.
V: QSL-card. (Email rpt to manager_phillippines@phi.ibb.gov)

POLAND (POL)

RADIO POLAND (Pub)
Al. Niepodleglosci 77/85, 00-977 Warszawa, Poland.
☎ +48 22 6453302. 🖷 +48 22 6453952.
E: zagranica@polskieradio.pl; ru@polskieradio.pl (Russian)
W: external.polskieradio.pl; www.radiopolsha.pl (Russian); www.radyjo.net (Belarusian)
Webcast: D/L/P Web-only languages: English, German, Polish, Ukrainian, Hebrew.
W: www.thenews.pl (English)
L.P: Editor-in-Chief: Michal Maliszewski.
SAT: Eutelsat Hot Bird 13C.
kHz: 738, 1386, 1395

Winter Schedule 2015/2016

Belarusian	Days	Area	kHz
0400-0500	daily	BLR	1386sit
Russian	**Days**	**Area**	**kHz**
0100-0130	daily	RUS	738msk*
0300-0330	daily	RUS	738msk*
0600-0630	daily	RUS	738msk*
0930-1000	daily	RUS	738msk*
1400-1430	daily	RUS	738msk
1630-1700	daily	RUS,BLR,UKR	1386sit
1700-1730	daily	RUS	738msk
1830-1900	daily	RUS,Cau	1395erv
1900-1930	daily	RUS	738msk*
2130-2200	daily	RUS	738msk*

Key: * Repeat of 1400 broadcast.
Ann: Russian: "Radio Polsha".
V: QSL-card.
Notes: External Sce of the public broadcaster Polskie Radio. The transmissions on 738kHz (via the local WRN relay in Moscow) are part of the WRN Russian language feed, and are intended for listeners in Moscow and Moscow region.

RADIODIENST POLSKA
ul. Grójecka 42/39, 02-320 Warszawa, Poland.
E: via website. **W:** www.radiodienst.pl
Webcast: L (www.shortwaveservice.com)
kHz: 3985

Winter Schedule 2015/2016

German	Days	Area	kHz
2000-2030	.....s.	Eu	3985kll

Notes: Produced by the foundation BelVoxTon Polonia, founded 2014 by staff of the former German External Service section of the Polish public broadcaster Polskie Radio.

ROMANIA (ROU)

RADIO ROMANIA INTERNATIONAL (RRI) (Pub)
P.O. Box 1-111, 014700 Bucuresti, Romania.
☎ +40 21 3031357; +40 21 3031465. 🖷 +40 21 2232613.
E: rri@rri.ro **W:** www.rri.ro
Webcast: L/P
L.P: Secretary General: Eugen Cojocariu.
MW/SW: Leased from Radiocom.
SAT: Eutelsat 16A.
kHz: 5910, 5920, 5930, 5935, 5940, 5945, 5955, 5975, 5990, 6010, 6015, 6020, 6030, 6040, 6090, 6125, 6145, 6170, 7220, 7235, 7310, 7320, 7325, 7330, 7335, 7340, 7345, 7350, 7360, 7370, 7375, 7380, 7395, 7400, 7405, 9470, 9525, 9600, 9620, 9655, 9680, 9730, 9770, 9790, 9800, 9880, 11660, 11760, 11790, 11845, 11945, 11975, 11985, 13580, 13660, 13730, 15150, 15170, 15200, 15220, 15255, 15260, 15330, 15370, 15380, 15400, 15430, 15460, 17640, 17745, 17765, 17775, 17780, 17810, 17850, 17860, 17870, 21580

Winter Schedule 2015/2016

Arabic	Days	Area	kHz
0730-0800	daily	NAf	15200gal
0730-0800	daily	ME	11660gal, 15330tig, 17810tig
1300-1330	daily	ME	11945gal, 13660tig
1300-1330	daily	NAf	15400tig, 15460gal, 17810tig
1630-1700	daily	ME	9680tig, 11760tig
1630-1700	daily	NAf	11975gal, 15170gal
Aromanian	**Days**	**Area**	**kHz**
1530-1600	daily	Eu	5955tig*
1730-1800	daily	Eu	5955tig*
1930-2000	daily	Eu	5945tig*
Chinese	**Days**	**Area**	**kHz**
0500-0530	daily	EAs	15220tig, 17640tig+
1330-1400	daily	EAs	11855tig, 13660tig
English	**Days**	**Area**	**kHz**
0100-0200	daily	NAm	6145gal, 7325gal
0400-0500	daily	ME	11790tig, 13730tig
0400-0500	daily	NAm	6020gal, 7340gal
0630-0700	daily	AUS,NZL	17780gal, 21580tig
0630-0700	daily	Eu	7345tig, 9600gal+
1200-1300	daily	Af	15150gal, 17765gal
1200-1300	daily	Eu	13580tig, 15460tig
1800-1900	daily	Eu	6090tig, 7350tig+
2130-2200	daily	Eu	6030gal+, 7375gal
2130-2200	daily	NAm	6170tig, 7310tig
2300-2400	daily	Eu	6015gal, 7220gal
2300-2400	daily	EAs	7395tig, 9620tig
French	**Days**	**Area**	**kHz**
0200-0300	daily	NAm	5975gal, 7395gal
0600-0630	daily	Eu	6040gal+, 7360gal
0600-0630	daily	Af	9770tig, 11790tig
1100-1200	daily	Eu	15255gal, 17870gal, 21580tig
1100-1200	daily	NAf	17640tig
1700-1800	daily	Eu	5935tig, 7400tig
2100-2130	daily	Eu	6030gal+, 7375gal
German	**Days**	**Area**	**kHz**
0700-0730	daily	Eu	6020tig+, 7345tig
1500-1600	daily	Eu	6040tig, 7330tig
1900-2000	daily	Eu	6010tig, 7405tig+
Italian	**Days**	**Area**	**kHz**
1500-1530	daily	Eu	5955tig*
1700-1730	daily	Eu	5955tig*
1900-1930	daily	Eu	5945tig+,*
Romanian	**Days**	**Area**	**kHz**
0100-0300	daily	NAm	5910tig, 7340tig
0500-0600	daily	Eu	6145gal, 7220gal
0800-0900	.....s	ME	15370tig, 15430gal, 17850gal, 17860tig
0900-1000	.....s	ME	15430tig, 17775tig
0900-1000	.....s	NAf	15380gal, 17745gal
1000-1100	.....s	Eu	15260gal, 17870gal

Romanian	Days	Area	kHz
1000-1100	......s	NAf	17640tig, 21580tig
1300-1400	daily	Eu	9880tig*
1400-1600	daily	Eu	9655gal, 11975gal
1700-1800	daily	ME	5920gal, 7370gal
1800-2100	daily	Eu	5990gal, 7375gal
Russian	**Days**	**Area**	**kHz**
0530-0600	daily	Eu	5940tig+, 7320tig
1400-1500	daily	RUS	9880tig, 11985tig
1600-1630	daily	Eu	5930tig+, 9800tig
Serbian	**Days**	**Area**	**kHz**
1630-1700	daily	Eu	5955tig*
1830-1900	daily	Eu	5945tig*
2030-2100	daily	Eu	6030tig*
Spanish	**Days**	**Area**	**kHz**
0000-0100	daily	SAm	7325tig, 7335gal, 9525gal, 9730tig
0300-0400	daily	CAs	7345gal
0300-0400	daily	SAm	6125gal, 7335tig, 9470tig
2000-2100	daily	Eu	7235tig
2000-2100	daily	NAf	6010tig
2200-2300	daily	SAm	7380tig, 9790tig
Ukrainian	**Days**	**Area**	**kHz**
1600-1630	daily	Eu	5955tig*
1800-1830	daily	Eu	5945tig*
2000-2030	daily	Eu	6030tig*

Key: + DRM; * From Saftica site.
Ann: English: "You are tuned to Radio Romania International, broadcasting from Bucharest".
V: QSL-card. (Online reception report form available)
Notes: Radio Romania International is the External Sce of the public broadcaster Radio Romania. Romanian language prgrs include relays of Home Sce networks. Transmissions may be shortened, or cancelled, at times.

RADIOCOM (Tx Operator)
✉ sos. Oltenitei nr. 103, sector 4, 041303 Bucuresti, Romania.
☎ +40 31 5003001. 🖷 +40 31 5003013.
E: office@radiocom.ro **W:** www.radiocom.ro
L.P: DG: Gabriel Grecu.
SW: [GAL] Bacau, Galbeni: 2 x 300kW; [TIG] Bucuresti, two sites: Tiganesti (G.C. 44N45 026E06): 3 x 300kW; Saftica (G.C. 44N38 026E05): 1 x 100kW.
Notes: Radiocom is the national transmitter network owner.

RUSSIA (RUS)

GTRK "ADYGEYA" (Gov)
✉ ul. Zhukovskogo 24, 385000 Maykop, Russia.
☎ +7 8772 522615.
E: adigradio@mail.ru **W:** www.adygtv.ru/radio
Webcast: D
L.P: Dir: Vyacheslav Zhachemuk.
SW: Leased from RTRN.
kHz: 6000

	Winter Schedule 2015/2016		
Adyghe	**Days**	**Area**	**kHz**
1900-2000	......s	ME	6000arm
Adyghe*	**Days**	**Area**	**kHz**
1800-1900	mt.....	ME	6000arm

Key: * Mondays also in Arabic and Turkish.
Notes: Special prgr for Circassian communities in the Near East, produced by the regional state broadcasting company GTRK "Adygeya". Prgrs for domestic audience: see National Radio section.

VESTI FM (Gov)
✉ Contact details see National Radio Section.
kHz: 1413

	Winter Schedule 2015/2016		
Russian	**Days**	**Area**	**kHz**
0000-2400	daily	UKR	1413kch

Notes: Relay of domestic prgr, produced by the national broadcasting company VGTRK.

RADIOAGENCY–M (Broker)
✉ 123308 Moskva, ul. Demyana Bednogo 24, Russia.
☎ +7 499 1919161. 🖷 +7 499 1918591.
E: abat@radioagency.ru
L.P: Dir: Aleksey A. Titov.
V: QSL-card. (For brokered stns)
Notes: Radioagency-M brokers air time for SW txs in Moldova (Pridnestrovian Moldavian Republic) and Uzbekistan.

RUSSIAN TELEVISION AND RADIO BROADCASTING NETWORK (RTRN) (Tx Operator)
✉ ul. Nikolskaya 7, 109012 Moscow, Russia.
☎ +7 495 6480111. 🖷 +7 495 6480111.
E: press@rtrn.ru **W:** www.rtrs.ru; www.rtrn.ru
L.P: DG: Viktor Konin.
MW: [MSK] Moskva 738kHz 5kW.
SW: [ARM] Krasnodar, Tbilisskaya: 1 x 100kW.
Notes: RTRN is the national transmitter network operator in Russia. RTRN also owns the transmitting centre Maiac in Moldova (Transnistria).

SÃO TOMÉ E PRÍNCIPE (STP)

IBB RELAY STATION SÃO TOMÉ
✉ IBB Transmitting Station, CP 522, São Tomé, São Tomé e Príncipe.
☎ +239 2223406. 🖷 +239 2223406.
L.P: SM: Kenneth Tripp.
MW: [SAO] Pinheira: 1530kHz 100/600kW.
SW: [SAO] Pinheira: 5 x 100kW.
V: QSL-card. (Email rpt to Secretary of SM, Helena de Menezes hmenezes@bbg.gov)

SAUDI ARABIA (ARS)

SAUDI INTERNATIONAL RADIO (Gov)
✉ P.O. Box 60059, Riyadh-11545, Saudi Arabia.
☎ +966 1 4425170. 🖷 +966 1 4041692.
E: via website (Arabic) **W:** international.sr.sa; www.sr.sa
Webcast: L (sm.gov.sa)
L.P: Minister, Culture and Information: Adel bin Zaid Al Toraifi.
SW: [RIY] Riyadh: 4 x 350, 8 x 500kW.
SAT: Arabsat 5A/C, AsiaSat 5, Badr 4/5, Eutelsat Hot Bird 13B, Galaxy 19, Hispasat 1C.
kHz: 7240, 9555, 9675, 9695, 9715, 9870, 9885, 11820, 11915, 11930, 11935, 13710, 13775, 15120, 15170, 15205, 15225, 15285, 15380, 15435, 15490, 17560, 17570, 17615, 17625, 17660, 17705, 17730, 17740, 17805, 17895, 21505, 21670

	Winter Schedule 2015/2016		
Arabic	**Days**	**Area**	**kHz**
0300-0600	daily	Eu,CAs	15170riy*
0300-0800	daily	CAs,EAs	17895riy*
0300-1000	daily	ME	9715riy*,^
0600-0900	daily	Eu	17740riy**
0600-0900	daily	ME	15380riy*
0600-0900	daily	NAf	17730riy**
0900-1200	daily	Eu	15490riy**
0900-1200	daily	SAs,SEA	17615riy*
0900-1200	daily	ME	11935riy*
0900-1200	daily	EAs,SEA	17570riy*
0900-1200	daily	NAf	17805riy**
1200-1400	daily	ME	15380riy*
1200-1400	daily	SAs,SEA	17625riy*
1200-1500	daily	NAf	17895riy*, 21505riy**
1200-1500	daily	Eu	17705riy**
1300-1600	daily	SAf	17615riy*
1500-1800	daily	NAf	13710riy*, 15225riy**
1500-1800	daily	Eu	15435riy**
1600-1800	daily	Eu	15205riy*
1600-1800	daily	WAf,CAf	17560riy*
1800-2300	daily	Eu	9870riy**, 11820riy*
1800-2300	daily	NAf	9555riy**, 11915riy*
1800-2300	daily	WAf,CAf	11930riy*
Bengali	**Days**	**Area**	**kHz**
1200-1500	daily	SAs	15120riy

French	Days	Area	kHz
1400-1800	daily	WAf	17660riy
Indonesian	**Days**	**Area**	**kHz**
0900-1200	daily	SEA	21670riy
Pashto	**Days**	**Area**	**kHz**
1400-1600	daily	WAs	9695riy
Persian	**Days**	**Area**	**kHz**
1500-1800	daily	ME	7240riy
Swahili	**Days**	**Area**	**kHz**
0400-0700	daily	EAf	15285riy
Tajik/Turkmen/			
Uyghur/Uzbek	**Days**	**Area**	**kHz**
1500-1800	daily	CAs	9885riy
Turkish	**Days**	**Area**	**kHz**
1800-2100	daily	ME	9675riy
Urdu	**Days**	**Area**	**kHz**
1200-1500	daily	SAs	13775riy

Key: * Quran prgr; ** General prgr; ^ Low power.
Ann: Arabic: "Idha'at ar-Riyadh" (General Prgr); "Idha-atu'l-Koran al-Kareem min al-mamlakah al-arabiyah t'il-saydiah" (Quran Prgr).
IS: 'Ud' (Oriental Lute). Opens and closes with National Anthem.
V: No longer issues QSL-cards.
Notes: The SW transmissions in Arabic are relays of Home Sce prgrs.

SERBIA (SRB)

INTERNATIONAL RADIO SERBIA ‡ (Gov)
Notes: The External Service International Radio Serbia was produced by the governmental broadcasting company SJU Radio-Jugoslavija. The station was closed and dissolved on 31 July 2015.

SINGAPORE (SNG)

TWR ASIA (Rlg)
✉ 85 Playfair Road #04-01, Tong Yuan Industrial Building, Singapore 368000.
☎ +65 65015150. 🖨 +65 64443053.
E: info@twr.asia **W:** www.twr.asia
Webcast: D
L.P: Int Dir: Sebastian Chan.
SW: Via TWR Guam relay station (KTWR) & leased foreign relays.
kHz: 9910, 9975, 11580, 11840, 11965, 12120, 15225, 15235, 15390

Winter Schedule 2015/2016

Assamese	Days	Area	kHz
1315-1345	mtwtf.s	SEA	15225twr
Burmese	**Days**	**Area**	**kHz**
1200-1230	mtwtf..	SEA	15390twr
1200-1245	.....s.	SEA	15390twr
1200-1300	......s	SEA	15390twr
Cantonese	**Days**	**Area**	**kHz**
1115-1130	daily	EAs	12120twr
1245-1300	mtwtf..	EAs	9910twr
1400-1430	mtwtf..	EAs	9975twr
Chinese	**Days**	**Area**	**kHz**
1000-1015	daily	EAs	15235twr
1015-1100	mtwtfs.	EAs	15235twr
1100-1115	daily	EAs	12120twr
1100-1130	mtwtf..	EAs	9910twr
1115-1130	.....s.	EAs	9910twr
1130-1230	daily	EAs	9910twr
1215-1245	.twt...	EAs	9975twr
1230-1245	mtwtf..	EAs	9910twr, 9910twr
1330-1400	mtwtf.s	EAs	9975twr
1345-1400	.....s.	EAs	9975twr
1430-1445	daily	EAs	9975twr
English	**Days**	**Area**	**kHz**
1000-1015	.....s.	AUS,NZL,Pac	11840twr
1000-1025	mtwtf..	AUS,NZL,Pac	11840twr
1030-1100	m......	SEA	11965twr
1030-1110	.twtf..	SEA	11965twr
1215-1245	m...fs.	EAs	9975twr+
1530-1545	.....s.	EAs	12120twr
1530-1550	mtwtf..	EAs	12120twr

Hakka	Days	Area	kHz
1130-1200	daily	EAs	12120twr
Hui	**Days**	**Area**	**kHz**
1400-1430	.....ss	EAs	9975twr
Indonesian	**Days**	**Area**	**kHz**
0930-1000	......s	INS	11965twr
Japanese	**Days**	**Area**	**kHz**
1215-1245	......s	J	9975twr
Karen (S'gaw)	**Days**	**Area**	**kHz**
1300-1315	.....s.	As	15390twr
1300-1330	mtwtf.s	As	15390twr
Korean	**Days**	**Area**	**kHz**
1345-1415	.....s.	EAs	9910twr
1345-1445	......s	EAs	9910twr
1345-1500	mtwtf..	EAs	9910twr
Madurese	**Days**	**Area**	**kHz**
0930-1000	mtwtf..	SEA	11965twr
Sundanese	**Days**	**Area**	**kHz**
1000-1030	mtwtf.s	SEA	11965twr
Vietnamese	**Days**	**Area**	**kHz**
1245-1330	mtwtf.s	SEA	11580twr
1245-1345	.....s.	SEA	11580twr
Yi (Sichuan)	**Days**	**Area**	**kHz**
1200-1215	daily	SEA	11580twr

Key: + DRM.
V: QSL-card. (Online form on website)
Notes: TWR regional branch for Asia. For corporate details, see under TWR (USA).

BBC FAR EASTERN RELAY STATION
✉ 51 Turut Track, Singapore 718930.
☎ +65 67937511. 🖨 +65 67937834.
L.P: Stn Mgr: Cindy Yao; Chief Eng: Tam Lam Soon.
SW: [SNG] Singapore: 4 x 100, 5 x 250kW.
V: QSL-card. (For direct report)
Notes: Owned by the BBC and operated by Babcock Media Services (see under United Kingdom).

SLOVAKIA (SVK)

RADIO SLOVAKIA INTERNATIONAL (Pub)
✉ Mýtna 1, P.O. Box 55, 817 55 Bratislava 15, Slovak Republic.
☎ +421 2 57273734. 🖨 +421 2 52496282.
E: drahoslava.valocka@slovakradio.sk; englishsection@slovakradio.sk
W: rsi.rtvs.sk
Webcast: L. Webcast languages: English, French, German, Russian, Slovak, Spanish.
L.P: Dir: Mária Mikušová.
SW: Leases airtime on WRMI (See under USA).
SAT: Astra 3B.
kHz: 738, 3985, 5850, 6005, 7310, 7570, 9560, 9955, 11580

Winter Schedule 2015/2016

English	Days	Area	kHz
0030-0100	daily	NAm	5850yfr
0030-0100	daily	Eu,NAm	11580yfr
1300-1330	daily	Eu	9560kll
1300-1330	mtwtf..	LAm	9955yfr
1530-1600	daily	Eu	7310kll
2000-2030	daily	Eu	3985kll
2100-2130	.....ss	NAm	7570yfr
French	**Days**	**Area**	**kHz**
0730-0800	daily	Eu	7310kll
1330-1400	daily	Eu	9560kll
1430-1500	daily	Eu	6005kll
1930-2000	daily	Eu	3985kll
German	**Days**	**Area**	**kHz**
0700-0730	daily	Eu	7310kll
1400-1430	daily	Eu	6005kll
1900-1930	daily	Eu	3985kll
Russian	**Days**	**Area**	**kHz**
0130-0200	daily	RUS	738msk
0500-0530	mtwtf..	RUS	738msk
0900-0930	mtwt.ss	RUS	738msk
1130-1200	daily	RUS	738msk

Russian	Days	Area	kHz
1300-1330	.twtfs.	RUS	738msk
1430-1500	daily	RUS	738msk
1630-1700	daily	RUS	738msk
1930-2000	mtwt..s	RUS	738msk
2300-2330	daily	RUS	738msk
Slovak	**Days**	**Area**	**kHz**
0000-0030	daily	Eu,NAm	11580yfr
0000-0030	daily	NAm	5850yfr
Spanish	**Days**	**Area**	**kHz**
0330-0400	daily	LAm	9955yfr
0530-0600	daily	LAm	9955yfr
1130-1200	mtwtfs.	LAm	9955yfr

Ann: English: "You are listening to Radio Slovakia International".
V: QSL-card.
Notes: Began broadcasting in 1993. Radio Slovakia International is the External Sce of the public-service Slovak Radio (Slovenský Rozhlas). Russian prgrs can be heard on MW in Moscow and Moscow region via the local WRN relay.

SOUTH AFRICA (AFS)

CHANNEL AFRICA (Pub)
✉ P.O. Box 91313, Auckland Park 2006, South Africa.
☎ +27 11 7142255. 📠 +27 11 7142072.
E: phetoess@sabc.co.za (General Manager); dawetimj@sabc.co.za (Prgr Manager) **W:** www.channelafrica.co.za
Webcast: D/L/P
LP: GM: Solly Phetoe; Managing Editor: Moshongwa Matsena; Prgr Mgr: Lungi Daweti.
SW: Leased from Sentech.
SAT: Intelsat 20.
kHz: 3345, 6155, 7230, 9625, 15235, 15255, 17770

Winter Schedule 2015/2016

English	Days	Area	kHz
0300-0400	mtwtf..	EAf	6155mey
0300-0500	mtwtf..	SAf	3345mey
0500-0700	mtwtf..	SAf	7230mey
0600-0700	mtwtf..	WAf	15255mey
0700-1200	mtwtf..	SAf	9625mey
1500-1600	mtwtf..	SAf	9625mey
1700-1800	mtwtf..	WAf	15235mey
French	**Days**	**Area**	**kHz**
1600-1700	mtwtf..	WAf	15235mey
Lozi	**Days**	**Area**	**kHz**
1300-1400	mtwtf..	SAf	9625mey
Nyanja	**Days**	**Area**	**kHz**
1200-1300	mtwtf..	SAf	9625mey
Portuguese	**Days**	**Area**	**kHz**
1400-1500	mtwtf..	SAf	9625mey
Swahili	**Days**	**Area**	**kHz**
1500-1600	mtwtf..	EAf	17770mey

Ann: English: "You're listening to Channel Africa coming to you from Johannesburg"; "You are listening to Channel Africa, the voice of the African Renaissance, broadcasting live from Johannesburg, South Africa".
IS: Birds chirping and native melody.
V: Does not verify. Rpts should be sent to Sentech.
Notes: Channel Africa is the External Sce of the public-service South African Broadcasting Corporation (SABC).

TWR AFRICA (Rlg)
✉ P.O. Box 4232, Kempton Park, 1620, South Africa.
☎ +27 11 9742885. 📠 +27 11 9749960.
E: info@twrafrica.org **W:** www.twrafrica.org
Webcast: D/L/P
✉ San Croy Business Park, Die Agora Rd., Kempton Park, 1619, South Africa.
LP: Dir: Sphiwe Nxumalo; Dir (Tech Sces) James Burnett.
MW: Via TWR Benin relay station.
SW: Via TWR Swaziland relay station & leased foreign relays.
SAT: Intelsat 20.
kHz: 1170, 1566, 3200, 3240, 4760, 4775, 5965, 6025, 6120, 6130, 7300, 7315, 9475, 9500, 9585, 9940, 11660, 12025, 15105, 17680

Winter Schedule 2015/2016

Afar	Days	Area	kHz
1300-1315	...tfss	EAf	17680dha
Amharic	**Days**	**Area**	**kHz**
1630-1645	m....s	EAf	11660man
1700-1715	.....s	EAf	11660man
1700-1730	mtwtf.s	EAf	11660man
1830-1900	......s	EAf	5965dha
Arabic (Juba)	**Days**	**Area**	**kHz**
1847-1902	mtwt..s	Af	9500man
Bambara	**Days**	**Area**	**kHz**
2025-2040	...f..	WAf	1566par
Chokwe	**Days**	**Area**	**kHz**
1850-1905	daily	SAf	6130man
Dendi	**Days**	**Area**	**kHz**
2010-2025	m....s	WAf	1566par
Ditamari	**Days**	**Area**	**kHz**
1925-1940	.....s.	WAf	1566par
English	**Days**	**Area**	**kHz**
0255-0325	......s	SAf	3200man
0315-0330	mtwtf..	WAf	1566par
0335-0345	.....ss	WAf	1566par
0430-0500	daily	WAf	1566par
0500-0800	daily	SAf	4775man
0501-0800	daily	Af	6120man
0530-0545	daily	WAf	1566par
1425-1455	daily	SAf	6025man
1525-1555	.....ss	SAf	6025man
1745-1820	daily	WAf	1566par
1802-1832	daily	Af	9500man
1830-2155	daily	SAf	1170man
1832-1847	.twt...	Af	9500man
1832-1902	...fs.	Af	9500man
Ewe	**Days**	**Area**	**kHz**
0515-0530	.....ss	WAf	1566par
Fiote	**Days**	**Area**	**kHz**
1935-1950	...f..	SAf	6130man
Fon	**Days**	**Area**	**kHz**
1855-1910	.....s	WAf	1566par
1940-2010	mtwtf..	WAf	1566par
Fongbe	**Days**	**Area**	**kHz**
1725-1745	daily	WAf	1566par
2010-2025	.tw....	WAf	1566par
French	**Days**	**Area**	**kHz**
1455-1525	.....s.	WAf	9585man
1935-2005	daily	WAf	9940man
2040-2215	daily	WAf	1566par
2215-2230	mtwtf..	WAf	1566par
Fulfulde	**Days**	**Area**	**kHz**
1940-2010	.....ss	WAf	1566par
German	**Days**	**Area**	**kHz**
0400-0430	mtwtf..	SAf	3200man, 4775man
0400-0500	.....ss	SAf	4775man
0430-0500	.....ss	SAf	3200man
Hadiyya	**Days**	**Area**	**kHz**
1645-1700	...fs.	EAf	11660man
Hausa	**Days**	**Area**	**kHz**
0330-0430	mtwtf..	WAf	1566par
0345-0430	.....ss	WAf	1566par
1855-1910	mtwtf..	WAf	1566par
Igbo	**Days**	**Area**	**kHz**
2025-2040	.....ss	WAf	1566par
Jula	**Days**	**Area**	**kHz**
2025-2040	...t...	WAf	1566par
Kambaata	**Days**	**Area**	**kHz**
1630-1645	...fs.	EAf	11660man
Kanuri	**Days**	**Area**	**kHz**
1910-1925	daily	WAf	1566par
KiKongo	**Days**	**Area**	**kHz**
1920-1935	mtwtf..	SAf	6130man
Kimbundu	**Days**	**Area**	**kHz**
2020-2035	daily	SAf	6130man

Kirundi	Days	Area	kHz
1557-1627	mtwtf..	Af	15105man
Kotokoli	**Days**	**Area**	**kHz**
1925-1940	mtwtf..	WAf	1566par
Kuanyama	**Days**	**Area**	**kHz**
1935-1950	.....s	SAf	6130man
Kunama	**Days**	**Area**	**kHz**
1800-1830	.....s	EAf	5965dha
Lingala	**Days**	**Area**	**kHz**
1905-1935	daily	Af	9940man
Lomwe	**Days**	**Area**	**kHz**
0342-0357	daily	SAf	4775man
Lopka	**Days**	**Area**	**kHz**
1925-1940	.....s	WAf	1566par
Luchazi	**Days**	**Area**	**kHz**
1935-1950	..w....	SAf	6130man
Lunyaneka	**Days**	**Area**	**kHz**
1935-1950	.....s.	SAf	6130man
Luvale	**Days**	**Area**	**kHz**
1935-1950	...t...	SAf	6130man
Makasar	**Days**	**Area**	**kHz**
1418-1453	daily	SAf	7315man
Malagasy	**Days**	**Area**	**kHz**
1455-1525	mtwtf.s	SAf	9585man
Moore	**Days**	**Area**	**kHz**
2025-2040	mtw....	WAf	1566par
Ndau	**Days**	**Area**	**kHz**
0325-0340	daily	SAf	3240man
Ndebele	**Days**	**Area**	**kHz**
0255-0310	.....s.	SAf	3200man
0255-0325	mtwtf..	SAf	3200man
1455-1510	m......	SAf	6025man
1525-1555	mtwtf..	SAf	6025man
Oromo	**Days**	**Area**	**kHz**
1630-1700	.twt...	EAf	11660man
1645-1700	m.....s	EAf	11660man
1730-1800	mtwtf..	EAf	11660man
Portuguese	**Days**	**Area**	**kHz**
1630-1645	.....s	SAf	4760man
1920-1935	.....ss	SAf	6130man
1935-1950	mt.....	SAf	6130man
1950-2020	daily	SAf	6130man
Shona	**Days**	**Area**	**kHz**
0255-0325	daily	SAf	3240man
1455-1510	.twtfss	SAf	6025man
1510-1525	daily	SAf	6025man
1555-1625	daily	SAf	6025man
Somali	**Days**	**Area**	**kHz**
1630-1645	.....s	EAf	12025dha
1630-1657	mtwtfs.	EAf	12025dha
Songhai	**Days**	**Area**	**kHz**
2010-2025	.....s.	WAf	1566par
Swahili	**Days**	**Area**	**kHz**
1745-1815	mtwtf.s	Af	9475man
1800-1815	.....s.	Af	9475man
1832-1847	m......	Af	9500man
1832-1902	.....s	Af	9500man
Tigre	**Days**	**Area**	**kHz**
1800-1830	.....s.	EAf	5965dha
Tigrinya	**Days**	**Area**	**kHz**
1800-1815	..wt...	EAf	5965dha
1815-1845	mtwtf..	EAf	5965dha
Turkana	**Days**	**Area**	**kHz**
1745-1800	.....s.	Af	9475man
Twi	**Days**	**Area**	**kHz**
0500-0515	.....ss	WAf	1566par
0500-0530	mtwtf..	WAf	1566par
Umbundu	**Days**	**Area**	**kHz**
1820-1850	mtwtf..	SAf	6130man
1905-1920	daily	SAf	6130man
Yao	**Days**	**Area**	**kHz**
1700-1730	daily	Af	7300man

Yoruba	Days	Area	kHz
1820-1855	daily	WAf	1566par
1855-1910	.....s.	WAf	1566par
Zulu	**Days**	**Area**	**kHz**
1800-1830	daily	SAf	1170man

Ann: English: "Trans World Radio" or "TWR".
IS: Last bar of "We've a story to tell the Nations", played on hand bells.
V: QSL-folder. Rp. (IRCs appreciated, 3 IRCs for airmail reply)
Notes: TWR regional division for Africa. For corporate details, see under TWR (USA). TWR Africa administrates the TWR transmitting stations in Benin and Swaziland.

AMATEUR RADIO TODAY
✉ P.O. Box 90438, Garsfontein 0042, South Africa.
☎ +27 11 6752393. ▤ +27 11 6752793.
E: artoday@sarl.org.za **W:** ww.amateurradio.org.za/ARTODAY2.htm; www.sarl.org.za/public/armi/armi.asp (outdated)
Webcast: P
SW: Leased from Sentech.
kHz: *4895, 7205, 17760*

Winter Schedule 2015/2016			
English	**Days**	**Area**	**kHz**
0800-0900	.....s	SAf	7205mey
0800-0900	.....s	EAf	17760mey
1630-1730	m......	SAf	4895mey

V: V: Does not verify, Rpts should be sent to Sentech (Pty) Ltd, see entry below.
Notes: Amateur Radio Today (previously known as Amateur Radio Mirror International) is a weekly prgr about amateur radio, short-wave listening and electronics, produced by the South African Radio League.

SENTECH (PTY) LTD. (Tx Operator)
✉ Private Bag X06, Honeydew 2040, South Africa.
☎ +27 11 4388883. ▤ +27 11 6917107.
E: support@sentechsa.com **W:** www.sentech.co.za
✉ P.O. Box 234, Meyerton 1960, South Africa. (Transmitter site)
☎ +27 16 3661055. ▤ +27 16 3660709.
L.P: Chmn: Magatho Mello; CEO: Setumo Mohapi; HF Coverage Planning: Sikander Hoosen.
SW: [MEY] Meyerton, Bloemendal: 7 x 100, 4 x 250kW.
V: QSL-letter (for relayed prgrs). Email rpt to hoosens@sentech.co.za (Sikander Hoosen).
Notes: Sentech (Pty) Ltd. is the operator of the transmitter networks in South Africa.

SPAIN (E)

RADIO EXTERIOR DE ESPAÑA (REE) (Pub)
✉ Casa de la Radio, Avenida de la Radio y la Televisión 4, Pozuelo de Alarcón, 28223 Madrid, Spain.
☎ +34 91 5817000.
E: ree@rtve.es; secretariatecnica.ree@rtve.es
W: www.rtve.es/radio/radio-exterior
Webcast: D/L/P Web languages: Arabic, English, French, Russian, Portuguese, Sefardi, Spanish.
L.P: Dir: Antonio Szigriszt.
SW: [NOB] Noblejas: 6 x 250kW.
SAT: Astra 1M, Eutelsat 5WA, EchoStar 9, Galaxy 23.
kHz: *738, 9690, 11530, 15390, 15500*

Winter Schedule 2015/2016			
Russian	**Days**	**Area**	**kHz**
0030-0100	.....s	RUS	738msk
0500-0530	.....s	RUS	738msk
0800-0830	.....s	RUS	738msk
1300-1330	m......	RUS	738msk
1930-2000	.....s.	RUS	738msk
Spanish	**Days**	**Area**	**kHz**
1500-1900	.....ss	SAm	15390nob
1500-1900	.....ss	ME,SAs	15500nob
1500-1900	.....ss	CAm,NAm	9690nob
1500-1900	.....ss	Af,Atl	11530nob
1900-2300	daily	SAm	15390nob
1900-2300	daily	ME,SAs	15500nob

Spanish

	Days	Area	kHz
1900-2300	daily	CAm,NAm	9690nob
1900-2300	daily	Af,Atl	11530nob

V: QSL-card.
Notes: REE is the External Sce of the public broadcaster Radio Nacional de España. Has resumed SW transmissions, in Spanish only, and is relayed via WRN, in Russian, on MW for listeners in Moscow and the surrounding area.

RADIO MI AMIGO INTERNATIONAL (Comm)

Avda. de Europa 85, Urb.La Marina, 03177 San Fulgencio, Alicante, Spain.
☎ +34 96 6790195.
E: info@radiomiamigo.es **W:** www.radiomiamigointernational.com; www.radiomiamigo.es/shortwave
Webcast: L
L.P: Dir (R. Mi Amigo): Kord Lemkau.
kHz: *1485, 3985, 6005, 7310, 9560*

Winter Schedule 2005/2006

Dutch	Days	Area	kHz
0800-0900	......s	Eu	6005kll
1000-1100	......s	Eu	6005kll, 9560kll
1200-1300	......s	Eu	7310kll, 9560kll
1200-1300	.....s.	Eu	6005kll, 9560kll
1400-1500	......s	Eu	7310kll
1600-1700	...t...	Eu	6005kll
1700-1800	...t...	Eu	3985kll
2000-2100	......s	LVA	1485rme
2200-2300	....ss	LVA	1485rme
English	**Days**	**Area**	**kHz**
0700-0800	......s	Eu	6005kll
0800-0900	.....s.	Eu	6005kll, 9560kll
0900-1000	......s	Eu	6005kll, 9560kll
1100-1200	......s	Eu	6005kll, 7310kll, 9560kll
1300-1400	......s	Eu	7310kll
1600-1700	mt..f..	Eu	6005kll
1700-1800	mt..f..	Eu	3985kll
1900-2000	......s	LVA	1485rme
2100-2200	......s	LVA	1485rme
German	**Days**	**Area**	**kHz**
0700-0800	.....s.	Eu	6005kll, 9560kll
0900-1200	.....s.	Eu	6005kll, 9560kll
1600-1700	..w....	Eu	6005kll
1600-1900	.....s.	LVA	1485rme
1700-1800	..w....	Eu	3985kll
2100-2200	.....s.	LVA	1485rme

Ann: English: "Radio Mi Amigo".
V: QSL-card.
Notes: Radio Mi Amigo International is a 24/7 Internet channel, produced with support of the German language radio station R. Mi Amigo that broadcasts on FM for listeners along the Costa Blanca coast of Spain. The prgr consists of music shows by German, Dutch and English DJs The relay on MW is broadcast via the local station R. Merkurs in Riga, Latvia (1.25kW), see Nat. Radio section for contact details.

SRI LANKA (CLN)

SRI LANKA BROADCASTING CORPORATION (SLBC) (Pub)

P.O. Box 574, Colombo 7, Sri Lanka.
☎ +94 11 2697491. ▤ +94 11 2691568.
E: chmnslbc@slbc.lk (Chairman); ddge@slbc.lk (Dir, Engineering) **W:** www.slbc.lk
Webcast: L
Independence Square, Colombo 7, Sri Lanka. (Studio)
☎ +94 26 2222097.
L.P: Chmn: Nanda Muruttetuwegama; DG: Erananda Hettiarachchi; Dir, Engineering: H. M. Jackson.
MW: [PUT] Puttalam: 873/882kHz 400kW (882 leased to TWR India, 873 leased to other customers), 1125kHz 50kW; [TRM] Trincomalee, Perkara (Former DW Relay Station): 1548kHz 400kW (leased to foreign customers).
SW: [TRM] Trincomalee, Perkara (Former DW Relay Station): 1 x 250, 3 x 300kW.

kHz: *9720, 11750, 11905*

Winter Schedule 2015/2016

Bengali	Days	Area	kHz
0115-0130	daily	SAs	11905trm
Hindi	**Days**	**Area**	**kHz**
0130-0230	daily	SAs	11905trm*
1115-1130	daily	SAs	9720trm
1145-1200	daily	SAs	9720trm
Malayalam	**Days**	**Area**	**kHz**
1130-1145	daily	SAs	9720trm
Sinhala	**Days**	**Area**	**kHz**
1630-1830	mtw..s	ME	11750trm
Tamil	**Days**	**Area**	**kHz**
1200-1215	daily	SAs	9720trm

Key: * Includes Christian prgs in English.
Ann: English: "This is the Sri Lanka Broadcasting Corporation".
IS: Melody on drums.
V: QSL-card. Rp.

IBB RELAY STATION SRI LANKA

IBB Transmitting Station, P.O. Box 14, Negombo, Sri Lanka.
☎ +94 32 2255931. ▤ +94 32 2255822.
L.P: SM:William S.Martin.
SW: [IRA] Iranawila: 3 x 250, 4 x 500kW.
V: QSL-card. (Email rpt to manager_srilanka@sri.ibb.gov)

SUDAN (SDN)

VOICE OF AFRICA – SUDAN RADIO (Gov)

P.O.Box 572, Omdurman, Sudan.
☎ +249 1 87572956. ▤ +249 1 87556006.
E: voiceofafrica@sudanradio.info **W:** www.sudanradio.info
L.P: DG (Sudan Radio): Mutasim Fadul.
SW: [ALF] Khartoum, Al Fitahab: 1 x 100kW
kHz: *9505*

Winter Schedule 2015/2016

Amharic	Days	Area	kHz
0630-0700	daily	Af	9505alf†
English	**Days**	**Area**	**kHz**
0800-0900	daily	Af	9505alf†
1730-1830	daily	Af	9505alf†
French	**Days**	**Area**	**kHz**
1630-1730	daily	Af	9505alf†
Hausa	**Days**	**Area**	**kHz**
1830-1930	daily	Af	9505alf†
Swahili	**Days**	**Area**	**kHz**
0700-0800	daily	Af	9505alf†

Key: † Irregular.
Ann: English: "This is the Voice of Africa from Sudan Radio"; French: "La Voix de L'Afrique, Radio National de Soudan".
Notes: The Voice of Africa is the external prgr of the state controlled Sudan Radio and Television Corporation (SRTC). Began test transmissions, consisting of Sudanese music and multilingual identifications, in October 2012.

SWAZILAND (SWZ)

TWR RELAY STATION

P.O. Box 64, Manzini, Swaziland.
☎ +268 25052781. ▤ +268 25055333.
L.P: Chief Engineer (interim): Klaus Schiller.
MW: [MAN] Manzini, Mpangela Ranch: 1170kHz 50kW.
SW: [MAN] Manzini, Mpangela Ranch: 3 x 100kW.
Notes: Owned by TWR. For corporate details, see under USA. For schedule, see TWR Africa, under South Africa.

SWEDEN (S)

IBRA RADIO (Rlg)

P.O.Box 15144, SE-16715 Bromma, Sweden.
☎ +46 8 6089680. ▤ +46 8 6089650.
E: info@ibra.se **W:** www.ibra.org (English); ibra.se (Swedish)
P.O. Box 2899, Stoke-on-Trent, ST4 9EL, United Kingdom.
☎ +44 1782 623759.
E: info@ibra.co.uk **W:** ibra.uk

LP: Mgr, IBRA Media: Pontus Fridolfsson; Public Relations: Birger Thureson.
kHz: 5905, 5940, 6180, 7235, 7265, 7510, 9390, 9445, 9540, 9635, 9820, 11610, 11655, 12065, 12125, 15260

Winter Schedule 2015/2016

Afar	Days	Area	kHz
1600-1630	daily	Af	11655dha
Amharic	**Days**	**Area**	**kHz**
1600-1700	daily	Af	12125erv
Arabic	**Days**	**Area**	**kHz**
0800-0830	daily	Af	15260wof
1700-1830	daily	Af	12065wof
1900-1930	daily	Af	7265wof
Bambara	**Days**	**Area**	**kHz**
1945-2000	.....ss	Af	7235wof
Beja	**Days**	**Area**	**kHz**
1730-1830	daily	Af	9635wof
Bengali	**Days**	**Area**	**kHz**
0000-0030	daily	As	5905tac
1500-1530	daily	As	9390tac
Dari	**Days**	**Area**	**kHz**
0230-0300	daily	WAs	5940dha
1500-1530	daily	WAs	9445erv
Dyula/Malinke	**Days**	**Area**	**kHz**
1930-1945	m.....s	Af	7235wof
Fulfulde	**Days**	**Area**	**kHz**
1900-1930	mtwtf..	Af	7235wof
Fur	**Days**	**Area**	**kHz**
1830-1900	daily	Af	9635wof
Hausa	**Days**	**Area**	**kHz**
1945-2000	mtwtf..	Af	7235wof
Kanuri	**Days**	**Area**	**kHz**
1915-1930	.....ss	Af	7235wof
Oromo	**Days**	**Area**	**kHz**
1700-1730	daily	Af	9540dha
Pular	**Days**	**Area**	**kHz**
1900-1915	.....ss	Af	7235wof
Silte	**Days**	**Area**	**kHz**
1730-1800	daily	Af	7510erv
Somali	**Days**	**Area**	**kHz**
1700-1730	daily	Af	6180dha
1730-1800	daily	Af	6180dha
Tamajeq	**Days**	**Area**	**kHz**
1930-1945	...tfs.	Af	7235wof
Tigrinya	**Days**	**Area**	**kHz**
1630-1700	daily	Af	9820dha
1700-1730	daily	Af	11610mey
1730-1757	daily	Af	9540dha
Zarma	**Days**	**Area**	**kHz**
1930-1945	.tw....	Af	7235wof

V: QSL-card.
Notes: IBRA Radio (part of IBRA Media), is the radio ministry of the Swedish Pentecostal Movement. On air since July 1955.

RADIO REVIVAL SWEDEN
✉ Vita Huset, Svartsjövägen 3A, S-17995 Svartsjö, Sweden.
☎ +49 8 56041050.
E: radiorevivalsweden@hotmail.com; info@rock.x.se
W: www.radiorevivalsweden.blogspot.com
LP: Licence Owner: Ronny Forslund (A.K.A. "Ronny B. Goode").
SW: [SLS] Sala, Ringvalla: 1 x 5, 1 x 10kW.
kHz: 6060, 9405

Winter Schedule 2015/2016

	Days	Area	kHz
English/Swedish			
1200-1300	.....s.	Eu	6060sls*, 9405sls*

Key: * Schedule variable, based on airtime bookings.
Ann: English: "This is Radio Revival, from Sweden".
V: QSL-email.
Notes: Operating on a series of 2 week temporary licences (Swedish broadcasting regulation allows temporary stns for a maximum duration of 2 weeks/month).

SWITZERLAND (SUI)

RADIO FREUNDES–DIENST (RIg)
✉ Missionswerk Freundes-Dienst International, Quellmattweg 2, CH-5023 Biberstein, Switzerland.
☎ +41 62 8272727. 🖷 +41 62 8393003.
E: info@freundesdienst.org **W:** www.freundesdienst.org
Webcast: D
LP: Pres (Freundes-Dienst International): Joseph Schmid.
kHz: 1440

Winter Schedule 2015/2016

German	Days	Area	kHz
0600-0630	.....s	Eu	1440mrn*
1830-1900	daily	Eu	1440mrn*

Key: * Until 31 Dec 2015.
V: QSL-card.
Notes: The prgr "Licht und Leben" (Radio Freundes-Dienst) is produced by the evangelical missionary organisation Freundes-Dienst International since 1959.

SYRIA (SYR)

RADIO DAMASCUS (Gov)
✉ P.O. Box 4702, Damascus, Syria.
☎ +963 11 2720700. 🖷 +963 11 2234336.
E: radiodamascusenglish@yahoo.com
W: www.syriaonline.sy/?f=Radio-Damascus; www.radio-damascus.net (unofficial)
Webcast: L/D (www.syriaonline.sy); P (English: radiodamascusenglish.podomatic.com; Spanish: aquidamasco.podomatic.com). Web languages: Arabic, English, French, German, Hebrew, Spanish, Turkish, Russian.
LP: DG (ORTAS): Mohammad Ramez Al-Torjan; Dir, Radio: Mahmoud Al Joma'at; Dir, Public Rel: Nawaem Salman.
MW: [TTS] Tartus: 783kHz 300kW.
SAT: Eutelsat 7WA.
kHz: 783

Winter Schedule 2015/2016

Hebrew	Days	Area	kHz
0400-0630	daily	ME	783ttst
Russian	**Days**	**Area**	**kHz**
0630-0700	daily	ME	783ttst

Key: † Irregular.
Ann: Arabic: "Idha'atu-l-jumhuriyati-l'arabiyya as-suriyya min dimashq"; English: "You are listening to Radio Damascus, the External Service of the Syrian Broadcasting System", "Welcome to the Broadcasting Service of the Syrian Arab Republic calling from Damascus"; French: "Ici Damas"; Hebrew: "Kol Damesek".
IS: Guitar.
V: QSL-card.
Notes: Radio Damascus is the External Sce of the state broadcaster Organisme de la Radio-TV Arabe Syrienne (ORTAS).

TAIWAN (Rep. of China) (TWN)

RADIO TAIWAN INTERNATIONAL (RTI) (Gov)
✉ 55 Pei An Road, Taipei 10462, Taiwan. or P.O. Box 123-199, Taipei 11199, Taiwan.
☎ +886 2 28856168. 🖷 +886 2 28862382.
E: rti@rti.org.tw **W:** www.rti.org.tw
Webcast: D/L/P
✉ Post Box 4914, P.O. Safdarjung Enclave, New Delhi 110029 India. (RTI India)
LP: Chmn: Sunshine Kuang; Pres: Lai Hsiang-Wei.
MW: [FAN] Fangliao: 1359/1503kHz 600kW; [KOU] Kouhu: 1098/1557kHz 300kW; [LUK] Lugang: 612kHz 500kW; [MIN] Minxiong: 1206kHz 100kW, 1422kHz 50kW.
SW: [KOU] Kouhu: 3 x 100kW; [PAO] Baozhong: 3 x 100kW; [TNN] Tainan 3 x 250kW; [TSH] Tanshui: 4 x 300kW.
kHz: 612, 1098, 1206, 1359, 1422, 1503, 1557, 3955, 5010, 6075, 6105, 6145, 6180, 7200, 7300, 7380, 7385, 7445, 7730, 9450, 9590, 9625, 9660, 9680, 9685, 9735, 9895, 11605, 11635, 11640, 11655, 11765, 11915, 11920, 11985, 15265, 15270, 15290, 15320, 15465

Winter Schedule 2015/2016

Amoy	Days	Area	kHz
0100-0200	mtwtf..	EAs	1422min

Amoy	Days	Area	kHz
0700-0900	daily	EAs	1422min
0800-0900	..w...	EAs	15290pao***
1000-1100	daily	EAs	1206min, 15465pao
1200-1300	daily	EAs	1206min
1300-1400	daily	EAs	11915tnn

Cantonese	Days	Area	kHz
0400-0430	mtwtf.s	SEA	15320tnn
0900-1000	.....ss	EAs	15465pao
1000-1030	daily	SEA	9735tnn, 15270pao
1200-1230	daily	EAs	6105kou, 9735tnn
1500-1530	daily	SEA	11605tnn
1500-1600	.....ss	EAs	7380pao

Chinese	Days	Area	kHz
0000-0300	daily	EAs	9660kou*
0200-0300	mtwtf..	EAs	1422min
0400-0500	daily	EAs	1422min
0400-0600	mtwtf.s	EAs	11640kou
0600-0700	mtwtf..	EAs	1422min
0900-1000	daily	EAs	1422min
0900-1000	mtwtf..	EAs	15465pao
0900-1700	daily	EAs	1557kou**
1000-1100	mtwtf..	EAs	1422min
1000-1200	daily	EAs	6105kou
1000-1300	daily	EAs	7200tsh
1000-1400	daily	EAs	9660kou, 11640kou
1000-1700	daily	EAs	6180tsh
1100-1200	daily	EAs	1206min, 11915tnn
1100-1400	daily	EAs	1503fan, 9680tsh
1200-1300	daily	EAs	11985tsh
1200-1500	daily	EAs	7445pao
1200-1705	daily	EAs	612luk
1300-1400	daily	EAs	1422min, 6105kou, 15265tnn
1300-1705	daily	EAs	1098kou, 7385tsh
1400-1700	daily	EAs	6075kou*, 6145kou*
1500-1700	mtwtf..	EAs	7380pao
1500-1705	daily	EAs	7300tsh
1600-1705	daily	EAs	1503fan
2200-2400	daily	EAs	1422min, 5010kou, 6105kou, 9450tsh
2200-2400	daily	SEA	11635tnn
2300-2400	daily	EAs	9685tsh

English	Days	Area	kHz
0300-0400	daily	SEA	15320tnn
1100-1200	daily	SEA	1359fan, 7445pao

French	Days	Area	kHz
1900-2000	daily	Eu	9895dha

German	Days	Area	kHz
1900-2000	daily	Eu	3955wof

Hakka	Days	Area	kHz
0400-0430	.....s.	SEA	15320tnn
0430-0500	daily	SEA	15320tnn
1030-1100	daily	SEA	9735tnn, 15270pao
1230-1300	daily	EAs	6105kou, 9735tnn
1530-1600	daily	SEA	11605tnn

Indonesian	Days	Area	kHz
0300-0400	daily	EAs	1422min
0900-1100	daily	SEA	11915tnn
1200-1300	daily	EAs	1422min
1200-1300	daily	SEA	11915tnn
1400-1500	daily	SEA	9735tnn

Japanese	Days	Area	kHz
0800-0900	daily	EAs	11605tnn
1100-1200	daily	EAs	9735tnn
1300-1400	daily	EAs	9735tnn
2200-2300	daily	EAs	9735tnn

Russian	Days	Area	kHz
1100-1200	daily	EAs	11985tsh
1400-1500	daily	Eu,CAs	9590tsh

Spanish	Days	Area	kHz
0200-0300	daily	LAm	11920yfr
0300-0400	daily	CAm	7730yfr

Thai	Days	Area	kHz
0000-0100	daily	EAs	1422min

Thai	Days	Area	kHz
1400-1500	daily	EAs	1422min
1400-1600	daily	SEA	9660kou
1500-1600	daily	SEA	1503fan, 7445pao
2200-2400	daily	SEA	7445tnn

Vietnamese	Days	Area	kHz
0500-0600	daily	EAs	1422min
0900-1000	daily	SEA	15270pao
1100-1200	daily	EAs	1422min
1200-1300	daily	SEA	11765pao
1300-1400	daily	EAs	1206min
1400-1500	daily	SEA	9625tnn
2300-2400	daily	SEA	11655pao

Key: * Mainland Network; ** Music Network; *** Relay of Yuyeh Broadc. St (Fishery R. Station) prgr.
Ann: Chinese: "Cheli shih Chungyang Kuangpo Tientai, Taiwan chih Yin"; English: "This is Radio Taiwan International"; Indonesian: "Inilah Radio Taiwan Internasional"; Japanese: "Kochirawa Taiwan Kokusai Hoso, RTI, Chukaminkoku Chuohosokyoku no nihongobangumi desu".
V: QSL-card. Rec. acc.
Notes: Formed in 1998, when the former Central Broadcasting System (owned by the Ministry of Defense) was joined with the international section of the Broadcasting Corporation of China (Voice of Free China). Schedule includes some CBS networks. Programmes to mainland China are jammed by "China National Radio (CNR)" 1st programme transmissions (usually). Transmissions from Tainan (code: tnn) will be completely replaced by Paochung (code: pao), until the end of 2015.

PCJ RADIO INTERNATIONAL (Comm)

✉ 8th FL, No. 47, Lane 31, Section 1, Sanmin Road, Panchiao Ward, New Taipei, 22070 Taiwan.
☎ +886 9 38408592. (cellphone)
E: pcjmedia@gmail.com **W:** www.pcjmedia.com
L.P: Director: Keith Perron.
kHz: 11580

	Winter Schedule 2015/2016		
English	Days	Area	kHz
0900-1000	.....s.	WEu	11580yfr*

Key: * to Dec. 26, 2015.
Ann: English: "This is PCJ Radio International".
V: E-QSL-card.
Notes: Broadcasts a variety of own and brokered programming.

TAJIKISTAN (TJK)

VOICE OF TAJIK (OVOZI TOJIK) (Gov)

✉ Chapaev St. 31, 734025 Dushanbe, Tajikistan.
☎ +992 37 2277417.
E: info@ktr.tj **W:** www.ktr.tj
Webcast: L (available on the tunein.com streaming portal)
L.P: Chmn (State Committee for Radio & TV): Asadulloi Rahmon.
MW/SW: Leased from Teleradiokom.
SAT: ABS 2.
kHz: 1143, 7245

	Winter Schedule 2015/2016		
Arabic	Days	Area	kHz
1200-1300	daily	ME	1143dsb, 7245dsb
Dari	Days	Area	kHz
0600-0800	daily	WAs	1143dsb, 7245dsb
English	Days	Area	kHz
1300-1400	daily	WAs	1143dsb, 7245dsb
Farsi	Days	Area	kHz
0400-0600	daily	ME	1143dsb, 7245dsb
1600-1800	daily	ME	1143dsb, 7245dsb
Hindi	Days	Area	kHz
1100-1200	daily	As	1143dsb, 7245dsb
Russian	Days	Area	kHz
0800-1000	daily	CAs	1143dsb, 7245dsb
Tajik	Days	Area	kHz
0200-0400	daily	CAs	1143dsb, 7245dsb
1400-1600	daily	CAs	1143dsb, 7245dsb
Uzbek	Days	Area	kHz
1000-1100	daily	CAs	1143dsb, 7245dsb

V: QSL-letter.
Notes: External Sce of the State Committee for TV and Radio Broadcasting.

TELERADIOKOM (Tx Operator)
✉ Internatsionalnaya Street 85, 734001 Dushanbe, Tajikistan.
☎ +992 37 2210912. 📠 +992 37 2217974.
E: info@teleradiocom.tj **W:** www.teleradiocom.tj
L.P: DG: Suhrob Aliyev.
MW: [DSB] Two sites: Dushanbe, Yangiyul (G.C: 38N29 068E48): 1143kHz 150kW, 1251kHz 100kW; Orzu (G.C: 37N32 068E48): 648/801kHz 1000kW, 927kHz 300kW; 972/1503kHz 500kW. Operated on behalf of IBB (USA): 972kHz 800kW.
SW: [DSB] Two sites: Dushanbe, Yangiyul (G.C: 38N29 068E48): 1 x 50, 5 x 100kW; Orzu (G.C: 37N32 068E48): 2 x 1000kW. Operated on behalf of IBB (USA): 1 x 250, 1 x 500kW.
Notes: Teleradiokom, a subsidiary of the Telecommunications Ministry, is the national transmitter network owner.

TANZANIA (TZA)

ZANZIBAR BROADCASTING CORPORATION (Pub)
✉ P.O. Box 314, Zanzibar, Tanzania.
☎ +255 24 2330000. 📠 +255 24 2330000.
E: karumehouse@tvz.co.tz **W:** zbc.co.tz
L.P: DG: Hassan Abdallah Massawi; Dir (Radio): Rafi Haji Makame.
SW: [DOL] Zanzibar City; Dole: 1 x 50kW.
kHz: 6015, 11735

	Winter Schedule 2015/2016		
Swahili	**Days**	**Area**	**kHz**
0300-0600	daily	EAf	6015dol†
1500-2100	daily	EAf,ME	11735dol†

Key: † Irregular.
Ann: English: "Zanzibar Broadcasting Corporation"; "ZBC".
Notes: Relay of domestic service (see National Radio section). News in English 1800-1810.

THAILAND (THA)

RADIO SARANROM (Gov)
✉ 443 Sri Ayudhya Road, Bangkok 10400, Thailand.
☎ +66 26435094. 📠 +66 26435093.
E: radio_saranrom@mfa.go.th; information05@mfa.go.th
W: saranrom.mfa.go.th
Webcast: D
L.P: Dir, Broadcasting Division (Information Dept): Jesda Katavetin.
MW: Uses tx operated by IBB.
kHz: 1575

	Winter Schedule 2015/2016		
English	**Days**	**Area**	**kHz**
1100-1130	m......	SEA	1575bph
2230-2300	.t.....	SEA	1575bph
Thai	**Days**	**Area**	**kHz**
1030-1100	daily	SEA	1575bph
1100-1130	.twtf..	SEA	1575bph
1200-1230	mtwtf..	SEA	1575bph
1500-1530	daily	SEA	1575bph
2230-2400	...tfss	SEA	1575bph

V: QSL-card.
Notes: Service for Thai's living in South East Asia, produced by the Information Department of the Thai Ministry of Foreign Affairs.

RADIO THAILAND WORLD SERVICE (HSK9) (Gov)
✉ Public Relations Department, Royal Thai Government, 236 Vibhavadi Rangsit Road, Ding Daeng, Bangkok 10400, Thailand.
☎ +66 22771814. 📠 +66 22776139.
E: english@hsk9.org; feedback@hsk9.org
W: www.hsk9.org; www.facebook.com/RadioThailandWorldService.
Webcast: D/L
L.P: Dir: Mrs Kasemsiri Pengpis.
SW: Uses txs operated by IBB.
SAT: Thaicom 5.
kHz: 5875, 9390, 13745, 17630, 17640

	Winter Schedule 2015/2016		
Burmese	**Days**	**Area**	**kHz**
1145-1200	daily	SEA	5875udo
Chinese	**Days**	**Area**	**kHz**
1315-1330	daily	EAs	9390udo
English	**Days**	**Area**	**kHz**
0000-0100	daily	NAm	13745udo
0200-0230	daily	NAm	13745udo
0530-0600	daily	Eu	17640udo
1230-1300	daily	As,Pac	9390udo
1400-1430	daily	As,Pac	9390udo
1900-2000	daily	Eu	9390udo
2030-2045	daily	Eu	9390udo
German	**Days**	**Area**	**kHz**
2000-2015	daily	Eu	9390udo
Japanese	**Days**	**Area**	**kHz**
1300-1315	daily	EAs	9390udo
Khmer	**Days**	**Area**	**kHz**
1115-1130	daily	SEA	5875udo
Lao	**Days**	**Area**	**kHz**
1130-1145	daily	SEA	5875udo
Malay	**Days**	**Area**	**kHz**
1200-1215	daily	SEA	9390udo
Thai	**Days**	**Area**	**kHz**
0100-0200	daily	NAm	13745udo
0230-0330	daily	NAm	13745udo
1000-1100	daily	ME	17630udo
1330-1400	daily	SEA	9390udo
1800-1900	daily	Eu	9390udo
2045-2115	daily	Eu	9390udo
Vietnamese	**Days**	**Area**	**kHz**
1100-1115	daily	SEA	5875udo

Ann: English: "This is HSK9, Radio Thailand's World Service broadcasting from the Public Relations Department in Bangkok".
IS: Gongs and chimes.
V: QSL-card.
Notes: Radio Thailand World Service is the External Sce and is produced by the Thai Government Public Relations Department.

AWR ASIA/PACIFIC (RIg)
✉ EIS Building B, Unit 1101, 71/15 Soi Pridi Banomyong 37, Sukhumvit 71 Road, Klongton Nua, Vadhana District, Bangkok 10110, Thailand.
☎ +66 223818869.
E: asia@awr.org
L.P: Dir, Asia/Pacific Region: Surachet Insom.
kHz: 9565, 9720, 9800, 9810, 9880, 9890, 11730, 11750, 11935, 11955, 12035, 15150, 15180, 15195, 15215, 15250, 15255, 15320, 15325, 15360, 15365, 15400, 15430, 15435, 15445, 15450, 15480, 15490, 15495, 15605, 15625, 15660, 15665, 15670, 15680, 15685, 15710, 15745, 17520, 17540, 17580, 17650, 17670, 17720, 17730, 17770, 17880

	Winter Schedule 2015/2016		
Amoy	**Days**	**Area**	**kHz**
0100-0130	mtwt..s	CHN	15625trm, 17650sda, 17880sda
1200-1230	mtwt..s	CHN	9800sda, 15180sda, 15195sda
Asho	**Days**	**Area**	**kHz**
1400-1430	daily	SEA	15150sda
Assamese	**Days**	**Area**	**kHz**
1330-1400	..w...s	As	15660sda
Bangla	**Days**	**Area**	**kHz**
1230-1300	mt.t.s.	As	15430trm
1300-1330	daily	As	15215sda
Batak	**Days**	**Area**	**kHz**
2230-2300	daily	INS	15435sda
Burmese	**Days**	**Area**	**kHz**
0000-0030	daily	SEA	9810trm
1430-1500	daily	SEA	15660sda
Cantonese	**Days**	**Area**	**kHz**
0130-0200	mtwt..s	CHN	15625trm, 17650sda, 17880sda
1230-1300	mtwt..s	CHN	9800sda, 15180sda, 15195sda
Chinese	**Days**	**Area**	**kHz**
0000-0100	daily	CHN	17520sda, 17880sda
0100-0200	....fs.	CHN	15625trm, 17650sda, 17880sda
1000-1100	daily	CHN	15325sda, 17580sda
1100-1200	daily	CHN	11730sda, 15180sda, 15195sda

Chinese	Days	Area	kHz
1200-1300	....fs.	CHN	9800sda, 15180sda, 15195sda
1300-1330	mtwtf..	CHN	15480nau
1300-1500	daily	CHN	11935sda
1330-1500	daily	CHN	15480nau
1400-1500	daily	CHN	15495sda
2100-2200	daily	CHN	9565sda, 9720sda
2200-2300	daily	CHN	15215sda, 15685sda
2300-2400	daily	CHN	17520sda, 17720sda

English	Days	Area	kHz
1300-1330	daily	As	15430sda
1600-1630	daily	SEA	15660sda
2200-2230	.t.t..s	As	15435sda
2330-2400	.....ss	SEA	15320sda

Gujarati	Days	Area	kHz
1530-1600	daily	As	15490sda

Hindi	Days	Area	kHz
1530-1600	daily	As	11955trm, 15250nau

Hmong	Days	Area	kHz
1330-1400	...tf..	SEA	15660sda

Ilocano	Days	Area	kHz
1030-1100	....f.s	SEA	17540sda

Indonesian	Days	Area	kHz
1100-1130	daily	INS	15495sda
2200-2230	daily	INS	15320sda

Isan	Days	Area	kHz
1300-1330	mtw.f.s	SEA	17770trm

Javanese	Days	Area	kHz
1130-1200	m.w.f..	INS	15495sda
2230-2300	daily	INS	15320sda

Kachin	Days	Area	kHz
1300-1330	daily	SEA	15670sda

Kannada	Days	Area	kHz
1530-1600	daily	As	15665sda

Karen	Days	Area	kHz
0030-0100	daily	SEA	9810trm
1430-1500	daily	SEA	17650trm

Khmer	Days	Area	kHz
1300-1330	daily	SEA	15150trm
1330-1400	......s	SEA	15150trm
2300-2330	daily	SEA	15365sda
2330-2400	......s	SEA	15365sda

Korean	Days	Area	kHz
1200-1300	daily	EAs	9880sda
2100-2200	daily	EAs	9890sda

Lao	Days	Area	kHz
1300-1330	...t.s	SEA	17770trm
2330-2400	...t.s	SEA	15365sda

Malay	Days	Area	kHz
1330-1400	mt...s.	SEA	15660sda

Malayalam	Days	Area	kHz
1530-1600	daily	SEA	15680mdc

Marathi	Days	Area	kHz
1530-1600	daily	As	12035trm

Meitei	Days	Area	kHz
1230-1300	..w.f.s	As	15430trm

Mizo	Days	Area	kHz
1500-1530	daily	As	15605sda

Mon	Days	Area	kHz
1200-1230	daily	SEA	15400trm

Mongolian	Days	Area	kHz
1030-1100	daily	EAs	17730sda

Nepali	Days	Area	kHz
1500-1530	daily	EAs	15745trm

Oriya	Days	Area	kHz
1530-1600	daily	As	15710sda

Pwo	Days	Area	kHz
1430-1500	daily	SEA	15150trm

Shan	Days	Area	kHz
1130-1200	daily	SEA	15605sda

Sindhi	Days	Area	kHz
1630-1700	.t.t.ss	As	15360trm

Sinhala	Days	Area	kHz
1400-1430	daily	As	15255sda

Sundanese	Days	Area	kHz
1130-1200	.t.t.ss	INS	15495sda
2200-2230	m.w.fs.	INS	15435sda

Tagalog	Days	Area	kHz
1030-1100	mtwt.s.	SEA	17540sda

Tamil	Days	Area	kHz
1500-1530	daily	As	15665sda

Telugu	Days	Area	kHz
1500-1530	daily	As	15490sda

Thai	Days	Area	kHz
0000-0030	daily	SEA	17650sda
1330-1357	daily	SEA	15450sda
2330-2400	mtw.f..	SEA	15365sda

Tibetan	Days	Area	kHz
1530-1558	...tf..	EAs	11750nau

Uighur	Days	Area	kHz
1300-1330	.....ss	CHN	15480nau

Vietnamese	Days	Area	kHz
0100-0200	.....s.	VTN	15445tsh
1400-1500	daily	VTN	17670trm
2300-2330	.....ss	VTN	15320sda
2300-2400	mtwtf..	VTN	15320sda

V: QSL-card.

Notes: Regional branch of Adventist Broadcasting Service, Inc (USA), see USA for corporate details. In 2014, this branch was moved to Thailand after having been based in Indonesia in earlier years. The individual AWR prgrs are produced by a large number of partner studios within the region.

BBC ASIA RELAY STATION
P.O. Box 20, Muang, Nakhon Sawan 60000, Thailand.
☎ +66 56227275. 🖷 +66 56227277.
SW: [NAK] Nakhon Sawan: 4 x 250kW.
V: QSL-card. (For direct report)
Notes: Owned by the BBC and operated by Babcock Media Services (see under United Kingdom).

IBB RELAY STATIONS THAILAND
IBB Transmitting Station, Rangsit-Bangpoon Road, Bangkok, Thailand.
☎ +66 25815191.
IBB Transmitting Station (Udon Thani), P.O. Box 99, Amphur Muang, Udon Thani 41000, Thailand.
L.P: SM: Dennis G.Brewer.
MW: [BPH] Ban Phachi, Rasom: 1575kHz 1000kW.
SW: [UDO] Udon Thani (Udorn), Ban Dung: 7 x 500kW.
V: QSL-card. (Email to manager_thailand@tha.ibb.gov)

TURKEY (TUR)

VOICE OF TURKEY (VOT) (Pub)
P.O. Box 333, Yenisehir, Ankara 06443, Turkey.
☎ +90 312 4909809. 🖷 +90 312 4909845.
E: tsr@trt.net.tr **W:** trtvotworld.com
Webcast: D/L/P
TRT/Oran Sitesi A Blok No: 427, Ankara 06109, Turkey. (Studio)
☎ +90 312 4633372. (English Desk)
L.P: Head (TRT External Services Department): Süleyman Erdal.
MW: [MER] Mersin: 630kHz 300kW.
SW: [EMR] Emirler: 5 x 500kW.
SAT: Eutelsat Hot Bird 13D, Galaxy 19, Türksat 3A/4A.
kHz: 630, 5960, 5965, 5970, 5980, 6000, 6050, 6120, 6185, 7205, 7240, 7245, 9410, 9460, 9495, 9530, 9610, 9650, 9655, 9665, 9700, 9785, 9820, 9840, 11680, 11730, 11795, 11815, 11835, 11925, 11955, 11965, 11985, 12035, 12045, 13625, 13685, 15200, 15350, 15360, 15480, 17755

Winter Schedule 2015/2016

Arabic	Days	Area	kHz
1000-1100	daily	ME,NAf	11955emr
1500-1600	daily	ME	9665emr
1500-1600	daily	NAf	15200emr
1800-1900	daily	ME	630mer*

Arabic	Days	Area	kHz
1900-2000	daily	ME	630mer

Azeri	Days	Area	kHz
0800-0900	daily	ME	11835emr
1630-1730	daily	ME	5965emr

Bulgarian	Days	Area	kHz
1200-1230	daily	Eu	7245emr

Chinese	Days	Area	kHz
1200-1300	daily	EAs	12045emr

Dari	Days	Area	kHz
1600-1630	daily	WAs	11680emr

English	Days	Area	kHz
0400-0500	daily	ME,NAf	7240emr
0400-0500	daily	Eu,NAm	9655emr
1330-1430	daily	Eu	12035emr
1730-1830	daily	CAs,SAs	11730emr
1930-2030	daily	Eu	6050emr
2130-2230	daily	SAs,Pac	9610emr
2300-2400	daily	Eu,NAm	5960emr

Farsi	Days	Area	kHz
0930-1100	daily	ME	11795emr
1600-1700	daily	ME	9530emr

French	Days	Area	kHz
1830-1930	daily	CAf	9620emr
2030-2130	daily	Eu	5970emr
2030-2130	daily	NAf,WAf	6050emr

Georgian	Days	Area	kHz
1100-1200	daily	Cau	9840emr

German	Days	Area	kHz
1230-1330	daily	Eu	17755emr
1830-1930	daily	Eu	7205emr

Italian	Days	Area	kHz
1500-1530	daily	Eu	6185emr

Kazakh	Days	Area	kHz
1430-1500	daily	CAs	9785emr

Pashto	Days	Area	kHz
1630-1700	daily	WAs	11680emr

Russian	Days	Area	kHz
1400-1500	daily	RUS	9410emr

Spanish	Days	Area	kHz
0200-0300	daily	CAm,Eu	9650emr
0200-0300	daily	SAm,Eu	9410emr
1730-1830	daily	Eu	9495emr

Tatar	Days	Area	kHz
1100-1130	daily	Eu,CAs	15360emr

Turkish	Days	Area	kHz
0100-0300	daily	CAs	6000emr
0500-0700	daily	ME	9820emr
0500-0700	daily	Eu	9700emr
0700-1000	daily	ME	11925emr
0700-1300	daily	ME,NAf	15480emr
0700-1400	daily	Eu	15350emr
1400-1700	daily	Eu	11815emr
1700-2200	daily	Eu	5980emr
1700-2200	daily	ME,NAf	6120emr

Turkmen	Days	Area	kHz
1300-1330	daily	CAs	11965emr

Urdu	Days	Area	kHz
1300-1400	daily	SAs	11985emr

Uyghur	Days	Area	kHz
0300-0400	daily	CAs	9460emr
1330-1430	daily	CAs	13685emr

Uzbek	Days	Area	kHz
1130-1200	daily	CAs	13625emr
1700-1730	daily	CAs	11680emr

Key: * Relay of TRT Arabic TV programme audio.
Ann: English: "This is the Voice of Turkey's English transmission"; German: "Hier ist der Kurzwellensender Die Stimme der Türkei"; Spanish: "Esta es La Voz de Turquia"; Turkish: "Burasi Türkiye'nin Sesi Radyosu".
V: QSL-card.
Notes: The Voice of Turkey is the External Sce of the public service Turkish Radio-TV Corporation, TRT (Türkiye Radyo-Televizyon Kurumu).

UKRAINE (UKR)

RADIO UKRAINE INTERNATIONAL (RUI) (Gov)
✉ vul. Kreshchatyk 26, 01001 Kyiv, Ukraine
☎ +380 44 2791757.
E: rus@nrcu.gov.ua (Russian language department) **W:** nrcu.gov.ua
Webcast: L. Webcast languages: English, German, Romanian, Ukrainian.
LP: Dir: Zhanna Mishcherska.
SAT: Astra 4A.
kHz: 837, 1278, 1431, 5850, 11580

Winter Schedule 2015/2016			
English	Days	Area	kHz
2330-2400	daily	NAm	5850yfr, 11580yfr
Russian	Days	Area	kHz
1700-2100	daily	RUS,UKR	837khr*, 1278pka*, 1431smf

Key: * Planned.
V: QSL-card.
Notes: Produced by the state broadcasting company Vsesvitna sluzhba "Ukrainske telebachennia i radiomovlennia" (VSU). This company is to be merged with the planned new state enterprise Inomovna teleradiokompaniia Ukrainy "Ukraine Tomorrow" (INTU).

CONCERN RRT (Tx Operator)
✉ vul. Dorohozhytska 10, 04112 Kyiv, Ukraine.
☎ +380 44 2262260. 🖷 +380 44 4408722.
E: rrt@rrt.ua **W:** www.rrt.ua
LP: DG: Volodymyr Ishchuk.
MW: [KHR] Kharkiv, Taranivka 837kHz 150kW; [PKA] Petrivka: 1278kHz 100kW; [SMF] Mykolaiv, Luch: 1431kHz 1200kW (run at 800kW).
Notes: Concern RRT is the national transmitter network operator.

UNITED ARAB EMIRATES (UAE)

ABU DHABI MEDIA (Tx Operator)
✉ 4th St, sector 18, Abu Dhabi, United Arab Emirates.
☎ +971 2 4144000. 🖷 +971 2 4144001.
E: communications@admedia.ae **W:** www.admedia.ae
LP: Chmn/MD: Mohamed Ebraheem Al Mahmod; Dir, Radio: Abdulrahman Awadh Al Harti.
MW: [DHA] Dhabbaya: 1575kHz 800kW.
SW: [DHA] Dhabbaya: 4 x 500kW.
Notes: Abu Dhabi Media is a state media company and transmitter operator. Under special appointment, the Dhabbaya transmitting station is currently operated and maintained by Babcock Media Services (UK).

UNITED KINGDOM (G)

BBC WORLD SERVICE (Pub)
✉ Broadcasting House, Portland Place, London W1A 1AA, United Kingdom.
☎ +44 20 72403456. 🖷 +44 20 75571258.
E: worldservice.letters@bbc.co.uk
W: www.bbc.co.uk/worldserviceradio
Webcast: D/L/P. Web only languages (some of which may also be broadcast on local FM affiliate stns): Azeri, Russian, Turkish, Ukrainian, Vietnamese.
LP: Dir (World Service Group): Francesca Unsworth.
MW/SW: Uses txs provided by Babcock Media Services & foreign relays.
SAT: AsiaSat 5, Astra 1N, Badr 4, Eutelsat 7A/36B/Hot Bird 13D, Intelsat 10-02/19/20/805, Koreasat 6, Nilesat 201, Palapa D, SES 7, Sirius FM5, Superbird C2, Telstar 12, Thaicom 5, XM3/4, Y1A.
kHz: 198, 639, 675, 702, 720, 1251, 1413, 3255, 3915, 3955, 4790, 5845, 5855, 5875, 5890, 5905, 5910, 5930, 5945, 5960, 5970, 5975, 5980, 6005, 6095, 6135, 6175, 6180, 6190, 6195, 7265, 7285, 7305, 7325, 7350, 7395, 7435, 7445, 7465, 7485, 7490, 7505, 7510, 7565, 7600, 9410, 9440, 9460, 9490, 9505, 9510, 9540, 9560, 9590, 9670, 9695, 9740, 9790, 9810, 9870, 9880, 9900, 9915, 9920, 11660, 11770, 11785, 11810, 11875, 11895, 11910, 11945, 11955, 11965, 11970, 11975, 11995, 12025, 12035, 12045, 12065, 12070, 12095, 13660, 13760, 13865, 15105, 15285, 15310, 15400, 15420, 15490, 15510, 15530, 15755, 15790, 17510, 17640, 17720, 17745, 17760, 17780, 17790, 17830, 17870, 17880, 17885, 21470, 21630

Winter Schedule 2015/2016

Arabic	Days	Area	kHz
0300-0400	daily	NAf	5875wof, 7285dha
0300-0700	daily	ME	639zak, 720zak
0400-0500	daily	NAf	7285wof
0500-0700	daily	NAf	17790sla
1500-2100	daily	ME	702sla
1700-2000	daily	NAf	12095dha
1700-2100	daily	ME	720zak
1800-2100	daily	ME	639zak
2000-2100	daily	NAf	11875sla

Bengali	Days	Area	kHz
0030-0100	daily	SAs	5875nak, 7510nak, 9790sng
0130-0200	daily	SAs	9790nak, 11995sng
1330-1400	daily	SAs	5855nak, 7565nak, 12065sng
1630-1700	daily	SAs	5875nak, 7485sng, 9540sng

Burmese	Days	Area	kHz
0000-0030	daily	SEA	5875nak, 9510sng, 12025sng
0200-0230	daily	SEA	9510nak, 11995sng, 12070nak
1345-1430	daily	SEA	7485sng, 9900sng, 11945sng
1430-1515	mtwtf..	SEA	7485sng, 11945sng

Dari	Days	Area	kHz
0030-0100	daily	WAs	1413sla, 5930sla, 7435wof
0130-0200	daily	WAs	5930mos, 6195sla, 7445wof
0230-0300	daily	WAs	6195sla, 7445sla, 15755nak
0830-0900	daily	WAs	15310sla, 17720nak
0930-1000	daily	WAs	15310sla, 17720nak
1030-1100	daily	WAs	15310sla, 17720nak
1400-1500	daily	WAs	5975dha, 9810sla
1600-1700	daily	WAs	9810sla, 12045nak
1700-1730	daily	WAs	5875nak, 5910sla, 9810wof
1800-1900	daily	WAs	5875nak, 5910sla, 7505nak
1830-1900	daily	CAs	1251dsb
1830-1900	daily	WAs	1413sla

English	Days	Area	kHz
0000-0100	daily	SAs	5970sla, 9410nak
0000-0200	daily	SAs	12095sng
0000-2400	daily	CHN	675hkg
0100-0300	daily	SAs	15310nak
0100-0520	daily	Eu	198dro
0130-0230	daily	SAs	1413sla
0200-0300	daily	SAs	12095sla
0300-0400	daily	ME	6195sla, 9410sla
0400-0500	daily	EAf	9460mey, 12095dha
0400-0500	daily	ME	9410sla, 12035sla
0500-0600	daily	CAf	5875asc
0500-0600	daily	EAf	12095mey
0500-0600	daily	ME	1413sla
0500-0600	daily	SAf	3255mey, 7445asc
0500-0700	daily	WAf	6005asc
0500-0800	daily	EAf	15420dha
0500-0800	daily	SAf	6190mey
0600-0700	daily	CAf	12095mey
0600-0700	daily	Eu	3955wof+
0600-0700	daily	WAf	9460asc
0600-0800	daily	EAf	17640mdc
0600-0800	daily	SAf	9410mey
0600-0800	daily	WAf	9915asc
0700-0800	daily	CAf	12095asc, 17830mey
0700-0800	daily	WAf	11770asc
0800-0900	daily	SAs	17790nak+
1000-1100	daily	FE	9740nak, 17760nak
1000-1200	daily	FE	15285sng
1000-1300	daily	FE	11895nak
1000-1400	daily	FE	9740sng

English	Days	Area	kHz
1000-1400	daily	SEA	6195sng
1200-1400	daily	FE	5875nak
1300-1400	daily	SAs	1413sla, 15310nak
1300-1500	daily	SAs	9410sla
1400-1700	daily	SAs	7465sng
1400-1800	daily	SAs	5845nak+
1430-1500	daily	SAs	1413sla
1500-1700	daily	EAf	12095mdc
1500-1700	daily	SAs	9410sng
1500-1800	daily	EAf	15420mey
1500-1800	daily	ME	9505sla
1500-1900	daily	ME	6195sla
1600-1700	daily	SAf	17640asc
1600-1800	daily	CAf	17830asc
1600-2000	daily	SAf	3255mey, 6190mey
1700-1730	mtwtf..	CAs	1251dsb
1700-1800	daily	EAf	9410dha
1700-1800	daily	SAs	1413sla
1700-1800	daily	WAf	17780asc
1700-1800	.....ss	CAs	1251dsb
1700-2000	daily	EAf	7445mdc
1700-2000	daily	WAf	15400asc
1800-1900	daily	ME	5945sla
1800-2000	daily	EAf	9410dha
1800-2000	daily	WAf	9915wof
1800-2100	daily	CAf	11810asc
1900-2100	daily	ME	1413sla
2000-2100	daily	WAf	12095asc
2100-2200	mtwtf..	CAf	11810asc
2100-2400	mtwtf..	WAf	9915asc, 12095asc
2200-2300	daily	FE	5905nak, 5960sla
2200-2300	daily	SEA	3915sng, 5890nak
2200-2400	daily	FE	7490nak
2200-2400	daily	FE,SEA	5875nak, 6195sng
2300-0000	daily	SEA	11955sng
2300-0000	daily	FE,SEA	9740sng

Farsi	Days	Area	kHz
0330-0430	daily	ME	1251dsb, 6095dha, 7445kch, 9695sla
0330-0500	daily	ME	1413sla
0430-0530	daily	ME	9440kch, 9670dha, 13660tac
1600-1700	daily	ME	1413sla, 11995nak, 13660wof

French	Days	Area	kHz
0430-0500	daily	CAf	6135asc, 7305asc
0430-0500	daily	EAf	17640dha
0600-0630	daily	WAf	7305asc
0600-0630	daily	CAf	9870asc
0600-0630	daily	NAf	6135wof, 7325wof
0700-0730	daily	CAf	17880mey
0700-0730	daily	WAf	9440asc
1200-1230	daily	CAf	21630asc
1200-1230	daily	NAf	17830wof
1200-1230	daily	WAf	17640asc
1800-1830	daily	CAf	11785asc
1800-1830	daily	NAf	7265wof
1800-1830	daily	SAf	7465mey
1800-1830	daily	WAf	11975asc, 15105asc

Hausa	Days	Area	kHz
0530-0600	daily	WAf	5975wof, 6135asc, 7305asc
0630-0700	daily	WAf	7305asc, 9440asc, 9870wof
1400-1430	mtwtf..	WAf	17640dha, 17780asc, 21630asc
1430-1700	.....s.	WAf	17780asc
1930-2000	daily	WAf	11660asc, 15105asc, 17885asc
2000-2030	....f..	WAf	11660asc, 15105asc, 17885asc

Hindi	Days	Area	kHz
0100-0130	daily	SAs	1413sla, 5980dha, 7395sla, 11995sng, 15510nak

Hindi

	Days	Area	kHz
0230-0300	daily	SAs	7350dha, 9560dha, 15510nak, 17510sng
1400-1430	daily	SAs	1413sla, 7565tac, 7600nak, 9510nak, 12065sng
1600-1630	daily	SAs	7485nak, 9490sla, 9540sng, 12065dha

Kinyarwanda/ Kirundi

	Days	Area	kHz
0500-0600	.....s.	EAf	11945mey, 15490mey
0530-0600	.....s	EAf	11945mey, 15490mey
1630-1700	mtwtf..	EAf	15790mdc, 17870mey

Pashto

	Days	Area	kHz
0100-0130	daily	WAs	5930mos, 6195sla, 7445wof
0200-0230	daily	WAs	6195sla, 7445sla, 15755nak
0300-0330	daily	WAs	7445erv, 9880erv, 11970sla
0900-0930	daily	WAs	15310sla, 17720nak
1000-1030	daily	WAs	15310sla, 17720nak
1000-1030	m.....s	WAs	1251dsb
1100-1130	daily	WAs	15310sla, 17720nak
1500-1600	daily	WAs	9810sng, 12045nak
1730-1800	daily	WAs	5875nak, 5910sla, 9810wof
1800-1830	daily	WAs	1413sla

Russian

	Days	Area	kHz
1000-1030	.twtfs.	CAs	1251dsb
1730-1800	mtwtf..	CAs	1251dsb

Sinhala

	Days	Area	kHz
1630-1700	daily	SAs	7600nak, 9900sng, 11965wof

Somali

	Days	Area	kHz
0400-0430	daily	EAf	11995mdc, 15490dha
1100-1130	daily	EAf	15530dha, 17780sla
1400-1500	daily	EAf	12095mdc, 17745sla, 21470dha
1500-1700	.....s.	EAf	17745mey, 21470asc
1800-1830	daily	EAf	6180dha, 9590mey, 11875mey

Tajik

	Days	Area	kHz
0200-0230	daily	CAs	1251dsb
0930-1000	daily	CAs	1251dsb
1400-1500	daily	CAs	1251dsb
1800-1830	daily	CAs	1251dsb

Tamil

	Days	Area	kHz
1545-1615	daily	SAs	7600nak, 9900sng, 11965wof

Urdu

	Days	Area	kHz
1500-1600	daily	SAs	1413sla, 6175sla, 9920nak, 11910nak, 12065sng

Uzbek

	Days	Area	kHz
1300-1330	daily	CAs	4790dsb, 13865sla, 15510nak, 17780sla
1300-1400	daily	CAs	1251dsb

Key: + DRM
Ann: English: "BBC World Service"; "This is the BBC".
V: Does not verify reception reports.
Notes: BBC World Service is produced by the Global News division of the British Broadcasting Corp. Prgrs in English and other languages are relayed by local stns in many countries. Transmissions in some Asian languages are jammed.

AWR AFRICA/EUROPE (Rlg)

1 Milbanke Court, Milbanke Way, Bracknell, Berks. RG12 1RP, United Kingdom.
☎ +44 1344 401401. 🖷 +44 1344 401419.
E: africa@awr.org (Africa Region only)
L.P: Dir, Africa Region: Ray Allen.
kHz: 5970, 5975, 5985, 6045, 6055, 6145, 7220, 7315, 9460, 9515, 9535, 9610, 9630, 9760, 9770, 9830, 9850, 11680, 11750, 11780, 11860, 11880, 11910, 11955, 11975, 11980, 15145, 15150, 15155, 15160, 15230, 15290, 15360, 15440, 15480, 15490, 15500, 15700, 17510, 17605, 17720, 17780, 17800

Winter Schedule 2015/2016

Afar

	Days	Area	kHz
1430-1500	daily	EAf	17605mos

Amharic

	Days	Area	kHz
0330-0400	daily	EAf	15500trm
1700-1730	daily	EAf	17510nau

Arabic

	Days	Area	kHz
0500-0600	daily	NAf,ME	17780trm
0600-0700	daily	NAf	11880mos
0700-0800	daily	NAf,ME	15230nau
1800-1900	daily	NAf	11680mos
1900-2000	daily	NAf,ME	9535nau, 15480mdc

Bulgarian

	Days	Area	kHz
0400-0430	daily	Eu	5975iss
1600-1630	daily	Eu	9830nau

Dyula

	Days	Area	kHz
2000-2030	daily	WAf	9770mos

English

	Days	Area	kHz
1530-1558	mtw..ss	EAs	11750nau
1600-1630	daily	As	11780trm
1630-1700	m.w.f..	ME	15360trm
1830-1900	daily	Af	15155trm
2100-2130	daily	WAf	11980mos

French

	Days	Area	kHz
0430-0500	daily	NAf	6045mos
0600-0630	daily	WAf	7220iss, 15700nau
0700-0730	daily	WAf	11880iss
0800-0830	daily	NAf	15145nau
1930-2000	daily	CAf	17510mos
2000-2030	daily	WAf	9515nau
2030-2100	daily	WAf	11980mos

Fulfulde

	Days	Area	kHz
1930-2000	daily	WAf	17800mey

Hausa

	Days	Area	kHz
0500-0530	daily	Af	9630mos
1900-1930	daily	WAf	11975mos

Ibo

	Days	Area	kHz
1930-2000	daily	Af	11750mey

Italian

	Days	Area	kHz
1000-1100	......s	Eu	9610nau

Kabyle

	Days	Area	kHz
0800-0830	daily	NAF	15160nau
1730-1800	daily	NAf	11860nau

Malagasy

	Days	Area	kHz
0300-0400	daily	SAf	6055mdc
1400-1500	daily	SAf	6055mdc

Masai

	Days	Area	kHz
1730-1800	daily	EAf	15490mey

Oromo

	Days	Area	kHz
0300-0330	daily	EAf	15500trm
1730-1800	daily	EAf	15155nau

Persian

	Days	Area	kHz
0330-0400	daily	ME	6145nau
1630-1700	daily	ME	9830mos

Punjabi

	Days	Area	kHz
0230-0300	daily	WAs	5970mos
1500-1530	daily	WAs	15150nau
1530-1600	daily	WAs	15290mos

Russian

	Days	Area	kHz
1100-1130	daily	RUS	9460sda
2000-2030	daily	RUS	9760sda

Somali

	Days	Area	kHz
1630-1700	daily	EAf	17510nau

Swahili

	Days	Area	kHz
1700-1730	daily	EAf	15480mey, 17720mdc

Tachelhit

	Days	Area	kHz
0830-0900	daily	NAf	15145nau
1930-2000	daily	NAf	9850nau

Tigrinya

	Days	Area	kHz
0300-0330	daily	EAf	7315nau
1630-1700	daily	EAf	15490nau

Turkish

	Days	Area	kHz
0400-0428	daily	ME	5985mos
1500-1530	daily	ME	11955mos

Urdu	Days	Area	kHz
0200-0230	daily	As	5970mos
1400-1430	daily	As	15440mos
1600-1630	daily	As	11910mos, 15360trm
Wolof	**Days**	**Area**	**kHz**
1900-1930	daily	WAf	11680nau
Yoruba	**Days**	**Area**	**kHz**
2030-2100	daily	Af	11750mey

Notes: Regional branch of Adventist Broadcasting Service, Inc (USA), covering Africa and formerly Europe. See USA for corporate details. The individual AWR prgrs are produced by a large number of partner studios within the region. Earlier, this branch also managed transmissions to Europe, they are now administered by the HQ in the USA (see USA entry). For the reader's convenience, the remaining transmissions to Europe continue to be listed under this header.

END TIMES COMING RADIO (Rlg)
✉ ETC Ministry, c/o Pennywise, 15a St. Andrews Court, Bolton BL1 1LD, United Kingdom.
W: www.excatholicsforchrist.com; www.endtimescoming.com
L.P: Host: G. Patrick Battell.
kHz: 11600, 15770

	Winter Schedule 2015/2016		
English	**Days**	**Area**	**kHz**
1800-1830	.....ss	Eu	11600sof
2100-2130	.....ss	Eu,NAf	15770yfr

Key: D/L/P
Ann: English: "End Times Coming"; "ETC Radio".
Notes: "End Times Coming" is a Bible Study broadcast with G. Patrick Battell.

WRN BROADCAST LTD
Notes: WRN Broadcast Ltd was purchased by Babcock Media Services (under United Kindom) on 9 Feb 2015. Broadcasts, however, continue to identify as being via "WRN".

BABCOCK MEDIA SERVICES (Tx Operator)
✉ Wyvil Court, 10 Wyvil Road, London SW8 2TG, United Kingdom.
☎ +44 20 78969000. 🖷 +44 20 7355 5360.
E: via website.
W: babcock.media; www.babcockinternational.com (corp.)
✉ Blue Fin Building, 110 Southwark Street, London, SE1 0TA, United Kingdom. (Media Management Centre)
☎ +44 20 79690000. 🖷 +44 20 73555360.
L.P: Dir: Leah Holding; Dir, Broadcast Operations: Paul Firth.
SW: [WOF] Woofferton: 6 x 250, 4 x 300kW.
Notes: Babcock Media Services is a division of Babcock International Group PLC. Babcock is the owner and operator of the shortwave transmitting centres in the UK, it also operates the BBC overseas relay stations, under a management contract. On 9 Feb 2015, Babcock acquired WRN Broadcast Ltd.

UNITED STATES OF AMERICA (USA)

BBG – AFIA DARFUR RADIO (Gov)
✉ 7600 Boston Boulevard, Springfield, VA 22153, USA.
☎ +1 703 8529000. 🖷 +1 703 9125499..
E: info@afiadarfur.com **W:** www.afiadarfur.com
Webcast: D
L.P: Dir (Middle East Broadcasting Networks): Brian Conniff.
SW: Via txs provided by IBB, plus other relays.
kHz: 7215, 9510, 9645, 9780, 9820, 11615, 12075

	Winter Schedule 2015/2016		
Arabic	**Days**	**Area**	**kHz**
0300-0330	daily	SDN	7215sao, 9510smg, 9820bot
1800-1830	daily	SDN	9645wof, 11615bot, 12075smg
1900-1930	daily	SDN	9780bot, 9820wof, 11615udo

Ann: Arabic: "Afia Darfur".
V: QSL-card
Notes: BBG funded service for listeners in the Darfur region of Sudan and Eastern Chad, launched on 29 Sept 2008. Produced in the studios of Middle East Broadcasting Network, Inc.

BBG – RADIO FARDA (Gov)
✉ 1201 Connecticut Avenue NW, Washington, D.C. 20036, USA.

☎ +1 202 8287220. 🖷 +1 202 8287235.
E: comment@radiofarda.com; info@radiofarda.com
W: www.radiofarda.com
Webcast: D/L/P
✉ Vinohradská 159A, 100 00 Prague 10, Czech Republic. (Studio)
☎ +420 2 21124113. 🖷 +420 2 21122622.
L.P: Dir: Armand Mostofi.
MW/SW: Via txs provided by IBB, plus other relays.
SAT: AsiaSat 7, Badr 4, Eutelsat Hot Bird 7A/13B, Nilesat 101, NSS 12, SES 6, Telstar 12, Türksat 3A.
kHz: 1575, 5865, 7585, 9990, 12005, 13710, 13765, 15690

	Winter Schedule 2015/2016		
Farsi	**Days**	**Area**	**kHz**
0000-0100	daily	ME	5865kwt
0000-2400	daily	ME	1575dha
0100-0300	daily	ME	5865lam
0230-0400	daily	ME	7585ira
0300-0400	daily	ME	5865kwt
0400-0530	daily	ME	13710ira
0400-0830	daily	ME	7585kwt
0430-0730	daily	ME	15690bib
0530-0730	daily	ME	13710lam
0630-1530	daily	ME	12005bib
0730-0930	daily	ME	13710lam
0730-1300	daily	ME	15690ira
0830-1300	daily	ME	9990kwt
0930-1100	daily	ME	13710ira
1100-1200	daily	ME	13710lam
1200-1500	daily	ME	13765lam
1300-1330	daily	ME	9990kwt
1300-1400	daily	ME	15690bib
1330-1430	daily	ME	9990ira
1400-1530	daily	ME	15690bib
1530-1700	daily	ME	5865ira
1530-1800	daily	ME	12005bib
1700-1900	daily	ME	5865kwt
1900-2000	daily	ME	5865ira
2000-2230	daily	ME	5865kwt
2230-2400	daily	ME	5865kwt

Ann: Farsi: "Radyo Farda".
V: QSL-card.
Notes: BBG funded station for listeners in Iran, launched in December 2002. 24h on satellite & FM. Transmissions on medium wave are jammed.

BBG – RADIO FREE ASIA (RFA) (Gov)
✉ 2025 M Street NW, Suite 300, Washington, D.C. 20036, USA.
☎ +1 202 5304900. 🖷 +1 202 5307794.
E: contact@rfa.org; info@rfa.org **W:** www.rfa.org
Webcast: D/L/P
L.P: Chmn (BBG/RFA): Jeffrey Shell; Pres: Libby Liu; Vice Pres, Government Relations & Corporate Communications: John A. Estrella; Dir, Programme & Ops Support: A.J. Janitschek.
MW/SW: Via txs provided by IBB, plus other relays.
SAT: NSS 12, Telstar 18.
kHz: 1098, 1188, 1503, 5825, 5830, 5855, 5905, 6020, 6095, 6120, 7210, 7415, 7445, 7455, 7460, 7470, 7480, 7540, 9405, 9410, 9415, 9455, 9480, 9495, 9535, 9570, 9670, 9690, 9720, 9825, 9850, 9860, 9890, 9900, 9940, 9985, 9995, 11540, 11560, 11660, 11695, 11720, 11750, 11775, 11795, 11805, 11850, 11980, 12050, 12055, 12105, 12115, 13645, 13650, 13655, 13665, 13685, 13695, 13705, 13735, 13795, 15270, 15340, 15375, 15665, 15685, 15700, 17510, 17525, 17675, 17690, 17750, 17810, 17815, 21480, 21680, 21700

	Winter Schedule 2015/2016		
Burmese	**Days**	**Area**	**kHz**
0030-0130	daily	BRM	12115ira, 15700tin, 17510tin
1230-1400	daily	BRM	13735tin
1230-1430	daily	BRM	11795tin, 12105sai
1630-1730	daily	BRM	9940tin
Cantonese	**Days**	**Area**	**kHz**
1400-1500	.....s	CHN	13645tin
1400-1500	.....s.	CHN	13695tin
1400-1500	.t.t..	CHN	13665tin

Cantonese	Days	Area	kHz
1400-1500	m.w.f..	CHN	13655tin
2200-2300	......s	CHN	9995sai
2200-2300	.....s.	CHN	9940sai
2200-2300	.t.t...	CHN	9415sai
2200-2300	m.w.f..	CHN	9720sai

Chinese	Days	Area	kHz
0300-0700	daily	CHN	11980dsb, 15340sai, 17690sai
0500-0700	daily	CHN	21700tin
1500-1600	daily	CHN	9495sai, 9850kwt
1500-2100	daily	CHN	7415tin
1600-1700	daily	CHN	6120tin
1600-2100	daily	CHN	9455sai
1700-2000	daily	CHN	9860sai
1700-2200	daily	CHN	6020tin
1900-2000	daily	CHN	6095kwt
1900-2200	daily	CHN	1098kou
2000-2100	daily	CHN	6095tin, 7445kwt
2000-2200	daily	CHN	9410sai
2100-2200	daily	CHN	7415kwt, 9455sit
2300-2400	daily	CHN	9825sit, 9900sai, 11775tin

Khmer	Days	Area	kHz
1230-1330	daily	CBG	11750sai
2230-2330	daily	CBG	11850ira

Korean	Days	Area	kHz
1500-1700	daily	KRE	7210tin, 9985sai
1500-1900	daily	KRE	1188seo, 5855tin
1700-1900	daily	KRE	9985ira
2100-2200	daily	KRE	7460uba, 9860tin, 9985tin

Lao	Days	Area	kHz
0000-0100	daily	LAO	15685sai
1100-1200	daily	LAO	13685sai

Tibetan	Days	Area	kHz
0100-0200	daily	CHN	13795sai, 15270tin
0100-0300	daily	CHN	9670dsb, 11695kwt, 17750uba
0200-0300	daily	CHN	9570kwt, 17525tin
0600-0700	daily	CHN	17675tin, 17815dsb, 21480tin, 21680dha
1000-1100	daily	CHN	9690dha, 15665lam, 17810lam
1100-1200	daily	CHN	11540kwt, 15375dha
1100-1400	daily	CHN	7470uba, 9940dsb
1200-1300	daily	CHN	11560kwt, 12055tin
1200-1400	daily	CHN	15375dsb
1300-1400	daily	CHN	12050kwt, 13650kwt
1500-1600	daily	CHN	5825dsb, 9940tin, 11660dha, 11805kwt
2200-2300	daily	CHN	7480kwt, 9890kwt
2200-2400	daily	CHN	7470dsb
2300-2400	daily	CHN	5905dha, 7540kwt, 9535kwt

Uyghur	Days	Area	kHz
0100-0200	daily	CHN	7480dsb, 9405sit, 9480kwt, 9690dha, 13705tin
1600-1700	daily	CHN	5830dsb, 7455kwt, 9720dha, 11720tin

Vietnamese	Days	Area	kHz
1400-1430	daily	VTN	1503fan
1400-1500	daily	VTN	11850sai, 13735tin
2330-0030	daily	VTN	11695tin

Ann: At the start of the transmission period on each frequency in English: "This is Radio Free Asia. The following program is in ...".
V: QSL-card. (Rpt to 'Reception Reports', Radio Free Asia, 2025 M. Street NW, Washington, DC 20036, USA or by email to qsl@rfa.org. Online rpt submission: www.techweb.rfa.org)
Notes: BBG funded station (R. Free Asia, Inc), launched in September 1996 and aimed at listeners in East & South East Asia. Transmissions are jammed in parts of the target area. Burmese language prgr includes segments in Arakanese, Chin Kachin, Karen, Karenni, Mon and Shan. Many frequencies are variable, to avoid jamming.

BBG – RADIO FREE EUROPE/RADIO LIBERTY (RFE/RL) (Gov)

🖃 1201 Connecticut Avenue NW, Washington, D.C. 20036, USA. (Corporate Office)
☎ +1 202 4576900. 🖺 +1 202 4576992.
E: levisonj@rferl.org **W:** www.rferl.org
Webcast: D/L Web-only languages (some of which may also be broadcast on local FM affiliate stns): Albanian (Kosovo), Armenian, Bosnian, Georgian, Macedonian, Montenegrin, Serbian, Ukrainian.
🖃 Vinohradská 159A, 100 00 Prague 10, Czech Republic. (HQ/Studios)
☎ +420 2 21121111. 🖺 +420 2 21123013.
E: knappj@rferl.org **W:** Most language services have own dedicated websites, see www.rferl.org for details.
LP: Chmn (BBG/RFE-RL): Jeffrey Shell; Vice Pres/Editor-in-Chief/Acting CEO: Nenad Pejic; Dir of Communications (Prague): Joanna Levison; Deputy Dir of Communications (Washington, D.C.): Martins Zvaners.
MW/SW: Via txs provided by IBB, plus other relays.
SAT: AsiaSat 7, Eutelsat Hot Bird 13B, Intelsat 907, NSS 12.
kHz: *1386, 5885, 5925, 6060, 6105, 6120, 7305, 7435, 7475, 7485, 7550, 9520, 9585, 9605, 9610, 9635, 9645, 9790, 9840, 11800, 11830, 11890, 11985, 12025, 12055, 13630, 15130, 15265, 17530, 17770*

Winter Schedule 2015/2016

Avar	Days	Area	kHz
0400-0420	daily	Cau	5885bib, 9520lam
1600-1620	daily	Cau	9605lam, 11800bib

Belarusian	Days	Area	kHz
0300-0330	daily	BLR	1386sit
0400-0500	daily	BLR	6105bib, 6120lam
1500-1700	daily	BLR	5885lam, 9645bib
1700-1800	daily	BLR	5885lam, 9645bib
1900-2100	daily	BLR	1386sit

Chechen	Days	Area	kHz
0420-0440	daily	Cau	5885bib, 9520lam
1620-1640	daily	Cau	9605lam, 11800bib

Circassian	Days	Area	kHz
0440-0500	daily	Cau	5885bib, 9520lam
1640-1700	daily	Cau	9605lam, 11800bib

Russian	Days	Area	kHz
0400-0500	daily	RUS	9635lam
0400-0700	daily	RUS	7435lam, 17770udo
0500-0800	daily	RUS	17530kwt
0700-0800	daily	RUS	9635lam, 12025bib
0900-1000	daily	RUS	17770udo
0900-1100	daily	RUS	12025bib
1000-1100	daily	RUS	17530lam
1300-1400	daily	RUS	9610tin
1300-1600	daily	RUS	15130lam
1400-1500	daily	RUS	11890pht
1500-1700	daily	RUS	11890lam
1500-1800	daily	RUS	11985bib
1600-1900	daily	RUS	9790lam
1700-1800	daily	Cau	9585wof*, 11800bib*
1700-2000	daily	RUS	9840lam
1800-1900	daily	RUS	1386sit, 7305bib
1900-2000	daily	RUS	7305udo
1900-2100	daily	RUS	7485bib
2000-2200	daily	RUS	5885udo
2000-2200	daily	RUS	5925lam
2100-0300	daily	RUS	1386sit
2100-2200	daily	RUS	7485kwt

Tajik	Days	Area	kHz
1400-1700	daily	TJK	7475udo, 11830lam

Turkmen	Days	Area	kHz
1400-1600	daily	TKM	6060kwt, 12055bib

Uzbek	Days	Area	kHz
1400-1500	daily	UZB	13630ira, 15265lam
1600-1700	daily	UZB	7550ira, 12055bib

Key: * Special service for Caucaus: "Ekho Kavkaza" ("Echo of the Caucasus").
Ann: Radio Liberty: Belarusian: "Havoryc Radyjo Svaboda"; Russian: "Govorit Radio Svoboda"; Tajik: "Injo Radioi Ozodi"; Turkmen: "Gepleýär Azatlyk Radiosy"; Uzbek: "Ozodlik Radiosidan gapiramiz".
V: QSL-card.

Notes: BBG funded station for listeners in Eastern Europe and the successor states to the former USSR. Radio Free Europe (launched 1949, targeting Eastern Europe incl. prgrs in Baltic languages) and Radio Liberty (launched 1953, targeting the USSR) merged into a single broadcaster, RFE/RL Inc, in 1976. Since the 1990s, the task of RFE/RL has been expanded to produce services targeting the Middle East, Afghanistan and Pakistan, see BBG-Radio Farda, BBG-Radio Free Afghanistan, BBG-Radio Mashaal. The following schedule lists Russian language segments that are broadcast within other language transmissions: Tajik: 1635-1700 Sun; Turkmen: 1435-1500, 1535-1600; Uzbek: 1435-1500, 1635-1700 Sat.

BBG – RADIO MARTÍ (Gov)
⌨ 4201 NW 77th Avenue, Miami, FL 33166, USA.
☎ +1 305 4377000. 🖷 +1 305 4377016.
E: info@martinoticias.com **W:** www.martinoticias.com
Webcast: L/P
⌨ Sister Creek Island, Sombrero Blvd, Marathon, FL 33050, USA. (MW tx site)
L.P: Dir: Carlos A García-Pérez.
MW: [MTH] Marathon, FL: 1180kHz 100kW.
SW: Via txs provided by IBB.
SAT: Hispasat 1C, NSS 806.
kHz: *1180, 5980, 6030, 7365, 7405, 9565, 11930, 13820*

Winter Schedule 2015/2016

Spanish	Days	Area	kHz
0000-0400	daily	CUB	7365grv
0000-1200	daily	CUB	6030grv
0000-2400	daily	CUB	1180mth
0400-0700	daily	CUB	7405grv
0700-1300	daily	CUB	5980grv
1100-1300	daily	CUB	5980grv
1200-1400	daily	CUB	7405grv
1300-1400	daily	CUB	11930grv
1400-2000	daily	CUB	13820grv
1400-2200	daily	CUB	11930grv
2000-2400	daily	CUB	9565grv
2200-2400	daily	CUB	7405grv

Ann: Spanish: "Radio Martí, retransmitiendo para Cuba desde Miami, Estados Unidos de America".
V: QSL-card.
Notes: BBG funded station for listeners in Cuba, launched in May 1985. Produced by Office of Cuba Broadcasting (OCB). Jammed.

BBG – RADIO MASHAAL (Gov)
⌨ 1201 Connecticut Avenue NW, Washington, D.C. 20036, USA.
☎ +1 202 4576900. 🖷 +1 202 4576992.
E: mashaalradio@rferl.org
W: www.mashaalradio.com; www.mashaalradio.org
Webcast: L/D/P
⌨ Vinohradská 159A, 100 00 Prague 10, Czech Republic. (Studio)
☎ +420 2 21121111. 🖷 +420 2 21123013.
L.P: Dir: Amanullah Ghilzai.
MW/SW: Via txs provided by IBB, plus other relays.
FM/DAB: See National Radio section. (Afghanistan)
SAT: Eutelsat Hot Bird 13B.
kHz: *621, 12130, 13580, 15760, 17880*

Winter Schedule 2015/2016

Pashto	Days	Area	kHz
0400-0800	daily	AFG,PAK	13580udo
0400-1300	daily	AFG,PAK	621kho, 12130kwt, 15760ira
0800-1100	daily	AFG,PAK	13580kwt
1100-1300	daily	AFG,PAK	17880ira

Ann: Pashto: "Daa Mashaal Radyo".
V: QSL-card.
Notes: BBG funded service of RFE/FL for Pashto speaking listeners in the Pakistani border region with Afghanistan. 24h on satellite and Internet. Radio Mashaal was launched on 15 January 2010 in order to counter the growing number of Islamic extremist radio stations in the region.

BBG – RADIO SAWA (Gov)
⌨ 7600 Boston Boulevard, Springfield, VA 22153, USA.
☎ +1 703 6885200. 🖷 +1 703 6885255.
E: comments@alhurra.com **W:** www.radiosawa.com

Webcast: L
L.P: Managing Editor: Maha Rabie.
MW: Via txs provided by IBB, plus other relays.
SAT: Badr 4, Eutelsat Hot Bird 13B, Intelsat 907, Nilesat 201, NSS 12.
kHz: *990, 1431, 1548, 1593*

Winter Schedule 2015/2016

Arabic	Days	Area	kHz
0000-2400	daily	IRQ	1593kwt
0000-2400	daily	ARS,YEM	1548kwt
0100-2200	daily	ME,NAf	990cgr
1645-0400	daily	SDN	1431dji
2200-0100	m.wtfss	ME,NAf	990cgr

Ann: Arabic: "Radio Sawa".
V: QSL-card.
Notes: BBG funded station for young Arab listeners in the Middle East & North Africa, launched on 23 March 2002. Produced in the studios of Middle East Broadcasting Network, Inc. 24h on satellite, FM, Internet.

BBG – VOA ASHNA RADIO (Gov)
⌨ Room 3200, 330 Independence Avenue SW, Washington, D.C. 20237, USA.
☎ +1 202 6193136 (Dari); +1 202 0327619. (Pashto) 🖷 +1 202 3825193 (Dari); +1 202 2125260. (Pashto)
E: dari@voanews.com (Dari); pashto@voanews.com (Pashto)
W: www.darivoa.com; www.pashtovoa.com
Webcast: D/L/P
L.P: Chief (VOA Afghanistan Service): Beth Mendelson.
MW/SW: Via txs provided by IBB, plus other relays.
FM/DAB: See National Radio section. (Afghanistan)
kHz: *1296, 7290, 7495, 9775, 11860, 12075, 12140*

Winter Schedule 2015/2016

Dari	Days	Area	kHz
0100-0130	daily	WAs	1296kab, 7290bib, 7495kwt
0200-0230	daily	WAs	1296kab, 7495kwt, 12140udo
1500-1530	daily	WAs	1296kab, 11860kwt, 12075wof, 12140kwt
Dari/Pashto	**Days**	**Area**	**kHz**
1530-1600	daily	WAs	12075smg
1530-1630	daily	WAs	1296kab, 11860kwt, 12140kwt
1600-1630	daily	WAs	12075kwt
Pashto	**Days**	**Area**	**kHz**
0030-0100	daily	WAs	1296kab, 7290bib, 7495kwt
0130-0200	daily	WAs	1296kab, 7495kwt, 12140udo
1430-1500	daily	WAs	1296kab, 11860kwt, 12075wof, 12140kwt
1630-1730	daily	WAs	1296kab, 9775udo, 12075kwt, 12140kwt

Ann: Dari: "In Radyoi Ashna"; Pashto: "Da VOA Ashna Radyo".
V: QSL-card.
Notes: BBG funded service for listeners in Afghanistan, launched April 2004. Produced in the VOA studios.

BBG – VOA DEEWA RADIO (Gov)
⌨ 330 Independence Avenue SW, Washington, D.C. 20237, USA.
☎ +1 202 2050403. 🖷 +1 202 3825218.
E: deewaradio@voanews.com **W:** www.voadeewaradio.com
Webcast: D/L
L.P: Managing Editor: Nafees Talkar.
MW/SW: Via txs provided by IBB, plus other relays.
FM/DAB: See National Radio section. (Afghanistan)
SAT: Eutelsat Hot Bird 13B.
kHz: *621, 7495, 7540, 9355, 9370, 9765, 12005, 12025, 13590*

Winter Schedule 2015/2016

Pashto	Days	Area	kHz
0100-0300	daily	AFG,PAK	12025udo
0100-0400	daily	AFG,PAK	621kho, 9765kwt, 12005ira

Pashto	Days	Area	kHz
0300-0400	daily	AFG,PAK	12025kwt
1300-1400	daily	AFG,PAK	7495udo
1300-1700	daily	AFG,PAK	13590ira
1300-1900	daily	AFG,PAK	621kho, 9355udo, 9370ira
1400-1500	daily	AFG,PAK	7495udo
1500-1900	daily	AFG,PAK	7495udo
1700-1900	daily	AFG,PAK	7540kwt

Ann: Pashto: "Deewa Radio".
V: QSL-card.
Notes: BBG funded service for Pashto speaking listeners in the Afghanistan-Pakistan border area. Launched 29 September 2006. Produced in the VOA studios.

BBG – VOA RADIO AAP KI DUNYAA (Gov)

☞ 330 Independence Avenue SW, Washington, D.C. 20237, USA.
☎ +1 202 6191933. 🖅 +1 202 6190339.
E: urdu@voanews.com **W:** www.urduvoa.com
Webcast: D/L/P
LP: Chief (VOA Urdu Service): Faiz Rehman.
MW: Via relay tx provided by Teleradiokom (Tajikistan), on behalf of IBB.
kHz: 972

Winter Schedule 2015/2016

Urdu	Days	Area	kHz
1400-0200	daily	SAs	972dsb

Ann: Urdu: "Radyo Aap ki Dunyaa".
V: QSL-card.
Notes: BBG funded station for listeners in Pakistan, launched May 2004. Produced in the VOA studios. Between 1900-0100 a trilingual service is carried, consisting of VOA news in English, VOA R. Aap Ki Dunyaa in Urdu and VOA Deewa R. in Pashto.

BBG – VOA STUDIO 7 (Gov)

☞ Voice of America, Africa Division, 330 Independence Avenue SW, Washington, D.C. 20237, USA.
☎ +1 202 2059942. (Then select #11) 🖅 +1 202 2034230.
E: studio7@voanews.com **W:** www.voazimbabwe.com
Webcast: D/P
LP: Dir (Africa Division): Negussie Mengesha.
MW/SW: Via txs provided by IBB.
kHz: 909, 4930, 13860, 15460

Winter Schedule 2015/2016

English	Days	Area	kHz
1720-1740	.....ss	ZWE	909bot, 4930bot, 13860sao, 15460sao
1730-1800	mtwt...	ZWE	909bot, 4930bot, 13860sao, 15460sao

English/Ndebele/ Shona	Days	Area	kHz
1800-1830	....f..	ZWE	909bot, 4930bot, 13860sao, 15460sao
1830-1900	mtwtf..	ZWE	909bot, 13860sao, 15460sao

Ndebele	Days	Area	kHz
1730-1800	....f..	ZWE	909bot, 4930bot, 13860sao, 15460sao
1740-1800	.....ss	ZWE	909bot, 4930bot, 13860sao, 15460sao
1800-1830	mtwt...	ZWE	909bot, 4930bot, 13860sao, 15460sao

Shona	Days	Area	kHz
1700-1720	.....ss	ZWE	909bot, 4930bot, 13860sao, 15460sao
1700-1730	mtwtf..	ZWE	909bot, 4930bot, 13860sao, 15460sao

Ann: English: "You're listening to Studio 7 for Zimbabwe, coming to you live from the Voice of America in Washington".
V: QSL-card.
Notes: BBG funded station for listeners in Zimbabwe, launched in April 2003. Produced in the VOA studios.

BBG – VOICE OF AMERICA (VOA) (Gov)

☞ 330 Independence Avenue SW, Washington, D.C. 20237, USA.
☎ +1 202 2034959. (Public Relations) 🖅 +1 202 2034960.

E: askvoa@voanews.com
W: www.voanews.com; www.insidevoa.com
Webcast: D/L/P. Web only languages (some of which may also be broadcast on local FM affiliate stns): Armenian, Bosnian, Creole, Greek, Indonesian, Macedonian, Russian, Serbian, Thai, Turkish, Ukrainian.
LP: Acting Dir: Kelu Chao; Associate Dir, Operations: Mark L. Prahl; Managing Editor: Clara Dominguez.
MW/SW: Via txs provided by IBB, plus other relays.
SAT: AsiaSat 7, Eutelsat Hot Bird 13B, Intelsat 20, Nilesat 201, NSS 12, SES 6, Superbird C2, Telstar 12.
kHz: *909, 1188, 1431, 1530, 1575, 4930, 4940, 4960, 5745, 5865, 5875, 5885, 6020, 6035, 6040, 6045, 6080, 6150, 6180, 7235, 7275, 7315, 7445, 7455, 7460, 7480, 7485, 7545, 7560, 7580, 9335, 9390, 9435, 9470, 9485, 9490, 9510, 9515, 9530, 9550, 9590, 9605, 9645, 9700, 9755, 9760, 9780, 9820, 9825, 9880, 9885, 11570, 11615, 11650, 11655, 11670, 11695, 11750, 11820, 11850, 11855, 11870, 11900, 11910, 11945, 11965, 12030, 12045, 12070, 12075, 12140, 13580, 13590, 13630, 13650, 13670, 13735, 13745, 13765, 13830, 13860, 13865, 15110, 15120, 15150, 15160, 15180, 15265, 15300, 15425, 15460, 15480, 15560, 15580, 15600, 15610, 15620, 15670, 15715, 15730, 15750, 15780, 17585, 17600, 17655, 17680, 17700, 17830, 17850, 17865, 17870, 17885, 17895, 21600, 21620, 21760, 21795*

Winter Schedule 2015/2016

Amharic	Days	Area	kHz
1600-1630	mtwtf..	EAf	1431dji
1800-1900	daily	EAf	9485wof, 9755smg, 11900mey, 11965lam, 12140kwt

Bambara	Days	Area	kHz
2130-2200	mtwtf..	WAf	5885smg, 9490sao, 13670bot, 15120asc

Bengali	Days	Area	kHz
1600-1700	daily	SAs	1575bph

Burmese	Days	Area	kHz
0000-0030	daily	SEA	1575bph
0130-0230	daily	SEA	9335udo, 11820ira, 15110pht
1200-1230	daily	SEA	11965ira, 15560pht, 17680pht
1430-1500	daily	SEA	1575bph
1430-1530	daily	SEA	17680pht
1430-1630	daily	SEA	9335pht, 11870pht
1530-1600	daily	SEA	1575bph
2330-0030	daily	SEA	6150udo, 7480ira, 9335pht

Cantonese	Days	Area	kHz
1300-1500	daily	EAs,SEA	7545pht

Chinese	Days	Area	kHz
0000-0100	daily	EAs	7560udo, 9880udo, 11945pht, 15425pht
0900-1000	daily	EAs	11855udo
0900-1100	daily	EAs	11650udo, 13765udo
0900-1200	daily	EAs	15150udo
0900-1500	daily	EAs	9530pht
1000-1100	daily	EAs	9825pht
1100-1200	daily	EAs	12045pht
1100-1500	daily	EAs	9825sai
1200-1400	daily	EAs	6045udo, 11655udo
1400-1500	daily	EAs	9605pht, 11655tin
2200-2300	daily	EAs	7445udo, 9390pht

English	Days	Area	kHz
0230-0300	......s	NAm	5745grv*
0300-0400	daily	Af	6080smg
0300-0430	daily	Af	1530sao
0300-0500	daily	Af	15580kwt
0300-0600	daily	Af	4930bot
0300-0700	daily	Af	909bot
0400-0500	daily	Af	4960sao
0400-0500	daily	Af	6080sao
0500-0700	daily	Af	15580bot
0600-0700	daily	Af	1530sao, 9550sao
0930-1000	.....s.	NAm	5865grv*
1400-1600	daily	Af	17885sao
1400-1700	daily	Af	4930bot

English	Days	Area	kHz
1400-2000	daily	Af	15580bot
1500-1600	daily	Af	6080bot
1600-1630	.....s.	Eu	17580grv*
1600-1700	daily	Af	909bot, 1530sao
1600-1800	daily	Af	6080sao, 17895smg
1630-1700	mtwtf..	SDN	11900mey**, 13865wof**, 15180smg**
1700-1730	daily	Af	13590kwt
1730-1800	daily	Af	13590sao
1800-1830	.....ss	Af	4930bot
1800-1900	.....ss	Af	909bot
1800-1900	daily	Af	13590lam
1830-2100	daily	Af	4930bot
1900-2000	daily	Af	13590sao
1900-2100	daily	Af	909bot
1930-2000	.....s	Eu	15670grv*
2000-2100	daily	Af	15580smg
2000-2200	daily	Af	1530sao, 6080sao
2030-2100	.....ss	Af	4940sao
2100-2200	daily	Af	15580grv

French	Days	Area	kHz
0530-0600	mtwtf..	Af	1530sao
0530-0630	mtwtf..	Af	4960sao, 6180sao, 9885bot, 13830bot
1100-1130	.....s.	Af	12030sao, 13735sao, 15715bot, 17850smg
1830-1930	daily	Af	15730smg
1830-2000	daily	Af	1530sao
1830-2030	daily	Af	12075bot
1900-2000	daily	Af	9590sao
1930-2030	daily	Af	11900sao, 15730grv
2000-2030	daily	Af	9490kwt
2030-2100	.....s	Af	11900sao, 15730bot
2030-2100	.....ss	Af	9490bot, 12075sao
2100-2130	mtwtf..	Af	5885smg, 9490bot, 12075smg

Hausa	Days	Area	kHz
0500-0530	daily	WAf	1530sao, 4960sao, 6020sao, 6035asc
0700-0730	daily	WAf	4960sao, 12070sao, 17700smg
1500-1530	daily	WAf	9765sao, 11850sao, 17700bot
1530-1600	mtwtf..	WAf	9765sao, 11850sao, 17700bot
2030-2100	mtwtfs.	WAf	6040sao
2030-2100	.....s.	WAf	11900sao, 15730bot
2030-2100	mtwtf..	WAf	4940sao, 9765wof, 11850bot, 12075sao

Khmer	Days	Area	kHz
1330-1430	daily	SEA	1575bph, 11695pht
2200-2230	daily	SEA	1575bph, 7460pht, 9435ira

Kinyarwanda/ Kirundi	Days	Area	kHz
0330-0400	daily	EAf,CAf	7275sao
0330-0430	daily	EAf,CAf	7460bot, 9885sao
0400-0430	daily	EAf,CAf	7275bot
0430-0530	mtwtf..	EAf,CAf	7275bot, 7460bot, 9885sao
1400-1500	.....ss	EAf,CAf	9470sao, 13860bot, 15300sao
1600-1630	daily	EAf,CAf	11750smg, 13630sao, 15460sao
1830-1900	mtwtf..	EAf,CAf	11850bot, 13630sao
1930-2000	mtwtf..	EAf,CAf	9470bot, 11615sao, 12140kwt

Korean	Days	Area	kHz
1100-1500	daily	EAs	1188seo
1200-1300	daily	EAs	9490pht
1200-1400	daily	EAs	11570pht
1200-1500	daily	EAs	7235tin
1300-1500	daily	EAs	9800pht
1400-1500	daily	EAs	11570tin

Korean	Days	Area	kHz
1900-2100	daily	EAs	5875pht, 9700udo, 9800tin

Kurdish	Days	Area	kHz
1400-1500	daily	ME	15600wof, 17870lam
1700-1800	daily	ME	7485ira, 9390lam, 9605lam
1900-2000	daily	ME	7315bib, 7455ira, 9515lam

Lao	Days	Area	kHz
1230-1300	daily	SEA	1575bph

Oromo	Days	Area	kHz
1730-1800	mtwtf..	EAf	9485dha, 9755udo, 11900mey, 11965smg, 12140kwt

Portuguese	Days	Area	kHz
1630-1700	...f..	Af	11850sao, 13630bot, 17655smg
1630-1730	...f..	Af	9485sao, 15480asc, 15730grv
1700-1800	daily	Af	1530sao, 13630bot, 17655grv
1800-1830	mtwtf..	Af	13630bot, 17655grv

Somali	Days	Area	kHz
0330-0400	daily	Af	11750bot
0330-0400	daily	EAf	9510smg, 9820lam
1030-1100	daily	EAf	13650bot, 15620sao, 17550bot
1300-1400	daily	EAf	15620bot, 17600sao
1600-1630	.....ss	EAf	1431dji
1600-1800	daily	EAf	13580bot, 15620wof

Swahili	Days	Area	kHz
1630-1700	daily	EAf	13745kwt, 15265mey, 15460sao

Tibetan	Days	Area	kHz
0000-0100	daily	SAs	5885ira, 7580kwt, 9645udo
0300-0400	daily	SAs	21600pht, 21795pht
0300-0600	daily	SAs	17865pht
0400-0500	daily	SAs	15610udo, 21620pht
0500-0600	daily	SAs	15560udo, 21760pht
1400-1500	daily	SAs	11910kwt, 15160kwt, 17585bib, 17830pht
1600-1700	daily	SAs	7580pht, 9760udo, 11670pht

Tigrinya	Days	Area	kHz
1900-1930	mtwtf..	EAf	9485wof, 9755smg, 11900dha, 11965sao, 12140kwt

Vietnamese	Days	Area	kHz
1300-1330	daily	SEA	1575bph

Key: * Digital modes experimental transmission; ** Special service for Sudan.

Ann: At the start and end of the transmission period on each frequency, English: "This is the Voice of America, Washington D.C., signing on/off". Before all foreign language programs: "This is the Voice of America. The following program is in... (language)".

V: QSL-card. (Email to: letters@voa.gov)

Notes: Launched in 1942, under the roof of the U.S. Foreign Information Service (FIS). From 1953-1994, financed by the U.S. Information Agency (USIA). BBG funded since April 1994. Some transmissions in Asian languages are jammed. Some programmes in Portuguese, directed to Angola, are from the "Vision Angola/VOA Multipress" service.

BROADCASTING BOARD OF GOVERNORS (BBG) (Gov)

⌨ 330 Independence Avenue SW, Washington, D.C. 20237, USA.
☎ +1 202 2034400. 🖷 +1 202 2034585.
E: publicaffairs@bbg.gov W: www.bbg.gov
L.P: Chmn: Jeff Shell; CEO: John Lansing; Chief Financial Officer: Leslie Hyland.
Notes: On 1 October 1999, the Broadcasting Board of Governors (BBG) became the independent, autonomous entity responsible for all U.S. government and government sponsored, non-military, international broadcasting.

INTERNATIONAL BROADCASTING BUREAU (IBB) (Gov)

✉ 330 Independence Avenue SW, Washington, D.C. 20237, USA.
☎ +1 202 4017000. 🖷 +1 202 6191241.
E: pubaff@ibb.gov
✉ 3919 VOA Site B Road, Grimesland, NC 27837, USA (Edward R. Murrow Transmitting Station).
L.P: Deputy Dir: Jeffrey N. Trimble; Dir, Office of Technology, Services and Innovation: André V. Mendes; Chief of Staff: Marie Skiba Lennon; SM, Edward R. Murrow Transmitting Station (Greenville): Tom Moore.
SW: [GRV] Greenville, NC: 3 x 250, 5 x 500kW.
V: QSL-card.
Notes: Under the supervision of the Broadcasting Board of Governors (BBG), the International Broadcasting Bureau (IBB) provides administrative, engineering, and marketing support for U.S. government funded non-military international broadcast services. The IBB Office of Technology, Services and Innovation manages, operates, and maintains a network of domestic and overseas transmitting stations in Botswana, Djibouti, Germany, Kuwait, Philippines, Northern Mariana Islands*, São Tomé & Príncipe, Sri Lanka, Thailand and continental USA (* operation outsourced to a third party). The Greenville site is also known as the "Edward R. Morrow" Transmitting Station.

RADIO AZADI (EX RADIO FREE AFGHANISTAN) (Gov)

✉ 1201 Connecticut Avenue NW, Washington, D.C. 20036, USA.
☎ +1 202 4576900. 🖷 +1 202 4576992.
E: azadiweb@rferl.org **W:** www.azadiradio.org; pa.azadiradio.org (Pashto); da.azadiradio.org (Dari)
Webcast: D/L/P
✉ Vinohradská 159A, 100 00 Prague 10, Czech Republic. (Studio)
☎ +420 2 21122370. 🖷 +420 2 21123245.
L.P: Dir: Hashem Mohmand.
MW/SW: Via txs provided by IBB, plus other relays.
FM/DAB: See National Radio section. (Afghanistan)
SAT: Eutelsat Hot Bird 13B.
kHz: 1296, 12075, 12140, 13860, 19010

Winter Schedule 2015/2016

Dari	Days	Area	kHz
0300-0330	daily	AFG	1296kab, 12140kwt, 13860udo
0430-0530	daily	AFG	1296kab, 12140kwt, 19010kwt
0630-0730	daily	AFG	1296kab, 12140kwt, 19010kwt
0830-0930	daily	AFG	1296kab, 12140kwt, 19010kwt
1030-1130	daily	AFG	1296kab, 12140kwt, 19010kwt
1230-1330	daily	AFG	1296kab, 12075kwt, 12140kwt
1400-1430	daily	AFG	1296kab, 12075kwt, 12140kwt

Pashto	Days	Area	kHz
0230-0300	daily	AFG	1296kab, 12140kwt, 13860udo
0330-0430	daily	AFG	1296kab, 12140kwt, 13860udo
0530-0630	daily	AFG	1296kab, 12140kwt, 19010kwt
0730-0830	daily	AFG	1296kab, 12140kwt, 19010kwt
0930-1030	daily	AFG	1296kab, 12140kwt, 19010kwt
1130-1230	daily	AFG	1296kab, 12140kwt, 19010kwt
1330-1400	daily	AFG	1296kab, 12075kwt, 12140kwt

Ann: Dari: "Inja Radyoi Azadi"; Pashto: "Da Azadi Radyo".
V: QSL-card.
Notes: BBG funded station for listeners in Afghanistan, launched in January 2002 as "R. Free Afghanistan". Produced in the RFE/RL studios in Prague, Czech Republic.

ADVENTIST WORLD RADIO (AWR) (Rlg)

✉ 12501 Old Columbia Pike, Silver Spring, ML 20904-6600, USA.
☎ +1 301 6806304. 🖷 +1 301 6806303.
E: info@awr.org **W:** www.awr.org
Webcast: D/L/P
L.P: Pres: Dowell W. Chow; Freq Manager: Claudius Dedio.
kHz: 5950

Winter Schedule 2015/2016

English	Days	Area	kHz
1130-1200	daily	CAm	5950yfr
2330-2400	daily	CAm	5950yfr
Spanish	**Days**	**Area**	**kHz**
1100-1130	daily	CAm	5950yfr
2300-2330	daily	CAm	5950yfr

IS: Various arrangements of the melody "Lift Up the Trumpet".
V: QSL-card.
Notes: AWR the international broadcast ministry of the Seventh-day Adventist Church. Produced by Adventist Broadcasting Service, Inc. which also is the owner of the SW transmitting station KSDA in Guam. For schedules, see AWR Asia/Pacific (Indonesia), AWR Africa/Europe (United Kingdom).

ELECTRONIC BIBLE FELLOWSHIP (MEIGUO BINZHOU DIANZI SHENGJING TUANQI) ‡ (Rlg)

✉ P.O. Box 1393, Sharon Hill, PA 19079-0593, USA.
☎ +1 484 4978689.
E: contactus@ebiblefellowship.com **W:** www.ebiblefellowship.com
Webcast: L (English only).
L.P: Head of organisation: Christopher McCann.
Key: ‡ Inactive at time of publication.
Notes: Produced by the Christian organisation Electronic Bible Fellowship, Inc.

ETERNAL GOOD NEWS (Rlg)

✉ P.O. Box 5333, Edmond, OK 73083-5333, USA.
☎ +1 405 3591235.
E: gabry@cox.net **W:** www.eternalgoodnews.info
Webcast: D (limited archive only).
kHz: 6030, 7315, 7365, 7385, 9715, 9930, 11635, 11705, 15525, 21480, 21600

Winter Schedule 2015/2016

English	Days	Area	kHz
0200-0215	m......	NAm	7385hri
0445-0500	.....s.	Af	11635hri
1115-1130	.....s	EAs	21480mdc
1130-1145	....f..	SAs	15525dha
1230-1245	.....s	EAs	9930hbn
1730-1745	.....s.	Af	21600hri
1800-1815	.....s.	ME	9715mos
1815-1830	.....s.	ME	7365nau
1930-1945	....s.	Eu	6030nau
2100-2115	.....s	Eu	11705nau
2345-2400	.....s	CAm	7315hri

V: QSL-letter.
Notes: Produced by the religious organisation "Eternal Good News".

FAMILY RADIO (Rlg)

✉ 290 Hegenberger Rd., Oakland, CA 94621, USA.
☎ +1 510 5686200. 🖷 +1 510 4300893.
E: info@familyradio.org
W: www.familyradio.org; www.familyradio.com
Webcast: D/L
L.P: Pres: Tom Evans.
SAT: Yamal 401.
kHz: 5950, 11920

Winter Schedule 2015/2016

Spanish	Days	Area	kHz
0100-0200	daily	SAm	11920yfr
2200-2300	daily	CAm	5950yfr
2300-2400	daily	CAm,Car	5950yfr

Ann: English: "You are listening to Family Radio, the Sound of the New Life".
V: QSL-card.
Notes: Owned by Family Stations, Inc. Established in 1959, first SW broadcasts in 1973.

FAR EAST BROADCASTING COMPANY INC (FEBC) (Rlg)

✉ P.O. Box 1, La Mirada, CA 90637-0001, USA.

☎ +1 562 9474651. 🖷 +1 562 9430160.
E: info@febc.org **W:** www.febc.org
Webcast: D
🖃 FEBC International Ltd, 30 Lorong Ampas, #07-01 Skywaves Industrial Bldg., Singapore 328783.
☎ +65 63923154. 🖷 +65 63923156.
E: info@febcintl.org **W:** www.febcintl.org
L.P: Chmn: Dr Douglas Pennoyer; Pres: Edward W. Cannon.
V: QSL-email for transmissions by FEBC branches. Printed QSL-cards are available only directly from the FEBC branches in South Korea and the Philippines.
Notes: Far East Broadcasting Company, Inc (FEBC) is a global evangelical media enterprise. For schedules, see FEBC Philippines (Philippines), FEBC Korea (South Korea) and FEBA India (India). FEBC owns transmitting stations in several countries, incl. the Philippines and South Korea.

FOLLOW THE BIBLE MINISTRIES (Rlg)
🖃 P.O.Box 1332, Alameda, CA 94501, USA.
☎ +1 510 7480504.
E: followthebibleministries@yahoo.com
W: www.followthebibleministries.com; www.isannihilationtrue.com/ftbm
Webcast: D
🖃 3374 Washington Court, Alameda, CA 94501, USA.
L.P: Host: David Hoff.
kHz: *11830*

Winter Schedule 2015/2016
English	Days	Area	kHz
1900-1930	......s	WAf	11830asc

Notes: Bible Study prgr produced by the Christian organisation "Follow The Bible Ministries".

KVOH – VOICE OF HOPE (Rlg)
🖃 P.O. Box 102, Los Angeles, CA 90078, USA.
☎ +1 805 3380075. 🖷 +1 805 2736905.
E: mail@kvoh.net (general); studio@kvoh.net (live prgr response)
W: www.kvoh.net
Webcast: L
L.P: Pres (Strategic Communications Group): Rev. John D. Tayloe; Dir, Engineering: Brent Jaybush; Ops Mgr: Ray Robinson.
SW: [VOH] Rancho Simi, CA: 2 x 50, 1 x 100kW.
kHz: *9975, 11775*

Winter Schedule 2015/2016
English	Days	Area	kHz
0000-0400	mtwtf..	CAm,SAm	9975voh
0100-0400	.....ss	CAm,SAm	9975voh
Spanish	**Days**	**Area**	**kHz**
1400-1900	mtwtf..	CAm,SAm	11775voh

Ann: English: "This is KVOH, the Voice of Hope"; Spanish: "Esta es KVOH, la Voz de Esperanza".
V: QSL-card. Email rpt to qsl@kvoh.net
Notes: Owned by the charitable organisation Strategic Communications Group (SCG). Initially began broadcasting in November 1986 under the ownership of High Adventures Ministries. In the near future, SCG plans to start broadcasting also from its newly acquired SW transmitting station in Africa, see Voice of Hope - Africa, under Zambia.

PAN AMERICAN BROADCASTING (Rlg)
🖃 Suite 250, 7011 Koll Center Parkway, Pleasanton CA 94566-3253 USA.
☎ +1 925 4629800. 🖷 +1 925 4629808.
E: info@panambc.com **W:** www.panamericanbroadcasting.com; www.panambc.com; www.radiopanam.com
Webcast: L (unrelated to SW broadcasts)
L.P: Pres: Jeff Bernald.
kHz: *9685, 15205, 21675*

Winter Schedule 2015/2016
English	Days	Area	kHz
1000-2300	daily	Af	21675yfr
1400-1445	......s	ME	15205nau
1415-1430	mtwtfs.	ME	15205nau
1930-2000	......s	NAf	9685nau

V: QSL-card. Online form available.
Notes: Pan American Broadcasting, Inc sells air time for religious paid programming, broadcast via international tx providers and via its service 'Radio Africa'.

RADIO PAYAM–E DOOST (Rlg)
🖃 P.O. Box 765, Great Falls, VA 22066, USA.

☎ +1 703 6718888.
E: payam@bahairadio.org **W:** www.bahairadio.org
Webcast: D/L
SAT: Eutelsat Hot Bird 13B, Galaxy 19.
kHz: *7460, 7480*

Winter Schedule 2015/2016
Farsi	Days	Area	kHz
0230-0315	daily	ME	7460kch
1800-1845	daily	ME	7480kch

Ann: Farsi: "Payam-e Doost".
Notes: Payam-e Doost ("Message from a friend") is an Internet/satellite radio station run by members of the Baha'i Faith in the USA. Regular relays on shortwave started 21 April 2001 and on satellite from May 2002. Jammed.

REACH BEYOND (Rlg)
🖃 1065 Garden of the Gods Road, Colorado Springs, CO 80907, USA.
☎ +1 719 5909800. 🖷 +1 719 5909801.
E: info@reachbeyond.org **W:** reachbeyond.org
Webcast: P
L.P: Pres/CEO: Wayne Pederson; Frequency Mgr: Douglas Weber.
kHz: *1251, 7300, 9530, 11900, 13740*

Winter Schedule 2015/2016
Arabic	Days	Area	kHz
2115-2145	daily	NAf	7300wof
Chechen	**Days**	**Area**	**kHz**
1600-1630	.....s.	RUS	11900nau, 13740nau
Dari	**Days**	**Area**	**kHz**
1530-1600	m..tfss	CAs	1251dsb
Pulaar	**Days**	**Area**	**kHz**
2145-2215	mt.tfss	Af	9530asc
Russian	**Days**	**Area**	**kHz**
1530-1600	.....s.	RUS	11900nau, 13740nau
Tachelhit	**Days**	**Area**	**kHz**
2100-2115	daily	NAf	7300wof
Turkmen	**Days**	**Area**	**kHz**
1545-1600	.tw....	CAs	1251dsb
1600-1615	daily	CAs	1251dsb
Uzbek	**Days**	**Area**	**kHz**
1530-1545	.tw....	CAs	1251dsb

V: QSL-card.
Notes: Reach Beyond (previously known as HCJB Global Voice) is the media ministry of World Radio Missionary Fellowship, Inc. See Australia, Ecuador and Germany for shortwave stations run by Reach Beyond partner organisations.

SUAB XAA MOO ZOO (Rlg)
🖃 Hmong District, 12287 Pennsylvania St, Thornton, CO 80241-3113, USA.
☎ +1 303 2521793. 🖷 +1 303 2527911.
E: suabxaamoozoo@yahoo.com **W:** www.sxmzradioministry.com
Webcast: D
E: radio@hmongdistrict.org **W:** www.hmongdistrict.org
L.P: Head, Radio Ministry (Hmong District): Num Nyaj Hawj.
kHz: *7530, 11570*

Winter Schedule 2015/2016
Hmong	Days	Area	kHz
1130-1200	daily	SEA	11570tsh
2230-2300	daily	SEA	7530tsh

V: QSL-card.
Notes: Christian missionary programming targeting Hmong listeners, produced by the Hmong District of the Christian & Missionary Alliance.

THE OVERCOMER MINISTRY (Rlg)
🖃 P.O. Box 691, Walterboro, SC 29488, USA.
☎ +1 843 5384202. 🖷 +1 843 5384202.
E: lastime@overcomerministry.org **W:** www.overcomerministry.org
Webcast: L
L.P: Owner (Faith Cathedral Fellowship, Inc) & Radio Host: Ralph G. Stair.
SAT: Amos 3, Echostar 9&Galaxy 23, Eutelsat 25B/Hot Bird 13D, Galaxy 19, Optus D2, Thaicom 5.
kHz: *3185, 5050, 5110, 5890, 5920, 7315, 7355, 7490, 7570, 9370, 9505, 9840, 9955, 9980, 11580, 11825, 15770, 17530, 17610, 21600, 21610, 21675*

Winter Schedule 2015/2016

English	Days	Area	kHz
0000-0100	m......	Eu,ME	5920hri
0000-1300	daily	NAm	3185wrb, 5050wrbt
0100-0200	......s	NAm,CAm	7490bcq
0200-0400	..w....	NAm,CAm	5110bcq*
0200-0400	mt.tfss	NAm,CAm	7490bcq
0300-1300	daily	NAm	11580yfr
0300-2300	.....ss	NAm,Af	9980wcr
0400-0500	.....s	NAm,CAm	7490bcq
0400-1300	mtwtf..	NAm,Af	5890wcr
0500-1300	.....ss	NAm,Af	5890wcr
0600-0700	daily	Eu,ME	7315hri
0600-1100	daily	NAm	9955yfr
0700-0800	daily	Eu,ME	7355hri
1000-1400	daily	Af	21675yfr
1000-2200	daily	NAm	11825yfr
1200-1300	......s	NAm	9840hri
1300-1400	.....ss	WAf,CAf	21610hri
1300-2000	mtwtf..	NAm,Af	9980wcr
1300-2100	daily	Eu,NAf	15770yfr
1300-2400	daily	NAm	9370wrb
1400-1500	...s.	SEu,NAf	21600hri
1400-1600	.....s.	NAm	9840hri
1600-1800	daily	NAm	9840hri
1800-1900	mtwtf..	WAf,CAf	21600hri
1800-2200	daily	NAm	17530hri
1900-2000	......s	NAm	9840hri
1900-2000	mtwtf..	NAm	17610hri
2100-2300	daily	NAm	11580yfr
2200-1000	daily	NAm	7570yfr
2200-2300	..w....	NAm	9955yfr
2200-2400	mt.....	NAm	9955yfr
2200-2400	mtwtf..	Eu,ME	9505hri
2300-0000	mtwtf..	NAm,CAm	7490bcq
2300-2400	mtwtf..	NAm,Af	9980wcr

Ann: English: "You have been listening to the International Broadcast - The Overcomer".
V: QSL-card.
Notes: Owned by Faith Cathedral Fellowship, Inc. Schedule is subject to change.

TRUNEWS RADIO (Rlg)
P.O. Box 690069, Vero Beach, FL 32969-0069, USA.
☎ +1 772 5698880.
E: info@trunews.com **W:** www.trunews.com
Webcast: D
L.P: Founder/Host: Rick Wiles.
SAT: Sirius XM (via Family Talk channel)
kHz: 5850, 5920, 7455, 9395, 9975, 11565

Winter Schedule 2015/2016

English	Days	Area	kHz
0000-0100	.twtfs.	CAm,SAm	9975voh
0000-2400	daily	NAm	9395yfr
0100-0200	.twtfs.	NAm,Eu	5920hri
0100-0700	daily	NAm	5850yfr
0100-0700	daily	CAm	7455yfr
0300-0400	.twtfs.	CAm,SAm	9975voh
0900-1000	.....s.	AUS,NZL,Pac	11565hri

Notes: "Trunews with Rick Wiles" is a Christian radio show hosted by the Religious Right activist and End Times broadcaster Rick Wiles. It is also carried by various local stns in the USA.

TWR (Rlg)
P.O. Box 8700, Cary, NC 27512, USA.
☎ +1 919 4603700. 🖷 +1 919 4603702.
E: info2@twr.org **W:** www.twr.org; www.twr360.org
Webcast: D/L
L.P: Chmn: Dr Thomas J. Lowell; Pres/CEO: Lauren Libby.
V: QSL-card.
Notes: Trans World Radio, Inc (TWR) is a global Christian media enterprise. For TWR's regional divisions and schedules, see under Austria (TWR Europe), India (TWR India), Singapore (TWR Asia) and South Africa (TWR Africa). TWR owns transmitting facilities in Benin, Bonaire, Guam and Swaziland.

UNIVERSITY NETWORK (Rlg)
P.O. Box 1, Los Angeles, CA 90053-0001, USA.
☎ +1 818 2408151.
E: pastor@pastormelissascottvideos.com
W: www.pastormelissascott.com; www.drgenescott.com
Webcast: L
MW/SW: See "Caribbean Beacon", under Anguilla.
kHz: 5935, 6090, 11775, 13845

Winter Schedule 2015/2016

English	Days	Area	kHz
0100-1300	daily	Af	5935wcr
1000-2200	daily	NAm	11775aiat
1300-0100	daily	NAm,Eu	13845wcr
2200-1000	daily	NAm	6090aiat

Key: t Irregular.
V: Does not verify reception reports.
Notes: Run by (Pastor) Melissa Scott, who took over the operation in 2005 after the death of her husband, (Pastor) Dr. William Eugene "Gene" Scott. The service consists of 24/7 broadcasts of sermons by Melissa Scott and archived material from the period of Gene Scott.

VOICE OF HOPE AFRICA ‡ (Rlg)
P.O. Box 102, Los Angeles, CA 90078, USA. (Strategic Communications Group)
E: mail@kvoh.net (KVOH) **W:** kvoh.net (KVOH)
L.P: Pres (Strategic Communications Group): Rev. John D. Tayloe.
SW: [LUS] Lusaka, Makeni Ranch: 2 x 100kW.
Key: ‡ Inactive at time of publication.
Notes: Run by Strategic Communications Group (SCG), USA (see under USA for sister station KVOH). In 2014, SCG purchased the former Christian Vision (UK) transmitting centre near Lusaka, Zambia. The new service is due to start in the near future.

WEWN – EWTN SHORTWAVE RADIO (Rlg)
5817 Old Leeds Rd., Irondale, AL 35210-2164, USA.
☎ +1 205 2712900. 🖷 +1 205 2712926.
E: radio@ewtn.com **W:** www.ewtn.com
Webcast: D/L/P
P.O. Box 157, Station A, Etobicoke, ON M9C 4V2, Canada.
L.P: Chmn/CEO: Michael P. Warsaw; Pres/COO: Doug Keck; Vice Pres, Engineering: Terry L Borders; Freq Mgr: Glen Tapley.
SW: [EWN] Vandiver, AL: 3 x 500kW. Backup tx: 1 x 500kW.
SAT: Galaxy 15, Intelsat 19/20/21, Sirius FM 5, XM3/4.
kHz: 5810, 7515, 11520, 11550, 11870, 12050, 13830, 15610

Winter Schedule 2015/2016

English	Days	Area	kHz
0000-0900	daily	Af	11520ewn
0900-1300	daily	EAs	11520ewn
1300-1500	daily	EAs	15610ewn
1500-1900	daily	ME	15610ewn
1900-2400	daily	Af	15610ewn
Spanish	**Days**	**Area**	**kHz**
0000-0500	daily	CAm	5810ewn
0000-1000	daily	SAm	11870ewn
0500-1300	daily	CAm	7515ewn
1000-1700	daily	SAm	12050ewn
1300-1800	daily	CAm	11550ewn
1700-2400	daily	SAm	13830ewn
1800-2400	daily	CAm	12050ewn

Ann: English: "This is WEWN, Global Catholic Radio, Birmingham, Alabama, USA".
V: QSL-card. (Online reception rpt form available)
Notes: Owned by the Eternal Word TV Network, Inc. Catholic station, began broadcasting in December 1992.

WHRI – WORLD HARVEST RADIO (WHR) (Rlg)
61300 Ironwood Rd, South Bend, IN 46614, USA.
☎ +1 574 2918200. 🖷 +1 574 2919043.
E: whr@lesea.com **W:** lesea.com/whr
Webcast: L
L.P: (LeSEA Broadcasting) Pres/CEO: Peter Sumrall; Dir, Engineering: Ves Hylton.
SW: [HRI] Furman, SC: 1 x 100, 3 x 500kW.
SAT: Galaxy 19.

kHz: 5920, 7315, 7385, 7520, 9505, 9840, 11565, 11635, 11705, 11790, 17610, 21600

Winter Schedule 2015/2016

English	Days	Area	kHz
0000-0030	.twtfs.	LAm,Car	7315hri
0000-0100	daily	NAm	7385hri
0015-0030	.twtfs.	Eu,ME	5920hri
0015-0030	m.....s	LAm,Car	7315hri
0030-0100	.twtfss	Eu,ME	5920hri
0030-0100	.twtfss	LAm,Car	7315hri
0100-0130	.twtfss	NAm	7385hri
0100-0200	......s	LAm,Car	7315hri
0100-0200	m.....s	NAm	7385hri
0200-0230	m.....s	LAm,Car	7315hri
0200-0300	daily	Eu,ME	5920hri
0200-0300	.twtfss	NAm	7385hri
0300-0400	mtwtfs.	Eu,ME	7520hri
0300-0400	m.....s	NAm	7385hri
0300-0400	mtwtf..	NAm, NEu,As	5920hri
0330-0400	.twtfs.	NAm	7385hri
0400-0500	daily	NAm	7385hri
0500-0600	daily	Eu,ME	11635hri
0900-1000	mtwtf.s	CAm,Pac	11565hri
1100-1130	daily	LAm,Car	7385hri
1100-1130	mtwtfs.	LAm,SAm	7315hri
1100-1200	......s	LAm,SAm	7315hri
1130-1200	mtwtf.s	NAm	7385hri
1130-1200	.....s.	LAm,SAm	7315hri
1200-1230	.....s.	LAm,Car	7385hri
1200-1300	.....ss	LAm,Car	11790hri
1300-1400	.....ss	NAm, NEu,As	9840hri
1400-1500	......s	NAm, NEu,As	9840hri
1400-1500	......s	SEu,NAf,ME	21600hri
1500-1600	.....ss	CAf	21600hri
1530-1600	......s	NAm, NEu,As	9840hri
1630-1700	mtwtfs.	CAf	21600hri
1745-1800	.....s	CAf	21600hri
1900-2100	.....s	CAf	17610hri
2000-2100	......s	Eu,ME	11705hri
2100-2130	mtwtf..	Eu,ME	11705hri
2100-2200	.....s.	Eu,ME	11705hri
2115-2130	......s	Eu,ME	11705hri
2130-2200	mtwtf.s	Eu,ME	11705hri
2200-2300	.....s.	Eu,ME	9505hri
2300-2315	.....s.	Eu,ME	9505hri
2300-2320	mtwtf..	LAm,Car	7315hri
2300-2400	.....s.	LAm,Car	7315hri
2315-2330	......s	LAm,Car	7315hri
2330-2345	.....s.	Eu,ME	9505hri
2330-2400	mtwtf..	LAm,Car	7315hri

French	Days	Area	kHz
0430-0500	mtwtf.s	Eu,ME	11635hri
0500-0515	...f...	Eu,ME	11635hri

Russian	Days	Area	kHz
0330-0400	......s	Eu,ME	7520hri

Ann: English: "This is World Harvest Radio".
V: QSL-card. (Online reception report form)
Notes: World Harvest Radio is a service of LeSEA Broadcasting Corp. and part of the LeSEA Broadcasting Network. On air since 25 Dec 1985. LeSEA Broadcasting Corp. owns the shortwave transmitting stations WHRI (Furman, SC) and T8WH (Palau). WHR transmits mainly own and paid religious programming; certain airtime is leased to non-religious broadcasters or prgr producers. Actual schedule may vary during the course of the season, depending on airtime sales.

WINB (Rlg)
✉ P.O. Box 88, Red Lion, PA 17356, USA.
☎ +1 717 2445360. 🖂 +1 717 2460363.
E: sally@winb.com **W:** www.winb.com
Webcast: D/L
L.P: Sales/Frequency Mgr: Hans Johnson.
SW: [INB] Red Lion, PA: 1 x 50kW.
kHz: 9265

Winter Schedule 2015/2016

English/Spanish	Days	Area	kHz
1230-0500	daily	CAm	9265inb

Ann: English: "This is WINB, Red Lion, Pennsylvania, USA".
V: QSL-card.
Notes: Owned by World International Broadcasters, Inc. Operational since October 1962. The station transmits religious paid programming. Schedule varies, depending on airtime sales.

WJHR RADIO INTERNATIONAL (Rlg)
✉ 5920 Oak Manor Drive, Milton, FL 32570, USA.
☎ +1 850 6235405.
E: wjhr@usa.com **W:** calvaryscall.org/whbr-radio
L.P: Owner: George Scott Mock.
SW: [JHR] Milton, FL: 1 x 0.25kW (run at 1kW PEP). F.pl: 1 x 50kW
kHz: 15555

Winter Schedule 2015/2016

English	Days	Area	kHz
1400-2200	daily	NAm	15555jhr*

Key: * USB (J3E mode)
Ann: English: "WJHR Radio International, located in the city of Milton, Florida".
V: QSL-email.
Notes: WJHR ("John Hill Radio") is owned by George Scott Mock (dba "Hill Radio International"), and operated by members of the Mt. Calvary Baptist Church. On the air since November 2009.

WORLD CHRISTIAN BROADCASTING INC. (Rlg)
✉ 605 Bradley Court, Franklin, TN 37067, USA.
☎ +1 615 3718707.
E: info@worldchristian.org **W:** www.worldchristian.org
L.P: Chmn: Dr. Frank Harrell; Pres: Charles H. Caudill; Vice Pres, Development: Andy Baker; Vice Pres/Dir, Engineering: Kevin K. Chambers.
Notes: World Christian Broadcasting, Inc owns and runs the SW transmitting station KNLS (see under Alaska), and a SW transmitting station in Southern Africa (see under Madagascar).

WRNO WORLDWIDE (Rlg)
✉ P.O. Box 895, Fort Worth, TX 76101, USA.
☎ +1 817 8509990. 🖂 +1 817 8509994.
E: wrnoradio@mailup.net **W:** wrnoworldwide.com
Webcast: L
L.P: Chmn, Good News World Outreach: Robert E. Mawire.
SW: [RNO] New Orleans, LA: 1 x 50kW.
kHz: 7506

Winter Schedule 2015/2016

English	Days	Area	kHz
0200-0500	daily	NAm,CAm	7506rno†

Key: † Irregular.
Ann: English: "This is WRNO Worldwide".
IS: "When the Saints go marching in".
V: QSL-card. Rp. (2 IRCs).
Notes: Owned by Good News World Outreach. The station transmits religious paid programming. Office is being relocated to Nashville, TN.

WTWW (Rlg)
✉ 131 Hiwassee Rd, Lebanon, TN 37087, USA.
E: email@wtww.us **W:** wtww.us
Webcast: L
✉ 6611 Ormond Dr, Nashville, TN 37205, USA. (HQ)
☎ +1 615 3528682.
L.P: Pres/Chief Operator: George McClintock; SM: Dan Dixon.
SW: [TWW] Lebanon, TN: 1 x 50, 2 x 100kW.
kHz: 5830, 9475, 12105

Winter Schedule 2015/2016

Arabic	Days	Area	kHz
1500-2100	daily	NAm,Eu	12105tww†
English	**Days**	**Area**	**kHz**
0200-1400	daily	NAm,Eu,Af	5830tww
0500-0800	.twtfs.	NAm	5830tww*
1400-0200	daily	NAm,Eu	9475tww‡
French	**Days**	**Area**	**kHz**
2100-2400	daily	NAm,Eu	12105tww†
Portuguese	**Days**	**Area**	**kHz**
0300-0500	daily	NAm,Eu	12105tww†
Russian	**Days**	**Area**	**kHz**
1400-1500	daily	NAm,Eu	12105tww†

Spanish

	Days	Area	kHz
0000-0300	daily	NAm,Eu	12105twwt

Key: ‡ Inactive at time of publication; † Irregular, schedule varies; * "Midnight in the Desert" programme with Art Bell.
Ann: English: "This is WTWW, Lebanon, Tennessee, USA".
V: QSL-card.
Notes: Owned by Leap of Faith, Inc. On the air since Feb 2010 (tests during Jan 2010). WTWW ("We Transmit World Wide") transmits own and paid religious programming.

WWCR – WORLDWIDE CHRISTIAN RADIO (Rlg)
🖃 1300 WWCR Avenue, Nashville, TN 37218, USA.
☎ +1 615 2551300. 📠 +1 615 2551311.
E: wwcr@wwcr.com **W:** www.wwcr.com
LP: GM: Eric Westenberger; Chief Engineer: Phil Patton; Ops Mgr: Brady Murray; Frequency Mgr: Dr Jerry Plummer.
SW: [WCR] Nashville, TN: 4 x 100kW.
kHz: 3195, 3215, 4840, 5070, 5890, 5935, 6115, 6875, 7490, 7520, 9350, 9980, 12160, 13845, 15795, 15825

Winter Schedule 2015/2016

English	Days	Area	kHz	
0000-0300	daily	NAm,CAm,Af	7520wcr*, 7520wcr**	
0000-1200	daily	Af	5935wcr**	
0000-1200	daily	NAm,Eu	4840wcr**	
0100-0400	daily	NAm,CAm,Af	6115wcr**	
0100-0900	daily	NAm,Eu,NAf,ME		3215wcr**
0100-1200	daily	NAm,CAm,Af	5890wcr**	
0100-1300	daily	NAm,Eu	4840wcr*	
0100-1300	daily	Af	5935wcr*	
0200-0400	daily	NAm,CAm,Af	6115wcr*	
0200-1100	daily	NAm,Eu,NAf,ME		3215wcr*
0300-1300	daily	NAm,CAm,Af	5890wcr*	
0600-1000	daily	NAm,Eu,NAf,ME		3195wcr*,
				3195wcr**
0700-1200	daily	NAm,CAm,Af	5070wcr*, 5070wcr**	
0900-1100	daily	NAm,Eu,NAf,ME		6875wcr**,
				7490wcr**
0900-1300	daily	NAm,Eu,NAf,ME	15795wcr**	
0900-2200	daily	NAm,Eu,NAf,ME	15825wcr**	
1000-1200	daily	NAm,Eu,NAf,ME		6875wcr*,
				7490wcr**
1000-1200	daily	NAm	6115wcr*, 6115wcr**	
1000-1400	daily	NAm,Eu,NAf,ME	15795wcr**	
1100-2200	daily	NAm,Eu,NAf,ME	15825wcr**	
1200-1500	daily	Af	7490wcr**	
1200-2400	daily	NAm,CAm,Af	9980wcr**	
1200-2400	daily	NAm,Eu	13845wcr**	
1300-0100	daily	NAm,Eu	13845wcr*	
1300-1600	daily	Af	7490wcr*	
1300-2400	daily	NAm,CAm,Af	9980wcr*	
1500-2000	daily	Af	12160wcr**	
1600-2100	daily	Af	12160wcr*	
2000-2400	daily	Af	9350wcr**	
2100-0100	daily	Af	9350wcr*	
2100-0100	daily	NAm,Eu,NAf,ME		3195wcr**
2100-0200	daily	NAm	6115wcr*	
2100-0200	daily	NAm,Eu,NAf,ME		6875wcr*,
				6875wcr**
2200-0100	daily	NAm	6115wcr**	

Key: * to 12 Mar 2016; ** From 13 Mar 2016.
Ann: English: "This is World Wide Christian Radio-WWCR, Nashville, Tennessee, USA".
V: QSL-card. Rp. preferred (1 IRC). Rec. acc.
Notes: Owned by F.W. Robert Broadcasting Co., Inc. The station transmits religious paid programming.

WBCQ – THE PLANET
🖃 274 Britton Road, Monticello, ME 04760, USA.
☎ +1 207 5389180.
E: wbcq@wbcq.com **W:** www.wbcq.com
Webcast: D/L
LP: Owners/GMs: Allan & Jennifer Weiner; Chief Engineer: Tim Smith.
SW: [BCQ] Monticello, ME: 4 x 50kW.
kHz: 5110, 7490, 9330, 15420

Winter Schedule 2015/2016

English	Days	Area	kHz
0000-0100	mtwtf.s	NAm,CAm	7490bcq
0000-0200	.....s.	NAm,CAm	7490bcq
0000-0500	....ss	NAm,CAm	5110bcq*
0100-0200	mtwtf..	NAm,CAm	7490bcq
0100-0200	daily	NAm,CAm	9330bcq*
0100-0200	....f..	NAm,CAm	5110bcq*
0200-0230	...t..	NAm,CAm	9330bcq*
0200-0300	..tf..	NAm,CAm	5110bcq*
0200-0400	..w....	NAm,CAm	7490bcq
0400-0500	mtwtf.s	NAm,CAm	7490bcq
1200-2300	daily	NAm,CAm	15420bcq*‡
2000-2100	.t.....	NAm,CAm	7490bcq
2100-2200	mtwtf..	NAm,CAm	7490bcq
2200-2300	mtwtf.s	NAm,CAm	7490bcq
2300-0000	.....ss	NAm,CAm	7490bcq

Key: ‡ Inactive at time of publication; * H3E (AM/U) mode
Ann: English: "This is WBCQ, Monticello, Maine, USA".
V: QSL-card. (SASE)
Notes: Owned by A. Weiner/Becker Broadcast Systems, Inc. Leases air time to religious and other prgr producers. Schedule is subject to daily variation (according to bookings) and start/end times are approximate. On air since 8 September 1998.

WRMI – RADIO MIAMI INTERNATIONAL
🖃 175 Fontainebleau Blvd., Suite 1N4, Miami, FL 33172, USA.
☎ +1 305 5599764. 📠 +1 305 5598186.
E: info@wrmi.net **W:** www.wrmi.net
Webcast: L
LP: GM: Jeff White; Dir, Technical: Jose Raul Mena.
SW: [YFR] Okeechobee, FL: 1 x 50, 12 x 100kW.
kHz: 5850, 7455, 7570, 9955, 11580, 15770

Winter Schedule 2015/2016

English	Days	Area	kHz
0000-0100	m......	CAm	7455yfr
0100-0300	daily	NAm	11580yfr
0700-0800	m......	CAm	7455yfr
1000-1100	.....s	NAm	7570yfr
1300-1400	.....s	NAm	11580yfr
2000-2100	.....s	NAm	11580yfr
2100-2200	daily	Eu,NAf	15770yfr
2300-2400	daily	NAm	5850yfr, 11580yfr

English/Spanish	Days	Area	kHz
2200-1500	daily	CAm,SAm	9955yfr

Ann: English: "This is WRMI, Radio Miami International".
V: QSL-card.
Notes: Owned by Radio Miami International, Inc. On air since June 1994 from the original SW site in Hialeah, FL (Miami). In 2013, Radio Miami International, Inc purchased the SW transmitting station WYFR Okeechobee, FL from Family Station, Inc. In December 2013, all transmissions from the Hialeah site were transferred to Okeechobee, including transfer of the callsign WRMI. WRMI provides air time for prgrs by various production companies and rebroadcasts international radio stations. See WRMI web site for detailed schedule. Some prgrs aimed at a Cuban audience are jammed.

WWRB
🖃 Airline Transport Communications Inc., Listener Services, P.O. Box 7, Manchester, TN 37349-0007, USA.
☎ +1 931 7286063. 📠 +1 931 7286087.
E: dfrantz@wwrb.org **W:** www.wwrb.org
Webcast: L
🖃 6755 Shady Grove Road, Morrison, TN 37355, USA. (Studio)
LP: Owner & CE: Dave Frantz.
SW: [WRB] Manchester, TN: 4 x 100kW. (plus 1 x 100kW backup tx).
kHz: 3185, 3195, 3215, 5050, 9370

Winter Schedule 2015/2016

English	Days	Area	kHz
0000-1300	daily	NAm	3185wrb
0100-0400	daily	NAm	3195wrb‡
1300-2400	daily	NAm	9370wrb
2100-0100	daily	NAm	3215wrb‡ **
2100-0200	daily	NAm	3215wrb‡ *
2200-1300	daily	NAm	5050wrb

Key: ‡ Inactive at time of publication; * to 12 Mar 2016; ** From 13 Mar 2016.
V: QSL-card. (Email rpts not accepted)
Notes: A subsidiary of Airline Transport Communications Inc. The station transmits religious paid programming. Frequency usage varies, depending on airtime sales. Occ uses unregistered freqs such as 3145kHz.

ALYX & YEYI (TECHNICAL SERVICE PROVIDER) (Broker)
✉ 5201 Blue Lagoon Drive, 8th Floor, Miami, FL 33126, USA.
☎ +1 305 5728070.
E: info@alyx-yeyi.com **W:** www.alyx-yeyi.com
LP: MD: Ludo Maes.
Notes: Alyx & Yeyi is a Technical Service Provider and brokers airtime for programs on shortwave, satellite and the internet, for radio stations with political, religious, commercial and NGO background. Latest broadcasting schedule can be found at www.airtime.org/schedule.asp

RED TELECOM (Broker)
✉ 300 East 75th Street, Suite 50, New York, NY 10021, USA.
☎ +1 917 5392494. 🖷 +1 208 4603547.
E: d.robinson@dtholdings.com; sales@dtholdings.com
W: www.dtholdings.com
LP: MD: Daniel Robinson.
Notes: Red Telecom brokers air time for transmitter facilities in Tajikistan and Uzbekistan.

UZBEKISTAN (UZB)

RADIOALOQA, RADIOESHITTIRISH VA TELEVIDENIYE MARKAZI (RRTM) (Tx Operator)
✉ Amir Timur Street 109a, 100202 Toshkent, Uzbekistan.
☎ +998 71 2356516. 🖷 +998 71 2344517.
E: gabulhona@crrt.uz **W:** www.crrt.uz
LP: GD: G'olibsher M. Ziyaev.
SW: [TAC] Toshkent: 11 x 100kW.
Notes: RRTM, a division of the State Communications and Information Agency of Uzbekistan, is the national transmitter network operator in Uzbekistan.

VATICAN CITY STATE (CVA)

VATICAN RADIO (Rlg)
✉ Piazza Pia 3, I-00120 Vatican City.
☎ +39 06 69883945. 🖷 +39 06 69883463.
E: english@vatiradio.va **W:** www.radiovaticana.va
Webcast: D/L/P
LP: GD: Fr Federico Lombardi; PD: Fr Andrzej Koprowski; Dir, Technical: Sandro Piervenanzi; Int Rel: Giacomo Ghisani.
MW: [VAT] Vatican City: 585/1260kHz 5kW.
SW: [SMG] Santa Maria di Galeria: 4 x 100, 5 x 500kW.
SAT: Eutelsat Hot Bird 13B, Optus D2.
kHz: *3975, 6070, 6185, 7250, 7275, 7305, 7360, 7410, 9560, 9600, 9610, 9645, 9660, 9695, 9755, 9850, 11625, 11695, 11715, 11740, 11875, 11890, 11935, 13765, 15470, 15595, 15775, 17590, 21550, 21560, 21570*

Winter Schedule 2015/2016

Amharic	Days	Area	kHz
0400-0415	daily	Af	7360smg
1630-1645	daily	Af	11625mdc, 13765smg

Amharic/Arabic/ Armenian/ Russian (Liturgy)	Days	Area	kHz
0930-1050	......s	Af	17590smg
0930-1050	......s	Af,Eu,ME	15595smg

Arabic	Days	Area	kHz
0500-0530	daily	NAf,ME	9645smg, 11715smg
0745-0805	mtwtfs.	Eu	7250smg
0745-0805	mtwtfs.	NAf	11740smg
0745-0805	mtwtfs.	NAf,ME	9645smg, 15595smg
1630-1700	daily	NAf,ME	11935smg, 15595smg
2140-2200	daily	Eu,NAf	6070smg
2140-2200	daily	NAf,ME	9755smg
2140-2200	daily	Eu	3975smg

Armenian	Days	Area	kHz
0310-0330	daily	Eu	6185smg, 7275smg
1650-1710	daily	Eu	6185smg, 7360smg

Belarusian	Days	Area	kHz
1800-1820	daily	Eu	6185smg

Chinese	Days	Area	kHz
0400-0430	daily	As	15470tin
1230-1300	mtwtf.s	As	11875pug, 15470pht
1230-1315	......s	As	11875pug, 15470pht
2200-2230	daily	As	7410pht, 9600pht, 15470tin

English	Days	Area	kHz
0140-0200	daily	As	7410smg, 9560smg
0300-0330	daily	As	15470pht
0300-0330	daily	Af	7360smg, 9660mdc
0500-0530	daily	Af	7360smg, 11625mdc
0630-0700	daily	Af	9660smg, 11625smg
0730-0745	mtwtfs.	Af	15595smg
0800-1130	daily	Af	21550smg
1530-1550	......s	Af	15470pug
1530-1550	mtwtf.s	As	15775smg+
1530-1600	......s	As	15775smg+
1530-1600	daily	Af	11695pht
1530-1600	mtwtf.s	Af	15470pug
1715-1730	daily	NAf,ME	11935smg
1730-1800	daily	Af	9660mdc, 11625smg, 13765smg
2000-2030	daily	Af	9660smg, 11625smg

English (Liturgy)	Days	Area	kHz
1130-1200	....f..	ME	21560smg
1130-1200	....f..	Eu	17590smg

French	Days	Area	kHz
0430-0500	daily	Af	11625mdc
0430-0500	daily	Eu	7360smg
0600-0630	mtwtfs.	Af	9660smg, 11625smg
0715-0730	mtwtfs.	Af	15595smg
0800-1130	daily	Af	21570smg
1700-1715	daily	NAf,ME	11935smg
1700-1730	daily	Af	11625smg, 13765smg
2030-2100	daily	Af	9660smg, 11625smg

Hindi	Days	Area	kHz
0040-0100	daily	As	7410smg, 9560smg
0200-0220	daily	As	15470pht
1430-1450	daily	As	11695pht, 15470pug

Italian	Days	Area	kHz
0700-0715	mtwtf..	Eu	15595smg
1300-1320	daily	Eu	17590smg

Italian (Angelus)	Days	Area	kHz
1050-1130	......s	Af	21560smg, 21560smg
1050-1130	......s	Eu	9645smg
1050-1130	......s	Eu,NAf	11740smg, 15595smg
1300-1320	daily	Af	21560smg

Italian (Liturgy)	Days	Area	kHz
0830-0930	......s	Eu	7250smg

Italian (Papal Audience)	Days	Area	kHz
0905-1100	..w....	Eu	7250smg

Latin (Liturgy)	Days	Area	kHz
1940-2000	daily	Af	9660smg, 11625smg
1940-2000	daily	Eu	3975smg
1940-2015	daily	ME	9755smg
1940-2015	daily	Eu	6070smg

Latin (Mass)	Days	Area	kHz
0630-0700	daily	Eu	3975smg
0630-0710	daily	Eu	15595smg
0630-0715	daily	Eu	6070smg

Malayalam	Days	Area	kHz
0120-0140	daily	As	7410smg, 9560smg
0240-0300	daily	As	15470pht
1510-1530	daily	As	11695pht, 15470pug

Portuguese	Days	Area	kHz
0530-0600	daily	Af	7360smg, 11625smg, 13765mdc
0800-1050	......s	Af	21560smg

Portuguese	Days	Area	kHz
0800-1130	mtwtfs.	Af	21560smg
1800-1830	daily	Af	9660smg, 11625smg, 13765smg

Romanian (Liturgy)	Days	Area	kHz
0715-0830	......s	Eu	7250smg, 9645smg

Russian	Days	Area	kHz
1330-1400	daily	RUS	9695pht, 11875pht
1710-1740	daily	RUS	6185smg, 7360smg

Somali	Days	Area	kHz
0345-0400	......s	Af	7360smg, 9660mdc
1615-1630	.....s.	Af	11625mdc, 13765smg

Spanish	Days	Area	kHz
0150-0245	daily	SAm	7305grv
1230-1300	daily	SAm	9610grv
1900-1930	.....s.	Af	9660smg

Swahili	Days	Area	kHz
0330-0345	......s	Af	7360smg, 9660mdc
0330-0400	mtwtfs.	Af	7360smg, 9660mdc
1600-1615	.....s.	Af	11625mdc, 13765smg
1600-1630	mtwtf.s	Af	11625mdc, 13765smg

Tamil	Days	Area	kHz
0100-0120	daily	As	7410smg, 9560smg
0220-0240	daily	As	15470pht
1450-1510	daily	As	11695pht, 15470pug

Tigrinya	Days	Area	kHz
0415-0430	daily	Af	7360smg, 9660smg
1645-1700	daily	Af	11625mdc, 13765smg

Ukrainian	Days	Area	kHz
1740-1800	daily	Eu	6185smg, 7360smg

Ukrainian (Liturgy)	Days	Area	kHz
0710-0845	......s	Eu	9850smg, 11740smg

Vietnamese	Days	Area	kHz
1315-1400	daily	SEA	11890tin, 15470pht
2315-2400	daily	SEA	9600pht, 15470tin

Key: + DRM.
Ann: Before all transmissions: Latin: "Laudetur Jesus Christus" (Praised be Jesus Christ), repeated in the language of the broadcast, then station identification. English: "This is the English program of Vatican Radio".
V: QSL-card.
Notes: On air since 12 Feb 1931. Certain schedule variations apply on Catholic Holy Days.

VIETNAM (VTN)

VOICE OF VIETNAM (OVERSEAS SERVICE) (VOV) (Gov)
🖃 45 Ba Trieu Street, Hanoi, Vietnam.
☎ +84 4 38266809. 🖷 +84 4 38266707..
E: vovworld@vov.org.vn **W:** vovworld.vn; tnvn.gov.vn; vov.vn
Webcast: L
LP: Dir (VOV5): Doan Thi Trung.
MW: [OMO] Can Tho, Ô Môn: 1242kHz 2000kW (Run at lower power - est. approx 100kW) .
SW: [VNI] Son Tay: 11 x 100kW & via leased foreign relays.
FM/DAB: FM: 105.5MHz (Hanoi); 105.7MHz (Ho Chi Minh City).
SAT: Eutelsat Hot Bird 13D, Vinasat 1.
kHz: *1242, 5955, 6135, 6175, 7220, 7280, 7285, 9550, 9730, 9840, 12000, 12020*

Winter Schedule 2015/2016

Chinese	Days	Area	kHz
1100-1130	daily	As	7220vni, 12000vni
1200-1230	daily	As	7220vni, 12000vni
1300-1330	daily	As	7220vni, 12000vni
2200-2230	daily	As	7220vni, 12000vni
2230-2300	daily	As	9840vni, 12020vni

English	Days	Area	kHz
0100-0130	daily	NAm	6175wof
0230-0300	daily	NAm	6175wof
0330-0400	daily	NAm	6175hri
1000-1030	daily	As	9840vni, 12020vni
1130-1200	daily	As	9840vni, 12020vni

English	Days	Area	kHz
1230-1300	daily	As	9840vni, 12020vni
1330-1400	daily	As	9840vni, 12020vni
1500-1530	daily	As	9840vni, 12020vni
1600-1630	daily	Eu	7280vni, 9730vni
1600-1630	daily	ME	7220vni, 9550vni
1800-1830	daily	Eu	5955mos
1900-1930	daily	Eu	7280vni, 9730vni
2030-2100	daily	Eu	7280vni, 9730vni
2030-2100	daily	ME	7220vni, 9550vni
2330-2400	daily	As	9840vni, 12020vni

French	Days	Area	kHz
1200-1230	daily	As	7285vni
1300-1330	daily	As	7285vni
1630-1700	daily	ME	7220vni, 9550vni
1830-1900	daily	Eu	7280vni, 9730vni
1930-2000	daily	Eu	5955mos, 7280vni, 9730vni
2100-2130	daily	ME	7220vni, 9550vni
2100-2130	daily	Eu	7280vni, 9730vni

German	Days	Area	kHz
2030-2100	daily	Eu	6175dha
2100-2130	daily	Eu	6175dha

Indonesian	Days	Area	kHz
1030-1100	daily	As	9840vni, 12020vni
1300-1330	daily	As	9840vni, 12020vni
1430-1500	daily	As	9840vni, 12020vni
2300-2330	daily	As	9840vni, 12020vni

Japanese	Days	Area	kHz
1100-1130	daily	As	9840vni, 12020vni
1200-1230	daily	As	9840vni, 12020vni
1400-1430	daily	As	9840vni, 12020vni
2200-2230	daily	As	9840vni, 12020vni

Lao	Days	Area	kHz
1100-1200	daily	As	7285vni
1330-1430	daily	SEA	1242omo

Russian	Days	Area	kHz
1130-1200	daily	As	7220vni, 12000vni
1230-1300	daily	As	7220vni, 12000vni
1630-1700	daily	Eu	7280vni, 9730vni
2000-2030	daily	Eu	6135wof, 7280vni, 9730vni

Spanish	Days	Area	kHz
0300-0330	daily	NAm	6175hri
0400-0430	daily	NAm	6175hri
1800-1830	daily	Eu	7280vni, 9730vni

Thai	Days	Area	kHz
1230-1300	daily	As	7285vni
1430-1500	daily	SEA	1242omo

Vietnamese	Days	Area	kHz
0130-0230	daily	NAm	6175wof
1500-1600	daily	ME	7220vni, 9550vni
1500-1600	daily	SEA	1242omo
1700-1800	daily	Eu	7280vni, 9730vni
1830-1930	daily	Eu	5955mos

Ann: English: "You are listening to Radio The Voice of Vietnam".
V: QSL-card.
Notes: The External Sce (VOV5) of the national broadcaster, Voice of Vietnam. Chinese programme has some segments in Cantonese.

YEMEN (YEM)

REPUBLIC OF YEMEN RADIO/RADIO SANA'A
🖃 See National Radio section.
SW: [SAN] Sana'a: 1 x 50, 1 x 100kW.‡
kHz: *11860*

Winter Schedule 2015/2016

Arabic	Days	Area	kHz
0400-0900	daily	ME	11860
1800-2300	daily	ME	11860

Ann: Arabic: "Radio Sana'a".
Key: Inactive at time of publication.
Notes: Reported to be using transmitters located in Saudi Arabia. Further details of this operation were not available at time of publication. 711kHz is apparently under the control of rebel forces.

CLANDESTINE AND OTHER TARGET BROADCASTS

Clandestine Broadcasts (Clan) are politically-motivated broadcasts produced by groups opposed to the government of the target country.
Other Target Broadcasts can be produced by either governmental or non-governmental organisations and are targetted at zones of regional or local conflict.
Most COTBs are transmitted via the facilities of international transmitter operators.
The following symbols are used in this section: † Irregular transmsission; ‡ Inactive at editorial deadline. ± Variable frequency.
Where a station is no longer broadcasting, the inactive symbol (‡) appears next to the station name. If a station has been inactive for the past two seasons and remains inactive, it is removed from the listing.

Target: CAMBODIA (CBG)

VOICE OF KHMER M'CHAS SROK
☐ 1050 Connecticut Avenue NW, 10th Floor, Washington DC 20026, USA.
☎ +1 202 7723100.
E: khmer.mchas.srok@gmail.com **W:** www.khmer-mchas-srok.org
Webcast: L/D
L.P: KMS Representative in USA: Hassan A. Kassem.
kHz: *17860*

Winter Schedule 2015/2016

Khmer	Days	Area	kHz
1130-1200	...t..s	CBG	17860dsb

V: QSL Email. Rpts to: kms.usa.representative@gmail.com
Notes: 24/7 internet radio station, founded by the former R. Free Asia journalist Hassan A. Kassem. Produced by the U.S. based NGO Khmer M'Chas Srok (KMS). On SW since 14 Feb 2014.

Target: CAMEROON (CME)

SAWTU LINJIILA (VOICE OF THE GOSPEL) (Rlg)
Notes: Since only a very small part of the target audience of this prgr (Fulani speakers in West Africa) lives in Cameroon, the complete entry was moved to the International Radio section (Cameroon).

Target: CHINA (CHN)

STREAM OF PRAISE MUSIC MINISTRIES (Rlg)
☐ 1165 Warner Avenue, Tustin, CA 92780, USA.
☎ +1 714 2581165. ▤ +1 714 2581166.
E: ely@sop.org; info@sop.org **W:** www.sop.org
Webcast: D/P
L.P: Pres/CEO: Rev. Sandy Yu.
kHz: *7530*

Winter Schedule 2015/2016

Cantonese/ Chinese	Days	Area	kHz
2100-2130	daily	CHN	7530tac

Notes: The religious organisation Stream of Praise Music Ministries was founded 1993.

SOUND OF HOPE RADIO INTERNATIONAL
☐ : 6-4, Lane 84, Guotai St, North District, Taichung 404, Taiwan.
E: contact@soundofhope.org; allenz@soundofhope.org
W: www.soundofhope.org
Webcast: D/L/P
☐ 333 Kearny St, San Francisco, CA 94108, USA. (HQ)
☎ +1 415 3988009. ▤ +1 415 2765861.
L.P: Pres (Sound of Hope Radio Network, Inc): Allen Yong Zeng.
kHz: *6230, 6370, 6730, 6900, 7210, 7280, 7310, 7580, 7600, 7730, 7800, 9180, 9200, 9230, 9255, 9320, 9360, 9635, 9730, 9850, 9930, 9970, 10820, 10870, 10960, 11070, 11100, 11150, 11300, 11370, 11410, 11470, 11500, 11530, 11580, 11600, 11715, 11765, 11775,*
11970, 12150, 12190, 12230, 12370, 12500, 12560, 12800, 12910, 12950, 12980, 13200, 13230, 13530, 13640, 13680, 13775, 13820, 13890, 13920, 13980, 14370, 14800, 14870, 14920, 14980, 15070, 15340, 15775, 15800, 15840, 15870, 15970, 16100, 16160, 16250, 16300, 16600, 16750, 16775, 16980, 17000, 17200, 17400, 17440, 18870

Winter Schedule 2015/2016

Chinese	Days	Area	kHz
0000-2400	daily	CHN	6370tsu±*,6730tsu±*, 6900tsu±*,7730tsu±*, 7800tsu±*
2300-1600	daily	CHN	6230tsu±*,7210tsu±*, 7280tsu±*,7310tsu±*, 7580tsu±*,7600tsu±*, 9180tsu±*, 9200tsu±*, 9230tsu±**,9255tsu±*, 9320tsu±**, 9360tsu±*, 9635tsu±*, 9730tsu±*, 9850tsu±**, 9930tsu±*, 9970tsu±*, 10820tsu±*, 10870tsu±*,10960tsu±*, 11070tsu±*,11100tsu±** 11150tsu±*,11300tsu±*, 11370tsu±*,11410tsu±*, 11470tsu±*,11500tsu±*, 11530tsu±*,11580tsu±*, 11600tsu±**,11715tsu±* 11765tsu±*, 11775tsu±*, 11970tsu±*,12150tsu±*, 12190tsu±**,12230tsu±* 12370tsu±*,12500tsu±*, 12560tsu±*, 12800tsu±*, 12910tsu±*, 12950tsu±*, 12980tsu±*, 13200tsu±*, 13230tsu±*,13530tsu±*, 13640tsu±**,13680tsu±*

Key: ± Variable frequency; *Includes also segment of Cantonese 1500-1600. Times variable; **Relay of R. Free Asia (RFA). Includes Cantonese 1400-1500. Times variable.
Ann: Chinese: "Xiwang zhi sheng guoji guangbo diantai".
V: QSL-card.
Notes: Established in June 2003. Falun Gong-related Sound of Hope Radio International is the shortwave programme of Sound of Hope Radio Network, Inc (USA). The organisation is a provider of Chinese language news and cultural programming for the worldwide Chinese community. SW broadcasts are subject to Chinese music jammers (also known in the DX community as 'Firedragon' or 'Firedrake'). At the top of the hour the jammers are off air for 15 minutes.

VOICE OF TIBET
☐ Voice of Tibet Foundation, Kirkegata 5, 0153 Oslo, Norway. (Administration)
☎ +47 22111209; +47 22112700.
E: oystalme@gmail.com **W:** www.vot.org
Webcast: D
☐ Ratoe Chuwar Labrang, Phuntsok Gyatsal House, Session Road, Dharamsala 176215, Distt Kangra H.P., India (Main Editorial Office)

☎ +91 1892 228179; +91 1892 222384. 🖹 +91 1892 224913.
L.P: Dir: Øystein Alme; Editor-in-Chief: Tenzin Paldon.
SAT: Intelsat 20.
kHz: *7598, 15538, 15543, 15548, 15565, 15568*

Winter Schedule 2015/2016

Chinese	Days	Area	kHz
1200-1230	daily	CHN	15538dsb±
1300-1400	daily	CHN	15543dsb±
Tibetan	**Days**	**Area**	**kHz**
1230-1400	daily	CHN	15568dsb±
1400-1430	daily	CHN	15548dsb±,
			15565mdc±
2300-2330	daily	CHN	7598dsb±

Key: ± Variable frequency.
Ann: Chinese: "Zheli shi Nuowei Xizang zhi Sheng Guangbo Diantai huayu jiemu"; Tibetan: "Di nor we bod kyi rlung 'phrin khang yin".
V: QSL-card.
Notes: On air since July 1996. Licensed radio station in Norway, run by the "Voice of Tibet Foundation". Established by the organisations "Worldview Rights", the "Norwegian Human Rights House" and the "Norwegian Tibet Committee". Frequencies are often changed due to jamming.

VOICE OF CHINA (Clan)
🖹 2261 Morello Avenue, Suite A, Pleasant Hill, CA 94523, USA.
☎ +1 510 6872354. 🖹 +1 510 6877396.
L.P: Exec Producer: Hu Juying (Lily Hu).
kHz: *7270*

Winter Schedule 2015/2016

Chinese	Days	Area	kHz
1400-1500	daily	CHN	7270tsh
2300-2400	daily	CHN	7270tsh

Ann: Chinese: "Zhongguo zhi yin".
V: QSL-card.
Notes: On air since April 1991. Produced by the "Foundation for China in the 21st Century", a U.S.-based non-profit organisation. Jammed.

Target: CUBA (CUB)

WRMI – RADIO MIAMI INTERNATIONAL
🖹 See International Radio section, under 'USA'.
SW: See International Radio section, under 'USA'.
Notes: WRMI relays a number of anti-Government broadcasts to Cuba, in Spanish, from various programmme producers. For full programme details, see www.wrmi.net

RADIO REPÚBLICA (Clan)
🖹 P.O. Box 110235, Hialeah, FL 33011, USA.
☎ +1 305 2794416.
E: info@directorio.org (Directorio Democrático Cubano)
W: www.directorio.org (Directorio Democrático Cubano)
kHz: *9490*

Winter Schedule 2015/2016

Spanish	Days	Area	kHz
0100-0300	daily	CUB	9490iss

Ann: Spanish: "Esta es Radio República. La voz del Directorio Democrático Cubano", "Radio República, la voz de Cuba libre".
V: QSL-email. Rpt to Maria Lima (Special Assistant to Program Coordinator) marialima@directorio.org
Notes: On air since August 2005. Produced by Directorio Democrático Cubano. Jammed. Freqs/schedules may be changed without notice to avoid jamming.

Target: ERITREA (ERI)

ERITREAN FORUM RADIO
🖹 Based in Washington, D.C., USA.
☎ +1 202 8887866.
E: arabic@forumeritrea.org (Arabic); tig@forumeritrea.org (Tigrinya)
W: forumeritrea.org; www.facebook.com/ForumEritrea
Webcast: D
SAT: Eutelsat 8WB.
kHz: *11720*

Winter Schedule 2015/2016

Arabic	Days	Area	kHz
1700-1800	..w....	ERI	11720iss
1800-1900	.....s.	ERI	11720iss
Tigrinya	**Days**	**Area**	**kHz**
1700-1800	.t..f.s	ERI	11720iss

Notes: Produced by the oppositional group "Eritrean Forum for National Dialogue" (EFND/Medrek). On SW since 15 October 2013.

RADIO ERENA
🖹 3, rue Henri Becque, F-75013 Paris, France.
☎ +33 145896451. 🖹 +33 145896451.
E: radioerena@gmail.com; radioerena@yahoo.com **W:** erena.org
Webcast: L (www.ustream.tv/user/radio_erena)
SAT: Eutelsat 8WA.
kHz: *11855*

Winter Schedule 2015/2016

Arabic	Days	Area	kHz
1730-1800	daily	ERI	11855sof
Tigrinya	**Days**	**Area**	**kHz**
1700-1730	daily	ERI	11855sof

Ann: Tigrinya: "Radio Erena".
Notes: Independent online radio station run by Eritrean exile journalists, supported by 'Reporters Without Borders'. On SW since November 2012.

DIMTSI WEGAHTA (VOICE OF THE DAWN) (Clan)
🖹 Based in Mekelle, Ethiopia.
E: selamwegahta@sallina.com **W:** www.sallina.com
Webcast: D
kHz: *918*

Winter Schedule 2015/2016

Arabic/Tigrinya	Days	Area	kHz
0250-0600	daily	ERI	918mek
1400-2000	daily	ERI	918mek

Ann: Tigrinya: "Dimtsi Wegahta".
Notes: Established on 19 July 2007. Mahbersebawit Dimtsi Wegahta ("Community Voice of Dawn") is produced by the oppositional "Charity of Civic Society of Eritrea". Successor station to "Eastern Radio", which transmitted via a tx in Sudan 2006-2007.

VOICE OF ASSENNA (Clan)
🖹 Assenna Foundation Ltd, 145-157 St John Street, London, EC1V 4PW, United Kingdom.
E: aseye.asena@gmail.com **W:** assenna.com
Webcast: D
L.P: Dir: Amanuel Eyasu.
kHz: *11720*

Winter Schedule 2015/2016

Tigrinya	Days	Area	kHz
1700-1800	m..t.s	ERI	11720iss

Ann: Tigrinya: "Ezi dimtsi Asena Eyu".
V: QSL-email.
Notes: Started broadcasts on 16 Feb 2009. Produced by Assenna Foundation Ltd. Also referred to as "Radio Asena".

VOICE OF DEMOCRATIC ALLIANCE (Clan)
🖹 c/o Eritrean Democratic Alliance, P.O. Box 13043, Khartoum, Sudan.
E: erit_alliance_2008@yahoo.com
W: www.erit-alliance.com (EDA)
SW: Via txs of the Ethiopian state broadcaster: Ethiopian Broadcasting Corp. (EBC).
kHz: *7236*

Winter Schedule 2015/2016

Afar	Days	Area	kHz
1530-1600	.t.t.s.	EAf	7236gjw±,†
Arabic	**Days**	**Area**	**kHz**
1500-1530	m.w.f.s	EAf	7236gjw±,†
Kunama	**Days**	**Area**	**kHz**
1530-1600	m.w.f..	EAf	7236gjw±,†
Tigrinya	**Days**	**Area**	**kHz**
1500-1530	.t.t.s.	EAf	7236gjw±,†
1530-1600	.....s	EAf	7236gjw±,†

Key: ± Variable frequency; † Irregular.

Ann: Arabic: "Sawt al-Tahalufa al-Dimuqrati".
Notes: On air since April 2005. Produced by the "Eritrean Democratic Alliance" (EDA), an umbrella organisation for around a dozen opposition political parties and groups.

VOICE OF ERITREA (Clan)
E: hizbawii@gmail.com **W:** www.harnnet.org (EPDP)
Webcast: D
SW: Via txs of the Ethiopian state broadcaster, Ethiopian Broadcasting Corp (EBC).
kHz: 7236

Winter Schedule 2015/2016

Tigrinya	Days	Area	kHz
0400-0430	.t.t.s.	ERI	7236gjw±,†
1800-1830	.t.t.s.	ERI	7236gjw±,†

Key: ± Variable frequency; † irregular.
Ann: Tigrinya: "Dimtsi Ertrai".
V: QSL-email.
Notes: Produced by "Eritrean People's Democratic Party" (EPDP). Formerly produced by the "Eritrean Democratic Party" (EPM), which in 2010 merged with other oppositional organisations to form the EPDP).

VOICE OF PEACE AND DEMOCRACY OF ERITREA (Clan)
c/o Radio Ethiopia, P.O. Box 1020, Addis Ababa, Ethiopia.
SW: Via txs of the Ethiopian state broadcaster, Ethiopian Broadcasting Corp (EBC).
kHz: 7236

Winter Schedule 2015/2016

Tigrinya	Days	Area	kHz
0400-0500	m.w.f..	ERI	7236gjw±,†
1800-1830	m.w.f..	ERI	7236gjw±,†

Key: ± Variable frequency; † Irregular.
Ann: Tigrinya: "Yeh Radio Demtsi Selaman Demokratia Ertrai".
Notes: On air since February 1999.

Target: ETHIOPIA (ETH)

RISALA INTERNATIONAL ‡ (RIg)
Based in Minneapolis, MN, USA.
☎ +1 612 4071236.
E: risalaint@live.com; radiorisala@live.com
W: risalainternational.org; www.facebook.com/RaadiyooRisaalaa
Webcast: D
Key: ‡ No SW broadcasts at time of publication.
Ann: Oromo:"Segalee Raadiyoo Risaalaa".
Notes: Islamic, Internet-based programme. SW broadcasts began on 20 Feb 2015.

OROMO VOICE RADIO (OVR)
1610 Columbia Rd NW, Washington DC, 20009, USA.
☎ +31 6 86266057; +61 466 521524.
E: ovr@oromovoice.org (OVR); info@oromovoice.org (MWMF)
W: oromovoice.org
Webcast: D
L.P: Exec Dir (MWMF): Aliye Geleto.
kHz: 17850

Winter Schedule 2015/2016

English	Days	Area	kHz
1615-1630	m......	ETH	17850iss

Oromo	Days	Area	kHz
1600-1615	m......	ETH	17850iss
1600-1630	..w..s.	ETH	17850iss

Ann: Oromo: "Raadiyoo Sagalee Oromoo".
Notes: Produced by the U.S. based NGO Madda Walaabuu Media Foundation (MWMF), which was founded in Nov 2013. On SW since 1st Jan 2014.

RADIO ABISINIA ‡
P.O. Box 56533, Washington DC 20040, USA.
☎ +1 202 3297709.
E: radioabisinia@yahoo.com **W:** www.radioabisinia.com
Webcast: D/L
6500 Luzon Avenue NW, Washington DC 20012, USA.

Key: ‡ No SW broadcasts at time of publication.
Notes: Radio Abisinia was founded 2004 as a non-profit organisation serving the Ethiopian community in the Washington, DC metropolitan area.

GINBOT 7 DIMTS RADIO (Clan)
P.O. Box 56281, London, N4 9BH, United Kingdom.
☎ +44 20 32869661.
E: g7radio@ginbot7.org; info@ginbot7.org **W:** www.ginbot7.org
Webcast: D
SW: Broadcast via txs of "The Voice of the Broad Masses of Eritrea" in Asmara, Eritrea.
kHz: 837, 7175

Winter Schedule 2015/2016

Amharic	Days	Area	kHz
0500-0530	.t.t...	ETH	837asm, 7175asm‡
0530-0600	.....s.	ETH	837asm, 7175asm‡
1430-1500	.t.t.s.	ETH	837asm, 7175asm‡

Key: ‡ Inactive at time of publication.
Ann: Amharic: "Yeh Ginbot Sabat Dimtse now".
V: QSL-email.
Notes: On air since September 2008. Produced by the Ethiopian oppositional party "Ginbot 7 - Movement for Justice, Freedom and Democracy".

RADIO XORIYO (Clan)
P.O. Box 27618, Toronto, ON M3A 3B8, Canada.
E: raadioxoriyo@yahoo.com
Webcast: D
kHz: 17630, 17850

Winter Schedule 2015/2016

Somali	Days	Area	kHz
1600-1630	m.w..s.	ETH	17850iss
1600-1630	.t...s.	ETH	17630iss

Ann: Somali: "Ku soo dhawaada Radio Xoriyo codkii ummadda Ogadeniya".
V: QSL-email.
Notes: On air, intermittently, since May 2000. Produced by the "Ogaden National Liberation Front" (ONLF).

VOICE OF OROMO LIBERATION (Clan)
Postfach 510620, D-13366 Berlin, Germany.
☎ +49 30 4943372. +49 30 4943372.
E: sbo.radio88@gmail.com
W: www.oromoliberationfront.org/sbo.html
Webcast: D
kHz: 17630

Winter Schedule 2015/2016

Amharic	Days	Area	kHz
1730-1800	..w....	ETH	17630iss

Oromo	Days	Area	kHz
1700-1730	..w....	ETH	17630iss
1700-1800	......s	ETH	17630iss

Ann: Amharic: "Radio Bilisummaa Oromoo"; Oromo: "Kun Sagalee Bilisummaa Oromoo".
V: QSL-letter.
Notes: On air since July 1988 (transmitted from outside of Ethiopian territory since 1996). Produced by the "Oromo Liberation Front" (OLF). Also carried via "Voice of the Broad Masses of Eritrea" transmitters (Eritrea).

Target: INDIA (IND)

VOICE OF JAMMU & KASHMIR FREEDOM MOVEMENT (Clan)
P.O. Box 102, Muzaffarabad 13100, Pakistan.
Webcast: L (www.kmsnews.org (Kashmir Media Service))
L.P: PM: J. Rehan.
SW: via tx of Pakistan Broadcasting Corp. in Rewat (Islamabad), Pakistan.
kHz: 3995

Winter Schedule 2015/2016

Kashmiri/Urdu	Days	Area	kHz
1300-1430	daily	IND	3995isl†

Key: † Irregular (Running at low power and with variable times).
Ann: Urdu: "Ye Sadayee Hurriyat Jammu Kashmir hai".
V: QSL-letter. No rp.
Notes: On air since 1999. Produced by the "Jammu and Kashmir Freedom Movement" (JKFM).

Target: IRAN (IRN)

RADIO RANGINKAMAN
Based in Los Angeles, California, USA.
☎ +1 818 6499406.
E: radioranginkaman@gmail.com **W:** radioranginkaman.org
Webcast: D
SAT: Eutelsat Hot Bird 13D (via Globecast Persian sat-feed R.Jahani).
kHz: 7575, 15630

Winter Schedule 2015/2016
Persian	Days	Area	kHz
1600-1630	m...f..	ME	7575tac, 15630sof

Notes: Prgr targetting the LGBT (lesbian, gay, bisexual and transgender) communities in Iran, Afghanistan and Tajikistan. The name translates in English as 'Radio Rainbow'. On SW since 24 September 2012. Also carried by KIRN Simi Valley, CA 670kHz (USA).

Target: KOREA, (D.P.R.) (KRE)

VOICE OF THE MARTYRS (Rlg)
#101, Deokseong B/D, 236-1 Mapo-dong, Mapo-gu, Seoul 121-050, Republic of Korea.
☎ +82 2 20650703. 🖹 +82 2 20650704.
E: mdillmuth@vomkorea.kr **W:** vomkorea.co.kr
5550 Tech Center Dr, Colorado Springs, CO 80919, USA. (New Horizons Foundation, Inc)
☎ +1 719 2601213. 🖹 +1 719 26640604.
E: via website. **W:** newhorizonsfoundation.com
L.P: Project Coordinator: Pastor Tim Dillmuth.
kHz: 7520

Winter Schedule 2015/2016
Korean	Days	Area	kHz
1630-1800	daily	EAs	7520tac±

Key: ± Variable frequency, to avoid jamming.
Ann: Korean: "I-bangsong-oen Daehan-Minguk Seoul-eseo bonae-deurineun Sungyo sori Tansaeng sori bangsong-imnida" (Translation: "This broadcast from Republic of Korea, Seoul. This is Voice of Martyrdom-Voice of the Birth").
V: QSL-email.
Notes: On air since 31 October 2009. Produced by the U.S. charity organisation New Horizons Foundation, Inc. Initially funded by the charity organisation Seoul USA. Earlier transmitted under the label "Voice of Free Radio" between 8 March 2008 and 30 September 2009.

VOICE OF WILDERNESS (Rlg)
208 Hannam-dong, Yongsan-gu, Seoul, 140-889, Republic of Korea.
☎ +82 2 7968846. 🖹 +82 2 7927567.
E: main@cornerstone.or.kr **W:** www.cornerstone.or.kr
Webcast: D
Cornerstone Ministries Int., P.O. Box 4002, Tustin, CA 92781, USA.
☎ +1 714 4840042. 🖹 +1 714 4840046.
E: info@cornerstoneusa.org (USA) **W:** cornerstoneusa.org
L.P: CEO (Cornerstone): Lee Saac; Chief Producer: Lee Saiah.
MW: For tx details see FEBC Korea, under Korea (Rep).
FM/DAB: FM: Relayed via FEBC Jeju (Sammaebong), Republic of Korea: HLAZ-SFM 101.1MHz 1kW.
kHz: 7615

Winter Schedule 2015/2016
Korean	Days	Area	kHz
1330-1530	daily	EAs	7615dsb

Ann: Korean: "Gwangya-e Sori Bangsong-imnida".
Notes: Produced by Cornerstone Ministries International. Initially listed in WRTH as "North Korea Missionary Broadcast".

FURUSATO NO KAZE/ILBON–E BARAM (WIND FROM JAPAN)
Policy Planning Division, Headquarters for the Abduction Issue, Cabinet Secretariat, 6-1 Nagata-cho 1-chome, Chiyoda-ku, Tokyo 100-8968, Japan.
☎ +81 3 52532111. 🖹 +81 3 3592 2300.
E: info@rachi.go.jp **W:** www.rachi.go.jp/jp/shisei/radio
Webcast: D
kHz: 9950, 9960, 9965, 9975

Winter Schedule 2015/2016
Japanese	Days	Area	kHz
1330-1400	daily	KRE	9950tsh
1430-1500	daily	KRE	9960hbn
1600-1630	daily	KRE	9975hbn
Korean	**Days**	**Area**	**kHz**
1300-1330	daily	KRE	9950tsh
1500-1530	daily	KRE	9975hbn
1530-1600	daily	KRE	9965hbn

Ann: Japanese: "Furusato no Kaze"; Korean "Ilbon-e Baram".
V: QSL-letter.
Notes: Produced by the Japanese government agency "Headquarters for the Abduction Issue", targeting abducted Japanese citizens in North Korea. On the air since July 2007. "Furusato no Kaze" is the name of the Japanese broadcast; "Ilbon-e-Baram" is the name of the Korean broadcast (translated to Japanese: "Nippon no Kaze").

NATIONAL UNITY RADIO (EX–RADIO FREE CHOSUN)
3rd Floor, 384-20 Mangwon-dong, Mapo-gu, Seoul 121-821, Republic of Korea.
☎ +82 505 8702012. 🖹 +82 505 8702012.
E: rfchosun@rfchosun.org **W:** www.rfchosun.org
Webcast: D
W: nknet.org
L.P: Pres: Lee Kwang Baek.
kHz: 7515

Winter Schedule 2015/2016
Korean	Days	Area	kHz
1300-1500	daily	KRE	7515tac

V: QSL-email.
Notes: Radio Free Chosun (RFC) begun broadcasts on SW on 5 December 2005. Produced by the NGO "Network for North Korean Democracy and Human Rights" (NKnet). The project is funded through U.S. Government / U.S. Congress grants. On November 26, 2014, RFC, Open Radio for North Korea (ONK) and the Daily NK made the consortium called the 'Unification Media Group' (UMG)'. RFC changed their name to 'National Unity Radio' in broadcasts since October 22, 2015.

SHIOKAZE (SEA BREEZE)
c/o COMJAN, Dairoku Matsuya Building 301, 3-8, Koraku 2-chome, Bunkyo-ku, Tokyo 112-0004, Japan.
☎ +81 3 56845058. 🖹 +81 3 56845059.
E: chosakai@circus.ocn.ne.jp **W:** www.chosa-kai.jp/SWR.html
Webcast: D (very limited archive)
L.P: Dir, COMJAN & Producer/Editor: Tatsuru Murao.
kHz: 5990, 7400

Winter Schedule 2015/2016
Chinese	Days	Area	kHz
1300-1330	m......	KRE	7400yam*
1600-1630	m......	KRE	5990yam*
English	**Days**	**Area**	**kHz**
1300-1400	...t...	KRE	7400yam*
1600-1700	...t...	KRE	5990yam*
Japanese	**Days**	**Area**	**kHz**
1300-1330	.....s	KRE	7400yam*
1300-1400	.t.....	KRE	7400yam*
1330-1400	....s	KRE	7400yam*
1600-1630	.....s	KRE	5990yam*
1600-1700	.t.....	KRE	5990yam*
1630-1700	....s	KRE	5990yam*
Korean	**Days**	**Area**	**kHz**
1300-1330	.....s.	KRE	7400yam*
1300-1400	..w.f..	KRE	7400yam*

Korean	Days	Area	kHz
1330-1400	m.....s	KRE	7400yam*
1600-1630	.....s	KRE	5990yam*
1600-1700	..w.f..	KRE	5990yam*
1630-1700	m.....s	KRE	5990yam*

Key: * Alt freqs: 5910/5955/5975/5985/6070/6085/6110/6135/6165/6185/7220/7240/7245/7260/7435.
Ann: Chinese: "Zheshi Shiokaze, Chaofeng Bosong"; English: "JSR. This is Shiokaze, Sea Breeze, the shortwave radio programme from Tokyo, Japan. This programme is broadcast by the Japanese private organisation COMJAN"; Japanese: "JSR, Kochirawa Shiokaze desu"; Korean: "Yeogineun Shiokaze, Badatbaramimnida".
V: QSL-card. (Issued if a $10 (US) money order donation is sent together with report)
Notes: Operational since 20 October 2006, produced by the "Investigation Commission on Missing Japanese Probably Related to North Korea" (COMJAN). Aimed at reaching Japanese citizens believed to have been abducted to North Korea. Jammed. Frequencies subject to change without notice. Chinese is broadcast, irregularly, twice a month.

VOICE OF FREEDOM
1, 3-ga, Yongsan-dong, Yongsan-gu, Seoul, Republic of Korea.
+82 2 7484662.
SW: [UIW] Suwon, Uiwang, Gyonggi-do Prefecture: 1 x10kW (presumed)
FM/DAB: FM: 101.7MHz (Baengnyeongdo), 103.1MHz (Ganghwado/Daeamsan), 107.3MHz (Hwaaksan), all in Republic of Korea.
kHz: 6135

Winter Schedule 2015/2016
Korean	Days	Area	kHz
0300-0500	daily	KRE	6135uiw*
0800-2000	daily	KRE	6135uiw*
2100-2400	daily	KRE	6135uiw*

Key: * Jammed.
Ann: Korean: "Yeogineun Jayu-eui Sori Bang-imnida".
Notes: Station re-activated on 24 May 2010 on FM and in 2013 on SW. Reported to be administered by the Republic of Korea Government Defense Department. 6135kHz has been added since 1 May, 2014. Claiming to be broadcast from Seoul, Republic of Korea. Operates to the following daily schedule, in Korean, targeting the Democratic People's Republic of Korea: 0300-0500, 0800-2000 and 2100-2400 on 101.7MHz, 103.1MHz and 107.3MHz FM and SW.

ECHO OF HOPE (VOH) (Clan)
c/o National Intelligence Service (NIS), Seongnam, Sinchondong, Seoul, Rep. of Korea.
W: www.nis.go.kr (NIS); eng.nis.go.kr (NIS, English)
SW: [SUW] Suwon, Osan, Gyonggi-do Prefecture: 4 x 100kW.
kHz: 3985, 6003, 6250, 6348

Winter Schedule 2015/2016
Korean	Days	Area	kHz
0600-2400	daily	KRE	3985suw, 6003suw, 6250suw, 6348suw

Ann: Korean: "Huimang-e meari pangsong-imnida, VOH".
Notes: Echo of Hope (alternative translation: Voice of Hope - VOH) was broadcast under the name "The Voice of Reunification" prior to 1973. Operated by the South Korean National Intelligence Service (NIS), though claiming to be a prgr of the (non-existent) "General Union of Overseas Compatriots". Jammed. Since Feb 2014 a 2nd transmitter site, in an unknown location, has been used for the 3985, 6260 and 6348kHz transmissions.

FREE NORTH KOREA RADIO (Clan)
#208, Daeryong Dream Tower 1-cha, 684-3 Deungchon-dong, Gangseo-gu, Seoul, 157-930, Republic of Korea.
+82 2 26990977. +82 2 26990978.
E: mini6915@hanmail.net **W:** www.fnkradio.com
Webcast: D
L.P: Dir: Kim Seong Min.
kHz: 9470

Winter Schedule 2015/2016
Korean	Days	Area	kHz
1200-1300	daily	KRE	9470tac

Ann: Korean: "Daehan Minguk Seoul-eso bonaeneun Jayu Bukhan Bangsong-imnida".
V: QSL-letter.
Notes: Founded on 20 April 2004 by North Korean defectors, on SW since 7 December 2005. Produced by the "North Korea People's Liberation Front" (NKPLF).

FREEDOM FM RADIO (Clan)
c/o National Intelligence Service (NIS), Seongnam, Sinchondong, Seoul, Republic of Korea.
W: www.nis.go.kr (NIS); en.nis.go.kr (NIS, English)
FM/DAB: FM: 94.5MHz, 97.7MHz, 100.6MHz, 103.1MHz, All presumed to be in South Korea, near to the DMZ.
Notes: Station was first heard in May, 1999 and confirmed the name on 15 June, 2004. Broadcasting in Korean and targeting North Korea: 0600-0300. Operated by the South Korean National Intelligence Service (NIS), though claiming to be a prgr of the (non-existent) "Young Men's Hangyeore Fellowship Association (Hangyeore Sarang Cheongnyen Moim)", until around 2014.

NORTH KOREA REFORM RADIO (Clan)
290-96, Sindang 6-dong, Jung-gu, Seoul 100-824, Republic of Korea.
+82 2 22426512. +82 2 22426512.
E: nkreform@naver.com **W:** www.nkreform.com
Webcast: D
L.P: Pres: Kim Seung Cheol.
kHz: 7590

Winter Schedule 2015/2016
Korean	Days	Area	kHz
1430-1530	daily	KRE	7590tac

Ann: Korean: "Inmini baraneun saeroun sesang-ul hamgge ggumgguneun Joseon Gyaehyeok Bangsong-imnida".
V: QSL-card.
Notes: On SW since December 2007. Produced by the NGO "North Korea Reform Institute" (NKRI). The project is funded through U.S. government / U.S. Congress grants.

OPEN RADIO FOR NORTH KOREA (Clan)
P.O. Box 158, Mapo-dong, Mapo-gu, Seoul, 121-600, Republic of Korea.
+82 505 4707470; +82 10 71512785. +82 505 4717470.
E: nkradio@nkradio.org; nkradio@naver.com; opennk@naver.com
W: www.nkradio.org; english.nkradio.org
Webcast: D/L (L: www.chmbc.co.kr (MBC Chuncheon), 1900-2000 broadcast only)
L.P: Pres: Young Howard (Tae Kung Ha).
MW: Relayed via MBC Chuncheon, Republic of Korea.
FM/DAB: FM: Broadcast from MBC Chuncheon, Republic of Korea: HLAN-FM 92.3MHz 3kW.
kHz: 774

Winter Schedule 2015/2016
Korean	Days	Area	kHz
1800-1955	daily	KRE	774chc

Ann: Korean: "Jayue gwangjang, huimang-e sori, Yeollin Bukhan Bangsong-imnida".
Notes: On air since 7 December 2005, targeting listeners in North Korea and the Korean minority in the NE of P.R.China. The project is funded thru U.S. Government / U.S. Congress grants.

RADIO FREE KOREA (Clan)
c/o National Intelligence Service (NIS), Seongnam, Sinchondong, Seoul, Rep. of Korea.
W: www.nis.go.kr (NIS); en.nis.go.kr (NIS, English)
MW: [GOY] Goyang, Gyonggi-do Prefecture. Power unknown (est 100kW).
kHz: 1143

Winter Schedule 2015/2016
Korean	Days	Area	kHz
1200-2100	daily	KRE	1143goy

Ann: Korean: "Radio Free Korea"; "RFK"; "Eseo Bonae Deulin Radio Free Korea Jayu Koria Bangsong Eul Deul-eu Syeossseubnida".
Notes: Radio Free Korea was first heard on 4 July, 2014. Operated by the South Korean National Intelligence Service (NIS), though claiming to be a prgr of the (non-existent) "Korea Future Solidarity".

VOICE OF THE PEOPLE (Clan)
Based in, and transmitted from, Republic of Korea.
SW: [GOY] Goyang, Gyeonggi-do: 6 x 50kW (presumed power).
kHz: *3480, 3912, 4450, 4557, 6518, 6600*

Winter Schedule 2015/2016

Korean	Days	Area	kHz
0530-2330	daily	KRE	3480goy, 3912goy, ‡4450goy, 4557goy, 6518goy, 6600goy

Ann: Korean: "Inmin-e sori pangsong-imnida".
Notes: On air since June 1985. Claims to be run by the Korean Workers Union, but is operated by the South Korean National Intelligence Service. Jammed.

Target: KOREA, Rep. of (KOR)

ECHO OF UNIFICATION (TONG–IL–E MEARI PANGSONG) (Clan)
Pyongyang, Democratic People's Republic of Korea.
W: www.tongilvoice.com
Webcast: D/P
MW/SW: Uses txs provided by the Ministry of Post & Telecommunications.
FM/DAB: FM: 97.8MHz Haeju (D.P.R. Korea) 10kW (Tx provided by the Ministry of Post & Telecommunications).
kHz: *684, 1080, 3964, 6250*

Winter Schedule 2015/2016

Korean	Days	Area	kHz
0430-0630	daily	KOR	684sag±, 1080hju, 3964chj±,†, 6250pyo
1230-1430	daily	KOR	684sag±, 1080hju, 3964chj±,†, 6250pyo
2230-0030	daily	KOR	684sag±, 1080hju, 3964chj±,†, 6250pyo

Key: ± Variable frequency; † Irregular.
Ann: Korean: "Yeogineun Tong-il-e Meari Pangsong-imnida".
IS: "We Are One".
Notes: The station has been operated by 'Committee for the Peaceful Reunification of the Fatherland' since Dec. 1, 2012. 3970kHz is also announced, but not confirmed in use, yet. The FM broadcasts follow the same schedule as MW/SW.

Target: MALAYSIA (MLA)

RADIO FREE SARAWAK
Based in London, United Kingdom.
☎ +60 82 237191. (Malaysia)
E: info@radiofreesarawak.org **W:** radiofreesarawak.org
Webcast: D
L.P: Founder/Executive Editor: Clare Rewcastle Brown.
SAT: Palapa D.
kHz: *15420*

Winter Schedule 2015/2016

Iban	Days	Area	kHz
1030-1200	mtwtf..	MLA	15420pug±

Key: ± Variable frequency.
Ann: Iban: "Radio Free Sarawak".
V: QSL-email.
Notes: On air since November 2010. Oppositional prgr for listeners in rural Sarawak. Linked with Sarawak tycoon and former MP S'ng Chee Hua.

Target: NIGERIA (NIG)

MANARA RADIO (Rlg)
Based in Abuja, Nigeria.
☎ +234 909 4440403.
E: Manaratv1@gmail.com
W: www.facebook.com/ManaraRadio; www.manaratv.com
Webcast: L

L.P: Chmn, JIBWIS: Skeikh Bala Lau.
kHz: *15440, 17765*

Winter Schedule 2015/2016

Hausa	Days	Area	kHz
0730-0830	daily	NIG	15440iss
1600-1700	daily	NIG	17765iss

Notes: Produced by the religious broadcasting company Manara Radio & Television, initiated by the Nigerian Islamic organization JIBWIS (Jama'atu Izalatul Bidah Wa Iqamatis Sunnah).

DANDAL KURA (Clan)
c/o Freedom Radio, Freedom House, Plot 47, Sharada Industrial Estate, Kano, 700234, Nigeria.
☎ +234 64 942777. 📠 +234 64 660907.
E: via website (dandalkura.com) **W:** dandalkura.com; www.facebook.com/dandalkura; freedomradionig.com (Freedom R.)
Webcast: D
L.P: GM/Editor-in-Chief (Freedom R.): Umar Saidu Tudunwada.
kHz: *7415, 12050, 15480*

Winter Schedule 2015/2016

Kanuri	Days	Area	kHz
0500-0700	daily	NIG	7415asc
0700-0800	daily	NIG	15480wof
1800-2100	daily	NIG	12050asc

Notes: Funded by the USAID and produced by Freedom Radio, an independent local radio network in Northern Nigeria and VOA affiliate, owned by Film Lab & Production Services Ltd. Target audience is the Kanuri and Hausa speaking population affected by Boko Haram in Nigeria, Chad, Niger and Cameroon. On SW since January 2015. Dandal Kura translates as "meeting place".

RADIO BIAFRA ‡ (Clan)
Community Hall, Homerton High St, London E9 6BP. United Kingdom.
☎ +44 2081339976
E: Via website. **W:** www.radiobiafra.co
Webcast: D/L
L.P: Dir: Nnamdi Kanu.
Key: ‡ Inactive at time of publication (Broadcasts reported to have been forcefully terminated).
Ann: English: "This is Radio Biafra".
IS: Anthem: "All Hail Biafra".
Notes: Opposition station. Produced by "Indegenous People of Biafra (IPOB)".

Target: PAKISTAN (PAK)

RADIO SEDAYEE KASHMIR (Clan)
c/o All India Radio (AIR), Akashvani Bhavan, Sansad Marg, New Delhi-110001, India.
kHz: *4870, 6100*

Winter Schedule 2015/2016

Dogri	Days	Area	kHz
0310-0330	daily	PAK	4870del
0810-0830	daily	PAK	6100del
1510-1530	daily	PAK	4870del
Kashmiri	**Days**	**Area**	**kHz**
0230-0310	daily	PAK	4870del
0730-0810	daily	PAK	6100del
1430-1510	daily	PAK	4870del

Ann: Urdu: "Ye Radio Sedayee Kashmir".
Notes: On air since early 2003. Radio Sedayee Kashmir is a prgr representing the views of the Indian government in the dispute with Pakistan over Kashmir.

Target: RWANDA (RRW)

RADIO INYABUTATU
☎ +44 20 32875143. (UK)
E: editor@radioinyabutatu.com; admin@radioinyabutatu.com

W: www.radioinyabutatu.com
Webcast: L
kHz: *17605*

Winter Schedule 2015/2016

Kinyarwanda	Days	Area	kHz
1600-1700	.....s.	RRW	17605iss

Notes: Internet radio station of the oppositional group "Rwandanese Protocol to Return the Kingdom" (RPRK). On SW since 31 August 2013.

Target: SOMALIA (SOM)

RADIO ERGO
✉ P.O.Box 2234, 00621 Nairobi, Kenya.
☎ +254 20 4002102.
E: info@radioergo.org **W:** www.radioergo.org
Webcast: D/P
✉ Nørregade 18, DK-1165 København K, Denmark. (IMS)
☎ +45 88327000. 🖷 +45 33120099.
E: info@mediasupport.org **W:** www.mediasupport.org
L.P: Exec. Dir, IMS: Jesper Højberg.
kHz: *17845*

Winter Schedule 2015/2016

Somali	Days	Area	kHz
1200-1300	daily	SOM	17845dha

Ann: Somali: "Halkalee Walanta Somalia Radio Ergo".
Notes: Produced by IMS Productions Aps (a branch of IMS - International Media Support). Originally aired under the name "IRIN Radio" by the UN Office for the Coordination of Humanitarian Affairs (OCHA) since 2008. IMS Productions took over the operation on 1 July 2011 and rebranded the service "Radio Ergo".

VOICE OF KHAATUMO
✉ Based in London, United Kingdom.
☎ +44 330 3326522 (UK); +1 712 4322943 (USA & Canada).
E: info@voiceofkhaatumo.com **W:** voiceofkhaatumo.com
kHz: *17580*

Winter Schedule 2015/2016

Arabic	Days	Area	kHz
1700-1730	mtwtf..	SOM	17580iss

Key: D
Ann: Somali: "Codka Khaatumo".
Notes: On SW since late October 2014.

Target: SOUTH SUDAN (SSD)

RADIO MIRAYA ‡
✉ See National Radio Section.
Webcast: D/L (www.radiomiraya.org)
Key: ‡ Inactive at time of publication.
Ann: English: "Radio Miraya".

Target: SUDAN (SDN)

RADIO DABANGA
✉ c/o Free Press Unlimited, Weesperstraat 3, 1018 DN Amsterdam, The Netherlands.
☎ +31 20 80000470.
E: radiodabanga@gmail.com **W:** www.radiodabangasudan.org
Webcast: D
W: www.freepressunlimited.org
L.P: Dir: Hildebrand Bijleveld.
kHz: *7315, 13800, 15550*

Winter Schedule 2015/2016

Arabic (Darfuri)	Days	Area	kHz
0430-0530	daily	SDN	15550mdc±
0430-0600	daily	SDN	7315smg±
0530-0600	daily	SDN	15550smg±
1530-1600	daily	SDN	13800mdc±
1530-1630	daily	SDN	15550smg±
1600-1630	daily	SDN	13800smg±

Key: ± Frequencies may be varied to avoid jamming.
Ann: All languages: "Radio Dabanga".
V: QSL-card.
Notes: On air since 15 November 2008, produced by the Dutch NGO "Press Unlimited" (a merger of the NGOs "Press Now" and "Free Voice"). Radio Dabanga is aimed at listeners in the Darfur area in Western Sudan. The broadcasts are in Standard Arabic, Darfuri Arabic, Fur, Masalit and Zaghawa.

RADIO TAMAZUJ
✉ c/o Free Press Unlimited, Weesperstraat 3, 1018 DN Amsterdam, The Netherlands.
☎ +31 20 8000400. 🖷 +31 20 7173648.
E: info@freepressunlimited.org **W:** radiotamazuj.org
Webcast: D
L.P: Dir: Hildebrand Bijleveld.
kHz: *7315, 9600, 13800, 15400, 15550*

Winter Schedule 2015/2016

Arabic	Days	Area	kHz
0400-0430	daily	SDN	7315smg±, 9600iss±, 15550mdc±
1500-1530	daily	SDN	13800mdc±, 15400iss±, 15550smg±

Key: ± Frequencies may be varied to avoid jamming.
Notes: Produced by the Dutch foundation "Free Press Unlimited". Daily broadcasts began in January 2012 and targets audiences in The Republic of Sudan and Republic of Southern Sudan, with an emphasis on the conflict affected regions.

Target: SYRIA (SYR)

AL-BAYAN RADIO (Clan)
FM/DAB: FM: 89.4MHz Mosul plus another, as yet unknown frequency, in Fallujah (both Iraq); 99.9MHz Raqqa (Syria) and 95.5MHz in Dema (Libya).
Ann: Arabic: "Idha'at Al-Bayan".
Notes: 'Islamic State of Iraq and the Levant (ISIL, ISIS or IS)' backed news bulletins, targetting Islamic State supporters in Iraq and Syria. Broadcasts in Arabic, Russian and English.

Target: TURKEY (TUR)

DENGÊ KURDISTANÊ
✉ Stiftelsen Kurdisk Media, Tre Kronors väg 33, S-13131 Nacka, Sweden.
☎ +46 8 6562038. 🖷 +46 8 6567919.
E: info@denge-kurdistane.com **W:** www.denge-kurdistane.com
Webcast: D/L
kHz: *9400*

Winter Schedule 2015/2016

Kurdish	Days	Area	kHz
0400-0800	daily	ME	9400kch
0800-1200	daily	ME	9400erv
1200-1500	daily	ME	9400kch
1500-1700	daily	ME	9400sof
1700-2000	daily	ME	9400iss
2000-2200	daily	ME	9400kch

Ann: Kurdish: "Era Dengê Kurdistanê".
Notes: Dengê Kurdistanê ("Voice of Kurdistan") is produced under the roof of the foundation Kurdisk Media. The prgr was launched on 1 Sep 2012 (on shortwave since 7 Sep), replacing Dengê Mezopotamya. The station broadcasts in various Kurdish dialects and is targeting Kurdish listeners across the Near East (Turkey, Iran, Iraq, Syria).

Target: VIETNAM (VTN)

QUÊ ME RADIO
✉ BP 60063, F-94472 Boissy Saint Léger Cedex, France.
☎ +33 145983085. 🖷 +33 145983261.

E: queme.democracy@gmail.com; queme@free.fr
W: www.queme.net
Webcast: D
kHz: *9930*

	Winter Schedule 2015/2016		
Vietnamese	Days	Area	kHz
1200-1230	....f..	VTN	9930hbn

V: QSL-email.
Notes: Produced by the non-profit organisation "Action for Democracy in Vietnam" and its international organ "Vietnam Committee on Human Rights".

RADIO DLSN

Vietnam Democracy Radio, P.O. Box 612882, San Jose, CA 95161, USA.
☎ +1 408 6639860.
E: lienlac.dlsn@gmail.com
W: radiodlsn.com; www.facebook.com/radiodlsn
Webcast: D
W: www.thedemocracyforvietnam.org (The Democracy for Vietnam Foundation)
kHz: *1503*

	Winter Schedule 2015/2016		
Vietnamese	Days	Area	kHz
1430-1500	daily	SEA	1503fan

Ann: Vietnamese: "Đây là đây phát thanh Đáp Lời Sông Núi".
Notes: On air since 15 May 2011. The airtime for the MW transmissions of Radio DLSN (Đáp Lời Sông Núi - "Fatherland") is booked with assistance of the UK-based "The Democracy for Vietnam Foundation".

Target: WESTERN SAHARA (AOE)

NATIONAL RADIO OF THE SAHARAN ARAB DEMOCRATIC REPUBLIC

BP 470, 37000 Tindouf, Algeria.
☎ +213 49 923525.
Webcast: D
c/o Mission de la R.A.S.D., BP 10, El Mouradia, 16000 Algiers, Algeria.
MW: [RBN] Rabouni (Algeria): 1550kHz 50kW (estimated power).
SW: [RBN] Rabouni (Algeria): 1 x 20kW. ‡
kHz: *1550*

	Winter Schedule 2015/2016		
Arabic	Days	Area	kHz
1800-2330	daily	NAf	1550rbn†
Spanish	Days	Area	kHz
1700-1800	daily	NAf	1550rbn†

Key: † Irregular.
Ann: Arabic: "Huna el-estudiohaay al-markaziya al-wataniya, Sowt al-sha'ab a-Sahraui al-mukafa"; Spanish: "Ésta es la Radio Nacional de la República Arabe Saharaui Democrática".
V: QSL-letter.
Notes: On air since 28 December 1975, founded by the "Polisario Front". Operated by the Ministry of Information of the government-in-exile of the Sahrawi Arab Democratic Republic, with approval by the Algerian authorities. Jammed.

Target: ZIMBABWE (ZWE)

RADIO DIALOGUE ‡

Box FM 100, Famona, Bulawayo, Zimbabwe.
☎ +263 9 884858. 🖷 +263 9 884828.
E: radio@radiodialogue.com; radio@radiodialogue.co.zw
W: www.radiodialogue.com
Physical address: 9th Floor, Pioneer House, Corner 8th Ave / Fife Street, Bulawayo, Zimbabwe.
W: www.zacraszim.org (ZACRAS)
LP: Dir: Mrs. Debra Mabunda; Dir (ZACRAS): Henry Masuku.
Key: ‡ Inactive at time of publication.
Ann: English: "Radio Dialogue - giving you a voice".
Notes: Produced by the Zimbabwe Association of Community Radio Stations (ZACRAS).

Religious Broadcasters Cross Reference Table

This table shows the names of religious broadcasters in the International Radio and COTB sections, together with a cross reference to enable the station and/or schedule to be looked up, by country. Where '✓' appears in the **Admin/Relay** column, this means that the entry contains corporate details of the broadcaster and is usually the company HQ. If the word '**Relay**' appears in that column, this indicates that this is just a transmitting site, the schedule can be found under the parent station, as indicated. '✗' indicates that the schedule is located elsewhere (such as a regional outlet), the HQ/Admin station entry will give details of where these schedules are listed. '‡' indicates a broadcaster that was inactive at editorial deadline (and, therefore, will not have a schedule).

Station Name	Country	Code	Schedule	Admin/Relay	Section
Adventist World Radio (AWR)	United States of America	USA	✗	✓	International Radio
Athmik Yatra Radio	India	IND	✓		International Radio
Awr Africa/europe	United Kingdom	G	✓		International Radio
AWR Asia/pacific	Indonesia	INS	✓		International Radio
Bible Voice Broadcasting (BVB)	Canada	CAN	✓		International Radio
Christian Science Herald	United States of America	USA	✓		International Radio
CVC The Voice Asia	United Kingdom	G	✓		International Radio
Electronic Bible Fellowship (Meiguo Binzhou Dianzi Shengjing Tuanqi)	United States of America	USA	✓		International Radio
Eternal Good News	United States of America	USA	✓		International Radio
Evangelische Missions-Gemeinden	Germany	D	✓		International Radio
Family Radio	United States of America	USA	✓		International Radio
Far East Broadcasting Company Inc (FEBC)	United States of America	USA	✗	✓	International Radio
FEBA India	India	IND	✓		International Radio
FEBA Radio	United Kingdom	G	✗	✓	International Radio
FEBC Korea	Korea, Rep. Of	KOR	✓		International Radio
FEBC Philippines	Philippines	PHL	✓		International Radio
HCJB - La Voz De Los Andes	Ecuador	EQA	✓		International Radio
Ibra Radio	Sweden	S	✓		International Radio
KJES Radio	United States of America	USA	✓		International Radio
KNLS International	Alaska	ALS	✓		International Radio
KSDA (AWR Asia/Pacific Relay Station)	Guam	GUM	✗	Relay	International Radio
KTWR(TWR Relay Station)	Guam	GUM	✗	Relay	International Radio
KVOH - Voice Of Hope	United States of America	USA	✓		International Radio
Lutherische Stunde	Germany	D	✓		International Radio
Madagascar World Voice ‡	Madagascar	MDG	✗	✓	International Radio
Missionswerk Heukelbach	Germany	D	✓		International Radio
Pan American Broadcasting	United States of America	USA	✓		International Radio
Radio Freundes-dienst	Switzerland	SUI	✓		International Radio
Radio HCJB Deutschland	Germany	D	✓		International Radio
Radio Payam-e Doost	United States of America	USA	✓		International Radio
Radio Veritas Asia	Philippines	PHL	✓		International Radio
Reach Beyond (ex Hcjb Global Voice)	United States of America	USA	✓		International Radio
Reach Beyond Australia (ex HCJB Global Voice Australia)	Australia	AUS	✓		International Radio
Sawtu Linjiila (Voice of the Gospel)	Cameroon	CME	✓		COTB
Shortwave Relay Service	Kyrgyzstan	KGZ	✓		International Radio
Stimme Des Trostes	Switzerland	SUI	✓		International Radio
Suab Xaa Moo Zoo	United States of America	USA	✓		International Radio
T8WH - World Harvest Radio (WHR)	Palau	PLW	✓		International Radio
Tartu Pereraadio	Estonia	EST	✗	✓	International Radio
The Overcomer Ministry	United States of America	USA	✓		International Radio
Trunews Radio	United States of America	USA	✓		International Radio
TWR	United States of America	USA	✗	✓	International Radio
TWR Africa	South Africa	AFS	✓		International Radio
TWR Asia	Singapore	SNG	✓		International Radio
TWR Bonaire	Bonaire	BES	✓		International Radio
TWR Europe	Austria	AUT	✓		International Radio
TWR India	India	IND	✓		International Radio
TWR Relay Station	Benin	BEN	✗	Relay	International Radio
TWR Relay Station	Swaziland	SWZ	✗	Relay	International Radio
Unidentified Station	China	CHN	✓		COTB
University Network	United States of America	USA	✓		International Radio
Vatican Radio	Vatican City State	CVA	✓		International Radio
Voice Of Khaatumo	Somalia	SOM	✓		COTB
Voice of the Martyrs	Korea, (D.P.R.)	KRE	✓		COTB
Voice of Wilderness	Korea, (D.P.R.)	KRE	✓		COTB
WEWN - Ewtn Shortwave Radio	United States of America	USA	✓		International Radio
WHRI - World Harvest Radio (WHR)	United States of America	USA	✓		International Radio
WINB	United States of America	USA	✓		International Radio
WJHR Radio International	United States of America	USA	✓		International Radio
WMLK ‡	United States of America	USA	✗	✓	International Radio
World Christian Broadcasting Inc.	United States of America	USA	✗	✓	International Radio
WRNO Worldwide	United States of America	USA	✓		International Radio
WTWW	United States of America	USA	✓		International Radio
WWCR - Worldwide Christian Radio	United States of America	USA	✓		International Radio
WWRB	United States of America	USA	✓		International Radio

FREQUENCY LISTS

Section Contents

Features & Reviews

National Radio

International Radio

Frequency Lists

(For country codes and transmitter codes, please see the decode tables in the Reference section)

Please note that the North America MW listing has been removed in order to increase the number of MW stations in the main USA listing

National Television

Reference

EUROPE, AFRICA & MIDDLE EAST

kHz	kW	Ctry	Station, location
25	300	BLR	STFT Station, Vileyka (CW)
25	300	BLR	STFT Station, Vileyka (CW)
	900	RUS	STFT Station, 3 stns (CW)
60	15	G	STFT Station, Anthorn (CW)
66.66	10	RUS	STFT Station, Moscow (AM)
77.5	50	D	STFT Station, Mainflingen (CW/PSK)
153	2000/1000	ALG	R. Algérienne 1, Béchar (low power)
	100	NOR	NRK P1/Troms og Finnmark, Ingøy
	200	ROU	Antena Satelor, Brasov
162	2000/1000	F	France Inter, Allouis
171	1600	MRC	Medi 1, Nador
177	150	D	R. Andernach, Zehlendorf (DRM tests)
183	2000	D	Europe 1, Felsberg
189	300	ISL	RUV Rás 1/2, Gufuskálar
198	2000/1000	ALG	R. Algérienne 1, Ouargla (low power)
	50	G	BBC R4, Burghead
	500	G	BBC R4, Droitwich
	50	G	BBC R4, Westerglen
207	100	ISL	RUV Rás 1/2, Eidar
	400	MRC	SNRT National Netw, Azilal
216	900	F	RMC Info, Roumoules
225	1000	POL	Polskie R. 1, Solec Kujawski
234	1500	LUX	RTL, Beidweiler
243	50	DNK	DR P4 news & weather, Kalundborg
252	1500/750	ALG	R. Algérienne 3, Tipaza
	300	IRL	RTE Radio 1, Summerhill (Clarkstown)
270	50	CZE	CRo 1, Uherské Hradište
279	500	BLR	BR 1, Sasnovy
531	600	ALG	R. Algérienne Jil FM, F'Kirina
	10	ARS	SBC Quran prgr, Bisha
	50	BOT	R. Botswana, Maun
	10	E	RNE R. 5, Cordoba
	20	E	RNE R. 5, Oviedo
	10	E	RNE R. 5, Pamplona
	10	E	RNE R. 5, Pontevedra
	15	FRO	Kringvarp Føroya Útvarpið, Akraberg
	0.001	G	RSLs
	500	IRN	IRIB R. Iran, Azarshahr
	600	IRN	IRIB R. Iran, Iranshahr
	50	ISR	KI Reshet Alef, Yavne
	0.8	POL	Twoje R, Wlodawa
	15	ROU	Antena Satelor, Urziceni
	15	ROU	R. România Actualitati, Petrosani
540	100	AFS	Sport 540 AM, Gauteng (F.P.I.)
	50	E	OCR Catalunya, Barcelona
	1000	HNG	MR Kossuth R, Solt
	200	IRN	IRIB R. Iran, Mashhad
	600	KWT	R. Kuwait Main prgr, Kabd
	600	MRC	SNRT National Netw./Reg, Sidi Bennour
	10	MWI	MBC R. 1, Mangochi
	50	NIG	Sokoto State BC "Rima R. ", Sokoto
	50	SDN	South Darfur State R, Nyala
549	600	ALG	R. Algérienne 1/R. Ouargla, Sidi Hamadouche
	51	ARS	SBC R. Riyadh, Qurayyat +3 stns
	20	GAB	RTG 2, Oyem
	25	IRL	Spirit R, Carrickroe
	400/100	IRN	IRIB R. Iran, Sirjan
	25	NIG	Broadc. Sce of the Ekiti State, Ado
	10	RKS	RTK R. Kosova, Prishtinë (inactive)
	15	SVN	R. Koper, Beli Kriz
	500	UKR	UR1, Mykolaiv
558	10	ALG	R. Algérienne 1/R. Ouargla, Touggourt
	5	ARS	SBC Quran prgr, Abha
	50	BOT	R. Botswana, Muchenje
	20	E	RNE R. 5, A Coruña
	20	E	RNE R. 5, San Sebastián
	50	E	RNE R. 5, Valencia
	100	EGY	ERTU Educ. prgr, Cairo (Abu Zaabal)
	1	G	Spectrum Radio, London
	1000	IRN	IRIB R. Farhang, Gheslagh
	25	KEN	KBC Western Sce, Kapsimotwa
	10	MWI	MBC R. 1, Karonga
	500	OMA	R. Sultanate of Oman, Bidiya
	400	ROU	R. Românía Actualitati, Tirgu Jiu
		SSD	South Sudan R, Bentiu (inactive)
	10	SVN	MMR / R. Slovenija 1, Nemcavci
567	25	AFS	Cape Talk, Cape Town
	15	ARS	SBC Quran prgr, Afif
	200	ARS	SBC Quran prgr, Jeddah (Bahrah)
	50	E	RNE R. 5, Murcia
	1	I	Challenger R, Villa Estense
	50	KEN	KBC R. Taifa, Garissa
	50	NIG	FRCN Ibadan, Alaho
	50	NIG	Imo BC, Owerri
	100	ROU	R. Românía Actualitati, Brasov/Satu Mare
	300	SYR	Syrian R. 1, Damascus Adra
576	50	AFS	R. Veritas, Meyerton
	400/200	ALG	R. Algérienne R. Béchar
	20	ARS	SBC Quran prgr, Gizan (Ahawagerh)
	400	BUL	Horizont/Turkish Sce, Vidin Gramada
	20	CNR	RNE R. Nacional, Las Palmas
	100	E	RNE R. 5, Barcelona
	50	IRN	IRIB R. Urmia, Maku
	600	IRN	VOIRI, Mahshahr
	25	NIG	FRCN Ibadan, Moniya
	100	OMA	R. Sultanate of Oman, Haima
	100	UGA	UBC West/Star FM, Mityana
584	5	AFG	R. Badakhsan, Faizabad (inactive)
585	1200	ARS	SBC R. Riyadh, Riyadh
	5	CVA	Vatican R, Vatican City
	600	E	RNE R. Nacional, Madrid
	2	G	BBC R. Scotland, Dumfries
	600	IRN	IRIB R. Quran, Tehran
	350	TUN	ERTT National prgr, Gafsa
	50	TZA	Zanzibar BC, Chumbuni
594	5	AFG	R. Faryab, Maimana
	2000	ARS	SBC R. Riyadh, Duba + 1 stn
	50	ARS	SBC R. Riyadh/Pilgrimage prgr, Makkah
	100	ETH	R. Ethiopia, Bahir Dar
	100	IRN	IRIB R. Iran, Zahedan
	30	MWI	MBC R. 1, Lilongwe
	200	NIG	FRCN Kaduna, Jaji
595	50	MRC	SNRT A/R, Oujda (alt. on 594kHz)
603	100	CYP	CyBC 3, Nicosia
	10	E	RNE R. 5, Palencia
	50	E	RNE R. 5, Sevilla
	50	EGY	ERTU Koran prgr, Sohag
	2	G	BBC R. 4, Newcastle
	0.4	G	Smooth R, Littlebourne
	400	IRN	IRIB R. Fars, Shiraz (Dehnow)
	10	IRN	IRIB R. Mashhad, Bajgiran
	50	NIG	Borno R. & TV Corp, Maiduguri
	25	NIG	Ogun State BC, Abeokuta
	30	ROU	Antena Satelor, Bucuresti
	100	ROU	R. Românía Actualitati, Botosani/Oradea
	15	ROU	R. Românía Actualitati, Drobeta-T. Severin
	100/10	TZA	TBC Taifa, Dodoma
612	20	ARS	SBC Quran prgr, Al-Aflaj/Hail
	100	BHR	R. Bahrain Quran prgr, Manama
	10	E	RNE R. Nacional, Lleida
	10	E	RNE R. Nacional, Vitoria
	600	IRN	VOIRI, Qasr-e-Shirin
	100	JOR	R. Jordan Main prgr, Shobak
	100	KEN	KBC R. Taifa, Ngong
	300	MRC	SNRT National Netw, Sebaa-Aioun
	50	NIG	Kwara State BC, Ilorin

kHz	kW	Ctry	Station, location
	20	RUS	R. Radonezh/Narodnoye R., Kurkino (Moskva)
621	200	AFG	BBG Deewa R. /R. Mashal, Khost
	300	BEL	RTBF International, Wavre
	100	BOT	R. Botswana, Selebi-Phikwe
	100	CNR	RNE R. Nacional, Santa Cruz de Tenerife
	10	E	RNE R. Nacional, Avila
	10	E	RNE R. Nacional, Jaén
	10	E	RNE R. Nacional, Palma de Mallorca
	1000	EGY	ERTU VO Arabs, Batra (Al-Mansura)
	200	IRN	IRIB R. Birjand, Birjand (Bojd)
	50	IRN	IRIB R. Khalij e Fars, Bandar Abbas
	150	MDA	Pridnestrovskaya GTRK R. 1, Grigoriopol
630	10	ARS	SBC Quran prgr, Najran
	20	ARS	SBC R. Jeddah, Gizan
	2	G	BBC R. Cornwall, Redruth
	0.2	G	BBC Three Counties R, Luton
	10	KWT	R. Kuwait Quran prgr, Kuwait city
	50	MDG	RNM, Antananarivo (irreg.)
	12	POR	RTP Antena 1, Montemor-o-Velho/ Miranda da Douro
	50	ROU	Antena Satelor, Voinesti
	400	ROU	R. Timisoara/R. R. Act, Ortisoara
	300	TUN	ERTT National prgr, Tunis Djedeida
	300	TUR	TRT 1/VOT, Mersin Kazanli
639	500	CYP	BBC Arabic Sce, Zakaki (Ladies Mile)
	780	CZE	CRo 2/CRo Plus, Praha (Liblice) + Ostrava
	300	E	RNE R. Nacional, A Coruña
	10	E	RNE R. Nacional, Albacete
	20	E	RNE R. Nacional, Almeria
	50	E	RNE R. Nacional, Bilbao
	50	E	RNE R. Nacional, Zaragoza
	400	IRN	VOIRI, Bonab
	50	KEN	KBC Somali Sce, Garissa
	100	LSO	LNBS R. Lesotho, Lancer's Gap
	50	NIG	Kaduna State Media Corp, Katabu
	100	OMA	R. Sultanate of Oman, Buraimi
	10	SDN	North Kordofan State R, Al-Ubayyid
648	2000	ARS	SBC R. Riyadh, Jeddah Khumra (low power)
	50	BOT	R. Botswana, Mopipi
	50	E	RNE R. Nacional, Badajoz
	50	IRN	IRIB R. Iran, Sefiddasht (Shahrekord)
	10	SVN	R. Murski Val, Nemcavci
	100/10	TZA	TBC Taifa, Nachingwea
657	50	AFS	R. Pulpit/R. Kansel, Meyerton
	20	ARS	SBC Quran prgr, Rafha
	50	E	RNE R. 5, Madrid
	0.5	G	BBC R. Cornwall, Bodmin
	2	G	BBC R. Wales, Wrexham
	100	I	RAI Radiouno/Reg, Pisa
	100	IRN	IRIB R. Gilan, Kiashahr
	100	IRN	IRIB R. Zahedan, Zahedan
	100	ISR	KI Reshet Bet, Yavne
	100	NIG	FRCN Ibadan, Ibadan
	100	TZA	TBC Taifa, Dar es Salaam
	100	UAE	Asianet R, Al-Dhabbiya
	25	UKR	UR3, Chernivtsi
666	10	ALG	R. Algérienne 1/R. Tindouf
	50	E	SER R. Barcelona, Barcelona
	0.5	G	R. York, Fulford
	50	IRN	IRIB R. Iran, Shushtar
	52	POR	RTP Antena 1, 5 stns
	20	REU	R. Réunion, St. Pierre
	10	SDN	Kassala State R, Kassala
	50	SYR	Syrian R. 2, Damascus Adra
675	25	ARS	SBC R. Riyadh, Abha/Afif
	60	IRN	IRIB R. Hamadan, Hamadan
	50	KEN	KBC R. Taifa, Marsabit
	100	LBY	R. Free Libya, Benghazi (inactive)
	50	MWI	MBC R. 1, Ekwendeni
	600	QAT	Qatar RTC, Al Arish
	0.5	SRB	RTS Beograd 1, Bosilegrad
684	200	ARS	SBC R. Jeddah, Jeddah (Bahrah)
	10	ARS	SBC R. Jeddah, Riyadh

kHz	kW	Ctry	Station, location
	200	E	RNE R. Nacional, Sevilla
	100	ETH	R. Ethiopia, Metu
	100	IRN	IRIB R. Mashhad, Mashhad
	10	MAU	MBC R. Maurice, Malherbes
	10	RUS	R. Radonezh, Sankt-Peterburg
	10	SRB	RTS Beograd 1, Aleksinac
	10	TUN	ERTT National prgr, Medenine
693	10	ALG	R. Algérienne 1/R. Adrar, Reggane
	5	ALG	RA 2, Aboudid (Ain el Hammam)
	20	ARS	SBC Quran prgr, Tabuk
	3	AZR	RDP Açores, Santa Barbara
	25	BOT	R. Botswana, Shakawe
	5	E	RNE R. Nacional, Boal
	20	E	RNE R. Nacional, Toledo
	10	E	RNE R. Nacional, Tortosa
	50/1	G	BBC R. 5 Live, 10 stns
	150	G	BBC R. 5 Live, Droitwich
	100	IRN	IRIB R. Khalij e Fars, Bandar Lengeh
	1	SOM	R. Hargeisa, Hargeisa
	0.6	SRB	RTS Beograd 1, Negotin
	40	SSD	South Sudan R, Juba
702	50	AFS	LM Radio, Welgedacht (F.PI.)
	25	ALG	R. Algérienne 1/R. Laghouat
	50	ARS	SBC R. Jeddah, Bisha/Duba
	10	EGY	ERTU Reg./Koran prgr, Asswan
	10	EGY	ERTU Reg./Koran/Sports, El Kharga
	500	IRN	VOIRI, Kiashahr
	800	OMA	BBC Arabic Service, A'Seela
	5	SVK	SR R. Patria/Devín, Kosice
	600	TUR	TRT 1, Istanbul Catalca
711	25	E	COPE Murcia
	100	EGY	ERTU Youth & Sports prgr, Tanta
	400	IRN	IRIB R. Ahvaz, Ahvaz
	300	MRC	SNRT National Netw./R, Laâyoune (‡)
	50	ROU	R. România Actualitati, Sighetul Marmatiei
	0.5	SRB	RTS Beograd 1/R. Niš
	100/10	TZA	TBC Taifa, Kigoma
	40	UKR	UR1, Dokuchaievsk
	200	YEM	YRTC General prgr, San'a
720	400	IRN	VO the Islamic Rep. of Iran, Tayebad
	10	CNR	RNE R. 5, Santa Cruz de Tenerife
	500	CYP	BBC Arabic Sce, Zakaki (Ladies Mile)
	10/0.3	G	BBC R. 4, Lisnagarvey + 2 stns
	750	IRN	IRIB R. Iran, Mahidasht
	400	IRN	IRIB R. Mashhad/VOIRI, Taybad
	50	POR	RTP Antena 1, 5 stns
	40	ROU	R. România Actualitati, Isaccea + 2 stns
	50/10	TZA	TBC Taifa, Mwanza
729	25	AFS	Cape Pulpit, Cape Town
	10	E	RNE R. Nacional, Alicante
	10	E	RNE R. Nacional, Cuenca
	20	E	RNE R. Nacional, Logroño
	20	E	RNE R. Nacional, Málaga
	100	E	RNE R. Nacional, Oviedo
	10	E	RNE R. Nacional, Valladolid
	0.2	G	BBC Essex, Manningtree
	100	GRC	ERT1, Athína Bogiati
	50	NIG	Kano State BC, Jogana
738	5	ALG	R. Algérienne 1/R. Illizi, In Amenas
	600	E	RNE R. Nacional, Barcelona
	0.04	G	BBC Hereford & W, Worcester
	50	IRN	IRIB R. Bushehr, Dayyer
	10	ISR	KI Arabic prgr, Akko (Acre)
	50	MOZ	Antena Nacional, Maputo
	100	OMA	R. Sultanate of Oman, Salalah
	5	RUS	KBS World R. (WRN Rel.), Kurkino (Moskva)
	5	RUS	R. Exterior de España (WRN Rel.), Kurkino (Moskva)
	5	RUS	R. Japan (WRN Rel.), Kurkino (Moskva)
	5	RUS	R. Poland (WRN Rel.), Kurkino (Moskva)
	5	RUS	R. Slovakia Int. (WRN Rel.), Kurkino (Moskva)
747	10	ARS	SBC R. Jeddah, Buraidah

kHz	kW	Ctry	Station, location
	10	ARS	SBC R. Riyadh, Najran
	25	CNR	RNE R. 5, Las Palmas
	10	E	RNE R. 5, Cádiz
	600	IRN	IRIB R. Iran, Gonbad-e Qabus
	150	IRN	IRIB R. Kerman, Sirjan
	100	KEN	KBC Central Sce, Ngong
	60	NIG	Nagarta R, Kaduna
	10	SDN	Khartoum State R, Khartoum
	5	SDN	Red Sea State R, Port Sudan
756	10	EGY	ERTU Reg./Koran prgr, Qena
	2	G	BBC R 4, Redruth
	1	G	R. Cumbria, Carlisle
	3	IRQ	R. Dar as-Salam, Basra
	50	ISR	Galei Tzahal, Metula
	10	MWI	MBC R. 1, Blantyre
	100	NIG	R. Oyo, Ibadan
	2	POR	RTP Antena 1, Lamego
	400	ROU	R. România Actualitati, Lugoj (Boldur)
765	50	ARS	SBC Quran prgr, 3 stns
	0.5	G	BBC Essex, Chelmsford
	600	IRN	IRIB R. Iran/VOIRI, Chabahar
	200/50	IRN	IRIB R. Jahanbin, Shahr-e-Kord
	50	MOZ	EP de Nampula, Nampula
	50	SDN	SRTC General prgr, Omdurman
	0.7	SRB	RTS Beograd 1, Medvedja
	40	UKR	R. Maiak, Odesa (Petrivka)
774	50	AGL	EP de Benguela, Benguela
	40	E	RNE R. Nacional, 4 stns
	60	E	RNE R. Nacional, Cáceres
	20	E	RNE R. Nacional, Ourense
	50	E	RNE R. Nacional, San Sebastián
	100	E	RNE R. Nacional, Valencia
	1000	EGY	ERTU Middle East prgr, Alexandria (Abis)
	1	G	BBC R4, Enniskillen/Plymouth
	0.7	G	R. Kent, Littlebourne
	0.5	G	R. Leeds/BBC Asian Network, Farnley
	0.1	G	Smooth R, Gloucester
	100	IRN	IRIB R. Markazi, Arak
783	5	ALG	R. Algérienne 1/R. Illizi, Djanet
	10	ALG	R. Algérienne 1/R. Souf, El Oued
	100	ARS	SBC Call of Islam, Ras al-Khair
	50	E	COPE, Barcelona
	150	IRN	IRIB R. Zahedan, Iranshahr
	50	MTN	R. Mauritanie, Nouakchott
	5	SDN	River Nile State R, Atbara
	300	SYR	Syrian R. 1/Ext. Sce, Tartus
792	50	ARS	SBC Quran prgr, Jeddah (An Nuziah)
	50	E	SER R. Sevilla
	1	G	BBC R. Foyle, Londonderry
	0.3	G	Smooth R, Bedford
	50	IRN	IRIB R. Zanjan, Sohravard
		IRQ	IMN Republic of Iraq R, Baghdad
801	150	AZE	Azärbaycan R, Haciqabul (Pirsaat)
	100	BHR	R. Bahrain General prgr, Manama
	10	E	RNE R. Nacional, Burgos
	10	E	RNE R. Nacional, Castello
	25	E	RNE R. Nacional, Ciudad Real
	10	E	RNE R. Nacional, Girona
	20	E	RNE R. Nacional, Lugo
	10	E	RNE R. Nacional, Zamora
	100	ETH	VO Amhara State, Bahir Dar
	2	G	R. Devon, Barnstaple
	50	IRN	IRIB R. Mashhad, Kashmar
	1	NIG	R. Kebbi, Zuru
	20	NIG	Yobe BC, Damaturu
810	20	ARS	SBC R. Jeddah, Abha
	20	E	SER R. Madrid
	100	G	BBC R. Scotland, Burghead
	5	G	BBC R. Scotland, Redmoss
	100	G	BBC R. Scotland, Westerglen
	100	IRN	IRIB R. Lorestan, Khorramabad
	5/2.5	IRQ	R. Um al-Qura, Baghdad
	100	MKD	MR1/R. Makedonija, Sveti Nikole
	50	MOZ	EP de Gaza, Xai-Xai
	10	MWI	MBC R. 1, Bangula

kHz	kW	Ctry	Station, location
	50	UAE	Abu Dhabi R, Maqtaa
	200	UAE	Pravasi Bharathi (F.P.I.)
819	1000	EGY	ERTU General prgr, Batra (Al-Mansura)
	30	IRN	IRIB R. Tabaristan, Sari
	10	IRQ	R. Al-Amal, Basra
	10	MAU	MBC R. Mauritius, Malherbes
	10	SDN	Northern State R, Dongola
	7	UKR	R. Bukovyna, Novodnistrovsk
828	25	AFS	Magic 828, Cape Town
	20	ARS	SBC R. Riyadh, Medinah
	1	AZR	RDP Açores, Monte das Cruzes
	5	E	Hit FM Catalunya, Terrassa
	100	ETH	R. Ethiopia, Arba Minch
	0.2	G	BBC Asian Network, Sedgley
	0.1	G	R. Aire 2, Leeds
	0.3	G	Smooth R, Bournemouth
	0.2	G	Smooth R, Luton
	50	IRN	IRIB R. Birjand, Tabas
	100	NIG	FRCN Enugu
	10	RUS	Rgazeta Slovo/Pravoslavnoye R, Skt-P.
	200	SYR	Syrian R. 1, Deir-ez-Zor
	1	UAE	Abu Dhabi R, Al-Ain
837	5	ALG	R. Algérienne 3, Béchar
	10	CNR	COPE Las Palmas, Gran Canaria
	10	E	COPE, Burgos
	5	E	COPE, El Ferrol
	10	E	COPE, Sevilla
	100	ERI	Vo the Broad Masses 2/Ginbot 7 Dimts R., Asmara
	100	ETH	R. Oromiya, Robe (Bale)
	0.5	G	BBC Asian Netw, Freemen's Common
	1	G	R. Cumbria, Barrow
	300	IRN	IRIB R. Isfahan, Habibabad
	1	TZA	TBC Taifa, Dar es Salaam
	30	UKR	R. Bukovyna, Chernivtsi
	150	UKR	UR1, Kharkiv (Taranivka)
838	30	YEM	YRTC General prgr, San'a
840	20	TCD	ONRTV, N'djamena-Gredia (inactive)
846	20	AFS	SABC Umhlobo Wenene FM, Komga
	20	ARS	SBC Quran prgr, Buraida
	1	I	Challenger R, Villa Estense
	1	IRL	R. North, Redcastle
	50	IRN	IRIB R. Tabriz, Mianeh
	20	UAE	Holy Quran R, Umm al Qiwain
855	100	ARS	SBC Quran prgr, Ras al-Khair
	55	E	RNE R. Nacional, 6 stns
	300	E	RNE R. Nacional, Murcia
	20	E	RNE R. Nacional, Pontevedra
	50	E	RNE R. Nacional, Santander
	20	E	RNE R. Nacional, Tarragona
	100	ETH	R. Ethiopia, Harar
	1	G	BBC R. Lancashire, Preston
	1.5	G	BBC R. Norfolk, Postwick
	0.2	G	Sunshine R, Ludlow
	10	JOR	R. Jordan Quran prgr, Amman
	400	ROU	R. România Actualitati, Tancabesti
864	1000	ARM	TWR Europe, Gavar
	10	E	RNE R. Nacional, Socuellamos
	500	EGY	ERTU Koran prgr, Santah
	50	IRN	IRIB R. Kermanshah, Qasr-e Shirin
873	10	ALG	R. Algérienne 1/R. Ghardaïa
	10	ARS	SBC Quran prgr, Ar-Rass
	50	BOT	R. Botswana, Gantsi
	10	E	SER R. Galicia, Stgo. de Compostela
	25	E	SER R. Zaragoza
	100	ETH	R. Ethiopia, Addis Ababa
	0.3	G	BBC R. Norfolk, West Lynn
	1	G	BBC R. Ulster, Enniskillen
	40	HNG	Magyar R. 4, Lakihegy/Pécs
	50	IRN	IRIB R. Bojnurd, Bojnurd
	50	MDA	R. Moldova Actualitati, Chisinau
	50	MOZ	EP de Sofala, Beira
	10	SDN	Al-Gezira State R, Wad Madani
	5	SDN	Northern State R, Wadi Halfa
	2.5	UKR	R. Mryia, Dnipropetrovsk

kHz	kW	Ctry	Station, location
882	100	ARS	SBC Quran prgr, Dammam
	20	CNR	COPE Tenerife, La Laguña
	10	E	COPE, Alicante
	5	E	COPE, Gijón
	5	E	COPE, Málaga
	5	E	COPE, Valladolid
	10	EGY	ERTU General prgr, Matruh
	10/5/1	G	BBC Wales, Penmon/Tywyn/Forden
	100	G	BBC Wales, Washford
	60	IRN	IRIB R. Mahabad, Mahabad
	5	IRQ	R. Dar as-Salam, Mosul
	10	ISR	KI Reshet Bet, She'ar Yashuv
	5	MNE	R. Crne Gore 1, Podgorica
891	600/300	ALG	R. Algérienne 1, Ouled Fayet (inactive)
	30	AZE	Azärbaycan R, Baki
	100	ETH	R. Ethiopia, Dese
	20	HOL	R. 538, Hulsberg
	50	IRN	IRIB R. Dena, Dehdasht
	50	IRN	IRIB R. Dena, Yasuj
	50	LSO	LNBS Ultimate FM, Lancer's Gap
	1	POR	R. Sim, Vilamoura
	5	SDN	Sennar State R, Singa
	300	TUR	TRT 1, Antalya
900	1000	ARS	SBC R. Riyadh, Qurayyat II
	5	E	COPE, Granada
	5	E	COPE, Vigo
	10	E	R. Popular, Bilbao
	100/50	I	RAI Radiouno/Reg, Milano
	600	IRN	IRIB R. Iran, Tehran + 1 stn
909	10	AFG	R. Kunduz
	0.05	AFG	R. Paktia, Gardez
	10	ALG	R. Algérienne 1, Tamanrasset
	600	BOT	VOA, Mopeng Hill (Selebi-Phikwe)
	5	E	RNE R. 5, Palma de Mallorca
	50/1	G	BBC R. 5 Live, 9 stns
	150	G	BBC R. 5 Live, Brookmans Park
	200	G	BBC R. 5 Live,Moorside Edge
	50	NIG	FRCN Abuja, Gwagwalada
	200	ROU	R. Cluj, Jucu
	25	ROU	R. Constanta, Valu lui Traian
	50	ROU	R. România Actualitati, Timisoara
	20	UGA	UBC West Nile FM, Kampala
917	50	NIG	R. Gotel, Yola
918	20	E	R. Intereconomia, Madrid
	10	EGY	ERTU General prgr, Bawiti
	100	ETH	Dimtsi Wegahta (Vo the Dawn), Mekele
	50	IRN	IRIB R. Kerman, Jiroft
	50	NIG	R. Benue, Makurdi
	50	RUS	R. Mayak/Reg, Makhachkala
	300	SVN	R. Slovenija 1, Domzale
927	10	ALG	R. Algérienne 1/R. Adrar, Timimoun
	20	ARS	SBC R. Jeddah, Al-Hufuf
	50	IRN	IRIB R. Lorestan, Dorud
	200	TUR	TRT 1, Izmir
936	10	AFG	R. Zabul, Qalat
	100	ARS	SBC Quran prgr, Makkah/Riyadh
	20	E	RNE R. 5, Alicante
	20	E	RNE R. 5, Valladolid
	20	E	RNE R. 5, Zaragoza
	10	EGY	ERTU General prgr, Salum
	50	EGY	ERTU Om Kalthoum prgr, Cairo
	0.1	G	Dales R, Hawes
	0.2	G	Smooth R, Naish Hill
	10/5	I	RAI Radiouno/Reg, Venezia
	300	IRN	IRIB R. Urmia, Miandoab
	50	IRN	IRIB R. Urmia, Urmia
	20	IRQ	R. As-Safir, Basra
	100	MRC	SNRT C/R, Agadir (inactive)
	5	RUS	R. Rossii/Reg, Matveyevka
945	25	AGL	RNA N'Gola Yetu/Int. Sce, Mulenvos
	5	ARS	SBC R. Riyadh, Hail
	25	BOT	R. Botswana, Mmathethe
	100	ERI	Vo the Broad Masses 1, Asmara
	0.2	G	Gold, Derby
	0.7	G	Smooth R, Bexhill

kHz	kW	Ctry	Station, location
	100	IRN	IRIB R. Kordestan, Dehgolan
	100	ISR	Galei Tzahal, Yavne
	10	NIG	R. Kebbi, Birnin Kebbi
	15	ROU	R. România Actualitati, Miercurea Ciuc
	5	SDN	South Kordofan State R, Al-Fulah
	20	STP	R. Nacional, Pinheira
954	250	CZE	CRo 2/CRo Plus, Dobrochov (Brno) + 2 stns
	50	E	Onda Cero R, Madrid
	3	ETH	R. Sidama, Yirgalem
	300	TUR	TRT 1, Trabzon
963	100	CYP	CyBC 1, Nicosia
	0.2	G	Asian Sound R, Haslingden
	1	G	Sunrise R, East London
	200	IRN	IRIB R. Iran, Birjand (Bojd)
	20	KWT	R. Kuwait Multilingual/Main prgr, K. City
	50	MOZ	EP de Tete, Tete
	0.1	POL	Twoje R, Lipsko
	1	POR	R. Sim, Seixal
	100	SDN	SRTC Peace R. /Koran prgr, Khartoum
	100	TUN	ERTT International channel, Tunis Djedeida
972		BOT	R. Botswana, Takotokwane
	5	E	RNE R. Nacional, Cabra
	2	E	RNE R. Nacional, Monforte de Lemos
	100	ETH	R. Ethiopia, Robe (Bale)
	1	G	Sunrise R, West London
	100	IRN	IRIB R. Ilam, Ilam
	5	MEL	RNE R. Nacional, Mellilla
	25	NIG	Katsina State R, Katsina
	10	NIG	R. Kogi, Otite
981	100	ALG	R. Algérienne 2, Ouled Fayet (Algér)
	20	ARS	SBC Quran prgr, Madinah
	15	CZE	R. Český Impuls, Praha Libeznice/Moravské Budejovice
	2	EGY	ERTU General prgr, Abu Simbel/Baris
	10	EGY	ERTU Reg./Koran prgr, Assiut
	20/10	I	RAI Reg. "Trst A", Trieste
	1	IRL	R. Star Country, Emmyvale
	100	IRN	IRIB R. Iran, Hamadan
	3	POR	R. Sim, Coimbra
989	1	ETH	R. Ethiopia FS relay, Addis Ababa
990	50	AGL	EP do Bié, Kuito
	600	CYP	R. Sawa, Cape Greco
	10	E	SER R. Bilbao
	5	E	SER R. Cádiz
	1	G	BBC R. 5 Live, Tywyn
	1	G	BBC R. Devon, Exeter
	1	G	BBC R. Nan Gaidheal, Redmoss
	0.1	G	Free R. 80s, Wolverhampton
	0.3	G	Hallam 2, Doncaster
	400	IRN	IRIB R. Iran, Shiraz (Dehnow)
	50	NIG	Bauchi R. Corp, Bauchi
	10	NIG	Lagos State BC, Ikeja
	100/10	TZA	TBC Taifa, Songea
999	5	AFG	R. Helmand, Lashkar Ga (inactive)
	20	ARS	SBC Quran prgr, Duba
	50	E	COPE, Madrid
	0.3	G	Gold, Nottingham
	1	G	R. Solent, Fareham
	0.8	G	Rock 2, Preston
	50/10	I	RAI Radiouno/Reg, Torino
	50	IRN	IRIB R. Sanandaj, Baneh
	20	IRQ	R. Bilad, Baghdad
	500	MDA	TWR, Grigoriopol
	5	MLT	R. Malta, Bizbizja
	100	UGA	UBC R, Kabale (irR.)
1008	10	CNR	Grupo R, Las Palmas
	5	E	SER R. Alicante
	5	E	SER R. Extremadura, Badajoz
	10	E	SER R. Girona
	100	EGY	ERTU Palestine/Hebrew prgr, El Arish
	10	EGY	ERTU Reg. prgr, El Fayoum
	100	HOL	Groot Nieuws R, Zeewolde
	100	IRN	IRIB R. Semnan, Semnan
	20	IRQ	Sowt al-Fadhila, Najaf

kHz	kW	Ctry	Station, location
	50	MOZ	EP de Maputo, Maputo
	10	NIG	Niger State Media Corp, Kontagora
	10	NIG	Osun State BC, Iree
	0.5	SRB	RTS Beograd 2/3, Beograd
1017	10	AFG	R. Ghazni
	20	ARS	SBC Pilgrimage R, Madinah
	10	E	RNE R. 5, Burgos
	10	E	RNE R. 5. Granada
	0.6	G	Free R. 80s, Shrewsbury
	1	I	Media Veneta Broadcast, Piove di Sacco (†)
	50	IRN	IRIB R. Iran, Bandar Abbas
	10	IRQ	R. Karbala, Karbala
1026	10	ALG	RA 1/R. Ouargla, Hassi Messaoud
	5	E	SER R. Asturias, Oviedo
	5	E	SER R. Jaén
	5	E	SER R. Jerez, J. de la Frontera
	10	E	SER R. Reus
	5	E	SER R. Salamanca
	5	E	SER R. Vigo
	0.5	G	BBC R. Cambrigeshire, Chesterton Fen
	1	G	BBC R. Jersey, Trinity
	1.7	G	Downtown R, Belfast
	200	IRN	IRIB R. Tabriz, Azarshahr
	50	MOZ	EP de Manica, Chimoio
	25	NIG	Jigawa BC, Dutse
	5	SDN	Blue Nile State R, Al-Damazin
1035	20	ARS	SBC R. Jeddah, Yanbu al-Bahr
	100/200	EST	R. Eli/TWR Europe, Tartu
	10	ETH	R. Oromiya, Adama (Nazret)
	1	G	BBC R. Sheffield/Asian Netw, Sheffield
	1	G	Lyca Dilse, London
	0.8	G	Northsound 2, Aberdeen
	0.3	G	Westsound, Ayr
	1	I	Media Veneta Broadcast (alt. 1040kHz)
	100	IRN	IRIB R. Yazd, Yazd
	20	JOR	R. Jordan Main prgr, Amman
1044	7	AFG	R. Farah (inactive)
	10	E	SER R. San Sebastian, Donostia-S.S.
	5	E	SER R. Valladolid
	200	ETH	R. Ethiopia, Mekele
	50	IRN	IRIB R. Ilam, Dehloran
	300	MRC	SNRT C, Sebaa-Aioun (inactive)
	1	UKR	UR1/Reg, Verkhovyna
1053	5	E	COPE, Vila Real
	25	E	COPE, Zaragoza
	100	ETH	R. Oromiya, Nekemte
	500	G	TalkSport, Droitwich + 12 stns
	100	IRN	IRIB R. Iran, Khorramabad
	30	IRN	IRIB R. Iran, Saravan
	3	IRQ	R. As-Salam, Baghdad
	100	LBY	VO Homeland, Tripoli
	400	ROU	R. Iasi, Uricani
	10	RUS	R. Mariya, Sankt-Peterburg
1062	20/1	CZE	Country R, Praha
	10/6	I	RAI Radiouno/Reg, Ancona
	60/10	I	RAI Radiouno/Reg, Cagliari
	20/2	I	RAI Radiouno/Reg, Catania
	200	IRN	IRIB R. Kerman, Kerman
	0.8	POL	R. AM, Pulawy
	0.8	POL	Twoje R, Cmolas
	0.5	POL	Twoje R, Jaroslaw
	300	TUR	TRT Kurdî, Diyarbakir
1071	5	ALG	R. Algérienne 1, Illizi
	20	ARS	SBC R. Riyadh, Bisha
	25	BOT	R. Botswana, Jwaneng
	100	EGY	ERTU Adults/Wadi al Nil, Cairo (Abu Zaabal)
	1	G	TalkSport, Clipstone/Newcastle
	100	IRN	IRIB R. Ma'aref, Alborz (Qom)
	100	SYR	R. Al-Nour (LBN) relay, Tartus
1080	10	ARS	SBC R. Jeddah, Najran
	10	E	Onda Cero R, Toledo
	5	E	SER R. Coruña, A Coruña
	5	E	SER R. Granada
	10	E	SER R. Huesca

kHz	kW	Ctry	Station, location
	5	E	SER R. Mallorca, Palma de M.
	20	EGY	ERTU General prgr, El Minya/Luxor
	3	ETH	R. Fana, Addis Ababa
	600	IRN	VOIRI, Mahshahr
	50	ISR	KI Arabic prgr, Yavne
1088	25	AGL	RNA Canal A, Mulenvos
1089	10	ALG	R. Algérienne 1/R. Adrar
	20	ARS	SBC R. Jeddah, Qurayyat
	400	G	TalkSport, Brookmans Park
	400	G	TalkSport, Moorside Edge
	80/1	G	TalkSport, Washford + 4 stns
	125	G	TalkSport, Westerglen
	50	IRN	IRIB R. Semnan, Shahrud
	50	RUS	R. Teos, Krasnyy Bor (Sankt-Peterburg)
1098	100	ARS	SBC R. Jeddah, Dammam
	10	CYP	Bayrak Radyo 1, Iskele
	25	E	RNE R. 5, Almeria
	10	E	RNE R. 5, Avila
	5	E	RNE R. 5, Huelva
	20	E	RNE R. 5, Lugo
	200/100	IRN	VOIRI, Zabol
	10	SVK	SR R. Patria/Devín, Nitra
1107	400	AFG	RTV Afghanistan, Pol-e-Charkhi
	10	D	AFN Bavaria, Vilseck
	20	E	RNE R. 5, Caceres
	20	E	RNE R. 5, Camargo
	25	E	RNE R. 5, Logroño
	10	E	RNE R. 5, Ponferrada
	10	E	RNE R. 5, Teruel
	1.5	G	Moray Firth R. 2, Inverness
	2/0.5	G	TalkSport, 6 stns
	10	I	RAI Radiouno/Reg, Roma
	50	IRN	IRIB R. Mashhad, Sabzevar
	100	KEN	KBC R. Taifa, Maralal
	25	NIG	FRCN Kaduna, Jaji
	0.6	SRB	RTN, rel. of Beograd 1, Orlovat
1116	20	ARS	SBC R. Jeddah, Madinah
	5	E	SER R. Albacete
	5	E	SER R. Pontevedra
	1	G	BBC R Derby/Asian N, Burnaston Lane
	0.5	G	BBC R. Guernsey, Rohais
	20	HNG	MR Dankó Rádió, Miskolc/ Mosonmagyaróvár
	0.5	HOL	R. Bloemendaal, Bloemendaal
	10	I	RAI Radiouno/Reg, Palermo
	200	IRN	IRIB R. Iran, Ardekan
	20	IRQ	R. Dar as-Salam, Baghdad
1125	9	BEL	RTBF Vivacité, Wavre
	5	E	RNE R. 5, Badajoz
	10	E	RNE R. 5, Castelló
	10	E	RNE R. 5, Soria
	10	E	RNE R. 5, Toledo
	10	E	RNE R. 5, Vitoria
	1	G	R. Wales, Llandrindod Wells
	50	IRN	IRIB R. Qazvin, Qazvin
	20	NGR	ORTN La Voix du Sahel, Niamey
1126	500	LBY	R. Free Libya, El Beida (inactive)
1134	10	AGL	EP do Bengo, Mulenvos
	5	E	COPE, Jerez de la Frontera
	5	E	COPE, Pamplona
	10	E	COPE, Salamanca
	0.003	G	BFBS Gurkha R, 3 sites
	0.001	G	LPAMs
	50	IRN	IRIB R. Iran, Bojnurd
	10	IRN	IRIB R. Tabriz, Kalibar
	100	KWT	R. Kuwait Sports/Main prgr, Kabd
	20	NIG	Cross River State BC, Ugaga
	20	RUS	R. Teos, Kurkino (Moskva)
1143	1	D	AFN Benelux, Mönchengladbach
	5	E	COPE, Jaén
	2	E	COPE, Ourense
	50	IRN	IRIB R. Iran, Yasuj
1152	10	AGL	EP do Zaire, Mbanza Congo
	10	E	RNE R. 5, Albacete
	10	E	RNE R. 5, Cartagena

kHz	kW	Ctry	Station, location
	10	E	RNE R. 5, Lleida
	20	E	RNE R. 5, Málaga
	10	E	RNE R. 5, Zamora
	4	G	Clyde 2, Glasgow
	3	G	Free R. 80s, Birmingham
	1.5	G	Key 2, Manchester
	24	G	LBC News, London
	2	G	Metro R. 2, Newcastle
	0.8	G	Smooth R, Norwich
	0.3	G	Smooth R, Plymouth
	50	KEN	KBC R. Taifa, Wajir
	400	ROU	R. România Actualitati, Cluj (Jucu)
	200	UAE	Voice of Kerala, Ras al-Khaimah
1161	5	ALG	RA 1/R. Tamanrasset, In Salah
	100	EGY	ERTU Reg. prgr, Tanta
	1	G	BBC Sussex, Bexhill
	0.1	G	BBC Three Counties R, Bedford
	0.2	G	Smooth R, Swindon
	1	G	Tay 2, Dundee
	0.4	G	Viking 2, Hull
	600	IRN	VOIRI, Qasr-e Shirin
1170	25	AGL	EP do Huambo, Huambo
	700	BLR	R. Belarus, Sasnovy
	0.2	G	Signal Two, Stoke-on-Trent
	0.3	G	Smooth R, Ipswich
	0.1	G	Smooth R, Portsmouth
	0.6	G	Swansea Sound, Swansea
	0.3	G	TFM 2, Stockton
	750	IRN	IRIB R. Iran, Abadan
	15	SVN	R. Capodistria, Beli Kriz
	50	SWZ	TWR Mpangela Ranch (Manzini)
		UAE	Abu Dhabi R, Al-Dhabbaya (irreg.)
1179	25	CNR	SER R. Club Tenerife, Santa Cruz
	2	E	SER R. Rioja, Logroño
	50	E	SER R. València
	10	EGY	ERTU General prgr, Qena
	0.05	G	R. BGWS, Farnborough
	50	IRN	IRIB R. Golestan, Gorgan
	50	IRN	IRIB R. Iran, Chabahar
	30	IRQ	R. Voice of Iraq, Baghdad
	50	MOZ	EP da Zambézia, Quelimane
	400	ROU	R. România Actualitati, Bacau (Galbeni)
	10	ROU	R. România Actualitati, Resita
	0.005	S	Hörby Radioförening, Hörby
1188	400	HNG	Magyar R. 4, Marcali/Szolnok
	300	IRN	IRIB R. Payam, Tehran
1197	10	AGL	EP de Malange, Malange
	6	G	Absolute R, 9 stns
	50	IRN	IRIB R. Ardabil, Moghan
	50	IRN	IRIB R. Fars, Dasht-e Qir
	1	IRQ	R. Dar as-Salam, Kirkuk
	50	LSO	LNBS Ultimate FM, Lancer's Gap
	15	ROU	R. Târgu Mures, Brasov
1200	0.5	AFG	R. Day Kundi, Nili (inactive)
1206	10	IRN	IRIB R. Birjand, Nehbandan
	50	ISR	KI Reshet Bet, Akko (Acre)
	50	MOZ	EP de Inhambane, Inhambane
	1	ROD	Mauritius BC R. Rodrigues, Citronelle
1215	20	ARS	SBC R. Jeddah, Madinah
	50	BOT	R. Botswana, Mahalapye
	5	E	COPE, Córdoba
	5	E	COPE, Léon
	5	E	COPE, Santander
	660	G	Absolute R, 14 stns
	60	IRN	IRIB R. Tabaristan, Chalus
	5	REU	R. Réunion, St. André
	10	TZA	TBC Taifa, Arusha
1224	5	E	COPE, Almería
	5	E	COPE, Huelva
	5	E	COPE, Lleida
	5	E	COPE, Lugo
	5	E	COPE, Palma de Mallorca
	0.01	HOL	R. Paradijs, Utrecht
	50	IRN	IRIB R. Iran, Kerman
	400	IRN	VOIRI, Kish Island

kHz	kW	Ctry	Station, location
	20	ISR	Galei Tzahal, Beersheba
	50	MOZ	EP de Cabo Delgado, Pemba
1233	600	CYP	Monte-Carlo Doualiya/TWR, Cape Greco
	20	CZE	R. Dechovka, Praha (Libeznice) + 4 stns
	2.4	G	Absolute R, 4 stns
	50	IRN	IRIB R. Fars, Abadeh
	50	KEN	KBC English/Eastern Sce, Marsabit
1242	4	G	Absolute R, 4 stns
	0.3	G	Smooth R, Maidstone
	50	IRN	IRIB R. Iran, Zanjan
	500	OMA	R. Sultanate of Oman, Barka (Seeb)
1251	0.001	G	BFBS Gurkha R, York
	0.001	G	LPAMs
	0.8	G	Smooth R, Bury St. Edmunds
	50	HNG	MR Dankó Rádió, Nyíregyháza/Szombathely
	100	IRN	IRIB R. Iran, Kiashahr
	200	LBY	R. Libya, Tripoli (inactive)
	2	POR	R. Sim, Castelo Branco/Chaves
1260	10	AGL	EP do Kuanza Norte, N'dalatando
	500	ARS	SBC R. Riyadh, Dammam
	2.5	CVA	Vatican R, Vatican City
	5	E	SER R. Algeciras
	5	E	SER R. Murcia
	1.5	G	Absolute R, Lydd/Guildford
	0.5	G	BBC R. York, Scarborough
	0.3	G	Sabras R, Leicester
	2	G	Smooth R, Bristol
	0.6	G	Smooth R, Wrexham
	10	IRN	IRIB R. Isfahan, Khur
	50	MOZ	EP do Niassa, Lichinga
1269	2	AFS	Arrowline Chinese R, Edenvale
	5	E	COPE, Badajoz
	5	E	COPE, Zamora
	50	IRN	IRIB R. Ardabil, Khalkhal
	100	KWT	R. Kuwait Classical music, Kabd
	10	NIG	Taraba State BS, Jalingo
	5	SRB	RTN Serbian Sce, Srbobran
1278	25	AGL	EP de Cabinda, Tenda
	10	EGY	ERTU General prgr, Asswan
	0.002	G	BFBS Gurkha R, Folkestone/Stafford
	0.001	G	LPAMs/RSLs
	0.4	G	Pulse 2, Bradford
	300	IRN	IRIB R. Kermanshah, Kermanshah
	100	OMA	R. Sultanate of Oman, Bahla
	100	UKR	UR1, Odesa (Petrivka)
1287	5	ARS	SBC Quran prgr, Makkah
	5	E	SER R. Castilla, Burgos
	10	E	SER R. Lleida
	5	E	SER R. Lugo
	0.003	G	BFBS Gurkha R, 3 sites
	0.002	G	BFBS UK, 2 sites
	0.001	G	LPAMs
	0.004	G	R. Clan Clwyd, Bodelwyddan
	60	IRN	IRIB R. Fars, Darab
	50	IRN	IRIB R. Fars, Lamerd
	50	IRN	IRIB R. Fars, Lar
	2	POR	RTP Antena 1, Portalegre
1290	1	AGL	EP do Zaire, Soyo
1296	400	AFG	R. Free Afgh./VOA, Pol-e-Charkhi
	10	AGL	EP do Uíge, Uíge
		AZE	VO Azerbaijan, Haciqabul (Pirsaat)
	50	E	COPE, Valencia
	10	G	R. XL, Birmingham
	50	IRN	IRIB R. Zahedan, Zabol
	600	SDN	SRTC General prgr, Sennar (Reiba)
	7	SRB	RTS Beograd 1, Vranje
1305	10	AFG	R. Kandahar
	1	ARS	SBC R. Jeddah, Taif
	20	E	RNE R. 5, Bilbao
	20	E	RNE R. 5, Ciudad Real
	10	E	RNE R. 5, León
	25	E	RNE R. 5, Ourense
	10	EGY	ERTU General prgr, Assiut
	0.2	G	Hallam 2, Barnsley

kHz	kW	Ctry	Station, location
	0.5	G	Premier Christian R, Chingford/Epsom
	0.2	G	Smooth R, Newport
	50	IRN	IRIB R. Bushehr, Bushehr
	50	ISR	Galei Tzahal, Rosh-Pina
	50	KEN	KBC Somali Sce, Wajir
1314	10	AGL	EP do Namibe, Namibe
	1000	ARM	Public R. of Armenia FS, Gavar
	20	E	RNE R. 5, Cuenca
	10	E	RNE R. 5, Salamanca
	10	E	RNE R. 5, Tarragona
	1	EGY	ERTU General prgr, Nag Hamadi
	1	EGY	ERTU Reg./Koran prgr, Abu Simbel
	10	GRC	ERT1, Tripoli
	50	IRN	IRIB R. Iran, Ardabil + 1 stn
	0.18	NOR	Bergen Kringkaster/R. Northern Star, Bergen, Erdal
	50	ROU	Antena Satelor, Constanta (Valu lui Traian)
	25	ROU	Antena Satelor, Timisoara
	15	ROU	R. Oltenia Craiova, Craiova
	50	SYR	Syrian R. 1, Aleppo
1323	0.02	G	Akash R, Leeds
	0.5	G	Smooth R, Brighton
	1	I	R. Base 101, Vigonza di Padova (irR.)
	50	IRN	VOIRI/R. Tabriz, Jolfa
	15	ROU	R. Târgu Mures
	10	TZA	R. One Swahili channel, Moshi
1332	50	CZE	CRoZ/CRo Plus, Moravské Budejovice
	0.4	G	BBC R. Wiltshire, Lacock
	1	G	Premier Christian R, London
	0.6	G	Smooth R, Peterborough
	0.002	HOL	R. Paradijs, Nieuwegein
	300	IRN	IRIB Tehran City R, Tehran
	50	ROU	R. România Actualitati, Galati
1341	10	E	Onda Cero R, Almeria
	5	E	Onda Cero R, Ciudad Real
	5	E	SER R. León
	100	EGY	ERTU Cult./Songs prgr, Cairo (Abu Zaabal)
	20	EGY	ERTU General prgr, Idfu/Siwa
	10	EGY	ERTU Koran/Educ./Sports prgr, Bawiti
	100	G	BBC R. Ulster, Lisnagarvey
	20	IRN	IRIB R. Kerman, Bam
	100	KWT	R. Kuwait Quran/2nd prgr, Magwa
1350	1000	ARM	TWR Europe, Gavar
	50	BOT	R. Botswana, Tshabong
	10	EGY	ERTU General prgr, Quseir
	0.001	G	LPAMs
	30	GEO	Abkhaz State R, Sokhumi
	5	HNG	Magyar R. 4, Györ
	5	I	R. I AM, Milano (irR.)
1359	100	ETH	VO Tigray Revolution, Mekele
	0.8	G	BBC R. Solent, Bournemouth
	0.3	G	Free R. 80s, Coventry
	0.2	G	Smooth R, Cardiff
	0.3	G	Smooth R, Chelmsford
1368	10	EGY	ERTU General prgr, El Kharga
	2	G	BBC R. Lincolnshire, Lincoln
	0.1	G	BBC R. Wiltshire, Swindon
	0.5	G	BBC Surrey, Duxhurst
	20	G	Manx Radio, Foxdale
	10	I	Challenger R, Villa Estense
	150	IRN	IRIB R. Golestan, Gonbad-e Qabus
	20	ISR	Galei Tzahal, Shivta
	10	SEY	SBC Radio, Victoria
1377	1000	ARM	TWR Europe, Gavar
	0.1	G	Asian Sound R, Ashton Moss
	50	IRN	IRIB R. Iran, Paveh
	50	IRN	IRIB R. Zahedan, Chabahar
	50	TZA	R. Free Africa, Mwanza
	7	UKR	R. Khvylia, Vinnytsia
	5	UKR	R. Mykolaiv
1386	5	AFG	R. Paktin Voice, Shakin
	10	AGL	EP da Lunda Sul, Saurimo
	10	EGY	ERTU Reg./Koran prgr, Luxor
	0.001	G	LPAMs
	0.01	G	R Jcom, Leeds
	100	KEN	KBC English/Eastern Sce, Maralal
	75	LTU	RFE/RL/R. Japan/R. Poland (rel. via R. Baltic Waves Int), Sitkunai
1395	500	ALB	R. Tirana/TWR relay, Fllakë
	500	ARM	Polskie R. dla Zagranicy, Gavar
	50	IRN	IRIB R. Khalij e-Fars, Hajiabad
		IRN	VOIRI, unknown location
	5	RUS	R. Rossii/Reg, Buguruslan
1404	10	AGL	EP do Bié, Kuito
	0.001	G	LPAMs/RSLs
	100	GRC	ERT1, Komotini
	1	I	Gruppo R. Luna 106, Chiozza di Scandiano
	10	IRN	IRIB R. Iran, Dasht-e Qir
		IRQ	R. Kull al-Iraq, Maysan
	10	MWI	MBC R. 1, Chitipa
	15	ROU	R. România Actualitati, Sibiu
	50	ROU	R. Cluj/R. Sighet, Sighetu Marmatiei
	10	UKR	UR1, Izmail
1413	5	E	RNE R. 5, Girona
	10	E	RNE R. 5, Jaén
	20	E	RNE R. 5, Vigo
	1	G	BBC R. Gloucestershire, 2 stns
	1	G	Premier Christian R, 2 stns
	10	IRN	IRIB R. Fars, Estahban
	500	MDA	Vesti FM, Grigoriopol
	800	OMA	BBC World Sce, A'Seela
1422	1	AFS	Hellenic R, Bedfordview
	50	ALG	R. Algérienne C, Ouled Fayet (Algér)
	20	ARS	SBC Call of Islam, Riyadh
	10	EGY	ERTU Reg./Koran prgr, Salum
	10	MWI	MBC R. 1, Matiya
	10	ROU	R. România Actualitati, Olanesti
1431	600	DJI	R. Sawa/VOA, Djibouti (Pk 12)
	0.001	G	LPAMs
	0.35	G	Smooth R, Southend
	0.35	GRC	1431 AM, Thessaloniki
	5/2	I	RAI Radiouno/Reg, Foggia
	200	IRN	IRIB R. Iran, Habibabad (Isfahan)
	800	UKR	R. Ukraine Int, Mykolaiv
1440	10	AFG	R. Nangarhar, Jalalabad
	10	AGL	EP da Lunda Norte, Dundo
	1600	ARS	SBC R. Riyadh, Ras al-Khair
	10	CAF	R. Centrafrique, Bangui (F.P.I.)
	10	NIG	Adamawa BC, Yola
	10	TZA	R. One English channel, Dar es Salaam
1449	200	ARS	SBC R. Riyadh, Jeddah (Bahrah)
	0.2	G	BBC Asian Network, Gunthorpe
	2	G	BBC R. 4, Redmoss
	0.001	G	LPAMs
	2	I	RAI Radiouno/Reg, Belluno
	400	IRN	VOIRI, Bandar Torkaman
1458	10	AGL	EP do Moxico, Luena
	500	ALB	R. Tirana, Fllakë
	10	BHR	R. Bahrain General prgr, Manama
	5	G	BBC Asian Network, Langley Mill
	2	G	BBC Newcastle, Wrekenton
	0.5	G	BBC R. Cumbria, Whitehaven
	2	G	BBC R. Devon, Torquay
	5	G	Gold, Manchester
	125	G	Lyca R. 1458, London
	4	GIB	GBC R. Gibraltar, Wellington Front
	10	IRN	IRIB R. Birjand, Ghayen
	20	ISR	KI Reshet Alef, Eilat/She'ar Yashuv
	5	MYT	Mayotte Première, Pamanzi
	100	ROU	R. România Actualitati, Constanta
1467	10	AGL	EP de Kuando-Kubango, Menongue
	50	ARS	SBC R. Riyadh, Hafar Al-Batin
	40	F	R. Maria France, Col de la Madone
	1000	F	TWR Europe, Roumoules
	100	IRN	IRIB R. Qom, Alborz (Qom)
1476	10	EGY	ERTU Reg./Koran prgr, El Minya
	5	I	R. Treviso (tests)

kHz	kW	Ctry	Station, location
	50	IRN	IRIB R. Kurdistan, Marivan
1485	1	AFS	R. Today, Honeydew
	10	AGL	EP do Kuanza Sul, Sumbe
	5	E	COPE, Vilanova (inactive)
	5	E	SER R. Alcoi
	10	E	SER R. Santander
	10	E	SER R. Zamora
	10	ETH	R. Ethiopia, Negele Borana
	1	G	BBC R 4, Carlisle
	2	G	BBC R. Humberside, Hull
	2	G	BBC R. Merseyside, Wallasey
	1	G	BBC Sussex, Brighton
	100	IRN	IRIB R. Abadan, Jamshidabad
	10	IRN	IRIB R. Fars, Jahrom
	10	IRN	IRIB R. Iran, Damghan
	10	IRN	IRIB R. Urmia, Khoy
	2/1.25	LVA	R. Merkurs/R. Mi Amigo Int., Riga
	1	MEL	SER R. Melilla, Melilla
	1	NOR	NRK P1/Troms og Finnmark, Longyearbyen
	3	ROU	R. Vocea Sperantei, 3 sites
	12	SDN	Al-Qadarif State R, Al-Qadarif
	0.5	SRB	RTN Serbian Sce, Novi Sad
	0.5	SRB	RTS Beograd 1, Crna Trava
	0.5	SRB	RTS Beograd 1/R. Tutin
1494	10	IRN	IRIB R. Mashhad, Taybad
	50	MDA	R. Moldova Actualitati, Cahul/Edinet
1500	0.1	AFG	R. Nuristan
	0.1	AFG	R. Samangan, Aybak (inactive)
	-	AFG	R. Sar-e-Pol
	6	AFG	RTA R. Badghis, Qalay-e-Naw
1503	10	AGL	EP de Benguela, Benguela
	0.1	AZR	AFN, Lajes
	1	BIH	R. 1503 Zavidovici, Zavidovici
	5	E	RNE R. 5, La Linea
	2	E	RNE R. 5, Monforte de Lemos
	25	EGY	ERTU Reg. prgr, El Arish
	1	G	BBC R. Stoke, Sideway
	0.1	G	Betar Bangla, East London
	200	IRN	IRIB R. Iran, Bushehr
	10	SRB	RTS Beograd 202, Beograd
1512	1000	ARS	SBC Quran prgr, Jeddah Khurma
	100	GRC	ERT1, Hania
	50	IRN	IRIB R. Ardabil, Ardabil
1521	2000	ARS	SBC R. Riyadh, Duba
	10	BHR	R. Bahrain 2nd prgr, Manama
	5	E	SER R. Castelló
	0.07	G	Flame Christian & Community R, Wirral
1530	10	AGL	EP de Cabinda, Tenda
	0.2	G	BBC Essex, Southend-on-Sea
	0.7	G	Pulse 2, Huddersfield
	50	IRN	IRIB R. Iran, Yazd
	3	MDR	Posto Emissor do Funchal, Poiso
	15	ROU	R. România Actualitati, Radauti
	15	ROU	R. Constanta, Mahmudia (Nufaru)
	600	STP	VOA, Pinheira
1539	6	E	SER R. Elche, Elx
	5	E	SER R. Manresa (irregular)
	0.4	IRL	Energy, Dublin (alt. fq 1395)
	50	IRN	IRIB R. Golestan, Derazno
	10	IRN	IRIB R. Iran, Garmsar
		UAE	Quran Kareem, Al-Dhabbaya (during Ramadan)
1548	10	AFS	R. Islam, Lenasia
	5	G	BBC R. Bristol, Mangotsfield
	2	G	Forth 2, Edinburgh
	97	G	Gold, London
	0.7	G	Hallam 2, Sheffield
	1	G	R. City 2, Liverpool
	10	IRN	IRIB R. Birjand, Ferdows
	15	IRN	IRIB R. Dena, Gachsaran
	20	IRN	IRIB R. Iran, 2 sites
	10	IRN	IRIB R. Mazandaran, Larijan
	600	KWT	R. Sawa, Kuwait

kHz	kW	Ctry	Station, location
	500	MDA	TWR, Grigoriopol
1550	0.1	AFG	R. Herat
	50	ALG	R. Nacional de la RASD, Rabouni
1557	0.3	G	R. Lancashire, Oxcliffe
	0.8	G	Smooth R, Northampton
	0.5	G	Smooth R, Southampton
	50	IRN	IRIB R. Iran, Zabol
1566	100	BEN	TWR Africa, Parakou
	0.6	G	BBC Somerset, Taunton
	0.8	G	Premier Christian R, Guildford
	1	HOL	Vahon Hindustani R, Haag
	1	I	R. Kolbe, Schio (irR.)
	100	IRN	IRIB R. Iran, Bandar Abbas
1575	10	AFG	R. Kunar, Asadabad
	5	E	SER R. Córdoba
	10	E	SER R. Pamplona
	10	EGY	ERTU Koran/Educ./Sports, Quseir
	0.001	G	LPAMs/RSLs
	50/30	I	RAI Radiouno/Reg, Genova
	400/800	IRN	IRIB R. Iran, Abadan
	2	MAU	BBC WS, Bigara
	800	UAE	R. Farda, Al-Dhabbiya
1584	10	AFG	R. Balkh, Mazar-e-Sharif
	0.5	AFG	R. Ghor, Chaghcharan
	2	AFG	R. Nimroz, Zaranj
	0.25	AFS	R 1584, Pretoria
	1	BHR	R. Bahrain English prgr, Manama
	1	BIH	R. Bosanski Petrovac
	5	CEU	SER Radiolé, Ceuta
	5	E	SER R. Gandía
	5	E	SER R. Ourense
	10	EGY	ERTU Reg./Koran prgr, Idfu
	1	EGY	ERTU Reg./Koran/Sports prgr, Baris
	0.3	G	BBC Hereford & Worcester, Woofferton
	0.25	G	BBC R. Kent, Rusthall
	1	G	BBC R. Nottingham, Clipstone
	0.2	G	Panjab R, N. London
	0.2	G	Tay 2, Perth
	1	GRC	RS Amaliadas, Kastro
	0.15	HOL	R. Paradijs, Utrecht
	2.5/12	I	R. Studio X, Momigno
	50/10	IRN	IRIB R. Semnan, Biarjmand
	0.1	POL	Twoje 9, Andrychów
	4	ROU	R. Vocea Sperantei, 4 sites
	0.4	RUS	R. MTUCI, Moskva (inactive)
	5	SDN	White Nile State R, Kosti
1593	10	EGY	ERTU Reg./Koran prgr, Matruh
	10/5	F	Bretagne 5, Saint-Gouéno
	150	KWT	R. Sawa, Kuwait
	10	ROU	Antena Sibiului/R. Cluj, Sibiu
	15	ROU	R. Cluj, Oradea
	15	ROU	R. Constanta, Ion Corvin
	15	ROU	R. Târgu Mures, Miercurea Ciuc
	0.01	RUS	R. SPBGUT/Bonch, Sankt-Peterburg (†)
	0.005	TUR	AFN Incirlik (Adana)
1602	5	E	SER R. Cartagena
	5	E	SER R. Linares
	5	E	SER R. Ontinyent
	5	E	SER R. Segovia
	10/1	EGY	ERTU Reg./Koran prgr, Nag Hamadi
	10	EGY	ERTU Reg./Koran/Sports, Siwa
	0.4	FIN	Scandinavian Weekend R, Virrat
	0.1	G	Desi R, Southall
	0.001	G	RSLs
	1	HOL	KBC R. /R. Seagull, Pietersbierum
	10	IRN	IRIB R. Ahvaz, Dezful
	10	IRN	IRIB R. Fars, Kazerun
	10	IRN	IRIB R. Iran, Bahabad
	20	IRN	IRIB R. Semnan, Damghan/Garmsar
	0.5	POL	R. AM, Kraków
	2	ROU	R. Vocea Sperantei, Bistrita/Piatra Neamt
	5	SDN	South Kordofan State R, Kadugli
	0.5	SRB	RTS Beograd 1, Sjenica
1611	0.18	NOR	Bergen Kringkaster, Bergen, Erdal (Test)

ASIA & PACIFIC
(excluding Middle East)

Abbreviations peculiar to the Asia & Pacific section of MW freq. lists: AF = allocated freq. C. = City. PO = Present operation on. Proj. = Projected station. Rptr. = repeater. Trtr = translator.
Australia: The numeral preceding the call letters indicates the state: 2 = New South Wales. 3 = Victoria. 4 = Queensland. 5 = South Australia. 6 = Western Australia. 7 = Tasmania. 8 = Northern Territory. ACT = Australian Capital Territory. **China, P.R:** If several locations are listed for one frequency, the power listed applies to the first entry. For full details see country section. **Indonesia:** Only RRI stns included. For details of other stns see country section. **Philippines:** Province Abbreviations: Ag Nte = Agusan del Norte; Ag Sur = Agusan del Sur; Ant = Antique; Boh = Bohol; Bat = Batangas; Buk = Bukidnon; Bul = Bulacan; Cag = Cagayan; Cam Nte = Camarines Norte; Cam Sur = Camarines Sur; Dvo Nte = Davao del Norte; Dvo Sur = Davao del Sur; Isa = Isabela; I.Nte = Ilocos Norte; I.Sur = Ilocos Sur; LU = La Union; Lanao Nte = Lanao del Norte; Lanao Sur = Lanao del Sur; Mag = Maguindanao; Mas = Masbate; M Octal = Mindoro Occidental; Mind Or = Mindoro Oriental; Mis Octal = Misamis Occidental; Mis Or = Misamis Oriental; Mt Prov = Mountain Province; Neg Occ = Negros Occidental; Neg Or = Negros Oriental; Nva Viz = Nueva Vizcaya; Pam = Pampanga; Pang = Pangasinan; Que = Quezon; Riz = Rizal; S Cot = South Cotabato; S Leyte = Southern Leyte; S Sur = Surigao del Sur; Sor = Sorsogon; Tar = Tarlac; Z Nte = Zamboanga del Norte; Z Sib = Zamboanga Sibugay; Z Sur = Zamboanga del Sur; Zamb = Zambales. **Russia:** Regions in the Asian parts of Russia: Sib. = Siberia. FE = Far East.

kHz	kW	Ctry	Call	Station, location
164	500	MNG		MRT (1), Ulaanbaatar
164	500	MNG		MRT (1), Ulaanbaatar
209	75	MNG		MRT (1), Dalanzadgad/Choybalsan
	75	MNG		MRT (1), Ölgiy
227	75	MNG		MRT (1)/Altay Public Radio, Altay
279	150	TKM		Turkmen Radio (1), Asgabat
531	10	AUS	6DL	ABC (LR), Dalwallinu
	5	AUS	4KZ	Innisfail
	5	AUS	2PM	Kempsey
	0.5	AUS	5RTI	R. Italiana, Adelaide (HPONS)
	5	AUS	3GG	Warragul
	10	CHN		ZJ
	300	IND		AIR, Jodhpur A
	10	J	JOQG	NHK (1), Morioka
	1	J		NHK (1), Nago
	5	NZL		531pi, Auckland
	2	NZL		More FM, Alexandra
	5	PHL	DZBR	Kumintang Bc. System, Batangas C, Bat.
	5	PHL	DXGH	Pacific Bc. System, Gen. Santos C, S Cot
	5	RUS		Avtoradio, Yuzhno-Sakhalinsk, FE
	25	THA		R. Thailand, Maha Sarakham
	10	TWN	BED57	BCC (L), Taipei (Tucheng)
540	10	AUS	4QL	ABC (LR), Longreach
	5	AUS	7SD	Scottsdale
	50	CHN		AH (CNR1); LN (CNR1)
	10	CHN		QH; NM (2 stns)
	20	IND		AIR, Aizawl
	10	INS		RRI, Bandung (4)
	1	J	JOSK	NHK (1), Kitakyushu
	1	J		NHK (1), Matsumoto
	5	J	JOMG	NHK (1), Miyazaki
	1	J		NHK (1), Nanao/Ishigaki
	5	J	JOJG	NHK (1), Yamagata
	10	KOR		KBS, Hongseong
	1	KOR		KBS, Jangsu/Jangheung/Jeomchon
	2	NZL		Rhema, Christchurch
	3	NZL		Rhema, New Plymouth
	5	NZL		Rhema, Tauranga
	300	PAK		PBC (1), Peshawar
	1	PHL	DYRB	DWRL Radio, Inc., Cebu C
	10	PHL	DZWT	Mt. Province BC, Baguio C, Benguet
	5	SMO		National Radio 2AP, Apia
	5	THA		Yaan Kraw, Bangkok
549	50	AUS	2CR	ABC (LR), Orange
	25	CHN		EN; NM (2 stns)
	1200	CHN		FJ (CNR5)
	100	IND		AIR, Ranchi A
	10	J	JOAP	NHK (1), Okinawa
	1	NZL		R. Sport, Nelson
	3	NZL		Rhema, Kaitaia
	1	NZL		TAB Trackside R., Napier-Hastings
	5	PHL	DXHM	Catholic Media Netw., Madong, Mind Or
	10	PHL	DWRB	Philippine Bc. Sce., Naga C, Cam. Sur
	10	THA		R. Thailand, Mukdahan
	100	THA		SoR. WoR. Sor, Lampang
	40	TJK		TR (2), Dushanbe
	200	VTN		Hung Yen (1), My Hao
550	5	HWA	KNUI	Wailuku, Maui
558	50	AUS	6WA	ABC (LR), Wagin
	5	AUS	4AM	Atherton
	2	AUS	7BU	Burnie
	5	AUS	4GY	Gympie
	100	BGD		Bangladesh Betar, Khulna
	120	CHN		XJ + 7 stns
	10	FJI		Fiji Bc. Corp. Ltd. (RF1), Suva
	100	IND		AIR, Mumbai B
	20	J	JOCR	CRK, Kobe
	250	KOR	HLQH	KBS, Daegu (2)
	5	NZL		R. Sport, Invercargill
	40	PHL	DZXL	R. Mindanao Netw., Pasig C, NCR
	10	THA		R. Thailand, Kanchanaburi
	1	TWN	BEH7	Fu Hsing BS (1), Taipei
	100	VTN		Ho Chi Min C. (2), Quan Tre
567	10	AUS	4JK	ABC (LR), Julia Creek
	0.1	AUS	6...	ABC (LR), W. A., 4 stns
	0.5	AUS	2BH	Broken Hill
	10	CHN		JS (CNR1)
	20	CHN		TJ; EN
	10	GUM	KGUM	Agana
	20	HKG		RTHK (3), Golden Hill
	300	IND		AIR, Dibrugarh
	100	J	JOIK	NHK (1), Sapporo
	100	KOR	HLKF	KBS, Jeonju
	200	LAO		Lao National Radio (N), Vientiane (kM 49)
	50	NZL		RNZ (N), Wellington
	300	PAK		PBC, Khuzdar
	5	PHL	DXCH	Pacific Bc. System, Cotabato C, Mag.
	5	THA		JoR. SoR. 5, Chaiyaphum
570	1	HWA	KUAI	Eleele, Kauai
576	50	AUS	2RN	ABC (RN), Sydney
	100	BRM		Myanma Radio, Yangon
	200	CHN		YN; ZJ(v); EN; FJ
	200	IND		AIR, Alappuzha
	1	J	JODG	NHK (1), Hamamatsu
	10	J	JOHG	NHK (1), Kagoshima
	40	KGZ		R. DDD, Osh
	5	KOR		AFNK, Munsan
	1	KOR		KBS, Suncheon (3)
	100	NPL		R. Nepal, Surkhet
	2.5	NZL		Star, Hamilton
	5	PHL	DZHR	Cebu Bc. Co., Tuguegarao, Cag.
	10	PHL	DXMF	People's Bc. Sce., Davao C, Dvo Sur

kHz	kW	Ctry	Station, location
	10	PHL	DYMR Philippine Bc. Sce., Cebu C
	10	PHL	DZMQ Philippine Bc. Sce., Dagupan C, Pang.
	5	THA	ToR. ChoR. DoR., Bangkok
	150	TKM	Turkmen Radio (2), Asgabat
	50	VTN	Khanh Hoa (2/P), Nha Trang
585	10	AUS	6PB ABC (PNN), Perth
	10	AUS	7RN ABC (RN), Hobart
	10	AUS	2WEB Bourke (PBS)
	50	CHN	JS + 11 stns
	200	CHN	Southeast BC, FJ
	300	IND	AIR, Nagpur A
	50	INS	RRI, Surabaya (4)
	10	J	JOPG NHK (1), Kushiro
	20	LAO	Lao National Radio (P), Khantabouly
	2	NZL	R. Ngati Porou, Ruatoria
	500	PAK	PBC, Islamabad
	5	PHL	DXCP Catholic Media Netw., Gen. Santos C, S Cot
	1	PHL	DYLL Philippine Bc. Sce., Iloilo C
	10	PNG	NBC Port Moresby
	5	THA	ThoR. PhoR. 3, Phrae
	5	THA	WoR. PoR. Tho. 15, Chumphon
590	7.5	HWA	KSSK Honolulu, Oahu
594	50	AUS	3WV ABC (LR), Horsham
	200	BRM	Myanma Radio, Naypyidaw
	300	CHN	XZ; SD (2 stns)
	1000	IND	AIR, Chinsurah, FS
	300	J	JOAK NHK (1), Tokyo
	10	KOR	KBS, Yeongju
	2	NZL	Rhema, Wanagnui
	5	NZL	Star, Timaru
	5	PHL	DXDB Catholic Media Netw., Malaybalay, Buk.
	20	PHL	DZBB GMA Network, Inc., Quezon C, NCR
	5	THA	Phon. PoR. ThoR. OR., Bangkok
	10	TWN	BEH44 Fu Hsing BS (1), Kaohsiung
	5	TWN	BEH38 Fu Hsing BS (2), Taichung
	10	TWN	BEH2 Fu Hsing BS (2), Taipei
	50	VTN	Danang (1), An Hai
603	10	AUS	4CH ABC (LR), Charleville
	2	AUS	6PH ABC (LR), Port Hedland
	10	AUS	2RN ABC (RN), Nowra
	100	CHN	EN + 41 stns
	600	CHN	HA (CRI)
	200	IND	AIR, Ajmer
	5	J	JOOG NHK (1), Obihiro
	5	J	JOKK NHK (1), Okayama
	500	KOR	HLSA KBS, Namyang (Seoul)
	5	NZL	R. Waatea, Auckland
	10	PHL	DZLL Bicol Bc. System, Naga C, Cam Sur
	5	PHL	DZVV Consolidated Bc. Syst., Inc., Vigan, I. Sur
	5	PHL	DXPR R. Mindanao Netw., Pagadian C, Z Sur
	5	THA	WoR. PoR. Tho. 12, Khon Kaen
610	200	VTN	Ho Chi Minh C. (H), Tang Nhon Phu
612	50	AUS	4QR ABC (LR), Brisbane
	10	AUS	6RN ABC (RN), Dalwallinu
	10	CHN	FJ; LN; SC; SD
	200	IND	AIR, Bengaluru A
	100	J	JOLK NHK (1), Fukuoka
	150	KGZ	Kyrgyz R. (1), Bishkek
	2	NZL	Star, Christchurch
	1.5	NZL	Star, Nelson
	5	PHL	DWSP Philippine Bc. Corp., Itogon, Benguet
	10	PHL	DYHP R. Mindanao Netw., Cebu C
	5	THA	MoR. KoR., Chiang Mai
	5	THA	WoR. SoR. PoR., Lop Buri
	500	TWN	RTI, Lukang
620	5	HWA	KHNU Hilo, Hawaii
	10	HWA	KHNU Kalaoa, Hawaii
	5	HWA	KHNU Naalehu, Hawaii
621	50	AUS	3RN ABC (RN), Melbourne
	2	AUS	6EL Bunbury
	200	CHN	HL; QH; HB; SC; SD
	20	HKG	RTHK (P), Golden Hill
	100	IND	AIR, Patna A
	3	J	JOCG NHK (1), Asahikawa

kHz	kW	Ctry	Station, location
	1	J	NHK (1), Iida/Nobeoka
	10	KOR	KBS, Seogwipo
	10	KOR	KBS, Taebaek
	1	KOR	KBS, Yeongdong
	500	KRE	Pyongyang BS/VoK, Chongjin
	2	NZL	Rhema, Dunedin
	2	NZL	Rhema, Whangarei
	1	PHL	DZVC Philippine Bc. Sce., Virac, Catanduanes
	10	PHL	DXDC R. Mindanao Netw., Davao C, Dvo Sur
	5	PHL	DZTG R. Philippines Netw., Tuguegarao, Cag.
	100	THA	SoR. WoR. Sor, Khon Kaen
	5	TUV	R. Tuvalu, Funafuti
	1	TWN	Taiwan BC, Tahsi
630	5	AUS	6AL ABC (LR), Albany
	50	AUS	4QN ABC (LR), Townsville
	10	AUS	2PB ABC (PNN), Sydney
	0.4	AUS	7RN ABC (RN), Queenstown
	100	BGD	Bangladesh Betar (B), Dhaka
	200	CHN	JX (CNR2); HEN (CNR2)
	2.5	CKH	R. Cook Is. AM, Rarotonga
	10	GUM	KUAM Agana
	100	IND	AIR, Thrissur
	50	INS	RRI, Makassar
	5	KOR	KBS, Inje
	10	KOR	KBS, Yeosu
	10	NZL	RNZ (N), Napier-Hastings
	100	PAK	PBC (1), Lahore
	35	PHL	DZMM ABS-CBN Bc. Corp., Quezon C, NCR
	10/5	PHL	DYWB Consolidated Bc. Syst., Inc., Bacolod C, Neg. Occ.
	5	THA	MoR. ThoR. BoR. 11, Bangkok
	10	TWN	BED65 BCC (N), Ilan
	10	TWN	Taiwan BC, Sungling
	200	VTN	Quang Binh (1), Dong Hoi
639	1	AUS	4MS ABC (LR), Mossman
	10	AUS	5CK ABC (LR), Port Pirie
	2	AUS	8RN ABC (RN), Katherine
	5	AUS	2HC Coff's Harbour
	50	BRM	Thazin Radio
	200	CHN	BJ (CNR1); SC (CNR1)
	100	IND	AIR, Kohima
	5	J	JOIP NHK (1), Oita
	10	J	JOPB NHK (2), Shizuoka
	5	J	JOWN STV, Hakodate
	2	NZL	RNZ (N), Alexandra
	100	PAK	PBC (2), Karachi (Landhi)
	5	PHL	DXKR R. Mindanao Netw., Koronadal, Cot. Sur
	1	PHL	DZRL R. Philippines Netw., Batac, I. Nte
	10	THA	R. Thailand, Chiang Mai
	20	THA	R. Thailand, N. Si Thammarat
648	2	AUS	6GF ABC (LR), Kalgoorlie
	10	AUS	2NU ABC (LR), Tamworth
	150	CHN	GD + 4 stns
	200	IND	AIR, Indore A
	10	J	AFN, Okinawa C.
	5	J	JOIG NHK (1), Toyama
	1	KOR	KBS, Boseong
	100	NPL	R. Nepal, Dhankuta
	5	PHL	DYRC Manila Bc. Co., Cebu C
	10	PHL	DWRH Pacific Bc. System, Santiago C, Isa.
	10	PHL	DWRM Philippine Bc. Sce., Pto. Princesa, Palawan
	3	PHL	DXMB R. Mindanao Netw., Malaybalay, Buk.
	25	THA	R. Thailand, Khon Kaen
	1000	TJK	Various relays, Orzu
	20	TWN	BED34 BCC (N), Taipei (Tucheng)
	50	VTN	Binh Dinh (1), An Nhon
650	5	HWA	KPRP Honolulu, Oahu
657	10	AUS	2BY ABC (LR), Byrock
	2	AUS	8RN ABC (RN), Darwin
	2	AUS	6RF Niche R. Netw., Perth (HPONS)
	300	CHN	EN; JL; ZJ
	200	IND	AIR, Kolkata A
	50	KOR	HLKM KBS, Chuncheon
	1500	KRE	Pyongyang BS, Kangnam

kHz	kW	Ctry	Call	Station, location
	10	NZL		RNZ (AM)/Star, Tauranga
	50	NZL		RNZ (AM)/Star, Wellington
	5	PHL	DXDD	Dan-ag sa Dakbayan Bc. Corp., Ozamis C, Mis. Occ.
	1	PHL	DYES	Philippine Bc. Sce., Borongan, E. Samar
	5	PHL	DWRN	Philippine R. Corp., Naga C, Cam. Sur
	5	PHL	DYVR	R. Mindanao Netw., Roxas C, Capiz
	1	PHL	DZLU	Satellite Bc. Corp., S. Fernando C, LU
	5	THA		JoR. SoR. 1, Bangkok
	20	TWN	BEV59	Cheng Sheng BC (2), Taichung
	100	VTN		Ho Chi Minh C. (1), Quan Tre
666	5	AUS	2CN	ABC (LR), Canberra
	2	AUS	4CC	Biloela (trtr)
	1	AUS	6LN	Carnarvon
	2	AUS	4LM	Mt. Isa
	200	CHN		QH + 11 stns
	600	CHN		VO Strait, FJ
	100	IND		AIR, New Delhi B
	100	J	JOBK	NHK (1), Osaka
	20	NCL		NouvelleCaledonie 1ère, Noumea
	35	PHL	DZRH	Manila Bc. Co., Makati C, NCR
	10	PHL	DXRP	Philippine Bc. Sce., Davao C, Dvo Sur
	5	THA		ThoR. PhoR. 2, Surin
	5	THA		ThoR. PhoR. 3, Tak
	50	VTN		Khanh Hoa (1), Nha Trang
670	5	HWA	KPUA	Hilo, Hawaii
675	10	AUS	2CO	ABC (LR), Albury
	5	AUS	6BE	ABC (LR), Broome
	1	CHN		BBCWS, Hongkong, Peng Chau
	200	CHN		NM + 4 stns
	10	HKG		RTHK (6), Peng Chau
	20	IND		AIR, Bhadravathi
	20	IND		AIR, Chhatarpur
	100	IND		AIR, Itanagar
	5	J	JOVK	NHK (1), Hakodate
	5	J	JOUG	NHK (1), Yamaguchi
	10	KOR		KBS, Jeonju (3)
	10	NZL		RNZ (N), Christchurch
	5	PHL	DYKC	R. Philippines Netw., Mandaue, Cebu
	1	PHL	DXGD	Sulu Tawi-Tawi Bc. Found., Bongao, Tawi-Tawi
	10	PNG		NBC Morobe, Lae
	10	PNG		NBC Wewak
	5	THA		SoR. ThoR. RoR. 2, Bangkok
	150	TKM		Turkmen R. (1), Asgabat
	10	TKM		Turkmen R. (2), Türkmenbasy
	5	TWN		Cheng Sheng BC, Peikang
	500	VTN		Hung Yen (1), My Hao
684	5	AUS	6BS	ABC (LR), Busselton
	10	AUS	2KP	ABC (LR), Kempsey
	1	AUS	8RN	ABC (RN), Tennant Creek
	600	CHN		China Radio Int., Dongfang, Hainan prov.
	1200	CHN		FJ (CNR6)
	200	CHN		GS + 9 stns
	200	IND		AIR, Kargil A
	100	IND		AIR, Kozhikode A
	100	IND		AIR, Port Blair
	5	J	JODF	IBC, Morioka
	1	J	JOLO	IBC, Ofunato
	5	J	JOAG	NHK (1), Nagasaki
	250	KRE		Pyongyang BS/Echo of Unification, Samgo
	100	NPL		R. Nepal, Pokhara
	5	NZL		Rhema, Gisborne
	5	PHL	DZCV	Filipinas Bc. Netw.,, Tuguegarao, Cag.
	5	PHL	DWJJ	Kaissar Bc. Netw., Cabanatuan, Nva. Ecija
	10	PHL	DYEZ	Manila Bc. Co., Bacolod, Neg. Occ.
	5	THA		ThoR. PhoR. 4, N. Si Thammarat
	5	THA		Yaan Kraw, Udon Thani
	10	TWN	BEC22	VO Han Bc. Netw., Taipei
690	10	HWA	KHNR	Honolulu, Oahu
693	2	AUS	5SY	ABC (LR), Streaky Bay
	10/5	AUS	4KQ	Brisbane
	0.5	AUS	4LM	Cloncurry (trtr)
	5	AUS	6WR	Kununurra (PBS)
	5	AUS	3AW	Melbourne
	0.5	AUS	4KZ	Tully (trtr)
	1000	BGD		Bangladesh Betar (A), Dhaka
	300	CHN		SN; HL
	500	J	JOAB	NHK (2), Tokyo
	5	NZL		R. Sport, Dunedin
	1	PHL	DYKX	Manila Bc. Co., Kalibo, Aklan
	10	PHL	DYPH	Manila Bc. Co., Pto. Princesa, Palawan
	10	PHL	DXBC	R. Mindanao Netw., Butuan, Ag. Nte
	1	PHL	DXDX	R. Philippines Netw., Gen. Santos C, S. Cot.
	10/5	PHL	DZTP	Tirad Pass R/TV Bc. Netw., Candon, I. Sur
	5	THA		Siang Adison, Saraburi
	8	TWN	BEC32	VO Han Bc. Netw., Tainan
	10	TWN	BEC25	VO Han Bc. Netw., Taoyuan
702	10	AUS	6KP	ABC (LR), Karratha
	50	AUS	2BL	ABC (LR), Sydney
		CHN		GD (CRI DS)
	200	CHN		JS + 8 stns
	200/300	IND		AIR, Jalandhar A, FS
	10	INS		RRI, Manokwari
	10	J	JOFB	NHK (2), Hiroshima
	10	J	JOKD	NHK (2), Kitami
	50	KRE		Korean Central BS (C/R), Chongjin
	10	NZL		Magic, Auckland
	1	NZL		R. Sport, Ashburton
	50	PHL	DZAS	FEBC, Valenzuela, NCR
	150	TJK		TR (1), Orzu
	50	VTN		Danang (2/Q/D), An Hai
705	10	LAO		Lao National Radio (P), Luang Prabang
711	10	AUS	4QW	ABC (LR), Roma/St. George
	400	BRM		Myanma Radio, Naypyidaw
	10	CHN		QH + 8 stns
	200	IND		AIR, Siliguri
	500	KOR	HLKA	KBS, Sorae (Seoul)
	5	NZL		TAB Trackside R., Wellington
	100	PAK		PBS, Dera Ismail Khan
	5	PHL	DZVR	Newsounds Bc. Netw., Laoag, I. Nte
	5	PHL	DXIC	R. Mindanao Netw., Iligan C, Lanao Nte
	5	PHL	DXRD	Swara Sug Media Corp., Davao C, Dvo. Sur
	5	PHL	DZYI	Swara Sug Media Corp., Ilagan, Isa.
	20	THA		SoR. WoR. Sor, U. Ratchathani
	5	THA		WoR. PoR. ThoR., Chiang Mai
	5	THA		WoR. SoR. PoR., Lop Buri
	10	TWN	BED92	BCC (C), Tainan
	250	TWN		VO Kuanghua, Hsinfeng
	500	VTN		Can Tho (1), Thoi Long
720	4	AUS	4AT	ABC (LR), Atherton
	0.4	AUS	2ML	ABC (LR), Murwillumbah
	2	AUS	3MT	ABC (LR), Omeo
	50	AUS	6WF	ABC (LR), Perth
	0.05	AUS	2RN	ABC (RN), Armidale
	200	CHN		BJ (CNR16)
	50	CHN		FJ (CNR2)
	1	CHN		SC; AH (2 stns)
		CHN		XJ (CNR13) (2 stns)
	5	HWA	KQNG	Kekaha, Kauai
	200	IND		AIR, Chennai A
	10	INS		RRI, Ambon
	1	J	JOIL	KBC, Kitakyushu
	500	KRE		Korean Central BS (C/R), Wiwon (Kanggye)
	10	NZL		RNZ (N), Invercargill
	5	PHL	DZJO	Bayanihan Bc. Corp., San Juan, NCR
	1	PHL	DYOK	Manila Bc. Co., Iloilo C
	5	PHL	DZSO	Newsounds Bc. Netw., San Fernando, LU
	10	THA		R. Thailand, Krabi (R. inactive)
	5	THA		SoR. ThoR. RoR. 5, Chon Buri
	1	TKM		Turkmen Radio (1), Ekarça/Etrek
	10	TWN	BED58	BCC (N), Taichung
729	50	AUS	5RN	ABC (RN), Adelaide
	100	BRM		Myanma Radio, Yangon
	200	CHN		JX; EN
	100	IND		AIR, Guwahati A
	10	INS		RRI, Nabire
	50	J	JOCK	NHK (1), Nagoya
	50	KRE		Pyongyang BS, Sepo

kHz	kW	Ctry	Call	Station, location
	5	NCL		NouvelleCaledonie 1ère, Touho
	0.1	NZL		Burn 729AM, Ranfurly
	3	NZL		R. Sport, Whangarei
	2.5	NZL		RNZ (N), Tokoroa
	10	PHL	DXIF	Newsounds Bc. Netw., Cagayan de Oro C, Mis. OR.
	5	PHL	DXOR	Pedro N. Roa Bc., Cagayan de Oro C, Mis. OR.
	5	PHL	DZGB	People's Bc. Netw., Legaspi C, Albay
	10	PHL	DWPE	Philippine Bc. Sce., Tuguegarao, Cag.
	5	PHL	DXMY	R. Mindanao Netw., Cotabato C, Mag.
	25	THA		R. Thailand, N. Ratchasima
	0.5	TWN	BEE43	Shih Hsin BS, Taipei
	200	VTN		Quang Binh (2), Dong Hoi
738	50	AUS	2NR	ABC (LR), Grafton
	5	AUS	6MJ	ABC (LR), Manjimup
	200	CHN		HN + 5 stns
	200	IND		AIR, Hyderabad A
	1	J		KNB, Takaoka
	5	J	JOLR	KNB, Toyama
	10	J	JORR	RBC, Naha, Okinawa
	100	KOR	HLKG	KBS, Daegu
	10	MAC		R. Vilaverde
	5	NZL		Magic, Christchurch
	20	OCE		R. Polynesie 1ère, Mahina
	60	PHL	DZRB	Philippine Bc. Sce., Quezon C, NCR
	50	RUS		R. Radonnezh, Tavrichanka, Sib.
	40	RUS		R. Rossii + Reg., Chelyabinsk, Sib.
	25	RUS		R. Rossii + Reg., Palana, FE
	5	THA		WoR. PoR. Tho. 2, Chiang Mai
	5	THA		WoR. PoR. Tho. 5, Songkhla
	100	TWN	BEL2	Yuyeh BS, Penghu
740	5	HWA	KCIK	Kihei, Maui
	50	VTN		Binh Dinh (2/P), An Nhon
747	0.2	AUS	8JB	ABC (LR), Jabiru
	10	AUS	4QS	ABC (LR), Toowoomba
	3.5	AUS	7PB	ABC (PNN), Hobart
	5	AUS	6SE	Esperance
	1	AUS	6FMS	Exmouth
	10	CHN		BJ (CNR12)
	200	CHN		SC + 29 stns
	300	IND		AIR, Lucknow A
	10	INS		RRI, Bengkulu
	500	J	JOIB	NHK (2), Sapporo
	100	KOR	HLKH	KBS, Gwangju
	0.4	NZL		NewstalkZB, Rotorua
	10	PHL	DZJC	Manila Bc. Co., Laoag C, I. Nte
	5	PHL	DXND	Notre Dame Bc. Co., Kidapawan, N. Cot.
	10	PHL	DYHB	R. Mindanao Netw., Bacolod, Neg. Occ.
	5	SMO		National Radio 2AP, Apia
	5	THA		RoR. DoR., Bangkok
	5	THA		ThoR. PhoR. 2, Udon Thani
750	1	CHN		SX
756	2	AUS	2TR	ABC (LR), Taree
	10	AUS	3RN	ABC (RN), Wangaratta
	2	AUS	6TZ	Margaret River
	150	CHN		HL (CNR1)
	100	IND		AIR, Jagdalpur
	10	INS		RRI, Purwokerto
	10	J	JOGK	NHK (1), Kumamoto
	100	KOR		KBS, Yeoju
	0.8	NZL		Puketapu R., Palmerston
	10	NZL		RNZ (N), Auckland
	150	PAK		PBC, Quetta (Yaru)
	10	PHL	DXBZ	Baganian Bc. Corp., Pagadiani, Z Sur
	1	PHL	DWHL	Beta Bc. Syst., Olongapo C, Zamb.
	10	PHL	DWRS	Philippine Bc. Sce., Tayug, Pang.
	2	PHL	DXJM	R. Corp. of the Philippines, Butuan C, Ag. Nte
	5	THA		KoR. WoR. SoR. 1, Surin
	5	THA		NoR. ThoR. PhoR., Narathiwat
	1	TWN		Sheng Li chih Sheng BC, Makung
	10	VTN		Long An (P), Tan An
760	10	HWA	KGU	Honolulu, Oahu
765	5	AUS	2EC	Bega
	0.5	AUS	4GC	Hughenden (trtr)
	0.5	AUS	8HOT	Katherine (trtr)
	5	AUS	5CC	Port Lincoln
	0.1	AUS	6SAT	Tom Price/Paraburdoo (trtr)
	10	CHN		EN + 5 stns
	600	CHN		FJ (CNR5)
	200	IND		AIR, Dharwad A
	1	INS		RRI, Tual
	5	J	JOPF	KRY, Shunan
	5	J	JOJF	YBS, Kofu
	10	KOR	HLCQ	MBC, Daejeon
	50	KRE		Korean Central BS (C/R), Hyesan
	2.5	NZL		R. Kahngungu, Napier-Hastings
	5	PHL	DXGS	DWRL Radio, Inc., Gen. Santos C, S. Cot.
	10	PHL	DYAP	Palawan Bc. Corp., Pto. Princesa, Palawan
	5	PHL	DYAR	Swara Sug Media Corp., Cebu C
	5	PHL	DZYT	Swara Sug Media Corp., Tuguegarao, Cag.
	5	RUS		R. Vostok Rossii, Bikin, FE (sync)
	20	RUS		R. Vostok Rossii, Khabarovsk, FE (sync)
	5	THA		Neung. PoR. NoR., Lampang
	5	THA		ThoR. OR. 2, Lop Buri
774	50	AUS	3LO	ABC (LR), Melbourne
	10	CHN		BJ (Beijing Foreign)
	200	CHN		HB; LN; SX; XJ
	100	IND		AIR, Shimla
		INS		RRI, Fak-Fak
	500	J	JOUB	NHK (2), Akita
	10	KOR	HLAN	MBC, Chuncheon
	10	KOR	HLAJ	MBC, Jeju
	5	NZL		R. Sport, New Plymouth
	25	PHL	DWWW	Interactive Bc. Media, Inc., Quezon C, NCR
	10	PHL	DXSM	Philippine Bc. Sce., Jolo, Sulu
	10	PHL	DXSO	Philippine Bc. Sce., Marawi C, Lanao Sur
	10	PHL	DYRI	R. Mindanao Netw., Iloilo C
	5	THA		Phon. MoR. 2, Rayong
	5	THA		SoR. SoR. SoR., Udon Thani
	20	TWN	BEV88	Hsien Sheng BC, Taoyuan
	5	TWN	BEV56	Sheng Li chih Sheng BC (1), Tainan
	20	TWN	BEV94	Taiwan BC, Taichung
783	2	AUS	8AL	ABC (LR), Alice Springs
	2	AUS	6VA	Albany
	100	CHN		EB (4 stns); GD
	600	CHN		VO Strait, FJ
	20	HKG		RTHK (5), Golden Hill
	20	IND		AIR, Chennai C
	10	INS		RRI, Ende
	10	KOR		KBS, Yeongwol
	10	NZL		Wellington Access R/Samoan CR, Wellington
	5	PHL	DYME	Masbate Comm. Bc. Co., Masbate C
	5	PHL	DZNL	Philippine Bc. Corp., San Fernando, LU
	10	PHL	DXRA	RMC Bc. Co., Inc., Davao C, Dvo Sur
	10	THA		R. Thailand, Ranong
	5	THA		ThoR. PhoR. 3, Kamphaeng Phet
	500	VTN		Can Tho (2), Thoi Long
790	5	HWA	KKON	Kealakekua, Hawaii
792	25	AUS	4RN	ABC (RN), Brisbane
	200	CHN		GX + 7 stns
	100	IND		AIR, Pune A
	1	J		NHK (1), Takada/Naze
	1	J		NHK (1), Takayama/Enbetsu
	50	KOR	HLSQ	Seoul Bc. System, Goyang (Seoul)
	100	NPL		R. Nepal, Kathmandu
	5	NZL		R. Sport, Hamilton
	150	PAK		Azad Kashmir Radio, Muzaffarabad (r. ‡)
	5	PHL	DWGV	GV Bc. System, Angeles C, Pampanga
	5	PHL	DYRR	Ormoc Bc. Co., Ormoc C, Leyte
	5	PHL	DXPD	People's Bc. Sce., Pagadian, Z. Sur
	10	PHL	DXBN	Philippine Bc. Sce., Butuan, Ag. Nte
	5	PHL	DWES	Rolin Bc. Enterprises, Narra, Palawan
	20	THA		WoR. PoR. ThoR., Bangkok
	1	TWN	BEV79	Keelung BS, Keelung
	10	TWN	BEC33	VO Han Bc. Netw., Hualien
801	2	AUS	4QY	ABC (LR), Cairns

kHz	kW	Ctry	Call	Station, location
	2	AUS	5RM	Berri
	5	AUS	2RF	Niche R. Netw., Gosford (HPONS)
	50	CHN		GD + 27 stns
	10	GUM	KTWG	Agana
	200	IND		AIR, Jabalpur
	1/50	INS		RRI, Medan (4)
	10	INS		RRI, Semarang
	500	KRE		Pyongyang BS, Kimchaek
	10	MLA		RTM Labuan, Kudat
	2	NZL		Rhema, Nelson
	5	PHL	DYKA	Catholic Media Netw., San José, Ant.
	5	PHL	DXES	Consolidated Bc. Syst., Inc., Gen. Santos C, S. Cot.
	5	PHL	DYWC	Franciscan Bc. Corp., Dumaguete, Neg. OR.
	10	PHL	DZNC	Newsounds Bc. Netw., Cauayan, Isa.
	1	PHL	DXBL	Swara Sug Media Corp., Bislig, Surigao S.
	5	THA		MoR. ThoR. BoR. No. 31, N. Sawan
	5	THA		ThoR. OR. 15, Chiang Rai
	5	THA		ThoR. OR. 8, U. Ratchathani
	1000	TJK		Various relays, Orzu
	1	TWN		Chien Kuo BS, Hsinhua
	250	TWN		VO Kuanghua, Kuanyin
810	10	AUS	2BA	ABC (LR), Bega
	20	AUS	6RN	ABC (RN), Perth
	200	CHN		ZJ + 6 stns
	300	IND		AIR, Rajkot A
	7.5	INS		RRI, Merauke
	50	J		AFN, Tokyo
	20	KOR	HLCT	MBC, Daegu
	50	KRE		Korean Central BS (C/R), Kaesong
	10	NPL		R. Nepal, Dipayal
	2	NZL		BBC WS NZ, Auckland
	10	NZL		RNZ (N), Dunedin
	1	PHL	DXRG	Philippine Bc. Sce., Gingoog C, Mis. OR.
	10	PHL	DZRJ	Rajah Bc. Netw., Manila, NCR
	2	PNG		NBC Rabaul
	20	THA		R. Thailand, Nong Khai
	10	THA		R. Thailand, Sangkhlaburi
	10	TWN	BEV54	Kuo Sheng BC, Changhua
819	10	AUS	2GL	ABC (LR), Glen Innes
	5	AUS	6KW	ABC (LR), Kununurra
	200	CHN		SX; SD; XJ(2 stns)
	200	IND		AIR, New Delhi A
	5	J	JONK	NHK (1), Nagano
	20	KOR	HLCN	MBC, Gwangju
	500	KRE		Korean Central BS (C), Pyongyang
	10	NZL		RNZ (N), Tauranga
	10	PHL	DYVL	Manila Bc. Co., Tacloban, Leyte
	5	PHL	DWAR	Swara Sug Media Corp., Laoag C, I. Nte
	10	PHL	DXUM	Univ. of Mindanao Bc. Netwk, Davao C, Dvo Sur
	1	PHL	DWMG	Vanguard R. Netw., Solano, Nva Viz
	10	THA		R. Thailand, Pathum Thani
	15	TJK		TR (1), Khujand
	10	TWN	BED28	BCC (N), Taitung
	5	TWN	BEV35	Cheng Sheng BC, Taipei
	20	VTN		Dac Lac (4), Buon Ma Tuhot
828	10	AUS	6GN	ABC (LR), Geraldton
	10	AUS	3GI	ABC (LR), Sale
	1	AUS	4GC	Charters Towers
	50	CHN		BJ + 6 stns
	20	IND		AIR, Panaji B
	20	IND		AIR, Silchar
	300	J	JOBB	NHK (2), Osaka
	2	NZL		TAB Trackside R., Palmerston No.
	100	PAK		PBC (1), Karachi
	1	PHL	DZTC	Govt of Tarlac Prov., Tarlac C
	5	PHL	DWZR	Hypersonic Bc. Center, Legaspi C, Albay
	10	PHL	DXCC	R. Mindanao Netw., Cagayan de Oro C, Mis. OR.
	5	THA		ThoR. PhoR. 3, Sukhothai
	5	THA		WoR. PoR. Tho. 4, N. Si Thammarat
	50	VTN		Son La (P)
830	10	HWA	KHVH	Honolulu, Oahu
837	1	AUS	6ED	ABC (LR), Esperance
	10	AUS	4RK	ABC (LR), Rockhampton
	0.5	AUS	7XS	Queenstown
	1000	CHN		FJ (CNR5)
	50	CHN		HL + 6 stns
	100	IND		AIR, Vijayawada A
	1	J		NHK (1), Nayoro
	10	J	JOQK	NHK (1), Niigata
	50	KOR	HLKY	CBS, Seoul
	2	NZL		RNZ (N), Kaitaia
	2.5	NZL		RNZ (N), Whangarei
	10	PHL	DYFM	Consolidated Bc. Syst., Inc., Iloilo C
	10	PHL	DXJS	Philippine Bc. Sce., Tandag, S Sur
	5	PHL	DXRE	Swara Sug Media Corp., Gen. Santos C, S. Cotab.
	5	THA		NoR. ThoR. PhoR., Sakon Nakhon
	10	THA		R. Thailand, Pathum Thani
	10	VTN		Can Tho (P)
846	2.5	AUS	6CA	ABC (LR), Carnarvon
	10	AUS	2RN	ABC (RN), Canberra
	5	AUS	4EL	Cairns
	100	BGD		Bangladesh Betar, Rajshahi (Bogra)
	10	CHN		BJ (CRI DS4)
	50	CHN		EN + 30 stns
	200	IND		AIR, Ahmedabad A
	5	J		NHK (1), Koriyama
	1	J		NHK (1), Uwajima/Hitoyoshi
	5	KOR		KBS, Yanggu
	10	KOR	HLAU	MBC, Ulsan
	2	NZL		NewstalkZB, Masterton
	50	PHL	DZRV	R. Veritas, Quezon C, NCR
	10	THA		R. Thailand, Phetchabun
	10	TWN	BEH56	Fu Hsing BS (2), Kaohsiung
	10	TWN	BEC38	VO Han Bc. Netw., Penghu
	250	TWN		VO Kuanghua, Kuanyin
	10	VTN		Thanh Hoa (P)
850	5	HWA	KHLO	Hilo, Hawaii
855	10	AUS	4QO	ABC (LR), Eidsvold
	10	AUS	4QB	ABC (LR), Pialba
	2	AUS	3CR	Melbourne (PBS)
	50	CHN		YN (CNR2); XJ (CNR13); NM
	50	INS		RRI, Mataram
	10	KOR	HLCX	MBC, Jeonju
	500	KRE		Pyongyang BS, Sangwon
	2	NZL		Rhema, Hamilton
	5	PHL	DXZH	Cebu Bc. Co., Zamboanga C, Z. Sur
	10	PHL	DZGE	Filipinas Bc. Netw.,. Naga C, Cam. Sur
	5	PHL	DXGO	Pacific Bc. System, Davao C, Dvo Sur
	5	THA		MoR. ThoR. BoR. 12, Prachin Buri
	10	TWN	BED27	BCC (N), Hualien
	1	TWN	BEV72	Cheng Sheng BC, Chia-i
	1	TWN	BEV24	Min Pen BC (2), Taipei
864	2	AUS	7RPH	Hobart (PBS)
	2	AUS	6AM	Northam
	2	AUS	4GR	Toowoomba
	50	CHN		AH; EB; EN; SD; ZJ (2 stns)
	10	HKG		Hong Kong Comm. Bc. Co., Peng Chau
	100	IND		AIR, Shillong
	10	INS		RRI, Cirebon
	1	J	JOXN	CRT, Nasu
	5	J	JOPR	FBC, Fukui
	3	J	JOHE	HBC, Asahikawa
	1	J		HBC, Enbetsu
	3	J	JOQF	HBC, Muroran
	10	J	JOXR	ROK, Naha, Okinawa
	1	J	JOSO	SBC, Matsumoto
	100	KOR	HLKR	KBS, Gangneung
	10	NZL		NewstalkZB, Invercargill
	5	PHL	DZWM	Alaminos City Bc. Corp., Alaminos, Pang.
	10	PHL	DYHH	Philippine Air Force, Bogo, Cebu
	10	PHL	DZIP	R. Palaweño, Pto. Princesa, Palawan
	5	PHL	DZSP	Swara Sug Media Corp., San Pablo C, Laguna
	5	PHL	DWSI	Swara Sug Media Corp., Santiago, Isa.
	10	PNG		NBC Madang
	10	THA		R. Thailand, Si Sa Ket

kHz	kW	Ctry	Call	Station, location
	10	THA		R. Thailand, Tak
	10	TWN	BED25	BCC (N), Kaohsiung
873	2	AUS	6DB	ABC (LR), Derby
	2	AUS	4AY	Innisfail (HPONS)
	5	AUS	2GB	Sydney
	100	BGD		Bangladesh Betar, Chittagong
	200	CHN		China Huayi BC, FJ
	100	CHN		HL + 7 stns
	200	CLN		FEBA India (SLBC rel.), Puttalam
	300	IND		AIR, Jalandhar B
	500	J	JOGB	NHK (2), Kumamoto
	250	KRE		Korean Central BS (C/R), Sinuiju
	1	NZL		Newstalk ZB, Ashburton
	1	NZL		TAB Trackside R., Tauranga
	5	PHL	DZPA	Abra Comm. Bc. Corp., Bangued, Abra
	5	PHL	DZRC	Filipinas Bc. Netw.,. Legaspi C, Albay
	5	PHL	DXRB	Swara Sug Media Corp., Butuan C, Ag. Nte
	5	PHL	DYUP	Univ. of the Philippines in the Visyas, Miagao, Iloilo
	5	THA		WoR. KoR. ThoR. MoR.., Bangkok
	500	VTN		Can Tho (1/3/4), Thoi Long
880	2	HWA	KHCM	Honolulu, Oahu
882	5	AUS	4BH	Brisbane
	10	AUS	6PR	Perth
	2	AUS	3YB	Warrnambool
	200	CHN		FJ + 13 stns
	400	CLN		TWR India rel., Puttalam
	300	IND		AIR, Imphal
	10	J	JOPK	NHK (1), Shizuoka
	1	J		STV, Esashi
	3	J	JOWS	STV, Kushiro
	20	KOR	HLKI	KBS, Daejeon
	250	KRE		Korean Central BS (C/R), Wonsan
	75	MNG		MRT (1), Mörön
	10	NZL		RNZ (AM)/Star, Auckland
	50	PHL	DWIZ	Aliw Bc. Corp., Navotas, NCR
	10	PHL	DXMS	Notre Dame Bc. Corp., Cotabato C, Mag.
	10	PHL	DYOG	Philippine Bc. Sce., Calbayog, W. Samar
	10	TWN	BEG77	BCC (N), Hsinchu
	1	TWN		Feng Ming BC, Penghu
891	50	AUS	5AN	ABC (LR), Adelaide
	5	AUS	4TAB	R. TAB, Townsville (HPONS)
	200	CHN		NX; LN; NM; SD; XJ
	20	IND		AIR, Rampur
	10	INS		RRI Ternate
	10	INS		RRI, Malang (R. inactive)
	20	J	JOHK	NHK (1), Sendai
	250	KOR	HLKB	KBS, Busan
	5	NZL		Magic, Wellington
	5	PHL	DZGR	People's Bc. Sce., Tuguegarao, Cag.
	1000	THA		R. Thailand, Sara Buri
	10	TWN	BED24	BCC (L), Tainan
900	2	AUS	8HA	Alice Springs
	2	AUS	6BY	Bridgetown
	2	AUS	7AD	Devonport
	5	AUS	2LM	Lismore
	5	AUS	2LT	Lithgow
		CHN		BJ (CRI DS5)
	10	CHN		QH (CNR2)
	100	CHN		YN (CRI)
	100	CHN		YN + 41 stns
	5	HWA	KMVI	Kahului, Maui
	100	IND		AIR, Kadapa
	5	J	JOHF	BSS, Yonago
	5	J	JOHO	HBC, Hakodate
	5	J	JOZR	RKC, Kochi
	50	KOR	HLKV	MBC, Seoul
	2.5	NZL		Coast, Whangarei
	10	NZL		RNZ (AM)/Star, Dunedin
	5	PHL	DYOW	Consolidated Bc. Syst., Inc., Roxas, Capiz
	5	PHL	DWNE	Nueva Ecija Prov. Gov., Cabanatuan C, Nva Viz.
	5	PHL	DXRZ	R. Mindanao Netw., Zamboanga C, Z . Sur
	10	PNG		NBC Kimbe
	10	VTN		Kon Tum (1/P)
909	300	CHN		FJ (CNR6)
	100	CHN		SC + 5 stns
	100	IND		AIR, Gorakhpur
	10	INS		RRI, Sorong
	10	J	JOCB	NHK (2), Nagoya
	5	J	JOVX	STV, Abashiri
	10	KOR		KBS, Gumi
	5	NZL		RNZ (AM)/Star, Napier-Hastings
	5	PHL	DZEA	Catholic Media Netw., Laoag C, I. Nte
	5	PHL	DYSP	Republic Bc. System, Pto. Princesa, Palawan
	5	PHL	DYLA	Visayas Mindanao C. of TU, Cebu C
	10	THA		R. Thailand, Dansai (Loei)
	25	THA		R. Thailand, Surin
	10	TWN	BEH3	Fu Hsing BS (1), Taipei
918	2/2.5	AUS	4VL	Charleville
	2	AUS	2XL	Cooma
	2	AUS	6NA	Narrogin
	200	CHN		SD
	300	IND		AIR, Suratgarh
	1	J	JOPN	KRY, Iwakuni
	1	J	JOPM	KRY, Shimonoseki
	1	J		YBC, Tsuruoka/Yonezawa/Shinjo
	5	J	JOEF	YBC, Yamagata
	50	KOR		KBS, Yeoncheon
	2.5	NZL		RNZ (N), New Plymouth
	2.5	NZL		RNZ (N), Timaru
	50	PHL	DZSR	Philippine Bc. Sce., Quezon C, NCR
	5	PHL	DXRS	R. Mindanao Netw., Surigao C, S. Nte
	100	THA		R. Thailand, Bangkok
	10	THA		SoR. WoR. PhoR. 1, Chiang Mai
927	5	AUS	4CC	Gladstone
	5	AUS	3UZ	Melbourne
	100	CHN		FJ (CNR6)
	200	CHN		GZ + 25 stns
	100	IND		AIR, Visakhapatnam
	25	INS		RRI, Pekanbaru (4)
	5	J	JOFG	NHK (1), Fukui
	5	J	JOKG	NHK (1), Kofu
	1	J		NHK (1), Wakkanai/Tsuyama
	10	KOR		KBS, Buyeo
	1	KOR		KBS, Hongcheon/Hadong
	50	KRE		Korean Central BS (C/R), Hwangju (Sariwon)
	2	NZL		NewstalkZB, Palmerston No.
	100	PAK		PBS, Khairpur (R. inactive)
	5	PHL	DXDA	Office of the Governor, San Francisco, Ag. Sur
	5	PHL	DZLG	People's Bc. Sce., Legaspi, Albay
	5	PHL	DXMD	R. Mindanao Netw., Gen. Santos C, S. Cot.
	5	PHL	DWRS	Solidnorth Bc.Syst., Vigan, I. Sur
	5	PHL	DXMM	Sulu Tawi-Tawi Bc. Found., Jolo,Sulu
	20	THA		SoR. WoR. Sor, Chanthaburi
	300	TJK		R. Japan rel., Dushanbe
	10	TWN	BED43	BCC (C), Taichung
930		CHN		ZJ
936	10	AUS	7ZR	ABC (LR), Hobart
	10	AUS	4PB	ABC (PNN), Brisbane
	5	AUS	6FX	Fitzroy Crossing (PBS)
	200	CHN		AH; NM
	100	IND		AIR, Tiruchirapalli A
	5	J	JOTR	ABS, Akita
	1	J		MRT, 4 stns
	5	J	JONF	MRT, Miyazaki
	10	KOR		KBS, Changwon (3)
	1	NZL		New Supremo, Auckland
	100	PAK		Azad Kashmir Radio, Mirpur
	5	PHL	DWIM	Insular Bc. System, Calapan, Mind. OR.
	10	PHL	DXIM	Philippine Bc. Sce., Cagayan de Oro C, Mis. OR.
	1	PHL	DZXT	R. Corp. of the Philippines, Tarlac C
	1	PHL	DYCC	R. Mindanao Netw., Calbayog C, W. Samar
	1	PHL	DYKW	R. Philippines Netw., Binalgaban, Neg. Occ.
	5	PHL	DXDN	Univ. of Mindanao, Tagum C, Dvo Nte

kHz	kW	Ctry	Call	Station, location
	50	THA		SoR. WoR. Sor, N. Sawan
	10	THA		ThoR. PhoR. 4, Pattani
	1	TWN	BEV98	Cheng Kung BS, Kaohsiung
	5	TWN		VO Han Bc. Netw., Taoyuan
940	10	HWA	KKNE	Honolulu, Oahu
945	1	AUS	4HI	Dysart (trtr)
	2	AUS	3UZ	RSN, Bendigo (HPONS)
	50	CHN		HL; HB (2 stns)
	400	CHN		JL (CNR 1)
	10	CHN		XJ (CNR13)
	100	IND		AIR, Sambalpur
	1	J		NHK (1), Fukue
	1	J	JOQP	NHK (1), Hikone
	3	J	JOIQ	NHK (1), Muroran
	5	J	JOXK	NHK (1), Tokushima
	10	KOR		KBS, Boeun
	2	NZL		NewstalkZB, Gisborne
	5	PHL	DXRO	Swara Sug Media Corp., Cotabato C, Mag.
	10	PHL	DXDV	Vismin R. and TV Bc. Net, Butuan C, Ag. Nte
	10	THA		ThoR. OR. 1, Bangkok
	10	THA		ThoR. PhoR. 2, Kalasin
954	0.35	AUS	4EL	Gordonvale (trtr)
	5	AUS	2UE	Sydney
	50	CHN		NM + 7 stns
	200	IND		AIR, Najibabad
	10	INS		RRI, Kendari
	100	J	JOKR	TBS Radio, Tokyo
	1	NZL		Coast, Dunedin
	2	NZL		TAB Trackside R., Hamilton
	40	PHL	DZEM	Christian Era Bc. Sce., Quezon City, NCR
	10	PHL	DWFB	Philippine Bc. Sce., Laoag C, I. Nte
	1	PHL	DXJT	Philippine Bc. Sce., Tangub C, Mis Octal
	10	THA		ThoR. OR. 10, Phitsanulok
	10	THA		ThoR. OR. 16, Chantaburi
	10	TWN	BEV85	Chien Kuo BS, Hsinying
963	2	AUS	6TZ	Bunbury
	5	AUS	2RG	Griffith
	5	AUS	5SE	Mt. Gambier
	5	AUS	4WK	Warwick
	20	BGD		Bangladesh Betar, Sylhet
	600	CHN		JL (CRI)
	50	CHN		LN; EB; HB; XJ (2 stns); ZJ
	20	IND		AIR, Jalgaon
	10	INS		RRI, Jember
	5	J	JOTG	NHK (1), Aomori
	5	J	JOZK	NHK (1), Matsuyama
	1	J	JOSP	NHK (1), Saga
	1	J		NHK (1), Yonago/Hagi
	10	KOR	HLCR	KBS, Andong
	10	KOR	HLKS	KBS, Jeju
	10	NZL		RNZ (AM)/Star, Christchurch
	5	PHL	DZNS	Archdiocese of Nueva Segovia, Vigan, I. Sur
	10	PHL	DYMF	People's Bc. Sce., Cebu C
	5	PHL	DXYZ	Swara Sug Media Corp., Zamboanga C, Z. Sur
	10	THA		Phon MoR. 2, Bangkok
	25	THA		SoR. WoR. Sor, Krabi
	20	TWN	BED55	BCC (C), Taipei (Tucheng)
	10	TWN	BEV84	Taiwan BC, Chunghsing
972	2	AUS	5PB	ABC (PNN), Adelaide
	0.3	AUS	2DU	Cobar (trtr)
	5	AUS	2MW	Murwillumbah
	150	CHN		EN; HL; XJ
	300	IND		AIR, Cuttack A
	50	INS		RRI, Surakarta
	1500	KOR	HLCA	KBS, Dangjin
	5	NZL		Rhema, Wellington
	5	PHL	DXKH	Cebu Bc. Co., Cagayan de Oro C, Mis. OR.
	1	PHL	DYSM	Cebu Bc. Co., Catarman, N. Samar
	5	PHL	DWTI	Katigbak Enterprises, Lucena C, Que.
	5	PHL	DWFR	Philippine Bc. Sce., Bontoc, Mt. Prov.
	10	THA		NoR. ThoR. PhoR., Phetchabun
	800	TJK		VOA R. Aap Ki Dunyaa, Dushanbe

kHz	kW	Ctry	Call	Station, location
	10	VTN		Quang Ngai (1/P)
981	2	AUS	3HA	Hamilton
	2	AUS	6KG	Kalgoorlie
	5	AUS	2NM	Muswellbrook
	200	CHN		JL (CNR1); JX (CNR1)
	5	CHN		SD
	100	IND		AIR, Raipur
	1	J		NHK (1), Kisofukushima/Sasebo
	2.5	NZL		Rhema, Timaru
	2	NZL		RNZ (N), Kaikohe
	10	PHL	DXBR	Consolidated Bc. Syst., Inc., Butuan C, Ag. Nte
	10	PHL	DYBQ	Intercontinental Bc. Corp., Iloilo C
	5	PHL	DWMT	Philippine Bc. Corp., Naga C, Cam. Sur
	5	PHL	DXDR	R. Mindanao Netw., Dipolog, Z. Nte
	10	PHL	DXOW	R. Pilipino Corp., Davao C, Dvo Sur
	5	PHL	DZRD	Swara Sug Media Corp., Dagupan C, Pang.
	10	THA		Mahaawittayalai Thammasat, Pathum Thani
	25	THA		R. Thailand, Mae Hong Son
	20	THA		R. Thailand, Nakhon Phanom
	25	THA		R. Thailand, Yala
	3	TWN	BEV68	Feng Ming BC (2), Kaohsiung
	250	TWN		VO Kuanghua, Hsinfeng
990	0.5	AUS	8GO	ABC (LR), Gove
	0.5	AUS	3RN	ABC (RN), Albury-Wodonga
	5	AUS	6RPH	Perth (PBS)
	5	AUS	4RO	Rockhampton
	100	CHN		SH; EB; NM (2 stns); YN
		FJI		Fiji Bc. Corp. Ltd. (late 2015)
	5	HWA	KIKI	Honolulu, Oahu
	300	IND		AIR, Jammu A
	10	J	JORK	NHK (1), Kochi
	10	KOR	HLAP	MBC, Changwon
	1	NZL		Apna 990, Auckland
	1	NZL		TAB Trackside R., Nelson
	5	PHL	DZMT	Pacific Bc. System, Laoag, I. Nte
	5	PHL	DYTH	Pacific Bc. System, Tacloban C, Leyte
	5	PHL	DXBM	Republic Bc. System, Cotabato C, Mag.
	10	PHL	DZIQ	Trans-Radio Bc. Corp., Makati C, NCR
	10	THA		SoR. WoR. PhoR. 2, N. Ratchasima
	20	TWN	BEV58	Cheng Sheng BC (1), Taichung
999	2	AUS	2NB	ABC (LR), Broken Hill
	5	AUS	2ST	Nowra
	10	BGD		Bangladesh Betar, Thakurgaon
	200	CHN		LN + 8 stns
	1	FSM	V6AF	Baptist R. Pohnpei, Kolonia
	1	IND		AIR, Almora
	20	IND		AIR, Coimbatore
	150	INS		RRI, Jakarta (3)
	1	J		NHK (1), Fukuyama/Hachinoe
	1	J		NHK (1), Nakamura
	10	KOR	HLCL	CBS, Gwangju
	250	KRE		Korean Central BS (C/R), Hamhung
	1.5	NZL		Manawatu Access R., Palmerston No.
	5	PHL	DWMI	Katigbak Enterprises, Calapan, Mind. OR.
	5	PHL	DZEQ	Philippine Bc. Sce., Baguio C, Benguet
	1	PHL	DXPT	Philippine Bc. Sce., Bongao, Tawi-Tawi
	1	PHL	DXHP	R. Mindanao Netw., Bislig, S. Sur
	5	PHL	DYSS	Republic Bc. System, Cebu C
	10	THA		Phon. Neung RoR. OR., Bangkok
	10	THA		ThoR. PhoR. 3, Chiang Rai
	1	TWN	BEV92	Tien Nan BS, Taipei
1008	10	AUS	4TAB	Brisbane
	5	AUS	7TAB	R. TAB, Launceston (HPONS)
	0.3	AUS	2TAB	Sky Sports R., Canberra (HPONS)
		AUS	6TAB	TAB R., Geraldton (HPONS)
	1	CHN		BJ (CNR DS3)
	50	CHN		TJ + 21 stns
	3	CHN		XJ (CNR DS)
	200	CHN		YN (CNR1)
	100	IND		AIR, Kolkata B
	10	INS		RRI, Gorontalo
	10	INS		RRI, Madiun
	50	J	JONR	ABC, Osaka

kHz	kW	Ctry	Call	Station, location
	50	KOR		KBS, Gangneung (3)
	10	NZL		NewstalkZB, Tauranga
	120	PAK		PBC (city), Hyderabad
	5	PHL	DWBS	Catholic Media Netw., Sto. Domingo, Albay
	10	PHL	DXXX	R. Philippines Netw., Zamboanga C, Z. Sur (±)
	5	PHL	DWGO	Subic Bc. Corp., Olongapo C, Zamb.
	10	THA		WoR. PoR. Tho 3, N. Ratchasima
	10	TWN	BED88	BCC (C), Taitung
	1	TWN	BEV60	Cheng Sheng BC, Kaohsiung
1017	0.5	AUS	6WH	ABC (LR), Wyndham
	5	AUS	2KY	Sydney
	1	AUS	6TAB	Vision ChR. R., Bunbury (HPONS)
	50	CHN		GD; EB
	600/100	CHN		JL(CNR8/CRI)
		CHN		ZJ (CNR1)
	20	IND		AIR, Chennai B
	10	IND		AIR, New Delhi
	50	J	JOLB	NHK (2), Fukuoka
	10	KOR	HLAW	MBC, Andong
	2.5	NZL		R. Sport/NewstalkZB, Christchurch
	10	PHL	DWDC	Intercontinental Bc. Corp., Dagupan C, Pang.
	10	PHL	DXRR	Kalayaan Bc. System, Davao C, Dvo Sur
	10	PHL	DWLC	Philippine Bc. Sce., Lucena C, Que.
	5	PHL	DXSN	Silangan Bc. Corp., Surigao C, S. Nte
	10	THA		ThoR. OR. 5, Prachuap KK
	10	TON	A3Z	Tonga Bc. Comm., Nuku'alofa
	10	TWN	BED53	BCC (C), Hsinchu
1026	14.5	AUS	3PB	ABC (PNN), Melbourne
	5	AUS	4AA	Mackay
	2	AUS	6NW	Port Hedland
	200	CHN		GZ; BJ + 4 stns
	20	IND		AIR, Allahabad A
	5	INS		RRI, Serui
	1	KOR		KBS, Geochang/Hwacheon
	2	NZL		Newstalk ZB, Kaitaia/Whangarei
	2.5	NZL		Star, Invercargill
	5	PHL	DXMC	People's Bc. Sce., Koronadal, S. Cot.
	10	PHL	DZAR	Swara Sug Media Corp., Quezon C, NCR
	10	THA		R. Thailand, Betong (Yala)
	25	THA		R. Thailand, Phitsanulok
	1	TWN	BEV51	Chung Hua BC (2), Sanchung
	1	TWN		Tien Sheng BS, Yuanli
1035	2	AUS	2EA	Wollongong (SBS)
	50	CHN		HB (CNR1); LN (CNR1)
	20	IND		AIR, Guwahati B
	5	INS		RRI, Bandar Lampung
		INS		RRI, Palu
	1	J	JOHD	NHK (2), Takamatsu
	1	J	JOIC	NHK (2), Toyama
	1	J		NHK (2), Tsuruoka
	10	KOR	HLCP	KBS, Pohang
	20	NZL		Newstalk ZB, Wellington
	120	PAK		PBC, Multan
	5	PHL	DZWX	Consolidated Bc. Syst., Inc., Baguio C, Benguet
	10	PHL	DYRL	R. Pilipino Corp., Bacolod C, Neg. Occ.
	5/1	PHL	DXUZ	Univ. de Zamboanga, Ipil, Z. Sib
	6	SLM		SIBC (R. Happy Isles), Honiara
	10	THA		Phaak Phiset, Bangkok
	10	TWN	BED26	BCC (C), Chia-i
1040	10	HWA	KLHT	Honolulu, Oahu
1044	1	AUS	6BR	ABC (LR), Bridgetown
	2	AUS	2UH	ABC (LR), Muswellbrook
	0.5	AUS	4WP	ABC (LR), Weipa
	2	AUS	5AU	Port Pirie
	600	CHN		JS (CRI)
	10	CHN		XJ (2 stns); YN
	10	HKG		Metro Bc. Corp., Peng Chau
	100	IND		AIR, Mumbai A
	10	INS		RRI Tahuna
	2	INS		RRI, Biak
	10	INS		RRI, Sibolga
	1	KOR		AFNK, Chuncheon
	10	KOR		KBS, Samcheok/Jecheon
	10	NZL		NewstalkZB, Dunedin
	5	PHL	DYMS	Cebu Bc. Co., Catbalogan, W. Samar (v)
	10	PHL	DZNG	Newsounds Bc. Netw., Naga C, Cam. Sur (±)
	5	PHL	DXCO	R. Pilipino Corp., Cayagan de Oro, Mis. OR.
	5	PHL	DXLL	R. T. Bc. Specialists Phil., Zamboanga C, Z. Sur
	10	THA		KoR. WoR. SoR. 5, Khon Kaen
	10	THA		ThoR. PhoR. 4, N. Si Thammarat
	5	TWN	BEV64	Yen Sheng BS (1), Hualien
1050		CHN		ZJ
1053	5	AUS	2CA	Canberra, ACT
	0.5	AUS	4RF	R. Rhythm, Brisbane (HPONS)
	10	BGD		Bangladesh Betar, Rangpur
	10	CHN		BJ (CNR 10)
	50	CHN		LN + 15 stns
	20	IND		AIR, Leh
	200	IND		AIR, Tuticorin, FS
	10	INS		RRI, Jayapura
	50	J	JOAR	CBC, Nagoya
	500	KRE		Pyongyang BS, Haeju
	2	NZL		NewstalkZB, New Plymouth
	10	PHL	DXKD	R. Philippines Netw., Dipolog, Z. Nte
	5	PHL	DYSA	Univ. of San Agustin, Iloilo C
	10	THA		MoR. ThoR. BoR. 11, Bangkok
1060	5	HWA	KIPA	Hilo, Hawaii (R. silent)
1062	2	AUS	5MV	ABC (LR), Renmark/Loxton
	2	AUS	4TI	ABC (LR), Thursday Isl.
	150	CHN		Zhujiang EBS; HL
	100	IND		AIR, Passighat
	50	KOR	HLKQ	KBS, Cheongju
	1	NZL		R. Sport, Wanganui
	40	PHL	DZEC	Eagle Bc. Corp., Quezon C, NRC
	5	PHL	DXKI	FEBC, Koronadal C, S. Cot.
	10/5	PHL	DYEC	Puerto Princesa Bc.Co., Pto Princesa C, Palawan
	10	THA		R. Thailand, Phuket
	10	THA		ThoR. OR. 9, Udon Thani
	10	TWN	BED23	BCC (L), Taichung
	1	TWN	BEV82	Cheng Sheng BC, Ilan
	5	TWN	BEV74	Min Li BS, Pingtung
	1	TWN		Taiwan BC, Kuanhsi
1071	2	AUS	6WB	Katanning
	2	AUS	4SB	Kingaroy
	5	AUS	3EL	Maryborough
	100	CHN		XJ + 8 stns
	870	IND		AIR, Rajkot, FS
	20	J	JOFK	NHK (1), Hiroshima
	5	J	JOWM	STV, Obihiro
	100	KAZ		Shygyz Qazaqstan OTRK, Ösqemen
	2.5	NZL		RNZ (N), Masterton
	1	NZL		TAB Trackside R., Ashburton
	5	PHL	DXKT	R. Philippines Netw., Davao C, Dvo Sur
	1	PHL	DZSL	S. O. L. Telebc. Station, Talisay, Cam Nte
	1	PHL	DYXT	Universal Bc. System, Tagbilaran C, Bohol
	10	THA		SW Rattasapha, Bangkok
	1	TWN	BEV96	Tien Sheng BS, Tainan
1080	2	AUS	2MO	Gunnedah
	2	AUS	6IX	Perth
	5	AUS	7TAB	R. TAB, Hobart (HPONS)
	10	BGD		Bangladesh Betar, Rajshahi
	600	CHN		CRI, Xuanwei, YN
	10	CHN		JS + 5 stns
	5	HWA	KWAI	Honolulu, Oahu
	10	INS		RRI, Singaraja
	10	KOR	HLAT	MBC, Yeosu
	1500	KRE		Echo of Unification, Haeju
	5	MRA	KCNM	Choice Bc. Comp., Chalan Kiya, Saipan
	10	NZL		NewstalkZB, Auckland
	5	PHL	DWRL	DWRL Radio, Inc., Legaspi C, Albay
	5	PHL	DWIN	Eagle Bc. Corp., Dagupan C, Pang.
	5	PHL	DYBH	Pacific Bc. System, Bacolod C, Neg Occ
	1	PHL	DXKS	R. Philippines Netw., Surigao, S. Nte

kHz	kW	Ctry	Call	Station, location
	10	THA		WoR. PoR. Tho. 10, Chiang Rai
	10	THA		WoR. PoR. Tho. 16, Yala
	10	THA		WoR. PoR. Tho. 9, N. Sawan
	5	TKM		Turkmen Radio (1), Serhetabat
1089	5	AUS	3WM	Horsham
	5	AUS	2EL	Orange
	600	CHN		FJ (CNR6)
	200	CHN		LN; HN
	20	IND		AIR, Naushera
	20	IND		AIR, Udipi
	10	J	JOHB	NHK (2), Sendai
	10	KOR	HLCH	KBS, Chungju
	2.5	NZL		R. Sport, Palmerston No.
	10	PHL	DXCM	Univ. of Mindanao, Cotabato C, Mag.
	10	THA		MoR. SoR. Thor, Udon Thani
	10	TWN	BEH34	Fu Hsing BS (2), Taichung
	5	TWN	BEH5	Fu Hsing BS (2), Taipei
	10	TWN	BEG28	Kaohsiung BS, Kaohsiung
	10	TWN	BEC31	VO Han Bc. Netw., Yunlin
	10	VTN		Cao Bang (P)
	10	VTN		Kien Giang (P), Rach Gia
1098	0.2	AUS	2RN	ABC (RN), Goulburn
	2	AUS	4LG	Longreach
	2	AUS	6MD	Merredin
	1000	CHN		QH (CNR1/11)
	50	CHN		TJ + 26 stns
	10	INS		RRI, Jambi
	10	INS		RRI, Sumenep
	1	J	JOMF	NBC, Sasebo
	5	J	JOGF	OBS, Oita
	5	J	JOWO	RFC, Koriyama
	1	J	JOSW	SBC, Iida
	5	J	JOSR	SBC, Nagano
	20	KOR	HLCJ	KBS, Jinju
	25	MHL	V7AB	R. Marshalls, Majuro (R. 0.25kW)
	5	NZL		NewstalkZB, Christchurch
	10	PHL	DWAD	Crusaders Bc. System, Mandaluyong C, NCR
	5	PHL	DXCL	Swara Sug Media Corp., Cagayan de Oro C, Mis. OR.
	10	THA		R. Thailand, Mae Sot
	10	THA		SoR. WoR. PhoR. 3, Songkhla
	250	TWN		R. Free Asia, Kouhu
	300	TWN		RTI, Kouhu
	10	VTN		Binh Thuan (1/P), Phan Thiet
	10	VTN		Thua Tien Hue (P), Hue
1107	5	AUS	2EA	Sydney (SBS)
	120	CHN		XJ + 8 stns
	20	IND		AIR, Gulbarga
	5	INS		RRI, Kupang
	10	INS		RRI, Yogyakarta (4)
	1	J		MBC, Akune/Oguchi/Sendai
	20	J	JOCF	MBC, Kagoshima
	5	J	JOMR	MRO, Kanazawa
	1	J		MRO, Nanao
	10	KOR	HLAV	MBC, Pohang
	1	NZL		R. Live, Tauranga/Rotorua
	1	PHL	DZOM	Ben Viduya, Calapan C, Mind. OR.
	5	PHL	DYIN	Inter-Island Broadc. Corp., Kalibo, Aklan
	10	PHL	DWDY	Northeastern Bc. Sce., Cauayan, Isa.
	5	PHL	DXBB	Sarangani Bc. Network, Gen. Santos C, S. Cot.
	10	THA		MoR. KoR., Samut Sakhon
	10	THA		ThoR. PhoR. 2, Khon Kaen
1110	5	HWA	KAOI	Kihei, Maui
1116	6.3/17	AUS	4BC	Brisbane
	2	AUS	6MM	Mandurah
	5	AUS	3AK	Melbourne
	600	CHN		FJ (CNR5)
	120	CHN		HL (CNR2)
	200	CHN		SC; AH; HA; SD
	300	IND		AIR, Srinagar A
	5	J	JODR	BSN, Niigata
	5	J	JOAF	RNB, Matsuyama
	1	J	JOAL	RNB, Niihama

kHz	kW	Ctry	Call	Station, location
	1	J	JOAM	RNB, Uwajima
	2.5	NZL		RNZ (N), Nelson
	5	PHL	DYAG	Cadiz R. And TV Netw., Cadiz C, Neg. Occ.
	5	PHL	DXAS	FEBC, Zamboanga C, Z. Sur
	10	PHL	DYTR	Tagbilaran Bc. Corp., Tagbilaran C, Bohol
	5	PHL	DZLB	Univ. of the Philippines, Los Banos, Laguna
	10	THA		R. Thailand, Takua Pa (Phang Nga)
	10	THA		ThoR. PhoR. 3, Phitsanulok
	3.5	TWN	BED72	BCC (N), Yuli
	10	TWN	BEC30	VO Han Bc. Netw., Ilan
	10	TWN	BEC22	VO Han Bc. Netw., Taipei
1125	2	AUS	1RPH	Canberra (PBS)
	5	AUS	5MU	Murray Bridge
	50	CHN		HB (2 stns); EB
	50	CLN		FEBA India/WRN relay, Puttalam
	20	IND		AIR, Tezpur
	20	IND		AIR, Udaipur
	1	J		NHK (2), Hagi/Nayoro
	1	J	JOIZ	NHK (2), Muroran
	10	J	JOAD	NHK (2), Naha, Okinawa
	1	J	JOOC	NHK (2), Obihiro
	1	J		NHK (2), Takayama
	1	J	JOLC	NHK (2), Tottori
	1	NZL		R. Hauraki, Dunedin
	1	NZL		R. Sport, Napier-Hastings
	10	PHL	DZWN	Consolidated Bc. Syst., Inc., Dagupan C, Pang.
	10	PHL	DXGL	PEC Bc. Corp., Butuan C, Ag. Nte
	5	PHL	DXGM	Republic Bc. System, Davao C, Dvo. Sur
	25	THA		R. Thailand, Chanthaburi
	20	TKM		Turkmen Radio (1), Asgabat
	5	TWN	BEV36	Cheng Sheng BC, Yunlin
	5	VTN		Tay Ninh (P)
	2.5	VUT		R. Vanuatu (VBTC), Emten Lagoon
1130	1	HWA	KPHI	Honolulu, Oahu
1134	2	AUS	2AD	Armidale
	5	AUS	3CS	Colac
	2	AUS	6TZ	Collie(trtr)
	10	CHN		GD + 5 stns
	1000	IND		AIR, Chinsurah (Mogra) N, FS
	25	INS		RRI, Banjarmasin (4) (R. inactive)
	100	J	JOQR	NCB, Tokyo
	500	KOR	HLKC	KBS, Hwaseong
	2	NZL		RNZ (N), Queenstown
	100	PAK		PBC (city), Quetta
	10	PHL	DWDD	Dept. of Nat. Defence, Quezon C, NCR
	1	PHL	DWBT	Philippine Bc. Sce., Basco, Batanes
	1	PHL	DYRM	Philippine R. Corp., Dumaguete, Neg. OR. (±)
	10	PHL	DXOS	Publ.Affairs Service, AFP, Basilan Isl., Basilan
	5	PHL	DWJS	Rolin Bc. Enterprises, Roxas, Palawan
	5	PHL	DXMV	Univ. of Mindanao, Valencia, Buk.
	10	THA		R. Thailand, Lampang
	10	THA		ThoR. PhoR. 2, N. Ratchasima
	10	TWN	BEG26	Taipei BS, Taipei
1143	5	AUS	4HI	Emerald
	2	AUS	2HD	Newcastle
	10	CHN		BJ (CNR8)
	50	CHN		EN + 36 stns
	20	IND		AIR, Ratnagiri
	20	IND		AIR, Rohtak
	20	J	JOBR	KBS, Kyoto
	100	KOR		R. Free Korea, Goyang
	10	NPL		R. Nepal, Bardibas
	2.5	NZL		RNZ (N), Hamilton
	10	PHL	DYAF	Diocese of Bacolod, Bacolod, Neg. Occ.
	10	PHL	DZMR	FEBC, Santiago C, Isa
	10	THA		OR. SoR. MoR. ThoR., Bangkok
	150	TJK		TR (2)/Vo Tajik (Ovozi Tojik), Yangiyul
	100	TWN	BEL3	Yuyeh BS, Penghu
1152	10	AUS	6PB	ABC (PNN), Busselton
	2	AUS	2WG	Wagga Wagga
	150	CHN		HN; LN; NM (2 stns)
	10	IND		AIR, Kavaratti

kHz	kW	Ctry	Call	Station, location
	10	J	JORB	NHK (2), Kochi
	10	J	JOPC	NHK (2), Kushiro
	10	KOR	HLCW	KBS, Wonju
	2	NZL		Newstalk ZB, Timaru
	100	PAK		PBC, Rawalpindi
	5	PHL	DYCM	Masbate Comm. Bc. Co., Bogo, Cebu
	10	THA		RoR. DoR., Chiang Mai
	10	THA		RoR. DoR., Khon Kaen
	1	TWN	BED68	BCC (C), Puli
	5	TWN	BEV70	Hua Sheng BC (1), Taipei
1161	1	AUS	7FG	ABC (LR), Fingal
	10	AUS	5PA	ABC (LR), Naracoorte
	2	AUS	4FC	Maryborough
	10	BGD		Bangladesh Betar, Rangamati
		CHN		CNR1
	10	CHN		SD + 4 stns
	20	IND		AIR, Trivandrum
	0.25	KOR		AFNK, Uijeongbu
	20	KOR	HLKU	MBC, Busan
	5	NZL		Te Upoko o te Ika, Wellington
	5	PHL	DYRD	Bohol Chronicle R. Corp., Tagbilaran C, Bohol
	5	PHL	DZMD	People's Bc. Netw., Daet, Cam. Nte
	10	PHL	DWCM	Philippine Bc. Corp., Dagupan C, Pang.
	5	PHL	DYKR	R. Mindanao Netw., Kalibo, Aklan
	1	PHL	DXDS	Univ. of Mindanao, Davao C, Dvo. Sur
	10	THA		SoR. ThoR. RoR. 9, U. Ratchathani
	20	THA		WoR. SoR. SoR., Bangkok
	40	TJK		TR (2), Orzu
	10	TWN	BED86	BCC (C), Ilan
	10	TWN	BED89	BCC (C), Miaoli
	1.2	TWN	BEV67	Feng Ming BC (1), Kaohsiung
1170	5	AUS	2CH	Sydney
	20	BGD		Bangladesh Betar (C), Dhaka
	600	CHN		JX (CNR1)
	10	CHN		SD (2 stns) + 7 stns
	1	IND		AIR, Hyderabad (stand-by)
	500	KOR	HLSR	KBS, Gimje
	5	MHL		Eagle Christian Radio, Majuro (R. silent)
	1.25	NZL		Te Kuiti (f.pl. 2016; irR. tests)
	100	PAK		PBS (3), Peshawar
	10	PHL	DYSL	FEBC, Sogod, S Leyte
	1000	PHL		IBB Relay Stn., Poro Pt, Luzon (R. inactive)
	10	PHL	DXMR	Philippine Bc. Sce., Zamboanga C, Z. Sur
	10	THA		SoR. ThoR. RoR. 4, Chantaburi
	10	THA		SoR. ThoR. RoR. 8, Phitsanulok
	10	VTN		An Giang (P), Long Xuyen
1179	5	AUS	3RPH	Melbourne (PBS)
	100	CHN		HB; HL; JS; XJ
	20	IND		AIR, Rewa
	10	INS		RRI, Padang
	50	J	JOOR	MBS, Osaka
	5	NZL		Ake, Auckland
	10	PHL	DWET	End-Time Mission Bc.Sce., Santiago C, Isa.
	5	PHL	DYSB	GMA Netw., Inc., Bacolod C, Neg. Occ
	5	PHL	DYCX	Newsounds Bc. Netw., S. J. de Buenavista, Antique
	1	PHL	DZRS	R. Sorsogon Netw., Inc., Sorsogon C
	5	PHL	DXYK	Republic Bc. System, Butuan C, Ag. Nte
	10	THA		NoR. ThoR. Phor, Chiang Rai
	10	THA		SoR. SoR. SoR., Bangkok
	2.5	TWN		Kuo Sheng BC, Erhlin
	10	VUT		R. Vanuatu (VBTC), Santo (R. silent)
1188	2	AUS	6XM	ABC (LR), Exmouth
	2	AUS	2NZ	Inverell
	300	CHN		CRI, Kunming, Anning, Yunnan
	10	CHN		EB(2 stns), JL
	50	IND		AIR, Mumbai C
	10	INS		RRI, Manado (4)
	10	J	JOKP	NHK (1), Kitami
	100	KOR	HLKX	RFA/VOA, Seoul
	0.4	NZL		RNZ (N), Rotorua
	5	PHL	DXLX	Consolidated Bc. Syst., Inc., Iligan, Lanao Nte
	5	PHL	DZLT	R. Corp. of the Philippines, Lucena C, Que.

kHz	kW	Ctry	Call	Station, location
	5	PHL	DZXO	Vanguard R. Netw., Cabanatuan, Nva. Ecija
	10	THA		KoR. WoR. SoR. 3, Sakon Nakhon
	10	THA		ThoR. PhoR. 1, Sa Kaeo
	10	THA		ThoR. PhoR. 3, Phitsanulok
	10	TWN	BED32	BCC (C), Hualien
	1	TWN	BEV57	Sheng Li chih Sheng BC (2), Tainan
	1	TWN	BEV46	Taiwan BC (2), Taipei
1197	2	AUS	5RPH	Adelaide (PBS)
	0.5/1	AUS	4BI	Brisbane (PBS)
	10	CHN		HL; FJ(v); SD; SH; YN
	1	IND		AIR, Shillong (stand-by)
	20	IND		AIR, Tirunelveli
	10	INS		RRI, Palangkaraya
	5	J	JOYF	IBS, Mito
	1	J	JOFO	RKB, Kitakyushu
	1	J		RKC, Nakamura
	1	J		RKK, 3 stns
	10	J	JOBF	RKK, Kumamoto
	1	J		STV, 3 stns
	3	J	JOWL	STV, Asahikawa
	1	KOR		AFNK, Dongducheon
	2	NZL		NewstalkZB, Wanganui
	5	PHL	DXFE	FEBC, Davao C, Dvo Sur
	5	PHL	DWBA	Satellite Bc. Corp., Bangued, Abra
	10	THA		JoR. ToR. Lor, Lop Buri
1206	5/5	AUS	2CC	Canberra, ACT
	5	AUS	2GF	Grafton
	2	AUS	6TAB	TAB R., Perth (HPONS)
	200	CHN		JL + 10 stns
	200	IND		AIR, Bhawanipatna
	1	KOR		KBS, Jeongseon/Cheongsong
	2	NZL		TAB Trackside R., Dunedin
	10	THA		ThoR. PhoR. 1, Prachuap KK
	100	TWN		RTI, Minhsiung
	10	TWN	BEV62	Taiwan BC, Hsinchu
1210	1	HWA	KZOO	Honolulu, Oahu
1215	0.5	AUS	6NM	ABC (LR), Northam
	0.35	AUS	2TAB	KIX Country, Bowral (HPONS)
	0.25	AUS	4HI	Moranbah (trtr)
	50	CHN		GD (CNR7)
	50	CHN		HL; HB; XJ
	20	CHN		LN (CNR2)
	20	IND		AIR, New Delhi (Kingsway) N
	20	IND		AIR, Pudducherri
		INS		RRI, Bandung (3)
	10	INS		RRI, Samarinda
	1	J	JOBW	KBS, Hikone
	2	J	JOBO	KBS, Maizuru
	10	KOR	HLAK	MBC, Jinju
	2	NZL		NewstalkZB, Kaikohe
	10	PHL	DYRF	Word Bc. Corp., Cebu C
	10	THA		KoR. WoR. SoR. 2, Phrae
	25	THA		R. Thailand, Surat Thani
	10	THA		ThoR. PhoR. 2, U. Ratchathani
	1	TWN		Tien Sheng BS, Pengshan
1224	5	AUS	3EA	Melbourne (SBS)
	5	AUS	2RPH	Sydney (PBS)
	100	CHN		FJ (CNR6)
	100	CHN		GX; JS; NM
	10	IND		AIR Srinagar C
	10	J	JOJK	NHK (1), Kanazawa
	20	KOR		KBS, Gwangju (3)
	2	NZL		TAB Trackside R., Invercargill
	10	PHL	DXED	Eagle Bc. Corp., Davao C, Dvo Sur
	5	PHL	DWSR	Manila Bc. Co., Lucena, Que.
	10	PHL	DZAG	Philippine Bc. Sce., Agoo, LU
	5	RUS		R. Rossii + Reg., Nikolayevsk-na-Amure, Sib.
	10	THA		ThoR. OR. 15, Chiang Rai
	10	THA		ThoR. OR. 4, N. Sawan
	10	TWN	BED52	BCC (C), Kaohsiung
	1	TWN	BEV71	Hua Sheng BC (2), Taipei
1233	10	AUS	2NC	ABC (LR), Newcastle
	120	CHN		XJ (2stns); HN (2 stns); JS
	20	IND		AIR, Tura

kHz	kW	Ctry	Call	Station, location
	5	INS		RRI, Pontianak
	5	J	JOUR	NBC, Nagasaki
	5	J	JOGR	RAB, Aomori
	1	KOR		KBS, Pyeongchang
	2	NZL		R. Live, Wellington
	5	PHL	DYVS	FEBC, Bacolod, Neg. Occ.
	5	PHL	DWRV	R. Veritas, Bayombong, Nva Viz.
	10	THA		ThoR. OR. 1, Bangkok
	10	THA		WoR. PoR. Tho. 7, Udon Thani
	40	TKM		Turkmen Radio (1), Syrttagta
	1	TWN		Chung Hua BC, Juifang
1242	2	AUS	5AU	Port Augusta
	2	AUS	8TAB	R. TAB, Darwin (HPONS)
	5	AUS	3GV	Sale
	2	AUS	4AK	Toowoomba
	100	CHN		YN + 5 stns
	100	IND		AIR, Varanasi
	10	INS		RRI, Bogor
	100	J	JOLF	NBS, Tokyo
	10	KOR	HLSB	MBC, Wonju
	2	NZL		One Double X, Whakatane
	1	NZL		TAB Trackside R., Timaru
	5	PHL	DXZB	DXZB/TV13 Coop., Inc., Zamboanga C, Z. Sur
	20	PHL	DWBL	FBS R. Netw., Pasig C, NCR
	5	PHL	DXSY	Times Bc. Corp., Ozamis C, Mis. Occ.
	50	THA		SoR. WoR. Sor, Surat Thani
	10	THA		ThoR. PhoR. 3, Phetchabun
	1	TWN		Yen Sheng BS (2), Hualien
	500	VTN		VO Vietnam, Can Tho
1250	1	CHN		ZJ
1251	1	FSM		Joy Family R., Colonia, Yap
	2	AUS	2DU	Dubbo
		CHN		BJ (CRI DS1)
	200	CHN		QH + 27 stns
	20	IND		AIR, Sangli
	10	INS		RRI, Banda Aceh
	10	KOR	HLKT	CBS, Daegu
	5	NZL		Rhema, Auckland
	6.3	NZL		Taupo (f.pl. 2016)
	10	PAK		PBC, Loralai
	1	PHL	DYRG	Intercontinental Bc. Corp., Kalibo, Aklan
	2.5	PHL	DZMS	People's Bc. Netw., Sorsogon C
	10	THA		JoR. SoR. 3, Roi Et
	5	THA		ThoR. OR. 6, Bangkok
	100	TJK		BBCWS/Reach Beyond, Dushanbe
	10	TWN		VO Han Bc. Netw., Kaohsiung
1260	1	AUS	6KA	Karratha
	2	AUS	3SR	Shepparton
	2	AUS	4MW	Thursday Island (PBS)
	10	CHN		LN; HN; XZ
	20	IND		AIR, Ambikapur
	20	J	JOIR	TBC, Sendai
	5	KOR		AFNK, Busan
	10	KOR		KBS, Namwon
	2	NZL		TAB Trackside R., Christchurch
	400	PAK		PBS (2), Peshawar
	5	PHL	DZEL	Eagle Bc. Corp., Lucena C, Que.
	5	PHL	DWMC	Magiliw Comm. Bc. Co., Rosales, Pang.
	5	PHL	DXRF	Manila Bc. Co., Davao C, Dvo Sur
	10	PHL	DYDD	Siam Bc. Netw. Corp., Lapu-Lapu C, Cebu
	25	THA		R. Thailand, Chiang Rai
	1	TWN		Cheng Sheng BC, Taipao
1269	5	AUS	6RN	ABC (RN), Busselton
	5	AUS	2SM	Sydney
	600	CHN		CRI, Xuanwei, Yunnan
	10	CHN		SX (2 stns); JL; JS
	20	IND		AIR, Agartala
	20	IND		AIR, Madurai
	1	J	JOFM	HBC, Esashi
	5	J	JOHW	HBC, Obihiro
	1	J		JRT, Ikeda
	5	J	JOJR	JRT, Tokushima
	1	KOR		KBS, Gurye
	10	KOR		KBS, Yangju

kHz	kW	Ctry	Call	Station, location
	0.4	NZL		The Hits, Takaka
	10	PHL	DWRC	Republic Bc. System, San Nicolas, I. Nte
	10	THA		Kho. SoR. ThoR. BoR., Bangkok
	10	THA		MoR. Kor, Songkhla
	1	TWN	BEV37	Cheng Sheng BC, Taitung
	10	TWN	BEC44	VO Han Bc. Netw., Penghu
	50	UZB		UZR (2), Zarafshon
1270	5	HWA	KNDI	Honolulu, Oahu
1278	5	AUS	3EE	Melbourne
	100	CHN		EB (2 stns); FJ; HL; JX
	10	IND		AIR, Lucknow C
	50	J	JOFR	RKB, Fukuoka
	1	KOR		KBS, Hapcheon
	2	NZL		Newstalk ZB, Napier-Hastings
	10	PHL	DZRM	Philippine Bc. Sce., Quezon C, NCR
	5	RUS		R. Rossii + Reg., Bagdarin, Sib. (cd 1st quarter 2016)
	1	TWN		Fuhsingkang BS, Peitou
1287	2	AUS	2TM	Tamworth
	10	BGD		Bangladesh Betar, Barishal
	10	CHN		FJ (CNR1)
	25	CHN		GD + 8 stns
	100	IND		AIR, Panaji A
	25	INS		RRI, Palembang
	50	J	JOHR	HBC, Sapporo
	150	KGZ		TWR Europe, Bishkek
	10	KOR	HLAX	MBC, Cheongju
	10	KOR	HLAF	MBC, Gangneung
	2	NZL		Newstalk ZB, Westport
	5	PHL	DZZH	Manila Bc. Corp., Sorsogon C
	10	THA		SoR. OR. ThoR., Samut Prakan (Bangkok)
	10	THA		WoR. PoR. Tho. 6, U. Ratchathani
	1	TWN		Min Li BS, Fangliao
	10	TWN	BEC27	VO Han Bc. Netw., Taichung
1296	10	AUS	6RN	ABC (RN), Wagin
	5	AUS	4RPH	Brisbane (PBS)
	300	CHN		CRI, Kunming,YN
	25	CHN		SH + 5 stns
	10	IND		AIR, Darbhanga
	10	J	JOTK	NHK (1), Matsue
	500	KGZ		R. Rossii relay, Bishkek
	2.5	NZL		NewstalkZB, Hamilton
	10	PHL	DXAB	ABS-CBN Bc. Corp., Davao C, Dvo Sur
	5	PHL	DYJJ	Intercontinental Bc. Corp., Roxas C, Capiz
	5	PHL	DWPR	Multipoint Broadc. Netwk., Dagupan C, Pang.
	300	TJK		R. Rossii relay, Orzu
	10	TWN	BED47	BCC (N), Tainan
	1	TWN	BEV23	Min Pen BC (1), Taipei
1305	2	AUS	5RN	ABC (RN), Renmark/Loxton
	10	CHN		QH (CNR2)
	10	CHN		SD; NM
	20	IND		AIR, Parbhani
	10	KOR		KBS, Uljin
	2.5	NZL		R. Dunedin
	10	THA		Yaan Kraw, Sara Buri
1314	5	AUS	3BT	Ballarat
	5	AUS	2TAB	Sky Sports R., Wollongong (HPONS)
	10	BGD		Bangladesh Betar, Cox's Bazar
	50	CHN		CQ + 6 stns
	20	IND		AIR, Bhuj
	1	IND		AIR, Cuttack B
	50	J	JOUF	OBC, Osaka
	10	KOR	HLCM	CBS, Jeonbuk
	5	NZL		RNZ (AM)/Star, Invercargill
	2	NZL		RNZ (N), Gisborne
	10	PHL	DWXI	Delta Bc. System, Parañaque, NCR
	10	THA		MoR. KoR., Khon Kaen
	1	TWN	BEP33	Ching Cha BS, Tainan
	10	TWN	BEV76	Tien Sheng BS, Chunan
1322	5	PHL	DXAD	Mindanao DMPC, Marawi, Lanao Sur (v)
1323	3.3/5	AUS	5DN	Adelaide
	0.4	AUS	1--	Star AM, Canberra (HPONS)
	200	CHN		HL(CRI)
	600	CHN		JL (CRI)

kHz	kW	Ctry	Call	Station, location
	500	CHN		XJ (CRI)
	20	CHN		ZJ + 5 stns
	20	IND		AIR, Kolkata C
	1	J	JOFP	NHK (1), Fukushima
	1	J		NHK (1), Yamada
	1	KOR		KBS, Yeonggwang/Ulleung
	3	NZL		Coast, Hawera
	10	PHL	DXHR	Gateway UHF Bc., Butuan C, Ag. Nte. (v)
	10	PHL	DYSI	GMA Netw., Inc., Iloilo C
	10	PHL	DZRK	Philippine Bc. Sce., Tabuk, Kalinga
	10	THA		ThoR. OR. 13, Chiang Mai
	10	THA		ThoR. OR. 7, Surat Thani
	7	TJK		Tajik R1, Dushanbe
	1	TWN	BEV45	Taiwan BC (1), Taipei
1332	5	AUS	4BU	Bundaberg
	2	AUS	3SH	Swan Hill
	100	CHN		EN (4 stns) + 4 stns
	10	IND		AIR, Tezu
	10	INS		RRI, Jakarta (4)
	50	J	JOSF	Tokai R., Nagoya
	10	KOR	HLAO	MBC, Chungju
	10	NZL		R. Sport, Auckland
	100	PAK		PBC (city), Lahore
	1	PHL	DZKI	R. Philippines Netw., Iriga C, Cam. Sur
	5	PHL	DWAY	Swara Sug Media Corp., Cabanatuan, Nva. Ecija
	10	THA		OR. SoR., Bangkok
	10	THA		ThoR. OR. 14, Maha Sarakham
	1	TWN		Taiwan BC, Puli
	10	TWN	BEC36	VO Han Bc. Netw., Kaohsiung
1341	5	AUS	3CW	Geelong (HPONS)
	5	AUS	2TAB	Sky Sports R., Newcastle (HPONS)
	300	CHN		GD (CRI/CNR 1)
	100	CHN		HL + 6 stns
	1	IND		AIR, Kohima
	5	INS		RRI, Tanjung Pinang
	1	J		NHK (1), Iwaki/Minamata
	25	KAZ		Qazaq Radiosi, Aqtaw
	2	NZL		NewstalkZB, Nelson
	10	PAK		PBC, Bahawalpur
	20	THA		R. Thailand, Loei
	10	THA		R. Thailand, Phangnga
	25	THA		R. Thailand, Ubon Ratchathani
1350	5	AUS	2LF	Young
	50	CHN		YN + 6 stns
	1	FSM	V6A	Baptist Church, Weno, Chuuk
	0.25	GUM		Agana
	1	IND		AIR, Jalandhar C
	20	IND		AIR, Kupwara
	10	INS		RRI, Tarakan
	20	J	JOER	RCC, Hiroshima
	10	KOR	HLAQ	MBC, Samcheok
	1	NZL		R. Sport, Rotorua
	10	PHL	DWUN	Prog.Bc.Corp., Quezon, C, NCR
	5	RUS		R. Rossii + Reg., Ust-Kan/Ulagan, Sib. (cd end of 2015)
	10	THA		Phon. Neung RoR. OR., Bangkok
	10	THA		WoR. PoR. Tho. 17, Trang
	10	TWN	BED63	BCC (N), Chia-i
	2.5	TWN	BEV50	Chung Hua BC (1), Sanchung
1359	0.2	AUS	3UZ	RSN, Mildura (HPONS)
	0.25	AUS	4WK	Toowoomba City (trtr)
		CHN		CNR1; YN (2 stns)
	2.5	NZL		Coast, New Plymouth
	1	NZL		More FM, Queenstown
	1	PHL	DYSJ	Inter-Island Broadc. Corp., S. J. de Buenavista, Antique
	5	PHL	DZYR	Philippine Bc. Corp., S. Fernando, LU
	10	THA		ThoR. PhoR. 2, Sakhon Nakhon
	600	TWN		RTI, Fangliao
	5	TWN	BEC40	VO Han Bc. Netw., Hualien
1368	2	AUS	2GN	Goulburn
	10	CHN		HL; FJ (v); HB (2 stns)
	20	IND		AIR, New Delhi C
	1	J	JOTS	HBC, Wakkanai

kHz	kW	Ctry	Call	Station, location
	5	J	JOHP	NHK (1), Takamatsu
	1	J	JOLG	NHK (1), Tottori
	1	J		NHK (1), Tsuruoka
	1	KOR		KBS, Muju
	2	KRE		Korean Central BS (E), Pyongyang
	1	NZL		R. Live, Napier-Hastings
	0.8/0.1	NZL		Village R., Tauranga
	1	PHL	DZRA	Catanduanes State College, Virac, Catanduanes
	2.5	PHL	DZBS	R. Philippines Netw., Baguio C, Benguet
	10	PHL	DXKO	R. Philippines Netw., Cagayan de Oro C, Mis. OR.
	10	THA		R. Thailand, Buri Ram
	25	THA		R. Thailand, Nan
	10	THA		ThoR. OR. 12, N. Pathom
	1	TWN		Chin Hsi BC, Kaohsiung
1370	6.2	HWA	KUPA	Pearl City, Oahu
1377	5	AUS	3MP	Melbourne
	600	CHN		HEN (CNR1)
	100	CHN		XZ + 5 stns
	20	IND		AIR, Hyderabad B
	10	INS		RRI, Tolitoli
	1	J		NHK (2), Hachinohe
	1	J	JOAC	NHK (2), Nagasaki
	5	J	JOUC	NHK (2), Yamaguchi
	2	NZL		R. Sport, Levin
	3	NZL		Star, Dunedin
	10	PHL	DXKP	R. Philippines Netw., Pagadian C, Z. Sur
	10	THA		R. Thailand, Chumphon
	10	THA		WoR. Phon 4, Phitsanulok
1386	50	CHN		TJ + 6 stns
	20	IND		AIR, Gwalior
	10	J	JOHC	NHK (2), Kagoshima
	10	J	JOJB	NHK (2), Kanazawa
	10	J	JOQC	NHK (2), Morioka
	5	J	JOKB	NHK (2), Okayama
	10	KOR	HLAM	MBC, Mokpo
	10	NZL		R. Tarana, Auckland
	5	PHL	DYVW	Catholic Media Netw., Borongan, E. Samar
	10	PHL	DXCR	Mt. View College, Valencia, Buk.
	10	THA		SW Pheua Kaan Kaset, Bangkok (Pathum Thani)
	3.5	TWN	BED74	BCC (C), Yuli
1395	0.2	AUS	2LG	ABC (LR), Lithgow
	5	AUS	5AA	Adelaide
	50	CHN		AH (3 stns) + 5 stns
	20	IND		AIR, Bikaner
	1	INS		RRI, Wamena
	1	J	JOCE	CRK, Toyooka
	1	J	JOWE	RFC, Wakamatsu
	10	KOR		KBS, Cheorwon
	2	NZL		NewstalkZB, Oamaru
	5	PHL	DZVT	Apostolic Vicariate of S. J., San Jose, Min. Occ.
	10	PHL	DYCH	Cebu Bc. Co., Talisay C, Cebu
	10	THA		NoR. ThoR. PhoR., Chiang Rai
	1	TWN		Cheng Sheng BC, Tafa
1404	2	AUS	2PK	Parkes/Forbes
	4	AUS	6TAB	TAB R., Busselton (HPONS)
	50	CHN		FJ (2 stns); HB (3 stns); LN; ZJ
	20	IND		AIR, Gangtok
	5	J	JOQL	HBC, Kushiro
	1	J	JOVO	SBS, Hamamatsu
	10	J	JOVR	SBS, Shizuoka
	7	KGZ		KGR (1), Aydarken/Naryn
	1	KGZ		KGR (1), Cholponata
	20	KGZ		KGR (1), Dödömöl
		KGZ		KGR (1), Orgochor
	10	KOR	HLKP	CBS, Busan
	5	NZL		Rhema, Invercargill
		PHL		End Time Mission, Lucena C, Que
	1	PHL	DYKB	R. Philippines Netw., Bacolod, Neg. Occ.
	10	THA		JoR. SoR. 4, Yasothon
	25	THA		R. Thailand, Songkhla
	10	THA		ThoR. PhoR. 1, Suphan Buri

kHz	kW	Ctry	Call	Station, location
	2.5/5	TLS		R. Timor Kmanek, Díli
	10	TWN	BEV78	Yi Shih BS, Keelung
1413	5	AUS	2EA	Newcastle (SBS)
	0.5	AUS	3UCB	Vison ChR. R., Shepparton (HPONS)
	10	BGD		Bangladesh Betar, Comilla
	5	CHN		XJ + 7 stns
	20	IND		AIR, Kota
	5	INS		RRI, Sungai Liat
	50	J	JOIF	KBC, Fukuoka
	2	NZL		NewstalkZB, Tokoroa
	1	NZL		R. Ferrymead, Christchurch
	5	PHL	DYXW	Filipinas Bc. Netw.,. Tacloban C, Leyte
	5	PHL	DWRA	Republic Bc. System, Bauio C, Benguet
	10	TWN	BED54	BCC (N), Miaoli
	1	TWN	BED67	BCC (N), Puli
1420	5	HWA	KKEA	Honolulu, Oahu
1422	1	AUS	4AM	Port Douglas (trtr)
	2	AUS	6GS	R. Great Southern, Wagin (HPONS)
	5	AUS	3XY	R. Helias, Melbourne (HPONS)
	20	CHN		SH (2 stns); SX (2 stns); SC
	600	CHN		XJ (CNR1/8/13/CRI)
	0.5	CHR	6ABCRN	ABC Radio National relay, Phosphate Hill
	50	J	JORF	RF, Yokohama
	5	PHL	DXMU	Central Mindanao Univ., Musuan, Buk.
	10	THA		Phon. Neung RoR. OR., Bangkok
	10	THA		R. Thailand, Amnat Charoen
	1	TWN		Chien Kuo BS, Kuanyin
	50	TWN		RTI, Minhsiung
1431	2	AUS	2RN	ABC (RN), Wollongong
	2	AUS	6TAB	Vision ChR. R., Kalgoorlie (HPONS)
	10	BGD		Bangladesh Betar, Bandorban
	10	CHN		EB + 6 stns
	1	J		BSS, Izumo
	1	J	JOHL	BSS, Tottori
	5	J	JOZF	GBS, Gifu
	1	J		NBC, Fukue
	1	J	JOWW	RFC, Iwaki
	5	J	JOVF	WBS, Wakayama
	40	KGZ		KGR1, Jalalabat
	2	NZL		R. Kidnappers, Napier-Hastings
	5	THA		SoR. ThoR. RoR. 6, Songkhla
	10	THA		ThoR. OR. 3, N. Ratchasima
1440	2	AUS	1SBS	Canberra (SBS)
	50	CHN		NM (2); GX; LN
	1	IND		AIR, Kurseong
	3	J		STV, Muroran
	50	J	JOWF	STV, Sapporo
	1	J		STV, Tomakomai
	10	KIR		R. Kiribati, Bairiki
	5-0.25	KOR		AFNK, 4 stns
	1.1	MRA	KKMP	Blue Continent Comm., Rota
	0.2	NZL		Moana AM, Tauranga
	10	PHL	DWDH	Manila Bc. Co., Dagupan C, Pang.
	0.01	PHL	DXSI	So. Inst. of Tech., Cagayan de Oro C, Mis. OR.
	5	RUS		R. Rossii + Reg., Ust-Koksa/Turochak, Sib. (cd end of 2015)
	10	THA		ThoR. PhoR. 2, N. Phanom
	10	THA		WoR. PoR. Tho. 8, Samut Sakhon
1449	5	AUS	2MG	Mudgee
	2	AUS	6TAB	TAB R., Mandurah (HPONS)
	20	CHN		JX; FJ; SD(2 stns)
	10	FSM	V6AH	FSMBS R. Pohnpei, Kolonia
	5	J	JOQM	HBC, Abashiri
	1	J		RNC, Marugame
	5	J	JOKF	RNC, Takamatsu
	10	KOR	HLQB	KBS, Ulsan
	5	MLD		Raajje Radio, Malé
	2.5	NZL		RNZ (N), Palmerston No.
	10	PAK		PBC, Zhob
	5	PHL	DXSA	Mindanao Bc. Co., Inc., Marawi C, Lanao Sur
	10	THA		ThoR. PhoR. 3, Phichit
	10	THA		WoR. SoR. PoR., Chumphon
1458	2	AUS	2PB	ABC (PNN), Newcastle
	200	CHN		NM; EN; JS; LN
	20	IND		AIR, Barmer
	20	IND		AIR, Bhagalpur
	1	J		IBS, Sekijo
	1	J	JOYL	IBS, Tsuchiura
	1	J	JOUO	NBC, Saga
	1	J		RCC, Shobara
	1	J	JOWR	RFC, Fukushima
	1	KOR		KBS, Hamyang/Bonghwa
	2.5	NZL		RNZ (N), Westport
	10	PHL	DYZZ	Siam Bc. Netw. Corp., Gihulngan, Neg. Occ.
	10	PHL	DZJV	ZOE Bc. Netw., Calamba, Laguna
	10	THA		JoR. SoR. 6, Si Sa Ket
	10	THA		SoR. ThoR. RoR. 3, Phuket
1460	5	HWA	KRHA	Honolulu, Oahu
1467	2	AUS	3ML	Mildura
	10	CHN		EB; JX; SD
	100	IND		AIR, Jeypore
	1	J	JOVB	NHK (2), Hakodate
	1	J	JOMC	NHK (2), Miyazaki
	1	J	JONB	NHK (2), Nagano
	1	J	JOID	NHK (2), Oita
	1	J		NHK (2), Wakkanai
	500	KGZ		TWR India, Bishkek, Krasnaya Rechka
	50	KOR	HLKN	KBS, Mokpo
	1	PHL	DWVR	R. Veritas, San Jose C, Nva Ecija
	5	PHL	DXVP	RCA-ZBN, Zamboanga C, Z. Sur
	100	THA		SoR. WoR. Sor, Pathum Thani
1476	1	AUS	5MG	ABC (LR), Mt. Gambier
	2	AUS	4ZR	Roma
	50	CHN		HL (3 stns) + 7 stns
	1	IND		AIR, Jaipur A
	1	J		NHK (2), Iida
	5	NZL		TAB Trackside R., Auckland
	10	PAK		PBC, Faisalabad
	1	PHL	DZYA	R. Pilipino Corp., Angeles C, Pamp.
	10	PHL	DXRJ	Rajah Bc. Netw., Iligan C, Lanao Nte
	1	PHL	DWRB	Ribbon Bc. Netw., Lipa C, Bat
	50	THA		R. Thailand, Chiang Mai
	10	TKM		Turkmen R. (1), Türkmenbasy
1485	0.05-0.2	AUS		ABC (LR), 2 stns
	0.1	AUS	2RN	ABC (RN), Wilcannia
	0.15	AUS	2EA	Shellharbour (SBS)
	10	CHN		HB + 16 stns
	0.25	DGA		AFRTS, Diego Garcia
	1	IND		AIR, 11 stns
	1	J	JOPL	KRY, Hagi
	1	J	JOGO	RAB, Hachinohe
	1	KOR		KBS, Gongju/Goheung
	1	NZL		TAB Trackside R., Gisborne
	5	PHL	DYDH	Pacific Bc. System, Iloilo C
1494	2	AUS	2AY	Albury
	1	CHN		AH + 6 stns
	5	FSM	V6AI	FSMBS R. Yap, Colonia
	1	J	JOTL	HBC, Nayoro
	1	J		RSK, 5 stns
	10	J	JOYR	RSK, Okayama
	2.5	NZL		R. Sport, Timaru
	2.5	NZL		RNZ (AM)/Star, Hamilton
	5	PHL	DXOC	DWRL Radio, Inc., Ozamis C, Mis. Occ.
	10	PHL	DWSS	Supreme Bc. Systems DWSS, Pasig C, NCR
	10	THA		OR. SoR. MoR. ThoR., Bangkok
	10	TWN	BEE34	Chiao Yu Bc. System, Changhua
	10	TWN	BEE32	Chiao Yu Bc. System, Taipei
1500	10	HWA	KHKA	Honolulu, Oahu
1503	5	AUS	2BS	Bathurst
	5	AUS	3KND	Melbourne (PBS)
	10	CHN		HN + 4 stns
	1	FSM	V6AJ	FSMBS R. Kosrae, Tofol
	10	J	JOUK	NHK (1), Akita
	1	J		NHK (1), Aso

kHz	kW	Ctry	Call	Station, location
	1	KOR		KBS, Gimcheon
	2.5	NZL		R. Sport, Christchurch
	5	NZL		R. Sport, Wellington
	10	THA		JoR. SoR. 2, Surat Thani
	600	TWN		RTI/RFA/R. DLSN, Fangliao
1512	10	AUS	2RN	ABC (RN), Newcastle
	5	AUS	6BAY	Morawa
	10	CHN		GS; NM; SD
	20	IND		AIR, Kokrajhar
	10	INS		RRI, Bukittinggi
	1	J		NHK (2), Koriyama/Matsumoto
	5	J	JOZB	NHK (2), Matsuyama
	1-0.1	KOR		AFNK, 5 stns
	10	PAK		PBC, Gilgit
	10	PHL	DYAB	ABS-CBN Bc. Corp., Cebu C
	10	PHL	DZAT	End Time Mission, Lucena C, Que
	10	THA		KoR. WoR. SoR. 4, Phayao
	10	THA		ThoR. OR. 11, Songkhla
	10	TWN		Ching Cha BS, Hsinchu
1521	2	AUS	2QN	Deniliquin
	500	CHN		CRI, Ürümqi, Xinjiang
	25	CHN		EB (2 stns) + 24 stns
	20	IND		AIR, Tawang
	1	J	JOTC	NHK (2), Aomori
	1	J	JOFC	NHK (2), Fukui
	1	J	JODC	NHK (2), Hamamatsu
	1	J		NHK (2), Ishigaki/Nakamura
	1	J	JOJC	NHK (2), Yamagata
	1	J		NHK (2), Yonago
	1	NZL		R. Sport, Tauranga
	10	THA		NoR. ThoR. Phor, Bangkok
1530	2	AUS	2VM	Moree
	50	CHN		ZJ; JL; SX
	0.25	GUM		Agana
	20	IND		AIR, Agra
	1	J	JODO	BSN, Joetsu
	5	J	JOXF	CRT, Utsunomiya
	1	J	JOEO	RCC, Fukuyama
	1	J		RCC, Mihara
	5	KOR		AFNK, Seoul (Yongsan)
	1	NZL		The Wireless Station, Napier-Hastings
	25	PHL	DZME	Capitol Bc. Center, Quezon C, NCR
	10	THA		ThoR. PhoR. 1, Chanthaburi
	10	THA		WoR. PoR. Tho. 14, Uttaradit
1539	1	AUS	2RF	Niche R. Netw., Sydney (HPONS)
	5	AUS	5TAB	R. TAB, Adelaide (HPONS)
	100	CHN		QH (CNR1)
	1	KOR		KBS, Gosan
	0.4	NZL		The Hits, Picton
	5	PHL	DZYM	Philippine R. Corp., San José, Mind. Occ.
	10	THA		Phon RoR. Kao, Kanchanaburi
1540	5	HWA	KREA	Honolulu, Oahu
1548	50	AUS	4QD	ABC (LR), Emerald
	200	CHN		SD
	400	CLN		Athmik Yatra Radio, Trincomalee
	1	NZL		Coast, Palmerston No
	0.9	NZL		TAB Trackside R., Rotorua
	5	PHL	DYDM	Catholic Media Netw., Maasin C, So. Leyte
	10	PHL	DZSD	GMA Netw., Inc., Dagupan C, Pang.
1557	0.5	AUS	5TAB	KIX Country, Renmark/Loxton (HPONS)
	2	AUS	2RE	Taree
	25	CHN		EB (2 stns)
		KGZ		Qazaq Radiosi, Lepsi
	2	NZL		Hokonui R., Hawera
	10	PAK		PBC, Skardu
	10	THA		R. Thailand, Trat
	10	THA		Siang Adison, Phetchabun
	300	TWN		RTI, Kouhu
1566	0.2	AUS	4GM	ABC (LR), Gympie
	5	AUS	3NE	Wangaratta
	10	CHN		EB + 5 stns
	1000	IND		AIR, Nagpur (Buttibori) N

kHz	kW	Ctry	Call	Station, location
	250	KOR	HLAZ	FEBC, Jeju
	0.1	NFK	VL2NI	R. Norfolk
	15.3	NZL		Wellington (f.pl. 2016)
	10	PHL	DXID	Ass. of Islamic Dev. Coop., Pagadian C, Z. Sur
1570	15	HWA	KUAU	Haiku, Maui
1575	5	AUS	2RF	Niche R. Netw., Wollongong (HPONS)
	2	CHN		LN; GX; JL
	1	J		AFN, Iwakuni
	0.6	J		AFN, Misawa
	0.25	J		AFN, Sasebo
	2.5	NZL		OAR 105.4 FM, Dunedin
	1000	THA		R. Saranrom/VOA, Ban Phachi, Rasom
1584	0.05-0.1	AUS		ABC (LR), 3 stns
	0.2	AUS	4VL	Cunnamulla (trtr)
	0.2	AUS	2EC	Narooma (trtr)
	0.5	AUS	4CC	Rockhampton (trtr)
	10	CHN		SX (3 stns) + 8 stns
	0.1	HKG		RTHK (3), Chung Hom Kok
	1	IND		AIR, 12 stns
	1	KOR		KBS, Danyang/Geumsan/Sancheong
	1	NZL		Coast, Napier-Hastings
	0.25	PAK		PBC, Chitral/Sibi
	1	PHL	DWBR	Dawnbreaker's Found., Talavera, Nva Ecija
	5	PLW	T8AA	Voice of Palau, Malakal Island, Koror
	1	RUS		R. Rossii + Reg., Taksimo, Sib. (cd 1st quarter 2016)
1593	5	AUS	3RG	Niche R. Netw., Melbourne (HPONS)
	0.2	AUS	2TAB	Sky Sports R., Murwillumbah (HPONS)
	10	CHN		HL (2 stns); XJ
	600	CHN		JS (CNR1)
	5	FSM	V6AK	FSMBS R. Chuuk, Weno
	10	IND		AIR, Bhopal A
	10	J	JOTB	NHK (2), Matsue
	10	J	JOQB	NHK (2), Niigata
	2.5	NZL		Coast, Christchurch
	5	NZL		R. Samoa, Auckland
	10	PHL	DXSK	Ranao Radio & TV Bc. Sys. Corp, Marawi C, Lanao Sur
	10	THA		R. Thailand, Ratchaburi
	10	TWN		Yuyeh BS, Ilan
1602	0.05-0.25	AUS		ABC (LR), 3 stns
	1	CHN		Jiangsu N,JS
	1	IND		AIR, 10 stns
	1	J		NHK (2), 6 stns
	1	J	JOCC	NHK (2), Asahikawa
	1	J	JOFD	NHK (2), Fukushima
	1	J	JOSB	NHK (2), Kitakyushu
	1	J	JOKC	NHK (2), Kofu
	1	KOR		KBS, Sabuk
	2.5	NZL		R. Reading Service, Levin
	0.25	PAK		PBC, Abbottabad
	1	PHL	DZUP	Univ. of the Philippines, Quzon C, NCR
	1	RUS		R. Rossii + Reg., Novoilinsk, Sib. (cd 1st quarter 2016)
	1	RUS		R. Rossii + Reg., Ust-Barguzin, Sib.(cd 1st quarter 2016)
1610		KRE		Frontline Soldiers Radio (±)
1611	0.05-0.4	AUS		22 stns (HPONS)
1620	0.4	AUS		7 stns (HPONS)
1629	0.1-0.4	AUS		11 stns (HPONS)
1638	0.4	AUS		4 stns (HPONS)
	0.6	PHL	DWGI	Guzman Inst. Of Tech., Manila, NCR
1647	0.4	AUS	4---	Vision ChR. R., Mackay (HPONS)
1656	0.4	AUS		4 stns (HPONS)
1665	0.4	AUS		2 stns (HPONS)
1674	0.4	AUS		2 stns (HPONS)
	1	PHL	DZBF	Mun. of Marikina, Marikina C, NCR
1683	0.4	AUS		2 stns (HPONS)
1692	0.4	AUS		2 stns (HPONS)
1701	0.1-0.4	AUS		3 stns (HPONS)

NORTH AMERICA

The North American MW frequency listing has been removed in order to make space for over 1,000 extra MW stations and their addresses in the main USA listing. To find the stations previously listed here, please go to the entries for Alaska, Canada, Hawaii and the United States of America in the National Radio section.

CENTRAL AMERICA, CARIBBEAN, BERMUDA & MEXICO

Abbreviations: Broadc.=Broadcasting, Corp.=Corporation, Em=Emisora, LV=La Voz, Nal=Nacional, Nat=National, Sce=Service.
Call signs: Costa Rica TI_, Cuba CM_, Dominican Republic HI_, El Salvador YS_, Guatemala TG_, Honduras HR_, Mexico XE_, Nicaragua YN_, Panama HO_

kHz	kW	Ctry	Call	Station, location
530		CTR	CAL	R. La Negrita, Cartago
	10	CUB	BQ	R. Enciclopedia, HA
		CUB	BA	R. Rebelde, Caribe, IJ
	1	CUB	BA	R. Rebelde, Guantánamo, GU
		TCA		R. Vision Cristiana, South Caicos
540	10	CUB	BA	R. Rebelde, Maisí, GU
	1	CUB	BA	R. Rebelde, Sancti Spíritus, SS
	5	DOM	B20	R. ABC, Sto Domingo
	0.02	GTM		R. Amistad, San Pedro de Laguna
	20/2.5	MEX	WF	La Bestia Grupera, Tlalmanalco
	5/2.5	MEX	HS	La Mejor, Los Mochis
	4/1	MEX	TX	La TX/La Ranchera de Paquimé, N. Casas Grandes
	1. 5/1	MEX	WA	Los 40 Principales, Monterrey
	150	MEX	WA	Los 40 Principales, S.L. Potosí
	5/1	MEX	MIT	R. IMER, Comitán
	0.1	MEX	SURF	R. Zion, Tijuana
	25	NCG	A3OW	R. Corporación, Managua
	10	PNR	PU	R. Lider, Panamá
	5	SLV	HV	La Estación de la Palabra, San Salvador
550	5	CTR	SCL	R. Santa Clara, Cd. Quesada
	12	CUB	BA	R. Rebelde, Pinar del Río, PR
	1	HND	XT	ABC Radio, Tegucigalpa
	0.5	HND	XD	R. Manantial, San Marcos
	5/0.15	MEX	PL	La Super Estación, Cd. Cuauhtémoc
	1.5/0.25	MEX	HLL	Los40 Principales, Salina Cruz
	2. 5/1	MEX	ZK	Poder 55, Tepatitlán
	2.5/0.15	MEX	TNC	R.Aztlán, Tepic
	5	PTR	WPAB	WPAB 550, Ponce
	2	SLV	FG	R. Cristo Te Llama, Sonsonate
560	10	CUB	BA	R. Rebelde, Ciego de Avila, CA
	1	GTM		R. Quetzal, Malacatán
	1	HND	KL	R. Reloj, San Pedro Sula
	1	HND	RZ	VRZ R. Juticalpa, Juticalpa
	1.4/0.25	MEX	GIK	LaAcerera, Monclova
	5/1	MEX	QAA	La Poderosa, Chetumal
	10/1	MEX	SRD	La Tremenda, Santiago Papasquiaro
	5/1	MEX	XZ	Lupe, Zacatecas
	0.75/0.5	MEX	OC	R.Chapultepec, México
	1/0.5	MEX	YO	R. Lobo, Huatabampo
	10/1	MEX	MZA	Sol FM, Manzanillo
	3	PNR	H2	RPC R., Colón
570	5	CTR	ELR	R. Libertad, San José
	1	CUB	BA	R. Rebelde, Pilón, GR
	25	CUB	BD	R. Reloj, Santa Clara, VC
	10/5	DOM	B22	R. Cristal, Sto Domingo
	1	GTM	PA	R. Palmeras, Escuintla
	2/1.7	MEX	LQ	Candela, Morelia
	5/2.5	MEX	OA	La Mexicana, Oaxaca
	0.5/0.25	MEX	UK	LaUK, Caborca
	1	MEX	TJ	Los 40 Principales, Gómez Palacio
	5/0.5	MEX	BJB	Nueva Vida, Monterrey
	5/1	MEX	TD	R. Red, Tecuala
	0.5	MEX	VJP	R. Xicotepec, Xicotepec de Juárez
	5	NCG	A2RQ	R. Veritas 5-70, Chinandega
	5	PNR	S	R. Soberana, Panamá
580	2.5	CUB	BA	R. Rebelde, Mabujabo, GU
	5	DOM	B23	R. Montecristi, Montecristi
	5	GTM	Y	R. Progreso, Guatemala
	3	HND	ZQ	R. Cadena Voces, Tegucigalpa
	3	HND	EO	Super Estrella de Occidente, Sta Rosa de Copán
	10/1	MEX	AV	Canal 58, Guadalajara
	1/0.5	MEX	DZ	Imagen R, Córdoba
	1	MEX	HP	La Más Prendida, Cd.Victoria
	5/2.5	MEX	MU	La Rancherita del Aire, Piedras Negras
	1/0.25	MEX	HO	Máxima, Cd. Obregón
	1/0.25	MEX	YI	Mix FM, Cancún
	5/0.7	MEX	FI	R. Mexicana, Chihuahua
	0.25	MEX	UAQ	R. UAQ 89.5, Querétaro
	10	NCG	A3LP	R. 5-80, Managua
	10	PNR	H4	RPC R., David
	10/5	PTR	WKAQ	R. KAQ, San Juan
590	25	CUB	BF	R. Musical Nacional, La Julia, MB
	10	CUB	BA	R. Rebelde, Guantánamo, GU
	10/5	DOM	B24	R. Santa María, La Vega
	5	GTM	RQ	R. Quiché, Sta Cruz del Quiché
	10	HND	LP3	R. América, San Pedro Sula
	1	HND	LP3	R. América, Tela
	10/5	MEX	CJU	La Explosiva 590, Puerto Vallarta
	1	MEX	BH	La Mejor, Hermosillo
	5/0.5	MEX	FD	La Mejor, Reynosa

kHz	kW	Ctry	Call	Station, location
	5/1	MEX	ZZZ	Los 40 Principales, Tapachula
	1	MEX	E	R. Fórmula Durango, Durango
	2.5	MEX	PH	Sabrosita 590, México
	10/0.25	MEX	GTO	TuRecuerdo, León
	10	PNR	H3	RPC R., Chitré
600	5	CUB	BC	R. Progreso, Santiago de Cuba, SC
	50	CUB	BA	R. Rebelde, San Germán, HO
		DOM	C85	Celestial 600, Santo Domingo
		DOM	B25	R. Santo Domingo, El Seybo
	1	MEX	TA	600 Solo Hits, Zitácuaro
	1	MEX	DN	Ke Buena, Gómez Palacio
	10/0.5	MEX	OCH	K'in Radio, Ococingo
	5/1	MEX	BB	La 101.5, La Comadre, Puros Éxitos, Acapulco
	5/1	MEX	CV	La Gran Compañía, Cd.Valles
	5/0.5	MEX	LAZ	La Mejor, Cd. Guzmán
	5/1	MEX	HW	La Mejor, Rosario
	1/0.5	MEX	MN	La Regiomontana, Monterrey
	5/1	MEX	Z	R. Fórmula, Segunda Cadena, Mérida
	10	NCG	A3MD	La Nueva R. Ya, Managua
	5	PTR	WYEL	Mayagüez
	3	SLV	NK	R. Cristo Viene, San Salvador
610	10	CUB	BA	R. Rebelde, Bueycito, GR
	1	CUB	BA	R. Rebelde, Cienfuegos, CI
	10	CUB	BA	R. Rebelde, Guane, PR
	1	CUB	BD	R. Reloj, Trinidad, SS
	5	DOM	B21	R. Amanecer, Santiago
	5	GTM	GA	R. Alianza, Guatemala
	1	HND		R. América, Gracias
	3	HND	LP	R. América, Santa Rosa de Copán
	10	HND	LD	R. América,Tegucigalpa
	5/0.5	MEX	BX	BX La Primera, Sabinas
	10/0.2	MEX	UM	Candela FM, Valladolid
	6/1	MEX	GS	La GS, Guasave
	5/1	MEX	UF	La Mexicana, Uruapan
	1/0.5	MEX	KZ	La Poderosa, Tehuantepec
	1/0.9	MEX	SAC	R. Lobo, Saltillo
	10	PNR	HM	RPC R., Panamá
	1/0.25	PTR	WEXS	X-AM, Patillas
620	25	CUB	BA	R. Rebelde, Colón, MA
	10	DOM	B28	R. Santo Domingo, Sto Domingo
	5	GTM	PQ	R. 6-20, San Cristóbal
	1	HND	LP	R. América, Juticalpa
	10	HND		R. América, Siguatepeque
	1	HND	LP17	R. Continental, San Pedro Sula
	5	MEX	SS	ESPN Deportes, Ensenada
	1/0.25	MEX	GH	La Lupe, Reynosa
	5/1	MEX	BU	La Norteñita, Chihuahua
	5/1	MEX	OO	Los 40 Principales, Tepic
	1/0.5	MEX	CK	Pop FM, Durango
	50/5	MEX	NK	R. 6-20, México
	2.5/0.5	MEX	WZ	R. Novedades, S. L. Potosí
	50	NCG	N	R. Nicaragua, Managua
630	5	CUB	BC	R. Progreso, Camagüey, CM
		GTM	EL	R. Cultural Porvenir, Sta Elena
	3.5	HND	LP	R. América, Choluteca
	5	HND	LP7	R. América, La Ceiba
	1/0.25	MEX	FX	Amor 101, Guaymas
	10/0.5	MEX	JB	C7 Radio, Guadalajara
	5/2.5	MEX	JR	Coral 630, Zihuatanejo
	14/0.25	MEX	OPE	ExaFM, Mazatlán
	10	MEX	FB	La FB 630, Monterrey
	10/0.75	MEX	FU	LaNueva Voz, Cosamaloapan
	0.5	MEX	CCQ	La Z, Cancún
	1/0.15	MEX	ERO	R. Tamaulipas, Esteros
	2	PNR	J35	R. Provincias, Chitré
	5	PTR	WUNO	NotiUno, San Juan
	10	SLV	LN	R. Santa Sion, San Salvador
640	20	CTR	ALY	R. Rica, San José
	50	CUB	BC	R. Progreso, Guanabacoa, CH
	10	CUB	BC	R. Progreso, Las Tunas, LT
	40	GLP		Guadeloupe Première, Point-à-Pitre
	1	HND	UP	R. Centro, Tegucigalpa
	5	MEX	JUA	BM R. 6-40, Cd.Juárez
	5/1	MEX	TAM	Ke Buena, Cd.Victoria
	50/25	MEX	NQ	La NQ, Tulancingo
	5/1	MEX	YQ	La Tremenda, Fresnillo
	10/1	MEX	HHI	Los 40 Principales, Hidalgo del Parral
	1	MEX	HDL	O AM, Huajuapan de León
	10	NCG	A4LR	La Mera Mera , Managua
	2.5	PNR	K22	CPR, Colón
	2.5	PNR		R. Panamá, La Palma
650	10	CUB	BC	R. Progreso, Ciego de Avila, CA
	5	CUB	BA	R. Rebelde, Santiago de Cuba, SC
	15/5	DOM	B31	R. Universal, Sto Domingo
	1	HND	LP	R. América, Danlí
	2.5	HND		R. América, Olanchito
	1	HND		R. América, Tocoa
	2.5	HND	VS	R. Católica de Olancho, Juticalpa
	25	HND	VS	R. Nuestra Señora de la Esperanza, S. P. S.
	5/0.25	MEX	CHH	Capital Máxima, Chilpancingo
	1	MEX	RCG	D-Rock, Cd. Acuña
	10	MEX	EJ	La Patrona, Puerto Vallarta
	5/1	MEX	ZM	La Zamorana, Zamora
	5/0.2	MEX	PX	LV de Ángel, Puerto Ángel
	1/0.5	MEX	VILL	Notícias, Villahermosa
	5/1	MEX	TNT	R. 65 FM, Los Mochis
	2.5/0.02	MEX	VG	R.Fórmula, Primera Cad, Mérida
	1/0.25	MEX	VSS	Romántica, Hermosillo
	10/8	NCG	RD	R. Diriangén, Granada
	5	NCG	A6RS	R. Muzun, Matagalpa
	5	PNR	S22	R. Mía, Panamá
660	12	CUB	BC	R. Progreso, Jovellanos, MA
	3	DOM	B32	R. Visión Cristiana, Santiago
	3	GTM	Q	LV de Quetzaltenango
	3	HND	NN18	LV de Honduras, La Ceiba
	5	HTI		R. Lumière, Port-au-Prince
	10/1	MEX	FZ	ABC R., Monterrey
	1/0.5	MEX	WX	Ke Buena, Durango
	2.5/0.25	MEX	SJC	KVOZ,San José del Cabo
	1/0.5	MEX	YG	La Consentida, Matías Romero
	50/10	MEX	EY	La Kaliente, Aguascalientes
	5	MEX	AR	La Mexicana, Tampico
	5	MEX	ACB	R. 6-60/La Tremenda N:o Uno, Cd. Delicias
	30	MEX	CPR	R. Chan Santa Cruz, Felipe Carillo Puerto
	50	MEX	DTL	R. Ciudadana, México
	5	NCG		R. Máxima, Managua
	5	PNR		La Nueva Exitosa, Sabana Grande
	1	PNR	H5	RPC R., Bocas del Toro
	10	SLV	UES	R. Universitaria, San Salvador
670	10	CTR	TNT	R. Managua, San José
	1	CUB	BQ	R. Enciclopedia, Cárdenas, MA
	50	CUB	BA	R. Rebelde, Arroyo Arenas, CH
	5	CUB	BA	R. Rebelde, Bahía Honda, PR
	10	CUB	BA	R. Rebelde, C. Brasil, CM
	10	CUB	BA	R. Rebelde, Camagüey, CM
		CUB	BA	R. Rebelde, Caribe, IJ
	5	CUB	BA	R. Rebelde, Ciego de Avila, CA
	5	CUB	BA	R. Rebelde, Circunvalación, MA
	10	CUB	BA	R. Rebelde, El Coco, HO
	1	CUB	BA	R. Rebelde, Los Palacios, PR
		CUB	BA	R. Rebelde, Mayarí, HO
	1	CUB	BA	R. Rebelde, Pinar del Río, PR
	50	CUB	BA	R. Rebelde, Santa Clara, VC
	1	CUB	BA	R. Rebelde, Santa Lucía, PR
	10	CUB	BA	R. Rebelde, Victoria de LT, LT
	5	DOM	B33	R. Dial, San Pedro de Macorís
	1	HND	NN20	LV de Honduras, Sta Rosa de Copán
	10	HND	N	LV de Honduras, Tegucigalpa
	5/1	MEX	IS	La Rancherita Consentida, Cd. Guzmán
	1/0.25	MEX	TOR	R. Ranchito, Torreón
		NCG	RC	R. Caribe, Pto Cabezas
680	3	DOM	B38	R. Zamba, San Ignacio de Sabaneta
	10	GTM	VP	R. Norte, Cobán
	1	HND	NN7	LV de Honduras, Danlí

kHz	kW	Ctry	Call	Station, location
	1	HND	NN10	LV de Honduras, Juticalpa
	10	HND	NN8	LV de Honduras, San Pedro Sula
	10	HND	NN2	LV de Honduras, Siguatepeque
	1/0.25	MEX	FO	Éxtasis Digital, Chihuahua
	1	MEX	SON	Éxtasis, Hermosillo
	5/3	MEX	KQ	Fiesta Mexicana, Tapachula
	1/0.1	MEX	FJ	La FJ, R. Teziutlán, Teziutlán
	1/0.5	MEX	ORO	La Mera Jefa, Guasave
	1	MEX	OAX	O AM, Oaxaca
	5/2.5	MEX	CHG	W Radio, Chilpancingo
	10/2	NCG	AM	R. La Primerísima, Managua
	5	PNR	F32	Mujer AM, David
	5	PNR		Voz Sin Fronteras, Metetí
	0.4	PTR	WA2XPA	Arecibo
	10	PTR	WAPA	Cadena WAPA R., San Juan
690	10	CUB	BC	R. Progreso, Santa Clara, VC
	5	CUB	BC	R. Progreso, Santiago de Cuba, SC
	10	DOM	B39	R. Guarachita, Sto Domingo
	1	GTM	VB	R. Tamazulapa, Jutiapa
	1	HND	NN3	LV de Honduras, Choluteca
	50/5	MEX	N	La 69, México
	2.5	MEX	XL	La Ley, Pátzcuaro
	50/2	MEX	MA	La Mejor Zacatecas, Fresnillo
	5/1	MEX	CS	La Mejor, Manzanillo
	10/1	MEX	RG	RG La Deportiva, Monterrey
	2/0.25	MEX	ST	Romántica, Mazatlán
	78/50	MEX	WW	W R. América, Tijuana
	10/5	NCG	RH	R. Hermanos, Matagalpa
	5	PNR		R. Evangelio Vivo, Panamá
700	10	CTR	JC	R. Sonora, San José
	0.5	DOM	B40	R. Mao, Valverde Mao
	1	GTM	AJ	R. Inspiración, Escuintla
	15	GTM	HR	R. Mundial, Guatemala
	5	HND	KL	Cadena Radial Reloj, Tegucigalpa
	5	MEX	LX	La Ke Buena, Zitácuaro
	2.5/0.1	MEX	VC	La Más Buena, Córdoba
	5/0.25	MEX	GD	La Poderosa, Hidalgo del Parral
	5	MEX	ETCH	LV de los Tres Ríos, Etchojoa
	5	MEX	XPUJ	LV del Corazón de la Selva, X'pujil
	10/0.15	MEX	DKR	R.Red, Guadalajara
	30	NCG	MM	R. La Poderosa, Managua
	12	SLV	JW	R. Mi Gente, San Miguel
	12	SLV	JW	R. Mi Gente, San Salvador
710	10	CUB	AM	R. Guamá, La Palma, PR
	50	CUB	BA	R. Rebelde, Cacocúm, HO
	25	CUB	BA	R. Rebelde, Camagüey, CM
	200	CUB	BA	R. Rebelde, Chambas, CA
	50	CUB	BA	R. Rebelde, La Julia, MB
	50	CUB	BA	R. Rebelde, Martí, MA
	50	CUB	BA	R. Rebelde, Santa Clara, VC
	1	CUB	BA	R. Rebelde, Yaguajay, SS
		DOM	B41	Ondas del Caribe, San Cristóbal
		DOM		Red Nacional Cristiana, Santo Domingo
	1	GTM	XL	R. Tecún Umán, Quetzaltenango
	2.5	HND	SG	R. LV de la Libertad, Catacamas
	1	MEX	RK	Fusión FM, Tepic
	1	MEX	OLA	Huasteca, Tampico
	5/0.25	MEX	BL	La Ke Buena, Culiacán
	10	MEX	MP	La Nueva 710, Mexico
	7/0.1	MEX	DP	La Ranchera de Cuauhtémoc, Cd. Cuauhtémoc
	1	MEX	RL	La RL, Colima
	1/0.25	MEX	PS	La Super Grupera, Guaymas
	5	MEX	RPO	La Z, Oaxaca
	1	MEX	MAR	R. Disney, Acapulco
	1/0.25	MEX	LZ	RCG R, Torreón
	10	PNR	Q51	KW R. Continente, Panamá
	5	PNR	B52	Ondas del Caribe, Bocas del Toro
	10/0.75	PTR	WKJB	KJB,Mayagüez
720	2.5	CUB	BC	R. Progreso, Mabujabo, GU
	5	DOM	B48	R. Cayacoa, Higüey
	1.5	DOM	B42	R. Norte, Santiago
	1	HND	NN3	R. Caribe, La Ceiba
	1	HTI		R. Lumière, Petite Riviere
	1/0.5	MEX	VU	Éxtasis Digital, Mazatlán
	1	MEX	JCC	Extremo 7-20, Cd. Juárez
	8/0.25	MEX	DE	La Kaliente, Saltillo
	5	MEX	KN	La Z, Huetamo
	1/0.4	MEX	QZ	Ritmo 720, San Juan de los Lagos
	25	NCG	A3RC	R. Católica, Managua
	10	PNR	B50	R. República, Chitré
	1	SLV	RA	Qué Buena, San Salvador
730	1	CTR		R. Pacífico, Puntarenas
	10	CUB	BC	R. Progreso, La Fe, IJ
	10	DOM	B43	R. HIZ
	10	GTM	N	R. Cultural, Guatemala
	1	HND	NN4	R. Exitos, Tegucigalpa
	1/0.25	MEX	EBC	Ke Buena, Ensenada
	50/1	MEX	HB	Ke Buena, Hidalgo del Parral
	5/1	MEX	PQ	La 73/La Sabrosita, Cd.Muzquiz
	5/1	MEX	GDL	La Explosiva, Guadalajara
	2/0.3	MEX	SOS	La Ranchera, Agua Prieta
	10	MEX	PET	LV de los Mayas, Peto
	10/1	MEX	LBC	R. La Giganta 730 AM, Loreto
	100	MEX	X	TDW R., México
	20	TRD		Inspirational 7-30 AM, Port of Spain
740	10	CUB	KO	R. Angulo, Sagua de Tanamo, HO
	1	HND	IH	La Super Grande, Juticalpa
	2.5	HND	VC	LV Evangélica, Olanchito
	1	HND	QQ	R. Intibucá, La Esperanza
	1	HND	TG2	R. Satélite, San Pedro Sula
	1	HTI		R. Lumière, Pignon
	1	MEX	VAY	Amor, Puerto Vallarta
	5/1	MEX	OF	Hit 101.9, Celaya
	20/10	MEX	CAQ	R. Fórmula QR Cancún, Cancún
	10/1	MEX	QN	R. Fórmula, Torreón
	5/1	MEX	CW	R. Variedades, Los Mochis
	5/1	MEX	POR	T-Prende, Putla de Guerrero
	50	NCG	A3LS	R. Sandino, Managua
	2.6	PNR	R44	La Exitosa de Chorrera, La Chorrera
	5	PNR	N26	R. Cristal, David
	0.5/0.1	PTR	WIAC	740 La Original, Ponce
	10	PTR	WIAC	740 La Original, San Juan
750	10	CUB	BC	R. Progreso, Palmira, CI
	5	DOM	B44	R. Jesús AM, Santiago
	1/0.1	MEX	RASA	Candela 750, San Luis Potosí
	5/0.25	MEX	KOK	Éxtasis Digital, Acapulco
	5/0.25	MEX	CSI	Éxtasis Digital, Culiacán
	1/0.1	MEX	CORO	Ke Buena, Loma Bonita
	10/0.25	MEX	TI	LaHuasteca, Tempoal
	1/0.25	MEX	MG	La Ke Buena, Arriaga
	1/0.75	MEX	OH	La Pantera, Camargo
	10/0.5	MEX	URM	Los 40 Principales, Uruapan
	10	MEX	JMN	LV de los Cuatro Pueblos, Jesús María
	5	PNR		R. Inolvidable, Chitré
760	5	CTR	LX	R. Columbia, San José
	10	CUB	BC	R. Progreso, Guane, PR
		CUB	BC	R. Progreso, Mayarí Arriba, SC
	5	DOM	B45	Global AM, Santo Domingo
	2.5	HND	XW	R. Comayagüela, Tegucigalpa
	2	HTI		R. Lumière, Les Cayes
	70/10	MEX	ABC	ABC Radio, México
	10	MEX	ES	Antena Musical 7-60, Chihuahua
	5/0.5	MEX	DGO	La Mejor, Durango
	5/1	MEX	EB	Preciosa, Cd.Obregón
	5/1	MEX	ZZ	R. Gallito, Guadalajara
	5/0.5	MEX	RA	R. Uno, San Cristóbal las Casas
	5/0.1	MEX	NY	R. Xeny, Nogales
	10	NCG	A3AR	R. Magic, Managua
	5	PNR	XO	LV del Istmo, Panamá
	5	PTR	WORA	NotiUno, Mayagüez
	5	SLV	KL	YSKL La Poderosa, San Miguel

kHz	kW	Ctry	Call	Station, location
	1	SLV	KL	YSKL La Poderosa, Sonsonate
		SLV	KL	YSKL La Poderosa, Zacateluca
770	10	CUB	BA	R. Rebelde, Victoria de LT, LT
	5	DOM	B46	R. Águila, Santiago
	1	HND	RD	R. Majestad, Juticalpa
	10	HND	NN21	R. Norte, San Pedro Sula
	5/1.5	MEX	ML	La Ranchera, Apatzingán
	5/0.1	MEX	REV	Los 40 Principales, Los Mochis
	10	MEX	ANT	LV de las Huastecas, Tancanhuitz de Santos
	1	MEX	MRO	OAM, Matías Romero
	1	MEX	HUA	OAM, Santa Cruz Huatulco
	7	MEX	ACH	R. Fórmula Monterrey, Monterrey
	5/1	MEX	SUR	Tu Ritmo Musical, Chilapa
	10	SLV	KL	YSKL La Poderosa, San Salvador
780	10	CTR	RA	R. América, San José
	0.5	DOM	B47	R. Constanza, Constanza
	1	GTM	CK	Sultana La Cristiana, Zacapa
	1	HND	SE	Alabanza Estéreo, Choluteca
	5/1	MEX	ZN	EXA FM, Celaya
	10/0.25	MEX	WGR	ExaFM, Monclova
	5/0.5	MEX	TS	Ke Buena, Tapachula
	5/1	MEX	SFT	La Poderosa, San Fernando
	10	MEX	GLO	LV de la Sierra Juárez, Guelatao de Juárez
	2. 5/1	MEX	XY	LV del Balsas, Cd.Altamirano
	5/0.5	MEX	LD	R. Costa, Autlán
	5	PNR		R. Recuerdo, Panamá
	1	SLV	KL	YSKL La Poderosa, Sta Ana
	1	SLV	KL	YSKL La Poderosa, Usulután
	10	VRG	ZBVI	ZBVI R., Tortola
790	10	CUB	BD	R. Reloj, Holguín, HO
	25	CUB	BD	R. Reloj, Pinar del Río, PR
	5	DOM	B49	R. Millón, Sto Domingo
	3	HND	TG	R. Satélite, Tegucigalpa
	50/1	MEX	RC	Formato 21, México
	1/0.25	MEX	SU	La Dinámica, Mexicali
	1/0.5	MEX	FE	La Pegajosa, Nuevo Laredo
	1	MEX	GZ	Milenio R, Torreón
	10/5	MEX	BI	R. B-I, Aguascalientes
	0.25	MEX	GAJ	R. Fórmula, Primera Cadena, Guadalajara
	5/0.75	MEX	NT	R. La Paz/R. Fórmula, La Paz
	5/0.4	MEX	RPC	R. Ranchito, Chihuahua
	6	PNR		R. Panamá, Santiago
800	100	BES	PJB	Trans World R., Kralendijk
	3	CTR	SD	R. Gigante, San José
	1	DOM	B50	R. Bonao, Bonao
	1	HND	DL	R. Corporación, Comayagua
	3	HND	MA	R. Moderna, San Pedro Sula
	0.5/0.25	MEX	SPN	Cadena800 AM, Tijuana
	10/2.5	MEX	DD	Delta FM, Montemorelos
	5/1	MEX	GX	Fiesta Mexicana, S. L. de la Paz
	1	MEX	QT	La Poderosa, Veracruz
	5/2.5	MEX	AN	La Ribereña, Ocotlán
	2	MEX	ZR	La Traviesa de Coahuila, Zaragoza
	5	MEX	ZV	LV de la Montaña, Tlapa de Comonfort
	50	MEX	ROK	R. Cañón, Cd.Juárez
	50	NCG	A3RO	R. 800, Managua
	3	PNR		Tropical 800, Los Santos
	12	SLV	AX	R. María El Salvador, San Salvador
810	10	BAH		ZNS3, Freeport
	10	CUB	BC	R. Progreso, Guantánamo, GU
	5	DOM	B52	R. Salvación Internacional, Baní
		GTM		R. Circuito San Juan, San Juan
		GTM	END	R. Constelación, San Marcos
		GTM		R. Moapán, Sta Elena
	6	HND	VC	LV Evangélica, La Ceiba
	3	HND	LP24	R. Valle, Choluteca
	10/0.25	MEX	UX	CapitalFM, Tepic
	5/1	MEX	ZC	La Grande, Río Grande
	1/0.5	MEX	IM	La Vecina, Saltillo
	7/0.6	MEX	AGR	R. Fórmula, Acapulco
	5/1	MEX	HT	R. Huamantla, Huamantla
	0.1	MEX	IC	R. I-C, Campeche
	1/0.5	MEX	EMM	R. La Salmantina, Salamanca
	1/0.25	MEX	MAX	R. Max, Tecomán
	1	MEX	SB	R. Mexicana/La S B, Santa Bárbara
	1/0.1	MEX	RI	R. Rey, Reynosa
	2.5/0.25	MEX	RB	SolEstéreo, Cozumel
	5	MEX	RSV	Tribuna R., Cd. Obregón
	1	PNR	G	R. 10, Panamá
	50	PTR	WKVM	R. Paz 810 AM, San Juan
	1.5	SLV	DA	R. Imperial, Sonsonate
	2	SLV	FA	R. Lorenzana, San Vicente
820	2.5	CTR	GC	8-20, San José
	10	CUB	BU	R. Ciudad de la Habana, Arroyo Arenas, CH
	10	CUB	IB	R. Progreso, Ciego de Avila, CA
	10	CUB	BC	R. Progreso, Ciego de Avila, CA
	1	CUB	BC	R. Progreso, Moa, HO
	3	DOM	B53	R. Vida, Santiago
	10	GTM	TO	R. Kyrios/R. Internacional, Guatemala
	5	HND	LP16	R. Moderna, Tegucigalpa
	7/3	HND	KW	R. Sultana, Sta Rosa de Copán
	10/1	MEX	BA	La Consentida, Guadalajara
	2.5/0.1	MEX	KG	La Dorada, Córdoba
	10/1	MEX	BM	La Mera Mera, San Luis Potosí
	1/0.5	MEX	YN	Los 40 Principales, Oaxaca
	3.5/0.5	MEX	ABCA	R. Frontera, Mexicali
	1/0.25	MEX	UDO	R. Universidad de Occidente, Los Mochis
	1	MEX	GRC	RTG R, Coyuca de Catalán
	10/0.5	MEX	DRD	W R., Durango
	20	NCG	FAOL	R. Ondas de Luz, Managua
	3	PNR	F28	R. Ritmo Chiriquí, David
	50	SCN		R. Paradise, Conaree, St. Kitts
830		CUB	BD	R. Reloj, Mayarí Arriba, SC
	10	DOM	B54	HIJB Radio, Sto Domingo
	5	GTM	AV	R. Satélite, Mazatenango
	1	HND	JB	Cadena Radial Impacto, Comayagua
	1	HND	RU	R. Uno, San Pedro Sula
	5/1	MEX	VQ	Amor, Culiacán
	1	MEX	DQ	Amor, San Andrés Tuxtla
	2.5	MEX	DR	Digital 99.5, Guaymas
	10/0.5	MEX	LK	Digital, Zacatecas
	5/0.25	MEX	LN	La Caliente, Linares
	1/0.5	MEX	TLX	La Poderosa, Tlaxiaco
	8	MEX	PUR	LV de los P'urhepechas, Cheran
	10/5	MEX	ITE	R. Capital, México
	5	PNR	R56	R. Península, Macaracas
840	10	CUB	E	R. CMHW, Santa Clara, VC
	1	CUB	KC	R. Revolución, Palma Soriano, SC
		GTM		R. Idea 840, Jutiapa
	2.5	GTM		R. Luz, San Pedro Carchá
	3	HND		LV Evangélica, Tela
	10	HTI		R. 4VEH, Cap Haitien
	5/1	MEX	XXX	Fiesta Mexicana, Tamazula
	2.5/0.1	MEX	PV	La Fiera Grupera, Papantla
	1	MEX	MY	La Jefa, Cd.Mante
	5/0.5	MEX	FG	La Mejor, Celaya
	1/0.25	MEX	TEY	R. Sensación, Tepic
	5	NCG	A3NT	R. Noticias, Managua
	10	PNR	L80	R. Nacional, Panamá
	5/1	PTR	WXEW	R. Victoria, Yabucoa
	10	SLV	FB	R. Santa Biblia, San Salvador
850	2	CTR	RDR	R. Cartago, Cartago
	1	CUB	BC	R. Progreso, Trinidad, SS
	1	CUB	BD	R. Reloj, Nueva Gerona, IJ
	5	DOM	B57	R. Guarocuya, Barahona
	0.25	MEX	ZF	Ke Buena, Mexicali
	3/1	MEX	MIA	La 850 AM, Guadalajara
	1/0.1	MEX	JAQ	La Jefa, Jalpan
	1	MEX	ZI	Maxistar, Zacapu
	1/0.2	MEX	US	R. Univ. de Sonora, Hermosillo
	5/1	MEX	M	Renacimiento 850 , Chihuahua
	5	PNR	T61	La Exitosa de Chiriquí, David

kHz	kW	Ctry	Call	Station, location
	1	PNR		La Exitosa, Colón
	5/1	PTR	WABA	Waba, Aguadilla
860		CUB	BD	R. Reloj, Bolondrón, MA
	5	CUB	BD	R. Reloj, Jovellanos, MA
	10	CUW	PJZ-86	Z-86 R. Curom, Willemstad
	10	DOM	B58	R. Clarín, Sto Domingo
	0.5	HND	LS	R. Dinorama, La Paz
	1.5	HND	BV	R. Piedra Blanca, Catacamas
	0.5	HND		R. Río de Dios, Olanchito
	10/7.5	MEX	MO	8-60 La Poderosa, Tijuana
	5/0.25	MEX	DB	Extremo Grupero, Tonalá
	2.5	MEX	PLA	La Mexicana, Aguascalientes
	5/0.8	MEX	HX	La Mía, Cd.Obregón
	1/0.25	MEX	TW	Latina, Tampico
	1/0.25	MEX	NW	Máxima 103, Culiacán
	5	MEX	CCN	R. Caribe, Cancún
	10/1	MEX	CTL	R. Chetumal, Chetumal
	5/0.1	MEX	AL	R. Fórmula, Manzanillo
	1/0.5	MEX	ZOL	R. Noticias 860, Cd.Juárez
	5/1.5	MEX	NL	R. Recuerdo, Monterrey
	4.5	MEX	UN	R. UNAM, México
	1/0.5	MEX	DU	XEDU, la que le gusta a Usted, Durango
	5	NCG	A3CO	La Gran Cadena, Managua
	10	PNR	L55	R. Reforma, Chitré
	10	SCN		Voice of Nevis, Nevis
870	10	CTR	UCR	R. 870 UCR, San Pedro Montes de Oca
	10	CUB	BD	R. Reloj, Baracoa, GU
	10	CUB	BD	R. Reloj, Bueycito, GR
	1	CUB	BD	R. Reloj, Sancti Spíritus, SS
	4	DOM	B59	R. La Vega, La Vega
	0.5	GTM	L	R. Victoria, Mazatenango
	1/0.1	MEX	NG	Canal 87, Huauchinango
	1/0.1	MEX	LY	Candela, Morelia
	1/0.5	MEX	AMO	Éxitos 98.9, Irapuato
	1/0.25	MEX	FIL	La Sinaloense, Mazatlán
	10	MEX	TAR	LV de la Sierra Tarahumara, Guachochi
	10/0.25	MEX	ACC	LVdel Puerto, Puerto Escondido
	1	MEX	GRO	RTG R, Chilpancingo
	10	NCG	CD	R. Centro, Juigalpa
	5.5	PNR	HO	R. Libre, Panamá
	5	PTR	WQBS	Vintage 870, San Juan
880	12	CUB	BC	R. Progreso, Mantua, PR
		CUB	BD	R. Reloj, Mayarí Arriba, SC
	10	HND	H	R. Nacional de Honduras, Tegucigalpa
	20/1	MEX	AAA	ESNE R, Guadalajara
	10/1	MEX	TC	Kiuu, Torreón
	5/1	MEX	EM	La M Mexicana, Río Verde
	1	MEX	RTP	La Poderosa, S. M. Texmelucan
	10/2	MEX	PNK	Planeta, Los Mochis:
	5/0.25	MEX	V	R. Fórmula, Chihuahua
	10	NCG	A3EP	R. El Pensamiento, Managua
	2.5	PNR		R. Panamá, Bocas del Toro
	2.5	PNR		R. Panamá, Chiriquí
	1	PNR	B51	R. Visión Panamá, Colón
	1/0.5	PTR	WYKO	La Poderosa 880, Sabana Grande
	1	SLV	CD	R. Ritmo, Stgo de María
890	10	CTR	BAS	R. Heredia, Heredia
	200	CUB	BC	R. Progreso, Chambas, CA
		CUB	KC	R. Revolución, Santiago de Cuba, SC
	3	DOM		R. 8-90/La Consentida, Valverde
	1	GTM	HU	R. Escuintla, Escuintla
	1/0.3	MEX	BY	Extasis Digital, Tuxpan
	10/0.5	MEX	NZ	La Sinaloense, Culiacán
	5/0.5	MEX	AK	R. Consentida, Acámbaro
	10/1	MEX	FRT	R. Frontera, Comitán
	1/0.25	MEX	PNA	Romántica, Tepic
	5/1	MEX	PC	Sonido Estrella, Zacatecas
	5	PNR	Q62	R. Ritmo Stereo, Chitré
	0.25	PTR	WFAB	La Nave 890, Ceiba
	3	SLV	LA	R. Renacimiento, Sta Ana
900	5	BRB		CBC, St Michael
	50	CUB	BC	R. Progreso, San Germán, HO
		DOM	B62	R. Amanecer, Neyba
	5/1	DOM	B63	R. Puerto Plata, Puerto Plata
	1	GTM	MA	R. Amatique, Puerto Barrios
	1	HND	UP	R. Centro, Choluteca
	1	HND	UP6	R. Satélite, La Ceiba
	5/1	MEX	DT	Hits FM, Cuauhtémoc
	1	MEX	ED	La Líder, Ameca
	50/10	MEX	WB	Los 40 Principales, Veracruz
	10/2.5	MEX	OK	OK Noticias, Monterrey
	250	MEX	W	W R., México
	5	NCG	A3RT	R. Tiempo, Managua
	10	PNR	HA	CD Radio, Panamá
	2	SLV	QJ	R. Cristo Te Llama, San Salvador
910	10	CTR	UM	BBN, San José/San Carlos
	25	CUB	HA	R. Cadena Agramonte, Camagüey, CM
	5	CUB	BL	R. Metropolitana, V. María, CH
	5	CUB	BD	R. Reloj, Bolondron, MA
	3	DOM	B64	Tiempo 910, Bonao
	10	GTM	KL	R. Fe y Esperanza, Guatemala
	10	HND	VS	R. Católica, Tegucigalpa
	10/1	MEX	NAY	Los 40 Principales, Puerto Vallarta
	10/2.5	MEX	OL	R. Impacto, Teziutlán
	0.25	MEX	AO	R. Mexicana, Mexicali
	5	NCG		R. Jinotega, Jinotega
	4.4	PTR	WPRP	NotiUno, Ponce
920	1	CUB	BC	R. Progreso, Pilón, GR
	10	DOM	B65	R. 9-20 AM-Stereo, Sto Domingo
	0.2	GTM	RS	R. Cultural, Escuintla
	5	HND	SK	R. Catacamas, Catacamas
	1	HND	RM	R. Sistema, Comayagua
	1	HND	ZV	Voz Que Clama en el Desierto, S. P. Sula
	1	MEX	ZAR	Éxtasis Digital, Puebla
	1/0.25	MEX	MJ	FM Globo, Piedras Negras
	5/1	MEX	RE	La Comadre, Puros Éxitos, Celaya
	5/0.5	MEX	CQ	La Nueva Nueva Ranchera, Culiacán
	10	MEX	LE	La Preferida, Tampico
	5/0.2	MEX	RCA	Planeta Rojo, Torreón
	5/1	MEX	HQ	R. Capital, Hermosillo
	1/0.125	MEX	PNX	R.Costa, Pinotepa Nacional
	10/1	MEX	LT	R. María, Tlaquepaque
	5/2.5	MEX	LCM	R. Mexicana, Cd.Lázaro Cárdenas
	1/0.25	MEX	QD	R. Noticias 920, Chihuahua
	1.5/0.5	MEX	TEB	Voces, Campeche
	10	NCG	W	R. Mundial, Managua
	5	PNR	S56	R. Mía, Los Santos
930	5	CTR	RCR	R. Costa Rica, Guadalupe
	1	CUB	BD	R. Reloj, Cienfuegos, CI
	1	CUB	BD	R. Reloj, La Jaiba, MA
	1	CUB	BD	R. Reloj, Stgo de Cuba, SC
	10	CUB	IP	R. Surco, Ciego de Ávila, CA
	3	HND	CQ	Cadena R. Samaritano, La Ceiba
	2.5	HND	LD	R. Estéreo Leed, Nacaome
	2/1	MEX	CY	Banda 930, Huejutla
	1	MEX	ZU	Candela, Zacapu
	1	MEX	TTT	Capital FM, Colima
	1/0.25	MEX	SHT	La Más Buena, Saltillo
	5/2.5	MEX	MK	La Mexicana, Huixtla
	5	MEX	TLA	LV de la Mixteca, Tlaxiaco
	10/3	MEX	QS	Romántica, Fresnillo
	10	PNR	R46	La Nueva Exitosa, Panamá
	2	PNR	K85	R. Mi Preferida,Pto Armuelles
	2.5	PTR	WYAC	740 La Original, Cabo Rojo
		SLV		R. San José, San Salvador
940	1	CUB	BC	R. Progreso, Sancti Spíritus, SS
	10	GTM	TL	Eventos Católicos R., S. Pedro Sacatepéquez
	1	HND	CR	Dif. Cristiana de R.
	1/0.1	MEX	MMM	940 AM Oldies, Mexicali
	50	MEX	Q	Ke Buena 9-40, México
	10/0.1	MEX	YJ	La Fiera Musical, Nueva Rosita
	1	MEX	HE	La Voz, Atotonilco

kHz	kW	Ctry	Call	Station, location
	10/1	MEX	RLA	R. Santa Rosalía, Santa Rosalía
	1	MEX	RKS	Romántica 9-40, Reynosa
	10	PTR	WIPR	Máxima 940 AM, San Juan
950	1	CUB	KC	R. R. Revolución, Mayarí Arriba, SC
	10	CUB	BD	R. Reloj, Arroyo Arenas, HA
	10	CUB	BD	R. Reloj, Camagüey, CM
	10	DOM	B68	R. Popular, Sto Domingo
	1	GTM	AF	R. Indiana, Mazatenango
	1	HND	QL	R. Centro de Honduras, Siguatepeque
	10/1	MEX	CEL	Él y Ella, Celaya
	10/0.1	MEX	PB	Grupera 93.1, Hermosillo
	5/0.5	MEX	MEX	La Mexicana, Cd.Guzmán
	3/0.9	MEX	MAB	La Poderosa, Cd. del Carmen
	1/0.5	MEX	FA	La Poderosa, Chihuahua
	2. 5/1	MEX	ZE	La Poderosa, Santiago Ixcuintla
	4/0.5	MEX	ORF	La Rancherita, Los Mochis
	10	MEX	OJN	LV de la Chinantla, San Lucas Ojitlán
	20/5	MEX	KAM	R. Fórmula Californias, Tijuana
	5/1	MEX	ACA	R. Fórmula, Acapulco
	5/1	MEX	RN	R. Naranjera, Monterrey
	5/2	MEX	TO	Romántica, Tampico
	1	SLV	HG	R. Chaparrastique, San Miguel
960	10	CUB	BD	R. Reloj, Guantánamo, GU
	5/1	DOM	B70	LV del Atlántico, Puerto Plata
	1	HND	YF	R. Fergusón, Choluteca
	1. 5/1	MEX	XC	ABC R. 960, Taxco
	1	MEX	CZ	ABC R., San Luis Potosí
	1/0.25	MEX	OZ	Amor, Xalapa
	1/0.5	MEX	IQ	Futura R, Cd.Obregón
	5/1	MEX	K	La Estación Grande, Nuevo Laredo
	1/0.5	MEX	UQ	La Poderosa, Zihuatanejo
	5	MEX	TPH	Las Tres Voces de Durango, Santa María Ocotán
	10/2.5	MEX	HK	LV de Guadalajara, Guadalajara
	1	MEX	MM	Mix, Morelia
	10/1	MEX	FAMA	R. Fama, Cd.Camargo
	0.5/0.1	MEX	KS	Super KS, Saltillo
	2.5	NCG	ACTH	LV del Trópico Húmedo, San Carlos
	1	PNR	M33	AM Tropical, David
	1	PNR		R. Capital, Panamá
	1/1.7	PTR	WDNO	La Radio Que Te Bendice, Quebradillas
970	5	CUB	AM	R. Guamá, Los Palacios, PR
	1	CUB	BA	R. Rebelde, Trinidad, SS
	5/1	DOM	B72	R. Barahona, Barahona
	6	DOM	B71	R. Olímpica, La Vega
	5	GTM	AX	R. Continental, Guatemala
	2	HND	LY	R. Millenium, Tegucigalpa
	1/0.5	MEX	ZAZ	Amor, Zacatecas
	5/0.5	MEX	MH	Candela FM, Mérida
	1	MEX	BJ	Di Hit All, Cd. Victoria
	5/0.4	MEX	VOX	Fiesta Mexicana, Mazatlán
	10/5	MEX	J	La J Mexicana, Cd.Juárez
	5/0.25	MEX	EZ	La Mejor, Caborca
	1/0.5	MEX	MF	La Mejor, Monclova
	1	MEX	O	NotiGape 970 AM, Matamoros
	1/0.25	MEX	CJ	R. Apatzingán, Apatzingán
	50/4	MEX	RFR	R. Fórmula, Primera Cadena, México
	1/0.5	MEX	SW	R. Madera/La Mera Mera, Cd. Madera
	1	MEX	UG	R. Universidad de Guanajuato, Guanajuato
	3	PNR	S97	Ondas Centrales, Santiago
	5/1	VIR	WSTX	WSTX-AM, St Croix
980	2.5	CUB	B	R. COCO, El Sapo, CH
	1	CUB	BD	R. Reloj, Moa, HO
	5	HND	VC	LV Evangélica, Comayagua
	2	HND	ZC	R. Rhema, San Pedro Sula
	1	HND	AO	R. Tocoa, Tocoa
	5/0.2	MEX	LC	Dual Stereo, La Piedad
	1/0.25	MEX	KE	KE, Navojoa
	1	MEX	XT	La Caliente, Tepic
	2.5/0.5	MEX	FQ	La FQ, Cananea
	5	MEX	FS	La Mexicana, Izúcar de Matamoros
	1	MEX	JK	La Poderosa, Cd.Delicias
	5/0.5	MEX	NR	La Que Gusta Más, Nueva Rosita
	10/1	MEX	TU	Tu Recuerdo, Tampico
	1	NCG	A3NO	R. Redención Internac., Managua
990	25	CUB	AM	R. Guamá, Pinar del Río, PR
	1	DOM	B74	R. Cibao, Santiago
	5/1	DOM	C84	R. Eternidad, Sto Domingo
	1	GTM	AL	R. Perla de Oriente, Chiquimula
	3.5	HND	PR	R. Paz, Choluteca
	2. 5/1	MEX	IU	Amor, Oaxaca
	20/1	MEX	TG	Extremo, Tuxtla Gutiérrez
	5/0.25	MEX	HZ	HZ La Pura Sabrosura, La Paz
	20/5	MEX	PI	Ke Buena, Chilpancingo
	1/0.1	MEX	BC	La Buena Onda, Cd.Guzmán
	50	MEX	T	La T Grande, Monterrey
	10/3	MEX	FP	R. Alegría, Xalpa
	1	MEX	ATM	R. Fórmula, Morelia
	5/0.25	MEX	ER	R. Lobo, Cd.Cuauhtémoc
	1.4/3	MEX	CL	Rockola 990, Mexicali
	5	PNR		W Radio, Panamá
	0.91	PTR	WPRA	La Primera, Mayagüez
1000	10	CUB	SW	R. Artemisa, Artemisa, AR
	5	CUB	NM	R. Granma, Media Luna, GR
	25	CUB	AM	R. Guamá, Pinjar del Río, PR
		GTM		R. Cultural y Educativa, Patzún
		GTM		R. Revelación y Verdad, Guatemala
	1	HND	XZ	HCH Radio, Tegucigalpa
	3	HND	CY	R. Congolón, Gracias
	10/1	MEX	TAC	Exa FM, Tapachula
	1	MEX	MMS	La Ke Buena, Mazatlán
	1	MEX	FV	La Rancherita, Cd.Juárez
	3.5	MEX	GQ	La Reyna, Los Reyes
	5/0.35	MEX	MYL	Los 40 Principales, Mérida
	1	MEX	CSV	Máxima FM, Coatzacoalcos
	1/0.1	MEX	NLT	R. Fórmula Nuevo Laredo, Nuevo Laredo
	50/20	MEX	OY	R. Mil, México
	1/0.5	MEX	HPC	R. Mil/R. Fórmula, Hidalgo del Parral
	1/0.25	MEX	MIL	Romántica, Los Mochis
	1/0.5	MEX	RZ	W R., León
	10	NCG	FF	Hosanna R, Managua
	10	PNR	K36	R. Poderosa, Aguadulce
	5/1	VIR	WVWI	R. One, Charlotte Amalie, St Thomas
1010	10	CUB	BD	R. Reloj, Victoria de Las Tunas, LT
	10	DOM	B76	R. Comercial, Sto Domingo
	1	GTM		R. Caribe, Izabal
	1	GTM	XI	R. Ixil, Nebaj
	1	HND	CD	R. Constelación. Juticalpa
	1	HND	LL	R. Visión Cristiana, Tocoa
	2/0.5	MEX	DX	Cadena 1010 AM, Ensenada
	0.5/0.25	MEX	KD	Digital,Cd.Acuña
	5/0.5	MEX	LO	Exa FM, Chihuahua
	1	MEX	HGO	Hidalgo R, Huejutla
	20/2	MEX	PA	Ke Buena, Puebla
	5	MEX	TUMI	LV de la Sierra Oriente, Tuxpan
	0.5/0.2	MEX	XN	R. Ures, Ures
	5/1	MEX	WS	Romántica, Culiacán
	5/0.5	MEX	FM	Romántica, Veracruz
	50/5	MEX	HL	TDW, Guadalajara
	5/1	MEX	VK	Tu Recuerdo, Gómez Palacio
	5	NCG	FAVP	R. LV del Pinar, Ocotal
1020		CUB	AM	R. Artemisa, AR
	10	CUB	AM	R. Guamá, Bahía Honda, PR
	10	CUB	M	R. Guantánamo, Baracoa, GU
	5	GTM	CM	R. Frontera, Pajapita
	3	HND	PN	R. Visión Cristiana Internacional, Marcovia
	1/0.25	MEX	WO	97.7, Chetumal
	1	MEX	PIC	Éxtasis Digital, Tepic
	5/1	MEX	OU	La Mejor FM, Huajuapan de León
	1	MEX	VE	La Mexicana, Colima
	5/0.5	MEX	PR	Los 40 Principales, Poza Rica
	5	MEX	KH	Top Music, Querétaro

kHz	kW	Ctry	Call	Station, location
	5	PNR		R. Ancón, Panamá
	1/0.28	PTR	WOQI	R. Coquí/La Señal de la Montaña, Adjuntas
	5	SLV	CA	R. Int. /La Máxima, San Salvador
1030	5	DOM	B78	R. Novedades, La Vega
	10	GTM	UX	R. Panamericana, Guatemala
	1	HND	RJ	R. Ticante, Ocotepeque
	10/1	MEX	MPM	Exa FM, Los Mochis
	0.5/0.2	MEX	TEKA	Ke Buena, Juchitán
	20/2	MEX	LJ	Ke Buena, Lagos de Moreno
	1/0.25	MEX	BCC	La Mejor, Cd. del Carmen
	1/0.5	MEX	VP	La Mexicana, Acapulco
	1/0.5	MEX	PAV	La Picuda, Tampico
	5	MEX	SDD	La Tremenda, Ensenada
	10/0.25	MEX	VFS	LVde la Frontera Sur, Las Margaritas
	5	MEX	NKA	LV del Gran Pueblo, Felipe Carillo Puerto
	50/5	MEX	QR	R. Centro, México
	5/0.5	MEX	YC	R. Fórmula, Cd.Juárez
	5/1	MEX	IE	Stereo 1030, Matehuala
	1	SLV	RM	R. Frontera, Ahuachapán
1040	2	CTR	HG	R. Nosara, Hojancha
		CTR		R. Pilarcita, La Garita
	10	CUB	CL	R. Mayabeque, Güines, MB
	10	DOM	B79	CDN AM, Sto Domingo
	1	GTM	JP	R. Oriental, Jalapa
	1	HND	VC	LV Evangélica, Danlí
	5	HND	VC	LV Evangélica, Juticalpa
	5/0.75	MEX	CH	R. Capital 1040, Toluca
	5/0.25	MEX	SAG	R. Lobo Bajío, Irapuato
	10/1	MEX	BBB	R. Mujer, Guadalajara
	5/0.5	MEX	PLE	R. Palanque, Palenque
	5/0.25	MEX	HES	Radiorama Siglo XXI, Chihuahua
	5/0.25	MEX	GYS	Radiovisa, Guaymas
	2	NCG	VJ	LV de Jinotega, Jinotega
	2.5	PNR	J2	Ondas del Canajagua, Las Tablas
	9/0.25	PTR	WZNA	Zona 1040, Moca
1050	1	CUB	AM	R. Guamá, Santa Lucía, PR
	10	CUB	LL	R. Victoria, Victoria de Las Tunas, LT
	1.5	DOM	B80	R. Hispaniola, Santiago
	5/1	GTM	SL	LV de los Cuchumatanes, Huehuetenango
	15	MEX	ZUM	ABC R., Chilpancingo
	1	MEX	DC	Amor, Aguascalientes
	3 5/2.5	MEX	QOO	Imagen, Cancún
	10	MEX	D	La Gran D, Mexicali
	5	MEX	RIO	La Nayarita, Ixtlán del Río
	1	MEX	IP	La Poderosa, Uruapán
	10/1	MEX	BCS	La Radio de Sudcalifornia, La Paz
	100	MEX	G	La Ranchera 1050, Monterrey
	5	MEX	JF	R. Max, Tierra Blanca
	3	NCG	LL	R. Masaya, Masaya
1060	1	CTR	LX	R. Columbia, San Isidro del General
	25	CUB	DL	R. 26, Jovellanos, MA
		DOM	B81	R. Amanecer, San Pedro de Macorís
	1	DOM	B82	R. Azua, Azua
	7/2.5	MEX	RDO	La Raza 1060, Reynosa
	100/20	MEX	EP	R. Educación, México
	1	NCG		LV del Atlántico, Bluefields
	3.5	PNR	J60	LV de Panamá, Panamá
	5/0.5	PTR	WCGB	Rock R. Netw., Juana Díaz
1070	10	CUB	AM	R. Guamá, Guane, PR
	10	CUB	M	R. Guantánamo, Guantánamo, GU
	5/1	DOM	B83	HIBI R. 1070, San Francisco de Macorís
	3/2	GTM	D	LV de Occidente, Quetzaltenango
	1	HND	LE	R. Unica AM, San Pedro Sula
	3	HND	BB	R. Unidad Evangélica, Catacamas
	1/0.2	MEX	AGS	Amor, Acapulco
	1/0.25	MEX	IT	Exa FM, Cd. del Carmen
	1/0.25	MEX	GY	La Mejor, Tehuacán
	1/0.1	MEX	SP	R. Notícias 10-70, Guadalajara
	1/0.25	MEX	OBS	Xtasis, Cd.Obregón
	3	PNR		R. Estéreo Mi Favorita, Penonomé
	0.5/2.5	PTR	WMIA	R. Arecibo del Norte, Arecibo
1080	1	CTR	FC	Faro del Caribe, San José

kHz	kW	Ctry	Call	Station, location
	5	CUB	CH	R. Cadena Habana, V. María, CH
	1	DOM	B84	R. RPQ Sport, Sto Domingo
	1	GTM	LU	R. Novedad, Zacapa
	3	HND	IE	R. Senda de Vida, Nacaome
	5	MEX	JLV	C7 R., Puerto Vallarta
	1/0.13	MEX	UU	La Mejor, Colima
	1/0.5	MEX	CN	Los 40 Principales, Irapuato
	0.5/0.25	MEX	PAB	R.Celebridad, La Paz
	5/0.5	MEX	AX	R. Fórmula Oaxaca, Oaxaca
	5/0.25	MEX	TUL	R. Mexiquense Valle de México, Tultitlán
	1/0.25	MEX	DY	Río Digital, San Luis Río Colorado
	10	NCG	A3LC	R. 15 de Septiembre, Managua
	5	PNR	J24	R. Mundo Internacional, Panamá
	0.25	PTR	WLEY	R. Isla 1080, Cayey
	6	SLV	ME	R. CRET, San Salvador
1090	1	CUB	LL	R. Victoria, Amancio, LT
	2.5	DOM	B85	R. Amistad, Santiago
	1	HND	CQ	Cadena Radial Samaritano, Tegucigalpa
	5/1	MEX	LB	Candela, La Barca
	2. 5/1	MEX	XE	Íntegra 2 siete, Querétaro
	10	MEX	MCA	La Grande de las Huastecas, Pánuco
	1	MEX	HR	La HR, Puebla
	1/0.5	MEX	IL	La Nueva Mix, Veracruz
	1	MEX	WL	La Romántica, Nuevo Laredo
	5/0.5	MEX	AU	Milenio R, Monterrey
	50	MEX	PRS	XX Sports 1090 AM/Mighty 1090, Rosarito
	5	NCG	HAAL	R. Alma Latina, Estelí
	0.25/0.7	PTR	WSOL	LaNueva Sol 1090, San Germán
	3	SLV	MG	R. 1090, Atiquizaya
	1	SLV		R. CRET, Sta Ana
	0.25	VIR	WUVI	R. Charlotte Amalie, St Thomas
1100	5	CTR	SCR	R. Chorotega, Santa Cruz
	1	CUB	KO	R. Angulo, Mayarí, HO
	1	DOM	B89	R. Comercial, Nagua
	1	DOM	B88	R. Jimaní, Jimaní
	1	DOM	B87	R. Ocoa, San José de Ocoa
	1	DOM	B86	R. Oriente, San Pedro de Macorís
	1	GTM	SR	R. Superior, Coatepeque
	5	HND	AJ	R. Antena 5, Catacamas
	1	HND	ND	R. Esperanza, La Esperanza
	1	HND	VA	R. Tiempo, San Pedro Sula
	1/0.5	MEX	NAS	95.5 Sin Límites, Navojoa
	1/0.25	MEX	PO	Imagen, San Luis Potosí
	5	MEX	BV	R. Alegría, Moroleón
	1	MEX	BAC	R. Asunción/R. Sur California, Bahía Asunción
	5/0.5	MEX	TGO	R. Cañón, Tlaltenango
	1	MEX	GRM	RTG R, Ometepec
	5	PNR	M92	R. Sabrosa, Panamá
1110	10	CUB	KO	R. Angulo, Holguín, HO
	2.5	DOM	B90	R. Jarabacoa, Jarabacoa
	1/0.5	DOM	B91	R. Marién, Dajabón
	1	GTM	MK	R. Verapaz, Cobán
	1/0.5	MEX	WR	Cristo Rey Radio, Ciudad Juarez
	1/0.2	MEX	PVJ	Ke Buena, Puerto Vallarta
	10	MEX	HTY	La Mejor, Tlapacayan
	0.25	MEX	PU	La P-U, Monclova
	5/1	MEX	LEO	La Rancherita, León
	1/0.25	MEX	VS	Maxima 96-3, Hermosillo
	1	MEX	OQ	Notigape 11-10/R. Fórmula, Reynosa
	0.4	MEX	TEO	O AM, Teotitlán de Flores Magon
	0.5	MEX	TUX	O AM, Tuxtepec
	100	MEX	RED	R. Red, México
	1	NCG	F2MT	R. Momotombo, La Paz Centro
	2.5/0.5	PTR	WVJP	R. Caguas, Caguas
1120	1	CTR	ACE	R. Alajuela, Alajuela
		DOM	B93	R. Antillas, Barahona
		DOM	C86	R. Metro Hit, Samaná
	10	DOM	B92	R. Metro Hit, Sto Domingo
	0.5	GTM	C	R. Poderosa, Guatemala
	2	HND	TL	R. Fiesta, Tegucigalpa
	5	MEX	POP	Fórmula 11-20 AM, Puebla
	1/0.5	MEX	GV	La Nueva Mix, Querétaro

kHz	kW	Ctry	Call	Station, location
	5/0.5	MEX	TQE	La R. de Tabasco, Tenosique
	0.4/0.1	MEX	MX	MIC R., Mexicali
	1	MEX	TR	R. Panorámica, Cd.Valles
	1	MEX	RUY	R. Universidad, Mérida
	0.5	MEX	UNO	R. Uno La Popular , Guadalajara
	5	NCG	A3CP	R. CEPAD, Managua
	5	PNR	M21	R. Sonora, Panamá
	2.6/5	PTR	WMSW	R. Once, Hatillo
	3	SLV	LR	R. Elohim, San Salvador
1130		CUB	BA	R. Rebelde, Imías, GU
	10/1	DOM	B94	CDN AM, Santiago
	1	GTM	VR	Em. Unidas LV de la Costa Sur, Retalhuleu
	1	HND	HP	R. Pinares, Siguatepeque
	5	HND	PL	R. Progreso, El Progreso
	1/0.25	MEX	MOS	Éxtasis Digital, Los Mochis
	10/5	MEX	TOL	La Comadre, Toluca
	10/2.5	MEX	YZ	La Poderosa, Aguascalientes
	1/0.1	MEX	FN	Moderna R, Uruapan
	1	MEX	LUP	R. Lupita, Las Varas
	1	MEX	HN	Toño, Nogales
	0.5	NCG		Voz Evangélica de Jalapa, Jalapa
	2.5	PNR	U80	Vox MN, Aguadulce
	0.2/0.7	PTR	WOIZ	R. Antillas, Guayanilla
	1	SLV	AJ	R. Moderna, Sta Ana
1140	5	CTR	DKN	R. Nueva, Guápiles
	1	CUB	NL	R. Bayamo, Media Luna, GR
	1	CUB	BQ	R. Camagüey, Camagüey,CM
	1	CUB	DP	R. Ciudad Bandera, Cárdenas, MA
		CUB		R. Ciudad del Mar, Cienfuegos, CI
	25	CUB	CL	R. Mayabeque, La Salud, MB
	10	CUB	BF	R. Musical Nacional, Santa Clara, VC
	10	CUB	BA	R. Rebelde, Aguada, CI
		CUB	BA	R. Rebelde, Caribe, IJ
	5	CUB	BA	R. Rebelde, Circunvalación, MA
		CUB	BA	R. Rebelde, Guantánamo, GU
	25	CUB	BA	R. Rebelde, Morón, CA
		CUB		R. Surco, Morón, CA
	5	DOM	B95	R. Anacaona, San Juan de la Maguana
	3	HND	VC	LV Evangélica, Choluteca
	1	HND	UL	R. Pico Bonito, La Ceiba
	5	MEX	TE	Ella, Tehuacán
	5/0.5	MEX	LIA	Grupera 93.1, Morelia
	1	MEX	PEC	Hidalgo R., San Bartolo Tutotepec
	50	MEX	MR	R. Esperanza, Monterrey
	1/0.5	MEX	TEC	R. Tecpatán, Tecpatán
	5	PNR	B49	R. Panamericana, Panamá
	10	PTR	WQII	Once Q Cadena Nacional, San Juan
1150	10	CUB	NL	R. Bayamo, Entronque Bueycito, GR
	5	DOM	B96	Onda Musical HIAS, Sto Domingo
	10	GTM	T	R. Sonora, Guatemala
	5	HND	AV	Ondas del Ulúa, Sta Bárbara
	1	HND	LP12	R. Universal, Tegucigalpa
	50/10	MEX	JP	El Fonógrafo, México
	5/0.3	MEX	SO	Fiesta Mexicana, Cd.Obregón
	10/1	MEX	XP	La Mejor, Tuxtepec
	1.5/0.5	MEX	TVR	La Nueva Azul, Tuxpan
	0.25	MEX	WU	La Poderosa, Matehuala
	2. 5/1	MEX	BF	La Poderosa, San Pedro
	1/0.5	MEX	JS	R. Exitos/JS Digital, Hidalgo del Parral
	1	MEX	RM	R. Fórmula, Mexicali
	5/1	MEX	XM	R. Jerez, Jerez de García Salinas
	50/1	MEX	AD	R. Metrópoli, Guadalajara
	10/0.15	MEX	UAS	R.UAS, Culiacán
	1	SLV	CF	R. María Zona Oriental, San Miguel
1160	10	ATG		Caribbean R. Lighthouse, St John's
	1	CTR	CA	R. Columbia, Puntarenas
	1	CUB	NL	R. Bayamo, Pilón, GR
	5	DOM	B97	Radiolandia, Santiago
	1	GTM	RI	R. Izabal, Morales
	1	HND	VZ	R. Juan Pablo II, Siguatepeque
	1	HND	HZ	R. Liberación, Tocoa
	5	HND	FJ	R. País, Progreso
	1/0.1	MEX	IW	Canal Stereo Juvenil, Uruapan
	10	MEX	QIN	LV del Valle, San Quintín
	1/0.1	MEX	GI	R. Reyna, Tamazunchale
	2.5/0.5	MEX	VW	Stereo Sensación, Acámbaro
	1	NCG	HM	R. Satélite, Estelí
	5	PNR	C20	Ondas Chiricanas, David
	10	PNR	WK	R. Metrópolis, Panamá
	5/2.5	PTR	WBQN	Super Borinquén, Barceloneta-Manatí
1170	10	CUB	M	R. Guantánamo, Maisí, GU
		DOM	B98	Cadena Espacial, Azua
	5	GTM	RL	R. Cadena Landívar, Quetzaltenango
	2	HND	AF	R. Campeonísima, Choluteca
	10/2.5	MEX	CD	Ciudad W, Puebla
	5	MEX	RT	Ke Buena, Reynosa
	1/0.5	MEX	MDA	La Mera Ley, Monclova
	1/0.1	MEX	JTF	La Tremenda, Zacoalco de Torres
	5/0.1	MEX	FEM	R. Disney, Hermosillo
	2.5/1	MEX	ZS	R. Hit, Coatzacoalcos
	1	MEX	IB	Radiovisa, Caborca
	1/0.25	MEX	RLK	Super Stereo Miled, Atlacomulco
	10/2.5	MEX	UVA	UVA, Aguascalientes
	0.2	PTR	WLEO	R. Leo, Ponce
	0.5	SLV	CB	R. Pentecostés, Sonsonate
1180	5	CTR	PJ	R. Victoria, Heredia
	1	CUB	DX	R. Baracoa CMDX, Mabujabo, GU
		CUB	BQ	R. Enciclopedia, Santiago de Cuba, SC
	10	CUB	BA	R. Rebelde, Arroyo Arenas, CH
	10	CUB	BA	R. Rebelde, Artemisa, AR
	5	CUB	BA	R. Rebelde, Bahía Honda, PR
	1	CUB	BA	R. Rebelde, Banes, HO
		CUB	BA	R. Rebelde, Bolondrón, MA
	10	CUB	BA	R. Rebelde, C. Brasil, CM
	50	CUB	BA	R. Rebelde, Cacocúm, HO
	50	CUB	BA	R. Rebelde, Camagüey, CM
	5	CUB	BA	R. Rebelde, Cárdenas, MA
	50	CUB	BA	R. Rebelde, Chambas, CA
	1	CUB	BA	R. Rebelde, Ciego de Avila, CA
	1	CUB	BA	R. Rebelde, Cienfuegos, CI
	25	CUB	BA	R. Rebelde, Colón, MA
		CUB	BA	R. Rebelde, Corralillo, SC
	50	CUB	BA	R. Rebelde, Guáimaro, CM
	50	CUB	BA	R. Rebelde, Guanabacoa, CH
	1	CUB	BA	R. Rebelde, Guantánamo, GU
	10	CUB	BA	R. Rebelde, Güines, MB
		CUB	BA	R. Rebelde, Hectómetro, MB
	5	CUB	BA	R. Rebelde, Ja Jaiba, MA
	10	CUB	BA	R. Rebelde, La Palma, PR
	10	CUB	BA	R. Rebelde, Los Palacios, PR
	200	CUB	BA	R. Rebelde, Martí, MA
	1	CUB	BA	R. Rebelde, Mayarí Arriba, SC
	1	CUB	BA	R. Rebelde, Mayarí Arriba, SC
	1	CUB	BA	R. Rebelde, Moa, HO
	5	CUB	BA	R. Rebelde, Nueva Gerona, IJ
	10	CUB	BA	R. Rebelde, Pinar del Río (III), PR
	10	CUB	BA	R. Rebelde, Pinar del Río, PR
	1	CUB	BA	R. Rebelde, Puerto Padre, LT
	5	CUB	BA	R. Rebelde, Sagua de Tánamo, HO
	1	CUB	BA	R. Rebelde, San Cristóbal, AR
	1	CUB	BA	R. Rebelde, Sancti Spíritus, SS
	10	CUB	BA	R. Rebelde, Santa Clara, VC
	1	CUB	BA	R. Rebelde, Santa Lucía, PR
	10	CUB	BA	R. Rebelde, Sta Cruz del Norte, MB
	5	CUB	BA	R. Rebelde, Tulipán, CI
	10	CUB	BA	R. Rebelde, Victoria de LT, LT
	10	DOM	B99	R. Mil, Sto Domingo
	1	HND	AZ	R. El Tigre, Tegucigalpa
	1	HND		R. Río de Dios, Belén
	0.5	MEX	AH	Hits, Juchitán
	5/1.5	MEX	DCH	Ke Buena, Cd. Delicias
	1/0.8	MEX	YA	La Picosa, Irapuato
	10/5	MEX	FR	R. Felicidad, México
	10	MEX	UBS	R. Univ. Autonoma de Baja California Sur,

kHz	kW	Ctry	Call	Station, location
				La Paz
	10	PNR	U	AM Original, Santiago
	10	PNR		R. Chinavisión, Panamá
	5	SLV	VG	R. VEA, San Salvador
1190	10	CUB	JD	R. Coral/R. Revolución, Chivirico, SC
	1	CUB	GL	R. Sancti Spíritus, Trinidad, SS
	5	HND	VW3	R. Cadena Voces, El Progreso
	8/0.125	MEX	TOT	ABCR., Tampico
	0.25/0.1	MEX	MBC	Cadena1190 AM, Mexicali
	10/0.1	MEX	CT	Contacto 11-90, Monterrey
	5	MEX	PP	La Comadre, Orizaba
	5	MEX	JPA	La Mexicana, Cuernavaca
	5/0.1	MEX	PZ	R. Norteña, Cd.Juárez
	5/2.5	MEX	SOL	R. Sol, la pura ley, Cd.Hidalgo
	2.5/1	MEX	XQ	R. Universidad, San Luís Potosí
	50/10	MEX	WK	W R. /W Guadalajara, Guadalajara
	1	NCG	A6RB	R. Bendición, Cayanlipe
	10/5	PTR	WBMJ	Rock R. Netw., San Juan
1200	5	CTR	TQ	R. Cucú, San José
	1	CUB	GL	R. Sancti Spíritus, Yaguajay, SS
	1	DOM	C21	R. Caracol, Azua
		DOM	C23	R. VEN, Sto Domingo
	12	GTM	RJ	R. Unción, Jutiapa
	1	HND	SI	R. Impacto, Tela
	2.5	MEX	QY	La Bestia Grupera, Toluca
	1/0.25	MEX	YF	R. Fórmula, Hermosillo
	1	MEX	PAS	R. Punta Abreojos, Punta Abreojos
	5	MEX	QJAL	R. y Televisión Querétaro, Jalpán
	1/0.25	MEX	WT	W R., Culiacán
		NCG	A3AC	1200 La R., Managua
	0.25/1	PTR	WGDL	La mejor AM, Lares
1210		CUB		R. Rebelde, Jobabo, LT
	10	CUB	GL	R. Sancti Spíritus, Sancti Spíritus, SS
	5	DOM		R. Merengue, San Francisco de Macorís
	10/5	GTM	MX	R. Miel, Guatemala
	2	HND	VC	LV Evangélica, Sta Barbara
	5	MEX	COPA	LV de los Vientos, Copainalá
	5/1	MEX	PUE	Méxicana 12-10 AM, Puebla
	1	MEX	ITC	R. Tecnológico, Celaya
	1	PNR	E91	R. Diez, Panamá
	1	PTR	WHOY	La Señal Activa de PR, Salinas
	1	SLV	CG	R. América/R. La Paz, Zacatecoluca
1220	1	CTR	Q	R. Fe y Poder, Limón
	10	CUB	BY	R. Caribe, La Fe, IJ
		DOM	C24	R. HIN, Sto Domingo
	1	HND	OP	R. Costeña Ebenezer, San Pedro Sula
	3	HND	SD	R. Destellos de Luz, Sabá
	1	HND	YS	R. Suari, Marcala
	100	MEX	B	La B Grande, México
	4.5	MEX	SAL	R. Universidad Agraria, Saltillo
	1	NCG	A3RA	R. América, Managua
1230		CUB	BC	R. Progreso, Bayamo, GR
		CUB	BC	R. Progreso, La Palma, PR
		GTM		R. América, Cuyotenango
	1	GTM	AT	R. Atlántida, Puerto Barrios
	0.25	HND	CQ	Cad. R. Samaritano, San Marcos de Colón
	20/1	MEX	TVH	La Radio de Tabasco, Villahermosa
	1	MEX	TCP	Los 40 Principales, Tehuacán
	10/2	MEX	EX	R. Fórmula, Culiacán
	1/0.25	MEX	DKN	R. Fórmula, Segunda Cadena, Guadalajara
	10/1	MEX	IZ	R. Fórmula, Tercera Cadena, Monterrey
	1	MEX	LP	R. Pía, La Piedad
	5	NCG	MNG	R. Manantial, Nueva Guinea
	1	PTR	WNIK	Única R., Arecibo
1240	1	CTR	WC	R. Corobicí, Cañas
	1	DOM	C26	R. María, Santo Domingo
	5	GTM	K	R. Luz, Guatemala
	1	HND	ZC	R. Vanguardia, Tegucigalpa
	1	MEX	WG	Cambio 1240, Cd.Juárez
	1	MEX	BQ	FM 105, Guaymas
	2.5/1	MEX	CE	Ke Buena, Oaxaca
	1	MEX	VM	La 100.9 FM, Piedras Negras
	1	MEX	RD	La Comadre, Pachuca
	1	MEX	SI	La Mejor, Santiago Ixcuintla
	4 1/2	MEX	RPA	R. Ranchito, Morelia
	1/0.25	MEX	S	R. Unción, Tampico
	1	MEX	BN	Radiola, Cd.Delicias
	1	MEX	CG	Romántica, Nogales
	5	NCG	A3RR	R. Vida Managua
	3	PNR	M56	Ondas de Vida, David
	1	PNR		R. Infantil, Panamá
	1/5	PTR	WALO	R. Oriental/Cad. R. Puerto Rico, Humacao
	0.5	SLV	MT	R. Metapán, Metapán
	1	SLV	QN	R. Norteña, San Miguel
1250	1	CUB	M	R. Playita, Imías, GU
	5	DOM	C28	LV del Progreso, San Francisco de Macorís
	5	DOM	C29	R. Juventud, La Romana
	1	GTM		LV Cristiana, Totonicapán
	1	GTM	PY	R. Payakí, Esquipulas
	1	HND	DG	R. Cadena Oriental, Danlí
	1	HND		R. Garzel, Juticalpa
	1	HND	YF	R. Renacimiento, Comayagua
	1/0.5	MEX	DL	Activa R, Hermosillo
	10/1	MEX	DK	DK 12-50, Guadalajara
	1/0.5	MEX	SC	La 97.7, Sabinas
	5/0.25	MEX	AT	La Caliente, Hidalgo del Parral
	5/0.5	MEX	ZT	La Mejor 12-50 AM, Puebla
	10	MEX	TF	R. Fórmula Segunda Cadena, Veracruz
	1/0.25	MEX	TEJ	R. Mexiquense, Tejupilco
	5/0.5	MEX	SJ	SJ, Saltillo
	2.5	NCG	CR	Cad. Radial Samaritano, Condega
	0.25/1	PTR	WJIT	R. Hit, Sabana
1260	5	CTR	DIO	R. Emaús, San Vito de Coto Brus
	2.5	CUB	BC	R. Progreso, Media Luna, GR
	1	HND	FP	R. Amistad, San Marcos de Colón
	1	MEX	QL	Catedral de la Música, Zamora
	1/0.25	MEX	MW	Dimensión 1260, San Luis Río Colorado
	5/0.5	MEX	SA	Exa FM, Culiacán
	1/0.25	MEX	R	Hits FM, Linares
	1	MEX	TBV	Ke Buena, Tierra Blanca
	20/10	MEX	L	La Comadre, México
	1/0.25	MEX	ZH	La Estación que se Escucha, Salamanca
	5/1	MEX	JY	La Mejor, Autlán
	10	MEX	JAM	LV de la Costa Chica, Santiago Jamiltepec
	1	MEX	MTV	R. Lobo de Mina, Minatitlán
	5/1	MEX	XR	R. Mensajera, Cd.Valles
	5/0.25	MEX	OG	R. Ranchito, Ojinaga
	2.5/0.9	PTR	WI3XSO	Cadena WAPA R, Aguadilla
	5/1.8	PTR	WIZXSO	Cadena WAPA R, Mayagüez
	2.5/2	PTR	WISO	Cadena WAPA R, Ponce
	12	SLV	AA	R. Abba, San Salvador
1270	1	DOM	C32	R. Ambiente, Baní
	1.2	DOM	C31	R. Metro-Hit 12-70, Santiago
	2.5	GTM	CQ	R. Exclusiva, Guatemala
	0.5/0.15	MEX	WN	ElFonógrafo, Torreón
	10/0.15	MEX	RPL	LaPoderosa RPL, León
	0.5	MEX	AZ	La Z, Tijuana
	1.5/0.4	MEX	HD	R. Universidad, Durango
	1/0.5	MEX	GL	R. XEGL, Navojoa
	1/0.25	MEX	RRR	Romántica, Papantla
	2/0.5	MEX	RRT	Voz, Cd.Madero
	3	NCG	RA	R. Amistad, Matagalpa
	3	PNR	J22	R. Tipy Q, Panamá
1280		CTR		R. Visión, San José
		CUB	BQ	R. Enciclopedia, Varadero, MA
	1	CUB	JN	R. Mambí, Santiago de Cuba, SC
	10	CUB		R. Trinidad Digital, Trinidad, SS
	1	HND	OW	R. LV de la Victoria, Juticalpa
	1	HND	BN	R. San Miguel, Marcala
	1/0.5	MEX	EG	ABC Radio, Puebla
	10/1	MEX	AW	AW, Involvidable, Monterrey
	2. 5/1	MEX	CAM	Kiss FM, Campeche
	1/0.5	MEX	BW	Palabra Viva, Chihuahua
	0.5/0.25	MEX	BON	R.Fórmula, Tercera Cadena, Guadalajara

kHz	kW	Ctry	Call	Station, location
2. 5/1	MEX	SQ	R. San Miguel, S. M. de Allende
	1	MEX	TUT	R. Tamaulipas, Tula
	5/1	PTR	WCMN	NotiUno, Arecibo
	1	SLV	MQ	R. Emaús, San Vicente
1290		GTM		R. Miramundo, Zacapa
	1	HND	NN26	R. Choluteca, Choluteca
	1/0.5	MEX	IX	La Pantera, Sahuayo
	5/0.25	MEX	FAC	La Poderosa, Salvatierra
	10/1	MEX	NX	R. Mujer, Mazatlán
	20/5	MEX	DA	R. Trece, México
	1/0.25	MEX	AP	Romántica, Cd.Obregón
	3	PNR	S23	R. Única, Chiriqui
	5.5	PNR		R. Única, Los Santos
	5	PNR		R. Unica, Panama
	1	SLV	MA	R. Chalatenango, Chalatenango
1300	1	CTR	GL	R. La Fuente Musical, Cartago
	1	CUB	KO	R. Angulo, Banes, HO
	5	HND	IV	CCI Radio, Tegucigalpa
	5	HND	LR	R. Santa Rosa, Sta Rosa de Copán
	1/0.1	MEX	XW	Ke Buena, Nogales
	1	MEX	KW	Kiss FM, Morelia
	1/0.25	MEX	JL	La 130, Guamuchil
	10/0.75	MEX	XV	LaZ, León
	38/0.2	MEX	P	R. 13/R. Centro, Cd.Juárez
	1/0.25	MEX	AWL	R. Jacala/Hidalgo R.,Jacala
	1	NCG	A2CC	Canal 130 AM, Managua
	5	PNR	I417	R. Baha'ís, Boca del Monte
	1	PTR	WTIL	R. Util, Mayagüez
		SLV	KG	R. Llanera, San Miguel
	6	SLV	LV	W-LV de la Verdad, San Salvador
	1	SXM	PJD-2	The Voice of St. Maarten, Philipsburg
1310	1	CUB	BQ	R. Enciclopedia, Nueva Gerona, IJ
	1	DOM	C36	R. Real, La Vega
	1	GTM	AN	R. LV de los Altos, Quetzaltenango
	2.5	HND	VC	LV Evangélica, San Pedro Sula
	1	HND	RL	R. Libertad, Marcala, La Paz
	5	HND	CM	R. Universidad de Agricultura, Catacamas
	1/0.25	MEX	AM	La Mandona, Matamoros
	5/0.25	MEX	VB	Mujer 1310.com, Monterrey
	1	MEX	BTS	R. Bahía de Tortugas, Bahía de Tortugas
	1	MEX	C	R. Enciso, Tijuana
	5/1	MEX	HIT	R. Felicidad, Puebla
	1	MEX	LPZ	R. La Paz, La Paz
	1	MEX	FH	R. Plan, Agua Prieta
	10/1	MEX	TIA	R. Vital, Guadalajara
	1	MEX	GRT	RTG R, Taxco
	5	MRT		Martinique Première, Lamentin
	10/1	NCG	SC	R. San Cristóbal, Chinandega
	5	SLV	RV	R. Veritas, Stgo de María
1320	1	CTR	LX	R. Columbia, San Carlos
		CUB		Ecos de Sagua, Sagua de Tánamo, HO
	1	CUB	DL	R. 26, La Jaiba, MA
	1	CUB	BA	R. Rebelde, San Cristóbal, AR
	1/0.5	DOM	C37	R. Centro, San Juan de la Maguana
	0.5	GTM	ME	R. Quezada, Jutiapa
	1	HND	MG	R. Bahía, La Ceiba
	10/2	MEX	UH	Ke Buena, Tuxtepec
	2.5/0.25	MEX	JZ	LaCampera/R. Fórmula, Cd.Jimenez:
	5/0.5	MEX	RJ	La Nueva RJ, Mazatlán
	10/0.1	MEX	CPN	La Poderosa, Piedras Negras
	0.5/0.25	MEX	SR	R.Cachanía, Santa Rosalia
	1/0.5	MEX	NM	Romance, Aguascalientes
	10/1	MEX	NI	Stereo Vida, Uruapán
	5/2.3	PTR	WSKN	R. Isla 1320, San Juan
1330	3	DOM	C38	R. Visión Cristiana, Sto Domingo
	5	GTM	MU	Unión R., Guatemala
	1	HND		R. Emisora Evangélica, Tegucigalpa
	1/0.1	MEX	RP	Boom FM, Cd.Madero
	10	MEX	MAC	La Poderosa, Manzanillo
	5/0.9	MEX	AJ	La Primera, Saltillo
	4/0.25	MEX	WQ	La Super Estación, Monclova
	0.5	MEX	EV	R. Capital, Izúcar de Matamoros

kHz	kW	Ctry	Call	Station, location
	5/1	MEX	BO	R. Variedades, Irapuato
	5	NCG	A6RM	R. Matagalpa, Matagalpa
	5	PNR		LV Poderosa, Panamá
	2/1.4	PTR	WENA	La Buena del Sur, Yauco
1340	5	CTR	HR	R. Sideral, San Ramón
	0.25	CUB	-	AFRTS, Guantánamo Bay
	10	CUB	FL	R. Ciudad del Mar, Palmira, CI
	1	HND	CQ	Cadena Radial Samaritano, Comayagua
	10	HND	TQ	Ebenezer 1340, San Pedro Sula
	1	MEX	AA	13-40 AM, Mexicali
	1	MEX	APM	Candela, Apatzingán
	1/0.5	MEX	RCH	Estéreo Romance, Ojinaga
	1	MEX	DH	Exa FM, Cd.Acuña
	5	MEX	ASM	Éxtasis Digital, Cuernavaca
	1	MEX	CI	Hit FM, Acapulco
	10/5	MEX	LU	Ke Buena Puebla, Cd. Serdán
	1	MEX	QB	La Divertida, Tulancingo
	1	MEX	QE	La Kañona, Escuinapa
	1	MEX	BK	La Raza, Nuevo Laredo
	1	MEX	CR	La Zeta, Morelia
	1	MEX	RPV	LV de Victoria, Cd.Victoria
	0.6	MEX	MT	Nostalgia, Matamoros
	1/0.64	MEX	OS	R. Mujer, Cd.Obregón
	5/1	MEX	DKT	R. Ranchito, Guadalajara
	1	MEX	NV	Romántica 1340, Monterrey
	1	NCG	OS	R. Ondas Sonoras, Managua
	2.5	PNR		R. Tipikal, Las Tablas
	0.95	PTR	WMNA	R. Una 1340, Aguadilla
	1	VIR	WSTA	R. Charlotte Amalie, St Thomas
1350	10	CUB	FL	R. Ciudad del Mar, Aguada, CI
	1	CUB	LM	R. Libertad, Puerto Padre, LT
	1	DOM	C41	Ondas del Yuna, Bonao
	1	DOM	C42	R. Rutas Musical, La Romana
	1	GTM	MC	R. Monja Blanca, Cobán
	1	HND	EL	R. Estelar, La Ceiba
	0.25	MEX	ZD	La Incondicional, Camargo
	5/1	MEX	CAH	La Popular, LV de Soconusco, Cacahoatán
	10	MEX	CTZ	LV de la Sierra Norte, Cuetzalán
	8	MEX	LBL	R. Centro, San Luis Río Colorado
	5/0.5	MEX	TB	R. Laguna, Torreón
	5/1	MEX	QK	Tropicalísima 13-50, México
	5	PNR	Z38	BBN R., Panamá
	2.5	PTR	WEGA	Faro de Santidad, Vega Baja
1360		DOM	C43	R. Tropical, Sto Domingo
	10	GTM	LK	R. Tic Tac, Guatemala
	1	HND	BS	R. San Pedro, Tegucigalpa
	5	HND	BH	R. Sta Bárbara, Sta Bárbara
	1/0.4	MEX	DI	La Nueva, Chihuahua
	1	MEX	KF	La Z, Iguala
	1/0.25	MEX	Y	Los 40 Principales, Celaya
	10	MEX	ZON	LV de la Sierra, Zongolica
1370	1	CUB		R. Guantánamo, Imías, GU
	5	DOM	C45	R. Seybo, El Seybo
	1	GTM	AC	LV de Colomba, Colomba
	5	HND	UN	LV de Catacamas, Catacamas
	1	HND	SQ	R. El Shaddai R., Siguatepeque
	5/0.5	MEX	GNK	Fiesta Mexicana, Nuevo Laredo
	10/1	MEX	PJ	Frecuencia Deportiva, Guadalajara
	1/0.25	MEX	RPU	La Z, Durango
	5	MEX	HF	R. Fórmula, Nogales
	10/0.4	MEX	MON	R. Fórmula, Segunda Cadena, Monterrey
	5/0.5	MEX	SV	R. Nicolaita, Morelia
	0.5	MEX	HG	Super, Mexicali
	1	NCG	AARS	R. Fronteras, Somoto
	5/1	PTR	WIVV	Rock Radio Netw.,Vieques Isl.
	1	SLV	KO	R. Lluvias de Bendición, San Miguel
1380	1	CTR	MS	R. Guanacaste, Liberia
	1	DOM	C47	R. Nacional, Santiago
	0.5	GTM	EB	R. Momostenango Educativa, Momost.
	0.5	HND	AH	R. Redención, Jutiapa
	1/0.5	MEX	RS	Éxtasis Digital, Gómes Palacio
	5/1	MEX	GW	Imagen, Cd.Victoria

kHz	kW	Ctry	Call	Station, location
	1/0.1	MEX	VD	R. Sensaciónal Digital, Allende
	50/5	MEX	CO	Romántica AM Digital, México
	10/1	MEX	TP	Sensación FM, Xalapa
	10	PNR		Mujer AM, Panamá
	1	PTR	WOLA	Prócer, Voz de la Montaña, Barranquitas
1390	1	DOM	C48	R. San Cristóbal
	1	HND	VC	LV Evangélica, Sta Rosa de Copán
	10/5	HND	VC	LV Evangélica, Tegucigalpa
	1/0.15	MEX	QC	La Reyna del Mar, Puerto Peñasco
	5/1	MEX	XO	La Super Buena, Cd.Mante
	5/0.1	MEX	KT	La Súper KT, Tecate
	10/2.5	MEX	TY	Los 40 Principales, Tecomán
	1	MEX	OR	NotiGape 1390 AM, Reynosa
	10/0.25	MEX	RW	RFórmula, León
	5/1	MEX	TL	R. Ola, Tuxpan
	1	MEX	CTA	Visión 90.9, Cuautla
	5	PNR		R. Mundo Internacional, Colón
	1	PTR	WISA	740 La Original, Isabela
		SLV		R. Fraternidad de Jesucristo, Chalchuapa
	1	SLV	JU	R. Getsemani, La Unión
	1	SLV	JS	Sinaí R., LV del Rey de Gloria, Soyapango
1400	1	CUB		R. Sagua, Sagua La Grande, VC
	1	DOM	C49	Ondas del Valle, La Vega
	5	GRD		Harbour Light of the Windwards, Carriacou
	1	HND	YT	R. Estrella de Oro, San Pedro Sula
	2.5/1	MEX	XI	Capital Máxima, Ixtapan de la Sal
	1	MEX	VI	EXA FM 99.1, San Juan del Río
	1	MEX	AC	Ke Buena, Aguascalientes
	5/1	MEX	I	Máxima 100.9, Morelia
	1	MEX	OJ	R. Horizonte/R. Fórmula, Cd.Lázaro Cárdenas
	51	MEX	SH	R. Sabinas, Cd.Sabinas
	0.25	MEX	AB	R. Santa Ana, Santa Ana
	1	MEX	UBJ	R. Universidad, Oaxaca
	1	MEX	KJ	Vida, Acapulco
	1	MEX	PF	Vida, Ensenada
	10	NCG	A3MA	R. María, Managua
	10	PNR	T40	Digital R. Luz, La Chorrera
	1	PTR	WIDA	R. Vida AM, Carolina.
	1	SLV	JI	LV del Litoral, Usulután
1410	3/0.5	DOM		R. 14-10 Cristiana, Barahona
	1/0.5	DOM	C52	R. Grí-Grí, Río San Juan
	1	DOM	C50	R. Tricolor, Sto Domingo
	5	GTM	GH	Nueva R. Xelajú, Quetzaltenango
	2/1	MEX	ZHO	Aquamarina R., Zihuatanejo
	1/0.25	MEX	AS	Ke Buena, Nuevo Laredo
	2.5	MEX	KB	La 1410, Guadalajara
	10/0.5	MEX	CF	La Mexicana, Los Mochis
	7	MEX	BS	Perrona 14-10, México
	1/0.25	MEX	CUA	R. Universidad, Campeche
	5/0.5	MEX	IR	Stereo Bit, Cd.Valles
	3/1	NCG	RA	La Estación de la Amistad, León
	5	PNR	H779	R. Mensabé, Las Tablas
	1	PTR	WRSS	R. Progreso, San Sebastián
1420	1	CTR	RPN	R. Pampa, Liberia
	1.5	DOM	C53	R. Oro, Cotuí
	10/1	MEX	WE	La Estación Familiar, Irapuato
	5/0.4	MEX	H	La H, Antología Vallenata, Monterrey
	5/0.5	MEX	F	R. Activa, Cd.Juárez
	10/2	MEX	XX	Vida, Tijuana
	1	MEX	EW	W1420/LV del Bajo Bravo, Matamoros
	1	PTR	WUKQ	Ponce
1430	3	CTR	RDVC	R. San Carlos, Cd. Quesada
	5	DOM	C54	R. Emanuel, Santiago
	1.2	GTM	AG	LV de Huehuetenango
	1	HND	FO	LV Evangélica, Puerto Cortés
	1	HND	QV	R. Futura, Olanchito
	1	HND	VM	R. Maranatha, La Paz
	1	MEX	COC	Amor, Colima
	5/0.5	MEX	OX	Exa FM, Cd.Obregón
	5/0.15	MEX	WD	La Grande, Cd. Miguel Alemán
	5/1	MEX	TT	R. Tlaxcala, La Doble TTlaxcala

kHz	kW	Ctry	Call	Station, location
	5	NCG	AARL	R. Liberación, Estelí
	7.5	PNR		R. Kids, Panamá
	5	PTR	WNEL	R. Tiempo/NotiUno, Caguas
1440	5	DOM	C55	R. Impactante, Sto Domingo
	5	DOM	C56	R. San Juan, San Juan de la Maguana
	0.5	GTM	MS	R. Nacional, Mazatenango
	5	HND	RD	R. Belén, La Ceiba
	10/1	MEX	ABCJ	La Estrella del Caribe, Guadalajara
	25/5	MEX	EST	Quiéreme 14-40, México
	25	NCG	A3MR	R. Maranatha, Managua
1450	1	CUB	LN	R. Maboas, Amancio Rodríguez, LT
	1	CUB	CL	R. Mayabeque, Santa Cruz del Norte, MB
	10	DOM	M20	R. Util, Salcedo
	1	GTM	LG	R. Hosanna, Guatemala
	1	MEX	CM	Bonita, Cd.Mante
	5/1	MEX	JM	La Caliente, Monterrey
	1	MEX	BP	La Más Buena, Gómez Palacio
	2/1	MEX	RY	La Poderosa V del Sur, Arcelia
	10/1	MEX	CU	La Z, Los Mochis
	0.4	MEX	PNO	O AM, Santiago Pinotepa Nacional
	1	MEX	RNB	R. Impacto, Sahuayo y Jiquilpan
	1/0.25	MEX	ARE	R. Pegüís/R. Lobo, Ojinaga
	5	PNR		R. Melodía, Panamá
	1	PTR	WCPR	R. Coamo, Coamo
	1	SLV	KR	R. Restauración, San Miguel
1460	1	CTR	LX	R. Columbia, Ciudad Quesada
		CUB		R. 8SF, Mayarí Arriba, SC
	5	DOM	C59	R. Renacimiento, Hato Mayor del Rey
	2.5	GTM	RN	R. Petén, Flores
	0.5	HND	CX	LV de Patuca, Catacamas
	2.5	HND	GC	R. Reino, San Pedro Sula
	1/0.1	MEX	JH	ABC R., Xalapa
	5/0.5	MEX	KC	Planeta, Oaxaca
	10/0.25	MEX	CB	R.Ranchito, San Luis Río Colorado
	0.5	PNR	D42	LV de Almirante, Bocas del Toro
	0.5	PTR	WLRP	R. Raíces, San Sebastián
	0.5/0.3	PTR	WRRE	Sonido Santidad, Juncos
1470	1	CUB	LM	R. Chaparra, Puerto Padre, LT
	1	DOM	C60	LV de la Alabanza, S.Francisco de Macorís
		DOM		R. Barahona, Provincia Independencia
		DOM	C61	R. Vibra, Barahona
	5/1	MEX	CAV	Exa FM, Durango
	50/5	MEX	AI	Fórmula Femenina, México
	1	MEX	IRG	La Campirana, Irapuato
	10/0.25	MEX	HI	LaConsentida, Ciudad Miguel Alemán
	1/0.5	MEX	IND	LV Sierra Hidalguense, Tlanchinol
	1/0.1	MEX	ACE	R. Fórmula Mazatlán, Mazatlán
	2.5/0.1	MEX	BAL	R. Voz Maya de México, Bécal
	10/5	MEX	RCN	Uniradio 14-70, Tijuana
	1	NCG	RY	R. Yarrince, Boaco
	5	PNR		La Primerísima, Panamá
	2/4	PTR	WKCK	R. Cumbre, Orocovis
1480	5	DOM	C63	R. Villa, Sto Domingo
	5	GTM	HB	R. Horizontes, Guatemala
	1	HND	EZ	LV de Misiones, Comayagüela
	20/1	MEX	ZJ	Ciudad 14-80, Guadalajara
	1/0.5	MEX	HM	La Caliente, Cd.Delicias
	1/0.1	MEX	XU	La Poderosa, Cd.Frontera
	10/1	MEX	TKR	La TKR, Rancherita y Regional, Monterrey
	5	MEX	CARH	LV del Pueblo Hña-hñu, Cárdonal
	5/0.15	MEX	VIC	R. Tamaulipas, Cd.Victoria
	1/0.25	MEX	NS	Z107.1, Navojoa
	5	PTR	WMDD	El 14-80 AM, Fajardo
1490	1	CUB	KN	R. Mayarí, Mayarí, HO
	1	GTM	RE	R. Modelo, Retalhuleu
	1	HND	HY	R. Boquerón, Juticalpa
	0.25	MEX	AQ	La Caliente, Agua Prieta
	1/0.25	MEX	SK	La Super K/La Costeñita, Cd.Ruiz
	1	MEX	MS	R. Mexicana, Matamoros
	1	MEX	CJC	R. Net, Cd.Juárez
	1/0.25	MEX	FF	R. Norteña, Matehuala

kHz	kW	Ctry	Call	Station, location
	1	MEX	YT	R. Teocelo, Teocelo
	5/1	MEX	GT	W R., Zamora
	3	PNR		Asamblea Nacional, Cocle
	5/1	PTR	WDEP	R. Isla, Ponce
1500	0.5	DOM	C65	R. Higüey, Higüey
	3	DOM		R. Juan Pablo Duarte, Elías Piña
	0.4	MEX	JQ	La Explosiva, Parras
	50	MEX	DF	R. Fórmula 1500, Segunda Cadena, México
	1/0.5	MEX	FL	R. Santa Fe, Guanajuato
	1	NCG	PT	R. Minuto, Managua
	1/0.25	PTR	WMNT	R. Atenas, Manatí
	1	SLV	CS	R. Pentecostal Bethel, Usulután
1510	10/3	DOM	C67	R. Pueblo, Sto Domingo
	1	HND	EM	R. Emanuel, Ocotepeque
	1	HND	PG	R. Gualcho, Tegucigalpa
	10	MEX	QI	La Nueva Radio, Monterrey
	0.25	MEX	HUI	R. Huichapán, Huichapán
	5	PNR	A95	Hosanna R., Panamá
	1	PTR	WBSG	R. Voz, Lajas
1520	1	CTR	LX	R. Columbia, Cartago
		CUB	KZ	R. Baraguá, Palma Soriano, SC
	1	DOM	C68	R. Samaná, Samaná
		GTM		R. Taysal, Sta Elena de la Cruz
	1	HND	DF	Estéreo Kabod, Siguatepeque
	5	HND	MQ	R. Manantial de Vida Eterna, Juticalpa
	1/0.5	MEX	YP	Imagen, Cd. Mante
	1	MEX	VO	La Furia, San Rafael
	1	MEX	VUC	La Norteñita, Allende
	1	MEX	EH	La Primera, San Luis Río Colorado
	1/0.25	MEX	ATL	R. Mexiquense, Atlacomulco
	2	MEX	ART	Señal 152, Jojutla
	25	PTR	WVOZ	Salud 1520 AM, San Juan
1530	0.5	DOM	C69	R. 15-30
	2.5	HND		R. La Guarachera, Choluteca
	10/0.1	MEX	SD	Arroba FM, Silao
	50/1	MEX	UR	Éxtasis Digital, México
	0.5	NCG	A4TS	LV de Sta Teresa, Sta Teresa
	10	PNR		R. Avivamiento, Panamá
	1/0.25	PTR	WUPR	Exitos 15-30, Utuado
1540	50	BAH		ZNS1, Nassau
	1	DOM	C71	LV de la Romana, La Romana
	2.5	HND	VK	R. Nuevo Mundo, Tegucigalpa
	1/0.25	MEX	NC	Fiesta Mexicana, Celaya
	5	MEX	HOS	La Invasora, Hermosillo
	5/0.5	MEX	STN	R. Red, Monterrey
	4	PNR		Festival AM Digital, Santiago
	1	PTR	WIBS	R. Voz/R. Caribe, Guayama
1550		CUB	BC	R. Progreso, La Palma, PR
	5	CUB	BA	R. Rebelde, Cárdenas, MA
	5	CUB	BA	R. Rebelde, Circunvalación, MA
		CUB	BA	R. Rebelde, Corralillo, VC
		CUB	BA	R. Rebelde, Guáimaro, CM
	1	CUB	BA	R. Rebelde, Guantánamo, GU
		CUB	BA	R. Rebelde, Hectómetro, MB
		CUB	BA	R. Rebelde, Jayama, CM
	1	CUB	BA	R. Rebelde, Sagua La Grande, VC
		CUB	BA	R. Rebelde, San Cristóbal, AR
	10	CUB	BA	R. Rebelde, Santa Clara, VC
		CUB	BA	R. Rebelde, Trinidad, SC
	5	CUB	BA	R. Rebelde, Tulipán, CI
	1	CUB	BA	R. Rebelde, Yaguajay, SS
	1	HND		R. Miel, Saba
	1	MEX	BG	Cadena 1550 AM, Tijuana
	5/0.25	MEX	NU	La Rancherita, Nuevo Laredo
	1	MEX	REL	R. Michoacán, Morelia
	10	MEX	RUV	R. Universidad Veracruzana, Xalapa
	0.25	PTR	WKFE	La Isla/R. Café Dinámica Yauco
	5	SLV		R. Sanidad Divina, San Salvador
1560	5	CTR	OAR	R. Nicoya, Nicoya
	1/0.5	DOM	C74	R. Pedernales, Pedernales

kHz	kW	Ctry	Call	Station, location
	1	DOM	C73	R. Única, Santiago
		GTM		R. Inspiración, Quetzaltenango
	50/10	MEX	INFO	15-60 AM, México
	5/1	MEX	LAC	R. Azul/LV del Balsas, Cd.Lázaro Cárdenas
	20/0.15	MEX	CHZ	R.Lagarto/LV Viva de Chiapas, Chiapa de Corzo
	1	MEX	JPV	R. Viva, Cd. Juárez
	1/0.25	MEX	MAS	WE, Salamanca
	10	PNR		R. Adventista, Panamá
	5/0.75	PTR	WRSJ	La Bachatera del Norte, Bayamón
1570	10	GTM	VE	VEA, Guatemala
	2.5	HND	RF	R. Cadena Nac. de Noticias, Tegucigalpa
	100	MEX	RF	La Poderosa, Cd.Acuña
	1/0.1	PTR	WPPC	R. Felicidad, Peñuelas
1580	0.25	CTR	RCLC	R. Cultural de La Cruz
	0.25	CTR	RCL	R. Cultural de Los Chiles
	0.25	CTR		R. Cultural de Pérez Zeledón
	0.5	CTR	RCS	R. Cultural de Puriscal
	0.25	CTR	RCVT	R. Cultural de Talamanca
	0.25	CTR		R. Cultural de Tilarán
	0.25	CTR	RCLS	R. Cultural Los Santos
	0.25	CTR	RSCM	R. Cultural Maleku
	10	DOM	C75	R. Amanecer, Sto Domingo
	1	DOM	C76	R. Neyba, Neyba
	1/0.5	MEX	AF	Éxtasis Digital, Celaya
	10	MEX	DM	Mix, Hermosillo
	1/0.25	MEX	LI	Super 94.7, Chilpancingo
	20	MEX	VAB	Super Stereo Miled, Valle del Bravo
	1	PNR		Hosanna Oeste, Panamá
	5/2.5	PTR	WEKO	R. Eko, Morovis
1590	1.5	CTR	LGJ	R. 16, Grecia
	1	DOM	C73	R. Libertad, Santiago
	1	GTM	XC	R. Triunfadora, Chimaltenango
	5	HND	BX	R. Perla, El Progreso
	1/0.25	MEX	BZ	Éxtasis Digital, Cd.Delicias
	1	MEX	HC	La Bestia Grupera, Ensenada
	20/10	MEX	VOZ	R. Mexicana, México
	1	PTR	WGYA	Guayama
1600	2.5	CTR	CC	R. Buenísima, Puerto Golfito
	0.25	CTR	RCBA	R. Cultural de Buenos Aires
	0.25	CTR		R. Cultural de Pital
	0.25	CTR	RCT	R. Cultural de Turrialba
	0.25	CTR	RCU	R. Cultural de Upala
	0.25	CTR	RSCN	R. Cultural Nicoyano, Nicoya
	1.5	CTR	MQ	R. Pococí, Guápiles
	0.5	CTR	RPQ	R. Quepos, Pto Quepos
	5	DOM	C78	R. Revelación en América, Sto Domingo
	1	HND	PC	R. Luz y Vida, San Luís
	5	MEX	GEM	R. Mexiquense, Metepec
	1	MEX	TPA	RTG R, Tlapa de Comonfort
	5	PTR	WCMA	Cima 103.7, Bayamón
		SLV	MV	R. Maya Visión, San Salvador
1610	50	AIA		Caribbean Beacon, The Valley
	5	MEX	UACH	R. Chapingo, Chapingo
1620		CUB	NL	R. Bayamo, Bayamo GR
		CUB	BA	R. Rebelde, El Sapo, CH
	5	CUB	BA	R. Rebelde, Guanabacoa, CH
	1	CUB	BA	R. Rebelde, Guantánamo, GU
		DOM	C79	R. Taina/Planeta, San Pedro de Macorís
	10/1	VIR	WDHP	WDHP, Christiansted, St Croix
1630	10/1	MEX	UT	UABC R, Mexicali
1640	1/0.5	DOM	C80	R. Juventus Don Bosco, Sto Domingo
1650	5	MEX	ARZ	ZER R. 16-50, México
1660	10/1	PTR	WGIT	Faro de Santidad, Canóvanas
1670	3	DOM	C81	LV del Yuna, Bonao
	1	MEX	ANAH	R. Anáhuac, Huixquilucan
1680	1	DOM	C82	R. Senda 1680 AM, San Pedro de Macorís
1690	0.9	VIR	WIGT	R. Charlotte Amalie, St Thomas
1700	10	MEX	PE	ESPN R., Tecate
	50/1	MEX	FCSM	XEFCSM

SOUTH AMERICA
(excluding Brazil)

NB: Brazil has been excluded to save space – see country entry for frequencies

Abbreviations: Dif=Difusora, Em=Emisora, LV=La Voz, Nal=Nacional, SF=Santafé.

kHz	kW	Ctry	Call	Station, location
530	25/5	ARG		R. Madre, Buenos Aires
	15	FLK		Falkland Islands R. Service, Stanley
540	10/5	ARG	LU17	R. Golfo Nuevo, Pto. Madryn
		ARG		R. Italia, Villa Martelli
	2.5/1	ARG	LRA14	R. Nal, Santa Fé
	10	ARG	LRA25	R. Nal,Tartagal
	25/5	ARG		Ushuaia
		BOL	LP77)	Radiodifusora Victoria, La Paz
	1	CHL	CB54	R. Ignacio Serrano, Melipilla
	10	CLM	KA	R. Auténtica Básica, Bogotá
	25	EQA	FA2	R. Santiago, Guayaquil
	10	PRU	OBX4E	R. Inca del Perú, Lima
	1	PRU	OCX2D	R. San Antonio, El Porvenir
	10	VEN		LV de Manapiare, San Juan de Manapiare
	50/25	VEN	OY	R. Perijá, La Villa del Rosario
550	5/0.5	ARG		AM 550 La Primera, Neuquen
	2	CHL	CC55	R. Corporación, Concepción
	1	CHL	CD55	R. Voz de la Tierra, Angol
	50	CLM	HF	R. Nac. de Colombia, Medellín
	30	CLM	R36	Vida, Mitú
	20/12	PRG	ZP16	R. Parque, Ciudad del Este
	1	PRU	OBU6W	R. Bacan Sat, Pocollay
	25	URG	CW1	R. Colonia, Colonia
	50	VEN	KE	R. Mundial, Caracas
560	25/5	ARG	LV1	R. Colón, San Juan
	10/3	ARG	LT15	R. del Litoral, Concordia
	25/1	ARG	LRA9	R. Nal, Esquel
	25/5	ARG	LRA13	R. Nal., Bahia Blanca
	25	ARG	LRA16	R. Nal., La Quiaca
	15	BOL	LP03)	R. El Mundo, La Paz
	25/10	CLM	PF	LV de la Pampa, Maicao
	10	CLM	GS	R. Nac. de Colombia, Tunja
	25	EQA	RN2	C. R. E. Satelital, Guayaquil
	10	GUY		Nat. Communications Netw., Georgetown
	1	PRU	OBU4M	R. La Luz, Sicaya
	5	PRU	OBZ4L	R. Oriente, Lima
	5	PRU	OBX1H	Radiomar, Chiclayo
	50	VEN	RH	RNV El Informativo, Pto.Ordaz
570	5	ARG		R. Argentina, Buenos Aires
	100	CLM	ND	R. Nac. de Colombia, Bogotá
	30	CLM	C61	Vida, Puerto Carreño
	10	EQA	CE1	R. El Sol, Quito
	1	PRG	ZP15	R. LV del Amambay, Pedro Juan Caballero
	12	PRG	ZP39	R. San Roque, Ayolas
	3	PRU	OAM2M	R. Antena 9, Huamachuco
	1	PRU	OAM5I	R. OAM5I, Salas
	3	PRU	OAU1M	R. Univ. Nal. Pedro Ruiz Gallo, Lambayeque
	100	VEN	LX	R. La Villa, Villa de Cura
580	3	ARG		R. Andina, San Rafael
	20	ARG	LU20	R. Chubut, Trelew
	25/5	ARG	LW1	R. Univ. Nal. de Córdoba, Córdoba
	10	BOL	LP01)	R. Panamericana, La Paz
	50/10	CLM	HP	R. Nac. de Colombia, Cali
	10	EQA	PC2	R. Uno, Guayaquil
	1	PRU	OCY2L	R. El Sol, La Esperanza
	10	PRU	OAX2E	R. Marañón, Jaén
	12	PRU	OAX4M	R. Maria, Lima
	1	PRU	OAM7N	R. Publica, Puno
	2	URG	CX58	R. Clarín, Montevideo
	50/10	VEN	MJ	LV de la Fe, Maracaibo
		VEN		RNV El Informativo, Barinas
590	19/2	ARG	LS4	R. Continental, Buenos Aires
	4/1	ARG	LV12	R. Independencia, San Miguel de Tucumán
	25/1	ARG	LRA30	R. Nal., San Carlos de Bariloche
	1	CHL	CC59	CARACOL 590, Concepción
	10	CHL	CD59	R. Pingüino, Punta Arenas
	50	CLM	CR	W Radio, Medellín
	10	EQA	SP1	Super K 800, Quito
	5	PRG	ZP32	R. Ycuámandyyú, San Pedro
	1	PRU	OCX6V	NSE R., Arequipa
	1	PRU	OAM5E	R. OAM5E, Chincha
	20	VEN	KL	R. Continente, Caracas
600	25/1	ARG	LU5	R. Neuquén, Neuquén
	10	BOL	CH01)	R. ACLO, Sucre
		BOL	SC55)	R. Familiar, Santa Cruz
	1	BOL	LP35)	Radioemisoras del Recobro, La Paz
	10	CHL	CB60	R. Vida Nueva, Santiago
	1	CLM	Z95	LV de los Awas, Ricaurte el Diviso
	50	CLM	HJ	R. Libertad, Barranquilla
	50	EQA	XY2	R. Ciudadana, Guayaquil
	10	PRU	OBZ4W	R. Cora, Lima
	1	PRU	OCU1K	R. Frias, Frias
	1	PRU	OBX2B	R. Ondas de Paz, Trujillo
	15	VEN	SW	R. Alto Llano, Sta Bárbara de Barinas
610	5	ARG		R. General San Martin, San Martin
	1	ARG	LRK201	R. Solidaridad, Añatuya
	30	CLM	KL	La Cariñosa, Bogotá
	50	CLM	D90	R. Nac. de Colombia, Riohacha
	10	EQA	MJ1	R. Caravana, Quito
	50	PRG	ZP30	LV del Chaco Paraguayo, Filadelfia
	1	PRU	OBU6V	R. OBU6V, Pocollay
	6	PRU	OCY2I	R. Santa Monica, Chota
	50	URG	CX4	R. Rural, Montevideo
	10	VEN	XY	R. Centro, Cantaura
	10	VEN	SE	R. Cristal, Barquisimeto
620	25	ARG	LRA26	R. Nal,. Resistencia
	25	ARG	LRA18	R. Nal., Río Turbio
	25/5	ARG	LT17	R. Provincia de Misiones, Posadas
	25/5	ARG	LV4	R. San Rafael, San Rafael
	10	BOL	LP02)	R. San Gabriel, El Alto
	10	CHL	CC62	R. Bío-Bío, Concepción
	1	CHL	CA62	R. Norte Verde, Ovalle
	50/20	CLM	EL	Colmundo, Cali
	10	CLM	VP	Colmundo, Cartagena
	10	EQA	HA2	Ondas Quevedeñas, Quevedo
	50	EQA	XY3	R. Ciudadana, Loja
	5	PRG	ZP40	R. Ñasaindý, San Estanislao
	0.4	PRU	OAX2M	R. Chepen, Chepen
	1	PRU	OCX6K	R. Maria, Uchumayo, Aqp
	10	PRU	OBU4B	R. Ovación, San Isidro
	50/25	VEN	ZC	R. Fe y Alegría,Guasdualito
	10	VEN	NO	R. Libertad, Cabimas
630	10/5	ARG	LU4	R. Patagonia Argentina,Comodoro Rivadavia
	25/5	ARG	LS5	R. Rivadavia, Buenos Aires
	25/5	ARG	LW8	R. San Salvador de Jujuy
	10	CHL	CB63	R. Stela Maris, Valparaíso
	10	CLM	E69	LV del Guainía, Puerto Inírida
	10	CLM	FD	R. Manizales, Manizales
	1	PRU	OBU7I	Chaski R., Urubamba
	18	PRU	OBX1U	R. Cutivalú, Castilla
	50/25	VEN	KA	RNV El Informativo, Caracas
640	10	ARG	LU18	R. El Valle, GeneralRoca
	25/5	ARG	LRA24	R. Nal., Río Grande
	10/5	ARG	LV15	R. Villa Mercedes
		BOL	TA12)	R. ALCO, Tarija
	1	CHL	CD64	R. Cooperativa AM, Temuco
	0.25	CHL	CC64	R. Portales, Curico

kHz	kW	Ctry	Call	Station, location
	10	CLM	BJ	RCN, Santa Marta
	50	EQA	XY1	R. Ciudadana, Quito
		EQA	X	R. Morena, Guayaquil
	15	PRG	ZP19	R. Caaguazú, Coronel Oviedo
	10	PRU	0AZ4K	R. Del Pacifico, Lima
	3	PRU	0AU1Y	R. La Luz, José Leonardo Ortiz
	10	PRU	0BX7B	R. Onda Azul, Puno
	30	VEN	QO	Deportes Unión R., Puerto La Cruz
	10/5	VEN	MU	R. Carora, Carora
650	3	ARG		Belgrano AM 650, Buenos Aires
	15	BOL	LP11)	R. Dif. Integración, El Alto
	50	CLM	KH	RCN Antena 2, Bogotá
	5	EQA	FD4	R. Visión, Manta
	50	PRG	ZP4	R. Uno, Asunción
	1.5	PRU	0BU2P	R. Bendición Cristiana, Huambos
		PRU	0AU9D	R. Kampagkis, Nieva
	1	PRU	0BM7C	R. 0BM7C, Sandia
	1	PRU	0CU5Q	R. 0CU5Q, Pueblo Nuevo
	1	PRU	0CU6L	R. 0CU6L, Alto de la Alianza
	1	PRU	0AX2N	R. Regional del Norte, Trujillo
	25	URG	CX6	Rad. Nacional del Uruguay, Montevideo
660	1	ARG		Amplitud 660, Ciudad Evita
	1/0.5	ARG	LT41	R. LV del Sur Entrerriano, Gualeguaychú
	1	BOL	SC10)	R. ABC, Santa Cruz
		BOL	LP150)	R. Taller de Historia Oral Andina, La Paz
	50	CHL	CB66	R. UC, Santiago
	25	CLM	QS	Colmundo, Cúcuta
	10	CLM	EZ	R. Auténtica, Cali
	5	PRG	ZP26	R. Itapirú, Cd. del Este
	10	PRG	ZP74	R. Regional, Concepción
	3	PRU	0CX1U	R. J.H.C., Chiclayo
	10	PRU	0CX4R	R. La Inolvidable, Lima
	3	PRU	0AZ7J	R. Santa Monica, Wanshaq
	10	VEN	NA	Ondas de los Medanos, Coro
	10	VEN	QZ	R. Anaco, Anaco
670	1	ARG	LT4	R. Dif. Misiones, Posadas
	25/5	ARG	LRI209	R. Mar del Plata, Mar del Plata
	10	ARG	LRA52	R. Nal., Chos Malal
	25/5	ARG	LRA11	R. Nal., Comodoro Rivadavia
	4	ARG		R. Republica, Ciudad Evita
		BOL	LP147)	R. Comunitaria Cadena Provincial, Jihuacuta
	10	CLM	R33	R. U.I.S, Bucaramanga
	50	CLM	PL	RCN Antena 2, Medellín
	12/5	EQA	FF1	R. Jesus del Gran Poder, Quito
	10	PRU	0AX7H	R. Nal.. del Perú, Puno
	100	VEN	LL	R. Rumbos, Caracas
680	5	ARG	LT3	R. Cerealista, Rosario
	2	ARG		R. Magna, Villa Martelli
	15	ARG	LV6	R. Nihuil, Mendoza
	1	ARG		R. Popular, Claypole
	25/5	ARG	LU12	R. Río Gallegos, Río Gallegos
		BOL	PO28)	R. ACLO, Potosi
	5	BOL	LP27)	R. Andina, La Paz
	10	BOL	LP155)	R. Jallalla Coca, Chulumani
	10	CHL	CC68	R. Cooperativa, Concepción
	50	CLM	ZO	R. Nac. de Colombia, Barranquilla
	25/12	EQA	VP2	R. Atalaya, Guayaquil
	50	PRG	ZP11	R. Caritas, Asunción
	5	PRU	0AX5E	Emisora del Pacifico, Ica
	0.5	PRU	0BX2L	R. Amauta, Chócope
	5	PRU	0AM4B	R. 0AM4B, Chaupimarca
	5	PRU	0CY2Y	R. San Luis, Jaén
	1	PRU	0BU7G	R. Vida, Cusco
	20	PRU	0BX4A	RBC Satelital, San Isidro
	1	URG	CW68	R. Young, Young
	10	VEN	QR	R. Continente, Cumaná
690	2	ARG		R. AM 690 - K-24, Buenos Aires
	10/3	ARG	LU19	R. LV de Comahue, Cipolletti
	25/5	ARG	LRA4	R. Nal. Salta
	10	CHL	CD69	R. Estrella del Mar, Ancud
	10	CHL	CB69	R. Santiago, Santiago
	1	CLM	Z73	Emisora Embera Chami y Zenu de la Palma
	35	CLM	CZ	W Radio, Bogotá
	50	EQA	JB1	LV de los Andes, Quito

kHz	kW	Ctry	Call	Station, location
	1	PRU	0AM7C	R. Altiva, Yanaoca
	25	URG	CX8	R. Sarandí, Montevideo
	50/20	VEN	MR	R. Barquisimeto, Barquisimeto
700	25/5	ARG	LV3	Cadena 3 - R. Córdoba
		BOL	LP116)	R. Pacha Kamasa, El Alto
	1	CHL	CD70	Nueva R. Valdivia, Valdivia
	5	CHL	CD70A	R. Magallanes, Punta Arenas
	30	CLM	CX	W Radio, Cali
	50	EQA	RS2	R. Sucre, Guayaquil
	1	GUY		Nat. Communications Netw., Linden
	12	PRG	ZP12	R. Carlos Antonio López, Pilar
	10	PRU	0AU9A	R. Canal Catolica San Gabriel, Moyobamba
	3	PRU	0BU4J	R. La Luz, El Tambo
	1	PRU	0BU7K	R. La Salle, Maras
	25	PRU	0BZ4H	R. R. Integridad, San Miguel
	1	PRU	0BU2T	R. Sausal Superior, Ascope
	10	VEN	MH	R. Popular, Maracaibo
	5/2	VEN	PQ	R. Sur, Puerto Ordaz
710	19/2	ARG	LRL202	R. Diez, Buenos Aires
	25/5	ARG	LRA19	R. Nal., Pto. Iguazú
	25/1	ARG	LRA17	R. Nal., Zapala
	10	BOL	PO40)	R. Pío XII, Siglo Veinte
	1	CLM	YD	R. La Paz, Paipa
	10	CLM	NX	R. Red RCN, Medellín
	8	EQA	ER5	Escuelas Radiofónicas Populares, Riobamba
	1	PRU	0AU6L	R. Amor, Socabaya, Aqp
	10	PRU	0CX7I	R. Nacional del Peru, Puerto Maldonado
	5	PRU	0BX5Q	R. Programas del Perú, Ica
	50/20	VEN	KY	R. Capital, Caracas
720	50/5	ARG	LV10	R. de Cuyo, Mendoza
	25/1	ARG	LRA59	R. Nac., Gobernador Gregores
	10	BOL	LP06)	R. La Cruz del Sur, La Paz
	1	CHL	CA72	R. Portales, Iquique
	30	CLM	AN	Emisoras Unidas, Barranquilla
	25	CLM	VO	Transmisora Quindío, Armenia
	10	EQA	GB4	LV de Portoviejo, Portoviejo
	5	EQA	IC1	R. Municipal, Quito
	10	EQA	UE3	R. Única, Machala
	50	PRG	ZP17	R. Pai Puku, Teniente Irala Fernández
	3	PRU	0BU7D	NSE Radio, Santiago
	0.5	PRU	0AU10	R. Frecuencia Oceánica, San José
	25	PRU	0AX2J	R. Nal.. del Perú, Trujillo
	2	PRU	0CU7J	R. Noticias, Puno
	10	PRU	0AU4E	R. Sideral, La Oroya
	10	VEN	XE	R. Elorza, Elorza
	50	VEN	QE	R. Venezuela Oriente, Porlamar
730	10/5	ARG		R. Concepto, Gregorio de Laferrere
	20/1	ARG	LU23	R. Lago Argentino, El Calafate
	25/5	ARG	LRA27	R. Nal., Catamarca
	20/5	ARG	LRA3	R. Nal., Santa Rosa
	2.5	BOL	LP05)	R. Yungas, Chulumani
	1	CHL	CD73	R. Angelina, Los Angeles
	10	CHL	CB73	R. Cooperativa AM, Valparaíso
	10	CLM	CU	Melodía Estéreo, Bogotá
	15	CLM	TJ	R. Uno, Montería
	50	PRG	ZP7	R. Cardinal, Lambaré
	1	PRU	0AM7X	R. Altura, Macusani
	10	PRU	0AX1D	R. del Pacifico, Piura
	2.5	PRU	0BU2Q	R. Maria, Cajamarca
	1	PRU	0CU6G	R. 0CU6G, Tacna
	50	PRU	0AX4G	R. Programas del Perú, San Isidro
	5/2.5	URG	CX10	R. Continente, Montevideo
	10	VEN	MT	R. Universo, Barquisimeto
740	10	ARG		AM 740 La Carretera, Allen
	10/1	ARG	LRI200	R. Municipal
	1	ARG	LRA55	R. Nal., Alto Río Senguer
	25/5	ARG	LRH251	R. Provincia de Chaco, Resistencia
		ARG		R. Rebelde, Buenos Aires
		BOL	LP151)	R. Pueblo de Dios, La Paz
	10	CLM	HB	Ecos de Pasto, Pasto
	50	CLM	NS	R. Guatapurí, Valledupar
	10	EQA	SE4	R. Libertad, Chone
	10	EQA	GC1	R. Melodía, Quito
	1/0.5	PRG	ZP38	R. Hechizo, Caazapá

kHz	kW	Ctry	Call	Station, location
	10	PRU	OAX6C	R. Continental, Paucarpat Aqp
	1	PRU	OCX2X	R. El Puerto, Pascamayo
	5	PRU	OBX2U	R. Ilucan, Cutervo
	1	PRU	OBU7C	R. La Rompa, Cusco
	1	PRU	OAM7R	R. OAM7R, Juliaca
	3	PRU	OCU4X	R. Vision, Huancayo
	5	URG	CW27	R. Tabaré, Salto
	50	VEN	NQ	R. Caroni, Puerto Ordaz
	10	VEN	NC	Unión R., Maracaibo
750	1/0.25	ARG	LRL203	R. AM 7-50, Lomas de Zamora
	100/10	ARG	LRA7	R. Nal., Córdoba
	50	CLM	DK	Caracol R, Medellín
	5	CLM	LH	LV de Yopal, Yopal
	30	EQA	RC2	R. Caravana, Guayaquil
	5	PRG	ZP42	R. LV de la Policía, Asunción
	10	PRU	OCX4X	R. Altura, Cerro de Pasco
	1	PRU	OBU6I	R. Bacan Sat 2, Pocollay
	1	PRU	OAM5D	R. OAM5D, Chincha
	5	PRU	OAU9G	R. OAU9G, Bellavista
	1	PRU	OCU7Q	R. OCU7Q, Yanaoca
	100	VEN	KS	RCR 750 Radio Caracas Radio, Caracas
760	25/5	ARG	LU6	Emisora Atlántica, Mar del Plata
	50	BOL	LP07)	R. Fides, La Paz
	50	CHL	CB76	R. Cooperativa, Santiago
	25	CLM	AJ	RCN La Radio, Barranquilla
	25	EQA	QR1	R. Quito, Quito
	25/10	PRG	ZP80	R. Encarnación, Encarnación
	0.5	PRU	OBX2K	R. Andino, Otuzco
	1	PRU	OAM7Q	R. Azángaro, Azángaro
	10	PRU	OCU4G	R. Mar Plus, Chorillos
	1	PRU	OBU5B	R. Municipal, Chincheros
	10	VEN	SO	R. Simpática 760, Trujillo
770	5/1	ARG		R. Cooperativa, Valentín Alsina
	5	BOL	CO02)	R. Cosmos, Cochabamba
	1	CHL	CD77	R. Cooperativa, Castro
	5	CHL	CD127	R. Agricultura, Temuco
	100	CLM	JX	RCN La Radio, Bogotá
	25/12	EQA	MF2	R. Revolución, Guayaquil
	2.5	PRU	OBX6H	R. La Inolvidable, Caiama, Aqp
	2.5	PRU	OAU7D	R. LV del Allinccapac, Macusani
	3	PRU	OCX1T	R. Vision, José Leonardo Ortiz
	1	PRU	OCU7K	R. R. LV Evangelica, Urcos
	100/25	URG	CX12	R. Oriental, Montevideo
	50/20	VEN	KK	RNV El Informativo, Valencia
780	25/5	ARG	LV8	R. Libertador, Mendoza
	25/5	ARG	LRA12	R. Nal., Santo Tomé
	7	ARG	LRA10	R. Nal., Ushuaía
	10/5	ARG	LRF210	R. Tres, Trelew
		BOL	SC44)	R. Sol, Santa Cruz
	10	CHL	CD78	R. Sago, Osorno
	10	CLM	C21	Antena del Río, Barrancabermeja
	10	CLM	ZG	LV del Valle, Cali
	30	CLM	ZW	R. Almirante, Riohacha
	5	CLM	FV	R. Viva, Pasto
	10/2	EQA	CM1	R. Colón R., Quito
	30	PRG	ZP70	R. Primero de Marzo, Asunción
	1	PRU	OBU2N	R. Coremarca, Bambamarca
	10	PRU	OAX1K	R. Nal. del Perú, Tumbes
	10	PRU	OAZ7S	R. Nuevo Tiempo, Juliaca
	2	PRU	OCU5L	R. OCU5L, Ayacucho
	3	PRU	OAX4X	R. Victoria,Lima
	50/20	VEN	OD	Ecos del Torbes, San Cristóbal
	15	VEN	MN	R. Coro, Coro
790	10	ARG	LV19	R. Malargüe
	25/5	ARG	LR6	R. Mitre, Buenos Aires
	25/5	ARG	LRA22	R. Nal, San Salvador de Jujuy
	1	CLM	NC	Ecos del Combeima, Ibagué
	15	CLM	DC	Múnera Eastman R, Medellín
		EQA		Su Radio 790 AM, Otavalo
	3	PRU	OAZ7H	R. La Luz, Cusco
	10	PRU	OAX2I	R. Programas del Perú, Trujillo
	2.5	PRU	OBU6D	R. Uno, Tacna
	50	VEN	XM	R. Minuto, Barquisimeto
	10	VEN	KC	R. Venezuela, Caracas
		VEN		RNV El Informativo, Cd. Bolívar

kHz	kW	Ctry	Call	Station, location
800	5	ARG	LT43	R. Mocoví, Charata
	1/0.25	ARG	LV23	R. Rio Atuel, General Alvear
	25/2	ARG	LU15	R. Viedma
	5	BOL	LP08)	R. Play, La Paz
	5/1	CHL	CB80	R. Maria, Viña del Mar
	1	CLM	JH	R. Ciudad Milagro, Armenia
	100	CLM	BW	RCN, Bucaramanga
	5	EQA	FB1	R. Sensación 800, Quito
	25	EQA	ML2	Super K 800, Guayaquil
	5	PRG	ZP23	La Union R800, Asunción
	5/3	PRG	ZP27	R. Mbaracayú, Salto del Guairá
	0.3	PRU	OBX6A	Contacto Sur, Cerro Colorado, Aqp
	0.5	PRU	OAU4H	R. La Luz, Huaral
	0.5	PRU	OBX5B	R. Sur, Ica
	1	PRU	OBU4D	R. Vida, Huancayo
	3	PRU	OCU2Y	R. Vision, Cajamarca
	1	PRU	OCX1P	Telecom del Norte, Piura
810	10/1	ARG		R. Mitre AM 810, Córdoba
		ARG		R. Federal, CF Buenos Aires
	60	CLM	CY	Caracol R, Bogotá
	5	EQA	VT2	R. Atalaya, Milagro
	1	PRU	OAU2G	R. Apocali, Trujillo
	3	PRU	OCU5Z	R. Asociación Cultural Tintaya, Cotabambas
	5	PRU	OAM7E	R. Jerusalen, Cusco
	1.5	PRU	OBU5E	R. OBU5E, Huamanga
	1	PRU	OCU2V	R. OCU2V, Jaen
	2	PRU	OCU6Q	R. OCU6Q, Moquegua
	10	PRU	OAX7T	R. Programas del Perú, Juliaca
	50/25	URG	CX14	R. El Espectador, Montevideo
820	2/0.5	ARG	LRI208	Estacion 820, Lomas de Zamora
	25/5	ARG	LRA8	R. Nal., Formosa
	5/1	ARG	LU24	R. Tres Arroyos
	10	BOL	LP10)	R. Altiplano Advenir, La Paz
	10/5	CHL	CB82	R. Carabineros, Santiago
	1	CHL	CD82	R. Concordia, La Unión
	10/1	CHL	CA82B	R. Portales Corporacion, La Serena
	1	CHL	CC82	R. UCSC, Concepción
	50	CLM	ED	Caracol R, Cali
	10	CLM	AD	R. Vigía, Cartagena
	5	EQA	VI5	R. LV de Ingapirca, Cañar
	25	EQA	UP1	R. Unión, Quito
	20	PRU	OAX4O	R. Libertad, Lima
	0.5	PRU	OBX2J	R. Nuevo Continente, Cajamarca
		PRU	OBU1X	R. Vision, Piura
	1/0.5	URG	CW23	R. Cultural, Salto
	50	VEN	SH	R. Guayana, Upata
830	5	ARG		R. Del Pueblo, Villa Forito
	1/0.5	ARG	LT21	R. Municipal, Alvear
	25/5	ARG	LV18	R. Municipal, San Rafael
	25	ARG	LU14	R. Provincia de Santa Cruz,Río Gallegos
	10/5	ARG	LT8	R. Rosario, Rosario
	15	CLM	DM	Q'hubo Radio, Medellín
	25	EQA	RM2	R. Huancavilca, Guayaquil
	10	PRU	OAU4C	R. Capital, El Tambo
	1	PRU	OCU2M	R. Ebenezer, Bambamarca
	5	PRU	OAM2A	R. Educacion, Trujillo
	1	PRU	OAZ7U	R. Inti Raimi, Santiago
	10	PRU	OAX6D	R. Nacional del Perú, Tacna
	1	PRU	OAM7W	R. OAM7W, Macusani
	25	VEN	LT	R. Sensación, Caracas
840	25/5	ARG	LU2	R. Bahía Blanca, Bahía Blanca
	5	ARG		R. General Belgrano, Buenos Aires
	10/5	ARG	LT12	R. General Madariaga, Paso de los Libres
	25/5	ARG	LV9	R. Salta AM 840, Salta
	3	BOL	LP75)	R. Atipiri, El Alto
	10	CHL	CB84	R. Portales, Valparaíso
	10	CHL	CD84	R. Santa María, Coyhaique
	30	CLM	KK	HJKK Sistema INRAI, Neiva
	10	CLM	BI	Ondas del Caribe, Santa Marta
	5	CLM	NA	R. Robledo, Cartago
	1	EQA	EM4	R. Costa Azul, Portoviejo
	50	EQA	PN1	R. Vigía, Quito
	5	PRG	ZP6	R. Guairá, Villarrica
	1	PRU	OBX6Y	R. Azul, Cayama Aqp

kHz	kW	Ctry	Call	Station, location
	1	PRU	OCU1C	R. Campesina de Ayabaca, Ayabaca
		PRU		R. Campesina, Huari
	1	PRU	OAU2E	R. Nuevo Continente, San Ignacio
	1	PRU	OCU5N	R. OCU5N, Abancay
	1	PRU	OCU7I	R. Santa Cruz, Kunturkanki
	1	PRU	OAU3Q	R. Vision, Casma
	10	VEN	MY	8-40 AM, Barquisimeto
	10/5	VEN	UZ	Guarapiche 8-40, Maturín
850	1	ARG		R. La Gauchita, Morón
	5	BOL	SC03)	R. María, Montero
	35	CLM	KC	Candela AM, Bogotá
	20/12	EQA	VS2	R. San Francisco, Guayaquil
	5	PRU	OAM7I	R. Lorena, San Sebastian
	1	PRU	OBU1M	R. Nal. del Peru, Ayabaca
	40	PRU	OAX4A	R. Nal. del Perú, Lima
		PRU	OAU6S	R. Nal. del Peru, Tarata
	1	PRU	OBU3B	R. OBU3B. Cerro Jactay
	1	PRU	OBX9W	R. OBX9W, Chachapoyas
		PRU	OBU7Z	R. Pachamama, Puno
	1	PRU	OCU1Y	R. OCU1Y, Chiclayo
	50	URG	CX16	R. Carve, Montevideo
	10	VEN	ZC	R. Fe y Alegría, Maracaibo
	10	VEN	RV	RV-850, Valencia
860	0.5	ARG		R. Digital, Lanus
	1	ARG	LRA56	R. Nal., Perito Moreno
		BOL	CO86)	R. FM Colores, Cochabamba
	10	BOL	LP12)	R. Nueva America, La Paz
	10	CHL	CC86	R. Inés de Suárez, Concepción
	10	CLM	DV	Voces de Occidente, Buga
	50	CLM	NJ	W Radio, Valledupar
	10	EQA	PC1	R. Positiva AM, Quito
	1	PRG	ZP28	LV de la Cordillera, Caacupé
		PRU	OCY2A	R. Norandina, Celendin
	3	PRU	OCX1M	R. Nuevo Norte, Sullana
		PRU	OBM7B	R. OBM7B, Sandia
	20/10	VEN	YE	Enlace 8-60, Valle de la Pascua
	10	VEN	OL	R. Mundial, San Cristóbal
870	100	ARG	LRA1	R. Nal., Buenos Aires
	10	CLM	LA	Bésame, Ibagué
	1	CLM	GD	Em. Reina de Colombia, Chiquinquirá
	5	CLM	ZH	Vida, Medellín
	20	EQA	NY2	R. Cristal, Guayaquil
	1	EQA	GS6	R. Píllaro, Píllaro
	2.5	PRU	OCX4D	R. Huancayo, El Tambo
	2.5	PRU	OCX6F	R. Impacto Universal, Uchumayo Aqp
	5	PRU	OAU7O	R. Libertad, Puno
	1	PRU	OCX7R	R. Mundo, Wanchaq
	10	PRU	OBX1F	R. Programas del Perú, Chiclayo
	10	VEN	MP	Unión R. Notícias, Barquisimeto
880		ARG		R. Democracia, Longchamps
	10	ARG	LU14	R. Provincia de Santa Cruz, Las Heras
	1/0.25	ARG		R. Provincial de Sierra Colorada, Sierra Colorada
		BOL	LP42)	R. Nueva Jacha, El Alto
		BOL	SC39)	Rdif. Oriente, Santa Cruz
	10	CHL	CB88	R. Colo Colo, Santiago
	20	CLM	GE	Caracol R, Bucaramanga
	10	CLM	FH	R. Regional Independiente, Anserma
	50/40	EQA	RP1	R. Católica Nacional, Quito
	5	PRU	OCU4S	R. Cumbre, Chaupimarca
	1	PRU	OBU5W	R. OBU5W,
	2	PRU	OAX2P	R. Sintonia, Trujillo
	50	PRU	OBZ4N	R. Union, Lima
	10	VEN		R. Paraguaná, Punto Fijo
	20/10	VEN	ZD	R. Venezuela Barinas, Barinas
	10	VEN	KV	RNV Musical, Caracas
890	25/5	ARG	LV11	Em. Santiago del Estero, Santiago del Estero
	25/1	ARG	LU33	Emisora Pampeana, Santa Rosa
	10	ARG		R. Libre, Villa Caraza
	1	CHL	CC89	R. Interamericana, Concepción
	20	CHL	CD89	R. Nacional., Punta Arenas
	10	CLM	CE	R. Continental, Bogotá
	0.25	CLM	HKO93	R. Ecos de Soledad, Soledad
	20	CLM	PM	R. Galeón, Santa Marta
	25/20	EQA	RS3	R. Superior, Machala
	5/0.5	PRG	ZP33	R. Tres de Febrero, Itá
	3	PRU	OBX7S	R. Bahá'í del Lago Titicaca, Chiucuito
	1	PRU	OCU5J	R. Cielo, San Pedro de Cachora
	1	PRU	OCU7C	R. Laramani, Espinar
	1	PRU	OCU5W	R. OCU5W, Ica
	1	PRU	OAU2N	R. Panorama, Cajamarca
	50/10	URG	CX18	R. Sport 890, Montevideo
	25	VEN	LW	Reloj R. América, Valencia
900	1	ARG		R. Municipal, 25 de Mayo
	25/5	ARG	LT7	R. Provincia de Corrientes, Corrientes
	5/0.1	BOL	LP36)	La Popular, La Paz
		BOL	PO39)	R. Dios es Amor Universal, Potosi
	0.25	BOL	TA01)	R. LV Nacional, Tarija
		BOL	CH31)	R. Tomina la Frontera, Villa Tomina
	1	CHL	CD90	R. LV de la Costa, Osorno
	1	CHL	CC90	R. Nuble, Chillán
	1	CHL	CB90	Viña del Mar
	10	CLM	EY	LV de Cali, Cali
	10	CLM	DD	RCN Fiesta, Cúcuta
	10	EQA	VA1	R. Sucre, Quito
	10	PRU	OBX4X	R. Felicidad, Lima
	3	PRU	OBX6K	R. Nevada, Uchumayo, Aqp
		PRU	OAX3E	R. Ribereña, Aucaycu
	1	PRU	OCU1P	R. Huarmaca, Huarmaca
	3	URG	CW17	R. Frontera, Artigas
	25	VEN	MD	R. Venezuela Mara Ritmo, Maracaibo
902	1	BOL	CO33)	R. Central Misionera, Cochabamba
910	150	ARG	LR5	R. La Red, Ituzaingó
	50/5	ARG	LRA23	R. Nal.,San Juan
	1	CHL	CC91	R. Tropical Latina, Talca
	15	CLM	S52	Colombia Estereo, Florencia
	10	CLM	DO	LV del Rio Grande, Medellín
	1	CLM	TT	Ondas del Porvenir, Samacá
	30	CLM	MY	RCN, San Andrés
	20	CLM	C84	Vida, Puerto Inírida
	2	EQA	BO2	Futbol FM, Guayaquil
	5	EQA	GE5	R. Mundial, Riobamba
	1	PRU	OAU5M	R. Estacion Wari, Ayacucho
	1	PRU	OAU7M	R. Regional - R. Quechua, Sicuani
	1	PRU	OAU7G	R. Vision del Altiplano, Juliaca
	50/20	VEN	RQ	RQ 910 AM Center, Caracas
920		BOL	LP88)	R. Bartolina Sisa, El Alto
		BOL	CO85)	R. Dios es Amor Universal, Cochabamba
		BOL	SC46)	R. El Mana, Santa Cruz
	3	BOL	CH11)	R. Encuentro, Sucre
	1	BOL	LP65)	R. San Andres de Topohoco, Topohoco
	1	CHL	CD92	R. 920, Temuco
	10	CLM	SJ	Colmundo, Ibagué
	10	CLM	AA	Em. Fuentes, Cartagena
	10	CLM	JN	Ondas del Mayo, Pasto
	10	EQA	RU3	CRO - Compañía Radiofónica Orense, Machala
	1	EQA	AB1	R. Democracia, Quito
	100	PRG	ZP1	R. Nal. del Paraguay, Asunción
	1	PRU	OAM7H	CVC La Voz, Cusco
		PRU		R. Campesina, Juli
	1	PRU	OAX9V	R. Marginal, Tocache
	1	PRU	OCU7W	R. OCU7W, Tambopata
	1	PRU	OBX2S	R. Ollantay, Virú
	10	PRU	OBX1J	R. Programas del Peru, Piura
	1	PRU	OCX5C	R. Stelar, Chinca Alta
	2.5	PRU	OBU6M	R. Uno, Tacna
	3	PRU	OAM2G	R. Vision, Samangay
	20	VEN	QX	R. Nueva Esparta, Porlamar
	10/5	VEN	QU	R. San Carlos, San Carlos
930	1/1	ARG		R. Excelsior, Monte Grande
	5	ARG		R. Nativa, Ciudad Evita
	25/5	ARG	LV7	R. Tucumán, San Miguel de Tucumán
	5/1	ARG	LV28	R. Villa María, Villa María
	10	CHL	CB93	R. Nuevo Mundo, Santiago
	10	CHL	CD93	R. Reloncaví, Puerto Montt
	10	CLM	CS	LV de Bogotá, Bogotá
	5	EQA	BA6	R. Ambato, Ambato
	3	PRU	OBU7T	R. Cadena Colca, Juliaca

kHz	kW	Ctry	Call	Station, location
	1	PRU	OAM7J	R. Cadena Sur, Espinar
	1	PRU	OCX2V	R. Inti, Chepén
	5	PRU	OAX4E	R. Moderna, Lima
	3	PRU	OCU1O	R. Nor Andina, Olmos
	1	PRU	OBU5S	R. OBU5S, Pucar del Sara Sara
	5	PRU	OBX9V	R. OBX9V, Huambo
	5	PRU	OBX6T	R. Yaravi, Cerro Colorado, Aqp.
	50	URG	CX20	R. Monte Carlo, Montevideo
	10	VEN	LJ	R. Maracay, Maracay
940	3/5	ARG	LRH200	R. Chajarí, Chajarí
	20/5	ARG	LRJ241	R. Dimensión, San Luís
	1	BOL	CH13)	R. Chuquisaca XXI, Sucre
		BOL	LP13)	R. Metropolitana, La Paz
		BOL	SC53)	R. Pan de de Vida, Santa Cruz
	1	CHL	CB94	R. Valentín Letelier, Valparaíso
	5	CLM	A76	Frecuencia U, Medellín
	10	CLM	GB	R. Calima, Cali
	25	CLM	TL	RCN, Cúcuta
		EQA		R. Austral del Ecuador, Cuenca
	5	EQA	BZ1	Rdif Casa de la Cultura Ecuatoriana, Quito
	1.5	PRU	OBX7P	R. Las Vegas - W Radio, Wanchaq
	1	PRU	OBU4E	R. Luz, Jauja
	1	PRU	OBU6G	R. OBU6G, Cotahuasi
	1	PRU	OBU1Y	R. Studio Satelite, Tambo Grande
	10	VEN	LU	R. Fe y Alegría, El Tigre
	10	VEN	NN	R. Punto Fijo, Punto Fijo
950	25/5	ARG	LR3	R. Belgrano, Buenos Aires
	25/5	ARG	LT16	R. Sáenz Peña , Roque Saénz Peña
	5	CLM	UJ	Armonias Boyacenses, Tunja
	15	CLM	FN	Caracol R, Pereira
	10	EQA	DE2	GRD R. Internacional, Guayaquil
	3	EQA	UE5	LV de AIIECH, Colta
		EQA		R. Chaskis del Norte, Ibarra
	1.5	PRU	OAM2H	Onda Popular, Bambamarca
		PRU		R. Campesina, Tarata
	1	PRU	OAM7S	R. OAM7S, Juliaca
	1	PRU	OBU5N	R. OBU5N, Paucar del Sara Sara
	1	PRU	OBU5R	R. OBU5R, Cotabambas
	1	PRU	OBX3S	R. Programas del Perú, Chimbote
960	25/5	ARG	LRA6	R. Nal., Mendoza
	10/1	ARG	LU13	R. Necochea, Necochea
	1	BOL	LP43)	R. Huayna Potosí, Milluni
	1	BOL	PO02)	R. Kollasuyo, Potosí
	10	BOL	SC04)	R. Santa Cruz, Santa Cruz
	10	CHL	CB96	R. Carrera, Santiago
	10	CHL	CD96	R. Polar, Punta Arenas
	5	CLM	HX	Bluradio, Bucaramanga
	15	CLM	R31	Candela, San Andrés
	10	CLM	HN	Caracol R, Magangué
	1	EQA	JX6	R. LV del Santuario, Baños
	1	EQA	SA5	R. Sonoonda Internacional, Cuenca
	1	PRU	OBU7P	R. Concierto Santa Monica, Espinar
	18	PRU	OBX6S	R. El Pueblo 960, Mariano Melgar, Aqp
	1	PRU	OCY4V	R. Manantial, Chilca
	10	PRU	OAX4D	R. Panamericana, Lima
	3	PRU	OBX1Y	R. WSP, Chiclayo
	2/1	URG	CW96	R. Yi, Durazno
	50/20	VEN	RB	R. Monagas, Maturín
	10	VEN	SS	R. San Sebastián, San Cristóbal
970	25/5	ARG	LV2	R. Cooperativa, Córdoba
	3	ARG		R. Génesis, Valentin Alsina
	1/0.25	ARG	LT25	R. Guaraní, Curuzú Cuatiá
	25	ARG	LRA43	R. Nal., Neuquén
	1	CHL	CD97	R. Austral, Valdivia
	1	CHL	CC97	R. Lautaro, Talca
	1	CHL	CD97A	R. Patagonia Chilena, Coyhaique
	15	CLM	VK	Armonias del Caquetá, Florencia
	1	CLM	HKX59	Ecos del Cacique, Calarca
	10	CLM	CI	R. Red RCN, Bogotá
	10	CLM	ME	RCN Guajira, Maicao
	1	EQA	MB1	R. Imperio, Ibarra
	80	PRG	ZP9	R. 9-70 , Asunción
	1	PRU	OBX5A	R. Comericial Sonora, Ica
	1.5	PRU	OBX1V	R. La Capullana, Sullana
	1	PRU	OAU2K	R. Lider del Norte, Cajamarca
	5	PRU	OAU7A	R. Tropicana, Wanchaq
	1	PRU	OBU7B	R. Union Qollasuyo, Juliaca
	20/3	URG	CX22	R. Universal, Montevideo
	10	VEN	LR	R. Continente 970, Maracay
	15	VEN	SD	R. Turismo, Valera
980	3/1	ARG	LU37	R. General Pico
	1	ARG	LRG387	R. Luján, Valcheta
	5	ARG	LT39	R. Victoria, Victoria
	25/5	ARG		Rio Gallegos
	5/1	ARG		San Salvador de Jujuy
	3	BOL	CO04)	R. Esperanza, Aiquile
		BOL	CH26)	R. La Bohemia, Sucre
	2.5	BOL	LP14)	R. Mar, La Paz
		BOL	OR41)	R. dif. Concordia, Oruro
	1	CHL	CA98	La Serena
	5	CHL	CB98	Valparaíso
	15	CLM	JV	Oxígeno, Cúcuta
	100	CLM	ES	RCN, Cali
	5	EQA	CL3	R. Cariamanga, Cariamanga
	1	EQA	JI5	R. El Prado, Riobamba
	5	PRG	ZP31	R. Mburucuyá, Pedro Juan Caballero
	1	PRU	OCX2R	Andina R., Chota
	1	PRU	OBU1N	R. Campesina, Huancabamba
		PRU		R. Comercial Cosmos, La Peca
	1	PRU	OBU5K	R. LV de Huamanga, Huamanga
	1	PRU	OBU4H	R. OBU4H, Huancayo
	1	PRU	OAU1N	R. Primavera, Lambayeque
	1	PRU	OCU7X	R. R. Caden Sur, Sicuani
	1.5	PRU	OAU6F	R. Universidad, Arequipa
	10	VEN	QM	Unión R. Notícias, El Tigre
990	25/5	ARG	LRH203	AM 990, Formosa
	1	ARG	LRJ201	R. Calingasta, Tamberías
	25/5	ARG	LR4	R. Splendid AM 990, Villa Domínico
		BOL	PO30)	R. Municipal de Colcha
	5	CLM	HI	LV de Garagoa, Garagoa
	50	CLM	CH	RCN, Medellín
	25	EQA	GH1	R. Tarquí, Quito
	3	PRU	OCU1H	R. Bendicion Cristiana, Piura
	10	PRU	OAX6K	R. Continental, Tacna
	0.5	PRU	OBX2M	R. Contumaza, Contumaza
	12	PRU	OBX4J	R. Latina, Miraflores
	2.5	PRU	OCU7T	R. OCU7T, Juliaca
		PRU	OCU4A	R. Oro, Huayllay
		PRU	OBX3L	R. Peruana, Chimbote
	20	VEN	RT	R. Tropical, Caracas
1000	5/1	ARG		Comodoro Rivadavia
	10/1	ARG		La Rioja
	5	ARG	LT42	R. Del Iberá, Mercedes
	3	ARG	LU16	R. Río Negro, Villa Regina
	1	ARG		R. Sintonia, José C.Paz
		BOL	CO84)	FM Unica, Cochabamba
	10	BOL	OR03)	R. Bahá'í de Bolivia, Oruro
		BOL	LP115)	R. LV del Arrebatamiento, Guaqui
	1	BOL	LP44)	R. Taypi, La Paz
	1	BOL	SC33)	Rdif. del Oriente, Santa Cruz
	10	CHL	CB100	BBN R., Santiago
	10	CLM	JG	R. Nac. de Colombia, Manizales
	15	CLM	AQ	RCN, Cartagena
	20	CLM	Q98	Vida, San José del Guaviare
	5/0.5	PRG	ZP36	R. Mil, San Antonio
	2.5	PRU	OBX6R	R. Edesa, Cerro Colorado, Aqp
	1	PRU	OBX3V	R. Huanuco
	1	PRU	OBX5W	R. Lircay, Lircay
	1	PRU	OBU4Z	R. OBU4Z, Pariahuanaca
	7	PRU	OCU1N	R. OCU1N, San José
	2	PRU	OAZ7P	R. Prensa al Dia, Cusco
	10	VEN	OA	Deportes Unión R, San Cristóbal
	10	VEN	NM	R. Caribeña Mil AM, Morón
1010	1/0.25	ARG	LW2	R. Emis. Tartagal
	4	ARG		R. Onda Latina, Buenos Aires
	20/10	ARG	LV16	R. Rio Cuarto, Rio Cuarto
	10	CHL	CD101	Temuco
	10	CLM	CC	Acuario Estéreo, Bogotá
	15	CLM	JR	Caracol R, Neiva
	10/5	CLM	BN	LV del Galeras, Pasto

kHz	kW	Ctry	Call	Station, location
	15	CLM	ZD	R. Panzenú, Montería
	10	CLM	IX	R. Yarima, Barrancabermeja
	10	CLM	OP	W Radio, Barranquilla
	3	EQA	RZ2	R. Sport, Guayaquil
	2.5	EQA	RV5	R. Visión AM, Cuenca
	15	EQA	NR6	TSB R. Líder, Ambato
	1	PRU	OBU1L	LV de las Huarinjas, Huancabamba
	10	PRU	OAX4U	R. Cielo, Lima
	1	PRU	OBX9T	R. Fé, Bagua Grande
	1	PRU	OCU7P	R. Nac. del Peru, Juli
	1	PRU	OBU5T	R. OBU5T, Cotabambas
	1.5	PRU	OBX2P	R. San Francisco, Cajamarca
	1	PRU	OBZ1C	R. Sonora, Tumbes
	1	PRU	OBU6L	R. Orcopampa, Orcopampa
	25	URG	CX24	R. 1010AM, Montevideo
	10	VEN	PC	R. Aragua, Cagua
	10	VEN	QF	R. Venezuela Bolívar, Cd. Bolívar
1020	25/5	ARG	LRJ214	AM 1020, San Juan
	1	ARG	LRA58	R. Nal., Río Mayo
	10/5	ARG	LT10	R. Univ. Nal. del Litoral, Santa Fé
		BOL	LP89)	R. Illimani - R. Patria Nueva, Achacachi
		BOL	LP133)	R. Illimani - R. Patria Nueva, Asunta
		BOL	CH35)	R. Illimani - R. Patria Nueva, Azurduy
		BOL	TA14)	R. Illimani - R. Patria Nueva, Bermejo
		BOL	SC42)	R. Illimani - R. Patria Nueva, Camiri
		BOL	LP90)	R. Illimani - R. Patria Nueva, Carabuco
		BOL	OR36)	R. Illimani - R. Patria Nueva, Caracolla
		BOL	LP92)	R. Illimani - R. Patria Nueva, Caranavi
		BOL	PO08)	R. Illimani - R. Patria Nueva, Catavi
		BOL	CO61)	R. Illimani - R. Patria Nueva, Chapare
		BOL	LP93)	R. Illimani - R. Patria Nueva, Chulumani
		BOL	PA10)	R. Illimani - R. Patria Nueva, Cobija
		BOL	CO57)	R. Illimani - R. Patria Nueva, Cochabamba
		BOL	CO70)	R. Illimani - R. Patria Nueva, Colomi
		BOL	LP91)	R. Illimani - R. Patria Nueva, Copacabana
		BOL	LP140)	R. Illimani - R. Patria Nueva, Corocoro
		BOL	LP136)	R. Illimani - R. Patria Nueva, Desaguadero
		BOL	TA19)	R. Illimani - R. Patria Nueva, Entre Rios
		BOL	LP135)	R. Illimani - R. Patria Nueva, Escoma
		BOL	LP94)	R. Illimani - R. Patria Nueva, Guaqui
		BOL	OR37)	R. Illimani - R. Patria Nueva, Huanuni
		BOL	LP124)	R. Illimani - R. Patria Nueva, Huarina
		BOL	CO68)	R. Illimani - R. Patria Nueva, Independencia
		BOL	CO62)	R. Illimani - R. Patria Nueva, Kami
	10	BOL	LP15)	R. Illimani - R. Patria Nueva, La Paz
		BOL	PO34)	R. Illimani - R. Patria Nueva, Llica
		BOL	CH36)	R. Illimani - R. Patria Nueva, Machareti
		BOL	OR29)	R. Illimani - R. Patria Nueva, Oruro
		BOL	PO07)	R. Illimani - R. Patria Nueva, Potosi
		BOL	LP132)	R. Illimani - R. Patria Nueva, Qhurpa
		BOL	BE24)	R. Illimani - R. Patria Nueva, Riberalta
		BOL	BE22)	R. Illimani - R. Patria Nueva, San Borja
		BOL	SC40)	R. Illimani - R. Patria Nueva, Santa Cruz
		BOL	CH32)	R. Illimani - R. Patria Nueva, Sopachuy
		BOL	CH21)	R. Illimani - R. Patria Nueva, Sucre
		BOL	LP129)	R. Illimani - R. Patria Nueva, Tapichulla
		BOL	LP128)	R. Illimani - R. Patria Nueva, Taraco
		BOL	TA13)	R. Illimani - R. Patria Nueva, Tarija
		BOL	LP130)	R. Illimani - R. Patria Nueva, Tiawanaku
		BOL	LP126)	R. Illimani - R. Patria Nueva, Topohoco
		BOL	BE21)	R. Illimani - R. Patria Nueva, Trinidad
		BOL	PO35)	R. Illimani - R. Patria Nueva, Tupiza
		BOL	PO32)	R. Illimani - R. Patria Nueva, Unica
		BOL	PO35)	R. Illimani - R. Patria Nueva, Uyuni
		BOL	CO59)	R. Illimani - R. Patria Nueva, Valle Alto
		BOL	SC41)	R. Illimani - R. Patria Nueva, Vallegrande
		BOL	LP127)	R. Illimani - R. Patria Nueva, Vilaque
		BOL	TA16)	R. Illimani - R. Patria Nueva, Villamontes
		BOL	PO33)	R. Illimani - R. Patria Nueva, Villazon
		BOL	TA18)	R. Illimani - R. Patria Nueva, Yacuiba
		BOL	SC43)	R. Illimani - R. Patria Nueva, Yapacani
		BOL	CO60)	R. Illimani - R. Patria Nueva. Tarata
	5	CHL	CC102	Talca
	10	CLM	DQ	Emisora Claridad, Medellín

kHz	kW	Ctry	Call	Station, location
	10	CLM	FT	La FM, Ibagué
	10	CLM	KS	LV del Llano, Villavicencio
	15	CLM	DZ	R. Primavera, Bucaramanga
	10	CLM	FQ	RCN, Pereira
	5/3	EQA	CR6	R. Surcos, Guaranda
	5	EQA	HR1	RTU Radio, Quito
	25	PRG	ZP14	R. Ñandutí, Asunción
	0.5	PRU	OBU5M	R. AM Vida, Huamanga
	2	PRU	OAU2P	R. Bambamarca, Bambamarca
	1	PRU	OBU4F	R. Cristo Vive, Huancayo
	1	PRU	OBU7O	R. Informes, Sicuani
	1	PRU	OAU6J	R. Internacional, Tacna
	1	PRU	OBU1D	R. La Luz, Piura
	1	PRU	OCU1M	R. OCU1M, José Leonardo Ortiz
	5	PRU	OAM7Y	R. Kinsachata Tintaya, Espinar
	0.1	URG	CW102	R. Libertadores, Salto
	25	VEN	TW	R. Alegría, Chivacoa
	50/10	VEN	MX	R. Calendario Zulia, Maracaibo
	10	VEN	RS	R. Mundial Margarita, La Asunción
1030	25/5	ARG	LS10	R. del Plata, Buenos Aires
		BOL	CO51)	R. 24 de Junio Totora
	3	BOL	BE20)	R. Comunitaria Riberalte , Riberalta
	3	BOL	OR26)	R. de los Pueblos Originarios , Orinaca
	3	BOL	CO48)	R. Independencia , Independencia
		BOL	CH19)	R. Mojocoya AM , Mojocoya
	10	CHL	CC103	R. Chilena, Concepción
	1	CHL	CD103	R. Chiloé, Castro
	1	CHL	CD103A	R. Payne AM, Puerto Natales
	1	CHL	CB103	R. Progreso, Talagante
	1	CLM	GX	CARACOL, Lorica
	10	CLM	DJ	La Cariñosa/Antena 2, Duitama
	15	CLM	RF	Ondas del Cesar, Aguachica
	5	CLM		Ondas del Vaupés, Mitú
	30	CLM	DT	RCN Antena 2, Cali
	5	EQA	RF2	R. Ecuantena, Guayaquil
	5	PRU	OAM2E	R. Cajamarca Viva, Cajamarca
	1	PRU	OCX6L	R. Cumbia, Arequipa
	1	PRU	OCX7O	R. HG-AM, Cusco
	5	PRU	OAU2U	R. Los Andes, Huamachuco
	1	PRU	OAX7N	R. LV del Altiplano, Puno
	1	PRU	OBX9Z	R. OBX9Z, San Ramon
	20	VEN	QY	R. Onda 1030, Guanare
	25/10	VEN	TD	R. Valles del Tuy, Ocumare del Tuy
1040		ARG		R. Revolution, Luján
		BOL	CH18	R. 12 de Marzo , Tarabuco
	0.25	BOL	OR14)	R. Atlántida, Oruro
	1	BOL	LP45)	R. Bolivianíssima, La Paz
		BOL	TA11)	R. Comunitaria Libertad , Villamontes
		BOL	SC37)	R. Nanduti , Camiri
		BOL	OR42)	R. Qaqachaca , Qaqachaca
		BOL	SC30)	R. San José , San José de Chiquitos
		BOL	SC38)	R. San Julián , San Julián
	0.25	BOL	CO20)	R. Sipe Sipe, Quillacollo
	15	CLM	CJ	Colmundo, Bogotá
	15	CLM	UB	Colmundo, Pasto
	15	CLM	FM	LV de Armenia, Armenia
	15	CLM	BF	LV del Norte, Cúcuta
	10	CLM	SY	R. 1040/La Caucana 10-40, Popayán
	15	CLM	AI	R. Tropical, Barranquilla
	3	EQA	CW1	LV del Valle, Machachi
	3	EQA	GB6	R. Colosal, Ambato
	10/3	EQA	EV5	R. Splendid, Cuenca
	5	PRG	ZP43	R. Arapysandú, San Ignacio
	1	PRU	OBX5U	R. La Luz, Ica
	1	PRU	OAU7H	R. Los Andes, Espinar
	10	PRU	OBX4O	R. Metropolitana, Miraflores
	1	PRU	OAU3P	R. Nueva Vida, Chimbote
	1	PRU	OAM2L	R. OAM2L, Pomahuaca
	1	PRU	OAZ1D	R. Vecinal, Piura
	20	VEN	LB	LV de Carabobo, Valencia
	20/10	VEN	ON	R. Mundial Los Andes, Mérida
1050	1.3	ARG		R. General Güemes, Villa Lynch
	10	ARG	LV27	R. San Francisco, San Francisco
		BOL	PO26)	R. Caiza D , Caiza D
		BOL	PO27)	R. Colquechaca, Colquechaca

kHz	kW	Ctry	Call	Station, location
		BOL	CH33)	R. Comunitaria, Villa Huaca
	3	BOL	OR27)	R. Sabaya Sabaya
	1	CHL	CD105	Osorno
	10	CLM	BB	Caracol R, Valledupar
	15	CLM	S62	Cusiana R., Yopal
	10	CLM	FZ	La Cariñosa del Centro, Antena 2, Espinal
	5	CLM	IO	LV de la Conquista, Granada
	10	CLM	E73	LV del Cinaruco/Caracol, Arauca
	10	CLM	GU	R. Bucarica, Bucaramanga
	5	CLM	NG	R. Palmira, Palmira
	10	CLM	DR	R. Unica, Medellín
	10	CLM	AW	RCN La Radio, Montería
	5/3	EQA	IM1	LV de Imbabura, Ibarra
	5	EQA	RQ2	R. Águila, Guayaqui
	1	PRU	OBZ4J	Bethel R., Huancayo
	3	PRU	OBX6B	Bethel Radio, Uchumayo, Aqp
	3	PRU	OCU1E	R. Bendición Cristiana, Chiclayo
	1	PRU	OCU2N	R. Campesina, Cajamarca
	1	PRU	OAZ7Q	R. Noticias, Juliaca
	1	PRU	OAZ1C	R. Superior, Chulucanas
	25	URG	CX26	Rad. Nacional del Uruguay, Montevideo
	20	VEN	PO	RNV El Informativo, Cabudare
1060		ARG		R. Las Naciones, Monte Grande
	1	BOL	CH02)	R. Dif. Colosal, Sucre
	1.5	BOL	OR01)	R. Noticias, Oruro
	10	BOL	LP38)	R. Presencia de Dios, La Paz
		BOL	LP95)	R. Qhana Amazonía, Caranavi
	100	CHL	CB106	R. Maria, Santiago
	1	CLM	YX	R. Caracolí, Sincelejo
	10	CLM	LY	R. Delfín, Riohacha
	10	CLM	MV	R. Furatena, Chiquinquirá
	1	CLM	MG	R. Litoral, Turbo
	15	CLM	OV	R. Surcolombiana, Neiva
	15	CLM	FJ	RCN Caldas, Manizales
	5	EQA	MG6	R. Ecos del Pueblo, Saquisilí
		EQA		R. Fiesta, Machala
		EQA		R. Richi, El Empalme
	1	PRU	OAU5P	Estacion Wari, Huamanga
	1	PRU	OAU7U	R. Estudio 1060, Cusco
	1	PRU	OCY4D	R. Exito, Lima
	1	PRU	OBU6O	R. Municipilidad, Omate
	3	PRU	OAU3S	R. R. Cielo, Chimbote
	2	PRU	OBU5Q	R. Restauracion, Andahuaylas
		PRU	OBU1F	R. Studio 1060. Piura
	5	PRU	OCY2O	R. Sudamerica, Cutervo
	1	PRU	OCU7V	Tambopata
	10	VEN	LN	R. Guárico, San Juan de los Morros
	10	VEN	OE	Unión R. Noticias, San Cristóbal
1070	25/5	ARG	LR1	R. El Mundo, Buenos Aires
	20	CLM	AH	Em. Atlántico, Barranquilla
	15	CLM	VR	Nueva R. Super, Popayán
	30	CLM	CG	Q'hubo R. /R. Santa Fe, Bogotá
	5	EQA	CJ5	LV del Tomebamba, Cuenca
	1	EQA	VP1	R. Libertad, Quito
	3	PRG	ZP51	AM 1070 R., Puerto Triunfo
	3	PRU	OBX9J	R. Andes, Tarapoto
	1	PRU	OAU3N	R. OAU3N, Huánuco
	0.2	PRU	OAX5A	R. San Juan, San Juan de Marcona
	1	PRU	OAU6K	R. Trinidad, Paucarpata, Aqp.
	1	PRU	OAU1J	R. Vida, José Leonardo Ortiz
	1	PRU	OBX4G	R. Visión, San Ramón
	25	VEN		Contacto 1070, Ospino
	10	VEN	MA	R. Mundial Zulia, Maracaibo
	10	VEN		Superior 1070 Biruaca, S. Fernando de Apure
1080	25/5	ARG	LU3	Ondas del Sur, Bahía Blanca
	10/1	ARG		Paso de los Libres
		ARG		R. Claridad, Monte Grande
	0.25	ARG	LW4	R. Orán/R. Maria
		BOL	LP76)	LV de la Mayoria , Caranavi
		BOL	CO83)	R. Cultura, Cochabamba
		BOL	CH34)	R. Comunitaria, Juana Azurduy
		BOL	CH30)	R. Comunitario, Sopachuy
		BOL	CH40)	R. Comunitario, Carama

kHz	kW	Ctry	Call	Station, location
	1	CHL	CD108	R. Los Confines, Angol
	1	CHL	CA108	Vicuña
	10	CLM	AX	LV de la Nostalgia, Medellín
	10	CLM	AW	LV de Montería, Montería
	10	CLM	KT	R. Autentica, Villavicencio
	10	CLM	JF	R. Eco, Cali
	10	CLM	MH	R. Melodía, Bucaramanga
	15	CLM	JS	R. Uno, La Dorada
	1	EQA	AB4	R. Contacto, Manta
	10	EQA	BH6	R. Latacunga AM, Latacunga
	10	EQA	KD2	Sistema 2, Guayaquil
	10	PRG	ZP25	R. Monumental, Luque
	10	PRU	OAU4I	R. La Luz, Lima
	1.5	PRU	OBX1D	R. La Luz, Piura
	1	PRU	OBU6H	R. LV del Sur, Moquegua
	5	PRU	OCU4O	R. Mineria, Chaupimarca
	1	PRU	OCU7O	R. Nacional, Ayaviri
	1	PRU	OAU2L	R. Nueva Vida, Cajamarca
	1	PRU	OBU4W	R. OBU4W, Huancayo
	2.2	PRU	OAX7S	R. Salkantay, Cusco
	10	VEN	QJ	R. Barcelona, Barcelona
	10	VEN	NR	R. Venezuela, Maracay
1090	1	ARG		Libertad AM 1100, Rosario
	3	ARG		R. Décadas, José León Suárez
	2	ARG		R. Popular, Valentín Alsina
		BOL	LP110)	R. Comunitaria Pachakuti
		BOL	CO63)	R. Cultura , Cliza
	5	CHL	CD109	Castro
	5/1	CHL	CC109	R. Chilena del Maule, Talca
	5	CLM	OM	Bluradio, Cartagena
	15	CLM	BC	Caracol R, Cúcuta
	8	CLM	IH	Caracol R, Sogamoso
	10	CLM	JB	HJKK Sistema INRAI, El Guamo
	10	CLM	IG	R. Autentica, Florencia
	10	CLM	IA	W Radio, Manizales
	5	EQA	VI1	R. Irfeyal, Quito
	1	PRU	OBX6X	R. Amistad, Arequipa
	1	PRU	OAU5F	R. Inti Andina, Aucara
	15	URG	CX28	R. Imparcial, Montevideo
	20	VEN	SZ	Deportes Unión R., Caracas
	10	VEN	PB	R. Yaracuy, S. Felipe
1100	1	ARG		R. Estilo, Quito
	10/0.5	ARG		R. Mitre, Corrientes
		BOL	LP29)	R. Cultural Chaka, Pucarani
		BOL	CO76)	R. Raqaypampa, Raqaypampa
	1	BOL	OR06)	R. Universidad de Oruro
		BOL	LP153)	Universal Radio Conciencia, El Alto
	10	CHL	CB110	BBN R., Viña del Mar
	10	CLM	CN	BBN R, Bogotá
	15	CLM	AT	Caracol R, Barranquilla
	5	CLM	MK	Emisora Ideal, Planeta Rica
	15	CLM	YZ	La FM, Neiva
	1	CLM	GI	LV de Colombia, Socorro
	5	CLM	GQ	Transmisora Surandes, Andes
	1.5	EQA	LE7	R. Oriental, Tena
	5/2	EQA	GR6	Solo Deportes R. Novedades, Latacunga
	5	PRG	ZP71	R. Ñú Verá, Capitán Bado
		PRU	OCU2E	R. 1000, Julcan
	1	PRU	OBX7Z	R. LTC, Juliaca
	1	PRU	OCU4N	R. OCU4N, Cañete
	1	PRU	OBX1L	R. Ondas de Paz, Chiclayo
	1	PRU	OAZ4W	R. Programas del Peru - RPP, Barranca
	1	PRU	OCY4G	Sonorama R., Huancayo
	10	VEN	SV	R. Angostura, Cd.Bolívar
1110	25/5	ARG	LS1	R. de la Ciudad, Dique Luján
	10	CHL	CD111	R. La Frontera, Temuco
	1	CLM	PA	R. de las Islas, San Andrés
	5	CLM	GP	LV del Río Arauca, Arauca
	10	CLM	EW	Q'hubo Radio, Cali
	3	CLM	DI	R. Bolivariana, Medellín
	15	CLM	ZE	R. Piragua, Sincelejo
	10	CLM	JP	RCN, Villavicencio
	10	EQA	JR1	R. Arpeggio, Quito
	5	EQA	JC5	R. Ondas Azuayas, Cuenca
	1	PRU	OBU6F	R. Austral, Ilo

kHz	kW	Ctry	Call	Station, location
	0.5	PRU	OCX1R	R. Centro Popular, La Union
	3	PRU	OAU3R	R. Cielo, Huánuco
	1	PRU	OAU4J	R. Feliz, Lima
	1	PRU	OCX2U	R. Jaén, Jaén
	5	PRU	OCX7T	R. Machupicchu, Cusco
	3	URG	CX111	R. Paso de los Toros, Paso de los Toros
	10	VEN	RX	Deportes Unión R., Valencia
	10	VEN	QT	R. Venezuela, Carúpano
1120	2	ARG		AM Tango, Villa Dominico
	1	ARG		Em. Santiago y Copla, Ciudad Evita
	1	ARG	LRK204	R. 21, Yerba Buena
	25/5	ARG	LV5	R. Sarmiento, San Juan
	1	ARG		R. Sudamericana, San Martin
		BOL	LP96)	R. Celestial, El Alto
		BOL	CO53)	R. El Porvenir, Tiquipaya
		BOL	LP97)	R. Wiñay Khantatt, Tiawuanaku
	10	CLM	KQ	Caracol, Tunja
	5	CLM	Q92	Colombia Mía, Yopal, CS
	15	CLM	GH	Q'hubo R, Bucaramanga
	5	CLM	JC	Vida, Pereira
	10	CLM	TI	Vox Dei, Cúcuta
	10	PRG	ZP24	La Deportiva, Lambaré, San Lorenzo
	3	PRU	OAM2F	R. Bambamarca - Frecuencia Lider, Chota
	1	PRU	OCU4E	R. Bendición, Barranca
	1.5	PRU	OBX2I	R. Dinamica, Trujillo
	0.5	PRU	OAU5W	R. Huayllahuara
	1	PRU	OCX6U	R. Municipal, Cerro Colorado, Aqp
	5	PRU	OAX8A	R. Nacional, Iquitos
	1	PRU	OBX8R	R. OAX8A, Campoverde
	1	PRU	OAU5H	R. Quispillaccta, Ayacucho
		PRU		R. San Bartolome, Junin
	10	URG	CW31	R. Salto, Salto
	20/10	VEN	SK	R. Dif.del Sur, San Fernando de Apure
	5	VEN	XZ	R. República, Maturín
1130	5/1	ARG	LRG203	R. Capital, Santa Rosa
	25/5	ARG	LRA21	R. Nal., Santiago del Estero
	3	ARG		R. Show, Isidro Casanova
	10	CLM	AC	Em. Riomar, Barranquilla
	1	CLM	NN	Ondas del Río, Magangué
	10	CLM	QQ	Oxígeno, Pasto
	15	CLM	VA	Vida, Bogotá
	5	EQA	PV6	R. Centro, Ambato
		EQA		R. Romántica, Machala
		EQA		R. Sibimbe AM, Ventanas
	2.6	PRU	OAX4N	R. Bacán, Lima
	1.2	PRU	OAX2V	R. Los Andes, Cjamarca
		PRU	OAM4K	R. OAM4K, Junin
	3	PRU	OBU6Q	R. OBU6Q, Moquegua
	1	PRU	OCU1R	R. OCU1R, Huarmaca
	1	PRU	OAU7B	R. Onda Popular, Juliaca
	5	PRU	OAM7F	R. Túpac Amaru, San Sebastian
	20	URG	CX30	R. Nacional, Montevideo
	20/10	VEN	RL	R. Ideal, Maiquetía
	10	VEN	KQ	R. Popular, Barquisimeto
1140	1	ARG		R. La Luna, El Palomar
	10/1	ARG	LU22	R. Tandil, Tandil
		BOL	CO82)	FM Fiesta, Cochabamba
		BOL	CO69)	R. San Isidro, Colomi
		BOL	LP99)	R. Sol Poder de Dios, Huanca
		BOL	LP98)	R. Sol Poder de Dios, La Paz
	100	CHL	CB114	R. Nal., Santiago
	10	CLM	E67	Caracol R, Villavicencio
	10	CLM	KO	R. Esperanza, Cartagena
	10	CLM	DL	R. Paisa la Cariñosa, Medellín
	10	CLM	CL	R. Panamericana, Girardot
		CLM		R. Piendamo, Piendamo
	10	CLM	RN	RCN, Barbosa
	1	EQA	AZ5	R. Alpha Musical, Cuenca
	5	EQA	IR1	R. Raíz, Quito
	5/2	PRG	CP22	R. Central de Notícias, Atyrá
		PRU	OCU2D	Chami R., Otuzco
	1	PRU	OAU3C	R. Bahia, Chimbote
	1	PRU	OAX6L	R. Capital, Cerro Colorado, Aqp
	0.5	PRU	OAX5W	R. Chinchaysuyo, Chinca Alta
	5	PRU	OAU1T	R. Fraternal, Ferreñafe

kHz	kW	Ctry	Call	Station, location
	5	PRU	OAM2O	R. Maria, Chota
	1.5	PRU	OBX1W	R. Piura, Piura
	1	PRU	OCY4C	R. Programas del Perú, Pilcomayo
1150	60	ARG	LT9	R. Brigadier López, Santa Fé
	5	ARG	LRA51	R. Nal., Jáchal
	25	ARG	LRA2	R. Nal., Viedma
	0.1	ARG		R. Sagrada Familia, Ciudad Madero
	50	ARG	LRH202	R. Tupá Mbaé, Posadas
	0.3	BOL	LP50)	R. Guaqui, Puerto de Guaqui
	15	CLM	FI	Caracol R, Armenia
	1	CLM	TE	LV del Chocó, Quibdó
	10	CLM	BT	R. Catatumbo, Ocaña
	10	CLM	FP	RCN, Neiva
	1	CLM	GJ	W Radio, Duitama
	10	EQA	GB5	LV de Riobamba, Riobamba
	10	EQA	AV3	R. Luz y Vida, Loja
	0.5	PRU	OCY2E	R. Chasquillacta, Pedro Galvez
	2.5	PRU	OAU7X	R. La Sureña, Juliaca
	5	PRU	OBU4K	R. Mineria, Cerro de Pasco
	2.5	PRU	OCX7Q	R. Universal, Wanchaq
	10	VEN	QD	Ecos del Orinoco, Cd.Bolívar
	10	VEN	MV	R. Venezuela Caribe, Punto Fijo
1160	5/10	ARG	LRH253	R. Cataratas, Pto. Iguazú
	10/2.5	ARG	LU32	R. Coronel Olavarría, Olavarría
	1	ARG		R. Independencia, Remedios de Escalada
		ARG		R. La Más Santiagueña, Gregorio de Laferrere
	5/1	ARG	LRA57	R. Nal., El Bolsón
	5/1	ARG		Salta
	5	BOL	SC11)	R. Centenario, Sta. Cruz
	10	BOL	LP33)	R. Continental, La Paz
	1	BOL	CH03)	R. Nuevo Mundo, Sucre
	3/1	BOL	CO08)	R. RTC Deportiva, Cochabamba
	1	CHL	CC116	R. Ancoa, Linares
	1	CHL	CD116A	R. Baha'i, Temuco
	1	CHL	CD116	R. America, La Serena
	10	CLM	S31	Colombia Mía, Barrancabermeja
	5	CLM	AZ	Frecuencia Bolivariana, Montería
	15	CLM	OC	Fuego AM, Bogotá
	15	CLM	AU	Ondas del Orteguaza, Florencia
	10	CLM	BL	R. Aeropuerto, Barranquilla
	10	CLM	EC	R. San José de Cúcuta, Cúcuta
	10	CLM	EV	R. Unica, Cali
	5	CLM	ZV	RCN R. Las Lajas, Ipiales
		EQA		LV del Pueblo, Azogue
	1	EQA	UR6	R. Runatacuyaj, Latacunga
	2	EQA	VR3	R. Vía, Machala
	5	EQA	CP1	Super Auténtica, Quito
	10	PRG	ZP72	R. Antena Dos, Asunción
	5	PRU	OAX4C	R. 1160/R. Onda Cero Lima
	1	PRU	OCX7Z	R. del Sur, Tambopata
	1	PRU	OBX5O	R. Huanta 2000, Huanta
	0.3	PRU	OAX2C	R. Libertad Mundo, Trujillo
	1	PRU	OCU1Q	R. LV Campesino, Huarmaca
	1	PRU	OCU4V	R. Maranatha, Huancayo
	1	PRU	OBX6G	R. Nac. del Perú, Moquegua
	1	PRU	OAU2T	R. Siglo 21, Chota
	1	PRU	OCX1S	Radiales Nor Oriental del Marañon, Chiclayo
	2/1	URG	CW116	R. Agraria del Uruguay, Cerro Chato
	20/10	VEN	RR	R. Industrial, Guarenas
	1	VEN	OK	R. Universidad, Mérida
1170	1	ARG		R. Luz del Mundo, Rafael Calzada
	5	ARG		R. Mi País, Hurlingham
	10	ARG	LRA29	R. Nal., San Luis
	5	CHL	CD117	R. Natales, Puerto Natales
	10	CLM	NW	Caracol R, Cartagena
	10	CLM	E74	Meridiano 70, Arauca
	10	CLM	PB	Ondas de Macondo, Valledupar
	10	CLM	BX	Ondas del Meta, Villavicencio
	10	CLM	FW	R. Nutibara, Medellín
	1	CLM	JE	RCN, Tuluá
	10	CLM	GA	Vida, Tunja
	5	EQA	RV2	R. Filadelfia, Guayaquil
	1	PRU	OBU7F	Bethel Radio, Cusco

kHz	kW	Ctry	Call	Station, location
	0.5	PRU	OCX7Y	R. Constelación, Puno
	1	PRU	OAM4I	R. COSAT, Satipo
	1	PRU	OAU4N	R. Horizonte La Voz del Agro, Pueblo Nuevo
	1	PRU	OAU2M	R. Layzon, Cajamarca
	1	PRU	OAZ3K	R. Nor Peruana Chimbote
	1	PRU	OAM7A	R. OAM4E, Paramonga
	2	PRU	OAM5B	R. OAM5B, Acobamba
	10	PRU	OBX6L	R. Programas del Perú, Uchumayo, Aqp
	10	URG	CX32	Radiomundo, Montevideo
	10	VEN	KW	R. Bolivariana, Maiquetía
1180	0.25	ARG	AM	San Ponciano, Abasto
		ARG	LRI230	R. de la Sierra, Tandil
	1	BOL	CO09)	R. Independencia, Quillacollo
	1	BOL	LP18)	R. Ingavi, Viacha
		BOL	OR40)	R. Sajama Estero, Oruro
	50	CHL	CB118	R. Portales, Santiago
	15	CLM	FX	Caracol R, Manizales
		CLM		Em. Coorpurabá, Apartadó
	5	CLM	WA	LV del Guaviare, San José del Guaviare
	20	CLM	GK	R. Santander 2, Bucaramanga
	10/5	CLM	JT	RCN, Ibagué
		EQA		LV del Volante, Portoviejo
	12.5	EQA	LR1	Nueva Em. Central, Quito
	4	EQA	DP5	R. Cuenca, Cuenca
	5/1	PRG	ZP52	R. Coronel Oviedo, Coronel Oviedo
	1	PRU	OAM2K	Municipalidad Provincial de Jaen, Jaen
	10	PRU	OCU4K	NSE Radio, Lima
	1	PRU	OCU6N	R. Bacan Sat 2, Pocollay
	1	PRU	OCY4Z	R. Libertad , Junin
	2.5	PRU	OAZ1H	R. Vencinal, Piura
	10	URG	CX118	LV de Artigas, Artigas
	10	VEN	OR	R. Maturín, Maturín
	10	VEN	LQ	Super Suave 11-80, La Victoria
1190	25/5	ARG	LR9	R. América, Buenos Aires
	25	ARG	LRA15	R. Nal., San Miguel de Tucumán
		BOL	LP122)	R. Comunitara, Guaqui
	10	CLM	CT	LV de la Costa, Barranquilla
	15	CLM	EO	Ondas del Valle, Cartago
	10	CLM	CV	R. Cordillera, Bogotá
	10	CLM	KG	R. Mira, Tumaco
	1	EQA	RF6	R. El Sol, Pujilí
	2	EQA	DE2	UCSG Radio, Guayaquil
	5	PRG	ZP45	LV de la Libertad, Henendarias
	10	PRU	OAX1E	Bravasa R., Chiclayo
	5	PRU	OBX3D	R. Ancash, Huaraz
	1	PRU	OCX6G	R. Central de Noticias, Miraflores Aqp
	3	PRU	OAM7V	R. Cielo, Tambopata
	3	PRU	OCU1S	R. Cielo. Tumbes
	2	PRU	OAX7B	R. Tawantinsuyo, Cusco
	2	PRU	OBU5U	R. OBU5U, Huamanga
	10	VEN	ZD	La Cultural del Táchira, San Cristóbal
	20/10	VEN	PF	Ondas de Libertad, San Felix
1195		CLM		Ondas del Ranchería, Barrancas
1200		ARG		La Radio del Chamamé, Morón
	10/1	ARG	LRF203	R. 3
	1	ARG	LT6	R. Goya, Goya
	25/5	ARG		Rio Grande
		BOL	LP100)	Cuarzo Comunicaciones, La Paz
	0.25	BOL	CO10)	R. 24 de Noviembre, Arani
		BOL	OR31)	R. Capital, Oruro
		BOL	LP115)	R. Carlos Palenque, La Paz
		BOL	LP117)	R. Maria de la Candelaria, Copacabana
	5	BOL	SC12)	R. Oriental, Santa Cruz
		BOL	CO81)	R. San Simón, Cochabamba
	10	CHL	CD120	R. Agricultura, Los Angeles
	10	CLM	CD	Em. Nueva Epoca, Fusagasugá
	10	CLM	BZ	Ondas del Riohacha, Riohacha
	15	CLM	IJ	R. 1200, Medellín
	10	CLM	BV	R. Príncipe, Cartagena
	10	CLM	NF	R. Red RCN, Cali
	10	CLM	GC	RCN La Radio, Sogamoso
	5	EQA	RE2	LV del Trópico, Quevedo
	5	EQA	RM5	R. El Mercurio, Cuenca
	5	EQA	CS1	R. Super K, Sangolquí
	10	PRG	ZP44	R. Libre, Fernando de la Mora
	3	PRU	OAX4B	Cadena R. 1200, Lima
	1	PRU	OAU2A	LV de Cumbe, Cajamarca
	3	PRU	OAU4G	R. Andes, Huancayo
	1	PRU	OBX5X	R. Comercial, Abancay
		PRU	OCX7S	R. Continental, Juliaca
	1	PRU	OCU1A	R. Fe, Piura
	3	PRU	OAU6P	R. La Luz, Tacna
		PRU		R. Master Mix, Huancavelica
	1	PRU	OAM7O	R. Universidad, Puno
	1	URG	CW33	La Nueva R., Florida
	10	VEN	SF	R. Dimensión, Caripito
	10	VEN	OZ	R. Tiempo, Caracas
1210		ARG		R. del Promesero, José C. Paz
	5	ARG		R. La Luz, Lomas de Mirador
	1/0.5	ARG	LRI229	R. Las Flores, Las Flores
		ARG		R. Mailin, Gregorio de Laferrere
	1	CHL	CD121	Puerto Montt
	1	CHL	CC121	R. Universidad de Talca, Talca
		CHL	CB121	R. Valparaiso, Valparaiso
	10	CLM	E65	La Cariñosa, Antena 2, Cúcuta
	10	CLM	BQ	La Cariñosa, Pereira
	10	CLM	FR	Oxígeno, Neiva
	10	EQA	VC3	R. Centinela del Sur, Loja
	20	EQA	BJ2	R. El Mundo, Guayaquil
	3	EQA	JM6	R. Sira, Ambato
	1	PRU	OCY4T	R. Galaxia, Satipo
	1	PRU	OBU3D	R. OBU3D, Chimbote
	1	PRU	OCU2W	R. OCU2W, Querocoto
	1	PRU	OBX3X	R. Ondas de Paz, Huanuco
	1	PRU	OCU7B	R. Qorilazo, Chumbivilcas
	1	PRU	OAX7M	R. Quillabamba, Quillabamba
	1	PRU	OAX2Q	R. Universo, Trujillo
	2/1	URG	CX121	Difusora Soriano, Mercedes
	0.25	URG	CW121	R. El Libertador, Villa Vergara
	2./1	URG	CV121	R. RBC, Piriápolis
1220	5/1	ARG		Eco R. AM 1210, Buenos Aires
	1	ARG		LRC Radio, Pres. Roque Sanez Peña
	10/5	ARG	LRI224	R. Onda Marina, Mar del Plata
	1	BOL	OR09)	R. Batallión Topátar, Oruro
		BOL	LP134)	R. La Asunta, Asunta
		BOL	LP143)	R. La Voz Cristiana, Achacachi
	1	BOL	LP19)	R. Nueva Splendid, La Paz
		BOL	CO80)	R. Progreso La Luz del Alba, Cochabamba
	10	CHL	CD122	R. Maria, Temuco
		CLM		Emisora 1220, Barranquilla
	10	CLM	KR	R. María, Bogotá
	10	CLM	AV	R. Uno, Montería
	10	CLM	NM	R. Viva Cultural Bolívar, Ipiales
	10	CLM	MT	RCN La Radio, San Gil
	10	EQA	AP1	R. Marañón, Quito
		PRU	OBU5I	R. Amor y Paz, San Clemente
		PRU	OCU4H	R. Fe, Lima
	3	PRU	OCX1X	R. Libertad, Chiclayo
	10	PRU	OAX6X	R. Melodia, Hunter, Aqp
	1.5	PRU	OCU4W	R. OCU4W, Huancayo
	1	PRU	OAU7N	R. Universidad de San Antonio Abad, Cusco
	1/0.5	URG	CX122	R. Reconquista, Rivera
	10	VEN	RD	LV de Apure, San Fernando de Apure
	20/10	VEN	ZO	R. Aeropuerto 1220, Maracaibo
	10/5	VEN	VM	Valencia 1220 - Circuito R. Venezuela, Valencia
1230	1	ARG		R. Creativa, CA Buenos Aires
	25/5	ARG	LT2	R. Gen. San Martín, Rosario
	5/1	ARG	LW5	R. Libertador, General San Martin
	1	ARG		R. Litoral, Ciudad Evita
	15	CLM	EH	Colmundo, Bucaramanga
	10	CLM	IL	Minuto de Dios, Medellín
	6	CLM	BR	Oxígeno, Tunja
	10	CLM	LK	R. Calidad, Cali
	1	CLM	TP	R. Colina, Girardot
	1	CLM	MJ	RCN Antena 2, Maicao
	3	EQA	RI1	CRI-Centro Radiofónico de Imbabura, Ibarra
	1	EQA	RL6	LV de Saquisilí, Saquisilí
	15	EQA	FV2	R. Galáctica, Guayaquil
	3	EQA	MV5	R. Popular, Cuenca

kHz	kW	Ctry	Call	Station, location
	1	PRU	OAM2B	R. Fé, Cajamarca
		PRU	OCU4C	R. La Luz, Huacho
	1	PRU	OBX4Z	R. LV de Oxapampa, Oxapampa
	1	PRU	OBU6T	R. OBU6T, Moquegua
	1	PRU	OBZ4Y	R. Selecciones,Tarma
	1	PRU	OAU7V	R. Surupana, Caminca
	2.5	PRU	OAM7T	R. Tambopata, Tambopata
	10	VEN	OH	R. Valera, Valera
1240	1	ARG		R. Cadena Uno, Paso del Rey
	1	ARG	LRI218	R. Universidad Nal. del Sur, Bahia Blanca
		BOL	LP154)	R, Zaráte Willka, La Paz
		BOL	PO29)	R. Indoamerica, Potosi
	2	BOL	TA03)	R. Los Andes, Tarija
		BOL	LP131)	R. Nueva Generación, Qhurpa
		BOL	LP51)	Rdif. Achocalla, Achocalla
	25	CHL	CB124	R. Universidad de Santiago, Santiago
	5	CLM	GN	R. Barrancabermeja, Barrancabermeja
	3	CLM	JA	R. Buenaventura, Buenaventura
	1	CLM	GO	R. Caribabare, Saravena
	10	CLM	FG	RCN, Calarcá
	5	EQA	RF3	R. Fenix, Zaruma
	1	EQA	PA1	R. Metropolitana, Yaraquí
	1	PRU	OAU9B	R. Bagua Grande, Chachapoyas
		PRU	OCX1C	R. Campesina, Ayaviri
	1	PRU	OAU5U	R. Eco, Ica
	1	PRU	OAZ1A	R. Ferreñafe, Ferrañafe
	1	PRU	OAU3L	R. La Luz, Chimbote
	15	PRU	OAU6D	R. Lider, Socabaya, Aqp
	12	PRU	OAU4V	R. Maria, Huancayo
	1	PRU	OAU2Y	R. Nor Andino, Santiago de Chuco
	5	PRU	OCU7Z	R. Pachatusán, Sicuani
	1	PRU	OCX1C	R. Sechura, Sechura
	5/1	URG	CW35	R. Paysandú, Paysandú
1250		ARG		New licence. Puerto Madryn
	10	ARG		R. Estirpe Nacional., San Justo
		BOL	LP146)	R. Comunitaria Compi, Capilaya
	0.1	BOL	PA01)	R. Frontera, Cobija
	2.5	BOL	CH04)	R. La Plata, Sucre
	10	CHL	CD125	R. Pilmaiquen, Valdivia
	10	CLM	CA	Capital Radio, Bogotá
	10	CLM	OK	Em. ABC, Barranquilla
	1	CLM	EM	LV de Corozal, Corozal
	15	CLM	HS	W Radio, Cúcuta
	10	EQA	EM1	Ondas Carchenses, Tulcán
	5	PRG	ZP3	R. Asunción, Asunción
	1	PRU	OAU2V	HGV, Santa Cruz
	1	PRU	OAX9C	R. Americana, Nueva Cajamarca
	1	PRU	OAU6I	R. Campesina, Omate
	3	PRU	OBX8S	R. Cielo, Calleria
	1.5	PRU	OBZ1B	R. Dif. BNS, Talara Alta
	5	PRU	OAX4L	R. Miraflores, Miraflores
	3	PRU	OBX7A	R. Solar, Cusco
	5	URG	CW125	R. Bella Unión, Bella Unión
	10	URG	CX36	R. Centenario, Montevideo
	20/10	VEN	PZ	Latina 12-50, Pto Ordaz
1260	2	ARG		R. Amor, Villa Tesel
	10/5	ARG	LT14	R. General Urquiza, Paraná
	9	ARG		R. Oliva, Gneral Rodriguez
		ARG		R. Sendero de Verdad, El Jagüel
		ARG		R. y Television del Neuquén, Neuquén
		BOL	SC52)	R. Amboro, Santa Cruz
		BOL	TA21)	R. Dios es Amor Universal, Tarija
		BOL	CO54)	R. LV de la Esperanza, Quillacollo
	10	BOL	OR20)	R. Nacional de Huanuni, Hunanuni
		BOL	SC54)	R. Sararenda, Camiri
		BOL	LP137)	R. SERVIR, Caranavi
	1	CHL	CC126	R. Condell, Curicó
	10	CHL	CD126	R. Maria, Punta Arenas
	10	CHL	CA126	R. Nacional, Arica
	5	CLM	CO	Caracol R, Ibagué
	1	CLM	HU	Caracol R, San Andrés
	5	CLM	LX	Minuto de Dios Eco Llanero, Villavicencio
	2	CLM	OU	Ondas del Amazonas, Leticia
	5	CLM	NO	Oxígeno, Duitama
	5	CLM	DA	R. Auténtica, Medellín

kHz	kW	Ctry	Call	Station, location
	5	CLM	ET	R. María, Cali
	5	CLM	TM	R. Sonar, Ocaña
	5	CLM	OH	RCN Cesar, Valledupar
	10	EQA	MO1	LV del Santuario del Quinche, Quito
	1	EQA	RB3	R. Benemérita, Sta Rosa
	3	EQA	RO6	R. Calidad, Ambato
	2	EQA	PB5	R. Contacto XG, Cuenca
	5	PRG	ZP34	R. Panambi Vera, Villarrica
	1	PRU	OCU4F	R. Corazón Andino, El Tambo
	3	PRU	OAU3G	R. El Pregonero Cristiano, Chimbote
	1	PRU	OAU3F	R. La Luz, Huanuco
	3	PRU	OCU4B	R. La Luz, San Vicente de Cañete
	1	PRU	OBX6D	R. Manahaim, Uchumayo Aqp
	0.3	PRU	OBX5S	R. Nac. del Perú, Ayacucho
	1	PRU	OCX10	R. Nova, Chiclayo
		PRU	OBX2C	R. Otuzco, Otuzco
	3	URG	CW37	Dif. Rochense, Rocha
	10	VEN	RM	BBN R, Caracas
1270	25/5	ARG	LRA20	R. Nal., Las Lomitas
	100	ARG	LS11	R. Provincia de Buenos Aires, La Plata
		BOL	LP125)	R. Comunitaria Norte, Puerto Acosta
	5	CHL	CB127	R. Festival, Viña del Mar
	5	CLM	TX	Bésame, Bucaramanga
	1	CLM	IM	Colmundo, Pereira
	5	CLM	Q99	Colombia Mía, San José del Guaviare
	2	CLM	AR	La Cariñosa, Cartagena
	1.5	CLM	KJ	LV de Curumaní, Curumaní
	1	CLM	SV	LV de Orito, Orito
	5	CLM	BM	R. Internacional, Honda
	1	CLM	XQ	Vida, Ubaté
	3	EQA	LD4	R. Junín, Junín
	15	EQA	UM2	R. Universal, Guayaquil
		PRU		R. Ebenezer, Bambamarca
	1	PRU	OCX2Z	R. Estacion Latina, Cepén
	2	PRU	OAU7S	R. Horizonte - LV de Agro, Cusco
	0.4	PRU	OAZ4H	R. Huacho, Huacho
	0.4	PRU	OBZ4T	R. La Merced, Chanchamayo
	1	PRU	OAU1S	R. Nor Peru, Paita
	2	PRU	OAM5A	R. OAM5A, Huancavelica
	3	PRU	OBU6N	R. OBU6N, Tacna
	1	PRU	OBU6P	R. San Antonio, Callalli
	4/2	URG	CV127	R. Cuareim, Artigas
	10	VEN	OU	R. Ondas Panamericanas, El Vigía
1280		ARG		El Sonido de la Gente, Gregorio de Laferrere
	6	ARG		R. Cadena Eco, CA Buenos Aires
	10/5	ARG	LU11	R. Trenque Lauquén, TR. Lauquén
		BOL	LP142)	R. Altar de Dios, Achacachi
		BOL	CO65)	R. Comunitaria del Sur, Cochabamba
		BOL	LP68)	R. Comunitaria Ondas del Titicaca, Huarina
		BOL	TA17)	R. Fronera, Yacuiba
	1	CHL	CD128	R. la Palabra, Osorno
	5	CLM	LR	Caracol R, Pasto
	5	CLM	RP	Ecos de Tibú, Tibú
	5	CLM	CM	HJKK Sistema INRAI, Pitalito
	5	CLM	HO	Impacto Popular, San Juan del Cesar
	1	CLM	NQ	LV del Río Suárez, Barbosa
	5	CLM	TK	R. Ciudad Centinela, Caicedonia
	5	CLM	SO	R. Playa Mendoza, Barranquilla
	5	CLM	MB	R. Suroeste, Concordia
	5	CLM	KN	R. Única, Bogotá
		EQA		R. Universitaria, Quito
	10/0.25	PRG	ZP53	LVdel Este, Cd. del Este
	1	PRU	OAU1R	Bethel R., San Jose
	2.5	PRU	OCU7S	R. Altura, Macusani
		PRU		R. Bethel, Chaquimarca
		PRU	OBX3C	R. El Puerto, Chimbote
	1	PRU	OCU7R	R. Fé, Sicuani
	0.5	PRU	OBX6P	R. Fénix, Camaná
	1	PRU	OAX3Y	R. La Selva, Rupa-Rupa
	1	PRU	OBX2F	R. Moderna, Cajamarca
	3	PRU	OBU5J	Yeshua R., Chinca Alta
	3/1	URG	CX128	R. Tacuarembó, Tacuarembó
	10	VEN	OF	R. Trujillo, Trujillo

kHz	kW	Ctry	Call	Station, location
	10/5	VEN	QS	R. Zaraza, Zaraza
1290	1/0.5	ARG	LRI371	R. Amanecer, Reconquista
	1	ARG		R. Interactiva, Ciudad Madero
	5/1	ARG	LRJ212	R. Murialdo, Villa Nueva de Guaymallén
	1	ARG		R. Provinciana, San Miguel
		BOL	LP148)	R. Comunitaria Alaxpacha, Canaviri
		BOL	PO31)	R. Tomas Katari de America, Ocuri
	1	BOL	OR12)	Radiodifusoras Minería, Oruro
	0.25	CHL	CA129	R. Coya, Los Angeles
	5	CLM	SZ	Colombia Mía, Saravena, AR
	5	CLM	TH	LV de las Estrellas, Medellín
	5	CLM	NE	LV del Ariari, Granada
	5	CLM	EB	LV del Turismo, Santa Marta
	5	CLM	OI	R. Chacurí, Después
	5	CLM	MC	R. Viva 12-90, Cali
	5	CLM	KY	RCN, Girardot
	3	EQA	JA5	LV del Río Tarqui, Cuenca
	1	EQA	NS1	R. Popular, Atuntaqui
	5	PRU	OCX6B	R. Cielo, Cerro Colorado Aqp
		PRU	OAM2C	R. Estelar, Chota
	1	PRU	OBU4S	R. Exito, La Oroya
	0.35	PRU	OAX7X	R. Juliaca, Juliaca
	1	PRU	OBU5V	R. OBU5V, Ayacucho
	1	PRU	OCX1Q	R. Programas del Perú, Tumbes
	1	PRU	OBU2D	R. Sonorama, Trujillo
	1	PRU	OBU4Q	S & RD, Hualmay
	1	PRU	OCU4P	San Vicente de Cañete
	10	URG	CX38	Rad. Nacional del Uruguay, Montevideo
	10	VEN	LF	R. Puerto Cabello, Puerto Cabello
1300		ARG		Plus Radio, Lanús
	2	ARG		R. Identidad, Buenos Aires
		ARG		R. Juventud, Florencio Varela
	10/1	ARG	LRA5	R. Nal., Rosario
	5	BOL	BE18)	R. Bandera Beniana, Trinidad
		BOL	PO38)	R. Fides, Potosi
	1	BOL	SC16)	R. Fuerzas Armadas, Sta. Cruz
	2.5	BOL	CH05)	R. Loyola, Sucre
		BOL	CO72)	R. San Simón, Cochabamba
	15/6	BOL	LP23)	R. Sol Poder de Diós, El Alto
		BOL	OR39)	Sistem de Comuncacion "Perez", Oruro
	1	CHL	CB130	R. Conexiones, Santiago
	5	CLM	RB	CRB Cadena Radial Boyacense, Tunja
	5	CLM	OG	LV de las Antillas, Cartagena
	5	CLM	NB	Onda 5, Bucaramanga
	5	CLM	LD	Q'hubo Radio, Pereira
	5	CLM	IN	R. Eucha, Belalcázar
	5	CLM	EA	R. Lumbí, Mariquita
	5	CLM	UA	R. Sindamanoy, Mocoa
	5	EQA	DC2	R. Cenit, Guayaquil
	5	EQA	RV1	R. Festival, Sto Domingo de los Colorados
		EQA		R. La Paz, Guaranda
	2/1	EQA	RS7	R. Sucumbios, Nueva Loja
	5	PRG	ZP53	R. Fe y Alegria, Villa Hayes
	3	PRU	OBU6X	R. Candarave, Ilabaya
	5	PRU	OAX4S	R. Comas, Comas
	1	PRU	OAU1U	R. Frecuencia Lider, Morro
	0.5	PRU	OAX3O	R. Huascarán, Independencia
	0.35	PRU	OAX7X	R. Juliaca, Juliaca
	1	PRU	OBX9P	R. La Luz, Tarapoto
	1	PRU	OAZ8B	R. Nuevo Mundo, Pucallpa
	2.5	PRU	OCU4R	R. OCU4R, Ahuac
	5	PRU	OAX7P	R. Onda Imperial, Cusco
	1	PRU	OAU2I	R. Paraiso, Cajabamba
	10/8	VEN	KH	R. Recuerdos AM Center, Caracas
	10	VEN	NS	R. Reloj, Maracaibo
1310	0.25	ARG		Gesell Radio, Villa Gesell
	0.5	ARG		R. DR. Gregorio Alvarez, Piedra del Aguila
	10	ARG	LRA42	R. Nal., Gualeguaychú
	1	ARG		Rdif. Antártica Argentina, Buenos Aires
	10	BOL	CO14)	R. San Rafael, Cochabamba
	5	CLM	JZ	Aviva 2, Bogotá
	5	CLM	DG	Caracol R, Monteria
	5	CLM	TQ	G12 Radio, Cúcuta
	5	CLM	AK	LV de la Patria Celestial, Barranquilla
	5	CLM	WD	Micrófono Civico, Palermo

kHz	kW	Ctry	Call	Station, location
	5	CLM	LM	R. Santa Bárbara
	5	CLM	IR	RCN Urabá, Apartadó
	0.5	EQA	AI5	Eco de los Andes, Cumanda
	1	EQA	CP3	LV de El Oro, Pasaje
	3	EQA	CI5	R. Internacional TVO, Biblián
	20	EQA	GB1	R. Nal. Espejo, Quito
	10/0.25	PRG	ZP53	LVdel Este, Cd. del Este
	3	PRU	OBU5X	Ayacucho
	3	PRU	OCU1D	Bethel R., Piura
	1	PRU	OBX2D	R. Chota, Chota
	1	PRU	OBX4L	R. Irvisa, Huacho
	6	PRU	OAU6N	R. Libertad, Alto Selva Alegre Aqp
	5	PRU	OAU3T	R. OAU3T, Rupa Rupa
	12	PRU	OBX8L	R. Vision Amazonia, Iquitos
	5	VEN	TS	R. Andina, Isnotú
	10	VEN	SM	RNV El Informativo, Barcelona
	1	VEN	SL	RNV El Informativo, Guri
		VEN		RNV El Informativo, Sta. Elena
1320	0.25	ARG	LV24	R. Andina, Tunuyán
	10	ARG	LU10	R. Azul, Azul
	1	ARG		R. Máster, Luján
		ARG		R. Area Uno, Caseros
		BOL	LP53)	R. Comunitaria Tawantinsuyo, Taraco
		BOL	LP111)	R. Em. Septima Voz, Achocalla
		BOL	CH25)	R. Sucre, Sucre
		BOL	LP121)	R. Comunitaria La Lumberia, La Paz
	1	CHL	CD132	R. Lincoyan, Mulchén
	5	CLM	NV	La Cariñosa, Girardot
	5	CLM	HT	R. Guateque, Guateque
	10	CLM	QI	R. Leda Int., San Andrés
	1	CLM	NK	R. Luna, Palmira
	5	CLM	TA	R. María, Medellín
	5	CLM	LV	R. Onda Fantastica, Fundación
	5	CLM	MS	RCN La Radio, Barrancabarmeja
	1	EQA	VO4	R. Carrizal, Calceta
	10	EQA	JD6	R. Continental, Ambato
	3	EQA	FR2	R. Guayaquil, Babahoyo
	1	PRU	OBU5L	La Luz del Mundo, Pueblo Nuevo
	2.5	PRU	OCU4T	R. Bacan, Huancayo
	1	PRU	OBU1S	R. Frecuencia Popular, Olmos
		PRU	OAX4I	R. La Cronica, Lima
	0.5	PRU	OBU6B	R. Majes
	5	PRU	OAU3W	R. OAU3W, La Caleta
	1	PRU	OBU6A	R. OBU6A, Tacna
	5	PRU	OCU5V	R. Cultural Tintaya, Cotabambas
	3	PRU	OAU7W	R. TV Peru, Juliaca
	1/0.5	URG	CW132	R. Fortaleza, Rocha
	1/0.5	URG	CW39	R. LV de Paysandú, Paysandú
	10/5	VEN	WP	R. Apolo, Turmero
	10	VEN	SG	R. Colonial, El Tocuyo
1330	1/0.25	ARG		AM 1330, Rosario
	3/1.5	CHL	CD133	Puerto Montt
	3	CHL	CB133	R. La Perla del Dial, Santiago
	0.25	CLM	HKR33	Alcadía de Salamina, Salamina
	5	CLM	FE	Antena 2, Pereira
	5	CLM	LS	Caracol R, Popayán
	5	CLM	NR	La Caliente 13-30, San Gil
	1	CLM	MP	LV de Aguachica, Aguachica
	5	CLM	AP	R. Auténtica, Cartagena
	1	CLM	RD	R. Fénix de Oriente 1330 AM, El Peñol
	5	EQA	RV3	Nacional El Oro, Machala
	2	EQA	LW5	R. Visión Cristiana, Cuenca
	3	EQA		R. Visión Cristiana, Quito
	10	PRG	ZP13	R. Chaco Boreal, Asunción
	0.5	PRU	OBU5P	Bethel R., Huamanga
	1	PRU	OAU1A	R. Amistad, Chiclayo
	1	PRU	OAM2D	R. Fé, La Esperanza
	5	PRU	OCX6E	R. Frecuencia 1330, Cayma Aqp
	1	PRU	OCU1J	R. Frecuencia Ideal, Frias
	1	PRU	OCX7K	R. San Miguel, Wanchaq
	1	PRU	OBX9Y	R. Fé, Tarapoto
	5	URG	CX40	R. Fénix, Montevideo
	5	VEN	OY	R. Los Llanos, Calabozo
		VEN		RNV El Informativo, La Paragua
1340	0.8	ARG		AM Renacer, Moreno

kHz	kW	Ctry	Call	Station, location
	1/0.25	ARG		Goya
	1	ARG		R. Mediterránea, Rosario del Tala
		ARG		R. Tradicional Conurbano Norte, Florida
		BOL	LP145)	R. Comunitaria La Voz de Valle, Sococoni
	0.5	BOL	LP39)	R. Copacabana, Copacabana
	1	BOL	SC17)	R. Grigotá, Santa Cruz
	0.5	BOL	LP40)	R. Jach'a Suyu, Corocoro
		BOL	LP152)	R. La Mision, La Paz
		BOL	CO79)	TV Sist. de Comunicacione Mundial, Cochabama
	10	CHL	CB134	R. Colo Colo, Valparaíso
	1	CHL	CC134	R. La Discusión, Chillán
	1	CHL	CD134	R. Vida Nueva, Panguipulli
	5	CLM	FB	Amor Estereo, Bogotá
	0.5	CLM	VL	Brisas del Catatumbo, Tibú
	5	CLM	KD	La Cariñosa/Antena 2, Neiva
	5	CLM	FA	R. Alegre, Barranquilla
	1	CLM	NP	R. Comunal, Nariño
	5	CLM	IS	R. El Sol, Buenaventura
	5	CLM	PY	R. Lemas, Cúcuta
	4	CLM	NY	R. Unica, Bucaramanga
	5	CLM	HA	RCN Nariño, Pasto
	5	CLM	HY	RCN Sucre, Sincelejo
		EQA		LV de su Amigo, Esmeraldas
	1	EQA		Ondas de Esperanza, Loja
	5	EQA	RT6	R. Paz y Bien, Ambato
	10	PRU	OAU4Q	R. Alegria, Pucasana
	0.5	PRU	OAX5D	R. Chincha, Chincha Alta
		PRU		R. Choque, Chumbivilcas
	1	PRU	OAU4N	R. Jauja, Jauja
	1	PRU	OBU3C	R. OBU3C, Casma
	1	PRU	OBX1K	R. San Francisco, Piura
	1	PRU	OAU2S	R. Shalom, Cajamarca
	1	PRU	OBU7V	R. Sudamericana, Juliaca
	10/1	URG	CW53	LV de Melo, Melo
		VEN		R Mundial, Barinas
	10	VEN	NE	R. Uno, Caracas
1350	1/0.25	ARG		Juan José Castelli, Chaco
	10/5	ARG	LS6	R. Buenos Aires, Burzaco
	5/1	ARG	LRJ747	R. Sucesos, Villa Carlos Paz
		BOL	CH06)	R. America, Sucre
	2.5	BOL	CO05)	R. Cochabamba, Cochabamba
		BOL	LP113)	R. Comunitario Inti, Contorno/Viacha
		BOL	LP123)	R. Llacxa, Achocalla
	0.02	CHL	CD135	Puerto Montt
	1	CHL	CA135	R. Riquelme, Coquimbo
	1	CLM	HW	Em. Ecos del Río, Puerto Boyacá
	5	CLM	DS	Ondas de la Montaña, Medellín
	5	CLM	HL	Oxígeno, Ibagué
	5	CLM	EN	R. Armonía, Cali
	1	CLM	MN	R. Perijá, Codazzi
	5	CLM	OA	R. Uno, Santa Marta
	5	CLM	LO	RCN Antena 2/La Cariñosa, Caucasia
	2/1	CLM	SF5	LV de San Fernando, San Fernando
	3	EQA	VP2	Teleradio 13-50 AM Digital , Guayaquil
	1	PRU	OBU5O	R. Atlantis, Huamanga
	1	PRU	OCU1I	R. Fé, Tumbes
	1	PRU	OAU3X	R. OAU3X, Pillco Marca
	3	PRU	OCU6D	R. OCU6D, Ichuña
	1	PRU	OAM4H	R. Paraiso, Huacho
		PRU	OBX8D	R. Super, Pucallpa
	1	PRU	OAU1H	R. Vision, Chiclayo
	5	VEN	ZZ	R. Eclipse, El Tigrito
	5	VEN	TJ	R. Falcón, Puerto Cumarebo
1355	0.25	BOL	CO15)	R. Armonía, Cliza
1360	0.4	ARG		R. Nuestra Señora de Itatí, Morón
	1	ARG		R. Cooperativa Estirpe Entrerriana, Maria Grande
		BOL	OR32)	Cadena Coral, Oruro
		BOL	SC47)	R. 24 de Septiembre, Santa Cruz
		BOL	LP103)	R. Em. Tunupa, Tiawuanaku
		BOL	PO37)	R. La Cruz del Sur, Potosi
		BOL	SC49)	R. TV Salesiana, Yapacani
	5	BOL	LP16)	R. Cordiale, El Alto
	5	CHL	CC136	R. Universidad Bio Bio, Concepcion
	5	CLM	RA	Ecos 13-60 Radio, Pereira
	10/5	CLM	PK	LV de Abejorral, Abejorral
	5	CLM	UO	Oxígeno, Cartagena
	5	CLM	MI	R. Auténtica, Melgar
	1	CLM	KV	R. Láser, Zapatoca
	0.5	CLM		R. Segovia, Segovia
	5	EQA	HG3	R. Jerusalem AM, Machala
	3	EQA	MT	R. Oyambaro, Tumbaco
	1	PRG	ZP37	R. Yby Ya'u, Ybu Ya'u
	10	PRU	OCU4I	R. Bienestar, Lima
	2.5	PRU	OUA7L	R. Continente, Juliaca
	1	PRU	OBZ5Z	R. Cruz del Sur, Palpa
	1	PRU	OBZ1A	R. del Norte, Sullana
	1	PRU	OAU3A	R. Intercontinental, Yungay
	2	PRU	OCU2Z	R. OCU2Z, Querocotillo
	3	PRU	OCX6T	R. Popular, Mariano Melgar
	2.5	PRU	OAX7R	R. Sicuani, Sicuani
	1	PRU	OAU4O	R. Sudamericana, Tarma
	2.5	URG	CW41	R. 41, San José
	1	URG	CW136	R. Río Branco, Río Branco
	5	VEN	TZ	R. Armonía, Charallave
1370	1/0.25	ARG		Aire de Santa FeRafaela
	3	ARG		AM Trece-70, González Catan
		ARG		Junin
	10	ARG	LRA54	R. Nal., Ingeniero Jacobacci
	0.15	BOL	CO16)	R. Libertad, Cliza
	1	CHL	CD137	R. Emaus, Temuco
	5	CLM	BO	Minuto de Dios, Barranquilla
	1	CLM	BD	R. Guaimaral, Cúcuta
	5	CLM	KI	R. Mundial, Bogotá
	1	CLM	NI	R. Sabana, Sincelejo
	1	CLM	JQ	RCN Antena 2, Zarzal
	5	CLM	EQ	RCN Cauca, Popayán
	2.5	CLM	NU	RCN, Rionegro
	2	EQA	JS1	Ecos Andinos, Pimampiro
	5	EQA	VO2	LV de Milagro, Milagro
	12	EQA	A05	R. El Rocio, Biblián
	1	PRU	OCX5A	Inti R., Abanacy
	10	PRU	OCU4U	R. Altura, Cerro de Pasco
		PRU	OAX6T	R. Moquegua, Moquegua
	5	PRU	OAU9E	R. OAU9E, Moyobamba
	1	PRU	OBU6Y	R. OBU6Y, Viraco
	3	PRU	OCU5Y	R. OCU5Y, Chalhuahuacho
	3	PRU	OAM7G	R. Qosqo Wayra, Cusco
	5.3/2.5	URG	CX42	Em. Ciudad de Montevideo
	1/0.5	URG	CW137	Nueva R. San Javier, San Javier
	0.5	URG	CV137A	R. Real, Minas de Corrales
	10	VEN	JI	R. Continente Cumbre, Mérida
	5	VEN	SV	RNV Portuguesa, Acarigua
	5	VEN	OQ	Unión R. Notícias, Valle de la Pascua
1380	5/1	ARG	LRI231	LV del Sudeste, Necochea
	0.5	ARG		R. AM Súper Sport, Temperley
	2	ARG		R. Buenas Nuevas, Merlo
	0.5	ARG		R. Los Toldos, Los Toldos
	1.5	BOL	CO34)	R. Bandera Tricolor, Cochabamba
		BOL	CH22)	R. Global, Sucre
		BOL	OR33)	R. Horizontes, Huanuni
	0.5	BOL	TA06)	R. Luis de Fuentes, Tarija
		BOL	LP104)	R. Maria, La Paz
		BOL	SC51)	R. Maria, Santa Cruz
		BOL	LP141)	R. TV Minera Matilde, Carabuco
	50	CHL	CB138	R. Corporación, Santiago
	1	CLM	EJ	Armonías del Palmar, Palmira
	3	CLM	LG	LV de La Dorada, La Dorada
	3	CLM	JD	NSE Radio, Medellín
	5	CLM	ID	R. Potencia Latina, La Plata
	5	CLM	EE	RCN, Tunja
	5	CLM	MM	Vida, Valledupar
	5	EQA	CV1	R. Cristal, Quito
	1	EQA	OA3	R. Estelar La Mejor, Balsas
	5	EQA		R. Mera, Ambato
	1	PRG	ZP8	R. Concepción, Concepción
	1	PRU	OAX2W	R. Atahualpa, Cajamarca
	1	PRU	OBZ1D	R. Bellavista, Bellavista
		PRU	OBU4L	R. Chilca,Chilca

kHz	kW	Ctry	Call	Station, location
	1	PRU	OCY4U	R. Nuevo Tiempo, Lima
	1	PRU	OAM5E	R. OAM5E, Salas
	1	PRU	OCU7U	R. OCU7U, Tambopata
	1	PRU	OBX3I	R. Pilco Mozo, Huanuco
	1	PRU	OAU3U	R. R. dif San Juan, Chimbote
	3	PRU	OAX6O	R. San Martin, Arequipa
	10	VEN	NG	Ondas del Mar, Puerto Cabello
	5	VEN	ME	R. Revelación, Cd.Bolivar
1390		ARG		La Rocha Azul AM 1390, Libertad
		ARG		R. General Paz, José C. Paz
	10	ARG	LR11	R. Univ. Nacional, La Plata
		BOL	CO50)	R. Andina , Pongo Khasa
	1	CLM	ZY	La Primera, Bucaramanga
	5	CLM	FY	Oxígeno R. Avendia, Espinal
	5	CLM	YW	R. Auténtica, Pacho
	5	CLM	FO	Red de los Andes,Manizales
	5	EQA	EA5	R. Tropicana, Cuenca
	0.5	PRU	OBU2U	Frequencia del Norte, Santa Cruz
	2.5	PRU	OCU5C	R. Cielo, Ayacucho
	1	PRU	OAU7T	R. Enlace, Kunturkanki
	3	PRU	OAM7A	R. Exitosa, Sicuani
		PRU	OCU1G	R. Fe, Pimentel
	3	PRU	OAU2Z	R. La Luz, Trujillo
	5	URG	CW45	Dif. Treinta y Tres, Treinta y Tres
	20	VEN	ZA	R. Fe y Alegría, Caracas
	10	VEN	ZO	R. Lumen, Maracaibo
1400		ARG		AM 1400, Luján
	1/0.25	ARG		AM del NEA, Charata
	5/1	ARG	LRG202	R. Cumbre, Neuquén
		ARG		R. Punto, Buenos Aires
	0.25	ARG		Red 24, Rosario
		BOL	CH20)	R. Antena 2000, Sucre
	0.25	BOL	OR38)	R. Atlantida, Oruro
	5	BOL	LP25)	R. Nacional de Bolivia, La Paz
		BOL	CO71)	R. Tricolor, Villa Tunari
	3	CHL	CD140	R. La Amistad, Los Angeles
	5	CHL	CD140A	R. Maria, Puerto Montt
	0.25	CLM	HKZ22	Alcaldía de Majagual, Majagual
	0.25	CLM	HKZ25	Alcaldía de Ovejas, Ovejas
	0.25	CLM		Brisas del Sinú, Tierralta
	1	CLM	ER	Ecos del Atrato, Quibdó
	5	CLM	KM	Em. Mariana, Bogotá
	5	CLM	HM	La Cariñosa de Armenia, Calarcá
	1	CLM	D31	LV de Cimitarra, Cimitarra
	1	CLM	BK	LV de la Gran Colombia, Cúcuta
	1	CLM	WY	LV de los Samanes
	5	CLM	DF	LV de Niquel, Montelíbano
	1.5	CLM		LV de Samaniego, Samaniego
	0.45	CLM		R. Cañaveral, Morales
	1	CLM	JJ	R. Ipiales, Ipiales
	5	CLM	AS	RCN Antena 2, Barranquilla
	1	CLM	LL	RCN Antena 2, Santa Bárbara
	10	EQA	FL2	R. Z Uno, Guayaquil
	2.5	PRU	OBX4W	R. Callao Super, Lima
	1	PRU	OAX7I	R. La Hora - IPDA, Cuzco
	1	PRU	OBX4H	R. Luz, Tarma
	1	PRU	OAU2H	R. Nueva Campesina, Cajamarca
	1	PRU	OAM5G	R. OAM5G, Ica
	1	PRU	OBU3E	R. OBU3E, Chimbote
	1	PRU	OCU6F	R. OCU6F, Calano
	25	URG	CX140	R. Zorrilla de San Martín, Tacuarembó
	1	VEN	NF	R. Sabana, El Sombrero
1410	5/1	ARG		R. Folclorismo, José Léon Suárez
	0.5	ARG		R. Fundacion, Rafael Calzada
	1	ARG		R. Lider, Mendoza
		ARG		R. María de La Paz, Villa Mercedes
	1	ARG		R. Cope, Chivilcoy
	1	CHL	CD141	R. Loncoche, Loncoche
	5	CHL	CB141	Valparaíso
	0.25	CLM	HKP86	Alcaldía de Chiquinquira, Chiquinquira
	5	CLM	DU	Em. Cultural Univ. de Antioquia, Medellín
	1	CLM	TY	LV del Carare, Vélez
	2	CLM	P79	R. Evangélica, Bogotá
	5	CLM	EI	R. Guadalajara, Buga
	1	CLM	HKP79	R. Universidad, Tunja
	5	CLM	FS	RCN, Honda
	1	EQA	FR4	LV de Quinindé, Quinindé
	1	EQA		Ondas Cisnerinas, Riobamba
	1	EQA	GC5	R. Centro Gualaceo, Gualaceo
	1	EQA	EC1	R. El Tiempo, Quito
	1	EQA	CQ2	R. Net AM, Milagro
	1	PRU	OBZ4V	Bethel R., Huacho
	1	PRU	OBX8I	Dif. Comercial, Pucallpa
	3	PRU	OCU5G	R. Genesis, Huanta
	1	PRU	OAU3Y	R. Ke Buena, Paucarbambilia
	1	PRU	OBU7A	R. La Luz, Juliaca
	3	PRU	OBU1H	R. La Luz, Tumbes
	1	PRU	OBU1G	R. Olmos, Olomos
	1	PRU	OCU2Q	R. San Marcos, Pedro Galvez
	10/5	URG	CX44	AM Libre, Montevideo
	2/0.5	URG	CW141	R. 1410, Salto
	10	VEN	SP	R. Simpatía, Valera
	5	VEN	ST	R. Turén, Turén
1420	1/0.25	ARG	LRK221	R. Ciudad Perico, Perico
	1/0.25	ARG	LRI220	R. Dime, Villa Martelli
	1	ARG		R. Génesis 2000, General Conesa
	1	BOL	CO18)	R. Centro, Cochabamba
		BOL	SC50)	R. Comunitaria, José Ballivian
		BOL	LP114)	R. Creo en Milagros, Murillo
	1.5	BOL	TA05)	R. Guadalquivir, Tarija
		BOL	LP105)	R. Omasuyos Andina, Achacachi
	1	BOL	CH15)	R. Real Audiencia, Sucre
	1	CHL	CB142	R. Panamericana, Santiago
	1	CLM	D23	Ecos de Frontino, Frontino
	1	CLM	LE	La Cariñosa, Antena 2, Ibagué
	2	CLM	SN	R. Lenguerque, Zapatoca
	5	CLM	BH	R. Magdalena, Santa Marta
	5	CLM	HK	Vida, Manizales
		EQA		Corazón AM, Machala
		EQA	VN7	LV del Napo, Tena
	5	PRG	ZP42	R. Güyrá Campana, Horqueta
	1	PRU	OBU6C	R. Fe, Arequipa
	0.5	PRU	OBU5H	R. la Luz, Salas
	5	PRU	OAM2P	R. La Positiva, Bambamarca
	2	PRU	OCU1F	R. OCU1F, Tambo Grande
	1	PRU	OBZ4G	R. San Isidro, Lima
	1/0.5	URG	CX142	R. Felicidad, Paysandú
	5	URG	CW43	R. Lavalleja, Minas
	10/5	VEN	RW	R. Cardenal, Carora
	1	VEN		R. Sintonia, Caracas
1430	1/0.25	ARG	LV26	Cadena 26, Río Tercero
	0.25	ARG	LRI235	R. Balcarce, Balcarce
	1	ARG		R. Cunumi Guazú, Rafael Castillo
	0.5	ARG		R. Shekinah, Merlo
	1	ARG		Red Pampeana, General Pico
	1/0.25	ARG	LT24	SN24, San Nicolás
	1	CHL	CC143	Rancagua -
	1	CLM	IU	Armonías del Ingrumá, Riosucio
	5	CLM	PW	Colmundo, Barranquilla
	0.25	CLM	X61	L U FM Estéreo, Armenia
	5	CLM	MF	La Ribereña, Puerto Berrío
	1	CLM	EG	LV de Belalcázar, Popayán
	0.5	CLM	G42	R. Alejandría, Alejandría
	2	CLM	BP	R. Cariongo, Pamplona
	1	CLM	HKX73	R. Ciudad de Pereira, Pereira
	5	CLM	QX	R. Majagual, Sincelejo
	0.5	CLM	HKK38	R. Manantial, Sibundoy
	1	CLM	CK	R. Sensación, Yarumal
	5	CLM	KU	Uniminuto R., Bogotá
	10	EQA	MB2	R. Federal, Virgen de Fátima
	3.5	EQA	GF1	R. Futura, Quito
	2	PRG	ZP35	R. Mangore, S. Juan Bautista
	1	PRU	OCU4L	Chilca, Cañete
	1	PRU	OAZ3H	R. Chavin, Chimbote
	1	PRU	OAU6M	R. Lider, Tacna
	1	PRU	OAZ7M	R. OAZ7M, Cusco
	1	PRU	OCU2U	R. OCU2U, Jaen
	3	PRU	OBU7U	R. Red Andina, Juliaca
	0.5	PRU	OAZ4V	R. Universal, El Tambo
	1	PRU	OBX9H	R. Utcubamba, Bagua Grande

kHz	kW	Ctry	Call	Station, location
	20/5	URG	CW25	R. Durazno, Durazno
	10	VEN	NB	Llanerísima, Guacara
	25	VEN	TP	R. Bahía, Puerto La Cruz
	10/5	VEN	TM	R. Caicara, Caicara del Orinoco
1440	1	ARG	LU36	R. Coronel Suárez, Coronel Suárez
	0.25	ARG		R. Cristo Viene, Mar del Plata
		ARG		R. FEDETUR Turismo, Mar de Ajó
	5/1	ARG	LRI221	R. General Obligado, Reconquista
	2	ARG		R. Impacto, Ciudad Madero
	1/0.25	ARG	LV20	R. Laboulaye, Laboulaye
	5	ARG	LRA53	R. Nal., San Martín de los Andes
	0.25	ARG		Villa Gesell
		BOL	CO74)	LV de Juno , Tiraque
	1	BOL	LP26)	R. Batallón Colorados, La Paz
	0.25	BOL	CO42)	R. Bolivia, Cochabamba
		BOL	LP139)	R. Comunitaria Eco Saywani, Carabuco
		BOL	BE02)	R. Dif. Tropico, Trinidad
	1	BOL	OR13)	R. Em. Bolivia, Oruro
	2/1	BOL	SC21)	R. Yaguary, Vallegrande
		BOL	CH39)	Sistema de Comunicaciones Horizontes, Sucre
	1	CHL	CC144	R. El Sembrador, Chillán
	1	CHL	C144A	R. Agricultura, La Serene
	0.25	CLM	HKT58	Alcaldía de Ubala, Ubala
	5	CLM	EK	Caracol R, Tuluá
	5	CLM	NZ	Colmundo, Medellín
	5	CLM	IB	R. Uno, Florencia
	5	CLM	GM	RCN Fiesta, Sogamoso
	2.8	EQA	OV5	Ondas del Volante, Azogues
	5	EQA	DF1	R. Panorama, Ibarra
	3	PRU	OCU5P	R. Cielo, Ica
	2	PRU	OBX1T	R. Cooperativa Tumán, , Tumán
	2	PRU	OAU2O	R. Frecuencia VH, Celendin
	1	PRU	OAX4K	R. Imperial 2, Lima
	1	PRU	OBU1Z	R. OBU1Z, Vice
	2.5	PRU	OCU5K	R. OCU5K, Ayacucho
	2.5	PRU	OAX6R	R. Santa Monica, Hunter, Aqp
	3	PRU	OAM7L	R. Solar, Espinar
	3/0.5	URG	CX144	R. Rivera, Rivera
	10	VEN	ZI	R. Estelar 14-40, Guanare
	5	VEN	RF	R. Orituco, Altagracia del Orituco
1450	5/1	ARG		Corrientes
	5	ARG		R. Banderas, Moreno
	1.32	ARG	LRI213	R. El Sol, Porción Quilmes
	1/0.25	ARG	LRI211	R. Las 40, Villa Aberastain
	0.5	BOL	CO39)	R. Magnal, Capinota
	1	CHL	CB145	R. Universidad Técnica , Valparaíso
	4	CHL	CC145	R. Tropical LatinaL, Curicó
	5	CLM	NL	La Cariñosa, Manizales
	0.5	CLM		LV del Cauca, El Bordo
	5	CLM	BY	Olímpica, Flandes
	5	CLM	HH	R. Católica Metropolitana, Bucaramanga
	1	CLM	MX	R. Mancomoján, Carmen de Bolívar
	1	CLM	E20	R. María, Urrao
	1	EQA	SC1	AS La Radio, Tabacundo
	1	EQA	SE2	R. Santa Elena, Santa Elena
	5	PRG	ZP29	R. Vallemi, Vallemi
	1	PRU	OBX4K	R. Fortaleza, Barranca
	1	PRU	OBU4Y	R. La Nueva Andina, Huancayo
		PRU		R. Libertad, Bambamarca
		PRU	OAU2W	R. Manantial de Vida, Cajamarca
	1	PRU	OAM4A	R. OAM4A, Tinyahuarco
	1	PRU	OBU6K	R. OBU6K, Chivay
	1	PRU	OCU6E	R. OCU6E, Ichuña
	1	PRU	OCX2J	R. San Juan, Trujillo
	10/5	URG	CX46	R. América, Montevideo
	1/0.25	URG	CW145	R. Arapey, Salto
	10/8	VEN	KJ	R. María, Caracas
	10/5	VEN	XC	R. Mega Visión, San Felix
1460	1	ARG		R. Contacto, San Antonio de Padua
		ARG		R. Jerusalén, Monte Grande
	0.25	ARG	LU30	R. Maipú, Maipú
	0.1	ARG	LU34	R. Pigüé, Pigüé
	1/0.25	ARG	LT29	R. Venado Tuerto, Venado Tuerto
		BOL	CO78)	R. Canal de Television Quillacollo

kHz	kW	Ctry	Call	Station, location
		BOL	LP138)	R. Jiwasa, Carabuco
		BOL	LP106)	R. Plenitud de Vida, El Alto
	1	CHL	CC146	R. Armonía, Talcahuano
	1	CHL	CB146	R. Palabra Viva, Santiago
	1	CLM	FL	Agustiniana Minuto de Dios, San Agustín
	0.25	CLM	HKY73	Alcaldía de San Andrés, San Andrés
		CLM	HKR44	Alcaldía de Victoria, Victoria
	5	CLM	JW	Em. Nuevo Continente, Bogotá
	5	CLM	ZU	La Cariñosa, Pasto
	1	CLM	MU	LV de Amalfi, Amalfi
	1	CLM	E26	R. Capiro, La Ceja
	5	CLM	TN	R. María, Turbo
	1	CLM	IW	R. Monumental, Cúcuta
	1	CLM	AL	R. Sincelejo, Sincelejo
	5	CLM	VH	R. Uno, Barranquilla
	5	EQA	IC6	R. Nuevos Horizontes, Latacunga
	1	PRU	OBU6R	R. Bahia, Mollendo
	0.5	PRU	OCY4I	R. Imperial, Junin
	1	PRU	OAZ4F	R. La Oroya, La Oroya
	2.5	PRU	OAU3V	R. Municipal, Cabana
		PRU	OBU7M	R. OBU7M, Marcapata
	10	PRU	OAX7W	R. Sol de los Andes, Juliaca
	1	PRU	OAX1V	R. Sullana, Sullana
	1	PRU	OCU4Y	R. Voz Cristiana, Chongo Bajo
	1	PRU	OAM5C	Rdif. Disaga, Pueblo Nuevo
	1	URG	CX146	R. Carmelo, Carmelo
	0.25	URG	CV146	R. José Batlle y Ordoñez, José Batlle y Ordoñez
	5	VEN	RJ	R. Jardín, Boconó
1470	0.7	ARG		Cadena 1470, Remedios de Escalada
	0.25	ARG	LU26	La Dorrego AM 1470, Coronel Dorrego
	1/0.25	ARG	LT20	R. Junín, Junin
		ARG		R. Lider, Mariano Acosta
	1	ARG		R. Mburucuya, José León Suarez
	1	ARG		R. Municipal, Luis Beltrán
	1/0.25	ARG	LT26	R. Nuevo Mundo, Colón
	1/0.25	ARG	LT28	R. Rafaela, Rafaela
		BOL	LP109)	R. Em. Ayni, Corapata
	1	BOL	CH29)	R. Integración, Padilla
		BOL	CO44)	R. Morochata , Morochata
	1	CHL	CB147	R. Sargento Aldea, San Antonio
	0.25	CLM	HKO96	Alcaldía de Baranoa, Baranoa
	5	CLM	PX	Colmundo, Cartagena
	0.25	CLM	JS20	Ecos de Palo Cabildo, Palo Cabildo
	5	CLM	TB	Ondas de Ibagué, Ibagué
	5	CLM	HQ	R. Futurama, Pacho
	5	CLM	NT	R. Huellas, Cali
	5	CLM	II	R. Popular, Medellín
	1	CLM	JIF	R. Tres Fronteras, Puerto Asís
	1	CLM	HJB63	R. Uno, Iza
	1.5	EQA	LD2	R. Ecos de Naranjito, Naranjito
	5	EQA	JC1	Rdif. Ecos de Cayambe, Cayambe
	1	PRU	OAU1P	R. California, Lambayeque
	20	PRU	OAU4B	R. Capital, Lima
	1	PRU	OAX7G	R. Cusco, Cusco
	1	PRU	OCY2G	R. Occidental, Quiruvilca
	0.8	PRU	OAX6M	R. Tacna, Tacna
	2.5	PRU	OAU6E	R. Victoria, Alto Selva Alegre Aqp
	1	PRU	OCU4Y	R. Voz Cristiana, Chongo Bajo
	2	URG	CX147	R. Cristal del Uruguay,Las Piedras
	1	URG	CW147	R. Maria, Melo
	10	VEN	JW	Union R. Cultural, Valencia
	10	VEN	SY	Union R. Vibración, Carúpano
1480	1	ARG	LU27	R. Centro, Dolores
	1	ARG		R. Sensaciones, Tapiales
		BOL	LP108)	LV de los Andes, Carabuco
		BOL	LP58)	R. Amor de Diós, La Paz
		BOL	PA09)	R. Bendita Trinidad y Espiritu Santo, Cobija
		BOL	CO66)	R. Bendita Trinidad y Espiritu Santo, Cochabamba
		BOL	SC48)	R. Bendita Trinidad y Espiritu Santo, Santa Cruz
	0.1	BOL	PO12)	R. Cadena Sur, Potosi
		BOL	CH24)	R. Charcas-Mundial, Sucre

kHz	kW	Ctry	Call	Station, location
	1/0.8	BOL	CO32)	R. Chiwalaqui, Vacas
		BOL	LP107)	R. Comunitaria Waley, Deaguadero
		BOL	CO40)	R. Domingo Savio, Independencia
	1	BOL	OR15)	R. San José, San José, Oruro
	1	CHL	CC148	R. La Amistad de Tomé, Tomé
	1	CHL	CA148	R. Comunicativa, Ovalle
	5	CLM	FC	R. Matecaña/R. Única, Pereira
	5	CLM	OD	R. Rodadero, Santa Marta
	1	CLM	TC	R. Sonsón, Sonsón
	5	CLM	TZ	RCN Antena 2, Bucaramanga
	3	EQA	JV4	R. LV de Jipijapa, Jipijapa
	5	EQA	CY6	R. Popular de la Maná, La Maná
	5	PRG	ZP20	R. América, Nemby
	1	PRG	ZP23	R. Dos Fronteras, Bella Vista Norte
	0.6	PRU	OCX2C	R. Comercial San Pedro, Virú
	1	PRU	OAZ7G	R. Espinar, Yauri
	1	PRU	OAU4A	R. Mineria, Santa Rosa de Sacco
	1	PRU	OAM4F	R. OAM4F, Barranca
	0.2	PRU	OBU2H	R. Santa Ana, Cutervo
	1	URG	CX148	Difusora Rio Negro, Young
	3/0.5	URG	CW43B	R. Internacional, Rivera
	3	URG	CW148	R. Universo, Castillos
		VEN		R. Cumarebo, Cumarebo
1490		ARG		AM Vida en el Espiritu, Mar del Plata
		ARG		R. AM Vida, Córdoba
		ARG		R. Ciudad de Caá Cati, José C. Paz
		ARG		R. Dif, Emanuel, Partido de Ezieza
	1.5	ARG		R. Gama, Lanús
	1/0.25	ARG	LV22	R. Huinca Renancó, Huinca Renancó
	1/0.25	ARG		Rivadavia
		BOL	LP144)	R. Wiñay Jatha, El Alto
	0.25	CHL	CB149	El Canelo, San Bernardo
	1	CHL	CA149	R. Alicanto, El Salvador
	5	CHL	CD149	R. Malleco, Victoria
	0.2	CLM	J76	Alcaldía de El Peñon, El Peñon
	0.2	CLM	HKW24	Alcaldía de Guaitarilla, Guaitarilla
	4	CLM	BS	Em. Punto Cinco, Bogotá
	1	CLM	JO	LV de San Marcos, San Marcos
	1	CLM	E62	R. Garzón, Garzón
	5	CLM	AY	R. Vida Nueva, Barranquilla
	5	CLM	ZB	Robles 14-90, La Nueva, Tuluá
	1	EQA	VY2	R. Dinámica, Guayaquil
		EQA		R. La Poderosa, Quito
	5	EQA	SM5	R. Santa María, Azogues
	2.5	EQA	AE4	R. Unión, Esmeraldas
	1	PRU	OAX8F	R. Atlántiada, Iquitos
	1.3	PRU	OAX6Q	R. Fidelidad, Cerro Colorado, Aqp
	1	PRU	OAX1L	R. Imperio, Chiclayo
	0.5	PRU	OCX4P	R. La Luz, Cerro de Pasco
	1	PRU	OAX5N	R. Nazca, Nazca
	2.5	PRU	OCU7Y	R. Nuevo Tiempo, Cusco
	1	PRU	OAM7P	R. OAM7P, Capachica
		PRU		R. Patron Santiago, Challhuacho
	2.5	PRU	OBU5C	Radiodifusora los Chankas, Andahuaylas
	1/0.25	URG	CV149	R. del Centro, Baltasar Brum
	5	URG	CX149	R. del Oeste, Nueva Helvecia
	10	VEN	XD	R. Dinámica, Caracas
	1	VEN	SQ	R. Mérida 14-90, Mérida
1500		ARG		AM Entre Mares, San Clemente del Tuyú
		ARG		Frecuencia On, La Reja
		ARG		R. 20 de Agosto, Longchamps
	2	ARG	LRI214	R. Bonaerense, Lavallol
	0.25	ARG	LT34	R. Nuclear, Zárate
	0.25	ARG		R. Olivera, General Rodriguez
		ARG		R. Vida, Río Cuarto
	5/1	BOL	LP31)	R. Chuquisaca, El Alto
		BOL	OR43)	R. Jacinto Rodriguez, Ciudad
		BOL	CO77)	R. Litoral, Cochabamba
	1	BOL	SC25)	R. Sagrado Corazón, Mineros
		BOL	TA15)	R. Universidad Juan Misael Saracho, Villamontes
	1	CHL	CC150	R. Centenario
	1	CHL	CD150	R. Tierra del Fuego, Porvenir
	1	CHL	CB150	R. Trasandina, Los Andes
	5	CLM	TW	Kirios R, Fusagasugá
	1	CLM	HKT71	Macheta
	5	CLM	UW	R. María, Manizales
	5	CLM	LJ	Sonora, La Voz de la Red, Cali
	1	EQA	RO1	R. Otavalo, Otavalo
	1	PRU	OAU6B	R. Bulevar, Tacna
	0.5	PRU	OBX2X	R. Comercial, Trujillo
	1	PRU	OBX3J	R. Luz y Sonido, Huanuco
	2	PRU	OBU2J	R. San Pablo, San Pablo
	18	PRU	OBX4I	R. Santa Rosa, Lima
	1	PRU	OCU4Q	R. Scala de Oro, Huancayo
	1	PRU	OAM7B	R. TV Cristiana, Sicuani
	10/5	VEN	RZ	R. 2000, Cumaná
1510		ARG		LV del Oeste,Libertad
		ARG		R. Alabanza, Guernica
	1/0.25	ARG	LRI253	R. Belgrano, Suardi
	2	ARG		R. Nueva Bolivia, Ciudad Madero
	1	ARG		R. RBN, Lomas de Zamora
	1/0.5	CHL	CA151	R. Luís Alvarez Sierra, Illapel
	1	CHL	CC151	R. Poder Pentecostal, Rancagua
	0.05	CHL	CD151	R. Loncoche, Loncoche
	0.25	CLM	HKZ94	Alcaldía de Buenaventura, Buenaventura
	1	CLM	HKZ93	Alcaldía de Versalles, Versalles
	1	CLM	HX	Candela AM, Bucaramanga
	1	CLM	HKY41	Colombia Mía, Barrancabermeja, SS
	5	CLM	D24	LV de La Unión, La Unión
	1	CLM	A22	LV de San Luis, San Luis de Gaceno
	1	CLM	ZA	R. Cristal, Armenia
	2	EQA	RC5	LV de la Juventud, Cañar
	5	EQA		R. Monumental, Quito
	0.5	EQA	HD2	R. Naval, Guayaquil
	1	EQA	RY6	R. Runacunapac Yachana, Simiátug
	3	PRU	OCX6Q	R. Alegria, Mariano Melgar, Aqp
	1	PRU	OBX8K	R. Centro de los Medios, Sepahua
	1	PRU	OBX7P	R. Las Vegas, Wanchaq
	1	PRU	OCU4M	R. OCU4M, San Vicente de Cañete
	1	PRU	OBU1B	R. Super Real, Olmos
	1	PRU	OCX4J	R. Tarma, Tarma
	1	PRU	OCX1V	R. Tumbes, Tumbes
	0.5	URG	CW151	R. Ibirapitá, San Gregorio de Polanco
	1/0.5	URG	CX151	R. Rincón, Fray Bentos
	2/0.5	URG	CW57	R. San Carlos, San Carlos
		VEN		RNV El Informativo, Güigüe
1520		ARG		Cadena D, Monte Chingolo
	2	ARG		LV del Sur, Luis Guillón
	5/1	ARG		R. Chascomús, Chascomús
	3	ARG		R. Cielo Nuevo, Isidro Casanova
	0.25	ARG	LT38	R. Gualeguay, Gualeguay
	1	ARG		R. Metropolitana, Ciudadela
	2	ARG		R. Norteña, Los Polvorines
	1	BOL	CO64)	R. la Chiwana, Cochabamba
		BOL	LP59)	R. La Luz del Tiempo, El Alto
	0.25	BOL	PO10)	R. Litoral, Llica
		BOL	CO73)	R. Rural, Tarata
		BOL	CO67)	R. Salesiana, Kami
		BOL	LP120)	R. San Pedro, Tiawuanaku
		BOL	CH38)	R. Universidad Juan Misael Saracho, Sucre
		BOL	CH38)	R. Universidad Juan Misael Saracho, Sucre
	1	CHL	CB152	R. Integración, San Antonio
	1	CHL	CC152	R. Soberanía, Linares
	0.25	CLM	HKT20	Alcaldía de Montería, Montería
	0.1	CLM	HKW43	Alcaldía de Tangua, Tangua
	1	CLM	RL	Antena de los Andes, Santa Rosa de Cabal
	0.3	CLM		Brisas del Palmar, Caucasia
	0.25	CLM	T21	Colombia Mía, Tierralta, CO
	1	CLM	MZ	Ecos de la Sierra Flor, Sincelejo
	1	CLM	J98	Em. Una Voz de la Frontera, Puerto Santander
	5	CLM	LI	Libertad, Bogotá
	1	CLM	MA	LV de Suroeste, Jericó
	1	CLM	AM	R. Altamizal, Dolores
	0.5	CLM	HKS24	R. Cristalares Timbío, Timbío
	5	CLM	LQ	R. Minuto, Barranquilla

kHz	kW	Ctry	Call	Station, location
	1	CLM	HKW37	R. Universidad, Pasto
		CLM		Sonoradio 1520 AM, Viterbo
	2.5	EQA	RI5	LV de Guamote, Guamote
	1	EQA	RN2	LV de Naranjal, El Naranjal
	1	EQA	TI1	R. Ibarra, Ibarra
		PRU		R Andina, Lampa
	1	PRU	OAX1C	R. Cristal, Chiclayo
	1	PRU	OCU1T	R. LV del Campesino, Ayabacha
	3	PRU	OBU5Z	R. Municipal, Castrovirreyna
		PRU	OAM4C	R. OAM4C, San Juan
	6	PRU	OBU6Z	R. OBU6Z, Mascal Nieto
	2	PRU	OCU5F	R. OCU5F, Huanta
	1	PRU	OBU7X	R. Voz Evangelica, Espinar
	2	URG	CX152	R. Acuarela, Melo
	1/0.5	URG	CV152	R. Paz, Guichón
1530	5	ARG		LV del Futuro, Merlo
	0.25	ARG	LRJ200	R. Centro Morteros, Morteros
	1.5	ARG		R. Esencia, San Miguel Oeste
	0.5	BOL	BE07)	R. Em. Ballivián, San Borja
	0.25	CHL	CD153	Puerto Montt
	1	CHL	CB153	R. Nexo, Quillota
	1	CHL	CA153	R. Vida Nueva, Copiapó
	0.25	CLM	HKN85	Alcaldía de Anza, Anza
	0.1	CLM	HKS58	Alcaldía de El Copey, El Copey
	0.25	CLM	HKN57	Alcaldía de San Juan de Uraba, San Juan de Uraba
	0.25	CLM	HKN79	Alcaldía de Uramita, Uramita
	1	CLM	HKV82	Alcaraván Radio, Puerto Lleras
	1	CLM	EU	Caracol Sevilla, Sevilla
	0.25	CLM	HKN65	Colombia Mía, Caucasia, AN
	1	CLM	HKR73	Ecos del Pacífico, Guapí
		CLM	HKS56	Fascinación AM, Becerril
	5	CLM	OZ	LV de la Prov. de Padilla, San Juan del Cesar
		CLM		R. Integración, Morales
	5	CLM	DN	Yeshu'a LV de Jesucristo, Medellín
	5	EQA	MP2	LV de la Península, La Libertad
	1	EQA	MZ6	R. Dorado Deportes, Pelileo
	3	EQA	VP5	R. LV de Pallatanga, Pallatanga
	5	EQA	CC5	R. Universitaria Católica, Azogues
	1	PRU	OBZ4S	R. 15-50, Huancayo
	1	PRU	OAM2Q	R. Charles, Bambamarca
	10	PRU	OBU4C	R. Milenia, Lima
	1	PRU	OBU7N	R. Ondas del Sur Oriente, Quillabamba
	3	PRU	OBX2R	R. Oriental, Jaén
	1	PRU	OAU5R	R. Universidad San Juan Bautista, Subtanjalla
	0.5	PRU	OAZ7F	Rdif. Espinar , Yauri
	0.25	URG	CW153	Em. Cono Sur, Nueva Palmira
	10	VEN	NP	R. San Felipe el Fuerte, San Felipe
1540	1	ARG		R. AM Líder, Benavidez
	1	ARG		R. Amanecer, Ciudad Evita
	0.25	ARG	LT35	R. Mon, Pergamino
	0.25	ARG	LU28	R. Tuyú
		ARG		R. Zorobabel, Esteban Echeverría
		BOL	LP67)	R. Bendita Trinidad y Espiritu Santo, El Alto
		BOL	CH37)	R. Comunitaria Rio Chico, Sucre
		BOL	LP112)	R. Comunitario Tutuka, Vilaque
	0.8	BOL	LP34)	R. Sariri, Escoma
	1	CHL	CC154	Chillán
	1	CHL	CD154	R. San José de Alcudia, Río Bueno
	1	CHL	CB154	R. Sudamérica, Santiago
	0.25	CHL	HKP50	Alcaldía de Arjona, Arjona
	0.15	CLM	HKR80	Alcaldía de Sacama, Sacama
	1	CLM	HKZ52	Colombia Mía, Chaparral, TO
	1	CLM	A26	Em. Brisas del Río Chico, Belmira
	1	CLM	HD	LV del Petróleo, Barrancabermeja
	2	CLM	RQ	R. Austral, Túquerres
	5	CLM	ZF	R. Cóndor, Manizales
	1	EQA	DP1	R. Caracol, Quito
	3	EQA	FM2	R. Cristal de Ventanas, Babahoyo
	0.25	EQA	VB7	R. LV del Upano, Macas
	1	PRU	OAM4G	R. Angie@Net, Barranca
	0.3	PRU	OBX4N	R. Corporacion, Cerro de Pasco
	1	PRU	OCX7V	R. Los Andes, Cusco
	1	PRU	OBX1B	R. LV de la Frontera, Tumbes
	1	PRU	OAU6A	R. Milenio Universal, Alto Selva Alegre
	2	PRU	OBU2A	R. Mundial AM, Trujillo
	1	PRU	OCU6H	R. OCU6H, Pocollay
	5	PRU	OCU2X	R. Turbomix, Cajamarca
	1	URG	CV154	R. Centro, Cardona
	0.1	URG	CW154	R. Charrúa, Paysandú
	0.5/0.25	URG	CX154	R.Patria, Treinta y Tres
1550		ARG		Estacion Quince Cincuenta, Villa Florito
	0.25	ARG	LT32	R. Chivilcoy, Chivilcoy
		ARG		R. Esperanza, Gregorio de Laferrere
		ARG		R. La Amistad, José C. Paz
	1	ARG	LT40	R. LV de la Paz, La Paz
		ARG		R. Popular, José León Suárez
	5/0.25	ARG	LT23	R. Regional, San Jenaro Norte
	10	BOL	LP28)	R. Caranavi, Caranavi
	1	CHL	CC155	R. Manuel Rodríguez, San Fernando
	1	CHL	CB155	R. Provincial AM, Putaendo
	0.1	CLM	HKW53	Alcaldía de El Tablón, El Tablón
	0.1	CLM	HKW55	Alcaldía de Guachucal, Guachucal
	0.25	CLM	HKW50	Alcaldía de Mallama, Mallama
	1	CLM	HKV38	Colombia Mía, Pitalito, HU
	5	CLM	HKX29	Colombia Mía, Tibú, NS
	5	CLM	LT	Em. Revivir en Cristo, Cali
	5	CLM	ZI	G12 Radio, Bogotá
	5	CLM	UN	LV del Río Arma, Aguadas
	5	CLM	CB	R. El Sol, Barranquilla
	5	CLM	QD	Vida, Calarcá
	5	EQA	AD5	LV de Chaguarurco, Santa Isabel
	2	EQA	AD2	LV del Triunfo, El Triunfo
	1	PRU	OAM7D	R . San Sebastian, Livitaca
	1	PRU	OAU3D	R. Cruz, Chimbote
	5	PRU	OBX4P	R. Independencia, Independencia
	1	PRU	OCU1B	R. La Clave, Castilla
	3	PRU	OAU5Z	R. La Luz del Mundo, Subtanjalla
	1	PRU	OBX5J	R. Maria, Huamanaga
	1	PRU	OCU1W	R. OCU1W, Monsefú
	0.25	URG	CV155	R. Agraciada, Mercedes
	2/0.5	URG	CW155	R. Sarandí del Yí, Sarandí del Yí
	10/5	VEN	XO	R. Impacto La Poderosa, Cd. Ojeda
1560	05/0.25	ARG		AM 1560, Tandil
	1/0.25	ARG		Mendoza
	0.25	ARG	LT33	R. 9 de Julio, 9 de Julio
	1	ARG		R. Antena, Lobos
	1.5	ARG		R. Castañares, Ituzaingó
	2.5/1.5	ARG	LT11	R. Gral. Francisco Ramírez, Concepción del Uruguay
		ARG		R. Restauración, Llavallol
	5	BOL	LP149)	R. Luz del Mundo, La Paz
	1	BOL	OR19)	R. Occidental, Oruro
	0.5	BOL	CO27)	R. Urkupiña, Quillacollo
	1	CHL	CB156	R. Manantial, Talagante
	5/3	CHL	CA156	R. Parinacota, Putre
	1	CHL	CD156	R. Parque, Villarrica
	0.25	CLM	HK035	Alcaldía de Cañasgordas, Cañasgordas
	0.25	CLM	HKV90	Alcaldía de Villavicencio, Villavicencio
	5	CLM	LP	La Cariñosa, Antena 2, Tuluá
	1	CLM	PZ	R. Codazzi, Codazzi
	0.5	CLM	HKS65	R. Tamalameque, Tamalameque
	5	CLM	CP	RCN Antena 2, Arbeláez
	5	CLM	XZ	Santa María de la Paz R., Medellín
	5	CLM	HE	Voces Rovirenses, Málaga
	1.5	EQA	ZD1	Ecos Culturales de Urcuquí, Urcuquí
	1	PRU	OAZ7N	R. Maria, Wanchaq
	1	PRU	OAM2I	R. OAM2I, Cajabamba
	2.5	PRU	OCU4Z	R. OCU4Z, Hualhuas
	1	PRU	OCU6K	R. OCU6K, Alto de la Alianza
	1	PRU	OCX6N	R. Sabor, Marino Melgar, Aqp
	2/0.5	URG	CX156	Dif. Americana, Trinidad
	3/0.5	URG	CW51	R. Maldonado, Maldonado
	1	URG	CV156	R. Vichadero
	10/5	VEN	LZ	RNV El Informativo, Mérida
1570		ARG		R. Alegría Regional, Luis Palacio
	1	ARG		R. AM Rocha, Tolosa

kHz	kW	Ctry	Call	Station, location
		ARG		R. La Morena de Itati, Grand Bourg
	2.5	ARG		R. Melody, Remedios de Escalada
		BOL	LP101)	R. Comunitaria Tawantinsuyo, Taraco
		BOL	BE23)	R. Pedro Ignacio Muiba
	1	CHL	CC157	R. Cristo Llama Al Pecador, Rancagua
	1	CHL	CC157A	R. Familia del Maule, Talca
	0.25	CLM	HKX78	Alcaldía de Balboa, Balboa
	0.15	CLM	HKU42	Alcaldía de Cajica, Cajica
	0.25	CLM	HKQ83	Alcaldía de Maripi, Maripi
	0.25	CLM	HKQ82	Alcaldía de Sta María, Sta María
	0.25	CLM	HKP58	Alcaldía de Sta Rosa Sur, Sta Rosa Sur
	2	CLM	HKX52	Arc. Armada de Colombia, Pto Leguizamo
	1	CLM	E96	Colombia Mía, Palmira, VA
	1	CLM	E70	R. Auténtica, Manizales
	1	CLM	HK022	R. Ciudad Dabeiba, Dabeiba
	1	CLM	TG	R. María, Machetá
	0.1	CLM	HKX80	R. Marsella, Marsella
	0.2	CLM	HKR66	R. Universidad de la Amazonia, Florencia
	0.5	CLM	HJR66	Timbiqui Estéreo, Timbiqui
	1	EQA		R. LV Espíritu Santo de Dios, Manta
	25	PRU	OCU4J	Bethel R., Lima
	1	PRU	OAU7Z	R. Carraviz, Juliaca
		PRU	OBU2L	R. Colonial, Contumaza
	1	PRU	OCX1Z	R. La Nueva Esperanza, Tambo Grande
	2.5	PRU	OCU5O	R. Musuq Chaski Radio, Huamanga
	1	PRU	OAM5H	R. OAM5H, Chinca Alta
	1	PRU	OBU3A	R. OBU3A. Cerro Jactay
	1	PRU	OCU7L	R. Vilcanota, Sicuani
	1	PRU	OCU2C	Radiodifusora Julcan, Otuzco
	1	URG	CW157A	Em. Celeste, Tomás Gomensoro
	2/0.5	URG	CX157	R. Canelones
1580	1	ARG		R. 26. de Julio, Longchamps
	0.25	ARG	LT36	R. Chacabuco, Chacabuco
		ARG		R. Cóndor, Moreno
	1	ARG		R. La Cueva, 25 de Mayo
	1	ARG	LT27	R. LV del Montiel, Villaguay
		ARG		R. Provincial de Sierra Colorada, Sierra Colorada
	2	ARG		R. Tradición, San Martín
		BOL	CO75)	LV del Valle, Valle Alto
	1	BOL	SC29)	R. Adonai, Santa Cruz
	3	BOL	TA07)	R. Bermejo, Bermejo
		BOL	OR35)	R. Comunitaria Jacinto Rodriguez, Caracolla
		BOL	CH28)	R. Contacto, Sucre
		BOL	LP62)	R. El Fuego del Espíritu Santo, El Alto
		BOL	TA20)	R. Magazine Tarija, Tarija
	1	CHL	CC158	R. Colchagua, Santa Cruz
	0.25	CLM	HKU42	Alcaldía de Cajica, Cajica
	0.1	CLM	HKW74	Alcaldía de Pupiales, Pupiales
	0.25	CLM	HKT34	Alcaldía de San Antero, San Antero
		CLM		Alcaldía de Yaguará, Yaguará
	5	CLM	RM	Caracol R, Sincelejo
	1	CLM	E66	Celestial 15-80, Rovira
	1	CLM	LC	LV del Banco, El Banco
	0.15	CLM	HKS46	R. Alcaldía de Padilla, Padilla
	5	CLM	QZ	R. María, Barranquilla
	1	CLM	KB	R. Zulima, Villa del Rosario
	5	CLM	QT	Verdad R, Bogotá
	3	EQA	TP5	Ecos del Portete, Girón
	1	EQA	LF1	R. Orellana, Machachi
	1	PRU	OBX1M	R. Naylamp, Lambayeque
	1	PRU	OBU6S	R. OBU6S, Orcopampa
	1	PRU	OAU4P	R. San Juan, Tarma
	1	PRU	OAU5J	R. Virgen del Carmen, Huancavelica
	2/0.5	URG	CW54	Emisoras del Este, Minas
	1/0.5	URG	CW158	R. San Salvador, Dolores
	10/5	VEN	YV	R. Venezolana, Calabozo
1590	1	ARG		R. Dolores, Dolores

kHz	kW	Ctry	Call	Station, location
	1	ARG		R. Sin Fronteras, Merlo
		ARG		R. Stentor, Buenos Aires
		BOL	LP61)	R. Kollasuyo Marka, Tiawanaku
	1	BOL	CO24)	R. Wayana Songo, Pongo K´asa
	0.1	CHL	CC159A	Parral
	1	CHL	CB159	R. Aconcagua, San Felipe
		CLM	HKS72	Alcaldía de La Gloria, La Gloria
	5	CLM	IP	BBN 15-90 R., Envigado
	1	CLM	QM	Ecos de la Miel, Samaná
	5	CLM	WB	Em Nuestra Sra del Socorro, Socorro
	1	EQA	RZ1	R. Mensaje, Cayambe
	1	EQA	QT6	R. Panamericana, Quero
	1	PRU	OAU7C	R. Asillo, Azangaro
	1	PRU	OBU2C	R. Bendicion, Trujillo
	1	PRU	OCX6S	R. Mundo, Arequipa
		PRU		R. Municipal, San Marcos
	1	PRU	OBU5F	R. OBU5F, Lucanas
	1.5	PRU	OAZ4Z	R. Vida, Lima
	1/0.25	URG	CW159	R. Nueva R. Lascano, Lascano
	1	URG	CX159	R. Real, Colonia
	10	VEN	UD	R. Deporte, Caracas
1600	0.25	ARG		AM 1600 Del Centro, Montes de Oca
	1	ARG		R. Armonia, Caseros
	1	BOL	LP63)	R. LV del Espíritu Santo, El Alto
	0.5	BOL	CO28)	R. P.C.A., Punata
	0.25	CHL	CD160	R. Alternativa, Temuco
	0.25	CHL	CC160	R. Llacolén, Concepción
	0.25	CHL	CB160	R. Nuevo Tiempo, Santiago
	0.25	CHL	CB160A	R. Positiva, Viña del Mar
	0.15	CLM	HKZ79	Alcaldía de Cajamarca, Cajamarca
	0.25	CLM	HKO63	Alcaldía de Jardín, Jardín
	0.25	CLM	HKX83	Alcaldía de La Celia, Celia
	0.25	CLM	HKT39	Alcaldía de Valencia, Valencia
	0.15	CLM	HKZ77	Alcaldía de Venadillo, Venadillo
	5	CLM	HJO72	Colombia Mía, Carepa, AN
	5	CLM	HV	Emisora Armoniaz, Zipaquirá
	0.25	CLM	HKR52	LV de Colina, Risaralda
	0.25	CLM	F33	R. Restauración, Cali
		PRU		R. Andina, Velille
	2.5	PRU	OBU4R	R. Nuevo Tiempo, Huancayo
	3	PRU	OBM7A	R. OBM7A, Wanchaq
	1	URG	CV160	R. Continental, Pando
	1	URG	CX160	R. Litoral, Fray Bentos
1610	0.5	ARG		R. Comunitaria Regional, Laboulaye
	0.2	ARG		R. Fósil, Rosario
	1	ARG		R. Guabiyú, Gregorio de Laferrere
	0.5	PRU	OAU6O	R. Flor de los Andes, Paucarpata
		PRU		R. Inka, Acora
1620	10/1	ARG		AM 16-20 La Radio, Mar del Plata
		ARG		R. Sentires,Merlo
	2	ARG		R. Vida, Monte Grande
1630	10	ARG		AM Diagonal, La Plata
	1	ARG		R. Restauración, Hurlingham
	1/0.25	ARG		R. America, San José
1640	1	ARG		R. Hosanna Argentina, Isidro Casanova
		PRU		R. Kalikanto, Chamaca
1650	1/0.5	ARG	LRI227	Antares AM 1650, Pilar
		ARG		R. El Mensajero, Rafael Castillo
		ARG		R. Fenix. Temperley
1660	5/0.25	ARG		Nogoyá
	1/0.25	ARG		Paso de los Libres
	1	ARG		R. Revivir, Gregorio de la Ferrere
1670		ARG		R. Bethel, Banfield
		ARG		R. Gratitud, Glew
1680		ARG		R. Santa Fe, Canning
1690	1	ARG		R. Cristo la Solución, San Justo
1700	5/1	ARG		R. Fantastico, Tigre
		ARG		R. Imagen, Castelar
1710	0.3	ARG		AM 1710/R. Urquiza, Buenos Aires

SHORTWAVE STATIONS
OF THE WORLD

November 2015 - World Copyright WRTH Publications Ltd

For country and site codes, see relevant tables in reference section. Stations marked as '**dom**' in the site column are domestic/national broadcasts. Stations marked with '**STF**' in the site column are Standard Time/Frequency transmissions. The column '**N**' indicates Notes. Symbols used in the '**N**' column are '**+**', indicating DRM transmissions; '**±**' which indicates variable frequency; '**†**' for irregular transmissions and **‡** for frequencies that were inactive at the editorial deadline.

kHz	N	kW	Ctry	Site	Station, location
2325		50	AUS	dom	N. Terr. SW Sce, Tennant Creek
2350	†	5	KRE	dom	KCBS/Reg., Sariwon
2368	†	0.4	AUS	dom	R. Symban, Sydney
2380	†	0.25	B	dom	R. Educadora, Limeira
2485		50	AUS	dom	N. Terr. SW Sce, Katherine
2500		10	CHN	STF	BPM, Kinshan
		2.5	USA	STF	WWV NIST, Fort Collins, CO
		5	HWA	STF	WWVH NIST, Kauai, HI
2850		50	KRE	dom	KCBS, Pyongyang
3185		100	USA	WRB	The Overcomer Ministry
		100	USA	WRB	WWRB
3195		100	USA	WCR	WWCR
	‡	100	USA	WRB	WWRB
3200		25	SWZ	MAN	TWR Africa
		50	SWZ	MAN	TWR Africa
3205	‡	10	PNG	dom	NBC Sandaun, Vanimo
3215		100	USA	WCR	WWCR
	‡	100	USA	WRB	WWRB
3220		5	KRE	dom	KCBS/Reg., Hamhung
3235	‡	10	PNG	dom	NBC West New Britain, Kimbe
3240		50	SWZ	MAN	TWR Africa
3250		100	KRE	PYO	Pyongyang Broadcasting Stn.
	‡	1	HND	dom	R. Luz y Vida, San Luís
		100	KRE	PYO	Voice of Korea
3255		100	AFS	MEY	BBC World Service
3260	†	10	PNG	dom	NBC Madang, Madang
3275	†	10	PNG	dom	NBC Sthn Highlands, Mendi
3280	‡	2	EQA	dom	LV del Napo, Tena
3290	‡	10	PNG	dom	NBC Central, Port Moresby
	†	1	GUY	dom	NCN VO Guyana, Georgetown
3305	‡	10	PNG	dom	NBC Western, Daru
3310		10	BOL	dom	R. Mosoj Chaski, Cochabamba
3315	‡	10	PNG	dom	NBC Manus, Lorengau
3320		50	KRE	PYO	Pyongyang Broadcasting Stn.
		100	AFS	dom	R. Sonder Grense, Meyerton
3325	‡	10	PNG	dom	NBC Bougainville, Buka
	†	10	INS	dom	RRI, Palangkaraya
3330		3	CAN	STF	CHU, Ottawa
		5	PRU	dom	R. Ondas de Huallaga, Huánuco
3335	‡	10	PNG	dom	NBC East Sepik, Wewak
3340	‡	2	HND	dom	R. Misiones Int., Comayagüela
3345		100	AFS	MEY	Channel Africa
	‡	10	PNG	dom	NBC Northern, Popondetta
3355	‡	10	PNG	dom	NBC Simbu, Kundiawa
3365	†	10	PNG	dom	NBC Milne Bay, Alotau
		1	B	dom	R. Cultura, Araraquara
3375	†	1	B	dom	R. Municipal, São Gabriel Cach.
3385	‡	10	PNG	dom	NBC E. New Britain, Rabaul
3480		50	KOR	GOY	Voice of the People
3900		5	CHN	dom	Hulun Buir PBS, Hailar
3905	‡	10	PNG	dom	NBC New Ireland, Kavieng

kHz	N	kW	Ctry	Site	Station, location
3912		50	KOR	GOY	Voice of the People
3915		100	SNG	SNG	BBC World Service
	‡	1	PNG	dom	R. Fly, Kiunga
3925		10	J	dom	R. Nikkei 1, Sapporo
3945		10	J	dom	R. Nikkei 2, Tokyo
	†	1	VUT	dom	R. Vanuatu, Port Vila
3950		100	CHN	dom	Xinjiang PBS, Urumqi
3955	+	250	G	WOF	BBC World Service
		250	G	WOF	KBS World Radio
		250	G	WOF	Radio Taiwan International
3959		5	KRE	dom	KCBS/Reg., Kanggye
3964	±†	5	KRE	CHJ	Echo of Unification
3965	+	1	F	ISS	Radio France Int. (RFI)
3970	±	5	KRE	dom	KCBS/Reg., Wonsan
3975		100	CVA	SMG	Vatican Radio
3985		100	CHN	dom	CNR2 Business R, Golmud
		100	KOR	SUW	Echo of Hope (VOH)
		1	D	KLL	R. Mi Amigo Int.
		1	D	KLL	Radio 700
		1	D	KLL	Radio Belarus
		1	D	KLL	Radio Bulgaria
		1	D	KLL	Radio Slovakia Int.
		1	D	KLL	RadioDienst Polska
		1	D	KLL	Voice of Mongolia
3990	†	15	CHN	dom	Gannan PBS, Hezuo
		100	CHN	dom	Xinjiang PBS, Urumqi
3995		1.5	D	WNM	HCJB Deutschland
		1.5	D	WNM	Lutherische Stunde
		1.5	D	WNM	Missionwerk Heukelbach
	†	100	PAK	ISL	VO Jammu Kashmir Fr Mov.
4010		100	KGZ	dom	KGR1, Bishkek
4055	†	0.7	GTM	dom	R. Verdad, Chiquimula
4363		10	F	MCR	Radio Monaco
4410	†	0.5	BOL	dom	R. Eco, Reyes
4450	‡	50	KOR	GOY	Voice of the People
4451		1	BOL	dom	R. Santa Ana, SA del Yacuma
4500		50	CHN	dom	Xinjiang PBS, Urumqi
4557		50	KOR	GOY	Voice of the People
4700		1	BOL	dom	R. San Miguel, Riberalta
4717		1	BOL	dom	R. Yura, Yura
4750	†	100	BGD	dom	Bangladesh Betar, Savar
		100	CHN	dom	CNR1 VO China, Hailar
	†	1	UGA	dom	Dunamis SW, Mukono
	†	50	INS	dom	RRI, Makassar
4751	±	0.5	PRU	dom	R. Huanta 2000, Huanta
4755	‡	10	B	dom	R. Imaculada Conceição, C. Grande
4756	†	1	FSM	dom	PMA The Cross, Kolonia
4760	†	10	IND	dom	AIR Leh
	†	4	IND	dom	AIR Port Blair
	‡	1	LBR	dom	ELWA R, Monrovia
		50	SWZ	MAN	TWR Africa

kHz	N	kW	Ctry	Site	Station, location
4765	†	10	B	dom	R. Integração, Cruzeiro do Sul
		50	CUB	dom	R. Progreso, Bejucal
	†	10	B	dom	R. Rural, Santarem
		50	TJK	dom	Tajik R, Yangiyul
4775	‡	50	IND	dom	AIR Imphal
	†	1	B	dom	R. Congonhas, Congonhas
	†	1	PRU	dom	R. Tarma, Tarma
		50	SWZ	MAN	TWR Africa
4780	‡	50	DJI	dom	RTD, Djibouti
4782	‡	3	EQA	dom	R. Oriental, Tena
4785	†	10	B	dom	R. Caiari, Porto Velho
4790		100	TJK	DSB	BBC World Service
		0.5	PRU	dom	R. Visión, Chiclayo
4800	†	50	IND	dom	AIR Hyderabad
		100	CHN	dom	CNR1 VO China, Golmud
	‡	1	MEX	dom	R. Transcontinental, México
4805		5	B	dom	R. Dif. do Amazonas, Manaus
4810		50	IND	dom	AIR Bhopal
		100	ARM	ERV	Public Radio of Armenia (FS)
		1	PRU	dom	R. Logos, Chazuta
4815		10	B	dom	R. Dif. Londrina, Londrina
4820		50	IND	dom	AIR Kolkata
		15	KGZ	dom	KGR1, Bishkek
		100	CHN	dom	Xizang PBS, Lhasa
4824		10	PRU	dom	LV de la Selva, Iquitos
4825	†	10	B	dom	R. Canção Nova, Cach. Paulista
	‡	5	B	dom	R. Educadora, Bragança
4827		0.3	PRU	dom	R. Sicuani, Sicuani
4830	‡	10	MNG	dom	Mongolian R. 1, Altay
		50	CHN	dom	VO Strait, Fuzhou
4835		10	IND	dom	AIR Gangtok
		50	AUS	dom	N. Terr. SW Sce, Alice Springs
		1	PRU	dom	Ondas del Suroriente, Quillab.
4840		100	USA	WCR	WWCR
4845		10	B	dom	R. Cultura, Manaus
	†	1	B	dom	R. Met. Paulista, Ibitinga
4850	†	50	IND	dom	AIR Kohima
		100	CHN	dom	Xinjiang PBS, Urumqi
4851		1	PRU	dom	R. Genesis, Huanta
4860	‡	50	IND	dom	AIR Shimla
4865	†	5	B	dom	R. Alvorada, Londrina
		5	B	dom	R. Verdes Florestas, Cruzeiro
4870		100	IND	DEL	All India Radio (AIR)
		100	IND	DEL	Radio Sedayee Kashmir
		10	INS	dom	RRI, Wamena
4875		10	B	dom	R. Dif. Roraima, Boa Vista
4880		50	IND	dom	AIR Lucknow
	‡		PRU	dom	R. JPJ, Lima
4885	†	1	B	dom	A Voz do Coração Im., Anápolis
		2	B	dom	R. Clube do Pará, Belém
	†	5	B	dom	R. Dif. Acreana, Rio Branco
4895		50	IND	dom	AIR Kurseong
		100	AFS	MEY	Amateur R. Today
	‡	10	MNG	dom	Mongolian R. 2, Mörön
	‡	5	B	dom	R. Novo Tempo, Campo Grande
4900	‡	1	GUI	dom	R. Familia, Timbi-Madina
4905		5	B	dom	Nova R. Relógio, Rio de Janeiro
	‡	1	B	dom	R. Anhanguera, Araguaína
		100	CHN	dom	Xizang PBS, Lhasa
4910		50	IND	dom	AIR Jaipur
		50	AUS	dom	N. Terr. SW Sce, Tennant Creek
4915		10	B	dom	R. Daqui, Goiânia
	†	10	B	dom	R. Dif, Macapá
4920		50	IND	dom	AIR Chennai
		100	CHN	dom	Xizang PBS, Lhasa
4925		5	B	dom	R. Educação Rural, Tefé
4930		100	BOT	BOT	BBG - VO America (VOA)
		100	BOT	BOT	BBG - VOA Studio 7
4940		100	STP	SAO	BBG - VO America (VOA)
	†	1	PRU	dom	R. San Antonio, Villa Atalaya
		50	CHN	dom	VO Strait News Ch, Fuzhou
4950	†	50	IND	dom	AIR Kashmir, Srinagar
		25	AGL	dom	R. Nal de Angola, Mulenvos
4955	‡	5	PRU	dom	R. Cultural Amauta, Huanta
4958	†	3	BOL	dom	R. Tropico, Trinidad
4960		100	STP	SAO	BBG - VO America (VOA)
4965		5	B	dom	R. Alvorada, Parintins
4970		50	IND	dom	AIR Shillong
4975		10	CHN	dom	Fujian PBS, Fuzhou
	†	5	PRU	dom	Pacífico R, Lima
	†	1	B	dom	R. Apolo, São Paulo
4976	‡	10	UGA	dom	UBC R. Red channel, Kampala
4980		100	CHN	dom	Xinjiang PBS, Urumqi
4985	†	10	B	dom	R. Brasil Central, Goiânia
4986	±	1	PRU	dom	R. Voz Cristiana, Huancayo
4990		10	CHN	dom	Hunan PBS, Xiangtan
	†	1	SUR	dom	R. Apintie, Paramaribo
4996		5	RUS	STF	RWM, Moscow
5000		20	CHN	STF	BPM, Kinshan
		2	KOR	STF	HLA Daejeon
		10	USA	STF	WWV NIST, Fort Collins, CO
		10	HWA	STF	WWVH NIST, Kauai, HI
5005	†	50	GNE	dom	Rdif Guinea Ecuatorial, Bata
5010		50	IND	dom	AIR, Thiruvananthapuram
		100	TWN	KOU	Radio Taiwan International
5011	†±	10	MDG	dom	R. Nal Malagasy, Ambohidrano
5014		1	PRU	dom	R. Altura, Cerro de Pasco
5015		1	B	dom	R. Cultura AM, Cuiabá
5020		10	SLM	dom	Solomon Islands BC, Honiara
5025		50	AUS	dom	N. Terr. SW Sce, Katherine
		5	PRU	dom	R. Quillabamba, Quillabamba
		50	CUB	dom	R. Rebelde, Bauta
5030	‡	100	BFA	dom	RTB, Ouagadougou
5035	†	5	B	dom	R Educação Rural, Coari
		10	B	dom	R. Aparecida, Aparecida
	Pl.	10	CAF	dom	R. Centrafrique, Bangui
5039	‡	1	PRU	dom	R. Libertad, Junín
5040		50	IND	dom	AIR Jeypore
		100	CUB	HAB	Radio Habana Cuba
5050	†	10	IND	dom	AIR Aizawl
		50	CHN	NNN	Beibu Bay Radio
	†	100	USA	WRB	The Overcomer Ministry
		100	USA	WRB	WWRB
5060	‡	1	PRU	dom	LV de Huarinjas, Huancabamba
		100	CHN	dom	Xinjiang PBS, Urumqi
5066		1	COD	dom	R. Télé Candip, Bunia
5070		100	USA	WCR	WWCR
5110		50	USA	BCQ	The Overcomer Ministry
		50	USA	BCQ	WBCQ
5130	†	15	KGZ	BIS	Shortwave Relay Sce.
5460	†		PRU	dom	R. Bolivar, Ciudad Bolivar
5580		† 0.25	BOL	dom	R. San José, SJ de Chiquitos
5688		† 0.03	URG	dom	Em. Chaná, Tacuarembó
5745		250	USA	GRV	BBG - VO America (VOA)
5810		250	USA	EWN	WEWN - EWTN Shortwave
5820		125	MDG	MDC	RTÉ Radio Worldwide
5825		200	TJK	DSB	BBG - R. Free Asia (RFA)
5830		200	TJK	DSB	BBG - R. Free Asia (RFA)

kHz	N	kW	Ctry	Site	Station, location
		100	USA	TWW	WTWW
5845	+	100	THA	NAK	BBC World Service
5850		100	USA	YFR	FG Radio (ex EUNN)
		100	USA	YFR	Radio Slovakia Int.
		100	USA	YFR	Radio Ukraine Int. (RUI)
		100	USA	YFR	Trunews Radio
		100	USA	YFR	WRMI - R. Miami Int.
5855		250	THA	NAK	BBC World Service
		250	MRA	TIN	BBG - R. Free Asia (RFA)
5865		250	CLN	IRA	BBG - R. Farda
		100	D	LAM	BBG - R. Farda
		250	KWT	KWT	BBG - R. Farda
		250	USA	GRV	BBG - VO America (VOA)
		500	F	ISS	Radio Algeriénne
5875		250	ASC	ASC	BBC World Service
		250	G	WOF	BBC World Service
		250	THA	NAK	BBC World Service
		300	THA	NAK	BBC World Service
		250	PHL	PHT	BBG - VO America (VOA)
		250	THA	UDO	R. Thailand World Service
5885		100	D	BIB	BBG - RFE/RL
		100	D	LAM	BBG - RFE/RL
		250	THA	UDO	BBG - RFE/RL
		250	CLN	IRA	BBG - VO America (VOA)
		250	CVA	SMG	BBG - VO America (VOA)
	‡	100	PAK	ISL	Radio Pakistan
5890		250	THA	NAK	BBC World Service
		100	USA	WCR	The Overcomer Ministry
		100	USA	WCR	WWCR
5895		0.05	NOR	ERD	LKB LLB Bergen Kringkaster
		0.05	NOR	ERD	R. Northern Star
5900		500	IRN	KAM	VO the Islamic Rep. of Iran
5905		250	THA	NAK	BBC World Service
		500	UAE	DHA	BBG - R. Free Asia (RFA)
		100	CHN	KAS	China Radio Int. (CRI)
		10	D	PIN	Deutscher Wetterdienst (DWD)
		100	UZB	TAC	IBRA Radio
5910	†	5	CLM	dom	Alcaraván R, Puerto Lleras
		250	OMA	SLA	BBC World Service
		500	CHN	BEI	China Radio Int. (CRI)
		100	LTU	SIT	Radio Japan (NHK World)
		300	ROU	TIG	Radio Romania International
		100	AUT	MOS	TWR Europe
5915		100	CHN	HUH	China Radio Int. (CRI)
		100	CHN	KAS	China Radio Int. (CRI)
		500	CHN	BEI	China Radio Int. (CRI)
		50	BRM	dom	Myanma R., Naypyitaw
	†	100	ZMB	dom	ZNBC R. One, Lusaka
5920		300	ROU	GAL	Radio Romania International
		250	USA	HRI	The Overcomer Ministry
		250	USA	HRI	Trunews Radio
		500	IRN	KAM	VO the Islamic Rep. of Iran
		250	USA	HRI	WHRI - World Harvest R.
5921		1	PRU	dom	Bethel R, Arequipa
5925		100	D	LAM	BBG - RFE/RL
		100	CHN	dom	CNR5 VO Zhonghua, Beijing
		500	F	ISS	Radio France Int. (RFI)
		500	IRN	SIR	VO the Islamic Rep. of Iran
		50	VTN	dom	VO Vietnam 2, Xuan Mai
5930		300	AUT	MOS	BBC World Service
		250	OMA	SLA	BBC World Service
	+	300	ROU	TIG	Radio Romania International
		500	IRN	KAM	VO the Islamic Rep. of Iran
5935		300	ROU	TIG	Radio Romania International

kHz	N	kW	Ctry	Site	Station, location
		100	USA	WCR	University Network
		500	IRN	SIR	VO the Islamic Rep. of Iran
		100	USA	WCR	WWCR
		100	CHN	dom	Xizang PBS, Lhasa
5940		250	D	NAU	Bible Voice Broadcasting (BVB)
		250	UAE	DHA	IBRA Radio
	+	300	ROU	TIG	Radio Romania International
		500	IRN	SIR	VO the Islamic Rep. of Iran
		10	B	dom	Voz Missionária, Camboriú
5945		250	OMA	SLA	BBC World Service
		100	CHN	dom	CNR1 VO China, Beijing
	+	100	ROU	TIG	Radio Romania International
		100	ROU	TIG	Radio Romania International
		75	ROU	TIG	Radio Romania International
		500	IRN	SIR	VO the Islamic Rep. of Iran
5950		100	USA	YFR	Adventist World R. (AWR)
		100	D	NAU	Bible Voice Broadcasting (BVB)
		100	USA	YFR	Family Radio
		500	F	ISS	KBS World Radio
		500	IRN	KAM	VO the Islamic Rep. of Iran
		500	IRN	SIR	VO the Islamic Rep. of Iran
		100	ETH	dom	VO Tigray Revolution, Geja
5952		5	BOL	dom	R. Pío XII, Siglo Veinte
5955		150	CHN	BEI	China Radio Int. (CRI)
		500	CHN	XIA	China Radio Int. (CRI)
		100	ROU	TIG	Radio Romania International
		100	AUT	MOS	Voice of Vietnam (VOV)
5960		250	OMA	SLA	BBC World Service
		150	ALB	CER	China Radio Int. (CRI)
		500	F	ISS	Radio Japan (NHK World)
		500	TUR	EMR	Voice of Turkey (VOT)
		100	CHN	dom	Xinjiang PBS, Urumqi
5965		500	CHN	BEI	China Radio Int. (CRI)
		500	CHN	XIA	China Radio Int. (CRI)
	†	8	B	dom	R. Transmundial, Santa Maria
	†	50	MLA	dom	RTM R. Klasik, Kajang
		250	UAE	DHA	TWR Africa
		500	IRN	SIR	VO the Islamic Rep. of Iran
		500	TUR	EMR	Voice of Turkey (VOT)
5970		300	AUT	MOS	AWR Africa/Europe
		250	OMA	SLA	BBC World Service
		150	ALB	CER	China Radio Int. (CRI)
		15	CHN	dom	Gannan PBS, Hezuo
		500	TUR	EMR	Voice of Turkey (VOT)
5975		100	F	ISS	AWR Africa/Europe
		250	G	WOF	BBC World Service
		250	UAE	DHA	BBC World Service
		500	CHN	BEI	China Radio Int. (CRI)
		100	CHN	dom	CNR8, Beijing
		300	ROU	GAL	Radio Romania International
		50	VTN	dom	VO Vietnam 1, Hanoi
5980		250	UAE	DHA	BBC World Service
		125	USA	GRV	BBG - R. Martí
		125	D	NAU	Bible Voice Broadcasting (BVB)
		500	CHN	XIA	China Radio Int. (CRI)
		1	PRU	dom	R. Chaski, Urubamba
		0.1	FIN	VIR	Scandinavian Weekend R.
		250	TUR	EMR	Voice of Turkey (VOT)
5985		300	AUT	MOS	AWR Africa/Europe
		150	ALB	CER	China Radio Int. (CRI)
		500	CHN	BEI	China Radio Int. (CRI)
		500	CHN	XIA	China Radio Int. (CRI)
		50	BRM	dom	Myanmar R., Yangon
		50	BRM	YAN	Radio Japan (NHK World)

kHz	N	kW	Ctry	Site	Station, location
		100	USA	YFR	Radio Japan (NHK World)
5990		250	IND	DEL	All India Radio (AIR)
		100	CHN	HUH	China Radio Int. (CRI)
		250	CUB	HAB	China Radio Int. (CRI)
	†	50	CHN	dom	Qinghai PBS, Xining
		300	ROU	GAL	Radio Romania International
		300	J	YAM	Shiokaze
5995		50	MLI	dom	R. Mali, Bamako (Kati)
		500	IRN	KAM	VO the Islamic Rep. of Iran
6000		10	IND	dom	AIR Leh
		100	CHN	dom	CNR1 VO China, Beijing
		100	RUS	ARM	GTRK "Adygeya"
	†	10	B	dom	R. Guaíba, Porto Alegre
		100	CUB	HAB	Radio Habana Cuba
		250	CUB	HAB	Radio Habana Cuba
		500	TUR	EMR	Voice of Turkey (VOT)
6003		100	KOR	SUW	Echo of Hope (VOH)
6005		250	ASC	ASC	BBC World Service
		1	D	KLL	R. Gloria International
		1	D	KLL	R. Mi Amigo Int.
		1	D	KLL	Radio 700
		1	D	KLL	Radio Belarus
		1	D	KLL	Radio Bulgaria
		1	D	KLL	Radio Slovakia Int.
		500	IRN	SIR	VO the Islamic Rep. of Iran
		1	D	KLL	Voice of Mongolia
6010		500	CHN	BEI	China Radio Int. (CRI)
		500	CHN	URU	China Radio Int. (CRI)
		100	CHN	dom	CNR11 Tibetan Sce, Xi'an
	†	5	CLM	dom	LV Conciencia, Puerto Lleras
	†	5	B	dom	R. Inconfidência, Belo Horizonte
		300	ROU	TIG	Radio Romania International
6015		100	KOR	HWA	KBS World Radio
		300	ROU	GAL	Radio Romania International
		100	CHN	dom	Xinjiang PBS, Urumqi
	†	50	TZA	DOL	Zanzibar Broadcasting Corp.
6019		3	PRU	dom	R. Victoria, Lima
6020	‡	50	IND	dom	AIR Shimla
		250	MRA	TIN	BBG - R. Free Asia (RFA)
		100	STP	SAO	BBG - VO America (VOA)
		300	ALB	CER	China Radio Int. (CRI)
		100	CHN	KAS	China Radio Int. (CRI)
		500	CHN	SZG	China Radio Int. (CRI)
	†	10	B	dom	R. Gaucha, Porto Alegre
		300	ROU	GAL	Radio Romania International
	+	300	ROU	TIG	Radio Romania International
		20	VTN	dom	VO Vietnam 1, Buôn Ma Thuôt
6025		500	CHN	XIA	China Radio Int. (CRI)
	‡	1	DOM	dom	R. Amanecer Int., Sto Domingo
		10	BOL	dom	Red Patria Nueva, La Paz
		100	SWZ	MAN	TWR Africa
		100	CHN	dom	Xizang PBS, Lhasa
6030		250	IND	dom	AIR Delhi
		125	USA	GRV	BBG - R. Martí
		100	D	NAU	Bible Voice Broadcasting (BVB)
	†	0.1	CAN	dom	CFVP Calgary AB
		100	CHN	dom	CNR1 VO China, Beijing
		100	D	NAU	Eternal Good News
		1	CAF	dom	R. ICDI, Boali
		1	CAF	dom	R. Ndeke Luka, Boali
		100	ETH	dom	R. Oromiya, Geja
		100	ROU	TIG	Radio Romania International
	+	300	ROU	GAL	Radio Romania International
		50	BRM	dom	Thazin R, Pyin U Lwin

kHz	N	kW	Ctry	Site	Station, location
6035		250	ASC	ASC	BBG - VO America (VOA)
	†	30	BTN	dom	Bhutan BS, Thimpu
	‡	5	CLM	dom	LV Guaviare, San José del G
		50	CHN	SHA	Yunnan PBS
6040	‡	50	IND	dom	AIR Jeypore
		100	STP	SAO	BBG - VO America (VOA)
		500	CHN	URU	China Radio Int. (CRI)
		500	CHN	XIA	China Radio Int. (CRI)
		150	CHN	dom	CNR2 Business R, Beijing
		50	CHN	dom	Nei Menggu-Mo, Hohhot
	†	7.5	B	dom	R. RB2, Curitiba
	+	300	ROU	GAL	Radio Romania International
		300	ROU	TIG	Radio Romania International
		500	IRN	SIR	VO the Islamic Rep. of Iran
6045		300	AUT	MOS	AWR Africa/Europe
		250	THA	UDO	BBG - VO America (VOA)
		250	G	WOF	KBS World Radio
	‡	0.45	MEX	dom	R. Universidad, San Luis Potosí
6047	†	10	PRU	dom	R. Santa Rosa, Lima
6050		1	LBR	dom	ELWA R, Monrovia
		50	MLA	dom	RTM Asyik FM, Kajang
		250	TUR	EMR	Voice of Turkey (VOT)
		500	TUR	EMR	Voice of Turkey (VOT)
		10	EQU	QUI	Vozandes Media
		100	CHN	dom	Xizang PBS, Lhasa
6055		100	MDG	MDC	AWR Africa/Europe
		150	ALB	CER	China Radio Int. (CRI)
		100	CHN	NNN	China Radio Int. (CRI)
		125	D	NAU	Ev. Missions-Gemeinden
	†	10	BOL	dom	R. Fides, La Paz
		50	J	dom	R. Nikkei 1, Tokyo
		500	IRN	KAM	VO the Islamic Rep. of Iran
6060	†		PRU	dom	Aroma Café R, Pichanaqui
		250	KWT	KWT	BBG - RFE/RL
		150	CHN	KUN	China Radio Int. (CRI)
		10	S	SLS	R. Revival Sweden
		100	CUB	HAB	Radio Habana Cuba
		50	ARG	BUE	Rdif. Argentina al Exterior
		15	CHN	dom	Sichuan PBS, Xichang
		500	IRN	ZAH	VO the Islamic Rep. of Iran
6065	†	50	IND	dom	AIR Kohima
		100	CHN	KAS	China Radio Int. (CRI)
		150	CHN	dom	CNR2 Business R, Beijing
6070	†	1	CAN	dom	CFRX Toronto ON
	†	0.01	D	ROB	Channel 292
		500	CHN	BEI	China Radio Int. (CRI)
		500	CHN	KAS	China Radio Int. (CRI)
		500	CHN	XIA	China Radio Int. (CRI)
		0.01	D	ROB	Radio DARC
		100	CVA	SMG	Vatican Radio
		250	CVA	SMG	Vatican Radio
		200	KRE	KNG	Voice of Korea
6075		100	CHN	KAS	China Radio Int. (CRI)
	‡	1	URG	dom	LV de Artigas, Artigas
		50	CUB	HAB	Radio Habana Cuba
		300	J	YAM	Radio Japan (NHK World)
		100	TWN	KOU	Radio Taiwan International
		500	IRN	SIR	VO the Islamic Rep. of Iran
6080		100	BOT	BOT	BBG - VO America (VOA)
		250	CVA	SMG	BBG - VO America (VOA)
		100	STP	SAO	BBG - VO America (VOA)
		150	BLR	dom	Belaruskaje R. 1, Minsk
		100	BLR	MNS	Belaruskaje Radyjo
		500	CHN	BEI	China Radio Int. (CRI)

kHz	N	kW	Ctry	Site	Station, location
		100	CHN	dom	CNR1 VO China, Golmud
		7	CHN	dom	Hulun Buir PBS, Hailar
		10	B	dom	R. Marumby, Curitiba
6085		500	IRN	SIR	VO the Islamic Rep. of Iran
6089	‡	1.5	PRU	dom	R. Universal, Wanchaq
6090		100	ETH	dom	Amhara State Regional R, Geja
		150	CHN	KUN	China Radio Int. (CRI)
		500	CHN	URU	China Radio Int. (CRI)
		500	CHN	XIA	China Radio Int. (CRI)
		100	CHN	dom	CNR2 Business R, Golmud
	†	50	NIG	dom	FRCN, Kaduna
	‡	10	B	dom	R. Bandeirantes, São Paulo
		300	J	YAM	Radio Japan (NHK World)
		300	ROU	TIG	Radio Romania International
	†	100	AIA	AIA	University Network
		500	IRN	SIR	VO the Islamic Rep. of Iran
6095		250	UAE	DHA	BBC World Service
		250	KWT	KWT	BBG - R. Free Asia (RFA)
		250	MRA	TIN	BBG - R. Free Asia (RFA)
		500	CHN	KAS	China Radio Int. (CRI)
		100	KOR	KIM	KBS World Radio
		250	KOR	KIM	KBS World Radio
	‡	100	PAK	ISL	Radio Pakistan
		100	D	NAU	The Mighty KBC
		100	D	NAU	Transport Radio
6100		50	IND	dom	AIR Delhi (DRM)
		100	CHN	URU	China Radio Int. (CRI)
		150	CHN	KUN	China Radio Int. (CRI)
		500	CHN	BEI	China Radio Int. (CRI)
		500	CHN	XIA	China Radio Int. (CRI)
	†	125	KRE	dom	KCBS, Kanggye
		100	CUB	HAB	Radio Habana Cuba
		250	IND	DEL	Radio Sedayee Kashmir
		500	IRN	KAM	VO the Islamic Rep. of Iran
6105		100	D	BIB	BBG - RFE/RL
	‡	0.25	MEX	dom	Candela FM, Mérida
		500	CHN	SZG	China Radio Int. (CRI)
		5	B	dom	R. Cult. Filadélfia, Foz de Iguaçu
	†	10	BOL	dom	R. Panamericana, La Paz
		100	TWN	KOU	Radio Taiwan International
6110	‡	50	IND	dom	AIR Kashmir, Srinagar
		500	CHN	XIA	China Radio Int. (CRI)
	†	100	ETH	dom	R. Fana, Geja
		250	IRN	AHW	VO the Islamic Rep. of Iran
		500	IRN	KAM	VO the Islamic Rep. of Iran
		500	IRN	SIR	VO the Islamic Rep. of Iran
		100	CHN	dom	Xizang PBS, Lhasa
6115		500	CHN	BEI	China Radio Int. (CRI)
	†	50	COG	dom	R. Congo, Brazzaville
		50	J	dom	R. Nikkei 2, Tokyo
		250	PHL	PUG	Radio Veritas Asia
		50	CHN	dom	VO Strait, Fuzhou
		100	USA	WCR	WWCR
6120		250	MRA	TIN	BBG - R. Free Asia (RFA)
		100	D	LAM	BBG - RFE/RL
		10	B	dom	Super R. Deus é Amor, São Paulo
		50	SWZ	MAN	TWR Africa
		500	IRN	KAM	VO the Islamic Rep. of Iran
		500	TUR	EMR	Voice of Turkey (VOT)
		100	CHN	dom	Xinjiang PBS, Urumqi
6125		100	CHN	dom	CNR1 VO China, Beijing
		100	CHN	dom	CNR1 VO China, Shijiazhuang
		250	AFS	MEY	Deutsche Welle
	†	0.3	URG	dom	R. Uruguay, Montevideo

kHz	N	kW	Ctry	Site	Station, location
		300	ROU	GAL	Radio Romania International
6130		50	LAO	VIE	Lao National Radio
		50	LAO	dom	R. Nationale Lao, Vientiane
		100	SWZ	MAN	TWR Africa
		100	CHN	dom	Xizang PBS, Lhasa
6135		250	ASC	ASC	BBC World Service
		300	G	WOF	BBC World Service
		500	CHN	BEI	China Radio Int. (CRI)
	†	10	B	dom	R. Aparecida, Aparecida
	†	30	MDG	dom	R. Nal Malagasy, Ambohidrano
		10	BOL	dom	R. Santa Cruz, Santa Cruz
		500	IRN	KAM	VO the Islamic Rep. of Iran
		10	KOR	UIW	Voice of freedom
		300	G	WOF	Voice of Vietnam (VOV)
6140		100	CHN	KAS	China Radio Int. (CRI)
		100	CHN	KUN	China Radio Int. (CRI)
	†	10	SOM	dom	Puntland R, Garowe
		250	IRN	AHW	VO the Islamic Rep. of Iran
6145		250	IND	ALG	All India Radio (AIR)
		300	AUT	MOS	AWR Africa/Europe
		150	CHN	BEI	China Radio Int. (CRI)
	†	50	CHN	dom	Qinghai PBS, Xining
		500	F	ISS	Radio Algériénne
		300	ROU	GAL	Radio Romania International
		100	TWN	KOU	Radio Taiwan International
		500	IRN	SIR	VO the Islamic Rep. of Iran
6150		250	THA	UDO	BBG - VO America (VOA)
		500	CHN	SZG	China Radio Int. (CRI)
	†	10	D	DAT	Europa 24
6155		250	IND	dom	AIR Delhi
		250	AFS	MEY	Channel Africa
		500	CHN	BEI	China Radio Int. (CRI)
		150	CHN	dom	CNR2 Business R, Beijing
		100	KOR	KIM	KBS World Radio
		300	AUT	MOS	Radio Ö1 International
6160		1	CAN	dom	CBU, Vancouver BC
		1	CAN	dom	CFGB-FM, St. John's NL
		500	CHN	XIA	China Radio Int. (CRI)
	†	10	B	dom	R. Boa Vontade, Porto Alegre
	†	10	B	dom	R. Rio Mar, Manaus
6165		250	IND	DEL	All India Radio (AIR)
		250	CHN	BEI	China Radio Int. (CRI)
		500	CHN	URU	China Radio Int. (CRI)
		100	CHN	dom	CNR6 VO Shenzhou, Beijing
	‡	250	TCD	dom	ONRT du Tchad, N'Djamena
		100	CUB	HAB	Radio Habana Cuba
		50	BRM	dom	Thazin R, Pyin U Lwin
		50	VTN	dom	VO Vietnam Min, Xuan Mai
	‡	100	ZMB	dom	ZNBC R. Two, Lusaka
6170		300	ROU	TIG	Radio Romania International
		0.1	FIN	VIR	Scandinavian Weekend R.
		200	KRE	KUJ	Voice of Korea
6174		1	PRU	dom	R. Tawantinsuyo, Cusco
6175		250	OMA	SLA	BBC World Service
		150	ALB	CER	China Radio Int. (CRI)
		100	CHN	NNN	China Radio Int. (CRI)
		100	CHN	dom	CNR1 VO China, Beijing
		500	IRN	KAM	VO the Islamic Rep. of Iran
		500	IRN	SIR	VO the Islamic Rep. of Iran
		250	G	WOF	Voice of Vietnam (VOV)
		250	UAE	DHA	Voice of Vietnam (VOV)
		250	USA	HRI	Voice of Vietnam (VOV)
6180		250	UAE	DHA	BBC World Service
		100	STP	SAO	BBG - VO America (VOA)

kHz	N	kW	Ctry	Site	Station, location
		100	CHN	KAS	China Radio Int. (CRI)
		100	CHN	KUN	China Radio Int. (CRI)
		150	CHN	KUN	China Radio Int. (CRI)
		500	CHN	URU	China Radio Int. (CRI)
		100	CHN	dom	CNR1 VO China, Lingshi
		100	CHN	dom	CNR8, Lingshi
		250	UAE	DHA	IBRA Radio
	†	250	B	dom	R. Nal da Amazônia, Brasília
		300	TWN	TSH	Radio Taiwan International
6185		15	CHN	dom	China Huayi BC, Fuzhou
		150	ALB	CER	China Radio Int. (CRI)
		500	CHN	XIA	China Radio Int. (CRI)
		10	MEX	dom	R. Educación, México
		100	CVA	SMG	Vatican Radio
		200	KRE	KUJ	Voice of Korea
		500	TUR	EMR	Voice of Turkey (VOT)
6190		100	AFS	MEY	BBC World Service
		100	CHN	dom	CNR2 Business R, Golmud
		1	D	GOH	Hamburger Lokalradio
		100	ALS	NLS	KNLS International
		300	J	YAM	Radio Japan (NHK World)
		50	CHN	dom	Xinjiang PBS, Urumqi
6195		250	OMA	SLA	BBC World Service
		250	SNG	SNG	BBC World Service
		250	USA	HRI	Radio Japan (NHK World)
		500	IRN	KAM	VO the Islamic Rep. of Iran
6200		50	CHN	dom	VO Jinling, Nanjing
		100	CHN	dom	Xizang PBS, Lhasa
6210	‡	1	COD	dom	R. Kahuzi, Bukavu
6230	±	1	TWN	TSU	Sound of Hope Radio Int.
6250		100	KOR	SUW	Echo of Hope (VOH)
		50	KRE	PYO	Echo of Unification
	‡	20	GNE	dom	Rdif Guinea Ecuatorial, Malabo
6260		100	UZB	TAC	Bible Voice Broadcasting (BVB)
6348		100	KOR	SUW	Echo of Hope (VOH)
6370	±	1	TWN	TSU	Sound of Hope Radio Int.
6400	†	50	KRE	KNG	Pyongyang Broadcasting Stn.
6518		50	KOR	GOY	Voice of the People
6600		50	KOR	GOY	Voice of the People
6730	±	1	TWN	TSU	Sound of Hope Radio Int.
6875		100	USA	WCR	WWCR
6900	‡	1	TWN	TSU	Sound of Hope Radio Int.
7120	†	100	SOM	dom	R. Hargeisa
7125	‡	50	GUI	dom	R. Guineé, Conakry
7175	‡	100	ERI	ASM	Ginbot 7 Dimts Radio
	†	100	ERI	dom	VO Broad Masses 2, Asmara
7195	‡	10	UGA	dom	UBC R. Red channel, Kampala
7200		50	BRM	dom	Myanma R., Yangon
		300	TWN	TSH	Radio Taiwan International
	†	100	ERI	dom	VO Broad Masses 1, Asmara
7205		100	AFS	MEY	Amateur R. Today
		100	CHN	KAS	China Radio Int. (CRI)
		150	CHN	BEI	China Radio Int. (CRI)
		500	CHN	BEI	China Radio Int. (CRI)
		500	CHN	XIA	China Radio Int. (CRI)
		500	F	ISS	Radio France Int. (RFI)
	†	100	SDN		SRTC, Khartoum
		250	TUR	EMR	Voice of Turkey (VOT)
		100	CHN	dom	Xinjiang PBS, Urumqi
7210		50	IND	dom	AIR Kolkata
		250	MRA	TIN	BBG - R. Free Asia (RFA)
		150	ALB	CER	China Radio Int. (CRI)
		100	CHN	URU	China Radio Int. (CRI)
		150	CHN	BEI	China Radio Int. (CRI)
		500	CHN	URU	China Radio Int. (CRI)
	±	1	TWN	TSU	Sound of Hope Radio Int.
		20	VTN	dom	VO Vietnam 1, Buôn Ma Thuột
		200	KRE	KUJ	Voice of Korea
		20	CHN	dom	Yunnan PBS, Kunming
7215		250	D	NAU	Athmik Yatra Radio
		100	STP	SAO	BBG - Afia Darfur Radio
		150	ALB	CER	China Radio Int. (CRI)
		500	CHN	BEI	China Radio Int. (CRI)
		500	CHN	JIN	China Radio Int. (CRI)
		500	CHN	KUN	China Radio Int. (CRI)
		500	CHN	SZG	China Radio Int. (CRI)
		500	CHN	XIA	China Radio Int. (CRI)
		100	CHN	dom	CNR1 VO China, Shijiazhuang
		100	KOR	KIM	KBS World Radio
		100	D	NAU	TWR Europe
7220		250	F	ISS	AWR Africa/Europe
		100	D	NAU	Bible Voice Broadcasting (BVB)
		150	ALB	CER	China Radio Int. (CRI)
		500	CHN	JIN	China Radio Int. (CRI)
		500	CHN	XIA	China Radio Int. (CRI)
		100	CHN	dom	CNR2 Business R, Golmud
	Pl.	10	CAF	dom	R. Centrafrique, Bangui
		300	ROU	GAL	Radio Romania International
		500	IRN	SIR	VO the Islamic Rep. of Iran
		200	KRE	KUJ	Voice of Korea
		100	VTN	VNI	Voice of Vietnam (VOV)
7225		500	CHN	BEI	China Radio Int. (CRI)
		500	CHN	URU	China Radio Int. (CRI)
		10	CHN	dom	Sichuan PBS, Chengdu
		500	IRN	KAM	VO the Islamic Rep. of Iran
		500	IRN	SIR	VO the Islamic Rep. of Iran
7230		50	IND	dom	AIR Kurseong
		100	AFS	MEY	Channel Africa
		100	CHN	dom	CNR1 VO China, Xi'an
	‡	100	BFA	dom	RTB, Ouagadougou
		50	CHN	dom	Xinjiang PBS, Urumqi
7235		250	MRA	TIN	BBG - VO America (VOA)
		100	CHN	KAS	China Radio Int. (CRI)
		500	CHN	KAS	China Radio Int. (CRI)
		300	G	WOF	IBRA Radio
		300	G	WOF	KBS World Radio
		300	ROU	TIG	Radio Romania International
		200	KRE	KUJ	Voice of Korea
7236	±†	100	ETH	GJW	Radio Ethiopia (EBC)
	±†	100	ETH	GJW	VO Peace & Dem. of Eritrea
	±†	100	ETH	GJW	Voice of Democratic Alliance
	±†	100	ETH	GJW	Voice of Eritrea
7240		100	CHN	KAS	China Radio Int. (CRI)
		500	ARS	RIY	Saudi Int. Radio
		500	TUR	EMR	Voice of Turkey (VOT)
		100	CHN	dom	Xizang PBS, Lhasa
7245		150	CHN	BJI	China Radio Int. (CRI)
		500	CHN	KAS	China Radio Int. (CRI)
		500	CHN	XIA	China Radio Int. (CRI)
		150	CHN	dom	CNR2 Business R, Beijing
	‡	20	MDG	dom	R. Nal Malagasy, Ambohidrano
		100	TJK	DSB	Voice of Tajik (Ovozi Tojik)
		250	TUR	EMR	Voice of Turkey (VOT)
7250		100	IND	dom	AIR Delhi
		100	IND	DEL	All India Radio (AIR)
		250	BGD	DKA	Bangladesh Betar
		100	CHN	KAS	China Radio Int. (CRI)
		500	CHN	URU	China Radio Int. (CRI)

kHz	N	kW	Ctry	Site	Station, location
		100	CVA	SMG	Vatican Radio
		250	CVA	SMG	Vatican Radio
7255		250	BLR	MNS	Belaruskaje Radyjo
		150	CHN	BEI	China Radio Int. (CRI)
		150	CHN	BJI	China Radio Int. (CRI)
		500	CHN	KAS	China Radio Int. (CRI)
		500	CHN	KUN	China Radio Int. (CRI)
		500	CHN	SZG	China Radio Int. (CRI)
		500	CHN	XIA	China Radio Int. (CRI)
		100	CHN	dom	CNR2 Business R, Baoji
	†	250	NIG	AJA	Voice of Nigeria
		100	CHN	dom	Xizang PBS, Lhasa
7260		100	CHN	KAS	China Radio Int. (CRI)
		500	CHN	URU	China Radio Int. (CRI)
		500	CHN	XIA	China Radio Int. (CRI)
		50	MNG	dom	Mongolian R. 2, Ulaanbaatar
	†	1	VUT	dom	R. Vanuatu, Port Vila
		100	CHN	dom	Xinjiang PBS, Urumqi
7265	†	100	PAK	dom	Azad Kashmir R., Islamabad
		300	G	WOF	BBC World Service
		100	CHN	KAS	China Radio Int. (CRI)
		500	CHN	BEI	China Radio Int. (CRI)
		500	CHN	KUN	China Radio Int. (CRI)
		500	CHN	URU	China Radio Int. (CRI)
		100	CHN	dom	CNR2 Business R, Baoji
		1	D	GOH	Hamburger Lokalradio
		250	G	WOF	IBRA Radio
		1	D	GOH	MV Baltic Radio
		1	D	GOH	R. Gloria International
7270		100	IND	dom	AIR Chennai
		100	IND	CNI	All India Radio (AIR)
		50	CHN	dom	Nei Menggu-Mo, Hohhot
		500	IRN	KAM	VO the Islamic Rep. of Iran
		100	TWN	TSH	Voice of China
		300	TWN	TSH	Voice of China
7275		100	BOT	BOT	BBG - VO America (VOA)
		100	STP	SAO	BBG - VO America (VOA)
		500	CHN	URU	China Radio Int. (CRI)
		100	CHN	dom	CNR1 VO China, Beijing
		250	KOR	KIM	KBS World Radio
		100	CVA	SMG	Vatican Radio
		100	CHN	dom	Xinjiang PBS, Urumqi
7280	±	1	TWN	TSU	Sound of Hope Radio Int.
		100	UZB	TAC	TWR India
		500	IRN	SIR	VO the Islamic Rep. of Iran
		100	VTN	VNI	Voice of Vietnam (VOV)
7285		250	G	WOF	BBC World Service
		250	UAE	DHA	BBC World Service
		150	ALB	CER	China Radio Int. (CRI)
		100	CHN	KAS	China Radio Int. (CRI)
		500	CHN	BEI	China Radio Int. (CRI)
		500	CHN	KUN	China Radio Int. (CRI)
		500	CHN	XIA	China Radio Int. (CRI)
		50	MLI	dom	R. Mali, Bamako (Kati)
		100	AFS	dom	R. Sonder Grense, Meyerton
		500	IRN	KAM	VO the Islamic Rep. of Iran
		100	VTN	VNI	Voice of Vietnam (VOV)
7290		50	IND	dom	AIR, Thiruvananthapuram
		100	D	BIB	BBG - VOA Ashna Radio
		100	CHN	KAS	China Radio Int. (CRI)
		500	CHN	SZG	China Radio Int. (CRI)
		500	CHN	XIA	China Radio Int. (CRI)
		100	CHN	dom	CNR1 VO China, Beijing
		100	BUL	SOF	IRRS Shortwave
		10	INS	dom	RRI, Nabire
		500	IRN	SIR	VO the Islamic Rep. of Iran
7295	†	10	IND	dom	AIR Aizawl
		500	CHN	KAS	China Radio Int. (CRI)
		100	MLI	BKO	China Radio Int. (CRI)
		500	F	ISS	Radio Algeriénnne
		500	F	ISS	Radio France Int. (RFI)
		100	CHN	dom	Xinjiang PBS, Urumqi
7300		100	CHN	KAS	China Radio Int. (CRI)
		500	CHN	KAS	China Radio Int. (CRI)
		500	CHN	URU	China Radio Int. (CRI)
		300	TWN	TSH	Radio Taiwan International
		250	G	WOF	Reach Beyond
		100	SWZ	MAN	TWR Africa
		100	D	NAU	TWR Europe
		500	IRN	SIR	VO the Islamic Rep. of Iran
7305		250	ASC	ASC	BBC World Service
		100	D	BIB	BBG - RFE/RL
		250	THA	UDO	BBG - RFE/RL
		150	CHN	BEI	China Radio Int. (CRI)
		500	CHN	URU	China Radio Int. (CRI)
		100	CHN	dom	CNR1 VO China, Shijiazhuang
		250	USA	GRV	Vatican Radio
		500	IRN	SIR	VO the Islamic Rep. of Iran
7310		1	D	KLL	R. Gloria International
		1	D	KLL	R. Mi Amigo Int.
		1	D	KLL	Radio 700
		1	D	KLL	Radio Bulgaria
		300	ROU	TIG	Radio Romania International
		1	D	KLL	Radio Slovakia Int.
	±	1	TWN	TSU	Sound of Hope Radio Int.
		1	D	KLL	Voice of Mongolia
		100	CHN	dom	Xinjiang PBS, Urumqi
7315		50	IND	dom	AIR Shillong
		250	D	NAU	AWR Africa/Europe
		100	D	BIB	BBG - VO America (VOA)
		100	CHN	KUN	China Radio Int. (CRI)
		500	CHN	KAS	China Radio Int. (CRI)
		500	CHN	KUN	China Radio Int. (CRI)
		150	CHN	dom	CNR2 Business R, Xi'an
		250	USA	HRI	Eternal Good News
	±	250	CVA	SMG	Radio Dabanga
	±	250	CVA	SMG	Radio Tamazuj
		250	USA	HRI	The Overcomer Ministry
		50	SWZ	MAN	TWR Africa
		500	IRN	KAM	VO the Islamic Rep. of Iran
		250	USA	HRI	WHRI - World Harvest R.
7320		500	CHN	KUN	China Radio Int. (CRI)
		300	ROU	TIG	Radio Romania International
		100	AUT	MOS	TWR Europe
		500	IRN	SIR	VO the Islamic Rep. of Iran
7325		50	IND	dom	AIR Jaipur
		250	G	WOF	BBC World Service
		250	D	NAU	Bible Voice Broadcasting (BVB)
		100	CHN	KAS	China Radio Int. (CRI)
		150	CHN	KUN	China Radio Int. (CRI)
		500	CHN	BEI	China Radio Int. (CRI)
		500	CHN	JIN	China Radio Int. (CRI)
		500	CHN	KUN	China Radio Int. (CRI)
		500	CHN	SZG	China Radio Int. (CRI)
		500	CHN	URU	China Radio Int. (CRI)
		500	CHN	XIA	China Radio Int. (CRI)
		300	ROU	GAL	Radio Romania International
		300	ROU	TIG	Radio Romania International

kHz	N	kW	Ctry	Site	Station, location
		500	IRN	KAM	VO the Islamic Rep. of Iran
	‡	1	PNG	dom	Wantok R. Light, Port Moresby
7330		500	CHN	KAS	China Radio Int. (CRI)
		500	CHN	XIA	China Radio Int. (CRI)
	+	50	NZL	RAN	R. New Zealand Int. (RNZI)
		100	UZB	TAC	Radio Japan (NHK World)
		100	AUT	MOS	Radio Joystick
		300	ROU	TIG	Radio Romania International
		500	IRN	KAM	VO the Islamic Rep. of Iran
7335	‡	50	IND	dom	AIR Imphal
		500	CHN	BEI	China Radio Int. (CRI)
		500	CHN	JIN	China Radio Int. (CRI)
		500	CHN	SZG	China Radio Int. (CRI)
		100	CHN	dom	CNR2 Business R, Baoji
		300	ROU	GAL	Radio Romania International
		300	ROU	TIG	Radio Romania International
7340		100	IND	dom	AIR Mumbai
		100	IND	MUM	All India Radio (AIR)
		500	CHN	KAS	China Radio Int. (CRI)
		300	ROU	GAL	Radio Romania International
		300	ROU	TIG	Radio Romania International
		100	CHN	dom	Xinjiang PBS, Urumqi
7345		150	ALB	CER	China Radio Int. (CRI)
		500	CHN	KAS	China Radio Int. (CRI)
		100	CHN	dom	CNR1 VO China, Beijing
		300	ROU	GAL	Radio Romania International
		300	ROU	TIG	Radio Romania International
		250	IRN	AHW	VO the Islamic Rep. of Iran
7350		250	IND	ALG	All India Radio (AIR)
		250	UAE	DHA	BBC World Service
		100	CHN	KAS	China Radio Int. (CRI)
		500	CHN	KAS	China Radio Int. (CRI)
		500	CHN	URU	China Radio Int. (CRI)
		100	CHN	dom	CNR11 Tibetan Sce, Xi'an
	+	300	ROU	TIG	Radio Romania International
		500	IRN	KAM	VO the Islamic Rep. of Iran
7355		100	ALS	NLS	KNLS International
		250	USA	HRI	The Overcomer Ministry
7360		150	ALB	CER	China Radio Int. (CRI)
		100	CHN	KUN	China Radio Int. (CRI)
		100	CHN	dom	CNR11 Tibetan Sce, Xi'an
		300	ROU	GAL	Radio Romania International
		100	CVA	SMG	Vatican Radio
		250	CVA	SMG	Vatican Radio
		500	IRN	KAM	VO the Islamic Rep. of Iran
		500	IRN	SIR	VO the Islamic Rep. of Iran
		500	IRN	ZAH	VO the Islamic Rep. of Iran
7365		125	USA	GRV	BBG - R. Martí
		100	D	NAU	Bible Voice Broadcasting (BVB)
		500	CHN	BEI	China Radio Int. (CRI)
		100	D	NAU	Eternal Good News
		1	D	WNM	HCJB Deutschland
		1	D	WNM	Lutherische Stunde
		1	D	WNM	Missionwerk Heukelbach
7370		100	IND	DEL	All India Radio (AIR)
		100	CHN	KAS	China Radio Int. (CRI)
		100	CHN	NNN	China Radio Int. (CRI)
		150	CHN	dom	CNR2 Business R, Beijing
		300	ROU	GAL	Radio Romania International
		500	IRN	KAM	VO the Islamic Rep. of Iran
7375		150	CHN	dom	CNR2 Business R, Beijing
		300	ROU	GAL	Radio Romania International
		100	D	NAU	TWR Europe
		500	IRN	KAM	VO the Islamic Rep. of Iran

kHz	N	kW	Ctry	Site	Station, location
7380		50	IND	dom	AIR Chennai
		150	ALB	CER	China Radio Int. (CRI)
		300	ROU	TIG	Radio Romania International
		100	TWN	PAO	Radio Taiwan International
		500	IRN	AHW	VO the Islamic Rep. of Iran
		500	IRN	SIR	VO the Islamic Rep. of Iran
7385		150	ALB	CER	China Radio Int. (CRI)
		500	CHN	KAS	China Radio Int. (CRI)
		250	USA	HRI	Eternal Good News
		300	TWN	TSH	Radio Taiwan International
		100	USA	HRI	WHRI - World Harvest R.
		100	CHN	dom	Xizang PBS, Lhasa
7390	†	4	IND	dom	AIR Port Blair
		100	CHN	HUH	China Radio Int. (CRI)
		150	CHN	BEI	China Radio Int. (CRI)
		500	CHN	JIN	China Radio Int. (CRI)
		500	CHN	XIA	China Radio Int. (CRI)
		500	F	ISS	Radio France Int. (RFI)
		100	ALB	SHI	RadioTirana
		500	IRN	KAM	VO the Islamic Rep. of Iran
7395		250	OMA	SLA	BBC World Service
		100	CHN	NNN	China Radio Int. (CRI)
		500	CHN	KAS	China Radio Int. (CRI)
		500	CHN	KUN	China Radio Int. (CRI)
		500	CHN	URU	China Radio Int. (CRI)
		500	CHN	XIA	China Radio Int. (CRI)
		150	CHN	dom	CNR2 Business R, Xianyang
		250	MDG	MDC	Radio Japan (NHK World)
		300	ROU	GAL	Radio Romania International
		300	ROU	TIG	Radio Romania International
		125	D	NAU	The Mighty KBC
7400		100	CHN	KUN	China Radio Int. (CRI)
		500	CHN	XIA	China Radio Int. (CRI)
		300	ROU	TIG	Radio Romania International
		300	J	YAM	Shiokaze
		500	IRN	SIR	VO the Islamic Rep. of Iran
7405		125	USA	GRV	BBG - R. Martí
		250	USA	GRV	BBG - R. Martí
		100	CHN	HUH	China Radio Int. (CRI)
		500	CHN	BEI	China Radio Int. (CRI)
		500	CHN	XIA	China Radio Int. (CRI)
	+	300	ROU	TIG	Radio Romania International
7410		100	CHN	KAS	China Radio Int. (CRI)
		500	CHN	BEI	China Radio Int. (CRI)
		500	CHN	JIN	China Radio Int. (CRI)
		500	CHN	SZG	China Radio Int. (CRI)
		100	CHN	dom	CNR5 VO Zhonghua, Beijing
		100	PHL	BOC	FEBC Philippines
		250	CVA	SMG	Vatican Radio
		250	PHL	PHT	Vatican Radio
7415		250	KWT	KWT	BBG - R. Free Asia (RFA)
		250	MRA	TIN	BBG - R. Free Asia (RFA)
		500	CHN	KAS	China Radio Int. (CRI)
		500	CHN	URU	China Radio Int. (CRI)
		500	CHN	XIA	China Radio Int. (CRI)
		100	CHN	dom	CNR5 VO Zhonghua, Beijing
		250	ASC	ASC	Dandal Kura
7420		100	IND	dom	AIR Delhi
		50	IND	dom	AIR Hyderabad
		150	CHN	KUN	China Radio Int. (CRI)
		500	CHN	URU	China Radio Int. (CRI)
		100	CHN	dom	Nei Menggu-Ch, Hohhot
7425		100	CHN	KAS	China Radio Int. (CRI)
		150	CHN	dom	CNR2 Business R, Xianyang

kHz	N	kW	Ctry	Site	Station, location
		500	IRN	KAM	VO the Islamic Rep. of Iran
		500	IRN	SIR	VO the Islamic Rep. of Iran
7430		50	IND	dom	AIR Bhopal
		500	CHN	JIN	China Radio Int. (CRI)
7435		250	G	WOF	BBC World Service
		100	D	LAM	BBG - RFE/RL
		500	CHN	BEI	China Radio Int. (CRI)
		500	CHN	JIN	China Radio Int. (CRI)
		500	CHN	KUN	China Radio Int. (CRI)
		500	CHN	SZG	China Radio Int. (CRI)
		500	CHN	XIA	China Radio Int. (CRI)
		50	VTN	dom	VO Vietnam 1, Son Tay
7440		50	IND	dom	AIR Lucknow
		100	CHN	NNN	China Radio Int. (CRI)
		500	CHN	BEI	China Radio Int. (CRI)
		500	CHN	JIN	China Radio Int. (CRI)
7445		300	ARM	ERV	BBC World Service
		250	ASC	ASC	BBC World Service
		250	G	WOF	BBC World Service
		300	MDA	KCH	BBC World Service
		250	MDG	MDC	BBC World Service
		250	OMA	SLA	BBC World Service
		250	KWT	KWT	BBG - R. Free Asia (RFA)
		250	THA	UDO	BBG - VO America (VOA)
		500	CHN	KUN	China Radio Int. (CRI)
		500	CHN	URU	China Radio Int. (CRI)
		100	TWN	PAO	Radio Taiwan International
		250	TWN	TNN	Radio Taiwan International
		500	IRN	KAM	VO the Islamic Rep. of Iran
		500	IRN	SIR	VO the Islamic Rep. of Iran
7450		100	CHN	dom	Xizang PBS, Lhasa
7455		250	KWT	KWT	BBG - R. Free Asia (RFA)
		250	CLN	IRA	BBG - VO America (VOA)
		100	USA	YFR	Trunews Radio
		100	USA	YFR	WRMI - R. Miami Int.
7460		250	MNG	UBA	BBG - R. Free Asia (RFA)
		100	BOT	BOT	BBG - VO America (VOA)
		250	PHL	PHT	BBG - VO America (VOA)
		500	MDA	KCH	Radio Payam-e Doost
7465		250	AFS	MEY	BBC World Service
		250	SNG	SNG	BBC World Service
		100	ALB	SHI	RadioTirana
7470		250	MNG	UBA	BBG - R. Free Asia (RFA)
		250	TJK	DSB	BBG - R. Free Asia (RFA)
	‡	100	PAK	ISL	Radio Pakistan
		100	ALB	SHI	RadioTirana
7475		250	THA	UDO	BBG - RFE/RL
7480		250	KWT	KWT	BBG - R. Free Asia (RFA)
		200	TJK	DSB	BBG - R. Free Asia (RFA)
		250	CLN	IRA	BBG - VO America (VOA)
		500	MDA	KCH	Radio Payam-e Doost
7485		100	SNG	SNG	BBC World Service
		250	THA	NAK	BBC World Service
		100	D	BIB	BBG - RFE/RL
		250	KWT	KWT	BBG - RFE/RL
		250	CLN	IRA	BBG - VO America (VOA)
7490		250	THA	NAK	BBC World Service
		50	USA	BCQ	The Overcomer Ministry
		50	USA	BCQ	WBCQ
		100	USA	WCR	WWCR
7495		250	KWT	KWT	BBG - VOA Ashna Radio
		250	THA	UDO	BBG - VOA Deewa Radio
7505		100	IND	DEL	All India Radio (AIR)
		250	IND	PAN	All India Radio (AIR)
		250	THA	NAK	BBC World Service
		100	UZB	TAC	TWR India
7506	†	50	USA	RNO	WRNO Worldwide
7510		250	THA	NAK	BBC World Service
		300	ARM	ERV	IBRA Radio
7515		100	UZB	TAC	National Unity Radio
		250	USA	EWN	WEWN - EWTN Shortwave
7520		250	IND	DEL	All India Radio (AIR)
	±	100	UZB	TAC	Voice of the Martyrs
		250	USA	HRI	WHRI - World Harvest R.
		100	USA	WCR	WWCR
7530		100	UZB	TAC	Stream of Praise Mus. Min.
		100	TWN	TSH	Suab Xaa Moo Zoo
7540		250	KWT	KWT	BBG - R. Free Asia (RFA)
		250	KWT	KWT	BBG - VOA Deewa Radio
7545		250	PHL	PHT	BBG - VO America (VOA)
7550	+	200	IND	BGL	All India Radio (AIR)
		250	CLN	IRA	BBG - RFE/RL
7555		100	IND	DEL	All India Radio (AIR)
7560		250	THA	UDO	BBG - VO America (VOA)
7565		250	THA	NAK	BBC World Service
		100	UZB	TAC	BBC World Service
7570		100	USA	YFR	FG Radio (ex EUNN)
		100	USA	YFR	Radio Slovakia Int.
		100	USA	YFR	The Overcomer Ministry
		200	KRE	KUJ	Voice of Korea
		100	USA	YFR	WRMI - R. Miami Int.
7575		100	UZB	TAC	Radio Ranginkaman
7580		250	KWT	KWT	BBG - VO America (VOA)
		250	PHL	PHT	BBG - VO America (VOA)
	±	1	TWN	TSU	Sound of Hope Radio Int.
		200	KRE	KUJ	Voice of Korea
7585		250	CLN	IRA	BBG - R. Farda
		250	KWT	KWT	BBG - R. Farda
7590		100	UZB	TAC	North Korea Reform Radio
7598	±	100	TJK	DSB	Voice of Tibet
7600		250	THA	NAK	BBC World Service
	±	1	TWN	TSU	Sound of Hope Radio Int.
7615		200	TJK	DSB	Voice of Wilderness
7730		100	USA	YFR	Radio Taiwan International
	±	1	TWN	TSU	Sound of Hope Radio Int.
7800	±	1	TWN	TSU	Sound of Hope Radio Int.
7850		5	CAN	STF	CHU, Ottawa, ON
8728		10	F	MCR	Radio Monaco
9180	±	1	TWN	TSU	Sound of Hope Radio Int.
9200	±	1	TWN	TSU	Sound of Hope Radio Int.
9230	±	1	TWN	TSU	Sound of Hope Radio Int.
9255	±	1	TWN	TSU	Sound of Hope Radio Int.
9265		50	USA	INB	WINB
9320	±	1	TWN	TSU	Sound of Hope Radio Int.
9330		50	USA	BCQ	WBCQ
9335		250	PHL	PHT	BBG - VO America (VOA)
		250	THA	UDO	BBG - VO America (VOA)
9345		100	PHL	IBA	FEBC Philippines
9350		100	USA	WCR	WWCR
9355		250	THA	UDO	BBG - VOA Deewa Radio
9360	±	1	TWN	TSU	Sound of Hope Radio Int.
9370		250	CLN	IRA	BBG - VOA Deewa Radio
		100	USA	WRB	The Overcomer Ministry
		100	USA	WRB	WWRB
9380	†	250	IND	dom	AIR Aligarh
		500	F	ISS	Radio Algeriénnne
9390		100	D	LAM	BBG - VO America (VOA)
		250	PHL	PHT	BBG - VO America (VOA)

kHz	N	kW	Ctry	Site	Station, location
		100	UZB	TAC	IBRA Radio
		250	THA	UDO	R. Thailand World Service
9395		100	USA	YFR	Radio Japan (NHK World)
		100	USA	YFR	Trunews Radio
9400		300	ARM	ERV	Dengê Kurdistanê
		100	BUL	SOF	Dengê Kurdistanê
		250	F	ISS	Dengê Kurdistanê
		300	MDA	KCH	Dengê Kurdistanê
		100	PHL	IBA	FEBC Philippines
9405		100	LTU	SIT	BBG - R. Free Asia (RFA)
		100	PHL	BOC	FEBC Philippines
		5	S	SLS	R. Revival Sweden
9410		250	AFS	MEY	BBC World Service
		250	OMA	SLA	BBC World Service
		100	SNG	SNG	BBC World Service
		250	THA	NAK	BBC World Service
		250	UAE	DHA	BBC World Service
		100	MRA	SAI	BBG - R. Free Asia (RFA)
		500	CHN	KAS	China Radio Int. (CRI)
		100	CHN	dom	CNR5 VO Zhonghua, Beijing
	†	10	TWN	dom	Fu Hsing BS, Kuanyin
		250	TUR	EMR	Voice of Turkey (VOT)
		500	TUR	EMR	Voice of Turkey (VOT)
9415		100	MRA	SAI	BBG - R. Free Asia (RFA)
		500	CHN	BEI	China Radio Int. (CRI)
		500	CHN	XIA	China Radio Int. (CRI)
9420		100	CHN	dom	CNR1 VO China, Lingshi
		100	CHN	dom	CNR13 Uyghur Sce, Lingshi
	‡	170	GRC	AVL	ERT (i Foni tis Elladas)
9425		150	CHN	BEI	China Radio Int. (CRI)
		500	CHN	JIN	China Radio Int. (CRI)
		200	KRE	KUJ	Voice of Korea
9430		500	CHN	KAS	China Radio Int. (CRI)
		100	PHL	BOC	FEBC Philippines
9435		250	CLN	IRA	BBG - VO America (VOA)
		100	CHN	KUN	China Radio Int. (CRI)
		500	CHN	KAS	China Radio Int. (CRI)
		500	CHN	XIA	China Radio Int. (CRI)
		250	EGY	ABS	Radio Cairo
		200	KRE	KUJ	Voice of Korea
9440		250	ASC	ASC	BBC World Service
		300	MDA	KCH	BBC World Service
		125	D	NAU	Bible Voice Broadcasting (BVB)
		100	CHN	NNN	China Radio Int. (CRI)
		150	CHN	KUN	China Radio Int. (CRI)
		500	CHN	KUN	China Radio Int. (CRI)
		500	CHN	XIA	China Radio Int. (CRI)
9445		250	IND	DEL	All India Radio (AIR)
		500	IND	BGL	All India Radio (AIR)
		300	ARM	ERV	IBRA Radio
		500	IRN	KAM	VO the Islamic Rep. of Iran
		200	KRE	KUJ	Voice of Korea
9450		250	D	NAU	Bible Voice Broadcasting (BVB)
		100	CHN	KAS	China Radio Int. (CRI)
		100	CHN	URU	China Radio Int. (CRI)
		500	CHN	KAS	China Radio Int. (CRI)
		300	TWN	TSH	Radio Taiwan International
9455		250	BGD	DKA	Bangladesh Betar
		100	LTU	SIT	BBG - R. Free Asia (RFA)
		100	MRA	SAI	BBG - R. Free Asia (RFA)
		150	CHN	KUN	China Radio Int. (CRI)
		100	CHN	dom	CNR1 VO China, Lingshi
9460		100	GUM	SDA	AWR Africa/Europe
		100	AFS	MEY	BBC World Service
9460		250	ASC	ASC	BBC World Service
		150	ALB	CER	China Radio Int. (CRI)
		100	CHN	KAS	China Radio Int. (CRI)
		100	CHN	NNN	China Radio Int. (CRI)
		150	CHN	KUN	China Radio Int. (CRI)
		500	CHN	URU	China Radio Int. (CRI)
		50	BRM	dom	Thazin R, Pyin U Lwin
		500	TUR	EMR	Voice of Turkey (VOT)
9465		100	PHL	BOC	FEBC Philippines
		250	D	NAU	Missionswerk Friedensstimme
9470		100	BOT	BOT	BBG - VO America (VOA)
		100	STP	SAO	BBG - VO America (VOA)
		250	D	NAU	Bible Voice Broadcasting (BVB)
		100	CHN	XIA	China Radio Int. (CRI)
		100	CHN	dom	CNR1 VO China, Beijing
		100	UZB	TAC	Free North Korea Radio
		300	ROU	TIG	Radio Romania International
		100	AUT	MOS	TWR Europe
		100	CHN	dom	Xinjiang PBS, Urumqi
9475		100	SWZ	MAN	TWR Africa
	‡	100	USA	TWW	WTWW
9480		250	KWT	KWT	BBG - R. Free Asia (RFA)
		100	CHN	dom	CNR11 Tibetan Sce, Xi'an
		250	IRN	AHW	VO the Islamic Rep. of Iran
		500	IRN	SIR	VO the Islamic Rep. of Iran
9485		300	G	WOF	BBG - VO America (VOA)
		100	STP	SAO	BBG - VO America (VOA)
		250	UAE	DHA	BBG - VO America (VOA)
		1	D	GOH	Hamburger Lokalradio
		1	D	GOH	MV Baltic Radio
		1	D	GOH	R. Gloria International
9490		250	OMA	SLA	BBC World Service
		100	BOT	BOT	BBG - VO America (VOA)
		250	KWT	KWT	BBG - VO America (VOA)
		250	PHL	PHT	BBG - VO America (VOA)
		100	STP	SAO	BBG - VO America (VOA)
		100	CHN	KAS	China Radio Int. (CRI)
		150	CHN	KUN	China Radio Int. (CRI)
		250	F	ISS	Radio República
		500	IRN	KAM	VO the Islamic Rep. of Iran
		100	CHN	dom	Xizang PBS, Lhasa
9495		100	MRA	SAI	BBG - R. Free Asia (RFA)
		250	TUR	EMR	Voice of Turkey (VOT)
9500		100	CHN	dom	CNR1 VO China, Shijiazhuang
		100	SWZ	MAN	TWR Africa
		500	IRN	SIR	VO the Islamic Rep. of Iran
9505		250	OMA	SLA	BBC World Service
	†	100	SDN	dom	SRTC, Khartoum
		250	USA	HRI	The Overcomer Ministry
	†	100	SDN	ALF	VO Africa
		50	CHN	dom	VO Strait News Ch, Fuzhou
		250	USA	HRI	WHRI - World Harvest R.
9510		250	SNG	SNG	BBC World Service
		250	THA	NAK	BBC World Service
		250	CVA	SMG	BBG - Afia Darfur Radio
		125	CVA	SMG	BBG - VO America (VOA)
		100	BUL	SOF	IRRS Shortwave
		500	IRN	KAM	VO the Islamic Rep. of Iran
		50	CHN	dom	Xinjiang PBS, Urumqi
9515		100	D	NAU	AWR Africa/Europe
		100	D	LAM	BBG - VO America (VOA)
		250	D	NAU	Bible Voice Broadcasting (BVB)
		100	CHN	KAS	China Radio Int. (CRI)
		150	CHN	dom	CNR2 Business R, Beijing

kHz	N	kW	Ctry	Site	Station, location
		250	KOR	KIM	KBS World Radio
		10	B	dom	R. Marumby, Curitiba
		500	IRN	KAM	VO the Islamic Rep. of Iran
9520		250	D	NAU	Athmik Yatra Radio
		100	D	LAM	BBG - RFE/RL
		50	CHN	dom	Nei Menggu-Ch, Hohhot
		250	PHL	PUG	Radio Veritas Asia
9525		500	CHN	KAS	China Radio Int. (CRI)
		300	ROU	GAL	Radio Romania International
9526	†	250	INS	JAK	Voice of Indonesia
9530		250	PHL	PHT	BBG - VO America (VOA)
		100	CHN	dom	CNR11 Tibetan Sce, Xi'an
	†	10	B	dom	R. Transmundial, Santa Maria
		250	ASC	ASC	Reach Beyond
		50	VTN	dom	VO Vietnam 1, Xuan Mai
		500	TUR	EMR	Voice of Turkey (VOT)
9535		100	D	NAU	AWR Africa/Europe
		250	KWT	KWT	BBG - R. Free Asia (RFA)
		100	CHN	KUN	China Radio Int. (CRI)
		150	CHN	BJI	China Radio Int. (CRI)
		500	CHN	XIA	China Radio Int. (CRI)
		100	CUB	HAB	Radio Habana Cuba
9540		250	SNG	SNG	BBC World Service
		500	CHN	BEI	China Radio Int. (CRI)
		500	CHN	KUN	China Radio Int. (CRI)
		100	UZB	TAC	FEBA India
		250	UAE	DHA	IBRA Radio
		500	F	ISS	Radio France Int. (RFI)
		100	OMA	THU	Radio Sultanate of Oman
9545		10	SLM	dom	Solomon Islands BC, Honiara
		500	IRN	KAM	VO the Islamic Rep. of Iran
9550		100	STP	SAO	BBG - VO America (VOA)
		150	CHN	KUN	China Radio Int. (CRI)
		500	CHN	BEI	China Radio Int. (CRI)
		10	B	dom	R. Boa Vontade, Porto Alegre
		250	CUB	HAB	Radio Habana Cuba
		500	IRN	KAM	VO the Islamic Rep. of Iran
		100	VTN	VNI	Voice of Vietnam (VOV)
9555		150	ALB	CER	China Radio Int. (CRI)
		150	CHN	BEI	China Radio Int. (CRI)
		500	ARS	RIY	Saudi Int. Radio
9560		250	UAE	DHA	BBC World Service
		100	CHN	KAS	China Radio Int. (CRI)
		500	CHN	URU	China Radio Int. (CRI)
		1	D	KLL	R. Mi Amigo Int.
		300	J	YAM	Radio Japan (NHK World)
		1	D	KLL	Radio Slovakia Int.
		250	CVA	SMG	Vatican Radio
		100	CHN	dom	Xinjiang PBS, Urumqi
9565		100	GUM	SDA	AWR Asia/Pacific
		250	USA	GRV	BBG - R. Martí
		150	ALB	CER	China Radio Int. (CRI)
		20	B	dom	Super R. Deus é Amor, Curitiba
9570		250	KWT	KWT	BBG - R. Free Asia (RFA)
		300	ALB	CER	China Radio Int. (CRI)
		100	CHN	KAS	China Radio Int. (CRI)
		500	CHN	BEI	China Radio Int. (CRI)
		250	CUB	HAB	China Radio Int. (CRI)
		100	CHN	dom	CNR2 Business R, Golmud
		100	KOR	KIM	KBS World Radio
		250	EGY	ABS	Radio Cairo
9575		500	IND	BGL	All India Radio (AIR)
		300	J	YAM	Radio Japan (NHK World)
		250	MRC	NAD	Radio Méditerranée Int.

kHz	N	kW	Ctry	Site	Station, location
9580		100	AUS	SHP	ABC Radio Australia
		250	CUB	HAB	China Radio Int. (CRI)
		250	KOR	KIM	KBS World Radio
		250	IRN	AHW	VO the Islamic Rep. of Iran
		100	CHN	dom	Xizang PBS, Lhasa
9585		300	G	WOF	BBG - RFE/RL
		500	CHN	KAS	China Radio Int. (CRI)
		10	B	dom	Super R. Deus é Amor, São Paulo
		100	SWZ	MAN	TWR Africa
		500	IRN	SIR	VO the Islamic Rep. of Iran
9590		250	AFS	MEY	BBC World Service
		100	STP	SAO	BBG - VO America (VOA)
		150	ALB	CER	China Radio Int. (CRI)
		150	CHN	KUN	China Radio Int. (CRI)
		500	CHN	KAS	China Radio Int. (CRI)
		500	CHN	SZG	China Radio Int. (CRI)
		300	TWN	TSH	Radio Taiwan International
		50	BRM	dom	Thazin R, Pyin U Lwin
		500	IRN	KAM	VO the Islamic Rep. of Iran
9595		500	IND	BGL	All India Radio (AIR)
		50	J	dom	R. Nikkei 1, Tokyo
9600		150	CHN	BJI	China Radio Int. (CRI)
		150	CHN	KUN	China Radio Int. (CRI)
		500	CHN	KAS	China Radio Int. (CRI)
	+	300	ROU	GAL	Radio Romania International
	±	250	F	ISS	Radio Tamazuj
		250	PHL	PHT	Vatican Radio
		100	CHN	dom	Xinjiang PBS, Urumqi
9605		100	D	LAM	BBG - RFE/RL
		100	D	LAM	BBG - VO America (VOA)
		250	PHL	PHT	BBG - VO America (VOA)
		250	USA	HRI	KBS World Radio
9610		100	D	NAU	AWR Africa/Europe
		250	MRA	TIN	BBG - RFE/RL
		100	CHN	KAS	China Radio Int. (CRI)
		100	CHN	KUN	China Radio Int. (CRI)
		150	CHN	KUN	China Radio Int. (CRI)
		100	CHN	dom	CNR8, Beijing
		250	USA	GRV	Vatican Radio
		500	TUR	EMR	Voice of Turkey (VOT)
9615		500	CHN	URU	China Radio Int. (CRI)
		100	ALS	NLS	KNLS International
9620		250	IND	ALG	All India Radio (AIR)
		500	CHN	KAS	China Radio Int. (CRI)
		150	CHN	dom	CNR2 Business R, Beijing
		100	CHN	dom	CNR6 VO Shenzhou, Beijing
		250	D	NAU	Radio Japan (NHK World)
		300	ROU	TIG	Radio Romania International
		500	TUR	EMR	Voice of Turkey (VOT)
9625		100	AFS	MEY	Channel Africa
	‡	10	BOL	dom	R. Fides, La Paz
		300	J	YAM	Radio Japan (NHK World)
		100	PLW	HBN	Radio Japan (NHK World)
		250	TWN	TNN	Radio Taiwan International
		100	AUS	KNX	Reach Beyond Australia
9630		300	AUT	MOS	AWR Africa/Europe
		100	CHN	dom	CNR1 VO China, Golmud
		100	CHN	dom	CNR1 VO China, Lingshi
		100	CHN	dom	CNR8, Lingshi
		10	B	dom	R. Aparecida, Aparecida
		500	IRN	KAM	VO the Islamic Rep. of Iran
9635		250	IND	ALG	All India Radio (AIR)
		100	D	LAM	BBG - RFE/RL
		250	G	WOF	IBRA Radio

kHz	N	kW	Ctry	Site	Station, location
		50	MLI	dom	R. Mali, Bamako (Kati)
	±	1	TWN	TSU	Sound of Hope Radio Int.
	±	100	VTN	dom	VO Vietnam 1, Son Tay
9640		500	CHN	KAS	China Radio Int. (CRI)
		100	KOR	KIM	KBS World Radio
		50	CUB	HAB	Radio Habana Cuba
9645		300	G	WOF	BBG - Afia Darfur Radio
		100	D	BIB	BBG - RFE/RL
		250	THA	UDO	BBG - VO America (VOA)
		500	CHN	BEI	China Radio Int. (CRI)
		500	CHN	KUN	China Radio Int. (CRI)
		100	CHN	dom	CNR1 VO China, Beijing
		250	KOR	KIM	KBS World Radio
	‡	8	B	dom	R. Bandeirantes, São Paulo
		250	PHL	PUG	Radio Veritas Asia
		100	CVA	SMG	Vatican Radio
		250	CVA	SMG	Vatican Radio
9650		100	AFS	dom	R. Sonder Grense, Meyerton
		200	KRE	KUJ	Voice of Korea
		500	TUR	EMR	Voice of Turkey (VOT)
9655		100	CHN	KAS	China Radio Int. (CRI)
		100	CHN	KUN	China Radio Int. (CRI)
		100	CHN	NNN	China Radio Int. (CRI)
		150	CHN	KUN	China Radio Int. (CRI)
		500	CHN	KUN	China Radio Int. (CRI)
		100	CHN	dom	CNR13 Uyghur Sce, Lingshi
		100	ALS	NLS	KNLS International
		300	ROU	GAL	Radio Romania International
		500	TUR	EMR	Voice of Turkey (VOT)
9660		100	TWN	KOU	Radio Taiwan International
		100	CVA	SMG	Vatican Radio
		250	CVA	SMG	Vatican Radio
		250	MDG	MDC	Vatican Radio
9665		100	CHN	KAS	China Radio Int. (CRI)
		500	CHN	JIN	China Radio Int. (CRI)
		500	CHN	KUN	China Radio Int. (CRI)
		500	CHN	XIA	China Radio Int. (CRI)
		100	CHN	dom	CNR5 VO Zhonghua, Beijing
		50	KRE	dom	KCBS, Pyongyang
		500	F	ISS	Radio France Int. (RFI)
		250	TUR	EMR	Voice of Turkey (VOT)
		10	B	dom	Voz Missionária, Camboriú
9670		250	UAE	DHA	BBC World Service
		250	TJK	DSB	BBG - R. Free Asia (RFA)
		300	J	YAM	Radio Japan (NHK World)
	†	250	PAK	ISL	Radio Pakistan
		250	PHL	PUG	Radio Veritas Asia
9675		150	CHN	KUN	China Radio Int. (CRI)
		500	CHN	KAS	China Radio Int. (CRI)
		100	CHN	dom	CNR1 VO China, Beijing
	†	5	PRU	dom	Pacífico R, Lima
		500	F	ISS	Radio France Int. (RFI)
		500	ARS	RIY	Saudi Int. Radio
9677		5	AZE	dom	Ictimai R. relay, Stepanakert
9680		100	ALS	NLS	KNLS International
		300	J	YAM	Radio Japan (NHK World)
		300	ROU	TIG	Radio Romania International
		300	TWN	TSH	Radio Taiwan International
	‡	250	INS	dom	RRI Prgr. 4, Jakarta
9685		150	CHN	BJI	China Radio Int. (CRI)
		500	CHN	KAS	China Radio Int. (CRI)
		500	CHN	KUN	China Radio Int. (CRI)
		500	CHN	URU	China Radio Int. (CRI)
		500	CHN	XIA	China Radio Int. (CRI)
		250	D	NAU	Pan American Broadcasting
		300	TWN	TSH	Radio Taiwan International
9690		500	IND	BGL	All India Radio (AIR)
		500	UAE	DHA	BBG - R. Free Asia (RFA)
		150	CHN	KUN	China Radio Int. (CRI)
		350	E	NOB	China Radio Int. (CRI)
		250	KOR	KIM	KBS World Radio
		200	E	NOB	R. Exterior de España (REE)
	†	250	NIG	AJA	Voice of Nigeria
9695		250	OMA	SLA	BBC World Service
		500	CHN	JIN	China Radio Int. (CRI)
		500	CHN	KUN	China Radio Int. (CRI)
	†	8	B	dom	R. Rio Mar, Manaus
		100	AUS	KNX	Reach Beyond Australia
		500	ARS	RIY	Saudi Int. Radio
		250	PHL	PHT	Vatican Radio
9700		250	THA	UDO	BBG - VO America (VOA)
		100	NZL	RAN	R. New Zealand Int. (RNZI)
		300	J	YAM	Radio Japan (NHK World)
	‡	100	PAK	ISL	Radio Pakistan
		500	TUR	EMR	Voice of Turkey (VOT)
9705		250	IND	PAN	All India Radio (AIR)
		500	CHN	KAS	China Radio Int. (CRI)
	‡	100	ETH	dom	R. Ethiopia, Geja
		100	CHN	dom	Xinjiang PBS, Urumqi
9710		500	CHN	KAS	China Radio Int. (CRI)
		100	CHN	dom	CNR1 VO China, Shijiazhuang
		100	CUB	HAB	Radio Habana Cuba
		500	IRN	SIR	VO the Islamic Rep. of Iran
9715		100	AUT	MOS	Bible Voice Broadcasting (BVB)
		100	D	NAU	Bible Voice Broadcasting (BVB)
		100	AUT	MOS	Eternal Good News
	^	500	ARS	RIY	Saudi Int. Radio
9720		100	GUM	SDA	AWR Asia/Pacific
		100	MRA	SAI	BBG - R. Free Asia (RFA)
		500	UAE	DHA	BBG - R. Free Asia (RFA)
		500	CHN	URU	China Radio Int. (CRI)
		500	CHN	XIA	China Radio Int. (CRI)
		150	CHN	dom	CNR2 Business R, Baoji
		250	PHL	PUG	Radio Veritas Asia
		100	AUS	KNX	Reach Beyond Australia
		125	CLN	TRM	Sri Lanka Broadcasting Corp.
9725	†	10	B	dom	R. RB2, Curitiba
9730		100	CHN	KAS	China Radio Int. (CRI)
		100	CHN	KUN	China Radio Int. (CRI)
		500	CHN	BEI	China Radio Int. (CRI)
		500	CHN	KAS	China Radio Int. (CRI)
		100	CHN	dom	CNR6 VO Shenzhou, Beijing
		50	BRM	dom	Myanmar R., Yangon
		50	BRM	YAN	Radio Japan (NHK World)
		300	ROU	TIG	Radio Romania International
	±	1	TWN	TSU	Sound of Hope Radio Int.
		200	KRE	KUJ	Voice of Korea
		100	VTN	VNI	Voice of Vietnam (VOV)
9735		250	TWN	TNN	Radio Taiwan International
9740		250	SNG	SNG	BBC World Service
		250	THA	NAK	BBC World Service
		250	KOR	KIM	KBS World Radio
		500	IRN	KAM	VO the Islamic Rep. of Iran
9745		500	CHN	URU	China Radio Int. (CRI)
		10	BHR	ABH	Radio Bahrain
		250	EGY	ABS	Radio Cairo
	‡	100	PAK	ISL	Radio Pakistan
	‡	250	TWN	dom	Voice of Kuanghua, Kuanyin

kHz	N	kW	Ctry	Site	Station, location
9750		50	CHN	dom	Nei Menggu-Mo, Hohhot
		300	J	YAM	Radio Japan (NHK World)
9755		250	CVA	SMG	BBG - VO America (VOA)
		250	THA	UDO	BBG - VO America (VOA)
		100	CHN	dom	CNR2 Business R, Baoji
		250	CVA	SMG	Vatican Radio
		500	IRN	KAM	VO the Islamic Rep. of Iran
9760		100	GUM	SDA	AWR Africa/Europe
		250	THA	UDO	BBG - VO America (VOA)
		500	CHN	KUN	China Radio Int. (CRI)
	+	90	G	WOF	KBS World Radio
		50	J	dom	R. Nikkei 2, Tokyo
	+	90	G	WOF	Radio Japan (NHK World)
9765		250	G	WOF	BBG - VO America (VOA)
		100	STP	SAO	BBG - VO America (VOA)
		250	KWT	KWT	BBG - VOA Deewa Radio
		100	CHN	NNN	China Radio Int. (CRI)
		150	CHN	BJI	China Radio Int. (CRI)
		100	NZL	RAN	R. New Zealand Int. (RNZI)
		250	D	NAU	Radio Japan (NHK World)
9770		300	AUT	MOS	AWR Africa/Europe
		500	CHN	KAS	China Radio Int. (CRI)
		100	KOR	KIM	KBS World Radio
		500	F	ISS	Radio Japan (NHK World)
		300	ROU	TIG	Radio Romania International
9774	‡	10	TWN	dom	Fu Hsing BS, Kuanyin
9775		250	THA	UDO	BBG - VOA Ashna Radio
		150	CHN	dom	CNR2 Business R, Beijing
		125	CLN	TRM	FEBA India
9780		100	BOT	BOT	BBG - Afia Darfur Radio
	†	50	CHN	dom	Qinghai PBS, Xining
	+	50	NZL	RAN	R. New Zealand Int. (RNZI)
9785		150	CHN	KUN	China Radio Int. (CRI)
		500	CHN	JIN	China Radio Int. (CRI)
		100	CHN	dom	CNR8, Beijing
		500	TUR	EMR	Voice of Turkey (VOT)
9790		250	SNG	SNG	BBC World Service
		250	THA	NAK	BBC World Service
		100	D	LAM	BBG - RFE/RL
		250	CUB	HAB	China Radio Int. (CRI)
		500	F	ISS	Radio France Int. (RFI)
		300	ROU	TIG	Radio Romania International
9795		500	CHN	URU	China Radio Int. (CRI)
		100	PHL	IBA	FEBC Philippines
	‡	100	PAK	ISL	Radio Pakistan
9800		250	IND	DEL	All India Radio (AIR)
		100	GUM	SDA	AWR Asia/Pacific
		250	MRA	TIN	BBG - VO America (VOA)
		250	PHL	PHT	BBG - VO America (VOA)
		500	CHN	KAS	China Radio Int. (CRI)
		250	AFS	MEY	Deutsche Welle
		500	F	ISS	Deutsche Welle
		300	ROU	TIG	Radio Romania International
		500	F	ISS	Sawtu Linjiila
		500	IRN	SIR	VO the Islamic Rep. of Iran
9805		100	KOR	KIM	KBS World Radio
		250	KOR	KIM	KBS World Radio
		500	F	ISS	Radio France Int. (RFI)
9810		250	IND	PAN	All India Radio (AIR)
		125	CLN	TRM	AWR Asia/Pacific
		250	G	WOF	BBC World Service
		250	OMA	SLA	BBC World Service
		250	SNG	SNG	BBC World Service
		100	CHN	dom	CNR1 VO China, Nanning
		100	CHN	dom	CNR2 Business R, Baoji
9820		250	IND	DEL	All India Radio (AIR)
		100	BOT	BOT	BBG - Afia Darfur Radio
		300	G	WOF	BBG - Afia Darfur Radio
		100	D	LAM	BBG - VO America (VOA)
		15	CHN	NNN	Beibu Bay Radio
		150	CHN	dom	CNR2 Business R, Xianyang
		250	UAE	DHA	IBRA Radio
		10	B	dom	R. Nove de Julho, São Paulo
		100	CUB	HAB	Radio Habana Cuba
		250	TUR	EMR	Voice of Turkey (VOT)
9825		100	LTU	SIT	BBG - R. Free Asia (RFA)
		100	MRA	SAI	BBG - VO America (VOA)
		250	PHL	PHT	BBG - VO America (VOA)
		100	CHN	KAS	China Radio Int. (CRI)
9830		300	AUT	MOS	AWR Africa/Europe
		100	D	NAU	AWR Africa/Europe
		100	CHN	dom	CNR1 VO China, Beijing
		100	STP	SAO	Deutsche Welle
9835		100	IND	DEL	All India Radio (AIR)
	†	100	MLA	dom	RTM Sarawak FM, Kajang
		100	CHN	dom	Xinjiang PBS, Urumqi
9840		100	D	LAM	BBG - RFE/RL
		250	UAE	DHA	KBS World Radio
		250	USA	HRI	The Overcomer Ministry
		250	TUR	EMR	Voice of Turkey (VOT)
		100	VTN	VNI	Voice of Vietnam (VOV)
		250	USA	HRI	WHRI - World Harvest R.
9845		100	CHN	dom	CNR1 VO China, Beijing
9850		100	D	NAU	AWR Africa/Europe
		250	KWT	KWT	BBG - R. Free Asia (RFA)
	†	50	CHN	dom	Qinghai PBS, Xining
		100	CUB	HAB	Radio Habana Cuba
	±	1	TWN	TSU	Sound of Hope Radio Int.
		100	CVA	SMG	Vatican Radio
		500	IRN	KAM	VO the Islamic Rep. of Iran
		100	VTN	dom	VO Vietnam Min, Xuan Mai
		200	KRE	KUJ	Voice of Korea
9855		500	CHN	BEI	China Radio Int. (CRI)
		250	MDG	MDC	Radio Japan (NHK World)
9860		100	MRA	SAI	BBG - R. Free Asia (RFA)
		250	MRA	TIN	BBG - R. Free Asia (RFA)
		500	CHN	JIN	China Radio Int. (CRI)
		500	CHN	KAS	China Radio Int. (CRI)
		100	CHN	dom	CNR1 VO China, Beijing
		250	EGY	ABS	Radio Cairo
9865		500	CHN	KUN	China Radio Int. (CRI)
9870		500	IND	dom	AIR Bengaluru
		250	ASC	ASC	BBC World Service
		250	G	WOF	BBC World Service
		500	CHN	XIA	China Radio Int. (CRI)
		500	ARS	RIY	Saudi Int. Radio
9875		500	CHN	KAS	China Radio Int. (CRI)
		500	IRN	SIR	VO the Islamic Rep. of Iran
		200	KRE	KUJ	Voice of Korea
9880		100	GUM	SDA	AWR Asia/Pacific
		100	ARM	ERV	BBC World Service
		250	THA	UDO	BBG - VO America (VOA)
		100	CHN	KUN	China Radio Int. (CRI)
		100	CHN	NNN	China Radio Int. (CRI)
		500	CHN	BEI	China Radio Int. (CRI)
		100	ROU	TIG	Radio Romania International
		300	ROU	TIG	Radio Romania International
9885		100	BOT	BOT	BBG - VO America (VOA)

kHz	N	kW	Ctry	Site	Station, location
		100	STP	SAO	BBG - VO America (VOA)
		250	EGY	ABS	Radio Cairo
		500	ARS	RIY	Saudi Int. Radio
9890		100	GUM	SDA	AWR Asia/Pacific
		250	KWT	KWT	BBG - R. Free Asia (RFA)
		100	CHN	dom	CNR1 VO China, Lingshi
		100	CHN	dom	CNR13 Uyghur Sce, Lingshi
		200	KRE	KUJ	Voice of Korea
9895		250	UAE	DHA	Radio Taiwan International
		500	IRN	ZAH	VO the Islamic Rep. of Iran
9900		100	SNG	SNG	BBC World Service
		100	MRA	SAI	BBG - R. Free Asia (RFA)
		250	EGY	ABS	Radio Cairo
9910		250	IND	ALG	All India Radio (AIR)
		250	IND	DEL	All India Radio (AIR)
		100	GUM	TWR	TWR Asia
		200	GUM	TWR	TWR Asia
9915		250	ASC	ASC	BBC World Service
		250	G	WOF	BBC World Service
9920		250	THA	NAK	BBC World Service
		100	PHL	IBA	FEBC Philippines
9925		100	BUL	SOF	Bible Voice Broadcasting (BVB)
		250	PHL	PHT	Radyo Pilipinas Overseas
9930		100	PLW	HBN	Eternal Good News
		100	PLW	HBN	Quê Me Radio
	±	1	TWN	TSU	Sound of Hope Radio Int.
		100	PLW	HBN	T8WH - World Harvest Radio Int
9935	‡	100	GRC	AVL	ERT (i Foni tis Elladas)
9940		100	IND	dom	AIR Delhi
		100	IND	DEL	All India Radio (AIR)
		500	IND	BGL	All India Radio (AIR)
		100	MRA	SAI	BBG - R. Free Asia (RFA)
		250	MRA	TIN	BBG - R. Free Asia (RFA)
		200	TJK	DSB	BBG - R. Free Asia (RFA)
		100	PHL	BOC	FEBC Philippines
		100	SWZ	MAN	TWR Africa
9950	+	100	IND	DEL	All India Radio (AIR)
		500	IND	BGL	All India Radio (AIR)
		100	TWN	TSH	Furustato/Ilbon-E Baram
9955		100	USA	YFR	FG Radio (ex EUNN)
		100	USA	YFR	Radio Prague
		100	USA	YFR	Radio Slovakia Int.
		100	USA	YFR	The Overcomer Ministry
		100	USA	YFR	WRMI - R. Miami Int.
9960		100	PLW	HBN	Furustato/Ilbon-E Baram
9965		100	PLW	HBN	Furustato/Ilbon-E Baram
		250	EGY	ABS	Radio Cairo
9970	±	1	TWN	TSU	Sound of Hope Radio Int.
9975		100	PLW	HBN	Furustato/Ilbon-E Baram
		50	USA	VOH	KVOH - Voice of Hope
		50	USA	VOH	Trunews Radio
		100	GUM	TWR	TWR Asia
		200	GUM	TWR	TWR Asia
	+	60	GUM	TWR	TWR Asia
9980		100	USA	WCR	The Overcomer Ministry
		100	USA	WCR	WWCR
9985		250	CLN	IRA	BBG - R. Free Asia (RFA)
		100	MRA	SAI	BBG - R. Free Asia (RFA)
		250	MRA	TIN	BBG - R. Free Asia (RFA)
9990		250	CLN	IRA	BBG - R. Farda
		250	KWT	KWT	BBG - R. Farda
9995		100	MRA	SAI	BBG - R. Free Asia (RFA)
9996		5	RUS	STF	RWM, Moscow
10000		20	CHN	STF	BPM, Kinshan
		2	ARG	STF	LOL, Buenos Aires
		1	B	STF	Observatório Nal, Rio de Janeiro
		10	USA	STF	WWV NIST, Fort Collins, CO
		10	HWA	STF	WWVH NIST, Kauai, HI
10820 ±		1	TWN	TSU	Sound of Hope Radio Int.
10870 ±		1	TWN	TSU	Sound of Hope Radio Int.
10960 ±		1	TWN	TSU	Sound of Hope Radio Int.
11070 ±		1	TWN	TSU	Sound of Hope Radio Int.
11100 ±		1	TWN	TSU	Sound of Hope Radio Int.
11150 ±		1	TWN	TSU	Sound of Hope Radio Int.
11300 ±		1	TWN	TSU	Sound of Hope Radio Int.
11370 ±		1	TWN	TSU	Sound of Hope Radio Int.
11410 ±		1	TWN	TSU	Sound of Hope Radio Int.
11470 ±		1	TWN	TSU	Sound of Hope Radio Int.
11500 ±		1	TWN	TSU	Sound of Hope Radio Int.
11520		250	USA	EWN	WEWN - EWTN Shortwave
11530		200	E	NOB	R. Exterior de España (REE)
	‡	250	PAK	ISL	Radio Pakistan
	±	1	TWN	TSU	Sound of Hope Radio Int.
11540		250	KWT	KWT	BBG - R. Free Asia (RFA)
11550		250	USA	EWN	WEWN - EWTN Shortwave
11560		250	IND	PAN	All India Radio (AIR)
		250	KWT	KWT	BBG - R. Free Asia (RFA)
11565		250	USA	HRI	Trunews Radio
		250	USA	HRI	WHRI - World Harvest R.
11570		250	MRA	TIN	BBG - VO America (VOA)
		250	PHL	PHT	BBG - VO America (VOA)
	‡	250	PAK	ISL	Radio Pakistan
		100	TWN	TSH	Suab Xaa Moo Zoo
11580		100	USA	YFR	FG Radio (ex EUNN)
		100	USA	YFR	PCJ R. International
		100	USA	YFR	Radio France Int. (RFI)
		100	USA	YFR	Radio Slovakia Int.
		100	USA	YFR	Radio Ukraine Int. (RUI)
	±	1	TWN	TSU	Sound of Hope Radio Int.
		100	USA	YFR	The Overcomer Ministry
		100	GUM	TWR	TWR Asia
		100	USA	YFR	WRMI - R. Miami Int.
11600		100	BUL	SOF	ETC Radio
	†	250	PAK	ISL	Radio Pakistan
	±	1	TWN	TSU	Sound of Hope Radio Int.
11605		250	TWN	TNN	Radio Taiwan International
11610		150	CHN	KUN	China Radio Int. (CRI)
		500	CHN	URU	China Radio Int. (CRI)
		150	CHN	dom	CNR2 Business R, Beijing
		100	AFS	MEY	IBRA Radio
11615		100	BOT	BOT	BBG - Afia Darfur Radio
		250	THA	UDO	BBG - Afia Darfur Radio
		100	STP	SAO	BBG - VO America (VOA)
11620		250	IND	dom	AIR Delhi
	+	200	IND	BGL	All India Radio (AIR)
		250	IND	DEL	All India Radio (AIR)
		500	IND	BGL	All India Radio (AIR)
		100	CHN	dom	CNR5 VO Zhonghua, Beijing
11625		250	CVA	SMG	Vatican Radio
		250	MDG	MDC	Vatican Radio
11630		100	CHN	dom	CNR1 VO China, Lingshi
		100	CHN	dom	CNR8, Lingshi
11635		500	CHN	BEI	China Radio Int. (CRI)
		250	USA	HRI	Eternal Good News
		250	TWN	TNN	Radio Taiwan International
		200	KRE	KUJ	Voice of Korea
		250	USA	HRI	WHRI - World Harvest R.
11640		100	CHN	KAS	China Radio Int. (CRI)

kHz	N	kW	Ctry	Site	Station, location
		100	CHN	KUN	China Radio Int. (CRI)
		150	CHN	KUN	China Radio Int. (CRI)
		500	CHN	BEI	China Radio Int. (CRI)
		500	CHN	JIN	China Radio Int. (CRI)
		500	CHN	XIA	China Radio Int. (CRI)
		100	MLI	BKO	China Radio Int. (CRI)
		100	TWN	KOU	Radio Taiwan International
		250	PHL	PUG	Radio Veritas Asia
11645	+	100	IND	DEL	All India Radio (AIR)
	‡	100	GRC	AVL	ERT (i Foni tis Elladas)
		200	KRE	KUJ	Voice of Korea
11650		250	THA	UDO	BBG - VO America (VOA)
		100	CHN	KUN	China Radio Int. (CRI)
		150	CHN	KUN	China Radio Int. (CRI)
		500	CHN	BEI	China Radio Int. (CRI)
		500	CHN	URU	China Radio Int. (CRI)
		100	PHL	BOC	FEBC Philippines
		100	OMA	THU	Radio Sultanate of Oman
11655		250	MRA	TIN	BBG - VO America (VOA)
		250	THA	UDO	BBG - VO America (VOA)
		250	UAE	DHA	IBRA Radio
		100	TWN	PAO	Radio Taiwan International
11660		250	ASC	ASC	BBC World Service
		500	UAE	DHA	BBG - R. Free Asia (RFA)
		150	CHN	dom	CNR2 Business R, Xi'an
		300	ROU	GAL	Radio Romania International
		100	SWZ	MAN	TWR Africa
11665		500	CHN	URU	China Radio Int. (CRI)
		250	EGY	ABS	Radio Cairo
		300	J	YAM	Radio Japan (NHK World)
	†	100	MLA	dom	RTM Wai FM, Kajang
11670		250	IND	ALG	All India Radio (AIR)
		500	IND	BGL	All India Radio (AIR)
		250	PHL	PHT	BBG - VO America (VOA)
		150	CHN	dom	CNR2 Business R, Beijing
		100	CUB	HAB	Radio Habana Cuba
11675		500	IRN	KAM	VO the Islamic Rep. of Iran
11680		300	AUT	MOS	AWR Africa/Europe
		250	D	NAU	AWR Africa/Europe
		100	CHN	NNN	China Radio Int. (CRI)
		100	KRE	dom	KCBS, Kanggye
		250	TUR	EMR	Voice of Turkey (VOT)
11685		100	CHN	dom	CNR11 Tibetan Sce, Xi'an
		250	SNG	SNG	Radio Japan (NHK World)
		100	UZB	TAC	Radio Japan (NHK World)
11690		500	CHN	XIA	China Radio Int. (CRI)
	+	50	NZL	RAN	R. New Zealand Int. (RNZI)
		0.1	FIN	VIR	Scandinavian Weekend R.
11695		250	KWT	KWT	BBG - R. Free Asia (RFA)
		250	MRA	TIN	BBG - R. Free Asia (RFA)
		250	PHL	PHT	BBG - VO America (VOA)
		250	PHL	PHT	Vatican Radio
11700		100	BUL	SOF	Bible Voice Broadcasting (BVB)
		100	CHN	KAS	China Radio Int. (CRI)
		100	CHN	KUN	China Radio Int. (CRI)
		150	CHN	KUN	China Radio Int. (CRI)
		500	F	ISS	Radio France Int. (RFI)
11705		250	USA	HRI	Eternal Good News
		250	USA	HRI	WHRI - World Harvest R.
11710		250	IND	DEL	All India Radio (AIR)
		100	CHN	NNN	China Radio Int. (CRI)
		500	CHN	URU	China Radio Int. (CRI)
		100	CHN	dom	CNR1 VO China, Beijing
		100	ARG	BUE	Rdif. Argentina al Exterior

kHz	N	kW	Ctry	Site	Station, location
		200	KRE	KUJ	Voice of Korea
11715		250	IND	DEL	All India Radio (AIR)
	±	1	TWN	TSU	Sound of Hope Radio Int.
		100	CVA	SMG	Vatican Radio
11720		250	MRA	TIN	BBG - R. Free Asia (RFA)
		150	CHN	BJI	China Radio Int. (CRI)
		100	CHN	dom	CNR1 VO China, Shijiazhuang
		250	F	ISS	Eritrean Forum Radio
		0.1	FIN	VIR	Scandinavian Weekend R.
		500	IRN	KAM	VO the Islamic Rep. of Iran
	†	100	VTN	dom	VO Vietnam 1, Son Tay
		250	F	ISS	Voice of Assenna
11725		150	ALB	CER	China Radio Int. (CRI)
	†	10	B	dom	R. Marumby, Curitiba
		100	NZL	RAN	R. New Zealand Int. (RNZI)
11730		100	GUM	SDA	AWR Asia/Pacific
		500	CHN	KUN	China Radio Int. (CRI)
		150	BLR	MNS	Radio Belarus
		250	BLR	MNS	Radio Belarus
		500	F	ISS	Radio Japan (NHK World)
		100	UZB	TAC	Radio Japan (NHK World)
		500	IRN	KAM	VO the Islamic Rep. of Iran
		500	TUR	EMR	Voice of Turkey (VOT)
11735	†	50	B	dom	R. Transmundial, Santa Maria
		200	KRE	KUJ	Voice of Korea
	†	50	TZA	DOL	Zanzibar Broadcasting Corp.
11740		250	IND	PAN	All India Radio (AIR)
		100	CHN	dom	CNR2 Business R, Lingshi
		250	SNG	SNG	Radio Japan (NHK World)
		100	CVA	SMG	Vatican Radio
		250	CVA	SMG	Vatican Radio
11750		250	AFS	MEY	AWR Africa/Europe
		250	D	NAU	AWR Africa/Europe
		250	D	NAU	AWR Asia/Pacific
		100	MRA	SAI	BBG - R. Free Asia (RFA)
		100	BOT	BOT	BBG - VO America (VOA)
		250	CVA	SMG	BBG - VO America (VOA)
		150	ALB	CER	China Radio Int. (CRI)
		500	CHN	BEI	China Radio Int. (CRI)
		100	CHN	dom	CNR1 VO China, Shijiazhuang
		100	PHL	BOC	FEBC Philippines
		250	EGY	ABS	Radio Cairo
		250	PHL	PUG	Radio Veritas Asia
		125	CLN	TRM	Sri Lanka Broadcasting Corp.
11760		500	CHN	KUN	China Radio Int. (CRI)
		100	CHN	dom	CNR1 VO China, Shijiazhuang
		100	CUB	HAB	Radio Habana Cuba
		300	ROU	TIG	Radio Romania International
		500	IRN	KAM	VO the Islamic Rep. of Iran
		500	IRN	SIR	VO the Islamic Rep. of Iran
11765		100	TWN	PAO	Radio Taiwan International
	±	1	TWN	TSU	Sound of Hope Radio Int.
		20	B	dom	Super R. Deus é Amor, Curitiba
11770		250	ASC	ASC	BBC World Service
		100	CHN	KAS	China Radio Int. (CRI)
		100	CHN	NNN	China Radio Int. (CRI)
		500	CHN	BEI	China Radio Int. (CRI)
		100	CHN	dom	Xinjiang PBS, Urumqi
11775		250	IND	PAN	All India Radio (AIR)
		250	MRA	TIN	BBG - R. Free Asia (RFA)
		50	USA	VOH	KVOH - Voice of Hope
		500	F	ISS	Radio Algériénnne
	±	1	TWN	TSU	Sound of Hope Radio Int.
	†	100	AIA	AIA	University Network

kHz	N	kW	Ctry	Site	Station, location
11780		125	CLN	TRM	AWR Africa/Europe
		500	CHN	JIN	China Radio Int. (CRI)
		250	B	dom	R. Nal da Amazônia, Brasília
		500	IRN	SIR	VO the Islamic Rep. of Iran
11785		250	ASC	ASC	BBC World Service
		150	ALB	CER	China Radio Int. (CRI)
		150	CHN	BJI	China Radio Int. (CRI)
		500	CHN	KAS	China Radio Int. (CRI)
11790		125	MDG	MDC	Bible Voice Broadcasting (BVB)
		100	CHN	KAS	China Radio Int. (CRI)
		500	CHN	XIA	China Radio Int. (CRI)
		250	EGY	ABS	Radio Cairo
		300	J	YAM	Radio Japan (NHK World)
		300	ROU	TIG	Radio Romania International
		100	USA	HRI	WHRI - World Harvest R.
11795		250	MRA	TIN	BBG - R. Free Asia (RFA)
		100	CHN	KAS	China Radio Int. (CRI)
		250	KOR	KIM	KBS World Radio
		500	TUR	EMR	Voice of Turkey (VOT)
11800		100	D	BIB	BBG - RFE/RL
		150	CHN	dom	CNR2 Business R, Beijing
		250	AFS	MEY	Radio Japan (NHK World)
11805		250	KWT	KWT	BBG - R. Free Asia (RFA)
		100	CHN	KUN	China Radio Int. (CRI)
	‡	100	PAK	ISL	Radio Pakistan
11810		250	ASC	ASC	BBC World Service
		100	CHN	dom	CNR8, Beijing
		250	MDG	MDC	Deutsche Welle
		250	KOR	KIM	KBS World Radio
		500	IRN	SIR	VO the Islamic Rep. of Iran
11815	†	8	B	dom	R. Brasil Central, Goiânia
		300	J	YAM	Radio Japan (NHK World)
		250	TUR	EMR	Voice of Turkey (VOT)
11820		250	CLN	IRA	BBG - VO America (VOA)
		500	CHN	XIA	China Radio Int. (CRI)
		500	ARS	RIY	Saudi Int. Radio
11825		100	PHL	BOC	FEBC Philippines
		100	USA	YFR	The Overcomer Ministry
		500	IRN	SIR	VO the Islamic Rep. of Iran
11830		100	D	LAM	BBG - RFE/RL
		250	ASC	ASC	Follow The Bible Ministries
		500	IRN	KAM	VO the Islamic Rep. of Iran
		500	IRN	SIR	VO the Islamic Rep. of Iran
11835		150	CHN	dom	CNR2 Business R, Xianyang
		250	TUR	EMR	Voice of Turkey (VOT)
11840		250	IND	DEL	All India Radio (AIR)
		250	CUB	HAB	Radio Habana Cuba
		100	GUM	TWR	TWR Asia
11845		250	IND	DEL	All India Radio (AIR)
		150	CHN	dom	CNR2 Business R, Xianyang
11850		100	IND	DEL	All India Radio (AIR)
		250	CLN	IRA	BBG - R. Free Asia (RFA)
		100	MRA	SAI	BBG - R. Free Asia (RFA)
		100	BOT	BOT	BBG - VO America (VOA)
		100	STP	SAO	BBG - VO America (VOA)
		250	PHL	PUG	Radio Veritas Asia
11855		250	THA	UDO	BBG - VO America (VOA)
		150	ALB	CER	China Radio Int. (CRI)
	†	10	B	dom	R. Aparecida, Aparecida
		100	BUL	SOF	Radio Erena
		300	ROU	TIG	Radio Romania International
		250	PHL	PUG	Radio Veritas Asia
11860		100	D	NAU	AWR Africa/Europe
		250	KWT	KWT	BBG - VOA Ashna Radio
		500	CHN	KUN	China Radio Int. (CRI)
	‡	100	PAK	ISL	Radio Pakistan
			ARS	-	Republic of Yemen Radio/R. Sana'a
		100	CHN	dom	Xizang PBS, Lhasa
11870		250	PHL	PHT	BBG - VO America (VOA)
		100	CHN	KAS	China Radio Int. (CRI)
		250	PHL	PUG	Radio Veritas Asia
		250	USA	EWN	WEWN - EWTN Shortwave
11875		100	AFS	MEY	BBC World Service
		250	OMA	SLA	BBC World Service
		100	D	NAU	Bible Voice Broadcasting (BVB)
		100	CHN	NNN	China Radio Int. (CRI)
		500	CHN	BEI	China Radio Int. (CRI)
		500	CHN	KUN	China Radio Int. (CRI)
	‡	100	PAK	ISL	Radio Pakistan
		250	PHL	PHT	Vatican Radio
		250	PHL	PUG	Vatican Radio
11880		300	AUT	MOS	AWR Africa/Europe
		250	F	ISS	AWR Africa/Europe
		100	CUB	HAB	Radio Habana Cuba
		500	IRN	SIR	VO the Islamic Rep. of Iran
11885		500	CHN	XIA	China Radio Int. (CRI)
		100	CHN	dom	Xinjiang PBS, Urumqi
11890		100	D	LAM	BBG - RFE/RL
		250	PHL	PHT	BBG - RFE/RL
		250	MRA	TIN	Vatican Radio
11895		250	THA	NAK	BBC World Service
		100	CHN	KAS	China Radio Int. (CRI)
		100	CHN	NNN	China Radio Int. (CRI)
	†	10	B	dom	R. Boa Vontade, Porto Alegre
11900		100	AFS	MEY	BBG - VO America (VOA)
		100	STP	SAO	BBG - VO America (VOA)
		250	UAE	DHA	BBG - VO America (VOA)
		150	CHN	BEI	China Radio Int. (CRI)
		500	CHN	BEI	China Radio Int. (CRI)
		100	D	NAU	Reach Beyond
11905		100	CHN	dom	CNR6 VO Shenzhou, Beijing
	†	250	PAK	ISL	Radio Pakistan
		125	CLN	TRM	Sri Lanka Broadcasting Corp.
11910		300	AUT	MOS	AWR Africa/Europe
		250	THA	NAK	BBC World Service
		250	KWT	KWT	BBG - VO America (VOA)
		500	CHN	BEI	China Radio Int. (CRI)
		300	J	YAM	Radio Japan (NHK World)
		200	KRE	KUJ	Voice of Korea
11915		250	D	NAU	Bible Voice Broadcasting (BVB)
		100	CHN	dom	CNR2 Business R, Baoji
	†	10	B	dom	R. Gaucha, Porto Alegre
		250	TWN	TNN	Radio Taiwan International
		500	ARS	RIY	Saudi Int. Radio
11920		150	ALB	CER	China Radio Int. (CRI)
		100	USA	YFR	Family Radio
		100	USA	YFR	Radio Taiwan International
11925		100	CHN	dom	CNR1 VO China, Lingshi
		100	PLW	HBN	Radio Japan (NHK World)
		500	IRN	KAM	VO the Islamic Rep. of Iran
		500	TUR	EMR	Voice of Turkey (VOT)
11930		125	USA	GRV	BBG - R. Martí
		250	BLR	MNS	Radio Belarus
		500	ARS	RIY	Saudi Int. Radio
11935		100	IND	MUM	All India Radio (AIR)
		100	GUM	SDA	AWR Asia/Pacific
		100	CHN	dom	CNR5 VO Zhonghua, Beijing
		10	B	dom	R. RB2, Curitiba

kHz	N	kW	Ctry	Site	Station, location
		250	PHL	PUG	Radio Veritas Asia
		500	ARS	RIY	Saudi Int. Radio
		100	CVA	SMG	Vatican Radio
		250	CVA	SMG	Vatican Radio
11940		500	IRN	KAM	VO the Islamic Rep. of Iran
11945		250	AFS	MEY	BBC World Service
		100	SNG	SNG	BBC World Service
		250	PHL	PHT	BBG - VO America (VOA)
		100	CHN	KUN	China Radio Int. (CRI)
		150	CHN	KUN	China Radio Int. (CRI)
		500	F	ISS	Radio Japan (NHK World)
		300	ROU	GAL	Radio Romania International
		250	PHL	PUG	Radio Veritas Asia
11950		100	CUB	HAB	Radio Habana Cuba
		100	CHN	dom	Xizang PBS, Lhasa
11955		300	AUT	MOS	AWR Africa/Europe
		125	CLN	TRM	AWR Asia/Pacific
		100	SNG	SNG	BBC World Service
		100	CHN	KUN	China Radio Int. (CRI)
		500	CHN	KUN	China Radio Int. (CRI)
		500	IRN	KAM	VO the Islamic Rep. of Iran
		500	TUR	EMR	Voice of Turkey (VOT)
11960		100	CHN	dom	CNR1 VO China, Beijing
11965		250	G	WOF	BBC World Service
		300	G	WOF	BBC World Service
		250	CLN	IRA	BBG - VO America (VOA)
		250	CVA	SMG	BBG - VO America (VOA)
		100	D	LAM	BBG - VO America (VOA)
		100	STP	SAO	BBG - VO America (VOA)
		100	GUM	TWR	TWR Asia
		250	TUR	EMR	Voice of Turkey (VOT)
11970		250	OMA	SLA	BBC World Service
	±	1	TWN	TSU	Sound of Hope Radio Int.
11975		300	AUT	MOS	AWR Africa/Europe
		250	ASC	ASC	BBC World Service
		500	CHN	KUN	China Radio Int. (CRI)
		500	F	ISS	Radio Japan (NHK World)
		300	ROU	GAL	Radio Romania International
		100	CHN	dom	Xinjiang PBS, Urumqi
11980		300	AUT	MOS	AWR Africa/Europe
		250	TJK	DSB	BBG - R. Free Asia (RFA)
		100	CHN	KAS	China Radio Int. (CRI)
		100	CHN	KUN	China Radio Int. (CRI)
		150	CHN	KUN	China Radio Int. (CRI)
	†	0.3	UKR	dom	Dniprovska Khvylia, Zaporizhia
11985		250	IND	DEL	All India Radio (AIR)
		100	D	BIB	BBG - RFE/RL
		500	F	ISS	Radio Algeriénnne
		300	ROU	TIG	Radio Romania International
		300	TWN	TSH	Radio Taiwan International
		500	TUR	EMR	Voice of Turkey (VOT)
11990		100	CHN	NNN	China Radio Int. (CRI)
		500	CHN	XIA	China Radio Int. (CRI)
11995		250	MDG	MDC	BBC World Service
		250	SNG	SNG	BBC World Service
		250	THA	NAK	BBC World Service
		500	F	ISS	Radio France Int. (RFI)
12000		100	VTN	VNI	Voice of Vietnam (VOV)
12005		100	D	BIB	BBG - R. Farda
		250	CLN	IRA	BBG - VOA Deewa Radio
		500	F	ISS	Deutsche Welle
12015		100	CHN	KAS	China Radio Int. (CRI)
		500	CHN	URU	China Radio Int. (CRI)
		250	ASC	ASC	Radio Japan (NHK World)

kHz	N	kW	Ctry	Site	Station, location
		200	KRE	KUJ	Voice of Korea
		250	MNG	UBA	Voice of Mongolia
12020		100	VTN	VNI	Voice of Vietnam (VOV)
12025		100	IND	PAN	All India Radio (AIR)
		250	SNG	SNG	BBC World Service
		100	D	BIB	BBG - RFE/RL
		250	KWT	KWT	BBG - VOA Deewa Radio
		250	THA	UDO	BBG - VOA Deewa Radio
		250	UAE	DHA	TWR Africa
		300	ARM	ERV	TWR India
12030		100	STP	SAO	BBG - VO America (VOA)
12035		125	CLN	TRM	AWR Asia/Pacific
		250	OMA	SLA	Voice of Mongolia
		500	CHN	XIA	China Radio Int. (CRI)
		250	MNG	UBA	Voice of Mongolia
		500	TUR	EMR	Voice of Turkey (VOT)
12040		500	IRN	KAM	VO the Islamic Rep. of Iran
		500	IRN	SIR	VO the Islamic Rep. of Iran
12045		250	THA	NAK	BBC World Service
		250	PHL	PHT	BBG - VO America (VOA)
		100	CHN	dom	CNR1 VO China, Beijing
		500	TUR	EMR	Voice of Turkey (VOT)
12050		250	KWT	KWT	BBG - R. Free Asia (RFA)
		250	ASC	ASC	Dandal Kura
		250	USA	EWN	WEWN - EWTN Shortwave
12055		250	MRA	TIN	BBG - R. Free Asia (RFA)
		100	D	BIB	BBG - RFE/RL
		100	CHN	dom	CNR1 VO China, Lingshi
		100	CHN	dom	CNR8, Lingshi
		100	PHL	BOC	FEBC Philippines
12065		100	AUS	SHP	ABC Radio Australia
		250	SNG	SNG	BBC World Service
		250	UAE	DHA	BBC World Service
		250	G	WOF	IBRA Radio
12070		250	THA	NAK	BBC World Service
		100	STP	SAO	BBG - VO America (VOA)
		500	CHN	XIA	China Radio Int. (CRI)
		100	PHL	IBA	FEBC Philippines
		250	EGY	ABS	Radio Cairo
12075		250	CVA	SMG	BBG - Afia Darfur Radio
		100	BOT	BOT	BBG - VO America (VOA)
		250	CVA	SMG	BBG - VO America (VOA)
		100	STP	SAO	BBG - VO America (VOA)
		250	CVA	SMG	BBG - VOA Ashna Radio
		300	G	WOF	BBG - VOA Ashna Radio
		250	KWT	KWT	BBG - VOA Ashna Radio
		250	KWT	KWT	Radio Azadi
12080		100	CHN	dom	CNR2 Business R, Baoji
12085		100	AUS	SHP	ABC Radio Australia
12095		100	AFS	MEY	BBC World Service
		250	AFS	MEY	BBC World Service
		125	ASC	ASC	BBC World Service
		250	ASC	ASC	BBC World Service
		250	MDG	MDC	BBC World Service
		250	OMA	SLA	BBC World Service
		250	SNG	SNG	BBC World Service
		250	UAE	DHA	BBC World Service
		100	PHL	BOC	FEBC Philippines
12105		100	MRA	SAI	BBG - R. Free Asia (RFA)
	†	100	USA	TWW	WTWW
12115		250	CLN	IRA	BBG - R. Free Asia (RFA)
12120		100	PHL	BOC	FEBC Philippines
		250	PHL	PHT	Radyo Pilipinas Overseas
		100	GUM	TWR	TWR Asia

kHz	N	kW	Ctry	Site	Station, location
12125		300	ARM	ERV	IBRA Radio
12130		250	KWT	KWT	BBG - Radio Mashaal
12140		250	KWT	KWT	BBG - VO America (VOA)
		250	KWT	KWT	BBG - VOA Ashna Radio
		250	THA	UDO	BBG - VOA Ashna Radio
		250	KWT	KWT	Radio Azadi
12150	±	1	TWN	TSU	Sound of Hope Radio Int.
12160		100	USA	WCR	WWCR
12190	±	1	TWN	TSU	Sound of Hope Radio Int.
12230	±	1	TWN	TSU	Sound of Hope Radio Int.
12370	±	1	TWN	TSU	Sound of Hope Radio Int.
12500	±	1	TWN	TSU	Sound of Hope Radio Int.
12560	±	1	TWN	TSU	Sound of Hope Radio Int.
12800	±	1	TWN	TSU	Sound of Hope Radio Int.
12910	±	1	TWN	TSU	Sound of Hope Radio Int.
12950	±	1	TWN	TSU	Sound of Hope Radio Int.
12980	±	1	TWN	TSU	Sound of Hope Radio Int.
13146	‡	10	F	MCR	Radio Monaco
13200	±	1	TWN	TSU	Sound of Hope Radio Int.
13230	±	1	TWN	TSU	Sound of Hope Radio Int.
13530	±	1	TWN	TSU	Sound of Hope Radio Int.
13570		500	CHN	XIA	China Radio Int. (CRI)
		500	IRN	KAM	VO the Islamic Rep. of Iran
13580		250	BGD	DKA	Bangladesh Betar
		250	KWT	KWT	BBG - Radio Mashaal
		250	THA	UDO	BBG - Radio Mashaal
		100	BOT	BOT	BBG - VO America (VOA)
		500	CHN	BEI	China Radio Int. (CRI)
		500	CHN	KUN	China Radio Int. (CRI)
		250	EGY	ABS	Radio Cairo
		300	ROU	TIG	Radio Romania International
13590		100	D	LAM	BBG - VO America (VOA)
		250	KWT	KWT	BBG - VO America (VOA)
		100	STP	SAO	BBG - VO America (VOA)
		250	CLN	IRA	BBG - VOA Deewa Radio
		500	CHN	BEI	China Radio Int. (CRI)
13600		150	CHN	KUN	China Radio Int. (CRI)
		500	CHN	XIA	China Radio Int. (CRI)
		100	OMA	THU	Radio Sultanate of Oman
13605	+	200	IND	BGL	All India Radio (AIR)
		500	IND	BGL	All India Radio (AIR)
13610		500	CHN	XIA	China Radio Int. (CRI)
		100	CHN	dom	CNR1 VO China, Nanning
		500	F	ISS	Deutsche Welle
13625		500	TUR	EMR	Voice of Turkey (VOT)
13630		250	CLN	IRA	BBG - RFE/RL
		100	BOT	BOT	BBG - VO America (VOA)
		100	STP	SAO	BBG - VO America (VOA)
		100	D	NAU	Bible Voice Broadcasting (BVB)
13640		500	IND	BGL	All India Radio (AIR)
		100	CHN	KAS	China Radio Int. (CRI)
		250	UAE	DHA	Radio Japan (NHK World)
	±	1	TWN	TSU	Sound of Hope Radio Int.
13645		250	IND	ALG	All India Radio (AIR)
		250	MRA	TIN	BBG - R. Free Asia (RFA)
		500	CHN	XIA	China Radio Int. (CRI)
13650		250	KWT	KWT	BBG - R. Free Asia (RFA)
		100	BOT	BOT	BBG - VO America (VOA)
		250	CUB	HAB	China Radio Int. (CRI)
		300	J	YAM	Radio Japan (NHK World)
		200	KRE	KUJ	Voice of Korea
13655		250	MRA	TIN	BBG - R. Free Asia (RFA)
		500	CHN	XIA	China Radio Int. (CRI)
13660		250	G	WOF	BBC World Service

kHz	N	kW	Ctry	Site	Station, location
		500	CHN	XIA	China Radio Int. (CRI)
		300	ROU	TIG	Radio Romania International
13665		250	MRA	TIN	BBG - R. Free Asia (RFA)
		150	ALB	CER	China Radio Int. (CRI)
13670		100	BOT	BOT	BBG - VO America (VOA)
		150	ALB	CER	China Radio Int. (CRI)
		500	CHN	KAS	China Radio Int. (CRI)
		250	EGY	ABS	Radio Cairo
		100	CHN	dom	Xinjiang PBS, Urumqi
13680	±	1	TWN	TSU	Sound of Hope Radio Int.
		500	IRN	SIR	VO the Islamic Rep. of Iran
13685		100	MRA	SAI	BBG - R. Free Asia (RFA)
		500	F	ISS	Radio France Int. (RFI)
		500	TUR	EMR	Voice of Turkey (VOT)
13695		500	IND	BGL	All India Radio (AIR)
		250	MRA	TIN	BBG - R. Free Asia (RFA)
		500	F	ISS	Radio France Int. (RFI)
13700		100	CHN	dom	CNR1 VO China, Lingshi
		100	CHN	dom	CNR13 Uyghur Sce, Lingshi
13705		250	MRA	TIN	BBG - R. Free Asia (RFA)
13710		500	IND	BGL	All India Radio (AIR)
		250	CLN	IRA	BBG - R. Farda
		100	D	LAM	BBG - R. Farda
		500	CHN	KAS	China Radio Int. (CRI)
		250	D	NAU	Missionswerk Friedensstimme
		500	ARS	RIY	Saudi Int. Radio
13715		100	CHN	KAS	China Radio Int. (CRI)
13720		100	CHN	KAS	China Radio Int. (CRI)
		500	CHN	XIA	China Radio Int. (CRI)
13725		500	F	ISS	Radio Japan (NHK World)
13730		100	CHN	KAS	China Radio Int. (CRI)
		250	MDG	MDC	Radio Japan (NHK World)
		300	ROU	TIG	Radio Romania International
		500	IRN	SIR	VO the Islamic Rep. of Iran
13735		250	MRA	TIN	BBG - R. Free Asia (RFA)
		100	STP	SAO	BBG - VO America (VOA)
		500	IRN	KAM	VO the Islamic Rep. of Iran
13740		100	CHN	KAS	China Radio Int. (CRI)
		500	F	ISS	Radio France Int. (RFI)
		100	CUB	HAB	Radio Habana Cuba
		100	D	NAU	Reach Beyond
		500	IRN	KAM	VO the Islamic Rep. of Iran
13745		250	KWT	KWT	BBG - VO America (VOA)
		250	THA	UDO	R. Thailand World Service
13750		500	CHN	KUN	China Radio Int. (CRI)
		500	F	ISS	Radio France Int. (RFI)
		500	IRN	KAM	VO the Islamic Rep. of Iran
		500	IRN	SIR	VO the Islamic Rep. of Iran
13760		100	UZB	TAC	BBC World Service
		200	KRE	KUJ	Voice of Korea
13765		100	D	LAM	BBG - R. Farda
		250	THA	UDO	BBG - VO America (VOA)
		100	CVA	SMG	Vatican Radio
		250	CVA	SMG	Vatican Radio
		250	MDG	MDC	Vatican Radio
13770		500	CHN	XIA	China Radio Int. (CRI)
13775		500	ARS	RIY	Saudi Int. Radio
	±	1	TWN	TSU	Sound of Hope Radio Int.
13780		100	CHN	KAS	China Radio Int. (CRI)
		500	CHN	KUN	China Radio Int. (CRI)
		500	IRN	KAM	VO the Islamic Rep. of Iran
13785		500	IRN	SIR	VO the Islamic Rep. of Iran
13790		500	CHN	URU	China Radio Int. (CRI)
		500	IRN	KAM	VO the Islamic Rep. of Iran

kHz	N	kW	Ctry	Site	Station, location
		500	IRN	SIR	VO the Islamic Rep. of Iran
13795		500	IND	BGL	All India Radio (AIR)
		100	MRA	SAI	BBG - R. Free Asia (RFA)
13800		100	CHN	KAS	China Radio Int. (CRI)
	†	10	SOM	dom	Puntland R, Garowe
	±	250	CVA	SMG	Radio Dabanga
	±	250	MDG	MDC	Radio Dabanga
	±	250	MDG	MDC	Radio Tamazuj
13810		100	CHN	KAS	China Radio Int. (CRI)
13820		250	USA	GRV	BBG - R. Martí
	±	1	TWN	TSU	Sound of Hope Radio Int.
		500	IRN	KAM	VO the Islamic Rep. of Iran
13830		100	BOT	BOT	BBG - VO America (VOA)
		250	IRN	AHW	VO the Islamic Rep. of Iran
		250	USA	EWN	WEWN - EWTN Shortwave
13840		100	NZL	RAN	R. New Zealand Int. (RNZI)
		250	MDG	MDC	Radio Japan (NHK World)
13845		100	USA	WCR	University Network
		100	USA	WCR	WWCR
13850		500	CHN	BEI	China Radio Int. (CRI)
13855		500	CHN	KAS	China Radio Int. (CRI)
13860		100	BOT	BOT	BBG - VO America (VOA)
		100	STP	SAO	BBG - VOA Studio 7
		250	THA	UDO	Radio Azadi
13865		250	OMA	SLA	BBC World Service
		300	G	WOF	BBG - VO America (VOA)
		500	IRN	SIR	VO the Islamic Rep. of Iran
13870		250	UAE	DHA	Radio Japan (NHK World)
13890	±	1	TWN	TSU	Sound of Hope Radio Int.
13920	±	1	TWN	TSU	Sound of Hope Radio Int.
13980	±	1	TWN	TSU	Sound of Hope Radio Int.
14370	±	1	TWN	TSU	Sound of Hope Radio Int.
14670		3	CAN	STF	CHU, Ottawa, ON
14800	±	1	TWN	TSU	Sound of Hope Radio Int.
14870	±	1	TWN	TSU	Sound of Hope Radio Int.
14920	±	1	TWN	TSU	Sound of Hope Radio Int.
14980	±	1	TWN	TSU	Sound of Hope Radio Int.
14996		5	RUS	STF	RWM, Moscow
15000		20	CHN	STF	BPM, Kinshan
		10	USA	STF	WWV NIST, Fort Collins, CO
		10	HWA	STF	WWVH NIST, Kauai, HI
15030		250	IND	ALG	All India Radio (AIR)
15040 +		200	IND	BGL	All India Radio (AIR)
15050 +		100	IND	DEL	All India Radio (AIR)
15070	±	1	TWN	TSU	Sound of Hope Radio Int.
15085		500	IRN	KAM	VO the Islamic Rep. of Iran
15105		250	BGD	DKA	Bangladesh Betar
		250	ASC	ASC	BBC World Service
		100	SWZ	MAN	TWR Africa
		200	KRE	KUJ	Voice of Korea
15110		250	PHL	PHT	BBG - VO America (VOA)
		100	CHN	KAS	China Radio Int. (CRI)
		500	CHN	URU	China Radio Int. (CRI)
15120 +		200	IND	BGL	All India Radio (AIR)
		500	IND	BGL	All India Radio (AIR)
		250	ASC	ASC	BBG - VO America (VOA)
		500	CHN	BEI	China Radio Int. (CRI)
		250	CUB	HAB	China Radio Int. (CRI)
		500	ARS	RIY	Saudi Int. Radio
	+	250	NIG	AJA	Voice of Nigeria
15125		500	CHN	BEI	China Radio Int. (CRI)
		100	MLI	BKO	China Radio Int. (CRI)
15130		100	D	LAM	BBG - RFE/RL
		150	CHN	BEI	China Radio Int. (CRI)
		500	F	ISS	Radio Japan (NHK World)
15135		100	CHN	KUN	China Radio Int. (CRI)
		500	CHN	KAS	China Radio Int. (CRI)
		500	CHN	KUN	China Radio Int. (CRI)
15140		250	IND	DEL	All India Radio (AIR)
		500	CHN	BEI	China Radio Int. (CRI)
		100	OMA	THU	Radio Sultanate of Oman
		500	IRN	KAM	VO the Islamic Rep. of Iran
15145		100	D	NAU	AWR Africa/Europe
		100	CHN	KAS	China Radio Int. (CRI)
		500	CHN	XIA	China Radio Int. (CRI)
15150		250	D	NAU	Athmik Yatra Radio
		250	D	NAU	AWR Africa/Europe
		125	CLN	TRM	AWR Asia/Pacific
		100	GUM	SDA	AWR Asia/Pacific
		250	THA	UDO	BBG - VO America (VOA)
		300	ROU	GAL	Radio Romania International
15155		250	CLN	TRM	AWR Africa/Europe
		250	D	NAU	AWR Africa/Europe
15160		250	D	NAU	AWR Africa/Europe
		250	KWT	KWT	BBG - VO America (VOA)
		100	CHN	NNN	China Radio Int. (CRI)
		500	CHN	JIN	China Radio Int. (CRI)
		100	KOR	KIM	KBS World Radio
15170		100	CHN	KAS	China Radio Int. (CRI)
		500	CHN	JIN	China Radio Int. (CRI)
		300	ROU	GAL	Radio Romania International
		500	ARS	RIY	Saudi Int. Radio
		500	IRN	SIR	VO the Islamic Rep. of Iran
15175		250	IND	PAN	All India Radio (AIR)
		500	IRN	KAM	VO the Islamic Rep. of Iran
15180		100	GUM	SDA	AWR Asia/Pacific
		250	CVA	SMG	BBG - VO America (VOA)
		200	KRE	KUJ	Voice of Korea
15185		250	IND	PAN	All India Radio (AIR)
		100	CHN	KAS	China Radio Int. (CRI)
15190		500	CHN	KAS	China Radio Int. (CRI)
		50	BUL	SOF	IRRS Shortwave
	†	5	B	dom	R. Inconfidência, Belo Horizonte
		250	PHL	PHT	Radyo Pilipinas Overseas
15195		100	GUM	SDA	AWR Asia/Pacific
		300	J	YAM	Radio Japan (NHK World)
15200		300	ROU	GAL	Radio Romania International
		500	TUR	EMR	Voice of Turkey (VOT)
15205		500	CHN	KAS	China Radio Int. (CRI)
		100	D	NAU	Pan American Broadcasting
		250	D	NAU	Pan American Broadcasting
		500	ARS	RIY	Saudi Int. Radio
15210		250	IND	PAN	All India Radio (AIR)
		500	CHN	KUN	China Radio Int. (CRI)
15215		100	GUM	SDA	AWR Asia/Pacific
		250	CLN	TRM	Deutsche Welle
15220		500	CHN	KAS	China Radio Int. (CRI)
		300	ROU	TIG	Radio Romania International
		500	IRN	SIR	VO the Islamic Rep. of Iran
15225		500	CHN	KAS	China Radio Int. (CRI)
		250	PHL	PUG	Radio Veritas Asia
		500	ARS	RIY	Saudi Int. Radio
		100	GUM	TWR	TWR Asia
		100	GUM	TWR	TWR India
15230		100	D	NAU	AWR Africa/Europe
		250	CUB	HAB	Radio Habana Cuba
15235		250	D	NAU	Athmik Yatra Radio
		250	AFS	MEY	Channel Africa

kHz	N	kW	Ctry	Site	Station, location
		200	GUM	TWR	TWR Asia
15240		100	AUS	SHP	ABC Radio Australia
		100	GUM	TWR	TWR India
		125	GUM	TWR	TWR India
		500	IRN	SIR	VO the Islamic Rep. of Iran
15245		200	KRE	KUJ	Voice of Korea
15250		250	D	NAU	AWR Asia/Pacific
		100	CHN	KUN	China Radio Int. (CRI)
15255		100	GUM	SDA	AWR Asia/Pacific
		250	AFS	MEY	Channel Africa
		300	ROU	GAL	Radio Romania International
		250	PHL	PUG	Radio Veritas Asia
15260		250	G	WOF	IBRA Radio
		300	ROU	GAL	Radio Romania International
15265		100	D	LAM	BBG - RFE/RL
		250	AFS	MEY	BBG - VO America (VOA)
		250	TWN	TNN	Radio Taiwan International
		250	PHL	PUG	Radio Veritas Asia
15270		250	MRA	TIN	BBG - R. Free Asia (RFA)
		150	CHN	dom	CNR2 Business R, Beijing
		100	TWN	PAO	Radio Taiwan International
15275		250	AFS	MEY	Deutsche Welle
		250	CLN	TRM	Deutsche Welle
		500	F	ISS	Deutsche Welle
		250	MDG	MDC	Deutsche Welle
15280		250	PHL	PUG	Radio Veritas Asia
		100	GUM	TWR	TWR India
15285		250	D	NAU	Athmik Yatra Radio
		250	SNG	SNG	BBC World Service
		100	EGY	ABZ	Radio Cairo
		500	ARS	RIY	Saudi Int. Radio
15290		300	AUT	MOS	AWR Africa/Europe
		100	EGY	ABZ	Radio Cairo
		500	F	ISS	Radio Japan (NHK World)
		300	TWN	PAO	Radio Taiwan International
15300		100	STP	SAO	BBG - VO America (VOA)
		100	EGY	ABZ	Radio Cairo
		500	F	ISS	Radio France Int. (RFI)
		500	IRN	KAM	VO the Islamic Rep. of Iran
15310		250	OMA	SLA	BBC World Service
		250	THA	NAK	BBC World Service
15315		500	F	ISS	Radio France Int. (RFI)
15320		100	GUM	SDA	AWR Asia/Pacific
		250	TWN	TNN	Radio Taiwan International
15325		100	GUM	SDA	AWR Asia/Pacific
15330		100	PHL	BOC	FEBC Philippines
		300	ROU	TIG	Radio Romania International
		250	CVA	SMG	Radio Veritas Asia
		500	IRN	SIR	VO the Islamic Rep. of Iran
15335		100	D	NAU	Bible Voice Broadcasting (BVB)
		500	CHN	KAS	China Radio Int. (CRI)
15340		100	MRA	SAI	BBG - R. Free Asia (RFA)
		500	CHN	XIA	China Radio Int. (CRI)
		100	AUS	KNX	Reach Beyond Australia
±		1	TWN	TSU	Sound of Hope Radio Int.
15345		250	EGY	ABS	Radio Cairo
		100	ARG	BUE	Rdif. Argentina al Exterior
15350		100	CHN	KAS	China Radio Int. (CRI)
		500	TUR	EMR	Voice of Turkey (VOT)
15355		250	PHL	PUG	Radio Veritas Asia
15360		125	CLN	TRM	AWR Africa/Europe
		125	CLN	TRM	AWR Asia/Pacific

kHz	N	kW	Ctry	Site	Station, location
		500	F	ISS	Radio France Int. (RFI)
		100	SWZ	MAN	TWR India
		500	IRN	KAM	VO the Islamic Rep. of Iran
		500	IRN	SIR	VO the Islamic Rep. of Iran
		500	TUR	EMR	Voice of Turkey (VOT)
15365		100	GUM	SDA	AWR Asia/Pacific
15370		100	CHN	dom	CNR1 VO China, Shijiazhuang
		100	CUB	HAB	Radio Habana Cuba
		300	ROU	TIG	Radio Romania International
15375		250	TJK	DSB	BBG - R. Free Asia (RFA)
		500	UAE	DHA	BBG - R. Free Asia (RFA)
15380		100	CHN	dom	CNR1 VO China, Beijing
		300	ROU	GAL	Radio Romania International
		500	ARS	RIY	Saudi Int. Radio
15390		100	CHN	dom	CNR1 VO China, Lingshi
		100	CHN	dom	CNR13 Uyghur Sce, Lingshi
		200	E	NOB	R. Exterior de España (REE)
		100	GUM	TWR	TWR Asia
15400		125	CLN	TRM	AWR Asia/Pacific
		125	ASC	ASC	BBC World Service
		300	ROU	TIG	Radio Romania International
±		250	F	ISS	Radio Tamazuj
		100	AUS	KNX	Reach Beyond Australia
		500	IRN	KAM	VO the Islamic Rep. of Iran
15410		250	IND	PAN	All India Radio (AIR)
		500	IND	BGL	All India Radio (AIR)
15415		100	AUS	SHP	ABC Radio Australia
15420		100	AFS	MEY	BBC World Service
		250	UAE	DHA	BBC World Service
±		125	PHL	PUG	Radio Free Sarawak
‡		50	USA	BCQ	WBCQ
15425		250	PHL	PHT	BBG - VO America (VOA)
		500	CHN	XIA	China Radio Int. (CRI)
15430		125	CLN	TRM	AWR Asia/Pacific
		100	GUM	SDA	AWR Asia/Pacific
		100	CHN	KAS	China Radio Int. (CRI)
		250	UAE	DHA	Deutsche Welle
		300	ROU	GAL	Radio Romania International
		300	ROU	TIG	Radio Romania International
		100	AUS	KNX	Reach Beyond Australia
15435		100	GUM	SDA	AWR Asia/Pacific
		500	CHN	XIA	China Radio Int. (CRI)
		100	PHL	BOC	FEBC Philippines
		500	ARS	RIY	Saudi Int. Radio
15440		300	AUT	MOS	AWR Africa/Europe
		500	CHN	KUN	China Radio Int. (CRI)
		150	F	ISS	Manara Radio
15445		100	TWN	TSH	AWR Asia/Pacific
		500	CHN	KAS	China Radio Int. (CRI)
15450		100	GUM	SDA	AWR Asia/Pacific
		100	PHL	BOC	FEBC Philippines
		100	PHL	IBA	FEBC Philippines
		100	EGY	ABZ	Radio Cairo
		250	PHL	PUG	Radio Veritas Asia
		500	IRN	KAM	VO the Islamic Rep. of Iran
15455		500	F	ISS	Radio France Int. (RFI)
15460		100	STP	SAO	BBG - VO America (VOA)
		100	STP	SAO	BBG - VOA Studio 7
		300	ROU	GAL	Radio Romania International
		300	ROU	TIG	Radio Romania International
		500	IRN	SIR	VO the Islamic Rep. of Iran
15465		100	CHN	KAS	China Radio Int. (CRI)

kHz	N	kW	Ctry	Site	Station, location
		100	TWN	PAO	Radio Taiwan International
15470		250	MRA	TIN	Vatican Radio
		250	PHL	PHT	Vatican Radio
		250	PHL	PUG	Vatican Radio
15476	†	10	ATA	LRA	RNASG (LRA36)
15480		250	AFS	MEY	AWR Africa/Europe
		250	MDG	MDC	AWR Africa/Europe
		250	D	NAU	AWR Asia/Pacific
		250	ASC	ASC	BBG - VO America (VOA)
		100	CHN	dom	CNR1 VO China, Beijing
		300	G	WOF	Dandal Kura
		500	TUR	EMR	Voice of Turkey (VOT)
15490		250	AFS	MEY	AWR Africa/Europe
		250	D	NAU	AWR Asia/Pacific
		100	GUM	SDA	AWR Asia/Pacific
		250	AFS	MEY	BBC World Service
		250	UAE	DHA	BBC World Service
		500	ARS	RIY	Saudi Int. Radio
		500	IRN	SIR	VO the Islamic Rep. of Iran
15495		250	GUM	SDA	AWR Asia/Pacific
15500		125	CLN	TRM	AWR Africa/Europe
		150	CHN	dom	CNR2 Business R, Beijing
		200	E	NOB	R. Exterior de España (REE)
15505		250	BGD	DKA	Bangladesh Betar
		100	MLI	BKO	China Radio Int. (CRI)
15510		250	THA	NAK	BBC World Service
15515		50	BUL	SOF	IRRS Shortwave
15520		250	MDG	MDC	Deutsche Welle
15525		500	CHN	URU	China Radio Int. (CRI)
		250	UAE	DHA	Eternal Good News
		100	AUS	KNX	Reach Beyond Australia
		500	IRN	KAM	VO the Islamic Rep. of Iran
15530		250	UAE	DHA	BBC World Service
		500	F	ISS	Deutsche Welle
		250	PHL	PUG	Radio Veritas Asia
		500	IRN	KAM	VO the Islamic Rep. of Iran
15535		250	EGY	ABS	Radio Cairo
15538	±	100	TJK	DSB	Voice of Tibet
15543	±	100	TJK	DSB	Voice of Tibet
15548	±	100	TJK	DSB	Voice of Tibet
15550		100	CHN	KAS	China Radio Int. (CRI)
		100	CHN	dom	CNR1 VO China, Beijing
	±	250	CVA	SMG	Radio Dabanga
	±	250	MDG	MDC	Radio Dabanga
	±	250	CVA	SMG	Radio Tamazuj
	±	250	MDG	MDC	Radio Tamazuj
		100	AUS	KNX	Reach Beyond Australia
15555		1	USA	JHR	WJHR Radio International
15560		250	PHL	PHT	BBG - VO America (VOA)
		250	THA	UDO	BBG - VO America (VOA)
		500	CHN	XIA	China Radio Int. (CRI)
		500	F	ISS	Deutsche Welle
		250	UAE	DHA	Deutsche Welle
		100	PHL	BOC	FEBC Philippines
15565		100	PLW	HBN	T8WH - World Harvest Radio Int
	±	250	MDG	MDC	Voice of Tibet
15568	±	100	TJK	DSB	Voice of Tibet
15570		100	CHN	dom	CNR11 Tibetan Sce, Xi'an
15575		250	KOR	KIM	KBS World Radio
15580		100	BOT	BOT	BBG - VO America (VOA)
		250	CVA	SMG	BBG - VO America (VOA)
		250	KWT	KWT	BBG - VO America (VOA)

kHz	N	kW	Ctry	Site	Station, location
		250	USA	GRV	BBG - VO America (VOA)
		100	PHL	BOC	FEBC Philippines
15590		300	J	YAM	Radio Japan (NHK World)
15595		100	CVA	SMG	Vatican Radio
		250	CVA	SMG	Vatican Radio
15600		250	G	WOF	BBG - VO America (VOA)
15605		100	GUM	SDA	AWR Asia/Pacific
15610		250	THA	UDO	BBG - VO America (VOA)
		250	EGY	ABZ	Radio Cairo
		250	USA	EWN	WEWN - EWTN Shortwave
15615		500	IRN	KAM	VO the Islamic Rep. of Iran
15620		100	BOT	BOT	BBG - VO America (VOA)
		250	G	WOF	BBG - VO America (VOA)
		100	STP	SAO	BBG - VO America (VOA)
		500	CHN	KAS	China Radio Int. (CRI)
		100	PHL	BOC	FEBC Philippines
		250	CVA	SMG	Radio Veritas Asia
15625		125	CLN	TRM	AWR Asia/Pacific
15630		50	BUL	SOF	Radio Ranginkaman
15640		100	PHL	BOC	FEBC Philippines
		250	PHL	PHT	Radyo Pilipinas Overseas
15660		100	GUM	SDA	AWR Asia/Pacific
15665		100	GUM	SDA	AWR Asia/Pacific
		100	D	LAM	BBG - R. Free Asia (RFA)
		500	CHN	URU	China Radio Int. (CRI)
15670		100	GUM	SDA	AWR Asia/Pacific
		125	USA	GRV	BBG - VO America (VOA)
15680		125	MDG	MDC	AWR Asia/Pacific
15685		100	GUM	SDA	AWR Asia/Pacific
		100	MRA	SAI	BBG - R. Free Asia (RFA)
15690		250	CLN	IRA	BBG - R. Farda
		100	D	BIB	BBG - R. Farda
15700		250	D	NAU	AWR Africa/Europe
		250	MRA	TIN	BBG - R. Free Asia (RFA)
		250	CUB	HAB	China Radio Int. (CRI)
15710		100	GUM	SDA	AWR Asia/Pacific
		100	CHN	dom	CNR6 VO Shenzhou, Beijing
		250	EGY	ABS	Radio Cairo
15715		100	BOT	BOT	BBG - VO America (VOA)
15720		100	NZL	RAN	R. New Zealand Int. (RNZI)
	+	50	NZL	RAN	R. New Zealand Int. (RNZI)
		250	MDG	MDC	Radio Japan (NHK World)
15725	†	250	PAK	ISL	Radio Pakistan
15730		100	BOT	BOT	BBG - VO America (VOA)
		250	CVA	SMG	BBG - VO America (VOA)
		125	USA	GRV	BBG - VO America (VOA)
		250	USA	GRV	BBG - VO America (VOA)
	†	250	PAK	ISL	Radio Pakistan
15745		125	CLN	TRM	AWR Asia/Pacific
15750		500	IRN	ZAH	VO the Islamic Rep. of Iran
15755		250	THA	NAK	BBC World Service
		100	UZB	TAC	TWR India
15760		250	CLN	IRA	BBG - Radio Mashaal
15770		250	IND	DEL	All India Radio (AIR)
		500	IND	PAN	All India Radio (AIR)
		100	CHN	dom	CNR2 Business R, Lingshi
		100	USA	YFR	ETC Radio
		100	USA	YFR	FG Radio (ex EUNN)
		100	USA	YFR	Radio France Int. (RFI)
		100	USA	YFR	The Overcomer Ministry
		100	USA	YFR	WRMI - R. Miami Int.
15775	±	1	TWN	TSU	Sound of Hope Radio Int.

kHz	N	kW	Ctry	Site	Station, location
	+	125	CVA	SMG	Vatican Radio
15790		250	MDG	MDC	BBC World Service
15795		100	USA	WCR	WWCR
15800	±	1	TWN	TSU	Sound of Hope Radio Int.
15825		100	USA	WCR	WWCR
15840	±	1	TWN	TSU	Sound of Hope Radio Int.
15870	±	1	TWN	TSU	Sound of Hope Radio Int.
15896	+	0.1	D	dom	BiteXpress, Erlangen
15970	±	1	TWN	TSU	Sound of Hope Radio Int.
16100	±	1	TWN	TSU	Sound of Hope Radio Int.
16160	±	1	TWN	TSU	Sound of Hope Radio Int.
16250	±	1	TWN	TSU	Sound of Hope Radio Int.
16300	±	1	TWN	TSU	Sound of Hope Radio Int.
16600	±	1	TWN	TSU	Sound of Hope Radio Int.
16750	±	1	TWN	TSU	Sound of Hope Radio Int.
16775	±	1	TWN	TSU	Sound of Hope Radio Int.
16980	±	1	TWN	TSU	Sound of Hope Radio Int.
17000	±	1	TWN	TSU	Sound of Hope Radio Int.
17200	±	1	TWN	TSU	Sound of Hope Radio Int.
17400	±	1	TWN	TSU	Sound of Hope Radio Int.
17440	±	1	TWN	TSU	Sound of Hope Radio Int.
17485		500	CHN	KAS	China Radio Int. (CRI)
17490		500	CHN	BEI	China Radio Int. (CRI)
		500	CHN	KAS	China Radio Int. (CRI)
17510		250	IND	DEL	All India Radio (AIR)
		300	AUT	MOS	AWR Africa/Europe
		250	D	NAU	AWR Africa/Europe
		250	SNG	SNG	BBC World Service
		250	MRA	TIN	BBG - R. Free Asia (RFA)
		250	F	ISS	Bible Voice Broadcasting (BVB)
		500	CHN	KAS	China Radio Int. (CRI)
		500	CHN	XIA	China Radio Int. (CRI)
17520		100	GUM	SDA	AWR Asia/Pacific
		100	CHN	KAS	China Radio Int. (CRI)
17525		250	MRA	TIN	BBG - R. Free Asia (RFA)
17530		100	D	LAM	BBG - RFE/RL
		250	KWT	KWT	BBG - RFE/RL
		100	USA	HRI	The Overcomer Ministry
17540		100	GUM	SDA	AWR Asia/Pacific
		125	D	NAU	Bible Voice Broadcasting (BVB)
		500	CHN	BEI	China Radio Int. (CRI)
		250	USA	HRI	Radio Japan (NHK World)
17550		100	BOT	BOT	BBG - VO America (VOA)
		100	CHN	dom	CNR1 VO China, Beijing
17560		500	CHN	XIA	China Radio Int. (CRI)
		500	ARS	RIY	Saudi Int. Radio
		500	IRN	KAM	VO the Islamic Rep. of Iran
		500	IRN	SIR	VO the Islamic Rep. of Iran
17565		100	CHN	dom	CNR1 VO China, Beijing
17570		500	CHN	KAS	China Radio Int. (CRI)
		500	CHN	URU	China Radio Int. (CRI)
		500	ARS	RIY	Saudi Int. Radio
17580		100	GUM	SDA	AWR Asia/Pacific
		250	USA	GRV	BBG - VO America (VOA)
		100	CHN	dom	CNR1 VO China, Lingshi
		100	CUB	HAB	Radio Habana Cuba
		250	F	ISS	VO Khaatumo
17585		100	D	BIB	BBG - VO America (VOA)
		300	J	YAM	Radio Japan (NHK World)
17590		100	CVA	SMG	Vatican Radio
		250	CVA	SMG	Vatican Radio

kHz	N	kW	Ctry	Site	Station, location
17595		100	CHN	dom	CNR1 VO China, Shijiazhuang
17600		100	STP	SAO	BBG - VO America (VOA)
17605		300	AUT	MOS	AWR Africa/Europe
		100	CHN	dom	CNR1 VO China, Beijing
		100	F	ISS	R. Inyabutatu
17610		100	USA	HRI	The Overcomer Ministry
		250	USA	HRI	WHRI - World Harvest R.
17615		500	CHN	URU	China Radio Int. (CRI)
		500	F	ISS	Radio France Int. (RFI)
		500	ARS	RIY	Saudi Int. Radio
17620		500	F	ISS	Radio France Int. (RFI)
17625		150	CHN	dom	CNR2 Business R, Beijing
		500	ARS	RIY	Saudi Int. Radio
17630		100	MLI	BKO	China Radio Int. (CRI)
		250	THA	UDO	R. Thailand World Service
		500	F	ISS	R. Xoriyo
		100	F	ISS	Voice of Oromo Liberation
17640		250	ASC	ASC	BBC World Service
		250	MDG	MDC	BBC World Service
		250	UAE	DHA	BBC World Service
		500	CHN	XIA	China Radio Int. (CRI)
		250	THA	UDO	R. Thailand World Service
	+	300	ROU	TIG	Radio Romania International
		300	ROU	TIG	Radio Romania International
		500	IRN	KAM	VO the Islamic Rep. of Iran
17650		125	CLN	TRM	AWR Asia/Pacific
		100	GUM	SDA	AWR Asia/Pacific
		500	CHN	KAS	China Radio Int. (CRI)
17655		250	CVA	SMG	BBG - VO America (VOA)
		250	USA	GRV	BBG - VO America (VOA)
17660		500	F	ISS	Radio France Int. (RFI)
		500	ARS	RIY	Saudi Int. Radio
		500	IRN	SIR	VO the Islamic Rep. of Iran
17670		250	IND	DEL	All India Radio (AIR)
		125	CLN	TRM	AWR Asia/Pacific
		500	CHN	KAS	China Radio Int. (CRI)
		500	CHN	KUN	China Radio Int. (CRI)
		500	IRN	SIR	VO the Islamic Rep. of Iran
17675		250	MRA	TIN	BBG - R. Free Asia (RFA)
	+	50	NZL	RAN	R. New Zealand Int. (RNZI)
17680		250	PHL	PHT	BBG - VO America (VOA)
		100	CHN	KUN	China Radio Int. (CRI)
		150	CHN	KUN	China Radio Int. (CRI)
		250	UAE	DHA	TWR Africa
17685		500	F	ISS	Radio France Int. (RFI)
		500	IRN	KAM	VO the Islamic Rep. of Iran
17690		100	MRA	SAI	BBG - R. Free Asia (RFA)
		500	CHN	JIN	China Radio Int. (CRI)
		100	CHN	dom	CNR1 VO China, Nanning
		500	IRN	SIR	VO the Islamic Rep. of Iran
17700		100	BOT	BOT	BBG - VO America (VOA)
		250	CVA	SMG	BBG - VO America (VOA)
	‡	250	PAK	ISL	Radio Pakistan
		250	PHL	PHT	Radyo Pilipinas Overseas
17705		500	IND	BGL	All India Radio (AIR)
		500	ARS	RIY	Saudi Int. Radio
17710		500	CHN	BEI	China Radio Int. (CRI)
		500	CHN	JIN	China Radio Int. (CRI)
		250	AFS	MEY	Deutsche Welle
		250	UAE	DHA	Deutsche Welle
		500	IRN	SIR	VO the Islamic Rep. of Iran

kHz	N	kW	Ctry	Site	Station, location
17715	+	100	IND	DEL	All India Radio (AIR)
		500	IRN	SIR	VO the Islamic Rep. of Iran
17720		250	MDG	MDC	AWR Africa/Europe
		100	GUM	SDA	AWR Asia/Pacific
		250	THA	NAK	BBC World Service
		500	CHN	KAS	China Radio Int. (CRI)
17725		100	PLW	HBN	T8WH - World Harvest Radio Int
17730		100	GUM	SDA	AWR Asia/Pacific
		500	CHN	XIA	China Radio Int. (CRI)
		100	CUB	HAB	Radio Habana Cuba
		50	CUB	HAB	Radio Habana Cuba
		500	ARS	RIY	Saudi Int. Radio
17735		100	CHN	KUN	China Radio Int. (CRI)
17740		500	CHN	XIA	China Radio Int. (CRI)
		500	ARS	RIY	Saudi Int. Radio
17745		250	AFS	MEY	BBC World Service
		250	OMA	SLA	BBC World Service
		300	ROU	GAL	Radio Romania International
17750		250	MNG	UBA	BBG - R. Free Asia (RFA)
		500	CHN	XIA	China Radio Int. (CRI)
		250	CUB	HAB	Radio Habana Cuba
17755		500	TUR	EMR	Voice of Turkey (VOT)
17760		250	AFS	MEY	Amateur R. Today
		250	THA	NAK	BBC World Service
		100	AUS	KNX	Reach Beyond Australia
17765		150	F	ISS	Manara Radio
		300	ROU	GAL	Radio Romania International
17770		125	CLN	TRM	AWR Asia/Pacific
		250	THA	UDO	BBG - RFE/RL
		250	AFS	MEY	Channel Africa
17775		300	ROU	TIG	Radio Romania International
17780		250	CLN	TRM	AWR Africa/Europe
		250	ASC	ASC	BBC World Service
		250	OMA	SLA	BBC World Service
		300	ROU	GAL	Radio Romania International
17790		250	OMA	SLA	BBC World Service
	+	100	THA	NAK	BBC World Service
17800		250	AFS	MEY	AWR Africa/Europe
		250	ASC	ASC	Deutsche Welle
		500	F	ISS	Deutsche Welle
		250	UAE	DHA	Deutsche Welle
17805		500	ARS	RIY	Saudi Int. Radio
17810		100	D	LAM	BBG - R. Free Asia (RFA)
		300	J	YAM	Radio Japan (NHK World)
		300	ROU	TIG	Radio Romania International
17815		200	TJK	DSB	BBG - R. Free Asia (RFA)
17820		100	UZB	TAC	Bible Voice Broadcasting (BVB)
		250	PHL	PHT	Radyo Pilipinas Overseas
		500	IRN	SIR	VO the Islamic Rep. of Iran
17830		250	AFS	MEY	BBC World Service
		250	ASC	ASC	BBC World Service
		250	G	WOF	BBC World Service
		250	PHL	PHT	BBG - VO America (VOA)
17840		100	AUS	SHP	ABC Radio Australia
17845		100	CHN	dom	CNR1 VO China, Shijiazhuang
		250	UAE	DHA	Radio ERGO
17850		250	CVA	SMG	BBG - VO America (VOA)
		100	F	ISS	Oromo Voice Radio (OVR)
		250	F	ISS	R. Xoriyo
		500	F	ISS	Radio France Int. (RFI)
		300	ROU	GAL	Radio Romania International
17855		500	CHN	BEI	China Radio Int. (CRI)
17860		100	UZB	TAC	Bible Voice Broadcasting (BVB)
		300	ROU	TIG	Radio Romania International
		250	PHL	PUG	Radio Veritas Asia
		200	TJK	DSB	VO Khmer M'Chas Srok
17865		250	PHL	PHT	BBG - VO America (VOA)
		500	IRN	KAM	VO the Islamic Rep. of Iran
17870		250	AFS	MEY	BBC World Service
		100	D	LAM	BBG - VO America (VOA)
		300	ROU	GAL	Radio Romania International
17875		500	IND	BGL	All India Radio (AIR)
17880		100	GUM	SDA	AWR Asia/Pacific
		250	AFS	MEY	BBC World Service
		250	CLN	IRA	BBG - Radio Mashaal
17885		250	ASC	ASC	BBC World Service
		100	STP	SAO	BBG - VO America (VOA)
17890		100	CHN	dom	CNR1 VO China, Beijing
17895	+	200	IND	BGL	All India Radio (AIR)
		250	CVA	SMG	BBG - VO America (VOA)
		500	ARS	RIY	Saudi Int. Radio
18870	±	1	TWN	TSU	Sound of Hope Radio Int.
19010		250	KWT	KWT	Radio Azadi
20000		2.5	USA	STF	WWV NIST, Fort Collins, CO
21470		250	ASC	ASC	BBC World Service
		250	UAE	DHA	BBC World Service
21480		250	MRA	TIN	BBG - R. Free Asia (RFA)
		125	MDG	MDC	Bible Voice Broadcasting (BVB)
		125	MDG	MDC	Eternal Good News
21505		500	ARS	RIY	Saudi Int. Radio
21510		500	IRN	KAM	VO the Islamic Rep. of Iran
21520		500	IRN	SIR	VO the Islamic Rep. of Iran
21550		250	CVA	SMG	Vatican Radio
21560		100	CVA	SMG	Vatican Radio
		250	CVA	SMG	Vatican Radio
21570		250	CVA	SMG	Vatican Radio
21580		500	F	ISS	Radio France Int. (RFI)
		300	ROU	TIG	Radio Romania International
21600		250	PHL	PHT	BBG - VO America (VOA)
		250	USA	HRI	Eternal Good News
		250	USA	HRI	The Overcomer Ministry
		500	IRN	SIR	VO the Islamic Rep. of Iran
		250	USA	HRI	WHRI - World Harvest R.
21610		250	USA	HRI	The Overcomer Ministry
21620		250	PHL	PHT	BBG - VO America (VOA)
		500	F	ISS	Radio France Int. (RFI)
21630		250	ASC	ASC	BBC World Service
21670		500	ARS	RIY	Saudi Int. Radio
21675		100	USA	YFR	Pan American Broadcasting
		100	USA	YFR	The Overcomer Ministry
21680		500	UAE	DHA	BBG - R. Free Asia (RFA)
21690		500	F	ISS	Radio France Int. (RFI)
		250	MDG	MDC	Radio France Int. (RFI)
21700		250	MRA	TIN	BBG - R. Free Asia (RFA)
21760		250	PHL	PHT	BBG - VO America (VOA)
21780		250	UAE	DHA	Deutsche Welle
21795		250	PHL	PHT	BBG - VO America (VOA)
25000		0.1	FIN	STF	Centre for Metrology, Espoo
25900	‡	0.4	RUS	dom	R. MTUCI, Moskva
26060	+	0.2	CVA	dom	Raiway, Vatican City

International Broadcasts in English, French, German, Portuguese and Spanish

English			

0000	English	Area	kHz
0000-0030	R. Australia	SEA	12005sng
0000-0030	WHRI	LAm,Car	7315hri
0000-0100	BBC World Sce	SAs	5970sla, 9410nak
0000-0100	CRI	SAs	7425kas
0000-0100	CRI	EAs	9425bei
0000-0100	R. Habana Cuba	CAm	5040hab
0000-0100	R. Thailand WS	NAm	13745udo
0000-0100	Overcomer Min.	Eu,ME	5920hri
0000-0100	Trunews Radio	CAm,SAm	9975voh
0000-0100	WBCQ	NAm,CAm	7490bcq
0000-0100	WHRI	NAm	7385hri
0000-0100	WRMI	CAm	7455yfr
0000-0200	BBC World Sce	SAs	12095sng
0000-0200	CRI	SEA	11885xia, 15125bei
0000-0200	CRI	NAm	6020cer, 9570cer
0000-0200	CRI	SAs	6075kas, 6180kas
0000-0200	WBCQ	NAm,CAm	7490bcq
0000-0300	WWCR	NAm,CAm,Af	7520wcr*, 7520wcr**
0000-0400	KVOH	CAm,SAm	9975voh
0000-0500	WBCQ	NAm,CAm	5110bcq*
0000-0900	WEWN	Af	11520ewn
0000-1200	WWCR	NAm,Eu	4840wcr**
0000-1200	WWCR	Af	5935wcr**
0000-1300	Overcomer Min.	NAm	3185wrb, 5050wrb†
0000-1300	WWRB	NAm	3185wrb
0000-2400	BBC World Sce	CHN	675hkg
0000-2400	Trunews Radio	NAm	9395yfr
0015-0030	WHRI	Eu,ME	5920hri
0015-0030	WHRI	LAm,Car	7315hri
0030-0045	TWR India	SAs	882put
0030-0100	R. Slovakia Int	Eu,NAm	11580yfr
0030-0100	R. Slovakia Int	NAm	5850yfr
0030-0100	WHRI	Eu,ME	5920hri
0030-0100	WHRI	LAm,Car	7315hri
0100	**English**		
0100-0130	VO Vietnam	NAm	6175wof
0100-0130	WHRI	NAm	7385hri
0100-0200	CRI	SAs	7370kas
0100-0200	CRI	NAm	9580hab
0100-0200	CRI	Eu	9675kas
0100-0200	RFI	NAm	11580yfr
0100-0200	R.Romania Int	NAm	6145gal, 7325gal
0100-0200	Overcomer Min.	NAm,CAm	7490bcq
0100-0200	Trunews Radio	NAm,Eu	5920hri
0100-0200	WBCQ	NAm,CAm	5110bcq*
0100-0200	WBCQ	NAm,CAm	7490bcq
0100-0200	WBCQ	NAm,CAm	9330bcq*

0100	English	Area	kHz
0100-0200	WHRI	LAm,Car	7315hri
0100-0200	WHRI	NAm	7385hri
0100-0300	BBC World Sce	SAs	15310nak
0100-0300	T8WH - WHR Int	SEA,CAf	17725hbn
0100-0300	WRMI	NAm	11580yfr
0100-0400	KVOH	CAm,SAm	9975voh
0100-0400	WWCR	NAm,CAm,Af	6115wcr**
0100-0400	WWRB	NAm	3195wrb‡
0100-0520	BBC World Sce	Eu	198dro
0100-0700	R. Habana Cuba	NAm	6000hab, 6165hab
0100-0700	Trunews Radio	NAm	5850yfr
0100-0700	Trunews Radio	CAm	7455yfr
0100-0900	WWCR	NAm,Eu,NAf	3215wcr**
0100-1200	WWCR	NAm,CAm,Af	5890wcr**
0100-1300	University Net.	Af	5935wcr
0100-1300	WWCR	NAm,Eu	4840wcr*
0100-1300	WWCR	Af	5935wcr*
0115-0130	FG Radio	NAm	11580yfr
0115-0130	TWR India	SAs	882put
0130-0200	R. Prague	LAm	9955yfr
0130-0230	BBC World Sce	SAs	1413sla
0140-0200	Vatican Radio	As	7410smg, 9560smg
0200	**English**		
0200-0215	BVB	SAs	11790mdc
0200-0215	Etrn.Good News	NAm	7385hri
0200-0230	BVB	SAs	11790mdc
0200-0230	R. Thailand WS	NAm	13745udo
0200-0230	WBCQ	NAm,CAm	9330bcq*
0200-0230	WHRI	LAm,Car	7315hri
0200-0300	BBC World Sce	SAs	12095sla
0200-0300	BVB	SAs	11790mdc
0200-0300	CRI	SAs	9610kas
0200-0300	KBS World R.	SAm	9580kim
0200-0300	KBS World R.	SEA	9690kim
0200-0300	RFI	NAm	11580yfr
0200-0300	WBCQ	NAm,CAm	5110bcq*
0200-0300	WHRI	Eu,ME	5920hri
0200-0300	WHRI	NAm	7385hri
0200-0330	R. Cairo	NAm	9860abs
0200-0330	R. Pilipinas	ME	15640pht, 17700pht, 17820pht
0200-0400	CRI	SAs	11770kas
0200-0400	Overcomer Min.	NAm,CAm	5110bcq*
0200-0400	Overcomer Min.	NAm,CAm	7490bcq
0200-0400	WBCQ	NAm,CAm	7490bcq
0200-0400	WWCR	NAm,CAm,Af	6115wcr*
0200-0500	WRNO	NAm,CAm	7506rno†
0200-1100	WWCR	NAm,Eu,NAf	3215wcr*
0200-1400	WTWW	NAm,Eu,Af	5830tww
0215-0230	FG Radio	NAm	11580yfr

0200	English	Area	kHz
0230-0300	All India R.	SAs	7505del
0230-0300	BBG-VOA	NAm	5745grv*
0230-0300	R. Tirana	NAm	7470shi
0230-0300	VO Vietnam	NAm	6175wof
0245-0300	FG Radio	LAm	9955yfr
0250-0400	RNZI	Pac	17675ran+
0255-0325	TWR Africa	SAf	3200man
0300	**English**		
0300-0330	Vatican Radio	As	15470pht
0300-0330	Vatican Radio	Af	7360smg, 9660mdc
0300-0400	BBC World Sce	ME	6195sla, 9410sla
0300-0400	BBG-VOA	Af	6080smg
0300-0400	Channel Africa	EAf	6155mey
0300-0400	CRI	SAs	13800kas
0300-0400	CRI	NAm	9790hab
0300-0400	R. Sult.of Oman	EAf	9540thu
0300-0400	R.Taiwan Int.	SEA	15320tnn
0300-0400	T8WH - WHR Int	SEA,CAf	17725hbn
0300-0400	Trunews Radio	CAm,SAm	9975voh
0300-0400	WHRI	NAm, NEu,As	5920hri
0300-0400	WHRI	NAm	7385hri
0300-0400	WHRI	Eu,ME	7520hri
0300-0430	BBG-VOA	Af	1530sao
0300-0500	BBG-VOA	Af	15580kwt
0300-0500	Channel Africa	SAf	3345mey
0300-0500	CRI	EAs	13570xia, 13590bei, 15120bei
0300-0600	BBG-VOA	Af	4930bot
0300-0700	BBG-VOA	Af	909bot
0300-1300	Overcomer Min.	NAm	11580yfr
0300-1300	WWCR	NAm,CAm,Af	5890wcr*
0300-2300	Overcomer Min.	NAm,Af	9980wcr
0315-0330	TWR Africa	WAf	1566par
0320-0420	VOIRI	NAm	7325kam**, 9710sir**
0330-0400	VO Vietnam	NAm	6175hri
0330-0400	WHRI	NAm	7385hri
0335-0345	TWR Africa	WAf	1566par
0400	**English**		
0400-0430	R. Prague	LAm	9955yfr
0400-0500	BBC World Sce	ME	9410sla, 12035sla
0400-0500	BBC World Sce	EAf	9460mey, 12095dha
0400-0500	BBG-VOA	Af	4960sao
0400-0500	Deutsche Welle	EAf	9800mey, 11810mdc
0400-0500	R.Romania Int	ME	11790tig, 13730tig
0400-0500	R.Romania Int	NAm	6020gal, 7340gal
0400-0500	Overcomer Min.	NAm,CAm	7490bcq
0400-0500	VO Turkey	ME,NAf	7240emr
0400-0500	VO Turkey	Eu,NAm	9655emr
0400-0500	WBCQ	NAm,CAm	7490bcq
0400-0500	WHRI	NAm	7385hri
0400-0600	CRI	CAs,Eu	17730xia
0400-0600	CRI	CAs	17855bei
0400-0700	BBG-VOA	Af	6080sao
0400-1300	Overcomer Min.	NAm,Af	5890wcr
0430-0500	TWR Africa	WAf	1566par
0430-0530	VO Korea	LAm	11735kuj, 13760kuj, 15180kuj
0430-0530	VO Korea	EAs	7220kuj, 9445kuj, 9730kuj
0445-0500	Etrn.Good News	Af	11635hri
0445-0515	BVB	ME	5980nau
0500	**English**		
0500-0530	R. Japan	Eu	13640dha
0500-0530	R. Japan	SAf	9770iss

0500	English	Area	kHz
0500-0530	Vatican Radio	Af	7360smg, 11625mdc
0500-0600	BBC World Sce	EAf	12095mey
0500-0600	BBC World Sce	ME	1413sla
0500-0600	BBC World Sce	SAf	3255mey, 7445asc
0500-0600	BBC World Sce	CAf	5875asc
0500-0600	Deutsche Welle	SAf	9800mey, 15520mdc
0500-0600	WHRI	Eu,ME	11635hri
0500-0700	BBC World Sce	WAf	6005asc
0500-0700	BBG-VOA	Af	15580bot
0500-0700	Channel Africa	SAf	7230mey
0500-0700	CRI	SAs	15430kas
0500-0700	CRI	ME,NAf	17510kas
0500-0700	R. Habana Cuba	NAm	6060hab, 6100hab
0500-0800	BBC World Sce	EAf	15420dha
0500-0800	BBC World Sce	SAf	6190mey
0500-0800	RNZI	Pac	11725ran
0500-0800	TWR Africa	SAf	4775man
0500-0800	WTWW	NAm	5830tww*
0500-0900	CRI	SAs	11895kas, 15465kas
0500-1100	CRI	SAs	15350kas
0500-1300	Overcomer Min.	NAm,Af	5890wcr
0500-1700	HCJB Deutsch	Eu	3995wnm
0501-0800	TWR Africa	Af	6120man
0515-0530	FG Radio	LAm	9955yfr
0530-0545	TWR Africa	WAf	1566par
0530-0600	R. Thailand WS	Eu	17640udo
0530-0630	VO Korea	SEA	13650kuj, 15105kuj
0600	**English**		
0600-0700	BBC World Sce	CAf	12095mey
0600-0700	BBC World Sce	Eu	3955wof+
0600-0700	BBC World Sce	WAf	9460asc
0600-0700	BBG-VOA	Af	1530sao, 9550sao
0600-0700	Channel Africa	WAf	15255mey
0600-0700	CRI	NAf	11750cer
0600-0700	CRI	ME	11870kas, 15145kas
0600-0700	CRI	SEA	13645xia
0600-0700	RFI	WAf,CAf	9675iss, 13695iss
0600-0700	R. Habana Cuba	CAm	5040hab
0600-0700	Overcomer Min.	Eu,ME	7315hri
0600-0800	BBC World Sce	EAf	17640mdc
0600-0800	BBC World Sce	SAf	9410mey
0600-0800	BBC World Sce	WAf	9915asc
0600-0800	CRI	SEA	17710bei
0600-0800	LKE LLB Bergen	Eu	1314erd*, 5895erd*
0600-1000	WWCR	NAm,Eu,NAf	3195wcr*, 3195wcr**
0600-1100	Overcomer Min.	NAm	9955yfr
0630-0700	R. Australia	Pac	15240shp, 15415shp, 17840shp
0630-0700	R.Romania Int	AUS,NZL	17780gal, 21580tig
0630-0700	R.Romania Int	Eu	7345tig, 9600gal+
0630-0700	Vatican Radio	Af	9660smg, 11625smg
0630-0730	VO Korea	EAs	7220kuj, 9445kuj, 9730kuj
0650-0800	RNZI	Pac	11690ran+
0700	**English**		
0700-0800	R. Australia	Pac	15240shp, 15415shp, 17840shp
0700-0800	BBC World Sce	WAf	11770asc
0700-0800	BBC World Sce	CAf	12095asc, 17830mey
0700-0800	CRI	SEA	13660xia
0700-0800	Deutsche Welle	WAf	15530iss, 17800dha
0700-0800	R. Mi Amigo Int	Eu	6005kll
0700-0800	Overcomer Min.	Eu,ME	7355hri
0700-0800	WRMI	CAm	7455yfr

0700	English	Area	kHz
0700-0900	CRI	Eu	11785cer
0700-0900	CRI	ME,NAf	17670kas
0700-1000	CRI	SAs	15185kas
0700-1200	Channel Africa	SAf	9625mey
0700-1200	WWCR	NAm,CAm,Af	5070wcr*, 5070wcr**
0700-1300	CRI	Eu	17490kas
0710-0725	R. Japan	SEA	9730yan*
0730-0745	Vatican Radio	Af	15595smg
0800	**English**		
0800-0805	R. Australia	Pac	15240shp, 15415shp, 17840shp
0800-0815	T8WH - WHR Int	As	9930hbn
0800-0830	BVB	WEu	7220nau
0800-0830	VO Mongolia	Eu	7310kll*
0800-0900	Amateur R.Today	EAf	17760mey
0800-0900	Amateur R.Today	SAf	7205mey
0800-0900	BBC World Sce	SAs	17790nak+
0800-0900	KBS World R.	SEA	9570kim
0800-0900	KNLS Int.	EAs	9615nls
0800-0900	R. Mi Amigo Int	Eu	6005kll, 9560kll
0800-0900	VO Africa	Af	9505alf†
0800-0900	VO Nigeria	WAf	7255aja†,*
0800-1000	CRI	EAs	9415xia
0800-1100	RNZI	Pac	9765ran
0800-1130	Vatican Radio	Af	21550smg
0805-0900	R. Australia	Pac	15240shp, 15415shp, 17840shp
0815-0830	T8WH - WHR Int	As	9930hbn
0830-0900	T8WH - WHR Int	As	9930hbn
0900	**English**		
0900-0930	R. Australia	Pac	9580shp, 12065shp, 12085shp
0900-0930	VO Mongolia	As	12035uba
0900-1000	BVB	NAf	17540nau
0900-1000	CRI	Eu	17570uru, 17650kas
0900-1000	IRRS Shortwave	Eu,ME,NAf	9510sof
0900-1000	PCJ R. Int.	WEu	11580yfr*
0900-1000	R. Mi Amigo Int	Eu	6005kll, 9560kll
0900-1000	T8WH - WHR Int	As	9930hbn
0900-1000	Trunews Radio	AUS,NZL,Pac	11565hri
0900-1000	WHRI	CAm,Pac	11565hri
0900-1100	CRI	Pac	15210kun, 17690jin
0900-1100	WWCR	NAm,Eu,NAf	6875wcr**, 7490wcr**
0900-1300	WEWN	EAs	11520ewn
0900-1300	WWCR	NAm,Eu,NAf	15795wcr**
0900-1600	The Mighty KBC	Eu	6095nau
0900-2200	WWCR	NAm,Eu,NAf	15825wcr**
0930-1000	BBG-VOA	NAm	5865grv*
0930-2100	R. Australia	Pac	9580shp, 12065shp, 12085shp
1000	**English**		
1000-1015	TWR Asia	AUS,NZL,Pac	11840twr
1000-1025	TWR Asia	AUS,NZL,Pac	11840twr
1000-1030	R. Japan	Pac	9625yam
1000-1030	VO Vietnam	As	9840vni, 12020vni
1000-1100	All India R.	SAs	1053tut, 7270cni
1000-1100	All India R.	EAs	13605bgl, 15030alg, 15410bgl
1000-1100	All India R.	Pac	13695bgl, 17510del, 17895bgl+
1000-1100	BBC World Sce	FE	9740nak, 17760nak
1000-1100	CRI	SAs	15190kas
1000-1100	CRI	EAs	5955xia, 7215xia, 11635bei

1000	English	Area	kHz
1000-1100	FEBC Korea	As	1188seo
1000-1100	KNLS Int.	EAs	9615nls
1000-1100	VO Indonesia	As,Pac	9526jakt†
1000-1100	WRMI	NAm	7570yfr
1000-1200	BBC World Sce	FE	15285sng
1000-1200	CRI	SEA	13590bei, 13720xia
1000-1200	WWCR	NAm	6115wcr*, 6115wcr**
1000-1200	WWCR	NAm,Eu,NAf	6875wcr*, 7490wcr*
1000-1300	BBC World Sce	FE	11895nak
1000-1400	BBC World Sce	SEA	6195sng
1000-1400	BBC World Sce	FE	9740sng
1000-1400	T8WH - WHR Int	As	9930hbn
1000-1400	Overcomer Min.	Af	21675yfr
1000-1400	WWCR	NAm,Eu,NAf	15795wcr*
1000-2200	Overcomer Min.	NAm	11825yfr
1000-2200	University Net.	NAm	11775aia†
1000-2300	PanAm Bc	Af	21675yfr
1020-1120	VOIRI	SAs	17560kam, 21510kam
1020-1120	VOIRI	ME	702kia
1030-1100	TWR Asia	SEA	11965twr
1030-1110	TWR Asia	SEA	11965twr
1030-1130	VO Korea	LAm	6170kuj, 9435kuj
1030-1130	VO Korea	SEA	6185kuj, 9850kuj
1030-1300	IRRS Shortwave	Eu,ME,NAf	9510sof
1100	**English**		
1100-1130	KBS World R.	Eu	9760wof+
1100-1130	R. Japan	Eu	9760wof+
1100-1130	R. Saranrom	SEA	1575bph
1100-1130	WHRI	LAm,SAm	7315hri
1100-1130	WHRI	LAm,Car	7385hri
1100-1200	CRI	SAs	11795kas
1100-1200	R. Mi Amigo Int	Eu	7310kll, 9560kll
1100-1200	R.Taiwan Int.	SEA	1359fan, 7445pao
1100-1200	WHRI	LAm,SAm	7315hri
1100-1300	CRI	SEA	1269xuw
1100-1300	CRI	Eu	13665cer
1100-1300	CRI	SAs	7250kas, 11650uru, 12015kas
1100-1300	RNZI	Pac	13840ran
1100-1600	CRI	EAs	5955bei
1100-2200	WWCR	NAm,Eu,NAf	15825wcr*
1115-1130	BVB	FE	21480mdc
1115-1130	Etrn.Good News	EAs	21480mdc
1115-1130	Reach Bey. Aus	As	15430knx
1130-1145	Etrn.Good News	SAs	15525dha
1130-1145	Reach Bey. Aus	As	15430knx
1130-1200	AWR	CAm	5950yfr
1130-1200	VO Vietnam	As	9840vni, 12020vni
1130-1200	WHRI	LAm,SAm	7315hri
1130-1200	WHRI	NAm	7385hri
1200	**English**		
1200-1215	BVB	SEA	17820tac**, 17860tac**
1200-1215	TWR India	SAs	882put
1200-1230	BVB	FE	21480mdc
1200-1230	R. Japan	SEA	11740sng
1200-1230	WHRI	LAm,Car	7385hri
1200-1300	BVB	FE	21480mdc
1200-1300	CRI	CAs	11690xia
1200-1300	CRI	SEA	684dof, 1188kun, 9600kun, 9645bei, 9730kun
1200-1300	CRI	SAs	9460kas
1200-1300	CRI	Pac	9760kun

1200	English	Area	kHz
1200-1300	KNLS Int.	EAs	7355nls, 9615nls
1200-1300	R.Romania Int	Eu	13580tig, 15460tig
1200-1300	R.Romania Int	Af	15150gal, 17765gal
1200-1300	Overcomer Min.	NAm	9840hri
1200-1300	WHRI	LAm,Car	11790hri
1200-1400	BBC World Sce	FE	5875nak
1200-1400	CRI	Pac	11760kun
1200-1400	CRI	SEA	1341hdu, 11980kun
1200-1400	CRI	Eu	13790uru
1200-1500	WWCR	Af	7490wcr**
1200-2300	WBCQ	NAm,CAm	15420bcq*‡
1200-2400	WWCR	NAm,Eu	13845wcr**
1200-2400	WWCR	NAm,CAm,Af	9980wcr**
1215-1230	TWR India	SAs	882put
1215-1245	TWR Asia	EAs	9975twr+
1230-1245	Etrn.Good News	EAs	9930hbn
1230-1245	FG Radio	LAm	9955yfr
1230-1245	TWR India	SAs	882put
1230-1300	Bangladesh Bet.	SEA	15105dka
1230-1300	R. Thailand WS	As,Pac	9390udo
1230-1300	VO Vietnam	As	9840vni, 12020vni
1230-1330	KBS World R.	EAs	6095kim
1300	**English**		
1300-0100	University Net.	NAm,Eu	13845wcr
1300-0100	WWCR	NAm,Eu	13845wcr*
1300-1330	AWR As/Pacific	As	15430sda
1300-1330	R. Prague	LAm	9955yfr
1300-1330	R. Slovakia Int	Eu	9560kll
1300-1330	R. Slovakia Int	LAm	9955yfr
1300-1400	BBC World Sce	SAs	1413sla, 15310nak
1300-1400	CRI	Pac	11900bei
1300-1400	CRI	Eu	13670kas
1300-1400	CRI	SAs	7300kas, 9655kas
1300-1400	CRI	NAm	9570hab
1300-1400	CRI	SEA	9730bei, 11910bei
1300-1400	KBS World R.	NAm	15575kim
1300-1400	KBS World R.	SEA	9570kim
1300-1400	R. Mi Amigo Int	Eu	7310kll
1300-1400	Shiokaze	KRE	7400yam*
1300-1400	Overcomer Min.	WAf,CAf	21610hri
1300-1400	VO Indonesia	As,Pac	9526jak†
1300-1400	VO Tajik	WAs	1143dsb, 7245dsb
1300-1400	WHRI	NAm, NEu,As	9840hri
1300-1400	WRMI	NAm	11580yfr
1300-1500	BBC World Sce	SAs	9410sla
1300-1500	CRI	CAs,Eu	9765bji
1300-1500	LKE LLB Bergen	Eu	1314erd*, 5895erd*
1300-1500	WEWN	EAs	15610ewn
1300-1600	CRI	SEA	9870xia
1300-1600	WWCR	Af	7490wcr*
1300-1745	RNZI	Pac	9700ran
1300-2000	Overcomer Min.	NAm,Af	9980wcr
1300-2100	Overcomer Min.	Eu,NAf	15770yfr
1300-2400	Overcomer Min.	NAm	9370wrb
1300-2400	WWCR	NAm,CAm,Af	9980wcr*
1300-2400	WWRB	NAm	9370wrb
1330-1345	FEBA India	As	9775trm
1330-1345	Reach Bey. Aus	As	9720knx, 15340knx
1330-1400	VO Vietnam	As	9840vni, 12020vni
1330-1430	VO Korea	Eu	7570kuj, 12015kuj
1330-1430	VO Korea	NAm	9435kuj, 11710kuj
1330-1430	VO Turkey	Eu	12035emr
1330-1500	All India R.	SEA	9690bgl, 11620del, 13710bgl

1400	English	Area	kHz
1400-0200	WTWW	NAm,Eu	9475tww‡
1400-1415	FG Radio	LAm	9955yfr
1400-1430	BVB	SAs	6260tac
1400-1430	Lao National R.	SEA	567vie, 6130vie
1400-1430	R. Japan	SAs	11685tac
1400-1430	R. Japan	SEA	11925hbn
1400-1430	R. Thailand WS	As,Pac	9390udo
1400-1445	PanAm Bc	ME	15205nau
1400-1500	BVB	SAs	17510iss
1400-1500	CRI	CAs,Eu	11665uru
1400-1500	CRI	SAs	7300uru, 9460uru
1400-1500	CRI	Eu	9795uru, 13710kas
1400-1500	KBS World R.	SEA	9640kim
1400-1500	KNLS Int.	EAs	9615nls
1400-1500	R. Sult.of Oman	Eu,ME	15140thu
1400-1500	Overcomer Min.	SEu,NAf	21600hri
1400-1500	WHRI	SEu,NAf,ME	21600hri
1400-1500	WHRI	NAm, NEu,As	9840hri
1400-1600	BBG-VOA	Af	17885sao
1400-1600	CRI	NAm	15700hab
1400-1600	CRI	EAf,WAf	17630bko
1400-1600	Overcomer Min.	NAm	9840hri
1400-1700	BBC World Sce	SAs	7465sng
1400-1700	BBG-VOA	Af	4930bot
1400-1800	BBC World Sce	SAs	5845nak+
1400-2000	BBG-VOA	Af	15580bot
1400-2200	WJHR	NAm	15555jhr*
1415-1430	PanAm Bc	ME	15205nau
1425-1455	TWR Africa	SAf	6025man
1430-1500	BBC World Sce	SAs	1413sla
1430-1530	T8WH - WHR Int	SEA,CAf	15565hbn
1445-1500	FG Radio	LAm	9955yfr
1445-1500	TWR Europe	CAs	1287bis
1445-1600	Reach Bey. Aus	As	15340knx
1500	**English**		
1500-1530	VO Mongolia	Eu	6005kll*
1500-1530	VO Vietnam	As	9840vni, 12020vni
1500-1600	BBG-VOA	Af	6080bot
1500-1600	Channel Africa	SAf	9625mey
1500-1600	CRI	SAs	1188kun, 7395uru, 9785jin
1500-1600	CRI	NAf,ME	6095kas, 9720uru
1500-1600	CRI	SEA	7325bei
1500-1600	CRI	Eu	9525kas
1500-1600	IRRS Shortwave	ME,As,AUS	15190sof
1500-1600	WHRI	As	21600hri
1500-1700	BBC World Sce	EAf	12095mdc
1500-1700	BBC World Sce	SAs	9410sng
1500-1700	CRI	Eu	9435kas
1500-1800	BBC World Sce	EAf	15420mey
1500-1800	BBC World Sce	ME	9505sla
1500-1800	CRI	SAs	1323uru
1500-1800	CRI	SEA	9880nnn
1500-1900	BBC World Sce	ME	6195sla
1500-1900	WEWN	ME	15610ewn
1500-2000	WWCR	Af	12160wcr**
1515-1545	BVB	SAs	13630nau
1520-1620	VOIRI	SAs,SEA	11940kam, 13785sir
1525-1555	TWR Africa	SAf	6025man
1530-1545	All India R.	EAf	7555del
1530-1545	TWR Asia	EAs	12120twr
1530-1550	TWR Asia	EAs	12120twr
1530-1550	Vatican Radio	Af	15470pug
1530-1550	Vatican Radio	As	15775smg+

1500	English	Area	kHz
1530-1558	AWR Af/Eu	EAs	11750nau
1530-1600	All India R.	SAs	1053tut
1530-1600	R. Slovakia Int	Eu	7310kll
1530-1600	T8WH - WHR Int	SEA,CAf	15565hbn
1530-1600	Vatican Radio	Af	11695pht
1530-1600	Vatican Radio	Af	15470pug
1530-1600	Vatican Radio	As	15775smg+
1530-1600	VO Mongolia	As	12015uba
1530-1600	WHRI	NAm, NEu,As	9840hri
1530-1630	VO Korea	Eu	7570kuj, 12015kuj
1530-1630	VO Korea	NAm	9435kuj, 11710kuj
1540-1600	R. Japan	SEA	5985yan*
1545-1615	TWR India	SAs	882put
1550-1650	RNZI	Pac	7330ran+
1600	**English**		
1600-1630	AWR Af/Eu	As	11780trm
1600-1630	AWR As/Pacific	SEA	15660sda
1600-1630	BBG-VOA	Eu	17580grv*
1600-1630	VO Vietnam	ME	7220vni, 9550vni
1600-1630	VO Vietnam	Eu	7280vni, 9730vni
1600-1640	R. Cairo	ISR	1008ela
1600-1700	BBC World Sce	SAf	17640asc
1600-1700	BBG-VOA	Af	909bot, 1530sao
1600-1700	CRI	SEA	6060kun
1600-1700	CRI	NAf,ME	7420uru
1600-1700	CRI	Eu	9875kas
1600-1700	R. Ethiopia EBC	EAf,ME	7236gjw±,†
1600-1700	KBS World R.	Eu	9515kim
1600-1700	KBS World R.	SEA	9640kim
1600-1700	R. Mi Amigo Int	Eu	6005kll
1600-1700	Shiokaze	KRE	5990yam*
1600-1800	BBC World Sce	CAf	17830asc
1600-1800	BBG-VOA	Af	6080sao, 17895smg
1600-1800	CRI	SEA	1080xuw, 6175nnn
1600-1800	CRI	SAs	7235kas
1600-1800	CRI	Eu	7255kas
1600-1800	CRI	SAf	7435jin, 9570bei
1600-1800	R. Cairo	CAf,SAf	15345abs
1600-1800	Overcomer Min.	NAm	9840hri
1600-2000	BBC World Sce	SAf	3255mey, 6190mey
1600-2100	WWCR	Af	12160wcr*
1615-1630	Oromo Voice R.	ETH	17850iss
1630-1700	AWR Af/Eu	ME	15360trm
1630-1700	BBG-VOA	SDN	11900mey**, 13865wof**, 15180smg**
1630-1700	WHRI	CAf	21600hri
1630-1730	Amateur R.Today	SAf	4895mey
1630-1730	VO Korea	ME,NAf	9890kuj, 11645kuj
1650-1745	RNZI	Pac	9780ran+
1700	**English**		
1700-1730	BBC World Sce	CAs	1251dsb
1700-1730	BBG-VOA	Af	13590kwt
1700-1800	BBC World Sce	CAs	1251dsb
1700-1800	BBC World Sce	SAs	1413sla
1700-1800	BBC World Sce	WAf	17780asc
1700-1800	BBC World Sce	EAf	9410dha
1700-1800	Channel Africa	WAf	15235mey
1700-1800	CRI	SEA	6090kun, 7420kun
1700-1800	CRI	SAs	6140kas, 7410kas
1700-1800	CRI	ME	6165bei
1700-1800	R. Mi Amigo Int	Eu	3985kll
1700-1900	CRI	Eu	6100bei
1700-2000	BBC World Sce	WAf	15400asc

1700	English	Area	kHz
1700-2000	BBC World Sce	EAf	7445mdc
1715-1730	Vatican Radio	NAf,ME	11935smg
1720-1740	VOA Studio7	ZWE	909bot, 4930bot, 13860sao, 15460sao
1730-1745	Etrn.Good News	Af	21600hri
1730-1800	VOA Studio7	ZWE	909bot, 4930bot, 13860sao, 15460sao
1730-1800	BBG-VOA	Af	13590sao
1730-1800	Vatican Radio	Af	9660mdc, 11625smg, 13765smg
1730-1830	VO Africa	Af	9505alf†
1730-1830	VO Turkey	CAs,SAs	11730emr
1730-2000	HCJB Deutsch	Eu	3995wnm
1745-1800	WHRI	CAf	21600hri
1745-1820	TWR Africa	WAf	1566par
1745-1900	Bangladesh Bet.	Eu	13580dka
1745-1945	All India R.	EAf	11935mum, 13695bgl, 17670del
1745-1945	All India R.	NAf,WAf	9445del
1745-1945	All India R.	Eu	9950del+, 11670bgl
1745-1950	RNZI	Pac	11690ran+
1745-2150	RNZI	Pac	11725ran
1800	**English**		
1800-1815	Etrn.Good News	ME	9715mos
1800-1830	BBG-VOA	Af	4930bot
1800-1830	BVB	ME	9715nau
1800-1830	ETC Radio	Eu	11600sof
1800-1830	R. Japan	CAf	11800mey
1800-1830	R. Japan	Am	9395yfr
1800-1830	VO Vietnam	Eu	5955mos
1800-1845	BVB	ME	9715nau
1800-1900	BBC World Sce	ME	5945sla
1800-1900	BBG-VOA	Af	13590lam
1800-1900	BBG-VOA	Af	909bot
1800-1900	BVB	ME	9715mos
1800-1900	CRI	Eu	7405bei
1800-1900	KBS World R.	Eu	7275kim
1800-1900	R.Romania Int	Eu	6090tig, 7350tig+
1800-1900	RAE	Eu	15345bue
1800-1900	Overcomer Min.	WAf,CAf	21600hri
1800-1930	VO Nigeria	Eu	15120aja+,†
1800-1930	VO Nigeria	WAf	7255aja†,*
1800-2000	BBC World Sce	EAf	9410dha
1800-2000	BVB	ME	9715nau
1800-2100	BBC World Sce	CAf	11810asc
1800-2100	BBC World Sce	WAf	9915wof
1800-2200	Overcomer Min.	NAm	17530hri
1802-1832	TWR Africa	Af	9500man
1815-1830	BVB	IRN	7365nau
1815-1830	Etrn.Good News	ME	7365nau
1830-1900	AWR Af/Eu	Af	15155trm
1830-1930	VO Korea	Eu	7570kuj, 12015kuj
1830-2000	BVB	EEu,RUS	6030nau
1830-2100	BBG-VOA	Af	4930bot
1830-2155	TWR Africa	SAf	1170man
1832-1847	TWR Africa	Af	9500man
1832-1902	TWR Africa	Af	9500man
1900	**English**		
1900-1930	FTB Ministry	WAf	11830asc
1900-1930	VO Vietnam	Eu	7280vni, 9730vni
1900-2000	BBG-VOA	Af	13590sao
1900-2000	BVB	ME	9715nau
1900-2000	IRRS Shortwave	Eu,ME,NAf	7290sof
1900-2000	R. Mi Amigo Int	LVA	1485rme

1900	English	Area	kHz
1900-2000	R. Thailand WS	Eu	9390udo
1900-2000	Overcomer Min.	NAm	17610hri
1900-2000	Overcomer Min.	NAm	9840hri
1900-2000	VO Indonesia	Eu,NAf,ME	9526jak†
1900-2000	R. Cairo	WAf	15290abz
1900-2100	BBC World Sce	ME	1413sla
1900-2100	BBG-VOA	Af	909bot
1900-2100	CRI	ME,NAf	7295kas, 9440kun
1900-2100	WHRI	CAf	17610hri
1900-2400	WEWN	Af	15610ewn
1915-1945	BVB	ME	9470nau
1920-2020	VOIRI	SAf	13735kam, 15460sir
1920-2020	VOIRI	Eu	6040sir, 7425kam
1930-1945	BVB	EEu,RUS	6030nau
1930-1945	Etrn.Good News	Eu	6030nau
1930-2000	BBG-VOA	Eu	15670grv*
1930-2000	PanAm Bc	NAf	9685nau
1930-2015	BVB	ME	9925sof
1930-2030	VO Korea	SAf	7210kuj, 11910kuj
1930-2030	VO Korea	ME,NAf	9875kuj, 11635kuj
1930-2030	VO Turkey	Eu	6050emr
1950-2150	RNZI	Pac	15720ran+

2000	English		
2000-2030	R. Slovakia Int	Eu	3985kll
2000-2030	Vatican Radio	Af	9660smg, 11625smg
2000-2030	VO Mongolia	Eu	3985kll*
2000-2100	BBC World Sce	WAf	12095asc
2000-2100	BBG-VOA	Af	15580smg
2000-2100	CRI	SAf	5985bei
2000-2100	R. Habana Cuba	NAm	11670hab
2000-2100	WBCQ	NAm,CAm	7490bcq
2000-2100	WHRI	Eu,ME	11705hri
2000-2100	WRMI	NAm	11580yfr
2000-2200	BBG-VOA	Af	1530sao, 6080sao
2000-2200	CRI	Eu	5960cer, 7285cer, 7415kas, 9600kas
2000-2200	R. Belarus	Eu	11730mns, 11930mns
2000-2400	WWCR	Af	9350wcr**
2020-2200	R. Belarus	Eu	11730mns, 11930mns
2030-2045	R. Thailand WS	Eu	9390udo
2030-2100	BBG-VOA	Af	4940sao
2030-2100	VO Vietnam	ME	7220vni, 9550vni
2030-2100	VO Vietnam	Eu	7280vni, 9730vni
2030-2300	HCJB Deutsch	Eu	3995wnm
2045-2230	All India R.	Eu	9445bgl, 9950del+, 11670bgl
2045-2230	All India R.	Pac	9910alg, 11620bgl, 11740pan

2100	English		
2100-0100	WWCR	NAm,Eu,NAf	3195wcr**
2100-0100	WWCR	Af	9350wcr*
2100-0100	WWRB	NAm	3215wrb‡**
2100-0200	WWCR	NAm	6115wcr*
2100-0200	WWCR	S	6875wcr*, 6875wcr**
2100-0200	WWRB	NAm	3215wrb‡*
2100-0630	R. Australia	Pac	15240shp, 15415shp, 17840shp
2100-2115	Etrn.Good News	Eu	11705hri
2100-2115	FG Radio	NAm	7570yfr, 15770yfr
2100-2130	AWR Af/Eu	WAf	11980mos
2100-2130	ETC Radio	Eu,NAf	15770yfr
2100-2130	R. Slovakia Int	NAm	7570yfr
2100-2130	R. Tirana	Eu	7465shi
2100-2130	WHRI	Eu,ME	11705hri

2100	English	Area	kHz
2100-2200	BBC World Sce	CAf	11810asc
2100-2200	BBG-VOA	Af	15580grv
2100-2200	CRI	SAf	7205xia, 7325bei
2100-2200	RFI	NAm	15770yfr
2100-2200	R. Mi Amigo Int	LVA	1485rme
2100-2200	WBCQ	NAm,CAm	7490bcq
2100-2200	WHRI	Eu,ME	11705hri
2100-2200	WRMI	Eu,NAf	15770yfr
2100-2300	Overcomer Min.	NAm	11580yfr
2100-2400	BBC World Sce	WAf	9915asc, 12095asc
2115-2130	WHRI	Eu,ME	11705hri
2115-2200	RFI	NAm	15770yfr
2115-2245	R. Cairo	Eu	9900abs
2130-2200	RFI	NAm	15770yfr
2130-2200	R.Romania Int	Eu	6030gal+, 7375gal
2130-2200	R.Romania Int	NAm	6170tig, 7310tig
2130-2200	WHRI	Eu,ME	11705hri
2130-2230	VO Korea	Eu	7570kuj, 12015kuj
2130-2230	VO Turkey	SAs,Pac	9610emr
2145-2200	FG Radio	NAm	15770yfr
2150-0500	RNZI	Pac	15720ran

2200	English		
2200-0100	WWCR	NAm	6115wcr**
2200-0800	LKE LLB Bergen	Eu	1314erd*, 5895erd*
2200-1000	Overcomer Min.	NAm	7570yfr
2200-1000	University Net.	NAm	6090aia†
2200-1300	WWRB	NAm	5050wrb
2200-2230	AWR As/Pacific	As	15435sda
2200-2300	Angolan Nat R.	SAf	945mul
2200-2300	BBC World Sce	SEA	3915sng, 5890nak
2200-2300	BBC World Sce	FE	5905nak, 5960sla
2200-2300	CRI	EAs	5915bei
2200-2300	KBS World R.	Eu	11810kim
2200-2300	R. Habana Cuba	Af	11880hab
2200-2300	Overcomer Min.	NAm	9955yfr
2200-2300	WBCQ	NAm,CAm	7490bcq
2200-2300	WHRI	Eu,ME	9505hri
2200-2400	BBC World Sce	FE,SEA	5875nak, 6195sng
2200-2400	BBC World Sce	FE	7490nak
2200-2400	Overcomer Min.	Eu,ME	9505hri
2200-2400	Overcomer Min.	NAm	9955yfr
2230-2300	R. Saranrom	SEA	1575bph
2245-0045	All India R.	EAs	9690bgl, 11645del+, 13605bgl+
2245-0045	All India R.	SEA	9705pan, 11710del
2255-0200	RNZI	Pac	17675ran+

2300	English		
2300-0000	BBC World Sce	SEA	11955sng
2300-0000	BBC World Sce	FE,SEA	9740sng
2300-0000	Overcomer Min.	NAm,CAm	7490bcq
2300-0000	WBCQ	NAm,CAm	7490bcq
2300-0030	R. Cairo	NAm	9965abs
2300-0030	TWR Bonaire	SAm	800twb
2300-0100	CRI	SEA	11790xia
2300-0200	CRI	Eu	7350kas
2300-2300	The Mighty KBC	NAm	7395nau
2300-2315	FG Radio	NAm	5850yfr, 11580yfr •
2300-2315	WHRI	Eu,ME	9505hri
2300-2320	WHRI	LAm,Car	7315hri
2300-2400	CRI	SAs	5915kas, 7410kas
2300-2400	CRI	NAm,CAm	5990hab
2300-2400	CRI	EAs	6145bei
2300-2400	CRI	SEA	9535kun
2300-2400	R.Romania Int	Eu	6015gal, 7220gal

2300	English	Area	kHz
2300-2400	R.Romania Int	EAs	7395tig, 9620tig
2300-2400	Overcomer Min.	NAm,Af	9980wcr
2300-2400	VO Turkey	Eu,NAm	5960emr
2300-2400	WHRI	LAm,Car	7315hri
2300-2400	WRMI	NAm	5850yfr, 11580yfr
2315-2330	WHRI	LAm,Car	7315hri
2330-2345	WHRI	Eu,ME	9505hri
2330-2400	AWR	CAm	5950yfr
2330-2400	AWR As/Pacific	SEA	15320sda
2330-2400	R. Ukraine Int.	NAm	5850yfr, 11580yfr
2330-2400	VO Vietnam	As	9840vni, 12020vni
2330-2400	WHRI	LAm,Car	7315hri
2345-2400	Etrn.Good News	CAm	7315hri
1100	**English (Liturgy)**		
1130-1200	Vatican Radio	Eu	17590smg
1130-1200	Vatican Radio	ME	21560smg
0600	**English/Finnish**		
0600-0900	Scan.Weekend R.	Eu	5980vir
0800			
0800-1400	Scan.Weekend R.	Eu	11720vir
0900			
0900-1500	Scan.Weekend R.	Eu	6170vir
1400			
1400-1700	Scan.Weekend R.	Eu	11690vir
1500			
1500-1900	Scan.Weekend R.	Eu	5980vir
1700			
1700-1900	Scan.Weekend R.	Eu	11720vir
1900			
1900-2200	Scan.Weekend R.	Eu	6170vir, 11690vir
2200			
2200-0600	Scan.Weekend R.	Eu	6170vir
2200-2200	Scan.Weekend R.	Eu	1602vir
2200-2300	Scan.Weekend R.	Eu	11720vir
2300			
2300-0800	Scan.Weekend R.	Eu	11690vir
0700	**English/German**		
0700-0800	R. Gloria Int.	Eu	9485goh*
0800			
0800-0900	R. Gloria Int.	Eu	7265goh*
0900			
0900-1000	R. Gloria Int.	Eu	9485goh*
1100			
1100-1200	R. Gloria Int.	Eu	7310kll*
1600			
1600-1700	R. Gloria Int.	Eu	6005kll*
0200	**English/Hindi**		
0230-0300	All India R.	SAs	594kkt
1500			
1515-1600	All India R.	SAs	1134kkt
1900	**English/Irish Gaelic**		
1930-2000	RTÉ R.Worldwide	Af	5820mdc
1800	**English/Ndebele/Shona**		
1800-1830	VOA Studio7	ZWE	909bot, 4930bot, 13860sao, 15460sao
1830-1900	VOA Studio7	ZWE	909bot, 13860sao, 15460sao
0100	**English/Norwegian**		
0100-0200	R. Nthn. Star	Eu	1314erd*, 5895erd*
0800			
0800-0815	R. Nthn. Star	Eu	1314erd*, 5895erd*
0900			
0900-0920	R. Nthn. Star	Eu	1314erd*, 5895erd*
1000			
1000-1130	R. Nthn. Star	Eu	1314erd*, 5895erd*

1800	Eng/Norwegian	Area	kHz
1800-1900	R. Nthn. Star	Eu	1314erd*, 5895erd*
1900			
1900-1945	R. Nthn. Star	Eu	1314erd*, 5895erd*
2000			
2000-2200	R. Nthn. Star	Eu	1314erd*, 5895erd*
1200	**English/Spanish**		
1230-0500	WINB	CAm	9265inb
2200			
2200-1500	WRMI	CAm,SAm	9955yfr
2300	**English/Thai/Khmer**		
2300-2400	Beibu Bay Radio	SEA	5050nnn, 9820nnn

0000	French	Area	kHz
0000-2400	RFI	Eu	3965iss+
0100	**French**		
0130-0200	R. Habana Cuba	Car	5040hab
0200	**French**		
0200-0300	R.Romania Int	NAm	5975gal, 7395gal
0400	**French**		
0400-0600	RFI	CAf,EAf	7390iss, 9790iss
0400-2310	RTBF Int.	WEu	621wav
0430-0500	AWR Af/Eu	NAf	6045mos
0430-0500	BBC World Sce	EAf	17640dha
0430-0500	BBC World Sce	CAf	6135asc, 7305asc
0430-0500	Vatican Radio	Af	11625mdc
0430-0500	Vatican Radio	Eu	7360smg
0430-0500	WHRI	Eu,ME	11635hri
0430-0530	VO Korea	SEA	13650kuj, 15105kuj
0500	**French**		
0500-0515	WHRI	Eu,ME	11635hri
0500-0600	RFI	CAf,EAf	11700iss
0530-0600	BBG-VOA	Af	1530sao
0530-0600	R. Japan	CAf,WAf	11730iss, 13840mdc
0530-0630	BBG-VOA	Af	4960sao, 6180sao, 9885bot, 13830bot
0600	**French**		
0600-0630	AWR Af/Eu	WAf	7220iss, 15700nau
0600-0630	BBC World Sce	NAf	6135wof, 7325wof
0600-0630	BBC World Sce	WAf	7305asc
0600-0630	BBC World Sce	CAf	9870asc
0600-0630	R.Romania Int	Eu	6040gal+, 7360gal
0600-0630	R.Romania Int	Af	9770tig, 11790tig
0600-0630	Vatican Radio	Af	9660smg, 11625smg
0600-0700	RFI	CAf,EAf	11700iss**
0600-0700	RFI	NAf,WAf	5925iss*, 7390iss*
0600-0700	RFI	WAf	9790iss**
0600-0800	CRI	Eu	15220kas
0600-0900	RFI	Af	15300iss
0620-0720	VOIRI	Eu,NAf	15450kam, 17865kam
0630-0730	VO Korea	LAm	11735kuj, 13760kuj, 15180kuj
0700	**French**		
0700-0730	AWR Af/Eu	WAf	11880iss
0700-0730	BBC World Sce	CAf	17880mey
0700-0730	BBC World Sce	WAf	9440asc
0700-0730	VO Nigeria	WAf	7255aja†,*
0700-0800	RFI	WAf,CAf	11700iss, 13695iss*
0700-0800	RFI	NAf,WAf	9790iss
0700-0900	RFI	CAf	17850iss
0715-0730	Vatican Radio	Af	15595smg
0730-0800	R. Slovakia Int	Eu	7310kll

0800	French	Area	kHz
0800-0805	R. Australia	Pac	15240shp, 15415shp, 17840shp
0800-0830	AWR Af/Eu	NAf	15145nau
0800-0900	RFI	NAf,WAf	13695iss
0800-0900	RFI	CAf	21580iss
0800-1130	Vatican Radio	Af	21570smg
1100	**French**		
1100-1130	BBG-VOA	Af	12030sao, 13735sao, 15715bot, 17850smg
1100-1200	R.Romania Int	Eu	15255gal, 17870gal, 21580tig
1100-1200	R.Romania Int	NAf	17640tig
1130-1230	VO Korea	LAm	6170kuj, 9435kuj
1130-1230	VO Korea	SEA	6185kuj, 9850kuj
1200	**French**		
1200-1203	R. Monaco	Atl,Med	4363mcr*, 8728mcr*, 13146mcr*,‡
1200-1230	BBC World Sce	WAf	17640asc
1200-1230	BBC World Sce	NAf	17830wof
1200-1230	BBC World Sce	CAf	21630asc
1200-1230	VO Vietnam	As	7285vni
1200-1300	RFI	NAf,WAf	17620iss
1200-1300	RFI	WAf,CAf	17660iss
1200-1300	RFI	CAf	21580iss, 21690mdc
1200-1400	CRI	Eu	15205kas
1300	**French**		
1300-1330	VO Vietnam	As	7285vni
1300-1400	CRI	Eu	17650kas
1330-1400	R. Slovakia Int	Eu	9560kll
1400	**French**		
1400-1600	CRI	WAf	11920cer, 13670cer
1400-1800	Saudi Int. R.	WAf	17660riy
1430-1500	Lao National R.	SEA	567vie, 6130vie
1430-1500	R. Slovakia Int	Eu	6005kll
1430-1530	VO Korea	Eu	7570kuj, 12015kuj
1430-1530	VO Korea	NAm	9435kuj, 11710kuj
1455-1525	TWR Africa	WAf	9585man
1600	**French**		
1600-1700	Channel Africa	WAf	15235mey
1600-1800	CRI	Eu	7350kas
1630-1700	VO Vietnam	ME	7220vni, 9550vni
1630-1730	VO Africa	Af	9505alf†
1630-1730	VO Korea	Eu	7570kuj, 12015kuj
1630-1730	VO Korea	NAm	9435kuj, 11710kuj
1640-1700	R. Cairo	ISR	1008ela
1700	**French**		
1700-1715	Vatican Radio	NAf,ME	11935smg
1700-1730	Vatican Radio	Af	11625smg, 13765smg
1700-1800	Deutsche Welle	Af	15275iss, 15560iss, 17800asc
1700-1800	R. Ethiopia EBC	EAf,ME	7236gjw±,†
1700-1800	RFI	WAf,CAf	17620iss
1700-1800	RFI	CAf	17850iss, 21580iss
1700-1800	R.Romania Int	Eu	5935tig, 7400tig
1700-1900	RFI	NAf,WAf	13740iss
1700-2000	RFI	WAf,CAf	15300iss
1800	**French**		
1800-1830	BBC World Sce	CAf	11785asc
1800-1830	BBC World Sce	WAf	11975asc, 15105asc
1800-1830	BBC World Sce	NAf	7265wof
1800-1830	BBC World Sce	SAf	7465mey
1800-2000	CRI	Eu	5970cer, 7360cer
1800-2000	CRI	NAf,WAf	6055cer, 7385cer
1800-2100	RFI	WAf,CAf	11995iss

1800	French	Area	kHz
1820-1920	VOIRI	WAf	11955kam
1820-1920	VOIRI	Eu	5935sir, 6135kam
1830-1900	R. Tirana	Eu	7465shi
1830-1900	VO Vietnam	Eu	7280vni, 9730vni
1830-1930	BBG-VOA	Af	15730smg
1830-1930	VO Korea	SAf	7210kuj, 11910kuj
1830-1930	VO Korea	ME,NAf	9875kuj, 11635kuj
1830-1930	VO Turkey	CAf	9620emr
1830-2000	BBG-VOA	Af	1530sao
1830-2030	BBG-VOA	Af	12075bot
1830-2030	CRI	WAf	7350uru, 9645kun
1900	**French**		
1900-2000	BBG-VOA	Af	9590sao
1900-2000	RFI	WAf,CAf	13695iss
1900-2000	R.Taiwan Int.	Eu	9895dha
1900-2200	RFI	WAf,CAf	9790iss
1930-2000	AWR Af/Eu	CAf	17510mos
1930-2000	R. Habana Cuba	Eu	15370hab
1930-2000	R. Slovakia Int	Eu	3985kll
1930-2000	VO Vietnam	Eu	5955mos, 7280vni, 9730vni
1930-2030	BBG-VOA	Af	11900sao, 15730grv
1935-2005	TWR Africa	WAf	9940man
1940-2000	R. Belarus	Eu	11730mns, 11930mns
1945-2030	All India R.	NAf,WAf	9620alg, 11710del, 13640bgl
2000	**French**		
2000-2030	AWR Af/Eu	WAf	9515nau
2000-2030	BBG-VOA	Af	9490kwt
2000-2100	KBS World R.	Af	5950iss
2000-2100	RAE	Eu	15345bue
2000-2100	VO Indonesia	Eu,NAf,ME	9526jak†
2000-2115	R. Cairo	Eu	9900abs
2000-2200	RFI	WAf,CAf	7205iss
2030-2100	AWR Af/Eu	WAf	11980mos
2030-2100	BBG-VOA	Af	11900sao, 15730bot
2030-2100	BBG-VOA	Af	9490bot, 12075sao
2030-2100	R. Japan	WAf	9855mdc
2030-2100	Vatican Radio	Af	9660smg, 11625smg
2030-2130	VO Korea	Eu	7570kuj, 12015kuj
2030-2130	VO Turkey	Eu	5970emr
2030-2130	VO Turkey	NAf,WAf	6050emr
2030-2230	CRI	Eu	6115bei, 7350uru
2040-2215	TWR Africa	WAf	1566par
2100	**French**		
2100-2130	BBG-VOA	Af	5885smg, 9490bot, 12075smg
2100-2130	R. Habana Cuba	NAm	11670hab
2100-2130	R. Habana Cuba	Af	11880hab
2100-2130	R.Romania Int	Eu	6030gal+, 7375gal
2100-2130	VO Vietnam	ME	7220vni, 9550vni
2100-2130	VO Vietnam	Eu	7280vni, 9730vni
2100-2200	Angolan Nat R.	SAf	945mul
2100-2200	KBS World R.	Eu	3955wof
2100-2300	R. Cairo	WAf	13580abs
2100-2400	WTWW	NAm,Eu	12105tww†
2200	**French**		
2215-2230	TWR Africa	WAf	1566par
2230-2300	R. Habana Cuba	SAm	17730hab
1900	**French/Hindi**		
1945-2030	All India R.	Eu	7550bgl+*
1800	**French/Macedonian**		
1830-1900	R. Makedonija	Eu	810sko

GERMAN

0400	German	Area	kHz
0400-0430	TWR Africa	SAf	3200man, 4775man
0400-0500	TWR Africa	SAf	4775man
0400-0600	RTL Radio	Eu	1440mrn*
0400-0700	RTL Radio	Eu	1440mrn*
0430-0500	TWR Africa	SAf	3200man
0500	**German**		
0500-1700	HCJB Deutsch	Eu	7365wnm
0600	**German**		
0600-0630	DWD	Eu	5905pin*
0600-0630	Miss.Heukelbach	Eu	3995wnm, 7365wnm
0600-0630	R. Freundes-D.	Eu	1440mrn*
0600-0715	R. Öl Int.	Eu,NAf,ME	6155mos
0600-0800	CRI	Eu	17615uru, 17720kas
0600-1100	CRI	Eu	1440mrn**
0630-0700	RTL Radio	Eu	1440mrn*
0700	**German**		
0700-0730	R.Romania Int	Eu	6020tig+, 7345tig
0700-0730	R. Slovakia Int	Eu	7310kll
0700-0800	R. Mi Amigo Int	Eu	6005kll, 9560kll
0700-0900	R. Belarus	Eu	3985kll*
0700-0900	R. Belarus	Eu	6005kll*
0700-1800	Europa 24	Eu	6150datt
0720-0820	VOIRI	Eu	15175kam, 17690sir
0725-0730	Lutherische Std	Eu	7365wnm
0800	**German**		
0830-0900	R. Bulgaria	Eu	7310kll*
0900	**German**		
0900-1000	R. 700	Eu	7310kll
0900-1200	R. Mi Amigo Int	Eu	6005kll, 9560kll
0900-1400	R. 700	Eu	6005kll
0900-1530	R. 700	Eu	7310kll
0900-1730	R. 700	Eu	3985kll
1000	**German**		
1000-1100	Radio DARC	Eu	6070rob
1000-1100	R. Mi Amigo Int	Eu	6005kll
1100	**German**		
1100-1200	R. 700	Eu	6005kll
1100-1200	R. Joystick	Eu	7330mos*
1130-1200	Ev.Miss.Gemeind	Eu	6055nau
1200	**German**		
1200-1210	RTL Radio	Eu	1440mrn*
1200-1230	DWD	Eu	5905pin*
1230-1330	VO Turkey	Eu	17755emr
1300	**German**		
1300-1400	R. 700	Eu	6005kll
1400	**German**		
1400-1430	R. Slovakia Int	Eu	6005kll
1500	**German**		
1500-1530	R. 700	Eu	7310kll
1500-1600	R.Romania Int	Eu	6040tig, 7330tig
1530-1600	R. Bulgaria	Eu	6005kll*
1600	**German**		
1600-1700	Radio DARC	Eu	6070rob
1600-1700	R. Mi Amigo Int	Eu	6005kll
1600-1800	CRI	Eu	5970cer, 7380cer
1600-1800	R. 700	Eu	6005kll
1600-1900	R. Mi Amigo Int	LVA	1485rme
1630-1700	Miss.Heukelbach	Eu	3995wnm, 7365wnm
1630-1730	VO Korea	Eu	6170kuj, 9425kuj
1655-1830	RTL Radio	Eu	1440mrn*

1700	German	Area	kHz
1700-1800	R. 700	Eu	6005kll
1700-1800	R. Mi Amigo Int	Eu	3985kll
1700-1800	RAE	Eu	15345bue
1720-1820	VOIRI	Eu	5900kam, 7425sir
1730-1800	R. Bulgaria	Eu	3985kll*
1730-2000	HCJB Deutsch	Eu	7365wnm
1800	**German**		
1800-1900	R. 700	Eu	3985kll
1800-1900	VO Indonesia	Eu	9526jakt
1800-1940	R. Belarus	Eu	11730mns, 11930mns
1800-2000	CRI	Eu	6160xia, 7395kas, 9615uru
1800-2000	R. Belarus	Eu	11730mns, 11930mns
1800-2300	CRI	Eu	1440mrn**
1825-1830	Lutherische Std	Eu	1440mrn*
1830-1900	R. Freundes-D.	Eu	1440mrn*
1830-1900	VO Turkey	Eu	7205emr
1830-2030	VO Korea	Eu	6170kuj, 9425kuj
1855-1900	Lutherische Std	Eu	3995wnm
1900	**German**		
1900-1930	R. Slovakia Int	Eu	3985kll
1900-2000	R. Cairo	Eu	9570abs
1900-2000	R.Romania Int	Eu	6010tig, 7405tig+
1900-2000	R.Taiwan Int.	Eu	3955wof
2000	**German**		
2000-2015	R. Thailand WS	Eu	9390udo
2000-2030	RadioDienst Pol	Eu	3985kll
2000-2100	KBS World R.	Eu	3955wof
2000-2100	Radio DARC	Eu	6070rob
2030-0400	HCJB Deutsch	Eu	7365wnm
2030-2100	R. Tirana	Eu	7465shi
2030-2100	VO Vietnam	Eu	6175dha
2100	**German**		
2100-2130	VO Vietnam	Eu	6175dha
2100-2200	R. Mi Amigo Int	LVA	1485rme
2100-2200	RAE	Eu	15345bue
2100-2300	R. Belarus	Eu	3985kll*
2300	**German**		
2300-0700	R. 700	Eu	3985kll
1700	**German (Low)**		
1700-1730	HCJB Deutsch	Eu	3995wnm, 7365wnm
2000			
2000-2030	HCJB Deutsch	Eu	3995wnm, 7365wnm
0700	**German/Dutch/English**		
0700-1300	R. Mi Amigo Int	Eu	6005kll
0900			
0900-1300	R. Mi Amigo Int	Eu	9560kll
1100			
1100-1500	R. Mi Amigo Int	Eu	7310kll
1600			
1600-1700	R. Mi Amigo Int	Eu	6005kll
1800			
1800-1900	R. Mi Amigo Int	Eu	3985kll
0000	**German/English**		
0000-2400	Channel 292	Eu	6070robt*
0700	**German/Various**		
0700-0900	Hamburger LR	Eu	7265goh
0800			
0800-0900	MV Baltic Radio	Eu	7265goh*
0900			
0900-1000	MV Baltic Radio	Eu	9485goh*
0900-1200	Hamburger LR	Eu	6190goh
1200			
1200-1600	Hamburger LR	Eu	7265goh

1200	German/Various	Area	kHz
1200-1600	Hamburger LR	Eu	9485goh

PORTUGUESE

0000	Portuguese	Area	kHz
0000-0100	CRI	SAm	9710kas
0300	**Portuguese**		
0300-0500	WTWW	NAm,Eu	12105tww†
0500	**Portuguese**		
0530-0600	Vatican Radio	Af	7360smg, 11625smg, 13765mdc
0700	**Portuguese**		
0700-0845	TWR Bonaire	SAm	800twb
0700-0900	TWR Bonaire	SAm	800twb
0800	**Portuguese**		
0800-1050	Vatican Radio	Af	21560smg
0800-1130	Vatican Radio	Af	21560smg
0900	**Portuguese**		
0900-0930	R. Japan	SAm	6195hri
1400	**Portuguese**		
1400-1500	Channel Africa	SAf	9625mey
1600	**Portuguese**		
1630-1645	TWR Africa	SAf	4760man
1630-1700	BBG-VOA	Af	11850sao, 13630bot, 17655smg
1630-1730	BBG-VOA	Af	9485sao, 15480asc, 15730grv
1700	**Portuguese**		
1700-1730	RFI	CAf	17685iss
1700-1800	BBG-VOA	Af	1530sao, 13630bot, 17655grv
1800	**Portuguese**		
1800-1830	BBG-VOA	Af	13630bot, 17655grv
1800-1830	Vatican Radio	Af	9660smg, 11625smg, 13765smg
1900	**Portuguese**		
1900-1930	RFI	CAf	15360iss
1900-2000	CRI	SAf	5985bei, 7365bei, 7405xia, 9535bji
1900-2000	CRI	Eu	7335jin, 9730kas
1920-1935	TWR Africa	SAf	6130man
1935-1950	TWR Africa	SAf	6130man
1950-2020	TWR Africa	SAf	6130man
2000	**Portuguese**		
2000-2030	R. Habana Cuba	Eu	15370hab
2100	**Portuguese**		
2130-2200	R. Habana Cuba	Af	11880hab
2130-2200	R. Japan	SAm	17540hri
2200	**Portuguese**		
2200-2300	CRI	Eu	6175cer, 7260uru
2200-2300	CRI	SAm	9410kas, 9685kas
2300	**Portuguese**		
2300-0100	CRI	SAm	6100bei
2300-2400	Angolan Nat R.	SAf	945mul
2300-2400	CRI	SAm	13650hab
2300-2400	R. Habana Cuba	SAm	15230hab
2330-2400	R. Habana Cuba	SAm	17730hab

SPANISH

0000	Spanish	Area	kHz
0000-0100	CRI	SAm	15120hab
0000	**Spanish**	**Area**	**kHz**
0000-0100	CRI	NAm,CAm	5990hab
0000-0100	R. Habana Cuba	NAm	6000hab*, 11950hab*
0000-0100	R.Romania Int	SAm	7325tig, 7335gal, 9525gal, 9730tig
0000-0300	WTWW	NAm,Eu	12105tww†
0000-0400	BBG-R.Martí	CUB	7365grv
0000-0500	R. Habana Cuba	NAm	6060hab
0000-0500	WEWN	CAm	5810ewn
0000-0600	R. Habana Cuba	SAm	11670hab
0000-0700	R. Habana Cuba	SAm	15230hab
0000-1000	WEWN	SAm	11870ewn
0000-1200	BBG-R.Martí	CUB	6030grv
0000-2400	BBG-R.Martí	CUB	1180mth
0020-0220	VOIRI	LAm	9445kam
0020-0320	VOIRI	LAm,Eu	7225kam
0030-0700	TWR Bonaire	SAm	800twb
0045-0200	R. Cairo	LAm	11750abs, 12070abs
0045-0200	R. Cairo	NAm	9860abs
0100	**Spanish**		
0100-0200	Family Radio	SAm	11920yfr
0100-0200	KBS World R.	SAm	9605hri, 11810kim
0100-0300	CRI	SAm	9710kas
0100-0300	R. República	CUB	9490iss
0130-0500	Vozandes Media	LAm	6050qui
0150-0245	Vatican Radio	SAm	7305grv
0200	**Spanish**		
0200-0300	KBS World R.	NAm	15575kim
0200-0300	R.Taiwan Int.	LAm	11920yfr
0200-0300	VO Turkey	SAm,Eu	9410emr
0200-0300	VO Turkey	CAm,Eu	9650emr
0200-0600	R. Habana Cuba	CAm	5040hab
0300	**Spanish**		
0300-0330	R. Prague	LAm	9955yfr
0300-0330	VO Vietnam	NAm	6175hri
0300-0400	R.Romania Int	SAm	6125gal, 7335tig, 9470tig
0300-0400	R.Romania Int	CAs	7345gal
0300-0400	R.Taiwan Int.	CAm	7730yfr
0300-0500	Vozandes Media	LAm	6050qui
0330-0400	R. Slovakia Int	LAm	9955yfr
0330-0430	VO Korea	LAm	11735kuj, 13760kuj, 15180kuj
0400	**Spanish**		
0400-0430	R. Japan	LAm	5985yfr, 6195hri
0400-0430	VO Vietnam	NAm	6175hri
0400-0700	BBG-R.Martí	CUB	7405grv
0500	**Spanish**		
0500-1300	WEWN	CAm	7515ewn
0520-0620	VOIRI	Eu	13865sir, 15530kam
0530-0600	R. Slovakia Int	LAm	9955yfr
0530-0630	VO Korea	LAm	11735kuj, 13760kuj, 15180kuj
0600	**Spanish**		
0600-0800	CRI	Eu	15135kas
0700	**Spanish**		
0700-1300	BBG-R.Martí	CUB	5980grv
0900	**Spanish**		
0900-1230	TWR Bonaire	SAm	800twb
0930-1000	R. Japan	SAm	6195hri
1000	**Spanish**		
1000-1700	WEWN	SAm	12050ewn
1100	**Spanish**		
1100-1130	AWR	CAm	5950yfr

1100	Spanish	Area	kHz
1100-1130	R. Prague	LAm	9955yfr
1100-1200	KBS World R.	SAm	11795kim
1100-1300	BBG-R.Martí	CUB	5980grv
1100-1500	Vozandes Media	LAm	6050qui
1130-1200	R. Slovakia Int	LAm	9955yfr
1130-1500	Vozandes Media	LAm	6050qui
1200	**Spanish**		
1200-1400	BBG-R.Martí	CUB	7405grv
1200-1400	R. Habana Cuba	Am	6000hab
1200-1400	R. Habana Cuba	NAm	9850hab
1200-1500	R. Habana Cuba	SAm	17580hab
1200-1500	R. Habana Cuba	NAm	9710hab
1200-1600	R. Habana Cuba	Am	11760hab
1200-1600	R. Habana Cuba	SAm	17730hab, 17750hab
1200-1600	R. Habana Cuba	Car	9640hab
1200-1600	R. Habana Cuba	CAm	9820hab
1200-1900	R. Habana Cuba	Am	11760hab
1230-1300	Vatican Radio	SAm	9610grv
1300	**Spanish**		
1300-1400	BBG-R.Martí	CUB	11930grv
1300-1530	RAE	Eu	15345bue
1300-1530	RAE	SAm	6060bue
1300-1800	WEWN	CAm	11550ewn
1400	**Spanish**		
1400-1500	R. Habana Cuba	CAm	9550hab
1400-1600	R. Habana Cuba	NAm	15370hab
1400-1900	KVOH	CAm,SAm	11775voh
1400-2000	BBG-R.Martí	CUB	13820grv
1400-2200	BBG-R.Martí	CUB	11930grv
1500	**Spanish**		
1500-1900	REE	Af,Atl	11530nob
1500-1900	REE	SAm	15390nob
1500-1900	REE	ME,SAs	15500nob
1500-1900	REE	CAm,NAm	9690nob
1600	**Spanish**		
1630-1900	R. Habana Cuba	Am	11760hab
1700	**Spanish**		
1700-1800	Nat Rad of SADR	NAf	1550rbn†
1700-1800	VO Indonesia	Eu	9526jak†
1700-2400	WEWN	SAm	13830ewn
1730-1830	VO Turkey	Eu	9495emr
1800	**Spanish**		
1800-0000	RAE	Am	15345bue*
1800-0000	RAE	SAm	6060bue*
1800-1830	VO Vietnam	Eu	7280vni, 9730vni
1800-1900	KBS World R.	Eu,Af	9740kim
1800-2400	WEWN	CAm	12050ewn
1830-2130	RNASG (LRA36)	SAm	15476lra†
1900	**Spanish**		
1900-1930	Vatican Radio	Af	9660smg
1900-2130	Vozandes Media	LAm	6050qui
1900-2300	REE	Af,Atl	11530nob
1900-2300	REE	SAm	15390nob
1900-2300	REE	ME,SAs	15500nob
1900-2300	REE	CAm,NAm	9690nob
1900-2400	Vozandes Media	LAm	6050qui
1930-2030	VO Korea	Eu	7570kuj, 12015kuj
2000	**Spanish**		
2000-2020	R. Belarus	Eu	11730mns, 11930mns
2000-2100	R.Romania Int	NAf	6010tig
2000-2100	R.Romania Int	Eu	7235tig

2100	Spanish	Area	kHz
2000-2400	BBG-R.Martí	CUB	9565grv
2020-2120	VOIRI	Eu	6195kam, 7400sir
2100-2300	CRI	Eu	6020szg, 9640kas
2130-2300	TWR Bonaire	SAm	800twb
2200	**Spanish**		
2200-0300	R. Habana Cuba	Am	11760hab
2200-0500	R. Habana Cuba	SAm	13740hab
2200-0500	R. Habana Cuba	CAm	9535hab
2200-0600	R. Habana Cuba	SAm	11840hab
2200-0600	R. Habana Cuba	Car	6075hab
2200-2300	CRI	SAm	6100bei
2200-2300	Family Radio	CAm	5950yfr
2200-2300	R.Romania Int	SAm	7380tig, 9790tig
2200-2330	Vozandes Media	LAm	6050qui
2200-2400	BBG-R.Martí	CUB	7405grv
2200-2400	CRI	Eu	7210cer, 7250uru
2200-2400	R. Habana Cuba	Eu	15370hab
2200-2400	R. Habana Cuba	CAm	5040hab
2200-2400	RAE	Am	11710bue
2200-2400	RAE	Eu	15345bue
2200-2400	RAE	SAm	6060bue
2230-2330	VO Korea	Eu	7570kuj, 12015kuj
2300	**Spanish**		
2300-0100	CRI	SAm	9800kas
2300-0300	CRI	SAm	9590kas
2300-2330	AWR	CAm	5950yfr
2300-2400	CRI	Eu	6175cer
2300-2400	Family Radio	CAm,Car	5950yfr

NB: not all broadcasts are daily, please check main schedules under the appropriate country for full details. Language combinations are only shown for broadcasts where English, French, German, Portuguese or Spanish is listed as the first language in the combination. English etc. may appear in parts of other language combinations not shown here, (see full schedule under main station entry).

For *, ** and *** please see Notes under the Country entry for that station in the International Radio section

Key: + = DRM broadcast, † = irregular; ‡ = inactive at time of publication.

© WRTH Publications Ltd, November 2015

Notes

DRM International Broadcasts

0000	Language	Area	Station	kHz, site
0000-2400	French	Eu	RFI	3965iss
0200				
0250-0400	English	Pac	RNZI	17675ran
0300				
0315-0415	Hindi	EAf	All India R.	15120bgl
0315-0415	Hindi	EAf	All India R.	17715del
0400				
0415-0430	Gujarati	EAf	All India R.	17715del
0430-0530	Hindi	EAf	All India R.	17715del
0500				
0500-0530	Chinese	EAs	R.Romania Int	17640tig
0530-0600	Russian	Eu	R.Romania Int	5940tig
0600				
0630-0700	English	Eu	R.Romania Int	9600gal
0650-0800	English	Pac	RNZI	11690ran
0600-0700	English	Eu	BBC World Sce	3955wof
0600-0630	French	Eu	R.Romania Int	6040gal
0700				
0700-0730	German	Eu	R.Romania Int	6020tig
0800				
0800-0900	English	SAs	BBC World Sce	17790nak
1000				
1000-1100	English	Pac	All India R.	17895bgl
1100				
1145-1315	Chinese	EAs	All India R.	15040bgl
1100-1130	English	Eu	KBS World R.	9760wof
1100-1130	English	Eu	R. Japan	9760wof
1130-1200	Russian	Eu	R. Japan	9760wof
1200				
1215-1245	English	EAs	TWR Asia	9975twr
1215-1330	Tibetan	SAs	All India R.	15040bgl
1300				
1300-1500	Sinhala	SAs	All India R.	15050del
1400				
1400-1800	English	SAs	BBC World Sce	5845nak
1500				
1530-1600	English	As	Vatican Radio	15775smg
1550-1650	English	Pac	RNZI	7330ran
1530-1550	English	As	Vatican Radio	15775smg
1600				
1650-1745	English	Pac	RNZI	9780ran
1600-1630	Russian	Eu	R.Romania Int	5930tig
1615-1715	Russian	Eu	All India R.	11620bgl
1700				
1745-1945	English	Eu	All India R.	9950del
1745-1950	English	Pac	RNZI	11690ran
1745-1945	Hindi/			
	English	Eu	All India R.	7550bgl
1800				
1800-1930	English	Eu	VO Nigeria	15120aja
1800-1900	English	Eu	R.Romania Int	7350tig
1900				
1950-2150	English	Pac	RNZI	15720ran
1945-2030	French/			
	Hindi	Eu	All India R.	7550bgl

1900	Language	Area	Station	kHz, site
1900-2000	German	Eu	R.Romania Int	7405tig
1945-2045	Hindi	Eu	All India R.	9950del
1900-1930	Italian	Eu	R.Romania Int	5945tig
2000				
2045-2230	English	Eu	All India R.	9950del
2045-2230	Hindi/			
	English	Eu	All India R.	7550bgl
2100				
2130-2200	English	Eu	R.Romania Int	6030gal
2100-2130	French	Eu	R.Romania Int	6030gal
2200				
2255-0200	English	Pac	RNZI	17675ran
2245-0045	English	EAs	All India R.	11645del
2245-0045	English	EAs	All India R.	13605bgl

NB: Not all broadcasts are daily. Please refer to individual station schedules for full details. Where two languages are shown for a single broadcast, this means that the first/primary language is broadcast on DRM channel 1 and the second or secondary language is 'simulcast' (i.e. broadcast at the same time) on DRM channel 2. Some DRM transmissions may be test broadcasts and subject to change or interruptions during the broadcast.

© WRTH Publications Ltd. November 2015.

NATIONAL TELEVISION

Section Contents

Initial entries for each letter,
see Main Index for full details

Features & Reviews

National Radio

International Radio

Frequency Lists

National Television
(incl. Radio via DTT)

Reference

CHARACTERISTICS OF ANALOGUE TELEVISION SYSTEMS
(Recommendation ITU-R BT.470-6, Revision 2005)

System	Number of lines	Channel width MHz.	Vision band-width MHz.	Vision/Sound separation MHz.	Vestigial side-band MHz.	Vision mod.	Sound mod.
B	625	7	5	+5.5	0.75	Neg.	FM
B1	625	8	5	+5.5	0.75	Neg.	FM
D	625	8	6	+6.5	0.75	Neg.	FM
D1	625	8	5	+6.5	0.75	Neg.	FM
G	625	8	5	+5.5	0.75	Neg.	FM
H	625	8	5	+5.5	1.25	Neg.	FM
I	625	8	5.5	+5.996	1.25	Neg.	FM
I1	625	8	5.5	+5.996	1.25	Neg.	FM
K	625	8	6	+6.5	0.75	Neg.	FM
K1	625	8	5	+6.5	0.75	Neg.	FM
L	625	8	6	+6.5	1.25	Pos.	AM
M	525	6	4.2	+4.5	0.75	Neg.	FM
N	625	6	4.2	+4.5	0.75	Neg.	FM

ANALOGUE CHANNEL INFORMATION
(Vision carrier frequencies in MHz)
(† = being phased out)

VHF Channels

[A] Channels

(Americas, parts of Asia & Pacific)

A2 = 55.25	A6 = 83.25	A10 = 193.25
A3 = 61.75	A7 = 175.25	A11 = 199.25
A4 = 67.25	A8 = 181.25	A12 = 205.25
A5 = 77.25	A9 = 187.25	A13 = 211.25

[E] Channels

(Most of Europe, Greenland, Africa, most of Asia & Pacific)

E2 = 48.25	E6 = 182.25	E11 = 217.25
E3 = 55.25	E7 = 189.25	E12 = 224.25
E4 = 62.25	E9 = 203.25	
E5 = 175.25	E10= 210.25	

[K] Channels

(Parts of Africa)

K4 = 175.25	K7 = 199.25	K10 = 223.25
K5 = 183.25	K8 = 207.25	
K6 = 191.25	K9 = 215.25	

[R] Channels

(Parts of Europe, Russia, parts of Asia)

R1 = 49.75	R5 = 93.25	R9 = 199.25
R2 = 59.25	R6 = 175.25	R10 = 207.25
R3 = 77.25	R7 = 183.25	R11 = 215.25
R4 = 85.25	R8 = 191.25	R12 = 223.25

Specific national parameters:

Morocco (†)

M4 = 163.25	M7 = 187.25	M9 = 203.25
M5 = 171.25	M8 = 195.25	M10 = 211.25
M6 = 179.25		

South Africa & Namibia

SA4 = 175.25	SA7 = 199.25	SA10 = 223.25
SA5 = 183.25	SA8 = 207.25	SA11 = 231.25
SA6 = 191.25	SA9 = 215.25	SA13 = 247.43

Japan

J1 = 91.25	J5 = 177.25	J9 = 199.25
J2 = 97.25	J6 = 183.25	J10 = 205.25
J3 = 103.25	J7 = 189.25	J11 = 211.25
J4 = 171.25	J8 = 193.25	J12 = 217.25

China (P.R.)

DS1 = 49.75	DS5 = 85.25	DS9 = 192.25
DS2 = 57.75	DS6 = 168.25	DS10 = 200.25
DS3 = 65.75	DS7 = 176.25	DS11 = 208.25
DS4 = 77.25	DS8 = 184.25	DS12 = 216.25

Australia & parts of Pacific

AU0 = 46.25 (†)	AU5 = 102.25 (†)	AU9 = 196.25
AU1 = 57.25 (†)	AU5A = 138.25 (†)	AU9A = 203.25
AU2 = 64.25 (†)	AU6 = 175.25	AU10 = 209.25
AU3 = 86.25 (†)	AU7 = 182.25	AU11 = 216.25
AU4 = 95.25 (†)	AU8 = 189.25	AU12 = 224.25

New Zealand (†) & parts of Pacific

NZ1 = 45.25	NZ5 = 182.25	NZ9 = 210.25
NZ2 = 55.25	NZ6 = 189.25	NZ10 = 217.25
NZ3 = 62.25	NZ7 = 196.25	NZ11 = 224.25
NZ4 = 175.25	NZ8 = 203.25	

UHF Channels

"A" Channels
(Americas, parts of Asia & Pacific)

14 = 471.25	33 = 585.25	52 = 699.25
15 = 477.25	34 = 591.25	53 = 705.25
16 = 483.25	35 = 597.25	54 = 711.25
17 = 489.25	36 = 603.25	55 = 717.25
18 = 495.25	37 = 609.25	56 = 723.25
19 = 501.25	38 = 615.25	57 = 729.25
20 = 507.25	39 = 621.25	58 = 735.25
21 = 513.25	40 = 627.25	59 = 741.25
22 = 519.25	41 = 633.25	60 = 747.25
23 = 525.25	42 = 639.25	61 = 753.25
24 = 531.25	43 = 645.25	62 = 759.25
25 = 537.25	44 = 651.25	63 = 765.25
26 = 543.25	45 = 657.25	64 = 771.25
27 = 549.25	46 = 663.25	65 = 777.25
28 = 555.25	47 = 669.25	66 = 783.25
29 = 561.25	48 = 675.25	67 = 789.25
30 = 567.25	49 = 681.25	68 = 795.25
31 = 573.25	50 = 687.25	69 = 801.25
32 = 579.25	51 = 693.25	

[E], [R] Channels
(Europe, Greenland, Russia, Africa, most of Asia & Pacific)

21 = 474.25	38 = 607.25	55 = 743.25
22 = 479.25	39 = 615.25	56 = 751.25
23 = 487.25	40 = 623.25	57 = 759.25
24 = 495.25	41 = 631.25	58 = 767.25
25 = 503.25	42 = 639.25	59 = 775.25
26 = 511.25	43 = 647.25	60 = 783.25
27 = 519.25	44 = 655.25	61 = 791.25
28 = 527.25	45 = 663.25	62 = 799.25
29 = 535.25	46 = 671.25	63 = 807.25
30 = 543.25	47 = 679.25	64 = 815.25
31 = 551.25	48 = 687.25	65 = 823.25
32 = 559.25	49 = 695.25	66 = 831.25
33 = 567.25	50 = 703.25	67 = 839.25
34 = 575.25	51 = 711.25	68 = 847.25
35 = 583.25	52 = 719.25	69 = 855.25
36 = 591.25	53 = 727.25	
37 = 599.25	54 = 735.25	

[J] Channels
(Japan)

13 = 471.25	30 = 573.25	47 = 675.25
14 = 477.25	31 = 579.25	48 = 681.25
15 = 483.25	32 = 585.25	49 = 687.25
16 = 489.25	33 = 591.25	50 = 693.25
17 = 495.25	34 = 597.25	51 = 699.25
18 = 501.25	35 = 603.25	52 = 705.25
19 = 507.25	36 = 609.25	53 = 711.25
20 = 513.25	37 = 615.25	54 = 717.25
21 = 519.25	38 = 621.25	55 = 723.25
22 = 525.25	39 = 627.25	56 = 729.25
23 = 531.25	40 = 633.25	57 = 735.25
24 = 537.25	41 = 639.25	58 = 741.25
25 = 543.25	42 = 645.25	59 = 747.25
26 = 549.25	43 = 651.25	60 = 753.25
27 = 555.25	44 = 657.25	61 = 759.25
28 = 561.25	45 = 663.25	62 = 765.25
29 = 567.25	46 = 669.25	

[NZ] Channels
(New Zealand & parts of Pacific)

27 = 519.25	42 = 639.25	57 = 759.25
28 = 527.25	43 = 647.25	58 = 767.25
29 = 535.25	44 = 655.25	59 = 775.25
30 = 543.25	45 = 663.25	60 = 783.25
31 = 551.25	46 = 671.25	61 = 791.25
32 = 559.25	47 = 679.25	62 = 799.25
33 = 567.25	48 = 687.25	
34 = 575.25	49 = 695.25	
35 = 583.25	50 = 703.25	
36 = 591.25	51 = 711.25	
37 = 599.25	52 = 719.25	
38 = 607.25	53 = 727.25	
39 = 615.25	54 = 735.25	
40 = 623.25	55 = 743.25	
41 = 631.25	56 = 751.25	

[DS] Channels
(China, P.R., exc. SAR Macau, SAR Hong Kong)

13 = 471.25	36 = 695.25	59 = 879.25
14 = 479.25	37 = 703.25	60 = 887.25
15 = 487.25	38 = 711.25	61 = 895.25
16 = 495.25	39 = 719.25	62 = 903.25
17 = 503.25	40 = 727.25	
18 = 511.25	41 = 735.25	
19 = 519.25	42 = 743.25	
20 = 527.25	43 = 751.25	
21 = 534.25	44 = 759.25	
22 = 543.25	45 = 767.25	
23 = 551.25	46 = 775.25	
24 = 559.25	47 = 783.25	
25 = 607.25	48 = 791.25	
26 = 615.25	49 = 799.25	
27 = 623.25	50 = 807.25	
28 = 631.25	51 = 815.25	
29 = 639.25	52 = 823.25	
30 = 647.25	53 = 831.25	
31 = 655.25	54 = 839.25	
32 = 663.25	55 = 847.25	
33 = 671.25	56 = 855.25	
34 = 679.25	57 = 863.25	
35 = 687.25	58 = 871.25	

DIGITAL TERRESTRIAL TELEVISION (DTT) SYSTEMS

ATSC
ATSC (**A**dvanced **T**elevision **S**ystems **C**ommittee) is the digital television standard developed in the USA. ATSC transmits with MPEG-2 video- and audio compression. It produces wide screen 16:9 images up to 1920×1080 pixels in size; up to six standard TV channels can be broadcast from a single TV transmitter using an existing 6MHz channel. ATSC uses the Dolby Digital AC-3 format to provide 5.1-channel surround sound. Numerous auxiliary services can also be provided, incl. radio programmes.

DTMB
DTMB (**D**igital **T**errestrial **M**ultimedia **B**roadcast) is the DTT standard of the P.R. China. It is understood to be a fusion of TDS-OFDM (**T**ime **D**omain **S**ynchronous OFDM), developed by the Beijing Tsinghua university and based on the standard used by multi-carriers (similar to DVB-T), and ADTB-T (**A**dvanced **D**igital **T**elevision **B**roadcast - **T**errestrial) developed by the Shanghai Jiatong University.

DVB-T / DVB-T2
DVB-T (**D**igital **V**ideo **B**roadcasting - **T**errestrial) is the standard of the European DVB consortium for the transmission of digital terrestrial television. This system transmits a compressed digital audio/video stream, using OFDM modulation with concatenated channel coding (COFDM). The source coding methods are MPEG-2 and MPEG-4. The modulation method in DVB-T is COFDM with either 64 or 16 state Quadrature Amplitude Modulation (QAM). 16 and 64QAM constellations can be combined in a single multiplex, providing a controllable degradation for more important programme streams. Several radio programmes can be transmitted as well.

ISDB-T / ISDB-TB
ISDB-T (**I**ntegrated **S**ervices **D**igital **B**roadcasting - **T**errestrial) was developed in Japan and works similar to the European DVB-T. It uses COFDM modulation with PSK/QAM.The compression system is MPEG2. ISDB-T can also transmit radio programmes in addition to TV channels. ISDB-TB or SBTVD (**S**istema **B**rasileiro de **T**elevisão **D**igital) is a version of ISDB-T developed in Brazil, with MPEG4 compression.

T-DMB
T-DMB (**T**errestrial **D**igital **M**ultimedia **B**roadcast) is the DTT standard developed in the Republic of Korea.

INTRODUCTION

The TV section contains information about terrestrial TV stations and radio prgrs via DTT, in a compact format. If applicable, each country entry is devided into subsections: "National Stations", "Regional Stations", "Local Stations", "Foreign TV Relays", "Foreign Military Stations". The subsection "DTT Tx Networks" contains details of DTT transmitter operators or licensees, and DTT transmitters. Contact info for domestic prgrs included in the DTT multiplexes is found in the subsections mentioned above.
Keys: "Systems": # = txs to be phased out, § = analogue txs are being phased out (tx details no longer listed) ⍿= analogue shutdown date; [A], [DS], [E], [J], [K], [R], [AU], [NZ], [SA] refer to the channel characteristics as shown in the "Channel Information" table. Tx networks for national stations are listed either with main txs (power limit applied) or with key tx(s). Local Stations (if included) are listed in full; if no tx location is given, the site refers to the city of the station's headquarters. (-) = tx details not received at editorial deadline.

AFGHANISTAN

Systems: # PAL-B/G [E]; DVB-T2 (MPEG4) [E]

National Stations
RTA TV (Gov) ⌨ P.O.Box 544, Kabul ☎ +93 20 2102487 🖷 +93 20 2101086 E: info@rta.org.af Web: www.rta.org.af L.P: DG (RTA): Zarin Anzor Txs: Kabul ch11 (2kW) & relay txs. NB: Local stations in Herat, Kandahar, Khost. – AFGHAN TV (Comm)⌨ Kabul ☎ +93 777 555566 🖷 +93 798 555566 L.P: Dir: Ahmed Shah Afghanzai. Txs: Kabul ch24 & relay txs. – ARIANA TELEVISION NETWORK (ATN) (Comm) ⌨ 318, Darulaman Street, Carte 3, Kabul ☎ +93 700 111113 E: marketing@arianatelevision.com W: arianatelevision.com L.P: MD: Arral Azizullah Txs: Kabul ch4 & relay txs. – TOLO TV (Comm)⌨ P.O.Box 225, Kabul E: info@tolo.tv W: www.tolo.tv L.P: Dir: Saad Mohseni Txs: Kabul ch9 & relay txs.

Local Stations not shown.

DTT Tx Network (under construction)
Tx Operator: Asia Consultancy Group M: RTA TV, multiprgr Txs: Kabul & nationwide network under construction

ALASKA (USA)

System: ATSC [A]

Local Stations*
KAKM (Pub) 3877 University Dr, Anchorage, AK 99508-4676. Tx: Anchorage ch8 (50kW). KATN (Comm): 516 2nd Ave Ste 400, Fairbanks, AK 99701-4729. Tx: ch18 (16kW). KDMD (Comm): 1310 E 66th Ave, Anchorage, AK 99518-1915. Tx: ch32 (17.2kW). KFXF (Comm): 3650 Braddock St Ste 2, Fairbanks, AK 99701-7617. Tx: ch22 (11kW). KIMO (Comm): 2700 E Tudor Rd, Anchorage, AK 99507-1136. Tx: ch12 (41kW). KJNP-TV (Rlg): 2501 Mission Rd, North Pole, AK 99705-6361. Tx: ch20 (15kW). KJUD (Comm) 175 S Franklin St, Juneau, AK 99801-1384. Tx: ch11 (0.14kW). KTBY (Comm): 440 E Benson Blvd Ste 1, Anchorage, AK 99503-4121. Tx: ch20 (234.4kW). KTNL-TV (Comm): 520 Lake St, Sitka, AK 99835-7403. Tx: ch2 (1kW). KTOO-TV (Pub): 360 Egan Dr, Juneau, AK 99801-1748. Tx: ch10 (1kW). KTUU-TV (Comm): 701 E Tudor Rd Ste 220, Anchorage, AK 99503-7488. Tx: ch10 (21kW). KTVA (Comm): 1007 W 32nd Ave, Anchorage, AK 99503-3728. Tx: ch28 (28.9kW). KTVF (Comm): 3528 International Way, Fairbanks, AK 99701-7382. Tx: ch26 (12kW). KUAC-TV (Pub): 312 Tanana Dr, Fairbanks, AK 99775-2004. Tx: ch24 (69kW). KYES-TV (Comm) 3700 Woodland Dr Ste 800, Anchorage, AK 99517-2588. Tx: ch6 (45kW). KYUK-TV (Pub) 640 Radio St, Bethel, AK 99559. Tx: ch3 (4.68kW).
*) Full power licenses (lp licenses not listed)

ALBANIA

System: DVB-T2 (MPEG4) [E]

National Stations
RADIOTELEVISIONI SHQIPTAR (RTSH) (Pub) ⌨ Rr. "Ismail Qemali" 11, Tirana ☎ +355 4 2256059 🖷 +355 4 2227745 W: www.rtsh.al L.P: DG: Martin Leka Chs: TVSH1, TVSH2. – TOP CHANNEL (Comm) ⌨ Blv. "Deshmoret e Kombit, Qendra Nderbombetare e Kultures", Tirana ☎ +355 4 2253177 🖷 +355 4 2253178 E: info@top-channel.tv W: www.top-channel.tv – TV KLAN (Comm) ⌨ Rr. "Aleksander Moisiu" 97, Tirana ☎ +355 4 2347805 🖷 +355 4 2347808 E: info@tvklan.al W: www.tvklan.al.

Local Stations not shown.

DTT Tx Networks
Licensee: RTSH Mux: TVSH1, TVSH2 Txs: MFN – Licensee: DigitALB ⌨ Rr. "Themistokli Germenji" 10, Tirana ☎+355 4 2255813 🖷 +355 4 2274831 E: info@digitalb.al W: www.digitalb.al Mux 1-5✪: multiprgr Txs: Mux 1: ch62 (SFN), Mux 2: ch64 (SFN), Mux 3: ch67 (SFN), Mux 4: ch69 (SFN). Mux 5 (DVB-H): ch38 (Tirana). – Licensee: Tring Digital ⌨ Kompleksi Don Bosko, Kulla 7, kati II, Tirana ☎+355 4 4800008 🖷 +355 4 4800001 E: info@tring.tv W: www.tring.tv Mux 1+2✪: multiprgr Txs: Mux 1: ch47 (Dajt) Mux 2: ch59 (Dajt).

ALGERIA

Systems: DVB-T (MPEG4) [E], § PAL-B [E]. Sahrawi Refugee Camps: PAL-B [E]

EPTV TÉLÉVISION ALGÉRIENNE (Pub)⌨ 21, Boulevard des Martyrs, Alger ☎ +213 21 602300 🖷 +213 21 230914 E: alger-contact@entv.dz W: www.entv.dz L.P: DG (EPTV): Toufik Kheladi Chs: EPTV Terrestre, Canal Algérie, A3, Algérie 4 (Tamazight), Algérie 5 (Kannat el-Coraän), Regional stns.

DTT Tx Network
Tx Operator: Télédiffusion d'Algérienne (TDA) ⌨ BP 50, 16340 Bouzareah ☎ +213 21 901717 🖷 +213 21 902424 E: tnt@tda.dz W: www.tda.dz M: EPTV, Canal Algérie, A3, Algérie 4 (Tamazight), Algérie 5 (Kannat el-Coraän), Regional stns ✖ Chaîne I, II, III

Location	ch	kW	Location	ch	kW
Adrar	21	1.5	Bouzaréah	32	1.5
Tamanrasset	21	1.5	Zerga	32	1.5
Filfila	22	1.2	Akfadou	33	2
Timimoun	22	1.5	Antar	35	1.5
Ain Salah	22	1.5	Bechar	37	1.5
Doukhane	22	1.5	Meghress	41	1.5
El Oued	22	1.5	Ain N'sour	41	1.5
DJ Khar	23	1.5	M'Cid	42	1.5
Hassi R'Mel	23	1.5	Hassi Messaoud	42	1.5
Ouargla	23	1.5	Chrea	43	1.2
Bordj El Bahri	24	1.5	Tessala	43	1.2
Dirah	25	1.5	Mahouna	44	1.5
Nador	25	1.5	Bouzizi	45	1.5
Mezghitane	27	1.5	Sbaa Mokrane	49	1.2
Kef lekhel	28	1.5			

+ txs below 1.2kW.

Sahrawi Refugee Camps

RASD TV (Gov) ⌨ BP 470, 37000 Tindouf ☎ +213 49 923525 W: www.rasd-tv.com Tx: Rabouni ªch22 (10kW). Rel. Al Aoula (Morocco) & own prgrs (ª=analogue)

ANDORRA

System: DVB-T (MPEG2) [E]

RÀDIO I TELEVISIÓ D'ANDORRA (Pub)⌨ Baixada del Molí 24, AD500 Andorra la Vella ☎ +376 873777 🖷 +376 863242 E: rtva@rtva.ad W: www.andorradifusio.ad L.P: DG: Xavier Mujal Ch: ATV.

DTT Tx Networks
Licensee: Andorra Telecom ⌨ Mossèn LLuís Pujol 8-14, AD500 Santa Coloma ☎ +376 875274 🖷 +376 863667 E: comunicacio@andorratele-com.ad W: www.andorratelecom.ad Mux 1: Direct8, Teledeporte, TV1 Internacional, 8TV Mux 2: Arte, BBC World News, RTPi, Telecinco, 3/24 Mux 3: CNN Int., Cuatro, La Sexta, NRJ 12, 33 Mux 4: ATV, La 2, M6, TF1, TV3 Mux 5: Antena 3, France 2, France 3, La 1, Super3/3XL Mux 6: Esport3, Euronews, Pirineus TV, TV5 Monde

Location	M1	M2	M3	M4	M5	M6
SFN	25	28	36	42	45	57

ANGOLA

Systems: # PAL-I [E]; ISDB-TB [E]

TELEVISÃO PÚBLICA DE ANGOLA (Pub) ⌨ CP 2604, Luanda ☎ +244 222 320326 🖷 +244 222 323622 **W:** tpa.sapo.ao **L.P:** Pres: Hélder Manuel Bárber Dias dos Santos **Chs:** TPA1, TPA2 **Txs: TPA 1:** Luanda ch9 (13kW) & relay txs. **TPA2:** Luanda ch4 & relay txs.

Local Station
TV Zimbo: Avenida de Talatona, Luanda Sul; ch45.

DTT Tx Networks (under construction)
Tx Operator: TPA **M:** TPA1, TPA2, TV Zimbo **Txs:** ch31 (Luanda) & nationwide network under construction

ANGUILLA (UK)

System: NTSC-M [A]

KREATIVE COMMUNICATIONS NETWORK (KCN) (Comm)⌨ P.O.Box 154, The Valley ☎ +1 264 5843519 🖷 +1 264 4973367 **E:** kcn@caribcable.com **W:** kcntv4.hotel-parapel.com **L.P:** CEO: Carlton Pickering **Stns:** ZJF-TV3 ch3 (0.003kW), ZJF-TV9 ch9 (0.03kW).

ANTARCTICA

NB: No terrestrial TV station.

ANTIGUA & BARBUDA

System: NTSC-M [A]

ABS-TV (Gov) ⌨ Cross St., St. John's, Antigua ☎ +1 268 4620010 🖷 +1 268 4624442 **E:** abstv@antigua.gov.ag **L.P:** SM: Trevor Parker. **Tx:** ch10V (5kW).

ARGENTINA

Systems: # PAL-N [A] ⇩1 Sep 2019; ISDB-TB [A]

National Stations
TV PÚBLICA (CANAL 7) (Gov)⌨Avenida Figueroa Alcorta 2977, 1425 Buenos Aires ☎+54 11 8026001 **W:** www.tvpublica.com.ar **Txs:** ch7 (212kW) & relay txs. – **CANAL 9 (Comm)**⌨ Av. Dorrego 1708, 1414 Buenos Aires ☎ +54 11 50936838 **W:** www.canal9.com.ar **Txs:** ch9 (62kW) & relay txs. – **EL TRECE (Comm)**⌨ Lima 1261, Constitucion, Capital Federal ☎+54 11 3050013 🖷 +54 11 3318559 **W:** www.eltrecetv. com.ar **Txs:** ch13 (116kW) & relay txs. – **TELEFE (Comm)**⌨ Pavón 2495, 1248 Buenos Aires ☎+54 11 43080145 🖷 +54 11 4301522 **W:** telefe.com **Txs:** ch11 (180kW) & relay txs. **NB:** all tx sites above = Buenos Aires.

Local Stations not shown.

DTT Tx Networks
Licensee: Radio y Televisión Argentina **Mux 1:** Encuentro, Encuentro Movil, Paka Paka, TaTeTi **Txs:** ch22 (Buenos Aires) & netw. **Mux 2:** TV Pública HD, TV Pública Movil, Construir TV **Txs:** ch23 (Buenos Aires) & netw. **Mux 3:** Gol TV, Go TV Movil, V!vra, Suri TV, Video Éxito **Txs:** ch24 (Buenos Aires) & netw. **Mux 4:** CN23, C5N, Telesur, 360 TV **Txs:** ch25 (Buenos Aires) & netw. – **Licensee:** Telefe **M:** Telefe, Telefe HD **Tx:** ch34 (Buenos Aires) & netw. – **Licensee:** El Trece **M:** El Trece **Tx:** ch33 (Buenos Aires) & netw. – **Licensee:** Canal 9 **M:** Canal 9, Canal9 HD,Canal 9 Movil **Txs:** ch35 (Buenos Aires) & netw.
Local licensees not shown.**NB:** Some local Tx Operators use DVB-T (MPEG2) and will migrate to ISDB-TB.

ARMENIA

Systems: DVB-T (MPEG4) [E]

National Stations
ARMENIAN PUBLIC TELEVISION (Pub)⌨ 26, G. Hovsepyan St., Nork 47, 0047 Yerevan ☎ +374 10 650015 **E:** International@ armtv.com **W:** www.1tv.am **L.P:** CEO: Margarita Grigoryan **Ch:** H1 – **ARMENIA TV (Comm)**⌨ 1, Yeghvard Highway, 0054 Yerevan ☎ +374 10 369344 🖷 +374 10 366852 **E:** info@armeniatv.am **W:** www. armeniatv.am – **h2 (Comm)**⌨ 3/1, Quarter # G-3, 0088 Yerevan ☎ +374 10 398831 🖷 +374 10 395640 **E:** lraber@tv.am **W:** www.tv.am **L.P:** DG: Samvel Mayrapetyan.

Local Stations not shown.

DTT Tx Network
Tx Operator: Television and Radio Broadcasting Network of Armenia **W:** tna.am **M1:** H1, Armenia TV, Shant TV, Shoghakat, ATV, ArmNews TV **M2:** Yerkir Media, Ar TV, Kentron TV, h2, Laym **M3:** Pervyy, RTR Planeta, Rossiya K, TV Mir, XXI, CNN Int. **M4:** 1TV, Armenia TV, Shant TV, Yerkir Media, h2, Shoghakat, Kentron TV, RTR Planeta, local stns

Location	1	2	3	4
Yerevan	23	28	35	43

+ nationwide network

ARUBA (Netherlands)

Systems: # NTSC-M [A]; DVB-T (MPEG2) planned

ARUBA BROADCASTING CO. N.V. (ATV) (Comm)⌨ P.O.Box 5040, Oranjestad ☎+297 5838150 🖷 +297 5838110 **W:** www.15atv.com **Tx:** Oranjestad ch15. – **CANAL 22 (Comm)** ⌨ Oranjestad. ☎+297 5859500 **Tx:** Oranjestad ch22. – **TELEARUBA (Comm)**⌨ P.O.Box 392, Oranjestad ☎ +297 5857302 🖷 + 297 5851683 **E:** info@telearuba.aw **W:** www.telea-ruba.aw **L.P:** Dir: Toko Winklaar. **Tx:** Oranjestad ch13 (3kW H).

ASCENSION ISLAND (UK)

System: PAL-I [E]

BFBS-TV (British Mil)⌨ Chalfont Grove, Narcot Lane, Chalfont St Peter, Buckinghamshire, SL9 8TN, United Kingdom. **Txs: BBC One:** Travellers Hill ch64, Cross Hill ch50 & ch61 **ITV:** Travellers Hill ch64, Cross Hill ch46.

AUSTRALIA

System: DVB-T (MPEG2) [VHF=AU, UHF=E]

National Stations
AUSTRALIAN BROADCASTING CORPORATION (ABC) (Pub)⌨ ABC Ultimo Centre, 700 Harris St, Ultimo, NSW 2007 ☎ +61 2 83331500 🖷 +61 2 83335305 **E:** comments@your.abc.net.au **W:** www. abc.net.au **L.P:** MD: Mark Scott **Chs (terr.):** ABC1, ABC2, ABC3, ABC Kids, ABC News 24. – **SPECIAL BROADCASTING SERVICE (SBS) (Pub)**⌨ Locked bag 028, Crows Nest, NSW 1585 ☎ +61 2 94302828 🖷 +61 2 94303700 **E:** comments@sbs.com.au **W:** www.sbs.com.au **L.P:** MD: Michael Ebeid – **NATIONAL INDIGIOUS TELEVISION (NITV) (Pub)**⌨ 5 Parsons Street, Alice Springs, NT 0870 ☎ +61 8 89534763 🖷 +61 8 89534764 **E:** admin@nitv.org.au **W:** www.nitv.org. au – **SEVEN NETWORK (Comm)**⌨ Television Centre, Mobbs Lane, Epping, NSW 2121 ☎ +61 2 8587777 🖷 +61 2 8587888 **W:** au.tv.yahoo. com **L.P:** CEO: Tim Worner – **NINE NETWORK (Comm)**⌨ P.O.Box 27, Willoughby, NSW 2068 ☎ +61 2 99069999 🖷 +61 2 99582279 **W:** channelnine.ninemsn.com.au **L.P:** CEO: David Gyngell – **TEN NETWORK (Comm)**⌨ P.O. Box 10, Lane Cove, NSW 2066 ☎ +61 2 8870222 **W:** tenplay.com.au **L.P:** CEO: Hamish McLennan

Regional Stations
IMPARJA TELEVISION (Pub)⌨ P.O.Box 2924, Alice Springs, NT 0871 ☎ +61 89 523744, 🖷 +61 89 531014 **W:** www.imparja.com.au – **PRIME TELEVISION (Comm)**⌨ PO Box 878, Dickson, ACT 2602 ☎ +61 2 62423700 🖷 +61 2 62423764 **W:** au.prime7.yahoo.com – **SOUTHERN CROSS TELEVISION (Comm)**⌨ 70 Park Street, South Melbourne, VIC 3205 ☎ +61 3 92432100 🖷 +61 3 96825158 **W:** www. southerncrosstelevision.com.au – **WIN TELEVISION (Comm)**⌨ Television Ave, Mt St Thomas, Wollongong, NSW 2500 ☎ +61 2 42234199 🖷 +61 2 42273682 **W:** www.wintv.com.au.

Local Stations not shown.

DTT Tx Networks (National Stations)
Licensee: ABC **M:** ABC1, ABC2/ABC Kids, ABC3, ABC News 24 ⌘ ABC Double J, ABC Jazz – **Licensee:** Seven Network **M:** 7 Digital, 7Two, 7mate, TV4ME, Racing.com – **Licensee:** Nine Network **M:** Nine Digital, GEM, eXtra, eXtra 2, GO! – **Licensee:** Ten Network **M:** Ten Digital, One, Eleven, TVSN, Spree TV – **Licensee:** SBS **M:** SBS, SBS HD, SBS2, SBS 3, Food Network, NITV ⌘ SBS Radio 1-3.

Location	ABC	7N	9N	10N	SBS	kW
Sydney	12	6	8	11	34	50

+ nationwide tx networks

AUSTRIA

System: DVB-T (MPEG2), DVB-T2 (MPEG4) [E]

National Stations
ÖSTERREICHISCHER RUNDFUNK (ORF) (Pub)⌨ Würzburgasse 30, 1136 Wien ☎ +43 1 878780 **E:** presse@orf.at **W:** orf.at **LP:** DG: Dr.Alexander Wrabetz **Chs:** ORF eins, ORF2 incl. reg. stns: a) ORF Burgenland (Buchgraben 51, 7000 Eisenstadt), b) ORF Kärnten (Sponheimer Straße 13, 9020 Klagenfurt), c) ORF Niederösterreich (Radioplatz 1, 3109 St.Pölten), d) ORF Oberösterreich (Europaplatz 3, 4010 Linz), e) ORF Salzburg (Nonntaler Hauptstraße 49d, 5020 Salzburg), f) ORF Steiermark (Marburgerstr. 20, 8042 Graz), g) ORF Tirol (Rennweg 14, 6010 Innsbruck), h) ORF Vorarlberg (Höchsterstraße 38, 6850 Dornbirn), i) ORF Wien (Argentinierstr. 30a, 1040 Wien), ORF III – **ATV (Comm)**⌨ Aspernbrückengasse 2, 1020 Wien ☎ +43 1 213640 🖷 +43 1 21364999 **E:** atv@atv.at **W:** atv.at **LP:** CEO: Martin Gastinger. – **PULS 4 (Comm)** ⌨ Maria Jacobi Gasse 1, 1030 Wien ☎ +43 1 999880 🖷 +43 1 999888888 **W:** www.puls4.com **LP:** CEO: Markus Breitenecker. – **SERVUS TV (Comm)** ⌨ Ludwig-Bieringer-Platz 1, 5073 Wals-Himmelreich 🖷 +43 662 84224428181 **E:** kontakt@servustv.at **W:** www.servustv.com **LP:** CEO: Martin Blank.

Local Stations not shown (via Mux 3 txs).

DTT Tx Networks (DVB-T2/MPEG4 exc. *= DVB-T/MPEG2)
Operator: Österreichische Sender GmbH & Co KG (ORS) ⌨ Würzburggasse 309, 1136 Wien **W:** www.ors.at **Mux 1*:** ORF eins, ORF2 incl. reg. prgrs, ATV **Mux 2*:** ORF III, ORF Sport+, 3sat, Puls 4, ServusTV. **Licensee Mux 3*:** Regional licensees (not shown). **Mux 4✪:** ORF 2 HD, ORF eins HD, ARD-alpha, DMAX, Nickelodeon, n-tv, Phoenix, RTLNITRO, Servus TV HD, SRF zwei, Super RTL. **Mux 5✪:** Das Erste HD, ZDF HD,Bayerisches Fernsehen, KiKa, ZDFneo, ARTE, Eurosport, Kabel eins, RTL 2, Sixx, SPORT 1, Playboy TV **Mux 6✪:** RTL HD, Sat.1 HD, ProSieben HD, Vox HD, Deluxe Music, CNN Int., Disney Channel, Puls 4 HD.

Location	M1	M2	M3	M4	M5	M6	kW
Bregenz (Pfänder)**	24	21	55	31	59	42	70
Bruck a.d.M. (Mugel)	41	25	-	-	-	-	71/63
Graz (Schöckl)	26	23	-	47	39	50	75
Innsbruck (Patscherkofel)**	23	27	36	37	24	22	3x63/3x100
Klagenfurt (Dobratsch)	24	23	-	48	30	51	2x150/3x125
Linz (Lichtenberg)	43	37	51	41	45	24	2x100/6.3/3x65
Mattersburg (Heuberg)	52V	30V-		36V	02V	53V	18/30/3x25
Rechnitz (Hirschenstein)	43V	23V-	-	-	-	-	31/10
Salzburg (Gaisberg)	32	29	55	47	59	55	2x80/3.2/3x80
Semmering (Sonnwendstein)	52	21	-	-	-	-	18/12
Semmering (Sonnwendstein)	41	-	-	-	-	-	14
St.Pölten (Jauerling)	31	21	-	38	55	58	2x100/3x80
Schärding (Schardenberg)	43	-	-	-	-	-	17.5
Schladming (Hauser Kaibling)	34	39	-	-	-	-	38
Viktring (Stifterkogel)	24	23	-	48	30	51	2x22/3x20
Waidhofen/Ybbs (Sonntagbg.)	43	-	-	-	-	-	15
Weitra (Wachberg)	31	-	-	-	-	-	20
Wien (Kahlenberg)**	24	34	41	36	60	53	2x80/5/3x63

+ sites with txs below 10kW. **) additional SFN sites in use
NB: All muxes are being changed to DVB-T2; muxes will be substantially re-arranged.

Systems: DVB-T2 (MPEG4) [E]; Mountainous Karabagh: # PAL-D/K [R]

National Stations
AZÄRBAYCAN TELEVIZIYA VÄ RADIO VERISLÄRI (Gov)⌨ Mehdi Hüseyn St. 1, AZ 1011 Baki ☎ +994 12 4984720 🖷 +994 12 4972020 **E:** info@aztv.az **W:** www.aztv.az **LP:** Chmn: Arif Alisanov . **Chs:** AzTV, Idman Azärbaycan, Mädäniyyät TV. – **ICTIMAI TELEVIZIYA (ITV) (Pub)**⌨ Särizadä St. 241, AZ 1012 Baki ☎ +994 12 4335525 🖷 +994 12 4302958 **E:** info@itv.az **W:** www.itv.az **LP:** Dir: Cämil Quliyev. – **ANS-TV (Comm)** ⌨Matbuat ave. 28/11, Baki ☎ +994 12 4977267 🖷 +994 12 4989498 **E:** info@anstv.ws **W:** www.anstv.ws – **AZAD AZÄRBAYCAN TV (ATV) (Comm)** ⌨Särizadä St. 10, AZ 1012 Baki ☎ +994 12 4977274 🖷 +994 12 4989498 **E:** info@atv.az **W:** www.atv.az – **LIDER TV (Comm)** ⌨ Ä.Äläkbärov St. 83/23, AZ 1141 Baki ☎ +994 12 4978899 🖷 +994 12 4978898 **E:** mail@lidermedia.az **W:** www.lidertv.com – **SPACE TV (Comm)** ⌨ Hüseyn Cavid ave. 8, AZ 1073 Baki ☎ +994 12 4921256 🖷 +994 12 4927665 **E:** info@spacetv.az **W:** www.spacetv.az – **XÄZÄR TV (Comm)** ⌨ Atatürk ave. 28, AZ 1000 Baki ☎ +994 12 5621647 🖷 +994 12 5621623 **E:** info@xazar.tv **W:** www.xazar.tv.

Local Stations not shown.

DTT Tx Networks

Tx Operator: RITN Teleradio IB ⌨ A.Abbaszadä 2, AZ 1073 Baki ☎ +994 12 4988066 🖷 +994 12 4988397 **E:** info@teleradio.az **W:** www.teleradio.az **Mux 1:** AzTV, Idman Azärbaycan, Mädäniyyät TV, ITV, Lider TV, ANS, Space TV, ATV, Xäzär TV, TRT1, local stns **Mux 2:** multiprgr.

Location	M1	M2	kW
Baki	37	48	0.8/1.2

+ nationwide network

MOUNTAINOUS KARABAGH

LERNAYIN GHARABAGH HANRAYIN HERUSTARADIOYIN KERUTYUN ⌨ Tigran Mets St. 23a, Stepanakert (mail via Armenia) ☎ +374 47 945261 **E:** artv_or@ktsurf.net **W:** www.artsakh.tv **LP:** Chmn: Norek A. Gasparyan **Txs:** (-).

System: DVB-T (MPEG4) [E]

RTP AÇORES (Pub)⌨ Rua Ernesto do Canto 40, 9500-312 Ponta Delgada ☎ +351 296202700 🖷 +351 296202771 **E:** rtpa@rtp.pt **W:** www.rtp.pt/acores **LP:** Dir: Lorina Bernardo.

DTT Tx Network
Licensee: Portugal Telecom **M:** RTP1, RTP2, RTP Açores/RTP3, SIC, TVI, ARTV **Txs:** ch47 (São Jorge), ch48 (S.Miguel, Graciosa), ch49 (Faial), ch54 (Terceira, S.Maria, Flores, Corvo), ch56 (Pico).

Systems: ATSC [A]

ZNS TV (Pub)⌨ P.O.Box N-1347, Nassau ☎ +1 242 5023800 🖷 +1 242 3226598 **E:** info@znsbahamas.com **W:** www.znsbahamas.com **LP:** GM: Edwin Lightbourn **Tx:** Nassau ch13 (50kW).

System: # PAL-B/G [E]; DVB-T [E] planned

BAHRAIN TELEVISION (BTV) (Gov)⌨ P.O.Box 1075, Bahrain ☎ +973 17686000 🖷 +973 17681544 **LP:** DG (Bahrain Radio & TV): Bassam Al-Dhawadi **Chs:** BTV, Channel 44, Channel 55 (English) **Txs: BTV:** ch4 (5kW), **Channel 44:** ch44* (500kW), **Channel 55:** ch55 (0.03kW).*) tx to be converted to DVB-T.

Foreign TV Relay
BBC World News (UK): ch57 (1kW)

Systems: # PAL-B [E]; DVB-T [E]

BANGLADESH TELEVISION (BTV) (Pub)⌨ TV Bhaban, Rampura, Dhaka 1219 ☎ +880 2 8618606 🖷 +880 2 8312927 **W:** www.btv.gov. bd **LP:** DG: Abdul Mannan. **Chs (terr.):** BTV, BTV World, Sangsad Bangadesh TV **Txs: BTV:** Dhaka ch9 (20kW) & netw. – **EKUSHEY TELEVISION (ETV) (Comm)**⌨ Jahangir Tower, 10, Karwan Bazar, Dhaka 1215 ☎ +880 2 8126535 🖷 +880 2 8121270 **E:** info@ekushey-tv.com **W:** ekushey-tv.com **LP:** Chmn: Abdus Salam **Txs:** Dhaka ch6 (20kW) & netw.

DTT Tx Networks (under construction)
Tx Operator: BTV **M:** BTV, BTV World, Sangsad Bangladesh TV **Txs:** ch(-) Dhaka, Chittagong, Khulna (3.5kW)

System: NTSC-M [A]

CARIBBEAN BROADCASTING CORP. (CBC-TV) (Gov)⌨ P.O. Box 900, Pine Hill, Bridgetown ☎ +1 246 4675400 🖷 +1 246 4294795 **W:** www.cbc.bb **LP:** CEO: Rodwell London **Txs:** Bridgetown ch8 (60kW).

System: DVB-T (MPEG4), DVB-T2 (MPEG4) [E]

National Stations
BELARUSKAJE TELEBACANNE (BT) (Gov) Makaionka St. 9, 220807 Minsk ☎ +375 17 2634301 🖷 +375 17 2648182 **E:** pr@tvr. by **W:** www.tvr.by **Chs (terr.):** Belarus 1 (incl. reg prgrs), Belarus 2, Belarus 3, Belarus 4 (Regional Stns). – **OBSHCHENATSIONALNOYE TELEVIDENIYE (ONT) (Gov)** Kamunistycny St. 6, 220029 Minsk ☎ +375 17 2170424 **E:** w@ont.by **W:** ont.by **LP:** Pres: Grigoriy L. Kisel. – **STOLICHNOYE TV (STV) (Gov)** Kamunistycny St. 6, 220029 Minsk ☎ +375 17 2906272 🖷 +375 17 2906432 **E:** reklama@ ctv.by **W:** www.ctv.by **LP: DG:** Yuriy Kozatko.

DTT Tx Networks
Licensee Mux 1: Belteleradyjo **M1:** Belarus 1 (incl. reg prgrs), Belarus 2, Belarus 3, Belarus 4, ONT, STV, NTV-Belarus, RTR-Belarus, TV Mir ✳Belaruskaje R. 1, 2, R. Stalica, Radyus FM – **Licensee Mux 2+3:** Beltelekom **M2 (DVB-T2)✪:** Russkiy illyuzion, Evrokino, Detskiy mir/Teleklub, Belarus 5, VTV, 8 kanal, Nashe kino, TV-3, S*TV, Europa Plus TV, Karusel, Shanson, Moya planeta, Rossiya K, Okhota i rybalka, Usadba, Setanta Sport, KKhL **M3 (DVB-T2)✪:** Sovereshhenno sekretno, 24 Tekhno, Kuhknya TV, BelMuzTV, RTVi, TVXXI, Soyuz, Shest, TRO, Tiji, Gulli, Detskiy, Multimaniya, Viasat TV1000, Viasat TV1000 Action, Viasat TV1000 Russkoye kino, NTV Kinohit, Indiya TV.

Location	1	2	3	kW	Location	1	2	3	kW
Asipovicy	49	51	38	2	Masty	21	25	36	1
Astryna	42	37	51	1	Mazyr	48	41	31	1
Asveja	33	30	42	1	Miadziel	44	51	34	2
Aziareck	25	36	38	1	Minsk	48	32	57	1
Babrujsk	47	52	40	2	Mscisláuĺ	49	56	33	2
Baranavicy	39	26	31	2	Myta	49	29	33	2
Barisaú	48	23	57	1	Navaselle	48	32	57	1
Berazino	41	46	58	2	Pinsk	56	50	50	2
Biahoml	40	47	50	1	Radaškovicy	48	32	57	1
Biarecca	43	58	35	1	Rakitnica	51	53	47	2
Brahin	43	39	21	2	Salihorsk	34	43	47	2
Braslaú	43	53	21	1	Saltanoú	51	30	38	1
Ciachcin	43	46	58	2	Sianno	25	36	38	2
Drahicyn	57	58	35	2	Sinkevicy	58	35	37	2
Drycyn	44	51	38	2	Slaúharad	50	59	39	2
Hara	33	30	42	2	Slonim	41	36	31	2
Heraniony	49	29	33	2	Smiatanicy	46	41	31	1
Homiel	51	30	38	2	St. Darohi	44	51	38	2
Hrodna	42	37	51	2	Stoúbcy	34	43	47	1
Ivanava Slabada	42	35	37	2	Strelcyky	59	25	23	1
Kapyl	34	43	47	1	Sviclac	21	25	36	2
Kašalioú	41	26	31	1	Ušacy	40	47	50	1
Kastjukovicy	50	51	39	2	V. Cucavicy	56	50	33	1
Kreva	59	25	23	1	Valosavicy	46	41	31	2
Krupski	41	46	58	2	Viciebsk	43	31	48	1
Krycaú	50	59	39	1	Vorša	25	36	38	1
Kuplin	51	53	47	2	Zaščobje	43	39	31	1
Ljuban	44	51	34	1	Zitkovicy	42	35	37	2
Luki	41	26	31	2	Zlobin	57	52	40	2
Mahilioú	49	56	33	2	+ sites with txs below 1kW				

Local licensee: Kosmos TV Minsk **M✪:** Okhota i rybalka, Usadba, Cinema, Russkaya noch, Kinohit, Dom kino, TiJi, Eurosport, Shanson TV, Euronews, Dscovery Channel, Europa Plus TV **Tx:** ch29 (Minsk 1kW).

BELGIUM

System: DVB-T (MPEG2) [E]

Flanders
National Station
VLAAMSE RADIO EN TELEVISIEOMROEP (VRT) (Pub) A. Reyerslaan 52, 1043 Brussel ☎ +32 2 7413111 🖷 +32 2 7349351 **E:** info@vrt.be **W:** www.vrt.be **LP:** CEO: Leo Hellemans **Chs (terr.):** (in Flemish) Éen, Canvas, Ketnet.

DTT Tx Network
Licensee: VRT **M:** Éen, Canvas, Ketnet ✳ VRT Radio 1, 2, Klara, Klara continuo, Studio Brussel, MNM, MNM Hits, nieuws+

Location	Ch	kW	Location	Ch	kW
Brussel	22V	10	Antwerpen	25V	10
Egem	22V	20	Genk	25	20
St.Pieters-Leew	22V	20	Schoten	25V	20
Veltem	22V	20			
+ txs below 10kW					

Wallonia
National Stations
RADIO TÉLÉVISION BELGE DE LA COMMUNAUTÉ FRANÇAISE (RTBF) (Pub) Boulevard Reyers 52, 1044 Bruxelles ☎ +32 2 7372111 🖷 +32 2 7374210 **W:** www.rtbf.be **LP:** Dir TV: François Tron **Chs (terr.):** (in French) La une, La deux, La troix. – **BELGISCHER RUNDFUNK (BRF) (Pub)** Kehrweg 11, 4700 Eupen ☎ +32 87 591111 🖷 +32 87 591199 **E:** info@brf.be **W:** brf.be **LP:** Dir: Toni Wimmer. **Ch:** (News-magazine in German) Blickpunkt.

DTT Tx Networks
Tx Operator: RTBF **M:** La Une, La Deux, La Troix, Euronews (via Liège tx: Euronews/BRF Blickpunkt) ✳ RTBF La Première, VivaCité, Musiq3, Classic 21, Pure FM, BRF1.

Location	Ch	kW	Location	Ch	kW
Liège	45	100	Wavre	56	80
Anderlues	56	80	Léglise	66	100
Profondville	56	50	Marche-en-Famene	66	13
Tournai	56V	40			
+ txs below 10kW					

Local Licensees: Télé Bruxelles (TLB) rue Gabrielle Petit 32/34, 1080 Bruxelles ☎ +32 2 4212121 🖷 +32 2 4212122 **E:** contact@telebruxelles. net **W:** www.telebruxelles.net **M:** TLB **Tx:** ch60V (Bruxelles 8kW).

BELIZE

Systems: NTSC-M [A]. BFBS-TV: DVB-T (MPEG4) [E]

BELIZE BROADCASTING NETWORK (Comm) Belize City ☎ +501 2232008 **E:** ramon@bbn9.com **W:** www.bbn9.com **LP:** Chmn/CEO: Ramon Vasquez **Tx:** ch9. – **CHANNEL 5 (Comm)** P.O.Box 679, Belize City ☎ +501 2277781 🖷 +501 2274936 **E:** gbtz@btl.net **W:** edition. channel5belize.com **Tx:** ch5. – **CHANNEL 7 (Comm)** P.O.Box 89, Belize City ☎ +501 2277246 🖷 +501 2275040 **E:** tvseven@btl.net **W:** www.7newsbelize.com **Tx:** ch7. – **TBN (Rlg)** Belize City **Tx:** ch13.

Foreign Military Station
BFBS-TV (British Mil) BFBS Belize, Airport Camp, BFPO 12, United Kingdom. **M✪:** BBC One*, BBC Two/CBBC*, ITV*, BFBS Extra/ Cbeebies*, BFBS Sport, Sky News, Sky Sports 1, Sky Sports 2, Nepali TV* (*=time-shifted) ✳ BFBS R. (Belize), BFBS R.2, BFBS Gurkha R. **Tx:** ch27 (Price Barracks).

BENIN

System: DVB-T2 (MPEG4) [E]

National Stations
OFFICE DE RADIODIFFUSION ET TÉLÉVISION DU BÉNIN (ORTB) (Gov) BP 366, Cotonou ☎+229 21301096 🖷 +229 21301437 **E:** ortb@intnet.bj **W:** www.ortb.info **LP:** Dir: Stéphane Todomè – **LC2 (Comm)** 05 BP 427 Cotonou. ☎+229 21334749 🖷 +229 21334675 **E:** lc2@intnet.bj **W:** www.lc2international.tv

Local Stations
Canal 3: 02 BP 371, Cotonou **Carrefour TV:** 01BP 440 Bohicon **Golfe TV:** 06 BP 1624, Cotonou **Imalè Africa:** Puerto-Novo

DTT Tx Network
Licensee: StarTimes Benin (GoTV) **Mux 1+2(partly✪):** multiprgr **Txs:** MFN.

BERMUDA (UK)

Systems: NTSC-M [A]; DVB-T [A]

BERMUDA BROADCASTING CO. LTD. (Gov) P.O.Box HM 452, Hamilton HMBX ☎ +1 441 2952828 🖷 +1 441 2954282 **E:** contactus@bermudabroadcasting.com **W:** bermudabroadcasting.com **Chs:** ZFB-TV (ABC affiliate), ZBM-TV (CBS affiliate) **Txs:** ZFB-TV: Hamilton ch7 (32.5kW); ZBM-TV: Hamilton ch9 (17.5kW) – **VSB-TV (Comm)** P.O.Box HM 1450, Hamilton HMFX ☎ +1 441 2920050 🖷 +1 441 2951658 **E:** info@vsb.bm **W:** vsb.bm **LP:** Ops Mgr: Lynn Jefferson **Tx:** Hamilton ch11 (NBC affiliate, also relays BBC World News).

DTT Tx Networks
Licensee: The World in Wireless Ltd. Church Street, Washington Mall Phase II, Hamilton HM 12 ☎ +1 441 2921969 🖷 +1 441 2921979 **E:** info@wow.bm **W:** www.wowbda.com **M✪:** multiprgr **Txs:** (-).

BHUTAN

Systems: PAL-B/G [E]; DVB-T planned

BHUTAN BROADCASTING SERVICE (BBS) (Pub)☑ P.O.Box 101, Thimphu ☎ +975 2 323580 🖷 +975 2 323073 **E:** md@bbs.bt **W:** www. bbs.bt **L.P:** CEO: Pema Choden **Chs:** BBS 1, BBS 2 **Txs: BBS 1:** Thimpu ch5 (1kW) & relay txs. **BBS 2:** Thimpu ch7.

BOLIVIA

Systems: ISDB-TB [A]; § NTSC-M [A] ⏻2016

National Stations (ᵃ=analogue)
TELEVISIÓN BOLIVIANA (TVB) (Gov)☑ Av. Camacho 1485, Ed. La Urbana, La Paz ☎ +591 2 2203404 🖷 +591 2 2203015 **W:** www.bolivia tv.bo **Txs: TVB:** La Paz ch7 & relay txs; **TVB HD:** La Paz ch16. – **TELEVISIÓN UNIVERSITARIA (Educ)** ☑ Av. 6 de Agosto No. 2170, 13383 La Paz ☎ +591 2 359297 🖷 +591 2 359491 **E:** canal13@umsa.bo **W:** www.tyu. umsa.bo. **Txs:** La Paz ᵃch13 (10kW) & relay txs – **ATB (ASOCIACIÓN TELEVISIÓN BOLIVIANO) (Comm)**☑ Av. Argentina 2057, La Paz ☎ +591 2 2229922 🖷 +591 2 227935 **E:** atbcbb@atb.com.bo **W:** www.atb.com.bo **Tx:** La Paz ᵃch9 & relay txs. – **BOLIVISIÓN (Comm)**☑ Av Santa Cruz esq, Tres pasos al frente, Santa Cruz ☎ +591 3 3524544 🖷 +591 3 3530707 **W:** www.redbolivision.tv.bo **Tx:** La Paz ᵃch5 & relay txs. – **RED UNO DE BOLIVIA (Comm)**☑ Romecin Campos 592, Sopocachi, 14976 La Paz ☎ +591 2 2421111 🖷 +591 2 2415101 **E:** notivision@reduno.com.bo **W:** www. reduno.com.bo **Tx:** La Paz ᵃch11 & relay txs. – **UNITEL (UNIVERSAL DE TELEVISIÓN) (Comm)**☑ A83 La Paz ☎ +591 2 359297 🖷 +591 2 359491 **W:** www.unitel.tv. **Txs:** La Paz ᵃch2 (10kW) & relay txs.

Local Stations not shown.

BONAIRE (Netherlands)

System: DVB-T (MPEG2) [E]

TELECURAÇAO RELAY (Curaçao): ch(-).

BOSNIA & HERZEGOVINA

Systems: DVB-T (MPEG4) [E]; § PAL-B/G [E]

National (Federal) Station
RADIO TELEVIZIJA BOSNE I HERCEGOVINE (BHRT) (Pub)☑ Bulevar Meše Selimovica 12, 71000 Sarajevo ☎ +387 33 455124 🖷 +387 33 461523 **E:** sptrgov@bhrt.ba **W:** www.bhrt.ba **L.P:** DG: Belmin Karamehmedovic **Ch:** BHT1.

Federacija Bosna i Hercegovina

National Station
FTV (Pub)☑ Bulevar Meše Selimovica 12, 71000 Sarajevo ☎ +387 33 461539 🖷 +387 33 461539 **E:** press@rtvfbih.ba **W:** www.rtvbih.ba **L.P:** DG (RTVFBiH): Dzemal Šabic.

Local Stations not shown.

DTT Tx Network (under construction)
Licensee: n/a **M1:** BHT1, FTV, RTRS **M2:** multiprgr.

Location	M1	M2	Location	M1	M2
Bjelašnica	30	24	Tušenica	38	44
Majevica	25	31	Velez	26	36
Plješevica	24	47	Vlašic	22	46
Trovrh	38	33			

Republika Srpska

National Station
RADIO TELEVIZIJA REPUBLIKE SRPSKE (RTRS) (Pub)☑ ul. Kralja Petra I Karadordevica 129, 78000 Banja Luka ☎ +387 51 301660 **E:** tv@rtrs.tv **W:** www.rtrs.tv **L.P:** DG: Draško Milinovic.

Local Stations not shown.

DTT Tx Network (under construction)
Licensee: n/a **M1:** BHT1, FTV, RTRS **M2:** multiprgr.

Location	M1	M2	Location	M1	M2
Kozara	32	48	Leotar	46	40

BOTSWANA

Systems: # PAL-I [E]; ISDB-TB [E] planned

BOTSWANA TV (BTV) (Gov) ☑ P.O.Box 0060, Gaborone ☎ +267 3658000 🖷 +267 3900051 **E:** marketing@btv.gov.bw **W:** www.btv.gov.bw **L.P:** GM: Molefhe Sejoe. **Txs:** (-). – **E-BOTSWANA (Comm)** ☑ P.O.Box 921, Gaborone **E:** info@ebotswana.co.bw **W:** www.ebotswana.co.bw **L.P:** GM: David Coles; **Txs:** Gaborone ch23 & relay txs.

BRAZIL

Systems: ISDB-TB [A]; § PAL-M [A] ⏻2018

National Stations
TV BRAZIL (Pub) ☑ An. Gomes Freire 474, Centro, 20231-010 Rio de Janeiro, RJ ☎ +55 21 21176208 **E:** contacto@tvbrasil.org.br **W:** tvbrasil. ebc.com.br – **CENTRAL NACIONAL DE TELEVISÃO (CNT) (Comm)** ☑ Rua Francisco Caron 29, Pilarzinho, 82120-200 Curitiba, PR ☎ +55 41 3383377 🖷 +55 41 3384878 **E:** cnt@cnt.com.br **W:** www.cnt.com.br – **REDE BRASIL DE TELEVISÃO (RBTV) (Comm)** ☑ Alameda dos Uapés, 313 - Saúde, 04067-030 São Paulo, SP **W:** rbtv.com.br – **REDE GLOBO (Comm)** ☑ Rua Lopes Quintas 303, Jardim Botanico, 22460-010 Rio de Janeiro, RJ ☎ +55 21 25402000 🖷 +55 21 22942092 **E:** wm@redeglobo.com.br **W:** redeglobo.globo.com – **REDE RECORD (Comm)** ☑ Rua da Várzea 240, 01140-080 São Paulo, SP ☎ +55 11 36604761 🖷 +55 11 36604756 **E:** tvrecord@rederecord.com.br **W:** rederecord.r7.com – **SISTEMA BRASILEIRO DE TELEVISÃO (SBT) (Comm)** ☑ Av. das Comunicações 4, Vila Jaraguá, 06278-905 Osasco, SP ☎ +55 11 70873000 🖷 +55 11 70873509 **E:** marketing@sbt.com.br **W:** www.sbt.com.br – **TV CULTURA (Non-Comm)** ☑ Rua Vladimir Herzog 75, Agua Branca, SP 05036-900 São Paulo ☎ +55 11 38743122 🖷 +55 11 36112014 **E:** dirprog@tvcultura.com.br **W:** tvcultura. cmais.com.br.

Local Stations not shown.

DTT Tx Networks
Nationwide & local multiprgr MFNs under construction.

BRITISH INDIAN OCEAN TERRITORY

System: DVB-T (MPEG4) [E]

BFBS-TV (British Mil) ☑ BFBS Diego Garcia **M:** BBC One*, BBC Two/CBBC*, ITV*, BFBS Extra/Cbeebies*, Sky News, Nepali TV* (*=time-shifted) ⌘ BFBS R., BFBS R.2, BFBS Gurkha R. **Tx:** ch27.

BRUNEI

Systems: DVB-T (MPEG4), DVB-T2 (MPEG4) [E]

RADIO TELEVISYEN BRUNEI (RTB) (Gov) ☑ Bandar Seri Begawan, BS8610, Negara ☎ +673 2243111 🖷 +673 2220884 **E:** rtbdir@rtb.gov.bn **W:** www.rtb.gov.bn **L.P:** Dir: Hj Muhd. Suffian Bin Hj. Bungsu **Chs:** RTB1, RTB2, RTB3, RTB4, RTB5.

DTT Tx Network (DVB-T2 exc. *=DVB-T)
Tx Operator: RTB **Mux:** RTB1, RTB2, RTB3, RTB4, RTB5 **Txs:** ch28* (Bt. Subok), ch30 (Bt. Subok 5kW, Bt. Andulau 5kW).

BULGARIA

System: DVB-T (MPEG4) [E]

BALGARSKA NATSIONALNA TELEVIZIYA (BNT) (Pub) ☑ ul. San Stefano 29, 1504 Sofiya ☎ +359 2 9661149 🖷 +359 2 9634045 **E:** press@bnt.bg **W:** bnt.bg **L.P:** DG: Vyara Ankova **Chs (terr.):** BNT1, BNT2, BNT HD & reg. studios. – **BTV (Comm)** ☑ Natsionalen Dvorets na Kulturata, 1463 Sofiya ☎ +359 2 9176800 🖷 +359 2 9176886 **E:** pr@btv.bg **W:** www.btv.bg **L.P:** DG (bTV Media Group): Pavel Stanchev – **BULGARIA ON AIR (Comm)** ☑ bul. Bryuksel 1, 1540 Sofiya ☎ +359 2 4484070 **E:** office@bulgarionair.bg **W:** bgonair. bg **L.P:** DG (Bulgaria On Air Media Group): Viktoriya Mitkova – **NOVA TELEVIZIYA (Comm)**☑ bul. Hristofor Kolumb 41, 1592 Sofiya ☎ +359 2 805000 **E:** office@novatv.bg **W:** novatv.bg **L.P:** CEO: Didier Stoessel – **TV7 (Comm)** ☑ bul. Tsar Boris III 159, 1618 Sofiya ☎ +359 2 8162740 **E:** tv7@tv7.bg **W:** tv7.bg **L.P:** CEO: Nikolay Barekov.

DTT Tx Networks

Licensee Mux 1+2: NURTS Digital ☑ bul. P. Yavorov 2, 1164 Sofiya **W:** www.nurts.bg **Mux 1:** tbd **Mux 2:** bTV, Bulgaria On Air, Nova Televiziya, TV7 – **Licensee Mux 3:** First Digital ☑ ul. Budapeshta 92, 1202 Sofiya **E:** office@first-digital.bg **W:** www.first-digital.bg **Mux 3:** BNT1, BNT1 HD, BNT2, BNT HD & regional prgrs.

Location	M1*	M2	M3	kW
Belogradchik	32	49	53	5
Dobrich	22	29	64	5
Goce Delchev	31	29	33	5
Kardzhali	26	42	45	5
Plovdiv	25	35	41	5
Ruse	26	49	64	5
Sliven	22	37	64	5
Smolyan	34	49	58	5
Sofiya	23	40	52	5
St. Zagora	22	37	64	5
Shumen	28	40	51	5
Varna	22	29	27	5
Vidin	32	49	53	2

+ sites with txs below 2kW. *) currently not in use
NB. Local test muxes not shown.

BURKINA FASO

Systems: DVB-T2 (MPEG4) [E]; § SECAM-K1 [K]

National Station
RADIODIFFUSION TÉLÉVISION DU BURKINA (RTB) (Gov) ☑ 01 BP 2530, Ouagadougou 01 ☎ +226 50318353 ▤ +226 50318393 **E:** television@rtb.bf **W:** www.rtb.bf **L.P:** Dir: Alfred Nikièma **Chs:** RTB, RTB2 (Regional).

Local Stations not shown.

DTT Tx Network (under construction)
Tx Operator: Société Burkinabè de Télédiffusion **M:** RTB, RTB2 (Regional) **Txs:** nationwide MFN.

BURUNDI

Systems: DVB-T (MPEG2) [E]; § SECAM-K1 [K]

TÉLÉVISION NATIONALE DU BURUNDI (Gov) ☑ BP 1900, Bujumbura ☎ +257 22224760 ▤ +257 22244877 **E:** rtnb@cbinf.com **W:** www.rtnbdi.bi **L.P:** Dir: Nestor Bankumukunzi.

Local stations
Héritage TV: BP 4251, Bujumbura. **Rema TV:** 29, Rue de la Mission, Bujumbara. **Télé 10:** 9, boulevard patrice Lumumba Rohero 1, Bujumbura. **Télé Renaissance:** BP 2986, Bujumbura. **TV Salama:** BP 2607, Bujumbura.

DTT Tx Network (under construction)
Tx Operator: StarTimes Burundi (GoTV) **M✪:** multiprgr **Txs:** MFN.

CAMBODIA

Systems: DVB-T (MPEG4) [E]; § PAL-B [E]

National Stations
NATIONAL TV OF CAMBODIA (TVK) (Gov) ☑ 62 Preah Monivong Boulevard, Sangkat Sras Chork, Khan Daun Penh, Phnon Penh 12202 ☎ +855 23 430827 ▤ +855 23 430752 **E:** info@tvk.gov.kh **W:** www.tvk. gov.kh **L.P:** DG: Kem Gunnawadh – **BAYON TV (Comm)** ☑ National Road No 1, Boeung Snoa, Chbar Ampeou, Phnon Penh 12357 ☎ +855 23 363695 ▤ +855 23 726619 **E:** bayontv@camnet.gov.kh **W:** bayontv. com.kh – **CAMBODIAN TV NETWORK (CTN) (Comm)** ☑ National Highway 5, Phum Krol Ko, Sangkat Kilomet 6, Khan Russei Keo, Phnom Penh 12104 ☎ +855 12 800800 ▤ +855 12 801801 **E:** wmaster@ctn-cambodia.com **W:** www.ctn.com.kh **Chs:** CTN, MyTV. – **TV3 (Comm)** ☑ 2 Bvd Confédération de la Russie (Rue 112), Sangat Monorom, Khan 7 Makra, Phnom Penh ☎ +855 23 360800 **W:** www.tv3.com. kh – **TV FARK (Comm)** ☑ rue 169, Borei Keila, Phnom Penh 12253 ☎ +855 23 366061 ▤ +855 23 366063.

Local Stations (ª=analogue)
Apsara TV (Comm): 69, rue 57, Sangat Beung Keng Kang 1, Khan Chamcarmon, Phnom Penh; ªch11 (10kW). **CTV9 (Comm):** 18 rue 562, Toul Kok, Phnom Penh 12151; ªch9 (10kW).

DTT Tx Network
Licensee: PPCTV **W:** www.ppctv.com.kh **M:** multiprgr **Tx:** MFN.

CAMEROON

Systems: DVB-T2 (MPEG4) [E]; § PAL-B [E]

National Stations
CAMEROON RADIO AND TELEVISION (CRTV) (Gov) ☑ BP 1634, Yaoundé ☎ +237 2214088 ▤ +237 2204340 **E:** infos@crtv.cm **W:** crtv.cm **L.P:** DG: Amadou Vamoulké – **SPECTRUM TELEVISION (STV) (Comm)** ☑ BP 4883, Douala ☎ +237 3433045 ▤ +237 3433048 **E:** spectrum1@camnet.cm **W:** www.stvgroup.com **Chs:** STV1, STV2.

Local Stations (all Comm)
Equinoxe Télévision (E.TV): BP 15333, Douala. **RTV Lumière:** Yaoundé. **TV Max:** BP 4527, Douala.

DTT Tx Network (under construction)
Tx Operator: n/a **M:** multiprgr **Txs:** nationwide MFN.

CANADA

Systems: ATSC [A]; § NTSC-M [A] (small markets only)

National Networks (ª=analogue, to be replaced by DTT)
CANADIAN BROADCASTING CORP. (CBC/RADIO-CANADA) (Pub) ☑ 181 Queen St, Box 3220 Stn C, Ottawa ON K1Y 1E4 ☎ +1 613 2886000 **W:** www.cbc.radio-canada.ca **L.P:** Pres/CEO: Hubert T. Lacroix. **Chs:** National English and French networks. **English Network (CBC Television):** ☑ 250 Front St W, Box 500 Stn A, Toronto ON M5W 1E6 ☎ +1 416 2053311 **W:** www.cbc.ca **L.P:** Exec. Vice Pres. (English Networks): Heather Conway **Stations:** CBAT-DT Fredericton NB ch31 (7.36kW), CBCT-DT Charlottetown PE ch13 (13kW), CBET-DT Windsor ON ch9 (26kW), CBHT-DT Halifax NS ch39 (157.54kW), CBIT-DT Sydney NS ch39 (157.54kW), CBKT-DT Regina SK ch9 (60kW), CBLT-DT Toronto ON ch20 (106.9kW), CBMT-DT Montréal QC ch21 (107kW), CBNT-DT St. John's NF ch8 (14.54kW), CBOT-DT Ottawa ON ch25 (165kW), CBRT-DT Calgary AB ch21 (23.5kW), CBUT-DT Vancouver BC ch43 (103.34kW), CBWT-DT Winnipeg MB ch27 (42kW), CBXT-DT Edmonton AB ch42 (131.71kW) & relay txs. **French Network (ICI Radio-Canada Télé):** ☑ 1400 René-Lévesque Boul. E, Box 6000, Montréal PQ H3C 3A8 ☎ +1 514 5976000 **W:** ici.radio-canada.ca **L.P:** Exec. Vice Pres. (French Networks): Louis Lalande. **Stations:** CBAFT-DT Moncton NB ch11 (17.65kW), CBFT-DT Montréal QC ch19 (290kW), CBKFT-DT Regina SK ch13 (27.1kW), CBOFT-DT Ottawa ON ch9 (3.5kW), CBVT-DT Québec QC ch25 (2.45kW), CBUFT-DT Vancouver BC ch26 (27.52kW), CBWFT-DT Winnipeg MB ch51 (7.6kW), CBXFT-DT Edmonton AB ch47 (15.18kW) & relay txs. – **CTV TELEVISION NETWORK (Comm)** (Div. of Bell Media) ☑ 9 Channel Nine Court, Scarborough ON M1S 4B5 ☎ +1 416 3325000 ▤ +1 416 3325283 **E:** bellmediapr@bellmedia.ca **W:** www.ctv.ca **L.P:** Pres (Bell Media): Mary Ann Turcke. **Stations:** CFCF-DT Montréal QC ch12 10.6kW), CFCN-DT Calgary AB ch29 (220kW), CFCN-DT-5 Lethbridge AB ch13 (139kW), CFQC-DT Saskatoon SK ch8 (13kW), CFPL-DT London ON ch10 (45kW), CFRN-DT Edmonton AB ch12 (25kW), CFTO-DT Toronto ON ch9 (10.2kW), CHBX Sault Ste. Marie ON ªch2 (100kW), CHRO Ottawa/Pembroke ON ªch5 (100kW)/ch43 (50kW), CHWI-DT Windsor ON ch16 (3.4kW), CICC Yorkton SK ªch10 (56kW), CICI Sudbury ON ªch5 (100kW), CIPA Prince Albert SK ªch9 (325kW), CITO Timmins ON ªch3 (100kW), CIVI-DT Victoria BC ch23 (1.5kW), CIVT-DT Vancouver BC ch32 (33kW), CJCB Sydney NS ªch4 (180kW), CJCH-DT Halifax NS ch48 (400kW), CJOH-DT Ottawa ON ch19 (19kW), CKCK-DT Regina SK ch8 (23kW), CKCO-DT Kitchener ON ch13 (12kW), CKCW-DT Moncton NB ch29 (390kW), CKLT-DT St. John NB ch9 (7.6kW), CKNY North Bay ON ªch10 (132.6kW), CKVR-DT Barrie ON ch10 (11kW), CKY-DT Winnipeg MB ch7 (24kW) & smaller txs. – **GLOBAL TV NETWORK (Comm)** (Div. of Shaw Media Inc.) ☑ 121 Bloor St. East, Toronto, ON M4W 3M5 ☎ +1 416 0671174 **E:** corporate.inquiries@ shawmedia.ca **W:** www.globaltv.com **L.P:** Pres (Shaw Media): Barbara Williams. **Stations:** CFRE-DT Regina SK ch11 (17.3kW), CFSK-DT Saskatoon SK ch42 (30kW), CHAN-DT Vancouver BC ch22 (40kW), CHBC-DT Kelowna BC ch27 (32.6kW), CICT-DT Calgary AB ch41 (50kW), CIHF-DT Halifax/Dartmouth NS ch8 (1kW), CIHF-DT-2 St. John NB ch12 (6kW), CIII-DT Toronto ON ch41 (100kW), CISA-DT Lethbridge AB ch7 (19.7kW), CITV-DT Edmonton AB ch13 (25kW), CKMI-DT Québec PQ ch15 (8kW), CKMI-DT-1 Montréal/Sherbrooke PQ ch11 (1kW), CKND-DT Winnipeg MB ch40 (25.1kW) & relay txs.

Major Regional Networks (ª=analogue)
SOCIÉTÉ DE TÉLÉDIFFUSION DU QUEBEC (TÉLÉ-QUÉBEC) (Pub)

✉ 1000 rue Fullum, Montréal QC H2K 3L7 ☎ +1 514 5212424 🖳 +1 514 5255511 **W:** www.telequebec.tv **L.P:** Pres/DG: Marie Collin. **Stations (French):** CIVM-DT Montréal QC ch26 (269kW) & relay txs (QC only). – **TVO (Pub)** ✉ Box 200 Stn Q, Toronto ON M4T 2T1 ☎ +1 416 4842600 🖳 +1 416 4847771 **W:** www.tvo.org **L.P:** CEO: Lisa de Wilde. **Stations:** CICA-DT Toronto ON ch19 (107kW) & relay txs (ON only). – **CHANNEL ZERO INC. (Comm)** ✉ Box 6143 Stn A, Toronto ON M5W 1P6 ☎ +1 416 4921595 🖳 +1 416 4929539 **W:** www.tvchannelzero.com **L.P:** Chmn/CEO: Romen Podzhyhun. **Station:** CHCH-DT Hamilton ON ch15 (132kW) – **CORUS ENTERTAINMENT INC. (Comm)** ✉ 630-3rd Ave SW Suite 501, Calgary AB T2P 4L4 ☎+1 403 4444244 🖳 +1 403 4444242 **W:** www.corusent.com **L.P:** Pres/CEO: Doug Murphy. **Stations:** CKWS-DT (CTV affiliate) Kingston ON ch11 (9.4kW), CHEX-DT (CTV affiliate) Peterborough ON ch12 (20kW) & relay txs (ON only). – **GROUPE TVA INC. (Comm)** (Div. of Québecor Media) ✉ 1600 boul. de Maisonneuve Est, Montréal PQ H2L 4P2 ☎ +1 514 5269251 **W:** tva.canoe.com **L.P:** Pres/CEO (Québecor Media): Pierre Dion. **Stations (French):** CFCM-DT Québec QC ch17 (210kW), CFEM-DT Rouyn-Noranda QC ch13 (22kW), CFER Rimouski QC °ch11 (325kW), CFTM-DT Montréal QC ch10 (11kW), CHAU-DT Carleton-sur-Mer QC ch5 (9.85kW), CHEM -DT Trois-Rivières QC ch8 (325kW), CHLT-DT Sherbrooke QC ch7 (300kW), CHOT-DT Hull QC ch40 (111.5kW), CIMT-DT Rivière-du-Loup QC ch9 (275.4kW), CJPM-DT Chicoutimi QC ch46 (89.3kW) & relay txs. – **JIM PATTISON BROADCAST GROUP (Comm)** ✉ 460 Pemberton Terrace, Kamloops BC V2C 1T5 ☎ +1 250 3723322 🖳 +1 250 3740445 **W:** www.jimpattison.com **L.P:** Pres: Rod Schween. **Stations:** CKPG Prince George BC °ch2 (8.3kW), CFJC Kamloops BC °ch4 (3.7kW), CHAT Medicine Hat AB °ch6 (58kW) & relay txs (AB & BC only). – **NEWFOUNDLAND BROADCASTING CO. LTD (Comm)** ✉ Box 2020, St. John's NL, A1C 5S2 ☎ +1 709 7225015 🖳 +1 709 7265107 **W:** www.ntv.ca **L.P:** Pres: Scott Stirling. **Stations:** CJON-DT St. John's NL ch21 (482.3kW) & relay txs (NL only). – **ROGERS MEDIA INC. (Comm)** (Div. of Rogers Communications) ✉ 333 Bloor St. E, 7th flr, Toronto ON M4W 1G9 ☎ +1 416 9358200 **W:** www.rogersmedia.com **L.P:** Pres: Keith Pelley. **Stations:** CFMT-DT Toronto ON ch47 (22.2kW), CHMI-DT Portage LaPrairie/Winnipeg MB ch13 (8.3kW), CHNM-DT Vancouver BC ch20 (8.3kW), CITY-DT Toronto ON ch44 (15kW), CJMT-DT Toronto ON ch51 (15kW), CJCO-DT Calgary AB ch38 (25kW), CJEO-DT Edmonton AB ch44 (58kW), CKAL-DT Calgary AB ch49 (100kW), CKEM-DT Edmonton AB ch17 (107kW), CKVU-DT Vancouver BC ch33 (8.3kW), CJNT-DT Montréal QC ch49 (4kW) & relay txs. – **V (Comm)** ✉ 612, rue St-Jacques bureau 100, Montréal QC H3C 5R1 ☎ +1 514 3906035 **W:** vtele.ca **L.P:** CEO: Maxime Rémillard **Stations (French):** CFJP-DT Montréal QC ch35 (13.9kW) & relay txs (QC only).

Other Regional Networks & Local Stations not shown.

CANARY ISLANDS (Spain)

System: DVB-T (MPEG2, MPEG4) [E]

National (Regional) Stations
TELEVISIÓN ESPAÑOLA EN CANARIAS (TVE) (Pub) ✉ Plazoleta de Milton 1, 35005 Las Palmas de Gran Canaria ☎ +34 928 293096. – **RADIOTELEVISIÓN CANARIA (RTCV) (Pub)** ✉Mariucha 2, 35012 Las Palmas de Gran Canaria ☎ +34 928 280188 **W:** www.rtvc. es. **Chs:** TV Canaria, TV Canaria Dos.

Local Stations not shown.

DTT Tx Networks
Operator: n/a **Mux 1:** La 1, La 1 HD, La 2, 24h, Clan ✳ RNE R. Nacional, RNE R.5. **Txs:** ch28 (Las Palmas) & netw. **Mux 2:** TDP, TDP HD ✳ RNE R. Clásica HD, RNE R.3, RNE R. Exterior **Txs:** ch36 (Las Palmas) & netw. **Mux 3:** Discovery MAX, Disney Channel, Paramount Channel ✳ Cope, R. Maria, R. Marca, Vaughn R., eRadio **Txs:** ch35 (Las Palmas) & netw. **Mux 4:** Antena 3, Antena 3 HD, laSexta, laSexta HD, Neox, Nova **Txs:** ch32 (Las Palmas) & netw. **Mux 5:** Telecinco, Telecinco HD, Cuatro, Cuatro HD, FDF, Divinity **Txs:** ch32 (Las Palmas) & netw. **Mux 6:** Boing, Energy, Mega ✳ Europa FM, Melodia FM, Onda Cero **Txs:** ch50 (Las Palmas) & netw. **Mux 7:** tbd **Txs:** ch25 (Las Palmas) & netw.
Local muxes not shown.

CAPE VERDE

Systems: # SECAM-K1 [VHF=K]; DVB-T (MPEG2) [E]

TELEVISÃO DE CABO VERDE (TCV) (Pub) ✉ Rua 13 de Janeiro, 1-A, Achada Santo António, Praia ☎ +238 2605200 🖳 +238 2605256 **E:** tcv@rtc.cv **W:** www.rtc.cv **L.P:** Dir: Júlio Rodrigues **Txs:** Praia ch9 (0.5kW H) & relay txs.

Foreign TV Relay
RTP África (Portugal): (-).

DTT Tx Network
Licensee: CV Telecom **W:** www.cvtelecom.cv **Mux:** Televisão de Cabo Verde, SIC Noticias, TV Record, Rai Uno, BBC World, TV5, TV Galicia, Infinito, Fox Life, Fashion TV, Euronews, Eurosport, Extreme Sport, TVE Internacional, CNBC, MCM, RTP África, Lusomundo Premium, Lusomundo Gallery, Playboy, SportTv, RTP1, RTP2, SIC, TVI. **Txs:** (-)

CAYMAN ISLANDS (UK)

System: NTSC-M [A]

CAYMAN INTERNATIONAL TV NETWORK (CITN) (Comm) ✉ P.O. Box 30563 SMB, Grand Cayman ☎ +1 345 9452739 🖳 +1 345 9490021 **E:** citn@cayman27.com.ky **W:** www.cayman27.com.ky **Tx:** ch27. – **CAYMAN TELEVISION SERVICE (CTS) (Comm)** ✉ P.O.Box 3117 SMB, Grand Cayman. **Tx:** ch24. – **CAYMAN ADVENTIST TELEVISION NETWORK (CATN) (Rlg)** ✉ P.O.Box 515 GT, Grand Cayman. **E:** mission@candw.ky **Tx:** ch30. Rel. 3ABN (USA). – **CAYMAN CHRISTIAN TELEVISION (CCT) (Rlg)** ✉ Grand Cayman. **Tx:** ch21. Rel. TBN (USA).

CENTRAL AFRICAN REPUBLIC

Systems: DVB-T2 (MPEG4) [E]; § SECAM-K1 [VHF=K]

National Station
TÉLÉVISION CENTRAFRICAINE (TVCA) (Gov) ✉ BP 940, Bangui ☎ +236 75501412 🖳 +236 21615985 **L.P:** DG: David Dotté Koimara **Txs:** Bangui ch9 (2kW) & relay txs.

Local Station
RTV Tropic: PK12, Bangui; ch6.

DTT Tx Network (under construction)
Tx Operator: Star Times **M✪:** multiprgr **Txs:** MFN.

CHAD

System: # SECAM-K1 [VHF=K, UHF=E]; DTT planned

TÉLÉ TCHAD (Gov) ✉ BP 5123, N'Djamena ☎ +235 22522923 🖳 +235 22525163 **E:** tele.tchad@intnet.td **W:** www.onrtv.org **L.P:** DG (ONRTV): Doubaye Kleoutouin **Txs:** N'Djamena ch6V (50kW) & relay txs.

CHILE

Systems: ISDB-TB [A]; § NTSC-M [A] ⇓2017

National Stations (°=analogue)
TVN CHILE (Gov) ✉ Bellavista 0990, Providencia, Santiago ☎ +56 2 7077130 **E:** tvngprog@tvn.cl **W:** www.tvchile.cl **Txs:** Santiago °ch7/ch33 & relay txs. – **CANAL 13 (Rlg, Comm)** ✉ Inés Matte Urrejola 0825, Providencia, Santiago ☎ +56 2 6302356 **E:** mailbag@13.cl **W:** www.13.cl **Txs:** Santiago °ch13/ch24 & relay txs. – **CHILEVISIÓN (CHV) (Comm)** ✉ Inés Matte Urrejola 0890, Providencia, Santiago ☎ +56 2 4615100 **E:** rcarmi@chilevision.cl **W:** www.chilevision.cl. **Txs:** Santiago °ch11 (60kW)/ch30 & relays txs. – **MEGA (Comm)** ✉ Av. Vicuña Mackenna 1348, Santiago ☎ +56 2 8108000 **E:** mega@mega.cl **W:** www.mega.cl **Txs:** Santiago °ch9/ch27 & relays. – **RED TV (Comm)** ✉ Avenida Quilín 3750, Macul, Santiago ☎ +56 2 23854000 **E:** lared@lared.cl **W:** lared.cl **Txs:** Santiago °ch4 & relay txs. – **TELECANAL (Comm)** ✉ Nueva Tajamar 481, Oficina 201, Torre Central, Las Condes, Santiago ☎ +56 2 4115600 **E:** telecanal@telecanal.cl **W:** www.telecanal.cl **Tx:** Santiago °ch2 & relays txs – **UCV TV (Comm)** ✉ Av. 11 Septiembre 2155 Of. 1402, Edificio Panorámico Torre A, Santiago ☎ +56 2 5864350 **E:** direccion@ucv.cl **W:** www.ucvmedios.cl **Txs:** Santiago °ch5/ch26 & relay txs.

Local Stations not shown.

CHINA (People's Rep. of)

Systems: DTMB [DS]; § PAL-D [DS] ⇓2018

National Stations
CHINA CENTRAL TELEVISION (CCTV) (Gov) ✉ 11 Fuxing Lu,

Haidian Qu, Beijing 100859 ☎ +86 10 68500114 📠 +86 10 68508743 **W:** www.cntv.cn **L.P:** Pres: Nie Chenxi. **Chs:** 22 FTA chs, 18 encrypted chs – **CHINA EDUCATION TELEVISION (CETV) (Gov)** 🖳 160 Fuxingmennei Dajie, Xicheng Qu, Beijing 100031 ☎ +86 10 66419055. 📠 +86 10 66084298 **L.P:** Pres: Yuan Xiaoping **W:** www.centv.cn **Chs:** CETV1, CETV2, CETV3, CETV4.

Regional Stations (all Gov)
AH) Anhui TV: 355 Tongcheng Nanlu, Hefei, Anhui 230011 **W:** www. ahtv.cn **BJ)** Beijing TV: 98 A Jianguo Lu, Chaoyang Qu, Beijing 100022 **W:** www.brtn.cn **CQ)** Chongqing TV: 68 Yuzhou Lu, Chongqing 400041 **W:** www.cbg.cn **EB)** Hebei TV: 100 Jianhua Nandajie, Shijiazhuang, Hebei 050031 **W:** www.hebtv.com **EN)** Henan TV: 18 Zhenghua Lu, Zhengzhou, Henan 450008 **W:** www.hntv.tv **FJ)** Fujian TV: 128 Xihuan Nanlu, Fuzhou, Fujian 350004 **W:** www.fjtv.net **GD)** Guangdong TV: 331 Huangshi Donglu, Guangzhou, Guangdong 510066 **W:** www.gdtv.cn **GS)** Gansu TV: 561 Zhangsutan, Chengguan Qu, Lanzhou, Gansu 730010 **W:** www.gntv.tv **GX)** Guangxi TV: 73 Minzu Dadao, Nanning, Guangxi 530022 **W:** www.gxtv. cn **GZ)** Guizhou TV: 261 Qingyun Lu, Guiyang, Guizhou 550002 **W:** www. gzstv.com **HA)** Hainan TV: 61 Nansha Lu, Haikou, Hainan 570206 **W:** www. hnntv.cn **HB)** Hubei TV: Zijin Cun, Liangdao Jun, Wuchang Qu, Wuhan, Hubei 430071 **W:** www.hbtv.com.cn **HL)** Heilongjiang TV: 181 Zhongshan Lu, Harbin, Heilongjiang 150001 **W:** www.hljtv.com **HN)** Hunan TV: Liuyang He Daqiao Dong, Changsha, Hunan 410003 **W:** zixun.hunantv.com **JL)** Jilin TV: 2066 Weixing Lu, Changchun, Jilin 130051 **W:** www.jilintv.cn **JS)** Jiangsu TV: 48 Xi Citang Xiang, Zhongshan Donglu, Nanjing, Jiangsu 210002 **W:** www.jstv.com **JX)** Jiangxi TV: 207 Hongdu Zhong Dadao, Nanchang, Jiangxi 330046 **W:** www.jxntv.cn **LN)** Liaoning TV: 79 Wenhua Lu, Heping Qu, Shenyang, Liaoning 110003 **W:** www.lntv.com.cn **NM)** Nei Menggu TV: 71 Xinhua Dajie, Hohhot, Nei Menggu 010058 **W:** www.nmtv.cn **NX)** Ningxia TV: 66 Beijing Zhonglu, Jinfeng Qu, Yinchuan, Ningxia 75000135 **W:** www.nxtv.com.cn **QH)** Qinghai TV: 6 Kunlun Lu, Xining, Qinghai 810001 **W:** www.qhbtv.com **SD)** Shandong TV: 81 Jingshi Lu, Jinan, Shandong 250062 **W:** www.sdtv.cn **SC)** Sichuan TV: 40 Dongsheng Jie, Chengdu, Sichuan 610015 **W:** www.sctv.com **SH)** Shanghai TV: 651 Nanjing Xilu, Shanghai 200041 **W:** www.smg.cn **SN)** Shaanxi TV: 336 Chang'an Nanlu, Xi'an, Shaanxi 710061 **W:** www.sxtvs.com **SX)** Shanxi TV: 318 Yingze Dajie, Taiyuan, Shanxi 030001 **W:** www.sxrtv.com **TJ)** Tianjin TV: 143 Weijin Lu, Heping Qu, Tianjin 300071 **W:** www.tjtv.com.cn **XJ)** Xinjiang TV: 84 Tuanjie Lu, Urumqi, Xinjiang 830044 **W:** www.xjtvs.com.cn **XZ)** Xizang TV: 149 Beijing Zhonglu, Lhasa, Xizang 850000 **W:** www.vtibet.com/ds **YN)** Yunnan TV: 182 Renmin Xilu, Kunming, Yunnan 650031 **W:** www.yntv.cn **ZJ)** Zhejiang TV: 111 Moganshan Lu, Hangzhou, Zhejiang 310005 **W:** www. cztv.com **NB:** Keys to regional codes - see National radio section.

DTT Tx Networks (under construction)
Tx Operator: SARFT **Mux 1:** multiprgr **Mux 2:** multiprgr (NB: The content of muxes 1+2 may vary from region to region)

Location	M1	M2
Beijing	33	32

+ national network under construction
Local muxes not shown.

NB: No terrestrial TV station.

NB: No terrestrial TV station.

COLOMBIA

Systems: # NTSC-M [A] ⇩2017; DVB-T2 (MPEG4) [A]

National Stations
RADIO TELEVISIÓN NACIONAL DE COLOMBIA (RTVC) (Pub) 🖳 Avenida El Dorado No. 46 - 76, Bogotá ☎+57 1 2200700 📠 +57 1 2222765 **E:** info@rtvc.gov.co **W:** www.rtvc.gov.co **Chs:** Canal Uno, Canal Institucional, Señal Colombia. **Txs: Canal Uno:** Bogotá ch8 & relay txs, **Canal Institucional:** Bogotá ch13 & relay txs, **Señal Colombia:** Bogotá ch11 & relay txs. – **CARACOL TELEVISION (Comm)** 🖳 Calle 103 #69 B 43, Bogotá ☎ +57 1 6430430 📠 +57 1 6430444 **E:** serviciocliente@caracol.com.co **W:** www.caracoltv.com **Txs:** Bogotá ch5 & relay txs. – **RCN TELEVISIÓN (Comm)** 🖳 Av Americas 65-82, Bogotá ☎ +57 1 4269292 📠 +57 1 4140412 **W:** www.canalrcnmsn.com **Txs:** Bogotá ch4 & relay txs.

Local Stations not shown.

DTT Tx Networks

Location	RTVC*	Caracol	RCN
Bogotá	16	14	15

+ nationwide netw. under construction
*) M: Canal Uno, Canal Institucional, Señal Columbia
Local muxes not shown.

COMOROS

Systems: DTMB [E]; § SECAM-K1 [VHF=K]

National Station
OFFICE DE RADIO ET TÉLÉVISION DES COMORES (ORTC) (Pub) 🖳 BP 250, Moroni ☎ +269 7744045 📠 +269 7731079 **W:** www.ortc. fr **L.P:** DG: Abdulla Saad.

Local Stations (all Comm)
Djabal TV: Iconi. **Kartala RTV:** Moroni. **TV-Sha:** Moroni. **MTV:** Moroni. **RTV Anjouanaise (RTA):** Mbouyoujou-Ouani, Ile Autonome d'Anjouan.

DTT Tx Network
Tx Operator: n/a **M:** multiprgr **Txs:** nationwide MFN under constr.

CONGO (Dem. Rep. of)

Systems: DVB-T (MPEG4) [E]; § SECAM-K1 [VHF=K]

National Station
RADIOTÉLÉVISION NATIONALE CONGOLAISE (RTNC) (Pub) 🖳 BP 3164, Gombe, Kinshasa ☎ +243 1 5260601 📠 +243 1 5220655 **E:** ica@ic.cd **L.P:** DG: Christophe Kolomoni N'djibu **Chs:** RTNC1, RTNC2, RTNC3. **Txs: RTNC1:** Kananga ch4 (2kW), Kamina ch4 (2kW), Kinshasa ch5 (27kW), Kolwezi ch5 (1kW), Mbuji Mayi ch6 (2kW). **RTNC2:** Kinshasa ch37.

Local Stations not shown.

DTT Tx Network (Trial)
Tx Operator: RTCN **M:** RTNC3, Tropicana TV, La chaîne du Sénat, Télé 50, Raga TV, B-Ones **Txs:** ch26 (Kinshasa 0.5kW).

CONGO (Rep. of)

Systems: # SECAM-K1 [VHF=K, UHF=E]; DVB-T [E] planned

TÉLÉ CONGO (Gov) 🖳 BP 1046, Brazzaville ☎ +242 222810116 📠 +242 222814128 **L.P:** DG: Jean Obambi **Txs:** (pol.H): Loubomo ch5 (1kW), Brazzaville ch7 (9kW), Pointe Noire ch9 (4.7kW) & relay txs. – **DRTV (Comm)** 🖳 Case J 421V.OCH Moungali III, BP 1974, Brazzaville **E:** info@drtv-congo.com **W:** www.drtv-congo.com **Txs:** Brazzaville ch40 & relay txs.

COOK ISLANDS

System: PAL-B [NZ]

COOK ISLANDS TELEVISION (CITV) (Comm) 🖳 P.O.Box 126, Avarua, Rarotonga ☎ +682 29460 📠 +682 21907 **E:** watchus@citv.co.ck **W:** www. citv.co.ck **L.P:** CEO: Jeane Matenga **Txs:** Airport ch4, Works Depot, TV studio, Mauke ch5, Matavera ch6, Titikaveka ch7, Aitutaki & Rarotonga ch9, Tu Papa ch10, Hospital & Ngatangiia ch11.

COSTA RICA

Systems: # NTSC-M [A] ⇩2018; ISDB-TB [A]

National Stations (ᵃ=analogue)
SISTEMA NACIONAL DE RADIO Y TELEVISIÓN (SINART) (Pub) 🖳 Apt 7-1908-1000, San José ☎ +506 22313333 📠 +506 22200072 **E:** canal13@sinart.go.cr **W:** www.sinart.go.cr **L.P:** DG: Pablo Cárdenas **Txs:** San José ch13 & relay txs. – **REPRETEL (Comm)** 🖳 Apartado 2860, 1000 San José ☎ +506 22906665 📠 +506 22324203 **E:** info@ repretel.com **W:** www.repretel.com **Chs:** Canal 4, 6, 11. **Txs:** San José ᵃch4, ch6, ᵃch11, ch6. – **TELETICA (Comm)** 🖳 Sabana Oeste, San José ☎ +506 22101201 📠 +506 22321107 **E:** info@teletica.com **W:** www.teletica.com **Tx:** San José ᵃch7/ch14.

Local Stations not shown.

CROATIA

System: DVB-T (MPEG2, MPEG4), DVB-T2 (MPEG4) [E]

National Stations
HRVATSKA RADIO-TELEVIZIJA (HRT) (Pub) ✎ Prisavlje 3, 10000 Zagreb. ☎ + 385 1 6163366 🖷 + 385 1 6163392 **W:** www.hrt. hr **L.P:** DG: Goran Radman. **Chs:** HRT1, HRT2, HRT3, HRT4 – **NOVA TV (Comm)** ✎ Remetinecka cesta 139, 10000 Zagreb ☎ +385 1 6008300 🖷 +385 1 6008333 **E:** novatv@novatv.hr **W:** www.novatv.hr **L.P:** DG: Drazen Mavric **Chs:** Nova TV, Doma TV. – **RTL TELEVIZIJA (Comm)** ✎ Krapinska 45, 10000 Zagreb ☎ +385 1 3660000 🖷 +385 1 3660609 **E:** rtl@rtl.hr **W:** www.rtl.hr **L.P:** Pres/CEO: Henning Tewes. **Chs (terr.):** RTL, RTL2.

Local Stations (via Mux 4, DTT regions: a-i)
Gradska TV: Molatska bb, 23000 Zadar (g) **Kanal RI:** Trg rijecke rezolucije 3, 51000 Rijeka (e). **Nezavisna Istarska Televizija (NIT):** Trg pod lipom 1, 52000 Pazin (e). **RI-TV:** Uzarska 17/3, 51000 Rijeka (e). **Slavonskobrodska Televizija:** Mile Budaka 1/IV, 35 000 Slavonski Brod (b). **TV Cakovec:** Kralja Tomislava 6, 40000 Cakovec (c). **TV Jadran:** Split (h). **TV Nova:** M. Laginje 5, 52100 Pula (e). **TV Slavonije i Baranje:** Hrvatske republike 20, 31000 Osijek (a). **Varazdinska Televizija (VTV):** Kralja P. Kresimira IV 6a, 42000 Varazdin (c). **Vinkovacka Televizija (VKTV):** Trg dr.F.Tudjmana 2, Vinkovci (a).

DTT Tx Networks (DVB-T/MPEG2 exc. where indicated)
Tx Operator: OIV ✎ ul. grada Vukovara 269d, 10000 Zagreb ☎ +385 1 6186000 🖷 +385 1 6186100 **E:** dvbt@oiv.hr **W:** www.oiv.hr **Mux 1:** HRT1, HRT2, RTL, Nova TV **Mux 2:** HRT3, HRT4, RTL2, Doma TV **Mux 3 (DVB-T2)**✪: tbd **Mux 4:** Local stns. **Mux 5 (DVB-T2)**✪: tbd

Location	M1	M2	M3	M4°	M5
Belje	38	44	51	21a	56
Biokovo	33	53	-	34h	-
Borinci	38	44	51	21a	56
Brac	33	53	23	53h	41
Celevac	51	59	-	31g	-
Drenovci	36	-	-	-	-
Gruda	51	59	-	-	-
Ivanšcica	44V	48V	28V	36Vc	53V
Kalnik	44	48	-	-	-
Krk	28	53	-	45	-
Labinštica	33	53	23	34h	41
Lastovo	33	-	-	-	-
Licka Plješevica	30	44	-	54	-
Mali Losinj	28	53	-	-	-
Mirkovica	30	44	-	54	-
Moslavacka Gora	23	39	-	-	-
Pag	51	59	-	-	-
Papuk	23	39	-	58	-
Petrova Gora	25	48	-	-	-
Promina	51	59	-	31g	-
Psunj	23	39	-	58	-
Pula	28	53	-	45e	-
Razromir	28	53	-	-	-
Rota	33	53	-	-	-
Sljeme	25	48	28	42d	53
Srdj	51	59	22	28i	45
Stipanov Gric	30	44	36	54	34
Sveta Gera	25	48	-	-	-
Sveta Nedjelja	25	48	-	42	-
Šibenik	51	59	21	31g	45
Ucka	28	53	57	29e	39
Ugljan	51	59	21	31g	45
Uljenje	51	59	-	-	-
Zagreb (HRT HQ)	25	48	-	-	-

+ repeaters. °) DTT regions a-i, see under "Local Stations".

CUBA

Systems: DTMB [A]; § NTSC-M [A] ↻2021

National Station (ᵃ=analogue)
INSTITUTO CUBANO DE RADIO Y TELEVISIÓN (ICRT) (Gov) ✎ Televisión Cubana, Calle 23 #258 e/L y M, Vedado, La Habana 10400 ☎ +53 7 8309705 🖷 +53 7 8309705 **E:** tvcubana@icrt.cu **W:** www.tvcubana.icrt.cu **L.P:** Pres (ICRT): Danylo Sirio Lopéz **Chs:** Canal Educativo, Canal Educativo 2, Cubavisión, Tele Rebelde, Multivisión, Canal Habana, Canal Clave. **Txs: Canal Educativo:** La Habana

ᵃch4 & network; **Canal Educativo 2:** La Habana ᵃch15 & network; **Cubavisión:** La Habana ᵃch6 & network; **Tele Rebelde:** La Habana ᵃch2 & network **Multivisión:** La Habana ᵃch21 & network.

Local Stations not shown.

DTT Tx Network (under construction)
Tx Operator: Radiocuba **M:** Canal Educativo, Canal Educativo 2, Cubavisión, Multivisión, Tele Rebelde, Canal Habana, Canal Clave **Txs:** ch38 (La Habana) & nationwide MFN netw.

CURAÇAO (Netherlands)

System: DVB-T (MPEG2) [E]

TELECURAÇAO (Gov) ✎ Berg Ararat zn., Willemstad ☎ +599 9 7771688 🖷 +599 9 4614138 **E:** info@telecuracao.com **W:** www.telecuracao.com **L.P:** GM: Hugo Lew Jen Tai **Tx:(-).**

CYPRUS

Systems: DVB-T (MPEG4) [E]. § PAL-B/G [E] (No. Cyprus only)

National Stations
CYPRUS BROADCASTING CORP. (CYBC) (Pub) ✎ P.O.Box 24824, 1397 Lefkosia ☎ +357 22862000 🖷 +357 22314050 **E:** rik@cybc.com.cy **W:** www.riknews.com.cy **L.P:** DG (acting): Costas Nikolaides **Chs:** RIK1, RIK 2 – **ANT1 (Comm)** ✎ P.O.Box 20923, 1665 Lefkosia ☎+357 22200200 🖷 +357 22200210 **E:** hr@antenna.com.cy **W:** www.ant1iwo.com – **CAPITAL TV (Comm)** ✎ P.O.Box 55633, 3781 Limassol ☎ +357 25577577 🖷 +357 25568122 **W:** www.capital-tv.com – **EXTRA TV (Comm)** ✎ P.O.Box 70651, 3801 Limassol ☎ +357 25715111 🖷 +357 25715333 **E:** harnic@cytanet.com.cy **W:** www.extratv.com.cy – **MEGA TV (Comm)** ✎ P.O.Box 27400, 1644 Lefkosia ☎ +357 22477777 🖷 +357 22355138 **E:** newsdpt@megatv.com **W:** www.megatv.com – **PLUS TV (Comm)** ✎ Neas Engomis St. 8, 2409 Lefkosia ☎ +357 22600600 🖷 +357 22600512 – **SIGMA TV (Comm)** ✎ P.O.Box 21836, 1513 Lefkosia ☎ +357 22580100 🖷 +357 22580252 **E:** info@sigmatv.com **W:** www.sigmatv.com.

Local stations not shown.

DTT Tx Networks
Tx Operator Mux 1: CYBC **M:** RIK1, RIK2, RIK HD, ERT1, Euronews ⌘ RIK1-4 **Tx Operator Mux 2:** Velister ✎ Evaggelistrias St. 68, Helen Hall, 2057 Strovolos ☎ +357 22267222 🖷 +357 22267233 **E:** info@velister.com.cy **W:** www.velister.com.cy **M:** ANT1, Sigma, Plus TV, Extra TV, Capital TV, Mad TV, Music TV**.**

Location	M1	M2	kW
Madari	33	49	5
Vavatsinia	33	49	5

+ txs below 5kW

NORTHERN CYPRUS

National Station
BAYRAK RADIO TELEVISYON KURUMU (BRTK) (Gov) ✎ Dr. Fazil Küçük Bulvari, BRT Sitesi, Lefkosa (mail: via Mersin 10, Turkey) ☎ +90 392 2254577 🖷 +90 392 2254577 **E:** info@brtk.net **W:** www.brtk.net **L.P:** DG: Mete Tümerkan **Chs:** BRT1, BRT2, BRT HD.

Local Stations not shown.

DTT Tx Networks
Tx Operator: BRTK **Mux 1+2:** multiprgr **Txs: M1:** ch41 (SFN) **M2:** ch33 (SFN).

AKROTIRI & DHEKELIA (UK)

System: DVB-T (MPEG2) [E]

BFBS-TV Relay (British Mil) ✎ BFPO 57, Dhekelia Mil 381 ☎ +357 24748518 **Mux**✪: BBC One, BBC Two/CBBC, ITV, BFBS Extra/Cbeebies, BFBS Sport, BFBS Movies, Sky News, Sky Sports 1, Sky Sports 2, Sky Sports 3, Nepali TV ⌘ BFBS R. (Cyprus), BFBS R.2, BFBS Gurkha R. **Txs:** ch27 (SFN).

CZECH REPUBLIC

System: DVB-T (MPEG2, MPEG4) [E]
National Stations
CESKÁ TELEVIZE (CT) (Pub) ✎ Kavcí Hory, 14070 Praha 4 ☎ +420

261131111 ▤ +420 261212891 **E**: info@ceskatelevize.cz **W**: www.
ceskatelevize.cz **L.P**: DG: Petr Dvorak **Chs**: CT1, CT2, Reg prgrs, CT24,
CT Art, CT Décko, sport – **PRIMA TV (Comm)** ▣ Na Žertvách 24,
18000 Praha 8 ☎ +420 266700111 ▤ +420 266700201 **E**: informace@
iprima.cz **W**: www.iprima.cz **Chs**: TV Prima, Prima COOL, Prima love,
Zoom – **TV NOVA (Comm)** ▣ Kříženeckého nám. 5, 15252 Praha 5
☎ +420 233100111 ▤ +420 242424525 **E**: info@nova.cz **W**: tv.nova.
cz **L.P**: DG: Christoph Mainusch – **TV BARRANDOV (Comm)** ▣
Kříženeského nám. 322, 15200 Praha 5 ▤ +420 267071771 **W**: www.
barrandov.tv – **TV ÓCKO (Comm)** ▣ Vrchlického 29, 15000 Praha ☎
+420 257222256 ▤ +420 257222094 **E**: ocko@ocko.tv **W**: ocko.tv.

Regional & Local Stations not shown (via DTT regional muxes)

DTT Tx Networks (MPEG2 exc. where stated)
Licensee Mux 1: České Televize **M**: CT1, CT2 (incl. reg. prgrs), CT24,
sport **Licensee Mux 2**: České Radiokomunikace a.s. ▣ Mahlerovy sady
1, 13000 Praha 3 ▤ +420 242411111 **E**: digital@radiokomunikace.cz **W**:
www.radiokomunikace.cz **M**: TV Nova, Nova Cinema, Prima TV, Prima
COOL, TV Barrandov – **Licensee Mux 3**: Czech Digital Group a.s. ▣
Skokanská 2117/1, 16900 Praha 6 ☎+420 242411411 **E**: mail@digitv.cz
W: www.digitv.cz **M**: CT Art, CT Décko, Prima love, Ócko, Zoom, Slágr
TV, Ocko Gold, Barrandov Kino, Barrandov Gold – **Licensee Mux 4**:
Digital Broadcasting s.r.o. ▣ Stavební 992/1, 70800 Ostrava **W**: www.
multiplex4.cz **M (MPEG4)**: Nova Cinema, TV Relax-Prohoda, TV Rebel,
Telka, Nova Smíchov, TV Fanda, TV Mnam – **Licensee Mux 7**: Progress
Digital s.r.o. ▣ Stavební 992/1, 70800 Ostrava **W**: www.progressdigital.
cz **M (MPEG4)**: CT1 HD, CT2 HD, sport HD, CT Art, CT Décko, Regionální
Televize, Cesty krajem. **Regional licensees/muxes** not shown.

Location	M1	M2	M3	M4	M7	kW
Benešov (Kozmice)	-	-	-	44	23	10
Brno (Barvicova)	-	-	-	46V	47V	10
Brno (Jihlavská)	-	-	-	-	47	10
Brno (Kojál)	29	40	59	-	-	100
Brno (Hády)	29	40	59	-	-	10
Brno (mesto)	29V	40V	59V	-	-	10
C.Budejovice (Klet')	49	39	22	25	32	4x100/63
Cheb (Zelená hora)	36	35	-	-	-	20
Chomutov (Jedlová hora)	33	58	-	-	-	32
Domazlice (Vraní vrch)	34	48	-	-	-	10
Frenštát (Velký Javorník)	-	-	42	-	-	10
Frýdek (Lysá hora)	54	37	-	-	-	25
Hlubocec (Hurka)	-	-	-	63	-	40
Hodonín (Kapansko)	-	-	-	46	-	10
Hradec Kralové (Chlum)	-	-	-	45	-	10
Jablonec nad Nisou	-	-	-	25	-	10
Jáchymov (Klínovec)	36	35	-	45	50	2x50/2x40
Jeseník (Praded)	36	53	51	-	-	100
Jihlava (Javorice)	33	35	30	-	-	100
Jihlava (Vetrny Jenikov)	-	-	42	-	-	10
Kraslice (Snezná)	36	35	-	-	-	10/0.01
Liberec (Ještěd)	43	52	60	-	-	2x50/20
Mariánské Lázne (Dylen)	-	-	-	45	-	50
Mikolov (Devín)	29	40	-	-	-	25
Olomouc (Slavonín)	-	-	-	44	50	100
Ostrava (Hoštálkovice)	54	37	48	-	-	100
Ostrava (Hladnov)	54	37	48	-	-	10
Ostrava (Lanová)	-	-	-	45	38	10
Pardubice	32	39	34	-	-	2x100/10
Plzen	-	-	-	-	38	32
Plzen (Krašov)	34	48	52	-	-	100
Praha (Cukrák)	53	41	59	-	-	100
Praha (Ládví)	-	-	-	42	37	20
Praha (Novodvorská)	-	-	-	-	37	10
Praha (Olšanská)	-	-	-	42V	-	10
Praha (Zizkov)	53V	41V	59V	-	-	32
Rakovník (Loukštín)	-	-	-	44	-	32
Sušice (Svatobor)	49	48	52	56	-	100/71/100/20
Svitavy (Hrebecov)	-	-	-	21	-	10
Teplice	-	-	-	30	-	10
Trutnov (Cerná hora)	40	61	60	-	-	100
Trutnov (Rozhledna)	-	-	-	21	-	20
Uherské Hradiště (Rovnina)	-	-	-	42	41	10
Ústí n.L. (Buková hora)	33	58	55	-	-	100
Ústí n.L. (Krušnohorská)	-	-	-	21	-	10
Ústí n. Orlící	-	-	-	45	-	10
Valašské Klobouky	33	49	-	-	-	25
Velké Popovice (Batošky)	-	-	-	64	-	20
Vimperk	49	39	-	-	-	20
Votice (Mezivrata)	53	41	-	-	-	32
Zlín (Jizní svahy)	-	-	-	42	-	10
Zlín (Tlustá hora)	33	49	25	-	-	2x100/10

Location	M1	M2	M3	M4	M7	kW
Znojmo (Deblínek)	-	-	-	46	-	10

+ sites with txs below 10kW. **Regional muxes** not shown.

System: DVB-T (MPEG4), DVB-T2 (MPEG4) [E]

National Stations
DR (Pub) ▣ TV Byen, Emil Holms Kanal 20, 0999 København C ☎
+45 35203040 ▤ +45 35202644 **E**: presse@dr.dk **W**: www.dr.dk **L.P**:
DG: Maria Rørbye Rønn **Chs**: DR1, DR2, DR3, DR K, DR Ramasjang,
DR Ultra. – **TV 2 DANMARK (Pub)** ▣ Rugaardsvej 25, 5100
Odense C ☎ +45 65919191 ▤ +45 65913322 **E**: tv2@tv2.dk **W**: tv2.
dk **L.P**: CEO: Merete Eldrup. Regional stns (**W**: www.tv2regionerne.
dk): a) TV 2/Bornholm (Brovangen 1, 3720 Aakirkeby), b) TV 2/Fyn
(Olfert Fischers Vej 31, 5220 Odense SØ), c) TV 2/Lorry (Allégade
7-9, 2000 Frederiksberg), d) TV/Midt-Vest (Søvej 2, 7500 Holstebro),
e) TV 2/Nord (Søparken 4, 9440 Åbybro), f) TV Syd (El-vej 2 B, Seest,
6000 Kolding), g) TV2 Øst (Kildemarksvej 7, 4760 Vordingborg), h)
TV 2 / Østjylland (Skejbyparken 1, 8200 Århus N) **Chs (terr.)**: TV 2,
TV 2 Regional Stations, TV 2 Charlie, TV 2 Fri, TV 2 NEWS, TV 2
Sportskanal, TV 2 Zulu.

DTT Tx Networks (DVB-T exc. where indicated)
Licensee Mux 1+2: DIGI-TV I/S ▣ Banestrøget 21, 2630 Taastrup
E: info@digi-tv.dk **W**: www.digi-tv.dk **M1**: DR1, DR2, TV 2 Regional
stns **M2**: DR3, DR K, DR Ramasjang, DR Ultra, Folketinget. – **Licensee
Mux 3-6**: Boxer TV A/S ▣ Langebrogade 6E, 1411 København K **E**:
info@boxertv.dk **W**: www.boxertv.dk **M3✪**: Animal Planet, BBC World
News, Canal 9, Discovery Science, Disney Channel, Disney XD, History
Channel, Kanal 4, Kanal 5, TLC, TV 2 (incl. reg. prgrs), TV3 **M4✪**: 6'eren,
Discovery, DK4, MTV, Nickelodeon, TV 2 Charlie, TV 2 NEWS, TV 2 Zulu,
TV 2 Sportskanal, TV3 Puls, TV3 Sport 1, VH1 Classic **M5 (DVB-T2)✪**:
6'eren HD, Eurosport, National Geographic, TV 2 HD, TV 2 Norge, TV 4
Malmø, TV3+ HD, VH1, ZDF **M6 (DVB-T2)✪**: Kanal 5 HD, TV 2 Fri HD,
TV 2 Sportskanal HD, TV3 HD, TV3 Sport 1 HD.

Location	M1*	M2	M3*	M4	M5	M6	kW
Hadsten	26h	44	24h	56	55	36	50
Hedensted	30f	44	46f	33	55	36	50
Jyderup	58g	51	42g	31	48	23	50
København (1)	53c	51	54c	31	59	23	50
København (2)	53c	51	54c	31	59	23	10
Nakskov	58g	34	42g	38	48	60	10
Nibe	29e	57	50e	37	35	39	50
Rø	59a	56	31a	39	51	32	25
Svendborg	25b	43	27b	22	49	41	25
Thisted	31dV	42V	21dV	43V	22V	49V	25
Tolne	29e	57	50e	37	35	39	10
Tommerup	25b	43	27b	22	49	41	50
Varde	30f	54	46f	33	53	28	50
Viborg	40d	59	21d	56	52	45	50
Videbæk	40d	59	34d	48	52	28	50
Vordingborg	58g	34	42g	38	48	60	50
Åbenrå	37f	50	32f	22	49	41	50

+ sites with txs below 10kW. (1) Søborg (2) Gladsaxe *) incl. TV 2
Reg stns (a-h)

Systems: DVB-T2 (MPEG4); § SECAM-B [E]

RADIODIFFUSION TÉLÉVISION DJIBOUTI (RTD) (Gov) ▣ BP 97,
Djibouti ☎ +253 21352294 ▤ +253 21356502 **E**: rtd@intnet.dj **W**:
www.rtd.dj **L.P**: DG: Abdoulkader Ahmed Idriss **Ch**: Télé Djibouti 1.

DTT Tx Network
Tx Operator: Djibouti Télécom **M**: Télé Djibouti 1 **Txs**: MFN.

NB: No terrestrial TV stations.

System: ATSC [A]

National Station
CORPORACIÓN ESTATAL DE RADIO Y TV (CERTV) (Pub) ▣ Av.

Dr. Tejeda Florentino 8, Sto. Domingo ☎ +1 829 6891220 📠+1 829 6886208 **W:** www.certvdominicana.com **L.P:** Dir: Héctor Olivo. **Txs:** Sto. Domingo ch4 & relay txs.

Local Stations not shown.

EASTER ISLAND (Chile)

System: NTSC-M [A]

TV RAPA NUI ⌨ Hanga Roa, Isla de Pascua. **Tx:** ch13.

ECUADOR

Systems: ISDB-TB [A]; § NTSC-M [A] ⬇2018

National Stations (ᵃ=analogue)
SISTEMA ECUATORIANA DE RADIO Y TELEVISIÓN (Pub)⌨ San Salvador E6-49 y Eloy Alfaro, Edificio Medias Públicos, Quito. **W:** www.tctelevision.com; www.gamatv.com.ec; www.ecuadortv.ec **Chs:** TC Televisión, Ecuador TV, Gama TV. **Txs: TC Televisión:** Quito ᵃch10/ch36 & relay txs, **Gama TV:** Quito ᵃch2/ch30 & relay txs, **Ecuador TV:** Quito ch26 & relay txs. – **CANAL UNO (Comm)** ⌨ Av. del Bosque Mz 112, Ciudadela Kennedy Norte, Guayaquil ☎ +593 4 2680200 📠 +593 4 2680185 **E:** relad_sa@canal1tv.com **W:** www.canal1tv.com. **Txs:** Quito ᵃch13/ch12 & relay txs. – **ECUAVISA (Comm)** ⌨ Bosmediano 447, José Carb, Quito 1 ☎ +593 2 2995300 📠 +593 2 2445488 **W:** www.ecuavisa.com. **Txs:** Quito ᵃch8/ch36 & relay txs. – **RTS (RED TELESISTEMA) (Comm)** ⌨ Av. de los Shyris y Suecia, Edificio Renazzo Plaza #202, Quito ☎ +593 2 2272086 📠 +593 2 2272086 **E:** rts@rts.com.ec **W:** www.rts.com.ec. **Txs:** Quito ᵃch5/ch34 & relay txs. – **RTU (RADIO Y TELEVISIÓN UNIDAS) (Comm)** ⌨ Carrión E5-55 y Juan León Mera, Quito. **E:** noticias@rtunoticias.com **W:** www.rtunoticias.com. **Txs:** Quito ch46 & relay txs. – **TELEAMAZONAS (Comm)** ⌨ Av. A. Granda C. 529 y Av. Brasil, Quito ☎ +593 2 2430350 📠 +593 2 2441620 **E:** contactenos@teleamazonas.com **W:** www.teleamazonas.com. **Txs:** Quito ᵃch4/ch32 & relay txs.

Local Stations not shown.

EGYPT

Systems: # PAL-B/G [E]; DVB-T2 (MPEG4) [E]

EGYPTIAN RADIO AND TV UNION (ERTU) (Pub) ⌨ TV Bldg, Corniche El Nil, Cairo 11511 ☎ +20 2 25757155 📠 +20 2 25746989 **E:** tvinfo@ertu.org **W:** ertu.org **L.P:** Head of TV: Magdi Lashin **Chs (terr.):** Channel 1 & Channel 2 (National), Prgr 3-8 (Regional), Nile TV, Nile Comedy, Nile Culture, Nile Drama, Nile Family, Nile Life, Nile News, Nile Sport

Location	1	2	kW	Location	1	2	kW
Abu Znima	26	29	15.5	Halayeb	9V	11V	31.6
Alexandria	6	11	110	Hassana	34	31	35.5
Aswan	5	9	67	Hurghada	5V	7V	89
Asyut	10	6	60	Idfu	8	11	165
Baris	7V	5V	10	Ismailia	11V	9V	260
Barnis	24	29	830	Kom Ombo	10	7	40
Beni Ali	6V	9V	5	Luxor	11	7	19
Beni Suef	11V	7V	110	Matruh	10	8	39.2
Cairo	5	9	200	Nag Hammadi	5	8	17
Dahab	6V	8V	9.3	Natron	41	44	36.4
Dumyat	58	61	15.2	Port Said	5V	7V	200
El Amain	46	48	126	Qena	9	6	30
El Arish	6V	10V	182	Rafah	45	48	350
El Bawiti	10	8	22.4	Ras El Hekma	32	35	31.6
El Dakhla	8	6	23	Ras Gharib	9	11	66
El Farafra	5V	7V	10	Ras Sedr	58	61	66.2
El Hammam	39	42	69.2	Safaga	11V	9V	50
El Kharga	10V	8V	40	Sallum	9	11	6
El Mahalla	8	10	1600	Sharm El Sheikh	27	33	8.9
El Minya	8V	5V	165	Sidy Barany	49	52	74
El Negila	22	25	74	Siwa	6V	8V	10
El Quseyr	7	5	50	Sohag	7	11	52
El Tur	10	8	33	Suez	7	5	200
Esna	9	18	Taba		32	37	25.7

+ sites with txs below 5kW. 1/2=Channel 1, Channel 2
ERTU El Mahrousa Regional Services
Prgr 3 (Cairo): Cairo ch7 (200kW) **Prgr 4 (Ismailia):** Negila ch28

(74kW), Suez ch30 (20.3kW), Ismailia ch33V (79.4kW), Port Said ch42V (20.3kW), Zagazig ch52 (158kW) **Prgr 5 (Alexandria):** Matruh ch5 (11kW), Siwa ch7V (11kW), Negila ch28 (74kW), Alexandria ch36 (678kW), Ras Hekma ch39 (31.6kW), Hammam ch51 (69kW), Sidi Barany ch55 (74kW) **Prgr 6 (Tanta):** Mahalla ch49 (321kW) **Prgr 7 (El Minya):** Beni Ali ch22V (13.2kW), El Minya ch39V (56kW), Asyut ch48 (117kW), Beni Suef ch51V (43kW), Fayoum ch55 (107kW) **Prgr 8 (Asswan):** Aswan ch21 (67.6kW), Luxor ch22 (69.2kW), Sohag ch27 (340kW), .Kom Ombo ch29 (33.9kW), Qena ch30 (85.1kW), Nag Hamady ch32 (77.6kW), Idfu ch40 (66kW), Isna ch49 (70.9kW).
ERTU Nile Television Network (NTN)
Nile TV: Sharm El Sheikh ch31 (79.4kW), Cairo ch46 (282kW) **Nile Cinema:** Alexandria ch21 (74kW), Sohag ch23 (340kW), Aswan ch24 (67.6kW), Luxor ch25 (69.2kW), Cairo ch28 (282kW), Ismailia ch31 (20.7kW) **Nile Comedy:** Cairo ch30 (282kW) **Nile Culture:** Cairo ch43 (91kW) **Nile Drama:** Cairo ch34 (282kW) **Nile Family:** Cairo ch40 (89kW) **Nile Life:** Cairo ch22 (282kW) **Nile News:** Alexandria ch24 (74kW); Cairo ch26 (282kW) **Nile Sport:** Cairo ch38 (316kW). (Txs below 5kW not mentioned; Pol=H exc. where indicated)

DTT Tx Networks (under construction)
Tx Operator: ERTU **Mux 1:** multiprgr **Tx:** ch27 (Alexandria 10kW), ch32 (Cairo 50kW) **Mux 2:** multiprgr **Tx:** ch36 (Cairo 30kW)

EL SALVADOR

Systems: # NTSC-M [A] ⬇1 Jan 2019; ATSC [A]

National Stations
TELEVISION CULTURAL EDUCATIVA CANAL 10 (Pub) ⌨ Ap. Postal No. 104, Neuva San Salvador ☎ +503 2280499 📠 +503 2280973 **E:** tydiez@es.com.sv **W:** www.tencanal10.tv **Tx:** S.Salvador ch10 (109kW). – **CANAL 12 (Comm)** ⌨ Carretera Panaméricana #12, Antiguo Custatlan, La Libertad, San Salvador ☎ +503 25601212 📠 +503 25101222 **E:** canal12@canal12.com.sv **W:** www.canal12.com. sv **Tx:** S.Salvador ch12. – **TELECORPORACIÓN SALVADOREÑA (TCS) (Comm)** ⌨ Alameda Manuel Enrique Araújo, Edifício Canales 2, 4 y 6, San Salvador ☎ +503 22092000 📠 +503 22092065 **W:** www.esmitv.com **L.P:** CEO: Boris Eserski. **Chs:** Teledos, Canal Cuatro, Canal Seis. **Txs:** S.Salvador Teledos ch2 (100kW), Canal Cuatro ch4 (75kW), Canal Seis ch6 (150kW). – **AGAPE TV CANAL 8 (Rlg)** ⌨ Calle Gerardo Barrios No. 1511, Col. Cucumacayán, Santa Salvador ☎ +503 22812828 📠 +503 22110799 **E:** info@agapetv8.com **W:** www.agapetv8.com **Tx:** S.Salvador ch8 (109kW).

Local Stations not shown.

EQUATORIAL GUINEA

System: PAL-B/G [E]

TELEVISIÓN GUINEA ECUATORIAL (TVGE) (Pub) ⌨ Calle 3 Augusto, Malabo ☎ +240 222515335 **E:** info@rtvge.tv **W:** www.rtvge.tv **L.P:** DG: Téobaldo Nchaso. **Txs:** Santa Isabel ch2 (50kW H) & relay txs. – **ASONGA TELEVISIÓN (Comm)** ⌨ Malabo. **E:** rrhh@rtvasonga.tv **W:** www.asongatv.com **Txs:** (-).

ERITREA

System: PAL-B/G [E]

ERITREA TELEVISION (ERI-TV) (Gov) ⌨ Asmara ☎ +291 1 116033 📠 +291 1 124847 **E:** aslmelashe@yahoo.com **W:** www.eri.tv **L.P:** DG: Asmelash Abraha **Chs:** ERI-TV1, ERI-TV2, ERI-TV3 **Txs: ERI-TV1:** (Pol.=H) Asmara ch5 (5kW), Assab ch11 (5kW) & relay txs. **ERI-TV2:** (-). **ERI-TV3:** (-).

ESTONIA

System: DVB-T (MPEG4), DVT-T2 (MPEG4) [E]

EESTI TELEVISIOON (ETV) (Pub) ⌨ Faehlmanni 12, 15029 Tallinn ☎ +372 6284133 📠 +372 6284155 **E:** etv@etv.ee **W:** etv.err.ee **L.P:** Chmn (ERR): Margus Allikmaa. **Chs:** ETV, ETV2, ETV+ – **TALLINNA TV (TTV) (Municipal)** ⌨Rävala pst 12, 10143 Tallinn ☎ +372 6005523 **E:** info@tallinnatv.eu **W:** www.tallinnatv.eu **L.P:** Chmn: Allan Alaküla – **AS KANAL 2 (Comm)** ⌨ Maakri 23a, 10145 Tallinn ☎ +372 6662450 📠 +372 6662451 **L.P:** DG: Urmas Oru **Chs:** Kanal 2, Kanal 11,

Kanal 12 – **AS TV3 (Comm)** ✉ Peterburi tee 81, 11415 Tallinn ☎ +372 6220200 🖷 +372 6220201 **L.P:** CEO: Priit Leito **Chs:** TV3, TV6.

DTT Tx Networks (DVB-T/MPEG4 except where indicated)
Licensee Mux 1, 4, 6+7: Levira AS ✉ Kloostrimetsa tee 58 A, 15026 Tallinn ☎ +372 6804000 🖷 +372 6804001 **E:** levira@levira.ee **W:** www.levira.ee **M1:** ETV, ETV2, Kanal 2, Tallinna TV. **M4:** tbd **M6:** ETV+, France 24, TV3 **M7 (DVB-T2):** ETV HD, ETV2 HD. – **Licensee Mux 2+3:** Starman AS ✉ Akadeemia tee 28, 12618 Tallinn ☎ +372 6779977 🖷 +372 6779907 **E:** pressiinfo@starman.ee **W:** www.starman.ee **M2✪:** Animal Planet, Discovery, Eurosport, History, Kanal 12, Kidzone TV, NTV Mir, PBK Estonia, REN TV Estonia, RTL TV, Setana Sports, Sony TV, Sony Turbo, TV3+, TV6 **M3✪:** ETV+, Euronews, Eurosport 2, Filmzone, Filmzone+, Fox, Fox Life, Hustler TV, ID Discovery, National Geographic, Pingviniukas, Seitse, TLC, Travel.

Location	M1	M2	M3	M4	M6	M7	kW
Ellamaa	28	-	-	-	-	-	8.8
Koeru	39	27	57	41	44	60	5/2x1.6/2/6/2.5
Kohtla-Nõmme	33	48	58	34	29	46	15/2x2/1/2x2
Pehka	28V	-	-	37V	-	-	6.6/3.3
Pärnu	26	56	53	36	32	49	18/2x20/15.5/2x7
Tallinn (TV-tower)	28	59	45	37	30	42	19/2x15/6/20/8.5
Valgjärve	23	52	47	55	40	35	20/2x7/6/17/8

+ sites with txs below 5kW **NB:** Mux 5 is currently not assigned.

ETHIOPIA

Systems: # PAL-B/G [E] ↻2016; DVB-T2 (MPEG4) [E]

National Station
ETHIOPIAN BROADCASTING CORP. (EBC) (Gov) ✉ P.O.Box 5544, Addis Ababa ☎ +251 11 5505483 🖷 +251 11 5505174 **W:** www.ebc. et **L.P:** GM: Berhane Kidanemariam **Chs (terr.):** EBC1, EBC2, EBC3, reg. stns **Txs:** EBC1: (pol.H) Shashemene ch5 (1kW), Debrebirhan ch6 (1kW), Debre Markos ch6 (1kW), Goba ch6 (1kW), Addis Ababa ch7 (25kW), Harar ch7 (1kW), Mekele ch7 (1kW), Gambella ch8 (1kW), Araminch ch9 (1kW), Assaita ch9 (1kW), Axum ch9 (1kW), Dessie ch9 (1kW), Godie ch9 (1kW), Assosa ch11 (1kW), Nazereth ch11 (1kW) & txs below 1kW; **EBC2:** Addis Ababa ch(-) (25kW); **EBC3:** Addis Ababa ch42 (10kW), to be converted to DTT.

Local Stations (all Gov)
Dire TV: Dire Dawa; ch9. **Harari TV:** Harar; tx: (-). **Oromia Radio & TV (ORTV):** P.O.Box 2919, Adama; Adama ch9 & netw. **Somali TV:** Jijiga; tx: (-).

DTT Tx Network (under construction)
Tx Operator: EBC **Mux:** EBC1, EBC2, EBC3, EBC4 **Txs:** ch42 (Addis Ababa 10kW) & network.

FALKLAND ISLANDS (UK)

System: DVB-T (MPEG4) [E]

BFBS-TV (British Mil) ✉ BFBS Falkland Islands, Mt. Pleasant, BFPO 655 ☎ +500 32179 🖷 +500 32193 **E:** falklands@bfbs.com **M:** BBC One*, BBC Two/CBBC*, ITV*, BFBS Extra/Cbeebies*, Sky News, Nepali TV* (*=time-shifted) ✖ BFBS R. (Falkland Islands), BFBS R.2, BFBS Gurkha R. **Txs:** ch27 (SFN).

FAROE ISLANDS (Denmark)

System: DVB-T (MPEG4) [E]

KRINGVARP FØROYA - SJÓNVARP (KVF) (Pub) ✉ P.O.Box 1299, 110 Tórshavn ☎ +298 347500 🖷 +298 347501 **E:** kringvarp@kvf.fo **W:** kvf.fo **L.P:** GM: Dia Midjord – **IKTUS (RIg)** ✉ c/o Anja Hansen, Landsvegur 9, 511 Gøtugjógv **E:** iktus@iktus.fo **W:** iktus.fo.

DTT Tx Networks (*=MPEG2)
Licensee Mux 1-4: Televarpið ✉ P.O.Box 3128, 110 Tórshavn ☎ +298 340340 🖷 +298 340341 **E:** televarp@televarp.fo **W:** tv.fo **M1✪:** TV3+, National Geographic, BBC Entertainment, BBC World News, Kanal 4, Kanal 5, Visjon Norge **M2 (partly✪):** KVF, DR1, DR2, TV3, TV3 Puls, NRK1 **M3✪:** DR Ramasjang, Viasat Action, Viasat Drama, Viasat Family, Viasat Film, Discovery, MTV, Nick jr./VH1 **M4✪:** TV2 Danmark, TV3 Sport, Eurosport, Animal Planet, Disney Channel, Kanal 6, Rás 1. **Licensee Mux 5:** R2 Net ✉ Sølðarfjarðarvefur 11, 660 Sølðarfjørður ☎ +298 559997 **E:** r2net@r2net.fo **W:** r2net.fo **M5:** 10'arin, IKTUS.

Location	M1	M2	M3	M4	M5	kW
Brúnaskarð	57	59	65	67	-	0.25
Klakkur	60	66	68	58	31	0.25
Knúkur	53	55	61	63	-	0.04
Stongin	52	50	48	46	34	0.04
Støðlafjall	52	50	48	46	-	0.04
Velbastaður	52V	50V	48V	46V	-	0.04

+ repeaters.

FIJI

Systems: DVB-T2 (MPEG4) [NZ]; § PAL-B [NZ]

FIJI BROADCASTING CORP. (FBC) (Pub) ✉ 69 Gladstone Rd, Suva ☎ +679 3314333 🖷 +679 3220990 **E:** infocenter@fbc.com.fj **W:** www. fbc.com.fj **L.P:** CEO: Riyaz Sayed-Khaiyum. **Ch:** FBC TV. – **FIJI ONE (Comm)** ✉ P.O.Box 150, 04201 Kerava ☎ +679 3305100 🖷 +679 3304630 **E:** fijitv@is.com.fj **W:** fijione.tv **L.P:** CEO (Fiji TV Ltd): Geoffrey Smith. – **MAI TV (Comm)** ✉ Grantham Rd, Suva ☎ +679 3275051 **E:** info@ tv.com.fj **W:** www.tv.com.fj **L.P:** CEO: Richard Broadbridge.

DTT Tx Network (under construction)
Tx Operator: FBC **M:** FBC TV, Fiji One, Mai TV **Txs:** nationwide MFN

FINLAND

System: DVB-T (MPEG2), DVB-T2 (MPEG4) [E]

National Stations
YLEISRADIO OY (Pub) ✉ Radiokatu 5, 00024 Helsinki ☎ +358 9 14801 🖷 +358 9 14805148 **W:** www.yle.fi **L.P:** CEO: Lauri Kivinen. **Chs:** Yle TV1, Yle TV2, Yle Teema; Yle Fem (in Swedish). – **ALFA TV (Comm)** ✉ P.O.Box 150, 04201 Kerava ☎ +358 10 3273000 **E:** info@alfatv.fi **W:** www.alfatv.fi **L.P:** Chmn/CEO: Hannu Haukka – **CANAL DIGITAL (Comm)** ✉ P.O.Box 2, 00381 Helsinki ☎ +358 9 54264200 🖷 +358 9 54264270 **E:** asiakaspalvelu@canaldigital.fi **W:** www.canaldigital.fi – **MTV3 (Comm)** ✉ Ilmalankatu 2, 00240 Helsinki ☎ +358 10 300300 🖷 +358 10 3005164 **W:** www.mtv3.fi **L.P:** CEO (MTV3 Media): Heikki Rotko **Chs (terr.):** MTV3, MTV3 Max, MTV3 Max Sport 1/2, JIM, Sub, MTV3 Juniori, MTV3 Leffa – **NELONEN (Comm)** ✉ Tehtaankatu 27-29D, 00150 Helsinki ☎ +358 9 4545414 **W:** www.nelonen.fi **L.P:** Pres (Nelonen Media): Pia Kalsta. **Chs (terr.):** Nelonen, Liv, Nelonen Prime, Nelonen Maailma, Nelonen Nappula, Nelonen Pro 1, Nelonen Pro 2. – **SBS DISCOVERY TELEVISION OY (Comm)** ✉ Tallberginkatu 1C, 00180 Helsinki ☎ +358 20 7870850 🖷 +358 9 75154188 **E:** info_dnf@discovery.com **W:** kutonen.fi **Chs:** TV5, Kutonen, Frii.

DTT Tx Networks (DVB-T2 except °= DVB-T/MPEG2)
Licensee: Mux 1-6 Digita Oy ✉ P.O.Box 135, 00521 Helsinki ☎ +358 20 411711 **E:** info@digita.fi **W:** www.digita.fi **M1°:** Yle TV1, Yle TV2, Yle Teema, Yle Fem/SVT World, Alfa TV, AVA ✖ Yle Klassinen, Yle Puhe, Yle Mondo **M2°:** MTV3, Nelonen, Sub, Liv, Estradi, MTV3 Max✪, MTV3 Juniori✪, MTV3 Leffa✪ **M3°(✪exc.*):** Hero*, Iskelmä TV/Harju & Pöntinen*, FOX, Frii, C More First, C More Series, Disney Channel, Nelonen Pro 1, Nelonen Pro 2, MTV3 Max Sport 1, Digiviihde **M4:** Eurosport 2, Animal Planet, National Geographic, Discovery ID, Disney Jr, Disney XD, MTV3 Fakta, MTV3 Sport 2, C More Hits, Viasat Sport, Viasat Golf, Viasat Sport Finland, Viasat XTRA, Viasat Film, Viasat History, Viasat NHL Xtra 1-7, Nelonen Pro 3-8 **M5°(✪exc.*):** TV5*, JIM*, Kutonen*, Discovery Channel, Eurosport, MTV, Nick jr., Nelonen Prime, Nelonen Maailma, Nelonen Nappula. **M6:** HD Life, TV Etusivu, AdultTV.fi HD, Alfa TV HD, Iskelmä TV/Harju & Pöntinen HD – **Licensee Mux 7-9:** DNA Oy ✉ P.O.Box 135, 00521 Helsinki ☎ +358 20 411711 **E:** info@digita.fi **W:** www.digita.fi **M7(✪exc.*):** Yle 1 HD*, Yle TV2 HD*, Yle Teema HD*, Yle Fem HD*, MTV3 HD **M8✪:** C More First HD, MTV MAX HD, MTV Sport 2 HD, Nelonen Pro 1 HD, Nelonen Pro 2 HD, Viasat Film Family HD **M9✪:** Viasat Sport Finland HD, Viasat Sport 1 HD, Viasat Hockey HD, Viasat Golf HD, Viasat Film HD.

Location	M1	M2	M3	M4	M5	M6	M7	M8	M9	kW
Anjalankoski	22	27	53	56	41	-	-	-	-	50
Espoo	32	44	46	53	35	26	6	8	5	5x50/3x1.9
Eurajoki	38	45	52	55	36	-	9	7	6	5x50/3x1.9
Fiskars	32	44	46	58	-	-	-	-	-	10
Haapavesi	34	42	53	57	-	-	-	-	-	50
Iisalmi	26	38	-	-	-	-	-	-	-	30
Inari	48	25	-	-	-	-	-	-	-	12
Joutseno	47	35	57	32	26	-	-	-	-	50
Jyväskylä	30	60	55	41	25	35	11	9	5	5x50/3x3.5
Kerimäki	30	37	33	58	-	-	-	-	-	50
Kiihtelysvaara	26	59	-	-	-	-	-	-	-	30

Location	M1	M2	M3	M4	M5	M6	M7	M8	M9	kW
Koli	25	40	47	51	-	-	-	-	-	60
Kruunupyy	27	22	41	44	30	-	-	-	-	50
Kuopio	24	31	39	52	46	-	6	7	8	5x50/3x3.5
Lahti	33	47	57	51	40	48	7	9	5	5x50/2x3/2
Lapua	38	37	55	48	24	-	9	5		5x50/2x3/2
Mikkeli	29	43	59	38	-	-	10	9	12	4x50/3x3.4
Oulu	41	51	54	37	24	33	-	-	-	50
Pernaja	23	50	-	39	-	-	-	-	-	10
Pihtipudas	50	45	58	-	-	-	-	-	-	80
Posio	31	39	-	-	-	-	-	-	-	14
Pyhätunturi	60	41	-	-	-	-	-	-	-	16
Pyhävuori	28	41	-	35	-	-	-	-	-	10
Rovaniemi	43	46	-	53	-	-	-	-	-	10
Ruka	33	48	59	-	-	-	-	-	-	10
Taivalkoski	32	38	-	-	-	-	-	-	-	14
Tammela	22	27	50	43	30	-	-	-	-	60
Tampere	34	23	58	59	42	46	-	-	-	50
Tervola	40	42	-	44	-	-	-	-	-	18
Turku	51	54	57	60	29	49	-	-	-	4x100/50
Vaasa	38	37	-	57	-	-	11	7	5	3x10/3x4.4
Vuokatti	30	52	55	59	-	-	-	-	-	80
Ylläs	30	36	-	-	-	-	-	-	-	14
Ähtäri	52	44	-	-	-	-	-	-	-	50

+ sites with txs below 10kW.

Licensee Local Mux: Anvia Oyj ⌨ Silmukkatie 6, 65100 Vaasa ☎ +358 64 114111 📠+358 63170146 **E:** info@anvia.fi **W:** www.anvia. fi **Mux✪:** SVT1, SVT2, SVTB/SVT24, SVT Kunskapskanalen, TV3, TV4, BotniaTV, När-TV, Krs-TV **Txs:** ch31 (Vaasa 3.5kW + SFN), ch33 (SFN), ch35 (SFN).

Åland

ÅLANDS RADIO/TV AB (Pub) ⌨ Ålandsvägen 24, 22101 Mariehamn ☎ +358 18 26060 📠 +358 18 26520 **E:** info@radiotv.ax **W:** www.radiotv. ax **LP:** Chmn: Jesper Eliasson – **ÅLAND 24 (Comm)** ⌨ Uppgårdsvägen 6, 22101 Mariehamn **E:** +358 18 23440 **W:** www.aland24.ax.

DTT Tx Network

Licensee: Ålands Radio/TV AB **M1:** SVT1, SVT2, SVTB/SVT24, SVT Kunskapskanalen, Ålandskanalen, Åland 24 **M2:** Yle TV1, Yle TV2, YLE Fem, TV4 **Txs: M1:** ch25 (Smedsböle 30kW) **M2:** ch35 (Smedsböle 30kW).

System: DVB-T (MPEG2 until 5 Apr; MPEG4) [E]; DVB-T2 (MPEG4) [E]

National Stations

FRANCE 24 (Pub) ⌨ 80 rue Camille Desmoulins, 92130 Issy-les-Moulineaux **LP:** Pres/DG: Marie-Christine Saragosse **W:** www.france24. com **NB:** terrestrially available in all French overseas territories, and via ch33 (Paris/Tour Eiffel 5kW) in the Île-de-France region. – **FRANCE TÉLÉVISIONS (Pub)** ⌨ 7 esplanade Henri de France, 75907 Paris CEDEX 15 ☎ +33 156226000 **W:** www.francetelevisions.fr; www.francetv.fr **LP:** Pres: Delphine Ernotte Cunci ⌨ France 5: 10 rue Horace Vernet, 92123 Issy-les-Moulineaux CEDEX 9 ☎ +33 156229191. ⌨ France Ô/La 1ère: 35/37 rue Danton, 92240 Malakoff ☎ +33 155227100. **Chs: La 1ère** (for French overseas territories, www.la1ere.fr), **France 2** (www.france2. fr), **France 3** (www.france3.fr) & regional prgrs, **France 4** (www.france4. fr), **France 5** (www.france5.fr), **France Ô** (www.franceo.fr) – **ARTE (Pub)** ⌨ 8 rue Marceau, 92785 Issy-les-Moulineaux CEDEX 9 ☎ +33 155007777 **W:** www.arte.tv **LP:** Pres: Véronique Cayla – **LA CHAÎNE PARLEMENTAIRE – ASSEMBLÉE NATIONALE (LCP) (Pub)** ⌨ 106 rue de l'Université, 75007 Paris ☎ +33 140639050 **W:** www.lcp.fr **LP:** Pres/DG: Marie-Eve Malouines – **PUBLIC SÉNAT (Pub)** ⌨ 92 boulevard Raspail, 75006 Paris ☎ +33 142344400 📠 +33 142344469 **W:** www. publicsenat.fr **LP:** Pres/DG: Emmanuel Kessler – **6TER (Comm)** ⌨ 89/91 avenue Charles de Gaulle, 92200 Neuilly-sur-Seine ☎ +33 141926666 **W:** www.6ter.fr **LP:** DG: Catherine Schöfer – **BFM TV (Comm)** ⌨ 12 rue d'Oradour-sur-Glane, 75740 Paris CEDEX 15 ☎ +33 171191181 **W:** www.bfmtv.com **LP:** Pres: Alain Weill – **CANAL+ (Comm)** ⌨ 1 place du spectacle, 92863 Issy-les-Moulineaux CEDEX 9 ☎ +33 171353535 **W:** www.canalplus.fr **LP:** Pres.: Bertrand Meheut. **Chs (terr.):** Canal+, Canal+ Cinéma, Canal+ Sport. – **CHERIE 25 (Comm)** ⌨ 46/50 avenue Théophile Gautier, 75016 Paris ☎ +33 140713929 **W:** www.cherie25.fr **LP:** Pres: Vincent Broussard – **D8 / D17 (Comm)** ⌨ 1 place du spectacle, 92863 Issy les Moulineaux CEDEX 9 ☎ +33 171353535 **W:** www.d8.tv / www. d17.tv **LP:** DG: Xavier Gandon – **GULLI (Comm)** ⌨ 28 rue François 1er, 75008 Paris ☎+33 156365555 **W:** www.gulli.fr **LP:** Pres: Gérald-Brice

Viret – **I>TELE (Comm)** ⌨ 1 rue les Enfants du Paradis, Batiment C, 92652 Boulogne-Billancourt CEDEX ☎ +33 171355555 **W:** www.itele.fr **LP:** DG: Cécilia Ragueneau – **L'ÉQUIPE 21 (Comm)** ⌨ 4 cours de l'Île Seguin, 92102 Boulogne-Billancourt CEDEX ☎ +33 140932020 **W:** www.lequipe21. fr **LP:** Pres: Xavier Spender – **LCI (Comm)** ⌨ 54 avenue de la Voie Lactée, 92656 Boulogne-Billancourt CEDEX ☎ +33 141412345 **W:** lci.tf1.fr **LP:** Pres: Catherine Nayle – **M6 (Comm)** ⌨ 89/91 avenue Charles de Gaulle, 92575 Neuilly-sur-Seine CEDEX ☎ +33 141926666 📠 +33 141926610 **W:** www.m6.fr **LP:** Pres: Nicolas de Tavernost – **NRJ 12 (Comm)** ⌨ 46/50 av. Théophile Gautier, 75016 Paris ☎ +33 140713929 **W:** www.nrj12.fr **LP:** DG: Vincent Broussard – **NUMERO 23 (Comm)** ⌨ 17 rue du Pont-aux-Choux, 75003 Paris ☎ +33 176214610 **W:** www.numero23.fr **LP:** Pres: Pascal Houzelot (NB: Stn will cease on 30 June 2016) – **PARIS PREMIÈRE (Comm)** ⌨ 89/91 avenue Charles de Gaulle, 92575 Neuilly-sur-Seine CEDEX ☎ +33 141925717 **W:** www.paris-premiere.fr **LP:** Pres: Philippe Bony – **PLANÈTE+ (Comm)** ⌨ 1 place du Spectacle, 92823 Issy-les-Moulineaux CEDEX 9 ☎ +33 171353535 **W:** www.planeteplus.com **LP:** DG: René Saal – **RMC DÉCOUVERTE (Comm)** ⌨ 12 rue d'Oradour sur Glane, 75015 Paris ☎ +33 171191035 **W:** www.rmcdecouverte.com **LP:** DG: Alain Weill – **TF1 / HD1 / NT1 / TMC (Comm)** ⌨ 1 quai du Point du Jour, 92656 Boulogne-Billancourt, CEDEX ☎ +33 141411234 **W:** www. tf1.fr **LP:** Pres: Nonce Paolini (TF1), Jean-François Lancelier (HD1/NT1), Jean Pastorelli (TMC) – **W9 (Comm)** ⌨ 89/91 avenue Charles de Gaulle, 92575 Neuilly-sur-Seine CEDEX ☎ +33 141927373 **W:** www.w9.fr **LP:** DG: Jérôme Fouqueray.

Local/Regional Stations

Txs: (a-s) or (#) = via txs of (National) Mux 1 (a-s via txs of 10kW & above, see main tx table, # via txs below 10kW, txs not shown); all others = via txs of the (Regional) Mux 15 (txs not shown).

Alsace 20: 333A avenue de Colmar, 67100 Strasbourg (a). **Angers Télé:** 3 rue de la Rame, 49100 Angers (#). **Azur TV:** 16 avenue Edouard Grinda, 06200 Nice (r). **BDM TV:** 51 avenue de Flandres, 75019 Paris. **BFM Business Paris:** 12 rue d'Oradour sur Glane, 75015 Paris (n). **BIP TV:** Rue des Noues Chaudes, 36105 Issoudun CEDEX (#). **Canal 32:** 7 rue Raymond Aron, 10120 Saint André les Vergers. **CINAPS TV:** 17 rue des Tiphoines, 91240 Saint Michel sur Orge. **D!CI TV:** ZA La Grande Île Nord, 05230 Chorges (#). **Demain IDF:** 1 rue Patry, 92220 Bagneux. **Grand Lille TV:** 1 rue Archimède, 59200 Villeneuve d'Ascq. **IDF1:** 7 rue des Bretons, 93210 La Plaine Saint-Denis. **La Chaîne Normande:** 4 passage de la Luciline, Le Vauban - Immeuble A, 76000 Rouen (b). **LDVTV:** Lycée Léonard de Vinci, Le Mazel, 43120 Monistrol-sur-Loire. **LM TV Sarthe:** 21/25 rue Pasteur, 72000 Le Mans (c). **Matélé:** Espace Créatis, 6 avenue Archimède, 02100 Saint Quentin (o). **Mirabelle TV:** 2 rue Saint Vincent, 57140 Woippy (d). **Tébéo:** 19 rue Jean Macé, 29200 Brest (f). **TébéSud:** 8 rue Auguste Nayel, 56100 Lorient (j). **Télénantes:** 10 rue Voltaire, 44000 Nantes (e). **Télé Bocal:** 12 villa Ribérolle, 75020 Paris. **TéléGrenoble:** 109 rue Hilaire de Chardonnet, 38100 Grenoble (#). **TéléPaese:** 36 chemin de Palazzi, 20220 Sant-Reparata-di-Balagna. **TELIM TV:** 15 rue du Général Catroux, 87000 Limoges (s). **TLC (Télévision Locale du Choletais):** ZI la Bergerie, rue Amère, 49280 La Séguinière. **TLM (Télé Lyon Métropole):** 227 cours Lafayette, 69006 Lyon CEDEX 7 (#). **TL7 Horizon Numérique:** Rue Jules Verne, 42530 Saint Genest Lerpt. **TV Sud Camargue Cévennes:** 240 rue Le Corbusier, 30000 Nîmes. **TV Sud Montpellier:** 753 avenue de la Pompignane, 34170 Castelnau-le-Lez (q). **TV Sud PO:** 753 avenue de la Pompignane, 34170 Castelnau-le-Lez (#).**TV Sud Provence:** 37/41 rue Guibal, 13303 Marseille CEDEX 3 (#). **TV Tours:** 232 avenue de Grammont, 37019 Tours CEDEX 1 (h). **TV Vendée:** ZI le Séjour, 13 rue Thomas Edison, 85170 Dompierre sur Yon. **TVPI:** 1 rue Contresta, 64210 Bidart (m). **TV7 Bordeaux:** 73 avenue Thiers, 33100 Bordeaux (i). **TV8 Mont-Blanc:** Route des Pontets, 74320 Sevrier CEDEX. **TVR Rennes 35 Bretagne:** 19 rue de la Quintaine, 35000 Rennes (g). **Vosges Télévision Images Plus:** 2 rue de la Chipotte, 88007 Épinal (k). **Wéo La Télé Nord Pas de Calais:** 8 place du Général de Gaulle, 59023 Lille CEDEX (l).

DTT Tx Networks ([1]until 5 Apr 2016, [2]from 5 Apr 2016) **Licensee Mux 1:** Société de gestion du réseau R1 ⌨ 7 esplanade Henri-de-France, 75015 Paris ☎ +33 156226000 📠 +33 156229961 **M:** France 2, France 3 + reg prgrs, France 4[2], France Ô, local stations, (France 5[1], LCP/Public Sénat[1]) – **Licensee Mux 2:** Nouvelles télévisions numériques ⌨ 1 place du Spectacle, 92130 Issy-les-Moulineaux ☎ +33 171354839 **M:** BFM TV, D8, D17, Gulli, i>TELE, (France 4[1]) – **Licensee Mux 3:** Compagnie du numérique hertzien ⌨ 1 place du Spectacle, 92863 Issy-les-Moulineaux ☎ +33 171350151 **M✪:** Canal+°, Canal+ Cinéma, Canal+ Sport°, LCP², Paris Premiere°², Planète+ – **Licensee Mux 4:** Multi 4 ⌨ 89 avenue Charles de Gaulle, 92200 Neuilly-sur-Seine ☎ +33 141926140 **M:** 6Ter², Arte, France 5², M6², NT1, W9, (Paris Première✪°[1]) – **(Licensee Mux 5[1]:** MR5 ⌨ 89 avenue Charles de Gaulle, 92200 Neuilly-sur-Seine ☎ +33 141926666 **M:** TF1, France 2, M6) – **Licensee Mux 6:** SMR6 ⌨ 1 quai du Point-du-Jour, 92100 Boulogne-Billancourt ☎ +33 141411234 **M:** Arte, LCP/Public Sénat², NRJ 12, TF1², TMC, (LCI✪[1]) – **Licensee Mux 7:**

MHD7 ✆1 quai du Point-du-Jour, 92100 Boulogne-Billancourt ☎ +33 141411234 **M:** Chérie 25, HD1, L'Équipe 21, Numero 23³, RMC Découverte² – **(Licensee Mux 8':** Société R8 ✆ 89 avenue Charles de Gaulle, 92200 Neuilly-sur-Seine ☎ +33 141926666 **M:** 6ter, RMC Découverte, Numéro 23) – **Licensees Local/Regional Mux 15:** various local/regional licensees **M:** various local/regional stns (depending on region, see chapter "Regional/Local Stations"). **NB:** HD versions not indicated. Until 5 Apr 2016: MPEG2 exc. M5,7+8 & HD versions on other muxes; from 5 Apr 2016: all muxes MPEG4 °) incl. unencrypted sequences (on Canal+ Sport; in MPEG2) ³) until 30 June 2016.

Location	1	2	3	4	(5)	6	7	(8)	kW
Abbeville	57	28	33	55	58	39	22	35	4x80/30/3x80
Ajaccio	21	51	34	44	37	31	24	53	64
Amiens	41	52	49	47	60	44	50	59	40/29/6x40
Aurillac (Labastide)	54	45	43	51	42	48	39	52	40/35.2/6x40
Autun	48	51	54	35	42	32	53	45	4x40/36/3x40
Auxerre	52	50	49	31	60	44	23	55	4x40/13/3x40
Avignon	45	36	33	47	39	42	57	51	50/33/6x50
Bar-le-Duc	48	30	57	22	44	50	51	28	13
Bastia	21	51	34	44	37	31	24	53	32/2x37/2x32/36/2x32
Bayonne	56	m42	45	49	57	58	43	51	25
Bergerac	33	41	56	31	35	58	59	53	40
Besançon (Lomont)	29	44	54	23	45	47	26	41	50
Besançon (Montf.)	29	44	54	23	60	47	26	41	25
Bordeaux	23i	37	60	39	57	30	55	45	63/37/6x63
Bourges	56	46	43	24	40	36	33	55	4x63/40/2x63/46
Brest	43f	58	35	39	30	34	46	37	(*)
Caen	25	42	22	29	45	28	30	39	100/50/100/94/3x100/88
Carcassonne	60	31	43	57	42	56	41	46	50/27/6x50
Chambéry	23	29	51	54	57	26	-	-	13
Charleville-Méz.	44	32	26	22	34	23	40	36	100/27/51/54/4x50
Chartres	47	21	49	50	55	44	52	40	4x25/11/3x25
Cherbourg-Octev.	35	34	59	37	60	36	30	50	10/7/2x11/8/11/2x10
Clermont-Ferrand	25n	47	22	30	52	28	29	41	50
Corte	21	51	34	44	37	31	24	53	10/6/6x10
Dijon	37	50	59	33	28	32	53	39	32
Dunkerque	42	52	27	45	31	21	25	28	13/6/2x13/4/3x13
Gex	45	21	57	55	58	24	39	63	69
Hirson	48o	32	27	51	35	54	39	25	80/3x22/3x80
Laval	33	58	43	57	60	51	35	53	9/14/4x10/8/9
Le Havre	43	44	57	32	41	46	47	35	20/15/6x30/20/13/20
Le Mans	26c	34	22	59	37	36	35	46	3x80/67/32/80/2x32
Lille	24l	23	27	26	31	21	30	59	80/20/80/14/3x80/30
Limoges	49	47	50	34	44	29	46	26	100/70/6x100
Longwy	47d	59	31	22	39	25	33	58	2x10/5/10/2x7/2x10
Lyon (Mt Pilat)	43	44	59	40	49	46	57	41	126
Marseille	23p	59	30	35	27	26	29	38	2x100/32/10/4x100
Metz	36d	59	31	22	39	37	34	58	100/90/80/85/62/3x90
Montpellier	40q	52	51	53	49	56	41	55	(**)
Mulhouse	24a	27	54	37	53	21	50	41	100
Nancy	53d	26	23	22	29	52	51	28	50/31/6x50
Nantes	47e	23	30	54	44	29	32	39	98/2x65/83/4x65
Niort	25	52	22	40	27	28	43	36	7x70/27
Paris	35n	25	22	30	28	32	42	58	50
Parthenay	48	49	33	55	60	36	43	57	5x13/6/2x13
Reims	53	56	43	46	34	45	40	36	80
Rennes	21g	40	27	49	55	24	46	31	7x80/40
Rouen	26b	34	33	53	23	51	37	40	45/20/10/5x40
Saint-Raphaël	39r	54	28	25	22	48	45	43	63
Sarrebourg	50d	26	23	22	56	25	34	47	50/20/40/4x50/40/3x50
Sens	47	50	49	31	60	44	23	55	4x10/7/3x10
Strasbourg	48a	40	43	22	56	25	51	47	50/2x20/10/4x20
Toulon	58	54	28	25	22	48	29	43	10
Toulouse	21	38	24	27	25	36	34	32	50
Tours	42h	23	45	24	37	29	58	31	50/42/2x50/20/2x50/20
Troyes	26	21	27	24	29	36	23	41	4x100/63/3x100
Ussel	23s	27	24	55	44	36	40	26	10/6/6x10
Vannes	57j	25	53	48	22	50	28	33	2x20/2x34/20/22/2x20
Verdun	47	59	31	22	39	23	33	58	2x100/4x65/2x100
Vittel	55k	58	59	37	45	32	42	40	2x10/7/5x10

+ sites with txs below 10kW. Pol.=H. (*)191/144/107/140/120/118/2x 100kW (**)100/32/35/100/32/100/80 1-8=National Muxes 1-8 **NB:** In preparation of the re-assignment of the 700MHz band to mobile services, muxes 5+8 will close on 5 Apr 2016 (prgrs will be moved to other muxes). Txs on chs 49-60 will gradually move to lower chs until 30 June 2019. – DVB-T2 (MPEG4) trials not shown.

FRENCH GUIANA

System: DVB-T (MPEG4) [E]

GUYANE 1ÈRE (Pub) ✆ Boulevard du docteur Lama, F-97354 Rémire-Montjoly ☎ +594 594256700 🖷 +594 594302649 **W:** guyane.la1ere.fr **LP:** Dir: Gérald Prufer. – **ANTENNE TÉLÉ GUYANE (ATV) (Comm)** ✆

Boute de la Madeleine, Immeuble Verriers, F-97300 Cayenne ☎ +594 594256940 🖷 +594 594256947 **W:** www.myatg.tv **LP:** Pres: Jean-Paul Le Pelletier – **KOUROU TV (KTV) (Comm)** ✆ 100 Avenue Boudinot, F-97310 Kourou ☎ +594 594222130 **LP:** Pres: Emmanuel Toko.

DTT Tx Networks
Tx Operator: TDF **Mux:** Guyane 1ère, France 2-5, France Ô, France 24, Arte, ATV, KTV **Txs:** MFN.

FRENCH POLYNESIA

System: DVB-T (MPEG4) [E]

POLYNÉSIE 1ÈRE (Pub) ✆ BP 60125, F-98702 Faa'a ☎ +689 689861616 🖷 +689 689861611 **W:** polynesie.la1ere.fr **LP:** Dir: Jean-Philippe Pascal. – **TAHITI NUI TV (TNTV) (Comm)** ✆ BP 348, F-98713 Papeete ☎ +689 689473636 🖷 +689 689532721 **E:** tntv@ tntv.pf **W:** www.tntv.pf **LP:** Pres: Jean-Paul Barral.

DTT Tx Networks
Tx Operator: TDF **Mux:** Polynésie 1ère, France 2-5, France Ô, France 24, Arte, TNTV **Txs:** MFN.

FRENCH SO. & ANTARTIC LANDS

NB: No terrestrial TV station.

GABON

Systems: DVB-T (MPEG2); § SECAM-K1 [VHF=K]

GABON TÉLÉVISION (Gov) ✆ BP 10150, Libreville ☎ +241 1732152 🖷 +241 1732153 **E:** ggabontelevisions@gmail.com **W:** www. facebook.com/GabonTelevision **Chs:** RTG1, RTG2. – **TV+ CHAÎNE 3 (Comm)** ✆BP 8344, Libreville ☎ +241 1775740 🖷 +241 1729204.

DTT Tx Networks
Tx Operator: Digital TV ✆ BP 7331, Libreville ☎ +241 6663666 **W:** www.tntafrica.com **Muxes 1-6 (partly ◑):** multiprgr **Txs:** MFN.

GALAPAGOS ISLANDS (Ecuador)

System: NTSC-M [A]

TELE GALÁPAGOS (Rlg) ✆ Misión Franciscana, Puerto Baquerizo Moreno, Isla San Cristobal, Galapagos, Ecuador ☎ +593 5 2520144 **Tx:** ch13.

GAMBIA

System: # PAL-I [E]; DVB-T2 (MPEG4) [E] planned

GAMBIA RADIO & TELEVISION (Gov) ✆ P.O.Box 2380, Serekunda ☎ +220 4374251 🖷 +220 4374242 **E:** grts@gamtel.gm **W:** www.grts. gm **LP:** DG: Lamin Manga **Txs:** Banjul ch11V (100kW) & relay txs.

GEORGIA

Systems: DVB-T2 (MPEG4) [E]; Abkhazia & South Ossetia: # SECAM-D/K [R]; # PAL-D/K [R]

National Stations
GEORGIAN PUBLIC BROADCASTER (Pub) ✆ M. Kostava St. 68, 0171 Tbilisi ☎ +995 32 2362294 🖷 +995 32 2368665 **E:** info@gpb. ge **W:** www.gpb.ge **LP:** DG: George Barashvili **Chs:** GPB TV1, GPB TV2. **Regional Station: Ajara Radio & TV,** Memed Abashidze Ave. 41, 6000 Batumi. – **GDS TV (Comm)** ✆ Kojori Lane 6, 0105 Tbilisi ☎ +995 32 2557070 **W:** gds.tv – **IMEDI TV (Comm)** ✆ Lubliana St. 5, 0159 Tbilisi ☎+995 32 2463041 **E:** contact@imedi.ge **W:** www.imedi.ge – **KOMEDIA TV (Comm)** ✆ Tbilisi. – **TABULA TV (Comm)** ✆ M. Kostava St. 75, 0171 Tbilisi ☎ +995 32 2420300 **E:** info@tabula.ge **W:** www.tabula.ge – **RUSTAVI 2 (Comm)** ✆ Sandro Euli St.. Sa, 0186 Tbilisi ☎ +995 32 2201111 🖷 +995 32 2200012 **E:** tv@rustavi2.com **W:** rustavi2.com.

Local Stations not shown.

DTT Tx Networks
Licensee Mux 1: Georgian Teleradio Center **W:** www.tvrcenter.ge **M1:** GPB TV1, GPB TV2, GPB Ajara TV **Licensee Mux 2-4** Stereo+ Ltd **M2:** GDS TV, Imedi TV, Komedia TV, Rustavi 2 TV, Tabula TV **M3+4◑:**

multiprgr **Txs: M1:** ch63 (Tbilisi 1kW) & nationwide MFN. **M2-4:** ch(-) (Tbilisi) & nationwide MFN. **Local licensees/muxes not shown.**

ABKHAZIA

APSUA XÖYNTKARRATÄ TELERADIOKOMPANIA ✉ Lasuria St. 16, Sokhumi (mail via Russia) ☎ +7 840 2266144 🖷 +7 840 2266144 **E:** info@apsua.tv **W:** www.apsua.tv **LP:** Dir: Alxas Colokwua **Txs:** Sokhumi ªch26 & netw. (ª=analogue)

SOUTH OSSETIA

PTRK "IR" ✉ Geroev St. 48, Tskhinvali (mail via Russia) ☎ +7 9974 451218 **E:** radio-ir@yandex.ru **LP:** Dir: Robert Kulumbegov **Txs:** (-)

GERMANY

System: DVB-T (MPEG2, MPEG4) [E], DVB-T2 (MPEG4) [E]

National Stations
ARBEITSGEMEINSCHAFT DER ÖFFENTLICH-RECHTLICHEN RUNDFUNKANSTALTEN DEUTSCHLANDS (ARD) (Pub) ✉ Arnulfstrasse 42, 80335 München ☎ +49 89 590001 🖷 +49 89 59003249 **LP:** Chmn: Lutz Marmor **W:** www.ard.de; www.daserste.de **Chs (terr.):** Das Erste, regional stns, EinsPlus, tagesschau24, Einsfestival, Phoenix, KiKa (KiKa is jointly produced with ZDF). **NB.** ARD is the head organisation for the regional public service broadcasters: **Bayerischer Rundfunk (BR)**: Rundfunkplatz 1, 80335 München ☎ +49 89 59002433 **W:** www.br.de **Hessischer Rundfunk (HR):** Bertramstrasse 8, 60320 Frankfurt ☎ +49 69 1551 **W:** www.hr-online.de **Mitteldeutscher Rundfunk (MDR)**, Kantstrasse 71-73, 04275 Leipzig ☎ +49 341 22760 **W:** www.mdr.de **Norddeutscher Rundfunk (NDR)**, Rothenbaumchaussee 132, 20149 Hamburg ☎ +49 40 4131 **W:** www.ndr.de **Rundfunk Berlin-Brandenburg (RBB)** Masurenallee 8-14, 14057 Berlin ☎ +49 30 9799330141 **W:** www.rbb-online.de **Radio Bremen Fernsehen (RB)**, Diepenau 10, 28195 Bremen ☎ +49 421 2460 **W:** www.radiobremen.de **Saarländischer Rundfunk (SR)**, Funkhaus Halberg, 66100 Saarbrücken ☎ +49 681 6020 **W:** www.sr-online.de **Südwestrundfunk (SWR)**, Neckarstrasse 230, 70190 Stuttgart ☎ +49 711 92910001 **W:** www.swr.de **Westdeutscher Rundfunk (WDR)**, Appellhoffplatz 1, 50667 Köln ☎ +49 221 2202100 **W:** www.wdr.de – **ZWEITES DEUTSCHES FERNSEHEN (ZDF) (Pub)** ✉ Postfach 4040, 55030 Mainz ☎ +49 6131 701 🖷 +49 6131 702157 **E:** info@zdf.de **W:** www.zdf.de **LP:** DG: Thomas Bellut **Chs (terr.):** ZDF, ZDFneo, ZDFinfo, 3sat (3sat is jointly produced with ARD) – **MEDIENGRUPPE RTL DEUTSCHLAND GMBH (Comm)** ✉ Picassoplatz 1, 50679 Köln ☎ +49 221 45600 🖷 +49 221 45669999 **E:** info@mediengruppe-rtl.de **W:** www.mediengruppe-rtl.de **LP:** CEO: Anke Schäferkordt **Chs (terr.):** RTL Television, RTL II, SuperRTL, Vox, n-tv. – **N24 (Comm)** ✉ Axel-Springer-Straße 65, 10888 Berlin ☎ +49 30 20902400 🖷 +49 30 20902499 **E:** info@n24.de **W:** www.n24.de **LP:** Editor-in-Chief: Arne Teetz – **PROSIEBENSAT.1 MEDIA AG (Comm)** ✉ Medienallee 7, 85774 Unterföhring ☎ +49 89 950710 🖷 +49 89 950711227 **W:** www.prosiebensat1.com **LP:** CEO: Thomas Ebeling **Chs (terr.):** ProSieben, Sat.1, Kabel eins.

Local Stations not shown.

DTT Tx Networks (DVB-T/MPEG2)
Licensee Mux 1+2: ARD **Mux 1*:** Das Erste, other public service channels **Mux 2*:** Das Erste (MV only), regional public service stns. – **Licensee Mux 3:** ZDF **M:** ZDF, 3Sat, KiKa/ZDFneo, ZDFinfo. – **Licensee Mux 4:** ProSiebenSat.1 Media **M*:** Sat.1 (incl. reg. prgrs), ProSieben, Kabel eins, N24 – **Licensee Mux 5:** Mediengruppe RTL Deutschland **M*:** RTL Television (incl. reg. prgrs), RTL II, SuperRTL, Vox. **NB:** *=The content of the muxes is licensed individually by each federal state and may vary.

RE	Location	M1	M2	M3	M4	M5	kW
BB	Cottbus (Calau)	53	57	36	-	-	100
BB	Frankfurt/O.	53V	57V	33V	-	-	50
BE	Berlin (Alexanderplatz)	27	47	33	-	-	120/100/50
BE	Berlin (Scholzplatz)	27	47	-	-	-	10
BE	Berlin (Schäferberg)	27	47	33	-	-	50/5/50
BW	Aalen	59	50	23	-	-	50
BW	Baden-Baden	60	49	33	-	-	50
BW	Bad Mergentheim	26	50	23	-	-	5/10/5
BW	Brandenkopf	52	39	33	-	-	50
BW	Donaueschingen	54	41	22	-	-	50
BW	Freiburg	52	39	33	-	-	50
BW	Heidelberg	60	49	21	-	-	50
BW	Hochrhein	52	39	33	-	-	50

RE	Location	M1	M2	M3	M4	M5	kW
BW	Pforzheim	60	49	33	-	-	50
BW	Ravensburg	43	40	22	-	-	50
BW	Raichberg	43	40	22	-	-	50
BW	Stuttgart	26	50	23	-	-	50
BW	Ulm	43	40	22	-	-	50
BW	Waldenburg	26	50	23	-	-	50
BY	Augsburg	36	25	44	-	-	100
BY	Bamberg	29	40	34	-	-	50
BY	Brotjacklriegel	40V	27V	33V	-	-	25/100/50
BY	Büttelberg	55	47	-	-	-	50
BY	Dillberg	55V	47V	34V	-	-	25/2x50
BY	Gelbelsee	36	25	44	-	-	50
BY	Grünten	45	46	28	-	-	50
BY	Hirschau	29	28	23	-	-	50
BY	Hohe Linie	42V	28V	53V	-	-	25/2x100
BY	Hoher Bogen	42V	28V	33V	-	-	25/100/50
BY	Hohenpeißenberg	47	53	28	-	-	2x100/50
BY	Landshut	40	27	33	-	-	20
BY	München	54V	56V	35V	48V	-	20/5x100
BY	Nürnberg	55V	47V	34V	52V	-	25/2x50/20
BY	Ochsenkopf	29	40	23	-	-	50
BY	Pfaffenberg	36	46	25	-	-	2x100/50
BY	Pfaffenhofen	36	25	44	-	-	50
BY	Pfarrkirchen	40	27	33	-	-	50
BY	Pfänder°	45	-	46	-	-	10
BY	Rhön	36	46	25	-	-	2x100/50
BY	Wassertrüdingen	55	47	44	-	-	2x100/50
BY	Wendelstein	54V	56V	35V	48V	-	25/4x100
BY	Würzburg	36	46	25	-	-	25/2x50
HB	Bremerhaven	22	29	32	49	42	2x10/3x5
HB	Bremen (Walle)	22	29	32	49	42	40/50/32/2x50
HE	Angelburg	32	24	45	-	-	50
HE	Frankfurt (Ginnheim)	37V	59V	22V	54V	34V	50/20/3x50
HE	Großer Feldberg	37V	59V	22V	54V	34V	50/10/3x50
HE	Habichtswald	32	55	42	-	-	50
HE	Heidelstein	43	35	25	-	-	50
HE	Hohe Wurzel	37V	59V	22V	54V	34V	100/20/2x100
HE	Hoher Meißner	32	55	42	-	-	50
HE	Rimberg	32	35	22	-	-	50
HE	Würzberg	31	53	21	-	-	50
HH	Hamburg	33	54	23	30	40	3x50/2x100
HH	Hamburg (Rahlstedt)	33	54	23	30	40	20/25/3x20
HH	Hamburg (Moorfleet)	-	54V	-	-	-	25
MV	Garz	-	29	40	-	-	20
MV	Helpterberg	-	22	23	-	-	20
MV	Rostock	-	26V	24V	-	-	40/20
MV	Schwerin	-	26	54	-	-	50
NI	Aurich	48	43	35	-	-	2x50/20
NI	Braunschweig	47V	36V	23V	44V	24V	10/8/3x5
NI	Braunschweig (Broitzem)	47V	36V	23V	44V	24V	2x10/3x5
NI	Cuxhaven	26	29	31	-	-	2x10/5
NI	Dannenberg	43	58	-	-	-	10/2
NI	Göttingen	59	21	42	-	-	50
NI	Göttingen (Hetjersh.)	59V	21V	-	-	-	40/25
NI	Hannover (Buchholz)	47	36	23	44	24	10/4x20
NI	Hildesheim	47V	36V	23V	-	-	10/8/5
NI	Lingen	41	37	59	-	-	20
NI	Osnabrück	41	37	59	-	-	50
NI	Rosengarten	33	56	23	-	-	5/20/5
NI	Stadthagen	47	36	-	-	-	10
NI	Steinkimmen	55	29	32	49	42	100/4x5
NI	Torfhaus	59V	46V	-	-	-	32
NI	Uelzen	43	58	27	-	-	20/2x50
NI	Visselhövede	43V	58V	27V	-	-	20
NW	Aachen	50V	37V	26V	-	-	2x10/5
NW	Aachen (Stolberg)	50V	37V	26V	-	-	2x50/20
NW	Bielefeld	26	31	33	-	-	20
NW	Bonn	50V	49V	26V	53V	29V	3x50/2x20
NW	Dortmund	48V	25V	35V	55V	29V	50
NW	Düsseldorf	48V	46V	35V	55V	29V	50
NW	Düsseldorf	46V	-	-	-	-	50
NW	Essen	48V	57V	35V	55V	29V	50
NW	Hochsauerland	60	27	30	-	-	50
NW	Köln	50V	49V	26V	53V	29V	3x50/2x20
NW	Langenberg	48V	46V	35V	55V	29V	50
NW	Langenberg	46V	25v	-	-	-	50
NW	Münster	21V	45V	59V	-	-	50
NW	Nordhelle	60V	27V	30V	-	-	100/2x50

RE	Location	M1	M2	M3	M4	M5	kW
NW	Siegen	60	27	30	-	-	20
NW	Teutoburger Wald	26V	31V	33V	-	-	50
NW	Wesel	48V	46V	35V	55V	29V	50
NW	Wesel	46V	-	-	-	-	50
NW	Wuppertal	48	22	35	-	-	50
RP	Ahrweiler	56	33	28	-	-	10
RP	Bad Marienberg	56	33	28	-	-	20
RP	Donnersberg	57	44	30	-	-	50
RP	Eifel	46	48	30	-	-	50
RP	Haardtkopf	46	48	30	-	-	50
RP	Kaiserslautern	57	44	30	-	-	20
RP	Kettrichshof	60	44	30	-	-	50
RP	Koblenz	56	33	28	-	-	50
RP	Saarburg	46	48	30	-	-	50
SH	Bredstedt	26	24	31	-	-	25
SH	Bungsberg	47V	39V	21V	-	-	50
SH	Flensburg	47V	39V	21V	-	-	2x50/20
SH	Heide	26	24	31	-	-	32/2x20
SH	Kiel	47	39	21	35	45	2x50/20
SH	Lübeck (Berkenthin)	33	28	23	30	40	20
SH	Lübeck (Stockelsdorf)	33V	28V	23V	30V	40V	20
SH	Mölln	-	28	-	-	-	10
SH	Neumünster	-	28	-	-	-	50
SH	Wedel	-	28	-	-	-	25
SL	Göttelborner Höhe	42V	44V	30V	-	-	50
SL	Schocksberg	42V	-	30V	-	-	20
SL	Spiesen	42V	-	-	-	-	25
ST	Brocken	29V	34V	30V	-	-	50
ST	Dequede	41V	34V	31V	-	-	50
ST	Halle	24V	35V	22V	-	28V	50
ST	Magdeburg	29V	34V	30V	-	-	2x100/50
ST	Wittenberg	24V	38V	30V	-	-	50
SN	Chemnitz	25V	32V	22V	-	-	2x20/5
SN	Geyer	25V	32V	22V	-	-	50
SN	Dresden	39V	29V	36V	-	-	100
SN	Leipzig	24V	37V	22V	-	28V	100
SN	Löbau	39V	27V	36V	-	-	50
SN	Schöneck	25V	32V	22V	-	-	50
TH	Erfurt	21V	27V	50V	-	-	50
TH	Gera	25V	27V	22V	-	-	50
TH	Inselsberg	53V	48V	50V	-	-	50
TH	Jena	21V	27V	50V	-	-	2x10/5
TH	Sonneberg	21V	27V	50V	-	-	2x10/20
TH	Weimar	21V	27V	50V	-	-	25

+ sites with txs below 10kW. °) tx located in Austria

Regional & Local Licensees not shown.

RE) Region codes (federal states): BB=Brandenburg, BE=Berlin, BW=Baden-Württemberg, BY=Bayern, HB=Bremen, HE=Hessen, HH=Hamburg, MV=Mecklenburg-Vorpommern, NI=Niedersachsen, NW=Nordrhein-Westfalen, RP=Rheinland-Pfalz, SH=Schleswig-Holstein, SL=Saarland, ST=Sachsen-Anhalt, SN=Sachsen, TH=Thüringen.

GHANA

Systems: DVB-T2 (MPEG4) [E]; § PAL-B [E] ⇩March 2017

GHANA BROADCASTING CORP. (GBC) (Gov) ☑ P.O. Box 1633, Accra ☎ +233 30 2221161 ▤ +233 30 2773240 **E:** info@gbcghana. comh **W:** www.gbcghana.com **L.P:** DG: Albert Don-Chebe. **Chs:** GTV, GBC 24, GBC Life, GTV Sports+ – **E.TV GHANA (Comm)** ☑ P.O.Box CT 5976, Accra ☎ +233 30 2912071 **E:** info@etvghana.com **W:** www.etvghana.com – **METRO TV (Semi-Gov, Comm)** 59 Josiah Tongogara Street, Labone, Accra ▤ +233 30 2765701 ▤ +233 30 2765703 **W:** www.mymetrotv.tv – **TV3 (Comm)** ☑ Box M83, Accra ☎ +233 30 2763458 ▤ +233 30 2763450 **E:** info@tv3network.com **W:** tv3network.com **L.P:** CEO: Santokh Singh – **TV AFRICA (Comm)** ☑ P.O.Box 7151, Accra-North ▤ +233 30 2224323 ▤ +233 30 2223320 **E:** info@tvafricaonline.com **W:** www.tvafricaonline.com – **VIASAT1 (Comm)** ☑ House 25/8 Abafun Crescent, North Labone, Accra ☎ +233 30 2760516 **E:** u2us@ viasat1.com.gh **W:** www.viasat1.com.gh **L.P:** CEO: Maame Arhin.

DTT Tx Networks
Tx Operator: GBC **Mux 1:** GTV, GBC 24, GBC Life, GTV Sports+,TV3, Viasat1, TV Africa, NET2, BBC World News, God TV, FOX Entertainment✪, Showtime✪, Hi Nolly✪, Homebase✪, Setanta Africa✪, Kiss✪, KidsCo✪ **Mux 2✪:** Skyy One, Music World, Channel D, Sports24, Cinimax, Heaven, Planet Kidz, Fiesta, Skyy World, e.TV Ghana ⌘ Skyy Power FM, Citi FM **Txs:** (-).

GIBRALTAR (UK)

Systems: DVB-T (MPEG2), DVB-T2 (MPEG4) [E]

GBC TELEVISION ☑ Broadcasting House, 18 So. Barrack Rd, Gibraltar ☎ +350 20048990 ▤ +350 20078673 **E:** television@gbc.gi **W:** www.gbc.gi **L.P:** CEO (Gibraltar Broadcasting Corp): Gerard Teuma.

DTT Tx Networks
Tx Operator: Arqiva **Muxes 1+2:** GBC TV ⌘ R. Gibraltar 1. **Txs: Mux 1 (DVB-T2/MPEG4):** ch30 (Upper Rock) **Mux 2 (DVB-T/ MPEG2):** ch56 (Upper Rock).

GREECE

System: DVB-T (MPEG2, MPEG4) [E]

National Stations
ELLINIKI RADIOFONIA TILEORASI A.E. (ERT) (Pub) ☑ TV studios: Mesogeion Ave. 136, 11527 Athina ☎ +30 2106066000 ▤+30 2106066109 **E:** info@ert.gr **W:** www.ert.gr **L.P:** MD: Lambis Tagmatarchis **Chs:** ERT1, ERT HD, ERT2, ERT3 – **VOULI TILEORASI (Pub)** ☑ Vasilisis Amalias Ave. 14, 10557 Athina ☎ +30 2103735302 ▤ +30 2103735014 **E:** kanali@parliament.gr **W:** www.hellenicparliament.gr/Enimerosi/Vouli-Tileorasi – **ALPHA TV (Comm)** ☎ +30 40.2km Attikis Odou, SEA Mesogeion, Building 6, 19002 Paiania ☎ +30 2122124000 ▤ +30 2122124356 **E:** pr@alphatv.gr **W:** www.alphatv. gr **L.P:** Owner: Dimitris Kontominas – **ANTENNA TV (ANT1) (Comm)** ☑ Kifisias Ave. 10-12, 15125 Marousi ☎ +30 2106886100 ▤ +30 2106890304 **E:** pr@antenna.gr **W:** www.antenna.gr **L.P:** CEO (Antenna Group): Theodore Kyriakou – **ART TV (Comm)** ☑Praxitelous 58, 17674 Kallithea ☎+30 2109407000 ▤+30 2109407024 **E:** arttileorasi@gmail. com **W:** www.arttv.info – **E TV (Comm)** ☑ Stountiou 10-12, 15126 Marousi ☎ +30 2112122000 ▤ +30 2112122062 **E:** pr@epsilontv.gr **W:** www.epsilontv.gr **L.P:** CEO: Dimitris Mpeis – **m. (MAKEDONIA TV) (Comm)** ☑ 26chs Oktovriou 90, 54627 Thessaloniki ☎ +30 2310504300 ▤ +30 2310504344 **E:** info@maktv.gr **W:** www.maktv. gr **L.P:** GM: George Zois – **MEGA CHANNEL (Comm)** ☑ Rousou 4, 11526 Ambelokipoi ☎ +30 2106903000 ▤ +30 2106983600 **E:** publ_rel@megatv.com **W:** www.megatv.com **L.P:** CEO: Elias Tsigas – **SKAI TV (Comm)** ☑ Ethnarchou Makariou & Falireos 2, 18547 Neo Faliro ☎ +30 2104800170 ▤ +30 2104800120 **E:** technicaltv@ skai.gr **W:** www.skai.gr **L.P:** CEO (Skai Group): Ioannis Alafouzos – **STAR CHANNEL (Comm)** ☑ Viltanioti 36, 14564 Kifisia ☎ +30 2111891000 ▤ +30 2111892000 **E:** info@star.gr **W:** www.star.gr **L.P:** GM: Karolos Alkalai.

Regional & Local Stations not shown.

DTT Tx Networks (MPEG4 exc. where stated)
Licensee M1+2: ERT M1: ERT1, ERT HD, ERT2, ERT3, Vouli ⌘ ERT Radio 1/2/3, Kosmos, Voice of Greece **M2 (MPEG2):** BBC World News, DW, RIK Sat, TV5 Monde Europe – **Licensee M3+4, R1-R3:** Digea ☑ Sorou 26, 15125 Marousi ☎ +30 2106838700 ▤ +30 2106823205 **E:** info@digea.gr **W:** www.digea.gr **M3:** Alpha TV, ANT1, Art TV, E TV **M4:** m. (Makedonia TV), Mega Channel, Skai TV, Star Channel **Muxes R1-3:** Various regional/local stns

Location	M1	M2	M3	M4	R1	R2	R3
Agrinio (Akarnanika Mts.)	23	32	27	28	46	51	-
Alexandroupoli (Plaka)	31	24	27	30	43	48	-
Athina (SFN 1)	21	28	22	27	45	52	54
Athina (SFN 2)	23	-	24	31	38	49	50
Dodecanese Isl. (SFN)	39	-	24	26	41	-	-
Halkidiki (Polygiros)	25	38	31	34	50	54	-
Hania (SFN)	21	38	31	34	54	-	-
Igoumenitsa (SFN)	45	33	22	26	48	59	-
Ioannina (SFN)	24	31	25	30	52	54	-
Iraklio (SFN)	39	-	25	37	55	-	-
Kalamata (SFN)	29	37	31	32	48	51	-
Karpenisi (SFN)	24	-	26	29	47	-	-
Kastellorizo Isl.	49	-	27	33	51	-	-
Kastoria/Florina (SFN)	44	-	26	32	47	52	-
Kavala (SFN)	22	-	23	37	47	51	-
Kefalonia (SFN)	21	36	22	33	59	60	-
Kerkira (SFN)	37	-	30	34	54	54	-
Korinthos (SFN)	26	43	29	41	51	56	-
Kozani/Grevena (SFN)	41	-	28	29	50	54	-
Lamia (SFN)	39	-	33	35	53	-	-
Larissa (SFN)	22	40	35	38	52	-	-

Location	M1	M2	M3	M4	R1	R2	R3
Lasithi/E. Crete (SFN)	38	-	28	31	40	-	-
Lesvos Isl. (SFN)	39	-	25	33	53	-	-
Mytilini/Hios/Limnos (SFN)	21	-	25	33	53	-	-
Nafplio/Argos (SFN)	33	55	35	39	58	59	-
Orestiada (Pithio)	25	-	32	35	51	56	-
Paros (SFN)	42	-	33	39	53	-	-
Patra (SFN)	24	34	25	31	44	53	-
Pyrgos (SFN)	49	-	30	38	52	56	-
Samos/Ikaria (SFN)	38	-	31	34	44	-	-
Santorini (SFN)	51	-	33	39	53	-	-
Serres/Drama (SFN)	35	-	32	40	52	53	-
Sparti (SFN)	40	-	25	27	52	57	-
Syros/Mykonos (SFN)	46	-	29	37	48	-	-
Thessaloniki (SFN)	24	36	27	30	55	56	-
Tripoli (SFN)	21	-	23	24	50	60	-
Volos (SFN)	21	37	26	29	47	-	-

GREENLAND (Denmark)

System: DVB-T (MPEG2, MPEG4) [E]

National Station
KNR-TV (Pub) ✉ P.O.Box 1007, 3900 Nuuk ☎ +299 361500 🖷 +299 325042 **E:** knr@knr.gl **W:** knr.gl **L.P:** Dir (KNR): Jacob Abelsen **Chs:** KNR1, KNR2.

DTT Tx Networks
Tx Operator: TELE Greenland **M (MPEG4):** KNR1, KNR2, DR1, DR2, DR Ultra ✂ KNR Radio, DR P1, DR P2, DR P3 **Txs:** Nationwide MFN. – **Local Licencees:** not shown.

GRENADA

System: NTSC-M [A]

GBN-TV (Gov) ✉ P.O.Box 535, St. George's ☎ +1 473 4445521 **E:** grenadabroadcastingnetwork@gmail.com **W:** www.gbn.gd **L.P:** GM: Ruel Edwards **Txs:** North/East ch7 (4kW), St. George's ch11 (5kW). – **MEANINGFUL TELEVISION (MTV) (Comm)** ✉Lagoon Road, St. George ☎ 1 473 4408442 **E:** mtvgrenada@gmail.com **Txs:** Saint George's 9 & netw. – **GFN-TV (Rlg)** ✉ P.O.Box 2747, St. Paul's, St. George ☎ +1 473 4354297 **W:** www.globalfamilynetwork.net **L.P:** Project Dir: John Bartels **Tx:** St. George's ch4.

GUADELOUPE (France)

System: DVB-T (MPEG4) [E]

GUADELOUPE 1ÈRE (Pub) ✉ BP 180, F-97122 Baie-Mahault ☎ +590 590939696 🖷 +590 590939682 **W:** guadeloupe.la1ere.fr **L.P:** Dir: Sylvie Gengoul – **CANAL 10 (Comm)** ✉ 21, Bd Marquisart De Houelbourg, F-97122 Baie-Mahault ☎ +590 590267303 🖷 +590 590266125 **E:** contact@canal10-tv.com **W:** www.canal10-tv.com **L.P:** Pres: Lisa Rodriguez – **ÉCLAIR TÉLÉVISION (ETV) (Comm)** ✉ 12, rue Alfred Lumière, Bureau n° 6, F-97122 Baie-Mahaut. ☎ +590 590328080 🖷 +590 590601533 **W:** www.efm-etv.com **L.P:** Pres: Mario Constant Moradel.

DTT Tx Networks
Tx Operator: TDF **M:** Guadeloupe 1ère, France 2-5, France Ô, France 24, Arte, Canal 10, Éclair Télévision **Txs:** MFN.

GUAM (USA)

System: ATSC [A]

Local Stations*
KGTF (Pub): P.O.Box 21449, GMF, Agana, GU 96921. Tx: Agana ch5 (8.26kW). **KTGM (Comm):** 692 N Marine Dr, Tamuning, GU 96913-4454. Tx: Tamuning ch17 (2kW). **KUAM-TV (Comm):** 600 Harmon Loop Rd, #102, Dededo, GU 96912-2536. Tx: Agana ch2 (0.035kW). *) Full power licenses (lp licenses not listed).

GUATEMALA

Systems: # NTSC-M [A]; ISDB-TB [A] planned

National Stations
GUATEVISIÓN (Pub) ✉ Calzada Roosevelt 22-43, Zona 11, Edificio Tikal Futura, Torre Sol 4o, Nivel, Guatemala ☎ +502 23286000 **E:** info@guatevjsion.com **W:** www.guatevision.com **Txs:** ch25 – **RADIO Y TELEVISIÓN DE GUATEMALA (Comm)** ✉ 30, Av. 3-40, Zona 11, 01011 Guatemala ☎ +502 25945320 **Chs:** Canal 19, El Súper Canal, Televisiete **W:** www.facebook.com/elsupercanal; www.canal7.com.gt; www.facebook.com/Trecevision **El Súper Canal:** ch3 (240kW); **Televisiete:** ch7 (180kW); **TeleOnce:** ch11 (316kW); **Trecevisión:** ch13 (25kW) – **AZTECA GUATEMALA (Comm)** ✉ 12 Avenida 1-96, Zona 2 de Mixco, Colonia Alvarado, Guatemala ☎ +502 24111140 🖷 +502 24111200 **E:** festrada@tvaguatemala.tv **W:** www.azteca.com.gt **Tx:** ch31. – **MAZATELEVISIÓN (Comm)** ✉ Guatemala. **Tx:** ch58. – **TV USAC (Educ)** ✉ Guatemala **W:** www.usac.edu.gt **Tx:** ch33. – **CANAL 27 (Rlg)** ✉ Carretera Vieja a Antigua 2 Calle 23-70, Zona 1 de Mixco, Guatemala ☎ +502 24213434 **E:** canal27@motivacioncristiana.org **W:** www.canal27.org **Tx:** ch27. – **CANAL 63 (Rlg)** ✉ Guatemala. **W:** www.canalcatolico.tv **Tx:** ch63. – **CANAL 65 (Rlg)** ✉ Guatemala. **Tx:** ch65. Rel. ETWN (USA). – **ENLACE CANAL 21 (Rlg)** ✉ Guatemala. **Tx:** ch21. Rel. TBN (USA).

Local Stations not shown.

GUINEA

Systems: # PAL-K1 [VHF=K, UHF=E]; DVB-T2 (MPEG2) [E]

TÉLÉVISION NATIONALE DE GUINÉE (Pub) ✉ BP 391, Conakry. ☎ +224 30452786 🖷 +224 30451408 **L.P:** DG (RTG): Yamoussa Sidibé **Chs:** RTG1, RTG2 **Txs:** **RTG1:** Kindia ch4 (0.2kW), Conakry ch5 (1kW), Faranah ch5 (0.5kW), Labé ch7 (8kW), Mamou ch9 (0.2kW), Kankan ch9 (1kW) **RTG2:** Conakry ch(-).

DTT Tx Network
Tx Operator: Star Times **M✿:** multiprgr **Txs:** MFN.

GUINEA-BISSAU

Systems: # PAL-B/G [E]; DVB-T (MPEG2) [E]

TELEVISÃO DA GUINÉ-BISSAU (TGB) (Gov) ✉ CP 178, Bissau ☎ +245 5000000 **W:** www.guine-bissau.tv **L.P:** DG: Paula Silva Melo **Txs:** Nhacra ch7 (200kW) & relay txs.

Foreign TV Relay
RTP África (Portugal): (-).

DTT Tx Network
Tx Operator: Phoenix TV **M✿:** multiprgr **Txs:** MFN.

GUYANA

System: # NTSC-M [A]; ATSC [A] planned

National Station
NATIONAL COMMUNICATIONS NETWORK (NCN) (Gov) ✉ Homestretch Ave, Durban Backland, Georgetown ☎ +592 2235162 🖷 +592 2235163 **E:** ceo@ncnguyana.com **W:** ncnguyana.com **L.P:** CEO: Molly Hassan **Tx:** ch10.

Local Stations not shown.

HAITI

System: ATSC [A]

National Station
RADIO TÉLÉVISION NATIONALE D'HAITI (RTNH) (Pub) ✉ BP 13400, Delmas 33, Port-au-Prince ☎ +509 2460200 🖷 +509 2463889 **E:** info@rtnh.ht **W:** www.rtnh.ht **L.P:** DG: Hérold Israël **Txs:** Port-au-Prince ch8 (0.3kW) & nationwide network.

Local Stations not shown.

HAWAII (USA)

System: ATSC [A]

Local Stations*
KAAH-TV (Rlg): 1152 Smith St, Honolulu, HI 96817-5101. Tx: ch27 (262kW). **KAII-TV (Comm):** satellite of KHON-TV. Tx: Wailuku 36

(50kW). **KALO (Rlg):** 875 Waimanu St, Ste 110, Honolulu, HI 96813-5271. Tx: ch10 (21kW). **KBFD (Comm):** 1188 Bishop St PH-1, Honolulu, HI 96813-3300. Tx: ch33 (108kW). **KFVE (Comm):** 150-B Puuhale Rd, Honolulu, HI 96819-2233. Tx: ch23 (50kW). **KGMB (Comm):** 1534 Kapiolani Blvd, Honolulu, HI 96814-3715. Tx: ch22 (1000kW). **KGMD-TV (Comm):** satellite of KGMB. Tx: Hilo ch8 (3.2kW). **KGMV (Comm):** satellite of KGMB. Tx: Wailuku ch24 (72.4kW). **KHAW-TV (Comm):** satellite of KHON-TV. Tx: Hilo ch21 (50kW). **KHBC-TV (Comm):** satellite of KHNL. Tx: Hilo ch22 (8kW). **KHET (Pub):** 2350 Dole St, Honolulu, HI 96822-2410. Tx: ch18 (9.5kW). **KHNL (Comm):** 150-B Puuhale Rd, Honolulu, HI 96819-2233. Tx: ch35 (5.9kW). **KHON-TV (Comm):** 88 Piikoi St, Honolulu, HI 96814-4245. Tx: ch8 (7.2kW). **KHVO (Comm):** satellite of KITV. Tx: Hilo ch18 (50kW). **KIKU (Comm):** 737 Bishop St Ste 1430, Honolulu, HI 96813-3204. Tx: ch19 (60.7kW). **KITV (Comm):** 801 S King St, Honolulu, HI 96813-3013. Tx: ch40 (85kW). **KKAI (Rlg):** 875 Waimanu St, Ste 110, Honolulu, HI 96813-5271. Tx: Kailua ch15 (19kW). **KLEI (Comm):** satellite of KPXO. Tx: Kailua-Kona ch25 (700kW). **KMAU (Comm):** satellite of KITV. Tx: Wailuku ch29 (51.2kW). **KMEB (Pub):** satellite of KHET. Tx: Wailuku ch30 (50kW). **KOGG (Comm):** satellite of KHNL. Tx: Wailuku ch16 (50kW). **KPXO (Comm):** 875 Waimanu St Ste 630, Honolulu, HI 96813-5267. Tx: Kane'ohe ch41 (34kW). **KUPU (Rlg):** 1188 Bishop St Ste 502, Honolulu, HI 96813-3302. Tx: Waimanalo ch23 (19kW). **KWBN (Rlg):** 3901 S Hwy 121 S, Bedford, TX 76021-2066. Tx: ch43 (6.46kW). **KWHE (Rlg):** 1188 Bishop St Ste 502, Honolulu, HI 96813-3302. Tx: ch31 (20.1kW). **KWHH (Rlg):** satellite of KWHE. Tx: Hilo ch23 (14.9kW). **KWHM (Rlg):** rel. KWHE. Tx: Wailuku 45 (87kW).*) Full power license (lp licenses not listed)
NB: Tx sites are Honolulu unless mentioned otherwise.

HONDURAS

Systems: # NTSC-M [A] ⇩2015; ISDB-TB [A]

National Stations (°=analogue)
TELEVISIÓN NACIONAL DE HONDURAS (TNH) (Gov) ✉ Edificio Ejecutivo #2 - 4 nivel Frente Casa Presidencial Tegucigalpa, M.D.C., Tegucigalpa **E:** info@tnh.gob.hn **W:** www.tnh.gob.hn **LP:** Chmn: Víctor G. Hémela **Txs:** Tegucigalpa °ch20 & relays. – **CANAL 6 (Comm)** ✉ 5ta Cll, 26 y 27 Ave., Bo. Río de Piedras, San Pedro Sula ☎ +504 25505009 🗎 +504 25531810 **W:** canal6.com.hn **Tx:** Tegucigalpa °ch6 & relays. – **CANAL 11 (Comm)** ✉ 5ta Cll, 26 y 27 Ave., Bo. Río de Piedras, San Pedro Sula **W:** canal11.hn **Tx:** San Pedro Sula & relays. – **HONDURED (Comm)** ✉ Casilla 3424, Tegucigalpa. **W:** www.hondured.tv **Txs:** Tegucigalpa °ch13 & relays. – **TELEPROGRESO (Comm)** ✉ 9 Ave 12 St. N, Edificio Turiplaza, El Progreso 23201 ☎ +504 26482222 **E:** micanal@teleprogreso.tv **W:** www.teleprogreso.tv **Txs:** Tegucigalpa °ch48 & relays – **TELEVICENTRO (Comm)** ✉ Boulevard Suyapa, Tegucigalpa ☎ +504 22327835 🗎 +504 2320097 **W:** televicentro.hn **Chs:** Canal Cinco, Canal 3, Cadena 7/4 **Txs:** Tegucigalpa °ch3 (Canal 3), Tegucigalpa °ch5 (Canal Cinco), Tegucigalpa °ch7 (Cadena 7/4) & relays.– **VTV (Comm)** ✉ 9 Cll. 10 Ave, N.O. Bo. Guamalito, San Pedro Sula **W:** www.vtv.com.hn **Txs:** Tegucigalpa °ch9 & relays.

Local Stations not shown.

HONG KONG (China, SAR)

Systems: DTMB [E]; § PAL-I [E] ⇩2020

RADIO TELEVISION HONG KONG (RTHK) (Pub) ✉ 30 Broadcast Drive, Kowloon, Hong Kong ☎ +852 23396330 🗎 +852 23800279 **E:** ccu@rthk.hk **W:** www.rthk.hk **LP:** Dir of Broadcasting: Roy Tang. **Chs:** RTHK TV1, RTHK TV2, RTHK TV3 & airtime on ATV and TVB. – **ASIA TELEVISION LTD. (ATV) (Comm)** ✉ 25-31 Dai Shing Street, Tai Po, Hong Kong ☎ +852 31682288 🗎 +852 27191654 **E:** atv@hkatv.com **W:** www.hkatv.com **LP:** CEO: Ip Ka Po **Chs:** ATV Home, ATV Asia, ATV World (English), ATV Classic, ATV HD. – **TELEVISION BROADCASTS LTD. (TVB) (Gov)** ✉ TV City, 77 Chun Choi Street, Tseung Kwan O Industrial Estate, Kowloon Hong Kong ☎ +852 23359123 🗎+852 23581300 **E:** tvbpr@tvb.com.hk **W:** www.tvb.com **LP:** Chmn: Run Run Shaw.

DTT Tx Networks
Licensee: RTHK **Mux 1:** RTHK TV1 **Mux 2** RTHK TV2 (Legislative Council meetings) **Mux 3:** RTHK TV3 (CCTV9 relay) – **Licensee:** ATV **Mux 4:** ATV, ATV World, ATV Asia, ATV Financial News Channel, ATV Home, CCTV1, SZTV. **Mux 5:** ATV HD. – **Licensee:** TVB **Mux 6:** TVB Jade, TVB Pearl, TVB iNews. **Mux 7:** TVB Jade J2, TVB Jade HD.

Location	M1	M2	M3	M4	M5	M6	M7
SFN	31	32	33	37	43	22	35

HUNGARY

System: DVB-T (MPEG4) [E]

National Stations
MÉDIOSZOLGÁLTATÁS-TÁMOGATÓ ÉS VAGYONKEZELÖ ALAP (MTVA) (Pub) ✉ Kunigunda útja 64, 1037 Budapest ☎ +36 1 7595050 **E:** corporate@mtva.hu **W:** www.mtva.hu; www.mediaklikk.hu **LP:** DG: Miklós Vaszily. **NB:** MTVA is the media holding for the Hungarian public broadcasters, incl. Magyar Televízió (MTV) and Duna Televízió. Studios: ✉ Szabadság tér 17, 1810 Budapest 5 (MTV); Mészáros u. 48-54, 1016 Budapest (Duna TV). **Chs: MTV:** M1, M2, M3 Anno, M4 Sport, reg. prgrs: a) Budapesti stúdió, b) Debreceni stúdió, c) Miskolci stúdió, d) Pécsi stúdió, e) Soproni stúdió, f) Szegedi stúdió; **Duna TV:** Duna, Duna World. – **RTL KLUB (Comm)** ✉ Nagytétényi út 29, 1222 Budapest ☎ +36 1 3828283 **E:** rtlklub@rtl.hu **W:** rtl.hu **LP:** CEO: Gabriella Vidus. – **TV2 (Comm)** ✉ Róna u. 174, 1145 Budapest ☎ +36 1 4676400 **E:** info@tv2.hu **W:** tv2.hu **LP:** CEO: Zsolt Simon.

Local Stations not shown.

DTT Tx Networks
Tx Operator: Antenna Hungária ✉ Petzvál József u. 31-33, 1119 Budapest ☎ +36 1 2036060 🗎 +36 1 4642525 **E:** antennadigital@ahrt.hu **W:** ahrt.hu **Mux 1:** M1 HD (incl. reg prgrs), M4 Sport HD, Duna HD, Duna World ✳ Kossuth R., Petöfi R., Bartók R., Dankó R. **Mux 2 (✪ exc.*):** Echo TV, Viasat 3, RTL+, Muzsika TV, DaVinci Learning Channel, Comedy Central, Nickelodeon, Cartoon Network, National Geographic, Filmbox, Eurosport, Dorcel TV, C8*, TV Paprika **Mux 3 (✪ exc.*):** M2 HD*, M3 Anno, RTL Klub*, TV2*, Cool TV, Film+, AXN, FEM3, ATV, HírTV **Mux 4✪:** FOX, DIGI Sport 1, RTL2, Super TV2, Sláger TV, Disney Channel, Spektrum, Paramount Channel, Discovery Channel, TLC, Viasat 6, Viasat History, Ozone Network, Story4 **Mux 5✪:** DIGI Sport 2, Eurosport 2, Fishing & Hunting, Brazzers TV, Animal Planet, Discovery Science, NatGeo Wild, Viasat Explore, Filmbox Premium, Filmbox Family, HBO, Pax TV, Bonum TV, Euronews, Sportklub.

Location	M1	M2	M3	M4	M5	kW
Aggtelek	45c	31	28	48	35	39/4x50
Budapest	38a	55	58	41	24	100/39/100/58/42
Csávoly	45f	25	28	42		76/56/50/69
Csengöd	45f	25	28	42		42/38/43/42
Debrecen	46b	51	49	32	29	2x13/12/13.5/14
Fehérgyarmat	58b	24	38	41		85/26/15.5/76
Gerecse	26e	29	59	41		15/16/42/11
Györ	42e	35	22	46	51	32/29.5/27.5/36/33
Kabhegy	57e	35	22	46	51	2x100/83/98/83
Kékes	53c	39	44	36		89/79/16/74
Komádi	46b	51	49	32		79/87/71/51
Nagykanizsa	24e	55	54	60	31	2x50/53/52.5/60
Pécs	52d	37	47	32		72/18/78/60
Salgótarján	38e	55	46	36	24	17/15/18/14/13.5
Sopron	42e	40	49	32	33	83/81/83/72/74
Szeged	23f	26	60	57	22	3x20/18/20
Szentes	23f	26	60	57		83/87/2x100
Szolnok	53c	30	59	36		24.5/19/24.5/18
Szombathely	38e	58	49	32		14.5/17/14/13
Tokaj	43c	31	43	26	35	43/13/18/65/66
Úzd	52d	37	47	32	50	56/50/3x55
Vásvar	52d	37	49	32	33	76/39/88/69/69

+ site with txs below 10kW. °) incl. reg prgrs (a-f), see above
Local licensees not shown.

ICELAND

System: DVB-T2 (MPEG4) [E]

National Stations
RÚV (Pub) ✉ Efstaleiti 1, 150 Reykjavík ☎ +354 5153000 🗎 +354 5153010 **E:** istv@ruv.is **W:** www.ruv.is **LP:** DG: Magnús Geir Þórðarsson – **365 MIÐLAR (Comm)** ✉ Skaftahlíð 24, 105 Reykjavík ☎ +354 5156000 **E:** 365@365.is **W:** www.365.is **LP:** Chair: Ingibjörg S. Pálmadóttir **Chs:** Stöð 2, Stöð 2 Gull, Stöð 3, Krakkar, Popptíví, Stöð 2 Sport, Stöð 2 Sport 2, Stöð 2 Bíó – **SKJÁREINN (Comm)** ✉ Ármúla 25, 108 Reykjavík ☎ +354 5956000 **E:** auglysingar@skjarinn.is **W:** www.skjareinn.is.

DTT Tx Networks
Licensee: Vodafone ✉Skútuvogi 2, 104 Reykjavík **E:** vodafone@vodafone.is **W:** vodafone.is **Mux 1✪exc.*:** RÚV HD*, RÚV*, Stöð 2, Stöð 3, Bíóstöðin, Krakkastöðin, Stöð 2 Sport, Stöð 2 Sport 2, Skjáreinn ✳ RÚV Rás 1*, Rás 2*, Rondó* **Mux 2✪:** Stöð 2 Sport 3,

Stöd 2 Sport 4, Gullstöðin, ÍNN, Skjár Sport, DR1, Discovery, Cartoon Network, Sky News, E! Entertainment, Blue Hustler.

Location	M1	M2	kW
Reykjavík	27	28	0.3

+ nationwide MFN

INDIA

Systems: DVB-T (MPEG2) [E], DVB-T2 (MPEG4) [E]

DOORDARSHAN (DD) (Pub) ✉ Doordarshan Bhawan, Copernicus Marg, New Delhi-110001 ☎ +91 11 23386055 📠 +91 11 23385843 **E:** dddirect@dd.nic.in **W:** www.ddindia.gov.in **L.P:** DG: Vijaya Laxmi Chabbra **Chs (terr.):** DD-National, DD-News, DD-Sports, DD-Bharati, DD-Kendra (Regional Channels).

DTT Tx Networks (under construction)
Tx Operator: Doordarshan **M1:** DD-National, DD-News, DD-Sports, DD-Barathi, DD-Regional **M2 (DVB-T2/MPEG4):** multiprgr **M3 (DVB-H):** multiprgr (16 prgrs).

Location	M1	M2	M3	kW
New Delhi	32	29	26	6/50

+ nationwide netw., mainly Mux 1 (ca. 230 HP sites)

INDONESIA

Systems: # PAL-B/G [E] ⇩2018; DVB-T2 (MPEG4) [E]

National Stations
TELEVISI REPUBLIK INDONESIA (TVRI) (Gov) ✉ Jalan Gerbang Pemuda, Senayan, Jakarta 10270 ☎ +62 21 3846740 📠 +62 21 5737152 **E:** wmaster@tvri.co.id **W:** www.tvri.co.id **L.P:** MD: Farhat Syukri **Chs:** TVRI Nasional, TVRI Sumut. **Txs:** TVRI1: Jakarta ch6 (5kW) & network; TVRI2: Jakarta ch9. – **TELEVISIE EDUKASIE (TVE) (Gov)** ✉ JI. RE. Martadinata Km. 5.5 Ciputat, Tangerang 15411. ☎ +62 21 7418808 **W:** tve.kemdikbud.go.id **Chs:** Channel 1, Channel 2 **Txs:** via DTT & relays in provinces. – **ANTV (PT CAKRAWALA ANDALAS TELEVISI) (Comm)** ✉ Mulia Center Building, 19th Floor, JI. HR Rasuna Said Kav. X-6 No.8, Jakarta 12940 ☎ +62 21 5222084 📠 +62 62 215222087 **E:** sales@anteve.co.id **W:** www.an.tv **Txs:** Jakarta ch47 (40kW) & network. – **GLOBAL TV (PT GLOBAL INFORMASI BERMUTU) (Comm)** ✉Wisma Indovision Lantai 17, Jalan Raya Panjang Z/III, Green Garden, Jakarta 11520 ☎ +62 21 5828555 📠 +62 21 5823636 **E:** globaltv@globaltv.co.id **W:** www.globaltv.co.id **Txs:** Jakarta ch51 (120kW) & network. – **INDOSIAR (PT. INDOSIAR VISUAL MANDIRI) (Comm)** ✉ JI. Damai No 11, Daan Mogot, Jakarta 11510 ☎ +62 21 5672222 📠 +62 21 5652221 **E:** program@indosiar.com **W:** www.indosiar.com **Txs:** Jakarta ch41 (120kW) & network. – **METRO TV (PT MEDIA TELEVISI INDONESIA)** ✉ JI. Pilar Mas Raya Kav. A-D., Kedoya, Kebon Jeruk, Jakarta 11520 ☎ +62 21 58300077 📠 +62 21 5816365 **E:** info@metrotvnews.com **W:** www.metrotvnews.com **Txs:** Jakarta ch57 & network. – **MNC TV (PT MEDIA NUSANTARA CITRA TV) (Comm)** ✉ Jalan Pintu II, Taman Mini Indonesia Indah, Pondok Gede, Jakarta 13810 ☎ +62 21 8412473 📠 +62 21 8412471 **E:** info@mnctv.com **W:** www.mnctv.com **Txs:** Jakarta ch37 (80kW) & network. – **RCTI (PT RAJAWALI CITRA TELEVISI INDONESIA) (Comm)** ✉ JI. Raya Perjuangan No. 3, kb. Jeruk, Jakarta 11000 ☎ +62 21 5303540 📠 +62 21 5493852 **E:** pr@rcti.tv **W:** www.rcti.tv **Txs:** Jakarta ch43 & network. – **SCTV (PT SURYA CITRA TELEVISI) (Comm)** ✉ Graha SCTV 2nd floor, JI. Gatot Subroto Kav 21, Jakarta 12930 ☎ +62 21 5225555 📠 +62 21 5224777 **E:** pr@sctv.co.id **W:** www.sctv.co.id **Txs:** Jakarta ch45 (120kW) & network. – **TRANS TV (PT TELEVISI TRANSFORMASI INDONESIA) (Comm)** ✉ JI. Kapten Tendean Kav. 12-14A, Jakarta 12790 ☎ +62 21 7944240 📠 +62 21 7992600 **E:** wmaster@transtv.co.id **W:** www.transtv.co.id **Txs:** Jakarta ch29 (80kW) & network. – **TRANS 7 (PT DUTA VISUAL NUSANTARA TIVI TUJUH) (Comm)** ✉ Menara Bank Mega Lt. 20, JI. Kapt. P. Tendean Kav.12-14A, Jakarta 12790 ☎ +62 21 79177000 📠 +62 21 79184684 **E:** info@trans7.co.id **W:** www.trans7.co.id **Txs:** Jakarta ch49 (60kW) & network. – **TVONE (PT LATIVI MEDIA KARYA (Comm)** ✉ Kawasan Industri Pulo Gadung, JI Rawa Teratai II No 2, Jakarta Timur 13260 ☎ +62 21 4613545 📠 +62 21 4616255 **E:** info@tvone.co.id **W:** www.tvone.co.id **Txs:** Jakarta ch53 & network.

Local Stations not shown.

DTT Tx Networks (under construction)
Licensee: TVRI/PT Telekom **Mux 1:** TVRI Nasional, TVRI Sumut, TV Edukasi, MNC TV/Global TV – **Licensee:** Televisi Digital Indonesie

W: tvdigital.kominfo.go.id **Mux 2:** SCTV, ANTV, tvOne, Trans TV, Trans7, Metro TV

Location	M1	M2	kW
Jakarta	42	46	1.5/5

+ nationwide netw. under construction

IRAN

Systems: DVB-T (MPEG4) [E]; § PAL-B/G [E]

ISLAMIC REPUBLIC OF IRAN BROADCASTING (IRIB) (Gov) ✉ P.O.Box 19395 3333, 19395 Tehran ☎ +98 21 22041093 📠 +98 21 22014802 **E:** tv@irib.ir **W:** iribtvnews.ir **L.P:** Pres: Mohammad Sarafraz **Chs (terr.):** IRIB TV1-TV4, IRIB HD, Amouzesh, Bazaar, IFilm, IRINN, Jame Jam 1, Mostanad, Namayesh, Nasim, Ostaniha, Pooya, Quran, Shoma, Tamasha, Varzesh, IRIB Provincial stations, Al-Alam (Arabic)

DTT Tx Network
Tx Operator: IRIB **M1:** IRIB TV1-TV4, Amouzesh, IRINN, Nasim, Ostaniha, Quran, Tamasha, IRIB Provincial stations. **M2:** Bazaar, IFilm, Jame Jam 1, Mostanad, Namayesh, Pooya, Shoma, Varzesh, Al-Alam. **M3:** IRIB HD, Ofogh.

Location	M1	M2	M3
Tehran	37	43	34

+ nationwide MFN

IRAQ

Systems: PAL-B/G [E]; DVB-T (MPEG4) [E]

National Station
IRAQI MEDIA NETWORK (IMN) (Pub) ✉ Salhiya, Baghdad ☎ +964 1 8844412 📠 +964 1 5410480 **W:** www.imn.iq **L.P:** DG: Mohammad Abdul Jabbar Al Shaboot **Chs:** Al-Iraqiya TV, Al-Iraqiya Sports TV, Al-Forqan TV. **Txs:** **Al-Iraqiya TV:** Baghdad ch9 & netw. **Al-Iraqiya Sports TV:** Baghdad ch7 & netw. **Al-Forqan TV:** Baghdad ch37 & netw.

Local Stations & Foreign TV Relays not shown.

Iraqi Kurdistan

DTT Tx Network
Tx Operator: Mix Media ✉ House No 635, Italian City Compound, Erbil ☎ +964 750 6421919 **E:** info@mixmediya.net **W:** www.mixmedya.net **Mux:** multiprgr **Txs:** Erbil & regional MFN.

IRELAND

System: DVB-T (MPEG4) [E]

RTÉ TELEVISION (Pub) ✉ Donnybrook, Dublin 4 ☎ +353 1 2083111 📠 +353 1 2082772 **E:** info@rte.ie **W:** www.rte.ie **L.P:** DG (RTÉ): Noel Curran **Chs:** RTÉ One, RTÉ2, RTÉ News Now, RTÉjr. – **TG4 (Pub)** ✉ Baile na hAbhann, Co. Galway ☎ +353 91 505050 📠 +353 91 505021 **E:** info@tg4.ie **W:** www.tg4.ie **L.P:** DG: Pól Ó Gallchóir – **TV3 (Comm)** ✉ Westgate Business Park, Ballymount, Dublin 24 ☎ +353 1 4193333 📠 +353 1 4193300 **E:** info@tv3.ie **W:** www.tv3.ie **L.P:** CEO (TV3 Group): David McRedmond **Chs:** TV3, 3e.

DTT Tx Networks
Tx Operator: RTÉ Network Ltd **M1:** RTÉ2 HD, RTÉ News Now, 3e, TV3, TG4 ⌘ RTÉ R. 1, R. 1 Extra, 2FM, Lyric FM, Raidió na Gaeltachta, Pulse, 2XM, Choice, Gold, Junior/Chill. **M2:** RTÉ One HD, RTÉ One +1, RTÉjr, UTV Ireland.

Location	M1	M2	kW	Location	M1	M2	kW
Cairn Hill	47	44	160	Mount Leinster	23	26	160
Clermont Carn	52V	56V	160	Mullaghanish	21	24	200
Dungarvan	55	59	10	Spur Hill	45	49	50
Holywell Hill	30	33	20	Three Rock	30	33	126
Kippure	54	58	63	Truskmore	53	57	160
Maghera	48	55	160	Woodcock Hill	47	44	10

+ sites with txs below 10kW.

ISRAEL

System: DVB-T (MPEG4) [E]; DVB-T2 (MPEG4) planned

ISRAEL BROADCASTING AUTHORITY (IBA) (Pub) (In liquidation) ✉161 Jaffa Road, Jerusalem 91280 **L.P:** CEO: Yona Wiesenthal **W:**

www.iba.org.il **Chs:** Channel 1, Channel 33. **Channel 1** ⌧ P.O.Box 7139, Jerusalem 91071 ☎ +972 2 5301333 ≣ +972 2 6291862 **E:** tvdep@iba.org.il **Channel 33** ⌧ P.O.Box 13172, Jerusalem 91131 ☎ +972 2 5013800 **E:** arutz33@iba.org.il – **ISRAEL EDUCATIONAL TELEVISION (IETV) (Pub)** ⌧ 14 Klausner St., Ramat Aviv, 69011 Tel Aviv **W:** www.23tv.co.il ☎ +972 3 6466650 ≣ +972 3 6466523 **L.P:** Dir: Eldad Koblenz **NB:** IBA is to be dissolved in 2016 and to be replaced by a new public broadcasting entity, together with IETV, producing three national TV channels. – **THE SECOND AUTHORITY FOR TELEVISION AND RADIO (Pub)** ⌧ P.O.Box 3445, Jerusalem ☎+972 2 6556222 ≣ +972 2 6556287 **E:** rashut@rashut2.org.il **W:** www.rashut2.org.il **L.P:** Chmn: Eva Madjiboj. **NB:** The Second Authority for Television and Radio supervises the commercial TV channels Channel 2, Channel 10. **Channel 2 (Comm)** ⌧P.O.Box 34122, Jerusalem 95464 ☎ +972 2 6556222 ≣ +972 2 6556286 **W:** reshet.tv. **Channel 10 (Comm)** ⌧53 Derech Hashalom St., Givatayim 53454 ☎ +972 3 7331000 ≣ +972 3 7331040 **W:** www.nana10.co.il **L.P:** CEO: Yossi Varshavsky. – **CHANNEL 99 (KNESSET CHANNEL) (Gov)** ⌧ Kiryat Ben-Gurion, Jerusalem 91950 ☎ +972 2 6541636 **E:** feedback@knesset.gov.il **W:** www.knesset.gov.il.

DTT Tx Networks
Tx Operator: Bezeq ⌧ P.O.Box 1088, Jerusalem 91010 ☎ +972 36 264562 ≣ +972 36 264559 **W:** www.bezeq.co.il **Mux:** IBA Channel 1, IBA Channel 33, Channel 2, Channel 10, The Educational Channel, Channel 99 **Txs:** ch26 (SFN, Central Israel), ch29 (SFN, Northern/ Southern Israel).

WEST BANK & GAZA STRIP
(Palestinian Authority/State of Palestine)

Systems: # PAL-B/G [E]; DVB-T2 (MPEG4) [E]

National Station
PALESTINE PUBLIC BROADCASTING CORP. ⌧ P.O.Box 984, Ramallah Albereih, West Bank ☎ +970 2 2987903 ≣ +970 2 29879031 **E:** pbcinfo@pbc.ps **W:** www.pbc.ps **L.P:** Chmn: Riyad Al-Hassan **Txs:** Nablus ch5, Khan Yunis ch21, Ariha (Jericho) ch21, Kasser-Elhakim (Gaza) ch23, Ramallah ch25, Halhul ch30, Jenin ch31, Betjala ch34.

Local Stations not shown.

DTT Tx Network
Tx Operator: Starcom for Media Services ⌧ Gaza **M:** multiprgr **Tx:** ch34 (Gaza)

ITALY

System: DVB-T (MPEG2), DVB-T2 (MPEG4) [E]

National Stations
RADIOTELEVISIONE ITALIANA (RAI) (Pub) ⌧ Direzione Centrale TV, Viale Mazzini 14, 00195 Roma (RM) ☎ +39 06 36864046 ≣ +39 06 36226422 **E:** portale@rai.it **W:** www.rai.it **L.P:** DG: Antonio Campo Dall'Orto **Chs (terr.):** Rai 1, Rai 2, Rai 3, Rai 4, Rai News 24, Rai Sport 1, Rai Sport 2, Rai Movie, Rai Gulp, Rai YoYo, Rai Scuola, Rai Storia – **LA 7 (Comm)** ⌧ Via della Pineta Sacchetti 229, 00166 Roma (RM) ☎ +39 06 35584 ≣ +39 06 355 84257 **E:** la7@la7.tv **W:** www.la7.tv – **MEDIASET (Comm)** ⌧ Viale Europa 48, Palazzo dei Cigni, 20093 Cologno Monzese (MI) ☎ +39 02 21021 ≣ +39 02 85414283 **W:** www. mediaset.it.

Local Stations not shown.

DTT Tx Networks (DVB-T except where noted)
Licensee: Rai M1: Rai 1, Rai 2, Rai 3, Rai News 24 ✻ Rai R.1-3 **Txs:** Roma (Monte Cavo) ch11 & netw. **M2:** Rai Sport 1, Rai Sport 2, Rai Scuola, TV2000 ✻ Rai radiofd4, Rai radiofd5, GR Parlamento, Rai Isoradio **Txs:** Roma (SFN) ch30 & netw. **M3:** Rai 4, Rai Gulp, Rai Movie, Rai Premium, Rai YoYo **Txs:** Roma (SFN) ch26 & netw. **M4:** Rai 5, Rai HD, Rai Storia **Txs:** Roma (SFN) ch40 & netw. **M5 (DVB-H):** Rai 1, Rai 2, Rai 3, Rai News 24, Rai Storia **Txs:** Roma (SFN) ch25 & netw. – **Licensee:** Dfree **W:** www.dfree.tv **M(✪ exc.*):** Sportitalia*, Premium Cinema HD, Premium Cinema 2 HD, Disney Channel, Disney Jr **Txs:** Roma (SFN) ch50 & netw. – **Licensee:** Mediaset **M1✪:** Premium Menù, Premium Play, Premium Action +24, Premium Cinema 2 +24, Disney Channel +1, Cartoon Network, Premium Sport, Premium Calcio, Premium Calcio 1-6 **Txs:** Roma (SFN) ch52 & netw. **M2✪:** QVC, Mediaset Extra, Italia 2, TOPCrime, Boing, Cartoonito, Fine Living, Rete 4 HD **Txs:** Roma (SFN) ch36 & netw. **M3✪:** Premium Comedy, Premium Calcio HD, Premium Sport HD, Eurosport, Eurosport 2 **Txs:** Roma (SFN) ch38 & netw. **M4✪:** Rete4, Canale5, Italia1,

Iris, La 5, TGCOM24, Rewind, Infinity **Txs:** Roma (SFN) ch49 & netw. **M5✪:** Premium Crime +24, Premium Joi, Premium Stories, Discovery World, BBC Knowledge, Premium Cinema +24, Premium Energy, Premium Emotion, Studio Universal **Txs:** Roma (SFN) ch56 & netw. – **Licensee:** Persidera **W:** www.persidera.it **M1:** Real Time, Agon Channel, RTL 102.5 TV, HSE24, Giallo, DMAX, Entertainment Fact, CuboVision ✻ RTL 102.5 **Txs:** Roma (SFN) ch47 & netw. **M2:** Super!, Gazzetta TV, Sport 2, Telecampione, Mediatext.it, Alice, Leonardo, Marcopolo, Alice Kochen, Italia Channel, Pianeta TV **Txs:** Roma (SFN) ch55 & netw. **M3:** La7, La 7D, K2, Frisbee, Sport 1, MTV, MTV Music, VOD **Txs:** Roma (SFN) ch48 & netw. **M4:** Deejay TV, Cielo, Sky TG24, Iaeffe, Focus, Winga Tv, Radio Italia TV ✻ R. Italia SMI, R. Maria, R. Deejay, R. Capital, m2o **Txs:** Roma (SFN) ch44 & netw. **M5:** Nuvolari, RadioCapitalTivù, Deejay TV +1, Gold TV Italia, La4 Italia, Channel 24, Rete Italia, Italia+, Juwelo, Linea Italia, Padre Pio TV, m2o TV, Onda Latina, TLC Italia, Luci Rosse TV1-TV3 **Txs:** Roma (SFN) ch39 & netw. – **Licensee:** Canale Italia **W:** www.cana-leitalia.it **M1:** Italia 53/83/84/121/126/127/135/136/142/156/159/160, France 24, Cantando Ballando, Italia TV, Top Italia, Canale Italia 2 **Txs:** Roma (SFN) ch39 & netw. **M2:** Italia 3/4/6/53/84, DTV, Canale Italia Musica, Serenissima, Nitegate Vetrina, Nitegate 1✪, Nitegate 2✪ **Txs:** Roma (SFN) ch22 & netw. – **Licensee:** H3G **W:** www.tre.it **M(✪ exc.*):** Canale5 HD, Italia1 HD*, Premium Action HD, Premium Crime HD, Premium Calcio HD **Txs:** Roma (SFN) ch37 & netw. – **Licensee:** Cairo Communication **M:** www.cairocommunication.it **M:** Test **Txs:** Roma (SFN) ch25 & netw. – **Licensee:** Europa 7 **W:** www.europa7.it **M✪ (DVB-T2):** R. 105 TV, R. Montecarlo TV, FLY, Sentimental, Classic, PPV Movie 1k, PPV Movie 2, Dorcel Sex 3D/HD, Dragon TV **Txs:** Roma (SFN) ch8 & netw.
Other licensees: Regional and licensees not shown (except below).

South Tyrol

Regional Licensee: Rundfunk-Anstalt Südtirol (RAS) ⌧ Europallee 164A, 39100 Bozen ☎ +39 0471 546666 ≣ +39 0471 200378 **E:** info@ ras.bz.it **W:** www.ras.bz.it **M1:** ORF eins, ORF2, Das Erste, ZDF, 3Sat, ORF III **M2:** SRF1, SRF2, BR, Kika, Arte, RSI LA1, **M3*:** ZDF HD, SRF1 HD, SRF2 HD **M4*:** ORF eins HD, ORF2 HD, Das Erste HD **Txs: M1:** ch34 (SFN), **M2:** ch51 (SFN) **M3:** ch27 (SFN) **M4:** ch59 (SFN). (*=MPEG4)

IVORY COAST

Systems: # SECAM-K1 [VHF=K]; DVB-T2 (MPEG4) [E] planned

TÉLÉVISION IVOIRIENNE (Gov) ⌧ 08 BP 883, Abidjan 08 ☎ +225 22449039 ≣ +225 22447339 **E:** dgrti@aviso.ci **W:** www.rti.ci **L.P:** DG: Ahmadou Bakayoko **Chs:** RTI1, RTI2. **Txs: RTI1:** Koun ch4 (10kW), Tiémé ch4 (10kW), Séguéla ch5 (10kW), Digo ch5 (2kW), Dimbroko ch6 (2kW), Touba ch6 (1kW), Man ch7 (10kW), Dabakala ch7 (2kW), Abidjan ch8 (10kW), Niangbo ch8 (10kW), Niangué ch8 (10kW), Bouaflé ch9 (10kW) & repeaters. **RTI2:** (-).

JAMAICA

Systems: # NTSC-M [A]; ATSC [A] planned

PUBLIC BROADCASTING CORP. OF JAMAICA (Pub) ⌧ 5-9 South Odeon Avenue, Kingston ☎ +1 876 7549123 ≣ +1 876 9060435 **E:** info@ pbcjamaica.org **W:** www.pbcjamaica.org **Txs:** (-) – **CVM TELEVISION LTD (Comm)** ⌧ 69 Constant Spring Rd, Kingston 10 ☎ +1 876 9319400 ≣ +1 876 9311573 **E:** customerservice@cvmtv.com **W:** www.cvmtv. com **L.P:** CEO: Andre McGlone **Txs:** Marley Hill ch4, Coopers Hill ch9, Ochos Rios ch10, Montego Bay ch11, Cabbage Hill ch12, Port Antonio ch13. – **TELEVISION JAMAICA LTD (TVJ) (Comm)** ⌧ P.O.Box 100, Kingston 10. ☎ +1 876 9265620 ≣ +1 876 9291029 **E:** tvjadmin@ cwjamaica.com **W:** www.televisionjamaica.com **L.P:** GM: Claire C. Grant **Txs:** ZQI-TV: Coopers Hill ch7, Port Antonio ch8, Yallahs ch9, Montego Bay ch9, Kingston ch11, Oracabessa ch12, Spur Tree ch13. – **LOVE TV (Rlg)** ⌧ 81 Hagley Park Road, Kingston 10 ☎ +1 876 9689596 ≣ +1 876 9685379 **L.P:** GM: Moya Thomas **Txs:** Montego Bay ch2, Ochos Rios ch3, Kingston ch6, Huntley ch8, Kingston ch17.

JAPAN

System: ISDB-T [J]

National Stations
NIPPON HOSO KYOKAI (NHK) (Pub) ⌧ 2-1, Jinnan 2-chome, Shibuya-ku, Tokyo 150-8001 ☎ +81 3 34651111 **W:** www.nhk. or.jp **Chs:** NHK General TV, NHK Educational TV **L.P:** Pres: Katsuto Momii – **ALL-NIPPON NEWS NETWORK (ANN) (Comm)** ⌧ 9-1,

Roppongi 6-chome, Minato-ku, Tokyo 106-8001 ☎ +81 3 64061111 **W:** www.tv-asahi.co.jp **LP:** Pres: Shinichi Yoshida. – **FUJI TELEVISION NETWORK (FTN) (Comm)** ▣ 4-8, Daiba 2-chome, Minato-ku, Tokyo 137-8088 ☎ +81 3 55008888 **W:** www.fujitv.co.jp; www.fnn-news.com **LP:** Chmn: Hisashi Hieda. – **JAPAN NEWS NETWORK (JNN) (Comm)** ▣ 3-6, Akasaka 5-chome, Minato-ku, Tokyo 107-8006. ☎ +81 3 37461111 **W:** www.tbs.co.jp **LP:** Chmn: Hiroshi Inoue – **NIPPON NEWS NETWORK (NNN) (Comm)** ▣ 6-1, Higashi Shimbashi 1-chome, Minato-ku, Tokyo 105-7444 ☎ +81 3 62154444 **W:** www.ntv.co.jp; www.news24.jp **LP:** Pres: Yoshio Okubo – **TV TOKYO NETWORK (TXN) (Comm)** ▣ 3-12, Toranomon 4-chome, Minato-ku, Tokyo 105-8012 ☎ +81 3 54707777 **W:** www.tv-tokyo. co.jp **LP:** Pres/CEO: Masayuki Shimada.
NB. Commercial stns are relayed nationwide via local affiliates.

Local Stations not shown.

DTT Tx Networks (National Stations)

Location	NHK¹	NHK²	ANN	FTN	JNN	NNN	TXN
Tokyo (Tokyo Skytree)	27	26	24	21	22	25	23

+ nationwide tx networks ¹) NHK General TV ²) NHK Educational TV

JORDAN

Systems: DVB-T2 (MPEG4) [E]

JORDAN RADIO & TELEVISION (JRTV) (Pub) ▣ P.O.Box 1041, 11118 Amman ☎ +962 6 4749171 ▣ +962 6 4778578 **E:** tv@jrtv. gov.jo **W:** www.jrtv.jo **LP:** DG: Mohammad Tarawneh **Chs:** JTV1, JTV2, JTV3.

DTT Tx Network
Tx Operator: JRTV **Mux:** JTV1, JTV2, JTV3 **Txs:** nationwide MFN.

KAZAKHSTAN

Systems: DVB-T2 (MPEG4) [E]; § SECAM-D/K [R], § PAL-D/K [R]

National Stations
QAZAQ TELEVIZIYASY (Gov) ▣ Jeltoqsan 177, 050013 Almati ☎ +7 727 2635579 ▣ +7 727 2631207 **W:** kaztv.kaztrk.kz **Chs:** Qazaqstan, KAZsport, Balapan, Regional Stations. – **XABAR (Gov)** ▣ Jeltoqsan 185, 050013 Almati ☎ +7 727 2700001 ▣ +7 727 2627805 **E:** khabar@khabar.kz **W:** khabar.kz **Chs:** Xabar, Yel Arna, Kazakh TV, 24 kz – **KTK (Comm)** ▣ Respwblïk alana 13, 050013 Almati ☎ +7 727 2583657 ▣ +7 727 2583693 **E:** ktk@ktk.kz **W:** www.ktk.kz **LP:** DG: Arman Shuraev. – **NTK (Comm)** ▣ Respwblïk alana 13, 050013 Almati ☎ +7 727 2672750 ▣ +7 727 2721154 **E:** office@ntk.kz **W:** www.ntk.kz **LP:** GD: Saida Igenbek – **31 ARNA (Comm)** ▣ Tajibaev 155, 050060 Almati ☎ +7 727 3153131 **E:** tv_31@31.kz **W:** 31.kz.

Local Stations, Foreign TV Relays not shown.

DTT Tx Networks (under construction)
Tx Operator: Kazteleradio **M1:** Qazaqstan, KAZsport, Balapan, Xabar, Yel Arna, Kazakh TV, Bilim, 24 kz, Astana TV, 1 Kanal Evrazia, KTK, NTK, 31 kanal, Sedmoy kanal, Mir **M2:** Balapan HD, Tan, STV, MuzZone, HitTV, 7 news, regional stns **Txs: M1:** ch47 (Almaty) & MFN under construction. **M2:** MFN under construction.

KENYA

Systems: DVB-T2 (MPEG4) [E]

National Stations
KENYA BROADCASTING CORP. (Gov) ▣ P.O.Box 30456, Harry Thuku Road, 00100 Nairobi ☎ +254 20 334567 ▣ +254 20 220675 **E:** kbctv@swiftkenya.com **W:** www.kbc.co.ke **LP:** Chmn: Charles Musyoki Muoki **Chs:** Channel 1, Channel 2, Metro TV. – **CITIZEN TV (Comm)** ▣ P.O.Box 7468, 00300 Nairobi ☎ +254 20 2721415 ▣ +254 20 2724220 **E:** news@royalmedia.co.ke **W:** www.citizentv. co.ke – **KENYA TELEVISION NETWORK (KTN) (Comm)** ▣ P.O.Box 56985, 00100 Nairobi ☎ +254 20 227122 ▣ +254 20 214467 **E:** admin@ktnkenya.com **W:** www.standardmedia.co.ke **LP:** Chmn: Mwakio Sio. – **K24 (Comm)** ▣ 3rd Floor, Longonot Place, Kijabe St., 00100 Nairobi. ☎ +254 20 2444800 **W:** www.news24.co.ke – **NATION TV (NTV) (Comm)** ▣ P.O.Box 49010, Nairobi 00100 GPO ☎ +254 20 3208000 **E:** views@ntv.co.ke **W:** www.ntv.co.ke – **OXYGEN TV (Comm)** ▣ P.O.Box 48445, 00100 Nairobi. **E:** info@odtv.co.ke **LP:** MD: Kass Khimji. – **STELLA VISION (STV) (Comm)** ▣ P.O. Box 20190, Nairobi ☎ +254 20 2712982 ▣ +254 20 2713146.– **FAMILY**

TV (Rlg) ▣ P.O.Box 2330 KNH, Nairobi ☎ +254 20 4200000 ▣ +254 20 4200100 **E:** info@familykenya.com **W:** familymedia.tv

Local Stations not shown.

DTT Tx Networks
Licensee: Signet Ltd (KBC) **M:** KBC Channel One, KBC Channel 2, Metro TV, NTV, KTN, CNBC Africa, K24, STV, EATN, EATV, Oxygen TV, Family TV, God TV, Kiss TV, Classic TV, Citizen TV, GBS ⌘ KBC English Service, KBC Idha FM, Metro FM, Coro FM **Txs:** ch57 (Nairobi 2.5kW) & nationwide netw. – **Licensee:** Pan-Africa Network Group Co. Ltd ▣ P.O.Box 29538, 00100 Nairobi **E:** info@pang.co.ke **W:** www.pang. co.ke **Mux✪:** multiprgr **Txs:** MFN – **Licensee:** Star Times **M✪:** multiprgr **Txs:** MFN.

KIRIBATI

NB: No terrestrial TV station.

KOREA, North (D.P.R. of Korea)

Systems: # PAL-D/K [R]; DTT planned

CENTRAL BROADCASTING COMMITTEE (Gov) ▣ Jonsung-dong, Moranbong District, Pyongyang ☎ +850 2 816035 ▣ +850 2 812100 **LP:** Chmn: Yong Bo Hwang **Chs:** Korean Central Television (KCTV), Mansudae Television Broadcasting Station (MTBS), Ryongnamsan Television Broadcasting Station (RTBS), Sports Television Broadcasting Station (STBS). **Txs: KCTV:** Sangmasan ch1 (10kW), Chayubong ch2 (30kW), Suryongsan ch2 (30kW), Pegebong ch3 (30kW), Hamhung ch3 (70kW), Wonsan ch4 (10kW), Songjinsan ch4 (20kW), Jajiryong ch5 (30kW), Peakam ch5 (10kW), Sambongsan ch5 (10kW), Kangryong ch5 (30kW), Kumgungsan ch5 (30kW), Chongjin ch6 (70kW), Hyangsan ch6 (10kW), Sepo ch6 (70kW), Sinuiju ch6 (70kW), Sariwon ch7 (30kW), Chayubong ch8 (30kW), Haksongsan ch8 (20kW), Kanggye ch8 (70kW), Jaedoksan ch9 (30kW), Unjubong ch9 (70kW), Wangjesan ch9 (30kW), Sepo ch9 (70kW), Sinyang ch9 (30kW), Wonsan ch10 (70kW), Haeju ch11 (70kW), Sambongsan ch11 (10kW), Jonchon ch11 (10kW), Songsan ch12 (10kW), Jajiryong ch12 (30kW), Chongjin ch12 (30kW), Haksongsan ch12 (20kW), Misan ch12 (70kW), Pyongyang ch12 (700kW), Rimbong ch12 (10kW), Robaeksan ch12 (30kW), Tokusan ch12 (20kW) & relay txs below 10kW; **MTBS:** Pyongyang ch5 (350kW); **RTBS:** Kaesong ch8 (30kW), Pyongyang ch9 (140kW); **STBS:** ch(-). **NB:** UHF in Pyongyang: ch25 & 31 (prgrs unconfirmed).

DTT Tx Network (planned)
Tx Operator: Ministry of Post and Telecommunication **M:** KCTV, MTBS, RTBS, STBS **Txs:** (-)

KOREA, South (Rep. of Korea)

System: ATSC [A]

National Stations
EDUCATIONAL BROADCASTING SYSTEM (EBS) (Pub) ▣ 35, Baumoe-ro 1-gil, Seocho-gu, Seoul 06762 ☎ +82 2 5211586 ▣ +82 2 5210241 **W:** www.ebs.co.kr **LP:** Pres: Shin Yong Seb. **Chs:** EBS1, EBS2 – **KOREAN BROADCASTING SYSTEM (KBS) (Pub)** ▣ 113, Yeouigongwon-ro, Yeoungdeungpo-gu, Seoul 07235 ☎ +82 2 7812001 ▣ +82 2 7812099 **W:** www.kbs.co.kr **LP:** Pres: Cho Dae-hyun **Chs:** KBS1, KBS2. – **MUNHWA BROADCASTING CORP. (MBC) (Comm)** ▣ 267, Seongam-ro, Mapo-gu, Seoul 03925 ☎ +82 2 7890011 ▣ +82 2 7823094 **W:** www.imbc.com **LP:** Pres/CEO: Gwang-Han Ahn. – **SEOUL BROADCASTING SYSTEM (SBS) (Comm)** ▣ 161, Mokdongseo-ro, Yangcheon-gu, Seoul 07996 ☎ +82 2 20610006 ▣ +82 2 21133169 **W:** www.sbs.co.kr **LP:** Chmn: Woong-Mo Lee. **Affiliates:** CJB (Cheongju), GTB (Chuncheon), JIBS (Jeju), JTV (Jeonju), KBC (Gwangju), KNN (Busan), TBC (Daegu), TJB (Daejeon), UBC (Ulsan).

Local Stations not shown.

DTT Tx Networks (National Stations)

Location	EBS*	KBS1	KBS2	MBC	SBS
Seoul	18	15	17	14	16

+ nationwide tx network *) Multiplex includes EBS1, EBS2

KOSOVO

Systems: DVB-T2 (MPEG4); § PAL-B/G [E]

National Stations
RADIOTELEVIZIONI I KOSOVËS (RTK) (Pub) ⌨ Rr. "Xhemail Prishtina" nr. 12, 10000 Prishtinë ☎+381 38 230102 🖷 +381 38 235336 **E:** post@rtklive.com **W:** www.rtklive.com **L.P:** Chmn: Ismet Bexheti **Chs (terr.):** RTK1-4 **Txs:** Cërnusha ch7, Zatriq ch9, Maja e Gjelbërt ch12, Prishtinë ch23. – **KOHAVISION TV (KTV) (Comm)** ⌨ Rr. Nene Tereza, 10000 Prishtinë ☎ +381 38 248014 🖷 +381 38 248015 **E:** kohavision@koha.net **W:** www.kohavision.net **Txs:** Cërnusha ch44 & netw. – **TV 21 (Comm)** ⌨ Pallati i Mediave, Aneks II, 10000 Prishtinë ☎ +381 38 241526 🖷 +381 38 241526 **E:** lajmet@rtv21.tv **W:** rtv21.tv **Txs:** Cërnusha ch48 & network.

Local Stations
TV Besa: Rr. Kater Kullat n.n., 20000 Prizereni; ch30. **TV Dukagjini:** Rr. Fehmi Agani 16, Pejë; ch36. **TV Festina:** Rr. Deshmoret e Kombit n.n., Ferizaj; ch40. **TV Herc:** 73000 Shterpcë; ch35. **TV Iliria:** Rr. Hoxhë Jonuzi n.n., 61000 Viti; ch28. **TV Liria:** Rr. Reçak n.n., Ferizaj; ch29. **TV Men:** Rr. Nene Tereza 52, Gjilan; ch47. **TV Mir:** Rr. Vojske Jugoslavije n.n., Leposaviq; ch23. **TV Mitrovica:** Mitrovicë; ch42. **TV Most:** Rr. Nemanjica 14, Zveqan; ch61. **TV Opinion:** Rr. Asdreni 1, 20000 Prizereni; Zym ch28. **TV Prizren:** Rr. Papa Gjon Pali II 1A, Prizereni; ch60. **TV Puls:** Shillovë; Gjilan ch36. **TV Syri Vision:** Rr. Sadik Pozhegu 28, Gjakovë; ch33. **TV Tema:** Rr. Sadik Bega n.n., Ferizaj; ch50. **TV Vali:** Pasjak; Gjilan ch39. **TV Zoom:** Kuvcë e Epërme; ch43. **TV Yeni Donem:** Rr. Gjeravica 13A, 20000 Prizereni; ch53. **TV 3K:** 38217 Soqanicë; ch52.

DTT Tx Networks
Tx Operator: n/a **M1:** RTK 1, RTK 2, RTK 3 i RTK 4, RTK HD, Rrokum HD, KLAN Kosova, TVSH **M2:** RTV21 HD, 21 Plus HD, 21 Popullore, 21 Junior, 21 Mix, 21 Business **M3:** Agon Channel, Vision Plus, Tring Fantasy, Tring Max, Jolly HD, KTV. **Txs:** nationwide MFN under construction.

Systems: DVB-T2 (MPEG4) [E]. BFBS-TV: DVB-T (MPEG4) [E]

KUWAIT TELEVISION (Gov) ⌨ P.O. Box 621, 13007 Safat ☎ +965 22415300 🖷 +965 22454233 **W:** www.media.gov.kw **Chs:** KTV1, KTV2, KTV3, KTV4.

DTT Tx Network
Tx Operator: Ministry of Information **M:** KTV1-4 **Txs:** SFN.

Foreign Military Station
BFBS-TV (British Mil) ⌨ Chalfont Grove, Narcot Lane, Chalfont St Peter, Buckinghamshire, SL9 8TN, United Kingdom. **Mux❂:** BBC One, BBC Two/CBBC, ITV, BFBS Extra/Cbeebies, BFBS Sport, BFBS Movies, Sky News, Sky Sports 1, Sky Sports 2, Sky Sports 3, Nepali TV ⌘ BFBS R., BFBS R.2, BFBS Gurkha R. **Tx:** ch27 (Camp Beuhring)

Systems: DVB-T2 (MPEG4) [E]; § SECAM-D/K [R], § PAL-D/K [R]

National Stations
KOOMDUK TELERADIO BERÜÜ KORPORATSIYASY (KTRK) ⌨ Jash Gvardiya blvd. 59, 720010 Bishkek ☎ +996 312 392059 **E:** public@ktrk.kg **W:** www.ktrk.kg **L.P:** DG: Ilim Karypbekov **Ch:** 1 Kanal Kyrgyzstan – **ELTR (Pub)** ⌨ blvd. Erkindik 122, 720040 Bishkek ☎ +996 312 906144 **L.P:** Dir: Shayyrbek Abdrakhmanov **E:** eltr@ktnet.kg – **5 KANAL (Pub)** ⌨ Ibraimov St 24, 720000 Bishkek ☎ +996 312 592066 **E:** koordinator@5tv.kg **W:** 5tv.kg.

Local Stations, Foreign TV Relays not shown.

DTT Tx Networks
Tx Operator: Kyrgyztelecom ⌨ Chui avenue 96, 720000 Bishkek ☎ +996 312 681616 🖷 +996 312 662424 **E:** info@kt.kg **W:** www.kt.kg **M:** 1 Kanal Kyrgyzstan, ELTR, 5 Kanal, 1 Kanal Russia, Rossiya 1, Rossiya 24, TV Mir **Txs:** ch25 (Bishkek) & nationwide netw.

Systems: DTMB [E]; § PAL-B [E]

National Station
LAO NATIONAL TELEVISION (LNTV) (Gov) ⌨ P.O.Box 5635, Vientiane ☎ +856 21 710643 🖷 +856 21 710182 **E:** laotv1@gmail.

com **W:** www.tnl.gov.la **L.P:** DG: Bounchom Vongphet. **Chs:** TV1, TV3, Provincial stns.

DTT Tx Networks
Licensee: Lao Digital TV Co. Ltd **W:** ldtv-lao.com **Mux 1-3(partly❂):** multiprgr **Txs: Mux 1:** ch21 (Savannakhet 2.5kW) & MFN **Mux 2:** ch23 (Savannakhet 2.5kW) & MFN **Mux 3:** ch25 (Savannakhet 2.5kW) & MFN

System: DVB-T (MPEG4) [E]

National Stations
LATVIJAS TELEVIZIJA (LTV) (Pub) ⌨ Zakusalas krastmala 3, 1509 Riga ☎ +371 67200316 🖷 +371 67200025 **E:** ltv@ltv.lv **W:** ltv.lsm.lv **L.P:** Chmn: Ivars Belte **Chs:** LTV1, LTV7 – **LATVIJAS REGIONU TELEVIZIJA (RE:TV) (Comm)** ⌨ Purva iela 12a, 4201 Valmiera ☎ +371 64219043 🖷 +371 64250881 **E:** redakcija@retv.lv **W:** www.retv.lv **L.P:** Dir: Aiva Logina – **LATVIJAS ŠLAGERKANALS (Comm)** ⌨ Elizabetes iela 57a-22, 1050 Riga ☎ +371 67296345 **E:** info@slageris.lv **W:** www.slageris.lv – **MTG TV LATVIA (Comm)** ⌨ Dzelzavas iela 120g, 1021 Riga ☎ +371 67479100 **E:** pasts@skaties.lv. **W:** skaties.lv **L.P:** CEO: Baiba Zuzena **Chs:** Kanals 2, LNT, TV3, TV5, TV6 – **RIGA TV 24 (Comm)** ⌨ Blaumana iela 32, 1011 Riga ☎ +371 67630301 **E:** reklama@rigatv24.lv **W:** rigatv24.lv **L.P:** Dir: Klavs Kalninš.

Local Station
Vidusdaugavas Televizija (Comm): Brivibas iela 2d, 5201 Jekabpils; ch55 (0.5 kW.

DTT Tx Networks
Licensee: Lattelecom SIA ⌨ Dzirnavu iela 105, 1011 Riga **E:** lat-telecom@lattelecom.lv **W:** www.lattelecom.lv **Mux 1:** LTV1, LTV7, Re:TV, Riga TV 24 **Mux 2❂:** 3+, 360TV, E! Entertainment, Eurosport, Kanals 2, National Geographic, PBK, REN Baltija, STV, TV3, TV5 **Mux 3❂:** Cartoon Network, Euronews, iConcerts, Latvijas Šlagerkanals, LNT, MTV Music 24, NTV Mir, Outdoor Channel, PBMK, RTR Planeta, TV XXI, TV6 **Mux 4❂:** Animal Planet, BBC Entertainment, CNN International, Discovery Channel, Discovery Science, DiscoveryID, DiscoveryWorld, MTV Europe, Nickelodeon, TLC, TravelChannel **Mux 5❂:** AMC, CTC Baltic, Dom Kino, FilmBox, Fox, Fox Life, Hustler TV, Sony Entertainment Television, Sony Turbo, VH1 Europe **Mux 6❂:** Best4Sport, Disney Channel, Disney Junior, Disney XD, Eurosport 2, JimJam, KHL, KidZone, Motors TV, NBA TV, Sport 1 **Mux 7❂:** Discovery HD Showcase, Eurosport HD, MTV HD.

Location	M1	M2	M3	M4	M5	M6	M7	kW
Cesvaine	22	46	41	58	30	24	-	75/2x120/110/2x100
Daugavpils	27	51	64	47	39	40	-	65/80/65/100/2x80
Dundaga	30	-	-	-	-	-	-	15
Kuldiga	30	40	47	52	25	35	-	65/5x80
Liepaja	21	23	39	26	33	35	-	50
Limbazi	21	-	-	-	-	-	-	25
Rezekne	44	50	56	27	39	37	-	5x100/5
Riga	28	31	43	45	48	44	59	5x85/74/80
Valmiera	21	51	54	50	33	37	-	65/3x80/65/25
Viesite	38	46	60	53	26	23	-	16

+ sites with txs below 10kW.

Systems: # PAL-B/G [E]; DVB-T2 (MPEG4) [E]

TÉLÉ-LIBAN (Pub) ⌨ Tallet El Khayat, Corniche canal 7, P.O.Box 4848, Beirut ☎ +961 1 786930 🖷 +961 1 786931 **W:** www.teleliban.com.lb **L.P:** CEO: Talal El Makdessi **Chs:** Channel 1, Channel 2 **Txs: Channel 1:** Beirut ch7 (50kW) & netw., **Channel 2:** Beirut ch9 & netw. – **AL-JADEED TV (Comm)** ⌨ BP 110, 5958 Beirut ☎ +961 1 303300 🖷 +961 1 303300 **E:** info@aljadeed.tv **W:** www.aljadeed.tv. **Txs:** (-). – **AL-MANAR TV** ⌨ BP 354/25, Beirut ☎ +961 1 276000 🖷 +961 1 823794 **E:** info@almanar.com.lb **W:** www.almanar.com.lb **Txs:** (-). – **FUTURE TELEVISION (Comm)** ⌨ BP 13-6052, Sanayeh, Beirut ☎ +961 1 355355 🖷 +961 1 753232 **W:** www.futuretvnetwork.com **Txs:** (-). – **LEBANESE BROADCASTING CORP. (LBC) (Comm)** ⌨ BP 165853, Zouk 111, Beirut ☎ +961 9 850850 🖷 +961 9 850916 **E:** info@lbcgroup.tv **W:** www.lbceurope.com **L.P:** SM: Pierre Al Daher. **Txs:**(-). – **MURR TELEVISION (MTV) (Comm)** ⌨ Ashrafieh Fouad Chehab Street, RML Building, Beirut ☎ +961 1 841020 🖷 +961 1 841029 **W:** mtv.com.lb **L.P:** Chmn/CEO: Michel El Murr. **Txs:** (-). – **NATIONAL BROADCASTING NETWORK (NBN) (Comm)** ⌨ BP

13-6633 Chouran, Beirut ☎ +961 1 841020 🖷 +961 1 841029 **E:** info@nbn.com.lb **W:** www.nbn.com.lb **Txs:** (-).

LESOTHO

Systems: DVB-T2 (MPEG4) [E]; § PAL-I [E]

LESOTHO TELEVISION (LTV) (Gov) 🖃 P.O.Box 552, Maseru 0100 ☎ +266 22323808 🖷 +266 22323808 **W:** www.lnbs.org.ls

Foreign TV Relay (ª=analogue)
TBN (USA): Berea Plateau ªch21, Leribe ªch41.

DTT Tx Network (under construction)
Tx Operator: LNBS **M:** LTV **Txs:** nationwide network.

LIBERIA

System: PAL-B [E]

LIBERIA BROADCASTING SYSTEM (Pub) 🖃 P.O.Box 594, Paynesville ☎ +231 88 6669808 **E:** lbs@yahoo.com **W:** www.facebook.com/Liberia-Broadcasting-System-569460933080763 **LP:** DG: Darryl Ambrose Nmah **Txs:**(-) – **CLAR TV (Comm)** 🖃 Pegasus Building, Mechlin St. 231, Monrovia ☎ +231 6522511 **E:** royalcommedia@yahoo.com **W:** www.royal.com.lr **LP:** SM: Ahmed Pabai **Tx:** Monrovia ch5. – **DCTV (Comm)** 🖃 P.O.Box 1312, Monrovia. **Tx:** Monrovia ch11. – **POWER TV (Comm)** 🖃 Broad & Gurley St., Monrovia ☎ +231 6514343 **Tx:** Monrovia ch9. – **REAL TV (Comm)** 🖃 Ashmun St., Monrovia ☎ +231 6518418 **E:** abkollie2002@yahoo.com **LP:** SM: Aaron Kollie **Tx:** Monrovia ch3.

LIBYA

System: PAL-B/G [E]

LIBYA NATIONAL CHANNEL (LNC) (Gov) 🖃 P.O.Box 80237, Tripoli ☎ +218 21 3402153 🖷 +218 21 3403458 **LP:** DG: Tareq Abdessalam Al Houni **Txs:** (pol.H) Tripoli ch6 (20kW) & network.

Local Stations not shown.

LIECHTENSTEIN

NB: No terrestrial TV station.

LITHUANIA

System: DVB-T (MPEG2, MPEG4) [E]

National Stations
LIETUVOS NACIONALINIS RADIJAS IR TELEVIZIJA (LRT) (Pub) 🖃 Konarskio g. 49, 03123 Vilnius ☎ +370 5 2363100 🖷 +370 5 2363208 **E:** lrt@lrt.lt **W:** www.lrt.lt **LP:** DG: Audrius Siaurusevicius. **Chs (terr.):** LRT Televizija, LRT Kultura. – **LIETUVOS RYTAS TV (Comm)** 🖃 Gedimino pr. 12 A, 01103 Vilnius ☎ +370 5 2743718 🖷 +370 5 2657338 **E:** tv@lrytas.lt **W:** tv.lrytas.lt **LP:** Dir: Linas Ryškus – **UAB TELE-3 (Comm)** 🖃 Kalvariju g. 143, 08221 Vilnius ☎ +370 5 2030101 🖷 +370 5 2030103 **E:** info@tv3.lt **W:** www.tv3.lt **LP:** Dir: Laura Blazeviciute. **Chs:** TV3, TV6, TV8. – **UAB LAISVAS IR NEPRIKLAUSOMAS KANALAS (Comm)** 🖃 Šeškines g. 20, 07156 Vilnius ☎ +370 5 2431058 🖷 +370 5 2123924 **E:** lnk@lnk.lt **W:** lnk.alfa.lt **LP:** DG: Zita Sarakiene. BTV: 🖃 Laisves pr. 60, 05120 Vilnius **Chs** LNK, TV1, Info TV, BTV, Liuks!

Local Stations (all Comm)
Dzukijos televizija: Pramones g. 9, 62175 Alytus; ch55 (3.2kW). **Kedainiu krašto televizija:** Basanavicius g. 36, 57288 Kedainiai; ch46 (1kW). **LN Televizija:** Plateliu g. 17, Plunge; ch40 (0.9kW). **Marijampoles televizija:** Gedimino g. 11, 68307 Marijampole; ch41 (1kW). **Pukas-TV:** Ringuvos g. 61, 45242 Kaunas; ch54 (Juragiai 0.8kW). **PTV:** Peršekininku kaimas, Miroslavo sen., 64262 Alytaus r.; ch49 (Peršekininkai 0.2kW). **Raseiniu krašto televizija:** Vaižganto g. 20, 60130 Raseiniai; ch40 (0.6kW). **Šiauliu televizija:** Liejyklos g. 10, 78147 Šiauliai; ch30 (Bubai 0.9kW). **S Plius:** Tilzes g. 74, 78140 Šiauliai; ch30 (Bubai 0.9kW). **TV7:** Chemiku g. 138a, 55218 Jonava; ch40 (0.3kW). **Ventos regionine televizija:** Ventos g. 32a, Venta, 85316 Akmenes r.; ch37 (Venta 2kW).

DTT Tx Networks
Licensee Mux 1+2: Lietuvos radijo ir televizijos centras (LRTC) 🖃 Sausio 13-osios g. 10, 04347 Vilnius ☎ +370 5 2621511 🖷 +370

5 2040396 **E:** info@telecentras.lt **W:** www.telecentras.lt **M1:** LRT Televizija, LRT Kultura, LNK, TV3, TV1, BTV, TV6, TV8, Info TV, Liuks! **M2 (✪exc.*):** Lietuvos rytas TV*, BBC World News, RTR Planeta, VH1, Pervyy Baltiyskiy, Dozhd, KidZone, RTL, Cartoon Network, Sport 1, Balticum Auksinis. – **Licensee Mux 3+4:** Teo LT 🖃 Savanoriu pr. 28, 03501 Vilnius ☎ +370 5 2621511 🖷 +370 5 2126665 **E:** info@teo.lt **W:** www.teo.lt **M3✪:** TLC, Sony Entertainment, Sony Turbo, Animal Planet, FOX, National Geographic, Discovery, Travel Channel/Playboy TV, Eurosport. **M4 (✪exc.*):** TVP Polonia*, Nickelodeon, CNN, Euronews, Discovery World, FOX Life, MTV Hits, Eurosport 2, Discovery Science – **Licensee Mux B:** Balticum TV 🖃 Taikos pr. 101, 94198 Klaipeda ☎ +370 46 390709 🖷 +370 46 342815 **E:** info@balticum.lt **W:** www.balticum.lt **Mux✪ (MPEG2):** Balticum TV, Balticum Auksinis, Balticum Platinum, Cartoon Channel, Discovery, Eurosport, Pervyy Baltiyskiy, NTV Mir, NatGeo Wild.

Location	M1	M2	M3	M4	B	kW
Bubiai	22	57	51	55	-	20.1/3x17.8
Giruliai	60	36	38	53	45	18.6/10.5/14.1/11/1
Juragiai	44	33	59	45	-	18.6/17.4/2x22
Pazagieniai	29	58	36	37	-	8.7/9.3/2x7
Taurage	60	27	38	-	-	6.8/6/5
Utena	28	22	45	-	-	6.5/6.1/3
Viešintos	49	58	36	-	-	6.8/5.9/4
Vilnius	57	26	50	38	53	31.6/6/23/25/6.3

+ sites with txs below 5kW

LORD HOWE ISLAND (Australia)

NB: No terrestrial TV station.

LUXEMBOURG

System: DVB-T (MPEG2) [E]

RTL GROUP (Comm) 🖃 45, blvd Pierre Frieden, 1543 Luxembourg ☎ +352 24865200 🖷 +352 24865139 **W:** www.rtlgroup.com; www.rtl.lu **LP:** Chmn (RTL Group): Thomas Rabe. **NB:** RTL Group is the company holding for several radio & TV enterprises. Prgrs distributed terrestrially via txs in Luxembourg: **RTL Télé Lëtzebuerg, den 2ten RTL** (in Luxembourgish); **RTL4, RTL5, RTL7, RTL8** (in Dutch, for viewers in the Netherlands); **Club RTL** (in Flemish, for viewers in Belgium); **Plug RTL, RTL TVI** (in French, for viewers in Belgium); **M6** (in French, for viewers in France).

DTT Tx Networks
Tx Operator: BCE **Mux 1:** Club RTL, Plug RTL, RTL TVI, RTL4, RTL5, RTL7 **Tx:** ch24 (Dudelange 40kW) **Mux 2:** RTL Télé Lëtzebuerg, RTL Télé Lëtzebuerg HD, den 2ten RTL **Tx:** ch27 (Dudelange 145kW) **Mux 3:** RTL8, M6 ✂ RTL France **Tx:** ch7 (Dudelange 25kW).

MACAU (China, SAR)

Systems: DTMB (MPEG2) [E]; # PAL-I [E] ⇩2020

TELEDIFUSÃO DE MACAU S.A. (TDM) (Gov) 🖃 CP 446, Macau ☎ +853 28520206 🖷 +853 28520208 **E:** tdmadm@tdm.com.mo **W:** www.tdm.com.mo **LP:** Chmn: Manuel Pires **Txs:** Canal Macau (Portuguese): Monte da Guia ch30 (0.2kW) & 1 repeater; Canal Ou Mun (Chinese): Monte da Guia ch32 (0.2kW) & 1 repeater.

DTT Tx Networks
Tx Operator: TDM **Mux 1:** Canal Macau, Canal Ou Mun, TDM Informação, Strait TV **Mux 2:** CCTV-9, CCTV-13, CCTV News (English), Fujian TV, Hunan TV **Mux 3:** TDM HD, TDM Desporto

Location	M1	M2	M3
SFN	24	43	48

MACEDONIA

System: DVB-T (MPEG4) [E]

National Stations
MAKEDONSKA RADIO-TELEVIZIJA (MRT) (Pub) 🖃 ul. Dolno Nerezi bb, 1000 Skopje ☎ +389 2 258230 🖷 +389 2 3112578 **W:** www.mtv.com.mk **LP:** DG: Julijana Spirovska **Chs:** MRT1, MRT2, MRT3, MRT Sobraniski kanal. – **ALFA (Comm)** 🖃 Gradski stadion, 1000 Skopje ☎ +389 2 3217170 🖷 +389 2 3213795 **W:** www.alfa.mk – **ALSAT-M (Comm)** 🖃 ul. Krste Misirkov 7, DTC Mavrovka lom. C kat 9, 1000 Skopje ☎ +389 2 3290364 🖷 +389 2 3290365 **W:**

alsat.mk – **KANAL 5 (Comm)** ⌨ ul. Skupi bb, 1000 Skopje ☎ +389 2 3091551 🖷 +389 2 3091560 **E:** kanal5@kanal5.com.mk **W:** kanal5.com.mk – **TV SITEL (Comm)** ⌨ ul. Gradski stadion bb, 1000 Skopje ☎ +389 2 3116566 🖷 +389 2 3229799 **E:** marketing@sitel.com.mk **W:** www.sitel.com.mk – **TV TELMA (Comm)** ⌨ ul. Nikola Parapunov bb, 1000 Skopje ☎ +389 2 3076677 🖷 +389 2 3070040 **E:** telma@telma.com.mk **W:** telma.com.mk.

Local Stations not shown.

DTT Tx Networks
Licensee Mux 1-3, 6+7: ONE Telecommunication Services ⌨ bul. Kuzman Josifovski Pitu 15, 1000 Skopje ☎ +389 2 441000 🖷 +389 2 441122 **E:** info@one.mk **W:** www.one.mk **Mux 1-3:** multiprgr **Mux 6:** Alfa, Alsat-M, Kanal 5, TV Telma, TV Sitel. **Mux 7:** local stns – **Licensee Mux 4+5:** MRT **Mux 4:** MRT1, MRT2, MRT3, MRT Sobraniski kanal **Mux 5:** MRT1 HD.

Location	M1	M2	M3	M4	M5	M6	M7
Boskija	21	37	49	34	41	50	54
Crn Vrv	26	28	30	23	52	40	47
Mali Vlaj	32	39	41	26	36	44	50
Pelister	25	29	33	22	37	38	42
Popova Šapka	24	34	38	27	36	41	50
Stracin	21	41	46	37	42	50	56
Turtel	22	32	43	24	39	38	44

MADAGASCAR

Systems: DVB-T2 (MPEG4) [E]; § SECAM-K1 [VHF=K]

National Station
TELEVISIONA MALAGASY (TVM) (Pub) ⌨ BP 271, 101 Antananarivo ☎ +261 20 2221784 🖷 +261 20 2232815 **E:** webtvmalagasy@gmail.com **W:** www.televiziona-malagasy.com **LP:** DG: Lanto Rasata.

Local Stations not shown.

DTT Tx Network
Licensee: Star Times **M(partly◑):** multiprgr **Txs:** MFN.

MADEIRA (Portugal)

System: DVB-T (MPEG4) [E]

RTP MADEIRA (Pub) ⌨ Rua Caminho de Santo António 145, 9020-002 Funchal ☎ +351 291709100 🖷 +351 291741859 **E:** martim.santos@rtp.pt **W:** www.rtp.pt/rtpmadeira **LP:** Dir: Martim Santos.

DTT Tx Network
Licensee: Portugal Telecom **Mux:** RTP1, RTP2, RTP Madeira/RTP3, SIC, TVI, ARTV **Txs:** ch54 (SFN).

MALAWI

Systems: DVB-T2 (MPEG4) [E]; § PAL-I [E] ⇩2016

National Station
MALAWI BROADCASTING CORP. (Pub) ⌨ P.O.Box 30133, Chichiri, Blantyre 3 ☎ +265 1871971 🖷 +265 1871257 **E:** tvmalawi@malawi.net **W:** www.mbc.mw **LP:** DG: Benson Tembo.

Local Stations not shown.

DTT Tx Network
Licensee: Multichoice Malawi **M(partly◑):** MBC TV + multiprgr **Txs:** nationwide MFN netw.

MALAYSIA

Systems: # PAL-B/G [E] ⇩2018; DVB-T (MPEG4) [E]

RADIO TELEVISYEN MALAYSIA (RTM) (Gov) ⌨ Dept. of Broadc, Angkasapuri, Kuala Lumpur 50614 ☎ +60 3 22825333 🖷 +60 3 22825103 **E:** aduan@rtm.gov.my **W:** www.rtm.gov.my **LP:** DG: Dato Norhyati Ismail **Chs:** TV1, TV2, TVi, regional stns. **Txs: TV1:** Kuala Lumpur ch50 & netw.; **TV2:** Kuala Lumpur ch53 & netw. – **METROPOLITAN TV (8TV)** ⌨ Metropolitan TV sdn bhd, Sri Pentas, 3 Persiaran Bandar Utama, 47800 Petaling Jaya, Selangor Darul Ehsan ☎ +60 3 77288282 🖷 +60 3 77268282 **E:** info@8tv.com.my **W:** www.8tv.com.my. **Txs:** Kuala Lumpur ch58 & netw. – **NTV7 (Comm)** ⌨ 7, Jalan Jurubina U1/18, Hicom-Glenmarie Industrial Park, 40000 Shah Alam, Selangor Darul Ehsan ☎ +60 3 55691777 🖷 +60 3 55692515 **E:** feedback@ntv7.com.my **W:** www.ntv7.com.my. **Txs:** Kuala Lumpur ch7 & netw. – **SYSTEM TV MALAYSIA BERHAD (TV3)** ⌨ Sri Pentas (Ground Floor, South Wing) No. 3, Persiaran Banjar Utama, 47800 Petaling Jaya Selangor Darul Ehsan ☎ +60 3 7166333 🖷 +60 3 77278455 **E:** query@tv3.com.my **W:** www.tv3.com.my **LP:** MD: Hisham Abdul Rahman. **Txs:** Kuala Lumpur ch12 & netw. – **TV9 (Comm)** ⌨ Lot 31, Jalan Pelukis U1/46, Temasya Industrial Park, 40150 Shah Alam, Selangor Darul Ehsan ☎ +60 3 55685999 **W:** www.tv9.com.my. **Txs:** Kuala Lumpur ch33 & netw.

DTT Tx Networks (under construction)
Licensee: RTM **Mux:** TV1, TV2, TVi, regional stns **Txs:** ch44 (Kuala Lumpur) & nationwide netw. under construction. – **Licensee:** U Television ⌨ 3rd Floor, KL Plaza, 179 Jalan Bukit Bintang, 55100 Kuala Lumpur **Mux◑:** multiprgr. **Txs:** MFN.

MALDIVES

Systems: # PAL-B [E] ⇩2018; ISDB-T [E] planned

PUBLIC SERVICE MEDIA (PSM) ⌨ Radio Building, Ameenee Magu, Malé, 20331 ☎ +960 3323105 🖷 +960 3325083 **W:** psmnews.mv **LP:** Chmn: Ibrahim Umar Manik **Chs:** TVM One, TVM Plus. **Txs: TVM One:** Malé ch7 (1kW H); **TVM Plus◑** : (-).

MALI

Systems: # SECAM-B/G [VHF=K, UHF=E]; DVB-T (MPEG2) [E]

RADIODIFFUSION TÉLÉVISION DU MALI (ORTM) (Pub) ⌨ BP 171, Bamako ☎ +223 20210737 🖷 +223 20214205 **E:** info@ortm.ml **W:** ortm.ml **LP:** Dir (TV): Youssouf Touré **Chs:** ORTM, TM2 **Txs: ORTM:** Bamako ªch4 (10kW) & relay txs; **TM2:** Bamako ªch49. (ª=analogue)

DTT Tx Network (under construction)
Tx Operator: n/a **M:** ORTM, TM2, TV5 Monde **Txs:** nationwide MFN.

MALTA

System: DVB-T (MPEG2) [E]

PUBLIC BROADCASTING SERVICES LTD (PBS) (Pub) ⌨ 75, Triq San Luqa, Gwardamangia, Pieta', PTA 1022 ☎ +356 21225051 🖷 +356 21244601 **E:** info@tvm.com.mt **W:** www.tvm.com.mt **LP:** Chmn: Tonio Portughese. **Chs:** TVM, TVM2 – **F LIVING CHANNEL (Comm)** ⌨ BME Studios, Gudja Road, Luqa, LQA 2022 ☎ +356 21664566 🖷 +356 21822792 **E:** flivingchannel@gmail.com **W:** fliving.tv **LP:** Dir's (Bonaci Media Entertainment): Karl & Romina Bonaci – **NET TV (Comm)** ⌨ Media.Link Communications, Dar Centrali, Triq Herbert Ganado, Pieta', PTA 1450 ☎ +356 21243641 🖷 +356 21242886 **E:** news@media.link.com.mt **W:** www.nettv.com.mt **LP:** Chmn: Joe Saliba – **ONE TV (Comm)** ⌨ ONE Productions Ltd., A28b, Qasam Industrijali, Marsa, MRS 3000 ☎ +356 25682568 🖷 +356 21248249 **E:** info@one.com.mt **W:** www.one.com.mt **LP:** Chmn: Jason Micallef – **SMASH TV (Comm)** ⌨ 4, Triq Tax-Xewk, Paola, PLA 1341 ☎ +356 21697829 🖷 +356 21697830 **E:** info@smashmalta.com **W:** www.smash.com.mt **LP:** Dir: Joseph Baldacchino – **XEJK TV (Comm)** ⌨ 28, New Street in Valletta Road, Luqa, LQA 6000 ☎ +356 21578022 🖷 +356 21578026 **E:** info@xejkmalta.com **W:** www.xejkmalta.com.

DTT Tx Networks
Licensee: PBS **Mux 1:** TVM, TVM2, F Living Channel, Net TV, One TV, Smash TV, Xejk TV **Mux 2:** TVM HD, TVM2 HD **Txs: M1:** ch66 (SFN), **M2:** ch5 (Valetta). – **Licensee:** GO ⌨ Gnien Spencer, Marsa, MRS 1990 ☎ +356 21212121 🖷 +356 21248925 **E:** info@go.com.mt **W:** www.go.com.mt **Muxes◑:** multiprgr **Txs:** MFN.

MARSHALL ISLANDS (USA associated)

NB: No terrestrial TV station.

MARTINIQUE (France)

System: DVB-T (MPEG4) [E]

MARTINIQUE 1ÈRE (Pub) ⌨ BP 662, F-97263 Fort-de-France

CEDEX ☎ +596 596595200 🖷 +596 596595226 **W:** martinique.la1ere. fr **L.P:** Dir: Augustin Hoareau – **ANTILLES TÉLÉVISION (ATV) (Comm)** 🖃 2 Habitation la Trompeuse, F-97232 Le Lamentin ☎ +596 596754444 🖷 +596 596755565 **E:** accueil@atv.mq **W:** atv.mq **L.P:** DG: Patrick Jean-Pierre – **KANAL MARTINIQUE TÉLÉVISION (KMT) (Comm)** 🖃 Voie n° 7, Renéville, F-97200 Fort-de-France ☎ +596 596718604 🖷 +596 596636485 **E:** webmaster@kmttelevision. com **W:** kmttelevision.com **L.P:** Pres: Roland Laouchez – **ZOUK TV (Comm)** 🖃 Rue de la Pointe Simon, F-97200 Fort-de-France ☎ +596 596712727 🖷 +596 596712728 **E:** contact@zouktv.com **W:** zouktv.com **L.P:** Pres: Emmanuel Granier.

DTT Tx Network
Tx Operator: TDF **M:** Martinique 1ère, France 2-5, France Ô, France 24, Arte, ATV, KMT, Zouk TV **Txs:** ch21 (Riviere Pilote), ch25 (La Trinite), ch37 (Fort-de-France), ch43 (Morne Rouge).

MAURITANIA

Systems: DVB-T (MPEG2) [E]; § SECAM-B [E] ⬇2020

TÉLÉDIFFUSION DE MAURITANIE (TDM) (Pub) 🖃 Ilot A lot Nr 627/TV-Zeina, BP 5176, Nouakchott ☎ +222 45255548 🖷 +222 45255547 **E:** tdm@tdm.mr **W:** www.tdm.mr **L.P:** DG: Mohamed Dieh Ould Sidaty **Chs:** TVM1 TVM Plus **Txs: TVM:** Nouakchott °ch5 (2kW H) & relay txs; **TVM Plus:** (-). (°=analogue)

DTT Tx Network (under construction)
Tx Operator: TDM **M:** TVM1, TVM Plus **Txs:** nationwide MFN.

MAURITIUS

System: DVB-T (MPEG2) [E]

MAURITIUS BROADCASTING CORP. (MBC) (Pub) 🖃 BP 48, Curepipe ☎ +230 6755001 🖷 +230 6757332 **E:** dirgen@mbc.intnet. mu **W:** www.mbcradio.tv **L.P:** DG: Vijay Pritam Purmessur.

DTT Tx Networks
Licensee: Multi Carrier Mauritius Ltd 🖃 Clement Charoux Street, Malherbes, Curepipe ☎ +230 6753234 🖷 +230 6746547 **E:** mcml@ multi-carrier.net **W:** www.multi-carrier.net **M1:** MBC1, MBC2, MBC3, MBC Digital 4, Cine 12, TV5 Monde, Zoom TV ✖ RM1, RM2, Kool FM **M2:** Sports 11, CCTV-9, France 24, MBC Knowledge, Bhojpuri Channel, BBC World News **M3:** Senn Kreol, DD Podhigai, DD Sahyadri, DD Saptagiri, DD Urdu Channel ✖ Best FM **Txs:** MFN

MAYOTTE (France)

System: DVB-T (MPEG4) [E]

MAYOTTE 1ÈRE (Pub) 🖃 BP 660, F-97600 Kaweni, Ile de Mayotte ☎ +262 269601017 🖷 +262 269601852 **W:** mayotte.la1ere.fr **L.P:** Dir: Eric Baraud – **KWEZI TÉLÉVISION (KTV) (Comm)** 🖃 F-97610 Dzaoudzi, Ile de Mayotte **W:** www.linfokwezi.fr – **TÉLÉMANTE (Comm)** 🖃 1, Bahoni Ld Pamandzi, F-97615 Dzaoudzi, Ile de Mayotte ☎ +262 639694792.

DTT Tx Network
Tx Operator: TDF **Mux:** Mayotte 1ère, France 2-5, France Ô, France 24, Arte, KTV, Télémante **Txs:** ch27 (SFN), ch41 (SFN), ch44 (SFN).

MEXICO

Systems: ATSC [A]

National Stations
AZTECA SA DE C.V. (Comm) 🖃 Periférico Sur 4121, Col. Fuentes del Pedregal, México, D.F. 14140 ☎ +52 55 30991313 🖷 +52 55 30991418 **E:** webtv@tvazteca.com **W:** www.tvazteca.com **L.P:** CEO: Benjamin Salinas Sada. **Chs:** Azteca 7, Azteca Trece. **Txs: Azteca 7:** XHIMT-TV Ciudad de México ch24 & relay txs; **Azteca Trece:** XHDF-TV Ciudad de México ch25 & relay txs. – **TELEVISA SA DE C.V. (Comm)** 🖃 2000 Avenida Vasco De Quiroga Santa Fe, México, D.F. 01210 ☎ +52 55 52612000 🖷 +52 55 52612494 **W:** www.televisa.com **L.P:** CEO: Emilio Azcárraga Jean. **Chs:** Canal de las Estrellas, Canal 5, Gala TV, FOROtv. **Txs: Canal de las Estrellas:** XEW-TV Ciudad de México ch48 & relay txs; **Canal 5:** XHGC-TV Ciudad de México ch50 & relay txs; **FOROtv:** XHTV Ciudad de México ch49 & relay txs; **Gala TV:** XEQ-TV Ciudad de México ch44 & relay txs.

Regional/Local Stations not shown.

MICRONESIA (USA associated)

System: NTSC-M [A]

KPON-TV (Comm)🖃 Central Micronesia Communications, P.O.Box 460, Kolonia, Pohnpei, FM 96941. **L.P:** Pres: Bernard Hegenberger. **Tx:** Pohnpei ch7 (1kW). – **TTTK-TV (Comm)** 🖃 Chuuk, FM 96942. **Tx:** Moen ch7 (0.1kW). – **WAAB-TV (Gov)** 🖃 Department of Youth and Civic Affairs, P.O.Box 30, Colonia, Yap, FM 96943 ☎ +1 691 3502502 **Tx:** ch7 (1kW).

MOLDOVA

Systems: DVB-T2 (MPEG4) [E]; § SECAM-D/K [R], § PAL-D/K [R]

National Stations
TELERADIO-MOLDOVA (Pub) 🖃 str. Hâncesti nr. 64, 2018 Chisinau ☎ +373 22 723380 🖷 +373 22 723329 **E:** tvdir@trm.md **W:** www.trm. md **L.P:** Dir (TV) Mircea Surdu **Ch:** Moldova 1 – **ALT TV (Comm)** 🖃 sos.Hîncesti nr. 61, 2028 Chisinau ☎ +373 22 220193 🖷 +373 22 224020 **E:** info@alttv.md **W:** alttv.md – **CANAL 2 (Comm)** 🖃 bd. D.Cantemir nr. 1/1, 2001 Chisinau ☎+373 22 809112 🖷 +373 22 809110 **W:** www.canal2.md – **CANAL 3 (Comm)** 🖃 Str. Banulescu-Bodoni nr. 57/1, 2102 Chisinau ☎ +373 22 854615 **E:** info@media-production.md **W:** canal3.md – **JURNAL TV (Comm)** 🖃 str. Vlaicu Pârcalab 63, 2012 Chisinau ☎ +373 22 235008 🖷 +373 22 234230 **E:** contact@jurnaltv.md **W:** jurnaltv.md – **N4 (Comm)** 🖃 str. Mihai Eminescu, 41/1, 2012 Chisinau ☎ +373 22 821801 **E:** office@n4.md **W:** n4.md – **PRIME (Comm)** 🖃str. Banulescu-Bodoni nr. 57/1, 2005 Chisinau ☎ +373 22 244746 🖷 +373 22 244746 **E:** info@prime.md **W:** prime.md – **PRO TV (Comm)** 🖃str. Maior Petru nr. 7, 2001 Chisinau ☎+373 22 213645 🖷 +373 22 213642 **E:** office@protv.md **W:** protv. md – **PUBLICA TV (Comm)** 🖃str. Ghioceilor nr. 1, 2071 Chisinau ☎+373 22 815555 🖷: +373 22 221722 **W:** www.publika.md – **RU TV (Comm)** 🖃 sos. Hîncesti nr. 59/1, 2028 Chisinau ☎ +373 22 202503 **E:** info@rutv.md **W:** rutv.md – **SUPER TV (Comm)** 🖃bd. Moscova nr. 21, sectia 3, 2068 Chisinau ☎ +373 22 601715 **W:** super-tv.md (Rel. SET, Russia) – **TVC-21 (Comm)** 🖃 str. A. Russo nr. 1, 2068 Chisinau ☎ +373 22 438118 🖷 +373 22 498814 **E:** admin@tvc21.md **W:** tvc21. md – **TV7 (Comm)** 🖃 str. Alecu Russo nr. 1, of. 21, 2068 Chisinau ☎+373 22 438434 🖷: +373 22 438434 **E:** office@amg.md **W:** www. tv7.md (Rel. NTV, Russia).

Local Stations (all analogue)
Albasat TV: str. Suveranitatii nr. 1, 6401 Nisporeni; ch8 (0.2kW). **ART-TV:** str. Eminescu nr.37, 3736 Straseni; Zubresti ch7 (0.01kW). **AVM:** str. Puskin nr. 16, 4601 Edinet; ch25 (0.1kW). **Bas-TV:** str. K. Marx nr. 67, 7401 Basarabeasca; ch26 (0.3kW). **Canal-X:** bd. Independentei nr. 48, 4701 Briceni; ch3 (0.1kW). **Drochia TV:** str. Sorocii nr. 44, ap. 7, 5201 Drochia; ch28 (0.3kW). **Elita TV:** str. 1 mai nr. 2, 5400 Rezina; Rezina ch21 (0.3kW), Soldanesti ch45 (0.4kW). **EuroNova:** str. Suveranitatii nr. 1, 6401 Nisporeni; Ungheni ch39 (5kW). **Flor-TV:** str. Stefan cel Mare nr. 30 A, 5003 Floresti; Vadeni ch38 (0.2kW), Floresti ch48 (0.1kW). **Impuls TV:** str. 31 august nr. 1, of. 304, 7201 Soldanesti; ch7 (0.3kW). **Media TV:** str. Stefan cel Mare nr. 14, 4101 Cimislia; ch43 (0.4kW). **NTS:** str. Mira nr. 12/67, 7401 Taraclia; Ciumai ch38 (0.3kW), Taraclia ch41 (0.3kW). **Realitatea TV:** str. Vlaicu Pârcalab 45, 2012 Chisinau; ch53 (0.3kW). **Sor-TV:** str. Banulescu-Bodoni nr. 2, 3000 Soroca; ch43 (0.3kW). **Studio-L:** bd. M. Eminescu nr. 23, 4301 Causeni; ch35 (0.2kW). **TV Prim:** str. Suveranitatii nr. 5, of. 94, 4901 Glodeni; ch35 (0.4kW). **TV6:** str. 31 August nr. 20-B, 3121 Balti; ch26 (0.3kW).
Gagauzia: TV GAGAUZIA (Pub): str. Lenin nr. 134, 3802 Comrat; Vulcanesti ch24 (0.2kW), Comrat ch36 (0.2kW), Copceac ch47 (0.03kW). – **Aiîn-Aciîc:** str. Cikalov, nr. 59/7, 6101 Ceadîr-Lunga; ch37 (0.03kW). **ATV:** str. Tretiacov nr. 4, of. 36, 3801 Comrat; ch38 (0.2kW). **Eni Ai:** str. Tretiacov nr. 4, 3801 Comrat; ch23 (0.1kW).

DTT Tx Network (under construction)
Tx Operator: Radiocomunicatii 🖃 str. Drumul Viilor nr. 28/2, 2021 Chisinau ☎ +373 22 733914 🖷 +373 22 733874 **E:** office@radiocom. md **W:** www.radiocom.md **M1:** Moldova 1 **M2:** Pro TV, Muz TV, TVC-21, TV7, Canal 3, Canal 2, Jurnal TV, Moldova 1, Prime, N4, Alt TV, Publica TV, RU TV, Noroc TV

Location	M1	M2	Location	M1	M2
Cahul	36	-	Edinet	30	-
Causeni	21	-	Mindesti Noi	22	-
Chisinau	56	58	Straseni	31	-
Cimislia	36	-	Trifesti	28	-

Location	M1	M2	Location	M1	M2
Ungheni	22	-			

TRANSNISTRIA

PRIDNESTROVSKAYA GTRK (PGTRK) ✆ per. Khristoforovo 5, 3300 Tiraspol ☎ +373 533 25708 **W:** tv.pgtrk.ru **L.P:** Dir: Irina Dementyeva **Ch:** Pervyy Pridnestrovskiy **Txs:** Maiac ch5 (1kW), Dnestrovsc ch6, Grigoriopol ch6, Bender & Camenca ch10, Dubasari ch12, Tiraspol ch31, Ribnita ch35. – **TSV (Comm)** ✆ul. Karl Libknekhta 1/2, 3300 Tiraspol ☎ +373 533 63632 🖹 +373 533 63632 **E:** inform@tsv-tv.idknet.com **Txs:** Ribnita ch44, Camenca & Dubasari ch45, Maiac ch47, Dnestrovsc ch49, Tiraspol ch54.

Local Station
BTV (TV Bender): ul. Lenina 17, 3200 Bender; ch26 (0.3kW) (Rel. Domashniy, Russia)

DTT Tx Networks (under construction)
Tx Operator: Ministry of Communications **M1:** NTV, TNT, MTV Russia, Rossiya 1, Rossiya K, STS, TV Zvezda, Rossiya 24 **M2:** Pervyy kanal, Euronews, Pervyy Pridnestrovskiy, Rossiya 2, TVTsi, Karusel **M3:** TV3, 8 kanal, TRO, TV Mir, Ren TV, Europa Plus TV **M4:** Muz-TV, Ru Music, STsi, Otkrytyy Mir, Vsegda s toboy, Domashnyy, 360 Podmoskovye, 7TV **M5:** Sport 2, ReMusic, Sarafan, Shanson, Znanye, DTV, RVTs-TV.

Location	M1	M2	M3	M4	M5
SFN	59	61	63	44	56

Local muxes not shown.

MONACO

System: DVB-T (MPEG2) [E]

TÉLÉ MONTE-CARLO (TMC) (Comm) ✆ 6 Quai Antoine 1er, 98000 Monaco ☎ +377 93151415 🖹 +377 92165481 **E:** tmc@fr.multithematiques.com **W:** www.tmc.tv **L.P:** Pres: Jean Pastorelli.

DTT Tx Networks
Tx Operator: Monaco Telecom ✆ 25 Boulevard de Suisse, 98000 Monaco ☎ +377 99663497 **E:** a.segala@monaco-telecom.mc **W:** www.monaco-telecom.mc **Mux:** TMC, Monaco Info, TF1, France 2-5, M6, Arte, Canal+ (unencrypted sequences), BFM TV, I>télé, Euronews, RAI 1-3, Canale 5, CNBC **Tx:**ch10 (Mont Agel).

MONGOLIA

Systems: DVB-T2 (MPEG4) [E]

National Station
MONGOLIN ÜNDESNIY OLON NIYTIYN RADIO TELEVIZ (MÜONRT) (Pub) ✆ Bayangol district, 11th subdistrict, Huvisgalin Rd. 3, Ulaanbaatar ☎ +976 11 323801 🖹 +976 11 327234 **E:** info@mnb.mn **W:** www.mnb.mn **L.P:** Chmn: Balgansuren Batsukh.

Local Stations not shown.

DTT Tx Networks
Tx Operator: MRTBN **Mux 1-3:** multiprgr **Local Muxes L1-L4 (Ulaanbaatar):** multiprgr.

Location	M1	M2	M3	L1	L2	L3	L4
Ulaanbaatar	39	49	51	31	33	35	37

+ nationwide MFN

MONTENEGRO

System: DVB-T2 (MPEG4) [E]

National Stations
RADIO I TELEVIZIJA CRNE GORE (RTCG) (Pub) ✆ Bul. Dzordza Vašingtona bb, 81000 Podgorica ☎ +382 20 225999 🖹 +382 20 225930 **E:** kontakt@rtcg.me **W:** www.rtcg.me **L.P:** DG: Rade Vojvodic **Chs (terr.):** TVCG1, TVCG2 – **TV PINK M (Comm)** ✆ Bul. Ivana Crnojevica 97, 81000 Podgorica ☎ +382 20 403505 🖹 +382 20 403501 **E:** kabinet@pinkm.co.me **W:** www.pinkm.co.me **L.P:** Dir: Goran Radenovic – **TV PRVA (Comm)** ✆ Bul. Dzordza Vašingtona (Zgr.Unistan, kula C), 81000 Podgorica ☎ +382 20 234840 🖹 +382 20 234838 **E:** vladimir.bukilic@protv.me **W:** www.protv.me **L.P:** Dir: Aleksandar Boškovic – **TV VIJESTI (Comm)** ✆ Trg Republike bb, 81000 Podgorica ☎ +382 20 404601 🖹 +382 20 404636 **E:** desk@vijesti.me **W:** www.vijesti.me **L.P:** Dir: Slavoljub Šcekic.

Local Stations not shown.

DTT Tx Networks
Tx Operator: Radio-difuzni centar d.o.o. ✆ Bulevar Svetlog Petra Cetinjskog 130/V, 81000 Podgorica ☎ +382 20 408000 🖹 +382 20 408005 **E:** rdc@rdc.co.me **W:** www.rdc.co.me **M1:** TVCG1, TVCG2, TV Prva, TV Vijesti, TV Pink M ✖ R. Crne Gore, R. 98 **M2✪:** tbd **M3:** Local stns

Location	M1	M2	M3	kW	Location	M1	M2	M3	kW
Bjelasica	43	25	-	50	Tovic	35	-	-	10
Lovcen	35	27	-	50	Trvdaš	49	22	26	5
Sjenica	24	-	21	10					

+ sites with txs below 5kW.

MONTSERRAT (UK)

System: NTSC-M [A]

ZJB-TV (Gov) ✆ Sweeney's, Montserrat. ☎ +1 664 4912885 🖹 +1 664 4919250 **E:** zjb@gov.ms **W:** zjb.gov.ms **Tx:** Chance Pic ch13. – **ANTILLES TV LTD (Comm)** ✆ P.O. Box 342, Plymouth, Montserrat ☎ +1 664 4912226 🖹 +1 664 4914511 **Tx:** Chance Pic ch7 (48kW).

MOROCCO

Systems: DVB-T (MPEG2) [E]

SOCIÉTÉ NATIONALE DE RADIODIFFUSION ET DE TÉLÉVISION (SNRT) (Gov) ✆ BP 1042, Rabat ☎ +212 37700319 🖹 +212 37722047 **W:** www.snrt.ma **L.P:** DG: Faiçal Laraichi. **Chs (terr.):** Al Aoula, Arriyadia, Arrabia, Assadissa, Aflam, Tamazight, Laayoune TV – **TÉLÉVISION 2M (Semi-Gov, Comm)** ✆ Km 7,3 route de Rabat Ain Sebaa, Casablanca 20250 ☎ +212 22354444 🖹 +212 22343390 **W:** www.2m.ma **L.P:** DG: Salim Cheikh.

DTT Tx Networks
Tx Operator: SNRT **Mux 1:** Al Aoula, 2M, Arriyadia, Arrabia, Assadissa, Aflam **Mux 2:** Al Aoula HD, Aflam, Tamazight, Laayoune TV

Location	M1	M2
Rabat	30	23

+ nationwide network

CEUTA (Spain)

System: DVB-T (MPEG2, MPEG4) [E]

Local Stations
Radio Televisión de Ceuta (RTVCE) (Pub): Alcalde Sanchez Prados n° 5, 51001 Ceuta. **Ceuta Televisión (Comm):** Ceuta.

DTT Tx Networks
Operator: n/a **Mux 1:** La 1, La 1 HD, La 2, 24h, Clan ✖ RNE R. Nacional, RNE R.5. **Txs:** ch52. **Mux 2:** TDP, TDP HD ✖ RNE R. Clásica HQ, RNE R.3 HQ, RNE R. Exterior **Txs:** ch55. **Mux 3:** Discovery MAX, Disney Channel, Paramount Channel ✖ Cope, R. Maria, R. Marca, Vaughn R., eRadio **Txs:** ch53. **Mux 4:** Antena 3, Antena 3 HD, laSexta, laSexta HD, Neox, Nova **Txs:** ch44. **Mux 5:** Telecinco, Telecinco HD, Cuatro, Cuatro HD, FDF, Divinity **Txs:** ch49. **Mux 6:** Boing, Energy, Mega ✖ Europa FM, Melodia FM, Onda Cero **Txs:** ch35. **Mux 7:** tbd **Txs:** ch25. **Local Mux Ceuta:** RTVCE, Ceuta TV, Canal Sur ✖ Radio Ceuta **Tx:** ch37.

MELILLA (Spain)

System: DVB-T (MPEG2, MPEG4) [E]

Local Stations
TV Melilla (TVM) (Pub): Miguel Zazo, 31, 2° 52004 Pontevedra. **Melilla Televisión (Comm):** Los Castaños, Urb Los Balandros n° 33, Aguadulce, 04720 Roquetas de Mar.

DTT Tx Networks
Operator: n/a **Mux 1:** La 1, La 1 HD, La 2, 24h, Clan ✖ RNE R. Nacional, RNE R.5. **Txs:** ch27. **Mux 2:** TDP, TDP HD ✖ RNE R. Clásica HQ, RNE R.3 HQ, RNE R. Exterior **Txs:** ch24. **Mux 3:** Discovery MAX, Disney Channel, Paramount Channel ✖ Cope, R. Maria, R. Marca, Vaughn R., eRadio **Txs:** ch21. **Mux 4:** Antena 3, Antena 3 HD, laSexta, laSexta HD, Neox, Nova **Txs:** ch41. **Mux 5:** Telecinco, Telecinco HD, Cuatro, Cuatro HD, FDF, Divinity **Txs:** ch45. **Mux 6:** Boing, Energy, Mega ✖ Europa FM, Melodia FM, Onda Cero **Txs:** ch38. **Mux 7:** tbd **Txs:** ch36. **Local Mux Melilla:** TV Melilla, Popular TV, Canal Sur, Canal Sur 2. **Tx:** ch43.

MOZAMBIQUE

Systems: DVB-T2 (MPEG4) [E]; § PAL-G [E]

TELEVISÃO DE MOÇAMBIQUE (TVM) (Gov) ✉ CP 2675, Maputo ☎ +258 21 308117 📠 +258 21 308122 **E:** tvm@tvm.co.mz **W:** www.tvm.co.mz **LP:** Chmn: Jaime Alfredo Cuambe **Chs:** TVM, TVM2 – **KTV (Comm)** ✉ Av. Julius Nyerere 390, Maputo ☎ +258 21 491744 📠 +258 21 491745 **E:** ktvcomercial@hotmail.com **LP:** DG: Izilda Kayroniss Mussa – **SOICO TELEVISÃO (STV) (Comm)** ✉ Rua de Timor Leste 108, Maputo ☎ +258 21 315117 📠 +258 21 301865 **E:** stv@soico.co.mz **W:** www.stv.co.mz **LP:** DG: Daniel David. – **TELEVISÃO MIRAMAR (Comm)** ✉ Av. Orlando Mendes 213, R/C, Sommerchield. ☎📠 +258 21 498440 **E:** comercial@miramar.co.mz **W** www.miramar.co.mz.

DTT Tx Networks
Licensee: TVM **M:** TVM, TVM2, RTP África **Txs:** (-) – **Licensee:** Multichoice Moçambique SA ✉ Av. Vladimir Lenine 3071, Maputo ☎ +258 21 416130 **MO:** multiprgr **Txs:** (-) – **Licensee:** StarTimes ✉ Av. Alberth Lithuli 934, Maputo ☎ +258 21 342400 **W:** www.startimes.co.mz **MO:** multiprgr. **Txs:** (-)

MYANMAR

Systems: # NTSC-M [A] ⇩2020; DVB-T2 (MPEG4) [E]

MYANMA RADIO AND TELEVISION (MRTV) (Gov) ✉ Naypyidaw ☎ +95 67 79483 **E:** mrtv@mptmail.net.mm **W:** www.mrtv.gov.mm **Chs:** MRTV, MRTV Entertainment, MRTV-4, Channel7, Readers Channel, Farmer Channel, Hluttaw Channel, MITV, MNTV **Txs: MRTV1:** Yangon ch6 (17kW H) & relay txs. – **MYAWADY TV (Mil)** ✉ Yangon **W:** www.myawady.com.mm **Chs:** MWD1, MWD2, MWD3, MWD4 **Txs:** (-).

DTT Tx Networks
Licensee: MRTV **M:** MRTV, MRTV Entertainment, MRTV-4, Channel7, Readers Channel, Farmer Channel, Hluttaw Channel, MITV, MNTV **Txs:** Nationwide MFN under construction. – **Licensee:** Myawady TV **M:** MWD1, MWD2, MWD3, MWD4 **Tx:** Nationwide MFN under construction.

NAMIBIA

Systems: DVB-T2 (MPEG4) [SA]; § PAL-I [SA] ⇩2016

NAMIBIAN BROADCASTING CORP. (NBC) (Gov) ✉ P.O.Box 321, Windhoek 9000 ☎ +264 61 2913111 📠 +264 61 216209 **E:** pr@nbc.na **W:** www.nbc.na **LP:** DG (acting): Verzenga Kauraisa **Chs:** NBC1, NBC2, NBC3 – **EDU TV (Educ)** ✉ Windhoek. – **ONE AFRICA TV (Comm)** ✉ Storch House, Storch St., Windhoek ☎ +264 61 253190 📠 +264 61 220410 **E:** paul@mac.com.na **W:** www.oneafrica.tv **LP:** MD: Paul van Schalkwyk – **THIS TV (Rlg)** ✉ Windhoek **W:** www.thistv.com.na – **TBN NAMIBIA (Rlg)** ✉ P.O.Box 1587, Swakopmund ☎ +264 64 401100 📠 +264 64 403752 **E:** comments@tbnnamibia.tv **W:** www.tbnnamibia.tv.

DTT Tx Networks
Licensee: NBC **M:** NBC, NBC 1, 2 and 3, One Africa TV, TBN, EDU TV, This TV ✖ 10 NBC Radio prgrs **Txs:** Nationwide MFN – **Licensee:** MultiChoice Namibia Pty. ✉ P.O.Box 2662, Windhoek ☎ +264 61 2705111 📠 +264 61 2705247 **MO:** M-Net, SuperSport 1, SABC Africa, Discovery, Channel O. **Txs:** Windhoek ch13 (0.06kW) & netw.

NAURU

System: PAL-B [NZ]

NAURU TELEVISION (NTV) (Gov) ✉ Government Offices, Yaren District ☎ +674 4443113 📠 +674 4443153 **Txs:** Command Ridge ch4 (0.1kW), NTV studio building ch10 (0.01kW).

NEPAL

Systems: # PAL-B/G [E] ⇩2017; DVB-T2 (MPEG4) [E] planned

NEPAL TELEVISION (Gov) ✉ P.O.Box 3826, Singha Durbar, Kathmandu ☎ +977 1 4200348 📠 +977 1 4200212 **E:** info@ntv.org.np **W:** www.ntv.org.np **LP:** GM: Laxman Humagain **Chs:** NTV, NTV Plus **Txs:** **NTV:** Kathmandu (Pulchowki) ch5 (5kW), Namje ch5 (2kW), Chamere

Danda ch5 (1kW), Sarangkot ch7 (5kW), Jaleshwar ch11 (2kW), Ilam ch12 (5kW) + txs below 1kW; **NTV Plus:** Kathmandu (Pulchowki) ch21 (1kW). – **KANTIPUR TELEVISION (Comm)** ✉ P.O.Box 7368, Subidhanagar, Kathmandu ☎ +977 1 4466300 📠 +977 1 4466321 **E:** info@kantipurtv.com **W:** kantipurtv.com **LP:** MD: Kailash Sirohiya **Txs:** Lalitpur ch23 (5kW), Namje ch23 (5kW).

Local Stations not shown.

NETHERLANDS

System: DVB-T (MPEG2) [E]

National Stations
NEDERLANDSE PUBLIEKE OMROEP (NPO) (Pub) ✉ P.O.Box 26444, 1202 JJ Hilversum ☎ +31 35 6779222 📠 +31 35 6774188 **E:** voorlichting@npo.nl **W:** www.npo.nl **LP:** Chmn: Henk Hagoort. **Chs (terr.):** NPO 1, NPO 2, NPO 3. Prgrs for the NPO are provided by **Nederlandse Omroep Stichting (NOS):** Sumatralaan 45, 1217 GP Hilversum; **NTR:** P.O.Box 29000, 1202 MA Hilversum; and the following broadcasting organizations: **AVROTROS:** Postbus 2, 1200 JA Hilversum; **BNN-VARA:** Postbus 175 1200 AD Hilversum; **EO:** P.O.Box 21000, 1202 BB Hilversum; **KRO-NCRV:** Postbus 200, 1200 AE Hilversum; **MAX:** P.O.Box 554, 2700 AM Hilversum; **VPRO:** P.O.Box 11, 1200 JC Hilversum – **RTL NEDERLAND (Comm)** ✉ P.O.Box 15016, 1200 TV Hilversum ☎ +31 35 6718718 📠 + 31 35 6236892 **E:** info@rtl.nl **W:** www.rtl.nl **Chs (terr.):** RTL4, RTL5, RTL7, RTL8 – **SBS BROADCASTING B.V. (Comm)** ✉ P.O.Box 18179, 1001 ZB Amsterdam ☎ +31 20 8007000 📠 +31 20 8007109 **E:** info@sbs.nl **W:** www.sbs.nl **Chs (terr.):** NET5, SBS6, Veronica TV.

Regional Stations (Pub) (via DTT Mux 1)
a) L1TV: P.O.Box 31, 6200 AA Maastricht; **b) Omroep Brabant TV:** Postbus 108, 5600 AC Eindhoven; **c) Omroep Fryslân TV:** P.O.Box 7600, 8903 JP Leeuwarden; **d) Omroep Zeeland TV:** P.O.Box 1090, 4388 ZH Oost-Souburg; **e) Regio TV Utrecht:** P.O.Box 9043, 3506 GA Utrecht; **f) TV Drenthe:** P.O.Box 999, 9400 AZ Assen; **g) TV Flevoland:** P.O.Box 567, 8200 AN Lelystad; **h) TV Gelderland:** P.O.Box 747, 6800 AS Arnhem; **i) TV Noord:** P.O.Box 30101, 9701 BH Groningen; **j) TV Noord-Holland:** P.O.Box 9823, 1006 AM Amsterdam; **k) TV Oost:** P.O.Box 1000, 7550 BA Hengelo; **l) TV Rijmond:** P.O.Box 350, 3000 AJ Rotterdam; **m) TV West:** P.O.Box 24012, 2490 AA Den Haag.

Local Stations
AT5: P.O.Box 3976, 1001 AT Amsterdam; via DTT Mux 3. **Haarlem 105:** P.O.Box 3355, 2001 DJ Haarlem; ch46V (0.025kW).

DTT Tx Networks
Licensee: KPN ✉ P.O.Box 30000, 2516 CK Den Haag ☎ +31 70 3434343 **W:** www.kpn.com **M1:** NPO 1, NPO 2, NPO 3, Public Regional Stations (a-m) ✖ NPO R.1, 2, 3FM, 4, 5, 6, FunX, Public reg. radio stns **M2O:** RTL4, RTL5, RTL7, NET5, SBS6 ✖ Classic FM, R. 10, Q-Music, R.Veronica, Sky R. 101 FM, Slam!FM, 100%NL **M3O:** BBC One, BBC Two, MTV, NGC, TLC, FOX Eredivisie Live 1, FOX Sports 3/Cartoon Netw./AT5, 24Kitchen ✖ Arrow Classic Rock, BNR Nieuwsradio, R.538 **M4O:** Eén, Canvas, Discovery Channel, Eurosport, Comedy Central, RTL8, Veronica TV/Disney HD, Meiden van Holland Hard **M5O:** CNN, Nickelodeon/TeenNick, Xite, FOX, Investigation Discovery, Ketnet/OP12 ✖ BBC Radio 1-4, SubLime FM, VRT R.1, R.2, Klara, Studio Brussel, MNM.

Location	M1*	M2	M3	M4	M5	kW
Alkmaar	39j	45	34	35	44	20
Alphen a.d.R.	52m	49	57	24	27	10/15/3x2
Amsterdam	39j	49	57	24	27	10
Apeldoorn	42h	36	58	53	28	20
Arnhem	42h	36	58	53	28	20/2x40/2x20
Breda	30b	60	31	32	33	2x20/3x15
Den Bosch	30b	60	31	56	33	2x10/5/10/5
Den Haag	52m	49	57	24	27	10
Den Haag (Zichtenb.)	52m	49	57	24	27	10
Deventer	22k	36	23	47	28	10
Doetinchem	42h	36	58	53	28	20/100/2x20
Eindhoven (Tongelre)	30b	60	31	56	33	15/10/3x15
Eindhoven (Croy)	30b	60	31	56	33	4x10/5
Enschede	22k	36	23	47	28	10/4x20
Goes	54d	48	29	32	35	10
Groningen	46i	30	54	33	25	20
Haarlem	39j	49	57	24	27	20
Heerlen	54a	34	51	51	27	40/20/2x40/20
Helmond	30b	60	31	56	33	20
Hengelo	22k	36	23	47	28	3x40/2x20

Location	M1*	M2	M3	M4	M5	kW
Hilversum	39j	49	57	24	27	15
Ijsselstein	50e	49	57	24	27	3x15/10
Krimpen a.d.IJ.	21l	49	57	24	27	10
Leeuwarden	32c	55	34	21	44	20
Lelystad	26g	36	23	47	44	2x20/10/2x20
Loon op Zand	30b	60	31	56	33	15
Maarssen	50e	49	57	24	27	10
Maastricht	54a	34	51	51	27	20/2x10/15/10
Nijmegen	42h	60	31	56	33	10/20/10/20/15
Oegstgeest	52m	49	57	24	27	15
Oss	42h	60	31	56	33	20/4x10
Oss	30b	-	-	-	-	10
Roermond	54a	34	24	51	27	20
Rosendaal	30b	48	29	32	35	20
Rotterdam (Waalhaven)	21l	49	57	24	27	10
Sittard	54a	34	24	51	27	20
Sliedrecht	21l	49	57	24	27	10
Smilde	60f	30	54	33	25	3x40/30/40
Utrecht	50e	49	57	24	27	10/5/3x4
Veenendaal	50e	36	58	53	28	10
Veenendaal	42h	-	-	-	-	20
Venlo	54a	34	31	56	27	20/40/20/40/20
Zoetermeer	52m	49	57	24	27	10
Zwolle	22k	36	23	47	28	20

+ sites with txs below 10kW. Pol=V. *) incl. regional stns (see above).

NEW CALEDONIA (France)

System: DVB-T (MPEG4) [E]

NOUVELLE CALEDONIE 1ÈRE (Pub) ☞ 1, rue Maréchal Leclerc, F-98848 Nouméa CEDEX ☎ +687 687274327 🖷 +687 687281252 **W:** nouvellecaledonie.la1ere.fr **L.P:** Dir: Wallès Kotra.

DTT Tx Networks
Tx Operator: TDF **Mux:** Nouvelle Caledonie 1ère, France 2-5, France Ô, France 24, Arte **Txs:** MFN

NEW ZEALAND

System: DVB-T (MPEG4), DVB-T2 (MPEG4) [NZ]

National Stations
MAORI TELEVISION (Pub) ☞ P.O.Box 113-017, Newmarket, Auckland 1149 ☎ +64 9 5397000 🖷 +64 9 5397199 **W:** www.maoritelevision.com – **TELEVISION NEW ZEALAND (TVNZ) (Pub)** ☞ P.O.Box 3819, Auckland ☎ +64 9 9167000 🖷 +64 9 9167934 **W:** tvnz.co.nz **L.P:** Chmn: Sir John Anderson **Chs:** TV One, TV One Plus 1, TV2, TV2 +1, TNVZ Pop-up – **MEDIAWORKS TV (Comm)** ☞ P.O.Box 92624, Symonds St., Auckland 1150 ☎ +64 9 9289000 **E:** replies@mediaworks.co.nz **W:** www.mediaworks.co.nz **Chs:** TV3, TV3+, Four, C4, The Edge TV – **PRIME TELEVISION (Comm)** ☞ 1 John Glenn Ave., North Harbour, Auckland ☎ +64 9 4140700 🖷 +64 9 4140701 **E:** info@primetv.co.nz **W:** www.primetv.co.nz.

Local Stations not shown.

DTT Tx Networks (DVB-T except where stated otherwise)
Licensee Mux 1: TVNZ **Mux:** TV One, TV One Plus 1, TV2, TV2 +1, TVNZ Pop-up – **Licensee Mux 2:** MediaWorks **Mux:** TV3, TV3+, C4, Four, The Edge TV – **Licensee Mux 3:** Kordia ☞ P.O.Box 2495, Auckland ☎ +64 9 9166400 🖷 +64 9 9166403 **W:** www.kordiasolutions.com **Mux:** Parliament TV, Maori Television, CTV8, Prime, Choice TV. – **Licensee Mux 4:** IGLOO Ltd ☞ P.O.Box 68700, Newton, Auckland **W:** www.igloo.co.nz **Mux✪ (DVB-T2/MPEG4)** multiprgr.

Location	M1	M2	M3	M4
Auckland (Waiatarua)	29	33	45	31

+ nationwide tx network

NICARAGUA

Systems: # NTSC-M [A]; ISDB-TB [A] planned

CANAL 6 (Comm) ☞ 3 1/2 Carretera Sur Contig o Shell, Managua ☎ +505 22660118🖷 +505 22666522 **E:** info@canal6.com.ni **W:** www.canal6.com.ni **Tx:** Managua ch6 (25kW). – **CANAL 10 (Comm)** ☞ Hotel Mansión Teodolinda, 2c, Abajo ☎ +505 22227788 **W:** canal10.com.ni **Tx:** Managua ch10. – **CANAL 15 (Comm)** ☞ Lomas de Tiscapa, frente al Hospital Militar, Managua ☎ +505 22669086 **E:** info@canal15.com.ni **W:** 100noticias.com.ni **Tx:** Managua ch15.

– **CANAL DE NOTICIAS DE NICARAGUA (CDNN) (Comm)** ☞ Carretera a Masaya Km. 4½, Motorama ½c al Su, Managua ☎ +505 22670170 **W:** www.cdnn23.com **Tx:** Managua ch23. – **MULTINOTICIAS (CANAL 4)** ☞ Del Montoya, 1c al Sur, 1c al Este, Managua ☎ +505 22663420 🖷 +505 22663467 **W:** www.multinoticiastv4.com **Tx:** Managua ch4. – **NICAVISIÓN (Comm)** ☞ Apdo 2766, Managua ☎ +505 22660691 🖷 +505 22661424 **Tx:** ch12. – **TELENICA (CANAL 8) (Comm)** ☞ Apdo Postal 3611, Hotel Mansión Teodolinda 1c al Sur, y ½ Abajo ☎ +505 22665021 🖷 +505 22665024 **W:** www.tn8.tv **Tx:** Managua ch8. – **TELEVICENTRO (CANAL 2) (Comm)** ☞ Apdo Postal 688, Managua ☎ +505 22682222 **E:** canal2@canal2.com.ni **W:** www.canal2.com.ni **Tx:** Managua ch2 (25kW). – **ENLACE NICARAGUA (CANAL 21) (Rlg)** ☞ 12 Avenida SO, Distrito II, Managua ☎ +505 22512000 **E:** nicaragua@enlace.org **W:** www.enlace.org/nicaragua **Tx:** Managua ch21. Rel. TBN (USA).

Local Stations not shown.

NIGER

Systems: DVB-T2 (MPEG4); § SECAM-K1 [VHF=K]

TÉLÉ-SAHEL (Gov) ☞ BP 309, Niamey ☎ +227 20723686 🖷 +227 20723153 **E:** ortny@intnet.net **W:** www.ortn.ne **L.P:** Dir TV: Moussa Abdou Saley. **Chs:** Télé Sahel, Tal TV. **Txs:** (pol.H exc. where stated) **Télé Sahel:** Agadez ch4 (10kW), Dosso ch4 (10kW), Zinder ch5 (10kW), Arlit ch6 (1kW), Maradi ch7V (10kW), Dogondoutchi ch7 (1kW), Gaya ch8V (1kW), Niamey ch9 (10kW), Konni ch9 (10kW), Diffa ch9 (10kW) & repeaters. **Tal TV:** (-). – **TÉNÉRÉ TV (Comm)** ☞ BP 13600, Niamey ☎ +227 20736576 🖷 +227 20737775 **E:** tenerefm@intnet.net **Txs:** (-).

DTT Tx Network (under construction)
Tx Operator: n/a **M:** Télé Sahel, Tal TV, Ténéré TV **Txs:** MFN.

NIGERIA

Systems: DVB-T2 (MPEG4) [E]; § PAL-B [E]

National Station
NIGERIAN TELEVISION AUTHORITY (NTA) (Pub) ☞ P.M.B 113, Garki, Abuja ☎ +234 9 2346907 🖷 +234 9 2345914 **E:** servicom@nta.com.ng **W:** www.nta.com.ng **L.P:** Chmn: Patrick Ogbu **Chs:** NTA, NTA2, reg. stns.

Local Stations
DBN Television (Comm): The Dream Centre, Durosinmi etti Drive, Lekki Phase 1, Lagos. **Galaxy TV (Comm):** Lagos. – **Lagos TV (Comm)** Lagos. – **Minaj Broadcast International (MBI) (Comm)** ☞ P.O.Box 3975, Mushin, Lagos.

DTT Tx Network
Tx Operator: NTA **M:** NTA, NTA2, regional stns **Txs:** nationwide MFN.

NIUE

System: PAL-B [NZ]

TV NIUE ☞ P.O.Box 68, Alofi ☎ +683 4026 🖷 +683 4217 **E:** gm.bcn@mail.gov.nu **L.P:** GM: Trever Tiakia **Txs:** Makefu ch4 (0.01kW), Alofi ch6 (0.75kW), Mutulau ch8 (0.04kW).

NORFOLK ISLAND (Australia)

Systems: DVB-T (MPEG2) [NZ]

TV NORFOLK ISLAND (TVNI) ☞ Taylors Road, Norfolk Island 2899, Australia ☎ +672 3 52500 **Txs:** TVNI: ch10 (Mt. Pitt); **Rel. Hope Channel (USA):** ch7V (Mt. Pitt 0.02kW).

DTT Tx Network
Tx Operator: Norfolk Telecom **Mux 1:** ABC, ABC2, ABC News 24 ⌘ ABC Jazz R., ABC Double J. **Mux 2:** Seven, Imparja, SBS One, SBS Two **Txs: Mux 1:** ch25 (Mt. Pitt 0.02kW), **Mux 2:** ch32 (Mt. Pitt 0.02kW)

N. MARIANA IS (USA associated)

NB: No terrestrial TV station.

NORWAY

System: DVB-T (MPEG4) [E]

National Stations
NORSK RIKSKRINGKASTING (NRK) (Pub) ✉ 0340 Oslo ☎ +47 23047000 🖷 +47 23047799 **E:** info@nrk.no **W:** www.nrk.no **L.P:** DG: Thor Gjermund Eriksen. **Chs:** NRK1 (incl. regional prgrs), NRK2, NRK3/ NRK Super – **CANAL DIGITAL (Comm)** ✉4896 Grimstad ☎ +47 81559600 🖷 +47 22939305 **E:** kundeservice@canaldigital.no **W:** www. canaldigital.no – **TV2 (Comm)** ✉ Postboks 7222, 5020 Bergen ☎ +47 55908070 🖷 +47 55908090 **E:** info@tv2.no **W:** www.tv2.no **L.P:** CEO: Olav T. Sandnes. – **TV NORGE (Comm)** ✉ Postboks 4800 Nydalen, 0422 Oslo ☎ +47 21022000 🖷 +47 22051000 **E:** tvnorge@tvnorge.no **W:** www.tvnorge.no **L.P:** CEO: Harald Strømme.

Local Stations (all Comm) (via Mux 3)
a) TKTV: P.O.Box 8, 6501 Kristiansund; **b) TV Haugaland:** P.O.Box 408, 5501 Haugesund; **c) TV Nord:** P.O.Box 1193, 9504 Alta; **d) TV Telemark:** P.O.Box 2833, 3702 Skien; **e) TV Vest:** Lervigsveien 16, 4095 Stavanger; **f) TV Vestfold:** Bjellandveien 24, 3172, Tønsberg; **g) TV Øst:** Hjellumveien 89, 2322 Ridabu.

DTT Tx Networks
Licensee: Norges televisjon AS ✉ P.O.Box 313, 0511 Oslo ☎ +47 22883780 🖷 +47 22883781 **E:** info@ntv.no **W:** www.ntv.no **M1:** NRK1 (incl. reg prgrs), NRK2, NRK3/NRK Super ⌘ NRK P1, P1+, P3, P13, mP3, Super, Alltid Nyheter, Jazz, Klassisk, Folkemusikk, Sport, Sámi R. **M2** (⊘exc.*):** TV2 HD*, TV2 Humor, TV2 Livsstil, TV2 Nyhetskanalen, TV2 Sportskanalen, TV2 Sport Premium, TV2 Sport Premium 2 **M3** (⊘exc.*):** BBC World News, C More Live 2, Eurosport, FEM, FOX, Frikanalen/Local Stations*, MTV, National Geographic, TV6, TV Norge HD ⌘ R. 1, R. Norge **M4⊘:** Animal Planet, C More First, C More Fotball, C More Live, C More Series, Discovery Channel, Disney Channel, MAX, TLC, TV3, Viasat 4 **M5⊘:** BBC Brit, Disney Junior, Disney XD, History, SVT1, TNT, TV2 Sport Premium 2, TV2 Zebra HD, Visjon Norge, VOX.

Location	M1	M2	M3*	M4	M5	kW
Bagn	32	39	42g	22	59	50
Bergen	33	49	39	43	53	50
Bjerkreim	23	26	30e	27	34	50
Bokn	36	54	57b	44	35	50
Bremager	25	28	31	46	52	50
Førde	35	45	48	22	32	10
Gamlemsveten	37	38	54a	24	34	50
Gausta	25	27	35	32	42	10
Greipstad	51	54	47	36	60	50
Grong	21	31	35	24	34	50
Gulen	37	42	26	29	23	50
Hadsel	45	48	58	25	38	50
Halden	32	42	31	38	45	60
Hammerfest	33	37	48c	41	26	50
Hemnes	42	45	48	29	39	50
Hovdefjell	41	52	48	55	58	40
Jetta	45	48	58g	41	51	50
Kistefjell	26	46	43	23	36	50
Kongsberg	60	34	51	43	44	50
Kongsvinger	24	48	55	28	41	50
Kopparen	26	40	45	23	36	50
Lyngdal	25	53	47	32	33	50
Lønahorgi	31	41	44	46	54	50
Melhus	55	28	25	30	33	50
Mosvik	44	47	46	37	41	50
Narvik	21	27	37	24	34	50
Nordfjordeid	40	44	33	27	30	10
Nordhue	33	43	56g	27	31	50
Nordkapp	30	40	43c	23	53	50
Oslo	52	58	46	30	40	50
Reinsfjell	39	42	35a	25	53	50
Salten	50	43	60	30	33	50
Skien	60	34	54d	24	44	50
Sogndal	21	24	34	38	57	50
Steigen	31	41	44	47	55	50
Stord	55	58	60b	47	50	50
Trolltind	27	39	42	34	22	50
Tron	26	34	49g	23	40	50
Varanger	28	33	50c	35	41	50
Vega	25	32	37	22	28	50

+ sites with txs below 10kW. *) incl. local stns (see above)

OMAN

Systems: # PAL-B/G [E]; DVB-T2 (MPEG4)

SULTANATE OF OMAN TELEVISION (Gov) ✉ P.O.Box 600, 113 Muscat, Oman ☎ +968 24603888 🖷 +968 24604629 **E:** tvradio@ omantel.net.om **W:** www.oman-tv.gov.om **L.P:** DG: Abdullah Bin Said Al Abri **Txs:** Bahlah ch5 (4kW), Shinas ch5 (7kW), Sur ch7 (15kW), Thamret ch8V (100kW), Al-Amirat ch10, Nizwa ch10 (100kW), Saham ch11 (200kW), Al-Berami ch12, Ibra ch12 (6kW), Maserah ch24, Dhank ch25 (2kW), Haima ch28, Adam ch40, Madha ch48, Barka ch51, Ibri ch55, Jabal Qahwi ch60 & low power txs.

DTT Tx Network (under construction)
Tx Operator: Ministry of Transport and Communications **M:** multiprgr **Txs:** national network planned

PAKISTAN

System: PAL-B/G [E]

PAKISTAN TELEVISION CORP. LTD (PTV) (Gov) ✉ P.O.Box 1221, Islamabad 44000 ☎ +92 51 9208651 🖷 +92 51 9203406 **E:** ptvhq@ hotmail.com **W:** www.ptv.com.pk **L.P:** MD: Muhammad Malick **Chs (terr.):** PTV Home, PTV News, regional stns, PTV Bolan, AJK TV **Txs:** **PTV Home:** Islamabad ch6 (50kW) & network; **PTV News:** (-) – **ATV (Comm)** ✉ 11 -F, Model Town, Lahore ☎ +92 42 5853669 🖷 +92 42 5853668 **E:** info@atv.com.pk **W:** www.atv.com.pk **Txs:** (-).

PALAU (USA associated)

NB: No terrestrial TV station.

PANAMA

Systems: # NTSC-M [A] ⇩2017; DVB-T (MPEG2) [A]

National Stations
SYSTEMA ESTATAL DE RADIO Y TELEVISIÓN (SERT) (Pub) ✉ Apt. 0843-0256, Curundu, diagonal al Ministerio de Obras Públicas, Panamá ☎ +507 5071500 🖷 +507 2362987 **E:** administracion@ sertv.gob.pa **W:** www.sertv.gob.pa **Chs:** SERTV **Txs:** Panamá ch11 & relays. – **FETV (CANAL 5) (Educ)** ✉Ave Ricardo J. Alfaro Contiguo al Gimnasio de la USMA, Apdo.6-7295, El Dorado, Panamá ☎ +507 2308000 🖷+507 2301955 **W:** www.fetv.org **L.P:** DG: Manuel Santiago Blanquer i Planells **Txs:** Panamá ch5 (30kW) & relays. – **COMPAÑIA DIGITAL DE TELEVISIÓN, S.A (NEXTV) (Comm)** ✉ Via Espana Sector de Carrasquilla, Apdo. postal 87-1989, Zona 7, Panamá **W:** nextvpanama.com **Txs:** Panamá ch21 (20kW) & relays. – **RPC TELEVISIÓN (CANAL 4) (Comm)** ✉Ave 12 de Octubre, Apartado 1-1425, Panamá 8 ☎ +507 2104104 **W:** www.rpctv.com **Txs:** Panamá ch4 (30kW) & relays. – **TELEMETRO (CANAL 13) (Comm)** ✉ Ave 12 de Octubre, Apartado 0827-00116, Panamá ☎ +507 2106845 🖷 +507 2106929 **W:** www.telemetro.com **L.P:** Pres: Fernando Eleta Almarán **Txs:** Panamá ch13 (30kW) & relays. **TELEVISORA NACIONAL S.A (TVN) (Comm)** ✉ Apt. 0819-07129, El Dorado, Panamá ☎ +507 2793700 🖷 +507 2362987 **E:** tvn@tvn-2.com **W:** www.tvn-2.com **L.P:** DG: Agustin De La Guardia **Chs:** TVN, TVN HD, TVMAX **Txs: TVN:** Panamá ch2 (18kW) & relays; **TVMAX:** Panamá ch9.

Local Stations not shown.

DTT Tx Networks (under construction)
Tx Operator: n/a **M1:** SERTV ⌘ R. Nacional, Crisol FM **M2:** RPC, Telemetro HD, Mall TV **Mux 3:** TVN HD, TVN +, TVMAX HD **Mux 4:** Hosanna Vision ⌘ Hosanna R. **Mux 5:** FETV **Mux 6:** NEXtv, +23 ⌘ RCM R.

Location	M1	M2	M3	M4	M5	M6
Panamá	41	42	45	47	48	49

+ nationwide network under construction

PAPUA NEW GUINEA

Systems: # PAL-B/G [NZ] ⇩2017; DVB-T2 (MPEG4) [NZ]

EMTV (Comm) ✉ P.O.Box 443, Boroko NCD 111 ☎ +675 3257322 🖷 +675 3254450 **E:** emtv@datec.com.pg **W:** www.emtv.com.pg **L.P:** CEO (Media Niugini Ltd): Bhanu Sud. **Txs:** Burns Peak ch9 (1.1kW), Air Niugini Hill ch31 (0.17kW), Garden City ch68 (0.02kW) [all Port

Moresby area).

DTT Tx Network (under construction)
Tx Operator: Digicel **M:** EMTV **Txs:** national network planned

PARAGUAY

Systems: # PAL-N [A] ⇩2022; ISDB-TB [A]

National Stations (ª=analogue)
TV PÚBLICA PARAGUAY (Pub) ☐ Avda. Alberdi 633 c/Gral Díaz, Asunción ☎ +595 21 494000 **E:** info@tvpublica.com.py **W:** www.tvpublica.com.py **Txs:** Asunción ªch14/ch15 – **LATELE (Comm)** ☐ Av. Eusebio Ayala 2995, Esq. Pasaje Tembetary, Asunción ☎ +595 21 4157400 **E:** info@latele.com.py **W:** www.latele.com.py **Txs:** Asunción ªch11 (40kW) & relays. – **PARAVISION (Comm)** ☐ Av. Mariscal López esq. Bélgica, Asunción ☎ +595 21 664380 **E:** info@paravision.com.py **W:** www.paravision.com.py **Txs:** Asunción ªch5 (20kW) & relays. – **RED GUARANI (Comm)** ☐ Gral. Santos 1024 c/Concordia, Asunción ☎ +595 21 205444 **E:** info@redguarani.com.py **W:** www.red-guarani.com.py **Txs:** Asunción ªch2 (20kW) & relays. – **RED PRIVADA DE COMUNICACIÓN (RPC) (Comm)** ☐ Calles Comendador Nicolás Bó y Guaranies, Lambaré, Asunción ☎ +595 21 332823 ☐ +595 21 331695 **E:** commercial@rpc.com.py **W:** www.rpc.com.py **Txs:** Asunción ªch13 (40kW) & relays. – **SISTEMA NACIONAL DE TELEVISIÓN (SNT) (Comm)** ☐ Av. Carlos Antonio Lopez 572, Asunción ☎ +595 21 424222 ☐ +595 21 480230 **E:** snt@snt.com.py **W:** www.snt.com.py **Txs:** Asunción ªch9 (40kW) & relays. – **TELEFUTURO (Comm)** ☐ Andrade c/ O'Higgins, Villa Morra, Asunción ☎ +595 21 608756 **W:** www.telefuturo.com.py **Txs:** Asunción ªch4 (60kW) & relays.

Local Stations not shown.

PERU

Systems: # NTSC-M [A] ⇩2020; ISDB-TB [A]

National Stations (ª=analogue)
TV PERÚ (Gov) ☐ Av. Jose Galvez 1040, Santa Beatriz, Líma ☎ +51 1 6190707 ☐ +51 1 6190711 **W:** www.typeru.gob.pe **Txs:** Líma ªch7 (10kW)/ch16 (0.24kW) & relays txs. – **AMERICA TELEVISIÓN (Comm)** ☐ Montero Rosas 1099, Santa Beatriz, Líma ☎ +51 1 2657361 ☐ +51 1 2656976 **E:** americanoticias@americatv.com.pe **W:** www.americatv.com.pe **LP:** CEO: Eric Jurgensen **Txs:** Líma ªch4 (2kW)/ch24 (0.24kW) & relay txs. – **ATV (ANDINA DE RADIODIFUSIÓN) (Comm)** ☐ Arequipa 3570, San Isidro, Apartado 270077, Líma ☎ +51 1 2212261 ☐ +51 1 4217263 **W:** www.atv.pe **Txs:** Líma ªch9 (315kW)/ch18 (1kW) & relay txs. – **FRECUENCIA LATINA (Comm)** ☐ Av. San Felipe 968, Jesús Mariá, Líma 11 ☎ +51 1 4707272 ☐ +51 1 4712688 **E:** info@latina.pe **W:** www.latina.pe **Txs:** Líma ªch2 (22,5kW)/ch20 (0.24kW) & relays txs. – **PANAMERICANA TELEVISIÓN (Comm)** ☐ Av. Arequipa 1110, Líma ☎ +51 1 4113200 ☐ +51 1 4113309 **W:** www.panamericana.pe **Txs:** Líma ªch5 (290kW)/ch26 (0.24kW)& relay txs. – **RBC TELEVISIÓN (Comm)** ☐ Manco Capac 333, La Victoria, Líma ☎ +51 1 4337674 ☐ +51 1 4331237 **W:** www.rbctelevision.com **Txs:** Líma ªch11 (30kW)/ch38 (0.24kW) & relays.

Local Stations not shown.

PHILIPPINES

Systems: ISDB-TB [A]; # NTSC-M [A] ⇩2018

National Stations (ª=analogue)
INTERCONTINENTAL BROADCASTING CORP. (IBC) (Gov) ☐ Broadcast City, Capitol Hills, Diliman, Quezon City ☎ +63 2 9318781 ☐ +63 2 9324611 **LP:** Pres/CEO: Manolito Ocampo-Cruz. **Txs:** DZTV-TV Manila ªch13 (50kW) & relay stns. – **PEOPLE'S TELEVISION NETWORK, INC (PTV) (Gov)** ☐ Broadcast Complex, Visayas Ave, Quezon City 1100 ☎ +63 2 9206521 ☐ +63 2 9204342 **W:** ptv.ph **LP:** GM: Renato Caluag. **Txs:** DGWT-TV Manila ªch4 (50kW)/ch48 & relay stns. – **PROGRESSIVE BROADCASTING CORP. (UNTV) (Pub)** ☐ #907 ESDA Philam, Quezon City. **W:** www.untvweb.com **LP:** Pres: Alfredo L. Henares. **Txs:** DWAO-TV Manila ªch37 (2058kW)/38 & relay stns. – **9MEDIA CORP., INC. (Comm)** ☐ Broadcast City, Capitol Hills, Quezon City ☎+63 2 9315080 ☐ +63 2 9321470 **LP:** Pres/CEO: Reggie Galura **Txs:** DZKB-TV Manila ªch9 (50kW) & relay stns. – **ABC DEVELOPMENT CORP. (TV5) (Comm)** ☐ AMPC Bldg., 136 Amorsolo cor. Gamboa Sts., Legaspi Village, Makati City ☎+63 2 8923801 ☐ +63 2 8154314 **W:** www.tv5.com.ph **LP:** Chmn: Manny V. Pangilinan. **Txs:** DWET-TV Manila ªch5 (55kW)/42 & relay stns. – **ABS-CBN BROADCASTING CORP. (Comm)** ☐Eugenio Lopez Jnr

St, Quezon C. ☎+63 2 4111166 ☐ +63 2 4152272 **W:** www.abs-cbn.com **LP:** Chmn/CEO: Eugenio Lopez III. **Txs:** **ABS-CBN:** DWAC-TV Manila ªch23 (1125kW)/ch47 & relay stns, **ABS-CBN Sports+Action:** DWAC-TV Manila ªch23 (1126kW) & relay stns. – **GMA NETWOR, INC (Comm)** ☐ EDSA, Diliman, Quezon City, Metro Manila ☎ +63 2 9285041 ☐ +63 2 9285041 **W:** www.gmanetwork.com **LP:** Chmn/CEO: Felipe Gozon. **Txs:** DZBB-TV Manila ªch7 (100kW)/ch27 & relay stns. – **RADIO MINDANAO NETWORK (RMN TV) (Comm)** ☐ 4F State Condominium I, Salcedo St., Legaspi Village, Makati City ☎ +63 2 8120540 ☐ +63 2 8163680 **W:** rmn.ph **LP:** Pres/CEO: Eric S. Canoy. **Txs:** DWKC-TV Manila ªch31 (50kW) & relay stns (rel. BEAM TV). – **RAJAH BROADCASTING NETWORK, INC. (2ND AVENUE/RJTV) (Comm)** ☐ 3/F Save-A-Lot Mall, 2284 Pasong Tamo Ext., Makati City ☎ +63 2 8933404 ☐ +63 2 8932360 **E:** rjofc@compass.com.ph **W:** www.rjplanet.com **LP:** Owner: Ramon Jacinto **Txs:** DZRJ-TV Manila ªch29 (1354kW) & relay stns. – **SOUTHERN BROADCASTING NETWORK, INC. (SBN/ETC NEWS CHANNEL) (Comm)** ☐ Suite 2901 Jollibee Plaza, Emerald Ave., Ortigas Center, Pasig City ☎ +63 2 6363286 ☐ +63 2 6363288 **E:** genceo@sbnphilippines.net **W:** www.solarentertainmentcorp.com **LP:** Pres/CEO: Teofilo A. Henson **Txs:** DWCP-TV Manila ªch21 (40kW) & relay stns. – **GATEWAY UHF BROADCASTING (3ABN) (RIg)** ☐ Sumulong Highway, Block 5, Brgy. Sta. Cruz, Antipolo City **Txs:** DWVN-TV Manila ªch45 (5kW) & relay stns. – **SONSHINE MEDIA NETWORK INTERNATIONAL (SMNI) (RIg)** ☐ Suite 3102 31/F Jollibee Plaza, F. Ortigas Jr. Road, Ortigas Center, Pasig City, 1600 ☎ +63 2 6830772 ☐ +63 2 6830775 **E:** sonshine@sonshine-media.com **W:** www.smni.com **Txs:** DWBP-TV Manila ªch39 (50kW)/28 & relay stns. – **ZOE BROADCASTING NETWORK, INC. (RIg)** ☐ 22F Strata 2000 Bldg., F. Ortigas Road, Ortigas Ctr, Pasig City ☎ +63 6383469 **W:** www.lightnetwork.ph **LP:** Chmn: Eddie Villanueva. **Txs:** DZOZ-TV Manila ªch33 & relay stns (rel. Light 33 TV); DZOE-TV Manila ªch11 & relay stns (rel. GMA News TV).

Local Stations not shown.

PITCAIRN ISLANDS (UK)

System: PAL-G [NZ]

Foreign TV Relay
Hope Channel (USA): ch29 (0.0035kW).

POLAND

System: DVB-T (MPEG4), DVB-T2 (MPEG4) [E]

National Stations
TELEWIZJA POLSKA S.A. (TVP) (Pub) ☐ ul. Woronicza 17, 00-999 Warszawa ☎ +48 225478000 ☐ +48 225478000 **E:** tvp@tvp.pl **W:** www.tvp.pl **LP:** Pres: Janusz Daszczynski **Chs (terr.):** TVP1, TVP2, TVP INFO, TVP Regionalna, TVP ABC, TVP Historia, TVP Kultura, TVP Polonia, TVP Rozrywka – **TVN S.A. (Comm)** ☐ ul. Wiertnicza 166, 02-952 Warszawa ☎ +48 228566060 ☐ +48 228566666 **E:** widzowie@tvn.pl **W:** www.tvn.pl **LP:** Chmn: Markus Tellenbach. – **TELEWIZJA POLSAT SP.Z.O.O. (Comm)** ☐ ul. Ostrobramska 77, 04-175 Warszawa ☎ +48 225145533 ☐ +48 225145550 **E:** poczta@polsat.pl **W:** www.polsat.pl **LP:** Chmn: Tomasz Gillner-Gorywoda. **Chs (terr.):** TV Polsat, TV4-Czworka, Polsat Film, Polsat News, Polsat Sport – **TV PULS (Comm)** ☐ ul. Chelmska 21, 00-724 Warszawa ☎ +48 225597300 ☐ +48 225597305 **E:** recepcja@pulstv.pl **W:** tvpuls.pl **LP:** Chmn: Dariusz Dabski.

DTT Tx Networks (DVB-T/MPEG4)
Tx Operator: EmiTel ☐ ul. Woloska 22, 02-675 Warszawa ☎ +48 225783301 ☐ +48 225678328 **E:** sekretariat@emitel.pl **W:** www.emitel.pl **Mux 1:** TVP ABC, TV Trwam, Stopklatka TV, Fokus TV, TTV, ATM Rozrywka, Eska TV, Polo TV **Mux 2:** Polsat, TVN, TV 4 Czwórka, TV Puls, TVN7, Polsat Sport News, TV 6, TV Puls 2 **Mux 3:** TVP 1 HD, TVP 2 HD, TVP INFO, TVP Regionalna, TVP Kultura, TVP Historia, TVP Polonia, TVP Rozrywka **Mux 4 (DVB-H) (✪exc.*)** TVP 1*, TVP 2*, Polsat*, TVN*, TV 4 Czwórka*, TV Puls*, Polsat News, Polsat Film, TVP Seriale, Kino Polska, Comedy Central, Polsat Sport, Polsat Sport Extra, Nickelodeon ⌘ RMF FM, RMF MAXXX, R. PIN, R. ZET, Antyradio, R. Plus, TOK FM, R. Roxy, R. Zlote Przeboje, Eska Rock, R. Bajka, Moje Polskie R.

Location	M1	M2	M3	M4*	kW
Bialogard (Slaworborze)	45	50	60	-	50
Bialystok (Krynice)	46	49	22	30	58/63/100/5
Bydgoszcz (Trzeciewiec)	41	32	36	-	100
Ciechanów	25	57	39	-	2x5/10
Czestochowa (Bleszno)	35	39	41	-	2x100/80
Elblag (Jagodnik)	43	25	26	-	10

Location	M1	M2	M3	M4*	kW
Gdansk (Chwaszczyno)	37	35	48	-	100
Gizycko (Milki)	43	48	50	-	2x100/90
Gorlice	45	36	34	-	20
Ilawa (Kisielice)	38	24	48	-	2x100/50
Jelenia Gora (Sniezne Kotly)	30	35	49	-	100
Kalisz (Mikstat)	38	44	31	-	100
Katowice (Kosztowy)	55	49	41	-	25/63/100
Kielce (Swiety Krzyz)	30	37	47	-	2x100/150
Klodzko (Czarna Góra)	55	58	25	-	50
Konin (Zolwieniec)	55	45	27	-	2x100/15
Konin (Zolwieniec)	-	-	36	-	40
Koronowo (Okole)	-	-	-	39V	10
Koszalin (Gologóra)	44	47	23	-	100
Kraków (Choragwica)	25	23	50	-	100
Kraków (Choragwica)	-	-	47	-	35
Krosno (Sucha Góra)	52	32	29	-	100
Lebork (Skórowo Nowe)	37	25	23	-	10
Lezajsk (Giedlarowa)	43	59	26	-	2x100/70
Lodz	46	24	43	-	2x100/170
Luban (Nowa Karczma)	-	-	49	-	20
Lublin (Piaski)	33	21	23	-	100
Olsztyn (Komin MPEC)	-	-	-	53V	10
Olsztyn (Pieczewo)	28	33	26	-	100
Opole (Chrzelice)	46	23	34	-	100
Ostroleka (Rozan)	40	41	42	-	2x6/30
Plock (Rachocin)	25	57	39	-	100
Poznan (Komin EC Karolin)	-	-	-	36V	10
Poznan (Srem)	23	39	27	-	2x100/110
Przemysl (Tatarska Góra)	43	59	26	-	20
Przysucha (Kozlowiec)	30	37	26	-	2x50/10
Rabka (G. Lubon Wielki)	43	36	34	-	2x10/9.8
Radom (Wacyn)	-	-	42	-	50
Ryki (Janiszewska)	22	24	52	-	20
Siedlce (Losice)	36	43	52	-	20/50/100
Sokolów Podlaski	36	-	56	-	5/10
Solina (Góra Jawor)	52	32	29	-	20
Suwalki (G. Krzemianucha)	43	29	58	-	20
Swinoujscie (Chrobrego)	58	34	-	-	10
Szczawnica (Góra Prehyba)	45	36	34	-	2x20/22
Szczecin (Kolowo)	41	34	48	-	100
Szczecin	-	-	-	55V	10
Tarnów (G. Sw.Marcina)	45	23	50	-	50
Tarnów (Góra Wal)	-	-	-	55V	10
Torun (Komin Cergia)	-	-	36	39V	12/2.5
Wagrowiec (Chojna)	42	43	31	-	2x20/23
Walcz (Rusinowo)	42	43	31	-	100
Warszawa (PKiN)	58	48	27	37V	2x3/10/2.2
Warszawa (Raszyn)	58	48	55	-	2x100/130
Wisla (G. Skrzyczne)	55	58	41	-	2x100/60
Wroclaw (G. Sleza)	55	58	25	-	100
Zagan (Wichów)	45	41	32	-	50
Zakopane (G. Gubalówka)	43	36	34	-	20
Zamosc (Tarnawatka)	50	53	36	-	50
Zielona Góra (G. Wilkanowska)	-	-	-	28V	10
Zielona Góra (Jemiolów)	45	46	32	-	2x80/100

+ sites with txs below 10kW. Pol.=H exc. where stated otherwise
Local muxes/DVB-T2 trials not shown

PORTUGAL

System: DVB-T (MPEG4) [E]

RÁDIO E TELEVISÃO DE PORTUGAL, S.A. (RTP) (Pub) ⊡ Av. Marechal Gomes da Costa 37, 1849-030 Lisboa ☎ +351 217947000 🖷 +351 217947570 **E:** rtp@rtp.pt **W:** www.rtp.pt **LP:** Pres: Gonçalo Reis **Chs (terr.):** RTP1, RTP2, RTP3, RTP Açores and RTP Madeira (see Azores, Madeira) (see Cape Verde, Guinea-Bissau, Mozambique, São Tomé e Príncipe). – **SOCIEDADE INDEPENDENTE DE COMUNICAÇÃO, S.A. (SIC) (Comm)** ⊡ Estrada da Outurela 119, 2794-052 Carnaxide ☎ +351 214179550 🖷 +351 214173118 **E:** contacto@siconline.pt **W:** sic.sapo.pt **LP:** Pres: Pedro Norton de Matos. – **TELEVISÃO INDEPENDENTE, S.A. (TVI) (Comm)** ⊡ R. Mário Castelhano, 40, Queluz de Baixo, 2749-502 Barcarena ☎ +351 214347500 🖷 +351 214355076 **E:** relacoes.exteriores@iol.pt **W:** www.tvi.iol.pt **LP:** DG: Luís Cunha Velho. – **ARTV (CANAL PARLAMENTO)** ⊡ Palácio de S. Bento, 1249-068 Lisboa ☎ +351 213919663 **E:** canal.parlamento@ar.parlamento.pt **W:** www.canal.parlamento.pt

DTT Tx Networks
Licensee: Portugal Telecom ⊡ Av. Fontes Pereira de Melo 40,

1069-300 Lisboa ☎ +351 215002000 🖷 +351 213308160 **E:** contact@telecom.pt **W:** www.telecom.pt **Mux:** RTP1, RTP2, SIC, TVI, ARTV **Txs:** ch56 (SFN), exc. ch42 (Monte da Virgem), ch46 (Lousã), ch49 (Montejunto).

PUERTO RICO (USA Commonwealth)

System: ATSC [A]

Local Stations*
WAPA-TV (Comm): Carr 19 Kilometro 0.5, Guaynabo, PR 00966. Tx: ch27 (1000kW). **WCCV-TV (Rlg):** Carr No 2 K92.6, Camuy, PR 00627-2348. Tx: Arecibo ch46 (50kW). **WDWL (Rlg):** Ave Sabana Seca Section 5, Toa Baja, PR 00949. °TBN. Tx: Bayamon ch30 (50kW). **WECN (Rlg):** Carr 167 KM 18.9, Bayamon, PR 00957. Tx: Naranjito ch18 (23kW). **WELU (Rlg):** Carr #2 Km162.8, Hormigueros, PR 00660. Tx: ch34 (250kW). **WIDP (Rlg):** Loma Verde San Jose 1820, Rio Piedras, PR 00926. Tx: ch45 (50.1kW). **WIMN-CA (Comm):** PO Box 1350, Hatillo, PR 00659. Tx: Arecibo ch20 (0.035kW). **WIPM-TV (Pub):** satellite of WIPR-TV. Tx: Mayagüez ch35 (620kW). **WIPR-TV (Pub):** 570 Ave. Hostos U.Baldrich, Hato Rey, PR 00918. °PBS. Tx: ch43 (790kW). **WIRS (Comm):** satellite of WJPX. Tx: Jauco ch41 (185kW). **WJPX (Comm):** Carr 19 Kilometro 0.5, Guaynabo, PR 00966. °CaribeVisión. Tx: ch21 (1000kW). **WJWN-TV (Comm):** satellite of WJPX. Tx: San Sebastán ch39 (700kW). **WKAQ-TV (Comm):** 383 Roosevelt Ave, Hato Rey, PR 00919. °Telemundo Tx: ch28 (924kW). **WKPV (Comm):** satellite of WJPX. Tx: Ponce ch19 (700kW). **WLII (Comm):** Calle Carazo 62, Guaynabo, PR 00969. °Univision. Tx: Caguas ch56 (71kW). **WMEI (Comm):** 1095 Avenida Wilson, Edificio Puerta del Condado, Suite 2, San Juan, PR 00907. Tx: Arecibo ch14 (50kW). **WMTJ (Pub):** Isodoro Colon Estatal176, San Juan, PR 00928-1345. °PBS. Tx: ch16 (140kW). **WNJX-TV (Comm):** satellite of WAPA-TV. Tx: Mayagüez ch23 (400kW). Mux: WAPA-TV, El Canal del Tiempo. **WOLE-TV (Comm):** Carr 111 Bario Palmar, Aguadilla, PR 00603-5125. Repeater for WKAQ-TV. Tx: Aguadilla ch69 (120kW). **WORA-TV (Comm):** satellite of WLII. Tx: Mayagüez ch29 (650kW). **WORO-TV (Rlg):** Ave Iturreguy/ Baldorioti, Carolina, PR 00902. °ABC. Tx: ch33 (6kW). **WQHA (Rlg):** satellite of WUJA. Tx: Aguada ch50 (50kW). **WQQZ-CA (Comm):** satellite of WMEI. Tx: Ponce ch33 (3kW). **WQTO (Pub):** satellite of WMTJ. Tx: Ponce ch25 (200kW). **WRFB (Comm):** #21Clle B Sabana Abajo Ind, Carolina, PR 00982. Tx: ch51 (16kW). **WRUA (Rlg):** satellite of WECN. Tx: Fajardo ch33 (37kW). **WSJN-CA (Rlg):** Carr 861 KM 4.4, Toa Alta, PR 00953. Tx: ch15 (38.8kW). **WSJU-TV (Comm):** 1508 Calle Bori Urb Antonsant, San Juan, PR 00927-6116. Tx: ch31 (66kW). **WSTE (Comm):** Calle Carazo 64, Guaynabo, PR 00969. Tx: Ponce ch8 (50kW). Boosters in San Juan (WSTE1), Mayagüez (WSTE2), Arecibo (WSTE3). **WSUR-TV (Comm):** satellite of WLII. Tx: Ponce 43 (68kW). **WTCV (Comm):** Calle Bori # 1554, San Juan, PR 00927-6113. Tx: ch32 (50kW). **WTIN (Comm):** satellite of WAPA-TV. Tx: Ponce ch15 (380.2kW). Mux: WAPA-TV, El Canal del Tiempo. **WUJA (Rlg):** Calle B #24 Urb Ind, Sabana Abajo Carolina, PR 00984-4039. Tx: Caguas ch48 (2.5kW). **WVEO (Comm):** satellite of WTCV. Tx: Aguadilla ch17 (42kW). **WVOZ-TV (Comm):** satellite of WTCV. Tx: Ponce ch47 (50.1kW). **WVSN (Rlg):** Satellite of WCCV-TV. Tx: Humaco ch49 (46kW).
*) Full power licenses (lp licenses not shown). °) Network affiliation. Tx sites are San Juan, unless indicated otherwise.

QATAR

System: DVB-T2 (MPEG4) [E]

QATAR GENERAL BROADCASTING AND TELEVISION CORP. (Pub) ⊡ P.O.Box 1944, Doha ☎ +974 44894444 🖷 +974 44864611 **E:** contact@qna.org.qa **W:** www.qatarbroadcast.qa; www.qtv.qa **Chs:** Qatar TV, Al Rayan TV, Al Dawri/Al Kass, Jeem TV, Baraem TV, Al Bidda TV.

DTT Tx Networks
Tx Operator: Qatar Media Corp. **M:** Qatar TV, Al Rayan TV, Al Dawri/Al Kass, Jeem TV, Baraem TV, Al Bidda TV **Txs:** ch53 (Doha) & nationwide MFN. – **Local Licensees** not shown.

RÉUNION (France)

System: DVB-T (MPEG4) [E]

RÉUNION 1ÈRE (Pub) ⊡ 12 rue René Demarne F-97490 Saint Denis ☎ +262 262406767 🖷 +262 262406771 **W:** reunion.1ere.fr **LP:** Dir: Jean-Claude Ho-Tin-Noé– **ANTENNE RÉUNION (Comm)** ⊡ BP 80001, F-97801 Saint-Denis CEDEX 009 ☎ +262 262482828 🖷 +262 262482829

W: www.antennereunion.fr **LP:** DG: Christophe Ducasse – **TÉLÉ KRÉOL (Comm)** ⌧ 16 rue du Fangourin, F-97460 Savannah ☎ +262 262452017 **E:** contact@telekreol.fr **W:** www.kreol.tv **LP:** Pres: M. Thierry Araye.

DTT Tx Network
Tx Operator: TDF **Mux:** Réunion 1ère, France 2-5, France Ô, France 24, Arte, Antenne Réunion, Télé Kréol **Txs:** MFN.

ROMANIA

Systems: DVB-T2 (MPEG4) [E]; § PAL-D/G [R/E] ⇩ 31 Dec 2016

National Stations
TELEVIZIUNEA ROMÂNA (TVR) (Pub)⌧ Calea Dorobantilor nr. 191, sector 1, 010565 Bucuresti ☎ +40 21 3199112 ▤ +40 21 3199264 **E:** office@tvr.ro **W:** www.tvr.ro **LP:** DG (acting): Irina Radu. **Chs (terr.):** TVR1, TVR2, TVR3, TVR HD, Regional stns. – **INTACT MEDIA GROUP (Comm)** ⌧ Str. Garlei no. 1B, sector 1, 013721 Bucuresti ☎ +40 21 4091861 ▤ +40 21 2030357 **E:** headoffice@intactmediagroup. ro **W:** www.intactmediagroup.ro **LP:** CEO: Alessandra Stoicescu Chs (terr.): Antena 1, Antena 3 – **NATIONAL TV (Comm)** ⌧ Str. Fabricii nr. 46B, Sector 6, 060825 Bucuresti ☎ +40 21 4042570 ▤ +40 21 4042429 **E:** office@nationaltv.ro **W:** www.nationaltv.ro **LP:** Dir: Calin Mircea Popa – **PRO TV (Comm)** ⌧ Bd. Pache Protopopescu 109, sector 2, 021409 Bucuresti ☎ +40 21 2501430 ▤ +40 21 3124218 **E:** doinita@protv.ro **W:** www.protv.ro **LP:** DG: Aleksander Cesnavicius – **REALITATEA TV (Comm)** ⌧ Sos. Dudesti Pantelimon 1-3, sector 3, 033091 Bucuresti ☎ +40 21 3160019 ▤ +40 21 3160019 **E:** office@ realitatea.net **W:** www.realitatea.net **LP:** DG: Rares Bogdan.

Local/Regional Stations not shown.

DTT Tx Networks (under construction)
Licensee Mux 1/2+4: Radiocom ⌧ Bd. Libertatii 14, sector 5, 050706 Bucuresti ☎ +40 31 5003007 ▤ +40 31 5003013 **W:** www. radiocom.ro **M1:** TVR1, TVR2, TVR HD, TVR3 **M2:** Antena 1, Antena 3, Realitatea TV, National TV **M4:** tbd – **Licensee Mux 3:** Media Pro **M:** Pro TV HD, sport.ro HD

Location	M1	M2	M3	M4
Alexandria	31	60	-	-
Arad	50	67	-	-
Bacau	39	63	-	45
Bistrita	34	22	-	-
Botosani	54	61	-	45
Brasov	59	58	-	-
Bucuresti (Herastrau)	54	59	30	-
Buzau	52	56	-	-
Calarasi	31	65	-	-
Cluj-Napoca	31	60	-	-
Comanesti	46	36	-	-
Constanta	48	55	-	-
Craiova	37	34	-	-
Deva	32	23	-	-
Drobeta-Turnu Severin	60	61	-	-
Focsani	51	56	-	21
Galati	58	60	-	-
Iasi	58	62	-	34
Oradea	25	45	-	-
Paltinis	54	47	-	-
Piatra Neamt	55	26	-	-
Ploiesti	21	62	-	-
Ramnicu Valcea	49	23	-	-
Satu Mare	50	21	-	-
Sibiu	54	64	-	-
Suceava	38	41	-	-
Targu Mures	27	61	-	-
Timisoara	50	68	-	-
Tulcea	38	63	-	-
+ translators				

Local/Regional muxes not shown.

RUSSIA

Systems: DVB-T2 (MPEG4) [E]; § SECAM-D/K [R] ⇩ 2020

National Stations
VSEROSSIYSKAYA GOSUDARSTVENNAYA TELEVIZIONNAYA I RADIOVESHCHATELNAYA KOMPANIYA (VGTRK) (Gov) ⌧ 125040 Moskva, ul. Yamskogo Polya ul. 19/21 ☎ +7 495 2326333 **W:** www.vgtrk.com **LP:** DG: Oleg B. Dobrodeyev. ⌧Studios: Rossiya 1, Rossiya 24, Match TV: 15162 Moskva, ul. Shabolovka 37; Rossiya K:

119902 Moskva, ul. Zubovskiy bul. 4; Karusel: 127427 Moskva, ul. Ak. Korolyova 19. **Chs:** Rossiya 1, Rossiya K, Rossiya 24, Karusel, Match TV; Regional Stations (see chapter below) **Txs: Rossiya 1:** Moskva ch11 (60kW) & network; **Rossiya 24:** via DTT; **Rossiya K:** Moskva ch33 (20kW) & network; **Karusel:** via DTT; **Match TV:** Moskva ch6 (1kW) & network.

VGTRK Regional Services: AD) GTRK "Adygeya": 385000 Maykop, ul. Zhukovskogo 24. **AK)** GTRK "Altay": 656045 Barnaul, Zmeinogorskiy trakt 27a. **AM)** GTRK "Amur": 675000 Blagoveshchensk, per. Svyatitelya Innokentiya 15. **AR)** GTRK "Pomorye": 163061 Arkhangelsk, ul. Popova 2. **AS)** GTRK "Lotos": 414000 Astrakhan, ul. Molodoy Gvardii 17. **BA)** GTRK "Bashkortostan": 450076 Ufa, ul. Gafuri 9/1. **BE)** GTRK "Belgorod": 308000 Belgorod, pr. Slavy 60. **BR)** GTRK "Bryansk": 241033 Bryansk, ul. Stanke Dimitrova 77. **BU)** GTRK "Buryatiya": 670000 Ulan-Ude, ul. Erbanova 7. **CB)** GTRK "Yuzhnyy Ural": 454000 Chelyabinsk, ul. Ordzhonikidze 54b. **CC)** GTRK "Vaynakh": 364000 Groznyy, ul. B.Khmelnitskogo 147, korpus 5. **CK)** GTRK "Chukotka": 686710 Anadyr, ul. Lenina 18. **CV)** GTRK "Chuvashiya": 428003 Cheboksary, ul. Nikolayeva 4. **DA)** GTRK "Dagestan": 367032 Makhachkala, ul. Magomeda Gadzhieva 182. **IN)** GTRK "Ingushetiya": 366720 Nazran, pr. Bazorkina 72. **IR)** GTRK "Irkutsk": 664003 Irkutsk, ul. Gorkogo 15. **IV)** GTRK "Ivteleradio": 153647 Ivanovo, ul. Teatralnaya 31. **KA)** GTRK "Kaliningrad": 236016 Kaliningrad, ul. Klinicheskaya 19. **KB)** GTRK "Kabardino-Balkariya": 360000 Nalchik, per. Lenina 3. **KC)** GTRK "Karachayevo-Cherkesiya": 357100 Cherkessk, ul. Krasnoarmeyskaya 51. **KD)** GTRK "Kuban": 350038 Krasnodar, ul. Radio 5. **KE)** GTRK "Kuzbass": 650099 Kemorovo, ul. Krasnoarmeyskaya 137a. **KG)** GTRK "Kurgan": 640018 Kurgan, ul. Sovetskaya 105. **KH)** GTRK "Dalnevostochnaya": 682632 Khabarovsk, ul. Lenina 4. **KL)** GTRK "Kaluga": 248021 Kaluga, Pole Svobody 40a. **KM)** GTRK "Kamchatka": 683000 Petropavlovsk-Kamchatskiy, ul. Sovetskaya 62. **KN)** GTRK "Krasnoyarsk": 660028 Krasnoyarsk, ul. Mechnikova 44a. **KO)** GTRK "Komi Gor": 167610 Syktyvkar, Oktyabrskiy pr. 164. **KS)** GTRK "Kostroma": 156005 Kostroma, ul. Nikitskaya 10. **KT)** GTRK "Kareliya": 185630 Petrozavodsk, ul. Pirogova 2. **KU)** GTRK "Kursk": 305016 Kursk, ul. Sovetskaya 32. **KV)** GTRK "Vyatka": 610002 Kirov, ul. Uritskogo 34. **KX)** GTRK "Kalmykiya": 358000 Elista, ul. M. Gorkogo 34. **KY)** GTRK "Yugoriya": 626200 Khanty-Mansiysk, ul. Mira 7. **LI)** GTRK "Lipetsk": 398050 Lipetsk, pl. Plekhanova 1. **MA)** GTRK "Magadan": 685024 Magadan, ul. Kommuny 8/12. **MD)** GTRK "Mordoviya": 430000 Saransk, ul. Dokuchayeva 29. **ME)** GTRK "Mariy-El": 424014 Yoshkar-Ola, ul. Osipenko 50. **MU)** GTRK "Murman": 183032 Murmansk, per. Rusanova 7. **NE)** Territorialnoye otdeleniya GTRK "Pomorye", 164700 Naryan-Mar, ul. Smidovicha 19. **NN)** GTRK "Nizhniy Novgorod": 603600 Nizhniy Novgorod, ul. Belinskogo 9a. **NO)** GTRK "Slaviya": 173620 Velikiy Novgorod, ul. B.Moskovskaya 106. **NS)** GTRK "Novosibirsk": 630048 Novosibirsk, ul. Rimskogo-Korsakova 9. **OB)** GTRK "Orenburg": 460024 Orenburg, per. Televizionnyy 3. **OL)** GTRK "Oryol": 302028 Oryol, ul. 7 Noyabrya 43. **OM)** GTRK "Irtysh": 644050 Omsk, pr. Mira 2. **PM)** GTRK "Vladivostok": 690091 Vladivostok, ul. Uborevicha 20a. **PR)** GTRK "Perm": 614070 Perm, ul. Tekhnicheskaya 7. **PS)** GTRK "Pskov": 180000 Pskov, ul. Nekrasova 50. **PZ)** GTRK "Penza": 440602 Penza, ul. Lermontova 39. **RA)** GTRK "Gornyy Altay": 659700 Gorno-Altaysk, ul. Choros-Gurkina 38. **RK)** GTRK "Khakasiya": 662000 Abakan, ul. Vyatkina 12. **RO)** GTRK "Don-TR": 344101 Rostov-na-Donu, ul. 1-ya Barrikadnaya 18. **RS)** GTRK "Sakha": 677007 Yakutsk, ul. Ordzhonikidze 48. **RT)** GTRK "Tyva": 667003 Kyzyl, ul. Gornaya 31. **RY)** GTRK "Oka": 390006 Ryazan, ul. Skomoroshinskaya 20. **SA)** GTRK "Samara": 443011 Samara, ul. Sovetskoy Armii 205. **SL)** GTRK "Sakhalin": 693000 Yuzhno-Sakhalinsk, ul. Komsomolskaya 209. **SM)** GTRK "Smolensk": 214025 Smolensk, ul. Nakhimova 1. **SO)** GTRK "Alaniya": 362007 Vladikavkaz, Osetinskaya gorka 2. **SP)** GTRK "Sankt-Peterburg": 197022 St.Peterburg, nab. reki Karpovki 43. **SR)** GTRK "Saratov": 410004 Saratov, 2-ya Sadovaya ul. 7. **ST)** GTRK "Stavropolye": 355000 Stavropol, ul. Artema 35a. **SV)** GTRK "Ural": 620026 Yekaterinburg, ul. Lunacharskogo 212. **TA)** GTRK "Tambov": 392720 Tambov, ul. Michurinskaya 8a. **TL)** GTRK "Tula": 300600 Tula, Staronikitskaya ul. 1. **TO)** GTRK "Tomsk": 634050 Tomsk, ul. Pushkina 19. **TS)** GTRK "Tatarstan": 420015 Kazan, ul. M. Gorkogo 15. **TV)** GTRK "Tver": 170000 Tver, ul. Vagzhanova 9. **TY)** GTRK "Region-Tyumen": 625013 Tyumen, ul. Permyakova 6. **UD)** GTRK "Udmurtiya": 426004 Izhevsk, ul. Komunarov 216. **UL)** GTRK "Volga": 432030 Ulyanovsk, ul. Simbirskaya 5. **VG)** GTRK "Volgograd-TRV": 400066 Volgograd, ul. Mira 9. **VL)** GTRK "Vladimir": 600000 Vladimir, ul. Bol. Moskovskaya 62. **VN)** GTRK "Voronezh": 394625 Voronezh, ul. Karl Marksa 114. **VO)** GTRK "Vologda": 160000 Vologda, ul. Predtecheskaya 32. **YA)** GTRK "Yaroslaviya": 150014 Yaroslavl, ul. Bogdanovicha 20. **YN)** GTRK "Yamal": 626600 Salekhard, ul. Lambinykh 3. **YV)** GTRK "Bira": 679016 Birobidzhan, ul. Oktyabrskaya 15. **ZB)** GTRK "Chita": 672090 Chita, ul.

Kostyushko-Grigorovicha 27.
NB. Keys to region codes: see National Radio section.

MIR TV (Gov) ▣ 107076 Moskva, ul. Krasnobogatyrskaya 44 ☎🖨
+7 495 6480792 **E:** mir24@mirtv.ru **W:** www.mirtv.ru **Txs:** via DTT
LP: Chmn: Radik Batyshin – **TV ZVEZDA (Gov)** ▣ 129110 Moskva,
Suvorovskaya pl. 2 ☎ +7 495 6316883 **E:** info@tvzvezda.ru **W:**
tvzvezda.ru **LP:** DG: Aleksey Pimanov. **Txs:** Moskva ch57 (5kW) &
netw. – **PERVYY KANAL (Semi-Gov)** ▣ 127000 Moskva, ul. Ak.
Korolyova 12 ☎ +7 495 2179838 🖨 +7 495 2151976. **E:** dip@1tv.
ru **W:** www.1tv.ru **LP:** DG: Konstantin Ernst. **Txs:** Moskva ch1
(40kW) & netw. – **TV TSENTR (Municipal)** ▣ 115184 Moskva, ul.
Bolshaya Tatarskaya 33-1 ☎ +7 495 9593900 **E:** press@tvc.ru **W:**
www.tvc.ru **LP:** DG: Yuliya Bystritskaya. **Txs:** Moskva ch3 (40kW)
& netw.– **OBSHCHESTVENNOYE TELEVIDENIYE ROSSII (OTR)
(Pub)** ▣ 127427 Moskva, ul. Ak. Korolyova 19 **E:** press@otr-online.ru
W: otr-online.ru **LP:** DG: Anatoliy Lysenko. **Txs:** via DTT. – **5 KANAL
(Comm)** ▣ 197376 St.Peterburg, ul. Chapygina 6 ☎ +7 812 3351560
🖨 +7 812 2343846 **E:** trk@spbtv.ru **W:** www.5-tv.ru **LP:** DG: Aleksey
Brodskiy. **Txs:** St.Peterburg ch3 (50kW) & netw. – **CHE (Comm)**
▣ 129226 Moskva, Leningradskiy pr. 31a ☎ +7 495 7856347 **W:**
chetv.ru **LP:** DG: Ruben Oganesyan. **Txs:** Moskva ch23 (10kW) &
netw. – **DOMASHNIY (Comm)** ▣ 125124 Moskva, ul. Pravdy 15a
☎ +7 495 7856333 🖨 +7 495 6429451 **E:** info@domashniy.ru **W:**
tv.domashniy.ru **LP:** DG: Lika Blank **Txs:** Moskva ch31 (20kW) & netw.
– **MUZ-TV (Comm)** ▣ 105066 Moskva, ul. Olkhovskaya 4 ☎ +7 495
2131888 🖨 +7 495 2131867 **E:** info@muz-tv.ru **W:** muz-tv.ru **LP:** DG:
Armen Davletyanov **Txs:** via DTT – **NTV (Comm)** ▣ 127000 Moskva,
ul. Ak. Korolyova 12 ☎ +7 495 2177895 🖨 +7 495 2175103 **E:** ntv@ntv.
ru **W:** www.ntv.ru **LP:** DG: Aleksey Zemskiy. **Txs:** Moskva ch8 (40kW)
& netw. – **PYATNITSA (Comm)** ▣ 129090 Moskva, Olimpiyskiy pr.
14 ☎ +7 495 7832306 **E:** info@friday.ru **W:** www.friday.ru **LP:** DG:
Nikolay Kartoziya. **Txs:** Moskva ch38 (10kW) & netw. – **REN-
TV (Comm)** ▣ 119847 Moskva, Zubovskiy bul. 17-1 ☎ +7 495
2465933.🖨 +7 495 2460655. **E:** press@ren-tv.com **W:** ren.tv **LP:** DG:
Vladimir Tyulin. **Txs:** Moskva ch49 (20kW) & netw. – **STS (Comm)** ▣
125254 Moskva, Leningradskiy pr. 31 ☎ +7 495 7856347 🖨 +7 495
7974101 **E:** ctc@ctc.ru **W:** ctc.ru **LP:** DG: Vyacheslav Murugov. **Txs:**
Moskva ch27 (5kW) & netw. – **TNT (Comm)** ▣ 129272 Moskva, ul.
Trifonovskaya 57-3 ☎ +7 495 2178188 🖨 +7 495 7481490 **E:** info@tnt-
tv.ru **W:** tnt-online.ru **LP:** DG: Igor Mishin. **Txs:** Moskva ch35 (5kW)
& network. – **TV-3 (Comm)** ▣ 117105 Moskva, Varshavskoye shosse
9 ☎ +7 495 9374039 **E:** info@tv3.ru **W:** tv3.ru **LP:** DG: Darya Fialko.
Txs: Moskva ch46 (5kW) & netw. – **SPAS (Rlg)** ▣ 129515 Moskva,
ul. Ak. Korolyova 13 ☎ +7 495 6510829 🖨 +7 495 6510790 **E:** office@
spas-tv.ru **W:** www.spastv.ru **LP:** DG: Boris Kostenko. **Txs:** via DTT.

Other Regional & Local Stations not shown.

DTT Tx Networks (under construction)
Tx Operator: RTRS ▣ 129515 Moskva, ul. Ak. Korolyova 13 ☎
+7 495 6480111 🖨 +7 495 6480111 **E:** rtrn@rtrn.ru **W:** www.rtrs.
ru **M1:** Rossiya 1, Rossiya 24, Rossiya K, Karusel, Match TV, Pervyy
kanal, NTV, OTR, 5-kanal, TV Tsentr, VGTRK Regional TV stns ⌘ R.
Rossii, Mayak, Vesti FM. **M2:** Domashniy, TV Zvezda, Mir TV, Muz-TV,
Pyatnitsa, REN TV, Spas, STS, TNT, TV-3

Re	Location	M1	M2	Re	Location	M1	M2
AD	Maykop	45	22	NN	N.Novgorod	28	53
AK	Barnaul	27	58	NO	V.Novgorod	30	56
AM	Blagoveshchensk	34	36	OB	Orenburg	22	31
AR	Arkhangelsk	33	44	OL	Oryol	26	44
BA	Ufa	31	43	OM	Omsk	31	49
BE	Belgorod	46	43	PM	Vladivostok	37	56
BR	Bryansk	39	23	PR	Perm	23	58
BU	Ulan-Ude	30	56	PS	Pskov	49	56
CB	Chelyabinsk	59	40	PZ	Penza	44	53
CC	Groznyy	57	59	RA	Gorno-Altaysk	24	32
CK	Anadyr	32	34	RK	Abakan	24	60
CV	Cheboksary	46	57	RO	Rostov-na-Donu	37	38
DA	Makhachkala	22	53	RS	Yakutsk	51	58
IN	Nazran	38	46	RT	Kyzyl	33	37
IR	Irkutsk	33	57	RY	Ryazan	43	27
IV	Ivanovo	59	57	SA	Samara	27	57
KA	Kaliningrad	47	41	SL	Yu-Sakhalinsk	21	51
KB	Nalchik	34	59	SM	Smolensk	39	46
KC	Cherkessk	58	59	SO	Vladikavkaz	35	50
KD	Krasnodar	60	56	SP	Sankt-Peterburg	35	45
KE	Kemerovo	23	56	SR	Saratov	56	40
KH	Khabarovsk	30	38	ST	Stavropol	57	32
KL	Kaluga	46	44	SV	Yekaterinburg	60	46
KM	Petropavlovsk-K.	22	26	TA	Tambov	46	56

Re	Location	M1	M2	Re	Location	M1	M2
KN	Krasnoyarsk	25	53	TL	Tula	60	56
KO	Syktyvkar	26	34	TO	Tomsk	21	44
KS	Kostroma	46	43	TS	Kazan	36	53
KT	Petrozavodsk	25	39	TV	Tver	47	58
KU	Kursk	24	53	TY	Tyumen	35	59
KV	Kirov	44	51	UD	Izhevsk	57	36
KX	Elista	46	39	UL	Ulyanovsk	56	59
KY	Khanty-Mansiysk	38	44	VG	Volgograd	44	60
LI	Lipetsk	30	40	VL	Vladimir	58	36
MA	Magadan	27	29	VN	Voronezh	52	43
MD	Saransk	43	46	VO	Vologda	34	35
ME	Yoshkar-Ola	34	56	YA	Yaroslavl	56	36
MO	Moskva	34	24	YN	Nakhodka	21	22
MU	Murmansk	23	34	YV	Birobidzhan	34	58
NE	Naryan-Mar	26	30	ZB	Chita	24	34

NB: Only txs in top-level administrative capitals shown.
Regional/Local licensees not shown.

CRIMEA

NB: The station listing can be found at the end of the "Ukraine" chapter.

RWANDA

System: DVB-T2 (MPEG4) [E]

RWANDA TV (RTV) (Gov) ▣ BP 83, Kigali ☎ +250 72577519
🖨 +250 72577520 **E:** info@rba.co.rw **W:** www.rba.co.rw – **TV10
(Comm)** ▣ BP 4307, Kigali ☎ +250 786022804 **E:** info@tv10rwanda.
com **W:** www.tv10rwanda.com; www.tele10group.com **LP:** CEO:
Eugene Nyagahene.

DTT Tx Networks
Licensee: RBA **M:** RTV, TV10, CNN, TV5 Monde, France 24 Français,
France 24 English, Al Jazeera, True Movies **Txs:** Nationwide MFN
network. – **Licensee:** TV10 **M⚙:** multiprgr **Txs:** MFN. – **Licensee:**
Star Times **M⚙:** multiprgr **Txs:** MFN.

SABA (Netherlands)

Systems: # NTSC-M [A]; DVB-T (MPEG2) planned

ATV RELAY (Aruba Broadcasting Co., Aruba): ch11

SAMOA

System: PAL-B [E]

STAR TV (Comm) ▣P.O.Box 1321, Apia **E:** talamuaeditor@gmail.
com **LP:** GM: Apulu Lance Polu **Txs:** (-). – **TV1 (Comm)** ▣ P.O.Box
3691, Apia ☎ +685 24790 🖨 +685 24789 **E:** ceo@sbcl.ws **LP:** GM:
Galumalemana Faiesea Matafeo **Txs:** Mount Aflau ch4 (0.05kW), Api
Park ch5 (0.005kW), Mount Fiamoe ch6 (0.01kW), Mount Vaea ch8
(0.05kW), Faleasiu ch10 (0.01kW), Apia ch11 (0.01kW) – **TV2 (Comm)**
▣P.O.Box 96, Apia ☎ +685 27882 🖨 +685 21923 **LP:** CEO: Tofilau
Elijah Ryan **Txs:** (-). – **TV3 (Comm)** ▣ Taufusi, Apia ☎ +685 33330
🖨 +685 22810 **E:** tvsamoa3@ipasifika.net **LP:** CEO: Atanoa Herbert
Crichton **Txs:** (-). – **KINGDOM TV (Rlg)** ▣Sogi, Apia ☎ +685 24966
🖨 +685 20657 **E:** afeleti@ymail.com **LP:** GM: Rev. Afereti Lui **Txs:** (-).

Foreign TV Relay
CCTV-9 (P.R.China): (-).

SAMOA (AMERICAN) (USA)

Systems: ATSC [A]; lp stns only: § NTSC-M [A]

KVZK-TV (Gov) ▣ P.O.Box 3511, Pago Pago AS 96799, USA ☎ +1
684 6334191 🖨 +1 684 6331044 **E:** kvzk-tv@samoatelco.com **LP:** Dir:
Fagafaga Daniel Langkilde **Tx:** Pago Pago ch5. **M:** KVZK-TV, KGMB/
CBS, PBS, BBC World. **NB:** Full power license (lp licenses not listed)

SAN MARINO

System: DVB-T (MPEG2) [E]

SAN MARINO RTV (Pub) ▣ Viale J.F.Kennedy 13, SM-47890 San

Marino ☎ +378 0549 882000 ▤ +378 0549 882850 **E**: amministrazione@sanmarinortv.sm **W**: www.smtvsanmarino.sm **L.P**: DG: Carlo Romeo **Tx**: San Marino ch51 (10kW).

SÃO TOMÉ & PRÍNCIPE

System: DVB-T (MPEG2) [E]

TELEVISÃO SÃO-TOMENSE (TVS) (Pub) ▤ CP 420, Bairro da Quinta do Santo António, 420 São Tomé ☎ +239 2221041 ▤ +239 2221942 **E**: tvs@cstome.net **W**: www.facebook.com/tvs.st **L.P**: Dir: Frederico Umbelina.

DTT Tx Network
Tx Operator: TVS **M**: TVS, RTP Africa **Txs**: MFN

SAUDI ARABIA

Systems: DVB-T, DVB-T2 (MPEG4) [E]

SAUDI ARABIAN TELEVISION (Gov) ▤ P.O.Box 570, Riyadh 11421 ☎ +966 1 4014440 ▤ +966 1 4044192 **W**: www.sm.gov.sa **Chs (Terr.)**: TV 1, TV2, Al-Riyadih, Al-Ekhbariya, Al-Eqtisadiyah, Al-Thakafiyah, Ajyal, Al-Sunna, A-Quran.

DTT Tx Networks (DVB-T2 exc. *=DVB-T)
Tx Operator: Ministry of Culture and Information **Mux 1**: TV1, TV2, Al-Riyadih, Al-Ekhbariya, Al-Eqtisadiyah, Al-Thakafiyah, Ajyal, Al-Sunna, A-Quran ✆ General prgr, Second prgr, R.Quran, European prgr **Mux 2**: Sindo TV, B Channel **Mux 3**: O Channel, Kompas TV) **Mux 4**: MBC1, MBC4, MBC Action **Mux 5**: Fox **Mux 6**: LBC Sat **Mux 7**: Al Jazeera **Mux 8**: ITV1, ITV2 **Mux 9**: OSN First, OSN News, Al Yawm, Series Channel **Mux 10**: ABP News, ABP Majha, ABP Ananda. (NB: Local variations may apply)

Location	M1	M2	M3	M4	M5	M6	M7	M8	M9	M10
Jeddah	30	21*	23*	25	29	31	35	41	43	45*

+ nationwide network.

SENEGAL

Systems: DVB-T2 (MPEG4) [E]; § SECAM-K1 [VHF=K, UHF=E]

RADIODIFFUSION TÉLÉVISION SÉNÉGALAISE (Pub) ▤ BP 1765, Dakar ☎ +221 338217801 ▤ +221 338223490 **E**: rts@rts.sn **W**: www.rts.sn **L.P**: DG: Racine Talla **Chs**: RTS1, SN2. – **TÉLÉ FUTURS MÉDIAS (TFM) (Comm)** ▤ BP 17795, Dakar ☎ +221 338491644 **W**: igfm.sn **L.P**: DG: Mamoudou Ibra Kane.

DTT Tx Network (under construction)
Tx Operator: Excaf Telecom Group **M**: RTS1, SN2, multiprgr **Txs**: nationwide MFN network.

SERBIA

System: DVB-T2 (MPEG4) [E]

National Stations
RADIO-TELEVIZIJA SRBIJE (RTS) (Pub) ▤ Takovska 10, 11000 Beograd ☎ +381 11 3212000 ▤ +381 11 3212211 **E**: rtstv@rts.rs **W**: www.rts.rs **L.P**: DG: Dragan Bujoševic **Chs (terr.)**: RTS1, RTS2, RTS3 – **NACIONALNA TELEVIZIJA HAPPY (Comm)** ▤ Aleksandra Dubceka 14, 11080 Zemun ☎ +381 11 3778373 ▤ +381 11 3778053 **E**: office@happytv.rs **W**: www.happytv.rs **L.P**: DG: Aleksandra Krstic – **PRVA SRPSKA TELEVIZIJA (Comm)** ▤ Autoput 22, 11080 Zemun ☎ +381 11 2091000 ▤ +381 11 2091001 **E**: produkcija@prva.rs **W**: www.prva.rs **L.P**: Dir: Dragan Nenadovic – **B92 (Comm)** ▤ Autoput 22, 11080 Zemun ☎ +381 11 3012000 ▤ +381 11 3012001 **E**: tvpitanja@b92.net **W**: www.b92.net **L.P**: CEO: Veran Matic – **TV PINK (Comm)** ▤ Neznanog junaka 1, 11000 Beograd ☎ +381 11 3063400 ▤ +381 11 3063500 **E**: marketing@rtvpink.com **W**: www.rtvpink.com **L.P**: DG (Pink Int.): Zeljko Mitrovic.

Local Stations (via DTT regions a-i*)
Belle Amie: Trg Kralja Milana 6-8, 18000 Niš (b,e,i). **Regionalna TV Novi Pazar**: Stane Bacanin 29, 36300 Novi Pazar (f). **Sat TV**: Boze Dimitrijevica 130a, 12000 Pozarevac (a). **Studio B**: Masarikova 5, 11000 Beograd (a). **TMS TV Telemark**: Sinceliceva bb, 32000 Cacak (g). **TV Best**: Ljube Nešica 38, 19000 Zajecar (d). **TV Bor**: Moše Pijade 19, 19210 Bor (d). **TV Enigma**: Valterova 133, 31300 Prijepolje (f). **TV Istok**: Jasikovacka petlja bb, 19224

Salaš (d). **TVK 9**: Miloja Pavlovica 8, 34000 Kragujevac (h). **TV Kraljevo**: Konarevo bb, 36000 Kraljevo (e,g). **TV Kragujevac**: Branka Radicevica 9, 34000 Kragujevac (h). **TV Kruševac**: Trg kosovskih junaka 6, 37000 Kruševac (e). **TV Lav Plus**: Ljube Stojanovica 3, 31000 Uzice (g). **TV Metropolis**: Terazije 27, 11000 Beograd (a). **TV Palma Plus**: Zeleznicka bb, 35000 Jagodina (h). **TV Pirot**: Branka Radicevica bb, 18300 Pirot (i). **TV Raška**: Dušanova 6, 36350 Raška (f). **TV Šabac**: Kneza Lazara 1, 15000 Šabac (c). **TV Vranje**: Partizanska 17a, 17500 Vranje (b). **TV Vujic**: Uzicka 25, 14104 Valjevo (c). *) local stns transmitted exclusively in lp DTT regions not listed

DTT Tx Network
Tx Operator: JP Emisiona Technika i Veze (ETV) ▤ Jovana Ristica 1, 11000 Beograd ☎+381 11 3693251 ▤ +381 11 3693260 **E**: office@etv.rs **W**: www.etv.rs **M1**: RTS1, RTS2, RTS3, Happy TV, Prva, TV B92, TV Pink, RTV1 (DTT Region "a" only) **M2**: Local stns **M3**: tbd

Location	M1	M2*	M3	kW
Avala	22	28a	45	100
Besna Kobila	35	39b	43	50
Deli Jovan	23	43d	41	10
Jastrebac	27	38e	42	50
Kopaonik	24	32f	34	50
Maljen	32	34c	37	10
Ovcar	23	36g	39	80
Rudnik	26	29h	35	32
Tupiznica	22	25i	28	50

+ sites with txs below 10kW *) Local stns a-i, see above

Vojvodina

RADIO-TELEVIZIJA VOJVODINE (RTV) (Pub) ▤ Sutjecka 1, 21000 Novi Sad ☎ +381 21 422829 ▤ +381 21 420139 **E**: office@rtv.rs **W**: www.rtv.rs **L.P**: DG: Srdjan Mihajlovic **Chs**: RTV1, RTV2

Local Stations (via DTT regions j-l)
RTV Panonija: Hajduk Veljkova 11, 21000 Novi Sad (j). **TV Banat**: Omladinski trg 17, 26300 Vršac (l). **TV Most**: Arse Teodorovica 5, 21000 Novi Sad (j). **TV Santos**: Koce Kolarova 29, 23000 Zrenjanin (k). **TV Sremska**: Zlatka Šnajdera 2, 22240 Šid (k).

DTT Tx Network
Tx Operator: JP Emisiona Technika i Veze (ETV) **M1**: RTS1, RTS2, RTS3, RTV1, RTV2, Happy TV, Prva, TV B92, TV Pink **M2**: Local stns **M3**: tbd

Location	M1	M2*	M3	kW
Crveni Cot	24	30k	41	100
Kikinda	32	55	29	10
Subotica	40	43j	29	50
Vršac	25	31l	37	50

*) Local stns j-l, see above

SEYCHELLES

System: DVB-T2 (MPEG4) [E]

SEYCHELLES BROADCASTING CORP. (SBC-TV) (Pub) ▤ P.O.Box 321, Victoria, Mahé ☎ +248 4289611 **E**: tv@sbc.sc **W**: www.sbc.sc **L.P**: CEO: Antoine Onezime **Txs**: (-)

SIERRA LEONE

System: # PAL-G [E]; DVB-T2 (MPEG4) [E] planned

SIERRA LEONE BROADCASTING CORP. (SLBC-TV) (Pub) ▤ New England Ville, Freetown ☎ +232 22 240123 ▤ +232 22 240922 **E**: contactus@slbc.sl **W**: www.slbc.sl **L.P**: DG: Elvis Gbanabom Hallowell **Txs**: Freetown ch24 & relay txs.

SINGAPORE

Systems: # PAL-B/G [E] ⬇2018; DVB-T (MPEG2), DVB-T2 (MPEG4) [E]

MEDIACORP PTE. LTD (Comm) ▤ Caldecott Broadcast Centre, Andrew Rd. Singapore, 299939 ☎ +65 63333888 ▤ +65 62538119 **W**: www.mediacorp.sg **L.P**: CEO: Shaun Seow. **Txs**: Channel 5 (English): Bukit Batok ch5 (120kW); Channel 8 (Chinese): Bukit Batok ch8 (120kW); Suria (Malay): ch12 (120kW); Vasantham: ch24; Channel U: ch28; okto: ch30; NewsAsia: ch32.

DTT Tx Networks (DVB-T2 exc. *=DVB-T/MPEG2)

Tx Operator: Mediacorp **M1:** Channel U, okto, NewsAsia. **M2:** Channel 5 HD, Suria HD **M3:** Channel 8 HD, Vasantham HD **M4:** Channel 8 HD +1 **M5:** Channel 5, Channel 5 HD, Channel 8, Channel News Asia.

Location	M1	M2	M3	M4	*M5
SFN	27	29	31	33	38

Systems: DVB-T (MPEG2, MPEG4), DVB-T2 (MPEG4) [E]

National Stations
ROZHLAS A TELEVÍZIA SLOVENSKÁ (RTVS) (Pub) ✉ Mlynská Dolina 28, 84545 Bratislava ☎ +421 2 60611111 **E:** press@rtvs.sk **W:** www.rtvs.sk; www.rtvs.org **L.P:** DG: Václav Mika. **Chs:** STV1, STV2, reg prgrs. – **TA3 (Comm)** ✉ Gagarinova 12, 82015 Bratislava 215 ☎ 421 2 48203511 ▤ + 421 2 48203549 **E:** ta3@ta3.com **W:** www. ta3.com. **L.P:** DG: Martin Ilavský. – **TV JOJ (Comm)** ▤ P.O.Box 33, 83007 Bratislava 37 ☎ +421 2 59888111 ▤ +421 2 59888112 **E:** joj@ joj.sk **W:** www.joj.sk **L.P:** CEO: Fratišek Borovský. **Chs:** TV JOJ, Plus. – **TV MARKÍZA (Comm)** ✉ Bratislavská 1/a, 84356 Bratislava 48 ☎ +421 2 68274111 ▤ +421 2 65956824 **E:** sekretariatgr@markiza. sk **W:** www.markiza.sk **L.P:** DG: Matthias Settele **Chs:** TV Markíza, Doma.

Local Stations not shown.

DTT Tx Networks (DVB-T/MPEG2, MPEG4)
Tx Operator: Towercom, a.s. ✉ Cesta na Kamzík 14, 831 01 Bratislava ☎ +421 2 49220111 ▤ +421 2 44461042 **E:** info@ towercom.sk **W:** www.towercom.sk **M1:** WAU, Dajto, TV Lux, Senzi, TV8 **M2:** TV JOJ, Plus, TV Markíza, Doma, TA3 **M3:** STV1, STV1 HD, STV2 **M4❂:** CT1, CT2, Sport 2, Eurosport 1, Eurosport 2, Film Plus, Nickelodeon, VH1, Viasat Explorer, Viasat History, Viasat Nature

Location	M1	M2	M3	M4	kW
Banská Bystrica (Laskomer)	49	51	33	40	50/20/2x25
Banská Štiavnica (Sitno)	50	21	48	31	2/50/35/13
Bardejov (Magura)	49	40	54	46	32/2x16/10
Borský Mikuláš (Dubník)	-	56	27	-	20/22
Bratislava (Kamzík)	44	56	27	39	50
Hranovnica	-	55	-	-	20
Košice (Dubník)	57	-	25	22	13/31/10
Košice (Heringeš)	50	59	25	21	20/17/20
Košice (Makovica)	-	59	-	-	16
Královský Chlmec	-	59	-	-	14
Lucenec (Blatný vrch)	49	60	33	32	32/16/20/10
Námestovo (Magurka)	-	59	26	-	20/10
Nitra (Zobor)	50	21	-	31	2/44/16
Nové Mesto n.V. (V.Javorina)	55	56	57	23	3x50/25
Poprad (Hranovnica)	41	56	24	39	2x50/2x20
Roznava	-	27	54	-	10/14
Ruzomberok (Úložisko)	44	59	26	46	50/3x20
Snina (Magura)	-	59	25	-	21/20
Stará L'ubovna (Kolník)	-	55	-	-	25
Trencin	-	52	57	-	40/50
Zilina (Krížava)	35	52	32	-	2/18/5

+ sites with txs below 10kW. Pol=V.
Test muxes (DVB-T2) & Local licensees not shown.

System: DVB-T (MPEG4) [E]

National Stations
RADIOTELEVIZIJA SLOVENIJA (RTVSLO) (Pub) ✉ Kolodvorska 2-4, 1000 Ljubljana ☎ +386 1 4752121 ▤ +386 1 4752020 **E:** info@ rtvslo.si **W:** www.rtvslo.si **L.P:** DG: Marko Filli **Chs:** RTVSLO1, RTVSLO2, RTVSLO3, TV Koper/Capodistria, Tele M. – **POP TV (Comm)** ✉ Kranjceva 26, 1113 Ljubljana ☎ +386 1 5893200 ▤ +386 1 5893200 **E:** info@pop-tv.si **W:** pro-plus.si – **TV3 MEDIAS (Comm)** ✉ Šmartinska cesta 152, 1000 Ljubljana ☎ +386 8 3874404 ▤ +386 8 3874402 **E:** info@tv3-medias.si **W:** www.tv3m.si.

Local Stations not shown.

DTT Tx Networks
Licensee: RTVSLO **Mux 1:** RTVSLO1, RTVSLO1 HD, RTVSLO2, RTVSLO2 HD, RTVSLO3, ¹TV Koper/Capodistria, ²Tele M, local stns **Mux 2:** Pop TV, Kanal A, Planet TV, Golica TV, Pink S.

Location	M1*	M2	kW	Location	M1*	M2	kW
Beli Kriz	27¹	33	5	Golo Brdo	27¹	-	5
Boc	27²	37	5	Krim	32	38	5

Location	M1*	M2	kW	Location	M1*	M2	kW
Krvavec	32	38	100	Pohorje	27²	37	100
Kuk	27¹	22	5	Skalnica	27¹	33	5
Kum	32	38	5	Slavnik	27¹	22	5
Nanos	27¹	22	200	Tinjan	27¹	33	5
Pecarovci	27²	37	5	Trdinov vrh	32	38	20
Plešivec	27²	37	25	Trstelj	27¹	33	25

+ sites with txs below 5kW *) Incl. reg. channels: ¹ ² see above
Local licensees not shown.

NB: No terrestrial TV station.

System: PAL-B/G [E]

National Station
SOMALI NATIONAL TELEVISION (SNTV) (Pub) ✉ Mogadishu. **W:** sntv.gov.so **Txs:** (-).

Regional/Local Stations not shown.

Systems: DVB-T2 (MPEG4) [SA]; § PAL-I [SA] ⇩2016

SOUTH AFRICAN BROADCASTING CORP. (SABC) (Pub) ✉ Private Bag XI, Auckland Park 2006 ☎ +27 11 7149111 ▤ +27 11 7143106 **E:** info@sabc.co.za **W:** www.sabc.co.za **L.P:** CEO: Frans Matlala. **Chs:** SABC1, SABC2, SABC3. – **E.TV (Comm)** ✉ Private Bag x9944, Sandton 2146 ☎ +27 21 4814500 ▤ +27 21 4814510 **E:** info@etv.co.za **W:** www.etv.co.za. – **M-NET (Comm)** ❂ ✉ P.O.Box 4950, Randburg 2125 ☎ +27 11 2893000 ▤ +27 11 7875763 **E:** inquiries@mnet.co.za **W:** m-net.dstv.com **L.P:** CEO: Yolisa Phahle.

DTT Tx Networks (under construction)
Licensee: Sentech **W:** www.sentech.co.za **Mux:** SABC1, SABC2, SABC3, e.tv **Txs:** ch65 (Johannesburg) & netw. – **Licensee:** Multichoice **W:** www.multichoice.co.za **Mux❂:** multiprgr (Orbicom/ M-Net) **Txs:** ch62V (Johannesburg, Kyalami, Helderkruin) & netw.
NB: Nationwide networks with 2 multiplexes under construction.

System: PAL-B/G [E]

National Station
SOUTH SUDAN BROADCASTING CORP. (SSBC) (Gov) ✉ Juba ☎ +211 912 452275. **Txs:** (-)

Local Stations not shown.

System: DVB-T (MPEG2, MPEG4) [E]

National Stations
TELEVISION ESPAÑOLA (TVE) (Pub) ✉ Prado del Rey, 28223 Pozuelo de Alarcon (Madrid) ☎ +34 91 5817000 ▤ +34 91 5815476 **E:** direccion.comunicacion@rtve.es **W:** www.rtve.es **L.P:** Dir: José Ramon Diez. **Chs:** La 1, La 2, 24h, Clan, TDP – **ANTENA 3 (Comm)** ✉ Carretera San Sebastian de los Reyes, 28700 Madrid ☎ +34 1 6320500 ▤ +34 1 6327144 **W:** www.antena3.com – **CUATRO (Comm)** ✉ Avenida de los Artesanos 6, 28760 Madrid ☎ +34 91 7367000 **E:** internet@cuatro.com **W:** www.cuatro.com – **LA SEXTA (Comm)** ✉ C/ Virgilio, 2 Edificio 4, 28223 Pozuelo de Alarcón ☎ +34 91 8382966 **E:** rr.hh@lasexta.com **W:** www.lasexta.com – **TELECINCO (Comm)** ✉ Ctra de Irún, Km 11,700, 28049 Madrid ☎ +34 902 155555 **E:** inversores@telecinco.es **W:** www.telecinco.es.

Regional Stations (Pub)
AN) Radio y Televisión de Andalucía (RTVA): Edificio Cana Sur, Avda. Josó Gálvez 1, 41092 Isla de la Cartuja (Sevilla) **W:** www.canalsur.es. Chs: Canal Sur, Canal Sur 2, Andalusía TV. **AR)** Corporación Aragonesa de Radio y Televisión (CARTV): Avda. Maria Zambrano 2, 50018 Zaragoza. **W:** www.cartv.es. Chs: Aragón TV. **AS)** Radioelevisión del Principado de Asturias (RTPA): Edificio RTPA, Parque Científico y Tecnológico de Gijon, c/

Luis Blanco 82, 33203 Gijon. **W:** www.rtpa.es. Chs: TPA7, TPA8. **BA)** Ente Público de Radiotelevisión de la Islas Baleares (EPRTVIB): c/ Madalena, 21 Polígon Son Bugadelles, 07180 Santa Ponça **W:** ib3tv.com. Ch: IB3 TV. **CA)** Corporació Catalana de Mitjans Audivisuals (CCMA): HQ: Via Augusta 252, 4a planta, 08817 Barcelona; Televisió de Catalunya: Carrer de la TV3, s/n, 08970 Sant Joan Despi (Barcelona) **W:** www.ccma.cat. Chs: TV3, TV3 HD, 33, Canal Super3, 324, Canal 3XL, Esport 3. **CL)** Radio Televisión de Castilla y León: c/Monasterio San Millán de la Cogolla 30, 47015 Valladoid **W:** www.rtvcyl.es Chs: CyLTV, La 8. **CM)** Radio Televisión de Castilla-La Mancha (RTVCM): C/ Río Alberche, s/n Polígono Santa Mª de Benquerencia, 45007 Toledo **W:** www.rtvcm.es. Chs: CMT, CMT 2. **EU)** Euskal Irrati Telebista (EITB): Capuchinos de Basurto 2, 48013 Bilbao **W:** www.eitb.eus Chs: ETB1, ETB2, ETB3. **GA)** Compañía de Radio-Televisión de Galicia (CRTVG): Bando - San Marcos s/n, 15820 Santiago de Compostela **W:** www.crtvg.es. Chs: TVG, tvG2. **MA)** Ente Público Radio Televisión Madrid (EPRTVM): Paseo del Príncipe 3, 28223 Pozuelo de Alarcón (Madrid). **W:** www.telemadrid.es. Chs: Telemadrid, Telemadrid HD, LaOtra. **MU)** Radiotelevisión de la Región de Murcia (RTRM): Plaza de San Agustín 5, 30005 Murcia. **W:** www.rtrm.es Chs: 7RM, 7RM HD. **VA)** Ràdiotelevisió Valenciana (RTVV): Polígon Accés Ademús s/n; 46100 Burjassot, València. **W:** www.rtvv.es. Chs: Canal Nou, Canal Nou Dos, Canal Nou 24. **NB.** Keys to region codes see National radio section.

Local Stations not shown.

DTT Tx Networks
Operator: n/a **Mux 1:** La 1, La 1 HD, La 2, 24h, Clan ✳ RNE R. Nacional, RNE R.5 **Txs:** ch58 (Madrid) & netw. **Mux 2:** TDP, TDP HD ✳ RNE R. Clásica HQ, RNE R. 3 HQ, RNE R. Exterior **Txs:** ch41 (Madrid) & netw. **Mux 3:** Discovery MAX, Disney Channel, Paramount Channel ✳ Cope, R. Maria, R. Marca, Vaughn R., esRadio **Txs:** ch33 (Madrid) & netw. **Mux 4:** Antena 3, Antena 3 HD, laSexta, laSexta HD, Neox, Nova **Txs:** ch59 (Madrid) & netw. **Mux 5:** Telecinco, Telecinco HD, Cuatro, Cuatro HD, FDF, Divinity **Txs:** ch49 (Madrid) & netw. **Mux 6:** Boing, Energy, Mega ✳ Europa FM, Melodia FM, Onda Cero **Txs:** ch26 (Madrid) & netw. **Mux 7:** tbd **Txs:** ch22 (Madrid) & netw.
Regional/Local muxes not shown.

SRI LANKA

Systems: # PAL-B/G [E] ⇓2020; DVB-T2 (MPEG4) [E]

National Stations
SRI LANKA RUPAVAHINI CORP. (SLRC) (Pub) ✉ P.O. Box 2204, Colombo 7 ☎ +94 11 2697491 🖷 +94 11 2695488 **L.P:** CEO: Gamini Somachandra Rasaputhra **E:** dg@rupavahini.lk **W:** www.rupavahini.lk **Chs:** Rupavahini, Channel Eye/Nethra TV, NTV. **Txs: Rupavahini:** Pidurutalagala ch5 (20kW), Kokavil ch8 (20 kW) & relay txs; **Channel Eye/Nethra TV:** Pidurutalagala ch7 (20kW) & network; **NTV:** Colombo ch52. – **INDEPENDENT TELEVISION NETWORK (ITN) (Comm)** ✉ Wickramasinghepura, Battaramulla ☎ +94 11 2774424 🖷 +94 11 2774591 **E:** itnadm@slt.lk **W:** www.itn.lk **Chmn:** Rosmund Senaratne **Chs:** Prime TV (English)/ Vasantham TV (Tamil) **Txs:** Deniyaya ch9 (20kW), Colombo ch12 (100kW), Yatiyantota ch12 (100kW), Nayabedde ch12 (100kW). – **MTV CHANNEL (PVT) LTD. (Comm)** ✉ 7, Braybrook Pl., Colombo 2 ☎ +94 11 4792600 🖷 +94 11 2447308 **E:** info@media.maharaja.lk **L.P:** CEO: Gayirika Perusignhe. **Chs:** MTV (English), Shakthi TV (Tamil), Sirasa TV (Singalese). **Txs:** Channel One/Shakthi: Colombo ch25 (5kW) & network; **Sirasa:** Colombo ch23 (5kW) & network. – **SWARNAVAHINI (EAP BROADCASTING CO. LTD.) (Comm)** ✉ 676 Galle Rd, Colombo 3 ☎ +94 11 2599642 🖷 +94 11 2503788 **E:** admin@swarnavahini.lk **W:** www.swarnavahini.lk **L.P:** Chmn: Dayanath Jayasuriya. **Txs:** Colombo ch34 (5kW) & network. – **TELSHAN NETWORK (PVT) LTD. (TNL) (Comm)** ✉ Innagale Estate Dampe-Piliyandala ☎ +94 11 2501681 🖷 +94 11 2575436 **E:** tnltvr@slt.lk **W:** www.tnltvisira.com **L.P:** Chmn/MD: Shantilal Nilkant Wickremesinghe **Txs:** Piliyandala ch3 (20kW), Polgahawela ch3 (1kW), Nuweraeliya ch4 (40kW), Colombo ch21 (22kW), Hantana (Kandy) ch21 (22kW), Piliyandala ch26 (22kW), Ratnapura ch26 (1kW). – **TV LANKA (Comm)** ✉ 68 Attidiya Road, Ratmalana ☎ +94 11 4213771 🖷 +94 11 4213980 **Txs:** Colombo & Matale & Matara ch48, Badulla & Kandy & Vauniya ch53.

Local Stations
Art TV: 451 Kandy Road, Kelaniya; Colombo ch28, Kandy ch52. **Derana TV:** 1072/1 5th Lane, Kotte Road, Rajagiriya; Matale ch28, Matara ch31, Badulla ch32, Nuwara Eliya ch36, Colombo ch37, Kalutara ch56. **Extra Terrestrial Vision:** 31 Shady Grove Avenue, Colombo 08; Colombo ch35, Kalutara ch40. **Max TV:** 221 Stanley Thilakaratne Mawatha, Nugedoga; Colombo ch30, Ratnapura ch32, Karagahatenna ch46, Nayabedda ch47, Hunnasgiriya & Kandy ch56.

TV2: Media House, 594/1 Galle Road, Colombo 03; Karagahatenna ch42, Colombo ch53. **Voice of Asia Networks:** Manila. Chs: Siyatha TV (Sinhala), Vettri TV (Tamil); Siyatha TV: Gongala ch28, Gammaduwa ch31, Colombo ch32, Kandy ch35; Vettri TV: Colombo ch46.

DTT Tx Network (Trial)
Licensee: Dialog Telekom PLC ✉ 475, Union Place, Colombo 02 ☎ +94 11 2678700 **W:** www.dialog.lk **M❂:** Rupavahini, ITN, Channel C, CSN, Citi Hitz, Kalaignar TV, The Buddhist **Txs:** ch50 (Colombo).

ST BARTHÉLEMY (France)

System: DVB-T (MPEG4) [E]

CARRIB'IN TV (INTV) (Comm) ✉ BP 658 Gustavia CEDEX, F-97099 Saint-Barthélemy ☎ +590 590874362 🖷 +590 590510787 **E:** contact@caribintv.com **W:** www.caribintv.com

DTT Tx Networks
Tx Operator: TDF **Mux:** Guadeloupe 1ère, France 2-5, France Ô, France 24, Arte, INTV **Txs:** ch41 (SFN).

ST EUSTATIUS (Netherlands)

NB: No terrestrial TV station.

ST HELENA (UK)

System: DVB-T2 (MPEG4) [E]

DTT Tx Network
Tx Operator: Sure South Atlantic Ltd. ✉ P.O.Box 2, Bishop's Rooms, Jamestown, St. Helena Island, South Atlantic Ocean STHL 1ZZ **E:** service@sure.co.sh **W:** www.sure.co.sh **Mux❂:** multiprgr (incl. Local TV1, Local TV2) ✳ Two radio prgrs **Txs:** (-).

ST KITTS & NEVIS

System: NTSC-M [A]

ZIZ BROADCASTING CORP. (Gov) ✉ P.O.Box 331, Basseterre, St. Kitts ☎ +1 869 4652621 🖷 +1 869 4652159 **E:** info@zizonline.com **W:** zizonline.com **L.P:** Chmn: Douglas Wattley **Txs:** (pol.H) Bayfords (St. Kitts) ch5 (20kW) & netw.

ST LUCIA

System: NTSC-M [A]

HELEN TELEVISION (HTS) (Comm) ✉ P.O. Box 621, The Morne, Castries ☎ +1 758 4524982 🖷 +1 758 4531737 **E:** news@htsstlucia.org **W:** www.htsstlucia.org **L.P:** MD: Linford Fevrier. **Txs:** Castries ch4 (20kW H) & ch5 (20kW H).

ST MAARTEN (Netherlands)

System: DVB-T (MPEG2) [E]

LEEWARD BROADCASTING CORP. (LBC) ✉ P.O.Box 375, Philipsburg. **Tx:**(-).

ST MARTIN (France)

System: DVB-T (MPEG4) [E]

DTT Tx Network
Tx Operator: TDF **Mux:** Guadeloupe 1ère, France 2-5, France Ô, France 24, Arte, INTV **Txs:** ch41 (Terre Basse), ch43 (Pic Paradis).

ST PIERRE & MIQUELON (France)

System: DVB-T (MPEG4) [E]

SAINT-PIERRE ET MIQUELON 1ÈRE (Pub) ✉ BP 4227, F-97500 Saint-Pierre et Miquelon ☎ +508 508411111 🖷 +508 508412219 **W:** saintpierremiquelon.la1ere.fr **L.P:** Dir: Gérard Hoareau.

DTT Tx Network
Tx Operator: TDF **Mux:** Saint-Pierre et Miquelon 1ère, France 2-,5, France Ô, France 24, Arte **Txs:** ch35 (Phare de Galantry), ch37 (Cap à l'Aigle), ch41 (Pointe au Cheval).

ST VINCENT & THE GRENADINES

System: NTSC-M [A]

SVGTV (Gov) P.O.Box 705, Kingstown, St. Vincent ☎ +1 784 4561078 **E:** svgbc@vincysurf.com **W:** www.svg-tv.com **L.P:** MD: R. Paul MacLeish. **Txs:** (pol.H) Dorsetshirehill ch9 (0.4kW), Layouhill ch7 (0.04kW), Maroonhill ch7 (0.04kW), Belleislehill ch11 (0.06kW), Mustique ch11 (0.06kW), Bequia ch13 (0.06kW).

Foreign TV Relay
TBN (USA): Kingstown ch4.

SUDAN

System: PAL-B/G [E]

SUDAN TELEVISION (Gov) P.O.Box 1094, Omdurman ☎ +249 183557398 +249 183553538 **E:** sudantvlive@sudanmail.net **W:** www.sudantv.net **Txs:** Omdurman ch5 (5kW H), Gezira ch7 (10kW) & relay txs.

SURINAME

Systems: # NTSC-M [A]; DVB-T2 (MPEG4)

National Stations
SURINAAMSE TELEVISIE STICHTING (STVS) (Gov) P.O.Box 535, Paramaribo ☎ +597 473032 +597 477216 **E:** info@stvs.sr **W:** www.stvs.sr **Txs:** Wageningen ch7 (0.10kW), Paramaribo ch8 (1kW), Moango ch9 (0.01kW), Caranis ch10 (0.10kW), Nickerie ch11 (1kW). –
ALGEMENE TELEVISIE VERZORGING (ATV) (Comm) P.O.Box 1839, Paramaribo ☎ +597 404611 +597 402660 **E:** info@atv.sr **W:** www.atv.sr **Txs:** Borokopondo ch2 (1kW), Wageningen ch6 (0.25kW), Moengo ch7, Paramaribo ch12 (0.4kW), Nickerie ch13 (0.5kW).

Local Stations (all Comm)
Ampies Broadcasting Corp: P.O.Box 885, Paramaribo; ch4 (1kW). **Garuda TV:** Goudstraat 20, Paramaribo; ch23. **Radika TV:** P.O.Box 1083, Paramaribo; ch14 (1kW). **Rapar Broadcasting Network (RBN):** P.O.Box 975, Paramaribo. Tx: ch5 (2kW). **Rasonic:** Bataviastraat 2, Nickerie; ch7 (1kW). **TV Apinti:** P.O.Box 595, Paramaribo; ch10 (1kW). **TV Sookha:** Batavaiastraat 25, Nickerie; tx: (-).

DTT Tx Networks
Licensee: Divitel **M:** multiprgr **Txs:** MFN. – **Licensee:** RBN **M:** multiprgr **Txs:** MFN.

SWAZILAND

Systems: DVB-T (MPEG2) [E]; § PAL-B [E]

SWAZI TV (Gov) Private Bag A146, Mbabane ☎ +268 24043036 +268 24042093 **E:** info@swazitv.co.sz **W:** www.swazitv.co.sz **L.P:** CEO: Austin B. Dlamini.

DTT Tx Network (under construction)
Tx Operator: n/a **M:** Swazi TV **Txs:** nationwide MFN network

SWEDEN

System: DVB-T (MPEG2), DVB-T2 (MPEG4) [E]

National Stations
SVERIGES TELEVISION AB (SVT) (Pub) Oxenstiernsgatan 26-34, 105 10 Stockholm ☎ +46 8 7840000 +46 8 7841500 **E:** info@svt. se **W:** www.svt.se **L.P:** MD: Eva Hamilton. **Chs (terr.):** SVT1, SVT2, Kunskapskanalen, SVTB/SVT24, regional prgrs. – **CANAL DIGITAL (Comm)** Tegeluddsvägen 7, 115 80 Stockholm ☎ +46 8 7722700 +46 8 7722555 **E:** kundservice@canaldigital.se **W:** www.canaldigital. se. – **TV4 AB (Comm)** Tegeluddsvägen 3-5, 115 79 Stockholm ☎ +46 8 4594000 +46 8 4594444 **E:** info@tv4.se **W:** www.tv4.se **L.P:** CEO (TV4 Group): Casten Almqvist – **VIASAT AB (Comm)** P.O.Box 17104, 104 62 Stockholm ☎ +46 8 56241060 +46 8 56202330 **E:**

info@viasat.se **W:** www.viasat.se **L.P:** CEO: Jonas Martin Karlén.

Local Stations not shown.

DTT Tx Networks (DVB-T/MPEG2 or °MPEG4 except where stated)
Licensee: Boxer TV Access AB Esplanaden 3c, 3 tr, 172 67 Sundbyberg ☎ +46 8 58789900 +46 8 58789999 **E:** kundtjanst@ boxer.se **W:** www.boxer.se **M1:** SVT1 (incl. reg. prgrs), SVT2 (incl. reg. prgrs), Kunskapskanalen, SVTB/SVT24 **M2(✪exc.*):** TV4*, TV4 Fakta/TV4 Film, Sjuan, TV6*, TV11, CNN International **M3✪:** TV3, Kanal 5, TV8, Disney Channel/Paramount Channel, C More First, SF-kanalen/C More Sport, Investigation Discovery° **M4✪:** Eurosport, Discovery Channel, Nickelodeon/Comedy Central, Kanal 9, MTV, TLC, TV10, Eurosport 2°, History°, Al Jazeera°, Horse 1° **M5(✪exc.*):** Axess TV°, BBC World News°, C More Series°, Animal Planet°, Disney XD/BBC Earth°, TNT, Cartoon Network°, Boomerang/TCM°, TV12, Fox°, Local stations*, Yle TV Finland* (Stockholm region only). **M6(✪exc.*) (DVB-T2):** SVT1 HD (incl. reg. prgrs)*, SVT2 HD (incl. reg. prgrs)*, TV3 HD, TV4 HD, Kanal 5 HD **M7✪(DVB-T2):** C More Live HD/C More Hits HD, TV4 Sport HD, National Geographic HD, C More Football/Hockey/Emotion, BBC Brit, Nick Jr./Travel Channel.

Location	M1	M2	M3	M4	M5	M6	M7	kW[1]
Arvidsjaur (Julträsk)	21	24	30	34	42	57	51	50
Bollnäs	29	49	34	39	23	53	6	50
Borlänge (Idkerberget)	47	52	43	41	54	60	28	50
Borås (Dalsjöfors)	44	54	29	42	55	36	41	50
Bäckefors	26	22	35	25	56	49	5	50
Emmaboda (Bälshult)	21	28	46	25	53	47	8	50
Filipstad (Klockarhöjden)	33	23	30	42	40	27	59	50
Finnveden	26	56	52	60	48	58	7	50
Gällivare	33	26	40	28	46	43	22	50
Gävle (Skogmur)	27	24	32	30	46	50	9	50
Göteborg (Brudaremossen)	30	27	46	40	43	33	9	50
Halmstad (Oskarström)	21	28	38	45	47	32	7	10
Helsingborg (Olympia)	33	43	41	25	22	30	10	10
Hudiksvall (Forsa)	31	44	34	39	23	53	60	50
Hörby (Sallerup)	33	43	41	25	22	30	10	50
Jönköping (Bondberget)	31	28	35	33	51	45	6	50
Kalix	35	29	60	55	50	58	27	50
Karlshamn	27	24	42	55	26	49	8	50
Karlskrona (Vämö)	27	24	42	55	26	49	8	50
Karlstad (Sörmon)	43	46	30	42	40	27	59	50
Kiruna (Kirunavaara)	39	35	32	49	42	29	44	50
Kisa	29	55	50	56	59	49	6	50
Lycksele (Knaften)	45	53	22	28	48	58	38	50
Malmö (Jägersro)	33	43	41	25	22	27	10	50
Mora (Eldris)	22	25	35	42	44	51	38	50
Motala (Ervasteby)	27	40	21	42	52	39	53	50
Norrköping (Krokek)	36	46	60	28	54	32	5	50
Nässjö	22	23	35	33	51	25	6	50
Pajala	34	23	31	37	54	47	51	50
Skellefteå	23	26	49	43	59	46	6	50
Skövde	37	24	32	34	57	60	47	50
Sollefteå (Multrå)	46	24	31	26	44	49	59	50
Stockholm (Nacka)	23	42	56	50	55	59	53	50
Storuman	33	43	36	46	56	60	49	50
Sundsvall (S Stadsberget)	47	27	30	43	56	58	50	50
Sunne (Blåbärskullen)	36	39	50	53	47	60	7	50
Sveg (Brickan)	21	24	46	41	36	59	32	50
Trollhättan	23	28	31	25	56	53	9	50
Tåsjö	37	40	51	41	50	57	30	50
Uddevalla (Herrestad)	23	28	31	25	56	53	9	50
Uppsala (Vedyxa)	40	21	43	49	33	58	52	50
Varberg (Grimeton)	21	28	38	45	47	32	7	10
Visby (Follingbo)	41	44	48	37	58	51	9	50
Vislanda (Nydala)	40	50	34	37	39	57	4	50
Vännäs (Granlundsberget)	47	50	56	36	52	60	39	50
Västervik (Fårhult)	26	34	24	30	40	43	57	50
Västerås (Lillhärad)	37	31	22	34	38	51	57	50
Västerås (Lillhärad)	44	-	-	-	-	-	-	50
Ånge (Snöberg)	42	37	57	28	55	52	22	50
Älvsbyn	36	39	47	32	38	52	56	50
Örebro (Lockhyttan)	29	25	49	55	58	48	50	50
Örnsköldsvik (Ås)	23	21	34	25	42	29	39	50
Östersund (Brattåsen)	27	45	58	53	54	56	48	50
Östhammar (Valö)	40	21	43	26	48	58	6	50
Överkalix	45	48	60	55	50	58	27	50

+ sites with txs below 10kW. [1] Power refers to UHF chs

SWITZERLAND

System: DVB-T (MPEG2) [E]

SRG SSR (Pub) Giacomettistrasse 1, 3000 Bern 31 ☎ +41 31 3509111 +41 31 3509256 **E:** info@srgssr.ch **W:** www.srgssr.ch

L.P: Pres: Viktor Baumeler (interim); DG: Roger de Weck **NB:** SRG SSR is the administrative holding for the regional branches SRF, RTR, RTS and RSI.
Schweizer Radio und Fernsehen (SRF) ✉ Fernsehstrasse 1-4, 8052 Zürich ☎+41 44 3056611 🖷 +41 44 3055635 **E:** srf@srf.ch **W:** www.srf.ch **L.P:** Dir: Rudolf Matter. **Chs (in Swiss German/German):** SRF1, SRF Zwei, SRF Info. **Radiotelevisiun Svizra Rumantscha (RTR)** ✉ Via da Masans 2, 7002 Cuira ☎+41 81 2557575 🖷 +41 81 2557500 **W:** www.rtr.ch **L.P:** Dir: Ladina Heimgartner. **Ch (in Rumantsch):** via SRF1. **Radio Télévision Suisse (RTS)** ✉ Quai Ernest-Ansermet 20, 1211 Genève 8 ☎+41 58 2367444 🖷 +41 58 2367454 **E:** manon.romerio@rts.ch **W:** www.rts.ch **L.P:** Dir: Gilles Marchand **Chs (in French):** RTS Un, RTS Deux. **Radiotelevisione svizzera (RSI)** ✉ Via Canevascini 5, 6900 Lugano ☎+41 91 8035111 🖷 +41 91 8035355 **E:** info@rsi.ch **W:** www.rsi.ch **L.P:** Dir: Maurizio Canetta. **Chs (in Italian):** LA 1, LA 2.

DTT Tx Networks
Tx Operator: Swisscom **Mux 1:** SRF 1, SRF Zwei, SRF Info, RTS Un, LA 1 **Mux 2:** RTS Un, RTS Deux, SRF 1, LA 1 **Mux 3:** LA 1, LA 2, SRF 1, RTS Un

Location	M1	M2	M3	kW
Altstätten (Hoher Kasten)	34	-	-	21.5
Arth (Rigi-Kulm)	32	-	-	16.3
Bolligen (Bantiger)	48	51	-	10
Bonvillars (Champ Lequet)	-	56	-	14.3
Chardonne (Mt. Pèlerin)	-	34	47	10
Cudrefin (Tremblex)	-	56	-	10
Höfen (Beisseren)	49	-	-	10
Montmagny	-	56	-	10
Carona (Monte San Salvatore)	-	-	57	40
Nods (Chasseral)	48	56	-	10
Bourrignon (Les Ordons)	-	56	-	10
Premier (Buclards)	-	34	-	10
Rivera (Mt. Ceneri)	-	-	49	13.5
Semione (Pizzo Matro)	-	-	29H	14
Sorens (Gibloux)	-	56	-	11
Visperterminen (Gebidem)	45	-	-	10
Wildhaus (Säntis)	34	-	-	42
Winterthur (Brüelberg)	32	-	-	10
Zürich (Uetliberg)	32	-	-	45

+ sites with txs below 10kW. Pol.=V except where noted
Local/regional Licensees not shown.

SYRIA

System: PAL-B/G [E]

National Stations
ORGANIZATION OF SYRIAN ARAB RADIO & TELEVISION (Gov) ✉ Ommayad Square, Damascus ☎ +963 11 2720700 🖷 +963 11 2234930 **L.P:** Dir (TV): Diana Jabbour **E:** srtv@rtv.gov.sy **W:** rtv.gov.sy **Txs:** (pol.H) **Prgr 1:** Damascus ch4 (100kW) & netw.; **Prgr 2:** Damascus ch32 & netw. – **ADDOUNIA TV (Comm)** ✉ Damascus **W:** www.addounia.tv **Txs:** (-).

Local Station: Ugarit TV (Gov), Latakia; tx:(-).

TAIWAN

System: DVB-T (MPEG2, MPEG4) [A]

CHINESE TELEVISION SYSTEM (CTS) (Pub) ✉ 100, Kuang Fu South Rd, Taipei 106 ☎ +886 2 27510321 🖷 +886 2 27775414 **E:** wwwpub@mail.cts.com.tw **W:** www.cts.com.tw **L.P:** Chair: Yaly Chao. **Chs (terr.):** CTS, CTS HD, CTS Education, CTS Recreation. – **PUBLIC TELEVISION SERVICE (PTS) (Pub)** ✉ 50, Lane 75, Kang-Ning Rd., Section 3, Taipei 114 ☎ 886 2 26339122 🖷 +886 2 26338124 **E:** pub@mail.pts.org.tw **W:** www.pts.org.tw **L.P:** Chair: Yaly Chao **Chs (terr.):** PTS, PTS2, Hakka TV. – **CHINA TELEVISION CO., LTD (CTV) (Comm)** ✉ 120, Chung-Yang Rd, Taipei 115 ☎ +886 2 27838308 🖷 +886 2 2782 6007 **E:** pubr@mail.chinatv.com.tw **W:** www.ctv.com.tw **L.P:** Chmn: Shengfen Lin. **Chs:** CTV, CTV HD, CTV News, CTV MyLife. – **FORMOSA TELEVISION, INC. (FTV) (Comm)** ✉ 24/F, 30, Pa Te Road, Section 3, Taipei 105 ☎ +886 2 25702570 🖷 +886 2 25796633 **E:** service@ftv.com.tw **W:** www.ftv.com.tw **Chs:** FTV, FTV HD, FTV News, Follow Me TV. **L.P:** Chairman: Tien Tsai-ting – **TAIWAN TELEVISION ENTERPRISE CO., LTD (TTV) (Comm)** ✉ 10, Pa Te Rd, Section 3, Taipei 10560 ☎ +886 2 25781515 🖷 +886 2 25799625 **E:** ref@email.ttv.com.tw **W:** www.ttv.

com.tw **L.P:** Chairman: Huang Sung. **Chs (terr.):** TTV, TTV HD, TTV Finance, TTV Health.

DTT Tx Networks (MPEG2 exc. *=MPEG4)
Licensee: CTS **Mux:** CTS, CTS HD*, CTS Education, CTS Recreation. – **Licensee:** PTS **Mux 1:** PTS, PTS2, Hakka TV **Mux 2*:** PTS HD. – **Licensee:** CTV **Mux:** CTV, CTV HD*, CTV News, CTV MyLife. – **Licensee:** FTV **Mux:** FTV, FTV HD*, FTV News, Follow Me TV, ⌘ Formosa Network. – **Licensee:** TTV **Mux:** TTV, TTV HD*, TTV Finance, TTV Health.

Location	PTS M1	PTS M2	CTS	CTV	FTV	TTV
SFN	26	30	34	24	28	32

TAJIKISTAN

Systems: DVB-T2 (MPEG4); § SECAM-D/K [R], § PAL-D/K [R]

National Station
KUMITAI TELEVIZION VA RADIOI (Gov) ✉ TV studios: Bekhzod St. 7a, 734013 Dushanbe ☎ +992 37 2224357 🖷 +992 37 2213459 info@ktr.tj **W:** www.ktr.tj **L.P:** Chmn: Asadulloi Rahmon **Chs:** Shabakai 1, TV Safina, TV Bakhoriston, Jahonnamo.

Local Stations, Foreign TV Relays not shown.

DTT Tx Networks (under construction)
Tx Operator: Teleradiokom **M:** Shabakai 1, TV Safina, TV Bakhoriston, Jahonnamo & others **Txs:** ch46 (Dushanbe 2.5kW), ch49 (Khujand) + nationwide MFN.

TANZANIA

System: DVB-T2 (MPEG4) [E]

National Stations
TANZANIA BROADCASTING CORP. (TBC) (Gov) ✉ P.O.Box 31519, Dar es Salaam ☎ +255 22 2700062 🖷 +255 22 2121315 **E:** info@tbc.go.tz **W:** www.tbc.go.tz **L.P:** DG: Clement Mshana **Ch:** TBC1, TBC2 – **CHANNEL 10 TV (Comm)** ✉ P.O.Box 19045, Dar es Salaam ☎ +255 22 2116341 🖷 +255 22 2113112 **E:** info@channelten.co.tz **W:** www.channelten.co.tz – **INDEPENDENT TV (ITV) (Comm)** ✉ P.O.Box 4374, Dar es Salaam ☎ +255 22 2775914 🖷 +255 22 2775915 **E:** info@itv.co.tz **W:** www.itv.co.tz – **STAR TV (Comm)** ✉ P.O.Box 1732, Mwanza ☎ +255 28 2503262 🖷 +255 28 2500713 **E:** marketing@startvtz.com **W:** www.startvtz.com.

Local Stations not shown.

DTT Tx Networks
Licensee: Basic Transmissions Ltd **M:** multiprgr **Txs:** MFN – **Licensee:** Star Media Tanzania Ltd **M⊕:** multiprgr **Txs:** MFN – **Licensee:** Agape Associates Limited **M⊕:** multiprgr **Txs:** MFN.

THAILAND

Systems: # PAL-B/G [E] ⇩2018; DVB-T2 (MPEG4) [E]

MCOT PLC (MODERNINE TV) (Gov) ✉ 63/1 Rama IX Road, Huay Khwang, Bangkok 10320 ☎ +66 2 22016000 🖷 +66 2 22451960 **W:** www.mcot.net **Txs:** Bangkok ch9 (20kW) & network. – **NATIONAL BROADCASTING SERVICES OF THAILAND (NBT) (Gov)** ✉ 90-91 New Phetchaburi Road, Huay Khwang, Bangkok 10320 ☎ +66 2 3182110 🖷 +66 2 3182991 **W:** nbttv.prd.go.th **Txs:** Bangkok ch11 (200kW) & relays. – **ROYAL ARMY TELEVISION (TV5) (Gov)** ✉ 210 Phaholyothin Rd, Sanam Pao, Bangkok 10400 ☎ +66 2 22710060 🖷 +66 2 22712515 **E:** army@tv5.co.th **W:** www.tv5.co.th **Txs:** Bangkok ch5 (20kW) & network. – **THAI PUBLIC BROADCASTING SERVICE (TPBS) (Pub)** ✉ 1010 Shinawatra Tower III, 13 Vibhavadi Rangsit Road, Chatchuchak, Bangkok 10900 ☎ +66 2 27911000 🖷 +66 2 27911010 **E:** webmaster@thaipbs.or.th **W:** www.thaipbs.or.th **Txs:** Bangkok ch29 (1000kW) & network. – **BANGKOK BROADCASTING & TELEVISION (BBTV) (Comm)** ✉ P.O.Box 4-56, Bangkok 10900 ☎ +66 2 2720010 🖷 +66 2 27202106 **E:** marketing@ch7.com **W:** www.ch7.com. **Txs:** Bangkok ch7 (20kW) & network. – **BANGKOK ENTERTAINMENT CO. LTD. (CHANNEL 3) (Comm)** ✉ Floors 7, 15, 16, The Emporium Tower, Sukhumvit Road, Khlong Tan, Khlong Toey, Bangkok 10110 ☎ +66 2 22623333 🖷 +66 2 22041384 **W:** www.thaitv3.com **Txs:** Bangkok ch32 (650kW) & network.

DTT Tx Networks (under construction)
Licensee: MCOT **Mux 1:** multiprgr **Txs:** ch56 (Bangkok SFN) & nationwide MFN **Mux 2:** multiprgr **Txs:** ch43 (Bangkok SFN) & nationwide

MFN **Mux 3:** multiprgr **Txs:** ch40 (Bangkok SFN) & nationwide MFN

TIMOR-LESTE

System: PAL-B [E]

RADIO TELEVISAUN TIMOR-LESTE (RTTL) (Pub) ✉ Estrada Mercado Municipal, Caicoli. Dili **E:** info@rttlep.tl **W:** rttlep.tl ☎ +670 3321827 **LP:** Pres: Expedito Dias Ximenes **Txs:** Dili ch7 (1.5 kW), Baucau ch12.

TOGO

Systems: DVB-T2 (MPEG4) [E]; § SECAM-K1 [VHF=K]

National Stations
TÉLÉVISION TOGOLAISE (Gov) ✉ BP 3286, Lomé ☎ +228 22215357 🖷 +228 22215786 **E:** televisiontogolaise@yahoo.fr **W:** tvt. tg **LP:** DG: Kuessan Yovodévi – **TV2 (Comm)** ✉ Lomé ☎ +228 22514993 **LP:** DG: Eudoxie Théophane.

Local Station
TV7: BP 81104, Lomé.

DTT Tx Network (under construction)
Tx Operator: n/a **M:** multiprgr **Txs:** MFN

TOKELAU (New Zealand)

NB: No terrestrial TV station.

TONGA

System: DVB-T (MPEG4) [NZ]

TONGA BROADCASTING COMMISSION (Gov) ✉ P.O.Box 36, Nuku'alofa ☎ +676 23555 🖷 +676 24417 **E:** news@tonga-broadcasting. net **W:** tonga-broadcasting.net **LP:** GM: Nanise Fifita **Chs:** TV Tonga, TV Tonga 2 (incl. relay CCTV-9), TV Vava'u. – **DOULOS BROADCASTING NETWORK (Rlg)** ✉ P.O.Box 91, Nuku'alofa ☎ +676 23314 🖷 +676 23658 **W:** doulostv.com **LP:** Dir: Gerhard Taukolo Taukolo.

DTT Tx Networks
Tx Operator: DigiTV (Tonga) Ltd. ✉ P.O.Box 875, Nuku'alofa **E:** customercare.tonga@digicelgroup.com **W:** www.digiceltonga.com **Mux✪:** multiprgr **Tx:** ch45V (Nuku'alofa 1kW).

TRINIDAD & TOBAGO

Systems: # NTSC-M [A]; DVB-T (MPEG4) [A]

TV4 (Gov) ✉ P.O. Box 665, Port-of-Spain, Trinidad ☎ +1 868 62241414 🖷 +1 868 6220344 **E:** marketing@gisltd.tt **W:** www.gisltd. tt/tv-4 **Txs:** ch4, ch16. – **ADVANCED COMMUNITY TV STATION (ACTS) (Pub)** ✉ 53B, Circular Road, San Fernando, Trinidad ☎ +1 868 6524855 **E:** info@acts25tt.com **W:** www.acts25tt.com **LP:** CEO/Pres: Nelson Sammy-Guilarte **Tx:** ch25. – **CCN-TV6 (Comm)** ✉ 35 Independence Sq, Port-of-Spain, Trinidad ☎ +1 868 6278806 🖷 +1 868 6271451 **W:** www.tv6tnt.com **LP:** CEO: Dawn Thomas **Txs:** ch6 (25kW) & ch18 (1kW) (Trinidad), ch19 (Tobago). – **C TELEVISION (CNMG) (Comm)** ✉ 11A Maraval Road, Port-of-Spain, Trinidad **W:** www.ctntworld.com **LP:** CEO: Ken Ali **Txs:** ch9, ch13. – **GAYELLE TV (Comm)** ✉ 13 Southern Main Road, Curepe, Trinidad and Tobago, Curepe Village, Saint George, Trinidad ☎ +1 868 2906880 **E:** gayel-letv@gmail.com **W:** www.facebook.com/GayelleTheChannel **LP:** CEO: Dwayne Cambridge **Tx:** ch23. – **WIN TV (Comm)** ✉ Corner Henry & Bonito Streets, Chaguanas, Trinidad ☎ +1 809 6726429 **E:** info@winhd. tt **W:** winhd.tt **LP:** Chmn: Mohan Jaikaran **Tx:** ch37, ch39.

DTT Tx Networks
Licensee: Green Dot Ltd ✉ 61 Mucurapo Road, St James, Trinidad ☎ +868 6284388 🖷 +868 6285197 **E:** info@gd.tt **W:** www.gd.tt **Mux 1-4:** multiprgr **Txs:** SFN.

TRISTAN DA CUNHA (UK)

NB: No terrestrial TV station.

TUNISIA

Systems: DVB-T (MPEG4) [E]

ENTREPRISE DE LA TÉLÉVISION TUNISIENNE (ETT) (Gov) ✉ Avenue de la Ligue Arabe, 1002 Tunis ☎ +216 71800844 🖷 +216 71781058 **E:** info@watania1.tn; info@.watania2.tn **W:** www. watania1.tn; www.watania2.tn **LP:** DG: Mustafa Ben Latif **Chs:** Al Watania 1; Al Watanya 2. – **EL HIWAR ETTOUNSI (Comm)** ✉ Avenue Habib Bourguiba, 1000 Tunis ☎ +216 71844855 **E:** contact@ elhiwarettounsi.tv **W:** www.elhiwarettounsi.com. – **HANNIBAL TV (HTV) (Comm)** ✉ 85 Avenue du 13 Aout, Choutrana 2 - La Soukra, 2036 Tunis ☎ +216 70944944 🖷 +216 70944411 **E:** info@hannibaltv. com.tn **W:** www.hannibaltv.com.tn. – **NESSMA (Comm)** ✉ 75 Av. Mohamed V, 1002 Tunis ☎ +216 71465560 **W:** www.nessma.tv. – **TUNISIA FIRST TV (Comm)** ✉ Rue Haroun Errachid, Z.I. Ksar Said, 2086 Tunis ☎ +216 70663791 🖷 +216 70663790 **W:** www. firsttv.tn.

DTT Tx Networks
Tx Operator: Office National de la Télédiffusion (ONT) ✉ BP 399, 1080 Tunis ☎ +216 71801177 🖷 +216 71781927 **E:** ont@teledif-fusion.net.tn **W:** www.telediffusion.net.tn **Mux:** Al Watanya 1, Al Watanya 2, HTV, Nessma, Ettounsi, Tunesia First TV, RAI 1.

Location	ch	Location	ch
Trozza	21	Zarzis	28
Kchabta	23	Nefta	28
Ain Draham	28	Chaambi	29
Kef Errand	30	Souk Ejomaa	44
Zaghouan	36	Boukornine	45
Remada	36	Broumet	51
Biadha	37	Goraa	52
Ksour Essaf	38	Tozeur	55
Ghraba	41		

TURKEY

Systems: DVB-T2 (MPEG4) [E]; § PAL-B/G [E]

National Stations
TÜRKIYE RADYO TELEVIZYON KURUMU (TRT) (Pub) ✉ TRT-TV Department, TRT Sitesi A Blok 427 Oran, 06109 Ankara ☎ +90 312 4901058 🖷 +90 312 4901109 **E:** genel.sekreterlik@trt.net.tr **W:** www. trt.net.tr. **LP:** Head of TV Dept: Tuncay Yürekli **Chs (terr.):** TRT1, TRT Haber, TRT3-Spor, TRT Çocuk, TRT Kurdî, TRT Avaz, TRT Türk, TRT Belgesel, TRT Müzik, TRT Diyanet, TRT Okul, Regional stns. – **ATV (Comm)** ✉ Barbaros Bulvari 125, Cam Han, Besiktas, Istanbul ☎ +90 216 4742020 **E:** editor@atv.com.tr **W:** www.atv.com.tr – **CINE 5 (Comm)** ✉ Halaskargazi Cad. 180, Pangalti, Istanbul ☎ +90 212 3361515 🖷 +90 212 2171986 **E:** cine5@cine5.com.tr **W:** www.cine5. com.tr – **CNBC-E (Comm)** ✉ Eskibüyükdere Cad. 61, USO Center, Maslak, 80660 Istanbul ☎ +90 212 3350000 🖷 +90 212 3350035 **E:** insankaynaklari@cnbce.com **W:** www.cnbce.tv; www.ntvpara.com – **CNN TÜRK (Comm)** ✉ Hürriyet Media Towers, Evren Mah. Günesli, Bagcilar, 34204 Istanbul ☎ +90 212 4785856 🖷 +90 212 5500239 **E:** info@cnnturk.com.tr **W:** www.cnnturk.com – **FLASH TV (Comm)** ✉ Catmamescit Mah., Tepebasi Cad., Elektrik Sok. 11, Istanbul ☎ +90 212 2568282 🖷 +90 212 2569992 **E:** flashtv-w@flashtv.com.tr **W:** www.flashtv.com.tr – **FOX (Comm)** ✉ Kazliçesme Mah. Kennedy Cad 44, Zeytinburnu, 34020 Istanbul ☎ +90 212 4149000 **E:** info@fox. com.tr **W:** www.fox.com.tr – **HABER TÜRK (Comm)** ✉ Tevfik Bey Mah. 20 Temmuz Cad 24, Sefaköy-Küçükçekmece, Istanbul ☎ +90 212 5805267 🖷 +90 212 4264241 **W:** www.haberturk.com – **KANAL A (Comm)** ✉ Subayevleri Güzin Sokak 40, Kiçiören, Ankara ☎ +90 313 3186970 🖷 +90 312 3181752 **E:** iletisim@kanala.com.tr **W:** www.kanala.com.tr – **KANAL D (Comm)** ✉ Kanal D TV Center, 100. Yil Mahallesi, Bagcilar, 34204 Istanbul ☎ +90 212 4135111 🖷 +90 212 4135550 **E:** bizeyazin@kanald.com.tr **W:** www.kanald.com. tr – **KANAL 7 (Comm)** ✉ Otakçilar Cad. 78, Eyüp, 34030 Istanbul ☎ +90 212 4378080 🖷 +90 212 4378599 **E:** kanal7@kanal7com **W:** www.kanal7.com – **MELTEM (Comm)** ✉ Imönü Cad. 96, Besyol, Florya, 34295 Istanbul ☎ +90 212 6240999 🖷 +90 212 4246977 **E:** bilgi@meltemtv.com.tr **W:** www.meltemtv.com.tr – **NTV (Comm)** ✉ Eskibüyükdere Cad. 61, Uso Center, Maslak, 80660 Istanbul ☎ +90 212 3350000 🖷 +90 212 3350099 **W:** www.ntv.com.tr **Chs:** NTV, NTV Spor – **SHOW TV (Comm)** ✉ AKS Televizyon, Yapi Kredi Plaza, E Blok 1, Levent, 80620 Istanbul ☎ +90 212 3550101 🖷 +90 212 2806302 **E:** info@showtvnet.com **W:** www.showtv.com.tr – **STAR TV (Comm)** ✉ Dogan TV Center, 100. Yil Mahallesi, 34204 Bagcilar,

Istanbul ☎: +90 212 4135000 **E:** izleyicitemsilcisi@startv.com.tr **W:** www.startv.com.tr – **SAMANYOLU TV (Comm)** ☑ Ferah Mah. Resatbey Sok. 12, Büyükçamlica, 34692 Istanbul ☎ +90 216 5249524 🗎 +90 216 3443803 **E:** haber@samanyolu.tv **W:** www.samanyolu. tv – **TNT (Comm)** ☑ Türkali Mah. Odalar Sok 9, Besiktas, Istanbul **Txs:** Ankara (Çankaya) ch53 & netw. – **TV8 (Comm)** ☑ Ihlamurdere Cad., Yesilçimen Sok. 5, OTIM, Besiktas, 80820 Istanbul ☎ +90 212 2885152 🗎 +90 212 2880413 **E:** tv8@tv8.com.tr **W:** www.tv8.com.tr.

Local Stations not shown.

DTT Tx Networks (under construction)
Tx Operator: Anten A.S. **W:** www.antenas.com.tr **Mux 1-6:** multiprgr.

Location	M1	M2	M3	M4	M5	M6
Ankara (Çankaya)	7	24	28	34	37	38

+ nationwide MFN under construction.

TURKMENISTAN

Systems: DVB-T2 (MPEG4); § SECAM-D/K [R], § PAL-D/K [R]

TELEWIDENIÝE, RADIOGEPLESIKLER WE KINEMATOGRAFIÝA BARAKDY DÖWLET KOMITET (Gov) ☑ Magtymguly köçesi 89, 744000 Asgabat ☎ +993 12 351515 🗎 +993 12 394470 **L.P:** Chmn: A. Kakaýewi **TV Studios:** ☑ 2003 St. 3, 744000 Asgabat **Chs:** Altyn Asyr Türkmenistan, Miras, Ýaslyk, TV4-Türkmenistan, Türkmen Owaz, Asgabat.

DTT Tx Networks (under construction)
Tx Operator: Ministry of Communications **Mux 1**: Altyn Asyr Türkmenistan, Miras, Ýaslyk, TV4-Türkmenistan, Türkmen Owaz, Asgabat (+ two HD simulcasts) **Mux 2-6**: multiprgr

Location	M1	M2	M3	M4	M5	M6	kW
Asgabat	n/a	43	48	58	60	62	1.3

+ nationwide network under construction.

TURKS & CAICOS ISLANDS (UK)

NB: No terrestrial TV station.

TUVALU

System: PAL-B [E]

TUVALU MEDIA CORP. (TMC) (Pub) ☑ Private Mail Bag, Funafuti ☎ +688 20139 🗎 +688 20732 **E:** media@tuvalu.tv **Tx:** Funafuti ch n/a (0.02kW).

UGANDA

System: DVB-T2 (MPEG4) [E]

National Stations
UGANDA BROADCASTING CORP. (UBC) (Pub) ☑ P.O.Box 2038, Kampala ☎ +256 41 4257034 🗎 +256 41 4257252 **E:** customerservice@ubc.ug **W:** ubc.ug **L.P:** MD: Apollo Nkeza – **WBS TELEVISION (Comm)** ☑ P.O.Box 5914, Kampala ☎ +256 41 4344313 🗎 +256 41 4345672 **E:** inquiry@wbs.ug **W:** www.wbs.ug.

Local Stations not shown.

DTT Tx Networks
Licensee: Multichoice Uganda ☑ Plot 1/13, Jinja Road, Shop No.2 ground Floor, Kampala **M:** KBC, NTV, QTV, KTN, Citizen, K24, Kiss TV **Txs:** MFN – **Licensee:** Zuku TV **M✪:** multiprgr **Txs:** MFN – **Licensee:** Star DTV Uganda ☑ First Floor, Soliz House, Plot 23, Lumumba Avenue, P.O.Box 2300 Nakasero, Kampala, **M✪:** multiprgr **Txs:** MFN.

UKRAINE

Systems: DVB-T (MPEG2, MPEG4) [E], DVB-T2 (MPEG4) [E]; § SECAM-D/K [R], § PAL-D/K [R] ⇩ 31 Dec 2016

National Stations
NATSIONALNA TELEKOMPANIA UKRAINY (NTKU) (Gov) ☑ vul. Melnykova 42, 04119 Kyiv ☎ +380 44 2413909 🗎 +380 44 2468848 **W:** 1tv.com.ua **L.P:** GD: Zurab Alasaniia. **Chs (terr.):** UA:Pershyi – **1+1 (Comm)** ☑ vul. Kyrylivska 23, 04080 Kyiv ☎ +380 44 4900101 🗎 +380 44 4907097 **E:** feedback@1plus1.ua **W:** www.1plus1.ua **L.P:** DG (1+1 Media): Oleksandr Tkachenko – **INTER (Comm)** ☑ vul. Dmytrivska 30,

01601 Kyiv ☎ +380 44 4906765 🗎 +380 44 4906765 **E:** program@inter. ua **W:** inter.ua **L.P:** CEO (U.A. Inter Media Group) Hanna Bezliudna – **5 KANAL (Comm)** ☑ vul. Elektrykiv 26, 04176 Kyiv ☎ +380 44 3517720 🗎 +380 44 3517725 **E:** box@5.ua **W:** www.5.ua.

Local Stations not shown.

DTT Tx Networks (under construction) (DVB-T2)
Licensee Mux 1-3, 5: Zeonbud ☑ P.O.Box 110, 01054 Kyiv. **E:** office@zeonbud.com.ua **W:** www.zeonbud.com.ua **M1:** Pershyi, Inter, 1+1, Ukraina, NTN, ICTV, Enter-Film **M2:** Zoom, Indigo TV, STB, TET, K2, Novyi kanal, M1, 5 kanal **M3:** Mega, Piksel TV, NLO-TV, 2+2, Dobro, Business, Espreso TV **M5:** Tonis TV, Vintage, Eskulap TV, IVF-ODTRK, RAI, 112 Ukraina HD, OTB, Halychyna, Hlas, UA:TV, Kultura.
Local licensees (DVB-T/MPEG2, MPEG4) not shown. **NB:** Mux 4 is currently vacant.

Location	M1	M2	M3	M5	kW
Andriivka	50	40	43	42	3x4.9/4.9
Bershad	35	53	54	51	4.9
Bilopillia	55	42	51	33	5.5x
Buky	62	61	29	37	1.26/2x0.4/1
Cherkasy	48	28	21	53	5.5
Chernihiv	22	34	35	61	5.7
Dnipropetrovsk	26	35	25	40	5.5
Ivano-Frankivsk	42	41	31	58	0.9/2x2.8/
Izium	26	39	25	43	2.7
Kamianets-Podilskyi	22	29	51	44	2x1.1/2x2.3
Kamianske	22	40	55	28	0.5/2x1.1/1.1
Kharkiv	31	35	48	58	4.9
Kherson	34	58	39	44	3x2.6/1
Khmelnytskyi	22	29	51	50	5.2
Kholmy	22	49	54	61	2.4
Khust	39	53	56	61	2.7
Kirovohrad	49	53	22	47	5.4
Kotovsk	62	43	54	40	5.4
Kovel	44	27	59	52	4.9/2.5/2x4.9
Krasnohorivka	26	37	41	51	3/2/2x1
Krasnoperekopsk	24	31	43	53	1.1
Kryvyi Rih	41	51	54	38	5.5
Kuibysheve	33	32	36	53	2.4
Kyiv	26	31	49	29	12
Lviv	22	28	40	33	6.4
Mariupol	39	42	34	24	5
Melitopol	33	26	28	50	5.4/3x5.9
Mykolaiv	34	58	39	48	0.4/5.3/2x1
Novodnistrovsk	60	34	64	25	2.7/0.5/2x2.7
Odesa	43	32	39	23	4.5
Olevsk	51	52	53	43	2.8
Pryluky	52	27	56	32	5.1
Rivne	38	42	40	33	4.9
Shostka	24	59	58	60	5.2
Starobilsk	32	55	62	58	2.4
Ternopil	25	39	23	37	4.8
Trostianets	54	49	51	30	5.2
Vasylivka	29	41	57	36	4.7
Vinnytsia	39	32	31	49	3.6
Zaporizhzhia	43	31	49	57	3x3.1/2.9
Zhovten	35	41	47	33	3x5.4/5.4

+ sites with only txs below 1kW.

NB: Txs in **Donets Basin** not shown.

CRIMEA
(under Russian administration)

Systems: DVB-T2 (MPEG4) [E]; § SECAM-D/K [R], § PAL-D/K [R]

TRK "KRYM" (Gov) ☑ 295001 Simferopol, ul. Studencheskaya 14 ☎ +7 652 546406 **W:** 1tvcrimea.ru **Ch:** 1 Krym **Txs:** Simferopol ch12 (1kW) & netw. **OBSHCHESTVENNAYA KRYMSKO-TATARSKAYA TRK (OKTT) (Pub)** ☑ 295011 Simferopol, ul. Kozlova 45a **L.P:** DG: Seyran Mambetov.

Other Regional Stations/Local Stations not shown.

DTT Tx Networks
Tx Operator: RTPTs Respubliki Krym **M1:** Rossiya 1, Rossiya 24, Rossiya K, Karusel, Match TV, Pervyy kanal, NTV, OTR, 5-kanal, TV Tsentr ✖ R. Rossii, Mayak, Vesti FM. **M2:** Domashniy, TV Zvezda, Mir TV, Muz-TV, Pyatnitsa, REN TV, Spas, STS, TNT, TV-3 **M3:** Krym 1, OKTT + multiprgr **M4:** 1 Krym – **Local muxes** not shown.

Location	M1	M2	M3	kW
Simferopol	36	37	58	0.2
+network				

UNITED ARAB EMIRATES

System: DVB-T2 (MPEG4) [E]

ABU DHABI TV (Gov) ▭ P.O.Box 637, Abu Dhabi ☎ +971 2 44451111 **E:** adtv@emi.co.ae **W:** www.adtv.ae **Chs: Prgr 1, Prgr 2 – AJMAN TV (Gov)** ▭ P.O.Box 422, Ajman ☎ +971 6 7465000 🖷 +971 6 7465135 **E:** progajtv@ajmantv.com **W:** www.ajmantv.com **– DUBAI TV (Gov)** ▭ P.O.Box 1695, Dubai ☎ +971 4 3077245 🖷 +971 4 3374111 **W:** www.dmi.ae **Chs:** Prgr 1, Prgr 2 – **SHARJAH TV (Gov)** ▭ P.O.Box 111, Sharjah ☎ +971 6 5661111 🖷 +971 6 5669999 **W:** smc.ae **Chs:** Prgr 1 (Arabic), Prgr 2 (English).

DTT Tx Networks
Tx Operator: Abu Dhabi TV **M:** multiprgr **Txs:** (-) **Tx Operator:** Ajman TV **M:** multiprgr **Txs:** (-) **Tx Operator:** Dubai TV **M:** multiprgr **Txs:** (-) **Tx Operator:** Sharjah TV **M:** multiprgr **Txs:** (-)

UNITED KINGDOM

Systems: DVB-T (MPEG2), DVB-T2 (MPEG4) [E]

National Stations
BRITISH BROADCASTING CORP. (BBC) (Pub) ▭ BBC Television Centre, 80 Wood Lane, London W12 4RJ ☎ +44 20 87438000 🖷 +44 20 87497520 **W:** www.bbc.co.uk/tv **L.P:** DG: Tony Hall. **Chs (terr.):** BBC One (incl. regional prgrs), BBC Two, BBC Three, BBC Four, CBBC, CBeebies, BBC News, BBC Parliament, Alba **Reg: a) BBC Cambridgeshire:** Broadcasting House, Cambridge Business Park, Cowley Rd, Cambridge, CB4 0WZ; **b) BBC Channel Islands:** 18-21 Parade Rd, St Helier JE2 3PL; **c) BBC East:** The Forum, Millennium Plain, Norwich NR2 1BH; **d) BBC East Midlands:** London Rd, Nottingham NG2 4UU; **e) BBC East Yorkshire & Lincolnshire:** Queen's Court, Hull HU1 3RH; **f) BBC London:** Marylebone High St., London W1A 6FL; **g) BBC North East & Cumbria:** Broadcasting Centre, Barrack Rd, Newcastle upon Tyne NE99 2NE; **h) BBC North West:** New Broadcasting House, Oxford Rd, Manchester M60 1SJ; **i) BBC Northern Ireland:** Ormeau Avenue, Belfast BT2 8HQ; **j) BBC Oxford:** 269 Banbury Rd, Summertown, Oxford, OX2 7DW; **k) BBC Scotland:** 40 Pacific Quay, Glasgow G51 1DA; **l) BBC South:** Broadcasting House, 10 Havelock Rd, Southampton SO14 7PU; **m) BBC South East:** The Great Hall, Mount Pleasant Rd, Tunbridge Wells TN1 1QQ; **n) BBC South West:** Broadcasting House, Seymour Rd, Plymouth PL3 5BD; **o) BBC Wales:** Llantrisant Rd, Cardiff CF5 2YQ; **p) BBC West:** Broadcasting House, Whiteladies Rd, Bristol BS8 2LR; **q) BBC West Midlands:** Level 7, The Mailbox, Birmingham B1 1RF; **r) BBC Yorkshire:** 2 St Peter's Square, Leeds LS9 8AH **– CHANNEL FOUR TELEVISION CORP. (Pub)** ▭ 124 Horseferry Rd, London SW1P 2TX ☎ +44 20 73964444 🖷 +44 20 73068366 **W:** www.channel4.com **L.P:** CEO: David Abraham. – **S4C (WELSH FOURTH CHANNEL AUTHORITY) (Pub)** ▭ Park Ty Glas, Llanishen, Caerdydd/Cardiff CF14 5DU ☎ +44 2920 747444 🖷 +44 2920 754444 **E:** s4c@s4c.co.uk **W:** www.s4c.co.uk **L.P:** CEO: Ian Jones – **INDEPENDENT TELEVISION NETWORK (ITV) (Comm)** ▭ London Television Centre, Upper Ground, London SE1 9LT ☎ +44 20 76201620 **W:** www.itv.com **L.P:** CEO: Adam Crozier. **Chs:** ITV1 (incl. regional prgrs), ITV2, ITV3, ITV4. **Reg: a) ITV Anglia:** Anglia House, Norwich NR1 3JG; **b) ITV Border:** 1 Clifford Court, Cooper Way, Parkhouse, Carlisle CA3 0JG; **c) ITV Central:** Central Court, Gas Street, Birmingham B1 2JT; **d) ITV Channel Islands:** The Television Centre, St Helier, Jersey, Channel Islands JE1 3ZD; **e) ITV Cymru Wales:** T3 Assembly Square, Britannia Quay, Cardiff Bay CF10 4PL; **f) ITV Granada:** Quay St., Manchester M60 9EA; **g) ITV London:** 200 Gray's Inn Rd, London WC1X 8HF; **h) ITV Meridian:** New Cut Road, Vinters Park, Maidstone, Kent ME14 5NZ; **i) ITV Tyne Tees:** Television House, The Watermark, Gateshead, NE11 9SZ; **j) ITV West Country:** 470 Bath Rd, Bristol BS4 3HG; **k) ITV Yorkshire:** The Television Centre, 104 Kirkstall Rd, Leeds LS3 1JS Emley Moor: ITV Calendar; **l) STV:** Pacific Quay, Glasgow G51 1PQ **W:** www.stv.tv; **m) UTV:** Havelock House, Ormeau Rd, Belfast BT7 1EB **W:** www.u.tv. – **CHANNEL 5 BROADCASTING LTD (Comm)** ▭ 22 Long Acre, London WC2E 9LY ☎ +44 20 75505555 🖷 +44 20 75505554 **W:** www.channel5.com – **BRITISH SKY BROADCASTING LTD (Comm)** ▭ Grant Way, Isleworth, London TW7 5QD ☎ +44 20 77053000 🖷 +44 20 77053453 **W:** www.sky.com **L.P:** CEO: Jeremy Darroch.

DTT Tx Networks (DVB-T/MPEG2 except where indicated otherwise)

Licensee Mux 1+3: BBC **M1:** BBC One (incl. reg. prgrs a-r), BBC Two, BBC Three, BBC Four, CBBC, CBeebies, BBC News, BBC Parliament ⌘ BBC R.1, 1Xtra, R.2, R.3, R.4, R.4 Extra, R.5 Live, R.5 Live Sports Extra, R.6 Music, BBC Asian Network, BBCWS, BBC Local stations **M3 (DVB-T2/MPEG4):** BBC One HD, BBC Two HD, BBC Three HD, CBBC HD, ITV1 HD, Channel 4 HD ⌘The Space – **Licensee Mux 2:** Digital 3&4 Ltd. **M2:** ITV1 (incl. reg. prgrs a-m), ITV1 +1, ITV2, Channel 4, Channel 5, Channel 4 +1, More4, E4, Film 4 – **Licensee Mux 4:** SDN Ltd. **M4:** ITV 3, Drama, 5USA, ITV Be, ITV 2 +1, 5*, ITV 3 +1, Quest, Channel 5 +1, Channel 5 +24, ITV Be +1, True Entertainment, ITV 4 +1, CBS Reality, CBS Drama, Vintage TV, Christian, Peace TV, Playboy TV Chat, Bluebird 1, QVC, The Store, TJC, ADULT Section❂, Television X❂, Xpanded TV❂, ADULYXXX❂, ADULT Sin TV❂, Holidays TV❂, Rabbit❂, Gay Rabbit❂, 1-2-1 Dating, CONNECT 4, VuTV, TV Player, Vision TV, JSTV, kykNET ⌘ Capital FM, Absolute R., Heart – **Licensee Mux 5-8:** Arqiva **M5:** Pick, Dave, Really, E4 +1, Movie Mix, Quest +1, Food Network, Challenge, Movies4Men, truTV, truTV +1, YourTV, Tiny Pop, Sky News, Create and Craft, Gems TV, TBN, ADULT smileTV3❂, ADULT PARTY❂, ADULT Blue❂, ADULT Babestation2❂, Kiss Me TV, Proud Dating, KISS FRESH, kiss, KISS STORY ⌘ Magic, Kerrang!, TalkSport, Insight R., Classic FM, LBC **M6:** 4Music, Yesterday, Dave ja vu, Spike, ITV 3 +1, Quest +1, Travel Channel, 4Seven, CBS Action, Horror Channel, YourTV +1, CITV, Al Jazeera English, RT HD, Dating, Q, Propeller TV, Ideal World, QVC Beauty, Rocks and Co, ADULT smileTV2, Babestation, ADULT Section, Connect 1, CCTV, Connect, Racing UK, SonLife ⌘The Hits R., heat, Smooth R., Premier R. **M7 (DVB-T2/MPEG4):** Motors TV, BBC Four HD, BBC News HD, Al Jazeera English HD, Community Channel, Channel 4+1 HD, 4seven HD, CBeebies HD, Al Jazeera Arabic, Daystar TV, Arise News, Rishtey, Planet Knowledge, VIVA HD **M8 (DVB-T2/MPEG4):** QVC +1 HD, QVC Beauty HD. **NB:** Some regional variations may apply. **Local/regional muxes** not shown.

Location	1°	2°	3	4	5	6	7	8	kW
Angus	60k	53l	57	54	58	49	31	37	3x20/3x10/2x4.5
Beacon Hill	60n	53j	57	42	45	51	33	34	3x20/3x10/4/1
Belmont	22e	25k	28	30	53	60	33	35	(*)
Bilsdale	26g	29i	23	43	46	40	31	37	3x100/3x50/18.5/5
Black Hill	46k	43l	40	41	44	47	32	35	6x100/43/12.5
Blaenplwyf	27o	24e	21	25	22	28	-	-	3x40/3x10
Bluebell Hill	46m	43h	40	45	39	54	32	34	3x20/4/1.5
Brougher Mt.	28i	22m	25	21	24	27	-	-	20
Caldbeck	25g	28b	30	23	26	29	32	35	3x100/3x50/5/4
Caldbeck	27k	24l	22	-	-	-	-	-	2x50/100
Caradon Hill	28n	25j	22	21	24	27	-	-	3x100/3x50
Carmel	60o	53e	57	54	58	49	-	-	3x20/3x10
Chatton	45g	42i	49	41	44	47	-	-	3x20/3x10
Craigkelly	27k	24l	21	42	45	39	33	34	3x20/3x10/11/3
Crystal Palace	23f	26g	30	25	22	28	33	35	6x200/43/13.5
Darvel	22k	25l	28	23	26	29	31	37	3x20/3x10/2x2.5
Divis	27i	21m	24	23	26	29	31	33	3x20/3x50/12.5/3.5
Dover	50m	51h	53	55	59	48	-	-	3x80/3x40
Durris	28k	25l	22	23	26	29	32	35	3x20/3x50/2x12.5
Emley More	47r	44k	41	51	52	48	32	34	5x174/87/55/17
Hannington	45l	42h	39	41	44	47	32	34	3x20/3x25/37/5.5
Heathfield	52m	49h	47	42	44	41	-	-	20
Huntshaw Cross	50n	59j	55	48	52	56	-	-	3x20/3x10
Keelylang Hill	46k	43l	50	42	45	49	-	-	3x20/3x10
Knockmore	26k	23l	29	53	57	60	-	-	3x20/3x10
Limavady	50i	59m	55	54	58	49	-	-	3x20/3x10
Llanddona	57o	60e	53	43	46	50	-	-	3x20/3x10
Mendip	49p	54j	58	48	56	52	33	35	6x100/72/17.5
Midhurst	55l	58k	54	59	50	-	-	-	3x20/3x10
Moel-y-Parc	45o	49e	42	51	52	48	32	34	3x20/3x10/16.5/6
Oxford	53l	60h	57	50	59	55	31	37	3x20/3x50/16.5/6
Pontop Pike	58g	54i	49	50	59	55	33	34	3x20/3x50/34/9.5
Preseli	43o	46e	50	42	45	49	-	-	3x20/3x10
Redruth	44n	41j	47	48	52	51	-	-	3x20/3x10
Ridge Hill	28q	25c	22	21	24	27	32	34	3x20/3x10/10.5/4
Ridge Hill	-	29j	-	-	-	-	-	-	20
Rosemarkie	45k	49l	42	43	46	50	-	-	3x20/3x10
Rowridge	24l	27h	21	25	22	28	31	37	3x200/3x50/24.5/25¹
Rumster Forest	27k	24l	21	30	59	55	-	-	3x20/3x10
Sandy Heath	27a	24a	21	51	52	48	32	34	3x180/3x170/50/8.5
Selkirk	50k	59l	55	57	53	60	-	-	3x10/3x5
Stockland Hill	26n	23j	29	25	22	28	-	-	3x50/3x25
Sudbury	44c	41a	47	58	60	56	-	-	100
Sutton Coldfield	43q	46c	40	42	45	39	33	35	6x200/89/8
Talconeston	55c	59a	62	42	45	50	31	37	6x100/27.5/10
The Wrekin	26q	23c	30	41	44	47	-	-	3x20/3x10
Waltham	49d	54c	58	29	56	57	31	37	3x50/3x25/10/1.5
Wenvoe	41o	44e	47	42	45	49	31	37	3x10/3x50/47/12
Winter Hill	50h	59f	54	58	49	55	31	37	6x100/14/1

+ sites with txs below 10kW. Pol=H °) incl. reg. prgrs (NB: subregional prgrs not indicated) (*) 3x150/50x2x100/37/15kW

UNITED STATES OF AMERICA

Systems: ATSC [A]; § NTSC-M [A] (some lps only)

Main National Networks (O&O = owned-and-operated)
(*= Spanish-language networks)
PUBLIC BROADCASTING SERVICE (PBS) (Pub) ✉ 1320 Braddock Place, Alexandria, VA 22314-1698 ☎ +1 703 7395000 🖷 +1 703 7390775 **W:** www.pbs.org **L.P:** Pres/CEO: Paula A. Kerger. **Member Stations:** ca 350. – **ABC, Inc. (Comm)** (Subsidiary of Walt Disney Co.) ✉ 77 W. 66th St., New York, NY 10023-6298 ☎ +1 212 4567777 🖷 +1 212 4566850 **W:** abc.go.com **L.P:** Pres: John Hare. **O&O Stations:** KABC-TV Los Angeles, CA: ch7 (28.7kW); KFSN-TV Fresno, CA: ch30 (260kW); KGO-TV San Francisco, CA: ch53 (24kW); KTRK-TV Houston, TX: ch13 (32.4kW); WABC-TV New York, NY: ch7 (34kW); WLS-TV Chicago, IL: ch44 (1000kW); WPVI-TV Philadelphia, PA: ch6 (30kW); WTVD Durham, NC: ch11 (46kW). **Full Power Affiliates:** ca 220. – **CBS BROADCASTING, Inc. (Comm)** (Subsidiary of CBS Corporation) ✉ 51 W. 52nd St, New York, NY 10019-6119 ☎ +1 212 9754321 🖷 +1 212 9754516 **W:** www.cbs.com **L.P:** Pres/CEO (CBS Corp.): Leslie Moonves. **O&O Stations:** KCBS-TV Los Angeles, CA: ch43 (1000kW); KCNC-TV Denver, CO: ch35 (1000kW); KDKA-TV Pittsburgh, PA: ch25 (1000kW); KOVR-TV Sacramento, CA: ch25 (760kW); KPIX-TV San Francisco, CA: ch29 (1000kW); KTVT-TV Dallas, TX: ch19 (1000kW); KYW-TV Philadelphia, PA: ch26 (790kW); WBBM-TV Chicago, IL: ch12 (8kW); WBZ-TV Boston, MA: ch30 (825kW); WCBS-TV New York, NY: ch33 (349kW); WCCO-TV Minneapolis, MN: ch32 (1000kW); WFOR-TV Miami, FL: ch22 (1000kW); WJZ-TV Baltimore, MD: ch13 (28.8kW); WWJ-TV Detroit, MI: ch44 (425kW). **Full Power Affiliates:** ca 210. – **FOX BROADCASTING CO. (Comm)** (Subsidiary of Twenty-First Century Fox, Inc.) ✉ 10201 W. Pico Blvd., Los Angeles, CA 90035 ☎ +1 310 3693716 🖷 +1 310 9693300 **W:** www.fox.com **L.P:** Chmn (Fox Networks Group): Peter Rice **O&O Stations:** KDFW Dallas, TX: ch35 (857kW); KMSP-TV Minneapolis, MN: ch9 (30kW); KRIV Houston, TX: ch26 (1000kW); KSAZ-TV Phoenix, AZ: ch10 (1000kW); KTBC Austin, TX: ch7 (98.6kW); KTTV Los Angeles, CA: ch11 (115kW); WAGA Atlanta, GA: ch27 (1000kW); WFLD Chicago, IL: ch31 (1000kW); WFXT Boston, MA: ch31 (780kW); WHBQ-TV Memphis, TN: ch13 (95kW); WJBK Detroit, MI: ch7 (27kW); WJZY Charlotte, NC ch47 (1000kW); WOFL Orlando, FL: ch22 (607kW); WOGX Ocala, FL: ch31 (500kW); WNYW New York, NY: ch44 (246kW); WTTG Washington, D.C.: ch36 (1000kW); WTVT Tampa Bay, FL: ch12 (72.3kW); WTXF-TV Philadelphia, PA: ch42 (1000kW). **Full Power Affiliates:** ca 220. – **MYNETWORKTV, Inc. (Comm)** (Subsidiary of Twenty-First Century Fox, Inc.) ✉ 110201 W Pico Blvd Los Angeles, CA 90064-2606 **W:** www.mynetworktv.com **O&O Stations:** KCOP-TV Los Angeles, CA: ch13 (120kW); KDFI-TV Dallas, TX: ch36 (1000kW); KUTP Phoenix, AZ: ch26 (1000kW); KTXH Houston, TX: ch19 (421kW); WDCA Washington, D.C: ch35 (500kW); WFTC Minneapolis, MI: ch29 (1000kW); WMYT-TV Charlotte, NC: ch39 (225kW); WPWR-TV Gary, IN: ch51 (1000kW); WRBW Orlando, FL: ch41 (763kW); WWOR-TV Secaucus, NJ: ch38 (170kW). **Full Power Affiliates:** ca 200. – **NBC UNIVERSAL, LLC (Comm)** (Division of Comast Corp.) ✉ 30 Rockefellar Plaza, New York, NY 10112 ☎ +1 212 6644444 🖷 +1 212 6644085 **W:** www.nbc.com **L.P:** CEO: Stephen B. Burke. **O&O Stations:** KNBC Los Angeles, CA: ch36 (380kW); KNSD San Diego, CA: ch40 (370kW); KNTV San Francisco, CA: ch12 (103.1kW); KXAS-TV Dallas/Fort Worth, TX: ch41 (891kW); WCAU Philadelphia, PA: ch34 (700kW); WMAQ-TV Chicago, IL: ch29 (350kW); WNBC New York, NY: ch28 (200.2kW); WRC-TV Washington, D.C.: ch48 (813kW); WTVJ Miami, FL: ch31 (1000kW); WVIT Hartford, CT: ch35 (250kW). **Full Power Affiliates:** ca 220. – **THE CW NETWORK, LLC (Comm)** (Subsidiary of Warner Bros. Entertainment, Inc. and CBS Corporation) ✉ 4000 Warner Blvd., Burbank, CA 91522 ☎ +1 818 9775000 🖷 +1 818 9778310 **W:** www.cwtv.com **L.P:** Pres: Mark Pedowitz. **O&O Stations:** KBCW San Francisco, CA: ch45 (500kW); KMAX-TV Sacramento, CA: ch21 (1000kW); KSTW Tacoma, WA: ch11 (100kW); WKBD-TV Detroit, MI: ch14 (185kW); WPCW Jeannette, PA: ch11 (30kW); WPSG Philadelphia, PA: ch32 (250kW); WTOG St. Petersburg, FL: ch44 (550kW); WUPA Atlanta, GA: ch43 (1000kW). **Full Power Affiliates:** ca 200. – **TELEMUNDO NETWORK GROUP, LLC (TELEMUNDO*) (Comm)** (Subsidiary of Telemundo Holdings, Inc.) ✉ 2290 West 8th Avenue, Hialeah, FL 33010 ☎ +1 305 8848200 🖷 +1 305 8897950 **W:** www.telemundo.com **L.P:** Pres/CEO (Telemundo Holdings, Inc): Donald V. Browne. **O&O Stations:** KBLR Las Vegas, NV: ch40 (230kW); KDEN-TV Denver, CO: ch29 (540kW); KHRR Tucson, AZ: ch40 (396kW); KNSO Fresno, CA: ch11 (45kW); KSTS San Jose, CA: ch49 (257kW); KTAZ Phoenix, AZ: ch39 (550kW); KTMD Galveston, TX: ch48 (1000kW); KVEA Corona, CA: ch39 (1000kW); KVDA San Antonio,

TX ch38 (1000kW); KXTX-TV Dallas, TX: ch40 (1000kW); WNEU Merrimack, NH: ch34 (80kW); WNJU Linden, NJ: ch36 (650kW); WSNS-TV Chicago, IL: ch45 (665kW); WSCV Fort Lauderdale, FL: ch30 (1000kW). **Full Power Affiliates:** ca 45. – **UNIMÁS* (Comm)** (Subsidiary of Univision Communications, Inc.) ✉ 9405 NW 41st Street, Miami, FL 33178-2301 ☎ +1 305 4713900 🖷 +1 305 4714065 **W:** www.unimas.com **L.P:** Pres/CEO (Univision Communications, Inc.): Randy Falco. **O&O Stations:** KBTF-CD Bakersfield, CA: ch31 (15kW); KFPH-DT Phoenix, AZ: ch13 (240kW); KFTH-DT Alvin, TX ch36 (1000kW); KFSF-DT Vallejo, CA: ch34 (150kW); KFTR-DT Los Angeles, CA: ch29 (400kW); KFTU-DT Douglas, AZ: ch36 (5kW); KNIC-DT Blanco, TX: ch18 (400kW); KSTR-DT Irving, TX: ch48 (225kW); KTFD-DT Boulder, CO: ch15 (200kW); KTFB-CA Bakersfield, CA: ch44 (0.25kW); KTFF-DT Porterville, CA: ch48 (197kW); KTFK-DT Stockton, CA: ch26 (850kW); KTFO-CD Austin, TX: ch36 (15kW); KTFQ-DT Albuquerque, NM: ch22 (1000kW); WAMI-DT Hollywood, FL: ch47 (1000kW); WFPA-CA Philadelphia, PA: ch28 (15kW); WFTT-DT Tampa, FL: ch47 (650kW); WFUT-DT Newark, NJ: ch30 (200kW); WOTF-DT Melbourne, FL: ch43 (1000kW); WTNC-LD Raleigh, NC: ch40 (15kW); WUTF-DT Marlborough, MA: ch27 (100kW); WUVG-DT Athens, GA: ch48 (1000kW); WXFT-DT Aurora,IL: ch50 (172kW). **Full Power Affiliates:** ca 35. – **UNIVISION* (Comm)** (Subsidiary of Univision Communications, Inc.) ✉ 9405 NW 41 St., Miami, FL 33178-2301 ☎ +1 305 4713900 🖷 +1 305 4714065 **W:** www.univision.com. **L.P:** Pres/CEO (Univision Communications, Inc.): Randy Falco. **O&O Stations:** KABE-CD Bakersfield, CA: ch39 (15kW); KAKW-DT Killeen, TX: ch13 (45kW); KDTV-DT San Francisco, CA: ch51 (476.3kW); KFTV-DT Hanford, CA: ch20 (350kW); KMEX-DT Los Angeles, CA: ch34 (392kW); KTVW-DT Phoenix, AZ: ch33 (470kW); KUTH-DT Provo, UT: ch32 (194kW); KUVE-DT Green Valley, AZ: ch46 (70.8kW); KUVN-DT Garland, TX: ch23 (1000kW); KUVS-DT Modesto, CA: ch18 (500kW); KWEX-DT San Antonio, TX: ch41 (580kW); KXLN-DT Rosenberg, TX: ch45 (1000kW); WFDC-DT Arlington, VA: ch15 (325kW); WGBO-DT Joliet, IL: ch38 (600kW); WQHS-DT Cleveland, OH: ch34 (525kW); WLTV-DT Miami, FL: ch23 (535kW); WXTV-DT Paterson, NJ: ch40 (300kW); WUVC-DT Fayetteville, NC: ch38 (500kW); WUVG-DT Athens, GA: ch48 (1000kW), see also UniMás; WUVP-DT Vineland, NJ: ch29 (335kW). **Full Power Affiliates:** ca 45.

Other Networks (*= Spanish-language networks)
CREATE (Pub) ✉ American Public Television: 55 Summer St., 4th Floor, Boston, MA 02110 **W:** createtv.com – **MHZ WORLDVIEW (Pub)** ✉ 8101A Lee Highway, Falls Church, VA 22042 **W:** www.mhznetworks. org – **V-ME* (Pub)** ✉ V-me Media, Inc.: 1001 Brickell Bay Drive Suite 1208 Miami, FL 33131 **W:** www.vmetv.com – **WORLD (Pub)** ✉ American Public Television: 55 Summer St., 4th Floor, Boston, MA 02110 **W:** worldchannel.org – **ACCUWEATHER CHANNEL (Comm)** ✉ AccuWeather, Inc.: 385 Science Park Road, State College, PA 16803 **W:** www.accuweather.com – **AMERICA ONE (Comm)** ✉ONE Media Corp.: 6125 Airport Fwy, Fort Worth, TX 76117 **W:** www. americaone.com – **ANTENNA TV (Comm)** ✉ Tribune Broadcasting: 435 N. Michigan Ave., 6th Floor, Chicago, IL 60611 **W:** www.antennatv.tv – **AZTECA AMÉRICA* (Comm)** ✉ 601 Clearwater Park Road, West Palm Beach, FL 33401 **W:** aztecaamerica.com – **BOUNCE (Comm)** ✉ Bounce Media, LLC: P.O. Box 673252, Marietta, GA 30006 **W:** www.bouncetv.com – **CBSN (Comm)** ✉ CBS Broadcasting, Inc.: 51 W. 52nd St, New York, NY 10019-6119 **W:** www.cbsnews. com – **COMET (Comm)** (Joint-venture of Metro-Goldwyn-Mayer and Sinclair Television Group, Inc.) ✉ Sinclair Television Group, Inc.: 10706 Beaver Dam Rd, Cockeysville, MD 21030 **W:** comettv.com – **COZI TV (Comm)** ✉ NBC Universal Media, LLC: 30 Rockefeller Plaza, New York, NY 10112 **W:** www.cozitv.com – **DECADES (Comm)** (Joint-venture of CBS Television Studios and Weigel Broadcasting Co.) ✉ : Weigel Broadcasting Co.: 26 North Halsted, Chicago, IL 60661 **W:** www.decades.com – **ESCAPE (Comm)** ✉ Escape Media, LLC: 3500 Piedmont Road, Suite 400, Atlanta, GA 30305 **W:** www.escapetv.com – **ESTRELLA TV* (Comm)** ✉ Liberman Broadcasting, Inc.: 1845 Empire Avenue, Burbank, CA 91504 **W:** www.estrellatv.com – **EXITOS TV* (Comm)** ✉ Telemundo Network Group: 2290 West 8th Avenue, Hialeah, FL 33010 – **GET TV (Comm)** ✉ CPE US Networks, Inc.: 10202 West Washington Boulevard, Culver City, CA 90232 **W:** get.tv – **GRIT (Comm)** ✉ GRIT Media, LLC: 1080 West Peachtree St, #309 Atlanta, GA 30309 **W:** www.grittv.com – **HSN (Comm)** ✉ HSN, Inc.: 2501 118th Ave N, St Petersburg, FL 33716 **W:** www.hsn.com – **ION LIFE (Comm)** ✉ ION Media Networks, Inc.: 601 Clearwater Park Road, West Palm Beach, FL 33401 **W:** www.ionlife.com – **ION TELEVISION (Comm)** ✉ ION Media Networks, Inc.: 601 Clearwater Park Road, West Palm Beach, FL 33401 **W:** www.iontelevision.com – **JUSTICE NETWORK (Comm)** ✉ Justice Network, LLC: 318 E Bond Ave, West Memphis, AR 72301 **W:** www.justicenetworktv.com – **LAFF (Comm)** ✉ Laff Media, LLC: Suite 400, 3500 Piedmont Road NE, Atlanta,

GA 30305 **W:** www.laff.com – **LATV* (Comm)** ⌧ LATV Networks, LLC: 2323 Corinth Avenue, Los Angeles, CA 90064 **W:** www.latv.com – **ME-TV NETWORK (Comm)** ⌧ Weigel Broadcasting Co.: 26 North Halsted, Chicago, IL 60661 **W:** metvnetwork.com – **MICASA (Comm)** ⌧MCB Network Corp.: 3120 Rogerdale Rd, Houston, TX 77042 **W:** www.mcbntv.com – **MOVIES! (Comm)** (Joint-venture of Weigel Broadcasting Co. and Twenty-First Century Fox, Inc.) ⌧ Weigel Broadcasting Co.: 26 North Halsted, Chicago, IL 60661 **W:** moviestvnetwork.com – **MUNDOMAX* (Comm)** ⌧ Mundo TV, LLC: 1440 South Sepulveda Blvd, Los Angeles, CA 90025 **W:** www.mundomax.com – **QUBO (Comm)** Qubo Venture LLC: 601 Clearwater Park Road, West Palm Beach, FL 33401 **W:** www.qubo.com – **QVC (Comm)** ⌧ QVC, Inc.: 1200 Wilson Drive, West Chester, PA 19380 **W:** www.qvc.com – **RETRO TV (Comm)** ⌧ Retro Television, Inc.: P.O.Box 11409, Chattanooga, TN 37401 **W:** www.myretrotv.com – **TELEXCITOS* (Comm)** ⌧ Telemundo Network Group: 2290 West 8th Avenue, Hialeah, FL, 33010. **W:** www.telexitos.com – **THE FAMILY CHANNEL (Comm)** ⌧ ValCom, Inc.: 429 Rockaway Valley Road, Boonton Township, NJ 07005 **W:** www.myfamilytv.tv – **THIS TV (Comm)** ⌧ This TV, LLC: 10250 Constellation Boulevard, Los Angeles, CA 90067-6241 **W:** thistv.com – **TUFF TV (Comm)** ⌧ TUFF TV Network, LLC: 3340 Peachtree Road, N.E., Suite 1800, Atlanta, GA 30326 **W:** www.tufftv.com – **WEATHER NATION (Comm)** ⌧ WeatherNation, Inc.: 8101 E. Prentice Ave #700, Greenwood Village, CO 80111 **W:** weathernationtv.com – **ALMAVISION* (Rlg)** Almavision TV, Inc.: 759 S. Central Ave. City, Los Angeles, CA 90021 **W:** almavision.com – **CORNERSTONE TV (Rlg)** ⌧ Cornerstone Television, Inc.: 1 Signal Hill Dr, Wall, PA 15148 **W:** www.ctvn.org – **DAYSTAR TV (Rlg)** ⌧ God Fellowship, Inc.: 3901 Hwy 121, Bedford, TX 76021 **W:** www.daystar.com – **ENLACE* (Rlg)** ⌧ Trinity Broadcasting Network, Inc.: 2823 West Irving Blvd., Irving, TX 75061 **W:** www.enlace.org – **JUCE TV (Rlg)** ⌧ Trinity Broadcasting Network, Inc.: 2442 Michelle Dr, Tustin, CA 92780 **W:** www.jctv.org – **SMILE OF A CHILD TV (Rlg)** ⌧ AMC Networks, Inc.: P.O.Box 10700, Santa Ana, CA 92711-0700 **W:** www.smileofachildtv.org – **THE CHURCH CHANNEL (Rlg)** ⌧ Trinity Broadcasting Network: 14171 Chambers Rd., Tustin, CA 92780 **W:** www.churchchannel.tv – **THREE ANGELS BROADCASTING NETWORK (3ABN) (Rlg)** ⌧ Three Angels Broadcasting, Inc.: 17466 Route 37,Johnston City, IL 62951 **W:** 3abn.org – **TRINITY BROADCASTING NETWORK (TBN) (Rlg)** ⌧ 2442 Michelle Drive, Tustin, CA 92780 **W:** www.tbn.org.

Local Stations

There are about 9000 txs operated by local TV stations in the USA. Station listings in top TV markets (Rated by audience size):

1. New York, NY

ch	kW	Location	Station
2	0.3	New York, NY	WKOB-LD
3	7	Middletown,NJ	WJLP
7	34	New York, NY	WABC-TV
8	41	New Brunswick, NJ	WNJB
11	7.5	New York, NY	WPIX
12	0.3	Amityville, NY	WPXU-LD
13	9.3	Newark, NY	WNET
17	0.3	Manhattan, NY	WEBR-CD
18	1000	Newton, NJ	WMBC-TV
20	15	Hempstead, NY	W20CQ-D
21	20	Garden City, NY	WLIW
22	15	Plainview, NY	WCBS-TV
22	15	Newburgh. NY	WEPT-CD
23	7	Edison, NJ	WDVB-CD
23	655	Smithtown, NY	WFTY-DT
24	151	New York, NY	WNYE-TV
25	15	Port Jervis, NY	WASA-LD
25	2.4	Monticello, NY	W25DY-D
26	0.6	New York, NY	WYXN-LD
27	1000	Poughkeepsie, NY	WTBY-TV
28	200	New York, NY	WNBC
29	200	West Milford, NJ	WNYJ-TV
30	200	Newark, NJ	WFUT-DT
31	180	New York, NY	WPXN-TV
32	7.5	New York, NY	WXNY-LD
33	284	New York, NY	WCBS-TV
34	3.5	East Orange, NJ	WPXO-LD
36	750	Linden, NJ	WNJU
38	170	Secaucus, NJ	WWOR-TV
39	3	New York, NY	WNYN-LD
40	300	Paterson, NJ	WXTV-DT
41	3.2	New York, NY	W41DO-D
42	780	Bridgeport, CT	WZME
43	4	New York, NY	WNXY-LD
44	990	New York, NY	WNYW
45	15	Mineola, NY	WMUN-CD
46	15	New York, NY	WMBQ-CD

ch	kW	Location	Station
47	1000	Riverhead, NY	WLNY-TV
48	946	Kingston, NY	WRNN-TV
49	170	Bridgeport, CT	WEDW
50	1.7	New York, NY	WBQM-LD
51	200	Montclair, NJ	WNJN

2. Los Angeles, CA

ch	kW	Location	Station
2	3	Los Angeles, CA	KHIZ-LD
7	29	Los Angeles, CA	KABC-TV
8	3	Los Angeles, CA	KFLA-LD
9	25	Los Angeles, CA	KCAL-TV
10	3	Los Angeles, CA	KIIO-LD
11	115	Los Angeles, CA	KTTV
12	1	Los Angeles, CA	KTBV-LD
13	120	Los Angeles, CA	KCOP-TV
18	700	Long Beach, CA	KSCI
22	8	Los Angeles, CA	KSFV-CD
23	150	Twentynine Palms, CA	KVMD
23	1.5	Ventura, CA	KIMG-LP
23	15	Los Angeles, CA	KSMV-LD
24	1000	Oxnard, CA	KBEH
25	13	Los Angeles, CA	KNET-CD
26	475	San Bernardino, CA	KVCR-DT
27	8	Los Angeles, CA	KHTV-CD
28	220	Los Angeles, CA	KCET
29	370	Ontario, CA	KFTR-DT
30	10	San Bernardino, CA	KSGA-LP
31	1000	Los Angeles, CA	KTLA
32	1000	Anaheim, CA	KDOC-TV
33	1000	Santa Ana, CA	KTBN-TV
34	500	Los Angeles, CA	KMEX-DT
35	1000	Riverside, CA	KRCA
36	665	Los Angeles, CA	KNBC
38	1000	San Bernardino, CA	KPXN-TV
39	1000	Corona, CA	KVEA
40	10	Glendale, CA	KVHD-LD
41	1000	Los Angeles, CA	KLCS
42	486	Los Angeles, CA	KWHY-TV
43	540	Los Angeles, CA	KCBS-TV
44	170	Barstow, CA	KILM
45	1	Van Nuys, VA	KSKJ-CD
46	15	Altadena, CA	KTAV-LD
47	350	Avalon, CA	KAZA-TV
48	1000	Huntington Beach, CA	KOCE-TV
49	1000	Ventura, CA	KJLA
50	15	Los Angeles, CA	KNLA-CD
51	1000	Rancho Palos Verdes, CA	KXLA

3. Chicago, IL

ch	kW	Location	Station
4	0.9	Chicago, IL	WOCK-CD
10	80	La Salle, IL	WWTO-TV
12	8	Chicago, IL	WBBM-TV
17	300	Gary, IN	WYIN
18	15	Gary, IN	WHNW-LD
19	645	Chicago, IL	WGN-TV
20	15	Chicago, IL	WPVN-CD
21	99	Chicago, IL	WYCC
24	6	Arlington Heights, IL	WRJK-LP
25	12.5	Arbury Hills, IL	W25DW-D
27	550	Chicago, IL	WCIU-TV
29	350	Chicago, IL	WMAQ-TV
30	15	Chicago, IL	WDCI-LD
31	1000	Chicago, IL	WFLD
32	15	Chicago, IL	WMEU-CD
33	15	Chicago, IL	WCHU-LD
34	4.3	Arlington Heights, IL	WEDE-CD
35	15	Plano, IL	WLPD-CD
36	145	Hammond, IN	WJYS
38	600	Joliet, IL	WGBO-DT
39	15	Chicago, IL	WWME-LD
40	6	Chicago, IL	WESV-LD
40	15	Sugar Grove, IL	W40CN-D
43	200	Chicago, IL	WCPX-TV
44	1000	Chicago, IL	WLS-TV
45	665	Chicago, IL	WSNS-TV
47	300	Chicago, IL	WTTW
49	15	Chicago, IL	WOCH-CD
50	230	Aurora, IL	WXFT-DT
51	1000	Gary, IN	WPWR-TV

4. Philadelphia, PA

ch	kW	Location	Station
2	9.4	Wilmington, DE	KJWP
4	10	Atlantic City, NJ	WACP
6	34	Philadelphia, PA	WPVI-TV

ch	kW	Location	Station
7	0.025	Allentown, PA	W07DC-D
9	81	Bethlehem, PA	WBPH-TV
12	30	Wilmington, DE	WHYY-TVP
17	645	Philadelphia, PA	WPHL-TV
22	145	Camden, NJ	WNJS
23	15	Philadelphia, PA	WTSD-CD
24	15	Philadelphia, PA	WPHA-CD
25	0.8	Reading, PA	WTVE
26	790	Philadelphia, PA	KYW-TV
27	160	Burlington, NJ	WGTW-TV
29	335	Vineland, NJ	WUVP-DT
30	10	Philadelphia, PA	WELL-LD
31	200	Wilmington, DE	WPPX-TV
32	250	Philadelphia, PA	WPSG
33	3	Philadelphia, PA	WZPA-LD
34	700	Philadelphia, PA	WCAU
35	450	Philadelphia, PA	WYBE
36	1	Darby, PA	W36DO-D
38	6	Hammonton, NJ	WPSJ-CD
39	52	Allentown, PA	WLVT-TV
42	620	Philadelphia, PA	WTXF-TV
43	59	Trenton, NJ	WNJT
44	200	Atlantic City, NJ	WMCN-TV
45	0.17	Allentown, PA	WFMZ-TV
46	800	Allentown, PA	WFMZ-TV
48	10	Philadelphia, PA	WEFG-LD
49	860	Atlantic City, NJ	WWSI
50	5.55	Trenton, NJ	WPHY-CD

5. Dallas - Ft. Worth, TX

ch	kW	Location	Station
2	0.13	Dallas, TX	KSFW-LD
8	55	Dallas, TX	WFAA
9	13	Fort Worth, TX	KFWD
14	975	Dallas, TX	KERA-TV
18	15	Keene, TX	KGSW-LD
18	15	Dallas, TX	KPFW-LD
19	1000	Fort Worth, TX	KTVT
20	15	Dallas, TX	KBOP-LD
21	15	Mineral Wells, TX	K21KJ-D
21	2	Dallas, TX	KWDA-LD
23	1000	Garland, TX	KUVN-DT
25	15	Corsicana, TX	K25FW-D
26	4.45	Dallas, TX	K26KC-D
27	15	Britton, TX	KODF-LD
27	15	Stephenville, TX	K27LU-D
28	15	De Soto, TX	KHPK-LD
29	1000	Fort Worth, TX	KTXA
30	1000	Decatur, TX	KMPX
31	8	De Soto, TX	K31GL-D
32	780	Dallas, TX	KDAF
34	15	Dallas, TX	KJJM-LD
35	1000	Dallas, TX	KDFW
36	1000	Dallas, TX	KDFI
38	15	Fort Worth, TX	KVFW-LD
39	1000	Lake Dallas, TX	KAZD
40	1000	Dallas, TX	KXTX-TV
41	891	Fort Worth, TX	KXAS-TV
42	1000	Arlington, TX	KPXD-TV
43	1000	Denton, TX	KDTN
44	15	Dallas, TX	KLEG-CD
45	15	Dallas, TX	KDTX-TV
46	600	Greenville	KTXD-TV
47	15	Mineral Wells, TX	K47NT-D
48	1000	Irving, TX	KSTR-DT
50	15	Mesquite, TX	KATA-CD
51	15	Dallas, TX	KHFD-LD

6. San Francisco - Oakland - San Jose, CA

ch	kW	Location	Station
2	3	Middletown, CA	KFTY-LD
3	0.1	Santa Rosa, CA	K03IC-D
3	2.5	San Francisco, CA	K03HY-D
7	24	San Francisco, CA	KGO-TV
8	0.2	San Francisco, CA	KDTS-LD
12	103	San Jose, CA	KNTV
14	12	Concord, CA	KTNC-TV
19	568	San Francisco, CA	KOFY-TV
20	0.7	Greenfield, CA	KSCZ-LD
20	3.6	Modesto, CA	KEXT-LD
23	105	Cotati, CA	KRCB
26	2	Santa Rosa, CA	KUKR-LD
27	858	San Francisco, CA	KTSF
28	15	San Francisco, CA	KFTL-CD
28	4	Santa Rosa, CA	KDTV-CD
29	1000	San Francisco, CA	KPIX-TV

ch	kW	Location	Station
30	1000	San Francisco, CA	KQED
32	20	Santa Rosa, CA	KEMO-TV
33	480	San Francisco, CA	KMTP-TV
34	370	Vallejo, CA	KFSF-DT
35	12	San Francisco, CA	KGO-TV
36	550	San Jose, CA	KICU-TV
38	1000	San Francisco, CA	KRON-TV
39	1000	San Francisco, CA	KCNS
40	3	San Francisco, CA	KMMC-LD
41	1000	San Jose, CA	KKPX-TV
42	12.5	San Jose, CA	KAXT-CD
43	500	San Mateo, CA	KCSM-TV
44	1000	Oakland, CA	KTVU
45	1000	San Francisco, CA	KBCW
47	1000	Novato, CA	KTLN-TV
48	3.5	Oakland, CA	KTVU
49	257	San Jose, CA	KSTS
49	1	Santa Rosa, CA	K49KS-D
50	310	San Jose, CA	KQEH
51	476	San Francisco, CA	KDTV-DT

7. Boston, MA

ch	kW	Location	Station
3	0.06	Nashua, NH	WORK-LP
4	0.06	Concord, NH	W39AR
7	0.06	Manchester, NH	W07DR-D
9	6.5	Manchester, NH	WMUR-TV
10	5	Norwell, MA	WWDP
11	30	Durham, NH	WENH-TV
18	1000	Lawrence, MA	WMFP
19	700	Boston, MA	WGBH-TV
20	625	Boston, MA	WCVB-TV
25	15	Boston, MA	WFXZ-CD
27	400	Marlborough. MA	WUTF-DT
29	270	Worcester, MA	WUNI
30	825	Boston, MA	WBZ-TV
31	780	Boston, MA	WFXT
32	300	Boston, MA	WBPX-TV
33	100	Concord, NH	WPXG-TV
34	80	Merrimack, NH	WNEU
35	7	Derry, NH	WBIN-TV
36	15	Nashua, NH	WYCN-LP
39	135	Boston, MA	WSBK-TV
40	3.5	Vineyard Haven, MA	WDPX-TV
41	690	Cambridge, MA	WLVI
42	1000	Boston, MA	WHDH
43	500	Boston, MA	WGBX-TV
45	15	Boston, MA	WCEA-LD
47	365	Worcester, MA	WYDN

8. Washington, D.C

ch	kW	Location	Station
7	52	Washington, D.C	WJLA-TV
8	0.2	Washington, D.C	WMDO-LD
9	52	Washington, D.C	WUSA
12	23	Martinsburg, WV	WWPX-TV
14	15	Washington, D.C	WWTD-LD
15	1000	Arlington, VA	WFDC-DT
20	7	Lake Shore, MD	WQAW-LP
23	10	Washington, D.C	WDDN-LD
23	15	Dale City, VA	WDWA-LP
24	160	Fairfax. VA	WNVC
25	7	Washington, D.C	WZDC-CD
27	108	Washington, D.C	WETA-TV
28	41	Frederick, VA	WFPT
30	160	Goldvein, VA	WNVT
33	152	Washington, D.C	WHUT-TV
34	1000	Manassas, VA	WPXW-TV
35	500	Washington, D.C	WDCA
36	1000	Washington, D.C	WTTG
42	516	Annapolis, MD	WMPT
44	12	Washington, D.C	WIAV-LD
45	15	Washington, D.C	W45DN-D
48	813	Washington, D.C	WRC-TV
50	1000	Washington, D.C	WDCW

9. Atlanta, GA

ch	kW	Location	Station
8	21	Athens, GA	WGTV
8	0.15	Toccoa, GA	W08EG-D
10	80	Atlanta, GA	WXIA-TV
12	0.5	Athens, GA	W12DO-D
13	0.14	Carrollton, GA	W13DJ-D
14	10	Atlanta, GA	WAGC-LD
15	15	Gainesville, GA	WGGD-LD
16	4	Atlanta, GA	WYGA-CD
17	15	Athens, GA	WUVG-DT

ch	kW	Location	Station
19	1000	Atlanta, GA	WGCL-TV
20	1000	Atlanta, GA	WPCH-TV
21	55	Atlanta, GA	WPB
22	15	Atlanta, GA	WSKC-CD
24	240	Toccoa, GA	WUGA-TV
25	500	Atlanta, GA	WATL
26	2	Cumming, GA	WLVO-LD
26	3	Athens, GA	W26EM-D
27	1000	Athens, GA	WAGA-TV
29	15	Athens, GA	W29DN-D
29	14	Atlanta, GA	WANN-CD
30	15	Atlanta, GA	WTBS-LD
31	9	Atlanta, GA	WSB-TV
32	6	Gainesville, GA	W32DT-D
35	15	Atlanta, GA	WDTA-LD
38	1.5	Athens, GA	W38EP-D
40	15	Atlanta, GA	WIRE-CD
39	1000	Atlanta, GA	WSB-TV
41	330	Atlanta, GA	WATC-DT
42	7	Atlanta, GA	WTHC-LD
43	1000	Atlanta, GA	WUPA
44	1000	Monroe, GA	WHSG-TV
45	15	Atlanta, GA	W45DX-D
46	5	Atlanta, GA	WSB-TV
47	12.5	Norcross, GA	WKTB-CD
48	1	Gainesville, GA	W48DR-D
48	1000	Athens, GA	WUVG-DT
51	1000	Rome, GA	WPXA-TV
56	50	Atlanta, GA	WQJY980

10. Houston, TX

ch	kW	Location	Station
7	0.3	Houston, TX	KDHU-LD
8	65	Houston, TX	KUHT
11	60	Houston, TX	KHOU
13	32	Houston, TX	KTRK-TV
15	15	Houston, TX	KVVV-LD
19	1000	Houston, TX	KTXH
20	4	Houston, TX	KQHO-LD
21	10.5	Houston, TX	KVQT-LD
22	15	Bay City, TX	K22JW-D
22	15	Missouri City, TX	KUVM-LD
23	350	Galveston, TX	KLTJ
24	1000	Houston, TX	KETH-TV
25	15	Livingston, TX	KCTL-LD
26	800	Houston, TX	KRIV
28	15	Houston, TX	KUGB-CD
30	15	Houston, TX	KCVH-LD
32	1000	Conroe, TX	KPXB-TV
34	15	Missouri City, TX	KUVM-LD
35	1000	Houston, TX	KPRC-TV
36	1000	Alvin, TX	KFTH-DT
38	1000	Houston, TX	KIAH
39	15	Houston, TX	KZHO-LD
41	1000	Baytown, TX	KUBE-TV
42	1000	Conroe, TX	KTBU
43	60	Houston, TX	KHLM-LD
44	1000	Houston, TX	KZJL
45	1000	Rosenberg, TX	KXLN-DT
46	15	Houston, TX	KBPX-LD
47	1000	Katy, TX	KYAZ
48	1000	Galveston, TX	KTMD
49	5	Houston, TX	KEHO-LD

11. Phoenix, AZ

ch	kW	Location	Station
8	40	Phoenix, AZ	KAET
10	48	Phoenix, AZ	KSAZ-TV
12	39	Mesa, AZ	KPNX
15	458	Phoenix, AZ	KNXV-TV
16	15	Phoenix, AZ	KPHE-LD
17	1000	Phoenix, AZ	KPHO-TV
20	1000	Phoenix, AZ	KPAZ-TV
22	15	Phoenix, AZ	KTVP-LD
24	1000	Phoenix, AZ	KTVK
26	1000	Phoenix, AZ	KUTP
33	470	Phoenix, AZ	KTVW-DT
35	12	Phoenix, AZ	KFPH-CD
36	15	Phoenix, AZ	KAZT-CD
38	15	Phoenix, AZ	K38IZ-D
39	550	Phoenix, AZ	KTAZ
40	14	Phoenix, AZ	KEJR-LD
41	5	Phoenix, AZ	KPDF-CA
42	15	Phoenix, AZ	KVPA-LD
46	15	Phoenix, AZ	KDPH-LD
49	531	Phoenix, AZ	KASW

ch	kW	Location	Station
50	15	Globe, AZ	KFPB-LD
51	1000	Tolleson, AZ	KPPX-TV

12. Detroit, MI

ch	kW	Location	Station
7	27	Detroit, MI	WJBK
14	180	Detroit, MI	WKBD-TV
18	14	Detroit, MI	WDWO-CD
20	15	Detroit, MI	WHNE-LD
21	500	Detroit, MI	WMYD
23	15	Detroit, MI	WUDT-LD
28	500	Flint, MI	WCMZ-TV
34	185	Jackson. MI	WHTV
39	1000	Mount Clemens, MI	WADL
40	2	Detroit, MI	WLPC-CD
41	1000	Detroit, MI	WXYZ-TV
43	600	Detroit, MI	WTVS
44	425	Detroit, MI	WWJ-TV
45	872	Detroit, MI	WDIV-TV
47	3	Detroit, MI	W47DL-D
50	345	Ann Arbor, MI	WPXD-TV

13. Tampa - St. Petersburg, FL

ch	kW	Location	Station
7	32	Tampa, FL	WFLA-TV
10	69	St. Petersburg, FL	WTSP
12	72	Tampa, FL	WTVT
13	25	Tampa, FL	WEDU
14	3.5	Largo, FL	WPDS-LD
15	5	Orient City, FL	W15CM-D
18	5	Tampa, FL	WSVT-LD
19	1000	Lakeland, FL	WMOR-TV
20	15	Tampa, FL	WARP-CD
21	1000	Clearwater, FL	WCLF
23	5.5	Sebring, FL	W23CN-D
24	90	Sarasota, FL	WWSB
25	750	Venice, FL	WVEA-TV
26	5	Inverness, FL	W26DP-D
28	15	Tampa, FL	WTAM-LD
29	1000	Tampa, FL	WFTS-TV
31	12	Tampa, FL	W31CZ-D
32	1000	St. Petersburg, FL	WTTA
34	475	Tampa, FL	WUSF-TV
36	0.07	St. Petersburg, FL	WDNP-LP
38	15	St. Petersburg, FL	WSPF-CD
40	3	St. Petersburg, FL	W40CU-D
42	257	Bradenton, FL	WXPX-TV
43	15	Lealman, FL	W43CE-D
44	550	St. Petersburg, FL	WTOG
47	650	Tampa, FL	WFTT-DT
49	15	Tampa, FL	WRMD-CD

14. Seattle - Tacoma, WA

ch	kW	Location	Station
8	0.25	Seattle, WA	K08OU-D
9	22	Seattle, WA	KCTS-TV
11	100	Tacoma, WA	KSTW
13	30	Tacoma, WA	KCPQ
14	90	Tacoma, WA	KTBW-TV
16	1	Tacoma, WA	KBTC-TV
17	0.5	Everett, WA	K17IZ-D
19	187	Centralia, WA	KCKA
19	165	Bellingham, WA	KBCB
22	15	Seattle, WA	KCPQ
24	4	Seattle, WA	KRUM-LD
25	8	Aberdeen, WA	K25CG-D
25	1000	Seattle, WA	KZJO
25	6	North Bend, WA	K25CH-D
26	1	Bremerton, WA	K26IC-D
27	100	Tacoma, WA	KBTC-TV
28	0.5	Mt. Vernon, WA	KIRO-TV
29	2	Centralia, WA	K29IA-D
29	2	Everett, WA	K29ED-D
31	700	Everett, WA	KONG
33	400	Bellevue, WA	KWPX-TV
34	0.5	Olympia, WA	KIRO-TV
35	580	Bellingham, WA	KVOS-TV
38	1000	Seattle, WA	KOMO-TV
39	1000	Seattle, WA	KIRO-TV
42	6	Centralia, WA	K42CM-D
42	144	Tacoma, WA	KWDK
44	169	Seattle, WA	KFFV
46	0.5	Seattle, WA	KUSE-LD
47	1	Point Pulley, WA	K47LG-D
48	960	Seattle, WA	KING-TV
49	2	Puyallup, WA	K49IX-D
50	1000	Bellevue, WA	KUNS-TV

ch	kW	Location	Station
51	1	Issaquah, WA	KIRO-TV

15. Minneapolis-St. Paul MI

ch	kW	Location	Station
9	30	Minneapolis, MN	KMSP-TV
11	45	Minneapolis, MN	KARE
16	15	St. Paul, MN	K16HY-D
17	15	Minneapolis, MN	WUMN-LD
22	1000	Minneapolis, MN	WUCW
23	325	St. Paul, MN	KTCI-TV
24	1.5	Grantsburg, WI	W24CL-D
25	15	Minneapolis, MN	KJNK-LD
27	291	Menomonie, WI	WHWC-TV
29	1000	Minneapolis, MN	WFTC
31	15	Minneapolis, MN	WDMI-LD
32	1000	Minneapolis, MN	WCCO-TV
33	15	Minneapolis, MN	K33LN-D
34	662	St. Paul, MN	KTCA-TV
35	755	St. Paul, MN	KSTP-TV
40	1000	St. Cloud, MN	KPXM-TV
43	15	Minneapolis, MN	K43HB-D
45	1000	Minneapolis, MN	KSTC-TV
47	1.6	River Falls, MN	W47CO-D
48	15	Minneapolis, MN	KHVM-LD
50	15	Minneapolis, MN	KTCJ-LD

16. Miami - Ft. Lauderdale, FL

ch	kW	Location	Station
7	158	Miami, FL	WSVN
9	3	Miami, FL	WDGT-LD
10	128	Miami, FL	WPLG
11	3	Miami, FL	WDFL-LD
16	3	West Gate, FL	W16CC-D
17	15	Miami, FL	W17DG-D
18	1000	Miami, FL	WPBT
19	1000	Miami, FL	WSFL-TV
20	870	Miami, FL	WLRN-TV
21	15	Pompano Beach, FL	WDLP-CD
22	1000	Miami, FL	WFOR-TV
23	1000	Miami, FL	WLTV-DT
25	15	Miami, FL	WIMP-CD
29	1	Miami, FL	WEYS-LD
30	1000	Fort Lauderdale, FL	WSCV
31	1000	Miami, FL	WTVJ
32	1000	Miami, FL	WBFS-TV
33	15	Miami, FL	WTXI-LD
35	242	Miami, FL	WPXM-TV
38	5	Miami, FL	WPMF-CD
39	6	Brownsville, FL	WMLD-LD
40	1000	Boca Raton, FL	WBEC-TV
41	15	Miami, FL	WJAN-CD
43	15	Matecumbe, FL	W43CB-D
45	15	Miami, FL	WGEN-LD
46	1000	Miami, FL	WHFT-TV
47	1000	Hollywood, FL	WAMI-DT
48	15	Miami, FL	WFUN-LD
50	15	Miami, etc.	WSBS-CD
51	15	Miami, FL	WLMF-LD

17. Denver, CO

ch	kW	Location	Station
5	1.5	Cripple Creek, CO	K05MD-D
7	54	Denver, CO	KMGH-TV
9	45	Denver, CO	KUSA
10	0.5	Steamboat Springs, CO	KRMZ
11	16	Cheyenne, CO	KQCK
13	34	Broomfield, CO	KBDI-TV
15	1000	Boulder, CO	KTFD-DT
16	15	Denver, CO	KHDT-LD
17	15	Denver, CO	KZCO-LD
18	1000	Denver, CO	KRMA-TV
19	1000	Denver, CO	KTVD
20	0.1	Ft. Morgan, CO	K20KE-D
21	50	Ft. Collins, CO	KFCT
23	1000	Sterling, CO	KCDO-TV
24	0.25	Boulder, CO	K24HQ-D
24	7.5	Ft. Collins, CO	KMLN-LD
25	0.1	Ft. Morgan, CO	K25LA-D
26	15	Denver, CO	KZDN-LD
27	0.2	Boulder, CO	K27MA-D
28	15	Denver, CO	KLPD-LD
29	800	Longmont, CO	KDEN-TV
32	1000	Denver, CO	KDVR
33	1.6	Denver, CO	KMAS-LD
34	1000	Denver, CO	KWGN-TV
34	1.5	Sidney, NE	KCDO-TV
35	1000	Denver, CO	KCNC-TV

ch	kW	Location	Station
38	1000	Greeley, CO	KPJR-TV
39	1	Denver, CO	KQDK-CD
40	75	Denver, CO	KRMT
41	15	Denver, CO	KSBS-CD
43	1000	Denver, CO	KPXC-TV
44	45	Ft. Collins, CO	KDNF-LD
45	100	Castle Rock, CO	KETD
47	1000	Ft. Collins, CO	KRMA-TV
48	15	Boulder, CO	K48MN-D
50	15	Denver, CO	KDEO-LD
50	1	Laramie, CO	KHDE-LD
51	990	Denver, CO	KCEC

URUGUAY

System: ISDB-TB [A]

National Station
TELEVISIÓN NACIONAL URUGUAY (TNU) (Gov) ✉ Bvrd. Artigas 2552,11600 Montevideo ☎ +598 2 4871129 **E:** contacto@tnu.com.uy **W:** www.tnu.com.uy **LP:** Dir: Virginia Martínez **Tx:** Montevideo ch30 & network.

Key Local Stations
MONTE CARLO TELEVISIÓN (Comm) ✉ Paraguay 2253, 11800 Montevideo ☎ +598 2 9247924 🖷 +598 2 9244444 **W:** www.monte-carlotv.com.uy **Tx:** Montevideo ch29. – **SAETA CANAL 10 (Comm)** ✉ Lorenzo Carnelli 1234, 11200 Montevideo ☎ +598 2 4002120 🖷 +598 2 4095812 **W:** www.canal10.com.uy **Tx:** Montevideo ch31. – **TELEDOCE (Comm)** ✉ Enriqueta Compte y Rique 1276, 11800 Montevideo ☎ +598 2 2083363 🖷 +598 2 2083555 **E:** teledoce@teledoce.com **W:** www.teledoce.com **Tx:** Montevideo ch28.

Other Local Stations not shown.

UZBEKISTAN

Systems: DVB-T (MPEG4) [E]; § SECAM-D/K [R], § PAL-D/K [R]

National Stations
UZBEK TELEVISION (Gov) ✉ Navoiy St. 69, 100011 Toshkent ☎+998 71 1141250 🖷 +998 71 1441332 **E:** info@mtrk.uz **W:** www.mtrk.uz **LP:** Chmn: Alisher Djuraqulovich Xadjayev. **Chs:** O'zbekiston, Yoshlar, Toshkent, Sport TV, Madaniyat va ma'rifat, Dunyo bo'ylab, Bolajon, regional stns.

Local Stations, Foreign TV Relays not shown.

DTT Tx Networks
Licensee: Uzdigital TV ✉ Amir Timur St. 109-A, 100084 Toshkent ☎ +998 71 1299000 🖷 +998 71 1505884 **E:** info@uzdtv.uz **W:** uzdtv.uz **Mux 1:** O'zbekiston, Yoshlar, Toshkent, Sport TV, Madaniyat va ma'rifat, Dunyo bo'ylab, Bolajon, Forum TV, UzHD (SD version), NTT TvMarkaz, SoftS **Mux 2❂:** n/a **Mux 3❂:** n/a **Mux 4❂:** UzHD

Location	M1	M2	M3	M4	kW
Toshkent	42	41	37	29	2

+ national network under construction

VANUATU

System: PAL-B [E]

TV BLONG VANUATU (Gov) ✉ P.M.B. 049, Port Vila **W:** www.facebook.com/TelevisionBlongVanuatu **LP:** Acting GM (VBTC): Fred Vurobaravu. **Txs:** (-).

Foreign TV Relay
CCTV-9 (P.R.China): Santo ch(-).

VATICAN CITY STATE

System: DVB-T (MPEG4) [E]

CENTRO TELEVISIVO VATICANO (CTV) ✉ Via del Pellegrino, I-00120 Vatican City ☎ +39 06 69885467 🖷 +39 06 69885192 **E:** ctv@ctv.va **W:** www.ctv.va **LP:** Dir: Mons. Dario Edoardo Viganò **Mux:** CTV HD ✂ R. Vaticana 105 Live, R. Vaticana Europa/America, R. Vaticana Africa/Asia **Tx:** ch45 (Castel Gandolfo).

VENEZUELA

Systems: # NTSC-M [A] ⇩2020; ISDB-TB [A]

National Stations (ᵃ=analogue)
TVES (TELEVISORA VENEZOLANA SOCIAL) (Gov) ⌨ Caraças **W:** www.tves.gob.ve **Txs:** Caracas ᵃch2 & relay txs. – **VIVE (VISIÓN VENEZUELA) (Gov)** ⌨ Final Av. Panteón, Foro Libertador, Edf. Biblioteca Nacional, AP-4, Altagracia, Caracas ☎+58 212 5051611 E: atencionciudadana@vive.gob.ve **W:** www.vive.gob.ve **Txs:** Caracas ᵃch25 & relay tx. – **VTV (VENEZOLANA DE TELEVISION) (Gov)** ⌨ Ap. 2979, Caracas 1050. ☎ +58 212 2349581 **E:** atencionciudadano@ vtv.gob.ve **W:** www.vtv.gob.ve **Txs:** Caracas ᵃch8 (190kW) & relay txs. – **TELESUR (Pub)** ⌨ Calle Vargas con Calle Santa Clara, edificio TeleSUR, Boleíta Norte, Caracas ☎ +58 212 6000202 **E:** contactenos@ telesurtv.net **W:** www.telesurtv.net **Txs:** Caracas ᵃch49 & relay txs. – **GLOBOVISIÓN (Comm)** ⌨ av. Los Pinos, cruce con Calle Alameda, Qta. Globovisión, Urb. Alta Florida, Caracas ☎ +58 212 7301134 **E:** info@globovision.com **W:** globovision.com. **Txs:** Caracas ᵃch33 & relay txs. – **MERIDIANO TELEVISIÓN (Comm)** ⌨ Final av. San Martin con Av. La Paz, Edificio Bloque De Armas, Caracas ☎ +58 212 4064516 🖷 +58 212 4515627 **E:** meridianotv@internet.ve **W:** www.meridiano.com. ve **Txs:** Caracas ᵃch39 & relay txs. – **TELEVEN (Comm)** ⌨ Av. Romulo Gallegos con 4ta. transversal de horizonte, Edificio Televen, Caracas 1071 ☎ +58 212 2800151 **E:** webmaster@televen.com. **W:** www. televen.com. **Txs:** Caracas ᵃch10 & relay txs. – **VENEVISIÓN (Comm)** ⌨ Av. La Salle, Edif, Venevisíon,Colinas de Los Caobos, Caracas 1050 ☎ +58 212 7089444 **W:** www.venevision.net. **Txs:** Caracas ᵃch4 (132kW) & relay txs. – **VALE TV (Rlg)** ⌨ Final Av. La Salle, Quinta ValeTV, Colinas de los Caobos, Caracas ☎ +58 212 7939215 🖷 +58 212 7089743 **E:** webmaster@valetv.com **W:** www.valetv.com **Txs:** Caracas ᵃch5 (210kW) & relay txs.

Local Stations (Comm. exc. where stated)
Amavision (Rlg): Calle Selesiano, Colegio Pio XI, Puerto Ayacucho, Amazonas; Puerto Ayacucho ᵃch7 (6kW). **La Tele:** Calle Republica Dominicana, Boleita Sur, Caracas; ᵃch12. **Canal Metropolitano de Televisión:** Av. Circumvalacion El Sol, Centro Professional Santa Paula, Torre B, Piso 4, Santa Paula, Caracas;ᵃ ch51. **NCTV:** Urv. La Paz, Avenida 57 y Maracaibo, Maracaibo; ᵃch11 (108kW). **Omnivision:** Calle Milan, Edif. Omnivision, Los Ruices Sur, Caracas. Puma TV: Av. Sanatorio del Avila, Boleíta Norte, Caracas 1071; Maracaibo ᵃch53, Caracas ᵃch57. **Televisora Andina de Merida (Rlg):** Av. Bolivar, Calle 23 entre Av. 4-5, Merida 5101; Tachira ᵃch3 (33kW), Merida ᵃch6 (20kW). **Tele Bocono (Cult)** Calle 3, Qta. Caleuche, El Saman. Bocono; Trujillo ᵃch13 (4kW). **Telecaribe:** Centro Banaven (Cubo Negro), Torre C, Piso 1, of C-12, Chuao, Caracas; Anzoategui ᵃch9 (50kW), Nueva Esparta ᵃch12 (30kW). **Telecentro:** Avenide Pedro León Torres, esquina de la calle 47, Edificio Telecentro, Barquisimeto, (3001) Lara; ᵃch11 (100kW). **TV Guyana:** Puerto Ordaz, Bolivar; ch12 (125kW). **Telesol:** Calle Sucre no 15, Cumana, Sucre; ᵃch7 (12kW). **Televisora Regional del Tachira:** Av. Libertador, edif. Servicios Unidos, Piso 3, San Cristobal, Tachira; ᵃch6 (144kW). **Televisora de Oriente (TVO):** Puerto la Cruz, Anzoategui; ᵃch5 (50kW).

DTT Tx Networks (under construction)
Licensee: n/a **Mux 1:** VTV, 123TV, Colombeia, Venevisión, Alba TV **Mux 2:** ViVe, TeleSUR, Venevisión, Meridiano TV, Televen, TV ConCiencia **Mux 3:** TVes, ANTV, SIBCI HD **Mux 4:** CCTV, Ávila TV, PDVSA TV, RT en español.

Location	M1	M2	M3	M4
Caracas	22	23	24	25

+ nationwide network under construction.

VIETNAM

Systems: # PAL-D/K [R] ⇩2020; DVB-T2 (MPEG2) [E]

National Stations
VIETNAM TELEVISION (Gov) ⌨ 43 Nguyen Chi Thanh, Ba Dinh District, Hanoi ☎ +84 8 8224403 🖷 +84 8 8223422 **E:** banbientap@vtv. vn **W:** www.vtv.vn **LP:** DG: Tran Binh Minh **Chs (terr.):** VTV1-16, VTV3 HD, VTV6 HD **Txs:** VTV1: Hanoi ch9 (10kW) & netw. **VTV2:** Hanoi ch11 (10kW) & netw. **VTV3:** Hanoi ch22 (20kW) & netw.

Regional and Local Stations not shown.

DTT Tx Networks (under construction)
Licensee: Vietnam Multimedia Corporation ⌨ 67B Ham Long Street, Hoan Kiem District, Hanoi ☎ +84 4 9433409 🖷 +84 4 9439867 **M:** VTV1-16, VTV3 HD, VTV6 HD, Hanoi TV 1, HTV1 **Txs:** ch26 (Hanoi 1.3kW) & nationwide netw. under construction.

VIRGIN ISLANDS (American) (USA)

Systems: ATSC [A]
Local Stations*
WCVI-TV (Comm): 1 k Little Princess, St. Croix, VI 00820-4027. Tx: St. Croix ch23 (0.66kW). **WSVI (Comm):** Sunny Isle Shopping Cente, St Croix, VI 00820-4493. Tx: St. Croix ch20 (459kW). **WTJX-TV (Pub):** 58-158A Hay Place Hill S, St. Thomas, VI 20801. Tx: Charlotte Amalie ch44 (50kW). **WVIF (Comm):** 4200 United Shipping Plaza #3, St Croix, VI 00820. Tx: Christiansted ch15 (16.2kW). **WVXF (Comm):** 8000 Nisky Center, Suite 714, Saint Thomas, VI 00802. Tx: Charlotte Amalie ch48 (50kW). **WZVI (Comm):** satellite of WSVI. Tx: Charlotte Amalie ch43 (1.4kW). *) Full power licenses (lp licenses not listed)

VIRGIN ISLANDS (British) (UK)

System: NTSC-M [A]

CARRIBEAN BROADCAST NETWORK LTD (Comm) ⌨ 2nd Floor, Chevelle Center Main Street, Road Town, Tortola VG1110 ☎ +1 284 3463633 **E:** info@cbnbvi.com **W:** www.cbnbvi.com **Tx:** ch5 (30kW).

WAKE ISLAND (USA)

NB: No terrestrial TV station.

WALLIS & FUTUNA (France)

System: DVB-T (MPEG4) [E]

WALLIS ET FUTUNA 1ÈRE (Pub) ⌨ BP 102, Pointe Matala, F-98600 Mata Utu ☎ +681 681722020 🖷 +681 681722346 **W:** wallisfutuna.la1ere.fr **L:P** Dir: Jean-Michel Fontaine.
DTT Tx Network
Tx Operator: TDF **M:** Wallis et Futuna 1ère, France 2-5, France Ô, France 24, Arte **Txs:** ch34 (SFN).

YEMEN

System: PAL-B [E]

YEMEN GENERAL CORP. FOR RADIO & TV (Gov) ⌨ P.O.Box 1140, al-Guraf, Sana'a ☎ +967 1 332001 🖷 +967 1 332086 **E:** gm@ yemenrtv.net **W:** www.yemenrtv.net **L:P:** GM: Hussein Mukbel **Chs:** Channel 1, Channel 2, Sheba TV, Al Iman TV ⌨**Channel 2:** P.O.Box 1264, Tawahi, Aden ☎ +967 2 202481 🖷 +967 2 221121. **Txs:** (-).

ZAMBIA

System: DVB-T2 (MPEG4) [E]

National Stations
ZAMBIA NATIONAL BROADCASTING CORP. (Gov) ⌨ P.O.Box 50015, Lusaka 10101 ☎ +260 21 1254989 🖷 +260 21 1254317 **E:** znbctv@znbc.co.zm **W:** www.znbc.co.zm **LP:** DG: Richard Mwanza **Chs:** ZNBC TV1, ZNBC TV2 – **MUVI TV (Comm)** ⌨ P.O.Box 33932, Lusaka 10101 ☎ +260 21 1253271 **E:** frontoffice@muvitv.com **W:** www.muvitv.com.

Local Stations (all Comm)
CBC: 22nd Floor, Findeco House, Lusaka. **Copperbelt Broadcasting Services:** Ndola. **Mobi TV:** 25 Mwambula Rd, Lusaka. **Northrise TV:** Lusaka.

DTT Tx Network
Licensee: Multichoice Zambia ⌨ P.O.Box 320011, Lusaka ☎ +260 21 1368300 🖷 +260 21 1261533 **E:** mczambia@zambia.multichoice. co.za **M(partly☉):** multiprgr **Txs:** MFN.

ZIMBABWE

Systems: DVB-T2 (MPEG4) [E]; § PAL-B [E]

ZIMBABWE TELEVISION (ZTV) (Gov) ⌨ P.O.Box HG 444, Highlands, Harare ☎ +263 4 498610 🖷 +263 4 498613 **E:** zbc@zbc. co.zw **W:** www.zbc.co.zw **LP:** CEO (Zimbabwe Broadcasting Corp.): Happison Muchechetere **Chs:** ZTV1, ZTV2.
DTT Tx Network (under construction)
Licensee: Multichoice Zimbabwe **M(partly☉):** multiprgr **Txs:** MFN.

REFERENCE

Section Contents

Features & Reviews

National Radio

International Radio

Frequency Lists

National Television

Reference

MAIN COUNTRY INDEX

	Nat	Int	CTB	TV		Nat	Int	CTB	TV
Afghanistan	66	450		608	Djibouti	184	462		617
Alaska	66	450		608	Dominica	184			617
Albania	67	450		608	Dominican Republic	185			617
Algeria	68	451		608	Easter Island	186			618
Andorra	69			608	Ecuador	186	462		618
Angola	69	451		608	Egypt	190	463		618
Anguilla	70	451		609	El Salvador	191			618
Antarctica	70	451		609	Equatorial Guinea	192			618
Antigua & Barbuda	70			609	Eritrea	192		509	618
Argentina	71	451		609	Estonia	192	463		618
Armenia	79	451		609	Ethiopia	193	463	510	619
Aruba	79			609	Falkland Islands	193			619
Ascension Island	80	452		609	Faroe Islands	194			619
Australia	80	452		609	Fiji	194			619
Austria	89	453		609	Finland	195	463		619
Azerbaijan	90	454		610	France	196	464		620
Azores	90			610	French Guiana	205			621
Bahamas	91			610	French Polynesia	205			621
Bahrain	92	454		610	French So. & Antarctic Lands..	206			621
Bangladesh	92	454		610	Gabon	206			621
Barbados	93			610	Galapagos Islands	206			621
Belarus	93	455		610	Gambia	206			621
Belgium	94	455		611	Georgia	206			621
Belize	96			611	Germany	207	465		622
Benin	97	456		611	Ghana	221			623
Bermuda	97			611	Gibraltar	222			623
Bhutan	97			612	Greece	222	467		623
Bolivia	98			612	Greenland	224			624
Bonaire	102	456		612	Grenada	224			624
Bosnia & Herzegovina	102			612	Guadeloupe	224			624
Botswana	103	456		612	Guam	225	467		624
Brazil	104			612	Guatemala	225			624
British Indian Ocean Territory .	135			612	Guinea	227			624
Brunei	135			612	Guinea-Bissau	227			624
Bulgaria	136	456		612	Guyana	227			624
Burkina Faso	137			613	Haiti	227			624
Burundi	137			613	Hawaii	228			624
Cambodia	137		508	613	Honduras	230			625
Cameroon	139	456	508	613	Hong Kong	232			625
Canada	139	456		613	Hungary	233			625
Canary Islands	146			614	Iceland	234			625
Cape Verde	147			614	India	234	467	510	626
Cayman Islands	148			614	Indonesia	240	472		626
Central African Rep.	148			614	Iran	244	472	511	626
Chad	148			614	Iraq	245			626
Chile	149			614	Ireland	247	474		626
China	151	456	508	614	Israel	249			627
Christmas Island	168			615	Italy	250	474		629
Cocos Islands	168			615	Ivory Coast	252			627
Colombia	168			615	Jamaica	252			627
Comoros	174			615	Japan	253	474		627
Congo (Dem. Rep.)	174			615	Jordan	256			628
Congo (Rep. of)	175			615	Kazakstan	257			628
Cook Islands	175			615	Kenya	257			628
Costa Rica	175			615	Kiribati	258			628
Croatia	176			616	Korea (DPR) (North)	259	475	511	628
Cuba	178	461	509	616	Korea (Rep) (South)	259	476	513	628
Curaçao	180			616	Kosovo	263			628
Cyprus	180	462		616	Kuwait	264	477		629
Czech Republic	181	462		616	Kyrgyzstan	264	477		629
Denmark	183			617	Laos	264	477		629

	Nat	Int	CTB	TV		Nat	Int	CTB	TV
Latvia	265			629	San Marino	354			640
Lebanon	265			629	São Tomé	354	484		640
Lesotho	265			630	Saudi Arabia	354	484		640
Liberia	267			630	Senegal	355			640
Libya	267			630	Serbia	356	485		641
Liechtenstein	267			630	Seychelles	357			641
Lithuania	268	477		630	Sierra Leone	357			641
Lord Howe Island	269			630	Singapore	357	485		641
Luxembourg	269	478		630	Slovakia	358	485		642
Macau	269			630	Slovenia	359			642
Macedonia	269	478		630	Solomon Islands	360			642
Madagascar	269	478		631	Somalia	360		514	642
Madeira	270			631	South Africa	361	486		642
Malawi	270			631	South Sudan	364		514	642
Malaysia	271		513	631	Spain	364	487		642
Maldives	273			631	Sri Lanka	373	488		643
Mali	274	478		631	St Barthélemy	373			643
Malta	274			631	St Eustatius	373			643
Marshall Islands	274			631	St Helena	373			643
Martinique	275			631	St Kitts & Nevis	374			643
Mauritania	275			632	St Lucia	374			643
Mauritius	275			632	St Maarten	374			643
Mayotte	275			632	St Martin	374			643
Mexico	276			632	St Pierre & Miquelon	375			643
Micronesia	286			632	St Vincent	375			644
Moldova	286	478		632	Sudan	375	488	514	644
Monaco	287	478		633	Suriname	375			644
Mongolia	288	479		633	Swaziland	376	488		644
Montenegro	289			633	Sweden	376	488		644
Montserrat	289			633	Switzerland	377	489		644
Morocco	289	479		633	Syria	379	489	514	645
Mozambique	290			634	Taiwan (Rep. of China)	379	489		645
Myanmar	291			634	Tajikistan	382	490		645
Namibia	291			634	Tanzania	383	491		645
Nauru	292			634	Thailand	383	491		645
Nepal	292			634	Timor-Leste	386			646
Netherlands	294	479		634	Togo	387			646
New Caledonia	296			635	Tokelau	387			646
New Zealand	297	479		635	Tonga	387			646
Nicaragua	302			635	Trinidad & Tobago	388			646
Niger	303			635	Tristan da Cunha	388			646
Nigeria	303	480	513	635	Tunisia	388			646
Niue	304			635	Turkey	389	492	514	646
Norfolk Island	304			635	Turkmenistan	390			647
Northern Mariana Is	305	480		635	Turks & Caicos Is	391			647
Norway	305	480		636	Tuvalu	391			647
Oman	306	480		636	Uganda	391			647
Pakistan	307	481	513	636	Ukraine	392	493		647
Palau	308	481		636	United Arab Emirates	395	493		648
Panama	308			636	United Kingdom	396	493		648
Papua New Guinea	309			636	United States of America	404	496		649
Paraguay	311			637	Uruguay	439			653
Peru	312			637	Uzbekistan	442	506		653
Philippines	322	481		637	Vanuatu	442			653
Pitcairn Islands	326			637	Vatican City State	442	506		653
Poland	326	483		637	Venezuela	443			654
Portugal	330			638	Vietnam	446	507	514	654
Puerto Rico	333			638	Virgin Is (American)	447			654
Qatar	334			638	Virgin Is (British)	447			654
Réunion	334			638	Wake Island	447			654
Romania	335	483		639	Wallis & Futuna	447			654
Russia	337	484		639	West Bank & Gaza (Palestine)	249			627
Rwanda	353		513	640	Western Sahara			515	
Saba	353			640	Yemen	448	507		654
Samoa	353			640	Zambia	448			654
Samoa (American)	354			640	Zimbabwe	448		515	654

GEOGRAPHICAL AREA CODES USED IN WRTH

Codes assigned by the International Telecommunications Union ITU (except * = WRTH code)

Code	Country	Code	Country	Code	Country	Code	Country
ABW	Aruba	D	Germany	LBY	Libya	SDN	Sudan
AFG	Afghanistan	DGA	Diego Garcia	LCA	St. Lucia	SEN	Senegal
AFS	South Africa	DJI	Djibouti	LHW*	Lord Howe Island	SEY	Seychelles
AGL	Angola	DMA	Dominica	LIE	Liechtenstein	SHN	St. Helena
AIA	Anguilla	DNK	Denmark	LSO	Lesotho	SLM	Solomon Islands
ALB	Albania	DOM	Dominican Republic	LTU	Lithuania	SLV	El Salvador
ALG	Algeria	E	Spain	LUX	Luxembourg	SMA	American Samoa
ALS	Alaska	EGY	Egypt	LVA	Latvia	SMO	Samoa
AND	Andorra	EQA	Ecuador	MAC	Macao	SMR	San Marino
AOE	Western Sahara	ERI	Eritrea	MAF	St. Martin	SNG	Singapore
ARG	Argentina	EST	Estonia	MAU	Mauritius	SOM	Somalia
ARM	Armenia	ETH	Ethiopia	MCO	Monaco	SPM	St. Pierre & Miquelon
ARS	Saudi Arabia	F	France	MDA	Moldova	SRB	Serbia
ASC	Ascension Island	FIN	Finland	MDG	Madagascar	SRL	Sierra Leone
ATA	Antarctica	FJI	Fiji	MDR	Madeira	SSD	South Sudan
ATG	Antigua & Barbuda	FLK	Falkland Islands	MEX	Mexico	STP	São Tomé & Príncipe
AUS	Australia	FRO	Faroe Islands	MHL	Marshall Islands	SUI	Switzerland
AUT	Austria	FSA*	French So. & Ant. Lands	MKD	Macedonia	SUR	Suriname
AZE	Azerbaijan	FSM	Micronesia	MLA	Malaysia	SVK	Slovakia
AZR	Azores	G	United Kingdom	MLD	Maldives	SVN	Slovenia
B	Brazil	GAB	Gabon	MLI	Mali	SWZ	Swaziland
BAH	Bahamas	GAL*	Galapagos Islands	MLT	Malta	SXM	St Maarten
BDI	Burundi	GEO	Georgia	MNE	Montenegro	SYR	Syria
BEL	Belgium	GHA	Ghana	MNG	Mongolia	TCA	Turks & Caicos Islands
BEN	Benin	GIB	Gibraltar	MOZ	Mozambique	TCD	Chad
BER	Bermuda	GLP	Guadeloupe	MRA	Northern Mariana Is	TGO	Togo
BES	Bonaire / St Eustatius /	GMB	Gambia	MRC	Morocco	THA	Thailand
	Saba	GNB	Guinea-Bissau	MRT	Martinique	TJK	Tajikistan
BFA	Burkina Faso	GNE	Equatorial Guinea	MSR	Montserrat	TKM	Turkmenistan
BGD	Bangladesh	GRC	Greece	MTN	Mauritania	TKL	Tokelau
BHR	Bahrain	GRD	Grenada	MWI	Malawi	TLS	Timor-Leste
BIH	Bosnia & Herzegovina	GRL	Greenland	MYT	Mayotte	TON	Tonga
BIO	British Indian Ocean	GTM	Guatemala	NCG	Nicaragua	TRC	Tristan da Cunha
	Territory	GUF	French Guiana	NCL	New Caledonia	TRD	Trinidad & Tobago
BLM	St. Barthélemy	GUI	Guinea	NFK	Norfolk Island	TUN	Tunisia
BLR	Belarus	GUM	Guam	NGR	Niger	TUR	Turkey
BLZ	Belize	GUY	Guyana	NIG	Nigeria	TUV	Tuvalu
BOL	Bolivia	HKG	Hong Kong	NIU	Niue	TWN*	Taiwan
BOT	Botswana	HND	Honduras	NMB	Namibia	TZA	Tanzania
BRB	Barbados	HNG	Hungary	NOR	Norway	UAE	United Arab Emirates
BRM	Myanmar	HOL	Netherlands	NPL	Nepal	UGA	Uganda
BRU	Brunei	HRV	Croatia	NRU	Nauru	UKR	Ukraine
BTN	Bhutan	HTI	Haiti	NZL	New Zealand	URG	Uruguay
BUL	Bulgaria	HWA	Hawaii	OCE	French Polynesia	USA	United States of America
CAF	Central African Republic	I	Italy	OMA	Oman	UZB	Uzbekistan
CAN	Canada	ICO	Cocos (Keeling) Islands	PAK	Pakistan	VCT	St. Vincent &
CBG	Cambodia	IND	India	PAQ	Easter Island		the Grenadines
CHL	Chile	INS	Indonesia	PHL	Philippines	VEN	Venezuela
CHN	China (People's Rep. of)	IRL	Ireland	PLW	Palau	VIR	Virgin Islands
CHR	Christmas Island	IRN	Iran	PNG	Papua New Guinea	VRG	British Virgin Islands
CKH	Cook Islands	IRQ	Iraq	PNR	Panama	VTN	Vietnam
CLM	Colombia	ISL	Iceland	POL	Poland	VUT	Vanuatu
CLN	Sri Lanka	ISR	Israel	POR	Portugal	WAL	Wallis & Futuna
CME	Cameroon	J	Japan	PRG	Paraguay	WAK	Wake Island
CNR	Canary Islands	JMC	Jamaica	PRU	Peru	XGZ	Gaza Strip[1]
COD	Congo (Dem. Rep. of the)	JOR	Jordan	PSE*	Palestine[1]	XWB	West Bank[1]
COG	Congo (Rep. of the)	KAZ	Kazakhstan	PTC	Pitcairn Islands	YEM	Yemen
COM	Comoros	KEN	Kenya	PTR	Puerto Rico	ZMB	Zambia
CPV	Cape Verde	KER	Iles Kerguelen	QAT	Qatar	ZWE	Zimbabwe
CTI	Côte d'Ivoire	KGZ	Kyrgyzstan	REU	Réunion		
CTR	Costa Rica	KIR	Kiribati	RKS*	Kosovo		
CUB	Cuba	KOR	Korea, South	ROD	Rodrigues		
CUW	Curaçao	KRE	Korea, North	ROU	Romania		
CVA	Vatican City State	KWT	Kuwait	RRW	Rwanda		
CYM	Cayman Islands	LAO	Laos	RUS	Russia		
CYP	Cyprus	LBN	Lebanon	S	Sweden		
CZE	Czech Republic	LBR	Liberia	SCN	St. Kitts & Nevis		

[1] The code "PSE" is used as target designation in the "COTB" section of "International Radio/ COTB"; otherwise the codes "XGZ"/"XWB" are used.

ABBREVIATIONS & SYMBOLS USED IN WRTH

⌨	= Address	DST	= Daylight Saving Time	LV	= La Voz, La Voce	Rep.	= Republic
☎	= Telephone	DTT	= Digital Terrestrial TV	LW	= Longwave	Rev.	= Reverend
🖹	= Fax	DVB	= Digital Video Broadc.	max.	= maximum	rlg	= religious
✪	= encrypted	DX	= Long Distance	M:	= Multiplex	Rp.	= Return Postage
⌘	= Radio via DTT		(Reception)	MD	= Managing Director	Rpt.	= (Reception) Report
†	= irregular	E	= English	MF	= Mondays-Fridays	S.	= San(ta), Sán, Santo
‡	= inactive	E:	= Email	MFN	= Multi Freq. Netw.	s/off	= sign off
±	= variable frequency	E.C	= Electric Current	Mgr	= Manager	s/on	= sign on
		Ea.	= East(ern)	MHz	= MegaHertz	SAE	= Self Addressed
acc.	= accepted	Edif.	= Edificio	mil.	= military		Envelope
Admin.	= Administration	Educ.	= Education(al),	Min.	= Ministry, Ministerio,	SAR	= Special Administrative
alt.	= alternate, alternative		Educación		Ministério		Region
AM	= Amplitude Modulation	e.g.	= for example	min(s)	= minute(s)	Sat	= Saturday, satellite
Ann.	= Announcement	Em.	= Emis(s)ora	Mon	= Monday	Sce.	= Service
Ap.	= Apartado	Eng.	= Engineer(ing)	Mpal.	= Municipal	Sched.	= Schedule
approx.	= approximate(ly)	ERP	= Effective Radiated	Mpo.	= Município	SE	= South East(ern)
Assoc.	= Association		Power	Mt	= Mount, Mountain	Secr.	= Secretary
Asst.	= Assistant	Esq.	= Esquina	MW	= Mediumwave	Sen.	= Senior
Ave	= Avenue, Avenida	est.	= estimated	N.	= News	SFN	= Single Freq. Netw.
B.P.	= Boîte Postale	Est.	= Estado	NB	= Note (Nota Bene)	Sist.	= Sistema
B'caster	= Broadcaster	exc.	= except	n.f.	= nominal frequency	SM	= Station Manager
Bldg	= Building	excl.	= excluding	n/a	= not available, not	So.	= South(ern)
Bo	= Barrio/Bairro	exec.	= executive		applicable	Soc.	= Sociedad(e)
Broadc.	= Broadcast(ing)	ext.	= external	nal.	= nacional	Sp.	= Spanish
BS	= Broadc. Stn/Sce	F	= French	nat.	= national	SS	= Sat/Sun
C	= Chinese	F.Pl.	= Future Plan(s)	nd	= nondirectional antenna	SSB	= Single Side Band
C.P.	= Case/Caixa Postal,	fed.	= federal	NE	= North East(ern)	St	= Saint, Street
	Construction Permit	FM	= Frequency Modulation	Netw.	= Network	Stn	= Station
Ca	= Calle	Fr.	= Father	No.	= North(ern), Number	Str.	= Street, Straße
Cad.	= Cadena	Freq.	= Frequency	nom.	= nominal	Su.	= Summer
Cas.	= Casilla	Fri	= Friday	Nte	= Norte	Sun	= Sunday
Cd.	= Ciudad	FS	= Foreign Service	NW	= North West(ern)	Superv.	= Supervisor
Ce.	= Central	Ft.	= Fort	occ.	= occasional(ly)	SW	= Shortwave
CEO	= Chief Exec. Officer	G	= German	Op(s)	= Operation(s)		South West(ern)
cf.	= refer to	G.C	= Geographical	Org.	= Organisation	Syst.	= System
Ch.	= Channel		Coordinates	Ote.	= Oeste	tbd	= to be defined
Chmn.	= Chairman/Chair	GD	= General Director	P	= Portuguese	TD	= Technical Director
Cl.	= Club(e)	gen.	= general	P.O.	= Post Office	techn.	= technical
Clan.	= Clandestine	GM	= General Manager	P.R.	= Public Relations,	terr.	= terrestrial
Co.	= Company	Gov.	= Government(al)		People's Republic	Thu	= Thursday
Com.	= Comunicações	Gte.	= Gerente	PD	= Programme Director	tr(s)	= transmission(s)
comm.	= commercial	H	= Horizontal Pol.	pl.	= planned	TRP	= Transmitter Power
Contr.	= Controller	h(rs)	= hour(s)	Pol.	= Polarisation	Tue	= Tuesday
Corp.	= Corporation	HD	= High Definition	Pop.	= Population	tx(s)	= transmitter(s)
Cra.	= Carrera	HQ	= Headquarters	Pr.	= Praça	ul.	= ulitsa, ulica
Cult.	= Cultura, Cultural	HS	= Home Service	Pr.L	= Principal Language(s)	u.c.	= under construction
D	= Daily	I	= Italian	Pres.	= President	Univ.	= University
d	= directional antenna	ID	= (Station) Identification	Priv.	= Private	unk.	= unknown
D.Prgr	= Daily Programme(s)	i.e.	= that is	Prgr(s).	= Programme(s)	UHF	= Ultra High Frequency
DAB	= Digital Audio Broadc.	Inc.	= Incorporated	Prod.	= Production	USB	= Upper Side Band
DMB	= Digital Multimedia	incl.	= including	Prov.	= Province, Provincial	UTC	= Coordinated
	Broadcasting	Inf.	= Information	Pt.	= Point		Universal Time
Dem.	= Democratic	int.	= international	Pte.	= Presidente	V	= Vertical Pol.
Dep.	= Deputy	IRC	= Int. Reply Coupon	Pto.	= Puerto	V.	= Verification
Dept.	= Department	irr.	= irregular	Pub	= Public service	v.	= varying/variable
Depto.	= Departamento	IS	= Interval Signal	Pub(s)	= Publication(s)	VHF	= Very High Frequency
Desp.	= Despacho	I./Is	= Island/Islands	QSL	= Reception Confirmation	VO	= Voice of
DG	= Director General	kHz	= kiloHertz	R.	= Radio, Rádio, Rádió	W	= Weekdays (Mon-Sat)
Dif.	= Difusão, Difusão	L	= Local		Radyjo, Radyo	W:	= Web
Diff.	= Diffusion	L.P	= Leading Personnel	r.	= reported, repeater	We.	= West(ern)
Dir.	= Director	L.T	= Local Time	Rdif.	= Radiodifusion	Wed	= Wednesday
Div.	= Division	Langs.	= Languages	R. Dif.	= Radio Difusora	Wi.	= Winter
dom	= domestic	Lp.	= Low power (transmitter)	Rec.	= Recording(s)	Wrp.	= Weather Report
DRM	= Digital Radio Mondiale	LSB	= Lower Side Band	Reg.	= Region(al)		
DSB	= Double Side Band	Ltd	= Limited	Rel.	= Relay(s), Relations		

TRANSMITTER SITES
Location & Decode Tables

INTERNATIONAL TRANSMITTER SITES

Code	Site	Ctry	Lat	Long	SW	MW
-	Unidentified	-	-	-	✗	✗
ABH	Abu Hayan	BHR	26N02	050E37	✓	✗
ABS	Abis	EGY	31N08	030E04	✓	✗
ABZ	Abu Zaabal	EGY	30N16	031E22	✓	✗
AHW	Ahwaz, Bandar-e Mahshar	IRN	30N37	049E12	✓	✓
AIA	The Valley	AIA	18N13	063W01	✓	✓
AJA	Abuja, Lugbe	NIG	08N58	007E22	✓	✗
ALF	Khartoum, Al Fitahab	SDN	15N35	032E27	✓	✗
ALG	Aligarh	IND	28N00	078E06	✓	✗
ARM	Krasnodar, Tbilisskaya	RUS	45N28	040E06	✓	✗
ASC	English Bay	ASC	07S54	014W23	✓	✗
ASM	Asmara	ERI	15N13	038E52	✓	✓
AVL	Vathy (Avlida municipality)	GRC	38N23	023E36	✓	✗
BCQ	Monticello, ME	USA	46N20	067W49	✓	✗
BEC	Béchar ‡	ALG	31N34	002W21	✓	✗
BEI	Beijing, Doudian	CHN	39N38	116E06	✓	✗
BGL	Bengaluru, Doddaballapur	IND	13N15	077E29	✓	✗
BIB	Biblis	D	49N41	008E29	✓	✗
BIS	Bishkek, Krasnaya Rechka	KGZ	42N53	074E59	✓	✓
BJI	Baoji, Qishan, Shaanxi prov.	CHN	34N42	106E57	✓	✗
BKO	Bamako, Kati	MLI	12N45	008W03	✓	✗
BNB	Bonab	IRN	37N18	046E03	✗	✓
BNT	Bandar-e Torkaman	IRN	36N54	054E03	✗	✓
BOC	Bocaue, Bulacan prov.	PHL	14N48	120E55	✓	✗
BOT	Selebi-Phikwe, Moepeng Hill	BOT	21S57	027E38	✓	✓
BPH	Ban Phachi, Rasom	THA	14N24	100E47	✗	✓
BUE	Buenos Aires,					
	General Pacheco	ARG	34S26	058W37	✓	✗
CAH	Changchun, Jilin prov.	CHN	43N44	125E24	✓	✗
CDM	Col de La Madone ‡	F	43N47	007E25	✗	✓
CER	Cërrik, Shtërmen	ALB	41N00	020E00	✓	✗
CGR	Cape Gkreko	CYP	34N58	034E05	✗	✓
CHB	Chabahar	IRN	25N29	060E32	✗	✓
CHC	MBC Chuncheon (HLAN)	KOR	37N56	127E43	✗	✓
CHJ	Chongjin	KRE	41N45	129E42	✗	✓
CNI	Chennai	IND	13N08	080E07	✓	✗
DAN	Dangjin (HLCA) ‡	KOR	36N58	126E37	✗	✓
DAT	Datteln	D	51N39	007E20	✗	✓
DEH	Luxi, Dehong pref.,					
	Yunnan prov.	CHN	24N27	098E36	✓	✗
DEL	Delhi	IND	28N43	077E12	✓	✗

Code	Site	Ctry	Lat	Long	SW	MW
DHA	Dhabbaya	UAE	24N10	054E15	✓	✓
DJI	Djibouti, Dorale	DJI	11N34	043E04	✗	✓
DKA	Dhaka, Khabirpur	BGD	24N00	090E15	✓	✗
DOF	Dongfang, Hainan prov.	CHN	18N53	108E39	✗	✓
DOL	Dole	TZA	06S06	039E15	✓	✓
DRO	Droitwich	G	52N18	002W06	✗	✓
DSB	Dushanbe	TJK	38N29	068E48	✓	✓
ELA	El Arish	EGY	31N07	033E42	✗	✓
EMR	Emirler	TUR	39N24	032E51	✓	✗
ERD	Bergen, Erdal	NOR	60N27	005E13	✓	✗
ERV	Gavar, Noratus	ARM	40N25	045E11	✓	✗
EWN	Vandiver, AL	USA	33N30	086W29	✓	✗
FAN	Fangliao	TWN	22N23	120E34	✗	✓
FLA	Fllaka	ALB	41N22	019E30	✓	✗
GAL	Bacau, Galbeni	ROU	46N45	026E51	✓	✗
GJW	Geja	ETH	08N47	038E39	✓	✗
GOH	Göhren	D	53N32	011E37	✓	✗
GOY	Goyang,					
	Gyonggi-do Prefecture	KOR	37N36	126E51	✓	✓
GRV	Greenville, NC	USA	35N28	077W12	✓	✗
HAB	La Habana	CUB	22N57	082W33	✓	✗
HBN	Medorm, Babeldaob Island	PLW	07N27	134E29	✓	✗
HDN	Huadian, Jilin prov.	CHN	43N07	126E31	✗	✓
HDU	Guangzhou, Liantang,					
	Huadu dist.,	CHN	23N24	113E14	✗	✓
HEI	Shuangyashan,					
	Heilongjiang prov.	CHN	46N43	131E13	✗	✓
HJU	Haeju	KRE	38N02	125E43	✗	✓
HKG	Hongkong, Peng Chau	CHN	22N17	114E03	✗	✓
HKG	Hongkong, Peng Chau	CHN	22N17	114E03	✗	✓
HNL	Changzhou, Henglin,					
	Jiangsu prov.	CHN	31N42	120E07	✗	✓
HQB	Haciqabul, Pirsaat	AZE	40N03	049E03	✗	✓
HRI	Furman, SC	USA	32N41	081W08	✓	✗
HUH	Hohhot, Bikeqi,					
	Nei Menggu aut. reg.	CHN	40N48	111E12	✓	✗
HWA	Hwaseong,					
	Gyonggi-do Prefecture	KOR	37N13	126E47	✓	✓
HWD	Kimchaek, Hwadae county ‡	KRE	40N41	129E12	✗	✓
IBA	Iba, Zambales prov.	PHL	15N22	119E57	✓	✗
IKO	Ikorodu ‡	NIG	06N36	003E30	✓	✗

Code	Site	Ctry	Lat	Long	SW	MW
INB	Red Lion, PA	USA	39N54	076W35	✓	✗
IRA	Iranawila	CLN	07N30	079E48	✓	✗
ISL	Islamabad, Rawat	PAK	33N28	073E12	✓	✗
ISS	Issoudun	F	46N56	001E53	✓	✗
JAK	Jakarta, Cimanggis	INS	06S24	106E52	✓	✗
JAL	Jalandhar	IND	31N09	075E47	✗	✓
JEJ	Jeju (HLAZ)	KOR	33N29	126E23	✗	✓
JHR	Milton, FL	USA	30N39	087W05	✓	✗
JIN	Jinhua, Lanxi, Zhejiang prov.	CHN	29N07	119E19	✓	✗
JOL	Jolfa	IRN	38N56	045E36	✗	✓
KAB	Kabul	AFG	34N32	069E20	✓	✓
KAC	Karachi, Landhi ‡	PSK	24N55	067E00	✓	✗
KAM	Tehran, Kamalabad	IRN	35N50	050E52	✓	✗
KAN	Kangnam	KRE	38N50	125E40	✗	✓
KAS	Kashgar (Kashi), Sayibage, Xinjiang Uighur	CHN	39N21	075E46	✓	✓
KBD	Kuwait, Kabd ‡	KWT	29N09	047E46	✓	✗
KCH	Grigoriopol, Maiac	MDA	47N17	029E25	✓	✓
KHO	Khost, Tani	AFG	33N20	069N56	✗	✓
KHR	Kharkiv, Taranivka	UKR	49N38	036E07	✗	✓
KIA	Bandar e-Kiashahr	IRN	37N25	050E01	✗	✓
KIH	Kish Island	IRN	26N34	053E56	✗	✓
KIM	Gimje	KOR	35N49	126E52	✓	✓
KKT	Chinsurah	IND	23N02	088E21	✗	✓
KLL	Kall, Krekel	D	50N29	006E31	✓	✗
KNG	Kanggye	KRE	41N01	126E39	✓	✗
KNX	Kununurra	AUS	15S49	128E40	✓	✗
KOU	Kouhu	TWN	23N32	120E10	✓	✗
KUJ	Kujang	KRE	40N05	126E07	✓	✗
KUN	Kunming, Anning, Yunnan prov.	CHN	24N53	102E30	✓	✓
KWT	Kuwait, Umm Al-Rimam	KWT	29N31	047E40	✓	✓
LAM	Lampertheim	D	49N36	008E32	✓	✗
LRA	Base Antártica Esperanza	ATA	63S24	057W00	✓	✗
LUK	Lugang	TWN	24N03	120E25	✗	✓
LUS	Lusaka, Makeni Ranch ‡	ZMB	15S32	028E00	✓	✗
MAN	Manzini, Mpangela Ranch	SWZ	26S20	031E36	✓	✓
MCR	Fontbonne, Mont Agel (Naya Utility Stn)	F	43N46	007E26	✓	✗
MDC	Talata Volonondry	MDG	18S45	047E37	✓	✗
MEK	Mek'ele	ETH	13N30	039E29	✗	✓
MER	Mersin	TUR	36N49	034E44	✗	✓
MEY	Meyerton, Bloemendal	AFS	26S35	028E08	✓	✗
MIN	Minxiong	TWN	23N34	120E26	✗	✓
MNS	Minsk, Kalodziscy	BLR	53N58	027E47	✗	✓
MOS	Moosbrunn	AUT	48N00	016E28	✓	✗
MRN	Marnach	LUX	50N03	006E05	✗	✓
MSK	Moskva	RUS	55N45	037E37	✗	✓
MTH	Marathon Key, FL	USA	24N42	081W05	✗	✓
MUL	Luanda, Mulenvos	AGL	08S51	013E19	✓	✓
MUM	Mumbai	IND	19N11	072E48	✓	✗
MWV	Mahajanga ‡	MDG	15S43	046E26	✓	✗
NAD	Nador	MRC	35N03	002W55	✓	✓
NAK	Nakhon Sawan	THA	15N49	100E04	✓	✗
NAU	Nauen	D	52N39	012E55	✓	✗
NLS	Anchor Point, AK	ALS	59N45	151W44	✓	✗
NNN	Nanning, Guangxi Zhuang aut. reg.	CHN	22N48	108E11	✓	✗
NOB	Noblejas	E	39N57	003W26	✓	✗
OMO	Can Tho, Ô Môn	VTN	10N07	105E34	✗	✓
ORG	Ourgla ‡	ALG	31N55	005E04	✓	✗
PAN	Panaji	IND	15N27	073E51	✓	✗
PAO	Baozhong	TWN	23N43	120E18	✓	✗
PAR	Parakou	BEN	09N21	002E37	✓	✓
PHT	Tinang	PHL	15N22	120E37	✓	✗
PIN	Pinneberg	D	53N40	009E48	✓	✗
PKA	Petrivka	UKR	49N59	030E55	✗	✓
PUG	Palauig	PHL	15N28	119E55	✓	✗
PUT	Puttalam	CLN	07N58	079E48	✗	✓
PYO	Pyongyang	KRE	39N03	125E42	✓	✗
QSH	Qasr-e Shirin	IRN	34N27	045E37	✗	✓
QUI	Quito, Mount Pichincha	EQU	00S10	078W32	✓	✗
RAJ	Rajkot	IND	22N30	070E31	✗	✓
RAN	Rangitaiki	NZL	38S51	176E26	✓	✗
RBN	Rabouni	ALG	27N33	008W06	✓	✓
RIY	Riyadh	ARS	24N49	046E52	✓	✗
RME	Riga (Daugavgriva), (R. Merkurs)	LVA	57N02	024E01	✗	✓
RNO	New Orleans, LA	USA	29N50	090W07	✓	✗
ROB	Rohrbach	D	48N36	011E33	✓	✗
ROU	Roumoules	F	43N48	006E10	✗	✓
SAG	Samgo	KRE	38N02	126E32	✓	✗
SAI	Saipan, Agingan Point	MRA	15N07	145E42	✓	✗
SAN	Sana'a ‡	YEM	15N23	044E12	✓	✓
SAO	Pinheira	STP	00N18	006E45	✓	✓
SAS	Sasnovy	BLR	53N25	028E31	✗	✓
SDA	Agat, Facpi Point	GUM	13N20	144E39	✓	✗
SEO	Seoul, Incheon (HLKX)	KOR	37N25	126E45	✗	✓
SEP	Sepo ‡	KRE	38N40	127E22	✗	✓
SHA	Kunming, Shalang, Yunnan prov.	CHN	25N41	102E41	✓	✗
SHI	Shijak	ALB	41N20	019E33	✓	✗
SHP	Shepparton	AUS	36S19	145E25	✓	✗
SIR	Sirjan	IRN	29N36	055E47	✓	✗
SIT	Kaunas, Sitkunai	LTU	55N03	023E49	✓	✗
SKO	Skopje, Sveti Nikole	MKD	41N47	021E53	✗	✓
SLA	A'Seela	OMA	21N55	059E37	✓	✗
SLS	Sala, Ringvalla	S	16E30	059N55	✓	✗
SMF	Mykolaiv, Luch	UKR	46N49	032E13	✗	✓
SMG	Santa Maria di Galeria	CVA	42N03	012E19	✓	✗
SNG	Singapore	SNG	01N25	103E43	✓	✗
SOF	Sofia, Kostinbrod	BUL	42N49	023E11	✓	✗
SUW	Suwon, Osan, Gyonggi-do Prefecture	KOR	37N09	127E00		✗
SWO	Sangwon	KRE	38N53	126E06	✗	✓
SZG	Shijiazhuang,					

Code	Site	Ctry	Lat	Long	SW	MW
	Nanpozhuang, Hebei prov.	CHN	38N13	114E06	✓	✗
TAC	Toshkent	UZB	41N13	069E09	✓	✗
THU	Thumrait	OMA	17N38	053E56	✓	✗
TIG	Bucuresti	ROU	44N45	026E06	✓	✗
TIN	Tinian	MRA	15N03	145E36	✓	✗
TNN	Tainan	TWN	23N03	120E10	✓	✗
TRM	Trincomalee,					
	Perkara (Former DW Relay)	CLN	08N45	081E08	✓	✓
TSH	Tanshui	TWN	25N11	121E25	✓	✗
TSU	Taiwan (exact site unknown)	TWN	-	-	✓	✓
TTS	Tartus	SYR	34N57	035E53	✗	✓
TTU	Tartu, Kavastu	EST	58N25	027E06	✗	✓
TUT	Tuticorin	IND	08N49	078E05	✗	✓
TWB	Bonaire, Belnem	BES	12N06	068W17	✗	✓
TWR	Merizo	GUM	13N17	144E40	✓	✗
TWW	Lebanon, TN	USA	36N17	086W06	✓	✗
TYB	Tayebad	IRN	34N44	060E48	✗	✓
UBA	Ulaanbaatar, Honhor	MNG	47N48	107E11	✓	✓
UDO	Udon Thani (Udorn),					
	Ban Dung.	THA	17N40	103E12	✓	✗
UIW	Suwon, Uiwang,					
	Gyonggi-do Prefecture	KOR	37N18	126E58	✓	✗
URU	Ürümqi, Hutubi,					
	Xinjiang Uighur aut. reg.	CHN	44N09	086E54	✓	✓
VAT	Vatican City ‡	CVA	41N54	012E27	✓	✓
VIE	Vientiane	LAO	18N00	102E38	✓	✗
VIR	Virrat, Liedenpohja	FIN	62N23	023E37	✓	✓
VNI	Son Tay	VTN	21N12	105E22	✓	✗
VOH	Rancho Simi, CA	USA	34N15	118W39	✓	✗
WAV	Wavre	BEL	50N45	004E35	✗	✓
WCR	Nashville, TN	USA	36N12	086W54	✓	✗
WNM	Weenermoor	D	53N12	007E19	✓	✗
WOF	Woofferton	G	52N19	002W43	✓	✗
WRB	Manchester, TN	USA	35N37	086W01	✓	✗
XIA	Xi'an, Xianyang,					
	Shaanxi prov.	CHN	34N22	108E37	✓	✗
XUW	Xuanwei, Yunnan prov.	CHN	26N08	104E01	✓	✓
YAM	Koga, Yamata,					
	Ibaraki prefecture	J	36N10	139E49	✓	✗

Code	Site	Ctry	Lat	Long	SW	MW
YAN	Yangon, Mayangon					
	(R. Myanmar)	BRM	16N52	096E10	✓	✗
YFR	Okeechobee, FL	USA	27N27	080W56	✓	✗
ZAB	Zabol	IRN	31N02	061E33	✗	✓
ZAH	Zahedan	IRN	29N28	060E52	✓	✗
ZAK	Zakaki (located at Lady's					
	Mile, Akrotiri SBA)	CYP	34N37	033E00	✗	✓

NB: Where the symbol ‡ is shown after a transmitter site name, this indicates that the site was not being used for international MW or SW broadcasts at the time of publication. Some inactive sites are in the process of being constructed, or repaired, while others are simply dormant and could possibly be used again.
If a site on the list is known to have been dismantled or decommissioned it will be removed.

TARGET AREA CODES

Code	Target Area	Code	Target Area	Code	Target Area	Code	Target Area
Af	Africa	Cau	Caucasia	ME	Middle East	SAs	Southern Asia
Am	Americas	EAf	Eastern Africa	Med	Mediterranean	SEA	South East Asia
As	Asia	EAs	Eastern Asia	NAf	Northern Africa	WAf	Western Africa
Atl	Atlantic Ocean	EEu	Eastern Europe	NAm	North America	WAs	West Asia
CAf	Central Africa	Eu	Europe	NEu	Northern Europe	WEu	Western Europe
CAm	Central America	FE	Far East	Pac	Pacific Ocean		
Car	Caribbean	IOc	Indian Ocean	SAf	Southern Africa		
CAs	Central Asia	LAm	Latin America	SAm	South America		

DOMESTIC SW TRANSMITTER SITES

Coordinate System: WGS84 (rounded)

NB: For coordinates of sites that are jointly used for National and International/COTB services, see the International Transmitter Sites table

Ctry	Site	Lat	Long	Ctry	Site	Lat	Long
AUS	Alice Springs	23S42	133E53	BOL	Tumupasa	14S09	067W55
AUS	Katherine	14S28	132E16	BOL	Uyuni	20S27	066W49
AUS	Tennant Creek	19S40	134E10	BOL	Yura	20S02	066W10
AZE	Stepanakert	39N49	046E44	BRM	Naypyitaw	19N45	096E11
B	Aparecida	23S00	045W00	BRM	Pyin U Lwin	22N01	096E33
B	Araguaína	07S16	048W18	BRM	Yangon	16N52	096E09
B	Araraquara	21S47	048W10	BTN	Thimphu	27N29	089E37
B	Belém	01S27	048W29	CAN	Calgary	50N54	113W53
B	Belo Horizonte	19S54	043W54	CAN	St. John's	47N34	052W49
B	Boa Vista	02N51	060W43	CAN	Toronto	43N30	079W38
B	Bragança	01S02	046W46	CAN	Vancouver	49N08	123W12
B	Brasilía	15S36	048W08	CHL	Putre	18S12	069W35
B	Cachoeira Paulista	22S39	045W01	CHL	Temuco	38S41	072W35
B	Camboriú	26S59	048W38	CHN	Fuzhou	26N06	119E24
B	Campo Grande	20S24	054W35	CHN	Guiyang	26N25	106E36
B	Coari	04S08	063W07	CHN	Hailar	49N02	119E45
B	Congonhas	20S30	043W53	CHN	Hezuo	35N06	102E54
B	Cruzeiro do Sul	07S40	072W39	CHN	Lingshi	36N52	111E56
B	Cuiabá	15S36	056W06	CHN	Xichang	27N49	102E14
B	Curitiba	25S23	049W10	CHN	Xining	36N38	101E36
B	Foz do Iguaçu	25S31	054W34	CLM	Puerto Lleras	03N16	073W22
B	Goiânia	16S43	049W18	CLM	S. José del Guaviare	02N34	072W38
B	Ibitinga	21S43	048W47	COD	Bunia	01N32	030E11
B	Limeira	22S34	047W25	D	Erlangen	49E58	011E00
B	Londrina	23S18	051W13	D	Hannover	52N22	009E44
B	Macapá	00N04	051W04	EQA	Quito	00S11	078W32
B	Manaus	03S04	060W00	EQA	Saraguro	03S42	079W18
B	Parintins	02S38	056W44	EQA	Tena	01S00	077W48
B	Porto Alegre	30S03	051W10	ERI	Asmara	15N13	038E53
B	Porto Velho	08S45	063W54	ETH	Addis Ababa	08N58	038E43
B	Rio Branco	09S58	067S49	ETH	Geja Dera	08N46	038E40
B	Rio de Janeiro	22S57	043W13	FSM	Ninseitamw	06N58	158E12
B	Santa Maria	29S44	053W33	GEO	Sokhumi	43N00	041E04
B	São Gonçalo	22S49	043W04	GNE	Malabo	03N45	008E47
B	Santarém	02S27	054W43	GTM	Chiquimula	14N48	089W32
B	S. Gabriel da Cachoeira	00S09	067W03	GUY	Georgetown	06N46	058W14
B	São Paulo	23S33	046W39	IND	Aizawl	23N43	092E43
B	Tefé	03S24	064W45	IND	Bhopal	23N15	077E29
B	Xapuri	10S40	068W30	IND	Gangtok	27N20	088E40
BGD	Shavar	23N52	090E16	IND	Guwahati	26N09	091E39
BOL	Camargo	20S38	065W15	IND	Hyderabad	17N20	078E34
BOL	Cochabamba	17S23	066W11	IND	Imphal	24N37	093E54
BOL	La Paz	16S30	068W08	IND	Itanagar	27N05	093E35
BOL	Reyes	14S18	067W23	IND	Jaipur	26N55	075E45
BOL	Riberalta	10S59	066W06	IND	Jammu	32N47	074E49
BOL	S. Ignacio de Velasco	16S22	060W57	IND	Jeypore	18N55	082E34
BOL	S. José de Chiquitos	17S53	060W45	IND	Kohima	25N43	094E02
BOL	S. Ana del Yacuma	13S45	065W32	IND	Kolkata	22N22	088E17
BOL	Santa Cruz	17S46	063W11	IND	Kurseong	26N55	088E19
BOL	Siglo Veinte	18S23	066W38	IND	Leh	34N07	077E35
BOL	Trinidad	14S50	064W54	IND	Lucknow	26N53	081E03

Ctry	Site	Lat	Long	Ctry	Site	Lat	Long
IND	Port Blair	11N37	092E45	PRU	Pichanaki	10S55	074W52
IND	Shillong	25N34	091E56	PRU	Puerto Maldonado	12S37	069W11
IND	Shimla	31N10	077E12	PRU	Quillabamba	12S49	072W41
IND	Srinagar	34N02	074E54	PRU	Santiago de Chuco	08S09	078W10
IND	Thiruvananthapuram	08N27	076E56	PRU	Sicuani	14S15	071W12
INS	Makassar	05S10	119E25	PRU	Tarma	11S28	075W41
INS	Merauke	08S30	140E24	PRU	Urubamba	13N18	072W07
INS	Nabire	03S22	135E29	SLM	Honiara	09S25	160E03
INS	Palangkaraya	02S12	113E50	SOM	Garoowe	08N24	048E29
INS	Palu	00S51	119E53	SOM	Hargaysa	09N34	44E04
INS	Wamena	04S06	138E57	TWN	Kuanyin	25N02	121E06
J	Nagara	35N28	140E12	UGA	Kampala	00N19	032E37
J	Nemuro	43N17	145E34	UGA	Mukono	00N21	032E45
KRE	Hamhung	39N55	127E31	UKR	Zaporizhzhia	47N51	035E09
KRE	Hyesan	41N23	128E10	URG	Artigas	30S25	056W29
KRE	Pyongsong	40N14	125E49	URG	Castillos	34S16	053W56
KRE	Sariwon	38N31	125E46	URG	Montevideo	34S50	056W18
LBR	Monrovia	06N14	010W42	VTN	Buôn Mê Thuôt	12N40	108E12
MDG	Ambohidrano	18S47	047E29	VTN	Xuân Mai	20N53	105E34
MEX	México	19N26	099W08	VUT	Port-Vila	17S45	168E22
MNG	Altay	46N19	096E15	ZMB	Lusaka	15S30	028E15
MNG	Mörön	49N37	100E10				
NIG	Kaduna	10N45	007E33				
NPL	Khumaltar	27N39	085E20				
PNG	Alotau	10S18	150E28				
PNG	Buka	05S25	154E40				
PNG	Daru	09S05	143E10				
PNG	Kavieng	02S34	150E48				
PNG	Kerema	07S59	145E46				
PNG	Kimbe	05S36	150E10				
PNG	Kiunga	06S07	141E17				
PNG	Kundiawa	06S00	144E57				
PNG	Lae	06S41	146E54				
PNG	Lorengau	02S01	147E15				
PNG	Madang	05S14	145E45				
PNG	Mendi	06S13	143E39				
PNG	Popondetta	08S45	148E15				
PNG	Port Moresby	09S26	147E11				
PNG	Rabaul	04S13	152E07				
PNG	Tabubil	05S17	141E14				
PNG	Vanimo	02S42	141E18				
PNG	Wabag	05S28	143E40				
PNG	Wewak	03S35	143E40				
PRU	Arequipa	16S25	071W32				
PRU	Atalaya	10S44	073W45				
PRU	Bolívar	07S16	077W47				
PRU	Cerro de Pasco	10S41	076W16				
PRU	Chachapoyas	06S10	077W50				
PRU	Chazuta	06S34	076W08				
PRU	Chiclayo	06S47	079W47				
PRU	Cusco	13S32	071W57				
PRU	Huancabamba	05S14	079W24				
PRU	Huancavelica	12S45	075W03				
PRU	Huancayo	12S05	075W12				
PRU	Huanta	12S54	074W13				
PRU	Huánuco	09S56	076W15				
PRU	Huaraz	09S33	077W31				
PRU	Iquitos	03S51	073W13				
PRU	Junín	11S11	076W00				
PRU	Líma	12S06	077W03				

CLUBS FOR DXERS & INTERNATIONAL LISTENERS

This section lists non-commercial hobby clubs serving international radio enthusiasts. Most clubs are orientated to DXing, the reception of distant radio stations, some are oriented to programme listening. Many clubs produce bulletins on a regular basis. Sample copies of club periodicals are often available in pdf-format, or mailed upon request per post for return postage (contact the club for payment details). For officially multilingual countries, the language(s) used in club publications (and/or activities) is indicated when known; for non-English speaking countries also if a publication is partly or entirely in English: EE = English, FF = French, GG = German, II = Italian, JJ = Japanese, SS = Spanish. This list does not include clubs run by commercial publications or by individual broadcasters.

EUROPE

European DX Council (EDXC) (Umbrella organization of DX Clubs in Europe) c/o Kari Kivekäs, Parmaajanpolku 3 B 11, 00750 Helsinki Finland. General Secretary: Kari Kivekäs (**E:** ksk@sdxl.org), Assistant General Secretary: Jan-Mikael Nurmela, Finland (**E:** jmn@sdxl.org) **W:** edxcnews.wordpress.com

AUSTRIA: Austrian DX Board (ADXB-OE) (Club der Freunde elektronischer Medien - Rundfunk global), Postfach 1000, 1082 Wien. **E:** office@adxb-oe.org **W:** www.adxb-oe.org Pub: *Rundbrief* (quarterly). Annual DX camp. Member of AGDX (Germany); club members receive the monthly AGDX publication *Radio-Kurier - weltweit hören*.

BELGIUM: DX-Antwerp, Steynstraat 104, 2660 Hoboken. (Flemish) **E:** info@dx-antwerp.com **W:** www.dx-antwerp.com Pub: *DXA-Bulletin* (quarterly, pdf)

CZECH REPUBLIC/SLOVAKIA: Czechoslovak DX Club (CSDXC), c/o Václav Dosoudil, Horní 9, 768 21 Kvasice, Czech Republic. **E:** mail@dx.cz **W:** www.dx.cz Pub: *Radio* (pdf)

DENMARK: Danish Shortwave Club International (DSWCI), Tavleager 31, 2670 Greve. **E:** kaj.bredahl@mail.dk **W:** www.dswci. org Pub (all EE): Pub: *Shortwave News*, *DX-Window* (bi-weekly by email), *Tropical Bands Monitor* (pdf, updated monthly), *Domestic Broadcasting Survey* (Annual, pdf) **NB:** The club will be dissolved by December 2016 – **Dansk DX Lytter Klub (DDXLK)**, P.O.Box 112, 8960 Randers SØ. **E:** ddxlk@ddxlk.dk **W:** www.ddxlk.dk Pub: *DX-AKTUELLT* (Swedish/Danish, joint publication with SDXF, Sweden; bimonthly, printed & pdf)

FINLAND: Finlands Svenska DX-Förbund rf (FSDXF), P.O.Box 9, 68601 Jakobstad (Umbrella organization of Swedish language DX clubs in Finland). **W:** uk.groups.yahoo.com/neo/groups/fsdxf/info (newsgroup) – **Suomen DX-liitto ry (SDXL)**, Annankatu 31-33, C 49 c, 00100 Helsinki (Umbrella organization of Finnish language DX clubs) **E:** toimisto@sdxl.fi **W:** www.sdxl.fi Pub (Finnish/EE): *Radiomaailma* (by post), *DX-clusive* (by email)

FRANCE: Radio Club des Écouteurs Lorraine, 19 rue des Jeux, 54570 Foug. **E:** alinco54@orange.fr **W:** www.rcdel.fr – **Radio Club du Perche**, 82 bis, Coat Canton, 29140 Rosporden. **E:** g.lelouet@orange.fr **W:** radioclub.perche.free.fr – **Radio DX Club d'Auvergne**, Centre Municipal P. et M. Curie, 2 bis, Rue du Clos Perret, 63100 Clermont-Ferrand. **E:** radiodxclub63@gmail.com **W:** www.radiodx.fr – **Union des Écouteurs Français**, BP 31, 92242 Malakoff Cédéx. **E:** tsfinfo@u-e-f.net **W:** www.u-e-f.net

GERMANY: Arbeitsgemeinschaft DX e.V. (AGDX), Postfach 1214, 61282 Bad Homburg (Umbrella organization for the German DX clubs adxb-DL, UKW/TV Arbeitskreis der AGDX, Worldwide DX Club, and for the Austrian DX-Board) **E:** mail@agdx.de **W:** www. agdx.de Pub: see ADDX. – **Assoziation Deutschsprachiger Kurzwellenhörer e.V. (ADDX)**, Scharsbergweg 14, 41189

Mönchengladbach. **E:** kurier@addx.de **W:** www.addx.de Pub (jointly for members of ADDX & AGDX, and ADXB-OE in Austria): *Radio-Kurier - weltweit hören* (monthly; printed & pdf) – **Assoziation Junger DXer e.V. (adxb-DL)**, c/o Thomas Schubaur, Neufnachstr. 30, 86850 Fischach. **E:** dl1ts@t-online.de **W:** www.adxb-dl.de – **Deutscher Welt-Radioclub e.V. (DWRC)**, c/o Bernd Schilling, Hüling 11, 53332 Bornheim. – **Eastside DX (EDX)**, c/o Jens Adolph, 04159 Leipzig-Wahren (Pittler) **E:** eastsidedx@mail.com – **Freundeskreis Berliner Empfangsamateure e.V.**, Postfach 200113, 13511 Berlin. **E:** berliner-empfangsamateure@t-online. de – **Hamburger Freunde des Rundfunkfernempfangs**, c/o Dieter Schäfer, Am Sportplatz 18, 24629 Kisdorf. **E:** dl1lad@darc. de – **Kurzwellenfreunde Brand**, c/o Hans-Jürgen Schmelzer, Mitterteicher Str. 15, 95643 Tirschenreuth. **E:** hugotir@t-online. de – **Kurzwellenclub Schwalmtal e.V.**, c/o Helmut Reitzer Jr, Willy-Rösler-Str. 41, 41366 Schwalmtal. **E:** dk0kws@qsl.net **W:** www.qsl.net/dk0kws – **Kurzwellenfreunde Rhein/Ruhr e.V.**, c/o U. Schnelle, Kurfürstenstr. 37, 45883 Gelsenkirchen. **E:** kwfr-web@ kwfr.de **W:** www.kwfr.de – **Kurzwellenfreunde Sachsen (KWFS)**, c/o AGDX e.V., Postfach 1214, 61282 Bad Homburg. **E:** dk5tl@ qsl.net – **Kurzwellenfreunde Wuppertal (KWFW)**, c/o Werner Kortmann, Postfach 220342, 42373 Wuppertal – **Oldenburger Kurzwellenfreunde**, c/o Olaf C. Hänßler, Sandweg 98, 26135 Oldenburg. **E:** olaf.haenssler@gmail.com **W:** www.member.uni-oldenburg.de/olaf.haenssler/olaf/OKF – **Radiofreunde NRW**, c/o Christof Proft, Kurfürstenstr. 15, 52066 Aachen. **E:** radiofreunde. nrw@gmail.com **W:** www.radiofreunde-nrw.de – **Radio Japan Club Brilon (RJCB)**, c/o Reinhard Reese, Niederbeckstr. 23, 40472 Düsseldorf. **E:** rreese@gmx.net **W:** radio-japan-club-brilon.gmx-home.de – **Rhein-Main-Radio-Club e.V. (RMRC)**, Am Gänsborn 9, 61476 Kronberg. **E:** mail@rmrc.de **W:** www.rmrc.de – **UKW/TV Arbeitskreis der AGDX**, c/o H.-J. Kuhlo, Wilhelm-Leuschner-Str. 293B, 64347 Griesheim. (FM/TV only) **E:** sekretariat@ukwtv.de **W:** www.ukwtv.de Pub: *Reflexion* (pdf) – **Worldwide DX Club (WWDXC)**, Postfach 1214, 61282 Bad Homburg. **E:** mail@wwdxc.de **W:** www.wwdxc.de. Pub: *DX-Magazine* (EE)

HUNGARY: Hungarian DX Club, c/o Tibor Szilagyi **E:** tiszi2035@ yahoo.com.

IRELAND: Irish DX Club, c/o Edward Dunne, 17 Anville Drive, Kilmacud, Stillorgan, Co. Dublin **E:** irishdxclub@live.ie Pub: *MediaWatch* (by email)

ITALY: Associazione Italiana Radioascolto (AIR), C.P. 1338, 10100 Torino (AD). **E:** redazione@air-radio.it **W:** www.air-radio.it Pub: *Radiorama* (monthly, pdf) – **BCL Sicilia Club**, c/o Roberto Scaglione, C.P. 119, Succursale 34, 90144 Palermo (PA). **E:** info@bclnews.it **W:** www.bclnews.it – **Coordinamento del Radioascolto (Co.Rad)**, c/o Dario Monferini (Web-based umbrella organisation of various Italian DX clubs) **E:** info@corad.net **W:** www. corad.net – **FM-DX Italy**, c/o Fabrizio Carnevalini (Web-based, FM-TV DX only) **E:** fabrizio58it@yahoo.it **W:** www.fmdx.altervista. org – **Gruppo d'Ascolto Radio dello Stretto**, c/o Giovanni Sergi, Via Sibari 40, 98149 Messina (CI). (II) **E:** gsergi5050@hotmail.com **W:** www.polistenaweb.it/gars Pub: *Radio Notizie* (quarterly, printed & pdf) – **Gruppo d'Ascolto Radio Televisivo della Sicilia**, c/o Gioacchino Stallone, Via G.Falcone 11, Lotto 27, interno 3, 91025 Marsala (TP). (local activity) – **Gruppo Radio Ascolto Bologna**, c/o Elio Antonucci, Bologna (Web-based) **E:** radioascolto@elio.org **W:** www.elio.org/radioascolto – **Gruppo Radio Ascolto Utility World**, c/o Quirino Tirelli, Via T. Rossi 6, 82100 Benevento **E:** qtirell@hotmail.it – **Play-DX**, c/o Dario Monferini, Via Davanzati 8, 20158 Milano (MI). (II/EE/SS) (specialises in difficult DX) **E:** info@ playdx.com **W:** www.playdx.com Pub: *PLAY-DX* (weekly)

NETHERLANDS: Benelux DX Club (BDXC), Rietdekkerstraat 40, 1445 KG Purmerend. **E:** secretaris@bdxc.nl **W:** www.bdxc.nl Pub: *BDXC-Bulletin* (Dutch/EE, printed and pdf)

RUSSIA: Club of DX-ers, c/o Vadim Alexeew, Moscow **E:** rts-center@mtu-net.ru **W:** dxing.ru Pub: *MIDXB* (by email) – **Novosibirsk DX Club**, c/o Igor Yaremenko, Novosibirsk. **E:** dxer@yandex.ru **W:** www.novosibdx.info – **Russian DX League**, c/o Anatoly Klepov, Moscow **E:** rusdx@yandex.ru **W:** rusdx.narod.ru Pub: *RUS-DX* (separate RR/EE versions, by email) – **Sankt-Peterburg DX Club**, c/o Alexander Beryozkin, St.Peterburg **E:** dxspb@nrec.spb.ru – **Tomsk DX Club**, c/o Vladimir Kovalenko, Tomsk. **E:** tomskdx@sibmail.com

SPAIN: Asociación DX Barcelona (ADXB), P.O. Box 335, 08080 Barcelona. **E:** info@mundodx.net **W:** www.mundodx.net Pub: *MundoDX-MundiMedia* (SS/Catalan) – **Asociación Española de Radioescucha (AER)**, Apartado 10014, 50080 Zaragoza. **E:** general@aer.org.es **W:** aer.org.es Pub: *El Dial (D), El Dial (FM)* (by email) – **S500 DX Club**, c/o Álvaro López Osuma, c/ Santa Micaela, 1 2° Derecha, 18015 Granada. **E:** alvak7@yahoo.es **W:** www.clubs500.es

SWEDEN: Arctic Radio Club (ARC), c/o Tore Larsson, Frejagatan 14A, 52143 Falköping (MW only) **E:** tore.larsson@beta.telenordia.se **W:** arcticradioclub.blogspot.com Pub: *MV-Eko* (Swedish/EE, by email) – **Sveriges DX Förbund (SDXF)**, Box 1097, 40523 Göteborg (Umbrella organization; list of local member clubs: see website). **E:** registrator@sdxf.se **W:** www.sdxf.se Pub: *DX-aktuellt* (Swedish/ Danish, joint publication with DDXLD, Denmark; bi-monthly, printed & pdf)

SWITZERLAND: Radio- und Fernseh- Club Basel und Umgebung (RFCB), c/o Hans-Peter Strub, Bündnerstrasse 65, 4055 Basel. (GG) **E:** hb9b@rfcb.ch **W:** www.rfcb.ch

UNITED KINGDOM: British DX Club (BDXC), 10 Hemdean Hill, Caversham, Reading RG4 7SB. **E:** bdxc@bdxc.org.uk **W:** www.bdxc.org.uk Pub: *Communication* (printed & pdf) – **International Shortwave League (ISWL)**, c/o Peter Lewis, 18 Bittaford Wood, Ivybridge, Devon, PL21 0ET. **E:** vfgnsu@yahoo.co.uk **W:** www.iswl.org.uk Pub: *Monitor* (pdf) – **Medium Wave Circle (MWC)**, c/o Herman Boel, Papeveld 3, 9320 Erembodegem-Aalst, Belgium (LW/MW only) **E:** herman@hermanboel.eu **W:** www.mwcircle.org Pub: *MW News* (pdf)

AFRICA

IVORY COAST: DX-Ivoire, c/o Jibirila Liasu, B.P. 197, Abidjan 20. (FF)

KENYA: DX Listeners' Club, c/o Oscar Machuki, PO Box 646, Kisii 4-0200. (EE/Swahili) (SW only) ☎ +254 721 534171 **E:** oscarmogire@yahoo.com

NIGERIA: Africa DX Association, c/o Mr. Friday I. Okoloise, NITEL, P.M.B. 23, Lafia, Plateau State. (EE) – **International DX Club**, Emmanuel Ezeani, P.O.Box 1633, Sokoto, Sokoto State. (EE) **E:** emmanuel_ezeani@yahoo.com

RÉUNION: Club DX de La Réunion, **E:** contest@rallye-dx.com **W:** www.rallye-dx.com (SW)

SÃO TOMÉ & PRÍNCIPE: Clube DX-STP, c/o Petter Leal Bouças, Av. 12 de Julho, Vila Maria (C.P. 490), São Tomé. **E:** petterboudx@hotmail.com

TANZANIA: Kemogemba DX Listeners Club, c/o Ras Franz Manko Ngogo, P.O.Box 71, Tarime, Mara. (EE/Swahili) ☎ + 255 755 814704 **E:** kemogemba@yahoo.com

TOGO: Club Inter Amitié Radio, CCF, B.P. 2090, Lomé. (FF) – **Groupe Endoc**, B.P. 2667, Lomé. (FF)

TUNISIA: Club des Auditeurs et de l'Amitié, c/o De Riadh Sakka, Route de Gremda Merkez Sahnoun, 3012 Sfax. (FF)

UGANDA: International DX Club of East Africa, c/o Samuel Ouma, P.B.Box 565, Iganga. (EE) ☎ +256 77 2444201 **E:** samuel.ouma@talk21.com **W:** www.facebook.com/idxeastafrica

ASIA

BANGLADESH: Aurora Listeners' Club, c/o Miss Kakali Rani, Harida Khalsi-6403, Madhnagar-Natore-6400 – **Basupara DX Listeners Club**, c/o Asfaqul Alam, Basupara, Nandangachi, Rajshahi 6260. **E:** bdxls@uymail.com – **International Radio Listeners Club**, Konabari, P.O.Nilnagor, Gazipur, Dhaka. (EE/Bengali) – **Online DX Forum**, c/o MD Azizul Alam Al-Amin, Gourhanga, Ghoramara, Rajshahi 6100. **E:** mtech@rajbd.com – **Wave Surfers' Association**, c/o Ashik Eqbal Tokon, Mohammadpur, Dhaka. **E:** rosedwlc@yahoo.com **W:** wsabd.webs.com; rosedwlc.webs.com. Pub: *DX-Net* (Bengali, quarterly)

INDIA: Apollo DX International, c/o Deepak Kumar Das, Dholi Sakra 843105, Dist. Muzaffarpur, Bihar – **Ardic DX Club**, c/o Jaisakthivel, T., Dept of Communication, Manonmaniam Sundranar University, Abishekapatti Post, Tirunelveli 627012, Tamil Nadu. ☎ +91 98413 66086 Pub: *DXers Guide* (EE quartely), *Sarvadesa Vanoli* (Tamil monthly). DX Prgr: Vaanoli Ulagam on AIR (Tamil). **E:** ardicdxclub@yahoo.co.in **W:** dxersguide.blogspot.com – **Asian DX League**, c/o Partha Sarathi Goswami, Kishalaya Book Stall, College Road, Siliguri 734001, West Bengal **E:** dxing@india.com **W:** www.dxinginfo.com – **Chaudhary Srota Sangh**, c/o Santosh Kumar (President), Kharauna Jairam, Kharauna Dih 843113, Dist. Muzaffarpur, Bihar – **Chaitak Listener Club**, P.O. Belga Nabodaypally Dt, Paschim, Medinipur 721424 **E:** sbchanu@gmail.com – **Chennai DX Club**, c/o K. Raja, 21 JP Koil St, Old Washermenpet, Chennai 600021, Tamil Nadu. **E:** chennaidxclub@gmail.com – **Foreign Radio Listeners' Club,** c/o Prasenjit Bhakat, 313/8 Ghoradhara, P.O Jhargram 721507, West Bengal. ☎ +91 3221 256084 **E:** frlclub@gmail.com – **Globe Radio DX Club (GRDXC)**, c/o Harjot Singh Brar, P.O.Box 158, Chandigarh 160017, Chandigarh. **E:** grdxc@yahoo.co.in – **Indian DX Club International**, GPO Box 646, Kolkata 700001, West Bengal. **E:** idxc.international@gmail.com **W:** www.idxci.in – **International DX Association**, c/o Bedanta Das, 1-No,Galiahati, Near Night School, Barpeta 781301, Assam. ☎ +91 3665 236267 **E:** das884@gmail.com Pub: *DX Times* (EE) – **Metali Listeners' Club**, c/o Mr Shivendu Paul, 49/36, Dr SG Dhar Lane, P.O. Khagra, Dist. Murshidabad 742103, West Bengal. **E:** metalilistenersclub@gmail.com ☎ +91 94348 58497 – **Minnakkal Kurinji DX Club**, c/o E. Selvaraj, Choolaimedu Street, Minnakkal, Dist. Namakkal 637505, Tamil Nadu. **E:** selvarajminnakkal@gmail.com – **Paribar Bandhu SWL Club**, c/o Mr Anand Mohan Bain, UCO Bank, 47/6, Nehru Nagar, P.O. Nehru Nagar, Bhilai, Dist. Durg 490020, Chattisgarh. **E:** anand_mohan10@yahoo.com ☎ +91 94255 21083, +91 78840 31648. – **Pollachi DX Club**, c/o Mr. N. Lakshmanan, Sri Mugha Bhavan, 44/77 Lac Colony, Dr Ansari Street, Pollachi 642001, Tamil Nadu. ☎ +91 98650 16402 **W:** pollachiradioclub.blogspot.com – **Span Radio Listeners' Club**, c/o A Ragu, Nandavankula Theru, Vedaraniam 614810, Tamil Nadu. ☎ +91 4369 318808 – **Utkarna Shrota Sangha**, c/o Mr. Rajib Bandopadhyay, Amrita Bhaban, P.O. Makardah 711409, Dist. Howrah, West Bengal ☎ +91 94334 28609, **E:** ussrajib@gmail.com – **World DX Club & Library**, c/o Baidyanath Upadhyaya, At Khairabarigaon, P.O. Khawrang, Udalguri 784509, Darrang, Assam. – **World DXing Club**, c/o Mr Madhab Ch. Sagour, 93/1, Mitrapara Road, P.O. Naihati 743 165, 24 Parganas (North), West Bengal. – **World Radio Club**, c/o Mr. Biswanath Mandal, Chak Harharia, P.O. Islampur 742304, Dist. Murshidabad, West Bengal. ☎ +91 3481 236534 **E:** bmandalwrc@rediffmail.com – **Young Stars Radio Club**, c/o Mr Hari Madugula, 40 Hastinapura Colony, Raghavendra Residency-FF4, Sainikpuri, Hyderabad 500094, Andhra Pradesh. **W:** ysrc.webs.com – **Youth International Radio Listeners' Club**, c/o Mr. Pranab Kumar Roy, Shyamnagar, 741 155, Nadia, West Bengal. ☎ +91 3471 252163 **E:** etherbarta@gmail.com Pub: *Etherbarta* (Bengali), *Radio Monitors' Guide* (EE)

INDONESIA: Borneo Listeners Club, Jalan Penjajap Timur 3A, Pemangkat, Kalimantan Barat 79453. (Indonesian/EE). **E:** h.rudi@yahoo.co.id **W:** www.bielsiklub.blogspot.com Pub: *Mediator* – **Indonesian DX Club (IDXC)**, P.O.Box 50, Kutoarjo 54201. (EE/Indonesian). **E:** contact@idxc.org **W:** www.idxc.org – **MAPEM Club**, c/o M. Jayadi D., 02 Tromolpos Pringgabaya, East Lombok, West Nusa Tenggara 83654. **E:** mapemclub2020@gmail.com **W:** mapemclub.org – **Media Monitoring Club**, c/o Summase A. Sanjaya, P.O.Box 1157 MKS, Makassar 90000. **E:** monitoringclub@yahoo.co.id **W:** monitoringclub.org

JAPAN: Asian Broadcasting Institute (ABI), P.O.Box 2334, Ginza Branch, Japan Post, Tokyo 100-8698. **E:** info@abiweb.jp **W:** www.abiweb.jp – **Japan Short Wave Club (JSWC)**, P.O.Box 44, Kamakura 248-8691. (JJ/EE) ☎▤ +81 467 43 2167 **W:** wwww5a.biglobe.ne.jp/~BCLSWL/jswc.html **E:** jswchq@live.jp Pub: *SW DX Guide* (JJ/EE) – **Nagoya DXers Circle (NDXC)**, c/o Shigenori Aoki, 2-51 Kasumori-cho, Nakamura-ku, Nagoya 453-0855. **W:** www.ndxc.org

KOREA (SOUTH): Northeast Asian Broadcasting Institute (NEABI), c/o SeKyung Park, #103-302, Geumho Apt, 240-32 Yeomchang-dong, Gangseo-gu, Seoul 157-861. **E:** neabipress@gmail.com **W:** www.neabi.com Pub: *Reports* (Korean, monthly)

NEPAL: Friendship Radio Club, c/o Mr Umesh Regmi, Tanki Sinuwari 5, District Morang, Biratnagar. **E:** friendshipradioclub@yahoo.com – **Listeners' Club of Nepal** (Reg. No.144), P.O.Box 126, Biratnagar-4. – **Small Giant Radio Listener Club** (Reg. No.17), P.O.Box 21110, Kathmandu

PAKISTAN: International Radio Listeners Club, Karachi. **E:** irlclub@hotmail.com **W:** sites.google.com/site/irlclub – **National Society of Pakistani DXers**, c/o Liaqat Ali, E-161/1, Iqbal Park, opposite Adil Hospital, Defence Housing Society Rd, Lahore Cantt. – **Pakistani Shortwave Listeners' Association**, c/o Muhammad Imran Mehr, 38/2 Habib Colony, Bahawalpur 63108, Punjab. ☎ +92 334 6865847, +92 300 6801719. **E:** imran.mehr@gmail.com Pub: *Radio World* (bi-monthly by email) – **Shortwave Listeners Club**, c/o Israr Ahmad Chaudhary, Street #2, Madina Park, Sheikhupura 39350, Punjab. **E:** pals_swlc@yahoo.com **W:** www.pals2000.webs.com – **Wonderful World of Shortwave (WWSW)**, c/o Baber Shehzad, 43 Habib Colony, Bahawalpur 63108, Punjab. **E:** baber73@yahoo.com. Pub: *News Letter of Pakistani DX-ers* (by email)

SRI LANKA: Union of Asian DXers (UADX), c/o Victor Goonetilleke, "Shangri-La" 298 Kolamunne, Piliyandala. **E:** victor.goonetileke@gmail.com **W:** dxasia-uadx.blogspot.com (EE)

PACIFIC

AUSTRALIA: Australian Radio DX Club (ARDXC), c/o John Wright, 29 Milford Road, Peakhurst, NSW 2210. **E:** dxer1234@gmail.com **W:** www.ardxc.info Pub: *Australian DX News Magazine* (printed & pdf) – **Electronic DX Press Radio Monitoring Association (EDXP)**, c/o Bob Padula, 404 Mont Albert Road, Mont Albert, VIC 3127. (Web-based club). **E:** bobpadula@mydesk.net.au **W:** edxp.yolasite.com

NEW ZEALAND: New Zealand Radio DX League, P.O. Box 178, Mangawhai 0540. **E:** secretary@radiodx.com **W:** www.radiodx.com Pub: *NZ DX Times* (monthly)

NORTH AMERICA

CANADA: Canadian International DX Club (CIDX), P.O.Box 67063-Lemoyne, St. Lambert, QC J4R 2T8. **E:** cidxclub@yahoo.com **W:** www.cidx.ca Pub: *The Messenger* (pdf, monthly) – **Club d'Ondes Courtes du Québec**, 5120, 35ème rue, Grand Mere, PO G9T 3N6. **E:** dduplessis@infoteck.qc.ca – **Ontario DX Association (ODXA)**, 3211 Centennial Drive, Apt. 23, Vernon, BC V1T 2T8. **E:** odxa@rogers.com **W:** www.odxa.on.ca – **Vancouver Shortwave Association**, P.O.Box 500, Vancouver, BC V5L 1C.

MEXICO: Audio Pico DX Club, c/o César Granillo, Ap. Postal 309, 94301 Orizaba, Veracruz – **Club DX Miguel Auza**, c/o Luis Antero Aguilar, Ap. Postal 38, 98330 Miguel Auza, Zacatecas – **Consultorio DX**, c/o Miguel Angel Rocha Gámez, Ap. Postal 31, 31820 Ascensión, Chihuahua – **Nayarit DX Club**, Ap. Postal 62, 63001 Tepic, Nayarit. **W:** www.naydx.8m.com – **Sociedad de Ingenieros Radioescuchas**, c/o Rafael Gustavo Grajeda Rosado, Ap. Postal 203, Admon. No.1, 91701 Veracruz, Veracruz. **E:** rggr681121@hotmail.com

USA: American Shortwave Listeners Club (ASWLC), c/o Stewart MacKenzie, 16182 Ballad Lane, Huntington Beach, CA 92649. – **Boston Area DXers**, c/o Paul Graveline, 9 Stirling St., Andover, MA 01810-1408 – **Central Indiana Shortwave Club**, c/o Steve Hammer, 2517 E. DePauw Road, Indianapolis, IN 46227-4404. – **Chicago Area DX Club**. Now defunct. **W:** home.earthlink.

net/~dxchicago. Website with article archive; updated & maintained by Christos Rigas (**E:** dxchicago@earthlink.net) – **DecalcoMania**, c/o Phil Bytheway, 9705 Mary NW, Seattle, WA 98117-2334. (Club for collectors of station promo, items and airchecks). **E:** phil_tekno@yahoo.com **W:** www.anarc.org/decal Pub: *DecalcoMania* – **Hampton Roads DX Association**, c/o Dr. Marc Fink, P.O.Box 2681, Chesapeake, VA 23327-2681. ☎ +1 757 547 3668 **E:** familyfoot@msn.com (LW, MW, SW, FM/TV) – **Indiana Recording Club**, c/o Bill Davies, 1729 E. 77th St., Indianapolis, IN 46240. (Club for airchecks and recordings of mediumwave stations). – **International Radio Club of America (IRCA)**, P.O.Box 60241, Lafayette, LA 70596. (MW only) **E:** ircamember@ircaonline.org **W:** www.ircaonline.org Pub: *DX Monitor* (by online or hardcopy subscription) – **Longwave Club of America (LWCA)**, 45 Wildflower Road, Levittown, PA 19057. **E:** billoliver@verizon.net **W:** www.lwca.org Pub: *The Lowdown* – **Miami Valley DX Club (MVDXC)**, P.O.Box 292132, Columbus, OH 43229. **W:** www.anarc.org/mvdxc Pub: *DX World.* – **Michigan Area Radio Enthusiasts Inc**, P.O.Box 200, Manchester, MI 48158. **E:** mare.radio@gmail.com – **Minnesota DX Club (MDXC)** c/o James Dale, 16330 Germane Ct W, Rosemount, MN 55068. **E:** mndxclub@charter.net **W:** www.frontiernet.net/~jadale Pub: *MDXC Newsletter* – **National Radio Club Inc (NRC)**, P.O.Box 473251, Aurora, CO 80047-3251. (MW only) **E:** sales@nrcdxas.org **W:** www.nrcdxas.org Pub: *DX News* (printed; bi-weekly in winter, monthly in summer), *E-DXN* (pdf) – **North American Shortwave Association (NASWA)**, 45 Wildflower Road, Levittown, PA 19057. **E:** billoliver@verizon.net **W:** www.naswa.net Pub: *The Journal* (by post) and *Flashsheet* (by email) – **Pacific Northwest/British Columbia DX Club**, c/o Bruce Portzer, 6546 19th Ave NE, Seattle WA 98115. **E:** phil_tekno@yahoo.com **W:** www.anarc.org/pnbcdxc Pub: *PNBCDXC newsletter* (every one or two months) – **Puna DX Club**, c/o Jerry Witham, P.O.Box 596, Keaau, HI 96749. – **Rocky Mountain Radio Listeners**, c/o Mike Curta, P.O.Box 470776, Aurora, CO 80047-0776. – **Southern California Area DXers**, c/o Bill Fisher Sr., 6398 Pheasant Drive, Buena Park, CA 90620-1356. **E:** williamfishersr@gmail.com – **Worldwide TV-FM DX Association (WFTDA)**, P.O.Box 501, Somersville, CT 06072 (FM/TV only). **E:** sales@wtfda.org **W:** www.wtfda.org Pub: *VUD* (via download).

SOUTH AMERICA

ARGENTINA: Grupo Radioescucha Argentino (GRA), c/o Marcelo A. Cornachioni, Alvarez Thomas 248, B1832DNF Lomas de Zamora, Buenos Aires. **E:** info@conexiongra.com.ar **W:** gruporadioescuchaargentino.wordpress.com

BRAZIL: Associação DX do Brasil, C.P. 4, 58300-970 Santa Rita, Paraíba. **E:** cartas@adxb.com.br **W:** www.adxb.com.br – **DX Clube do Brasil (DXCP)**, C.P. 1594, 09571-970 São Caetano do Sul (SP). **E:** dxcb@bol.com.br **W:** www.ondascurtas.com – **DX Clube Sem Fronteiras**, C.P. 77, 55002-970 Caruaru (PE). **W:** www.dxclubesem-fronteiras.com

CHILE: Club Diexista de Chile, Calle 3 Ponienta 55, Talca. **E:** chiledxclub@mixmail.com **W:** www.galeon.com/chiledxclub Pub: *Radiograma* – **Federación de Clubes de Radioaficionados de Chile (FEDERACHI)**, c/o Héctor Frías Jofre, Dr. Eduardo Cruz Coke 389, Oficina C, Casilla 9570, Santiago 21. **E:** federachi@federachi.cl **W:** www.federachi.cl

COLOMBIA: Grupo Internacional de Diexistas y Radioaficionados, c/o Miguel Bayona. **E:** m-bayona@hotmail.com

URUGUAY: DX Club Montevideo, Calle Batovi 2068, 11800 Montevideo. **E:** diexman@adinet.com.uy, diexman@montevideo.com.uy **W:** groups.yahoo.com/neo/groups/dxclubmontevideo/info (newsgroup)

VENEZUELA: Asociación Diexista de Venezuela, Ap. Postal 65657, Caracas 1066-A. **E:** marl1@hotmail.com – **Club Diexistas de la Amistad (CDXA)**, c/o Ing. Santiago San Gil Gonzáles, Ap. Postal 202, Barinas 5201-A, Estado Barinas. **E:** cdxainternacional@gmail.com **W:** diexismovenezolano.blogspot.com – **Venezuelan QSL Help**, c/o Winter Monges, Ap. Postal 1.116, Barquisimeto 3001-A, Lara. (SS/EE) **E:** venezuelanqslhelp@yahoo.com **W:** winter-monges.tripod.com/index-2.html

STANDARD TIME & FREQUENCY TRANSMISSIONS

What are STFTs?

Standard Time and Frequency Transmissions (STFTs) are transmissions aimed at testing and calibrating radio receivers and synchronizing clocks. When broadcast on shortwave, STFTs usually consist of continuous AM and/or SSB transmissions of 'beeps' or 'pips' every second (often referred to as 'Time Signals'), with the time in UTC (or local time) announced at certain intervals. Some stations broadcast for 24 hours a day while other stations run for up to a few hours daily or on certain days of the week.

Also listed in this chapter is a selection of standard broadcast and VLF utility stations that broadcast regular timechecks in modes other than AM/SSB. The VLF transmitters of the maritime navigation networks Loran-C/Chayka on 100kHz and similar VLF txs primarily used for navigation purposes, except for txs of the "Beta" system of the Russian Navy and BPL in P.R. China, are not included.

Using STFTs

STFTs are invaluable aids for the SW radio user. Not only do they allow listeners to synchronise clocks to UTC but they are also a handy tool for checking propagation and reception paths. Their most useful role for serious shortwave listeners, however, is for checking that equipment is performing as it should and to test for receiver frequency calibration errors.

Checking Performance

It is possible to carry out tests on a variety of frequencies ranging from 2500 to 20000kHz. First select an appropriate set of STFTs, perhaps by saving them into a set of memory channels if your radio has the facility. A quick check can be made for the characteristic ticks and pulses to ensure that there is a good reception path and that the STFT is currently active, before moving on to the tests themselves. Don't forget that it is essential to allow the radio to warm up for at least one hour before starting these tests.

The object of the exercise is to mix the incoming STFT signal with an internally generated signal from the radio's Beat Frequency Oscillator (BFO) and then tune the radio until the resulting whistle, or heterodyne as it is known, drops down to zero. This process of tuning for 'zero beat' then ensures that the radio is on exactly the same frequency as the transmission – any error shown on the dial will be the receiver error and any drift in tone will be receiver drift.

For most radios it will suffice to select either upper or lower sideband mode with a wide filter setting and use a loudspeaker or pair of headphones with a good low frequency audio performance. Many SW receivers have internal speakers which are not good when it comes to reproducing low notes so are useless for this procedure.

As you carefully tune down and hear the note drop, you should find that the S-meter needle starts to fluctuate. This means that you are very close to 'zero beat'. The lower the rate of S-meter needle movement, the nearer you are to the end point. At this stage you will probably not be able to hear much in the headphones apart from a near silent carrier, and the meter will be your best guide as it will be indicating the 'phase error' between the STFT and your BFO. When your needle moves at its slowest rate, you have reached zero beat. Make a note of the dial reading as this will show the receiver error.

For those radios with particularly good filters, which may prevent a 'zero beat' approach, a similar technique can be used by switching to CW mode. This method requires the use of an audio digital frequency meter – ask around at your radio club and you will probably find one. First of all, refer to the manual and find the 'CW offset' frequency. This is the audio frequency which the receiver will produce when it is exactly tuned to the carrier of the STFT. Common values are 600Hz to 800Hz. Some radios allow the user to programme the CW offset, so make sure that it has not been changed before you start the tests.

The procedure is essentially the same as has just been described, except that you will be tuning the radio until the DFM reads 600Hz exactly, then the receiver dial will show you any error. By repeating this test on a number of frequencies, you can be confident that your radio is accurate, or at least be aware of any errors or developing problems, and of course these are handy techniques for testing a radio you are considering buying.

STFT Stations, Schedules and Contact Information

ARGENTINA

📧 Servicio de Hidrografía Naval, Observatorio Naval, Av. España 2099, 1107 Buenos Aires, Argentina ☎ +54 11 43611162 📠 +54 11 43611162 **E**: onba@hidro.gov.ar **W**: www.hidro.gov.ar

Location	Call	kHz	kW	Mode	Schedule
Buenos Aires	LOL	10000	2	AM	1400-1500 (MF)

BELARUS

📧 43-y uzel svyazi Voenno-morskogo Flota RF, Vileyka, Belarus.

Location	Call	kHz	kW	Mode	Schedule
Vileyka	RJH69	*25	300	CW	0706-0747

Key: *) :06-:25 on 25.0, :27-:30 on 25.1, :32-:35 on 25.5, :38-:41 on 23.0, :44-:47 on 20.5kHz.
NB: Site is operated by Russian Navy; see Russia for HQ.

BRAZIL

📧 Divisão Serviço da Hora (DSHO), Observatório Nacional, R. Gal. José Cristino 77, São Cristóvão, Rio de Janeiro, CEP 20921-400, Brazil ☎ +55 21 35049100 📠 +55 21 25806041 **E**: dsh@on.br **W**: www.horalegalbrasil.mct.on.br

Location	Call	kHz	kW	Mode	Schedule
Rio de Janeiro	PPE	10000	1	AM/U	24h

CANADA

📧 National Research Council Canada (NRC), 1200 Montreal Road, Bldg M-36, Ottawa, Ontario, K1A 0R6, Canada ☎ +1 613 9935698 📠 +1 613 9521394 **E:** radio.chu@nrc-cnrc.gc.ca **W:** www.nrc-cnrc.gc.ca

Location	Call	kHz	kW	Mode	Schedule
Ottawa	CHU	3330	3	AM/U	24h
	CHU	7850	5	AM/U	24h
	CHU	14670	3	AM/U	24h

CHINA (P.R.)

📧 National Time Service Center (NTSC), Chinese Academy of Sciences, P.O.Box 18, Lintong 710600, Shaanxi, P.R.China ☎ +86 29 83890326 📠 +86 29 83890196 **E:** kyc@ntsc.ac.cn **W:** www.ntsc.ac.cn

Location	Call	kHz	kW	Mode	Schedule
Shangqiu	BPC	68.5	90	CW	0000-2100
Lintong	BPL	100	800	-	0530-1330
Lintong	BPM	2500	10	AM	0730-0100
	BPM	5000	20	AM	24h
	BPM	10000	20	AM	24h
	BPM	15000	20	AM	0100-0900

FINLAND

📧 VTT Technical Research Centre of Finland Ltd, Centre for Metrology MIKES, P.O.Box 1000, 02044 VTT, Finland ☎ +358 20

72211 **E:** kalevi.kalliomaki@mikes.fi **W:** www.mikes.fi

Location	Call	kHz	kW	Mode	Schedule
Espoo	(none)	25000	0.2	CW	24h

NB: Tx is intended for local service only.

FRANCE

▣ Laboratoire national de métrologie et d'essais - Système de Références Temps-Espace (LNE-SYRTE), 61 avenue de l'Observatoire, 75014 Paris, France ☎+33 140512070 🖹 +33 143255542 **E:** info. syrte@obspm.fr **W:** syrte.obspm.fr

Location	Call	kHz	kW	Mode	Schedule
Allouis	(none)	162	2000*	PSK	24h

Key: *) 1000kW evening/nighttime
NB: Tx is provided by Télédiffusion de France (TDF) and carries the France Inter radio prgr.

GERMANY

▣ Physikalisch-Technische Bundesanstalt (PTB), Bundesallee 100, 38116 Braunschweig, Germany ☎ +49 531 59230 **E:** time@ptb.de **W:** www.ptb.de

Location	Call	kHz	kW	Mode	Schedule
Mainflingen	DCF77	77.5	50	CW/PSK	24h

NB: Tx is leased from Media Broadcast.

HAWAII (USA)

▣ NIST radio station WWVH, P.O.Box 417, Kekaha, HI 96752, USA **E:** wwvh@boulder.nist.gov

Location	Call	kHz	kW	Mode	Schedule
Kekaha, HI	WWVH	2500	5	AM	24h
	WWVH	5000	10	AM	24h
	WWVH	10000	10	AM	24h
	WWVH	15000	10	AM	24h

NB: Time announced in female voice. NIST HQ: see USA.

JAPAN

▣ National Institute of Information and Communications Technology (NICT), Applied Electromagnetic Research Institute, Japan Standard Time Group, 4-2-1, Nukui-Kitamachi, Koganei, Tokyo 184-8795, Japan ☎ +81 42 3277567 🖹 +81 42 3276689 **E:** horonet@nict.go.jp **W:** jjy.nict.go.jp

Location	Call	kHz	kW	Mode	Schedule
Mt. Ohtakadoya	JJY	40	10	CW	24h
Mt. Hagane	JJY	60	10	CW	24h

KOREA, SOUTH

▣ Center for Time and Frequency, Korea Research Institute of Standards & Science (KRISS), 267 Gajeong-ro, Yuseong-gu, Daejeon 305-340, Rep. of Korea ☎ +82 42 8685145 🖹 +82 42 8685287 **E:** dhyu@kriss.re.kr **W:** www.kriss.re.kr

Location	Call	kHz	kW	Mode	Schedule
Daejeon	HLA	5000	2	AM	24h

KYRGYZSTAN

▣ Sukhoputnyy uzel svyazi Tikhookeanskogo flota VMF RF, Chaldybar, Kyrgyzstan.

Location	Call	kHz	kW	Mode	Schedule
Chaldybar	RJH66	*25	300	CW	0406-0447,1006-1047

Key: *) :06-:25 on 25.0, :27-:30 on 25.1, :32-:35 on 25.5, :38-:41 on 23.0, :44-:47 on 20.5kHz.
NB: Site is operated by Russian Navy; see Russia for HQ.

RUSSIA

▣ Generalniy Shtab Voenno-morskogo Flota RF (Russian Navy), St.Petersburg, Russia **W:** www.navy.ru

Location	Call	kHz	kW	Mode	Schedule
Arkhangelsk	RJH77	*25	300	CW	0906-0947
Khabarovsk	RAB99	**25	300	CW	0206-0236, 0606-0636
Krasnodar	RJH63	**25	300	+CW	1106-1140
N.Novgorod	RJH90	*25	300	CW	0806-0847

Key: *) :06-:25 on 25.0, :27-:30 on 25.1, :32-:35 on 25.5, :38-:41 on

23.0, :44-:47 on 20.5kHz; **) :06-:20 on 25.0, :21-:23 on 25.1, :24-:26 on 25.5, :27-:31 on 23.0, :32-:36(40) on 20.5kHz; +) also in FSK mode :36-:40 on 20.5kHz.

▣ Main Metrological Center of the State Service for Time, Frequency and Earth rotation parameters determination (SSTF), National Research Institute for Physicotechnical and Radio Engineering Measurements (FSUE "VNIIFTRI"), Moscow Region, 141570 Mendeleevo, Russia ☎+7 495 5350836 🖹 +7 495 5350871 **E:** office@vniiftri.ru **W:** www.vniiftri.ru

Location	Call	kHz	kW	Mode	Schedule
Taldom	RBU	66.66	50	CW	24h
Taldom	RWM	4996	10	CW	24h
Taldom	RWM	9996	10	CW	24h
Taldom	RWM	14996	10	CW	24h

NB: Txs are leased from RTRS.

▣ East Siberian Branch of FSUE "VNIIFTRI", 664056 Irkutsk, ul. Borodina 57, Russia ☎+7 3952 468303 🖹 +7 3952 463848 **E:** office@niiftri.irk.ru **W:** www.vniiftri-irk.ru

Location	Call	kHz	kW	Mode	Schedule
Angarsk	RTZ	50	10	CW	2000-1900

NB: Tx is leased from RTRS.

SPAIN

▣ Real Instituto y Observatorio de la Armada (ROA), Calle Cecilio Pujazón s/n, 11110 San Fernando, Spain ☎+34 956545590 🖹 +34 956599366 **W:** www.armada.mde.es

Location	Call	kHz	kW	Mode	Schedule
San Fernando	EBC	4998	1	CW	1030-1055 (MF)
		15006	1	CW	1000-1025 (MF)

TAIWAN

▣ National Time and Frequency Standard Laboratory, 12, Lane 551, Min-Tsu Road, Sec. 5, Yang-Mei, Taoyuan, 326, Rep. of China ☎+886 3 4244066 🖹 +886 3 4245474 **E:** linht@cht.com.tw **W:** www.stdtime.gov.tw

Location	Call	kHz	kW	Mode	Schedule
Chung-Li	BSF	77.5	1	CW	24h

UNITED KINGDOM

▣ National Physical Laboratory, Hampton Road, Teddington, Middlesex, TW11 0LW, United Kingdom ☎ +44 20 89773222 **E:** time@npl.co.uk **W:** www.npl.co.uk

Location	Call	kHz	kW	Mode	Schedule
Anthorn*	MSF	60	15	CW	24h
Droitwich**	(none)	198	500	PSK	24h
Burghead**	(none)	198	50	PSK	24h
Westerglen**	(none)	198	50	PSK	24h

Key: *) Tx is leased from Babcock; **) Txs are provided by Arqiva and carry the BBC Radio 4/BBCWS prgrs.

UNITED STATES OF AMERICA

▣ National Institute of Standards and Technology (NIST), Physical Masurement Laboratory, Time & Frequency Division, 325 Broadway, M/S 847, Boulder, CO 80305-3328, USA ☎ +1 303 4973295 🖹 +1 303 4976461 **E:** inquiries@nist.gov **W:** www.nist.gov

▣ NIST radio stations WWV/WWVB, 2000 East County Rd. 58, Ft. Collins, CO 80524 **E:** nist.radio@boulder.nist.gov **W:** wwv@nist.gov

Location	Call	kHz	kW	Mode	Schedule
Ft. Collins, CO	WWVB	60	50	CW	24h
	WWV	2500	2.5	AM	24h
	WWV	5000	10	AM	24h
	WWV	10000	10	AM	24h
	WWV	15000	10	AM	24h
	WWV	20000	2.5	AM	24h
	WWV	25000	2.5	AM	24h*

Key: *) Experimental broadcast, trs may be interrupted or suspended without notice
NB: WWV: Time announced in male voice. See also under Hawaii.

INTERNATIONAL BROADCASTING ORGANISATIONS & INSTITUTES

ARAB STATES BROADCASTING UNION (ASBU)
CP 250, 1080 Tunis Cedex, Tunisia. Street address: Rue 8840, centre urban nord, Tunis, Tunisia
☎ +216 71849000 ▦ +216 71843054
E: asbu@asbu.net **W:** www.asbu.net
L.P: Pres: Ismail Al-Shishtawi

ASIA-PACIFIC BROADCASTING UNION (ABU)
P.O.Box 12287, 50772 Kuala Lumpur, Malaysia
☎ +60 3 22823592 ▦ +60 3 22825292
E: info@abu.org.my **W:** www.abu.org.my
L.P: Pres: Cho Dae-hyun; Secr. General: Javad Mottaghi

ASIA-PACIFIC INSTITUTE FOR BROADCASTING DEVELOPMENT (AIBD)
P.O.Box 12066, 50766 Kuala Lumpur, Malaysia. Street address: Angkasapuri, Jalan Pantai Dalam, 50614 Kuala Lumpur, Malaysia
☎ +60 3 22824618 ▦ +60 3 22822761
E: info@aibd.org.my **W:** www.aibd.org.my
L.P: Dir: Chang Jin

ASIA-PACIFIC SATELLITE COMMUNICATIONS COUNCIL (APSCC)
Suite T-1602 Poonglim Iwantplus, 255-1 Seohyun-dong, Bundang-gu, Seongnam, Gyeonggi-do 463-862, Republic of Korea
☎ +82 31 7836244 ▦ +82 31 7836249
E: info@apscc.or.kr **W:** www.apscc.or.kr
L.P: Pres: Paul Brown-Kenyoni

ASOCIACIÓN INTERNACIONAL DE RADIODIFUSIÓN (AIR)
Carlos Quijano 1264, 11100 Montevideo, Uruguay ☎ +598 2 9011319 ▦ +598 2 9080458
E: mail@airiab.com **W:** www.airiab.com
L.P: Pres: Alexandre Jobin; DG: Juan Andres Lerena

CARIBBEAN BROADCASTING UNION (CBU)
Caribbean Media Centre, Suite 1B, Building #6A, Harbour Industrial Estate, Harbour Road, St. Michael, 11145, Barbados
☎ +1 246 4301007 ▦ +1 246 2289524
E: info@caribroadcastunion.org **W:** caribroadcastunion.org
L.P: Pres: Shida Bolai; Secr. General: Sonia Gill

DIGITAL RADIO MONDIALE (DRM)
DRM Project Office (London), c/o BBC Global News, 3rd Floor, Brock House, 19 Langham St., London W1A 1AA, United Kingdom
☎ +44 20 36142310 ▦ +44 20 36142330
E: projectoffice@drm.org **W:** www.drm.org
L.P: Chmn (DRM Consortium)/Pres (DRM Association): Ruxandra Obeja

EUROPEAN BROADCASTING UNION (EBU)
L'Ancienne-Route 17A, CH-1218 Grand-Saconnex, Switzerland
☎ +41 22 7172111 ▦ +41 22 7474000
E: ebu@ebu.ch **W:** www.ebu.ch
L.P: Pres: Jean-Paul Philippot; DG: Ingrid Deltenre

HIGH FREQUENCY CO-ORDINATION CONFERENCE (HFCC)
Vinohradská 2516/28, 12000 Praha 2, Czech Republic
E: info@hfcc.org **W:** www.hfcc.org
L.P: Chmn: Jeff White

INTERNATIONAL INSTITUTE OF COMMUNICATIONS (IIC)
Highlands House, 165 The Broadway, London, SW19 1NE, United Kingdom
☎ +44 20 85448076 ▦ +44 20 85448077
E: enquiries@iicom.org **W:** www.iicom.org
L.P: Pres: Fabio Colasanti

INTERNATIONAL TELECOMMUNICATIONS UNION (ITU)
Place des Nations, 1211 Genève 20, Switzerland
☎ +41 22 7305111 ▦ +41 22 7337256
E: itumail@itu.int **W:** www.itu.int
L.P: Secr. General: Houlin Zhao; Deputy Secr. General: Malcolm Johnson

NORTH AMERICAN BROADCASTERS ASSOCIATION (NABA)
P.O.Box 500, Station A, Toronto, Ontario, M5W 1E6, Canada
☎ +1 416 5989877 ▦ +1 416 5989774
E: contact@nabanet.com **W:** www.nabanet.com
L.P: Pres: Robert J. Ross; DG: Michael McEwen

PUBLIC MEDIA ALLIANCE
Arts 1.80, DEV, University of East Anglia, Norwich NR4 7TJ, United Kingdom
☎ +44 1603 592335
E: info@publicmediaalliance.org **W:** publicmediaalliance.org
L.P: Pres: Moneeza Hashimi; Secr. General: Sally-Ann Wilson

SOUTHERN AFRICAN BROADCASTING ASSOCIATION (SABA)
Postnet Suite No. 210, Private Bag X9, Melville 2109, South Africa
☎ +27 11 8884472 ▦ +27 11 8884489
E: dantagonanuses@gmail.com **W:** www.sabaorg.com
L.P: Pres: Albertus Aochamub; Secr. General: Ellen Nanuses

UNION AFRICAINE DE RADIODIFFUSION (UAR)
BP 3237, Dakar, Senegal. Street address: Avenue Carde, Immeuble CSS, Dakar, Senegal
☎ +221 338211625 ▦ +221 338225113
W: www.aub-uar.org
L.P: Pres: Amara Latrous; DG: Lawrence Addo-Yao Atiase

WORLD ASSOCIATION OF COMMUNITY RADIO BROADCASTERS (AMARC)
International Secretariat, 2 rue Sainte-Catherine Est, suite 102, Montréal, Quebec, H2X 1K4, Canada
☎ +1 514 9820351 ▦ +1 514 8497129
E: secretariat@si.amarc.org **W:** www.amarc.org
L.P: Pres: María Pía Matta; Secr. General: Francesco Diasio

WORLD DAB
WorldDAB Project Office, 6th Floor, 55 New Oxford Street, London, WC1A 1BS, United Kingdom
☎ +44 20 70100742 ▦ +44 20 72884643
E: info@worlddab.org **W:** www.worlddab.org
L.P: Pres: Patrick Hannon